is presented to

by

on

Church Record

EVENT

MINISTER

CHURCH

DATE

EVENT

MINISTER

CHURCH

DATE

EVENT

MINISTER

CHURCH

DATE

EVENT

MINISTER

CHURCH

DATE

EVENT

MINISTER

CHURCH

DATE

EVENT

MINISTER

CHURCH

DATE

Marriages

HUSBAND

WIFE

PLACE DATE

HUSBAND

WIFE

PLACE DATE

HUSBAND

WIFE

PLACE DATE

HUSBAND

WIFE

PLACE DATE

HUSBAND

WIFE

PLACE DATE

HUSBAND

WIFE

PLACE DATE

Wife's Family Tree

NAME

BIRTHPLACE DATE

BROTHERS AND SISTERS

PARENTS

FATHER

NAME

BIRTHPLACE DATE

MOTHER

NAME

BIRTHPLACE DATE

GRANDPARENTS

PATERNAL

GRANDFATHER

BIRTHPLACE DATE

GRANDMOTHER

BIRTHPLACE DATE

MATERNAL

GRANDFATHER

BIRTHPLACE DATE

GRANDMOTHER

BIRTHPLACE DATE

GREAT-GRANDPARENTS

PATERNAL

GRANDFATHER'S FATHER

BIRTHPLACE DATE

GRANDFATHER'S MOTHER

BIRTHPLACE DATE

GRANDMOTHER'S FATHER

BIRTHPLACE DATE

GRANDMOTHER'S MOTHER

BIRTHPLACE DATE

MATERNAL

GRANDFATHER'S FATHER

BIRTHPLACE DATE

GRANDFATHER'S MOTHER

BIRTHPLACE DATE

GRANDMOTHER'S FATHER

BIRTHPLACE DATE

GRANDMOTHER'S MOTHER

BIRTHPLACE DATE

Husband's Family Tree

NAME

BIRTHPLACE DATE

BROTHERS AND SISTERS

PARENTS

FATHER

NAME

BIRTHPLACE DATE

MOTHER

NAME

BIRTHPLACE DATE

GRANDPARENTS

PATERNAL

GRANDFATHER

BIRTHPLACE DATE

GRANDMOTHER

BIRTHPLACE DATE

MATERNAL

GRANDFATHER

BIRTHPLACE DATE

GRANDMOTHER

BIRTHPLACE DATE

GREAT-GRANDPARENTS

PATERNAL

GRANDFATHER'S FATHER

BIRTHPLACE DATE

GRANDFATHER'S MOTHER

BIRTHPLACE DATE

GRANDMOTHER'S FATHER

BIRTHPLACE DATE

GRANDMOTHER'S MOTHER

BIRTHPLACE DATE

MATERNAL

GRANDFATHER'S FATHER

BIRTHPLACE DATE

GRANDFATHER'S MOTHER

BIRTHPLACE DATE

GRANDMOTHER'S FATHER

BIRTHPLACE DATE

GRANDMOTHER'S MOTHER

BIRTHPLACE DATE

Births

NAME DATE

BORN TO

NAME DATE

BORN TO

NAME DATE

BORN TO

NAME DATE

BORN TO

NAME DATE

BORN TO

NAME DATE

BORN TO

NAME DATE

BORN TO

NAME DATE

BORN TO

NAME DATE

BORN TO

Deaths

NAME

DATE

NAME

DATE

NAME

DATE

NAME

DATE

NAME

DATE

NAME

DATE

NAME

DATE

NAME

DATE

NAME

DATE

EVENT

PLACE DATE

EVENT

PLACE DATE

EVENT

PLACE DATE

EVENT

PLACE DATE

EVENT

PLACE DATE

EVENT

PLACE DATE

HOLY BIBLE

New Revised Standard Version

containing the
OLD AND NEW TESTAMENTS
with the
APOCRYPHAL / DEUTEROCANONICAL BOOKS

ZONDERVAN BIBLE PUBLISHERS
GRAND RAPIDS, MICHIGAN

Published by Zondervan Publishing House, Grand Rapids, Michigan 49530, U.S.A.
Printed in the United States of America

93 94 95 96 97 98 99 7 6 5 4 3 2 1

RRD

The Names And Order Of The

BOOKS OF THE BIBLE

The Old Testament

The Apocryphal / Deuterocanonical Books

The New Testament

MAPS AND CHARTS

The Old Testament

The New Testament

ABBREVIATIONS

The following abbrevations are used for the books of the Bible:

The Old Testament

Gen	Genesis	2 Chr	2 Chronicles	Dan	Daniel
Ex	Exodus	Ezra	Ezra	Hos	Hosea
Lev	Leviticus	Neh	Nehemiah	Joel	Joel
Num	Numbers	Esth	Esther	Am	Amos
Deut	Deuteronomy	Job	Job	Ob	Obadiah
Josh	Joshua	Ps	Psalms	Jon	Jonah
Judg	Judges	Prov	Proverbs	Mic	Micah
Ruth	Ruth	Eccl	Ecclesiastes	Nah	Nahum
1 Sam	1 Samuel	Song	Song of Solomon	Hab	Habakkuk
2 Sam	2 Samuel	Isa	Isaiah	Zeph	Zephaniah
1 Kings	1 Kings	Jer	Jeremiah	Hag	Haggai
2 Kings	2 Kings	Lam	Lamentations	Zech	Zechariah
1 Chr	1 Chronicles	Ezek	Ezekiel	Mal	Malachi

The Apocryphal / Deuterocanonical Books

Tob	Tobit	Song of Thr	Prayer of Azariah and the Song of the Three Jews
Jdt	Judith	Sus	Susanna
Add Esth	Additions to Esther	Bel	Bel and the Dragon
Wis	Wisdom	1 Macc	1 Maccabees
Sir	Sirach (Ecclesiasticus)	2 Macc	2 Maccabees
Bar	Baruch	3 Macc	3 Maccabees
1 Esd	1 Esdras	4 Macc	4 Maccabees
2 Esd	2 Esdras	Pr Man	Prayer of Manasseh
Let Jer	Letter of Jeremiah		

The New Testament

Mt	Matthew	Eph	Ephesians	Heb	Hebrews
Mk	Mark	Phil	Philippians	Jas	James
Lk	Luke	Col	Colossians	1 Pet	1 Peter
Jn	John	1 Thess	1 Thessalonians	2 Pet	2 Peter
Acts	Acts of the Apostles	2 Thess	2 Thessalonians	1 Jn	1 John
Rom	Romans	1 Tim	1 Timothy	2 Jn	2 John
1 Cor	1 Corinthians	2 Tim	2 Timothy	3 Jn	3 John
2 Cor	2 Corinthians	Titus	Titus	Jude	Jude
Gal	Galatians	Philem	Philemon	Rev	Revelation

In the notes to the books of the Old Testament the following abbreviations are used:

Ant.	Josephus, *Antiquities of the Jews*
Aram	Aramaic
Ch, chs	Chapter, chapters
Cn	Correction; made where the text has suffered in transmission and the versions provide no satisfactory restoration but where the Standard Bible Committee agrees with the judgment of competent scholars as to the most probable reconstruction of the original text.
Gk	Septuagint, Greek version of the Old Testament
Heb	Hebrew of the consonantal Masoretic Text of the Old Testament
Josephus	Flavius Josephus (Jewish historian, about A.D. 37 to about 95)
Macc.	The book(s) of the Maccabees
Ms(s)	Manuscript(s)
MT	The Hebrew of the pointed Masoretic Text of the Old Testament
OL	Old Latin
Q Ms(s)	Manuscript(s) found at Qumran by the Dead Sea
Sam	Samaritan Hebrew text of the Old Testament
Syr	Syriac Version of the Old Testament
Syr H	Syriac Version of Origen's Hexapla
Tg	Targum
Vg	Vulgate, Latin Version of the Old Testament

Cross References

The center column of each page of this Bible contains references that connect one text of the Bible with others that have a similar theme. By using this system, difficult or obscure passages of the Bible can be clarified by other Scripture references. The cross references for each verse are listed in the sequence of their relevance to the material in that verse.

The cross reference system for the Old and New Testaments was developed by Harold Lindsell. The cross reference system for the Apocrypha was developed by Verlyn D. Verbrugge.

In the Apocrypha, the texts in the cross reference column connect verses of the Apocrypha to other verses within the Apocrypha and to verses in the Old and New Testaments. No cross references, however, direct the reader from the Old Testament or New Testament into the Apocrypha.

In Matthew, Mark, Luke, and John, parallel passages are also listed within the cross reference system. These references direct the reader to other passages that tell of the same or very similar events. Such parallel passages are indicated in the center column by an abbreviation of "pp" following the reference.

To The Reader

This preface is addressed to you by the Committee of translators, who wish to explain, as briefly as possible, the origin and character of our work. The publication of our revision is yet another step in the long, continual process of making the Bible available in the form of the English language that is most widely current in our day. To summarize in a single sentence: the New Revised Standard Version of the Bible is an authorized revision of the Revised Standard Version, published in 1952, which was a revision of the American Standard Version, published in 1901, which, in turn, embodied earlier revisions of the King James Version, published in 1611.

In the course of time, the King James Version came to be regarded as "the Authorized Version." With good reason it has been termed "the noblest monument of English prose," and it has entered, as no other book has, into the making of the personal character and the public institutions of the English-speaking peoples. We owe to it an incalculable debt.

Yet the King James Version has serious defects. By the middle of the nineteenth century, the development of biblical studies and the discovery of many biblical manuscripts more ancient than those on which the King James Version was based made it apparent that these defects were so many as to call for revision. The task was begun, by authority of the Church of England, in 1870. The (British) Revised Version of the Bible was published in 1881-1885; and the American Standard Version, its variant embodying the preferences of the American scholars associated with the work, was published, as was mentioned above, in 1901. In 1928 the copyright of the latter was acquired by the International Council of Religious Education and thus passed into the ownership of the churches of the United States and Canada that were associated in this Council through their boards of education and publication.

The Council appointed a committee of scholars to have charge of the text of the American Standard Version and to undertake inquiry concerning the need for further revision. After studying the questions whether or not revision should be undertaken, and if so, what its nature and extent should be, in 1937 the Council authorized a revision. The scholars who served as members of the Committee worked in two sections, one dealing with the Old Testament and one with the New Testament. In 1946 the Revised Standard Version of the New Testament was published. The publication of the Revised Standard Version of the Bible, containing the Old and New Testaments, took place on September 30, 1952. A translation of the Apocryphal/Deuterocanonical Books of the Old Testament followed in 1957. In 1977 this collection was issued in an expanded edition, containing three additional texts received by Eastern Orthodox communions (3 and 4 Maccabees and Psalm 151). Thereafter the Revised Standard Version gained the distinction of being officially authorized for use by all major Christian churches: Protestant, Anglican, Roman Catholic, and Eastern Orthodox.

The Revised Standard Version Bible Committee is a continuing body, comprising about thirty members, both men and women. Ecumenical in representation, it includes scholars affiliated with various Protestant denominations, as well as several Roman Catholic members, an Eastern Orthodox member, and a Jewish member who serves in the Old Testament section. For a period of time the Committee included several members from Canada and from England.

Because no translation of the Bible is perfect or is acceptable to all groups of readers, and because discoveries of older manuscripts and further investigation of linguistic features of the text continue to become available, renderings of the Bible have proliferated. During the years following the publication of the Revised Standard Version, twenty-six other English translations and revisions of the Bible were produced by committees and by individual scholars—not to mention twenty-five other translations and revisions of the New Testament alone. One of the latter was the second edition of the RSV New Testament, issued in 1971, twenty-five years after its initial publication.

Following the publication of the RSV Old Testament in 1952, significant advances were made in the discovery and interpretation of documents in Semitic languages related to Hebrew. In addition to the information that had become available in the late 1940s from the Dead Sea texts of Isaiah and Habakkuk, subsequent acquisitions from the same area brought to light many other early copies of all the books of the Hebrew Scriptures (except Esther), though most of these copies are fragmentary. During the same period early Greek manuscript copies of books of the New Testament also became available.

In order to take these discoveries into account, along with recent studies of documents in Semitic languages related to Hebrew, in 1974 the Policies Committee of the Revised Standard Version, which is a standing committee of the National Council of the Churches of Christ in the U.S.A., authorized the preparation of a revision of the entire RSV Bible.

For the Old Testament the Committee has made use of the *Biblia Hebraica Stuttgartensia* (1977; ed. sec. emendata, 1983). This is an edition of the Hebrew and Aramaic text as current early in the Christian era and fixed by Jewish scholars (the "Masoretes") of the sixth to the ninth centuries. The vowel signs, which were added by the Masoretes, are accepted in the main, but where a more probable and convincing reading can be obtained by assuming different vowels, this has been done. No notes are given in such cases, because the vowel points are less ancient and reliable than the consonants. When an alternative reading given by the Masoretes is translated in a footnote, this is identified by the words "Another reading is."

Departures from the consonantal text of the best manuscripts have been made only where it seems clear that errors in copying had been made before the text was standardized. Most of the corrections adopted are based on the ancient versions (translations into Greek, Aramaic, Syriac, and Latin), which were made prior to the time of the work of the Masoretes and which therefore may reflect earlier forms of the Hebrew text. In such instances a footnote specifies the version or versions from which the correction has been derived and also gives a translation of the Masoretic Text. Where it was deemed appropriate to do so, information is supplied in footnotes from subsidiary Jewish traditions concerning other textual readings (the *Tiqqune Sopherim*, "emendations of the scribes"). These are identified in the footnotes as "Ancient Heb tradition."

Occasionally it is evident that the text has suffered in transmission and that none of the versions provides a satisfactory restoration. Here we can only follow the best judgment of competent scholars as to the most probable reconstruction of the original text. Such reconstructions are indicated in footnotes by the abbreviation Cn ("Correction"), and a translation of the Masoretic Text is added.

For the Apocryphal/Deuterocanonical Books of the Old Testament the Committee has made use of a number of texts. For most of these books the basic

Greek text from which the present translation was made is the edition of the Septuagint prepared by Alfred Rahlfs and published by the Württemberg Bible Society (Stuttgart, 1935). For several of the books the more recently published individual volumes of the Göttingen Septuagint project were utilized. For the book of Tobit it was decided to follow the form of the Greek text found in codex Sinaiticus (supported as it is by evidence from Qumran); where this text is defective, it was supplemented and corrected by other Greek manuscripts. For the three Additions to Daniel (namely, Susanna, the Prayer of Azariah and the Song of the Three Jews, and Bel and the Dragon) the Committee continued to use the Greek version attributed to Theodotion (the so-called "Theodotion-Daniel"). In translating Ecclesiasticus (Sirach), while constant reference was made to the Hebrew fragments of a large portion of this book (those discovered at Qumran and Masada as well as those recovered from the Cairo Geniza), the Committee generally followed the Greek text (including verse numbers) published by Joseph Ziegler in the Göttingen Septuagint (1965). But in many places the Committee has translated the Hebrew text when this provides a reading that is clearly superior to the Greek; the Syriac and Latin versions were also consulted throughout and occasionally adopted. The basic text adopted in rendering 2 Esdras is the Latin version given in *Biblia Sacra*, edited by Robert Weber (Stuttgart, 1971). This was supplemented by consulting the Latin text as edited by R. L. Bensly (1895) and by Bruno Violet (1910), as well as by taking into account the several Oriental versions of 2 Esdras, namely, the Syriac, Ethiopic, Arabic (two forms, referred to as Arabic 1 and Arabic 2), Armenian, and Georgian versions. Finally, since the Additions to the Book of Esther are disjointed and quite unintelligible as they stand in most editions of the Apocrypha, we have provided them with their original context by translating the whole of the Greek version of Esther from Robert Hanhart's Göttingen edition (1983).

For the New Testament the Committee has based its work on the most recent edition of *The Greek New Testament*, prepared by an interconfessional and international committee and published by the United Bible Societies (1966; 3rd ed. corrected, 1983; information concerning changes to be introduced into the critical apparatus of the forthcoming 4th edition was available to the Committee). As in that edition, double brackets are used to enclose a few passages that are generally regarded to be later additions to the text, but which we have retained because of their evident antiquity and their importance in the textual tradition. Only in very rare instances have we replaced the text or the punctuation of the Bible Societies' edition by an alternative that seemed to us to be superior. Here and there in the footnotes the phrase, "Other ancient authorities read," identifies alternative readings preserved by Greek manuscripts and early versions. In both Testaments, alternative renderings of the text are indicated by the word "Or."

As for the style of English adopted for the present revision, among the mandates given to the Committee in 1980 by the Division of Education and Ministry of the National Council of Churches of Christ (which now holds the copyright of the RSV Bible) was the directive to continue in the tradition of the King James Bible, but to introduce such changes as are warranted on the basis of accuracy, clarity, euphony, and current English usage. Within the constraints set by the original texts and by the mandates of the Division, the Committee has followed the maxim, "As literal as possible, as free as necessary." As a consequence, the New Revised Standard Version (NRSV) remains essentially a literal translation. Paraphrastic renderings have been adopted only sparingly, and then chiefly to compensate for a deficiency in the English language—the lack of a common gender third person singular pronoun.

During the almost half a century since the publication of the RSV, many in the churches have become sensitive to the danger of linguistic sexism arising from the inherent bias of the English language towards the masculine gender, a bias that in the case of the Bible has often restricted or obscured the meaning of the original text. The mandates from the Division specified that, in references to men and women, masculine-oriented language should be eliminated as far as this can be done without altering passages that reflect the historical situation of ancient patriarchal culture. As can be appreciated, more than once the Committee found that the several mandates stood in tension and even in conflict. The various concerns had to be balanced case by case in order to provide a faithful and acceptable rendering without using contrived English. Only very occasionally has the pronoun "he" or "him" been retained in passages where the reference may have been to a woman as well as to a man; for example, in several legal texts in Leviticus and Deuteronomy. In such instances of formal, legal language, the options of either putting the passage in the plural or of introducing additional nouns to avoid masculine pronouns in English seemed to the Committee to obscure the historic structure and literary character of the original. In the vast majority of cases, however, inclusiveness has been attained by simple rephrasing or by introducing plural forms when this does not distort the meaning of the passage. Of course, in narrative and in parable no attempt was made to generalize the sex of individual persons.

Another aspect of style will be detected by readers who compare the more stately English rendering of the Old Testament with the less formal rendering adopted for the New Testament. For example, the traditional distinction between *shall* and *will* in English has been retained in the Old Testament as appropriate in rendering a document that embodies what may be termed the classic form of Hebrew, while in the New Testament the abandonment of such distinctions in the usage of the future tense in English reflects the more colloquial nature of the koine Greek used by most New Testament authors except when they are quoting the Old Testament.

Careful readers will notice that here and there in the Old Testament the word LORD (or in certain cases GOD) is printed in capital letters. This represents the traditional manner in English versions of rendering the Divine Name, the "Tetragrammaton" (see the notes on Exodus 3.14, 15), following the precedent of the ancient Greek and Latin translators and the long established practice in the reading of the Hebrew Scriptures in the synagogue. While it is almost if not quite certain that the Name was originally pronounced "Yahweh," this pronunciation was not indicated when the Masoretes added vowel sounds to the consonantal Hebrew text. To the four consonants YHWH of the Name, which had come to be regarded as too sacred to be pronounced, they attached vowel signs indicating that in its place should be read the Hebrew word *Adonai* meaning "Lord" (or *Elohim* meaning "God"). Ancient Greek translators employed the word *Kyrios* ("Lord") for the Name. The Vulgate likewise used the Latin word *Dominus* ("Lord"). The form "Jehovah" is of late medieval origin; it is a combination of the consonants of the Divine Name and the vowels attached to it by the Masoretes but belonging to an entirely different word. Although the American Standard Version (1901) had used "Jehovah" to render the Tetragrammaton (the sound of Y being represented by J and the sound of W by V, as in Latin), for two reasons the Committees that produced the RSV and the NRSV returned to the more familiar usage of the King James Version. (1) The word "Jehovah" does not accurately represent any form of the Name ever used in Hebrew. (2) The use of any proper name for the one and only God, as though there were other gods from whom the true God had to be distinguished, began to be discontinued in Judaism before the Christian era and is inappropriate for the universal faith of the Christian Church.

It will be seen that in the Psalms and in other prayers addressed to God the archaic second person singular pronouns (*thee*, *thou*, *thine*) and verb forms (*art*, *hast*, *hadst*) are no longer used. Although some readers may regret this change, it should be pointed out that in the original languages neither the Old Testament nor the New makes any linguistic distinction between addressing a human being and addressing the Deity. Furthermore, in the tradition of the King James Version one will not expect to find the use of capital letters for pronouns that refer to the Deity — such capitalization is an unnecessary innovation that has only recently been introduced into a few English translations of the Bible. Finally, we have left to the discretion of the licensed publishers such matters as section headings, cross-references, and clues to the pronunciation of proper names.

This new version seeks to preserve all that is best in the English Bible as it has been known and used through the years. It is intended for use in public reading and congregational worship, as well as in private study, instruction, and meditation. We have resisted the temptation to introduce terms and phrases that merely reflect current moods, and have tried to put the message of the Scriptures in simple, enduring words and expressions that are worthy to stand in the great tradition of the King James Bible and its predecessors.

In traditional Judaism and Christianity, the Bible has been more than a historical document to be preserved or a classic of literature to be cherished and admired; it is recognized as the unique record of God's dealings with people over the ages. The Old Testament sets forth the call of a special people to enter into covenant relation with the God of justice and steadfast love and to bring God's law to the nations. The New Testament records the life and work of Jesus Christ, the one in whom "the Word became flesh," as well as describes the rise and spread of the early Christian Church. The Bible carries its full message, not to those who regard it simply as a noble literary heritage of the past or who wish to use it to enhance political purposes and advance otherwise desirable goals, but to all persons and communities who read it so that they may discern and understand what God is saying to them. That message must not be disguised in phrases that are no longer clear, or hidden under words that have changed or lost their meaning; it must be presented in language that is direct and plain and meaningful to people today. It is the hope and prayer of the translators that this version of the Bible may continue to hold a large place in congregational life and to speak to all readers, young and old alike, helping them to understand and believe and respond to its message.

For the Committee,

BRUCE M. METZGER

THE HEBREW SCRIPTURES
commonly called

THE OLD TESTAMENT

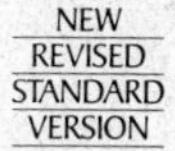

Genesis

Title and Background

The first phrase in the Hebrew text of Genesis 1.1 means "In the beginning." The book of Genesis is about many beginnings–the beginning of the universe, the beginning of man and woman, the beginning of human sin, and the beginning of God's promises and plans for salvation.

Author and Date of Writing

Traditionally, Jews and Christians alike have held that Moses was the author/compiler of Genesis, the first of the five books of the Old Testament known as the Pentateuch (meaning "five-volumed book"). More recently, scholars have suggested that though Moses may have written parts of the Pentateuch, these five books did not take their final form until later on in Israelite history.

There are two possibilities for the historical period during which Moses lived. The older view puts Moses in the fifteenth century B.C.; this is based primarily on 1 Kings 6.1, which states that "the fourth year of Solomon's reign over Israel" was the same as "the four hundred eightieth year after the Israelites came out of the land of Egypt." The other view, based largely on archaeological evidence for the date of the exodus, places Moses in the thirteenth century B.C.

Theme and Message

The message of Genesis is rich and complex but it is mainly a book of relationships–between God and nature, between God and the human race, and between various people. It stresses the fact that the one true God is sovereign over all that exists, whether good or evil. It introduces us to the way in which God initiates and enters into covenants with his chosen people, pledging his love and faithfulness to them.

Outline

- I. Primeval History: Four Great Events (1.1–11.32)
  - A. The Creation of the Universe, Adam, and Eve (1.1–2.25)
  - B. The Human Race's First Sin and Its Results (3.1–5.32)
  - C. The Great Flood (6.1–9.29)
  - D. The Scattering of the Nations (10.1–11.32)
- II. Patriarchal History: Four Great Characters (12.1–50.26)
  - A. The Life of Abraham (12.1–20.18)
  - B. The Life of Isaac (21.1–26.35)
  - C. The Life of Jacob (27.1–37.1)
  - D. The Life of Joseph (37.2–50.26)

Six Days of Creation and the Sabbath

1 In the beginning when God
created[a] the heavens and the
earth, 2 the earth was a formless
void and darkness covered the face
of the deep, while a wind from
God[b] swept over the face of the
waters. 3 Then God said, "Let there
be light"; and there was light. 4 And
God saw that the light was good;
and God separated the light from
the darkness. 5 God called the light
Day, and the darkness he called

1.1 Jn 1.1,2; Ps 8.3; Isa 44.24; 42.5; 45.18 **1.2** Jer 4.23; Ps 104.30 **1.3** Ps 33.6,9; 2 Cor 4.6

1.4 Isa 45.7 **1.5** Ps 74.16

[a] Or *when God began to create* or *In the beginning God created* [b] Or *while the spirit of God* or *while a mighty wind*

Night. And there was evening and
there was morning, the first day.
6 And God said, "Let there be a
dome in the midst of the waters,
and let it separate the waters from
the waters." 7 So God made the
dome and separated the waters
that were under the dome from the
waters that were above the dome.
And it was so. 8 God called the
dome Sky. And there was evening
and there was morning, the second
day.
9 And God said, "Let the waters
under the sky be gathered together
into one place, and let the dry land
appear." And it was so. 10 God
called the dry land Earth, and the
waters that were gathered together
he called Seas. And God saw that it
was good. 11 Then God said, "Let
the earth put forth vegetation:
plants yielding seed, and fruit trees
of every kind on earth that bear
fruit with the seed in it." And it was
so. 12 The earth brought forth vegetation: plants yielding seed of every
kind, and trees of every kind bearing fruit with the seed in it. And
God saw that it was good. 13 And
there was evening and there was
morning, the third day.
14 And God said, "Let there be
lights in the dome of the sky to separate the day from the night; and
let them be for signs and for seasons and for days and years, 15 and
let them be lights in the dome of
the sky to give light upon the
earth." And it was so. 16 God made
the two great lights—the greater
light to rule the day and the lesser
light to rule the night—and the
stars. 17 God set them in the dome
of the sky to give light upon the
earth, 18 to rule over the day and
over the night, and to separate the
light from the darkness. And God
saw that it was good. 19 And there
was evening and there was morning, the fourth day.
20 And God said, "Let the waters bring forth swarms of living
creatures, and let birds fly above
the earth across the dome of the
sky." 21 So God created the great
sea monsters and every living crea-

1.6 Jer 10.12
1.7 Prov 8.28; Ps 148.4
1.9 Job 26.10; Prov 8.29; Jer 5.22; 2 Pet 3.5
1.10 Ps 33.7
1.11 Lk 6.44
1.14 Ps 74.16; 104.19
1.16 Ps 136.8,9; Job 38.7
1.18 Jer 31.35
1.21 Ps 104.25, 26
1.22 Gen 8.17
1.25 Jer 27.5
1.26 Ps 100.3; Acts 17.26, 28,29; Col 3.10
1.27 1 Cor 11.7; Gen 5.2; Mt 19.4
1.28 Gen 9.1,7; Lev 26.9
1.29 Ps 104.14, 15; 136.25
1.30 Ps 145.15; Job 38.41
1.31 Ps 104.24

ture that moves, of every kind, with
which the waters swarm, and every
winged bird of every kind. And God
saw that it was good. 22 God blessed
them, saying, "Be fruitful and multiply and fill the waters in the seas,
and let birds multiply on the
earth." 23 And there was evening
and there was morning, the fifth
day.
24 And God said, "Let the earth
bring forth living creatures of every
kind: cattle and creeping things
and wild animals of the earth of every kind." And it was so. 25 God
made the wild animals of the earth
of every kind, and the cattle of every kind, and everything that
creeps upon the ground of every
kind. And God saw that it was
good.
26 Then God said, "Let us make
humankind[c] in our image, according to our likeness; and let them
have dominion over the fish of the
sea, and over the birds of the air,
and over the cattle, and over all the
wild animals of the earth,[d] and
over every creeping thing that
creeps upon the earth."
27 So God created humankind[c]
in his image,
in the image of God he
created them;[e]
male and female he
created them.
28 God blessed them, and God said
to them, "Be fruitful and multiply,
and fill the earth and subdue it;
and have dominion over the fish of
the sea and over the birds of the air
and over every living thing that
moves upon the earth." 29 God said,
"See, I have given you every plant
yielding seed that is upon the face
of all the earth, and every tree with
seed in its fruit; you shall have
them for food. 30 And to every beast
of the earth, and to every bird of the
air, and to everything that creeps
on the earth, everything that has
the breath of life, I have given every
green plant for food." And it was
so. 31 God saw everything that he

[c] Heb *adam* [d] Syr: Heb *and over all the earth* [e] Heb *him*

had made, and indeed, it was very
good. And there was evening and
there was morning, the sixth day.

2 Thus the heavens and the
earth were finished, and all
their multitude. 2 And on the seventh day God finished the work
that he had done, and he rested on
the seventh day from all the work
that he had done. 3 So God blessed
the seventh day and hallowed it,
because on it God rested from all
the work that he had done in creation.

4 These are the generations of
the heavens and the earth when
they were created.

Another Account of the Creation

In the day that the LORD God
made the earth and the heavens,
5 when no plant of the field was yet
in the earth and no herb of the field
had yet sprung up—for the LORD
God had not caused it to rain upon
the earth, and there was no one to
till the ground; 6 but a stream
would rise from the earth, and water the whole face of the ground—
7 then the LORD God formed man
from the dust of the ground,[f] and
breathed into his nostrils the
breath of life; and the man became
a living being. 8 And the LORD God
planted a garden in Eden, in the
east; and there he put the man
whom he had formed. 9 Out of the
ground the LORD God made to grow
every tree that is pleasant to the
sight and good for food, the tree of
life also in the midst of the garden,
and the tree of the knowledge of
good and evil.

10 A river flows out of Eden to
water the garden, and from there it
divides and becomes four
branches. 11 The name of the first is
Pishon; it is the one that flows
around the whole land of Havilah,
where there is gold; 12 and the gold
of that land is good; bdellium and
onyx stone are there. 13 The name
of the second river is Gihon; it is
the one that flows around the
whole land of Cush. 14 The name of
the third river is Tigris, which flows

2.1 Ps 33.6 **2.2** Ex 20.11; Heb 4.4 **2.3** Isa 58.13 **2.5** Gen 1.12; Job 38.26-28 **2.7** Gen 3.19; Ps 103.14; Job 33.4; Acts 17.25; 1 Cor 15.45 **2.8** Isa 51.3; Gen 3.24; 4.16 **2.9** Ezek 31.8; Gen 3.22; Rev 2.7; 22.2,14 **2.12** Num 11.7 **2.14** Dan 10.4

2.17 Deut 30.15, 19,20; Rom 6.23; Jas 1.15 **2.18** 1 Cor 11.9 **2.19** Gen 1.20, 24; Ps 8.7 **2.21** 1 Sam 26.12 **2.23** Eph 5.30; 1 Cor 11.8 **2.24** Mt 19.5; Mk 10.7,8; 1 Cor 6.16; Eph 5.31 **2.25** Gen 3.7,10, 11 **3.1** 2 Cor 11.3; Rev 12.9; 20.2

east of Assyria. And the fourth river
is the Euphrates.

15 The LORD God took the man
and put him in the garden of Eden
to till it and keep it. 16 And the LORD
God commanded the man, "You
may freely eat of every tree of the
garden; 17 but of the tree of the
knowledge of good and evil you
shall not eat, for in the day that you
eat of it you shall die."

18 Then the LORD God said, "It
is not good that the man should be
alone; I will make him a helper as
his partner." 19 So out of the ground
the LORD God formed every animal
of the field and every bird of the air,
and brought them to the man to
see what he would call them; and
whatever the man called every living creature, that was its name.
20 The man gave names to all cattle,
and to the birds of the air, and to
every animal of the field; but for
the man[g] there was not found a
helper as his partner. 21 So the LORD
God caused a deep sleep to fall
upon the man, and he slept; then
he took one of his ribs and closed
up its place with flesh. 22 And the
rib that the LORD God had taken
from the man he made into a woman and brought her to the man.
23 Then the man said,

"This at last is bone of my
bones
and flesh of my flesh;
this one shall be called
Woman,[h]
for out of Man[i] this one
was taken."

24 Therefore a man leaves his father
and his mother and clings to his
wife, and they become one flesh.
25 And the man and his wife were
both naked, and were not
ashamed.

The First Sin and Its Punishment

3 Now the serpent was more
crafty than any other wild animal that the LORD God had made.
He said to the woman, "Did God

[f] Or *formed a man* (Heb *adam*) *of dust from the ground* (Heb *adamah*) [g] Or *for Adam* [h] Heb *ishshah* [i] Heb *ish*

say, 'You shall not eat from any tree
in the garden'?" 2 The woman said
to the serpent, "We may eat of the
fruit of the trees in the garden; 3 but
God said, 'You shall not eat of the
fruit of the tree that is in the middle of the garden, nor shall you
touch it, or you shall die.' " 4 But
the serpent said to the woman,
"You will not die; 5 for God knows
that when you eat of it your eyes
will be opened, and you will be like
God,[j] knowing good and evil." 6 So
when the woman saw that the tree
was good for food, and that it was
a delight to the eyes, and that the
tree was to be desired to make one
wise, she took of its fruit and ate;
and she also gave some to her husband, who was with her, and he
ate. 7 Then the eyes of both were
opened, and they knew that they
were naked; and they sewed fig
leaves together and made loin-
cloths for themselves.

8 They heard the sound of the
LORD God walking in the garden at
the time of the evening breeze, and
the man and his wife hid themselves from the presence of the
LORD God among the trees of the
garden. 9 But the LORD God called
to the man, and said to him,
"Where are you?" 10 He said, "I
heard the sound of you in the garden, and I was afraid, because I was
naked; and I hid myself." 11 He
said, "Who told you that you were
naked? Have you eaten from the
tree of which I commanded you not
to eat?" 12 The man said, "The
woman whom you gave to be with
me, she gave me fruit from the tree,
and I ate." 13 Then the LORD God
said to the woman, "What is this
that you have done?" The woman
said, "The serpent tricked me, and
I ate." 14 The LORD God said to the
serpent,

"Because you have done this,
cursed are you among all
animals
and among all wild
creatures;
upon your belly you shall go,
and dust you shall eat
all the days of your life.

3.3 2 Cor 11.3
3.4 Jn 8.44
3.6 1 Tim 2.14
3.8 Job 31.33; Jer 23.24
3.10 1 Jn 3.20
3.12 Prov 28.13
3.13 2 Cor 11.3; 1 Tim 2.14
3.14 Isa 65.25; Mic 7.17
3.15 Jn 8.44; Acts 13.10; 1 Jn 3.8; Isa 7.14; Mt 1.23; Rom 16.20; Rev 12.7
3.16 Isa 13.8; Gen 4.7; 1 Cor 11.3; Eph 5.22
3.17 1 Sam 15.23; Gen 2.17; Rom 8.20-22
3.18 Ps 104.14
3.19 Gen 2.7; Ps 90.3; 104.29; Eccl 12.7
3.22 Rev 22.2
3.23 Gen 4.2

15 I will put enmity between
you and the woman,
and between your offspring
and hers;
he will strike your head,
and you will strike his
heel."
16 To the woman he said,
"I will greatly increase your
pangs in childbearing;
in pain you shall bring
forth children,
yet your desire shall be for
your husband,
and he shall rule over you."
17 And to the man[k] he said,
"Because you have listened
to the voice of your
wife,
and have eaten of the tree
about which I commanded
you,
'You shall not eat of it,'
cursed is the ground because
of you;
in toil you shall eat of it all
the days of your life;
18 thorns and thistles it shall
bring forth for you;
and you shall eat the
plants of the field.
19 By the sweat of your face
you shall eat bread
until you return to the
ground,
for out of it you were
taken;
you are dust,
and to dust you shall
return."

20 The man named his wife
Eve,[l] because she was the mother
of all living. 21 And the LORD God
made garments of skins for the
man[m] and for his wife, and clothed
them.

22 Then the LORD God said,
"See, the man has become like one
of us, knowing good and evil; and
now, he might reach out his hand
and take also from the tree of life,
and eat, and live forever"—
23 therefore the LORD God sent him
forth from the garden of Eden, to

[j] Or *gods* [k] Or *to Adam* [l] In Heb *Eve* resembles the word for *living* [m] Or *for Adam*

till the ground from which he was
taken. 24 He drove out the man; and
at the east of the garden of Eden he
placed the cherubim, and a sword
flaming and turning to guard the
way to the tree of life.

Cain Murders Abel

4 Now the man knew his wife
Eve, and she conceived and
bore Cain, saying, "I have produced[n] a man with the help of the
LORD." 2 Next she bore his brother
Abel. Now Abel was a keeper of
sheep, and Cain a tiller of the
ground. 3 In the course of time Cain
brought to the LORD an offering of
the fruit of the ground, 4 and Abel
for his part brought of the firstlings
of his flock, their fat portions. And
the LORD had regard for Abel and
his offering, 5 but for Cain and his
offering he had no regard. So Cain
was very angry, and his countenance fell. 6 The LORD said to Cain,
"Why are you angry, and why has
your countenance fallen? 7 If you
do well, will you not be accepted?
And if you do not do well, sin is
lurking at the door; its desire is for
you, but you must master it."

8 Cain said to his brother Abel,
"Let us go out to the field."[o] And
when they were in the field, Cain
rose up against his brother Abel,
and killed him. 9 Then the LORD
said to Cain, "Where is your brother Abel?" He said, "I do not know;
am I my brother's keeper?" 10 And
the LORD said, "What have you
done? Listen; your brother's blood
is crying out to me from the
ground! 11 And now you are cursed
from the ground, which has opened
its mouth to receive your brother's
blood from your hand. 12 When you
till the ground, it will no longer
yield to you its strength; you will be
a fugitive and a wanderer on the
earth." 13 Cain said to the LORD,
"My punishment is greater than I
can bear! 14 Today you have driven
me away from the soil, and I shall
be hidden from your face; I shall be
a fugitive and a wanderer on the
earth, and anyone who meets me
may kill me." 15 Then the LORD said
to him, "Not so![p] Whoever kills
Cain will suffer a sevenfold vengeance." And the LORD put a mark
on Cain, so that no one who came
upon him would kill him. 16 Then
Cain went away from the presence
of the LORD, and settled in the land
of Nod,[q] east of Eden.

Beginnings of Civilization

17 Cain knew his wife, and she
conceived and bore Enoch; and he
built a city, and named it Enoch after his son Enoch. 18 To Enoch was
born Irad; and Irad was the father
of Mehujael, and Mehujael the father of Methushael, and Methushael the father of Lamech. 19 Lamech took two wives; the name of
the one was Adah, and the name of
the other Zillah. 20 Adah bore Jabal;
he was the ancestor of those who
live in tents and have livestock.
21 His brother's name was Jubal; he
was the ancestor of all those who
play the lyre and pipe. 22 Zillah bore
Tubal-cain, who made all kinds of
bronze and iron tools. The sister of
Tubal-cain was Naamah.

23 Lamech said to his wives:
"Adah and Zillah, hear my
voice;
you wives of Lamech, listen
to what I say:
I have killed a man for
wounding me,
a young man for striking
me.
24 If Cain is avenged sevenfold,
truly Lamech
seventy-sevenfold."

25 Adam knew his wife again,
and she bore a son and named him
Seth, for she said, "God has appointed[r] for me another child instead of Abel, because Cain killed
him." 26 To Seth also a son was
born, and he named him Enosh. At
that time people began to invoke
the name of the LORD.

3.24 Gen 2.8,9
4.2 Lk 11.50,51
4.3 Num 18.12
4.4 Num 18.17; Lev 3.16; Heb 11.4
4.5 Isa 3.9; Jude 11
4.8 Mt 23.35; 1 Jn 3.12
4.10 Heb 12.24; Rev 6.10
4.12 v. 14
4.14 Ps 51.11; Gen 9.6; Num 35.19, 21,27
4.15 Ps 79.12; Ezek 9.4,6
4.17 Ps 49.11
4.18 Gen 5.25, 28,30
4.23 Ex 20.13; Lev 19.18; Deut 32.35; Lk 3.36; v. 18
4.24 v. 15
4.25 Gen 5.3; v. 8
4.26 1 Kings 18.24; Ps 116.17; Joel 2.32; Zeph 3.9; 1 Cor 1.2

[n] The verb in Heb resembles the word for *Cain* [o] Sam Gk Syr Compare Vg: MT lacks *Let us go out to the field* [p] Gk Syr Vg: Heb *Therefore* [q] That is *Wandering* [r] The verb in Heb resembles the word for *Seth*

Adam's Descendants to Noah and His Sons

5 This is the list of the descendants of Adam. When God created humankind,[s] he made them[t]
in the likeness of God. 2 Male and
female he created them, and he
blessed them and named them
"Humankind"[s] when they were
created.
3 When Adam had lived one
hundred thirty years, he became
the father of a son in his likeness,
according to his image, and named
him Seth. 4 The days of Adam after
he became the father of Seth were
eight hundred years; and he had
other sons and daughters. 5 Thus
all the days that Adam lived were
nine hundred thirty years; and he
died.
6 When Seth had lived one hundred five years, he became the father of Enosh. 7 Seth lived after the
birth of Enosh eight hundred seven
years, and had other sons and
daughters. 8 Thus all the days of
Seth were nine hundred twelve
years; and he died.
9 When Enosh had lived ninety
years, he became the father of Kenan. 10 Enosh lived after the birth
of Kenan eight hundred fifteen
years, and had other sons and
daughters. 11 Thus all the days of
Enosh were nine hundred five
years; and he died.
12 When Kenan had lived seventy years, he became the father of
Mahalalel. 13 Kenan lived after the
birth of Mahalalel eight hundred
and forty years, and had other sons
and daughters. 14 Thus all the days
of Kenan were nine hundred and
ten years; and he died.
15 When Mahalalel had lived
sixty-five years, he became the father of Jared. 16 Mahalalel lived after the birth of Jared eight hundred
thirty years, and had other sons
and daughters. 17 Thus all the days
of Mahalalel were eight hundred
ninety-five years; and he died.
18 When Jared had lived one
hundred sixty-two years he became
the father of Enoch. 19 Jared lived
after the birth of Enoch eight hundred years, and had other sons and
daughters. 20 Thus all the days of
Jared were nine hundred sixty-two
years; and he died.
21 When Enoch had lived sixty-
five years, he became the father of
Methuselah. 22 Enoch walked with
God after the birth of Methuselah
three hundred years, and had other
sons and daughters. 23 Thus all the
days of Enoch were three hundred
sixty-five years. 24 Enoch walked
with God; then he was no more, because God took him.
25 When Methuselah had lived
one hundred eighty-seven years, he
became the father of Lamech.
26 Methuselah lived after the birth
of Lamech seven hundred eighty-
two years, and had other sons and
daughters. 27 Thus all the days of
Methuselah were nine hundred
sixty-nine years; and he died.
28 When Lamech had lived one
hundred eighty-two years, he became the father of a son; 29 he
named him Noah, saying, "Out of
the ground that the LORD has
cursed this one shall bring us relief
from our work and from the toil of
our hands." 30 Lamech lived after
the birth of Noah five hundred
ninety-five years, and had other
sons and daughters. 31 Thus all the
days of Lamech were seven hundred seventy-seven years; and he
died.
32 After Noah was five hundred
years old, Noah became the father
of Shem, Ham, and Japheth.

The Wickedness of Humankind

6 When people began to multiply on the face of the ground,
and daughters were born to them,
2 the sons of God saw that they
were fair; and they took wives for
themselves of all that they chose.
3 Then the LORD said, "My spirit
shall not abide[u] in mortals forever,
for they are flesh; their days shall
be one hundred twenty years."
4 The Nephilim were on the earth in
those days—and also afterward—

5.1 Gen 1.26; Eph 4.24; Col 3.10
5.2 Gen 1.27
5.3 Gen 4.25
5.5 Gen 3.19; Heb 9.27
5.6 Gen 4.26
5.7 Lk 3.38
5.11 1 Chr 1.1
5.12 1 Chr 1.2
5.15 1 Chr 1.2
5.18 Jude 14,15
5.21 1 Chr 1.3; Lk 3.37; Jude 14
5.24 2 Kings 2.11; Heb 11.5
5.26 Lk 3.36
5.29 Gen 3.17-19
5.32 Gen 6.10; 10.21
6.1 Gen 1.28
6.2 Deut 7.1-4
6.3 1 Pet 3.19; Ps 78.39

[s] Heb *adam* [t] Heb *him* [u] Meaning of Heb uncertain

when the sons of God went in to
the daughters of humans, who bore
children to them. These were the
heroes that were of old, warriors of
renown.
5 The LORD saw that the wickedness of humankind was great in the
earth, and that every inclination of
the thoughts of their hearts was
only evil continually. 6 And the
LORD was sorry that he had made
humankind on the earth, and it
grieved him to his heart. 7 So the
LORD said, "I will blot out from the
earth the human beings I have
created—people together with animals and creeping things and birds
of the air, for I am sorry that I have
made them." 8 But Noah found favor in the sight of the LORD.

Noah Pleases God

9 These are the descendants of
Noah. Noah was a righteous man,
blameless in his generation; Noah
walked with God. 10 And Noah had
three sons, Shem, Ham, and Japheth.
11 Now the earth was corrupt in
God's sight, and the earth was
filled with violence. 12 And God saw
that the earth was corrupt; for all
flesh had corrupted its ways upon
the earth. 13 And God said to Noah,
"I have determined to make an end
of all flesh, for the earth is filled
with violence because of them;
now I am going to destroy them
along with the earth. 14 Make yourself an ark of cypress[v] wood; make
rooms in the ark, and cover it inside and out with pitch. 15 This is
how you are to make it: the length
of the ark three hundred cubits, its
width fifty cubits, and its height
thirty cubits. 16 Make a roof[w] for
the ark, and finish it to a cubit
above; and put the door of the ark
in its side; make it with lower, second, and third decks. 17 For my
part, I am going to bring a flood of
waters on the earth, to destroy
from under heaven all flesh in
which is the breath of life; everything that is on the earth shall die.
18 But I will establish my covenant
with you; and you shall come into

6.5 Gen 8.21
6.6 1 Sam 15.11, 29; 2 Sam 24.16; Mal 3.6; Jas 1.17; Isa 63.10
6.8 Gen 19.19; Ex 33.12; Lk 1.30; Acts 7.46
6.9 Gen 17.1; Ezek 14.14, 20; Heb 11.7; 2 Pet 2.5; Gen 5.22
6.10 Gen 5.32
6.11 Rom 2.13; Ezek 8.17
6.12 Ps 14.1-3
6.13 Ezek 7.2,3; v. 17
6.14 Heb 11.7; 1 Pet 3.20
6.17 Gen 7.4, 21-23
6.18 Gen 7.1,7, 13; 1 Pet 3.20; 2 Pet 2.5
6.19 Gen 7.8,9, 15,16
6.20 Gen 7.9,15
6.22 Heb 11.7; Gen 7.5
7.1 Mt 24.38; Lk 17.26
7.2 Lev ch. 11; 10.10; Ezek 44.23
7.7 Gen 6.22; v. 1
7.11 Gen 8.2; Prov 8.28; Ezek 26.19

the ark, you, your sons, your wife,
and your sons' wives with you.
19 And of every living thing, of all
flesh, you shall bring two of every
kind into the ark, to keep them
alive with you; they shall be male
and female. 20 Of the birds according to their kinds, and of the animals according to their kinds, of
every creeping thing of the ground
according to its kind, two of every
kind shall come in to you, to keep
them alive. 21 Also take with you every kind of food that is eaten, and
store it up; and it shall serve as
food for you and for them." 22 Noah
did this; he did all that God commanded him.

The Great Flood

7 Then the LORD said to Noah,
"Go into the ark, you and all
your household, for I have seen
that you alone are righteous before
me in this generation. 2 Take with
you seven pairs of all clean animals, the male and its mate; and a
pair of the animals that are not
clean, the male and its mate; 3 and
seven pairs of the birds of the air
also, male and female, to keep
their kind alive on the face of all
the earth. 4 For in seven days I will
send rain on the earth for forty days
and forty nights; and every living
thing that I have made I will blot
out from the face of the ground."
5 And Noah did all that the LORD
had commanded him.
6 Noah was six hundred years
old when the flood of waters came
on the earth. 7 And Noah with his
sons and his wife and his sons'
wives went into the ark to escape
the waters of the flood. 8 Of clean
animals, and of animals that are
not clean, and of birds, and of everything that creeps on the ground,
9 two and two, male and female,
went into the ark with Noah, as
God had commanded Noah. 10 And
after seven days the waters of the
flood came on the earth.
11 In the six hundredth year of
Noah's life, in the second month,
on the seventeenth day of the

[v] Meaning of Heb uncertain [w] Or *window*

month, on that day all the fountains of the great deep burst forth,
and the windows of the heavens
were opened. 12 The rain fell on the
earth forty days and forty nights.
13 On the very same day Noah with
his sons, Shem and Ham and Japheth, and Noah's wife and the
three wives of his sons entered the
ark, 14 they and every wild animal of
every kind, and all domestic animals of every kind, and every creeping thing that creeps on the earth,
and every bird of every kind—every
bird, every winged creature. 15 They
went into the ark with Noah, two
and two of all flesh in which there
was the breath of life. 16 And those
that entered, male and female of
all flesh, went in as God had commanded him; and the LORD shut
him in.

17 The flood continued forty
days on the earth; and the waters
increased, and bore up the ark, and
it rose high above the earth. 18 The
waters swelled and increased
greatly on the earth; and the ark
floated on the face of the waters.
19 The waters swelled so mightily
on the earth that all the high
mountains under the whole heaven
were covered; 20 the waters swelled
above the mountains, covering
them fifteen cubits deep. 21 And all
flesh died that moved on the earth,
birds, domestic animals, wild animals, all swarming creatures that
swarm on the earth, and all human
beings; 22 everything on dry land in
whose nostrils was the breath of
life died. 23 He blotted out every living thing that was on the face of the
ground, human beings and animals
and creeping things and birds of
the air; they were blotted out from
the earth. Only Noah was left, and
those that were with him in the ark.
24 And the waters swelled on the
earth for one hundred fifty days.

The Flood Subsides

8 But God remembered Noah
and all the wild animals and
all the domestic animals that were
with him in the ark. And God made
a wind blow over the earth, and the
waters subsided; 2 the fountains of
the deep and the windows of the
heavens were closed, the rain from
the heavens was restrained, 3 and
the waters gradually receded from
the earth. At the end of one hundred fifty days the waters had abated; 4 and in the seventh month, on
the seventeenth day of the month,
the ark came to rest on the mountains of Ararat. 5 The waters continued to abate until the tenth month;
in the tenth month, on the first day
of the month, the tops of the
mountains appeared.

6 At the end of forty days Noah
opened the window of the ark that
he had made 7 and sent out the raven; and it went to and fro until the
waters were dried up from the
earth. 8 Then he sent out the dove
from him, to see if the waters had
subsided from the face of the
ground; 9 but the dove found no
place to set its foot, and it returned
to him to the ark, for the waters
were still on the face of the whole
earth. So he put out his hand and
took it and brought it into the ark
with him. 10 He waited another sev-
en days, and again he sent out the
dove from the ark; 11 and the dove
came back to him in the evening,
and there in its beak was a freshly
plucked olive leaf; so Noah knew
that the waters had subsided from
the earth. 12 Then he waited another seven days, and sent out the
dove; and it did not return to him
any more.

13 In the six hundred first year,
in the first month, the first day of
the month, the waters were dried
up from the earth; and Noah removed the covering of the ark, and
looked, and saw that the face of the
ground was drying. 14 In the second
month, on the twenty-seventh day
of the month, the earth was dry.
15 Then God said to Noah, 16 "Go
out of the ark, you and your wife,
and your sons and your sons' wives
with you. 17 Bring out with you every living thing that is with you of
all flesh—birds and animals and
every creeping thing that creeps
on the earth—so that they may

7.12 vv. 4,17
7.13 vv. 1,7; 6.18
7.15 Gen 6.20
7.16 vv. 2,3
7.17 vv. 4,12
7.18 Ps 104.26
7.21 Gen 6.13,17
7.22 Gen 2.7
7.23 1 Pet 3.20; 2 Pet 2.5
7.24 Gen 8.3
8.1 Gen 19.29; Ex 2.24; 1 Sam 1.19; Ex 14.21; Job 12.15; Ps 29.10; Isa 44.27; Nah 1.4
8.2 Gen 7.11; Job 38.37
8.3 Gen 7.24
8.4 Jer 51.27
8.6 2 Pet 2.5
8.7 1 Kings 17.4, 6
8.11 Mt 10.16
8.13 2 Pet 3.5,6
8.16 Gen 7.13
8.17 Gen 1.22

abound on the earth, and be fruitful and multiply on the earth." 18 So
Noah went out with his sons and
his wife and his sons' wives. 19 And
every animal, every creeping thing,
and every bird, everything that
moves on the earth, went out of the
ark by families.

God's Promise to Noah

20 Then Noah built an altar to
the LORD, and took of every clean
animal and of every clean bird, and
offered burnt offerings on the altar.
21 And when the LORD smelled the
pleasing odor, the LORD said in his
heart, "I will never again curse the
ground because of humankind, for
the inclination of the human heart
is evil from youth; nor will I ever
again destroy every living creature
as I have done.
22 As long as the earth endures,
seedtime and harvest, cold
and heat,
summer and winter, day and
night,
shall not cease."

The Covenant with Noah

9 God blessed Noah and his
sons, and said to them, "Be
fruitful and multiply, and fill the
earth. 2 The fear and dread of you
shall rest on every animal of the
earth, and on every bird of the air,
on everything that creeps on the
ground, and on all the fish of the
sea; into your hand they are delivered. 3 Every moving thing that
lives shall be food for you; and just
as I gave you the green plants, I give
you everything. 4 Only, you shall
not eat flesh with its life, that is, its
blood. 5 For your own lifeblood I
will surely require a reckoning:
from every animal I will require it
and from human beings, each one
for the blood of another, I will require a reckoning for human life.
6 Whoever sheds the blood of
a human,
by a human shall that
person's blood be shed;
for in his own image
God made humankind.
7 And you, be fruitful and multiply,

8.20 Gen 12.7,8; 13.18; 22.9; 7.2; 22.2; Ex 10.25
8.21 Lev 1.9; 2 Cor 2.15; Gen 3.17; 6.17; 9.11,15
8.22 Isa 54.9; Jer 33.20,25
9.1 v. 7; Gen 1.28
9.3 Deut 12.15; Gen 1.29
9.4 Lev 17.10-16; Deut 12.23; 1 Sam 14.33
9.5 Ex 21.28; Gen 4.9,10
9.6 Ex 21.12, 14; Lev 24.17; Mt 26.52; Gen 1.27
9.7 vv. 1,19
9.9 Gen 6.18; Isa 54.9
9.10 Ps 149.9
9.11 Isa 54.9
9.12 Gen 17.11
9.13 Ezek 1.28; Rev 4.3
9.15 Lev 26.42, 45; Deut 7.9
9.16 Gen 17.13, 19
9.18 Gen 10.6
9.19 Gen 5.32
9.23 Ex 20.12

abound on the earth and multiply
in it."
8 Then God said to Noah and to
his sons with him, 9 "As for me, I
am establishing my covenant with
you and your descendants after
you, 10 and with every living creature that is with you, the birds, the
domestic animals, and every animal of the earth with you, as many
as came out of the ark.[x] 11 I establish my covenant with you, that
never again shall all flesh be cut off
by the waters of a flood, and never
again shall there be a flood to destroy the earth." 12 God said, "This
is the sign of the covenant that I
make between me and you and every living creature that is with you,
for all future generations: 13 I have
set my bow in the clouds, and it
shall be a sign of the covenant between me and the earth. 14 When I
bring clouds over the earth and the
bow is seen in the clouds, 15 I will
remember my covenant that is between me and you and every living
creature of all flesh; and the waters
shall never again become a flood to
destroy all flesh. 16 When the bow is
in the clouds, I will see it and remember the everlasting covenant
between God and every living creature of all flesh that is on the
earth." 17 God said to Noah, "This
is the sign of the covenant that I
have established between me and
all flesh that is on the earth."

Noah and His Sons

18 The sons of Noah who went
out of the ark were Shem, Ham,
and Japheth. Ham was the father of
Canaan. 19 These three were the
sons of Noah; and from these the
whole earth was peopled.
20 Noah, a man of the soil, was
the first to plant a vineyard. 21 He
drank some of the wine and became drunk, and he lay uncovered
in his tent. 22 And Ham, the father
of Canaan, saw the nakedness of
his father, and told his two brothers outside. 23 Then Shem and Japheth took a garment, laid it on
both their shoulders, and walked

[x] Gk: Heb adds *every animal of the earth*

backward and covered the nakedness of their father; their faces
were turned away, and they did not
see their father's nakedness.
24 When Noah awoke from his wine
and knew what his youngest son
had done to him, 25 he said,
"Cursed be Canaan;
lowest of slaves shall he be
to his brothers."
26 He also said,
"Blessed by the LORD my God
be Shem;
and let Canaan be his
slave.
27 May God make space for[y]
Japheth,
and let him live in the
tents of Shem;
and let Canaan be his
slave."
28 After the flood Noah lived
three hundred fifty years. 29 All the
days of Noah were nine hundred
fifty years; and he died.

Nations Descended from Noah

10 These are the descendants
of Noah's sons, Shem,
Ham, and Japheth; children were
born to them after the flood.
2 The descendants of Japheth:
Gomer, Magog, Madai, Javan, Tubal, Meshech, and Tiras. 3 The descendants of Gomer: Ashkenaz,
Riphath, and Togarmah. 4 The
descendants of Javan: Elishah,
Tarshish, Kittim, and Rodanim.[z]
5 From these the coastland peoples
spread. These are the descendants
of Japheth[a] in their lands, with
their own language, by their families, in their nations.
6 The descendants of Ham:
Cush, Egypt, Put, and Canaan.
7 The descendants of Cush: Seba,
Havilah, Sabtah, Raamah, and Sab-
teca. The descendants of Raamah:
Sheba and Dedan. 8 Cush became
the father of Nimrod; he was the
first on earth to become a mighty
warrior. 9 He was a mighty hunter
before the LORD; therefore it is said,
"Like Nimrod a mighty hunter before the LORD." 10 The beginning of
his kingdom was Babel, Erech, and
Accad, all of them in the land of
Shinar. 11 From that land he went
into Assyria, and built Nineveh,
Rehoboth-ir, Calah, and 12 Resen
between Nineveh and Calah; that
is the great city. 13 Egypt became
the father of Ludim, Anamim, Lehabim, Naphtuhim, 14 Pathrusim,
Casluhim, and Caphtorim, from
which the Philistines come.[b]
15 Canaan became the father of
Sidon his firstborn, and Heth,
16 and the Jebusites, the Amorites,
the Girgashites, 17 the Hivites, the
Arkites, the Sinites, 18 the Arvad-
ites, the Zemarites, and the Ha-
mathites. Afterward the families of
the Canaanites spread abroad.
19 And the territory of the Canaanites extended from Sidon, in the direction of Gerar, as far as Gaza, and
in the direction of Sodom, Gomorrah, Admah, and Zeboiim, as far as
Lasha. 20 These are the descendants of Ham, by their families,
their languages, their lands, and
their nations.
21 To Shem also, the father of
all the children of Eber, the elder
brother of Japheth, children were
born. 22 The descendants of Shem:
Elam, Asshur, Arpachshad, Lud,
and Aram. 23 The descendants of
Aram: Uz, Hul, Gether, and Mash.
24 Arpachshad became the father of
Shelah; and Shelah became the father of Eber. 25 To Eber were born
two sons: the name of the one was
Peleg,[c] for in his days the earth
was divided, and his brother's
name was Joktan. 26 Joktan became the father of Almodad, Sheleph, Hazarmaveth, Jerah, 27 Hadoram, Uzal, Diklah, 28 Obal,
Abimael, Sheba, 29 Ophir, Havilah,
and Jobab; all these were the descendants of Joktan. 30 The territory in which they lived extended
from Mesha in the direction of Se-
phar, the hill country of the east.
31 These are the descendants of
Shem, by their families, their lan-

9.25 Deut 27.16
9.26 Ps 144.15
9.27 Eph 2.13, 14; 3.6
10.2 1 Chr 1.5-7
10.5 Gen 5.32
10.6 1 Chr 1.8-10
10.9 Mic 5.6
10.10 Mic 5.6
10.13 1 Chr 1.8, 11
10.15 1 Chr 1.13
10.18 1 Chr 1.16; 18.3
10.19 Num 34.2-12
10.22 1 Chr 1.17; Gen 14.1,9; 2 Kings 15.29; Gen 11.10; Isa 66.19
10.23 Job 1.1
10.24 Gen 11.12; Lk 3.35
10.25 1 Chr 1.19
10.26-29 1 Chr 1.20-23

[y] Heb *yapht*, a play on *Japheth*
[z] Heb Mss Sam Gk See 1 Chr 1.7: MT *Dodanim*
[a] Compare verses 20, 31. Heb lacks *These are the descendants of Japheth*
[b] Cn: Heb *Casluhim, from which the Philistines come, and Caphtorim*
[c] That is *Division*

guages, their lands, and their nations.

32 These are the families of Noah's sons, according to their genealogies, in their nations; and from these the nations spread abroad on the earth after the flood.

The Tower of Babel

11 Now the whole earth had one language and the same words. 2 And as they migrated from the east,[d] they came upon a plain in the land of Shinar and settled there. 3 And they said to one another, "Come, let us make bricks, and burn them thoroughly." And they had brick for stone, and bitumen for mortar. 4 Then they said, "Come, let us build ourselves a city, and a tower with its top in the heavens, and let us make a name for ourselves; otherwise we shall be scattered abroad upon the face of the whole earth." 5 The LORD came down to see the city and the tower, which mortals had built. 6 And the LORD said, "Look, they are one people, and they have all one language; and this is only the beginning of what they will do; nothing that they propose to do will now be impossible for them. 7 Come, let us go down, and confuse their language there, so that they will not understand one another's speech." 8 So the LORD scattered them abroad from there over the face of all the earth, and they left off building the city. 9 Therefore it was called Babel, because there the LORD confused[e] the language of all the earth; and from there the LORD scattered them abroad over the face of all the earth.

Descendants of Shem

10 These are the descendants of Shem. When Shem was one hundred years old, he became the father of Arpachshad two years after the flood; 11 and Shem lived after the birth of Arpachshad five hundred years, and had other sons and daughters.

12 When Arpachshad had lived thirty-five years, he became the father of Shelah; 13 and Arpachshad lived after the birth of Shelah four hundred three years, and had other sons and daughters.

14 When Shelah had lived thirty years, he became the father of Eber; 15 and Shelah lived after the birth of Eber four hundred three years, and had other sons and daughters.

16 When Eber had lived thirty-four years, he became the father of Peleg; 17 and Eber lived after the birth of Peleg four hundred thirty years, and had other sons and daughters.

18 When Peleg had lived thirty years, he became the father of Reu; 19 and Peleg lived after the birth of Reu two hundred nine years, and had other sons and daughters.

20 When Reu had lived thirty-two years, he became the father of Serug; 21 and Reu lived after the birth of Serug two hundred seven years, and had other sons and daughters.

22 When Serug had lived thirty years, he became the father of Nahor; 23 and Serug lived after the birth of Nahor two hundred years, and had other sons and daughters.

24 When Nahor had lived twenty-nine years, he became the father of Terah; 25 and Nahor lived after the birth of Terah one hundred nineteen years, and had other sons and daughters.

26 When Terah had lived seventy years, he became the father of Abram, Nahor, and Haran.

Descendants of Terah

27 Now these are the descendants of Terah. Terah was the father of Abram, Nahor, and Haran; and Haran was the father of Lot. 28 Haran died before his father Terah in the land of his birth, in Ur of the Chaldeans. 29 Abram and Nahor took wives; the name of Abram's wife was Sarai, and the name of Nahor's wife was Milcah. She was the daughter of Haran the father of

10.32 v. 1
11.2 Ex 1.11,14; 5.7-19
11.4ff Deut 1.28
11.5 Gen 18.21
11.6 Acts 17.26; Gen 9.19
11.7 Gen 1.26; 42.23; Ex 4.11; 1 Cor 14.2, 11
11.8 Lk 1.51; Gen 10.25, 32
11.9 Gen 10.10
11.10 Gen 10.22; 1 Chr 1.17
11.12 Lk 3.36
11.16 1 Chr 1.19
11.20 Lk 3.35
11.24 Lk 3.34
11.26 Josh 24.2
11.29 Gen 24.10; 17.15; 20.12; 22.20

[d] Or *migrated eastward* [e] Heb *balal*, meaning *to confuse*

Milcah and Iscah. 30 Now Sarai was
barren; she had no child.
31 Terah took his son Abram
and his grandson Lot son of Haran,
and his daughter-in-law Sarai, his
son Abram's wife, and they went
out together from Ur of the Chaldeans to go into the land of Canaan;
but when they came to Haran, they
settled there. 32 The days of Terah
were two hundred five years; and
Terah died in Haran.

The Call of Abram

12 Now the LORD said to
Abram, "Go from your
country and your kindred and your
father's house to the land that I will
show you. 2 I will make of you a
great nation, and I will bless you,
and make your name great, so that
you will be a blessing. 3 I will bless
those who bless you, and the one
who curses you I will curse; and in
you all the families of the earth
shall be blessed."[f]
4 So Abram went, as the LORD
had told him; and Lot went with
him. Abram was seventy-five years
old when he departed from Haran.
5 Abram took his wife Sarai and his
brother's son Lot, and all the possessions that they had gathered,
and the persons whom they had acquired in Haran; and they set forth
to go to the land of Canaan. When
they had come to the land of Canaan, 6 Abram passed through the
land to the place at Shechem, to
the oak[g] of Moreh. At that time
the Canaanites were in the land.
7 Then the LORD appeared to
Abram, and said, "To your offspring[h] I will give this land." So he
built there an altar to the LORD,
who had appeared to him. 8 From
there he moved on to the hill country on the east of Bethel, and
pitched his tent, with Bethel on the
west and Ai on the east; and there
he built an altar to the LORD and
invoked the name of the LORD.
9 And Abram journeyed on by
stages toward the Negeb.

Abram and Sarai in Egypt

10 Now there was a famine in
the land. So Abram went down to
Egypt to reside there as an alien,
for the famine was severe in the
land. 11 When he was about to enter
Egypt, he said to his wife Sarai, "I
know well that you are a woman
beautiful in appearance; 12 and
when the Egyptians see you, they
will say, 'This is his wife'; then they
will kill me, but they will let you
live. 13 Say you are my sister, so that
it may go well with me because of
you, and that my life may be spared
on your account." 14 When Abram
entered Egypt the Egyptians saw
that the woman was very beautiful.
15 When the officials of Pharaoh
saw her, they praised her to Pharaoh. And the woman was taken
into Pharaoh's house. 16 And for
her sake he dealt well with Abram;
and he had sheep, oxen, male donkeys, male and female slaves, female donkeys, and camels.
17 But the LORD afflicted Pharaoh and his house with great
plagues because of Sarai, Abram's
wife. 18 So Pharaoh called Abram,
and said, "What is this you have
done to me? Why did you not tell
me that she was your wife? 19 Why
did you say, 'She is my sister,' so
that I took her for my wife? Now
then, here is your wife, take her,
and be gone." 20 And Pharaoh gave
his men orders concerning him;
and they set him on the way, with
his wife and all that he had.

Abram and Lot Separate

13 So Abram went up from
Egypt, he and his wife, and
all that he had, and Lot with him,
into the Negeb.
2 Now Abram was very rich in
livestock, in silver, and in gold. 3 He
journeyed on by stages from the
Negeb as far as Bethel, to the place
where his tent had been at the beginning, between Bethel and Ai,
4 to the place where he had made
an altar at the first; and there
Abram called on the name of the
LORD. 5 Now Lot, who went with

11.30 Gen 16.1
11.31 Gen 15.7; Neh 9.7; Acts 7.4
12.1 Acts 7.3; Heb 11.8
12.2 Gen 15.5; 17.4,5; 18.18; 22.17; 28.14; 32.12; 35.11; 46.3
12.3 Gen 27.29; Ex 23.22; Num 24.9; Gen 18.18; 22.18; 26.4; Acts 3.25; Gal 3.8
12.4 Gen 11.27, 31
12.5 Gen 14.14; 11.31
12.6 Heb 11.9; Deut 11.30; Gen 10.18, 19
12.7 Gen 17.1; 13.15; 17.8; Ps 105.9; Gen 13.4
12.8 Gen 13.4
12.12 Gen 20.11
12.13 Gen 20.5,13
12.15 Gen 20.2
12.16 Gen 20.14
12.17 Gen 20.18; 1 Chr 16.21; Ps 105.14
12.18 Gen 20.9,10
12.20 Prov 21.1
13.1 Gen 12.9
13.3 Gen 12.8,9
13.4 Gen 12.7,8

[f] Or *by you all the families of the earth shall bless themselves* [g] Or *terebinth*
[h] Heb *seed*

Abram, also had flocks and herds
and tents, 6 so that the land could
not support both of them living together; for their possessions were
so great that they could not live together, 7 and there was strife between the herders of Abram's livestock and the herders of Lot's
livestock. At that time the Canaanites and the Perizzites lived in the
land.
8 Then Abram said to Lot, "Let
there be no strife between you and
me, and between your herders and
my herders; for we are kindred. 9 Is
not the whole land before you?
Separate yourself from me. If you
take the left hand, then I will go to
the right; or if you take the right
hand, then I will go to the left."
10 Lot looked about him, and saw
that the plain of the Jordan was
well watered everywhere like the
garden of the LORD, like the land of
Egypt, in the direction of Zoar; this
was before the LORD had destroyed
Sodom and Gomorrah. 11 So Lot
chose for himself all the plain of
the Jordan, and Lot journeyed
eastward; thus they separated from
each other. 12 Abram settled in the
land of Canaan, while Lot settled
among the cities of the Plain and
moved his tent as far as Sodom.
13 Now the people of Sodom were
wicked, great sinners against the
LORD.
14 The LORD said to Abram, after
Lot had separated from him,
"Raise your eyes now, and look
from the place where you are,
northward and southward and
eastward and westward; 15 for all
the land that you see I will give to
you and to your offspring[i] forever.
16 I will make your offspring like the
dust of the earth; so that if one can
count the dust of the earth, your
offspring also can be counted.
17 Rise up, walk through the length
and the breadth of the land, for I
will give it to you." 18 So Abram
moved his tent, and came and settled by the oaks[j] of Mamre, which
are at Hebron; and there he built
an altar to the LORD.

13.7 Gen 26.20 **13.8** Prov 15.18; 20.3 **13.10** Gen 19.17-29; Deut 34.3; Gen 2.8; 47.6; 14.8 **13.12** Gen 19.29 **13.13** Gen 18.20; 2 Pet 2.7,8 **13.14** Gen 28.14; Deut 3.27 **13.15** Gen 12.7; 17.8; Deut 34.3; Acts 7.5; 2 Chr 20.7 **13.16** Gen 16.10; 28.14 **13.17** Num 13.17-24 **13.18** Gen 14.13; 35.27

14.1 Isa 11.11; Dan 8.2 **14.2** Gen 10.19; Deut 29.23; Gen 13.10 **14.3** Num 34.12; Deut 3.17; Josh 3.16 **14.5** Gen 15.20; Deut 2.20 **14.6** Deut 2.12, 22 **14.7** 2 Chr 20.2 **14.11** vv. 16,21 **14.12** Gen 12.5; 13.12 **14.13** Gen 13.18; v. 24

Lot's Captivity and Rescue

14 In the days of King Amraphel of Shinar, King Arioch
of Ellasar, King Chedorlaomer of
Elam, and King Tidal of Goiim,
2 these kings made war with King
Bera of Sodom, King Birsha of Gomorrah, King Shinab of Admah,
King Shemeber of Zeboiim, and the
king of Bela (that is, Zoar). 3 All
these joined forces in the Valley of
Siddim (that is, the Dead Sea).[k]
4 Twelve years they had served
Chedorlaomer, but in the thirteenth year they rebelled. 5 In the
fourteenth year Chedorlaomer and
the kings who were with him came
and subdued the Rephaim in
Ashteroth-karnaim, the Zuzim in
Ham, the Emim in Shaveh-
kiriathaim, 6 and the Horites in the
hill country of Seir as far as El-
paran on the edge of the wilderness; 7 then they turned back and
came to En-mishpat (that is, Kadesh), and subdued all the country
of the Amalekites, and also the
Amorites who lived in Hazazon-
tamar. 8 Then the king of Sodom,
the king of Gomorrah, the king of
Admah, the king of Zeboiim, and
the king of Bela (that is, Zoar) went
out, and they joined battle in the
Valley of Siddim 9 with King Chedorlaomer of Elam, King Tidal of
Goiim, King Amraphel of Shinar,
and King Arioch of Ellasar, four
kings against five. 10 Now the Valley
of Siddim was full of bitumen pits;
and as the kings of Sodom and Gomorrah fled, some fell into them,
and the rest fled to the hill country.
11 So the enemy took all the goods
of Sodom and Gomorrah, and all
their provisions, and went their
way; 12 they also took Lot, the son
of Abram's brother, who lived in
Sodom, and his goods, and departed.
13 Then one who had escaped
came and told Abram the Hebrew,
who was living by the oaks[j] of
Mamre the Amorite, brother of
Eshcol and of Aner; these were al-

[i] Heb *seed* [j] Or *terebinths* [k] Heb *Salt Sea*

lies of Abram. 14 When Abram
heard that his nephew had been
taken captive, he led forth his
trained men, born in his house,
three hundred eighteen of them,
and went in pursuit as far as Dan.
15 He divided his forces against
them by night, he and his servants,
and routed them and pursued them
to Hobah, north of Damascus.
16 Then he brought back all the
goods, and also brought back his
nephew Lot with his goods, and the
women and the people.

Abram Blessed by Melchizedek

17 After his return from the defeat of Chedorlaomer and the kings
who were with him, the king of
Sodom went out to meet him at the
Valley of Shaveh (that is, the King's
Valley). 18 And King Melchizedek of
Salem brought out bread and wine;
he was priest of God Most High.[l]
19 He blessed him and said,

"Blessed be Abram by God
Most High,[l]
maker of heaven and earth;
20 and blessed be God Most
High,[l]
who has delivered your
enemies into your
hand!"

And Abram gave him one tenth of
everything. 21 Then the king of Sodom said to Abram, "Give me the
persons, but take the goods for
yourself." 22 But Abram said to the
king of Sodom, "I have sworn to the
LORD, God Most High,[l] maker of
heaven and earth, 23 that I would
not take a thread or a sandal-thong
or anything that is yours, so that
you might not say, 'I have made
Abram rich.' 24 I will take nothing
but what the young men have eat-
en, and the share of the men who
went with me—Aner, Eshcol, and
Mamre. Let them take their share."

God's Covenant with Abram

15 After these things the word
of the LORD came to Abram
in a vision, "Do not be afraid,
Abram, I am your shield; your reward shall be very great." 2 But
Abram said, "O Lord GOD, what
will you give me, for I continue
childless, and the heir of my house
is Eliezer of Damascus?"[m] 3 And
Abram said, "You have given me no
offspring, and so a slave born in my
house is to be my heir." 4 But the
word of the LORD came to him,
"This man shall not be your heir;
no one but your very own issue
shall be your heir." 5 He brought
him outside and said, "Look toward heaven and count the stars, if
you are able to count them." Then
he said to him, "So shall your descendants be." 6 And he believed
the LORD; and the LORD[n] reckoned
it to him as righteousness.

7 Then he said to him, "I am the
LORD who brought you from Ur of
the Chaldeans, to give you this land
to possess." 8 But he said, "O Lord
GOD, how am I to know that I shall
possess it?" 9 He said to him,
"Bring me a heifer three years old,
a female goat three years old, a ram
three years old, a turtledove, and a
young pigeon." 10 He brought him
all these and cut them in two, laying each half over against the other; but he did not cut the birds in
two. 11 And when birds of prey
came down on the carcasses,
Abram drove them away.

12 As the sun was going down, a
deep sleep fell upon Abram, and a
deep and terrifying darkness descended upon him. 13 Then the
LORD[n] said to Abram, "Know this
for certain, that your offspring shall
be aliens in a land that is not
theirs, and shall be slaves there,
and they shall be oppressed for
four hundred years; 14 but I will
bring judgment on the nation that
they serve, and afterward they shall
come out with great possessions.
15 As for yourself, you shall go to
your ancestors in peace; you shall
be buried in a good old age. 16 And
they shall come back here in the
fourth generation; for the iniquity
of the Amorites is not yet complete."

17 When the sun had gone down

[l] Heb *El Elyon* [m] Meaning of Heb uncertain [n] Heb *he*

14.14 Gen 13.8; 15.3 **14.16** vv. 11,12 **14.17** 1 Sam 18.6, 18 **14.18** Heb 7.1; Ps 110.4; Heb 5.6,10 **14.19** v. 22; Mt 11.25 **14.20** Gen 24.27; Heb 7.4 **14.22** Dan 12.7; v. 19 **14.23** 2 Kings 5.16 **15.1** Dan 10.1; Gen 21.17; 26.24; Deut 33.29; Prov 11.8 **15.2f** Acts 7.5 **15.3** Gen 14.14 **15.4** Gal 4.28 **15.5** Ps 147.4; Jer 33.22; Gen 22.17; Rom 4.18; Heb 11.12 **15.7** Gen 11.31; 13.15,17 **15.8** Lk 1.18 **15.10** Jer 34.18; Lev 1.17 **15.12** Gen 2.21 **15.13** Acts 7.6; Ex 12.40 **15.14** Ex 12.36 **15.15** Gen 25.8 **15.16** 1 Kings 21.26 **15.17** Jer 34.18,19

and it was dark, a smoking fire pot
and a flaming torch passed between these pieces. 18 On that day
the LORD made a covenant with
Abram, saying, "To your descendants I give this land, from the river
of Egypt to the great river, the river
Euphrates, 19 the land of the Kenites, the Kenizzites, the Kadmon-
ites, 20 the Hittites, the Perizzites,
the Rephaim, 21 the Amorites, the
Canaanites, the Girgashites, and
the Jebusites."

The Birth of Ishmael

16 Now Sarai, Abram's wife,
bore him no children. She
had an Egyptian slave-girl whose
name was Hagar, 2 and Sarai said to
Abram, "You see that the LORD has
prevented me from bearing children; go in to my slave-girl; it may
be that I shall obtain children by
her." And Abram listened to the
voice of Sarai. 3 So, after Abram had
lived ten years in the land of Canaan, Sarai, Abram's wife, took Hagar the Egyptian, her slave-girl, and
gave her to her husband Abram as
a wife. 4 He went in to Hagar, and
she conceived; and when she saw
that she had conceived, she looked
with contempt on her mistress.
5 Then Sarai said to Abram, "May
the wrong done to me be on you! I
gave my slave-girl to your embrace,
and when she saw that she had
conceived, she looked on me with
contempt. May the LORD judge between you and me!" 6 But Abram
said to Sarai, "Your slave-girl is in
your power; do to her as you
please." Then Sarai dealt harshly
with her, and she ran away from
her.
7 The angel of the LORD found
her by a spring of water in the wilderness, the spring on the way to
Shur. 8 And he said, "Hagar, slave-
girl of Sarai, where have you come
from and where are you going?"
She said, "I am running away from
my mistress Sarai." 9 The angel of
the LORD said to her, "Return to
your mistress, and submit to her."
10 The angel of the LORD also said to
her, "I will so greatly multiply your

15.18 Gen 24.7; 12.7; Ex 23.31; Num 34.3; Deut 11.24; Josh 1.4
16.1 Gen 11.30; 21.9; Gal 4.24
16.2 Gen 30.3,4, 9,10
16.3 Gen 12.5
16.5 Gen 31.53
16.7 Gen 21.17, 18; 22.11,15; 31.11; 20.1
16.10 Gen 17.20
16.11 Ex 3.7,9
16.12 Gen 25.18
16.13 Gen 32.30
16.15 Gal 4.22
17.1 Gen 28.3; Ex 6.3; Deut 18.13
17.2 Gen 15.18
17.4 Gen 35.11; 48.19
17.5 Neh 9.7; Rom 4.17
17.6 Gen 35.11; Mt 1.6
17.7 Gal 3.17; Gen 26.24; 28.13; Rom 9.8

offspring that they cannot be
counted for multitude." 11 And the
angel of the LORD said to her,
"Now you have conceived
and shall bear a son;
you shall call him
Ishmael,[o]
for the LORD has given heed
to your affliction.
12 He shall be a wild ass of a
man,
with his hand against
everyone,
and everyone's hand
against him;
and he shall live at odds
with all his kin."
13 So she named the LORD who
spoke to her, "You are El-roi";[p] for
she said, "Have I really seen God
and remained alive after seeing
him?"[q] 14 Therefore the well was
called Beer-lahai-roi;[r] it lies between Kadesh and Bered.
15 Hagar bore Abram a son; and
Abram named his son, whom Hagar bore, Ishmael. 16 Abram was
eighty-six years old when Hagar
bore him[s] Ishmael.

The Sign of the Covenant

17 When Abram was ninety-
nine years old, the LORD appeared to Abram, and said to him,
"I am God Almighty;[t] walk before
me, and be blameless. 2 And I will
make my covenant between me
and you, and will make you exceedingly numerous." 3 Then
Abram fell on his face; and God
said to him, 4 "As for me, this is my
covenant with you: You shall be the
ancestor of a multitude of nations.
5 No longer shall your name be
Abram,[u] but your name shall be
Abraham;[v] for I have made you the
ancestor of a multitude of nations.
6 I will make you exceedingly fruitful; and I will make nations of you,
and kings shall come from you. 7 I
will establish my covenant be-

[o] That is *God hears* [p] Perhaps *God of seeing* or *God who sees* [q] Meaning of Heb uncertain [r] That is *the Well of the Living One who sees me* [s] Heb *Abram* [t] Traditional rendering of Heb *El Shaddai* [u] That is *exalted ancestor* [v] Here taken to mean *ancestor of a multitude*

tween me and you, and your offspring after you throughout their
generations, for an everlasting covenant, to be God to you and to your
offspring[w] after you. 8 And I will
give to you, and to your offspring
after you, the land where you are
now an alien, all the land of Canaan, for a perpetual holding; and
I will be their God."
9 God said to Abraham, "As for
you, you shall keep my covenant,
you and your offspring after you
throughout their generations.
10 This is my covenant, which you
shall keep, between me and you
and your offspring after you: Every
male among you shall be circumcised. 11 You shall circumcise the
flesh of your foreskins, and it shall
be a sign of the covenant between
me and you. 12 Throughout your
generations every male among you
shall be circumcised when he is
eight days old, including the slave
born in your house and the one
bought with your money from any
foreigner who is not of your offspring. 13 Both the slave born in
your house and the one bought
with your money must be circumcised. So shall my covenant be in
your flesh an everlasting covenant.
14 Any uncircumcised male who is
not circumcised in the flesh of his
foreskin shall be cut off from his
people; he has broken my covenant."
15 God said to Abraham, "As for
Sarai your wife, you shall not call
her Sarai, but Sarah shall be her
name. 16 I will bless her, and moreover I will give you a son by her. I
will bless her, and she shall give
rise to nations; kings of peoples
shall come from her." 17 Then Abraham fell on his face and laughed,
and said to himself, "Can a child be
born to a man who is a hundred
years old? Can Sarah, who is ninety
years old, bear a child?" 18 And
Abraham said to God, "O that Ishmael might live in your sight!"
19 God said, "No, but your wife Sarah shall bear you a son, and you
shall name him Isaac.[x] I will establish my covenant with him as an everlasting covenant for his offspring
after him. 20 As for Ishmael, I have
heard you; I will bless him and
make him fruitful and exceedingly
numerous; he shall be the father of
twelve princes, and I will make him
a great nation. 21 But my covenant
I will establish with Isaac, whom
Sarah shall bear to you at this season next year." 22 And when he had
finished talking with him, God
went up from Abraham.
23 Then Abraham took his son
Ishmael and all the slaves born in
his house or bought with his money, every male among the men of
Abraham's house, and he circumcised the flesh of their foreskins
that very day, as God had said to
him. 24 Abraham was ninety-nine
years old when he was circumcised
in the flesh of his foreskin. 25 And
his son Ishmael was thirteen years
old when he was circumcised in the
flesh of his foreskin. 26 That very
day Abraham and his son Ishmael
were circumcised; 27 and all the
men of his house, slaves born in
the house and those bought with
money from a foreigner, were circumcised with him.

A Son Promised to Abraham and Sarah

18 The LORD appeared to Abraham[y] by the oaks[z] of
Mamre, as he sat at the entrance of
his tent in the heat of the day. 2 He
looked up and saw three men
standing near him. When he saw
them, he ran from the tent entrance to meet them, and bowed
down to the ground. 3 He said, "My
lord, if I find favor with you, do not
pass by your servant. 4 Let a little
water be brought, and wash your
feet, and rest yourselves under the
tree. 5 Let me bring a little bread,
that you may refresh yourselves,
and after that you may pass on—
since you have come to your servant." So they said, "Do as you
have said." 6 And Abraham hastened into the tent to Sarah, and
said, "Make ready quickly three

17.8 Gen 12.7; Ps 105.9,11; Gen 23.4; 28.4; Ex 6.7; Lev 26.12
17.10 Acts 7.8
17.11 Ex 12.48; Deut 10.16; Rom 4.11
17.12 Lev 12.3; Lk 2.21
17.14 Ex 4.24
17.16 Gen 18.10; 35.11; Gal 4.31
17.17 Gen 18.12; 21.6
17.19 Gen 18.10; 21.2; 26.2-5
17.20 Gen 16.10; 25.12,16
17.23 Gen 14.14
17.24 Rom 4.11
18.1 Gen 13.18; 14.13
18.2 vv. 16,22; Gen 32.24; Josh 5.13; Judg 13.6-11
18.4 Gen 19.2; 43.24
18.5 Judg 6.18, 19; 13.15,16

w Heb *seed* x That is *he laughs*
y Heb *him* z Or *terebinths*

measures[a] of choice flour, knead
it, and make cakes." 7 Abraham ran
to the herd, and took a calf, tender
and good, and gave it to the servant, who hastened to prepare it.
8 Then he took curds and milk and
the calf that he had prepared, and
set it before them; and he stood by
them under the tree while they ate.
9 They said to him, "Where is
your wife Sarah?" And he said,
"There, in the tent." 10 Then one
said, "I will surely return to you in
due season, and your wife Sarah
shall have a son." And Sarah was
listening at the tent entrance behind him. 11 Now Abraham and Sarah were old, advanced in age; it had
ceased to be with Sarah after the
manner of women. 12 So Sarah
laughed to herself, saying, "After I
have grown old, and my husband is
old, shall I have pleasure?" 13 The
Lord said to Abraham, "Why did
Sarah laugh, and say, 'Shall I indeed bear a child, now that I am
old?' 14 Is anything too wonderful
for the Lord? At the set time I will
return to you, in due season, and
Sarah shall have a son." 15 But Sarah denied, saying, "I did not
laugh"; for she was afraid. He said,
"Oh yes, you did laugh."

Judgment Pronounced on Sodom

16 Then the men set out from
there, and they looked toward Sodom; and Abraham went with them
to set them on their way. 17 The
Lord said, "Shall I hide from Abraham what I am about to do, 18 seeing that Abraham shall become a
great and mighty nation, and all
the nations of the earth shall be
blessed in him?[b] 19 No, for I have
chosen[c] him, that he may charge
his children and his household after him to keep the way of the Lord
by doing righteousness and justice;
so that the Lord may bring about
for Abraham what he has promised
him." 20 Then the Lord said, "How
great is the outcry against Sodom
and Gomorrah and how very grave
their sin! 21 I must go down and see
whether they have done altogether

18.8 Gen 19.3 **18.10** Rom 9.9 **18.11** Gen 17.17; Rom 4.19 **18.12ff** 1 Pet 3.6 **18.14** Jer 32.17, 27; Zech 8.6; Mt 3.9; Lk 1.37 **18.18** Gal 3.8 **18.19** Deut 4.9,10; 6.7; Josh 24.15; Eph 6.4 **18.20** Gen 19.13; Ezek 16.49, 50 **18.21** Gen 11.5

18.22 Gen 19.1 **18.23** Heb 10.22; Num 16.22 **18.24** Jer 5.1 **18.25** Job 8.20; Isa 3.10,11; Rom 3.6 **18.27** Gen 3.19; Job 4.19; 30.19; 42.6; 2 Cor 5.1 **18.32** Judg 6.39; Jas 5.16

according to the outcry that has
come to me; and if not, I will
know."
22 So the men turned from
there, and went toward Sodom,
while Abraham remained standing
before the Lord.[d] 23 Then Abraham
came near and said, "Will you indeed sweep away the righteous
with the wicked? 24 Suppose there
are fifty righteous within the city;
will you then sweep away the place
and not forgive it for the fifty righteous who are in it? 25 Far be it from
you to do such a thing, to slay the
righteous with the wicked, so that
the righteous fare as the wicked!
Far be that from you! Shall not the
Judge of all the earth do what is
just?" 26 And the Lord said, "If I
find at Sodom fifty righteous in the
city, I will forgive the whole place
for their sake." 27 Abraham answered, "Let me take it upon myself to speak to the Lord, I who am
but dust and ashes. 28 Suppose five
of the fifty righteous are lacking?
Will you destroy the whole city for
lack of five?" And he said, "I will
not destroy it if I find forty-five
there." 29 Again he spoke to him,
"Suppose forty are found there."
He answered, "For the sake of forty
I will not do it." 30 Then he said,
"Oh do not let the Lord be angry if
I speak. Suppose thirty are found
there." He answered, "I will not do
it, if I find thirty there." 31 He said,
"Let me take it upon myself to
speak to the Lord. Suppose twenty
are found there." He answered,
"For the sake of twenty I will not
destroy it." 32 Then he said, "Oh do
not let the Lord be angry if I speak
just once more. Suppose ten are
found there." He answered, "For
the sake of ten I will not destroy it."
33 And the Lord went his way, when
he had finished speaking to Abraham; and Abraham returned to his
place.

[a] Heb *seahs* [b] Or *and all the nations of the earth shall bless themselves by him* [c] Heb *known* [d] Another ancient tradition reads *while the Lord remained standing before Abraham*

The Depravity of Sodom

19 The two angels came to
Sodom in the evening, and
Lot was sitting in the gateway of
Sodom. When Lot saw them, he
rose to meet them, and bowed
down with his face to the ground.
2 He said, "Please, my lords, turn
aside to your servant's house and
spend the night, and wash your
feet; then you can rise early and go
on your way." They said, "No; we
will spend the night in the square."
3 But he urged them strongly; so
they turned aside to him and entered his house; and he made them
a feast, and baked unleavened
bread, and they ate. 4 But before
they lay down, the men of the city,
the men of Sodom, both young and
old, all the people to the last man,
surrounded the house; 5 and they
called to Lot, "Where are the men
who came to you tonight? Bring
them out to us, so that we may
know them." 6 Lot went out of the
door to the men, shut the door after
him, 7 and said, "I beg you, my
brothers, do not act so wickedly.
8 Look, I have two daughters who
have not known a man; let me
bring them out to you, and do to
them as you please; only do nothing to these men, for they have
come under the shelter of my roof."
9 But they replied, "Stand back!"
And they said, "This fellow came
here as an alien, and he would play
the judge! Now we will deal worse
with you than with them." Then
they pressed hard against the man
Lot, and came near the door to
break it down. 10 But the men inside reached out their hands and
brought Lot into the house with
them, and shut the door. 11 And
they struck with blindness the men
who were at the door of the house,
both small and great, so that they
were unable to find the door.

Sodom and Gomorrah Destroyed

12 Then the men said to Lot,
"Have you anyone else here? Sons-
in-law, sons, daughters, or anyone
you have in the city—bring them
out of the place. 13 For we are about
to destroy this place, because the
outcry against its people has become great before the LORD, and
the LORD has sent us to destroy it."
14 So Lot went out and said to his
sons-in-law, who were to marry his
daughters, "Up, get out of this
place; for the LORD is about to destroy the city." But he seemed to
his sons-in-law to be jesting.
15 When morning dawned, the
angels urged Lot, saying, "Get up,
take your wife and your two daughters who are here, or else you will
be consumed in the punishment of
the city." 16 But he lingered; so the
men seized him and his wife and
his two daughters by the hand, the
LORD being merciful to him, and
they brought him out and left him
outside the city. 17 When they had
brought them outside, they[e] said,
"Flee for your life; do not look back
or stop anywhere in the Plain; flee
to the hills, or else you will be consumed." 18 And Lot said to them,
"Oh, no, my lords; 19 your servant
has found favor with you, and you
have shown me great kindness in
saving my life; but I cannot flee to
the hills, for fear the disaster will
overtake me and I die. 20 Look, that
city is near enough to flee to, and it
is a little one. Let me escape
there—is it not a little one?—and
my life will be saved!" 21 He said to
him, "Very well, I grant you this favor too, and will not overthrow the
city of which you have spoken.
22 Hurry, escape there, for I can do
nothing until you arrive there."
Therefore the city was called
Zoar.[f] 23 The sun had risen on the
earth when Lot came to Zoar.
24 Then the LORD rained on Sodom and Gomorrah sulfur and fire
from the LORD out of heaven; 25 and
he overthrew those cities, and all
the Plain, and all the inhabitants of
the cities, and what grew on the
ground. 26 But Lot's wife, behind
him, looked back, and she became
a pillar of salt.
27 Abraham went early in the
morning to the place where he had

19.1 Gen 18.22; 18.1ff **19.2** Heb 13.2; Gen 18.4 **19.3** Gen 18.8 **19.5** Isa 3.9; Judg 19.22; Rom 1.24 **19.6** Judg 19.23 **19.8** Judg 19.24 **19.9** 2 Pet 2.7, 8; Ex 2.14 **19.11** 2 Kings 6.18; Acts 13.11 **19.12** Gen 7.1; 2 Pet 2.7,9 **19.13** Gen 18.20; 1 Chr 21.15

19.14 Num 16.21; Ex 9.21; Lk 17.28 **19.15** Num 16.24, 26; Rev 18.4 **19.16** Lk 18.13; Ps 34.22 **19.17** 1 Kings 19.3; Jer 48.6; v. 26 **19.21** Job 42.8,9; Ps 145.9 **19.24** Deut 29.23; Isa 13.19; Lk 17.29; Jude 7 **19.25** Ps 107.34 **19.26** Lk 17.32 **19.27** Gen 18.22

[e] Gk Syr Vg: Heb *he* [f] That is *Little*

stood before the LORD; [28]and he
looked down toward Sodom and
Gomorrah and toward all the land
of the Plain and saw the smoke of
the land going up like the smoke of
a furnace.
29 So it was that, when God destroyed the cities of the Plain, God
remembered Abraham, and sent
Lot out of the midst of the overthrow, when he overthrew the cities in which Lot had settled.

The Shameful Origin of Moab and Ammon

30 Now Lot went up out of Zoar
and settled in the hills with his two
daughters, for he was afraid to stay
in Zoar; so he lived in a cave with
his two daughters. [31]And the firstborn said to the younger, "Our father is old, and there is not a man
on earth to come in to us after the
manner of all the world. [32]Come,
let us make our father drink wine,
and we will lie with him, so that we
may preserve offspring through our
father." [33]So they made their father drink wine that night; and the
firstborn went in, and lay with her
father; he did not know when she
lay down or when she rose. [34]On
the next day, the firstborn said to
the younger, "Look, I lay last night
with my father; let us make him
drink wine tonight also; then you
go in and lie with him, so that we
may preserve offspring through our
father." [35]So they made their father drink wine that night also; and
the younger rose, and lay with him;
and he did not know when she lay
down or when she rose. [36]Thus
both the daughters of Lot became
pregnant by their father. [37]The
firstborn bore a son, and named
him Moab; he is the ancestor of the
Moabites to this day. [38]The younger also bore a son and named him
Ben-ammi; he is the ancestor of
the Ammonites to this day.

Abraham and Sarah at Gerar

20 From there Abraham journeyed toward the region of
the Negeb, and settled between
Kadesh and Shur. While residing in
Gerar as an alien, [2]Abraham said of
his wife Sarah, "She is my sister."
And King Abimelech of Gerar sent
and took Sarah. [3]But God came to
Abimelech in a dream by night, and
said to him, "You are about to die
because of the woman whom you
have taken; for she is a married
woman." [4]Now Abimelech had not
approached her; so he said, "Lord,
will you destroy an innocent people? [5]Did he not himself say to me,
'She is my sister'? And she herself
said, 'He is my brother.' I did this in
the integrity of my heart and the
innocence of my hands." [6]Then
God said to him in the dream, "Yes,
I know that you did this in the integrity of your heart; furthermore it
was I who kept you from sinning
against me. Therefore I did not let
you touch her. [7]Now then, return
the man's wife; for he is a prophet,
and he will pray for you and you
shall live. But if you do not restore
her, know that you shall surely die,
you and all that are yours."
8 So Abimelech rose early in the
morning, and called all his servants
and told them all these things; and
the men were very much afraid.
[9]Then Abimelech called Abraham,
and said to him, "What have you
done to us? How have I sinned
against you, that you have brought
such great guilt on me and my
kingdom? You have done things to
me that ought not to be done."
[10]And Abimelech said to Abraham,
"What were you thinking of, that
you did this thing?" [11]Abraham
said, "I did it because I thought,
There is no fear of God at all in this
place, and they will kill me because
of my wife. [12]Besides, she is indeed
my sister, the daughter of my father
but not the daughter of my mother;
and she became my wife. [13]And
when God caused me to wander
from my father's house, I said to
her, 'This is the kindness you must
do me: at every place to which we
come, say of me, He is my brother.' " [14]Then Abimelech took
sheep and oxen, and male and female slaves, and gave them to
Abraham, and restored his wife

19.28 Rev 9.2; 18.9
19.29 2 Pet 2.7
19.31 Gen 38.8,9; Deut 25.5
19.32 Mk 12.19
19.37 Deut 2.9
19.38 Deut 2.19
20.1 Gen 18.1; 16.7,14; 26.6
20.2 v. 12; Gen 12.13, 15
20.3 Ps 105.14; Job 33.15; Gen 26.11
20.5 1 Kings 9.4; 2 Kings 20.3
20.7 1 Sam 7.5; Job 42.8
20.9 Gen 26.10; Ex 32.21; Josh 7.25; Gen 34.7
20.11 Ps 36.1; Gen 12.12; 26.7
20.13 v. 5
20.14 Gen 12.16

Sarah to him. 15 Abimelech said,
"My land is before you; settle
where it pleases you." 16 To Sarah
he said, "Look, I have given your
brother a thousand pieces of silver;
it is your exoneration before all
who are with you; you are completely vindicated." 17 Then Abraham prayed to God; and God
healed Abimelech, and also healed
his wife and female slaves so that
they bore children. 18 For the LORD
had closed fast all the wombs of
the house of Abimelech because of
Sarah, Abraham's wife.

The Birth of Isaac

21 The LORD dealt with Sarah
as he had said, and the
LORD did for Sarah as he had promised. 2 Sarah conceived and bore
Abraham a son in his old age, at the
time of which God had spoken to
him. 3 Abraham gave the name
Isaac to his son whom Sarah bore
him. 4 And Abraham circumcised
his son Isaac when he was eight
days old, as God had commanded
him. 5 Abraham was a hundred
years old when his son Isaac was
born to him. 6 Now Sarah said,
"God has brought laughter for me;
everyone who hears will laugh with
me." 7 And she said, "Who would
ever have said to Abraham that Sarah would nurse children? Yet I have
borne him a son in his old age."

Hagar and Ishmael Sent Away

8 The child grew, and was
weaned; and Abraham made a
great feast on the day that Isaac
was weaned. 9 But Sarah saw the
son of Hagar the Egyptian, whom
she had borne to Abraham, playing
with her son Isaac.[g] 10 So she said
to Abraham, "Cast out this slave
woman with her son; for the son of
this slave woman shall not inherit
along with my son Isaac." 11 The
matter was very distressing to
Abraham on account of his son.
12 But God said to Abraham, "Do
not be distressed because of the
boy and because of your slave
woman; whatever Sarah says to
you, do as she tells you, for it is
through Isaac that offspring shall
be named for you. 13 As for the son
of the slave woman, I will make a
nation of him also, because he is
your offspring." 14 So Abraham rose
early in the morning, and took
bread and a skin of water, and gave
it to Hagar, putting it on her shoulder, along with the child, and sent
her away. And she departed, and
wandered about in the wilderness
of Beer-sheba.

15 When the water in the skin
was gone, she cast the child under
one of the bushes. 16 Then she went
and sat down opposite him a good
way off, about the distance of a
bowshot; for she said, "Do not let
me look on the death of the child."
And as she sat opposite him, she
lifted up her voice and wept. 17 And
God heard the voice of the boy; and
the angel of God called to Hagar
from heaven, and said to her,
"What troubles you, Hagar? Do not
be afraid; for God has heard the
voice of the boy where he is.
18 Come, lift up the boy and hold
him fast with your hand, for I will
make a great nation of him."
19 Then God opened her eyes and
she saw a well of water. She went,
and filled the skin with water, and
gave the boy a drink.

20 God was with the boy, and he
grew up; he lived in the wilderness,
and became an expert with the
bow. 21 He lived in the wilderness
of Paran; and his mother got a wife
for him from the land of Egypt.

Abraham and Abimelech Make a Covenant

22 At that time Abimelech, with
Phicol the commander of his army,
said to Abraham, "God is with you
in all that you do; 23 now therefore
swear to me here by God that you
will not deal falsely with me or with
my offspring or with my posterity,
but as I have dealt loyally with you,
you will deal with me and with the
land where you have resided as an
alien." 24 And Abraham said, "I
swear it."

25 When Abraham complained

20.15 Gen 13.9 **20.17** Num 12.13; Job 42.9 **20.18** Gen 12.17 **21.1** 1 Sam 2.21; Gen 17.16, 21; Gal 4.23 **21.2** Acts 7.8; Gal 4.22; Heb 11.11; Gen 17.21 **21.3** Gen 17.19 **21.4** Gen 17.12; Acts 7.8 **21.5** Gen 17.17 **21.6** Ps 126.2; Isa 54.1 **21.7** Gen 18.13 **21.9** Gen 16.15; Gal 4.29 **21.10** Gal 4.30 **21.11** Gen 17.18 **21.12** Rom 9.7; Heb 11.18

21.13 v. 18; Gen 16.10; 17.20 **21.17** Ex 3.7 **21.18** v. 13 **21.19** Num 22.31 **21.20** Gen 28.15; 39.2,3,21 **21.21** Gen 24.4 **21.22** Gen 20.2; 26.26,28 **21.25** Gen 26.15, 18,20-22

g Gk Vg: Heb lacks *with her son Isaac*

to Abimelech about a well of water
that Abimelech's servants had
seized, 26 Abimelech said, "I do not
know who has done this; you did
not tell me, and I have not heard of
it until today." 27 So Abraham took
sheep and oxen and gave them to
Abimelech, and the two men made
a covenant. 28 Abraham set apart
seven ewe lambs of the flock.
29 And Abimelech said to Abraham,
"What is the meaning of these sev-
en ewe lambs that you have set
apart?" 30 He said, "These seven
ewe lambs you shall accept from
my hand, in order that you may be
a witness for me that I dug this
well." 31 Therefore that place was
called Beer-sheba;[h] because there
both of them swore an oath.
32 When they had made a covenant
at Beer-sheba, Abimelech, with
Phicol the commander of his army,
left and returned to the land of the
Philistines. 33 Abraham[i] planted a
tamarisk tree in Beer-sheba, and
called there on the name of the
LORD, the Everlasting God.[j] 34 And
Abraham resided as an alien many
days in the land of the Philistines.

The Command to Sacrifice Isaac

22 After these things God tested Abraham. He said to
him, "Abraham!" And he said,
"Here I am." 2 He said, "Take your
son, your only son Isaac, whom you
love, and go to the land of Moriah,
and offer him there as a burnt offering on one of the mountains that I
shall show you." 3 So Abraham rose
early in the morning, saddled his
donkey, and took two of his young
men with him, and his son Isaac;
he cut the wood for the burnt offering, and set out and went to the
place in the distance that God had
shown him. 4 On the third day
Abraham looked up and saw the
place far away. 5 Then Abraham
said to his young men, "Stay here
with the donkey; the boy and I will
go over there; we will worship, and
then we will come back to you."
6 Abraham took the wood of the
burnt offering and laid it on his son
Isaac, and he himself carried the

21.27 Gen 26.31
21.30 Gen 31.48, 52
21.31 Gen 26.33
21.33 Gen 4.26; Deut 33.27
22.2 Heb 11.17; 2 Chr 3.1
22.6 Jn 19.17
22.7 Jn 1.29,36; Rev 13.8
22.9 Heb 11.17-19
22.12 Gen 26.5; 1 Sam 15.22
22.16 Heb 6.13,14
22.17 Gen 15.5; 26.4; 32.12; 24.60
22.18 Gal 3.8,16; Acts 3.25; Gen 18.19

fire and the knife. So the two of
them walked on together. 7 Isaac
said to his father Abraham, "Father!" And he said, "Here I am, my
son." He said, "The fire and the
wood are here, but where is the
lamb for a burnt offering?" 8 Abraham said, "God himself will provide the lamb for a burnt offering,
my son." So the two of them
walked on together.
9 When they came to the place
that God had shown him, Abraham
built an altar there and laid the
wood in order. He bound his son
Isaac, and laid him on the altar, on
top of the wood. 10 Then Abraham
reached out his hand and took the
knife to kill[k] his son. 11 But the angel of the LORD called to him from
heaven, and said, "Abraham, Abraham!" And he said, "Here I am."
12 He said, "Do not lay your hand on
the boy or do anything to him; for
now I know that you fear God,
since you have not withheld your
son, your only son, from me."
13 And Abraham looked up and saw
a ram, caught in a thicket by its
horns. Abraham went and took the
ram and offered it up as a burnt offering instead of his son. 14 So Abraham called that place "The LORD
will provide";[l] as it is said to this
day, "On the mount of the LORD it
shall be provided."[m]
15 The angel of the LORD called
to Abraham a second time from
heaven, 16 and said, "By myself I
have sworn, says the LORD: Because
you have done this, and have not
withheld your son, your only son,
17 I will indeed bless you, and I will
make your offspring as numerous
as the stars of heaven and as the
sand that is on the seashore. And
your offspring shall possess the
gate of their enemies, 18 and by
your offspring shall all the nations
of the earth gain blessing for themselves, because you have obeyed
my voice." 19 So Abraham returned

[h] That is *Well of seven* or *Well of the oath*
[i] Heb *He* [j] Or *the LORD, El Olam*
[k] Or *to slaughter* [l] Or *will see*; Heb traditionally transliterated *Jehovah Jireh*
[m] Or *he shall be seen*

to his young men, and they arose and went together to Beer-sheba; and Abraham lived at Beer-sheba.

The Children of Nahor

20 Now after these things it was told Abraham, "Milcah also has borne children, to your brother Nahor: 21 Uz the firstborn, Buz his brother, Kemuel the father of Aram, 22 Chesed, Hazo, Pildash, Jidlaph, and Bethuel." 23 Bethuel became the father of Rebekah. These eight Milcah bore to Nahor, Abraham's brother. 24 Moreover, his concubine, whose name was Reumah, bore Tebah, Gaham, Tahash, and Maacah.

Sarah's Death and Burial

23 Sarah lived one hundred twenty-seven years; this was the length of Sarah's life. 2 And Sarah died at Kiriath-arba (that is, Hebron) in the land of Canaan; and Abraham went in to mourn for Sarah and to weep for her. 3 Abraham rose up from beside his dead, and said to the Hittites, 4 "I am a stranger and an alien residing among you; give me property among you for a burying place, so that I may bury my dead out of my sight." 5 The Hittites answered Abraham, 6 "Hear us, my lord; you are a mighty prince among us. Bury your dead in the choicest of our burial places; none of us will withhold from you any burial ground for burying your dead." 7 Abraham rose and bowed to the Hittites, the people of the land. 8 He said to them, "If you are willing that I should bury my dead out of my sight, hear me, and entreat for me Ephron son of Zohar, 9 so that he may give me the cave of Machpelah, which he owns; it is at the end of his field. For the full price let him give it to me in your presence as a possession for a burying place." 10 Now Ephron was sitting among the Hittites; and Ephron the Hittite answered Abraham in the hearing of the Hittites, of all who went in at the gate of his city, 11 "No, my lord, hear me; I give you the field, and I give you the cave that is in it; in the presence of my people I give it to you; bury your dead." 12 Then Abraham bowed down before the people of the land. 13 He said to Ephron in the hearing of the people of the land, "If you only will listen to me! I will give the price of the field; accept it from me, so that I may bury my dead there." 14 Ephron answered Abraham, 15 "My lord, listen to me; a piece of land worth four hundred shekels of silver—what is that between you and me? Bury your dead." 16 Abraham agreed with Ephron; and Abraham weighed out for Ephron the silver that he had named in the hearing of the Hittites, four hundred shekels of silver, according to the weights current among the merchants.

17 So the field of Ephron in Machpelah, which was to the east of Mamre, the field with the cave that was in it and all the trees that were in the field, throughout its whole area, passed 18 to Abraham as a possession in the presence of the Hittites, in the presence of all who went in at the gate of his city. 19 After this, Abraham buried Sarah his wife in the cave of the field of Machpelah facing Mamre (that is, Hebron) in the land of Canaan. 20 The field and the cave that is in it passed from the Hittites into Abraham's possession as a burying place.

The Marriage of Isaac and Rebekah

24 Now Abraham was old, well advanced in years; and the LORD had blessed Abraham in all things. 2 Abraham said to his servant, the oldest of his house, who had charge of all that he had, "Put your hand under my thigh 3 and I will make you swear by the LORD, the God of heaven and earth, that you will not get a wife for my son from the daughters of the Canaanites, among whom I live, 4 but will go to my country and to my kindred and get a wife for my son Isaac." 5 The servant said to him, "Perhaps the woman may not be

22.23 Gen 24.15
23.2 Josh 14.15; v. 19; Gen 13.18
23.4 1 Chr 29.15; Ps 105.12; Heb 11.9,13
23.6 Gen 14.14; 24.35
23.8 Gen 25.9
23.10 Gen 24.20, 24; Ruth 4.4
23.11 2 Sam 24.21-24
23.15 Ex 30.13; Ezek 45.12
23.16 Jer 32.9; Zech 11.12
23.17 Gen 25.9; 49.30-32; 50.13; Acts 7.16
24.1 v. 35; Gen 13.2
24.2 Gen 47.29
24.3 Gen 14.22; 10.18,19; 26.34,35; 28.1,2,8
24.4 Gen 28.2; 12.1

willing to follow me to this land;
must I then take your son back to
the land from which you came?"
6 Abraham said to him, "See to it
that you do not take my son back
there. 7 The LORD, the God of heav-
en, who took me from my father's
house and from the land of my
birth, and who spoke to me and
swore to me, 'To your offspring I
will give this land,' he will send his
angel before you, and you shall
take a wife for my son from there.
8 But if the woman is not willing to
follow you, then you will be free
from this oath of mine; only you
must not take my son back there."
9 So the servant put his hand under
the thigh of Abraham his master
and swore to him concerning this
matter.
10 Then the servant took ten of
his master's camels and departed,
taking all kinds of choice gifts from
his master; and he set out and went
to Aram-naharaim, to the city of
Nahor. 11 He made the camels
kneel down outside the city by the
well of water; it was toward evening, the time when women go out
to draw water. 12 And he said,
"O LORD, God of my master Abraham, please grant me success today and show steadfast love to my
master Abraham. 13 I am standing
here by the spring of water, and the
daughters of the townspeople are
coming out to draw water. 14 Let
the girl to whom I shall say, 'Please
offer your jar that I may drink,' and
who shall say, 'Drink, and I will water your camels'—let her be the
one whom you have appointed for
your servant Isaac. By this I shall
know that you have shown steadfast love to my master."
15 Before he had finished
speaking, there was Rebekah, who
was born to Bethuel son of Milcah,
the wife of Nahor, Abraham's
brother, coming out with her water
jar on her shoulder. 16 The girl was
very fair to look upon, a virgin,
whom no man had known. She
went down to the spring, filled her
jar, and came up. 17 Then the servant ran to meet her and said,

24.7 Gen 12.7; 13.15; 15.18; Ex 23.20,23
24.9 v. 2
24.10 Gen 11.31, 32; 27.43
24.11 1 Sam 9.11
24.12 v. 27; Gen 26.24; Ex 3.6
24.13 v. 43
24.14 Judg 6.17, 37; 1 Sam 6.7
24.15 v. 45; Gen 22.20, 23
24.16 Gen 26.7
24.18 vv. 14,16
24.19 v. 14
24.21 vv. 12-14; 56
24.22 v. 47
24.24 v. 15
24.26 vv. 48,52
24.27 vv. 42,48,21
24.29 Gen 29.5,13
24.31 Gen 26.29
24.32 Gen 43.24; Judg 19.21

"Please let me sip a little water
from your jar." 18 "Drink, my lord,"
she said, and quickly lowered her
jar upon her hand and gave him a
drink. 19 When she had finished giving him a drink, she said, "I will
draw for your camels also, until
they have finished drinking." 20 So
she quickly emptied her jar into
the trough and ran again to the well
to draw, and she drew for all his
camels. 21 The man gazed at her in
silence to learn whether or not the
LORD had made his journey successful.
22 When the camels had finished drinking, the man took a gold
nose-ring weighing a half shekel,
and two bracelets for her arms
weighing ten gold shekels, 23 and
said, "Tell me whose daughter you
are. Is there room in your father's
house for us to spend the night?"
24 She said to him, "I am the daughter of Bethuel son of Milcah, whom
she bore to Nahor." 25 She added,
"We have plenty of straw and fodder and a place to spend the night."
26 The man bowed his head and
worshiped the LORD 27 and said,
"Blessed be the LORD, the God of
my master Abraham, who has not
forsaken his steadfast love and his
faithfulness toward my master. As
for me, the LORD has led me on the
way to the house of my master's
kin."
28 Then the girl ran and told her
mother's household about these
things. 29 Rebekah had a brother
whose name was Laban; and Laban
ran out to the man, to the spring.
30 As soon as he had seen the nose-
ring, and the bracelets on his sister's arms, and when he heard the
words of his sister Rebekah, "Thus
the man spoke to me," he went to
the man; and there he was, standing by the camels at the spring.
31 He said, "Come in, O blessed of
the LORD. Why do you stand outside
when I have prepared the house
and a place for the camels?" 32 So
the man came into the house; and
Laban unloaded the camels, and
gave him straw and fodder for the
camels, and water to wash his feet

and the feet of the men who were
with him. 33 Then food was set before him to eat; but he said, "I will
not eat until I have told my er-
rand." He said, "Speak on."
34 So he said, "I am Abraham's
servant. 35 The LORD has greatly
blessed my master, and he has become wealthy; he has given him
flocks and herds, silver and gold,
male and female slaves, camels
and donkeys. 36 And Sarah my master's wife bore a son to my master
when she was old; and he has given
him all that he has. 37 My master
made me swear, saying, 'You shall
not take a wife for my son from the
daughters of the Canaanites, in
whose land I live; 38 but you shall go
to my father's house, to my kindred, and get a wife for my son.' 39 I
said to my master, 'Perhaps the
woman will not follow me.' 40 But
he said to me, 'The LORD, before
whom I walk, will send his angel
with you and make your way successful. You shall get a wife for my
son from my kindred, from my father's house. 41 Then you will be
free from my oath, when you come
to my kindred; even if they will not
give her to you, you will be free
from my oath.'
42 "I came today to the spring,
and said, 'O LORD, the God of my
master Abraham, if now you will
only make successful the way I am
going! 43 I am standing here by the
spring of water; let the young woman who comes out to draw, to
whom I shall say, "Please give me a
little water from your jar to drink,"
44 and who will say to me, "Drink,
and I will draw for your camels
also"—let her be the woman whom
the LORD has appointed for my master's son.'
45 "Before I had finished speaking in my heart, there was Rebekah
coming out with her water jar on
her shoulder; and she went down to
the spring, and drew. I said to her,
'Please let me drink.' 46 She quickly
let down her jar from her shoulder,
and said, 'Drink, and I will also water your camels.' So I drank, and
she also watered the camels.

24.35 v. 1; Gen 13.2
24.36 Gen 21.2, 10; 25.5
24.37 vv. 2-4
24.38 v. 4
24.39 v. 5
24.40 v. 7
24.41 v. 8
24.42 vv. 11,12
24.43 vv. 13,14
24.45 vv. 15,17; 1 Sam 1.13
24.46 v. 18
24.47 vv. 23,24
24.48 vv. 26,27
24.49 Gen 47.29; Josh 2.14
24.50 Ps 118.23; Gen 31.24
24.52 v. 26
24.53 vv. 10,22
24.54 vv. 56,59
24.59 Gen 35.8
24.60 Gen 17.16; 22.17

47 Then I asked her, 'Whose daughter are you?' She said, 'The daughter of Bethuel, Nahor's son, whom
Milcah bore to him.' So I put the
ring on her nose, and the bracelets
on her arms. 48 Then I bowed my
head and worshiped the LORD, and
blessed the LORD, the God of my
master Abraham, who had led me
by the right way to obtain the
daughter of my master's kinsman
for his son. 49 Now then, if you will
deal loyally and truly with my master, tell me; and if not, tell me, so
that I may turn either to the right
hand or to the left."
50 Then Laban and Bethuel answered, "The thing comes from the
LORD; we cannot speak to you anything bad or good. 51 Look, Rebekah is before you, take her and go,
and let her be the wife of your master's son, as the LORD has spoken."
52 When Abraham's servant
heard their words, he bowed himself to the ground before the LORD.
53 And the servant brought out jewelry of silver and of gold, and garments, and gave them to Rebekah;
he also gave to her brother and to
her mother costly ornaments.
54 Then he and the men who were
with him ate and drank, and they
spent the night there. When they
rose in the morning, he said, "Send
me back to my master." 55 Her
brother and her mother said, "Let
the girl remain with us a while, at
least ten days; after that she may
go." 56 But he said to them, "Do not
delay me, since the LORD has made
my journey successful; let me go
that I may go to my master."
57 They said, "We will call the girl,
and ask her." 58 And they called Rebekah, and said to her, "Will you go
with this man?" She said, "I will."
59 So they sent away their sister Rebekah and her nurse along with
Abraham's servant and his men.
60 And they blessed Rebekah and
said to her,

"May you, our sister, become
thousands of myriads;
may your offspring gain
possession
of the gates of their foes."

61 Then Rebekah and her maids
rose up, mounted the camels, and
followed the man; thus the servant
took Rebekah, and went his way.
62 Now Isaac had come from[n]
Beer-lahai-roi, and was settled in
the Negeb. 63 Isaac went out in the
evening to walk[o] in the field; and
looking up, he saw camels coming.
64 And Rebekah looked up, and
when she saw Isaac, she slipped
quickly from the camel, 65 and said
to the servant, "Who is the man
over there, walking in the field to
meet us?" The servant said, "It is
my master." So she took her veil
and covered herself. 66 And the servant told Isaac all the things that
he had done. 67 Then Isaac brought
her into his mother Sarah's tent.
He took Rebekah, and she became
his wife; and he loved her. So Isaac
was comforted after his mother's
death.

Abraham Marries Keturah

25 Abraham took another
wife, whose name was Ke-
turah. 2 She bore him Zimran, Jokshan, Medan, Midian, Ishbak, and
Shuah. 3 Jokshan was the father of
Sheba and Dedan. The sons of Dedan were Asshurim, Letushim, and
Leummim. 4 The sons of Midian
were Ephah, Epher, Hanoch, Abida, and Eldaah. All these were the
children of Keturah. 5 Abraham
gave all he had to Isaac. 6 But to the
sons of his concubines Abraham
gave gifts, while he was still living,
and he sent them away from his
son Isaac, eastward to the east
country.

The Death of Abraham

7 This is the length of Abraham's life, one hundred seventy-
five years. 8 Abraham breathed his
last and died in a good old age, an
old man and full of years, and was
gathered to his people. 9 His sons
Isaac and Ishmael buried him in
the cave of Machpelah, in the field
of Ephron son of Zohar the Hittite,
east of Mamre, 10 the field that
Abraham purchased from the Hittites. There Abraham was buried,
with his wife Sarah. 11 After the
death of Abraham God blessed his
son Isaac. And Isaac settled at
Beer-lahai-roi.

Ishmael's Descendants

12 These are the descendants of
Ishmael, Abraham's son, whom
Hagar the Egyptian, Sarah's slave-
girl, bore to Abraham. 13 These are
the names of the sons of Ishmael,
named in the order of their birth:
Nebaioth, the firstborn of Ishmael;
and Kedar, Adbeel, Mibsam,
14 Mishma, Dumah, Massa, 15 Hadad, Tema, Jetur, Naphish, and
Kedemah. 16 These are the sons of
Ishmael and these are their names,
by their villages and by their encampments, twelve princes according to their tribes. 17 (This is the
length of the life of Ishmael, one
hundred thirty-seven years; he
breathed his last and died, and was
gathered to his people.) 18 They settled from Havilah to Shur, which is
opposite Egypt in the direction of
Assyria; he settled down[p] alongside of[q] all his people.

The Birth and Youth of Esau and Jacob

19 These are the descendants of
Isaac, Abraham's son: Abraham
was the father of Isaac, 20 and Isaac
was forty years old when he married Rebekah, daughter of Bethuel
the Aramean of Paddan-aram, sister of Laban the Aramean. 21 Isaac
prayed to the LORD for his wife, because she was barren; and the LORD
granted his prayer, and his wife Rebekah conceived. 22 The children
struggled together within her; and
she said, "If it is to be this way, why
do I live?"[r] So she went to inquire
of the LORD. 23 And the LORD said to
her,

"Two nations are in your
womb,
and two peoples born of
you shall be divided;
the one shall be stronger
than the other,

24.62 Gen 16.14; 25.11; 20.1
24.63 Ps 1.2; 77.12; 119.15; 143.5; 145.5
24.67 Gen 29.18; 23.1,2; 25.20
25.2 1 Chr 1.32, 33
25.5 Gen 24.35, 36
25.8 Gen 15.15; 35.29; 49.29, 33
25.10 Gen 23.16
25.11 Gen 24.62
25.12 Gen 16.15
25.13 1 Chr 1.29-31
25.16 Gen 17.20
25.17 v. 8
25.18 Gen 16.12
25.20 Gen 24.15, 29
25.21 1 Sam 1.17; Ps 127.3
25.23 Gen 17.16; Num 20.14; Gen 27.29; Mal 1.3; Rom 9.12

[n] Syr Tg: Heb *from coming to* [o] Meaning of Heb word is uncertain [p] Heb *he fell* [q] Or *down in opposition to* [r] Syr: Meaning of Heb uncertain

the elder shall serve the
younger."
24 When her time to give birth was
at hand, there were twins in her
womb. 25 The first came out red, all
his body like a hairy mantle; so
they named him Esau. 26 Afterward
his brother came out, with his hand
gripping Esau's heel; so he was
named Jacob.[s] Isaac was sixty
years old when she bore them.
27 When the boys grew up, Esau
was a skillful hunter, a man of the
field, while Jacob was a quiet man,
living in tents. 28 Isaac loved Esau,
because he was fond of game; but
Rebekah loved Jacob.

Esau Sells His Birthright

29 Once when Jacob was cooking a stew, Esau came in from the
field, and he was famished. 30 Esau
said to Jacob, "Let me eat some of
that red stuff, for I am famished!"
(Therefore he was called Edom.[t])
31 Jacob said, "First sell me your
birthright." 32 Esau said, "I am
about to die; of what use is a birthright to me?" 33 Jacob said, "Swear
to me first."[u] So he swore to him,
and sold his birthright to Jacob.
34 Then Jacob gave Esau bread and
lentil stew, and he ate and drank,
and rose and went his way. Thus
Esau despised his birthright.

Isaac and Abimelech

26 Now there was a famine in
the land, besides the former famine that had occurred in
the days of Abraham. And Isaac
went to Gerar, to King Abimelech
of the Philistines. 2 The LORD appeared to Isaac[v] and said, "Do not
go down to Egypt; settle in the land
that I shall show you. 3 Reside in
this land as an alien, and I will be
with you, and will bless you; for to
you and to your descendants I will
give all these lands, and I will fulfill
the oath that I swore to your father
Abraham. 4 I will make your offspring as numerous as the stars of
heaven, and will give to your offspring all these lands; and all the
nations of the earth shall gain
blessing for themselves through
your offspring, 5 because Abraham
obeyed my voice and kept my
charge, my commandments, my
statutes, and my laws."
6 So Isaac settled in Gerar.
7 When the men of the place asked
him about his wife, he said, "She is
my sister"; for he was afraid to say,
"My wife," thinking, "or else the
men of the place might kill me for
the sake of Rebekah, because she
is attractive in appearance."
8 When Isaac had been there a long
time, King Abimelech of the Philistines looked out of a window and
saw him fondling his wife Rebekah.
9 So Abimelech called for Isaac,
and said, "So she is your wife! Why
then did you say, 'She is my sister'?" Isaac said to him, "Because I
thought I might die because of
her." 10 Abimelech said, "What is
this you have done to us? One of
the people might easily have lain
with your wife, and you would have
brought guilt upon us." 11 So Abimelech warned all the people, saying, "Whoever touches this man or
his wife shall be put to death."
12 Isaac sowed seed in that
land, and in the same year reaped
a hundredfold. The LORD blessed
him, 13 and the man became rich;
he prospered more and more until
he became very wealthy. 14 He had
possessions of flocks and herds,
and a great household, so that the
Philistines envied him. 15 (Now the
Philistines had stopped up and
filled with earth all the wells that
his father's servants had dug in the
days of his father Abraham.) 16 And
Abimelech said to Isaac, "Go away
from us; you have become too powerful for us."
17 So Isaac departed from there
and camped in the valley of Gerar
and settled there. 18 Isaac dug again
the wells of water that had been
dug in the days of his father Abraham; for the Philistines had
stopped them up after the death of
Abraham; and he gave them the
names that his father had given

25.25 Gen 27.11 **25.26** Hos 12.3; Gen 27.36 **25.27** Gen 27.3,5 **25.33** Heb 12.16 **26.1** Gen 12.10; 20.1,2 **26.2** Gen 12.7; 17.1; 18.1; 19.1 **26.3** Gen 20.1; 12.2,7; 13.15; 15.18; 22.16-18 **26.4** Gen 15.5; 22.17; Ex 32.15; Gen 12.3; 22.18; Gal 3.8

26.7 Gen 12.13; 20.2,12,13 **26.10** Gen 20.9 **26.12** v. 3 **26.14** Gen 24.35; 37.11 **26.15** Gen 21.25, 30 **26.18** Gen 21.31

[s] That is *He takes by the heel* or *He supplants*
[t] That is *Red* [u] Heb *today* [v] Heb *him*

them. 19 But when Isaac's servants
dug in the valley and found there a
well of spring water, 20 the herders
of Gerar quarreled with Isaac's
herders, saying, "The water is
ours." So he called the well Esek,[w]
because they contended with him.
21 Then they dug another well, and
they quarreled over that one also;
so he called it Sitnah.[x] 22 He
moved from there and dug another
well, and they did not quarrel over
it; so he called it Rehoboth,[y] saying, "Now the LORD has made room
for us, and we shall be fruitful in
the land."
23 From there he went up to
Beer-sheba. 24 And that very night
the LORD appeared to him and said,
"I am the God of your father Abraham; do not be afraid, for I am with
you and will bless you and make
your offspring numerous for my
servant Abraham's sake." 25 So he
built an altar there, called on the
name of the LORD, and pitched his
tent there. And there Isaac's servants dug a well.
26 Then Abimelech went to him
from Gerar, with Ahuzzath his ad-
viser and Phicol the commander of
his army. 27 Isaac said to them,
"Why have you come to me, seeing
that you hate me and have sent me
away from you?" 28 They said, "We
see plainly that the LORD has been
with you; so we say, let there be an
oath between you and us, and let
us make a covenant with you 29 so
that you will do us no harm, just as
we have not touched you and have
done to you nothing but good and
have sent you away in peace. You
are now the blessed of the LORD."
30 So he made them a feast, and
they ate and drank. 31 In the morning they rose early and exchanged
oaths; and Isaac set them on their
way, and they departed from him in
peace. 32 That same day Isaac's servants came and told him about the
well that they had dug, and said to
him, "We have found water!" 33 He
called it Shibah;[z] therefore the
name of the city is Beer-sheba[a] to
this day.

26.22 Gen 17.6
26.24 Gen 17.7; 24.12; Ex 3.6
26.25 Gen 12.7,8; 13.4,18; Ps 116.17
26.26 Gen 21.22
26.27 v. 16
26.28 Gen 21.22, 23
26.31 Gen 21.31
26.33 Gen 21.31
26.34 Gen 28.8; 36.2
26.35 Gen 27.46
27.1 Gen 48.10; 1 Sam 3.2
27.2 Gen 47.29
27.3 Gen 25.27, 28
27.4 v. 27; Gen 48.9, 15; 49.28
27.8 v. 13
27.11 Gen 25.25
27.12 vv. 21,22
27.13 v. 8; Mt 27.25

Esau's Hittite Wives

34 When Esau was forty years
old, he married Judith daughter of
Beeri the Hittite, and Basemath
daughter of Elon the Hittite; 35 and
they made life bitter for Isaac and
Rebekah.

Isaac Blesses Jacob

27 When Isaac was old and his
eyes were dim so that he
could not see, he called his elder
son Esau and said to him, "My
son"; and he answered, "Here I
am." 2 He said, "See, I am old; I do
not know the day of my death.
3 Now then, take your weapons,
your quiver and your bow, and go
out to the field, and hunt game for
me. 4 Then prepare for me savory
food, such as I like, and bring it to
me to eat, so that I may bless you
before I die."
5 Now Rebekah was listening
when Isaac spoke to his son Esau.
So when Esau went to the field to
hunt for game and bring it, 6 Rebekah said to her son Jacob, "I heard
your father say to your brother
Esau, 7 'Bring me game, and prepare for me savory food to eat, that
I may bless you before the LORD before I die.' 8 Now therefore, my son,
obey my word as I command you.
9 Go to the flock, and get me two
choice kids, so that I may prepare
from them savory food for your father, such as he likes; 10 and you
shall take it to your father to eat, so
that he may bless you before he
dies." 11 But Jacob said to his
mother Rebekah, "Look, my brother Esau is a hairy man, and I am a
man of smooth skin. 12 Perhaps my
father will feel me, and I shall seem
to be mocking him, and bring a
curse on myself and not a blessing." 13 His mother said to him,
"Let your curse be on me, my son;
only obey my word, and go, get
them for me." 14 So he went and got
them and brought them to his
mother; and his mother prepared

[w] That is *Contention* [x] That is *Enmity* [y] That is *Broad places* or *Room* [z] A word resembling the word for *oath* [a] That is *Well of the oath* or *Well of seven*

savory food, such as his father
loved. 15 Then Rebekah took the
best garments of her elder son
Esau, which were with her in the
house, and put them on her younger son Jacob; 16 and she put the
skins of the kids on his hands and
on the smooth part of his neck.
17 Then she handed the savory
food, and the bread that she had
prepared, to her son Jacob.

18 So he went in to his father,
and said, "My father"; and he said,
"Here I am; who are you, my son?"
19 Jacob said to his father, "I am
Esau your firstborn. I have done as
you told me; now sit up and eat of
my game, so that you may bless
me." 20 But Isaac said to his son,
"How is it that you have found it so
quickly, my son?" He answered,
"Because the LORD your God granted me success." 21 Then Isaac said
to Jacob, "Come near, that I may
feel you, my son, to know whether
you are really my son Esau or not."
22 So Jacob went up to his father
Isaac, who felt him and said, "The
voice is Jacob's voice, but the
hands are the hands of Esau." 23 He
did not recognize him, because his
hands were hairy like his brother
Esau's hands; so he blessed him.
24 He said, "Are you really my son
Esau?" He answered, "I am."
25 Then he said, "Bring it to me,
that I may eat of my son's game and
bless you." So he brought it to him,
and he ate; and he brought him
wine, and he drank. 26 Then his father Isaac said to him, "Come near
and kiss me, my son." 27 So he
came near and kissed him; and he
smelled the smell of his garments,
and blessed him, and said,

"Ah, the smell of my son
is like the smell of a field
that the LORD has
blessed.
28 May God give you of the dew
of heaven,
and of the fatness of the
earth,
and plenty of grain and
wine.
29 Let peoples serve you,
and nations bow down to
you.
Be lord over your brothers,
and may your mother's
sons bow down to you.
Cursed be everyone who
curses you,
and blessed be everyone
who blesses you!"

27.15 v. 27 **27.19** v. 4 **27.21** v. 12 **27.23** v. 16 **27.25** vv. 4,10,19, 31 **27.27** Heb 11.20; Song 4.11 **27.28** Deut 33.13, 28; Gen 45.18 **27.29** Gen 9.25; 25.23; 49.8; 12.3; Num 24.9; Zeph 2.8

Esau's Lost Blessing

30 As soon as Isaac had finished
blessing Jacob, when Jacob had
scarcely gone out from the presence of his father Isaac, his brother
Esau came in from his hunting.
31 He also prepared savory food,
and brought it to his father. And he
said to his father, "Let my father sit
up and eat of his son's game, so
that you may bless me." 32 His father Isaac said to him, "Who are
you?" He answered, "I am your
firstborn son, Esau." 33 Then Isaac
trembled violently, and said, "Who
was it then that hunted game and
brought it to me, and I ate it all[b]
before you came, and I have
blessed him?—yes, and blessed he
shall be!" 34 When Esau heard his
father's words, he cried out with an
exceedingly great and bitter cry,
and said to his father, "Bless me,
me also, father!" 35 But he said,
"Your brother came deceitfully,
and he has taken away your blessing." 36 Esau said, "Is he not rightly
named Jacob?[c] For he has sup-
planted me these two times. He
took away my birthright; and look,
now he has taken away my blessing." Then he said, "Have you not
reserved a blessing for me?"
37 Isaac answered Esau, "I have already made him your lord, and I
have given him all his brothers as
servants, and with grain and wine I
have sustained him. What then can
I do for you, my son?" 38 Esau said
to his father, "Have you only one
blessing, father? Bless me, me also,
father!" And Esau lifted up his
voice and wept.

39 Then his father Isaac answered him:

27.31 v. 4 **27.32** v. 18 **27.33** Gen 28.3,4; Rom 11.29 **27.34** Heb 12.17 **27.37** vv. 28,29 **27.38** Heb 12.17 **27.39** v. 28

[b] Cn: Heb *of all* [c] That is *He supplants* or *He takes by the heel*

"See, away from[d] the fatness
of the earth shall your
home be,
and away from[e] the dew of
heaven on high.
40 By your sword you shall live,
and you shall serve your
brother;
but when you break loose,[f]
you shall break his yoke
from your neck."

Jacob Escapes Esau's Fury

41 Now Esau hated Jacob because of the blessing with which his father had blessed him, and Esau said to himself, "The days of mourning for my father are approaching; then I will kill my brother Jacob." 42 But the words of her elder son Esau were told to Rebekah; so she sent and called her younger son Jacob and said to him, "Your brother Esau is consoling himself by planning to kill you. 43 Now therefore, my son, obey my voice; flee at once to my brother Laban in Haran, 44 and stay with him a while, until your brother's fury turns away— 45 until your brother's anger against you turns away, and he forgets what you have done to him; then I will send, and bring you back from there. Why should I lose both of you in one day?"

46 Then Rebekah said to Isaac, "I am weary of my life because of the Hittite women. If Jacob marries one of the Hittite women such as these, one of the women of the land, what good will my life be to me?"

28 Then Isaac called Jacob and blessed him, and charged him, "You shall not marry one of the Canaanite women. 2 Go at once to Paddan-aram to the house of Bethuel, your mother's father; and take as wife from there one of the daughters of Laban, your mother's brother. 3 May God Almighty[g] bless you and make you fruitful and numerous, that you may become a company of peoples. 4 May he give to you the blessing of Abraham, to you and to your offspring with you, so that you may take possession of the land where you now live as an alien—land that God gave to Abraham." 5 Thus Isaac sent Jacob away; and he went to Paddan-aram, to Laban son of Bethuel the Aramean, the brother of Rebekah, Jacob's and Esau's mother.

Esau Marries Ishmael's Daughter

6 Now Esau saw that Isaac had blessed Jacob and sent him away to Paddan-aram to take a wife from there, and that as he blessed him he charged him, "You shall not marry one of the Canaanite women," 7 and that Jacob had obeyed his father and his mother and gone to Paddan-aram. 8 So when Esau saw that the Canaanite women did not please his father Isaac, 9 Esau went to Ishmael and took Mahalath daughter of Abraham's son Ishmael, and sister of Nebaioth, to be his wife in addition to the wives he had.

Jacob's Dream at Bethel

10 Jacob left Beer-sheba and went toward Haran. 11 He came to a certain place and stayed there for the night, because the sun had set. Taking one of the stones of the place, he put it under his head and lay down in that place. 12 And he dreamed that there was a ladder[h] set up on the earth, the top of it reaching to heaven; and the angels of God were ascending and descending on it. 13 And the LORD stood beside him[i] and said, "I am the LORD, the God of Abraham your father and the God of Isaac; the land on which you lie I will give to you and to your offspring; 14 and your offspring shall be like the dust of the earth, and you shall spread abroad to the west and to the east and to the north and to the south; and all the families of the earth shall be blessed[j] in you and in

27.40 Gen 25.23; 2 Kings 8.20-22
27.41 Gen 32.3-11
27.43 vv. 8,13; Gen 24.29
27.46 Gen 26.34, 35
28.1 Gen 24.3,4
28.2 Gen 25.20
28.3 Gen 17.1,6
28.4 Gen 12.2; 17.8
28.6 v. 1
28.8 Gen 24.3; 26.35
28.9 Gen 36.3
28.12 Jn 1.51
28.13 Gen 35.1; 48.3; 26.24; 13.15; 35.12
28.14 Gen 13.14-16; 22.17; 12.3; 18.18; 22.18; 26.4

[d] Or *See, of* [e] Or *and of* [f] Meaning of Heb uncertain [g] Traditional rendering of Heb *El Shaddai* [h] Or *stairway* or *ramp* [i] Or *stood above it* [j] Or *shall bless themselves*

your offspring. 15 Know that I am
with you and will keep you wherever you go, and will bring you back
to this land; for I will not leave you
until I have done what I have promised you." 16 Then Jacob woke from
his sleep and said, "Surely the LORD
is in this place—and I did not know
it!" 17 And he was afraid, and said,
"How awesome is this place! This
is none other than the house of
God, and this is the gate of heav-
en."

18 So Jacob rose early in the
morning, and he took the stone
that he had put under his head and
set it up for a pillar and poured oil
on the top of it. 19 He called that
place Bethel;[k] but the name of the
city was Luz at the first. 20 Then Jacob made a vow, saying, "If God
will be with me, and will keep me
in this way that I go, and will give
me bread to eat and clothing to
wear, 21 so that I come again to my
father's house in peace, then the
LORD shall be my God, 22 and this
stone, which I have set up for a pillar, shall be God's house; and of all
that you give me I will surely give
one tenth to you."

Jacob Meets Rachel

29 Then Jacob went on his
journey, and came to the
land of the people of the east. 2 As
he looked, he saw a well in the field
and three flocks of sheep lying
there beside it; for out of that well
the flocks were watered. The stone
on the well's mouth was large,
3 and when all the flocks were gathered there, the shepherds would
roll the stone from the mouth of
the well, and water the sheep, and
put the stone back in its place on
the mouth of the well.

4 Jacob said to them, "My
brothers, where do you come
from?" They said, "We are from Haran." 5 He said to them, "Do you
know Laban son of Nahor?" They
said, "We do." 6 He said to them,
"Is it well with him?" "Yes," they
replied, "and here is his daughter
Rachel, coming with the sheep."
7 He said, "Look, it is still broad
daylight; it is not time for the animals to be gathered together. Water the sheep, and go, pasture
them." 8 But they said, "We cannot
until all the flocks are gathered together, and the stone is rolled from
the mouth of the well; then we water the sheep."

9 While he was still speaking
with them, Rachel came with her
father's sheep; for she kept them.
10 Now when Jacob saw Rachel, the
daughter of his mother's brother
Laban, and the sheep of his mother's brother Laban, Jacob went up
and rolled the stone from the well's
mouth, and watered the flock of his
mother's brother Laban. 11 Then
Jacob kissed Rachel, and wept
aloud. 12 And Jacob told Rachel
that he was her father's kinsman,
and that he was Rebekah's son;
and she ran and told her father.

13 When Laban heard the news
about his sister's son Jacob, he ran
to meet him; he embraced him and
kissed him, and brought him to his
house. Jacob[l] told Laban all these
things, 14 and Laban said to him,
"Surely you are my bone and my
flesh!" And he stayed with him a
month.

Jacob Marries Laban's Daughters

15 Then Laban said to Jacob,
"Because you are my kinsman,
should you therefore serve me for
nothing? Tell me, what shall your
wages be?" 16 Now Laban had two
daughters; the name of the elder
was Leah, and the name of the
younger was Rachel. 17 Leah's eyes
were lovely,[m] and Rachel was
graceful and beautiful. 18 Jacob
loved Rachel; so he said, "I will
serve you seven years for your
younger daughter Rachel." 19 Laban said, "It is better that I give her
to you than that I should give her to
any other man; stay with me." 20 So
Jacob served seven years for Rachel, and they seemed to him but a
few days because of the love he had
for her.

28.15 Gen 26.3; Num 6.24; Ps 121.7,8; Gen 48.21; Deut 31.6,8
28.16 Ex 3.5; Josh 5.15
28.18 Gen 35.14; Lev 8.10-12
28.19 Judg 1.23, 26; Hos 4.15
28.20ff Gen 31.13; v. 15; 1 Tim 6.8
28.21 Judg 11.31; 2 Sam 19.24, 30; Deut 26.17; 2 Sam 15.8
28.22 Gen 35.7, 14; Lev 27.30
29.1 Judg 6.3,33
29.4 Gen 28.10
29.5 Gen 24.24, 29
29.6 Gen 43.27
29.9 Ex 2.16
29.10 Ex 2.17
29.12 Gen 13.8; 14.14,16; 24.28
29.13 Gen 24.29, 31; 33.4
29.14 Judg 9.2
29.18 Hos 12.12

[k] That is *House of God* [l] Heb *He*
[m] Meaning of Heb uncertain

21 Then Jacob said to Laban,
"Give me my wife that I may go in
to her, for my time is completed."
22 So Laban gathered together all
the people of the place, and made
a feast. 23 But in the evening he
took his daughter Leah and
brought her to Jacob; and he went
in to her. 24 (Laban gave his maid
Zilpah to his daughter Leah to be
her maid.) 25 When morning came,
it was Leah! And Jacob said to Laban, "What is this you have done to
me? Did I not serve with you for Rachel? Why then have you deceived
me?" 26 Laban said, "This is not
done in our country—giving the
younger before the firstborn.
27 Complete the week of this one,
and we will give you the other also
in return for serving me another
seven years." 28 Jacob did so, and
completed her week; then Laban
gave him his daughter Rachel as a
wife. 29 (Laban gave his maid Bilhah to his daughter Rachel to be
her maid.) 30 So Jacob went in to
Rachel also, and he loved Rachel
more than Leah. He served Laban[n]
for another seven years.

31 When the LORD saw that Leah
was unloved, he opened her womb;
but Rachel was barren. 32 Leah conceived and bore a son, and she
named him Reuben;[o] for she said,
"Because the LORD has looked on
my affliction; surely now my husband will love me." 33 She conceived again and bore a son, and
said, "Because the LORD has
heard[p] that I am hated, he has giv-
en me this son also"; and she
named him Simeon. 34 Again she
conceived and bore a son, and said,
"Now this time my husband will be
joined[q] to me, because I have
borne him three sons"; therefore
he was named Levi. 35 She conceived again and bore a son, and
said, "This time I will praise[r] the
LORD"; therefore she named him
Judah; then she ceased bearing.

30 When Rachel saw that she
bore Jacob no children, she
envied her sister; and she said to
Jacob, "Give me children, or I shall
die!" 2 Jacob became very angry
with Rachel and said, "Am I in the
place of God, who has withheld
from you the fruit of the womb?"
3 Then she said, "Here is my maid
Bilhah; go in to her, that she may
bear upon my knees and that I too
may have children through her."
4 So she gave him her maid Bilhah
as a wife; and Jacob went in to her.
5 And Bilhah conceived and bore
Jacob a son. 6 Then Rachel said,
"God has judged me, and has also
heard my voice and given me a
son"; therefore she named him
Dan.[s] 7 Rachel's maid Bilhah conceived again and bore Jacob a second son. 8 Then Rachel said, "With
mighty wrestlings I have wrestled[t]
with my sister, and have prevailed"; so she named him Naphtali.

9 When Leah saw that she had
ceased bearing children, she took
her maid Zilpah and gave her to Jacob as a wife. 10 Then Leah's maid
Zilpah bore Jacob a son. 11 And
Leah said, "Good fortune!" so she
named him Gad.[u] 12 Leah's maid
Zilpah bore Jacob a second son.
13 And Leah said, "Happy am I! For
the women will call me happy"; so
she named him Asher.[v]

14 In the days of wheat harvest
Reuben went and found mandrakes in the field, and brought
them to his mother Leah. Then Rachel said to Leah, "Please give me
some of your son's mandrakes."
15 But she said to her, "Is it a small
matter that you have taken away
my husband? Would you take away
my son's mandrakes also?" Rachel
said, "Then he may lie with you tonight for your son's mandrakes."
16 When Jacob came from the field
in the evening, Leah went out to
meet him, and said, "You must
come in to me; for I have hired you
with my son's mandrakes." So he
lay with her that night. 17 And God
heeded Leah, and she conceived
and bore Jacob a fifth son. 18 Leah

29.21 Judg 15.1 **29.22** Judg 14.10; Jn 2.1,2 **29.27** Judg 14.12 **29.30** vv. 17,18 **29.31** Ps 127.3; Gen 30.1 **29.32** Gen 16.11; 31.42 **29.34** Gen 49.5 **29.35** Gen 49.8; Mt 1.2 **30.1** 1 Sam 1.5, 6 **30.2** Gen 20.18; 29.31

30.3 Gen 16.2 **30.4** Gen 16.3,4 **30.6** Lam 3.59 **30.8** Mt 4.13 **30.9** v. 4 **30.13** Prov 31.28 **30.14** Gen 25.30 **30.15** Num 16.9, 13

[n] Heb *him* [o] That is *See, a son*
[p] Heb *shama* [q] Heb *lawah*
[r] Heb *hodah* [s] That is *He judged*
[t] Heb *niphtal* [u] That is *Fortune* [v] That is *Happy*

said, "God has given me my hire[w]
because I gave my maid to my husband"; so she named him Issachar.
19 And Leah conceived again, and
she bore Jacob a sixth son. 20 Then
Leah said, "God has endowed me
with a good dowry; now my husband will honor[x] me, because I
have borne him six sons"; so she
named him Zebulun. 21 Afterwards
she bore a daughter, and named
her Dinah.
22 Then God remembered Rachel, and God heeded her and
opened her womb. 23 She conceived and bore a son, and said,
"God has taken away my reproach"; 24 and she named him Joseph,[y] saying, "May the LORD add
to me another son!"

Jacob Prospers at Laban's Expense

25 When Rachel had borne Joseph, Jacob said to Laban, "Send
me away, that I may go to my own
home and country. 26 Give me my
wives and my children for whom I
have served you, and let me go; for
you know very well the service I
have given you." 27 But Laban said
to him, "If you will allow me to say
so, I have learned by divination
that the LORD has blessed me because of you; 28 name your wages,
and I will give it." 29 Jacob said to
him, "You yourself know how I
have served you, and how your cattle have fared with me. 30 For you
had little before I came, and it has
increased abundantly; and the
LORD has blessed you wherever I
turned. But now when shall I provide for my own household also?"
31 He said, "What shall I give you?"
Jacob said, "You shall not give me
anything; if you will do this for me,
I will again feed your flock and
keep it: 32 let me pass through all
your flock today, removing from it
every speckled and spotted sheep
and every black lamb, and the spotted and speckled among the goats;
and such shall be my wages. 33 So
my honesty will answer for me later, when you come to look into my
wages with you. Every one that is

30.20 Mt 4.13
30.22 1 Sam 1.19, 20; Gen 29.31
30.23 Isa 4.1; Lk 1.25
30.24 Gen 35.17
30.25 Gen 24.54, 56
30.26 Gen 29.20, 30; Hos 12.12
30.27 Gen 39.3,5
30.28 Gen 29.15
30.29 Gen 31.38-40
30.30 1 Tim 5.8
30.32 Gen 31.8
30.33 Ps 37.6
30.37 Gen 31.9-12
30.43 Gen 12.16; 13.2; 24.35; 26.13,14

not speckled and spotted among
the goats and black among the
lambs, if found with me, shall be
counted stolen." 34 Laban said,
"Good! Let it be as you have said."
35 But that day Laban removed the
male goats that were striped and
spotted, and all the female goats
that were speckled and spotted, every one that had white on it, and
every lamb that was black, and put
them in charge of his sons; 36 and
he set a distance of three days'
journey between himself and Jacob, while Jacob was pasturing the
rest of Laban's flock.
37 Then Jacob took fresh rods
of poplar and almond and plane,
and peeled white streaks in them,
exposing the white of the rods.
38 He set the rods that he had
peeled in front of the flocks in the
troughs, that is, the watering
places, where the flocks came to
drink. And since they bred when
they came to drink, 39 the flocks
bred in front of the rods, and so the
flocks produced young that were
striped, speckled, and spotted.
40 Jacob separated the lambs, and
set the faces of the flocks toward
the striped and the completely
black animals in the flock of Laban; and he put his own droves
apart, and did not put them with
Laban's flock. 41 Whenever the
stronger of the flock were breeding,
Jacob laid the rods in the troughs
before the eyes of the flock, that
they might breed among the rods,
42 but for the feebler of the flock he
did not lay them there; so the feebler were Laban's, and the stronger
Jacob's. 43 Thus the man grew exceedingly rich, and had large
flocks, and male and female slaves,
and camels and donkeys.

Jacob Flees with Family and Flocks

31 Now Jacob heard that the
sons of Laban were saying,
"Jacob has taken all that was our
father's; he has gained all this
wealth from what belonged to our

[w] Heb *sakar* [x] Heb *zabal* [y] That is *He adds*

father." 2And Jacob saw that Laban did not regard him as favorably
as he did before. 3Then the LORD
said to Jacob, "Return to the land
of your ancestors and to your kindred, and I will be with you." 4So
Jacob sent and called Rachel and
Leah into the field where his flock
was, 5and said to them, "I see that
your father does not regard me as
favorably as he did before. But the
God of my father has been with me.
6You know that I have served your
father with all my strength; 7yet
your father has cheated me and
changed my wages ten times, but
God did not permit him to harm
me. 8If he said, 'The speckled shall
be your wages,' then all the flock
bore speckled; and if he said, 'The
striped shall be your wages,' then
all the flock bore striped. 9Thus
God has taken away the livestock
of your father, and given them to
me.

10 During the mating of the
flock I once had a dream in which
I looked up and saw that the male
goats that leaped upon the flock
were striped, speckled, and mottled. 11Then the angel of God said
to me in the dream, 'Jacob,' and I
said, 'Here I am!' 12And he said,
'Look up and see that all the goats
that leap on the flock are striped,
speckled, and mottled; for I have
seen all that Laban is doing to you.
13I am the God of Bethel,[z] where
you anointed a pillar and made a
vow to me. Now leave this land at
once and return to the land of your
birth.' " 14Then Rachel and Leah
answered him, "Is there any portion or inheritance left to us in our
father's house? 15Are we not regarded by him as foreigners? For he
has sold us, and he has been using
up the money given for us. 16All the
property that God has taken away
from our father belongs to us and
to our children; now then, do whatever God has said to you."

17 So Jacob arose, and set his
children and his wives on camels;
18and he drove away all his livestock, all the property that he had
gained, the livestock in his possession that he had acquired in
Paddan-aram, to go to his father
Isaac in the land of Canaan.

19 Now Laban had gone to
shear his sheep, and Rachel stole
her father's household gods. 20And
Jacob deceived Laban the Aramе-
an, in that he did not tell him that
he intended to flee. 21So he fled
with all that he had; starting out he
crossed the Euphrates,[a] and set
his face toward the hill country of
Gilead.

Laban Overtakes Jacob

22 On the third day Laban was
told that Jacob had fled. 23So he
took his kinsfolk with him and pursued him for seven days until he
caught up with him in the hill
country of Gilead. 24But God came
to Laban the Aramean in a dream
by night, and said to him, "Take
heed that you say not a word to Jacob, either good or bad."

25 Laban overtook Jacob. Now
Jacob had pitched his tent in the
hill country, and Laban with his
kinsfolk camped in the hill country
of Gilead. 26Laban said to Jacob,
"What have you done? You have
deceived me, and carried away my
daughters like captives of the
sword. 27Why did you flee secretly
and deceive me and not tell me? I
would have sent you away with
mirth and songs, with tambourine
and lyre. 28And why did you not
permit me to kiss my sons and my
daughters farewell? What you have
done is foolish. 29It is in my power
to do you harm; but the God of your
father spoke to me last night, saying, 'Take heed that you speak to
Jacob neither good nor bad.'
30Even though you had to go because you longed greatly for your
father's house, why did you steal
my gods?" 31Jacob answered Laban, "Because I was afraid, for I
thought that you would take your
daughters from me by force. 32But
anyone with whom you find your
gods shall not live. In the presence
of our kinsfolk, point out what I

31.3 Gen 28.15, 20,21; 32.9
31.5 vv. 3,42; Gen 48.15
31.7 v. 41; Job 19.3; Ps 37.28; 105.14
31.8 Gen 30.32
31.11 Gen 48.16
31.13 Gen 28.13, 18,20
31.14 Gen 29.15, 27
31.19 vv. 30,34; Judg 17.5; 1 Sam 19.13; Hos 3.4
31.21 Gen 37.25
31.23 Gen 13.8
31.24 Gen 20.3; Job 33.15; Gen 24.50
31.26 1 Sam 30.2
31.27 v. 55; Ruth 1.9,14; Acts 20.37
31.29 vv. 53,24
31.30 v. 19
31.32 Gen 44.9

z Cn: Meaning of Heb uncertain
a Heb *the river*

have that is yours, and take it."
Now Jacob did not know that Rachel had stolen the gods.[b]
33 So Laban went into Jacob's
tent, and into Leah's tent, and into
the tent of the two maids, but he
did not find them. And he went out
of Leah's tent, and entered Rachel's. 34 Now Rachel had taken the
household gods and put them in
the camel's saddle, and sat on
them. Laban felt all about in the
tent, but did not find them. 35 And
she said to her father, "Let not my
lord be angry that I cannot rise before you, for the way of women is
upon me." So he searched, but did
not find the household gods.
36 Then Jacob became angry,
and upbraided Laban. Jacob said
to Laban, "What is my offense?
What is my sin, that you have hotly
pursued me? 37 Although you have
felt about through all my goods,
what have you found of all your
household goods? Set it here before my kinsfolk and your kinsfolk,
so that they may decide between us
two. 38 These twenty years I have
been with you; your ewes and your
female goats have not miscarried,
and I have not eaten the rams of
your flocks. 39 That which was torn
by wild beasts I did not bring to
you; I bore the loss of it myself; of
my hand you required it, whether
stolen by day or stolen by night.
40 It was like this with me: by day
the heat consumed me, and the
cold by night, and my sleep fled
from my eyes. 41 These twenty years
I have been in your house; I served
you fourteen years for your two
daughters, and six years for your
flock, and you have changed my
wages ten times. 42 If the God of my
father, the God of Abraham and the
Fear[c] of Isaac, had not been on my
side, surely now you would have
sent me away empty-handed. God
saw my affliction and the labor of
my hands, and rebuked you last
night."

Laban and Jacob Make a Covenant

43 Then Laban answered and
said to Jacob, "The daughters are
my daughters, the children are my
children, the flocks are my flocks,
and all that you see is mine. But
what can I do today about these
daughters of mine, or about their
children whom they have borne?
44 Come now, let us make a covenant, you and I; and let it be a witness between you and me." 45 So
Jacob took a stone, and set it up as
a pillar. 46 And Jacob said to his
kinsfolk, "Gather stones," and they
took stones, and made a heap; and
they ate there by the heap. 47 Laban
called it Jegar-sahadutha:[d] but Jacob called it Galeed.[e] 48 Laban
said, "This heap is a witness between you and me today." Therefore he called it Galeed, 49 and the
pillar[f] Mizpah,[g] for he said, "The
LORD watch between you and me,
when we are absent one from the
other. 50 If you ill-treat my daughters, or if you take wives in addition
to my daughters, though no one
else is with us, remember that God
is witness between you and me."
51 Then Laban said to Jacob,
"See this heap and see the pillar,
which I have set between you and
me. 52 This heap is a witness, and
the pillar is a witness, that I will not
pass beyond this heap to you, and
you will not pass beyond this heap
and this pillar to me, for harm.
53 May the God of Abraham and the
God of Nahor"—the God of their
father—"judge between us." So Jacob swore by the Fear[c] of his father Isaac, 54 and Jacob offered a
sacrifice on the height and called
his kinsfolk to eat bread; and they
ate bread and tarried all night in
the hill country.
55 [h]Early in the morning Laban
rose up, and kissed his grandchildren and his daughters and blessed
them; then he departed and returned home.

32

Jacob went on his way and
the angels of God met him;

31.35 Ex 20.12; Lev 19.32
31.39 Ex 22.10-13
31.41 Gen 29.27, 30; v. 7
31.42 Ps 124.1,2; v. 53; Isa 8.13; Gen 29.32; 1 Chr 12.17
31.44 Gen 21.27, 32; 26.28; Josh 24.27
31.45 Gen 28.18
31.48 Josh 24.27
31.49 Judg 11.29; 1 Sam 7.5
31.53 Gen 16.5; 21.23; 28.13; v. 42
31.55 Gen 18.33; 30.25
32.1 Ps 34.7; 91.11; Heb 1.14

[b] Heb *them* [c] Meaning of Heb uncertain
[d] In Aramaic *The heap of witness*
[e] In Hebrew *The heap of witness*
[f] Compare Sam: MT lacks *the pillar* [g] That is *Watchpost* [h] Ch 32.1 in Heb

JACOB'S JOURNEYS

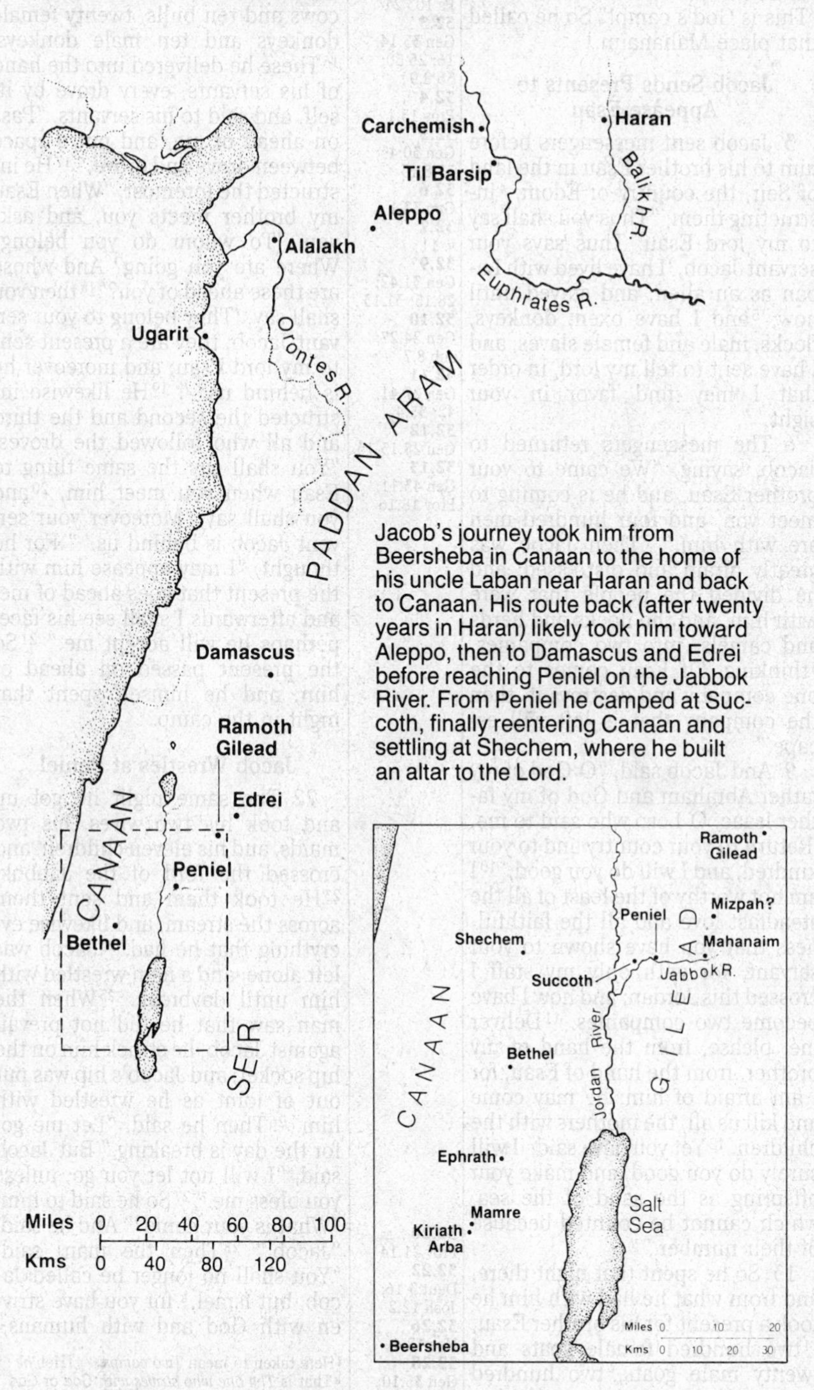

Jacob's journey took him from Beersheba in Canaan to the home of his uncle Laban near Haran and back to Canaan. His route back (after twenty years in Haran) likely took him toward Aleppo, then to Damascus and Edrei before reaching Peniel on the Jabbok River. From Peniel he camped at Succoth, finally reentering Canaan and settling at Shechem, where he built an altar to the Lord.

2 and when Jacob saw them he said,
"This is God's camp!" So he called
that place Mahanaim.[i]

Jacob Sends Presents to Appease Esau

3 Jacob sent messengers before
him to his brother Esau in the land
of Seir, the country of Edom, 4 instructing them, "Thus you shall say
to my lord Esau: Thus says your
servant Jacob, 'I have lived with Laban as an alien, and stayed until
now; 5 and I have oxen, donkeys,
flocks, male and female slaves; and
I have sent to tell my lord, in order
that I may find favor in your
sight.' "
6 The messengers returned to
Jacob, saying, "We came to your
brother Esau, and he is coming to
meet you, and four hundred men
are with him." 7 Then Jacob was
greatly afraid and distressed; and
he divided the people that were
with him, and the flocks and herds
and camels, into two companies,
8 thinking, "If Esau comes to the
one company and destroys it, then
the company that is left will escape."
9 And Jacob said, "O God of my
father Abraham and God of my father Isaac, O LORD who said to me,
'Return to your country and to your
kindred, and I will do you good,' 10 I
am not worthy of the least of all the
steadfast love and all the faithfulness that you have shown to your
servant, for with only my staff I
crossed this Jordan; and now I have
become two companies. 11 Deliver
me, please, from the hand of my
brother, from the hand of Esau, for
I am afraid of him; he may come
and kill us all, the mothers with the
children. 12 Yet you have said, 'I will
surely do you good, and make your
offspring as the sand of the sea,
which cannot be counted because
of their number.' "
13 So he spent that night there,
and from what he had with him he
took a present for his brother Esau,
14 two hundred female goats and
twenty male goats, two hundred
ewes and twenty rams, 15 thirty
milch camels and their colts, forty
cows and ten bulls, twenty female
donkeys and ten male donkeys.
16 These he delivered into the hand
of his servants, every drove by itself, and said to his servants, "Pass
on ahead of me, and put a space
between drove and drove." 17 He instructed the foremost, "When Esau
my brother meets you, and asks
you, 'To whom do you belong?
Where are you going? And whose
are these ahead of you?' 18 then you
shall say, 'They belong to your servant Jacob; they are a present sent
to my lord Esau; and moreover he
is behind us.' " 19 He likewise instructed the second and the third
and all who followed the droves,
"You shall say the same thing to
Esau when you meet him, 20 and
you shall say, 'Moreover your servant Jacob is behind us.' " For he
thought, "I may appease him with
the present that goes ahead of me,
and afterwards I shall see his face;
perhaps he will accept me." 21 So
the present passed on ahead of
him; and he himself spent that
night in the camp.

Jacob Wrestles at Peniel

22 The same night he got up
and took his two wives, his two
maids, and his eleven children, and
crossed the ford of the Jabbok.
23 He took them and sent them
across the stream, and likewise everything that he had. 24 Jacob was
left alone; and a man wrestled with
him until daybreak. 25 When the
man saw that he did not prevail
against Jacob, he struck him on the
hip socket; and Jacob's hip was put
out of joint as he wrestled with
him. 26 Then he said, "Let me go,
for the day is breaking." But Jacob
said, "I will not let you go, unless
you bless me." 27 So he said to him,
"What is your name?" And he said,
"Jacob." 28 Then the man[j] said,
"You shall no longer be called Jacob, but Israel,[k] for you have striv-
en with God and with humans,[l]

32.2 Ps 103.21
32.3 Gen 33.14, 16; 25.30; 36.8,9
32.4 Prov 15.1
32.5 Gen 30.43; 33.8,15
32.6 Gen 33.1
32.7 v. 11
32.9 Gen 31.42; 28.15; 31.13
32.10 Gen 24.27; Job 8.7
32.11 Gen 27.41, 42; 33.4
32.12 Gen 28.13-15
32.13 Gen 43.11; Prov 18.16
32.20 Prov 21.14
32.22 Deut 3.16; Josh 12.2
32.26 Hos 12.4
32.28 Gen 35.10; 1 Kings 18.31

[i] Here taken to mean *Two camps* [j] Heb *he*
[k] That is *The one who strives with God* or *God strives* [l] Or *with divine and human beings*

and have prevailed." 29 Then Jacob
asked him, "Please tell me your
name." But he said, "Why is it that
you ask my name?" And there he
blessed him. 30 So Jacob called the
place Peniel,[m] saying, "For I have
seen God face to face, and yet my
life is preserved." 31 The sun rose
upon him as he passed Penuel,
limping because of his hip.
32 Therefore to this day the Israelites do not eat the thigh muscle
that is on the hip socket, because
he struck Jacob on the hip socket
at the thigh muscle.

Jacob and Esau Meet

33 Now Jacob looked up and
saw Esau coming, and four
hundred men with him. So he divided the children among Leah and
Rachel and the two maids. 2 He put
the maids with their children in
front, then Leah with her children,
and Rachel and Joseph last of all.
3 He himself went on ahead of
them, bowing himself to the
ground seven times, until he came
near his brother.

4 But Esau ran to meet him, and
embraced him, and fell on his neck
and kissed him, and they wept.
5 When Esau looked up and saw the
women and children, he said,
"Who are these with you?" Jacob
said, "The children whom God has
graciously given your servant."
6 Then the maids drew near, they
and their children, and bowed
down; 7 Leah likewise and her children drew near and bowed down;
and finally Joseph and Rachel drew
near, and they bowed down. 8 Esau
said, "What do you mean by all this
company that I met?" Jacob answered, "To find favor with my
lord." 9 But Esau said, "I have
enough, my brother; keep what you
have for yourself." 10 Jacob said,
"No, please; if I find favor with you,
then accept my present from my
hand; for truly to see your face is
like seeing the face of God—since
you have received me with such favor. 11 Please accept my gift that is
brought to you, because God has
dealt graciously with me, and because I have everything I want." So
he urged him, and he took it.

12 Then Esau said, "Let us journey on our way, and I will go alongside you." 13 But Jacob said to him,
"My lord knows that the children
are frail and that the flocks and
herds, which are nursing, are a care
to me; and if they are overdriven for
one day, all the flocks will die.
14 Let my lord pass on ahead of his
servant, and I will lead on slowly,
according to the pace of the cattle
that are before me and according to
the pace of the children, until I
come to my lord in Seir."

15 So Esau said, "Let me leave
with you some of the people who
are with me." But he said, "Why
should my lord be so kind to me?"
16 So Esau returned that day on his
way to Seir. 17 But Jacob journeyed
to Succoth,[n] and built himself a
house, and made booths for his
cattle; therefore the place is called
Succoth.

Jacob Reaches Shechem

18 Jacob came safely to the city
of Shechem, which is in the land of
Canaan, on his way from Paddan-
aram; and he camped before the
city. 19 And from the sons of Hamor, Shechem's father, he bought
for one hundred pieces of money[o]
the plot of land on which he had
pitched his tent. 20 There he erected an altar and called it El-Elohe-
Israel.[p]

The Rape of Dinah

34 Now Dinah the daughter of
Leah, whom she had borne
to Jacob, went out to visit the wom-
en of the region. 2 When Shechem
son of Hamor the Hivite, prince of
the region, saw her, he seized her
and lay with her by force. 3 And his
soul was drawn to Dinah daughter
of Jacob; he loved the girl, and
spoke tenderly to her. 4 So Shechem spoke to his father Hamor,
saying, "Get me this girl to be my
wife."

32.29 Judg 13.17, 18
32.30 Gen 16.13; Ex 24.11; Num 12.8; Judg 6.22; 13.22
33.1 Gen 32.6
33.3 Gen 18.2; 42.6
33.4 Gen 45.14, 15
33.5 Gen 48.9; Ps 127.3; Isa 8.18
33.8 Gen 32.14-16
33.10 Gen 43.3; 2 Sam 3.13
33.11 1 Sam 25.27
33.14 Gen 32.3
33.15 Gen 34.11; 47.25; Ruth 2.13
33.17 Judg 8.5,14
33.18 Josh 24.1; Judg 9.1; Gen 25.20; 28.2
33.19 Josh 24.32; Jn 4.5
34.1 Gen 30.21
34.4 Judg 14.2

m That is *The face of God*
n That is *Booths*
o Heb *one hundred qesitah*
p That is *God, the God of Israel*

5 Now Jacob heard that Shechem[q] had defiled his daughter
Dinah; but his sons were with his
cattle in the field, so Jacob held his
peace until they came. 6 And Hamor the father of Shechem went
out to Jacob to speak with him,
7 just as the sons of Jacob came in
from the field. When they heard of
it, the men were indignant and very
angry, because he had committed
an outrage in Israel by lying with
Jacob's daughter, for such a thing
ought not to be done.
8 But Hamor spoke with them,
saying, "The heart of my son Shechem longs for your daughter;
please give her to him in marriage.
9 Make marriages with us; give your
daughters to us, and take our
daughters for yourselves. 10 You
shall live with us; and the land
shall be open to you; live and trade
in it, and get property in it." 11 Shechem also said to her father and to
her brothers, "Let me find favor
with you, and whatever you say to
me I will give. 12 Put the marriage
present and gift as high as you like,
and I will give whatever you ask
me; only give me the girl to be my
wife."
13 The sons of Jacob answered
Shechem and his father Hamor deceitfully, because he had defiled
their sister Dinah. 14 They said to
them, "We cannot do this thing, to
give our sister to one who is uncircumcised, for that would be a disgrace to us. 15 Only on this condition will we consent to you: that
you will become as we are and every male among you be circumcised. 16 Then we will give our
daughters to you, and we will take
your daughters for ourselves, and
we will live among you and become
one people. 17 But if you will not listen to us and be circumcised, then
we will take our daughter and be
gone."
18 Their words pleased Hamor
and Hamor's son Shechem. 19 And
the young man did not delay to do
the thing, because he was delighted with Jacob's daughter. Now he
was the most honored of all his
family. 20 So Hamor and his son
Shechem came to the gate of their
city and spoke to the men of their
city, saying, 21 "These people are
friendly with us; let them live in the
land and trade in it, for the land is
large enough for them; let us take
their daughters in marriage, and let
us give them our daughters. 22 Only
on this condition will they agree to
live among us, to become one people: that every male among us be
circumcised as they are circumcised. 23 Will not their livestock,
their property, and all their animals be ours? Only let us agree
with them, and they will live
among us." 24 And all who went out
of the city gate heeded Hamor and
his son Shechem; and every male
was circumcised, all who went out
of the gate of his city.

Dinah's Brothers Avenge Their Sister

25 On the third day, when they
were still in pain, two of the sons of
Jacob, Simeon and Levi, Dinah's
brothers, took their swords and
came against the city unawares,
and killed all the males. 26 They
killed Hamor and his son Shechem
with the sword, and took Dinah out
of Shechem's house, and went
away. 27 And the other sons of Jacob came upon the slain, and plundered the city, because their sister
had been defiled. 28 They took their
flocks and their herds, their donkeys, and whatever was in the city
and in the field. 29 All their wealth,
all their little ones and their wives,
all that was in the houses, they
captured and made their prey.
30 Then Jacob said to Simeon and
Levi, "You have brought trouble on
me by making me odious to the inhabitants of the land, the Canaanites and the Perizzites; my numbers
are few, and if they gather themselves against me and attack me, I
shall be destroyed, both I and my
household." 31 But they said,
"Should our sister be treated like a
whore?"

34.7 Deut 22.21; Josh 7.15; Judg 20.6; 2 Sam 13.12
34.10 Gen 13.9; 20.15
34.12 Ex 22.16; Deut 22.29; 1 Sam 18.25
34.14 Gen 17.14
34.19 1 Chr 4.9
34.24 Gen 23.10
34.25 Gen 49.5-7
34.30 Gen 49.6; Ex 5.21; Gen 36.26, 27

q Heb *he*

Jacob Returns to Bethel

35 God said to Jacob, "Arise, go up to Bethel, and settle there. Make an altar there to the God who appeared to you when you fled from your brother Esau." 2 So Jacob said to his household and to all who were with him, "Put away the foreign gods that are among you, and purify yourselves, and change your clothes; 3 then come, let us go up to Bethel, that I may make an altar there to the God who answered me in the day of my distress and has been with me wherever I have gone." 4 So they gave to Jacob all the foreign gods that they had, and the rings that were in their ears; and Jacob hid them under the oak that was near Shechem.

5 As they journeyed, a terror from God fell upon the cities all around them, so that no one pursued them. 6 Jacob came to Luz (that is, Bethel), which is in the land of Canaan, he and all the people who were with him, 7 and there he built an altar and called the place El-bethel,[r] because it was there that God had revealed himself to him when he fled from his brother. 8 And Deborah, Rebekah's nurse, died, and she was buried under an oak below Bethel. So it was called Allon-bacuth.[s]

9 God appeared to Jacob again when he came from Paddan-aram, and he blessed him. 10 God said to him, "Your name is Jacob; no longer shall you be called Jacob, but Israel shall be your name." So he was called Israel. 11 God said to him, "I am God Almighty:[t] be fruitful and multiply; a nation and a company of nations shall come from you, and kings shall spring from you. 12 The land that I gave to Abraham and Isaac I will give to you, and I will give the land to your offspring after you." 13 Then God went up from him at the place where he had spoken with him. 14 Jacob set up a pillar in the place where he had spoken with him, a pillar of stone; and he poured out a drink offering on it, and poured oil on it. 15 So Jacob called the place where God had spoken with him Bethel.

The Birth of Benjamin and the Death of Rachel

16 Then they journeyed from Bethel; and when they were still some distance from Ephrath, Rachel was in childbirth, and she had hard labor. 17 When she was in her hard labor, the midwife said to her, "Do not be afraid; for now you will have another son." 18 As her soul was departing (for she died), she named him Ben-oni;[u] but his father called him Benjamin.[v] 19 So Rachel died, and she was buried on the way to Ephrath (that is, Bethlehem), 20 and Jacob set up a pillar at her grave; it is the pillar of Rachel's tomb, which is there to this day. 21 Israel journeyed on, and pitched his tent beyond the tower of Eder.

22 While Israel lived in that land, Reuben went and lay with Bilhah his father's concubine; and Israel heard of it.

Now the sons of Jacob were twelve. 23 The sons of Leah: Reuben (Jacob's firstborn), Simeon, Levi, Judah, Issachar, and Zebulun. 24 The sons of Rachel: Joseph and Benjamin. 25 The sons of Bilhah, Rachel's maid: Dan and Naphtali. 26 The sons of Zilpah, Leah's maid: Gad and Asher. These were the sons of Jacob who were born to him in Paddan-aram.

The Death of Isaac

27 Jacob came to his father Isaac at Mamre, or Kiriath-arba (that is, Hebron), where Abraham and Isaac had resided as aliens. 28 Now the days of Isaac were one hundred eighty years. 29 And Isaac breathed his last; he died and was gathered to his people, old and full of days; and his sons Esau and Jacob buried him.

35.1 Gen 28.19, 13; 27.43 **35.2** Gen 31.19, 30,34; Ex 19.10,14 **35.3** Gen 32.7, 24; 28.20-22; 28.15 **35.4** Hos 2.13; Josh 24.26 **35.6** Gen 28.19; 48.3 **35.7** Gen 28.13 **35.8** Gen 24.59 **35.9** Hos 12.4; Gen 32.29 **35.10** Gen 32.28 **35.11** Gen 17.1; 28.3; 48.4; 17.6,16; 36.31 **35.12** Gen 13.15; 26.3; 28.13 **35.13** Gen 17.22 **35.14** Gen 28.18 **35.15** Gen 28.19 **35.17** Gen 30.24 **35.19** Gen 48.7; Ruth 1.2; Mic 5.2; Mt 2.6 **35.20** 1 Sam 10.2; 35.5; Ex 15.16; Deut 2.25; 11.25 **35.22** Gen 49.2; 1 Chr 5.1; 1 Cor 5.1 **35.27** Gen 18.1; 23.9 **35.29** Gen 25.8; 15.15

[r] That is *God of Bethel* [s] That is *Oak of weeping* [t] Traditional rendering of Heb *El Shaddai* [u] That is *Son of my sorrow* [v] That is *Son of the right hand* or *Son of the South*

Esau's Descendants

36 These are the descendants
of Esau (that is, Edom).
2 Esau took his wives from the Canaanites: Adah daughter of Elon
the Hittite, Oholibamah daughter
of Anah son[w] of Zibeon the Hivite,
3 and Basemath, Ishmael's daughter, sister of Nebaioth. 4 Adah bore
Eliphaz to Esau; Basemath bore
Reuel; 5 and Oholibamah bore Jeush, Jalam, and Korah. These are
the sons of Esau who were born to
him in the land of Canaan.
6 Then Esau took his wives, his
sons, his daughters, and all the
members of his household, his cattle, all his livestock, and all the
property he had acquired in the
land of Canaan; and he moved to a
land some distance from his brother Jacob. 7 For their possessions
were too great for them to live together; the land where they were
staying could not support them because of their livestock. 8 So Esau
settled in the hill country of Seir;
Esau is Edom.
9 These are the descendants of
Esau, ancestor of the Edomites, in
the hill country of Seir. 10 These are
the names of Esau's sons: Eliphaz
son of Adah the wife of Esau; Reuel, the son of Esau's wife Basemath. 11 The sons of Eliphaz were
Teman, Omar, Zepho, Gatam, and
Kenaz. 12 (Timna was a concubine
of Eliphaz, Esau's son; she bore
Amalek to Eliphaz.) These were
the sons of Adah, Esau's wife.
13 These were the sons of Reuel:
Nahath, Zerah, Shammah, and
Mizzah. These were the sons of
Esau's wife, Basemath. 14 These
were the sons of Esau's wife Oholibamah, daughter of Anah son[x] of
Zibeon: she bore to Esau Jeush, Jalam, and Korah.

Clans and Kings of Edom

15 These are the clans[y] of the
sons of Esau. The sons of Eliphaz
the firstborn of Esau: the clans[y]
Teman, Omar, Zepho, Kenaz,
16 Korah, Gatam, and Amalek;
these are the clans[y] of Eliphaz in
the land of Edom; they are the sons
of Adah. 17 These are the sons of
Esau's son Reuel: the clans[y] Nahath, Zerah, Shammah, and Mizzah; these are the clans[y] of Reuel
in the land of Edom; they are the
sons of Esau's wife Basemath.
18 These are the sons of Esau's wife
Oholibamah: the clans[y] Jeush, Jalam, and Korah; these are the
clans[y] born of Esau's wife Oholibamah, the daughter of Anah.
19 These are the sons of Esau (that
is, Edom), and these are their
clans.[y]
20 These are the sons of Seir the
Horite, the inhabitants of the land:
Lotan, Shobal, Zibeon, Anah, 21 Dishon, Ezer, and Dishan; these are
the clans[y] of the Horites, the sons
of Seir in the land of Edom. 22 The
sons of Lotan were Hori and Heman; and Lotan's sister was Timna.
23 These are the sons of Shobal: Al-
van, Manahath, Ebal, Shepho, and
Onam. 24 These are the sons of Zibeon: Aiah and Anah; he is the Anah
who found the springs[z] in the wilderness, as he pastured the donkeys of his father Zibeon. 25 These
are the children of Anah: Dishon
and Oholibamah daughter of Anah.
26 These are the sons of Dishon:
Hemdan, Eshban, Ithran, and Cheran. 27 These are the sons of Ezer:
Bilhan, Zaavan, and Akan. 28 These
are the sons of Dishan: Uz and
Aran. 29 These are the clans[y] of the
Horites: the clans[y] Lotan, Shobal,
Zibeon, Anah, 30 Dishon, Ezer, and
Dishan; these are the clans[y] of the
Horites, clan by clan[a] in the land
of Seir.
31 These are the kings who
reigned in the land of Edom, before
any king reigned over the Israelites.
32 Bela son of Beor reigned in
Edom, the name of his city being
Dinhabah. 33 Bela died, and Jobab
son of Zerah of Bozrah succeeded
him as king. 34 Jobab died, and Husham of the land of the Temanites
succeeded him as king. 35 Husham
died, and Hadad son of Bedad, who
defeated Midian in the country of

36.1 Gen 25.30
36.2 Gen 26.34; 28.9
36.6 Gen 12.5
36.7 Gen 13.6, 11; 17.8; 28.4
36.8 Gen 32.3
36.10 1 Chr 1.35
36.12 Ex 17.8,14
36.15 1 Chr 1.34
36.17 1 Chr 1.35, 37
36.18 v. 25; 1 Chr 1.52
36.20 Gen 14.6; Deut 2.12, 22; 1 Chr 1.38
36.25 v. 18; 1 Chr 1.52
36.27 1 Chr 1.42
36.31 1 Chr 1.43

[w] Sam Gk Syr: Heb *daughter* [x] Gk Syr: Heb *daughter* [y] Or *chiefs* [z] Meaning of Heb uncertain [a] Or *chief by chief*

Moab, succeeded him as king, the
name of his city being Avith. 36 Hadad died, and Samlah of Masrekah
succeeded him as king. 37 Samlah
died, and Shaul of Rehoboth on the
Euphrates succeeded him as king.
38 Shaul died, and Baal-hanan son
of Achbor succeeded him as king.
39 Baal-hanan son of Achbor died,
and Hadar succeeded him as king,
the name of his city being Pau; his
wife's name was Mehetabel, the
daughter of Matred, daughter of
Me-zahab.

40 These are the names of the
clans[b] of Esau, according to their
families and their localities by
their names: the clans[b] Timna, Alvah, Jetheth, 41 Oholibamah, Elah,
Pinon, 42 Kenaz, Teman, Mibzar,
43 Magdiel, and Iram; these are the
clans[b] of Edom (that is, Esau, the
father of Edom), according to their
settlements in the land that they
held.

Joseph Dreams of Greatness

37 Jacob settled in the land
where his father had lived
as an alien, the land of Canaan.
2 This is the story of the family of
Jacob.

Joseph, being seventeen years
old, was shepherding the flock with
his brothers; he was a helper to the
sons of Bilhah and Zilpah, his father's wives; and Joseph brought a
bad report of them to their father.
3 Now Israel loved Joseph more
than any other of his children, because he was the son of his old age;
and he had made him a long robe
with sleeves.[c] 4 But when his
brothers saw that their father loved
him more than all his brothers,
they hated him, and could not
speak peaceably to him.

5 Once Joseph had a dream, and
when he told it to his brothers, they
hated him even more. 6 He said to
them, "Listen to this dream that I
dreamed. 7 There we were, binding
sheaves in the field. Suddenly my
sheaf rose and stood upright; then
your sheaves gathered around it,
and bowed down to my sheaf."
8 His brothers said to him, "Are you
indeed to reign over us? Are you indeed to have dominion over us?"
So they hated him even more because of his dreams and his words.

9 He had another dream, and
told it to his brothers, saying,
"Look, I have had another dream:
the sun, the moon, and eleven stars
were bowing down to me." 10 But
when he told it to his father and to
his brothers, his father rebuked
him, and said to him, "What kind
of dream is this that you have had?
Shall we indeed come, I and your
mother and your brothers, and bow
to the ground before you?" 11 So his
brothers were jealous of him, but
his father kept the matter in mind.

Joseph Is Sold by His Brothers

12 Now his brothers went to
pasture their father's flock near
Shechem. 13 And Israel said to Joseph, "Are not your brothers pasturing the flock at Shechem?
Come, I will send you to them." He
answered, "Here I am." 14 So he
said to him, "Go now, see if it is
well with your brothers and with
the flock; and bring word back to
me." So he sent him from the valley
of Hebron.

He came to Shechem, 15 and a
man found him wandering in the
fields; the man asked him, "What
are you seeking?" 16 "I am seeking
my brothers," he said; "tell me,
please, where they are pasturing
the flock." 17 The man said, "They
have gone away, for I heard them
say, 'Let us go to Dothan.' " So Joseph went after his brothers, and
found them at Dothan. 18 They saw
him from a distance, and before he
came near to them, they conspired
to kill him. 19 They said to one another, "Here comes this dreamer.
20 Come now, let us kill him and
throw him into one of the pits; then
we shall say that a wild animal has
devoured him, and we shall see
what will become of his dreams."
21 But when Reuben heard it, he delivered him out of their hands, say-

36.39 1 Chr 1.50
36.40 1 Chr 1.51
37.1 Gen 17.8; 28.4
37.3 Gen 44.20
37.4 Gen 27.41; 49.22,23
37.7 Gen 42.6,9; 43.26; 44.14
37.8 Gen 49.26
37.10 Gen 27.29
37.11 Acts 7.9
37.14 Gen 35.27
37.17 2 Kings 6.13
37.18 1 Sam 19.1; Mt 27.1; Acts 23.12
37.21 Gen 42.22

[b] Or *chiefs* [c] Traditional rendering (compare Gk): *a coat of many colors*; Meaning of Heb uncertain

ing, "Let us not take his life."
22 Reuben said to them, "Shed no
blood; throw him into this pit here
in the wilderness, but lay no hand
on him"—that he might rescue
him out of their hand and restore
him to his father. 23 So when Joseph came to his brothers, they
stripped him of his robe, the long
robe with sleeves[d] that he wore;
24 and they took him and threw him
into a pit. The pit was empty; there
was no water in it.
25 Then they sat down to eat;
and looking up they saw a caravan
of Ishmaelites coming from Gilead,
with their camels carrying gum,
balm, and resin, on their way to
carry it down to Egypt. 26 Then Judah said to his brothers, "What
profit is it if we kill our brother and
conceal his blood? 27 Come, let us
sell him to the Ishmaelites, and not
lay our hands on him, for he is our
brother, our own flesh." And his
brothers agreed. 28 When some
Midianite traders passed by, they
drew Joseph up, lifting him out of
the pit, and sold him to the Ishmaelites for twenty pieces of silver.
And they took Joseph to Egypt.
29 When Reuben returned to
the pit and saw that Joseph was not
in the pit, he tore his clothes. 30 He
returned to his brothers, and said,
"The boy is gone; and I, where can
I turn?" 31 Then they took Joseph's
robe, slaughtered a goat, and
dipped the robe in the blood.
32 They had the long robe with
sleeves[d] taken to their father, and
they said, "This we have found; see
now whether it is your son's robe or
not." 33 He recognized it, and said,
"It is my son's robe! A wild animal
has devoured him; Joseph is without doubt torn to pieces." 34 Then
Jacob tore his garments, and put
sackcloth on his loins, and
mourned for his son many days.
35 All his sons and all his daughters
sought to comfort him; but he refused to be comforted, and said,
"No, I shall go down to Sheol to my
son, mourning." Thus his father
bewailed him. 36 Meanwhile the
Midianites had sold him in Egypt

37.25 vv. 28,36; Gen 43.11; Jer 8.22
37.26 v. 20; Gen 4.10; Job 16.18
37.27 Gen 42.21
37.28 Judg 6.3; Gen 45.4,5; Acts 7.9; Gen 39.1
37.29 Gen 44.13
37.30 Gen 42.13, 36
37.31 vv. 3,23
37.33 v. 20; Gen 44.28
37.34 v. 29; 2 Sam 3.31
37.35 2 Sam 12.17; Gen 42.38; 44.29,31
37.36 Gen 39.1

38.3 Gen 46.12; Num 26.19
38.7 1 Chr 2.3
38.8 Deut 25.5; Mt 22.24
38.9 Deut 25.6
38.11 Ruth 1.12, 13
38.12 Josh 15.10, 57

to Potiphar, one of Pharaoh's officials, the captain of the guard.

Judah and Tamar

38 It happened at that time
that Judah went down from
his brothers and settled near a certain Adullamite whose name was
Hirah. 2 There Judah saw the
daughter of a certain Canaanite
whose name was Shua; he married
her and went in to her. 3 She conceived and bore a son; and he
named him Er. 4 Again she conceived and bore a son whom she
named Onan. 5 Yet again she bore a
son, and she named him Shelah.
She[e] was in Chezib when she bore
him. 6 Judah took a wife for Er his
firstborn; her name was Tamar.
7 But Er, Judah's firstborn, was
wicked in the sight of the LORD, and
the LORD put him to death. 8 Then
Judah said to Onan, "Go in to your
brother's wife and perform the duty
of a brother-in-law to her; raise up
offspring for your brother." 9 But
since Onan knew that the offspring
would not be his, he spilled his semen on the ground whenever he
went in to his brother's wife, so
that he would not give offspring to
his brother. 10 What he did was displeasing in the sight of the LORD,
and he put him to death also.
11 Then Judah said to his daughter-
in-law Tamar, "Remain a widow in
your father's house until my son
Shelah grows up"—for he feared
that he too would die, like his
brothers. So Tamar went to live in
her father's house.
12 In course of time the wife of
Judah, Shua's daughter, died;
when Judah's time of mourning
was over,[f] he went up to Timnah
to his sheepshearers, he and his
friend Hirah the Adullamite.
13 When Tamar was told, "Your
father-in-law is going up to Timnah
to shear his sheep," 14 she put off
her widow's garments, put on a
veil, wrapped herself up, and sat
down at the entrance to Enaim,
which is on the road to Timnah.

[d] See note on 37.3 [e] Gk: Heb *He*
[f] Heb *when Judah was comforted*

She saw that Shelah was grown up,
yet she had not been given to him
in marriage. 15 When Judah saw
her, he thought her to be a prostitute, for she had covered her face.
16 He went over to her at the road
side, and said, "Come, let me come
in to you," for he did not know that
she was his daughter-in-law. She
said, "What will you give me, that
you may come in to me?" 17 He answered, "I will send you a kid from
the flock." And she said, "Only if
you give me a pledge, until you
send it." 18 He said, "What pledge
shall I give you?" She replied,
"Your signet and your cord, and the
staff that is in your hand." So he
gave them to her, and went in to
her, and she conceived by him.
19 Then she got up and went away,
and taking off her veil she put on
the garments of her widowhood.

20 When Judah sent the kid by
his friend the Adullamite, to recover the pledge from the woman, he
could not find her. 21 He asked the
townspeople, "Where is the temple
prostitute who was at Enaim by the
wayside?" But they said, "No prostitute has been here." 22 So he returned to Judah, and said, "I have
not found her; moreover the townspeople said, 'No prostitute has
been here.' " 23 Judah replied, "Let
her keep the things as her own,
otherwise we will be laughed at;
you see, I sent this kid, and you
could not find her."

24 About three months later Judah was told, "Your daughter-in-
law Tamar has played the whore;
moreover she is pregnant as a result of whoredom." And Judah
said, "Bring her out, and let her be
burned." 25 As she was being
brought out, she sent word to her
father-in-law, "It was the owner of
these who made me pregnant."
And she said, "Take note, please,
whose these are, the signet and the
cord and the staff." 26 Then Judah
acknowledged them and said, "She
is more in the right than I, since I
did not give her to my son Shelah."
And he did not lie with her again.

27 When the time of her delivery came, there were twins in her
womb. 28 While she was in labor,
one put out a hand; and the midwife took and bound on his hand a
crimson thread, saying, "This one
came out first." 29 But just then he
drew back his hand, and out came
his brother; and she said, "What a
breach you have made for yourself!" Therefore he was named Perez.[g] 30 Afterward his brother came
out with the crimson thread on his
hand; and he was named Zerah.[h]

Joseph and Potiphar's Wife

39 Now Joseph was taken
down to Egypt, and Poti-
phar, an officer of Pharaoh, the
captain of the guard, an Egyptian,
bought him from the Ishmaelites
who had brought him down there.
2 The LORD was with Joseph, and he
became a successful man; he was
in the house of his Egyptian master. 3 His master saw that the LORD
was with him, and that the LORD
caused all that he did to prosper in
his hands. 4 So Joseph found favor
in his sight and attended him; he
made him overseer of his house
and put him in charge of all that he
had. 5 From the time that he made
him overseer in his house and over
all that he had, the LORD blessed
the Egyptian's house for Joseph's
sake; the blessing of the LORD was
on all that he had, in house and
field. 6 So he left all that he had in
Joseph's charge; and, with him
there, he had no concern for anything but the food that he ate.

Now Joseph was handsome and
good-looking. 7 And after a time his
master's wife cast her eyes on Joseph and said, "Lie with me." 8 But
he refused and said to his master's
wife, "Look, with me here, my master has no concern about anything
in the house, and he has put everything that he has in my hand. 9 He
is not greater in this house than I
am, nor has he kept back anything
from me except yourself, because
you are his wife. How then could I
do this great wickedness, and sin

38.17 Ezek 16.33; v. 20
38.18 v. 25
38.19 v. 14
38.24 Lev 21.9; Deut 22.21
38.25 v. 18
38.26 1 Sam 24.17; v. 14
38.29 Gen 46.12; Num 26.20; Mt 1.3
39.1 Gen 37.28, 36; Ps 105.17
39.2 vv. 3,21,23
39.3 Gen 21.22; 26.28; Acts 7.9
39.4 vv. 8,22
39.5 Gen 30.27
39.7 2 Sam 13.11; Prov 7.15-20
39.9 Gen 20.6; 42.18; 2 Sam 12.13

[g] That is *A breach* [h] That is *Brightness*; perhaps alluding to the crimson thread

against God?" 10 And although she
spoke to Joseph day after day, he
would not consent to lie beside her
or to be with her. 11 One day, however, when he went into the house
to do his work, and while no one
else was in the house, 12 she caught
hold of his garment, saying, "Lie
with me!" But he left his garment
in her hand, and fled and ran outside. 13 When she saw that he had
left his garment in her hand and
had fled outside, 14 she called out
to the members of her household
and said to them, "See, my husband[i] has brought among us a Hebrew to insult us! He came in to me
to lie with me, and I cried out with
a loud voice; 15 and when he heard
me raise my voice and cry out, he
left his garment beside me, and
fled outside." 16 Then she kept his
garment by her until his master
came home, 17 and she told him the
same story, saying, "The Hebrew
servant, whom you have brought
among us, came in to me to insult
me; 18 but as soon as I raised my
voice and cried out, he left his garment beside me, and fled outside."
19 When his master heard the
words that his wife spoke to him,
saying, "This is the way your servant treated me," he became enraged. 20 And Joseph's master took
him and put him into the prison,
the place where the king's prisoners were confined; he remained
there in prison. 21 But the LORD was
with Joseph and showed him
steadfast love; he gave him favor in
the sight of the chief jailer. 22 The
chief jailer committed to Joseph's
care all the prisoners who were in
the prison, and whatever was done
there, he was the one who did it.
23 The chief jailer paid no heed to
anything that was in Joseph's care,
because the LORD was with him;
and whatever he did, the LORD
made it prosper.

The Dreams of Two Prisoners

40 Some time after this, the
cupbearer of the king of
Egypt and his baker offended their
lord the king of Egypt. 2 Pharaoh
was angry with his two officers, the
chief cupbearer and the chief baker, 3 and he put them in custody in
the house of the captain of the
guard, in the prison where Joseph
was confined. 4 The captain of the
guard charged Joseph with them,
and he waited on them; and
they continued for some time in
custody. 5 One night they both
dreamed—the cupbearer and the
baker of the king of Egypt, who
were confined in the prison—each
his own dream, and each dream
with its own meaning. 6 When Joseph came to them in the morning,
he saw that they were troubled. 7 So
he asked Pharaoh's officers, who
were with him in custody in his
master's house, "Why are your
faces downcast today?" 8 They said
to him, "We have had dreams, and
there is no one to interpret them."
And Joseph said to them, "Do not
interpretations belong to God?
Please tell them to me."
9 So the chief cupbearer told his
dream to Joseph, and said to him,
"In my dream there was a vine before me, 10 and on the vine there
were three branches. As soon as it
budded, its blossoms came out and
the clusters ripened into grapes.
11 Pharaoh's cup was in my hand;
and I took the grapes and pressed
them into Pharaoh's cup, and
placed the cup in Pharaoh's hand."
12 Then Joseph said to him, "This
is its interpretation: the three
branches are three days; 13 within
three days Pharaoh will lift up your
head and restore you to your office;
and you shall place Pharaoh's cup
in his hand, just as you used to do
when you were his cupbearer.
14 But remember me when it is well
with you; please do me the kindness to make mention of me to
Pharaoh, and so get me out of this
place. 15 For in fact I was stolen out
of the land of the Hebrews; and
here also I have done nothing that
they should have put me into the
dungeon."
16 When the chief baker saw

39.12 Prov 7.13-25
39.17 Ex 23.1; Ps 120.3
39.19 Prov 6.34,35
39.20 Ps 105.18
39.21 v.21; Ps 105.19; Ex 3.21; Dan 1.9
39.22 v. 4
39.23 vv. 2,3,8
40.1 vv. 11,13
40.3 Gen 39.20, 23
40.8 Gen 41.16; Dan 2.27,28
40.12 Gen 41.12, 25; Dan 2.36; 4.19
40.14 Lk 23.42; Josh 2.12
40.15 Gen 37.26-28

[i] Heb *he*

that the interpretation was favorable, he said to Joseph, "I also had
a dream: there were three cake baskets on my head, 17 and in the uppermost basket there were all sorts
of baked food for Pharaoh, but the
birds were eating it out of the basket on my head." 18 And Joseph answered, "This is its interpretation:
the three baskets are three days;
19 within three days Pharaoh will
lift up your head—from you!—and
hang you on a pole; and the birds
will eat the flesh from you."

20 On the third day, which was
Pharaoh's birthday, he made a
feast for all his servants, and lifted
up the head of the chief cupbearer
and the head of the chief baker
among his servants. 21 He restored
the chief cupbearer to his cupbear-
ing, and he placed the cup in Pharaoh's hand; 22 but the chief baker
he hanged, just as Joseph had interpreted to them. 23 Yet the chief
cupbearer did not remember Joseph, but forgot him.

Joseph Interprets Pharaoh's Dream

41 After two whole years,
Pharaoh dreamed that he
was standing by the Nile, 2 and
there came up out of the Nile seven
sleek and fat cows, and they grazed
in the reed grass. 3 Then seven other cows, ugly and thin, came up out
of the Nile after them, and stood by
the other cows on the bank of the
Nile. 4 The ugly and thin cows ate
up the seven sleek and fat cows.
And Pharaoh awoke. 5 Then he fell
asleep and dreamed a second time;
seven ears of grain, plump and
good, were growing on one stalk.
6 Then seven ears, thin and blighted by the east wind, sprouted after
them. 7 The thin ears swallowed up
the seven plump and full ears.
Pharaoh awoke, and it was a
dream. 8 In the morning his spirit
was troubled; so he sent and called
for all the magicians of Egypt and
all its wise men. Pharaoh told them
his dreams, but there was no one
who could interpret them to Pharaoh.

40.18 v. 12
40.19 v. 13
40.20 vv. 13,19
40.21 v. 13
40.22 v. 19
41.8 Dan 2.1,3; 4.5,19; Ex 7.11,22; Dan 2.27; 4.7
41.10 Gen 40.2,3.
41.11 Gen 40.5
41.12 Gen 40.12ff
41.13 Gen 40.21, 22
41.14 Ps 105.20; Dan 2.25; Ps 113.7,8
41.15 v. 12
41.16 Dan 2.30; Acts 3.12; 2 Cor 3.5; Gen 40.8
41.24 v. 8

9 Then the chief cupbearer said
to Pharaoh, "I remember my faults
today. 10 Once Pharaoh was angry
with his servants, and put me and
the chief baker in custody in the
house of the captain of the guard.
11 We dreamed on the same night,
he and I, each having a dream with
its own meaning. 12 A young Hebrew was there with us, a servant of
the captain of the guard. When we
told him, he interpreted our
dreams to us, giving an interpretation to each according to his
dream. 13 As he interpreted to us,
so it turned out; I was restored to
my office, and the baker was
hanged."

14 Then Pharaoh sent for Joseph, and he was hurriedly brought
out of the dungeon. When he had
shaved himself and changed his
clothes, he came in before Pharaoh. 15 And Pharaoh said to Joseph,
"I have had a dream, and there is
no one who can interpret it. I have
heard it said of you that when you
hear a dream you can interpret it."
16 Joseph answered Pharaoh, "It is
not I; God will give Pharaoh a favorable answer." 17 Then Pharaoh said
to Joseph, "In my dream I was
standing on the banks of the Nile;
18 and seven cows, fat and sleek,
came up out of the Nile and fed in
the reed grass. 19 Then seven other
cows came up after them, poor,
very ugly, and thin. Never had I
seen such ugly ones in all the land
of Egypt. 20 The thin and ugly cows
ate up the first seven fat cows,
21 but when they had eaten them no
one would have known that they
had done so, for they were still as
ugly as before. Then I awoke. 22 I
fell asleep a second time[j] and I
saw in my dream seven ears of
grain, full and good, growing on
one stalk, 23 and seven ears, withered, thin, and blighted by the east
wind, sprouting after them; 24 and
the thin ears swallowed up the sev-
en good ears. But when I told it to

[j] Gk Syr Vg: Heb lacks *I fell asleep a second time*

the magicians, there was no one
who could explain it to me."
25 Then Joseph said to Pharaoh, "Pharaoh's dreams are one
and the same; God has revealed to
Pharaoh what he is about to do.
26 The seven good cows are seven
years, and the seven good ears are
seven years; the dreams are one.
27 The seven lean and ugly cows
that came up after them are seven
years, as are the seven empty ears
blighted by the east wind. They are
seven years of famine. 28 It is as I
told Pharaoh; God has shown to
Pharaoh what he is about to do.
29 There will come seven years of
great plenty throughout all the
land of Egypt. 30 After them there
will arise seven years of famine,
and all the plenty will be forgotten
in the land of Egypt; the famine
will consume the land. 31 The plenty will no longer be known in the
land because of the famine that
will follow, for it will be very grievous. 32 And the doubling of Pharaoh's dream means that the thing
is fixed by God, and God will shortly bring it about. 33 Now therefore
let Pharaoh select a man who is
discerning and wise, and set him
over the land of Egypt. 34 Let Pharaoh proceed to appoint overseers
over the land, and take one-fifth of
the produce of the land of Egypt
during the seven plenteous years.
35 Let them gather all the food of
these good years that are coming,
and lay up grain under the authority of Pharaoh for food in the cities,
and let them keep it. 36 That food
shall be a reserve for the land
against the seven years of famine
that are to befall the land of Egypt,
so that the land may not perish
through the famine."

Joseph's Rise to Power

37 The proposal pleased Pharaoh and all his servants. 38 Pharaoh
said to his servants, "Can we find
anyone else like this—one in
whom is the spirit of God?" 39 So
Pharaoh said to Joseph, "Since
God has shown you all this, there is
no one so discerning and wise as
you. 40 You shall be over my house,
and all my people shall order themselves as you command; only with
regard to the throne will I be greater than you." 41 And Pharaoh said
to Joseph, "See, I have set you over
all the land of Egypt." 42 Removing
his signet ring from his hand, Pharaoh put it on Joseph's hand; he arrayed him in garments of fine lin-
en, and put a gold chain around his
neck. 43 He had him ride in the
chariot of his second-in-command;
and they cried out in front of him,
"Bow the knee!"[k] Thus he set him
over all the land of Egypt. 44 Moreover Pharaoh said to Joseph, "I am
Pharaoh, and without your consent
no one shall lift up hand or foot in
all the land of Egypt." 45 Pharaoh
gave Joseph the name Zaphenath-
paneah; and he gave him Asenath
daughter of Potiphera, priest of On,
as his wife. Thus Joseph gained authority over the land of Egypt.
46 Joseph was thirty years old
when he entered the service of
Pharaoh king of Egypt. And Joseph
went out from the presence of
Pharaoh, and went through all the
land of Egypt. 47 During the seven
plenteous years the earth produced
abundantly. 48 He gathered up all
the food of the seven years when
there was plenty[l] in the land of
Egypt, and stored up food in the
cities; he stored up in every city the
food from the fields around it. 49 So
Joseph stored up grain in such
abundance—like the sand of the
sea—that he stopped measuring it;
it was beyond measure.
50 Before the years of famine
came, Joseph had two sons, whom
Asenath daughter of Potiphera,
priest of On, bore to him. 51 Joseph
named the firstborn Manasseh,[m]
"For," he said, "God has made me
forget all my hardship and all my
father's house." 52 The second he
named Ephraim,[n] "For God has

41.25 vv. 28,32
41.27 2 Kings 8.1
41.28 vv. 25,32
41.29 v. 47
41.30 vv. 54,56; Gen 47.13
41.32 Num 23.19; Isa 46.10,11
41.35 v. 48
41.38 Num 27.18; Dan 4.8,18
41.40 Ps 105.21, 22; Acts 7.10
41.41 Gen 42.6
41.42 Esther 3.10; Dan 5.7,16, 29
41.43 Esther 6.9
41.44 Ps 105.22
41.46 Gen 37.2
41.50 Gen 46.20
41.52 Gen 17.6; 28.3; 49.22

[k] *Abrek*, apparently an Egyptian word similar in sound to the Hebrew word meaning *to kneel*
[l] Sam Gk: MT *the seven years that were*
[m] That is *Making to forget*
[n] From a Hebrew word meaning *to be fruitful*

made me fruitful in the land of my
misfortunes."
53 The seven years of plenty
that prevailed in the land of Egypt
came to an end; 54 and the seven
years of famine began to come, just
as Joseph had said. There was famine in every country, but throughout the land of Egypt there was
bread. 55 When all the land of Egypt
was famished, the people cried to
Pharaoh for bread. Pharaoh said to
all the Egyptians, "Go to Joseph;
what he says to you, do." 56 And
since the famine had spread over
all the land, Joseph opened all the
storehouses,[o] and sold to the
Egyptians, for the famine was severe in the land of Egypt. 57 Moreover, all the world came to Joseph
in Egypt to buy grain, because the
famine became severe throughout
the world.

Joseph's Brothers Go to Egypt

42 When Jacob learned that
there was grain in Egypt, he
said to his sons, "Why do you keep
looking at one another? 2 I have
heard," he said, "that there is grain
in Egypt; go down and buy grain for
us there, that we may live and not
die." 3 So ten of Joseph's brothers
went down to buy grain in Egypt.
4 But Jacob did not send Joseph's
brother Benjamin with his brothers, for he feared that harm might
come to him. 5 Thus the sons of Israel were among the other people
who came to buy grain, for the famine had reached the land of Canaan.
6 Now Joseph was governor over
the land; it was he who sold to all
the people of the land. And Joseph's brothers came and bowed
themselves before him with their
faces to the ground. 7 When Joseph
saw his brothers, he recognized
them, but he treated them like
strangers and spoke harshly to
them. "Where do you come from?"
he said. They said, "From the land
of Canaan, to buy food." 8 Although
Joseph had recognized his brothers, they did not recognize him.
9 Joseph also remembered the
dreams that he had dreamed about
them. He said to them, "You are
spies; you have come to see the nakedness of the land!" 10 They said
to him, "No, my lord; your servants
have come to buy food. 11 We are all
sons of one man; we are honest
men; your servants have never been
spies." 12 But he said to them, "No,
you have come to see the nakedness of the land!" 13 They said, "We,
your servants, are twelve brothers,
the sons of a certain man in the
land of Canaan; the youngest, however, is now with our father, and
one is no more." 14 But Joseph said
to them, "It is just as I have said to
you; you are spies! 15 Here is how
you shall be tested: as Pharaoh
lives, you shall not leave this place
unless your youngest brother
comes here! 16 Let one of you go
and bring your brother, while the
rest of you remain in prison, in order that your words may be tested,
whether there is truth in you; or
else, as Pharaoh lives, surely you
are spies." 17 And he put them all
together in prison for three days.
18 On the third day Joseph said
to them, "Do this and you will live,
for I fear God: 19 if you are honest
men, let one of your brothers stay
here where you are imprisoned.
The rest of you shall go and carry
grain for the famine of your households, 20 and bring your youngest
brother to me. Thus your words will
be verified, and you shall not die."
And they agreed to do so. 21 They
said to one another, "Alas, we are
paying the penalty for what we did
to our brother; we saw his anguish
when he pleaded with us, but we
would not listen. That is why this
anguish has come upon us."
22 Then Reuben answered them,
"Did I not tell you not to wrong the
boy? But you would not listen. So
now there comes a reckoning for
his blood." 23 They did not know
that Joseph understood them,
since he spoke with them through
an interpreter. 24 He turned away

41.54 v. 30; Ps 105.16; Acts 7.11
41.56 Gen 42.6
42.1 Acts 7.12
42.2 Gen 43.8
42.4 Gen 35.24
42.5 Gen 41.57; Acts 7.11
42.6 Gen 41.41, 55; 37.7
42.7 v. 30
42.9 Gen 37.6-9
42.13 Gen 43.7; 37.30
42.18 Lev 25.43
42.20 v. 34
42.21 Hos 5.15; Prov 21.13
42.22 Gen 37.22; 9.5,6
42.24 Gen 43.30; 45.14,15; 43.14,23

o Gk Vg Compare Syr: Heb *opened all that was in* (or, *among*) *them*

from them and wept; then he returned and spoke to them. And he
picked out Simeon and had him
bound before their eyes. 25 Joseph
then gave orders to fill their bags
with grain, to return every man's
money to his sack, and to give them
provisions for their journey. This
was done for them.

Joseph's Brothers Return to Canaan

26 They loaded their donkeys
with their grain, and departed.
27 When one of them opened his
sack to give his donkey fodder at
the lodging place, he saw his money at the top of the sack. 28 He said
to his brothers, "My money has
been put back; here it is in my
sack!" At this they lost heart and
turned trembling to one another,
saying, "What is this that God has
done to us?"
29 When they came to their father Jacob in the land of Canaan,
they told him all that had happened to them, saying, 30 "The
man, the lord of the land, spoke
harshly to us, and charged us with
spying on the land. 31 But we said to
him, 'We are honest men, we are
not spies. 32 We are twelve brothers, sons of our father; one is no
more, and the youngest is now with
our father in the land of Canaan.'
33 Then the man, the lord of the
land, said to us, 'By this I shall
know that you are honest men:
leave one of your brothers with me,
take grain for the famine of your
households, and go your way.
34 Bring your youngest brother to
me, and I shall know that you are
not spies but honest men. Then I
will release your brother to you,
and you may trade in the land.' "
35 As they were emptying their
sacks, there in each one's sack was
his bag of money. When they and
their father saw their bundles of
money, they were dismayed. 36 And
their father Jacob said to them, "I
am the one you have bereaved of
children: Joseph is no more, and
Simeon is no more, and now you
would take Benjamin. All this has
happened to me!" 37 Then Reuben
said to his father, "You may kill my
two sons if I do not bring him back
to you. Put him in my hands, and I
will bring him back to you." 38 But
he said, "My son shall not go down
with you, for his brother is dead,
and he alone is left. If harm should
come to him on the journey that
you are to make, you would bring
down my gray hairs with sorrow to
Sheol."

The Brothers Come Again, Bringing Benjamin

43 Now the famine was severe
in the land. 2 And when
they had eaten up the grain that
they had brought from Egypt, their
father said to them, "Go again, buy
us a little more food." 3 But Judah
said to him, "The man solemnly
warned us, saying, 'You shall not
see my face unless your brother is
with you.' 4 If you will send our
brother with us, we will go down
and buy you food; 5 but if you will
not send him, we will not go down,
for the man said to us, 'You shall
not see my face, unless your brother is with you.' " 6 Israel said, "Why
did you treat me so badly as to tell
the man that you had another
brother?" 7 They replied, "The man
questioned us carefully about ourselves and our kindred, saying, 'Is
your father still alive? Have you another brother?' What we told him
was in answer to these questions.
Could we in any way know that he
would say, 'Bring your brother
down'?" 8 Then Judah said to his
father Israel, "Send the boy with
me, and let us be on our way, so
that we may live and not die—you
and we and also our little ones. 9 I
myself will be surety for him; you
can hold me accountable for him.
If I do not bring him back to you
and set him before you, then let me
bear the blame forever. 10 If we had
not delayed, we would now have returned twice."
11 Then their father Israel said
to them, "If it must be so, then do
this: take some of the choice fruits
of the land in your bags, and carry

42.25 Gen 44.1; Rom 12.17, 20,21
42.26 Gen 37.31-35
42.30 v. 7
42.31 v. 11
42.33 Gen 15.19, 20
42.35 Gen 43.12, 15
42.36 Gen 43.14
42.38 Gen 37.33, 35; 44.31
43.1 Gen 41.56, 57
43.3 Gen 42.20; 44.23
43.7 v. 27; Gen 42.13
43.9 Gen 42.37; 44.32; Philem 18, 19
43.11 Gen 32.20; Prov 18.16; Gen 37.25; Jer 8.22

them down as a present to the
man—a little balm and a little honey, gum, resin, pistachio nuts, and
almonds. 12 Take double the money
with you. Carry back with you the
money that was returned in the top
of your sacks; perhaps it was an
oversight. 13 Take your brother
also, and be on your way again to
the man; 14 may God Almighty[p]
grant you mercy before the man, so
that he may send back your other
brother and Benjamin. As for me, if
I am bereaved of my children, I am
bereaved." 15 So the men took the
present, and they took double the
money with them, as well as Benjamin. Then they went on their way
down to Egypt, and stood before
Joseph.
16 When Joseph saw Benjamin
with them, he said to the steward
of his house, "Bring the men into
the house, and slaughter an animal
and make ready, for the men are to
dine with me at noon." 17 The man
did as Joseph said, and brought the
men to Joseph's house. 18 Now the
men were afraid because they were
brought to Joseph's house, and
they said, "It is because of the
money, replaced in our sacks the
first time, that we have been
brought in, so that he may have an
opportunity to fall upon us, to
make slaves of us and take our donkeys." 19 So they went up to the
steward of Joseph's house and
spoke with him at the entrance to
the house. 20 They said, "Oh, my
lord, we came down the first time
to buy food; 21 and when we came
to the lodging place we opened our
sacks, and there was each one's
money in the top of his sack, our
money in full weight. So we have
brought it back with us. 22 Moreover we have brought down with us
additional money to buy food. We
do not know who put our money in
our sacks." 23 He replied, "Rest assured, do not be afraid; your God
and the God of your father must
have put treasure in your sacks for
you; I received your money." Then
he brought Simeon out to them.
24 When the steward[q] had brought
the men into Joseph's house, and
given them water, and they had
washed their feet, and when he had
given their donkeys fodder, 25 they
made the present ready for Joseph's coming at noon, for they
had heard that they would dine
there.
26 When Joseph came home,
they brought him the present that
they had carried into the house,
and bowed to the ground before
him. 27 He inquired about their
welfare, and said, "Is your father
well, the old man of whom you
spoke? Is he still alive?" 28 They
said, "Your servant our father is
well; he is still alive." And they
bowed their heads and did obeisance. 29 Then he looked up and
saw his brother Benjamin, his
mother's son, and said, "Is this
your youngest brother, of whom
you spoke to me? God be gracious
to you, my son!" 30 With that, Joseph hurried out, because he was
overcome with affection for his
brother, and he was about to weep.
So he went into a private room and
wept there. 31 Then he washed his
face and came out; and controlling
himself he said, "Serve the meal."
32 They served him by himself, and
them by themselves, and the Egyptians who ate with him by themselves, because the Egyptians
could not eat with the Hebrews, for
that is an abomination to the Egyptians. 33 When they were seated before him, the firstborn according to
his birthright and the youngest according to his youth, the men
looked at one another in amazement. 34 Portions were taken to
them from Joseph's table, but Benjamin's portion was five times as
much as any of theirs. So they
drank and were merry with him.

Joseph Detains Benjamin

44 Then he commanded the
steward of his house, "Fill
the men's sacks with food, as much
as they can carry, and put each
man's money in the top of his sack.

43.12 Gen 42.35; vv. 21,22
43.14 Gen 17.1; 28.3; 35.11; Ps 106.46; Gen 42.24
43.16 Gen 44.1
43.20 Gen 42.3,10
43.21 Gen 42.35; vv. 12,15
43.23 Gen 42.24
43.24 Gen 18.4; 19.2; 24.32
43.26 Gen 37.7,10
43.27 v. 7; Gen 45.3
43.28 Gen 37.7,10
43.29 Gen 35.17, 18; 42.13; Num 6.25; Ps 67.1
43.30 Gen 42.24; 45.2,14,15; 46.29
43.31 Gen 45.1
43.32 Gen 46.34
43.34 Gen 45.22
44.1 Gen 42.25

[p] Traditional rendering of Heb *El Shaddai*
[q] Heb *the man*

2 Put my cup, the silver cup, in the
top of the sack of the youngest,
with his money for the grain." And
he did as Joseph told him. 3 As soon
as the morning was light, the men
were sent away with their donkeys.
4 When they had gone only a short
distance from the city, Joseph said
to his steward, "Go, follow after the
men; and when you overtake them,
say to them, 'Why have you returned evil for good? Why have you
stolen my silver cup?[r] 5 Is it not
from this that my lord drinks? Does
he not indeed use it for divination?
You have done wrong in doing
this.' "

6 When he overtook them, he
repeated these words to them.
7 They said to him, "Why does my
lord speak such words as these?
Far be it from your servants that
they should do such a thing! 8 Look,
the money that we found at the top
of our sacks, we brought back to
you from the land of Canaan; why
then would we steal silver or gold
from your lord's house? 9 Should it
be found with any one of your servants, let him die; moreover the
rest of us will become my lord's
slaves." 10 He said, "Even so; in accordance with your words, let it be:
he with whom it is found shall become my slave, but the rest of you
shall go free." 11 Then each one
quickly lowered his sack to the
ground, and each opened his sack.
12 He searched, beginning with the
eldest and ending with the youngest; and the cup was found in Benjamin's sack. 13 At this they tore
their clothes. Then each one loaded his donkey, and they returned to
the city.

14 Judah and his brothers came
to Joseph's house while he was still
there; and they fell to the ground
before him. 15 Joseph said to them,
"What deed is this that you have
done? Do you not know that one
such as I can practice divination?"
16 And Judah said, "What can we
say to my lord? What can we speak?
How can we clear ourselves? God
has found out the guilt of your servants; here we are then, my lord's
slaves, both we and also the one in
whose possession the cup has been
found." 17 But he said, "Far be it
from me that I should do so! Only
the one in whose possession the
cup was found shall be my slave;
but as for you, go up in peace to
your father."

Judah Pleads for Benjamin's Release

18 Then Judah stepped up to
him and said, "O my lord, let your
servant please speak a word in my
lord's ears, and do not be angry
with your servant; for you are like
Pharaoh himself. 19 My lord asked
his servants, saying, 'Have you a father or a brother?' 20 And we said to
my lord, 'We have a father, an old
man, and a young brother, the
child of his old age. His brother is
dead; he alone is left of his mother's children, and his father loves
him.' 21 Then you said to your servants, 'Bring him down to me, so
that I may set my eyes on him.'
22 We said to my lord, 'The boy cannot leave his father, for if he should
leave his father, his father would
die.' 23 Then you said to your servants, 'Unless your youngest brother comes down with you, you shall
see my face no more.' 24 When we
went back to your servant my father we told him the words of my
lord. 25 And when our father said,
'Go again, buy us a little food,'
26 we said, 'We cannot go down.
Only if our youngest brother goes
with us, will we go down; for we
cannot see the man's face unless
our youngest brother is with us.'
27 Then your servant my father said
to us, 'You know that my wife bore
me two sons; 28 one left me, and I
said, Surely he has been torn to
pieces; and I have never seen him
since. 29 If you take this one also
from me, and harm comes to him,
you will bring down my gray hairs
in sorrow to Sheol.' 30 Now therefore, when I come to your servant
my father and the boy is not with
us, then, as his life is bound up in

44.5 v. 15; Lev 19.26; Deut 18.10-14
44.8 Gen 43.21
44.9 Gen 31.32
44.13 Gen 37.29, 34; Num 14.6
44.14 Gen 37.7,10
44.15 v. 5
44.16 v. 9
44.18 Gen 37.7,8; 41.40-44
44.20 v. 30; Gen 43.8; 37.33; 42.13, 38
44.23 Gen 43.3
44.28 Gen 37.31-35
44.29 Gen 42.36, 38

[r] Gk Compare Vg: Heb lacks *Why have you stolen my silver cup?*

the boy's life, 31 when he sees that the boy is not with us, he will die; and your servants will bring down the gray hairs of your servant our father with sorrow to Sheol. 32 For your servant became surety for the boy to my father, saying, 'If I do not bring him back to you, then I will bear the blame in the sight of my father all my life.' 33 Now therefore, please let your servant remain as a slave to my lord in place of the boy; and let the boy go back with his brothers. 34 For how can I go back to my father if the boy is not with me? I fear to see the suffering that would come upon my father."

Joseph Reveals Himself to His Brothers

45 Then Joseph could no longer control himself before all those who stood by him, and he cried out, "Send everyone away from me." So no one stayed with him when Joseph made himself known to his brothers. 2 And he wept so loudly that the Egyptians heard it, and the household of Pharaoh heard it. 3 Joseph said to his brothers, "I am Joseph. Is my father still alive?" But his brothers could not answer him, so dismayed were they at his presence.

4 Then Joseph said to his brothers, "Come closer to me." And they came closer. He said, "I am your brother, Joseph, whom you sold into Egypt. 5 And now do not be distressed, or angry with yourselves, because you sold me here; for God sent me before you to preserve life. 6 For the famine has been in the land these two years; and there are five more years in which there will be neither plowing nor harvest. 7 God sent me before you to preserve for you a remnant on earth, and to keep alive for you many survivors. 8 So it was not you who sent me here, but God; he has made me a father to Pharaoh, and lord of all his house and ruler over all the land of Egypt. 9 Hurry and go up to my father and say to him, 'Thus says your son Joseph, God has made me lord of all Egypt; come

44.32 Gen 43.9
45.1 Acts 7.13
45.2 vv. 14,15; Gen 46.29
45.3 Gen 43.27
45.4 Gen 37.28
45.5 Isa 40.2; Gen 37.28; 44.20; 50.20
45.8 Gen 41.43
45.10 Gen 46.28, 34; 47.1
45.13 Acts 7.14
45.18 Gen 27.28; Num 18.12, 29
45.22 Gen 43.34

down to me, do not delay. 10 You shall settle in the land of Goshen, and you shall be near me, you and your children and your children's children, as well as your flocks, your herds, and all that you have. 11 I will provide for you there—since there are five more years of famine to come—so that you and your household, and all that you have, will not come to poverty.' 12 And now your eyes and the eyes of my brother Benjamin see that it is my own mouth that speaks to you. 13 You must tell my father how greatly I am honored in Egypt, and all that you have seen. Hurry and bring my father down here." 14 Then he fell upon his brother Benjamin's neck and wept, while Benjamin wept upon his neck. 15 And he kissed all his brothers and wept upon them; and after that his brothers talked with him.

16 When the report was heard in Pharaoh's house, "Joseph's brothers have come," Pharaoh and his servants were pleased. 17 Pharaoh said to Joseph, "Say to your brothers, 'Do this: load your animals and go back to the land of Canaan. 18 Take your father and your households and come to me, so that I may give you the best of the land of Egypt, and you may enjoy the fat of the land.' 19 You are further charged to say, 'Do this: take wagons from the land of Egypt for your little ones and for your wives, and bring your father, and come. 20 Give no thought to your possessions, for the best of all the land of Egypt is yours.' "

21 The sons of Israel did so. Joseph gave them wagons according to the instruction of Pharaoh, and he gave them provisions for the journey. 22 To each one of them he gave a set of garments; but to Benjamin he gave three hundred pieces of silver and five sets of garments. 23 To his father he sent the following: ten donkeys loaded with the good things of Egypt, and ten female donkeys loaded with grain, bread, and provision for his father on the journey. 24 Then he sent his

brothers on their way, and as they
were leaving he said to them, "Do
not quarrel[s] along the way."
25 So they went up out of Egypt
and came to their father Jacob in
the land of Canaan. 26 And they told
him, "Joseph is still alive! He is
even ruler over all the land of
Egypt." He was stunned; he could
not believe them. 27 But when they
told him all the words of Joseph
that he had said to them, and when
he saw the wagons that Joseph had
sent to carry him, the spirit of their
father Jacob revived. 28 Israel said,
"Enough! My son Joseph is still
alive. I must go and see him before
I die."

Jacob Brings His Whole Family to Egypt

46 When Israel set out on his
journey with all that he had
and came to Beer-sheba, he offered
sacrifices to the God of his father
Isaac. 2 God spoke to Israel in visions of the night, and said, "Jacob, Jacob." And he said, "Here I
am." 3 Then he said, "I am God,[t]
the God of your father; do not be
afraid to go down to Egypt, for I will
make of you a great nation there. 4 I
myself will go down with you to
Egypt, and I will also bring you up
again; and Joseph's own hand shall
close your eyes."
5 Then Jacob set out from Beer-
sheba; and the sons of Israel carried their father Jacob, their little
ones, and their wives, in the wagons that Pharaoh had sent to carry
him. 6 They also took their livestock and the goods that they had
acquired in the land of Canaan,
and they came into Egypt, Jacob
and all his offspring with him, 7 his
sons, and his sons' sons with him,
his daughters, and his sons' daughters; all his offspring he brought
with him into Egypt.
8 Now these are the names of
the Israelites, Jacob and his offspring, who came to Egypt. Reuben, Jacob's firstborn, 9 and the
children of Reuben: Hanoch, Pallu,
Hezron, and Carmi. 10 The children
of Simeon: Jemuel, Jamin, Ohad,
Jachin, Zohar, and Shaul,[u] the son
of a Canaanite woman. 11 The children of Levi: Gershon, Kohath, and
Merari. 12 The children of Judah:
Er, Onan, Shelah, Perez, and Zerah
(but Er and Onan died in the land
of Canaan); and the children of Perez were Hezron and Hamul. 13 The
children of Issachar: Tola, Puvah,
Jashub,[v] and Shimron. 14 The children of Zebulun: Sered, Elon, and
Jahleel 15 (these are the sons of
Leah, whom she bore to Jacob in
Paddan-aram, together with his
daughter Dinah; in all his sons and
his daughters numbered thirty-
three). 16 The children of Gad:
Ziphion, Haggi, Shuni, Ezbon, Eri,
Arodi, and Areli. 17 The children of
Asher: Imnah, Ishvah, Ishvi, Beriah, and their sister Serah. The children of Beriah: Heber and Malchiel
18 (these are the children of Zilpah,
whom Laban gave to his daughter
Leah; and these she bore to
Jacob—sixteen persons). 19 The
children of Jacob's wife Rachel: Joseph and Benjamin. 20 To Joseph in
the land of Egypt were born Manasseh and Ephraim, whom Asenath
daughter of Potiphera, priest of On,
bore to him. 21 The children of Benjamin: Bela, Becher, Ashbel, Gera,
Naaman, Ehi, Rosh, Muppim,
Huppim, and Ard 22 (these are the
children of Rachel, who were born
to Jacob—fourteen persons in all).
23 The children of Dan: Hashum.[w]
24 The children of Naphtali: Jahzeel, Guni, Jezer, and Shillem
25 (these are the children of Bilhah,
whom Laban gave to his daughter
Rachel, and these she bore to
Jacob—seven persons in all). 26 All
the persons belonging to Jacob
who came into Egypt, who were his
own offspring, not including the
wives of his sons, were sixty-six
persons in all. 27 The children of Joseph, who were born to him in
Egypt, were two; all the persons of
the house of Jacob who came into
Egypt were seventy.

46.1 Gen 28.10; 26.24; 28.13
46.2 Job 33.14, 15; Gen 22.11; 31.11
46.3 Gen 28.13; 12.2
46.4 Gen 28.15; 50.13,24,25; Ex 3.8; Gen 50.1
46.5 Gen 45.19, 21
46.6 Acts 7.15; Deut 26.5; Josh 24.4; Ps 105.23; Isa 52.4
46.8 Ex 1.1
46.10 Ex 6.15
46.11 1 Chr 6.1, 16
46.12 1 Chr 2.3; 4.21; 38.3,7, 10,29
46.17 1 Chr 7.30
46.18 Gen 30.10; 29.24
46.19 Gen 44.27
46.20 Gen 41.50
46.21 1 Chr 7.6; 8.1
46.23 1 Chr 7.12
46.24 1 Chr 7.13
46.25 Gen 30.5,7; 29.29
46.26 Ex 1.5
46.27 Deut 10.22; Acts 7.14

[s] Or *be agitated* [t] Heb *the God*
[u] Or *Saul* [v] Compare Sam Gk Num 26.24
1 Chr 7.1: MT *Iob* [w] Gk: Heb *Hushim*

Jacob Settles in Goshen

28 Israel[x] sent Judah ahead to
Joseph to lead the way before him
into Goshen. When they came to
the land of Goshen, 29 Joseph made
ready his chariot and went up to
meet his father Israel in Goshen.
He presented himself to him, fell
on his neck, and wept on his neck
a good while. 30 Israel said to Joseph, "I can die now, having seen
for myself that you are still alive."
31 Joseph said to his brothers and to
his father's household, "I will go up
and tell Pharaoh, and will say to
him, 'My brothers and my father's
household, who were in the land of
Canaan, have come to me. 32 The
men are shepherds, for they have
been keepers of livestock; and they
have brought their flocks, and their
herds, and all that they have.'
33 When Pharaoh calls you, and
says, 'What is your occupation?'
34 you shall say, 'Your servants have
been keepers of livestock from our
youth even until now, both we and
our ancestors'—in order that you
may settle in the land of Goshen,
because all shepherds are abhorrent to the Egyptians."

47 So Joseph went and told
Pharaoh, "My father and
my brothers, with their flocks and
herds and all that they possess,
have come from the land of Canaan; they are now in the land of
Goshen." 2 From among his brothers he took five men and presented
them to Pharaoh. 3 Pharaoh said to
his brothers, "What is your occupation?" And they said to Pharaoh,
"Your servants are shepherds, as
our ancestors were." 4 They said to
Pharaoh, "We have come to reside
as aliens in the land; for there is no
pasture for your servants' flocks because the famine is severe in the
land of Canaan. Now, we ask you,
let your servants settle in the land
of Goshen." 5 Then Pharaoh said to
Joseph, "Your father and your
brothers have come to you. 6 The
land of Egypt is before you; settle
your father and your brothers in the
best part of the land; let them live
in the land of Goshen; and if you
know that there are capable men
among them, put them in charge of
my livestock."

7 Then Joseph brought in his father Jacob, and presented him before Pharaoh, and Jacob blessed
Pharaoh. 8 Pharaoh said to Jacob,
"How many are the years of your
life?" 9 Jacob said to Pharaoh, "The
years of my earthly sojourn are one
hundred thirty; few and hard have
been the years of my life. They do
not compare with the years of the
life of my ancestors during their
long sojourn." 10 Then Jacob
blessed Pharaoh, and went out
from the presence of Pharaoh.
11 Joseph settled his father and his
brothers, and granted them a holding in the land of Egypt, in the best
part of the land, in the land of Rameses, as Pharaoh had instructed.
12 And Joseph provided his father,
his brothers, and all his father's
household with food, according to
the number of their dependents.

The Famine in Egypt

13 Now there was no food in all
the land, for the famine was very
severe. The land of Egypt and the
land of Canaan languished because
of the famine. 14 Joseph collected
all the money to be found in the
land of Egypt and in the land of Canaan, in exchange for the grain that
they bought; and Joseph brought
the money into Pharaoh's house.
15 When the money from the land of
Egypt and from the land of Canaan
was spent, all the Egyptians came
to Joseph, and said, "Give us food!
Why should we die before your
eyes? For our money is gone."
16 And Joseph answered, "Give me
your livestock, and I will give you
food in exchange for your livestock,
if your money is gone." 17 So they
brought their livestock to Joseph;
and Joseph gave them food in exchange for the horses, the flocks,
the herds, and the donkeys. That
year he supplied them with food in
exchange for all their livestock.
18 When that year was ended, they

46.28 Gen 47.1
46.29 Gen 45.14, 15
46.31 Gen 47.1
46.33 Gen 47.2,3
46.34 Gen 13.7,8; 26.20; 37.2; 45.10,18; Ex 8.26
47.1 Gen 46.31
47.3 Gen 46.33, 34
47.4 Gen 15.13; Deut 26.5; Gen 43.1; 46.34
47.6 v. 11; Gen 45.10, 18
47.8 Ps 39.12; Heb 11.9, 13; Job 14.1; Gen 25.7; 35.28
47.10 v. 7
47.11 Ex 1.11; 12.37; 6.27
47.13 Gen 41.30; Acts 7.11
47.14 Gen 41.56
47.15 v. 19

[x] Heb *He*

came to him the following year,
and said to him, "We can not hide
from my lord that our money is all
spent; and the herds of cattle are
my lord's. There is nothing left in
the sight of my lord but our bodies
and our lands. 19 Shall we die before your eyes, both we and our
land? Buy us and our land in exchange for food. We with our land
will become slaves to Pharaoh; just
give us seed, so that we may live
and not die, and that the land may
not become desolate."
20 So Joseph bought all the
land of Egypt for Pharaoh. All the
Egyptians sold their fields, because
the famine was severe upon them;
and the land became Pharaoh's.
21 As for the people, he made slaves
of them[y] from one end of Egypt to
the other. 22 Only the land of the
priests he did not buy; for the
priests had a fixed allowance from
Pharaoh, and lived on the allowance that Pharaoh gave them;
therefore they did not sell their
land. 23 Then Joseph said to the
people, "Now that I have this day
bought you and your land for Pharaoh, here is seed for you; sow the
land. 24 And at the harvests you
shall give one-fifth to Pharaoh, and
four-fifths shall be your own, as
seed for the field and as food for
yourselves and your households,
and as food for your little ones."
25 They said, "You have saved our
lives; may it please my lord, we will
be slaves to Pharaoh." 26 So Joseph
made it a statute concerning the
land of Egypt, and it stands to this
day, that Pharaoh should have the
fifth. The land of the priests alone
did not become Pharaoh's.

The Last Days of Jacob

27 Thus Israel settled in the
land of Egypt, in the region of Goshen; and they gained possessions
in it, and were fruitful and multiplied exceedingly. 28 Jacob lived in
the land of Egypt seventeen years;
so the days of Jacob, the years of
his life, were one hundred forty-
seven years.
29 When the time of Israel's
death drew near, he called his son
Joseph and said to him, "If I have
found favor with you, put your
hand under my thigh and promise
to deal loyally and truly with me.
Do not bury me in Egypt. 30 When I
lie down with my ancestors, carry
me out of Egypt and bury me in
their burial place." He answered, "I
will do as you have said." 31 And he
said, "Swear to me"; and he swore
to him. Then Israel bowed himself
on the head of his bed.

Jacob Blesses Joseph's Sons

48 After this Joseph was told,
"Your father is ill." So he
took with him his two sons, Manasseh and Ephraim. 2 When Jacob
was told, "Your son Joseph has
come to you," he[z] summoned his
strength and sat up in bed. 3 And
Jacob said to Joseph, "God Almighty[a] appeared to me at Luz in
the land of Canaan, and he blessed
me, 4 and said to me, 'I am going to
make you fruitful and increase your
numbers; I will make of you a company of peoples, and will give this
land to your offspring after you for
a perpetual holding.' 5 Therefore
your two sons, who were born to
you in the land of Egypt before I
came to you in Egypt, are now
mine; Ephraim and Manasseh shall
be mine, just as Reuben and Simeon are. 6 As for the offspring born to
you after them, they shall be yours.
They shall be recorded under the
names of their brothers with regard
to their inheritance. 7 For when I
came from Paddan, Rachel, alas,
died in the land of Canaan on the
way, while there was still some distance to go to Ephrath; and I buried
her there on the way to Ephrath"
(that is, Bethlehem).
8 When Israel saw Joseph's
sons, he said, "Who are these?"
9 Joseph said to his father, "They
are my sons, whom God has given
me here." And he said, "Bring them
to me, please, that I may bless
them." 10 Now the eyes of Israel

47.22 Ezra 7.24
47.24 Gen 41.34
47.25 Gen 33.15
47.26 v. 22
47.27 v. 11; Gen 46.3; Ex 1.7
47.29 Deut 31.14; Gen 24.2,49
47.30 Gen 49.29; 50.5,13
47.31 Gen 21.23, 24; 24.3; 31.53; 50.25
48.3 Gen 35.9-12; 28.19; 35.6
48.4 Gen 18.8
48.5 Gen 46.20; Josh 13.7; 14.4
48.7 Gen 33.18; 35.19,20
48.9 Gen 33.5
48.10 Gen 27.1,27

[y] Sam Gk Compare Vg: MT *He removed them to the cities* [z] Heb *Israel* [a] Traditional rendering of Heb *El Shaddai*

were dim with age, and he could
not see well. So Joseph brought
them near him; and he kissed them
and embraced them. 11 Israel said
to Joseph, "I did not expect to see
your face; and here God has let me
see your children also." 12 Then Joseph removed them from his father's knees,[b] and he bowed himself with his face to the earth.
13 Joseph took them both, Ephraim
in his right hand toward Israel's
left, and Manasseh in his left hand
toward Israel's right, and brought
them near him. 14 But Israel
stretched out his right hand and
laid it on the head of Ephraim, who
was the younger, and his left hand
on the head of Manasseh, crossing
his hands, for Manasseh was the
firstborn. 15 He blessed Joseph, and
said,

"The God before whom my
ancestors Abraham and
Isaac walked,
the God who has been my
shepherd all my life to
this day,
16 the angel who has redeemed
me from all harm, bless
the boys;
and in them let my name be
perpetuated, and the
name of my ancestors
Abraham and Isaac;
and let them grow into a
multitude on the
earth."

17 When Joseph saw that his father laid his right hand on the head
of Ephraim, it displeased him; so
he took his father's hand, to remove it from Ephraim's head to
Manasseh's head. 18 Joseph said to
his father, "Not so, my father!
Since this one is the firstborn, put
your right hand on his head." 19 But
his father refused, and said, "I
know, my son, I know; he also shall
become a people, and he also shall
be great. Nevertheless his younger
brother shall be greater than he,
and his offspring shall become a
multitude of nations." 20 So he
blessed them that day, saying,

"By you[c] Israel will invoke
blessings, saying,
'God make you[c] like
Ephraim and like
Manasseh.' "

So he put Ephraim ahead of Manasseh. 21 Then Israel said to Joseph, "I am about to die, but God
will be with you and will bring you
again to the land of your ancestors.
22 I now give to you one portion[d]
more than to your brothers, the
portion[d] that I took from the hand
of the Amorites with my sword and
with my bow."

Jacob's Last Words to His Sons

49 Then Jacob called his sons,
and said: "Gather around,
that I may tell you what will happen to you in days to come.

2 Assemble and hear, O sons
of Jacob;
listen to Israel your father.

3 Reuben, you are my
firstborn,
my might and the first
fruits of my vigor,
excelling in rank and
excelling in power.
4 Unstable as water, you shall
no longer excel
because you went up onto
your father's bed;
then you defiled it—you[e]
went up onto my
couch!

5 Simeon and Levi are
brothers;
weapons of violence are
their swords.
6 May I never come into their
council;
may I not be joined to their
company—
for in their anger they killed
men,
and at their whim they
hamstrung oxen.
7 Cursed be their anger, for it
is fierce,
and their wrath, for it is
cruel!

48.11 Gen 45.26 **48.14** v. 19 **48.15** Gen 17.1; Heb 11.21 **48.16** Gen 28.15; 31.11,13,24; 28.14; 46.3 **48.17** v. 14 **48.19** v. 14; Num 1.33, 35 **48.21** Gen 26.3; 28.15; 46.4; 50.24 **48.22** Josh 24.32; Jn 4.5 **49.1** Num 24.14 **49.3** Gen 29.32; Deut 21.17 **49.4** Gen 35.22; Deut 27.20 **49.5** Gen 34.25-30 **49.6** Prov 1.15; Eph 5.11; Gen 34.26 **49.7** Josh 19.1,9; 21.1-42

[b] Heb *from his knees* [c] *you* here is singular in Heb [d] Or *mountain slope* (Heb *shekem*, a play on the name of the town and district of Shechem) [e] Gk Syr Tg: Heb *he*

I will divide them in Jacob,
and scatter them in Israel.

8 Judah, your brothers shall praise you;
your hand shall be on the neck of your enemies;
your father's sons shall bow down before you.
9 Judah is a lion's whelp;
from the prey, my son, you have gone up.
He crouches down, he stretches out like a lion,
like a lioness—who dares rouse him up?
10 The scepter shall not depart from Judah,
nor the ruler's staff from between his feet,
until tribute comes to him;[f]
and the obedience of the peoples is his.
11 Binding his foal to the vine
and his donkey's colt to the choice vine,
he washes his garments in wine
and his robe in the blood of grapes;
12 his eyes are darker than wine,
and his teeth whiter than milk.

13 Zebulun shall settle at the shore of the sea;
he shall be a haven for ships,
and his border shall be at Sidon.

14 Issachar is a strong donkey,
lying down between the sheepfolds;
15 he saw that a resting place was good,
and that the land was pleasant;
so he bowed his shoulder to the burden,
and became a slave at forced labor.

16 Dan shall judge his people
as one of the tribes of Israel.
17 Dan shall be a snake by the roadside,
a viper along the path,
that bites the horse's heels
so that its rider falls backward.

18 I wait for your salvation, O LORD.

19 Gad shall be raided by raiders,
but he shall raid at their heels.

20 Asher's[g] food shall be rich,
and he shall provide royal delicacies.

21 Naphtali is a doe let loose
that bears lovely fawns.[h]

22 Joseph is a fruitful bough,
a fruitful bough by a spring;
his branches run over the wall.[i]
23 The archers fiercely attacked him;
they shot at him and pressed him hard.
24 Yet his bow remained taut,
and his arms[j] were made agile
by the hands of the Mighty One of Jacob,
by the name of the Shepherd, the Rock of Israel,
25 by the God of your father, who will help you,
by the Almighty[k] who will bless you
with blessings of heaven above,
blessings of the deep that lies beneath,
blessings of the breasts and of the womb.

49.8 Deut 33.7; 1 Chr 5.2
49.9 Ezek 19.5-7; Mic 5.8
49.10 Num 24.17; Ps 60.7; Lk 1.32; Isa 2.2; 11.1
49.13 Deut 33.18, 19; Josh 19.10, 11
49.16 Deut 33.22; Judg 18.1,2
49.17 Judg 18.26, 27
49.18 Ex 15.2; Ps 25.5; 119.166,174; Isa 25.9; Mic 7.7
49.19 Deut 33.20; 1 Chr 5.18
49.20 Deut 33.24, 25; Josh 19.24
49.21 Deut 33.23
49.22 Deut 33.13-17
49.23 Gen 37.4, 24,28
49.24 Ps 18.34; Isa 41.10; Ps 132.2,5; Isa 1.24; Ps 23.1; Isa 28.16; 1 Pet 2.6-8
49.25 Gen 28.3, 13; 32.9; 48.3; 27.28

f Or *until Shiloh comes* or *until he comes to Shiloh* or (with Syr) *until he comes to whom it belongs* g Gk Vg Syr: Heb *From Asher* h Or *that gives beautiful words* i Meaning of Heb uncertain j Heb *the arms of his hands* k Traditional rendering of Heb *Shaddai*

26 The blessings of your father
are stronger than the
blessings of the eternal
mountains,
the bounties[1] of the
everlasting hills;
may they be on the head of
Joseph,
on the brow of him who
was set apart from his
brothers.

27 Benjamin is a ravenous wolf,
in the morning devouring
the prey,
and at evening dividing the
spoil."

28 All these are the twelve
tribes of Israel, and this is what
their father said to them when he
blessed them, blessing each one of
them with a suitable blessing.

Jacob's Death and Burial

29 Then he charged them, saying to them, "I am about to be gathered to my people. Bury me with
my ancestors—in the cave in the
field of Ephron the Hittite, 30 in the
cave in the field at Machpelah,
near Mamre, in the land of Canaan,
in the field that Abraham bought
from Ephron the Hittite as a burial
site. 31 There Abraham and his wife
Sarah were buried; there Isaac and
his wife Rebekah were buried; and
there I buried Leah— 32 the field
and the cave that is in it were purchased from the Hittites." 33 When
Jacob ended his charge to his sons,
he drew up his feet into the bed,
breathed his last, and was gathered
to his people.

50 Then Joseph threw himself
on his father's face and
wept over him and kissed him. 2 Joseph commanded the physicians in
his service to embalm his father. So
the physicians embalmed Israel;
3 they spent forty days in doing this,

49.26 Deut 33.15, 16
49.28 Gen 23.16-20
49.29 Gen 25.8; 47.30
49.30 Gen 23.16
49.31 Gen 23.19; 25.9; 35.29
49.33 Gen 25.8; Acts 7.15; v. 29
50.1 Gen 46.4
50.2 v. 26
50.3 v. 10; Num 20.29; Deut 34.8

[1] Cn Compare Gk: Heb *of my progenitors to the boundaries*

THE TRIBES OF ISRAEL

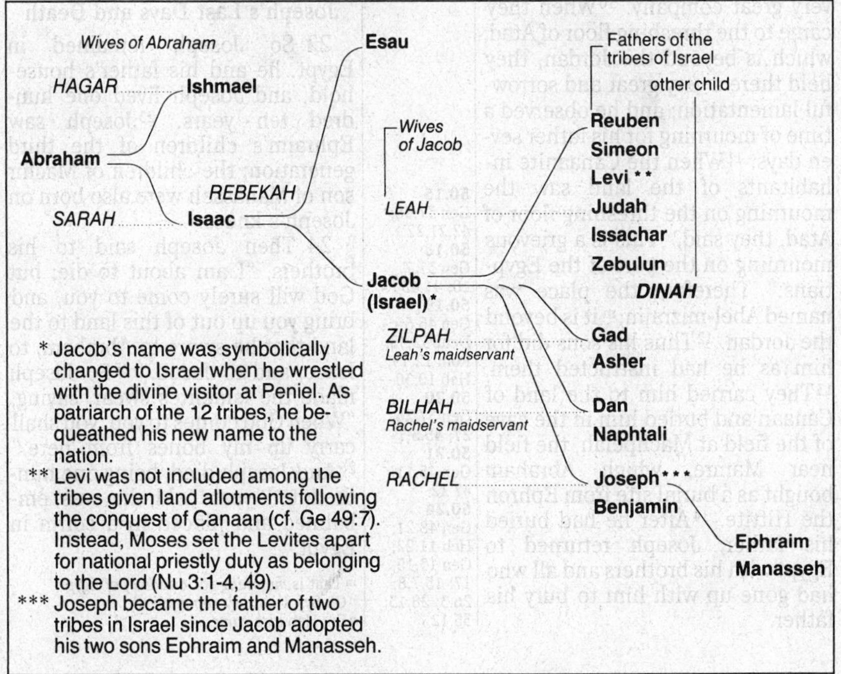

* Jacob's name was symbolically changed to Israel when he wrestled with the divine visitor at Peniel. As patriarch of the 12 tribes, he bequeathed his new name to the nation.

** Levi was not included among the tribes given land allotments following the conquest of Canaan (cf. Ge 49:7). Instead, Moses set the Levites apart for national priestly duty as belonging to the Lord (Nu 3:1-4, 49).

*** Joseph became the father of two tribes in Israel since Jacob adopted his two sons Ephraim and Manasseh.

for that is the time required for em-
balming. And the Egyptians wept
for him seventy days.
4 When the days of weeping for
him were past, Joseph addressed
the household of Pharaoh, "If now
I have found favor with you, please
speak to Pharaoh as follows: 5 My
father made me swear an oath; he
said, 'I am about to die. In the
tomb that I hewed out for myself in
the land of Canaan, there you shall
bury me.' Now therefore let me go
up, so that I may bury my father;
then I will return." 6 Pharaoh answered, "Go up, and bury your
father, as he made you swear to
do."
7 So Joseph went up to bury his
father. With him went up all the
servants of Pharaoh, the elders of
his household, and all the elders of
the land of Egypt, 8 as well as all the
household of Joseph, his brothers,
and his father's household. Only
their children, their flocks, and
their herds were left in the land of
Goshen. 9 Both chariots and charioteers went up with him. It was a
very great company. 10 When they
came to the threshing floor of Atad,
which is beyond the Jordan, they
held there a very great and sorrowful lamentation; and he observed a
time of mourning for his father sev-
en days. 11 When the Canaanite inhabitants of the land saw the
mourning on the threshing floor of
Atad, they said, "This is a grievous
mourning on the part of the Egyptians." Therefore the place was
named Abel-mizraim;[m] it is beyond
the Jordan. 12 Thus his sons did for
him as he had instructed them.
13 They carried him to the land of
Canaan and buried him in the cave
of the field at Machpelah, the field
near Mamre, which Abraham
bought as a burial site from Ephron
the Hittite. 14 After he had buried
his father, Joseph returned to
Egypt with his brothers and all who
had gone up with him to bury his
father.

50.5 Gen 47.29-31 **50.8** Ex 8.22 **50.10** 2 Sam 1.17; 1 Sam 31.13; Job 2.13 **50.13** Gen 49.29, 30; 23.16

Joseph Forgives His Brothers

15 Realizing that their father
was dead, Joseph's brothers said,
"What if Joseph still bears a grudge
against us and pays us back in full
for all the wrong that we did to
him?" 16 So they approached[n] Joseph, saying, "Your father gave this
instruction before he died, 17 'Say
to Joseph: I beg you, forgive the
crime of your brothers and the
wrong they did in harming you.'
Now therefore please forgive the
crime of the servants of the God of
your father." Joseph wept when
they spoke to him. 18 Then his
brothers also wept,[o] fell down before him, and said, "We are here as
your slaves." 19 But Joseph said to
them, "Do not be afraid! Am I in
the place of God? 20 Even though
you intended to do harm to me,
God intended it for good, in order
to preserve a numerous people, as
he is doing today. 21 So have no
fear; I myself will provide for you
and your little ones." In this way he
reassured them, speaking kindly to
them.

Joseph's Last Days and Death

22 So Joseph remained in
Egypt, he and his father's household; and Joseph lived one hundred ten years. 23 Joseph saw
Ephraim's children of the third
generation; the children of Machir
son of Manasseh were also born on
Joseph's knees.
24 Then Joseph said to his
brothers, "I am about to die; but
God will surely come to you, and
bring you up out of this land to the
land that he swore to Abraham, to
Isaac, and to Jacob." 25 So Joseph
made the Israelites swear, saying,
"When God comes to you, you shall
carry up my bones from here."
26 And Joseph died, being one hundred ten years old; he was embalmed and placed in a coffin in
Egypt.

50.15 Gen 37.28; 42.21,22 **50.18** Gen 37.7, 10; 41.43 **50.19** Gen 45.5; Deut 32.35; Rom 12.19; Heb 10.30 **50.20** Gen 37.26, 27; 45.5,7 **50.21** Gen 45.11; 47.12 **50.24** Gen 48.21; Heb 11.22; Gen 13.15, 17; 15.7,8; 26.3; 28.13; 35.12

[m] That is *mourning* (or *meadow*) *of Egypt*
[n] Gk Syr: Heb *they commanded*
[o] Cn: Heb *also came*

Exodus

Title and Background

Exodus is a Latin word (derived from the Greek) that means "exit," "departure." This book describes the greatest miracle in the Old Testament record of Israel's history–their "going out" from Egypt and slavery. While the story of the Israelites began with Abraham in Genesis, Exodus is the history of their early years as God's chosen nation, committed to him according to the terms of the Mosaic covenant given at Mount Sinai. The book of Exodus was not intended to exist separately, but was thought of as a continuation of a narrative that began in Genesis and moves on through Leviticus, Numbers, and Deuteronomy.

Author and Date of Writing

Several verses in Exodus state that Moses wrote certain sections of the book (see 17.14; 24.4; 34.27). The New Testament also mentions Mosaic authorship for various passages in Exodus (see, e.g., Mk 7.10; 12.26; Lk 2.22-23). It seems likely, however, that the final form of Exodus took place at a later time in Israel's history.

Using 1 Kings 6.1 as a basis for dating places the exodus at approximately 1446 B.C. This date is by no means certain, however, for a significant amount of archaeological evidence tends to date Moses and the exodus in the thirteenth century B.C.

Theme and Message

Exodus lays the foundation for a theology of God's revelation of his name, his attributes, his redemption, his law, and his worship. It also reports the appointment and work of the first covenant mediator (Moses), describes the beginning of the priesthood, defines the role of the prophet, and relates how the ancient covenant relationship between God and his people came under a new administration (the Sinai covenant).

Outline

I. Preparation for Israel's Deliverance from Slavery (1.1–4.31)
II. Israel's Deliverance from Egyptian Slavery (5.1–18.27)
   A. Pharaoh's Resistance and the Lord's Reassurance (5.1–6.27)
   B. The Ten Plagues on Egypt (6.28–12.36)
   C. The Exodus: From Egypt to Mount Sinai (12.37–18.27)
III. The Covenant at Sinai (19.1–24.18)
IV. The Tabernacle for Worship (25.1–40.38)

---

1 These are the names of the
sons of Israel who came to
Egypt with Jacob, each with his
household: 2 Reuben, Simeon,
Levi, and Judah, 3 Issachar, Zebulun, and Benjamin, 4 Dan and
Naphtali, Gad and Asher. 5 The total number of people born to Jacob
was seventy. Joseph was already in
Egypt. 6 Then Joseph died, and all
his brothers, and that whole generation. 7 But the Israelites were

1.1 Gen 46.8-27
1.5 Gen 46.27
1.6 Gen 50.26
1.7 Gen 46.3; 47.27; Acts 7.17
1.8 Acts 7.18,19
1.9 Ps 105.24, 25

fruitful and prolific; they multiplied and grew exceedingly strong,
so that the land was filled with
them.

The Israelites Are Oppressed

8 Now a new king arose over
Egypt, who did not know Joseph.
9 He said to his people, "Look, the
Israelite people are more numerous and more powerful than we.
10 Come, let us deal shrewdly with

them, or they will increase and, in
the event of war, join our enemies
and fight against us and escape
from the land." 11 Therefore they
set taskmasters over them to oppress them with forced labor. They
built supply cities, Pithom and
Rameses, for Pharaoh. 12 But the
more they were oppressed, the
more they multiplied and spread,
so that the Egyptians came to
dread the Israelites. 13 The Egyptians became ruthless in imposing
tasks on the Israelites, 14 and made
their lives bitter with hard service
in mortar and brick and in every
kind of field labor. They were ruthless in all the tasks that they imposed on them.

15 The king of Egypt said to the
Hebrew midwives, one of whom
was named Shiphrah and the other
Puah, 16 "When you act as midwives to the Hebrew women, and
see them on the birthstool, if it is a
boy, kill him; but if it is a girl, she
shall live." 17 But the midwives
feared God; they did not do as the
king of Egypt commanded them,
but they let the boys live. 18 So the
king of Egypt summoned the midwives and said to them, "Why have
you done this, and allowed the
boys to live?" 19 The midwives said
to Pharaoh, "Because the Hebrew
women are not like the Egyptian
women; for they are vigorous and
give birth before the midwife
comes to them." 20 So God dealt
well with the midwives; and the
people multiplied and became very
strong. 21 And because the midwives feared God, he gave them
families. 22 Then Pharaoh commanded all his people, "Every boy
that is born to the Hebrews[a] you
shall throw into the Nile, but you
shall let every girl live."

Birth and Youth of Moses

2 Now a man from the house of
Levi went and married a Levite
woman. 2 The woman conceived
and bore a son; and when she saw
that he was a fine baby, she hid him
three months. 3 When she could
hide him no longer she got a papyrus basket for him, and plastered it
with bitumen and pitch; she put
the child in it and placed it among
the reeds on the bank of the river.
4 His sister stood at a distance, to
see what would happen to him.

5 The daughter of Pharaoh
came down to bathe at the river,
while her attendants walked beside
the river. She saw the basket
among the reeds and sent her maid
to bring it. 6 When she opened it,
she saw the child. He was crying,
and she took pity on him, "This
must be one of the Hebrews' children," she said. 7 Then his sister
said to Pharaoh's daughter, "Shall
I go and get you a nurse from the
Hebrew women to nurse the child
for you?" 8 Pharaoh's daughter said
to her, "Yes." So the girl went and
called the child's mother. 9 Pharaoh's daughter said to her, "Take
this child and nurse it for me, and
I will give you your wages." So the
woman took the child and nursed
it. 10 When the child grew up, she
brought him to Pharaoh's daughter, and she took him as her son.
She named him Moses,[b] "because," she said, "I drew him out[c]
of the water."

Moses Flees to Midian

11 One day, after Moses had
grown up, he went out to his people
and saw their forced labor. He saw
an Egyptian beating a Hebrew, one
of his kinsfolk. 12 He looked this
way and that, and seeing no one he
killed the Egyptian and hid him in
the sand. 13 When he went out the
next day, he saw two Hebrews
fighting; and he said to the one
who was in the wrong, "Why do you
strike your fellow Hebrew?" 14 He
answered, "Who made you a ruler
and judge over us? Do you mean to
kill me as you killed the Egyptian?"
Then Moses was afraid and
thought, "Surely the thing is
known." 15 When Pharaoh heard of
it, he sought to kill Moses.

But Moses fled from Pharaoh.
He settled in the land of Midian,

1.11 Ex 3.7; 5.6 **1.14** Ps 81.6 **1.16** Acts 7.19 **1.17** v. 21 **1.20** v. 12; Isa 3.10 **1.21** 1 Sam 2.35 **1.22** Acts 7.19 **2.1** Ex 6.19,20 **2.2** Acts 7.20; Heb 11.23

2.4 Ex 15.20; Num 26.59 **2.10** Acts 7.21 **2.11** Acts 7.23; Heb 11.24-26 **2.12** Acts 7.24 **2.13** Acts 7.26-28 **2.14** Gen 19.9; Acts 7.27 **2.15** Acts 7.29; Gen 24.11; 29.2

[a] Sam Gk Tg: Heb lacks *to the Hebrews*
[b] Heb *Mosheh* [c] Heb *mashah*

and sat down by a well. 16 The
priest of Midian had seven daughters. They came to draw water, and
filled the troughs to water their father's flock. 17 But some shepherds
came and drove them away. Moses
got up and came to their defense
and watered their flock. 18 When
they returned to their father Reuel,
he said, "How is it that you have
come back so soon today?" 19 They
said, "An Egyptian helped us
against the shepherds; he even
drew water for us and watered the
flock." 20 He said to his daughters,
"Where is he? Why did you leave
the man? Invite him to break
bread." 21 Moses agreed to stay
with the man, and he gave Moses
his daughter Zipporah in marriage.
22 She bore a son, and he named
him Gershom; for he said, "I have
been an alien[d] residing in a foreign
land."

23 After a long time the king of
Egypt died. The Israelites groaned
under their slavery, and cried out.
Out of the slavery their cry for help
rose up to God. 24 God heard their
groaning, and God remembered his
covenant with Abraham, Isaac, and
Jacob. 25 God looked upon the Israelites, and God took notice of
them.

Moses at the Burning Bush

3 Moses was keeping the flock
of his father-in-law Jethro, the
priest of Midian; he led his flock
beyond the wilderness, and came
to Horeb, the mountain of God.
2 There the angel of the LORD appeared to him in a flame of fire out
of a bush; he looked, and the bush
was blazing, yet it was not consumed. 3 Then Moses said, "I must
turn aside and look at this great
sight, and see why the bush is not
burned up." 4 When the LORD saw
that he had turned aside to see,
God called to him out of the bush,
"Moses, Moses!" And he said,
"Here I am." 5 Then he said, "Come
no closer! Remove the sandals from
your feet, for the place on which
you are standing is holy ground."
6 He said further, "I am the God of
your father, the God of Abraham,
the God of Isaac, and the God of
Jacob." And Moses hid his face, for
he was afraid to look at God.

7 Then the LORD said, "I have
observed the misery of my people
who are in Egypt; I have heard their
cry on account of their taskmasters. Indeed, I know their sufferings, 8 and I have come down to deliver them from the Egyptians, and
to bring them up out of that land to
a good and broad land, a land flowing with milk and honey, to the
country of the Canaanites, the Hittites, the Amorites, the Perizzites,
the Hivites, and the Jebusites.
9 The cry of the Israelites has now
come to me; I have also seen how
the Egyptians oppress them. 10 So
come, I will send you to Pharaoh to
bring my people, the Israelites, out
of Egypt." 11 But Moses said to
God, "Who am I that I should go to
Pharaoh, and bring the Israelites
out of Egypt?" 12 He said, "I will be
with you; and this shall be the sign
for you that it is I who sent you:
when you have brought the people
out of Egypt, you shall worship God
on this mountain."

The Divine Name Revealed

13 But Moses said to God, "If I
come to the Israelites and say to
them, 'The God of your ancestors
has sent me to you,' and they ask
me, 'What is his name?' what shall
I say to them?" 14 God said to Moses, "I AM WHO I AM."[e] He said further, "Thus you shall say to the Israelites, 'I AM has sent me to you.' "
15 God also said to Moses, "Thus
you shall say to the Israelites, 'The
LORD,[f] the God of your ancestors,
the God of Abraham, the God of
Isaac, and the God of Jacob, has
sent me to you':

This is my name forever,
and this my title for all
generations.

16 Go and assemble the elders of Israel, and say to them, 'The LORD,

2.16 Ex 3.1; 18.12; Gen 24.13, 19
2.17 Gen 29.3,10
2.18 Ex 3.1; Num 10.29
2.20 Gen 31.54
2.21 Acts 7.29; Gen 4.25; 18.2
2.22 Ex 18.3; Heb 11.13, 14
2.23 Acts 7.30; Deut 26.7; Ex 3.9; Jas 5.4
2.24 Ex 6.5; Ps 105.8,42; Gen 22.16-18
2.25 Ex 4.31; 3.7; 4.27; 18.5
3.1 Ex 2.18
3.2 Deut 33.16; Mk 12.26
3.3 Acts 7.31
3.5 Josh 5.15; Acts 7.33
3.6 Mt 22.31, 32; Mk 12.26; Lk 20.37; Acts 7.32
3.7 Ex 2.25; Neh 9.9; Acts 7.34
3.8 Gen 50.24, 25; v. 17; Josh 24.11
3.9 Ex 2.23; 1.13,14
3.10 Mic 6.4
3.12 Gen 31.3; Josh 1.5
3.14 Ex 6.3; Jn 8.58; Heb 13.8
3.15 Ps 135.13; Hos 12.5

[d] Heb *ger* [e] Or *I AM WHAT I AM* or *I WILL BE WHAT I WILL BE* [f] The word "LORD" when spelled with capital letters stands for the divine name, *YHWH,* which is here connected with the verb *hayah,* "to be"

the God of your ancestors, the God
of Abraham, of Isaac, and of Jacob,
has appeared to me, saying: I have
given heed to you and to what has
been done to you in Egypt. 17 I declare that I will bring you up out of
the misery of Egypt, to the land of
the Canaanites, the Hittites, the
Amorites, the Perizzites, the Hivites, and the Jebusites, a land
flowing with milk and honey.'
18 They will listen to your voice; and
you and the elders of Israel shall go
to the king of Egypt and say to him,
'The LORD, the God of the Hebrews,
has met with us; let us now go a
three days' journey into the wilderness, so that we may sacrifice to
the LORD our God.' 19 I know, however, that the king of Egypt will not
let you go unless compelled by a
mighty hand.[g] 20 So I will stretch
out my hand and strike Egypt with
all my wonders that I will perform
in it; after that he will let you go. 21 I
will bring this people into such favor with the Egyptians that, when
you go, you will not go empty-
handed; 22 each woman shall ask
her neighbor and any woman living
in the neighbor's house for jewelry
of silver and of gold, and clothing,
and you shall put them on your
sons and on your daughters; and so
you shall plunder the Egyptians."

Moses' Miraculous Power

4 Then Moses answered, "But
suppose they do not believe
me or listen to me, but say, 'The
LORD did not appear to you.' " 2 The
LORD said to him, "What is that in
your hand?" He said, "A staff."
3 And he said, "Throw it on the
ground." So he threw the staff on
the ground, and it became a snake;
and Moses drew back from it.
4 Then the LORD said to Moses,
"Reach out your hand, and seize it
by the tail"—so he reached out his
hand and grasped it, and it became
a staff in his hand— 5 "so that they
may believe that the LORD, the God
of their ancestors, the God of Abraham, the God of Isaac, and the God
of Jacob, has appeared to you."
6 Again, the LORD said to him,
"Put your hand inside your cloak."
He put his hand into his cloak; and
when he took it out, his hand was
leprous,[h] as white as snow. 7 Then
God said, "Put your hand back into
your cloak"—so he put his hand
back into his cloak, and when he
took it out, it was restored like the
rest of his body— 8 "If they will not
believe you or heed the first sign,
they may believe the second sign.
9 If they will not believe even these
two signs or heed you, you shall
take some water from the Nile and
pour it on the dry ground; and the
water that you shall take from the
Nile will become blood on the dry
ground."
10 But Moses said to the LORD,
"O my Lord, I have never been eloquent, neither in the past nor even
now that you have spoken to your
servant; but I am slow of speech
and slow of tongue." 11 Then the
LORD said to him, "Who gives
speech to mortals? Who makes
them mute or deaf, seeing or blind?
Is it not I, the LORD? 12 Now go, and
I will be with your mouth and teach
you what you are to speak." 13 But
he said, "O my Lord, please send
someone else." 14 Then the anger of
the LORD was kindled against Moses and he said, "What of your
brother Aaron, the Levite? I know
that he can speak fluently; even
now he is coming out to meet you,
and when he sees you his heart will
be glad. 15 You shall speak to him
and put the words in his mouth;
and I will be with your mouth and
with his mouth, and will teach you
what you shall do. 16 He indeed
shall speak for you to the people;
he shall serve as a mouth for you,
and you shall serve as God for him.
17 Take in your hand this staff, with
which you shall perform the signs."

Moses Returns to Egypt

18 Moses went back to his
father-in-law Jethro and said to
him, "Please let me go back to my
kindred in Egypt and see whether

3.17 Gen 15.14, 16; Josh 24.11
3.18 Ex 4.31; 5.1,3
3.19 Ex 5.2; 6.1
3.20 Ex 6.6; 9.15; Deut 6.22; Neh 9.10; Ex 12.31
3.21 Ex 11.3; 12.36
3.22 Ex 11.2,3; 12.35,36
4.1 Ex 3.18; 6.30
4.2 vv. 17,20
4.6 Num 12.10; 2 Kings 5.27
4.7 Num 12.13, 14; Deut 32.39; 2 Kings 5.14; Mt 8.3
4.9 Ex 7.19
4.10 Ex 6.12; Jer 1.6
4.11 Ps 94.9; Mt 11.5
4.12 Isa 50.4; Jer 1.9; Mt 10.19; Mk 13.11; Lk 12.11,12; 21.14,15
4.14 v. 27
4.15 Ex 7.1,2; Num 23.5, 12,16; Deut 5.31
4.17 v. 2; Ex 7.9-20

[g] Gk Vg: Heb *no, not by a mighty hand* [h] A term for several skin diseases; precise meaning uncertain

they are still living." And Jethro
said to Moses, "Go in peace."
19 The LORD said to Moses in Midian, "Go back to Egypt; for all those
who were seeking your life are
dead." 20 So Moses took his wife
and his sons, put them on a donkey
and went back to the land of Egypt;
and Moses carried the staff of God
in his hand.

21 And the LORD said to Moses,
"When you go back to Egypt, see
that you perform before Pharaoh
all the wonders that I have put in
your power; but I will harden his
heart, so that he will not let the
people go. 22 Then you shall say to
Pharaoh, 'Thus says the LORD: Israel is my firstborn son. 23 I said to
you, "Let my son go that he may
worship me." But you refused to let
him go; now I will kill your firstborn son.' "

24 On the way, at a place where
they spent the night, the LORD met
him and tried to kill him. 25 But
Zipporah took a flint and cut off her
son's foreskin, and touched Moses'[i] feet with it, and said, "Truly
you are a bridegroom of blood to
me!" 26 So he let him alone. It was
then she said, "A bridegroom of
blood by circumcision."

27 The LORD said to Aaron, "Go
into the wilderness to meet Moses." So he went; and he met him at
the mountain of God and kissed
him. 28 Moses told Aaron all the
words of the LORD with which he
had sent him, and all the signs with
which he had charged him. 29 Then
Moses and Aaron went and assembled all the elders of the Israelites.
30 Aaron spoke all the words that
the LORD had spoken to Moses, and
performed the signs in the sight of
the people. 31 The people believed;
and when they heard that the LORD
had given heed to the Israelites and
that he had seen their misery, they
bowed down and worshiped.

Bricks without Straw

5 Afterward Moses and Aaron
went to Pharaoh and said,
"Thus says the LORD, the God of Israel, 'Let my people go, so that they

4.19 Ex 2.15,23
4.20 Ex 17.9; Num 20.8
4.21 Ex 7.3,13; 9.12,35; 10.1; 14.8; Deut 2.30; Jn 12.40; Rom 19.18
4.22 Isa 63.16; 64.8; Hos 11.1; Rom 9.4; Jer 31.9
4.23 Ex 5.1; 6.11; 7.16; 12.29
4.24ff Num 22.22; Gen 17.14
4.25 Josh 5.2,3
4.27 v. 14; Ex 3.1
4.28 vv. 15,16; 8.9
4.29 Ex 3.16
4.30 v. 16
4.31 v. 8,9; Ex 3.18; 2.25; 3.7; 12.27
5.1 Ex 3.18; 4.23; 10.9
5.2 Job 21.15; Ex 3.19
5.3 Ex 3.18
5.4 Ex 1.11; 2.11; 6.6,7
5.5 Ex 1.7,9
5.6 Ex 1.11; 3.7
5.8 v. 17
5.10 v. 6
5.14 v. 6; Isa 10.24

may celebrate a festival to me in
the wilderness.' " 2 But Pharaoh
said, "Who is the LORD, that I
should heed him and let Israel go?
I do not know the LORD, and I will
not let Israel go." 3 Then they said,
"The God of the Hebrews has revealed himself to us; let us go a
three days' journey into the wilderness to sacrifice to the LORD our
God, or he will fall upon us with
pestilence or sword." 4 But the king
of Egypt said to them, "Moses and
Aaron, why are you taking the people away from their work? Get to
your labors!" 5 Pharaoh continued,
"Now they are more numerous
than the people of the land[j] and
yet you want them to stop working!" 6 That same day Pharaoh
commanded the taskmasters of the
people, as well as their supervisors,
7 "You shall no longer give the people straw to make bricks, as before;
let them go and gather straw for
themselves. 8 But you shall require
of them the same quantity of bricks
as they have made previously; do
not diminish it, for they are lazy;
that is why they cry, 'Let us go and
offer sacrifice to our God.' 9 Let
heavier work be laid on them; then
they will labor at it and pay no attention to deceptive words."

10 So the taskmasters and the
supervisors of the people went out
and said to the people, "Thus says
Pharaoh, 'I will not give you straw.
11 Go and get straw yourselves,
wherever you can find it; but your
work will not be lessened in the
least.' " 12 So the people scattered
throughout the land of Egypt, to
gather stubble for straw. 13 The
taskmasters were urgent, saying,
"Complete your work, the same
daily assignment as when you were
given straw." 14 And the supervisors
of the Israelites, whom Pharaoh's
taskmasters had set over them,
were beaten, and were asked, "Why
did you not finish the required
quantity of bricks yesterday and today, as you did before?"

[i] Heb *his* [j] Sam: Heb *The people of the land are now many*

15 Then the Israelite supervisors came to Pharaoh and cried, "Why do you treat your servants like this? 16 No straw is given to your servants, yet they say to us, 'Make bricks!' Look how your servants are beaten! You are unjust to your own people."[k] 17 He said, "You are lazy, lazy; that is why you say, 'Let us go and sacrifice to the LORD.' 18 Go now, and work; for no straw shall be given you, but you shall still deliver the same number of bricks." 19 The Israelite supervisors saw that they were in trouble when they were told, "You shall not lessen your daily number of bricks." 20 As they left Pharaoh, they came upon Moses and Aaron who were waiting to meet them. 21 They said to them, "The LORD look upon you and judge! You have brought us into bad odor with Pharaoh and his officials, and have put a sword in their hand to kill us."

22 Then Moses turned again to the LORD and said, "O LORD, why have you mistreated this people? Why did you ever send me? 23 Since I first came to Pharaoh to speak in your name, he has mistreated this people, and you have done nothing at all to deliver your people."

Israel's Deliverance Assured

6 Then the LORD said to Moses, "Now you shall see what I will do to Pharaoh: Indeed, by a mighty hand he will let them go; by a mighty hand he will drive them out of his land."

2 God also spoke to Moses and said to him: "I am the LORD. 3 I appeared to Abraham, Isaac, and Jacob as God Almighty,[l] but by my name 'The LORD'[m] I did not make myself known to them. 4 I also established my covenant with them, to give them the land of Canaan, the land in which they resided as aliens. 5 I have also heard the groaning of the Israelites whom the Egyptians are holding as slaves, and I have remembered my covenant. 6 Say therefore to the Israelites, 'I am the LORD, and I will free you from the burdens of the Egyptians and deliver you from slavery to them. I will redeem you with an outstretched arm and with mighty acts of judgment. 7 I will take you as my people, and I will be your God. You shall know that I am the LORD your God, who has freed you from the burdens of the Egyptians. 8 I will bring you into the land that I swore to give to Abraham, Isaac, and Jacob; I will give it to you for a possession. I am the LORD.' " 9 Moses told this to the Israelites; but they would not listen to Moses, because of their broken spirit and their cruel slavery.

10 Then the LORD spoke to Moses, 11 "Go and tell Pharaoh king of Egypt to let the Israelites go out of his land." 12 But Moses spoke to the LORD, "The Israelites have not listened to me; how then shall Pharaoh listen to me, poor speaker that I am?"[n] 13 Thus the LORD spoke to Moses and Aaron, and gave them orders regarding the Israelites and Pharaoh king of Egypt, charging them to free the Israelites from the land of Egypt.

The Genealogy of Moses and Aaron

14 The following are the heads of their ancestral houses: the sons of Reuben, the firstborn of Israel: Hanoch, Pallu, Hezron, and Carmi; these are the families of Reuben. 15 The sons of Simeon: Jemuel, Jamin, Ohad, Jachin, Zohar, and Shaul,[o] the son of a Canaanite woman; these are the families of Simeon. 16 The following are the names of the sons of Levi according to their genealogies: Gershon,[p] Kohath, and Merari, and the length of Levi's life was one hundred thirty-seven years. 17 The sons of Gershon:[p] Libni and Shimei, by their families. 18 The sons of Kohath: Amram, Izhar, Hebron, and Uzziel, and the length of Kohath's life was one hundred thirty-three years. 19 The

5.17 v. 8
5.21 Ex 14.11; 15.24; Gen 16.5; 34.30
5.22 Num 11.11; Jer 4.10
5.23 Ex 3.8
6.1 Ex 3.19,20; 7.4,5; 12.31, 33,39
6.3 Ps 68.4; 83.18; Isa 52.6; Jer 16.21; Ezek 37.6, 13
6.4 Gen 15.18; 28.4
6.5 Ex 2.24
6.6 Deut 26.8
6.7 Deut 4.20; 26.8; Ps 81.6; Ex 16.12; Isa 41.20
6.8 Gen 15.18
6.14 Gen 46.9; Num 26.5-11
6.15 Gen 46.10; 1 Chr 4.24
6.16 Gen 46.11; Num 3.17
6.17 1 Chr 6.17
6.18 1 Chr 6.2, 18
6.19 1 Chr 6.19

[k] Gk Compare Syr Vg: Heb *beaten, and the sin of your people* [l] Traditional rendering of Heb *El Shaddai* [m] Heb *YHWH*; see note at 3.15 [n] Heb *me? I am uncircumcised of lips* [o] Or *Saul* [p] Also spelled *Gershom*; see 2.22

sons of Merari: Mahli and Mushi.
These are the families of the Levites according to their genealogies. 20 Amram married Jochebed
his father's sister and she bore him
Aaron and Moses, and the length of
Amram's life was one hundred
thirty-seven years. 21 The sons of Izhar: Korah, Nepheg, and Zichri.
22 The sons of Uzziel: Mishael, Elzaphan, and Sithri. 23 Aaron married Elisheba, daughter of Amminadab and sister of Nahshon, and
she bore him Nadab, Abihu, Eleazar, and Ithamar. 24 The sons of Korah: Assir, Elkanah, and Abiasaph;
these are the families of the Korahites. 25 Aaron's son Eleazar married
one of the daughters of Putiel, and
she bore him Phinehas. These are
the heads of the ancestral houses
of the Levites by their families.
26 It was this same Aaron and
Moses to whom the LORD said,
"Bring the Israelites out of the land
of Egypt, company by company."
27 It was they who spoke to Pharaoh
king of Egypt to bring the Israelites
out of Egypt, the same Moses and
Aaron.

Moses and Aaron Obey God's Commands

28 On the day when the LORD
spoke to Moses in the land of
Egypt, 29 he said to him, "I am the
LORD; tell Pharaoh king of Egypt all
that I am speaking to you." 30 But
Moses said in the LORD's presence,
"Since I am a poor speaker,[q] why
would Pharaoh listen to me?"
7 The LORD said to Moses, "See,
I have made you like God to
Pharaoh, and your brother Aaron
shall be your prophet. 2 You shall
speak all that I command you, and
your brother Aaron shall tell Pharaoh to let the Israelites go out of
his land. 3 But I will harden Pharaoh's heart, and I will multiply my
signs and wonders in the land of
Egypt. 4 When Pharaoh does not
listen to you, I will lay my hand
upon Egypt and bring my people
the Israelites, company by company, out of the land of Egypt by great
acts of judgment. 5 The Egyptians
shall know that I am the LORD,
when I stretch out my hand against
Egypt and bring the Israelites out
from among them." 6 Moses and
Aaron did so; they did just as the
LORD commanded them. 7 Moses
was eighty years old and Aaron
eighty-three when they spoke to
Pharaoh.

Aaron's Miraculous Rod

8 The LORD said to Moses and
Aaron, 9 "When Pharaoh says to
you, 'Perform a wonder,' then you
shall say to Aaron, 'Take your staff
and throw it down before Pharaoh,
and it will become a snake.' " 10 So
Moses and Aaron went to Pharaoh
and did as the LORD had commanded; Aaron threw down his staff before Pharaoh and his officials, and
it became a snake. 11 Then Pharaoh
summoned the wise men and the
sorcerers; and they also, the magicians of Egypt, did the same by
their secret arts. 12 Each one threw
down his staff, and they became
snakes; but Aaron's staff swallowed up theirs. 13 Still Pharaoh's
heart was hardened, and he would
not listen to them, as the LORD had
said.

The First Plague: Water Turned to Blood

14 Then the LORD said to Moses,
"Pharaoh's heart is hardened; he
refuses to let the people go. 15 Go to
Pharaoh in the morning, as he is
going out to the water; stand by at
the river bank to meet him, and
take in your hand the staff that was
turned into a snake. 16 Say to him,
'The LORD, the God of the Hebrews,
sent me to you to say, "Let my people go, so that they may worship
me in the wilderness." But until
now you have not listened.' 17 Thus
says the LORD, "By this you shall
know that I am the LORD." See, with
the staff that is in my hand I will
strike the water that is in the Nile,
and it shall be turned to blood.
18 The fish in the river shall die, the
river itself shall stink, and the
Egyptians shall be unable to drink

6.20 Ex 2.1,2; Num 26.59
6.21 Num 16.1; 1 Chr 6.37,38
6.22 Lev 10.4; Num 3.30
6.24 Num 26.11
6.25 Josh 24.33; Num 25.7-11; Ps 106.30
6.29 v. 11; Ex 7.2
6.30 v. 12; Ex 4.10
7.1 Ex 4.16
7.2 Ex 4.15
7.3 Ex 4.21; 11.9
7.4 Ex 3.19,20; 10.1; 11.9; 12.51; 13.3,9; 6.6
7.5 v. 17; Ex 8.19; 3.20
7.6 v. 2
7.7 Deut 34.7; Acts 7.23,30
7.9 Isa 7.11; Jn 2.18; Ex 4.2,17
7.10 v. 9; Ex 4.3
7.11 Gen 41.8; v. 22; Ex 8.7,18
7.13 v. 4; Ex 4.21
7.14 Ex 8.15; 10.1,20,27
7.15 v. 10; Ex 4.2,3
7.16 Ex 3.12,18; 5.1,3
7.17 v. 5; Ex 5.2; 4.9; Rev 11.6; 16.4,6
7.18 vv. 21,24

[q] Heb *am uncircumcised of lips*; see 6.12

water from the Nile.' " 19 The LORD
said to Moses, "Say to Aaron, 'Take
your staff and stretch out your
hand over the waters of Egypt—
over its rivers, its canals, and its
ponds, and all its pools of water—
so that they may become blood;
and there shall be blood throughout the whole land of Egypt, even
in vessels of wood and in vessels of
stone.' "
20 Moses and Aaron did just as
the LORD commanded. In the sight
of Pharaoh and of his officials he
lifted up the staff and struck the
water in the river, and all the water
in the river was turned into blood,
21 and the fish in the river died. The
river stank so that the Egyptians
could not drink its water, and there
was blood throughout the whole
land of Egypt. 22 But the magicians
of Egypt did the same by their secret arts; so Pharaoh's heart remained hardened, and he would
not listen to them; as the LORD had
said. 23 Pharaoh turned and went
into his house, and he did not take
even this to heart. 24 And all the
Egyptians had to dig along the Nile
for water to drink, for they could
not drink the water of the river.
25 Seven days passed after the
LORD had struck the Nile.

The Second Plague: Frogs

8 [r] Then the LORD said to Moses,
"Go to Pharaoh and say to
him, 'Thus says the LORD: Let my
people go, so that they may worship me. 2 If you refuse to let them
go, I will plague your whole country
with frogs. 3 The river shall swarm
with frogs; they shall come up into
your palace, into your bedchamber
and your bed, and into the houses
of your officials and of your people,[s] and into your ovens and your
kneading bowls. 4 The frogs shall
come up on you and on your people
and on all your officials.' " 5 [t] And
the LORD said to Moses, "Say to
Aaron, 'Stretch out your hand with
your staff over the rivers, the canals, and the pools, and make frogs
come up on the land of Egypt.' "
6 So Aaron stretched out his hand
over the waters of Egypt; and the
frogs came up and covered the land
of Egypt. 7 But the magicians did
the same by their secret arts, and
brought frogs up on the land of
Egypt.
8 Then Pharaoh called Moses
and Aaron, and said, "Pray to the
LORD to take away the frogs from
me and my people, and I will let the
people go to sacrifice to the LORD."
9 Moses said to Pharaoh, "Kindly
tell me when I am to pray for you
and for your officials and for your
people, that the frogs may be removed from you and your houses
and be left only in the Nile." 10 And
he said, "Tomorrow." Moses said,
"As you say! So that you may know
that there is no one like the LORD
our God, 11 the frogs shall leave you
and your houses and your officials
and your people; they shall be left
only in the Nile." 12 Then Moses
and Aaron went out from Pharaoh;
and Moses cried out to the LORD
concerning the frogs that he had
brought upon Pharaoh.[u] 13 And the
LORD did as Moses requested: the
frogs died in the houses, the court-
yards, and the fields. 14 And they
gathered them together in heaps,
and the land stank. 15 But when
Pharaoh saw that there was a respite, he hardened his heart, and
would not listen to them, just as
the LORD had said.

The Third Plague: Gnats

16 Then the LORD said to Moses,
"Say to Aaron, 'Stretch out your
staff and strike the dust of the
earth, so that it may become gnats
throughout the whole land of
Egypt.' " 17 And they did so; Aaron
stretched out his hand with his
staff and struck the dust of the
earth, and gnats came on humans
and animals alike; all the dust of
the earth turned into gnats
throughout the whole land of
Egypt. 18 The magicians tried to
produce gnats by their secret arts,
but they could not. There were

7.19 Ex 8.5,6,16; 9.22; 10.12, 21; 14.21,26
7.20 Ps 78.44; 105.29
7.21 v. 18
7.22 v. 11; Ex 8.7
8.1 Ex 3.12,18
8.3 Ps 105.30
8.5 Ex 7.19
8.6 Ps 78.45; 105.30
8.7 Ex 7.11
8.8 vv. 25,28; Ex 9.27,28; 10.17
8.10 Ex 9.14; Deut 33.26; Ps 86.8; Isa 46.9; Jer 10.6,7
8.12 v. 30; Ex 9.33; 10.18
8.15 Ex 7.4
8.17 Ps 105.31
8.18 Ex 7.11

[r] Ch 7.26 in Heb [s] Gk: Heb *upon your people* [t] Ch 8.1 in Heb [u] Or *frogs, as he had agreed with Pharaoh*

gnats on both humans and animals. 19 And the magicians said to
Pharaoh, "This is the finger of
God!" But Pharaoh's heart was
hardened, and he would not listen
to them, just as the LORD had said.

The Fourth Plague: Flies

20 Then the LORD said to Moses,
"Rise early in the morning and
present yourself before Pharaoh, as
he goes out to the water, and say to
him, 'Thus says the LORD: Let my
people go, so that they may worship me. 21 For if you will not let my
people go, I will send swarms of
flies on you, your officials, and your
people, and into your houses; and
the houses of the Egyptians shall
be filled with swarms of flies; so
also the land where they live. 22 But
on that day I will set apart the land
of Goshen, where my people live,
so that no swarms of flies shall be
there, that you may know that I the
LORD am in this land. 23 Thus I will
make a distinction[v] between my
people and your people. This sign
shall appear tomorrow.'" 24 The
LORD did so, and great swarms of
flies came into the house of Pharaoh and into his officials' houses;
in all of Egypt the land was ruined
because of the flies.
25 Then Pharaoh summoned
Moses and Aaron, and said, "Go,
sacrifice to your God within the
land." 26 But Moses said, "It would
not be right to do so; for the sacrifices that we offer to the LORD our
God are offensive to the Egyptians.
If we offer in the sight of the Egyptians sacrifices that are offensive to
them, will they not stone us? 27 We
must go a three days' journey into
the wilderness and sacrifice to the
LORD our God as he commands us."
28 So Pharaoh said, "I will let you go
to sacrifice to the LORD your God in
the wilderness, provided you do
not go very far away. Pray for me."
29 Then Moses said, "As soon as I
leave you, I will pray to the LORD
that the swarms of flies may depart
tomorrow from Pharaoh, from his
officials, and from his people; only
do not let Pharaoh again deal falsely by not letting the people go to
sacrifice to the LORD."
30 So Moses went out from
Pharaoh and prayed to the LORD.
31 And the LORD did as Moses asked:
he removed the swarms of flies
from Pharaoh, from his officials,
and from his people; not one remained. 32 But Pharaoh hardened
his heart this time also, and would
not let the people go.

The Fifth Plague: Livestock Diseased

9 Then the LORD said to Moses,
"Go to Pharaoh, and say to
him, 'Thus says the LORD, the God
of the Hebrews: Let my people go,
so that they may worship me. 2 For
if you refuse to let them go and still
hold them, 3 the hand of the LORD
will strike with a deadly pestilence
your livestock in the field: the
horses, the donkeys, the camels,
the herds, and the flocks. 4 But the
LORD will make a distinction between the livestock of Israel and
the livestock of Egypt, so that nothing shall die of all that belongs to
the Israelites.'" 5 The LORD set a
time, saying, "Tomorrow the LORD
will do this thing in the land." 6 And
on the next day the LORD did so; all
the livestock of the Egyptians died,
but of the livestock of the Israelites
not one died. 7 Pharaoh inquired
and found that not one of the livestock of the Israelites was dead.
But the heart of Pharaoh was hardened, and he would not let the people go.

The Sixth Plague: Boils

8 Then the LORD said to Moses
and Aaron, "Take handfuls of soot
from the kiln, and let Moses throw
it in the air in the sight of Pharaoh.
9 It shall become fine dust all over
the land of Egypt, and shall cause
festering boils on humans and animals throughout the whole land of
Egypt." 10 So they took soot from
the kiln, and stood before Pharaoh,
and Moses threw it in the air, and
it caused festering boils on humans
and animals. 11 The magicians

8.19 Ex 7.5; 10.7
8.20 Ex 9.13; 7.15; v. 1
8.22 Ex 9.4,6,26; 10.23; 11.6,7
8.24 Ps 78.45; 105.31
8.27 Ex 3.18; 5.3
8.28 vv. 8,15,29, 32
8.29 vv. 8,15
8.32 vv. 8,15; Ex 4.21
9.1 Ex 8.1
9.2 Ex 8.2
9.4 Ex 8.22
9.6 Ex 11.5; v. 4
9.7 Ex 7.14; 8.32
9.9 Rev 16.2

[v] Gk Vg: Heb *will set redemption*

could not stand before Moses because of the boils, for the boils afflicted the magicians as well as all
the Egyptians. 12 But the LORD hardened the heart of Pharaoh, and he
would not listen to them, just as
the LORD had spoken to Moses.

The Seventh Plague: Thunder and Hail

13 Then the LORD said to Moses,
"Rise up early in the morning and
present yourself before Pharaoh,
and say to him, 'Thus says the
LORD, the God of the Hebrews: Let
my people go, so that they may
worship me. 14 For this time I will
send all my plagues upon you yourself, and upon your officials, and
upon your people, so that you may
know that there is no one like me
in all the earth. 15 For by now I
could have stretched out my hand
and struck you and your people
with pestilence, and you would
have been cut off from the earth.
16 But this is why I have let you live:
to show you my power, and to make
my name resound through all the
earth. 17 You are still exalting yourself against my people, and will not
let them go. 18 Tomorrow at this
time I will cause the heaviest hail
to fall that has ever fallen in Egypt
from the day it was founded until
now. 19 Send, therefore, and have
your livestock and everything that
you have in the open field brought
to a secure place; every human or
animal that is in the open field and
is not brought under shelter will
die when the hail comes down
upon them.' " 20 Those officials of
Pharaoh who feared the word of the
LORD hurried their slaves and livestock off to a secure place. 21 Those
who did not regard the word of the
LORD left their slaves and livestock
in the open field.

22 The LORD said to Moses,
"Stretch out your hand toward
heaven so that hail may fall on the
whole land of Egypt, on humans
and animals and all the plants of
the field in the land of Egypt."
23 Then Moses stretched out his
staff toward heaven, and the LORD
sent thunder and hail, and fire
came down on the earth. And the
LORD rained hail on the land of
Egypt; 24 there was hail with fire
flashing continually in the midst of
it, such heavy hail as had never fall-
en in all the land of Egypt since it
became a nation. 25 The hail struck
down everything that was in the
open field throughout all the land
of Egypt, both human and animal;
the hail also struck down all the
plants of the field, and shattered
every tree in the field. 26 Only in the
land of Goshen, where the Israelites were, there was no hail.

27 Then Pharaoh summoned
Moses and Aaron, and said to
them, "This time I have sinned; the
LORD is in the right, and I and my
people are in the wrong. 28 Pray to
the LORD! Enough of God's thunder
and hail! I will let you go; you need
stay no longer." 29 Moses said to
him, "As soon as I have gone out of
the city, I will stretch out my hands
to the LORD; the thunder will cease,
and there will be no more hail, so
that you may know that the earth is
the LORD's. 30 But as for you and
your officials, I know that you do
not yet fear the LORD God." 31 (Now
the flax and the barley were ruined,
for the barley was in the ear and the
flax was in bud. 32 But the wheat
and the spelt were not ruined, for
they are late in coming up.) 33 So
Moses left Pharaoh, went out of the
city, and stretched out his hands to
the LORD; then the thunder and the
hail ceased, and the rain no longer
poured down on the earth. 34 But
when Pharaoh saw that the rain
and the hail and the thunder had
ceased, he sinned once more and
hardened his heart, he and his officials. 35 So the heart of Pharaoh was
hardened, and he would not let the
Israelites go, just as the LORD had
spoken through Moses.

The Eighth Plague: Locusts

10 Then the LORD said to Moses, "Go to Pharaoh; for I
have hardened his heart and the
heart of his officials, in order that I
may show these signs of mine

9.12 Ex 4.21 **9.13** Ex 8.20 **9.14** Ex 8.10 **9.15** Ex 3.20 **9.16** Rom 9.17 **9.18** vv. 23,24 **9.20** Prov 13.13 **9.22** Rev 16.21 **9.23** Gen 19.24; Josh 10.11; Ps 78.47; Isa 30.30; Ezek 38.22; Rev 8.7 **9.25** v. 19; Ps 78.47; 105.32,33 **9.26** Ex 8.22; 9.4,6; 10.23; 11.7; 12.13 **9.27** Ex 8.8; 10.16,17; 2 Chr 12.6; Ps 129.4 **9.28** Ex 8.8; 10.17 **9.29** 1 Kings 8.22; Ps 143.6; Ex 8.22; 19.5; 20.11; Ps 24.1 **9.35** Ex 4.21 **10.1** Ex 4.21; 7.14

among them, 2 and that you may
tell your children and grandchildren how I have made fools of the
Egyptians and what signs I have
done among them—so that you
may know that I am the LORD."
3 So Moses and Aaron went to
Pharaoh, and said to him, "Thus
says the LORD, the God of the Hebrews, 'How long will you refuse to
humble yourself before me? Let my
people go, so that they may worship me. 4 For if you refuse to let my
people go, tomorrow I will bring locusts into your country. 5 They
shall cover the surface of the land,
so that no one will be able to see
the land. They shall devour the last
remnant left you after the hail, and
they shall devour every tree of
yours that grows in the field. 6 They
shall fill your houses, and the
houses of all your officials and of
all the Egyptians—something that
neither your parents nor your
grandparents have seen, from the
day they came on earth to this
day.'" Then he turned and went
out from Pharaoh.
7 Pharaoh's officials said to
him, "How long shall this fellow be
a snare to us? Let the people go, so
that they may worship the LORD
their God; do you not yet understand that Egypt is ruined?" 8 So
Moses and Aaron were brought
back to Pharaoh, and he said to
them, "Go, worship the LORD your
God! But which ones are to go?"
9 Moses said, "We will go with our
young and our old; we will go with
our sons and daughters and with
our flocks and herds, because we
have the LORD's festival to celebrate." 10 He said to them, "The
LORD indeed will be with you, if ever
I let your little ones go with you!
Plainly, you have some evil purpose in mind. 11 No, never! Your
men may go and worship the LORD,
for that is what you are asking."
And they were driven out from
Pharaoh's presence.
12 Then the LORD said to Moses,
"Stretch out your hand over the
land of Egypt, so that the locusts
may come upon it and eat every
plant in the land, all that the hail
has left." 13 So Moses stretched out
his staff over the land of Egypt, and
the LORD brought an east wind
upon the land all that day and all
that night; when morning came,
the east wind had brought the locusts. 14 The locusts came upon all
the land of Egypt and settled on the
whole country of Egypt, such a
dense swarm of locusts as had never been before, nor ever shall be
again. 15 They covered the surface
of the whole land, so that the land
was black; and they ate all the
plants in the land and all the fruit
of the trees that the hail had left;
nothing green was left, no tree, no
plant in the field, in all the land of
Egypt. 16 Pharaoh hurriedly summoned Moses and Aaron and said,
"I have sinned against the LORD
your God, and against you. 17 Do
forgive my sin just this once, and
pray to the LORD your God that at
the least he remove this deadly
thing from me." 18 So he went out
from Pharaoh and prayed to the
LORD. 19 The LORD changed the wind
into a very strong west wind, which
lifted the locusts and drove them
into the Red Sea;[w] not a single locust was left in all the country of
Egypt. 20 But the LORD hardened
Pharaoh's heart, and he would not
let the Israelites go.

The Ninth Plague: Darkness

21 Then the LORD said to Moses,
"Stretch out your hand toward
heaven so that there may be darkness over the land of Egypt, a darkness that can be felt." 22 So Moses
stretched out his hand toward
heaven, and there was dense darkness in all the land of Egypt for
three days. 23 People could not see
one another, and for three days
they could not move from where
they were; but all the Israelites had
light where they lived. 24 Then
Pharaoh summoned Moses, and
said, "Go, worship the LORD. Only
your flocks and your herds shall remain behind. Even your children
may go with you." 25 But Moses

10.2 Ex 12.26, 27; 13.8,14, 15; Deut 4.9; Ps 44.1; Ex 7.5,15
10.3 Jas 4.10; 1 Pet 5.6; Ex 4.23
10.4 Rev 9.3
10.5 Ex 9.32; Joel 1.4; 2.25
10.6 Ex 8.3,21
10.7 Ex 7.5; 8.19; 12.33
10.8 Ex 8.8,25
10.9 Ex 12.37, 38; v. 26; Ex 5.1
10.11 v. 28
10.12 Ex 7.19; vv. 4,5
10.14 Ps 78.46; 105.34; Joel 2.1-11
10.15 v. 5; Ps 105.35
10.16 Ex 9.27
10.17 Ex 8.8,29
10.20 Ex 4.21; 11.10
10.21 Deut 28.29
10.22 Ps 105.28
10.24 vv. 8,10

[w] Or *Sea of Reeds*

said, "You must also let us have
sacrifices and burnt offerings to
sacrifice to the LORD our God.
26 Our livestock also must go with
us; not a hoof shall be left behind,
for we must choose some of them
for the worship of the LORD our
God, and we will not know what to
use to worship the LORD until we
arrive there." 27 But the LORD hardened Pharaoh's heart, and he was
unwilling to let them go. 28 Then
Pharaoh said to him, "Get away
from me! Take care that you do not
see my face again, for on the day
you see my face you shall die."
29 Moses said, "Just as you say! I
will never see your face again."

Warning of the Final Plague

11 The LORD said to Moses, "I
will bring one more plague
upon Pharaoh and upon Egypt; afterwards he will let you go from
here; indeed, when he lets you go,
he will drive you away. 2 Tell the
people that every man is to ask his
neighbor and every woman is to ask
her neighbor for objects of silver
and gold." 3 The LORD gave the people favor in the sight of the Egyptians. Moreover, Moses himself
was a man of great importance in
the land of Egypt, in the sight of
Pharaoh's officials and in the sight
of the people.

4 Moses said, "Thus says the
LORD: About midnight I will go out
through Egypt. 5 Every firstborn in
the land of Egypt shall die, from
the firstborn of Pharaoh who sits
on his throne to the firstborn of the
female slave who is behind the
handmill, and all the firstborn of
the livestock. 6 Then there will be a
loud cry throughout the whole land
of Egypt, such as has never been or
will ever be again. 7 But not a dog
shall growl at any of the
Israelites—not at people, not at
animals—so that you may know
that the LORD makes a distinction
between Egypt and Israel. 8 Then
all these officials of yours shall
come down to me, and bow low to
me, saying, 'Leave us, you and all
the people who follow you.' After

10.26 v. 9
10.27 v. 20
10.28 v. 11
10.29 Heb 11.27
11.1 Ex 12.31, 33,39
11.2 Ex 3.22; 12.35,36
11.3 Ex 3.21; 12.36; Deut 34.10-12
11.4 Ex 12.29
11.5 Ex 12.12, 29; Ps 78.51; 105.36; 135.8; 136.10
11.6 Ex 12.30
11.7 Ex 8.22
11.8 Ex 12.31-33
11.9 Ex 7.3,4
11.10 Ex 4.21; 10.20,27
12.2 Ex 13.4; Deut 16.1
12.5 Lev 22.18-20
12.6 Lev 23.5; Num 9.3; Deut 16.1,6
12.8 Ex 34.25; Num 9.11, 12; Deut 16.7
12.10 Ex 23.18; 34.25
12.11 v. 27
12.12 Ex 11.4,5; Num 33.4

that I will leave." And in hot anger
he left Pharaoh.

9 The LORD said to Moses,
"Pharaoh will not listen to you, in
order that my wonders may be multiplied in the land of Egypt." 10 Moses and Aaron performed all these
wonders before Pharaoh; but the
LORD hardened Pharaoh's heart,
and he did not let the people of Israel go out of his land.

The First Passover Instituted

12 The LORD said to Moses and
Aaron in the land of Egypt:
2 This month shall mark for you the
beginning of months; it shall be the
first month of the year for you.
3 Tell the whole congregation of Israel that on the tenth of this month
they are to take a lamb for each
family, a lamb for each household.
4 If a household is too small for a
whole lamb, it shall join its closest
neighbor in obtaining one; the
lamb shall be divided in proportion
to the number of people who eat of
it. 5 Your lamb shall be without
blemish, a year-old male; you may
take it from the sheep or from the
goats. 6 You shall keep it until the
fourteenth day of this month; then
the whole assembled congregation
of Israel shall slaughter it at twilight. 7 They shall take some of the
blood and put it on the two doorposts and the lintel of the houses in
which they eat it. 8 They shall eat
the lamb that same night; they
shall eat it roasted over the fire
with unleavened bread and bitter
herbs. 9 Do not eat any of it raw or
boiled in water, but roasted over
the fire, with its head, legs, and inner organs. 10 You shall let none of
it remain until the morning; anything that remains until the morning you shall burn. 11 This is how
you shall eat it: your loins girded,
your sandals on your feet, and your
staff in your hand; and you shall eat
it hurriedly. It is the passover of the
LORD. 12 For I will pass through the
land of Egypt that night, and I will
strike down every firstborn in the
land of Egypt, both human beings
and animals; on all the gods of

HEBREW CALENDAR AND SELECTED EVENTS

Sacred Sequence Begins	Hebrew Name	Modern Equivalent	Biblical References	Agriculture	Feasts
1	**Abib; Nisan**	March-April	Ex 12:2; 13:4; 23:15; 34:18; Dt 16:1; Ne 2:1; Est 3:7	Spring (later) rains; barley and flax harvest begins	Passover; Unleavened Bread; Firstfruits
2	**Ziv (Iyyar)***	April-May	1 Ki 6:1,37	Barley havest; dry season begins	
3	**Sivan**	May-June	Est 8:9	Wheat harvest	Pentecost (Weeks)
4	**(Tammuz)***	June-July		Tending vines	
5	**(Ab)***	July-August		Ripening of grapes, figs and olives	
6	**Elul**	August-September	Ne 6:15	Processing grapes, figs and olives	
7	**Ethanim (Tishri)***	September-October	1 Ki 8:2	Autumn (early) rains begin; plowing	Trumpets; Atonement; Tabernacles (Booths)
8	**Bul (Marcheshvan)***	October-November	1 Ki 6:38	Sowing of wheat and barley	
9	**Kislev**	November-December	Ne 1:1, Zec 7:1	Winter rains begin (snow in some areas)	Hanukkah ("Dedication")
10	**Tebeth**	December-January	Est 2:16		
11	**Shebat**	January-February	Zec 1:7		
12	**Adar**	February-March	Ezr 6:15; Est 3:7,13; 8:12; 9:1,15,17,19,21	Almond trees bloom; citrus fruit harvest	Purim
	(Adar Sheni)* Second Adar	This intercalary month was added about every three years so the lunar calendar would correspond to the solar year.			

* Names in parentheses are not in the Bible

Egypt I will execute judgments: I
am the LORD. 13 The blood shall be
a sign for you on the houses where
you live: when I see the blood, I will
pass over you, and no plague shall
destroy you when I strike the land
of Egypt.

14 This day shall be a day of remembrance for you. You shall celebrate it as a festival to the LORD;
throughout your generations you
shall observe it as a perpetual ordinance. 15 Seven days you shall eat
unleavened bread; on the first day
you shall remove leaven from your
houses, for whoever eats leavened
bread from the first day until the
seventh day shall be cut off from
Israel. 16 On the first day you shall
hold a solemn assembly, and on
the seventh day a solemn assembly; no work shall be done on those
days; only what everyone must eat,
that alone may be prepared by you.
17 You shall observe the festival of
unleavened bread, for on this very
day I brought your companies out
of the land of Egypt: you shall observe this day throughout your generations as a perpetual ordinance.
18 In the first month, from the evening of the fourteenth day until the
evening of the twenty-first day, you
shall eat unleavened bread. 19 For
seven days no leaven shall be found
in your houses; for whoever eats
what is leavened shall be cut off
from the congregation of Israel,
whether an alien or a native of the
land. 20 You shall eat nothing leavened; in all your settlements you
shall eat unleavened bread.

21 Then Moses called all the elders of Israel and said to them,
"Go, select lambs for your families,
and slaughter the passover lamb.
22 Take a bunch of hyssop, dip it in
the blood that is in the basin, and
touch the lintel and the two doorposts with the blood in the basin.
None of you shall go outside the
door of your house until morning.
23 For the LORD will pass through to
strike down the Egyptians; when
he sees the blood on the lintel and
on the two doorposts, the LORD will
pass over that door and will not allow the destroyer to enter your
houses to strike you down. 24 You
shall observe this rite as a perpetual ordinance for you and your children. 25 When you come to the land
that the LORD will give you, as he
has promised, you shall keep this
observance. 26 And when your children ask you, 'What do you mean
by this observance?' 27 you shall
say, 'It is the passover sacrifice to
the LORD, for he passed over the
houses of the Israelites in Egypt,
when he struck down the Egyptians but spared our houses.' " And
the people bowed down and worshiped.

28 The Israelites went and did
just as the LORD had commanded
Moses and Aaron.

The Tenth Plague: Death of the Firstborn

29 At midnight the LORD struck
down all the firstborn in the land of
Egypt, from the firstborn of Pharaoh who sat on his throne to the
firstborn of the prisoner who was in
the dungeon, and all the firstborn
of the livestock. 30 Pharaoh arose in
the night, he and all his officials
and all the Egyptians; and there
was a loud cry in Egypt, for there
was not a house without someone
dead. 31 Then he summoned Moses
and Aaron in the night, and said,
"Rise up, go away from my people,
both you and the Israelites! Go,
worship the LORD, as you said.
32 Take your flocks and your herds,
as you said, and be gone. And bring
a blessing on me too!"

The Exodus: From Rameses to Succoth

33 The Egyptians urged the people to hasten their departure from
the land, for they said, "We shall all
be dead." 34 So the people took
their dough before it was leavened,
with their kneading bowls wrapped
up in their cloaks on their shoulders. 35 The Israelites had done as
Moses told them; they had asked
the Egyptians for jewelry of silver
and gold, and for clothing, 36 and
the LORD had given the people favor

12.14 v. 6; Ex 13.9; v. 17; Ex 13.10
12.15 Ex 23.15; 34.18; Lev 23.5,6; Deut 16.3; v. 19; Num 9.13
12.16 Lev 23.7,8
12.17 v. 41; Ex 13.3
12.18 v. 2; Lev 23.5-8; Num 28.16-25
12.19 v. 15
12.21 Heb 11.28; v. 11; Num 9.4
12.22 v. 7
12.23 vv. 12,13
12.24 Ex 13.5,10
12.26 Ex 13.14, 15; Josh 4.6
12.27 v. 11; Ex 4.31
12.29 Ex 11.4; 4.23; 9.6; Ps 78.51; 105.36
12.30 Ex 11.6
12.31 Ex 8.8,25
12.32 Ex 10.9,26
12.33 v. 39; Ex 10.7; 11.1; Ps 105.38
12.35 Ex 3.21,22; 11.2,3
12.36 Ex 3.22

in the sight of the Egyptians, so
that they let them have what they
asked. And so they plundered the
Egyptians.
37 The Israelites journeyed
from Rameses to Succoth, about
six hundred thousand men on foot,
besides children. 38 A mixed crowd
also went up with them, and livestock in great numbers, both flocks
and herds. 39 They baked unleavened cakes of the dough that they
had brought out of Egypt; it was
not leavened, because they were
driven out of Egypt and could not
wait, nor had they prepared any
provisions for themselves.
40 The time that the Israelites
had lived in Egypt was four hundred thirty years. 41 At the end of
four hundred thirty years, on that
very day, all the companies of the
LORD went out from the land of
Egypt. 42 That was for the LORD a
night of vigil, to bring them out of
the land of Egypt. That same night
is a vigil to be kept for the LORD by
all the Israelites throughout their
generations.

Directions for the Passover

43 The LORD said to Moses and
Aaron: This is the ordinance for the
passover: no foreigner shall eat of
it, 44 but any slave who has been
purchased may eat of it after he has
been circumcised; 45 no bound or
hired servant may eat of it. 46 It
shall be eaten in one house; you
shall not take any of the animal
outside the house, and you shall
not break any of its bones. 47 The
whole congregation of Israel shall
celebrate it. 48 If an alien who resides with you wants to celebrate
the passover to the LORD, all his
males shall be circumcised; then
he may draw near to celebrate it; he
shall be regarded as a native of the
land. But no uncircumcised person
shall eat of it; 49 there shall be one
law for the native and for the alien
who resides among you.
50 All the Israelites did just as
the LORD had commanded Moses
and Aaron. 51 That very day the
LORD brought the Israelites out of
the land of Egypt, company by
company.

12.37 Num 33.3,4; Ex 38.26; Num 1.46; 11.21
12.38 Num 11.4; Ex 17.3
12.39 vv. 31-33; Ex 11.1
12.40 Gen 15.13; Acts 7.6; Gal 3.17
12.41 v. 17; Ex 3.8,10; 6.6
12.42 Ex 13.10; Deut 16.1
12.43 vv. 11,48
12.44 Gen 17.12, 13; Lev 22.11
12.46 Num 9.12; Jn 19.33,36
12.47 Num 9.13, 14
12.49 Num 15.15, 16; Gal 3.28
12.51 v. 41
13.2 vv. 12,13, 15; Ex 22.29; Lk 2.23
13.3 Ex 3.20; 6.1; 12.19
13.5 Ex 3.8; 12.25,26
13.6 Ex 12.15-20
13.8 v. 14; Ex 10.2
13.9 v. 16; Ex 12.14; Deut 6.8; 11.18
13.10 Ex 12.24,25
13.12 v. 2; Ex 22.29; 34.19
13.13 Ex 34.20; Num 18.15, 16

13 The LORD said to Moses:
2 Consecrate to me all the
firstborn; whatever is the first to
open the womb among the Israelites, of human beings and animals,
is mine.

The Festival of Unleavened Bread

3 Moses said to the people, "Remember this day on which you
came out of Egypt, out of the house
of slavery, because the LORD
brought you out from there by
strength of hand; no leavened
bread shall be eaten. 4 Today, in the
month of Abib, you are going out.
5 When the LORD brings you into the
land of the Canaanites, the Hittites, the Amorites, the Hivites,
and the Jebusites, which he swore
to your ancestors to give you, a land
flowing with milk and honey, you
shall keep this observance in this
month. 6 Seven days you shall eat
unleavened bread, and on the seventh day there shall be a festival to
the LORD. 7 Unleavened bread shall
be eaten for seven days; no leavened bread shall be seen in your
possession, and no leaven shall be
seen among you in all your territory. 8 You shall tell your child on that
day, 'It is because of what the LORD
did for me when I came out of
Egypt.' 9 It shall serve for you as a
sign on your hand and as a reminder on your forehead, so that the
teaching of the LORD may be on
your lips; for with a strong hand the
LORD brought you out of Egypt.
10 You shall keep this ordinance at
its proper time from year to year.

The Consecration of the Firstborn

11 "When the LORD has brought
you into the land of the Canaanites, as he swore to you and your
ancestors, and has given it to you,
12 you shall set apart to the LORD all
that first opens the womb. All the
firstborn of your livestock that are
males shall be the LORD's. 13 But every firstborn donkey you shall re-

deem with a sheep; if you do not
redeem it, you must break its neck.
Every firstborn male among your
children you shall redeem. [14]When
in the future your child asks you,
'What does this mean?' you shall
answer, 'By strength of hand the
LORD brought us out of Egypt, from
the house of slavery. [15]When Pharaoh stubbornly refused to let us go,
the LORD killed all the firstborn in
the land of Egypt, from human
firstborn to the firstborn of animals. Therefore I sacrifice to the
LORD every male that first opens the
womb, but every firstborn of my
sons I redeem.' [16]It shall serve as a
sign on your hand and as an emblem[x] on your forehead that by
strength of hand the LORD brought
us out of Egypt."

The Pillars of Cloud and Fire

17 When Pharaoh let the people
go, God did not lead them by way
of the land of the Philistines, although that was nearer; for God
thought, "If the people face war,
they may change their minds and
return to Egypt." [18]So God led the
people by the roundabout way of
the wilderness toward the Red
Sea.[y] The Israelites went up out of
the land of Egypt prepared for battle. [19]And Moses took with him the
bones of Joseph who had required
a solemn oath of the Israelites, saying, "God will surely take notice of
you, and then you must carry my
bones with you from here." [20]They
set out from Succoth, and camped
at Etham, on the edge of the wilderness. [21]The LORD went in front
of them in a pillar of cloud by day,
to lead them along the way, and in
a pillar of fire by night, to give them
light, so that they might travel by
day and by night. [22]Neither the pillar of cloud by day nor the pillar of
fire by night left its place in front of
the people.

Crossing the Red Sea

14 Then the LORD said to Moses: [2]Tell the Israelites to
turn back and camp in front of Pi-
hahiroth, between Migdol and the
sea, in front of Baal-zephon; you
shall camp opposite it, by the sea.
[3]Pharaoh will say of the Israelites,
'They are wandering aimlessly in
the land; the wilderness has closed
in on them.' [4]I will harden Pharaoh's heart, and he will pursue
them, so that I will gain glory for
myself over Pharaoh and all his
army; and the Egyptians shall
know that I am the LORD. And they
did so.

5 When the king of Egypt was
told that the people had fled, the
minds of Pharaoh and his officials
were changed toward the people,
and they said, "What have we done,
letting Israel leave our service?"
[6]So he had his chariot made ready,
and took his army with him; [7]he
took six hundred picked chariots
and all the other chariots of Egypt
with officers over all of them. [8]The
LORD hardened the heart of Pharaoh king of Egypt and he pursued
the Israelites, who were going out
boldly. [9]The Egyptians pursued
them, all Pharaoh's horses and
chariots, his chariot drivers and his
army; they overtook them camped
by the sea, by Pi-hahiroth, in front
of Baal-zephon.

10 As Pharaoh drew near, the Israelites looked back, and there
were the Egyptians advancing on
them. In great fear the Israelites
cried out to the LORD. [11]They said
to Moses, "Was it because there
were no graves in Egypt that you
have taken us away to die in the
wilderness? What have you done to
us, bringing us out of Egypt? [12]Is
this not the very thing we told you
in Egypt, 'Let us alone and let us
serve the Egyptians'? For it would
have been better for us to serve the
Egyptians than to die in the wilderness." [13]But Moses said to the people, "Do not be afraid, stand firm,
and see the deliverance that the
LORD will accomplish for you today;
for the Egyptians whom you see today you shall never see again.

13.14 Ex 12.26, 27; Deut 6.20; vv. 3,9
13.15 Ex 12.29
13.16 v. 9
13.17 Ex 14.11, 12; Num 14.1-4; Deut 17.16
13.19 Gen 50.25, 26; Josh 24.32; Acts 7.16
13.20 Num 33.6-8
13.21f Ex 14.19, 24; 33.9,10; Ps 78.14; 105.39; 1 Cor 10.1
14.2 Num 33.7,8
14.4 v. 17; Ex 4.21; 7.5
14.8 v. 4; Num 33.3; Acts 13.17
14.9 Ex 15.9
14.10 Neh 9.9
14.11 Ps 106.7,8
14.13 Gen 15.1; v. 30; Ex 15.2

[x] Or *as a frontlet*; Meaning of Heb uncertain
[y] Or *Sea of Reeds*

14 The LORD will fight for you, and
you have only to keep still."
15 Then the LORD said to Moses,
"Why do you cry out to me? Tell the
Israelites to go forward. 16 But you
lift up your staff, and stretch out
your hand over the sea and divide
it, that the Israelites may go into
the sea on dry ground. 17 Then I will
harden the hearts of the Egyptians
so that they will go in after them;
and so I will gain glory for myself
over Pharaoh and all his army, his
chariots, and his chariot drivers.
18 And the Egyptians shall know
that I am the LORD, when I have
gained glory for myself over Pharaoh, his chariots, and his chariot
drivers."
19 The angel of God who was
going before the Israelite army
moved and went behind them; and
the pillar of cloud moved from in
front of them and took its place behind them. 20 It came between the
army of Egypt and the army of Israel. And so the cloud was there with
the darkness, and it lit up the
night; one did not come near the
other all night.
21 Then Moses stretched out
his hand over the sea. The LORD
drove the sea back by a strong east
wind all night, and turned the sea
into dry land; and the waters were
divided. 22 The Israelites went into
the sea on dry ground, the waters
forming a wall for them on their
right and on their left. 23 The Egyptians pursued, and went into the
sea after them, all of Pharaoh's
horses, chariots, and chariot drivers. 24 At the morning watch the
LORD in the pillar of fire and cloud
looked down upon the Egyptian
army, and threw the Egyptian army
into panic. 25 He clogged[z] their
chariot wheels so that they turned
with difficulty. The Egyptians said,
"Let us flee from the Israelites, for
the LORD is fighting for them
against Egypt."

The Pursuers Drowned

26 Then the LORD said to Moses,
"Stretch out your hand over the
sea, so that the water may come
back upon the Egyptians, upon
their chariots and chariot drivers."
27 So Moses stretched out his hand
over the sea, and at dawn the sea
returned to its normal depth. As
the Egyptians fled before it, the
LORD tossed the Egyptians into the
sea. 28 The waters returned and
covered the chariots and the chariot drivers, the entire army of Pharaoh that had followed them into
the sea; not one of them remained.
29 But the Israelites walked on dry
ground through the sea, the waters
forming a wall for them on their
right and on their left.
30 Thus the LORD saved Israel
that day from the Egyptians; and
Israel saw the Egyptians dead on
the seashore. 31 Israel saw the great
work that the LORD did against the
Egyptians. So the people feared the
LORD and believed in the LORD and
in his servant Moses.

The Song of Moses

15 Then Moses and the Israelites sang this song to the
LORD:

"I will sing to the LORD, for
he has triumphed
gloriously;
horse and rider he has
thrown into the sea.
2 The LORD is my strength and
my might,[a]
and he has become my
salvation;
this is my God, and I will
praise him,
my father's God, and I will
exalt him.
3 The LORD is a warrior;
the LORD is his name.

4 "Pharaoh's chariots and his
army he cast into the
sea;
his picked officers were
sunk in the Red Sea.[b]
5 The floods covered them;
they went down into the
depths like a stone.
6 Your right hand, O LORD,
glorious in power—

14.14 Ex 15.3; Deut 1.30; 3.22; Isa 30.15 **14.16** Ex 4.17; Num 20.8,9, 11; Isa 10.26 **14.17** v. 4 **14.18** v. 25 **14.19** Ex 13.21,22 **14.21** v. 16; Ps 106.9; 114.3,5; Isa 63.12,13 **14.22** Ex 15.19; Neh 9.11; Heb 11.29 **14.24** Ex 13.21 **14.25** vv. 4,18 **14.27** Ex 15.1,7 **14.28** Ps 78.53; 106.11 **14.29** Ex 15.19; Neh 9.11; Heb 11.29 **14.30** Ps 106.8 **14.31** Ps 106.12 **15.1** Ps 106.12; Rev 15.3 **15.2** Ps 59.17; Ex 3.15,16 **15.3** Ps 24.8; 83.18 **15.4** Ex 14.6,7, 17,28 **15.5** v. 10; Neh 9.11 **15.6** Ps 118.15

[z] Sam Gk Syr: MT *removed* [a] Or *song*
[b] Or *Sea of Reeds*

your right hand, O LORD,
shattered the enemy.
7 In the greatness of your
majesty you overthrew
your adversaries;
you sent out your fury, it
consumed them like
stubble.
8 At the blast of your nostrils
the waters piled up,
the floods stood up in a
heap;
the deeps congealed in the
heart of the sea.
9 The enemy said, 'I will
pursue, I will overtake,
I will divide the spoil, my
desire shall have its fill
of them.
I will draw my sword, my
hand shall destroy
them.'
10 You blew with your wind, the
sea covered them;
they sank like lead in the
mighty waters.

11 "Who is like you, O LORD,
among the gods?
Who is like you, majestic
in holiness,
awesome in splendor,
doing wonders?
12 You stretched out your right
hand,
the earth swallowed them.

13 "In your steadfast love you
led the people whom
you redeemed;
you guided them by your
strength to your holy
abode.
14 The peoples heard, they
trembled;
pangs seized the
inhabitants of Philistia.
15 Then the chiefs of Edom
were dismayed;
trembling seized the
leaders of Moab;
all the inhabitants of
Canaan melted away.
16 Terror and dread fell upon
them;
by the might of your arm,
they became still as a
stone
until your people, O LORD,
passed by,
until the people whom you
acquired passed by.
17 You brought them in and
planted them on the
mountain of your own
possession,
the place, O LORD, that you
made your abode,
the sanctuary, O LORD, that
your hands have
established.
18 The LORD will reign forever
and ever."
19 When the horses of Pharaoh
with his chariots and his chariot
drivers went into the sea, the LORD
brought back the waters of the sea
upon them; but the Israelites
walked through the sea on dry
ground.

The Song of Miriam

20 Then the prophet Miriam,
Aaron's sister, took a tambourine
in her hand; and all the women
went out after her with tambourines and with dancing. 21 And Miriam sang to them:
"Sing to the LORD, for he has
triumphed gloriously;
horse and rider he has
thrown into the sea."

Bitter Water Made Sweet

22 Then Moses ordered Israel to
set out from the Red Sea,[c] and
they went into the wilderness of
Shur. They went three days in the
wilderness and found no water.
23 When they came to Marah, they
could not drink the water of Marah
because it was bitter. That is why it
was called Marah.[d] 24 And the people complained against Moses, saying, "What shall we drink?" 25 He
cried out to the LORD; and the LORD
showed him a piece of wood;[e] he
threw it into the water, and the water became sweet.

There the LORD[f] made for them
a statute and an ordinance and

15.7 Ex 14.27; Ps 78.49,50
15.8 Ex 14.22, 29; Ps 78.13
15.9 Ex 14.5
15.10 Ex 14.28
15.11 Ex 8.10; Deut 3.24; Isa 6.3; Rev 4.8;
Ps 22.23; 72.18
15.13 Neh 9.12; Ps 77.15; 78.54
15.14 Deut 2.25; Hab 3.7
15.15 Gen 36.15; Num 22.3; Josh 5.1
15.16 Ex 23.27; 1 Sam 25.37; Ps 74.2
15.17 Ps 44.2; 78.54
15.18 Ps 10.16
15.19 Ex 14.23,28
15.20 Judg 4.4; Num 26.59; 1 Sam 18.6; Ps 30.11; 150.4
15.21 v. 1
15.22 Ps 77.20; Num 33.8
15.23 Num 33.8
15.24 Ex 14.11; Ps 106.13
15.25 Ex 14.10; Ps 50.15

c Or *Sea of Reeds* d That is *Bitterness*
e Or *a tree* f Heb *he*

there he put them to the test. 26 He
said, "If you will listen carefully to
the voice of the LORD your God, and
do what is right in his sight, and
give heed to his commandments
and keep all his statutes, I will not
bring upon you any of the diseases
that I brought upon the Egyptians;
for I am the LORD who heals you."
27 Then they came to Elim,
where there were twelve springs of
water and seventy palm trees; and
they camped there by the water.

Bread from Heaven

16 The whole congregation of
the Israelites set out from
Elim; and Israel came to the wilderness of Sin, which is between
Elim and Sinai, on the fifteenth
day of the second month after they
had departed from the land of
Egypt. 2 The whole congregation of
the Israelites complained against
Moses and Aaron in the wilderness.
3 The Israelites said to them, "If
only we had died by the hand of the
LORD in the land of Egypt, when we
sat by the fleshpots and ate our fill
of bread; for you have brought us
out into this wilderness to kill this
whole assembly with hunger."
4 Then the LORD said to Moses,
"I am going to rain bread from
heaven for you, and each day the
people shall go out and gather
enough for that day. In that way I
will test them, whether they will
follow my instruction or not. 5 On
the sixth day, when they prepare
what they bring in, it will be twice
as much as they gather on other
days." 6 So Moses and Aaron said to
all the Israelites, "In the evening
you shall know that it was the LORD
who brought you out of the land of
Egypt, 7 and in the morning you
shall see the glory of the LORD, because he has heard your complaining against the LORD. For what are
we, that you complain against us?"
8 And Moses said, "When the LORD
gives you meat to eat in the evening
and your fill of bread in the morning, because the LORD has heard the
complaining that you utter against
him—what are we? Your complaining is not against us but against the
LORD."
9 Then Moses said to Aaron,
"Say to the whole congregation of
the Israelites, 'Draw near to the
LORD, for he has heard your complaining.' " 10 And as Aaron spoke
to the whole congregation of the Israelites, they looked toward the
wilderness, and the glory of the
LORD appeared in the cloud. 11 The
LORD spoke to Moses and said, 12 "I
have heard the complaining of the
Israelites; say to them, 'At twilight
you shall eat meat, and in the
morning you shall have your fill of
bread; then you shall know that I
am the LORD your God.' "
13 In the evening quails came
up and covered the camp; and in
the morning there was a layer of
dew around the camp. 14 When the
layer of dew lifted, there on the surface of the wilderness was a fine
flaky substance, as fine as frost on
the ground. 15 When the Israelites
saw it, they said to one another,
"What is it?"[g] For they did not
know what it was. Moses said to
them, "It is the bread that the LORD
has given you to eat. 16 This is what
the LORD has commanded: 'Gather
as much of it as each of you needs,
an omer to a person according to
the number of persons, all providing for those in their own tents.' "
17 The Israelites did so, some gathering more, some less. 18 But when
they measured it with an omer,
those who gathered much had
nothing over, and those who gathered little had no shortage; they
gathered as much as each of them
needed. 19 And Moses said to them,
"Let no one leave any of it over until morning." 20 But they did not listen to Moses; some left part of it
until morning, and it bred worms
and became foul. And Moses was
angry with them. 21 Morning by
morning they gathered it, as much
as each needed; but when the sun
grew hot, it melted.

15.26 Deut 7.12; 28.27
15.27 Num 33.9, 10
16.1 Num 33.11, 12
16.2 Ex 14.11; 1 Cor 10.10
16.3 Ex 17.3; Num 11.4,5
16.4 Jn 6.31; 1 Cor 10.3; Deut 8.2,16
16.5 v. 22
16.7 v. 12; Num 14.27; 16.11
16.9 Num 16.16
16.10 v. 7; Num 16.19
16.13 Num 11.31; Ps 78.27,28; 105.40
16.14 Num 11.7-9; v. 31
16.15 v. 4
16.18 2 Cor 8.15
16.19 v. 23; Ex 12.10; 23.18

g Or *"It is manna"* (Heb *man hu,* see verse 31)

22 On the sixth day they gathered twice as much food, two omers apiece. When all the leaders of the congregation came and told Moses, 23 he said to them, "This is what the LORD has commanded: 'Tomorrow is a day of solemn rest, a holy sabbath to the LORD; bake what you want to bake and boil what you want to boil, and all that is left over put aside to be kept until morning.' " 24 So they put it aside until morning, as Moses commanded them; and it did not become foul, and there were no worms in it. 25 Moses said, "Eat it today, for today is a sabbath to the LORD; today you will not find it in the field. 26 Six days you shall gather it; but on the seventh day, which is a sabbath, there will be none."

27 On the seventh day some of the people went out to gather, and they found none. 28 The LORD said to Moses, "How long will you refuse to keep my commandments and instructions? 29 See! The LORD has given you the sabbath, therefore on the sixth day he gives you food for two days; each of you stay where you are; do not leave your place on the seventh day." 30 So the people rested on the seventh day.

31 The house of Israel called it manna; it was like coriander seed, white, and the taste of it was like wafers made with honey. 32 Moses said, "This is what the LORD has commanded: 'Let an omer of it be kept throughout your generations, in order that they may see the food with which I fed you in the wilderness, when I brought you out of the land of Egypt.' " 33 And Moses said to Aaron, "Take a jar, and put an omer of manna in it, and place it before the LORD, to be kept throughout your generations." 34 As the LORD commanded Moses, so Aaron placed it before the covenant,[h] for safekeeping. 35 The Israelites ate manna forty years, until they came to a habitable land; they ate manna, until they came to the border of the land of Canaan. 36 An omer is a tenth of an ephah.

16.22 v. 5; Ex 34.31 **16.23ff** Ex 20.8; 23.12 **16.24** v. 20 **16.28** Ps 78.10 **16.31** Num 11.6-9 **16.33** Heb 9.4 **16.34** Ex 25.16,21 **16.35** Josh 5.12; Neh 9.20,21

17.1 Ex 16.1 **17.2** Num 20.3; Deut 6.16; 1 Cor 10.9 **17.3** Ex 16.2,3 **17.4** Ex 14.15; Num 14.10; 1 Sam 30.6 **17.5** Ex 3.16,18; 7.20 **17.6** Num 20.10; Ps 114.8; 1 Cor 10.4 **17.7** Ps 81.7 **17.8** Num 24.20; Deut 25.17-19 **17.9** Ex 4.20

Water from the Rock

17 From the wilderness of Sin the whole congregation of the Israelites journeyed by stages, as the LORD commanded. They camped at Rephidim, but there was no water for the people to drink. 2 The people quarreled with Moses, and said, "Give us water to drink." Moses said to them, "Why do you quarrel with me? Why do you test the LORD?" 3 But the people thirsted there for water; and the people complained against Moses and said, "Why did you bring us out of Egypt, to kill us and our children and livestock with thirst?" 4 So Moses cried out to the LORD, "What shall I do with this people? They are almost ready to stone me." 5 The LORD said to Moses, "Go on ahead of the people, and take some of the elders of Israel with you; take in your hand the staff with which you struck the Nile, and go. 6 I will be standing there in front of you on the rock at Horeb. Strike the rock, and water will come out of it, so that the people may drink." Moses did so, in the sight of the elders of Israel. 7 He called the place Massah[i] and Meribah,[j] because the Israelites quarreled and tested the LORD, saying, "Is the LORD among us or not?"

Amalek Attacks Israel and Is Defeated

8 Then Amalek came and fought with Israel at Rephidim. 9 Moses said to Joshua, "Choose some men for us and go out, fight with Amalek. Tomorrow I will stand on the top of the hill with the staff of God in my hand." 10 So Joshua did as Moses told him, and fought with Amalek, while Moses, Aaron, and Hur went up to the top of the hill. 11 Whenever Moses held up his hand, Israel prevailed; and whenever he lowered his hand, Amalek prevailed. 12 But Moses' hands grew weary; so they took a stone and put it under him, and he

[h] Or *treaty* or *testimony*; Heb *eduth* [i] That is *Test* [j] That is *Quarrel*

sat on it. Aaron and Hur held up his
hands, one on one side, and the
other on the other side; so his
hands were steady until the sun
set. 13 And Joshua defeated Amalek
and his people with the sword.
14 Then the LORD said to Moses,
"Write this as a reminder in a book
and recite it in the hearing of Joshua: I will utterly blot out the remembrance of Amalek from under
heaven." 15 And Moses built an altar and called it, The LORD is my
banner. 16 He said, "A hand upon
the banner of the LORD![k] The LORD
will have war with Amalek from
generation to generation."

Jethro's Advice

18 Jethro, the priest of Midian, Moses' father-in-law,
heard of all that God had done for
Moses and for his people Israel,
how the LORD had brought Israel
out of Egypt. 2 After Moses had sent
away his wife Zipporah, his father-
in-law Jethro took her back, 3 along
with her two sons. The name of the
one was Gershom (for he said, "I
have been an alien[l] in a foreign
land"), 4 and the name of the other,
Eliezer[m] (for he said, "The God of
my father was my help, and delivered me from the sword of Pharaoh"). 5 Jethro, Moses' father-in-
law, came into the wilderness
where Moses was encamped at the
mountain of God, bringing Moses'
sons and wife to him. 6 He sent
word to Moses, "I, your father-in-
law Jethro, am coming to you, with
your wife and her two sons." 7 Moses went out to meet his father-in-
law; he bowed down and kissed
him; each asked after the other's
welfare, and they went into the
tent. 8 Then Moses told his father-
in-law all that the LORD had done to
Pharaoh and to the Egyptians for
Israel's sake, all the hardship that
had beset them on the way, and
how the LORD had delivered them.
9 Jethro rejoiced for all the good
that the LORD had done to Israel, in
delivering them from the Egyptians.
10 Jethro said, "Blessed be the
LORD, who has delivered you from
the Egyptians and from Pharaoh.
11 Now I know that the LORD is
greater than all gods, because he
delivered the people from the
Egyptians,[n] when they dealt arrogantly with them." 12 And Jethro,
Moses' father-in-law, brought a
burnt offering and sacrifices to
God; and Aaron came with all the
elders of Israel to eat bread with
Moses' father-in-law in the presence of God.
13 The next day Moses sat as
judge for the people, while the people stood around him from morning until evening. 14 When Moses'
father-in-law saw all that he was
doing for the people, he said,
"What is this that you are doing for
the people? Why do you sit alone,
while all the people stand around
you from morning until evening?"
15 Moses said to his father-in-law,
"Because the people come to me to
inquire of God. 16 When they have a
dispute, they come to me and I decide between one person and another, and I make known to them
the statutes and instructions of
God." 17 Moses' father-in-law said
to him, "What you are doing is not
good. 18 You will surely wear yourself out, both you and these people
with you. For the task is too heavy
for you; you cannot do it alone.
19 Now listen to me. I will give you
counsel, and God be with you! You
should represent the people before
God, and you should bring their
cases before God; 20 teach them the
statutes and instructions and make
known to them the way they are to
go and the things they are to do.
21 You should also look for able
men among all the people, men
who fear God, are trustworthy, and
hate dishonest gain; set such men
over them as officers over thousands, hundreds, fifties and tens.
22 Let them sit as judges for the
people at all times; let them bring
every important case to you, but

17.14 Ex 34.27; Num 24.20; Deut 29.19
18.1 Ex 2.16; 3.1
18.2 Ex 4.25
18.3 Acts 7.29; Ex 2.22
18.5 Ex 3.1,12
18.7 Gen 43.26-28; Ex 4.27
18.8 Ps 81.7
18.10 Ps 68.19,20
18.11 Ex 12.12; 15.11; 1 Sam 2.3
18.15 Num 9.8; Deut 17.8-13
18.18 Num 11.14, 17
18.19 Ex 3.12; Num 27.5
18.20 Deut 1.18
18.21ff v. 25; Deut 1.13, 15
18.22 Deut 1.17, 18; Num 11.17

[k] Cn: Meaning of Heb uncertain
[l] Heb *ger* [m] Heb *Eli,* my God; *ezer,* help
[n] The clause *because . . . Egyptians* has been transposed from verse 10

decide every minor case themselves. So it will be easier for you,
and they will bear the burden with
you. 23 If you do this, and God so
commands you, then you will be
able to endure, and all these people will go to their home in peace."
24 So Moses listened to his
father-in-law and did all that he
had said. 25 Moses chose able men
from all Israel and appointed them
as heads over the people, as officers over thousands, hundreds, fifties, and tens. 26 And they judged
the people at all times; hard cases
they brought to Moses, but any minor case they decided themselves.
27 Then Moses let his father-in-law
depart, and he went off to his own
country.

The Israelites Reach Mount Sinai

19 On the third new moon after the Israelites had gone
out of the land of Egypt, on that
very day, they came into the wilderness of Sinai. 2 They had journeyed
from Rephidim, entered the wilderness of Sinai, and camped in the
wilderness; Israel camped there in
front of the mountain. 3 Then Moses went up to God; the LORD called
to him from the mountain, saying,
"Thus you shall say to the house of
Jacob, and tell the Israelites: 4 You
have seen what I did to the Egyptians, and how I bore you on eagles'
wings and brought you to myself.
5 Now therefore, if you obey my
voice and keep my covenant, you
shall be my treasured possession
out of all the peoples. Indeed, the
whole earth is mine, 6 but you shall
be for me a priestly kingdom and a
holy nation. These are the words
that you shall speak to the Israelites."
7 So Moses came, summoned
the elders of the people, and set before them all these words that the
LORD had commanded him. 8 The
people all answered as one: "Everything that the LORD has spoken we
will do." Moses reported the words
of the people to the LORD. 9 Then
the LORD said to Moses, "I am going
to come to you in a dense cloud, in
order that the people may hear
when I speak with you and so trust
you ever after."

The People Consecrated

When Moses had told the words
of the people to the LORD, 10 the
LORD said to Moses: "Go to the people and consecrate them today and
tomorrow. Have them wash their
clothes 11 and prepare for the third
day, because on the third day the
LORD will come down upon Mount
Sinai in the sight of all the people.
12 You shall set limits for the people
all around, saying, 'Be careful not
to go up the mountain or to touch
the edge of it. Any who touch the
mountain shall be put to death.
13 No hand shall touch them, but
they shall be stoned or shot with
arrows;[o] whether animal or human
being, they shall not live.' When
the trumpet sounds a long blast,
they may go up on the mountain."
14 So Moses went down from the
mountain to the people. He consecrated the people, and they washed
their clothes. 15 And he said to the
people, "Prepare for the third day;
do not go near a woman."
16 On the morning of the third
day there was thunder and lightning, as well as a thick cloud on the
mountain, and a blast of a trumpet
so loud that all the people who
were in the camp trembled. 17 Moses brought the people out of the
camp to meet God. They took their
stand at the foot of the mountain.
18 Now Mount Sinai was wrapped in
smoke, because the LORD had descended upon it in fire; the smoke
went up like the smoke of a kiln,
while the whole mountain shook
violently. 19 As the blast of the
trumpet grew louder and louder,
Moses would speak and God would
answer him in thunder. 20 When the
LORD descended upon Mount Sinai,
to the top of the mountain, the
LORD summoned Moses to the top
of the mountain, and Moses went
up. 21 Then the LORD said to Moses,
"Go down and warn the people not

18.25 Deut 1.15 **18.26** v. 22 **18.27** Num 10.29, 30 **19.2** Ex 17.1; 18.5 **19.3** Ex 20;21; Acts 7.38 **19.4** Deut 29.2; Isa 63.9 **19.5ff** Deut 5.2; 7.6; 10.14 **19.6** 1 Pet 2.5; Rev 1.6; 5.10; Deut 14.21; 26.19 **19.8** Ex 24.3,7 **19.9** v. 16; Ex 24.15

19.10 Lev 11.44, 45; Heb 10.22; Gen 35.2; Num 8.7; 19.19 **19.11** v. 16 **19.12** Heb 12.20 **19.13** v. 17 **19.16** Heb 12.18, 19; Ex 40.34 **19.18** Ps 104.32; Heb 12.18; Gen 19.28; Ps 68.7,8 **19.19** Heb 12.21; Ps 81.7 **19.21** Ex 3.5

o Heb lacks *with arrows*

to break through to the LORD to
look; otherwise many of them will
perish. 22 Even the priests who approach the LORD must consecrate
themselves or the LORD will break
out against them." 23 Moses said to
the LORD, "The people are not permitted to come up to Mount Sinai;
for you yourself warned us, saying,
'Set limits around the mountain
and keep it holy.' " 24 The LORD said
to him, "Go down, and come up
bringing Aaron with you; but do not
let either the priests or the people
break through to come up to the
LORD; otherwise he will break out
against them." 25 So Moses went
down to the people and told them.

The Ten Commandments

20 Then God spoke all these
words:
2 I am the LORD your God, who
brought you out of the land of
Egypt, out of the house of slavery;
3 you shall have no other gods before[p] me.
4 You shall not make for yourself an idol, whether in the form of
anything that is in heaven above, or
that is on the earth beneath, or that
is in the water under the earth.
5 You shall not bow down to them
or worship them; for I the LORD your
God am a jealous God, punishing
children for the iniquity of parents,
to the third and the fourth generation of those who reject me, 6 but
showing steadfast love to the thousandth generation[q] of those who
love me and keep my commandments.
7 You shall not make wrongful
use of the name of the LORD your
God, for the LORD will not acquit
anyone who misuses his name.
8 Remember the sabbath day,
and keep it holy. 9 Six days you
shall labor and do all your work.
10 But the seventh day is a sabbath
to the LORD your God; you shall not
do any work—you, your son or your
daughter, your male or female
slave, your livestock, or the alien
resident in your towns. 11 For in six
days the LORD made heaven and
earth, the sea, and all that is in
them, but rested the seventh day;
therefore the LORD blessed the sabbath day and consecrated it.
12 Honor your father and your
mother, so that your days may be
long in the land that the LORD your
God is giving you.
13 You shall not murder.[r]
14 You shall not commit adultery.
15 You shall not steal.
16 You shall not bear false witness against your neighbor.
17 You shall not covet your
neighbor's house; you shall not
covet your neighbor's wife, or male
or female slave, or ox, or donkey, or
anything that belongs to your
neighbor.
18 When all the people witnessed the thunder and lightning,
the sound of the trumpet, and the
mountain smoking, they were
afraid[s] and trembled and stood at
a distance, 19 and said to Moses,
"You speak to us, and we will listen; but do not let God speak to us,
or we will die." 20 Moses said to the
people, "Do not be afraid; for God
has come only to test you and to
put the fear of him upon you so
that you do not sin." 21 Then the
people stood at a distance, while
Moses drew near to the thick darkness where God was.

The Law concerning the Altar

22 The LORD said to Moses:
Thus you shall say to the Israelites:
"You have seen for yourselves that
I spoke with you from heaven.
23 You shall not make gods of silver
alongside me, nor shall you make
for yourselves gods of gold. 24 You
need make for me only an altar of
earth and sacrifice on it your burnt
offerings and your offerings of well-
being, your sheep and your oxen; in
every place where I cause my name
to be remembered I will come to
you and bless you. 25 But if you
make for me an altar of stone, do
not build it of hewn stones; for if
you use a chisel upon it you profane it. 26 You shall not go up by

19.22 Lev 10.3; 2 Sam 6.7 **19.23** v. 12 **20.1** Deut 5.22 **20.2** Deut 5.6; 7.8 **20.3** Jer 35.15 **20.4** Lev 26.1; Deut 4.15-19; Ps 97.7 **20.5** Isa 44.15, 19; Deut 4.24; Jer 32.18 **20.6** Deut 7.9 **20.7** Lev 19.12; Mt 5.33 **20.8** Ex 23.12; 31.15 **20.9** Ex 34.21; Lk 13.14 **20.11** Gen 2.2,3

20.12 Lev 19.3; Mt 15.4; Mk 7.10; Eph 6.2 **20.13** Rom 13.9 **20.14** Mt 19.18 **20.15** Mt 19.18 **20.16** Ex 23.1; Mt 19.18 **20.17** Rom 7.7; 13.9 **20.18** Heb 12.18; Ex 19.18 **20.19** Deut 5.23-27 **20.20** Ex 14.13; 15.25; Deut 4.10 **20.21** Deut 5.22 **20.22** Neh 9.13 **20.23** v. 3; Ex 32.1,2,4 **20.24** Lev 1.2; Deut 12.5; Gen 12.2 **20.25** Deut 27.5,6

[p] Or *besides* [q] Or *to thousands*
[r] Or *kill* [s] Sam Gk Syr Vg: MT *they saw*

steps to my altar, so that your nakedness may not be exposed on it."

The Law concerning Slaves

21 These are the ordinances that you shall set before them:

2 When you buy a male Hebrew slave, he shall serve six years, but in the seventh he shall go out a free person, without debt. [3]If he comes in single, he shall go out single; if he comes in married, then his wife shall go out with him. [4]If his master gives him a wife and she bears him sons or daughters, the wife and her children shall be her master's and he shall go out alone. [5]But if the slave declares, "I love my master, my wife, and my children; I will not go out a free person," [6]then his master shall bring him before God.[t] He shall be brought to the door or the doorpost; and his master shall pierce his ear with an awl; and he shall serve him for life.

7 When a man sells his daughter as a slave, she shall not go out as the male slaves do. [8]If she does not please her master, who designated her for himself, then he shall let her be redeemed; he shall have no right to sell her to a foreign people, since he has dealt unfairly with her. [9]If he designates her for his son, he shall deal with her as with a daughter. [10]If he takes another wife to himself, he shall not diminish the food, clothing, or marital rights of the first wife.[u] [11]And if he does not do these three things for her, she shall go out without debt, without payment of money.

The Law concerning Violence

12 Whoever strikes a person mortally shall be put to death. [13]If it was not premeditated, but came about by an act of God, then I will appoint for you a place to which the killer may flee. [14]But if someone willfully attacks and kills another by treachery, you shall take the killer from my altar for execution.

15 Whoever strikes father or mother shall be put to death.

21.1 Deut 4.14 **21.2** Lev 25.39-41; Deut 15.12-18 **21.6** Ex 22.8,9, 28 **21.7** Neh 5.5; vv. 2,3 **21.10** 1 Cor 7.3, 5 **21.12** Gen 9.6; Lev 24.17 **21.13** Num 35.22; Deut 19.4,5 **21.14** Deut 19.11, 12; Heb 10.26; 1 Kings 2.28-34

21.16 Deut 24.7 **21.17** Lev 20.9; Mt 15.4; Mk 7.10 **21.21** Lev 25.45, 46 **21.23ff** Lev 24.19 **21.24** Mt 5.38 **21.28** Gen 9.5

16 Whoever kidnaps a person, whether that person has been sold or is still held in possession, shall be put to death.

17 Whoever curses father or mother shall be put to death.

18 When individuals quarrel and one strikes the other with a stone or fist so that the injured party, though not dead, is confined to bed, [19]but recovers and walks around outside with the help of a staff, then the assailant shall be free of liability, except to pay for the loss of time, and to arrange for full recovery.

20 When a slaveowner strikes a male or female slave with a rod and the slave dies immediately, the owner shall be punished. [21]But if the slave survives a day or two, there is no punishment; for the slave is the owner's property.

22 When people who are fighting injure a pregnant woman so that there is a miscarriage, and yet no further harm follows, the one responsible shall be fined what the woman's husband demands, paying as much as the judges determine. [23]If any harm follows, then you shall give life for life, [24]eye for eye, tooth for tooth, hand for hand, foot for foot, [25]burn for burn, wound for wound, stripe for stripe.

26 When a slaveowner strikes the eye of a male or female slave, destroying it, the owner shall let the slave go, a free person, to compensate for the eye. [27]If the owner knocks out a tooth of a male or female slave, the slave shall be let go, a free person, to compensate for the tooth.

Laws concerning Property

28 When an ox gores a man or a woman to death, the ox shall be stoned, and its flesh shall not be eaten; but the owner of the ox shall not be liable. [29]If the ox has been accustomed to gore in the past, and its owner has been warned but has not restrained it, and it kills a man or a woman, the ox shall be stoned, and its owner also shall be

[t] Or *to the judges* [u] Heb *of her*

put to death. 30 If a ransom is imposed on the owner, then the owner shall pay whatever is imposed for
the redemption of the victim's life.
31 If it gores a boy or a girl, the owner shall be dealt with according to
this same rule. 32 If the ox gores a
male or female slave, the owner
shall pay to the slaveowner thirty
shekels of silver, and the ox shall
be stoned.
33 If someone leaves a pit open,
or digs a pit and does not cover it,
and an ox or a donkey falls into it,
34 the owner of the pit shall make
restitution, giving money to its
owner, but keeping the dead animal.
35 If someone's ox hurts the ox
of another, so that it dies, then they
shall sell the live ox and divide the
price of it; and the dead animal
they shall also divide. 36 But if it
was known that the ox was accustomed to gore in the past, and its
owner has not restrained it, the
owner shall restore ox for ox, but
keep the dead animal.

Laws of Restitution

22 [v] When someone steals an
ox or a sheep, and slaugh-
ters it or sells it, the thief shall pay
five oxen for an ox, and four sheep
for a sheep.[w] The thief shall make
restitution, but if unable to do so,
shall be sold for the theft. 4 When
the animal, whether ox or donkey
or sheep, is found alive in the
thief's possession, the thief shall
pay double.
2 [x]If a thief is found breaking in,
and is beaten to death, no bloodguilt is incurred; 3 but if it happens
after sunrise, bloodguilt is incurred.
5 When someone causes a field
or vineyard to be grazed over, or
lets livestock loose to graze in
someone else's field, restitution
shall be made from the best in the
owner's field or vineyard.
6 When fire breaks out and
catches in thorns so that the
stacked grain or the standing grain
or the field is consumed, the one
who started the fire shall make full
restitution.
7 When someone delivers to a
neighbor money or goods for safekeeping, and they are stolen from
the neighbor's house, then the
thief, if caught, shall pay double.
8 If the thief is not caught, the owner of the house shall be brought before God,[y] to determine whether
or not the owner had laid hands on
the neighbor's goods.
9 In any case of disputed ownership involving ox, donkey, sheep,
clothing, or any other loss, of
which one party says, "This is
mine," the case of both parties
shall come before God;[y] the one
whom God condemns[z] shall pay
double to the other.
10 When someone delivers to
another a donkey, ox, sheep, or any
other animal for safekeeping, and
it dies or is injured or is carried off,
without anyone seeing it, 11 an oath
before the LORD shall decide between the two of them that the one
has not laid hands on the property
of the other; the owner shall accept
the oath, and no restitution shall
be made. 12 But if it was stolen, restitution shall be made to its owner.
13 If it was mangled by beasts, let it
be brought as evidence; restitution
shall not be made for the mangled
remains.
14 When someone borrows an
animal from another and it is injured or dies, the owner not being
present, full restitution shall be
made. 15 If the owner was present,
there shall be no restitution; if it
was hired, only the hiring fee is
due.

Social and Religious Laws

16 When a man seduces a virgin
who is not engaged to be married,
and lies with her, he shall give the
bride-price for her and make her
his wife. 17 But if her father refuses
to give her to him, he shall pay an

21.30 v. 22
21.32 Zech 11.12, 13; Mt 26.15
21.33 Lk 14.5
22.1 2 Sam 12.6
22.2 Mt 24.43; Num 35.27
22.3 Ex 21.2
22.7 v. 4
22.8 v. 28; Ex 21.6; Deut 17.8,9; 19.17
22.9 vv. 8,28
22.11 Heb 6.16
22.12 Gen 31.39
22.16 Deut 22.28, 29
22.17 Deut 22.29

[v] Ch 21.37 in Heb [w] Verses 2, 3, and 4 rearranged thus: 3b, 4, 2, 3a [x] Ch 22.1 in Heb [y] Or *before the judges* [z] Or *the judges condemn*

amount equal to the bride-price for
virgins.
18 You shall not permit a female
sorcerer to live.
19 Whoever lies with an animal
shall be put to death.
20 Whoever sacrifices to any
god, other than the LORD alone,
shall be devoted to destruction.
21 You shall not wrong or oppress a resident alien, for you were
aliens in the land of Egypt. 22 You
shall not abuse any widow or orphan. 23 If you do abuse them,
when they cry out to me, I will surely heed their cry; 24 my wrath will
burn, and I will kill you with the
sword, and your wives shall become widows and your children orphans.
25 If you lend money to my people, to the poor among you, you
shall not deal with them as a creditor; you shall not exact interest
from them. 26 If you take your
neighbor's cloak in pawn, you shall
restore it before the sun goes down;
27 for it may be your neighbor's only
clothing to use as cover; in what
else shall that person sleep? And if
your neighbor cries out to me, I will
listen, for I am compassionate.
28 You shall not revile God, or
curse a leader of your people.
29 You shall not delay to make
offerings from the fullness of your
harvest and from the outflow of
your presses.[a]
The firstborn of your sons you
shall give to me. 30 You shall do the
same with your oxen and with your
sheep: seven days it shall remain
with its mother; on the eighth day
you shall give it to me.
31 You shall be people consecrated to me; therefore you shall
not eat any meat that is mangled by
beasts in the field; you shall throw
it to the dogs.

Justice for All

23 You shall not spread a false
report. You shall not join
hands with the wicked to act as a
malicious witness. 2 You shall not
follow a majority in wrongdoing;
when you bear witness in a lawsuit,

22.18 Lev 20.27; Deut 18.10
22.19 Lev 18.23; Deut 27.21
22.20 Deut 17.2,3, 5
22.21 Lev 19.33; Deut 10.19
22.22 Deut 24.17, 18
22.23 Deut 15.9; Lk 18.7; Ps 18.6
22.24 Ps 69.24; 109.9
22.25 Lev 25.35-37; Deut 23.19, 20
22.28 Lev 24.15, 16; Acts 23.5
22.29 Ex 23.16; 13.2,12
22.30 Deut 15.19; Lev 22.27
22.31 Lev 19.6; 22.8
23.1 Ex 20.16; Ps 35.11
23.2 Deut 16.19
23.4 Deut 22.1
23.5 Deut 22.4
23.6 vv. 2,3
23.7 Rom 1.18
23.8 Deut 10.17; 16.19
23.9 Ex 22.21
23.10 Lev 25.3
23.12 Ex 20.8-11
23.13 Ps 39.1; Eph 5.15
23.14 Ex 34.23
23.15 Ex 12.15; 34.20

you shall not side with the majority
so as to pervert justice; 3 nor shall
you be partial to the poor in a lawsuit.
4 When you come upon your enemy's ox or donkey going astray,
you shall bring it back.
5 When you see the donkey of
one who hates you lying under its
burden and you would hold back
from setting it free, you must help
to set it free.[a]
6 You shall not pervert the justice due to your poor in their lawsuits. 7 Keep far from a false charge,
and do not kill the innocent and
those in the right, for I will not acquit the guilty. 8 You shall take no
bribe, for a bribe blinds the officials, and subverts the cause of
those who are in the right.
9 You shall not oppress a resident alien; you know the heart of
an alien, for you were aliens in the
land of Egypt.

Sabbatical Year and Sabbath

10 For six years you shall sow
your land and gather in its yield;
11 but the seventh year you shall let
it rest and lie fallow, so that the
poor of your people may eat; and
what they leave the wild animals
may eat. You shall do the same
with your vineyard, and with your
olive orchard.
12 Six days you shall do your
work, but on the seventh day you
shall rest, so that your ox and your
donkey may have relief, and your
homeborn slave and the resident
alien may be refreshed. 13 Be attentive to all that I have said to you. Do
not invoke the names of other
gods; do not let them be heard on
your lips.

The Annual Festivals

14 Three times in the year you
shall hold a festival for me. 15 You
shall observe the festival of unleavened bread; as I commanded you,
you shall eat unleavened bread for
seven days at the appointed time in
the month of Abib, for in it you
came out of Egypt.

[a] Meaning of Heb uncertain

No one shall appear before me
empty-handed.
16 You shall observe the festival
of harvest, of the first fruits of your
labor, of what you sow in the field.
You shall observe the festival of ingathering at the end of the year,
when you gather in from the field
the fruit of your labor. 17 Three
times in the year all your males
shall appear before the Lord God.
18 You shall not offer the blood
of my sacrifice with anything leavened, or let the fat of my festival
remain until the morning.
19 The choicest of the first
fruits of your ground you shall
bring into the house of the Lord
your God.
You shall not boil a kid in its
mother's milk.

The Conquest of Canaan Promised

20 I am going to send an angel
in front of you, to guard you on the
way and to bring you to the place
that I have prepared. 21 Be attentive
to him and listen to his voice; do
not rebel against him, for he will
not pardon your transgression; for
my name is in him.
22 But if you listen attentively
to his voice and do all that I say,
then I will be an enemy to your enemies and a foe to your foes.
23 When my angel goes in front
of you, and brings you to the Amorites, the Hittites, the Perizzites,
the Canaanites, the Hivites, and
the Jebusites, and I blot them out,
24 you shall not bow down to their
gods, or worship them, or follow
their practices, but you shall utterly demolish them and break their
pillars in pieces. 25 You shall worship the Lord your God, and I[b] will
bless your bread and your water;
and I will take sickness away from
among you. 26 No one shall miscar-
ry or be barren in your land; I will
fulfill the number of your days. 27 I
will send my terror in front of you,
and will throw into confusion all
the people against whom you shall
come, and I will make all your enemies turn their backs to you. 28 And
I will send the pestilence[c] in front
of you, which shall drive out the Hivites, the Canaanites, and the Hittites from before you. 29 I will not
drive them out from before you in
one year, or the land would become
desolate and the wild animals
would multiply against you. 30 Little by little I will drive them out
from before you, until you have increased and possess the land. 31 I
will set your borders from the Red
Sea[d] to the sea of the Philistines,
and from the wilderness to the Euphrates; for I will hand over to you
the inhabitants of the land, and
you shall drive them out before
you. 32 You shall make no covenant
with them and their gods. 33 They
shall not live in your land, or they
will make you sin against me; for if
you worship their gods, it will surely be a snare to you.

The Blood of the Covenant

24 Then he said to Moses,
"Come up to the Lord, you
and Aaron, Nadab, and Abihu, and
seventy of the elders of Israel, and
worship at a distance. 2 Moses
alone shall come near the Lord; but
the others shall not come near, and
the people shall not come up with
him."
3 Moses came and told the people all the words of the Lord and all
the ordinances; and all the people
answered with one voice, and said,
"All the words that the Lord has
spoken we will do." 4 And Moses
wrote down all the words of the
Lord. He rose early in the morning,
and built an altar at the foot of the
mountain, and set up twelve pillars, corresponding to the twelve
tribes of Israel. 5 He sent young
men of the people of Israel, who offered burnt offerings and sacrificed
oxen as offerings of well-being to
the Lord. 6 Moses took half of the
blood and put it in basins, and half
of the blood he dashed against the
altar. 7 Then he took the book of
the covenant, and read it in the
hearing of the people; and they

23.16 Ex 34.22; Deut 16.13
23.17 Deut 16.16
23.18 Ex 34.25
23.19 Ex 22.29; Deut 14.21
23.20 Ex 32.34; 15.16,17
23.21 Num 14.11; Ps 78.40,56; Num 14.35
23.22 Gen 12.2
23.23 Josh 24.8, 11
23.24 Ex 20.5; Lev 18.3; Ex 34.13
23.25 Deut 6.13; Mt 4.10; Deut 28.5; Ex 15.26
23.26 Deut 7.14; Mal 3.11; Job 5.26
23.27 Ex 15.14, 16; Deut 7.23
23.28 Deut 7.20; Josh 24.12
23.29 Deut 7.22
23.31 Gen 15.18; Josh 21.44; 24.12,18
23.32 Deut 7.2; vv. 13,24
23.33 Deut 7.1-5, 16
24.1 Lev 10.1,2; Num 11.16
24.3 v. 7; Ex 19.8
24.4 Deut 31.9; Gen 28.18
24.6 Heb 9.18
24.7 Heb 9.19; v. 3

[b] Gk Vg: Heb *he* [c] Or *hornets*: Meaning of Heb uncertain [d] Or *Sea of Reeds*

said, "All that the LORD has spoken
we will do, and we will be obedient." 8 Moses took the blood and
dashed it on the people, and said,
"See the blood of the covenant that
the LORD has made with you in accordance with all these words."

On the Mountain with God

9 Then Moses and Aaron, Nadab, and Abihu, and seventy of the
elders of Israel went up, 10 and they
saw the God of Israel. Under his
feet there was something like a
pavement of sapphire stone, like
the very heaven for clearness.
11 God[e] did not lay his hand on the
chief men of the people of Israel;
also they beheld God, and they ate
and drank.
12 The LORD said to Moses,
"Come up to me on the mountain,
and wait there; and I will give you
the tablets of stone, with the law
and the commandment, which I
have written for their instruction."
13 So Moses set out with his assistant Joshua, and Moses went up
into the mountain of God. 14 To the
elders he had said, "Wait here for
us, until we come to you again; for
Aaron and Hur are with you; whoever has a dispute may go to them."
15 Then Moses went up on the
mountain, and the cloud covered
the mountain. 16 The glory of the
LORD settled on Mount Sinai, and
the cloud covered it for six days; on
the seventh day he called to Moses
out of the cloud. 17 Now the appearance of the glory of the LORD was
like a devouring fire on the top of
the mountain in the sight of the
people of Israel. 18 Moses entered
the cloud, and went up on the
mountain. Moses was on the
mountain for forty days and forty
nights.

Offerings for the Tabernacle

25 The LORD said to Moses:
2 Tell the Israelites to take
for me an offering; from all whose
hearts prompt them to give you
shall receive the offering for me.
3 This is the offering that you shall
receive from them: gold, silver, and
bronze, 4 blue, purple, and crimson
yarns and fine linen, goats' hair,
5 tanned rams' skins, fine leather,[f]
acacia wood, 6 oil for the lamps,
spices for the anointing oil and for
the fragrant incense, 7 onyx stones
and gems to be set in the ephod
and for the breastpiece. 8 And have
them make me a sanctuary, so that
I may dwell among them. 9 In accordance with all that I show you
concerning the pattern of the tabernacle and of all its furniture, so
you shall make it.

The Ark of the Covenant

10 They shall make an ark of
acacia wood; it shall be two and a
half cubits long, a cubit and a half
wide, and a cubit and a half high.
11 You shall overlay it with pure
gold, inside and outside you shall
overlay it, and you shall make a
molding of gold upon it all around.
12 You shall cast four rings of gold
for it and put them on its four feet,
two rings on the one side of it, and
two rings on the other side. 13 You
shall make poles of acacia wood,
and overlay them with gold. 14 And
you shall put the poles into the
rings on the sides of the ark, by
which to carry the ark. 15 The poles
shall remain in the rings of the ark;
they shall not be taken from it.
16 You shall put into the ark the
covenant[g] that I shall give you.
17 Then you shall make a mercy
seat[h] of pure gold; two cubits and
a half shall be its length, and a cubit and a half its width. 18 You shall
make two cherubim of gold; you
shall make them of hammered
work, at the two ends of the mercy
seat.[i] 19 Make one cherub at the
one end, and one cherub at the
other; of one piece with the mercy
seat[i] you shall make the cherubim
at its two ends. 20 The cherubim
shall spread out their wings above,
overshadowing the mercy seat[i]
with their wings. They shall face
one to another; the faces of the
cherubim shall be turned toward

24.8 Heb 9.20; 1 Pet 1.2
24.9 v. 1
24.10 Ezek 1.26; Rev 4.3; Mt 17.2
24.11 Ex 19.21; Gen 32.30; 31.54
24.12 vv. 2,15; Ex 32.15,16
24.13 Ex 17.9-14; 3.1
24.15 Ex 19.9
24.16 Ex 16.10
24.17 Ex 3.2; Deut 4.36; Heb 12.18, 29
24.18 Ex 34.28; Deut 9.9
25.2 Ex 35.5,21; 2 Cor 8.12; 9.7
25.6 Ex 27.20; 30.23,34
25.7 Ex 28.4,6, 15
25.8 Ex 36.1,3,4; Heb 9.1,2; Ex 29.45; Rev 21.3
25.9 v. 40; Acts 7.44; Heb 8.2,5
25.10 Ex 37.1-9
25.16 Deut 31.26; Heb 9.4
25.17 Ex 37.6; Rom 3.25; Heb 9.5
25.20 1 Kings 8.7; Heb 9.5

[e] Heb *He* [f] Meaning of Heb uncertain
[g] Or *treaty*, or *testimony*; Heb *eduth*
[h] Or *a cover* [i] Or *the cover*

the mercy seat.[j] 21 You shall put
the mercy seat[j] on the top of the
ark; and in the ark you shall put the
covenant[k] that I shall give you.
22 There I will meet with you, and
from above the mercy seat,[j] from
between the two cherubim that are
on the ark of the covenant,[k] I will
deliver to you all my commands for
the Israelites.

The Table for the Bread of the Presence

23 You shall make a table of
acacia wood, two cubits long, one
cubit wide, and a cubit and a half
high. 24 You shall overlay it with
pure gold, and make a molding of
gold around it. 25 You shall make
around it a rim a handbreadth
wide, and a molding of gold around
the rim. 26 You shall make for it four
rings of gold, and fasten the rings
to the four corners at its four legs.
27 The rings that hold the poles
used for carrying the table shall be
close to the rim. 28 You shall make
the poles of acacia wood, and overlay them with gold, and the table
shall be carried with these. 29 You
shall make its plates and dishes for
incense, and its flagons and bowls
with which to pour drink offerings;
you shall make them of pure gold.
30 And you shall set the bread of the
Presence on the table before me always.

The Lampstand

31 You shall make a lampstand
of pure gold. The base and the
shaft of the lampstand shall be
made of hammered work; its cups,
its calyxes, and its petals shall be
of one piece with it; 32 and there
shall be six branches going out of
its sides, three branches of the
lampstand out of one side of it and
three branches of the lampstand
out of the other side of it; 33 three
cups shaped like almond blossoms, each with calyx and petals,
on one branch, and three cups
shaped like almond blossoms,
each with calyx and petals, on the
other branch—so for the six
branches going out of the lampstand. 34 On the lampstand itself
there shall be four cups shaped like
almond blossoms, each with its calyxes and petals. 35 There shall be a
calyx of one piece with it under the
first pair of branches, a calyx of one
piece with it under the next pair of
branches, and a calyx of one piece
with it under the last pair of
branches—so for the six branches
that go out of the lampstand.
36 Their calyxes and their branches
shall be of one piece with it, the
whole of it one hammered piece of
pure gold. 37 You shall make the
seven lamps for it; and the lamps
shall be set up so as to give light on
the space in front of it. 38 Its snuffers and trays shall be of pure gold.
39 It, and all these utensils, shall be
made from a talent of pure gold.
40 And see that you make them according to the pattern for them,
which is being shown you on the
mountain.

The Tabernacle

26 Moreover you shall make
the tabernacle with ten
curtains of fine twisted linen, and
blue, purple, and crimson yarns;
you shall make them with cherubim skillfully worked into them.
2 The length of each curtain shall
be twenty-eight cubits, and the
width of each curtain four cubits;
all the curtains shall be of the same
size. 3 Five curtains shall be joined
to one another; and the other five
curtains shall be joined to one another. 4 You shall make loops of
blue on the edge of the outermost
curtain in the first set; and likewise
you shall make loops on the edge of
the outermost curtain in the second set. 5 You shall make fifty loops
on the one curtain, and you shall
make fifty loops on the edge of the
curtain that is in the second set;
the loops shall be opposite one another. 6 You shall make fifty clasps
of gold, and join the curtains to one
another with the clasps, so that the
tabernacle may be one whole.
7 You shall also make curtains

[j] Or *the cover* [k] Or *treaty,* or *testimony;* Heb *eduth*

25.21 Ex 26.34; v. 16
25.22 Ex 29.42, 43; 30.6,36; Num 7.89; Ps 80.1
25.23 Ex 37.10-16; Heb 9.2
25.29 Ex 37.16; Num 4.7
25.30 Lev 24.5-9
25.31 Ex 37.17; Heb 9.2; Rev 1.12
25.32 Ex 38.18
25.34 Ex 37.20
25.37 Ex 27.21; Lev 24.3,4
25.40 Ex 26.30; Acts 7.44; Heb 8.5
26.1 Ex 36.8
26.3 Ex 36.10
26.5 Ex 36.12
26.7 Ex 36.14

of goats' hair for a tent over the tabernacle; you shall make eleven curtains. 8 The length of each curtain shall be thirty cubits, and the width of each curtain four cubits; the eleven curtains shall be of the same size. 9 You shall join five curtains by themselves, and six curtains by themselves, and the sixth curtain you shall double over at the front of the tent. 10 You shall make fifty loops on the edge of the curtain that is outermost in one set, and fifty loops on the edge of the curtain that is outermost in the second set.

11 You shall make fifty clasps of bronze, and put the clasps into the loops, and join the tent together, so that it may be one whole. 12 The part that remains of the curtains of the tent, the half curtain that remains, shall hang over the back of the tabernacle. 13 The cubit on the one side, and the cubit on the other side, of what remains in the length of the curtains of the tent, shall hang over the sides of the tabernacle, on this side and that side, to cover it. 14 You shall make for the tent a covering of tanned rams' skins and an outer covering of fine leather.[l]

The Framework

15 You shall make upright frames of acacia wood for the tabernacle. 16 Ten cubits shall be the length of a frame, and a cubit and a half the width of each frame. 17 There shall be two pegs in each frame to fit the frames together; you shall make these for all the frames of the tabernacle. 18 You shall make the frames for the tabernacle: twenty frames for the south side; 19 and you shall make forty bases of silver under the twenty frames, two bases under the first frame for its two pegs, and two bases under the next frame for its two pegs; 20 and for the second side of the tabernacle, on the north side twenty frames, 21 and their forty bases of silver, two bases under the first frame, and two bases under the next frame; 22 and for the rear of the tabernacle westward you shall make six frames. 23 You shall make two frames for corners of the tabernacle in the rear; 24 they shall be separate beneath, but joined at the top, at the first ring; it shall be the same with both of them; they shall form the two corners. 25 And so there shall be eight frames, with their bases of silver, sixteen bases; two bases under the first frame, and two bases under the next frame.

26 You shall make bars of acacia wood, five for the frames of the one side of the tabernacle, 27 and five bars for the frames of the other side of the tabernacle, and five bars for the frames of the side of the tabernacle at the rear westward. 28 The middle bar, halfway up the frames, shall pass through from end to end. 29 You shall overlay the frames with gold, and shall make their rings of gold to hold the bars; and you shall overlay the bars with gold. 30 Then you shall erect the tabernacle according to the plan for it that you were shown on the mountain.

The Curtain

31 You shall make a curtain of blue, purple, and crimson yarns, and of fine twisted linen; it shall be made with cherubim skillfully worked into it. 32 You shall hang it on four pillars of acacia overlaid with gold, which have hooks of gold and rest on four bases of silver. 33 You shall hang the curtain under the clasps, and bring the ark of the covenant[m] in there, within the curtain; and the curtain shall separate for you the holy place from the most holy. 34 You shall put the mercy seat[n] on the ark of the covenant[m] in the most holy place. 35 You shall set the table outside the curtain, and the lampstand on the south side of the tabernacle opposite the table; and you shall put the table on the north side.

36 You shall make a screen for the entrance of the tent, of blue, purple, and crimson yarns, and of

26.11 Ex 36.18
26.14 Ex 36.19
26.15 Ex 36.20
26.20 Ex 36.23
26.25 Ex 36.30
26.30 Ex 25.9,40; 27.8; Acts 7.44; Heb 8.5
26.31 Ex 36.35; Mt 27.51; Heb 9.3
26.33 Ex 25.16; 40.21; Lev 16.2; Heb 9.2,3
26.34 Ex 25.21; 40.20; Heb 9.5
26.35 Ex 40.22, 24; Heb 9.2
26.36 Ex 36.37

[l] Meaning of Heb uncertain [m] Or *treaty*, or *testimony*; Heb *eduth* [n] Or *the cover*

fine twisted linen, embroidered
with needlework. 37 You shall make
for the screen five pillars of acacia,
and overlay them with gold; their
hooks shall be of gold, and you
shall cast five bases of bronze for
them.

The Altar of Burnt Offering

27 You shall make the altar of
acacia wood, five cubits
long and five cubits wide; the altar
shall be square, and it shall be
three cubits high. 2 You shall make
horns for it on its four corners; its
horns shall be of one piece with it,
and you shall overlay it with
bronze. 3 You shall make pots for it
to receive its ashes, and shovels
and basins and forks and firepans;
you shall make all its utensils of
bronze. 4 You shall also make for it
a grating, a network of bronze; and
on the net you shall make four
bronze rings at its four corners.
5 You shall set it under the ledge of
the altar so that the net shall extend halfway down the altar. 6 You
shall make poles for the altar, poles
of acacia wood, and overlay them
with bronze; 7 the poles shall be put
through the rings, so that the poles
shall be on the two sides of the altar when it is carried. 8 You shall
make it hollow, with boards. They
shall be made just as you were
shown on the mountain.

The Court and Its Hangings

9 You shall make the court of
the tabernacle. On the south side
the court shall have hangings of
fine twisted linen one hundred cubits long for that side; 10 its twenty
pillars and their twenty bases shall
be of bronze, but the hooks of the
pillars and their bands shall be of
silver. 11 Likewise for its length on
the north side there shall be hangings one hundred cubits long, their
pillars twenty and their bases
twenty, of bronze, but the hooks of
the pillars and their bands shall be
of silver. 12 For the width of the
court on the west side there shall
be fifty cubits of hangings, with ten
pillars and ten bases. 13 The width

26.37 Ex 36.38
27.1 Ex 38.1; Ezek 43.13
27.3 Num 4.14
27.8 Ex 25.40; 26.30
27.9 Ex 38.9
27.10 Ex 38.17
27.14 Ex 38.15
27.16 Ex 36.37
27.20 Lev 24.2
27.21 Ex 26.31, 33; 30.8; 28.43; Lev 3.17; 16.34
28.1 Num 18.7; Heb 5.1,4
28.2 Ex 29.5,29; 31.10
28.3 Ex 31.3,6
28.4 see vv. 6,15, 31,39

of the court on the front to the east
shall be fifty cubits. 14 There shall
be fifteen cubits of hangings on the
one side, with three pillars and
three bases. 15 There shall be fifteen cubits of hangings on the other side, with three pillars and three
bases. 16 For the gate of the court
there shall be a screen twenty cubits long, of blue, purple, and crimson yarns, and of fine twisted linen,
embroidered with needlework; it
shall have four pillars and with
them four bases. 17 All the pillars
around the court shall be banded
with silver; their hooks shall be of
silver, and their bases of bronze.
18 The length of the court shall be
one hundred cubits, the width fifty,
and the height five cubits, with
hangings of fine twisted linen and
bases of bronze. 19 All the utensils
of the tabernacle for every use, and
all its pegs and all the pegs of the
court, shall be of bronze.

The Oil for the Lamp

20 You shall further command
the Israelites to bring you pure oil
of beaten olives for the light, so
that a lamp may be set up to burn
regularly. 21 In the tent of meeting,
outside the curtain that is before
the covenant,[o] Aaron and his sons
shall tend it from evening to morning before the LORD. It shall be a
perpetual ordinance to be observed
throughout their generations by
the Israelites.

Vestments for the Priesthood

28 Then bring near to you your
brother Aaron, and his sons
with him, from among the Israelites, to serve me as priests—Aaron
and Aaron's sons, Nadab and Abihu, Eleazar and Ithamar. 2 You
shall make sacred vestments for
the glorious adornment of your
brother Aaron. 3 And you shall
speak to all who have ability, whom
I have endowed with skill, that they
make Aaron's vestments to consecrate him for my priesthood.
4 These are the vestments that they
shall make: a breastpiece, an

[o] Or *treaty*, or *testimony*; Heb *eduth*

ephod, a robe, a checkered tunic, a
turban, and a sash. When they
make these sacred vestments for
your brother Aaron and his sons to
serve me as priests, 5 they shall use
gold, blue, purple, and crimson
yarns, and fine linen.

The Ephod

6 They shall make the ephod of
gold, of blue, purple, and crimson
yarns, and of fine twisted linen,
skillfully worked. 7 It shall have two
shoulder-pieces attached to its two
edges, so that it may be joined together. 8 The decorated band on it
shall be of the same workmanship
and materials, of gold, of blue, purple, and crimson yarns, and of fine
twisted linen. 9 You shall take two
onyx stones, and engrave on them
the names of the sons of Israel,
10 six of their names on the one
stone, and the names of the remaining six on the other stone, in
the order of their birth. 11 As a gem-
cutter engraves signets, so you
shall engrave the two stones with
the names of the sons of Israel; you
shall mount them in settings of
gold filigree. 12 You shall set the
two stones on the shoulder-pieces
of the ephod, as stones of remembrance for the sons of Israel; and
Aaron shall bear their names before the LORD on his two shoulders
for remembrance. 13 You shall
make settings of gold filigree,
14 and two chains of pure gold,
twisted like cords; and you shall attach the corded chains to the settings.

The Breastplate

15 You shall make a breastpiece
of judgment, in skilled work; you
shall make it in the style of the
ephod; of gold, of blue and purple
and crimson yarns, and of fine
twisted linen you shall make it. 16 It
shall be square and doubled, a
span in length and a span in width.
17 You shall set in it four rows of
stones. A row of carnelian,[p] chrysolite, and emerald shall be the first
row; 18 and the second row a turquoise, a sapphire[q] and a moonstone; 19 and the third row a jacinth, an agate, and an amethyst;
20 and the fourth row a beryl, an
onyx, and a jasper; they shall be set
in gold filigree. 21 There shall be
twelve stones with names corresponding to the names of the sons
of Israel; they shall be like signets,
each engraved with its name, for
the twelve tribes. 22 You shall make
for the breastpiece chains of pure
gold, twisted like cords; 23 and you
shall make for the breastpiece two
rings of gold, and put the two rings
on the two edges of the breastpiece. 24 You shall put the two
cords of gold in the two rings at the
edges of the breastpiece; 25 the two
ends of the two cords you shall attach to the two settings, and so attach it in front to the shoulder-
pieces of the ephod. 26 You shall
make two rings of gold, and put
them at the two ends of the breastpiece, on its inside edge next to the
ephod. 27 You shall make two rings
of gold, and attach them in front to
the lower part of the two shoulder-
pieces of the ephod, at its joining
above the decorated band of the
ephod. 28 The breastpiece shall be
bound by its rings to the rings of
the ephod with a blue cord, so that
it may lie on the decorated band of
the ephod, and so that the breastpiece shall not come loose from the
ephod. 29 So Aaron shall bear the
names of the sons of Israel in the
breastpiece of judgment on his
heart when he goes into the holy
place, for a continual remembrance before the LORD. 30 In the
breastpiece of judgment you shall
put the Urim and the Thummim,
and they shall be on Aaron's heart
when he goes in before the LORD;
thus Aaron shall bear the judgment
of the Israelites on his heart before
the LORD continually.

Other Priestly Vestments

31 You shall make the robe of
the ephod all of blue. 32 It shall

28.6 Ex 39.2 **28.9** 1 Cor 9.22 **28.12** v. 29; Ex 39.7 **28.15** Ex 39.8 **28.17** Ex 39.10ff **28.21** Ex 39.14 **28.24** Ex 39.17 **28.26** Ex 39.17 **28.29** v. 12 **28.30** Lev 8.8; Num 27.21 **28.31** Ex 39.22

[p] The identity of several of these stones is uncertain [q] Or *lapis lazuli*

have an opening for the head in the
middle of it, with a woven binding
around the opening, like the opening in a coat of mail,[r] so that it
may not be torn. 33 On its lower
hem you shall make pomegranates
of blue, purple, and crimson yarns,
all around the lower hem, with
bells of gold between them all
around—34 a golden bell and a
pomegranate alternating all
around the lower hem of the robe.
35 Aaron shall wear it when he ministers, and its sound shall be heard
when he goes into the holy place
before the LORD, and when he
comes out, so that he may not die.
36 You shall make a rosette of
pure gold, and engrave on it, like
the engraving of a signet, "Holy to
the LORD." 37 You shall fasten it on
the turban with a blue cord; it shall
be on the front of the turban. 38 It
shall be on Aaron's forehead, and
Aaron shall take on himself any
guilt incurred in the holy offering
that the Israelites consecrate as
their sacred donations; it shall always be on his forehead, in order
that they may find favor before the
LORD.
39 You shall make the checker-
ered tunic of fine linen, and you
shall make a turban of fine linen,
and you shall make a sash embroidered with needlework.
40 For Aaron's sons you shall
make tunics and sashes and headdresses; you shall make them for
their glorious adornment. 41 You
shall put them on your brother Aaron, and on his sons with him, and
shall anoint them and ordain them
and consecrate them, so that they
may serve me as priests. 42 You
shall make for them linen undergarments to cover their naked
flesh; they shall reach from the
hips to the thighs; 43 Aaron and his
sons shall wear them when they go
into the tent of meeting, or when
they come near the altar to minister in the holy place; or they will
bring guilt on themselves and die.
This shall be a perpetual ordinance
for him and for his descendants after him.

28.36 Ex 39.30,31
28.38 v. 43; Lev 10.17; Num 18.1; Heb 9.28; 1 Pet 2.24
28.40 v. 4; Ex 39.27-29
28.41 Ex 29.7-9; 30.30; Lev ch. 8; Heb 7.28
28.42 Ex 39.28
28.43 Ex 20.26; Lev 20.19, 20; Ex 27.21; Lev 17.7

29.1 Lev 8.2
29.2 Lev 6.19-23
29.4 Ex 40.12; Heb 10.22
29.5 Ex 28.2,8
29.6 Lev 8.9
29.7 Lev 8.12
29.8 Lev 8.13
29.9 Num 18.7; Ex 28.41
29.10 Lev 1.4; 8.14
29.12 Lev 8.15; Ex 27.2
29.13 Lev 3.3
29.14 Lev 4.11,12, 21

The Ordination of the Priests

29 Now this is what you shall
do to them to consecrate
them, so that they may serve me as
priests. Take one young bull and
two rams without blemish, 2 and
unleavened bread, unleavened
cakes mixed with oil, and unleavened wafers spread with oil. You
shall make them of choice wheat
flour. 3 You shall put them in one
basket and bring them in the basket, and bring the bull and the two
rams. 4 You shall bring Aaron and
his sons to the entrance of the tent
of meeting, and wash them with
water. 5 Then you shall take the
vestments, and put on Aaron the
tunic and the robe of the ephod,
and the ephod, and the breastpiece, and gird him with the decorated band of the ephod; 6 and you
shall set the turban on his head,
and put the holy diadem on the turban. 7 You shall take the anointing
oil, and pour it on his head and
anoint him. 8 Then you shall bring
his sons, and put tunics on them,
9 and you shall gird them with
sashes[s] and tie headdresses on
them; and the priesthood shall be
theirs by a perpetual ordinance.
You shall then ordain Aaron and
his sons.
10 You shall bring the bull in
front of the tent of meeting. Aaron
and his sons shall lay their hands
on the head of the bull, 11 and you
shall slaughter the bull before the
LORD, at the entrance of the tent of
meeting, 12 and shall take some of
the blood of the bull and put it on
the horns of the altar with your finger, and all the rest of the blood
you shall pour out at the base of
the altar. 13 You shall take all the
fat that covers the entrails, and the
appendage of the liver, and the two
kidneys with the fat that is on
them, and turn them into smoke on
the altar. 14 But the flesh of the
bull, and its skin, and its dung, you
shall burn with fire outside the
camp; it is a sin offering.

[r] Meaning of Heb uncertain [s] Gk: Heb *sashes, Aaron and his sons*

15 Then you shall take one of
the rams, and Aaron and his sons
shall lay their hands on the head of
the ram, 16 and you shall slaughter
the ram, and shall take its blood
and dash it against all sides of the
altar. 17 Then you shall cut the ram
into its parts, and wash its entrails
and its legs, and put them with its
parts and its head, 18 and turn the
whole ram into smoke on the altar;
it is a burnt offering to the LORD; it
is a pleasing odor, an offering by
fire to the LORD.

19 You shall take the other ram;
and Aaron and his sons shall lay
their hands on the head of the ram,
20 and you shall slaughter the ram,
and take some of its blood and put
it on the lobe of Aaron's right ear
and on the lobes of the right ears of
his sons, and on the thumbs of
their right hands, and on the big
toes of their right feet, and dash the
rest of the blood against all sides of
the altar. 21 Then you shall take
some of the blood that is on the altar, and some of the anointing oil,
and sprinkle it on Aaron and his
vestments and on his sons and his
sons' vestments with him; then he
and his vestments shall be holy, as
well as his sons and his sons' vestments.

22 You shall also take the fat of
the ram, the fat tail, the fat that
covers the entrails, the appendage
of the liver, the two kidneys with
the fat that is on them, and the
right thigh (for it is a ram of ordination), 23 and one loaf of bread, one
cake of bread made with oil, and
one wafer, out of the basket of unleavened bread that is before the
LORD; 24 and you shall place all
these on the palms of Aaron and on
the palms of his sons, and raise
them as an elevation offering before the LORD. 25 Then you shall
take them from their hands, and
turn them into smoke on the altar
on top of the burnt offering of
pleasing odor before the LORD; it is
an offering by fire to the LORD.

26 You shall take the breast of
the ram of Aaron's ordination and
raise it as an elevation offering before the LORD; and it shall be your
portion. 27 You shall consecrate the
breast that was raised as an elevation offering and the thigh that was
raised as an elevation offering from
the ram of ordination, from that
which belonged to Aaron and his
sons. 28 These things shall be a perpetual ordinance for Aaron and his
sons from the Israelites, for this is
an offering; and it shall be an offering by the Israelites from their sacrifice of offerings of well-being,
their offering to the LORD.

29 The sacred vestments of Aaron shall be passed on to his sons
after him; they shall be anointed in
them and ordained in them. 30 The
son who is priest in his place shall
wear them seven days, when he
comes into the tent of meeting to
minister in the holy place.

31 You shall take the ram of ordination, and boil its flesh in a holy
place; 32 and Aaron and his sons
shall eat the flesh of the ram and
the bread that is in the basket, at
the entrance of the tent of meeting.
33 They themselves shall eat the
food by which atonement is made,
to ordain and consecrate them, but
no one else shall eat of them, because they are holy. 34 If any of the
flesh for the ordination, or of the
bread, remains until the morning,
then you shall burn the remainder
with fire; it shall not be eaten, because it is holy.

35 Thus you shall do to Aaron
and to his sons, just as I have commanded you; through seven days
you shall ordain them. 36 Also every
day you shall offer a bull as a sin
offering for atonement. Also you
shall offer a sin offering for the altar, when you make atonement for
it, and shall anoint it, to consecrate
it. 37 Seven days you shall make
atonement for the altar, and consecrate it, and the altar shall be most
holy; whatever touches the altar
shall become holy.

The Daily Offerings

38 Now this is what you shall offer on the altar: two lambs a year
old regularly each day. 39 One lamb

29.18 Gen 8.21
29.21 Ex 30.25, 31; v. 1; Heb 9.22
29.23 Lev 8.26
29.24 Lev 7.30
29.25 Lev 8.28
29.26 Lev 8.29
29.27 Lev 7.31,34; Deut 18.3
29.28 Lev 10.15
29.29 Num 20.26, 28; 18.8
29.30 Num 20.28; Lev 8.35; 9.1,8
29.31 Lev 8.31
29.32 Mt 12.4
29.33 Lev 10.14, 15,17; 22.10
29.34 Lev 8.32
29.35 Lev 8.33
29.36 Heb 10.11; Ex 40.10
29.37 Ex 40.10; Mt 23.19
29.38 Num 28.3

you shall offer in the morning, and the other lamb you shall offer in the evening; 40 and with the first lamb one-tenth of a measure of choice flour mixed with one-fourth of a hin of beaten oil, and one-fourth of a hin of wine for a drink offering. 41 And the other lamb you shall offer in the evening, and shall offer with it a grain offering and its drink offering, as in the morning, for a pleasing odor, an offering by fire to the LORD. 42 It shall be a regular burnt offering throughout your generations at the entrance of the tent of meeting before the LORD, where I will meet with you, to speak to you there. 43 I will meet with the Israelites there, and it shall be sanctified by my glory; 44 I will consecrate the tent of meeting and the altar; Aaron also and his sons I will consecrate, to serve me as priests. 45 I will dwell among the Israelites, and I will be their God. 46 And they shall know that I am the LORD their God, who brought them out of the land of Egypt that I might dwell among them; I am the LORD their God.

The Altar of Incense

30 You shall make an altar on which to offer incense; you shall make it of acacia wood. 2 It shall be one cubit long, and one cubit wide; it shall be square, and shall be two cubits high; its horns shall be of one piece with it. 3 You shall overlay it with pure gold, its top, and its sides all around and its horns; and you shall make for it a molding of gold all around. 4 And you shall make two golden rings for it; under its molding on two opposite sides of it you shall make them, and they shall hold the poles with which to carry it. 5 You shall make the poles of acacia wood, and overlay them with gold. 6 You shall place it in front of the curtain that is above the ark of the covenant,[t] in front of the mercy seat[u] that is over the covenant,[t] where I will meet with you. 7 Aaron shall offer fragrant incense on it; every morning when he dresses the lamps he shall offer it, 8 and when Aaron sets up the lamps in the evening, he shall offer it, a regular incense offering before the LORD throughout your generations. 9 You shall not offer unholy incense on it, or a burnt offering, or a grain offering; and you shall not pour a drink offering on it. 10 Once a year Aaron shall perform the rite of atonement on its horns. Throughout your generations he shall perform the atonement for it once a year with the blood of the atoning sin offering. It is most holy to the LORD.

The Half Shekel for the Sanctuary

11 The LORD spoke to Moses: 12 When you take a census of the Israelites to register them, at registration all of them shall give a ransom for their lives to the LORD, so that no plague may come upon them for being registered. 13 This is what each one who is registered shall give: half a shekel according to the shekel of the sanctuary (the shekel is twenty gerahs), half a shekel as an offering to the LORD. 14 Each one who is registered, from twenty years old and upward, shall give the LORD's offering. 15 The rich shall not give more, and the poor shall not give less, than the half shekel, when you bring this offering to the LORD to make atonement for your lives. 16 You shall take the atonement money from the Israelites and shall designate it for the service of the tent of meeting; before the LORD it will be a reminder to the Israelites of the ransom given for your lives.

The Bronze Basin

17 The LORD spoke to Moses: 18 You shall make a bronze basin with a bronze stand for washing. You shall put it between the tent of meeting and the altar, and you shall put water in it; 19 with the water[v] Aaron and his sons shall wash their hands and their feet. 20 When they go into the tent of meeting, or

29.42 Ex 30.8
29.43 1 Kings 8.11
29.44 Lev 21.15
29.45 Ex 25.8; Lev 26.12; Rev 21.3
29.46 Ex 20.2
30.1 Ex 37.25
30.6 Ex 25.21,22
30.7 vv. 34,35; Ex 27.21
30.9 Lev 10.1
30.10 Lev 16.18
30.12 Num 1.2,5; 31.50; Mt 20.28; 2 Sam 24.15
30.13 Mt 17.24
30.15 Prov 22.2
30.16 Ex 38.25; Num 16.40
30.18 Ex 38.8; 40.7,30
30.19 Ex 40.31,32

[t] Or *treaty*, or *testimony*; Heb *eduth*
[u] Or *the cover*
[v] Heb *it*

when they come near the altar to
minister, to make an offering by
fire to the LORD, they shall wash
with water, so that they may not
die. 21 They shall wash their hands
and their feet, so that they may not
die: it shall be a perpetual ordinance for them, for him and for his
descendants throughout their generations.

The Anointing Oil and Incense

22 The LORD spoke to Moses:
23 Take the finest spices: of liquid
myrrh five hundred shekels, and of
sweet-smelling cinnamon half as
much, that is, two hundred fifty,
and two hundred fifty of aromatic
cane, 24 and five hundred of
cassia—measured by the sanctuary
shekel—and a hin of olive oil;
25 and you shall make of these a sacred anointing oil blended as by
the perfumer; it shall be a holy
anointing oil. 26 With it you shall
anoint the tent of meeting and the
ark of the covenant,[w] 27 and the table and all its utensils, and the
lampstand and its utensils, and the
altar of incense, 28 and the altar of
burnt offering with all its utensils,
and the basin with its stand; 29 you
shall consecrate them, so that they
may be most holy; whatever
touches them will become holy.
30 You shall anoint Aaron and his
sons, and consecrate them, in order that they may serve me as
priests. 31 You shall say to the Israelites, "This shall be my holy
anointing oil throughout your generations. 32 It shall not be used in
any ordinary anointing of the body,
and you shall make no other like it
in composition; it is holy, and it
shall be holy to you. 33 Whoever
compounds any like it or whoever
puts any of it on an unqualified
person shall be cut off from the
people."
34 The LORD said to Moses: Take
sweet spices, stacte, and onycha,
and galbanum, sweet spices with
pure frankincense (an equal part of
each), 35 and make an incense
blended as by the perfumer, seasoned with salt, pure and holy;
36 and you shall beat some of it into
powder, and put part of it before
the covenant[w] in the tent of meeting where I shall meet with you; it
shall be for you most holy. 37 When
you make incense according to this
composition, you shall not make it
for yourselves; it shall be regarded
by you as holy to the LORD. 38 Whoever makes any like it to use as perfume shall be cut off from the people.

Bezalel and Oholiab

31 The LORD spoke to Moses:
2 See, I have called by name
Bezalel son of Uri son of Hur, of the
tribe of Judah: 3 and I have filled
him with divine spirit,[x] with ability, intelligence, and knowledge in
every kind of craft, 4 to devise artistic designs, to work in gold, silver,
and bronze, 5 in cutting stones for
setting, and in carving wood, in every kind of craft. 6 Moreover, I have
appointed with him Oholiab son of
Ahisamach, of the tribe of Dan; and
I have given skill to all the skillful,
so that they may make all that I
have commanded you: 7 the tent of
meeting, and the ark of the covenant,[w] and the mercy seat[y] that is
on it, and all the furnishings of the
tent, 8 the table and its utensils,
and the pure lampstand with all its
utensils, and the altar of incense,
9 and the altar of burnt offering
with all its utensils, and the basin
with its stand, 10 and the finely
worked vestments, the holy vestments for the priest Aaron and the
vestments of his sons, for their service as priests, 11 and the anointing
oil and the fragrant incense for the
holy place. They shall do just as I
have commanded you.

The Sabbath Law

12 The LORD said to Moses:
13 You yourself are to speak to the
Israelites: "You shall keep my sabbaths, for this is a sign between me
and you throughout your generations, given in order that you may
know that I, the LORD, sanctify you.

30.21 Ex 28.43 **30.25** Ex 37.29; 40.9 **30.26** Lev 8.10 **30.29** Ex 29.37 **30.30** Lev 8.12,30 **30.32** vv. 25,37 **30.33** v. 38; Ex 12.15 **30.35** v. 25

30.36 Ex 29.42; Lev 16.2; v. 32; Ex 29.37; Lev 2.3 **31.2** Ex 35.30-36.1 **31.6** Ex 35.34 **31.7** Ex 36.8; 37.1,6 **31.8** Ex 37.10,17 **31.11** Ex 30.25, 31; 37.29; 30.34 **31.13** Lev 19.3,30; Ezek 20.12, 20

[w] Or *treaty*, or *testimony*; Heb *eduth*
[x] Or *with the spirit of God* [y] Or *the cover*

14 You shall keep the sabbath, because it is holy for you; everyone
who profanes it shall be put to
death; whoever does any work on it
shall be cut off from among the
people. 15 Six days shall work be
done, but the seventh day is a sabbath of solemn rest, holy to the
LORD; whoever does any work on
the sabbath day shall be put to
death. 16 Therefore the Israelites
shall keep the sabbath, observing
the sabbath throughout their generations, as a perpetual covenant.
17 It is a sign forever between me
and the people of Israel that in six
days the LORD made heaven and
earth, and on the seventh day he
rested, and was refreshed."

The Two Tablets of the Covenant

18 When God[z] finished speaking with Moses on Mount Sinai, he
gave him the two tablets of the covenant,[a] tablets of stone, written
with the finger of God.

The Golden Calf

32 When the people saw that
Moses delayed to come
down from the mountain, the people gathered around Aaron, and
said to him, "Come, make gods for
us, who shall go before us; as for
this Moses, the man who brought
us up out of the land of Egypt, we
do not know what has become of
him." 2 Aaron said to them, "Take
off the gold rings that are on the
ears of your wives, your sons, and
your daughters, and bring them to
me." 3 So all the people took off the
gold rings from their ears, and
brought them to Aaron. 4 He took
the gold from them, formed it in a
mold,[b] and cast an image of a calf;
and they said, "These are your
gods, O Israel, who brought you up
out of the land of Egypt!" 5 When
Aaron saw this, he built an altar before it; and Aaron made proclamation and said, "Tomorrow shall be
a festival to the LORD." 6 They rose
early the next day, and offered
burnt offerings and brought sacrifices of well-being; and the people
sat down to eat and drink, and rose
up to revel.

7 The LORD said to Moses, "Go
down at once! Your people, whom
you brought up out of the land of
Egypt, have acted perversely; 8 they
have been quick to turn aside from
the way that I commanded them;
they have cast for themselves an
image of a calf, and have worshiped
it and sacrificed to it, and said,
'These are your gods, O Israel, who
brought you up out of the land of
Egypt!'" 9 The LORD said to Moses,
"I have seen this people, how stiff-
necked they are. 10 Now let me
alone, so that my wrath may burn
hot against them and I may consume them; and of you I will make
a great nation."

11 But Moses implored the LORD
his God, and said, "O LORD, why
does your wrath burn hot against
your people, whom you brought
out of the land of Egypt with great
power and with a mighty hand?
12 Why should the Egyptians say, 'It
was with evil intent that he brought
them out to kill them in the mountains, and to consume them from
the face of the earth'? Turn from
your fierce wrath; change your
mind and do not bring disaster on
your people. 13 Remember Abraham, Isaac, and Israel, your servants, how you swore to them by
your own self, saying to them, 'I
will multiply your descendants like
the stars of heaven, and all this
land that I have promised I will give
to your descendants, and they shall
inherit it forever.'" 14 And the LORD
changed his mind about the disaster that he planned to bring on his
people.

15 Then Moses turned and went
down from the mountain, carrying
the two tablets of the covenant[a] in
his hands, tablets that were written
on both sides, written on the front
and on the back. 16 The tablets
were the work of God, and the writing was the writing of God, engraved upon the tablets. 17 When

31.14 Ex 35.2; Num 15.32, 35
31.15 Ex 16.23; 20.9,10
31.17 v. 13; Gen 2.2,3
31.18 Ex 24.12; 32.15,16; 34.1,28
32.1 Ex 24.18; Deut 9.9; Acts 7.40; Ex 13.21
32.2 Ex 35.22
32.4 Deut 9.16; Acts 7.41
32.6 1 Cor 10.7
32.7 Deut 9.12; Dan 9.24; Gen 6.11,12
32.8 Ex 20.3,4, 23; 1 Kings 12.28
32.9 Num 14.11-20; Ex 33.3,5; 34.9; Acts 7.31
32.10 Deut 9.14; Num 14.12
32.11 Deut 9.18
32.12 Num 14.13; Deut 9.28; v. 14
32.13 Gen 22.16; Heb 6.13; Gen 12.7; 13.15; Ex 13.5
32.14 Ps 106.45
32.15 Deut 9.15
32.16 Ex 31.18

[z] Heb *he* [a] Or *treaty*, or *testimony*; Heb *eduth* [b] Or *fashioned it with a graving tool*; Meaning of Heb uncertain

Joshua heard the noise of the people as they shouted, he said to Moses, "There is a noise of war in the
camp." 18 But he said,

"It is not the sound made by
victors,
or the sound made by losers;
it is the sound of revelers
that I hear."

19 As soon as he came near the
camp and saw the calf and the
dancing, Moses' anger burned hot,
and he threw the tablets from his
hands and broke them at the foot
of the mountain. 20 He took the calf
that they had made, burned it with
fire, ground it to powder, scattered
it on the water, and made the Israelites drink it.

21 Moses said to Aaron, "What
did this people do to you that you
have brought so great a sin upon
them?" 22 And Aaron said, "Do not
let the anger of my lord burn hot;
you know the people, that they are
bent on evil. 23 They said to me,
'Make us gods, who shall go before
us; as for this Moses, the man who
brought us up out of the land of
Egypt, we do not know what has
become of him.' 24 So I said to
them, 'Whoever has gold, take it
off'; so they gave it to me, and I
threw it into the fire, and out came
this calf!"

25 When Moses saw that the
people were running wild (for Aaron had let them run wild, to the derision of their enemies), 26 then
Moses stood in the gate of the
camp, and said, "Who is on the
LORD's side? Come to me!" And all
the sons of Levi gathered around
him. 27 He said to them, "Thus says
the LORD, the God of Israel, 'Put
your sword on your side, each of
you! Go back and forth from gate to
gate throughout the camp, and
each of you kill your brother, your
friend, and your neighbor.' " 28 The
sons of Levi did as Moses commanded, and about three thousand
of the people fell on that day.
29 Moses said, "Today you have ordained yourselves[c] for the service
of the LORD, each one at the cost of
a son or a brother, and so have

32.19 Deut 9.16, 17
32.20 Deut 9.21
32.21 Gen 26.10
32.22 Deut 9.24
32.23 v. 1
32.24 v. 4
32.27 Num 25.7-13; Deut 33.9
32.30 1 Sam 12.20, 23; 2 Sam 16.12; Num 25.13
32.31 Deut 9.18; Ex 20.23
32.32 Ps 69.28; Rom 9.3; Dan 12.1; Rev 3.5; 13.8; 17.8; 21.27
32.33 Deut 29.20; Ps 9.5
32.34 Ex 3.17; 23.20; Ps 99.8
32.35 vv. 4,24,28
33.1 Ex 32.7,13; Gen 12.7
33.2 Ex 32.34; 23.27-31
33.3 Ex 3.8,17; 32.9,10
33.4 Num 14.1, 39
33.5 v. 3

brought a blessing on yourselves
this day."

30 On the next day Moses said
to the people, "You have sinned a
great sin. But now I will go up to
the LORD; perhaps I can make
atonement for your sin." 31 So Moses returned to the LORD and said,
"Alas, this people has sinned a
great sin; they have made for themselves gods of gold. 32 But now, if
you will only forgive their sin—but
if not, blot me out of the book that
you have written." 33 But the LORD
said to Moses, "Whoever has
sinned against me I will blot out of
my book. 34 But now go, lead the
people to the place about which I
have spoken to you; see, my angel
shall go in front of you. Nevertheless, when the day comes for punishment, I will punish them for
their sin."

35 Then the LORD sent a plague
on the people, because they made
the calf—the one that Aaron made.

The Command to Leave Sinai

33 The LORD said to Moses,
"Go, leave this place, you
and the people whom you have
brought up out of the land of Egypt,
and go to the land of which I swore
to Abraham, Isaac, and Jacob, saying, 'To your descendants I will
give it.' 2 I will send an angel before
you, and I will drive out the Canaanites, the Amorites, the Hittites, the Perizzites, the Hivites,
and the Jebusites. 3 Go up to a land
flowing with milk and honey; but I
will not go up among you, or I
would consume you on the way, for
you are a stiff-necked people."

4 When the people heard these
harsh words, they mourned, and no
one put on ornaments. 5 For the
LORD had said to Moses, "Say to the
Israelites, 'You are a stiff-necked
people; if for a single moment I
should go up among you, I would
consume you. So now take off your
ornaments, and I will decide what
to do to you.' " 6 Therefore the Isra-

[c] Gk Vg Compare Tg: Heb *Today ordain yourselves*

elites stripped themselves of their
ornaments, from Mount Horeb onward.

The Tent outside the Camp

7 Now Moses used to take the
tent and pitch it outside the camp,
far off from the camp; he called it
the tent of meeting. And everyone
who sought the LORD would go out
to the tent of meeting, which was
outside the camp. 8 Whenever Moses went out to the tent, all the
people would rise and stand, each
of them, at the entrance of their
tents and watch Moses until he had
gone into the tent. 9 When Moses
entered the tent, the pillar of cloud
would descend and stand at the entrance of the tent, and the LORD
would speak with Moses. 10 When
all the people saw the pillar of
cloud standing at the entrance of
the tent, all the people would rise
and bow down, all of them, at the
entrance of their tent. 11 Thus the
LORD used to speak to Moses face to
face, as one speaks to a friend.
Then he would return to the camp;
but his young assistant, Joshua son
of Nun, would not leave the tent.

Moses' Intercession

12 Moses said to the LORD, "See,
you have said to me, 'Bring up this
people'; but you have not let me
know whom you will send with me.
Yet you have said, 'I know you by
name, and you have also found favor in my sight.' 13 Now if I have
found favor in your sight, show me
your ways, so that I may know you
and find favor in your sight. Consider too that this nation is your
people." 14 He said, "My presence
will go with you, and I will give you
rest." 15 And he said to him, "If your
presence will not go, do not carry
us up from here. 16 For how shall it
be known that I have found favor in
your sight, I and your people, unless you go with us? In this way, we
shall be distinct, I and your people,
from every people on the face of
the earth."

17 The LORD said to Moses, "I
will do the very thing that you have
asked; for you have found favor in
my sight, and I know you by name."
18 Moses said, "Show me your glory,
I pray." 19 And he said, "I will make
all my goodness pass before you,
and will proclaim before you the
name, 'The LORD';[d] and I will be
gracious to whom I will be gracious, and will show mercy on
whom I will show mercy. 20 But," he
said, "you cannot see my face; for
no one shall see me and live."
21 And the LORD continued, "See,
there is a place by me where you
shall stand on the rock; 22 and
while my glory passes by I will put
you in a cleft of the rock, and I will
cover you with my hand until I have
passed by; 23 then I will take away
my hand, and you shall see my
back; but my face shall not be
seen."

Moses Makes New Tablets

34 The LORD said to Moses,
"Cut two tablets of stone
like the former ones, and I will
write on the tablets the words that
were on the former tablets, which
you broke. 2 Be ready in the morning, and come up in the morning to
Mount Sinai and present yourself
there to me, on the top of the
mountain. 3 No one shall come up
with you, and do not let anyone be
seen throughout all the mountain;
and do not let flocks or herds graze
in front of that mountain." 4 So Moses cut two tablets of stone like the
former ones; and he rose early in
the morning and went up on Mount
Sinai, as the LORD had commanded
him, and took in his hand the two
tablets of stone. 5 The LORD descended in the cloud and stood
with him there, and proclaimed the
name, "The LORD."[d] 6 The LORD
passed before him, and proclaimed,

"The LORD, the LORD,
a God merciful and gracious,
slow to anger,
and abounding in steadfast
love and faithfulness,

33.7 Ex 29.42, 43; Deut 4.29
33.8 Num 16.27
33.9 Ex 25.22; 31.18; Ps 99.7
33.11 Num 12.8; Deut 34.10; Ex 24.13
33.12 Ex 32.34; v. 17; Jer 1.5; Jn 10.14,15; 2 Tim 2.19
33.13 Ex 34.9; Ps 25.4; Deut 9.26, 29
33.14 Isa 63.9; Josh 22.4
33.16 Num 14.14; Ex 34.10
33.17 v. 12
33.18 vv. 20,23
33.19 Rom 9.15, 16,18
33.20 Gen 32.20; Isa 6.5
33.23 Jn 1.18
34.1 Ex 32.16, 19; v. 28
34.2 Ex 19.20
34.3 Ex 19.12, 13,21
34.5 Ex 33.19
34.6 Num 14.18; Neh 9.17; Ps 86.15; 103.8

[d] Heb *YHWH*; see note at 3.15

7 keeping steadfast love for the
thousandth
generation,[e]
forgiving iniquity and
transgression and sin,
yet by no means clearing the
guilty,
but visiting the iniquity of
the parents
upon the children
and the children's children,
to the third and the fourth
generation."
8 And Moses quickly bowed his
head toward the earth, and worshiped. 9 He said, "If now I have
found favor in your sight, O Lord, I
pray, let the Lord go with us. Although this is a stiff-necked people, pardon our iniquity and our
sin, and take us for your inheritance."

The Covenant Renewed

10 He said: I hereby make a covenant. Before all your people I will
perform marvels, such as have not
been performed in all the earth or
in any nation; and all the people
among whom you live shall see the
work of the LORD; for it is an awesome thing that I will do with you.
11 Observe what I command
you today. See, I will drive out before you the Amorites, the Canaanites, the Hittites, the Perizzites, the
Hivites, and the Jebusites. 12 Take
care not to make a covenant with
the inhabitants of the land to
which you are going, or it will become a snare among you. 13 You
shall tear down their altars, break
their pillars, and cut down their sacred poles[f] 14 (for you shall worship no other god, because the
LORD, whose name is Jealous, is a
jealous God). 15 You shall not make
a covenant with the inhabitants of
the land, for when they prostitute
themselves to their gods and sacrifice to their gods, someone among
them will invite you, and you will
eat of the sacrifice. 16 And you will
take wives from among their
daughters for your sons, and their
daughters who prostitute themselves to their gods will make your
sons also prostitute themselves to
their gods.
17 You shall not make cast
idols.
18 You shall keep the festival of
unleavened bread. Seven days you
shall eat unleavened bread, as I
commanded you, at the time appointed in the month of Abib; for in
the month of Abib you came out
from Egypt.
19 All that first opens the womb
is mine, all your male[g] livestock,
the firstborn of cow and sheep.
20 The firstborn of a donkey you
shall redeem with a lamb, or if you
will not redeem it you shall break
its neck. All the firstborn of your
sons you shall redeem.
No one shall appear before me
empty-handed.
21 Six days you shall work, but
on the seventh day you shall rest;
even in plowing time and in harvest
time you shall rest. 22 You shall observe the festival of weeks, the first
fruits of wheat harvest, and the festival of ingathering at the turn of
the year. 23 Three times in the year
all your males shall appear before
the LORD God, the God of Israel.
24 For I will cast out nations before
you, and enlarge your borders; no
one shall covet your land when you
go up to appear before the LORD
your God three times in the year.
25 You shall not offer the blood
of my sacrifice with leaven, and the
sacrifice of the festival of the passover shall not be left until the
morning.
26 The best of the first fruits of
your ground you shall bring to the
house of the LORD your God.
You shall not boil a kid in its
mother's milk.
27 The LORD said to Moses:
Write these words; in accordance
with these words I have made a
covenant with you and with Israel.
28 He was there with the LORD forty
days and forty nights; he neither
ate bread nor drank water. And he
wrote on the tablets the words of

34.7 Ex 20.6,7; Ps 103.3; Dan 9.9; Eph 4.32
34.8 Ex 4.31
34.9 Ex 33.3,15,16
34.10 Deut 5.2; 4.32
34.11 Deut 6.3; Ex 33.2
34.12 Ex 23.32,33
34.13 Ex 23.24; 2 Kings 18.4
34.14 Ex 20.3,5; Deut 4.24
34.15 Judg 2.17; Num 25.2; 1 Cor 8.4,7,10
34.16 Deut 7.3; Num 25.1
34.17 Ex 32.8
34.18 Ex 12.2,15-17; 13.4
34.19 Ex 13.2; 22.29
34.20 Ex 13.13; 23.15
34.21 Ex 20.9; Lk 13.14
34.22 Ex 23.16
34.23 Ex 23.14-17
34.25 Ex 23.18; 12.10
34.26 Ex 23.19
34.27 Ex 17.14; 24.4
34.28 Ex 24.18; 31.18; 34.1; Deut 4.13; 10.4

e Or *for thousands* f Heb *Asherim*
g Gk Theodotion Vg Tg: Meaning of Heb uncertain

the covenant, the ten commandments.[h]

The Shining Face of Moses

29 Moses came down from
Mount Sinai. As he came down
from the mountain with the two
tablets of the covenant[i] in his
hand, Moses did not know that the
skin of his face shone because he
had been talking with God. 30 When
Aaron and all the Israelites saw
Moses, the skin of his face was
shining, and they were afraid to
come near him. 31 But Moses called
to them; and Aaron and all the
leaders of the congregation returned to him, and Moses spoke
with them. 32 Afterward all the Israelites came near, and he gave them
in commandment all that the LORD
had spoken with him on Mount Sinai. 33 When Moses had finished
speaking with them, he put a veil
on his face; 34 but whenever Moses
went in before the LORD to speak
with him, he would take the veil
off, until he came out; and when he
came out, and told the Israelites
what he had been commanded,
35 the Israelites would see the face
of Moses, that the skin of his face
was shining; and Moses would put
the veil on his face again, until he
went in to speak with him.

Sabbath Regulations

35 Moses assembled all the
congregation of the Israelites and said to them: These are the
things that the LORD has commanded you to do:
2 Six days shall work be done,
but on the seventh day you shall
have a holy sabbath of solemn rest
to the LORD; whoever does any work
on it shall be put to death. 3 You
shall kindle no fire in all your
dwellings on the sabbath day.

Preparations for Making the Tabernacle

4 Moses said to all the congregation of the Israelites: This is the
thing that the LORD has commanded: 5 Take from among you an offering to the LORD; let whoever is of a
generous heart bring the LORD's offering: gold, silver, and bronze;
6 blue, purple, and crimson yarns,
and fine linen; goats' hair, 7 tanned
rams' skins, and fine leather;[j] acacia wood, 8 oil for the light, spices
for the anointing oil and for the fragrant incense, 9 and onyx stones
and gems to be set in the ephod
and the breastpiece.
10 All who are skillful among
you shall come and make all that
the LORD has commanded: the tabernacle, 11 its tent and its covering,
its clasps and its frames, its bars,
its pillars, and its bases; 12 the ark
with its poles, the mercy seat,[k] and
the curtain for the screen; 13 the table with its poles and all its utensils, and the bread of the Presence;
14 the lampstand also for the light,
with its utensils and its lamps, and
the oil for the light; 15 and the altar
of incense, with its poles, and the
anointing oil and the fragrant incense, and the screen for the entrance, the entrance of the tabernacle; 16 the altar of burnt offering,
with its grating of bronze, its poles,
and all its utensils, the basin with
its stand; 17 the hangings of the
court, its pillars and its bases, and
the screen for the gate of the court;
18 the pegs of the tabernacle and
the pegs of the court, and their
cords; 19 the finely worked vestments for ministering in the holy
place, the holy vestments for the
priest Aaron, and the vestments of
his sons, for their service as priests.

Offerings for the Tabernacle

20 Then all the congregation of
the Israelites withdrew from the
presence of Moses. 21 And they
came, everyone whose heart was
stirred, and everyone whose spirit
was willing, and brought the LORD's
offering to be used for the tent of
meeting, and for all its service, and
for the sacred vestments. 22 So they
came, both men and women; all
who were of a willing heart brought
brooches and earrings and signet
rings and pendants, all sorts of gold

34.29 Ex 32.15; Mt 17.2; 2 Cor 3.7, 13
34.32 Ex 24.3
34.33 2 Cor 3.13
34.34 2 Cor 3.16
35.1 Ex 34.32
35.2 Ex 31.15
35.3 Ex 16.23
35.4 Ex 25.1-9
35.10 Ex 31.6
35.11 Ex 26.1ff
35.13 Ex 25.23, 30; Lev 24.5,6
35.15 Ex 30.1
35.19 Ex 31.10
35.21 Ex 25.2

[h] Heb *words*
[i] Or *treaty*, or *testimony*; Heb *eduth*
[j] Meaning of Heb uncertain
[k] Or *the cover*

objects, everyone bringing an offering of gold to the LORD. 23 And everyone who possessed blue or purple or crimson yarn or fine linen or goats' hair or tanned rams' skins or fine leather,[1] brought them. 24 Everyone who could make an offering of silver or bronze brought it as the LORD's offering; and everyone who possessed acacia wood of any use in the work, brought it. 25 All the skillful women spun with their hands, and brought what they had spun in blue and purple and crimson yarns and fine linen; 26 all the women whose hearts moved them to use their skill spun the goats' hair. 27 And the leaders brought onyx stones and gems to be set in the ephod and the breastpiece, 28 and spices and oil for the light, and for the anointing oil, and for the fragrant incense. 29 All the Israelite men and women whose hearts made them willing to bring anything for the work that the LORD had commanded by Moses to be done, brought it as a freewill offering to the LORD.

Bezalel and Oholiab

30 Then Moses said to the Israelites: See, the LORD has called by name Bezalel son of Uri son of Hur, of the tribe of Judah; 31 he has filled him with divine spirit,[m] with skill, intelligence, and knowledge in every kind of craft, 32 to devise artistic designs, to work in gold, silver, and bronze, 33 in cutting stones for setting, and in carving wood, in every kind of craft. 34 And he has inspired him to teach, both him and Oholiab son of Ahisamach, of the tribe of Dan. 35 He has filled them with skill to do every kind of work done by an artisan or by a designer or by an embroiderer in blue, purple, and crimson yarns, and in fine linen, or by a weaver—by any sort of artisan or skilled designer.

36 Bezalel and Oholiab and every skillful one to whom the LORD has given skill and understanding to know how to do any work in the construction of the sanctuary shall work in accordance with all that the LORD has commanded.

2 Moses then called Bezalel and Oholiab and every skillful one to whom the LORD had given skill, everyone whose heart was stirred to come to do the work; 3 and they received from Moses all the freewill offerings that the Israelites had brought for doing the work on the sanctuary. They still kept bringing him freewill offerings every morning, 4 so that all the artisans who were doing every sort of task on the sanctuary came, each from the task being performed, 5 and said to Moses, "The people are bringing much more than enough for doing the work that the LORD has commanded us to do." 6 So Moses gave command, and word was proclaimed throughout the camp: "No man or woman is to make anything else as an offering for the sanctuary." So the people were restrained from bringing; 7 for what they had already brought was more than enough to do all the work.

Construction of the Tabernacle

8 All those with skill among the workers made the tabernacle with ten curtains; they were made of fine twisted linen, and blue, purple, and crimson yarns, with cherubim skillfully worked into them. 9 The length of each curtain was twenty-eight cubits, and the width of each curtain four cubits; all the curtains were of the same size.

10 He joined five curtains to one another, and the other five curtains he joined to one another. 11 He made loops of blue on the edge of the outermost curtain of the first set; likewise he made them on the edge of the outermost curtain of the second set; 12 he made fifty loops on the one curtain, and he made fifty loops on the edge of the curtain that was in the second set; the loops were opposite one another. 13 And he made fifty clasps of gold, and joined the curtains one to

35.23 1 Chr 29.8
35.25 Ex 28.3
35.27 1 Chr 29.6; Ezra 2.68
35.28 Ex 30.23
35.29 v. 21
35.30 Ex 31.1-6
35.35 v. 31
36.1 Ex 25.8
36.2 Ex 35.21, 26; 1 Chr 29.5
36.3 Ex 35.27
36.5 2 Chr 24.14; 31.6-10; 2 Cor 8.23
36.8 Ex 26.1-14
36.12 Ex 26.5

[1] Meaning of Heb uncertain [m] Or *the spirit of God*

the other with clasps; so the tabernacle was one whole.
14 He also made curtains of
goats' hair for a tent over the tabernacle; he made eleven curtains.
15 The length of each curtain was
thirty cubits, and the width of each
curtain four cubits; the eleven curtains were of the same size. 16 He
joined five curtains by themselves,
and six curtains by themselves.
17 He made fifty loops on the edge
of the outermost curtain of the one
set, and fifty loops on the edge of
the other connecting curtain. 18 He
made fifty clasps of bronze to join
the tent together so that it might be
one whole. 19 And he made for the
tent a covering of tanned rams'
skins and an outer covering of fine
leather.[n]
20 Then he made the upright
frames for the tabernacle of acacia
wood. 21 Ten cubits was the length
of a frame, and a cubit and a half
the width of each frame. 22 Each
frame had two pegs for fitting together; he did this for all the frames
of the tabernacle. 23 The frames for
the tabernacle he made in this way:
twenty frames for the south side;
24 and he made forty bases of silver
under the twenty frames, two bases
under the first frame for its two
pegs, and two bases under the next
frame for its two pegs. 25 For the
second side of the tabernacle, on
the north side, he made twenty
frames 26 and their forty bases of
silver, two bases under the first
frame and two bases under the
next frame. 27 For the rear of the
tabernacle westward he made six
frames. 28 He made two frames for
corners of the tabernacle in the
rear. 29 They were separate beneath, but joined at the top, at the
first ring; he made two of them in
this way, for the two corners.
30 There were eight frames with
their bases of silver: sixteen bases,
under every frame two bases.
31 He made bars of acacia
wood, five for the frames of the one
side of the tabernacle, 32 and five
bars for the frames of the other side
of the tabernacle, and five bars for

36.14 Ex 26.7
36.19 Ex 26.14
36.20 Ex 26.15-29
36.24 Ex 26.21
36.27 Ex 26.22
36.31 Ex 26.26
36.35 Ex 26.31-37
37.1 Ex 25.10-20
37.3 Ex 25.12
37.6 Ex 25.17

the frames of the tabernacle at the
rear westward. 33 He made the middle bar to pass through from end to
end halfway up the frames. 34 And
he overlaid the frames with gold,
and made rings of gold for them to
hold the bars, and overlaid the bars
with gold.
35 He made the curtain of blue,
purple, and crimson yarns, and fine
twisted linen, with cherubim skillfully worked into it. 36 For it he
made four pillars of acacia, and
overlaid them with gold; their
hooks were of gold, and he cast for
them four bases of silver. 37 He also
made a screen for the entrance to
the tent, of blue, purple, and crimson yarns, and fine twisted linen,
embroidered with needlework;
38 and its five pillars with their
hooks. He overlaid their capitals
and their bases with gold, but their
five bases were of bronze.

Making the Ark of the Covenant

37 Bezalel made the ark of
acacia wood; it was two
and a half cubits long, a cubit and
a half wide, and a cubit and a half
high. 2 He overlaid it with pure gold
inside and outside, and made a
molding of gold around it. 3 He cast
for it four rings of gold for its four
feet, two rings on its one side and
two rings on its other side. 4 He
made poles of acacia wood, and
overlaid them with gold, 5 and put
the poles into the rings on the sides
of the ark, to carry the ark. 6 He
made a mercy seat[o] of pure gold;
two cubits and a half was its length,
and a cubit and a half its width.
7 He made two cherubim of hammered gold; at the two ends of the
mercy seat[p] he made them, 8 one
cherub at the one end, and one
cherub at the other end; of one
piece with the mercy seat[p] he
made the cherubim at its two ends.
9 The cherubim spread out their
wings above, overshadowing the
mercy seat[p] with their wings. They
faced one another; the faces of the

[n] Meaning of Heb uncertain [o] Or *a cover*
[p] Or *the cover*

cherubim were turned toward the
mercy seat.[q]

Making the Table for the Bread of the Presence

10 He also made the table of
acacia wood, two cubits long, one
cubit wide, and a cubit and a half
high. 11 He overlaid it with pure
gold, and made a molding of gold
around it. 12 He made around it a
rim a handbreadth wide, and made
a molding of gold around the rim.
13 He cast for it four rings of gold,
and fastened the rings to the four
corners at its four legs. 14 The rings
that held the poles used for carrying the table were close to the rim.
15 He made the poles of acacia
wood to carry the table, and overlaid them with gold. 16 And he
made the vessels of pure gold that
were to be on the table, its plates
and dishes for incense, and its
bowls and flagons with which to
pour drink offerings.

Making the Lampstand

17 He also made the lampstand
of pure gold. The base and the
shaft of the lampstand were made
of hammered work; its cups, its calyxes, and its petals were of one
piece with it. 18 There were six
branches going out of its sides,
three branches of the lampstand
out of one side of it and three
branches of the lampstand out of
the other side of it; 19 three cups
shaped like almond blossoms,
each with calyx and petals, on one
branch, and three cups shaped like
almond blossoms, each with calyx
and petals, on the other branch—
so for the six branches going out of
the lampstand. 20 On the lampstand itself there were four cups
shaped like almond blossoms,
each with its calyxes and petals.
21 There was a calyx of one piece
with it under the first pair of
branches, a calyx of one piece with
it under the next pair of branches,
and a calyx of one piece with it under the last pair of branches.
22 Their calyxes and their branches
were of one piece with it, the whole
of it one hammered piece of pure
gold. 23 He made its seven lamps
and its snuffers and its trays of pure
gold. 24 He made it and all its utensils of a talent of pure gold.

Making the Altar of Incense

25 He made the altar of incense
of acacia wood, one cubit long, and
one cubit wide; it was square, and
was two cubits high; its horns were
of one piece with it. 26 He overlaid
it with pure gold, its top, and its
sides all around, and its horns; and
he made for it a molding of gold all
around, 27 and made two golden
rings for it under its molding, on
two opposite sides of it, to hold the
poles with which to carry it. 28 And
he made the poles of acacia wood,
and overlaid them with gold.

Making the Anointing Oil and the Incense

29 He made the holy anointing
oil also, and the pure fragrant incense, blended as by the perfumer.

Making the Altar of Burnt Offering

38 He made the altar of burnt
offering also of acacia
wood; it was five cubits long, and
five cubits wide; it was square, and
three cubits high. 2 He made horns
for it on its four corners; its horns
were of one piece with it, and he
overlaid it with bronze. 3 He made
all the utensils of the altar, the
pots, the shovels, the basins, the
forks, and the firepans: all its utensils he made of bronze. 4 He made
for the altar a grating, a network of
bronze, under its ledge, extending
halfway down. 5 He cast four rings
on the four corners of the bronze
grating to hold the poles; 6 he made
the poles of acacia wood, and overlaid them with bronze. 7 And he put
the poles through the rings on the
sides of the altar, to carry it with
them; he made it hollow, with
boards.

8 He made the basin of bronze
with its stand of bronze, from the
mirrors of the women who served

37.16 Ex 25.29
37.17 Ex 25.31-39
37.19 Ex 25.33
37.21 Ex 25.35
37.25 Ex 30.1-5
37.29 Ex 30.23,34
38.1 Ex 27.1-8
38.8 Ex 30.18

[q] Or *the cover*

at the entrance to the tent of meeting.

Making the Court of the Tabernacle

9 He made the court; for the
south side the hangings of the
court were of fine twisted linen,
one hundred cubits long; [10]its
twenty pillars and their twenty
bases were of bronze, but the
hooks of the pillars and their bands
were of silver. [11]For the north side
there were hangings one hundred
cubits long; its twenty pillars and
their twenty bases were of bronze,
but the hooks of the pillars and
their bands were of silver. [12]For the
west side there were hangings fifty
cubits long, with ten pillars and ten
bases; the hooks of the pillars and
their bands were of silver. [13]And for
the front to the east, fifty cubits.
[14]The hangings for one side of the
gate were fifteen cubits, with three
pillars and three bases. [15]And so
for the other side; on each side of
the gate of the court were hangings
of fifteen cubits, with three pillars
and three bases. [16]All the hangings
around the court were of fine twisted linen. [17]The bases for the pillars
were of bronze, but the hooks of
the pillars and their bands were of
silver; the overlaying of their capitals was also of silver, and all the
pillars of the court were banded
with silver. [18]The screen for the entrance to the court was embroidered with needlework in blue,
purple, and crimson yarns and fine
twisted linen. It was twenty cubits
long and, along the width of it, five
cubits high, corresponding to the
hangings of the court. [19]There were
four pillars; their four bases were of
bronze, their hooks of silver, and
the overlaying of their capitals and
their bands of silver. [20]All the pegs
for the tabernacle and for the court
all around were of bronze.

Materials of the Tabernacle

21 These are the records of the
tabernacle, the tabernacle of the
covenant,[r] which were drawn up
at the commandment of Moses,
the work of the Levites being under
the direction of Ithamar son of the
priest Aaron. [22]Bezalel son of Uri
son of Hur, of the tribe of Judah,
made all that the LORD commanded
Moses; [23]and with him was Oholiab son of Ahisamach, of the tribe of
Dan, engraver, designer, and embroiderer in blue, purple, and crimson yarns, and in fine linen.

24 All the gold that was used for
the work, in all the construction of
the sanctuary, the gold from the offering, was twenty-nine talents and
seven hundred thirty shekels, measured by the sanctuary shekel.
[25]The silver from those of the congregation who were counted was
one hundred talents and one thousand seven hundred seventy-five
shekels, measured by the sanctuary shekel; [26]a beka a head (that is,
half a shekel, measured by the
sanctuary shekel), for everyone
who was counted in the census,
from twenty years old and upward,
for six hundred three thousand,
five hundred fifty men. [27]The hundred talents of silver were for casting the bases of the sanctuary, and
the bases of the curtain; one hundred bases for the hundred talents,
a talent for a base. [28]Of the thousand seven hundred seventy-five
shekels he made hooks for the pillars, and overlaid their capitals and
made bands for them. [29]The
bronze that was contributed was
seventy talents, and two thousand
four hundred shekels; [30]with it he
made the bases for the entrance of
the tent of meeting, the bronze altar and the bronze grating for it and
all the utensils of the altar, [31]the
bases all around the court, and the
bases of the gate of the court, all
the pegs of the tabernacle, and all
the pegs around the court.

Making the Vestments for the Priesthood

39 Of the blue, purple, and
crimson yarns they made
finely worked vestments, for ministering in the holy place; they made
the sacred vestments for Aaron; as

38.9 Ex 27.9-19 **38.11** Ex 27.11 **38.14** Ex 27.14 **38.18** Ex 27.16 **38.21** Num 4.28, 33

38.22 Ex 31.2,6 **38.24** Ex 30.13 **38.25** Ex 30.11-16 **38.26** Ex 30.13, 15; Num 1.46 **38.27** Ex 26.19, 21,25,32 **39.1** Ex 35.23; 28.4

[r] Or *treaty*, or *testimony*; Heb *eduth*

the LORD had commanded Moses.
2 He made the ephod of gold, of
blue, purple, and crimson yarns,
and of fine twisted linen. 3 Gold
leaf was hammered out and cut
into threads to work into the blue,
purple, and crimson yarns and into
the fine twisted linen, in skilled design. 4 They made for the ephod
shoulder-pieces, joined to it at its
two edges. 5 The decorated band on
it was of the same materials and
workmanship, of gold, of blue, purple, and crimson yarns, and of fine
twisted linen; as the LORD had commanded Moses.
6 The onyx stones were prepared, enclosed in settings of gold
filigree and engraved like the engravings of a signet, according to
the names of the sons of Israel. 7 He
set them on the shoulder-pieces of
the ephod, to be stones of remembrance for the sons of Israel; as the
LORD had commanded Moses.
8 He made the breastpiece, in
skilled work, like the work of the
ephod, of gold, of blue, purple, and
crimson yarns, and of fine twisted
linen. 9 It was square; the breastpiece was made double, a span in
length and a span in width when
doubled. 10 They set in it four rows
of stones. A row of carnelian,[s]
chrysolite, and emerald was the
first row; 11 and the second row, a
turquoise, a sapphire,[t] and a
moonstone; 12 and the third row, a
jacinth, an agate, and an amethyst;
13 and the fourth row, a beryl, an
onyx, and a jasper; they were enclosed in settings of gold filigree.
14 There were twelve stones with
names corresponding to the names
of the sons of Israel; they were like
signets, each engraved with its
name, for the twelve tribes. 15 They
made on the breastpiece chains of
pure gold, twisted like cords; 16 and
they made two settings of gold filigree and two gold rings, and put
the two rings on the two edges of
the breastpiece; 17 and they put the
two cords of gold in the two rings at
the edges of the breastpiece. 18 Two
ends of the two cords they had attached to the two settings of fili-

39.2 Ex 28.6-12
39.6 Ex 28.9
39.7 Ex 28.12
39.8 Ex 28.15-28
39.11 Ex 28.18
39.14 Ex 28.21
39.16 Ex 28.24
39.19 Ex 28.26
39.22 Ex 28.31-34
39.27 Ex 28.39, 40,42
39.30 Ex 28.36,37

gree; in this way they attached it in
front to the shoulder-pieces of the
ephod. 19 Then they made two rings
of gold, and put them at the two
ends of the breastpiece, on its inside edge next to the ephod.
20 They made two rings of gold, and
attached them in front to the lower
part of the two shoulder-pieces of
the ephod, at its joining above the
decorated band of the ephod.
21 They bound the breastpiece by
its rings to the rings of the ephod
with a blue cord, so that it should
lie on the decorated band of the
ephod, and that the breastpiece
should not come loose from the
ephod; as the LORD had commanded Moses.
22 He also made the robe of the
ephod woven all of blue yarn; 23 and
the opening of the robe in the middle of it was like the opening in a
coat of mail,[u] with a binding
around the opening, so that it
might not be torn. 24 On the lower
hem of the robe they made pomegranates of blue, purple, and crimson yarns, and of fine twisted linen.
25 They also made bells of pure
gold, and put the bells between the
pomegranates on the lower hem of
the robe all around, between the
pomegranates; 26 a bell and a
pomegranate, a bell and a pomegranate all around on the lower
hem of the robe for ministering; as
the LORD had commanded Moses.
27 They also made the tunics,
woven of fine linen, for Aaron and
his sons, 28 and the turban of fine
linen, and the headdresses of fine
linen, and the linen undergarments
of fine twisted linen, 29 and the
sash of fine twisted linen, and of
blue, purple, and crimson yarns,
embroidered with needlework; as
the LORD had commanded Moses.
30 They made the rosette of the
holy diadem of pure gold, and
wrote on it an inscription, like the
engraving of a signet, "Holy to the
LORD." 31 They tied to it a blue cord,
to fasten it on the turban above; as

[s] The identification of several of these stones is uncertain [t] Or *lapis lazuli* [u] Meaning of Heb uncertain

the LORD had commanded Moses.

The Work Completed

32 In this way all the work of the
tabernacle of the tent of meeting
was finished; the Israelites had
done everything just as the LORD
had commanded Moses. 33 Then
they brought the tabernacle to Moses, the tent and all its utensils, its
hooks, its frames, its bars, its pillars, and its bases; 34 the covering of
tanned rams' skins and the covering of fine leather,[v] and the curtain for the screen; 35 the ark of the
covenant[w] with its poles and the
mercy seat;[x] 36 the table with all its
utensils, and the bread of the Presence; 37 the pure lampstand with its
lamps set on it and all its utensils,
and the oil for the light; 38 the gold-
en altar, the anointing oil and the
fragrant incense, and the screen for
the entrance of the tent; 39 the
bronze altar, and its grating of
bronze, its poles, and all its utensils; the basin with its stand; 40 the
hangings of the court, its pillars,
and its bases, and the screen for
the gate of the court, its cords, and
its pegs; and all the utensils for the
service of the tabernacle, for the
tent of meeting; 41 the finely
worked vestments for ministering
in the holy place, the sacred vestments for the priest Aaron, and the
vestments of his sons to serve as
priests. 42 The Israelites had done
all of the work just as the LORD had
commanded Moses. 43 When Moses saw that they had done all the
work just as the LORD had commanded, he blessed them.

The Tabernacle Erected and Its Equipment Installed

40 The LORD spoke to Moses:
2 On the first day of the first
month you shall set up the tabernacle of the tent of meeting. 3 You
shall put in it the ark of the covenant,[w] and you shall screen the ark
with the curtain. 4 You shall bring
in the table, and arrange its setting;
and you shall bring in the lampstand, and set up its lamps. 5 You
shall put the golden altar for incense before the ark of the covenant,[w] and set up the screen for
the entrance of the tabernacle.
6 You shall set the altar of burnt offering before the entrance of the
tabernacle of the tent of meeting,
7 and place the basin between the
tent of meeting and the altar, and
put water in it. 8 You shall set up
the court all around, and hang up
the screen for the gate of the court.
9 Then you shall take the anointing
oil, and anoint the tabernacle and
all that is in it, and consecrate it
and all its furniture, so that it shall
become holy. 10 You shall also
anoint the altar of burnt offering
and all its utensils, and consecrate
the altar, so that the altar shall be
most holy. 11 You shall also anoint
the basin with its stand, and consecrate it. 12 Then you shall bring Aaron and his sons to the entrance of
the tent of meeting, and shall wash
them with water, 13 and put on Aaron the sacred vestments, and you
shall anoint him and consecrate
him, so that he may serve me as
priest. 14 You shall bring his sons
also and put tunics on them, 15 and
anoint them, as you anointed their
father, that they may serve me as
priests: and their anointing shall
admit them to a perpetual priesthood throughout all generations to
come.

16 Moses did everything just as
the LORD had commanded him.
17 In the first month in the second
year, on the first day of the month,
the tabernacle was set up. 18 Moses
set up the tabernacle; he laid its
bases, and set up its frames, and
put in its poles, and raised up its
pillars; 19 and he spread the tent
over the tabernacle, and put the
covering of the tent over it; as the
LORD had commanded Moses. 20 He
took the covenant[w] and put it into
the ark, and put the poles on the
ark, and set the mercy seat[x] above
the ark; 21 and he brought the ark
into the tabernacle, and set up the
curtain for screening, and screened

39.32 vv. 42,43; Ex 25.40 **39.35** Ex 25.16; 30.6 **39.41** Ex 26.33 **39.43** Lev 9.22,23 **40.2** Ex 12.2; 13.4; v. 17 **40.3** vv. 21-30

40.9 Ex 30.26 **40.10** Ex 29.36,37 **40.12** Lev 8.1-13 **40.13** Ex 28.41 **40.15** Num 25.13 **40.20** Ex 25.16 **40.21** Ex 26.33; 35.12

[v] Meaning of Heb uncertain [w] Or *treaty*, or *testimony*; Heb *eduth* [x] Or *the cover*

the ark of the covenant;[y] as the
LORD had commanded Moses. 22 He
put the table in the tent of meeting, on the north side of the tabernacle, outside the curtain, 23 and
set the bread in order on it before
the LORD; as the LORD had commanded Moses. 24 He put the lampstand in the tent of meeting, opposite the table on the south side of
the tabernacle, 25 and set up the
lamps before the LORD; as the LORD
had commanded Moses. 26 He put
the golden altar in the tent of meeting before the curtain, 27 and offered fragrant incense on it; as the
LORD had commanded Moses. 28 He
also put in place the screen for the
entrance of the tabernacle. 29 He
set the altar of burnt offering at the
entrance of the tabernacle of the
tent of meeting, and offered on it
the burnt offering and the grain offering as the LORD had commanded
Moses. 30 He set the basin between
the tent of meeting and the altar,
and put water in it for washing,
31 with which Moses and Aaron and
his sons washed their hands and
their feet. 32 When they went into
the tent of meeting, and when they
approached the altar, they washed;
as the LORD had commanded Moses. 33 He set up the court around
the tabernacle and the altar, and
put up the screen at the gate of the
court. So Moses finished the work.

The Cloud and the Glory

34 Then the cloud covered the
tent of meeting, and the glory of
the LORD filled the tabernacle.
35 Moses was not able to enter the
tent of meeting because the cloud
settled upon it, and the glory of the
LORD filled the tabernacle. 36 Whenever the cloud was taken up from
the tabernacle, the Israelites would
set out on each stage of their journey; 37 but if the cloud was not tak-
en up, then they did not set out until the day that it was taken up.
38 For the cloud of the LORD was on
the tabernacle by day, and fire was
in the cloud[z] by night, before the
eyes of all the house of Israel at
each stage of their journey.

40.22 Ex 26.35
40.23 v. 4
40.25 Ex 25.37
40.26 v. 5
40.28 Ex 26.36
40.30 v. 7
40.32 Ex 30.19,20
40.34 Num 9.15-23
40.36 Num 9.17; 10.11; Neh 9.19
40.38 Ex 13.21; Num 9.15

[y] Or *treaty*, or *testimony*; Heb *eduth*
[z] Heb *it*

Leviticus

Title and Background

Leviticus receives its name from the Septuagint (the Greek translation of the Old Testament) and means "relating to the Levites." Although Leviticus does not deal only with the special duties of the Levites, it is so named because it is concerned mainly with the service of worship at the tabernacle. Exodus had given the directions for building the tabernacle. Leviticus gives the laws and regulations for worship at the tabernacle, along with instructions on ceremonial cleanness, moral laws, holy days, the sabbath year, the year of jubilee, etc.

Author and Date of Writing

Leviticus 1.1 states that the contents of Leviticus were given to Moses by God. In more than fifty places in the book it is said that the Lord spoke to Moses. For the date of Moses and the exodus, see the Introductions to Genesis and Exodus.

Theme and Message

The key thought of Leviticus is holiness–the holiness of God and his people. The command to be holy is stated in 11.45–"you shall be holy, for I am holy." The instructions or laws in the book were given to help the Israelites worship and live as God's holy people.

Some of the instructions deal with such things as offering sacrifices, handling everyday problems concerning cleanliness, and observing special holidays. The Levitical priests are given special instructions for making sacrifices and carrying out God's commands.

Outline

I. Laws and Instructions for Offerings (1.1–7.38)
II. Appointment of Aaron and His Sons as God's Priests (8.1–10.20)
III. Rules for Holy Living (11.1–15.33)
IV. The Day of Atonement (16.1-34)
V. Practical Holiness (17.1–22.33)
VI. The Sabbath, Festivals, and Seasons (23.1–25.55)
VII. Conditions for God's Blessings (26.1–27.34)

The Burnt Offering

1 The LORD summoned Moses
and spoke to him from the
tent of meeting, saying: 2 Speak to
the people of Israel and say to
them: When any of you bring an offering of livestock to the LORD, you
shall bring your offering from the
herd or from the flock.
3 If the offering is a burnt offering from the herd, you shall offer a
male without blemish; you shall
bring it to the entrance of the tent
of meeting, for acceptance in your
behalf before the LORD. 4 You shall
lay your hand on the head of the
burnt offering, and it shall be acceptable in your behalf as atonement for you. 5 The bull shall be
slaughtered before the LORD; and
Aaron's sons the priests shall offer
the blood, dashing the blood
against all sides of the altar that is
at the entrance of the tent of meeting. 6 The burnt offering shall be
flayed and cut up into its parts.
7 The sons of the priest Aaron shall
put fire on the altar and arrange
wood on the fire. 8 Aaron's sons the
priests shall arrange the parts, with
the head and the suet, on the wood

1.1 Num 7.89
1.2f Lev 22.18, 19
1.3 Deut 15.21; Heb 9.14; 1 Pet 1.19
1.4f Ex 29.10; Lev 9.7; Num 15.25
1.5 Ex 29.11; Heb 10.11; 12.24; 1 Pet 1.2
1.7 Lev 6.8-13

that is on the fire on the altar; 9 but
its entrails and its legs shall be
washed with water. Then the priest
shall turn the whole into smoke on
the altar as a burnt offering, an offering by fire of pleasing odor to the
LORD.

10 If your gift for a burnt offering is from the flock, from the
sheep or goats, your offering shall
be a male without blemish. 11 It
shall be slaughtered on the north
side of the altar before the LORD,
and Aaron's sons the priests shall
dash its blood against all sides of
the altar. 12 It shall be cut up into
its parts, with its head and its suet,
and the priest shall arrange them
on the wood that is on the fire on
the altar; 13 but the entrails and the
legs shall be washed with water.
Then the priest shall offer the
whole and turn it into smoke on
the altar; it is a burnt offering, an
offering by fire of pleasing odor to
the LORD.

14 If your offering to the LORD is
a burnt offering of birds, you shall
choose your offering from turtledoves or pigeons. 15 The priest shall
bring it to the altar and wring off its
head, and turn it into smoke on the
altar; and its blood shall be drained
out against the side of the altar.
16 He shall remove its crop with its
contents[a] and throw it at the east
side of the altar, in the place for
ashes. 17 He shall tear it open by its
wings without severing it. Then the
priest shall turn it into smoke on
the altar, on the wood that is on the
fire; it is a burnt offering, an offering by fire of pleasing odor to the
LORD.

Grain Offerings

2 When anyone presents a grain
offering to the LORD, the offering shall be of choice flour; the
worshiper shall pour oil on it, and
put frankincense on it, 2 and bring
it to Aaron's sons the priests. After
taking from it a handful of the
choice flour and oil, with all its
frankincense, the priest shall turn
this token portion into smoke on
the altar, an offering by fire of
pleasing odor to the LORD. 3 And
what is left of the grain offering
shall be for Aaron and his sons, a
most holy part of the offerings by
fire to the LORD.

4 When you present a grain offering baked in the oven, it shall be
of choice flour: unleavened cakes
mixed with oil, or unleavened wafers spread with oil. 5 If your offering is grain prepared on a griddle, it
shall be of choice flour mixed with
oil, unleavened; 6 break it in pieces,
and pour oil on it; it is a grain offering. 7 If your offering is grain prepared in a pan, it shall be made of
choice flour in oil. 8 You shall bring
to the LORD the grain offering that is
prepared in any of these ways; and
when it is presented to the priest,
he shall take it to the altar. 9 The
priest shall remove from the grain
offering its token portion and turn
this into smoke on the altar, an offering by fire of pleasing odor to the
LORD. 10 And what is left of the grain
offering shall be for Aaron and his
sons; it is a most holy part of the
offerings by fire to the LORD.

11 No grain offering that you
bring to the LORD shall be made
with leaven, for you must not turn
any leaven or honey into smoke as
an offering by fire to the LORD.
12 You may bring them to the LORD
as an offering of choice products,
but they shall not be offered on the
altar for a pleasing odor. 13 You
shall not omit from your grain offerings the salt of the covenant
with your God; with all your offerings you shall offer salt.

14 If you bring a grain offering of
first fruits to the LORD, you shall
bring as the grain offering of your
first fruits coarse new grain from
fresh ears, parched with fire. 15 You
shall add oil to it and lay frankincense on it; it is a grain offering.
16 And the priest shall turn a token
portion of it into smoke—some of
the coarse grain and oil with all its
frankincense; it is an offering by
fire to the LORD.

1.9 Num 15.8-10; Eph 5.2
1.11 v. 5
1.14 Lev 5.7
1.15 Lev 5.9
1.16 Lev 6.10
1.17 Lev 5.8; Gen 15.10
2.1 Lev 6.14
2.2 vv. 9,16; Lev 5.12; 6.15; Acts 10.4
2.3 Lev 6.16; 10.12,13
2.9 v. 2; Ex 29.18
2.10 v. 3
2.11 Lev 6.16,17; Ex 23.18; 34.25
2.12 Lev 7.13; 23.10,11
2.13 Mk 9.49; Num 18.19
2.14 Lev 23.10, 14
2.16 v. 2

[a] Meaning of Heb uncertain

Offerings of Well-Being

3 If the offering is a sacrifice of well-being, if you offer an animal of the herd, whether male or female, you shall offer one without blemish before the LORD. 2 You shall lay your hand on the head of the offering and slaughter it at the entrance of the tent of meeting; and Aaron's sons the priests shall dash the blood against all sides of the altar. 3 You shall offer from the sacrifice of well-being, as an offering by fire to the LORD, the fat that covers the entrails and all the fat that is around the entrails; 4 the two kidneys with the fat that is on them at the loins, and the appendage of the liver, which he shall remove with the kidneys. 5 Then Aaron's sons shall turn these into smoke on the altar, with the burnt offering that is on the wood on the fire, as an offering by fire of pleasing odor to the LORD.

6 If your offering for a sacrifice of well-being to the LORD is from the flock, male or female, you shall offer one without blemish. 7 If you present a sheep as your offering, you shall bring it before the LORD 8 and lay your hand on the head of the offering. It shall be slaughtered before the tent of meeting, and Aaron's sons shall dash its blood against all sides of the altar. 9 You shall present its fat from the sacrifice of well-being, as an offering by fire to the LORD: the whole broad tail, which shall be removed close to the backbone, the fat that covers the entrails, and all the fat that is around the entrails; 10 the two kidneys with the fat that is on them at the loins, and the appendage of the liver, which you shall remove with the kidneys. 11 Then the priest shall turn these into smoke on the altar as a food offering by fire to the LORD.

12 If your offering is a goat, you shall bring it before the LORD 13 and lay your hand on its head; it shall be slaughtered before the tent of meeting; and the sons of Aaron shall dash its blood against all sides of the altar. 14 You shall present as your offering from it, as an offering by fire to the LORD, the fat that covers the entrails, and all the fat that is around the entrails; 15 the two kidneys with the fat that is on them at the loins, and the appendage of the liver, which you shall remove with the kidneys. 16 Then the priest shall turn these into smoke on the altar as a food offering by fire for a pleasing odor.

All fat is the LORD's. 17 It shall be a perpetual statute throughout your generations, in all your settlements: you must not eat any fat or any blood.

Sin Offerings

4 The LORD spoke to Moses, saying, 2 Speak to the people of Israel, saying: When anyone sins unintentionally in any of the LORD's commandments about things not to be done, and does any one of them:

3 If it is the anointed priest who sins, thus bringing guilt on the people, he shall offer for the sin that he has committed a bull of the herd without blemish as a sin offering to the LORD. 4 He shall bring the bull to the entrance of the tent of meeting before the LORD and lay his hand on the head of the bull; the bull shall be slaughtered before the LORD. 5 The anointed priest shall take some of the blood of the bull and bring it into the tent of meeting. 6 The priest shall dip his finger in the blood and sprinkle some of the blood seven times before the LORD in front of the curtain of the sanctuary. 7 The priest shall put some of the blood on the horns of the altar of fragrant incense that is in the tent of meeting before the LORD; and the rest of the blood of the bull he shall pour out at the base of the altar of burnt offering, which is at the entrance of the tent of meeting. 8 He shall remove all the fat from the bull of sin offering: the fat that covers the entrails and all the fat that is around the entrails; 9 the two kidneys with the fat that is on them at the loins; and the

3.1 Lev 7.11,19; 22.21
3.2 Lev 1.4; Ex 29.11, 16,20
3.3 Ex 29.13,22
3.5 Lev 7.28-34; Ex 29.13
3.6 v. 1
3.7 Lev 17.8,9
3.8 Lev 1.4,5; v. 2
3.10 v. 4
3.11 vv. 5,16; Lev 21.6,8, 17
3.16 Lev 7.23-25
3.17 Gen 9.4; Lev 17.10, 14; Deut 12.16
4.2 Lev 5.15-18; Ps 19.12
4.3ff vv. 14,23,28
4.4 Lev 1.4
4.5 Lev 16.14
4.7 Lev 8.15; 9.9; Lev 5.9
4.8 Lev 3.3-5

OLD TESTAMENT SACRIFICES

Sacrifice	OT References	Elements	Purpose
BURNT OFFERING	Lev 1; 6:8-13; 8:18-21; 16:24	Bull, ram or male bird (dove or young pigeon for poor); wholly consumed; no defect	Voluntary act of worship; atonement for unintentional sin in general; expression of devotion, commitment and complete surrender to God
GRAIN OFFERING	Lev 2; 6:14-23	Grain, fine flour, olive oil, incense, baked bread (cakes or wafers), salt; no yeast or honey; accompanied burnt offering and fellowship offering (along with drink offering)	Voluntary act of worship; recognition of God's goodness and provisions; devotion to God
FELLOWSHIP OFFERING	Lev 3; 7:11-34	Any animal without defect from herd or flock; variety of breads	Voluntary act of worship; thanksgiving and fellowship (it included a communal meal)
SIN OFFERING	Lev 4:1-5:13; 6:24-30; 8:14-17; 16:3-22	1. Young bull: for high priest and congregation 2. Male goat: for leader 3. Female goat or lamb: for common person 4. Dove or pigeon: for the poor 5. Tenth of an ephah of fine flour: for the very poor	Mandatory atonement for specific unintentional sin; confession of sin; forgiveness of sin; cleansing from defilement
GUILT OFFERING	Lev 5:14-6:7; 7:1-6	Ram or lamb	Mandatory atonement for unintentional sin requiring restitution; cleansing from defilement; make restitution; pay 20% fine

When more than one kind of offering was presented (as in Nu 7:16, 17), the procedure was usually as follows: (1) sin offering or guilt offering, (2) burnt offering, (3) fellowship offering and grain offering (along with a drink offering). This sequence furnishes part of the spiritual significance of the sacrificial system. First, sin had to be dealt with (sin offering or guilt offering). Second, the worshiper committed himself completely to God (burnt offering and grain offering). Third, fellowship or communion between the Lord, the priest and the worshiper (fellowship offering) was established.

appendage of the liver, which he
shall remove with the kidneys,
10 just as these are removed from
the ox of the sacrifice of well-
being. The priest shall turn them
into smoke upon the altar of burnt
offering. 11 But the skin of the bull
and all its flesh, as well as its head,
its legs, its entrails, and its dung—
12 all the rest of the bull—he shall
carry out to a clean place outside
the camp, to the ash heap, and
shall burn it on a wood fire; at the
ash heap it shall be burned.

13 If the whole congregation of
Israel errs unintentionally and the
matter escapes the notice of the assembly, and they do any one of the
things that by the LORD's commandments ought not to be done
and incur guilt; 14 when the sin that
they have committed becomes
known, the assembly shall offer a
bull of the herd for a sin offering
and bring it before the tent of
meeting. 15 The elders of the congregation shall lay their hands on
the head of the bull before the
LORD, and the bull shall be slaughtered before the LORD. 16 The
anointed priest shall bring some of
the blood of the bull into the tent
of meeting, 17 and the priest shall
dip his finger in the blood and
sprinkle it seven times before the
LORD, in front of the curtain. 18 He
shall put some of the blood on the
horns of the altar that is before the
LORD in the tent of meeting; and the
rest of the blood he shall pour out
at the base of the altar of burnt offering that is at the entrance of the
tent of meeting. 19 He shall remove
all its fat and turn it into smoke on
the altar. 20 He shall do with the
bull just as is done with the bull of
sin offering; he shall do the same
with this. The priest shall make
atonement for them, and they shall
be forgiven. 21 He shall carry the
bull outside the camp, and burn it
as he burned the first bull; it is the
sin offering for the assembly.

22 When a ruler sins, doing unintentionally any one of all the
things that by commandments of
the LORD his God ought not to be

4.12 Lev 6.11; Heb 13.11
4.13 Num 15.24-26; Lev 5.2-4,17
4.14 vv. 3,23,28
4.15 Lev 1.4
4.17 v. 6
4.20 Rom 5.11; Heb 2.17; 10.10-12
4.22 vv. 2,13
4.23 v. 14
4.25 vv. 7,18,30, 34
4.26 vv. 19,20
4.27 v. 2
4.28 v. 23
4.29 Lev 1.4,5
4.32 v. 28

done and incurs guilt, 23 once the
sin that he has committed is made
known to him, he shall bring as his
offering a male goat without blemish. 24 He shall lay his hand on the
head of the goat; it shall be slaughtered at the spot where the burnt
offering is slaughtered before the
LORD; it is a sin offering. 25 The
priest shall take some of the blood
of the sin offering with his finger
and put it on the horns of the altar
of burnt offering, and pour out the
rest of its blood at the base of the
altar of burnt offering. 26 All its fat
he shall turn into smoke on the altar, like the fat of the sacrifice of
well-being. Thus the priest shall
make atonement on his behalf for
his sin, and he shall be forgiven.

27 If anyone of the ordinary
people among you sins unintentionally in doing any one of the
things that by the LORD's commandments ought not to be done
and incurs guilt, 28 when the sin
that you have committed is made
known to you, you shall bring a female goat without blemish as your
offering, for the sin that you have
committed. 29 You shall lay your
hand on the head of the sin offering; and the sin offering shall be
slaughtered at the place of the
burnt offering. 30 The priest shall
take some of its blood with his finger and put it on the horns of the
altar of burnt offering, and he shall
pour out the rest of its blood at the
base of the altar. 31 He shall remove
all its fat, as the fat is removed from
the offering of well-being, and the
priest shall turn it into smoke on
the altar for a pleasing odor to the
LORD. Thus the priest shall make
atonement on your behalf, and you
shall be forgiven.

32 If the offering you bring as a
sin offering is a sheep, you shall
bring a female without blemish.
33 You shall lay your hand on the
head of the sin offering; and it shall
be slaughtered as a sin offering at
the spot where the burnt offering is
slaughtered. 34 The priest shall take
some of the blood of the sin offering with his finger and put it on the

horns of the altar of burnt offering, and pour out the rest of its blood at the base of the altar. 35 You shall remove all its fat, as the fat of the sheep is removed from the sacrifice of well-being, and the priest shall turn it into smoke on the altar, with the offerings by fire to the LORD. Thus the priest shall make atonement on your behalf for the sin that you have committed, and you shall be forgiven.

5 When any of you sin in that you have heard a public adjuration to testify and—though able to testify as one who has seen or learned of the matter—does not speak up, you are subject to punishment. 2 Or when any of you touch any unclean thing—whether the carcass of an unclean beast or the carcass of unclean livestock or the carcass of an unclean swarming thing—and are unaware of it, you have become unclean, and are guilty. 3 Or when you touch human uncleanness—any uncleanness by which one can become unclean—and are unaware of it, when you come to know it, you shall be guilty. 4 Or when any of you utter aloud a rash oath for a bad or a good purpose, whatever people utter in an oath, and are unaware of it, when you come to know it, you shall in any of these be guilty. 5 When you realize your guilt in any of these, you shall confess the sin that you have committed. 6 And you shall bring to the LORD, as your penalty for the sin that you have committed, a female from the flock, a sheep or a goat, as a sin offering; and the priest shall make atonement on your behalf for your sin.

7 But if you cannot afford a sheep, you shall bring to the LORD, as your penalty for the sin that you have committed, two turtledoves or two pigeons, one for a sin offering and the other for a burnt offering. 8 You shall bring them to the priest, who shall offer first the one for the sin offering, wringing its head at the nape without severing it. 9 He shall sprinkle some of the blood of the sin offering on the side of the altar, while the rest of the blood shall be drained out at the base of the altar; it is a sin offering. 10 And the second he shall offer for a burnt offering according to the regulation. Thus the priest shall make atonement on your behalf for the sin that you have committed, and you shall be forgiven.

11 But if you cannot afford two turtledoves or two pigeons, you shall bring as your offering for the sin that you have committed one-tenth of an ephah of choice flour for a sin offering; you shall not put oil on it or lay frankincense on it, for it is a sin offering. 12 You shall bring it to the priest, and the priest shall scoop up a handful of it as its memorial portion, and turn this into smoke on the altar, with the offerings by fire to the LORD; it is a sin offering. 13 Thus the priest shall make atonement on your behalf for whichever of these sins you have committed, and you shall be forgiven. Like the grain offering, the rest shall be for the priest.

Offerings with Restitution

14 The LORD spoke to Moses, saying: 15 When any of you commit a trespass and sin unintentionally in any of the holy things of the LORD, you shall bring, as your guilt offering to the LORD, a ram without blemish from the flock, convertible into silver by the sanctuary shekel; it is a guilt offering. 16 And you shall make restitution for the holy thing in which you were remiss, and shall add one-fifth to it and give it to the priest. The priest shall make atonement on your behalf with the ram of the guilt offering, and you shall be forgiven.

17 If any of you sin without knowing it, doing any of the things that by the LORD's commandments ought not to be done, you have incurred guilt, and are subject to punishment. 18 You shall bring to the priest a ram without blemish from the flock, or the equivalent, as a guilt offering; and the priest shall make atonement on your behalf for

4.35 Lev 3.5; vv. 26,31
5.1 Prov 29.24; v. 17
5.2 Lev 11.24-39; Num 19.11-16
5.5 Lev 16.21; 26.40; Num 5.7; Prov 28.13
5.7 Lev 12.8; 14.21
5.8 Lev 1.15,17
5.9 Lev 4.7,18, 30,34
5.10 Lev 1.14-17
5.11 Lev 2.1,2
5.13 Lev 4.26; 2.3
5.14 Lev 22.14; 7.1-10; Ex 30.13
5.16 Lev 6.5; 22.14; Num 5.7,8; Lev 4.26
5.17 v. 15; 4.2, 13,22,27
5.18 vv. 15-17

the error that you committed unintentionally, and you shall be forgiven. 19 It is a guilt offering; you have incurred guilt before the LORD.

6 [b] The LORD spoke to Moses, saying: 2 When any of you sin and commit a trespass against the LORD by deceiving a neighbor in a matter of a deposit or a pledge, or by robbery, or if you have defrauded a neighbor, 3 or have found something lost and lied about it—if you swear falsely regarding any of the various things that one may do and sin thereby— 4 when you have sinned and realize your guilt, and would restore what you took by robbery or by fraud or the deposit that was committed to you, or the lost thing that you found, 5 or anything else about which you have sworn falsely, you shall repay the principal amount and shall add one-fifth to it. You shall pay it to its owner when you realize your guilt. 6 And you shall bring to the priest, as your guilt offering to the LORD, a ram without blemish from the flock, or its equivalent, for a guilt offering. 7 The priest shall make atonement on your behalf before the LORD, and you shall be forgiven for any of the things that one may do and incur guilt thereby.

Instructions concerning Sacrifices

8 [c] The LORD spoke to Moses, saying: 9 Command Aaron and his sons, saying: This is the ritual of the burnt offering. The burnt offering itself shall remain on the hearth upon the altar all night until the morning, while the fire on the altar shall be kept burning. 10 The priest shall put on his linen vestments after putting on his linen undergarments next to his body; and he shall take up the ashes to which the fire has reduced the burnt offering on the altar, and place them beside the altar. 11 Then he shall take off his vestments and put on other garments, and carry the ashes out to a clean place outside the camp. 12 The fire on the altar shall be kept burning; it shall not go out. Every morning the priest shall add wood to it, lay out the burnt offering on it, and turn into smoke the fat pieces of the offerings of well-being. 13 A perpetual fire shall be kept burning on the altar; it shall not go out.

14 This is the ritual of the grain offering: The sons of Aaron shall offer it before the LORD, in front of the altar. 15 They shall take from it a handful of the choice flour and oil of the grain offering, with all the frankincense that is on the offering, and they shall turn its memorial portion into smoke on the altar as a pleasing odor to the LORD. 16 Aaron and his sons shall eat what is left of it; it shall be eaten as unleavened cakes in a holy place; in the court of the tent of meeting they shall eat it. 17 It shall not be baked with leaven. I have given it as their portion of my offerings by fire; it is most holy, like the sin offering and the guilt offering. 18 Every male among the descendants of Aaron shall eat of it, as their perpetual due throughout your generations, from the LORD's offerings by fire; anything that touches them shall become holy.

19 The LORD spoke to Moses, saying: 20 This is the offering that Aaron and his sons shall offer to the LORD on the day when he is anointed: one-tenth of an ephah of choice flour as a regular offering, half of it in the morning and half in the evening. 21 It shall be made with oil on a griddle; you shall bring it well soaked, as a grain offering of baked[d] pieces, and you shall present it as a pleasing odor to the LORD. 22 And so the priest, anointed from among Aaron's descendants as a successor, shall prepare it; it is the LORD's—a perpetual due—to be turned entirely into smoke. 23 Every grain offering of a priest shall be wholly burned; it shall not be eaten.

24 The LORD spoke to Moses, saying: 25 Speak to Aaron and his

6.2 Num 5.6; Acts 5.4; Col 3.9; Ex 22.7,10; Prov 24.28
6.3 Deut 22.1-3
6.5 Lev 5.16; Num 5.7,8
6.6 Lev 5.16
6.7 Lev 4.26
6.10 Ex 28.39-41, 43; 39.27,28
6.14 Lev 2.1,2
6.16 Lev 2.3
6.17 Lev 2.11; vv. 26,29,30
6.18 v. 29; Num 18.10; v. 27
6.20 Ex 29.1,2
6.21 Lev 2.5
6.25 Lev 4.2,24, 29,33; 1.3,5, 11

[b] Ch 5.20 in Heb [c] Ch 6.1 in Heb
[d] Meaning of Heb uncertain

sons, saying: This is the ritual of
the sin offering. The sin offering
shall be slaughtered before the
LORD at the spot where the burnt
offering is slaughtered; it is most
holy. [26]The priest who offers it as a
sin offering shall eat of it; it shall
be eaten in a holy place, in the
court of the tent of meeting.
[27]Whatever touches its flesh shall
become holy; and when any of its
blood is spattered on a garment,
you shall wash the bespattered part
in a holy place. [28]An earthen vessel
in which it was boiled shall be broken; but if it is boiled in a bronze
vessel, that shall be scoured and
rinsed in water. [29]Every male
among the priests shall eat of it; it
is most holy. [30]But no sin offering
shall be eaten from which any
blood is brought into the tent of
meeting for atonement in the holy
place; it shall be burned with fire.
7 This is the ritual of the guilt
offering. It is most holy; [2]at
the spot where the burnt offering is
slaughtered, they shall slaughter
the guilt offering, and its blood
shall be dashed against all sides of
the altar. [3]All its fat shall be offered: the broad tail, the fat that
covers the entrails, [4]the two kidneys with the fat that is on them at
the loins, and the appendage of the
liver, which shall be removed with
the kidneys. [5]The priest shall turn
them into smoke on the altar as an
offering by fire to the LORD; it is a
guilt offering. [6]Every male among
the priests shall eat of it; it shall be
eaten in a holy place; it is most
holy.
7 The guilt offering is like the
sin offering, there is the same ritual
for them; the priest who makes
atonement with it shall have it.
[8]So, too, the priest who offers anyone's burnt offering shall keep the
skin of the burnt offering that he
has offered. [9]And every grain offering baked in the oven, and all that
is prepared in a pan or on a griddle,
shall belong to the priest who offers it. [10]But every other grain offering, mixed with oil or dry, shall

6.26 Lev 10.17, 18; v. 16
6.27 Ex 29.37
6.28 Ex 11.33; 15.12
6.29 vv. 18,25
6.30 Lev 4.1,7, 11,12,18,21
7.1 Lev 5.14-6.7
7.2 Lev 1.11
7.4 Lev 3.4
7.6 Lev 6.16-18; 2.3
7.7 Lev 6.25,26
7.9 Lev 2.3,10
7.14 Num 18.8, 11,19
7.15 Lev 22.30
7.16 Lev 19.6-8
7.18 Lev 19.7; Num 18.27
7.20 Lev 22.3
7.21 Lev 11.24, 28
7.23 Lev 3.17

belong to all the sons of Aaron
equally.

Further Instructions

11 This is the ritual of the sacrifice of the offering of well-being
that one may offer to the LORD. [12]If
you offer it for thanksgiving, you
shall offer with the thank offering
unleavened cakes mixed with oil,
unleavened wafers spread with oil,
and cakes of choice flour well
soaked in oil. [13]With your thanksgiving sacrifice of well-being you
shall bring your offering with cakes
of leavened bread. [14]From this you
shall offer one cake from each offering, as a gift to the LORD; it shall
belong to the priest who dashes the
blood of the offering of well-being.
[15]And the flesh of your thanksgiving sacrifice of well-being shall be
eaten on the day it is offered; you
shall not leave any of it until morning. [16]But if the sacrifice you offer
is a votive offering or a freewill offering, it shall be eaten on the day
that you offer your sacrifice, and
what is left of it shall be eaten the
next day; [17]but what is left of the
flesh of the sacrifice shall be
burned up on the third day. [18]If any
of the flesh of your sacrifice of well-
being is eaten on the third day, it
shall not be acceptable, nor shall it
be credited to the one who offers it;
it shall be an abomination, and the
one who eats of it shall incur guilt.
19 Flesh that touches any unclean thing shall not be eaten; it
shall be burned up. As for other
flesh, all who are clean may eat
such flesh. [20]But those who eat
flesh from the LORD's sacrifice of
well-being while in a state of uncleanness shall be cut off from
their kin. [21]When any one of you
touches any unclean thing—
human uncleanness or an unclean
animal or any unclean creature—
and then eats flesh from the LORD's
sacrifice of well-being, you shall be
cut off from your kin.
22 The LORD spoke to Moses,
saying: [23]Speak to the people of Israel, saying: You shall eat no fat of
ox or sheep or goat. [24]The fat of an

animal that died or was torn by
wild animals may be put to any use,
but you must not eat it. 25 If any one
of you eats the fat from an animal
of which an offering by fire may be
made to the LORD, you who eat it
shall be cut off from your kin.
26 You must not eat any blood whatever, either of bird or of animal, in
any of your settlements. 27 Any one
of you who eats any blood shall be
cut off from your kin.
28 The LORD spoke to Moses,
saying: 29 Speak to the people of Israel, saying: Any one of you who
would offer to the LORD your sacrifice of well-being must yourself
bring to the LORD your offering from
your sacrifice of well-being. 30 Your
own hands shall bring the LORD's
offering by fire; you shall bring the
fat with the breast, so that the
breast may be raised as an elevation offering before the LORD. 31 The
priest shall turn the fat into smoke
on the altar, but the breast shall
belong to Aaron and his sons.
32 And the right thigh from your
sacrifices of well-being you shall
give to the priest as an offering;
33 the one among the sons of Aaron
who offers the blood and fat of the
offering of well-being shall have
the right thigh for a portion. 34 For
I have taken the breast of the elevation offering, and the thigh that is
offered, from the people of Israel,
from their sacrifices of well-being,
and have given them to Aaron the
priest and to his sons, as a perpetual due from the people of Israel.
35 This is the portion allotted to
Aaron and to his sons from the offerings made by fire to the LORD,
once they have been brought forward to serve the LORD as priests;
36 these the LORD commanded to be
given them, when he anointed
them, as a perpetual due from the
people of Israel throughout their
generations.
37 This is the ritual of the burnt
offering, the grain offering, the sin
offering, the guilt offering, the offering of ordination, and the sacrifice of well-being, 38 which the LORD
commanded Moses on Mount Si-

7.26 Lev 17.10-14
7.29 Lev 3.1
7.31 v. 34
7.34 Num 18.18, 19
7.37 Lev 6.9,14, 20,25; vv. 1, 11
7.38 Lev 1.1,2

8.2 Ex 29.1-3; 28.2,4; 30.24, 25
8.6 Ex 29.4-6
8.8 Ex 28.30
8.9 Ex 28.36,37
8.10 v. 2
8.12 Ex 30.30; Ps 133.2
8.13 Ex 29.8,9
8.14 Ex 29.10; Lev 4.4
8.15 Lev 4.7; Heb 9.22

nai, when he commanded the people of Israel to bring their offerings
to the LORD, in the wilderness of Sinai.

The Rites of Ordination

8 The LORD spoke to Moses, saying: 2 Take Aaron and his sons
with him, the vestments, the
anointing oil, the bull of sin offering, the two rams, and the basket of
unleavened bread; 3 and assemble
the whole congregation at the entrance of the tent of meeting. 4 And
Moses did as the LORD commanded
him. When the congregation was
assembled at the entrance of the
tent of meeting, 5 Moses said to the
congregation, "This is what the
LORD has commanded to be done."
6 Then Moses brought Aaron
and his sons forward, and washed
them with water. 7 He put the tunic
on him, fastened the sash around
him, clothed him with the robe,
and put the ephod on him. He then
put the decorated band of the
ephod around him, tying the ephod
to him with it. 8 He placed the
breastpiece on him, and in the
breastpiece he put the Urim and
the Thummim. 9 And he set the turban on his head, and on the turban,
in front, he set the golden ornament, the holy crown, as the LORD
commanded Moses.
10 Then Moses took the anointing oil and anointed the tabernacle
and all that was in it, and consecrated them. 11 He sprinkled some
of it on the altar seven times, and
anointed the altar and all its utensils, and the basin and its base, to
consecrate them. 12 He poured
some of the anointing oil on Aaron's head and anointed him, to
consecrate him. 13 And Moses
brought forward Aaron's sons, and
clothed them with tunics, and fastened sashes around them, and
tied headdresses on them, as the
LORD commanded Moses.
14 He led forward the bull of sin
offering; and Aaron and his sons
laid their hands upon the head of
the bull of sin offering, 15 and it was
slaughtered. Moses took the blood

and with his finger put some on
each of the horns of the altar, purifying the altar; then he poured out
the blood at the base of the altar.
Thus he consecrated it, to make
atonement for it. 16 Moses took all
the fat that was around the entrails, and the appendage of the liver, and the two kidneys with their
fat, and turned them into smoke on
the altar. 17 But the bull itself, its
skin and flesh and its dung, he
burned with fire outside the camp,
as the LORD commanded Moses.
18 Then he brought forward the
ram of burnt offering. Aaron and
his sons laid their hands on the
head of the ram, 19 and it was
slaughtered. Moses dashed the
blood against all sides of the altar.
20 The ram was cut into its parts,
and Moses turned into smoke the
head and the parts and the suet.
21 And after the entrails and the
legs were washed with water, Moses turned into smoke the whole
ram on the altar; it was a burnt offering for a pleasing odor, an offering by fire to the LORD, as the LORD
commanded Moses.
22 Then he brought forward the
second ram, the ram of ordination.
Aaron and his sons laid their hands
on the head of the ram, 23 and it
was slaughtered. Moses took some
of its blood and put it on the lobe
of Aaron's right ear and on the
thumb of his right hand and on the
big toe of his right foot. 24 After Aaron's sons were brought forward,
Moses put some of the blood on
the lobes of their right ears and on
the thumbs of their right hands and
on the big toes of their right feet;
and Moses dashed the rest of the
blood against all sides of the altar.
25 He took the fat—the broad tail,
all the fat that was around the entrails, the appendage of the liver,
and the two kidneys with their
fat—and the right thigh. 26 From
the basket of unleavened bread
that was before the LORD, he took
one cake of unleavened bread, one
cake of bread with oil, and one wafer, and placed them on the fat and
on the right thigh. 27 He placed all

8.16 Lev 4.8
8.17 Lev 4.11,12
8.18 Ex 29.15
8.21 Ex 29.18
8.22 Ex 29.19,31
8.25 Ex 29.22
8.26 Ex 29.23
8.28 Ex 29.25
8.29 Ex 29.26
8.30 Ex 30.30; Num 3.3
8.31 Ex 29.31,32
8.32 Ex 29.34
8.33 Ex 29.30,35
8.34 Heb 7.16
9.2 Lev 8.18; Ex 29.1
9.3 Lev 4.23

these on the palms of Aaron and on
the palms of his sons, and raised
them as an elevation offering before the LORD. 28 Then Moses took
them from their hands and turned
them into smoke on the altar with
the burnt offering. This was an ordination offering for a pleasing
odor, an offering by fire to the LORD.
29 Moses took the breast and raised
it as an elevation offering before
the LORD; it was Moses' portion of
the ram of ordination, as the LORD
commanded Moses.
30 Then Moses took some of the
anointing oil and some of the blood
that was on the altar and sprinkled
them on Aaron and his vestments,
and also on his sons and their vestments. Thus he consecrated Aaron
and his vestments, and also his
sons and their vestments.
31 And Moses said to Aaron and
his sons, "Boil the flesh at the entrance of the tent of meeting, and
eat it there with the bread that is in
the basket of ordination offerings,
as I was commanded, 'Aaron and
his sons shall eat it'; 32 and what remains of the flesh and the bread
you shall burn with fire. 33 You shall
not go outside the entrance of the
tent of meeting for seven days, until the day when your period of ordination is completed. For it will
take seven days to ordain you; 34 as
has been done today, the LORD has
commanded to be done to make
atonement for you. 35 You shall remain at the entrance of the tent of
meeting day and night for seven
days, keeping the LORD's charge so
that you do not die; for so I am
commanded." 36 Aaron and his
sons did all the things that the LORD
commanded through Moses.

Aaron's Priesthood Inaugurated

9 On the eighth day Moses summoned Aaron and his sons and
the elders of Israel. 2 He said to Aaron, "Take a bull calf for a sin offering and a ram for a burnt offering,
without blemish, and offer them
before the LORD. 3 And say to the
people of Israel, 'Take a male goat
for a sin offering; a calf and a lamb,

yearlings without blemish, for a
burnt offering; 4and an ox and a
ram for an offering of well-being to
sacrifice before the LORD; and a
grain offering mixed with oil. For
today the LORD will appear to
you.' " 5They brought what Moses
commanded to the front of the tent
of meeting; and the whole congregation drew near and stood before
the LORD. 6And Moses said, "This is
the thing that the LORD commanded you to do, so that the glory of the
LORD may appear to you." 7Then
Moses said to Aaron, "Draw near to
the altar and sacrifice your sin offering and your burnt offering, and
make atonement for yourself and
for the people; and sacrifice the offering of the people, and make
atonement for them; as the LORD
has commanded."
8 Aaron drew near to the altar,
and slaughtered the calf of the sin
offering, which was for himself.
9The sons of Aaron presented the
blood to him, and he dipped his
finger in the blood and put it on the
horns of the altar; and the rest of
the blood he poured out at the base
of the altar. 10But the fat, the kidneys, and the appendage of the liver from the sin offering he turned
into smoke on the altar, as the LORD
commanded Moses; 11and the
flesh and the skin he burned with
fire outside the camp.
12 Then he slaughtered the
burnt offering. Aaron's sons
brought him the blood, and he
dashed it against all sides of the altar. 13And they brought him the
burnt offering piece by piece, and
the head, which he turned into
smoke on the altar. 14He washed
the entrails and the legs and, with
the burnt offering, turned them
into smoke on the altar.
15 Next he presented the people's offering. He took the goat of
the sin offering that was for the
people, and slaughtered it, and
presented it as a sin offering like
the first one. 16He presented the
burnt offering, and sacrificed it according to regulation. 17He presented the grain offering, and, taking a handful of it, he turned it into
smoke on the altar, in addition to
the burnt offering of the morning.
18 He slaughtered the ox and
the ram as a sacrifice of well-being
for the people. Aaron's sons
brought him the blood, which he
dashed against all sides of the altar, 19and the fat of the ox and of
the ram—the broad tail, the fat
that covers the entrails, the two
kidneys and the fat on them,[e] and
the appendage of the liver. 20They
first laid the fat on the breasts, and
the fat was turned into smoke on
the altar; 21and the breasts and the
right thigh Aaron raised as an elevation offering before the LORD, as
Moses had commanded.
22 Aaron lifted his hands toward the people and blessed them;
and he came down after sacrificing
the sin offering, the burnt offering,
and the offering of well-being.
23Moses and Aaron entered the
tent of meeting, and then came out
and blessed the people; and the
glory of the LORD appeared to all
the people. 24Fire came out from
the LORD and consumed the burnt
offering and the fat on the altar;
and when all the people saw it,
they shouted and fell on their
faces.

Nadab and Abihu

10 Now Aaron's sons, Nadab
and Abihu, each took his
censer, put fire in it, and laid incense on it; and they offered unholy fire before the LORD, such as he
had not commanded them. 2And
fire came out from the presence of
the LORD and consumed them, and
they died before the LORD. 3Then
Moses said to Aaron, "This is what
the LORD meant when he said,

'Through those who are near
me
I will show myself holy,
and before all the people
I will be glorified.' "

And Aaron was silent.
4 Moses summoned Mishael
and Elzaphan, sons of Uzziel the

9.6 v. 23
9.7 Heb 5.1,3
9.8 Lev 4.1-12
9.9 vv. 12,18
9.11 Lev 4.11; 8.17
9.15 Lev 4.27-31
9.16 Lev 1.3,10
9.17 Lev 2.1,2; 3.5
9.18 Lev 3.1-11
9.21 Lev 7.30-34
9.23 v. 6; Num 14.10
9.24 1 Kings 18.38, 39
10.1 Num 3.3,4; Lev 16.12; Ex 30.9
10.2 Num 3.4; 26.61
10.3 Ex 19.22; 30.30; Lev 21.6
10.4 Ex 6.18,22; Acts 5.6,9, 10

[e] Gk: Heb *the broad tail, and that which covers, and the kidneys*

uncle of Aaron, and said to them,
"Come forward, and carry your
kinsmen away from the front of the
sanctuary to a place outside the
camp." 5 They came forward and
carried them by their tunics out of
the camp, as Moses had ordered.
6 And Moses said to Aaron and to
his sons Eleazar and Ithamar, "Do
not dishevel your hair, and do not
tear your vestments, or you will die
and wrath will strike all the congregation; but your kindred, the whole
house of Israel, may mourn the
burning that the LORD has sent.
7 You shall not go outside the entrance of the tent of meeting, or
you will die; for the anointing oil of
the LORD is on you." And they did as
Moses had ordered.
8 And the LORD spoke to Aaron:
9 Drink no wine or strong drink,
neither you nor your sons, when
you enter the tent of meeting, that
you may not die; it is a statute forever throughout your generations.
10 You are to distinguish between
the holy and the common, and between the unclean and the clean;
11 and you are to teach the people
of Israel all the statutes that the
LORD has spoken to them through
Moses.
12 Moses spoke to Aaron and to
his remaining sons, Eleazar and
Ithamar: Take the grain offering
that is left from the LORD's offerings
by fire, and eat it unleavened beside the altar, for it is most holy;
13 you shall eat it in a holy place,
because it is your due and your
sons' due, from the offerings by fire
to the LORD; for so I am commanded. 14 But the breast that is elevated
and the thigh that is raised, you
and your sons and daughters as
well may eat in any clean place; for
they have been assigned to you and
your children from the sacrifices of
the offerings of well-being of the
people of Israel. 15 The thigh that is
raised and the breast that is elevated they shall bring, together with
the offerings by fire of the fat, to
raise for an elevation offering before the LORD; they are to be your
due and that of your children forever, as the LORD has commanded.
16 Then Moses made inquiry
about the goat of the sin offering,
and—it had already been burned!
He was angry with Eleazar and Ithamar, Aaron's remaining sons, and
said, 17 "Why did you not eat the sin
offering in the sacred area? For it is
most holy, and God[f] has given it to
you that you may remove the guilt
of the congregation, to make
atonement on their behalf before
the LORD. 18 Its blood was not
brought into the inner part of the
sanctuary. You should certainly
have eaten it in the sanctuary, as I
commanded." 19 And Aaron spoke
to Moses, "See, today they offered
their sin offering and their burnt offering before the LORD; and yet such
things as these have befallen me! If
I had eaten the sin offering today,
would it have been agreeable to the
LORD?" 20 And when Moses heard
that, he agreed.

Clean and Unclean Foods

11 The LORD spoke to Moses
and Aaron, saying to them:
2 Speak to the people of Israel, saying:
From among all the land animals, these are the creatures that
you may eat. 3 Any animal that has
divided hoofs and is cleft-footed
and chews the cud—such you may
eat. 4 But among those that chew
the cud or have divided hoofs, you
shall not eat the following: the
camel, for even though it chews the
cud, it does not have divided hoofs;
it is unclean for you. 5 The rock
badger, for even though it chews
the cud, it does not have divided
hoofs; it is unclean for you. 6 The
hare, for even though it chews the
cud, it does not have divided hoofs;
it is unclean for you. 7 The pig, for
even though it has divided hoofs
and is cleft-footed, it does not
chew the cud; it is unclean for you.
8 Of their flesh you shall not eat,
and their carcasses you shall not
touch; they are unclean for you.
9 These you may eat, of all that

10.6 Lev 21.1,10; Num 16.22, 46; Josh 7;1; 22.18-20
10.7 Lev 21.12
10.9 Ezek 44.21
10.10 Lev 11.47; 20.25; Ezek 22.26
10.11 Deut 24.8; Mal 2.7
10.12 Lev 6.14-18; 21.22
10.14 Ex 29.24, 26,27
10.15 Lev 7.29,30, 34
10.17 Lev 6.24-30
10.19 Lev 9.8,12
11.2 Deut 14.3-21
11.7 Isa 65.4; 66.3,17
11.8 Isa 52.11; Heb 9.10
11.9 Deut 14.9

[f] Heb *he*

are in the waters. Everything in the
waters that has fins and scales,
whether in the seas or in the
streams—such you may eat. 10 But
anything in the seas or the streams
that does not have fins and scales,
of the swarming creatures in the
waters and among all the other living creatures that are in the
waters—they are detestable to you
11 and detestable they shall remain.
Of their flesh you shall not eat, and
their carcasses you shall regard as
detestable. 12 Everything in the waters that does not have fins and
scales is detestable to you.

13 These you shall regard as detestable among the birds. They
shall not be eaten; they are an
abomination: the eagle, the vulture, the osprey, 14 the buzzard, the
kite of any kind; 15 every raven of
any kind; 16 the ostrich, the nighthawk, the sea gull, the hawk of any
kind; 17 the little owl, the cormorant, the great owl, 18 the water
hen, the desert owl,[g] the carrion
vulture, 19 the stork, the heron of
any kind, the hoopoe, and the
bat.[h]

20 All winged insects that walk
upon all fours are detestable to
you. 21 But among the winged insects that walk on all fours you may
eat those that have jointed legs
above their feet, with which to leap
on the ground. 22 Of them you may
eat: the locust according to its
kind, the bald locust according to
its kind, the cricket according to its
kind, and the grasshopper according to its kind. 23 But all other
winged insects that have four feet
are detestable to you.

Unclean Animals

24 By these you shall become
unclean; whoever touches the carcass of any of them shall be unclean until the evening, 25 and whoever carries any part of the carcass
of any of them shall wash his
clothes and be unclean until the
evening. 26 Every animal that has
divided hoofs but is not cleft-
footed or does not chew the cud is
unclean for you; everyone who

11.10 Lev 7.18; Deut 14.3
11.13 Deut 14.12
11.22 Mt 3.4; Mk 1.6
11.25 v. 40
11.29 Isa 66.17
11.32 Lev 15.12
11.33 Lev 6.28; 15.12

touches one of them shall be unclean. 27 All that walk on their
paws, among the animals that walk
on all fours, are unclean for you;
whoever touches the carcass of any
of them shall be unclean until the
evening, 28 and the one who carries
the carcass shall wash his clothes
and be unclean until the evening;
they are unclean for you.

29 These are unclean for you
among the creatures that swarm
upon the earth: the weasel, the
mouse, the great lizard according
to its kind, 30 the gecko, the land
crocodile, the lizard, the sand lizard, and the chameleon. 31 These
are unclean for you among all that
swarm; whoever touches one of
them when they are dead shall be
unclean until the evening. 32 And
anything upon which any of them
falls when they are dead shall be
unclean, whether an article of
wood or cloth or skin or sacking,
any article that is used for any purpose; it shall be dipped into water,
and it shall be unclean until the
evening, and then it shall be clean.
33 And if any of them falls into any
earthen vessel, all that is in it shall
be unclean, and you shall break the
vessel. 34 Any food that could be
eaten shall be unclean if water
from any such vessel comes upon
it; and any liquid that could be
drunk shall be unclean if it was in
any such vessel. 35 Everything on
which any part of the carcass falls
shall be unclean; whether an oven
or stove, it shall be broken in
pieces; they are unclean, and shall
remain unclean for you. 36 But a
spring or a cistern holding water
shall be clean, while whatever
touches the carcass in it shall be
unclean. 37 If any part of their carcass falls upon any seed set aside
for sowing, it is clean; 38 but if water
is put on the seed and any part of
their carcass falls on it, it is unclean for you.

39 If an animal of which you
may eat dies, anyone who touches

[g] Or *pelican* [h] Identification of several of the birds in verses 13-19 is uncertain

its carcass shall be unclean until
the evening. 40 Those who eat of its
carcass shall wash their clothes
and be unclean until the evening;
and those who carry the carcass
shall wash their clothes and be unclean until the evening.
41 All creatures that swarm
upon the earth are detestable; they
shall not be eaten. 42 Whatever
moves on its belly, and whatever
moves on all fours, or whatever has
many feet, all the creatures that
swarm upon the earth, you shall
not eat; for they are detestable.
43 You shall not make yourselves
detestable with any creature that
swarms; you shall not defile yourselves with them, and so become
unclean. 44 For I am the LORD your
God; sanctify yourselves therefore,
and be holy, for I am holy. You shall
not defile yourselves with any
swarming creature that moves on
the earth. 45 For I am the LORD who
brought you up from the land of
Egypt, to be your God; you shall be
holy, for I am holy.
46 This is the law pertaining to
land animal and bird and every living creature that moves through
the waters and every creature that
swarms upon the earth, 47 to make
a distinction between the unclean
and the clean, and between the living creature that may be eaten and
the living creature that may not be
eaten.

Purification of Women after Childbirth

12 The LORD spoke to Moses,
saying: 2 Speak to the people of Israel, saying:
If a woman conceives and bears
a male child, she shall be
ceremonially unclean seven days;
as at the time of her menstruation,
she shall be unclean. 3 On the
eighth day the flesh of his foreskin
shall be circumcised. 4 Her time of
blood purification shall be thirty-
three days; she shall not touch any
holy thing, or come into the sanctuary, until the days of her purification are completed. 5 If she bears a
female child, she shall be unclean
two weeks, as in her menstruation;
her time of blood purification shall
be sixty-six days.
6 When the days of her purification are completed, whether for a
son or for a daughter, she shall
bring to the priest at the entrance
of the tent of meeting a lamb in its
first year for a burnt offering, and a
pigeon or a turtledove for a sin offering. 7 He shall offer it before the
LORD, and make atonement on her
behalf; then she shall be clean
from her flow of blood. This is the
law for her who bears a child, male
or female. 8 If she cannot afford a
sheep, she shall take two turtledoves or two pigeons, one for a
burnt offering and the other for a
sin offering; and the priest shall
make atonement on her behalf,
and she shall be clean.

Leprosy, Varieties and Symptoms

13 The LORD spoke to Moses
and Aaron, saying:
2 When a person has on the skin
of his body a swelling or an eruption or a spot, and it turns into a
leprous[i] disease on the skin of his
body, he shall be brought to Aaron
the priest or to one of his sons the
priests. 3 The priest shall examine
the disease on the skin of his body,
and if the hair in the diseased area
has turned white and the disease
appears to be deeper than the skin
of his body, it is a leprous[i] disease;
after the priest has examined him
he shall pronounce him ceremonially unclean. 4 But if the spot is
white in the skin of his body, and
appears no deeper than the skin,
and the hair in it has not turned
white, the priest shall confine the
diseased person for seven days.
5 The priest shall examine him on
the seventh day, and if he sees that
the disease is checked and the disease has not spread in the skin,
then the priest shall confine him
seven days more. 6 The priest shall
examine him again on the seventh
day, and if the disease has abated

11.40 Lev 17.15; 22.8
11.41 v. 29
11.43 Lev 20.25
11.44 Ex 6.7; 19.6; Lev 19.2; 1 Pet 1.15, 16
11.45 Ex 6.7
11.47 Lev 10.10
12.2 Lev 15.19; 18.19
12.3 Gen 17.12
12.6 Lk 2.22
12.8 Lk 2.22-24; Lev 5.7; 4.26
13.2 Deut 24.8
13.4 v. 21
13.6 Lev 11.25; 14.8

[i] A term for several skin diseases; precise meaning uncertain

and the disease has not spread in
the skin, the priest shall pronounce
him clean; it is only an eruption;
and he shall wash his clothes, and
be clean. 7 But if the eruption
spreads in the skin after he has
shown himself to the priest for his
cleansing, he shall appear again
before the priest. 8 The priest shall
make an examination, and if the
eruption has spread in the skin, the
priest shall pronounce him unclean; it is a leprous[j] disease.
9 When a person contracts a
leprous[j] disease, he shall be
brought to the priest. 10 The priest
shall make an examination, and if
there is a white swelling in the skin
that has turned the hair white, and
there is quick raw flesh in the
swelling, 11 it is a chronic leprous[j]
disease in the skin of his body. The
priest shall pronounce him unclean; he shall not confine him, for
he is unclean. 12 But if the disease
breaks out in the skin, so that it
covers all the skin of the diseased
person from head to foot, so far as
the priest can see, 13 then the priest
shall make an examination, and if
the disease has covered all his
body, he shall pronounce him
clean of the disease; since it has all
turned white, he is clean. 14 But if
raw flesh ever appears on him, he
shall be unclean; 15 the priest shall
examine the raw flesh and pronounce him unclean. Raw flesh is
unclean, for it is a leprous[j] disease. 16 But if the raw flesh again
turns white, he shall come to the
priest; 17 the priest shall examine
him, and if the disease has turned
white, the priest shall pronounce
the diseased person clean. He is
clean.
18 When there is on the skin of
one's body a boil that has healed,
19 and in the place of the boil there
appears a white swelling or a
reddish-white spot, it shall be
shown to the priest. 20 The priest
shall make an examination, and if
it appears deeper than the skin and
its hair has turned white, the priest
shall pronounce him unclean; this
is a leprous[j] disease, broken out in
the boil. 21 But if the priest examines it and the hair on it is not
white, nor is it deeper than the skin
but has abated, the priest shall
confine him seven days. 22 If it
spreads in the skin, the priest shall
pronounce him unclean; it is diseased. 23 But if the spot remains in
one place and does not spread, it is
the scar of the boil; the priest shall
pronounce him clean.
24 Or, when the body has a burn
on the skin and the raw flesh of the
burn becomes a spot, reddish-
white or white, 25 the priest shall
examine it. If the hair in the spot
has turned white and it appears
deeper than the skin, it is a leprous[j] disease; it has broken out in
the burn, and the priest shall pronounce him unclean. This is a leprous[j] disease. 26 But if the priest
examines it and the hair in the spot
is not white, and it is no deeper
than the skin but has abated, the
priest shall confine him seven
days. 27 The priest shall examine
him the seventh day; if it is spreading in the skin, the priest shall pronounce him unclean. This is a leprous[j] disease. 28 But if the spot
remains in one place and does not
spread in the skin but has abated,
it is a swelling from the burn, and
the priest shall pronounce him
clean; for it is the scar of the burn.
29 When a man or woman has a
disease on the head or in the beard,
30 the priest shall examine the disease. If it appears deeper than the
skin and the hair in it is yellow and
thin, the priest shall pronounce
him unclean; it is an itch, a leprous[j] disease of the head or the
beard. 31 If the priest examines the
itching disease, and it appears no
deeper than the skin and there is
no black hair in it, the priest shall
confine the person with the itching
disease for seven days. 32 On the
seventh day the priest shall examine the itch; if the itch has not
spread, and there is no yellow hair
in it, and the itch appears to be no

13.7 Lk 5.14
13.10 Num 12.10; 2 Kings 5.27; 2 Chr 26.20
13.12 Lk 5.12
13.15 Mt 8.3
13.18 Ex 9.9
13.19 v. 43
13.21 Num 12.14, 15
13.25 v. 15
13.27 v. 5
13.29 v. 44
13.32 v. 5

[j] A term for several skin diseases; precise meaning uncertain

deeper than the skin, 33 he shall
shave, but the itch he shall not
shave. The priest shall confine the
person with the itch for seven days
more. 34 On the seventh day the
priest shall examine the itch; if the
itch has not spread in the skin and
it appears to be no deeper than the
skin, the priest shall pronounce
him clean. He shall wash his
clothes and be clean. 35 But if the
itch spreads in the skin after he
was pronounced clean, 36 the priest
shall examine him. If the itch has
spread in the skin, the priest need
not seek for the yellow hair; he is
unclean. 37 But if in his eyes the
itch is checked, and black hair has
grown in it, the itch is healed, he is
clean; and the priest shall pronounce him clean.

38 When a man or a woman has
spots on the skin of the body, white
spots, 39 the priest shall make an
examination, and if the spots on
the skin of the body are of a dull
white, it is a rash that has broken
out on the skin; he is clean.

40 If anyone loses the hair from
his head, he is bald but he is clean.
41 If he loses the hair from his forehead and temples, he has baldness
of the forehead but he is clean.
42 But if there is on the bald head or
the bald forehead a reddish-white
diseased spot, it is a leprous[k] disease breaking out on his bald head
or his bald forehead. 43 The priest
shall examine him; if the diseased
swelling is reddish-white on his
bald head or on his bald forehead,
which resembles a leprous[k] disease in the skin of the body, 44 he is
leprous,[k] he is unclean. The priest
shall pronounce him unclean; the
disease is on his head.

45 The person who has the leprous[k] disease shall wear torn
clothes and let the hair of his head
be disheveled; and he shall cover
his upper lip and cry out, "Unclean,
unclean." 46 He shall remain unclean as long as he has the disease;
he is unclean. He shall live alone;
his dwelling shall be outside the
camp.

47 Concerning clothing: when a
leprous[k] disease appears in it, in
woolen or linen cloth, 48 in warp or
woof of linen or wool, or in a skin
or in anything made of skin, 49 if the
disease shows greenish or reddish
in the garment, whether in warp or
woof or in skin or in anything made
of skin, it is a leprous[k] disease and
shall be shown to the priest. 50 The
priest shall examine the disease,
and put the diseased article aside
for seven days. 51 He shall examine
the disease on the seventh day. If
the disease has spread in the cloth,
in warp or woof, or in the skin,
whatever be the use of the skin,
this is a spreading leprous[k] disease; it is unclean. 52 He shall burn
the clothing, whether diseased in
warp or woof, woolen or linen, or
anything of skin, for it is a spreading leprous[k] disease; it shall be
burned in fire.

53 If the priest makes an examination, and the disease has not
spread in the clothing, in warp or
woof or in anything of skin, 54 the
priest shall command them to
wash the article in which the disease appears, and he shall put it
aside seven days more. 55 The priest
shall examine the diseased article
after it has been washed. If the diseased spot has not changed color,
though the disease has not spread,
it is unclean; you shall burn it in
fire, whether the leprous[k] spot is
on the inside or on the outside.

56 If the priest makes an examination, and the disease has abated
after it is washed, he shall tear the
spot out of the cloth, in warp or
woof, or out of skin. 57 If it appears
again in the garment, in warp or
woof, or in anything of skin, it is
spreading; you shall burn with fire
that in which the disease appears.
58 But the cloth, warp or woof, or
anything of skin from which the
disease disappears when you have
washed it, shall then be washed a
second time, and it shall be clean.

59 This is the ritual for a leprous[k] disease in a cloth of wool or

13.34 Lev 14.8 **13.36** v. 30 **13.40** Ezek 29.18 **13.44** v. 29 **13.45** Ezek 24.17, 22; Mic 3.7; Lam 4.15 **13.46** Num 5.2; 12.14; 2 Kings 7.3; 15.5; Lk 17.12

13.51 Lev 14.44 **13.52** Lev 14.44 **13.54** v. 4 **13.56** Lev 14.8

[k] A term for several skin diseases; precise meaning uncertain

linen, either in warp or woof, or in
anything of skin, to decide whether
it is clean or unclean.

Purification of Lepers and Leprous Houses

14 The LORD spoke to Moses,
saying: 2 This shall be the
ritual for the leprous[l] person at
the time of his cleansing:
He shall be brought to the priest;
3 the priest shall go out of the
camp, and the priest shall make an
examination. If the disease is
healed in the leprous[l] person,
4 the priest shall command that two
living clean birds and cedarwood
and crimson yarn and hyssop be
brought for the one who is to be
cleansed. 5 The priest shall command that one of the birds be
slaughtered over fresh water in an
earthen vessel. 6 He shall take the
living bird with the cedarwood and
the crimson yarn and the hyssop,
and dip them and the living bird in
the blood of the bird that was
slaughtered over the fresh water.
7 He shall sprinkle it seven times
upon the one who is to be cleansed
of the leprous[l] disease; then he
shall pronounce him clean, and he
shall let the living bird go into the
open field. 8 The one who is to be
cleansed shall wash his clothes,
and shave off all his hair, and bathe
himself in water, and he shall be
clean. After that he shall come into
the camp, but shall live outside his
tent seven days. 9 On the seventh
day he shall shave all his hair: of
head, beard, eyebrows; he shall
shave all his hair. Then he shall
wash his clothes, and bathe his
body in water, and he shall be
clean.
10 On the eighth day he shall
take two male lambs without blemish, and one ewe lamb in its first
year without blemish, and a grain
offering of three-tenths of an
ephah of choice flour mixed with
oil, and one log[m] of oil. 11 The
priest who cleanses shall set the
person to be cleansed, along with
these things, before the LORD, at
the entrance of the tent of meeting.

14.2 Mt 8.2,4; Mk 1.40,44; Lk 5.12,14; 17.14
14.4 vv. 6,49,51, 52; Num 19.6
14.7 2 Kings 5.10, 14
14.8 Lev 13.6; Num 8.7
14.10 Mt 8.4; Mk 1.44; Lk 5.14
14.12 Lev 5.2,8; 6.6,7; Ex 29.24
14.13 Lev 1.5,11; 6.24-30; 2.3; 7.6
14.14 Lev 8.23
14.18 Lev 4.26
14.19 v. 12
14.21 Lev 5.7,11; 12.8; v. 22
14.22 Lev 12.8; 15.14,15

12 The priest shall take one of the
lambs, and offer it as a guilt offering, along with the log[m] of oil, and
raise them as an elevation offering
before the LORD. 13 He shall slaughter the lamb in the place where the
sin offering and the burnt offering
are slaughtered in the holy place;
for the guilt offering, like the sin
offering, belongs to the priest: it is
most holy. 14 The priest shall take
some of the blood of the guilt offering and put it on the lobe of the
right ear of the one to be cleansed,
and on the thumb of the right
hand, and on the big toe of the
right foot. 15 The priest shall take
some of the log[m] of oil and pour it
into the palm of his own left hand,
16 and dip his right finger in the oil
that is in his left hand and sprinkle
some oil with his finger seven
times before the LORD. 17 Some of
the oil that remains in his hand the
priest shall put on the lobe of the
right ear of the one to be cleansed,
and on the thumb of the right
hand, and on the big toe of the
right foot, on top of the blood of the
guilt offering. 18 The rest of the oil
that is in the priest's hand he shall
put on the head of the one to be
cleansed. Then the priest shall
make atonement on his behalf before the LORD: 19 the priest shall offer the sin offering, to make atonement for the one to be cleansed
from his uncleanness. Afterward he
shall slaughter the burnt offering;
20 and the priest shall offer the
burnt offering and the grain offering on the altar. Thus the priest
shall make atonement on his behalf and he shall be clean.
21 But if he is poor and cannot
afford so much, he shall take one
male lamb for a guilt offering to be
elevated, to make atonement on
his behalf, and one-tenth of an
ephah of choice flour mixed with
oil for a grain offering and a log[m] of
oil; 22 also two turtledoves or two
pigeons, such as he can afford, one
for a sin offering and the other for

[l] A term for several skin diseases; precise meaning uncertain [m] A liquid measure

a burnt offering. 23 On the eighth day he shall bring them for his cleansing to the priest, to the entrance of the tent of meeting, before the LORD; 24 and the priest shall take the lamb of the guilt offering and the log[n] of oil, and the priest shall raise them as an elevation offering before the LORD. 25 The priest shall slaughter the lamb of the guilt offering and shall take some of the blood of the guilt offering, and put it on the lobe of the right ear of the one to be cleansed, and on the thumb of the right hand, and on the big toe of the right foot. 26 The priest shall pour some of the oil into the palm of his own left hand, 27 and shall sprinkle with his right finger some of the oil that is in his left hand seven times before the LORD. 28 The priest shall put some of the oil that is in his hand on the lobe of the right ear of the one to be cleansed, and on the thumb of the right hand, and the big toe of the right foot, where the blood of the guilt offering was placed. 29 The rest of the oil that is in the priest's hand he shall put on the head of the one to be cleansed, to make atonement on his behalf before the LORD. 30 And he shall offer, of the turtledoves or pigeons such as he can afford, 31 one[o] for a sin offering and the other for a burnt offering, along with a grain offering; and the priest shall make atonement before the LORD on behalf of the one being cleansed. 32 This is the ritual for the one who has a leprous[p] disease, who cannot afford the offerings for his cleansing.

33 The LORD spoke to Moses and Aaron, saying:

34 When you come into the land of Canaan, which I give you for a possession, and I put a leprous[p] disease in a house in the land of your possession, 35 the owner of the house shall come and tell the priest, saying, "There seems to me to be some sort of disease in my house." 36 The priest shall command that they empty the house before the priest goes to examine the disease, or all that is in the house will become unclean; and afterward the priest shall go in to inspect the house. 37 He shall examine the disease; if the disease is in the walls of the house with greenish or reddish spots, and if it appears to be deeper than the surface, 38 the priest shall go outside to the door of the house and shut up the house seven days. 39 The priest shall come again on the seventh day and make an inspection; if the disease has spread in the walls of the house, 40 the priest shall command that the stones in which the disease appears be taken out and thrown into an unclean place outside the city. 41 He shall have the inside of the house scraped thoroughly, and the plaster that is scraped off shall be dumped in an unclean place outside the city. 42 They shall take other stones and put them in the place of those stones, and take other plaster and plaster the house.

43 If the disease breaks out again in the house, after he has taken out the stones and scraped the house and plastered it, 44 the priest shall go and make inspection; if the disease has spread in the house, it is a spreading leprous[p] disease in the house; it is unclean. 45 He shall have the house torn down, its stones and timber and all the plaster of the house, and taken outside the city to an unclean place. 46 All who enter the house while it is shut up shall be unclean until the evening; 47 and all who sleep in the house shall wash their clothes; and all who eat in the house shall wash their clothes.

48 If the priest comes and makes an inspection, and the disease has not spread in the house after the house was plastered, the priest shall pronounce the house clean; the disease is healed. 49 For the cleansing of the house he shall take two birds, with cedarwood and crimson yarn and hyssop, 50 and

14.23 vv. 10,11
14.24 v. 12
14.25 v. 14
14.28 Lev 5.6
14.30 v. 22; Lev 15.15
14.31 Lev 5.7
14.34 Gen 17.8; Num 32.22; Deut 7.1
14.35 Ps 91.10; Prov 3.33
14.38 Num 12.15
14.40 v. 45
14.44 Lev 13.51
14.49 v. 4

[n] A liquid measure [o] Gk Syr: Heb *afford*, [31] *such as he can afford, one* [p] A term for several skin diseases; precise meaning uncertain

shall slaughter one of the birds
over fresh water in an earthen vessel, 51 and shall take the cedarwood
and the hyssop and the crimson
yarn, along with the living bird, and
dip them in the blood of the
slaughtered bird and the fresh water, and sprinkle the house seven
times. 52 Thus he shall cleanse the
house with the blood of the bird,
and with the fresh water, and with
the living bird, and with the cedarwood and hyssop and crimson
yarn; 53 and he shall let the living
bird go out of the city into the open
field; so he shall make atonement
for the house, and it shall be clean.
54 This is the ritual for any leprous[q] disease: for an itch, 55 for
leprous[q] diseases in clothing and
houses, 56 and for a swelling or an
eruption or a spot, 57 to determine
when it is unclean and when it is
clean. This is the ritual for leprous[q] diseases.

Concerning Bodily Discharges

15 The LORD spoke to Moses
and Aaron, saying: 2 Speak
to the people of Israel and say to
them:
When any man has a discharge
from his member,[r] his discharge
makes him ceremonially unclean.
3 The uncleanness of his discharge
is this: whether his member[r] flows
with his discharge, or his member[r]
is stopped from discharging, it is
uncleanness for him. 4 Every bed
on which the one with the discharge lies shall be unclean; and
everything on which he sits shall be
unclean. 5 Anyone who touches his
bed shall wash his clothes, and
bathe in water, and be unclean until the evening. 6 All who sit on anything on which the one with the
discharge has sat shall wash their
clothes, and bathe in water, and be
unclean until the evening. 7 All who
touch the body of the one with the
discharge shall wash their clothes,
and bathe in water, and be unclean
until the evening. 8 If the one with
the discharge spits on persons who
are clean, then they shall wash
their clothes, and bathe in water,

14.51 Ps 51.7
14.53 v. 20
14.54 Lev 13.30
14.56 Lev 13.2
15.2 Lev 22.4; Num 5.2; 2 Sam 3.29; Mt 9.20
15.7 Num 19.19
15.10 Num 19.10
15.12 Lev 6.28; 11.32,33
15.13 v. 28
15.14 Lev 14.22, 23
15.15 Lev 14.30, 31
15.16 Lev 22.4; Deut 23.10
15.18 1 Sam 21.4
15.19 Lev 12.2

and be unclean until the evening.
9 Any saddle on which the one with
the discharge rides shall be unclean. 10 All who touch anything
that was under him shall be unclean until the evening, and all
who carry such a thing shall wash
their clothes, and bathe in water,
and be unclean until the evening.
11 All those whom the one with the
discharge touches without his having rinsed his hands in water shall
wash their clothes, and bathe in
water, and be unclean until the
evening. 12 Any earthen vessel that
the one with the discharge touches
shall be broken; and every vessel of
wood shall be rinsed in water.
13 When the one with a discharge is cleansed of his discharge,
he shall count seven days for his
cleansing; he shall wash his
clothes and bathe his body in fresh
water, and he shall be clean. 14 On
the eighth day he shall take two
turtledoves or two pigeons and
come before the LORD to the entrance of the tent of meeting and
give them to the priest. 15 The
priest shall offer them, one for a sin
offering and the other for a burnt
offering; and the priest shall make
atonement on his behalf before the
LORD for his discharge.
16 If a man has an emission of
semen, he shall bathe his whole
body in water, and be unclean until
the evening. 17 Everything made of
cloth or of skin on which the semen
falls shall be washed with water,
and be unclean until the evening.
18 If a man lies with a woman and
has an emission of semen, both of
them shall bathe in water, and be
unclean until the evening.
19 When a woman has a discharge of blood that is her regular
discharge from her body, she shall
be in her impurity for seven days,
and whoever touches her shall be
unclean until the evening. 20 Everything upon which she lies during
her impurity shall be unclean; everything also upon which she sits

[q] A term for several skin diseases; precise meaning uncertain [r] Heb *flesh*

shall be unclean. 21 Whoever
touches her bed shall wash his
clothes, and bathe in water, and be
unclean until the evening. 22 Whoever touches anything upon which
she sits shall wash his clothes, and
bathe in water, and be unclean until the evening; 23 whether it is the
bed or anything upon which she
sits, when he touches it he shall be
unclean until the evening. 24 If any
man lies with her, and her impurity
falls on him, he shall be unclean
seven days; and every bed on which
he lies shall be unclean.

25 If a woman has a discharge of
blood for many days, not at the
time of her impurity, or if she has a
discharge beyond the time of her
impurity, all the days of the discharge she shall continue in uncleanness; as in the days of her impurity, she shall be unclean.
26 Every bed on which she lies during all the days of her discharge
shall be treated as the bed of her
impurity; and everything on which
she sits shall be unclean, as in the
uncleanness of her impurity.
27 Whoever touches these things
shall be unclean, and shall wash
his clothes, and bathe in water, and
be unclean until the evening. 28 If
she is cleansed of her discharge,
she shall count seven days, and after that she shall be clean. 29 On
the eighth day she shall take two
turtledoves or two pigeons and
bring them to the priest to the entrance of the tent of meeting. 30 The
priest shall offer one for a sin offering and the other for a burnt offering; and the priest shall make
atonement on her behalf before the
LORD for her unclean discharge.

31 Thus you shall keep the people of Israel separate from their uncleanness, so that they do not die
in their uncleanness by defiling my
tabernacle that is in their midst.

32 This is the ritual for those
who have a discharge: for him who
has an emission of semen, becoming unclean thereby, 33 for her who
is in the infirmity of her period, for
anyone, male or female, who has a
discharge, and for the man who lies
with a woman who is unclean.

The Day of Atonement

16 The LORD spoke to Moses
after the death of the two
sons of Aaron, when they drew near
before the LORD and died. 2 The
LORD said to Moses:

Tell your brother Aaron not to
come just at any time into the
sanctuary inside the curtain before
the mercy seat[s] that is upon the
ark, or he will die; for I appear in
the cloud upon the mercy seat.[s]
3 Thus shall Aaron come into the
holy place: with a young bull for a
sin offering and a ram for a burnt
offering. 4 He shall put on the holy
linen tunic, and shall have the lin-
en undergarments next to his body,
fasten the linen sash, and wear the
linen turban; these are the holy
vestments. He shall bathe his body
in water, and then put them on.
5 He shall take from the congregation of the people of Israel two
male goats for a sin offering, and
one ram for a burnt offering.

6 Aaron shall offer the bull as a
sin offering for himself, and shall
make atonement for himself and
for his house. 7 He shall take the
two goats and set them before the
LORD at the entrance of the tent of
meeting; 8 and Aaron shall cast lots
on the two goats, one lot for the
LORD and the other lot for Azazel.[t]
9 Aaron shall present the goat on
which the lot fell for the LORD, and
offer it as a sin offering; 10 but the
goat on which the lot fell for Azazel[t] shall be presented alive before
the LORD to make atonement over
it, that it may be sent away into the
wilderness to Azazel.[t]

11 Aaron shall present the bull
as a sin offering for himself, and
shall make atonement for himself
and for his house; he shall slaughter the bull as a sin offering for
himself. 12 He shall take a censer
full of coals of fire from the altar
before the LORD, and two handfuls
of crushed sweet incense, and he

15.21 v. 27
15.24 Lev 20.18
15.25 Mt 9.20; Mk 5.25; Lk 8.43
15.27 v. 21
15.29 Gen 15.9
15.31 Ezek 44.23; Num 5.3; 19.13,20; Ezek 5.11; 23.38
15.32 vv. 2,16
15.33 vv. 19,24,25
16.1 Lev 10.1,2
16.2 Ex 30.10; Heb 9.7; 10.19; Ex 25.21,22
16.3 Heb 9.7,12, 24,25; Lev 4.3
16.4 Ex 28.39, 42,43; v. 24
16.5 Lev 4.13-21
16.6 Lev 9.7; Heb 5.2; 7.27,28; 9.7
16.11 Heb 7.27; 9.7
16.12 Lev 10.1; Ex 30.34

[s] Or *the cover*
[t] Traditionally rendered *a scapegoat*

shall bring it inside the curtain
13 and put the incense on the fire
before the LORD, that the cloud of
the incense may cover the mercy
seat[u] that is upon the covenant,[v]
or he will die. 14 He shall take some
of the blood of the bull, and sprinkle it with his finger on the front of
the mercy seat,[u] and before the
mercy seat[u] he shall sprinkle the
blood with his finger seven times.
15 He shall slaughter the goat of
the sin offering that is for the people and bring its blood inside the
curtain, and do with its blood as he
did with the blood of the bull,
sprinkling it upon the mercy seat[u]
and before the mercy seat.[u]
16 Thus he shall make atonement
for the sanctuary, because of the
uncleannesses of the people of Israel, and because of their transgressions, all their sins; and so he
shall do for the tent of meeting,
which remains with them in the
midst of their uncleannesses. 17 No
one shall be in the tent of meeting
from the time he enters to make
atonement in the sanctuary until
he comes out and has made atonement for himself and for his house
and for all the assembly of Israel.
18 Then he shall go out to the altar
that is before the LORD and make
atonement on its behalf, and shall
take some of the blood of the bull
and of the blood of the goat, and
put it on each of the horns of the
altar. 19 He shall sprinkle some of
the blood on it with his finger seven
times, and cleanse it and hallow it
from the uncleannesses of the people of Israel.
20 When he has finished atoning for the holy place and the tent
of meeting and the altar, he shall
present the live goat. 21 Then Aaron
shall lay both his hands on the
head of the live goat, and confess
over it all the iniquities of the people of Israel, and all their transgressions, all their sins, putting them
on the head of the goat, and sending it away into the wilderness by
means of someone designated for
the task.[w] 22 The goat shall bear on
itself all their iniquities to a barren
region; and the goat shall be set
free in the wilderness.
23 Then Aaron shall enter the
tent of meeting, and shall take off
the linen vestments that he put on
when he went into the holy place,
and shall leave them there. 24 He
shall bathe his body in water in a
holy place, and put on his vestments; then he shall come out and
offer his burnt offering and the
burnt offering of the people, making atonement for himself and for
the people. 25 The fat of the sin offering he shall turn into smoke on
the altar. 26 The one who sets the
goat free for Azazel[x] shall wash his
clothes and bathe his body in water, and afterward may come into
the camp. 27 The bull of the sin offering and the goat of the sin offering, whose blood was brought in to
make atonement in the holy place,
shall be taken outside the camp;
their skin and their flesh and their
dung shall be consumed in fire.
28 The one who burns them shall
wash his clothes and bathe his
body in water, and afterward may
come into the camp.
29 This shall be a statute to you
forever: In the seventh month, on
the tenth day of the month, you
shall deny yourselves,[y] and shall
do no work, neither the citizen nor
the alien who resides among you.
30 For on this day atonement shall
be made for you, to cleanse you;
from all your sins you shall be
clean before the LORD. 31 It is a sabbath of complete rest to you, and
you shall deny yourselves;[y] it is a
statute forever. 32 The priest who is
anointed and consecrated as priest
in his father's place shall make
atonement, wearing the linen vestments, the holy vestments. 33 He
shall make atonement for the sanctuary, and he shall make atonement for the tent of meeting and
for the altar, and he shall make
atonement for the priests and for
all the people of the assembly.

16.13 Lev 22.9
16.14 Heb 9.13, 25; Lev 4.6, 17
16.15 Heb 9.3,7, 12
16.16 Ex 29.36; Heb 2.17
16.18 Lev 4.25; Ezek 43.20, 22
16.19 v. 14
16.21 Isa 53.6
16.22 Isa 53.11,12
16.23 v. 4; Ezek 42.14; 44.19
16.24 vv. 3-5
16.27 Lev 4.12,21; 6.30; Heb 13.11
16.29 Lev 23.27; Num 29.7
16.31 Lev 23.32; Isa 58.3,5
16.32 v. 4; Num 20.26, 28
16.33 vv. 6,16-18, 24

[u] Or *the cover* [v] Or *treaty*, or *testament*; Heb *eduth* [w] Meaning of Heb uncertain
[x] Traditionally rendered *a scapegoat*
[y] Or *shall fast*

34 This shall be an everlasting statute for you, to make atonement for the people of Israel once in the year for all their sins. And Moses did as the LORD had commanded him.

The Slaughtering of Animals

17 The LORD spoke to Moses: 2 Speak to Aaron and his sons and to all the people of Israel and say to them: This is what the LORD has commanded. 3 If anyone of the house of Israel slaughters an ox or a lamb or a goat in the camp, or slaughters it outside the camp, 4 and does not bring it to the entrance of the tent of meeting, to present it as an offering to the LORD before the tabernacle of the LORD, he shall be held guilty of bloodshed; he has shed blood, and he shall be cut off from the people. 5 This is in order that the people of Israel may bring their sacrifices that they offer in the open field, that they may bring them to the LORD, to the priest at the entrance of the tent of meeting, and offer them as sacrifices of well-being to the LORD. 6 The priest shall dash the blood against the altar of the LORD at the entrance of the tent of meeting, and turn the fat into smoke as a pleasing odor to the LORD, 7 so that they may no longer offer their sacrifices for goat-demons, to whom they prostitute themselves. This shall be a statute forever to them throughout their generations.

8 And say to them further: Anyone of the house of Israel or of the aliens who reside among them who offers a burnt offering or sacrifice, 9 and does not bring it to the entrance of the tent of meeting, to sacrifice it to the LORD, shall be cut off from the people.

Eating Blood Prohibited

10 If anyone of the house of Israel or of the aliens who reside among them eats any blood, I will set my face against that person who eats blood, and will cut that person off from the people. 11 For the life of the flesh is in the blood; and I have given it to you for making atonement for your lives on the altar; for, as life, it is the blood that makes atonement. 12 Therefore I have said to the people of Israel: No person among you shall eat blood, nor shall any alien who resides among you eat blood. 13 And anyone of the people of Israel, or of the aliens who reside among them, who hunts down an animal or bird that may be eaten shall pour out its blood and cover it with earth.

14 For the life of every creature—its blood is its life; therefore I have said to the people of Israel: You shall not eat the blood of any creature, for the life of every creature is its blood; whoever eats it shall be cut off. 15 All persons, citizens or aliens, who eat what dies of itself or what has been torn by wild animals, shall wash their clothes, and bathe themselves in water, and be unclean until the evening; then they shall be clean. 16 But if they do not wash themselves or bathe their body, they shall bear their guilt.

Sexual Relations

18 The LORD spoke to Moses, saying:

2 Speak to the people of Israel and say to them: I am the LORD your God. 3 You shall not do as they do in the land of Egypt, where you lived, and you shall not do as they do in the land of Canaan, to which I am bringing you. You shall not follow their statutes. 4 My ordinances you shall observe and my statutes you shall keep, following them: I am the LORD your God. 5 You shall keep my statutes and my ordinances; by doing so one shall live: I am the LORD.

6 None of you shall approach anyone near of kin to uncover nakedness: I am the LORD. 7 You shall not uncover the nakedness of your father, which is the nakedness of your mother; she is your mother, you shall not uncover her nakedness. 8 You shall not uncover the nakedness of your father's wife; it is the nakedness of your father.

16.34 Heb 9.7,25
17.4 Deut 12.5-21; Rom 5.13
17.6 Lev 3.2; Num 18.17
17.7 Ex 22.20; 32.8; 34.15; Deut 32.17; 2 Chr 11.15
17.9 v. 4
17.10 Lev 3.17; Deut 12.16, 23
17.11 v. 14; Gen 9.4; Heb 9.22
17.13 Lev 7.26; Deut 12.16
17.14 v. 11
17.15 Ex 22.31; Deut 14.21
18.2 Ex 6.7; Lev 11.44
18.3 Ezek 20.7,8; Ex 23.24; Lev 20.23
18.5 Ezek 20.11; Lk 10.28; Rom 10.5; Gal 3.12
18.7 Lev 20.11

9 You shall not uncover the nakedness of your sister, your father's
daughter or your mother's daughter, whether born at home or born
abroad. 10 You shall not uncover
the nakedness of your son's daughter or of your daughter's daughter,
for their nakedness is your own nakedness. 11 You shall not uncover
the nakedness of your father's
wife's daughter, begotten by your
father, since she is your sister.
12 You shall not uncover the nakedness of your father's sister; she is
your father's flesh. 13 You shall not
uncover the nakedness of your
mother's sister, for she is your
mother's flesh. 14 You shall not uncover the nakedness of your father's brother, that is, you shall not
approach his wife; she is your aunt.
15 You shall not uncover the nakedness of your daughter-in-law: she is
your son's wife; you shall not uncover her nakedness. 16 You shall
not uncover the nakedness of your
brother's wife; it is your brother's
nakedness. 17 You shall not uncover the nakedness of a woman and
her daughter, and you shall not
take[z] her son's daughter or her
daughter's daughter to uncover her
nakedness; they are your[a] flesh; it
is depravity. 18 And you shall not
take[z] a woman as a rival to her sister, uncovering her nakedness
while her sister is still alive.

19 You shall not approach a
woman to uncover her nakedness
while she is in her menstrual uncleanness. 20 You shall not have
sexual relations with your kinsman's wife, and defile yourself with
her. 21 You shall not give any of your
offspring to sacrifice them[b] to Molech, and so profane the name of
your God: I am the LORD. 22 You
shall not lie with a male as with a
woman; it is an abomination.
23 You shall not have sexual relations with any animal and defile
yourself with it, nor shall any woman give herself to an animal to have
sexual relations with it: it is perversion.

24 Do not defile yourselves in
any of these ways, for by all these
practices the nations I am casting
out before you have defiled themselves. 25 Thus the land became defiled; and I punished it for its iniquity, and the land vomited out its
inhabitants. 26 But you shall keep
my statutes and my ordinances and
commit none of these abominations, either the citizen or the alien
who resides among you 27 (for the
inhabitants of the land, who were
before you, committed all of these
abominations, and the land became defiled); 28 otherwise the
land will vomit you out for defiling
it, as it vomited out the nation that
was before you. 29 For whoever
commits any of these abominations shall be cut off from their
people. 30 So keep my charge not to
commit any of these abominations
that were done before you, and not
to defile yourselves by them: I am
the LORD your God.

Ritual and Moral Holiness

19 The LORD spoke to Moses,
saying:
2 Speak to all the congregation
of the people of Israel and say to
them: You shall be holy, for I the
LORD your God am holy. 3 You shall
each revere your mother and father, and you shall keep my sabbaths: I am the LORD your God. 4 Do
not turn to idols or make cast images for yourselves: I am the LORD
your God.

5 When you offer a sacrifice of
well-being to the LORD, offer it in
such a way that it is acceptable on
your behalf. 6 It shall be eaten on
the same day you offer it, or on the
next day; and anything left over until the third day shall be consumed
in fire. 7 If it is eaten at all on the
third day, it is an abomination; it
will not be acceptable. 8 All who eat
it shall be subject to punishment,
because they have profaned what is
holy to the LORD; and any such person shall be cut off from the people.

9 When you reap the harvest of
your land, you shall not reap to the

18.9 Lev 20.17
18.12 Lev 20.19
18.14 Lev 20.20
18.15 Lev 20.12
18.16 Lev 20.21
18.17 Lev 20.14
18.19 Lev 15.24; 20.18
18.20 Lev 20.10; Ex 20.14; Prov 6.32; Mt 5.27
18.21 Lev 20.2-5; 19.12; 21.6
18.22 Lev 20.13; Rom 1.27
18.23 Ex 22.19; Lev 20.15; Deut 27.21
18.24 v. 3; Lev 20.23
18.25 Lev 20.23; Deut 9.5; 18.12; v. 28
18.30 Lev 22.9; Deut 11.1; v. 2
19.2 1 Pet 1.16
19.3 Ex 20.8,12; Lev 11.44
19.4 Lev 26.1; Ps 96.5; Ex 20.23; 34.17
19.9 Lev 23.22; Deut 24.20-22

[z] Or *marry* [a] Gk: Heb lacks *your*
[b] Heb *to pass them over*

very edges of your field, or gather the gleanings of your harvest. 10You shall not strip your vineyard bare, or gather the fallen grapes of your vineyard; you shall leave them for the poor and the alien: I am the LORD your God.

11 You shall not steal; you shall not deal falsely; and you shall not lie to one another. 12And you shall not swear falsely by my name, profaning the name of your God: I am the LORD.

13 You shall not defraud your neighbor; you shall not steal; and you shall not keep for yourself the wages of a laborer until morning. 14You shall not revile the deaf or put a stumbling block before the blind; you shall fear your God: I am the LORD.

15 You shall not render an unjust judgment; you shall not be partial to the poor or defer to the great: with justice you shall judge your neighbor. 16You shall not go around as a slanderer[c] among your people, and you shall not profit by the blood[d] of your neighbor: I am the LORD.

17 You shall not hate in your heart anyone of your kin; you shall reprove your neighbor, or you will incur guilt yourself. 18You shall not take vengeance or bear a grudge against any of your people, but you shall love your neighbor as yourself: I am the LORD.

19 You shall keep my statutes. You shall not let your animals breed with a different kind; you shall not sow your field with two kinds of seed; nor shall you put on a garment made of two different materials.

20 If a man has sexual relations with a woman who is a slave, designated for another man but not ransomed or given her freedom, an inquiry shall be held. They shall not be put to death, since she has not been freed; 21but he shall bring a guilt offering for himself to the LORD, at the entrance of the tent of meeting, a ram as guilt offering. 22And the priest shall make atonement for him with the ram of guilt offering before the LORD for his sin that he committed; and the sin he committed shall be forgiven him.

23 When you come into the land and plant all kinds of trees for food, then you shall regard their fruit as forbidden;[e] three years it shall be forbidden[f] to you, it must not be eaten. 24In the fourth year all their fruit shall be set apart for rejoicing in the LORD. 25But in the fifth year you may eat of their fruit, that their yield may be increased for you: I am the LORD your God.

26 You shall not eat anything with its blood. You shall not practice augury or witchcraft. 27You shall not round off the hair on your temples or mar the edges of your beard. 28You shall not make any gashes in your flesh for the dead or tattoo any marks upon you: I am the LORD.

29 Do not profane your daughter by making her a prostitute, that the land not become prostituted and full of depravity. 30You shall keep my sabbaths and reverence my sanctuary: I am the LORD.

31 Do not turn to mediums or wizards; do not seek them out, to be defiled by them: I am the LORD your God.

32 You shall rise before the aged, and defer to the old; and you shall fear your God: I am the LORD.

33 When an alien resides with you in your land, you shall not oppress the alien. 34The alien who resides with you shall be to you as the citizen among you; you shall love the alien as yourself, for you were aliens in the land of Egypt: I am the LORD your God.

35 You shall not cheat in measuring length, weight, or quantity. 36You shall have honest balances, honest weights, an honest ephah, and an honest hin: I am the LORD your God, who brought you out of the land of Egypt. 37You shall keep all my statutes and all my ordinances, and observe them: I am the LORD.

19.11 Ex 20.15; Lev 6.2; Eph 4.25; Col 3.9
19.12 Ex 20.7; Lev 18.21
19.13 Ex 22.7-15; 21-27; Deut 24.15; Jas 5.4
19.14 Deut 27.18
19.15 Ex 23.6; Deut 1.17
19.16 Ps 15.3; Ezek 22.9; Ex 23.7
19.17 1 Jn 2.9, 11; 3.15; Lk 17.3; Gal 6.1
19.18 Rom 12.19; Ps 103.9; Mt 19.19; Mk 12.31; Rom 13.9
19.19 Deut 22.9, 11
19.21 Lev 5.15
19.24 Deut 12.17, 18; Prov 3.9
19.26 Lev 17.10; Deut 18.10
19.27 Lev 21.5
19.28 Lev 21.5
19.29 Deut 23.17
19.30 v. 3; Lev 26.2
19.31 Lev 20.6,27; Deut 18.10, 11
19.33 Ex 22.21
19.34 Ex 12.48, 49; Deut 10.19

[c] Meaning of Heb uncertain [d] Heb *stand against the blood* [e] Heb *as their uncircumcision* [f] Heb *uncircumcision*

Penalties for Violations of Holiness

20 The LORD spoke to Moses, saying: 2 Say further to the people of Israel:

Any of the people of Israel, or of the aliens who reside in Israel, who give any of their offspring to Molech shall be put to death; the people of the land shall stone them to death. 3 I myself will set my face against them, and will cut them off from the people, because they have given of their offspring to Molech, defiling my sanctuary and profaning my holy name. 4 And if the people of the land should ever close their eyes to them, when they give of their offspring to Molech, and do not put them to death, 5 I myself will set my face against them and against their family, and will cut them off from among their people, them and all who follow them in prostituting themselves to Molech.

6 If any turn to mediums and wizards, prostituting themselves to them, I will set my face against them, and will cut them off from the people. 7 Consecrate yourselves therefore, and be holy; for I am the LORD your God. 8 Keep my statutes, and observe them; I am the LORD; I sanctify you. 9 All who curse father or mother shall be put to death; having cursed father or mother, their blood is upon them.

10 If a man commits adultery with the wife of[g] his neighbor, both the adulterer and the adulteress shall be put to death. 11 The man who lies with his father's wife has uncovered his father's nakedness; both of them shall be put to death; their blood is upon them. 12 If a man lies with his daughter-in-law, both of them shall be put to death; they have committed perversion, their blood is upon them. 13 If a man lies with a male as with a woman, both of them have committed an abomination; they shall be put to death; their blood is upon them. 14 If a man takes a wife and her mother also, it is depravity; they shall be burned to death, both he and they, that there may be no depravity among you. 15 If a man has sexual relations with an animal, he shall be put to death; and you shall kill the animal. 16 If a woman approaches any animal and has sexual relations with it, you shall kill the woman and the animal; they shall be put to death, their blood is upon them.

17 If a man takes his sister, a daughter of his father or a daughter of his mother, and sees her nakedness, and she sees his nakedness, it is a disgrace, and they shall be cut off in the sight of their people; he has uncovered his sister's nakedness, he shall be subject to punishment. 18 If a man lies with a woman having her sickness and uncovers her nakedness, he has laid bare her flow and she has laid bare her flow of blood; both of them shall be cut off from their people. 19 You shall not uncover the nakedness of your mother's sister or of your father's sister, for that is to lay bare one's own flesh; they shall be subject to punishment. 20 If a man lies with his uncle's wife, he has uncovered his uncle's nakedness; they shall be subject to punishment; they shall die childless. 21 If a man takes his brother's wife, it is impurity; he has uncovered his brother's nakedness; they shall be childless.

22 You shall keep all my statutes and all my ordinances, and observe them, so that the land to which I bring you to settle in may not vomit you out. 23 You shall not follow the practices of the nation that I am driving out before you. Because they did all these things, I abhorred them. 24 But I have said to you: You shall inherit their land, and I will give it to you to possess, a land flowing with milk and honey. I am the LORD your God; I have separated you from the peoples. 25 You shall therefore make a distinction between the clean animal and the unclean, and between the unclean bird and the clean; you

20.2 Lev 18.21
20.3 Lev 15.31; 18.21
20.4 Deut 17.2,3, 5
20.6 Lev 19.31
20.7 1 Pet 1.16
20.8 Lev 19.37; Ex 31.13
20.9 Ex 21.17; Deut 27.16
20.10 Lev 18.20; Deut 22.22
20.11 Lev 18.7,8
20.12 Lev 18.15
20.13 Lev 18.22
20.14 Deut 27.23
20.15 Lev 18.23
20.17 Lev 18.9
20.18 Lev 18.19
20.19 Lev 18.12, 13
20.20 Lev 18.14
20.21 Lev 18.16
20.22 Lev 18.25, 26,28
20.23 Lev 18.3,24, 27,30
20.24 Ex 13.5; 33.3,16; v. 26
20.25 Lev 11.1-47; Deut 14.3-21

[g] Heb repeats *if a man commits adultery with the wife of*

shall not bring abomination on yourselves by animal or by bird or by anything with which the ground teems, which I have set apart for you to hold unclean. 26 You shall be holy to me; for I the LORD am holy, and I have separated you from the other peoples to be mine.

27 A man or a woman who is a medium or a wizard shall be put to death; they shall be stoned to death, their blood is upon them.

The Holiness of Priests

21 The LORD said to Moses: Speak to the priests, the sons of Aaron, and say to them:

No one shall defile himself for a dead person among his relatives, 2 except for his nearest kin: his mother, his father, his son, his daughter, his brother; 3 likewise, for a virgin sister, close to him because she has had no husband, he may defile himself for her. 4 But he shall not defile himself as a husband among his people and so profane himself. 5 They shall not make bald spots upon their heads, or shave off the edges of their beards, or make any gashes in their flesh. 6 They shall be holy to their God, and not profane the name of their God; for they offer the LORD's offerings by fire, the food of their God; therefore they shall be holy. 7 They shall not marry a prostitute or a woman who has been defiled; neither shall they marry a woman divorced from her husband. For they are holy to their God, 8 and you shall treat them as holy, since they offer the food of your God; they shall be holy to you, for I the LORD, I who sanctify you, am holy. 9 When the daughter of a priest profanes herself through prostitution, she profanes her father; she shall be burned to death.

10 The priest who is exalted above his fellows, on whose head the anointing oil has been poured and who has been consecrated to wear the vestments, shall not dishevel his hair, nor tear his vestments. 11 He shall not go where there is a dead body; he shall not defile himself even for his father or mother. 12 He shall not go outside the sanctuary and thus profane the sanctuary of his God; for the consecration of the anointing oil of his God is upon him: I am the LORD. 13 He shall marry only a woman who is a virgin. 14 A widow, or a divorced woman, or a woman who has been defiled, a prostitute, these he shall not marry. He shall marry a virgin of his own kin, 15 that he may not profane his offspring among his kin; for I am the LORD; I sanctify him.

16 The LORD spoke to Moses, saying: 17 Speak to Aaron and say: No one of your offspring throughout their generations who has a blemish may approach to offer the food of his God. 18 For no one who has a blemish shall draw near, one who is blind or lame, or one who has a mutilated face or a limb too long, 19 or one who has a broken foot or a broken hand, 20 or a hunchback, or a dwarf, or a man with a blemish in his eyes or an itching disease or scabs or crushed testicles. 21 No descendant of Aaron the priest who has a blemish shall come near to offer the LORD's offerings by fire; since he has a blemish, he shall not come near to offer the food of his God. 22 He may eat the food of his God, of the most holy as well as of the holy. 23 But he shall not come near the curtain or approach the altar, because he has a blemish, that he may not profane my sanctuaries; for I am the LORD; I sanctify them. 24 Thus Moses spoke to Aaron and to his sons and to all the people of Israel.

The Use of Holy Offerings

22 The LORD spoke to Moses, saying: 2 Direct Aaron and his sons to deal carefully with the sacred donations of the people of Israel, which they dedicate to me, so that they may not profane my holy name; I am the LORD. 3 Say to them: If anyone among all your offspring throughout your generations comes near the sacred donations, which the people of Israel

20.26 v. 24
20.27 Lev 19.31
21.1 Lev 19.28; Ezek 44.25
21.5 Deut 14.1; Ezek 44.20; Lev 19.27
21.6 Lev 18.21; 3.11
21.7 vv. 13,14
21.10 Lev 16.32; 10.6,7
21.11 Lev 19.28
21.12 Lev 10.7; Ex 29.6,7
21.13 v. 7; Ezek 44.22
21.17ff v. 6
21.18 Lev 22.23
21.20 Deut 23.1
21.21 v. 6
21.23 v. 12
22.3 Lev 7.20

dedicate to the LORD, while he is in
a state of uncleanness, that person
shall be cut off from my presence:
I am the LORD. 4 No one of Aaron's
offspring who has a leprous[h] disease or suffers a discharge may eat
of the sacred donations until he is
clean. Whoever touches anything
made unclean by a corpse or a man
who has had an emission of semen,
5 and whoever touches any swarming thing by which he may be made
unclean or any human being by
whom he may be made unclean—
whatever his uncleanness may
be— 6 the person who touches any
such shall be unclean until evening
and shall not eat of the sacred donations unless he has washed his
body in water. 7 When the sun sets
he shall be clean; and afterward he
may eat of the sacred donations,
for they are his food. 8 That which
died or was torn by wild animals he
shall not eat, becoming unclean by
it: I am the LORD. 9 They shall keep
my charge, so that they may not incur guilt and die in the sanctuary[i]
for having profaned it: I am the
LORD; I sanctify them.

10 No lay person shall eat of the
sacred donations. No bound or
hired servant of the priest shall eat
of the sacred donations; 11 but if a
priest acquires anyone by purchase, the person may eat of them;
and those that are born in his
house may eat of his food. 12 If a
priest's daughter marries a layman,
she shall not eat of the offering of
the sacred donations; 13 but if a
priest's daughter is widowed or divorced, without offspring, and returns to her father's house, as in
her youth, she may eat of her father's food. No lay person shall eat
of it. 14 If a man eats of the sacred
donation unintentionally, he shall
add one-fifth of its value to it, and
give the sacred donation to the
priest. 15 No one shall profane the
sacred donations of the people of
Israel, which they offer to the LORD,
16 causing them to bear guilt requir-
ing a guilt offering, by eating their
sacred donations: for I am the
LORD; I sanctify them.

22.4 Lev 14.1-32; Num 19.11, 12; 15.16,17
22.5 Lev 11.24, 43,44; 15.7, 19
22.8 Ex 22.31; Lev 17.15
22.9 Lev 18.30; v. 16
22.10 v. 13
22.13 v. 10
22.14 Lev 5.15,16
22.16 v. 9

Acceptable Offerings

17 The LORD spoke to Moses,
saying: 18 Speak to Aaron and his
sons and all the people of Israel
and say to them: When anyone of
the house of Israel or of the aliens
residing in Israel presents an offering, whether in payment of a vow or
as a freewill offering that is offered
to the LORD as a burnt offering, 19 to
be acceptable in your behalf it
shall be a male without blemish, of
the cattle or the sheep or the goats.
20 You shall not offer anything that
has a blemish, for it will not be acceptable in your behalf.

21 When anyone offers a sacrifice of well-being to the LORD, in
fulfillment of a vow or as a freewill
offering, from the herd or from the
flock, to be acceptable it must be
perfect; there shall be no blemish
in it. 22 Anything blind, or injured,
or maimed, or having a discharge or
an itch or scabs—these you shall
not offer to the LORD or put any of
them on the altar as offerings by
fire to the LORD. 23 An ox or a lamb
that has a limb too long or too short
you may present for a freewill offering; but it will not be accepted for
a vow. 24 Any animal that has its
testicles bruised or crushed or torn
or cut, you shall not offer to the
LORD; such you shall not do within
your land, 25 nor shall you accept
any such animals from a foreigner
to offer as food to your God; since
they are mutilated, with a blemish
in them, they shall not be accepted
in your behalf.

26 The LORD spoke to Moses,
saying: 27 When an ox or a sheep or
a goat is born, it shall remain seven
days with its mother, and from the
eighth day on it shall be acceptable
as the LORD's offering by fire. 28 But
you shall not slaughter, from the
herd or the flock, an animal with its
young on the same day. 29 When
you sacrifice a thanksgiving offering to the LORD, you shall sacrifice
it so that it may be acceptable in

22.19 Lev 1.3
22.20 Deut 15.21; 17.1; Heb 9.14; 1 Pet 1.19
22.21 Lev 3.1,6
22.25 Lev 21.6,17
22.27 Ex 22.30
22.28 Deut 22.6,7
22.29 Lev 7.12

[h] A term for several skin diseases; precise meaning uncertain [i] Vg: Heb *incur guilt for it and die in it*

your behalf. 30 It shall be eaten on
the same day; you shall not leave
any of it until morning: I am the
LORD.
31 Thus you shall keep my commandments and observe them: I
am the LORD. 32 You shall not profane my holy name, that I may be
sanctified among the people of Israel: I am the LORD; I sanctify you,
33 I who brought you out of the land
of Egypt to be your God: I am the
LORD.

Appointed Festivals

23 The LORD spoke to Moses,
saying: 2 Speak to the people of Israel and say to them: These
are the appointed festivals of the
LORD that you shall proclaim as
holy convocations, my appointed
festivals.

The Sabbath, Passover, and Unleavened Bread

3 Six days shall work be done;
but the seventh day is a sabbath of
complete rest, a holy convocation;
you shall do no work: it is a sabbath
to the LORD throughout your settlements.
4 These are the appointed festivals of the LORD, the holy convocations, which you shall celebrate at
the time appointed for them. 5 In
the first month, on the fourteenth
day of the month, at twilight,[j]
there shall be a passover offering to
the LORD, 6 and on the fifteenth day
of the same month is the festival of
unleavened bread to the LORD; sev-
en days you shall eat unleavened
bread. 7 On the first day you shall
have a holy convocation; you shall
not work at your occupations. 8 For
seven days you shall present the
LORD's offerings by fire; on the seventh day there shall be a holy convocation: you shall not work at your
occupations.

The Offering of First Fruits

9 The LORD spoke to Moses:
10 Speak to the people of Israel and
say to them: When you enter the
land that I am giving you and you
reap its harvest, you shall bring the
sheaf of the first fruits of your harvest to the priest. 11 He shall raise
the sheaf before the LORD, that you
may find acceptance; on the day after the sabbath the priest shall
raise it. 12 On the day when you
raise the sheaf, you shall offer a
lamb a year old, without blemish,
as a burnt offering to the LORD.
13 And the grain offering with it
shall be two-tenths of an ephah of
choice flour mixed with oil, an offering by fire of pleasing odor to the
LORD; and the drink offering with it
shall be of wine, one-fourth of a
hin. 14 You shall eat no bread or
parched grain or fresh ears until
that very day, until you have
brought the offering of your God: it
is a statute forever throughout your
generations in all your settlements.

The Festival of Weeks

15 And from the day after the
sabbath, from the day on which
you bring the sheaf of the elevation
offering, you shall count off seven
weeks; they shall be complete.
16 You shall count until the day after the seventh sabbath, fifty days;
then you shall present an offering
of new grain to the LORD. 17 You
shall bring from your settlements
two loaves of bread as an elevation
offering, each made of two-tenths
of an ephah; they shall be of choice
flour, baked with leaven, as first
fruits to the LORD. 18 You shall
present with the bread seven lambs
a year old without blemish, one
young bull, and two rams; they
shall be a burnt offering to the
LORD, along with their grain offering and their drink offerings, an offering by fire of pleasing odor to the
LORD. 19 You shall also offer one
male goat for a sin offering, and
two male lambs a year old as a sacrifice of well-being. 20 The priest
shall raise them with the bread of
the first fruits as an elevation offering before the LORD, together with
the two lambs; they shall be holy to
the LORD for the priest. 21 On that
same day you shall make proclamation; you shall hold a holy convocation; you shall not work at your

22.30 Lev 7.15
22.31 Lev 19.37
22.32 Lev 18.21; 10.3
22.33 Ex 6.7; Lev 11.45
23.2 vv. 4,37,44; Num 29.39
23.3 Lev 19.3; Ex 31.13-17; Deut 5.13
23.4 v. 2
23.5 Ex 12.18, 19; Num 28.16, 17
23.8 vv. 8,21,25, 35,36
23.10 Ex 23.16, 19; 34.22,26
23.13 Lev 2.14-16
23.15 Deut 16.9
23.16 Num 28.26
23.17 Lev 2.12; 7.13
23.19 Num 28.30; Lev 3.1
23.21 v. 7

[j] Heb *between the two evenings*

occupations. This is a statute forever in all your settlements
throughout your generations.
22 When you reap the harvest of
your land, you shall not reap to the
very edges of your field, or gather
the gleanings of your harvest; you
shall leave them for the poor and
for the alien: I am the LORD your
God.

The Festival of Trumpets

23 The LORD spoke to Moses,
saying: 24 Speak to the people of Israel, saying: In the seventh month,
on the first day of the month, you
shall observe a day of complete
rest, a holy convocation commem-
orated with trumpet blasts. 25 You
shall not work at your occupations;
and you shall present the LORD's offering by fire.

The Day of Atonement

26 The LORD spoke to Moses,
saying: 27 Now, the tenth day of this
seventh month is the day of atonement; it shall be a holy convocation
for you: you shall deny yourselves[k]
and present the LORD's offering by
fire; 28 and you shall do no work
during that entire day; for it is a day
of atonement, to make atonement
on your behalf before the LORD your
God. 29 For anyone who does not
practice self-denial[l] during that
entire day shall be cut off from the
people. 30 And anyone who does
any work during that entire day,
such a one I will destroy from the
midst of the people. 31 You shall do
no work: it is a statute forever
throughout your generations in all
your settlements. 32 It shall be to
you a sabbath of complete rest, and
you shall deny yourselves;[k] on the
ninth day of the month at evening,
from evening to evening you shall
keep your sabbath.

The Festival of Booths

33 The LORD spoke to Moses,
saying: 34 Speak to the people of Israel, saying: On the fifteenth day of
this seventh month, and lasting
seven days, there shall be the festival of booths[m] to the LORD. 35 The
first day shall be a holy convocation; you shall not work at your occupations. 36 Seven days you shall
present the LORD's offerings by fire;
on the eighth day you shall observe
a holy convocation and present the
LORD's offerings by fire; it is a solemn assembly; you shall not work
at your occupations.
37 These are the appointed festivals of the LORD, which you shall
celebrate as times of holy convocation, for presenting to the LORD offerings by fire—burnt offerings and
grain offerings, sacrifices and drink
offerings, each on its proper day—
38 apart from the sabbaths of the
LORD, and apart from your gifts, and
apart from all your votive offerings,
and apart from all your freewill offerings, which you give to the LORD.
39 Now, the fifteenth day of the
seventh month, when you have
gathered in the produce of the
land, you shall keep the festival of
the LORD, lasting seven days; a complete rest on the first day, and a
complete rest on the eighth day.
40 On the first day you shall take the
fruit of majestic[n] trees, branches
of palm trees, boughs of leafy trees,
and willows of the brook; and you
shall rejoice before the LORD your
God for seven days. 41 You shall
keep it as a festival to the LORD sev-
en days in the year; you shall keep
it in the seventh month as a statute
forever throughout your generations. 42 You shall live in booths for
seven days; all that are citizens in
Israel shall live in booths, 43 so that
your generations may know that I
made the people of Israel live in
booths when I brought them out of
the land of Egypt: I am the LORD
your God.
44 Thus Moses declared to the
people of Israel the appointed festivals of the LORD.

The Lamp

24 The LORD spoke to Moses,
saying: 2 Command the
people of Israel to bring you pure
oil of beaten olives for the lamp,

23.22 Lev 19.9
23.24 Num 29.1; Lev 25.9
23.27 Lev 16.29, 30
23.29 Gen 17.14
23.30 Lev 20.3,5,6
23.34 Ex 23.16; Num 29.12; vv. 42,43
23.36 Num 29.12-38
23.37 vv. 2,4
23.39 Ex 23.16; Deut 16.13
23.40 Neh 8.15; Deut 16.14, 15
23.42 Neh 8.14-16
23.44 vv. 2,37
24.2 Ex 27.20,21

[k] Or *shall fast* [l] Or *does not fast*
[m] Or *tabernacles*: Heb *succoth* [n] Meaning of Heb uncertain

that a light may be kept burning
regularly. 3 Aaron shall set it up in
the tent of meeting, outside the
curtain of the covenant,[o] to burn
from evening to morning before the
LORD regularly; it shall be a statute
forever throughout your generations. 4 He shall set up the lamps
on the lampstand of pure gold[p] before the LORD regularly.

The Bread for the Tabernacle

5 You shall take choice flour,
and bake twelve loaves of it; two-
tenths of an ephah shall be in each
loaf. 6 You shall place them in two
rows, six in a row, on the table of
pure gold.[q] 7 You shall put pure
frankincense with each row, to be a
token offering for the bread, as an
offering by fire to the LORD. 8 Every
sabbath day Aaron shall set them
in order before the LORD regularly
as a commitment of the people of
Israel, as a covenant forever. 9 They
shall be for Aaron and his descendants, who shall eat them in a holy
place, for they are most holy portions for him from the offerings by
fire to the LORD, a perpetual due.

Blasphemy and Its Punishment

10 A man whose mother was an
Israelite and whose father was an
Egyptian came out among the people of Israel; and the Israelite woman's son and a certain Israelite began fighting in the camp. 11 The
Israelite woman's son blasphemed
the Name in a curse. And they
brought him to Moses—now his
mother's name was Shelomith,
daughter of Dibri, of the tribe of
Dan— 12 and they put him in custody, until the decision of the LORD
should be made clear to them.

13 The LORD said to Moses, saying: 14 Take the blasphemer outside
the camp; and let all who were
within hearing lay their hands on
his head, and let the whole congregation stone him. 15 And speak to
the people of Israel, saying: Anyone
who curses God shall bear the sin.
16 One who blasphemes the name
of the LORD shall be put to death;
the whole congregation shall stone
the blasphemer. Aliens as well as
citizens, when they blaspheme the
Name, shall be put to death. 17 Anyone who kills a human being shall
be put to death. 18 Anyone who kills
an animal shall make restitution
for it, life for life. 19 Anyone who
maims another shall suffer the
same injury in return: 20 fracture for
fracture, eye for eye, tooth for
tooth; the injury inflicted is the injury to be suffered. 21 One who kills
an animal shall make restitution
for it; but one who kills a human
being shall be put to death. 22 You
shall have one law for the alien and
for the citizen: for I am the LORD
your God. 23 Moses spoke thus to
the people of Israel; and they took
the blasphemer outside the camp,
and stoned him to death. The people of Israel did as the LORD had
commanded Moses.

The Sabbatical Year

25 The LORD spoke to Moses
on Mount Sinai, saying:
2 Speak to the people of Israel and
say to them: When you enter the
land that I am giving you, the land
shall observe a sabbath for the
LORD. 3 Six years you shall sow your
field, and six years you shall prune
your vineyard, and gather in their
yield; 4 but in the seventh year
there shall be a sabbath of complete rest for the land, a sabbath for
the LORD: you shall not sow your
field or prune your vineyard. 5 You
shall not reap the aftergrowth of
your harvest or gather the grapes of
your unpruned vine: it shall be a
year of complete rest for the land.
6 You may eat what the land yields
during its sabbath—you, your male
and female slaves, your hired and
your bound laborers who live with
you; 7 for your livestock also, and
for the wild animals in your land all
its yield shall be for food.

The Year of Jubilee

8 You shall count off seven
weeks[r] of years, seven times seven

24.4 Ex 31.8; 39.37
24.5 Ex 25.30
24.6 Ex 25.24; 1 Kings 7.48
24.8 Num 4.7; 1 Chr 9.32; 2 Chr 2.4
24.9 Mt 12.4; Mk 2.26; Lk 6.4; Lev 8.31
24.11 v. 16
24.12 Num 15.34; Ex 18.15,16
24.14 Deut 13.9; 17.7; Lev 20.2,27; Deut 21.21
24.16 1 Kings 21.10, 13; Mt 12.31; Mk 3.28
24.17 Ex 21.12; Num 35.30, 31; Deut 19.11, 12
24.18 v. 21
24.20 Ex 21.23, 24; Deut 19.21; Mt 5.38
24.21 vv. 17,18
24.22 Ex 12.49; Num 15.16
25.2 Ex 23.10,11
25.6 vv. 20,21

[o] Or *treaty*, or *testament*; Heb *eduth*
[p] Heb *pure lampstand* [q] Heb *pure table*
[r] Or *sabbaths*

years, so that the period of seven
weeks of years gives forty-nine
years. 9 Then you shall have the
trumpet sounded loud; on the
tenth day of the seventh month—
on the day of atonement—you
shall have the trumpet sounded
throughout all your land. 10 And
you shall hallow the fiftieth year
and you shall proclaim liberty
throughout the land to all its inhabitants. It shall be a jubilee for
you: you shall return, every one of
you, to your property and every one
of you to your family. 11 That fiftieth year shall be a jubilee for you:
you shall not sow, or reap the aftergrowth, or harvest the unpruned
vines. 12 For it is a jubilee; it shall
be holy to you: you shall eat only
what the field itself produces.

13 In this year of jubilee you
shall return, every one of you, to
your property. 14 When you make a
sale to your neighbor or buy from
your neighbor, you shall not cheat
one another. 15 When you buy from
your neighbor, you shall pay only
for the number of years since the
jubilee; the seller shall charge you
only for the remaining crop years.
16 If the years are more, you shall
increase the price, and if the years
are fewer, you shall diminish the
price; for it is a certain number of
harvests that are being sold to you.
17 You shall not cheat one another,
but you shall fear your God; for I
am the LORD your God.

18 You shall observe my statutes and faithfully keep my ordinances, so that you may live on the
land securely. 19 The land will yield
its fruit, and you will eat your fill
and live on it securely. 20 Should
you ask, What shall we eat in the
seventh year, if we may not sow or
gather in our crop? 21 I will order my
blessing for you in the sixth year, so
that it will yield a crop for three
years. 22 When you sow in the
eighth year, you will be eating from
the old crop; until the ninth year,
when its produce comes in, you
shall eat the old. 23 The land shall
not be sold in perpetuity, for the
land is mine; with me you are but
aliens and tenants. 24 Throughout
the land that you hold, you shall
provide for the redemption of the
land.

25 If anyone of your kin falls
into difficulty and sells a piece of
property, then the next of kin shall
come and redeem what the relative
has sold. 26 If the person has no one
to redeem it, but then prospers and
finds sufficient means to do so,
27 the years since its sale shall be
computed and the difference shall
be refunded to the person to whom
it was sold, and the property shall
be returned. 28 But if there is not
sufficient means to recover it, what
was sold shall remain with the purchaser until the year of jubilee; in
the jubilee it shall be released, and
the property shall be returned.

29 If anyone sells a dwelling
house in a walled city, it may be
redeemed until a year has elapsed
since its sale; the right of redemption shall be one year. 30 If it is not
redeemed before a full year has
elapsed, a house that is in a walled
city shall pass in perpetuity to the
purchaser, throughout the generations; it shall not be released in the
jubilee. 31 But houses in villages
that have no walls around them
shall be classed as open country;
they may be redeemed, and they
shall be released in the jubilee.
32 As for the cities of the Levites,
the Levites shall forever have the
right of redemption of the houses
in the cities belonging to them.
33 Such property as may be redeemed from the Levites—houses
sold in a city belonging to them—
shall be released in the jubilee; because the houses in the cities of
the Levites are their possession
among the people of Israel. 34 But
the open land around their cities
may not be sold; for that is their
possession for all time.

35 If any of your kin fall into difficulty and become dependent on
you,[s] you shall support them; they
shall live with you as though resident aliens. 36 Do not take interest

25.9 Lev 23.24, 27
25.10 vv. 13,28,54
25.13 v. 10
25.14 Lev 19.13; 1 Sam 12.3, 4; 1 Cor 6.8
25.15 Lev 27.18, 23
25.17 v. 14; Lev 19.14, 32
25.18 Lev 19.37; 26.4,5
25.20 vv. 4,5
25.22 Lev 26.10
25.23 Ex 19.5; Gen 23.4; 1 Chr 29.15; Ps 39.12
25.25 Ruth 2.20; 4.4,6
25.27 vv. 50-52
25.28 v. 13
25.32 Num 35.1-8
25.35 Deut 15.7-11; Ps 37.26; Lk 6.35
25.36 Ex 22.25; Deut 23.19, 20

[s] Meaning of Heb uncertain

in advance or otherwise make a
profit from them, but fear your
God; let them live with you. 37 You
shall not lend them your money at
interest taken in advance, or provide them food at a profit. 38 I am
the LORD your God, who brought
you out of the land of Egypt, to give
you the land of Canaan, to be your
God.

39 If any who are dependent on
you become so impoverished that
they sell themselves to you, you
shall not make them serve as
slaves. 40 They shall remain with
you as hired or bound laborers.
They shall serve with you until the
year of the jubilee. 41 Then they and
their children with them shall be
free from your authority; they shall
go back to their own family and return to their ancestral property.
42 For they are my servants, whom I
brought out of the land of Egypt;
they shall not be sold as slaves are
sold. 43 You shall not rule over them
with harshness, but shall fear your
God. 44 As for the male and female
slaves whom you may have, it is
from the nations around you that
you may acquire male and female
slaves. 45 You may also acquire
them from among the aliens residing with you, and from their families that are with you, who have
been born in your land; and they
may be your property. 46 You may
keep them as a possession for your
children after you, for them to inherit as property. These you may
treat as slaves, but as for your fellow Israelites, no one shall rule
over the other with harshness.

47 If resident aliens among you
prosper, and if any of your kin fall
into difficulty with one of them and
sell themselves to an alien, or to a
branch of the alien's family, 48 after
they have sold themselves they
shall have the right of redemption;
one of their brothers may redeem
them, 49 or their uncle or their uncle's son may redeem them, or anyone of their family who is of their
own flesh may redeem them; or if
they prosper they may redeem
themselves. 50 They shall compute
with the purchaser the total from
the year when they sold themselves
to the alien until the jubilee year;
the price of the sale shall be applied to the number of years: the
time they were with the owner
shall be rated as the time of a hired
laborer. 51 If many years remain,
they shall pay for their redemption
in proportion to the purchase
price; 52 and if few years remain until the jubilee year, they shall compute thus: according to the years
involved they shall make payment
for their redemption. 53 As a laborer
hired by the year they shall be under the alien's authority, who shall
not, however, rule with harshness
over them in your sight. 54 And if
they have not been redeemed in
any of these ways, they and their
children with them shall go free in
the jubilee year. 55 For to me the
people of Israel are servants; they
are my servants whom I brought
out from the land of Egypt: I am the
LORD your God.

Rewards for Obedience

26 You shall make for yourselves no idols and erect no
carved images or pillars, and you
shall not place figured stones in
your land, to worship at them; for I
am the LORD your God. 2 You shall
keep my sabbaths and reverence
my sanctuary: I am the LORD.

3 If you follow my statutes and
keep my commandments and observe them faithfully, 4 I will give
you your rains in their season, and
the land shall yield its produce,
and the trees of the field shall yield
their fruit. 5 Your threshing shall
overtake the vintage, and the vintage shall overtake the sowing; you
shall eat your bread to the full, and
live securely in your land. 6 And I
will grant peace in the land, and
you shall lie down, and no one shall
make you afraid; I will remove dangerous animals from the land, and
no sword shall go through your
land. 7 You shall give chase to your
enemies, and they shall fall before
you by the sword. 8 Five of you shall
give chase to a hundred, and a hun-

25.38 Lev 11.45
25.39 Ex 21.2; Deut 15.12; 1 Kings 9.22
25.41 Ex 21.3; v. 28
25.43 vv. 46,53; Ex 1.13,14
25.45 Isa 56.3,6
25.46 v. 43
25.48 Neh 5.5
25.49 v. 26
25.50 Job 7.1; Isa 16.14; 21.16
25.51 Jer 32.7
25.54 vv. 10,13,28
26.1 Ex 20.4,5; Lev 19.4; Deut 5.8
26.2 Lev 19.30
26.3 Deut 28.1
26.5 Am 9.13; Lev 25.18, 19
26.6 Ps 29.11; 147.14; Zeph 3.13; vv. 22,25
26.8 Deut 32.30; Josh 23.10

dred of you shall give chase to ten
thousand; your enemies shall fall
before you by the sword. 9 I will
look with favor upon you and make
you fruitful and multiply you; and
I will maintain my covenant with
you. 10 You shall eat old grain long
stored, and you shall have to clear
out the old to make way for the
new. 11 I will place my dwelling in
your midst, and I shall not abhor
you. 12 And I will walk among you,
and will be your God, and you shall
be my people. 13 I am the LORD your
God who brought you out of the
land of Egypt, to be their slaves no
more; I have broken the bars of
your yoke and made you walk
erect.

Penalties for Disobedience

14 But if you will not obey me,
and do not observe all these commandments, 15 if you spurn my
statutes, and abhor my ordinances,
so that you will not observe all my
commandments, and you break my
covenant, 16 I in turn will do this to
you: I will bring terror on you; consumption and fever that waste the
eyes and cause life to pine away.
You shall sow your seed in vain, for
your enemies shall eat it. 17 I will
set my face against you, and you
shall be struck down by your enemies; your foes shall rule over you,
and you shall flee though no one
pursues you. 18 And if in spite of
this you will not obey me, I will
continue to punish you sevenfold
for your sins. 19 I will break your
proud glory, and I will make your
sky like iron and your earth like
copper. 20 Your strength shall be
spent to no purpose: your land
shall not yield its produce, and the
trees of the land shall not yield
their fruit.
21 If you continue hostile to me,
and will not obey me, I will continue to plague you sevenfold for your
sins. 22 I will let loose wild animals
against you, and they shall bereave
you of your children and destroy
your livestock; they shall make you
few in number, and your roads
shall be deserted.

26.9 Gen 17.6,7; 22.17; Neh 9.23
26.10 Lev 25.22
26.11 Ex 25.8; Ps 76.2
26.12 2 Cor 6.16
26.14 Deut 28.15; Mal 2.2
26.16 Deut 28.22; 1 Sam 2.33; Deut 28.35, 51
26.17 Lev 17.10; Deut 28.25; Ps 106.41; 53.5; vv. 36, 37
26.18 vv. 21,24,28
26.19 Isa 25.11; Deut 28.23
26.20 Isa 17.10, 11; Deut 11.17
26.21 vv. 18,24, 27,40
26.22 Deut 32.24
26.23 Jer 2.30; 5.3
26.24 vv. 21,28,41
26.25 Ezek 5.17; Num 14.12
26.26 Ps 105.16; Isa 3.1; Mic 6.14
26.28 vv. 24,41
26.29 Deut 28.53
26.30 2 Chr 34.3; Ezek 6.3-6, 13
26.31 Ps 74.7; Isa 63.18
26.32 Jer 9.11; 19.18
26.33 Deut 4.27; Ezek 12.15
26.34 v. 43; 2 Chr 36.21
26.36 Ezek 21.7
26.37 Josh 7.12, 13

23 If in spite of these punishments you have not turned back to
me, but continue hostile to me,
24 then I too will continue hostile to
you: I myself will strike you sevenfold for your sins. 25 I will bring the
sword against you, executing vengeance for the covenant; and if you
withdraw within your cities, I will
send pestilence among you, and
you shall be delivered into enemy
hands. 26 When I break your staff of
bread, ten women shall bake your
bread in a single oven, and they
shall dole out your bread by weight;
and though you eat, you shall not
be satisfied.
27 But if, despite this, you disobey me, and continue hostile to
me, 28 I will continue hostile to you
in fury; I in turn will punish you
myself sevenfold for your sins.
29 You shall eat the flesh of your
sons, and you shall eat the flesh of
your daughters. 30 I will destroy
your high places and cut down your
incense altars; I will heap your carcasses on the carcasses of your
idols. I will abhor you. 31 I will lay
your cities waste, will make your
sanctuaries desolate, and I will not
smell your pleasing odors. 32 I will
devastate the land, so that your enemies who come to settle in it shall
be appalled at it. 33 And you I will
scatter among the nations, and I
will unsheathe the sword against
you; your land shall be a desolation, and your cities a waste.
34 Then the land shall enjoy[t]
its sabbath years as long as it lies
desolate, while you are in the land
of your enemies; then the land
shall rest, and enjoy[t] its sabbath
years. 35 As long as it lies desolate,
it shall have the rest it did not have
on your sabbaths when you were
living on it. 36 And as for those of
you who survive, I will send faint-
ness into their hearts in the lands
of their enemies; the sound of a
driven leaf shall put them to flight,
and they shall flee as one flees from
the sword, and they shall fall
though no one pursues. 37 They

[t] Or *make up for*

shall stumble over one another, as
if to escape a sword, though no one
pursues; and you shall have no
power to stand against your enemies. 38 You shall perish among the
nations, and the land of your enemies shall devour you. 39 And those
of you who survive shall languish in
the land of your enemies because
of their iniquities; also they shall
languish because of the iniquities
of their ancestors.

40 But if they confess their iniquity and the iniquity of their ancestors, in that they committed
treachery against me and, moreover, that they continued hostile to
me— 41 so that I, in turn, continued
hostile to them and brought them
into the land of their enemies; if
then their uncircumcised heart is
humbled and they make amends
for their iniquity, 42 then will I remember my covenant with Jacob; I
will remember also my covenant
with Isaac and also my covenant
with Abraham, and I will remember
the land. 43 For the land shall be
deserted by them, and enjoy[u] its
sabbath years by lying desolate
without them, while they shall
make amends for their iniquity, because they dared to spurn my ordinances, and they abhorred my statutes. 44 Yet for all that, when they
are in the land of their enemies, I
will not spurn them, or abhor them
so as to destroy them utterly and
break my covenant with them; for I
am the LORD their God; 45 but I will
remember in their favor the covenant with their ancestors whom I
brought out of the land of Egypt in
the sight of the nations, to be their
God: I am the LORD.

46 These are the statutes and
ordinances and laws that the LORD
established between himself and
the people of Israel on Mount Sinai
through Moses.

Votive Offerings

27 The LORD spoke to Moses,
saying: 2 Speak to the people of Israel and say to them: When
a person makes an explicit vow to
the LORD concerning the equivalent
for a human being, 3 the equivalent
for a male shall be: from twenty to
sixty years of age the equivalent
shall be fifty shekels of silver by the
sanctuary shekel. 4 If the person is
a female, the equivalent is thirty
shekels. 5 If the age is from five to
twenty years of age, the equivalent
is twenty shekels for a male and ten
shekels for a female. 6 If the age is
from one month to five years, the
equivalent for a male is five shekels
of silver, and for a female the
equivalent is three shekels of silver. 7 And if the person is sixty years
old or over, then the equivalent for
a male is fifteen shekels, and for a
female ten shekels. 8 If any cannot
afford the equivalent, they shall be
brought before the priest and the
priest shall assess them; the priest
shall assess them according to
what each one making a vow can
afford.

9 If it concerns an animal that
may be brought as an offering to
the LORD, any such that may be giv-
en to the LORD shall be holy. 10 Another shall not be exchanged or
substituted for it, either good for
bad or bad for good; and if one animal is substituted for another, both
that one and its substitute shall be
holy. 11 If it concerns any unclean
animal that may not be brought as
an offering to the LORD, the animal
shall be presented before the
priest. 12 The priest shall assess it:
whether good or bad, according to
the assessment of the priest, so it
shall be. 13 But if it is to be redeemed, one-fifth must be added to the
assessment.

14 If a person consecrates a
house to the LORD, the priest shall
assess it: whether good or bad, as
the priest assesses it, so it shall
stand. 15 And if the one who consecrates the house wishes to redeem
it, one-fifth shall be added to its assessed value, and it shall revert to
the original owner.

16 If a person consecrates to the
LORD any inherited landholding, its
assessment shall be in accordance
with its seed requirements: fifty

26.38 Deut 4.26 **26.39** Deut 4.27; Ezek 4.17 **26.40ff** Jer 3.12-15; Lk 15.18; 1 Jn 1.9 **26.41** Ezek 44.9; 2 Chr 12.6, 7 **26.42** Gen 28.13-15; 26.2-5; 22.15-18 **26.43** vv. 34,35,15 **26.44** Deut 4.31; Rom 11.2 **26.45** Ex 6.6-8; Lev 25.38; Gen 17.7 **26.46** Lev 7.38; 27.34; 25.1

27.3 Ex 30.13 **27.6** Num 18.16 **27.8** v. 12 **27.12** v. 8 **27.13** vv. 15,19 **27.15** v. 20

[u] Or *make up for*

shekels of silver to a homer of barley seed. [17]If the person consecrates the field as of the year of jubilee, that assessment shall stand; [18]but if the field is consecrated after the jubilee, the priest shall compute the price for it according to the years that remain until the year of jubilee, and the assessment shall be reduced. [19]And if the one who consecrates the field wishes to redeem it, then one-fifth shall be added to its assessed value, and it shall revert to the original owner; [20]but if the field is not redeemed, or if it has been sold to someone else, it shall no longer be redeemable. [21]But when the field is released in the jubilee, it shall be holy to the LORD as a devoted field; it becomes the priest's holding. [22]If someone consecrates to the LORD a field that has been purchased, which is not a part of the inherited landholding, [23]the priest shall compute for it the proportionate assessment up to the year of jubilee, and the assessment shall be paid as of that day, a sacred donation to the LORD. [24]In the year of jubilee the field shall return to the one from whom it was bought, whose holding the land is. [25]All assessments shall be by the sanctuary shekel: twenty gerahs shall make a shekel.

26 A firstling of animals, however, which as a firstling belongs to the LORD, cannot be consecrated by anyone; whether ox or sheep, it is the LORD's. [27]If it is an unclean animal, it shall be ransomed at its assessment, with one-fifth added; if it is not redeemed, it shall be sold at its assessment.

28 Nothing that a person owns that has been devoted to destruction for the LORD, be it human or animal, or inherited landholding, may be sold or redeemed; every devoted thing is most holy to the LORD. [29]No human beings who have been devoted to destruction can be ransomed; they shall be put to death.

30 All tithes from the land, whether the seed from the ground or the fruit from the tree, are the LORD's; they are holy to the LORD. [31]If persons wish to redeem any of their tithes, they must add one-fifth to them. [32]All tithes of herd and flock, every tenth one that passes under the shepherd's staff, shall be holy to the LORD. [33]Let no one inquire whether it is good or bad, or make substitution for it; if one makes substitution for it, then both it and the substitute shall be holy and cannot be redeemed.

34 These are the commandments that the LORD gave to Moses for the people of Israel on Mount Sinai.

27.18 Lev 25.15, 16
27.21 Lev 25.10, 28,31; Num 18.14
27.23 v. 18
27.24 Lev 25.28
27.25 Ex 30.13
27.26 Ex 13.2,12
27.27 vv. 11,12
27.28 Josh 6.17-19
27.30 Gen 28.22; Mal 3.8,10
27.31 v. 13
27.33 v. 10
27.34 Lev 26.46; Deut 4.5

Numbers

Title and Background

The book of Numbers gets its name from the two numberings or countings of the people of Israel during their forty years of wandering in the desert. These countings are found in chapters 1 and 26. Numbers presents an account of that wandering in the desert following the establishment of the covenant at Sinai.

Author and Date of Writing

Numbers has been traditionally ascribed to Moses, though like the other books of the Pentateuch, the final form of the first five books of the Bible may not have taken place until later on in Israel's history. The New Testament consistently ascribes quotations from the Pentateuch to Moses (e.g., Mt 19.8; Jn 5.46-47; Rom 10.5).

Theme and Message

Numbers relates the story of Israel's journey from Mount Sinai to the plains of Moab on the border of Canaan. It tells of the murmuring and rebellion of God's people and of their subsequent judgment. They were condemned to live out their lives in the desert; only their children would enjoy the fulfillment of the promise that had originally been theirs.

Throughout the years in the desert, one thing became clear to Israel–God's constant care for them. Not only did he meet their needs but he also loved and forgave his people continually.

Outline

I. Israel at Sinai, Preparing to Go to Canaan (1.1–10.10)
II. From Sinai to Kadesh (10.11–12.16)
III. Israel at Kadesh, the Delay Resulting from Rebellion (13.1–20.13)
IV. From Kadesh to the Plains of Moab (20.14–22.1)
V. Israel on the Plains of Moab (22.2–32.42)
VI. Supplements Dealing with Various Matters (33.1–36.13)

The First Census of Israel

1 The LORD spoke to Moses in
the wilderness of Sinai, in the
tent of meeting, on the first day of
the second month, in the second
year after they had come out of the
land of Egypt, saying: 2 Take a census of the whole congregation of Israelites, in their clans, by ancestral
houses, according to the number of
names, every male individually;
3 from twenty years old and upward, everyone in Israel able to go
to war. You and Aaron shall enroll
them, company by company. 4 A
man from each tribe shall be with
you, each man the head of his ancestral house. 5 These are the
names of the men who shall assist
you:

From Reuben, Elizur son of Shedeur.
6 From Simeon, Shelumiel son of Zurishaddai.
7 From Judah, Nahshon son of Amminadab.
8 From Issachar, Nethanel son of Zuar.
9 From Zebulun, Eliab son of Helon.
10 From the sons of Joseph:
from Ephraim, Elishama son of Ammihud;
from Manasseh, Gamaliel son of Pedahzur.

1.1 Ex 19.1; 40.2,17 **1.2** Ex 38.26; Num 26.2 **1.4** v. 16

11 From Benjamin, Abidan son
of Gideoni.
12 From Dan, Ahiezer son of
Ammishaddai.
13 From Asher, Pagiel son of
Ochran.
14 From Gad, Eliasaph son of
Deuel.
15 From Naphtali, Ahira son of
Enan.
16 These were the ones chosen from
the congregation, the leaders of
their ancestral tribes, the heads of
the divisions of Israel.
17 Moses and Aaron took these
men who had been designated by
name, 18 and on the first day of the
second month they assembled the
whole congregation together. They
registered themselves in their
clans, by their ancestral houses,
according to the number of names
from twenty years old and upward,
individually, 19 as the LORD commanded Moses. So he enrolled
them in the wilderness of Sinai.
20 The descendants of Reuben,
Israel's firstborn, their lineage, in
their clans, by their ancestral
houses, according to the number of
names, individually, every male
from twenty years old and upward,
everyone able to go to war: 21 those
enrolled of the tribe of Reuben
were forty-six thousand five hundred.
22 The descendants of Simeon,
their lineage, in their clans, by
their ancestral houses, those of
them that were numbered, according to the number of names, individually, every male from twenty
years old and upward, everyone
able to go to war: 23 those enrolled
of the tribe of Simeon were fifty-
nine thousand three hundred.
24 The descendants of Gad,
their lineage, in their clans, by
their ancestral houses, according
to the number of the names, from
twenty years old and upward, everyone able to go to war: 25 those
enrolled of the tribe of Gad were
forty-five thousand six hundred fifty.
26 The descendants of Judah,
their lineage, in their clans, by

1.14 Num 2.14
1.16 Num 16.2; 26.9
1.20 Num 26.5-11
1.22 Num 26.12-14
1.24 Num 26.15-18
1.26 Num 26.19-22
1.28 Num 26.23-25
1.30 Num 26.26, 27
1.32 Num 26.35-37
1.34 Num 26.28-34
1.36 Num 26.38-41
1.38 Num 26.42, 43

their ancestral houses, according
to the number of names, from
twenty years old and upward, everyone able to go to war: 27 those
enrolled of the tribe of Judah were
seventy-four thousand six hundred.
28 The descendants of Issachar,
their lineage, in their clans, by
their ancestral houses, according
to the number of names, from
twenty years old and upward, everyone able to go to war: 29 those
enrolled of the tribe of Issachar
were fifty-four thousand four hundred.
30 The descendants of Zebulun,
their lineage, in their clans, by
their ancestral houses, according
to the number of names, from
twenty years old and upward, everyone able to go to war: 31 those
enrolled of the tribe of Zebulun
were fifty-seven thousand four
hundred.
32 The descendants of Joseph,
namely, the descendants of Ephraim, their lineage, in their clans, by
their ancestral houses, according
to the number of names, from
twenty years old and upward, everyone able to go to war: 33 those
enrolled of the tribe of Ephraim
were forty thousand five hundred.
34 The descendants of Manas-
seh, their lineage, in their clans, by
their ancestral houses, according
to the number of names, from
twenty years old and upward, everyone able to go to war: 35 those
enrolled of the tribe of Manasseh
were thirty-two thousand two hundred.
36 The descendants of Benja-
min, their lineage, in their clans, by
their ancestral houses, according
to the number of names, from
twenty years old and upward, everyone able to go to war: 37 those
enrolled of the tribe of Benjamin
were thirty-five thousand four hundred.
38 The descendants of Dan,
their lineage, in their clans, by
their ancestral houses, according
to the number of names, from
twenty years old and upward, ev-

eryone able to go to war: 39 those
enrolled of the tribe of Dan were
sixty-two thousand seven hundred.
40 The descendants of Asher,
their lineage, in their clans, by
their ancestral houses, according
to the number of names, from
twenty years old and upward, everyone able to go to war: 41 those
enrolled of the tribe of Asher were
forty-one thousand five hundred.
42 The descendants of Naphtali, their lineage, in their clans, by
their ancestral houses, according
to the number of names, from
twenty years old and upward, everyone able to go to war: 43 those
enrolled of the tribe of Naphtali
were fifty-three thousand four hundred.
44 These are those who were
enrolled, whom Moses and Aaron
enrolled with the help of the leaders of Israel, twelve men, each representing his ancestral house. 45 So
the whole number of the Israelites,
by their ancestral houses, from
twenty years old and upward, everyone able to go to war in Israel—
46 their whole number was six hundred three thousand five hundred
fifty. 47 The Levites, however, were
not numbered by their ancestral
tribe along with them.
48 The LORD had said to Moses:
49 Only the tribe of Levi you shall
not enroll, and you shall not take a
census of them with the other Israelites. 50 Rather you shall appoint
the Levites over the tabernacle of
the covenant,[a] and over all its
equipment, and over all that belongs to it; they are to carry the tabernacle and all its equipment, and
they shall tend it, and shall camp
around the tabernacle. 51 When the
tabernacle is to set out, the Levites
shall take it down; and when the
tabernacle is to be pitched, the Levites shall set it up. And any outsider who comes near shall be put to
death. 52 The other Israelites shall
camp in their respective regimental camps, by companies; 53 but the
Levites shall camp around the tabernacle of the covenant,[a] that
there may be no wrath on the congregation of the Israelites; and the
Levites shall perform the guard
duty of the tabernacle of the covenant.[a] 54 The Israelites did so; they
did just as the LORD commanded
Moses.

The Order of Encampment and Marching

2 The LORD spoke to Moses and
Aaron, saying: 2 The Israelites
shall camp each in their respective
regiments, under ensigns by their
ancestral houses; they shall camp
facing the tent of meeting on every
side. 3 Those to camp on the east
side toward the sunrise shall be of
the regimental encampment of Judah by companies. The leader of
the people of Judah shall be Nahshon son of Amminadab, 4 with a
company as enrolled of seventy-
four thousand six hundred. 5 Those
to camp next to him shall be the
tribe of Issachar. The leader of the
Issacharites shall be Nethanel son
of Zuar, 6 with a company as enrolled of fifty-four thousand four
hundred. 7 Then the tribe of Zebulun: The leader of the Zebulunites
shall be Eliab son of Helon, 8 with
a company as enrolled of fifty-
seven thousand four hundred.
9 The total enrollment of the camp
of Judah, by companies, is one
hundred eighty-six thousand four
hundred. They shall set out first on
the march.
10 On the south side shall be
the regimental encampment of
Reuben by companies. The leader
of the Reubenites shall be Elizur
son of Shedeur, 11 with a company
as enrolled of forty-six thousand
five hundred. 12 And those to camp
next to him shall be the tribe of
Simeon. The leader of the Simeonites shall be Shelumiel son of Zurishaddai, 13 with a company as enrolled of fifty-nine thousand three
hundred. 14 Then the tribe of Gad:
The leader of the Gadites shall be
Eliasaph son of Reuel, 15 with a
company as enrolled of forty-five
thousand six hundred fifty. 16 The
total enrollment of the camp of

1.40 Num 26.44-47
1.42 Num 26.48-50
1.44 Num 26.64
1.46 Num 2.32; 26.51; Ex 12.37; 38.26
1.47 Num 2.33; chs. 3,4; 26.57
1.50 Num 3.25-37
1.51 Num 4.1-33
1.52 Num 2.2
1.53 v. 50
2.2 Num 1.52
2.3 Num 10;14
2.5 Num 1.8
2.9 Num 10.14
2.10 Num 1.5
2.12 Num 1.6
2.14 Num 1.14,

[a] Or *treaty*, or *testimony*; Heb *eduth*

Reuben, by companies, is one hundred fifty-one thousand four hundred fifty. They shall set out second.

17 The tent of meeting, with the camp of the Levites, shall set out in the center of the camps; they shall set out just as they camp, each in position, by their regiments.

18 On the west side shall be the regimental encampment of Ephraim by companies. The leader of the people of Ephraim shall be Elishama son of Ammihud, 19 with a company as enrolled of forty thousand five hundred. 20 Next to him shall be the tribe of Manasseh. The leader of the people of Manasseh shall be Gamaliel son of Pedahzur, 21 with a company as enrolled of thirty-two thousand two hundred. 22 Then the tribe of Benjamin: The leader of the Benjaminites shall be Abidan son of Gideoni, 23 with a company as enrolled of thirty-five thousand four hundred. 24 The total enrollment of the camp of Ephraim, by companies, is one hundred eight thousand one hundred. They shall set out third on the march.

25 On the north side shall be the regimental encampment of Dan by companies. The leader of the Danites shall be Ahiezer son of Ammishaddai, 26 with a company as enrolled of sixty-two thousand seven hundred. 27 Those to camp next to him shall be the tribe of Asher. The leader of the Asherites shall be Pagiel son of Ochran, 28 with a company as enrolled of forty-one thousand five hundred. 29 Then the tribe of Naphtali: The leader of the Naphtalites shall be Ahira son of Enan, 30 with a company as enrolled of fifty-three thousand four hundred. 31 The total enrollment of the camp of Dan is one hundred fifty-seven thousand six hundred. They shall set out last, by companies.[b]

32 This was the enrollment of the Israelites by their ancestral houses; the total enrollment in the camps by their companies was six hundred three thousand five hundred fifty. 33 Just as the LORD had commanded Moses, the Levites were not enrolled among the other Israelites.

34 The Israelites did just as the LORD had commanded Moses: They camped by regiments, and they set out the same way, everyone by clans, according to ancestral houses.

The Sons of Aaron

3 This is the lineage of Aaron and Moses at the time when the LORD spoke with Moses on Mount Sinai. 2 These are the names of the sons of Aaron: Nadab the firstborn, and Abihu, Eleazar, and Ithamar; 3 these are the names of the sons of Aaron, the anointed priests, whom he ordained to minister as priests. 4 Nadab and Abihu died before the LORD when they offered illicit fire before the LORD in the wilderness of Sinai, and they had no children. Eleazar and Ithamar served as priests in the lifetime of their father Aaron.

The Duties of the Levites

5 Then the LORD spoke to Moses, saying: 6 Bring the tribe of Levi near, and set them before Aaron the priest, so that they may assist him. 7 They shall perform duties for him and for the whole congregation in front of the tent of meeting, doing service at the tabernacle; 8 they shall be in charge of all the furnishings of the tent of meeting, and attend to the duties for the Israelites as they do service at the tabernacle. 9 You shall give the Levites to Aaron and his descendants; they are unreservedly given to him from among the Israelites. 10 But you shall make a register of Aaron and his descendants; it is they who shall attend to the priesthood, and any outsider who comes near shall be put to death.

11 Then the LORD spoke to Moses, saying: 12 I hereby accept the Levites from among the Israelites as substitutes for all the firstborn that open the womb among the Is-

2.17 Num 1.53
2.20 Num 1.10
2.24 Num 10.22
2.25 Num 1.12
2.27 Num 1.13
2.31 Num 10.25
2.32 Num 1.46; Ex 38.26
2.33 Num 1.47
3.2 Num 26.60
3.4 Num 26.61
3.6 Num 8.6-22; 18.1-7
3.9 Num 18.6
3.10 Ex 29.9; Num 1.51
3.12 v. 41; Num 8.16; 18.6

b Compare verses 9, 16, 24: Heb *by their regiments*

raelites. The Levites shall be mine,
13 for all the firstborn are mine;
when I killed all the firstborn in the
land of Egypt, I consecrated for my
own all the firstborn in Israel, both
human and animal; they shall be
mine. I am the LORD.

A Census of the Levites

14 Then the LORD spoke to Moses in the wilderness of Sinai, saying: 15 Enroll the Levites by ancestral houses and by clans. You shall
enroll every male from a month old
and upward. 16 So Moses enrolled
them according to the word of the
LORD, as he was commanded. 17 The
following were the sons of Levi, by
their names: Gershon, Kohath, and
Merari. 18 These are the names of
the sons of Gershon by their clans:
Libni and Shimei. 19 The sons of
Kohath by their clans: Amram, Izhar, Hebron, and Uzziel. 20 The
sons of Merari by their clans: Mahli
and Mushi. These are the clans of
the Levites, by their ancestral
houses.

21 To Gershon belonged the
clan of the Libnites and the clan of
the Shimeites; these were the clans
of the Gershonites. 22 Their enrollment, counting all the males from
a month old and upward, was seven
thousand five hundred. 23 The
clans of the Gershonites were to
camp behind the tabernacle on the
west, 24 with Eliasaph son of Lael as
head of the ancestral house of the
Gershonites. 25 The responsibility
of the sons of Gershon in the tent
of meeting was to be the tabernacle, the tent with its covering, the
screen for the entrance of the tent
of meeting, 26 the hangings of the
court, the screen for the entrance
of the court that is around the tabernacle and the altar, and its
cords—all the service pertaining to
these.

27 To Kohath belonged the clan
of the Amramites, the clan of the
Izharites, the clan of the Hebronites, and the clan of the Uzzielites;
these are the clans of the Kohathites. 28 Counting all the males, from
a month old and upward, there
were eight thousand six hundred,
attending to the duties of the sanctuary. 29 The clans of the Kohathites were to camp on the south side
of the tabernacle, 30 with Elizaphan
son of Uzziel as head of the ancestral house of the clans of the Kohathites. 31 Their responsibility was
to be the ark, the table, the lampstand, the altars, the vessels of the
sanctuary with which the priests
minister, and the screen—all the
service pertaining to these. 32 Eleazar son of Aaron the priest was to
be chief over the leaders of the Levites, and to have oversight of those
who had charge of the sanctuary.

33 To Merari belonged the clan
of the Mahlites and the clan of the
Mushites: these are the clans of
Merari. 34 Their enrollment, counting all the males from a month old
and upward, was six thousand two
hundred. 35 The head of the ancestral house of the clans of Merari
was Zuriel son of Abihail; they were
to camp on the north side of the
tabernacle. 36 The responsibility
assigned to the sons of Merari was
to be the frames of the tabernacle,
the bars, the pillars, the bases, and
all their accessories—all the service pertaining to these; 37 also the
pillars of the court all around, with
their bases and pegs and cords.

38 Those who were to camp in
front of the tabernacle on the
east—in front of the tent of meeting toward the east—were Moses
and Aaron and Aaron's sons, having charge of the rites within the
sanctuary, whatever had to be done
for the Israelites; and any outsider
who came near was to be put to
death. 39 The total enrollment of
the Levites whom Moses and Aaron
enrolled at the commandment of
the LORD, by their clans, all the
males from a month old and upward, was twenty-two thousand.

The Redemption of the Firstborn

40 Then the LORD said to Moses:
Enroll all the firstborn males of the
Israelites, from a month old and
upward, and count their names.
41 But you shall accept the Levites

3.13 Ex 13.2,12,15; Num 8.17
3.15 v. 39
3.17 Ex 6.16-22
3.20 Gen 46.11
3.21 Ex 6.17
3.25 Num 4.24-26; Ex 25.9
3.27 1 Chr 26.23
3.29 Ex 6.18
3.33 Ex 6.19
3.36 Num 4.29-32
3.38 Num 18.5; vv. 7,8,10
3.39 Num 26.62
3.41 vv. 12,45

for me—I am the LORD—as substitutes for all the firstborn among the Israelites, and the livestock of the Levites as substitutes for all the firstborn among the livestock of the Israelites. 42 So Moses enrolled all the firstborn among the Israelites, as the LORD commanded him. 43 The total enrollment, all the firstborn males from a month old and upward, counting the number of names, was twenty-two thousand two hundred seventy-three.

44 Then the LORD spoke to Moses, saying: 45 Accept the Levites as substitutes for all the firstborn among the Israelites, and the livestock of the Levites as substitutes for their livestock; and the Levites shall be mine. I am the LORD. 46 As the price of redemption of the two hundred seventy-three of the firstborn of the Israelites, over and above the number of the Levites, 47 you shall accept five shekels apiece, reckoning by the shekel of the sanctuary, a shekel of twenty gerahs. 48 Give to Aaron and his sons the money by which the excess number of them is redeemed. 49 So Moses took the redemption money from those who were over and above those redeemed by the Levites; 50 from the firstborn of the Israelites he took the money, one thousand three hundred sixty-five shekels, reckoned by the shekel of the sanctuary; 51 and Moses gave the redemption money to Aaron and his sons, according to the word of the LORD, as the LORD had commanded Moses.

The Kohathites

4 The LORD spoke to Moses and Aaron, saying: 2 Take a census of the Kohathites separate from the other Levites, by their clans and their ancestral houses, 3 from thirty years old up to fifty years old, all who qualify to do work relating to the tent of meeting. 4 The service of the Kohathites relating to the tent of meeting concerns the most holy things.

5 When the camp is to set out, Aaron and his sons shall go in and take down the screening curtain, and cover the ark of the covenant[c] with it; 6 then they shall put on it a covering of fine leather,[d] and spread over that a cloth all of blue, and shall put its poles in place. 7 Over the table of the bread of the Presence they shall spread a blue cloth, and put on it the plates, the dishes for incense, the bowls, and the flagons for the drink offering; the regular bread also shall be on it; 8 then they shall spread over them a crimson cloth, and cover it with a covering of fine leather,[d] and shall put its poles in place. 9 They shall take a blue cloth, and cover the lampstand for the light, with its lamps, its snuffers, its trays, and all the vessels for oil with which it is supplied; 10 and they shall put it with all its utensils in a covering of fine leather,[d] and put it on the carrying frame. 11 Over the golden altar they shall spread a blue cloth, and cover it with a covering of fine leather,[d] and shall put its poles in place; 12 and they shall take all the utensils of the service that are used in the sanctuary, and put them in a blue cloth, and cover them with a covering of fine leather,[d] and put them on the carrying frame. 13 They shall take away the ashes from the altar, and spread a purple cloth over it; 14 and they shall put on it all the utensils of the altar, which are used for the service there, the firepans, the forks, the shovels, and the basins, all the utensils of the altar; and they shall spread on it a covering of fine leather,[d] and shall put its poles in place. 15 When Aaron and his sons have finished covering the sanctuary and all the furnishings of the sanctuary, as the camp sets out, after that the Kohathites shall come to carry these, but they must not touch the holy things, or they will die. These are the things of the tent of meeting that the Kohathites are to carry.

16 Eleazar son of Aaron the

3.43 v. 39
3.45 vv. 12,41
3.46 Ex 13.13; Num 18.15
3.47 Ex 30.13
3.50 vv. 46-48
4.3 Num 8.24; vv. 23,30,35
4.6 v. 25
4.7 Ex 25.23, 29,30; Lev 24.5-9
4.9 Ex 25.31, 37,38
4.11 Ex 30.1,3
4.15 Num 7.9; 2 Sam 6.6, 7
4.16 Lev 24.1-3; Ex 30.34; 29.40; 30.23

c Or *treaty*, or *testimony*; Heb *eduth*
d Meaning of Heb uncertain

priest shall have charge of the oil
for the light, the fragrant incense,
the regular grain offering, and the
anointing oil, the oversight of all
the tabernacle and all that is in it,
in the sanctuary and in its utensils.
17 Then the LORD spoke to Moses and Aaron, saying: 18 You must
not let the tribe of the clans of the
Kohathites be destroyed from
among the Levites. 19 This is how
you must deal with them in order
that they may live and not die when
they come near to the most holy
things: Aaron and his sons shall go
in and assign each to a particular
task or burden. 20 But the Kohathites[e] must not go in to look on the
holy things even for a moment; otherwise they will die.

The Gershonites and Merarites

21 Then the LORD spoke to Moses, saying: 22 Take a census of the
Gershonites also, by their ancestral
houses and by their clans; 23 from
thirty years old up to fifty years old
you shall enroll them, all who qualify to do work in the tent of meeting. 24 This is the service of the
clans of the Gershonites, in serving
and bearing burdens: 25 They shall
carry the curtains of the tabernacle, and the tent of meeting with its
covering, and the outer covering of
fine leather[f] that is on top of it,
and the screen for the entrance of
the tent of meeting, 26 and the
hangings of the court, and the
screen for the entrance of the gate
of the court that is around the tabernacle and the altar, and their
cords, and all the equipment for
their service; and they shall do all
that needs to be done with regard
to them. 27 All the service of the
Gershonites shall be at the command of Aaron and his sons, in all
that they are to carry, and in all
that they have to do; and you shall
assign to their charge all that they
are to carry. 28 This is the service of
the clans of the Gershonites relating to the tent of meeting, and their
responsibilities are to be under the
oversight of Ithamar son of Aaron
the priest.

4.19 vv. 4,15 **4.23** v. 3 **4.25** Num 3.25, 26 **4.27** Num 3.21

4.30 v. 3 **4.31** Num 3.36, 37 **4.33** v. 28 **4.34** v. 2 **4.37** Num 3.27 **4.38** Gen 46.11 **4.41** v. 22

29 As for the Merarites, you
shall enroll them by their clans and
their ancestral houses; 30 from thirty years old up to fifty years old you
shall enroll them, everyone who
qualifies to do the work of the tent
of meeting. 31 This is what they are
charged to carry, as the whole of
their service in the tent of meeting:
the frames of the tabernacle, with
its bars, pillars, and bases, 32 and
the pillars of the court all around
with their bases, pegs, and cords,
with all their equipment and all
their related service; and you shall
assign by name the objects that
they are required to carry. 33 This is
the service of the clans of the Merarites, the whole of their service relating to the tent of meeting, under
the hand of Ithamar son of Aaron
the priest.

Census of the Levites

34 So Moses and Aaron and the
leaders of the congregation enrolled the Kohathites, by their
clans and their ancestral houses,
35 from thirty years old up to fifty
years old, everyone who qualified
for work relating to the tent of
meeting; 36 and their enrollment by
clans was two thousand seven hundred fifty. 37 This was the enrollment of the clans of the Kohathites, all who served at the tent of
meeting, whom Moses and Aaron
enrolled according to the commandment of the LORD by Moses.
38 The enrollment of the Gershonites, by their clans and their
ancestral houses, 39 from thirty
years old up to fifty years old, everyone who qualified for work relating to the tent of meeting—
40 their enrollment by their clans
and their ancestral houses was two
thousand six hundred thirty.
41 This was the enrollment of the
clans of the Gershonites, all who
served at the tent of meeting,
whom Moses and Aaron enrolled
according to the commandment of
the LORD.
42 The enrollment of the clans
of the Merarites, by their clans and

[e] Heb *they* [f] Meaning of Heb uncertain

their ancestral houses, [43]from thirty years old up to fifty years old, everyone who qualified for work relating to the tent of meeting—
[44]their enrollment by their clans
was three thousand two hundred.
[45]This is the enrollment of the
clans of the Merarites, whom Moses and Aaron enrolled according
to the commandment of the LORD
by Moses.
46 All those who were enrolled
of the Levites, whom Moses and
Aaron and the leaders of Israel enrolled, by their clans and their ancestral houses, [47]from thirty years
old up to fifty years old, everyone
who qualified to do the work of service and the work of bearing burdens relating to the tent of meeting, [48]their enrollment was eight
thousand five hundred eighty.
[49]According to the commandment
of the LORD through Moses they
were appointed to their several
tasks of serving or carrying; thus
they were enrolled by him, as the
LORD commanded Moses.

Unclean Persons

5 The LORD spoke to Moses, saying: [2]Command the Israelites
to put out of the camp everyone
who is leprous,[g] or has a discharge, and everyone who is unclean through contact with a
corpse; [3]you shall put out both
male and female, putting them
outside the camp; they must not
defile their camp, where I dwell
among them. [4]The Israelites did
so, putting them outside the camp;
as the LORD had spoken to Moses,
so the Israelites did.

Confession and Restitution

5 The LORD spoke to Moses, saying: [6]Speak to the Israelites: When
a man or a woman wrongs another,
breaking faith with the LORD, that
person incurs guilt [7]and shall confess the sin that has been committed. The person shall make full restitution for the wrong, adding one
fifth to it, and giving it to the one
who was wronged. [8]If the injured
party has no next of kin to whom

4.45 v. 29
4.47 vv. 3,23,30
5.2ff Lev 13.3,46; 15.2; 19.11
5.3 Lev 26.11, 12; 2 Cor 6.16
5.6 Lev 6.2,3
5.7 Lev 5.5; 26.40; 6.5
5.8 Lev 6.6,7; 7.7
5.9 Lev 6.17,18, 26; 7.6-14
5.10 Lev 10.13
5.12 Ex 20.14
5.13 Lev 18.20
5.15 Ezek 29.16
5.18 1 Cor 11.6

restitution may be made for the
wrong, the restitution for wrong
shall go to the LORD for the priest,
in addition to the ram of atonement with which atonement is
made for the guilty party. [9]Among
all the sacred donations of the Israelites, every gift that they bring to
the priest shall be his. [10]The sacred
donations of all are their own;
whatever anyone gives to the priest
shall be his.

Concerning an Unfaithful Wife

11 The LORD spoke to Moses,
saying: [12]Speak to the Israelites
and say to them: If any man's wife
goes astray and is unfaithful to
him, [13]if a man has had intercourse
with her but it is hidden from her
husband, so that she is undetected
though she has defiled herself, and
there is no witness against her
since she was not caught in the act;
[14]if a spirit of jealousy comes on
him, and he is jealous of his wife
who has defiled herself; or if a spirit
of jealousy comes on him, and he is
jealous of his wife, though she has
not defiled herself; [15]then the man
shall bring his wife to the priest.
And he shall bring the offering required for her, one-tenth of an
ephah of barley flour. He shall pour
no oil on it and put no frankincense
on it, for it is a grain offering of jealousy, a grain offering of remembrance, bringing iniquity to remembrance.
16 Then the priest shall bring
her near, and set her before the
LORD; [17]the priest shall take holy
water in an earthen vessel, and
take some of the dust that is on the
floor of the tabernacle and put it
into the water. [18]The priest shall
set the woman before the LORD, dishevel the woman's hair, and place
in her hands the grain offering of
remembrance, which is the grain
offering of jealousy. In his own
hand the priest shall have the water of bitterness that brings the
curse. [19]Then the priest shall make
her take an oath, saying, "If no man

[g] A term for several skin diseases; precise meaning uncertain

has lain with you, if you have not
turned aside to uncleanness while
under your husband's authority, be
immune to this water of bitterness
that brings the curse. 20 But if you
have gone astray while under your
husband's authority, if you have
defiled yourself and some man other than your husband has had intercourse with you," 21 —let the
priest make the woman take the
oath of the curse and say to
the woman—"the LORD make you an
execration and an oath among your
people, when the LORD makes your
uterus drop, your womb discharge;
22 now may this water that brings
the curse enter your bowels and
make your womb discharge, your
uterus drop!" And the woman shall
say, "Amen. Amen."
23 Then the priest shall put
these curses in writing, and wash
them off into the water of bitterness. 24 He shall make the woman
drink the water of bitterness that
brings the curse, and the water that
brings the curse shall enter her and
cause bitter pain. 25 The priest shall
take the grain offering of jealousy
out of the woman's hand, and shall
elevate the grain offering before
the LORD and bring it to the altar;
26 and the priest shall take a handful of the grain offering, as its memorial portion, and turn it into
smoke on the altar, and afterward
shall make the woman drink the
water. 27 When he has made her
drink the water, then, if she has defiled herself and has been unfaithful to her husband, the water that
brings the curse shall enter into her
and cause bitter pain, and her
womb shall discharge, her uterus
drop, and the woman shall become
an execration among her people.
28 But if the woman has not defiled
herself and is clean, then she shall
be immune and be able to conceive
children.
29 This is the law in cases of
jealousy, when a wife, while under
her husband's authority, goes
astray and defiles herself, 30 or
when a spirit of jealousy comes on
a man and he is jealous of his wife;
then he shall set the woman before
the LORD, and the priest shall apply
this entire law to her. 31 The man
shall be free from iniquity, but the
woman shall bear her iniquity.

The Nazirites

6 The LORD spoke to Moses, saying: 2 Speak to the Israelites
and say to them: When either men
or women make a special vow, the
vow of a nazirite,[h] to separate
themselves to the LORD, 3 they shall
separate themselves from wine and
strong drink; they shall drink no
wine vinegar or other vinegar, and
shall not drink any grape juice or
eat grapes, fresh or dried. 4 All their
days as nazirites[i] they shall eat
nothing that is produced by the
grapevine, not even the seeds or
the skins.
5 All the days of their nazirite
vow no razor shall come upon the
head; until the time is completed
for which they separate themselves
to the LORD, they shall be holy; they
shall let the locks of the head grow
long.
6 All the days that they separate
themselves to the LORD they shall
not go near a corpse. 7 Even if their
father or mother, brother or sister,
should die, they may not defile
themselves; because their consecration to God is upon the head.
8 All their days as nazirites[i] they
are holy to the LORD.
9 If someone dies very suddenly
nearby, defiling the consecrated
head, then they shall shave the
head on the day of their cleansing;
on the seventh day they shall shave
it. 10 On the eighth day they shall
bring two turtledoves or two young
pigeons to the priest at the entrance of the tent of meeting, 11 and
the priest shall offer one as a sin
offering and the other as a burnt offering, and make atonement for
them, because they incurred guilt
by reason of the corpse. They shall
sanctify the head that same day,
12 and separate themselves to the
LORD for their days as nazirites,[i]

5.21 Josh 6.26; 1 Sam 14.24; Neh 10.29
5.22 Deut 27.15; Ps 109.18
5.25 Lev 8.27
5.27 Jer 29.18; 42.18; Zech 8.13
5.29 vv. 12,19
6.2 Judg 13.5; 16.17; Am 2.11,12
6.5 1 Sam 1.11
6.6 Lev 19.11-22; 21.1-3
6.10 Lev 5.7
6.12 Lev 5.6

[h] That is *one separated* or *one consecrated*
[i] That is *those separated* or *those consecrated*

and bring a male lamb a year old as
a guilt offering. The former time
shall be void, because the consecrated head was defiled.
13 This is the law for the nazirites[j] when the time of their consecration has been completed:
they shall be brought to the entrance of the tent of meeting, 14 and
they shall offer their gift to the
LORD, one male lamb a year old
without blemish as a burnt offering, one ewe lamb a year old without blemish as a sin offering, one
ram without blemish as an offering
of well-being, 15 and a basket of unleavened bread, cakes of choice
flour mixed with oil and unleavened wafers spread with oil,
with their grain offering and their
drink offerings. 16 The priest shall
present them before the LORD and
offer their sin offering and burnt offering, 17 and shall offer the ram as
a sacrifice of well-being to the
LORD, with the basket of unleavened bread; the priest also shall
make the accompanying grain offering and drink offering. 18 Then
the nazirites[j] shall shave the consecrated head at the entrance of
the tent of meeting, and shall take
the hair from the consecrated head
and put it on the fire under the sacrifice of well-being. 19 The priest
shall take the shoulder of the ram,
when it is boiled, and one unleavened cake out of the basket, and
one unleavened wafer, and shall
put them in the palms of the nazirites,[j] after they have shaved the
consecrated head. 20 Then the
priest shall elevate them as an elevation offering before the LORD;
they are a holy portion for the
priest, together with the breast that
is elevated and the thigh that is offered. After that the nazirites[j] may
drink wine.
21 This is the law for the nazirites[j] who take a vow. Their offering to the LORD must be in accordance with the nazirite[k] vow, apart
from what else they can afford. In
accordance with whatever vow they
take, so they shall do, following the
law for their consecration.

The Priestly Benediction

22 The LORD spoke to Moses,
saying: 23 Speak to Aaron and his
sons, saying, Thus you shall bless
the Israelites: You shall say to
them,

24 The LORD bless you and keep
you;
25 the LORD make his face to
shine upon you, and be
gracious to you;
26 the LORD lift up his
countenance upon you,
and give you peace.

27 So they shall put my name on
the Israelites, and I will bless them.

Offerings of the Leaders

7 On the day when Moses had
finished setting up the tabernacle, and had anointed and consecrated it with all its furnishings,
and had anointed and consecrated
the altar with all its utensils, 2 the
leaders of Israel, heads of their ancestral houses, the leaders of the
tribes, who were over those who
were enrolled, made offerings.
3 They brought their offerings before the LORD, six covered wagons
and twelve oxen, a wagon for every
two of the leaders, and for each one
an ox; they presented them before
the tabernacle. 4 Then the LORD
said to Moses: 5 Accept these from
them, that they may be used in doing the service of the tent of meeting, and give them to the Levites, to
each according to his service. 6 So
Moses took the wagons and the
oxen, and gave them to the Levites.
7 Two wagons and four oxen he
gave to the Gershonites, according
to their service; 8 and four wagons
and eight oxen he gave to the Merarites, according to their service, under the direction of Ithamar son of
Aaron the priest. 9 But to the Kohathites he gave none, because
they were charged with the care of
the holy things that had to be carried on the shoulders.
10 The leaders also presented
offerings for the dedication of the

6.13 Acts 21.26
6.14 Num 15.27; Lev 14.10
6.15 Num 15.1-7
6.18 v. 9; Acts 21.24
6.23 1 Chr 23.13
6.24 Deut 28.3-6
6.25 Ps 80.3,7, 19; 119.135; Gen 43.29
6.26 Ps 4.6; 44.3; Jn 14.27
6.27 Deut 28.10; 2 Chr 7.14
7.1 Ex 40.18
7.2 Num 1.5-16
7.7 Num 4.25
7.8 Num 4.28, 31,33
7.9 Num 4.5-15
7.10 2 Chr 7.9

[j] That is *those separated* or *those consecrated*
[k] That is *one separated* or *one consecrated*

altar at the time when it was
anointed; the leaders presented
their offering before the altar.
11 The LORD said to Moses: They
shall present their offerings, one
leader each day, for the dedication
of the altar.
12 The one who presented his
offering the first day was Nahshon
son of Amminadab, of the tribe of
Judah; 13 his offering was one silver
plate weighing one hundred thirty
shekels, one silver basin weighing
seventy shekels, according to the
shekel of the sanctuary, both of
them full of choice flour mixed
with oil for a grain offering; 14 one
golden dish weighing ten shekels,
full of incense; 15 one young bull,
one ram, one male lamb a year old,
for a burnt offering; 16 one male
goat for a sin offering; 17 and for the
sacrifice of well-being, two oxen,
five rams, five male goats, and five
male lambs a year old. This was the
offering of Nahshon son of Amminadab.
18 On the second day Nethanel
son of Zuar, the leader of Issachar,
presented an offering; 19 he presented for his offering one silver
plate weighing one hundred thirty
shekels, one silver basin weighing
seventy shekels, according to the
shekel of the sanctuary, both of
them full of choice flour mixed
with oil for a grain offering; 20 one
golden dish weighing ten shekels,
full of incense; 21 one young bull,
one ram, one male lamb a year old,
as a burnt offering; 22 one male goat
as a sin offering; 23 and for the sacrifice of well-being, two oxen, five
rams, five male goats, and five male
lambs a year old. This was the offering of Nethanel son of Zuar.
24 On the third day Eliab son of
Helon, the leader of the Zebulunites: 25 his offering was one silver
plate weighing one hundred thirty
shekels, one silver basin weighing
seventy shekels, according to the
shekel of the sanctuary, both of
them full of choice flour mixed
with oil for a grain offering; 26 one
golden dish weighing ten shekels,
full of incense; 27 one young bull,
one ram, one male lamb a year old,
for a burnt offering; 28 one male
goat for a sin offering; 29 and for the
sacrifice of well-being, two oxen,
five rams, five male goats, and five
male lambs a year old. This was the
offering of Eliab son of Helon.
30 On the fourth day Elizur son
of Shedeur, the leader of the Reubenites: 31 his offering was one silver plate weighing one hundred
thirty shekels, one silver basin
weighing seventy shekels, according to the shekel of the sanctuary,
both of them full of choice flour
mixed with oil for a grain offering;
32 one golden dish weighing ten
shekels, full of incense; 33 one
young bull, one ram, one male
lamb a year old, for a burnt offering; 34 one male goat for a sin offering; 35 and for the sacrifice of well-
being, two oxen, five rams, five
male goats, and five male lambs a
year old. This was the offering of
Elizur son of Shedeur.
36 On the fifth day Shelumiel
son of Zurishaddai, the leader of
the Simeonites: 37 his offering was
one silver plate weighing one hundred thirty shekels, one silver basin
weighing seventy shekels, according to the shekel of the sanctuary,
both of them full of choice flour
mixed with oil for a grain offering;
38 one golden dish weighing ten
shekels, full of incense; 39 one
young bull, one ram, one male
lamb a year old, for a burnt offering; 40 one male goat for a sin offering; 41 and for the sacrifice of well-
being, two oxen, five rams, five
male goats, and five male lambs a
year old. This was the offering of
Shelumiel son of Zurishaddai.
42 On the sixth day Eliasaph
son of Deuel, the leader of the Gadites: 43 his offering was one silver
plate weighing one hundred thirty
shekels, one silver basin weighing
seventy shekels, according to the
shekel of the sanctuary, both of
them full of choice flour mixed
with oil for a grain offering; 44 one
golden dish weighing ten shekels,
full of incense; 45 one young bull,
one ram, one male lamb a year old,

7.13 Num 3.47
7.14 Ex 30.34
7.17 Lev 3.1
7.18 Num 1.8
7.23 v. 18
7.24 Num 1.9
7.29 Lev 7.32
7.30 Num 1.5
7.34 Heb 10.4
7.36 Num 1.6
7.40 v. 34
7.42 Num 1.14

for a burnt offering; 46 one male
goat for a sin offering; 47 and for the
sacrifice of well-being, two oxen,
five rams, five male goats, and five
male lambs a year old. This was the
offering of Eliasaph son of Deuel.
48 On the seventh day Elishama
son of Ammihud, the leader of the
Ephraimites: 49 his offering was one
silver plate weighing one hundred
thirty shekels, one silver basin
weighing seventy shekels, according to the shekel of the sanctuary,
both of them full of choice flour
mixed with oil for a grain offering;
50 one golden dish weighing ten
shekels, full of incense; 51 one
young bull, one ram, one male
lamb a year old, for a burnt offering; 52 one male goat for a sin offering; 53 and for the sacrifice of well-
being, two oxen, five rams, five
male goats, and five male lambs a
year old. This was the offering of
Elishama son of Ammihud.
54 On the eighth day Gamaliel
son of Pedahzur, the leader of the
Manassites: 55 his offering was one
silver plate weighing one hundred
thirty shekels, one silver basin
weighing seventy shekels, according to the shekel of the sanctuary,
both of them full of choice flour
mixed with oil for a grain offering;
56 one golden dish weighing ten
shekels, full of incense; 57 one
young bull, one ram, one male
lamb a year old, for a burnt offering; 58 one male goat for a sin offering; 59 and for the sacrifice of well-
being, two oxen, five rams, five
male goats, and five male lambs a
year old. This was the offering of
Gamaliel son of Pedahzur.
60 On the ninth day Abidan son
of Gideoni, the leader of the Benjaminites: 61 his offering was one silver plate weighing one hundred
thirty shekels, one silver basin
weighing seventy shekels, according to the shekel of the sanctuary,
both of them full of choice flour
mixed with oil for a grain offering;
62 one golden dish weighing ten
shekels, full of incense; 63 one
young bull, one ram, one male
lamb a year old, for a burnt offering; 64 one male goat for a sin offering; 65 and for the sacrifice of well-
being, two oxen, five rams, five
male goats, and five male lambs a
year old. This was the offering of
Abidan son of Gideoni.
66 On the tenth day Ahiezer son
of Ammishaddai, the leader of the
Danites: 67 his offering was one silver plate weighing one hundred
thirty shekels, one silver basin
weighing seventy shekels, according to the shekel of the sanctuary,
both of them full of choice flour
mixed with oil for a grain offering;
68 one golden dish weighing ten
shekels, full of incense; 69 one
young bull, one ram, one male
lamb a year old, for a burnt offering; 70 one male goat for a sin offering; 71 and for the sacrifice of well-
being, two oxen, five rams, five
male goats, and five male lambs a
year old. This was the offering of
Ahiezer son of Ammishaddai.
72 On the eleventh day Pagiel
son of Ochran, the leader of the
Asherites: 73 his offering was one
silver plate weighing one hundred
thirty shekels, one silver basin
weighing seventy shekels, according to the shekel of the sanctuary,
both of them full of choice flour
mixed with oil for a grain offering;
74 one golden dish weighing ten
shekels, full of incense; 75 one
young bull, one ram, one male
lamb a year old, for a burnt offering; 76 one male goat for a sin offering; 77 and for the sacrifice of well-
being, two oxen, five rams, five
male goats, and five male lambs a
year old. This was the offering of
Pagiel son of Ochran.
78 On the twelfth day Ahira son
of Enan, the leader of the Naphtalites: 79 his offering was one silver
plate weighing one hundred thirty
shekels, one silver basin weighing
seventy shekels, according to the
shekel of the sanctuary, both of
them full of choice flour mixed
with oil for a grain offering; 80 one
golden dish weighing ten shekels,
full of incense; 81 one young bull,
one ram, one male lamb a year old,
for a burnt offering; 82 one male

7.46 v. 34
7.48 Num 1.10
7.52 Heb 10.4
7.54 Num 1.10
7.58 v. 52
7.60 Num 1.11
7.64 v. 52
7.66 Num 1.12
7.70 Heb 10.4
7.72 Num 1.13
7.76 v. 70
7.78 Num 1.15
7.82 v. 70

goat for a sin offering; 83 and for the
sacrifice of well-being, two oxen,
five rams, five male goats, and five
male lambs a year old. This was the
offering of Ahira son of Enan.

84 This was the dedication offering for the altar, at the time
when it was anointed, from the
leaders of Israel: twelve silver
plates, twelve silver basins, twelve
golden dishes, 85 each silver plate
weighing one hundred thirty shekels and each basin seventy, all the
silver of the vessels two thousand
four hundred shekels according to
the shekel of the sanctuary, 86 the
twelve golden dishes, full of incense, weighing ten shekels apiece
according to the shekel of the sanctuary, all the gold of the dishes being one hundred twenty shekels;
87 all the livestock for the burnt offering twelve bulls, twelve rams,
twelve male lambs a year old, with
their grain offering; and twelve
male goats for a sin offering; 88 and
all the livestock for the sacrifice of
well-being twenty-four bulls, the
rams sixty, the male goats sixty,
the male lambs a year old sixty.
This was the dedication offering for
the altar, after it was anointed.

89 When Moses went into the
tent of meeting to speak with the
LORD,[l] he would hear the voice
speaking to him from above the
mercy seat[m] that was on the ark of
the covenant[n] from between the
two cherubim; thus it spoke to
him.

7.84 vv. 1,10 **7.87** Gen 8.20 **7.89** Ex 33.9,11; 25.21,22 **8.2** Ex 25.37; Lev 24.2,4 **8.4** Ex 25.31-40; 25.18

The Seven Lamps

8 The LORD spoke to Moses, saying: 2 Speak to Aaron and say
to him: When you set up the lamps,
the seven lamps shall give light in
front of the lampstand. 3 Aaron did
so; he set up its lamps to give light
in front of the lampstand, as the
LORD had commanded Moses.
4 Now this was how the lampstand
was made, out of hammered work
of gold. From its base to its flowers,
it was hammered work; according
to the pattern that the LORD had
shown Moses, so he made the
lampstand.

8.7 Num 19.9, 17,18; Lev 14.8,9; v. 21 **8.8** Lev 2.1 **8.9** Lev 8.3 **8.12** Ex 29.10 **8.14** Num 3.12, 45 **8.15** vv. 11,13 **8.16** Num 3.12, 45

Consecration and Service of the Levites

5 The LORD spoke to Moses, saying: 6 Take the Levites from among
the Israelites and cleanse them.
7 Thus you shall do to them, to
cleanse them: sprinkle the water of
purification on them, have them
shave their whole body with a razor
and wash their clothes, and so
cleanse themselves. 8 Then let
them take a young bull and its
grain offering of choice flour mixed
with oil, and you shall take another
young bull for a sin offering. 9 You
shall bring the Levites before the
tent of meeting, and assemble the
whole congregation of the Israelites. 10 When you bring the Levites
before the LORD, the Israelites shall
lay their hands on the Levites,
11 and Aaron shall present the Levites before the LORD as an elevation offering from the Israelites,
that they may do the service of the
LORD. 12 The Levites shall lay their
hands on the heads of the bulls,
and he shall offer the one for a sin
offering and the other for a burnt
offering to the LORD, to make
atonement for the Levites. 13 Then
you shall have the Levites stand before Aaron and his sons, and you
shall present them as an elevation
offering to the LORD.

14 Thus you shall separate the
Levites from among the other Israelites, and the Levites shall be
mine. 15 Thereafter the Levites may
go in to do service at the tent of
meeting, once you have cleansed
them and presented them as an elevation offering. 16 For they are unreservedly given to me from among
the Israelites; I have taken them for
myself, in place of all that open the
womb, the firstborn of all the Israelites. 17 For all the firstborn among
the Israelites are mine, both human and animal. On the day that I
struck down all the firstborn in the
land of Egypt I consecrated them
for myself, 18 but I have taken the
Levites in place of all the firstborn

[l] Heb *him* [m] Or *the cover* [n] Or *treaty*, or *testimony*; Heb *eduth*

among the Israelites. 19 Moreover, I
have given the Levites as a gift to
Aaron and his sons from among the
Israelites, to do the service for the
Israelites at the tent of meeting,
and to make atonement for the Israelites, in order that there may be
no plague among the Israelites for
coming too close to the sanctuary.
20 Moses and Aaron and the
whole congregation of the Israelites did with the Levites accordingly; the Israelites did with the Levites just as the LORD had
commanded Moses concerning
them. 21 The Levites purified themselves from sin and washed their
clothes; then Aaron presented
them as an elevation offering before the LORD, and Aaron made
atonement for them to cleanse
them. 22 Thereafter the Levites
went in to do their service in the
tent of meeting in attendance on
Aaron and his sons. As the LORD
had commanded Moses concerning the Levites, so they did with
them.
23 The LORD spoke to Moses,
saying: 24 This applies to the Levites: from twenty-five years old
and upward they shall begin to do
duty in the service of the tent of
meeting; 25 and from the age of fifty
years they shall retire from the duty
of the service and serve no more.
26 They may assist their brothers in
the tent of meeting in carrying out
their duties, but they shall perform
no service. Thus you shall do with
the Levites in assigning their duties.

The Passover at Sinai

9 The LORD spoke to Moses in
the wilderness of Sinai, in the
first month of the second year after
they had come out of the land of
Egypt, saying: 2 Let the Israelites
keep the passover at its appointed
time. 3 On the fourteenth day of
this month, at twilight,[o] you shall
keep it at its appointed time; according to all its statutes and all its
regulations you shall keep it. 4 So
Moses told the Israelites that they
should keep the passover. 5 They
kept the passover in the first
month, on the fourteenth day of
the month, at twilight,[o] in the wilderness of Sinai. Just as the LORD
had commanded Moses, so the Israelites did. 6 Now there were certain people who were unclean
through touching a corpse, so that
they could not keep the passover
on that day. They came before Moses and Aaron on that day, 7 and
said to him, "Although we are unclean through touching a corpse,
why must we be kept from presenting the LORD's offering at its appointed time among the Israelites?" 8 Moses spoke to them,
"Wait, so that I may hear what the
LORD will command concerning
you."
9 The LORD spoke to Moses, saying: 10 Speak to the Israelites, saying: Anyone of you or your descendants who is unclean through
touching a corpse, or is away on a
journey, shall still keep the passover to the LORD. 11 In the second
month on the fourteenth day, at
twilight,[o] they shall keep it; they
shall eat it with unleavened bread
and bitter herbs. 12 They shall leave
none of it until morning, nor break
a bone of it; according to all the
statute for the passover they shall
keep it. 13 But anyone who is clean
and is not on a journey, and yet refrains from keeping the passover,
shall be cut off from the people for
not presenting the LORD's offering
at its appointed time; such a one
shall bear the consequences for the
sin. 14 Any alien residing among
you who wishes to keep the passover to the LORD shall do so according to the statute of the passover
and according to its regulation; you
shall have one statute for both the
resident alien and the native.

The Cloud and the Fire

15 On the day the tabernacle
was set up, the cloud covered the
tabernacle, the tent of the covenant;[p] and from evening until
morning it was over the tabernacle,

8.19 Num 1.53 **8.21** vv. 7,11,12 **8.24** Num 4.3 **9.1** Num 1.1 **9.2** Ex 12.6 **9.5** Josh 5.10

9.6 Num 19.11-22 **9.8** Ex 18.15; Num 27.5 **9.11** Ex 12.8 **9.12** Ex 12.10, 43,46; Jn 19.36 **9.13** v. 7; Ex 12.15 **9.14** Ex 12.48,49 **9.15** Ex 40.34; Neh 9.12, 19; Ps 78.4; Ex 13.21; 40.38

[o] Heb *between the two evenings*
[p] Or *treaty*, or *testimony*; Heb *eduth*

having the appearance of fire. 16 It was always so: the cloud covered it by day[q] and the appearance of fire by night. 17 Whenever the cloud lifted from over the tent, then the Israelites would set out; and in the place where the cloud settled down, there the Israelites would camp. 18 At the command of the LORD the Israelites would set out, and at the command of the LORD they would camp. As long as the cloud rested over the tabernacle, they would remain in camp. 19 Even when the cloud continued over the tabernacle many days, the Israelites would keep the charge of the LORD, and would not set out. 20 Sometimes the cloud would remain a few days over the tabernacle, and according to the command of the LORD they would remain in camp; then according to the command of the LORD they would set out. 21 Sometimes the cloud would remain from evening until morning; and when the cloud lifted in the morning, they would set out, or if it continued for a day and a night, when the cloud lifted they would set out. 22 Whether it was two days, or a month, or a longer time, that the cloud continued over the tabernacle, resting upon it, the Israelites would remain in camp and would not set out; but when it lifted they would set out. 23 At the command of the LORD they would camp, and at the command of the LORD they would set out. They kept the charge of the LORD, at the command of the LORD by Moses.

The Silver Trumpets

10 The LORD spoke to Moses, saying: 2 Make two silver trumpets; you shall make them of hammered work; and you shall use them for summoning the congregation, and for breaking camp. 3 When both are blown, the whole congregation shall assemble before you at the entrance of the tent of meeting. 4 But if only one is blown, then the leaders, the heads of the tribes of Israel, shall assemble before you. 5 When you blow an alarm, the camps on the east side shall set out; 6 when you blow a second alarm, the camps on the south side shall set out. An alarm is to be blown whenever they are to set out. 7 But when the assembly is to be gathered, you shall blow, but you shall not sound an alarm. 8 The sons of Aaron, the priests, shall blow the trumpets; this shall be a perpetual institution for you throughout your generations. 9 When you go to war in your land against the adversary who oppresses you, you shall sound an alarm with the trumpets, so that you may be remembered before the LORD your God and be saved from your enemies. 10 Also on your days of rejoicing, at your appointed festivals, and at the beginnings of your months, you shall blow the trumpets over your burnt offerings and over your sacrifices of well-being; they shall serve as a reminder on your behalf before the LORD your God: I am the LORD your God.

Departure from Sinai

11 In the second year, in the second month, on the twentieth day of the month, the cloud lifted from over the tabernacle of the covenant.[r] 12 Then the Israelites set out by stages from the wilderness of Sinai, and the cloud settled down in the wilderness of Paran. 13 They set out for the first time at the command of the LORD by Moses. 14 The standard of the camp of Judah set out first, company by company, and over the whole company was Nahshon son of Amminadab. 15 Over the company of the tribe of Issachar was Nethanel son of Zuar; 16 and over the company of the tribe of Zebulun was Eliab son of Helon.

17 Then the tabernacle was taken down, and the Gershonites and the Merarites, who carried the tabernacle, set out. 18 Next the standard of the camp of Reuben set out, company by company; and over the whole company was Elizur son of

9.17 Num 10.11, 12; Ex 40.36-38
9.18 1 Cor 10.1
9.19 Num 1.53; 3.8
9.22 Ex 40.36,37
10.3 Jer 4.5
10.5 v. 14
10.6 v. 18
10.8 Num 31.6
10.9 Num 31.6; Judg 2.18; Ps 106.4
10.10 Num 29.1; Lev 23.24; Ps 81.3-5
10.11 Num 9.17
10.13 Deut 1.6
10.14 Num 2.3-9
10.17 Num 4.21-32
10.18 Num 2.10-16

[q] Gk Syr Vg: Heb lacks *by day* [r] Or *treaty*, or *testimony*; Heb *eduth*

Shedeur. [19]Over the company of
the tribe of Simeon was Shelumiel
son of Zurishaddai, [20]and over the
company of the tribe of Gad was
Eliasaph son of Deuel.
21 Then the Kohathites, who
carried the holy things, set out; and
the tabernacle was set up before
their arrival. [22]Next the standard of
the Ephraimite camp set out, company by company, and over the
whole company was Elishama son
of Ammihud. [23]Over the company
of the tribe of Manasseh was Gamaliel son of Pedahzur, [24]and over
the company of the tribe of Benjamin was Abidan son of Gideoni.
25 Then the standard of the
camp of Dan, acting as the rear
guard of all the camps, set out,
company by company, and over the
whole company was Ahiezer son of
Ammishaddai. [26]Over the company of the tribe of Asher was Pagiel
son of Ochran, [27]and over the company of the tribe of Naphtali was
Ahira son of Enan. [28]This was the
order of march of the Israelites,
company by company, when they
set out.
29 Moses said to Hobab son of
Reuel the Midianite, Moses'
father-in-law, "We are setting out
for the place of which the LORD
said, 'I will give it to you'; come
with us, and we will treat you well;
for the LORD has promised good to
Israel." [30]But he said to him, "I will
not go, but I will go back to my own
land and to my kindred." [31]He said,
"Do not leave us, for you know
where we should camp in the wilderness, and you will serve as eyes
for us. [32]Moreover, if you go with
us, whatever good the LORD does for
us, the same we will do for you."
33 So they set out from the
mount of the LORD three days' journey with the ark of the covenant of
the LORD going before them three
days' journey, to seek out a resting
place for them, [34]the cloud of the
LORD being over them by day when
they set out from the camp.
35 Whenever the ark set out,
Moses would say,

10.21 Num 4.4-20
10.22 Num 2.18-24
10.25 Num 2.25-31; Josh 6.9,13
10.29 Judg 4.11; Ex 2.18; Gen 12.7; 32.12; Ex 3.8
10.32 Ps 22.27-31; Lev 19.34
10.33 v. 11; Deut 1.33; Isa 11.10
10.34 Num 9.15-23
10.35 Ps 68.1,2; Deut 7.10; 32.41
11.1 Num 14.2; 16.11; 17.5; 16.35; Lev 10.2
11.2 Num 21.7
11.4 Ex 12.38; Ps 78.18; 1 Cor 10.6
11.5 Ex 16.3
11.6 Lev 21.5
11.7 Ex 16.14,31
11.9 Ex 16.13,14
11.10 Ps 78.21
11.12 Isa 40.11; 49.23; Gen 26.3; Ex 13.5

"Arise, O LORD, let your
enemies be scattered,
and your foes flee before
you."
[36]And whenever it came to rest, he
would say,
"Return, O LORD of the ten
thousand thousands of
Israel."[s]

Complaining in the Desert

11 Now when the people complained in the hearing of
the LORD about their misfortunes,
the LORD heard it and his anger was
kindled. Then the fire of the LORD
burned against them, and consumed some outlying parts of the
camp. [2]But the people cried out to
Moses; and Moses prayed to the
LORD, and the fire abated. [3]So that
place was called Taberah,[t] because the fire of the LORD burned
against them.
4 The rabble among them had a
strong craving; and the Israelites
also wept again, and said, "If only
we had meat to eat! [5]We remember
the fish we used to eat in Egypt for
nothing, the cucumbers, the melons, the leeks, the onions, and the
garlic; [6]but now our strength is
dried up, and there is nothing at all
but this manna to look at."
7 Now the manna was like coriander seed, and its color was like
the color of gum resin. [8]The people
went around and gathered it,
ground it in mills or beat it in mortars, then boiled it in pots and
made cakes of it; and the taste of it
was like the taste of cakes baked
with oil. [9]When the dew fell on the
camp in the night, the manna
would fall with it.
10 Moses heard the people
weeping throughout their families,
all at the entrances of their tents.
Then the LORD became very angry,
and Moses was displeased. [11]So
Moses said to the LORD, "Why have
you treated your servant so badly?
Why have I not found favor in your
sight, that you lay the burden of all
this people on me? [12]Did I con-

[s] Meaning of Heb uncertain [t] That is *Burning*

ceive all this people? Did I give
birth to them, that you should say
to me, 'Carry them in your bosom,
as a nurse carries a sucking child,'
to the land that you promised on
oath to their ancestors? 13 Where
am I to get meat to give to all this
people? For they come weeping to
me and say, 'Give us meat to eat!'
14 I am not able to carry all this people alone, for they are too heavy for
me. 15 If this is the way you are going to treat me, put me to death at
once—if I have found favor in your
sight—and do not let me see my
misery."

The Seventy Elders

16 So the LORD said to Moses,
"Gather for me seventy of the elders of Israel, whom you know to
be the elders of the people and officers over them; bring them to the
tent of meeting, and have them
take their place there with you. 17 I
will come down and talk with you
there; and I will take some of the
spirit that is on you and put it on
them; and they shall bear the burden of the people along with you so
that you will not bear it all by yourself. 18 And say to the people: Consecrate yourselves for tomorrow,
and you shall eat meat; for you
have wailed in the hearing of the
LORD, saying, 'If only we had meat
to eat! Surely it was better for us in
Egypt.' Therefore the LORD will give
you meat, and you shall eat. 19 You
shall eat not only one day, or two
days, or five days, or ten days, or
twenty days, 20 but for a whole
month—until it comes out of your
nostrils and becomes loathsome to
you—because you have rejected
the LORD who is among you, and
have wailed before him, saying,
'Why did we ever leave Egypt?' "
21 But Moses said, "The people I am
with number six hundred thousand
on foot; and you say, 'I will give
them meat, that they may eat for a
whole month'! 22 Are there enough
flocks and herds to slaughter for
them? Are there enough fish in the
sea to catch for them?" 23 The LORD
said to Moses, "Is the LORD's power
limited?[u] Now you shall see
whether my word will come true for
you or not."
24 So Moses went out and told
the people the words of the LORD;
and he gathered seventy elders of
the people, and placed them all
around the tent. 25 Then the LORD
came down in the cloud and spoke
to him, and took some of the spirit
that was on him and put it on the
seventy elders; and when the spirit
rested upon them, they prophesied. But they did not do so again.
26 Two men remained in the
camp, one named Eldad, and the
other named Medad, and the spirit
rested on them; they were among
those registered, but they had not
gone out to the tent, and so they
prophesied in the camp. 27 And a
young man ran and told Moses,
"Eldad and Medad are prophesying
in the camp." 28 And Joshua son of
Nun, the assistant of Moses, one of
his chosen men,[v] said, "My lord
Moses, stop them!" 29 But Moses
said to him, "Are you jealous for my
sake? Would that all the LORD's
people were prophets, and that the
LORD would put his spirit on them!"
30 And Moses and the elders of Israel returned to the camp.

The Quails

31 Then a wind went out from
the LORD, and it brought quails
from the sea and let them fall beside the camp, about a day's journey on this side and a day's journey
on the other side, all around the
camp, about two cubits deep on
the ground. 32 So the people
worked all that day and night and
all the next day, gathering the
quails; the least anyone gathered
was ten homers; and they spread
them out for themselves all around
the camp. 33 But while the meat
was still between their teeth, before it was consumed, the anger of
the LORD was kindled against the
people, and the LORD struck the
people with a very great plague.
34 So that place was called Kibroth-

11.13 vv. 21,22; Jn 6.5-9
11.14 Ex 18.18
11.15 1 Kings 19.4; Jon 4.3
11.16 Ex 24.1,9; Deut 16.18
11.17 v. 25; Ex 19.20; 1 Sam 10.6; 2 Kings 2.15
11.18 Ex 19.10; 16.7; v. 5; Acts 7.39
11.19 Ps 78.29; 106.15; Num 21.5
11.22 Mt 15.33
11.23 Isa 50.2; 59.1; Num 23.19
11.24 v. 16
11.25 v. 17; Num 12.5; 1 Sam 10.5, 6,10; Acts 2.17,18
11.26 1 Sam 10.6; 20.26
11.28 Mk 9.38-40
11.29 1 Cor 14.5
11.31 Ex 16.13; Ps 78.26-28; 105.40
11.33 Ps 78.30,31; 106.15
11.34 Deut 9.22

[u] Heb *LORD's hand too short?* [v] Or *of Moses from his youth*

hattaavah,[w] because there they buried the people who had the craving. 35 From Kibroth-hattaavah the people journeyed to Hazeroth.

Aaron and Miriam Jealous of Moses

12 While they were at Hazeroth, Miriam and Aaron spoke against Moses because of the Cushite woman whom he had married (for he had indeed married a Cushite woman); 2 and they said, "Has the LORD spoken only through Moses? Has he not spoken through us also?" And the LORD heard it. 3 Now the man Moses was very humble,[x] more so than anyone else on the face of the earth. 4 Suddenly the LORD said to Moses, Aaron, and Miriam, "Come out, you three, to the tent of meeting." So the three of them came out. 5 Then the LORD came down in a pillar of cloud, and stood at the entrance of the tent, and called Aaron and Miriam; and they both came forward. 6 And he said, "Hear my words:

When there are prophets
among you,
I the LORD make myself
known to them in
visions;
I speak to them in dreams.
7 Not so with my servant
Moses;
he is entrusted with all my
house.
8 With him I speak face to
face—clearly, not in
riddles;
and he beholds the form of
the LORD.

Why then were you not afraid to speak against my servant Moses?" 9 And the anger of the LORD was kindled against them, and he departed.

10 When the cloud went away from over the tent, Miriam had become leprous,[y] as white as snow. And Aaron turned towards Miriam and saw that she was leprous. 11 Then Aaron said to Moses, "Oh, my lord, do not punish us[z] for a sin that we have so foolishly committed. 12 Do not let her be like one stillborn, whose flesh is half consumed when it comes out of its mother's womb." 13 And Moses cried to the LORD, "O God, please heal her." 14 But the LORD said to Moses, "If her father had but spit in her face, would she not bear her shame for seven days? Let her be shut out of the camp for seven days, and after that she may be brought in again." 15 So Miriam was shut out of the camp for seven days; and the people did not set out on the march until Miriam had been brought in again. 16 After that the people set out from Hazeroth, and camped in the wilderness of Paran.

Spies Sent into Canaan

13 The LORD said to Moses, 2 "Send men to spy out the land of Canaan, which I am giving to the Israelites; from each of their ancestral tribes you shall send a man, every one a leader among them." 3 So Moses sent them from the wilderness of Paran, according to the command of the LORD, all of them leading men among the Israelites. 4 These were their names: From the tribe of Reuben, Shammua son of Zaccur; 5 from the tribe of Simeon, Shaphat son of Hori; 6 from the tribe of Judah, Caleb son of Jephunneh; 7 from the tribe of Issachar, Igal son of Joseph; 8 from the tribe of Ephraim, Hoshea son of Nun; 9 from the tribe of Benjamin, Palti son of Raphu; 10 from the tribe of Zebulun, Gaddiel son of Sodi; 11 from the tribe of Joseph (that is, from the tribe of Manasseh), Gaddi son of Susi; 12 from the tribe of Dan, Ammiel son of Gemalli; 13 from the tribe of Asher, Sethur son of Michael; 14 from the tribe of Naphtali, Nahbi son of Vophsi; 15 from the tribe of Gad, Geuel son of Machi. 16 These were the names of the men whom Moses sent to spy out the land. And Moses changed

11.35 Num 33.17
12.1 Ex 2.21
12.2 Num 16.3
12.3 Mt 11.29
12.5 Num 11.25; 16.19
12.6 Gen 46.2; 31.10,11; 1 Kings 3.5
12.7 Ps 105.26; Heb 3.2,5
12.8 Ex 33.11; Deut 34.10; Ex 33.19
12.10 Deut 24.9; 2 Kings 5.27; 15.5
12.11 2 Sam 19.19; 24.10
12.14 Lev 13.46; Num 5.2,3
13.2 Deut 1.22
13.8 v. 16
13.16 v. 8

[w] That is *Graves of craving* [x] Or *devout*
[y] A term for several skin diseases; precise meaning uncertain [z] Heb *do not lay sin upon us*

the name of Hoshea son of Nun to
Joshua.
17 Moses sent them to spy out
the land of Canaan, and said to
them, "Go up there into the Negeb,
and go up into the hill country,
18 and see what the land is like, and
whether the people who live in it
are strong or weak, whether they
are few or many, 19 and whether the
land they live in is good or bad, and
whether the towns that they live in
are unwalled or fortified, 20 and
whether the land is rich or poor,
and whether there are trees in it or
not. Be bold, and bring some of the
fruit of the land." Now it was the
season of the first ripe grapes.
21 So they went up and spied
out the land from the wilderness of
Zin to Rehob, near Lebo-hamath.
22 They went up into the Negeb,
and came to Hebron; and Ahiman,
Sheshai, and Talmai, the Anakites,
were there. (Hebron was built sev-
en years before Zoan in Egypt.)
23 And they came to the Wadi Eshcol, and cut down from there a
branch with a single cluster of
grapes, and they carried it on a pole
between two of them. They also
brought some pomegranates and
figs. 24 That place was called the
Wadi Eshcol,[a] because of the cluster that the Israelites cut down
from there.

The Report of the Spies

25 At the end of forty days they
returned from spying out the land.
26 And they came to Moses and Aaron and to all the congregation of
the Israelites in the wilderness of
Paran, at Kadesh; they brought
back word to them and to all the
congregation, and showed them
the fruit of the land. 27 And they
told him, "We came to the land to
which you sent us; it flows with
milk and honey, and this is its fruit.
28 Yet the people who live in the
land are strong, and the towns are
fortified and very large; and besides, we saw the descendants of
Anak there. 29 The Amalekites live
in the land of the Negeb; the Hittites, the Jebusites, and the Amorites live in the hill country; and
the Canaanites live by the sea, and
along the Jordan."
30 But Caleb quieted the people
before Moses, and said, "Let us go
up at once and occupy it, for we are
well able to overcome it." 31 Then
the men who had gone up with him
said, "We are not able to go up
against this people, for they are
stronger than we." 32 So they
brought to the Israelites an unfavorable report of the land that they
had spied out, saying, "The land
that we have gone through as spies
is a land that devours its inhabitants; and all the people that we
saw in it are of great size. 33 There
we saw the Nephilim (the Anakites
come from the Nephilim); and to
ourselves we seemed like grasshoppers, and so we seemed to them."

The People Rebel

14 Then all the congregation
raised a loud cry, and the
people wept that night. 2 And all
the Israelites complained against
Moses and Aaron; the whole congregation said to them, "Would
that we had died in the land of
Egypt! Or would that we had died
in this wilderness! 3 Why is the LORD
bringing us into this land to fall by
the sword? Our wives and our little
ones will become booty; would it
not be better for us to go back to
Egypt?" 4 So they said to one another, "Let us choose a captain, and go
back to Egypt."
5 Then Moses and Aaron fell on
their faces before all the assembly
of the congregation of the Israelites. 6 And Joshua son of Nun and
Caleb son of Jephunneh, who were
among those who had spied out the
land, tore their clothes 7 and said to
all the congregation of the Israelites, "The land that we went
through as spies is an exceedingly
good land. 8 If the LORD is pleased
with us, he will bring us into this
land and give it to us, a land that
flows with milk and honey. 9 Only,
do not rebel against the LORD; and
do not fear the people of the land,

13.17 v. 21
13.20 Deut 1.24, 25; 31.6,23
13.22 Josh 15.13, 14; vv. 28, 33; Ps 78.12
13.26 v. 3; Num 20.1, 16; 32.8
13.27 Ex 3.8; Deut 1.25
13.28 Deut 1.28
13.29 Num 14.43
13.30 Num 14.6, 24
13.31 Deut 1.28
13.32 Num 14.36; Ps 106.24; Am 2.9
13.33 Deut 1.28; 9.2
14.2 Num 11.1,5
14.5 Num 16.4, 22
14.7 Num 13.27; Deut 1.25
14.8 Deut 10.15; Num 13.27
14.9 Deut 9.7,23, 24; 7.18; 20.1,3,4

[a] That is *Cluster*

for they are no more than bread for
us; their protection is removed
from them, and the LORD is with us;
do not fear them." 10 But the whole
congregation threatened to stone
them.

Then the glory of the LORD appeared at the tent of meeting to all
the Israelites. 11 And the LORD said
to Moses, "How long will this people despise me? And how long will
they refuse to believe in me, in
spite of all the signs that I have
done among them? 12 I will strike
them with pestilence and disinherit them, and I will make of you a
nation greater and mightier than
they."

Moses Intercedes for the People

13 But Moses said to the LORD,
"Then the Egyptians will hear of it,
for in your might you brought up
this people from among them,
14 and they will tell the inhabitants
of this land. They have heard that
you, O LORD, are in the midst of
this people; for you, O LORD, are
seen face to face, and your cloud
stands over them and you go in
front of them, in a pillar of cloud by
day and in a pillar of fire by night.
15 Now if you kill this people all at
one time, then the nations who
have heard about you will say, 16 'It
is because the LORD was not able to
bring this people into the land he
swore to give them that he has
slaughtered them in the wilderness.' 17 And now, therefore, let the
power of the LORD be great in the
way that you promised when you
spoke, saying,

18 'The LORD is slow to anger,
and abounding in steadfast
love,
forgiving iniquity and
transgression,
but by no means clearing the
guilty,
visiting the iniquity of the
parents
upon the children
to the third and the fourth
generation.'

19 Forgive the iniquity of this people according to the greatness of

14.10 Ex 17.4; 16.10; Lev 9.23
14.11 Deut 9.7,8; Ps 78.22; 106.24
14.12 Ex 32.10
14.13 Ps 106.23
14.14 Ex 15.14; Josh 2.9,10; Ex 13.21
14.16 Deut 9.28
14.18 Ex 34.6,7; Ps 103.8; Ex 20.5
14.19 Ex 34.9; Ps 106.45; 78.38
14.20 Ps 106.23
14.21 Ps 72.19
14.24 vv. 7-9; Num 32.12; Josh 14.6-15
14.25 Deut 1.40
14.27 Num 11.1; Ex 16.12
14.28 v. 21; Deut 1.35; see v. 2
14.29 Num 1.45; 26.64
14.30 v. 24; Deut 1.36
14.31 Deut 1.39; Ps 106.24
14.32 1 Cor 10.5
14.33 Num 32.13; Ps 107.40

your steadfast love, just as you
have pardoned this people, from
Egypt even until now."

20 Then the LORD said, "I do forgive, just as you have asked;
21 nevertheless—as I live, and as all
the earth shall be filled with the
glory of the LORD— 22 none of the
people who have seen my glory and
the signs that I did in Egypt and in
the wilderness, and yet have tested
me these ten times and have not
obeyed my voice, 23 shall see the
land that I swore to give to their ancestors; none of those who despised me shall see it. 24 But my
servant Caleb, because he has a different spirit and has followed me
wholeheartedly, I will bring into
the land into which he went, and
his descendants shall possess it.
25 Now, since the Amalekites and
the Canaanites live in the valleys,
turn tomorrow and set out for the
wilderness by the way to the Red
Sea."[b]

An Attempted Invasion is Repulsed

26 And the LORD spoke to Moses
and to Aaron, saying: 27 How long
shall this wicked congregation
complain against me? I have heard
the complaints of the Israelites,
which they complain against me.
28 Say to them, "As I live," says the
LORD, "I will do to you the very
things I heard you say: 29 your dead
bodies shall fall in this very wilderness; and of all your number, included in the census, from twenty
years old and upward, who have
complained against me, 30 not one
of you shall come into the land in
which I swore to settle you, except
Caleb son of Jephunneh and Joshua son of Nun. 31 But your little
ones, who you said would become
booty, I will bring in, and they shall
know the land that you have despised. 32 But as for you, your dead
bodies shall fall in this wilderness.
33 And your children shall be shepherds in the wilderness for forty
years, and shall suffer for your
faithlessness, until the last of your

b Or *Sea of Reeds*

dead bodies lies in the wilderness. 34 According to the number of the days in which you spied out the land, forty days, for every day a year, you shall bear your iniquity, forty years, and you shall know my displeasure." 35 I the LORD have spoken; surely I will do thus to all this wicked congregation gathered together against me: in this wilderness they shall come to a full end, and there they shall die.

36 And the men whom Moses sent to spy out the land, who returned and made all the congregation complain against him by bringing a bad report about the land— 37 the men who brought an unfavorable report about the land died by a plague before the LORD. 38 But Joshua son of Nun and Caleb son of Jephunneh alone remained alive, of those men who went to spy out the land.

39 When Moses told these words to all the Israelites, the people mourned greatly. 40 They rose early in the morning and went up to the heights of the hill country, saying, "Here we are. We will go up to the place that the LORD has promised, for we have sinned." 41 But Moses said, "Why do you continue to transgress the command of the LORD? That will not succeed. 42 Do not go up, for the LORD is not with you; do not let yourselves be struck down before your enemies. 43 For the Amalekites and the Canaanites will confront you there, and you shall fall by the sword; because you have turned back from following the LORD, the LORD will not be with you." 44 But they presumed to go up to the heights of the hill country, even though the ark of the covenant of the LORD, and Moses, had not left the camp. 45 Then the Amalekites and the Canaanites who lived in that hill country came down and defeated them, pursuing them as far as Hormah.

Various Offerings

15 The LORD spoke to Moses, saying: 2 Speak to the Israelites and say to them: When you come into the land you are to inhabit, which I am giving you, 3 and you make an offering by fire to the LORD from the herd or from the flock—whether a burnt offering or a sacrifice, to fulfill a vow or as a freewill offering or at your appointed festivals—to make a pleasing odor for the LORD, 4 then whoever presents such an offering to the LORD shall present also a grain offering, one-tenth of an ephah of choice flour, mixed with one-fourth of a hin of oil. 5 Moreover, you shall offer one-fourth of a hin of wine as a drink offering with the burnt offering or the sacrifice, for each lamb. 6 For a ram, you shall offer a grain offering, two-tenths of an ephah of choice flour mixed with one-third of a hin of oil; 7 and as a drink offering you shall offer one-third of a hin of wine, a pleasing odor to the LORD. 8 When you offer a bull as a burnt offering or a sacrifice, to fulfill a vow or as an offering of well-being to the LORD, 9 then you shall present with the bull a grain offering, three-tenths of an ephah of choice flour, mixed with half a hin of oil, 10 and you shall present as a drink offering half a hin of wine, as an offering by fire, a pleasing odor to the LORD.

11 Thus it shall be done for each ox or ram, or for each of the male lambs or the kids. 12 According to the number that you offer, so you shall do with each and every one. 13 Every native Israelite shall do these things in this way, in presenting an offering by fire, a pleasing odor to the LORD. 14 An alien who lives with you, or who takes up permanent residence among you, and wishes to offer an offering by fire, a pleasing odor to the LORD, shall do as you do. 15 As for the assembly, there shall be for both you and the resident alien a single statute, a perpetual statute throughout your generations; you and the alien shall be alike before the LORD. 16 You and the alien who resides with you shall have the same law and the same ordinance.

17 The LORD spoke to Moses,

14.34 Num 13.25; Ps 95.10
14.35 Num 23.19; 26.65
14.36 Num 13.4-16, 32
14.38 Josh 14.6
14.39 Ex 33.4
14.40 Deut 1.41
14.42 Deut 1.42
14.44 Deut 1.43
14.45 Deut 1.44; Num 21.3
15.2 v. 18
15.3 Lev 23.1-44
15.4 Lev 2.1; 6.14; Ex 29.40; Lev 23.13; 14.10; Num 28.5
15.5 Num 28.7, 14
15.6 Num 28.12, 14
15.8 Lev 7.11
15.9 Num 28.12, 14
15.15 v. 29; Num 9.14

saying: 18 Speak to the Israelites
and say to them: After you come
into the land to which I am bringing you, 19 whenever you eat of the
bread of the land, you shall present
a donation to the LORD. 20 From
your first batch of dough you shall
present a loaf as a donation; you
shall present it just as you present
a donation from the threshing
floor. 21 Throughout your generations you shall give to the LORD a
donation from the first of your
batch of dough.
22 But if you unintentionally
fail to observe all these commandments that the LORD has spoken to
Moses— 23 everything that the
LORD has commanded you by Moses, from the day the LORD gave
commandment and thereafter,
throughout your generations—
24 then if it was done unintentionally without the knowledge of the
congregation, the whole congregation shall offer one young bull for a
burnt offering, a pleasing odor to
the LORD, together with its grain offering and its drink offering, according to the ordinance, and one
male goat for a sin offering. 25 The
priest shall make atonement for all
the congregation of the Israelites,
and they shall be forgiven; it was
unintentional, and they have
brought their offering, an offering
by fire to the LORD, and their sin offering before the LORD, for their error. 26 All the congregation of the
Israelites shall be forgiven, as well
as the aliens residing among them,
because the whole people was involved in the error.
27 An individual who sins unintentionally shall present a female
goat a year old for a sin offering.
28 And the priest shall make atonement before the LORD for the one
who commits an error, when it is
unintentional, to make atonement
for the person, who then shall be
forgiven. 29 For both the native
among the Israelites and the alien
residing among them—you shall
have the same law for anyone who
acts in error. 30 But whoever acts
high-handedly, whether a native or

15.18 v. 2
15.19 Josh 5.11, 12
15.20 Deut 26.2, 10; Lev 2.14
15.22 Lev 4.2
15.24 Lev 4.13; vv. 8-10
15.25 Lev 4.20
15.27 Lev 4.27,28
15.28 Lev 4.35
15.29 v. 15
15.31 2 Sam 12.9; Lev 5.1; Ezek 18.20
15.32 Ex 31.14, 15; 35.2,3
15.34 Lev 24.12
15.35 Ex 31.14, 15; Lev 24.14; Acts 7.58
15.38 Deut 22.12; Mt 23.5
15.39 Deut 4.23; Ps 73.27
15.40 Lev 11.44; Rom 12.1; Col 1.22; 1 Pet 1.15, 16
16.1 Ex 6.21; Jude 11
16.2 Num 26.9

an alien, affronts the LORD, and
shall be cut off from among the
people. 31 Because of having despised the word of the LORD and
broken his commandment, such a
person shall be utterly cut off and
bear the guilt.

Penalty for Violating the Sabbath

32 When the Israelites were in
the wilderness, they found a man
gathering sticks on the sabbath
day. 33 Those who found him gathering sticks brought him to Moses,
Aaron, and to the whole congregation. 34 They put him in custody,
because it was not clear what
should be done to him. 35 Then the
LORD said to Moses, "The man shall
be put to death; all the congregation shall stone him outside the
camp." 36 The whole congregation
brought him outside the camp and
stoned him to death, just as the
LORD had commanded Moses.

Fringes on Garments

37 The LORD said to Moses:
38 Speak to the Israelites, and tell
them to make fringes on the corners of their garments throughout
their generations and to put a blue
cord on the fringe at each corner.
39 You have the fringe so that, when
you see it, you will remember all
the commandments of the LORD
and do them, and not follow the
lust of your own heart and your
own eyes. 40 So you shall remember
and do all my commandments, and
you shall be holy to your God. 41 I
am the LORD your God, who
brought you out of the land of
Egypt, to be your God: I am the
LORD your God.

Revolt of Korah, Dathan, and Abiram

16 Now Korah son of Izhar son
of Kohath son of Levi,
along with Dathan and Abiram
sons of Eliab, and On son of
Peleth—descendants of Reuben—
took 2 two hundred fifty Israelite
men, leaders of the congregation,
chosen from the assembly, well-

known men,[c] and they confronted
Moses. 3 They assembled against
Moses and against Aaron, and said
to them, "You have gone too far! All
the congregation are holy, everyone of them, and the LORD is among
them. So why then do you exalt
yourselves above the assembly of
the LORD?" 4 When Moses heard it,
he fell on his face. 5 Then he said to
Korah and all his company, "In the
morning the LORD will make known
who is his, and who is holy, and
who will be allowed to approach
him; the one whom he will choose
he will allow to approach him. 6 Do
this: take censers, Korah and all
your[d] company, 7 and tomorrow
put fire in them, and lay incense on
them before the LORD; and the man
whom the LORD chooses shall be
the holy one. You Levites have
gone too far!" 8 Then Moses said to
Korah, "Hear now, you Levites! 9 Is
it too little for you that the God of
Israel has separated you from the
congregation of Israel, to allow you
to approach him in order to perform the duties of the LORD's tabernacle, and to stand before the congregation and serve them? 10 He
has allowed you to approach him,
and all your brother Levites with
you; yet you seek the priesthood as
well! 11 Therefore you and all your
company have gathered together
against the LORD. What is Aaron
that you rail against him?"

12 Moses sent for Dathan and
Abiram sons of Eliab; but they said,
"We will not come! 13 Is it too little
that you have brought us up out of
a land flowing with milk and honey
to kill us in the wilderness, that
you must also lord it over us? 14 It is
clear you have not brought us into
a land flowing with milk and honey, or given us an inheritance of
fields and vineyards. Would you
put out the eyes of these men? We
will not come!"

15 Moses was very angry and
said to the LORD, "Pay no attention
to their offering. I have not taken
one donkey from them, and I have
not harmed any one of them."
16 And Moses said to Korah, "As for
you and all your company, be
present tomorrow before the LORD,
you and they and Aaron; 17 and let
each one of you take his censer,
and put incense on it, and each one
of you present his censer before the
LORD, two hundred fifty censers;
you also, and Aaron, each his censer." 18 So each man took his censer, and they put fire in the censers
and laid incense on them, and they
stood at the entrance of the tent of
meeting with Moses and Aaron.
19 Then Korah assembled the
whole congregation against them
at the entrance of the tent of meeting. And the glory of the LORD appeared to the whole congregation.

20 Then the LORD spoke to Moses and to Aaron, saying: 21 Separate yourselves from this congregation, so that I may consume them
in a moment. 22 They fell on their
faces, and said, "O God, the God of
the spirits of all flesh, shall one
person sin and you become angry
with the whole congregation?"

23 And the LORD spoke to Moses, saying: 24 Say to the congregation: Get away from the dwellings
of Korah, Dathan, and Abiram.
25 So Moses got up and went to Dathan and Abiram; the elders of Israel followed him. 26 He said to the
congregation, "Turn away from the
tents of these wicked men, and
touch nothing of theirs, or you will
be swept away for all their sins."
27 So they got away from the dwellings of Korah, Dathan, and Abiram;
and Dathan and Abiram came out
and stood at the entrance of their
tents, together with their wives,
their children, and their little ones.
28 And Moses said, "This is how you
shall know that the LORD has sent
me to do all these works; it has not
been of my own accord: 29 If these
people die a natural death, or if a
natural fate comes on them, then
the LORD has not sent me. 30 But if
the LORD creates something new,
and the ground opens its mouth
and swallows them up, with all that

16.3 Ps 106.16; Ex 19.6; Num 14.14
16.4 Num 14.5
16.5 Lev 10.3; Ps 65.4; Num 17.5,8
16.9 Num 3.6,9; 8.14; Deut 10.8
16.11 Ex 16.7,8; 1 Cor 10.10
16.13 Num 11.4-6; Ex 2.14; Acts 7.27,35
16.14 Lev 20.24
16.15 Gen 4.4,5; 1 Sam 12.3
16.16 vv. 6,7
16.19 v. 42; Num 14.10; Ex 16.7,10; Lev 9.6,23
16.21 v. 45; Ex 32.10,12
16.22 v. 45; Num 14.5
16.26 Gen 19.12, 14
16.28 Ex 3.12; Jn 5.36; Num 24.13; Jn 6.38
16.30 v. 33; Ps 55.15

[c] Cn: Heb *and they confronted Moses, and two hundred fifty men . . . well-known men*
[d] Heb *his*

belongs to them, and they go down
alive into Sheol, then you shall
know that these men have despised the LORD."
31 As soon as he finished speaking all these words, the ground under them was split apart. 32 The
earth opened its mouth and swallowed them up, along with their
households—everyone who belonged to Korah and all their
goods. 33 So they with all that belonged to them went down alive
into Sheol; the earth closed over
them, and they perished from the
midst of the assembly. 34 All Israel
around them fled at their outcry,
for they said, "The earth will swallow us too!" 35 And fire came out
from the LORD and consumed the
two hundred fifty men offering the
incense.
36 [e]Then the LORD spoke to Moses, saying: 37 Tell Eleazar son of
Aaron the priest to take the censers
out of the blaze; then scatter the
fire far and wide. 38 For the censers
of these sinners have become holy
at the cost of their lives. Make
them into hammered plates as a
covering for the altar, for they presented them before the LORD and
they became holy. Thus they shall
be a sign to the Israelites. 39 So Eleazar the priest took the bronze censers that had been presented by
those who were burned; and they
were hammered out as a covering
for the altar— 40 a reminder to the
Israelites that no outsider, who is
not of the descendants of Aaron,
shall approach to offer incense before the LORD, so as not to become
like Korah and his company—just
as the LORD had said to him through
Moses.
41 On the next day, however,
the whole congregation of the Israelites rebelled against Moses and
against Aaron, saying, "You have
killed the people of the LORD."
42 And when the congregation had
assembled against them, Moses
and Aaron turned toward the tent
of meeting; the cloud had covered
it and the glory of the LORD appeared. 43 Then Moses and Aaron
came to the front of the tent of
meeting, 44 and the LORD spoke to
Moses, saying, 45 "Get away from
this congregation, so that I may
consume them in a moment." And
they fell on their faces. 46 Moses
said to Aaron, "Take your censer,
put fire on it from the altar and lay
incense on it, and carry it quickly
to the congregation and make
atonement for them. For wrath has
gone out from the LORD; the plague
has begun." 47 So Aaron took it as
Moses had ordered, and ran into
the middle of the assembly, where
the plague had already begun
among the people. He put on the
incense, and made atonement for
the people. 48 He stood between
the dead and the living; and the
plague was stopped. 49 Those who
died by the plague were fourteen
thousand seven hundred, besides
those who died in the affair of Korah. 50 When the plague was
stopped, Aaron returned to Moses
at the entrance of the tent of meeting.

The Budding of Aaron's Rod

17 [f]The LORD spoke to Moses,
saying: 2 Speak to the Israelites, and get twelve staffs from
them, one for each ancestral
house, from all the leaders of their
ancestral houses. Write each man's
name on his staff, 3 and write Aaron's name on the staff of Levi. For
there shall be one staff for the head
of each ancestral house. 4 Place
them in the tent of meeting before
the covenant,[g] where I meet with
you. 5 And the staff of the man
whom I choose shall sprout; thus I
will put a stop to the complaints of
the Israelites that they continually
make against you. 6 Moses spoke to
the Israelites; and all their leaders
gave him staffs, one for each leader, according to their ancestral
houses, twelve staffs; and the staff
of Aaron was among theirs. 7 So
Moses placed the staffs before the
LORD in the tent of the covenant.[g]
8 When Moses went into the

16.31 Num 26.10
16.32 Num 26.11
16.35 Num 11.1-3; 26.10
16.38 Prov 20.2; Num 26.10
16.40 Num 3.10; 2 Chr 26.18
16.41 v. 3
16.42 Ex 40.34; v. 19; Num 20.6
16.45 vv. 21,24
16.46 Num 8.19; Ps 106.29
16.47 Num 25.7,8, 13
16.48 Ps 106.30
16.49 vv. 32,35
17.4 Ex 25.22; 29.42,43
17.5 Num 16.5, 11
17.7 Num 18.2; Acts 7.44

[e] Ch 17.1 in Heb [f] Ch 17.16 in Heb
[g] Or *treaty*, or *testimony*; Heb *eduth*

tent of the covenant[h] on the next
day, the staff of Aaron for the house
of Levi had sprouted. It put forth
buds, produced blossoms, and bore
ripe almonds. 9 Then Moses
brought out all the staffs from before the LORD to all the Israelites;
and they looked, and each man
took his staff. 10 And the LORD said
to Moses, "Put back the staff of
Aaron before the covenant,[h] to be
kept as a warning to rebels, so that
you may make an end of their complaints against me, or else they will
die." 11 Moses did so; just as the
LORD commanded him, so he did.
12 The Israelites said to Moses,
"We are perishing; we are lost, all
of us are lost! 13 Everyone who approaches the tabernacle of the
LORD will die. Are we all to perish?"

Responsibility of Priests and Levites

18 The LORD said to Aaron:
You and your sons and your
ancestral house with you shall bear
responsibility for offenses connected with the sanctuary, while you
and your sons alone shall bear responsibility for offenses connected
with the priesthood. 2 So bring with
you also your brothers of the tribe
of Levi, your ancestral tribe, in order that they may be joined to you,
and serve you while you and your
sons with you are in front of the
tent of the covenant.[h] 3 They shall
perform duties for you and for the
whole tent. But they must not approach either the utensils of the
sanctuary or the altar, otherwise
both they and you will die. 4 They
are attached to you in order to perform the duties of the tent of meeting, for all the service of the tent;
no outsider shall approach you.
5 You yourselves shall perform the
duties of the sanctuary and the duties of the altar, so that wrath may
never again come upon the Israelites. 6 It is I who now take your
brother Levites from among the Israelites; they are now yours as a
gift, dedicated to the LORD, to perform the service of the tent of
meeting. 7 But you and your sons
with you shall diligently perform
your priestly duties in all that concerns the altar and the area behind
the curtain. I give your priesthood
as a gift;[i] any outsider who approaches shall be put to death.

The Priests' Portion

8 The LORD spoke to Aaron: I
have given you charge of the offerings made to me, all the holy gifts
of the Israelites; I have given them
to you and your sons as a priestly
portion due you in perpetuity.
9 This shall be yours from the most
holy things, reserved from the fire:
every offering of theirs that they
render to me as a most holy thing,
whether grain offering, sin offering,
or guilt offering, shall belong to you
and your sons. 10 As a most holy
thing you shall eat it; every male
may eat it; it shall be holy to you.
11 This also is yours: I have given to
you, together with your sons and
daughters, as a perpetual due,
whatever is set aside from the gifts
of all the elevation offerings of the
Israelites; everyone who is clean in
your house may eat them. 12 All the
best of the oil and all the best of
the wine and of the grain, the
choice produce that they give to
the LORD, I have given to you. 13 The
first fruits of all that is in their land,
which they bring to the LORD, shall
be yours; everyone who is clean in
your house may eat of it. 14 Every
devoted thing in Israel shall be
yours. 15 The first issue of the
womb of all creatures, human and
animal, which is offered to the
LORD, shall be yours; but the firstborn of human beings you shall redeem, and the firstborn of unclean
animals you shall redeem. 16 Their
redemption price, reckoned from
one month of age, you shall fix at
five shekels of silver, according to
the shekel of the sanctuary (that is,
twenty gerahs). 17 But the firstborn
of a cow, or the firstborn of a sheep,
or the firstborn of a goat, you shall
not redeem; they are holy. You
shall dash their blood on the altar,

17.10 Heb 9.4; v. 5
17.13 Num 1.51, 53
18.1 Ex 28.38
18.2 Num 3.5-10
18.3 Num 3.25, 31,36; 4.15
18.4 Num 3.10
18.5 Num 16.46
18.6 Num 3.9,12, 45
18.7 Num 3.10; Heb 9.3,6
18.8 Lev 6.16,18; 7.6,32; Ex 29.29; 40.13,15
18.9 Lev 2.2,3; 10.12,13; 6.25,26; 7.7
18.10 Lev 6.16,26
18.11 Ex 29.27, 28; Lev 22.1-16
18.12 Ex 23.19; Deut 18.4; Neh 10.35; Ex 22.29
18.13 Ex 22.29; 23.19; 34.26
18.14 Lev 27.28
18.15 Ex 13.2; Lev 27.26; Ex 13.13
18.16 Lev 27.6
18.17 Lev 3.2,5

[h] Or *treaty*, or *testimony*; Heb *eduth*
[i] Heb *as a service of gift*

and shall turn their fat into smoke
as an offering by fire for a pleasing
odor to the LORD; 18 but their flesh
shall be yours, just as the breast
that is elevated and as the right
thigh are yours. 19 All the holy offerings that the Israelites present to
the LORD I have given to you, together with your sons and daughters, as a perpetual due; it is a covenant of salt forever before the LORD
for you and your descendants as
well. 20 Then the LORD said to Aaron: You shall have no allotment in
their land, nor shall you have any
share among them; I am your share
and your possession among the Israelites.

21 To the Levites I have given
every tithe in Israel for a possession
in return for the service that they
perform, the service in the tent of
meeting. 22 From now on the Israelites shall no longer approach the
tent of meeting, or else they will incur guilt and die. 23 But the Levites
shall perform the service of the tent
of meeting, and they shall bear responsibility for their own offenses;
it shall be a perpetual statute
throughout your generations. But
among the Israelites they shall
have no allotment, 24 because I
have given to the Levites as their
portion the tithe of the Israelites,
which they set apart as an offering
to the LORD. Therefore I have said of
them that they shall have no allotment among the Israelites.

25 Then the LORD spoke to Moses, saying: 26 You shall speak to
the Levites, saying: When you receive from the Israelites the tithe
that I have given you from them for
your portion, you shall set apart an
offering from it to the LORD, a tithe
of the tithe. 27 It shall be reckoned
to you as your gift, the same as the
grain of the threshing floor and the
fullness of the wine press. 28 Thus
you also shall set apart an offering
to the LORD from all the tithes that
you receive from the Israelites; and
from them you shall give the LORD's
offering to the priest Aaron. 29 Out
of all the gifts to you, you shall set
apart every offering due to the
LORD; the best of all of them is the
part to be consecrated. 30 Say also
to them: When you have set apart
the best of it, then the rest shall be
reckoned to the Levites as produce
of the threshing floor, and as produce of the wine press. 31 You may
eat it in any place, you and your
households; for it is your payment
for your service in the tent of meeting. 32 You shall incur no guilt by
reason of it, when you have offered
the best of it. But you shall not profane the holy gifts of the Israelites,
on pain of death.

Ceremony of the Red Heifer

19 The LORD spoke to Moses
and Aaron, saying: 2 This is
a statute of the law that the LORD
has commanded: Tell the Israelites
to bring you a red heifer without
defect, in which there is no blemish and on which no yoke has been
laid. 3 You shall give it to the priest
Eleazar, and it shall be taken outside the camp and slaughtered in
his presence. 4 The priest Eleazar
shall take some of its blood with
his finger and sprinkle it seven
times towards the front of the tent
of meeting. 5 Then the heifer shall
be burned in his sight; its skin, its
flesh, and its blood, with its dung,
shall be burned. 6 The priest shall
take cedarwood, hyssop, and crimson material, and throw them into
the fire in which the heifer is burning. 7 Then the priest shall wash his
clothes and bathe his body in water, and afterwards he may come
into the camp; but the priest shall
remain unclean until evening.
8 The one who burns the heifer[j]
shall wash his clothes in water and
bathe his body in water; he shall
remain unclean until evening.
9 Then someone who is clean shall
gather up the ashes of the heifer,
and deposit them outside the camp
in a clean place; and they shall be
kept for the congregation of the Israelites for the water for cleansing.
It is a purification offering. 10 The
one who gathers the ashes of the

18.19 v. 11; 2 Chr 13.5
18.20 Deut 10.9; 12.12; 14.27, 29; 18.1,2; Josh 13.33; Ezek 44.28
18.21 Lev 27.30-33
18.22 Num 1.51
18.23 Num 3.7; vv. 1,20
18.26 Neh 10.38
18.28 Ex 29.27
18.32 Lev 19.8; 22.2,15,16
19.2 Deut 21.3
19.3 Lev 4.12,21; 16.27
19.4 Lev 4.6; Heb 9.13
19.6 Lev 15.4,6, 49
19.7 Lev 11.25; 16.26,28; 22.6
19.9 Heb 9.13; vv. 13,20,21

j Heb *it*

heifer shall wash his clothes and be
unclean until evening.
This shall be a perpetual statute
for the Israelites and for the alien
residing among them. 11 Those who
touch the dead body of any human
being shall be unclean seven days.
12 They shall purify themselves
with the water on the third day and
on the seventh day, and so be
clean; but if they do not purify
themselves on the third day and on
the seventh day, they will not become clean. 13 All who touch a
corpse, the body of a human being
who has died, and do not purify
themselves, defile the tabernacle
of the LORD; such persons shall be
cut off from Israel. Since water for
cleansing was not dashed on them,
they remain unclean; their uncleanness is still on them.

14 This is the law when someone dies in a tent: everyone who
comes into the tent, and everyone
who is in the tent, shall be unclean
seven days. 15 And every open vessel with no cover fastened on it is
unclean. 16 Whoever in the open
field touches one who has been
killed by a sword, or who has died
naturally,[k] or a human bone, or a
grave, shall be unclean seven days.
17 For the unclean they shall take
some ashes of the burnt purification offering, and running water
shall be added in a vessel; 18 then a
clean person shall take hyssop, dip
it in the water, and sprinkle it on
the tent, on all the furnishings, on
the persons who were there, and
on whoever touched the bone, the
slain, the corpse, or the grave.
19 The clean person shall sprinkle
the unclean ones on the third day
and on the seventh day, thus purifying them on the seventh day.
Then they shall wash their clothes
and bathe themselves in water, and
at evening they shall be clean.
20 Any who are unclean but do not
purify themselves, those persons
shall be cut off from the assembly,
for they have defiled the sanctuary
of the LORD. Since the water for
cleansing has not been dashed on
them, they are unclean.

19.11 Num 5.2; Lev 21.1; Acts 21.26, 27
19.12 v. 19; Num 31.19
19.13 v. 20; Lev 15.31; v. 9; Num 8.7; Lev 7.20; 22.3
19.16 v. 11
19.17 v. 9
19.19 Ezek 36.25; Heb 10.22
19.20 v. 13
19.22 Hag 2.13,14
20.1 Num 33.36
20.2 Ex 17.1
20.3 Ex 17.2; Num 14.2,3; 16.31-35
20.4 Ex 17.3
20.6 Num 14.5, 10
20.8 Ex 17.5; Neh 9.15; Isa 43.20; 48.21
20.10 Ps 106.32, 33
20.11 Ps 78.16; Isa 48.21; 1 Cor 10.14

21 It shall be a perpetual statute
for them. The one who sprinkles
the water for cleansing shall wash
his clothes, and whoever touches
the water for cleansing shall be unclean until evening. 22 Whatever
the unclean person touches shall
be unclean, and anyone who
touches it shall be unclean until
evening.

The Waters of Meribah

20 The Israelites, the whole
congregation, came into
the wilderness of Zin in the first
month, and the people stayed in
Kadesh. Miriam died there, and
was buried there.

2 Now there was no water for
the congregation; so they gathered
together against Moses and against
Aaron. 3 The people quarreled with
Moses and said, "Would that we
had died when our kindred died before the LORD! 4 Why have you
brought the assembly of the LORD
into this wilderness for us and our
livestock to die here? 5 Why have
you brought us up out of Egypt, to
bring us to this wretched place? It
is no place for grain, or figs, or
vines, or pomegranates; and there
is no water to drink." 6 Then Moses
and Aaron went away from the assembly to the entrance of the tent
of meeting; they fell on their faces,
and the glory of the LORD appeared
to them. 7 The LORD spoke to Moses, saying: 8 Take the staff, and assemble the congregation, you and
your brother Aaron, and command
the rock before their eyes to yield
its water. Thus you shall bring water out of the rock for them; thus
you shall provide drink for the congregation and their livestock.

9 So Moses took the staff from
before the LORD, as he had commanded him. 10 Moses and Aaron
gathered the assembly together before the rock, and he said to them,
"Listen, you rebels, shall we bring
water for you out of this rock?"
11 Then Moses lifted up his hand
and struck the rock twice with his
staff; water came out abundantly,

[k] Heb lacks *naturally*

and the congregation and their
livestock drank. 12 But the LORD
said to Moses and Aaron, "Because
you did not trust in me, to show my
holiness before the eyes of the Israelites, therefore you shall not bring
this assembly into the land that
I have given them." 13 These are
the waters of Meribah,[l] where the
people of Israel quarreled with the
LORD, and by which he showed his
holiness.

Passage through Edom Refused

14 Moses sent messengers from
Kadesh to the king of Edom, "Thus
says your brother Israel: You know
all the adversity that has befallen
us: 15 how our ancestors went down
to Egypt, and we lived in Egypt a
long time; and the Egyptians oppressed us and our ancestors;
16 and when we cried to the LORD,
he heard our voice, and sent an angel and brought us out of Egypt;
and here we are in Kadesh, a town
on the edge of your territory. 17 Now
let us pass through your land. We
will not pass through field or vineyard, or drink water from any well;
we will go along the King's Highway, not turning aside to the right
hand or to the left until we have
passed through your territory."
18 But Edom said to him, "You
shall not pass through, or we will
come out with the sword against
you." 19 The Israelites said to him,
"We will stay on the highway; and
if we drink of your water, we and
our livestock, then we will pay for
it. It is only a small matter; just let
us pass through on foot." 20 But he
said, "You shall not pass through."
And Edom came out against them
with a large force, heavily armed.
21 Thus Edom refused to give Israel
passage through their territory; so
Israel turned away from them.

The Death of Aaron

22 They set out from Kadesh,
and the Israelites, the whole congregation, came to Mount Hor.
23 Then the LORD said to Moses and
Aaron at Mount Hor, on the border
of the land of Edom, 24 "Let Aaron
be gathered to his people. For he
shall not enter the land that I have
given to the Israelites, because you
rebelled against my command at
the waters of Meribah. 25 Take Aaron and his son Eleazar, and bring
them up Mount Hor; 26 strip Aaron
of his vestments, and put them on
his son Eleazar. But Aaron shall be
gathered to his people,[m] and shall
die there." 27 Moses did as the LORD
had commanded; they went up
Mount Hor in the sight of the
whole congregation. 28 Moses
stripped Aaron of his vestments,
and put them on his son Eleazar;
and Aaron died there on the top of
the mountain. Moses and Eleazar
came down from the mountain.
29 When all the congregation saw
that Aaron had died, all the house
of Israel mourned for Aaron thirty
days.

The Bronze Serpent

21 When the Canaanite, the
king of Arad, who lived in
the Negeb, heard that Israel was
coming by the way of Atharim, he
fought against Israel and took
some of them captive. 2 Then Israel
made a vow to the LORD and said,
"If you will indeed give this people
into our hands, then we will utterly
destroy their towns." 3 The LORD listened to the voice of Israel, and
handed over the Canaanites; and
they utterly destroyed them and
their towns; so the place was called
Hormah.[n]
4 From Mount Hor they set out
by the way to the Red Sea,[o] to go
around the land of Edom; but the
people became impatient on the
way. 5 The people spoke against
God and against Moses, "Why have
you brought us up out of Egypt to
die in the wilderness? For there is
no food and no water, and we detest this miserable food." 6 Then
the LORD sent poisonous[p] serpents
among the people, and they bit the
people, so that many Israelites
died. 7 The people came to Moses

20.12 Num 27.14; Deut 1.37; 3.26,27; Lev 10.3
20.13 Deut 33.8; Ps 95.8
20.14 Deut 2.4
20.15 Gen 46.6; Acts 7.15, 19; Ex 12.40; Deut 26.6
20.16 Ex 2.23; 14.19
20.19 Deut 2.6,28
20.21 Judg 11.17; Deut 2.8
20.22 Num 33.37; 21.4
20.24 Gen 25.8; v. 12
20.25 Num 33.38; Deut 32.50
20.28 Num 33.38; Deut 10.6
21.1 Num 33.40; Judg 1.16; Num 13.21
21.4 Num 20.22
21.5 Ps 78.19; Ex 16.3; 17.3; Num 11.6
21.6 Deut 8.15; 1 Cor 10.9
21.7 Ps 78.34

[l] That is *Quarrel* [m] Heb lacks *to his people*
[n] Heb *Destruction* [o] Or *Sea of Reeds*
[p] Or *fiery*; Heb *seraphim*

and said, "We have sinned by
speaking against the LORD and
against you; pray to the LORD to
take away the serpents from us."
So Moses prayed for the people.
8 And the LORD said to Moses,
"Make a poisonous[q] serpent, and
set it on a pole; and everyone who
is bitten shall look at it and live."
9 So Moses made a serpent of
bronze, and put it upon a pole; and
whenever a serpent bit someone,
that person would look at the serpent of bronze and live.

The Journey to Moab

10 The Israelites set out, and
camped in Oboth. 11 They set out
from Oboth, and camped at Iye-
abarim, in the wilderness bordering Moab toward the sunrise.
12 From there they set out, and
camped in the Wadi Zered. 13 From
there they set out, and camped on
the other side of the Arnon, in[r] the
wilderness that extends from the
boundary of the Amorites; for
the Arnon is the boundary of Moab,
between Moab and the Amorites.
14 Wherefore it is said in the Book
of the Wars of the LORD,

"Waheb in Suphah and the
wadis.
The Arnon 15 and the slopes of
the wadis
that extend to the seat of Ar,
and lie along the border of
Moab."[s]

16 From there they continued
to Beer;[t] that is the well of which
the LORD said to Moses, "Gather
the people together, and I will give
them water." 17 Then Israel sang
this song:

"Spring up, O well!—Sing to
it!—
18 the well that the leaders
sank,
that the nobles of the people
dug,
with the scepter, with the
staff."

From the wilderness to Mattanah,
19 from Mattanah to Nahaliel, from
Nahaliel to Bamoth, 20 and from
Bamoth to the valley lying in the
region of Moab by the top of Pisgah
that overlooks the wasteland.[u]

King Sihon Defeated

21 Then Israel sent messengers
to King Sihon of the Amorites, saying, 22 "Let me pass through your
land; we will not turn aside into
field or vineyard; we will not drink
the water of any well; we will go by
the King's Highway until we have
passed through your territory."
23 But Sihon would not allow Israel
to pass through his territory. Sihon
gathered all his people together,
and went out against Israel to the
wilderness; he came to Jahaz, and
fought against Israel. 24 Israel put
him to the sword, and took possession of his land from the Arnon to
the Jabbok, as far as to the Ammonites; for the boundary of the
Ammonites was strong. 25 Israel
took all these towns, and Israel settled in all the towns of the Amorites, in Heshbon, and in all its villages. 26 For Heshbon was the city
of King Sihon of the Amorites, who
had fought against the former king
of Moab and captured all his land
as far as the Arnon. 27 Therefore the
ballad singers say,

"Come to Heshbon, let it be
built;
let the city of Sihon be
established.
28 For fire came out from
Heshbon,
flame from the city of
Sihon.
It devoured Ar of Moab,
and swallowed up[v] the
heights of the Arnon.
29 Woe to you, O Moab!
You are undone, O people
of Chemosh!
He has made his sons
fugitives,
and his daughters captives,
to an Amorite king, Sihon.
30 So their posterity perished
from Heshbon[w] to Dibon,

21.9 2 Kings 18.4; Jn 3.14,15 **21.10** Num 33.43 **21.11** Num 33.44 **21.12** Deut 2.13 **21.15** v. 28; Deut 2.18, 29

21.21 Deut 2.26, 27 **21.22** Num 20.16, 17 **21.23** Num 20.21; Deut 2.32 **21.24** Deut 2.33; Josh 12.1,2; Ps 135.10, 11 **21.28** Jer 48.45, 46; Deut 2.9,18; Isa 15.1 **21.29** Judg 11.24; 1 Kings 11.7, 33; 2 Kings 23.13; Jer 48.7,13 **21.30** Num 32.3, 34; Jer 48.18,22

[q] Or *fiery*; Heb *seraph* [r] Gk: Heb *which is in* [s] Meaning of Heb uncertain [t] That is *Well* [u] Or *Jeshimon* [v] Gk: Heb *and the lords of* [w] Gk: Heb *we have shot at them; Heshbon has perished*

and we laid waste until fire
spread to Medeba."[x]

31 Thus Israel settled in the
land of the Amorites. 32 Moses sent
to spy out Jazer; and they captured
its villages, and dispossessed the
Amorites who were there.

King Og Defeated

33 Then they turned and went
up the road to Bashan; and King Og
of Bashan came out against them,
he and all his people, to battle at
Edrei. 34 But the LORD said to Moses, "Do not be afraid of him; for I
have given him into your hand,
with all his people, and all his land.
You shall do to him as you did to
King Sihon of the Amorites, who
ruled in Heshbon." 35 So they killed
him, his sons, and all his people,
until there was no survivor left;
and they took possession of his
land.

Balak Summons Balaam to Curse Israel

22 The Israelites set out, and
camped in the plains of
Moab across the Jordan from Jericho. 2 Now Balak son of Zippor saw
all that Israel had done to the Amorites. 3 Moab was in great dread of
the people, because they were so
numerous; Moab was overcome
with fear of the people of Israel.
4 And Moab said to the elders of
Midian, "This horde will now lick
up all that is around us, as an ox
licks up the grass of the field." Now
Balak son of Zippor was king of
Moab at that time. 5 He sent messengers to Balaam son of Beor at
Pethor, which is on the Euphrates,
in the land of Amaw,[y] to summon
him, saying, "A people has come
out of Egypt; they have spread over
the face of the earth, and they have
settled next to me. 6 Come now,
curse this people for me, since they
are stronger than I; perhaps I shall
be able to defeat them and drive
them from the land; for I know that
whomever you bless is blessed, and
whomever you curse is cursed."

21.32 Num 32.1; Jer 48.32
21.33 Deut 3.1-7; Josh 13.12
21.34 Deut 3.2; v. 24
22.1 Num 33.48
22.3 Ex 15.15
22.4 Num 31.1-3, 8
22.5 Num 23.7; Josh 24.9; Deut 23.4
22.6 v. 17; Num 23.7
22.7 Num 23.23; 24.1
22.8 v. 19
22.12 Num 23.20
22.17 v. 6
22.18 Num 24.13; 1 Kings 22.14; 2 Chr 18.13
22.20 v. 35; Num 23.12, 26; 24.13
22.21 2 Pet 2.15

7 So the elders of Moab and the
elders of Midian departed with the
fees for divination in their hand;
and they came to Balaam, and gave
him Balak's message. 8 He said to
them, "Stay here tonight, and I will
bring back word to you, just as the
LORD speaks to me"; so the officials
of Moab stayed with Balaam. 9 God
came to Balaam and said, "Who are
these men with you?" 10 Balaam
said to God, "King Balak son of
Zippor of Moab, has sent me this
message: 11 'A people has come out
of Egypt and has spread over the
face of the earth; now come, curse
them for me; perhaps I shall be
able to fight against them and drive
them out.' " 12 God said to Balaam,
"You shall not go with them; you
shall not curse the people, for they
are blessed." 13 So Balaam rose in
the morning, and said to the officials of Balak, "Go to your own
land, for the LORD has refused to let
me go with you." 14 So the officials
of Moab rose and went to Balak,
and said, "Balaam refuses to come
with us."

15 Once again Balak sent officials, more numerous and more
distinguished than these. 16 They
came to Balaam and said to him,
"Thus says Balak son of Zippor: 'Do
not let anything hinder you from
coming to me; 17 for I will surely do
you great honor, and whatever you
say to me I will do; come, curse this
people for me.' " 18 But Balaam replied to the servants of Balak, "Although Balak were to give me his
house full of silver and gold, I could
not go beyond the command of the
LORD my God, to do less or more.
19 You remain here, as the others
did, so that I may learn what more
the LORD may say to me." 20 That
night God came to Balaam and said
to him, "If the men have come to
summon you, get up and go with
them; but do only what I tell you to
do." 21 So Balaam got up in the
morning, saddled his donkey, and
went with the officials of Moab.

[x] Compare Sam Gk: Meaning of MT uncertain
[y] Or *land of his kinsfolk*

Balaam, the Donkey, and the Angel

22 God's anger was kindled because he was going, and the angel
of the LORD took his stand in the
road as his adversary. Now he was
riding on the donkey, and his two
servants were with him. 23 The donkey saw the angel of the LORD
standing in the road, with a drawn
sword in his hand; so the donkey
turned off the road, and went into
the field; and Balaam struck the
donkey, to turn it back onto the
road. 24 Then the angel of the LORD
stood in a narrow path between the
vineyards, with a wall on either
side. 25 When the donkey saw the
angel of the LORD, it scraped
against the wall, and scraped Balaam's foot against the wall; so he
struck it again. 26 Then the angel of
the LORD went ahead, and stood in
a narrow place, where there was no
way to turn either to the right or to
the left. 27 When the donkey saw
the angel of the LORD, it lay down
under Balaam; and Balaam's anger
was kindled, and he struck the
donkey with his staff. 28 Then the
LORD opened the mouth of the donkey, and it said to Balaam, "What
have I done to you, that you have
struck me these three times?"
29 Balaam said to the donkey, "Because you have made a fool of me!
I wish I had a sword in my hand! I
would kill you right now!" 30 But
the donkey said to Balaam, "Am I
not your donkey, which you have
ridden all your life to this day?
Have I been in the habit of treating
you this way?" And he said, "No."

31 Then the LORD opened the
eyes of Balaam, and he saw the angel of the LORD standing in the
road, with his drawn sword in his
hand; and he bowed down, falling
on his face. 32 The angel of the LORD
said to him, "Why have you struck
your donkey these three times? I
have come out as an adversary, because your way is perverse[z] before
me. 33 The donkey saw me, and
turned away from me these three
times. If it had not turned away
from me, surely just now I would
have killed you and let it live."
34 Then Balaam said to the angel of
the LORD, "I have sinned, for I did
not know that you were standing in
the road to oppose me. Now therefore, if it is displeasing to you, I will
return home." 35 The angel of the
LORD said to Balaam, "Go with the
men; but speak only what I tell you
to speak." So Balaam went on with
the officials of Balak.

36 When Balak heard that Balaam had come, he went out to
meet him at Ir-moab, on the
boundary formed by the Arnon, at
the farthest point of the boundary.
37 Balak said to Balaam, "Did I not
send to summon you? Why did you
not come to me? Am I not able to
honor you?" 38 Balaam said to Balak, "I have come to you now, but
do I have power to say just anything? The word God puts in my
mouth, that is what I must say."
39 Then Balaam went with Balak,
and they came to Kiriath-huzoth.
40 Balak sacrificed oxen and sheep,
and sent them to Balaam and to
the officials who were with him.

Balaam's First Oracle

41 On the next day Balak took
Balaam and brought him up to
Bamoth-baal; and from there he
could see part of the people of Isra-
23 el.[a] 1 Then Balaam said to
Balak, "Build me seven altars here, and prepare seven bulls
and seven rams for me." 2 Balak did
as Balaam had said; and Balak and
Balaam offered a bull and a ram on
each altar. 3 Then Balaam said to
Balak, "Stay here beside your burnt
offerings while I go aside. Perhaps
the LORD will come to meet me.
Whatever he shows me I will tell
you." And he went to a bare height.

4 Then God met Balaam; and
Balaam said to him, "I have arranged the seven altars, and have
offered a bull and a ram on each
altar." 5 The LORD put a word in Balaam's mouth, and said, "Return to
Balak, and this is what you must

22.23 2 Pet 2.16
22.24 Judg 6.12
22.28 2 Pet 2.16
22.29 Prov 12.10
22.30 2 Pet 2.16
22.31 Josh 5.13-15
22.34 Num 14.40; 1 Sam 15.24, 30; 2 Sam 12.13
22.35 v. 20
22.37 v. 17; Num 24.11
22.38 v. 18; Num 23.26; 24.13
22.41 Deut 12.2
23.1 v. 29
23.2 vv. 14,30
23.3 v. 15
23.4 v. 16
23.5 v. 16; Num 22.35; Deut 18.18; Jer 1.9

[z] Meaning of Heb uncertain [a] Heb lacks *of Israel*

say." 6 So he returned to Balak,[b]
who was standing beside his burnt
offerings with all the officials of
Moab. 7 Then Balaam[c] uttered his
oracle, saying:
"Balak has brought me from
Aram,
the king of Moab from the
eastern mountains:
'Come, curse Jacob for me;
Come, denounce Israel!'
8 How can I curse whom God
has not cursed?
How can I denounce those
whom the LORD has not
denounced?
9 For from the top of the crags
I see him,
from the hills I behold
him;
Here is a people living alone,
and not reckoning itself
among the nations!
10 Who can count the dust of
Jacob,
or number the dust-cloud[d]
of Israel?
Let me die the death of the
upright,
and let my end be like
his!"
11 Then Balak said to Balaam,
"What have you done to me? I
brought you to curse my enemies,
but now you have done nothing but
bless them." 12 He answered,
"Must I not take care to say what
the LORD puts into my mouth?"

Balaam's Second Oracle

13 So Balak said to him, "Come
with me to another place from
which you may see them; you shall
see only part of them, and shall not
see them all; then curse them for
me from there." 14 So he took him
to the field of Zophim, to the top of
Pisgah. He built seven altars, and
offered a bull and a ram on each
altar. 15 Balaam said to Balak,
"Stand here beside your burnt offerings, while I meet the LORD over
there. 16 The LORD met Balaam, put
a word into his mouth, and said,
"Return to Balak, and this is what
you shall say." 17 When he came to
him, he was standing beside his

23.7 v. 18; Num 24.3, 15,23; Job 27.1; 29.1; Ps 78.2; Num 22.6 **23.8** Num 22.12 **23.9** Ex 33.16; Deut 32.8; 33.28 **23.10** Gen 13.16; Ps 116.15 **23.11** Num 24.10 **23.12** Num 22.20, 38 **23.14** vv. 1,2 **23.16** Num 22.20

23.19 1 Sam 15.29; Mal 3.6; Rom 11.29; Titus 1.2; Jas 1.17 **23.20** Isa 43.13 **23.21** Ps 32.2,5; Rom 4.7,8; Isa 40.2; Ex 29.45, 46; Ps 89.15 **23.22** Num 24.8 **23.24** Gen 49.9,27 **23.26** v. 12; Num 22.38 **23.27** v. 13

burnt offerings with the officials of
Moab. Balak said to him, "What
has the LORD said?" 18 Then Balaam
uttered his oracle, saying:
"Rise, Balak, and hear;
listen to me, O son of
Zippor:
19 God is not a human being,
that he should lie,
or a mortal, that he should
change his mind.
Has he promised, and will he
not do it?
Has he spoken, and will he
not fulfill it?
20 See, I received a command
to bless;
he has blessed, and I
cannot revoke it.
21 He has not beheld
misfortune in Jacob;
nor has he seen trouble in
Israel.
The LORD their God is with
them,
acclaimed as a king among
them.
22 God, who brings them out of
Egypt,
is like the horns of a wild
ox for them.
23 Surely there is no
enchantment against
Jacob,
no divination against Israel;
now it shall be said of Jacob
and Israel,
'See what God has done!'
24 Look, a people rising up like
a lioness,
and rousing itself like a
lion!
It does not lie down until it
has eaten the prey
and drunk the blood of the
slain."
25 Then Balak said to Balaam,
"Do not curse them at all, and do
not bless them at all." 26 But Balaam answered Balak, "Did I not
tell you, 'Whatever the LORD says,
that is what I must do'?"
27 So Balak said to Balaam,
"Come now, I will take you to another place; perhaps it will please

[b] Heb *him* [c] Heb *he* [d] Or *fourth part*

God that you may curse them for
me from there." 28 So Balak took
Balaam to the top of Peor, which
overlooks the wasteland.[e] 29 Balaam said to Balak, "Build me sev-
en altars here, and prepare seven
bulls and seven rams for me." 30 So
Balak did as Balaam had said, and
offered a bull and a ram on each
altar.

Balaam's Third Oracle

24 Now Balaam saw that it
pleased the LORD to bless
Israel, so he did not go, as at other
times, to look for omens, but set
his face toward the wilderness.
2 Balaam looked up and saw Israel
camping tribe by tribe. Then the
spirit of God came upon him, 3 and
he uttered his oracle, saying:

"The oracle of Balaam son of
Beor,
the oracle of the man
whose eye is clear,[f]
4 the oracle of one who hears
the words of God,
who sees the vision of the
Almighty,[g]
who falls down, but with
eyes uncovered:
5 how fair are your tents,
O Jacob,
your encampments,
O Israel!
6 Like palm groves that stretch
far away,
like gardens beside a river,
like aloes that the LORD has
planted,
like cedar trees beside the
waters.
7 Water shall flow from his
buckets,
and his seed shall have
abundant water,
his king shall be higher than
Agag,
and his kingdom shall be
exalted.
8 God who brings him out of
Egypt,
is like the horns of a wild
ox for him;
he shall devour the nations
that are his foes
and break their bones.

23.29 v. 1 **24.1** Num 23.3, 15 **24.2** Num 11.25, 26; 1 Sam 10.10; 2 Chr 15.1 **24.3** Num 23.7, 18 **24.4** Num 22.20; 12.6 **24.6** Ps 1.3; 104.16 **24.7** v. 20; 1 Sam 15.8, 9; 2 Sam 5.12; 1 Chr 14.2 **24.8** Num 23.22, 24; Ps 2.9; 45.5; Jer 50.9,17

He shall strike with his
arrows.[h]
9 He crouched, he lay down
like a lion,
and like a lioness; who will
rouse him up?
Blessed is everyone who
blesses you,
and cursed is everyone who
curses you."

10 Then Balak's anger was kindled against Balaam, and he struck
his hands together. Balak said to
Balaam, "I summoned you to curse
my enemies, but instead you have
blessed them these three times.
11 Now be off with you! Go home! I
said, 'I will reward you richly,' but
the LORD has denied you any reward." 12 And Balaam said to Balak,
"Did I not tell your messengers
whom you sent to me, 13 'If Balak
should give me his house full of silver and gold, I would not be able to
go beyond the word of the LORD, to
do either good or bad of my own
will; what the LORD says, that is
what I will say'? 14 So now, I am going to my people; let me advise you
what this people will do to your
people in days to come."

Balaam's Fourth Oracle

15 So he uttered his oracle, saying:

"The oracle of Balaam son of
Beor,
the oracle of the man
whose eye is clear,[f]
16 the oracle of one who hears
the words of God,
and knows the knowledge
of the Most High,[i]
who sees the vision of the
Almighty,[g]
who falls down, but with
his eyes uncovered:
17 I see him, but not now;
I behold him, but not
near—
a star shall come out of
Jacob,

24.9 Gen 49.9; 12.3; 27.29 **24.11** Num 22.17, 37 **24.13** Num 22.18, 20 **24.14** Gen 49.1; Dan 2.28; Mic 6.5 **24.17** Rev 1.7; Mt 2.2; Gen 49.10

[e] Or *overlooks Jeshimon* [f] Or *closed* or *open* [g] Traditional rendering of Heb *Shaddai* [h] Meaning of Heb uncertain [i] Or *of Elyon*

and a scepter shall rise out
of Israel;
it shall crush the
borderlands[j] of Moab,
and the territory[k] of all the
Shethites.
18 Edom will become a
possession,
Seir a possession of its
enemies,[l]
while Israel does valiantly.
19 One out of Jacob shall rule,
and destroy the survivors of
Ir."

20 Then he looked on Amalek,
and uttered his oracle, saying:
"First among the nations was
Amalek,
but its end is to perish
forever."

21 Then he looked on the Kenite, and uttered his oracle, saying:
"Enduring is your dwelling
place,
and your nest is set in the
rock;
22 yet Kain is destined for
burning.
How long shall Asshur take
you away captive?"

23 Again he uttered his oracle,
saying:
"Alas, who shall live when
God does this?
24 But ships shall come from
Kittim
and shall afflict Asshur and
Eber;
and he also shall perish
forever."

25 Then Balaam got up and
went back to his place, and Balak
also went his way.

Worship of Baal of Peor

25 While Israel was staying at
Shittim, the people began
to have sexual relations with the
women of Moab. 2 These invited
the people to the sacrifices of their
gods, and the people ate and
bowed down to their gods. 3 Thus
Israel yoked itself to the Baal of
Peor, and the LORD's anger was kindled against Israel. 4 The LORD said
to Moses, "Take all the chiefs of
the people, and impale them in the

24.18 2 Sam 8.14
24.19 Gen 49.10; Mic 5.2
24.20 Ex 17.8,14, 16
24.24 Gen 10.4, 21; v. 20
24.25 Num 31.8
25.1 Mic 6.5; Num 31.16; 1 Cor 10.8; Rev 2.14
25.2 Ex 34.15; 20.5; 1 Cor 10.20
25.3 Ps 106.28, 29; Hos 9.10
25.4 Deut 4.3
25.7 Ps 106.30
25.9 Deut 4.3; 1 Cor 10.8
25.11 Ps 106.30; Ex 20.5; Deut 32.16, 21
25.12 Isa 54.10; Mal 2.4,5
25.13 Ex 40.15; Num 16.46; Heb 2.17
25.15 Num 31.8
25.17 Num 31.2
25.18 Num 31.16

sun before the LORD, in order that
the fierce anger of the LORD may
turn away from Israel." 5 And Moses said to the judges of Israel,
"Each of you shall kill any of your
people who have yoked themselves
to the Baal of Peor."
6 Just then one of the Israelites
came and brought a Midianite
woman into his family, in the sight
of Moses and in the sight of the
whole congregation of the Israelites, while they were weeping at
the entrance of the tent of meeting.
7 When Phinehas son of Eleazar,
son of Aaron the priest, saw it, he
got up and left the congregation.
Taking a spear in his hand, 8 he
went after the Israelite man into
the tent, and pierced the two of
them, the Israelite and the woman,
through the belly. So the plague
was stopped among the people of
Israel. 9 Nevertheless those that
died by the plague were twenty-
four thousand.
10 The LORD spoke to Moses,
saying: 11 "Phinehas son of Eleazar,
son of Aaron the priest, has turned
back my wrath from the Israelites
by manifesting such zeal among
them on my behalf that in my jealousy I did not consume the Israelites. 12 Therefore say, 'I hereby
grant him my covenant of peace.
13 It shall be for him and for his descendants after him a covenant of
perpetual priesthood, because he
was zealous for his God, and made
atonement for the Israelites.' "
14 The name of the slain Israelite man, who was killed with the
Midianite woman, was Zimri son of
Salu, head of an ancestral house
belonging to the Simeonites. 15 The
name of the Midianite woman who
was killed was Cozbi daughter of
Zur, who was the head of a clan, an
ancestral house in Midian.
16 The LORD said to Moses,
17 "Harass the Midianites, and defeat them; 18 for they have harassed
you by the trickery with which they
deceived you in the affair of Peor,

[j] Or *forehead* [k] Some Mss read *skull*
[l] Heb *Seir, its enemies, a possession*

and in the affair of Cozbi, the
daughter of a leader of Midian,
their sister; she was killed on the
day of the plague that resulted
from Peor."

A Census of the New Generation

26 After the plague the LORD
said to Moses and to Eleazar son of Aaron the priest, 2"Take
a census of the whole congregation
of the Israelites, from twenty years
old and upward, by their ancestral
houses, everyone in Israel able to
go to war." 3 Moses and Eleazar the
priest spoke with them in the
plains of Moab by the Jordan opposite Jericho, saying, 4"Take a census of the people,[m] from twenty
years old and upward," as the LORD
commanded Moses.
The Israelites, who came out of
the land of Egypt, were:
5 Reuben, the firstborn of Israel.
The descendants of Reuben: of Hanoch, the clan of the Hanochites;
of Pallu, the clan of the Palluites;
6 of Hezron, the clan of the Hezron-
ites; of Carmi, the clan of the Car-
mites. 7 These are the clans of the
Reubenites; the number of those
enrolled was forty-three thousand
seven hundred thirty. 8 And the descendants of Pallu: Eliab. 9 The descendants of Eliab: Nemuel, Dathan, and Abiram. These are the
same Dathan and Abiram, chosen
from the congregation, who rebelled against Moses and Aaron in
the company of Korah, when they
rebelled against the LORD, 10 and
the earth opened its mouth and
swallowed them up along with Korah, when that company died,
when the fire devoured two hundred fifty men; and they became a
warning. 11 Notwithstanding, the
sons of Korah did not die.
12 The descendants of Simeon
by their clans: of Nemuel, the clan
of the Nemuelites; of Jamin, the
clan of the Jaminites; of Jachin,
the clan of the Jachinites; 13 of Zerah, the clan of the Zerahites; of
Shaul, the clan of the Shaulites.[n]
14 These are the clans of the Simeonites, twenty-two thousand two
hundred.
15 The children of Gad by their
clans: of Zephon, the clan of the
Zephonites; of Haggi, the clan of
the Haggites; of Shuni, the clan of
the Shunites; 16 of Ozni, the clan
of the Oznites; of Eri, the clan of the
Erites; 17 of Arod, the clan of the Ar-
odites; of Areli, the clan of the Are-
lites. 18 These are the clans of the
Gadites: the number of those enrolled was forty thousand five hundred.
19 The sons of Judah: Er and
Onan; Er and Onan died in the land
of Canaan. 20 The descendants of
Judah by their clans were: of Shelah, the clan of the Shelanites; of
Perez, the clan of the Perezites; of
Zerah, the clan of the Zerahites.
21 The descendants of Perez were:
of Hezron, the clan of the Hezron-
ites; of Hamul, the clan of the Ha-
mulites. 22 These are the clans of
Judah: the number of those enrolled was seventy-six thousand
five hundred.
23 The descendants of Issachar
by their clans: of Tola, the clan of
the Tolaites; of Puvah, the clan of
the Punites; 24 of Jashub, the clan
of the Jashubites; of Shimron, the
clan of the Shimronites. 25 These
are the clans of Issachar: sixty-four
thousand three hundred enrolled.
26 The descendants of Zebulun
by their clans: of Sered, the clan of
the Seredites; of Elon, the clan of
the Elonites; of Jahleel, the clan
of the Jahleelites. 27 These are the
clans of the Zebulunites; the number of those enrolled was sixty
thousand five hundred.
28 The sons of Joseph by their
clans: Manasseh and Ephraim.
29 The descendants of Manasseh: of
Machir, the clan of the Machirites;
and Machir was the father of Gilead; of Gilead, the clan of the Gileadites. 30 These are the descendants of Gilead: of Iezer, the clan of
the Iezerites; of Helek, the clan of
the Helekites; 31 and of Asriel, the

26.2 Ex 30.12; 38.25,26; Num 1.2
26.5 Ex 6.14
26.9 Num 16.1,2
26.10 Num 16.32, 35,38
26.11 Deut 24.16
26.12 Ex 6.15; 1 Chr 4.24
26.13 Gen 46.10
26.15 Gen 46.16
26.16 Gen 46.16
26.17 Gen 46.16
26.18 Num 1.25
26.22 Num 1.27
26.24 Gen 46.13
26.25 Num 1.29
26.27 Num 1.31
26.30 see Josh 17.2

[m] Heb lacks *take a census of the people*: Compare verse 2 [n] Or *Saul . . . Saulites*

clan of the Asrielites; and of Shechem, the clan of the Shechemites;
32 and of Shemida, the clan of the
Shemidaites; and of Hepher, the
clan of the Hepherites. 33 Now Zelophehad son of Hepher had no
sons, but daughters: and the names
of the daughters of Zelophehad
were Mahlah, Noah, Hoglah, Milcah, and Tirzah. 34 These are the
clans of Manasseh; the number of
those enrolled was fifty-two thousand seven hundred.

35 These are the descendants of
Ephraim according to their clans:
of Shuthelah, the clan of the Shu-
thelahites; of Becher, the clan of
the Becherites; of Tahan, the clan
of the Tahanites. 36 And these are
the descendants of Shuthelah: of
Eran, the clan of the Eranites.
37 These are the clans of the Ephraimites: the number of those enrolled was thirty-two thousand five
hundred. These are the descendants of Joseph by their clans.

38 The descendants of Benjamin by their clans: of Bela, the clan
of the Belaites; of Ashbel, the clan
of the Ashbelites; of Ahiram, the
clan of the Ahiramites; 39 of She-
phupham, the clan of the Shu-
phamites; of Hupham, the clan of
the Huphamites. 40 And the sons of
Bela were Ard and Naaman: of Ard,
the clan of the Ardites; of Naaman,
the clan of the Naamites. 41 These
are the descendants of Benjamin
by their clans; the number of those
enrolled was forty-five thousand
six hundred.

42 These are the descendants of
Dan by their clans: of Shuham, the
clan of the Shuhamites. These are
the clans of Dan by their clans.
43 All the clans of the Shuhamites:
sixty-four thousand four hundred
enrolled.

44 The descendants of Asher by
their families: of Imnah, the clan of
the Imnites; of Ishvi, the clan of the
Ishvites; of Beriah, the clan of the
Beriites. 45 Of the descendants of
Beriah: of Heber, the clan of the
Heberites; of Malchiel, the clan of
the Malchielites. 46 And the name
of the daughter of Asher was Serah.
47 These are the clans of the Asherites: the number of those enrolled
was fifty-three thousand four hundred.

48 The descendants of Naphtali
by their clans: of Jahzeel, the clan
of the Jahzeelites; of Guni, the clan
of the Gunites; 49 of Jezer, the
clan of the Jezerites; of Shillem,
the clan of the Shillemites. 50 These
the Naphtalites[o] by their clans:
the number of those enrolled was
forty-five thousand four hundred.

51 This was the number of the
Israelites enrolled: six hundred
and one thousand seven hundred
thirty.

52 The LORD spoke to Moses,
saying: 53 To these the land shall be
apportioned for inheritance according to the number of names.
54 To a large tribe you shall give a
large inheritance, and to a small
tribe you shall give a small inheritance; every tribe shall be given its
inheritance according to its enrollment. 55 But the land shall be apportioned by lot; according to the
names of their ancestral tribes they
shall inherit. 56 Their inheritance
shall be apportioned according to
lot between the larger and the
smaller.

57 This is the enrollment of the
Levites by their clans: of Gershon,
the clan of the Gershonites; of Kohath, the clan of the Kohathites; of
Merari, the clan of the Merarites.
58 These are the clans of Levi: the
clan of the Libnites, the clan of the
Hebronites, the clan of the Mahlites, the clan of the Mushites, the
clan of the Korahites. Now Kohath
was the father of Amram. 59 The
name of Amram's wife was Jochebed daughter of Levi, who was born
to Levi in Egypt; and she bore to
Amram: Aaron, Moses, and their
sister Miriam. 60 To Aaron were
born Nadab, Abihu, Eleazar, and
Ithamar. 61 But Nadab and Abihu
died when they offered illicit fire
before the LORD. 62 The number of
those enrolled was twenty-three
thousand, every male one month

26.35 1 Chr 7.20
26.37 Num 1.33
26.38 Gen 46.21
26.39 Gen 46.21
26.40 1 Chr 8.3
26.41 Num 1.37
26.42 Gen 46.23
26.43 Num 1.39
26.47 Num 1.41
26.50 Num 1.43
26.53 Josh 11.23; 14.1
26.54 Num 33.54
26.55 Num 33.54; 34.13
26.59 Ex 6.20
26.60 Num 3.2
26.61 Lev 10.1,2; Num 3.4
26.62 Num 1.47; 18.20,23,24

o Heb *clans of Naphtali*

old and up; for they were not enrolled among the Israelites because there was no allotment given to them among the Israelites.

63 These were those enrolled by Moses and Eleazar the priest, who enrolled the Israelites in the plains of Moab by the Jordan opposite Jericho. 64 Among these there was not one of those enrolled by Moses and Aaron the priest, who had enrolled the Israelites in the wilderness of Sinai. 65 For the LORD had said of them, "They shall die in the wilderness." Not one of them was left, except Caleb son of Jephunneh and Joshua son of Nun.

The Daughters of Zelophehad

27 Then the daughters of Zelophehad came forward. Zelophehad was son of Hepher son of Gilead son of Machir son of Manasseh son of Joseph, a member of the Manassite clans. The names of his daughters were: Mahlah, Noah, Hoglah, Milcah, and Tirzah. 2 They stood before Moses, Eleazar the priest, the leaders, and all the congregation, at the entrance of the tent of meeting, and they said, 3 "Our father died in the wilderness; he was not among the company of those who gathered themselves together against the LORD in the company of Korah, but died for his own sin; and he had no sons. 4 Why should the name of our father be taken away from his clan because he had no son? Give to us a possession among our father's brothers."

5 Moses brought their case before the LORD. 6 And the LORD spoke to Moses, saying: 7 The daughters of Zelophehad are right in what they are saying; you shall indeed let them possess an inheritance among their father's brothers and pass the inheritance of their father on to them. 8 You shall also say to the Israelites, "If a man dies, and has no son, then you shall pass his inheritance on to his daughter. 9 If he has no daughter, then you shall give his inheritance to his brothers. 10 If he has no brothers, then you shall give his inheritance to his father's brothers. 11 And if his father has no brothers, then you shall give his inheritance to the nearest kinsman of his clan, and he shall possess it. It shall be for the Israelites a statute and ordinance, as the LORD commanded Moses."

Joshua Appointed Moses' Successor

12 The LORD said to Moses, "Go up this mountain of the Abarim range, and see the land that I have given to the Israelites. 13 When you have seen it, you also shall be gathered to your people, as your brother Aaron was, 14 because you rebelled against my word in the wilderness of Zin when the congregation quarreled with me.[p] You did not show my holiness before their eyes at the waters." (These are the waters of Meribath–Kadesh in the wilderness of Zin.) 15 Moses spoke to the LORD, saying, 16 "Let the LORD, the God of the spirits of all flesh, appoint someone over the congregation 17 who shall go out before them and come in before them, who shall lead them out and bring them in, so that the congregation of the LORD may not be like sheep without a shepherd." 18 So the LORD said to Moses, "Take Joshua son of Nun, a man in whom is the spirit, and lay your hand upon him; 19 have him stand before Eleazar the priest and all the congregation, and commission him in their sight. 20 You shall give him some of your authority, so that all the congregation of the Israelites may obey. 21 But he shall stand before Eleazar the priest, who shall inquire for him by the decision of the Urim before the LORD; at his word they shall go out, and at his word they shall come in, both he and all the Israelites with him, the whole congregation." 22 So Moses did as the LORD commanded him. He took Joshua and had him stand before Eleazar the priest and the whole congregation; 23 he laid his hands on him and commis-

26.64 Deut 2.14, 15
26.65 Num 14.28, 29; 1 Cor 10.5, 6; Num 14.30
27.1ff Num 26.33; 36.1
27.3 Num 26.64, 65; 26.33; 16.1,2
27.4 Josh 17.4
27.5 Num 9.8
27.6 Num 36.2
27.12 Num 33.47; Deut 32.49
27.13 Num 31.2
27.14 Num 20.12; Ex 17.7
27.16 Num 16.22
27.17 Deut 31.2; Mt 9.36; Mk 6.34
27.18 Num 11.25-29; Deut 34.9
27.19 Deut 31.3,7, 8,23
27.20 Josh 1.16, 17
27.21 Ex 28.30

[p] Heb lacks *with me*

sioned him—as the LORD had directed through Moses.

Daily Offerings

28 The LORD spoke to Moses,
saying: [2]Command the Israelites, and say to them: My offering, the food for my offerings by
fire, my pleasing odor, you shall
take care to offer to me at its appointed time. [3]And you shall say to
them, This is the offering by fire
that you shall offer to the LORD: two
male lambs a year old without
blemish, daily, as a regular offering. [4]One lamb you shall offer in
the morning, and the other lamb
you shall offer at twilight[q] [5]also
one-tenth of an ephah of choice
flour for a grain offering, mixed
with one-fourth of a hin of beaten
oil. [6]It is a regular burnt offering,
ordained at Mount Sinai for a
pleasing odor, an offering by fire to
the LORD. [7]Its drink offering shall
be one-fourth of a hin for each
lamb; in the sanctuary you shall
pour out a drink offering of strong
drink to the LORD. [8]The other lamb
you shall offer at twilight[q] with a
grain offering and a drink offering
like the one in the morning; you
shall offer it as an offering by fire,
a pleasing odor to the LORD.

Sabbath Offerings

9 On the sabbath day: two male
lambs a year old without blemish,
and two-tenths of an ephah of
choice flour for a grain offering,
mixed with oil, and its drink
offering— [10]this is the burnt offering for every sabbath, in addition to
the regular burnt offering and its
drink offering.

Monthly Offerings

11 At the beginnings of your
months you shall offer a burnt offering to the LORD: two young bulls,
one ram, seven male lambs a year
old without blemish; [12]also three-
tenths of an ephah of choice flour
for a grain offering, mixed with oil,
for each bull; and two-tenths of
choice flour for a grain offering,
mixed with oil, for the one ram;
[13]and one-tenth of choice flour
mixed with oil as a grain offering
for every lamb—a burnt offering of
pleasing odor, an offering by fire to
the LORD. [14]Their drink offerings
shall be half a hin of wine for a bull,
one-third of a hin for a ram, and
one-fourth of a hin for a lamb. This
is the burnt offering of every month
throughout the months of the year.
[15]And there shall be one male goat
for a sin offering to the LORD; it
shall be offered in addition to the
regular burnt offering and its drink
offering.

Offerings at Passover

16 On the fourteenth day of the
first month there shall be a passover offering to the LORD. [17]And on
the fifteenth day of this month is a
festival; seven days shall unleavened bread be eaten. [18]On the first
day there shall be a holy convocation. You shall not work at your occupations. [19]You shall offer an offering by fire, a burnt offering to
the LORD: two young bulls, one ram,
and seven male lambs a year old;
see that they are without blemish.
[20]Their grain offering shall be of
choice flour mixed with oil: three-
tenths of an ephah shall you offer
for a bull, and two-tenths for a ram;
[21]one-tenth shall you offer for each
of the seven lambs; [22]also one male
goat for a sin offering, to make
atonement for you. [23]You shall offer these in addition to the burnt
offering of the morning, which belongs to the regular burnt offering.
[24]In the same way you shall offer
daily, for seven days, the food of an
offering by fire, a pleasing odor to
the LORD; it shall be offered in addition to the regular burnt offering
and its drink offering. [25]And on the
seventh day you shall have a holy
convocation; you shall not work at
your occupations.

Offerings at the Festival of Weeks

26 On the day of the first fruits,
when you offer a grain offering of
new grain to the LORD at your festival of weeks, you shall have a holy

28.2 Lev 3.11 **28.3** Ex 29.38 **28.7** Ex 29.42 **28.10** v. 3 **28.11** Num 10.10; Ezek 45.17; 46.6 **28.12** Num 15.4-12

28.15 v. 3 **28.16** Ex 12.6,18; Lev 23.5; Deut 16.1 **28.17** Lev 23.6 **28.18** Ex 12.16; Lev 23.7 **28.23** v. 3 **28.25** Ex 12.16 **28.26** Ex 23.16; 34.22; Lev 23.10, 15; Deut 16.10

[q] Heb *between the two evenings*

convocation; you shall not work at your occupations. [27]You shall offer a burnt offering, a pleasing odor to the LORD: two young bulls, one ram, seven male lambs a year old. [28]Their grain offering shall be of choice flour mixed with oil, three-tenths of an ephah for each bull, two-tenths for one ram, [29]one-tenth for each of the seven lambs; [30]with one male goat, to make atonement for you. [31]In addition to the regular burnt offering with its grain offering, you shall offer them and their drink offering. They shall be without blemish.

Offerings at the Festival of Trumpets

29 On the first day of the seventh month you shall have a holy convocation; you shall not work at your occupations. It is a day for you to blow the trumpets, [2]and you shall offer a burnt offering, a pleasing odor to the LORD: one young bull, one ram, seven male lambs a year old without blemish. [3]Their grain offering shall be of choice flour mixed with oil, three-tenths of one ephah for the bull, two-tenths for the ram, [4]and one-tenth for each of the seven lambs; [5]with one male goat for a sin offering, to make atonement for you. [6]These are in addition to the burnt offering of the new moon and its grain offering, and the regular burnt offering and its grain offering, and their drink offerings, according to the ordinance for them, a pleasing odor, an offering by fire to the LORD.

Offerings on the Day of Atonement

7 On the tenth day of this seventh month you shall have a holy convocation, and deny yourselves;[r] you shall do no work. [8]You shall offer a burnt offering to the LORD, a pleasing odor: one young bull, one ram, seven male lambs a year old. They shall be without blemish. [9]Their grain offering shall be of choice flour mixed with oil, three-tenths of an ephah for the bull, two-tenths for the one ram, [10]one-tenth for each of the seven lambs; [11]with one male goat for a sin offering, in addition to the sin offering of atonement, and the regular burnt offering and its grain offering, and their drink offerings.

Offerings at the Festival of Booths

12 On the fifteenth day of the seventh month you shall have a holy convocation; you shall not work at your occupations. You shall celebrate a festival to the LORD seven days. [13]You shall offer a burnt offering, an offering by fire, a pleasing odor to the LORD: thirteen young bulls, two rams, fourteen male lambs a year old. They shall be without blemish. [14]Their grain offering shall be of choice flour mixed with oil, three-tenths of an ephah for each of the thirteen bulls, two-tenths for each of the two rams, [15]and one-tenth for each of the fourteen lambs; [16]also one male goat for a sin offering, in addition to the regular burnt offering, its grain offering and its drink offering.

17 On the second day: twelve young bulls, two rams, fourteen male lambs a year old without blemish, [18]with the grain offering and the drink offerings for the bulls, for the rams, and for the lambs, as prescribed in accordance with their number; [19]also one male goat for a sin offering, in addition to the regular burnt offering and its grain offering, and their drink offerings.

20 On the third day: eleven bulls, two rams, fourteen male lambs a year old without blemish, [21]with the grain offering and the drink offerings for the bulls, for the rams, and for the lambs, as prescribed in accordance with their number; [22]also one male goat for a sin offering, in addition to the regular burnt offering and its grain offering and its drink offering.

23 On the fourth day: ten bulls, two rams, fourteen male lambs a

28.31 vv. 3,19
29.1 Ex 23.16; 34.22; Lev 23.24
29.6 Num 28.3, 11
29.7 Lev 16.29-34; 23.26-32
29.11 Lev 16.3,5; Num 28.3
29.12 Lev 23.33-35
29.16 v. 11
29.18 vv. 3,4,9,10; Num 15.12; 28.7,14
29.22 Num 28.15

[r] Or *and fast*

year old without blemish, 24with
the grain offering and the drink offerings for the bulls, for the rams,
and for the lambs, as prescribed in
accordance with their number;
25also one male goat for a sin offering, in addition to the regular burnt
offering, its grain offering and its
drink offering.
26 On the fifth day: nine bulls,
two rams, fourteen male lambs a
year old without blemish, 27with
the grain offering and the drink offerings for the bulls, for the rams,
and for the lambs, as prescribed in
accordance with their number;
28also one male goat for a sin offering, in addition to the regular burnt
offering and its grain offering and
its drink offering.
29 On the sixth day: eight bulls,
two rams, fourteen male lambs a
year old without blemish, 30with
the grain offering and the drink offerings for the bulls, for the rams,
and for the lambs, as prescribed in
accordance with their number;
31also one male goat for a sin offering, in addition to the regular burnt
offering, its grain offering, and its
drink offerings.
32 On the seventh day: seven
bulls, two rams, fourteen male
lambs a year old without blemish,
33with the grain offering and the
drink offerings for the bulls, for the
rams, and for the lambs, as prescribed in accordance with their
number; 34also one male goat for a
sin offering, besides the regular
burnt offering, its grain offering,
and its drink offering.
35 On the eighth day you shall
have a solemn assembly; you shall
not work at your occupations.
36You shall offer a burnt offering,
an offering by fire, a pleasing odor
to the LORD: one bull, one ram, sev-
en male lambs a year old without
blemish, 37and the grain offering
and the drink offerings for the bull,
for the ram, and for the lambs, as
prescribed in accordance with their
number; 38also one male goat for a
sin offering, in addition to the regular burnt offering and its grain offering and its drink offering.

29.28 Num 15.24 **29.31** v. 22; Gen 8.20 **29.35** Lev 23.36

29.39 Lev 23.2; 1 Chr 23.31; 2 Chr 31.3; Lev 7.11,16 **30.2** Deut 23.21; Mt 5.23 **30.5** Eccl 5.4 **30.6** Ps 56.12 **30.8** Gen 3.16

39 These you shall offer to the
LORD at your appointed festivals, in
addition to your votive offerings
and your freewill offerings, as your
burnt offerings, your grain offerings, your drink offerings, and your
offerings of well-being.
40[s]So Moses told the Israelites
everything just as the LORD had
commanded Moses.

Vows Made by Women

30 Then Moses said to the
heads of the tribes of the
Israelites: This is what the LORD has
commanded. 2When a man makes
a vow to the LORD, or swears an oath
to bind himself by a pledge, he
shall not break his word; he shall
do according to all that proceeds
out of his mouth.
3 When a woman makes a vow
to the LORD, or binds herself by a
pledge, while within her father's
house, in her youth, 4and her father hears of her vow or her pledge
by which she has bound herself,
and says nothing to her; then all
her vows shall stand, and any
pledge by which she has bound
herself shall stand. 5But if her father expresses disapproval to her at
the time that he hears of it, no vow
of hers, and no pledge by which she
has bound herself, shall stand; and
the LORD will forgive her, because
her father had expressed to her his
disapproval.
6 If she marries, while obligated
by her vows or any thoughtless utterance of her lips by which she has
bound herself, 7and her husband
hears of it and says nothing to her
at the time that he hears, then her
vows shall stand, and her pledges
by which she has bound herself
shall stand. 8But if, at the time that
her husband hears of it, he expresses disapproval to her, then he
shall nullify the vow by which she
was obligated, or the thoughtless
utterance of her lips, by which she
bound herself; and the LORD will
forgive her. 9(But every vow of a
widow or of a divorced woman, by
which she has bound herself, shall

[s] Ch 30.1 in Heb

be binding upon her.) 10 And if she
made a vow in her husband's
house, or bound herself by a pledge
with an oath, 11 and her husband
heard it and said nothing to her,
and did not express disapproval to
her, then all her vows shall stand,
and any pledge by which she bound
herself shall stand. 12 But if her
husband nullifies them at the time
that he hears them, then whatever
proceeds out of her lips concerning
her vows, or concerning her pledge
of herself, shall not stand. Her husband has nullified them, and the
LORD will forgive her. 13 Any vow or
any binding oath to deny herself,[t]
her husband may allow to stand, or
her husband may nullify. 14 But if
her husband says nothing to her
from day to day,[u] then he validates
all her vows, or all her pledges, by
which she is obligated; he has vali-
dated them, because he said nothing to her at the time that he heard
of them. 15 But if he nullifies them
some time after he has heard of
them, then he shall bear her guilt.

16 These are the statutes that
the LORD commanded Moses concerning a husband and his wife,
and a father and his daughter while
she is still young and in her father's
house.

War against Midian

31 The LORD spoke to Moses,
saying, 2 "Avenge the Israelites on the Midianites; afterward
you shall be gathered to your people." 3 So Moses said to the people,
"Arm some of your number for the
war, so that they may go against
Midian, to execute the LORD's vengeance on Midian. 4 You shall send
a thousand from each of the tribes
of Israel to the war." 5 So out of the
thousands of Israel, a thousand
from each tribe were conscripted,
twelve thousand armed for battle.
6 Moses sent them to the war, a
thousand from each tribe, along
with Phinehas son of Eleazar the
priest,[v] with the vessels of the
sanctuary and the trumpets for
sounding the alarm in his hand.
7 They did battle against Midian, as
the LORD had commanded Moses,
and killed every male. 8 They killed
the kings of Midian: Evi, Rekem,
Zur, Hur, and Reba, the five kings
of Midian, in addition to others
who were slain by them; and they
also killed Balaam son of Beor with
the sword. 9 The Israelites took the
women of Midian and their little
ones captive; and they took all
their cattle, their flocks, and all
their goods as booty. 10 All their
towns where they had settled, and
all their encampments, they
burned, 11 but they took all the
spoil and all the booty, both people
and animals. 12 Then they brought
the captives and the booty and the
spoil to Moses, to Eleazar the
priest, and to the congregation of
the Israelites, at the camp on the
plains of Moab by the Jordan at
Jericho.

Return from the War

13 Moses, Eleazar the priest,
and all the leaders of the congregation went to meet them outside the
camp. 14 Moses became angry with
the officers of the army, the commanders of thousands and the
commanders of hundreds, who had
come from service in the war.
15 Moses said to them, "Have you
allowed all the women to live?
16 These women here, on Balaam's
advice, made the Israelites act
treacherously against the LORD in
the affair of Peor, so that the
plague came among the congregation of the LORD. 17 Now therefore,
kill every male among the little
ones, and kill every woman who
has known a man by sleeping with
him. 18 But all the young girls who
have not known a man by sleeping
with him, keep alive for yourselves.
19 Camp outside the camp seven
days; whoever of you has killed any
person or touched a corpse, purify
yourselves and your captives on the
third and on the seventh day. 20 You
shall purify every garment, every
article of skin, everything made of

30.12 Eph 5.22
30.15 Col 3.18
30.16 Ex 15.26
31.2 Num 25.1, 16,17; 27.13
31.6 Num 10.9
31.8 Josh 13.21, 22; v. 16
31.11 Deut 20.14
31.16 Num 25.1-9; 24.14; 2 Pet 2.15; Rev 2.14
31.17 Judg 21.11
31.19 Num 19.11-22

[t] Or *to fast* [u] Or *from that day to the next* [v] Gk: Heb adds *to the war*

goats' hair, and every article of wood."

21 Eleazar the priest said to the troops who had gone to battle: "This is the statute of the law that the LORD has commanded Moses: 22 gold, silver, bronze, iron, tin, and lead— 23 everything that can withstand fire, shall be passed through fire, and it shall be clean. Nevertheless it shall also be purified with the water for purification; and whatever cannot withstand fire, shall be passed through the water. 24 You must wash your clothes on the seventh day, and you shall be clean; afterward you may come into the camp."

Disposition of Captives and Booty

25 The LORD spoke to Moses, saying, 26 "You and Eleazar the priest and the heads of the ancestral houses of the congregation make an inventory of the booty captured, both human and animal. 27 Divide the booty into two parts, between the warriors who went out to battle and all the congregation. 28 From the share of the warriors who went out to battle, set aside as tribute for the LORD, one item out of every five hundred, whether persons, oxen, donkeys, sheep, or goats. 29 Take it from their half and give it to Eleazar the priest as an offering to the LORD. 30 But from the Israelites' half you shall take one out of every fifty, whether persons, oxen, donkeys, sheep, or goats—all the animals—and give them to the Levites who have charge of the tabernacle of the LORD."

31 Then Moses and Eleazar the priest did as the LORD had commanded Moses:

32 The booty remaining from the spoil that the troops had taken totaled six hundred seventy-five thousand sheep, 33 seventy-two thousand oxen, 34 sixty-one thousand donkeys, 35 and thirty-two thousand persons in all, women who had not known a man by sleeping with him.

36 The half-share, the portion of those who had gone out to war, was in number three hundred thirty-seven thousand five hundred sheep and goats, 37 and the LORD's tribute of sheep and goats was six hundred seventy-five. 38 The oxen were thirty-six thousand, of which the LORD's tribute was seventy-two. 39 The donkeys were thirty thousand five hundred, of which the LORD's tribute was sixty-one. 40 The persons were sixteen thousand, of which the LORD's tribute was thirty-two persons. 41 Moses gave the tribute, the offering for the LORD, to Eleazar the priest, as the LORD had commanded Moses.

42 As for the Israelites' half, which Moses separated from that of the troops, 43 the congregation's half was three hundred thirty-seven thousand five hundred sheep and goats, 44 thirty-six thousand oxen, 45 thirty thousand five hundred donkeys, 46 and sixteen thousand persons. 47 From the Israelites' half Moses took one of every fifty, both of persons and of animals, and gave them to the Levites who had charge of the tabernacle of the LORD; as the LORD had commanded Moses.

48 Then the officers who were over the thousands of the army, the commanders of thousands and the commanders of hundreds, approached Moses, 49 and said to Moses, "Your servants have counted the warriors who are under our command, and not one of us is missing. 50 And we have brought the LORD's offering, what each of us found, articles of gold, armlets and bracelets, signet rings, earrings, and pendants, to make atonement for ourselves before the LORD." 51 Moses and Eleazar the priest received the gold from them, all in the form of crafted articles. 52 And all the gold of the offering that they offered to the LORD, from the commanders of thousands and the commanders of hundreds, was sixteen thousand seven hundred fifty shekels. 53 (The troops had all taken plunder for themselves.) 54 So Moses and Eleazar the priest re-

31.23 Num 19.9, 17
31.24 Lev 11.25
31.28 Num 18.21-30
31.30 Num 3.7,8, 25; 18.3,4
31.32 Gen 49.27; Ex 15.9
31.37 vv. 38,41
31.41 Num 18.8,9
31.47 v. 30
31.50 Ex 30.12,16
31.53 v. 32; Deut 20.14
31.54 Ex 30.16

ceived the gold from the commanders of thousands and of hundreds, and brought it into the tent
of meeting as a memorial for the
Israelites before the LORD.

Conquest and Division of Transjordan

32 Now the Reubenites and
the Gadites owned a very
great number of cattle. When they
saw that the land of Jazer and the
land of Gilead was a good place for
cattle, 2 the Gadites and the Reubenites came and spoke to Moses,
to Eleazar the priest, and to the
leaders of the congregation, saying,
3 "Ataroth, Dibon, Jazer, Nimrah,
Heshbon, Elealeh, Sebam, Nebo,
and Beon — 4 the land that the LORD
subdued before the congregation
of Israel—is a land for cattle; and
your servants have cattle." 5 They
continued, "If we have found favor
in your sight, let this land be given
to your servants for a possession;
do not make us cross the Jordan."
6 But Moses said to the Gadites
and to the Reubenites, "Shall your
brothers go to war while you sit
here? 7 Why will you discourage the
hearts of the Israelites from going
over into the land that the LORD has
given them? 8 Your fathers did this,
when I sent them from Kadesh-
barnea to see the land. 9 When they
went up to the Wadi Eshcol and
saw the land, they discouraged the
hearts of the Israelites from going
into the land that the LORD had giv-
en them. 10 The LORD's anger was
kindled on that day and he swore,
saying, 11 'Surely none of the people who came up out of Egypt, from
twenty years old and upward, shall
see the land that I swore to give to
Abraham, to Isaac, and to Jacob,
because they have not unreservedly followed me— 12 none except
Caleb son of Jephunneh the Kenizzite and Joshua son of Nun, for
they have unreservedly followed
the LORD.' 13 And the LORD's anger
was kindled against Israel, and he
made them wander in the wilderness for forty years, until all the
generation that had done evil in
the sight of the LORD had disappeared. 14 And now you, a brood of
sinners, have risen in place of your
fathers, to increase the LORD's
fierce anger against Israel! 15 If you
turn away from following him, he
will again abandon them in the wilderness; and you will destroy all
this people."
16 Then they came up to him
and said, "We will build sheepfolds
here for our flocks, and towns for
our little ones, 17 but we will take
up arms as a vanguard[w] before the
Israelites, until we have brought
them to their place. Meanwhile our
little ones will stay in the fortified
towns because of the inhabitants
of the land. 18 We will not return to
our homes until all the Israelites
have obtained their inheritance.
19 We will not inherit with them on
the other side of the Jordan and beyond, because our inheritance has
come to us on this side of the Jordan to the east."
20 So Moses said to them, "If
you do this—if you take up arms to
go before the LORD for the war,
21 and all those of you who bear
arms cross the Jordan before the
LORD, until he has driven out his
enemies from before him 22 and the
land is subdued before the LORD—
then after that you may return and
be free of obligation to the LORD
and to Israel, and this land shall be
your possession before the LORD.
23 But if you do not do this, you
have sinned against the LORD; and
be sure your sin will find you out.
24 Build towns for your little ones,
and folds for your flocks; but do
what you have promised."
25 Then the Gadites and the
Reubenites said to Moses, "Your
servants will do as my lord commands. 26 Our little ones, our
wives, our flocks, and all our livestock shall remain there in the
towns of Gilead; 27 but your servants will cross over, everyone
armed for war, to do battle for the
LORD, just as my lord orders."
28 So Moses gave command

32.1 Ex 12.38; Num 21.32
32.7 Num 13.27-14.4
32.8 Num 13.3, 26
32.10 Num 14.11, 21; Deut 1.34
32.11 Num 14.28-30; Deut 1.35
32.12 Num 14.24; Deut 1.36
32.13 Num 14.33-35; 26.64,65
32.15 Deut 30.17, 18
32.17 Josh 4.12, 13
32.18 Josh 22.1-4
32.19 v. 33
32.20 Deut 3.18
32.22 Deut 3.12-20
32.24 vv. 16,34
32.26 Josh 1.14
32.27 Josh 4.12
32.28 Josh 1.13

[w] Cn: Heb *hurrying*

concerning them to Eleazar the
priest, to Joshua son of Nun, and to
the heads of the ancestral houses
of the Israelite tribes. 29 And Moses
said to them, "If the Gadites and
the Reubenites, everyone armed
for battle before the LORD, will
cross over the Jordan with you and
the land shall be subdued before
you, then you shall give them the
land of Gilead for a possession;
30 but if they will not cross over
with you armed, they shall have
possessions among you in the land
of Canaan." 31 The Gadites and the
Reubenites answered, "As the LORD
has spoken to your servants, so we
will do. 32 We will cross over armed
before the LORD into the land of Canaan, but the possession of our inheritance shall remain with us on
this side of[x] the Jordan."
33 Moses gave to them—to the
Gadites and to the Reubenites and
to the half-tribe of Manasseh son of
Joseph—the kingdom of King Sihon of the Amorites and the kingdom of King Og of Bashan, the land
and its towns, with the territories
of the surrounding towns. 34 And
the Gadites rebuilt Dibon, Ataroth, Aroer, 35 Atroth-shophan,
Jazer, Jogbehah, 36 Beth-nimrah,
and Beth-haran, fortified cities, and
folds for sheep. 37 And the Reubenites rebuilt Heshbon, Elealeh, Kiriathaim, 38 Nebo, and Baal-meon
(some names being changed), and
Sibmah; and they gave names to
the towns that they rebuilt. 39 The
descendants of Machir son of Manasseh went to Gilead, captured it,
and dispossessed the Amorites
who were there; 40 so Moses gave
Gilead to Machir son of Manasseh,
and he settled there. 41 Jair son of
Manasseh went and captured their
villages, and renamed them
Havvoth-jair.[y] 42 And Nobah went
and captured Kenath and its villages, and renamed it Nobah after
himself.

The Stages of Israel's Journey from Egypt

33 These are the stages by
which the Israelites went
out of the land of Egypt in military
formation under the leadership of
Moses and Aaron. 2 Moses wrote
down their starting points, stage by
stage, by command of the LORD;
and these are their stages according to their starting places. 3 They
set out from Rameses in the first
month, on the fifteenth day of the
first month; on the day after the
passover the Israelites went out
boldly in the sight of all the Egyptians, 4 while the Egyptians were
burying all their firstborn, whom
the LORD had struck down among
them. The LORD executed judgments even against their gods.
5 So the Israelites set out from
Rameses, and camped at Succoth.
6 They set out from Succoth, and
camped at Etham, which is on the
edge of the wilderness. 7 They set
out from Etham, and turned back
to Pi-hahiroth, which faces Baal-
zephon; and they camped before
Migdol. 8 They set out from Pi-
hahiroth, passed through the sea
into the wilderness, went a three
days' journey in the wilderness of
Etham, and camped at Marah.
9 They set out from Marah and
came to Elim; at Elim there were
twelve springs of water and seventy
palm trees, and they camped there.
10 They set out from Elim and
camped by the Red Sea.[z] 11 They
set out from the Red Sea[z] and
camped in the wilderness of Sin.
12 They set out from the wilderness
of Sin and camped at Dophkah.
13 They set out from Dophkah and
camped at Alush. 14 They set out
from Alush and camped at Rephidim, where there was no water for
the people to drink. 15 They set out
from Rephidim and camped in the
wilderness of Sinai. 16 They set out
from the wilderness of Sinai and
camped at Kibroth-hattaavah.
17 They set out from Kibroth-
hattaavah and camped at Hazeroth. 18 They set out from Hazeroth
and camped at Rithmah. 19 They
set out from Rithmah and camped

32.29 v. 1
32.33 Deut 3.12-17; Josh 12.1-6; Num 21.24, 33,35
32.41 Judg 10.4
33.1 Ps 77.20; Mic 6.4
33.3 Ex 12.37; 14.8
33.4 Ex 12.12
33.6 Ex 13.20
33.7 Ex 14.2,9
33.8 Ex 14.22
33.9 Ex 15.27
33.11 Ex 16.1
33.14 Ex 17.1
33.15 Ex 19.1
33.16 Num 11.34
33.17 Num 11.35

[x] Heb *beyond* [y] That is *the villages of Jair*
[z] Or *Sea of Reeds*

at Rimmon-perez. 20 They set out
from Rimmon-perez and camped at
Libnah. 21 They set out from Libnah and camped at Rissah. 22 They
set out from Rissah and camped at
Kehelathah. 23 They set out from
Kehelathah and camped at Mount
Shepher. 24 They set out from
Mount Shepher and camped at Ha-
radah. 25 They set out from Hara-
dah and camped at Makheloth.
26 They set out from Makheloth and
camped at Tahath. 27 They set out
from Tahath and camped at Terah.
28 They set out from Terah and
camped at Mithkah. 29 They set out
from Mithkah and camped at
Hashmonah. 30 They set out from
Hashmonah and camped at Moseroth. 31 They set out from Moseroth
and camped at Bene-jaakan.
32 They set out from Bene-jaakan
and camped at Hor-haggidgad.
33 They set out from Hor-haggidgad
and camped at Jotbathah. 34 They
set out from Jotbathah and
camped at Abronah. 35 They set out
from Abronah and camped at
Ezion-geber. 36 They set out from
Ezion-geber and camped in the wilderness of Zin (that is, Kadesh).
37 They set out from Kadesh and
camped at Mount Hor, on the edge
of the land of Edom.

38 Aaron the priest went up
Mount Hor at the command of the
LORD and died there in the fortieth
year after the Israelites had come
out of the land of Egypt, on the first
day of the fifth month. 39 Aaron was
one hundred twenty-three years
old when he died on Mount Hor.

40 The Canaanite, the king of
Arad, who lived in the Negeb in the
land of Canaan, heard of the coming of the Israelites.

41 They set out from Mount Hor
and camped at Zalmonah. 42 They
set out from Zalmonah and
camped at Punon. 43 They set out
from Punon and camped at Oboth.
44 They set out from Oboth and
camped at Iye-abarim, in the territory of Moab. 45 They set out from
Iyim and camped at Dibon-gad.
46 They set out from Dibon-gad and
camped at Almon-diblathaim.
47 They set out from Almon-
diblathaim and camped in the
mountains of Abarim, before Nebo.
48 They set out from the mountains
of Abarim and camped in the
plains of Moab by the Jordan at
Jericho; 49 they camped by the Jordan from Beth-jeshimoth as far as
Abel-shittim in the plains of Moab.

Directions for the Conquest of Canaan

50 In the plains of Moab by the
Jordan at Jericho, the LORD spoke
to Moses, saying: 51 Speak to the Israelites, and say to them: When
you cross over the Jordan into the
land of Canaan, 52 you shall drive
out all the inhabitants of the land
from before you, destroy all their
figured stones, destroy all their
cast images, and demolish all
their high places. 53 You shall take
possession of the land and settle in
it, for I have given you the land to
possess. 54 You shall apportion the
land by lot according to your clans;
to a large one you shall give a large
inheritance, and to a small one you
shall give a small inheritance; the
inheritance shall belong to the person on whom the lot falls; according to your ancestral tribes you
shall inherit. 55 But if you do not
drive out the inhabitants of the
land from before you, then those
whom you let remain shall be as
barbs in your eyes and thorns in
your sides; they shall trouble you in
the land where you are settling.
56 And I will do to you as I thought
to do to them.

The Boundaries of the Land

34 The LORD spoke to Moses,
saying: 2 Command the Is-
raelites, and say to them: When
you enter the land of Canaan (this
is the land that shall fall to you for
an inheritance, the land of Canaan,
defined by its boundaries), 3 your
south sector shall extend from the
wilderness of Zin along the side of
Edom. Your southern boundary
shall begin from the end of the
Dead Sea[a] on the east; 4 your

33.20 see Josh 10.29
33.30 Deut 10.6
33.33 Deut 10.7
33.35 Deut 2.8
33.36 Num 20.1
33.37 Num 20.16, 22; 21.4
33.38 Num 20.25, 28; Deut 10.6
33.40 Num 21.1
33.43 Num 21.10
33.44 Num 21.11
33.47 Num 27.12
33.48 Num 22.1
33.49 Num 25.1
33.52 Ex 23.24, 33; 34.13; Deut 7.2,5; 12.3; Josh 11.12
33.54 Num 26.53-55
33.55 Josh 23.13; Ps 106.34, 36
34.2 Gen 17.8; Deut 1.7; Ps 78.55; Ezek 47.15
34.3 Josh 15.1-3

[a] Heb *Salt Sea*

boundary shall turn south of the
ascent of Akrabbim, and cross to
Zin, and its outer limit shall be
south of Kadesh-barnea; then it
shall go on to Hazar-addar, and
cross to Azmon; 5 the boundary
shall turn from Azmon to the Wadi
of Egypt, and its termination shall
be at the Sea.

6 For the western boundary, you
shall have the Great Sea and its[b]
coast; this shall be your western
boundary.

7 This shall be your northern
boundary: from the Great Sea you
shall mark out your line to Mount
Hor; 8 from Mount Hor you shall
mark it out to Lebo-hamath, and
the outer limit of the boundary
shall be at Zedad; 9 then the boundary shall extend to Ziphron, and its
end shall be at Hazar-enan; this
shall be your northern boundary.

10 You shall mark out your eastern boundary from Hazar-enan to
Shepham; 11 and the boundary
shall continue down from Shepham to Riblah on the east side of
Ain; and the boundary shall go
down, and reach the eastern slope
of the sea of Chinnereth; 12 and the
boundary shall go down to the Jordan, and its end shall be at the
Dead Sea.[c] This shall be your land
with its boundaries all around.

13 Moses commanded the Israelites, saying: This is the land that
you shall inherit by lot, which the
LORD has commanded to give to the
nine tribes and to the half-tribe;
14 for the tribe of the Reubenites by
their ancestral houses and the tribe
of the Gadites by their ancestral
houses have taken their inheritance, and also the half-tribe of
Manasseh; 15 the two tribes and the
half-tribe have taken their inheritance beyond the Jordan at Jericho
eastward, toward the sunrise.

Tribal Leaders

16 The LORD spoke to Moses,
saying: 17 These are the names of
the men who shall apportion the
land to you for inheritance: the
priest Eleazar and Joshua son of
Nun. 18 You shall take one leader of
every tribe to apportion the land for
inheritance. 19 These are the names
of the men: Of the tribe of Judah,
Caleb son of Jephunneh. 20 Of the
tribe of the Simeonites, Shemuel
son of Ammihud. 21 Of the tribe of
Benjamin, Elidad son of Chislon.
22 Of the tribe of the Danites a leader, Bukki son of Jogli. 23 Of the Josephites: of the tribe of the Manassites a leader, Hanniel son of
Ephod, 24 and of the tribe of the
Ephraimites a leader, Kemuel son
of Shiphtan. 25 Of the tribe of the
Zebulunites a leader, Eli-zaphan
son of Parnach. 26 Of the tribe of
the Issacharites a leader, Paltiel
son of Azzan. 27 And of the tribe of
the Asherites a leader, Ahihud son
of Shelomi. 28 Of the tribe of the
Naphtalites a leader, Pedahel son
of Ammihud. 29 These were the
ones whom the LORD commanded
to apportion the inheritance for the
Israelites in the land of Canaan.

Cities for the Levites

35 In the plains of Moab by
the Jordan at Jericho, the
LORD spoke to Moses, saying:
2 Command the Israelites to give,
from the inheritance that they possess, towns for the Levites to live
in; you shall also give to the Levites
pasture lands surrounding the
towns. 3 The towns shall be theirs
to live in, and their pasture lands
shall be for their cattle, for their
livestock, and for all their animals.
4 The pasture lands of the towns,
which you shall give to the Levites,
shall reach from the wall of the
town outward a thousand cubits all
around. 5 You shall measure, outside the town, for the east side two
thousand cubits, for the south side
two thousand cubits, for the west
side two thousand cubits, and for
the north side two thousand cubits, with the town in the middle;
this shall belong to them as pasture
land for their towns.

6 The towns that you give to the
Levites shall include the six cities
of refuge, where you shall permit a
slayer to flee, and in addition to

34.5 Gen 15.18; Josh 15.4, 47
34.7 Ezek 47.15-17
34.8 Num 13.21
34.11 2 Kings 23.33; Deut 3.17; Josh 11.2
34.13 Josh 14.1,2
34.14 Num 32.33; Josh 14.2,3
34.17 Josh 14.1
34.18 Num 1.4,16

35.2 Lev 25.32-34; Josh 14.3,4
35.6 Josh 20.7-9; 21.3,13,21, 27,32,36,38

[b] Syr: Heb lacks *its* [c] Heb *Salt Sea*

them you shall give forty-two towns. 7 The towns that you give to the Levites shall total forty-eight, with their pasture lands. 8 And as for the towns that you shall give from the possession of the Israelites, from the larger tribes you shall take many, and from the smaller tribes you shall take few; each, in proportion to the inheritance that it obtains, shall give of its towns to the Levites.

Cities of Refuge

9 The LORD spoke to Moses, saying: 10 Speak to the Israelites, and say to them: When you cross the Jordan into the land of Canaan, 11 then you shall select cities to be cities of refuge for you, so that a slayer who kills a person without intent may flee there. 12 The cities shall be for you a refuge from the avenger, so that the slayer may not die until there is a trial before the congregation.

13 The cities that you designate shall be six cities of refuge for you: 14 you shall designate three cities beyond the Jordan, and three cities in the land of Canaan, to be cities of refuge. 15 These six cities shall serve as refuge for the Israelites, for the resident or transient alien among them, so that anyone who kills a person without intent may flee there.

Concerning Murder and Blood Revenge

16 But anyone who strikes another with an iron object, and death ensues, is a murderer; the murderer shall be put to death. 17 Or anyone who strikes another with a stone in hand that could cause death, and death ensues, is a murderer; the murderer shall be put to death. 18 Or anyone who strikes another with a weapon of wood in hand that could cause death, and death ensues, is a murderer; the murderer shall be put to death. 19 The avenger of blood is the one who shall put the murderer to death; when they meet, the avenger of blood shall execute the sentence. 20 Likewise, if someone pushes another from hatred, or hurls something at another, lying in wait, and death ensues, 21 or in enmity strikes another with the hand, and death ensues, then the one who struck the blow shall be put to death; that person is a murderer; the avenger of blood shall put the murderer to death, when they meet.

22 But if someone pushes another suddenly without enmity, or hurls any object without lying in wait, 23 or, while handling any stone that could cause death, unintentionally[d] drops it on another and death ensues, though they were not enemies, and no harm was intended, 24 then the congregation shall judge between the slayer and the avenger of blood, in accordance with these ordinances; 25 and the congregation shall rescue the slayer from the avenger of blood. Then the congregation shall send the slayer back to the original city of refuge. The slayer shall live in it until the death of the high priest who was anointed with the holy oil. 26 But if the slayer shall at any time go outside the bounds of the original city of refuge, 27 and is found by the avenger of blood outside the bounds of the city of refuge, and is killed by the avenger, no bloodguilt shall be incurred. 28 For the slayer must remain in the city of refuge until the death of the high priest; but after the death of the high priest the slayer may return home.

29 These things shall be a statute and ordinance for you throughout your generations wherever you live.

30 If anyone kills another, the murderer shall be put to death on the evidence of witnesses; but no one shall be put to death on the testimony of a single witness. 31 Moreover you shall accept no ransom for the life of a murderer who is subject to the death penalty; a murderer must be put to death.

35.8 Num 26.54; Lev 25.32-34; Josh 21.1-42
35.11 Deut 19.1-13; Ex 21.13
35.12 Josh 20.2-6
35.15 v. 11
35.16 Ex 21.12, 14; Lev 24.17
35.19 vv. 21,24,27
35.22 v. 11; Ex 21.13
35.24 v. 12
35.30 v. 16; Deut 17.6; 19.15; Mt 18.16; 2 Cor 13.1; Heb 10.28

[d] Heb *without seeing*

32 Nor shall you accept ransom for
one who has fled to a city of refuge,
enabling the fugitive to return to
live in the land before the death of
the high priest. 33 You shall not pollute the land in which you live; for
blood pollutes the land, and no expiation can be made for the land,
for the blood that is shed in it, except by the blood of the one who
shed it. 34 You shall not defile the
land in which you live, in which I
also dwell; for I the LORD dwell
among the Israelites.

Marriage of Female Heirs

36 The heads of the ancestral
houses of the clans of the
descendants of Gilead son of Machir son of Manasseh, of the Jo-
sephite clans, came forward and
spoke in the presence of Moses and
the leaders, the heads of the ancestral houses of the Israelites; 2 they
said, "The LORD commanded my
lord to give the land for inheritance
by lot to the Israelites; and my lord
was commanded by the LORD to
give the inheritance of our brother
Zelophehad to his daughters. 3 But
if they are married into another Israelite tribe, then their inheritance
will be taken from the inheritance
of our ancestors and added to the
inheritance of the tribe into which
they marry; so it will be taken away
from the allotted portion of our inheritance. 4 And when the jubilee
of the Israelites comes, then their
inheritance will be added to the inheritance of the tribe into which
they have married; and their inheritance will be taken from the inheritance of our ancestral tribe."

5 Then Moses commanded the
Israelites according to the word of
the LORD, saying, "The descendants
of the tribe of Joseph are right in
what they are saying. 6 This is what
the LORD commands concerning
the daughters of Zelophehad, 'Let
them marry whom they think best;
only it must be into a clan of their
father's tribe that they are married,

35.33 Ps 106.38; Gen 9.6
35.34 Lev 18.25; Ex 29.45,46
36.1 Num 26.29; 27.1
36.2 Num 26.55; 33.54; 27.1,7
36.4 Lev 25.10
36.6 v. 12

CITIES OF REFUGE

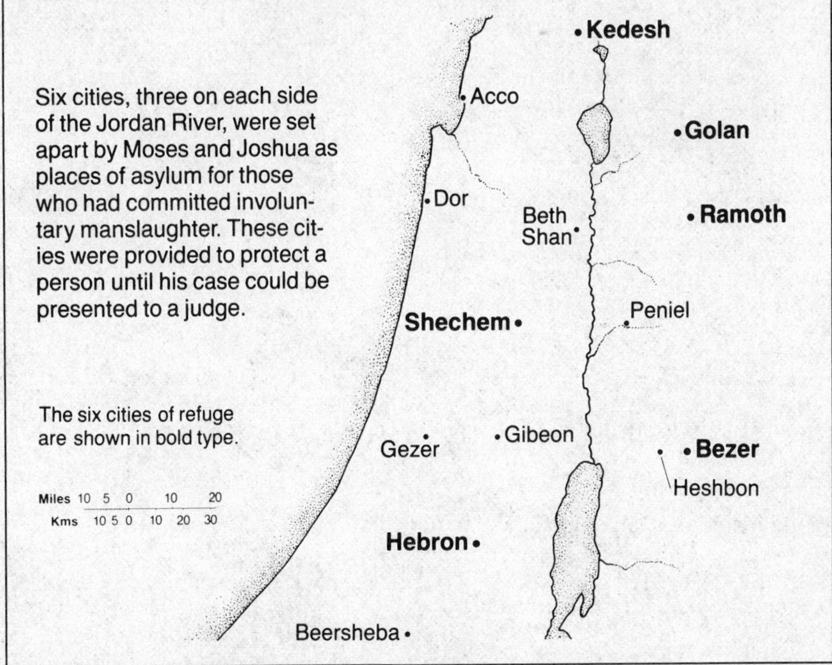

Six cities, three on each side of the Jordan River, were set apart by Moses and Joshua as places of asylum for those who had committed involuntary manslaughter. These cities were provided to protect a person until his case could be presented to a judge.

The six cities of refuge are shown in bold type.

7 so that no inheritance of the Israelites shall be transferred from one
tribe to another; for all Israelites
shall retain the inheritance of their
ancestral tribes. 8 Every daughter
who possesses an inheritance in
any tribe of the Israelites shall marry one from the clan of her father's
tribe, so that all Israelites may continue to possess their ancestral inheritance. 9 No inheritance shall be
transferred from one tribe to another; for each of the tribes of the
Israelites shall retain its own inheritance.' "
10 The daughters of Zelophehad did as the LORD had commanded Moses. 11 Mahlah, Tirzah, Hoglah, Milcah, and Noah, the
daughters of Zelophehad, married
sons of their father's brothers.
12 They were married into the clans
of the descendants of Manasseh
son of Joseph, and their inheritance remained in the tribe of their
father's clan.

13 These are the command-
ments and the ordinances that the
LORD commanded through Moses
to the Israelites in the plains of
Moab by the Jordan at Jericho.

36.8 1 Chr 23.22
36.11 Num 27.1
36.13 Num 22.1; Lev 26.46; 27.34

Deuteronomy

Title and Background

Deuteronomy means "repetition of the law." After forty years the Israelites were about to enter Canaan. But before they did, Moses wanted to remind them of their history, all that God had done for them, and the laws they had to continue to obey as God's chosen people.

Author and Date of Writing

This book is cast as a speech that Moses gave to the nation of Israel as they gathered on the other side of the Jordan, waiting for their entry into Canaan (1.5; 4.44; 5.1; 27.1). The time of this speech would be shortly before his death, recorded in the last chapter. See the Introductions to Genesis and Exodus for the two possible dates for Moses.

Theme and Message

Moses reminded the people of God's goodness to them through their journey and his giving them the land of Canaan. He also summarized God's laws, including the Ten Commandments. One subject that pervades the whole book is the love relationship of the Lord to his people and that of the people to the Lord as their sovereign God.

Outline

I. Preamble (1.1-5)
II. Historical Prologue (1.6–4.43)
III. Stipulations of the Covenant (4.44–26.19)
  A. Primary Demands (4.44–11.32)
  B. Additional Requirements (12.1–26.19)
IV. Curses and Blessings, and Renewal of the Covenant (27.1–30.20)
V. Succession under the Covenant (31.1-29)
VI. Moses' Song, Final Blessing, and Death (31.30–34.12)

Events at Horeb Recalled

1 These are the words that Moses spoke to all Israel beyond
the Jordan—in the wilderness, on
the plain opposite Suph, between
Paran and Tophel, Laban, Hazeroth, and Di-zahab. 2 (By the way of
Mount Seir it takes eleven days to
reach Kadesh-barnea from Horeb.)
3 In the fortieth year, on the first
day of the eleventh month, Moses
spoke to the Israelites just as the
LORD had commanded him to speak
to them. 4 This was after he had defeated King Sihon of the Amorites,
who reigned in Heshbon, and King
Og of Bashan, who reigned in Ashtaroth and[a] in Edrei. 5 Beyond the
Jordan in the land of Moab, Moses
undertook to expound this law as
follows:

6 The LORD our God spoke to us
at Horeb, saying, "You have stayed
long enough at this mountain.
7 Resume your journey, and go into
the hill country of the Amorites as
well as into the neighboring
regions—the Arabah, the hill
country, the Shephelah, the Negeb, and the seacoast—the land of
the Canaanites and the Lebanon,
as far as the great river, the river

1.3 Num 33.38
1.4 Num 21.24, 33
1.6 Ex 3.1; Num 10.11-13

[a] Gk Syr Vg Compare Josh 12.4: Heb lacks *and*

Euphrates. 8See, I have set the
land before you; go in and take possession of the land that I[b] swore to
your ancestors, to Abraham, to
Isaac, and to Jacob, to give to them
and to their descendants after
them."

Appointment of Tribal Leaders

9 At that time I said to you, "I
am unable by myself to bear you.
10The Lord your God has multiplied you, so that today you are as
numerous as the stars of heaven.
11May the Lord, the God of your
ancestors, increase you a thousand
times more and bless you, as he has
promised you! 12But how can I bear
the heavy burden of your disputes
all by myself? 13Choose for each of
your tribes individuals who are
wise, discerning, and reputable to
be your leaders." 14You answered
me, "The plan you have proposed is
a good one." 15So I took the leaders
of your tribes, wise and reputable
individuals, and installed them as
leaders over you, commanders of
thousands, commanders of hundreds, commanders of fifties, commanders of tens, and officials,
throughout your tribes. 16I charged
your judges at that time: "Give the
members of your community a fair
hearing, and judge rightly between
one person and another, whether
citizen or resident alien. 17You
must not be partial in judging: hear
out the small and the great alike;
you shall not be intimidated by
anyone, for the judgment is God's.
Any case that is too hard for you,
bring to me, and I will hear it." 18So
I charged you at that time with all
the things that you should do.

Israel's Refusal to Enter the Land

19 Then, just as the Lord our
God had ordered us, we set out
from Horeb and went through all
that great and terrible wilderness
that you saw, on the way to the hill
country of the Amorites, until we
reached Kadesh-barnea. 20I said to
you, "You have reached the hill
country of the Amorites, which the
Lord our God is giving us. 21See,
the Lord your God has given the
land to you; go up, take possession,
as the Lord, the God of your ancestors, has promised you; do not fear
or be dismayed."

22 All of you came to me and
said, "Let us send men ahead of us
to explore the land for us and bring
back a report to us regarding the
route by which we should go up
and the cities we will come to."
23The plan seemed good to me,
and I selected twelve of you, one
from each tribe. 24They set out and
went up into the hill country, and
when they reached the Valley of
Eshcol they spied it out 25and gathered some of the land's produce,
which they brought down to us.
They brought back a report to us,
and said, "It is a good land that the
Lord our God is giving us."

26 But you were unwilling to go
up. You rebelled against the command of the Lord your God; 27you
grumbled in your tents and said, "It
is because the Lord hates us that
he has brought us out of the land of
Egypt, to hand us over to the Amorites to destroy us. 28Where are we
headed? Our kindred have made
our hearts melt by reporting, 'The
people are stronger and taller than
we; the cities are large and fortified
up to heaven! We actually saw
there the offspring of the Anakim!'"
29I said to you, "Have no dread or
fear of them. 30The Lord your God,
who goes before you, is the one
who will fight for you, just as he did
for you in Egypt before your very
eyes, 31and in the wilderness,
where you saw how the Lord your
God carried you, just as one carries
a child, all the way that you traveled until you reached this place.
32But in spite of this, you have no
trust in the Lord your God, 33who
goes before you on the way to seek
out a place for you to camp, in fire
by night, and in the cloud by day,
to show you the route you should
take."

1.8 Gen 12.7; 15.18; 17.7,8; 26.4; 28.13
1.9 Ex 18.18
1.10 Gen 15.5; Deut 10.22
1.11 Gen 22.17; Ex 32.13
1.13 Ex 18.21
1.15 Ex 18.25
1.16 Deut 16.18; Lev 24.22
1.17 Lev 19.15; Jas 2.1; Ex 18.19-26
1.19 v. 2; Deut 8.15; Num 13.26
1.21 Josh 1.9
1.23 Num 13.1-3
1.24 Num 13.22-24
1.25 Num 13.27
1.26 Num 14.1-4
1.27 Deut 9.28; Ps 106.25
1.28 Num 13.28, 31-33; Deut 9.1,2
1.30 Ex 14.14; Deut 3.22
1.31 Deut 32.11, 12; Acts 13.18
1.32 Ps 106.24
1.33 Ex 13.21; Num 10.33

[b] Sam Gk: MT *the Lord*

The Penalty for Israel's Rebellion

34 When the LORD heard your
words, he was wrathful and swore:
35 "Not one of these—not one of
this evil generation—shall see the
good land that I swore to give to
your ancestors, 36 except Caleb son
of Jephunneh. He shall see it, and
to him and to his descendants I will
give the land on which he set foot,
because of his complete fidelity to
the LORD." 37 Even with me the LORD
was angry on your account, saying,
"You also shall not enter there.
38 Joshua son of Nun, your assistant, shall enter there; encourage
him, for he is the one who will secure Israel's possession of it. 39 And
as for your little ones, who you
thought would become booty, your
children, who today do not yet
know right from wrong, they shall
enter there; to them I will give it,
and they shall take possession of it.
40 But as for you, journey back into
the wilderness, in the direction of
the Red Sea."[c]
41 You answered me, "We have
sinned against the LORD! We are
ready to go up and fight, just as the
LORD our God commanded us." So
all of you strapped on your battle
gear, and thought it easy to go up
into the hill country. 42 The LORD
said to me, "Say to them, 'Do not
go up and do not fight, for I am not
in the midst of you; otherwise you
will be defeated by your enemies.' " 43 Although I told you, you
would not listen. You rebelled
against the command of the LORD
and presumptuously went up into
the hill country. 44 The Amorites
who lived in that hill country then
came out against you and chased
you as bees do. They beat you down
in Seir as far as Hormah. 45 When
you returned and wept before the
LORD, the LORD would neither heed
your voice nor pay you any attention.

The Desert Years

46 After you had stayed at Kadesh as many days as you did,

1.34 Num 14.22-30 **1.37** Num 20.12; Deut 3.26; Ps 106.32 **1.38** Num 14.30; Deut 3.28; 31.7 **1.39** Num 14.3, 31 **1.40** Num 14.25 **1.41** Num 14.40 **1.42** Num 14.42 **1.43** Num 14.44, 45 **1.44** Ps 118.12

2.1 Num 21.4 **2.4** Num 20.14 **2.5** Josh 24.4 **2.7** Deut 8.2-4 **2.8** Judg 11.18 **2.9** v. 18; Num 21.28; Gen 19.36, 37 **2.10ff** Gen 14.5; Num 13.22, 33 **2.12** v. 22

2 1 we journeyed back into the
wilderness, in the direction of
the Red Sea,[c] as the LORD had told
me and skirted Mount Seir for
many days. 2 Then the LORD said to
me: 3 "You have been skirting this
hill country long enough. Head
north, 4 and charge the people as
follows: You are about to pass
through the territory of your kindred, the descendants of Esau, who
live in Seir. They will be afraid of
you, so, be very careful 5 not to engage in battle with them, for I will
not give you even so much as a
foot's length of their land, since I
have given Mount Seir to Esau as a
possession. 6 You shall purchase
food from them for money, so that
you may eat; and you shall also buy
water from them for money, so that
you may drink. 7 Surely the LORD
your God has blessed you in all
your undertakings; he knows your
going through this great wilderness. These forty years the LORD
your God has been with you; you
have lacked nothing." 8 So we
passed by our kin, the descendants
of Esau who live in Seir, leaving behind the route of the Arabah, and
leaving behind Elath and Ezion-
geber.
When we had headed out along
the route of the wilderness of
Moab, 9 the LORD said to me: "Do
not harass Moab or engage them in
battle, for I will not give you any of
its land as a possession, since I
have given Ar as a possession to the
descendants of Lot." 10 (The
Emim—a large and numerous people, as tall as the Anakim—had formerly inhabited it. 11 Like the Anakim, they are usually reckoned as
Rephaim, though the Moabites call
them Emim. 12 Moreover, the Horim had formerly inhabited Seir,
but the descendants of Esau dispossessed them, destroying them
and settling in their place, as Israel
has done in the land that the LORD
gave them as a possession.)
13 "Now then, proceed to cross over
the Wadi Zered."

[c] Or *Sea of Reeds*

So we crossed over the Wadi Zered. 14 And the length of time we
had traveled from Kadesh-barnea
until we crossed the Wadi Zered
was thirty-eight years, until the entire generation of warriors had perished from the camp, as the LORD
had sworn concerning them. 15 Indeed, the LORD's own hand was
against them, to root them out
from the camp, until all had perished.

16 Just as soon as all the warriors had died off from among the
people, 17 the LORD spoke to me,
saying, 18 "Today you are going to
cross the boundary of Moab at Ar.
19 When you approach the frontier
of the Ammonites, do not harass
them or engage them in battle, for
I will not give the land of the Ammonites to you as a possession, because I have given it to the descendants of Lot." 20 (It also is usually
reckoned as a land of Rephaim.
Rephaim formerly inhabited it,
though the Ammonites call them
Zamzummim, 21 a strong and numerous people, as tall as the Anakim. But the LORD destroyed them
from before the Ammonites so that
they could dispossess them and
settle in their place. 22 He did the
same for the descendants of Esau,
who live in Seir, by destroying the
Horim before them so that they
could dispossess them and settle in
their place even to this day. 23 As
for the Avvim, who had lived in settlements in the vicinity of Gaza,
the Caphtorim, who came from
Caphtor, destroyed them and settled in their place.) 24 "Proceed on
your journey and cross the Wadi Arnon. See, I have handed over to you
King Sihon the Amorite of Heshbon, and his land. Begin to take
possession by engaging him in battle. 25 This day I will begin to put
the dread and fear of you upon the
peoples everywhere under heaven;
when they hear report of you, they
will tremble and be in anguish because of you."

Defeat of King Sihon

26 So I sent messengers from
the wilderness of Kedemoth to
King Sihon of Heshbon with the
following terms of peace: 27 "If you
let me pass through your land, I
will travel only along the road; I
will turn aside neither to the right
nor to the left. 28 You shall sell me
food for money, so that I may eat,
and supply me water for money, so
that I may drink. Only allow me to
pass through on foot— 29 just as
the descendants of Esau who live
in Seir have done for me and likewise the Moabites who live in Ar—
until I cross the Jordan into the
land that the LORD our God is giving
us." 30 But King Sihon of Heshbon
was not willing to let us pass
through, for the LORD your God had
hardened his spirit and made his
heart defiant in order to hand him
over to you, as he has now done.

31 The LORD said to me, "See, I
have begun to give Sihon and his
land over to you. Begin now to take
possession of his land." 32 So when
Sihon came out against us, he and
all his people for battle at Jahaz,
33 the LORD our God gave him over
to us; and we struck him down,
along with his offspring and all his
people. 34 At that time we captured
all his towns, and in each town we
utterly destroyed men, women, and
children. We left not a single survivor. 35 Only the livestock we kept as
spoil for ourselves, as well as the
plunder of the towns that we had
captured. 36 From Aroer on the
edge of the Wadi Arnon (including
the town that is in the wadi itself)
as far as Gilead, there was no citadel too high for us. The LORD our
God gave everything to us. 37 You
did not encroach, however, on the
land of the Ammonites, avoiding
the whole upper region of the Wadi
Jabbok as well as the towns of the
hill country, just as[d] the LORD our
God had charged.

Defeat of King Og

3 When we headed up the road
to Bashan, King Og of Bashan
came out against us, he and all his
people, for battle at Edrei. 2 The

2.14 Num 13.26; 14.29-35; 26.64; Deut 1.34, 35
2.15 Ps 106.26
2.19 v. 9
2.21 v. 10
2.22 Gen 36.8; v. 12
2.23 Josh 13.3; Gen 10.14; Am 9.7
2.24 Judg 11.18
2.25 Ex 15.14, 15; Deut 11.25; Josh 2.9,10
2.26 Deut 20.10
2.27 Num 21.21, 22
2.28 Num 20.19
2.30 Num 21.23
2.31 Deut 1.8
2.32 Num 21.23, 24; Deut 7.2; 20.16
2.34 Deut 3.6
2.36 Deut 3.12; 4.48; Ps 44.3
2.37 Num 21.24
3.1 Num 21.33-35
3.2 Num 21.34

[d] Gk Tg: Heb *and all*

LORD said to me, "Do not fear him,
for I have handed him over to you,
along with his people and his land.
Do to him as you did to King Sihon
of the Amorites, who reigned in
Heshbon." 3 So the LORD our God
also handed over to us King Og of
Bashan and all his people. We
struck him down until not a single
survivor was left. 4 At that time we
captured all his towns; there was
no citadel that we did not take
from them—sixty towns, the whole
region of Argob, the kingdom of Og
in Bashan. 5 All these were fortress
towns with high walls, double
gates, and bars, besides a great
many villages. 6 And we utterly destroyed them, as we had done to
King Sihon of Heshbon, in each
city utterly destroying men, wom-
en, and children. 7 But all the livestock and the plunder of the towns
we kept as spoil for ourselves.
8 So at that time we took from
the two kings of the Amorites the
land beyond the Jordan, from the
Wadi Arnon to Mount Hermon
9 (the Sidonians call Hermon Sirion, while the Amorites call it Senir), 10 all the towns of the tableland, the whole of Gilead, and all of
Bashan, as far as Salecah and Edrei, towns of Og's kingdom in Bashan. 11 (Now only King Og of Bashan was left of the remnant of the
Rephaim. In fact his bed, an iron
bed, can still be seen in Rabbah of
the Ammonites. By the common
cubit it is nine cubits long and four
cubits wide.) 12 As for the land that
we took possession of at that time,
I gave to the Reubenites and Gadites the territory north of Aroer,[e]
that is on the edge of the Wadi Arnon, as well as half the hill country
of Gilead with its towns, 13 and I
gave to the half-tribe of Manasseh
the rest of Gilead and all of Bashan,
Og's kingdom. (The whole region
of Argob: all that portion of Bashan
used to be called a land of Rephaim; 14 Jair the Manassite acquired
the whole region of Argob as far as
the border of the Geshurites and
the Maacathites, and he named
them—that is, Bashan—after himself, Havvoth-jair,[f] as it is to this
day.) 15 To Machir I gave Gilead.
16 And to the Reubenites and the
Gadites I gave the territory from
Gilead as far as the Wadi Arnon,
with the middle of the wadi as a
boundary, and up to the Jabbok,
the wadi being boundary of the
Ammonites; 17 the Arabah also,
with the Jordan and its banks, from
Chinnereth down to the sea of the
Arabah, the Dead Sea,[g] with the
lower slopes of Pisgah on the east.
18 At that time, I charged you as
follows: "Although the LORD your
God has given you this land to occupy, all your troops shall cross
over armed as the vanguard of your
Israelite kin. 19 Only your wives,
your children, and your livestock—
I know that you have much
livestock—shall stay behind in the
towns that I have given to you.
20 When the LORD gives rest to your
kindred, as to you, and they too
have occupied the land that the
LORD your God is giving them beyond the Jordan, then each of you
may return to the property that I
have given to you." 21 And I charged
Joshua as well at that time, saying:
"Your own eyes have seen everything that the LORD your God has
done to these two kings; so the
LORD will do to all the kingdoms
into which you are about to cross.
22 Do not fear them, for it is the
LORD your God who fights for you."

Moses Views Canaan from Pisgah

23 At that time, too, I entreated
the LORD, saying: 24 "O Lord GOD,
you have only begun to show your
servant your greatness and your
might; what god in heaven or on
earth can perform deeds and
mighty acts like yours! 25 Let me
cross over to see the good land beyond the Jordan, that good hill
country and the Lebanon." 26 But
the LORD was angry with me on your
account and would not heed me.
The LORD said to me, "Enough from
you! Never speak to me of this mat-

3.3 Num 21.35 **3.4** 1 Kings 4.13 **3.6** Deut 2.24, 34 **3.9** Ps 29.6 **3.11** Am 2.9; Gen 14.5; 2 Sam 12.26; Jer 49.2 **3.12** Deut 2.36; Num 32.32-38; Josh 13.8-13 **3.14** Num 32.41; 1 Chr 2.22

3.15 Num 32.39, 40 **3.17** Num 34.11; Josh 13.27 **3.18** Num 32.20 **3.20** Josh 22.4 **3.22** Deut 1.30 **3.24** Ex 15.11; Ps 86.8 **3.26** Deut 1.37; 31.2

e Heb *territory from Aroer* f That is *Settlement of Jair* g Heb *Salt Sea*

ter again! 27 Go up to the top of Pisgah and look around you to the west, to the north, to the south, and to the east. Look well, for you shall not cross over this Jordan. 28 But charge Joshua, and encourage and strengthen him, because it is he who shall cross over at the head of this people and who shall secure their possession of the land that you will see." 29 So we remained in the valley opposite Beth-peor.

Moses Commands Obedience

4 So now, Israel, give heed to the statutes and ordinances that I am teaching you to observe, so that you may live to enter and occupy the land that the LORD, the God of your ancestors, is giving you. 2 You must neither add anything to what I command you nor take away anything from it, but keep the commandments of the LORD your God with which I am charging you. 3 You have seen for yourselves what the LORD did with regard to the Baal of Peor—how the LORD your God destroyed from among you everyone who followed the Baal of Peor, 4 while those of you who held fast to the LORD your God are all alive today.

5 See, just as the LORD my God has charged me, I now teach you statutes and ordinances for you to observe in the land that you are about to enter and occupy. 6 You must observe them diligently, for this will show your wisdom and discernment to the peoples, who, when they hear all these statutes, will say, "Surely this great nation is a wise and discerning people!" 7 For what other great nation has a god so near to it as the LORD our God is whenever we call to him? 8 And what other great nation has statutes and ordinances as just as this entire law that I am setting before you today?

9 But take care and watch yourselves closely, so as neither to forget the things that your eyes have seen nor to let them slip from your mind all the days of your life; make them known to your children and your children's children— 10 how you once stood before the LORD your God at Horeb, when the LORD said to me, "Assemble the people for me, and I will let them hear my words, so that they may learn to fear me as long as they live on the earth, and may teach their children so"; 11 you approached and stood at the foot of the mountain while the mountain was blazing up to the very heavens, shrouded in dark clouds. 12 Then the LORD spoke to you out of the fire. You heard the sound of words but saw no form; there was only a voice. 13 He declared to you his covenant, which he charged you to observe, that is, the ten commandments;[h] and he wrote them on two stone tablets. 14 And the LORD charged me at that time to teach you statutes and ordinances for you to observe in the land that you are about to cross into and occupy.

15 Since you saw no form when the LORD spoke to you at Horeb out of the fire, take care and watch yourselves closely, 16 so that you do not act corruptly by making an idol for yourselves, in the form of any figure—the likeness of male or female, 17 the likeness of any animal that is on the earth, the likeness of any winged bird that flies in the air, 18 the likeness of anything that creeps on the ground, the likeness of any fish that is in the water under the earth. 19 And when you look up to the heavens and see the sun, the moon, and the stars, all the host of heaven, do not be led astray and bow down to them and serve them, things that the LORD your God has allotted to all the peoples everywhere under heaven. 20 But the LORD has taken you and brought you out of the iron-smelter, out of Egypt, to become a people of his very own possession, as you are now.

21 The LORD was angry with me because of you, and he vowed that I should not cross the Jordan and

3.27 Num 27.12
3.28 Num 27.18, 23; Deut 31.3,7
3.29 Deut 4.46; 34.6
4.1 Deut 5.33; 8.1; 16.20; 30.16,19
4.2 Deut 12.32; Josh 1.7; Rev 22.18, 19
4.3 Num 25.4; Ps 106.28, 29
4.6 Deut 30.19, 20; 32.46,47
4.7 2 Sam 7.23; Ps 46.1; Isa 55.6
4.9 Prov 4.23; Gen 18.19; Deut 6.7; 11.19; Ps 78.5,6; Eph 6.4
4.10 Ex 19.9,16
4.11 Ex 19.18; Heb 12.18, 19
4.12 Deut 5.4,22; Ex 20.22
4.13 Deut 9.9,11; Ex 34.28; 24.12; 31.18
4.16 Ex 32.7; 20.4,5; Deut 5.8
4.19 Deut 17.3; 2 Kings 17.16; Rom 1.25
4.20 1 Kings 8.51; Jer 11.4; Deut 9.29
4.21 Deut 1.37

[h] Heb *the ten words*

that I should not enter the good
land that the LORD your God is giving for your possession. 22 For I am
going to die in this land without
crossing over the Jordan, but you
are going to cross over to take possession of that good land. 23 So be
careful not to forget the covenant
that the LORD your God made with
you, and not to make for yourselves
an idol in the form of anything that
the LORD your God has forbidden
you. 24 For the LORD your God is a
devouring fire, a jealous God.
25 When you have had children
and children's children, and become complacent in the land, if
you act corruptly by making an idol
in the form of anything, thus doing
what is evil in the sight of the LORD
your God, and provoking him to anger, 26 I call heaven and earth to
witness against you today that you
will soon utterly perish from the
land that you are crossing the Jordan to occupy; you will not live
long on it, but will be utterly destroyed. 27 The LORD will scatter you
among the peoples; only a few of
you will be left among the nations
where the LORD will lead you.
28 There you will serve other gods
made by human hands, objects of
wood and stone that neither see,
nor hear, nor eat, nor smell.
29 From there you will seek the
LORD your God, and you will find
him if you search after him with all
your heart and soul. 30 In your distress, when all these things have
happened to you in time to come,
you will return to the LORD your
God and heed him. 31 Because the
LORD your God is a merciful God, he
will neither abandon you nor destroy you; he will not forget the
covenant with your ancestors that
he swore to them.
32 For ask now about former
ages, long before your own, ever
since the day that God created human beings on the earth; ask from
one end of heaven to the other: has
anything so great as this ever happened or has its like ever been
heard of? 33 Has any people ever
heard the voice of a god speaking
out of a fire, as you have heard, and
lived? 34 Or has any god ever attempted to go and take a nation for
himself from the midst of another
nation, by trials, by signs and wonders, by war, by a mighty hand and
an outstretched arm, and by terrifying displays of power, as the LORD
your God did for you in Egypt before your very eyes? 35 To you it was
shown so that you would acknowledge that the LORD is God; there is
no other besides him. 36 From
heaven he made you hear his voice
to discipline you. On earth he
showed you his great fire, while you
heard his words coming out of the
fire. 37 And because he loved your
ancestors, he chose their descendants after them. He brought you
out of Egypt with his own presence,
by his great power, 38 driving out
before you nations greater and
mightier than yourselves, to bring
you in, giving you their land for a
possession, as it is still today. 39 So
acknowledge today and take to
heart that the LORD is God in heav-
en above and on the earth beneath;
there is no other. 40 Keep his statutes and his commandments,
which I am commanding you today
for your own well-being and that of
your descendants after you, so that
you may long remain in the land
that the LORD your God is giving you
for all time.

Cities of Refuge East of the Jordan

41 Then Moses set apart on the
east side of the Jordan three cities
42 to which a homicide could flee,
someone who unintentionally kills
another person, the two not having
been at enmity before; the homicide could flee to one of these cities and live: 43 Bezer in the wilderness on the tableland belonging to
the Reubenites, Ramoth in Gilead
belonging to the Gadites, and Golan in Bashan belonging to the Manassites.

Transition to the Second Address

44 This is the law that Moses set

4.22 Deut 3.25,27
4.23 vv. 9,16; Ex 20.4,5
4.24 Ex 24.17; Deut 9.3; Heb 12.29; Deut 6.15
4.25 vv. 16,23; 2 Kings 17.17
4.26 Deut 30.18,19
4.27 Deut 28.62,64
4.28 Deut 28.64; 1 Sam 26.19; Ps 115.4,5
4.29 Deut 30.1-3; 2 Chr 15.4; Isa 55.6,7; Jer 29.12-14
4.31 2 Chr 30.9; Ps 116.5
4.32 Deut 32.7; Gen 1.27; Deut 28.64
4.33 Ex 20.22; Deut 5.24,26
4.34 Deut 7.19; Ex 7.3; 13.3; 6.6; Deut 26.8; 34.12
4.35 Deut 32.39; 1 Sam 2.2; Isa 45.5,18; Mk 12.29
4.36 Ex 19.9,19; Heb 12.18
4.37 Deut 10.15; Ex 13.3,9,14
4.38 Deut 7.1; 9.1,4,5
4.39 v. 35; Josh 2.11
4.40 Lev 22.31; Deut 5.16,29,33; Eph 6.2,3
4.41 Num 35.6

before the Israelites. 45 These are
the decrees and the statutes and
ordinances that Moses spoke to the
Israelites when they had come out
of Egypt, 46 beyond the Jordan in
the valley opposite Beth-peor, in
the land of King Sihon of the Amorites, who reigned at Heshbon,
whom Moses and the Israelites defeated when they came out of
Egypt. 47 They occupied his land
and the land of King Og of Bashan,
the two kings of the Amorites on
the eastern side of the Jordan:
48 from Aroer, which is on the edge
of the Wadi Arnon, as far as Mount
Sirion[i] (that is, Hermon), 49 together with all the Arabah on the
east side of the Jordan as far as the
Sea of the Arabah, under the slopes
of Pisgah.

The Ten Commandments

5 Moses convened all Israel, and
said to them:
Hear, O Israel, the statutes and
ordinances that I am addressing to
you today; you shall learn them
and observe them diligently. 2 The
LORD our God made a covenant
with us at Horeb. 3 Not with our ancestors did the LORD make this covenant, but with us, who are all of us
here alive today. 4 The LORD spoke
with you face to face at the mountain, out of the fire. 5 (At that time
I was standing between the LORD
and you to declare to you the
words[j] of the LORD; for you were
afraid because of the fire and did
not go up the mountain.) And he
said:
6 I am the LORD your God, who
brought you out of the land of
Egypt, out of the house of slavery;
7 you shall have no other gods before[k] me.
8 You shall not make for yourself an idol, whether in the form of
anything that is in heaven above, or
that is on the earth beneath, or that
is in the water under the earth.
9 You shall not bow down to them
or worship them; for I the LORD your
God am a jealous God, punishing
children for the iniquity of parents,
to the third and fourth generation
of those who reject me, 10 but
showing steadfast love to the thousandth generation[l] of those who
love me and keep my commandments.
11 You shall not make wrongful
use of the name of the LORD your
God, for the LORD will not acquit
anyone who misuses his name.
12 Observe the sabbath day and
keep it holy, as the LORD your God
commanded you. 13 Six days you
shall labor and do all your work.
14 But the seventh day is a sabbath
to the LORD your God; you shall not
do any work—you, or your son or
your daughter, or your male or female slave, or your ox or your donkey, or any of your livestock, or the
resident alien in your towns, so
that your male and female slave
may rest as well as you. 15 Remember that you were a slave in the
land of Egypt, and the LORD your
God brought you out from there
with a mighty hand and an outstretched arm; therefore the LORD
your God commanded you to keep
the sabbath day.
16 Honor your father and your
mother, as the LORD your God commanded you, so that your days may
be long and that it may go well with
you in the land that the LORD your
God is giving you.
17 You shall not murder.[m]
18 Neither shall you commit
adultery.
19 Neither shall you steal.
20 Neither shall you bear false
witness against your neighbor.
21 Neither shall you covet your
neighbor's wife.
Neither shall you desire your
neighbor's house, or field, or male
or female slave, or ox, or donkey, or
anything that belongs to your
neighbor.

Moses the Mediator of God's Will

22 These words the LORD spoke

4.46 Deut 3.29; Num 21.21-25
4.48 Deut 2.36; 3.12
5.2 Ex 19.5
5.4 Ex 19.9,19; Deut 4.33, 36
5.5 Ex 20.18,21
5.6 Ex 20.2-17
5.9 Ex 34.7
5.10 Jer 32.18
5.14 Gen 2.2; Ex 16.29,30
5.15 Deut 15.16; 4.34,37
5.21 Rom 7.7; 13.9
5.22 Ex 31.18; Deut 4.13

[i] Syr: Heb *Sion* [j] Q Mss Sam Gk Syr Vg Tg: MT *word* [k] Or *besides* [l] Or *to thousands* [m] Or *kill*

with a loud voice to your whole assembly at the mountain, out of the fire, the cloud, and the thick darkness, and he added no more. He wrote them on two stone tablets, and gave them to me. 23 When you heard the voice out of the darkness, while the mountain was burning with fire, you approached me, all the heads of your tribes and your elders; 24 and you said, "Look, the LORD our God has shown us his glory and greatness, and we have heard his voice out of the fire. Today we have seen that God may speak to someone and the person may still live. 25 So now why should we die? For this great fire will consume us; if we hear the voice of the LORD our God any longer, we shall die. 26 For who is there of all flesh that has heard the voice of the living God speaking out of fire, as we have, and remained alive? 27 Go near, you yourself, and hear all that the LORD our God will say. Then tell us everything that the LORD our God tells you, and we will listen and do it."

28 The LORD heard your words when you spoke to me, and the LORD said to me: "I have heard the words of this people, which they have spoken to you; they are right in all that they have spoken. 29 If only they had such a mind as this, to fear me and to keep all my commandments always, so that it might go well with them and with their children forever! 30 Go say to them, 'Return to your tents.' 31 But you, stand here by me, and I will tell you all the commandments, the statutes and the ordinances, that you shall teach them, so that they may do them in the land that I am giving them to possess." 32 You must therefore be careful to do as the LORD your God has commanded you; you shall not turn to the right or to the left. 33 You must follow exactly the path that the LORD your God has commanded you, so that you may live, and that it may go well with you, and that you may live long in the land that you are to possess.

5.24 Ex 19.19 **5.25** Deut 18.16 **5.26** Deut 4.33 **5.28** Deut 18.17 **5.29** Ps 81.13; Isa 48.18; Deut 4.40 **5.31** Ex 24.12 **5.32** Deut 17.20; 28.14; Josh 1.7; 23.6 **5.33** Deut 4.40

6.2 Ex 20.20; Deut 10.12, 13 **6.3** Deut 5.33; Gen 15.5; Ex 3.8 **6.4ff** Mk 12.29, 32; Jn 17.3; 1 Cor 8.4, 6 **6.5** Deut 10.12; Mt 22.37; Lk 10.27 **6.7** Deut 4.9; Eph 6.4 **6.8** Ex 13.9,16; Deut 11.18 **6.9** Deut 11.20 **6.10** Deut 9.1; Josh 24.13 **6.11** Deut 8.10 **6.13** Deut 10.20

The Great Commandment

6 Now this is the commandment—the statutes and the ordinances—that the LORD your God charged me to teach you to observe in the land that you are about to cross into and occupy, 2 so that you and your children and your children's children may fear the LORD your God all the days of your life, and keep all his decrees and his commandments that I am commanding you, so that your days may be long. 3 Hear therefore, O Israel, and observe them diligently, so that it may go well with you, and so that you may multiply greatly in a land flowing with milk and honey, as the LORD, the God of your ancestors, has promised you.

4 Hear, O Israel: The LORD is our God, the LORD alone.[n] 5 You shall love the LORD your God with all your heart, and with all your soul, and with all your might. 6 Keep these words that I am commanding you today in your heart. 7 Recite them to your children and talk about them when you are at home and when you are away, when you lie down and when you rise. 8 Bind them as a sign on your hand, fix them as an emblem[o] on your forehead, 9 and write them on the doorposts of your house and on your gates.

Caution against Disobedience

10 When the LORD your God has brought you into the land that he swore to your ancestors, to Abraham, to Isaac, and to Jacob, to give you—a land with fine, large cities that you did not build, 11 houses filled with all sorts of goods that you did not fill, hewn cisterns that you did not hew, vineyards and olive groves that you did not plant—and when you have eaten your fill, 12 take care that you do not forget the LORD, who brought you out of the land of Egypt, out of the house of slavery. 13 The LORD your God you shall fear; him you shall serve, and

n Or *The LORD our God is one LORD,* or *The LORD our God, the LORD is one,* or *The LORD is our God, the LORD is one* o Or *as a frontlet*

by his name alone you shall swear.
14 Do not follow other gods, any of
the gods of the peoples who are all
around you, 15 because the LORD
your God, who is present with you,
is a jealous God. The anger of the
LORD your God would be kindled
against you and he would destroy
you from the face of the earth.
16 Do not put the LORD your God
to the test, as you tested him at
Massah. 17 You must diligently
keep the commandments of the
LORD your God, and his decrees,
and his statutes that he has commanded you. 18 Do what is right and
good in the sight of the LORD, so
that it may go well with you, and so
that you may go in and occupy the
good land that the LORD swore to
your ancestors to give you,
19 thrusting out all your enemies
from before you, as the LORD has
promised.
20 When your children ask you
in time to come, "What is the
meaning of the decrees and the
statutes and the ordinances that
the LORD our God has commanded
you?" 21 then you shall say to your
children, "We were Pharaoh's
slaves in Egypt, but the LORD
brought us out of Egypt with a
mighty hand. 22 The LORD displayed
before our eyes great and awesome
signs and wonders against Egypt,
against Pharaoh and all his household. 23 He brought us out from
there in order to bring us in, to give
us the land that he promised on
oath to our ancestors. 24 Then the
LORD commanded us to observe all
these statutes, to fear the LORD our
God, for our lasting good, so as to
keep us alive, as is now the case.
25 If we diligently observe this entire commandment before the LORD
our God, as he has commanded us,
we will be in the right."

A Chosen People

7 When the LORD your God
brings you into the land that
you are about to enter and occupy,
and he clears away many nations
before you—the Hittites, the Girgashites, the Amorites, the Canaanites, the Perizzites, the Hivites, and the Jebusites, seven
nations mightier and more numerous than you— 2 and when the
LORD your God gives them over to
you and you defeat them, then you
must utterly destroy them. Make
no covenant with them and show
them no mercy. 3 Do not intermarry
with them, giving your daughters to
their sons or taking their daughters
for your sons, 4 for that would turn
away your children from following
me, to serve other gods. Then the
anger of the LORD would be kindled
against you, and he would destroy
you quickly. 5 But this is how you
must deal with them: break down
their altars, smash their pillars,
hew down their sacred poles,[p] and
burn their idols with fire. 6 For you
are a people holy to the LORD your
God; the LORD your God has chosen
you out of all the peoples on earth
to be his people, his treasured possession.
7 It was not because you were
more numerous than any other
people that the LORD set his heart
on you and chose you—for you
were the fewest of all peoples. 8 It
was because the LORD loved you
and kept the oath that he swore to
your ancestors, that the LORD has
brought you out with a mighty
hand, and redeemed you from the
house of slavery, from the hand of
Pharaoh king of Egypt. 9 Know
therefore that the LORD your God is
God, the faithful God who maintains covenant loyalty with those
who love him and keep his commandments, to a thousand generations, 10 and who repays in their
own person those who reject him.
He does not delay but repays in
their own person those who reject
him. 11 Therefore, observe diligently the commandment—the statutes, and the ordinances—that I
am commanding you today.

Blessings for Obedience

12 If you heed these ordinances,
by diligently observing them, the
LORD your God will maintain with

6.15 Deut 4.24
6.16 Mt 4.7; Ex 17.2,7
6.17 Deut 11.22
6.18 Deut 4.40
6.20 Ex 13.14
6.24 Deut 10.12
6.25 Deut 24.13
7.1 Deut 31.3; Acts 13.19
7.2 Ex 23.32; Deut 13.8
7.3 Ex 34.15,16
7.4 Deut 6.15
7.5 Ex 23.24
7.6 Ex 19.5,6; Deut 14.2
7.7 Deut 10.22
7.8 Deut 10.15; Ex 32.13; 13.3,14
7.9 Deut 4.35, 39; Neh 1.5
7.12 Lev 26.3; Deut 28.1; Ps 105.8,9

[p] Heb *Asherim*

you the covenant loyalty that he
swore to your ancestors; 13 he will
love you, bless you, and multiply
you; he will bless the fruit of your
womb and the fruit of your ground,
your grain and your wine and your
oil, the increase of your cattle and
the issue of your flock, in the land
that he swore to your ancestors to
give you. 14 You shall be the most
blessed of peoples, with neither
sterility nor barrenness among you
or your livestock. 15 The LORD will
turn away from you every illness;
all the dread diseases of Egypt that
you experienced, he will not inflict
on you, but he will lay them on all
who hate you. 16 You shall devour
all the peoples that the LORD your
God is giving over to you, showing
them no pity; you shall not serve
their gods, for that would be a
snare to you.

17 If you say to yourself, "These
nations are more numerous than I;
how can I dispossess them?" 18 do
not be afraid of them. Just remember what the LORD your God did to
Pharaoh and to all Egypt, 19 the
great trials that your eyes saw, the
signs and wonders, the mighty
hand and the outstretched arm by
which the LORD your God brought
you out. The LORD your God will do
the same to all the peoples of
whom you are afraid. 20 Moreover,
the LORD your God will send the
pestilence[q] against them, until
even the survivors and the fugitives
are destroyed. 21 Have no dread of
them, for the LORD your God, who is
present with you, is a great and
awesome God. 22 The LORD your
God will clear away these nations
before you little by little; you will
not be able to make a quick end of
them, otherwise the wild animals
would become too numerous for
you. 23 But the LORD your God will
give them over to you, and throw
them into great panic, until they
are destroyed. 24 He will hand their
kings over to you and you shall blot
out their name from under heaven;
no one will be able to stand against
you, until you have destroyed
them. 25 The images of their gods
you shall burn with fire. Do not
covet the silver or the gold that is
on them and take it for yourself,
because you could be ensnared by
it; for it is abhorrent to the LORD
your God. 26 Do not bring an abhorrent thing into your house, or you
will be set apart for destruction like
it. You must utterly detest and abhor it, for it is set apart for destruction.

7.13 Deut 28.4
7.14 Ex 23.26
7.15 Ex 15.26
7.16 v. 2; Ex 23.33
7.18 Deut 31.6
7.19 Deut 4.34
7.20 Ex 23.28; Josh 24.12
7.21 Deut 10.17
7.22 Ex 23.29,30
7.24 v. 16
7.25 1 Chr 14.12; Josh 7.1,21; Judg 8.27

A Warning Not to Forget God in Prosperity

8 This entire commandment
that I command you today you
must diligently observe, so that you
may live and increase, and go in
and occupy the land that the LORD
promised on oath to your ancestors. 2 Remember the long way that
the LORD your God has led you
these forty years in the wilderness,
in order to humble you, testing you
to know what was in your heart,
whether or not you would keep his
commandments. 3 He humbled you
by letting you hunger, then by feeding you with manna, with which
neither you nor your ancestors
were acquainted, in order to make
you understand that one does not
live by bread alone, but by every
word that comes from the mouth of
the LORD.[r] 4 The clothes on your
back did not wear out and your feet
did not swell these forty years.
5 Know then in your heart that as a
parent disciplines a child so the
LORD your God disciplines you.
6 Therefore keep the commandments of the LORD your God, by
walking in his ways and by fearing
him. 7 For the LORD your God is
bringing you into a good land, a
land with flowing streams, with
springs and underground waters
welling up in valleys and hills, 8 a
land of wheat and barley, of vines
and fig trees and pomegranates, a
land of olive trees and honey, 9 a
land where you may eat bread without scarcity, where you will lack
nothing, a land whose stones are
iron and from whose hills you may

8.1 Deut 4.1
8.2 Deut 29.5; 13.3
8.3 Ex 16.2,3, 12,14,35; Mt 4.4; Lk 4.7
8.4 Deut 29.5
8.5 Prov 3.12; Heb 12.5,6
8.6 Deut 5.33
8.7 Deut 11.10-12

[q] Or *hornets*: Meaning of Heb uncertain
[r] Or *by anything that the LORD decrees*

mine copper. 10 You shall eat your fill and bless the LORD your God for the good land that he has given you.

11 Take care that you do not forget the LORD your God, by failing to keep his commandments, his ordinances, and his statutes, which I am commanding you today. 12 When you have eaten your fill and have built fine houses and live in them, 13 and when your herds and flocks have multiplied, and your silver and gold is multiplied, and all that you have is multiplied, 14 then do not exalt yourself, forgetting the LORD your God, who brought you out of the land of Egypt, out of the house of slavery, 15 who led you through the great and terrible wilderness, an arid wasteland with poisonous[s] snakes and scorpions. He made water flow for you from flint rock, 16 and fed you in the wilderness with manna that your ancestors did not know, to humble you and to test you, and in the end to do you good. 17 Do not say to yourself, "My power and the might of my own hand have gotten me this wealth." 18 But remember the LORD your God, for it is he who gives you power to get wealth, so that he may confirm his covenant that he swore to your ancestors, as he is doing today. 19 If you do forget the LORD your God and follow other gods to serve and worship them, I solemnly warn you today that you shall surely perish. 20 Like the nations that the LORD is destroying before you, so shall you perish, because you would not obey the voice of the LORD your God.

The Consequences of Rebelling against God

9 Hear, O Israel! You are about to cross the Jordan today, to go in and dispossess nations larger and mightier than you, great cities, fortified to the heavens, 2 a strong and tall people, the offspring of the Anakim, whom you know. You have heard it said of them, "Who can stand up to the Anakim?" 3 Know then today that the LORD your God is the one who crosses over before you as a devouring fire; he will defeat them and subdue them before you, so that you may dispossess and destroy them quickly, as the LORD has promised you.

4 When the LORD your God thrusts them out before you, do not say to yourself, "It is because of my righteousness that the LORD has brought me in to occupy this land"; it is rather because of the wickedness of these nations that the LORD is dispossessing them before you. 5 It is not because of your righteousness or the uprightness of your heart that you are going in to occupy their land; but because of the wickedness of these nations the LORD your God is dispossessing them before you, in order to fulfill the promise that the LORD made on oath to your ancestors, to Abraham, to Isaac, and to Jacob.

6 Know, then, that the LORD your God is not giving you this good land to occupy because of your righteousness; for you are a stubborn people. 7 Remember and do not forget how you provoked the LORD your God to wrath in the wilderness; you have been rebellious against the LORD from the day you came out of the land of Egypt until you came to this place.

8 Even at Horeb you provoked the LORD to wrath, and the LORD was so angry with you that he was ready to destroy you. 9 When I went up the mountain to receive the stone tablets, the tablets of the covenant that the LORD made with you, I remained on the mountain forty days and forty nights; I neither ate bread nor drank water. 10 And the LORD gave me the two stone tablets written with the finger of God; on them were all the words that the LORD had spoken to you at the mountain out of the fire on the day of the assembly. 11 At the end of forty days and forty nights the LORD gave me the two stone tablets, the tablets of the covenant. 12 Then the LORD said

8.10 Deut 6.11, 12
8.14 Ps 106.21
8.15 Num 21.6; 20.11; Ps 78.15; 114.8
8.16 vv. 2,3; Ex 16.15
8.18 Prov 10.22; Hos 2.8
8.19 Deut 4.26; 30.18
9.1 Deut 11.31
9.2 Num 13.22, 28,32,33
9.3 Deut 31.3; 4.24; 7.23,24
9.4 Deut 8.17; 18.12; Lev 18.24, 25
9.5 Gen 12.7
9.6 v. 13; Ex 32.9; Deut 31.27
9.8 Ex 32.7-10
9.9 Ex 24.12, 15,18
9.10 Ex 31.18; Deut 4.13
9.12 Ex 32.7,8; Deut 31.29

s Or *fiery*; Heb *seraph*

to me, "Get up, go down quickly
from here, for your people whom
you have brought from Egypt have
acted corruptly. They have been
quick to turn from the way that I
commanded them; they have cast
an image for themselves." 13 Furthermore the LORD said to me, "I
have seen that this people is indeed a stubborn people. 14 Let me
alone that I may destroy them and
blot out their name from under
heaven; and I will make of you a
nation mightier and more numerous than they."
15 So I turned and went down
from the mountain, while the
mountain was ablaze; the two tablets of the covenant were in my two
hands. 16 Then I saw that you had
indeed sinned against the LORD
your God, by casting for yourselves
an image of a calf; you had been
quick to turn from the way that the
LORD had commanded you. 17 So I
took hold of the two tablets and
flung them from my two hands,
smashing them before your eyes.
18 Then I lay prostrate before the
LORD as before, forty days and forty
nights; I neither ate bread nor
drank water, because of all the sin
you had committed, provoking the
LORD by doing what was evil in his
sight. 19 For I was afraid that the anger that the LORD bore against you
was so fierce that he would destroy
you. But the LORD listened to me
that time also. 20 The LORD was so
angry with Aaron that he was ready
to destroy him, but I interceded
also on behalf of Aaron at that
same time. 21 Then I took the sinful
thing you had made, the calf, and
burned it with fire and crushed it,
grinding it thoroughly, until it was
reduced to dust; and I threw the
dust of it into the stream that runs
down the mountain.
22 At Taberah also, and at Massah, and at Kibroth-hattaavah, you
provoked the LORD to wrath. 23 And
when the LORD sent you from
Kadesh-barnea, saying, "Go up and
occupy the land that I have given
you," you rebelled against the command of the LORD your God, neither

9.13 Ex 32.9; v. 6
9.14 Ex 32.10; Deut 29.20; Num 14.12
9.15 Ex 32.15-19; 19.18
9.16 Ex 32.19
9.18 Ex 34.28
9.19 Ex 32.10-14
9.21 Ex 32.20
9.22 Num 11.3, 34; Ex 17.7
9.24 v. 7; Deut 31.27
9.25 v. 18
9.26 Ex 32.11-13
9.29 Deut 4.20, 34
10.1 Ex 34.1,2; 25.10
10.2 Deut 4.13; Ex 25.16,21
10.3 Ex 37.1; 34.4
10.4 Ex 20.1
10.5 Ex 40.20
10.6 Num 33.30, 31,38

trusting him nor obeying him.
24 You have been rebellious against
the LORD as long as he has[t] known
you.
25 Throughout the forty days
and forty nights that I lay prostrate
before the LORD when the LORD intended to destroy you, 26 I prayed to
the LORD and said, "Lord GOD, do
not destroy the people who are
your very own possession, whom
you redeemed in your greatness,
whom you brought out of Egypt
with a mighty hand. 27 Remember
your servants, Abraham, Isaac, and
Jacob; pay no attention to the stubbornness of this people, their wickedness and their sin, 28 otherwise
the land from which you have
brought us might say, 'Because the
LORD was not able to bring them
into the land that he promised
them, and because he hated them,
he has brought them out to let
them die in the wilderness.' 29 For
they are the people of your very
own possession, whom you
brought out by your great power
and by your outstretched arm."

The Second Pair of Tablets

10 At that time the LORD said
to me, "Carve out two tablets of stone like the former ones,
and come up to me on the mountain, and make an ark of wood. 2 I
will write on the tablets the words
that were on the former tablets,
which you smashed, and you shall
put them in the ark." 3 So I made an
ark of acacia wood, cut two tablets
of stone like the former ones, and
went up the mountain with the two
tablets in my hand. 4 Then he wrote
on the tablets the same words as
before, the ten commandments[u]
that the LORD had spoken to you on
the mountain out of the fire on the
day of the assembly; and the LORD
gave them to me. 5 So I turned and
came down from the mountain,
and put the tablets in the ark that
I had made; and there they are, as
the LORD commanded me.
6 (The Israelites journeyed from

[t] Sam Gk: MT *I have* [u] Heb *the ten words*

Beeroth-bene-jaakan[v] to Mose-
rah. There Aaron died, and there he
was buried; his son Eleazar succeeded him as priest. 7 From there
they journeyed to Gudgodah, and
from Gudgodah to Jotbathah, a
land with flowing streams. 8 At that
time the LORD set apart the tribe of
Levi to carry the ark of the covenant of the LORD, to stand before
the LORD to minister to him, and to
bless in his name, to this day.
9 Therefore Levi has no allotment
or inheritance with his kindred; the
LORD is his inheritance, as the LORD
your God promised him.)
10 I stayed on the mountain forty days and forty nights, as I had
done the first time. And once again
the LORD listened to me. The LORD
was unwilling to destroy you. 11 The
LORD said to me, "Get up, go on
your journey at the head of the people, that they may go in and occupy
the land that I swore to their ancestors to give them."

The Essence of the Law

12 So now, O Israel, what does
the LORD your God require of you?
Only to fear the LORD your God, to
walk in all his ways, to love him, to
serve the LORD your God with all
your heart and with all your soul,
13 and to keep the commandments
of the LORD your God[w] and his decrees that I am commanding you
today, for your own well-being.
14 Although heaven and the heaven
of heavens belong to the LORD your
God, the earth with all that is in it,
15 yet the LORD set his heart in love
on your ancestors alone and chose
you, their descendants after them,
out of all the peoples, as it is today.
16 Circumcise, then, the foreskin of
your heart, and do not be stubborn
any longer. 17 For the LORD your
God is God of gods and Lord of
lords, the great God, mighty and
awesome, who is not partial and
takes no bribe, 18 who executes justice for the orphan and the widow,
and who loves the strangers, providing them food and clothing.
19 You shall also love the stranger,
for you were strangers in the land

10.7 Num 33.32-34 **10.8** Num 3.6; 4.15; Deut 18.5; 21.5 **10.9** Num 18.20, 24 **10.10** Deut 9.18, 25; Ex 33.17 **10.12** Mic 6.8; Deut 6.13; 5.33; 6.5 **10.14** 1 Kings 8.27; Ex 19.5 **10.15** Deut 4.37 **10.16** Jer 4.4; Deut 9.6 **10.17** Josh 22.22; Rev 19.16; Acts 10.34 **10.18** Ps 68.5 **10.19** Lev 19.34

10.20 Mt 4.10; Deut 11.22; Ps 63.11 **10.21** Ex 15.2; Ps 106.21, 22 **10.22** Gen 46.27; Deut 1.10 **11.1** Deut 10.12; Zech 3.7 **11.2** Deut 8.5; 5.24 **11.4** Ex 14.27,28 **11.6** Num 16.31-33 **11.8** Josh 1.6,7 **11.9** Deut 4.40; 9.5; Ex 3.8

of Egypt. 20 You shall fear the LORD
your God; him alone you shall worship; to him you shall hold fast,
and by his name you shall swear.
21 He is your praise; he is your God,
who has done for you these great
and awesome things that your own
eyes have seen. 22 Your ancestors
went down to Egypt seventy persons; and now the LORD your God
has made you as numerous as the
stars in heaven.

Rewards for Obedience

11 You shall love the LORD
your God, therefore, and
keep his charge, his decrees, his ordinances, and his commandments
always. 2 Remember today that it
was not your children (who have
not known or seen the discipline of
the LORD your God), but it is you
who must acknowledge his greatness, his mighty hand and his outstretched arm, 3 his signs and his
deeds that he did in Egypt to Pharaoh, the king of Egypt, and to all
his land; 4 what he did to the Egyptian army, to their horses and chariots, how he made the water of the
Red Sea[x] flow over them as they
pursued you, so that the LORD has
destroyed them to this day; 5 what
he did to you in the wilderness, until you came to this place; 6 and
what he did to Dathan and Abiram,
sons of Eliab son of Reuben, how in
the midst of all Israel the earth
opened its mouth and swallowed
them up, along with their households, their tents, and every living
being in their company; 7 for it is
your own eyes that have seen every
great deed that the LORD did.
8 Keep, then, this entire commandment that I am commanding
you today, so that you may have
strength to go in and occupy the
land that you are crossing over to
occupy, 9 and so that you may live
long in the land that the LORD
swore to your ancestors to give
them and to their descendants, a
land flowing with milk and honey.

[v] Or *the wells of the Bene-jaakan* [w] Q Ms Gk Syr: MT lacks *your God* [x] Or *Sea of Reeds*

10 For the land that you are about to
enter to occupy is not like the land
of Egypt, from which you have
come, where you sow your seed
and irrigate by foot like a vegetable
garden. 11 But the land that you are
crossing over to occupy is a land of
hills and valleys, watered by rain
from the sky, 12 a land that the LORD
your God looks after. The eyes of
the LORD your God are always on it,
from the beginning of the year to
the end of the year.

13 If you will only heed his every
commandment[y] that I am commanding you today—loving the
LORD your God, and serving him
with all your heart and with all your
soul— 14 then he[z] will give the rain
for your land in its season, the early
rain and the later rain, and you will
gather in your grain, your wine, and
your oil; 15 and he[z] will give grass
in your fields for your livestock,
and you will eat your fill. 16 Take
care, or you will be seduced into
turning away, serving other gods
and worshiping them, 17 for then
the anger of the LORD will be kindled against you and he will shut
up the heavens, so that there will
be no rain and the land will yield
no fruit; then you will perish quickly off the good land that the LORD is
giving you.

18 You shall put these words of
mine in your heart and soul, and
you shall bind them as a sign on
your hand, and fix them as an emblem[a] on your forehead. 19 Teach
them to your children, talking
about them when you are at home
and when you are away, when you
lie down and when you rise.
20 Write them on the doorposts of
your house and on your gates, 21 so
that your days and the days of your
children may be multiplied in the
land that the LORD swore to your
ancestors to give them, as long as
the heavens are above the earth.

22 If you will diligently observe
this entire commandment that I
am commanding you, loving the
LORD your God, walking in all his
ways, and holding fast to him,
23 then the LORD will drive out all
these nations before you, and you
will dispossess nations larger and
mightier than yourselves. 24 Every
place on which you set foot shall be
yours; your territory shall extend
from the wilderness to the Lebanon and from the River, the river
Euphrates, to the Western Sea.
25 No one will be able to stand
against you; the LORD your God will
put the fear and dread of you on all
the land on which you set foot, as
he promised you.

26 See, I am setting before you
today a blessing and a curse: 27 the
blessing, if you obey the commandments of the LORD your God that I
am commanding you today; 28 and
the curse, if you do not obey the
commandments of the LORD your
God, but turn from the way that I
am commanding you today, to follow other gods that you have not
known.

29 When the LORD your God has
brought you into the land that you
are entering to occupy, you shall
set the blessing on Mount Gerizim
and the curse on Mount Ebal. 30 As
you know, they are beyond the Jordan, some distance to the west, in
the land of the Canaanites who live
in the Arabah, opposite Gilgal, beside the oak[b] of Moreh.

31 When you cross the Jordan to
go in to occupy the land that the
LORD your God is giving you, and
when you occupy it and live in it,
32 you must diligently observe all
the statutes and ordinances that I
am setting before you today.

Pagan Shrines to Be Destroyed

12 These are the statutes and
ordinances that you must
diligently observe in the land that
the LORD, the God of your ancestors, has given you to occupy all the
days that you live on the earth.

2 You must demolish completely all the places where the nations
whom you are about to dispossess
served their gods, on the mountain

11.11 Deut 8.7
11.13 v. 22; Deut 6.17; 10.12
11.14 Deut 28.12; Joel 2.23
11.15 Deut 6.11
11.16 Deut 29.18; 8.19
11.17 Deut 6.15; 1 Kings 8.35; Deut 4.26
11.18 Deut 6.6,8
11.19 Deut 4.9,10; 6.7
11.20 Deut 6.9
11.22 Deut 6.17; 10.20
11.23 Deut 9.1,5
11.24 Josh 1.3; Gen 15.18; Ex 23.31
11.25 Deut 7.24; Ex 23.27
11.26 Deut 30.1, 19
11.27 Deut 28.2
11.28 Deut 28.15
11.29 Deut 27.12; Josh 8.33
11.30 Josh 4.19; Gen 12.6
11.31 Deut 9.1; Josh 1.11
12.1 Deut 4.9,10

[y] Compare Gk: Heb *my commandments*
[z] Sam Gk Vg: MT *I* [a] Or *as a frontlet*
[b] Gk Syr: Compare Gen 12.6; Heb *oaks* or *terebinths*

heights, on the hills, and under every leafy tree. 3 Break down their altars, smash their pillars, burn their
sacred poles[c] with fire, and hew
down the idols of their gods, and
thus blot out their name from their
places. 4 You shall not worship the
LORD your God in such ways. 5 But
you shall seek the place that the
LORD your God will choose out of all
your tribes as his habitation to put
his name there. You shall go there,
6 bringing there your burnt offerings and your sacrifices, your tithes
and your donations, your votive
gifts, your freewill offerings, and
the firstlings of your herds and
flocks. 7 And you shall eat there in
the presence of the LORD your God,
you and your households together,
rejoicing in all the undertakings in
which the LORD your God has
blessed you.
8 You shall not act as we are acting here today, all of us according
to our own desires, 9 for you have
not yet come into the rest and the
possession that the LORD your God
is giving you. 10 When you cross
over the Jordan and live in the land
that the LORD your God is allotting
to you, and when he gives you rest
from your enemies all around so
that you live in safety, 11 then you
shall bring everything that I command you to the place that the
LORD your God will choose as a
dwelling for his name: your burnt
offerings and your sacrifices, your
tithes and your donations, and all
your choice votive gifts that you
vow to the LORD. 12 And you shall
rejoice before the LORD your God,
you together with your sons and
your daughters, your male and female slaves, and the Levites who
reside in your towns (since they
have no allotment or inheritance
with you).

A Prescribed Place of Worship

13 Take care that you do not offer your burnt offerings at any place
you happen to see. 14 But only at
the place that the LORD will choose
in one of your tribes—there you
shall offer your burnt offerings and

12.3 Deut 7.5
12.5 v. 11
12.7 Deut 14.26; vv. 12,18
12.10 Deut 11.31
12.11 v. 5
12.12 v. 7; Deut 10.9
12.14 v. 11
12.15 vv. 20-23; Deut 14.5
12.16 Lev 17.10-12
12.18 vv. 5,7,12
12.19 Deut 14.27
12.20 Gen 15.18
12.22 v. 15
12.23 v. 16; Lev 17.11, 14
12.25 Deut 4.40; 13.18
12.26 v. 17

there you shall do everything I
command you.
15 Yet whenever you desire you
may slaughter and eat meat within
any of your towns, according to the
blessing that the LORD your God has
given you; the unclean and the
clean may eat of it, as they would of
gazelle or deer. 16 The blood, however, you must not eat; you shall
pour it out on the ground like water. 17 Nor may you eat within your
towns the tithe of your grain, your
wine, and your oil, the firstlings of
your herds and your flocks, any of
your votive gifts that you vow, your
freewill offerings, or your donations; 18 these you shall eat in the
presence of the LORD your God at
the place that the LORD your God
will choose, you together with your
son and your daughter, your male
and female slaves, and the Levites
resident in your towns, rejoicing in
the presence of the LORD your God
in all your undertakings. 19 Take
care that you do not neglect the Levite as long as you live in your land.
20 When the LORD your God enlarges your territory, as he has
promised you, and you say, "I am
going to eat some meat," because
you wish to eat meat, you may eat
meat whenever you have the desire. 21 If the place where the LORD
your God will choose to put his
name is too far from you, and you
slaughter as I have commanded
you any of your herd or flock that
the LORD has given you, then you
may eat within your towns whenever you desire. 22 Indeed, just as gazelle or deer is eaten, so you may
eat it; the unclean and the clean
alike may eat it. 23 Only be sure that
you do not eat the blood; for the
blood is the life, and you shall not
eat the life with the meat. 24 Do not
eat it; you shall pour it out on the
ground like water. 25 Do not eat it,
so that all may go well with you and
your children after you, because
you do what is right in the sight of
the LORD. 26 But the sacred donations that are due from you, and

[c] Heb *Asherim*

your votive gifts, you shall bring to
the place that the LORD will choose.
27 You shall present your burnt offerings, both the meat and the
blood, on the altar of the LORD your
God; the blood of your other sacrifices shall be poured out beside[d]
the altar of the LORD your God, but
the meat you may eat.
28 Be careful to obey all these
words that I command you today,[e]
so that it may go well with you and
with your children after you forever, because you will be doing what
is good and right in the sight of the
LORD your God.

Warning against Idolatry

29 When the LORD your God has
cut off before you the nations
whom you are about to enter to dispossess them, when you have dispossessed them and live in their
land, 30 take care that you are not
snared into imitating them, after
they have been destroyed before
you: do not inquire concerning
their gods, saying, "How did these
nations worship their gods? I also
want to do the same." 31 You must
not do the same for the LORD your
God, because every abhorrent
thing that the LORD hates they have
done for their gods. They would
even burn their sons and their
daughters in the fire to their gods.
32[f] You must diligently observe everything that I command you; do
not add to it or take anything from
it.

13 [g] If prophets or those who divine by dreams appear
among you and promise you omens
or portents, 2 and the omens or the
portents declared by them take
place, and they say, "Let us follow
other gods" (whom you have not
known) "and let us serve them,"
3 you must not heed the words of
those prophets or those who divine
by dreams; for the LORD your God is
testing you, to know whether you
indeed love the LORD your God with
all your heart and soul. 4 The LORD
your God you shall follow, him
alone you shall fear, his commandments you shall keep, his voice you
shall obey, him you shall serve, and
to him you shall hold fast. 5 But
those prophets or those who divine
by dreams shall be put to death for
having spoken treason against the
LORD your God—who brought you
out of the land of Egypt and redeemed you from the house of
slavery—to turn you from the way
in which the LORD your God commanded you to walk. So you shall
purge the evil from your midst.
6 If anyone secretly entices
you—even if it is your brother, your
father's son or[h] your mother's son,
or your own son or daughter, or the
wife you embrace, or your most intimate friend—saying, "Let us go
worship other gods," whom neither
you nor your ancestors have
known, 7 any of the gods of the peoples that are around you, whether
near you or far away from you, from
one end of the earth to the other,
8 you must not yield to or heed any
such persons. Show them no pity or
compassion and do not shield
them. 9 But you shall surely kill
them; your own hand shall be first
against them to execute them, and
afterwards the hand of all the people. 10 Stone them to death for trying to turn you away from the LORD
your God, who brought you out of
the land of Egypt, out of the house
of slavery. 11 Then all Israel shall
hear and be afraid, and never again
do any such wickedness.
12 If you hear it said about one
of the towns that the LORD your God
is giving you to live in, 13 that
scoundrels from among you have
gone out and led the inhabitants of
the town astray, saying, "Let us go
and worship other gods," whom
you have not known, 14 then you
shall inquire and make a thorough
investigation. If the charge is established that such an abhorrent
thing has been done among you,
15 you shall put the inhabitants of
that town to the sword, utterly de-

12.28 v. 25; Deut 4.40
12.31 Deut 9.5; 18.10
12.32 Deut 4.2
13.1 Mt 24.24; Mk 13.22
13.2 vv. 6,13
13.3 Deut 8.2,16
13.4 2 Kings 23.3; Deut 10.20
13.5 Deut 18.20; 17.7
13.6 Deut 17.2-7; 29.18
13.9 Deut 17.5,7
13.11 Deut 19.20
13.13 vv. 2,6; see 1 Jn 2.19
13.15 Ex 22.20

[d] Or *on* [e] Gk Sam Syr: MT lacks *today*
[f] Ch 13.1 in Heb [g] Ch 13.2 in Heb
[h] Sam Gk Compare Tg: MT lacks *your father's son or*

stroying it and everything in it—even putting its livestock to the sword. 16 All of its spoil you shall gather into its public square; then burn the town and all its spoil with fire, as a whole burnt offering to the LORD your God. It shall remain a perpetual ruin, never to be rebuilt. 17 Do not let anything devoted to destruction stick to your hand, so that the LORD may turn from his fierce anger and show you compassion, and in his compassion multiply you, as he swore to your ancestors, 18 if you obey the voice of the LORD your God by keeping all his commandments that I am commanding you today, doing what is right in the sight of the LORD your God.

Pagan Practices Forbidden

14 You are children of the LORD your God. You must not lacerate yourselves or shave your forelocks for the dead. 2 For you are a people holy to the LORD your God; it is you the LORD has chosen out of all the peoples on earth to be his people, his treasured possession.

Clean and Unclean Foods

3 You shall not eat any abhorrent thing. 4 These are the animals you may eat: the ox, the sheep, the goat, 5 the deer, the gazelle, the roebuck, the wild goat, the ibex, the antelope, and the mountain-sheep. 6 Any animal that divides the hoof and has the hoof cleft in two, and chews the cud, among the animals, you may eat. 7 Yet of those that chew the cud or have the hoof cleft you shall not eat these: the camel, the hare, and the rock badger, because they chew the cud but do not divide the hoof; they are unclean for you. 8 And the pig, because it divides the hoof but does not chew the cud, is unclean for you. You shall not eat their meat, and you shall not touch their carcasses.

9 Of all that live in water you may eat these: whatever has fins and scales you may eat. 10 And whatever does not have fins and scales you shall not eat; it is unclean for you.

11 You may eat any clean birds. 12 But these are the ones that you shall not eat: the eagle, the vulture, the osprey, 13 the buzzard, the kite, of any kind; 14 every raven of any kind; 15 the ostrich, the nighthawk, the sea gull, the hawk, of any kind; 16 the little owl and the great owl, the water hen 17 and the desert owl,[i] the carrion vulture and the cormorant, 18 the stork, the heron, of any kind; the hoopoe and the bat.[j] 19 And all winged insects are unclean for you; they shall not be eaten. 20 You may eat any clean winged creature.

21 You shall not eat anything that dies of itself; you may give it to aliens residing in your towns for them to eat, or you may sell it to a foreigner. For you are a people holy to the LORD your God.

You shall not boil a kid in its mother's milk.

Regulations concerning Tithes

22 Set apart a tithe of all the yield of your seed that is brought in yearly from the field. 23 In the presence of the LORD your God, in the place that he will choose as a dwelling for his name, you shall eat the tithe of your grain, your wine, and your oil, as well as the firstlings of your herd and flock, so that you may learn to fear the LORD your God always. 24 But if, when the LORD your God has blessed you, the distance is so great that you are unable to transport it, because the place where the LORD your God will choose to set his name is too far away from you, 25 then you may turn it into money. With the money secure in hand, go to the place that the LORD your God will choose; 26 spend the money for whatever you wish—oxen, sheep, wine, strong drink, or whatever you desire. And you shall eat there in the presence of the LORD your God, you and your household rejoicing together. 27 As for the Levites resi-

[i] Or *pelican* [j] Identification of several of the birds in verses 12-18 is uncertain

13.16 Josh 6.24; 8.28
13.17 Num 25.4; Deut 30.3; 7.13
13.18 Deut 12.28
14.1 Rom 8;16; Lev 21.5
14.2 Deut 7.6
14.4 Lev 11.2-45; Acts 10.14
14.8 Lev 11.26, 27
14.9 Lev 11.9
14.12 Lev 11.3
14.19 Lev 11.20
14.21 Lev 17.15; v. 2; Ex 29.19; 34.26
14.22ff Lev 27.30
14.23 Deut 12.5-7; 4.10
14.24 Deut 12.5, 21
14.26 Deut 12.7, 18
14.27 Deut 12.12; Num 18.20

dent in your towns, do not neglect
them, because they have no allotment or inheritance with you.
28 Every third year you shall
bring out the full tithe of your produce for that year, and store it
within your towns; 29 the Levites,
because they have no allotment or
inheritance with you, as well as the
resident aliens, the orphans, and
the widows in your towns, may
come and eat their fill so that the
LORD your God may bless you in all
the work that you undertake.

Laws concerning the Sabbatical Year

15 Every seventh year you
shall grant a remission of
debts. 2 And this is the manner of
the remission: every creditor shall
remit the claim that is held against
a neighbor, not exacting it of a
neighbor who is a member of the
community, because the LORD's remission has been proclaimed. 3 Of
a foreigner you may exact it, but
you must remit your claim on
whatever any member of your community owes you. 4 There will, however, be no one in need among you,
because the LORD is sure to bless
you in the land that the LORD your
God is giving you as a possession to
occupy, 5 if only you will obey the
LORD your God by diligently observing this entire commandment that
I command you today. 6 When the
LORD your God has blessed you, as
he promised you, you will lend to
many nations, but you will not borrow; you will rule over many nations, but they will not rule over
you.
7 If there is among you anyone
in need, a member of your community in any of your towns within the
land that the LORD your God is giving you, do not be hard-hearted or
tight-fisted toward your needy
neighbor. 8 You should rather open
your hand, willingly lending
enough to meet the need, whatever
it may be. 9 Be careful that you do
not entertain a mean thought,
thinking, "The seventh year, the
year of remission, is near," and
therefore view your needy neighbor
with hostility and give nothing;
your neighbor might cry to the LORD
against you, and you would incur
guilt. 10 Give liberally and be un-
grudging when you do so, for on
this account the LORD your God will
bless you in all your work and in all
that you undertake. 11 Since there
will never cease to be some in need
on the earth, I therefore command
you, "Open your hand to the poor
and needy neighbor in your land."
12 If a member of your community, whether a Hebrew man or a
Hebrew woman, is sold[k] to you
and works for you six years, in the
seventh year you shall set that person free. 13 And when you send a
male slave[l] out from you a free
person, you shall not send him out
empty-handed. 14 Provide liberally
out of your flock, your threshing
floor, and your wine press, thus giving to him some of the bounty with
which the LORD your God has
blessed you. 15 Remember that you
were a slave in the land of Egypt,
and the LORD your God redeemed
you; for this reason I lay this command upon you today. 16 But if he
says to you, "I will not go out from
you," because he loves you and
your household, since he is well off
with you, 17 then you shall take an
awl and thrust it through his ear-
lobe into the door, and he shall be
your slave[m] forever.
You shall do the same with regard to your female slave.[n]
18 Do not consider it a hardship
when you send them out from you
free persons, because for six years
they have given you services worth
the wages of hired laborers; and the
LORD your God will bless you in all
that you do.

The Firstborn of Livestock

19 Every firstling male born of
your herd and flock you shall consecrate to the LORD your God; you
shall not do work with your firstling
ox nor shear the firstling of your
flock. 20 You shall eat it, you to-

14.28 Deut 26.12 **14.29** Deut 26.12; v. 27; Deut 15.10 **15.1** Deut 31.10 **15.5** Deut 28.1 **15.6** Deut 28.12, 13 **15.7** 1 Jn 3.17 **15.8** Lev 25.35 **15.9** v. 1; Deut 24.15

15.10 2 Cor 9.5, 7; Deut 24.19 **15.11** Mt 26.11; Mk 14.7; Jn 12.8 **15.12** Ex 21.2; Lev 25.39 **15.15** Deut 5.15; 16.12 **15.16** Ex 21.5,6 **15.19** Ex 13.2 **15.20** Deut 12.5-7, 17

[k] Or *sells himself or herself* [l] Heb *him*
[m] Or *bondman* [n] Or *bondwoman*

gether with your household, in the
presence of the LORD your God year
by year at the place that the LORD
will choose. 21 But if it has any
defect—any serious defect, such as
lameness or blindness—you shall
not sacrifice it to the LORD your
God; 22 within your towns you may
eat it, the unclean and the clean
alike, as you would a gazelle or
deer. 23 Its blood, however, you
must not eat; you shall pour it out
on the ground like water.

The Passover Reviewed

16 Observe the month[o] of
Abib by keeping the pass-
over for the LORD your God, for in
the month of Abib the LORD your
God brought you out of Egypt by
night. 2 You shall offer the passover
sacrifice for the LORD your God,
from the flock and the herd, at the
place that the LORD will choose as a
dwelling for his name. 3 You must
not eat with it anything leavened.
For seven days you shall eat unleavened bread with it—the bread
of affliction—because you came
out of the land of Egypt in great
haste, so that all the days of your
life you may remember the day of
your departure from the land of
Egypt. 4 No leaven shall be seen
with you in all your territory for sev-
en days; and none of the meat of
what you slaughter on the evening
of the first day shall remain until
morning. 5 You are not permitted to
offer the passover sacrifice within
any of your towns that the LORD
your God is giving you. 6 But at the
place that the LORD your God will
choose as a dwelling for his name,
only there shall you offer the passover sacrifice, in the evening at
sunset, the time of day when you
departed from Egypt. 7 You shall
cook it and eat it at the place that
the LORD your God will choose; the
next morning you may go back to
your tents. 8 For six days you shall
continue to eat unleavened bread,
and on the seventh day there shall
be a solemn assembly for the LORD
your God, when you shall do no
work.

The Festival of Weeks Reviewed

9 You shall count seven weeks;
begin to count the seven weeks
from the time the sickle is first put
to the standing grain. 10 Then you
shall keep the festival of weeks for
the LORD your God, contributing a
freewill offering in proportion to
the blessing that you have received
from the LORD your God. 11 Rejoice
before the LORD your God—you and
your sons and your daughters, your
male and female slaves, the Levites
resident in your towns, as well as
the strangers, the orphans, and the
widows who are among you—at the
place that the LORD your God will
choose as a dwelling for his name.
12 Remember that you were a slave
in Egypt, and diligently observe
these statutes.

The Festival of Booths Reviewed

13 You shall keep the festival of
booths[p] for seven days, when you
have gathered in the produce from
your threshing floor and your wine
press. 14 Rejoice during your festival, you and your sons and your
daughters, your male and female
slaves, as well as the Levites, the
strangers, the orphans, and the
widows resident in your towns.
15 Seven days you shall keep the
festival for the LORD your God at the
place that the LORD will choose; for
the LORD your God will bless you in
all your produce and in all your undertakings, and you shall surely
celebrate.

16 Three times a year all your
males shall appear before the LORD
your God at the place that he will
choose: at the festival of unleavened bread, at the festival of
weeks, and at the festival of
booths.[p] They shall not appear before the LORD empty-handed; 17 all
shall give as they are able, according to the blessing of the LORD your
God that he has given you.

Municipal Judges and Officers

18 You shall appoint judges and
officials throughout your tribes, in

15.21 Lev 22.19-25 **15.22** Deut 12.15, 22 **15.23** Deut 12.16, 23 **16.1** Ex 12.2,29, 42; 13.4 **16.2** Deut 12.5, 26 **16.3** Ex 12.8,15 **16.4** Ex 13.7; 12.10 **16.6** Deut 12.5; Ex 12.6 **16.7** Ex 12.8,9 **16.8** Ex 12.16

16.9 Ex 23.16; 34.22; Lev 23.15; Num 28.26 **16.11** Deut 12.7, 12 **16.12** Deut 15.15 **16.13** Ex 23.16; Lev 23.34 **16.14** v. 11 **16.15** Lev 23.39 **16.16** Ex 23.14-17; 34.20,23 **16.18** Deut 1.16

[o] Or *new moon* [p] Or *tabernacles*; Heb *succoth*

all your towns that the LORD your
God is giving you, and they shall
render just decisions for the people. 19 You must not distort justice;
you must not show partiality; and
you must not accept bribes, for a
bribe blinds the eyes of the wise
and subverts the cause of those
who are in the right. 20 Justice, and
only justice, you shall pursue, so
that you may live and occupy the
land that the LORD your God is giving you.

Forbidden Forms of Worship

21 You shall not plant any tree
as a sacred pole[q] beside the altar
that you make for the LORD your
God; 22 nor shall you set up a stone
pillar—things that the LORD your
God hates.

17 You must not sacrifice to
the LORD your God an ox or
a sheep that has a defect, anything
seriously wrong; for that is abhorrent to the LORD your God.

2 If there is found among you, in
one of your towns that the LORD
your God is giving you, a man or
woman who does what is evil in the
sight of the LORD your God, and
transgresses his covenant 3 by going to serve other gods and worshiping them—whether the sun or
the moon or any of the host of
heaven, which I have forbidden—
4 and if it is reported to you or you
hear of it, and you make a thorough
inquiry, and the charge is proved
true that such an abhorrent thing
has occurred in Israel, 5 then you
shall bring out to your gates that
man or that woman who has committed this crime and you shall
stone the man or woman to death.
6 On the evidence of two or three
witnesses the death sentence shall
be executed; a person must not be
put to death on the evidence of
only one witness. 7 The hands of
the witnesses shall be the first
raised against the person to execute the death penalty, and afterward the hands of all the people. So
you shall purge the evil from your
midst.

Legal Decisions by Priests and Judges

8 If a judicial decision is too difficult for you to make between one
kind of bloodshed and another,
one kind of legal right and another,
or one kind of assault and
another—any such matters of dispute in your towns—then you
shall immediately go up to the
place that the LORD your God will
choose, 9 where you shall consult
with the levitical priests and the
judge who is in office in those days;
they shall announce to you the decision in the case. 10 Carry out exactly the decision that they announce to you from the place that
the LORD will choose, diligently observing everything they instruct
you. 11 You must carry out fully the
law that they interpret for you or
the ruling that they announce to
you; do not turn aside from the decision that they announce to you,
either to the right or to the left.
12 As for anyone who presumes to
disobey the priest appointed to
minister there to the LORD your
God, or the judge, that person shall
die. So you shall purge the evil
from Israel. 13 All the people will
hear and be afraid, and will not act
presumptuously again.

Limitations of Royal Authority

14 When you have come into
the land that the LORD your God is
giving you, and have taken possession of it and settled in it, and you
say, "I will set a king over me, like
all the nations that are around
me," 15 you may indeed set over you
a king whom the LORD your God will
choose. One of your own community you may set as king over you;
you are not permitted to put a foreigner over you, who is not of your
own community. 16 Even so, he
must not acquire many horses for
himself, or return the people to
Egypt in order to acquire more
horses, since the LORD has said to
you, "You must never return that
way again." 17 And he must not ac-

16.19 Deut 1.17; Ex 23.8
16.21 Ex 34.13; Deut 7.5
17.1 Deut 15.21; Mal 1.8,13
17.2 Deut 13.6
17.4 Deut 13.12, 14
17.6 Num 35.30; Deut 19.15; Mt 18.16
17.7 Deut 13.5,9
17.8 Deut 12.5
17.9 Deut 19.17; Ezek 44.24
17.11 Deut 25.1
17.13 Deut 13.11; 19.20
17.14 Deut 11.31; 1 Sam 8.5, 19,20
17.15 Jer 30.21
17.16ff 1 Kings 4.26; 10.26,28; Isa 31.1; Ezek 17.15
17.17 cf. 1 Kings 11.3, 4

[q] Heb *Asherah*

quire many wives for himself, or
else his heart will turn away; also
silver and gold he must not acquire
in great quantity for himself.
18 When he has taken the throne of
his kingdom, he shall have a copy
of this law written for him in the
presence of the levitical priests.
19 It shall remain with him and he
shall read in it all the days of his
life, so that he may learn to fear the
LORD his God, diligently observing
all the words of this law and these
statutes, 20 neither exalting himself
above other members of the community nor turning aside from the
commandment, either to the right
or to the left, so that he and his descendants may reign long over his
kingdom in Israel.

Privileges of Priests and Levites

18 The levitical priests, the
whole tribe of Levi, shall
have no allotment or inheritance
within Israel. They may eat the sacrifices that are the LORD's portion[r]
2 but they shall have no inheritance
among the other members of the
community; the LORD is their inheritance, as he promised them.
3 This shall be the priests' due
from the people, from those offering a sacrifice, whether an ox or a
sheep: they shall give to the priest
the shoulder, the two jowls, and
the stomach. 4 The first fruits of
your grain, your wine, and your oil,
as well as the first of the fleece of
your sheep, you shall give him.
5 For the LORD your God has chosen
Levi[s] out of all your tribes, to
stand and minister in the name of
the LORD, him and his sons for all
time.
6 If a Levite leaves any of your
towns, from wherever he has been
residing in Israel, and comes to the
place that the LORD will choose
(and he may come whenever he
wishes), 7 then he may minister in
the name of the LORD his God, like
all his fellow-Levites who stand to
minister there before the LORD.
8 They shall have equal portions to
eat, even though they have income
from the sale of family possessions.[r]

Child-Sacrifice, Divination, and Magic Prohibited

9 When you come into the land
that the LORD your God is giving
you, you must not learn to imitate
the abhorrent practices of those
nations. 10 No one shall be found
among you who makes a son or
daughter pass through fire, or who
practices divination, or is a sooth-
sayer, or an augur, or a sorcerer,
11 or one who casts spells, or who
consults ghosts or spirits, or who
seeks oracles from the dead. 12 For
whoever does these things is abhorrent to the LORD; it is because of
such abhorrent practices that the
LORD your God is driving them out
before you. 13 You must remain
completely loyal to the LORD your
God. 14 Although these nations that
you are about to dispossess do give
heed to soothsayers and diviners,
as for you, the LORD your God does
not permit you to do so.

A New Prophet Like Moses

15 The LORD your God will raise
up for you a prophet[t] like me from
among your own people; you shall
heed such a prophet.[u] 16 This is
what you requested of the LORD
your God at Horeb on the day of the
assembly when you said: "If I hear
the voice of the LORD my God any
more, or ever again see this great
fire, I will die." 17 Then the LORD replied to me: "They are right in what
they have said. 18 I will raise up for
them a prophet[t] like you from
among their own people; I will put
my words in the mouth of the
prophet,[v] who shall speak to them
everything that I command. 19 Anyone who does not heed the words
that the prophet[w] shall speak in
my name, I myself will hold accountable. 20 But any prophet who
speaks in the name of other gods,
or who presumes to speak in my
name a word that I have not com-

17.18 Deut 31.24-26 **17.19** Josh 1.8 **17.20** Deut 5.32 **18.1** Deut 10.9; 1 Cor 9.13 **18.3** Lev 7.30-34 **18.4** Ex 22.29; Num 18.12 **18.5** Ex 28.1; Deut 10.8 **18.8** Neh 12.44, 47

18.9 Deut 12.29-31 **18.10** Deut 12.31; Lev 19.26, 31 **18.12** Deut 9.4 **18.15ff** Jn 1.21; Acts 3.22; 7.37 **18.16** Deut 5.23-27; Ex 20.19 **18.17** Deut 5.28 **18.18** v. 15; Isa 51.16; Jn 4.25,26 **18.19** Acts 3.23 **18.20** Deut 13.1,2, 5

r Meaning of Heb uncertain s Heb *him*
t Or *prophets* u Or *such prophets*
v Or *mouths of the prophets* w Heb *he*

manded the prophet to speak—
that prophet shall die." 21 You may
say to yourself, "How can we recognize a word that the LORD has not
spoken?" 22 If a prophet speaks in
the name of the LORD but the thing
does not take place or prove true, it
is a word that the LORD has not spoken. The prophet has spoken it presumptuously; do not be frightened
by it.

Laws concerning the Cities of Refuge

19 When the LORD your God
has cut off the nations
whose land the LORD your God is
giving you, and you have dispossessed them and settled in their
towns and in their houses, 2 you
shall set apart three cities in the
land that the LORD your God is giving you to possess. 3 You shall calculate the distances[x] and divide
into three regions the land that the
LORD your God gives you as a possession, so that any homicide can
flee to one of them.

4 Now this is the case of a homicide who might flee there and live,
that is, someone who has killed another person unintentionally when
the two had not been at enmity before: 5 Suppose someone goes into
the forest with another to cut
wood, and when one of them
swings the ax to cut down a tree,
the head slips from the handle and
strikes the other person who then
dies; the killer may flee to one of
these cities and live. 6 But if the distance is too great, the avenger of
blood in hot anger might pursue
and overtake and put the killer to
death, although a death sentence
was not deserved, since the two
had not been at enmity before.
7 Therefore I command you: You
shall set apart three cities.

8 If the LORD your God enlarges
your territory, as he swore to your
ancestors—and he will give you all
the land that he promised your ancestors to give you, 9 provided you
diligently observe this entire commandment that I command you today, by loving the LORD your God
and walking always in his ways—
then you shall add three more cities to these three, 10 so that the
blood of an innocent person may
not be shed in the land that the
LORD your God is giving you as an
inheritance, thereby bringing
bloodguilt upon you.

11 But if someone at enmity
with another lies in wait and attacks and takes the life of that person, and flees into one of these cities, 12 then the elders of the killer's
city shall send to have the culprit
taken from there and handed over
to the avenger of blood to be put to
death. 13 Show no pity; you shall
purge the guilt of innocent blood
from Israel, so that it may go well
with you.

Property Boundaries

14 You must not move your neighbor's boundary marker, set up by former generations, on the property that will be allotted to you in the land that the LORD your God is giving you to possess.

Law concerning Witnesses

15 A single witness shall not
suffice to convict a person of any
crime or wrongdoing in connection
with any offense that may be committed. Only on the evidence of
two or three witnesses shall a
charge be sustained. 16 If a malicious witness comes forward to accuse someone of wrongdoing,
17 then both parties to the dispute
shall appear before the LORD, before the priests and the judges who
are in office in those days, 18 and
the judges shall make a thorough
inquiry. If the witness is a false witness, having testified falsely
against another, 19 then you shall
do to the false witness just as the
false witness had meant to do to
the other. So you shall purge the
evil from your midst. 20 The rest
shall hear and be afraid, and a
crime such as this shall never again
be committed among you. 21 Show
no pity: life for life, eye for eye,

18.22 Jer 28.9; v. 20
19.1 Deut 12.29
19.2 Num 35.10, 14
19.4 Num 35.15
19.6 Num 35.12
19.9 Josh 20.7,8
19.10 Deut 21.1-9; Num 35.33
19.13 Deut 7.2
19.14 Deut 27.17
19.15 Num 35.30; Deut 17.6; Mt 18.16; 2 Cor 13.1
19.16 Ex 23.1; Ps 27.12
19.17 Deut 17.9
19.19 Prov 19.5,9
19.21 v. 13; Ex 21.23; Lev 24.20; Mt 5.38

[x] Or *prepare roads to them*

tooth for tooth, hand for hand, foot
for foot.

Rules of Warfare

20 When you go out to war
against your enemies, and
see horses and chariots, an army
larger than your own, you shall not
be afraid of them; for the LORD your
God is with you, who brought you
up from the land of Egypt. 2 Before
you engage in battle, the priest
shall come forward and speak to
the troops, 3 and shall say to them:
"Hear, O Israel! Today you are
drawing near to do battle against
your enemies. Do not lose heart, or
be afraid, or panic, or be in dread of
them; 4 for it is the LORD your God
who goes with you, to fight for you
against your enemies, to give you
victory." 5 Then the officials shall
address the troops, saying, "Has
anyone built a new house but not
dedicated it? He should go back to
his house, or he might die in the
battle and another dedicate it.
6 Has anyone planted a vineyard
but not yet enjoyed its fruit? He
should go back to his house, or he
might die in the battle and another
be first to enjoy its fruit. 7 Has anyone become engaged to a woman
but not yet married her? He should
go back to his house, or he might
die in the battle and another marry
her." 8 The officials shall continue
to address the troops, saying, "Is
anyone afraid or disheartened? He
should go back to his house, or he
might cause the heart of his comrades to melt like his own." 9 When
the officials have finished addressing the troops, then the commanders shall take charge of them.

10 When you draw near to a
town to fight against it, offer it
terms of peace. 11 If it accepts your
terms of peace and surrenders to
you, then all the people in it shall
serve you at forced labor. 12 If it
does not submit to you peacefully,
but makes war against you, then
you shall besiege it; 13 and when
the LORD your God gives it into your
hand, you shall put all its males to
the sword. 14 You may, however,
take as your booty the women, the
children, livestock, and everything
else in the town, all its spoil. You
may enjoy the spoil of your enemies, which the LORD your God has
given you. 15 Thus you shall treat all
the towns that are very far from
you, which are not towns of the nations here. 16 But as for the towns of
these peoples that the LORD your
God is giving you as an inheritance,
you must not let anything that
breathes remain alive. 17 You shall
annihilate them—the Hittites and
the Amorites, the Canaanites and
the Perizzites, the Hivites and the
Jebusites—just as the LORD your
God has commanded, 18 so that
they may not teach you to do all the
abhorrent things that they do for
their gods, and you thus sin against
the LORD your God.

19 If you besiege a town for a
long time, making war against it in
order to take it, you must not destroy its trees by wielding an ax
against them. Although you may
take food from them, you must not
cut them down. Are trees in the
field human beings that they
should come under siege from you?
20 You may destroy only the trees
that you know do not produce food;
you may cut them down for use in
building siegeworks against the
town that makes war with you, until it falls.

Law concerning Murder by Persons Unknown

21 If, in the land that the LORD
your God is giving you to
possess, a body is found lying in
open country, and it is not known
who struck the person down, 2 then
your elders and your judges shall
come out to measure the distances
to the towns that are near the body.
3 The elders of the town nearest the
body shall take a heifer that has
never been worked, one that has
not pulled in the yoke; 4 the elders
of that town shall bring the heifer
down to a wadi with running water,
which is neither plowed nor sown,
and shall break the heifer's neck
there in the wadi. 5 Then the

20.1 Deut 31.6,8
20.3 v. 1; Josh 23.10
20.4 Deut 1.30
20.6 1 Cor 9.7
20.7 Deut 24.5
20.8 Judg 7.3
20.10ff Lk 14.31
20.14 Josh 8.2; 22.8
20.16 Deut 7.1,2; Josh 11.14
20.18 Ex 23.33
21.1 Josh 1.6
21.5 Deut 17.8-11

priests, the sons of Levi, shall come
forward, for the LORD your God has
chosen them to minister to him
and to pronounce blessings in the
name of the LORD, and by their decision all cases of dispute and assault shall be settled. 6 All the elders of that town nearest the body
shall wash their hands over the
heifer whose neck was broken in
the wadi, 7 and they shall declare:
"Our hands did not shed this
blood, nor were we witnesses to it.
8 Absolve, O LORD, your people Israel, whom you redeemed; do not let
the guilt of innocent blood remain
in the midst of your people Israel."
Then they will be absolved of
bloodguilt. 9 So you shall purge the
guilt of innocent blood from your
midst, because you must do what is
right in the sight of the LORD.

21.8 Jon 1.8 **21.9** Deut 19.13 **21.12** Lev 14.8,9; Num 6.9 **21.16** 1 Chr 26.10

Female Captives

10 When you go out to war
against your enemies, and the LORD
your God hands them over to you
and you take them captive, 11 suppose you see among the captives a
beautiful woman whom you desire
and want to marry, 12 and so you
bring her home to your house: she
shall shave her head, pare her
nails, 13 discard her captive's garb,
and shall remain in your house a
full month, mourning for her father
and mother; after that you may go
in to her and be her husband, and
she shall be your wife. 14 But if you
are not satisfied with her, you shall
let her go free and not sell her for
money. You must not treat her as a
slave, since you have dishonored
her.

The Right of the Firstborn

15 If a man has two wives, one
of them loved and the other disliked, and if both the loved and the
disliked have borne him sons, the
firstborn being the son of the one
who is disliked, 16 then on the day
when he wills his possessions to
his sons, he is not permitted to
treat the son of the loved as the
firstborn in preference to the son of
the disliked, who is the firstborn.
17 He must acknowledge as firstborn the son of the one who is disliked, giving him a double portion[y]
of all that he has; since he is the
first issue of his virility, the right of
the firstborn is his.

21.17 Gen 49.3 **21.18** Isa 30.1 **21.21** Deut 13.5, 11 **21.23** Josh 8.29; 10.26,27; Jn 19.31; Gal 3.13 **22.1** Ex 23.4 **22.4** Ex 23.5

Rebellious Children

18 If someone has a stubborn
and rebellious son who will not
obey his father and mother, who
does not heed them when they discipline him, 19 then his father and
his mother shall take hold of him
and bring him out to the elders of
his town at the gate of that place.
20 They shall say to the elders of his
town, "This son of ours is stubborn
and rebellious. He will not obey us.
He is a glutton and a drunkard."
21 Then all the men of the town
shall stone him to death. So you
shall purge the evil from your
midst; and all Israel will hear, and
be afraid.

Miscellaneous Laws

22 When someone is convicted
of a crime punishable by death and
is executed, and you hang him on a
tree, 23 his corpse must not remain
all night upon the tree; you shall
bury him that same day, for anyone
hung on a tree is under God's
curse. You must not defile the land
that the LORD your God is giving you
for possession.

22 You shall not watch your
neighbor's ox or sheep
straying away and ignore them; you
shall take them back to their owner. 2 If the owner does not reside
near you or you do not know who
the owner is, you shall bring it to
your own house, and it shall remain with you until the owner
claims it; then you shall return it.
3 You shall do the same with a
neighbor's donkey; you shall do the
same with a neighbor's garment;
and you shall do the same with
anything else that your neighbor
loses and you find. You may not
withhold your help.
4 You shall not see your neighbor's donkey or ox fallen on the

[y] Heb *two-thirds*

road and ignore it; you shall help to
lift it up.
5 A woman shall not wear a
man's apparel, nor shall a man put
on a woman's garment; for whoever
does such things is abhorrent to
the LORD your God.
6 If you come on a bird's nest, in
any tree or on the ground, with
fledglings or eggs, with the mother
sitting on the fledglings or on the
eggs, you shall not take the mother
with the young. 7 Let the mother
go, taking only the young for yourself, in order that it may go well
with you and you may live long.
8 When you build a new house,
you shall make a parapet for your
roof; otherwise you might have
bloodguilt on your house, if anyone
should fall from it.
9 You shall not sow your vineyard with a second kind of seed, or
the whole yield will have to be forfeited, both the crop that you have
sown and the yield of the vineyard
itself.
10 You shall not plow with an ox
and a donkey yoked together.
11 You shall not wear clothes
made of wool and linen woven together.
12 You shall make tassels on
the four corners of the cloak with
which you cover yourself.

Laws concerning Sexual Relations

13 Suppose a man marries a
woman, but after going in to her, he
dislikes her 14 and makes up
charges against her, slandering her
by saying, "I married this woman;
but when I lay with her, I did not
find evidence of her virginity."
15 The father of the young woman
and her mother shall then submit
the evidence of the young woman's
virginity to the elders of the city at
the gate. 16 The father of the young
woman shall say to the elders: "I
gave my daughter in marriage to
this man but he dislikes her; 17 now
he has made up charges against
her, saying, 'I did not find evidence
of your daughter's virginity.' But
here is the evidence of my daughter's virginity." Then they shall
spread out the cloth before the elders of the town. 18 The elders of
that town shall take the man and
punish him; 19 they shall fine him
one hundred shekels of silver
(which they shall give to the young
woman's father) because he has
slandered a virgin of Israel. She
shall remain his wife; he shall not
be permitted to divorce her as long
as he lives.
20 If, however, this charge is
true, that evidence of the young
woman's virginity was not found,
21 then they shall bring the young
woman out to the entrance of her
father's house and the men of her
town shall stone her to death, because she committed a disgraceful
act in Israel by prostituting herself
in her father's house. So you shall
purge the evil from your midst.
22 If a man is caught lying with
the wife of another man, both of
them shall die, the man who lay
with the woman as well as the
woman. So you shall purge the evil
from Israel.
23 If there is a young woman, a
virgin already engaged to be married, and a man meets her in the
town and lies with her, 24 you shall
bring both of them to the gate of
that town and stone them to death,
the young woman because she did
not cry for help in the town and the
man because he violated his neighbor's wife. So you shall purge the
evil from your midst.
25 But if the man meets the engaged woman in the open country,
and the man seizes her and lies
with her, then only the man who
lay with her shall die. 26 You shall
do nothing to the young woman;
the young woman has not committed an offense punishable by
death, because this case is like that
of someone who attacks and murders a neighbor. 27 Since he found
her in the open country, the engaged woman may have cried for
help, but there was no one to rescue her.
28 If a man meets a virgin who is
not engaged, and seizes her and

22.6 Lev 22.28
22.7 Deut 4.40
22.9 Lev 19.19
22.11 Lev 19.19
22.12 Num 15.37-41; Mt 23.5
22.13 Deut 24.1
22.15 v. 23ff
22.21 Deut 23.17, 18; 13.5
22.22 Lev 20.10; Jn 8.5
22.24 vv. 21,22
22.25 Jn 8.1-11
22.28 Ex 22.16,17

lies with her, and they are caught in
the act, 29 the man who lay with her
shall give fifty shekels of silver to
the young woman's father, and she
shall become his wife. Because he
violated her he shall not be permitted to divorce her as long as he
lives.
30[z] A man shall not marry his father's wife, thereby violating his father's rights.[a]

Those Excluded from the Assembly

23 No one whose testicles are
crushed or whose penis is
cut off shall be admitted to the assembly of the LORD.
2 Those born of an illicit union
shall not be admitted to the assembly of the LORD. Even to the tenth
generation, none of their descendants shall be admitted to the assembly of the LORD.
3 No Ammonite or Moabite
shall be admitted to the assembly
of the LORD. Even to the tenth generation, none of their descendants
shall be admitted to the assembly
of the LORD, 4 because they did not
meet you with food and water on
your journey out of Egypt, and because they hired against you Balaam son of Beor, from Pethor of
Mesopotamia, to curse you. 5 (Yet
the LORD your God refused to heed
Balaam; the LORD your God turned
the curse into a blessing for you,
because the LORD your God loved
you.) 6 You shall never promote
their welfare or their prosperity as
long as you live.
7 You shall not abhor any of the
Edomites, for they are your kin.
You shall not abhor any of the
Egyptians, because you were an
alien residing in their land. 8 The
children of the third generation
that are born to them may be admitted to the assembly of the LORD.

Sanitary, Ritual, and Humanitarian Precepts

9 When you are encamped
against your enemies you shall
guard against any impropriety.
10 If one of you becomes unclean because of a nocturnal emission, then he shall go outside the
camp; he must not come within the
camp. 11 When evening comes, he
shall wash himself with water, and
when the sun has set, he may come
back into the camp.
12 You shall have a designated
area outside the camp to which you
shall go. 13 With your utensils you
shall have a trowel; when you relieve yourself outside, you shall dig
a hole with it and then cover up
your excrement. 14 Because the
LORD your God travels along with
your camp, to save you and to hand
over your enemies to you, therefore
your camp must be holy, so that he
may not see anything indecent
among you and turn away from
you.
15 Slaves who have escaped to
you from their owners shall not be
given back to them. 16 They shall
reside with you, in your midst, in
any place they choose in any one of
your towns, wherever they please;
you shall not oppress them.
17 None of the daughters of Israel shall be a temple prostitute;
none of the sons of Israel shall be
a temple prostitute. 18 You shall not
bring the fee of a prostitute or the
wages of a male prostitute[b] into
the house of the LORD your God in
payment for any vow, for both of
these are abhorrent to the LORD
your God.
19 You shall not charge interest
on loans to another Israelite, interest on money, interest on provisions, interest on anything that is
lent. 20 On loans to a foreigner you
may charge interest, but on loans
to another Israelite you may not
charge interest, so that the LORD
your God may bless you in all your
undertakings in the land that you
are about to enter and possess.
21 If you make a vow to the LORD
your God, do not postpone fulfilling it; for the LORD your God will
surely require it of you, and you
would incur guilt. 22 But if you re-

22.30 Deut 27.20
23.3 Neh 13.1,2
23.4 Num 22.5,6
23.7 Gen 25.24-26
23.10 Lev 15.16
23.14 Lev 26.12
23.17 Deut 22.21
23.19 Ex 22.25; Lev 25.36, 37
23.20 Deut 28.12
23.21 Num 30.2; Mt 5.33

[z] Ch 23.1 in Heb [a] Heb *uncovering his father's skirt* [b] Heb *a dog*

MAJOR SOCIAL CONCERNS IN THE COVENANT

1. PERSONHOOD
Everyone's person is to be secure (Ex 20:13; Dt 5:17; Ex 21:16-21, 26-31; Lev 19:14; Dt 24:7; 27:18).

2. FALSE ACCUSATION
Everyone is to be secure against slander and false accusation (Ex 20:16; Dt 5:20; Ex 23:1-3; Lev 19:16; Dt 19:15-21).

3. WOMAN
No woman is to be taken advantage of within her subordinate status in society (Ex 21:7-11, 20, 26-32; 22:16-17; Dt. 21:10-14; 22:13-30; 24:1-5).

4. PUNISHMENT
Punishment for wrongdoing shall not be excessive so that the culprit is dehumanized (Dt 25:1-5).

5. DIGNITY
Every Israelite's dignity and right to be God's freedman and servant are to be honored and safeguarded (Ex 21:2, 5-6; Lev 25; Dt 15:12-18).

6. INHERITANCE
Every Israelite's inheritance in the promised land is to be secure (Lev 25; Nu 27:5-7; 36:1-9; Dt 25:5-10).

7. PROPERTY
Everyone's property is to be secure (Ex 20:15; Dt 5:19; Ex 21:33-36; 22:1-15; 23:4-5; Lev 19:35-36; Dt 22:1-4; 25:13-15).

8. FRUIT OF LABOR
Everyone is to receive the fruit of his labors (Lev 19:13; Dt 24:14; 25:4).

9. FRUIT OF THE GROUND
Everyone is to share the fruit of the ground (Ex 23:10-11; Lev 19:9-10; 23:22; 25:3-55; Dt. 14:28-29; 24:19-21).

10. REST ON SABBATH
Everyone, down to the humblest servant and the resident alien, is to share in the weekly rest of God's Sabbath (Ex 20:8-11; Dt 5:12-15; Ex 23:12).

11. MARRIAGE
The marriage relationship is to be kept inviolate (Ex 20:14; Dt 5:18; see also Lev 18:6-23; 20:10-21; Dt 22:13-30).

12. EXPLOITATION
No one, however disabled, impoverished or powerless, is to be oppressed or exploited (Ex 22:21-27; Lev 19:14, 33-34; 25:35-36; Dt 23:19; 24:6, 12-15, 17; 27:18).

13. FAIR TRIAL
Everyone is to have free access to the courts and is to be afforded a fair trial (Ex 23:6,8; Lev 19:15; Dt 1:17; 10:17-18; 16:18-20; 17:8-13; 19:15-21).

14. SOCIAL ORDER
Every person's God-given place in the social order is to be honored (Ex 20:12; Dt 5:16; Ex 21:15, 17; 22:28; Lev 19:3, 32; 20:9; Dt 17:8-13; 21:15-21; 27:16).

15. LAW
No one shall be above the law, not even the king (Dt 17:18-20).

16. ANIMALS
Concern for the welfare of other creatures is to be extended to the animal world (Ex 23:5, 11; Lev 25:7, Dt 22:4, 6-7; 25:4).

frain from vowing, you will not incur guilt. 23 Whatever your lips utter you must diligently perform,
just as you have freely vowed to the
LORD your God with your own
mouth.
24 If you go into your neighbor's
vineyard, you may eat your fill of
grapes, as many as you wish, but
you shall not put any in a contain-
er.
25 If you go into your neighbor's
standing grain, you may pluck the
ears with your hand, but you shall
not put a sickle to your neighbor's
standing grain.

Laws concerning Marriage and Divorce

24 Suppose a man enters into
marriage with a woman,
but she does not please him because he finds something objec-
tionable about her, and so he
writes her a certificate of divorce,
puts it in her hand, and sends her
out of his house; she then leaves
his house 2 and goes off to become
another man's wife. 3 Then suppose the second man dislikes her,
writes her a bill of divorce, puts it
in her hand, and sends her out of
his house (or the second man who
married her dies); 4 her first husband, who sent her away, is not
permitted to take her again to be
his wife after she has been defiled;
for that would be abhorrent to the
LORD, and you shall not bring guilt
on the land that the LORD your God
is giving you as a possession.

Miscellaneous Laws

5 When a man is newly married,
he shall not go out with the army or
be charged with any related duty.
He shall be free at home one year,
to be happy with the wife whom he
has married.
6 No one shall take a mill or an
upper millstone in pledge, for that
would be taking a life in pledge.
7 If someone is caught kidnap-
ing another Israelite, enslaving or
selling the Israelite, then that kid-
naper shall die. So you shall purge
the evil from your midst.

23.25 Mt 12.1; Mk 2.23; Lk 6.1
24.1 Deut 22.13-21; Mt 5.31; 19.7; Mk 10.4
24.4 Jer 3.1
24.5 Deut 20.7
24.7 Ex 21.16

8 Guard against an outbreak of a
leprous[c] skin disease by being very
careful; you shall carefully observe
whatever the levitical priests instruct you, just as I have commanded them. 9 Remember what the
LORD your God did to Miriam on
your journey out of Egypt.
10 When you make your neighbor a loan of any kind, you shall not
go into the house to take the
pledge. 11 You shall wait outside,
while the person to whom you are
making the loan brings the pledge
out to you. 12 If the person is poor,
you shall not sleep in the garment
given you as[d] the pledge. 13 You
shall give the pledge back by sunset, so that your neighbor may
sleep in the cloak and bless you;
and it will be to your credit before
the LORD your God.
14 You shall not withhold the
wages of poor and needy laborers,
whether other Israelites or aliens
who reside in your land in one of
your towns. 15 You shall pay them
their wages daily before sunset, because they are poor and their liveli-
hood depends on them; otherwise
they might cry to the LORD against
you, and you would incur guilt.
16 Parents shall not be put to
death for their children, nor shall
children be put to death for their
parents; only for their own crimes
may persons be put to death.
17 You shall not deprive a resident alien or an orphan of justice;
you shall not take a widow's garment in pledge. 18 Remember that
you were a slave in Egypt and the
LORD your God redeemed you from
there; therefore I command you to
do this.
19 When you reap your harvest
in your field and forget a sheaf in
the field, you shall not go back to
get it; it shall be left for the alien,
the orphan, and the widow, so that
the LORD your God may bless you in
all your undertakings. 20 When you
beat your olive trees, do not strip

24.8 Lev 13.2; 14.2
24.9 Num 12.10
24.13 Ex 22.26; Deut 6.25
24.14 Lev 25.35-43; Deut 15.7-18
24.15 Lev 19.13; Jas 5.4; Deut 15.9
24.16 2 Kings 14.6; 2 Chr 25.4; Jer 31.29, 30; Ezek 18.20
24.17 Deut 1.17; 10.17; 16.19
24.18 Deut 16.12
24.19 Lev 19.9,10; 23.22
24.20 Lev 19.10

[c] A term for several skin diseases; precise meaning uncertain [d] Heb lacks *the garment given you as*

what is left; it shall be for the alien,
the orphan, and the widow.
21 When you gather the grapes
of your vineyard, do not glean what
is left; it shall be for the alien, the
orphan, and the widow. 22 Remember that you were a slave in the
land of Egypt; therefore I am commanding you to do this.

25 Suppose two persons have
a dispute and enter into litigation, and the judges decide between them, declaring one to be in
the right and the other to be in the
wrong. 2 If the one in the wrong deserves to be flogged, the judge shall
make that person lie down and be
beaten in his presence with the
number of lashes proportionate to
the offense. 3 Forty lashes may be
given but not more; if more lashes
than these are given, your neighbor
will be degraded in your sight.
4 You shall not muzzle an ox
while it is treading out the grain.

Levirate Marriage

5 When brothers reside together, and one of them dies and has no
son, the wife of the deceased shall
not be married outside the family
to a stranger. Her husband's brother shall go in to her, taking her in
marriage, and performing the duty
of a husband's brother to her, 6 and
the firstborn whom she bears shall
succeed to the name of the deceased brother, so that his name
may not be blotted out of Israel.
7 But if the man has no desire to
marry his brother's widow, then his
brother's widow shall go up to the
elders at the gate and say, "My husband's brother refuses to perpetuate his brother's name in Israel; he
will not perform the duty of a husband's brother to me." 8 Then the
elders of his town shall summon
him and speak to him. If he persists, saying, "I have no desire to
marry her," 9 then his brother's wife
shall go up to him in the presence
of the elders, pull his sandal off his
foot, spit in his face, and declare,
"This is what is done to the man
who does not build up his brother's
house." 10 Throughout Israel his
family shall be known as "the
house of him whose sandal was
pulled off."

Various Commands

11 If men get into a fight with
one another, and the wife of one
intervenes to rescue her husband
from the grip of his opponent by
reaching out and seizing his geni-
tals, 12 you shall cut off her hand;
show no pity.
13 You shall not have in your
bag two kinds of weights, large and
small. 14 You shall not have in your
house two kinds of measures, large
and small. 15 You shall have only a
full and honest weight; you shall
have only a full and honest measure, so that your days may be long
in the land that the LORD your God
is giving you. 16 For all who do such
things, all who act dishonestly, are
abhorrent to the LORD your God.
17 Remember what Amalek did
to you on your journey out of
Egypt, 18 how he attacked you on
the way, when you were faint and
weary, and struck down all who
lagged behind you; he did not fear
God. 19 Therefore when the LORD
your God has given you rest from
all your enemies on every hand, in
the land that the LORD your God is
giving you as an inheritance to possess, you shall blot out the remembrance of Amalek from under heav-
en; do not forget.

First Fruits and Tithes

26 When you have come into
the land that the LORD your
God is giving you as an inheritance
to possess, and you possess it, and
settle in it, 2 you shall take some of
the first of all the fruit of the
ground, which you harvest from the
land that the LORD your God is giving you, and you shall put it in a
basket and go to the place that the
LORD your God will choose as a
dwelling for his name. 3 You shall
go to the priest who is in office at
that time, and say to him, "Today I
declare to the LORD your God that I
have come into the land that the
LORD swore to our ancestors to give

24.22 v. 18
25.1 Deut 19.17; 1.16,17
25.3 2 Cor 11.24
25.4 1 Cor 9.9; 1 Tim 5.18
25.5ff Mt 22.24; Mk 12.19; Lk 20.28
25.6 Gen 38.9; Ruth 4.10
25.7 Ruth 4.1,2
25.8 Ruth 4.6
25.9f Ruth 4.7,11
25.13 Lev 19.35-37
25.16 Prov 11.1
25.17 Ex 17.8
25.19 1 Sam 15.2, 3
26.2 Ex 22.29; 23.16,19; Num 18.13

us." 4 When the priest takes the
basket from your hand and sets it
down before the altar of the LORD
your God, 5 you shall make this response before the LORD your God:
"A wandering Aramean was my ancestor; he went down into Egypt
and lived there as an alien, few in
number, and there he became a
great nation, mighty and populous.
6 When the Egyptians treated us
harshly and afflicted us, by imposing hard labor on us, 7 we cried to
the LORD, the God of our ancestors;
the LORD heard our voice and saw
our affliction, our toil, and our oppression. 8 The LORD brought us out
of Egypt with a mighty hand and an
outstretched arm, with a terrifying
display of power, and with signs
and wonders; 9 and he brought us
into this place and gave us this
land, a land flowing with milk and
honey. 10 So now I bring the first of
the fruit of the ground that you,
O LORD, have given me." You shall
set it down before the LORD your
God and bow down before the LORD
your God. 11 Then you, together
with the Levites and the aliens who
reside among you, shall celebrate
with all the bounty that the LORD
your God has given to you and to
your house.
12 When you have finished paying all the tithe of your produce in
the third year (which is the year of
the tithe), giving it to the Levites,
the aliens, the orphans, and the
widows, so that they may eat their
fill within your towns, 13 then you
shall say before the LORD your God:
"I have removed the sacred portion
from the house, and I have given it
to the Levites, the resident aliens,
the orphans, and the widows, in accordance with your entire commandment that you commanded
me; I have neither transgressed nor
forgotten any of your commandments: 14 I have not eaten of it
while in mourning; I have not removed any of it while I was unclean; and I have not offered any of
it to the dead. I have obeyed the
LORD my God, doing just as you
commanded me. 15 Look down
from your holy habitation, from
heaven, and bless your people Israel and the ground that you have giv-
en us, as you swore to our
ancestors—a land flowing with
milk and honey."

Concluding Exhortation

16 This very day the LORD your
God is commanding you to observe
these statutes and ordinances; so
observe them diligently with all
your heart and with all your soul.
17 Today you have obtained the
LORD's agreement: to be your God;
and for you to walk in his ways, to
keep his statutes, his commandments, and his ordinances, and to
obey him. 18 Today the LORD has obtained your agreement: to be his
treasured people, as he promised
you, and to keep his commandments; 19 for him to set you high
above all nations that he has made,
in praise and in fame and in honor;
and for you to be a people holy to
the LORD your God, as he promised.

The Inscribed Stones and Altar on Mount Ebal

27 Then Moses and the elders
of Israel charged all the
people as follows: Keep the entire
commandment that I am commanding you today. 2 On the day
that you cross over the Jordan into
the land that the LORD your God is
giving you, you shall set up large
stones and cover them with plaster.
3 You shall write on them all the
words of this law when you have
crossed over, to enter the land that
the LORD your God is giving you, a
land flowing with milk and honey,
as the LORD, the God of your ancestors, promised you. 4 So when you
have crossed over the Jordan, you
shall set up these stones, about
which I am commanding you today, on Mount Ebal, and you shall
cover them with plaster. 5 And you
shall build an altar there to the
LORD your God, an altar of stones
on which you have not used an iron
tool. 6 You must build the altar of
the LORD your God of unhewn[e]

26.5 Hos 12.12; Gen 43.1,2; 45.7,11; 46.27; Deut 10.22
26.6 Ex 1.11,14
26.7 Ex 2.23-25
26.8 Deut 4.34
26.9 Ex 3.8
26.11 Deut 12.7
26.12 Deut 14.28, 29; Heb 7.5, 9,10
26.13 Ps 119.141, 153,176
26.14 Lev 7.20; Hos 9.4
26.16 Deut 4.29
26.18 Deut 7.6
26.19 Deut 28.1; Ps 148.14; Deut 7.6
27.2 Josh 8.30-32
27.3 Deut 26.9
27.5 Ex 20.25; Josh 8.31

[e] Heb *whole*

stones. Then offer up burnt offerings on it to the LORD your God,
7 make sacrifices of well-being, and
eat them there, rejoicing before the
LORD your God. 8 You shall write on
the stones all the words of this law
very clearly.
9 Then Moses and the levitical
priests spoke to all Israel, saying:
Keep silence and hear, O Israel!
This very day you have become the
people of the LORD your God.
10 Therefore obey the LORD your
God, observing his commandments and his statutes that I am
commanding you today.

Twelve Curses

11 The same day Moses charged
the people as follows: 12 When you
have crossed over the Jordan, these
shall stand on Mount Gerizim for
the blessing of the people: Simeon,
Levi, Judah, Issachar, Joseph, and
Benjamin. 13 And these shall stand
on Mount Ebal for the curse: Reuben, Gad, Asher, Zebulun, Dan,
and Naphtali. 14 Then the Levites
shall declare in a loud voice to all
the Israelites:
15 "Cursed be anyone who
makes an idol or casts an image,
anything abhorrent to the LORD, the
work of an artisan, and sets it up in
secret." All the people shall respond, saying, "Amen!"
16 "Cursed be anyone who dishonors father or mother." All the
people shall say, "Amen!"
17 "Cursed be anyone who
moves a neighbor's boundary
marker." All the people shall say,
"Amen!"
18 "Cursed be anyone who misleads a blind person on the road."
All the people shall say, "Amen!"
19 "Cursed be anyone who deprives the alien, the orphan, and
the widow of justice." All the people shall say, "Amen!"
20 "Cursed be anyone who lies
with his father's wife, because he
has violated his father's rights."[f]
All the people shall say, "Amen!"
21 "Cursed be anyone who lies
with any animal." All the people
shall say, "Amen!"

27.9 Deut 26.18 **27.12** Josh 8.33-35 **27.15** Ex 20.4,23; 34.17 **27.16** Ex 21.17; Lev 20.9 **27.17** Lev 19.14 **27.18** Lev 19.14 **27.19** Deut 10.18; 24.17 **27.20** Lev 18.8; Deut 22.30 **27.21** Lev 18.23

27.22 Lev 18.9; 20.17 **27.23** Lev 20.14 **27.24** Lev 24.17; Num 35.31 **27.25** Ex 23.7,8 **27.26** Deut 28.15; Gal 3.10 **28.1** Deut 7.12-26; 26.19 **28.3** Gen 39.5; Ps 128.14 **28.4** Gen 49.25; Ps 107.38; Prov 10.22 **28.7** Lev 26.7,8 **28.9** Deut 7.6

22 "Cursed be anyone who lies
with his sister, whether the daughter of his father or the daughter of
his mother." All the people shall
say, "Amen!"
23 "Cursed be anyone who lies
with his mother-in-law." All the
people shall say, "Amen!"
24 "Cursed be anyone who
strikes down a neighbor in secret."
All the people shall say, "Amen!"
25 "Cursed be anyone who
takes a bribe to shed innocent
blood." All the people shall say,
"Amen!"
26 "Cursed be anyone who does
not uphold the words of this law by
observing them." All the people
shall say, "Amen!"

Blessings for Obedience

28 If you will only obey the
LORD your God, by diligently observing all his commandments
that I am commanding you today,
the LORD your God will set you high
above all the nations of the earth;
2 all these blessings shall come
upon you and overtake you, if you
obey the LORD your God:
3 Blessed shall you be in the
city, and blessed shall you be in the
field.
4 Blessed shall be the fruit of
your womb, the fruit of your
ground, and the fruit of your livestock, both the increase of your
cattle and the issue of your flock.
5 Blessed shall be your basket
and your kneading bowl.
6 Blessed shall you be when you
come in, and blessed shall you be
when you go out.
7 The LORD will cause your enemies who rise against you to be defeated before you; they shall come
out against you one way, and flee
before you seven ways. 8 The LORD
will command the blessing upon
you in your barns, and in all that
you undertake; he will bless you in
the land that the LORD your God is
giving you. 9 The LORD will establish
you as his holy people, as he has
sworn to you, if you keep the commandments of the LORD your God

[f] Heb *uncovered his father's skirt*

and walk in his ways. 10 All the peoples of the earth shall see that you
are called by the name of the LORD,
and they shall be afraid of you.
11 The LORD will make you abound
in prosperity, in the fruit of your
womb, in the fruit of your livestock,
and in the fruit of your ground in
the land that the LORD swore to
your ancestors to give you. 12 The
LORD will open for you his rich
storehouse, the heavens, to give
the rain of your land in its season
and to bless all your undertakings.
You will lend to many nations, but
you will not borrow. 13 The LORD
will make you the head, and not
the tail; you shall be only at the
top, and not at the bottom—if you
obey the commandments of the
LORD your God, which I am commanding you today, by diligently
observing them, 14 and if you do not
turn aside from any of the words
that I am commanding you today,
either to the right or to the left, following other gods to serve them.

Warnings against Disobedience

15 But if you will not obey the
LORD your God by diligently observing all his commandments and decrees, which I am commanding you
today, then all these curses shall
come upon you and overtake you:
16 Cursed shall you be in the
city, and cursed shall you be in the
field.
17 Cursed shall be your basket
and your kneading bowl.
18 Cursed shall be the fruit of
your womb, the fruit of your
ground, the increase of your cattle
and the issue of your flock.
19 Cursed shall you be when
you come in, and cursed shall you
be when you go out.
20 The LORD will send upon you
disaster, panic, and frustration in
everything you attempt to do, until
you are destroyed and perish
quickly, on account of the evil of
your deeds, because you have forsaken me. 21 The LORD will make
the pestilence cling to you until it
has consumed you off the land that
you are entering to possess. 22 The
LORD will afflict you with consumption, fever, inflammation, with fiery heat and drought, and with
blight and mildew; they shall pursue you until you perish. 23 The sky
over your head shall be bronze, and
the earth under you iron. 24 The
LORD will change the rain of your
land into powder, and only dust
shall come down upon you from
the sky until you are destroyed.
25 The LORD will cause you to be
defeated before your enemies; you
shall go out against them one way
and flee before them seven ways.
You shall become an object of horror to all the kingdoms of the earth.
26 Your corpses shall be food for every bird of the air and animal of the
earth, and there shall be no one to
frighten them away. 27 The LORD
will afflict you with the boils of
Egypt, with ulcers, scurvy, and
itch, of which you cannot be
healed. 28 The LORD will afflict you
with madness, blindness, and confusion of mind; 29 you shall grope
about at noon as blind people
grope in darkness, but you shall be
unable to find your way; and you
shall be continually abused and
robbed, without anyone to help.
30 You shall become engaged to a
woman, but another man shall lie
with her. You shall build a house,
but not live in it. You shall plant a
vineyard, but not enjoy its fruit.
31 Your ox shall be butchered before your eyes, but you shall not eat
of it. Your donkey shall be stolen in
front of you, and shall not be restored to you. Your sheep shall be
given to your enemies, without
anyone to help you. 32 Your sons
and daughters shall be given to another people, while you look on;
you will strain your eyes looking for
them all day but be powerless to do
anything. 33 A people whom you do
not know shall eat up the fruit of
your ground and of all your labors;
you shall be continually abused
and crushed, 34 and driven mad by
the sight that your eyes shall see.
35 The LORD will strike you on the
knees and on the legs with grievous
boils of which you cannot be

28.10 2 Chr 7.14
28.11 Deut 30.9
28.12 Lev 26.4; Deut 15.6
28.14 Deut 5.32
28.15 Lev 26.14; Josh 23.15; Mal 2.2
28.20 Deut 4.26
28.21 Lev 26.25; Jer 24.10
28.22 Lev 26.16; Am 4.9
28.23 Lev 26.19
28.25 Lev 26.17, 37; Jer 15.4
28.26 Jer 7.33; 16.4; 34.20
28.27 vv. 60,61
28.29 Job 5.14; Isa 59.10
28.30 Jer 8.10; 12.13; Am 5.11
28.32 v. 41
28.33 Jer 5.17
28.35 v. 27

healed, from the sole of your foot to
the crown of your head. 36 The LORD
will bring you, and the king whom
you set over you, to a nation that
neither you nor your ancestors
have known, where you shall serve
other gods, of wood and stone.
37 You shall become an object of
horror, a proverb, and a byword
among all the peoples where the
LORD will lead you.

38 You shall carry much seed
into the field but shall gather little
in, for the locust shall consume it.
39 You shall plant vineyards and
dress them, but you shall neither
drink the wine nor gather the
grapes, for the worm shall eat
them. 40 You shall have olive trees
throughout all your territory, but
you shall not anoint yourself with
the oil, for your olives shall drop
off. 41 You shall have sons and
daughters, but they shall not remain yours, for they shall go into
captivity. 42 All your trees and the
fruit of your ground the cicada
shall take over. 43 Aliens residing
among you shall ascend above you
higher and higher, while you shall
descend lower and lower. 44 They
shall lend to you but you shall not
lend to them; they shall be the
head and you shall be the tail.

45 All these curses shall come
upon you, pursuing and overtaking
you until you are destroyed, because you did not obey the LORD
your God, by observing the commandments and the decrees that
he commanded you. 46 They shall
be among you and your descendants as a sign and a portent forever.

47 Because you did not serve
the LORD your God joyfully and with
gladness of heart for the abundance of everything, 48 therefore
you shall serve your enemies whom
the LORD will send against you, in
hunger and thirst, in nakedness
and lack of everything. He will put
an iron yoke on your neck until he
has destroyed you. 49 The LORD will
bring a nation from far away, from
the end of the earth, to swoop
down on you like an eagle, a nation
whose language you do not understand, 50 a grim-faced nation showing no respect to the old or favor to
the young. 51 It shall consume the
fruit of your livestock and the fruit
of your ground until you are destroyed, leaving you neither grain,
wine, and oil, nor the increase of
your cattle and the issue of your
flock, until it has made you perish.
52 It shall besiege you in all your
towns until your high and fortified
walls, in which you trusted, come
down throughout your land; it shall
besiege you in all your towns
throughout the land that the LORD
your God has given you. 53 In the
desperate straits to which the enemy siege reduces you, you will eat
the fruit of your womb, the flesh of
your own sons and daughters
whom the LORD your God has given
you. 54 Even the most refined and
gentle of men among you will begrudge food to his own brother, to
the wife whom he embraces, and to
the last of his remaining children,
55 giving to none of them any of the
flesh of his children whom he is
eating, because nothing else remains to him, in the desperate
straits to which the enemy siege
will reduce you in all your towns.
56 She who is the most refined and
gentle among you, so gentle and refined that she does not venture to
set the sole of her foot on the
ground, will begrudge food to the
husband whom she embraces, to
her own son, and to her own daughter, 57 begrudging even the after-
birth that comes out from between
her thighs, and the children that
she bears, because she is eating
them in secret for lack of anything
else, in the desperate straits to
which the enemy siege will reduce
you in your towns.

58 If you do not diligently observe all the words of this law that
are written in this book, fearing
this glorious and awesome name,
the LORD your God, 59 then the LORD
will overwhelm both you and your
offspring with severe and lasting afflictions and grievous and lasting
maladies. 60 He will bring back

28.36 2 Kings 17.4, 6; 24.12,14; 25.7,11; Deut 4.28
28.37 Jer 24.9; Ps 44.14
28.38 Mic 6.15
28.41 v. 32
28.42 v. 38
28.43 v. 13
28.44 vv. 12,13
28.45 v. 15
28.47 Deut 32.15
28.48 Jer 28.13,14
28.49 Jer 5.15
28.51 v. 33
28.52 Jer 10.17, 18; Zeph 1.15, 16; Josh 1.4
28.53 Lev 26.29; Jer 19.9; Lam 2.20
28.56 v. 54
28.58 Ex 6.3
28.60 v. 27

upon you all the diseases of Egypt,
of which you were in dread, and
they shall cling to you. 61 Every other malady and affliction, even
though not recorded in the book of
this law, the LORD will inflict on you
until you are destroyed. 62 Although once you were as numerous
as the stars in heaven, you shall be
left few in number, because you
did not obey the LORD your God.
63 And just as the LORD took delight
in making you prosperous and numerous, so the LORD will take delight in bringing you to ruin and destruction; you shall be plucked off
the land that you are entering to
possess. 64 The LORD will scatter
you among all peoples, from one
end of the earth to the other; and
there you shall serve other gods, of
wood and stone, which neither you
nor your ancestors have known.
65 Among those nations you shall
find no ease, no resting place for
the sole of your foot. There the
LORD will give you a trembling
heart, failing eyes, and a languishing spirit. 66 Your life shall hang in
doubt before you; night and day
you shall be in dread, with no assurance of your life. 67 In the morning you shall say, "If only it were
evening!" and at evening you shall
say, "If only it were morning!"—
because of the dread that your
heart shall feel and the sights that
your eyes shall see. 68 The LORD will
bring you back in ships to Egypt, by
a route that I promised you would
never see again; and there you shall
offer yourselves for sale to your enemies as male and female slaves,
but there will be no buyer.

29 [g] These are the words of the
covenant that the LORD
commanded Moses to make with
the Israelites in the land of Moab,
in addition to the covenant that he
had made with them at Horeb.

The Covenant Renewed in Moab

2 [h] Moses summoned all Israel
and said to them: You have seen all
that the LORD did before your eyes
in the land of Egypt, to Pharaoh
and to all his servants and to all his
land, 3 the great trials that your
eyes saw, the signs, and those great
wonders. 4 But to this day the LORD
has not given you a mind to understand, or eyes to see, or ears to
hear. 5 I have led you forty years in
the wilderness. The clothes on your
back have not worn out, and the
sandals on your feet have not worn
out; 6 you have not eaten bread,
and you have not drunk wine or
strong drink— so that you may
know that I am the LORD your God.
7 When you came to this place,
King Sihon of Heshbon and King
Og of Bashan came out against us
for battle, but we defeated them.
8 We took their land and gave it as
an inheritance to the Reubenites,
the Gadites, and the half-tribe of
Manasseh. 9 Therefore diligently
observe the words of this covenant,
in order that you may succeed [i] in
everything that you do.

10 You stand assembled today,
all of you, before the LORD your
God—the leaders of your tribes, [j]
your elders, and your officials, all
the men of Israel, 11 your children,
your women, and the aliens who
are in your camp, both those who
cut your wood and those who draw
your water— 12 to enter into the
covenant of the LORD your God,
sworn by an oath, which the LORD
your God is making with you today;
13 in order that he may establish
you today as his people, and that
he may be your God, as he promised you and as he swore to your
ancestors, to Abraham, to Isaac,
and to Jacob. 14 I am making this
covenant, sworn by an oath, not
only with you who stand here with
us today before the LORD our God,
15 but also with those who are not
here with us today. 16 You know
how we lived in the land of Egypt,
and how we came through the
midst of the nations through which
you passed. 17 You have seen their
detestable things, the filthy idols of
wood and stone, of silver and gold,
that were among them. 18 It may be

28.61 Deut 4.25, 26
28.62 Deut 4.27; 10.22
28.63 Jer 12.14; 45.4
28.64 Deut 4.27, 28
28.65 Lev 26.16, 36
28.67 v. 34
29.1 Deut 5.2,3
29.2 Ex 19.4
29.4 Isa 6.9,10; Acts 28.26, 27; Eph 4.18
29.5 Deut 8.4
29.6 Deut 8.3
29.7 Num 21.21-24, 33-35; Deut 2.32; 3.1
29.8 Num 32.33; Deut 3.12, 13
29.9 Deut 4.6; Josh 1.7
29.11 Josh 9.21, 23,27
29.13 Deut 28.9; Ex 6.7; Gen 17.7
29.17 Deut 28.26
29.18 Deut 11.16; Heb 12.15

g Ch 28.69 in Heb
h Ch 29.1 in Heb
i Or *deal wisely*
j Gk Syr: Heb *your leaders, your tribes*

that there is among you a man or
woman, or a family or tribe, whose
heart is already turning away from
the LORD our God to serve the gods
of those nations. It may be that
there is among you a root sprouting
poisonous and bitter growth. 19 All
who hear the words of this oath and
bless themselves, thinking in their
hearts, "We are safe even though
we go our own stubborn ways"
(thus bringing disaster on moist
and dry alike)[k]— 20 the LORD will
be unwilling to pardon them, for
the LORD's anger and passion will
smoke against them. All the curses
written in this book will descend
on them, and the LORD will blot out
their names from under heaven.
21 The LORD will single them out
from all the tribes of Israel for calamity, in accordance with all the
curses of the covenant written in
this book of the law. 22 The next
generation, your children who rise
up after you, as well as the foreigner who comes from a distant country, will see the devastation of that
land and the afflictions with which
the LORD has afflicted it— 23 all its
soil burned out by sulfur and salt,
nothing planted, nothing sprouting, unable to support any vegetation, like the destruction of Sodom
and Gomorrah, Admah and Zeboiim, which the LORD destroyed in his
fierce anger— 24 they and indeed
all the nations will wonder, "Why
has the LORD done thus to this
land? What caused this great display of anger?" 25 They will con-
clude, "It is because they abandoned the covenant of the LORD,
the God of their ancestors, which
he made with them when he
brought them out of the land of
Egypt. 26 They turned and served
other gods, worshiping them, gods
whom they had not known and
whom he had not allotted to them;
27 so the anger of the LORD was kindled against that land, bringing on
it every curse written in this book.
28 The LORD uprooted them from
their land in anger, fury, and great
wrath, and cast them into another
land, as is now the case." 29 The secret things belong to the LORD our
God, but the revealed things belong to us and to our children forever, to observe all the words of
this law.

God's Fidelity Assured

30 When all these things have
happened to you, the blessings and the curses that I have set
before you, if you call them to mind
among all the nations where the
LORD your God has driven you, 2 and
return to the LORD your God, and
you and your children obey him
with all your heart and with all your
soul, just as I am commanding you
today, 3 then the LORD your God will
restore your fortunes and have
compassion on you, gathering you
again from all the peoples among
whom the LORD your God has scattered you. 4 Even if you are exiled to
the ends of the world,[l] from there
the LORD your God will gather you,
and from there he will bring you
back. 5 The LORD your God will
bring you into the land that your
ancestors possessed, and you will
possess it; he will make you more
prosperous and numerous than
your ancestors.
6 Moreover, the LORD your God
will circumcise your heart and the
heart of your descendants, so that
you will love the LORD your God
with all your heart and with all your
soul, in order that you may live.
7 The LORD your God will put all
these curses on your enemies and
on the adversaries who took advantage of you. 8 Then you shall again
obey the LORD, observing all his
commandments that I am commanding you today, 9 and the LORD
your God will make you abundantly prosperous in all your undertakings, in the fruit of your body, in
the fruit of your livestock, and in
the fruit of your soil. For the LORD
will again take delight in prospering you, just as he delighted in
prospering your ancestors, 10 when
you obey the LORD your God by observing his commandments and

29.20 Ps 74.1; 79.5; Deut 9.14; Ex 32.33
29.21 Mt 24.51
29.22 Jer 19.8
29.23 Gen 19.24; Isa 34.9; Jer 20.16
29.24 Jer 22.8,9
29.28 1 Kings 14.15; 2 Chr 7.20
30.1 vv. 15,19; Deut 11.26; 28.64; 29.28
30.2 Deut 4.29, 30
30.3 Jer 29.14; 32.37
30.4 Neh 1.9; Isa 43.6
30.6 Jer 32.39
30.9 Deut 28.11; Jer 32.41

[k] Meaning of Heb uncertain [l] Heb *of heaven*

decrees that are written in this
book of the law, because you turn
to the LORD your God with all your
heart and with all your soul.

Exhortation to Choose Life

11 Surely, this commandment
that I am commanding you today is
not too hard for you, nor is it too far
away. 12 It is not in heaven, that you
should say, "Who will go up to
heaven for us, and get it for us so
that we may hear it and observe
it?" 13 Neither is it beyond the sea,
that you should say, "Who will
cross to the other side of the sea for
us, and get it for us so that we may
hear it and observe it?" 14 No, the
word is very near to you; it is in your
mouth and in your heart for you to
observe.

15 See, I have set before you today life and prosperity, death and
adversity. 16 If you obey the commandments of the LORD your God[m]
that I am commanding you today,
by loving the LORD your God, walking in his ways, and observing his
commandments, decrees, and ordinances, then you shall live and
become numerous, and the LORD
your God will bless you in the land
that you are entering to possess.
17 But if your heart turns away and
you do not hear, but are led astray
to bow down to other gods and
serve them, 18 I declare to you today
that you shall perish; you shall not
live long in the land that you are
crossing the Jordan to enter and
possess. 19 I call heaven and earth
to witness against you today that I
have set before you life and death,
blessings and curses. Choose life
so that you and your descendants
may live, 20 loving the LORD your
God, obeying him, and holding fast
to him; for that means life to you
and length of days, so that you may
live in the land that the LORD swore
to give to your ancestors, to Abraham, to Isaac, and to Jacob.

Joshua Becomes Moses' Successor

31 When Moses had finished
speaking all[n] these words
to all Israel, 2 he said to them: "I am
now one hundred twenty years old.
I am no longer able to get about,
and the LORD has told me, 'You
shall not cross over this Jordan.'
3 The LORD your God himself will
cross over before you. He will destroy these nations before you, and
you shall dispossess them. Joshua
also will cross over before you, as
the LORD promised. 4 The LORD will
do to them as he did to Sihon and
Og, the kings of the Amorites, and
to their land, when he destroyed
them. 5 The LORD will give them
over to you and you shall deal with
them in full accord with the command that I have given to you. 6 Be
strong and bold; have no fear or
dread of them, because it is the
LORD your God who goes with you;
he will not fail you or forsake you."

7 Then Moses summoned Josh-
ua and said to him in the sight of all
Israel: "Be strong and bold, for you
are the one who will go with this
people into the land that the LORD
has sworn to their ancestors to give
them; and you will put them in possession of it. 8 It is the LORD who
goes before you. He will be with
you; he will not fail you or forsake
you. Do not fear or be dismayed."

The Law to Be Read Every Seventh Year

9 Then Moses wrote down this
law, and gave it to the priests, the
sons of Levi, who carried the ark of
the covenant of the LORD, and to all
the elders of Israel. 10 Moses commanded them: "Every seventh
year, in the scheduled year of remission, during the festival of
booths,[o] 11 when all Israel comes
to appear before the LORD your God
at the place that he will choose,
you shall read this law before all Israel in their hearing. 12 Assemble
the people—men, women, and
children, as well as the aliens residing in your towns—so that they
may hear and learn to fear the LORD

30.11 Isa 45.19 **30.12** Rom 10.6-8 **30.15** vv. 1,19 **30.18** Deut 4.26 **30.19** Deut 4.26; v. 1 **30.20** Deut 6.5; 10.20; Ps 27.1; Jn 11.25

31.2 Deut 34.7; 3.27 **31.3** Deut 9.3; 3.28 **31.5** Deut 7.2 **31.6** Josh 10.25; Deut 1.29; 20.4; Heb 13.5 **31.7** Deut 1.38; 3.28 **31.8** v. 6 **31.9** v. 25; Num 4.15 **31.10** Deut 15.1; Lev 23.34 **31.11** Deut 16.16; Josh 8.34, 35 **31.12** Deut 4.10

[m] Gk: Heb lacks *If you obey the commandments of the LORD your God*
[n] Q Ms Gk: MT *Moses went and spoke*
[o] Or *tabernacles*; Heb *succoth*

your God and to observe diligently
all the words of this law, 13 and so
that their children, who have not
known it, may hear and learn to
fear the LORD your God, as long as
you live in the land that you are
crossing over the Jordan to possess."

Moses and Joshua Receive God's Charge

14 The LORD said to Moses,
"Your time to die is near; call Joshua and present yourselves in the
tent of meeting, so that I may commission him." So Moses and Joshua went and presented themselves
in the tent of meeting, 15 and the
LORD appeared at the tent in a pillar
of cloud; the pillar of cloud stood at
the entrance to the tent.
16 The LORD said to Moses,
"Soon you will lie down with your
ancestors. Then this people will
begin to prostitute themselves to
the foreign gods in their midst, the
gods of the land into which they are
going; they will forsake me, breaking my covenant that I have made
with them. 17 My anger will be kindled against them in that day. I will
forsake them and hide my face
from them; they will become easy
prey, and many terrible troubles
will come upon them. In that day
they will say, 'Have not these troubles come upon us because our
God is not in our midst?' 18 On that
day I will surely hide my face on
account of all the evil they have
done by turning to other gods.
19 Now therefore write this song,
and teach it to the Israelites; put it
in their mouths, in order that this
song may be a witness for me
against the Israelites. 20 For when I
have brought them into the land
flowing with milk and honey,
which I promised on oath to their
ancestors, and they have eaten
their fill and grown fat, they will
turn to other gods and serve them,
despising me and breaking my covenant. 21 And when many terrible
troubles come upon them, this
song will confront them as a witness, because it will not be lost

31.13 Deut 11.2; Ps 78.6,7
31.14 Deut 32.49, 50; v. 23
31.15 Ex 33.9
31.16 Judg 2.11, 12; 10.6,13
31.17 Judg 2.14; 6.13; Deut 32.20; Num 14.42
31.20 Deut 6.10-12; 32.15-17; v. 16
31.21 v. 17; Hos 5.3
31.22 v. 19
31.23 v. 7; Josh 1.6
31.25 v. 9
31.26 v. 19
31.27 Deut 9.6,24
31.28 Deut 4.26
31.29 Deut 32.5; 28.15
32.1 Isa 1.2
32.2 Isa 55.10,11

from the mouths of their descendants. For I know what they are inclined to do even now, before I
have brought them into the land
that I promised them on oath."
22 That very day Moses wrote this
song and taught it to the Israelites.
23 Then the LORD commis-
sioned Joshua son of Nun and said,
"Be strong and bold, for you shall
bring the Israelites into the land
that I promised them; I will be with
you."
24 When Moses had finished
writing down in a book the words of
this law to the very end, 25 Moses
commanded the Levites who carried the ark of the covenant of the
LORD, saying, 26 "Take this book of
the law and put it beside the ark of
the covenant of the LORD your God;
let it remain there as a witness
against you. 27 For I know well how
rebellious and stubborn you are. If
you already have been so rebellious
toward the LORD while I am still
alive among you, how much more
after my death! 28 Assemble to me
all the elders of your tribes and
your officials, so that I may recite
these words in their hearing and
call heaven and earth to witness
against them. 29 For I know that after my death you will surely act corruptly, turning aside from the way
that I have commanded you. In
time to come trouble will befall
you, because you will do what is
evil in the sight of the LORD, provoking him to anger through the work
of your hands."

The Song of Moses

30 Then Moses recited the
words of this song, to the very end,
in the hearing of the whole assembly of Israel:

32 Give ear, O heavens, and
I will speak;
let the earth hear the
words of my mouth.
2 May my teaching drop like
the rain,
my speech condense like
the dew;
like gentle rain on grass,

like showers on new growth.
3 For I will proclaim the name of the LORD;
ascribe greatness to our God!
4 The Rock, his work is perfect,
and all his ways are just.
A faithful God, without deceit,
just and upright is he;
5 yet his degenerate children have dealt falsely with him,[p]
a perverse and crooked generation.
6 Do you thus repay the LORD,
O foolish and senseless people?
Is not he your father, who created you,
who made you and established you?
7 Remember the days of old,
consider the years long past;
ask your father, and he will inform you;
your elders, and they will tell you.
8 When the Most High[q] apportioned the nations,
when he divided humankind,
he fixed the boundaries of the peoples
according to the number of the gods;[r]
9 the LORD's own portion was his people,
Jacob his allotted share.

10 He sustained[s] him in a desert land,
in a howling wilderness waste;
he shielded him, cared for him,
guarded him as the apple of his eye.
11 As an eagle stirs up its nest,
and hovers over its young;
as it spreads its wings, takes them up,
and bears them aloft on its pinions,
12 the LORD alone guided him;
no foreign god was with him.
13 He set him atop the heights of the land,
and fed him with[t] produce of the field;
he nursed him with honey from the crags,
with oil from flinty rock;
14 curds from the herd, and milk from the flock,
with fat of lambs and rams;
Bashan bulls and goats,
together with the choicest wheat—
you drank fine wine from the blood of grapes.
15 Jacob ate his fill;[u]
Jeshurun grew fat, and kicked.
You grew fat, bloated, and gorged!
He abandoned God who made him,
and scoffed at the Rock of his salvation.
16 They made him jealous with strange gods,
with abhorrent things they provoked him.
17 They sacrificed to demons, not God,
to deities they had never known,
to new ones recently arrived,
whom your ancestors had not feared.
18 You were unmindful of the Rock that bore you;[v]
you forgot the God who gave you birth.

19 The LORD saw it, and was jealous[w]
he spurned[x] his sons and daughters.

32.3 Ex 33.19; Deut 3.24 **32.4** vv. 15,18, 30; Deut 7.9; Ps 92.15 **32.5** Deut 31.29; Lk 9.41 **32.6** Deut 1.31 **32.7** Ex 13.14 **32.8** Gen 11.8; Acts 17.26 **32.9** 1 Kings 8.51, 53; Jer 10.16 **32.10** Jer 2.6; Zech 2.8 **32.11** Ex 19.4; Isa 31.5 **32.12** v. 39 **32.13** Isa 58.14; Job 29.6 **32.14** Ps 147.14 **32.15** Deut 33.5, 26; Isa 1.4; vv. 6,4 **32.16** Ps 78.58; 1 Cor 10.22 **32.17** Ps 106.37; Deut 28.64; Judg 5.8 **32.18** Isa 17.10; Ps 106.21 **32.19** Ps 106.40; Jer 44.21-23

[p] Meaning of Heb uncertain [q] Traditional rendering of Heb *Elyon* [r] Q Ms Compare Gk Tg: MT *the Israelites* [s] Sam Gk Compare Tg: MT *found* [t] Sam Gk Syr Tg: MT *he ate* [u] Q Mss Sam Gk: MT lacks *Jacob ate his fill* [v] Or *that begot you* [w] Q Mss Gk: MT lacks *was jealous* [x] Cn: Heb *he spurned because of provocation*

20 He said: I will hide my face
from them,
I will see what their end
will be;
for they are a perverse
generation,
children in whom there is
no faithfulness.
21 They made me jealous with
what is no god,
provoked me with their
idols.
So I will make them jealous
with what is no people,
provoke them with a
foolish nation.
22 For a fire is kindled by my
anger,
and burns to the depths of
Sheol;
it devours the earth and its
increase,
and sets on fire the
foundations of the
mountains.
23 I will heap disasters upon
them,
spend my arrows against
them:
24 wasting hunger,
burning consumption,
bitter pestilence.
The teeth of beasts I will
send against them,
with venom of things
crawling in the dust.
25 In the street the sword shall
bereave,
and in the chambers terror,
for young man and woman
alike,
nursing child and old gray
head.
26 I thought to scatter them[y]
and blot out the memory of
them from humankind;
27 but I feared provocation by
the enemy,
for their adversaries might
misunderstand
and say, "Our hand is
triumphant;
it was not the LORD who
did all this."
28 They are a nation void of
sense;
there is no understanding
in them.
29 If they were wise, they would
understand this;
they would discern what
the end would be.
30 How could one have routed a
thousand,
and two put a myriad to
flight,
unless their Rock had sold
them,
the LORD had given them
up?
31 Indeed their rock is not like
our Rock;
our enemies are fools.[y]
32 Their vine comes from the
vinestock of Sodom,
from the vineyards of
Gomorrah;
their grapes are grapes of
poison,
their clusters are bitter;
33 their wine is the poison of
serpents,
the cruel venom of asps.

34 Is not this laid up in store
with me,
sealed up in my treasuries?
35 Vengeance is mine, and
recompense,
for the time when their
foot shall slip;
because the day of their
calamity is at hand,
their doom comes swiftly.

36 Indeed the LORD will
vindicate his people,
have compassion on his
servants,
when he sees that their
power is gone,
neither bond nor free
remaining.
37 Then he will say: Where are
their gods,
the rock in which they took
refuge,
38 who ate the fat of their
sacrifices,
and drank the wine of their
libations?

32.20 Deut 31.17, 29; v. 5
32.21 v. 16; Rom 10.19
32.22 Jer 15.14
32.23 Deut 29.21; Ezek 5.16
32.24 Deut 28.22; Lev 26.22; v. 33
32.25 Ezek 7.15; 2 Chr 36.17
32.26 Deut 4.27; Ps 34.16
32.27 Deut 9.26-28; Isa 10.13
32.29 Ps 81.13
32.30 Lev 26.7,8; v. 4
32.31 1 Sam 2.2; 4.8
32.33 Ps 58.4
32.34 Hos 13.12
32.35 Rom 12.19; Heb 10.30
32.36 Ps 135.14; 106.45; Judg 2.18; Joel 2.14
32.37 Jer 2.28

y Gk: Meaning of Heb uncertain

Let them rise up and help you,
let them be your protection!
39 See now that I, even I, am he;
there is no god besides me.
I kill and I make alive;
I wound and I heal;
and no one can deliver from my hand.
40 For I lift up my hand to heaven,
and swear: As I live forever,
41 when I whet my flashing sword,
and my hand takes hold on judgment;
I will take vengeance on my adversaries,
and will repay those who hate me.
42 I will make my arrows drunk with blood,
and my sword shall devour flesh—
with the blood of the slain and the captives,
from the long-haired enemy.

43 Praise, O heavens,[z] his people,
worship him, all you gods![a]
For he will avenge the blood of his children,[b]
and take vengeance on his adversaries;
he will repay those who hate him,[a]
and cleanse the land for his people.[c]

44 Moses came and recited all
the words of this song in the hearing of the people, he and Joshua[d]
son of Nun. 45 When Moses had finished reciting all these words to all
Israel, 46 he said to them: "Take to
heart all the words that I am giving
in witness against you today; give
them as a command to your children, so that they may diligently
observe all the words of this law.
47 This is no trifling matter for you,
but rather your very life; through it
you may live long in the land that
you are crossing over the Jordan to
possess."

Moses' Death Foretold

48 On that very day the LORD addressed Moses as follows: 49 "Ascend this mountain of the Abarim,
Mount Nebo, which is in the land
of Moab, across from Jericho, and
view the land of Canaan, which I
am giving to the Israelites for a possession; 50 you shall die there on
the mountain that you ascend and
shall be gathered to your kin, as
your brother Aaron died on Mount
Hor and was gathered to his kin;
51 because both of you broke faith
with me among the Israelites at the
waters of Meribath-kadesh in the
wilderness of Zin, by failing to
maintain my holiness among the
Israelites. 52 Although you may
view the land from a distance, you
shall not enter it—the land that I
am giving to the Israelites."

Moses' Final Blessing on Israel

33 This is the blessing with
which Moses, the man of
God, blessed the Israelites before
his death. 2 He said:

The LORD came from Sinai,
and dawned from Seir upon us;[e]
he shone forth from Mount Paran.
With him were myriads of holy ones;[f]
at his right, a host of his own.[g]
3 Indeed, O favorite among[h] peoples,
all his holy ones were in your charge;
they marched at your heels,
accepted direction from you.
4 Moses charged us with the law,

32.39 Isa 41.4; Ps 50.22 **32.41** Ezek 21.9, 10 **32.42** Jer 46.10 **32.43** Rom 15.10; Rev 19.2; Ps 85.1 **32.46** Deut 6.6; Ezek 40.4 **32.47** Deut 30.20 **32.49** Num 27.12-14 **32.51** Num 20.11-13; 27.14 **32.52** Deut 34.1-3; 1.37 **33.1** Josh 14.6 **33.2** Hab 3.3; Dan 7.10; Acts 7.53; Gal 3.19; Rev 5.11 **33.3** Hos 11.1; Deut 14.2 **33.4** Jn 1.17; Ps 119.111

z Q Ms Gk: MT *nations* a Q Ms Gk: MT lacks this line b Q Ms Gk: MT *his servants* c Q Ms Sam Gk Vg: MT *his land his people* d Sam Gk Syr Vg: MT *Hoshea* e Gk Syr Vg Compare Tg: Heb *upon them* f Cn Compare Gk Sam Syr Vg: MT *He came from Ribeboth-kodesh,* g Cn Compare Gk: meaning of Heb uncertain h Or *O lover of the*

as a possession for the assembly of Jacob.
5 There arose a king in Jeshurun,
when the leaders of the people assembled—
the united tribes of Israel.

6 May Reuben live, and not die out,
even though his numbers are few.

7 And this he said of Judah:
O LORD, give heed to Judah,
and bring him to his people;
strengthen his hands for him,[i]
and be a help against his adversaries.

8 And of Levi he said:
Give to Levi[j] your Thummim,
and your Urim to your loyal one,
whom you tested at Massah,
with whom you contended at the waters of Meribah;
9 who said of his father and mother,
"I regard them not";
he ignored his kin,
and did not acknowledge his children.
For they observed your word,
and kept your covenant.
10 They teach Jacob your ordinances,
and Israel your law;
they place incense before you,
and whole burnt offerings on your altar.
11 Bless, O LORD, his substance,
and accept the work of his hands;
crush the loins of his adversaries,
of those that hate him, so that they do not rise again.

12 Of Benjamin he said:
The beloved of the LORD rests in safety—
the High God[k] surrounds him all day long—
the beloved[l] rests between his shoulders.

13 And of Joseph he said:
Blessed by the LORD be his land,
with the choice gifts of heaven above,
and of the deep that lies beneath;
14 with the choice fruits of the sun,
and the rich yield of the months;
15 with the finest produce of the ancient mountains,
and the abundance of the everlasting hills;
16 with the choice gifts of the earth and its fullness,
and the favor of the one who dwells on Sinai.[m]
Let these come on the head of Joseph,
on the brow of the prince among his brothers.
17 A firstborn[n] bull—majesty is his!
His horns are the horns of a wild ox;
with them he gores the peoples,
driving them to[o] the ends of the earth;
such are the myriads of Ephraim,
such the thousands of Manasseh.

18 And of Zebulun he said:
Rejoice, Zebulun, in your going out;
and Issachar, in your tents.
19 They call peoples to the mountain;
there they offer the right sacrifices;

33.7 Gen 49.8-12 **33.8** Ex 28.30; 17.7 **33.9** Ex 32.26-29 **33.10** Deut 31.9-13; Ex 30.7,8; Ps 51.19 **33.11** 2 Sam 24.23; Ps 20.3

33.13 Gen 49.25; 27.28 **33.15** Gen 49.26 **33.16** Ex 3.2,4; Acts 7.30,35 **33.17** Num 23.22; Ps 44.5 **33.18** Gen 49.13-15 **33.19** Isa 2.3; Ps 4.5

[i] Cn: Heb *with his hands he contended*
[j] Q Ms Gk: MT lacks *Give to Levi*
[k] Heb *above him*
[l] Heb *he*
[m] Cn: Heb *in the bush*
[n] Q Ms Gk Syr Vg: MT *His firstborn*
[o] Cn: Heb *the peoples, together*

for they suck the affluence of
the seas
and the hidden treasures of
the sand.

20 And of Gad he said:
Blessed be the enlargement
of Gad!
Gad lives like a lion;
he tears at arm and scalp.
21 He chose the best for
himself,
for there a commander's
allotment was reserved;
he came at the head of the
people,
he executed the justice of
the LORD,
and his ordinances for
Israel.

22 And of Dan he said:
Dan is a lion's whelp
that leaps forth from
Bashan.

23 And of Naphtali he said:
O Naphtali, sated with favor,
full of the blessing of the
LORD,
possess the west and the
south.

24 And of Asher he said:
Most blessed of sons be
Asher;
may he be the favorite of
his brothers,
and may he dip his foot in
oil.
25 Your bars are iron and
bronze;
and as your days, so is your
strength.

26 There is none like God,
O Jeshurun,
who rides through the
heavens to your help,
majestic through the skies.
27 He subdues the ancient
gods,[p]
shatters[q] the forces of
old;[r]
he drove out the enemy
before you,
and said, "Destroy!"

33.20 Gen 49.19 **33.21** Num 32.1-5, 31,32; Josh 4.12; 22.1-3 **33.22** Gen 49.16 **33.23** Gen 49.21 **33.24** Gen 49.20; Job 29;6 **33.25** Deut 4.40; 32.49 **33.26** Ex 15.11; Ps 68.33,34 **33.27** Ps 90.1,2; Josh 24.18

33.28 Num 23.9; Gen 27.28 **33.29** Ps 144.15; 2 Sam 7.23; Ps 18.14; Deut 32.13 **34.1** Deut 32.49, 52 **34.4** Gen 12.7; 28.13 **34.5** Deut 32.50; Josh 1.1,2 **34.7** Deut 31.2 **34.9** Isa 11.2; Num 27.18, 23

28 So Israel lives in safety,
untroubled is Jacob's
abode[s]
in a land of grain and wine,
where the heavens drop
down dew.
29 Happy are you, O Israel! Who
is like you,
a people saved by the LORD,
the shield of your help,
and the sword of your
triumph!
Your enemies shall come
fawning to you,
and you shall tread on
their backs.

Moses Dies and Is Buried in the Land of Moab

34 Then Moses went up from
the plains of Moab to
Mount Nebo, to the top of Pisgah,
which is opposite Jericho, and the
LORD showed him the whole land:
Gilead as far as Dan, 2 all Naphtali,
the land of Ephraim and Manasseh, all the land of Judah as far as
the Western Sea, 3 the Negeb, and
the Plain—that is, the valley of Jericho, the city of palm trees—as far
as Zoar. 4 The LORD said to him,
"This is the land of which I swore to
Abraham, to Isaac, and to Jacob,
saying, 'I will give it to your descendants'; I have let you see it with
your eyes, but you shall not cross
over there." 5 Then Moses, the servant of the LORD, died there in the
land of Moab, at the LORD's command. 6 He was buried in a valley in
the land of Moab, opposite Beth-
peor, but no one knows his burial
place to this day. 7 Moses was one
hundred twenty years old when he
died; his sight was unimpaired and
his vigor had not abated. 8 The Israelites wept for Moses in the plains
of Moab thirty days; then the period of mourning for Moses was ended.
9 Joshua son of Nun was full of
the spirit of wisdom, because Moses had laid his hands on him; and

[p] Or *The eternal God is a dwelling place* [q] Cn: Heb *from underneath* [r] Or *the everlasting arms* [s] Or *fountain*

the Israelites obeyed him, doing as
the LORD had commanded Moses.
10 Never since has there arisen
a prophet in Israel like Moses,
whom the LORD knew face to face.
11 He was unequaled for all the
signs and wonders that the LORD
sent him to perform in the land of
Egypt, against Pharaoh and all his
servants and his entire land, 12 and
for all the mighty deeds and all the
terrifying displays of power that
Moses performed in the sight of all
Israel.

34.10 Num 12.6,8
34.11 Deut 4.34

Joshua

Title and Background

This book is named after its leading character, Joshua, whom God named as the leader of Israel before Moses' death. Where Deuteronomy ends the book of Joshua begins, with the tribes still camped on the east side of the Jordan River, ready to enter Canaan.

Author and Date of Writing

The earliest Jewish traditions (Talmud) claim that Joshua wrote his own book, except the final section about his funeral, which is assigned to Eleazar son of Aaron. Others think that Samuel may have shaped or compiled the materials of the book. However, we have no sure knowledge of who the author was. The book of Joshua was probably written, at least in its early form, sometime before 1000 B.C.

Theme and Message

The theme of this book is the establishment of the nation of Israel in the promised land. With God's help the people crossed the Jordan River and took possession of all the main areas of Canaan. Toward the end of the book Joshua reminded the people of God's covenant promises to them and instructed them to keep on loving and obeying God.

Outline

I. Preparation for Possession of Canaan (1.1–5.12)
II. The Conquest of Canaan (5.13–12.24)
III. The Distribution of Land to Tribes (13.1–21.45)
IV. Farewell and Death of Joshua (22.1–24.33)

God's Commission to Joshua

1 After the death of Moses the
servant of the LORD, the LORD
spoke to Joshua son of Nun, Moses' assistant, saying, 2 "My servant
Moses is dead. Now proceed to
cross the Jordan, you and all this
people, into the land that I am giving to them, to the Israelites. 3 Every place that the sole of your foot
will tread upon I have given to you,
as I promised to Moses. 4 From the
wilderness and the Lebanon as far
as the great river, the river Euphrates, all the land of the Hittites, to
the Great Sea in the west shall be
your territory. 5 No one shall be
able to stand against you all the
days of your life. As I was with Moses, so I will be with you; I will not
fail you or forsake you. 6 Be strong
and courageous; for you shall put
this people in possession of the
land that I swore to their ancestors
to give them. 7 Only be strong and
very courageous, being careful to
act in accordance with all the law
that my servant Moses commanded you; do not turn from it to the
right hand or to the left, so that you
may be successful wherever you go.
8 This book of the law shall not depart out of your mouth; you shall
meditate on it day and night, so
that you may be careful to act in
accordance with all that is written
in it. For then you shall make your
way prosperous, and then you shall
be successful. 9 I hereby command
you: Be strong and courageous; do
not be frightened or dismayed, for
the LORD your God is with you
wherever you go."

1.2 Num 12.7; Deut 34.5; v. 11
1.3 Deut 11.24
1.4 Gen 15.18
1.5 Deut 7.24; 31.6-8
1.7 Deut 5.32; 28.14
1.8 Deut 17.8,9; Ps 1.1-3
1.9 Deut 31.7,8, 23; Jer 1.8
1.11 Joel 3.2

Preparations for the Invasion

10 Then Joshua commanded
the officers of the people, 11 "Pass

through the camp, and command
the people: 'Prepare your provisions; for in three days you are to
cross over the Jordan, to go in to
take possession of the land that the
LORD your God gives you to possess.' "
12 To the Reubenites, the Gadites, and the half-tribe of Manasseh
Joshua said, 13 "Remember the
word that Moses the servant of the
LORD commanded you, saying, 'The
LORD your God is providing you a
place of rest, and will give you this
land.' 14 Your wives, your little
ones, and your livestock shall remain in the land that Moses gave
you beyond the Jordan. But all the
warriors among you shall cross over
armed before your kindred and
shall help them, 15 until the LORD
gives rest to your kindred as well as
to you, and they too take possession of the land that the LORD your
God is giving them. Then you shall
return to your own land and take
possession of it, the land that Moses the servant of the LORD gave you
beyond the Jordan to the east."
16 They answered Joshua: "All
that you have commanded us we
will do, and wherever you send us
we will go. 17 Just as we obeyed Moses in all things, so we will obey
you. Only may the LORD your God
be with you, as he was with Moses!
18 Whoever rebels against your orders and disobeys your words,
whatever you command, shall be
put to death. Only be strong and
courageous."

Spies Sent to Jericho

2 Then Joshua son of Nun sent
two men secretly from Shittim
as spies, saying, "Go, view the land,
especially Jericho." So they went,
and entered the house of a prostitute whose name was Rahab, and
spent the night there. 2 The king of
Jericho was told, "Some Israelites
have come here tonight to search
out the land." 3 Then the king of
Jericho sent orders to Rahab,
"Bring out the men who have come
to you, who entered your house, for
they have come only to search out
the whole land." 4 But the woman
took the two men and hid them.
Then she said, "True, the men
came to me, but I did not know
where they came from. 5 And when
it was time to close the gate at
dark, the men went out. Where the
men went I do not know. Pursue
them quickly, for you can overtake
them." 6 She had, however, brought
them up to the roof and hidden
them with the stalks of flax that
she had laid out on the roof. 7 So
the men pursued them on the way
to the Jordan as far as the fords. As
soon as the pursuers had gone out,
the gate was shut.
8 Before they went to sleep, she
came up to them on the roof 9 and
said to the men: "I know that the
LORD has given you the land, and
that dread of you has fallen on us,
and that all the inhabitants of the
land melt in fear before you. 10 For
we have heard how the LORD dried
up the water of the Red Sea[a] before you when you came out of
Egypt, and what you did to the two
kings of the Amorites that were beyond the Jordan, to Sihon and Og,
whom you utterly destroyed. 11 As
soon as we heard it, our hearts
melted, and there was no courage
left in any of us because of you. The
LORD your God is indeed God in
heaven above and on earth below.
12 Now then, since I have dealt
kindly with you, swear to me by the
LORD that you in turn will deal kindly with my family. Give me a sign of
good faith 13 that you will spare my
father and mother, my brothers
and sisters, and all who belong to
them, and deliver our lives from
death." 14 The men said to her,
"Our life for yours! If you do not tell
this business of ours, then we will
deal kindly and faithfully with you
when the LORD gives us the land."
15 Then she let them down by a
rope through the window, for her
house was on the outer side of the
city wall and she resided within the
wall itself. 16 She said to them, "Go
toward the hill country, so that the

1.12 Num 32.20-22
1.13 Deut 3.18-20
1.15 Josh 22.1-4
1.17 vv. 5,9
2.1 Num 25.1; Heb 11.31; Jas 2.25
2.6 Jas 2.25
2.9 Ex 23.27; Deut 2.25
2.10 Ex 14.21; Num 21.24, 34,35
2.11 Ex 15.14, 15; Josh 5.1; Deut 4.39
2.12 v. 18
2.14 Judg 1.24
2.16 Jas 2.25

[a] Or *Sea of Reeds*

pursuers may not come upon you.
Hide yourselves there three days,
until the pursuers have returned;
then afterward you may go your
way." 17 The men said to her, "We
will be released from this oath that
you have made us swear to you 18 if
we invade the land and you do not
tie this crimson cord in the window
through which you let us down,
and you do not gather into your
house your father and mother, your
brothers, and all your family. 19 If
any of you go out of the doors of
your house into the street, they
shall be responsible for their own
death, and we shall be innocent;
but if a hand is laid upon any who
are with you in the house, we shall
bear the responsibility for their
death. 20 But if you tell this business of ours, then we shall be released from this oath that you
made us swear to you." 21 She said,
"According to your words, so be it."
She sent them away and they departed. Then she tied the crimson
cord in the window.
22 They departed and went into
the hill country and stayed there
three days, until the pursuers returned. The pursuers had searched
all along the way and found nothing. 23 Then the two men came
down again from the hill country.
They crossed over, came to Joshua
son of Nun, and told him all that
had happened to them. 24 They said
to Joshua, "Truly the LORD has giv-
en all the land into our hands;
moreover all the inhabitants of the
land melt in fear before us."

Israel Crosses the Jordan

3 Early in the morning Joshua
rose and set out from Shittim
with all the Israelites, and they
came to the Jordan. They camped
there before crossing over. 2 At the
end of three days the officers went
through the camp 3 and commanded the people, "When you see the
ark of the covenant of the LORD
your God being carried by the levitical priests, then you shall set out
from your place. Follow it, 4 so that
you may know the way you should
go, for you have not passed this way
before. Yet there shall be a space
between you and it, a distance of
about two thousand cubits; do not
come any nearer to it." 5 Then Joshua said to the people, "Sanctify
yourselves; for tomorrow the LORD
will do wonders among you." 6 To
the priests Joshua said, "Take up
the ark of the covenant, and pass
on in front of the people." So they
took up the ark of the covenant and
went in front of the people.
7 The LORD said to Joshua, "This
day I will begin to exalt you in the
sight of all Israel, so that they may
know that I will be with you as I
was with Moses. 8 You are the one
who shall command the priests
who bear the ark of the covenant,
'When you come to the edge of the
waters of the Jordan, you shall
stand still in the Jordan.' " 9 Joshua
then said to the Israelites, "Draw
near and hear the words of the LORD
your God." 10 Joshua said, "By this
you shall know that among you is
the living God who without fail will
drive out from before you the Canaanites, Hittites, Hivites, Perizzites, Girgashites, Amorites, and
Jebusites: 11 the ark of the covenant of the Lord of all the earth is
going to pass before you into the
Jordan. 12 So now select twelve
men from the tribes of Israel, one
from each tribe. 13 When the soles
of the feet of the priests who bear
the ark of the LORD, the Lord of all
the earth, rest in the waters of the
Jordan, the waters of the Jordan
flowing from above shall be cut off;
they shall stand in a single heap."
14 When the people set out
from their tents to cross over the
Jordan, the priests bearing the ark
of the covenant were in front of the
people. 15 Now the Jordan overflows all its banks throughout the
time of harvest. So when those who
bore the ark had come to the Jordan, and the feet of the priests
bearing the ark were dipped in the
edge of the water, 16 the waters
flowing from above stood still, rising up in a single heap far off at
Adam, the city that is beside Zare-

2.17 Gen 24.8
2.18 v. 12; Josh 6.23
2.19 Ezek 33.4
2.24 v. 9; Josh 6.2
3.1 Josh 2.1
3.2 Josh 1.11
3.3 Deut 31.9
3.5 Ex 19.10, 14; Josh 7.13
3.7 Josh 4.7; 1.5
3.8 vv. 3,17
3.10 Deut 7.1
3.12 Josh 4.2
3.13 Ex 15.8; Ps 78.13
3.15 Josh 4.18
3.16 Ps 66.6; 74.15; v. 13

than, while those flowing toward
the sea of the Arabah, the Dead
Sea,[b] were wholly cut off. Then the
people crossed over opposite Jericho. 17 While all Israel were crossing over on dry ground, the priests
who bore the ark of the covenant of
the LORD stood on dry ground in the
middle of the Jordan, until the entire nation finished crossing over
the Jordan.

Twelve Stones Set Up at Gilgal

4 When the entire nation had
finished crossing over the Jordan, the LORD said to Joshua: 2 "Select twelve men from the people,
one from each tribe, 3 and command them, 'Take twelve stones
from here out of the middle of the
Jordan, from the place where the
priests' feet stood, carry them over
with you, and lay them down in the
place where you camp tonight.' "
4 Then Joshua summoned the
twelve men from the Israelites,
whom he had appointed, one from
each tribe. 5 Joshua said to them,
"Pass on before the ark of the LORD
your God into the middle of the
Jordan, and each of you take up a
stone on his shoulder, one for each
of the tribes of the Israelites, 6 so
that this may be a sign among you.
When your children ask in time to
come, 'What do those stones mean
to you?' 7 then you shall tell them
that the waters of the Jordan were
cut off in front of the ark of the covenant of the LORD. When it crossed
over the Jordan, the waters of the
Jordan were cut off. So these
stones shall be to the Israelites a
memorial forever."
8 The Israelites did as Joshua
commanded. They took up twelve
stones out of the middle of the Jordan, according to the number of
the tribes of the Israelites, as the
LORD told Joshua, carried them
over with them to the place where
they camped, and laid them down
there. 9 (Joshua set up twelve
stones in the middle of the Jordan,
in the place where the feet of the
priests bearing the ark of the covenant had stood; and they are there
to this day.)
10 The priests who bore the ark
remained standing in the middle of
the Jordan, until everything was
finished that the LORD commanded
Joshua to tell the people, according to all that Moses had commanded Joshua. The people
crossed over in haste. 11 As soon as
all the people had finished crossing
over, the ark of the LORD, and the
priests, crossed over in front of the
people. 12 The Reubenites, the
Gadites, and the half-tribe of Manasseh crossed over armed before
the Israelites, as Moses had ordered them. 13 About forty thousand armed for war crossed over
before the LORD to the plains of Jericho for battle.
14 On that day the LORD exalted
Joshua in the sight of all Israel; and
they stood in awe of him, as they
had stood in awe of Moses, all the
days of his life.
15 The LORD said to Joshua,
16 "Command the priests who bear
the ark of the covenant,[c] to come
up out of the Jordan." 17 Joshua
therefore commanded the priests,
"Come up out of the Jordan."
18 When the priests bearing the ark
of the covenant of the LORD came
up from the middle of the Jordan,
and the soles of the priests' feet
touched dry ground, the waters of
the Jordan returned to their place
and overflowed all its banks, as before.
19 The people came up out of
the Jordan on the tenth day of the
first month, and they camped in
Gilgal on the east border of Jericho. 20 Those twelve stones, which
they had taken out of the Jordan,
Joshua set up in Gilgal, 21 saying to
the Israelites, "When your children
ask their parents in time to come,
'What do these stones mean?'
22 then you shall let your children
know, 'Israel crossed over the Jordan here on dry ground.' 23 For the
LORD your God dried up the waters

3.17 Ex 14.29 **4.2** Josh 3.12 **4.3** vv. 19,20 **4.6** v. 21; Ex 12.26; 13.14 **4.7** Josh 3.13 **4.8** vv. 19,20 **4.9** Ex 28.21
4.12 Num 32.17 **4.14** Josh 3.7 **4.18** Josh 3.15 **4.19** Josh 5.9 **4.20** vv. 3,8 **4.21** v. 6 **4.22** Josh 3.17 **4.23** Ex 14.21

[b] Heb *Salt Sea* [c] Or *treaty*, or *testimony*; Heb *eduth*

of the Jordan for you until you crossed over, as the LORD your God did to the Red Sea,[d] which he dried up for us until we crossed over, [24]so that all the peoples of the earth may know that the hand of the LORD is mighty, and so that you may fear the LORD your God forever."

The New Generation Circumcised

5 When all the kings of the Amorites beyond the Jordan to the west, and all the kings of the Canaanites by the sea, heard that the LORD had dried up the waters of the Jordan for the Israelites until they had crossed over, their hearts melted, and there was no longer any spirit in them, because of the Israelites.

2 At that time the LORD said to Joshua, "Make flint knives and circumcise the Israelites a second time." [3]So Joshua made flint knives, and circumcised the Israelites at Gibeath-haaraloth.[e] [4]This is the reason why Joshua circumcised them: all the males of the people who came out of Egypt, all the warriors, had died during the journey through the wilderness after they had come out of Egypt. [5]Although all the people who came out had been circumcised, yet all the people born on the journey through the wilderness after they had come out of Egypt had not been circumcised. [6]For the Israelites traveled forty years in the wilderness, until all the nation, the warriors who came out of Egypt, perished, not having listened to the voice of the LORD. To them the LORD swore that he would not let them see the land that he had sworn to their ancestors to give us, a land flowing with milk and honey. [7]So it was their children, whom he raised up in their place, that Joshua circumcised; for they were uncircumcised, because they had not been circumcised on the way.

8 When the circumcising of all the nation was done, they remained in their places in the camp until they were healed. [9]The LORD said to Joshua, "Today I have rolled away from you the disgrace of Egypt." And so that place is called Gilgal[f] to this day.

The Passover at Gilgal

10 While the Israelites were camped in Gilgal they kept the passover in the evening on the fourteenth day of the month in the plains of Jericho. [11]On the day after the passover, on that very day, they ate the produce of the land, unleavened cakes and parched grain. [12]The manna ceased on the day they ate the produce of the land, and the Israelites no longer had manna; they ate the crops of the land of Canaan that year.

Joshua's Vision

13 Once when Joshua was by Jericho, he looked up and saw a man standing before him with a drawn sword in his hand. Joshua went to him and said to him, "Are you one of us, or one of our adversaries?" [14]He replied, "Neither; but as commander of the army of the LORD I have now come." And Joshua fell on his face to the earth and worshiped, and he said to him, "What do you command your servant, my lord?" [15]The commander of the army of the LORD said to Joshua, "Remove the sandals from your feet, for the place where you stand is holy." And Joshua did so.

Jericho Taken and Destroyed

6 Now Jericho was shut up inside and out because of the Israelites; no one came out and no one went in. [2]The LORD said to Joshua, "See, I have handed Jericho over to you, along with its king and soldiers. [3]You shall march around the city, all the warriors circling the city once. Thus you shall do for six days, [4]with seven priests bearing seven trumpets of rams' horns before the ark. On the seventh day you shall march around the city seven times, the priests blowing the trumpets. [5]When they

4.24 1 Kings 8.42, 43; Ps 89.13; Ex 14.31
5.1 Num 13.29; Josh 2.9-11
5.2 Ex 4.25
5.4 Deut 2.16
5.6 Deut 2.7,14; Num 14.23
5.10 Ex 12.6,8
5.12 Ex 16.35
5.13 Gen 18.2; 32.24; Num 22.31
5.14 Gen 17.3
5.15 Ex 3.5
6.2 Josh 2.9,24; Deut 7.24
6.4 Num 10.8
6.5 Lev 25.9

[d] Or *Sea of Reeds* [e] That is *the Hill of the Foreskins* [f] Related to Heb *galal* to roll

make a long blast with the ram's
horn, as soon as you hear the sound
of the trumpet, then all the people
shall shout with a great shout; and
the wall of the city will fall down
flat, and all the people shall charge
straight ahead." 6 So Joshua son of
Nun summoned the priests and
said to them, "Take up the ark of
the covenant, and have seven
priests carry seven trumpets of
rams' horns in front of the ark of
the LORD." 7 To the people he said,
"Go forward and march around the
city; have the armed men pass on
before the ark of the LORD."
8 As Joshua had commanded
the people, the seven priests carrying the seven trumpets of rams'
horns before the LORD went forward, blowing the trumpets, with
the ark of the covenant of the LORD
following them. 9 And the armed
men went before the priests who
blew the trumpets; the rear guard
came after the ark, while the trumpets blew continually. 10 To the
people Joshua gave this command:
"You shall not shout or let your
voice be heard, nor shall you utter
a word, until the day I tell you to
shout. Then you shall shout." 11 So
the ark of the LORD went around the
city, circling it once; and they came
into the camp, and spent the night
in the camp.
12 Then Joshua rose early in the
morning, and the priests took up
the ark of the LORD. 13 The seven
priests carrying the seven trumpets
of rams' horns before the ark of the
LORD passed on, blowing the trumpets continually. The armed men
went before them, and the rear
guard came after the ark of the
LORD, while the trumpets blew continually. 14 On the second day they
marched around the city once and
then returned to the camp. They
did this for six days.
15 On the seventh day they rose
early, at dawn, and marched
around the city in the same manner
seven times. It was only on that day
that they marched around the city
seven times. 16 And at the seventh
time, when the priests had blown
the trumpets, Joshua said to the
people, "Shout! For the LORD has
given you the city. 17 The city and
all that is in it shall be devoted to
the LORD for destruction. Only Rahab the prostitute and all who are
with her in her house shall live because she hid the messengers we
sent. 18 As for you, keep away from
the things devoted to destruction,
so as not to covet[g] and take any of
the devoted things and make the
camp of Israel an object for destruction, bringing trouble upon it.
19 But all silver and gold, and vessels of bronze and iron, are sacred
to the LORD; they shall go into the
treasury of the LORD." 20 So the people shouted, and the trumpets were
blown. As soon as the people heard
the sound of the trumpets, they
raised a great shout, and the wall
fell down flat; so the people
charged straight ahead into the city
and captured it. 21 Then they devoted to destruction by the edge of the
sword all in the city, both men and
women, young and old, oxen,
sheep, and donkeys.
22 Joshua said to the two men
who had spied out the land, "Go
into the prostitute's house, and
bring the woman out of it and all
who belong to her, as you swore to
her." 23 So the young men who had
been spies went in and brought Rahab out, along with her father, her
mother, her brothers, and all who
belonged to her—they brought all
her kindred out—and set them
outside the camp of Israel. 24 They
burned down the city, and everything in it; only the silver and gold,
and the vessels of bronze and iron,
they put into the treasury of the
house of the LORD. 25 But Rahab the
prostitute, with her family and all
who belonged to her, Joshua
spared. Her family[h] has lived in Israel ever since. For she hid the
messengers whom Joshua sent to
spy out Jericho.
26 Joshua then pronounced this
oath, saying,

6.7 Ex 14.15 **6.9** v. 13; Isa 52.12 **6.13** vv. 4,9
6.17 Lev 27.28; Josh 2.4 **6.18** Josh 7.1,25 **6.20** v. 5; Heb 11.30 **6.21** Deut 7.2; 20.16 **6.22** Josh 2.14; Heb 11.31 **6.23** Josh 2.13 **6.24** v. 19 **6.25** Heb 11.31 **6.26** 1 Kings 16.34

[g] Gk: Heb *devote to destruction* Compare 7.21
[h] Heb *She*

"Cursed before the LORD be
anyone who tries
to build this city—this
Jericho!
At the cost of his firstborn
he shall lay its
foundation,
and at the cost of his
youngest he shall set up
its gates!"

27 So the LORD was with Joshua;
and his fame was in all the land.

The Sin of Achan and Its Punishment

7 But the Israelites broke faith
in regard to the devoted
things: Achan son of Carmi son of
Zabdi son of Zerah, of the tribe of
Judah, took some of the devoted
things; and the anger of the LORD
burned against the Israelites.

2 Joshua sent men from Jericho
to Ai, which is near Beth-aven, east
of Bethel, and said to them, "Go up
and spy out the land." And the men
went up and spied out Ai. 3 Then
they returned to Joshua and said to
him, "Not all the people need go
up; about two or three thousand
men should go up and attack Ai.
Since they are so few, do not make
the whole people toil up there."
4 So about three thousand of the
people went up there; and they fled
before the men of Ai. 5 The men of
Ai killed about thirty-six of them,
chasing them from outside the gate
as far as Shebarim and killing them
on the slope. The hearts of the people melted and turned to water.

6 Then Joshua tore his clothes,
and fell to the ground on his face
before the ark of the LORD until the
evening, he and the elders of Israel;
and they put dust on their heads.
7 Joshua said, "Ah, Lord GOD! Why
have you brought this people
across the Jordan at all, to hand us
over to the Amorites so as to destroy us? Would that we had been
content to settle beyond the Jordan! 8 O Lord, what can I say, now
that Israel has turned their backs
to their enemies! 9 The Canaanites
and all the inhabitants of the land
will hear of it, and surround us, and
cut off our name from the earth.
Then what will you do for your
great name?"

10 The LORD said to Joshua,
"Stand up! Why have you fallen
upon your face? 11 Israel has
sinned; they have transgressed my
covenant that I imposed on them.
They have taken some of the devoted things; they have stolen, they
have acted deceitfully, and they
have put them among their own belongings. 12 Therefore the Israelites
are unable to stand before their enemies; they turn their backs to
their enemies, because they have
become a thing devoted for destruction themselves. I will be with
you no more, unless you destroy
the devoted things from among
you. 13 Proceed to sanctify the people, and say, 'Sanctify yourselves
for tomorrow; for thus says the
LORD, the God of Israel, "There are
devoted things among you,
O Israel; you will be unable to
stand before your enemies until
you take away the devoted things
from among you." 14 In the morning
therefore you shall come forward
tribe by tribe. The tribe that the
LORD takes shall come near by
clans, the clan that the LORD takes
shall come near by households,
and the household that the LORD
takes shall come near one by one.
15 And the one who is taken as having the devoted things shall be
burned with fire, together with all
that he has, for having transgressed
the covenant of the LORD, and for
having done an outrageous thing in
Israel.' "

16 So Joshua rose early in the
morning, and brought Israel near
tribe by tribe, and the tribe of Judah was taken. 17 He brought near
the clans of Judah, and the clan of
the Zerahites was taken; and he
brought near the clan of the Zerahites, family by family,[i] and Zabdi
was taken. 18 And he brought near
his household one by one, and
Achan son of Carmi son of Zabdi
son of Zerah, of the tribe of Judah,

6.27 Josh 1.5; 9.1,3 **7.1** Josh 6.17-19 **7.4** Lev 26.17; 28.25 **7.6** Job 2.12; Rev 18.19 **7.7** Ex 5.22 **7.9** Ex 32.12; Deut 9.28

7.11 v. 1; Josh 6.18, 19; Acts 5.1,2 **7.13** Josh 3.5; 6.18 **7.15** v. 11 **7.17** Num 26.20

[i] Mss Syr: MT *man by man*

was taken. 19 Then Joshua said to
Achan, "My son, give glory to the
LORD God of Israel and make confession to him. Tell me now what
you have done; do not hide it from
me." 20 And Achan answered Joshua, "It is true; I am the one who
sinned against the LORD God of Israel. This is what I did: 21 when I
saw among the spoil a beautiful
mantle from Shinar, and two hundred shekels of silver, and a bar of
gold weighing fifty shekels, then I
coveted them and took them. They
now lie hidden in the ground inside
my tent, with the silver underneath."
22 So Joshua sent messengers,
and they ran to the tent; and there
it was, hidden in his tent with the
silver underneath. 23 They took
them out of the tent and brought
them to Joshua and all the Israelites; and they spread them out before the LORD. 24 Then Joshua and
all Israel with him took Achan son
of Zerah, with the silver, the mantle, and the bar of gold, with his
sons and daughters, with his oxen,
donkeys, and sheep, and his tent
and all that he had; and they
brought them up to the Valley of
Achor. 25 Joshua said, "Why did you
bring trouble on us? The LORD is
bringing trouble on you today."
And all Israel stoned him to death;
they burned them with fire, cast
stones on them, 26 and raised over
him a great heap of stones that remains to this day. Then the LORD
turned from his burning anger.
Therefore that place to this day is
called the Valley of Achor.[j]

Ai Captured by a Stratagem and Destroyed

8 Then the LORD said to Joshua,
"Do not fear or be dismayed;
take all the fighting men with you,
and go up now to Ai. See, I have
handed over to you the king of Ai
with his people, his city, and his
land. 2 You shall do to Ai and its
king as you did to Jericho and its
king; only its spoil and its livestock
you may take as booty for yourselves. Set an ambush against the
city, behind it."
3 So Joshua and all the fighting
men set out to go up against Ai.
Joshua chose thirty thousand warriors and sent them out by night
4 with the command, "You shall lie
in ambush against the city, behind
it; do not go very far from the city,
but all of you stay alert. 5 I and all
the people who are with me will approach the city. When they come
out against us, as before, we shall
flee from them. 6 They will come
out after us until we have drawn
them away from the city; for they
will say, 'They are fleeing from us,
as before.' While we flee from
them, 7 you shall rise up from the
ambush and seize the city; for the
LORD your God will give it into your
hand. 8 And when you have taken
the city, you shall set the city on
fire, doing as the LORD has ordered;
see, I have commanded you." 9 So
Joshua sent them out; and they
went to the place of ambush, and
lay between Bethel and Ai, to the
west of Ai; but Joshua spent that
night in the camp.[k]
10 In the morning Joshua rose
early and mustered the people, and
went up, with the elders of Israel,
before the people to Ai. 11 All the
fighting men who were with him
went up, and drew near before the
city, and camped on the north side
of Ai, with a ravine between them
and Ai. 12 Taking about five thousand men, he set them in ambush
between Bethel and Ai, to the west
of the city. 13 So they stationed the
forces, the main encampment that
was north of the city and its rear
guard west of the city. But Joshua
spent that night in the valley.
14 When the king of Ai saw this, he
and all his people, the inhabitants
of the city, hurried out early in the
morning to the meeting place facing the Arabah to meet Israel in
battle; but he did not know that
there was an ambush against him
behind the city. 15 And Joshua and
all Israel made a pretense of being

7.19 Jer 13.16; Jn 9.24; Num 5.6,7; 1 Sam 14.43
7.20 Josh 22.20; 1 Chr 2.7
7.24 Josh 15.7
7.25 Josh 6.18; Deut 17.5
7.26 Deut 13.17; Isa 65.10; Hos 2.15
8.1 Deut 1.21; 7.18; Josh 1.9; 6.2
8.2 v. 27; Deut 20.14
8.4 Judg 20.29-32
8.8 v. 2
8.10 v. 33
8.14 Josh 3.16; Judg 20.34

[j] That is *Trouble* [k] Heb *among the people*

beaten before them, and fled in the
direction of the wilderness. 16 So all
the people who were in the city
were called together to pursue
them, and as they pursued Joshua
they were drawn away from the
city. 17 There was not a man left in
Ai or Bethel who did not go out after Israel; they left the city open,
and pursued Israel.
18 Then the LORD said to Joshua, "Stretch out the sword that is in
your hand toward Ai; for I will give
it into your hand." And Joshua
stretched out the sword that was in
his hand toward the city. 19 As soon
as he stretched out his hand, the
troops in ambush rose quickly out
of their place and rushed forward.
They entered the city, took it, and
at once set the city on fire. 20 So
when the men of Ai looked back,
the smoke of the city was rising to
the sky. They had no power to flee
this way or that, for the people who
fled to the wilderness turned back
against the pursuers. 21 When Joshua and all Israel saw that the ambush had taken the city and that
the smoke of the city was rising,
then they turned back and struck
down the men of Ai. 22 And the others came out from the city against
them; so they were surrounded by
Israelites, some on one side, and
some on the other; and Israel
struck them down until no one was
left who survived or escaped. 23 But
the king of Ai was taken alive and
brought to Joshua.
24 When Israel had finished
slaughtering all the inhabitants of
Ai in the open wilderness where
they pursued them, and when all of
them to the very last had fallen by
the edge of the sword, all Israel returned to Ai, and attacked it with
the edge of the sword. 25 The total
of those who fell that day, both
men and women, was twelve
thousand—all the people of Ai.
26 For Joshua did not draw back his
hand, with which he stretched out
the sword, until he had utterly destroyed all the inhabitants of Ai.
27 Only the livestock and the spoil
of that city Israel took as their booty, according to the word of the
LORD that he had issued to Joshua.
28 So Joshua burned Ai, and made it
forever a heap of ruins, as it is to
this day. 29 And he hanged the king
of Ai on a tree until evening; and at
sunset Joshua commanded, and
they took his body down from the
tree, threw it down at the entrance
of the gate of the city, and raised
over it a great heap of stones,
which stands there to this day.

Joshua Renews the Covenant

30 Then Joshua built on Mount
Ebal an altar to the LORD, the God
of Israel, 31 just as Moses the servant of the LORD had commanded
the Israelites, as it is written in the
book of the law of Moses, "an altar
of unhewn[l] stones, on which no
iron tool has been used"; and they
offered on it burnt offerings to the
LORD, and sacrificed offerings of
well-being. 32 And there, in the
presence of the Israelites, Joshua[m]
wrote on the stones a copy of the
law of Moses, which he had written. 33 All Israel, alien as well as citizen, with their elders and officers
and their judges, stood on opposite
sides of the ark in front of the levitical priests who carried the ark of
the covenant of the LORD, half of
them in front of Mount Gerizim
and half of them in front of Mount
Ebal, as Moses the servant of the
LORD had commanded at the first,
that they should bless the people
of Israel. 34 And afterward he read
all the words of the law, blessings
and curses, according to all that is
written in the book of the law.
35 There was not a word of all that
Moses commanded that Joshua
did not read before all the assembly of Israel, and the women, and
the little ones, and the aliens who
resided among them.

The Gibeonites Save Themselves by Trickery

9 Now when all the kings who
were beyond the Jordan in the
hill country and in the lowland all
along the coast of the Great Sea to-

8.18 v. 26; Ex 14.16; 17.9-13 **8.19** v. 8 **8.22** Deut 7.2 **8.25** Deut 20.16-18 **8.26** Ex 17.11,12 **8.27** v. 2; Num 31.22

8.28 Deut 13.16 **8.29** Deut 21.22, 23 **8.30** Deut 27.2-8 **8.31** Ex 20.24, 25; Deut 27.5,6 **8.32** Deut 27.2,8 **8.33** Deut 31.9, 12; 27.11-14 **8.34f** Deut 31.11; Josh 1.8 **8.35** Deut 31.12 **9.1** Josh 3.10

[l] Heb *whole* [m] Heb *he*

ward Lebanon—the Hittites, the Amorites, the Canaanites, the Perizzites, the Hivites, and the Jebusites—heard of this, 2 they gathered together with one accord to fight Joshua and Israel.

3 But when the inhabitants of Gibeon heard what Joshua had done to Jericho and to Ai, 4 they on their part acted with cunning: they went and prepared provisions,[n] and took worn-out sacks for their donkeys, and wineskins, worn-out and torn and mended, 5 with worn-out, patched sandals on their feet, and worn-out clothes; and all their provisions were dry and moldy. 6 They went to Joshua in the camp at Gilgal, and said to him and to the Israelites, "We have come from a far country; so now make a treaty with us." 7 But the Israelites said to the Hivites, "Perhaps you live among us; then how can we make a treaty with you?" 8 They said to Joshua, "We are your servants." And Joshua said to them, "Who are you? And where do you come from?" 9 They said to him, "Your servants have come from a very far country, because of the name of the LORD your God; for we have heard a report of him, of all that he did in Egypt, 10 and of all that he did to the two kings of the Amorites who were beyond the Jordan, King Sihon of Heshbon, and King Og of Bashan who lived in Ashtaroth. 11 So our elders and all the inhabitants of our country said to us, 'Take provisions in your hand for the journey; go to meet them, and say to them, "We are your servants; come now, make a treaty with us." ' 12 Here is our bread; it was still warm when we took it from our houses as our food for the journey, on the day we set out to come to you, but now, see, it is dry and moldy; 13 these wineskins were new when we filled them, and see, they are burst; and these garments and sandals of ours are worn out from the very long journey." 14 So the leaders[o] partook of their provisions, and did not ask direction from the LORD. 15 And Joshua made peace with them, guaranteeing their lives by a treaty; and the leaders of the congregation swore an oath to them.

16 But when three days had passed after they had made a treaty with them, they heard that they were their neighbors and were living among them. 17 So the Israelites set out and reached their cities on the third day. Now their cities were Gibeon, Chephirah, Beeroth, and Kiriath-jearim. 18 But the Israelites did not attack them, because the leaders of the congregation had sworn to them by the LORD, the God of Israel. Then all the congregation murmured against the leaders. 19 But all the leaders said to all the congregation, "We have sworn to them by the LORD, the God of Israel, and now we must not touch them. 20 This is what we will do to them: We will let them live, so that wrath may not come upon us, because of the oath that we swore to them." 21 The leaders said to them, "Let them live." So they became hewers of wood and drawers of water for all the congregation, as the leaders had decided concerning them.

22 Joshua summoned them, and said to them, "Why did you deceive us, saying, 'We are very far from you,' while in fact you are living among us? 23 Now therefore you are cursed, and some of you shall always be slaves, hewers of wood and drawers of water for the house of my God." 24 They answered Joshua, "Because it was told to your servants for a certainty that the LORD your God had commanded his servant Moses to give you all the land, and to destroy all the inhabitants of the land before you; so we were in great fear for our lives because of you, and did this thing. 25 And now we are in your hand: do as it seems good and right in your sight to do to us." 26 This is what he did for them: he saved them from the Israelites; and they did not kill them. 27 But on that day Joshua

9.3 Josh 10.2; 6.27
9.6 Josh 5.10
9.7 v. 2; Josh 11.19; Ex 23.32
9.8 Deut 20.11
9.9 Deut 20.15; vv. 16,17, 24; Josh 2.9,10
9.10 Num 21.24, 33
9.14 Num 27.21
9.15 Ex 23.32
9.17 Josh 18.25-28; Ezra 2.25
9.18 Ps 15.4; Eccl 5.2
9.21 v. 15
9.22 vv. 6.9,16, 17
9.23 Gen 9.25; vv. 21,27
9.24 Deut 7.1,2
9.25 Gen 16.6
9.27 vv. 21,23; Deut 12.5

[n] Cn: Meaning of Heb uncertain
[o] Gk: Heb *men*

made them hewers of wood and
drawers of water for the congregation and for the altar of the LORD, to
continue to this day, in the place
that he should choose.

The Sun Stands Still

10 When King Adoni-zedek of
Jerusalem heard how Josh-
ua had taken Ai, and had utterly
destroyed it, doing to Ai and its
king as he had done to Jericho and
its king, and how the inhabitants of
Gibeon had made peace with Israel
and were among them, 2 he[p] became greatly frightened, because
Gibeon was a large city, like one of
the royal cities, and was larger than
Ai, and all its men were warriors.
3 So King Adoni-zedek of Jerusalem
sent a message to King Hoham of
Hebron, to King Piram of Jarmuth,
to King Japhia of Lachish, and
to King Debir of Eglon, saying,
4 "Come up and help me, and let us
attack Gibeon; for it has made
peace with Joshua and with the Israelites." 5 Then the five kings of
the Amorites—the king of Jerusalem, the king of Hebron, the king of
Jarmuth, the king of Lachish, and
the king of Eglon—gathered their
forces, and went up with all their
armies and camped against Gibeon, and made war against it.
6 And the Gibeonites sent to
Joshua at the camp in Gilgal, saying, "Do not abandon your servants; come up to us quickly, and
save us, and help us; for all the
kings of the Amorites who live in
the hill country are gathered
against us." 7 So Joshua went up
from Gilgal, he and all the fighting
force with him, all the mighty warriors. 8 The LORD said to Joshua,
"Do not fear them, for I have handed them over to you; not one of
them shall stand before you." 9 So
Joshua came upon them suddenly,
having marched up all night from
Gilgal. 10 And the LORD threw them
into a panic before Israel, who inflicted a great slaughter on them at
Gibeon, chased them by the way of
the ascent of Beth-horon, and
struck them down as far as Azekah
and Makkedah. 11 As they fled before Israel, while they were going
down the slope of Beth-horon, the
LORD threw down huge stones from
heaven on them as far as Azekah,
and they died; there were more
who died because of the hailstones
than the Israelites killed with the
sword.
12 On the day when the LORD
gave the Amorites over to the Israelites, Joshua spoke to the LORD;
and he said in the sight of Israel,
"Sun, stand still at Gibeon,
and Moon, in the valley of
Aijalon."
13 And the sun stood still, and
the moon stopped,
until the nation took
vengeance on their
enemies.
Is this not written in the Book of
Jashar? The sun stopped in midheaven, and did not hurry to set for
about a whole day. 14 There has
been no day like it before or since,
when the LORD heeded a human
voice; for the LORD fought for Israel.
15 Then Joshua returned, and
all Israel with him, to the camp at
Gilgal.

Five Kings Defeated

16 Meanwhile, these five kings
fled and hid themselves in the cave
at Makkedah. 17 And it was told
Joshua, "The five kings have been
found, hidden in the cave at Makkedah." 18 Joshua said, "Roll large
stones against the mouth of the
cave, and set men by it to guard
them; 19 but do not stay there yourselves; pursue your enemies, and
attack them from the rear. Do not
let them enter their towns, for the
LORD your God has given them into
your hand." 20 When Joshua and
the Israelites had finished inflicting a very great slaughter on them,
until they were wiped out, and
when the survivors had entered
into the fortified towns, 21 all the
people returned safe to Joshua in
the camp at Makkedah; no one
dared to speak[q] against any of the
Israelites.

10.1 Josh 6.21; 8.22,26,28; 9.15
10.4 v. 1
10.5 Josh 9.2
10.8 Josh 1.5,9; 11.6
10.10 Deut 7.23
10.11 Ps 18.13,14; Isa 30.30
10.12 Hab 3.11
10.13 2 Sam 1.18; Isa 38.8
10.14 v. 42
10.15 v. 43
10.16 v. 5
10.20 Deut 20.16
10.21 Ex 11.7

[p] Heb *they* [q] Heb *moved his tongue*

22 Then Joshua said, "Open the
mouth of the cave, and bring those
five kings out to me from the cave."
23 They did so, and brought the five
kings out to him from the cave, the
king of Jerusalem, the king of Hebron, the king of Jarmuth, the king
of Lachish, and the king of Eglon.
24 When they brought the kings out
to Joshua, Joshua summoned all
the Israelites, and said to the chiefs
of the warriors who had gone with
him, "Come near, put your feet on
the necks of these kings." Then
they came near and put their feet
on their necks. 25 And Joshua said
to them, "Do not be afraid or dismayed; be strong and courageous;
for thus the LORD will do to all the
enemies against whom you fight."
26 Afterward Joshua struck them
down and put them to death, and
he hung them on five trees. And
they hung on the trees until evening. 27 At sunset Joshua commanded, and they took them down
from the trees and threw them into
the cave where they had hidden
themselves; they set large stones
against the mouth of the cave,
which remain to this very day.
28 Joshua took Makkedah on
that day, and struck it and its king
with the edge of the sword; he utterly destroyed every person in it;
he left no one remaining. And he
did to the king of Makkedah as he
had done to the king of Jericho.
29 Then Joshua passed on from
Makkedah, and all Israel with him,
to Libnah, and fought against Libnah. 30 The LORD gave it also and its
king into the hand of Israel; and he
struck it with the edge of the
sword, and every person in it; he
left no one remaining in it; and he
did to its king as he had done to the
king of Jericho.
31 Next Joshua passed on from
Libnah, and all Israel with him, to
Lachish, and laid siege to it, and
assaulted it. 32 The LORD gave Lachish into the hand of Israel, and
he took it on the second day, and
struck it with the edge of the
sword, and every person in it, as he
had done to Libnah.

10.22 Deut 7.24 **10.24** Ps 110.5; Isa 26.5,6; Mal 4.3 **10.25** v. 8 **10.26** Josh 8.29 **10.27** Deut 21.23; Josh 8.9 **10.28** Deut 20.16; Josh 6.21 **10.29** 1 Chr 6.57 **10.31** 2 Kings 14.19

10.36 Josh 14.13; 15.13; Judg 1.10 **10.38** Josh 15.15; Judg 1.11 **10.40** Deut 1.7; 7.24; 20.16, 17 **10.41** Josh 11.16; 15.51 **10.42** v. 14 **11.1** v. 10 **11.2** Josh 12.3ff

33 Then King Horam of Gezer
came up to help Lachish; and Joshua struck him and his people, leaving him no survivors.
34 From Lachish Joshua passed
on with all Israel to Eglon; and they
laid siege to it, and assaulted it;
35 and they took it that day, and
struck it with the edge of the
sword; and every person in it he utterly destroyed that day, as he had
done to Lachish.
36 Then Joshua went up with all
Israel from Eglon to Hebron; they
assaulted it, 37 and took it, and
struck it with the edge of the
sword, and its king and its towns,
and every person in it; he left no
one remaining, just as he had done
to Eglon, and utterly destroyed it
with every person in it.
38 Then Joshua, with all Israel,
turned back to Debir and assaulted
it, 39 and he took it with its king and
all its towns; they struck them with
the edge of the sword, and utterly
destroyed every person in it; he left
no one remaining; just as he had
done to Hebron, and, as he had
done to Libnah and its king, so he
did to Debir and its king.
40 So Joshua defeated the
whole land, the hill country and
the Negeb and the lowland and the
slopes, and all their kings; he left
no one remaining, but utterly destroyed all that breathed, as the
LORD God of Israel commanded.
41 And Joshua defeated them from
Kadesh-barnea to Gaza, and all the
country of Goshen, as far as Gibeon. 42 Joshua took all these kings
and their land at one time, because
the LORD God of Israel fought for Israel. 43 Then Joshua returned, and
all Israel with him, to the camp at
Gilgal.

The United Kings of Northern Canaan Defeated

11 When King Jabin of Hazor
heard of this, he sent to
King Jobab of Madon, to the king
of Shimron, to the king of Achshaph, 2 and to the kings who were
in the northern hill country, and in
the Arabah south of Chinneroth,

and in the lowland, and in
Naphoth-dor on the west, 3 to the
Canaanites in the east and the
west, the Amorites, the Hittites,
the Perizzites, and the Jebusites in
the hill country, and the Hivites
under Hermon in the land of Mizpah. 4 They came out, with all their
troops, a great army, in number
like the sand on the seashore, with
very many horses and chariots. 5 All
these kings joined their forces, and
came and camped together at the
waters of Merom, to fight with Israel.

6 And the LORD said to Joshua,
"Do not be afraid of them, for tomorrow at this time I will hand over
all of them, slain, to Israel; you
shall hamstring their horses, and
burn their chariots with fire." 7 So
Joshua came suddenly upon them
with all his fighting force, by the
waters of Merom, and fell upon
them. 8 And the LORD handed them
over to Israel, who attacked them
and chased them as far as Great Sidon and Misrephoth-maim, and
eastward as far as the valley of Mizpeh. They struck them down, until
they had left no one remaining.
9 And Joshua did to them as the
LORD commanded him; he hamstrung their horses, and burned
their chariots with fire.

10 Joshua turned back at that
time, and took Hazor, and struck
its king down with the sword. Before that time Hazor was the head
of all those kingdoms. 11 And they
put to the sword all who were in it,
utterly destroying them; there was
no one left who breathed, and he
burned Hazor with fire. 12 And all
the towns of those kings, and all
their kings, Joshua took, and
struck them with the edge of the
sword, utterly destroying them, as
Moses the servant of the LORD had
commanded. 13 But Israel burned
none of the towns that stood on
mounds except Hazor, which Joshua did burn. 14 All the spoil of these
towns, and the livestock, the Israelites took for their booty; but all
the people they struck down with
the edge of the sword, until they
had destroyed them, and they did
not leave any who breathed. 15 As
the LORD had commanded his servant Moses, so Moses commanded
Joshua, and so Joshua did; he left
nothing undone of all that the LORD
had commanded Moses.

Summary of Joshua's Conquests

16 So Joshua took all that land:
the hill country and all the Negeb
and all the land of Goshen and the
lowland and the Arabah and the
hill country of Israel and its lowland, 17 from Mount Halak, which
rises toward Seir, as far as Baal-gad
in the valley of Lebanon below
Mount Hermon. He took all their
kings, struck them down, and put
them to death. 18 Joshua made war
a long time with all those kings.
19 There was not a town that made
peace with the Israelites, except
the Hivites, the inhabitants of Gibeon; all were taken in battle. 20 For
it was the LORD's doing to harden
their hearts so that they would
come against Israel in battle, in order that they might be utterly destroyed, and might receive no mercy, but be exterminated, just as the
LORD had commanded Moses.

21 At that time Joshua came
and wiped out the Anakim from the
hill country, from Hebron, from
Debir, from Anab, and from all the
hill country of Judah, and from all
the hill country of Israel; Joshua
utterly destroyed them with their
towns. 22 None of the Anakim was
left in the land of the Israelites;
some remained only in Gaza, in
Gath, and in Ashdod. 23 So Joshua
took the whole land, according to
all that the LORD had spoken to Moses; and Joshua gave it for an inheritance to Israel according to their
tribal allotments. And the land had
rest from war.

The Kings Conquered by Moses

12 Now these are the kings of
the land, whom the Israelites defeated, whose land they occupied beyond the Jordan toward
the east, from the Wadi Arnon to
Mount Hermon, with all the Ara-

11.4 Judg 7.12
11.6 Josh 10.8; 2 Sam 8.4
11.8 Josh 13.6
11.9 v. 6
11.11 Deut 20.16, 17
11.14 Num 31.11, 12
11.15 Ex 34.11, 12; Deut 7.2; Josh 1.7
11.16 Josh 10.40, 41; v. 2
11.17 Josh 12.7; Deut 7.24
11.19 Josh 9.3,7
11.20 Deut 2.30; Rom 9.18; Deut 20.16, 17
11.21 Num 13.33; Deut 9.2
11.23 Num 34.2ff
12.1 Deut 3.8,9

bah eastward: 2 King Sihon of the
Amorites who lived at Heshbon,
and ruled from Aroer, which is on
the edge of the Wadi Arnon, and
from the middle of the valley as far
as the river Jabbok, the boundary
of the Ammonites, that is, half of
Gilead, 3 and the Arabah to the Sea
of Chinneroth eastward, and in the
direction of Beth-jeshimoth, to the
sea of the Arabah, the Dead Sea,[r]
southward to the foot of the slopes
of Pisgah; 4 and King Og[s] of Bashan, one of the last of the Rephaim, who lived at Ashtaroth and at
Edrei 5 and ruled over Mount Hermon and Salecah and all Bashan to
the boundary of the Geshurites and
the Maacathites, and over half of
Gilead to the boundary of King Sihon of Heshbon. 6 Moses, the servant of the LORD, and the Israelites
defeated them; and Moses the servant of the LORD gave their land for
a possession to the Reubenites and
the Gadites and the half-tribe of
Manasseh.

The Kings Conquered by Joshua

7 The following are the kings of
the land whom Joshua and the Israelites defeated on the west side
of the Jordan, from Baal-gad in the
valley of Lebanon to Mount Halak,
that rises toward Seir (and Joshua
gave their land to the tribes of Israel as a possession according to
their allotments, 8 in the hill country, in the lowland, in the Arabah,
in the slopes, in the wilderness,
and in the Negeb, the land of the
Hittites, Amorites, Canaanites,
Perizzites, Hivites, and Jebusites):

9 the king of Jericho one
the king of Ai, which is next to Bethel one
10 the king of Jerusalem one
the king of Hebron one
11 the king of Jarmuth one
the king of Lachish one
12 the king of Eglon one
the king of Gezer one
13 the king of Debir one
the king of Geder one
14 the king of Hormah one
the king of Arad one
15 the king of Libnah one
the king of Adullam one
16 the king of Makkedah one
the king of Bethel one
17 the king of Tappuah one
the king of Hepher one
18 the king of Aphek one
the king of Lasharon one
19 the king of Madon one
the king of Hazor one
20 the king of Shimron-meron one
the king of Achshaph one
21 the king of Taanach one
the king of Megiddo one
22 the king of Kedesh one
the king of Jokneam in Carmel one
23 the king of Dor in Naphath-dor one
the king of Goiim in Galilee,[t] one
24 the king of Tirzah one
thirty-one kings in all.

The Parts of Canaan Still Unconquered

13 Now Joshua was old and
advanced in years; and the
LORD said to him, "You are old and
advanced in years, and very much
of the land still remains to be possessed. 2 This is the land that still
remains: all the regions of the Philistines, and all those of the Geshurites 3 (from the Shihor, which is
east of Egypt, northward to the
boundary of Ekron, it is reckoned
as Canaanite; there are five rulers
of the Philistines, those of Gaza,
Ashdod, Ashkelon, Gath, and Ekron), and those of the Avvim, 4 in
the south, all the land of the Canaanites, and Mearah that belongs
to the Sidonians, to Aphek, to the
boundary of the Amorites, 5 and the
land of the Gebalites, and all Lebanon, toward the east, from Baal-
gad below Mount Hermon to Lebo-
hamath, 6 all the inhabitants of the
hill country from Lebanon to
Misrephoth-maim, even all the Sidonians. I will myself drive them
out from before the Israelites; only
allot the land to Israel for an inheritance, as I have commanded you.

12.2 Deut 2.33, 36 **12.3** Josh 11.2; 13.20 **12.4** Deut 3.11 **12.5** Deut 3.8ff **12.6** Num 21.24, 33; 32.29,33 **12.7** Josh 11.17, 23 **12.8** Josh 11.16 **12.9ff** Josh 6.2; 8.29 **12.12** Josh 10.33 **12.13** Josh 10.38 **12.24** Deut 7.24 **13.1** Josh 14.10 **13.3** Judg 3.3; Deut 2.23 **13.6** Josh 11.8

[r] Heb *Salt Sea* [s] Gk: Heb *the boundary of King Og* [t] Gk: Heb *Gilgal*

7 Now therefore divide this land for
an inheritance to the nine tribes
and the half-tribe of Manasseh."

The Territory East of the Jordan

8 With the other half-tribe of
Manasseh[u] the Reubenites and
the Gadites received their inheritance, which Moses gave them, beyond the Jordan eastward, as Moses the servant of the LORD gave
them: 9 from Aroer, which is on the
edge of the Wadi Arnon, and the
town that is in the middle of
the valley, and all the tableland
from[v] Medeba as far as Dibon;
10 and all the cities of King Sihon
of the Amorites, who reigned in
Heshbon, as far as the boundary of
the Ammonites; 11 and Gilead, and
the region of the Geshurites and
Maacathites, and all Mount Hermon, and all Bashan to Salecah;
12 all the kingdom of Og in Bashan,
who reigned in Ashtaroth and in
Edrei (he alone was left of the
survivors of the Rephaim); these
Moses had defeated and driven out.
13 Yet the Israelites did not drive
out the Geshurites or the Maacathites; but Geshur and Maacath
live within Israel to this day.
14 To the tribe of Levi alone
Moses gave no inheritance; the offerings by fire to the LORD God of
Israel are their inheritance, as he
said to them.

The Territory of Reuben

15 Moses gave an inheritance to
the tribe of the Reubenites according to their clans. 16 Their territory
was from Aroer, which is on the
edge of the Wadi Arnon, and the
town that is in the middle of
the valley, and all the tableland by
Medeba; 17 with Heshbon, and all
its towns that are in the tableland;
Dibon, and Bamoth-baal, and Beth-
baal-meon, 18 and Jahaz, and
Kedemoth, and Mephaath, 19 and
Kiriathaim, and Sibmah, and Ze-
reth-shahar on the hill of the valley, 20 and Beth-peor, and the
slopes of Pisgah, and Beth-
jeshimoth, 21 that is, all the towns
of the tableland, and all the kingdom of King Sihon of the Amorites,
who reigned in Heshbon, whom
Moses defeated with the leaders of
Midian, Evi and Rekem and Zur
and Hur and Reba, as princes of Sihon, who lived in the land. 22 Along
with the rest of those they put to
death, the Israelites also put to the
sword Balaam son of Beor, who
practiced divination. 23 And the
border of the Reubenites was the
Jordan and its banks. This was
the inheritance of the Reubenites,
according to their families with
their towns and villages.

The Territory of Gad

24 Moses gave an inheritance
also to the tribe of the Gadites, according to their families. 25 Their
territory was Jazer, and all the
towns of Gilead, and half the land
of the Ammonites, to Aroer, which
is east of Rabbah, 26 and from
Heshbon to Ramath-mizpeh and
Betonim, and from Mahanaim to
the territory of Debir,[w] 27 and in the
valley Beth-haram, Beth-nimrah,
Succoth, and Zaphon, the rest of
the kingdom of King Sihon of
Heshbon, the Jordan and its banks,
as far as the lower end of the Sea of
Chinnereth, eastward beyond the
Jordan. 28 This is the inheritance of
the Gadites according to their
clans, with their towns and villages.

The Territory of the Half-Tribe of Manasseh (East)

29 Moses gave an inheritance to
the half-tribe of Manasseh; it was
allotted to the half-tribe of the Manassites according to their families. 30 Their territory extended
from Mahanaim, through all Bashan, the whole kingdom of King
Og of Bashan, and all the settlements of Jair, which are in Bashan,
sixty towns, 31 and half of Gilead,
and Ashtaroth, and Edrei, the
towns of the kingdom of Og in Bashan; these were allotted to the
people of Machir son of Manasseh

13.8 Josh 12.1-6
13.9 v. 16
13.10 Num 21.24, 25
13.12 Deut 3.11; Num 21.24, 35
13.14 Deut 18.1,2
13.16 Josh 12.2
13.21 Num 31.8
13.22 Num 31.8
13.25 Num 21.32
13.27 Num 34.11
13.30 Num 32.41

[u] Cn: Heb *With it* [v] Compare Gk: Heb lacks *from* [w] Gk Syr Vg: Heb *Lidebir*

according to their clans—for half the Machirites.

32 These are the inheritances that Moses distributed in the plains of Moab, beyond the Jordan east of Jericho. 33 But to the tribe of Levi Moses gave no inheritance; the LORD God of Israel is their inheritance, as he said to them.

The Distribution of Territory West of the Jordan

14 These are the inheritances that the Israelites received in the land of Canaan, which the priest Eleazar, and Joshua son of Nun, and the heads of the families of the tribes of the Israelites distributed to them. 2 Their inheritance was by lot, as the LORD had commanded Moses for the nine and one-half tribes. 3 For Moses had given an inheritance to the two and one-half tribes beyond the Jordan; but to the Levites he gave no inheritance among them. 4 For the people of Joseph were two tribes, Manasseh and Ephraim; and no portion was given to the Levites in the land, but only towns to live in, with their pasture lands for their flocks and herds. 5 The Israelites did as the LORD commanded Moses; they allotted the land.

Hebron Allotted to Caleb

6 Then the people of Judah came to Joshua at Gilgal; and Caleb son of Jephunneh the Kenizzite said to him, "You know what the LORD said to Moses the man of God in Kadesh-barnea concerning you and me. 7 I was forty years old when Moses the servant of the LORD sent me from Kadesh-barnea to spy out the land; and I brought him an honest report. 8 But my companions who went up with me made the heart of the people melt; yet I wholeheartedly followed the LORD my God. 9 And Moses swore on that day, saying, 'Surely the land on which your foot has trodden shall be an inheritance for you and your children forever, because you have wholeheartedly followed the LORD my God.' 10 And now, as you see, the LORD has kept me alive, as he said, these forty-five years since the time that the LORD spoke this word to Moses, while Israel was journeying through the wilderness; and here I am today, eighty-five years old. 11 I am still as strong today as I was on the day that Moses sent me; my strength now is as my strength was then, for war, and for going and coming. 12 So now give me this hill country of which the LORD spoke on that day; for you heard on that day how the Anakim were there, with great fortified cities; it may be that the LORD will be with me, and I shall drive them out, as the LORD said."

13 Then Joshua blessed him, and gave Hebron to Caleb son of Jephunneh for an inheritance. 14 So Hebron became the inheritance of Caleb son of Jephunneh the Kenizzite to this day, because he wholeheartedly followed the LORD, the God of Israel. 15 Now the name of Hebron formerly was Kiriath-arba;[x] this Arba was[y] the greatest man among the Anakim. And the land had rest from war.

The Territory of Judah

15 The lot for the tribe of the people of Judah according to their families reached southward to the boundary of Edom, to the wilderness of Zin at the farthest south. 2 And their south boundary ran from the end of the Dead Sea,[z] from the bay that faces southward; 3 it goes out southward of the ascent of Akrabbim, passes along to Zin, and goes up south of Kadesh-barnea, along by Hezron, up to Addar, makes a turn to Karka, 4 passes along to Azmon, goes out by the Wadi of Egypt, and comes to its end at the sea. This shall be your south boundary. 5 And the east boundary is the Dead Sea,[z] to the mouth of the Jordan. And the boundary on the north side runs from the bay of the sea at the mouth of the Jordan; 6 and the boundary goes up to Beth-hoglah,

13.33 v. 14; Num 18.20; Deut 10.9; 18.1,2
14.1 Num 34.17, 18
14.2 Num 26.55
14.3 Num 32.33; Josh 13.14
14.4 Gen 48.5
14.6 Num 13.6, 26,30; 14.6, 24,30
14.7 Num 13.6; 14.6
14.8 Num 13.31, 32; 14.24
14.9 Deut 1.36
14.10 Num 14.30
14.12 Num 13.33
14.14 Josh 22.6; vv. 8,9
14.15 Josh 11.23
15.1 Num 34.3,4; 33.36
15.3 Num 34.4
15.4 Num 34.5
15.6 Josh 18.17, 19

[x] That is *the city of Arba* [y] Heb lacks *this Arba was* [z] Heb *Salt Sea*

and passes along north of Beth-
arabah; and the boundary goes up
to the Stone of Bohan, Reuben's
son; [7] and the boundary goes up to
Debir from the Valley of Achor, and
so northward, turning toward Gilgal, which is opposite the ascent of
Adummim, which is on the south
side of the valley; and the boundary
passes along to the waters of En-
shemesh, and ends at En-rogel;
[8] then the boundary goes up by the
valley of the son of Hinnom at the
southern slope of the Jebusites
(that is, Jerusalem); and the
boundary goes up to the top of the
mountain that lies over against the
valley of Hinnom, on the west, at
the northern end of the valley of
Rephaim; [9] then the boundary extends from the top of the mountain
to the spring of the Waters of Nephtoah, and from there to the towns
of Mount Ephron; then the boundary bends around to Baalah (that
is, Kiriath-jearim); [10] and the
boundary circles west of Baalah to
Mount Seir, passes along to the
northern slope of Mount Jearim
(that is, Chesalon), and goes down
to Beth-shemesh, and passes along
by Timnah; [11] the boundary goes
out to the slope of the hill north of
Ekron, then the boundary bends
around to Shikkeron, and passes
along to Mount Baalah, and goes
out to Jabneel; then the boundary
comes to an end at the sea. [12] And
the west boundary was the Mediterranean with its coast. This is the
boundary surrounding the people
of Judah according to their families.

Caleb Occupies His Portion

13 According to the commandment of the LORD to Joshua, he gave
to Caleb son of Jephunneh a portion among the people of Judah,
Kiriath-arba,[a] that is, Hebron
(Arba was the father of Anak).
[14] And Caleb drove out from there
the three sons of Anak: Sheshai,
Ahiman, and Talmai, the descendants of Anak. [15] From there he
went up against the inhabitants of
Debir; now the name of Debir formerly was Kiriath-sepher. [16] And
Caleb said, "Whoever attacks
Kiriath-sepher and takes it, to him
I will give my daughter Achsah as
wife." [17] Othniel son of Kenaz, the
brother of Caleb, took it; and he
gave him his daughter Achsah as
wife. [18] When she came to him, she
urged him to ask her father for a
field. As she dismounted from her
donkey, Caleb said to her, "What
do you wish?" [19] She said to him,
"Give me a present; since you have
set me in the land of the Negeb,
give me springs of water as well."
So Caleb gave her the upper springs
and the lower springs.

The Towns of Judah

20 This is the inheritance of the
tribe of the people of Judah according to their families. [21] The towns
belonging to the tribe of the people
of Judah in the extreme South, toward the boundary of Edom, were
Kabzeel, Eder, Jagur, [22] Kinah, Di-
monah, Adadah, [23] Kedesh, Hazor,
Ithnan, [24] Ziph, Telem, Bealoth,
[25] Hazor-hadattah, Kerioth-hezron
(that is, Hazor), [26] Amam, Shema,
Moladah, [27] Hazar-gaddah, Hesh-
mon, Beth-pelet, [28] Hazar-shual,
Beer-sheba, Biziothiah, [29] Baalah,
Iim, Ezem, [30] Eltolad, Chesil, Hormah, [31] Ziklag, Madmannah, San-
sannah, [32] Lebaoth, Shilhim, Ain,
and Rimmon: in all, twenty-nine
towns, with their villages.
33 And in the Lowland, Eshtaol,
Zorah, Ashnah, [34] Zanoah, En-
gannim, Tappuah, Enam, [35] Jarmuth, Adullam, Socoh, Azekah,
[36] Shaaraim, Adithaim, Gederah,
Gederothaim: fourteen towns with
their villages.
37 Zenan, Hadashah, Migdal-
gad, [38] Dilan, Mizpeh, Jokthe-el,
[39] Lachish, Bozkath, Eglon, [40] Cab-
bon, Lahmam, Chitlish, [41] Gederoth, Beth-dagon, Naamah, and
Makkedah: sixteen towns with
their villages.
42 Libnah, Ether, Ashan, [43] Iph-
tah, Ashnah, Nezib, [44] Keilah, Achzib, and Mareshah: nine towns
with their villages.

15.7 Josh 7.24
15.8 v. 63
15.9 Josh 18.15
15.10 Judg 14.1
15.12 v. 47
15.13 Jn 14.13-15
15.14 Josh 11.21, 22; Num 13.22
15.15 Josh 10.38
15.16 Judg 1.12, 13; 3.9
15.18 Judg 1.14
15.28 Gen 21.31
15.31 1 Sam 27.6
15.33 Judg 13.25; 16.31
15.35 1 Sam 22.1
15.38 2 Kings 14.7
15.39 Josh 10.3; 2 Kings 14.19

[a] That is *the city of Arba*

45 Ekron, with its dependencies
and its villages; 46 from Ekron to
the sea, all that were near Ashdod,
with their villages.
47 Ashdod, its towns and its villages; Gaza, its towns and its villages; to the Wadi of Egypt, and the
Great Sea with its coast.
48 And in the hill country, Shamir, Jattir, Socoh, 49 Dannah,
Kiriath-sannah (that is, Debir),
50 Anab, Eshtemoh, Anim, 51 Goshen, Holon, and Giloh: eleven
towns with their villages.
52 Arab, Dumah, Eshan, 53 Ja-
nim, Beth-tappuah, Aphekah,
54 Humtah, Kiriath-arba (that is,
Hebron), and Zior: nine towns with
their villages.
55 Maon, Carmel, Ziph, Juttah,
56 Jezreel, Jokdeam, Zanoah,
57 Kain, Gibeah, and Timnah: ten
towns with their villages.
58 Halhul, Beth-zur, Gedor,
59 Maarath, Beth-anoth, and Elte-
kon: six towns with their villages.
60 Kiriath-baal (that is, Kiriath-
jearim), and Rabbah: two towns
with their villages.
61 In the wilderness, Beth-
arabah, Middin, Secacah, 62 Nib-
shan, the City of Salt, and En-gedi:
six towns with their villages.
63 But the people of Judah
could not drive out the Jebusites,
the inhabitants of Jerusalem; so
the Jebusites live with the people
of Judah in Jerusalem to this day.

The Territory of Ephraim

16 The allotment of the Josephites went from the Jordan by Jericho, east of the waters
of Jericho, into the wilderness, going up from Jericho into the hill
country to Bethel; 2 then going
from Bethel to Luz, it passes along
to Ataroth, the territory of the Ar-
chites; 3 then it goes down westward to the territory of the Japhle-
tites, as far as the territory of Lower
Beth-horon, then to Gezer, and it
ends at the sea.
4 The Josephites—Manasseh
and Ephraim—received their inheritance.
5 The territory of the Ephraimites by their families was as follows: the boundary of their inheritance on the east was
Ataroth-addar as far as Upper Beth-
horon, 6 and the boundary goes
from there to the sea; on the north
is Michmethath; then on the east
the boundary makes a turn toward
Taanath-shiloh, and passes along
beyond it on the east to Janoah,
7 then it goes down from Janoah to
Ataroth and to Naarah, and
touches Jericho, ending at the Jordan. 8 From Tappuah the boundary
goes westward to the Wadi Kanah,
and ends at the sea. Such is the inheritance of the tribe of the Ephraimites by their families, 9 together
with the towns that were set apart
for the Ephraimites within the inheritance of the Manassites, all
those towns with their villages.
10 They did not, however, drive out
the Canaanites who lived in Gezer:
so the Canaanites have lived within
Ephraim to this day but have been
made to do forced labor.

The Other Half-Tribe of Manasseh (West)

17 Then allotment was made
to the tribe of Manasseh,
for he was the firstborn of Joseph.
To Machir the firstborn of Manasseh, the father of Gilead, were allotted Gilead and Bashan, because
he was a warrior. 2 And allotments
were made to the rest of the tribe of
Manasseh, by their families, Abiezer, Helek, Asriel, Shechem, Hepher, and Shemida; these were the
male descendants of Manasseh son
of Joseph, by their families.
3 Now Zelophehad son of Hepher son of Gilead son of Machir
son of Manasseh had no sons, but
only daughters; and these are the
names of his daughters: Mahlah,
Noah, Hoglah, Milcah, and Tirzah.
4 They came before the priest Eleazar and Joshua son of Nun and the
leaders, and said, "The LORD commanded Moses to give us an inheritance along with our male kin." So
according to the commandment of
the LORD he gave them an inheritance among the kinsmen of their

15.47 v. 4; Num 34.6
15.51 Josh 10.41; 11.16
15.60 Josh 18.14
15.63 Judg 1.21; 2 Sam 5.6
16.1 Josh 18.12
16.2 Josh 18.13
16.3 Josh 18.13; 2 Chr 8.5
16.5 Josh 18.13
16.6 Josh 17.7
16.7 1 Chr 7.28
16.8 Josh 17.8,9
16.10 Judg 1.29; 1 Kings 9.16; Josh 17.12, 13
17.1 Gen 41.41; 50.23; Deut 3.15
17.2 Num 26.29-32
17.3 Num 26.33; 27.1-7
17.4 Num 27.5-7

father. 5 Thus there fell to Manasseh ten portions, besides the land of Gilead and Bashan, which is on the other side of the Jordan, 6 because the daughters of Manasseh received an inheritance along with his sons. The land of Gilead was allotted to the rest of the Manassites.

7 The territory of Manasseh reached from Asher to Michmethath, which is east of Shechem; then the boundary goes along southward to the inhabitants of En-tappuah. 8 The land of Tappuah belonged to Manasseh, but the town of Tappuah on the boundary of Manasseh belonged to the Ephraimites. 9 Then the boundary went down to the Wadi Kanah. The towns here, to the south of the wadi, among the towns of Manasseh, belong to Ephraim. Then the boundary of Manasseh goes along the north side of the wadi and ends at the sea. 10 The land to the south is Ephraim's and that to the north is Manasseh's, with the sea forming its boundary; on the north Asher is reached, and on the east Issachar. 11 Within Issachar and Asher, Manasseh had Beth-shean and its villages, Ibleam and its villages, the inhabitants of Dor and its villages, the inhabitants of En-dor and its villages, the inhabitants of Taanach and its villages, and the inhabitants of Megiddo and its villages (the third is Naphath).[b] 12 Yet the Manassites could not take possession of those towns; but the Canaanites continued to live in that land. 13 But when the Israelites grew strong, they put the Canaanites to forced labor, but did not utterly drive them out.

The Tribe of Joseph Protests

14 The tribe of Joseph spoke to Joshua, saying, "Why have you given me but one lot and one portion as an inheritance, since we are a numerous people, whom all along the LORD has blessed?" 15 And Joshua said to them, "If you are a numerous people, go up to the forest, and clear ground there for yourselves in the land of the Perizzites and the Rephaim, since the hill country of Ephraim is too narrow for you." 16 The tribe of Joseph said, "The hill country is not enough for us; yet all the Canaanites who live in the plain have chariots of iron, both those in Beth-shean and its villages and those in the Valley of Jezreel." 17 Then Joshua said to the house of Joseph, to Ephraim and Manasseh, "You are indeed a numerous people, and have great power; you shall not have one lot only, 18 but the hill country shall be yours, for though it is a forest, you shall clear it and possess it to its farthest borders; for you shall drive out the Canaanites, though they have chariots of iron, and though they are strong."

The Territories of the Remaining Tribes

18 Then the whole congregation of the Israelites assembled at Shiloh, and set up the tent of meeting there. The land lay subdued before them.

2 There remained among the Israelites seven tribes whose inheritance had not yet been apportioned. 3 So Joshua said to the Israelites, "How long will you be slack about going in and taking possession of the land that the LORD, the God of your ancestors, has given you? 4 Provide three men from each tribe, and I will send them out that they may begin to go throughout the land, writing a description of it with a view to their inheritances. Then come back to me. 5 They shall divide it into seven portions, Judah continuing in its territory on the south, and the house of Joseph in their territory on the north. 6 You shall describe the land in seven divisions and bring the description here to me; and I will cast lots for you here before the LORD our God. 7 The Levites have no portion among you, for the priesthood of the LORD is their heritage; and Gad and Reuben and the half-tribe of Manasseh have received their inheritance beyond

17.6 Josh 13.30, 31
17.7 Josh 16.6
17.8 Josh 16.8
17.9 Josh 16.8,9
17.11 1 Chr 7.29
17.12 Judg 1.27, 28
17.13 Josh 16.10
17.14 Num 26.34, 37
17.16 Judg 1.19; 4.3
18.1 Josh 19.51; Jer 7.12; Judg 18.31
18.3 Judg 18.9
18.5 Josh 15.1; 16.1,4
18.7 Josh 13.33; 13.8

[b] Meaning of Heb uncertain

the Jordan eastward, which Moses
the servant of the LORD gave them."
8 So the men started on their
way; and Joshua charged those
who went to write the description
of the land, saying, "Go throughout
the land and write a description of
it, and come back to me; and I will
cast lots for you here before the
LORD in Shiloh." 9 So the men went
and traversed the land and set
down in a book a description of it
by towns in seven divisions; then
they came back to Joshua in the
camp at Shiloh, 10 and Joshua cast
lots for them in Shiloh before the
LORD; and there Joshua apportioned the land to the Israelites, to
each a portion.

The Territory of Benjamin

11 The lot of the tribe of Benjamin according to its families came
up, and the territory allotted to it
fell between the tribe of Judah and
the tribe of Joseph. 12 On the north
side their boundary began at the
Jordan; then the boundary goes up
to the slope of Jericho on the
north, then up through the hill
country westward; and it ends at
the wilderness of Beth-aven.
13 From there the boundary passes
along southward in the direction of
Luz, to the slope of Luz (that is,
Bethel), then the boundary goes
down to Ataroth-addar, on the
mountain that lies south of Lower
Beth-horon. 14 Then the boundary
goes in another direction, turning
on the western side southward
from the mountain that lies to the
south, opposite Beth-horon, and it
ends at Kiriath-baal (that is,
Kiriath-jearim), a town belonging
to the tribe of Judah. This forms
the western side. 15 The southern
side begins at the outskirts of
Kiriath-jearim; and the boundary
goes from there to Ephron,[c] to the
spring of the Waters of Nephtoah;
16 then the boundary goes down to
the border of the mountain that
overlooks the valley of the son of
Hinnom, which is at the north end
of the valley of Rephaim; and it
then goes down the valley of Hinnom, south of the slope of the Jebusites, and downward to En-rogel;
17 then it bends in a northerly direction going on to En-shemesh, and
from there goes to Geliloth, which
is opposite the ascent of Adummim; then it goes down to the
Stone of Bohan, Reuben's son;
18 and passing on to the north of the
slope of Beth-arabah[d] it goes down
to the Arabah; 19 then the boundary
passes on to the north of the slope
of Beth-hoglah; and the boundary
ends at the northern bay of the
Dead Sea,[e] at the south end of the
Jordan: this is the southern border.
20 The Jordan forms its boundary
on the eastern side. This is the inheritance of the tribe of Benjamin,
according to its families, boundary
by boundary all around.
21 Now the towns of the tribe of
Benjamin according to their families were Jericho, Beth-hoglah,
Emek-keziz, 22 Beth-arabah, Zemaraim, Bethel, 23 Avvim, Parah, Ophrah, 24 Chephar-ammoni, Ophni,
and Geba—twelve towns with their
villages: 25 Gibeon, Ramah, Beeroth, 26 Mizpeh, Chephirah, Mozah,
27 Rekem, Irpeel, Taralah, 28 Zela,
Haeleph, Jebus[f] (that is, Jerusalem), Gibeah[g] and Kiriath-
jearim[h]—fourteen towns with their
villages. This is the inheritance of
the tribe of Benjamin according to
its families.

The Territory of Simeon

19 The second lot came out
for Simeon, for the tribe of
Simeon, according to its families;
its inheritance lay within the inheritance of the tribe of Judah. 2 It had
for its inheritance Beer-sheba, Sheba, Moladah, 3 Hazar-shual, Balah,
Ezem, 4 Eltolad, Bethul, Hormah,
5 Ziklag, Beth-marcaboth, Hazar-
susah, 6 Beth-lebaoth, and
Sharuhen—thirteen towns with
their villages; 7 Ain, Rimmon,
Ether, and Ashan—four towns with
their villages; 8 together with all the

18.8 v. 1; Judg 18.31 **18.10** Josh 19.51 **18.13** Gen 28.19; Josh 16.3 **18.14** Josh 15.9 **18.15** Josh 15.5-9 **18.16** 2 Kings 23.10 **18.20** Josh 21.4, 17 **18.28** Josh 15.8 **19.1** v. 9 **19.5** 1 Sam 30.1

[c] Cn See 15.9. Heb *westward* [d] Gk: Heb *to the slope over against the Arabah* [e] Heb *Salt Sea* [f] Gk Syr Vg: Heb *the Jebusite* [g] Heb *Gibeath* [h] Gk: Heb *Kiriath*

villages all around these towns as
far as Baalath-beer, Ramah of the
Negeb. This was the inheritance of
the tribe of Simeon according to its
families. 9 The inheritance of the
tribe of Simeon formed part of the
territory of Judah; because the portion of the tribe of Judah was too
large for them, the tribe of Simeon
obtained an inheritance within
their inheritance.

The Territory of Zebulun

10 The third lot came up for the
tribe of Zebulun, according to its
families. The boundary of its inheritance reached as far as Sarid;
11 then its boundary goes up westward, and on to Maralah, and
touches Dabbesheth, then the
wadi that is east of Jokneam;
12 from Sarid it goes in the other direction eastward toward the sunrise to the boundary of Chisloth-
tabor; from there it goes to
Daberath, then up to Japhia;
13 from there it passes along on the
east toward the sunrise to Gath-
hepher, to Eth-kazin, and going on
to Rimmon it bends toward Neah;
14 then on the north the boundary
makes a turn to Hannathon, and it
ends at the valley of Iphtah-el;
15 and Kattath, Nahalal, Shimron,
Idalah, and Bethlehem—twelve
towns with their villages. 16 This is
the inheritance of the tribe of Zebulun, according to its families—
these towns with their villages.

The Territory of Issachar

17 The fourth lot came out for
Issachar, for the tribe of Issachar,
according to its families. 18 Its territory included Jezreel, Chesulloth,
Shunem, 19 Hapharaim, Shion,
Anaharath, 20 Rabbith, Kishion,
Ebez, 21 Remeth, En-gannim, En-
haddah, Beth-pazzez; 22 the boundary also touches Tabor, Shahazu-
mah, and Beth-shemesh, and its
boundary ends at the Jordan—
sixteen towns with their villages.
23 This is the inheritance of the
tribe of Issachar, according to its
families—the towns with their villages.

19.9 v. 1
19.11 Josh 21.34
19.15 Mic 5.2
19.17 2 Sam 2.9
19.28 Josh 11.8
19.30 Josh 21.31
19.34 Deut 33.23

The Territory of Asher

24 The fifth lot came out for the
tribe of Asher according to its families. 25 Its boundary included Helkath, Hali, Beten, Achshaph, 26 Al-
lammelech, Amad, and Mishal; on
the west it touches Carmel and
Shihor-libnath, 27 then it turns
eastward, goes to Beth-dagon, and
touches Zebulun and the valley of
Iphtah-el northward to Beth-emek
and Neiel; then it continues in the
north to Cabul, 28 Ebron, Rehob,
Hammon, Kanah, as far as Great
Sidon; 29 then the boundary
turns to Ramah, reaching to the
fortified city of Tyre; then the
boundary turns to Hosah, and it
ends at the sea; Mahalab,[i] Achzib,
30 Ummah, Aphek, and Rehob—
twenty-two towns with their villages. 31 This is the inheritance of
the tribe of Asher according to its
families—these towns with their
villages.

The Territory of Naphtali

32 The sixth lot came out for
the tribe of Naphtali, for the tribe
of Naphtali, according to its families. 33 And its boundary ran from
Heleph, from the oak in Zaanan-
nim, and Adami-nekeb, and Jabneel, as far as Lakkum; and it ended
at the Jordan; 34 then the boundary
turns westward to Aznoth-tabor,
and goes from there to Hukkok,
touching Zebulun at the south, and
Asher on the west, and Judah on
the east at the Jordan. 35 The fortified towns are Ziddim, Zer, Hammath, Rakkath, Chinnereth, 36 Adamah, Ramah, Hazor, 37 Kedesh,
Edrei, En-hazor, 38 Iron, Mig-
dal-el Horem, Beth-anath, and
Beth-shemesh—nineteen towns
with their villages. 39 This is the inheritance of the tribe of Naphtali
according to its families—the
towns with their villages.

The Territory of Dan

40 The seventh lot came out for
the tribe of Dan, according to its
families. 41 The territory of its inheritance included Zorah, Eshtaol,

[i] Cn Compare Gk: Heb *Mehebel*

Ir-shemesh, 42 Shaalabbin, Aijalon,
Ithlah, 43 Elon, Timnah, Ekron,
44 Eltekeh, Gibbethon, Baalath,
45 Jehud, Bene-berak, Gath-
rimmon, 46 Me-jarkon, and Rakkon
at the border opposite Joppa.
47 When the territory of the Danites
was lost to them, the Danites went
up and fought against Leshem, and
after capturing it and putting it to
the sword, they took possession of
it and settled in it, calling Leshem,
Dan, after their ancestor Dan.
48 This is the inheritance of the
tribe of Dan, according to their
families—these towns with their
villages.

Joshua's Inheritance

49 When they had finished dis-
tributing the several territories of
the land as inheritances, the Israelites gave an inheritance among
them to Joshua son of Nun. 50 By
command of the LORD they gave
him the town that he asked for,
Timnath-serah in the hill country
of Ephraim; he rebuilt the town,
and settled in it.

51 These are the inheritances
that the priest Eleazar and Joshua
son of Nun and the heads of the
families of the tribes of the Israelites distributed by lot at Shiloh before the LORD, at the entrance of the
tent of meeting. So they finished
dividing the land.

The Cities of Refuge

20 Then the LORD spoke to
Joshua, saying, 2 "Say to
the Israelites, 'Appoint the cities of
refuge, of which I spoke to you
through Moses, 3 so that anyone
who kills a person without intent or
by mistake may flee there; they
shall be for you a refuge from the
avenger of blood. 4 The slayer shall
flee to one of these cities and shall
stand at the entrance of the gate of
the city, and explain the case to the
elders of that city; then the fugitive
shall be taken into the city, and giv-
en a place, and shall remain with
them. 5 And if the avenger of blood
is in pursuit, they shall not give up
the slayer, because the neighbor
was killed by mistake, there having
been no enmity between them before. 6 The slayer shall remain in
that city until there is a trial before
the congregation, until the death of
the one who is high priest at the
time: then the slayer may return
home, to the town in which the
deed was done.' "

7 So they set apart Kedesh in
Galilee in the hill country of Naphtali, and Shechem in the hill country of Ephraim, and Kiriath-arba
(that is, Hebron) in the hill country
of Judah. 8 And beyond the Jordan
east of Jericho, they appointed Bezer in the wilderness on the tableland, from the tribe of Reuben, and
Ramoth in Gilead, from the tribe of
Gad, and Golan in Bashan, from
the tribe of Manasseh. 9 These were
the cities designated for all the Israelites, and for the aliens residing
among them, that anyone who
killed a person without intent
could flee there, so as not to die by
the hand of the avenger of blood,
until there was a trial before the
congregation.

Cities Allotted to the Levites

21 Then the heads of the families of the Levites came to
the priest Eleazar and to Joshua
son of Nun and to the heads of the
families of the tribes of the Israelites; 2 they said to them at Shiloh in
the land of Canaan, "The LORD
commanded through Moses that
we be given towns to live in, along
with their pasture lands for our
livestock." 3 So by command of the
LORD the Israelites gave to the Levites the following towns and pasture lands out of their inheritance.

4 The lot came out for the families of the Kohathites. So those Levites who were descendants of Aaron the priest received by lot
thirteen towns from the tribes of
Judah, Simeon, and Benjamin.

5 The rest of the Kohathites received by lot ten towns from the
families of the tribe of Ephraim,
from the tribe of Dan, and the half-
tribe of Manasseh.

6 The Gershonites received by

19.42 Judg 1.35 **19.47** Judg 18.27-31 **19.50** Josh 24.30 **19.51** Josh 14.1; 18.1,10 **20.2** Num 35.6-34; Deut 4.41; 19.2 **20.4** Ruth 4.1,2 **20.5** Num 35.12 **20.6** Num 35.25 **20.7** Josh 21.32; 1 Chr 6.76; Josh 21.11; Lk 1.39 **20.8** Josh 21.27, 36,38 **20.9** Num 35.15; v. 6 **21.1** Num 35.1-8 **21.2** Num 35.2 **21.4** vv. 8,19 **21.5** v. 20ff **21.6** v. 27ff

lot thirteen towns from the families of the tribe of Issachar, from
the tribe of Asher, from the tribe of
Naphtali, and from the half-tribe of
Manasseh in Bashan.
7 The Merarites according to
their families received twelve
towns from the tribe of Reuben, the
tribe of Gad, and the tribe of Zebulun.
8 These towns and their pasture
lands the Israelites gave by lot to
the Levites, as the LORD had commanded through Moses.
9 Out of the tribe of Judah and
the tribe of Simeon they gave the
following towns mentioned by
name, 10 which went to the descendants of Aaron, one of the families
of the Kohathites who belonged to
the Levites, since the lot fell to
them first. 11 They gave them
Kiriath-arba (Arba being the father
of Anak), that is Hebron, in the hill
country of Judah, along with the
pasture lands around it. 12 But the
fields of the town and its villages
had been given to Caleb son of Jephunneh as his holding.
13 To the descendants of Aaron
the priest they gave Hebron, the
city of refuge for the slayer, with its
pasture lands, Libnah with its pasture lands, 14 Jattir with its pasture
lands, Eshtemoa with its pasture
lands, 15 Holon with its pasture
lands, Debir with its pasture lands,
16 Ain with its pasture lands, Juttah
with its pasture lands, and Beth-
shemesh with its pasture lands—
nine towns out of these two tribes.
17 Out of the tribe of Benjamin:
Gibeon with its pasture lands,
Geba with its pasture lands, 18 Anathoth with its pasture lands, and
Almon with its pasture lands—four
towns. 19 The towns of the descendants of Aaron—the priests—were
thirteen in all, with their pasture
lands.
20 As to the rest of the Kohathites belonging to the Kohathite
families of the Levites, the towns
allotted to them were out of the
tribe of Ephraim. 21 To them were
given Shechem, the city of refuge
for the slayer, with its pasture

21.7 v. 34ff
21.8 v. 3
21.11 Josh 15.13, 14; 1 Chr 6.55
21.13 Josh 15.42, 54; 20.7; 1 Chr 6.57
21.15 Josh 15.49, 51; 1 Chr 6.58
21.16 Josh 15.10, 15; 1 Chr 6.59
21.18 1 Chr 6.60
21.21 Josh 20.7
21.27 v. 6
21.32 Josh 20.7
21.34 v. 7
21.36 Josh 20.8

lands in the hill country of Ephraim, Gezer with its pasture lands,
22 Kibzaim with its pasture lands,
and Beth-horon with its pasture
lands—four towns. 23 Out of the
tribe of Dan: Elteke with its pasture lands, Gibbethon with its pasture lands, 24 Aijalon with its pasture lands, Gath-rimmon with its
pasture lands—four towns. 25 Out
of the half-tribe of Manasseh: Taanach with its pasture lands, and
Gath-rimmon with its pasture
lands—two towns. 26 The towns of
the families of the rest of the Kohathites were ten in all, with their
pasture lands.
27 To the Gershonites, one of
the families of the Levites, were
given out of the half-tribe of Manasseh, Golan in Bashan with its
pasture lands, the city of refuge for
the slayer, and Beeshterah with its
pasture lands—two towns. 28 Out
of the tribe of Issachar: Kishion
with its pasture lands, Daberath
with its pasture lands, 29 Jarmuth
with its pasture lands, En-gannim
with its pasture lands—four towns;
30 Out of the tribe of Asher: Mishal
with its pasture lands, Abdon with
its pasture lands, 31 Helkath with
its pasture lands, and Rehob with
its pasture lands—four towns.
32 Out of the tribe of Naphtali: Kedesh in Galilee with its pasture
lands, the city of refuge for the
slayer, Hammoth-dor with its pasture lands, and Kartan with its pasture lands—three towns. 33 The
towns of the several families of the
Gershonites were in all thirteen,
with their pasture lands.
34 To the rest of the Levites—
the Merarite families—were given
out of the tribe of Zebulun: Jokneam with its pasture lands, Kartah
with its pasture lands, 35 Dimnah
with its pasture lands, Nahalal
with its pasture lands—four towns.
36 Out of the tribe of Reuben: Bezer
with its pasture lands, Jahzah with
its pasture lands, 37 Kedemoth with
its pasture lands, and Mephaath
with its pasture lands—four towns.
38 Out of the tribe of Gad: Ramoth
in Gilead with its pasture lands,

the city of refuge for the slayer, Mahanaim with its pasture lands, 39 Heshbon with its pasture lands, Jazer with its pasture lands—four towns in all. 40 As for the towns of the several Merarite families, that is, the remainder of the families of the Levites, those allotted to them were twelve in all.

41 The towns of the Levites within the holdings of the Israelites were in all forty-eight towns with their pasture lands. 42 Each of these towns had its pasture lands around it; so it was with all these towns.

43 Thus the LORD gave to Israel all the land that he swore to their ancestors that he would give them; and having taken possession of it, they settled there. 44 And the LORD gave them rest on every side just as he had sworn to their ancestors; not one of all their enemies had withstood them, for the LORD had given all their enemies into their hands. 45 Not one of all the good promises that the LORD had made to the house of Israel had failed; all came to pass.

The Eastern Tribes Return to Their Territory

22 Then Joshua summoned the Reubenites, the Gadites, and the half-tribe of Manasseh, 2 and said to them, "You have observed all that Moses the servant of the LORD commanded you, and have obeyed me in all that I have commanded you; 3 you have not forsaken your kindred these many days, down to this day, but have been careful to keep the charge of the LORD your God. 4 And now the LORD your God has given rest to your kindred, as he promised them; therefore turn and go to your tents in the land where your possession lies, which Moses the servant of the LORD gave you on the other side of the Jordan. 5 Take good care to observe the commandment and instruction that Moses the servant of the LORD commanded you, to love the LORD your God, to walk in all his ways, to keep his commandments, and to hold fast to him, and to serve him with all your heart and with all your soul." 6 So Joshua blessed them and sent them away, and they went to their tents.

7 Now to the one half of the tribe of Manasseh Moses had given a possession in Bashan; but to the other half Joshua had given a possession beside their fellow Israelites in the land west of the Jordan. And when Joshua sent them away to their tents and blessed them, 8 he said to them, "Go back to your tents with much wealth, and with very much livestock, with silver, gold, bronze, and iron, and with a great quantity of clothing; divide the spoil of your enemies with your kindred." 9 So the Reubenites and the Gadites and the half-tribe of Manasseh returned home, parting from the Israelites at Shiloh, which is in the land of Canaan, to go to the land of Gilead, their own land of which they had taken possession by command of the LORD through Moses.

A Memorial Altar East of the Jordan

10 When they came to the region[j] near the Jordan that lies in the land of Canaan, the Reubenites and the Gadites and the half-tribe of Manasseh built there an altar by the Jordan, an altar of great size. 11 The Israelites heard that the Reubenites and the Gadites and the half-tribe of Manasseh had built an altar at the frontier of the land of Canaan, in the region[k] near the Jordan, on the side that belongs to the Israelites. 12 And when the people of Israel heard of it, the whole assembly of the Israelites gathered at Shiloh, to make war against them.

13 Then the Israelites sent the priest Phinehas son of Eleazar to the Reubenites and the Gadites and the half-tribe of Manasseh, in the land of Gilead, 14 and with him ten chiefs, one from each of the tribal families of Israel, every one of them the head of a family among the clans of Israel. 15 They came to

21.41 Num 35.7
21.43ff Gen 13.15; Deut 11.31
21.44 Josh 1.13; 11.23; Deut 7.24
21.45 Josh 23.14
22.2 Num 32.20
22.4 Num 32.18; Deut 3.20
22.5 Deut 6.6,17; 10.12
22.7 Num 32.33; Josh 17.5
22.9 Num 32.1, 26,29
22.11 v. 19
22.12 Josh 18.1
22.13 Deut 13.14; Num 25.7

j Or *to Geliloth* k Or *at Geliloth*

the Reubenites, the Gadites, and
the half-tribe of Manasseh, in the
land of Gilead, and they said to
them, 16“Thus says the whole congregation of the LORD, ‘What is this
treachery that you have committed
against the God of Israel in turning
away today from following the
LORD, by building yourselves an altar today in rebellion against the
LORD? 17 Have we not had enough of
the sin at Peor from which even yet
we have not cleansed ourselves,
and for which a plague came upon
the congregation of the LORD,
18 that you must turn away today
from following the LORD! If you rebel against the LORD today, he will
be angry with the whole congregation of Israel tomorrow. 19 But now,
if your land is unclean, cross over
into the LORD's land where the
LORD's tabernacle now stands, and
take for yourselves a possession
among us; only do not rebel against
the LORD, or rebel against us[1] by
building yourselves an altar other
than the altar of the LORD our God.
20 Did not Achan son of Zerah break
faith in the matter of the devoted
things, and wrath fell upon all the
congregation of Israel? And he did
not perish alone for his iniquity!’ ”
21 Then the Reubenites, the
Gadites, and the half-tribe of Manasseh said in answer to the heads
of the families of Israel, 22 “The
LORD, God of gods! The LORD, God
of gods! He knows; and let Israel
itself know! If it was in rebellion or
in breach of faith toward the LORD,
do not spare us today 23 for building
an altar to turn away from following the LORD; or if we did so to offer
burnt offerings or grain offerings or
offerings of well-being on it, may
the LORD himself take vengeance.
24 No! We did it from fear that in
time to come your children might
say to our children, ‘What have you
to do with the LORD, the God of Israel? 25 For the LORD has made the
Jordan a boundary between us and
you, you Reubenites and Gadites;
you have no portion in the LORD.’
So your children might make our
children cease to worship the LORD.
26 Therefore we said, ‘Let us now
build an altar, not for burnt offering, nor for sacrifice, 27 but to be a
witness between us and you, and
between the generations after us,
that we do perform the service of
the LORD in his presence with our
burnt offerings and sacrifices and
offerings of well-being; so that your
children may never say to our children in time to come, “You have no
portion in the LORD.” ’ 28 And we
thought, If this should be said to us
or to our descendants in time to
come, we could say, ‘Look at this
copy of the altar of the LORD, which
our ancestors made, not for burnt
offerings, nor for sacrifice, but to
be a witness between us and you.’
29 Far be it from us that we should
rebel against the LORD, and turn
away this day from following the
LORD by building an altar for burnt
offering, grain offering, or sacrifice,
other than the altar of the LORD our
God that stands before his tabernacle!”
30 When the priest Phinehas
and the chiefs of the congregation,
the heads of the families of Israel
who were with him, heard the
words that the Reubenites and the
Gadites and the Manassites spoke,
they were satisfied. 31 The priest
Phinehas son of Eleazar said to the
Reubenites and the Gadites and
the Manassites, “Today we know
that the LORD is among us, because
you have not committed this
treachery against the LORD; now
you have saved the Israelites from
the hand of the LORD.”
32 Then the priest Phinehas son
of Eleazar and the chiefs returned
from the Reubenites and the Gadites in the land of Gilead to the
land of Canaan, to the Israelites,
and brought back word to them.
33 The report pleased the Israelites;
and the Israelites blessed God and
spoke no more of making war
against them, to destroy the land
where the Reubenites and the Gadites were settled. 34 The Reubenites
and the Gadites called the altar

22.16 v. 11; Deut 12.13, 14
22.17 Num 25.1-9
22.19 v. 11
22.20 Josh 7.1-26
22.22 Deut 10.17; 1 Kings 8.39
22.23 Deut 18.19; 1 Sam 20.16
22.27 Josh 24.27
22.29 Deut 12.13, 14
22.31 Lev 26.11, 12; 2 Chr 15.2
22.33 1 Chr 29.20
22.34 Josh 24.27

[1] Or *make rebels of us*

Witness;[m] "For," said they, "it is a
witness between us that the LORD is
God."

Joshua Exhorts the People

23 A long time afterward,
when the LORD had given
rest to Israel from all their enemies
all around, and Joshua was old and
well advanced in years, 2 Joshua
summoned all Israel, their elders
and heads, their judges and officers, and said to them, "I am now
old and well advanced in years;
3 and you have seen all that the
LORD your God has done to all these
nations for your sake, for it is the
LORD your God who has fought for
you. 4 I have allotted to you as an
inheritance for your tribes those
nations that remain, along with all
the nations that I have already cut
off, from the Jordan to the Great
Sea in the west. 5 The LORD your
God will push them back before
you, and drive them out of your
sight; and you shall possess their
land, as the LORD your God promised you. 6 Therefore be very steadfast to observe and do all that is
written in the book of the law of
Moses, turning aside from it neither to the right nor to the left, 7 so
that you may not be mixed with
these nations left here among you,
or make mention of the names of
their gods, or swear by them, or
serve them, or bow yourselves
down to them, 8 but hold fast to the
LORD your God, as you have done to
this day. 9 For the LORD has driven
out before you great and strong nations; and as for you, no one has
been able to withstand you to this
day. 10 One of you puts to flight a
thousand, since it is the LORD your
God who fights for you, as he promised you. 11 Be very careful, therefore, to love the LORD your God.
12 For if you turn back, and join the
survivors of these nations left here
among you, and intermarry with
them, so that you marry their wom-
en and they yours, 13 know assuredly that the LORD your God will not
continue to drive out these nations
before you; but they shall be a
snare and a trap for you, a scourge
on your sides, and thorns in your
eyes, until you perish from this
good land that the LORD your God
has given you.
14 "And now I am about to go
the way of all the earth, and you
know in your hearts and souls, all
of you, that not one thing has failed
of all the good things that the LORD
your God promised concerning
you; all have come to pass for you,
not one of them has failed. 15 But
just as all the good things that the
LORD your God promised concerning you have been fulfilled for you,
so the LORD will bring upon you all
the bad things, until he has destroyed you from this good land
that the LORD your God has given
you. 16 If you transgress the covenant of the LORD your God, which
he enjoined on you, and go and
serve other gods and bow down to
them, then the anger of the LORD
will be kindled against you, and
you shall perish quickly from the
good land that he has given to
you."

The Tribes Renew the Covenant

24 Then Joshua gathered all
the tribes of Israel to Shechem, and summoned the elders,
the heads, the judges, and the officers of Israel; and they presented
themselves before God. 2 And Joshua said to all the people, "Thus
says the LORD, the God of Israel:
Long ago your ancestors—Terah
and his sons Abraham and
Nahor—lived beyond the Euphrates and served other gods. 3 Then I
took your father Abraham from beyond the River and led him through
all the land of Canaan and made
his offspring many. I gave him
Isaac; 4 and to Isaac I gave Jacob
and Esau. I gave Esau the hill country of Seir to possess, but Jacob and
his children went down to Egypt.
5 Then I sent Moses and Aaron, and
I plagued Egypt with what I did in
its midst; and afterwards I brought
you out. 6 When I brought your ancestors out of Egypt, you came to

23.1 Josh 21.44; 13.1 **23.2** Josh 24.1 **23.3** Josh 10.14, 42 **23.5** Num 33.53 **23.6** Deut 5.32; Josh 1.7 **23.7** Ex 23.33; Deut 7.2,3; Ex 23.13; Ps 16.4 **23.8** Deut 10.20 **23.9** Deut 11.23; Josh 1.5 **23.10** Lev 26.8; v. 3; Deut 3.22 **23.12** Ex 34.15, 16; Deut 7.3 **23.13** Judg 2.3; Ex 23.33; Num 33.55 **23.14** 1 Kings 2.2; Josh 21.45 **23.15** Lev 26.16; Deut 28.15 **24.1** Josh 23.2 **24.2** Gen 11.27-32 **24.3** Gen 12.1; 15.5; 21.3 **24.4** Gen 25.25, 26; Deut 2.5; Gen 46.6,7 **24.5** Ex 3.10 **24.6** Ex 12.51; 14.2-31

m Cn Compare Syr: Heb lacks *Witness*

the sea; and the Egyptians pursued your ancestors with chariots and horsemen to the Red Sea.[n] 7 When they cried out to the LORD, he put darkness between you and the Egyptians, and made the sea come upon them and cover them; and your eyes saw what I did to Egypt. Afterwards you lived in the wilderness a long time. 8 Then I brought you to the land of the Amorites, who lived on the other side of the Jordan; they fought with you, and I handed them over to you, and you took possession of their land, and I destroyed them before you. 9 Then King Balak son of Zippor of Moab, set out to fight against Israel. He sent and invited Balaam son of Beor to curse you, 10 but I would not listen to Balaam; therefore he blessed you; so I rescued you out of his hand. 11 When you went over the Jordan and came to Jericho, the citizens of Jericho fought against you, and also the Amorites, the Perizzites, the Canaanites, the Hittites, the Girgashites, the Hivites, and the Jebusites; and I handed them over to you. 12 I sent the hornet[o] ahead of you, which drove out before you the two kings of the Amorites; it was not by your sword or by your bow. 13 I gave you a land on which you had not labored, and towns that you had not built, and you live in them; you eat the fruit of vineyards and oliveyards that you did not plant.

14 "Now therefore revere the LORD, and serve him in sincerity and in faithfulness; put away the gods that your ancestors served beyond the River and in Egypt, and serve the LORD. 15 Now if you are unwilling to serve the LORD, choose this day whom you will serve, whether the gods your ancestors served in the region beyond the River or the gods of the Amorites in whose land you are living; but as for me and my household, we will serve the LORD."

16 Then the people answered, "Far be it from us that we should forsake the LORD to serve other gods; 17 for it is the LORD our God who brought us and our ancestors up from the land of Egypt, out of the house of slavery, and who did those great signs in our sight. He protected us along all the way that we went, and among all the peoples through whom we passed; 18 and the LORD drove out before us all the peoples, the Amorites who lived in the land. Therefore we also will serve the LORD, for he is our God."

19 But Joshua said to the people, "You cannot serve the LORD, for he is a holy God. He is a jealous God; he will not forgive your transgressions or your sins. 20 If you forsake the LORD and serve foreign gods, then he will turn and do you harm, and consume you, after having done you good." 21 And the people said to Joshua, "No, we will serve the LORD!" 22 Then Joshua said to the people, "You are witnesses against yourselves that you have chosen the LORD, to serve him." And they said, "We are witnesses." 23 He said, "Then put away the foreign gods that are among you, and incline your hearts to the LORD, the God of Israel." 24 The people said to Joshua, "The LORD our God we will serve, and him we will obey." 25 So Joshua made a covenant with the people that day, and made statutes and ordinances for them at Shechem. 26 Joshua wrote these words in the book of the law of God; and he took a large stone, and set it up there under the oak in the sanctuary of the LORD. 27 Joshua said to all the people, "See, this stone shall be a witness against us; for it has heard all the words of the LORD that he spoke to us; therefore it shall be a witness against you, if you deal falsely with your God." 28 So Joshua sent the people away to their inheritances.

Death of Joshua and Eleazar

29 After these things Joshua son of Nun, the servant of the LORD, died, being one hundred ten years old. 30 They buried him in his own

24.8 Num 21.21-35
24.9 Num 22.2,5
24.11 Josh 3.16, 17; 6.1
24.12 Ex 23.28; Deut 7.20; Ps 44.3,6
24.13 Deut 6.10, 11
24.14 Deut 10.12; 18.13; 2 Cor 1.12
24.15 Ruth 1.15; 1 Kings 18.21; Ezek 20.39
24.19 Lev 19.2; Ex 20.5; 23.21
24.20 1 Chr 28.9; Josh 23.15
24.23 Judg 10.16
24.24 Ex 19.8; 24.3,7; Deut 5.27
24.25 Ex 24.8
24.27 Josh 22.27
24.29 Judg 2.8
24.30 Josh 19.50

[n] Or *Sea of Reeds* [o] Meaning of Heb uncertain

inheritance at Timnath-serah,
which is in the hill country of
Ephraim, north of Mount Gaash.
31 Israel served the LORD all the
days of Joshua, and all the days of
the elders who outlived Joshua and
had known all the work that the
LORD did for Israel.
32 The bones of Joseph, which
the Israelites had brought up from
Egypt, were buried at Shechem, in
the portion of ground that Jacob
had bought from the children of
Hamor, the father of Shechem, for
one hundred pieces of money;[p] it
became an inheritance of the descendants of Joseph.
33 Eleazar son of Aaron died;
and they buried him at Gibeah, the
town of his son Phinehas, which
had been given him in the hill
country of Ephraim.

24.31 Judg 2.7 **24.32** Gen 50.24, 25; Ex 13.19; Gen 33.19 **24.33** Josh 22.13

[p] Heb *one hundred qesitah*

Judges

Title and Background

The title describes the type of leaders Israel had from the time of the elders who outlived Joshua until the time of the monarchy. Their principal purpose for having these leaders is best expressed in 2.16. "Then the LORD raised up judges, who delivered them out of the power of those who plundered them." The book tells of Israel's history for the period between the death of Joshua and the ministry of Samuel.

Author and Date of Writing

According to tradition, Samuel wrote the book, but actual authorship is uncertain. It is possible that Samuel assembled some of the accounts from the period of the judges and that some of the prophets had a hand in shaping and editing the material (see 1Ch 29.29). The date of composition was undoubtedly sometime after 1000 B.C.

Theme and Message

On the one hand, the book of Judges tells how the Israelites frequently departed from the Lord to serve idols, provoking God's chastening. On the other hand, it is an account of urgent appeals to God in times of crisis, moving the Lord to raise up leaders (judges) through whom he threw off foreign oppressors and restored the land to peace. It contains several accounts of this recurring cycle (turning to idols, oppression, crying to the Lord, and deliverance). Judges reveals an age when "there was no king in Israel; all the people did what was right in their own eyes" (21.25).

Outline

I. Introduction: Incomplete Conquest and Apostasy (1.1–3.6)
  A. First Episode (1.1–2.5)
  B. Second Episode (2.6–3.6)
II. Oppression by Nations and Deliverance by Judges (3.7–16.31)
III. Epilogue: Religious and Moral Disorder (17.1–21.25)
  A. First Episode (17.1–18.31)
  B. Second Episode (19.1–21.25)

Israel's Failure to Complete the Conquest of Canaan

1 After the death of Joshua, the
Israelites inquired of the LORD,
"Who shall go up first for us against
the Canaanites, to fight against
them?" 2 The LORD said, "Judah
shall go up. I hereby give the land
into his hand." 3 Judah said to his
brother Simeon, "Come up with me
into the territory allotted to me,
that we may fight against the Canaanites;
then I too will go with
you into the territory allotted to
you." So Simeon went with him.

1.1 Num 27.21
1.3 v. 17
1.4 Gen 13.7

4 Then Judah went up and the LORD
gave the Canaanites and the Perizzites
into their hand; and they defeated
ten thousand of them at Bezek.
5 They came upon Adoni-bezek
at Bezek, and fought against him,
and defeated the Canaanites and
the Perizzites. 6 Adoni-bezek fled;
but they pursued him, and caught
him, and cut off his thumbs and big
toes. 7 Adoni-bezek said, "Seventy
kings with their thumbs and big
toes cut off used to pick up scraps
under my table; as I have done, so
God has paid me back." They

brought him to Jerusalem, and he
died there.
8 Then the people of Judah
fought against Jerusalem and took
it. They put it to the sword and set
the city on fire. 9 Afterward the people of Judah went down to fight
against the Canaanites who lived in
the hill country, in the Negeb, and
in the lowland. 10 Judah went
against the Canaanites who lived in
Hebron (the name of Hebron was
formerly Kiriath-arba); and they
defeated Sheshai and Ahiman and
Talmai.
11 From there they went against
the inhabitants of Debir (the name
of Debir was formerly Kiriath-
sepher). 12 Then Caleb said, "Whoever attacks Kiriath-sepher and
takes it, I will give him my daughter
Achsah as wife." 13 And Othniel son
of Kenaz, Caleb's younger brother,
took it; and he gave him his daughter Achsah as wife. 14 When she
came to him, she urged him to ask
her father for a field. As she dismounted from her donkey, Caleb
said to her, "What do you wish?"
15 She said to him, "Give me a
present; since you have set me in
the land of the Negeb, give me also
Gulloth-mayim."[a] So Caleb gave
her Upper Gulloth and Lower Gulloth.
16 The descendants of Hobab[b]
the Kenite, Moses' father-in-law,
went up with the people of Judah
from the city of palms into the wilderness of Judah, which lies in the
Negeb near Arad. Then they went
and settled with the Amalekites.[c]
17 Judah went with his brother Simeon, and they defeated the Canaanites who inhabited Zephath,
and devoted it to destruction. So
the city was called Hormah. 18 Judah took Gaza with its territory,
Ashkelon with its territory, and Ekron with its territory. 19 The LORD
was with Judah, and he took possession of the hill country, but
could not drive out the inhabitants
of the plain, because they had
chariots of iron. 20 Hebron was giv-
en to Caleb, as Moses had said; and
he drove out from it the three sons
of Anak. 21 But the Benjaminites
did not drive out the Jebusites who
lived in Jerusalem; so the Jebusites
have lived in Jerusalem among the
Benjaminites to this day.
22 The house of Joseph also
went up against Bethel; and the
LORD was with them. 23 The house
of Joseph sent out spies to Bethel
(the name of the city was formerly
Luz). 24 When the spies saw a man
coming out of the city, they said to
him, "Show us the way into the
city, and we will deal kindly with
you." 25 So he showed them the way
into the city; and they put the city
to the sword, but they let the man
and all his family go. 26 So the man
went to the land of the Hittites and
built a city, and named it Luz; that
is its name to this day.
27 Manasseh did not drive out
the inhabitants of Beth-shean and
its villages, or Taanach and its villages, or the inhabitants of Dor and
its villages, or the inhabitants of Ibleam and its villages, or the inhabitants of Megiddo and its villages;
but the Canaanites continued to
live in that land. 28 When Israel
grew strong, they put the Canaanites to forced labor, but did not in
fact drive them out.
29 And Ephraim did not drive
out the Canaanites who lived in
Gezer; but the Canaanites lived
among them in Gezer.
30 Zebulun did not drive out the
inhabitants of Kitron, or the inhabitants of Nahalol; but the Canaanites lived among them, and became
subject to forced labor.
31 Asher did not drive out the
inhabitants of Acco, or the inhabitants of Sidon, or of Ahlab, or of
Achzib, or of Helbah, or of Aphik,
or of Rehob; 32 but the Asherites
lived among the Canaanites, the
inhabitants of the land; for they did
not drive them out.
33 Naphtali did not drive out
the inhabitants of Beth-shemesh,
or the inhabitants of Beth-anath,
but lived among the Canaanites,

1.8 v. 21; Josh 15.63
1.10 Josh 15.13-19
1.13 Judg 3.9
1.14 Josh 15.18, 19
1.16 Judg 4.11, 17; Deut 34.3; Judg 3.13
1.17 v. 3; Num 21.3
1.19 v. 2; Josh 17.16, 18
1.20 Josh 14.9; 15.13,14; v. 10
1.21 Josh 15.63
1.23 Gen 28.19
1.25 Josh 6.25
1.27 Josh 17.11-13
1.29 Josh 16.10
1.31 Judg 10.6

[a] That is *Basins of Water* [b] Gk: Heb lacks *Hobab* [c] See 1 Sam 15.6: Heb *people*

the inhabitants of the land; nevertheless the inhabitants of Beth-
shemesh and of Beth-anath became subject to forced labor for
them.
34 The Amorites pressed the
Danites back into the hill country;
they did not allow them to come
down to the plain. 35 The Amorites
continued to live in Har-heres, in
Aijalon, and in Shaalbim, but the
hand of the house of Joseph rested
heavily on them, and they became
subject to forced labor. 36 The border of the Amorites ran from the ascent of Akrabbim, from Sela and
upward.

Israel's Disobedience

2 Now the angel of the LORD
went up from Gilgal to Bochim, and said, "I brought you up
from Egypt, and brought you into
the land that I had promised to
your ancestors. I said, 'I will never
break my covenant with you. 2 For
your part, do not make a covenant
with the inhabitants of this land;
tear down their altars.' But you
have not obeyed my command. See
what you have done! 3 So now I say,
I will not drive them out before
you; but they shall become adversaries[d] to you, and their gods shall
be a snare to you." 4 When the angel of the LORD spoke these words
to all the Israelites, the people lifted up their voices and wept. 5 So
they named that place Bochim,[e]
and there they sacrificed to the
LORD.

Death of Joshua

6 When Joshua dismissed the
people, the Israelites all went to
their own inheritances to take possession of the land. 7 The people
worshiped the LORD all the days of
Joshua, and all the days of the elders who outlived Joshua, who had
seen all the great work that the
LORD had done for Israel. 8 Joshua
son of Nun, the servant of the LORD,
died at the age of one hundred ten
years. 9 So they buried him within
the bounds of his inheritance in
Timnath-heres, in the hill country
of Ephraim, north of Mount Gaash.
10 Moreover, that whole generation
was gathered to their ancestors,
and another generation grew up after them, who did not know the
LORD or the work that he had done
for Israel.

Israel's Unfaithfulness

11 Then the Israelites did what
was evil in the sight of the LORD and
worshiped the Baals; 12 and they
abandoned the LORD, the God of
their ancestors, who had brought
them out of the land of Egypt; they
followed other gods, from among
the gods of the peoples who were
all around them, and bowed down
to them; and they provoked the
LORD to anger. 13 They abandoned
the LORD, and worshiped Baal and
the Astartes. 14 So the anger of the
LORD was kindled against Israel,
and he gave them over to plunderers who plundered them, and he
sold them into the power of their
enemies all around, so that they
could no longer withstand their enemies. 15 Whenever they marched
out, the hand of the LORD was
against them to bring misfortune,
as the LORD had warned them and
sworn to them; and they were in
great distress.
16 Then the LORD raised up
judges, who delivered them out of
the power of those who plundered
them. 17 Yet they did not listen
even to their judges; for they lusted
after other gods and bowed down
to them. They soon turned aside
from the way in which their ancestors had walked, who had obeyed
the commandments of the LORD;
they did not follow their example.
18 Whenever the LORD raised up
judges for them, the LORD was with
the judge, and he delivered them
from the hand of their enemies all
the days of the judge; for the LORD
would be moved to pity by their
groaning because of those who persecuted and oppressed them. 19 But
whenever the judge died, they
would relapse and behave worse

1.34 Ex 3.17
1.36 Josh 15.3
2.1 v. 5; Judg 6.11; Ex 20.2; Gen 17.7; Deut 7.9
2.2 Ex 23.32; 34.12,13
2.3 Josh 23.13; Judg 3.6; Deut 7.16; Ps 106.36
2.6 Josh 24.28-31
2.10 1 Sam 2.12; 1 Chr 28.9; Gal 4.8
2.11 Judg 3.7,12; 4.1; 6.1,25; 8.33; 10.6
2.12 Deut 31.16
2.13 Judg 10.6
2.14 Judg 3.8; Ps 106.40-42; Deut 28.25
2.16 Ps 106.43-45; Acts 13.20
2.17 v. 7
2.19 Judg 3.12; 4.1; 8.33

[d] OL Vg Compare Gk: Heb *sides* [e] That is *Weepers*

than their ancestors, following other gods, worshiping them and bowing down to them. They would not
drop any of their practices or their
stubborn ways. 20 So the anger of
the LORD was kindled against Israel;
and he said, "Because this people
have transgressed my covenant
that I commanded their ancestors,
and have not obeyed my voice, 21 I
will no longer drive out before
them any of the nations that Joshua left when he died." 22 In order to
test Israel, whether or not they
would take care to walk in the way
of the LORD as their ancestors did,
23 the LORD had left those nations,
not driving them out at once, and
had not handed them over to Joshua.

Nations Remaining in the Land

3 Now these are the nations that
the LORD left to test all those in
Israel who had no experience of
any war in Canaan 2 (it was only
that successive generations of Israelites might know war, to teach
those who had no experience of it
before): 3 the five lords of the Philistines, and all the Canaanites, and
the Sidonians, and the Hivites who
lived on Mount Lebanon, from
Mount Baal-hermon as far as Lebo-
hamath. 4 They were for the testing
of Israel, to know whether Israel
would obey the commandments of
the LORD, which he commanded
their ancestors by Moses. 5 So the
Israelites lived among the Canaanites, the Hittites, the Amorites, the
Perizzites, the Hivites, and the Jebusites; 6 and they took their daughters as wives for themselves, and
their own daughters they gave to
their sons; and they worshiped
their gods.

Othniel

7 The Israelites did what was
evil in the sight of the LORD, forgetting the LORD their God, and worshiping the Baals and the Ashe-
rahs. 8 Therefore the anger of the
LORD was kindled against Israel,
and he sold them into the hand of
King Cushan-rishathaim of Aram-
naharaim; and the Israelites
served Cushan-rishathaim eight
years. 9 But when the Israelites
cried out to the LORD, the LORD
raised up a deliverer for the Israelites, who delivered them, Othniel
son of Kenaz, Caleb's younger
brother. 10 The spirit of the LORD
came upon him, and he judged Israel; he went out to war, and the
LORD gave King Cushan-rishathaim
of Aram into his hand; and his
hand prevailed over Cushan-
rishathaim. 11 So the land had rest
forty years. Then Othniel son of
Kenaz died.

Ehud

12 The Israelites again did what
was evil in the sight of the LORD;
and the LORD strengthened King
Eglon of Moab against Israel, because they had done what was evil
in the sight of the LORD. 13 In alliance with the Ammonites and the
Amalekites, he went and defeated
Israel; and they took possession of
the city of palms. 14 So the Israelites served King Eglon of Moab
eighteen years.
15 But when the Israelites cried
out to the LORD, the LORD raised up
for them a deliverer, Ehud son of
Gera, the Benjaminite, a left-
handed man. The Israelites sent
tribute by him to King Eglon of
Moab. 16 Ehud made for himself a
sword with two edges, a cubit in
length; and he fastened it on his
right thigh under his clothes.
17 Then he presented the tribute to
King Eglon of Moab. Now Eglon
was a very fat man. 18 When Ehud
had finished presenting the tribute, he sent the people who carried
the tribute on their way. 19 But he
himself turned back at the sculptured stones near Gilgal, and said,
"I have a secret message for you,
O king." So the king said,[f] "Silence!" and all his attendants went
out from his presence. 20 Ehud
came to him, while he was sitting
alone in his cool roof chamber, and

2.20 v. 14; Josh 23.16
2.21 Josh 23.13
2.22 Judg 3.1,4
3.1 Judg 2.21, 22
3.3 Josh 13.3
3.4 Deut 8.2; Judg 2.22
3.6 Ex 34.16; Deut 7.3,4
3.7 Judg 2.11, 13; Deut 4.9
3.9 v. 15; Judg 1.13
3.10 Num 11.25, 29; 24.2; Judg 6.34
3.12 Judg 2.11, 14
3.13 Judg 1.16
3.15 Ps 107.13
3.17 v. 12

[f] Heb *he said*

said, "I have a message from God
for you." So he rose from his seat.
21 Then Ehud reached with his left
hand, took the sword from his right
thigh, and thrust it into Eglon's[g]
belly; 22 the hilt also went in after
the blade, and the fat closed over
the blade, for he did not draw the
sword out of his belly; and the dirt
came out.[h] 23 Then Ehud went out
into the vestibule,[i] and closed the
doors of the roof chamber on him,
and locked them.
24 After he had gone, the servants came. When they saw that
the doors of the roof chamber were
locked, they thought, "He must be
relieving himself[j] in the cool
chamber." 25 So they waited until
they were embarrassed. When he
still did not open the doors of the
roof chamber, they took the key
and opened them. There was their
lord lying dead on the floor.
26 Ehud escaped while they delayed, and passed beyond the
sculptured stones, and escaped to
Seirah. 27 When he arrived, he
sounded the trumpet in the hill
country of Ephraim; and the Israelites went down with him from the
hill country, having him at their
head. 28 He said to them, "Follow
after me; for the LORD has given
your enemies the Moabites into
your hand." So they went down after him, and seized the fords of the
Jordan against the Moabites, and
allowed no one to cross over. 29 At
that time they killed about ten
thousand of the Moabites, all
strong, able-bodied men; no one
escaped. 30 So Moab was subdued
that day under the hand of Israel.
And the land had rest eighty years.

Shamgar

31 After him came Shamgar son
of Anath, who killed six hundred of
the Philistines with an oxgoad. He
too delivered Israel.

Deborah and Barak

4 The Israelites again did what
was evil in the sight of the
LORD, after Ehud died. 2 So the LORD
sold them into the hand of King Jabin of Canaan, who reigned in Hazor; the commander of his army
was Sisera, who lived in Harosheth-
ha-goiim. 3 Then the Israelites
cried out to the LORD for help; for
he had nine hundred chariots of
iron, and had oppressed the Israelites cruelly twenty years.
4 At that time Deborah, a
prophetess, wife of Lappidoth, was
judging Israel. 5 She used to sit under the palm of Deborah between
Ramah and Bethel in the hill country of Ephraim; and the Israelites
came up to her for judgment. 6 She
sent and summoned Barak son of
Abinoam from Kedesh in Naphtali,
and said to him, "The LORD, the
God of Israel, commands you, 'Go,
take position at Mount Tabor,
bringing ten thousand from the
tribe of Naphtali and the tribe of
Zebulun. 7 I will draw out Sisera,
the general of Jabin's army, to
meet you by the Wadi Kishon with
his chariots and his troops; and I
will give him into your hand.' "
8 Barak said to her, "If you will go
with me, I will go; but if you will
not go with me, I will not go." 9 And
she said, "I will surely go with you;
nevertheless, the road on which
you are going will not lead to your
glory, for the LORD will sell Sisera
into the hand of a woman." Then
Deborah got up and went with Barak to Kedesh. 10 Barak summoned
Zebulun and Naphtali to Kedesh;
and ten thousand warriors went up
behind him; and Deborah went up
with him.
11 Now Heber the Kenite had
separated from the other Kenites,[k]
that is, the descendants of Hobab
the father-in-law of Moses, and had
encamped as far away as Elon-
bezaanannim, which is near Kedesh.
12 When Sisera was told that
Barak son of Abinoam had gone up
to Mount Tabor, 13 Sisera called out
all his chariots, nine hundred char-

3.24 1 Sam 24.3
3.25 2 Kings 2.17; 8.11
3.28 Judg 7.9,15, 24; 12.5
3.30 v. 11
3.31 Judg 5.6
4.1 Judg 2.19
4.2 Josh 11.1, 10; vv. 13, 16; Ps 83.9
4.3 Judg 1.19
4.6 Heb 11.32
4.7 Ps 83.9
4.9 v. 21
4.10 Judg 5.18; v. 14; Judg 5.15
4.11 Judg 1.16; v. 6
4.13 v. 3

[g] Heb *his* [h] With Tg Vg: Meaning of Heb uncertain [i] Meaning of Heb uncertain [j] Heb *covering his feet* [k] Heb *from the Kain*

iots of iron, and all the troops who
were with him, from Harosheth-ha-
goiim to the Wadi Kishon. 14 Then
Deborah said to Barak, "Up! For
this is the day on which the LORD
has given Sisera into your hand.
The LORD is indeed going out before
you." So Barak went down from
Mount Tabor with ten thousand
warriors following him. 15 And the
LORD threw Sisera and all his chariots and all his army into a panic[l]
before Barak; Sisera got down from
his chariot and fled away on foot,
16 while Barak pursued the chariots
and the army to Harosheth-ha-
goiim. All the army of Sisera fell by
the sword; no one was left.
17 Now Sisera had fled away on
foot to the tent of Jael wife of Heber the Kenite; for there was peace
between King Jabin of Hazor and
the clan of Heber the Kenite. 18 Jael
came out to meet Sisera, and said
to him, "Turn aside, my lord, turn
aside to me; have no fear." So he
turned aside to her into the tent,
and she covered him with a rug.
19 Then he said to her, "Please give
me a little water to drink; for I am
thirsty." So she opened a skin of
milk and gave him a drink and covered him. 20 He said to her, "Stand
at the entrance of the tent, and if
anybody comes and asks you, 'Is
anyone here?' say, 'No.' " 21 But
Jael wife of Heber took a tent peg,
and took a hammer in her hand,
and went softly to him and drove
the peg into his temple, until it
went down into the ground—he
was lying fast asleep from
weariness—and he died. 22 Then,
as Barak came in pursuit of Sisera,
Jael went out to meet him, and said
to him, "Come, and I will show you
the man whom you are seeking."
So he went into her tent; and there
was Sisera lying dead, with the tent
peg in his temple.
23 So on that day God subdued
King Jabin of Canaan before the Israelites. 24 Then the hand of the Israelites bore harder and harder on
King Jabin of Canaan, until they
destroyed King Jabin of Canaan.

4.14 Deut 9.3 **4.15** Josh 10.10 **4.16** Ps 83.9 **4.19** Judg 5.25 **4.21** Judg 5.26

5.1 Ex 15.1 **5.2** Deut 32.41 **5.3** Ps 27.6 **5.4** Deut 33.2; Ps 68.7-9 **5.5** Ps 97.5; Isa 64.1,3; Ps 68.8 **5.6** Judg 3.31; 4.17 **5.8** Deut 32.17

The Song of Deborah

5 Then Deborah and Barak son
of Abinoam sang on that day,
saying:
2 "When locks are long in
Israel,
when the people offer
themselves willingly—
bless[m] the LORD!

3 "Hear, O kings; give ear,
O princes;
to the LORD I will sing,
I will make melody to the
LORD, the God of Israel.

4 "LORD, when you went out
from Seir,
when you marched from
the region of Edom,
the earth trembled,
and the heavens poured,
the clouds indeed poured
water.
5 The mountains quaked
before the LORD, the
One of Sinai,
before the LORD, the God of
Israel.

6 "In the days of Shamgar son
of Anath,
in the days of Jael,
caravans ceased
and travelers kept to the
byways.
7 The peasantry prospered in
Israel,
they grew fat on plunder,
because you arose, Deborah,
arose as a mother in Israel.
8 When new gods were chosen,
then war was in the gates.
Was shield or spear to be
seen
among forty thousand in
Israel?
9 My heart goes out to the
commanders of Israel
who offered themselves
willingly among the
people.
Bless the LORD.

[l] Heb adds *to the sword*; compare verse 16
[m] Or *You who offer yourselves willingly among the people, bless*

10 "Tell of it, you who ride on
white donkeys,
you who sit on rich
carpets[n]
and you who walk by the
way.
11 To the sound of musicians[n]
at the watering places,
there they repeat the
triumphs of the LORD,
the triumphs of his
peasantry in Israel.

"Then down to the gates
marched the people of
the LORD.

12 "Awake, awake, Deborah!
Awake, awake, utter a
song!
Arise, Barak, lead away your
captives,
O son of Abinoam.
13 Then down marched the
remnant of the noble;
the people of the LORD
marched down for him[o]
against the mighty.
14 From Ephraim they set out[p]
into the valley,[q]
following you, Benjamin,
with your kin;
from Machir marched down
the commanders,
and from Zebulun those
who bear the marshal's
staff;
15 the chiefs of Issachar came
with Deborah,
and Issachar faithful to
Barak;
into the valley they rushed
out at his heels.
Among the clans of Reuben
there were great searchings
of heart.
16 Why did you tarry among the
sheepfolds,
to hear the piping for the
flocks?
Among the clans of Reuben
there were great searchings
of heart.
17 Gilead stayed beyond the
Jordan;
and Dan, why did he abide
with the ships?
Asher sat still at the coast of
the sea,
settling down by his
landings.
18 Zebulun is a people that
scorned death;
Naphtali too, on the
heights of the field.

19 "The kings came, they
fought;
then fought the kings of
Canaan,
at Taanach, by the waters of
Megiddo;
they got no spoils of silver.
20 The stars fought from
heaven,
from their courses they
fought against Sisera.
21 The torrent Kishon swept
them away,
the onrushing torrent, the
torrent Kishon.
March on, my soul, with
might!

22 "Then loud beat the horses'
hoofs
with the galloping,
galloping of his steeds.

23 "Curse Meroz, says the angel
of the LORD,
curse bitterly its
inhabitants,
because they did not come
to the help of the LORD,
to the help of the LORD
against the mighty.

24 "Most blessed of women be
Jael,
the wife of Heber the
Kenite,
of tent-dwelling women
most blessed.
25 He asked water and she gave
him milk,
she brought him curds in a
lordly bowl.
26 She put her hand to the tent
peg

5.11 1 Sam 12.7; Mic 6.5
5.12 Ps 57.8; 68.18
5.14 Judg 3.13, 27; Num 32.39
5.15 Judg 4.10
5.16 Num 32.1
5.17 Josh 13.24-28; 19.29,46
5.18 Judg 4.6,10
5.19ff Josh 11.1,2; Judg 1.27
5.20 Josh 10.11-14
5.21 Judg 4.7
5.24 Judg 4.17, 19-21
5.25 Judg 4.19
5.26 Judg 4.21

[n] Meaning of Heb uncertain [o] Gk: Heb *me*
[p] Cn: Heb *From Ephraim their root*
[q] Gk: Heb *in Amalek*

and her right hand to the
workmen's mallet;
she struck Sisera a blow,
she crushed his head,
she shattered and pierced
his temple.
27 He sank, he fell,
he lay still at her feet;
at her feet he sank, he fell;
where he sank, there he
fell dead.

28 "Out of the window she
peered,
the mother of Sisera
gazed[r] through the
lattice:
'Why is his chariot so long in
coming?
Why tarry the hoofbeats of
his chariots?'
29 Her wisest ladies make
answer,
indeed, she answers the
question herself:
30 'Are they not finding and
dividing the spoil?—
A girl or two for every man;
spoil of dyed stuffs for
Sisera,
spoil of dyed stuffs
embroidered,
two pieces of dyed work
embroidered for my
neck as spoil?'

31 "So perish all your enemies,
O LORD!
But may your friends be
like the sun as it rises
in its might."

And the land had rest forty years.

The Midianite Oppression

6 The Israelites did what was
evil in the sight of the LORD,
and the LORD gave them into the
hand of Midian seven years. 2 The
hand of Midian prevailed over Israel; and because of Midian the Israelites provided for themselves hiding places in the mountains, caves
and strongholds. 3 For whenever
the Israelites put in seed, the Midianites and the Amalekites and the
people of the east would come up
against them. 4 They would encamp against them and destroy the
produce of the land, as far as the
neighborhood of Gaza, and leave
no sustenance in Israel, and no
sheep or ox or donkey. 5 For they
and their livestock would come up,
and they would even bring their
tents, as thick as locusts; neither
they nor their camels could be
counted; so they wasted the land as
they came in. 6 Thus Israel was
greatly impoverished because of
Midian; and the Israelites cried out
to the LORD for help.
7 When the Israelites cried to
the LORD on account of the Midianites, 8 the LORD sent a prophet to
the Israelites; and he said to them,
"Thus says the LORD, the God of Israel: I led you up from Egypt, and
brought you out of the house of
slavery; 9 and I delivered you from
the hand of the Egyptians, and
from the hand of all who oppressed
you, and drove them out before
you, and gave you their land; 10 and
I said to you, 'I am the LORD your
God; you shall not pay reverence to
the gods of the Amorites, in whose
land you live.' But you have not giv-
en heed to my voice."

The Call of Gideon

11 Now the angel of the LORD
came and sat under the oak at
Ophrah, which belonged to Joash
the Abiezrite, as his son Gideon
was beating out wheat in the wine
press, to hide it from the Midianites. 12 The angel of the LORD appeared to him and said to him,
"The LORD is with you, you mighty
warrior." 13 Gideon answered him,
"But sir, if the LORD is with us, why
then has all this happened to us?
And where are all his wonderful
deeds that our ancestors recounted
to us, saying, 'Did not the LORD
bring us up from Egypt?' But now
the LORD has cast us off, and given
us into the hand of Midian."
14 Then the LORD turned to him and
said, "Go in this might of yours and
deliver Israel from the hand of Midian; I hereby commission you."

5.28 Prov 7.6
5.30 Ex 15.9
5.31 Ps 68.2; 92.9; 19.4,5; Judg 3.11
6.1 Judg 2.11, 19; Num 25.15-18; 31.1-3
6.3 Judg 3.13
6.4 Lev 26.16; Deut 28.30, 33,51
6.5 Judg 7.12
6.6 Judg 3.15
6.8 Judg 2.1,2
6.9 Ps 44.2,3
6.11 Josh 17.2
6.12 Josh 1.5
6.13 Ps 44.1; 2 Chr 15.2
6.14 Heb 11.32, 34; Judg 4.6

r Gk Compare Tg: Heb *exclaimed*

15 He responded, "But sir, how can I deliver Israel? My clan is the weakest in Manasseh, and I am the least in my family." 16 The LORD said to him, "But I will be with you, and you shall strike down the Midianites, every one of them." 17 Then he said to him, "If now I have found favor with you, then show me a sign that it is you who speak with me. 18 Do not depart from here until I come to you, and bring out my present, and set it before you." And he said, "I will stay until you return."

19 So Gideon went into his house and prepared a kid, and unleavened cakes from an ephah of flour; the meat he put in a basket, and the broth he put in a pot, and brought them to him under the oak and presented them. 20 The angel of God said to him, "Take the meat and the unleavened cakes, and put them on this rock, and pour out the broth." And he did so. 21 Then the angel of the LORD reached out the tip of the staff that was in his hand, and touched the meat and the unleavened cakes; and fire sprang up from the rock and consumed the meat and the unleavened cakes; and the angel of the LORD vanished from his sight. 22 Then Gideon perceived that it was the angel of the LORD; and Gideon said, "Help me, Lord GOD! For I have seen the angel of the LORD face to face." 23 But the LORD said to him, "Peace be to you; do not fear, you shall not die." 24 Then Gideon built an altar there to the LORD, and called it, The LORD is peace. To this day it still stands at Ophrah, which belongs to the Abiezrites.

25 That night the LORD said to him, "Take your father's bull, the second bull seven years old, and pull down the altar of Baal that belongs to your father, and cut down the sacred pole[s] that is beside it; 26 and build an altar to the LORD your God on the top of the stronghold here, in proper order; then take the second bull, and offer it as a burnt offering with the wood of the sacred pole[s] that you shall cut down." 27 So Gideon took ten of his servants, and did as the LORD had told him; but because he was too afraid of his family and the townspeople to do it by day, he did it by night.

Gideon Destroys the Altar of Baal

28 When the townspeople rose early in the morning, the altar of Baal was broken down, and the sacred pole[s] beside it was cut down, and the second bull was offered on the altar that had been built. 29 So they said to one another, "Who has done this?" After searching and inquiring, they were told, "Gideon son of Joash did it." 30 Then the townspeople said to Joash, "Bring out your son, so that he may die, for he has pulled down the altar of Baal and cut down the sacred pole[s] beside it." 31 But Joash said to all who were arrayed against him, "Will you contend for Baal? Or will you defend his cause? Whoever contends for him shall be put to death by morning. If he is a god, let him contend for himself, because his altar has been pulled down." 32 Therefore on that day Gideon[t] was called Jerubbaal, that is to say, "Let Baal contend against him," because he pulled down his altar.

33 Then all the Midianites and the Amalekites and the people of the east came together, and crossing the Jordan they encamped in the Valley of Jezreel. 34 But the spirit of the LORD took possession of Gideon; and he sounded the trumpet, and the Abiezrites were called out to follow him. 35 He sent messengers throughout all Manasseh, and they too were called out to follow him. He also sent messengers to Asher, Zebulun, and Naphtali, and they went up to meet them.

The Sign of the Fleece

36 Then Gideon said to God, "In order to see whether you will deliver Israel by my hand, as you have

6.15 Ex 3.11; 1 Sam 9.21
6.16 Ex 3.12; Josh 1.5
6.17 vv. 36,37; Isa 38.7,8
6.19 Gen 18.6-8
6.20 Judg 13.19
6.21 Lev 9.24
6.22 Judg 13.21
6.25 Ex 34.13; Deut 7.5
6.28 1 Kings 16.32
6.32 Judg 7.1; 1 Sam 12.11
6.33 v. 3; Josh 17.16
6.34 Judg 3.10, 27; 1 Chr 12.18; 2 Chr 24.20

s Heb *Asherah* t Heb *he*

said, 37 I am going to lay a fleece of wool on the threshing floor; if there is dew on the fleece alone, and it is dry on all the ground, then I shall know that you will deliver Israel by my hand, as you have said." 38 And it was so. When he rose early next morning and squeezed the fleece, he wrung enough dew from the fleece to fill a bowl with water. 39 Then Gideon said to God, "Do not let your anger burn against me, let me speak one more time; let me, please, make trial with the fleece just once more; let it be dry only on the fleece, and on all the ground let there be dew." 40 And God did so that night. It was dry on the fleece only, and on all the ground there was dew.

Gideon Surprises and Routs the Midianites

7 Then Jerubbaal (that is, Gideon) and all the troops that were with him rose early and encamped beside the spring of Harod; and the camp of Midian was north of them, below[u] the hill of Moreh, in the valley.

2 The LORD said to Gideon, "The troops with you are too many for me to give the Midianites into their hand. Israel would only take the credit away from me, saying, 'My own hand has delivered me.' 3 Now therefore proclaim this in the hearing of the troops, 'Whoever is fearful and trembling, let him return home.'" Thus Gideon sifted them out;[v] twenty-two thousand returned, and ten thousand remained.

4 Then the LORD said to Gideon, "The troops are still too many; take them down to the water and I will sift them out for you there. When I say, 'This one shall go with you,' he shall go with you; and when I say, 'This one shall not go with you,' he shall not go." 5 So he brought the troops down to the water; and the LORD said to Gideon, "All those who lap the water with their tongues, as a dog laps, you shall put to one side; all those who kneel down to drink, putting their hands to their mouths,[w] you shall put to the other side." 6 The number of those that lapped was three hundred; but all the rest of the troops knelt down to drink water. 7 Then the LORD said to Gideon, "With the three hundred that lapped I will deliver you, and give the Midianites into your hand. Let all the others go to their homes." 8 So he took the jars of the troops from their hands,[x] and their trumpets; and he sent all the rest of Israel back to their own tents, but retained the three hundred. The camp of Midian was below him in the valley.

9 That same night the LORD said to him, "Get up, attack the camp; for I have given it into your hand. 10 But if you fear to attack, go down to the camp with your servant Purah; 11 and you shall hear what they say, and afterward your hands shall be strengthened to attack the camp." Then he went down with his servant Purah to the outposts of the armed men that were in the camp. 12 The Midianites and the Amalekites and all the people of the east lay along the valley as thick as locusts; and their camels were without number, countless as the sand on the seashore. 13 When Gideon arrived, there was a man telling a dream to his comrade; and he said, "I had a dream, and in it a cake of barley bread tumbled into the camp of Midian, and came to the tent, and struck it so that it fell; it turned upside down, and the tent collapsed." 14 And his comrade answered, "This is no other than the sword of Gideon son of Joash, a man of Israel; into his hand God has given Midian and all the army."

15 When Gideon heard the telling of the dream and its interpretation, he worshiped; and he returned to the camp of Israel, and said, "Get up; for the LORD has given the army of Midian into your hand." 16 After he divided the three

6.37 Ex 4.3-7
6.39 Gen 18.32
7.1 Judg 6.32
7.2 Deut 8.17; Isa 10.13; 2 Cor 4.7
7.3 Deut 20.8
7.4 1 Sam 14.6
7.7 1 Sam 14.6
7.9 Josh 2.24; 10.8; 11.6
7.11 vv. 13-15
7.12 Judg 6.5; 8.10; Josh 11.4
7.14 v. 20
7.15 1 Sam 15.31

[u] Heb *from* [v] Cn: Heb *home, and depart from Mount Gilead'"* [w] Heb places the words *putting their hands to their mouths* after the word *lapped* in verse 6 [x] Cn: Heb *So the people took provisions in their hands*

hundred men into three companies, and put trumpets into the
hands of all of them, and empty
jars, with torches inside the jars,
17 he said to them, "Look at me,
and do the same; when I come to
the outskirts of the camp, do as I
do. 18 When I blow the trumpet, I
and all who are with me, then you
also blow the trumpets around the
whole camp, and shout, 'For the
LORD and for Gideon!' "
19 So Gideon and the hundred
who were with him came to the
outskirts of the camp at the beginning of the middle watch, when
they had just set the watch; and
they blew the trumpets and
smashed the jars that were in their
hands. 20 So the three companies
blew the trumpets and broke the
jars, holding in their left hands the
torches, and in their right hands
the trumpets to blow; and they
cried, "A sword for the LORD and for
Gideon!" 21 Every man stood in his
place all around the camp, and all
the men in camp ran; they cried out
and fled. 22 When they blew the
three hundred trumpets, the LORD
set every man's sword against his
fellow and against all the army; and
the army fled as far as Beth-shittah
toward Zererah,[y] as far as the border of Abel-meholah, by Tabbath.
23 And the men of Israel were called
out from Naphtali and from Asher
and from all Manasseh, and they
pursued after the Midianites.
24 Then Gideon sent messengers throughout all the hill country
of Ephraim, saying, "Come down
against the Midianites and seize
the waters against them, as far as
Beth-barah, and also the Jordan."
So all the men of Ephraim were
called out, and they seized the waters as far as Beth-barah, and also
the Jordan. 25 They captured the
two captains of Midian, Oreb and
Zeeb; they killed Oreb at the rock
of Oreb, and Zeeb they killed at the
wine press of Zeeb, as they pursued
the Midianites. They brought the
heads of Oreb and Zeeb to Gideon
beyond the Jordan.

7.18 vv. 14,20 **7.20** v. 14 **7.21** 2 Kings 7.7 **7.22** Josh 6.4; 16.20; 1 Sam 14.20 **7.23** Judg 6.35 **7.24** Judg 3.27, 28 **7.25** Judg 8.3,4; Ps 83.11; Isa 10.26

8.1 Judg 12.1 **8.3** Judg 7.24, 25 **8.5** Gen 33.17 **8.6** v. 15 **8.7** Judg 7.15 **8.8** Gen 32.30, 31 **8.9** v. 18 **8.12** Ps 83.11

Gideon's Triumph and Vengeance

8 Then the Ephraimites said to
him, "What have you done to
us, not to call us when you went to
fight against the Midianites?" And
they upbraided him violently. 2 So
he said to them, "What have I done
now in comparison with you? Is not
the gleaning of the grapes of Ephraim better than the vintage of Abiezer? 3 God has given into your
hands the captains of Midian, Oreb
and Zeeb; what have I been able to
do in comparison with you?" When
he said this, their anger against
him subsided.
4 Then Gideon came to the Jordan and crossed over, he and the
three hundred who were with him,
exhausted and famished.[z] 5 So he
said to the people of Succoth,
"Please give some loaves of bread
to my followers, for they are exhausted, and I am pursuing Zebah
and Zalmunna, the kings of Midian." 6 But the officials of Succoth
said, "Do you already have in your
possession the hands of Zebah and
Zalmunna, that we should give
bread to your army?" 7 Gideon replied, "Well then, when the LORD
has given Zebah and Zalmunna
into my hand, I will trample your
flesh on the thorns of the wilderness and on briers." 8 From there
he went up to Penuel, and made
the same request of them; and the
people of Penuel answered him as
the people of Succoth had answered. 9 So he said to the people of
Penuel, "When I come back victorious, I will break down this tower."
10 Now Zebah and Zalmunna
were in Karkor with their army,
about fifteen thousand men, all
who were left of all the army of the
people of the east; for one hundred
twenty thousand men bearing arms
had fallen. 11 So Gideon went up by
the caravan route east of Nobah
and Jogbehah, and attacked the
army; for the army was off its guard.
12 Zebah and Zalmunna fled; and

[y] Another reading is *Zeredah* [z] Gk: Heb *pursuing*

he pursued them and took the two
kings of Midian, Zebah and Zalmunna, and threw all the army into
a panic.
13 When Gideon son of Joash
returned from the battle by the ascent of Heres, 14 he caught a young
man, one of the people of Succoth,
and questioned him; and he listed
for him the officials and elders of
Succoth, seventy-seven people.
15 Then he came to the people of
Succoth, and said, "Here are Zebah
and Zalmunna, about whom you
taunted me, saying, 'Do you already have in your possession the
hands of Zebah and Zalmunna,
that we should give bread to your
troops who are exhausted?' " 16 So
he took the elders of the city and he
took thorns of the wilderness and
briers and with them he trampled[a]
the people of Succoth. 17 He also
broke down the tower of Penuel,
and killed the men of the city.
18 Then he said to Zebah and
Zalmunna, "What about the men
whom you killed at Tabor?" They
answered, "As you are, so were
they, every one of them; they re-
sembled the sons of a king." 19 And
he replied, "They were my brothers, the sons of my mother; as the
LORD lives, if you had saved them
alive, I would not kill you." 20 So he
said to Jether his firstborn, "Go kill
them!" But the boy did not draw his
sword, for he was afraid, because
he was still a boy. 21 Then Zebah
and Zalmunna said, "You come
and kill us; for as the man is, so is
his strength." So Gideon proceeded to kill Zebah and Zalmunna; and
he took the crescents that were on
the necks of their camels.

Gideon's Idolatry

22 Then the Israelites said to
Gideon, "Rule over us, you and
your son and your grandson also;
for you have delivered us out of the
hand of Midian." 23 Gideon said to
them, "I will not rule over you, and
my son will not rule over you; the
LORD will rule over you." 24 Then
Gideon said to them, "Let me
make a request of you; each of you

8.15 v. 6
8.16 v. 7
8.17 v. 9
8.18 Judg 4.6
8.21 Ps 83.11; v. 26
8.23 1 Sam 8.7; 10.19; 12.12
8.27 Judg 17.5; Ps 106.39; Deut 7.16
8.28 Judg 5.31
8.29 Judg 7.1
8.30 Judg 9.2,5
8.31 Judg 9.1
8.33 Judg 2.17, 19; 9.4,46
8.34 Judg 3.7; Deut 4.9
9.1 Judg 8.31

give me an earring he has taken as
booty." (For the enemy[b] had gold-
en earrings, because they were Ishmaelites.) 25 "We will willingly give
them," they answered. So they
spread a garment, and each threw
into it an earring he had taken as
booty. 26 The weight of the golden
earrings that he requested was one
thousand seven hundred shekels of
gold (apart from the crescents and
the pendants and the purple garments worn by the kings of Midian,
and the collars that were on the
necks of their camels). 27 Gideon
made an ephod of it and put it in
his town, in Ophrah; and all Israel
prostituted themselves to it there,
and it became a snare to Gideon
and to his family. 28 So Midian was
subdued before the Israelites, and
they lifted up their heads no more.
So the land had rest forty years in
the days of Gideon.

Death of Gideon

29 Jerubbaal son of Joash went
to live in his own house. 30 Now
Gideon had seventy sons, his own
offspring, for he had many wives.
31 His concubine who was in Shechem also bore him a son, and he
named him Abimelech. 32 Then
Gideon son of Joash died at a good
old age, and was buried in the tomb
of his father Joash at Ophrah of the
Abiezrites.
33 As soon as Gideon died, the
Israelites relapsed and prostituted
themselves with the Baals, making
Baal-berith their god. 34 The Israelites did not remember the LORD
their God, who had rescued them
from the hand of all their enemies
on every side; 35 and they did not
exhibit loyalty to the house of Jerubbaal (that is, Gideon) in return
for all the good that he had done to
Israel.

Abimelech Attempts to Establish a Monarchy

9 Now Abimelech son of Jerubbaal went to Shechem to his
mother's kinsfolk and said to them

[a] With verse 7, Compare Gk: Heb *he taught*
[b] Heb *they*

and to the whole clan of his mother's family, 2 “Say in the hearing of
all the lords of Shechem, ‘Which is
better for you, that all seventy of
the sons of Jerubbaal rule over you,
or that one rule over you?’ Remember also that I am your bone and
your flesh.” 3 So his mother's kinsfolk spoke all these words on his
behalf in the hearing of all the lords
of Shechem; and their hearts inclined to follow Abimelech, for
they said, “He is our brother.”
4 They gave him seventy pieces of
silver out of the temple of Baal-
berith with which Abimelech hired
worthless and reckless fellows,
who followed him. 5 He went to his
father's house at Ophrah, and
killed his brothers the sons of Jerubbaal, seventy men, on one stone;
but Jotham, the youngest son of
Jerubbaal, survived, for he hid himself. 6 Then all the lords of Shechem and all Beth-millo came together, and they went and made
Abimelech king, by the oak of the
pillar[c] at Shechem.

The Parable of the Trees

7 When it was told to Jotham,
he went and stood on the top of
Mount Gerizim, and cried aloud
and said to them, “Listen to me,
you lords of Shechem, so that God
may listen to you.

8 The trees once went out
to anoint a king over
themselves.
So they said to the olive tree,
‘Reign over us.’
9 The olive tree answered
them,
‘Shall I stop producing my
rich oil
by which gods and
mortals are honored,
and go to sway over the
trees?’
10 Then the trees said to the fig
tree,
‘You come and reign over
us.’
11 But the fig tree answered
them,
‘Shall I stop producing my
sweetness
and my delicious fruit,
and go to sway over the
trees?’
12 Then the trees said to the
vine,
‘You come and reign over
us.’
13 But the vine said to them,
‘Shall I stop producing my
wine
that cheers gods and
mortals,
and go to sway over the
trees?’
14 So all the trees said to the
bramble,
‘You come and reign over
us.’
15 And the bramble said to the
trees,
‘If in good faith you are
anointing me king over
you,
then come and take
refuge in my shade;
but if not, let fire come out
of the bramble
and devour the cedars of
Lebanon.’

16 “Now therefore, if you acted
in good faith and honor when you
made Abimelech king, and if you
have dealt well with Jerubbaal and
his house, and have done to him as
his actions deserved— 17 for my father fought for you, and risked his
life, and rescued you from the hand
of Midian; 18 but you have risen up
against my father's house this day,
and have killed his sons, seventy
men on one stone, and have made
Abimelech, the son of his slave
woman, king over the lords of
Shechem, because he is your
kinsman— 19 if, I say, you have acted in good faith and honor with Jerubbaal and with his house this day,
then rejoice in Abimelech, and let
him also rejoice in you; 20 but if not,
let fire come out from Abimelech,
and devour the lords of Shechem,
and Beth-millo; and let fire come
out from the lords of Shechem, and
from Beth-millo, and devour Abimelech.” 21 Then Jotham ran away

9.2 Judg 8.30; Gen 29.14
9.4 Judg 8.33
9.5 v. 2
9.7 Deut 11.29; 27.12; Jn 4.20
9.15 Isa 30.2; v. 20
9.16 Judg 8.35
9.18 vv. 5,6; Judg 8.31
9.19 Judg 8.35

c Cn: Meaning of Heb uncertain

and fled, going to Beer, where he
remained for fear of his brother
Abimelech.

The Downfall of Abimelech

22 Abimelech ruled over Israel
three years. 23 But God sent an evil
spirit between Abimelech and the
lords of Shechem; and the lords of
Shechem dealt treacherously with
Abimelech. 24 This happened so
that the violence done to the seventy sons of Jerubbaal might be
avenged[d] and their blood be laid
on their brother Abimelech, who
killed them, and on the lords of
Shechem, who strengthened his
hands to kill his brothers. 25 So, out
of hostility to him, the lords of Shechem set ambushes on the mountain tops. They robbed all who
passed by them along that way; and
it was reported to Abimelech.
26 When Gaal son of Ebed
moved into Shechem with his kinsfolk, the lords of Shechem put confidence in him. 27 They went out
into the field and gathered the
grapes from their vineyards, trod
them, and celebrated. Then they
went into the temple of their god,
ate and drank, and ridiculed Abimelech. 28 Gaal son of Ebed said,
"Who is Abimelech, and who are
we of Shechem, that we should
serve him? Did not the son of Jerubbaal and Zebul his officer serve
the men of Hamor father of Shechem? Why then should we serve
him? 29 If only this people were under my command! Then I would remove Abimelech; I would say[e] to
him, 'Increase your army, and
come out.' "
30 When Zebul the ruler of the
city heard the words of Gaal son of
Ebed, his anger was kindled. 31 He
sent messengers to Abimelech at
Arumah,[f] saying, "Look, Gaal son
of Ebed and his kinsfolk have come
to Shechem, and they are stirring
up[g] the city against you. 32 Now
therefore, go by night, you and the
troops that are with you, and lie in
wait in the fields. 33 Then early in
the morning, as soon as the sun
rises, get up and rush on the city;
and when he and the troops that
are with him come out against you,
you may deal with them as best you
can."
34 So Abimelech and all the
troops with him got up by night and
lay in wait against Shechem in four
companies. 35 When Gaal son of
Ebed went out and stood in the entrance of the gate of the city, Abimelech and the troops with him rose
from the ambush. 36 And when
Gaal saw them, he said to Zebul,
"Look, people are coming down
from the mountain tops!" And Zebul said to him, "The shadows on
the mountains look like people to
you." 37 Gaal spoke again and said,
"Look, people are coming down
from Tabbur-erez, and one company is coming from the direction of
Elon-meonenim."[h] 38 Then Zebul
said to him, "Where is your boast[i]
now, you who said, 'Who is Abimelech, that we should serve him?'
Are not these the troops you made
light of? Go out now and fight with
them." 39 So Gaal went out at the
head of the lords of Shechem, and
fought with Abimelech. 40 Abimelech chased him, and he fled before
him. Many fell wounded, up to the
entrance of the gate. 41 So Abimelech resided at Arumah; and Zebul
drove out Gaal and his kinsfolk, so
that they could not live on at Shechem.
42 On the following day the
people went out into the fields.
When Abimelech was told, 43 he
took his troops and divided them
into three companies, and lay in
wait in the fields. When he looked
and saw the people coming out of
the city, he rose against them and
killed them. 44 Abimelech and the
company that was[j] with him
rushed forward and stood at the entrance of the gate of the city, while
the two companies rushed on all
who were in the fields and killed
them. 45 Abimelech fought against

9.23 1 Sam 16.14; 18.9,10
9.24 vv. 56,57; Deut 27.25; Num 35.33
9.27 Judg 8.33
9.28 Gen 34.2,6
9.29 2 Sam 15.4
9.33 1 Sam 10.7
9.37 Ezek 38.12
9.38 vv. 28,29
9.39 Gen 35.4
9.45 v. 20; Deut 29.23

[d] Heb *might come* [e] Gk: Heb *and he said* [f] Cn See 9.41. Heb *Tormah* [g] Cn: Heb *are besieging* [h] That is *Diviners' Oak* [i] Heb *mouth* [j] Vg and some Gk Mss: Heb *companies that were*

the city all that day; he took the
city, and killed the people that
were in it; and he razed the city and
sowed it with salt.
46 When all the lords of the
Tower of Shechem heard of it, they
entered the stronghold of the temple of El-berith. 47 Abimelech was
told that all the lords of the Tower
of Shechem were gathered together. 48 So Abimelech went up to
Mount Zalmon, he and all the
troops that were with him. Abimelech took an ax in his hand, cut
down a bundle of brushwood, and
took it up and laid it on his shoulder. Then he said to the troops with
him, "What you have seen me do,
do quickly, as I have done." 49 So
every one of the troops cut down a
bundle and following Abimelech
put it against the stronghold, and
they set the stronghold on fire over
them, so that all the people of the
Tower of Shechem also died, about
a thousand men and women.
50 Then Abimelech went to
Thebez, and encamped against
Thebez, and took it. 51 But there
was a strong tower within the city,
and all the men and women and all
the lords of the city fled to it and
shut themselves in; and they went
to the roof of the tower. 52 Abimelech came to the tower, and fought
against it, and came near to the entrance of the tower to burn it with
fire. 53 But a certain woman threw
an upper millstone on Abimelech's
head, and crushed his skull. 54 Immediately he called to the young
man who carried his armor and
said to him, "Draw your sword and
kill me, so people will not say
about me, 'A woman killed him.' "
So the young man thrust him
through, and he died. 55 When the
Israelites saw that Abimelech was
dead, they all went home. 56 Thus
God repaid Abimelech for the
crime he committed against his father in killing his seventy brothers;
57 and God also made all the wickedness of the people of Shechem
fall back on their heads, and on
them came the curse of Jotham son
of Jerubbaal.

9.46 Judg 8.33 **9.48** Ps 68.14 **9.50** 2 Sam 11.21 **9.53** v. 50 **9.56** v. 24; Ps 94.23 **9.57** v. 20

10.1 Judg 2.16 **10.4** Num 32.41 **10.6** Judg 2.11-13; Deut 31.16, 17; 32.15 **10.7** Judg 2.14 **10.10** 1 Sam 12.10 **10.11** Ex 14.30; Num 21.21; 24.25; Judg 3.12, 13,31 **10.12** Judg 5.19; Ps 106.42, 43

Tola and Jair

10 After Abimelech, Tola son
of Puah son of Dodo, a man
of Issachar, who lived at Shamir in
the hill country of Ephraim, rose to
deliver Israel. 2 He judged Israel
twenty-three years. Then he died,
and was buried at Shamir.
3 After him came Jair the Gileadite, who judged Israel twenty-
two years. 4 He had thirty sons who
rode on thirty donkeys; and they
had thirty towns, which are in the
land of Gilead, and are called
Havvoth-jair to this day. 5 Jair died,
and was buried in Kamon.

Oppression by the Ammonites

6 The Israelites again did what
was evil in the sight of the LORD,
worshiping the Baals and the Astartes, the gods of Aram, the gods
of Sidon, the gods of Moab, the
gods of the Ammonites, and the
gods of the Philistines. Thus they
abandoned the LORD, and did not
worship him. 7 So the anger of the
LORD was kindled against Israel,
and he sold them into the hand of
the Philistines and into the hand of
the Ammonites, 8 and they crushed
and oppressed the Israelites that
year. For eighteen years they oppressed all the Israelites that were
beyond the Jordan in the land of
the Amorites, which is in Gilead.
9 The Ammonites also crossed the
Jordan to fight against Judah and
against Benjamin and against the
house of Ephraim; so that Israel
was greatly distressed.
10 So the Israelites cried to the
LORD, saying, "We have sinned
against you, because we have abandoned our God and have worshiped
the Baals." 11 And the LORD said to
the Israelites, "Did I not deliver
you[k] from the Egyptians and from
the Amorites, from the Ammonites
and from the Philistines? 12 The Sidonians also, and the Amalekites,
and the Maonites, oppressed you;
and you cried to me, and I delivered you out of their hand. 13 Yet
you have abandoned me and wor-

[k] Heb lacks *Did I not deliver you*

shiped other gods; therefore I will
deliver you no more. 14 Go and cry
to the gods whom you have chosen;
let them deliver you in the time of
your distress." 15 And the Israelites
said to the LORD, "We have sinned;
do to us whatever seems good to
you; but deliver us this day!" 16 So
they put away the foreign gods
from among them and worshiped
the LORD; and he could no longer
bear to see Israel suffer.
17 Then the Ammonites were
called to arms, and they encamped
in Gilead; and the Israelites came
together, and they encamped at
Mizpah. 18 The commanders of the
people of Gilead said to one another, "Who will begin the fight
against the Ammonites? He shall
be head over all the inhabitants of
Gilead."

Jephthah

11 Now Jephthah the Gileadite, the son of a prostitute,
was a mighty warrior. Gilead was
the father of Jephthah. 2 Gilead's
wife also bore him sons; and when
his wife's sons grew up, they drove
Jephthah away, saying to him,
"You shall not inherit anything in
our father's house; for you are the
son of another woman." 3 Then
Jephthah fled from his brothers
and lived in the land of Tob. Outlaws collected around Jephthah
and went raiding with him.
4 After a time the Ammonites
made war against Israel. 5 And
when the Ammonites made war
against Israel, the elders of Gilead
went to bring Jephthah from the
land of Tob. 6 They said to Jephthah, "Come and be our commander, so that we may fight with the
Ammonites." 7 But Jephthah said
to the elders of Gilead, "Are you
not the very ones who rejected me
and drove me out of my father's
house? So why do you come to me
now when you are in trouble?"
8 The elders of Gilead said to Jephthah, "Nevertheless, we have now
turned back to you, so that you may
go with us and fight with the Ammonites, and become head over us,
over all the inhabitants of Gilead."
9 Jephthah said to the elders of Gilead, "If you bring me home again to
fight with the Ammonites, and the
LORD gives them over to me, I will
be your head." 10 And the elders of
Gilead said to Jephthah, "The LORD
will be witness between us; we will
surely do as you say." 11 So Jephthah went with the elders of Gilead, and the people made him head
and commander over them; and
Jephthah spoke all his words before the LORD at Mizpah.
12 Then Jephthah sent messengers to the king of the Ammonites
and said, "What is there between
you and me, that you have come to
me to fight against my land?"
13 The king of the Ammonites answered the messengers of Jephthah, "Because Israel, on coming
from Egypt, took away my land
from the Arnon to the Jabbok and
to the Jordan; now therefore restore it peaceably." 14 Once again
Jephthah sent messengers to the
king of the Ammonites 15 and said
to him: "Thus says Jephthah: Israel
did not take away the land of Moab
or the land of the Ammonites,
16 but when they came up from
Egypt, Israel went through the wilderness to the Red Sea[1] and came
to Kadesh. 17 Israel then sent messengers to the king of Edom, saying, 'Let us pass through your
land'; but the king of Edom would
not listen. They also sent to the
king of Moab, but he would not
consent. So Israel remained at Kadesh. 18 Then they journeyed
through the wilderness, went
around the land of Edom and the
land of Moab, arrived on the east
side of the land of Moab, and
camped on the other side of the Arnon. They did not enter the territory of Moab, for the Arnon was the
boundary of Moab. 19 Israel then
sent messengers to King Sihon of
the Amorites, king of Heshbon;
and Israel said to him, 'Let us pass
through your land to our country.'
20 But Sihon did not trust Israel to

10.14 Deut 32.37
10.15 1 Sam 3.18
10.16 Josh 24.23; Jer 18.7,8; Deut 32.36; Ps 106.44, 45
10.17 Judg 11.29
10.18 Judg 11.8, 11
11.1 Heb 11.32
11.3 2 Sam 10.6, 8
11.4 Judg 10.9, 17
11.8 Judg 10.18
11.10 Jer 42.5
11.11 v. 8; Judg 10.17
11.13 Num 21.24-26
11.15 Deut 2.9,19
11.16 Num 14.25; 20.1,14-21
11.18 Num 21.4; Deut 2.1-9, 18,19
11.19 Num 21.21, 22; Deut 2.26, 27
11.20 Num 21.23; Deut 2.32

[1] Or *Sea of Reeds*

pass through his territory; so Sihon
gathered all his people together,
and encamped at Jahaz, and fought
with Israel. 21 Then the LORD, the
God of Israel, gave Sihon and all his
people into the hand of Israel, and
they defeated them; so Israel occupied all the land of the Amorites,
who inhabited that country. 22 They
occupied all the territory of the
Amorites from the Arnon to the
Jabbok and from the wilderness to
the Jordan. 23 So now the LORD, the
God of Israel, has conquered the
Amorites for the benefit of his people Israel. Do you intend to take
their place? 24 Should you not possess what your god Chemosh gives
you to possess? And should we not
be the ones to possess everything
that the LORD our God has conquered for our benefit? 25 Now are
you any better than King Balak son
of Zippor of Moab? Did he ever enter into conflict with Israel, or did
he ever go to war with them?
26 While Israel lived in Heshbon
and its villages, and in Aroer and its
villages, and in all the towns that
are along the Arnon, three hundred
years, why did you not recover
them within that time? 27 It is not I
who have sinned against you, but
you are the one who does me wrong
by making war on me. Let the LORD,
who is judge, decide today for the
Israelites or for the Ammonites."
28 But the king of the Ammonites
did not heed the message that
Jephthah sent him.

Jephthah's Vow

29 Then the spirit of the LORD
came upon Jephthah, and he
passed through Gilead and Manasseh. He passed on to Mizpah of Gilead, and from Mizpah of Gilead he
passed on to the Ammonites.
30 And Jephthah made a vow to the
LORD, and said, "If you will give the
Ammonites into my hand, 31 then
whoever comes out of the doors of
my house to meet me, when I return victorious from the Ammonites, shall be the LORD's, to be offered up by me as a burnt offering."
32 So Jephthah crossed over to the
Ammonites to fight against them;
and the LORD gave them into his
hand. 33 He inflicted a massive defeat on them from Aroer to the
neighborhood of Minnith, twenty
towns, and as far as Abel-keramim.
So the Ammonites were subdued
before the people of Israel.

Jephthah's Daughter

34 Then Jephthah came to his
home at Mizpah; and there was his
daughter coming out to meet him
with timbrels and with dancing.
She was his only child; he had no
son or daughter except her.
35 When he saw her, he tore his
clothes, and said, "Alas, my daughter! You have brought me very low;
you have become the cause of great
trouble to me. For I have opened
my mouth to the LORD, and I cannot
take back my vow." 36 She said to
him, "My father, if you have
opened your mouth to the LORD, do
to me according to what has gone
out of your mouth, now that the
LORD has given you vengeance
against your enemies, the Ammonites." 37 And she said to her father,
"Let this thing be done for me:
Grant me two months, so that I
may go and wander[m] on the mountains, and bewail my virginity, my
companions and I." 38 "Go," he said
and sent her away for two months.
So she departed, she and her companions, and bewailed her virginity
on the mountains. 39 At the end of
two months, she returned to her father, who did with her according to
the vow he had made. She had never slept with a man. So there arose
an Israelite custom that 40 for four
days every year the daughters of Israel would go out to lament the
daughter of Jephthah the Gileadite.

Intertribal Dissension

12 The men of Ephraim were
called to arms, and they
crossed to Zaphon and said to
Jephthah, "Why did you cross over
to fight against the Ammonites,
and did not call us to go with you?

11.21 Num 21.24, 25; Deut 2.33, 34
11.22 Deut 2.36
11.24 Num 21.29; 1 Kings 11.7; Josh 3.10
11.25 Num 22.2; Josh 24.9
11.26 Num 21.25; Deut 2.36
11.27 Gen 16.5; 18.25; 31.53; 1 Sam 24.12, 15
11.29 Judg 3.10
11.33 Ezek 27.17
11.34 Judg 10.17; Ex 15.20; 1 Sam 18.6; Jer 31.4
11.35 Num 30.2; Eccl 5.2,4,5
11.36 Num 30.2; 2 Sam 18.19, 31; Lk 1.38
12.1 Judg 8.1

[m] Cn: Heb *go down*

We will burn your house down over
you!" 2 Jephthah said to them, "My
people and I were engaged in conflict with the Ammonites who oppressed us[n] severely. But when I
called you, you did not deliver me
from their hand. 3 When I saw that
you would not deliver me, I took
my life in my hand, and crossed
over against the Ammonites, and
the LORD gave them into my hand.
Why then have you come up to me
this day, to fight against me?"
4 Then Jephthah gathered all the
men of Gilead and fought with
Ephraim; and the men of Gilead
defeated Ephraim, because they
said, "You are fugitives from
Ephraim, you Gileadites—in the
heart of Ephraim and Manasseh."[o]
5 Then the Gileadites took the fords
of the Jordan against the Ephraimites. Whenever one of the fugitives
of Ephraim said, "Let me go over,"
the men of Gilead would say to
him, "Are you an Ephraimite?"
When he said, "No," 6 they said to
him, "Then say Shibboleth," and
he said, "Sibboleth," for he could
not pronounce it right. Then they
seized him and killed him at the
fords of the Jordan. Forty-two
thousand of the Ephraimites fell at
that time.
7 Jephthah judged Israel six
years. Then Jephthah the Gileadite
died, and was buried in his town in
Gilead.[p]

Ibzan, Elon, and Abdon

8 After him Ibzan of Bethlehem
judged Israel. 9 He had thirty sons.
He gave his thirty daughters in
marriage outside his clan and
brought in thirty young women
from outside for his sons. He
judged Israel seven years. 10 Then
Ibzan died, and was buried at Bethlehem.
11 After him Elon the Zebulunite judged Israel; and he judged Israel ten years. 12 Then Elon the
Zebulunite died, and was buried at
Aijalon in the land of Zebulun.
13 After him Abdon son of Hillel
the Pirathonite judged Israel. 14 He
had forty sons and thirty grand-
sons, who rode on seventy donkeys; he judged Israel eight years.
15 Then Abdon son of Hillel the Pirathonite died, and was buried at
Pirathon in the land of Ephraim, in
the hill country of the Amalekites.

The Birth of Samson

13 The Israelites again did
what was evil in the sight of
the LORD, and the LORD gave them
into the hand of the Philistines forty years.
2 There was a certain man of Zorah, of the tribe of the Danites,
whose name was Manoah. His wife
was barren, having borne no children. 3 And the angel of the LORD
appeared to the woman and said to
her, "Although you are barren, having borne no children, you shall
conceive and bear a son. 4 Now be
careful not to drink wine or strong
drink, or to eat anything unclean,
5 for you shall conceive and bear a
son. No razor is to come on his
head, for the boy shall be a nazirite[q] to God from birth. It is he who
shall begin to deliver Israel from
the hand of the Philistines." 6 Then
the woman came and told her husband, "A man of God came to me,
and his appearance was like that of
an angel[r] of God, most awe-
inspiring; I did not ask him where
he came from, and he did not tell
me his name; 7 but he said to me,
'You shall conceive and bear a son.
So then drink no wine or strong
drink, and eat nothing unclean, for
the boy shall be a nazirite[q] to God
from birth to the day of his
death.' "
8 Then Manoah entreated the
LORD, and said, "O, LORD, I pray, let
the man of God whom you sent
come to us again and teach us what
we are to do concerning the boy
who will be born." 9 God listened to
Manoah, and the angel of God
came again to the woman as she
sat in the field; but her husband
Manoah was not with her. 10 So the

12.3 1 Sam 19.5; 28.21; Job 13.14
12.4 Judg 3.28; 7.24
12.5 Judg 3.28; 7.24; Josh 22.11
12.7 Heb 11.32
12.14 Judg 5.10; 10.4
13.1 Judg 2.11; 1 Sam 12.9
13.2 Josh 19.41
13.3 vv. 6,8,10; Judg 6.12
13.4 v. 14; Num 6.2,3
13.5 Lk 1.15; Num 6.2,5
13.6 1 Sam 2.27; Mt 28.3; vv. 17,18
13.8 vv. 3,7

[n] Gk OL, Syr H: Heb lacks *who oppressed us*
[o] Meaning of Heb uncertain: Gk omits *because . . . Manasseh*
[p] Gk: Heb *in the towns of Gilead*
[q] That is *one separated* or *one consecrated*
[r] Or *the angel*

woman ran quickly and told her
husband, "The man who came to
me the other day has appeared to
me." 11 Manoah got up and followed his wife, and came to the
man and said to him, "Are you the
man who spoke to this woman?"
And he said, "I am." 12 Then Manoah said, "Now when your words
come true, what is to be the boy's
rule of life; what is he to do?" 13 The
angel of the LORD said to Manoah,
"Let the woman give heed to all
that I said to her. 14 She may not eat
of anything that comes from the
vine. She is not to drink wine or
strong drink, or eat any unclean
thing. She is to observe everything
that I commanded her."
15 Manoah said to the angel of
the LORD, "Allow us to detain you,
and prepare a kid for you." 16 The
angel of the LORD said to Manoah,
"If you detain me, I will not eat
your food; but if you want to prepare a burnt offering, then offer it
to the LORD." (For Manoah did not
know that he was the angel of the
LORD.) 17 Then Manoah said to the
angel of the LORD, "What is your
name, so that we may honor you
when your words come true?"
18 But the angel of the LORD said to
him, "Why do you ask my name? It
is too wonderful."
19 So Manoah took the kid with
the grain offering, and offered it on
the rock to the LORD, to him who
works[s] wonders.[t] 20 When the
flame went up toward heaven from
the altar, the angel of the LORD ascended in the flame of the altar
while Manoah and his wife looked
on; and they fell on their faces to
the ground. 21 The angel of the LORD
did not appear again to Manoah
and his wife. Then Manoah realized that it was the angel of the
LORD. 22 And Manoah said to his
wife, "We shall surely die, for we
have seen God." 23 But his wife said
to him, "If the LORD had meant to
kill us, he would not have accepted
a burnt offering and a grain offering
at our hands, or shown us all these
things, or now announced to us
such things as these."

13.13 vv. 4,11
13.14 Num 6.4
13.15 v. 3
13.16 Judg 6.20
13.17 Gen 32.29
13.18 Isa 9.6
13.19 Judg 6.20, 21
13.20 Lev 9.24
13.21 v. 16
13.22 Judg 6.22; Deut 5.26
13.24 Heb 11.32; 1 Sam 3.19
13.25 Judg 3.10; 18.11
14.2 Gen 21.21; 34.4
14.4 Josh 11.20; Judg 13.1
14.6 Judg 3.10; 13.25
14.7 v. 3

24 The woman bore a son, and
named him Samson. The boy grew,
and the LORD blessed him. 25 The
spirit of the LORD began to stir him
in Mahaneh-dan, between Zorah
and Eshtaol.

Samson's Marriage

14 Once Samson went down
to Timnah, and at Timnah
he saw a Philistine woman. 2 Then
he came up, and told his father and
mother, "I saw a Philistine woman
at Timnah; now get her for me as
my wife." 3 But his father and
mother said to him, "Is there not a
woman among your kin, or among
all our[u] people, that you must go
to take a wife from the uncircumcised Philistines?" But Samson
said to his father, "Get her for me,
because she pleases me." 4 His father and mother did not know that
this was from the LORD; for he was
seeking a pretext to act against the
Philistines. At that time the Philistines had dominion over Israel.
5 Then Samson went down with
his father and mother to Timnah.
When he came to the vineyards of
Timnah, suddenly a young lion
roared at him. 6 The spirit of the
LORD rushed on him, and he tore
the lion apart barehanded as one
might tear apart a kid. But he did
not tell his father or his mother
what he had done. 7 Then he went
down and talked with the woman,
and she pleased Samson. 8 After a
while he returned to marry her, and
he turned aside to see the carcass
of the lion, and there was a swarm
of bees in the body of the lion, and
honey. 9 He scraped it out into his
hands, and went on, eating as he
went. When he came to his father
and mother, he gave some to them,
and they ate it. But he did not tell
them that he had taken the honey
from the carcass of the lion.
10 His father went down to the
woman, and Samson made a feast
there as the young men were accustomed to do. 11 When the people

[s] Gk Vg: Heb *and working* [t] Heb *wonders, while Manoah and his wife looked on*
[u] Cn: Heb *my*

saw him, they brought thirty companions to be with him. 12 Samson
said to them, "Let me now put a
riddle to you. If you can explain it
to me within the seven days of the
feast, and find it out, then I will
give you thirty linen garments and
thirty festal garments. 13 But if you
cannot explain it to me, then you
shall give me thirty linen garments
and thirty festal garments." So they
said to him, "Ask your riddle; let us
hear it." 14 He said to them,

"Out of the eater came
something to eat.
Out of the strong came
something sweet."

But for three days they could not
explain the riddle.

15 On the fourth[v] day they said
to Samson's wife, "Coax your husband to explain the riddle to us, or
we will burn you and your father's
house with fire. Have you invited
us here to impoverish us?" 16 So
Samson's wife wept before him,
saying, "You hate me; you do not
really love me. You have asked a
riddle of my people, but you have
not explained it to me." He said to
her, "Look, I have not told my father or my mother. Why should I
tell you?" 17 She wept before him
the seven days that their feast lasted; and because she nagged him,
on the seventh day he told her.
Then she explained the riddle to
her people. 18 The men of the town
said to him on the seventh day before the sun went down,

"What is sweeter than
honey?
What is stronger than a
lion?"

And he said to them,

"If you had not plowed with
my heifer,
you would not have found
out my riddle."

19 Then the spirit of the LORD
rushed on him, and he went down
to Ashkelon. He killed thirty men
of the town, took their spoil, and
gave the festal garments to those
who had explained the riddle. In
hot anger he went back to his father's house. 20 And Samson's wife
was given to his companion, who
had been his best man.

Samson Defeats the Philistines

15 After a while, at the time of
the wheat harvest, Samson
went to visit his wife, bringing
along a kid. He said, "I want to go
into my wife's room." But her father would not allow him to go in.
2 Her father said, "I was sure that
you had rejected her; so I gave her
to your companion. Is not her
younger sister prettier than she?
Why not take her instead?" 3 Samson said to them, "This time, when
I do mischief to the Philistines, I
will be without blame." 4 So Samson went and caught three hundred
foxes, and took some torches; and
he turned the foxes[w] tail to tail,
and put a torch between each pair
of tails. 5 When he had set fire to
the torches, he let the foxes go into
the standing grain of the Philistines, and burned up the shocks
and the standing grain, as well as
the vineyards and[x] olive groves.
6 Then the Philistines asked, "Who
has done this?" And they said,
"Samson, the son-in-law of the
Timnite, because he has taken
Samson's wife and given her to his
companion." So the Philistines
came up, and burned her and her
father. 7 Samson said to them, "If
this is what you do, I swear I will
not stop until I have taken revenge
on you." 8 He struck them down hip
and thigh with great slaughter; and
he went down and stayed in the
cleft of the rock of Etam.

9 Then the Philistines came up
and encamped in Judah, and made
a raid on Lehi. 10 The men of Judah
said, "Why have you come up
against us?" They said, "We have
come up to bind Samson, to do to
him as he did to us." 11 Then three
thousand men of Judah went down
to the cleft of the rock of Etam, and
they said to Samson, "Do you not
know that the Philistines are rulers
over us? What then have you done
to us?" He replied, "As they did to

14.12 1 Kings 10.2; Ezek 17.2; Gen 29.27
14.15 Judg 16.5; 15.6
14.18 v. 14
14.19 Judg 3.10
14.20 Judg 15.2; Jn 3.29
15.2 Judg 14.20
15.6 Judg 14.15
15.9 v. 19
15.11 Judg 13.1; 14.4

[v] Gk Syr: Heb *seventh* [w] Heb *them*
[x] Gk Tg Vg: Heb lacks *and*

me, so I have done to them."
12 They said to him, "We have come
down to bind you, so that we may
give you into the hands of the Philistines." Samson answered them,
"Swear to me that you yourselves
will not attack me." 13 They said to
him, "No, we will only bind you
and give you into their hands; we
will not kill you." So they bound
him with two new ropes, and
brought him up from the rock.
14 When he came to Lehi, the
Philistines came shouting to meet
him; and the spirit of the LORD
rushed on him, and the ropes that
were on his arms became like flax
that has caught fire, and his bonds
melted off his hands. 15 Then he
found a fresh jawbone of a donkey,
reached down and took it, and with
it he killed a thousand men. 16 And
Samson said,

"With the jawbone of a
donkey,
heaps upon heaps,
with the jawbone of a
donkey
I have slain a thousand
men."

17 When he had finished speaking,
he threw away the jawbone; and
that place was called Ramath-
lehi.[y]
18 By then he was very thirsty,
and he called on the LORD, saying,
"You have granted this great victory by the hand of your servant. Am
I now to die of thirst, and fall into
the hands of the uncircumcised?"
19 So God split open the hollow
place that is at Lehi, and water
came from it. When he drank, his
spirit returned, and he revived.
Therefore it was named En-
hakkore,[z] which is at Lehi to this
day. 20 And he judged Israel in the
days of the Philistines twenty
years.

Samson and Delilah

16 Once Samson went to
Gaza, where he saw a prostitute and went in to her. 2 The Ga-
zites were told,[a] "Samson has
come here." So they circled around
and lay in wait for him all night at
the city gate. They kept quiet all
night, thinking, "Let us wait until
the light of the morning; then we
will kill him." 3 But Samson lay
only until midnight. Then at midnight he rose up, took hold of the
doors of the city gate and the two
posts, pulled them up, bar and all,
put them on his shoulders, and carried them to the top of the hill that
is in front of Hebron.
4 After this he fell in love with a
woman in the valley of Sorek,
whose name was Delilah. 5 The
lords of the Philistines came to her
and said to her, "Coax him, and
find out what makes his strength so
great, and how we may overpower
him, so that we may bind him in
order to subdue him; and we will
each give you eleven hundred
pieces of silver." 6 So Delilah said
to Samson, "Please tell me what
makes your strength so great, and
how you could be bound, so that
one could subdue you." 7 Samson
said to her, "If they bind me with
seven fresh bowstrings that are not
dried out, then I shall become
weak, and be like anyone else."
8 Then the lords of the Philistines
brought her seven fresh bowstrings
that had not dried out, and she
bound him with them. 9 While men
were lying in wait in an inner
chamber, she said to him, "The
Philistines are upon you, Samson!"
But he snapped the bowstrings, as
a strand of fiber snaps when it
touches the fire. So the secret of
his strength was not known.
10 Then Delilah said to Samson, "You have mocked me and
told me lies; please tell me how you
could be bound." 11 He said to her,
"If they bind me with new ropes
that have not been used, then I
shall become weak, and be like
anyone else." 12 So Delilah took
new ropes and bound him with
them, and said to him, "The Philistines are upon you, Samson!" (The
men lying in wait were in an inner

15.14 Judg 14.19; 1 Sam 11.6
15.15 Lev 26.8; Josh 23.10; Judg 3.31
15.18 Judg 16.28
15.19 Gen 45.27; Isa 40.29
15.20 Heb 11.32; Judg 13.1; 16.31
16.2 Ps 118.10-12
16.5 Judg 14.15
16.10 vv. 13,15

[y] That is *The Hill of the Jawbone* [z] That is *The Spring of the One who Called*
[a] Gk: Heb lacks *were told*

chamber.) But he snapped the
ropes off his arms like a thread.
13 Then Delilah said to Samson, "Until now you have mocked
me and told me lies; tell me how
you could be bound." He said to
her, "If you weave the seven locks
of my head with the web and make
it tight with the pin, then I shall
become weak, and be like anyone
else." 14 So while he slept, Delilah
took the seven locks of his head
and wove them into the web,[b] and
made them tight with the pin.
Then she said to him, "The Philistines are upon you, Samson!" But
he awoke from his sleep, and
pulled away the pin, the loom, and
the web.
15 Then she said to him, "How
can you say, 'I love you,' when your
heart is not with me? You have
mocked me three times now and
have not told me what makes your
strength so great." 16 Finally, after
she had nagged him with her words
day after day, and pestered him, he
was tired to death. 17 So he told her
his whole secret, and said to her,
"A razor has never come upon my
head; for I have been a nazirite[c] to
God from my mother's womb. If my
head were shaved, then my
strength would leave me; I would
become weak, and be like anyone
else."
18 When Delilah realized that
he had told her his whole secret,
she sent and called the lords of the
Philistines, saying, "This time
come up, for he has told his whole
secret to me." Then the lords of the
Philistines came up to her, and
brought the money in their hands.
19 She let him fall asleep on her lap;
and she called a man, and had him
shave off the seven locks of his
head. He began to weaken,[d] and
his strength left him. 20 Then she
said, "The Philistines are upon
you, Samson!" When he awoke
from his sleep, he thought, "I will
go out as at other times, and shake
myself free." But he did not know
that the LORD had left him. 21 So the
Philistines seized him and gouged
out his eyes. They brought him
down to Gaza and bound him with
bronze shackles; and he ground at
the mill in the prison. 22 But the
hair of his head began to grow
again after it had been shaved.

Samson's Death

23 Now the lords of the Philistines gathered to offer a great sacrifice to their god Dagon, and to rejoice; for they said, "Our god has
given Samson our enemy into our
hand." 24 When the people saw
him, they praised their god; for
they said, "Our god has given our
enemy into our hand, the ravager of
our country, who has killed many
of us." 25 And when their hearts
were merry, they said, "Call Samson, and let him entertain us." So
they called Samson out of the prison, and he performed for them.
They made him stand between the
pillars; 26 and Samson said to the
attendant who held him by the
hand, "Let me feel the pillars on
which the house rests, so that I
may lean against them." 27 Now the
house was full of men and women;
all the lords of the Philistines were
there, and on the roof there were
about three thousand men and
women, who looked on while Samson performed.
28 Then Samson called to the
LORD and said, "Lord GOD, remember me and strengthen me only this
once, O God, so that with this one
act of revenge I may pay back the
Philistines for my two eyes."[e]
29 And Samson grasped the two
middle pillars on which the house
rested, and he leaned his weight
against them, his right hand on the
one and his left hand on the other.
30 Then Samson said, "Let me die
with the Philistines." He strained
with all his might; and the house
fell on the lords and all the people
who were in it. So those he killed at
his death were more than those he
had killed during his life. 31 Then

16.13 vv. 10,15 **16.15** Judg 14.16 **16.17** Mic 7.5; Num 6.5; Judg 13.5 **16.19** Prov 7.26,27 **16.20** Josh 7.12; 1 Sam 16.14; 18.12 **16.23** 1 Sam 5.2 **16.24** Dan 5.4 **16.25** Judg 9.27 **16.27** Deut 22.8 **16.28** Judg 15.18; Jer 15.15 **16.31** Judg 15.20

[b] Compare Gk: in verses 13-14, Heb lacks *and make it tight . . . into the web* [c] That is *one separated* or *one consecrated*
[d] Gk: Heb *She began to torment him*
[e] Or *so that I may be avenged upon the Philistines for one of my two eyes*

his brothers and all his family came
down and took him and brought
him up and buried him between
Zorah and Eshtaol in the tomb of
his father Manoah. He had judged
Israel twenty years.

Micah and the Levite

17 There was a man in the hill
country of Ephraim whose
name was Micah. 2 He said to his
mother, "The eleven hundred
pieces of silver that were taken
from you, about which you uttered
a curse, and even spoke it in my
hearing,—that silver is in my possession; I took it; but now I will return it to you."[f] And his mother
said, "May my son be blessed by
the LORD!" 3 Then he returned the
eleven hundred pieces of silver to
his mother; and his mother said, "I
consecrate the silver to the LORD
from my hand for my son, to make
an idol of cast metal." 4 So when he
returned the money to his mother,
his mother took two hundred
pieces of silver, and gave it to the
silversmith, who made it into an
idol of cast metal; and it was in the
house of Micah. 5 This man Micah
had a shrine, and he made an
ephod and teraphim, and installed
one of his sons, who became his
priest. 6 In those days there was no
king in Israel; all the people did
what was right in their own eyes.
7 Now there was a young man of
Bethlehem in Judah, of the clan of
Judah. He was a Levite residing
there. 8 This man left the town of
Bethlehem in Judah, to live wherever he could find a place. He came
to the house of Micah in the hill
country of Ephraim to carry on his
work.[g] 9 Micah said to him, "From
where do you come?" He replied, "I
am a Levite of Bethlehem in Judah,
and I am going to live wherever I
can find a place." 10 Then Micah
said to him, "Stay with me, and be
to me a father and a priest, and I
will give you ten pieces of silver a
year, a set of clothes, and your living."[h] 11 The Levite agreed to stay
with the man; and the young man
became to him like one of his sons.

17.3 Ex 20.4,23; 34.17; Lev 19.4
17.5 Judg 18.24; 8.27; 18.14; Gen 31.19
17.6 Judg 18.1; 19.1; Deut 12.8
17.7 Judg 19.1; Ruth 1.1,2; Mic 5.2; Mt 2.1
17.10 Judg 18.19
17.12 v. 5; Judg 13.25
18.1 Judg 17.6; 19.1; Josh 19.47
18.2 Judg 13.25; Josh 2.1; Judg 17.1
18.4 Judg 17.10, 12
18.5 1 Kings 22.5
18.6 1 Kings 22.6
18.7 vv. 27,28; Josh 19.47
18.8 v. 2

12 So Micah installed the Levite,
and the young man became his
priest, and was in the house of Micah. 13 Then Micah said, "Now I
know that the LORD will prosper
me, because the Levite has become
my priest."

The Migration of Dan

18 In those days there was no
king in Israel. And in those
days the tribe of the Danites was
seeking for itself a territory to live
in; for until then no territory
among the tribes of Israel had been
allotted to them. 2 So the Danites
sent five valiant men from the
whole number of their clan, from
Zorah and from Eshtaol, to spy out
the land and to explore it; and they
said to them, "Go, explore the
land." When they came to the hill
country of Ephraim, to the house of
Micah, they stayed there. 3 While
they were at Micah's house, they
recognized the voice of the young
Levite; so they went over and asked
him, "Who brought you here? What
are you doing in this place? What is
your business here?" 4 He said to
them, "Micah did such and such
for me, and he hired me, and I have
become his priest." 5 Then they
said to him, "Inquire of God that
we may know whether the mission
we are undertaking will succeed."
6 The priest replied, "Go in peace.
The mission you are on is under the
eye of the LORD."
7 The five men went on, and
when they came to Laish, they observed the people who were there
living securely, after the manner of
the Sidonians, quiet and unsuspecting, lacking[i] nothing on
earth, and possessing wealth.[j]
Furthermore, they were far from
the Sidonians and had no dealings
with Aram.[k] 8 When they came to
their kinsfolk at Zorah and Eshtaol,

[f] The words *but now I will return it to you* are transposed from the end of verse 3 in Heb
[g] Or *Ephraim, continuing his journey*
[h] Heb *living, and the Levite went*
[i] Cn Compare 18.10: Meaning of Heb uncertain [j] Meaning of Heb uncertain
[k] Symmachus: Heb *with anyone*

they said to them, "What do you report?" 9 They said, "Come, let us go
up against them; for we have seen
the land, and it is very good. Will
you do nothing? Do not be slow to
go, but enter in and possess the
land. 10 When you go, you will come
to an unsuspecting people. The
land is broad—God has indeed giv-
en it into your hands—a place
where there is no lack of anything
on earth."
11 Six hundred men of the Danite clan, armed with weapons of
war, set out from Zorah and Eshtaol, 12 and went up and encamped at
Kiriath-jearim in Judah. On this
account that place is called
Mahaneh-dan[l] to this day; it is
west of Kiriath-jearim. 13 From
there they passed on to the hill
country of Ephraim, and came to
the house of Micah.
14 Then the five men who had
gone to spy out the land (that is,
Laish) said to their comrades, "Do
you know that in these buildings
there are an ephod, teraphim, and
an idol of cast metal? Now therefore consider what you will do."
15 So they turned in that direction
and came to the house of the young
Levite, at the home of Micah, and
greeted him. 16 While the six hundred men of the Danites, armed
with their weapons of war, stood by
the entrance of the gate, 17 the five
men who had gone to spy out the
land proceeded to enter and take
the idol of cast metal, the ephod,
and the teraphim.[m] The priest was
standing by the entrance of the
gate with the six hundred men
armed with weapons of war.
18 When the men went into Micah's
house and took the idol of cast
metal, the ephod, and the teraphim, the priest said to them,
"What are you doing?" 19 They said
to him, "Keep quiet! Put your hand
over your mouth, and come with
us, and be to us a father and a
priest. Is it better for you to be
priest to the house of one person,
or to be priest to a tribe and clan in
Israel?" 20 Then the priest accepted
the offer. He took the ephod, the

18.9 Num 13.30; 1 Kings 22.3
18.10 vv. 7,27; Deut 8.9
18.12 Judg 13.25
18.13 v. 2
18.14 Judg 17.5
18.16 v. 11
18.17 vv. 2,14
18.19 Job 21.5; Judg 17.10
18.24 Judg 17.5
18.27 vv. 7,10; Josh 19.47
18.28 v. 7; 2 Sam 10.6
18.29 Josh 19.47
18.30 Judg 17.3,5; Ex 2.22
18.31 Josh 18.1

teraphim, and the idol, and went
along with the people.
21 So they resumed their journey, putting the little ones, the
livestock, and the goods in front of
them. 22 When they were some distance from the home of Micah, the
men who were in the houses near
Micah's house were called out, and
they overtook the Danites. 23 They
shouted to the Danites, who turned
around and said to Micah, "What is
the matter that you come with such
a company?" 24 He replied, "You
take my gods that I made, and the
priest, and go away, and what have
I left? How then can you ask me,
'What is the matter?' " 25 And the
Danites said to him, "You had better not let your voice be heard
among us or else hot-tempered fellows will attack you, and you will
lose your life and the lives of your
household." 26 Then the Danites
went their way. When Micah saw
that they were too strong for him,
he turned and went back to his
home.

The Danites Settle in Laish

27 The Danites, having taken
what Micah had made, and the
priest who belonged to him, came
to Laish, to a people quiet and unsuspecting, put them to the sword,
and burned down the city. 28 There
was no deliverer, because it was far
from Sidon and they had no dealings with Aram.[n] It was in the valley that belongs to Beth-rehob.
They rebuilt the city, and lived in
it. 29 They named the city Dan, after
their ancestor Dan, who was born
to Israel; but the name of the city
was formerly Laish. 30 Then the
Danites set up the idol for themselves. Jonathan son of Gershom,
son of Moses,[o] and his sons were
priests to the tribe of the Danites
until the time the land went into
captivity. 31 So they maintained as

[l] That is *Camp of Dan* [m] Compare 17.4, 5; 18.14: Heb *teraphim and the cast metal* [n] Cn Compare verse 7: Heb *with anyone* [o] Another reading is *son of Manasseh*

their own Micah's idol that he had
made, as long as the house of God
was at Shiloh.

The Levite's Concubine

19 In those days, when there
was no king in Israel, a certain Levite, residing in the remote
parts of the hill country of Ephraim, took to himself a concubine
from Bethlehem in Judah. 2 But his
concubine became angry with[p]
him, and she went away from him
to her father's house at Bethlehem
in Judah, and was there some four
months. 3 Then her husband set
out after her, to speak tenderly to
her and bring her back. He had
with him his servant and a couple
of donkeys. When he reached[q] her
father's house, the girl's father saw
him and came with joy to meet
him. 4 His father-in-law, the girl's
father, made him stay, and he remained with him three days; so
they ate and drank, and he[r] stayed
there. 5 On the fourth day they got
up early in the morning, and he
prepared to go; but the girl's father
said to his son-in-law, "Fortify
yourself with a bit of food, and after
that you may go." 6 So the two men
sat and ate and drank together; and
the girl's father said to the man,
"Why not spend the night and enjoy yourself?" 7 When the man got
up to go, his father-in-law kept
urging him until he spent the night
there again. 8 On the fifth day he
got up early in the morning to
leave; and the girl's father said,
"Fortify yourself." So they lingered[s] until the day declined, and
the two of them ate and drank.[t]
9 When the man with his concubine
and his servant got up to leave, his
father-in-law, the girl's father, said
to him, "Look, the day has worn on
until it is almost evening. Spend
the night. See, the day has drawn to
a close. Spend the night here and
enjoy yourself. Tomorrow you can
get up early in the morning for your
journey, and go home."
10 But the man would not
spend the night; he got up and departed, and arrived opposite Jebus
(that is, Jerusalem). He had with
him a couple of saddled donkeys,
and his concubine was with him.
11 When they were near Jebus, the
day was far spent, and the servant
said to his master, "Come now, let
us turn aside to this city of the Jebusites, and spend the night in it."
12 But his master said to him, "We
will not turn aside into a city of foreigners, who do not belong to the
people of Israel; but we will continue on to Gibeah." 13 Then he said to
his servant, "Come, let us try to
reach one of these places, and
spend the night at Gibeah or at Ramah." 14 So they passed on and
went their way; and the sun went
down on them near Gibeah, which
belongs to Benjamin. 15 They
turned aside there, to go in and
spend the night at Gibeah. He went
in and sat down in the open square
of the city, but no one took them in
to spend the night.
16 Then at evening there was an
old man coming from his work in
the field. The man was from the hill
country of Ephraim, and he was residing in Gibeah. (The people of
the place were Benjaminites.)
17 When the old man looked up and
saw the wayfarer in the open
square of the city, he said, "Where
are you going and where do you
come from?" 18 He answered him,
"We are passing from Bethlehem in
Judah to the remote parts of the
hill country of Ephraim, from
which I come. I went to Bethlehem
in Judah; and I am going to my
home.[u] Nobody has offered to take
me in. 19 We your servants have
straw and fodder for our donkeys,
with bread and wine for me and the
woman and the young man along
with us. We need nothing more."
20 The old man said, "Peace be to
you. I will care for all your wants;
only do not spend the night in the
square." 21 So he brought him into

19.1 Judg 18.1 **19.3** Gen 34.3; 50.21 **19.5** v. 8; Gen 18.5 **19.6** vv. 9,22 **19.10** 1 Chr 11.4, 5
19.11 Judg 1.21 **19.12** Heb 11.13 **19.15** Heb 13.2 **19.16** Ps 104.23; v. 14 **19.18** Judg 18.31; 20.18 **19.21** Gen 24.32, 33

[p] Gk OL: Heb *prostituted herself against* [q] Gk: Heb *she brought him* [r] Compare verse 7 and Gk: Heb *they* [s] Cn: Heb *Linger* [t] Gk: Heb lacks *and drank* [u] Gk Compare 19.29. Heb *to the house of the LORD*

his house, and fed the donkeys;
they washed their feet, and ate and
drank.

Gibeah's Crime

22 While they were enjoying
themselves, the men of the city, a
perverse lot, surrounded the house,
and started pounding on the door.
They said to the old man, the master of the house, "Bring out the
man who came into your house, so
that we may have intercourse with
him." 23 And the man, the master of
the house, went out to them and
said to them, "No, my brothers, do
not act so wickedly. Since this man
is my guest, do not do this vile
thing. 24 Here are my virgin daughter and his concubine; let me bring
them out now. Ravish them and do
whatever you want to them; but
against this man do not do such a
vile thing." 25 But the men would
not listen to him. So the man
seized his concubine, and put her
out to them. They wantonly raped
her, and abused her all through the
night until the morning. And as the
dawn began to break, they let her
go. 26 As morning appeared, the
woman came and fell down at the
door of the man's house where her
master was, until it was light.
27 In the morning her master
got up, opened the doors of the
house, and when he went out to go
on his way, there was his concubine lying at the door of the house,
with her hands on the threshold.
28 "Get up," he said to her, "we are
going." But there was no answer.
Then he put her on the donkey; and
the man set out for his home.
29 When he had entered his house,
he took a knife, and grasping his
concubine he cut her into twelve
pieces, limb by limb, and sent her
throughout all the territory of Israel. 30 Then he commanded the men
whom he sent, saying, "Thus shall
you say to all the Israelites, 'Has
such a thing ever happened[v] since
the day that the Israelites came up
from the land of Egypt until this
day? Consider it, take counsel, and
speak out.'"

19.22 Gen 19.4; Deut 13.13; Rom 1.26, 27
19.23 Gen 34.7; Deut 22.21; 2 Sam 13.12
19.24 Gen 19.8; Deut 21.14
19.28 Judg 20.5
19.29 1 Sam 11.7
19.30 Judg 20.7

20.1 Judg 21.5; 1 Sam 7.5
20.4 Judg 19.15
20.5 Judg 19.22, 25,26
20.6 Judg 19.29; Josh 7.15
20.7 Judg 19.30
20.12 Deut 13.14, 15

The Other Tribes Attack Benjamin

20 Then all the Israelites
came out, from Dan to
Beer-sheba, including the land of
Gilead, and the congregation assembled in one body before the
LORD at Mizpah. 2 The chiefs of all
the people, of all the tribes of Israel, presented themselves in the assembly of the people of God, four
hundred thousand foot-soldiers
bearing arms. 3 (Now the Benjaminites heard that the people of Israel had gone up to Mizpah.) And
the Israelites said, "Tell us, how
did this criminal act come about?"
4 The Levite, the husband of the
woman who was murdered, answered, "I came to Gibeah that belongs to Benjamin, I and my concubine, to spend the night. 5 The lords
of Gibeah rose up against me, and
surrounded the house at night.
They intended to kill me, and they
raped my concubine until she died.
6 Then I took my concubine and cut
her into pieces, and sent her
throughout the whole extent of Israel's territory; for they have committed a vile outrage in Israel. 7 So
now, you Israelites, all of you, give
your advice and counsel here."
8 All the people got up as one,
saying, "We will not any of us go to
our tents, nor will any of us return
to our houses. 9 But now this is
what we will do to Gibeah: we will
go up[w] against it by lot. 10 We will
take ten men of a hundred
throughout all the tribes of Israel,
and a hundred of a thousand, and
a thousand of ten thousand, to
bring provisions for the troops, who
are going to repay[x] Gibeah of Benjamin for all the disgrace that they
have done in Israel." 11 So all the
men of Israel gathered against the
city, united as one.
12 The tribes of Israel sent men
through all the tribe of Benjamin,
saying, "What crime is this that has
been committed among you?

[v] Compare Gk: Heb [30] *And all who saw it said, "Such a thing has not happened or been seen*
[w] Gk: Heb lacks *we will go up*
[x] Compare Gk: Meaning of Heb uncertain

13 Now then, hand over those
scoundrels in Gibeah, so that we
may put them to death, and purge
the evil from Israel." But the Benjaminites would not listen to their
kinsfolk, the Israelites. 14 The Benjaminites came together out of the
towns to Gibeah, to go out to battle
against the Israelites. 15 On that
day the Benjaminites mustered
twenty-six thousand armed men
from their towns, besides the inhabitants of Gibeah. 16 Of all this
force, there were seven hundred
picked men who were left-handed;
every one could sling a stone at a
hair, and not miss. 17 And the Israelites, apart from Benjamin, mustered four hundred thousand
armed men, all of them warriors.
18 The Israelites proceeded to
go up to Bethel, where they inquired of God, "Which of us shall
go up first to battle against the
Benjaminites?" And the LORD answered, "Judah shall go up first."
19 Then the Israelites got up in
the morning, and encamped
against Gibeah. 20 The Israelites
went out to battle against Benjamin; and the Israelites drew up the
battle line against them at Gibeah.
21 The Benjaminites came out of
Gibeah, and struck down on that
day twenty-two thousand of the Israelites. 23[y] The Israelites went up
and wept before the LORD until the
evening; and they inquired of the
LORD, "Shall we again draw near to
battle against our kinsfolk the Benjaminites?" And the LORD said, "Go
up against them." 22 The Israelites
took courage, and again formed the
battle line in the same place where
they had formed it on the first day.
24 So the Israelites advanced
against the Benjaminites the second day. 25 Benjamin moved out
against them from Gibeah the second day, and struck down eighteen
thousand of the Israelites, all of
them armed men. 26 Then all the Israelites, the whole army, went back
to Bethel and wept, sitting there
before the LORD; they fasted that
day until evening. Then they offered burnt offerings and sacrifices
of well-being before the LORD.
27 And the Israelites inquired of the
LORD (for the ark of the covenant of
God was there in those days, 28 and
Phinehas son of Eleazar, son of
Aaron, ministered before it in
those days), saying, "Shall we go
out once more to battle against our
kinsfolk the Benjaminites, or shall
we desist?" The LORD answered,
"Go up, for tomorrow I will give
them into your hand."
29 So Israel stationed men in
ambush around Gibeah. 30 Then
the Israelites went up against the
Benjaminites on the third day, and
set themselves in array against Gibeah, as before. 31 When the Benjaminites went out against the army,
they were drawn away from the
city. As before they began to inflict
casualties on the troops, along the
main roads, one of which goes up
to Bethel and the other to Gibeah,
as well as in the open country, killing about thirty men of Israel.
32 The Benjaminites thought,
"They are being routed before us,
as previously." But the Israelites
said, "Let us retreat and draw them
away from the city toward the
roads." 33 The main body of the Israelites drew back its battle line to
Baal-tamar, while those Israelites
who were in ambush rushed out of
their place west[z] of Geba. 34 There
came against Gibeah ten thousand
picked men out of all Israel, and
the battle was fierce. But the Benjaminites did not realize that disaster was close upon them.
35 The LORD defeated Benjamin
before Israel; and the Israelites destroyed twenty-five thousand one
hundred men of Benjamin that
day, all of them armed.
36 Then the Benjaminites saw
that they were defeated.[a]
The Israelites gave ground to
Benjamin, because they trusted to
the troops in ambush that they had
stationed against Gibeah. 37 The
troops in ambush rushed quickly
upon Gibeah. Then they put the

20.13 Judg 19.22 **20.16** Judg 3.15; 1 Chr 12.2 **20.18** vv. 23,26, 27; Num 27.21 **20.21** v. 25 **20.23** v. 18 **20.25** v. 21 **20.26** v. 23; Judg 21.2 **20.27** Josh 18.1 **20.28** Josh 24.33; Deut 18.5; Judg 7.9 **20.29** Josh 8.4 **20.31** Josh 8.16 **20.33** Josh 8.19 **20.34** Josh 8.14 **20.36** Josh 8.15 **20.37** Josh 8.19

[y] Verses 22 and 23 are transposed [z] Gk Vg: Heb *in the plain* [a] This sentence is continued by verse 45.

whole city to the sword. 38 Now the
agreement between the main body
of Israel and the men in ambush
was that when they sent up a cloud
of smoke out of the city 39 the main
body of Israel should turn in battle.
But Benjamin had begun to inflict
casualties on the Israelites, killing
about thirty of them; so they
thought, "Surely they are defeated
before us, as in the first battle."
40 But when the cloud, a column of
smoke, began to rise out of the city,
the Benjaminites looked behind
them—and there was the whole
city going up in smoke toward the
sky! 41 Then the main body of Israel
turned, and the Benjaminites were
dismayed, for they saw that disaster was close upon them. 42 Therefore they turned away from the Israelites in the direction of the
wilderness; but the battle overtook
them, and those who came out of
the city[b] were slaughtering them
in between.[c] 43 Cutting down[d] the
Benjaminites, they pursued them
from Nohah[e] and trod them down
as far as a place east of Gibeah.
44 Eighteen thousand Benjaminites
fell, all of them courageous fighters. 45 When they turned and fled
toward the wilderness to the rock
of Rimmon, five thousand of them
were cut down on the main roads,
and they were pursued as far as Gi-
dom, and two thousand of them
were slain. 46 So all who fell that
day of Benjamin were twenty-five
thousand arms-bearing men, all of
them courageous fighters. 47 But
six hundred turned and fled toward
the wilderness to the rock of Rimmon, and remained at the rock of
Rimmon for four months. 48 Meanwhile, the Israelites turned back
against the Benjaminites, and put
them to the sword—the city, the
people, the animals, and all that
remained. Also the remaining
towns they set on fire.

The Benjaminites Saved from Extinction

21 Now the Israelites had
sworn at Mizpah, "No one
of us shall give his daughter in marriage to Benjamin." 2 And the people came to Bethel, and sat there
until evening before God, and they
lifted up their voices and wept bitterly. 3 They said, "O LORD, the God
of Israel, why has it come to pass
that today there should be one
tribe lacking in Israel?" 4 On the
next day, the people got up early,
and built an altar there, and offered
burnt offerings and sacrifices of
well-being. 5 Then the Israelites
said, "Which of all the tribes of Israel did not come up in the assembly to the LORD?" For a solemn oath
had been taken concerning whoever did not come up to the LORD to
Mizpah, saying, "That one shall be
put to death." 6 But the Israelites
had compassion for Benjamin their
kin, and said, "One tribe is cut off
from Israel this day. 7 What shall we
do for wives for those who are left,
since we have sworn by the LORD
that we will not give them any of
our daughters as wives?"

8 Then they said, "Is there anyone from the tribes of Israel who
did not come up to the LORD to Mizpah?" It turned out that no one
from Jabesh-gilead had come to
the camp, to the assembly. 9 For
when the roll was called among the
people, not one of the inhabitants
of Jabesh-gilead was there. 10 So
the congregation sent twelve thousand soldiers there and commanded them, "Go, put the inhabitants
of Jabesh-gilead to the sword, including the women and the little
ones. 11 This is what you shall do;
every male and every woman that
has lain with a male you shall devote to destruction." 12 And they
found among the inhabitants of
Jabesh-gilead four hundred young
virgins who had never slept with a
man and brought them to the camp
at Shiloh, which is in the land of
Canaan.

13 Then the whole congregation
sent word to the Benjaminites who
were at the rock of Rimmon, and

20.38 Josh 8.20
20.39 v. 32
20.40 Josh 8.20
20.45 Judg 21.13
20.47 Judg 21.13
21.1 vv. 7,18
21.2 Judg 20.18, 26
21.4 2 Sam 24.25
21.7 v. 1
21.11 Num 31.17
21.13 Judg 20.47; Deut 20.10

[b] Compare Vg and some Gk Mss: Heb *cities*
[c] Compare Syr: Meaning of Heb uncertain
[d] Gk: Heb *Surrounding*
[e] Gk: Heb *pursued them at their resting place*

proclaimed peace to them. [14]Benjamin returned at that time; and they gave them the women whom they had saved alive of the women of Jabesh-gilead; but they did not suffice for them.

15 The people had compassion on Benjamin because the LORD had made a breach in the tribes of Israel. [16]So the elders of the congregation said, "What shall we do for wives for those who are left, since there are no women left in Benjamin?" [17]And they said, "There must be heirs for the survivors of Benjamin, in order that a tribe may not be blotted out from Israel. [18]Yet we cannot give any of our daughters to them as wives." For the Israelites had sworn, "Cursed be anyone who gives a wife to Benjamin." [19]So they said, "Look, the yearly festival of the LORD is taking place at Shiloh, which is north of Bethel, on the east of the highway that goes up from Bethel to Shechem, and south of Lebonah." [20]And they instructed the Benjaminites, saying, "Go and lie in wait in the vineyards, [21]and watch; when the young women of Shiloh come out to dance in the dances, then come out of the vineyards and each of you carry off a wife for himself from the young women of Shiloh, and go to the land of Benjamin. [22]Then if their fathers or their brothers come to complain to us, we will say to them, 'Be generous and allow us to have them; because we did not capture in battle a wife for each man. But neither did you incur guilt by giving your daughters to them.' " [23]The Benjaminites did so; they took wives for each of them from the dancers whom they abducted. Then they went and returned to their territory, and rebuilt the towns, and lived in them. [24]So the Israelites departed from there at that time by tribes and families, and they went out from there to their own territories.

25 In those days there was no king in Israel; all the people did what was right in their own eyes.

21.15 v. 6
21.18 v. 18
21.19 Judg 18.31; 1 Sam 1.3
21.21 Ex 15.20; Judg 11.34
21.22 vv. 1,18
21.23 Judg 20.48
21.25 Judg 17.6; 18.1; 19.1

Ruth

Title and Background

This book is named after the leading character whose story is told here. Ruth was the great-grandmother of David and was included in the genealogy of Jesus (Mt 1.1,5). The story is set in the time of the judges and reflects a temporary time of peace between Israel and Moab. It gives a series of intimate glances into the private lives of the members of an Israelite family and presents a delightful account of a remnant of true faith and piety during this period.

Author and Date of Writing

The author is unknown, although Jewish tradition points to Samuel. This is unlikely because the mention of David (4.17,22) implies a later date. The literary style of the Hebrew text suggests it was written during the monarchy, probably sometime after 1000 B.C.

Theme and Message

Redemption is a key concept throughout the book; the Hebrew word in its various forms occurs twenty-three times. The word shows how God is working out his plan of salvation. The book of Ruth also illustrates love and devotion–self-giving love that fulfills God's law, and God's love in blessing the lives of his children.

Outline

I. Introduction: Naomi Emptied (1.1-5)
II. Naomi Returns from Moab (1.6-22)
III. Ruth and Boaz Meet in the Harvest Fields (2.1-23)
IV. Ruth Goes to Boaz at the Threshing Floor (3.1-18)
V. Boaz Arranges to Marry Ruth (4.1-12)
VI. Conclusion: Naomi Filled (4.13-17)
VII. Epilogue: Genealogy of David (4.18-22)

Elimelech's Family Goes to Moab

1.1 Judg 2.16
1.2 Gen 35.19; Judg 3.30

1 In the days when the judges
ruled, there was a famine in
the land, and a certain man of
Bethlehem in Judah went to live in
the country of Moab, he and his
wife and two sons. 2 The name of
the man was Elimelech and the
name of his wife Naomi, and the
names of his two sons were Mahlon
and Chilion; they were Ephrathites
from Bethlehem in Judah. They
went into the country of Moab and
remained there. 3 But Elimelech,
the husband of Naomi, died, and
she was left with her two sons.
4 These took Moabite wives; the
name of the one was Orpah and the
name of the other Ruth. When they
had lived there about ten years,
5 both Mahlon and Chilion also
died, so that the woman was left
without her two sons and her husband.

Naomi and Her Moabite Daughters-in-Law

1.6 Ex 4.31
1.8 v. 5; Ruth 2.20

6 Then she started to return
with her daughters-in-law from the
country of Moab, for she had heard
in the country of Moab that the
LORD had considered his people
and given them food. 7 So she set
out from the place where she had
been living, she and her two
daughters-in-law, and they went on
their way to go back to the land of
Judah. 8 But Naomi said to her two

daughters-in-law, "Go back each of
you to your mother's house. May
the LORD deal kindly with you, as
you have dealt with the dead and
with me. 9 The LORD grant that you
may find security, each of you in
the house of your husband." Then
she kissed them, and they wept
aloud. 10 They said to her, "No, we
will return with you to your people." 11 But Naomi said, "Turn
back, my daughters, why will you
go with me? Do I still have sons in
my womb that they may become
your husbands? 12 Turn back, my
daughters, go your way, for I am too
old to have a husband. Even if I
thought there was hope for me,
even if I should have a husband tonight and bear sons, 13 would you
then wait until they were grown?
Would you then refrain from marrying? No, my daughters, it has been
far more bitter for me than for you,
because the hand of the LORD has
turned against me." 14 Then they
wept aloud again. Orpah kissed her
mother-in-law, but Ruth clung to
her.

15 So she said, "See, your sister-
in-law has gone back to her people
and to her gods; return after your
sister-in-law." 16 But Ruth said,

"Do not press me to leave
you
or to turn back from
following you!
Where you go, I will go;
where you lodge, I will
lodge;
your people shall be my
people,
and your God my God.
17 Where you die, I will die—
there will I be buried.
May the LORD do thus and so
to me,
and more as well,
if even death parts me from
you!"

18 When Naomi saw that she was
determined to go with her, she said
no more to her.

19 So the two of them went on
until they came to Bethlehem.
When they came to Bethlehem, the
whole town was stirred because of
them; and the women said, "Is this
Naomi?" 20 She said to them,

"Call me no longer Naomi,[a]
call me Mara,[b]
for the Almighty[c] has dealt
bitterly with me.
21 I went away full,
but the LORD has brought
me back empty;
why call me Naomi
when the LORD has dealt
harshly with[d] me,
and the Almighty[c] has
brought calamity upon
me?"

22 So Naomi returned together
with Ruth the Moabite, her
daughter-in-law, who came back
with her from the country of Moab.
They came to Bethlehem at the beginning of the barley harvest.

Ruth Meets Boaz

2 Now Naomi had a kinsman on
her husband's side, a prominent rich man, of the family of
Elimelech, whose name was Boaz.
2 And Ruth the Moabite said to Naomi, "Let me go to the field and
glean among the ears of grain, behind someone in whose sight I may
find favor." She said to her, "Go,
my daughter." 3 So she went. She
came and gleaned in the field behind the reapers. As it happened,
she came to the part of the field belonging to Boaz, who was of the
family of Elimelech. 4 Just then
Boaz came from Bethlehem. He
said to the reapers, "The LORD be
with you." They answered, "The
LORD bless you." 5 Then Boaz said
to his servant who was in charge of
the reapers, "To whom does this
young woman belong?" 6 The servant who was in charge of the reapers answered, "She is the Moabite
who came back with Naomi from
the country of Moab. 7 She said,
'Please, let me glean and gather
among the sheaves behind the
reapers.' So she came, and she has
been on her feet from early this

1.9 Ruth 3.1 **1.11** Deut 25.5 **1.13** Judg 2.15; Ps 32.4 **1.16** 2 Kings 2.2, 4,6; Ruth 2.11, 12 **1.18** Acts 21.14

1.20 Ex 6.3; Job 6.4 **1.21** Job 1.21 **1.22** Ex 9.31,32; Ruth 2.23 **2.1** Ruth 1.2; 3.2,12 **2.2** v. 7; Lev 19.9; Deut 24.19 **2.4** Ps 129.7,8; Lk 1.28 **2.6** Ruth 1.22

[a] That is *Pleasant* [b] That is *Bitter*
[c] Traditional rendering of Heb *Shaddai*
[d] Or *has testified against*

morning until now, without resting
even for a moment."[e]
8 Then Boaz said to Ruth, "Now
listen, my daughter, do not go to
glean in another field or leave this
one, but keep close to my young
women. 9 Keep your eyes on the
field that is being reaped, and follow behind them. I have ordered
the young men not to bother you. If
you get thirsty, go to the vessels
and drink from what the young
men have drawn." 10 Then she fell
prostrate, with her face to the
ground, and said to him, "Why have
I found favor in your sight, that you
should take notice of me, when I
am a foreigner?" 11 But Boaz answered her, "All that you have done
for your mother-in-law since the
death of your husband has been
fully told me, and how you left your
father and mother and your native
land and came to a people that you
did not know before. 12 May the
LORD reward you for your deeds,
and may you have a full reward
from the LORD, the God of Israel,
under whose wings you have come
for refuge!" 13 Then she said, "May
I continue to find favor in your
sight, my lord, for you have comforted me and spoken kindly to
your servant, even though I am not
one of your servants."
14 At mealtime Boaz said to
her, "Come here, and eat some of
this bread, and dip your morsel in
the sour wine." So she sat beside
the reapers, and he heaped up for
her some parched grain. She ate
until she was satisfied, and she had
some left over. 15 When she got up
to glean, Boaz instructed his young
men, "Let her glean even among
the standing sheaves, and do not
reproach her. 16 You must also pull
out some handfuls for her from the
bundles, and leave them for her to
glean, and do not rebuke her."
17 So she gleaned in the field
until evening. Then she beat out
what she had gleaned, and it was
about an ephah of barley. 18 She
picked it up and came into the
town, and her mother-in-law saw
how much she had gleaned. Then

2.10 1 Sam 25.23 **2.11** Ruth 1.14, 16,17 **2.12** 1 Sam 24.19; Ps 17.8; Ruth 1.16 **2.14** v. 18 **2.18** v. 14

2.19 v. 10 **2.20** Ruth 3.10; Prov 17.17; Ruth 3.9; 4.6 **2.23** Deut 16.9 **3.1** Ruth 1.9 **3.2** Deut 25.5-10; Ruth 2.8 **3.3** 2 Sam 14.2

she took out and gave her what was
left over after she herself had been
satisfied. 19 Her mother-in-law said
to her, "Where did you glean today?
And where have you worked?
Blessed be the man who took notice of you." So she told her
mother-in-law with whom she had
worked, and said, "The name of the
man with whom I worked today is
Boaz." 20 Then Naomi said to her
daughter-in-law, "Blessed be he by
the LORD, whose kindness has not
forsaken the living or the dead!"
Naomi also said to her, "The man
is a relative of ours, one of our nearest kin."[f] 21 Then Ruth the Moabite said, "He even said to me, 'Stay
close by my servants, until they
have finished all my harvest.' "
22 Naomi said to Ruth, her
daughter-in-law, "It is better, my
daughter, that you go out with his
young women, otherwise you
might be bothered in another
field." 23 So she stayed close to the
young women of Boaz, gleaning until the end of the barley and wheat
harvests; and she lived with her
mother-in-law.

Ruth and Boaz at the Threshing Floor

3 Naomi her mother-in-law said
to her, "My daughter, I need to
seek some security for you, so that
it may be well with you. 2 Now here
is our kinsman Boaz, with whose
young women you have been working. See, he is winnowing barley tonight at the threshing floor. 3 Now
wash and anoint yourself, and put
on your best clothes and go down
to the threshing floor; but do not
make yourself known to the man
until he has finished eating and
drinking. 4 When he lies down, observe the place where he lies; then,
go and uncover his feet and lie
down; and he will tell you what to
do." 5 She said to her, "All that you
tell me I will do."
6 So she went down to the

[e] Compare Gk Vg: Meaning of Heb uncertain
[f] Or *one with the right to redeem*

threshing floor and did just as her
mother-in-law had instructed her.
7 When Boaz had eaten and drunk,
and he was in a contented mood,
he went to lie down at the end of
the heap of grain. Then she came
stealthily and uncovered his feet,
and lay down. 8 At midnight the
man was startled, and turned over,
and there, lying at his feet, was a
woman! 9 He said, "Who are you?"
And she answered, "I am Ruth,
your servant; spread your cloak
over your servant, for you are next-
of-kin."[g] 10 He said, "May you be
blessed by the LORD, my daughter;
this last instance of your loyalty is
better than the first; you have not
gone after young men, whether
poor or rich. 11 And now, my daughter, do not be afraid, I will do for
you all that you ask, for all the assembly of my people know that you
are a worthy woman. 12 But now,
though it is true that I am a near
kinsman, there is another kinsman
more closely related than I. 13 Remain this night, and in the morning, if he will act as next-of-kin[g]
for you, good; let him do it. If he is
not willing to act as next-of-kin[g]
for you, then, as the LORD lives, I
will act as next-of-kin[g] for you. Lie
down until the morning."

14 So she lay at his feet until
morning, but got up before one person could recognize another; for he
said, "It must not be known that
the woman came to the threshing
floor." 15 Then he said, "Bring the
cloak you are wearing and hold it
out." So she held it, and he measured out six measures of barley,
and put it on her back; then he
went into the city. 16 She came to
her mother-in-law, who said, "How
did things go with you,[h] my daughter?" Then she told her all that the
man had done for her, 17 saying,
"He gave me these six measures of
barley, for he said, 'Do not go back
to your mother-in-law empty-
handed.' " 18 She replied, "Wait, my
daughter, until you learn how the
matter turns out, for the man will
not rest, but will settle the matter
today."

3.7 Judg 19.6,9, 22; 2 Sam 13.28 **3.9** v. 12; Ruth 2.20 **3.11** Prov 12.4 **3.12** v. 9; Ruth 4.1 **3.13** Ruth 4.5 **3.18** Ps 37.3-5

4.1 Ruth 3.12 **4.3** Lev 25.25 **4.4** Jer 32.7,8; Lev 25.25 **4.5ff** Deut 25.5,6 **4.6** Ruth 3.12, 13 **4.7** Deut 25.7,9 **4.10** Deut 25.6

The Marriage of Boaz and Ruth

4 No sooner had Boaz gone up
to the gate and sat down there
than the next-of-kin,[g] of whom
Boaz had spoken, came passing by.
So Boaz said, "Come over, friend;
sit down here." And he went over
and sat down. 2 Then Boaz took ten
men of the elders of the city, and
said, "Sit down here"; so they sat
down. 3 He then said to the next-of-
kin,[g] "Naomi, who has come back
from the country of Moab, is selling
the parcel of land that belonged to
our kinsman Elimelech. 4 So I
thought I would tell you of it, and
say: Buy it in the presence of those
sitting here, and in the presence of
the elders of my people. If you will
redeem it, redeem it; but if you will
not, tell me, so that I may know; for
there is no one prior to you to redeem it, and I come after you." So
he said, "I will redeem it." 5 Then
Boaz said, "The day you acquire
the field from the hand of Naomi,
you are also acquiring Ruth[i] the
Moabite, the widow of the dead
man, to maintain the dead man's
name on his inheritance." 6 At this,
the next-of-kin[g] said, "I cannot redeem it for myself without damag-
ing my own inheritance. Take my
right of redemption yourself, for I
cannot redeem it."

7 Now this was the custom in
former times in Israel concerning
redeeming and exchanging: to confirm a transaction, the one took off
a sandal and gave it to the other;
this was the manner of attesting in
Israel. 8 So when the next-of-kin[g]
said to Boaz, "Acquire it for yourself," he took off his sandal. 9 Then
Boaz said to the elders and all the
people, "Today you are witnesses
that I have acquired from the hand
of Naomi all that belonged to Elimelech and all that belonged to Chilion and Mahlon. 10 I have also acquired Ruth the Moabite, the wife
of Mahlon, to be my wife, to maintain the dead man's name on his

[g] Or *one with the right to redeem*
[h] Or *"Who are you,*
[i] OL Vg: Heb *from the hand of Naomi and from Ruth*

inheritance, in order that the name
of the dead may not be cut off from
his kindred and from the gate of his
native place; today you are witnesses." 11 Then all the people who
were at the gate, along with the elders, said, "We are witnesses. May
the LORD make the woman who is
coming into your house like Rachel
and Leah, who together built up
the house of Israel. May you produce children in Ephrathah and
bestow a name in Bethlehem;
12 and, through the children that
the LORD will give you by this young
woman, may your house be like the
house of Perez, whom Tamar bore
to Judah."

The Genealogy of David

13 So Boaz took Ruth and she
became his wife. When they came
together, the LORD made her conceive, and she bore a son. 14 Then
the women said to Naomi,
"Blessed be the LORD, who has not
left you this day without next-of-
kin;[j] and may his name be renowned in Israel! 15 He shall be to
you a restorer of life and a nourish-
er of your old age; for your
daughter-in-law who loves you,
who is more to you than seven
sons, has borne him." 16 Then Naomi took the child and laid him in
her bosom, and became his nurse.
17 The women of the neighborhood
gave him a name, saying, "A son
has been born to Naomi." They
named him Obed; he became the
father of Jesse, the father of David.

18 Now these are the descendants of Perez: Perez became the
father of Hezron, 19 Hezron of Ram,
Ram of Amminadab, 20 Amminadab of Nahshon, Nahshon of Salmon, 21 Salmon of Boaz, Boaz of
Obed, 22 Obed of Jesse, and Jesse
of David.

4.11 Ps 127.3
4.12 v. 18; Gen 38.29
4.13 Ruth 3.11; Gen 29.31; 33.5
4.14 Lk 1.58
4.15 Ruth 1.16, 17; 2.11,12
4.18 Mt 1.3-6

[j] Or *one with the right to redeem*

1 Samuel

Title and Background

1 and 2 Samuel are named after the individual whom God used to establish kingship in Israel. These two books were originally one book, but it was divided into two parts by the translators of the Septuagint (Greek version of the Old Testament). The book of 1 Samuel records the lives of Samuel and Saul, and most of the life of David before he became king.

Author and Date of Writing

Who the author was is uncertain because the book itself does not identify anyone. The author probably wrote some time after the division of the kingdom that followed upon the death of Solomon in 930 B.C. Some scholars place its composition as late as the exile (seventh century B.C.).

Theme and Message

1 Samuel portrays the establishment of kingship in Israel. When the people demanded a king, Samuel was led by God to anoint Saul as the first king of Israel. But Saul was disobedient to God, and God rejected him as king. Then Samuel secretly anointed David to take Saul's place. The struggles between Saul and David make up the rest of the book. The weaknesses and sins of these leaders of Israel are shown, but so are Samuel's and David's goodness and obedience to God.

Outline

I. Background for the Establishment of Kingship in Israel (1.1–7.17)
II. Establishment of Kingship in Israel (8.1–12.25)
III. Failure of Saul's Kingship (13.1–15.35)
IV. David and Saul (16.1–30.31)
V. Death of Saul (31.1-13)

Samuel's Birth and Dedication

1 There was a certain man of Ra-
mathaim, a Zuphite[a] from the
hill country of Ephraim, whose
name was Elkanah son of Jeroham
son of Elihu son of Tohu son of
Zuph, an Ephraimite. 2 He had two
wives; the name of the one was
Hannah, and the name of the other
Peninnah. Peninnah had children,
but Hannah had no children.
3 Now this man used to go up
year by year from his town to worship and to sacrifice to the LORD of
hosts at Shiloh, where the two sons
of Eli, Hophni and Phinehas, were
priests of the LORD. 4 On the day
when Elkanah sacrificed, he would
give portions to his wife Peninnah
and to all her sons and daughters;
5 but to Hannah he gave a double
portion,[b] because he loved her,
though the LORD had closed her
womb. 6 Her rival used to provoke
her severely, to irritate her, because the LORD had closed her
womb. 7 So it went on year by year;
as often as she went up to the
house of the LORD, she used to provoke her. Therefore Hannah wept
and would not eat. 8 Her husband
Elkanah said to her, "Hannah, why
do you weep? Why do you not eat?
Why is your heart sad? Am I not
more to you than ten sons?"
9 After they had eaten and
drunk at Shiloh, Hannah rose and
presented herself before the

1.1 Josh 17.17, 18; 1 Chr 6.27
1.2 Deut 21.15-17; Lk 2.36
1.3 Ex 34.23; Deut 12.5; Josh 18.1
1.4 Deut 12.17
1.5 Gen 16.1; 30.2
1.6 Job 24.21
1.8 Ruth 4.15
1.9 1 Sam 3.3

[a] Compare Gk and 1 Chr 6.35-36: Heb *Ramathaim-zophim* [b] Syr: Meaning of Heb uncertain

LORD.[c] Now Eli the priest was sitting on the seat beside the doorpost of the temple of the LORD.
10 She was deeply distressed and
prayed to the LORD, and wept bitterly. 11 She made this vow: "O LORD of
hosts, if only you will look on the
misery of your servant, and remember me, and not forget your servant,
but will give to your servant a male
child, then I will set him before you
as a nazirite[d] until the day of his
death. He shall drink neither wine
nor intoxicants,[e] and no razor
shall touch his head."
12 As she continued praying before the LORD, Eli observed her
mouth. 13 Hannah was praying silently; only her lips moved, but her
voice was not heard; therefore Eli
thought she was drunk. 14 So Eli
said to her, "How long will you
make a drunken spectacle of yourself? Put away your wine." 15 But
Hannah answered, "No, my lord, I
am a woman deeply troubled; I
have drunk neither wine nor strong
drink, but I have been pouring out
my soul before the LORD. 16 Do not
regard your servant as a worthless
woman, for I have been speaking
out of my great anxiety and vexation all this time." 17 Then Eli answered, "Go in peace; the God of
Israel grant the petition you have
made to him." 18 And she said, "Let
your servant find favor in your
sight." Then the woman went to
her quarters,[f] ate and drank with
her husband,[g] and her countenance was sad no longer.[h]
19 They rose early in the morning and worshiped before the LORD;
then they went back to their house
at Ramah. Elkanah knew his wife
Hannah, and the LORD remembered
her. 20 In due time Hannah conceived and bore a son. She named
him Samuel, for she said, "I have
asked him of the LORD."
21 The man Elkanah and all his
household went up to offer to the
LORD the yearly sacrifice, and to pay
his vow. 22 But Hannah did not go
up, for she said to her husband, "As
soon as the child is weaned, I will
bring him, that he may appear in
the presence of the LORD, and remain there forever; I will offer him
as a nazirite[d] for all time."[i] 23 Her
husband Elkanah said to her, "Do
what seems best to you, wait until
you have weaned him; only—may
the LORD establish his word."[j] So
the woman remained and nursed
her son, until she weaned him.
24 When she had weaned him, she
took him up with her, along with a
three-year-old bull,[k] an ephah of
flour, and a skin of wine. She
brought him to the house of the
LORD at Shiloh; and the child was
young. 25 Then they slaughtered
the bull, and they brought the child
to Eli. 26 And she said, "Oh, my
lord! As you live, my lord, I am the
woman who was standing here in
your presence, praying to the LORD.
27 For this child I prayed; and the
LORD has granted me the petition
that I made to him. 28 Therefore I
have lent him to the LORD; as long
as he lives, he is given to the LORD."
She left him there for[l] the LORD.

1.11 Gen 28.20; 29.32; Num 6.5; Judg 13.5 **1.13** Gen 24.42-45 **1.14** Acts 2.4,13 **1.15** Ps 62.8 **1.17** Judg 18.6; 1 Sam 25.35; Mk 5.34 **1.18** Ruth 2.13; Eccl 9.7 **1.19** Gen 4.1; 30.22 **1.20** Gen 41.51, 52; Ex 2.10, 22 **1.21** v. 3 **1.22** Lk 2.22; 1 Sam 2.11, 18 **1.23** Num 30.7; v. 17 **1.24** Deut 12.5; Josh 18.1 **1.25** Lev 1.5; Lk 2.22 **1.26** 2 Kings 2.2 **1.27** vv. 11-13 **1.28** vv. 11,22 **2.1** Lk 1.46-55; Ps 89.17; Isa 12.2,3 **2.2** Lev 19.2; 2 Sam 22.32; Deut 32.30, 31

Hannah's Prayer

2 Hannah prayed and said,
"My heart exults in the LORD;
my strength is exalted in my God.[m]
My mouth derides my enemies,
because I rejoice in my[n] victory.

2 "There is no Holy One like the LORD,
no one besides you;
there is no Rock like our God.

[c] Gk: Heb lacks *and presented herself before the LORD* [d] That is *one separated* or *one consecrated* [e] Cn Compare Gk Q Ms 1.22: MT *then I will give him to the LORD all the days of his life* [f] Gk: Heb *went her way* [g] Gk: Heb lacks *and drank with her husband* [h] Gk: Meaning of Heb uncertain [i] Cn Compare Q Ms: MT lacks *I will offer him as a nazirite for all time* [j] MT: Q Ms Gk Compare Syr *that which goes out of your mouth* [k] Q Ms Gk Syr: MT *three bulls* [l] Gk (Compare Q Ms) and Gk at 2.11: MT *And he* (that is, Elkanah) *worshiped there before* [m] Gk: Heb *the LORD* [n] Q Ms: MT *your*

[3] Talk no more so very
    proudly,
  let not arrogance come
    from your mouth;
for the LORD is a God of
    knowledge,
  and by him actions are
    weighed.
[4] The bows of the mighty are
    broken,
  but the feeble gird on
    strength.
[5] Those who were full have
    hired themselves out for
    bread,
  but those who were hungry
    are fat with spoil.
The barren has borne seven,
  but she who has many
    children is forlorn.
[6] The LORD kills and brings to
    life;
  he brings down to Sheol
    and raises up.
[7] The LORD makes poor and
    makes rich;
  he brings low, he also
    exalts.
[8] He raises up the poor from
    the dust;
  he lifts the needy from the
    ash heap,
to make them sit with
    princes
  and inherit a seat of
    honor.[o]
For the pillars of the earth
    are the LORD's,
  and on them he has set the
    world.

[9] "He will guard the feet of his
    faithful ones,
  but the wicked shall be cut
    off in darkness;
  for not by might does one
    prevail.
[10] The LORD! His adversaries
    shall be shattered;
  the Most High[p] will
    thunder in heaven.
The LORD will judge the ends
    of the earth;
  he will give strength to his
    king,
  and exalt the power of his
    anointed."

Eli's Wicked Sons

11 Then Elkanah went home to
Ramah, while the boy remained to
minister to the LORD, in the presence of the priest Eli.
12 Now the sons of Eli were
scoundrels; they had no regard for
the LORD [13] or for the duties of the
priests to the people. When anyone
offered sacrifice, the priest's servant would come, while the meat
was boiling, with a three-pronged
fork in his hand, [14] and he would
thrust it into the pan, or kettle, or
caldron, or pot; all that the fork
brought up the priest would take
for himself.[q] This is what they did
at Shiloh to all the Israelites who
came there. [15] Moreover, before the
fat was burned, the priest's servant
would come and say to the one who
was sacrificing, "Give meat for the
priest to roast; for he will not accept boiled meat from you, but
only raw." [16] And if the man said to
him, "Let them burn the fat first,
and then take whatever you wish,"
he would say, "No, you must give it
now; if not, I will take it by force."
[17] Thus the sin of the young men
was very great in the sight of the
LORD; for they treated the offerings
of the LORD with contempt.

The Child Samuel at Shiloh

18 Samuel was ministering before the LORD, a boy wearing a linen
ephod. [19] His mother used to make
for him a little robe and take it to
him each year, when she went up
with her husband to offer the yearly
sacrifice. [20] Then Eli would bless
Elkanah and his wife, and say,
"May the LORD repay[r] you with
children by this woman for the gift
that she made to[s] the LORD"; and
then they would return to their
home.
21 And[t] the LORD took note of
Hannah; she conceived and bore
three sons and two daughters. And

2.3 Prov 8.13; 1 Sam 16.7; 1 Kings 8.39; Prov 16.2; 24.12
2.4 Ps 76.3
2.5 Ps 113.9; Jer 15.9
2.6 Deut 32.39; Isa 26.19
2.7 Deut 8.17, 18; Job 5.11; Ps 75.6,7
2.8 Ps 113.7,8; Job 36.7; 38.4,5
2.9 Ps 91.11,12; Mt 8.12; Ps 33.16,17
2.10 Ps 2.9; 18.13; 96.13; 21.1,7; 89.24
2.11 1 Sam 3.1
2.12 Jer 2.8; 9.3, 6
2.13 Lev 7.29-34
2.15 Lev 3.3,4
2.17 Mal 2.7-9
2.18 vv. 11,28; 1 Sam 3.1
2.19 1 Sam 1.3
2.20 Lk 2.34; 1 Sam 1.11, 27,28
2.21 Gen 21.1; v. 26; 1 Sam 3.19; Lk 2.40

[o] Gk (Compare Q Ms) adds *He grants the vow of the one who vows, and blesses the years of the just* [p] Cn Heb *against him he* [q] Gk Syr Vg: Heb *with it* [r] Q Ms Gk: MT *give* [s] Q Ms Gk: MT *for the petition that she asked of* [t] Q Ms Gk: MT *When*

the boy Samuel grew up in the presence of the LORD.

Prophecy against Eli's Household

22 Now Eli was very old. He heard all that his sons were doing to all Israel, and how they lay with the women who served at the entrance to the tent of meeting. 23 He said to them, "Why do you do such things? For I hear of your evil dealings from all these people. 24 No, my sons; it is not a good report that I hear the people of the LORD spreading abroad. 25 If one person sins against another, someone can intercede for the sinner with the LORD;[u] but if someone sins against the LORD, who can make intercession?" But they would not listen to the voice of their father; for it was the will of the LORD to kill them.

26 Now the boy Samuel continued to grow both in stature and in favor with the LORD and with the people.

27 A man of God came to Eli and said to him, "Thus the LORD has said, 'I revealed[v] myself to the family of your ancestor in Egypt when they were slaves[w] to the house of Pharaoh. 28 I chose him out of all the tribes of Israel to be my priest, to go up to my altar, to offer incense, to wear an ephod before me; and I gave to the family of your ancestor all my offerings by fire from the people of Israel. 29 Why then look with greedy eye[x] at my sacrifices and my offerings that I commanded, and honor your sons more than me by fattening yourselves on the choicest parts of every offering of my people Israel?' 30 Therefore the LORD the God of Israel declares: 'I promised that your family and the family of your ancestor should go in and out before me forever'; but now the LORD declares: 'Far be it from me; for those who honor me I will honor, and those who despise me shall be treated with contempt. 31 See, a time is coming when I will cut off your strength and the strength of your ancestor's family, so that no one in your family will live to old age. 32 Then in distress you will look with greedy eye[y] on all the prosperity that shall be bestowed upon Israel; and no one in your family shall ever live to old age. 33 The only one of you whom I shall not cut off from my altar shall be spared to weep out his[z] eyes and grieve his[a] heart; all the members of your household shall die by the sword.[b] 34 The fate of your two sons, Hophni and Phinehas, shall be the sign to you—both of them shall die on the same day. 35 I will raise up for myself a faithful priest, who shall do according to what is in my heart and in my mind. I will build him a sure house, and he shall go in and out before my anointed one forever. 36 Everyone who is left in your family shall come to implore him for a piece of silver or a loaf of bread, and shall say, Please put me in one of the priest's places, that I may eat a morsel of bread.' "

Samuel's Calling and Prophetic Activity

3 Now the boy Samuel was ministering to the LORD under Eli. The word of the LORD was rare in those days; visions were not widespread.

2 At that time Eli, whose eyesight had begun to grow dim so that he could not see, was lying down in his room; 3 the lamp of God had not yet gone out, and Samuel was lying down in the temple of the LORD, where the ark of God was. 4 Then the LORD called, "Samuel! Samuel!"[c] and he said, "Here I am!" 5 and ran to Eli, and said, "Here I am, for you called me." But he said, "I did not call; lie down again." So he went and lay down. 6 The LORD called again, "Samuel!" Samuel got up and went to Eli, and said, "Here

2.22 Ex 38.8
2.24 1 Kings 15.26
2.25 Deut 1.17; Num 15.30; Josh 11.20
2.26 v. 21; Lk 2.52
2.27 1 Kings 13.1; Ex 4.14-16
2.28 Ex 28.1-4; Lev 8.7,8
2.29 vv. 13-17; Deut 12.5; Mt 10.37
2.30 Ex 29.9; Ps 91.14; Mal 2.9
2.31 1 Sam 4.11-18; 22.17-20
2.32 1 Kings 2.26, 27; Zech 8.4
2.34 1 Kings 13.3; 1 Sam 4.11
2.35 1 Kings 2.35; 2 Sam 7.11, 27; 1 Kings 11.38; 1 Sam 12.3; 16.13
2.36 1 Kings 2.27
3.1 1 Sam 2.11, 18; Ps 74.9; Am 8.11
3.2 1 Sam 4.15
3.3 Lev 24.2-4
3.4 Isa 6.8

[u] Gk Compare Q Ms: MT *another, God will mediate for him* [v] Gk Tg Syr: Heb *Did I reveal* [w] Q Ms Gk: MT lacks *slaves* [x] Q Ms Gk: MT *then kick* [y] Q Ms Gk: MT *will kick* [z] Q Ms Gk: MT *your* [a] Q Ms Gk: Heb *your* [b] Q Ms See Gk: MT *die like mortals* [c] Q Ms Gk See 3.10: MT *the LORD called Samuel*

I am, for you called me." But he
said, "I did not call, my son; lie
down again." 7 Now Samuel did not
yet know the LORD, and the word of
the LORD had not yet been revealed
to him. 8 The LORD called Samuel
again, a third time. And he got up
and went to Eli, and said, "Here I
am, for you called me." Then Eli
perceived that the LORD was calling
the boy. 9 Therefore Eli said to
Samuel, "Go, lie down; and if he
calls you, you shall say, 'Speak,
LORD, for your servant is listening.' " So Samuel went and lay
down in his place.
10 Now the LORD came and
stood there, calling as before,
"Samuel! Samuel!" And Samuel
said, "Speak, for your servant is listening." 11 Then the LORD said to
Samuel, "See, I am about to do
something in Israel that will make
both ears of anyone who hears of it
tingle. 12 On that day I will fulfill
against Eli all that I have spoken
concerning his house, from beginning to end. 13 For I have told him
that I am about to punish his house
forever, for the iniquity that he
knew, because his sons were blaspheming God,[d] and he did not restrain them. 14 Therefore I swear to
the house of Eli that the iniquity of
Eli's house shall not be expiated by
sacrifice or offering forever."
15 Samuel lay there until morning; then he opened the doors of
the house of the LORD. Samuel was
afraid to tell the vision to Eli. 16 But
Eli called Samuel and said, "Samuel, my son." He said, "Here I am."
17 Eli said, "What was it that he told
you? Do not hide it from me. May
God do so to you and more also, if
you hide anything from me of all
that he told you." 18 So Samuel told
him everything and hid nothing
from him. Then he said, "It is the
LORD; let him do what seems good
to him."
19 As Samuel grew up, the LORD
was with him and let none of his
words fall to the ground. 20 And all
Israel from Dan to Beer-sheba
knew that Samuel was a trustworthy prophet of the LORD. 21 The LORD
continued to appear at Shiloh, for
the LORD revealed himself to Samuel at Shiloh by the word of the
4 LORD. 1 And the word of Samuel came to all Israel.

The Ark of God Captured

In those days the Philistines
mustered for war against Israel,[e]
and Israel went out to battle
against them;[f] they encamped at
Ebenezer, and the Philistines encamped at Aphek. 2 The Philistines
drew up in line against Israel, and
when the battle was joined,[g] Israel
was defeated by the Philistines,
who killed about four thousand
men on the field of battle. 3 When
the troops came to the camp, the
elders of Israel said, "Why has the
LORD put us to rout today before the
Philistines? Let us bring the ark of
the covenant of the LORD here from
Shiloh, so that he may come
among us and save us from the
power of our enemies." 4 So the
people sent to Shiloh, and brought
from there the ark of the covenant
of the LORD of hosts, who is enthroned on the cherubim. The two
sons of Eli, Hophni and Phinehas,
were there with the ark of the covenant of God.
5 When the ark of the covenant
of the LORD came into the camp, all
Israel gave a mighty shout, so that
the earth resounded. 6 When the
Philistines heard the noise of the
shouting, they said, "What does
this great shouting in the camp of
the Hebrews mean?" When they
learned that the ark of the LORD had
come to the camp, 7 the Philistines
were afraid; for they said, "Gods
have[h] come into the camp." They
also said, "Woe to us! For nothing
like this has happened before.
8 Woe to us! Who can deliver us
from the power of these mighty
gods? These are the gods who
struck the Egyptians with every
sort of plague in the wilderness.
9 Take courage, and be men,

3.7 Acts 19.2
3.11 2 Kings 21.12; Jer 19.3
3.12 1 Sam 2.30-36
3.13 1 Sam 2.12, 17,22,29-31
3.14 Lev 15.30, 31; Isa 22.14
3.17 Ruth 1.17; 2 Sam 3.35
3.18 Job 2.10; Isa 39.8
3.19 1 Sam 2.21; Gen 21.22; 39.2; 1 Sam 9.6
3.20 Judg 20.1
3.21 v. 10
4.1 1 Sam 7.12
4.3 Josh 7.7,8; Num 10.35
4.4 2 Sam 6.2; Ex 25.18,22
4.5 Josh 6.5,20
4.6 Ex 15.14
4.9 1 Cor 16.13; Judg 13.1

[d] Another reading is *for themselves*
[e] Gk: Heb lacks *In those days the Philistines mustered for war against Israel*
[f] Gk: Heb *against the Philistines*
[g] Meaning of Heb uncertain
[h] Or *A god has*

O Philistines, in order not to become slaves to the Hebrews as they
have been to you; be men and
fight."
10 So the Philistines fought; Israel was defeated, and they fled,
everyone to his home. There was a
very great slaughter, for there fell of
Israel thirty thousand foot soldiers.
11 The ark of God was captured; and
the two sons of Eli, Hophni and
Phinehas, died.

Death of Eli

12 A man of Benjamin ran from
the battle line, and came to Shiloh
the same day, with his clothes torn
and with earth upon his head.
13 When he arrived, Eli was sitting
upon his seat by the road watching,
for his heart trembled for the ark of
God. When the man came into the
city and told the news, all the city
cried out. 14 When Eli heard the
sound of the outcry, he said, "What
is this uproar?" Then the man
came quickly and told Eli. 15 Now
Eli was ninety-eight years old and
his eyes were set, so that he could
not see. 16 The man said to Eli, "I
have just come from the battle; I
fled from the battle today." He
said, "How did it go, my son?"
17 The messenger replied, "Israel
has fled before the Philistines, and
there has also been a great slaughter among the troops; your two
sons also, Hophni and Phinehas,
are dead, and the ark of God has
been captured." 18 When he mentioned the ark of God, Eli[i] fell over
backward from his seat by the side
of the gate; and his neck was broken and he died, for he was an old
man, and heavy. He had judged Israel forty years.
19 Now his daughter-in-law, the
wife of Phinehas, was pregnant,
about to give birth. When she heard
the news that the ark of God was
captured, and that her father-in-
law and her husband were dead,
she bowed and gave birth; for her
labor pains overwhelmed her. 20 As
she was about to die, the women
attending her said to her, "Do not
be afraid, for you have borne a
son." But she did not answer or
give heed. 21 She named the child
Ichabod, meaning, "The glory has
departed from Israel," because the
ark of God had been captured and
because of her father-in-law and
her husband. 22 She said, "The glory has departed from Israel, for the
ark of God has been captured."

The Philistines and the Ark

5 When the Philistines captured
the ark of God, they brought it
from Ebenezer to Ashdod; 2 then
the Philistines took the ark of God
and brought it into the house of
Dagon and placed it beside Dagon.
3 When the people of Ashdod rose
early the next day, there was Dagon, fallen on his face to the
ground before the ark of the LORD.
So they took Dagon and put him
back in his place. 4 But when they
rose early on the next morning, Dagon had fallen on his face to the
ground before the ark of the LORD,
and the head of Dagon and both his
hands were lying cut off upon the
threshold; only the trunk of[j] Dagon was left to him. 5 This is why
the priests of Dagon and all who
enter the house of Dagon do not
step on the threshold of Dagon in
Ashdod to this day.
6 The hand of the LORD was
heavy upon the people of Ashdod,
and he terrified and struck them
with tumors, both in Ashdod and in
its territory. 7 And when the inhabitants of Ashdod saw how things
were, they said, "The ark of the
God of Israel must not remain with
us; for his hand is heavy on us and
on our god Dagon." 8 So they sent
and gathered together all the lords
of the Philistines, and said, "What
shall we do with the ark of the God
of Israel?" The inhabitants of Gath
replied, "Let the ark of God be
moved on to us."[k] So they moved
the ark of the God of Israel to
Gath.[l] 9 But after they had brought
it to Gath,[m] the hand of the LORD

4.10 v. 2; Deut 28.25; 2 Sam 18.17; 2 Kings 14.12
4.11 1 Sam 2.34; Ps 78.56-64
4.12 Josh 7.6; 2 Sam 1.2; Neh 9.1
4.13 v. 18; 1 Sam 1.9
4.15 1 Sam 3.2
4.16 2 Sam 1.4
4.18 v. 13
4.20 Gen 35.16-19
4.22 Jer 2.11; v. 11
5.1 1 Sam 4.1; 7.12
5.2 Judg 16.23
5.3 Isa 19.1; 46.1,2,7
5.4 Ezek 6.4,6
5.6 vv. 7,11; Ex 9.3; 1 Sam 6.5; Deut 28.27; Ps 78.66
5.8 v. 11
5.9 vv. 6,11; 1 Sam 7.13; Ps 78.66

[i] Heb *he* [j] Heb lacks *the trunk of*
[k] Gk Compare Q Ms: MT *They answered, "Let the ark of the God of Israel be brought around to Gath."* [l] Gk: Heb lacks *to Gath*
[m] Q Ms: MT lacks *to Gath*

was against the city, causing a very
great panic; he struck the inhabitants of the city, both young and
old, so that tumors broke out on
them. 10 So they sent the ark of the
God of Israel[n] to Ekron. But when
the ark of God came to Ekron, the
people of Ekron cried out, "Why[o]
have they brought around to us[p]
the ark of the God of Israel to kill
us[p] and our[q] people?" 11 They sent
therefore and gathered together all
the lords of the Philistines, and
said, "Send away the ark of the God
of Israel, and let it return to its own
place, that it may not kill us and
our people." For there was a deathly panic[r] throughout the whole
city. The hand of God was very
heavy there; 12 those who did not
die were stricken with tumors, and
the cry of the city went up to heav-
en.

The Ark Returned to Israel

6 The ark of the LORD was in the
country of the Philistines sev-
en months. 2 Then the Philistines
called for the priests and the diviners and said, "What shall we do
with the ark of the LORD? Tell us
what we should send with it to its
place." 3 They said, "If you send
away the ark of the God of Israel,
do not send it empty, but by all
means return him a guilt offering.
Then you will be healed and will be
ransomed;[s] will not his hand then
turn from you?" 4 And they said,
"What is the guilt offering that we
shall return to him?" They answered, "Five gold tumors and five
gold mice, according to the number of the lords of the Philistines;
for the same plague was upon all of
you and upon your lords. 5 So you
must make images of your tumors
and images of your mice that ravage the land, and give glory to the
God of Israel; perhaps he will light-
en his hand on you and your gods
and your land. 6 Why should you
harden your hearts as the Egyptians and Pharaoh hardened their
hearts? After he had made fools of
them, did they not let the people
go, and they departed? 7 Now then,
get ready a new cart and two milch
cows that have never borne a yoke,
and yoke the cows to the cart, but
take their calves home, away from
them. 8 Take the ark of the LORD
and place it on the cart, and put in
a box at its side the figures of gold,
which you are returning to him as a
guilt offering. Then send it off, and
let it go its way. 9 And watch; if it
goes up on the way to its own land,
to Beth-shemesh, then it is he who
has done us this great harm; but if
not, then we shall know that it is
not his hand that struck us; it happened to us by chance."

10 The men did so; they took
two milch cows and yoked them to
the cart, and shut up their calves at
home. 11 They put the ark of the
LORD on the cart, and the box with
the gold mice and the images of
their tumors. 12 The cows went
straight in the direction of Beth-
shemesh along one highway, lowing as they went; they turned neither to the right nor to the left, and
the lords of the Philistines went after them as far as the border of
Beth-shemesh.

13 Now the people of Beth-
shemesh were reaping their wheat
harvest in the valley. When they
looked up and saw the ark, they
went with rejoicing to meet it.[t]
14 The cart came into the field of
Joshua of Beth-shemesh, and
stopped there. A large stone was
there; so they split up the wood of
the cart and offered the cows as a
burnt offering to the LORD. 15 The
Levites took down the ark of the
LORD and the box that was beside
it, in which were the gold objects,
and set them upon the large stone.
Then the people of Beth-shemesh
offered burnt offerings and presented sacrifices on that day to the
LORD. 16 When the five lords of the
Philistines saw it, they returned
that day to Ekron.

17 These are the gold tumors,

5.11 vv. 6,8,9 **6.2** Gen 41.8; Ex 7.11; Isa 2.6 **6.3** Ex 23.15; Deut 16.16; Lev 5.15,16 **6.4** vv. 17,18; Josh 13.3; Judg 3.3 **6.5** 1 Sam 5.3-11; Josh 7.19; Isa 42.12 **6.6** Ex 8.15; 9.34; 12.31 **6.7** 2 Sam 6.3; Num 19.2

6.8 vv. 3-5 **6.9** Josh 15.10; v. 3 **6.12** v. 9; Num 20.19 **6.14** 2 Sam 24.22; 1 Kings 19.21 **6.16** Josh 13.3 **6.17** v. 4

[n] Q Ms Gk: MT lacks *of Israel* [o] Q Ms Gk: MT lacks *Why* [p] Heb *me* [q] Heb *my* [r] Q Ms reads *a panic from the LORD* [s] Q Ms Gk: MT *and it will be known to you* [t] Gk: Heb *rejoiced to see it*

which the Philistines returned as a
guilt offering to the LORD: one for
Ashdod, one for Gaza, one for Ashkelon, one for Gath, one for Ekron;
18 also the gold mice, according to
the number of all the cities of the
Philistines belonging to the five
lords, both fortified cities and unwalled villages. The great stone,
beside which they set down the ark
of the LORD, is a witness to this day
in the field of Joshua of Beth-
shemesh.

The Ark at Kiriath-jearim

19 The descendants of Jeconiah
did not rejoice with the people of
Beth-shemesh when they greeted[u]
the ark of the LORD; and he killed
seventy men of them.[v] The people
mourned because the LORD had
made a great slaughter among the
people. 20 Then the people of Beth-
shemesh said, "Who is able to
stand before the LORD, this holy
God? To whom shall he go so that
we may be rid of him?" 21 So they
sent messengers to the inhabitants
of Kiriath-jearim, saying, "The
Philistines have returned the ark of
the LORD. Come down and take it
7 up to you." 1 And the people of
Kiriath-jearim came and took
up the ark of the LORD, and brought
it to the house of Abinadab on the
hill. They consecrated his son, Eleazar, to have charge of the ark of
the LORD.

2 From the day that the ark was
lodged at Kiriath-jearim, a long
time passed, some twenty years,
and all the house of Israel lamented[w] after the LORD.

Samuel as Judge

3 Then Samuel said to all the
house of Israel, "If you are returning to the LORD with all your heart,
then put away the foreign gods and
the Astartes from among you. Direct your heart to the LORD, and
serve him only, and he will deliver
you out of the hand of the Philistines." 4 So Israel put away the Baals and the Astartes, and they
served the LORD only.

5 Then Samuel said, "Gather all
Israel at Mizpah, and I will pray to
the LORD for you." 6 So they gathered at Mizpah, and drew water
and poured it out before the LORD.
They fasted that day, and said, "We
have sinned against the LORD." And
Samuel judged the people of Israel
at Mizpah.

7 When the Philistines heard
that the people of Israel had gathered at Mizpah, the lords of the
Philistines went up against Israel.
And when the people of Israel
heard of it they were afraid of the
Philistines. 8 The people of Israel
said to Samuel, "Do not cease to
cry out to the LORD our God for us,
and pray that he may save us from
the hand of the Philistines." 9 So
Samuel took a sucking lamb and
offered it as a whole burnt offering
to the LORD; Samuel cried out to
the LORD for Israel, and the LORD answered him. 10 As Samuel was offering up the burnt offering, the Philistines drew near to attack Israel;
but the LORD thundered with a
mighty voice that day against the
Philistines and threw them into
confusion; and they were routed
before Israel. 11 And the men of Israel went out of Mizpah and pursued the Philistines, and struck
them down as far as beyond Beth-
car.

12 Then Samuel took a stone
and set it up between Mizpah and
Jeshanah,[x] and named it Ebenezer;[y] for he said, "Thus far the LORD
has helped us." 13 So the Philistines
were subdued and did not again
enter the territory of Israel; the
hand of the LORD was against the
Philistines all the days of Samuel.
14 The towns that the Philistines
had taken from Israel were restored
to Israel, from Ekron to Gath; and
Israel recovered their territory from
the hand of the Philistines. There
was peace also between Israel and
the Amorites.

15 Samuel judged Israel all the

6.18 vv. 14,15
6.19 Num 4.5,15, 20; 2 Sam 6.7
6.20 Lev 11.44, 45; 2 Sam 6.9
6.21 Josh 9.17; 15.9,60
7.1 2 Sam 6.3, 4
7.3 Joel 2.2; Josh 24.14; Judg 2.13; Deut 6.13; Mt 4.10
7.6 Ps 62.8; Neh 9.1; Judg 10.10
7.7 1 Sam 17.11
7.8 Isa 37.4
7.9 Ps 99.6; Jer 15.1
7.10 Josh 10.10; 1 Sam 2.10; 2 Sam 22.14, 15
7.12 Gen 35.14; Josh 4.9
7.13 Judg 13.1; 1 Sam 13.5
7.15 v. 6; 1 Sam 12.11

[u] Gk: Heb *And he killed some of the people of Beth-shemesh, because they looked into*
[v] Heb *killed seventy men, fifty thousand men*
[w] Meaning of Heb uncertain
[x] Gk Syr: Heb *Shen*
[y] That is *Stone of Help*

days of his life. 16 He went on a circuit year by year to Bethel, Gilgal,
and Mizpah; and he judged Israel
in all these places. 17 Then he
would come back to Ramah, for his
home was there; he administered
justice there to Israel, and built
there an altar to the LORD.

Israel Demands a King

8 When Samuel became old, he
made his sons judges over Israel. 2 The name of his firstborn son
was Joel, and the name of his second, Abijah; they were judges in
Beer-sheba. 3 Yet his sons did not
follow in his ways, but turned aside
after gain; they took bribes and
perverted justice.
4 Then all the elders of Israel
gathered together and came to
Samuel at Ramah, 5 and said to
him, "You are old and your sons do
not follow in your ways; appoint for
us, then, a king to govern us, like
other nations." 6 But the thing displeased Samuel when they said,
"Give us a king to govern us." Samuel prayed to the LORD, 7 and the
LORD said to Samuel, "Listen to the
voice of the people in all that they
say to you; for they have not rejected you, but they have rejected me
from being king over them. 8 Just as
they have done to me,[z] from the
day I brought them up out of Egypt
to this day, forsaking me and serving other gods, so also they are doing to you. 9 Now then, listen to
their voice; only—you shall solemnly warn them, and show them
the ways of the king who shall reign
over them."
10 So Samuel reported all the
words of the LORD to the people
who were asking him for a king.
11 He said, "These will be the ways
of the king who will reign over you:
he will take your sons and appoint
them to his chariots and to be his
horsemen, and to run before his
chariots; 12 and he will appoint for
himself commanders of thousands
and commanders of fifties, and
some to plow his ground and to
reap his harvest, and to make his
implements of war and the equipment of his chariots. 13 He will take
your daughters to be perfumers
and cooks and bakers. 14 He will
take the best of your fields and
vineyards and olive orchards and
give them to his courtiers. 15 He will
take one-tenth of your grain and of
your vineyards and give it to his officers and his courtiers. 16 He will
take your male and female slaves,
and the best of your cattle[a] and
donkeys, and put them to his work.
17 He will take one-tenth of your
flocks, and you shall be his slaves.
18 And in that day you will cry out
because of your king, whom you
have chosen for yourselves; but the
LORD will not answer you in that
day."

Israel's Request for a King Granted

19 But the people refused to listen to the voice of Samuel; they
said, "No! but we are determined
to have a king over us, 20 so that we
also may be like other nations, and
that our king may govern us and go
out before us and fight our battles." 21 When Samuel had heard all
the words of the people, he repeated them in the ears of the LORD.
22 The LORD said to Samuel, "Listen
to their voice and set a king over
them." Samuel then said to the
people of Israel, "Each of you return home."

Saul Chosen to Be King

9 There was a man of Benjamin
whose name was Kish son of
Abiel son of Zeror son of Becorath
son of Aphiah, a Benjaminite, a
man of wealth. 2 He had a son
whose name was Saul, a handsome
young man. There was not a man
among the people of Israel more
handsome than he; he stood head
and shoulders above everyone else.
3 Now the donkeys of Kish,
Saul's father, had strayed. So Kish
said to his son Saul, "Take one of
the boys with you; go and look for
the donkeys." 4 He passed through
the hill country of Ephraim and

7.17 1 Sam 1.19; 7.5; Judg 20.1; 1 Sam 8.6
8.1 Deut 16.18, 19
8.3 Ex 23.6,8; Deut 16.19; Ps 15.5
8.4 1 Sam 7.17
8.5ff Deut 17.14, 15
8.6 1 Sam 15.11
8.7 1 Sam 10.19; Ex 16.8
8.9 v. 11
8.11 1 Sam 14.52; 2 Sam 15.1
8.12 1 Sam 22.7
8.14 1 Kings 21.7; Ezek 46.18
8.18 Prov 1.25-28; Mic 3.4
8.20 v. 5
8.22 v. 7
9.1 1 Sam 14.51; 1 Chr 9.36-39
9.2 1 Sam 10.23, 24
9.4 Josh 24.33; 2 Kings 4.42; Josh 19.42

[z] Gk: Heb lacks *to me* [a] Gk: Heb *young men*

passed through the land of Shalishah, but they did not find them.
And they passed through the land
of Shaalim, but they were not
there. Then he passed through the
land of Benjamin, but they did not
find them.
5 When they came to the land of
Zuph, Saul said to the boy who was
with him, "Let us turn back, or my
father will stop worrying about the
donkeys and worry about us." 6 But
he said to him, "There is a man of
God in this town; he is a man held
in honor. Whatever he says always
comes true. Let us go there now;
perhaps he will tell us about the
journey on which we have set out."
7 Then Saul replied to the boy, "But
if we go, what can we bring the
man? For the bread in our sacks is
gone, and there is no present to
bring to the man of God. What have
we?" 8 The boy answered Saul
again, "Here, I have with me a
quarter shekel of silver; I will give it
to the man of God, to tell us our
way." 9 (Formerly in Israel, anyone
who went to inquire of God would
say, "Come, let us go to the seer";
for the one who is now called a
prophet was formerly called a
seer.) 10 Saul said to the boy,
"Good; come, let us go." So they
went to the town where the man of
God was.
11 As they went up the hill to
the town, they met some girls coming out to draw water, and said to
them, "Is the seer here?" 12 They
answered, "Yes, there he is just
ahead of you. Hurry; he has come
just now to the town, because the
people have a sacrifice today at the
shrine. 13 As soon as you enter
the town, you will find him, before
he goes up to the shrine to eat. For
the people will not eat until he
comes, since he must bless the
sacrifice; afterward those eat who
are invited. Now go up, for you
will meet him immediately." 14 So
they went up to the town. As they
were entering the town, they saw
Samuel coming out toward them on
his way up to the shrine.
15 Now the day before Saul
came, the LORD had revealed to
Samuel: 16 "Tomorrow about this
time I will send to you a man from
the land of Benjamin, and you shall
anoint him to be ruler over my people Israel. He shall save my people
from the hand of the Philistines;
for I have seen the suffering of[b] my
people, because their outcry has
come to me." 17 When Samuel saw
Saul, the LORD told him, "Here is
the man of whom I spoke to you.
He it is who shall rule over my people." 18 Then Saul approached
Samuel inside the gate, and said,
"Tell me, please, where is the
house of the seer?" 19 Samuel answered Saul, "I am the seer; go up
before me to the shrine, for today
you shall eat with me, and in the
morning I will let you go and will
tell you all that is on your mind.
20 As for your donkeys that were
lost three days ago, give no further
thought to them, for they have
been found. And on whom is all Israel's desire fixed, if not on you and
on all your ancestral house?"
21 Saul answered, "I am only a Benjaminite, from the least of the
tribes of Israel, and my family is the
humblest of all the families of the
tribe of Benjamin. Why then have
you spoken to me in this way?"
22 Then Samuel took Saul and
his servant-boy and brought them
into the hall, and gave them a place
at the head of those who had been
invited, of whom there were about
thirty. 23 And Samuel said to the
cook, "Bring the portion I gave you,
the one I asked you to put aside."
24 The cook took up the thigh and
what went with it[c] and set them
before Saul. Samuel said, "See,
what was kept is set before you.
Eat; for it is set[d] before you at the
appointed time, so that you might
eat with the guests."[e]
So Saul ate with Samuel that
day. 25 When they came down from
the shrine into the town, a bed was

9.5 1 Sam 10.2 **9.6** Deut 33.1; 1 Sam 3.19 **9.7** 1 Kings 14.3; 2 Kings 8.8 **9.9** 2 Sam 24.11; 1 Chr 26.28; Isa 30.10 **9.11** Gen 24.15 **9.12** Num 28.11-15; 1 Sam 7.17; 10.5 **9.16** 1 Sam 10.1; Ex 3.7,9 **9.17** 1 Sam 16.12 **9.20** v. 3; 1 Sam 8.5; 12.13 **9.21** 1 Sam 15.17; Judg 20.46, 48 **9.24** Lev 7.32,33; Num 18.18 **9.25** Deut 22.8; Acts 10.9

[b] Gk: Heb lacks *the suffering of* [c] Meaning of Heb uncertain [d] Q Ms Gk: MT *it was kept* [e] Cn: Heb *it was kept for you, saying, I have invited the people*

spread for Saul[f] on the roof, and
he lay down to sleep.[g] 26 Then at
the break of dawn[h] Samuel called
to Saul upon the roof, "Get up, so
that I may send you on your way."
Saul got up, and both he and Samuel went out into the street.

Samuel Anoints Saul

27 As they were going down to
the outskirts of the town, Samuel
said to Saul, "Tell the boy to go on
before us, and when he has passed
on, stop here yourself for a while,
that I may make known to you the
10 word of God." 1 Samuel
took a vial of oil and
poured it on his head, and kissed
him; he said, "The LORD has anointed you ruler over his people Israel.
You shall reign over the people of
the LORD and you will save them
from the hand of their enemies all
around. Now this shall be the sign
to you that the LORD has anointed
you ruler[i] over his heritage:
2 When you depart from me today
you will meet two men by Rachel's
tomb in the territory of Benjamin
at Zelzah; they will say to you, 'The
donkeys that you went to seek are
found, and now your father has
stopped worrying about them and
is worrying about you, saying: What
shall I do about my son?' 3 Then
you shall go on from there further
and come to the oak of Tabor; three
men going up to God at Bethel will
meet you there, one carrying three
kids, another carrying three loaves
of bread, and another carrying a
skin of wine. 4 They will greet you
and give you two loaves of bread,
which you shall accept from them.
5 After that you shall come to
Gibeath-elohim,[j] at the place
where the Philistine garrison is;
there, as you come to the town, you
will meet a band of prophets coming down from the shrine with
harp, tambourine, flute, and lyre
playing in front of them; they will
be in a prophetic frenzy. 6 Then the
spirit of the LORD will possess you,
and you will be in a prophetic frenzy along with them and be turned
into a different person. 7 Now when
these signs meet you, do whatever
you see fit to do, for God is with
you. 8 And you shall go down to Gilgal ahead of me; then I will come
down to you to present burnt offerings and offer sacrifices of well-
being. Seven days you shall wait,
until I come to you and show you
what you shall do."

Saul Prophesies

9 As he turned away to leave
Samuel, God gave him another
heart; and all these signs were fulfilled that day. 10 When they were
going from there[k] to Gibeah,[l] a
band of prophets met him; and the
spirit of God possessed him, and he
fell into a prophetic frenzy along
with them. 11 When all who knew
him before saw how he prophesied
with the prophets, the people said
to one another, "What has come
over the son of Kish? Is Saul also
among the prophets?" 12 A man of
the place answered, "And who is
their father?" Therefore it became
a proverb, "Is Saul also among the
prophets?" 13 When his prophetic
frenzy had ended, he went home.[m]

14 Saul's uncle said to him and
to the boy, "Where did you go?"
And he replied, "To seek the donkeys; and when we saw they were
not to be found, we went to Samuel." 15 Saul's uncle said, "Tell me
what Samuel said to you." 16 Saul
said to his uncle, "He told us that
the donkeys had been found." But
about the matter of the kingship, of
which Samuel had spoken, he did
not tell him anything.

Saul Proclaimed King

17 Samuel summoned the people to the LORD at Mizpah 18 and
said to them,[n] "Thus says the
LORD, the God of Israel, 'I brought
up Israel out of Egypt, and I rescued you from the hand of the
Egyptians and from the hand of all

10.1 1 Sam 16.13; 2 Kings 9.3, 6; Ps 2.12; Deut 32.9; Ps 78.71
10.2 Gen 35.19, 20; 1 Sam 9.3-5
10.3 Gen 28.22; 35.1,3,7,8
10.5 1 Sam 13.3; 9.12; 19.20; 2 Kings 3.15
10.6 Num 11.25, 29; v. 10; 1 Sam 19.23, 24
10.7 Josh 1.5; Judg 6.12
10.8 1 Sam 11.15; 13.8
10.9 v. 6
10.10 vv. 5,6; 1 Sam 19.20
10.11 1 Sam 19.24; Mt 13.54, 55; Jn 7.15
10.16 1 Sam 9.20
10.17 1 Sam 7.5, 6
10.18 Judg 6.8,9

[f] Gk: Heb *and he spoke with Saul*
[g] Gk: Heb lacks *and he lay down to sleep*
[h] Gk: Heb *and they arose early and at break of dawn*
[i] Gk: Heb lacks *over his people Israel. You shall . . . anointed you ruler*
[j] Or *the Hill of God*
[k] Gk: Heb *they came there*
[l] Or *the hill*
[m] Cn: Heb *he came to the shrine*
[n] Heb *to the people of Israel*

the kingdoms that were oppressing you.’ 19 But today you have rejected your God, who saves you from all your calamities and your distresses; and you have said, ‘No! but set a king over us.’ Now therefore present yourselves before the LORD by your tribes and by your clans.”

20 Then Samuel brought all the tribes of Israel near, and the tribe of Benjamin was taken by lot. 21 He brought the tribe of Benjamin near by its families, and the family of the Matrites was taken by lot. Finally he brought the family of the Matrites near man by man,[o] and Saul the son of Kish was taken by lot. But when they sought him, he could not be found. 22 So they inquired again of the LORD, “Did the man come here?”[p] and the LORD said, “See, he has hidden himself among the baggage.” 23 Then they ran and brought him from there. When he took his stand among the people, he was head and shoulders taller than any of them. 24 Samuel said to all the people, “Do you see the one whom the LORD has chosen? There is no one like him among all the people.” And all the people shouted, “Long live the king!”

25 Samuel told the people the rights and duties of the kingship; and he wrote them in a book and laid it up before the LORD. Then Samuel sent all the people back to their homes. 26 Saul also went to his home at Gibeah, and with him went warriors whose hearts God had touched. 27 But some worthless fellows said, “How can this man save us?” They despised him and brought him no present. But he held his peace.

Now Nahash, king of the Ammonites, had been grievously oppressing the Gadites and the Reubenites. He would gouge out the right eye of each of them and would not grant Israel a deliverer. No one was left of the Israelites across the Jordan whose right eye Nahash, king of the Ammonites, had not gouged out. But there were seven thousand men who had escaped from the Ammonites and had entered Jabesh-gilead.[q]

Saul Defeats the Ammonites

11 About a month later,[r] Nahash the Ammonite went up and besieged Jabesh-gilead; and all the men of Jabesh said to Nahash, “Make a treaty with us, and we will serve you.” 2 But Nahash the Ammonite said to them, “On this condition I will make a treaty with you, namely that I gouge out everyone’s right eye, and thus put disgrace upon all Israel.” 3 The elders of Jabesh said to him, “Give us seven days’ respite that we may send messengers through all the territory of Israel. Then, if there is no one to save us, we will give ourselves up to you.” 4 When the messengers came to Gibeah of Saul, they reported the matter in the hearing of the people; and all the people wept aloud.

5 Now Saul was coming from the field behind the oxen; and Saul said, “What is the matter with the people, that they are weeping?” So they told him the message from the inhabitants of Jabesh. 6 And the spirit of God came upon Saul in power when he heard these words, and his anger was greatly kindled. 7 He took a yoke of oxen, and cut them in pieces and sent them throughout all the territory of Israel by messengers, saying, “Whoever does not come out after Saul and Samuel, so shall it be done to his oxen!” Then the dread of the LORD fell upon the people, and they came out as one. 8 When he mustered them at Bezek, those from Israel were three hundred thousand, and those from Judah seventy[s] thousand. 9 They said to the messengers who had come, “Thus shall you say to the inhabitants of Jabesh-gilead: ‘Tomorrow, by the time the sun is hot, you shall have deliverance.’ ” When the messen-

10.19 1 Sam 8.6, 7; Josh 24.1
10.20 Josh 7.14, 16,17
10.22 1 Sam 23.2, 4,9-11
10.23 1 Sam 9.2
10.24 2 Sam 21.6; 1 Kings 1.25, 39
10.25 1 Sam 8.11-18; Deut 17.14-20
10.26 1 Sam 11.4
10.27 1 Kings 10.25; 2 Chr 17.5
11.1 1 Sam 12.12; Judg 21.8; 1 Kings 20.34; Ezek 17.13
11.2 Num 16.14; 1 Sam 17.26
11.4 1 Sam 10.26; 15.34; 30.4; Judg 2.4
11.6 Judg 3.10; 6.34; 13.25; 14.6; 1 Sam 10.10; 16.13
11.7 Judg 19.29; 21.5,8,10
11.8 Judg 1.5; 20.2

[o] Gk: Heb lacks *Finally . . . man by man*
[p] Gk: Heb *Is there yet a man to come here?*
[q] Q Ms Compare Josephus, *Antiquities* VI.v.1 (68-71): MT lacks *Now Nahash . . . entered Jabesh-gilead.*
[r] Q Ms Gk: MT lacks *About a month later*
[s] Q Ms Gk: MT *thirty*

gers came and told the inhabitants
of Jabesh, they rejoiced. 10 So the
inhabitants of Jabesh said, "Tomorrow we will give ourselves up to
you, and you may do to us whatever
seems good to you." 11 The next day
Saul put the people in three companies. At the morning watch they
came into the camp and cut down
the Ammonites until the heat of
the day; and those who survived
were scattered, so that no two of
them were left together.
12 The people said to Samuel,
"Who is it that said, 'Shall Saul
reign over us?' Give them to us so
that we may put them to death."
13 But Saul said, "No one shall be
put to death this day, for today the
LORD has brought deliverance to Israel."
14 Samuel said to the people,
"Come, let us go to Gilgal and there
renew the kingship." 15 So all the
people went to Gilgal, and there
they made Saul king before the
LORD in Gilgal. There they sacrificed offerings of well-being before
the LORD, and there Saul and all the
Israelites rejoiced greatly.

Samuel's Farewell Address

12 Samuel said to all Israel, "I
have listened to you in all
that you have said to me, and have
set a king over you. 2 See, it is the
king who leads you now; I am old
and gray, but my sons are with you.
I have led you from my youth until
this day. 3 Here I am; testify against
me before the LORD and before his
anointed. Whose ox have I taken?
Or whose donkey have I taken? Or
whom have I defrauded? Whom
have I oppressed? Or from whose
hand have I taken a bribe to blind
my eyes with it? Testify against
me[t] and I will restore it to you."
4 They said, "You have not defrauded us or oppressed us or taken anything from the hand of anyone."
5 He said to them, "The LORD is witness against you, and his anointed
is witness this day, that you have
not found anything in my hand."
And they said, "He is witness."
6 Samuel said to the people,
"The LORD is witness, who[u] appointed Moses and Aaron and
brought your ancestors up out of
the land of Egypt. 7 Now therefore
take your stand, so that I may enter
into judgment with you before the
LORD, and I will declare to you[v] all
the saving deeds of the LORD that he
performed for you and for your ancestors. 8 When Jacob went into
Egypt and the Egyptians oppressed
them,[w] then your ancestors cried
to the LORD and the LORD sent Moses and Aaron, who brought forth
your ancestors out of Egypt, and
settled them in this place. 9 But
they forgot the LORD their God; and
he sold them into the hand of Sisera, commander of the army of
King Jabin of[x] Hazor, and into the
hand of the Philistines, and into
the hand of the king of Moab; and
they fought against them. 10 Then
they cried to the LORD, and said,
'We have sinned, because we have
forsaken the LORD, and have served
the Baals and the Astartes; but now
rescue us out of the hand of our enemies, and we will serve you.'
11 And the LORD sent Jerubbaal and
Barak,[y] and Jephthah, and Samson,[z] and rescued you out of the
hand of your enemies on every
side; and you lived in safety. 12 But
when you saw that King Nahash of
the Ammonites came against you,
you said to me, 'No, but a king
shall reign over us,' though the
LORD your God was your king.
13 See, here is the king whom you
have chosen, for whom you have
asked; see, the LORD has set a king
over you. 14 If you will fear the LORD
and serve him and heed his voice
and not rebel against the commandment of the LORD, and if both
you and the king who reigns over
you will follow the LORD your God,
it will be well; 15 but if you will not
heed the voice of the LORD, but rebel against the commandment of

11.10 v. 3
11.11 Judg 7.16
11.12 1 Sam 10.27; Lk 19.27
11.13 2 Sam 19.22; Ex 14.13; 1 Sam 19.5
11.14 1 Sam 10.8, 25
11.15 1 Sam 10.8, 17
12.1 1 Sam 8.7, 9,22; 10.24; 11.14,15
12.2 1 Sam 8.1, 5,20
12.3 1 Sam 10.1; 24.6; 2 Sam 1.14; Num 16.15; Acts 20.33; Deut 16.19
12.5 Acts 23.9; 24.20; Ex 22.4
12.6 Ex 6.26
12.7 Isa 1.18; Mic 6.1-5
12.8 Ex 2.23; 3.10; 4.16
12.9 Judg 3.7; 4.2; 10.7; 13.1; 3.12
12.10 Judg 10.10; 2.13; 10.15
12.11 Judg 6.14, 32; 4.6; 11.1
12.12 1 Sam 11.1; 8.6,19; Judg 8.23
12.13 1 Sam 10.24; 8.5; Hos 13.11
12.14 Josh 24.14
12.15 Josh 24.20

[t] Gk: Heb lacks *Testify against me*
[u] Gk: Heb lacks *is witness, who*
[v] Gk: Heb lacks *and I will declare to you*
[w] Gk: Heb lacks *and the Egyptians oppressed them*
[x] Gk: Heb lacks *Jabin king of*
[y] Gk Syr: Heb *Bedan*
[z] Gk: Heb *Samuel*

the LORD, then the hand of the LORD
will be against you and your king.[a]
16 Now therefore take your stand
and see this great thing that the
LORD will do before your eyes. 17 Is
it not the wheat harvest today? I
will call upon the LORD, that he may
send thunder and rain; and you
shall know and see that the wickedness that you have done in the
sight of the LORD is great in demanding a king for yourselves."
18 So Samuel called upon the LORD,
and the LORD sent thunder and rain
that day; and all the people greatly
feared the LORD and Samuel.

19 All the people said to Samuel, "Pray to the LORD your God for
your servants, so that we may not
die; for we have added to all our
sins the evil of demanding a king
for ourselves." 20 And Samuel said
to the people, "Do not be afraid;
you have done all this evil, yet do
not turn aside from following the
LORD, but serve the LORD with all
your heart; 21 and do not turn aside
after useless things that cannot
profit or save, for they are useless.
22 For the LORD will not cast away
his people, for his great name's
sake, because it has pleased the
LORD to make you a people for himself. 23 Moreover as for me, far be it
from me that I should sin against
the LORD by ceasing to pray for you;
and I will instruct you in the good
and the right way. 24 Only fear the
LORD, and serve him faithfully with
all your heart; for consider what
great things he has done for you.
25 But if you still do wickedly, you
shall be swept away, both you and
your king."

Saul's Unlawful Sacrifice

13 Saul was . . .[b] years old
when he began to reign;
and he reigned . . . and two[c] years
over Israel.

2 Saul chose three thousand out
of Israel; two thousand were with
Saul in Michmash and the hill
country of Bethel, and a thousand
were with Jonathan in Gibeah of
Benjamin; the rest of the people he
sent home to their tents. 3 Jonathan defeated the garrison of the
Philistines that was at Geba; and
the Philistines heard of it. And Saul
blew the trumpet throughout all
the land, saying, "Let the Hebrews
hear!" 4 When all Israel heard that
Saul had defeated the garrison of
the Philistines, and also that Israel
had become odious to the Philistines, the people were called out to
join Saul at Gilgal.

5 The Philistines mustered to
fight with Israel, thirty thousand
chariots, and six thousand horsemen, and troops like the sand on
the seashore in multitude; they
came up and encamped at Michmash, to the east of Beth-aven.
6 When the Israelites saw that they
were in distress (for the troops
were hard pressed), the people hid
themselves in caves and in holes
and in rocks and in tombs and in
cisterns. 7 Some Hebrews crossed
the Jordan to the land of Gad and
Gilead. Saul was still at Gilgal, and
all the people followed him trembling.

8 He waited seven days, the
time appointed by Samuel; but
Samuel did not come to Gilgal, and
the people began to slip away from
Saul.[d] 9 So Saul said, "Bring the
burnt offering here to me, and the
offerings of well-being." And he offered the burnt offering. 10 As soon
as he had finished offering the
burnt offering, Samuel arrived; and
Saul went out to meet him and salute him. 11 Samuel said, "What
have you done?" Saul replied,
"When I saw that the people were
slipping away from me, and that
you did not come within the days
appointed, and that the Philistines
were mustering at Michmash, 12 I
said, 'Now the Philistines will
come down upon me at Gilgal, and
I have not entreated the favor of the
LORD'; so I forced myself, and offered the burnt offering." 13 Samuel

12.16 Ex 14.13,31
12.17 Prov 26.1; 1 Sam 7.9, 10; 8.7
12.18 Ex 14.31
12.19 v. 23; Ex 9.28; Jas 5.15
12.21 Deut 11.16; Jer 16.19; Hab 2.18
12.22 1 Kings 6.13; Josh 7.9; Deut 7.7,8
12.23 Rom 1.9; Col 1.9; 2 Tim 1.3; 1 Kings 8.36
12.24 Eccl 12.13; Deut 10.21
12.25 Josh 24.20; 1 Sam 31.1-5
13.2 1 Sam 10.26
13.3 1 Sam 10.5
13.5 Josh 11.4
13.6 Judg 6.2
13.8 1 Sam 10.8
13.9 2 Sam 24.25
13.10 1 Sam 15.13
13.11 vv. 2,5,16, 23
13.13 2 Chr 16.9; 1 Sam 15.11, 22

[a] Gk: Heb *and your ancestors*
[b] The number is lacking in the Heb text (the verse is lacking in the Septuagint). [c] *Two* is not the entire number; something has dropped out. [d] Heb *him*

said to Saul, "You have done foolishly; you have not kept the commandment of the LORD your God,
which he commanded you. The
LORD would have established your
kingdom over Israel forever, 14 but
now your kingdom will not continue; the LORD has sought out a man
after his own heart; and the LORD
has appointed him to be ruler over
his people, because you have not
kept what the LORD commanded
you." 15 And Samuel left and went
on his way from Gilgal.[e] The rest of
the people followed Saul to join the
army; they went up from Gilgal toward Gibeah of Benjamin.[f]

Preparations for Battle

Saul counted the people who
were present with him, about six
hundred men. 16 Saul, his son Jonathan, and the people who were
present with them stayed in Geba
of Benjamin; but the Philistines
encamped at Michmash. 17 And
raiders came out of the camp of the
Philistines in three companies; one
company turned toward Ophrah, to
the land of Shual, 18 another company turned toward Beth-horon,
and another company turned toward the mountain[g] that looks
down upon the valley of Zeboim toward the wilderness.

19 Now there was no smith to
be found throughout all the land of
Israel; for the Philistines said, "The
Hebrews must not make swords or
spears for themselves"; 20 so all the
Israelites went down to the Philistines to sharpen their plowshare,
mattocks, axes, or sickles;[h] 21 The
charge was two-thirds of a shekel[i]
for the plowshares and for the mattocks, and one-third of a shekel for
sharpening the axes and for setting
the goads.[j] 22 So on the day of the
battle neither sword nor spear was
to be found in the possession of
any of the people with Saul and
Jonathan; but Saul and his son
Jonathan had them.

Jonathan Surprises and Routs the Philistines

23 Now a garrison of the Philistines had gone out to the pass of

14 Michmash. 1 One day
Jonathan son of Saul said
to the young man who carried
his armor, "Come, let us go over
to the Philistine garrison on the
other side." But he did not
tell his father. 2 Saul was staying in
the outskirts of Gibeah under the
pomegranate tree that is at Migron;
the troops that were with him were
about six hundred men, 3 along
with Ahijah son of Ahitub, Ichabod's brother, son of Phinehas son
of Eli, the priest of the LORD in Shiloh, carrying an ephod. Now the
people did not know that Jonathan
had gone. 4 In the pass,[k] by which
Jonathan tried to go over to the
Philistine garrison, there was a
rocky crag on one side and a rocky
crag on the other; the name of the
one was Bozez, and the name of the
other Seneh. 5 One crag rose on the
north in front of Michmash, and
the other on the south in front of
Geba.

6 Jonathan said to the young
man who carried his armor, "Come,
let us go over to the garrison of
these uncircumcised; it may be
that the LORD will act for us; for
nothing can hinder the LORD from
saving by many or by few." 7 His
armor-bearer said to him, "Do all
that your mind inclines to.[l] I am
with you; as your mind is, so is
mine."[m] 8 Then Jonathan said,
"Now we will cross over to those
men and will show ourselves to
them. 9 If they say to us, 'Wait until
we come to you,' then we will stand
still in our place, and we will not go
up to them. 10 But if they say,
'Come up to us,' then we will go up;
for the LORD has given them into
our hand. That will be the sign for
us." 11 So both of them showed
themselves to the garrison of the
Philistines; and the Philistines

13.14 1 Sam 15.28; Acts 13.22
13.15 1 Sam 14.2
13.17 1 Sam 14.15
13.18 Josh 18.13, 14; Neh 11.34
13.19 2 Kings 24.14
13.22 Judg 5.8
14.2 1 Sam 13.15
14.3 1 Sam 22.9-12, 20; 4.21; 2.28
14.4 1 Sam 13.23
14.6 Judg 7.4,7; 1 Sam 17.46, 47
14.10 Gen 24.14; Judg 6.36, 37
14.11 1 Sam 13.6

[e] Gk: Heb *went up from Gilgal to Gibeah of Benjamin* [f] Gk: Heb lacks *The rest . . . of Benjamin* [g] Cn Compare Gk: Heb *toward the border* [h] Gk: Heb *plowshare* [i] Heb *was a pim* [j] Cn: Meaning of Heb uncertain [k] Heb *Between the passes* [l] Gk: Heb *Do all that is in your mind. Turn* [m] Gk: Heb lacks *so is mine*

said, "Look, Hebrews are coming
out of the holes where they have
hidden themselves." 12 The men of
the garrison hailed Jonathan and
his armor-bearer, saying, "Come up
to us, and we will show you something." Jonathan said to his armor-
bearer, "Come up after me; for the
LORD has given them into the hand
of Israel." 13 Then Jonathan
climbed up on his hands and feet,
with his armor-bearer following after him. The Philistines[n] fell before Jonathan, and his armor-
bearer, coming after him, killed
them. 14 In that first slaughter Jonathan and his armor-bearer killed
about twenty men within an area
about half a furrow long in an
acre[o] of land. 15 There was a panic
in the camp, in the field, and
among all the people; the garrison
and even the raiders trembled; the
earth quaked; and it became a very
great panic.

16 Saul's lookouts in Gibeah of
Benjamin were watching as the
multitude was surging back and
forth.[p] 17 Then Saul said to the
troops that were with him, "Call
the roll and see who has gone from
us." When they had called the roll,
Jonathan and his armor-bearer
were not there. 18 Saul said to Ahijah, "Bring the ark[q] of God here."
For at that time the ark[q] of God
went with the Israelites. 19 While
Saul was talking to the priest, the
tumult in the camp of the Philistines increased more and more;
and Saul said to the priest, "Withdraw your hand." 20 Then Saul and
all the people who were with him
rallied and went into the battle;
and every sword was against the
other, so that there was very great
confusion. 21 Now the Hebrews
who previously had been with the
Philistines and had gone up with
them into the camp turned and
joined the Israelites who were with
Saul and Jonathan. 22 Likewise,
when all the Israelites who had
gone into hiding in the hill country
of Ephraim heard that the Philistines were fleeing, they too followed closely after them in the battle. 23 So the LORD gave Israel the
victory that day.

The battle passed beyond Beth-
aven, and the troops with Saul
numbered altogether about ten
thousand men. The battle spread
out over the hill country of Ephraim.

Saul's Rash Oath

24 Now Saul committed a very
rash act on that day.[r] He had laid
an oath on the troops, saying,
"Cursed be anyone who eats food
before it is evening and I have been
avenged on my enemies." So none
of the troops tasted food. 25 All the
troops[s] came upon a honeycomb;
and there was honey on the
ground. 26 When the troops came
upon the honeycomb, the honey
was dripping out; but they did not
put their hands to their mouths, for
they feared the oath. 27 But Jonathan had not heard his father
charge the troops with the oath; so
he extended the staff that was in
his hand, and dipped the tip of it in
the honeycomb, and put his hand
to his mouth; and his eyes brightened. 28 Then one of the soldiers
said, "Your father strictly charged
the troops with an oath, saying,
'Cursed be anyone who eats food
this day.' And so the troops are
faint." 29 Then Jonathan said, "My
father has troubled the land; see
how my eyes have brightened because I tasted a little of this honey.
30 How much better if today the
troops had eaten freely of the spoil
taken from their enemies; for now
the slaughter among the Philistines has not been great."

31 After they had struck down
the Philistines that day from Michmash to Aijalon, the troops were
very faint; 32 so the troops flew
upon the spoil, and took sheep and
oxen and calves, and slaughtered
them on the ground; and the troops
ate them with the blood. 33 Then it
was reported to Saul, "Look, the

14.12 1 Sam 17.43, 44; 2 Sam 5.24
14.15 2 Kings 7.6, 7; 1 Sam 13.17
14.16 2 Sam 18.24
14.19 Num 27.21
14.20 Judg 7.22; 2 Chr 20.23
14.22 1 Sam 13.6
14.23 Ex 14.30; Ps 44.6,7; 1 Sam 13.5
14.24 Josh 6.26
14.27 1 Sam 30.12
14.29 1 Kings 18.18
14.32 1 Sam 15.19; Lev 17.10-14

[n] Heb *They* [o] Heb *yoke* [p] Gk: Heb *they went and there* [q] Gk *the ephod*
[r] Gk: Heb *The Israelites were distressed that day* [s] Heb *land*

troops are sinning against the LORD
by eating with the blood." And he
said, "You have dealt treacherously; roll a large stone before me
here."[t] 34 Saul said, "Disperse
yourselves among the troops, and
say to them, 'Let all bring their
oxen or their sheep, and slaughter
them here, and eat; and do not sin
against the LORD by eating with the
blood.'" So all of the troops
brought their oxen with them that
night, and slaughtered them there.
35 And Saul built an altar to the
LORD; it was the first altar that he
built to the LORD.

Jonathan in Danger of Death

36 Then Saul said, "Let us go
down after the Philistines by night
and despoil them until the morning light; let us not leave one of
them." They said, "Do whatever
seems good to you." But the priest
said, "Let us draw near to God
here." 37 So Saul inquired of God,
"Shall I go down after the Philistines? Will you give them into the
hand of Israel?" But he did not answer him that day. 38 Saul said,
"Come here, all you leaders of the
people; and let us find out how this
sin has arisen today. 39 For as the
LORD lives who saves Israel, even if
it is in my son Jonathan, he shall
surely die!" But there was no one
among all the people who answered him. 40 He said to all Israel,
"You shall be on one side, and I and
my son Jonathan will be on the
other side." The people said to
Saul, "Do what seems good to
you." 41 Then Saul said, "O LORD
God of Israel, why have you not answered your servant today? If this
guilt is in me or in my son Jonathan, O LORD God of Israel, give
Urim; but if this guilt is in your people Israel,[u] give Thummim." And
Jonathan and Saul were indicated
by the lot, but the people were
cleared. 42 Then Saul said, "Cast
the lot between me and my son
Jonathan." And Jonathan was tak-
en.
43 Then Saul said to Jonathan,
"Tell me what you have done."
Jonathan told him, "I tasted a little
honey with the tip of the staff that
was in my hand; here I am, I will
die." 44 Saul said, "God do so to me
and more also; you shall surely die,
Jonathan!" 45 Then the people said
to Saul, "Shall Jonathan die, who
has accomplished this great victory
in Israel? Far from it! As the LORD
lives, not one hair of his head shall
fall to the ground; for he has
worked with God today." So the
people ransomed Jonathan, and he
did not die. 46 Then Saul withdrew
from pursuing the Philistines; and
the Philistines went to their own
place.

Saul's Continuing Wars

47 When Saul had taken the
kingship over Israel, he fought
against all his enemies on every
side—against Moab, against the
Ammonites, against Edom, against
the kings of Zobah, and against the
Philistines; wherever he turned he
routed them. 48 He did valiantly,
and struck down the Amalekites,
and rescued Israel out of the hands
of those who plundered them.
49 Now the sons of Saul were
Jonathan, Ishvi, and Malchishua;
and the names of his two daughters
were these: the name of the firstborn was Merab, and the name of
the younger, Michal. 50 The name
of Saul's wife was Ahinoam daughter of Ahimaaz. And the name of
the commander of his army was
Abner son of Ner, Saul's uncle;
51 Kish was the father of Saul, and
Ner the father of Abner was the son
of Abiel.
52 There was hard fighting
against the Philistines all the days
of Saul; and when Saul saw any
strong or valiant warrior, he took
him into his service.

Saul Defeats the Amalekites but Spares Their King

15 Samuel said to Saul, "The
LORD sent me to anoint you
king over his people Israel; now
therefore listen to the words of the

14.35 1 Sam 7.17
14.37 1 Sam 10.22; 28.6
14.38 Josh 7.14; 1 Sam 10.19
14.39 2 Sam 12.5
14.41 Prov 16.33; Acts 1.24
14.43 Josh 7.19; v. 23
14.44 Ruth 1.17; v. 39
14.45 2 Sam 14.11; 1 Kings 1.52; Acts 27.34
14.47 1 Sam 11.1-13; 2 Sam 10.6; v. 52
14.48 1 Sam 15.3, 7
14.49 1 Sam 31.2; 1 Chr 8.33; 1 Sam 18.17-20
14.50 2 Sam 2.8
14.51 1 Sam 9.1
14.52 1 Sam 8.11
15.1 1 Sam 9.16

[t] Gk: Heb *me this day* [u] Vg Compare Gk: Heb [41] *Saul said to the LORD, the God of Israel*

LORD. 2 Thus says the LORD of hosts,
'I will punish the Amalekites for
what they did in opposing the Israelites when they came up out of
Egypt. 3 Now go and attack Amalek, and utterly destroy all that
they have; do not spare them, but
kill both man and woman, child
and infant, ox and sheep, camel
and donkey.' "
4 So Saul summoned the people, and numbered them in Telaim,
two hundred thousand foot soldiers, and ten thousand soldiers of
Judah. 5 Saul came to the city of
the Amalekites and lay in wait in
the valley. 6 Saul said to the Kenites, "Go! Leave! Withdraw from
among the Amalekites, or I will destroy you with them; for you
showed kindness to all the people
of Israel when they came up out of
Egypt." So the Kenites withdrew
from the Amalekites. 7 Saul defeated the Amalekites, from Havilah as
far as Shur, which is east of Egypt.
8 He took King Agag of the Amalekites alive, but utterly destroyed all
the people with the edge of the
sword. 9 Saul and the people spared
Agag, and the best of the sheep and
of the cattle and of the fatlings, and
the lambs, and all that was valuable, and would not utterly destroy
them; all that was despised and
worthless they utterly destroyed.

Saul Rejected as King

10 The word of the LORD came to
Samuel: 11 "I regret that I made
Saul king, for he has turned back
from following me, and has not carried out my commands." Samuel
was angry; and he cried out to the
LORD all night. 12 Samuel rose early
in the morning to meet Saul, and
Samuel was told, "Saul went to
Carmel, where he set up a monument for himself, and on returning
he passed on down to Gilgal."
13 When Samuel came to Saul, Saul
said to him, "May you be blessed
by the LORD; I have carried out the
command of the LORD." 14 But Samuel said, "What then is this bleat-
ing of sheep in my ears, and the
lowing of cattle that I hear?" 15 Saul

15.2 Ex 17.8-14; Num 24.20; Deut 25.17-19
15.3 Num 24.20; Deut 20.16-18; 1 Sam 22.19
15.6 Judg 1.16; 4.11; Ex 18.10, 19; Num 10.29-32
15.7 1 Sam 14.48; Gen 16.7; 25.17,18; Ex 15.22
15.8 1 Kings 20.34ff; 1 Sam 30.1
15.9 vv. 3,15
15.11 Gen 6.6,7; 2 Sam 24.16; 1 Kings 9.6, 7; 1 Sam 16.1
15.12 Josh 15.55
15.13 Gen 14.19; Judg 17.2
15.15 vv. 9,21; Gen 3.12
15.17 1 Sam 9.21
15.18 v. 3
15.19 1 Sam 14.32
15.20 v. 13
15.21 v. 15
15.22 Isa 1.11-13; Mic 6.6-8; Heb 10.6-9; Hos 6.6; Mk 12.33
15.23 1 Sam 13.14
15.24 2 Sam 12.13; Prov 29.25; Isa 51.12,13

said, "They have brought them
from the Amalekites; for the people spared the best of the sheep
and the cattle, to sacrifice to the
LORD your God; but the rest we have
utterly destroyed." 16 Then Samuel
said to Saul, "Stop! I will tell you
what the LORD said to me last
night." He replied, "Speak."
17 Samuel said, "Though you
are little in your own eyes, are you
not the head of the tribes of Israel?
The LORD anointed you king over Israel. 18 And the LORD sent you on a
mission, and said, 'Go, utterly destroy the sinners, the Amalekites,
and fight against them until they
are consumed.' 19 Why then did you
not obey the voice of the LORD?
Why did you swoop down on the
spoil, and do what was evil in the
sight of the LORD?" 20 Saul said to
Samuel, "I have obeyed the voice of
the LORD, I have gone on the mission on which the LORD sent me, I
have brought Agag the king of Amalek, and I have utterly destroyed
the Amalekites. 21 But from the
spoil the people took sheep and
cattle, the best of the things devoted to destruction, to sacrifice to
the LORD your God in Gilgal." 22 And
Samuel said,

"Has the LORD as great
delight in burnt
offerings and sacrifices,
as in obeying the voice of
the LORD?
Surely, to obey is better than
sacrifice,
and to heed than the fat of
rams.
23 For rebellion is no less a sin
than divination,
and stubbornness is like
iniquity and idolatry.
Because you have rejected
the word of the LORD,
he has also rejected you
from being king."

24 Saul said to Samuel, "I have
sinned; for I have transgressed the
commandment of the LORD and
your words, because I feared the
people and obeyed their voice.
25 Now therefore, I pray, pardon my
sin, and return with me, so that I

may worship the LORD." 26 Samuel
said to Saul, "I will not return with
you; for you have rejected the word
of the LORD, and the LORD has rejected you from being king over Israel." 27 As Samuel turned to go
away, Saul caught hold of the hem
of his robe, and it tore. 28 And Samuel said to him, "The LORD has torn
the kingdom of Israel from you this
very day, and has given it to a
neighbor of yours, who is better
than you. 29 Moreover the Glory of
Israel will not recant[v] or change
his mind; for he is not a mortal,
that he should change his mind."
30 Then Saul[w] said, "I have sinned;
yet honor me now before the elders
of my people and before Israel, and
return with me, so that I may worship the LORD your God." 31 So Samuel turned back after Saul; and
Saul worshiped the LORD.

32 Then Samuel said, "Bring
Agag king of the Amalekites here to
me." And Agag came to him halt-
ingly.[x] Agag said, "Surely this is
the bitterness of death."[y] 33 But
Samuel said,

"As your sword has made
women childless,
so your mother shall be
childless among
women."

And Samuel hewed Agag in pieces
before the LORD in Gilgal.

34 Then Samuel went to Ramah; and Saul went up to his house
in Gibeah of Saul. 35 Samuel did
not see Saul again until the day of
his death, but Samuel grieved over
Saul. And the LORD was sorry that
he had made Saul king over Israel.

David Anointed as King

16 The LORD said to Samuel,
"How long will you grieve
over Saul? I have rejected him from
being king over Israel. Fill your
horn with oil and set out; I will
send you to Jesse the Bethlehemite, for I have provided for myself a
king among his sons." 2 Samuel
said, "How can I go? If Saul hears of
it, he will kill me." And the LORD
said, "Take a heifer with you, and
say, 'I have come to sacrifice to the
LORD.' 3 Invite Jesse to the sacrifice,
and I will show you what you shall
do; and you shall anoint for me the
one whom I name to you." 4 Samuel
did what the LORD commanded,
and came to Bethlehem. The elders of the city came to meet him
trembling, and said, "Do you come
peaceably?" 5 He said, "Peaceably;
I have come to sacrifice to the
LORD; sanctify yourselves and come
with me to the sacrifice." And he
sanctified Jesse and his sons and
invited them to the sacrifice.

6 When they came, he looked on
Eliab and thought, "Surely the
LORD's anointed is now before the
LORD."[z] 7 But the LORD said to Samuel, "Do not look on his appearance or on the height of his stature,
because I have rejected him; for the
LORD does not see as mortals see;
they look on the outward appearance, but the LORD looks on the
heart." 8 Then Jesse called Abinadab, and made him pass before
Samuel. He said, "Neither has the
LORD chosen this one." 9 Then Jesse
made Shammah pass by. And he
said, "Neither has the LORD chosen
this one." 10 Jesse made seven of
his sons pass before Samuel, and
Samuel said to Jesse, "The LORD
has not chosen any of these."
11 Samuel said to Jesse, "Are all
your sons here?" And he said,
"There remains yet the youngest,
but he is keeping the sheep." And
Samuel said to Jesse, "Send and
bring him; for we will not sit down
until he comes here." 12 He sent
and brought him in. Now he was
ruddy, and had beautiful eyes, and
was handsome. The LORD said,
"Rise and anoint him; for this is the
one." 13 Then Samuel took the horn
of oil, and anointed him in the
presence of his brothers; and the
spirit of the LORD came mightily
upon David from that day forward.
Samuel then set out and went to
Ramah.

15.26 1 Sam 13.14
15.27 1 Kings 11.30, 31
15.28 1 Sam 28.17
15.29 1 Chr 29.11; Num 23.19; Ezek 24.14
15.30 Jn 12.43; Isa 29.13
15.33 Gen 9.6; Judg 1.7
15.34 1 Sam 7.17; 11.4
15.35 1 Sam 19.24; 16.1
16.1 1 Sam 15.23, 35; 9.16; 2 Kings 9.1; Ps 78.70; Acts 13.22
16.2 1 Sam 20.29
16.3 Ex 4.15; 1 Sam 9.16
16.4 Lk 2.4; 1 Kings 2.13; 2 Kings 9.22
16.5 Ex 19.10
16.6 1 Sam 17.13
16.7 Isa 55.8; 1 Kings 8.39; 1 Chr 28.9
16.8 1 Sam 17.13
16.9 1 Sam 17.13
16.11 1 Sam 17.12
16.12 1 Sam 17.42; 9.17
16.13 1 Sam 10.1, 6,9,10; Judg 11.29

[v] Q Ms Gk: MT *deceive* [w] Heb *he*
[x] Cn Compare Gk: Meaning of Heb uncertain
[y] Q Ms Gk: MT *Surely the bitterness of death is past* [z] Heb *him*

David Plays the Lyre for Saul

14 Now the spirit of the LORD departed from Saul, and an evil spirit
from the LORD tormented him.
15 And Saul's servants said to him,
"See now, an evil spirit from God is
tormenting you. 16 Let our lord now
command the servants who attend
you to look for someone who is
skillful in playing the lyre; and
when the evil spirit from God is
upon you, he will play it, and you
will feel better." 17 So Saul said to
his servants, "Provide for me someone who can play well, and bring
him to me." 18 One of the young
men answered, "I have seen a son
of Jesse the Bethlehemite who is
skillful in playing, a man of valor, a
warrior, prudent in speech, and a
man of good presence; and the
LORD is with him." 19 So Saul sent
messengers to Jesse, and said,
"Send me your son David who is
with the sheep." 20 Jesse took a
donkey loaded with bread, a skin of
wine, and a kid, and sent them by
his son David to Saul. 21 And David
came to Saul, and entered his service. Saul loved him greatly, and he
became his armor-bearer. 22 Saul
sent to Jesse, saying, "Let David remain in my service, for he has
found favor in my sight." 23 And
whenever the evil spirit from God
came upon Saul, David took the
lyre and played it with his hand,
and Saul would be relieved and feel
better, and the evil spirit would depart from him.

David and Goliath

17 Now the Philistines gathered their armies for battle;
they were gathered at Socoh, which
belongs to Judah, and encamped
between Socoh and Azekah, in
Ephes-dammim. 2 Saul and the Israelites gathered and encamped in
the valley of Elah, and formed
ranks against the Philistines. 3 The
Philistines stood on the mountain
on the one side, and Israel stood on
the mountain on the other side,
with a valley between them. 4 And
there came out from the camp of
the Philistines a champion named
Goliath, of Gath, whose height was
six[a] cubits and a span. 5 He had a
helmet of bronze on his head, and
he was armed with a coat of mail;
the weight of the coat was five
thousand shekels of bronze. 6 He
had greaves of bronze on his legs
and a javelin of bronze slung between his shoulders. 7 The shaft of
his spear was like a weaver's beam,
and his spear's head weighed six
hundred shekels of iron; and his
shield-bearer went before him. 8 He
stood and shouted to the ranks of
Israel, "Why have you come out to
draw up for battle? Am I not a Philistine, and are you not servants of
Saul? Choose a man for yourselves,
and let him come down to me. 9 If
he is able to fight with me and kill
me, then we will be your servants;
but if I prevail against him and kill
him, then you shall be our servants
and serve us." 10 And the Philistine
said, "Today I defy the ranks of Israel! Give me a man, that we may
fight together." 11 When Saul and
all Israel heard these words of the
Philistine, they were dismayed and
greatly afraid.

12 Now David was the son of an
Ephrathite of Bethlehem in Judah,
named Jesse, who had eight sons.
In the days of Saul the man was already old and advanced in years.[b]
13 The three eldest sons of Jesse
had followed Saul to the battle; the
names of his three sons who went
to the battle were Eliab the firstborn, and next to him Abinadab,
and the third Shammah. 14 David
was the youngest; the three eldest
followed Saul, 15 but David went
back and forth from Saul to feed
his father's sheep at Bethlehem.
16 For forty days the Philistine
came forward and took his stand,
morning and evening.

17 Jesse said to his son David,
"Take for your brothers an ephah of
this parched grain and these ten
loaves, and carry them quickly to
the camp to your brothers; 18 also
take these ten cheeses to the com-

16.14 Judg 16.20; 1 Sam 18.10
16.16 v. 23; 1 Sam 18.10; 19.9; 2 Kings 3.15
16.18 1 Sam 17.32-36; 3.19
16.20 1 Sam 10.27; Prov 18.16
16.21f Gen 41.46; Prov 22.29
16.23 vv. 14-16
17.1 1 Sam 13.5; 2 Chr 28.18
17.2 1 Sam 21.9
17.4 2 Sam 21.19; Josh 11.21, 22
17.6 v. 45
17.7 2 Sam 21.19; v. 41
17.8 1 Sam 8.17
17.10 vv. 26,36,45
17.12 Ruth 4.22; 1 Sam 16.18; Gen 35.19; 1 Sam 16.10, 11; 1 Chr 2.13-15
17.13 1 Sam 16.6, 8,9
17.15 1 Sam 16.19
17.18 Gen 37.14

[a] MT: Q Ms Gk *four* [b] Gk Syr: Heb *among men*

DAVID'S FAMILY TREE

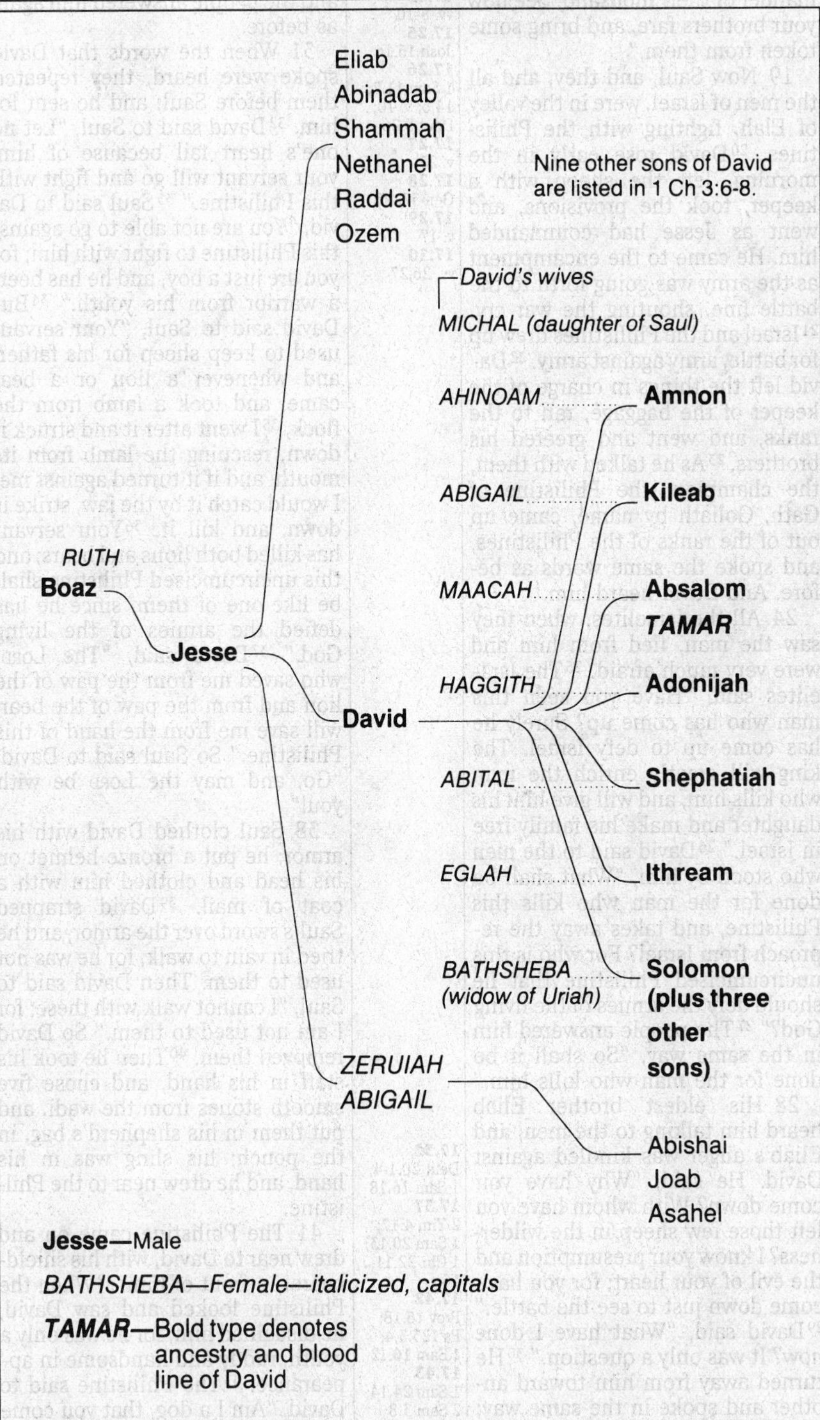

Eliab
Abinadab
Shammah
Nethanel
Raddai
Ozem
Nine other sons of David are listed in 1 Ch 3:6-8.
David's wives
MICHAL (daughter of Saul)
AHINOAM
Amnon
ABIGAIL
Kileab
RUTH
Boaz
MAACAH
Absalom
TAMAR
Jesse
HAGGITH
Adonijah
David
ABITAL
Shephatiah
EGLAH
Ithream
BATHSHEBA (widow of Uriah)
Solomon (plus three other sons)
ZERUIAH
ABIGAIL
Abishai
Joab
Asahel
Jesse—Male
BATHSHEBA—Female—italicized, capitals
TAMAR—Bold type denotes ancestry and blood line of David

mander of their thousand. See how your brothers fare, and bring some token from them."

19 Now Saul, and they, and all the men of Israel, were in the valley of Elah, fighting with the Philistines. 20 David rose early in the morning, left the sheep with a keeper, took the provisions, and went as Jesse had commanded him. He came to the encampment as the army was going forth to the battle line, shouting the war cry. 21 Israel and the Philistines drew up for battle, army against army. 22 David left the things in charge of the keeper of the baggage, ran to the ranks, and went and greeted his brothers. 23 As he talked with them, the champion, the Philistine of Gath, Goliath by name, came up out of the ranks of the Philistines, and spoke the same words as before. And David heard him.

24 All the Israelites, when they saw the man, fled from him and were very much afraid. 25 The Israelites said, "Have you seen this man who has come up? Surely he has come up to defy Israel. The king will greatly enrich the man who kills him, and will give him his daughter and make his family free in Israel." 26 David said to the men who stood by him, "What shall be done for the man who kills this Philistine, and takes away the reproach from Israel? For who is this uncircumcised Philistine that he should defy the armies of the living God?" 27 The people answered him in the same way, "So shall it be done for the man who kills him."

28 His eldest brother Eliab heard him talking to the men; and Eliab's anger was kindled against David. He said, "Why have you come down? With whom have you left those few sheep in the wilderness? I know your presumption and the evil of your heart; for you have come down just to see the battle." 29 David said, "What have I done now? It was only a question." 30 He turned away from him toward another and spoke in the same way; and the people answered him again as before.

31 When the words that David spoke were heard, they repeated them before Saul; and he sent for him. 32 David said to Saul, "Let no one's heart fail because of him; your servant will go and fight with this Philistine." 33 Saul said to David, "You are not able to go against this Philistine to fight with him; for you are just a boy, and he has been a warrior from his youth." 34 But David said to Saul, "Your servant used to keep sheep for his father; and whenever a lion or a bear came, and took a lamb from the flock, 35 I went after it and struck it down, rescuing the lamb from its mouth; and if it turned against me, I would catch it by the jaw, strike it down, and kill it. 36 Your servant has killed both lions and bears; and this uncircumcised Philistine shall be like one of them, since he has defied the armies of the living God." 37 David said, "The LORD, who saved me from the paw of the lion and from the paw of the bear, will save me from the hand of this Philistine." So Saul said to David, "Go, and may the LORD be with you!"

38 Saul clothed David with his armor; he put a bronze helmet on his head and clothed him with a coat of mail. 39 David strapped Saul's sword over the armor, and he tried in vain to walk, for he was not used to them. Then David said to Saul, "I cannot walk with these; for I am not used to them." So David removed them. 40 Then he took his staff in his hand, and chose five smooth stones from the wadi, and put them in his shepherd's bag, in the pouch; his sling was in his hand, and he drew near to the Philistine.

41 The Philistine came on and drew near to David, with his shield-bearer in front of him. 42 When the Philistine looked and saw David, he disdained him, for he was only a youth, ruddy and handsome in appearance. 43 The Philistine said to David, "Am I a dog, that you come

17.23 vv. 8-10
17.25 Josh 15.16
17.26 1 Sam 11.2; 14.6; v. 10; Deut 5.26
17.27 v. 25
17.28 Gen 37.4ff
17.29 v. 17
17.30 vv. 26,27
17.32 Deut 20.1-4; 1 Sam 16.18
17.37 2 Tim 4.17; 1 Sam 20.13; 1 Chr 22.11, 16
17.42 Prov 16.18; Ps 123.3,4; 1 Sam 16.12
17.43 1 Sam 24.14; 2 Sam 3.8

to me with sticks?" And the Philistine cursed David by his gods.
44 The Philistine said to David,
"Come to me, and I will give your
flesh to the birds of the air and to
the wild animals of the field."
45 But David said to the Philistine,
"You come to me with sword and
spear and javelin; but I come to you
in the name of the LORD of hosts,
the God of the armies of Israel,
whom you have defied. 46 This very
day the LORD will deliver you into
my hand, and I will strike you down
and cut off your head; and I will
give the dead bodies of the Philistine army this very day to the birds
of the air and to the wild animals of
the earth, so that all the earth may
know that there is a God in Israel,
47 and that all this assembly may
know that the LORD does not save
by sword and spear; for the battle is
the LORD's and he will give you into
our hand."
48 When the Philistine drew
nearer to meet David, David ran
quickly toward the battle line to
meet the Philistine. 49 David put
his hand in his bag, took out a
stone, slung it, and struck the Philistine on his forehead; the stone
sank into his forehead, and he fell
face down on the ground.
50 So David prevailed over the
Philistine with a sling and a stone,
striking down the Philistine and
killing him; there was no sword in
David's hand. 51 Then David ran
and stood over the Philistine; he
grasped his sword, drew it out of its
sheath, and killed him; then he cut
off his head with it.
When the Philistines saw that
their champion was dead, they
fled. 52 The troops of Israel and Judah rose up with a shout and pursued the Philistines as far as Gath[c]
and the gates of Ekron, so that the
wounded Philistines fell on the
way from Shaaraim as far as Gath
and Ekron. 53 The Israelites came
back from chasing the Philistines,
and they plundered their camp.
54 David took the head of the Philistine and brought it to Jerusalem;
but he put his armor in his tent.

17.44 1 Kings 20.10
17.45 2 Chr 32.8; Ps 124.8; Heb 11.34
17.46 1 Kings 18.36; 2 Kings 19.19; Isa 52.10
17.47 1 Sam 14.6; 2 Chr 14.11; Ps 44.6,7
17.51 1 Sam 21.9; Heb 11.34
17.52 Josh 15.36
17.55 1 Sam 16.21, 22
17.57 v. 54
17.58 v. 12
18.1 Gen 44.30; Deut 13.6; 1 Sam 20.17; 2 Sam 1.26
18.2 1 Sam 17.15
18.6 Ex 15.20; Judg 11.34; Ps 68.25
18.7 Ex 15.21; 1 Sam 21.11
18.8 1 Sam 15.8

55 When Saul saw David go out
against the Philistine, he said to
Abner, the commander of the
army, "Abner, whose son is this
young man?" Abner said, "As your
soul lives, O king, I do not know."
56 The king said, "Inquire whose
son the stripling is." 57 On David's
return from killing the Philistine,
Abner took him and brought him
before Saul, with the head of the
Philistine in his hand. 58 Saul said
to him, "Whose son are you, young
man?" And David answered, "I am
the son of your servant Jesse the
Bethlehemite."

Jonathan's Covenant with David

18 When David[d] had finished
speaking to Saul, the soul
of Jonathan was bound to the soul
of David, and Jonathan loved him
as his own soul. 2 Saul took him
that day and would not let him return to his father's house. 3 Then
Jonathan made a covenant with
David, because he loved him as his
own soul. 4 Jonathan stripped himself of the robe that he was wearing, and gave it to David, and his
armor, and even his sword and his
bow and his belt. 5 David went out
and was successful wherever Saul
sent him; as a result, Saul set him
over the army. And all the people,
even the servants of Saul, approved.
6 As they were coming home,
when David returned from killing
the Philistine, the women came
out of all the towns of Israel, singing and dancing, to meet King
Saul, with tambourines, with songs
of joy, and with musical instruments.[e] 7 And the women sang to
one another as they made merry,

"Saul has killed his
thousands,
and David his ten
thousands."

8 Saul was very angry, for this saying
displeased him. He said, "They
have ascribed to David ten thousands, and to me they have ascribed thousands; what more can

[c] Gk Syr: Heb *Gai* [d] Heb *he*
[e] Or *triangles,* or *three-stringed instruments*

he have but the kingdom?" [9]So
Saul eyed David from that day on.

Saul Tries to Kill David

10 The next day an evil spirit
from God rushed upon Saul, and he
raved within his house, while David
was playing the lyre, as he did day
by day. Saul had his spear in his
hand; [11]and Saul threw the spear,
for he thought, "I will pin David to
the wall." But David eluded him
twice.
12 Saul was afraid of David, because the LORD was with him but
had departed from Saul. [13]So Saul
removed him from his presence,
and made him a commander of a
thousand; and David marched out
and came in, leading the army.
[14]David had success in all his undertakings; for the LORD was with
him. [15]When Saul saw that he had
great success, he stood in awe of
him. [16]But all Israel and Judah
loved David; for it was he who
marched out and came in leading
them.

David Marries Michal

17 Then Saul said to David,
"Here is my elder daughter Merab;
I will give her to you as a wife; only
be valiant for me and fight the
LORD's battles." For Saul thought,
"I will not raise a hand against him;
let the Philistines deal with him."
[18]David said to Saul, "Who am I
and who are my kinsfolk, my father's family in Israel, that I should
be son-in-law to the king?" [19]But at
the time when Saul's daughter Merab should have been given to David, she was given to Adriel the Meholathite as a wife.
20 Now Saul's daughter Michal
loved David. Saul was told, and the
thing pleased him. [21]Saul thought,
"Let me give her to him that she
may be a snare for him and that the
hand of the Philistines may be
against him." Therefore Saul said
to David a second time,[f] "You
shall now be my son-in-law."
[22]Saul commanded his servants,
"Speak to David in private and say,
'See, the king is delighted with you,
and all his servants love you; now
then, become the king's son-in-
law.' " [23]So Saul's servants reported these words to David in private.
And David said, "Does it seem to
you a little thing to become the
king's son-in-law, seeing that I am
a poor man and of no repute?"
[24]The servants of Saul told him,
"This is what David said." [25]Then
Saul said, "Thus shall you say to
David, 'The king desires no marriage present except a hundred
foreskins of the Philistines, that he
may be avenged on the king's enemies.' " Now Saul planned to make
David fall by the hand of the Philistines. [26]When his servants told David these words, David was well
pleased to be the king's son-in-law.
Before the time had expired, [27]Da-
vid rose and went, along with his
men, and killed one hundred[g] of
the Philistines; and David brought
their foreskins, which were given in
full number to the king, that he
might become the king's son-in-
law. Saul gave him his daughter
Michal as a wife. [28]But when Saul
realized that the LORD was with David, and that Saul's daughter Michal loved him, [29]Saul was still
more afraid of David. So Saul was
David's enemy from that time forward.
30 Then the commanders of the
Philistines came out to battle; and
as often as they came out, David
had more success than all the servants of Saul, so that his fame became very great.

Jonathan Intercedes for David

19 Saul spoke with his son
Jonathan and with all his
servants about killing David. But
Saul's son Jonathan took great delight in David. [2]Jonathan told David, "My father Saul is trying to kill
you; therefore be on guard tomorrow morning; stay in a secret place
and hide yourself. [3]I will go out and
stand beside my father in the field
where you are, and I will speak to
my father about you; if I learn any-

[f] Heb *by two* [g] Gk Compare 2 Sam 3.14: Heb *two hundred*

18.10 1 Sam 16.14, 23; 19.9,23, 24 **18.11** 1 Sam 19.10; 20.33 **18.12** vv. 15,29; 1 Sam 16.13, 14,18 **18.13** v. 16; 2 Sam 5.2 **18.14** 1 Sam 16.18; Gen 39.2,3, 23 **18.16** v. 5 **18.17** 1 Sam 17.25; 25.28; vv. 21,25 **18.18** v. 23; 1 Sam 9.21; 2 Sam 7.18 **18.19** 2 Sam 21.8; Judg 7.22 **18.20** v. 28 **18.21** vv. 17,26

18.25 Ex 22.17; 1 Sam 14.24; v. 17 **18.26** v. 21 **18.27** v. 13; 2 Sam 3.14 **18.30** v. 5 **19.1** 1 Sam 18.1-3, 8,9 **19.3** 1 Sam 20.9, 13

thing I will tell you." 4 Jonathan
spoke well of David to his father
Saul, saying to him, "The king
should not sin against his servant
David, because he has not sinned
against you, and because his deeds
have been of good service to you;
5 for he took his life in his hand
when he attacked the Philistine,
and the LORD brought about a great
victory for all Israel. You saw it, and
rejoiced; why then will you sin
against an innocent person by killing David without cause?" 6 Saul
heeded the voice of Jonathan; Saul
swore, "As the LORD lives, he shall
not be put to death." 7 So Jonathan
called David and related all these
things to him. Jonathan then
brought David to Saul, and he was
in his presence as before.

Michal Helps David Escape from Saul

8 Again there was war, and David went out to fight the Philistines. He launched a heavy attack
on them, so that they fled before
him. 9 Then an evil spirit from the
LORD came upon Saul, as he sat in
his house with his spear in his
hand, while David was playing music. 10 Saul sought to pin David to
the wall with the spear; but he
eluded Saul, so that he struck the
spear into the wall. David fled and
escaped that night.

11 Saul sent messengers to David's house to keep watch over him,
planning to kill him in the morning. David's wife Michal told him,
"If you do not save your life tonight, tomorrow you will be killed."
12 So Michal let David down
through the window; he fled away
and escaped. 13 Michal took an
idol[h] and laid it on the bed; she
put a net[i] of goats' hair on its
head, and covered it with the
clothes. 14 When Saul sent messengers to take David, she said, "He is
sick." 15 Then Saul sent the messengers to see David for themselves. He said, "Bring him up to
me in the bed, that I may kill him."
16 When the messengers came in,
the idol[j] was in the bed, with the
covering[i] of goats' hair on its
head. 17 Saul said to Michal, "Why
have you deceived me like this, and
let my enemy go, so that he has escaped?" Michal answered Saul,
"He said to me, 'Let me go; why
should I kill you?' "

David Joins Samuel in Ramah

18 Now David fled and escaped;
he came to Samuel at Ramah, and
told him all that Saul had done to
him. He and Samuel went and settled at Naioth. 19 Saul was told,
"David is at Naioth in Ramah."
20 Then Saul sent messengers to
take David. When they saw the
company of the prophets in a frenzy, with Samuel standing in charge
of[i] them, the spirit of God came
upon the messengers of Saul, and
they also fell into a prophetic frenzy. 21 When Saul was told, he sent
other messengers, and they also
fell into a frenzy. Saul sent messengers again the third time, and they
also fell into a frenzy. 22 Then he
himself went to Ramah. He came
to the great well that is in Secu;[k]
he asked, "Where are Samuel and
David?" And someone said, "They
are at Naioth in Ramah." 23 He
went there, toward Naioth in Ramah; and the spirit of God came
upon him. As he was going, he fell
into a prophetic frenzy, until he
came to Naioth in Ramah. 24 He too
stripped off his clothes, and he too
fell into a frenzy before Samuel. He
lay naked all that day and all that
night. Therefore it is said, "Is Saul
also among the prophets?"

The Friendship of David and Jonathan

20 David fled from Naioth in
Ramah. He came before
Jonathan and said, "What have I
done? What is my guilt? And what
is my sin against your father that he
is trying to take my life?" 2 He said
to him, "Far from it! You shall not
die. My father does nothing either
great or small without disclosing it

19.4 1 Sam 20.32; Gen 42.22
19.5 1 Sam 17.49, 50; 11.13; 20.32
19.7 1 Sam 16.21; 18.2,13
19.9 1 Sam 16.14; 18.10,11
19.10 1 Sam 18.11
19.12 Josh 2.15; Acts 9.24,25
19.14 Josh 2.5
19.18 1 Sam 7.17
19.20 vv. 11,14; 1 Sam 10.5, 6; Num 11.25
19.23 Isa 20.2; 1 Sam 10.10-12
20.1 1 Sam 24.9

[h] Heb *took the teraphim* [i] Meaning of Heb uncertain [j] Heb *the teraphim*
[k] Gk reads *to the well of the threshing floor on the bare height*

to me; and why should my father
hide this from me? Never!" 3 But
David also swore, "Your father
knows well that you like me; and
he thinks, 'Do not let Jonathan
know this, or he will be grieved.'
But truly, as the LORD lives and as
you yourself live, there is but a step
between me and death." 4 Then
Jonathan said to David, "Whatever
you say, I will do for you." 5 David
said to Jonathan, "Tomorrow is the
new moon, and I should not fail to
sit with the king at the meal; but let
me go, so that I may hide in the
field until the third evening. 6 If
your father misses me at all, then
say, 'David earnestly asked leave of
me to run to Bethlehem his city; for
there is a yearly sacrifice there for
all the family.' 7 If he says, 'Good!'
it will be well with your servant; but
if he is angry, then know that evil
has been determined by him.
8 Therefore deal kindly with your
servant, for you have brought your
servant into a sacred covenant[l]
with you. But if there is guilt in me,
kill me yourself; why should you
bring me to your father?" 9 Jonathan said, "Far be it from you! If I
knew that it was decided by my father that evil should come upon
you, would I not tell you?" 10 Then
David said to Jonathan, "Who will
tell me if your father answers you
harshly?" 11 Jonathan replied to
David, "Come, let us go out into
the field." So they both went out
into the field.

12 Jonathan said to David, "By
the LORD, the God of Israel! When I
have sounded out my father, about
this time tomorrow, or on the third
day, if he is well disposed toward
David, shall I not then send and
disclose it to you? 13 But if my father intends to do you harm, the
LORD do so to Jonathan, and more
also, if I do not disclose it to you,
and send you away, so that you may
go in safety. May the LORD be with
you, as he has been with my father.
14 If I am still alive, show me the
faithful love of the LORD; but if I
die,[m] 15 never cut off your faithful
love from my house, even if the
LORD were to cut off every one of
the enemies of David from the face
of the earth." 16 Thus Jonathan
made a covenant with the house of
David, saying, "May the LORD seek
out the enemies of David." 17 Jonathan made David swear again by
his love for him; for he loved him as
he loved his own life.

18 Jonathan said to him, "Tomorrow is the new moon; you will
be missed, because your place will
be empty. 19 On the day after tomorrow, you shall go a long way
down; go to the place where you
hid yourself earlier, and remain beside the stone there.[m] 20 I will shoot
three arrows to the side of it, as
though I shot at a mark. 21 Then I
will send the boy, saying, 'Go, find
the arrows.' If I say to the boy,
'Look, the arrows are on this side of
you, collect them,' then you are to
come, for, as the LORD lives, it is
safe for you and there is no danger.
22 But if I say to the young man,
'Look, the arrows are beyond you,'
then go; for the LORD has sent you
away. 23 As for the matter about
which you and I have spoken, the
LORD is witness[n] between you and
me forever."

24 So David hid himself in the
field. When the new moon came,
the king sat at the feast to eat.
25 The king sat upon his seat, as at
other times, upon the seat by the
wall. Jonathan stood, while Abner
sat by Saul's side; but David's place
was empty.

26 Saul did not say anything
that day; for he thought, "Something has befallen him; he is not
clean, surely he is not clean." 27 But
on the second day, the day after the
new moon, David's place was empty. And Saul said to his son Jonathan, "Why has the son of Jesse not
come to the feast, either yesterday
or today?" 28 Jonathan answered
Saul, "David earnestly asked leave
of me to go to Bethlehem; 29 he
said, 'Let me go; for our family is
holding a sacrifice in the city, and

20.5 Num 10.10; 28.11; 1 Sam 19.2
20.6 1 Sam 17.58; Deut 12.5
20.8 1 Sam 18.3; 23.18; 2 Sam 14.32
20.13 1 Sam 3.17; Ruth 1.17; 1 Sam 17.37
20.15 2 Sam 9.1
20.17 1 Sam 18.1
20.18 vv. 5,25
20.19 1 Sam 19.2
20.22 v. 37
20.23 vv. 14,15; Gen 31.49, 53
20.25 v. 18
20.26 1 Sam 16.5; Lev 7.20,21
20.28 v. 6

[l] Heb *a covenant of the LORD* [m] Meaning of Heb uncertain [n] Gk: Heb lacks *witness*

my brother has commanded me to
be there. So now, if I have found
favor in your sight, let me get away,
and see my brothers.' For this reason he has not come to the king's
table."

30 Then Saul's anger was kindled against Jonathan. He said to
him, "You son of a perverse, rebellious woman! Do I not know that
you have chosen the son of Jesse to
your own shame, and to the shame
of your mother's nakedness? 31 For
as long as the son of Jesse lives
upon the earth, neither you nor
your kingdom shall be established.
Now send and bring him to me, for
he shall surely die." 32 Then Jonathan answered his father Saul,
"Why should he be put to death?
What has he done?" 33 But Saul
threw his spear at him to strike
him; so Jonathan knew that it was
the decision of his father to put David to death. 34 Jonathan rose from
the table in fierce anger and ate no
food on the second day of the
month, for he was grieved for David, and because his father had disgraced him.

35 In the morning Jonathan
went out into the field to the appointment with David, and with
him was a little boy. 36 He said to
the boy, "Run and find the arrows
that I shoot." As the boy ran, he
shot an arrow beyond him. 37 When
the boy came to the place where
Jonathan's arrow had fallen, Jonathan called after the boy and said,
"Is the arrow not beyond you?"
38 Jonathan called after the boy,
"Hurry, be quick, do not linger." So
Jonathan's boy gathered up the arrows and came to his master. 39 But
the boy knew nothing; only Jonathan and David knew the arrangement. 40 Jonathan gave his weapons to the boy and said to him, "Go
and carry them to the city." 41 As
soon as the boy had gone, David
rose from beside the stone heap[o]
and prostrated himself with his
face to the ground. He bowed three
times, and they kissed each other,
and wept with each other; David
wept the more.[p] 42 Then Jonathan
said to David, "Go in peace, since
both of us have sworn in the name
of the LORD, saying, 'The LORD shall
be between me and you, and between my descendants and your
descendants, forever.' " He got up
and left; and Jonathan went into
the city.[q]

20.30 Deut 21.20 **20.32** 1 Sam 19.5; Mt 27.23; Lk 23.22 **20.33** v. 7 **20.36** vv. 20,21 **20.37** v. 22 **20.42** 1 Sam 1.17; v. 22

David and the Holy Bread

21 [r] David came to Nob to the
priest Ahimelech. Ahime-
lech came trembling to meet David, and said to him, "Why are you
alone, and no one with you?" 2 David said to the priest Ahimelech,
"The king has charged me with a
matter, and said to me, 'No one
must know anything of the matter
about which I send you, and with
which I have charged you.' I have
made an appointment[s] with the
young men for such and such a
place. 3 Now then, what have you at
hand? Give me five loaves of bread,
or whatever is here." 4 The priest
answered David, "I have no ordinary bread at hand, only holy
bread—provided that the young
men have kept themselves from
women." 5 David answered the
priest, "Indeed women have been
kept from us as always when I go on
an expedition; the vessels of the
young men are holy even when it is
a common journey; how much
more today will their vessels be
holy?" 6 So the priest gave him the
holy bread; for there was no bread
there except the bread of the Presence, which is removed from before the LORD, to be replaced by hot
bread on the day it is taken away.

7 Now a certain man of the servants of Saul was there that day,
detained before the LORD; his name
was Doeg the Edomite, the chief of
Saul's shepherds.

8 David said to Ahimelech, "Is
there no spear or sword here with
you? I did not bring my sword or my
weapons with me, because the
king's business required haste."

21.1 1 Sam 22.19; 14.3; 16.4 **21.4** Lev 24.5-9; Mt 12.4 **21.5** Ex 19.14,15 **21.6** Mt 12.3,4; Mk 2.25,26; Lev 24.8,9 **21.7** 1 Sam 22.9

[o] Gk: Heb *from beside the south* [p] Vg: Meaning of Heb uncertain [q] This sentence is 21.1 in Heb [r] Ch 21.2 in Heb [s] Q Ms Vg Compare Gk: Meaning of MT uncertain

9 The priest said, "The sword of Goliath the Philistine, whom you
killed in the valley of Elah, is here
wrapped in a cloth behind the
ephod; if you will take that, take it,
for there is none here except that
one." David said, "There is none
like it; give it to me."

David Flees to Gath

10 David rose and fled that day
from Saul; he went to King Achish
of Gath. 11 The servants of Achish
said to him, "Is this not David the
king of the land? Did they not sing
to one another of him in dances,
'Saul has killed his
thousands,
and David his ten
thousands'?"
12 David took these words to heart
and was very much afraid of King
Achish of Gath. 13 So he changed
his behavior before them; he pretended to be mad when in their
presence.[t] He scratched marks on
the doors of the gate, and let his
spittle run down his beard.
14 Achish said to his servants,
"Look, you see the man is mad;
why then have you brought him to
me? 15 Do I lack madmen, that you
have brought this fellow to play the
madman in my presence? Shall this
fellow come into my house?"

David and His Followers at Adullam

22 David left there and escaped to the cave of Adullam; when his brothers and all his
father's house heard of it, they
went down there to him. 2 Everyone
who was in distress, and everyone
who was in debt, and everyone who
was discontented gathered to him;
and he became captain over them.
Those who were with him numbered about four hundred.
3 David went from there to Mizpeh of Moab. He said to the king of
Moab, "Please let my father and
mother come[u] to you, until I know
what God will do for me." 4 He left
them with the king of Moab, and
they stayed with him all the time
that David was in the stronghold.
5 Then the prophet Gad said to David, "Do not remain in the stronghold; leave, and go into the land of
Judah." So David left, and went
into the forest of Hereth.

Saul Slaughters the Priests at Nob

6 Saul heard that David and
those who were with him had been
located. Saul was sitting at Gibeah,
under the tamarisk tree on the
height, with his spear in his hand,
and all his servants were standing
around him. 7 Saul said to his servants who stood around him, "Hear
now, you Benjaminites; will the
son of Jesse give every one of you
fields and vineyards, will he make
you all commanders of thousands
and commanders of hundreds? 8 Is
that why all of you have conspired
against me? No one discloses to me
when my son makes a league with
the son of Jesse, none of you is sorry for me or discloses to me that my
son has stirred up my servant
against me, to lie in wait, as he is
doing today." 9 Doeg the Edomite,
who was in charge of Saul's servants, answered, "I saw the son of
Jesse coming to Nob, to Ahimelech
son of Ahitub; 10 he inquired of the
LORD for him, gave him provisions,
and gave him the sword of Goliath
the Philistine."
11 The king sent for the priest
Ahimelech son of Ahitub and for all
his father's house, the priests who
were at Nob; and all of them came
to the king. 12 Saul said, "Listen
now, son of Ahitub." He answered,
"Here I am, my lord." 13 Saul said to
him, "Why have you conspired
against me, you and the son of Jesse, by giving him bread and a
sword, and by inquiring of God for
him, so that he has risen against
me, to lie in wait, as he is doing
today?"
14 Then Ahimelech answered
the king, "Who among all your servants is so faithful as David? He is
the king's son-in-law, and is
quick[v] to do your bidding, and is

21.9 1 Sam 17.2, 51
21.11 1 Sam 18.7; 29.5
21.12 1 Sam 2.19
22.1 2 Sam 23.13
22.2 1 Sam 23.13; 25.13
22.5 2 Sam 24.11; 1 Chr 29.29; 2 Chr 29.25
22.7 1 Sam 8.14
22.8 1 Sam 18.3; 20.16
22.9 1 Sam 21.1; 14.3
22.10 1 Sam 10.22; 21.6,9
22.14 1 Sam 19.4, 5

[t] Heb *in their hands* [u] Syr Vg: Heb *come out* [v] Heb *and turns aside*

honored in your house. 15 Is today the first time that I have inquired of God for him? By no means! Do not let the king impute anything to his servant or to any member of my father's house; for your servant has known nothing of all this, much or little." 16 The king said, "You shall surely die, Ahimelech, you and all your father's house." 17 The king said to the guard who stood around him, "Turn and kill the priests of the LORD, because their hand also is with David; they knew that he fled, and did not disclose it to me." But the servants of the king would not raise their hand to attack the priests of the LORD. 18 Then the king said to Doeg, "You, Doeg, turn and attack the priests." Doeg the Edomite turned and attacked the priests; on that day he killed eighty-five who wore the linen ephod. 19 Nob, the city of the priests, he put to the sword; men and women, children and infants, oxen, donkeys, and sheep, he put to the sword.

20 But one of the sons of Ahimelech son of Ahitub, named Abiathar, escaped and fled after David. 21 Abiathar told David that Saul had killed the priests of the LORD. 22 David said to Abiathar, "I knew on that day, when Doeg the Edomite was there, that he would surely tell Saul. I am responsible[w] for the lives of all your father's house. 23 Stay with me, and do not be afraid; for the one who seeks my life seeks your life; you will be safe with me."

David Saves the City of Keilah

23 Now they told David, "The Philistines are fighting against Keilah, and are robbing the threshing floors." 2 David inquired of the LORD, "Shall I go and attack these Philistines?" The LORD said to David, "Go and attack the Philistines and save Keilah." 3 But David's men said to him, "Look, we are afraid here in Judah; how much more then if we go to Keilah against the armies of the Philistines?" 4 Then David inquired of the LORD again. The LORD answered him, "Yes, go down to Keilah; for I will give the Philistines into your hand." 5 So David and his men went to Keilah, fought with the Philistines, brought away their livestock, and dealt them a heavy defeat. Thus David rescued the inhabitants of Keilah.

6 When Abiathar son of Ahimelech fled to David at Keilah, he came down with an ephod in his hand. 7 Now it was told Saul that David had come to Keilah. And Saul said, "God has given[x] him into my hand; for he has shut himself in by entering a town that has gates and bars." 8 Saul summoned all the people to war, to go down to Keilah, to besiege David and his men. 9 When David learned that Saul was plotting evil against him, he said to the priest Abiathar, "Bring the ephod here." 10 David said, "O LORD, the God of Israel, your servant has heard that Saul seeks to come to Keilah, to destroy the city on my account. 11 And now, will[y] Saul come down as your servant has heard? O LORD, the God of Israel, I beseech you, tell your servant." The LORD said, "He will come down." 12 Then David said, "Will the men of Keilah surrender me and my men into the hand of Saul?" The LORD said, "They will surrender you." 13 Then David and his men, who were about six hundred, set out and left Keilah; they wandered wherever they could go. When Saul was told that David had escaped from Keilah, he gave up the expedition. 14 David remained in the strongholds in the wilderness, in the hill country of the Wilderness of Ziph. Saul sought him every day, but the LORD[z] did not give him into his hand.

David Eludes Saul in the Wilderness

15 David was in the Wilderness of Ziph at Horesh when he learned

22.17 Ex 1.17
22.18 1 Sam 2.18, 31
22.20 1 Sam 23.6, 9; 2.33
22.22 1 Sam 21.7
22.23 1 Kings 2.26
23.1 Josh 15.44
23.2 vv. 4,6,9; 2 Sam 5.19, 23
23.4 Josh 8.7; Judg 7.7
23.6 1 Sam 22.20
23.9 v. 6; 1 Sam 30.7
23.12 v. 20
23.13 1 Sam 22.2; 25.13
23.14 Josh 15.15; Ps 54.3,4

[w] Gk Vg: Meaning of Heb uncertain
[x] Gk Tg: Heb *made a stranger of*
[y] Q Ms Compare Gk: MT *Will the men of Keilah surrender me into his hand? Will*
[z] Q Ms Gk: MT *God*

that[a] Saul had come out to seek
his life. 16 Saul's son Jonathan set
out and came to David at Horesh;
there he strengthened his hand
through the LORD.[b] 17 He said to
him, "Do not be afraid; for the
hand of my father Saul shall not
find you; you shall be king over Israel, and I shall be second to you;
my father Saul also knows that this
is so." 18 Then the two of them
made a covenant before the LORD;
David remained at Horesh, and
Jonathan went home.

19 Then some Ziphites went up
to Saul at Gibeah and said, "David
is hiding among us in the strongholds of Horesh, on the hill of Hachilah, which is south of Jeshimon.
20 Now, O king, whenever you wish
to come down, do so; and our part
will be to surrender him into the
king's hand." 21 Saul said, "May
you be blessed by the LORD for
showing me compassion! 22 Go and
make sure once more; find out exactly where he is, and who has seen
him there; for I am told that he is
very cunning. 23 Look around and
learn all the hiding places where he
lurks, and come back to me with
sure information. Then I will go
with you; and if he is in the land, I
will search him out among all the
thousands of Judah." 24 So they set
out and went to Ziph ahead of Saul.

David and his men were in the
wilderness of Maon, in the Arabah
to the south of Jeshimon. 25 Saul
and his men went to search for
him. When David was told, he went
down to the rock and stayed in the
wilderness of Maon. When Saul
heard that, he pursued David into
the wilderness of Maon. 26 Saul
went on one side of the mountain,
and David and his men on the other
side of the mountain. David was
hurrying to get away from Saul,
while Saul and his men were closing in on David and his men to capture them. 27 Then a messenger
came to Saul, saying, "Hurry and
come; for the Philistines have
made a raid on the land." 28 So Saul
stopped pursuing David, and went
against the Philistines; therefore
that place was called the Rock of
Escape.[c] 29[d] David then went up
from there, and lived in the strongholds of En-gedi.

David Spares Saul's Life

24 When Saul returned from
following the Philistines,
he was told, "David is in the wilderness of En-gedi." 2 Then Saul took
three thousand chosen men out of
all Israel, and went to look for David and his men in the direction of
the Rocks of the Wild Goats. 3 He
came to the sheepfolds beside the
road, where there was a cave; and
Saul went in to relieve himself.[e]
Now David and his men were sitting in the innermost parts of the
cave. 4 The men of David said to
him, "Here is the day of which the
LORD said to you, 'I will give your
enemy into your hand, and you
shall do to him as it seems good to
you.' " Then David went and
stealthily cut off a corner of Saul's
cloak. 5 Afterward David was strick-
en to the heart because he had cut
off a corner of Saul's cloak. 6 He
said to his men, "The LORD forbid
that I should do this thing to my
lord, the LORD's anointed, to raise
my hand against him; for he is the
LORD's anointed." 7 So David scolded his men severely and did not
permit them to attack Saul. Then
Saul got up and left the cave, and
went on his way.

8 Afterwards David also rose up
and went out of the cave and called
after Saul, "My lord the king!"
When Saul looked behind him, David bowed with his face to the
ground, and did obeisance. 9 David
said to Saul, "Why do you listen to
the words of those who say, 'David
seeks to do you harm'? 10 This very
day your eyes have seen how the
LORD gave you into my hand in the
cave; and some urged me to kill
you, but I spared[f] you. I said, 'I
will not raise my hand against my
lord; for he is the LORD's anointed.'

23.16 1 Sam 30.6
23.17 1 Sam 20.31; 24.20
23.18 1 Sam 18.3; 20.16,42; 2 Sam 9.1; 21.7
23.19 1 Sam 26.1
23.20 v. 12
23.21 1 Sam 22.8
23.24 Josh 15.55; 1 Sam 25.2
23.26 Ps 17.9
23.29 2 Chr 20.2
24.1 1 Sam 23.28, 29
24.2 1 Sam 26.2
24.3 Judg 3.24
24.4 1 Sam 23.17; 25.28-30
24.5 2 Sam 24.10
24.6 1 Sam 26.11
24.8 1 Sam 25.23, 24

[a] Or *saw that* [b] Compare Q Ms Gk: MT *God* [c] Or *Rock of Division*; Meaning of Heb uncertain [d] Ch 24.1 in Heb [e] Heb *to cover his feet* [f] Gk Syr Tg Vg: Heb *it* (my eye) *spared*

11 See, my father, see the corner of
your cloak in my hand; for by the
fact that I cut off the corner of your
cloak, and did not kill you, you may
know for certain that there is no
wrong or treason in my hands. I
have not sinned against you,
though you are hunting me to take
my life. 12 May the LORD judge between me and you! May the LORD
avenge me on you; but my hand
shall not be against you. 13 As the
ancient proverb says, 'Out of the
wicked comes forth wickedness';
but my hand shall not be against
you. 14 Against whom has the king
of Israel come out? Whom do you
pursue? A dead dog? A single flea?
15 May the LORD therefore be judge,
and give sentence between me and
you. May he see to it, and plead my
cause, and vindicate me against
you."
16 When David had finished
speaking these words to Saul, Saul
said, "Is this your voice, my son David?" Saul lifted up his voice and
wept. 17 He said to David, "You are
more righteous than I; for you have
repaid me good, whereas I have repaid you evil. 18 Today you have explained how you have dealt well
with me, in that you did not kill me
when the LORD put me into your
hands. 19 For who has ever found an
enemy, and sent the enemy safely
away? So may the LORD reward you
with good for what you have done
to me this day. 20 Now I know that
you shall surely be king, and that
the kingdom of Israel shall be established in your hand. 21 Swear to
me therefore by the LORD that you
will not cut off my descendants after me, and that you will not wipe
out my name from my father's
house." 22 So David swore this to
Saul. Then Saul went home; but
David and his men went up to the
stronghold.

Death of Samuel

25 Now Samuel died; and all
Israel assembled and
mourned for him. They buried him
at his home in Ramah.

24.11 Ps 7.3; 35.7; 1 Sam 23.14, 23; 26.20
24.12 Gen 31.53; Judg 11.27; 1 Sam 26.10; Job 5.8
24.13 Mt 7.16-20
24.14 1 Sam 17.43; 26.20
24.15 v. 12; Ps 35.1; Mic 7.9
24.16 1 Sam 26.17
24.17 1 Sam 26.21; Mt 5.44
24.18 1 Sam 26.23
24.20 1 Sam 23.17
24.21 Gen 21.23; 2 Sam 21.6-8
24.22 1 Sam 23.29
25.1 1 Sam 28.3; Deut 34.8; 2 Chr 33.20; Gen 21.21
25.2 1 Sam 23.24; Josh 15.55
25.6 1 Chr 12.18
25.7 2 Sam 13.23, 24; vv. 15, 21
25.8 Neh 8.10-12
25.10 Judg 9.28
25.13 1 Sam 23.13; 30.24

Then David got up and went
down to the wilderness of Paran.

David and the Wife of Nabal

2 There was a man in Maon,
whose property was in Carmel. The
man was very rich; he had three
thousand sheep and a thousand
goats. He was shearing his sheep in
Carmel. 3 Now the name of the man
was Nabal, and the name of his
wife Abigail. The woman was clever
and beautiful, but the man was sur-
ly and mean; he was a Calebite.
4 David heard in the wilderness that
Nabal was shearing his sheep. 5 So
David sent ten young men; and David said to the young men, "Go up
to Carmel, and go to Nabal, and
greet him in my name. 6 Thus you
shall salute him: 'Peace be to you,
and peace be to your house, and
peace be to all that you have. 7 I
hear that you have shearers; now
your shepherds have been with us,
and we did them no harm, and they
missed nothing, all the time they
were in Carmel. 8 Ask your young
men, and they will tell you. Therefore let my young men find favor in
your sight; for we have come on a
feast day. Please give whatever you
have at hand to your servants and
to your son David.'"
9 When David's young men
came, they said all this to Nabal in
the name of David; and then they
waited. 10 But Nabal answered David's servants, "Who is David? Who
is the son of Jesse? There are many
servants today who are breaking
away from their masters. 11 Shall I
take my bread and my water and
the meat that I have butchered for
my shearers, and give it to men who
come from I do not know where?"
12 So David's young men turned
away, and came back and told him
all this. 13 David said to his men,
"Every man strap on his sword!"
And every one of them strapped on
his sword; David also strapped on
his sword; and about four hundred
men went up after David, while two
hundred remained with the baggage.
14 But one of the young men

told Abigail, Nabal's wife, "David
sent messengers out of the wilderness to salute our master; and he
shouted insults at them. 15 Yet the
men were very good to us, and we
suffered no harm, and we never
missed anything when we were in
the fields, as long as we were with
them; 16 they were a wall to us both
by night and by day, all the while
we were with them keeping the
sheep. 17 Now therefore know this
and consider what you should do;
for evil has been decided against
our master and against all his
house; he is so ill-natured that no
one can speak to him."
18 Then Abigail hurried and
took two hundred loaves, two skins
of wine, five sheep ready dressed,
five measures of parched grain, one
hundred clusters of raisins, and
two hundred cakes of figs. She
loaded them on donkeys 19 and said
to her young men, "Go on ahead of
me; I am coming after you." But
she did not tell her husband Nabal.
20 As she rode on the donkey and
came down under cover of the
mountain, David and his men
came down toward her; and she
met them. 21 Now David had said,
"Surely it was in vain that I protected all that this fellow has in the wilderness, so that nothing was
missed of all that belonged to him;
but he has returned me evil for
good. 22 God do so to David[g] and
more also, if by morning I leave so
much as one male of all who belong to him."
23 When Abigail saw David, she
hurried and alighted from the donkey, fell before David on her face,
bowing to the ground. 24 She fell at
his feet and said, "Upon me alone,
my lord, be the guilt; please let
your servant speak in your ears,
and hear the words of your servant.
25 My lord, do not take seriously
this ill-natured fellow, Nabal; for as
his name is, so is he; Nabal[h] is his
name, and folly is with him; but I,
your servant, did not see the young
men of my lord, whom you sent.
26 Now then, my lord, as the
LORD lives, and as you yourself live,
since the LORD has restrained you
from bloodguilt and from taking
vengeance with your own hand,
now let your enemies and those
who seek to do evil to my lord be
like Nabal. 27 And now let this
present that your servant has
brought to my lord be given to the
young men who follow my lord.
28 Please forgive the trespass of
your servant; for the LORD will certainly make my lord a sure house,
because my lord is fighting the battles of the LORD; and evil shall not
be found in you so long as you live.
29 If anyone should rise up to pursue you and to seek your life, the
life of my lord shall be bound in the
bundle of the living under the care
of the LORD your God; but the lives
of your enemies he shall sling out
as from the hollow of a sling.
30 When the LORD has done to my
lord according to all the good that
he has spoken concerning you, and
has appointed you prince over Israel, 31 my lord shall have no cause of
grief, or pangs of conscience, for
having shed blood without cause or
for having saved himself. And when
the LORD has dealt well with my
lord, then remember your servant."
32 David said to Abigail,
"Blessed be the LORD, the God of
Israel, who sent you to meet me today! 33 Blessed be your good sense,
and blessed be you, who have kept
me today from bloodguilt and from
avenging myself by my own hand!
34 For as surely as the LORD the God
of Israel lives, who has restrained
me from hurting you, unless you
had hurried and come to meet me,
truly by morning there would not
have been left to Nabal so much as
one male." 35 Then David received
from her hand what she had
brought him; he said to her, "Go up
to your house in peace; see, I have
heeded your voice, and I have
granted your petition."
36 Abigail came to Nabal; he
was holding a feast in his house,
like the feast of a king. Nabal's

25.15 v. 7
25.16 Ex 14.22
25.18 2 Sam 16.1; 1 Chr 12.40
25.19 Gen 32.16, 20
25.21 Ps 109.5
25.22 1 Sam 3.17; 20.13; 1 Kings 14.10
25.23 1 Sam 20.41
25.26 Heb 10.30; 2 Sam 18.32
25.27 Gen 33.11; 1 Sam 30.26
25.28 2 Sam 7.11, 27; 18.17; 24.11
25.29 Jer 10.18
25.30 1 Sam 13.14
25.32 Ex 18.10
25.33 v. 26
25.34 v. 26
25.35 1 Sam 20.42; 2 Kings 5.19; Gen 19.21
25.36 2 Sam 13.23

g Gk Compare Syr: Heb *the enemies of David*
h That is *Fool*

heart was merry within him, for he
was very drunk; so she told him
nothing at all until the morning
light. 37 In the morning, when the
wine had gone out of Nabal, his
wife told him these things, and his
heart died within him; he became
like a stone. 38 About ten days later
the LORD struck Nabal, and he died.
39 When David heard that Nabal was dead, he said, "Blessed be
the LORD who has judged the case
of Nabal's insult to me, and has
kept back his servant from evil; the
LORD has returned the evildoing of
Nabal upon his own head." Then
David sent and wooed Abigail, to
make her his wife. 40 When David's
servants came to Abigail at Carmel,
they said to her, "David has sent us
to you to take you to him as his
wife." 41 She rose and bowed down,
with her face to the ground, and
said, "Your servant is a slave to
wash the feet of the servants of my
lord." 42 Abigail got up hurriedly
and rode away on a donkey; her five
maids attended her. She went after
the messengers of David and became his wife.
43 David also married Ahinoam
of Jezreel; both of them became his
wives. 44 Saul had given his daughter Michal, David's wife, to Palti
son of Laish, who was from Gallim.

David Spares Saul's Life a Second Time

26 Then the Ziphites came to
Saul at Gibeah, saying,
"David is in hiding on the hill of
Hachilah, which is opposite Jeshimon."[i] 2 So Saul rose and went
down to the Wilderness of Ziph,
with three thousand chosen men of
Israel, to seek David in the Wilderness of Ziph. 3 Saul encamped on
the hill of Hachilah, which is opposite Jeshimon[i] beside the road.
But David remained in the wilderness. When he learned that Saul
came after him into the wilderness,
4 David sent out spies, and learned
that Saul had indeed arrived.
5 Then David set out and came to
the place where Saul had encamped; and David saw the place
where Saul lay, with Abner son of
Ner, the commander of his army.
Saul was lying within the encampment, while the army was encamped around him.
6 Then David said to Ahimelech
the Hittite, and to Joab's brother
Abishai son of Zeruiah, "Who will
go down with me into the camp to
Saul?" Abishai said, "I will go down
with you." 7 So David and Abishai
went to the army by night; there
Saul lay sleeping within the encampment, with his spear stuck in
the ground at his head; and Abner
and the army lay around him.
8 Abishai said to David, "God has
given your enemy into your hand
today; now therefore let me pin
him to the ground with one stroke
of the spear; I will not strike him
twice." 9 But David said to Abishai,
"Do not destroy him; for who can
raise his hand against the LORD's
anointed, and be guiltless?" 10 David said, "As the LORD lives, the
LORD will strike him down; or his
day will come to die; or he will go
down into battle and perish. 11 The
LORD forbid that I should raise my
hand against the LORD's anointed;
but now take the spear that is at his
head, and the water jar, and let us
go." 12 So David took the spear that
was at Saul's head and the water
jar, and they went away. No one
saw it, or knew it, nor did anyone
awake; for they were all asleep, because a deep sleep from the LORD
had fallen upon them.
13 Then David went over to the
other side, and stood on top of a
hill far away, with a great distance
between them. 14 David called to
the army and to Abner son of Ner,
saying, "Abner! Will you not answer?" Then Abner replied, "Who
are you that calls to the king?"
15 David said to Abner, "Are you not
a man? Who is like you in Israel?
Why then have you not kept watch
over your lord the king? For one of
the people came in to destroy your
lord the king. 16 This thing that you
have done is not good. As the LORD

25.39 1 Sam 24.15; vv. 26,34; 1 Kings 2.44
25.41 Ruth 2.10, 13; Mk 1.7
25.42 Gen 24.61-67
25.43 Josh 15.56; 1 Sam 27.3
25.44 2 Sam 3.14; Isa 10.30
26.1 1 Sam 23.19
26.2 1 Sam 13.2; 24.2
26.5 1 Sam 14.50; 17.55
26.6 1 Chr 2.16; Judg 7.10, 11
26.9 1 Sam 24.6, 7; 2 Sam 1.16
26.10 1 Sam 25.38; Deut 31.14; 1 Sam 31.6
26.11 1 Sam 24.6, 12
26.12 Gen 2.21; 16.12

[i] Or *opposite the wasteland*

lives, you deserve to die, because
you have not kept watch over your
lord, the LORD's anointed. See now,
where is the king's spear, or the water jar that was at his head?"
17 Saul recognized David's
voice, and said, "Is this your voice,
my son David?" David said, "It is
my voice, my lord, O king." 18 And
he added, "Why does my lord pursue his servant? For what have I
done? What guilt is on my hands?
19 Now therefore let my lord the
king hear the words of his servant.
If it is the LORD who has stirred you
up against me, may he accept an
offering; but if it is mortals, may
they be cursed before the LORD, for
they have driven me out today from
my share in the heritage of the
LORD, saying, 'Go, serve other
gods.' 20 Now therefore, do not let
my blood fall to the ground, away
from the presence of the LORD; for
the king of Israel has come out to
seek a single flea, like one who
hunts a partridge in the mountains."
21 Then Saul said, "I have done
wrong; come back, my son David,
for I will never harm you again, because my life was precious in your
sight today; I have been a fool, and
have made a great mistake." 22 David replied, "Here is the spear,
O king! Let one of the young men
come over and get it. 23 The LORD
rewards everyone for his righteousness and his faithfulness; for the
LORD gave you into my hand today,
but I would not raise my hand
against the LORD's anointed. 24 As
your life was precious today in my
sight, so may my life be precious in
the sight of the LORD, and may he
rescue me from all tribulation."
25 Then Saul said to David,
"Blessed be you, my son David!
You will do many things and will
succeed in them." So David went
his way, and Saul returned to his
place.

David Serves King Achish of Gath

27 David said in his heart, "I
shall now perish one day by
the hand of Saul; there is nothing
better for me than to escape to the
land of the Philistines; then Saul
will despair of seeking me any longer within the borders of Israel, and
I shall escape out of his hand." 2 So
David set out and went over, he and
the six hundred men who were
with him, to King Achish son of
Maoch of Gath. 3 David stayed with
Achish at Gath, he and his troops,
every man with his household, and
David with his two wives, Ahinoam
of Jezreel, and Abigail of Carmel,
Nabal's widow. 4 When Saul was
told that David had fled to Gath, he
no longer sought for him.
5 Then David said to Achish, "If
I have found favor in your sight, let
a place be given me in one of the
country towns, so that I may live
there; for why should your servant
live in the royal city with you?" 6 So
that day Achish gave him Ziklag;
therefore Ziklag has belonged to
the kings of Judah to this day. 7 The
length of time that David lived in
the country of the Philistines was
one year and four months.
8 Now David and his men went
up and made raids on the Geshurites, the Girzites, and the Amalekites; for these were the landed settlements from Telam[j] on the way
to Shur and on to the land of Egypt.
9 David struck the land, leaving neither man nor woman alive, but
took away the sheep, the oxen, the
donkeys, the camels, and the
clothing, and came back to Achish.
10 When Achish asked, "Against
whom[k] have you made a raid today?" David would say, "Against
the Negeb of Judah," or "Against
the Negeb of the Jerahmeelites,"
or, "Against the Negeb of the Kenites." 11 David left neither man
nor woman alive to be brought
back to Gath, thinking, "They
might tell about us, and say, 'David
has done so and so.'" Such was his
practice all the time he lived in the
country of the Philistines. 12 Achish
trusted David, thinking, "He has

26.17 1 Sam 24.16
26.18 1 Sam 24.9, 11-14
26.19 2 Sam 16.11
26.20 1 Sam 24.14
26.21 1 Sam 15.24; 24.17
26.22 1 Sam 24.12, 19
26.24 Ps 54.7
27.2 1 Sam 25.13; 21.10
27.3 1 Sam 30.3; 25.42,43
27.6 Josh 15.31; 19.5
27.7 1 Sam 29.3
27.8 Josh 13.2, 13; Ex 17.8; 1 Sam 15.7, 8; Ex 15.22
27.9 1 Sam 15.3
27.10 1 Chr 2.9, 25; Judg 1.16

[j] Compare Gk 15.4: Heb *from of old*
[k] Q Ms Gk Vg: MT lacks *whom*

made himself utterly abhorrent to
his people Israel; therefore he shall
always be my servant."

28 In those days the Philistines gathered their forces
for war, to fight against Israel.
Achish said to David, "You know,
of course, that you and your men
are to go out with me in the army."
2 David said to Achish, "Very well,
then you shall know what your servant can do." Achish said to David,
"Very well, I will make you my
bodyguard for life."

Saul Consults a Medium

3 Now Samuel had died, and all
Israel had mourned for him and
buried him in Ramah, his own city.
Saul had expelled the mediums
and the wizards from the land.
4 The Philistines assembled, and
came and encamped at Shunem.
Saul gathered all Israel, and they
encamped at Gilboa. 5 When Saul
saw the army of the Philistines, he
was afraid, and his heart trembled
greatly. 6 When Saul inquired of the
LORD, the LORD did not answer him,
not by dreams, or by Urim, or by
prophets. 7 Then Saul said to his
servants, "Seek out for me a woman who is a medium, so that I may
go to her and inquire of her." His
servants said to him, "There is a
medium at Endor."

8 So Saul disguised himself and
put on other clothes and went
there, he and two men with him.
They came to the woman by night.
And he said, "Consult a spirit for
me, and bring up for me the one
whom I name to you." 9 The woman
said to him, "Surely you know what
Saul has done, how he has cut off
the mediums and the wizards from
the land. Why then are you laying
a snare for my life to bring about
my death?" 10 But Saul swore to her
by the LORD, "As the LORD lives, no
punishment shall come upon you
for this thing." 11 Then the woman
said, "Whom shall I bring up for
you?" He answered, "Bring up
Samuel for me." 12 When the woman saw Samuel, she cried out with
a loud voice; and the woman said

28.1f 1 Sam 29.1
28.3 1 Sam 25.1; 7.17; 15.23; Lev 19.31; Deut 18.10, 11
28.4 2 Kings 4.8; 1 Sam 31.1
28.6 1 Chr 10.13, 14; Prov 1.28; Ex 28.30
28.7 Acts 16.16; Josh 17.11
28.8 Isa 8.19; Deut 18.10, 11
28.9 v. 3
28.14 1 Sam 15.27; 24.8
28.15 1 Sam 18.12; v. 6
28.17 1 Sam 15.28
28.18 1 Sam 15.9, 20,26
28.19 1 Sam 31.2
28.21 1 Sam 19.5; Judg 12.3

to Saul, "Why have you deceived
me? You are Saul!" 13 The king said
to her, "Have no fear; what do you
see?" The woman said to Saul, "I
see a divine being[1] coming up out
of the ground." 14 He said to her,
"What is his appearance?" She
said, "An old man is coming up; he
is wrapped in a robe." So Saul knew
that it was Samuel, and he bowed
with his face to the ground, and did
obeisance.

15 Then Samuel said to Saul,
"Why have you disturbed me by
bringing me up?" Saul answered, "I
am in great distress, for the Philistines are warring against me, and
God has turned away from me and
answers me no more, either by
prophets or by dreams; so I have
summoned you to tell me what I
should do." 16 Samuel said, "Why
then do you ask me, since the LORD
has turned from you and become
your enemy? 17 The LORD has done
to you just as he spoke by me; for
the LORD has torn the kingdom out
of your hand, and given it to your
neighbor, David. 18 Because you did
not obey the voice of the LORD, and
did not carry out his fierce wrath
against Amalek, therefore the LORD
has done this thing to you today.
19 Moreover the LORD will give Israel
along with you into the hands of
the Philistines; and tomorrow you
and your sons shall be with me; the
LORD will also give the army of Israel into the hands of the Philistines."

20 Immediately Saul fell full
length on the ground, filled with
fear because of the words of Samuel; and there was no strength in
him, for he had eaten nothing all
day and all night. 21 The woman
came to Saul, and when she saw
that he was terrified, she said to
him, "Your servant has listened to
you; I have taken my life in my
hand, and have listened to what
you have said to me. 22 Now therefore, you also listen to your servant;
let me set a morsel of bread before
you. Eat, that you may have

[1] Or *a god*; or *gods*

strength when you go on your way."
23 He refused, and said, "I will not
eat." But his servants, together
with the woman, urged him; and he
listened to their words. So he got
up from the ground and sat on the
bed. 24 Now the woman had a fatted
calf in the house. She quickly
slaughtered it, and she took flour,
kneaded it, and baked unleavened
cakes. 25 She put them before Saul
and his servants, and they ate.
Then they rose and went away that
night.

The Philistines Reject David

29 Now the Philistines gathered all their forces at
Aphek, while the Israelites were
encamped by the fountain that is
in Jezreel. 2 As the lords of the Philistines were passing on by hundreds and by thousands, and David
and his men were passing on in the
rear with Achish, 3 the commanders of the Philistines said, "What
are these Hebrews doing here?"
Achish said to the commanders of
the Philistines, "Is this not David,
the servant of King Saul of Israel,
who has been with me now for days
and years? Since he deserted to me
I have found no fault in him to this
day." 4 But the commanders of the
Philistines were angry with him;
and the commanders of the Philistines said to him, "Send the man
back, so that he may return to the
place that you have assigned to
him; he shall not go down with us
to battle, or else he may become an
adversary to us in the battle. For
how could this fellow reconcile
himself to his lord? Would it not be
with the heads of the men here? 5 Is
this not David, of whom they sing
to one another in dances,

'Saul has killed his
thousands,
and David his ten
thousands'?"

6 Then Achish called David and
said to him, "As the LORD lives, you
have been honest, and to me it
seems right that you should march
out and in with me in the campaign; for I have found nothing
wrong in you from the day of your
coming to me until today. Nevertheless the lords do not approve of
you. 7 So go back now; and go
peaceably; do nothing to displease
the lords of the Philistines." 8 David said to Achish, "But what have
I done? What have you found in
your servant from the day I entered
your service until now, that I
should not go and fight against the
enemies of my lord the king?"
9 Achish replied to David, "I know
that you are as blameless in my
sight as an angel of God; nevertheless, the commanders of the Philistines have said, 'He shall not go up
with us to the battle.' 10 Now then
rise early in the morning, you and
the servants of your lord who came
with you, and go to the place that
I appointed for you. As for the evil
report, do not take it to heart, for
you have done well before me.[m]
Start early in the morning, and
leave as soon as you have light."
11 So David set out with his men
early in the morning, to return to
the land of the Philistines. But the
Philistines went up to Jezreel.

David Avenges the Destruction of Ziklag

30 Now when David and his
men came to Ziklag on the
third day, the Amalekites had
made a raid on the Negeb and on
Ziklag. They had attacked Ziklag,
burned it down, 2 and taken captive
the women and all[n] who were in it,
both small and great; they killed
none of them, but carried them off,
and went their way. 3 When David
and his men came to the city, they
found it burned down, and their
wives and sons and daughters tak-
en captive. 4 Then David and the
people who were with him raised
their voices and wept, until they
had no more strength to weep.
5 David's two wives also had been
taken captive, Ahinoam of Jezreel,
and Abigail the widow of Nabal of

28.23 2 Kings 5.13
29.1 1 Sam 28.1; 4.1; Josh 12.18
29.2 1 Sam 28.1, 2
29.3 1 Sam 27.7; Dan 6.5
29.4 1 Chr 12.19; 1 Sam 14.21
29.5 1 Sam 18.7; 21.11
29.6 v. 3
29.9 2 Sam 14.17, 20; 19.27; v. 4
29.10 1 Chr 12.19, 22
30.1 1 Sam 29.4, 11; 15.7; 27.8
30.5 1 Sam 25.42, 43

[m] Gk: Heb lacks *and go to the place . . . done well before me*
[n] Gk: Heb lacks *and all*

Carmel. 6 David was in great danger; for the people spoke of stoning
him, because all the people were
bitter in spirit for their sons and
daughters. But David strengthened
himself in the LORD his God.
7 David said to the priest Abiathar son of Ahimelech, "Bring me
the ephod." So Abiathar brought
the ephod to David. 8 David inquired of the LORD, "Shall I pursue
this band? Shall I overtake them?"
He answered him, "Pursue; for you
shall surely overtake and shall
surely rescue." 9 So David set out,
he and the six hundred men who
were with him. They came to the
Wadi Besor, where those stayed
who were left behind. 10 But David
went on with the pursuit, he and
four hundred men; two hundred
stayed behind, too exhausted to
cross the Wadi Besor.
11 In the open country they
found an Egyptian, and brought
him to David. They gave him bread
and he ate, they gave him water to
drink; 12 they also gave him a piece
of fig cake and two clusters of raisins. When he had eaten, his spirit
revived; for he had not eaten bread
or drunk water for three days and
three nights. 13 Then David said to
him, "To whom do you belong?
Where are you from?" He said, "I
am a young man of Egypt, servant
to an Amalekite. My master left me
behind because I fell sick three
days ago. 14 We had made a raid on
the Negeb of the Cherethites and
on that which belongs to Judah
and on the Negeb of Caleb; and we
burned Ziklag down." 15 David said
to him, "Will you take me down to
this raiding party?" He said, "Swear
to me by God that you will not kill
me, or hand me over to my master,
and I will take you down to them."
16 When he had taken him
down, they were spread out all over
the ground, eating and drinking
and dancing, because of the great
amount of spoil they had taken
from the land of the Philistines and
from the land of Judah. 17 David attacked them from twilight until the
evening of the next day. Not one of
them escaped, except four hundred young men, who mounted
camels and fled. 18 David recovered
all that the Amalekites had taken;
and David rescued his two wives.
19 Nothing was missing, whether
small or great, sons or daughters,
spoil or anything that had been
taken; David brought back everything. 20 David also captured all the
flocks and herds, which were driv-
en ahead of the other cattle; people
said, "This is David's spoil."
21 Then David came to the two
hundred men who had been too exhausted to follow David, and who
had been left at the Wadi Besor.
They went out to meet David and
to meet the people who were with
him. When David drew near to the
people he saluted them. 22 Then all
the corrupt and worthless fellows
among the men who had gone with
David said, "Because they did not
go with us, we will not give them
any of the spoil that we have recovered, except that each man may
take his wife and children, and
leave." 23 But David said, "You shall
not do so, my brothers, with what
the LORD has given us; he has preserved us and handed over to us the
raiding party that attacked us.
24 Who would listen to you in this
matter? For the share of the one
who goes down into the battle shall
be the same as the share of the one
who stays by the baggage; they
shall share alike." 25 From that day
forward he made it a statute and an
ordinance for Israel; it continues to
the present day.
26 When David came to Ziklag,
he sent part of the spoil to his
friends, the elders of Judah, saying,
"Here is a present for you from the
spoil of the enemies of the LORD";
27 it was for those in Bethel, in Ramoth of the Negeb, in Jattir, 28 in
Aroer, in Siphmoth, in Eshtemoa,
29 in Racal, in the towns of the Jerahmeelites, in the towns of the
Kenites, 30 in Hormah, in Bor-
ashan, in Athach, 31 in Hebron, all
the places where David and his
men had roamed.

30.6 Ex 17.4; Ps 27.14; 56.3,4,11
30.7 1 Sam 23.9
30.8 1 Sam 23.2, 4; v. 18
30.9 1 Sam 27.2
30.10 vv. 9,21
30.12 Judg 15.19
30.14 vv. 1,16; 2 Sam 8.18; Ezek 25.16; Josh 14.13
30.16 v. 14
30.17 1 Sam 15.3
30.19 v. 8
30.20 vv. 26-31
30.21 v. 10
30.24 Num 31.27; Josh 22.8
30.27 Josh 15.30; 19.8; 15.48
30.28 Josh 13.16; 15.50
30.29 1 Sam 27.10; 15.16
30.30 Judg 1.17
30.31 Josh 14.13

The Death of Saul and His Sons

31 Now the Philistines fought against Israel; and the men of Israel fled before the Philistines, and many fell[o] on Mount Gilboa. 2 The Philistines overtook Saul and his sons; and the Philistines killed Jonathan and Abinadab and Malchishua, the sons of Saul. 3 The battle pressed hard upon Saul; the archers found him, and he was badly wounded by them. 4 Then Saul said to his armor-bearer, "Draw your sword and thrust me through with it, so that these uncircumcised may not come and thrust me through, and make sport of me." But his armor-bearer was unwilling; for he was terrified. So Saul took his own sword and fell upon it. 5 When his armor-bearer saw that Saul was dead, he also fell upon his sword and died with him. 6 So Saul and his three sons and his armor-bearer and all his men died together on the same day. 7 When the men of Israel who were on the other side of the valley and those beyond the Jordan saw that the men of Israel had fled and that Saul and his sons were dead, they forsook their towns and fled; and the Philistines came and occupied them.

8 The next day, when the Philistines came to strip the dead, they found Saul and his three sons fallen on Mount Gilboa. 9 They cut off his head, stripped off his armor, and sent messengers throughout the land of the Philistines to carry the good news to the houses of their idols and to the people. 10 They put his armor in the temple of Astarte;[p] and they fastened his body to the wall of Beth-shan. 11 But when the inhabitants of Jabesh-gilead heard what the Philistines had done to Saul, 12 all the valiant men set out, traveled all night long, and took the body of Saul and the bodies of his sons from the wall of Beth-shan. They came to Jabesh and burned them there. 13 Then they took their bones and buried them under the tamarisk tree in Jabesh, and fasted seven days.

31.1 1 Chr 10.1-12; 1 Sam 28.4
31.3 2 Sam 1.6
31.4 Judg 9.54; 2 Sam 1.6, 10
31.9 2 Sam 1.20
31.10 1 Sam 7.3; Judg 2.13; 2 Sam 21.12; Josh 17.11
31.11 1 Sam 11.3, 9,11
31.12 2 Sam 2.4-7; 2 Chr 16.14
31.13 2 Sam 21.12-14; 1 Sam 22.6; 2 Sam 1.12

o Heb *and they fell slain* p Heb plural

2 Samuel

Title and Background

1 and 2 Samuel were originally one book (see Introduction to 1 Samuel).

Author and Date of Writing

See Introduction to 1 Samuel.

Theme and Message

2 Samuel depicts David as a true (though imperfect) representative of the ideal theocratic king. Under David's rule the Lord caused the nation to prosper, and he helped the Israelites defeat their enemies. In chapter 7 God established his covenant with David and promised that David's dynasty would endure forever.

Outline

I. David Becomes King Over Judah (1.1–4.12)
II. David Becomes King Over All Israel (5.1-5)
III. David's Kingship: Its Accomplishments and Glory (5.6–9.12)
IV. David's Kingship: Its Weaknesses and Failures (10.1–20.16)
V. Final Reflections on David's Reign (21.1–24.25)

David Mourns for Saul and Jonathan

1 After the death of Saul, when
David had returned from defeating the Amalekites, David remained two days in Ziklag. 2 On the
third day, a man came from Saul's
camp, with his clothes torn and
dirt on his head. When he came to
David, he fell to the ground and did
obeisance. 3 David said to him,
"Where have you come from?" He
said to him, "I have escaped from
the camp of Israel." 4 David said to
him, "How did things go? Tell me!"
He answered, "The army fled from
the battle, but also many of the
army fell and died; and Saul and
his son Jonathan also died." 5 Then
David asked the young man who
was reporting to him, "How do you
know that Saul and his son Jonathan died?" 6 The young man reporting to him said, "I happened to
be on Mount Gilboa; and there was
Saul leaning on his spear, while the
chariots and the horsemen drew
close to him. 7 When he looked behind him, he saw me, and called to
me. I answered, 'Here sir.' 8 And he
said to me, 'Who are you?' I answered him, 'I am an Amalekite.'
9 He said to me, 'Come, stand over
me and kill me; for convulsions
have seized me, and yet my life still
lingers.' 10 So I stood over him, and
killed him, for I knew that he could
not live after he had fallen. I took
the crown that was on his head and
the armlet that was on his arm, and
I have brought them here to my
lord."
11 Then David took hold of his
clothes and tore them; and all the
men who were with him did the
same. 12 They mourned and wept,
and fasted until evening for Saul
and for his son Jonathan, and for
the army of the LORD and for the
house of Israel, because they had
fallen by the sword. 13 David said to
the young man who had reported to
him, "Where do you come from?"
He answered, "I am the son of a
resident alien, an Amalekite."
14 David said to him, "Were you not
afraid to lift your hand to destroy
the LORD's anointed?" 15 Then David called one of the young men

1.1 1 Sam 31.6; 30.17,26
1.2 1 Sam 4.10, 12
1.6 1 Sam 31.2-4
1.8 1 Sam 15.3
1.10 Judg 9.54
1.11 2 Sam 3.31; 13.31
1.12 2 Sam 3.35
1.13 v. 8
1.14 1 Sam 24.6; 26.9
1.15 2 Sam 4.10, 12

and said, "Come here and strike
him down." So he struck him down
and he died. 16 David said to him,
"Your blood be on your head; for
your own mouth has testified
against you, saying, 'I have killed
the LORD's anointed.' "
17 David intoned this lamentation over Saul and his son Jonathan. 18 (He ordered that The Song
of the Bow[a] be taught to the people of Judah; it is written in the
Book of Jashar.) He said:

19 Your glory, O Israel, lies
slain upon your high
places!
How the mighty have
fallen!
20 Tell it not in Gath,
proclaim it not in the
streets of Ashkelon;
or the daughters of the
Philistines will rejoice,
the daughters of the
uncircumcised will
exult.

21 You mountains of Gilboa,
let there be no dew or rain
upon you,
nor bounteous fields![b]
For there the shield of the
mighty was defiled,
the shield of Saul, anointed
with oil no more.

22 From the blood of the
slain,
from the fat of the mighty,
the bow of Jonathan did not
turn back,
nor the sword of Saul
return empty.

23 Saul and Jonathan, beloved
and lovely!
In life and in death they
were not divided;
they were swifter than
eagles,
they were stronger than
lions.

24 O daughters of Israel, weep
over Saul,
who clothed you with
crimson, in luxury,
who put ornaments of gold
on your apparel.

25 How the mighty have fallen
in the midst of the battle!

Jonathan lies slain upon
your high places.
26 I am distressed for you, my
brother Jonathan;
greatly beloved were you to
me;
your love to me was
wonderful,
passing the love of women.

27 How the mighty have fallen,
and the weapons of war
perished!

David Anointed King of Judah

2 After this David inquired of
the LORD, "Shall I go up into
any of the cities of Judah?" The
LORD said to him, "Go up." David
said, "To which shall I go up?" He
said, "To Hebron." 2 So David went
up there, along with his two wives,
Ahinoam of Jezreel, and Abigail
the widow of Nabal of Carmel. 3 David brought up the men who were
with him, every one with his household; and they settled in the towns
of Hebron. 4 Then the people of Judah came, and there they anointed
David king over the house of Judah.
When they told David, "It was
the people of Jabesh-gilead who
buried Saul," 5 David sent messengers to the people of Jabesh-gilead,
and said to them, "May you be
blessed by the LORD, because you
showed this loyalty to Saul your
lord, and buried him! 6 Now may
the LORD show steadfast love and
faithfulness to you! And I too will
reward you because you have done
this thing. 7 Therefore let your
hands be strong, and be valiant; for
Saul your lord is dead, and the
house of Judah has anointed me
king over them."

1.16 2 Sam 3.28, 29; v. 10
1.17 2 Chr 35.25
1.18 1 Sam 31.3; Josh 10.13
1.19 v. 27
1.20 1 Sam 31.9; Mic 1.10; Ex 15.20; 1 Sam 18.6; 31.4
1.21 1 Sam 31.1; Job 3.3,4; Isa 21.5
1.22 Isa 34.6; 1 Sam 18.4
1.23 Jer 4.13; Judg 14.18
1.25 vv. 19,27
1.26 1 Sam 18.1-4
1.27 vv. 19,25; 1 Sam 2.4
2.1 1 Sam 23.2, 4,9-12; 30.31
2.2 1 Sam 30.5
2.3 1 Sam 30.9; 1 Chr 12.1
2.4 2 Sam 5.3, 5; 1 Sam 31.11-13
2.5 1 Sam 23.21

[a] Heb *that The Bow* [b] Meaning of Heb uncertain

Ishbaal King of Israel

8 But Abner son of Ner, commander of Saul's army, had taken
Ishbaal[c] son of Saul, and brought
him over to Mahanaim. 9 He made
him king over Gilead, the Ashur-
ites, Jezreel, Ephraim, Benjamin,
and over all Israel. 10 Ishbaal,[c]
Saul's son, was forty years old
when he began to reign over Israel,
and he reigned two years. But the
house of Judah followed David.
11 The time that David was king in
Hebron over the house of Judah
was seven years and six months.

The Battle of Gibeon

12 Abner son of Ner, and the
servants of Ishbaal[c] son of Saul,
went out from Mahanaim to Gibeon. 13 Joab son of Zeruiah, and the
servants of David, went out and
met them at the pool of Gibeon.
One group sat on one side of the
pool, while the other sat on the
other side of the pool. 14 Abner said
to Joab, "Let the young men come
forward and have a contest before
us." Joab said, "Let them come forward." 15 So they came forward and
were counted as they passed by,
twelve for Benjamin and Ishbaal[c]
son of Saul, and twelve of the servants of David. 16 Each grasped his
opponent by the head, and thrust
his sword in his opponent's side; so
they fell down together. Therefore
that place was called Helkath-
hazzurim,[d] which is at Gibeon.
17 The battle was very fierce that
day; and Abner and the men of Israel were beaten by the servants of
David.

18 The three sons of Zeruiah
were there, Joab, Abishai, and Asahel. Now Asahel was as swift of foot
as a wild gazelle. 19 Asahel pursued
Abner, turning neither to the right
nor to the left as he followed him.
20 Then Abner looked back and
said, "Is it you, Asahel?" He answered, "Yes, it is." 21 Abner said to
him, "Turn to your right or to your
left, and seize one of the young
men, and take his spoil." But Asahel would not turn away from following him. 22 Abner said again to
Asahel, "Turn away from following
me; why should I strike you to the
ground? How then could I show my
face to your brother Joab?" 23 But
he refused to turn away. So Abner
struck him in the stomach with the
butt of his spear, so that the spear
came out at his back. He fell there,
and died where he lay. And all
those who came to the place where
Asahel had fallen and died, stood
still.

24 But Joab and Abishai pursued Abner. As the sun was going
down they came to the hill of Ammah, which lies before Giah on the
way to the wilderness of Gibeon.
25 The Benjaminites rallied around
Abner and formed a single band;
they took their stand on the top of
a hill. 26 Then Abner called to Joab,
"Is the sword to keep devouring
forever? Do you not know that the
end will be bitter? How long will it
be before you order your people to
turn from the pursuit of their kinsmen?" 27 Joab said, "As God lives, if
you had not spoken, the people
would have continued to pursue
their kinsmen, not stopping until
morning." 28 Joab sounded the
trumpet and all the people
stopped; they no longer pursued Israel or engaged in battle any further.

29 Abner and his men traveled
all that night through the Arabah;
they crossed the Jordan, and,
marching the whole forenoon,[e]
they came to Mahanaim. 30 Joab returned from the pursuit of Abner;
and when he had gathered all the
people together, there were missing of David's servants nineteen
men besides Asahel. 31 But the servants of David had killed of Benjamin three hundred sixty of Abner's
men. 32 They took up Asahel and
buried him in the tomb of his father, which was at Bethlehem.
Joab and his men marched all
night, and the day broke upon
them at Hebron.

2.8 2 Sam 14.50
2.9 Judg 1.32; 1 Sam 29.1
2.11 2 Sam 5.5
2.12 Josh 18.25
2.13 1 Chr 2.16
2.17 2 Sam 3.1
2.18 1 Chr 2.16; 12.8
2.22 2 Sam 3.27
2.23 2 Sam 3.27; 4.6; 20.10
2.24 Josh 10.41
2.27 v. 14
2.29 v. 8

[c] Gk Compare 1 Chr 8.33; 9.39: Heb *Ish-bosheth*, "man of shame" [d] That is *Field of Sword-edges* [e] Meaning of Heb uncertain

Abner Defects to David

3 There was a long war between
the house of Saul and the
house of David; David grew stronger and stronger, while the house
of Saul became weaker and weaker.
2 Sons were born to David at
Hebron: his firstborn was Amnon,
of Ahinoam of Jezreel; 3 his second,
Chileab, of Abigail the widow of
Nabal of Carmel; the third, Absalom son of Maacah, daughter of
King Talmai of Geshur; 4 the
fourth, Adonijah son of Haggith;
the fifth, Shephatiah son of Abital;
5 and the sixth, Ithream, of David's
wife Eglah. These were born to David in Hebron.
6 While there was war between
the house of Saul and the house of
David, Abner was making himself
strong in the house of Saul. 7 Now
Saul had a concubine whose name
was Rizpah daughter of Aiah. And
Ishbaal[f] said to Abner, "Why have
you gone in to my father's concubine?" 8 The words of Ishbaal[g]
made Abner very angry; he said,
"Am I a dog's head for Judah? Today I keep showing loyalty to the
house of your father Saul, to his
brothers, and to his friends, and
have not given you into the hand of
David; and yet you charge me now
with a crime concerning this woman. 9 So may God do to Abner and
so may he add to it! For just what
the LORD has sworn to David, that
will I accomplish for him, 10 to
transfer the kingdom from the
house of Saul, and set up the
throne of David over Israel and over
Judah, from Dan to Beer-sheba."
11 And Ishbaal[f] could not answer
Abner another word, because he
feared him.
12 Abner sent messengers to
David at Hebron,[h] saying, "To
whom does the land belong? Make
your covenant with me, and I will
give you my support to bring all Israel over to you." 13 He said, "Good;
I will make a covenant with you.
But one thing I require of you: you
shall never appear in my presence
unless you bring Saul's daughter
Michal when you come to see me."
14 Then David sent messengers to
Saul's son Ishbaal,[i] saying, "Give
me my wife Michal, to whom I became engaged at the price of one
hundred foreskins of the Philistines." 15 Ishbaal[i] sent and took
her from her husband Paltiel the
son of Laish. 16 But her husband
went with her, weeping as he
walked behind her all the way to
Bahurim. Then Abner said to him,
"Go back home!" So he went back.
17 Abner sent word to the elders
of Israel, saying, "For some time
past you have been seeking David
as king over you. 18 Now then bring
it about; for the LORD has promised
David: Through my servant David I
will save my people Israel from the
hand of the Philistines, and from
all their enemies." 19 Abner also
spoke directly to the Benjaminites;
then Abner went to tell David at
Hebron all that Israel and the
whole house of Benjamin were
ready to do.
20 When Abner came with
twenty men to David at Hebron,
David made a feast for Abner and
the men who were with him. 21 Abner said to David, "Let me go and
rally all Israel to my lord the king,
in order that they may make a covenant with you, and that you may
reign over all that your heart desires." So David dismissed Abner,
and he went away in peace.

Abner Is Killed by Joab

22 Just then the servants of David arrived with Joab from a raid,
bringing much spoil with them.
But Abner was not with David at
Hebron, for David[j] had dismissed
him, and he had gone away in
peace. 23 When Joab and all the
army that was with him came, it
was told Joab, "Abner son of Ner
came to the king, and he has dismissed him, and he has gone away
in peace." 24 Then Joab went to the

3.2 1 Chr 3.1-3; 1 Sam 25.42, 43
3.3 1 Sam 27.8; 2 Sam 13.37
3.4 1 Kings 1.5
3.7 2 Sam 21.8-11; 16.21
3.8 1 Sam 24.14; 2 Sam 9.8
3.9 1 Kings 19.2; 1 Sam 15.8
3.10 Judg 20.1; 1 Sam 3.20
3.13 Gen 43.3; 1 Sam 18.20
3.14 1 Sam 18.25, 27
3.15 1 Sam 25.44
3.16 2 Sam 16.5
3.18 1 Sam 9.16; 15.28
3.19 1 Sam 10.20, 21
3.21 vv. 10,12; 1 Kings 11.37
3.22 1 Sam 27.8

[f] Heb *And he* [g] Gk Compare 1 Chr 8.33; 9.39: Heb *Ish-bosheth*, "man of shame"
[h] Gk: Heb *where he was*
[i] Heb *Ish-bosheth* [j] Heb *he*

king and said, "What have you
done? Abner came to you; why did
you dismiss him, so that he got
away? 25 You know that Abner son
of Ner came to deceive you, and to
learn your comings and goings and
to learn all that you are doing."
26 When Joab came out from
David's presence, he sent messengers after Abner, and they brought
him back from the cistern of Sirah;
but David did not know about it.
27 When Abner returned to Hebron,
Joab took him aside in the gateway
to speak with him privately, and
there he stabbed him in the stomach. So he died for shedding[k] the
blood of Asahel, Joab's[l] brother.
28 Afterward, when David heard of
it, he said, "I and my kingdom are
forever guiltless before the LORD for
the blood of Abner son of Ner.
29 May the guilt[m] fall on the head of
Joab, and on all his father's house;
and may the house of Joab never be
without one who has a discharge,
or who is leprous,[n] or who holds a
spindle, or who falls by the sword,
or who lacks food!" 30 So Joab and
his brother Abishai murdered Abner because he had killed their
brother Asahel in the battle at Gibeon.
31 Then David said to Joab and
to all the people who were with
him, "Tear your clothes, and put on
sackcloth, and mourn over Abner."
And King David followed the bier.
32 They buried Abner at Hebron.
The king lifted up his voice and
wept at the grave of Abner, and all
the people wept. 33 The king lamented for Abner, saying,

"Should Abner die as a fool
dies?
34 Your hands were not bound,
your feet were not fettered;
as one falls before the
wicked
you have fallen."

And all the people wept over him
again. 35 Then all the people came
to persuade David to eat something
while it was still day; but David
swore, saying, "So may God do to
me, and more, if I taste bread or
anything else before the sun goes
down!" 36 All the people took notice of it, and it pleased them; just
as everything the king did pleased
all the people. 37 So all the people
and all Israel understood that day
that the king had no part in the killing of Abner son of Ner. 38 And the
king said to his servants, "Do you
not know that a prince and a great
man has fallen this day in Israel?
39 Today I am powerless, even
though anointed king; these men,
the sons of Zeruiah, are too violent
for me. The LORD pay back the one
who does wickedly in accordance
with his wickedness!"

Ishbaal Assassinated

4 When Saul's son Ishbaal[o]
heard that Abner had died at
Hebron, his courage failed, and all
Israel was dismayed. 2 Saul's son
had two captains of raiding bands;
the name of the one was Baanah,
and the name of the other Rechab.
They were sons of Rimmon a Benjaminite from Beeroth—for Beeroth is considered to belong to
Benjamin. 3 (Now the people of Beeroth had fled to Gittaim and are
there as resident aliens to this day).
4 Saul's son Jonathan had a son
who was crippled in his feet. He
was five years old when the news
about Saul and Jonathan came
from Jezreel. His nurse picked him
up and fled; and, in her haste to
flee, it happened that he fell and
became lame. His name was Mephibosheth.[p]
5 Now the sons of Rimmon the
Beerothite, Rechab and Baanah,
set out, and about the heat of the
day they came to the house of Ishbaal,[q] while he was taking his
noonday rest. 6 They came inside
the house as though to take wheat,
and they struck him in the stomach; then Rechab and his brother
Baanah escaped.[r] 7 Now they had
come into the house while he was
lying on his couch in his bedcham-

3.25 1 Sam 29.6; Isa 37.28
3.27 2 Sam 2.23; 4.6; 20.9,10; 1 Kings 2.5
3.29 1 Kings 2.32, 33; Lev 15.2
3.30 2 Sam 2.23
3.31 Gen 37.34; 2 Sam 1.2, 11
3.33 2 Sam 1.17
3.35 2 Sam 12.17; 1 Sam 3.17; 2 Sam 1.12
3.39 2 Sam 19.5-7; 1 Kings 2.5, 6,33,34
4.1 2 Sam 3.27; Ezra 4.4
4.2 Josh 18.25
4.3 Neh 11.33
4.4 2 Sam 9.3, 6; 1 Sam 31.1-4
4.5 2 Sam 2.8
4.6 2 Sam 2.23

[k] Heb lacks *shedding* [l] Heb *his*
[m] Heb *May it* [n] A term for several skin diseases; precise meaning uncertain
[o] Heb lacks *Ishbaal* [p] In 1 Chr 8.34 and 9.40, *Merib-baal* [q] Heb *Ish-bosheth*
[r] Meaning of Heb of verse 6 uncertain

ber; they attacked him, killed him,
and beheaded him. Then they took
his head and traveled by way of the
Arabah all night long. 8 They
brought the head of Ishbaal[s] to
David at Hebron and said to the
king, "Here is the head of Ishbaal,[s]
son of Saul, your enemy, who
sought your life; the LORD has
avenged my lord the king this day
on Saul and on his offspring."
9 David answered Rechab and
his brother Baanah, the sons of
Rimmon the Beerothite, "As the
LORD lives, who has redeemed my
life out of every adversity, 10 when
the one who told me, 'See, Saul is
dead,' thought he was bringing
good news, I seized him and killed
him at Ziklag—this was the reward
I gave him for his news. 11 How
much more then, when wicked
men have killed a righteous man
on his bed in his own house! And
now shall I not require his blood at
your hand, and destroy you from
the earth?" 12 So David commanded the young men, and they killed
them; they cut off their hands and
feet, and hung their bodies beside
the pool at Hebron. But the head of
Ishbaal[s] they took and buried in
the tomb of Abner at Hebron.

David Anointed King of All Israel

5 Then all the tribes of Israel
came to David at Hebron, and
said, "Look, we are your bone and
flesh. 2 For some time, while Saul
was king over us, it was you who led
out Israel and brought it in. The
LORD said to you: It is you who shall
be shepherd of my people Israel,
you who shall be ruler over Israel."
3 So all the elders of Israel came to
the king at Hebron; and King David
made a covenant with them at Hebron before the LORD, and they
anointed David king over Israel.
4 David was thirty years old when
he began to reign, and he reigned
forty years. 5 At Hebron he reigned
over Judah seven years and six
months; and at Jerusalem he
reigned over all Israel and Judah
thirty-three years.

Jerusalem Made Capital of the United Kingdom

6 The king and his men
marched to Jerusalem against the
Jebusites, the inhabitants of the
land, who said to David, "You will
not come in here, even the blind
and the lame will turn you back"—
thinking, "David cannot come in
here." 7 Nevertheless David took
the stronghold of Zion, which is
now the city of David. 8 David had
said on that day, "Whoever would
strike down the Jebusites, let him
get up the water shaft to attack the
lame and the blind, those whom
David hates."[t] Therefore it is said,
"The blind and the lame shall not
come into the house." 9 David occupied the stronghold, and named
it the city of David. David built the
city all around from the Millo inward. 10 And David became greater
and greater, for the LORD, the God
of hosts, was with him.
11 King Hiram of Tyre sent messengers to David, along with cedar
trees, and carpenters and masons
who built David a house. 12 David
then perceived that the LORD had
established him king over Israel,
and that he had exalted his kingdom for the sake of his people Israel.
13 In Jerusalem, after he came
from Hebron, David took more
concubines and wives; and more
sons and daughters were born to
David. 14 These are the names of
those who were born to him in Jerusalem: Shammua, Shobab, Nathan, Solomon, 15 Ibhar, Elishua,
Nepheg, Japhia, 16 Elishama, Eliada, and Eliphelet.

Philistine Attack Repulsed

17 When the Philistines heard
that David had been anointed king
over Israel, all the Philistines went
up in search of David; but David
heard about it and went down to
the stronghold. 18 Now the Philistines had come and spread out in
the valley of Rephaim. 19 David in-

4.8 1 Sam 23.15; 25.29
4.9 1 Kings 1.29
4.10 2 Sam 1.2, 4,15
4.11 Gen 9.5,6
4.12 2 Sam 1.15; 3.32
5.1 1 Chr 11.1; 2 Sam 19.13
5.2 1 Sam 18.13; 16.1,12; 25.30
5.3 1 Chr 11.3; 2 Sam 3.21; 2.4
5.4 Num 4.3; Lk 3.23; 1 Chr 26.31
5.5 2 Sam 2.11
5.6 Josh 15.63; Judg 1.8,21
5.8 v. 9; 2 Sam 6.12, 16; 1 Kings 2.10
5.9 v. 7
5.10 2 Sam 3.1
5.11 1 Chr 14.1
5.13 Deut 17.17; 1 Chr 3.9
5.14 1 Chr 3.5-8
5.17 2 Sam 23.14
5.18 Josh 15.18; 17.15; 18.16
5.19 1 Sam 23.2; 2 Sam 2.1

s Heb *Ish-bosheth* t Another reading is *those who hate David*

quired of the LORD, "Shall I go up
against the Philistines? Will you
give them into my hand?" The LORD
said to David, "Go up; for I will certainly give the Philistines into your
hand." 20 So David came to Baal-
perazim, and David defeated them
there. He said, "The LORD has burst
forth against[u] my enemies before
me, like a bursting flood." Therefore that place is called Baal-
perazim.[v] 21 The Philistines abandoned their idols there, and David
and his men carried them away.
22 Once again the Philistines
came up, and were spread out in
the valley of Rephaim. 23 When David inquired of the LORD, he said,
"You shall not go up; go around to
their rear, and come upon them opposite the balsam trees. 24 When
you hear the sound of marching in
the tops of the balsam trees, then
be on the alert; for then the LORD
has gone out before you to strike
down the army of the Philistines."
25 David did just as the LORD had
commanded him; and he struck
down the Philistines from Geba all
the way to Gezer.

David Brings the Ark to Jerusalem

6 David again gathered all the
chosen men of Israel, thirty
thousand. 2 David and all the people with him set out and went from
Baale-judah, to bring up from there
the ark of God, which is called by
the name of the LORD of hosts who
is enthroned on the cherubim.
3 They carried the ark of God on a
new cart, and brought it out of the
house of Abinadab, which was on
the hill. Uzzah and Ahio,[w] the sons
of Abinadab, were driving the new
cart 4 with the ark of God;[x] and
Ahio[w] went in front of the ark. 5 David and all the house of Israel were
dancing before the LORD with all
their might, with songs[y] and lyres
and harps and tambourines and
castanets and cymbals.
6 When they came to the threshing floor of Nacon, Uzzah reached
out his hand to the ark of God and
took hold of it, for the oxen shook
it. 7 The anger of the LORD was kindled against Uzzah; and God struck
him there because he reached out
his hand to the ark;[z] and he died
there beside the ark of God. 8 David
was angry because the LORD had
burst forth with an outburst upon
Uzzah; so that place is called Perez-
uzzah,[a] to this day. 9 David was
afraid of the LORD that day; he said,
"How can the ark of the LORD come
into my care?" 10 So David was unwilling to take the ark of the LORD
into his care in the city of David;
instead David took it to the house
of Obed-edom the Gittite. 11 The
ark of the LORD remained in the
house of Obed-edom the Gittite
three months; and the LORD blessed
Obed-edom and all his household.
12 It was told King David, "The
LORD has blessed the household of
Obed-edom and all that belongs to
him, because of the ark of God." So
David went and brought up the ark
of God from the house of Obed-
edom to the city of David with rejoicing; 13 and when those who bore
the ark of the LORD had gone six
paces, he sacrificed an ox and a fatling. 14 David danced before the
LORD with all his might; David was
girded with a linen ephod. 15 So David and all the house of Israel
brought up the ark of the LORD with
shouting, and with the sound of the
trumpet.
16 As the ark of the LORD came
into the city of David, Michal
daughter of Saul looked out of the
window, and saw King David leaping and dancing before the LORD;
and she despised him in her heart.
17 They brought in the ark of
the LORD, and set it in its place, inside the tent that David had
pitched for it; and David offered
burnt offerings and offerings of
well-being before the LORD. 18 When
David had finished offering the

5.20 Isa 28.21
5.21 1 Chr 14.12
5.22 v. 18
5.23 v. 19
5.24 2 Kings 7.6; Judg 4.14
5.25 Josh 12.12; 1 Chr 14.16
6.2 1 Chr 13.5, 6; Lev 24.16; 1 Sam 4.4
6.3 1 Sam 6.7
6.4 1 Sam 7.1
6.5 1 Sam 18.6, 7; 1 Chr 13.8
6.6 1 Chr 13.9; Num 4.15, 19,20
6.7 1 Sam 6.19
6.10 1 Chr 13.13
6.11 1 Chr 13.14
6.12 1 Chr 15.25; 1 Kings 8.1
6.14 Ex 15.20; 1 Sam 2.18
6.15 1 Chr 15.28
6.16 1 Chr 15.29
6.17 1 Chr 15.1; 16.1; 1 Kings 8.62-65
6.18 1 Kings 8.14, 15

[u] Heb *paraz* [v] That is *Lord of Bursting Forth* [w] Or *and his brother* [x] Compare Gk: Heb *and brought it out of the house of Abinadab, which was on the hill with the ark of God* [y] Q Ms Gk 1 Chr 13.8: Heb *fir-trees* [z] 1 Chr 13.10 Compare Q Ms: Meaning of Heb uncertain [a] That is *Bursting Out Against Uzzah*

burnt offerings and the offerings of
well-being, he blessed the people
in the name of the LORD of hosts,
19 and distributed food among all
the people, the whole multitude of
Israel, both men and women, to
each a cake of bread, a portion of
meat,[b] and a cake of raisins. Then
all the people went back to their
homes.
20 David returned to bless his
household. But Michal the daughter of Saul came out to meet David,
and said, "How the king of Israel
honored himself today, uncovering
himself today before the eyes of his
servants' maids, as any vulgar fellow might shamelessly uncover
himself!" 21 David said to Michal,
"It was before the LORD, who chose
me in place of your father and all
his household, to appoint me as
prince over Israel, the people of the
LORD, that I have danced before the
LORD. 22 I will make myself yet more
contemptible than this, and I will
be abased in my own eyes; but by
the maids of whom you have spoken, by them I shall be held in hon-
or." 23 And Michal the daughter of
Saul had no child to the day of her
death.

God's Covenant with David

7 Now when the king was settled in his house, and the LORD
had given him rest from all his enemies around him, 2 the king said to
the prophet Nathan, "See now, I
am living in a house of cedar, but
the ark of God stays in a tent." 3 Nathan said to the king, "Go, do all
that you have in mind; for the LORD
is with you."
4 But that same night the word
of the LORD came to Nathan: 5 Go
and tell my servant David: Thus
says the LORD: Are you the one to
build me a house to live in? 6 I have
not lived in a house since the day I
brought up the people of Israel
from Egypt to this day, but I have
been moving about in a tent and a
tabernacle. 7 Wherever I have
moved about among all the people
of Israel, did I ever speak a word
with any of the tribal leaders[c] of

6.20 vv. 14,16; 1 Sam 19.24 **6.21** 1 Sam 13.14; 15.28 **7.1** 1 Chr 17.1ff **7.2** 2 Sam 5.11; Acts 7.46; Ex 26.1 **7.3** 1 Kings 8.17, 18 **7.5** 1 Kings 5.3, 4; 8.19 **7.6** 1 Kings 8.16; Ex 40.18,34 **7.7** Lev 26.11, 12; Deut 23.14; 2 Sam 5.2 **7.8** 1 Sam 16.11, 12; Ps 78.70; 2 Sam 6.21 **7.9** 1 Sam 18.14; 2 Sam 5.10; Ps 18.37-42 **7.10** Ex 15.17; Isa 5.2,7; Ps 89.22; Isa 60.18 **7.11** Judg 2.16; 1 Sam 12.9-11; vv. 1,27; 1 Sam 25.28 **7.12** 1 Kings 2.1 **7.13** 1 Kings 5.5; Ps 89.4,29; 36.37; Isa 9.7 **7.14** Ps 89.26,27; Heb 1.5; Ps 89.30-33 **7.15** 1 Sam 15.23, 28 **7.16** Ps 89.36,37 **7.18** Ex 3.11; 1 Sam 18.18

Israel, whom I commanded to
shepherd my people Israel, saying,
"Why have you not built me a
house of cedar?" 8 Now therefore
thus you shall say to my servant
David: Thus says the LORD of hosts:
I took you from the pasture, from
following the sheep to be prince
over my people Israel; 9 and I have
been with you wherever you went,
and have cut off all your enemies
from before you; and I will make for
you a great name, like the name of
the great ones of the earth. 10 And I
will appoint a place for my people
Israel and will plant them, so that
they may live in their own place,
and be disturbed no more; and evildoers shall afflict them no more, as
formerly, 11 from the time that I appointed judges over my people Israel; and I will give you rest from all
your enemies. Moreover the LORD
declares to you that the LORD will
make you a house. 12 When your
days are fulfilled and you lie down
with your ancestors, I will raise up
your offspring after you, who shall
come forth from your body, and I
will establish his kingdom. 13 He
shall build a house for my name,
and I will establish the throne of
his kingdom forever. 14 I will be a
father to him, and he shall be a son
to me. When he commits iniquity,
I will punish him with a rod such as
mortals use, with blows inflicted by
human beings. 15 But I will not
take[d] my steadfast love from him,
as I took it from Saul, whom I put
away from before you. 16 Your
house and your kingdom shall be
made sure forever before me;[e]
your throne shall be established
forever. 17 In accordance with all
these words and with all this vision, Nathan spoke to David.

David's Prayer

18 Then King David went in and
sat before the LORD, and said, "Who
am I, O Lord GOD, and what is my
house, that you have brought me

[b] Vg: Meaning of Heb uncertain [c] Or *any of the tribes* [d] Gk Syr Vg 1 Chr 17.13: Heb *shall not depart* [e] Gk Heb Mss: MT *before you;* Compare 2 Sam 7.26, 29

thus far? 19 And yet this was a small
thing in your eyes, O Lord GOD; you
have spoken also of your servant's
house for a great while to come.
May this be instruction for the people,[f] O Lord GOD! 20 And what
more can David say to you? For you
know your servant, O Lord GOD!
21 Because of your promise, and according to your own heart, you
have wrought all this greatness, so
that your servant may know it.
22 Therefore you are great, O LORD
God; for there is no one like you,
and there is no God besides you,
according to all that we have heard
with our ears. 23 Who is like your
people, like Israel? Is there another[g] nation on earth whose God
went to redeem it as a people, and
to make a name for himself, doing
great and awesome things for
them,[h] by driving out[i] before his
people nations and their gods?[j]
24 And you established your people
Israel for yourself to be your people
forever; and you, O LORD, became
their God. 25 And now, O LORD God,
as for the word that you have spoken concerning your servant and
concerning his house, confirm it
forever; do as you have promised.
26 Thus your name will be magnified forever in the saying, 'The LORD
of hosts is God over Israel'; and the
house of your servant David will be
established before you. 27 For you,
O LORD of hosts, the God of Israel,
have made this revelation to your
servant, saying, 'I will build you a
house'; therefore your servant has
found courage to pray this prayer to
you. 28 And now, O Lord GOD, you
are God, and your words are true,
and you have promised this good
thing to your servant; 29 now therefore may it please you to bless the
house of your servant, so that it
may continue forever before you;
for you, O Lord GOD, have spoken,
and with your blessing shall the
house of your servant be blessed
forever."

David's Wars

8 Some time afterward, David
attacked the Philistines and
subdued them; David took Metheg-
ammah out of the hand of the Philistines.

2 He also defeated the Moabites
and, making them lie down on the
ground, measured them off with a
cord; he measured two lengths of
cord for those who were to be put
to death, and one length[k] for those
who were to be spared. And the
Moabites became servants to David and brought tribute.

3 David also struck down King
Hadadezer son of Rehob of Zobah,
as he went to restore his monument[l] at the river Euphrates. 4 David took from him one thousand
seven hundred horsemen, and
twenty thousand foot soldiers. David hamstrung all the chariot
horses, but left enough for a hundred chariots. 5 When the Arameans of Damascus came to help King
Hadadezer of Zobah, David killed
twenty-two thousand men of the
Arameans. 6 Then David put garrisons among the Arameans of Damascus; and the Arameans became
servants to David and brought tribute. The LORD gave victory to David
wherever he went. 7 David took the
gold shields that were carried by
the servants of Hadadezer, and
brought them to Jerusalem. 8 From
Betah and from Berothai, towns of
Hadadezer, King David took a great
amount of bronze.

9 When King Toi of Hamath
heard that David had defeated the
whole army of Hadadezer, 10 Toi
sent his son Joram to King David,
to greet him and to congratulate
him because he had fought against
Hadadezer and defeated him. Now
Hadadezer had often been at war
with Toi. Joram brought with him
articles of silver, gold, and bronze;
11 these also King David dedicated
to the LORD, together with the silver
and gold that he dedicated from all
the nations he subdued, 12 from

7.19 Isa 55.8
7.20 1 Sam 16.7; Jn 21.17
7.22 Ps 48.1; 86.10; Ex 15.11; Deut 3.24; Ps 44.1
7.23 Deut 4.7, 32-38; 10.21; 15.15; 9.26
7.24 Deut 26.18; Ps 48.14
7.26 Ps 72.18,19
7.27 v. 13
7.28 Jn 17.17
7.29 Num 6.24-26
8.2 Num 24.17
8.3 2 Sam 10.15-19
8.4 Josh 11.6,9
8.5 1 Kings 11.23-25
8.6 v. 14; 2 Sam 7.9
8.7 1 Kings 10.16
8.10 1 Chr 18.10
8.11 1 Kings 7.51; 1 Chr 18.11; 26.25

[f] Meaning of Heb uncertain [g] Gk: Heb *one* [h] Heb *you* [i] Gk 1 Chr 17.21: Heb *for your land* [j] Cn: Heb *before your people, whom you redeemed for yourself from Egypt, nations and its gods* [k] Heb *one full length* [l] Compare 1 Sam 15.12 and 2 Sam 18.18

Edom, Moab, the Ammonites, the
Philistines, Amalek, and from the
spoil of King Hadadezer son of Rehob of Zobah.
13 David won a name for himself. When he returned, he killed
eighteen thousand Edomites[m] in
the Valley of Salt. 14 He put garrisons in Edom; throughout all
Edom he put garrisons, and all the
Edomites became David's servants. And the LORD gave victory to
David wherever he went.

David's Officers

15 So David reigned over all Israel; and David administered justice and equity to all his people.
16 Joab son of Zeruiah was over the
army; Jehoshaphat son of Ahilud
was recorder; 17 Zadok son of Ahitub and Ahimelech son of Abiathar
were priests; Seraiah was secretary;
18 Benaiah son of Jehoiada was
over[n] the Cherethites and the Pelethites; and David's sons were
priests.

David's Kindness to Mephibosheth

9 David asked, "Is there still
anyone left of the house of
Saul to whom I may show kindness
for Jonathan's sake?" 2 Now there
was a servant of the house of Saul
whose name was Ziba, and he was
summoned to David. The king said
to him, "Are you Ziba?" And he
said, "At your service!" 3 The king
said, "Is there anyone remaining of
the house of Saul to whom I may
show the kindness of God?" Ziba
said to the king, "There remains a
son of Jonathan; he is crippled in
his feet." 4 The king said to him,
"Where is he?" Ziba said to the
king, "He is in the house of Machir
son of Ammiel, at Lo-debar."
5 Then King David sent and brought
him from the house of Machir son
of Ammiel, at Lo-debar. 6 Mephibosheth[o] son of Jonathan son of Saul
came to David, and fell on his face
and did obeisance. David said,
"Mephibosheth!"[o] He answered,
"I am your servant." 7 David said to
him, "Do not be afraid, for I will
show you kindness for the sake of
your father Jonathan; I will restore
to you all the land of your grandfather Saul, and you yourself shall
eat at my table always." 8 He did
obeisance and said, "What is your
servant, that you should look upon
a dead dog such as I?"
9 Then the king summoned
Saul's servant Ziba, and said to
him, "All that belonged to Saul and
to all his house I have given to your
master's grandson. 10 You and your
sons and your servants shall till the
land for him, and shall bring in the
produce, so that your master's
grandson may have food to eat; but
your master's grandson Mephibosheth[o] shall always eat at my table." Now Ziba had fifteen sons
and twenty servants. 11 Then Ziba
said to the king, "According to all
that my lord the king commands
his servant, so your servant will
do." Mephibosheth[o] ate at David's[p] table, like one of the king's
sons. 12 Mephibosheth[o] had a
young son whose name was Mica.
And all who lived in Ziba's house
became Mephibosheth's[q] servants. 13 Mephibosheth[o] lived in
Jerusalem, for he always ate at the
king's table. Now he was lame in
both his feet.

The Ammonites and Arameans Are Defeated

10 Some time afterward, the
king of the Ammonites
died, and his son Hanun succeeded
him. 2 David said, "I will deal loyally with Hanun son of Nahash, just
as his father dealt loyally with me."
So David sent envoys to console
him concerning his father. When
David's envoys came into the land
of the Ammonites, 3 the princes of
the Ammonites said to their lord
Hanun, "Do you really think that
David is honoring your father just
because he has sent messengers
with condolences to you? Has not
David sent his envoys to you to

8.13 2 Ki 14.7 **8.14** Gen 27.29, 37,40; Num 24.17, 18; v. 6 **8.16** 2 Sam 19.13; 1 Kings 4.3; 2 Kings 18.18, 37 **8.17** 1 Chr 24.3 **8.18** 1 Sam 30.14 **9.1** 1 Sam 20.14-17, 42 **9.2** 2 Sam 16.1-4; 19.17,29 **9.3** 1 Sam 20.14; 2 Sam 4.4 **9.4** 2 Sam 17.27 **9.6** 2 Sam 16.4; 19.24-30 **9.7** vv. 1,3; 2 Sam 12.8; 19.28 **9.8** 2 Sam 16.9 **9.9** 2 Sam 16.4; 19.29 **9.10** vv. 7,11,13; 2 Sam 19.28 **9.12** 1 Chr 8.34 **9.13** vv. 3,7,10 **10.1** 1 Chr 19.1ff

[m] Gk: Heb *returned from striking down eighteen thousand Arameans* [n] Syr Tg Vg 20.23; 1 Chr 18.17: Heb lacks *was over* [o] Or *Merib-baal*: See 4.4 note [p] Gk: Heb *my* [q] Or *Merib-baal's*: See 4.4 note

search the city, to spy it out, and to
overthrow it?" 4 So Hanun seized
David's envoys, shaved off half the
beard of each, cut off their garments in the middle at their hips,
and sent them away. 5 When David
was told, he sent to meet them, for
the men were greatly ashamed. The
king said, "Remain at Jericho until
your beards have grown, and then
return."
6 When the Ammonites saw
that they had become odious to
David, the Ammonites sent and
hired the Arameans of Beth-rehob
and the Arameans of Zobah, twenty
thousand foot soldiers, as well as
the king of Maacah, one thousand
men, and the men of Tob, twelve
thousand men. 7 When David heard
of it, he sent Joab and all the army
with the warriors. 8 The Ammonites
came out and drew up in battle array at the entrance of the gate; but
the Arameans of Zobah and of Rehob, and the men of Tob and Maacah, were by themselves in the
open country.
9 When Joab saw that the battle
was set against him both in front
and in the rear, he chose some of
the picked men of Israel, and arrayed them against the Arameans;
10 the rest of his men he put in the
charge of his brother Abishai, and
he arrayed them against the Ammonites. 11 He said, "If the Arameans are too strong for me, then you
shall help me; but if the Ammonites are too strong for you, then I
will come and help you. 12 Be
strong, and let us be courageous for
the sake of our people, and for the
cities of our God; and may the LORD
do what seems good to him." 13 So
Joab and the people who were with
him moved forward into battle
against the Arameans; and they
fled before him. 14 When the Ammonites saw that the Arameans
fled, they likewise fled before
Abishai, and entered the city. Then
Joab returned from fighting against
the Ammonites, and came to Jerusalem.
15 But when the Arameans saw
that they had been defeated by Israel, they gathered themselves together. 16 Hadadezer sent and
brought out the Arameans who
were beyond the Euphrates; and
they came to Helam, with Shobach
the commander of the army of
Hadadezer at their head. 17 When it
was told David, he gathered all Israel together, and crossed the Jordan, and came to Helam. The Arameans arrayed themselves against
David and fought with him. 18 The
Arameans fled before Israel; and
David killed of the Arameans seven
hundred chariot teams, and forty
thousand horsemen,[r] and wounded Shobach the commander of
their army, so that he died there.
19 When all the kings who were servants of Hadadezer saw that they
had been defeated by Israel, they
made peace with Israel, and became subject to them. So the Arameans were afraid to help the Ammonites any more.

David Commits Adultery with Bathsheba

11 In the spring of the year,
the time when kings go out
to battle, David sent Joab with his
officers and all Israel with him;
they ravaged the Ammonites, and
besieged Rabbah. But David remained at Jerusalem.
2 It happened, late one afternoon, when David rose from his
couch and was walking about on
the roof of the king's house, that he
saw from the roof a woman bathing; the woman was very beautiful.
3 David sent someone to inquire
about the woman. It was reported,
"This is Bathsheba daughter of Eliam, the wife of Uriah the Hittite."
4 So David sent messengers to get
her, and she came to him, and he
lay with her. (Now she was purifying herself after her period.) Then
she returned to her house. 5 The
woman conceived; and she sent
and told David, "I am pregnant."
6 So David sent word to Joab,
"Send me Uriah the Hittite." And
Joab sent Uriah to David. 7 When

[r] 1 Chr 19.18 and some Gk Mss read *foot soldiers*

10.4 Isa 15.2; 20.4
10.6 Gen 34.30; 2 Sam 8.3, 5; Judg 18.28
10.8 1 Chr 19.9; Judg 11.3,5
10.12 Deut 31.6; 1 Cor 16.13; 1 Sam 3.18
10.13 1 Kings 20.13-21
10.16 2 Sam 8.3; 1 Chr 19.16
10.18 1 Chr 19.18; 2 Sam 8.6
11.1 1 Chr 20.1; 1 Kings 20.22, 26; 2 Sam 12.26-28
11.2 Deut 22.8; Mt 5.28
11.3 2 Sam 23.39
11.4 Lev 15.19, 28; 18.19
11.5 Lev 20.10

Uriah came to him, David asked
how Joab and the people fared, and
how the war was going. [8]Then David said to Uriah, "Go down to your
house, and wash your feet." Uriah
went out of the king's house, and
there followed him a present from
the king. [9]But Uriah slept at the
entrance of the king's house with
all the servants of his lord, and did
not go down to his house. [10]When
they told David, "Uriah did not go
down to his house," David said to
Uriah, "You have just come from a
journey. Why did you not go down
to your house?" [11]Uriah said to David, "The ark and Israel and Judah
remain in booths;[s] and my lord
Joab and the servants of my lord
are camping in the open field; shall
I then go to my house, to eat and to
drink, and to lie with my wife? As
you live, and as your soul lives, I
will not do such a thing." [12]Then
David said to Uriah, "Remain here
today also, and tomorrow I will
send you back." So Uriah remained
in Jerusalem that day. On the next
day, [13]David invited him to eat and
drink in his presence and made
him drunk; and in the evening he
went out to lie on his couch with
the servants of his lord, but he did
not go down to his house.

David Has Uriah Killed

14 In the morning David wrote a
letter to Joab, and sent it by the
hand of Uriah. [15]In the letter he
wrote, "Set Uriah in the forefront of
the hardest fighting, and then draw
back from him, so that he may be
struck down and die." [16]As Joab
was besieging the city, he assigned
Uriah to the place where he knew
there were valiant warriors. [17]The
men of the city came out and
fought with Joab; and some of the
servants of David among the people fell. Uriah the Hittite was killed
as well. [18]Then Joab sent and told
David all the news about the fighting; [19]and he instructed the messenger, "When you have finished
telling the king all the news about
the fighting, [20]then, if the king's
anger rises, and if he says to you,

11.8 Gen 43.24; Lk 7.44
11.10 2 Sam 7.2, 6; 20.6
11.13 v. 9
11.14 1 Kings 21.8-10
11.15 2 Sam 12.9
11.17 v. 21
11.21 Judg 9.50-54
11.26 Deut 34.8; 1 Sam 31.13
11.27 2 Sam 12.9; Ps 51.4,5
12.1 2 Sam 14.4-7; 1 Kings 20.35-40

'Why did you go so near the city to
fight? Did you not know that they
would shoot from the wall? [21]Who
killed Abimelech son of Jerubbaal?[t] Did not a woman throw an
upper millstone on him from the
wall, so that he died at Thebez?
Why did you go so near the wall?'
then you shall say, 'Your servant
Uriah the Hittite is dead too.' "

22 So the messenger went, and
came and told David all that Joab
had sent him to tell. [23]The messenger said to David, "The men gained
an advantage over us, and came out
against us in the field; but we drove
them back to the entrance of the
gate. [24]Then the archers shot at
your servants from the wall; some
of the king's servants are dead; and
your servant Uriah the Hittite is
dead also." [25]David said to the
messenger, "Thus you shall say to
Joab, 'Do not let this matter trouble you, for the sword devours now
one and now another; press your
attack on the city, and overthrow
it.' And encourage him."

26 When the wife of Uriah heard
that her husband was dead, she
made lamentation for him. [27]When
the mourning was over, David sent
and brought her to his house, and
she became his wife, and bore him
a son.

Nathan Condemns David

But the thing that David had
12 done displeased the LORD,
[1]and the LORD sent Nathan
to David. He came to him, and said
to him, "There were two men in a
certain city, the one rich and the
other poor. [2]The rich man had very
many flocks and herds; [3]but the
poor man had nothing but one little ewe lamb, which he had bought.
He brought it up, and it grew up
with him and with his children; it
used to eat of his meager fare, and
drink from his cup, and lie in his
bosom, and it was like a daughter
to him. [4]Now there came a traveler
to the rich man, and he was loath
to take one of his own flock or herd

[s] Or *at Succoth* [t] Gk Syr Judg 7.1: Heb *Jerubbesheth*

to prepare for the wayfarer who had
come to him, but he took the poor
man's lamb, and prepared that for
the guest who had come to him."
5 Then David's anger was greatly
kindled against the man. He said to
Nathan, "As the LORD lives, the
man who has done this deserves to
die; 6 he shall restore the lamb four-
fold, because he did this thing, and
because he had no pity."

7 Nathan said to David, "You are
the man! Thus says the LORD, the
God of Israel: I anointed you king
over Israel, and I rescued you
from the hand of Saul; 8 I gave you
your master's house, and your master's wives into your bosom, and
gave you the house of Israel and of
Judah; and if that had been too little, I would have added as much
more. 9 Why have you despised the
word of the LORD, to do what is evil
in his sight? You have struck down
Uriah the Hittite with the sword,
and have taken his wife to be your
wife, and have killed him with the
sword of the Ammonites. 10 Now
therefore the sword shall never depart from your house, for you have
despised me, and have taken the
wife of Uriah the Hittite to be your
wife. 11 Thus says the LORD: I will
raise up trouble against you from
within your own house; and I will
take your wives before your eyes,
and give them to your neighbor,
and he shall lie with your wives in
the sight of this very sun. 12 For you
did it secretly; but I will do this
thing before all Israel, and before
the sun." 13 David said to Nathan,
"I have sinned against the LORD."
Nathan said to David, "Now the
LORD has put away your sin; you
shall not die. 14 Nevertheless, because by this deed you have utterly
scorned the LORD,[u] the child that is
born to you shall die." 15 Then Nathan went to his house.

Bathsheba's Child Dies

The LORD struck the child that
Uriah's wife bore to David, and it
became very ill. 16 David therefore
pleaded with God for the child; David fasted, and went in and lay all
night on the ground. 17 The elders
of his house stood beside him,
urging him to rise from the ground;
but he would not, nor did he eat
food with them. 18 On the seventh
day the child died. And the servants of David were afraid to tell
him that the child was dead; for
they said, "While the child was still
alive, we spoke to him, and he did
not listen to us; how then can we
tell him the child is dead? He may
do himself some harm." 19 But
when David saw that his servants
were whispering together, he perceived that the child was dead; and
David said to his servants, "Is the
child dead?" They said, "He is
dead."

20 Then David rose from the
ground, washed, anointed himself,
and changed his clothes. He went
into the house of the LORD, and
worshiped; he then went to his own
house; and when he asked, they set
food before him and he ate. 21 Then
his servants said to him, "What is
this thing that you have done? You
fasted and wept for the child while
it was alive; but when the child
died, you rose and ate food." 22 He
said, "While the child was still
alive, I fasted and wept; for I said,
'Who knows? The LORD may be gracious to me, and the child may
live.' 23 But now he is dead; why
should I fast? Can I bring him back
again? I shall go to him, but he will
not return to me."

Solomon Is Born

24 Then David consoled his wife
Bathsheba, and went to her, and
lay with her; and she bore a son,
and he named him Solomon. The
LORD loved him, 25 and sent a message by the prophet Nathan; so he
named him Jedidiah,[v] because of
the LORD.

The Ammonites Crushed

26 Now Joab fought against
Rabbah of the Ammonites, and
took the royal city. 27 Joab sent

12.5 1 Kings 20.39, 41
12.6 Ex 22.1; Lk 19.8
12.7 1 Kings 20.42; 1 Sam 16.13
12.9 1 Sam 15.19; 2 Sam 11.15-17, 27
12.10 2 Sam 13.28; 18.14; 1 Kings 2.25
12.11 Deut 28.30; 2 Sam 16.22
12.12 2 Sam 11.4-15; 16.22
12.13 1 Sam 15.24; 2 Sam 24.10; Prov 28.13; Mic 7.18
12.14 Isa 52.5; Rom 2.24
12.15 1 Sam 25.38
12.16 2 Sam 13.31
12.20 Job 1.20
12.22 Isa 38.1,5; Jon 3.9
12.23 Gen 37.35; Job 7.8-10
12.24 Mt 1.6; 1 Chr 22.9
12.26 1 Chr 20.1-3

[u] Ancient scribal tradition: Compare 1 Sam 25.22 note: Heb *scorned the enemies of the* LORD [v] That is *Beloved of the* LORD

messengers to David, and said, "I
have fought against Rabbah; moreover, I have taken the water city.
28 Now, then, gather the rest of the
people together, and encamp
against the city, and take it; or I
myself will take the city, and it will
be called by my name." 29 So David
gathered all the people together
and went to Rabbah, and fought
against it and took it. 30 He took the
crown of Milcom[w] from his head;
the weight of it was a talent of gold,
and in it was a precious stone; and
it was placed on David's head. He
also brought forth the spoil of the
city, a very great amount. 31 He
brought out the people who were in
it, and set them to work with saws
and iron picks and iron axes, or
sent them to the brickworks. Thus
he did to all the cities of the Ammonites. Then David and all the
people returned to Jerusalem.

Amnon and Tamar

13 Some time passed. David's
son Absalom had a beauti-
ful sister whose name was Tamar;
and David's son Amnon fell in love
with her. 2 Amnon was so tormented that he made himself ill because
of his sister Tamar, for she was a
virgin and it seemed impossible to
Amnon to do anything to her. 3 But
Amnon had a friend whose name
was Jonadab, the son of David's
brother Shimeah; and Jonadab was
a very crafty man. 4 He said to him,
"O son of the king, why are you so
haggard morning after morning?
Will you not tell me?" Amnon said
to him, "I love Tamar, my brother
Absalom's sister." 5 Jonadab said
to him, "Lie down on your bed, and
pretend to be ill; and when your father comes to see you, say to him,
'Let my sister Tamar come and give
me something to eat, and prepare
the food in my sight, so that I may
see it and eat it from her hand.' "
6 So Amnon lay down, and pretended to be ill; and when the king
came to see him, Amnon said to
the king, "Please let my sister Tamar come and make a couple of
cakes in my sight, so that I may eat
from her hand."
7 Then David sent home to Tamar, saying, "Go to your brother
Amnon's house, and prepare food
for him." 8 So Tamar went to her
brother Amnon's house, where he
was lying down. She took dough,
kneaded it, made cakes in his
sight, and baked the cakes. 9 Then
she took the pan and set them[x] out
before him, but he refused to eat.
Amnon said, "Send out everyone
from me." So everyone went out
from him. 10 Then Amnon said to
Tamar, "Bring the food into the
chamber, so that I may eat from
your hand." So Tamar took the
cakes she had made, and brought
them into the chamber to Amnon
her brother. 11 But when she
brought them near him to eat, he
took hold of her, and said to her,
"Come, lie with me, my sister."
12 She answered him, "No, my
brother, do not force me; for such a
thing is not done in Israel; do not
do anything so vile! 13 As for me,
where could I carry my shame? And
as for you, you would be as one of
the scoundrels in Israel. Now
therefore, I beg you, speak to the
king; for he will not withhold me
from you." 14 But he would not listen to her; and being stronger than
she, he forced her and lay with her.
15 Then Amnon was seized with
a very great loathing for her; indeed, his loathing was even greater
than the lust he had felt for her.
Amnon said to her, "Get out!"
16 But she said to him, "No, my
brother;[y] for this wrong in sending
me away is greater than the other
that you did to me." But he would
not listen to her. 17 He called the
young man who served him and
said, "Put this woman out of my
presence, and bolt the door after
her." 18 (Now she was wearing a
long robe with sleeves; for this is
how the virgin daughters of the
king were clothed in earlier

12.30 1 Chr 20.2
13.1 2 Sam 3.2, 3; 1 Chr 3.9
13.3 1 Sam 16.9
13.6 Gen 18.6
13.9 Gen 45.1
13.11 Gen 39.12
13.12 Lev 20.17; Judg 19.23; 20.6
13.13 Gen 20.12; Lev 18.9,11
13.14 Deut 22.25
13.18 Gen 37.3; Judg 5.30

[w] Gk See 1 Kings 11.5, 33: Heb *their kings*
[x] Heb *and poured* [y] Cn Compare Gk Vg: Meaning of Heb uncertain

times.[z]) So his servant put her out,
and bolted the door after her. 19 But
Tamar put ashes on her head, and
tore the long robe that she was
wearing; she put her hand on her
head, and went away, crying aloud
as she went.
20 Her brother Absalom said to
her, "Has Amnon your brother
been with you? Be quiet for now,
my sister; he is your brother; do not
take this to heart." So Tamar remained, a desolate woman, in her
brother Absalom's house. 21 When
King David heard of all these
things, he became very angry, but
he would not punish his son Amnon, because he loved him, for he
was his firstborn.[a] 22 But Absalom
spoke to Amnon neither good nor
bad; for Absalom hated Amnon,
because he had raped his sister Tamar.

Absalom Avenges the Violation of His Sister

23 After two full years Absalom
had sheepshearers at Baal-hazor,
which is near Ephraim, and Absalom invited all the king's sons.
24 Absalom came to the king, and
said, "Your servant has sheepshearers; will the king and his servants please go with your servant?"
25 But the king said to Absalom,
"No, my son, let us not all go, or
else we will be burdensome to
you." He pressed him, but he
would not go but gave him his
blessing. 26 Then Absalom said, "If
not, please let my brother Amnon
go with us." The king said to him,
"Why should he go with you?"
27 But Absalom pressed him until
he let Amnon and all the king's
sons go with him. Absalom made a
feast like a king's feast.[b] 28 Then
Absalom commanded his servants,
"Watch when Amnon's heart is
merry with wine, and when I say to
you, 'Strike Amnon,' then kill him.
Do not be afraid; have I not myself
commanded you? Be courageous
and valiant." 29 So the servants of
Absalom did to Amnon as Absalom
had commanded. Then all the
king's sons rose, and each mounted his mule and fled.
30 While they were on the way,
the report came to David that Absalom had killed all the king's
sons, and not one of them was left.
31 The king rose, tore his garments,
and lay on the ground; and all his
servants who were standing by tore
their garments. 32 But Jonadab, the
son of David's brother Shimeah,
said, "Let not my lord suppose that
they have killed all the young men
the king's sons; Amnon alone is
dead. This has been determined by
Absalom from the day Amnon[c]
raped his sister Tamar. 33 Now
therefore, do not let my lord the
king take it to heart, as if all the
king's sons were dead; for Amnon
alone is dead."
34 But Absalom fled. When the
young man who kept watch looked
up, he saw many people coming
from the Horonaim road[d] by the
side of the mountain. 35 Jonadab
said to the king, "See, the king's
sons have come; as your servant
said, so it has come about." 36 As
soon as he had finished speaking,
the king's sons arrived, and raised
their voices and wept; and the king
and all his servants also wept very
bitterly.
37 But Absalom fled, and went
to Talmai son of Ammihud, king of
Geshur. David mourned for his son
day after day. 38 Absalom, having
fled to Geshur, stayed there three
years. 39 And the heart of[e] the king
went out, yearning for Absalom; for
he was now consoled over the
death of Amnon.

Absalom Returns to Jerusalem

14 Now Joab son of Zeruiah
perceived that the king's
mind was on Absalom. 2 Joab sent
to Tekoa and brought from there a
wise woman. He said to her, "Pretend to be a mourner; put on
mourning garments, do not anoint

13.19 1 Sam 4.12; 2 Sam 1.2; Jer 2.37
13.20 2 Sam 14.24
13.22 Gen 31.24; Lev 19.17, 18
13.28 Judg 19.6,9, 22; 1 Sam 25.36
13.29 2 Sam 18.9; 1 Kings 1.33, 38
13.31 2 Sam 1.11; 12.16
13.32 v. 3
13.33 2 Sam 19.19
13.34 vv. 37,38; 2 Sam 18.24
13.37 v. 34; 2 Sam 3.3; 14.23,32
13.39 2 Sam 12.19-23
14.1 2 Sam 13.39
14.2 2 Chr 11.6; 1 Kings 20.35-43; 2 Sam 12.20

[z] Cn: Heb *were clothed in robes* [a] Q Ms Gk: MT lacks *but he would not punish . . . firstborn* [b] Gk Compare Q Ms: MT lacks *Absalom made a feast like a king's feast* [c] Heb *he* [d] Cn Compare Gk: Heb *the road behind him* [e] Q Ms Gk: MT *And David*

yourself with oil, but behave like a
woman who has been mourning
many days for the dead. 3 Go to the
king and speak to him as follows."
And Joab put the words into her
mouth.
4 When the woman of Tekoa
came to the king, she fell on her
face to the ground and did obeisance, and said, "Help, O king!"
5 The king asked her, "What is your
trouble?" She answered, "Alas, I
am a widow; my husband is dead.
6 Your servant had two sons, and
they fought with one another in the
field; there was no one to part
them, and one struck the other and
killed him. 7 Now the whole family
has risen against your servant.
They say, 'Give up the man who
struck his brother, so that we may
kill him for the life of his brother
whom he murdered, even if we destroy the heir as well.' Thus they
would quench my one remaining
ember, and leave to my husband
neither name nor remnant on the
face of the earth."
8 Then the king said to the
woman, "Go to your house, and I
will give orders concerning you."
9 The woman of Tekoa said to the
king, "On me be the guilt, my lord
the king, and on my father's house;
let the king and his throne be guiltless." 10 The king said, "If anyone
says anything to you, bring him to
me, and he shall never touch you
again." 11 Then she said, "Please,
may the king keep the LORD your
God in mind, so that the avenger of
blood may kill no more, and my son
not be destroyed." He said, "As the
LORD lives, not one hair of your son
shall fall to the ground."
12 Then the woman said,
"Please let your servant speak a
word to my lord the king." He said,
"Speak." 13 The woman said, "Why
then have you planned such a thing
against the people of God? For in
giving this decision the king convicts himself, inasmuch as the king
does not bring his banished one
home again. 14 We must all die; we
are like water spilled on the
ground, which cannot be gathered

14.3 v. 19
14.4 2 Sam 1.2; 2 Kings 6.26-28
14.5 2 Sam 12.1-7
14.7 Num 35.19; Deut 19.12; Mt 21.38
14.9 1 Sam 25.24; Mt 27.25; 1 Kings 2.33
14.11 Num 35.19; 1 Sam 14.45
14.13 2 Sam 12.7; 1 Kings 20.40-42; 2 Sam 13.37, 38
14.14 Job 34.15; Heb 9.27; Num 35.15, 25,28
14.17 v. 20; 2 Sam 19.27
14.19 v. 3
14.20 v. 17; 2 Sam 19.27
14.23 2 Sam 13.37, 38
14.24 2 Sam 3.13

up. But God will not take away a
life; he will devise plans so as not to
keep an outcast banished forever
from his presence.[f] 15 Now I have
come to say this to my lord the king
because the people have made me
afraid; your servant thought, 'I will
speak to the king; it may be that
the king will perform the request of
his servant. 16 For the king will
hear, and deliver his servant from
the hand of the man who would cut
both me and my son off from the
heritage of God.' 17 Your servant
thought, 'The word of my lord the
king will set me at rest'; for my lord
the king is like the angel of God,
discerning good and evil. The LORD
your God be with you!"
18 Then the king answered the
woman, "Do not withhold from me
anything I ask you." The woman
said, "Let my lord the king speak."
19 The king said, "Is the hand of
Joab with you in all this?" The
woman answered and said, "As
surely as you live, my lord the king,
one cannot turn right or left from
anything that my lord the king has
said. For it was your servant Joab
who commanded me; it was he who
put all these words into the mouth
of your servant. 20 In order to
change the course of affairs your
servant Joab did this. But my lord
has wisdom like the wisdom of the
angel of God to know all things that
are on the earth."
21 Then the king said to Joab,
"Very well, I grant this; go, bring
back the young man Absalom."
22 Joab prostrated himself with his
face to the ground and did obeisance, and blessed the king; and
Joab said, "Today your servant
knows that I have found favor in
your sight, my lord the king, in that
the king has granted the request of
his servant." 23 So Joab set off, went
to Geshur, and brought Absalom to
Jerusalem. 24 The king said, "Let
him go to his own house; he is not
to come into my presence." So Absalom went to his own house, and

[f] Meaning of Heb uncertain

did not come into the king's presence.

David Forgives Absalom

25 Now in all Israel there was no
one to be praised so much for his
beauty as Absalom; from the sole
of his foot to the crown of his head
there was no blemish in him.
26 When he cut the hair of his head
(for at the end of every year he used
to cut it; when it was heavy on him,
he cut it), he weighed the hair of
his head, two hundred shekels by
the king's weight. 27 There were
born to Absalom three sons, and
one daughter whose name was Tamar; she was a beautiful woman.
28 So Absalom lived two full
years in Jerusalem, without coming into the king's presence.
29 Then Absalom sent for Joab to
send him to the king; but Joab
would not come to him. He sent a
second time, but Joab would not
come. 30 Then he said to his servants, "Look, Joab's field is next to
mine, and he has barley there; go
and set it on fire." So Absalom's
servants set the field on fire.
31 Then Joab rose and went to Absalom at his house, and said to
him, "Why have your servants set
my field on fire?" 32 Absalom answered Joab, "Look, I sent word to
you: Come here, that I may send
you to the king with the question,
'Why have I come from Geshur? It
would be better for me to be there
still.' Now let me go into the king's
presence; if there is guilt in me, let
him kill me!" 33 Then Joab went to
the king and told him; and he summoned Absalom. So he came to the
king and prostrated himself with
his face to the ground before the
king; and the king kissed Absalom.

Absalom Usurps the Throne

15 After this Absalom got
himself a chariot and
horses, and fifty men to run ahead
of him. 2 Absalom used to rise early
and stand beside the road into the
gate; and when anyone brought a
suit before the king for judgment,
Absalom would call out and say,
"From what city are you?" When
the person said, "Your servant is of
such and such a tribe in Israel,"
3 Absalom would say, "See, your
claims are good and right; but there
is no one deputed by the king to
hear you." 4 Absalom said moreover, "If only I were judge in the
land! Then all who had a suit or
cause might come to me, and I
would give them justice." 5 Whenever people came near to do obeisance to him, he would put out his
hand and take hold of them, and
kiss them. 6 Thus Absalom did to
every Israelite who came to the
king for judgment; so Absalom
stole the hearts of the people of Israel.

7 At the end of four[g] years Absalom said to the king, "Please let
me go to Hebron and pay the vow
that I have made to the LORD. 8 For
your servant made a vow while I
lived at Geshur in Aram: If the LORD
will indeed bring me back to Jerusalem, then I will worship the LORD
in Hebron."[h] 9 The king said to
him, "Go in peace." So he got up,
and went to Hebron. 10 But Absalom sent secret messengers
throughout all the tribes of Israel,
saying, "As soon as you hear the
sound of the trumpet, then shout:
Absalom has become king at Hebron!" 11 Two hundred men from
Jerusalem went with Absalom;
they were invited guests, and they
went in their innocence, knowing
nothing of the matter. 12 While Absalom was offering the sacrifices,
he sent for[i] Ahithophel the Gilonite, David's counselor, from his
city Giloh. The conspiracy grew in
strength, and the people with Absalom kept increasing.

David Flees from Jerusalem

13 A messenger came to David,
saying, "The hearts of the Israelites
have gone after Absalom." 14 Then
David said to all his officials who
were with him at Jerusalem, "Get
up! Let us flee, or there will be no
escape for us from Absalom. Hurry,

14.25 Isa 1.6
14.26 Ezek 44.20
14.27 2 Sam 18.18
14.28 v. 24
14.32 1 Sam 20.8
14.33 Gen 33.4; Lk 15.20
15.1 2 Sam 12.11; 1 Kings 1.5
15.2 2 Sam 19.8
15.4 Judg 9.29
15.6 Rom 16.18
15.7ff 2 Sam 3.2, 3
15.8 2 Sam 13.37, 38; Gen 28.20, 21
15.11 1 Sam 9.13; 22.15
15.12 v. 31; Josh 15.51; Ps 3.1
15.13 v. 6; Judg 9.3
15.14 2 Sam 12.11; 19.9

[g] Gk Syr: Heb *forty* [h] Gk Mss: Heb lacks *in Hebron* [i] Or *he sent*

or he will soon overtake us, and
bring disaster down upon us, and
attack the city with the edge of the
sword." 15 The king's officials said
to the king, "Your servants are
ready to do whatever our lord the
king decides." 16 So the king left,
followed by all his household, except ten concubines whom he left
behind to look after the house.
17 The king left, followed by all the
people; and they stopped at the
last house. 18 All his officials
passed by him; and all the Cherethites, and all the Pelethites, and all
the six hundred Gittites who had
followed him from Gath, passed on
before the king.

19 Then the king said to Ittai
the Gittite, "Why are you also coming with us? Go back, and stay with
the king; for you are a foreigner,
and also an exile from your home.
20 You came only yesterday, and
shall I today make you wander
about with us, while I go wherever
I can? Go back, and take your kinsfolk with you; and may the LORD
show[j] steadfast love and faithfulness to you." 21 But Ittai answered
the king, "As the LORD lives, and as
my lord the king lives, wherever my
lord the king may be, whether for
death or for life, there also your servant will be." 22 David said to Ittai,
"Go then, march on." So Ittai the
Gittite marched on, with all his
men and all the little ones who
were with him. 23 The whole country wept aloud as all the people
passed by; the king crossed the
Wadi Kidron, and all the people
moved on toward the wilderness.

24 Abiathar came up, and Za-
dok also, with all the Levites, carrying the ark of the covenant of God.
They set down the ark of God, until
the people had all passed out of the
city. 25 Then the king said to Zadok,
"Carry the ark of God back into the
city. If I find favor in the eyes of the
LORD, he will bring me back and let
me see both it and the place where
it stays. 26 But if he says, 'I take no
pleasure in you,' here I am, let him
do to me what seems good to him."
27 The king also said to the priest
Zadok, "Look,[k] go back to the city
in peace, you and Abiathar,[l] with
your two sons, Ahimaaz your son,
and Jonathan son of Abiathar.
28 See, I will wait at the fords of the
wilderness until word comes from
you to inform me." 29 So Zadok and
Abiathar carried the ark of God
back to Jerusalem, and they remained there.

30 But David went up the ascent
of the Mount of Olives, weeping as
he went, with his head covered and
walking barefoot; and all the people who were with him covered
their heads and went up, weeping
as they went. 31 David was told that
Ahithophel was among the conspirators with Absalom. And David
said, "O LORD, I pray you, turn the
counsel of Ahithophel into foolishness."

Hushai Becomes David's Spy

32 When David came to the
summit, where God was worshiped, Hushai the Archite came to
meet him with his coat torn and
earth on his head. 33 David said to
him, "If you go on with me, you will
be a burden to me. 34 But if you return to the city and say to Absalom,
'I will be your servant, O king; as I
have been your father's servant in
time past, so now I will be your servant,' then you will defeat for me
the counsel of Ahithophel. 35 The
priests Zadok and Abiathar will be
with you there. So whatever you
hear from the king's house, tell it
to the priests Zadok and Abiathar.
36 Their two sons are with them
there, Zadok's son Ahimaaz and
Abiathar's son Jonathan; and by
them you shall report to me everything you hear." 37 So Hushai, David's friend, came into the city, just
as Absalom was entering Jerusalem.

David's Adversaries

16 When David had passed a
little beyond the summit,
Ziba the servant of Mephibosheth[m]

15.16 2 Sam 16.21, 22 **15.18** 2 Sam 8.18 **15.19** 2 Sam 18.2 **15.20** 1 Sam 23.13 **15.21** Ruth 1.16, 17 **15.24** 2 Sam 8.17; Num 4.15; 1 Sam 22.20 **15.25** Ps 43.3; Jer 25.30 **15.26** 2 Sam 22.20; 1 Kings 10.9; 1 Sam 3.18 **15.27** 1 Sam 9.6-9; 2 Sam 17.17 **15.28** 2 Sam 17.16 **15.30** Esther 6.12; 2 Sam 19.4; Isa 20.2-4; Ps 126.6 **15.31** v. 12; 2 Sam 16.23; 17.14,23 **15.32** Josh 16.2; 2 Sam 1.2 **15.33** 2 Sam 19.35 **15.34** 2 Sam 16.19 **15.35** 2 Sam 17.15, 16 **15.36** v. 27; 2 Sam 17.17 **15.37** 2 Sam 16.16, 17; 1 Chr 27.33 **16.1** 2 Sam 15.32; 9.2-13

[j] Gk Compare 2.6: Heb lacks *may the LORD show* [k] Gk: Heb *Are you a seer* or *Do you see?* [l] Cn: Heb lacks *and Abiathar* [m] Or *Merib-baal*: See 4.4 note

met him, with a couple of donkeys
saddled, carrying two hundred
loaves of bread, one hundred bunch-
es of raisins, one hundred of
summer fruits, and one skin of
wine. 2 The king said to Ziba, "Why
have you brought these?" Ziba answered, "The donkeys are for the
king's household to ride, the bread
and summer fruit for the young
men to eat, and the wine is for
those to drink who faint in the wilderness." 3 The king said, "And
where is your master's son?" Ziba
said to the king, "He remains in Jerusalem; for he said, 'Today the
house of Israel will give me back
my grandfather's kingdom.' "
4 Then the king said to Ziba, "All
that belonged to Mephibosheth[n] is
now yours." Ziba said, "I do obeisance; let me find favor in your
sight, my lord the king."

Shimei Curses David

5 When King David came to Bahurim, a man of the family of the
house of Saul came out whose
name was Shimei son of Gera; he
came out cursing. 6 He threw
stones at David and at all the servants of King David; now all the
people and all the warriors were on
his right and on his left. 7 Shimei
shouted while he cursed, "Out!
Out! Murderer! Scoundrel! 8 The
LORD has avenged on all of you the
blood of the house of Saul, in
whose place you have reigned; and
the LORD has given the kingdom
into the hand of your son Absalom.
See, disaster has overtaken you; for
you are a man of blood."

9 Then Abishai son of Zeruiah
said to the king, "Why should this
dead dog curse my lord the king?
Let me go over and take off his
head." 10 But the king said, "What
have I to do with you, you sons of
Zeruiah? If he is cursing because
the LORD has said to him, 'Curse
David,' who then shall say, 'Why
have you done so?' " 11 David said
to Abishai and to all his servants,
"My own son seeks my life; how
much more now may this Benjaminite! Let him alone, and let him
curse; for the LORD has bidden him.
12 It may be that the LORD will look
on my distress,[o] and the LORD will
repay me with good for this cursing
of me today." 13 So David and his
men went on the road, while Shimei went along on the hillside opposite him and cursed as he went,
throwing stones and flinging dust
at him. 14 The king and all the people who were with him arrived weary at the Jordan;[p] and there he refreshed himself.

The Counsel of Ahithophel

15 Now Absalom and all the Israelites[q] came to Jerusalem;
Ahithophel was with him. 16 When
Hushai the Archite, David's friend,
came to Absalom, Hushai said to
Absalom, "Long live the king! Long
live the king!" 17 Absalom said to
Hushai, "Is this your loyalty to your
friend? Why did you not go with
your friend?" 18 Hushai said to Absalom, "No; but the one whom the
LORD and this people and all the Israelites have chosen, his I will be,
and with him I will remain. 19 Moreover, whom should I serve? Should
it not be his son? Just as I have
served your father, so I will serve
you."

20 Then Absalom said to Ahithophel, "Give us your counsel; what
shall we do?" 21 Ahithophel said to
Absalom, "Go in to your father's
concubines, the ones he has left to
look after the house; and all Israel
will hear that you have made yourself odious to your father, and the
hands of all who are with you will
be strengthened." 22 So they
pitched a tent for Absalom upon
the roof; and Absalom went in to
his father's concubines in the sight
of all Israel. 23 Now in those days
the counsel that Ahithophel gave
was as if one consulted the oracle[r]
of God; so all the counsel of Ahithophel was esteemed, both by David
and by Absalom.

16.2 2 Sam 17.29
16.3 2 Sam 9.9, 10; 19.26,27
16.5 2 Sam 3.16-18; 19.16-23; 1 Kings 2.8
16.7 2 Sam 12.9
16.8 2 Sam 21.1-9
16.9 2 Sam 19.21; 9.8; Ex 22.28
16.10 2 Sam 19.22; 1 Pet 2.23; 2 Kings 18.25; Rom 9.20
16.11 2 Sam 12.11; Gen 45.5
16.12 Rom 8.28
16.15 2 Sam 15.37
16.16 2 Sam 15.37
16.17 2 Sam 19.25
16.19 2 Sam 15.34
16.21 2 Sam 15.16; 1 Sam 13.4; 2 Sam 2.7
16.22 2 Sam 12.11, 12
16.23 2 Sam 15.12

[n] Or *Merib-baal*: See 4.4 note [o] Gk Vg: Heb *iniquity* [p] Gk: Heb lacks *at the Jordan* [q] Gk: Heb *all the people, the men of Israel* [r] Heb *word*

17 Moreover Ahithophel said
to Absalom, "Let me
choose twelve thousand men, and I
will set out and pursue David tonight. 2 I will come upon him while
he is weary and discouraged, and
throw him into a panic; and all the
people who are with him will flee.
I will strike down only the king,
3 and I will bring all the people back
to you as a bride comes home to
her husband. You seek the life of
only one man,[s] and all the people
will be at peace." 4 The advice
pleased Absalom and all the elders
of Israel.

The Counsel of Hushai

5 Then Absalom said, "Call Hushai the Archite also, and let us
hear too what he has to say."
6 When Hushai came to Absalom,
Absalom said to him, "This is what
Ahithophel has said; shall we do as
he advises? If not, you tell us."
7 Then Hushai said to Absalom,
"This time the counsel that Ahithophel has given is not good." 8 Hushai continued, "You know that
your father and his men are warriors, and that they are enraged,
like a bear robbed of her cubs in
the field. Besides, your father is expert in war; he will not spend the
night with the troops. 9 Even now
he has hidden himself in one of the
pits, or in some other place. And
when some of our troops[t] fall at
the first attack, whoever hears it
will say, 'There has been a slaughter among the troops who follow
Absalom.' 10 Then even the valiant
warrior, whose heart is like the
heart of a lion, will utterly melt
with fear; for all Israel knows that
your father is a warrior, and that
those who are with him are valiant
warriors. 11 But my counsel is that
all Israel be gathered to you, from
Dan to Beer-sheba, like the sand by
the sea for multitude, and that you
go to battle in person. 12 So we shall
come upon him in whatever place
he may be found, and we shall light
on him as the dew falls on the
ground; and he will not survive, nor
will any of those with him. 13 If he
withdraws into a city, then all Israel will bring ropes to that city, and
we shall drag it into the valley, until not even a pebble is to be found
there." 14 Absalom and all the men
of Israel said, "The counsel of
Hushai the Archite is better than
the counsel of Ahithophel." For the
LORD had ordained to defeat the
good counsel of Ahithophel, so
that the LORD might bring ruin on
Absalom.

Hushai Warns David to Escape

15 Then Hushai said to the
priests Zadok and Abiathar, "Thus
and so did Ahithophel counsel Absalom and the elders of Israel; and
thus and so I have counseled.
16 Therefore send quickly and tell
David, 'Do not lodge tonight at the
fords of the wilderness, but by all
means cross over; otherwise the
king and all the people who are
with him will be swallowed up.' "
17 Jonathan and Ahimaaz were
waiting at En-rogel; a servant-girl
used to go and tell them, and they
would go and tell King David; for
they could not risk being seen entering the city. 18 But a boy saw
them, and told Absalom; so both of
them went away quickly, and came
to the house of a man at Bahurim,
who had a well in his courtyard;
and they went down into it. 19 The
man's wife took a covering,
stretched it over the well's mouth,
and spread out grain on it; and
nothing was known of it. 20 When
Absalom's servants came to the
woman at the house, they said,
"Where are Ahimaaz and Jonathan?" The woman said to them,
"They have crossed over the
brook[u] of water." And when they
had searched and could not find
them, they returned to Jerusalem.
21 After they had gone, the men
came up out of the well, and went
and told King David. They said to
David, "Go and cross the water
quickly; for thus and so has Ahithophel counseled against you." 22 So

17.2 2 Sam 16.14; 1 Kings 22.31
17.5 2 Sam 15.32-34
17.8 Hos 13.8; 1 Sam 16.18
17.10 Josh 2.11
17.14 2 Sam 15.31, 34
17.15 2 Sam 15.35
17.16 2 Sam 15.28
17.17 2 Sam 15.27, 36; Josh 15.7; 18.16
17.18 2 Sam 16.5
17.19 Josh 2.4-6
17.20 Josh 2.3-5; 1 Sam 19.12-17
17.21 vv. 15,16

[s] Gk: Heb *like the return of the whole (is) the man whom you seek* [t] Gk Mss: Heb *some of them* [u] Meaning of Heb uncertain

David and all the people who were
with him set out and crossed the
Jordan; by daybreak not one was
left who had not crossed the Jordan.
23 When Ahithophel saw that
his counsel was not followed, he
saddled his donkey and went off
home to his own city. He set his
house in order, and hanged himself; he died and was buried in the
tomb of his father.
24 Then David came to Mahanaim, while Absalom crossed the
Jordan with all the men of Israel.
25 Now Absalom had set Amasa
over the army in the place of Joab.
Amasa was the son of a man named
Ithra the Ishmaelite,[v] who had
married Abigal daughter of Nahash, sister of Zeruiah, Joab's
mother. 26 The Israelites and Absalom encamped in the land of Gilead.
27 When David came to Mahanaim, Shobi son of Nahash from
Rabbah of the Ammonites, and
Machir son of Ammiel from Lo-
debar, and Barzillai the Gileadite
from Rogelim, 28 brought beds, basins, and earthen vessels, wheat,
barley, meal, parched grain, beans
and lentils,[w] 29 honey and curds,
sheep, and cheese from the herd,
for David and the people with him
to eat; for they said, "The troops
are hungry and weary and thirsty in
the wilderness."

The Defeat and Death of Absalom

18 Then David mustered the
men who were with him,
and set over them commanders of
thousands and commanders of
hundreds. 2 And David divided the
army into three groups:[x] one third
under the command of Joab, one
third under the command of Abishai son of Zeruiah, Joab's brother,
and one third under the command
of Ittai the Gittite. The king said to
the men, "I myself will also go out
with you." 3 But the men said, "You
shall not go out. For if we flee, they
will not care about us. If half of us
die, they will not care about us. But
you are worth ten thousand of us;[y]
therefore it is better that you send
us help from the city." 4 The king
said to them, "Whatever seems
best to you I will do." So the king
stood at the side of the gate, while
all the army marched out by hundreds and by thousands. 5 The king
ordered Joab and Abishai and Ittai,
saying, "Deal gently for my sake
with the young man Absalom."
And all the people heard when the
king gave orders to all the commanders concerning Absalom.
6 So the army went out into the
field against Israel; and the battle
was fought in the forest of Ephraim. 7 The men of Israel were defeated there by the servants of David,
and the slaughter there was great
on that day, twenty thousand men.
8 The battle spread over the face of
all the country; and the forest
claimed more victims that day than
the sword.
9 Absalom happened to meet
the servants of David. Absalom was
riding on his mule, and the mule
went under the thick branches of a
great oak. His head caught fast in
the oak, and he was left hanging[z]
between heaven and earth, while
the mule that was under him went
on. 10 A man saw it, and told Joab,
"I saw Absalom hanging in an oak."
11 Joab said to the man who told
him, "What, you saw him! Why
then did you not strike him there to
the ground? I would have been glad
to give you ten pieces of silver and
a belt." 12 But the man said to Joab,
"Even if I felt in my hand the
weight of a thousand pieces of silver, I would not raise my hand
against the king's son; for in our
hearing the king commanded you
and Abishai and Ittai, saying: For
my sake protect the young man Absalom! 13 On the other hand, if I
had dealt treacherously against his
life[a] (and there is nothing hidden

17.23 2 Sam 15.12; 2 Kings 20.1; Mt 27.5
17.24 Gen 32.2; 2 Sam 2.8
17.25 2 Sam 19.13; 20.9-12
17.27 2 Sam 10.1, 2; 12.26,29; 19.31,32; 1 Kings 2.7
17.29 2 Sam 16.2
18.1 Ex 18.25; 1 Sam 22.7
18.2 1 Sam 11.11; 2 Sam 15.19
18.3 2 Sam 21.17
18.4 v. 24
18.5 v. 12
18.6 Josh 17.15, 18
18.9 2 Sam 14.26
18.12 v. 5

[v] 1 Chr 2.17: Heb *Israelite* [w] Heb *and lentils and parched grain* [x] Gk: Heb *sent forth the army* [y] Gk Vg Symmachus: Heb *for now there are ten thousand such as we* [z] Gk Syr Tg: Heb *was put* [a] Another reading is *at the risk of my life*

from the king), then you yourself
would have stood aloof." 14 Joab
said, "I will not waste time like this
with you." He took three spears in
his hand, and thrust them into the
heart of Absalom, while he was still
alive in the oak. 15 And ten young
men, Joab's armor-bearers, surrounded Absalom and struck him,
and killed him.

16 Then Joab sounded the
trumpet, and the troops came back
from pursuing Israel, for Joab restrained the troops. 17 They took
Absalom, threw him into a great pit
in the forest, and raised over him a
very great heap of stones. Meanwhile all the Israelites fled to their
homes. 18 Now Absalom in his lifetime had taken and set up for himself a pillar that is in the King's Valley, for he said, "I have no son to
keep my name in remembrance";
he called the pillar by his own
name. It is called Absalom's Monument to this day.

David Hears of Absalom's Death

19 Then Ahimaaz son of Zadok
said, "Let me run, and carry tidings
to the king that the LORD has delivered him from the power of his enemies." 20 Joab said to him, "You are
not to carry tidings today; you may
carry tidings another day, but today
you shall not do so, because the
king's son is dead." 21 Then Joab
said to a Cushite, "Go, tell the king
what you have seen." The Cushite
bowed before Joab, and ran.
22 Then Ahimaaz son of Zadok said
again to Joab, "Come what may, let
me also run after the Cushite." And
Joab said, "Why will you run, my
son, seeing that you have no reward[b] for the tidings?" 23 "Come
what may," he said, "I will run." So
he said to him, "Run." Then Ahimaaz ran by the way of the Plain, and
outran the Cushite.

24 Now David was sitting between the two gates. The sentinel
went up to the roof of the gate by
the wall, and when he looked up,
he saw a man running alone. 25 The
sentinel shouted and told the king.
The king said, "If he is alone, there
are tidings in his mouth." He kept
coming, and drew near. 26 Then the
sentinel saw another man running;
and the sentinel called to the gatekeeper and said, "See, another
man running alone!" The king said,
"He also is bringing tidings." 27 The
sentinel said, "I think the running
of the first one is like the running
of Ahimaaz son of Zadok." The king
said, "He is a good man, and comes
with good tidings."

28 Then Ahimaaz cried out to
the king, "All is well!" He prostrated himself before the king with his
face to the ground, and said,
"Blessed be the LORD your God,
who has delivered up the men who
raised their hand against my lord
the king." 29 The king said, "Is it
well with the young man Absalom?" Ahimaaz answered, "When
Joab sent your servant,[c] I saw a
great tumult, but I do not know
what it was." 30 The king said,
"Turn aside, and stand here." So he
turned aside, and stood still.

31 Then the Cushite came; and
the Cushite said, "Good tidings for
my lord the king! For the LORD has
vindicated you this day, delivering
you from the power of all who rose
up against you." 32 The king said to
the Cushite, "Is it well with the
young man Absalom?" The Cushite
answered, "May the enemies of my
lord the king, and all who rise up to
do you harm, be like that young
man."

David Mourns for Absalom

33 [d]The king was deeply moved,
and went up to the chamber over
the gate, and wept; and as he went,
he said, "O my son Absalom, my
son, my son Absalom! Would I had
died instead of you, O Absalom,
my son, my son!"

19 It was told Joab, "The king
is weeping and mourning
for Absalom." 2 So the victory that
day was turned into mourning for
all the troops; for the troops heard
that day, "The king is grieving for

18.14 2 Sam 14.30
18.16 2 Sam 2.28; 20.22
18.17 Josh 7.26; 8.29; 2 Sam 19.8
18.18 1 Sam 15.12; Gen 14.17; 2 Sam 14.27
18.19 2 Sam 15.36; v. 31
18.24 2 Sam 19.8; 13.34; 2 Kings 9.17
18.28 2 Sam 14.4; 1 Sam 25.23; 17.46
18.29 v. 22
18.31 v. 19; Judg 5.31
18.32 1 Sam 25.26
18.33 2 Sam 19.4; Ex 32.32; Rom 9.3
19.1 2 Sam 18.33

[b] Meaning of Heb uncertain
[c] Heb *the king's servant, your servant*
[d] Ch 19.1 in Heb

his son." 3 The troops stole into the city that day as soldiers steal in who are ashamed when they flee in battle. 4 The king covered his face, and the king cried with a loud voice, "O my son Absalom, O Absalom, my son, my son!" 5 Then Joab came into the house to the king, and said, "Today you have covered with shame the faces of all your officers who have saved your life today, and the lives of your sons and your daughters, and the lives of your wives and your concubines, 6 for love of those who hate you and for hatred of those who love you. You have made it clear today that commanders and officers are nothing to you; for I perceive that if Absalom were alive and all of us were dead today, then you would be pleased. 7 So go out at once and speak kindly to your servants; for I swear by the LORD, if you do not go, not a man will stay with you this night; and this will be worse for you than any disaster that has come upon you from your youth until now." 8 Then the king got up and took his seat in the gate. The troops were all told, "See, the king is sitting in the gate"; and all the troops came before the king.

David Recalled to Jerusalem

Meanwhile, all the Israelites had fled to their homes. 9 All the people were disputing throughout all the tribes of Israel, saying, "The king delivered us from the hand of our enemies, and saved us from the hand of the Philistines; and now he has fled out of the land because of Absalom. 10 But Absalom, whom we anointed over us, is dead in battle. Now therefore why do you say nothing about bringing the king back?"

11 King David sent this message to the priests Zadok and Abiathar, "Say to the elders of Judah, 'Why should you be the last to bring the king back to his house? The talk of all Israel has come to the king.[e] 12 You are my kin, you are my bone and my flesh; why then should you be the last to bring back the king?' 13 And say to Amasa, 'Are you not my bone and my flesh? So may God do to me, and more, if you are not the commander of my army from now on, in place of Joab.' " 14 Amasa[f] swayed the hearts of all the people of Judah as one, and they sent word to the king, "Return, both you and all your servants." 15 So the king came back to the Jordan; and Judah came to Gilgal to meet the king and to bring him over the Jordan.

16 Shimei son of Gera, the Benjaminite, from Bahurim, hurried to come down with the people of Judah to meet King David; 17 with him were a thousand people from Benjamin. And Ziba, the servant of the house of Saul, with his fifteen sons and his twenty servants, rushed down to the Jordan ahead of the king, 18 while the crossing was taking place,[g] to bring over the king's household, and to do his pleasure.

David's Mercy to Shimei

Shimei son of Gera fell down before the king, as he was about to cross the Jordan, 19 and said to the king, "May my lord not hold me guilty or remember how your servant did wrong on the day my lord the king left Jerusalem; may the king not bear it in mind. 20 For your servant knows that I have sinned; therefore, see, I have come this day, the first of all the house of Joseph to come down to meet my lord the king." 21 Abishai son of Zeruiah answered, "Shall not Shimei be put to death for this, because he cursed the LORD's anointed?" 22 But David said, "What have I to do with you, you sons of Zeruiah, that you should today become an adversary to me? Shall anyone be put to death in Israel this day? For do I not know that I am this day king over Israel?" 23 The king said to Shimei, "You shall not die." And the king gave him his oath.

19.4 2 Sam 15.30; 18.33
19.6 Mt 5.46
19.8 2 Sam 15.2; 18.4
19.9 2 Sam 8.1-14; 5.20; 15.14
19.12 2 Sam 5.1
19.13 2 Sam 17.25; 1 Kings 19.2; 8.16; vv. 5-7
19.14 Judg 20.1
19.15 Josh 5.9
19.16 2 Sam 16.5; 1 Kings 2.8
19.17 2 Sam 16.1, 2
19.19 1 Sam 22.15; 2 Sam 16.6-8; 13.33
19.20 2 Sam 16.5
19.21 2 Sam 16.7, 8; Ex 22.28
19.22 2 Sam 16.10; 1 Sam 11.13
19.23 1 Kings 2.8

[e] Gk: Heb *to the king, to his house*
[f] Heb *He* [g] Cn: Heb *the ford crossed*

David and Mephibosheth Meet

24 Mephibosheth[h] grandson of Saul came down to meet the king; he had not taken care of his feet, or trimmed his beard, or washed his clothes, from the day the king left until the day he came back in safety. 25 When he came from Jerusalem to meet the king, the king said to him, "Why did you not go with me, Mephibosheth?"[h] 26 He answered, "My lord, O king, my servant deceived me; for your servant said to him, 'Saddle a donkey for me,[i] so that I may ride on it and go with the king.' For your servant is lame. 27 He has slandered your servant to my lord the king. But my lord the king is like the angel of God; do therefore what seems good to you. 28 For all my father's house were doomed to death before my lord the king; but you set your servant among those who eat at your table. What further right have I, then, to appeal to the king?" 29 The king said to him, "Why speak any more of your affairs? I have decided: you and Ziba shall divide the land." 30 Mephibosheth[h] said to the king, "Let him take it all, since my lord the king has arrived home safely."

David's Kindness to Barzillai

31 Now Barzillai the Gileadite had come down from Rogelim; he went on with the king to the Jordan, to escort him over the Jordan. 32 Barzillai was a very aged man, eighty years old. He had provided the king with food while he stayed at Mahanaim, for he was a very wealthy man. 33 The king said to Barzillai, "Come over with me, and I will provide for you in Jerusalem at my side." 34 But Barzillai said to the king, "How many years have I still to live, that I should go up with the king to Jerusalem? 35 Today I am eighty years old; can I discern what is pleasant and what is not? Can your servant taste what he eats or what he drinks? Can I still listen to the voice of singing men and singing women? Why then should your servant be an added burden to my lord the king? 36 Your servant will go a little way over the Jordan with the king. Why should the king recompense me with such a reward? 37 Please let your servant return, so that I may die in my own town, near the graves of my father and my mother. But here is your servant Chimham; let him go over with my lord the king; and do for him whatever seems good to you." 38 The king answered, "Chimham shall go over with me, and I will do for him whatever seems good to you; and all that you desire of me I will do for you." 39 Then all the people crossed over the Jordan, and the king crossed over; the king kissed Barzillai and blessed him, and he returned to his own home. 40 The king went on to Gilgal, and Chimham went on with him; all the people of Judah, and also half the people of Israel, brought the king on his way.

41 Then all the people of Israel came to the king, and said to him, "Why have our kindred the people of Judah stolen you away, and brought the king and his household over the Jordan, and all David's men with him?" 42 All the people of Judah answered the people of Israel, "Because the king is near of kin to us. Why then are you angry over this matter? Have we eaten at all at the king's expense? Or has he given us any gift?" 43 But the people of Israel answered the people of Judah, "We have ten shares in the king, and in David also we have more than you. Why then did you despise us? Were we not the first to speak of bringing back our king?" But the words of the people of Judah were fiercer than the words of the people of Israel.

The Rebellion of Sheba

20 Now a scoundrel named Sheba son of Bichri, a Benjaminite, happened to be there. He sounded the trumpet and cried out,

19.24 2 Sam 9.6-10
19.25 2 Sam 16.17
19.26 2 Sam 9.3
19.27 2 Sam 16.3; 14.17,20
19.28 2 Sam 21.6-9; 9.7,10,13
19.31 1 Kings 2.7
19.32 1 Sam 17.27
19.35 Ps 90.10; Isa 5.11,12
19.37 v. 40; 1 Kings 2.7; Jer 41.17
19.39 Gen 31.55
19.41 v. 15
19.42 v. 12
19.43 1 Kings 11.30, 31
20.1 2 Sam 19.43; 1 Kings 12.16; 2 Chr 10.16

[h] Or *Merib-baal*: See 4.4 note [i] Gk Syr Vg: Heb *said, I will saddle a donkey for myself*

"We have no portion in
David,
no share in the son of Jesse!
Everyone to your tents,
O Israel!"
2 So all the people of Israel withdrew from David and followed Sheba son of Bichri; but the people of
Judah followed their king steadfastly from the Jordan to Jerusalem.
3 David came to his house at Jerusalem; and the king took the ten
concubines whom he had left to
look after the house, and put them
in a house under guard, and provided for them, but did not go in to
them. So they were shut up until
the day of their death, living as if in
widowhood.
4 Then the king said to Amasa,
"Call the men of Judah together to
me within three days, and be here
yourself." 5 So Amasa went to summon Judah; but he delayed beyond
the set time that had been appointed him. 6 David said to Abishai,
"Now Sheba son of Bichri will do
us more harm than Absalom; take
your lord's servants and pursue
him, or he will find fortified cities
for himself, and escape from us."
7 Joab's men went out after him,
along with the Cherethites, the
Pelethites, and all the warriors;
they went out from Jerusalem to
pursue Sheba son of Bichri. 8 When
they were at the large stone that is
in Gibeon, Amasa came to meet
them. Now Joab was wearing a soldier's garment and over it was a
belt with a sword in its sheath fastened at his waist; as he went forward it fell out. 9 Joab said to Amasa, "Is it well with you, my
brother?" And Joab took Amasa by
the beard with his right hand to
kiss him. 10 But Amasa did not notice the sword in Joab's hand; Joab
struck him in the belly so that his
entrails poured out on the ground,
and he died. He did not strike a
second blow.
Then Joab and his brother
Abishai pursued Sheba son of
Bichri. 11 And one of Joab's men
took his stand by Amasa, and said,
"Whoever favors Joab, and whoever
is for David, let him follow Joab."
12 Amasa lay wallowing in his blood
on the highway, and the man saw
that all the people were stopping.
Since he saw that all who came by
him were stopping, he carried Amasa from the highway into a field,
and threw a garment over him.
13 Once he was removed from the
highway, all the people went on after Joab to pursue Sheba son of
Bichri.
14 Sheba[j] passed through all
the tribes of Israel to Abel of Beth-
maacah;[k] and all the Bichrites[l]
assembled, and followed him inside. 15 Joab's forces[m] came and
besieged him in Abel of Beth-
maacah; they threw up a siege
ramp against the city, and it stood
against the rampart. Joab's forces
were battering the wall to break it
down. 16 Then a wise woman called
from the city, "Listen! Listen! Tell
Joab, 'Come here, I want to speak
to you.' " 17 He came near her; and
the woman said, "Are you Joab?"
He answered, "I am." Then she
said to him, "Listen to the words of
your servant." He answered, "I am
listening." 18 Then she said, "They
used to say in the old days, 'Let
them inquire at Abel'; and so they
would settle a matter. 19 I am one of
those who are peaceable and faithful in Israel; you seek to destroy a
city that is a mother in Israel; why
will you swallow up the heritage of
the LORD?" 20 Joab answered, "Far
be it from me, far be it, that I
should swallow up or destroy!
21 That is not the case! But a man of
the hill country of Ephraim, called
Sheba son of Bichri, has lifted up
his hand against King David; give
him up alone, and I will withdraw
from the city." The woman said to
Joab, "His head shall be thrown
over the wall to you." 22 Then the
woman went to all the people with
her wise plan. And they cut off the
head of Sheba son of Bichri, and
threw it out to Joab. So he blew the

20.3 2 Sam 15.16; 16.21,22
20.4 2 Sam 19.13
20.6 2 Sam 11.11; 1 Kings 1.33
20.7 2 Sam 8.18; 1 Kings 1.38; 2 Sam 15.18
20.9 Mt 26.49
20.10 2 Sam 2.23; 3.27; 1 Kings 2.5
20.15 1 Kings 15.20; 2 Kings 19.32
20.16 2 Sam 14.2
20.19 1 Sam 26.19; 2 Sam 21.3
20.21 v. 2
20.22 Eccl 9.13-16; v. 1

[j] Heb *He* [k] Compare 20.15: Heb *and Beth-maacah* [l] Compare Gk Vg: Heb *Berites* [m] Heb *They*

trumpet, and they dispersed from the city, and all went to their homes, while Joab returned to Jerusalem to the king.

23 Now Joab was in command of all the army of Israel;[n] Benaiah son of Jehoiada was in command of the Cherethites and the Pelethites; 24 Adoram was in charge of the forced labor; Jehoshaphat son of Ahilud was the recorder; 25 Sheva was secretary; Zadok and Abiathar were priests; 26 and Ira the Jairite was also David's priest.

David Avenges the Gibeonites

21 Now there was a famine in the days of David for three years, year after year; and David inquired of the LORD. The LORD said, "There is bloodguilt on Saul and on his house, because he put the Gibeonites to death." 2 So the king called the Gibeonites and spoke to them. (Now the Gibeonites were not of the people of Israel, but of the remnant of the Amorites; although the people of Israel had sworn to spare them, Saul had tried to wipe them out in his zeal for the people of Israel and Judah.) 3 David said to the Gibeonites, "What shall I do for you? How shall I make expiation, that you may bless the heritage of the LORD?" 4 The Gibeonites said to him, "It is not a matter of silver or gold between us and Saul or his house; neither is it for us to put anyone to death in Israel." He said, "What do you say that I should do for you?" 5 They said to the king, "The man who consumed us and planned to destroy us, so that we should have no place in all the territory of Israel— 6 let seven of his sons be handed over to us, and we will impale them before the LORD at Gibeon on the mountain of the LORD."[o] The king said, "I will hand them over."

7 But the king spared Mephibosheth,[p] the son of Saul's son Jonathan, because of the oath of the LORD that was between them, between David and Jonathan son of Saul. 8 The king took the two sons of Rizpah daughter of Aiah, whom she bore to Saul, Armoni and Mephibosheth;[p] and the five sons of Merab[q] daughter of Saul, whom she bore to Adriel son of Barzillai the Meholathite; 9 he gave them into the hands of the Gibeonites, and they impaled them on the mountain before the LORD. The seven of them perished together. They were put to death in the first days of harvest, at the beginning of barley harvest.

10 Then Rizpah the daughter of Aiah took sackcloth, and spread it on a rock for herself, from the beginning of harvest until rain fell on them from the heavens; she did not allow the birds of the air to come on the bodies[r] by day, or the wild animals by night. 11 When David was told what Rizpah daughter of Aiah, the concubine of Saul, had done, 12 David went and took the bones of Saul and the bones of his son Jonathan from the people of Jabesh-gilead, who had stolen them from the public square of Beth-shan, where the Philistines had hung them up, on the day the Philistines killed Saul on Gilboa. 13 He brought up from there the bones of Saul and the bones of his son Jonathan; and they gathered the bones of those who had been impaled. 14 They buried the bones of Saul and of his son Jonathan in the land of Benjamin in Zela, in the tomb of his father Kish; they did all that the king commanded. After that, God heeded supplications for the land.

Exploits of David's Men

15 The Philistines went to war again with Israel, and David went down together with his servants. They fought against the Philistines, and David grew weary. 16 Ishbi-benob, one of the descendants of the giants, whose spear weighed three hundred shekels of bronze, and who was fitted out

20.23 2 Sam 8.16-18
20.25 2 Sam 8.17
20.26 2 Sam 23.38
21.2 Josh 9.3, 15-17
21.3 2 Sam 20.19
21.4 Num 35.31, 32
21.5 1 Sam 10.24, 26
21.7 2 Sam 4.4; 9.10; 1 Sam 18.3; 20.8,15; 23.18
21.8 2 Sam 3.7
21.10 v. 8; Deut 21.23; 1 Sam 17.44, 46
21.12 1 Sam 31.10-13
21.14 Josh 18.28; 7.26; 2 Sam 24.25

[n] Cn: Heb *Joab to all the army, Israel*
[o] Cn Compare Gk and 21.9: Heb *at Gibeah of Saul, the chosen of the LORD*
[p] Or *Merib-baal*: See 4.4 note
[q] Two Heb Mss Syr Compare Gk: MT *Michal*
[r] Heb *them*

with new weapons,[s] said he would
kill David. 17 But Abishai son of
Zeruiah came to his aid, and attacked the Philistine and killed
him. Then David's men swore to
him, "You shall not go out with us
to battle any longer, so that you do
not quench the lamp of Israel."
18 After this a battle took place
with the Philistines, at Gob; then
Sibbecai the Hushathite killed
Saph, who was one of the descendants of the giants. 19 Then there
was another battle with the Philistines at Gob; and Elhanan son of
Jaare-oregim, the Bethlehemite,
killed Goliath the Gittite, the shaft
of whose spear was like a weaver's
beam. 20 There was again war at
Gath, where there was a man of
great size, who had six fingers on
each hand, and six toes on each
foot, twenty-four in number; he too
was descended from the giants.
21 When he taunted Israel, Jonathan son of David's brother Shimei,
killed him. 22 These four were descended from the giants in Gath;
they fell by the hands of David and
his servants.

David's Song of Thanksgiving

22 David spoke to the LORD
the words of this song on
the day when the LORD delivered
him from the hand of all his enemies, and from the hand of Saul.
2 He said:

The LORD is my rock, my
fortress, and my
deliverer,
3 my God, my rock, in whom
I take refuge,
my shield and the horn of
my salvation,
my stronghold and my
refuge,
my savior; you save me
from violence.
4 I call upon the LORD, who is
worthy to be praised,
and I am saved from my
enemies.

5 For the waves of death
encompassed me,
the torrents of perdition
assailed me;
6 the cords of Sheol entangled
me,
the snares of death
confronted me.

7 In my distress I called upon
the LORD;
to my God I called.
From his temple he heard
my voice,
and my cry came to his
ears.

8 Then the earth reeled and
rocked;
the foundations of the
heavens trembled
and quaked, because he
was angry.
9 Smoke went up from his
nostrils,
and devouring fire from his
mouth;
glowing coals flamed forth
from him.
10 He bowed the heavens, and
came down;
thick darkness was under
his feet.
11 He rode on a cherub, and
flew;
he was seen upon the
wings of the wind.
12 He made darkness around
him a canopy,
thick clouds, a gathering of
water.
13 Out of the brightness before
him
coals of fire flamed forth.
14 The LORD thundered from
heaven;
the Most High uttered his
voice.
15 He sent out arrows, and
scattered them
—lightning, and routed
them.
16 Then the channels of the sea
were seen,
the foundations of the
world were laid bare
at the rebuke of the LORD,

21.17 2 Sam 18.3; 6.17
21.18 1 Chr 20.4; 11.29
21.19 1 Chr 20.5
21.20 1 Chr 20.6
21.21 see 1 Sam 16.9
21.22 1 Chr 20.8
22.1 Ex 15.1; Judg 5.1; Ps 18.2-50
22.2 Deut 32.4; Ps 31.3; 71.3; 91.2; 144.2
22.3 Heb 2.13; Gen 15.1; Lk 1.69; Ps 9.9; 14.6; Jer 16.19
22.4 Ps 48.1
22.5 Ps 93.4; Jon 2.3; Ps 69.14,15
22.6 Ps 116.3
22.7 Ps 116.4; 120.1; 34.6, 15
22.8 Judg 5.4; Ps 77.18; Job 26.11
22.9 Ps 97.3; Heb 12.29
22.10 Ex 19.16; 1 Kings 8.12; Ps 97.2
22.11 Ps 104.3
22.12 Ps 97.2
22.13 v. 9
22.14 1 Sam 2.10
22.16 Hab 3.11

[s] Heb *was belted anew*

at the blast of the breath
of his nostrils.
17 He reached from on high, he
took me,
he drew me out of mighty
waters.
18 He delivered me from my
strong enemy,
from those who hated me;
for they were too mighty
for me.
19 They came upon me in the
day of my calamity,
but the LORD was my stay.
20 He brought me out into a
broad place;
he delivered me, because
he delighted in me.

21 The LORD rewarded me
according to my
righteousness;
according to the cleanness
of my hands he
recompensed me.
22 For I have kept the ways of
the LORD,
and have not wickedly
departed from my God.
23 For all his ordinances were
before me,
and from his statutes I did
not turn aside.
24 I was blameless before him,
and I kept myself from
guilt.
25 Therefore the LORD has
recompensed me
according to my
righteousness,
according to my cleanness
in his sight.

26 With the loyal you show
yourself loyal;
with the blameless you
show yourself
blameless;
27 with the pure you show
yourself pure,
and with the crooked you
show yourself perverse.
28 You deliver a humble people,
but your eyes are upon the
haughty to bring them
down.

22.17 Ps 144.7; 32.6 **22.19** Ps 23.4 **22.20** Ps 31.8; 22.8 **22.21** 1 Kings 8.32; Ps 24.4 **22.22** Gen 18.19; Ps 128.1 **22.23** Deut 6.6-9 **22.24** Gen 7.1; 17.1; Eph 1.4 **22.25** v. 21 **22.26** Mt 5.7 **22.27** Lev 26.23 **22.28** Ps 72.12; Isa 2.11,12, 17

22.29 Ps 27.1 **22.31** Deut 32.4; Mt 5.48; Ps 12.6; v. 3 **22.32** 1 Sam 2.2; v. 2 **22.33** Ps 27.1; Ps 101.2,6 **22.34** Hab 3.19; Deut 32.13 **22.35** Ps 144.1 **22.37** Prov 4.12 **22.39** Mal 4.3 **22.40** Ps 44.5 **22.41** Ex 23.27; Josh 10.24 **22.42** Ps 50.22; 1 Sam 28.6

29 Indeed, you are my lamp,
O LORD,
the LORD lightens my
darkness.
30 By you I can crush a troop,
and by my God I can leap
over a wall.
31 This God—his way is
perfect;
the promise of the LORD
proves true;
he is a shield for all who
take refuge in him.

32 For who is God, but the
LORD?
And who is a rock, except
our God?
33 The God who has girded me
with strength[t]
has opened wide my path.[u]
34 He made my[v] feet like the
feet of deer,
and set me secure on the
heights.
35 He trains my hands for war,
so that my arms can bend
a bow of bronze.
36 You have given me the shield
of your salvation,
and your help[w] has made
me great.
37 You have made me stride
freely,
and my feet do not slip;
38 I pursued my enemies and
destroyed them,
and did not turn back until
they were consumed.
39 I consumed them; I struck
them down, so that
they did not rise;
they fell under my feet.
40 For you girded me with
strength for the battle;
you made my assailants
sink under me.
41 You made my enemies turn
their backs to me,
those who hated me, and I
destroyed them.
42 They looked, but there was
no one to save them;

[t] Q Ms Gk Syr Vg Compare Ps 18.32: MT *God is my strong refuge* [u] Meaning of Heb uncertain [v] Another reading is *his* [w] Q Ms: MT *your answering*

they cried to the LORD, but he did not answer them.
43 I beat them fine like the dust of the earth,
I crushed them and stamped them down like the mire of the streets.

44 You delivered me from strife with the peoples;[x]
you kept me as the head of the nations;
people whom I had not known served me.
45 Foreigners came cringing to me;
as soon as they heard of me, they obeyed me.
46 Foreigners lost heart,
and came trembling out of their strongholds.

47 The LORD lives! Blessed be my rock,
and exalted be my God, the rock of my salvation,
48 the God who gave me vengeance
and brought down peoples under me,
49 who brought me out from my enemies;
you exalted me above my adversaries,
you delivered me from the violent.

50 For this I will extol you, O LORD, among the nations,
and sing praises to your name.
51 He is a tower of salvation for his king,
and shows steadfast love to his anointed,
to David and his descendants forever.

The Last Words of David

23 Now these are the last words of David:

22.43 Ps 18.42; Isa 10;6 **22.44** 2 Sam 3.1; Deut 28.13; Isa 55.5 **22.45** Ps 66.3 **22.46** Mic 7.17 **22.47** Ps 89.26 **22.48** Ps 94.1; 144.2 **22.49** Ps 44.5; 140.1 **22.50** Rom 15.9 **22.51** Ps 144.10; 89.20,29; 2 Sam 7.12-16 **23.1** 2 Sam 7.8, 9; Ps 78.70; 89.27; 1 Sam 16.12, 13; Ps 89.20 **23.2** 2 Pet 1.21 **23.3** Deut 32.4; 2 Sam 22.2, 32; Ex 18.21; 2 Chr 19.7, 9 **23.4** Judg 5.31; Ps 89.36 **23.5** Ps 89.29; Isa 55.3 **23.6** Mt 13.42

The oracle of David, son of Jesse,
the oracle of the man whom God exalted,[y]
the anointed of the God of Jacob,
the favorite of the Strong One of Israel:

2 The spirit of the LORD speaks through me,
his word is upon my tongue.
3 The God of Israel has spoken,
the Rock of Israel has said to me:
One who rules over people justly,
ruling in the fear of God,
4 is like the light of morning,
like the sun rising on a cloudless morning,
gleaming from the rain on the grassy land.

5 Is not my house like this with God?
For he has made with me an everlasting covenant,
ordered in all things and secure.
Will he not cause to prosper all my help and my desire?
6 But the godless are[z] all like thorns that are thrown away;
for they cannot be picked up with the hand;
7 to touch them one uses an iron bar
or the shaft of a spear.
And they are entirely consumed in fire on the spot.[a]

David's Mighty Men

8 These are the names of the
warriors whom David had: Josheb-
basshebeth a Tahchemonite; he
was chief of the Three;[b] he wield-

[x] Gk: Heb *from strife with my people*
[y] Q Ms: MT *who was raised on high*
[z] Heb *But worthlessness*
[a] Heb *in sitting*
[b] Gk Vg Compare 1 Chr 11.11: Meaning of Heb uncertain

ed his spear[c] against eight hundred whom he killed at one
time.
9 Next to him among the three
warriors was Eleazar son of Dodo
son of Ahohi. He was with David
when they defied the Philistines
who were gathered there for battle.
The Israelites withdrew, 10 but he
stood his ground. He struck down
the Philistines until his arm grew
weary, though his hand clung to
the sword. The LORD brought about
a great victory that day. Then the
people came back to him—but
only to strip the dead.
11 Next to him was Shammah
son of Agee, the Hararite. The Philistines gathered together at Lehi,
where there was a plot of ground
full of lentils; and the army fled
from the Philistines. 12 But he took
his stand in the middle of the plot,
defended it, and killed the Philistines; and the LORD brought about a
great victory.
13 Towards the beginning of
harvest three of the thirty[d] chiefs
went down to join David at the cave
of Adullam, while a band of Philistines was encamped in the valley of
Rephaim. 14 David was then in the
stronghold; and the garrison of the
Philistines was then at Bethlehem.
15 David said longingly, "O that
someone would give me water to
drink from the well of Bethlehem
that is by the gate!" 16 Then the
three warriors broke through the
camp of the Philistines, drew water
from the well of Bethlehem that
was by the gate, and brought it to
David. But he would not drink of it;
he poured it out to the LORD, 17 for
he said, "The LORD forbid that I
should do this. Can I drink the
blood of the men who went at the
risk of their lives?" Therefore he
would not drink it. The three warriors did these things.
18 Now Abishai son of Zeruiah,
the brother of Joab, was chief of
the Thirty.[e] With his spear he
fought against three hundred men
and killed them, and won a name
beside the Three. 19 He was the
most renowned of the Thirty,[f] and
became their commander; but he
did not attain to the Three.
20 Benaiah son of Jehoiada was
a valiant warrior[g] from Kabzeel, a
doer of great deeds; he struck down
two sons of Ariel[h] of Moab. He also
went down and killed a lion in a pit
on a day when snow had fallen.
21 And he killed an Egyptian, a
handsome man. The Egyptian had
a spear in his hand; but Benaiah
went against him with a staff,
snatched the spear out of the Egyptian's hand, and killed him with his
own spear. 22 Such were the things
Benaiah son of Jehoiada did, and
won a name beside the three warriors. 23 He was renowned among
the Thirty, but he did not attain to
the Three. And David put him in
charge of his bodyguard.
24 Among the Thirty were Asahel brother of Joab; Elhanan son of
Dodo of Bethlehem; 25 Shammah of
Harod; Elika of Harod; 26 Helez the
Paltite; Ira son of Ikkesh of Tekoa;
27 Abiezer of Anathoth; Mebunnai
the Hushathite; 28 Zalmon the Ahohite; Maharai of Netophah; 29 He-
leb son of Baanah of Netophah; Ittai son of Ribai of Gibeah of the
Benjaminites; 30 Benaiah of Pirathon; Hiddai of the torrents of Gaash; 31 Abi-albon the Arbathite; Azmaveth of Bahurim; 32 Eliahba of
Shaalbon; the sons of Jashen: Jonathan 33 son of[i] Shammah the Hararite; Ahiam son of Sharar the Hararite; 34 Eliphelet son of Ahasbai
of Maacah; Eliam son of Ahithophel the Gilonite; 35 Hezro[j] of Carmel; Paarai the Arbite; 36 Igal son of
Nathan of Zobah; Bani the Gadite;
37 Zelek the Ammonite; Naharai of
Beeroth, the armor-bearer of Joab
son of Zeruiah; 38 Ira the Ithrite;
Gareb the Ithrite; 39 Uriah the
Hittite—thirty-seven in all.

23.9 1 Chr 27.4
23.10 1 Chr 11.12-14
23.11 1 Chr 11.27
23.13 1 Sam 22.1; 2 Sam 5.18
23.14 1 Sam 22.4, 5
23.17 Lev 17.10
23.18 2 Sam 10.10, 14; 1 Chr 11.20
23.20 2 Sam 8.18; 20.33; Josh 15.21
23.23 2 Sam 8.18; 20.23
23.24 2 Sam 2.18
23.25 1 Chr 11.27
23.38 2 Sam 20.26
23.39 2 Sam 11.3, 6

[c] 1 Chr 11.11: Meaning of Heb uncertain
[d] Heb adds *head*
[e] Two Heb Mss Syr: MT *Three*
[f] Syr Compare 1 Chr 11.25: Heb *Was he the most renowned of the Three?*
[g] Another reading is *the son of Ish-hai*
[h] Gk: Heb lacks *sons of*
[i] Gk: Heb lacks *son of*
[j] Another reading is *Hezrai*

David's Census of Israel and Judah

24 Again the anger of the LORD
was kindled against Israel,
and he incited David against them,
saying, "Go, count the people of Israel and Judah." 2 So the king said
to Joab and the commanders of the
army,[k] who were with him, "Go
through all the tribes of Israel, from
Dan to Beer-sheba, and take a census of the people, so that I may
know how many there are." 3 But
Joab said to the king, "May the
LORD your God increase the number of the people a hundredfold,
while the eyes of my lord the king
can still see it! But why does my
lord the king want to do this?" 4 But
the king's word prevailed against
Joab and the commanders of the
army. So Joab and the commanders of the army went out from the
presence of the king to take a census of the people of Israel. 5 They
crossed the Jordan, and began
from[l] Aroer and from the city that
is in the middle of the valley, toward Gad and on to Jazer. 6 Then
they came to Gilead, and to Kadesh
in the land of the Hittites;[m] and
they came to Dan, and from Dan[n]
they went around to Sidon, 7 and
came to the fortress of Tyre and to
all the cities of the Hivites and Canaanites; and they went out to the
Negeb of Judah at Beer-sheba. 8 So
when they had gone through all the
land, they came back to Jerusalem
at the end of nine months and
twenty days. 9 Joab reported to the
king the number of those who had
been recorded: in Israel there were
eight hundred thousand soldiers
able to draw the sword, and those
of Judah were five hundred thousand.

Judgment on David's Sin

10 But afterward, David was
stricken to the heart because he
had numbered the people. David
said to the LORD, "I have sinned
greatly in what I have done. But
now, O LORD, I pray you, take away
the guilt of your servant; for I have
done very foolishly." 11 When David
rose in the morning, the word of
the LORD came to the prophet Gad,
David's seer, saying, 12 "Go and say
to David: Thus says the LORD: Three
things I offer[o] you; choose one of
them, and I will do it to you." 13 So
Gad came to David and told him;
he asked him, "Shall three[p] years
of famine come to you on your
land? Or will you flee three months
before your foes while they pursue
you? Or shall there be three days'
pestilence in your land? Now consider, and decide what answer I
shall return to the one who sent
me." 14 Then David said to Gad, "I
am in great distress; let us fall into
the hand of the LORD, for his mercy
is great; but let me not fall into human hands."

15 So the LORD sent a pestilence
on Israel from that morning until
the appointed time; and seventy
thousand of the people died, from
Dan to Beer-sheba. 16 But when the
angel stretched out his hand toward Jerusalem to destroy it, the
LORD relented concerning the evil,
and said to the angel who was
bringing destruction among the
people, "It is enough; now stay
your hand." The angel of the LORD
was then by the threshing floor of
Araunah the Jebusite. 17 When David saw the angel who was destroying the people, he said to the LORD,
"I alone have sinned, and I alone
have done wickedly; but these
sheep, what have they done? Let
your hand, I pray, be against me
and against my father's house."

David's Altar on the Threshing Floor

18 That day Gad came to David
and said to him, "Go up and erect
an altar to the LORD on the threshing floor of Araunah the Jebusite."
19 Following Gad's instructions,
David went up, as the LORD had
commanded. 20 When Araunah
looked down, he saw the king and

24.1 2 Sam 20.1, 2; 1 Chr 27.23, 24
24.2 2 Sam 3.10; Judg 20.1
24.5 Deut 2.36; Josh 13.9, 16; Num 32.1,3
24.6 Josh 19.28
24.7 Josh 11.3; Gen 21.22-33
24.9 1 Chr 21.5
24.10 1 Sam 24.5; 2 Sam 12.13; 1 Sam 13.13
24.11 1 Sam 22.5; 9.9; 1 Chr 29.29
24.12 1 Chr 21.12
24.14 Ps 103.8,13, 14
24.15 1 Chr 21.14; 27.24
24.16 Ex 12.23; Gen 6.6; 1 Sam 15.11
24.17 v. 10; 1 Chr 21.17
24.18 1 Chr 21.18ff

[k] 1 Chr 21.2 Gk: Heb *to Joab the commander of the army* [l] Gk Mss: Heb *encamped in Aroer south of* [m] Gk: Heb *to the land of Tahtim-hodshi* [n] Cn Compare Gk: Heb *they came to Dan-jaan and* [o] Or *hold over* [p] 1 Chr 21.12 Gk: Heb *seven*

his servants coming toward him;
and Araunah went out and prostrated himself before the king with
his face to the ground. 21 Araunah
said, "Why has my lord the king
come to his servant?" David said,
"To buy the threshing floor from
you in order to build an altar to the
LORD, so that the plague may be
averted from the people." 22 Then
Araunah said to David, "Let my
lord the king take and offer up what
seems good to him; here are the
oxen for the burnt offering, and the
threshing sledges and the yokes of
the oxen for the wood. 23 All this,
O king, Araunah gives to the king."
And Araunah said to the king,
"May the LORD your God respond
favorably to you."
24 But the king said to Araunah,
"No, but I will buy them from you
for a price; I will not offer burnt offerings to the LORD my God that
cost me nothing." So David bought
the threshing floor and the oxen for
fifty shekels of silver. 25 David built
there an altar to the LORD, and offered burnt offerings and offerings
of well-being. So the LORD answered his supplication for the
land, and the plague was averted
from Israel.

24.21 Num 16.48, 50
24.22 1 Kings 19.21
24.23 Ezek 20.40, 41
24.24 1 Chr 21.24, 25
24.25 2 Sam 21:14; v. 21

1 Kings

Title and Background

1 and 2 Kings (like 1,2 Samuel) are actually one literary work, called in Hebrew tradition simply "Kings." The division into two books was first done in the Septuagint (Greek translation of the Old Testament). Together Samuel and Kings relate the whole history of the monarchy, from its rise under the ministry of Samuel to its destruction at the hands of the Babylonians. Beginning with Solomon's reign, 1 Kings records the history of Israel through the divided kingdom to the death of Ahab.

Author and Date of Writing

There is little conclusive evidence as to the author of 1 and 2 Kings. Whoever the author may have been, this person was clearly familiar with the book of Deuteronomy–as were many of Israel's prophets. The book was probably written subsequent to Jehoiachin's release from prison (562 B.C.) and prior to the end of the Babylonian exile in 539.

Theme and Message

1 and 2 Kings contain no explicit statement of purpose or theme. In general, these two books describe the history of the kings of Israel and Judah in the light of God's covenants. The author was primarily concerned with Israel's faithfulness to the covenants, and consequently recorded the activities of each ruler as to his/her obedience to the covenant. Obedience to God brought peace and prosperity; disobedience and idol worship resulted in war and disaster. 1 Kings also carries stories of several prophets, notably Elijah.

Outline

I. Solomon's Reign (1.1–12.24)
II. Israel and Judah from Jeroboam/Rehoboam to Ahab/Asa (12.25–16.34)
III. Elijah and King Ahab (17.1–22.40)
IV. Jehoshaphat King of Judah (22.41-50)
V. Ahaziah King of Israel (22.51-53)

The Struggle for the Succession

1 King David was old and advanced in years; and although
they covered him with clothes, he
could not get warm. 2 So his servants said to him, "Let a young virgin be sought for my lord the king,
and let her wait on the king, and be
his attendant; let her lie in your bosom, so that my lord the king may
be warm." 3 So they searched for a
beautiful girl throughout all the
territory of Israel, and found Abishag the Shunammite, and brought
her to the king. 4 The girl was very
beautiful. She became the king's
attendant and served him, but the
king did not know her sexually.
5 Now Adonijah son of Haggith
exalted himself, saying, "I will be
king"; he prepared for himself
chariots and horsemen, and fifty
men to run before him. 6 His father
had never at any time displeased
him by asking, "Why have you done
thus and so?" He was also a very
handsome man, and he was born
next after Absalom. 7 He conferred
with Joab son of Zeruiah and with
the priest Abiathar, and they supported Adonijah. 8 But the priest
Zadok, and Benaiah son of Jehoiada, and the prophet Nathan, and

1.3 Josh 19.18
1.5 2 Sam 3.4; 15.1
1.6 2 Sam 3.3, 4
1.7 1 Chr 11.6; 2 Sam 20.25; 1 Kings 2.22, 28
1.8 2 Sam 20.25; 8.18; 12.1; 23.8

Shimei, and Rei, and David's own
warriors did not side with Adonijah.
9 Adonijah sacrificed sheep,
oxen, and fatted cattle by the stone
Zoheleth, which is beside En-rogel,
and he invited all his brothers, the
king's sons, and all the royal officials of Judah, 10 but he did not invite the prophet Nathan or Benaiah
or the warriors or his brother Solomon.
11 Then Nathan said to Bathsheba, Solomon's mother, "Have
you not heard that Adonijah son of
Haggith has become king and our
lord David does not know it? 12 Now
therefore come, let me give you advice, so that you may save your own
life and the life of your son Solomon. 13 Go in at once to King David, and say to him, 'Did you not,
my lord the king, swear to your servant, saying: Your son Solomon
shall succeed me as king, and he
shall sit on my throne? Why then is
Adonijah king?' 14 Then while you
are still there speaking with the
king, I will come in after you and
confirm your words."
15 So Bathsheba went to the
king in his room. The king was very
old; Abishag the Shunammite was
attending the king. 16 Bathsheba
bowed and did obeisance to the
king, and the king said, "What do
you wish?" 17 She said to him, "My
lord, you swore to your servant by
the LORD your God, saying: Your
son Solomon shall succeed me as
king, and he shall sit on my throne.
18 But now suddenly Adonijah has
become king, though you, my lord
the king, do not know it. 19 He has
sacrificed oxen, fatted cattle, and
sheep in abundance, and has invited all the children of the king, the
priest Abiathar, and Joab the commander of the army; but your servant Solomon he has not invited.
20 But you, my lord the king—the
eyes of all Israel are on you to tell
them who shall sit on the throne of
my lord the king after him. 21 Otherwise it will come to pass, when
my lord the king sleeps with his
ancestors, that my son Solomon
and I will be counted offenders."
22 While she was still speaking
with the king, the prophet Nathan
came in. 23 The king was told,
"Here is the prophet Nathan."
When he came in before the king,
he did obeisance to the king, with
his face to the ground. 24 Nathan
said, "My lord the king, have you
said, 'Adonijah shall succeed me as
king, and he shall sit on my
throne'? 25 For today he has gone
down and has sacrificed oxen, fatted cattle, and sheep in abundance, and has invited all the
king's children, Joab the commander[a] of the army, and the
priest Abiathar, who are now eating
and drinking before him, and saying, 'Long live King Adonijah!'
26 But he did not invite me, your
servant, and the priest Zadok, and
Benaiah son of Jehoiada, and your
servant Solomon. 27 Has this thing
been brought about by my lord the
king and you have not let your servants know who should sit on the
throne of my lord the king after
him?"

The Accession of Solomon

28 King David answered, "Summon Bathsheba to me." So she
came into the king's presence, and
stood before the king. 29 The king
swore, saying, "As the LORD lives,
who has saved my life from every
adversity, 30 as I swore to you by the
LORD, the God of Israel, 'Your son
Solomon shall succeed me as king,
and he shall sit on my throne in my
place,' so will I do this day."
31 Then Bathsheba bowed with her
face to the ground, and did obeisance to the king, and said, "May
my lord King David live forever!"
32 King David said, "Summon
to me the priest Zadok, the prophet
Nathan, and Benaiah son of Jehoiada." When they came before the
king, 33 the king said to them,
"Take with you the servants of your
lord, and have my son Solomon
ride on my own mule, and bring
him down to Gihon. 34 There let the

1.9 2 Sam 17.17 **1.10** 2 Sam 12.24 **1.11** 2 Sam 3.4 **1.13** v. 30; 1 Chr 22.9-13 **1.15** v. 1 **1.17** vv. 13,30 **1.19** v. 9 **1.21** Deut 31.16; 1 Kings 2.10

1.25 v. 9; 1 Sam 10.24 **1.26** vv. 8,10 **1.29** 2 Sam 4.9 **1.30** vv. 13,17 **1.31** Neh 2.3; Dan 2.4 **1.33** 2 Sam 20.6, 7 **1.34** 1 Sam 10.1; 16.3,12; 2 Sam 15.10; v. 25

a Gk: Heb *the commanders*

priest Zadok and the prophet Nathan anoint him king over Israel;
then blow the trumpet, and say,
'Long live King Solomon!' 35 You
shall go up following him. Let him
enter and sit on my throne; he shall
be king in my place; for I have appointed him to be ruler over Israel
and over Judah." 36 Benaiah son of
Jehoiada answered the king,
"Amen! May the LORD, the God of
my lord the king, so ordain. 37 As
the LORD has been with my lord the
king, so may he be with Solomon,
and make his throne greater than
the throne of my lord King David."
38 So the priest Zadok, the
prophet Nathan, and Benaiah son
of Jehoiada, and the Cherethites
and the Pelethites, went down and
had Solomon ride on King David's
mule, and led him to Gihon.
39 There the priest Zadok took the
horn of oil from the tent and
anointed Solomon. Then they blew
the trumpet, and all the people
said, "Long live King Solomon!"
40 And all the people went up following him, playing on pipes and
rejoicing with great joy, so that the
earth quaked at their noise.
41 Adonijah and all the guests
who were with him heard it as they
finished feasting. When Joab heard
the sound of the trumpet, he said,
"Why is the city in an uproar?"
42 While he was still speaking, Jonathan son of the priest Abiathar arrived. Adonijah said, "Come in, for
you are a worthy man and surely
you bring good news." 43 Jonathan
answered Adonijah, "No, for our
lord King David has made Solomon
king; 44 the king has sent with him
the priest Zadok, the prophet Nathan, and Benaiah son of Jehoiada,
and the Cherethites and the Pelethites; and they had him ride on
the king's mule; 45 the priest Zadok
and the prophet Nathan have
anointed him king at Gihon; and
they have gone up from there rejoicing, so that the city is in an uproar. This is the noise that you
heard. 46 Solomon now sits on the
royal throne. 47 Moreover the king's
servants came to congratulate our
lord King David, saying, 'May God
make the name of Solomon more
famous than yours, and make his
throne greater than your throne.'
The king bowed in worship on the
bed 48 and went on to pray thus,
'Blessed be the LORD, the God of Israel, who today has granted one of
my offspring[b] to sit on my throne
and permitted me to witness it.' "
49 Then all the guests of Adonijah got up trembling and went their
own ways. 50 Adonijah, fearing Solomon, got up and went to grasp the
horns of the altar. 51 Solomon was
informed, "Adonijah is afraid of
King Solomon; see, he has laid
hold of the horns of the altar, saying, 'Let King Solomon swear to me
first that he will not kill his servant
with the sword.' " 52 So Solomon responded, "If he proves to be a worthy man, not one of his hairs shall
fall to the ground; but if wickedness is found in him, he shall die."
53 Then King Solomon sent to have
him brought down from the altar.
He came to do obeisance to King
Solomon; and Solomon said to
him, "Go home."

David's Instruction to Solomon

2 When David's time to die drew
near, he charged his son Solomon, saying: 2 "I am about to go the
way of all the earth. Be strong, be
courageous, 3 and keep the charge
of the LORD your God, walking in
his ways and keeping his statutes,
his commandments, his ordinances, and his testimonies, as it is
written in the law of Moses, so that
you may prosper in all that you do
and wherever you turn. 4 Then the
LORD will establish his word that he
spoke concerning me: 'If your heirs
take heed to their way, to walk before me in faithfulness with all
their heart and with all their soul,
there shall not fail you a successor
on the throne of Israel.'
5 "Moreover you know also
what Joab son of Zeruiah did to me,
how he dealt with the two commanders of the armies of Israel, Abner son of Ner, and Amasa son of

1.37 Josh 1.5,17; 1 Sam 20.13; v. 47
1.38 vv. 8,33; 2 Sam 8.18
1.39 Ex 30.23-32; Ps 89.20; 1 Chr 29.22; v. 34
1.42 2 Sam 15.27, 36; 18.27
1.45 v. 40
1.46 1 Chr 29.23
1.47 v. 37; Gen 47.31
1.48 1 Kings 3.6; 2 Sam 7.12
1.50 1 Kings 2.28
1.52 1 Sam 14.45; 2 Sam 14.11
2.1 Gen 47.29; Deut 31.14
2.2 Josh 23.14; Deut 31.7, 23; Josh 1.6,7
2.3 Josh 1.7; 1 Chr 22.12, 13
2.4 2 Sam 7.25; Ps 132.12; 2 Kings 20.3; 2 Sam 7.12, 13
2.5 2 Sam 18.5, 12,14; 3.27; 20.10

[b] Gk: Heb *one*

Jether, whom he murdered, retali-
ating in time of peace for blood
that had been shed in war, and putting the blood of war on the belt
around his waist, and on the sandals on his feet. 6 Act therefore according to your wisdom, but do not
let his gray head go down to Sheol
in peace. 7 Deal loyally, however,
with the sons of Barzillai the Gileadite, and let them be among those
who eat at your table; for with such
loyalty they met me when I fled
from your brother Absalom. 8 There
is also with you Shimei son of Gera,
the Benjaminite from Bahurim,
who cursed me with a terrible curse
on the day when I went to Mahanaim; but when he came down to
meet me at the Jordan, I swore to
him by the LORD, 'I will not put you
to death with the sword.' 9 Therefore do not hold him guiltless, for
you are a wise man; you will know
what you ought to do to him, and
you must bring his gray head down
with blood to Sheol."

Death of David

10 Then David slept with his ancestors, and was buried in the city
of David. 11 The time that David
reigned over Israel was forty years;
he reigned seven years in Hebron,
and thirty-three years in Jerusalem. 12 So Solomon sat on the
throne of his father David; and his
kingdom was firmly established.

Solomon Consolidates His Reign

13 Then Adonijah son of Haggith came to Bathsheba, Solomon's mother. She asked, "Do you
come peaceably?" He said, "Peaceably." 14 Then he said, "May I have
a word with you?" She said, "Go
on." 15 He said, "You know that the
kingdom was mine, and that all Israel expected me to reign; however,
the kingdom has turned about and
become my brother's, for it was his
from the LORD. 16 And now I have
one request to make of you; do not
refuse me." She said to him, "Go
on." 17 He said, "Please ask King
Solomon—he will not refuse you—
to give me Abishag the Shunammite as my wife." 18 Bathsheba
said, "Very well; I will speak to the
king on your behalf."

19 So Bathsheba went to King
Solomon, to speak to him on behalf
of Adonijah. The king rose to meet
her, and bowed down to her; then
he sat on his throne, and had a
throne brought for the king's mother, and she sat on his right. 20 Then
she said, "I have one small request
to make of you; do not refuse me."
And the king said to her, "Make
your request, my mother; for I will
not refuse you." 21 She said, "Let
Abishag the Shunammite be given
to your brother Adonijah as his
wife." 22 King Solomon answered
his mother, "And why do you ask
Abishag the Shunammite for Adonijah? Ask for him the kingdom as
well! For he is my elder brother; ask
not only for him but also for the
priest Abiathar and for Joab son of
Zeruiah!" 23 Then King Solomon
swore by the LORD, "So may God do
to me, and more also, for Adonijah
has devised this scheme at the risk
of his life! 24 Now therefore as the
LORD lives, who has established me
and placed me on the throne of my
father David, and who has made
me a house as he promised, today
Adonijah shall be put to death."
25 So King Solomon sent Benaiah
son of Jehoiada; he struck him
down, and he died.

26 The king said to the priest
Abiathar, "Go to Anathoth, to your
estate; for you deserve death. But I
will not at this time put you to
death, because you carried the ark
of the Lord GOD before my father
David, and because you shared in
all the hardships my father endured." 27 So Solomon banished
Abiathar from being priest to the
LORD, thus fulfilling the word of the
LORD that he had spoken concerning the house of Eli in Shiloh.

28 When the news came to
Joab—for Joab had supported Adonijah though he had not supported Absalom—Joab fled to the tent
of the LORD and grasped the horns
of the altar. 29 When it was told

2.6 v. 6
2.7 2 Sam 19.31, 38; 9.7,10; 17.27
2.8 2 Sam 16.5-8; 19.18-23
2.9 v. 6
2.10 Acts 2.29; 2 Sam 5.7
2.11 2 Sam 5.4; 1 Chr 29.26, 27
2.12 1 Chr 29.23; 2 Chr 1.1
2.13 1 Sam 16.4
2.15 1 Kings 1.5; 1 Chr 22.9, 10; 28.5-7
2.17 1 Kings 1.3, 4
2.19 Ps 45.9
2.20 v. 16
2.21 1 Kings 1.3, 4
2.22 2 Sam 12.8; 1 Kings 1.6, 7
2.23 Ruth 1.17
2.24 2 Sam 7.11, 13; 1 Chr 22.10
2.26 Josh 21.18; 1 Sam 23.6; 2 Sam 15.24-29; 1 Sam 22.20-23
2.27 1 Sam 2.31-35
2.28 1 Kings 1.7, 50
2.29 v. 25

King Solomon, "Joab has fled to
the tent of the LORD and now is beside the altar," Solomon sent Benaiah son of Jehoiada, saying, "Go,
strike him down." 30 So Benaiah
came to the tent of the LORD and
said to him, "The king commands,
'Come out.'" But he said, "No, I
will die here." Then Benaiah
brought the king word again, saying, "Thus said Joab, and thus he
answered me." 31 The king replied
to him, "Do as he has said, strike
him down and bury him; and thus
take away from me and from my father's house the guilt for the blood
that Joab shed without cause.
32 The LORD will bring back his
bloody deeds on his own head, because, without the knowledge of
my father David, he attacked and
killed with the sword two men
more righteous and better than
himself, Abner son of Ner, commander of the army of Israel, and
Amasa son of Jether, commander
of the army of Judah. 33 So shall
their blood come back on the head
of Joab and on the head of his descendants forever; but to David,
and to his descendants, and to his
house, and to his throne, there
shall be peace from the LORD forevermore." 34 Then Benaiah son of Jehoiada went up and struck him
down and killed him; and he was
buried at his own house near the
wilderness. 35 The king put Benaiah
son of Jehoiada over the army in
his place, and the king put the
priest Zadok in the place of Abiathar.
36 Then the king sent and summoned Shimei, and said to him,
"Build yourself a house in Jerusalem, and live there, and do not go
out from there to any place whatever. 37 For on the day you go out, and
cross the Wadi Kidron, know for
certain that you shall die; your
blood shall be on your own head."
38 And Shimei said to the king,
"The sentence is fair; as my lord
the king has said, so will your servant do." So Shimei lived in Jerusalem many days.

2.31 Ex 21.14; Num 35.33; Deut 19.13
2.32 Judg 9.24, 57; Ps 7.16; 2 Chr 21.13; 2 Sam 3.27; 20.10
2.33 2 Sam 3.29; Prov 25.5
2.35 1 Kings 4.4; 1 Chr 29.22; v. 27
2.36 v. 8
2.37 2 Sam 15.23; Lev 20.9; 2 Sam 1.16
2.39 1 Sam 27.2
2.40 2 Sam 19.16-23
2.44 2 Sam 16.5-13; 1 Sam 25.39; Ezek 17.19
2.45 2 Sam 7.13
2.46 vv. 12,25, 34; 2 Chr 1.1
3.1 1 Kings 7.8; 9.24; 2 Sam 5.7; 1 Kings 7.1; ch. 6; 9.15,19
3.2 Lev 17.3-5; Deut 12.2,4, 5
3.3f Deut 6.5; Ps 31.23; 1 Kings 2.3; 9.4; 11.4,6,38
3.4 2 Chr 1.3; 1 Chr 16.39

39 But it happened at the end of
three years that two of Shimei's
slaves ran away to King Achish son
of Maacah of Gath. When it was
told Shimei, "Your slaves are in
Gath," 40 Shimei arose and saddled
a donkey, and went to Achish in
Gath, to search for his slaves;
Shimei went and brought his slaves
from Gath. 41 When Solomon was
told that Shimei had gone from Jerusalem to Gath and returned,
42 the king sent and summoned
Shimei, and said to him, "Did I not
make you swear by the LORD, and
solemnly adjure you, saying, 'Know
for certain that on the day you go
out and go to any place whatever,
you shall die'? And you said to me,
'The sentence is fair; I accept.'
43 Why then have you not kept your
oath to the LORD and the commandment with which I charged
you?" 44 The king also said to Shimei, "You know in your own heart all
the evil that you did to my father
David; so the LORD will bring back
your evil on your own head. 45 But
King Solomon shall be blessed,
and the throne of David shall be established before the LORD forever."
46 Then the king commanded Benaiah son of Jehoiada; and he went
out and struck him down, and he
died.

So the kingdom was established in the hand of Solomon.

Solomon's Prayer for Wisdom

3 Solomon made a marriage alliance with Pharaoh king of
Egypt; he took Pharaoh's daughter
and brought her into the city of David, until he had finished building
his own house and the house of the
LORD and the wall around Jerusalem. 2 The people were sacrificing
at the high places, however, because no house had yet been built
for the name of the LORD.
3 Solomon loved the LORD, walking in the statutes of his father David; only, he sacrificed and offered
incense at the high places. 4 The
king went to Gibeon to sacrifice
there, for that was the principal

high place; Solomon used to offer a
thousand burnt offerings on that
altar. 5 At Gibeon the LORD appeared to Solomon in a dream by
night; and God said, "Ask what I
should give you." 6 And Solomon
said, "You have shown great and
steadfast love to your servant my
father David, because he walked
before you in faithfulness, in righteousness, and in uprightness of
heart toward you; and you have
kept for him this great and steadfast love, and have given him a son
to sit on his throne today. 7 And
now, O LORD my God, you have
made your servant king in place of
my father David, although I am
only a little child; I do not know
how to go out or come in. 8 And
your servant is in the midst of the
people whom you have chosen, a
great people, so numerous they
cannot be numbered or counted.
9 Give your servant therefore an understanding mind to govern your
people, able to discern between
good and evil; for who can govern
this your great people?"
10 It pleased the Lord that Solomon had asked this. 11 God said to
him, "Because you have asked this,
and have not asked for yourself
long life or riches, or for the life of
your enemies, but have asked for
yourself understanding to discern
what is right, 12 I now do according
to your word. Indeed I give you a
wise and discerning mind; no one
like you has been before you and
no one like you shall arise after
you. 13 I give you also what you have
not asked, both riches and honor
all your life; no other king shall
compare with you. 14 If you will
walk in my ways, keeping my statutes and my commandments, as
your father David walked, then I
will lengthen your life."
15 Then Solomon awoke; it had
been a dream. He came to Jerusalem where he stood before the ark
of the covenant of the LORD. He offered up burnt offerings and offerings of well-being, and provided a
feast for all his servants.

3.5 1 Kings 9.2; 2 Chr 1.7; Num 12.6; Mt 1.20
3.6 2 Chr 1.8ff; 1 Kings 2.4; 9.4; 1.48
3.7 1 Chr 2.9-13; 29.1; Num 27.17
3.8 Deut 7.6; Gen 13.16; 15.5
3.9 2 Chr 1.10; Prov 2.3-9; Jas 1.5; Ps 72.1,2
3.11 Jas 4.3
3.12 1 Jn 5.14, 15; 1 Kings 4.29-31
3.13 Mt 6.33; 1 Kings 4.21-24
3.14 v. 6
3.15 Gen 41.7; 1 Kings 8.65; Esther 1.3; Dan 5.1; Mk 6.21
3.17 Num 27.2
3.20 Ruth 4.16
3.26 Gen 43.30; Isa 49.15; Jer 31.20
3.28 vv. 9,11,12

Solomon's Wisdom in Judgment

16 Later, two women who were
prostitutes came to the king and
stood before him. 17 The one woman said, "Please, my lord, this
woman and I live in the same
house; and I gave birth while she
was in the house. 18 Then on the
third day after I gave birth, this
woman also gave birth. We were together; there was no one else with
us in the house, only the two of us
were in the house. 19 Then this
woman's son died in the night, because she lay on him. 20 She got up
in the middle of the night and took
my son from beside me while your
servant slept. She laid him at her
breast, and laid her dead son at my
breast. 21 When I rose in the morning to nurse my son, I saw that he
was dead; but when I looked at him
closely in the morning, clearly it
was not the son I had borne." 22 But
the other woman said, "No, the living son is mine, and the dead son is
yours." The first said, "No, the
dead son is yours, and the living
son is mine." So they argued before
the king.
23 Then the king said, "The one
says, 'This is my son that is alive,
and your son is dead'; while the
other says, 'Not so! Your son is
dead, and my son is the living
one.' " 24 So the king said, "Bring
me a sword," and they brought a
sword before the king. 25 The king
said, "Divide the living boy in two;
then give half to the one, and half
to the other." 26 But the woman
whose son was alive said to the
king—because compassion for her
son burned within her— "Please,
my lord, give her the living boy; certainly do not kill him!" The other
said, "It shall be neither mine nor
yours; divide it." 27 Then the king
responded: "Give the first woman
the living boy; do not kill him. She
is his mother." 28 All Israel heard of
the judgment that the king had
rendered; and they stood in awe of
the king, because they perceived
that the wisdom of God was in him,
to execute justice.

Solomon's Administrative Officers

4 King Solomon was king over
all Israel, 2 and these were his
high officials: Azariah son of Zadok
was the priest; 3 Elihoreph and Ahijah sons of Shisha were secretaries;
Jehoshaphat son of Ahilud was recorder; 4 Benaiah son of Jehoiada
was in command of the army; Zadok and Abiathar were priests; 5 Azariah son of Nathan was over the
officials; Zabud son of Nathan was
priest and king's friend; 6 Ahishar
was in charge of the palace; and
Adoniram son of Abda was in
charge of the forced labor.

7 Solomon had twelve officials
over all Israel, who provided food
for the king and his household;
each one had to make provision for
one month in the year. 8 These were
their names: Ben-hur, in the hill
country of Ephraim; 9 Ben-deker, in
Makaz, Shaalbim, Beth-shemesh,
and Elon-beth-hanan; 10 Ben-
hesed, in Arubboth (to him belonged Socoh and all the land of
Hepher); 11 Ben-abinadab, in all
Naphath-dor (he had Taphath, Solomon's daughter, as his wife);
12 Baana son of Ahilud, in Taanach,
Megiddo, and all Beth-shean,
which is beside Zarethan below
Jezreel, and from Beth-shean to
Abel-meholah, as far as the other
side of Jokmeam; 13 Ben-geber, in
Ramoth-gilead (he had the villages
of Jair son of Manasseh, which are
in Gilead, and he had the region of
Argob, which is in Bashan, sixty
great cities with walls and bronze
bars); 14 Ahinadab son of Iddo, in
Mahanaim; 15 Ahimaaz, in Naphtali
(he had taken Basemath, Solomon's daughter, as his wife); 16 Baana son of Hushai, in Asher and Bealoth; 17 Jehoshaphat son of
Paruah, in Issachar; 18 Shimei son
of Ela, in Benjamin; 19 Geber son of
Uri, in the land of Gilead, the country of King Sihon of the Amorites
and of King Og of Bashan. And
there was one official in the land of
Judah.

Magnificence of Solomon's Rule

20 Judah and Israel were as numerous as the sand by the sea; they
ate and drank and were happy.
21[c] Solomon was sovereign over all
the kingdoms from the Euphrates to
the land of the Philistines, even to
the border of Egypt; they brought
tribute and served Solomon all the
days of his life.

22 Solomon's provision for one
day was thirty cors of choice flour,
and sixty cors of meal, 23 ten fat
oxen, and twenty pasture-fed cattle, one hundred sheep, besides
deer, gazelles, roebucks, and fatted
fowl. 24 For he had dominion over
all the region west of the Euphrates
from Tiphsah to Gaza, over all the
kings west of the Euphrates; and he
had peace on all sides. 25 During
Solomon's lifetime Judah and Israel lived in safety, from Dan even to
Beer-sheba, all of them under their
vines and fig trees. 26 Solomon also
had forty thousand stalls of horses
for his chariots, and twelve thousand horsemen. 27 Those officials
supplied provisions for King Solomon and for all who came to King
Solomon's table, each one in his
month; they let nothing be lacking.
28 They also brought to the required
place barley and straw for the
horses and swift steeds, each according to his charge.

Fame of Solomon's Wisdom

29 God gave Solomon very great
wisdom, discernment, and breadth
of understanding as vast as the
sand on the seashore, 30 so that Solomon's wisdom surpassed the wisdom of all the people of the east,
and all the wisdom of Egypt. 31 He
was wiser than anyone else, wiser
than Ethan the Ezrahite, and Heman, Calcol, and Darda, children
of Mahol; his fame spread throughout all the surrounding nations.
32 He composed three thousand
proverbs, and his songs numbered
a thousand and five. 33 He would
speak of trees, from the cedar that
is in the Lebanon to the hyssop

4.5 v. 7 **4.8** Josh 24.33 **4.9** Josh 1.35; 21.16 **4.10** Josh 15.35; 12.17 **4.11** Josh 11.1,2 **4.12** Josh 5.19; 17.11; 3.16; 1 Kings 19.16; 1 Chr 6.68 **4.13** Num 32.41; Deut 3.4 **4.14** Josh 13.26 **4.15** 2 Sam 15.27 **4.16** 2 Sam 15.32 **4.18** 1 Kings 1.8 **4.19** Deut 3.8-10 **4.20** Gen 32.12; 1 Kings 3.8 **4.21** 2 Chr 9.26; Gen 15.18; Ps 68.29; 72.10,11 **4.24** Ps 72.11; 1 Chr 22.9 **4.25** Jer 23.6; Mic 4.4; Zech 3.10; Judg 20.1 **4.26** 1 Kings 10.26; 2 Chr 1.14 **4.27** v. 7 **4.29** 1 Kings 3.12 **4.30** Gen 25.6; Acts 7.22 **4.31** 1 Kings 3.12; 1 Chr 15.19; 2.6; 6.33 **4.32** Prov 1.1; Eccl 12.9; Song 1.1

c Ch 5.1 in Heb

that grows in the wall; he would
speak of animals, and birds, and
reptiles, and fish. 34 People came
from all the nations to hear the wisdom of Solomon; they came from
all the kings of the earth who had
heard of his wisdom.

Preparations and Materials for the Temple

5[d] Now King Hiram of Tyre sent
his servants to Solomon, when
he heard that they had anointed
him king in place of his father; for
Hiram had always been a friend to
David. 2 Solomon sent word to Hiram, saying, 3 "You know that my
father David could not build a
house for the name of the LORD his
God because of the warfare with
which his enemies surrounded
him, until the LORD put them under
the soles of his feet.[e] 4 But now the
LORD my God has given me rest on
every side; there is neither adversary nor misfortune. 5 So I intend to
build a house for the name of the
LORD my God, as the LORD said to
my father David, 'Your son, whom
I will set on your throne in your
place, shall build the house for my
name.' 6 Therefore command that
cedars from the Lebanon be cut for
me. My servants will join your servants, and I will give you whatever
wages you set for your servants; for
you know that there is no one
among us who knows how to cut
timber like the Sidonians."

7 When Hiram heard the words
of Solomon, he rejoiced greatly,
and said, "Blessed be the LORD today, who has given to David a wise
son to be over this great people."
8 Hiram sent word to Solomon, "I
have heard the message that you
have sent to me; I will fulfill all
your needs in the matter of cedar
and cypress timber. 9 My servants
shall bring it down to the sea from
the Lebanon; I will make it into
rafts to go by sea to the place you
indicate. I will have them broken
up there for you to take away. And
you shall meet my needs by providing food for my household." 10 So
Hiram supplied Solomon's every
need for timber of cedar and cypress. 11 Solomon in turn gave Hiram twenty thousand cors of wheat
as food for his household, and
twenty cors of fine oil. Solomon
gave this to Hiram year by year.
12 So the LORD gave Solomon wisdom, as he promised him. There
was peace between Hiram and Solomon; and the two of them made a
treaty.

13 King Solomon conscripted
forced labor out of all Israel; the
levy numbered thirty thousand
men. 14 He sent them to the Lebanon, ten thousand a month in
shifts; they would be a month in
the Lebanon and two months at
home; Adoniram was in charge of
the forced labor. 15 Solomon also
had seventy thousand laborers and
eighty thousand stonecutters in
the hill country, 16 besides Solomon's three thousand three hundred supervisors who were over the
work, having charge of the people
who did the work. 17 At the king's
command, they quarried out great,
costly stones in order to lay the
foundation of the house with
dressed stones. 18 So Solomon's
builders and Hiram's builders and
the Gebalites did the stonecutting
and prepared the timber and the
stone to build the house.

Solomon Builds the Temple

6 In the four hundred eightieth
year after the Israelites came
out of the land of Egypt, in the
fourth year of Solomon's reign over
Israel, in the month of Ziv, which is
the second month, he began to
build the house of the LORD. 2 The
house that King Solomon built for
the LORD was sixty cubits long,
twenty cubits wide, and thirty cubits high. 3 The vestibule in front of
the nave of the house was twenty
cubits wide, across the width of the
house. Its depth was ten cubits in
front of the house. 4 For the house
he made windows with recessed
frames.[f] 5 He also built a structure
against the wall of the house, run-

4.34 1 Kings 10.1; 2 Chr 9.23
5.1 vv. 10,18; 2 Chr 2.3; 2 Sam 5.11; 1 Chr 14.1
5.3 1 Chr 22.8; 28.3
5.4 1 Kings 4.24; 1 Chr 22.9
5.5 2 Sam 7.12, 13; 1 Chr 17.12; 22.10
5.9 2 Chr 2.16; Ezra 3.7; Ezek 27.17; Acts 12.20
5.11 cf. 2 Chr 2.10
5.12 1 Kings 3.12
5.14 1 Kings 4.6
5.15 1 Kings 9.20-22; 2 Chr 2.17, 18
5.17 1 Chr 22.2
6.1 2 Chr 3.1, 2; Acts 7.47
6.2 cf. Ezek 41.1ff
6.4 Ezek 40.16; 41.16
6.5 Ezek 41.6; vv. 16, 19-21,31

[d] Ch 5.15 in Heb [e] Gk Tg Vg: Heb *my feet* or *his feet* [f] Gk: Meaning of Heb uncertain

ning around the walls of the house,
both the nave and the inner sanctuary; and he made side chambers
all around. 6 The lowest story[g] was
five cubits wide, the middle one
was six cubits wide, and the third
was seven cubits wide; for around
the outside of the house he made
offsets on the wall in order that the
supporting beams should not be inserted into the walls of the house.
7 The house was built with
stone finished at the quarry, so that
neither hammer nor ax nor any tool
of iron was heard in the temple
while it was being built.
8 The entrance for the middle
story was on the south side of the
house: one went up by winding
stairs to the middle story, and from
the middle story to the third. 9 So
he built the house, and finished it;
he roofed the house with beams
and planks of cedar. 10 He built the
structure against the whole house,
each story[h] five cubits high, and it
was joined to the house with timbers of cedar.
11 Now the word of the LORD
came to Solomon, 12 "Concerning
this house that you are building, if
you will walk in my statutes, obey
my ordinances, and keep all my
commandments by walking in
them, then I will establish my
promise with you, which I made to
your father David. 13 I will dwell
among the children of Israel, and
will not forsake my people Israel."
14 So Solomon built the house,
and finished it. 15 He lined the
walls of the house on the inside
with boards of cedar; from the floor
of the house to the rafters of the
ceiling, he covered them on the inside with wood; and he covered the
floor of the house with boards of
cypress. 16 He built twenty cubits of
the rear of the house with boards of
cedar from the floor to the rafters,
and he built this within as an inner
sanctuary, as the most holy place.
17 The house, that is, the nave in
front of the inner sanctuary, was
forty cubits long. 18 The cedar within the house had carvings of gourds
and open flowers; all was cedar, no

6.7 Deut 27.5,6
6.9 vv. 14,38
6.12 1 Kings 2.4; 9.4
6.13 Ex 25.8; Deut 31.6
6.14 vv. 9,38
6.16 Ex 26.33; Lev 16.2; 1 Kings 8.6; 2 Chr 3.8
6.18 1 Kings 7.24
6.22 Ex 30.1,3,6
6.23 2 Chr 3.10-12
6.27 Ex 25.20; 37.9; 1 Kings 8.7; 2 Chr 5.8

stone was seen. 19 The inner sanctuary he prepared in the innermost
part of the house, to set there the
ark of the covenant of the LORD.
20 The interior of the inner sanctuary was twenty cubits long, twenty
cubits wide, and twenty cubits
high; he overlaid it with pure gold.
He also overlaid the altar with cedar.[i] 21 Solomon overlaid the inside of the house with pure gold,
then he drew chains of gold across,
in front of the inner sanctuary, and
overlaid it with gold. 22 Next he
overlaid the whole house with gold,
in order that the whole house
might be perfect; even the whole
altar that belonged to the inner
sanctuary he overlaid with gold.

The Furnishings of the Temple

23 In the inner sanctuary he
made two cherubim of olivewood,
each ten cubits high. 24 Five cubits
was the length of one wing of the
cherub, and five cubits the length
of the other wing of the cherub; it
was ten cubits from the tip of one
wing to the tip of the other. 25 The
other cherub also measured ten cubits; both cherubim had the same
measure and the same form. 26 The
height of one cherub was ten cubits, and so was that of the other
cherub. 27 He put the cherubim in
the innermost part of the house;
the wings of the cherubim were
spread out so that a wing of one
was touching the one wall, and a
wing of the other cherub was
touching the other wall; their other
wings toward the center of the
house were touching wing to wing.
28 He also overlaid the cherubim
with gold.
29 He carved the walls of the
house all around about with carved
engravings of cherubim, palm
trees, and open flowers, in the inner and outer rooms. 30 The floor of
the house he overlaid with gold, in
the inner and outer rooms.
31 For the entrance to the inner
sanctuary he made doors of olivewood; the lintel and the doorposts

[g] Gk: Heb *structure* [h] Heb lacks *each story* [i] Meaning of Heb uncertain

were five-sided.[j] 32 He covered the
two doors of olivewood with carvings of cherubim, palm trees, and
open flowers; he overlaid them
with gold, and spread gold on the
cherubim and on the palm trees.
33 So also he made for the entrance to the nave doorposts of olivewood, four-sided each, 34 and
two doors of cypress wood; the two
leaves of the one door were folding,
and the two leaves of the other
door were folding. 35 He carved
cherubim, palm trees, and open
flowers, overlaying them with gold
evenly applied upon the carved
work. 36 He built the inner court
with three courses of dressed stone
to one course of cedar beams.
37 In the fourth year the foundation of the house of the LORD was
laid, in the month of Ziv. 38 In the
eleventh year, in the month of Bul,
which is the eighth month, the
house was finished in all its parts,
and according to all its specifica-
tions. He was seven years in building it.

Solomon's Palace and Other Buildings

7 Solomon was building his own
house thirteen years, and he
finished his entire house.
2 He built the House of the Forest of the Lebanon one hundred
cubits long, fifty cubits wide, and
thirty cubits high, built on four
rows of cedar pillars, with cedar
beams on the pillars. 3 It was roofed
with cedar on the forty-five rafters,
fifteen in each row, which were on
the pillars. 4 There were window
frames in the three rows, facing
each other in the three rows. 5 All
the doorways and doorposts had
four-sided frames, opposite, facing
each other in the three rows.
6 He made the Hall of Pillars fifty cubits long and thirty cubits
wide. There was a porch in front
with pillars, and a canopy in front
of them.
7 He made the Hall of the
Throne where he was to pronounce
judgment, the Hall of Justice, covered with cedar from floor to floor.

6.34 Ezek 41.23-25
6.36 1 Kings 7.12
6.37 v. 1
7.1 1 Kings 9.10; 2 Chr 8.1
7.2 1 Kings 10.17, 21
7.7 1 Kings 6.15, 16
7.8 1 Kings 3.1; 2 Chr 8.11
7.12 1 Kings 6.36; v. 6
7.13 2 Chr 4.11
7.14 2 Chr 2.14; 4.16; Ex 31.3-5; 35.31
7.15 2 Kings 25.17; 2 Chr 3.15

8 His own house where he
would reside, in the other court
back of the hall, was of the same
construction. Solomon also made a
house like this hall for Pharaoh's
daughter, whom he had taken in
marriage.
9 All these were made of costly
stones, cut according to measure,
sawed with saws, back and front,
from the foundation to the coping,
and from outside to the great court.
10 The foundation was of costly
stones, huge stones, stones of eight
and ten cubits. 11 There were costly
stones above, cut to measure, and
cedarwood. 12 The great court had
three courses of dressed stone to
one layer of cedar beams all
around; so had the inner court of
the house of the LORD, and the vestibule of the house.

Products of Hiram the Bronzeworker

13 Now King Solomon invited
and received Hiram from Tyre.
14 He was the son of a widow of the
tribe of Naphtali, whose father, a
man of Tyre, had been an artisan in
bronze; he was full of skill, intelligence, and knowledge in working
bronze. He came to King Solomon,
and did all his work.
15 He cast two pillars of bronze.
Eighteen cubits was the height of
the one, and a cord of twelve cubits
would encircle it; the second pillar
was the same.[k] 16 He also made
two capitals of molten bronze, to
set on the tops of the pillars; the
height of the one capital was five
cubits, and the height of the other
capital was five cubits. 17 There
were nets of checker work with
wreaths of chain work for the capitals on the tops of the pillars; sev-
en[l] for the one capital, and seven[l]
for the other capital. 18 He made
the columns with two rows around
each latticework to cover the capitals that were above the pomegranates; he did the same with the other capital. 19 Now the capitals that

[j] Meaning of Heb uncertain [k] Cn: Heb *and a cord of twelve cubits encircled the second pillar*; Compare Jer 52.21 [l] Heb: Gk *a net*

were on the tops of the pillars in
the vestibule were of lily-work, four
cubits high. 20 The capitals were on
the two pillars and also above the
rounded projection that was beside
the latticework; there were two
hundred pomegranates in rows all
around; and so with the other capital. 21 He set up the pillars at the
vestibule of the temple; he set up
the pillar on the south and called it
Jachin; and he set up the pillar on
the north and called it Boaz. 22 On
the tops of the pillars was lily-work.
Thus the work of the pillars was
finished.

23 Then he made the molten
sea; it was round, ten cubits from
brim to brim, and five cubits high.
A line of thirty cubits would encircle it completely. 24 Under its brim
were panels all around it, each of
ten cubits, surrounding the sea;
there were two rows of panels, cast
when it was cast. 25 It stood on
twelve oxen, three facing north,
three facing west, three facing
south, and three facing east; the
sea was set on them. The hindquarters of each were toward the inside.
26 Its thickness was a handbreadth;
its brim was made like the brim of
a cup, like the flower of a lily; it
held two thousand baths.[m]

27 He also made the ten stands
of bronze; each stand was four cubits long, four cubits wide, and
three cubits high. 28 This was the
construction of the stands: they
had borders; the borders were within the frames; 29 on the borders that
were set in the frames were lions,
oxen, and cherubim. On the
frames, both above and below the
lions and oxen, there were wreaths
of beveled work. 30 Each stand had
four bronze wheels and axles of
bronze; at the four corners were
supports for a basin. The supports
were cast with wreaths at the side
of each. 31 Its opening was within
the crown whose height was one
cubit; its opening was round, as a
pedestal is made; it was a cubit and
a half wide. At its opening there
were carvings; its borders were
four-sided, not round. 32 The four
wheels were underneath the borders; the axles of the wheels were
in the stands; and the height of a
wheel was a cubit and a half. 33 The
wheels were made like a chariot
wheel; their axles, their rims, their
spokes, and their hubs were all
cast. 34 There were four supports at
the four corners of each stand; the
supports were of one piece with the
stands. 35 On the top of the stand
there was a round band half a cubit
high; on the top of the stand, its
stays and its borders were of one
piece with it. 36 On the surfaces of
its stays and on its borders he
carved cherubim, lions, and palm
trees, where each had space, with
wreaths all around. 37 In this way he
made the ten stands; all of them
were cast alike, with the same size
and the same form.

38 He made ten basins of
bronze; each basin held forty
baths,[m] each basin measured four
cubits; there was a basin for each of
the ten stands. 39 He set five of the
stands on the south side of the
house, and five on the north side of
the house; he set the sea on the
southeast corner of the house.

40 Hiram also made the pots,
the shovels, and the basins. So Hiram finished all the work that he
did for King Solomon on the house
of the LORD: 41 the two pillars, the
two bowls of the capitals that were
on the tops of the pillars, the two
latticeworks to cover the two bowls
of the capitals that were on the
tops of the pillars; 42 the four hundred pomegranates for the two latticeworks, two rows of pomegranates for each latticework, to cover
the two bowls of the capitals that
were on the pillars; 43 the ten
stands, the ten basins on the
stands; 44 the one sea, and the
twelve oxen underneath the sea.

45 The pots, the shovels, and
the basins, all these vessels that
Hiram made for King Solomon for
the house of the LORD were of burnished bronze. 46 In the plain of the
Jordan the king cast them, in the

7.20 2 Chr 3.16; 4.13; Jer 52.23
7.21 2 Chr 3.17; 1 Kings 6.3
7.23 2 Kings 25.13; 2 Chr 4.2; Jer 52.17
7.24 1 Kings 6.18; 2 Chr 4.3
7.25 2 Chr 4.4, 5; Jer 52.20
7.27 v. 38; 2 Chr 4.14
7.30 2 Kings 16.17; 25.13,16
7.37 2 Chr 4.14
7.38 2 Chr 4.6
7.41 vv. 17,18
7.42 v. 20
7.44 vv. 23,25
7.45 2 Chr 4.16
7.46 2 Chr 4.17; Josh 13.27; 3.16

[m] A Heb measure of volume

clay ground between Succoth and Zarethan. 47 Solomon left all the vessels unweighed, because there were so many of them; the weight of the bronze was not determined.

48 So Solomon made all the vessels that were in the house of the LORD: the golden altar, the golden table for the bread of the Presence, 49 the lampstands of pure gold, five on the south side and five on the north, in front of the inner sanctuary; the flowers, the lamps, and the tongs, of gold; 50 the cups, snuffers, basins, dishes for incense, and firepans, of pure gold; the sockets for the doors of the innermost part of the house, the most holy place, and for the doors of the nave of the temple, of gold.

51 Thus all the work that King Solomon did on the house of the LORD was finished. Solomon brought in the things that his father David had dedicated, the silver, the gold, and the vessels, and stored them in the treasuries of the house of the LORD.

Dedication of the Temple

8 Then Solomon assembled the elders of Israel and all the heads of the tribes, the leaders of the ancestral houses of the Israelites, before King Solomon in Jerusalem, to bring up the ark of the covenant of the LORD out of the city of David, which is Zion. 2 All the people of Israel assembled to King Solomon at the festival in the month Ethanim, which is the seventh month. 3 And all the elders of Israel came, and the priests carried the ark. 4 So they brought up the ark of the LORD, the tent of meeting, and all the holy vessels that were in the tent; the priests and the Levites brought them up. 5 King Solomon and all the congregation of Israel, who had assembled before him, were with him before the ark, sacrificing so many sheep and oxen that they could not be counted or numbered. 6 Then the priests brought the ark of the covenant of the LORD to its place, in the inner sanctuary of the house, in the most holy place, underneath the wings of the cherubim. 7 For the cherubim spread out their wings over the place of the ark, so that the cherubim made a covering above the ark and its poles. 8 The poles were so long that the ends of the poles were seen from the holy place in front of the inner sanctuary; but they could not be seen from outside; they are there to this day. 9 There was nothing in the ark except the two tablets of stone that Moses had placed there at Horeb, where the LORD made a covenant with the Israelites, when they came out of the land of Egypt. 10 And when the priests came out of the holy place, a cloud filled the house of the LORD, 11 so that the priests could not stand to minister because of the cloud; for the glory of the LORD filled the house of the LORD.

12 Then Solomon said,
"The LORD has said that he
would dwell in thick
darkness.
13 I have built you an exalted
house,
a place for you to dwell in
forever."

Solomon's Speech

14 Then the king turned around and blessed all the assembly of Israel, while all the assembly of Israel stood. 15 He said, "Blessed be the LORD, the God of Israel, who with his hand has fulfilled what he promised with his mouth to my father David, saying, 16 'Since the day that I brought my people Israel out of Egypt, I have not chosen a city from any of the tribes of Israel in which to build a house, that my name might be there; but I chose David to be over my people Israel.' 17 My father David had it in mind to build a house for the name of the LORD, the God of Israel. 18 But the LORD said to my father David, 'You did well to consider building a house for my name; 19 nevertheless you shall not build the house, but your son who shall be born to you shall build the house for my name.' 20 Now the LORD has upheld the

7.48 Ex 37.10ff
7.49 Ex 31-38
7.51 2 Sam 8.11; 2 Chr 5.1
8.1 2 Chr 5.2; 2 Sam 6.17; 5.7,9
8.2 Lev 23.34; 2 Chr 7.8
8.3 Num 7.9
8.4 1 Kings 3.4; 2 Chr 1.3
8.5 2 Sam 6.13
8.6 2 Sam 6.17; 1 Kings 6.19, 27
8.8 Ex 25.14
8.9 Ex 25.21; Deut 10.2-5; Heb 9.4; Ex 24.7,8
8.10 Ex 40.34, 35; 2 Chr 7.1, 2
8.12 2 Chr 6.1; Ps 97.2
8.13 2 Sam 7.13; Ps 132.14
8.14 2 Sam 6.18
8.15 1 Chr 29.10, 20; Neh 9.5; 2 Sam 7.12, 13
8.16 2 Sam 7.4-6; Deut 12.11; 1 Sam 16.1; 2 Sam 7.8
8.17 2 Sam 7.2; 1 Chr 17.1
8.19 2 Sam 7.5; 12.13; 1 Kings 5.3, 5
8.20 1 Chr 28.5, 6

promise that he made; for I have
risen in the place of my father David; I sit on the throne of Israel, as
the LORD promised, and have built
the house for the name of the LORD,
the God of Israel. 21 There I have
provided a place for the ark, in
which is the covenant of the LORD
that he made with our ancestors
when he brought them out of the
land of Egypt."

Solomon's Prayer of Dedication

22 Then Solomon stood before
the altar of the LORD in the presence of all the assembly of Israel,
and spread out his hands to heav-
en. 23 He said, "O LORD, God of Israel, there is no God like you in heav-
en above or on earth beneath,
keeping covenant and steadfast
love for your servants who walk before you with all their heart, 24 the
covenant that you kept for your servant my father David as you declared to him; you promised with
your mouth and have this day fulfilled with your hand. 25 Therefore,
O LORD, God of Israel, keep for your
servant my father David that which
you promised him, saying, 'There
shall never fail you a successor before me to sit on the throne of Israel, if only your children look to
their way, to walk before me as you
have walked before me.' 26 Therefore, O God of Israel, let your word
be confirmed, which you promised
to your servant my father David.

27 "But will God indeed dwell
on the earth? Even heaven and the
highest heaven cannot contain
you, much less this house that I
have built! 28 Regard your servant's
prayer and his plea, O LORD my
God, heeding the cry and the
prayer that your servant prays to
you today; 29 that your eyes may be
open night and day toward this
house, the place of which you said,
'My name shall be there,' that you
may heed the prayer that your servant prays toward this place.
30 Hear the plea of your servant and
of your people Israel when they
pray toward this place; O hear in
heaven your dwelling place; heed
and forgive.

31 "If someone sins against a
neighbor and is given an oath to
swear, and comes and swears before your altar in this house, 32 then
hear in heaven, and act, and judge
your servants, condemning the
guilty by bringing their conduct on
their own head, and vindicating the
righteous by rewarding them according to their righteousness.

33 "When your people Israel,
having sinned against you, are defeated before an enemy but turn
again to you, confess your name,
pray and plead with you in this
house, 34 then hear in heaven, forgive the sin of your people Israel,
and bring them again to the land
that you gave to their ancestors.

35 "When heaven is shut up and
there is no rain because they have
sinned against you, and then they
pray toward this place, confess
your name, and turn from their sin,
because you punish[n] them, 36 then
hear in heaven, and forgive the sin
of your servants, your people Israel,
when you teach them the good way
in which they should walk; and
grant rain on your land, which you
have given to your people as an inheritance.

37 "If there is famine in the
land, if there is plague, blight, mildew, locust, or caterpillar; if their
enemy besieges them in any[o] of
their cities; whatever plague, whatever sickness there is; 38 whatever
prayer, whatever plea there is from
any individual or from all your people Israel, all knowing the afflictions of their own hearts so that
they stretch out their hands toward
this house; 39 then hear in heaven
your dwelling place, forgive, act,
and render to all whose hearts you
know—according to all their ways,
for only you know what is in every
human heart— 40 so that they may
fear you all the days that they live
in the land that you gave to our ancestors.

8.21 v. 9 **8.22** 2 Chr 6.12ff; Ex 9.33; Ezra 9.5 **8.23** 1 Sam 2.2; 2 Sam 7.22; Deut 7.9; Neh 1.5,9, 32 **8.25** 2 Sam 7.12, 16; 1 Kings 2.4 **8.26** 2 Sam 7.25 **8.27** 2 Chr 2.6; Isa 66.1; Jer 23.24; Acts 7.49 **8.29** Deut 12.11; Dan 6.10 **8.30** Neh 1.6 **8.31** Ex 22.11 **8.32** Deut 25.1 **8.33** Lev 26.17; Deut 28.25; Lev 26.39 **8.35** Lev 26.19; Deut 28.23 **8.36** 1 Sam 12.23; Ps 27.11; 94.12 **8.37** Lev 26.16, 25,26; Deut 28.21-23, 38-42 **8.39** 1 Sam 16.7; 1 Chr 28.9; Ps 11.4; Jer 17.10 **8.40** Ps 130.4

[n] Or *when you answer* [o] Gk Syr: Heb *in the land*

41 "Likewise when a foreigner,
who is not of your people Israel,
comes from a distant land because
of your name 42—for they shall
hear of your great name, your
mighty hand, and your outstretched arm—when a foreigner
comes and prays toward this
house, 43 then hear in heaven your
dwelling place, and do according to
all that the foreigner calls to you,
so that all the peoples of the earth
may know your name and fear you,
as do your people Israel, and so
that they may know that your name
has been invoked on this house
that I have built.
44 "If your people go out to battle against their enemy, by whatever way you shall send them, and
they pray to the LORD toward the
city that you have chosen and the
house that I have built for your
name, 45 then hear in heaven their
prayer and their plea, and maintain
their cause.
46 "If they sin against you—for
there is no one who does not sin—
and you are angry with them and
give them to an enemy, so that they
are carried away captive to the land
of the enemy, far off or near; 47 yet
if they come to their senses in the
land to which they have been taken
captive, and repent, and plead with
you in the land of their captors,
saying, 'We have sinned, and have
done wrong; we have acted wickedly'; 48 if they repent with all their
heart and soul in the land of their
enemies, who took them captive,
and pray to you toward their land,
which you gave to their ancestors,
the city that you have chosen, and
the house that I have built for your
name; 49 then hear in heaven your
dwelling place their prayer and
their plea, maintain their cause
50 and forgive your people who have
sinned against you, and all their
transgressions that they have committed against you; and grant them
compassion in the sight of their
captors, so that they may have
compassion on them 51 (for they are
your people and heritage, which
you brought out of Egypt, from the
midst of the iron-smelter). 52 Let
your eyes be open to the plea of
your servant, and to the plea of
your people Israel, listening to
them whenever they call to you.
53 For you have separated them
from among all the peoples of the
earth, to be your heritage, just as
you promised through Moses, your
servant, when you brought our ancestors out of Egypt, O Lord GOD."

Solomon Blesses the Assembly

54 Now when Solomon finished
offering all this prayer and this plea
to the LORD, he arose from facing
the altar of the LORD, where he had
knelt with hands outstretched toward heaven; 55 he stood and
blessed all the assembly of Israel
with a loud voice:
56 "Blessed be the LORD, who
has given rest to his people Israel
according to all that he promised;
not one word has failed of all his
good promise, which he spoke
through his servant Moses. 57 The
LORD our God be with us, as he was
with our ancestors; may he not
leave us or abandon us, 58 but incline our hearts to him, to walk in
all his ways, and to keep his commandments, his statutes, and his
ordinances, which he commanded
our ancestors. 59 Let these words of
mine, with which I pleaded before
the LORD, be near to the LORD our
God day and night, and may he
maintain the cause of his servant
and the cause of his people Israel,
as each day requires; 60 so that all
the peoples of the earth may know
that the LORD is God; there is no
other. 61 Therefore devote yourselves completely to the LORD our
God, walking in his statutes and
keeping his commandments, as at
this day."

Solomon Offers Sacrifices

62 Then the king, and all Israel
with him, offered sacrifice before
the LORD. 63 Solomon offered as sacrifices of well-being to the LORD
twenty-two thousand oxen and one
hundred twenty thousand sheep.
So the king and all the people of

8.42 Deut 3.24
8.43 1 Sam 17.46; 2 Kings 19.19; Ps 102.15
8.46 2 Chr 6.36; Prov 20.9; 1 Jn 1.8-10; Lev 26.34-39; Deut 28.36, 64
8.47 Lev 26.40; Neh 1.6; Ps 106.6; Dan 9.5
8.48 Jer 29.12-14; Dan 6.10
8.50 2 Chr 30.9; Ps 106.46
8.51 Deut 9.29; Neh 1.10; Deut 4.20; Jer 11.4
8.53 Ex 19.5; Deut 9.26-29
8.55 v. 14
8.56 Josh 21.45; 23.14
8.57 Josh 1.5; Rom 8.28; Heb 13.5
8.58 Ps 119.36
8.60 1 Kings 18.39; Jer 10.10-12
8.61 1 Kings 11.4; 15.3,14; 2 Kings 20.3
8.62 2 Chr 7.4ff

Israel dedicated the house of the
LORD. 64 The same day the king consecrated the middle of the court
that was in front of the house of the
LORD; for there he offered the burnt
offerings and the grain offerings
and the fat pieces of the sacrifices
of well-being, because the bronze
altar that was before the LORD was
too small to receive the burnt offerings and the grain offerings and the
fat pieces of the sacrifices of well-
being.
65 So Solomon held the festival
at that time, and all Israel with
him—a great assembly, people
from Lebo-hamath to the Wadi of
Egypt—before the LORD our God,
seven days.[p] 66 On the eighth day
he sent the people away; and they
blessed the king, and went to their
tents, joyful and in good spirits because of all the goodness that the
LORD had shown to his servant David and to his people Israel.

God Appears Again to Solomon

9 When Solomon had finished
building the house of the LORD
and the king's house and all that
Solomon desired to build, 2 the
LORD appeared to Solomon a second time, as he had appeared to
him at Gibeon. 3 The LORD said to
him, "I have heard your prayer and
your plea, which you made before
me; I have consecrated this house
that you have built, and put my
name there forever; my eyes and
my heart will be there for all time.
4 As for you, if you will walk before
me, as David your father walked,
with integrity of heart and uprightness, doing according to all that I
have commanded you, and keeping
my statutes and my ordinances,
5 then I will establish your royal
throne over Israel forever, as I
promised your father David, saying,
'There shall not fail you a successor on the throne of Israel.'
6 "If you turn aside from following me, you or your children, and
do not keep my commandments
and my statutes that I have set before you, but go and serve other
gods and worship them, 7 then I will

8.64 2 Chr 7.7; 4.1
8.65 v. 2; Lev 23.34; Num 34.8; Josh 13.5; Gen 15.18; 2 Chr 7.8
9.1 2 Chr 7.11ff; 1 Kings 7.1; 2 Chr 8.6
9.2 1 Kings 3.5
9.3 2 Kings 20.5; 1 Kings 8.29; Deut 11.12
9.4 Gen 17.1; 1 Kings 15.5
9.5 2 Sam 7.12, 16; 1 Kings 2.4; 1 Chr 22.10
9.6 2 Sam 7.14; 2 Chr 7.19, 20
9.7 2 Kings 17.23; 25.21; Jer 7.14; Deut 28.37; Ps 44.14
9.8 2 Chr 7.21; Deut 29.24-26; Jer 22.8,9
9.10 1 Kings 6.37, 38; 7.1; 2 Chr 8.1
9.11 2 Chr 8.2
9.13 Josh 19.27
9.15 1 Kings 5.13; v. 24; 2 Sam 5.9; Josh 19.36; 17.11; 16.10
9.16 Josh 16.10
9.17 Josh 16.3; 2 Chr 8.5

cut Israel off from the land that I
have given them; and the house
that I have consecrated for my
name I will cast out of my sight;
and Israel will become a proverb
and a taunt among all peoples.
8 This house will become a heap of
ruins;[q] everyone passing by it will
be astonished, and will hiss; and
they will say, 'Why has the LORD
done such a thing to this land and
to this house?' 9 Then they will say,
'Because they have forsaken the
LORD their God, who brought their
ancestors out of the land of Egypt,
and embraced other gods, worshiping them and serving them; therefore the LORD has brought this disaster upon them.' "
10 At the end of twenty years, in
which Solomon had built the two
houses, the house of the LORD and
the king's house, 11 King Hiram of
Tyre having supplied Solomon with
cedar and cypress timber and gold,
as much as he desired, King Solomon gave to Hiram twenty cities in
the land of Galilee. 12 But when Hiram came from Tyre to see the cities that Solomon had given him,
they did not please him. 13 Therefore he said, "What kind of cities
are these that you have given me,
my brother?" So they are called the
land of Cabul[r] to this day. 14 But
Hiram had sent to the king one
hundred twenty talents of gold.

Other Acts of Solomon

15 This is the account of the
forced labor that King Solomon
conscripted to build the house of
the LORD and his own house, the
Millo and the wall of Jerusalem,
Hazor, Megiddo, Gezer 16 (Pharaoh
king of Egypt had gone up and captured Gezer and burned it down,
had killed the Canaanites who
lived in the city, and had given it as
dowry to his daughter, Solomon's
wife; 17 so Solomon rebuilt Gezer),
Lower Beth-horon, 18 Baalath, Tamar in the wilderness, within the

[p] Compare Gk: Heb *seven days and seven days, fourteen days* [q] Syr Old Latin: Heb *will become high* [r] Perhaps meaning *a land good for nothing*

land, 19 as well as all of Solomon's
storage cities, the cities for his
chariots, the cities for his cavalry,
and whatever Solomon desired to
build, in Jerusalem, in Lebanon,
and in all the land of his dominion.
20 All the people who were left of
the Amorites, the Hittites, the Perizzites, the Hivites, and the Jebusites, who were not of the people of
Israel— 21 their descendants who
were still left in the land, whom the
Israelites were unable to destroy
completely—these Solomon conscripted for slave labor, and so they
are to this day. 22 But of the Israelites Solomon made no slaves; they
were the soldiers, they were his officials, his commanders, his captains, and the commanders of his
chariotry and cavalry.
23 These were the chief officers
who were over Solomon's work:
five hundred fifty, who had charge
of the people who carried on the
work.
24 But Pharaoh's daughter went
up from the city of David to her
own house that Solomon had built
for her; then he built the Millo.
25 Three times a year Solomon
used to offer up burnt offerings and
sacrifices of well-being on the altar
that he built for the LORD, offering
incense[s] before the LORD. So he
completed the house.

Solomon's Commercial Activity

26 King Solomon built a fleet of
ships at Ezion-geber, which is near
Eloth on the shore of the Red Sea,[t]
in the land of Edom. 27 Hiram sent
his servants with the fleet, sailors
who were familiar with the sea, together with the servants of Solomon. 28 They went to Ophir, and
imported from there four hundred
twenty talents of gold, which they
delivered to King Solomon.

Visit of the Queen of Sheba

10 When the queen of Sheba
heard of the fame of Solomon, (fame due to[u] the name of
the LORD), she came to test him
with hard questions. 2 She came to
Jerusalem with a very great retinue, with camels bearing spices,
and very much gold, and precious
stones; and when she came to Solomon, she told him all that was on
her mind. 3 Solomon answered all
her questions; there was nothing
hidden from the king that he could
not explain to her. 4 When the
queen of Sheba had observed all
the wisdom of Solomon, the house
that he had built, 5 the food of his
table, the seating of his officials,
and the attendance of his servants,
their clothing, his valets, and his
burnt offerings that he offered at
the house of the LORD, there was no
more spirit in her.
6 So she said to the king, "The
report was true that I heard in my
own land of your accomplishments
and of your wisdom, 7 but I did not
believe the reports until I came and
my own eyes had seen it. Not even
half had been told me; your wisdom and prosperity far surpass the
report that I had heard. 8 Happy are
your wives![v] Happy are these your
servants, who continually attend
you and hear your wisdom!
9 Blessed be the LORD your God,
who has delighted in you and set
you on the throne of Israel! Because the LORD loved Israel forever,
he has made you king to execute
justice and righteousness." 10 Then
she gave the king one hundred
twenty talents of gold, a great
quantity of spices, and precious
stones; never again did spices
come in such quantity as that
which the queen of Sheba gave to
King Solomon.
11 Moreover, the fleet of Hiram,
which carried gold from Ophir,
brought from Ophir a great quantity of almug wood and precious
stones. 12 From the almug wood the
king made supports for the house
of the LORD, and for the king's
house, lyres also and harps for the
singers; no such almug wood has
come or been seen to this day.
13 Meanwhile King Solomon
gave to the queen of Sheba every

9.19 1 Kings 4.26; v. 1
9.20 2 Chr 8.7
9.21 Judg 1.21, 27,29; Josh 15.63; 17.12; Judg 1.21; Gen 9.25, 26; Ezra 2.55,58
9.22 Lev 25.39
9.23 2 Chr 8.10
9.24 1 Kings 3.1; 7.8; 11.27; 2 Chr 32.5
9.25 2 Chr 8.12, 13,16
9.26 2 Chr 8.17, 18; Num 33.35; Deut 2.8; 1 Kings 22.48
9.27 1 Kings 10.11
9.28 1 Chr 29.4
10.1 2 Chr 9.1ff; Mt 12.42; Judg 14.12
10.5 1 Chr 26.16
10.9 1 Kings 5.7; 2 Sam 8.15
10.10 v. 2
10.11 1 Kings 9.27, 28
10.12 2 Chr 9.10, 11

[s] Gk: Heb *offering incense with it that was*
[t] Or *Sea of Reeds* [u] Meaning of Heb uncertain [v] Gk Syr: Heb *men*

desire that she expressed, as well
as what he gave her out of Solomon's royal bounty. Then she returned to her own land, with her
servants.

14 The weight of gold that came
to Solomon in one year was six
hundred sixty-six talents of gold,
15 besides that which came from
the traders and from the business
of the merchants, and from all the
kings of Arabia and the governors
of the land. 16 King Solomon made
two hundred large shields of beat-
en gold; six hundred shekels of
gold went into each large shield.
17 He made three hundred shields
of beaten gold; three minas of gold
went into each shield; and the king
put them in the House of the Forest of Lebanon. 18 The king also
made a great ivory throne, and
overlaid it with the finest gold.
19 The throne had six steps. The top
of the throne was rounded in the
back, and on each side of the seat
were arm rests and two lions standing beside the arm rests, 20 while
twelve lions were standing, one on
each end of a step on the six steps.
Nothing like it was ever made in
any kingdom. 21 All King Solomon's
drinking vessels were of gold, and
all the vessels of the House of the
Forest of Lebanon were of pure
gold; none were of silver—it was
not considered as anything in the
days of Solomon. 22 For the king
had a fleet of ships of Tarshish at
sea with the fleet of Hiram. Once
every three years the fleet of ships
of Tarshish used to come bringing
gold, silver, ivory, apes, and peacocks.[w]

23 Thus King Solomon excelled
all the kings of the earth in riches
and in wisdom. 24 The whole earth
sought the presence of Solomon to
hear his wisdom, which God had
put into his mind. 25 Every one of
them brought a present, objects of
silver and gold, garments, weaponry, spices, horses, and mules, so
much year by year.

26 Solomon gathered together
chariots and horses; he had fourteen hundred chariots and twelve

10.14 2 Chr 9.13-28
10.16 1 Kings 14.26-28
10.17 1 Kings 7.2
10.18 2 Chr 9.17ff
10.22 1 Kings 9.26-28; 22.48; 2 Chr 20.36
10.23 1 Kings 3.12, 13; 4.30
10.24 1 Kings 3.9, 12,28
10.26 1 Kings 4.26; 2 Chr 1.14; 9.25; 1 Kings 9.19
10.28 2 Chr 1.16; 9.28
10.29 2 Kings 7.6, 7
11.1 Neh 13.26; Deut 17.17
11.2 Ex 34.16; Deut 7.3,4
11.4 1 Kings 8.61; 9.4
11.5 v. 33; Judg 2.13; 2 Kings 23.13
11.7 Num 21.29; Judg 11.24; 2 Kings 23.13
11.9 vv. 2,3; 1 Kings 3.5; 9.2

thousand horses, which he stationed in the chariot cities and
with the king in Jerusalem. 27 The
king made silver as common in Jerusalem as stones, and he made cedars as numerous as the sycamores
of the Shephelah. 28 Solomon's import of horses was from Egypt and
Kue, and the king's traders received them from Kue at a price.
29 A chariot could be imported from
Egypt for six hundred shekels of
silver, and a horse for one hundred
fifty; so through the king's traders
they were exported to all the kings
of the Hittites and the kings of
Aram.

Solomon's Errors

11 King Solomon loved many
foreign women along with
the daughter of Pharaoh: Moabite,
Ammonite, Edomite, Sidonian,
and Hittite women, 2 from the nations concerning which the LORD
had said to the Israelites, "You
shall not enter into marriage with
them, neither shall they with you;
for they will surely incline your
heart to follow their gods"; Solomon clung to these in love.
3 Among his wives were seven hundred princesses and three hundred
concubines; and his wives turned
away his heart. 4 For when Solomon was old, his wives turned away
his heart after other gods; and his
heart was not true to the LORD his
God, as was the heart of his father
David. 5 For Solomon followed Astarte the goddess of the Sidonians,
and Milcom the abomination of
the Ammonites. 6 So Solomon did
what was evil in the sight of the
LORD, and did not completely follow the LORD, as his father David
had done. 7 Then Solomon built a
high place for Chemosh the abomination of Moab, and for Molech the
abomination of the Ammonites, on
the mountain east of Jerusalem.
8 He did the same for all his foreign
wives, who offered incense and
sacrificed to their gods.

9 Then the LORD was angry with
Solomon, because his heart had

[w] Or *baboons*

turned away from the LORD, the
God of Israel, who had appeared to
him twice, 10 and had commanded
him concerning this matter, that
he should not follow other gods;
but he did not observe what the
LORD commanded. 11 Therefore the
LORD said to Solomon, "Since this
has been your mind and you have
not kept my covenant and my statutes that I have commanded you, I
will surely tear the kingdom from
you and give it to your servant.
12 Yet for the sake of your father David I will not do it in your lifetime;
I will tear it out of the hand of your
son. 13 I will not, however, tear
away the entire kingdom; I will give
one tribe to your son, for the sake
of my servant David and for the
sake of Jerusalem, which I have
chosen."

Adversaries of Solomon

14 Then the LORD raised up an
adversary against Solomon, Hadad
the Edomite; he was of the royal
house in Edom. 15 For when David
was in Edom, and Joab the commander of the army went up to
bury the dead, he killed every male
in Edom 16 (for Joab and all Israel
remained there six months, until
he had eliminated every male in
Edom); 17 but Hadad fled to Egypt
with some Edomites who were servants of his father. He was a young
boy at that time. 18 They set out
from Midian and came to Paran;
they took people with them from
Paran and came to Egypt, to Pharaoh king of Egypt, who gave him a
house, assigned him an allowance
of food, and gave him land. 19 Hadad found great favor in the sight of
Pharaoh, so that he gave him his
sister-in-law for a wife, the sister of
Queen Tahpenes. 20 The sister of
Tahpenes gave birth by him to his
son Genubath, whom Tahpenes
weaned in Pharaoh's house; Genubath was in Pharaoh's house
among the children of Pharaoh.
21 When Hadad heard in Egypt that
David slept with his ancestors and
that Joab the commander of the
army was dead, Hadad said to
Pharaoh, "Let me depart, that I
may go to my own country." 22 But
Pharaoh said to him, "What do you
lack with me that you now seek to
go to your own country?" And he
said, "No, do let me go."

23 God raised up another adversary against Solomon,[x] Rezon son
of Eliada, who had fled from his
master, King Hadadezer of Zobah.
24 He gathered followers around
him and became leader of a marauding band, after the slaughter
by David; they went to Damascus,
settled there, and made him king
in Damascus. 25 He was an adversary of Israel all the days of Solomon, making trouble as Hadad did;
he despised Israel and reigned over
Aram.

Jeroboam's Rebellion

26 Jeroboam son of Nebat, an
Ephraimite of Zeredah, a servant of
Solomon, whose mother's name
was Zeruah, a widow, rebelled
against the king. 27 The following
was the reason he rebelled against
the king. Solomon built the Millo,
and closed up the gap in the wall[y]
of the city of his father David.
28 The man Jeroboam was very
able, and when Solomon saw that
the young man was industrious he
gave him charge over all the forced
labor of the house of Joseph.
29 About that time, when Jeroboam
was leaving Jerusalem, the prophet
Ahijah the Shilonite found him on
the road. Ahijah had clothed himself with a new garment. The two of
them were alone in the open country 30 when Ahijah laid hold of the
new garment he was wearing and
tore it into twelve pieces. 31 He
then said to Jeroboam: Take for
yourself ten pieces; for thus says
the LORD, the God of Israel, "See, I
am about to tear the kingdom from
the hand of Solomon, and will give
you ten tribes. 32 One tribe will remain his, for the sake of my servant
David and for the sake of Jerusalem, the city that I have chosen out
of all the tribes of Israel. 33 This is

11.10 1 Kings 6.12; 9.6,7
11.11 v. 31; 1 Kings 12.15, 16
11.13 2 Sam 7.15; 1 Kings 12.20; Deut 12.11
11.15 2 Sam 8.14; 1 Chr 18.12, 13
11.21 1 Kings 2.10
11.23 v. 14; 2 Sam 8.3
11.24 2 Sam 8.3; 10.8,18
11.26 1 Kings 12.2; 2 Chr 13.6; 2 Sam 20.21
11.27 1 Kings 9.24
11.29 1 Kings 14.2
11.30 1 Sam 15.27, 28
11.31 vv. 11-13
11.33 vv. 5-7

[x] Heb *him* [y] Heb lacks *in the wall*

because he has[z] forsaken me, worshiped Astarte the goddess of the
Sidonians, Chemosh the god of
Moab, and Milcom the god of the
Ammonites, and has[z] not walked
in my ways, doing what is right in
my sight and keeping my statutes
and my ordinances, as his father
David did. 34 Nevertheless I will not
take the whole kingdom away from
him but will make him ruler all the
days of his life, for the sake of my
servant David whom I chose and
who did keep my commandments
and my statutes; 35 but I will take
the kingdom away from his son and
give it to you—that is, the ten
tribes. 36 Yet to his son I will give
one tribe, so that my servant David
may always have a lamp before me
in Jerusalem, the city where I have
chosen to put my name. 37 I will
take you, and you shall reign over
all that your soul desires; you shall
be king over Israel. 38 If you will listen to all that I command you, walk
in my ways, and do what is right in
my sight by keeping my statutes
and my commandments, as David
my servant did, I will be with you,
and will build you an enduring
house, as I built for David, and I
will give Israel to you. 39 For this
reason I will punish the descendants of David, but not forever."
40 Solomon sought therefore to kill
Jeroboam; but Jeroboam promptly
fled to Egypt, to King Shishak of
Egypt, and remained in Egypt until
the death of Solomon.

Death of Solomon

41 Now the rest of the acts of
Solomon, all that he did as well as
his wisdom, are they not written in
the Book of the Acts of Solomon?
42 The time that Solomon reigned
in Jerusalem over all Israel was forty years. 43 Solomon slept with his
ancestors and was buried in the
city of his father David; and his son
Rehoboam succeeded him.

The Northern Tribes Secede

12 Rehoboam went to She-
chem, for all Israel had
come to Shechem to make him
king. 2 When Jeroboam son of Nebat heard of it (for he was still in
Egypt, where he had fled from King
Solomon), then Jeroboam returned
from[a] Egypt. 3 And they sent and
called him; and Jeroboam and all
the assembly of Israel came and
said to Rehoboam, 4 "Your father
made our yoke heavy. Now therefore lighten the hard service of your
father and his heavy yoke that he
placed on us, and we will serve
you." 5 He said to them, "Go away
for three days, then come again to
me." So the people went away.
6 Then King Rehoboam took
counsel with the older men who
had attended his father Solomon
while he was still alive, saying,
"How do you advise me to answer
this people?" 7 They answered him,
"If you will be a servant to this people today and serve them, and
speak good words to them when
you answer them, then they will be
your servants forever." 8 But he disregarded the advice that the older
men gave him, and consulted with
the young men who had grown up
with him and now attended him.
9 He said to them, "What do you advise that we answer this people
who have said to me, 'Lighten the
yoke that your father put on us'?"
10 The young men who had grown
up with him said to him, "Thus you
should say to this people who
spoke to you, 'Your father made
our yoke heavy, but you must light-
en it for us'; thus you should say to
them, 'My little finger is thicker
than my father's loins. 11 Now,
whereas my father laid on you a
heavy yoke, I will add to your yoke.
My father disciplined you with
whips, but I will discipline you with
scorpions.'"
12 So Jeroboam and all the people came to Rehoboam the third
day, as the king had said, "Come to
me again the third day." 13 The king
answered the people harshly. He
disregarded the advice that the older men had given him 14 and spoke

11.35 1 Kings 12.16, 17
11.36 v. 13; 1 Kings 15.4; 2 Kings 8.19
11.38 Josh 1.5; 2 Sam 7.11, 27
11.41 2 Chr 9.29
11.42 2 Chr9.30
11.43 2 Chr 9.31; 1 Kings 14.21
12.1 2 Chr 10.1ff
12.2 1 Kings 11.26, 40
12.4 1 Sam 8.11-18; 1 Kings 4.7
12.5 v. 12
12.7 2 Chr 10.7
12.8 Lev 19.32
12.12 v. 5
12.14 Ex 1.13,14; 5.5-9,16-18

[z] Gk Syr Vg: Heb *they have* [a] Gk Vg Compare 2 Chr 10.2: Heb *lived in*

to them according to the advice of
the young men, "My father made
your yoke heavy, but I will add to
your yoke; my father disciplined
you with whips, but I will discipline
you with scorpions." 15 So the king
did not listen to the people, because it was a turn of affairs
brought about by the LORD that he
might fulfill his word, which the
LORD had spoken by Ahijah the Shilonite to Jeroboam son of Nebat.
16 When all Israel saw that the
king would not listen to them, the
people answered the king,

"What share do we have in
David?
We have no inheritance in
the son of Jesse.
To your tents, O Israel!
Look now to your own
house, O David."

So Israel went away to their tents.
17 But Rehoboam reigned over the
Israelites who were living in the
towns of Judah. 18 When King Rehoboam sent Adoram, who was
taskmaster over the forced labor,
all Israel stoned him to death. King
Rehoboam then hurriedly mounted his chariot to flee to Jerusalem.
19 So Israel has been in rebellion
against the house of David to this
day.

First Dynasty: Jeroboam Reigns over Israel

20 When all Israel heard that
Jeroboam had returned, they sent
and called him to the assembly and
made him king over all Israel.
There was no one who followed the
house of David, except the tribe of
Judah alone.
21 When Rehoboam came to Jerusalem, he assembled all the
house of Judah and the tribe of
Benjamin, one hundred eighty
thousand chosen troops to fight
against the house of Israel, to restore the kingdom to Rehoboam
son of Solomon. 22 But the word of
God came to Shemaiah the man of
God: 23 Say to King Rehoboam of
Judah, son of Solomon, and to all
the house of Judah and Benjamin,
and to the rest of the people,
24 "Thus says the LORD, You shall
not go up or fight against your kindred the people of Israel. Let everyone go home, for this thing is from
me." So they heeded the word of
the LORD and went home again, according to the word of the LORD.

Jeroboam's Golden Calves

25 Then Jeroboam built Shechem in the hill country of Ephraim, and resided there; he went out
from there and built Penuel.
26 Then Jeroboam said to himself,
"Now the kingdom may well revert
to the house of David. 27 If this people continues to go up to offer sacrifices in the house of the LORD at
Jerusalem, the heart of this people
will turn again to their master,
King Rehoboam of Judah; they will
kill me and return to King Rehoboam of Judah." 28 So the king took
counsel, and made two calves of
gold. He said to the people,[b] "You
have gone up to Jerusalem long
enough. Here are your gods,
O Israel, who brought you up out of
the land of Egypt." 29 He set one in
Bethel, and the other he put in
Dan. 30 And this thing became a
sin, for the people went to worship
before the one at Bethel and before
the other as far as Dan.[c] 31 He also
made houses[d] on high places, and
appointed priests from among all
the people, who were not Levites.
32 Jeroboam appointed a festival on
the fifteenth day of the eighth
month like the festival that was in
Judah, and he offered sacrifices on
the altar; so he did in Bethel, sacrificing to the calves that he had
made. And he placed in Bethel the
priests of the high places that he
had made. 33 He went up to the altar that he had made in Bethel on
the fifteenth day in the eighth
month, in the month that he alone
had devised; he appointed a festival for the people of Israel, and he
went up to the altar to offer incense.

12.15 v. 24; Judg 14.4; 2 Chr 10.15; 22.7; 25.20; 1 Kings 11.11, 31
12.16 2 Sam 20.1
12.17 1 Kings 11.13, 36
12.18 1 Kings 4.6; 5.14
12.19 2 Kings 17.21
12.20 1 Kings 11.13, 32
12.21 2 Chr 11.1ff
12.24 v. 15
12.25 Judg 9.45; 8.17
12.27 Deut 12.5,6
12.28 2 Kings 10.29; 17.16; Ex 32.4,8
12.29 Gen 28.19; Judg 18.29
12.30 1 Kings 13.34; 2 Kings 17.21
12.31 1 Kings 13.32, 33; Num 3.10; 2 Kings 17.32
12.32 Lev 23.33, 34; Num 29.12; Am 7.13
12.33 1 Kings 13.1

[b] Gk: Heb *to them* [c] Compare Gk: Heb *went to the one as far as Dan* [d] Gk Vg Compare 13.32: Heb *a house*

A Man of God from Judah

13 While Jeroboam was standing by the altar to offer incense, a man of God came out of
Judah by the word of the Lord to
Bethel 2 and proclaimed against
the altar by the word of the Lord,
and said, "O altar, altar, thus says
the Lord: 'A son shall be born to
the house of David, Josiah by
name; and he shall sacrifice on you
the priests of the high places who
offer incense on you, and human
bones shall be burned on you.' "
3 He gave a sign the same day, saying, "This is the sign that the Lord
has spoken: 'The altar shall be torn
down, and the ashes that are on it
shall be poured out.' " 4 When the
king heard what the man of God
cried out against the altar at Bethel, Jeroboam stretched out his
hand from the altar, saying, "Seize
him!" But the hand that he
stretched out against him withered
so that he could not draw it back to
himself. 5 The altar also was torn
down, and the ashes poured out
from the altar, according to the
sign that the man of God had given
by the word of the Lord. 6 The king
said to the man of God, "Entreat
now the favor of the Lord your God,
and pray for me, so that my hand
may be restored to me." So the
man of God entreated the Lord;
and the king's hand was restored to
him, and became as it was before.
7 Then the king said to the man of
God, "Come home with me and
dine, and I will give you a gift."
8 But the man of God said to the
king, "If you give me half your kingdom, I will not go in with you; nor
will I eat food or drink water in this
place. 9 For thus I was commanded
by the word of the Lord: You shall
not eat food, or drink water, or return by the way that you came."
10 So he went another way, and did
not return by the way that he had
come to Bethel.

11 Now there lived an old
prophet in Bethel. One of his sons
came and told him all that the man
of God had done that day in Bethel;
the words also that he had spoken
to the king, they told to their father. 12 Their father said to them,
"Which way did he go?" And his
sons showed him the way that the
man of God who came from Judah
had gone. 13 Then he said to his
sons, "Saddle a donkey for me." So
they saddled a donkey for him, and
he mounted it. 14 He went after the
man of God, and found him sitting
under an oak tree. He said to him,
"Are you the man of God who came
from Judah?" He answered, "I am."
15 Then he said to him, "Come
home with me and eat some food."
16 But he said, "I cannot return with
you, or go in with you; nor will I eat
food or drink water with you in this
place; 17 for it was said to me by the
word of the Lord: You shall not eat
food or drink water there, or return
by the way that you came." 18 Then
the other[e] said to him, "I also am
a prophet as you are, and an angel
spoke to me by the word of the
Lord: Bring him back with you into
your house so that he may eat food
and drink water." But he was deceiving him. 19 Then the man of
God[e] went back with him, and ate
food and drank water in his house.

20 As they were sitting at the table, the word of the Lord came to
the prophet who had brought him
back; 21 and he proclaimed to the
man of God who came from Judah,
"Thus says the Lord: Because you
have disobeyed the word of the
Lord, and have not kept the commandment that the Lord your God
commanded you, 22 but have come
back and have eaten food and
drunk water in the place of which
he said to you, 'Eat no food, and
drink no water,' your body shall not
come to your ancestral tomb."
23 After the man of God[e] had eaten
food and had drunk, they saddled
for him a donkey belonging to the
prophet who had brought him
back. 24 Then as he went away, a
lion met him on the road and killed
him. His body was thrown in the
road, and the donkey stood beside

13.1 2 Kings 23.17; 1 Kings 12.32, 33
13.2 2 Kings 23.15, 16
13.3 Isa 7.14; Judg 6.17
13.6 Ex 8.8; 9.28; Acts 8.24; Lk 6.27,28
13.7 1 Sam 9.7, 8; 2 Kings 5.15
13.8 vv. 16,17; Num 22.18; 24.13
13.11 v. 25
13.16 vv. 8,9
13.17 1 Kings 20.35
13.21 1 Sam 15.26
13.24 1 Kings 20.36

[e] Heb *he*

it; the lion also stood beside the body. 25 People passed by and saw the body thrown in the road, with the lion standing by the body. And they came and told it in the town where the old prophet lived.

26 When the prophet who had brought him back from the way heard of it, he said, "It is the man of God who disobeyed the word of the LORD; therefore the LORD has given him to the lion, which has torn him and killed him according to the word that the LORD spoke to him." 27 Then he said to his sons, "Saddle a donkey for me." So they saddled one, 28 and he went and found the body thrown in the road, with the donkey and the lion standing beside the body. The lion had not eaten the body or attacked the donkey. 29 The prophet took up the body of the man of God, laid it on the donkey, and brought it back to the city,[f] to mourn and to bury him. 30 He laid the body in his own grave; and they mourned over him, saying, "Alas, my brother!" 31 After he had buried him, he said to his sons, "When I die, bury me in the grave in which the man of God is buried; lay my bones beside his bones. 32 For the saying that he proclaimed by the word of the LORD against the altar in Bethel, and against all the houses of the high places that are in the cities of Samaria, shall surely come to pass."

33 Even after this event Jeroboam did not turn from his evil way, but made priests for the high places again from among all the people; any who wanted to be priests he consecrated for the high places. 34 This matter became sin to the house of Jeroboam, so as to cut it off and to destroy it from the face of the earth.

Judgment on the House of Jeroboam

14 At that time Abijah son of Jeroboam fell sick. 2 Jeroboam said to his wife, "Go, disguise yourself, so that it will not be known that you are the wife of Jeroboam, and go to Shiloh; for the prophet Ahijah is there, who said of me that I should be king over this people. 3 Take with you ten loaves, some cakes, and a jar of honey, and go to him; he will tell you what shall happen to the child."

4 Jeroboam's wife did so; she set out and went to Shiloh, and came to the house of Ahijah. Now Ahijah could not see, for his eyes were dim because of his age. 5 But the LORD said to Ahijah, "The wife of Jeroboam is coming to inquire of you concerning her son; for he is sick. Thus and thus you shall say to her."

When she came, she pretended to be another woman. 6 But when Ahijah heard the sound of her feet, as she came in at the door, he said, "Come in, wife of Jeroboam; why do you pretend to be another? For I am charged with heavy tidings for you. 7 Go, tell Jeroboam, 'Thus says the LORD, the God of Israel: Because I exalted you from among the people, made you leader over my people Israel, 8 and tore the kingdom away from the house of David to give it to you; yet you have not been like my servant David, who kept my commandments and followed me with all his heart, doing only that which was right in my sight, 9 but you have done evil above all those who were before you and have gone and made for yourself other gods, and cast images, provoking me to anger, and have thrust me behind your back; 10 therefore, I will bring evil upon the house of Jeroboam. I will cut off from Jeroboam every male, both bond and free in Israel, and will consume the house of Jeroboam, just as one burns up dung until it is all gone. 11 Anyone belonging to Jeroboam who dies in the city, the dogs shall eat; and anyone who dies in the open country, the birds of the air shall eat; for the LORD has spoken.' 12 Therefore set out, go to your house. When your feet enter the city, the child shall die. 13 All

13.25 v. 11
13.26 v. 21
13.30 Jer 22.18
13.31 2 Kings 23.17, 18
13.32 v. 2; 2 Kings 23.16, 17,19; see 1 Kings 16.24
13.33 1 Kings 12.31, 32; 2 Chr 11.15; 13.9
13.34 1 Kings 12.30; 14.10
14.2 1 Sam 28.8; 2 Sam 14.2; 1 Kings 11.29-31
14.3 1 Sam 9.7, 8
14.4 1 Kings 11.29; 1 Sam 3.2; 4.15
14.5 2 Sam 14.2
14.7 1 Kings 11.28-31;16.2
14.8 1 Kings 11.31ff
14.9 1 Kings 12.28; 2 Chr 11.15; Ps 50.17; Ex 34.17; Ezek 23.35
14.10 1 Kings 15.29; 21.21; 2 Kings 9.8; Deut 32.36; 2 Kings 14.26
14.11 1 Kings 16.4; 21.24
14.12 v. 17
14.13 2 Chr 12.12

[f] Gk: Heb *he came to the town of the old prophet*

Israel shall mourn for him and bury
him; for he alone of Jeroboam's
family shall come to the grave, because in him there is found something pleasing to the LORD, the God
of Israel, in the house of Jeroboam.
14 Moreover the LORD will raise up
for himself a king over Israel, who
shall cut off the house of Jeroboam
today, even right now![g]
15 "The LORD will strike Israel,
as a reed is shaken in the water; he
will root up Israel out of this good
land that he gave to their ancestors, and scatter them beyond the
Euphrates, because they have
made their sacred poles,[h] provoking the LORD to anger. 16 He will give
Israel up because of the sins of Jeroboam, which he sinned and which
he caused Israel to commit."
17 Then Jeroboam's wife got up
and went away, and she came to
Tirzah. As she came to the threshold of the house, the child died.
18 All Israel buried him and
mourned for him, according to the
word of the LORD, which he spoke
by his servant the prophet Ahijah.

Death of Jeroboam

19 Now the rest of the acts of
Jeroboam, how he warred and how
he reigned, are written in the Book
of the Annals of the Kings of Israel.
20 The time that Jeroboam reigned
was twenty-two years; then he slept
with his ancestors, and his son Nadab succeeded him.

Rehoboam Reigns over Judah

21 Now Rehoboam son of Solomon reigned in Judah. Rehoboam
was forty-one years old when he began to reign, and he reigned seventeen years in Jerusalem, the city
that the LORD had chosen out of all
the tribes of Israel, to put his name
there. His mother's name was Naamah the Ammonite. 22 Judah did
what was evil in the sight of the
LORD; they provoked him to jealousy with their sins that they committed, more than all that their ancestors had done. 23 For they also built
for themselves high places, pillars,
and sacred poles[h] on every high
hill and under every green tree;
24 there were also male temple
prostitutes in the land. They committed all the abominations of the
nations that the LORD drove out before the people of Israel.
25 In the fifth year of King Rehoboam, King Shishak of Egypt
came up against Jerusalem; 26 he
took away the treasures of the
house of the LORD and the treasures
of the king's house; he took everything. He also took away all the
shields of gold that Solomon had
made; 27 so King Rehoboam made
shields of bronze instead, and committed them to the hands of the officers of the guard, who kept the
door of the king's house. 28 As often
as the king went into the house of
the LORD, the guard carried them
and brought them back to the
guardroom.
29 Now the rest of the acts of
Rehoboam, and all that he did, are
they not written in the Book of the
Annals of the Kings of Judah?
30 There was war between Rehoboam and Jeroboam continually.
31 Rehoboam slept with his ancestors and was buried with his ancestors in the city of David. His mother's name was Naamah the
Ammonite. His son Abijam succeeded him.

Abijam Reigns over Judah: Idolatry and War

15 Now in the eighteenth year
of King Jeroboam son of
Nebat, Abijam began to reign over
Judah. 2 He reigned for three years
in Jerusalem. His mother's name
was Maacah daughter of Abishalom. 3 He committed all the sins
that his father did before him; his
heart was not true to the LORD his
God, like the heart of his father David. 4 Nevertheless for David's sake
the LORD his God gave him a lamp
in Jerusalem, setting up his son after him, and establishing Jerusalem; 5 because David did what was
right in the sight of the LORD, and
did not turn aside from anything
that he commanded him all the

14.14 1 Kings 15.27-29
14.15 2 Kings 17.6; Josh 23.15, 16; 2 Kings 15.29; Ex 34.13; Deut 12.3,4
14.16 1 Kings 12.30; 13.34; 15.30, 34
14.17 1 Kings 16.6-9
14.18 v. 13
14.19 2 Chr 13.2-20
14.21 2 Chr 12.13; 1 Kings 11.32, 36; v. 31
14.22 2 Chr 12.1; Deut 32.21
14.23 Deut 12.2; Ezek 16.24, 25; 2 Kings 17.9, 10; Isa 57.5
14.24 Deut 23.17; 1 Kings 15.12; 2 Kings 23.7
14.25 1 Kings 11.40; 2 Chr 12.2, 9-11
14.26 1 Kings 15.18; 10.17
14.29 2 Chr 12.15
14.30 1 Kings 12.21-24; 15.6
14.31 2 Chr 12.16; v. 21
15.1 2 Chr 13.1, 2
15.3 1 Kings 11.4
15.4 1 Kings 11.36; 2 Chr 21.7
15.5 1 Kings 14.8; 2 Sam 11.4, 15-17; 12.9

[g] Meaning of Heb uncertain [h] Heb *Asherim*

days of his life, except in the matter of Uriah the Hittite. 6 The war
begun between Rehoboam and Jeroboam continued all the days of his
life. 7 The rest of the acts of Abijam,
and all that he did, are they not
written in the Book of the Annals of
the Kings of Judah? There was war
between Abijam and Jeroboam.
8 Abijam slept with his ancestors,
and they buried him in the city of
David. Then his son Asa succeeded
him.

Asa Reigns over Judah

9 In the twentieth year of King
Jeroboam of Israel, Asa began to
reign over Judah; 10 he reigned
forty-one years in Jerusalem. His
mother's name was Maacah daughter of Abishalom. 11 Asa did what
was right in the sight of the LORD, as
his father David had done. 12 He
put away the male temple prostitutes out of the land, and removed
all the idols that his ancestors had
made. 13 He also removed his
mother Maacah from being queen
mother, because she had made an
abominable image for Asherah;
Asa cut down her image and
burned it at the Wadi Kidron. 14 But
the high places were not taken
away. Nevertheless the heart of Asa
was true to the LORD all his days.
15 He brought into the house of the
LORD the votive gifts of his father
and his own votive gifts—silver,
gold, and utensils.

Alliance with Aram against Israel

16 There was war between Asa
and King Baasha of Israel all their
days. 17 King Baasha of Israel went
up against Judah, and built Ramah, to prevent anyone from going
out or coming in to King Asa of Judah. 18 Then Asa took all the silver
and the gold that were left in the
treasures of the house of the LORD
and the treasures of the king's
house, and gave them into the
hands of his servants. King Asa
sent them to King Ben-hadad son
of Tabrimmon son of Hezion of
Aram, who resided in Damascus,

15.6 1 Kings 14.30
15.7 2 Chr 13.2, 3,22
15.8 2 Chr 14.1
15.10 v. 2
15.11 2 Chr 14.2
15.12 1 Kings 14.24; 22.46
15.13 2 Chr 15.16-18; Ex 32.20
15.14 1 Kings 22.43; 2 Chr 15.17, 18; v. 3
15.15 1 Kings 7.51
15.16 v. 32
15.17 2 Chr 16.1ff; Josh 18.25; 1 Kings 12.27
15.18 v. 15; 2 Chr 16.2; 1 Kings 11.23, 24
15.20 2 Kings 15.29; Judg 18.29; 2 Sam 20.14
15.22 2 Chr 16.6; Josh 21.17
15.23 2 Chr 16.11-14
15.24 2 Chr 17.1
15.25 1 Kings 14.20
15.26 1 Kings 12.30; 14.16
15.27 1 Kings 14.14; Josh 19.44; 21.23
15.29 1 Kings 14.10, 14

saying, 19 "Let there be an alliance
between me and you, like that between my father and your father: I
am sending you a present of silver
and gold; go, break your alliance
with King Baasha of Israel, so that
he may withdraw from me." 20 Ben-
hadad listened to King Asa, and
sent the commanders of his armies
against the cities of Israel. He conquered Ijon, Dan, Abel-beth-
maacah, and all Chinneroth, with
all the land of Naphtali. 21 When
Baasha heard of it, he stopped
building Ramah and lived in Tirzah. 22 Then King Asa made a proclamation to all Judah, none was exempt: they carried away the stones
of Ramah and its timber, with
which Baasha had been building;
with them King Asa built Geba of
Benjamin and Mizpah. 23 Now the
rest of all the acts of Asa, all his
power, all that he did, and the cities that he built, are they not written in the Book of the Annals of the
Kings of Judah? But in his old age
he was diseased in his feet. 24 Then
Asa slept with his ancestors, and
was buried with his ancestors in
the city of his father David; his son
Jehoshaphat succeeded him.

Nadab Reigns over Israel

25 Nadab son of Jeroboam began to reign over Israel in the second year of King Asa of Judah; he
reigned over Israel two years. 26 He
did what was evil in the sight of the
LORD, walking in the way of his ancestor and in the sin that he caused
Israel to commit.

27 Baasha son of Ahijah, of the
house of Issachar, conspired
against him; and Baasha struck
him down at Gibbethon, which belonged to the Philistines; for Nadab and all Israel were laying siege
to Gibbethon. 28 So Baasha killed
Nadab[i] in the third year of King
Asa of Judah, and succeeded him.
29 As soon as he was king, he killed
all the house of Jeroboam; he left
to the house of Jeroboam not one
that breathed, until he had destroyed it, according to the word of

[i] Heb *him*

the LORD that he spoke by his servant Ahijah the Shilonite— 30 because of the sins of Jeroboam that
he committed and that he caused
Israel to commit, and because of
the anger to which he provoked the
LORD, the God of Israel.
31 Now the rest of the acts of
Nadab, and all that he did, are they
not written in the Book of the Annals of the Kings of Israel? 32 There
was war between Asa and King Baasha of Israel all their days.

Second Dynasty: Baasha Reigns over Israel

33 In the third year of King Asa
of Judah, Baasha son of Ahijah began to reign over all Israel at Tirzah; he reigned twenty-four years.
34 He did what was evil in the sight
of the LORD, walking in the way of
Jeroboam and in the sin that he
caused Israel to commit.

16 The word of the LORD came
to Jehu son of Hanani
against Baasha, saying, 2 "Since I
exalted you out of the dust and
made you leader over my people Israel, and you have walked in the
way of Jeroboam, and have caused
my people Israel to sin, provoking
me to anger with their sins, 3 therefore, I will consume Baasha and his
house, and I will make your house
like the house of Jeroboam son of
Nebat. 4 Anyone belonging to Baasha who dies in the city the dogs
shall eat; and anyone of his who
dies in the field the birds of the air
shall eat."
5 Now the rest of the acts of Baasha, what he did, and his power,
are they not written in the Book of
the Annals of the Kings of Israel?
6 Baasha slept with his ancestors,
and was buried at Tirzah; and his
son Elah succeeded him. 7 Moreover the word of the LORD came by
the prophet Jehu son of Hanani
against Baasha and his house, both
because of all the evil that he did in
the sight of the LORD, provoking
him to anger with the work of his
hands, in being like the house of
Jeroboam, and also because he destroyed it.

15.30 1 Kings 14.9, 16
15.31 v. 16
15.34 1 Kings 12.28, 29; 13.33; 14.16
16.1 v. 7; 2 Chr 19.2; 20.34
16.2 1 Kings 14.7; 15.34
16.3 v. 11; 1 Kings 14.10; 15.29
16.4 1 Kings 14.11
16.5 1 Kings 14.19; 15.31
16.6 1 Kings 14.17; 15.21
16.7 v. 1; 1 Kings 15.27, 29
16.9 2 Kings 9.30-33
16.12 v. 3; 2 Chr 19.2; 20.34
16.13 Deut 32.21; 1 Sam 12.21; Isa 41.29
16.14 v. 5
16.15 1 Kings 15.27
16.18 1 Sam 31.4, 5; 2 Sam 17.23
16.19 1 Kings 12.28; 15.26,34

Elah Reigns over Israel

8 In the twenty-sixth year of
King Asa of Judah, Elah son of Baasha began to reign over Israel in
Tirzah; he reigned two years. 9 But
his servant Zimri, commander of
half his chariots, conspired against
him. When he was at Tirzah, drinking himself drunk in the house of
Arza, who was in charge of the palace at Tirzah, 10 Zimri came in and
struck him down and killed him, in
the twenty-seventh year of King
Asa of Judah, and succeeded him.
11 When he began to reign, as
soon as he had seated himself on
his throne, he killed all the house
of Baasha; he did not leave him a
single male of his kindred or his
friends. 12 Thus Zimri destroyed all
the house of Baasha, according to
the word of the LORD, which he
spoke against Baasha by the prophet Jehu— 13 because of all the sins
of Baasha and the sins of his son
Elah that they committed, and that
they caused Israel to commit, provoking the LORD God of Israel to anger with their idols. 14 Now the rest
of the acts of Elah, and all that he
did, are they not written in the
Book of the Annals of the Kings of
Israel?

Third Dynasty: Zimri Reigns over Israel

15 In the twenty-seventh year of
King Asa of Judah, Zimri reigned
seven days in Tirzah. Now the
troops were encamped against Gibbethon, which belonged to the
Philistines, 16 and the troops who
were encamped heard it said,
"Zimri has conspired, and he has
killed the king"; therefore all Israel
made Omri, the commander of the
army, king over Israel that day in
the camp. 17 So Omri went up from
Gibbethon, and all Israel with him,
and they besieged Tirzah. 18 When
Zimri saw that the city was taken,
he went into the citadel of the
king's house; he burned down the
king's house over himself with fire,
and died— 19 because of the sins
that he committed, doing evil in
the sight of the LORD, walking in the

way of Jeroboam, and for the sin
that he committed, causing Israel
to sin. 20 Now the rest of the acts of
Zimri, and the conspiracy that he
made, are they not written in the
Book of the Annals of the Kings of
Israel?

Fourth Dynasty: Omri Reigns over Israel

21 Then the people of Israel
were divided into two parts; half of
the people followed Tibni son of
Ginath, to make him king, and half
followed Omri. 22 But the people
who followed Omri overcame the
people who followed Tibni son of
Ginath; so Tibni died, and Omri
became king. 23 In the thirty-first
year of King Asa of Judah, Omri began to reign over Israel; he reigned
for twelve years, six of them in Tirzah.

Samaria the New Capital

24 He bought the hill of Samaria from Shemer for two talents of
silver; he fortified the hill, and
called the city that he built, Samaria, after the name of Shemer, the
owner of the hill.
25 Omri did what was evil in the
sight of the LORD; he did more evil
than all who were before him.
26 For he walked in all the way of
Jeroboam son of Nebat, and in the
sins that he caused Israel to commit, provoking the LORD, the God of
Israel, to anger by their idols.
27 Now the rest of the acts of Omri
that he did, and the power that he
showed, are they not written in the
Book of the Annals of the Kings of
Israel? 28 Omri slept with his ancestors, and was buried in Samaria; his
son Ahab succeeded him.

Ahab Reigns over Israel

29 In the thirty-eighth year of
King Asa of Judah, Ahab son of
Omri began to reign over Israel;
Ahab son of Omri reigned over Israel in Samaria twenty-two years.
30 Ahab son of Omri did evil in the
sight of the LORD more than all who
were before him.

Ahab Marries Jezebel and Worships Baal

31 And as if it had been a light
thing for him to walk in the sins of
Jeroboam son of Nebat, he took as
his wife Jezebel daughter of King
Ethbaal of the Sidonians, and went
and served Baal, and worshiped
him. 32 He erected an altar for Baal
in the house of Baal, which he built
in Samaria. 33 Ahab also made a sacred pole.[j] Ahab did more to provoke the anger of the LORD, the God
of Israel, than had all the kings of
Israel who were before him. 34 In
his days Hiel of Bethel built Jericho; he laid its foundation at the
cost of Abiram his firstborn, and
set up its gates at the cost of his
youngest son Segub, according to
the word of the LORD, which he
spoke by Joshua son of Nun.

Elijah Predicts a Drought

17 Now Elijah the Tishbite, of
Tishbe[k] in Gilead, said to
Ahab, "As the LORD the God of Israel lives, before whom I stand, there
shall be neither dew nor rain these
years, except by my word." 2 The
word of the LORD came to him, saying, 3 "Go from here and turn eastward, and hide yourself by the
Wadi Cherith, which is east of the
Jordan. 4 You shall drink from the
wadi, and I have commanded the
ravens to feed you there." 5 So he
went and did according to the word
of the LORD; he went and lived by
the Wadi Cherith, which is east of
the Jordan. 6 The ravens brought
him bread and meat in the morning, and bread and meat in the evening; and he drank from the wadi.
7 But after a while the wadi dried
up, because there was no rain in
the land.

The Widow of Zarephath

8 Then the word of the LORD
came to him, saying, 9 "Go now to
Zarephath, which belongs to Sidon, and live there; for I have commanded a widow there to feed
you." 10 So he set out and went to
Zarephath. When he came to the

16.20 vv. 5,14,27 **16.23** 1 Kings 15.21 **16.24** 1 Kings 13.32; Jn 4.4 **16.26** Mic 6.16; v. 19 **16.30** v. 25; 1 Kings 14.9

16.31 Deut 7.3; 2 Kings 10.18; 17.16 **16.32** 2 Kings 10.21, 26,27 **16.33** 2 Kings 13.6; vv. 29,30 **16.34** Josh 6.26 **17.1** 2 Kings 3.14; Deut 10.8; 1 Kings 18.1; Jas 5.17; Lk 4.25 **17.9** Ob 20; Lk 4.26

j Heb *Asherah* k Gk: Heb *of the settlers*

gate of the town, a widow was there
gathering sticks; he called to her
and said, "Bring me a little water in
a vessel, so that I may drink." 11 As
she was going to bring it, he called
to her and said, "Bring me a morsel
of bread in your hand." 12 But she
said, "As the LORD your God lives, I
have nothing baked, only a handful
of meal in a jar, and a little oil in a
jug; I am now gathering a couple of
sticks, so that I may go home and
prepare it for myself and my son,
that we may eat it, and die." 13 Elijah said to her, "Do not be afraid;
go and do as you have said; but first
make me a little cake of it and
bring it to me, and afterwards make
something for yourself and your
son. 14 For thus says the LORD the
God of Israel: The jar of meal will
not be emptied and the jug of oil
will not fail until the day that the
LORD sends rain on the earth."
15 She went and did as Elijah said,
so that she as well as he and her
household ate for many days.
16 The jar of meal was not emptied,
neither did the jug of oil fail, according to the word of the LORD that
he spoke by Elijah.

Elijah Revives the Widow's Son

17 After this the son of the
woman, the mistress of the house,
became ill; his illness was so severe
that there was no breath left in
him. 18 She then said to Elijah,
"What have you against me, O man
of God? You have come to me to
bring my sin to remembrance, and
to cause the death of my son!"
19 But he said to her, "Give me your
son." He took him from her bosom,
carried him up into the upper
chamber where he was lodging,
and laid him on his own bed. 20 He
cried out to the LORD, "O LORD my
God, have you brought calamity
even upon the widow with whom I
am staying, by killing her son?"
21 Then he stretched himself upon
the child three times, and cried out
to the LORD, "O LORD my God, let
this child's life come into him
again." 22 The LORD listened to the
voice of Elijah; the life of the child
came into him again, and he revived. 23 Elijah took the child,
brought him down from the upper
chamber into the house, and gave
him to his mother; then Elijah said,
"See, your son is alive." 24 So the
woman said to Elijah, "Now I know
that you are a man of God, and that
the word of the LORD in your mouth
is truth."

Elijah's Message to Ahab

18 After many days the word
of the LORD came to Elijah,
in the third year of the drought,[1]
saying, "Go, present yourself to
Ahab; I will send rain on the earth."
2 So Elijah went to present himself
to Ahab. The famine was severe in
Samaria. 3 Ahab summoned Obadiah, who was in charge of the palace. (Now Obadiah revered the
LORD greatly; 4 when Jezebel was
killing off the prophets of the LORD,
Obadiah took a hundred prophets,
hid them fifty to a cave, and provided them with bread and water.)
5 Then Ahab said to Obadiah, "Go
through the land to all the springs
of water and to all the wadis; perhaps we may find grass to keep the
horses and mules alive, and not
lose some of the animals." 6 So they
divided the land between them to
pass through it; Ahab went in one
direction by himself, and Obadiah
went in another direction by himself.

7 As Obadiah was on the way,
Elijah met him; Obadiah recognized him, fell on his face, and
said, "Is it you, my lord Elijah?"
8 He answered him, "It is I. Go, tell
your lord that Elijah is here." 9 And
he said, "How have I sinned, that
you would hand your servant over
to Ahab, to kill me? 10 As the LORD
your God lives, there is no nation or
kingdom to which my lord has not
sent to seek you; and when they
would say, 'He is not here,' he
would require an oath of the kingdom or nation, that they had not
found you. 11 But now you say, 'Go,
tell your lord that Elijah is here.'
12 As soon as I have gone from you,

17.12 v. 1; 2 Kings 4.2-7 **17.14** Lk 4.25,26 **17.18** 2 Kings 3.13 **17.21** 2 Kings 4.34, 35; Acts 20.10 **17.22** Heb 11.25 **17.24** Jn 3.2; 16.30 **18.1** 1 Kings 17.1; Lk 4.25; Jas 5.17 **18.4** v. 13 **18.7** 2 Kings 1.6-8 **18.10** 1 Kings 17.1 **18.12** 2 Kings 2.16; Ezek 3.12, 14; Acts 8.39

[1] Heb lacks *of the drought*

the spirit of the LORD will carry you
I know not where; so, when I come
and tell Ahab and he cannot find
you, he will kill me, although I your
servant have revered the LORD from
my youth. 13 Has it not been told
my lord what I did when Jezebel
killed the prophets of the LORD,
how I hid a hundred of the LORD's
prophets fifty to a cave, and provided them with bread and water?
14 Yet now you say, 'Go, tell your
lord that Elijah is here'; he will
surely kill me." 15 Elijah said, "As
the LORD of hosts lives, before
whom I stand, I will surely show
myself to him today." 16 So Obadiah went to meet Ahab, and told
him; and Ahab went to meet Elijah.
17 When Ahab saw Elijah, Ahab
said to him, "Is it you, you troubler
of Israel?" 18 He answered, "I have
not troubled Israel; but you have,
and your father's house, because
you have forsaken the commandments of the LORD and followed the
Baals. 19 Now therefore have all Israel assemble for me at Mount Carmel, with the four hundred fifty
prophets of Baal and the four hundred prophets of Asherah, who eat
at Jezebel's table."

Elijah's Triumph over the Priests of Baal

20 So Ahab sent to all the Israelites, and assembled the prophets at
Mount Carmel. 21 Elijah then came
near to all the people, and said,
"How long will you go limping with
two different opinions? If the LORD
is God, follow him; but if Baal, then
follow him." The people did not
answer him a word. 22 Then Elijah
said to the people, "I, even I only,
am left a prophet of the LORD; but
Baal's prophets number four hundred fifty. 23 Let two bulls be given
to us; let them choose one bull for
themselves, cut it in pieces, and lay
it on the wood, but put no fire to it;
I will prepare the other bull and lay
it on the wood, but put no fire to it.
24 Then you call on the name of
your god and I will call on the name
of the LORD; the god who answers
by fire is indeed God." All the

18.13 v. 4
18.15 1 Kings 17.1
18.17 1 Kings 21.20; Josh 7.25; Acts 16.20
18.18 2 Chr 15.2; 1 Kings 16.31; 21.25,26
18.19 Josh 19.26; 1 Kings 16.33
18.21 2 Kings 17.41; Mt 6.24; Josh 24.15
18.22 1 Kings 19.10, 14; v. 19
18.24 v. 38; 1 Chr 21.26; Acts 20.10
18.26 Ps 115.5; Jer 10.5; 1 Cor 8.4; 12.2
18.28 Lev 19.28; Deut 14.1
18.29 v. 26
18.30 1 Kings 19.10, 14
18.31 Gen 32.28; 35.10; 2 Kings 17.34
18.32 Col 3.17
18.33 Gen 22.9; Lev 1.6-8
18.36 Ex 3.6; 1 Kings 8.43; 2 Kings 19.19; Num 16.28

people answered, "Well spoken!"
25 Then Elijah said to the prophets
of Baal, "Choose for yourselves one
bull and prepare it first, for you are
many; then call on the name of
your god, but put no fire to it." 26 So
they took the bull that was given
them, prepared it, and called on
the name of Baal from morning until noon, crying, "O Baal, answer
us!" But there was no voice, and no
answer. They limped about the altar that they had made. 27 At noon
Elijah mocked them, saying, "Cry
aloud! Surely he is a god; either he
is meditating, or he has wandered
away, or he is on a journey, or perhaps he is asleep and must be
awakened." 28 Then they cried
aloud and, as was their custom,
they cut themselves with swords
and lances until the blood gushed
out over them. 29 As midday
passed, they raved on until the
time of the offering of the oblation,
but there was no voice, no answer,
and no response.
30 Then Elijah said to all the
people, "Come closer to me"; and
all the people came closer to him.
First he repaired the altar of the
LORD that had been thrown down;
31 Elijah took twelve stones, according to the number of the tribes
of the sons of Jacob, to whom the
word of the LORD came, saying, "Israel shall be your name"; 32 with
the stones he built an altar in the
name of the LORD. Then he made a
trench around the altar, large
enough to contain two measures of
seed. 33 Next he put the wood in order, cut the bull in pieces, and laid
it on the wood. He said, "Fill four
jars with water and pour it on the
burnt offering and on the wood."
34 Then he said, "Do it a second
time"; and they did it a second
time. Again he said, "Do it a third
time"; and they did it a third time,
35 so that the water ran all around
the altar, and filled the trench also
with water.
36 At the time of the offering of
the oblation, the prophet Elijah
came near and said, "O LORD, God
of Abraham, Isaac, and Israel, let it

be known this day that you are God
in Israel, that I am your servant,
and that I have done all these
things at your bidding. 37 Answer
me, O LORD, answer me, so that
this people may know that you,
O LORD, are God, and that you have
turned their hearts back." 38 Then
the fire of the LORD fell and consumed the burnt offering, the
wood, the stones, and the dust, and
even licked up the water that was
in the trench. 39 When all the people saw it, they fell on their faces
and said, "The LORD indeed is God;
the LORD indeed is God." 40 Elijah
said to them, "Seize the prophets
of Baal; do not let one of them escape." Then they seized them; and
Elijah brought them down to the
Wadi Kishon, and killed them
there.

The Drought Ends

41 Elijah said to Ahab, "Go up,
eat and drink; for there is a sound
of rushing rain." 42 So Ahab went
up to eat and to drink. Elijah went
up to the top of Carmel; there he
bowed himself down upon the
earth and put his face between his
knees. 43 He said to his servant, "Go
up now, look toward the sea." He
went up and looked, and said,
"There is nothing." Then he said,
"Go again seven times." 44 At the
seventh time he said, "Look, a little
cloud no bigger than a person's
hand is rising out of the sea." Then
he said, "Go say to Ahab, 'Harness
your chariot and go down before
the rain stops you.' " 45 In a little
while the heavens grew black with
clouds and wind; there was a heavy
rain. Ahab rode off and went to Jezreel. 46 But the hand of the LORD
was on Elijah; he girded up his
loins and ran in front of Ahab to the
entrance of Jezreel.

Elijah Flees from Jezebel

19 Ahab told Jezebel all that
Elijah had done, and how
he had killed all the prophets with
the sword. 2 Then Jezebel sent a
messenger to Elijah, saying, "So
may the gods do to me, and more
also, if I do not make your life like
the life of one of them by this time
tomorrow." 3 Then he was afraid;
he got up and fled for his life, and
came to Beer-sheba, which belongs
to Judah; he left his servant there.
4 But he himself went a day's
journey into the wilderness, and
came and sat down under a solitary
broom tree. He asked that he might
die: "It is enough; now, O LORD,
take away my life, for I am no better
than my ancestors." 5 Then he lay
down under the broom tree and fell
asleep. Suddenly an angel touched
him and said to him, "Get up and
eat." 6 He looked, and there at his
head was a cake baked on hot
stones, and a jar of water. He ate
and drank, and lay down again.
7 The angel of the LORD came a second time, touched him, and said,
"Get up and eat, otherwise the
journey will be too much for you."
8 He got up, and ate and drank;
then he went in the strength of that
food forty days and forty nights to
Horeb the mount of God. 9 At that
place he came to a cave, and spent
the night there.
Then the word of the LORD came
to him, saying, "What are you doing
here, Elijah?" 10 He answered, "I
have been very zealous for the
LORD, the God of hosts; for the Israelites have forsaken your covenant,
thrown down your altars, and killed
your prophets with the sword. I
alone am left, and they are seeking
my life, to take it away."

Elijah Meets God at Horeb

11 He said, "Go out and stand
on the mountain before the LORD,
for the LORD is about to pass by."
Now there was a great wind, so
strong that it was splitting mountains and breaking rocks in pieces
before the LORD, but the LORD was
not in the wind; and after the wind
an earthquake, but the LORD was
not in the earthquake; 12 and after
the earthquake a fire, but the LORD
was not in the fire; and after the fire
a sound of sheer silence. 13 When
Elijah heard it, he wrapped his face
in his mantle and went out and

18.38 Lev 9.24; 1 Chr 21.26; 2 Chr 7.1
18.39 vv. 21,24
18.40 Deut 13.5; 18.20; 2 Kings 10.24, 25
18.42 vv. 19,20; Jas 5.17,18
18.46 2 Kings 3.15; 4.29
19.1 1 Kings 18.40
19.2 1 Kings 20.10; 2 Kings 6.31
19.4 Num 11.15; Jon 4.3,8
19.8 Ex 34.28; Deut 9.9-11, 18; Mt 4.2; Ex 3.1
19.10 Rom 11.3; 1 Kings 18.4, 22
19.11 Ex 24.12; Ezek 1.4; 37.7
19.13 Ex 3.6; v. 9

stood at the entrance of the cave.
Then there came a voice to him
that said, "What are you doing
here, Elijah?" 14 He answered, "I
have been very zealous for the
LORD, the God of hosts; for the Israelites have forsaken your covenant,
thrown down your altars, and killed
your prophets with the sword. I
alone am left, and they are seeking
my life, to take it away." 15 Then
the LORD said to him, "Go, return
on your way to the wilderness of
Damascus; when you arrive, you
shall anoint Hazael as king over
Aram. 16 Also you shall anoint Jehu
son of Nimshi as king over Israel;
and you shall anoint Elisha son of
Shaphat of Abel-meholah as
prophet in your place. 17 Whoever
escapes from the sword of Hazael,
Jehu shall kill; and whoever escapes from the sword of Jehu, Elisha shall kill. 18 Yet I will leave sev-
en thousand in Israel, all the knees
that have not bowed to Baal, and
every mouth that has not kissed
him."

Elisha Becomes Elijah's Disciple

19 So he set out from there, and
found Elisha son of Shaphat, who
was plowing. There were twelve
yoke of oxen ahead of him, and he
was with the twelfth. Elijah passed
by him and threw his mantle over
him. 20 He left the oxen, ran after
Elijah, and said, "Let me kiss my
father and my mother, and then I
will follow you." Then Elijah[m] said
to him, "Go back again; for what
have I done to you?" 21 He returned
from following him, took the yoke
of oxen, and slaughtered them; using the equipment from the oxen,
he boiled their flesh, and gave it to
the people, and they ate. Then he
set out and followed Elijah, and became his servant.

Ahab's Wars with the Arameans

20 King Ben-hadad of Aram
gathered all his army to-
gether; thirty-two kings were with
him, along with horses and chariots. He marched against Samaria,
laid siege to it, and attacked it.
2 Then he sent messengers into the
city to King Ahab of Israel, and said
to him: "Thus says Ben-hadad:
3 Your silver and gold are mine;
your fairest wives and children also
are mine." 4 The king of Israel answered, "As you say, my lord,
O king, I am yours, and all that I
have." 5 The messengers came
again and said: "Thus says Ben-
hadad: I sent to you, saying, 'Deliver to me your silver and gold, your
wives and children'; 6 nevertheless
I will send my servants to you tomorrow about this time, and they
shall search your house and the
houses of your servants, and lay
hands on whatever pleases them,[n]
and take it away."

7 Then the king of Israel called
all the elders of the land, and said,
"Look now! See how this man is
seeking trouble; for he sent to me
for my wives, my children, my silver, and my gold; and I did not refuse him." 8 Then all the elders and
all the people said to him, "Do not
listen or consent." 9 So he said to
the messengers of Ben-hadad,
"Tell my lord the king: All that you
first demanded of your servant I
will do; but this thing I cannot do."
The messengers left and brought
him word again. 10 Ben-hadad sent
to him and said, "The gods do so to
me, and more also, if the dust of
Samaria will provide a handful for
each of the people who follow me."
11 The king of Israel answered,
"Tell him: One who puts on armor
should not brag like one who takes
it off." 12 When Ben-hadad heard
this message—now he had been
drinking with the kings in the
booths—he said to his men, "Take
your positions!" And they took
their positions against the city.

Prophetic Opposition to Ahab

13 Then a certain prophet came
up to King Ahab of Israel and said,
"Thus says the LORD, Have you seen
all this great multitude? Look, I
will give it into your hand today;
and you shall know that I am the
LORD." 14 Ahab said, "By whom?"

19.14 v. 10 **19.15** 2 Kings 8.12, 13 **19.16** 2 Kings 9.1-3; vv. 19-21; 2 Kings 2.9, 15 **19.17** 2 Kings 8.12; 9.14ff; 13.3, 22 **19.18** Rom 11.4; Hos 13.2 **19.19** 2 Kings 2.8, 13 **19.20** Mt 8.21,22; Lk 9.61,62 **19.21** 2 Sam 24.22 **20.1** 1 Kings 15.18, 20; 2 Kings 6.24; 1 Kings 22.31; 2 Kings 6.24-29

20.7 2 Kings 5.7 **20.10** 1 Kings 19.2 **20.11** Prov 27.1 **20.12** v. 16 **20.13** v. 28

[m] Heb *he* [n] Gk Syr Vg: Heb *you*

He said, "Thus says the LORD, By
the young men who serve the district governors." Then he said,
"Who shall begin the battle?" He
answered, "You." 15 Then he mustered the young men who serve the
district governors, two hundred
thirty-two; after them he mustered
all the people of Israel, seven thousand.
16 They went out at noon, while
Ben-hadad was drinking himself
drunk in the booths, he and the
thirty-two kings allied with him.
17 The young men who serve the
district governors went out first.
Ben-hadad had sent out scouts,[o]
and they reported to him, "Men
have come out from Samaria."
18 He said, "If they have come out
for peace, take them alive; if they
have come out for war, take them
alive."
19 But these had already come
out of the city: the young men who
serve the district governors, and
the army that followed them.
20 Each killed his man; the Arameans fled and Israel pursued them,
but King Ben-hadad of Aram escaped on a horse with the cavalry.
21 The king of Israel went out, attacked the horses and chariots, and
defeated the Arameans with a great
slaughter.
22 Then the prophet ap-
proached the king of Israel and said
to him, "Come, strengthen yourself, and consider well what you
have to do; for in the spring the
king of Aram will come up against
you."

The Arameans Are Defeated

23 The servants of the king of
Aram said to him, "Their gods are
gods of the hills, and so they were
stronger than we; but let us fight
against them in the plain, and surely we shall be stronger than they.
24 Also do this: remove the kings,
each from his post, and put commanders in place of them; 25 and
muster an army like the army that
you have lost, horse for horse, and
chariot for chariot; then we will
fight against them in the plain, and

20.16 v. 12
20.18 2 Kings 14.8-12
20.22 vv. 13,26; 2 Sam 11.1
20.23 1 Kings 14.23
20.26 v. 22; 2 Kings 13.7
20.28 v. 13
20.30 v. 26; 1 Kings 22.25; 2 Chr 18.24
20.31 Gen 37.34
20.32 vv. 3-6
20.34 1 Kings 15.20

surely we shall be stronger than
they." He heeded their voice, and
did so.
26 In the spring Ben-hadad
mustered the Arameans and went
up to Aphek to fight against Israel.
27 After the Israelites had been
mustered and provisioned, they
went out to engage them; the people of Israel encamped opposite
them like two little flocks of goats,
while the Arameans filled the
country. 28 A man of God approached and said to the king of Israel, "Thus says the LORD: Because
the Arameans have said, 'The LORD
is a god of the hills but he is not a
god of the valleys,' therefore I will
give all this great multitude into
your hand, and you shall know that
I am the LORD." 29 They encamped
opposite one another seven days.
Then on the seventh day the battle
began; the Israelites killed one
hundred thousand Aramean foot
soldiers in one day. 30 The rest fled
into the city of Aphek; and the wall
fell on twenty-seven thousand men
that were left.
Ben-hadad also fled, and entered
the city to hide. 31 His servants said
to him, "Look, we have heard that
the kings of the house of Israel are
merciful kings; let us put sackcloth
around our waists and ropes on our
heads, and go out to the king of Israel; perhaps he will spare your
life." 32 So they tied sackcloth
around their waists, put ropes on
their heads, went to the king of Israel, and said, "Your servant Ben-
hadad says, 'Please let me live.' "
And he said, "Is he still alive? He is
my brother." 33 Now the men were
watching for an omen; they quickly
took it up from him and said, "Yes,
Ben-hadad is your brother." Then
he said, "Go and bring him." So
Ben-hadad came out to him; and
he had him come up into the chariot. 34 Ben-hadad[p] said to him, "I
will restore the towns that my father took from your father; and you
may establish bazaars for yourself
in Damascus, as my father did in

[o] Heb lacks *scouts* [p] Heb *He*

Samaria." The king of Israel responded,[q] "I will let you go on
those terms." So he made a treaty
with him and let him go.

A Prophet Condemns Ahab

35 At the command of the LORD
a certain member of a company of
prophets[r] said to another, "Strike
me!" But the man refused to strike
him. 36 Then he said to him, "Because you have not obeyed the
voice of the LORD, as soon as you
have left me, a lion will kill you."
And when he had left him, a lion
met him and killed him. 37 Then he
found another man and said,
"Strike me!" So the man hit him,
striking and wounding him. 38 Then
the prophet departed, and waited
for the king along the road, disguising himself with a bandage over his
eyes. 39 As the king passed by, he
cried to the king and said, "Your
servant went out into the thick of
the battle; then a soldier turned
and brought a man to me, and said,
'Guard this man; if he is missing,
your life shall be given for his life,
or else you shall pay a talent of silver.' 40 While your servant was busy
here and there, he was gone." The
king of Israel said to him, "So shall
your judgment be; you yourself
have decided it." 41 Then he quickly took the bandage away from his
eyes. The king of Israel recognized
him as one of the prophets. 42 Then
he said to him, "Thus says the
LORD, 'Because you have let the
man go whom I had devoted to destruction, therefore your life shall
be for his life, and your people for
his people.' " 43 The king of Israel
set out toward home, resentful and
sullen, and came to Samaria.

Naboth's Vineyard

21 Later the following events
took place: Naboth the Jezreelite had a vineyard in Jezreel,
beside the palace of King Ahab of
Samaria. 2 And Ahab said to Naboth, "Give me your vineyard, so
that I may have it for a vegetable
garden, because it is near my
house; I will give you a better vineyard for it; or, if it seems good to
you, I will give you its value in money." 3 But Naboth said to Ahab,
"The LORD forbid that I should give
you my ancestral inheritance."
4 Ahab went home resentful and
sullen because of what Naboth the
Jezreelite had said to him; for he
had said, "I will not give you my ancestral inheritance." He lay down
on his bed, turned away his face,
and would not eat.
5 His wife Jezebel came to him
and said, "Why are you so depressed that you will not eat?" 6 He
said to her, "Because I spoke to Naboth the Jezreelite and said to him,
'Give me your vineyard for money;
or else, if you prefer, I will give you
another vineyard for it'; but he answered, 'I will not give you my vineyard.' " 7 His wife Jezebel said to
him, "Do you now govern Israel?
Get up, eat some food, and be
cheerful; I will give you the vineyard of Naboth the Jezreelite."
8 So she wrote letters in Ahab's
name and sealed them with his
seal; she sent the letters to the elders and the nobles who lived with
Naboth in his city. 9 She wrote in
the letters, "Proclaim a fast, and
seat Naboth at the head of the assembly; 10 seat two scoundrels opposite him, and have them bring a
charge against him, saying, 'You
have cursed God and the king.'
Then take him out, and stone him
to death." 11 The men of his city,
the elders and the nobles who lived
in his city, did as Jezebel had sent
word to them. Just as it was written
in the letters that she had sent to
them, 12 they proclaimed a fast and
seated Naboth at the head of the
assembly. 13 The two scoundrels
came in and sat opposite him; and
the scoundrels brought a charge
against Naboth, in the presence of
the people, saying, "Naboth cursed
God and the king." So they took
him outside the city, and stoned
him to death. 14 Then they sent to

20.35 2 Kings 2.3-7; 1 Kings 13.17, 18
20.36 1 Kings 13.24
20.39 2 Kings 10.24
20.42 v. 39; 1 Kings 22.31-37
20.43 1 Kings 21.4
21.1 1 Kings 18.45, 46
21.2 1 Sam 8.14
21.3 Lev 25.23; Num 36.7; Ezek 46.18
21.4 1 Kings 20.43
21.7 1 Sam 8.14
21.8 Esther 3.12; 8.8,10
21.10 Ex 22.28; Lev 24.15, 16; Acts 6.11
21.13 2 Kings 9.26

[q] Heb lacks *The king of Israel responded*
[r] Heb *of the sons of the prophets*

Jezebel, saying, "Naboth has been
stoned; he is dead."
15 As soon as Jezebel heard that
Naboth had been stoned and was
dead, Jezebel said to Ahab, "Go,
take possession of the vineyard of
Naboth the Jezreelite, which he refused to give you for money; for Naboth is not alive, but dead." 16 As
soon as Ahab heard that Naboth
was dead, Ahab set out to go down
to the vineyard of Naboth the Jezreelite, to take possession of it.

Elijah Pronounces God's Sentence

17 Then the word of the LORD
came to Elijah the Tishbite, saying:
18 Go down to meet King Ahab of
Israel, who rules[s] in Samaria; he is
now in the vineyard of Naboth,
where he has gone to take possession. 19 You shall say to him, "Thus
says the LORD: Have you killed, and
also taken possession?" You shall
say to him, "Thus says the LORD: In
the place where dogs licked up the
blood of Naboth, dogs will also lick
up your blood."
20 Ahab said to Elijah, "Have
you found me, O my enemy?" He
answered, "I have found you. Because you have sold yourself to do
what is evil in the sight of the LORD,
21 I will bring disaster on you; I will
consume you, and will cut off from
Ahab every male, bond or free, in
Israel; 22 and I will make your house
like the house of Jeroboam son of
Nebat, and like the house of Baasha son of Ahijah, because you
have provoked me to anger and
have caused Israel to sin. 23 Also
concerning Jezebel the LORD said,
'The dogs shall eat Jezebel within
the bounds of Jezreel.' 24 Anyone
belonging to Ahab who dies in the
city the dogs shall eat; and anyone
of his who dies in the open country
the birds of the air shall eat."
25 (Indeed, there was no one
like Ahab, who sold himself to do
what was evil in the sight of the
LORD, urged on by his wife Jezebel.
26 He acted most abominably in going after idols, as the Amorites had

21.17 Ps 9.12
21.18 1 Kings 16.29
21.19 1 Kings 22.38; 2 Kings 9.8
21.20 1 Kings 18.17; v. 25
21.21 1 Kings 14.10; 2 Kings 9.8
21.22 1 Kings 15.29
21.23 2 Kings 9.10, 30-37
21.24 1 Kings 14.11; 16.4
21.25 v. 20; 1 Kings 16.30-33
21.26 Gen 15.16; Lev 18.25-30

21.27 2 Sam 3.31; 2 Kings 6.30
21.29 2 Kings 9.25
22.2 2 Chr 18.2ff; 1 Kings 15.24
22.3 Deut 4.43; Josh 21.38
22.4 2 Kings 3.7
22.6 1 Kings 18.19
22.7 2 Kings 3.11
22.10 v. 6

done, whom the LORD drove out before the Israelites.)
27 When Ahab heard those
words, he tore his clothes and put
sackcloth over his bare flesh; he
fasted, lay in the sackcloth, and
went about dejectedly. 28 Then the
word of the LORD came to Elijah the
Tishbite: 29 "Have you seen how
Ahab has humbled himself before
me? Because he has humbled himself before me, I will not bring the
disaster in his days; but in his son's
days I will bring the disaster on his
house."

Joint Campaign with Judah against Aram

22 For three years Aram and
Israel continued without
war. 2 But in the third year King Jehoshaphat of Judah came down to
the king of Israel. 3 The king of Israel said to his servants, "Do you
know that Ramoth-gilead belongs
to us, yet we are doing nothing to
take it out of the hand of the king
of Aram?" 4 He said to Jehoshaphat, "Will you go with me to battle
at Ramoth-gilead?" Jehoshaphat
replied to the king of Israel, "I am
as you are; my people are your people, my horses are your horses."
5 But Jehoshaphat also said to
the king of Israel, "Inquire first for
the word of the LORD." 6 Then the
king of Israel gathered the prophets together, about four hundred of
them, and said to them, "Shall I go
to battle against Ramoth-gilead, or
shall I refrain?" They said, "Go up;
for the LORD will give it into the
hand of the king." 7 But Jehoshaphat said, "Is there no other prophet of the LORD here of whom we may
inquire?" 8 The king of Israel said to
Jehoshaphat, "There is still one
other by whom we may inquire of
the LORD, Micaiah son of Imlah; but
I hate him, for he never prophesies
anything favorable about me, but
only disaster." Jehoshaphat said,
"Let the king not say such a thing."
9 Then the king of Israel summoned
an officer and said, "Bring quickly
Micaiah son of Imlah." 10 Now the

[s] Heb *who is*

king of Israel and King Jehoshaphat of Judah were sitting on their
thrones, arrayed in their robes, at
the threshing floor at the entrance
of the gate of Samaria; and all the
prophets were prophesying before
them. 11 Zedekiah son of Chenaanah made for himself horns of iron,
and he said, "Thus says the LORD:
With these you shall gore the Arameans until they are destroyed."
12 All the prophets were prophesying the same and saying, "Go up to
Ramoth-gilead and triumph; the
LORD will give it into the hand of the
king."

Micaiah Predicts Failure

13 The messenger who had
gone to summon Micaiah said to
him, "Look, the words of the
prophets with one accord are favorable to the king; let your word be
like the word of one of them, and
speak favorably." 14 But Micaiah
said, "As the LORD lives, whatever
the LORD says to me, that I will
speak."

15 When he had come to the
king, the king said to him, "Micaiah, shall we go to Ramoth-gilead
to battle, or shall we refrain?" He
answered him, "Go up and triumph; the LORD will give it into the
hand of the king." 16 But the king
said to him, "How many times
must I make you swear to tell me
nothing but the truth in the name
of the LORD?" 17 Then Micaiah[t]
said, "I saw all Israel scattered on
the mountains, like sheep that
have no shepherd; and the LORD
said, 'These have no master; let
each one go home in peace.' "
18 The king of Israel said to Jehoshaphat, "Did I not tell you that he
would not prophesy anything favorable about me, but only disaster?"

19 Then Micaiah[t] said, "Therefore hear the word of the LORD: I
saw the LORD sitting on his throne,
with all the host of heaven standing
beside him to the right and to the
left of him. 20 And the LORD said,
'Who will entice Ahab, so that he
may go up and fall at Ramoth-
gilead?' Then one said one thing,
and another said another, 21 until a
spirit came forward and stood before the LORD, saying, 'I will entice
him.' 22 'How?' the LORD asked him.
He replied, 'I will go out and be a
lying spirit in the mouth of all his
prophets.' Then the LORD[t] said,
'You are to entice him, and you
shall succeed; go out and do it.'
23 So you see, the LORD has put a
lying spirit in the mouth of all
these your prophets; the LORD has
decreed disaster for you."

24 Then Zedekiah son of Chenaanah came up to Micaiah, slapped
him on the cheek, and said,
"Which way did the spirit of the
LORD pass from me to speak to
you?" 25 Micaiah replied, "You will
find out on that day when you go in
to hide in an inner chamber."
26 The king of Israel then ordered,
"Take Micaiah, and return him to
Amon the governor of the city and
to Joash the king's son, 27 and say,
'Thus says the king: Put this fellow
in prison, and feed him on reduced
rations of bread and water until I
come in peace.' " 28 Micaiah said,
"If you return in peace, the LORD
has not spoken by me." And he
said, "Hear, you peoples, all of
you!"

Defeat and Death of Ahab

29 So the king of Israel and King
Jehoshaphat of Judah went up to
Ramoth-gilead. 30 The king of Israel
said to Jehoshaphat, "I will disguise myself and go into battle, but
you wear your robes." So the king
of Israel disguised himself and
went into battle. 31 Now the king of
Aram had commanded the thirty-
two captains of his chariots, "Fight
with no one small or great, but only
with the king of Israel." 32 When the
captains of the chariots saw Jehoshaphat, they said, "It is surely
the king of Israel." So they turned
to fight against him; and Jehoshaphat cried out. 33 When the captains of the chariots saw that it was
not the king of Israel, they turned
back from pursuing him. 34 But a
certain man drew his bow and un-

22.11 Zech 1.18-21; Deut 33.17
22.14 1 Kings 18.10, 15; Num 22.18; 24.13
22.15 v. 12
22.17 vv. 34-36
22.18 v. 8
22.19 Isa 6.1; Dan 7.9,10
22.22 Judg 9.23; 1 Sam 16.14; 18.10; 19.9; 2 Thes 2.11
22.23 Ezek 14.9
22.24 2 Chr 18.23
22.25 1 Kings 20.30
22.27 2 Chr 18.25-27
22.28 Deut 18.22
22.29 vv. 3,4
22.30 2 Chr 25.32
22.31 2 Chr 18.30
22.32 2 Chr 18.31

[t] Heb *he*

knowingly struck the king of Israel
between the scale armor and the
breastplate; so he said to the driver
of his chariot, "Turn around, and
carry me out of the battle, for I am
wounded." 35 The battle grew hot
that day, and the king was propped
up in his chariot facing the Arameans, until at evening he died; the
blood from the wound had flowed
into the bottom of the chariot.
36 Then about sunset a shout went
through the army, "Every man to
his city, and every man to his country!"
37 So the king died, and was
brought to Samaria; they buried
the king in Samaria. 38 They
washed the chariot by the pool of
Samaria; the dogs licked up his
blood, and the prostitutes washed
themselves in it,[u] according to the
word of the LORD that he had spoken. 39 Now the rest of the acts of
Ahab, and all that he did, and the
ivory house that he built, and all
the cities that he built, are they not
written in the Book of the Annals of
the Kings of Israel? 40 So Ahab slept
with his ancestors; and his son
Ahaziah succeeded him.

Jehoshaphat Reigns over Judah

41 Jehoshaphat son of Asa began to reign over Judah in the
fourth year of King Ahab of Israel.
42 Jehoshaphat was thirty-five years
old when he began to reign, and he
reigned twenty-five years in Jerusalem. His mother's name was Azubah daughter of Shilhi. 43 He
walked in all the way of his father
Asa; he did not turn aside from it,
doing what was right in the sight of
the LORD; yet the high places were
not taken away, and the people still
sacrificed and offered incense on
the high places. 44 Jehoshaphat
also made peace with the king of
Israel.
45 Now the rest of the acts of Jehoshaphat, and his power that he
showed, and how he waged war, are
they not written in the Book of the
Annals of the Kings of Judah?
46 The remnant of the male temple
prostitutes who were still in the
land in the days of his father Asa,
he exterminated.
47 There was no king in Edom;
a deputy was king. 48 Jehoshaphat
made ships of the Tarshish type to
go to Ophir for gold; but they did
not go, for the ships were wrecked
at Ezion-geber. 49 Then Ahaziah
son of Ahab said to Jehoshaphat,
"Let my servants go with your servants in the ships," but Jehoshaphat was not willing. 50 Jehoshaphat slept with his ancestors and
was buried with his ancestors in
the city of his father David; his son
Jehoram succeeded him.

Ahaziah Reigns over Israel

51 Ahaziah son of Ahab began
to reign over Israel in Samaria in
the seventeenth year of King Jehoshaphat of Judah; he reigned
two years over Israel. 52 He did what
was evil in the sight of the LORD,
and walked in the way of his father
and mother, and in the way of Jeroboam son of Nebat, who caused Israel to sin. 53 He served Baal and
worshiped him; he provoked the
LORD, the God of Israel, to anger,
just as his father had done.

22.38 1 Kings 21.19
22.39 Am 3.15
22.41 2 Chr 20.31
22.43 2 Chr 17.3; 1 Kings 15.14; 2 Kings 12.3
22.44 2 Chr 19.2
22.45 2 Chr 20.34
22.46 1 Kings 14.24; 15.12
22.47 2 Sam 8.14; 2 Kings 3.9
22.48 2 Chr 20.35ff; 1 Kings 10.22
22.50 2 Chr 21.1
22.51 v. 40
22.52 1 Kings 15.26; 21.25
22.53 1 Kings 16.30-32

[u] Heb lacks *in it*

2 Kings

Title and Background

See Introduction to 1 Kings.

Author and Date of Writing

See Introduction to 1 Kings.

Theme and Message

2 Kings continues the stories of the great prophets Elijah and Elisha. It also tells the history of the northern and southern kingdoms until they were both finally conquered. In both kingdoms God's prophets kept warning the people that God would punish them if they did not repent of their sins.

Outline

I. Elijah and Elisha (1.1–8.15)
II. Israel and Judah from Joram/Jehoram to Israel's Exile (8.16–17.41)
III. Judah from Hezekiah to the Babylonian Exile (18.1–25.30)

Elijah Denounces Ahaziah

1 After the death of Ahab, Moab
rebelled against Israel.
2 Ahaziah had fallen through
the lattice in his upper chamber in
Samaria, and lay injured; so he sent
messengers, telling them, "Go, inquire of Baal-zebub, the god of Ekron, whether I shall recover from
this injury." 3 But the angel of the
LORD said to Elijah the Tishbite,
"Get up, go to meet the messengers
of the king of Samaria, and say to
them, 'Is it because there is no God
in Israel that you are going to inquire of Baal-zebub, the god of Ekron?' 4 Now therefore thus says the
LORD, 'You shall not leave the bed
to which you have gone, but you
shall surely die.' " So Elijah went.
5 The messengers returned to
the king, who said to them, "Why
have you returned?" 6 They answered him, "There came a man to
meet us, who said to us, 'Go back
to the king who sent you, and say to
him: Thus says the LORD: Is it because there is no God in Israel that
you are sending to inquire of Baal-
zebub, the god of Ekron? Therefore
you shall not leave the bed to

1.1 2 Sam 8.2; 2 Kings 3.5 **1.2** vv. 3,6; Mt 10.25; 2 Kings 8.7-10 **1.4** vv. 6,16 **1.8** Zech 13.4; Mt 3.4 **1.10** 1 Kings 18.36-38; Lk 9.54

which you have gone, but shall
surely die.' " 7 He said to them,
"What sort of man was he who
came to meet you and told you
these things?" 8 They answered
him, "A hairy man, with a leather
belt around his waist." He said, "It
is Elijah the Tishbite."
9 Then the king sent to him a
captain of fifty with his fifty men.
He went up to Elijah, who was sitting on the top of a hill, and said to
him, "O man of God, the king says,
'Come down.' " 10 But Elijah answered the captain of fifty, "If I am
a man of God, let fire come down
from heaven and consume you and
your fifty." Then fire came down
from heaven, and consumed him
and his fifty.
11 Again the king sent to him
another captain of fifty with his fifty. He went up[a] and said to him,
"O man of God, this is the king's
order: Come down quickly!" 12 But
Elijah answered them, "If I am a
man of God, let fire come down
from heaven and consume you and
your fifty." Then the fire of God

[a] Gk Compare verses 9, 13: Heb *He answered*

came down from heaven and consumed him and his fifty.

13 Again the king sent the captain of a third fifty with his fifty. So the third captain of fifty went up, and came and fell on his knees before Elijah, and entreated him, "O man of God, please let my life, and the life of these fifty servants of yours, be precious in your sight. 14 Look, fire came down from heaven and consumed the two former captains of fifty men with their fifties; but now let my life be precious in your sight." 15 Then the angel of the LORD said to Elijah, "Go down with him; do not be afraid of him." So he set out and went down with him to the king, 16 and said to him, "Thus says the LORD: Because you have sent messengers to inquire of Baal-zebub, the god of Ekron,—is it because there is no God in Israel to inquire of his word?—therefore you shall not leave the bed to which you have gone, but you shall surely die."

Death of Ahaziah

17 So he died according to the word of the LORD that Elijah had spoken. His brother,[b] Jehoram succeeded him as king in the second year of King Jehoram son of Jehoshaphat of Judah, because Ahaziah had no son. 18 Now the rest of the acts of Ahaziah that he did, are they not written in the Book of the Annals of the Kings of Israel?

Elijah Ascends to Heaven

2 Now when the LORD was about to take Elijah up to heaven by a whirlwind, Elijah and Elisha were on their way from Gilgal. 2 Elijah said to Elisha, "Stay here; for the LORD has sent me as far as Bethel." But Elisha said, "As the LORD lives, and as you yourself live, I will not leave you." So they went down to Bethel. 3 The company of prophets[c] who were in Bethel came out to Elisha, and said to him, "Do you know that today the LORD will take your master away from you?" And he said, "Yes, I know; keep silent."

4 Elijah said to him, "Elisha, stay here; for the LORD has sent me to Jericho." But he said, "As the LORD lives, and as you yourself live, I will not leave you." So they came to Jericho. 5 The company of prophets[c] who were at Jericho drew near to Elisha, and said to him, "Do you know that today the LORD will take your master away from you?" And he answered, "Yes, I know; be silent."

6 Then Elijah said to him, "Stay here; for the LORD has sent me to the Jordan." But he said, "As the LORD lives, and as you yourself live, I will not leave you." So the two of them went on. 7 Fifty men of the company of prophets[c] also went, and stood at some distance from them, as they both were standing by the Jordan. 8 Then Elijah took his mantle and rolled it up, and struck the water; the water was parted to the one side and to the other, until the two of them crossed on dry ground.

9 When they had crossed, Elijah said to Elisha, "Tell me what I may do for you, before I am taken from you." Elisha said, "Please let me inherit a double share of your spirit." 10 He responded, "You have asked a hard thing; yet, if you see me as I am being taken from you, it will be granted you; if not, it will not." 11 As they continued walking and talking, a chariot of fire and horses of fire separated the two of them, and Elijah ascended in a whirlwind into heaven. 12 Elisha kept watching and crying out, "Father, father! The chariots of Israel and its horsemen!" But when he could no longer see him, he grasped his own clothes and tore them in two pieces.

Elisha Succeeds Elijah

13 He picked up the mantle of Elijah that had fallen from him, and went back and stood on the bank of the Jordan. 14 He took the mantle of Elijah that had fallen from him, and struck the water, saying, "Where is the LORD, the God

1.13 1 Sam 26.21; Ps 72.14
1.15 v. 3
1.16 v. 3
1.17 2 Kings 3.1; 8.16
2.1 Gen 5.24; Heb 11.5; 1 Kings 19.21
2.2 Ruth 1.15, 16; vv. 4,6; 1 Sam 1.26; 2 Kings 4.30
2.3 vv. 5,7,15; 2 Kings 4.1, 38
2.4 v. 2; Josh 6.26
2.5 v. 3
2.6 v. 3; Josh 3.8, 15-17
2.7 vv. 15,16
2.8 1 Kings 19.13, 19; v. 14; Ex 14.21,22
2.11 2 Kings 6.17; Ps 104.4
2.12 2 Kings 13.14
2.14 v. 8

[b] Gk Syr: Heb lacks *His brother*
[c] Heb *sons of the prophets*

of Elijah?" When he had struck the water, the water was parted to the one side and to the other, and Elisha went over.

15 When the company of prophets[d] who were at Jericho saw him at a distance, they declared, "The spirit of Elijah rests on Elisha." They came to meet him and bowed to the ground before him. [16]They said to him, "See now, we have fifty strong men among your servants; please let them go and seek your master; it may be that the spirit of the LORD has caught him up and thrown him down on some mountain or into some valley." He responded, "No, do not send them." [17]But when they urged him until he was ashamed, he said, "Send them." So they sent fifty men who searched for three days but did not find him. [18]When they came back to him (he had remained at Jericho), he said to them, "Did I not say to you, Do not go?"

Elisha Performs Miracles

19 Now the people of the city said to Elisha, "The location of this city is good, as my lord sees; but the water is bad, and the land is unfruitful." [20]He said, "Bring me a new bowl, and put salt in it." So they brought it to him. [21]Then he went to the spring of water and threw the salt into it, and said, "Thus says the LORD, I have made this water wholesome; from now on neither death nor miscarriage shall come from it." [22]So the water has been wholesome to this day, according to the word that Elisha spoke.

23 He went up from there to Bethel; and while he was going up on the way, some small boys came out of the city and jeered at him, saying, "Go away, baldhead! Go away, baldhead!" [24]When he turned around and saw them, he cursed them in the name of the LORD. Then two she-bears came out of the woods and mauled forty-two of the boys. [25]From there he went on to Mount Carmel, and then returned to Samaria.

2.15 v. 7
2.16 1 Kings 18.12; Acts 8.39
2.17 2 Kings 8.11
2.21 Ex 15.25; 2 Kings 4.41; 6.6
2.24 Neh 13.25-27
2.25 2 Kings 4.25; 1 Kings 18.19, 20

3.1 2 Kings 1.17
3.2 2 Kings 10.18, 26-28; 1 Kings 16.31, 32
3.3 1 Kings 12.28-32; 14.9,16
3.4 2 Sam 8.2; Isa 16.1
3.5 2 Kings 1.1
3.7 1 Kings 22.4
3.9 vv. 1,7; 1 Kings 22.47
3.11 1 Kings 22.7; 19.21

Jehoram Reigns over Israel

3 In the eighteenth year of King Jehoshaphat of Judah, Jehoram son of Ahab became king over Israel in Samaria; he reigned twelve years. [2]He did what was evil in the sight of the LORD, though not like his father and mother, for he removed the pillar of Baal that his father had made. [3]Nevertheless he clung to the sin of Jeroboam son of Nebat, which he caused Israel to commit; he did not depart from it.

War with Moab

4 Now King Mesha of Moab was a sheep breeder, who used to deliver to the king of Israel one hundred thousand lambs, and the wool of one hundred thousand rams. [5]But when Ahab died, the king of Moab rebelled against the king of Israel. [6]So King Jehoram marched out of Samaria at that time and mustered all Israel. [7]As he went he sent word to King Jehoshaphat of Judah, "The king of Moab has rebelled against me; will you go with me to battle against Moab?" He answered, "I will; I am with you, my people are your people, my horses are your horses." [8]Then he asked, "By which way shall we march?" Jehoram answered, "By the way of the wilderness of Edom."

9 So the king of Israel, the king of Judah, and the king of Edom set out; and when they had made a roundabout march of seven days, there was no water for the army or for the animals that were with them. [10]Then the king of Israel said, "Alas! The LORD has summoned us, three kings, only to be handed over to Moab." [11]But Jehoshaphat said, "Is there no prophet of the LORD here, through whom we may inquire of the LORD?" Then one of the servants of the king of Israel answered, "Elisha son of Shaphat, who used to pour water on the hands of Elijah, is here." [12]Jehoshaphat said, "The word of the LORD is with him." So the king of Israel and Jehoshaphat and the

[d] Heb *sons of the prophets*

king of Edom went down to him.
13 Elisha said to the king of Israel, "What have I to do with you?
Go to your father's prophets or to
your mother's." But the king of Israel said to him, "No; it is the LORD
who has summoned us, three
kings, only to be handed over to
Moab." 14 Elisha said, "As the LORD
of hosts lives, whom I serve, were it
not that I have regard for King Jehoshaphat of Judah, I would give
you neither a look nor a glance.
15 But get me a musician." And
then, while the musician was playing, the power of the LORD came on
him. 16 And he said, "Thus says the
LORD, 'I will make this wadi full of
pools.' 17 For thus says the LORD,
'You shall see neither wind nor
rain, but the wadi shall be filled
with water, so that you shall drink,
you, your cattle, and your animals.'
18 This is only a trifle in the sight of
the LORD, for he will also hand
Moab over to you. 19 You shall conquer every fortified city and every
choice city; every good tree you
shall fell, all springs of water you
shall stop up, and every good piece
of land you shall ruin with stones."
20 The next day, about the time of
the morning offering, suddenly water began to flow from the direction
of Edom, until the country was
filled with water.
21 When all the Moabites heard
that the kings had come up to fight
against them, all who were able to
put on armor, from the youngest to
the oldest, were called out and
were drawn up at the frontier.
22 When they rose early in the
morning, and the sun shone upon
the water, the Moabites saw the
water opposite them as red as
blood. 23 They said, "This is blood;
the kings must have fought together, and killed one another. Now
then, Moab, to the spoil!" 24 But
when they came to the camp of Israel, the Israelites rose up and attacked the Moabites, who fled before them; as they entered Moab
they continued the attack.[e] 25 The
cities they overturned, and on every good piece of land everyone
threw a stone, until it was covered;
every spring of water they stopped
up, and every good tree they felled.
Only at Kir-hareseth did the stone
walls remain, until the slingers surrounded and attacked it. 26 When
the king of Moab saw that the battle was going against him, he took
with him seven hundred swords-
men to break through, opposite the
king of Edom; but they could not.
27 Then he took his firstborn son
who was to succeed him, and offered him as a burnt offering on the
wall. And great wrath came upon
Israel, so they withdrew from him
and returned to their own land.

Elisha and the Widow's Oil

4 Now the wife of a member of
the company of prophets[f]
cried to Elisha, "Your servant my
husband is dead; and you know
that your servant feared the LORD,
but a creditor has come to take my
two children as slaves." 2 Elisha
said to her, "What shall I do for
you? Tell me, what do you have in
the house?" She answered, "Your
servant has nothing in the house,
except a jar of oil." 3 He said, "Go
outside, borrow vessels from all
your neighbors, empty vessels and
not just a few. 4 Then go in, and
shut the door behind you and your
children, and start pouring into all
these vessels; when each is full, set
it aside." 5 So she left him and shut
the door behind her and her children; they kept bringing vessels to
her, and she kept pouring. 6 When
the vessels were full, she said to her
son, "Bring me another vessel."
But he said to her, "There are no
more." Then the oil stopped flowing. 7 She came and told the man of
God, and he said, "Go sell the oil
and pay your debts, and you and
your children can live on the rest."

Elisha Raises the Shunammite's Son

8 One day Elisha was passing
through Shunem, where a wealthy
woman lived, who urged him to

3.13 Ezek 14.3-5; 1 Kings 18.19
3.14 1 Kings 17.1; 2 Kings 5.16
3.15 1 Sam 16.23; Ezek 1.3
3.19 v. 25
3.20 Ex 29.39,40
3.21 Gen 19.37
3.25 v. 19; Isa 16.7,11; Jer 48.31,36
3.27 Am 2.1; Mic 6.7
4.1 2 Kings 2.3; Lev 25.39; Mt 18.25
4.7 1 Kings 12.22
4.8 Josh 19.18

[e] Compare Gk Syr: Meaning of Heb uncertain
[f] Heb *the sons of the prophets*

have a meal. So whenever he
passed that way, he would stop
there for a meal. 9 She said to her
husband, "Look, I am sure that this
man who regularly passes our way
is a holy man of God. 10 Let us make
a small roof chamber with walls,
and put there for him a bed, a table, a chair, and a lamp, so that he
can stay there whenever he comes
to us."

11 One day when he came
there, he went up to the chamber
and lay down there. 12 He said to
his servant Gehazi, "Call the Shunammite woman." When he had
called her, she stood before him.
13 He said to him, "Say to her, Since
you have taken all this trouble for
us, what may be done for you?
Would you have a word spoken on
your behalf to the king or to the
commander of the army?" She answered, "I live among my own people." 14 He said, "What then may be
done for her?" Gehazi answered,
"Well, she has no son, and her husband is old." 15 He said, "Call her."
When he had called her, she stood
at the door. 16 He said, "At this season, in due time, you shall embrace
a son." She replied, "No, my lord,
O man of God; do not deceive your
servant."

17 The woman conceived and
bore a son at that season, in due
time, as Elisha had declared to her.

18 When the child was older, he
went out one day to his father
among the reapers. 19 He complained to his father, "Oh, my
head, my head!" The father said to
his servant, "Carry him to his
mother." 20 He carried him and
brought him to his mother; the
child sat on her lap until noon, and
he died. 21 She went up and laid
him on the bed of the man of God,
closed the door on him, and left.
22 Then she called to her husband,
and said, "Send me one of the servants and one of the donkeys, so
that I may quickly go to the man of
God and come back again." 23 He
said, "Why go to him today? It is
neither new moon nor sabbath."
She said, "It will be all right."
24 Then she saddled the donkey and
said to her servant, "Urge the animal on; do not hold back for me
unless I tell you." 25 So she set out,
and came to the man of God at
Mount Carmel.

When the man of God saw her
coming, he said to Gehazi his servant, "Look, there is the Shunammite woman; 26 run at once to meet
her, and say to her, Are you all
right? Is your husband all right? Is
the child all right?" She answered,
"It is all right." 27 When she came to
the man of God at the mountain,
she caught hold of his feet. Gehazi
approached to push her away. But
the man of God said, "Let her
alone, for she is in bitter distress;
the LORD has hidden it from me and
has not told me." 28 Then she said,
"Did I ask my lord for a son? Did I
not say, Do not mislead me?" 29 He
said to Gehazi, "Gird up your loins,
and take my staff in your hand, and
go. If you meet anyone, give no
greeting, and if anyone greets you,
do not answer; and lay my staff on
the face of the child." 30 Then the
mother of the child said, "As the
LORD lives, and as you yourself live,
I will not leave without you." So he
rose up and followed her. 31 Gehazi
went on ahead and laid the staff on
the face of the child, but there was
no sound or sign of life. He came
back to meet him and told him,
"The child has not awakened."

32 When Elisha came into the
house, he saw the child lying dead
on his bed. 33 So he went in and
closed the door on the two of them,
and prayed to the LORD. 34 Then he
got up on the bed[g] and lay upon
the child, putting his mouth upon
his mouth, his eyes upon his eyes,
and his hands upon his hands; and
while he lay bent over him, the
flesh of the child became warm.
35 He got down, walked once to and
fro in the room, then got up again
and bent over him; the child
sneezed seven times, and the child
opened his eyes. 36 Elisha[h] summoned Gehazi and said, "Call the

4.9 v. 7
4.12 vv. 29-31; 2 Kings 5.20-27; 8.4,5
4.16 Gen 18.10, 14; v. 28
4.21 vv. 7,32
4.23 Num 10.10; 28.11; 1 Chr 23.31
4.25 2 Kings 2.25
4.28 v. 16
4.29 1 Kings 18.46; 2 Kings 9.1; Lk 10.4; Ex 7.19; 14.16; 2 Kings 2.8, 14
4.30 2 Kings 2.2
4.33 v. 4; Mt 6.6; 1 Kings 17.20
4.34 1 Kings 17.21; Acts 20.10
4.35 1 Kings 17.21; 2 Kings 8.1, 5

[g] Heb lacks *on the bed* [h] Heb *he*

Shunammite woman." So he called
her. When she came to him, he
said, "Take your son." 37 She came
and fell at his feet, bowing to the
ground; then she took her son and
left.

Elisha Purifies the Pot of Stew

38 When Elisha returned to Gilgal, there was a famine in the land.
As the company of prophets was[i]
sitting before him, he said to his
servant, "Put the large pot on, and
make some stew for the company
of prophets."[j] 39 One of them went
out into the field to gather herbs;
he found a wild vine and gathered
from it a lapful of wild gourds, and
came and cut them up into the pot
of stew, not knowing what they
were. 40 They served some for the
men to eat. But while they were
eating the stew, they cried out,
"O man of God, there is death in
the pot!" They could not eat it.
41 He said, "Then bring some
flour." He threw it into the pot, and
said, "Serve the people and let
them eat." And there was nothing
harmful in the pot.

Elisha Feeds One Hundred Men

42 A man came from Baal-
shalishah, bringing food from the
first fruits to the man of God: twenty loaves of barley and fresh ears of
grain in his sack. Elisha said, "Give
it to the people and let them eat."
43 But his servant said, "How can I
set this before a hundred people?"
So he repeated, "Give it to the people and let them eat, for thus says
the LORD, 'They shall eat and have
some left.' " 44 He set it before
them, they ate, and had some left,
according to the word of the LORD.

The Healing of Naaman

5 Naaman, commander of the
army of the king of Aram, was
a great man and in high favor with
his master, because by him the
LORD had given victory to Aram.
The man, though a mighty warrior,
suffered from leprosy.[k] 2 Now the
Arameans on one of their raids had
taken a young girl captive from the
land of Israel, and she served Naaman's wife. 3 She said to her mistress, "If only my lord were with the
prophet who is in Samaria! He
would cure him of his leprosy."[k]
4 So Naaman[l] went in and told his
lord just what the girl from the land
of Israel had said. 5 And the king of
Aram said, "Go then, and I will
send along a letter to the king of
Israel."

He went, taking with him ten talents of silver, six thousand shekels
of gold, and ten sets of garments.
6 He brought the letter to the king
of Israel, which read, "When this
letter reaches you, know that I have
sent to you my servant Naaman,
that you may cure him of his leprosy."[k] 7 When the king of Israel read
the letter, he tore his clothes and
said, "Am I God, to give death or
life, that this man sends word to
me to cure a man of his leprosy?[k]
Just look and see how he is trying
to pick a quarrel with me."

8 But when Elisha the man of
God heard that the king of Israel
had torn his clothes, he sent a message to the king, "Why have you
torn your clothes? Let him come to
me, that he may learn that there is
a prophet in Israel." 9 So Naaman
came with his horses and chariots,
and halted at the entrance of Elisha's house. 10 Elisha sent a messenger to him, saying, "Go, wash in
the Jordan seven times, and your
flesh shall be restored and you
shall be clean." 11 But Naaman became angry and went away, saying,
"I thought that for me he would
surely come out, and stand and call
on the name of the LORD his God,
and would wave his hand over the
spot, and cure the leprosy![k] 12 Are
not Abana[m] and Pharpar, the rivers
of Damascus, better than all the
waters of Israel? Could I not wash
in them, and be clean?" He turned
and went away in a rage. 13 But his
servants approached and said to
him, "Father, if the prophet had

4.37 1 Kings 17.23; Heb 11.35
4.38 2 Kings 2.1, 3; 8.1; Lk 10.39; Acts 22.3
4.41 Ex 15.25; 2 Kings 2.21
4.42 1 Sam 9.4, 7
4.44 Mt 14.16-21; 15.32-38
5.1 Lk 4.27
5.5 1 Sam 9.8; 2 Kings 8.8, 9
5.7 Gen 37.29; 30.2; Deut 32.39; 1 Sam 2.6; 1 Kings 20.7
5.8 1 Kings 12.22
5.10 Jn 9.7
5.13 2 Kings 6.21; 8.9; 1 Sam 28.23

[i] Heb *sons of the prophets were*
[j] Heb *sons of the prophets* [k] A term for several skin diseases; precise meaning uncertain [l] Heb *he* [m] Another reading is *Amana*

commanded you to do something
difficult, would you not have done
it? How much more, when all he
said to you was, 'Wash, and be
clean'?" 14 So he went down and
immersed himself seven times in
the Jordan, according to the word
of the man of God; his flesh was
restored like the flesh of a young
boy, and he was clean.
15 Then he returned to the man
of God, he and all his company; he
came and stood before him and
said, "Now I know that there is no
God in all the earth except in Israel; please accept a present from
your servant." 16 But he said, "As
the LORD lives, whom I serve, I will
accept nothing!" He urged him to
accept, but he refused. 17 Then Naaman said, "If not, please let two
mule-loads of earth be given to
your servant; for your servant will
no longer offer burnt offering or
sacrifice to any god except the
LORD. 18 But may the LORD pardon
your servant on one count: when
my master goes into the house of
Rimmon to worship there, leaning
on my arm, and I bow down in the
house of Rimmon, when I do bow
down in the house of Rimmon, may
the LORD pardon your servant on
this one count." 19 He said to him,
"Go in peace."

Gehazi's Greed

But when Naaman had gone
from him a short distance, 20 Gehazi, the servant of Elisha the man of
God, thought, "My master has let
that Aramean Naaman off too
lightly by not accepting from him
what he offered. As the LORD lives,
I will run after him and get something out of him." 21 So Gehazi
went after Naaman. When Naaman
saw someone running after him, he
jumped down from the chariot to
meet him and said, "Is everything
all right?" 22 He replied, "Yes, but
my master has sent me to say, 'Two
members of a company of prophets[n] have just come to me from the
hill country of Ephraim; please give
them a talent of silver and two
changes of clothing.' " 23 Naaman
said, "Please accept two talents."
He urged him, and tied up two talents of silver in two bags, with two
changes of clothing, and gave them
to two of his servants, who carried
them in front of Gehazi.[o] 24 When
he came to the citadel, he took the
bags[p] from them, and stored them
inside; he dismissed the men, and
they left.
25 He went in and stood before
his master; and Elisha said to him,
"Where have you been, Gehazi?"
He answered, "Your servant has
not gone anywhere at all." 26 But he
said to him, "Did I not go with you
in spirit when someone left his
chariot to meet you? Is this a time
to accept money and to accept
clothing, olive orchards and vineyards, sheep and oxen, and male
and female slaves? 27 Therefore the
leprosy[q] of Naaman shall cling to
you, and to your descendants forever." So he left his presence leprous,[q] as white as snow.

The Miracle of the Ax Head

6 Now the company of prophets[n] said to Elisha, "As you
see, the place where we live under
your charge is too small for us. 2 Let
us go to the Jordan, and let us collect logs there, one for each of us,
and build a place there for us to
live." He answered, "Do so." 3 Then
one of them said, "Please come
with your servants." And he answered, "I will." 4 So he went with
them. When they came to the Jordan, they cut down trees. 5 But as
one was felling a log, his ax head
fell into the water; he cried out,
"Alas, master! It was borrowed."
6 Then the man of God said,
"Where did it fall?" When he
showed him the place, he cut off a
stick, and threw it in there, and
made the iron float. 7 He said, "Pick
it up." So he reached out his hand
and took it.

The Aramean Attack Is Thwarted

8 Once when the king of Aram

5.14 v. 10; Job 33.25; Lk 4.27
5.15 1 Sam 15.46, 47; Dan 2.47; 3.29; 1 Sam 25.27
5.16 2 Kings 3.14; vv. 20,26; Gen 14.22, 23
5.18 2 Kings 7.2, 17
5.20 2 Kings 4.12, 31,36
5.22 2 Kings 4.26; Josh 24.33
5.25 v. 22
5.26 v. 16
5.27 Ex 4.6; Num 12.10; 2 Kings 15.5
6.1 2 Kings 4.38
6.6 2 Kings 2.21

[n] Heb *sons of the prophets* [o] Heb *him*
[p] Heb lacks *the bags* [q] A term for several skin diseases; precise meaning uncertain

was at war with Israel, he took
counsel with his officers. He said,
"At such and such a place shall be
my camp." 9But the man of God
sent word to the king of Israel,
"Take care not to pass this place,
because the Arameans are going
down there." 10The king of Israel
sent word to the place of which the
man of God spoke. More than once
or twice he warned such a place[r]
so that it was on the alert.
11 The mind of the king of Aram
was greatly perturbed because of
this; he called his officers and said
to them, "Now tell me who among
us sides with the king of Israel?"
12Then one of his officers said, "No
one, my lord king. It is Elisha, the
prophet in Israel, who tells the king
of Israel the words that you speak
in your bedchamber." 13He said,
"Go and find where he is; I will
send and seize him." He was told,
"He is in Dothan." 14So he sent
horses and chariots there and a
great army; they came by night,
and surrounded the city.
15 When an attendant of the
man of God rose early in the morning and went out, an army with
horses and chariots was all around
the city. His servant said, "Alas,
master! What shall we do?" 16He
replied, "Do not be afraid, for there
are more with us than there are
with them." 17Then Elisha prayed:
"O LORD, please open his eyes that
he may see." So the LORD opened
the eyes of the servant, and he saw;
the mountain was full of horses
and chariots of fire all around Elisha. 18When the Arameans[s] came
down against him, Elisha prayed to
the LORD, and said, "Strike this
people, please, with blindness." So
he struck them with blindness as
Elisha had asked. 19Elisha said to
them, "This is not the way, and this
is not the city; follow me, and I will
bring you to the man whom you
seek." And he led them to Samaria.
20 As soon as they entered Samaria, Elisha said, "O LORD, open
the eyes of these men so that they
may see." The LORD opened their
eyes, and they saw that they were
inside Samaria. 21When the king of
Israel saw them he said to Elisha,
"Father, shall I kill them? Shall I
kill them?" 22He answered, "No!
Did you capture with your sword
and your bow those whom you
want to kill? Set food and water before them so that they may eat and
drink; and let them go to their master." 23So he prepared for them a
great feast; after they ate and
drank, he sent them on their way,
and they went to their master. And
the Arameans no longer came raiding into the land of Israel.

Ben-hadad's Siege of Samaria

24 Some time later King Ben-
hadad of Aram mustered his entire
army; he marched against Samaria
and laid siege to it. 25As the siege
continued, famine in Samaria became so great that a donkey's head
was sold for eighty shekels of silver,
and one-fourth of a kab of dove's
dung for five shekels of silver.
26Now as the king of Israel was
walking on the city wall, a woman
cried out to him, "Help, my lord
king!" 27He said, "No! Let the LORD
help you. How can I help you?
From the threshing floor or from
the wine press?" 28But then the
king asked her, "What is your complaint?" She answered, "This woman said to me, 'Give up your son;
we will eat him today, and we will
eat my son tomorrow.' 29So we
cooked my son and ate him. The
next day I said to her, 'Give up your
son and we will eat him.' But she
has hidden her son." 30When the
king heard the words of the woman
he tore his clothes—now since he
was walking on the city wall, the
people could see that he had sackcloth on his body underneath—
31and he said, "So may God do to
me, and more, if the head of Elisha
son of Shaphat stays on his shoulders today." 32So he dispatched a
man from his presence.
Now Elisha was sitting in his
house, and the elders were sitting
with him. Before the messenger arrived, Elisha said to the elders,

6.9 v. 12 **6.13** Gen 37.17 **6.16** 2 Chr 32.7, 8; Ps 55.18; Rom 8.31 **6.17** 2 Kings 2.11; Ps 68.17; Zech 6.1-7 **6.18** Gen 19.11 **6.20** v. 17

6.21 2 Kings 2.12; 5.13; 8.9 **6.22** Deut 20.11-16; Rom 12.20 **6.23** vv. 8,9; 2 Kings 5.2 **6.24** 1 Kings 20.1 **6.29** Lev 26.27-29; Deut 28.52, 53,57 **6.30** 1 Kings 21.27 **6.31** Ruth 1.17; 1 Kings 19.2 **6.32** Ezek 8.1; 20.1; 1 Kings 18.4, 13,14

[r] Heb *warned it* [s] Heb *they*

"Are you aware that this murderer
has sent someone to take off my
head? When the messenger comes,
see that you shut the door and hold
it closed against him. Is not the
sound of his master's feet behind
him?" 33 While he was still speaking with them, the king[t] came
down to him and said, "This trouble is from the LORD! Why should
I hope in the LORD any longer?"
7 1 But Elisha said, "Hear the
word of the LORD: thus says the
LORD, Tomorrow about this time a
measure of choice meal shall be
sold for a shekel, and two measures
of barley for a shekel, at the gate of
Samaria." 2 Then the captain on
whose hand the king leaned said to
the man of God, "Even if the LORD
were to make windows in the sky,
could such a thing happen?" But
he said, "You shall see it with your
own eyes, but you shall not eat
from it."

The Arameans Flee

3 Now there were four leprous[u]
men outside the city gate, who said
to one another, "Why should we sit
here until we die? 4 If we say, 'Let
us enter the city,' the famine is in
the city, and we shall die there; but
if we sit here, we shall also die.
Therefore, let us desert to the Aramean camp; if they spare our lives,
we shall live; and if they kill us, we
shall but die." 5 So they arose at
twilight to go to the Aramean
camp; but when they came to the
edge of the Aramean camp, there
was no one there at all. 6 For the
Lord had caused the Aramean army
to hear the sound of chariots, and
of horses, the sound of a great
army, so that they said to one another, "The king of Israel has hired
the kings of the Hittites and the
kings of Egypt to fight against us."
7 So they fled away in the twilight
and abandoned their tents, their
horses, and their donkeys leaving
the camp just as it was, and fled for
their lives. 8 When these leprous[u]
men had come to the edge of the
camp, they went into a tent, ate
and drank, carried off silver, gold,
and clothing, and went and hid
them. Then they came back, entered another tent, carried off
things from it, and went and hid
them.
9 Then they said to one another,
"What we are doing is wrong. This
is a day of good news; if we are silent and wait until the morning
light, we will be found guilty; therefore let us go and tell the king's
household." 10 So they came and
called to the gatekeepers of the
city, and told them, "We went to
the Aramean camp, but there was
no one to be seen or heard there,
nothing but the horses tied, the
donkeys tied, and the tents as they
were." 11 Then the gatekeepers
called out and proclaimed it to the
king's household. 12 The king got
up in the night, and said to his servants, "I will tell you what the Arameans have prepared against us.
They know that we are starving; so
they have left the camp to hide
themselves in the open country,
thinking, 'When they come out of
the city, we shall take them alive
and get into the city.' " 13 One of his
servants said, "Let some men take
five of the remaining horses, since
those left here will suffer the fate of
the whole multitude of Israel that
have perished already;[v] let us send
and find out." 14 So they took two
mounted men, and the king sent
them after the Aramean army, saying, "Go and find out." 15 So they
went after them as far as the Jordan; the whole way was littered
with garments and equipment that
the Arameans had thrown away in
their haste. So the messengers returned, and told the king.
16 Then the people went out,
and plundered the camp of the Arameans. So a measure of choice
meal was sold for a shekel, and two
measures of barley for a shekel, according to the word of the LORD.
17 Now the king had appointed the
captain on whose hand he leaned

6.33 Job 2.9
7.1 v. 18
7.2 vv. 17,19, 20; Mal 3.10
7.3 Lev 13.46
7.4 2 Kings 6.24
7.6 2 Sam 5.24; 19.7; 1 Kings 10.29
7.7 Ps 48.4-6
7.9 2 Sam 18.27
7.12 2 Kings 6.25-29
7.16 v. 1
7.17 v. 2; 2 Kings 6.32

[t] See 7.2: Heb *messenger* [u] A term for several skin diseases; precise meaning uncertain [v] Compare Gk Syr Vg: Meaning of Heb uncertain

to have charge of the gate; the people trampled him to death in the
gate, just as the man of God had
said when the king came down to
him. 18 For when the man of God
had said to the king, "Two measures of barley shall be sold for a
shekel, and a measure of choice
meal for a shekel, about this time
tomorrow in the gate of Samaria,"
19 the captain had answered the
man of God, "Even if the LORD were
to make windows in the sky, could
such a thing happen?" And he had
answered, "You shall see it with
your own eyes, but you shall not
eat from it." 20 It did indeed happen
to him; the people trampled him to
death in the gate.

The Shunammite Woman's Land Restored

8 Now Elisha had said to the
woman whose son he had restored to life, "Get up and go with
your household, and settle wherever you can; for the LORD has called
for a famine, and it will come on
the land for seven years." 2 So the
woman got up and did according to
the word of the man of God; she
went with her household and settled in the land of the Philistines
seven years. 3 At the end of the sev-
en years, when the woman returned from the land of the Philistines, she set out to appeal to the
king for her house and her land.
4 Now the king was talking with Gehazi the servant of the man of God,
saying, "Tell me all the great things
that Elisha has done." 5 While he
was telling the king how Elisha had
restored a dead person to life, the
woman whose son he had restored
to life appealed to the king for her
house and her land. Gehazi said,
"My lord king, here is the woman,
and here is her son whom Elisha
restored to life." 6 When the king
questioned the woman, she told
him. So the king appointed an official for her, saying, "Restore all
that was hers, together with all the
revenue of the fields from the day
that she left the land until now."

7.18 v. 1 **7.19** v. 2 **8.1** 2 Kings 4.35; Ps 105.16; Hag 1.11 **8.4** 2 Kings 4.12; 5.20-27 **8.5** 2 Kings 4.35

8.7 1 Kings 11.24; 2 Kings 6.24 **8.8** 1 Kings 19.15; 14.3; 2 Kings 1.2 **8.10** vv. 14,15 **8.12** 2 Kings 10.32; 12.17; 13.3,7; 15.16; Hos 13.16; Am 1.13 **8.13** 1 Sam 17.43; 1 Kings 19.15 **8.15** v. 10 **8.16** 2 Kings 1.17; 3.1; 2 Chr 21.3, 4 **8.17** 2 Chr 21.5-10

Death of Ben-hadad

7 Elisha went to Damascus
while King Ben-hadad of Aram was
ill. When it was told him, "The man
of God has come here," 8 the king
said to Hazael, "Take a present
with you and go to meet the man of
God. Inquire of the LORD through
him, whether I shall recover from
this illness." 9 So Hazael went to
meet him, taking a present with
him, all kinds of goods of Damascus, forty camel loads. When he entered and stood before him, he
said, "Your son King Ben-hadad of
Aram has sent me to you, saying,
'Shall I recover from this illness?' "
10 Elisha said to him, "Go, say to
him, 'You shall certainly recover';
but the LORD has shown me that he
shall certainly die." 11 He fixed his
gaze and stared at him, until he
was ashamed. Then the man of
God wept. 12 Hazael asked, "Why
does my lord weep?" He answered,
"Because I know the evil that you
will do to the people of Israel; you
will set their fortresses on fire, you
will kill their young men with the
sword, dash in pieces their little
ones, and rip up their pregnant
women." 13 Hazael said, "What is
your servant, who is a mere dog,
that he should do this great thing?"
Elisha answered, "The LORD has
shown me that you are to be king
over Aram." 14 Then he left Elisha,
and went to his master Ben-
hadad,[w] who said to him, "What
did Elisha say to you?" And he answered, "He told me that you
would certainly recover." 15 But the
next day he took the bed-cover and
dipped it in water and spread it
over the king's face, until he died.
And Hazael succeeded him.

Jehoram Reigns over Judah

16 In the fifth year of King Joram son of Ahab of Israel,[x] Jehoram son of King Jehoshaphat of Judah began to reign. 17 He was
thirty-two years old when he became king, and he reigned eight

[w] Heb lacks *Ben-hadad* [x] Gk Syr: Heb adds *Jehoshaphat being king of Judah,*

years in Jerusalem. 18 He walked in the way of the kings of Israel, as the house of Ahab had done, for the daughter of Ahab was his wife. He did what was evil in the sight of the LORD. 19 Yet the LORD would not destroy Judah, for the sake of his servant David, since he had promised to give a lamp to him and to his descendants forever.

20 In his days Edom revolted against the rule of Judah, and set up a king of their own. 21 Then Joram crossed over to Zair with all his chariots. He set out by night and attacked the Edomites and their chariot commanders who had surrounded him;[y] but his army fled home. 22 So Edom has been in revolt against the rule of Judah to this day. Libnah also revolted at the same time. 23 Now the rest of the acts of Joram, and all that he did, are they not written in the Book of the Annals of the Kings of Judah? 24 So Joram slept with his ancestors, and was buried with them in the city of David; his son Ahaziah succeeded him.

Ahaziah Reigns over Judah

25 In the twelfth year of King Joram son of Ahab of Israel, Ahaziah son of King Jehoram of Judah began to reign. 26 Ahaziah was twenty-two years old when he began to reign; he reigned one year in Jerusalem. His mother's name was Athaliah, a granddaughter of King Omri of Israel. 27 He also walked in the way of the house of Ahab, doing what was evil in the sight of the LORD, as the house of Ahab had done, for he was son-in-law to the house of Ahab.

28 He went with Joram son of Ahab to wage war against King Hazael of Aram at Ramoth-gilead, where the Arameans wounded Joram. 29 King Joram returned to be healed in Jezreel of the wounds that the Arameans had inflicted on him at Ramah, when he fought against King Hazael of Aram. King Ahaziah son of Jehoram of Judah went down to see Joram son of Ahab in Jezreel, because he was wounded.

Anointing of Jehu

9 Then the prophet Elisha called a member of the company of prophets[z] and said to him, "Gird up your loins; take this flask of oil in your hand, and go to Ramoth-gilead. 2 When you arrive, look there for Jehu son of Jehoshaphat, son of Nimshi; go in and get him to leave his companions, and take him into an inner chamber. 3 Then take the flask of oil, pour it on his head, and say, 'Thus says the LORD: I anoint you king over Israel.' Then open the door and flee; do not linger."

4 So the young man, the young prophet, went to Ramoth-gilead. 5 He arrived while the commanders of the army were in council, and he announced, "I have a message for you, commander." "For which one of us?" asked Jehu. "For you, commander." 6 So Jehu[a] got up and went inside; the young man poured the oil on his head, saying to him, "Thus says the LORD the God of Israel: I anoint you king over the people of the LORD, over Israel. 7 You shall strike down the house of your master Ahab, so that I may avenge on Jezebel the blood of my servants the prophets, and the blood of all the servants of the LORD. 8 For the whole house of Ahab shall perish; I will cut off from Ahab every male, bond or free, in Israel. 9 I will make the house of Ahab like the house of Jeroboam son of Nebat, and like the house of Baasha son of Ahijah. 10 The dogs shall eat Jezebel in the territory of Jezreel, and no one shall bury her." Then he opened the door and fled.

11 When Jehu came back to his master's officers, they said to him, "Is everything all right? Why did that madman come to you?" He answered them, "You know the sort and how they babble." 12 They said, "Liar! Come on, tell us!" So he said, "This is just what he said to me:

8.18 v. 27
8.19 2 Sam 7.13; 1 Kings 11.36; 2 Chr 21.7
8.20 1 Kings 22.4; 2 Kings 3.27; 2 Chr 21.8-10
8.21 2 Sam 18.17; 19.8
8.22 2 Chr 21.10
8.24 2 Chr 21.20; 22.1
8.25 2 Chr 22.1-6
8.28 v. 15; 1 Kings 22.3, 29
8.29 2 Kings 9.15; 2 Chr 22.6, 7
9.1 2 Kings 2.3; 4.29; 8.28,29
9.2 vv. 5,11
9.3 2 Chr 22.7
9.6 v. 3; 1 Kings 19.16; 2 Chr 22.7
9.7 Deut 32.35; 1 Kings 18.4; 21.15; vv. 32,37
9.8 2 Kings 10.17; 1 Kings 21.21; 1 Sam 25.22; Deut 32.36; 2 Kings 14.26
9.9 1 Kings 14.10; 15.29; 16.3-5, 11,12
9.10 vv. 35,36; 1 Kings 21.23
9.11 Jer 29.26; Jn 10.20; Acts 26.24

[y] Meaning of Heb uncertain [z] Heb *sons of the prophets* [a] Heb *he*

'Thus says the LORD, I anoint you
king over Israel.' " 13 Then hurriedly they all took their cloaks and
spread them for him on the bare[b]
steps; and they blew the trumpet,
and proclaimed, "Jehu is king."

Joram of Israel Killed

14 Thus Jehu son of Jehoshaphat son of Nimshi conspired
against Joram. Joram with all Israel had been on guard at Ramoth-
gilead against King Hazael of
Aram; 15 but King Joram had returned to be healed in Jezreel of
the wounds that the Arameans had
inflicted on him, when he fought
against King Hazael of Aram. So
Jehu said, "If this is your wish, then
let no one slip out of the city to go
and tell the news in Jezreel."
16 Then Jehu mounted his chariot
and went to Jezreel, where Joram
was lying ill. King Ahaziah of Judah
had come down to visit Joram.

17 In Jezreel, the sentinel
standing on the tower spied the
company of Jehu arriving, and said,
"I see a company." Joram said,
"Take a horseman; send him to
meet them, and let him say, 'Is it
peace?' " 18 So the horseman went
to meet him; he said, "Thus says
the king, 'Is it peace?' " Jehu responded, "What have you to do
with peace? Fall in behind me."
The sentinel reported, saying, "The
messenger reached them, but he is
not coming back." 19 Then he sent
out a second horseman, who came
to them and said, "Thus says the
king, 'Is it peace?' " Jehu answered, "What have you to do with
peace? Fall in behind me." 20 Again
the sentinel reported, "He reached
them, but he is not coming back. It
looks like the driving of Jehu son of
Nimshi; for he drives like a maniac."

21 Joram said, "Get ready." And
they got his chariot ready. Then
King Joram of Israel and King Ahaziah of Judah set out, each in his
chariot, and went to meet Jehu;
they met him at the property of Naboth the Jezreelite. 22 When Joram
saw Jehu, he said, "Is it peace,
Jehu?" He answered, "What peace
can there be, so long as the many
whoredoms and sorceries of your
mother Jezebel continue?" 23 Then
Joram reined about and fled, saying to Ahaziah, "Treason, Ahaziah!" 24 Jehu drew his bow with all
his strength, and shot Joram between the shoulders, so that the arrow pierced his heart; and he sank
in his chariot. 25 Jehu said to his
aide Bidkar, "Lift him out, and
throw him on the plot of ground belonging to Naboth the Jezreelite;
for remember, when you and I rode
side by side behind his father Ahab
how the LORD uttered this oracle
against him: 26 'For the blood of
Naboth and for the blood of his
children that I saw yesterday, says
the LORD, I swear I will repay you on
this very plot of ground.' Now
therefore lift him out and throw
him on the plot of ground, in accordance with the word of the LORD."

Ahaziah of Judah Killed

27 When King Ahaziah of Judah
saw this, he fled in the direction of
Beth-haggan. Jehu pursued him,
saying, "Shoot him also!" And they
shot him[c] in the chariot at the ascent to Gur, which is by Ibleam.
Then he fled to Megiddo, and died
there. 28 His officers carried him in
a chariot to Jerusalem, and buried
him in his tomb with his ancestors
in the city of David.

29 In the eleventh year of Joram
son of Ahab, Ahaziah began to
reign over Judah.

Jezebel's Violent Death

30 When Jehu came to Jezreel,
Jezebel heard of it; she painted her
eyes, and adorned her head, and
looked out of the window. 31 As
Jehu entered the gate, she said, "Is
it peace, Zimri, murderer of your
master?" 32 He looked up to the
window and said, "Who is on my
side? Who?" Two or three eunuchs
looked out at him. 33 He said,
"Throw her down." So they threw
her down; some of her blood spat-

9.13 Mt 21.7; 2 Sam 15.10; 1 Kings 1.34, 39
9.14 2 Kings 8.28
9.15 2 Kings 8.29
9.16 2 Kings 8.29
9.18 vv. 19,22
9.20 2 Sam 18.27; 1 Kings 19.17
9.21 2 Chr 22.7; v. 26; 1 Kings 21.1-7, 15-19
9.22 1 Kings 16.30-33; 18.19; 2 Chr 21.13
9.23 2 Kings 11.24
9.24 1 Kings 22.34
9.25 1 Kings 21.1, 19,24-29
9.26 1 Kings 21.19
9.27 2 Chr 22.9
9.28 2 Kings 23.30
9.30 Jer 4.30; Ezek 23.40
9.31 1 Kings 16.9-20

[b] Meaning of Heb uncertain [c] Syr Vg Compare Gk: Heb lacks *and they shot him*

tered on the wall and on the horses,
which trampled on her. 34 Then he
went in and ate and drank; he said,
"See to that cursed woman and
bury her; for she is a king's daughter." 35 But when they went to bury
her, they found no more of her than
the skull and the feet and the
palms of her hands. 36 When they
came back and told him, he said,
"This is the word of the LORD,
which he spoke by his servant Elijah the Tishbite, 'In the territory of
Jezreel the dogs shall eat the flesh
of Jezebel; 37 the corpse of Jezebel
shall be like dung on the field in
the territory of Jezreel, so that no
one can say, This is Jezebel.' "

Massacre of Ahab's Descendants

10 Now Ahab had seventy
sons in Samaria. So Jehu
wrote letters and sent them to Samaria, to the rulers of Jezreel,[d] to
the elders, and to the guardians of
the sons of[e] Ahab, saying, 2 "Since
your master's sons are with you
and you have at your disposal chariots and horses, a fortified city, and
weapons, 3 select the son of your
master who is the best qualified,
set him on his father's throne, and
fight for your master's house."
4 But they were utterly terrified and
said, "Look, two kings could not
withstand him; how then can we
stand?" 5 So the steward of the palace, and the governor of the city,
along with the elders and the
guardians, sent word to Jehu: "We
are your servants; we will do anything you say. We will not make
anyone king; do whatever you
think right." 6 Then he wrote them
a second letter, saying, "If you are
on my side, and if you are ready to
obey me, take the heads of your
master's sons and come to me at
Jezreel tomorrow at this time."
Now the king's sons, seventy persons, were with the leaders of the
city, who were charged with their
upbringing. 7 When the letter
reached them, they took the king's
sons and killed them, seventy persons; they put their heads in baskets and sent them to him at Jezre-

9.34 1 Kings 21.25; 16.31
9.36 1 Kings 21.23
9.37 Jer 8.1-3
10.1 1 Kings 16.24-29
10.5 1 Kings 20.4, 32
10.7 1 Kings 21.21
10.9 2 Kings 9.14-24; v. 6
10.10 2 Kings 9.7-10; 1 Kings 21.19-29
10.13 2 Kings 8.24, 29; 2 Chr 22.8
10.15 Jer 35.6ff; 1 Chr 2.55; Ezra 10.19
10.16 1 Kings 19.10
10.17 2 Kings 9.8; 2 Chr 22.8; v. 10

el. 8 When the messenger came and
told him, "They have brought the
heads of the king's sons," he said,
"Lay them in two heaps at the entrance of the gate until the morning." 9 Then in the morning when
he went out, he stood and said to
all the people, "You are innocent.
It was I who conspired against my
master and killed him; but who
struck down all these? 10 Know
then that there shall fall to the
earth nothing of the word of the
LORD, which the LORD spoke concerning the house of Ahab; for the
LORD has done what he said
through his servant Elijah." 11 So
Jehu killed all who were left of the
house of Ahab in Jezreel, all his
leaders, close friends, and priests,
until he left him no survivor.

12 Then he set out and went to
Samaria. On the way, when he was
at Beth-eked of the Shepherds,
13 Jehu met relatives of King Ahaziah of Judah and said, "Who are
you?" They answered, "We are kin
of Ahaziah; we have come down to
visit the royal princes and the sons
of the queen mother." 14 He said,
"Take them alive." They took them
alive, and slaughtered them at the
pit of Beth-eked, forty-two in all;
he spared none of them.

15 When he left there, he met
Jehonadab son of Rechab coming
to meet him; he greeted him, and
said to him, "Is your heart as true
to mine as mine is to yours?"[f] Jehonadab answered, "It is." Jehu
said,[g] "If it is, give me your hand."
So he gave him his hand. Jehu took
him up with him into the chariot.
16 He said, "Come with me, and see
my zeal for the LORD." So he[h] had
him ride in his chariot. 17 When he
came to Samaria, he killed all who
were left to Ahab in Samaria, until
he had wiped them out, according
to the word of the LORD that he
spoke to Elijah.

[d] Or *of the city*; Vg Compare Gk
[e] Gk: Heb lacks *of the sons of*
[f] Gk: Heb *Is it right with your heart, as my heart is with your heart?*
[g] Gk: Heb lacks *Jehu said*
[h] Gk Syr Tg: Heb *they*

Slaughter of Worshipers of Baal

18 Then Jehu assembled all the people and said to them, "Ahab offered Baal small service; but Jehu will offer much more. 19 Now therefore summon to me all the prophets of Baal, all his worshipers, and all his priests; let none be missing, for I have a great sacrifice to offer to Baal; whoever is missing shall not live." But Jehu was acting with cunning in order to destroy the worshipers of Baal. 20 Jehu decreed, "Sanctify a solemn assembly for Baal." So they proclaimed it. 21 Jehu sent word throughout all Israel; all the worshipers of Baal came, so that there was no one left who did not come. They entered the temple of Baal, until the temple of Baal was filled from wall to wall. 22 He said to the keeper of the wardrobe, "Bring out the vestments for all the worshipers of Baal." So he brought out the vestments for them. 23 Then Jehu entered the temple of Baal with Jehonadab son of Rechab; he said to the worshipers of Baal, "Search and see that there is no worshiper of the LORD here among you, but only worshipers of Baal." 24 Then they proceeded to offer sacrifices and burnt offerings.

Now Jehu had stationed eighty men outside, saying, "Whoever allows any of those to escape whom I deliver into your hands shall forfeit his life." 25 As soon as he had finished presenting the burnt offering, Jehu said to the guards and to the officers, "Come in and kill them; let no one escape." So they put them to the sword. The guards and the officers threw them out, and then went into the citadel of the temple of Baal. 26 They brought out the pillar[i] that was in the temple of Baal, and burned it. 27 Then they demolished the pillar of Baal, and destroyed the temple of Baal, and made it a latrine to this day.

28 Thus Jehu wiped out Baal from Israel. 29 But Jehu did not turn aside from the sins of Jeroboam son of Nebat, which he caused Israel to commit—the golden calves that were in Bethel and in Dan. 30 The LORD said to Jehu, "Because you have done well in carrying out what I consider right, and in accordance with all that was in my heart have dealt with the house of Ahab, your sons of the fourth generation shall sit on the throne of Israel." 31 But Jehu was not careful to follow the law of the LORD the God of Israel with all his heart; he did not turn from the sins of Jeroboam, which he caused Israel to commit.

Death of Jehu

32 In those days the LORD began to trim off parts of Israel. Hazael defeated them throughout the territory of Israel: 33 from the Jordan eastward, all the land of Gilead, the Gadites, the Reubenites, and the Manassites, from Aroer, which is by the Wadi Arnon, that is, Gilead and Bashan. 34 Now the rest of the acts of Jehu, all that he did, and all his power, are they not written in the Book of the Annals of the Kings of Israel? 35 So Jehu slept with his ancestors, and they buried him in Samaria. His son Jehoahaz succeeded him. 36 The time that Jehu reigned over Israel in Samaria was twenty-eight years.

Athaliah Reigns over Judah

11 Now when Athaliah, Ahaziah's mother, saw that her son was dead, she set about to destroy all the royal family. 2 But Jehosheba, King Joram's daughter, Ahaziah's sister, took Joash son of Ahaziah, and stole him away from among the king's children who were about to be killed; she put[j] him and his nurse in a bedroom. Thus she[k] hid him from Athaliah, so that he was not killed; 3 he remained with her six years, hidden in the house of the LORD, while Athaliah reigned over the land.

Jehoiada Anoints the Child Joash

4 But in the seventh year Jehoi-

10.18 1 Kings 16.31, 32
10.19 1 Kings 22.6
10.20 Joel 1.14; Ex 32.4-6
10.21 1 Kings 16.32; 2 Kings 11.18
10.24 1 Kings 20.39
10.25 1 Kings 18.40
10.26 1 Kings 14.23
10.27 Ezra 6.11; Dan 2.5; 3.29
10.29 1 Kings 12.28, 29
10.30 v. 35; 2 Kings 15.8, 12
10.31 v. 29
10.32 2 Kings 8.12
10.34 Am 1.3-5
11.1 2 Chr 22.10-12
11.4 2 Chr 23.1ff; v. 19

[i] Gk Vg Syr Tg: Heb *pillars* [j] With 2 Chr 22.11: Heb lacks *she put* [k] Gk Syr Vg Compare 2 Chr 22.11: Heb *they*

ada summoned the captains of the
Carites and of the guards and had
them come to him in the house of
the LORD. He made a covenant with
them and put them under oath in
the house of the LORD; then he
showed them the king's son. 5 He
commanded them, "This is what
you are to do: one-third of you,
those who go off duty on the sabbath and guard the king's house
6 (another third being at the gate
Sur and a third at the gate behind
the guards), shall guard the palace;
7 and your two divisions that come
on duty in force on the sabbath and
guard the house of the LORD[l]
8 shall surround the king, each with
weapons in hand; and whoever approaches the ranks is to be killed.
Be with the king in his comings and
goings."

9 The captains did according to
all that the priest Jehoiada commanded; each brought his men
who were to go off duty on the sabbath, with those who were to come
on duty on the sabbath, and came
to the priest Jehoiada. 10 The priest
delivered to the captains the spears
and shields that had been King David's, which were in the house of
the LORD; 11 the guards stood, every
man with his weapons in his hand,
from the south side of the house to
the north side of the house, around
the altar and the house, to guard
the king on every side. 12 Then he
brought out the king's son, put the
crown on him, and gave him the
covenant;[m] they proclaimed him
king, and anointed him; they
clapped their hands and shouted,
"Long live the king!"

Death of Athaliah

13 When Athaliah heard the
noise of the guard and of the people, she went into the house of the
LORD to the people; 14 when she
looked, there was the king standing
by the pillar, according to custom,
with the captains and the trumpeters beside the king, and all the people of the land rejoicing and blowing trumpets. Athaliah tore her
clothes and cried, "Treason! Treason!" 15 Then the priest Jehoiada
commanded the captains who were
set over the army, "Bring her out
between the ranks, and kill with
the sword anyone who follows
her." For the priest said, "Let her
not be killed in the house of the
LORD." 16 So they laid hands on her;
she went through the horses' entrance to the king's house, and
there she was put to death.

17 Jehoiada made a covenant
between the LORD and the king and
people, that they should be the
LORD's people; also between the
king and the people. 18 Then all
the people of the land went to the
house of Baal, and tore it down; his
altars and his images they broke in
pieces, and they killed Mattan, the
priest of Baal, before the altars.
The priest posted guards over the
house of the LORD. 19 He took the
captains, the Carites, the guards,
and all the people of the land; then
they brought the king down from
the house of the LORD, marching
through the gate of the guards to
the king's house. He took his seat
on the throne of the kings. 20 So all
the people of the land rejoiced; and
the city was quiet after Athaliah
had been killed with the sword at
the king's house.

21 [n]Jehoash[o] was seven years
old when he began to reign.

The Temple Repaired

12 In the seventh year of Jehu,
Jehoash began to reign; he
reigned forty years in Jerusalem.
His mother's name was Zibiah of
Beer-sheba. 2 Jehoash did what was
right in the sight of the LORD all his
days, because the priest Jehoiada
instructed him. 3 Nevertheless the
high places were not taken away;
the people continued to sacrifice
and make offerings on the high
places.

4 Jehoash said to the priests,
"All the money offered as sacred
donations that is brought into the
house of the LORD, the money for

11.5 1 Chr 9.25 **11.9** 2 Chr 23.8 **11.10** 2 Sam 8.7; 1 Chr 18.7 **11.12** 1 Sam 10.24 **11.13** 2 Chr 23.12ff **11.14** 2 Kings 23.3; 2 Chr 34.31; 1 Kings 1.39, 40; 2 Kings 9.23

11.17 2 Chr 23.16; 15.12-14; 2 Sam 5.3 **11.18** 2 Kings 10.26; Deut 12.3; 2 Chr 23.17ff **11.19** vv. 4,6 **11.21** 2 Chr 24.1 **12.3** 2 Kings 14.4; 15.35 **12.4** 2 Kings 22.4; Ex 35.5; 1 Chr 29.3-9

[l] Heb *the LORD to the king* [m] Or *treaty* or *testimony*; Heb *eduth* [n] Ch 12.1 in Heb
[o] Another spelling is *Joash*; see verse 19

which each person is assessed—the money from the assessment of persons—and the money from the voluntary offerings brought into the house of the LORD, 5 let the priests receive from each of the donors; and let them repair the house wherever any need of repairs is discovered." 6 But by the twenty-third year of King Jehoash the priests had made no repairs on the house. 7 Therefore King Jehoash summoned the priest Jehoiada with the other priests and said to them, "Why are you not repairing the house? Now therefore do not accept any more money from your donors but hand it over for the repair of the house." 8 So the priests agreed that they would neither accept more money from the people nor repair the house.

9 Then the priest Jehoiada took a chest, made a hole in its lid, and set it beside the altar on the right side as one entered the house of the LORD; the priests who guarded the threshold put in it all the money that was brought into the house of the LORD. 10 Whenever they saw that there was a great deal of money in the chest, the king's secretary and the high priest went up, counted the money that was found in the house of the LORD, and tied it up in bags. 11 They would give the money that was weighed out into the hands of the workers who had the oversight of the house of the LORD; then they paid it out to the carpenters and the builders who worked on the house of the LORD, 12 to the masons and the stonecutters, as well as to buy timber and quarried stone for making repairs on the house of the LORD, as well as for any outlay for repairs of the house. 13 But for the house of the LORD no basins of silver, snuffers, bowls, trumpets, or any vessels of gold, or of silver, were made from the money that was brought into the house of the LORD, 14 for that was given to the workers who were repairing the house of the LORD with it. 15 They did not ask an accounting from those into whose hand they delivered the money to pay out to the workers, for they dealt honestly. 16 The money from the guilt offerings and the money from the sin offerings was not brought into the house of the LORD; it belonged to the priests.

Hazael Threatens Jerusalem

17 At that time King Hazael of Aram went up, fought against Gath, and took it. But when Hazael set his face to go up against Jerusalem, 18 King Jehoash of Judah took all the votive gifts that Jehoshaphat, Jehoram, and Ahaziah, his ancestors, the kings of Judah, had dedicated, as well as his own votive gifts, all the gold that was found in the treasuries of the house of the LORD and of the king's house, and sent these to King Hazael of Aram. Then Hazael withdrew from Jerusalem.

Death of Joash

19 Now the rest of the acts of Joash, and all that he did, are they not written in the Book of the Annals of the Kings of Judah? 20 His servants arose, devised a conspiracy, and killed Joash in the house of Millo, on the way that goes down to Silla. 21 It was Jozacar son of Shimeath and Jehozabad son of Shomer, his servants, who struck him down, so that he died. He was buried with his ancestors in the city of David; then his son Amaziah succeeded him.

Jehoahaz Reigns over Israel

13 In the twenty-third year of King Joash son of Ahaziah of Judah, Jehoahaz son of Jehu began to reign over Israel in Samaria; he reigned seventeen years. 2 He did what was evil in the sight of the LORD, and followed the sins of Jeroboam son of Nebat, which he caused Israel to sin; he did not depart from them. 3 The anger of the LORD was kindled against Israel, so that he gave them repeatedly into the hand of King Hazael of Aram, then into the hand of Ben-hadad son of Hazael. 4 But Jehoahaz entreated the LORD, and the LORD

12.6 2 Chr 24.5
12.7 2 Chr 24.6
12.9 2 Chr 24.8; Mk 12.41; Lk 21.1
12.10 2 Kings 19.2
12.12 2 Kings 22.5, 6
12.13 2 Chr 24.14; 1 Kings 7.48, 50
12.15 2 Kings 22.7
12.16 Lev 5.15-18; 4.24,29; Num 18.9, 19
12.17 2 Kings 8.12; 2 Chr 24.23
12.18 1 Kings 15.18; 2 Kings 18.15, 16
12.20 2 Kings 14.5; 2 Chr 24.25; 1 Kings 11.27
12.21 2 Chr 24.26, 27; 2 Kings 14.1
13.2 1 Kings 12.26-33
13.3 Judg 2.14; 2 Kings 8.12; 12.17
13.4 Num 21.7-9; Ps 78.34; Ex 3.7; 2 Kings 14.26

heeded him; for he saw the oppression of Israel, how the king of Aram oppressed them. [5]Therefore the LORD gave Israel a savior, so that they escaped from the hand of the Arameans; and the people of Israel lived in their homes as formerly. [6]Nevertheless they did not depart from the sins of the house of Jeroboam, which he caused Israel to sin, but walked[p] in them; the sacred pole[q] also remained in Samaria. [7]So Jehoahaz was left with an army of not more than fifty horsemen, ten chariots and ten thousand footmen; for the king of Aram had destroyed them and made them like the dust at threshing. [8]Now the rest of the acts of Jehoahaz and all that he did, including his might, are they not written in the Book of the Annals of the Kings of Israel? [9]So Jehoahaz slept with his ancestors, and they buried him in Samaria; then his son Joash succeeded him.

Jehoash Reigns over Israel

10 In the thirty-seventh year of King Joash of Judah, Jehoash son of Jehoahaz began to reign over Israel in Samaria; he reigned sixteen years. [11]He also did what was evil in the sight of the LORD; he did not depart from all the sins of Jeroboam son of Nebat, which he caused Israel to sin, but he walked in them. [12]Now the rest of the acts of Joash, and all that he did, as well as the might with which he fought against King Amaziah of Judah, are they not written in the Book of the Annals of the Kings of Israel? [13]So Joash slept with his ancestors, and Jeroboam sat upon his throne; Joash was buried in Samaria with the kings of Israel.

Death of Elisha

14 Now when Elisha had fallen sick with the illness of which he was to die, King Joash of Israel went down to him, and wept before him, crying, "My father, my father! The chariots of Israel and its horsemen!" [15]Elisha said to him, "Take a bow and arrows"; so he took a bow and arrows. [16]Then he said to the king of Israel, "Draw the bow"; and he drew it. Elisha laid his hands on the king's hands. [17]Then he said, "Open the window eastward"; and he opened it. Elisha said, "Shoot"; and he shot. Then he said, "The LORD's arrow of victory, the arrow of victory over Aram! For you shall fight the Arameans in Aphek until you have made an end of them." [18]He continued, "Take the arrows"; and he took them. He said to the king of Israel, "Strike the ground with them"; he struck three times, and stopped. [19]Then the man of God was angry with him, and said, "You should have struck five or six times; then you would have struck down Aram until you had made an end of it, but now you will strike down Aram only three times."

20 So Elisha died, and they buried him. Now bands of Moabites used to invade the land in the spring of the year. [21]As a man was being buried, a marauding band was seen and the man was thrown into the grave of Elisha; as soon as the man touched the bones of Elisha, he came to life and stood on his feet.

Israel Recaptures Cities from Aram

22 Now King Hazael of Aram oppressed Israel all the days of Jehoahaz. [23]But the LORD was gracious to them and had compassion on them; he turned toward them, because of his covenant with Abraham, Isaac, and Jacob, and would not destroy them; nor has he banished them from his presence until now.

24 When King Hazael of Aram died, his son Ben-hadad succeeded him. [25]Then Jehoash son of Jehoahaz took again from Ben-hadad son of Hazael the towns that he had taken from his father Jehoahaz in war. Three times Joash defeated him and recovered the towns of Israel.

13.5 v. 25; 2 Kings 14.25, 27
13.6 v. 2; 1 Kings 16.33
13.7 Am 1.3
13.9 2 Kings 10.35
13.12 vv. 14-19; 2 Kings 14.8-15; 2 Chr 25.17ff
13.14 2 Kings 2.12
13.17 1 Kings 20.26
13.19 v. 25
13.20 2 Kings 3.7; 24.2
13.22 2 Kings 8.12
13.23 2 Kings 14.27; Ex 2.24,25; Gen 13.16, 17
13.25 2 Kings 10.32, 33; 14.25; vv. 18,19

[p] Gk Syr Tg Vg: Heb *he walked*
[q] Heb *Asherah*

Amaziah Reigns over Judah

14 In the second year of King
Joash son of Joahaz of Israel, King Amaziah son of Joash of
Judah, began to reign. 2 He was
twenty-five years old when he began to reign, and he reigned
twenty-nine years in Jerusalem.
His mother's name was Jehoaddin
of Jerusalem. 3 He did what was
right in the sight of the LORD, yet
not like his ancestor David; in all
things he did as his father Joash
had done. 4 But the high places
were not removed; the people still
sacrificed and made offerings on
the high places. 5 As soon as the
royal power was firmly in his hand
he killed his servants who had murdered his father the king. 6 But he
did not put to death the children of
the murderers; according to what is
written in the book of the law of
Moses, where the LORD commanded, "The parents shall not be put to
death for the children, or the children be put to death for the parents; but all shall be put to death
for their own sins."
7 He killed ten thousand Edomites in the Valley of Salt and took
Sela by storm; he called it Jokthe-
el, which is its name to this day.
8 Then Amaziah sent messengers to King Jehoash son of Jehoahaz, son of Jehu, of Israel, saying,
"Come, let us look one another in
the face." 9 King Jehoash of Israel
sent word to King Amaziah of Judah, "A thornbush on Lebanon
sent to a cedar on Lebanon, saying,
'Give your daughter to my son for a
wife'; but a wild animal of Lebanon
passed by and trampled down the
thornbush. 10 You have indeed defeated Edom, and your heart has
lifted you up. Be content with your
glory, and stay at home; for why
should you provoke trouble so that
you fall, you and Judah with you?"
11 But Amaziah would not listen. So King Jehoash of Israel went
up; he and King Amaziah of Judah
faced one another in battle at Beth-
shemesh, which belongs to Judah.
12 Judah was defeated by Israel; everyone fled home. 13 King Jehoash
of Israel captured King Amaziah of
Judah son of Jehoash, son of Ahaziah, at Beth-shemesh; he came to
Jerusalem, and broke down the
wall of Jerusalem from the Ephraim Gate to the Corner Gate, a distance of four hundred cubits. 14 He
seized all the gold and silver, and
all the vessels that were found in
the house of the LORD and in the
treasuries of the king's house, as
well as hostages; then he returned
to Samaria.
15 Now the rest of the acts that
Jehoash did, his might, and how he
fought with King Amaziah of Judah, are they not written in the
Book of the Annals of the Kings of
Israel? 16 Jehoash slept with his ancestors, and was buried in Samaria
with the kings of Israel; then his
son Jeroboam succeeded him.
17 King Amaziah son of Joash of
Judah lived fifteen years after the
death of King Jehoash son of Jehoahaz of Israel. 18 Now the rest of the
deeds of Amaziah, are they not
written in the Book of the Annals of
the Kings of Judah? 19 They made a
conspiracy against him in Jerusalem, and he fled to Lachish. But
they sent after him to Lachish, and
killed him there. 20 They brought
him on horses; he was buried in Jerusalem with his ancestors in the
city of David. 21 All the people of
Judah took Azariah, who was sixteen years old, and made him king
to succeed his father Amaziah.
22 He rebuilt Elath and restored it
to Judah, after King Amaziah[r]
slept with his ancestors.

Jeroboam II Reigns over Israel

23 In the fifteenth year of King
Amaziah son of Joash of Judah,
King Jeroboam son of Joash of Israel began to reign in Samaria; he
reigned forty-one years. 24 He did
what was evil in the sight of the
LORD; he did not depart from all the
sins of Jeroboam son of Nebat,
which he caused Israel to sin. 25 He
restored the border of Israel from
Lebo-hamath as far as the Sea of

14.1 2 Kings 13.10; 2 Chr 25.1
14.4 2 Kings 12.3; 16.4
14.5 2 Kings 12.20
14.6 Deut 24.16; Ezek 18.4, 20
14.7 2 Chr 25.11; 2 Sam 8.13; Josh 15.38
14.8 2 Chr 25.17-24
14.9 Judg 9.8-15
14.10 v. 7; Deut 8.14; 2 Chr 26.16; 32.25
14.11 Josh 19.38
14.12 2 Sam 18.17
14.13 Neh 8.16; 12.39; 2 Chr 25.23
14.14 2 Kings 12.18
14.15 2 Kings 13.12
14.17 2 Chr 25.25-28
14.19 Josh 10.31; 2 Kings 18.14, 17
14.22 2 Kings 16.6; 2 Chr 26.2
14.25 2 Kings 10.32; 1 Kings 8.65; Deut 3.17; Jon 1.1; Mt 12.39, 40; Josh 19.13

r Heb *the king*

the Arabah, according to the word
of the LORD, the God of Israel,
which he spoke by his servant Jonah son of Amittai, the prophet,
who was from Gath-hepher. 26 For
the LORD saw that the distress of Israel was very bitter; there was no
one left, bond or free, and no one to
help Israel. 27 But the LORD had not
said that he would blot out the
name of Israel from under heaven,
so he saved them by the hand of
Jeroboam son of Joash.
28 Now the rest of the acts of
Jeroboam, and all that he did, and
his might, how he fought, and how
he recovered for Israel Damascus
and Hamath, which had belonged
to Judah, are they not written in
the Book of the Annals of the Kings
of Israel? 29 Jeroboam slept with his
ancestors, the kings of Israel; his
son Zechariah succeeded him.

Azariah Reigns over Judah

15 In the twenty-seventh year
of King Jeroboam of Israel
King Azariah son of Amaziah of Judah began to reign. 2 He was sixteen years old when he began to
reign, and he reigned fifty-two
years in Jerusalem. His mother's
name was Jecoliah of Jerusalem.
3 He did what was right in the sight
of the LORD, just as his father Amaziah had done. 4 Nevertheless the
high places were not taken away;
the people still sacrificed and
made offerings on the high places.
5 The LORD struck the king, so that
he was leprous[s] to the day of his
death, and lived in a separate
house. Jotham the king's son was
in charge of the palace, governing
the people of the land. 6 Now the
rest of the acts of Azariah, and all
that he did, are they not written in
the Book of the Annals of the Kings
of Judah? 7 Azariah slept with his
ancestors; they buried him with his
ancestors in the city of David; his
son Jotham succeeded him.

Zechariah Reigns over Israel

8 In the thirty-eighth year of
King Azariah of Judah, Zechariah
son of Jeroboam reigned over Israel

14.26 2 Kings 13.4; Deut 32.36
14.27 2 Kings 13.5, 23
14.28 2 Sam 8.6; 1 Kings 11.24; 2 Chr 8.3
14.29 2 Kings 15.8
15.1 2 Kings 14.21; 2 Chr 26.1, 3,4
15.2 2 Chr 26.3, 4
15.4 2 Kings 12.3; 14.4
15.5 2 Chr 26.19-21
15.7 2 Chr 26.23
15.10 Am 7.9
15.12 2 Kings 10.30
15.13 vv. 1,8
15.14 1 Kings 14.17
15.16 1 Kings 4.24; 2 Kings 8.12
15.17 vv. 1,8,13
15.19 1 Chr 5.26

in Samaria six months. 9 He did
what was evil in the sight of the
LORD, as his ancestors had done. He
did not depart from the sins of Jeroboam son of Nebat, which he
caused Israel to sin. 10 Shallum son
of Jabesh conspired against him,
and struck him down in public and
killed him, and reigned in place of
him. 11 Now the rest of the deeds of
Zechariah are written in the Book
of the Annals of the Kings of Israel.
12 This was the promise of the LORD
that he gave to Jehu, "Your sons
shall sit on the throne of Israel to
the fourth generation." And so it
happened.

Shallum Reigns over Israel

13 Shallum son of Jabesh began
to reign in the thirty-ninth year of
King Uzziah of Judah; he reigned
one month in Samaria. 14 Then
Menahem son of Gadi came up
from Tirzah and came to Samaria;
he struck down Shallum son of Jabesh in Samaria and killed him; he
reigned in place of him. 15 Now the
rest of the deeds of Shallum, including the conspiracy that he
made, are written in the Book of
the Annals of the Kings of Israel.
16 At that time Menahem sacked
Tiphsah, all who were in it and its
territory from Tirzah on; because
they did not open it to him, he
sacked it. He ripped open all the
pregnant women in it.

Menahem Reigns over Israel

17 In the thirty-ninth year of
King Azariah of Judah, Menahem
son of Gadi began to reign over Israel; he reigned ten years in Samaria. 18 He did what was evil in the
sight of the LORD; he did not depart
all his days from any of the sins of
Jeroboam son of Nebat, which he
caused Israel to sin. 19 King Pul of
Assyria came against the land;
Menahem gave Pul a thousand talents of silver, so that he might help
him confirm his hold on the royal
power. 20 Menahem exacted the
money from Israel, that is, from all

[s] A term for several skin diseases; precise meaning uncertain

the wealthy, fifty shekels of silver
from each one, to give to the king of
Assyria. So the king of Assyria
turned back, and did not stay there
in the land. 21 Now the rest of the
deeds of Menahem, and all that he
did, are they not written in the
Book of the Annals of the Kings of
Israel? 22 Menahem slept with his
ancestors, and his son Pekahiah
succeeded him.

Pekahiah Reigns over Israel

23 In the fiftieth year of King
Azariah of Judah, Pekahiah son of
Menahem began to reign over Israel in Samaria; he reigned two years.
24 He did what was evil in the sight
of the LORD; he did not turn away
from the sins of Jeroboam son of
Nebat, which he caused Israel to
sin. 25 Pekah son of Remaliah, his
captain, conspired against him
with fifty of the Gileadites, and attacked him in Samaria, in the citadel of the palace along with Argob
and Arieh; he killed him, and
reigned in place of him. 26 Now the
rest of the deeds of Pekahiah, and
all that he did, are written in the
Book of the Annals of the Kings of
Israel.

Pekah Reigns over Israel

27 In the fifty-second year of
King Azariah of Judah, Pekah son
of Remaliah began to reign over Israel in Samaria; he reigned twenty
years. 28 He did what was evil in the
sight of the LORD; he did not depart
from the sins of Jeroboam son of
Nebat, which he caused Israel to
sin.

29 In the days of King Pekah of
Israel, King Tiglath-pileser of Assyria came and captured Ijon, Abel-
beth-maacah, Janoah, Kedesh, Hazor, Gilead, and Galilee, all the
land of Naphtali; and he carried
the people captive to Assyria.
30 Then Hoshea son of Elah made a
conspiracy against Pekah son of
Remaliah, attacked him, and killed
him; he reigned in place of him, in
the twentieth year of Jotham son of
Uzziah. 31 Now the rest of the acts
of Pekah, and all that he did, are

15.23 vv. 1,8,13, 17
15.25 1 Kings 16.18
15.27 v. 23; Isa 7.1
15.29 v. 19; 2 Kings 17.6; 1 Chr 5.26
15.32 2 Chr 27.1ff
15.34 v. 3; 2 Chr 26.4, 5
15.35 v. 4; 2 Chr 27.3
15.37 2 Kings 16.5; Isa 7.1; v. 27
16.1 2 Chr 28.1ff
16.3 Lev 18.21; 2 Kings 17.17; 21.6; Deut 12.31; 2 Kings 21.2, 11
16.4 Deut 12.2; 2 Kings 14.4
16.5 2 Kings 15.37; Isa 7.1; 2 Chr 28.5, 6
16.6 2 Kings 14.22; 2 Chr 26.2

written in the Book of the Annals of
the Kings of Israel.

Jotham Reigns over Judah

32 In the second year of King
Pekah son of Remaliah of Israel,
King Jotham son of Uzziah of Judah began to reign. 33 He was
twenty-five years old when he began to reign and reigned sixteen
years in Jerusalem. His mother's
name was Jerusha daughter of Zadok. 34 He did what was right in the
sight of the LORD, just as his father
Uzziah had done. 35 Nevertheless
the high places were not removed;
the people still sacrificed and
made offerings on the high places.
He built the upper gate of the
house of the LORD. 36 Now the rest
of the acts of Jotham, and all that
he did, are they not written in the
Book of the Annals of the Kings of
Judah? 37 In those days the LORD
began to send King Rezin of Aram
and Pekah son of Remaliah against
Judah. 38 Jotham slept with his ancestors, and was buried with his
ancestors in the city of David, his
ancestor; his son Ahaz succeeded
him.

Ahaz Reigns over Judah

16 In the seventeenth year of
Pekah son of Remaliah,
King Ahaz son of Jotham of Judah
began to reign. 2 Ahaz was twenty
years old when he began to reign;
he reigned sixteen years in Jerusalem. He did not do what was right
in the sight of the LORD his God, as
his ancestor David had done, 3 but
he walked in the way of the kings of
Israel. He even made his son pass
through fire, according to the
abominable practices of the nations whom the LORD drove out before the people of Israel. 4 He sacrificed and made offerings on the
high places, on the hills, and under
every green tree.

5 Then King Rezin of Aram and
King Pekah son of Remaliah of Israel came up to wage war on Jerusalem; they besieged Ahaz but
could not conquer him. 6 At that

time the king of Edom[t] recovered
Elath for Edom,[u] and drove the Judeans from Elath; and the Edomites came to Elath, where they live
to this day. 7 Ahaz sent messengers
to King Tiglath-pileser of Assyria,
saying, "I am your servant and your
son. Come up, and rescue me from
the hand of the king of Aram and
from the hand of the king of Israel,
who are attacking me." 8 Ahaz also
took the silver and gold found in
the house of the LORD and in the
treasures of the king's house, and
sent a present to the king of Assyria. 9 The king of Assyria listened to
him; the king of Assyria marched
up against Damascus, and took it,
carrying its people captive to Kir;
then he killed Rezin.

10 When King Ahaz went to Damascus to meet King Tiglath-
pileser of Assyria, he saw the altar
that was at Damascus. King Ahaz
sent to the priest Uriah a model of
the altar, and its pattern, exact in
all its details. 11 The priest Uriah
built the altar; in accordance with
all that King Ahaz had sent from
Damascus, just so did the priest
Uriah build it, before King Ahaz arrived from Damascus. 12 When the
king came from Damascus, the
king viewed the altar. Then the
king drew near to the altar, went up
on it, 13 and offered his burnt offering and his grain offering, poured
his drink offering, and dashed the
blood of his offerings of well-being
against the altar. 14 The bronze altar that was before the LORD he removed from the front of the house,
from the place between his altar
and the house of the LORD, and put
it on the north side of his altar.
15 King Ahaz commanded the priest
Uriah, saying, "Upon the great altar
offer the morning burnt offering,
and the evening grain offering, and
the king's burnt offering, and his
grain offering, with the burnt offering of all the people of the land,
their grain offering, and their drink
offering; then dash against it all the
blood of the burnt offering, and all
the blood of the sacrifice; but the
bronze altar shall be for me to inquire by." 16 The priest Uriah did
everything that King Ahaz commanded.

17 Then King Ahaz cut off the
frames of the stands, and removed
the laver from them; he removed
the sea from the bronze oxen that
were under it, and put it on a pedi-
ment of stone. 18 The covered por-
tal for use on the sabbath that had
been built inside the palace, and
the outer entrance for the king he
removed from[v] the house of the
LORD. He did this because of the
king of Assyria. 19 Now the rest of
the acts of Ahaz that he did, are
they not written in the Book of the
Annals of the Kings of Judah?
20 Ahaz slept with his ancestors,
and was buried with his ancestors
in the city of David; his son Hezekiah succeeded him.

Hoshea Reigns over Israel

17 In the twelfth year of King
Ahaz of Judah, Hoshea son
of Elah began to reign in Samaria
over Israel; he reigned nine years.
2 He did what was evil in the sight
of the LORD, yet not like the kings of
Israel who were before him. 3 King
Shalmaneser of Assyria came up
against him; Hoshea became his
vassal, and paid him tribute. 4 But
the king of Assyria found treachery
in Hoshea; for he had sent messengers to King So of Egypt, and offered no tribute to the king of Assyria, as he had done year by year;
therefore the king of Assyria confined him and imprisoned him.

Israel Carried Captive to Assyria

5 Then the king of Assyria invaded all the land and came to Samaria; for three years he besieged
it. 6 In the ninth year of Hoshea the
king of Assyria captured Samaria;
he carried the Israelites away to Assyria. He placed them in Halah, on
the Habor, the river of Gozan, and
in the cities of the Medes.

7 This occurred because the
people of Israel had sinned against
the LORD their God, who had

16.7 2 Chr 28.16ff; 2 Kings 15.29
16.8 2 Kings 12.17, 18
16.9 2 Chr 28.21; Am 1.3-5
16.10 2 Kings 15.29; Isa 8.2
16.14 2 Chr 4.1
16.15 Ex 29.39-41
16.17 1 Kings 7.23-28
16.20 2 Chr 28.27
17.1 2 Kings 15.30
17.3 2 Kings 18.9-12
17.5 Hos 13.16
17.6 Hos 13.16; Deut 28.64; 29.27,28; 1 Chr 5.26; 2 Kings 18.10, 11
17.7 Josh 23.16; Ex 14.15-30; Judg 6.10

[t] Cn: Heb *King Rezin of Aram* [u] Cn: Heb *Aram* [v] Cn: Heb lacks *from*

brought them up out of the land of Egypt from under the hand of Pharaoh king of Egypt. They had worshiped other gods 8 and walked in the customs of the nations whom the LORD drove out before the people of Israel, and in the customs that the kings of Israel had introduced.[w] 9 The people of Israel secretly did things that were not right against the LORD their God. They built for themselves high places at all their towns, from watchtower to fortified city; 10 they set up for themselves pillars and sacred poles[x] on every high hill and under every green tree; 11 there they made offerings on all the high places, as the nations did whom the LORD carried away before them. They did wicked things, provoking the LORD to anger; 12 they served idols, of which the LORD had said to them, "You shall not do this." 13 Yet the LORD warned Israel and Judah by every prophet and every seer, saying, "Turn from your evil ways and keep my commandments and my statutes, in accordance with all the law that I commanded your ancestors and that I sent to you by my servants the prophets." 14 They would not listen but were stubborn, as their ancestors had been, who did not believe in the LORD their God. 15 They despised his statutes, and his covenant that he made with their ancestors, and the warnings that he gave them. They went after false idols and became false; they followed the nations that were around them, concerning whom the LORD had commanded them that they should not do as they did. 16 They rejected all the commandments of the LORD their God and made for themselves cast images of two calves; they made a sacred pole,[y] worshiped all the host of heaven, and served Baal. 17 They made their sons and their daughters pass through fire; they used divination and augury; and they sold themselves to do evil in the sight of the LORD, provoking him to anger. 18 Therefore the LORD was very angry with Israel and removed them out of his sight; none was left but the tribe of Judah alone.

19 Judah also did not keep the commandments of the LORD their God but walked in the customs that Israel had introduced. 20 The LORD rejected all the descendants of Israel; he punished them and gave them into the hand of plunderers, until he had banished them from his presence.

21 When he had torn Israel from the house of David, they made Jeroboam son of Nebat king. Jeroboam drove Israel from following the LORD and made them commit great sin. 22 The people of Israel continued in all the sins that Jeroboam committed; they did not depart from them 23 until the LORD removed Israel out of his sight, as he had foretold through all his servants the prophets. So Israel was exiled from their own land to Assyria until this day.

Assyria Resettles Samaria

24 The king of Assyria brought people from Babylon, Cuthah, Avva, Hamath, and Sepharvaim, and placed them in the cities of Samaria in place of the people of Israel; they took possession of Samaria, and settled in its cities. 25 When they first settled there, they did not worship the LORD; therefore the LORD sent lions among them, which killed some of them. 26 So the king of Assyria was told, "The nations that you have carried away and placed in the cities of Samaria do not know the law of the god of the land; therefore he has sent lions among them; they are killing them, because they do not know the law of the god of the land." 27 Then the king of Assyria commanded, "Send there one of the priests whom you carried away from there; let him[z] go and live there, and teach them the law of the god of the land." 28 So one of the priests whom they had carried away from Samaria came

17.8 Lev 18.3; Deut 18.9; 2 Kings 16.3
17.9 2 Kings 18.8
17.10 Ex 34.12-14; 1 Kings 14.23; Mic 5.14
17.12 Ex 20.3,4
17.13 1 Sam 9.9; Jer 18.11; 25.5; 35.15
17.14 Ex 32.9; Deut 31.27; Acts 7.51
17.15 Jer 8.9; Deut 29.25; 32.21; Deut 12.30, 31
17.16 1 Kings 12.28; 14.15,23; 2 Kings 21.3; 1 Kings 16.31
17.17 Lev 19.26; 2 Kings 16.3; Deut 18.10-12; 1 Kings 21.20
17.18 v. 6; 1 Kings 11.13, 32,36
17.19 1 Kings 14.22, 23; 2 Kings 16.3
17.20 2 Kings 15.29
17.21 1 Kings 11.11, 31; 12.20, 28-33
17.23 vv. 6,13
17.24 Ezra 4.2,10; 2 Kings 18.34
17.27 Mic 3.11

[w] Meaning of Heb uncertain
[x] Heb *Asherim*
[y] Heb *Asherah*
[z] Syr Vg: Heb *them*

and lived in Bethel; he taught them
how they should worship the LORD.
29 But every nation still made
gods of its own and put them in the
shrines of the high places that the
people of Samaria had made, every
nation in the cities in which they
lived; 30 the people of Babylon
made Succoth-benoth, the people
of Cuth made Nergal, the people of
Hamath made Ashima; 31 the Av-
vites made Nibhaz and Tartak; the
Sepharvites burned their children
in the fire to Adrammelech and
Anammelech, the gods of Sepharvaim. 32 They also worshiped the
LORD and appointed from among
themselves all sorts of people as
priests of the high places, who sacrificed for them in the shrines of
the high places. 33 So they worshiped the LORD but also served
their own gods, after the manner of
the nations from among whom
they had been carried away. 34 To
this day they continue to practice
their former customs.
They do not worship the LORD
and they do not follow the statutes
or the ordinances or the law or the
commandment that the LORD commanded the children of Jacob,
whom he named Israel. 35 The LORD
had made a covenant with them
and commanded them, "You shall
not worship other gods or bow
yourselves to them or serve them or
sacrifice to them, 36 but you shall
worship the LORD, who brought you
out of the land of Egypt with great
power and with an outstretched
arm; you shall bow yourselves to
him, and to him you shall sacrifice.
37 The statutes and the ordinances
and the law and the commandment that he wrote for you, you
shall always be careful to observe.
You shall not worship other gods;
38 you shall not forget the covenant
that I have made with you. You
shall not worship other gods, 39 but
you shall worship the LORD your
God; he will deliver you out of the
hand of all your enemies." 40 They
would not listen, however, but they
continued to practice their former
custom.

17.30 v. 24
17.31 vv. 17,24
17.32 1 Kings 12.31
17.33 Zeph 1.5
17.34 Gen 32.28; 35.10
17.35 Judg 6.10; Ex 20.5
17.36 Ex 6.6; Deut 10.20
17.37 Deut 5.32
17.38 Deut 4.23
17.41 vv. 32,33
18.1 2 Kings 17.1; 2 Chr 28.27
18.2 2 Chr 29.1, 2
18.4 2 Chr 31.1; Num 21.8,9
18.5 2 Kings 19.10; 23.25
18.6 Deut 10.20
18.7 Gen 39.2,3; 1 Sam 18.14; 2 Kings 16.7
18.8 1 Chr 4.41; Isa 14.29; 2 Kings 17.9
18.9 2 Kings 17.3
18.10 2 Kings 17.6
18.11 2 Kings 17.6

41 So these nations worshiped
the LORD, but also served their
carved images; to this day their
children and their children's children continue to do as their ancestors did.

Hezekiah's Reign over Judah

18 In the third year of King
Hoshea son of Elah of Israel, Hezekiah son of King Ahaz of
Judah began to reign. 2 He was
twenty-five years old when he began to reign; he reigned twenty-
nine years in Jerusalem. His mother's name was Abi daughter of
Zechariah. 3 He did what was right
in the sight of the LORD just as his
ancestor David had done. 4 He removed the high places, broke down
the pillars, and cut down the sacred pole.[a] He broke in pieces the
bronze serpent that Moses had
made, for until those days the people of Israel had made offerings to
it; it was called Nehushtan. 5 He
trusted in the LORD the God of Israel; so that there was no one like
him among all the kings of Judah
after him, or among those who
were before him. 6 For he held fast
to the LORD; he did not depart from
following him but kept the commandments that the LORD commanded Moses. 7 The LORD was
with him; wherever he went, he
prospered. He rebelled against the
king of Assyria and would not serve
him. 8 He attacked the Philistines
as far as Gaza and its territory, from
watchtower to fortified city.
9 In the fourth year of King Hezekiah, which was the seventh year
of King Hoshea son of Elah of Israel, King Shalmaneser of Assyria
came up against Samaria, besieged
it, 10 and at the end of three years,
took it. In the sixth year of Hezekiah, which was the ninth year of
King Hoshea of Israel, Samaria was
taken. 11 The king of Assyria carried
the Israelites away to Assyria, settled them in Halah, on the Habor,
the river of Gozan, and in the cities
of the Medes, 12 because they did
not obey the voice of the LORD

[a] Heb *Asherah*

their God but transgressed his
covenant—all that Moses the servant of the LORD had commanded;
they neither listened nor obeyed.

Sennacherib Invades Judah

13 In the fourteenth year of
King Hezekiah, King Sennacherib
of Assyria came up against all the
fortified cities of Judah and captured them. 14 King Hezekiah of Judah sent to the king of Assyria at
Lachish, saying, "I have done
wrong; withdraw from me; whatever you impose on me I will bear."
The king of Assyria demanded of
King Hezekiah of Judah three hundred talents of silver and thirty talents of gold. 15 Hezekiah gave him
all the silver that was found in the
house of the LORD and in the treasuries of the king's house. 16 At that
time Hezekiah stripped the gold
from the doors of the temple of the
LORD, and from the doorposts that
King Hezekiah of Judah had overlaid and gave it to the king of Assyria. 17 The king of Assyria sent the
Tartan, the Rabsaris, and the Rabshakeh with a great army from Lachish to King Hezekiah at Jerusalem. They went up and came to
Jerusalem. When they arrived, they
came and stood by the conduit of
the upper pool, which is on the
highway to the Fuller's Field.
18 When they called for the king,
there came out to them Eliakim
son of Hilkiah, who was in charge
of the palace, and Shebnah the secretary, and Joah son of Asaph, the
recorder.
19 The Rabshakeh said to them,
"Say to Hezekiah: Thus says the
great king, the king of Assyria: On
what do you base this confidence
of yours? 20 Do you think that mere
words are strategy and power for
war? On whom do you now rely,
that you have rebelled against me?
21 See, you are relying now on
Egypt, that broken reed of a staff,
which will pierce the hand of anyone who leans on it. Such is Pharaoh king of Egypt to all who rely on
him. 22 But if you say to me, 'We
rely on the LORD our God,' is it not
he whose high places and altars
Hezekiah has removed, saying to
Judah and to Jerusalem, 'You shall
worship before this altar in Jerusalem'? 23 Come now, make a wager
with my master the king of Assyria:
I will give you two thousand horses,
if you are able on your part to set
riders on them. 24 How then can
you repulse a single captain among
the least of my master's servants,
when you rely on Egypt for chariots
and for horsemen? 25 Moreover, is it
without the LORD that I have come
up against this place to destroy it?
The LORD said to me, Go up against
this land, and destroy it."
26 Then Eliakim son of Hilkiah,
and Shebnah, and Joah said to the
Rabshakeh, "Please speak to your
servants in the Aramaic language,
for we understand it; do not speak
to us in the language of Judah
within the hearing of the people
who are on the wall." 27 But the
Rabshakeh said to them, "Has my
master sent me to speak these
words to your master and to you,
and not to the people sitting on the
wall, who are doomed with you to
eat their own dung and to drink
their own urine?"
28 Then the Rabshakeh stood
and called out in a loud voice in the
language of Judah, "Hear the word
of the great king, the king of Assyria! 29 Thus says the king: 'Do not let
Hezekiah deceive you, for he will
not be able to deliver you out of my
hand. 30 Do not let Hezekiah make
you rely on the LORD by saying, The
LORD will surely deliver us, and this
city will not be given into the hand
of the king of Assyria.' 31 Do not listen to Hezekiah; for thus says the
king of Assyria: 'Make your peace
with me and come out to me; then
every one of you will eat from your
own vine and your own fig tree, and
drink water from your own cistern,
32 until I come and take you away to
a land like your own land, a land of
grain and wine, a land of bread and
vineyards, a land of olive oil and
honey, that you may live and not
die. Do not listen to Hezekiah
when he misleads you by saying,

18.13 2 Chr 32.1ff; Isa 36.1ff
18.15 2 Kings 16.8
18.17 Isa 20.1; 7.3
18.18 2 Kings 19.2; Isa 22.15,20
18.19 2 Chr 32.10ff
18.21 Ezek 29.6,7
18.22 v. 4; 2 Chr 31.1; 32.12
18.24 Isa 31.1
18.26 Ezra 4.7
18.29 2 Chr 32.15
18.31 1 Kings 4.20, 25
18.32 Deut 8.7-9

The LORD will deliver us. 33 Has any
of the gods of the nations ever delivered its land out of the hand of
the king of Assyria? 34 Where are
the gods of Hamath and Arpad?
Where are the gods of Sepharvaim,
Hena, and Ivvah? Have they delivered Samaria out of my hand?
35 Who among all the gods of the
countries have delivered their
countries out of my hand, that the
LORD should deliver Jerusalem out
of my hand?' "
36 But the people were silent
and answered him not a word, for
the king's command was, "Do not
answer him." 37 Then Eliakim son
of Hilkiah, who was in charge of
the palace, and Shebna the secretary, and Joah son of Asaph, the recorder, came to Hezekiah with
their clothes torn and told him the
words of the Rabshakeh.

Hezekiah Consults Isaiah

19 When King Hezekiah heard
it, he tore his clothes, covered himself with sackcloth, and
went into the house of the LORD.
2 And he sent Eliakim, who was in
charge of the palace, and Shebna
the secretary, and the senior
priests, covered with sackcloth, to
the prophet Isaiah son of Amoz.
3 They said to him, "Thus says Hezekiah, This day is a day of distress,
of rebuke, and of disgrace; children
have come to the birth, and there is
no strength to bring them forth. 4 It
may be that the LORD your God
heard all the words of the Rabshakeh, whom his master the king of
Assyria has sent to mock the living
God, and will rebuke the words
that the LORD your God has heard;
therefore lift up your prayer for the
remnant that is left." 5 When the
servants of King Hezekiah came to
Isaiah, 6 Isaiah said to them, "Say
to your master, 'Thus says the
LORD: Do not be afraid because of
the words that you have heard,
with which the servants of the king
of Assyria have reviled me. 7 I myself will put a spirit in him, so that
he shall hear a rumor and return to
his own land; I will cause him to

18.33 2 Kings 19.12; 2 Chr 32.14; Isa 10.10,11
18.34 2 Kings 19.13; 17.24
18.37 vv. 18,26; 2 Kings 6.30
19.1 2 Chr 32.20-22; Isa 37.1-38; 2 Kings 18.37; 1 Kings 21.27
19.2 Isa 1.1; 2.1
19.4 2 Sam 16.12; 2 Kings 18.35; 1.9
19.6 Isa 37.6ff; 2 Kings 18.17ff
19.7 vv. 35-37
19.8 Josh 10.29; 2 Kings 18.14
19.10 2 Kings 18.5, 30
19.12 2 Kings 18.33
19.13 2 Kings 18.34
19.14 Isa 37.14
19.15 1 Sam 4.4; 1 Kings 18.39
19.16 Ps 31.2; 2 Chr 6.40; v. 4
19.18 Ps 115.4; Jer 10.3
19.19 Ps 83.18; v. 15

fall by the sword in his own land.' "

Sennacherib's Threat

8 The Rabshakeh returned, and
found the king of Assyria fighting
against Libnah; for he had heard
that the king had left Lachish.
9 When the king[b] heard concerning
King Tirhakah of Ethiopia,[c] "See,
he has set out to fight against you,"
he sent messengers again to Hezekiah, saying, 10 "Thus shall you
speak to King Hezekiah of Judah:
Do not let your God on whom you
rely deceive you by promising that
Jerusalem will not be given into
the hand of the king of Assyria.
11 See, you have heard what the
kings of Assyria have done to all
lands, destroying them utterly.
Shall you be delivered? 12 Have the
gods of the nations delivered them,
the nations that my predecessors
destroyed, Gozan, Haran, Rezeph,
and the people of Eden who were
in Telassar? 13 Where is the king of
Hamath, the king of Arpad, the
king of the city of Sepharvaim, the
king of Hena, or the king of Ivvah?"

Hezekiah's Prayer

14 Hezekiah received the letter
from the hand of the messengers
and read it; then Hezekiah went up
to the house of the LORD and spread
it before the LORD. 15 And Hezekiah
prayed before the LORD, and said:
"O LORD the God of Israel, who are
enthroned above the cherubim,
you are God, you alone, of all the
kingdoms of the earth; you have
made heaven and earth. 16 Incline
your ear, O LORD, and hear; open
your eyes, O LORD, and see; hear
the words of Sennacherib, which
he has sent to mock the living God.
17 Truly, O LORD, the kings of Assyria have laid waste the nations and
their lands, 18 and have hurled their
gods into the fire, though they were
no gods but the work of human
hands—wood and stone—and so
they were destroyed. 19 So now,
O LORD our God, save us, I pray
you, from his hand, so that all the
kingdoms of the earth may know

[b] Heb *he* [c] Or *Nubia*; Heb *Cush*

that you, O LORD, are God alone."
20 Then Isaiah son of Amoz sent
to Hezekiah, saying, "Thus says the
LORD, the God of Israel: I have
heard your prayer to me about King
Sennacherib of Assyria. 21 This is
the word that the LORD has spoken
concerning him:

She despises you, she scorns
you—
virgin daughter Zion;
she tosses her head—behind
your back,
daughter Jerusalem.

22 Whom have you mocked and
reviled?
Against whom have you
raised your voice
and haughtily lifted your
eyes?
Against the Holy One of
Israel!
23 By your messengers you have
mocked the Lord,
and you have said, 'With
my many chariots
I have gone up the heights of
the mountains,
to the far recesses of
Lebanon;
I felled its tallest cedars,
its choicest cypresses;
I entered its farthest retreat,
its densest forest.
24 I dug wells
and drank foreign waters,
I dried up with the sole of
my foot
all the streams of Egypt.'

25 Have you not heard
that I determined it long
ago?
I planned from days of old
what now I bring to pass,
that you should make
fortified cities
crash into heaps of ruins,
26 while their inhabitants,
shorn of strength,
are dismayed and
confounded;
they have become like plants
of the field
and like tender grass,
like grass on the housetops,

19.20 2 Kings 20.5; Isa 37.21
19.21 Lam 2.13; Job 16.4; Ps 22.7,8
19.22 vv. 4,6; Ps 71.22; Isa 5.24
19.23 2 Kings 18.17; Ps 20.7; Isa 10.18
19.24 Isa 19.6
19.25 Isa 45.7; 10.5
19.26 Ps 129.6
19.28 Job 41.2; Ezek 29.4; vv. 33,36
19.29 1 Sam 2.34; 2 Kings 20.8, 9; Lk 2.12
19.30 2 Chr 32.22, 23
19.31 Isa 9.7
19.33 v. 28
19.34 2 Kings 20.6; 1 Kings 11.12, 13
19.35 2 Chr 32.21; Isa 37.36
19.36 vv. 7,28,33; Jon 1.2
19.37 2 Chr 32.21; v. 7; Ezra 4.2

blighted before it is grown.

27 "But I know your rising[d] and
your sitting,
your going out and coming
in,
and your raging against me.
28 Because you have raged
against me
and your arrogance has
come to my ears,
I will put my hook in your
nose
and my bit in your mouth;
I will turn you back on the
way
by which you came.

29 "And this shall be the sign
for you: This year you shall eat
what grows of itself, and in the second year what springs from that;
then in the third year sow, reap,
plant vineyards, and eat their fruit.
30 The surviving remnant of the
house of Judah shall again take
root downward, and bear fruit upward; 31 for from Jerusalem a remnant shall go out, and from Mount
Zion a band of survivors. The zeal
of the LORD of hosts will do this.
32 "Therefore thus says the
LORD concerning the king of Assyria: He shall not come into this city,
shoot an arrow there, come before
it with a shield, or cast up a siege
ramp against it. 33 By the way that
he came, by the same he shall return; he shall not come into this
city, says the LORD. 34 For I will defend this city to save it, for my own
sake and for the sake of my servant
David."

Sennacherib's Defeat and Death

35 That very night the angel of
the LORD set out and struck down
one hundred eighty-five thousand
in the camp of the Assyrians; when
morning dawned, they were all
dead bodies. 36 Then King Sennacherib of Assyria left, went
home, and lived at Nineveh. 37 As
he was worshiping in the house of
his god Nisroch, his sons Adram-

[d] Gk Compare Isa 37.27 Q Ms: MT lacks *rising*

melech and Sharezer killed him
with the sword, and they escaped
into the land of Ararat. His son
Esar-haddon succeeded him.

Hezekiah's Illness

20 In those days Hezekiah became sick and was at the
point of death. The prophet Isaiah
son of Amoz came to him, and said
to him, "Thus says the LORD: Set
your house in order, for you shall
die; you shall not recover." 2 Then
Hezekiah turned his face to the
wall and prayed to the LORD: 3 "Remember now, O LORD, I implore
you, how I have walked before you
in faithfulness with a whole heart,
and have done what is good in your
sight." Hezekiah wept bitterly.
4 Before Isaiah had gone out of the
middle court, the word of the LORD
came to him: 5 "Turn back, and say
to Hezekiah prince of my people,
Thus says the LORD, the God of your
ancestor David: I have heard your
prayer, I have seen your tears; indeed, I will heal you; on the third
day you shall go up to the house of
the LORD. 6 I will add fifteen years to
your life. I will deliver you and this
city out of the hand of the king of
Assyria; I will defend this city for
my own sake and for my servant
David's sake." 7 Then Isaiah said,
"Bring a lump of figs. Let them take
it and apply it to the boil, so that he
may recover."
8 Hezekiah said to Isaiah,
"What shall be the sign that the
LORD will heal me, and that I shall
go up to the house of the LORD on
the third day?" 9 Isaiah said, "This
is the sign to you from the LORD,
that the LORD will do the thing that
he has promised: the shadow has
now advanced ten intervals; shall it
retreat ten intervals?" 10 Hezekiah
answered, "It is normal for the
shadow to lengthen ten intervals;
rather let the shadow retreat ten intervals." 11 The prophet Isaiah cried
to the LORD; and he brought the
shadow back the ten intervals, by
which the sun[e] had declined on
the dial of Ahaz.

Envoys from Babylon

12 At that time King Merodach-
baladan son of Baladan of Babylon
sent envoys with letters and a
present to Hezekiah, for he had
heard that Hezekiah had been sick.
13 Hezekiah welcomed them;[f] he
showed them all his treasure
house, the silver, the gold, the
spices, the precious oil, his armory,
all that was found in his storehouses; there was nothing in his
house or in all his realm that Hezekiah did not show them. 14 Then
the prophet Isaiah came to King
Hezekiah, and said to him, "What
did these men say? From where did
they come to you?" Hezekiah answered, "They have come from a far
country, from Babylon." 15 He said,
"What have they seen in your
house?" Hezekiah answered,
"They have seen all that is in my
house; there is nothing in my storehouses that I did not show them."
16 Then Isaiah said to Hezekiah, "Hear the word of the LORD:
17 Days are coming when all that is
in your house, and that which your
ancestors have stored up until this
day, shall be carried to Babylon;
nothing shall be left, says the LORD.
18 Some of your own sons who are
born to you shall be taken away;
they shall be eunuchs in the palace
of the king of Babylon." 19 Then
Hezekiah said to Isaiah, "The word
of the LORD that you have spoken is
good." For he thought, "Why not, if
there will be peace and security in
my days?"

Death of Hezekiah

20 The rest of the deeds of Hezekiah, all his power, how he made
the pool and the conduit and
brought water into the city, are
they not written in the Book of the
Annals of the Kings of Judah?
21 Hezekiah slept with his ancestors; and his son Manasseh succeeded him.

20.1 2 Chr 32.24; Isa 38.1; 2 Sam 17.23
20.3 Neh 13.22; 2 Kings 18.3-6
20.5 1 Sam 9.16; 10.1; 2 Kings 19.20; Ps 39.12
20.6 2 Kings 19.34
20.7 Isa 38.21
20.11 Josh 10.12-14
20.12 Isa 39.1ff
20.13 2 Chr 32.27
20.15 v. 13
20.17 2 Kings 24.13; 25.13; Jer 52.17
20.18 2 Kings 24.12; 2 Chr 33.1; Dan 1.3-7
20.19 1 Sam 3.18
20.20 2 Chr 32.32; Neh 3.16
20.21 2 Chr 32.33

[e] Syr See Isa 38.8 and Tg: Heb *it* [f] Gk Vg Syr: Heb *When Hezekiah heard about them*

Manasseh Reigns over Judah

21 Manasseh was twelve years old when he began to reign; he reigned fifty-five years in Jerusalem. His mother's name was Hephzibah. 2 He did what was evil in the sight of the LORD, following the abominable practices of the nations that the LORD drove out before the people of Israel. 3 For he rebuilt the high places that his father Hezekiah had destroyed; he erected altars for Baal, made a sacred pole,[g] as King Ahab of Israel had done, worshiped all the host of heaven, and served them. 4 He built altars in the house of the LORD, of which the LORD had said, "In Jerusalem I will put my name." 5 He built altars for all the host of heaven in the two courts of the house of the LORD. 6 He made his son pass through fire; he practiced soothsaying and augury, and dealt with mediums and with wizards. He did much evil in the sight of the LORD, provoking him to anger. 7 The carved image of Asherah that he had made he set in the house of which the LORD said to David and to his son Solomon, "In this house, and in Jerusalem, which I have chosen out of all the tribes of Israel, I will put my name forever; 8 I will not cause the feet of Israel to wander any more out of the land that I gave to their ancestors, if only they will be careful to do according to all that I have commanded them, and according to all the law that my servant Moses commanded them." 9 But they did not listen; Manasseh misled them to do more evil than the nations had done that the LORD destroyed before the people of Israel.

10 The LORD said by his servants the prophets, 11 "Because King Manasseh of Judah has committed these abominations, has done things more wicked than all that the Amorites did, who were before him, and has caused Judah also to sin with his idols; 12 therefore thus says the LORD, the God of Israel, I am bringing upon Jerusalem and Judah such evil that the ears of everyone who hears of it will tingle. 13 I will stretch over Jerusalem the measuring line for Samaria, and the plummet for the house of Ahab; I will wipe Jerusalem as one wipes a dish, wiping it and turning it upside down. 14 I will cast off the remnant of my heritage, and give them into the hand of their enemies; they shall become a prey and a spoil to all their enemies, 15 because they have done what is evil in my sight and have provoked me to anger, since the day their ancestors came out of Egypt, even to this day."

16 Moreover Manasseh shed very much innocent blood, until he had filled Jerusalem from one end to another, besides the sin that he caused Judah to sin so that they did what was evil in the sight of the LORD.

17 Now the rest of the acts of Manasseh, all that he did, and the sin that he committed, are they not written in the Book of the Annals of the Kings of Judah? 18 Manasseh slept with his ancestors, and was buried in the garden of his house, in the garden of Uzza. His son Amon succeeded him.

Amon Reigns over Judah

19 Amon was twenty-two years old when he began to reign; he reigned two years in Jerusalem. His mother's name was Meshullemeth daughter of Haruz of Jotbah. 20 He did what was evil in the sight of the LORD, as his father Manasseh had done. 21 He walked in all the way in which his father walked, served the idols that his father served, and worshiped them; 22 he abandoned the LORD, the God of his ancestors, and did not walk in the way of the LORD. 23 The servants of Amon conspired against him, and killed the king in his house. 24 But the people of the land killed all those who had conspired against King Amon, and the people of the land made his son Josiah king in place of him. 25 Now the rest of the acts of Amon that he did, are they not written in the

21.1 2 Chr 33.1ff
21.2 2 Kings 16.3
21.3 2 Kings 18.4; 1 Kings 16.32, 33; 2 Kings 17.16; Deut 17.3
21.4 Jer 32.34; 2 Sam 7.13; 1 Kings 8.29
21.6 Lev 18.21; 2 Kings 16.3; 17.17; Lev 19.26, 31; Deut 18.20, 11
21.7 1 Kings 8.29; 9.3; 2 Kings 23.27; Jer 32.34
21.8 2 Sam 7.10
21.9 Prov 29.12
21.11 2 Kings 24.3, 4; 1 Kings 21.26; v. 16
21.12 1 Sam 3.11; Jer 19.3
21.13 Isa 34.11; Am 7.7,8
21.16 2 Kings 24.4
21.17 2 Chr 33.11-19
21.18 2 Chr 33.20
21.19 2 Chr 33.21-23
21.20 vv. 2-6,11, 16
21.22 1 Kings 11.33
21.23 2 Chr 33.24, 25

g Heb *Asherah*

Book of the Annals of the Kings of
Judah? 26 He was buried in his
tomb in the garden of Uzza; then
his son Josiah succeeded him.

Josiah Reigns over Judah

22 Josiah was eight years old
when he began to reign; he
reigned thirty-one years in Jerusalem. His mother's name was Jedi-
dah daughter of Adaiah of Bozkath.
2 He did what was right in the sight
of the LORD, and walked in all the
way of his father David; he did not
turn aside to the right or to the left.

Hilkiah Finds the Book of the Law

3 In the eighteenth year of King
Josiah, the king sent Shaphan son
of Azaliah, son of Meshullam, the
secretary, to the house of the LORD,
saying, 4 "Go up to the high priest
Hilkiah, and have him count the
entire sum of the money that has
been brought into the house of the
LORD, which the keepers of the
threshold have collected from
the people; 5 let it be given into the
hand of the workers who have the
oversight of the house of the LORD;
let them give it to the workers who
are at the house of the LORD, repairing the house, 6 that is, to the carpenters, to the builders, to the masons; and let them use it to buy
timber and quarried stone to repair
the house. 7 But no accounting
shall be asked from them for the
money that is delivered into their
hand, for they deal honestly."
8 The high priest Hilkiah said to
Shaphan the secretary, "I have
found the book of the law in the
house of the LORD." When Hilkiah
gave the book to Shaphan, he read
it. 9 Then Shaphan the secretary
came to the king, and reported to
the king, "Your servants have emptied out the money that was found
in the house, and have delivered it
into the hand of the workers who
have oversight of the house of the
LORD." 10 Shaphan the secretary informed the king, "The priest Hilkiah has given me a book." Shaphan
then read it aloud to the king.

11 When the king heard the
words of the book of the law, he
tore his clothes. 12 Then the king
commanded the priest Hilkiah,
Ahikam son of Shaphan, Achbor
son of Micaiah, Shaphan the secretary, and the king's servant Asaiah,
saying, 13 "Go, inquire of the LORD
for me, for the people, and for all
Judah, concerning the words of
this book that has been found; for
great is the wrath of the LORD that
is kindled against us, because our
ancestors did not obey the words of
this book, to do according to all
that is written concerning us."
14 So the priest Hilkiah, Ahikam, Achbor, Shaphan, and Asaiah
went to the prophetess Huldah the
wife of Shallum son of Tikvah, son
of Harhas, keeper of the wardrobe;
she resided in Jerusalem in the
Second Quarter, where they consulted her. 15 She declared to them,
"Thus says the LORD, the God of Israel: Tell the man who sent you to
me, 16 Thus says the LORD, I will indeed bring disaster on this place
and on its inhabitants—all the
words of the book that the king of
Judah has read. 17 Because they
have abandoned me and have
made offerings to other gods, so
that they have provoked me to anger with all the work of their hands,
therefore my wrath will be kindled
against this place, and it will not be
quenched. 18 But as to the king of
Judah, who sent you to inquire of
the LORD, thus shall you say to him,
Thus says the LORD, the God of Israel: Regarding the words that you
have heard, 19 because your heart
was penitent, and you humbled
yourself before the LORD, when you
heard how I spoke against this
place, and against its inhabitants,
that they should become a desolation and a curse, and because you
have torn your clothes and wept
before me, I also have heard you,
says the LORD. 20 Therefore, I will
gather you to your ancestors, and
you shall be gathered to your grave
in peace; your eyes shall not see all
the disaster that I will bring on this

21.26 v. 18
22.1 2 Chr 34.1; Josh 15.39
22.2 Deut 5.32
22.3 2 Chr 34.8ff
22.4 2 Kings 12.4, 9,10
22.5 2 Kings 12.11-14
22.7 2 Kings 12.15
22.8 Deut 31.24-26; 2 Chr 34.14, 15
22.12 2 Kings 25.22; 2 Chr 34.20
22.13 Deut 29.27
22.14 2 Chr 34.22
22.17 Deut 29.25-27
22.19 Ps 51.17; Isa 57.15; 1 Kings 21.29; Lev 26.31; Jer 26.6

place." They took the message back to the king.

Josiah's Reformation

23 Then the king directed that all the elders of Judah and Jerusalem should be gathered to him. 2 The king went up to the house of the LORD, and with him went all the people of Judah, all the inhabitants of Jerusalem, the priests, the prophets, and all the people, both small and great; he read in their hearing all the words of the book of the covenant that had been found in the house of the LORD. 3 The king stood by the pillar and made a covenant before the LORD, to follow the LORD, keeping his commandments, his decrees, and his statutes, with all his heart and all his soul, to perform the words of this covenant that were written in this book. All the people joined in the covenant.

4 The king commanded the high priest Hilkiah, the priests of the second order, and the guardians of the threshold, to bring out of the temple of the LORD all the vessels made for Baal, for Asherah, and for all the host of heaven; he burned them outside Jerusalem in the fields of the Kidron, and carried their ashes to Bethel. 5 He deposed the idolatrous priests whom the kings of Judah had ordained to make offerings in the high places at the cities of Judah and around Jerusalem; those also who made offerings to Baal, to the sun, the moon, the constellations, and all the host of the heavens. 6 He brought out the image of[h] Asherah from the house of the LORD, outside Jerusalem, to the Wadi Kidron, burned it at the Wadi Kidron, beat it to dust and threw the dust of it upon the graves of the common people. 7 He broke down the houses of the male temple prostitutes that were in the house of the LORD, where the women did weaving for Asherah. 8 He brought all the priests out of the towns of Judah, and defiled the high places where the priests had made offerings, from Geba to Beer-sheba; he broke down the high places of the gates that were at the entrance of the gate of Joshua the governor of the city, which were on the left at the gate of the city. 9 The priests of the high places, however, did not come up to the altar of the LORD in Jerusalem, but ate unleavened bread among their kindred. 10 He defiled Topheth, which is in the valley of Ben-hinnom, so that no one would make a son or a daughter pass through fire as an offering to Molech. 11 He removed the horses that the kings of Judah had dedicated to the sun, at the entrance to the house of the LORD, by the chamber of the eunuch Nathan-melech, which was in the precincts;[i] then he burned the chariots of the sun with fire. 12 The altars on the roof of the upper chamber of Ahaz, which the kings of Judah had made, and the altars that Manasseh had made in the two courts of the house of the LORD, he pulled down from there and broke in pieces, and threw the rubble into the Wadi Kidron. 13 The king defiled the high places that were east of Jerusalem, to the south of the Mount of Destruction, which King Solomon of Israel had built for Astarte the abomination of the Sidonians, for Chemosh the abomination of Moab, and for Milcom the abomination of the Ammonites. 14 He broke the pillars in pieces, cut down the sacred poles,[j] and covered the sites with human bones.

15 Moreover, the altar at Bethel, the high place erected by Jeroboam son of Nebat, who caused Israel to sin—he pulled down that altar along with the high place. He burned the high place, crushing it to dust; he also burned the sacred pole.[k] 16 As Josiah turned, he saw the tombs there on the mount; and he sent and took the bones out of the tombs, and burned them on the altar, and defiled it, according to

23.1 2 Chr 34.29-32
23.2 Deut 31.10-13; 2 Kings 22.8
23.3 2 Kings 11.14, 17; Deut 13.4
23.4ff 2 Kings 21.3, 7
23.7 1 Kings 14.24; 15.12; Ezek 16.16
23.8 1 Kings 15.22
23.9 Ezek 44.10-14
23.10 Isa 30.33; Jer 7.31; Lev 18.21; Deut 18.10
23.12 Jer 19.13; Zeph 1.5; 2 Kings 21.5; vv. 4,6
23.13 1 Kings 11.7
23.14 Ex 23.24; Deut 7.5,25
23.15 1 Kings 12.28-33
23.16 1 Kings 13.2

[h] Heb lacks *image of* [i] Meaning of Heb uncertain [j] Heb *Asherim*
[k] Heb *Asherah*

the word of the LORD that the man
of God proclaimed,[l] when Jeroboam stood by the altar at the festival; he turned and looked up at the
tomb of the man of God who had
predicted these things. 17 Then he
said, "What is that monument that
I see?" The people of the city told
him, "It is the tomb of the man of
God who came from Judah and
predicted these things that you
have done against the altar at Bethel." 18 He said, "Let him rest; let no
one move his bones." So they let
his bones alone, with the bones of
the prophet who came out of Samaria. 19 Moreover, Josiah removed
all the shrines of the high places
that were in the towns of Samaria,
which kings of Israel had made,
provoking the LORD to anger; he did
to them just as he had done at
Bethel. 20 He slaughtered on the altars all the priests of the high
places who were there, and burned
human bones on them. Then he returned to Jerusalem.

The Passover Celebrated

21 The king commanded all the
people, "Keep the passover to the
LORD your God as prescribed in this
book of the covenant." 22 No such
passover had been kept since the
days of the judges who judged Israel, or during all the days of the
kings of Israel or of the kings of Judah; 23 but in the eighteenth year of
King Josiah this passover was kept
to the LORD in Jerusalem.

24 Moreover Josiah put away
the mediums, wizards, teraphim,[m]
idols, and all the abominations
that were seen in the land of Judah
and in Jerusalem, so that he established the words of the law that
were written in the book that the
priest Hilkiah had found in the
house of the LORD. 25 Before him
there was no king like him, who
turned to the LORD with all his
heart, with all his soul, and with all
his might, according to all the law
of Moses; nor did any like him arise
after him.

26 Still the LORD did not turn
from the fierceness of his great
wrath, by which his anger was kindled against Judah, because of all
the provocations with which Manasseh had provoked him. 27 The
LORD said, "I will remove Judah
also out of my sight, as I have removed Israel; and I will reject this
city that I have chosen, Jerusalem,
and the house of which I said, My
name shall be there."

Josiah Dies in Battle

28 Now the rest of the acts of
Josiah, and all that he did, are they
not written in the Book of the Annals of the Kings of Judah? 29 In his
days Pharaoh Neco king of Egypt
went up to the king of Assyria to
the river Euphrates. King Josiah
went to meet him; but when Pharaoh Neco met him at Megiddo, he
killed him. 30 His servants carried
him dead in a chariot from Megiddo, brought him to Jerusalem, and
buried him in his own tomb. The
people of the land took Jehoahaz
son of Josiah, anointed him, and
made him king in place of his father.

Reign and Captivity of Jehoahaz

31 Jehoahaz was twenty-three
years old when he began to reign;
he reigned three months in Jerusalem. His mother's name was Hamutal daughter of Jeremiah of Libnah. 32 He did what was evil in the
sight of the LORD, just as his ancestors had done. 33 Pharaoh Neco
confined him at Riblah in the land
of Hamath, so that he might not
reign in Jerusalem, and imposed
tribute on the land of one hundred
talents of silver and a talent of
gold. 34 Pharaoh Neco made Eliakim son of Josiah king in place of
his father Josiah, and changed his
name to Jehoiakim. But he took
Jehoahaz away; he came to Egypt,
and died there. 35 Jehoiakim gave
the silver and the gold to Pharaoh,
but he taxed the land in order to
meet Pharaoh's demand for money. He exacted the silver and the
gold from the people of the land,

23.17 1 Kings 13.1, 30
23.18 1 Kings 13.31
23.19 2 Chr 34.6, 7
23.20 2 Kings 10.25; 11.18; 2 Chr 34.5
23.21 2 Chr 35.1; Ex 12.3; Num 9.2; Deut 16.2
23.22 2 Chr 35.18, 19
23.24 2 Kings 21.6, 11,21; Deut 18.10-12
23.25 2 Kings 18.5
23.26 2 Kings 21.11, 12; Jer 15.4
23.27 2 Kings 18.11; 21.13,14
23.29 2 Chr 35.20; Zech 12.11
23.30 2 Chr 35.24; 36.1
23.31 1 Chr 3.15; Jer 22.11; 2 Kings 24.18
23.33 2 Kings 25.6; Jer 52.27; 2 Chr 36.3
23.34 2 Chr 36.4; 2 Kings 24.17; Ezek 19.3,4
23.35 v. 33

[l] Gk: Heb *proclaimed, who had predicted these things* [m] Or *household gods*

from all according to their assessment, to give it to Pharaoh Neco.

Jehoiakim Reigns over Judah

36 Jehoiakim was twenty-five years old when he began to reign; he reigned eleven years in Jerusalem. His mother's name was Zebidah daughter of Pedaiah of Rumah. 37 He did what was evil in the sight of the LORD, just as all his ancestors had done.

Judah Overrun by Enemies

24 In his days King Nebuchadnezzar of Babylon came up; Jehoiakim became his servant for three years; then he turned and rebelled against him. 2 The LORD sent against him bands of the Chaldeans, bands of the Arameans, bands of the Moabites, and bands of the Ammonites; he sent them against Judah to destroy it, according to the word of the LORD that he spoke by his servants the prophets. 3 Surely this came upon Judah at the command of the LORD, to remove them out of his sight, for the sins of Manasseh, for all that he had committed, 4 and also for the innocent blood that he had shed; for he filled Jerusalem with innocent blood, and the LORD was not willing to pardon. 5 Now the rest of the deeds of Jehoiakim, and all that he did, are they not written in the Book of the Annals of the Kings of Judah? 6 So Jehoiakim slept with his ancestors; then his son Jehoiachin succeeded him. 7 The king of Egypt did not come again out of his land, for the king of Babylon had taken over all that belonged to the king of Egypt from the Wadi of Egypt to the River Euphrates.

Reign and Captivity of Jehoiachin

8 Jehoiachin was eighteen years old when he began to reign; he reigned three months in Jerusalem. His mother's name was Nehushta daughter of Elnathan of Jerusalem. 9 He did what was evil in the sight of the LORD, just as his father had done.

10 At that time the servants of King Nebuchadnezzar of Babylon came up to Jerusalem, and the city was besieged. 11 King Nebuchadnezzar of Babylon came to the city, while his servants were besieging it; 12 King Jehoiachin of Judah gave himself up to the king of Babylon, himself, his mother, his servants, his officers, and his palace officials. The king of Babylon took him prisoner in the eighth year of his reign.

Capture of Jerusalem

13 He carried off all the treasures of the house of the LORD, and the treasures of the king's house; he cut in pieces all the vessels of gold in the temple of the LORD, which King Solomon of Israel had made, all this as the LORD had foretold. 14 He carried away all Jerusalem, all the officials, all the warriors, ten thousand captives, all the artisans and the smiths; no one remained, except the poorest people of the land. 15 He carried away Jehoiachin to Babylon; the king's mother, the king's wives, his officials, and the elite of the land, he took into captivity from Jerusalem to Babylon. 16 The king of Babylon brought captive to Babylon all the men of valor, seven thousand, the artisans and the smiths, one thousand, all of them strong and fit for war. 17 The king of Babylon made Mattaniah, Jehoiachin's uncle, king in his place, and changed his name to Zedekiah.

Zedekiah Reigns over Judah

18 Zedekiah was twenty-one years old when he began to reign; he reigned eleven years in Jerusalem. His mother's name was Hamutal daughter of Jeremiah of Libnah. 19 He did what was evil in the sight of the LORD, just as Jehoiakim had done. 20 Indeed, Jerusalem and Judah so angered the LORD that he expelled them from his presence.

The Fall and Captivity of Judah

Zedekiah rebelled against the king of Babylon.
25 1 And in the ninth year of his reign, in the tenth month, on the tenth

23.36 2 Chr 36.5
24.1 2 Chr 36.6; Jer 25.1
24.2 Jer 25.9; 35.11; 2 Kings 23.27
24.3 2 Kings 18.25; 23.26
24.4 2 Kings 21.16
24.6 Jer 22.18,19
24.7 Jer 37.5-7; 46.2
24.8 1 Chr 3.16; 2 Chr 36.9
24.10 Dan 1.1
24.12 Jer 24.1; 29.1,2; 25.1; 2 Kings 25.27; Jer 52.28
24.13 2 Kings 20.17; Isa 39.6; 2 Kings 25.13-15; Jer 20.5
24.14 Jer 24.1; 52.28; 2 Kings 25.12; Jer 40.7
24.15 2 Chr 36.10; Jer 22.24-28
24.16 Jer 52.28
24.17 Jer 37.1; 1 Chr 3.15; 2 Chr 36.4, 10
24.18 2 Chr 36.11; Jer 52.1ff; 2 Kings 23.31
24.19 2 Chr 36.12
24.20 2 Chr 36.13
25.1 2 Chr 36.13, 17-20; Jer 39.1-7; Ezek 24.1,2

day of the month, King Nebuchadnezzar of Babylon came with all his
army against Jerusalem, and laid
siege to it; they built siegeworks
against it all around. 2 So the city
was besieged until the eleventh
year of King Zedekiah. 3 On the
ninth day of the fourth month the
famine became so severe in the city
that there was no food for the people of the land. 4 Then a breach was
made in the city wall;[n] the king
with all the soldiers fled[o] by night
by the way of the gate between the
two walls, by the king's garden,
though the Chaldeans were all
around the city. They went in the
direction of the Arabah. 5 But the
army of the Chaldeans pursued
the king, and overtook him in the
plains of Jericho; all his army was
scattered, deserting him. 6 Then
they captured the king and brought
him up to the king of Babylon at
Riblah, who passed sentence on
him. 7 They slaughtered the sons of
Zedekiah before his eyes, then put
out the eyes of Zedekiah; they
bound him in fetters and took him
to Babylon.

8 In the fifth month, on the seventh day of the month—which was
the nineteenth year of King Nebuchadnezzar, king of Babylon—
Nebuzaradan, the captain of the
bodyguard, a servant of the king of
Babylon, came to Jerusalem. 9 He
burned the house of the LORD, the
king's house, and all the houses of
Jerusalem; every great house he
burned down. 10 All the army of the
Chaldeans who were with the captain of the guard broke down the
walls around Jerusalem. 11 Nebuzaradan the captain of the guard
carried into exile the rest of the
people who were left in the city and
the deserters who had defected to
the king of Babylon—all the rest of
the population. 12 But the captain
of the guard left some of the poorest people of the land to be vinedressers and tillers of the soil.

13 The bronze pillars that were
in the house of the LORD, as well as
the stands and the bronze sea that
were in the house of the LORD, the
Chaldeans broke in pieces, and
carried the bronze to Babylon.
14 They took away the pots, the
shovels, the snuffers, the dishes for
incense, and all the bronze vessels
used in the temple service, 15 as
well as the firepans and the basins.
What was made of gold the captain
of the guard took away for the gold,
and what was made of silver, for
the silver. 16 As for the two pillars,
the one sea, and the stands, which
Solomon had made for the house of
the LORD, the bronze of all these
vessels was beyond weighing.
17 The height of the one pillar was
eighteen cubits, and on it was a
bronze capital; the height of the
capital was three cubits; latticework and pomegranates, all of
bronze, were on the capital all
around. The second pillar had the
same, with the latticework.

18 The captain of the guard
took the chief priest Seraiah, the
second priest Zephaniah, and the
three guardians of the threshold;
19 from the city he took an officer
who had been in command of the
soldiers, and five men of the king's
council who were found in the city;
the secretary who was the commander of the army who mustered
the people of the land; and sixty
men of the people of the land who
were found in the city. 20 Nebuzaradan the captain of the guard took
them, and brought them to the
king of Babylon at Riblah. 21 The
king of Babylon struck them down
and put them to death at Riblah in
the land of Hamath. So Judah went
into exile out of its land.

Gedaliah Made Governor of Judah

22 He appointed Gedaliah son
of Ahikam son of Shaphan as governor over the people who remained in the land of Judah, whom
King Nebuchadnezzar of Babylon
had left. 23 Now when all the captains of the forces and their men
heard that the king of Babylon had
appointed Gedaliah as governor,

25.3 Jer 39.1,2
25.4 Jer 39.4-7
25.6 Jer 34.21, 22; 2 Kings 23.33
25.7 Jer 39.6,7; Ezek 12.13
25.8 Jer 52.12-14; 39.9
25.9 2 Chr 36.19; Ps 74.3-7; Am 2.5
25.10 Neh 1.3; Jer 52.14
25.11 2 Chr 36.20; Jer 39.9; 52.15
25.12 2 Kings 24.14; Jer 40.7
25.13 2 Chr 36.18
25.14 1 Kings 7.47-50
25.16 1 Kings 7.47
25.17 1 Kings 7.15-22
25.18 1 Chr 6.14; Ezra 7.1; Jer 21.1; 29.25
25.21 Deut 28.64; 2 Kings 23.27
25.22 Jer 40.5
25.23 Jer 40.7-9

[n] Heb lacks *wall* [o] Gk Compare Jer 39.4; 52.7: Heb lacks *the king* and lacks *fled*

they came with their men to Gedaliah at Mizpah, namely, Ishmael
son of Nethaniah, Johanan son of
Kareah, Seraiah son of Tanhumeth
the Netophathite, and Jaazaniah
son of the Maacathite. 24 Gedaliah
swore to them and their men, saying, "Do not be afraid because of
the Chaldean officials; live in the
land, serve the king of Babylon,
and it shall be well with you."
25 But in the seventh month, Ishmael son of Nethaniah son of
Elishama, of the royal family, came
with ten men; they struck down
Gedaliah so that he died, along
with the Judeans and Chaldeans
who were with him at Mizpah.
26 Then all the people, high and
low[p] and the captains of the forces
set out and went to Egypt; for they
were afraid of the Chaldeans.

25.25 Jer 41.1,2
25.26 Jer 43.4-7
25.27 Jer 52.31-34; Gen 40.13, 20
25.29 2 Sam 9.7

Jehoiachin Released from Prison

27 In the thirty-seventh year of
the exile of King Jehoiachin of Judah, in the twelfth month, on the
twenty-seventh day of the month,
King Evil-merodach of Babylon, in
the year that he began to reign, released King Jehoiachin of Judah
from prison; 28 he spoke kindly to
him, and gave him a seat above the
other seats of the kings who were
with him in Babylon. 29 So Jehoiachin put aside his prison clothes.
Every day of his life he dined regularly in the king's presence. 30 For
his allowance, a regular allowance
was given him by the king, a portion every day, as long as he lived.

p Or *young and old*

1 Chronicles

Title and Background

The Hebrew title can be translated "the events (or annals) of the days (or years)." The Septuagint translators dubbed the book "the things omitted," indicating that they regarded it as a supplement to Samuel and Kings.

Author and Date of Writing

According to ancient Jewish tradition, Ezra wrote Chronicles, but this cannot be established with certainty. A growing consensus dates Chronicles in the latter half of the fifth century B.C., thus possibly within Ezra's lifetime. It must be acknowledged that the author, if not Ezra, at least shared many basic concerns with that reforming priest.

Theme and Message

Chronicles was written for the exiles who had returned to Israel after the Babylonian captivity, to remind them that they were still God's chosen people. The burning issue was the question of continuity with the past: Is God still interested in us? Are his covenants still in force? Now that we have no Davidic king and are subject to Persia, do God's promises to David still have meaning for us?

Outline

I. Genealogies: From Creation to Restoration (1.1–9.44)
II. The Death of Saul (10.1-14)
III. The Reign of David (11.1–29.30)

From Adam to Abraham

1 Adam, Seth, Enosh; 2 Kenan,
Mahalalel, Jared; 3 Enoch,
Methuselah, Lamech; 4 Noah,
Shem, Ham, and Japheth.
5 The descendants of Japheth:
Gomer, Magog, Madai, Javan, Tubal, Meshech, and Tiras. 6 The descendants of Gomer: Ashkenaz, Di-
phath,[a] and Togarmah. 7 The
descendants of Javan: Elishah,
Tarshish, Kittim, and Rodanim.[b]
8 The descendants of Ham:
Cush, Egypt, Put, and Canaan.
9 The descendants of Cush: Seba,
Havilah, Sabta, Raama, and Sabte-
ca. The descendants of Raamah:
Sheba and Dedan. 10 Cush became
the father of Nimrod; he was the
first to be a mighty one on the
earth.
11 Egypt became the father of
Ludim, Anamim, Lehabim, Naphtuhim, 12 Pathrusim, Casluhim,
and Caphtorim, from whom the
Philistines come.[c]
13 Canaan became the father of
Sidon his firstborn, and Heth,
14 and the Jebusites, the Amorites,
the Girgashites, 15 the Hivites, the
Arkites, the Sinites, 16 the Arvad-
ites, the Zemarites, and the Ha-
mathites.
17 The descendants of Shem:
Elam, Asshur, Arpachshad, Lud,
Aram, Uz, Hul, Gether, and Meshech.[d] 18 Arpachshad became the
father of Shelah; and Shelah became the father of Eber. 19 To Eber
were born two sons: the name of
the one was Peleg (for in his days
the earth was divided), and the
name of his brother Joktan. 20 Joktan became the father of Almodad,
Sheleph, Hazarmaveth, Jerah,

1.1 Gen 4.25; 5.32
1.5 Gen 10.2-4
1.8 Gen 10.6ff
1.10 Gen 10.8, 13ff
1.17 Gen 10.22ff

[a] Gen 10.3 *Ripath*; See Gk Vg [b] Gen 10.4 *Dodanim*; See Syr Vg [c] Heb *Casluhim, from which the Philistines come, Caphtorim*; See Am 9.7, Jer 47.4 [d] *Mash* in Gen 10.23

21 Hadoram, Uzal, Diklah, 22 Ebal,
Abimael, Sheba, 23 Ophir, Havilah,
and Jobab; all these were the descendants of Joktan.
24 Shem, Arpachshad, Shelah;
25 Eber, Peleg, Reu; 26 Serug, Nahor, Terah; 27 Abram, that is, Abraham.

From Abraham to Jacob

28 The sons of Abraham: Isaac
and Ishmael. 29 These are their genealogies: the firstborn of Ishmael,
Nebaioth; and Kedar, Adbeel, Mibsam, 30 Mishma, Dumah, Massa,
Hadad, Tema, 31 Jetur, Naphish,
and Kedemah. These are the sons
of Ishmael. 32 The sons of Keturah,
Abraham's concubine: she bore
Zimran, Jokshan, Medan, Midian,
Ishbak, and Shuah. The sons of
Jokshan: Sheba and Dedan. 33 The
sons of Midian: Ephah, Epher, Hanoch, Abida, and Eldaah. All these
were the descendants of Keturah.
34 Abraham became the father
of Isaac. The sons of Isaac: Esau
and Israel. 35 The sons of Esau: Eliphaz, Reuel, Jeush, Jalam, and Korah. 36 The sons of Eliphaz: Teman,
Omar, Zephi, Gatam, Kenaz, Timna, and Amalek. 37 The sons of Reuel: Nahath, Zerah, Shammah, and
Mizzah.
38 The sons of Seir: Lotan, Shobal, Zibeon, Anah, Dishon, Ezer,
and Dishan. 39 The sons of Lotan:
Hori and Homam; and Lotan's sister was Timna. 40 The sons of Shobal: Alian, Manahath, Ebal, She-
phi, and Onam. The sons of
Zibeon: Aiah and Anah. 41 The sons
of Anah: Dishon. The sons of Dishon: Hamran, Eshban, Ithran, and
Cheran. 42 The sons of Ezer: Bilhan,
Zaavan, and Jaakan.[e] The sons of
Dishan:[f] Uz and Aran.
43 These are the kings who
reigned in the land of Edom before
any king reigned over the Israelites:
Bela son of Beor, whose city was
called Dinhabah. 44 When Bela
died, Jobab son of Zerah of Bozrah
succeeded him. 45 When Jobab
died, Husham of the land of the Temanites succeeded him. 46 When
Husham died, Hadad son of Bedad,

1.24 Gen 11.10ff
1.29 Gen 25.13-16
1.32 Gen 25.1-4
1.34 Gen 21.2,3; 25.25,26
1.35 Gen 36.9,10
1.38 Gen 36.20-28
1.43 Gen 36.31-43

2.1 Gen 35.23-26; 46.8-25
2.2 Gen 38.2-10
2.4 Gen 38.29, 30
2.5 Gen 46.12
2.6 Josh 7.1; 1 Kings 4.31
2.7 Josh 6.18; 7.1
2.10 Ruth 4.19, 20; Mt 1.4

who defeated Midian in the country of Moab, succeeded him; and
the name of his city was Avith.
47 When Hadad died, Samlah of
Masrekah succeeded him. 48 When
Samlah died, Shaul[g] of Rehoboth
on the Euphrates succeeded him.
49 When Shaul[g] died, Baal-hanan
son of Achbor succeeded him.
50 When Baal-hanan died, Hadad
succeeded him; the name of his
city was Pai, and his wife's name
Mehetabel daughter of Matred,
daughter of Me-zahab. 51 And Hadad died.
The clans[h] of Edom were:
clans[h] Timna, Aliah,[i] Jetheth,
52 Oholibamah, Elah, Pinon, 53 Kenaz, Teman, Mibzar, 54 Magdiel,
and Iram; these are the clans[h] of
Edom.

The Sons of Israel and the Descendants of Judah

2 These are the sons of Israel:
Reuben, Simeon, Levi, Judah,
Issachar, Zebulun, 2 Dan, Joseph,
Benjamin, Naphtali, Gad, and Asher. 3 The sons of Judah: Er, Onan,
and Shelah; these three the Canaanite woman Bath-shua bore to
him. Now Er, Judah's firstborn,
was wicked in the sight of the LORD,
and he put him to death. 4 His
daughter-in-law Tamar also bore
him Perez and Zerah. Judah had
five sons in all.
5 The sons of Perez: Hezron and
Hamul. 6 The sons of Zerah: Zimri,
Ethan, Heman, Calcol, and Dara,[j]
five in all. 7 The sons of Carmi:
Achar, the troubler of Israel, who
transgressed in the matter of the
devoted thing; 8 and Ethan's son
was Azariah.
9 The sons of Hezron, who were
born to him: Jerahmeel, Ram, and
Chelubai. 10 Ram became the father of Amminadab, and Amminadab became the father of Nahshon,
prince of the sons of Judah. 11 Nahshon became the father of Salma,
Salma of Boaz, 12 Boaz of Obed,

[e] Or *and Akan*; See Gen 36.27 [f] See 1.38: Heb *Dishon* [g] Or *Saul* [h] Or *chiefs* [i] Or *Alvah*; See Gen 36.40 [j] Or *Darda*; Compare Syr Tg some Gk Mss; See 1 Kings 4.31

RULERS OF ISRAEL AND JUDAH

Biblical References	Kings	Years of Reign	Dates of Reign	Notes
1. 1 Ki 12:1-24 14:21-31	***Rehoboam** (J)*	*17 years*	***930-913***	
2. 1 Ki 12:25–14:20	**Jeroboam I** (I)	22 years	**930-909**	
3. 1 Ki 15:1-8	***Abijah** (J)*	*3 years*	***913-910***	
4. 1 Ki 15:9-24	***Asa** (J)*	*41 years*	***910-869***	
5. 1 Ki 15:25-31	**Nadab** (I)	2 years	**909-908**	
6. 1 Ki 15:32–16:7	**Baasha** (I)	24 years	**908-886**	
7. 1 Ki 16:8-14	**Elah** (I)	2 years	**886-885**	
8. 1 Ki 16:15-20	**Zimri** (I)	7 days	**885**	
9. 1 Ki 16:21-22	**Tibni** (I)		**885-880**	Overlap with Omri
10. 1 Ki 16:23-28	**Omri** (I)		885	Made king by the people
			885-880	Overlap with Tibni
		12 years	**885-874**	Official reign = 11 actual years
11. 1 Ki 16:29–22:40	**Ahab** (I)	22 years	**874-853**	Official reign = 21 actual years
12. 1 Ki 22:41-50	***Jehoshaphat** (J)*		*872-869*	*Co-regency with Asa*
		25 years	*872-848*	*Official reign*
			869	*Beginning of sole reign*
			853-848	*Has Jehoram as regent*
13. 1 Ki 22:51– 2 Ki 1:18	**Ahaziah** (I)	2 years	**853-852**	Official reign = 1 yr. actual reign
14. 2 Ki 1:17	**Joram** (I)		852	
2 Ki 3:1–8:15		12 years	**852-841**	Official reign = 11 actual years
15. 2 Ki 8:16-24	***Jehoram** (J)*		***848***	*Beginning of sole reign*
		8 years	***848-841***	*Official reign = 7 actual years*
16. 2 Ki 8:25-29	***Ahaziah** (J)*	*1 year*	*841*	*Nonaccession-year reckoning*
2 Ki 9:29			*841*	*Accession-year reckoning*
17. 2 Ki 9:30–10:36	**Jehu** (I)	28 years	**841-814**	
18. 2 Ki 11	***Athaliah** (J)*	*7 years*	***841-835***	
19. 2 Ki 12	***Joash** (J)*	*40 years*	***835-796***	
20. 2 Ki 13:1-9	**Jehoahaz** (I)	17 years	**814-798**	
21. 2 Ki 13:10-25	**Jehoash** (I)	16 years	**798-782**	

Biblical References	Kings	Years of Reign	Dates of Reign	Notes
22. 2 Ki 14:1-22	***Amaziah** (J)*	*29 years*	**796-767**	
			792-767	*Overlap with Azariah*
23. 2 Ki 14:23-29	**Jeroboam II** (I)		**793-782**	Co-regency with Jehoash
		41 years	**793-753**	Total reign
24. 2 Ki 15:1-7	***Azariah** (J)*		792-767	*Overlap with Amaziah*
		52 years	**792-740**	*Total reign*
			767	*Beginning of sole reign*
25. 2 Ki 15:8-12	**Zechariah** (I)	6 months	**753**	
26. 2 Ki 15:13-15	**Shallum** (I)	1 month	**752**	
27. 2 Ki 15:16-22	**Menahem** (I)	10 years	**752-742**	Ruled in Samaria
28. 2 Ki 15:23-26	**Pekahiah** (I)	2 years	**742-740**	
29. 2 Ki 15:27-31	**Pekah** (I)		752-740	In Gilead; overlapping years
		20 years	**752-732**	Total reign
			740	Beginning of sole reign
30. 2 Ki 15:32-38 *2 Ki 15:30*	***Jotham** (J)*		750-740	*Co-regency with Azariah*
		16 years	**750-735**	*Official reign*
			750-732	*Reign to his 20th year*
			750	*Beginning of co-regency*
31. 2 Ki 16	***Ahaz** (J)*		735-715	*Total reign*
		16 years	**732-715**	*From 20th of Jotham*
32. 2 Ki 15:30 2 Ki 17	**Hoshea** (I)		732	20th of Jotham
		9 years	**732-722**	
33. 2 Ki 18:1–20:21	***Hezekiah** (J)*	*29 years*	**715-686**	
34. 2 Ki 21:1-18	***Manasseh** (J)*		**697-686**	*Co-regency with Hezekiah*
		55 years	**697-642**	*Total reign*
35. 2 Ki 21:19-26	***Amon** (J)*	*2 years*	**642-640**	
36. 2 Ki 22:1–23:30	***Josiah** (J)*	*31 years*	**640-609**	
37. 2 Ki 23:31-33	***Jehoahaz** (J)*	*3 months*	**609**	
38. 2 Ki 23:34–24:7	***Jehoiakim** (J)*	*11 years*	**609-598**	
39. 2 Ki 24:8-17	***Jehoiachin** (J)*	*3 months*	**598-597**	
40. 2 Ki 24:18–25:26	***Zedekiah** (J)*	*11 years*	**597-586**	

Data and dates in order of sequence
(J) Italics denote kings of ***Judah.*** (I) non-italic type denotes kings of **Israel.**
Adapted from: *A Chronology of the Hebrew Kings* by Edwin R. Thiele.

Obed of Jesse. 13 Jesse became the
father of Eliab his firstborn, Abinadab the second, Shimea the third,
14 Nethanel the fourth, Raddai the
fifth, 15 Ozem the sixth, David the
seventh; 16 and their sisters were
Zeruiah and Abigail. The sons of
Zeruiah: Abishai, Joab, and Asahel,
three. 17 Abigail bore Amasa, and
the father of Amasa was Jether the
Ishmaelite.
18 Caleb son of Hezron had
children by his wife Azubah, and by
Jerioth; these were her sons: Je-
sher, Shobab, and Ardon. 19 When
Azubah died, Caleb married Ephrath, who bore him Hur. 20 Hur became the father of Uri, and Uri became the father of Bezalel.
21 Afterward Hezron went in to
the daughter of Machir father of
Gilead, whom he married when he
was sixty years old; and she bore
him Segub; 22 and Segub became
the father of Jair, who had twenty-
three towns in the land of Gilead.
23 But Geshur and Aram took from
them Havvoth-jair, Kenath and its
villages, sixty towns. All these were
descendants of Machir, father of
Gilead. 24 After the death of Hezron, in Caleb-ephrathah, Abijah
wife of Hezron bore him Ashhur,
father of Tekoa.
25 The sons of Jerahmeel, the
firstborn of Hezron: Ram his firstborn, Bunah, Oren, Ozem, and Ahijah. 26 Jerahmeel also had another
wife, whose name was Atarah; she
was the mother of Onam. 27 The
sons of Ram, the firstborn of Jerahmeel: Maaz, Jamin, and Eker.
28 The sons of Onam: Shammai and
Jada. The sons of Shammai: Nadab
and Abishur. 29 The name of Abishur's wife was Abihail, and she
bore him Ahban and Molid. 30 The
sons of Nadab: Seled and Appaim;
and Seled died childless. 31 The
son[k] of Appaim: Ishi. The son[k] of
Ishi: Sheshan. The son[k] of Sheshan: Ahlai. 32 The sons of Jada,
Shammai's brother: Jether and
Jonathan; and Jether died childless. 33 The sons of Jonathan: Peleth and Zaza. These were the descendants of Jerahmeel. 34 Now
Sheshan had no sons, only daughters; but Sheshan had an Egyptian
slave, whose name was Jarha. 35 So
Sheshan gave his daughter in marriage to his slave Jarha; and she
bore him Attai. 36 Attai became the
father of Nathan, and Nathan of
Zabad. 37 Zabad became the father
of Ephlal, and Ephlal of Obed.
38 Obed became the father of Jehu,
and Jehu of Azariah. 39 Azariah became the father of Helez, and Helez of Eleasah. 40 Eleasah became
the father of Sismai, and Sismai of
Shallum. 41 Shallum became the father of Jekamiah, and Jekamiah of
Elishama.
42 The sons of Caleb brother of
Jerahmeel: Mesha[l] his firstborn,
who was father of Ziph. The sons of
Mareshah father of Hebron. 43 The
sons of Hebron: Korah, Tappuah,
Rekem, and Shema. 44 Shema became father of Raham, father of
Jorkeam; and Rekem became the
father of Shammai. 45 The son of
Shammai: Maon; and Maon was
the father of Beth-zur. 46 Ephah
also, Caleb's concubine, bore Haran, Moza, and Gazez; and Haran
became the father of Gazez. 47 The
sons of Jahdai: Regem, Jotham,
Geshan, Pelet, Ephah, and Shaaph.
48 Maacah, Caleb's concubine, bore
Sheber and Tirhanah. 49 She also
bore Shaaph father of Madmannah, Sheva father of Machbenah
and father of Gibea; and the daughter of Caleb was Achsah. 50 These
were the descendants of Caleb.
The sons[m] of Hur the firstborn
of Ephrathah: Shobal father of
Kiriath-jearim, 51 Salma father of
Bethlehem, and Hareph father
of Beth-gader. 52 Shobal father of
Kiriath-jearim had other sons: Ha-
roeh, half of the Menuhoth. 53 And
the families of Kiriath-jearim: the
Ithrites, the Puthites, the Shu-
mathites, and the Mishraites; from
these came the Zorathites and the
Eshtaolites. 54 The sons of Salma:
Bethlehem, the Netophathites,
Atroth-beth-joab, and half of the

2.13 1 Sam 16.6, 9
2.16 2 Sam 2.18
2.17 2 Sam 17.25
2.19 v. 50
2.20 Ex 31.2
2.21 Num 27.1
2.23 Num 32.41; Deut 3.14; Josh 13.30
2.24 1 Chr 4.5
2.31 vv. 34,35
2.36 1 Chr 11.41
2.42 1 Chr 2.18, 19
2.50 1 Chr 4.4

[k] Heb *sons* [l] Gk reads *Mareshah*
[m] Gk Vg: Heb *son*

Manahathites, the Zorites. 55 The
families also of the scribes that
lived at Jabez: the Tirathites, the
Shimeathites, and the Sucathites.
These are the Kenites who came
from Hammath, father of the house
of Rechab.

Descendants of David and Solomon

3 These are the sons of David
who were born to him in Hebron: the firstborn Amnon, by
Ahinoam the Jezreelite; the second
Daniel, by Abigail the Carmelite;
2 the third Absalom, son of Maacah, daughter of King Talmai of
Geshur; the fourth Adonijah, son of
Haggith; 3 the fifth Shephatiah, by
Abital; the sixth Ithream, by his
wife Eglah; 4 six were born to him
in Hebron, where he reigned for
seven years and six months. And he
reigned thirty-three years in Jerusalem. 5 These were born to him in
Jerusalem: Shimea, Shobab, Nathan, and Solomon, four by Bath-
shua, daughter of Ammiel; 6 then
Ibhar, Elishama, Eliphelet, 7 Nogah, Nepheg, Japhia, 8 Elishama,
Eliada, and Eliphelet, nine. 9 All
these were David's sons, besides
the sons of the concubines; and Tamar was their sister.
10 The descendants of Solomon: Rehoboam, Abijah his son,
Asa his son, Jehoshaphat his son,
11 Joram his son, Ahaziah his son,
Joash his son, 12 Amaziah his son,
Azariah his son, Jotham his son,
13 Ahaz his son, Hezekiah his son,
Manasseh his son, 14 Amon his son,
Josiah his son. 15 The sons of Josiah: Johanan the firstborn, the second Jehoiakim, the third Zedekiah,
the fourth Shallum. 16 The descendants of Jehoiakim: Jeconiah his
son, Zedekiah his son; 17 and the
sons of Jeconiah, the captive: Shealtiel his son, 18 Malchiram, Pedaiah, Shenazzar, Jekamiah, Hosha-
ma, and Nedabiah; 19 The sons of
Pedaiah: Zerubbabel and Shimei;
and the sons of Zerubbabel: Meshullam and Hananiah, and Shelomith was their sister; 20 and Hashu-
bah, Ohel, Berechiah, Hasadiah,
and Jushab-hesed, five. 21 The sons
of Hananiah: Pelatiah and Jeshaiah, his son[n] Rephaiah, his son[n]
Arnan, his son[n] Obadiah, his son[n]
Shecaniah. 22 The son[o] of Shecaniah: Shemaiah. And the sons of Shemaiah: Hattush, Igal, Bariah, Neariah, and Shaphat, six. 23 The sons
of Neariah: Elioenai, Hizkiah, and
Azrikam, three. 24 The sons of Elioenai: Hodaviah, Eliashib, Pelaiah,
Akkub, Johanan, Delaiah, and
Anani, seven.

Descendants of Judah

4 The sons of Judah: Perez, Hezron, Carmi, Hur, and Shobal.
2 Reaiah son of Shobal became the
father of Jahath, and Jahath became the father of Ahumai and La-
had. These were the families of the
Zorathites. 3 These were the sons[p]
of Etam: Jezreel, Ishma, and Id-
bash; and the name of their sister
was Hazzelelponi, 4 and Penuel was
the father of Gedor, and Ezer the
father of Hushah. These were the
sons of Hur, the firstborn of Ephrathah, the father of Bethlehem.
5 Ashhur father of Tekoa had two
wives, Helah and Naarah; 6 Naarah
bore him Ahuzzam, Hepher, Teme-
ni, and Haahashtari.[q] These were
the sons of Naarah. 7 The sons of
Helah: Zereth, Izhar,[r] and Ethnan.
8 Koz became the father of Anub,
Zobebah, and the families of Ahar-
hel son of Harum. 9 Jabez was honored more than his brothers; and
his mother named him Jabez, saying, "Because I bore him in pain."
10 Jabez called on the God of Israel,
saying, "Oh that you would bless
me and enlarge my border, and that
your hand might be with me, and
that you would keep me from hurt
and harm!" And God granted what
he asked. 11 Chelub the brother of
Shuhah became the father of Me-
hir, who was the father of Eshton.
12 Eshton became the father of
Beth-rapha, Paseah, and Tehinnah
the father of Ir-nahash. These are

2.55 Judg 1.16; Jer 35.2
3.1 2 Sam 3.2, 3; Josh 15.56
3.3 2 Sam 3.5
3.4 2 Sam 2.11; 5.5
3.5 2 Sam 5.14-16; 2 Sam 12.24; 11.3
3.9 2 Sam 13.1
3.10 1 Kings 11.43
3.16 Mt 1.11
3.22 Ezek 8.2
4.1 Gen 46.12
4.4 1 Chr 2.50
4.5 1 Chr 2.24
4.9 Gen 34.19

[n] Gk Compare Syr Vg: Heb *sons of*
[o] Heb *sons*
[p] Gk Compare Vg: Heb *the father*
[q] Or *Ahashtari*
[r] Another reading is *Zohar*

the men of Recah. 13 The sons of
Kenaz: Othniel and Seraiah; and
the sons of Othniel: Hathath and
Meonothai.[s] 14 Meonothai became
the father of Ophrah; and Seraiah
became the father of Joab father of
Ge-harashim,[t] so-called because
they were artisans. 15 The sons of
Caleb son of Jephunneh: Iru, Elah,
and Naam; and the son[u] of Elah:
Kenaz. 16 The sons of Jehallelel:
Ziph, Ziphah, Tiria, and Asarel.
17 The sons of Ezrah: Jether, Mered,
Epher, and Jalon. These are the
sons of Bithiah, daughter of Pharaoh, whom Mered married;[v] and
she conceived and bore[w] Miriam,
Shammai, and Ishbah father of
Eshtemoa. 18 And his Judean wife
bore Jered father of Gedor, Heber
father of Soco, and Jekuthiel father
of Zanoah. 19 The sons of the wife of
Hodiah, the sister of Naham, were
the fathers of Keilah the Garmite
and Eshtemoa the Maacathite.
20 The sons of Shimon: Amnon,
Rinnah, Ben-hanan, and Tilon. The
sons of Ishi: Zoheth and Ben-
zoheth. 21 The sons of Shelah son of
Judah: Er father of Lecah, Laadah
father of Mareshah, and the families of the guild of linen workers at
Beth-ashbea; 22 and Jokim, and the
men of Cozeba, and Joash, and Sa-
raph, who married into Moab but
returned to Lehem[x] (now the
records[y] are ancient). 23 These
were the potters and inhabitants of
Netaim and Gederah; they lived
there with the king in his service.

Descendants of Simeon

24 The sons of Simeon: Nemuel, Jamin, Jarib, Zerah, Shaul;[z]
25 Shallum was his son, Mibsam his
son, Mishma his son. 26 The sons of
Mishma: Hammuel his son, Zaccur
his son, Shimei his son. 27 Shimei
had sixteen sons and six daughters;
but his brothers did not have many
children, nor did all their family
multiply like the Judeans. 28 They
lived in Beer-sheba, Moladah,
Hazar-shual, 29 Bilhah, Ezem, To-
lad, 30 Bethuel, Hormah, Ziklag,
31 Beth-marcaboth, Hazar-susim,
Beth-biri, and Shaaraim. These
were their towns until David became king. 32 And their villages
were Etam, Ain, Rimmon, Tochen,
and Ashan, five towns, 33 along with
all their villages that were around
these towns as far as Baal. These
were their settlements. And they
kept a genealogical record.
34 Meshobab, Jamlech, Joshah
son of Amaziah, 35 Joel, Jehu son of
Joshibiah son of Seraiah son of Asiel, 36 Elioenai, Jaakobah, Jeshoha-
iah, Asaiah, Adiel, Jesimiel, Benaiah, 37 Ziza son of Shiphi son of
Allon son of Jedaiah son of Shimri
son of Shemaiah— 38 these mentioned by name were leaders in
their families, and their clans increased greatly. 39 They journeyed
to the entrance of Gedor, to the
east side of the valley, to seek pasture for their flocks, 40 where they
found rich, good pasture, and the
land was very broad, quiet, and
peaceful; for the former inhabitants there belonged to Ham.
41 These, registered by name, came
in the days of King Hezekiah of Judah, and attacked their tents and
the Meunim who were found there,
and exterminated them to this day,
and settled in their place, because
there was pasture there for their
flocks. 42 And some of them, five
hundred men of the Simeonites,
went to Mount Seir, having as their
leaders Pelatiah, Neariah, Rephaiah, and Uzziel, sons of Ishi; 43 they
destroyed the remnant of the Amalekites that had escaped, and they
have lived there to this day.

Descendants of Reuben

5 The sons of Reuben the firstborn of Israel. (He was the
firstborn, but because he defiled
his father's bed his birthright was
given to the sons of Joseph son of
Israel, so that he is not enrolled in
the genealogy according to the
birthright; 2 though Judah became
prominent among his brothers and

4.13 Josh 15.17 **4.14** Neh 11.35 **4.21** Gen 38.1,5 **4.24** Gen 29.33 **4.28** Josh 19.2 **4.30** 1 Chr 12.1 **4.40** Judg 18.7-10 **4.41** 2 Kings 18.8 **4.43** 1 Sam 15.8; 30.17; 2 Sam 8.12 **5.1f** Gen 29.32; 35.22; 49.4; 48.15,22 **5.2** Gen 49.8, 10; Mic 5.2; Mt 2.6

[s] Gk Vg: Heb lacks *and Meonothai* [t] That is *Valley of artisans* [u] Heb *sons* [v] The clause: *These are . . . married* is transposed from verse 18 [w] Heb lacks *and bore* [x] Vg Compare Gk: Heb *and Jashubi-lahem* [y] Or *matters* [z] Or *Saul*

a ruler came from him, yet the
birthright belonged to Joseph.)
3 The sons of Reuben, the firstborn
of Israel: Hanoch, Pallu, Hezron,
and Carmi. 4 The sons of Joel: Shemaiah his son, Gog his son, Shimei
his son, 5 Micah his son, Reaiah his
son, Baal his son, 6 Beerah his son,
whom King Tilgath-pilneser of Assyria carried away into exile; he
was a chieftain of the Reubenites.
7 And his kindred by their families,
when the genealogy of their generations was reckoned: the chief, Jeiel, and Zechariah, 8 and Bela son of
Azaz, son of Shema, son of Joel,
who lived in Aroer, as far as Nebo
and Baal-meon. 9 He also lived to
the east as far as the beginning of
the desert this side of the Euphrates, because their cattle had multiplied in the land of Gilead. 10 And
in the days of Saul they made war
on the Hagrites, who fell by their
hand; and they lived in their tents
throughout all the region east of
Gilead.

Descendants of Gad

11 The sons of Gad lived beside
them in the land of Bashan as far as
Salecah: 12 Joel the chief, Shapham
the second, Janai, and Shaphat in
Bashan. 13 And their kindred according to their clans: Michael,
Meshullam, Sheba, Jorai, Jacan,
Zia, and Eber, seven. 14 These were
the sons of Abihail son of Huri, son
of Jaroah, son of Gilead, son of Michael, son of Jeshishai, son of Jah-
do, son of Buz; 15 Ahi son of Abdiel,
son of Guni, was chief in their clan;
16 and they lived in Gilead, in Bashan and in its towns, and in all the
pasture lands of Sharon to their
limits. 17 All of these were enrolled
by genealogies in the days of King
Jotham of Judah, and in the days of
King Jeroboam of Israel.
18 The Reubenites, the Gadites,
and the half-tribe of Manasseh had
valiant warriors, who carried shield
and sword, and drew the bow, expert in war, forty-four thousand
seven hundred sixty, ready for service. 19 They made war on the Hagrites, Jetur, Naphish, and Nodab;
20 and when they received help
against them, the Hagrites and all
who were with them were given
into their hands, for they cried to
God in the battle, and he granted
their entreaty because they trusted
in him. 21 They captured their livestock: fifty thousand of their camels, two hundred fifty thousand
sheep, two thousand donkeys, and
one hundred thousand captives.
22 Many fell slain, because the war
was of God. And they lived in their
territory until the exile.

The Half-Tribe of Manasseh

23 The members of the half-
tribe of Manasseh lived in the land;
they were very numerous from Bashan to Baal-hermon, Senir, and
Mount Hermon. 24 These were the
heads of their clans: Epher,[a] Ishi,
Eliel, Azriel, Jeremiah, Hodaviah,
and Jahdiel, mighty warriors, famous men, heads of their clans.
25 But they transgressed against the
God of their ancestors, and prostituted themselves to the gods of the
peoples of the land, whom God had
destroyed before them. 26 So the
God of Israel stirred up the spirit of
King Pul of Assyria, the spirit of
King Tilgath-pilneser of Assyria,
and he carried them away, namely,
the Reubenites, the Gadites, and
the half-tribe of Manasseh, and
brought them to Halah, Habor,
Hara, and the river Gozan, to this
day.

Descendants of Levi

6 [b] The sons of Levi: Gershom,[c]
Kohath, and Merari. 2 The
sons of Kohath: Amram, Izhar, Hebron, and Uzziel. 3 The children of
Amram: Aaron, Moses, and Miriam. The sons of Aaron: Nadab, Abihu, Eleazar, and Ithamar. 4 Eleazar
became the father of Phinehas,
Phinehas of Abishua, 5 Abishua of
Bukki, Bukki of Uzzi, 6 Uzzi of Zerahiah, Zerahiah of Meraioth, 7 Meraioth of Amariah, Amariah of Ahitub, 8 Ahitub of Zadok, Zadok of
Ahimaaz, 9 Ahimaaz of Azariah, Az-

5.3 Gen 46.9; Num 26.5
5.7 v. 17
5.8 Josh 13.15, 16
5.9 Josh 22.9
5.10 vv. 18-21
5.11 Josh 13.11, 24
5.16 1 Chr 27.29
5.17 2 Kings 15.5, 32; 14.16,28
5.19 v. 10; 1 Chr 1.31
5.20 2 Chr 4.11-13; Ps 22.4,5
5.22 2 Kings 15.29; 17.6
5.25 2 Kings 17.7
5.26 2 Kings 15.19, 29; 17.6; 18.11
6.1 Ex 6.16; Num 26.57; 1 Chr 23.6
6.3 Lev 10.1
6.8 2 Sam 8.17; 15.27

[a] Gk Vg: Heb *and Epher* [b] Ch 5.27 in Heb
[c] Heb *Gershon*, variant of *Gershom*; See 6.16

ariah of Johanan, 10 and Johanan of
Azariah (it was he who served as
priest in the house that Solomon
built in Jerusalem). 11 Azariah became the father of Amariah, Amariah of Ahitub, 12 Ahitub of Zadok,
Zadok of Shallum, 13 Shallum of
Hilkiah, Hilkiah of Azariah, 14 Azariah of Seraiah, Seraiah of Jehozadak; 15 and Jehozadak went into exile when the LORD sent Judah and
Jerusalem into exile by the hand of
Nebuchadnezzar.

16 [d]The sons of Levi: Gershom,
Kohath, and Merari. 17 These are
the names of the sons of Gershom:
Libni and Shimei. 18 The sons of
Kohath: Amram, Izhar, Hebron,
and Uzziel. 19 The sons of Merari:
Mahli and Mushi. These are the
clans of the Levites according to
their ancestry. 20 Of Gershom: Libni his son, Jahath his son, Zimmah
his son, 21 Joah his son, Iddo his
son, Zerah his son, Jeatherai his
son. 22 The sons of Kohath: Amminadab his son, Korah his son,
Assir his son, 23 Elkanah his son,
Ebiasaph his son, Assir his son,
24 Tahath his son, Uriel his son, Uzziah his son, and Shaul his son.
25 The sons of Elkanah: Amasai and
Ahimoth, 26 Elkanah his son, Zo-
phai his son, Nahath his son, 27 Eliab his son, Jeroham his son, Elkanah his son. 28 The sons of Samuel:
Joel[e] his firstborn, the second Abijah.[f] 29 The sons of Merari: Mahli,
Libni his son, Shimei his son, Uzzah his son, 30 Shimea his son, Hag-
giah his son, and Asaiah his son.

Musicians Appointed by David

31 These are the men whom David put in charge of the service of
song in the house of the LORD, after
the ark came to rest there. 32 They
ministered with song before the
tabernacle of the tent of meeting,
until Solomon had built the house
of the LORD in Jerusalem; and they
performed their service in due order. 33 These are the men who
served; and their sons were: Of the
Kohathites: Heman, the singer,
son of Joel, son of Samuel, 34 son of
Elkanah, son of Jeroham, son of
Eliel, son of Toah, 35 son of Zuph,
son of Elkanah, son of Mahath, son
of Amasai, 36 son of Elkanah, son of
Joel, son of Azariah, son of Zephaniah, 37 son of Tahath, son of Assir,
son of Ebiasaph, son of Korah,
38 son of Izhar, son of Kohath, son
of Levi, son of Israel; 39 and his
brother Asaph, who stood on his
right, namely, Asaph son of Berechiah, son of Shimea, 40 son of Michael, son of Baaseiah, son of Malchijah, 41 son of Ethni, son of
Zerah, son of Adaiah, 42 son of
Ethan, son of Zimmah, son of
Shimei, 43 son of Jahath, son of
Gershom, son of Levi. 44 On the left
were their kindred the sons of Merari: Ethan son of Kishi, son of
Abdi, son of Malluch, 45 son of
Hashabiah, son of Amaziah, son of
Hilkiah, 46 son of Amzi, son of Bani,
son of Shemer, 47 son of Mahli, son
of Mushi, son of Merari, son of
Levi; 48 and their kindred the Levites were appointed for all the service of the tabernacle of the house
of God.

49 But Aaron and his sons made
offerings on the altar of burnt offering and on the altar of incense, doing all the work of the most holy
place, to make atonement for Israel, according to all that Moses the
servant of God had commanded.
50 These are the sons of Aaron: Eleazar his son, Phinehas his son,
Abishua his son, 51 Bukki his son,
Uzzi his son, Zerahiah his son,
52 Meraioth his son, Amariah his
son, Ahitub his son, 53 Zadok his
son, Ahimaaz his son.

Settlements of the Levites

54 These are their dwelling
places according to their settlements within their borders: to the
sons of Aaron of the families of
Kohathites—for the lot fell to
them first— 55 to them they gave
Hebron in the land of Judah and its
surrounding pasture lands, 56 but
the fields of the city and its villages

6.14 Neh 11.11 **6.15** 2 Kings 25.18 **6.16** Ex 6.16 **6.20** v. 42 **6.25** vv. 35,36 **6.26** v. 34 **6.31** 1 Chr 15.16-16.6 **6.37** Ex 6.24 **6.41** v. 21 **6.49** Ex 27.1-8; 30.1-7,10 **6.50** vv. 4-8 **6.54** Josh 21.4, 10 **6.55** Josh 21.11, 12 **6.56** Josh 14.13; 15.13

[d] Ch 6.1 in Heb [e] Gk Syr Compare verse 33 and 1 Sam 8.2: Heb lacks *Joel*
[f] Heb reads *Vashni, and Abijah* for *the second Abijah*, taking *the second* as a proper name

they gave to Caleb son of Jephunneh. 57 To the sons of Aaron they
gave the cities of refuge: Hebron,
Libnah with its pasture lands, Jattir, Eshtemoa with its pasture
lands, 58 Hilen[g] with its pasture
lands, Debir with its pasture lands,
59 Ashan with its pasture lands, and
Beth-shemesh with its pasture
lands. 60 From the tribe of Benjamin, Geba with its pasture lands,
Alemeth with its pasture lands,
and Anathoth with its pasture
lands. All their towns throughout
their families were thirteen.
61 To the rest of the Kohathites
were given by lot out of the family
of the tribe, out of the half-tribe,
the half of Manasseh, ten towns.
62 To the Gershomites according to
their families were allotted thirteen towns out of the tribes of Issachar, Asher, Naphtali, and Manasseh in Bashan. 63 To the Merarites
according to their families were allotted twelve towns out of the
tribes of Reuben, Gad, and Zebulun. 64 So the people of Israel gave
the Levites the towns with their
pasture lands. 65 They also gave
them by lot out of the tribes of Judah, Simeon, and Benjamin these
towns that are mentioned by name.
66 And some of the families of
the sons of Kohath had towns of
their territory out of the tribe of
Ephraim. 67 They were given the
cities of refuge: Shechem with its
pasture lands in the hill country of
Ephraim, Gezer with its pasture
lands, 68 Jokmeam with its pasture
lands, Beth-horon with its pasture
lands, 69 Aijalon with its pasture
lands, Gath-rimmon with its pasture lands; 70 and out of the half-
tribe of Manasseh, Aner with its
pasture lands, and Bileam with its
pasture lands, for the rest of the
families of the Kohathites.
71 To the Gershomites: out of
the half-tribe of Manasseh: Golan
in Bashan with its pasture lands
and Ashtaroth with its pasture
lands; 72 and out of the tribe of Issachar: Kedesh with its pasture
lands, Daberath[h] with its pasture
lands, 73 Ramoth with its pasture
lands, and Anem with its pasture
lands; 74 out of the tribe of Asher:
Mashal with its pasture lands, Abdon with its pasture lands, 75 Hu-
kok with its pasture lands, and Rehob with its pasture lands; 76 and
out of the tribe of Naphtali: Kedesh
in Galilee with its pasture lands,
Hammon with its pasture lands,
and Kiriathaim with its pasture
lands. 77 To the rest of the Merarites out of the tribe of Zebulun:
Rimmono with its pasture lands,
Tabor with its pasture lands, 78 and
across the Jordan from Jericho, on
the east side of the Jordan, out of
the tribe of Reuben: Bezer in the
steppe with its pasture lands, Jahzah with its pasture lands, 79 Kedemoth with its pasture lands, and
Mephaath with its pasture lands;
80 and out of the tribe of Gad: Ramoth in Gilead with its pasture
lands, Mahanaim with its pasture
lands, 81 Heshbon with its pasture
lands, and Jazer with its pasture
lands.

Descendants of Issachar

7 The sons[i] of Issachar: Tola,
Puah, Jashub, and Shimron,
four. 2 The sons of Tola: Uzzi, Rephaiah, Jeriel, Jahmai, Ibsam, and
Shemuel, heads of their ancestral
houses, namely of Tola, mighty
warriors of their generations, their
number in the days of David being
twenty-two thousand six hundred.
3 The son[j] of Uzzi: Izrahiah. And
the sons of Izrahiah: Michael, Obadiah, Joel, and Isshiah, five, all of
them chiefs; 4 and along with them,
by their generations, according to
their ancestral houses, were units
of the fighting force, thirty-six
thousand, for they had many wives
and sons. 5 Their kindred belonging
to all the families of Issachar were
in all eighty-seven thousand
mighty warriors, enrolled by genealogy.

Descendants of Benjamin

6 The sons of Benjamin: Bela,

6.57 Josh 21.13
6.61 vv. 66-70; Josh 21.5
6.63 Josh 21.7, 34
6.64 Josh 21.3, 41,42
6.65 vv. 57-60
6.66 v. 61
6.67 Josh 21.21
6.68 see Josh 21.22-35 where some names are differently given
6.73 Josh 21.29; 19.21
6.76 v. 62
6.77 v. 63
7.1 Gen 46.13; Num 26.23
7.2 2 Sam 24.1, 2
7.5 1 Chr 6.62, 72
7.6 Gen 46.21; Num 26.38; 1 Chr 8.1-40

[g] Other readings *Hilez, Holon*; See Josh 21.15 [h] Or *Dobrath* [i] Syr Compare Vg: Heb *And to the sons* [j] Heb *sons*

Becher, and Jediael, three. [7]The
sons of Bela: Ezbon, Uzzi, Uzziel,
Jerimoth, and Iri, five, heads of ancestral houses, mighty warriors;
and their enrollment by genealogies was twenty-two thousand
thirty-four. [8]The sons of Becher:
Zemirah, Joash, Eliezer, Elioenai,
Omri, Jeremoth, Abijah, Anathoth,
and Alemeth. All these were the
sons of Becher; [9]and their enrollment by genealogies, according to
their generations, as heads of their
ancestral houses, mighty warriors,
was twenty thousand two hundred.
[10]The sons of Jediael: Bilhan. And
the sons of Bilhan: Jeush, Benjamin, Ehud, Chenaanah, Zethan,
Tarshish, and Ahishahar. [11]All
these were the sons of Jediael according to the heads of their ancestral houses, mighty warriors, seventeen thousand two hundred, ready
for service in war. [12]And Shuppim
and Huppim were the sons of Ir,
Hushim the son[k] of Aher.

Descendants of Naphtali

13 The descendants of Naphtali: Jahziel, Guni, Jezer, and Shallum, the descendants of Bilhah.

Descendants of Manasseh

14 The sons of Manasseh: Asriel, whom his Aramean concubine
bore; she bore Machir the father of
Gilead. [15]And Machir took a wife
for Huppim and for Shuppim. The
name of his sister was Maacah.
And the name of the second was
Zelophehad; and Zelophehad had
daughters. [16]Maacah the wife of
Machir bore a son, and she named
him Peresh; the name of his brother was Sheresh; and his sons were
Ulam and Rekem. [17]The son[k] of
Ulam: Bedan. These were the sons
of Gilead son of Machir, son of Manasseh. [18]And his sister Hammole-
cheth bore Ishhod, Abiezer, and
Mahlah. [19]The sons of Shemida
were Ahian, Shechem, Likhi, and
Aniam.

Descendants of Ephraim

20 The sons of Ephraim: Shuthelah, and Bered his son, Tahath
his son, Eleadah his son, Tahath
his son, [21]Zabad his son, Shuthelah his son, and Ezer and Elead.
Now the people of Gath, who were
born in the land, killed them, because they came down to raid their
cattle. [22]And their father Ephraim
mourned many days, and his brothers came to comfort him. [23]Ephra-
im[l] went in to his wife, and she
conceived and bore a son; and he
named him Beriah, because disaster[m] had befallen his house. [24]His
daughter was Sheerah, who built
both Lower and Upper Beth-horon,
and Uzzen-sheerah. [25]Rephah was
his son, Resheph his son, Telah his
son, Tahan his son, [26]Ladan his
son, Ammihud his son, Elishama
his son, [27]Nun[n] his son, Joshua his
son. [28]Their possessions and settlements were Bethel and its
towns, and eastward Naaran, and
westward Gezer and its towns, Shechem and its towns, as far as Ayyah
and its towns; [29]also along the borders of the Manassites, Beth-shean
and its towns, Taanach and its
towns, Megiddo and its towns, Dor
and its towns. In these lived the
sons of Joseph son of Israel.

Descendants of Asher

30 The sons of Asher: Imnah,
Ishvah, Ishvi, Beriah, and their sister Serah. [31]The sons of Beriah:
Heber and Malchiel, who was the
father of Birzaith. [32]Heber became
the father of Japhlet, Shomer, Hotham, and their sister Shua. [33]The
sons of Japhlet: Pasach, Bimhal,
and Ashvath. These are the sons of
Japhlet. [34]The sons of Shemer:
Ahi, Rohgah, Hubbah, and Aram.
[35]The sons of Helem[o] his brother:
Zophah, Imna, Shelesh, and Amal.
[36]The sons of Zophah: Suah, Har-
nepher, Shual, Beri, Imrah, [37]Be-
zer, Hod, Shamma, Shilshah, Ithran, and Beera. [38]The sons of
Jether: Jephunneh, Pispa, and Ara.
[39]The sons of Ulla: Arah, Hanniel,
and Rizia. [40]All of these were men
of Asher, heads of ancestral
houses, select mighty warriors,

7.12 Num 26.39
7.13 Gen 46.24
7.17 1 Sam 12.11
7.20 Num 26.35
7.24 Josh 16.3,5
7.27 Ex 17.9-14; 24.13
7.28 Josh 16.7
7.30 Gen 46.17; Num 26.44
7.40 v. 30

[k] Heb *sons* [l] Heb *He* [m] Heb *beraah*
[n] Here spelled *Non*; see Ex 33.11
[o] Or *Hotham*; see 7.32

chief of the princes. Their number
enrolled by genealogies, for service
in war, was twenty-six thousand
men.

Descendants of Benjamin

8 Benjamin became the father
of Bela his firstborn, Ashbel
the second, Aharah the third, 2 Nohah the fourth, and Rapha the fifth.
3 And Bela had sons: Addar, Gera,
Abihud,[p] 4 Abishua, Naaman, Aho-
ah, 5 Gera, Shephuphan, and Huram. 6 These are the sons of Ehud
(they were heads of ancestral
houses of the inhabitants of Geba,
and they were carried into exile to
Manahath): 7 Naaman,[q] Ahijah,
and Gera, that is, Heglam,[r] who
became the father of Uzza and Ahihud. 8 And Shaharaim had sons in
the country of Moab after he had
sent away his wives Hushim and
Baara. 9 He had sons by his wife
Hodesh: Jobab, Zibia, Mesha, Malcam, 10 Jeuz, Sachia, and Mirmah.
These were his sons, heads of ancestral houses. 11 He also had sons
by Hushim: Abitub and Elpaal.
12 The sons of Elpaal: Eber, Mi-
sham, and Shemed, who built Ono
and Lod with its towns, 13 and Beriah and Shema (they were heads of
ancestral houses of the inhabitants
of Aijalon, who put to flight the inhabitants of Gath); 14 and Ahio,
Shashak, and Jeremoth. 15 Zebadiah, Arad, Eder, 16 Michael, Ish-
pah, and Joha were sons of Beriah.
17 Zebadiah, Meshullam, Hizki, Heber, 18 Ishmerai, Izliah, and Jobab
were the sons of Elpaal. 19 Jakim,
Zichri, Zabdi, 20 Elienai, Zillethai,
Eliel, 21 Adaiah, Beraiah, and Shim-
rath were the sons of Shimei. 22 Ish-
pan, Eber, Eliel, 23 Abdon, Zichri,
Hanan, 24 Hananiah, Elam, Antho-
thijah, 25 Iphdeiah, and Penuel
were the sons of Shashak. 26 Sham-
sherai, Shehariah, Athaliah, 27 Jaa-
reshiah, Elijah, and Zichri were the
sons of Jeroham. 28 These were the
heads of ancestral houses, according to their generations, chiefs.
These lived in Jerusalem.
29 Jeiel[s] the father of Gibeon
lived in Gibeon, and the name of
his wife was Maacah. 30 His firstborn son: Abdon, then Zur, Kish,
Baal,[t] Nadab, 31 Gedor, Ahio, Ze-
cher, 32 and Mikloth, who became
the father of Shimeah. Now these
also lived opposite their kindred in
Jerusalem, with their kindred.
33 Ner became the father of Kish,
Kish of Saul,[u] Saul[u] of Jonathan,
Malchishua, Abinadab, and Esh-
baal; 34 and the son of Jonathan
was Merib-baal; and Merib-baal
became the father of Micah. 35 The
sons of Micah: Pithon, Melech, Ta-
rea, and Ahaz. 36 Ahaz became the
father of Jehoaddah; and Jehoaddah became the father of Alemeth,
Azmaveth, and Zimri; Zimri became the father of Moza. 37 Moza
became the father of Binea; Ra-
phah was his son, Eleasah his son,
Azel his son. 38 Azel had six sons,
and these are their names: Azrikam, Bocheru, Ishmael, Sheariah,
Obadiah, and Hanan; all these
were the sons of Azel. 39 The sons of
his brother Eshek: Ulam his firstborn, Jeush the second, and Eliphelet the third. 40 The sons of Ulam
were mighty warriors, archers, having many children and grandchildren, one hundred fifty. All these
were Benjaminites.

9 So all Israel was enrolled by
genealogies; and these are
written in the Book of the Kings of
Israel. And Judah was taken into
exile in Babylon because of their
unfaithfulness. 2 Now the first to
live again in their possessions in
their towns were Israelites, priests,
Levites, and temple servants.

Inhabitants of Jerusalem after the Exile

3 And some of the people of Judah, Benjamin, Ephraim, and Manasseh lived in Jerusalem: 4 Uthai
son of Ammihud, son of Omri, son
of Imri, son of Bani, from the sons
of Perez son of Judah. 5 And of the
Shilonites: Asaiah the firstborn,
and his sons. 6 Of the sons of Zerah:

8.1 Gen 46.21; 1 Chr 7.6
8.6 1 Chr 2.52
8.13 v. 21
8.21 v. 13
8.29 1 Chr 9.35
8.33 1 Chr 9.35-38
8.34 2 Sam 9.12
9.1 1 Chr 5.25, 26
9.2 Neh 11.3-22; Ezra 2.43; 8.20
9.3 Neh 11.1

[p] Or *father of Ehud*; see 8.6 [q] Heb *and Naaman* [r] Or *he carried them into exile* [s] Compare 9.35: Heb lacks *Jeiel* [t] Gk Ms adds *Ner*; Compare 8.33 and 9.36 [u] Or *Shaul*

Jeuel and their kin, six hundred
ninety. 7 Of the Benjaminites: Sallu
son of Meshullam, son of Hodaviah, son of Hassenuah, 8 Ibneiah son
of Jeroham, Elah son of Uzzi, son
of Michri, and Meshullam son of
Shephatiah, son of Reuel, son of
Ibnijah; 9 and their kindred according to their generations, nine hundred fifty-six. All these were heads
of families according to their ancestral houses.

Priestly Families

10 Of the priests: Jedaiah, Jehoiarib, Jachin, 11 and Azariah son
of Hilkiah, son of Meshullam, son
of Zadok, son of Meraioth, son of
Ahitub, the chief officer of the
house of God; 12 and Adaiah son of
Jeroham, son of Pashhur, son of
Malchijah, and Maasai son of Adiel, son of Jahzerah, son of Meshullam, son of Meshillemith, son of
Immer; 13 besides their kindred,
heads of their ancestral houses,
one thousand seven hundred sixty,
qualified for the work of the service
of the house of God.

Levitical Families

14 Of the Levites: Shemaiah son
of Hasshub, son of Azrikam, son of
Hashabiah, of the sons of Merari;
15 and Bakbakkar, Heresh, Galal,
and Mattaniah son of Mica, son of
Zichri, son of Asaph; 16 and Obadiah son of Shemaiah, son of Galal,
son of Jeduthun, and Berechiah
son of Asa, son of Elkanah, who
lived in the villages of the Netophathites.

17 The gatekeepers were: Shallum, Akkub, Talmon, Ahiman; and
their kindred Shallum was the
chief, 18 stationed previously in the
king's gate on the east side. These
were the gatekeepers of the camp
of the Levites. 19 Shallum son of
Kore, son of Ebiasaph, son of Korah, and his kindred of his ancestral house, the Korahites, were in
charge of the work of the service,
guardians of the thresholds of the
tent, as their ancestors had been in
charge of the camp of the LORD,
guardians of the entrance. 20 And
Phinehas son of Eleazar was chief
over them in former times; the
LORD was with him. 21 Zechariah
son of Meshelemiah was gatekeeper at the entrance of the tent of
meeting. 22 All these, who were
chosen as gatekeepers at the
thresholds, were two hundred
twelve. They were enrolled by genealogies in their villages. David
and the seer Samuel established
them in their office of trust. 23 So
they and their descendants were in
charge of the gates of the house of
the LORD, that is, the house of the
tent, as guards. 24 The gatekeepers
were on the four sides, east, west,
north, and south; 25 and their kindred who were in their villages
were obliged to come in every sev-
en days, in turn, to be with them;
26 for the four chief gatekeepers,
who were Levites, were in charge of
the chambers and the treasures of
the house of God. 27 And they
would spend the night near the
house of God; for on them lay the
duty of watching, and they had
charge of opening it every morning.

28 Some of them had charge of
the utensils of service, for they
were required to count them when
they were brought in and taken
out. 29 Others of them were appointed over the furniture, and
over all the holy utensils, also over
the choice flour, the wine, the oil,
the incense, and the spices. 30 Others, of the sons of the priests, prepared the mixing of the spices,
31 and Mattithiah, one of the Levites, the firstborn of Shallum the
Korahite, was in charge of making
the flat cakes. 32 Also some of their
kindred of the Kohathites had
charge of the rows of bread, to prepare them for each sabbath.

33 Now these are the singers,
the heads of ancestral houses of
the Levites, living in the chambers
of the temple free from other service, for they were on duty day and
night. 34 These were heads of ancestral houses of the Levites, according to their generations; these
leaders lived in Jerusalem.

9.10 Neh 11.10-14
9.14 Neh 11.15-19
9.18 Ezek 46.1,2
9.20 Num 25.7-13
9.21 1 Chr 26.2, 14
9.22 1 Chr 26.1, 2; 2 Chr 31.15, 18
9.25 v. 16; 2 Kings 11.5, 7; 2 Chr 23.8
9.27 1 Chr 23.30-32
9.29 1 Chr 23.29
9.30 Ex 30.23-25
9.32 Lev 24.8
9.33 1 Chr 6.31; 25.1; Ps 134.1

The Family of King Saul

35 In Gibeon lived the father of Gibeon, Jeiel, and the name of his wife was Maacah. 36 His firstborn son was Abdon, then Zur, Kish, Baal, Ner, Nadab, 37 Gedor, Ahio, Zechariah, and Mikloth; 38 and Mikloth became the father of Shimeam; and these also lived opposite their kindred in Jerusalem, with their kindred. 39 Ner became the father of Kish, Kish of Saul, Saul of Jonathan, Malchishua, Abinadab, and Esh-baal; 40 and the son of Jonathan was Merib-baal; and Merib-baal became the father of Micah. 41 The sons of Micah: Pithon, Melech, Tahrea, and Ahaz;[v] 42 and Ahaz became the father of Jarah, and Jarah of Alemeth, Azmaveth, and Zimri; and Zimri became the father of Moza. 43 Moza became the father of Binea; and Rephaiah was his son, Eleasah his son, Azel his son. 44 Azel had six sons, and these are their names: Azrikam, Bocheru, Ishmael, Sheariah, Obadiah, and Hanan; these were the sons of Azel.

Death of Saul and His Sons

10 Now the Philistines fought against Israel; and the men of Israel fled before the Philistines, and fell slain on Mount Gilboa. 2 The Philistines overtook Saul and his sons; and the Philistines killed Jonathan and Abinadab and Malchishua, sons of Saul. 3 The battle pressed hard on Saul; and the archers found him, and he was wounded by the archers. 4 Then Saul said to his armor-bearer, "Draw your sword, and thrust me through with it, so that these uncircumcised may not come and make sport of me." But his armor-bearer was unwilling, for he was terrified. So Saul took his own sword and fell on it. 5 When his armor-bearer saw that Saul was dead, he also fell on his sword and died. 6 Thus Saul died; he and his three sons and all his house died together. 7 When all the men of Israel who were in the valley saw that the army[w] had fled and that Saul and his sons were dead, they abandoned their towns and fled; and the Philistines came and occupied them.

8 The next day when the Philistines came to strip the dead, they found Saul and his sons fallen on Mount Gilboa. 9 They stripped him and took his head and his armor, and sent messengers throughout the land of the Philistines to carry the good news to their idols and to the people. 10 They put his armor in the temple of their gods, and fastened his head in the temple of Dagon. 11 But when all Jabesh-gilead heard everything that the Philistines had done to Saul, 12 all the valiant warriors got up and took away the body of Saul and the bodies of his sons, and brought them to Jabesh. Then they buried their bones under the oak in Jabesh, and fasted seven days.

13 So Saul died for his unfaithfulness; he was unfaithful to the LORD in that he did not keep the command of the LORD; moreover, he had consulted a medium, seeking guidance, 14 and did not seek guidance from the LORD. Therefore the LORD[x] put him to death and turned the kingdom over to David son of Jesse.

David Anointed King of All Israel

11 Then all Israel gathered together to David at Hebron and said, "See, we are your bone and flesh. 2 For some time now, even while Saul was king, it was you who commanded the army of Israel. The LORD your God said to you: It is you who shall shepherd of my people Israel, you who shall be ruler over my people Israel." 3 So all the elders of Israel came to the king at Hebron, and David made a covenant with them at Hebron before the LORD. And they anointed David king over Israel, according to the word of the LORD by Samuel.

Jerusalem Captured

4 David and all Israel marched

9.35 1 Chr 8.29
9.39 1 Chr 8.33
9.41 1 Chr 8.35
10.1 1 Sam 31.1, 2
10.4 cf. 1 Sam 31.4-7
10.10 1 Sam 31.10
10.13 1 Sam 13.13; 15.23; 28.7
10.14 1 Sam 15.28; 1 Chr 12.23
11.1 2 Sam 5.1
11.2 2 Sam 5.2; Ps 78.71
11.3 2 Sam 5.3; 1 Sam 16.1, 12,13
11.4 Judg 1.21; 19.10

[v] Compare 8.35: Heb lacks *and Ahaz*
[w] Heb *they* [x] Heb *he*

to Jerusalem, that is Jebus, where
the Jebusites were, the inhabitants
of the land. 5 The inhabitants of Jebus said to David, "You will not
come in here." Nevertheless David
took the stronghold of Zion, now
the city of David. 6 David had said,
"Whoever attacks the Jebusites
first shall be chief and commander." And Joab son of Zeruiah went
up first, so he became chief. 7 David
resided in the stronghold; therefore it was called the city of David.
8 He built the city all around, from
the Millo in complete circuit; and
Joab repaired the rest of the city.
9 And David became greater and
greater, for the LORD of hosts was
with him.

David's Mighty Men and Their Exploits

10 Now these are the chiefs of
David's warriors, who gave him
strong support in his kingdom, together with all Israel, to make him
king, according to the word of the
LORD concerning Israel. 11 This is an
account of David's mighty warriors:
Jashobeam, son of Hachmoni,[y]
was chief of the Three;[z] he wielded his spear against three hundred
whom he killed at one time.
12 And next to him among the
three warriors was Eleazar son of
Dodo, the Ahohite. 13 He was with
David at Pas-dammim when the
Philistines were gathered there for
battle. There was a plot of ground
full of barley. Now the people had
fled from the Philistines, 14 but he
and David took their stand in the
middle of the plot, defended it, and
killed the Philistines; and the LORD
saved them by a great victory.
15 Three of the thirty chiefs
went down to the rock to David at
the cave of Adullam, while the
army of Philistines was encamped
in the valley of Rephaim. 16 David
was then in the stronghold; and the
garrison of the Philistines was then
at Bethlehem. 17 David said longingly, "O that someone would give
me water to drink from the well of
Bethlehem that is by the gate!"
18 Then the Three broke through
the camp of the Philistines, and
drew water from the well of Bethlehem that was by the gate, and they
brought it to David. But David
would not drink of it; he poured it
out to the LORD, 19 and said, "My
God forbid that I should do this.
Can I drink the blood of these men?
For at the risk of their lives they
brought it." Therefore he would
not drink it. The three warriors did
these things.
20 Now Abishai,[a] the brother of
Joab, was chief of the Thirty.[b]
With his spear he fought against
three hundred and killed them,
and won a name beside the Three.
21 He was the most renowned[c] of
the Thirty,[b] and became their
commander; but he did not attain
to the Three.
22 Benaiah son of Jehoiada was
a valiant man[d] of Kabzeel, a doer
of great deeds; he struck down two
sons of[e] Ariel of Moab. He also
went down and killed a lion in a pit
on a day when snow had fallen.
23 And he killed an Egyptian, a man
of great stature, five cubits tall. The
Egyptian had in his hand a spear
like a weaver's beam; but Benaiah
went against him with a staff,
snatched the spear out of the Egyptian's hand, and killed him with his
own spear. 24 Such were the things
Benaiah son of Jehoiada did, and
he won a name beside the three
warriors. 25 He was renowned
among the Thirty, but he did not
attain to the Three. And David put
him in charge of his bodyguard.
26 The warriors of the armies
were Asahel brother of Joab, Elhanan son of Dodo of Bethlehem,
27 Shammoth of Harod,[f] Helez the
Pelonite, 28 Ira son of Ikkesh of Tekoa, Abiezer of Anathoth, 29 Sibbecai the Hushathite, Ilai the Ahohite, 30 Maharai of Netophah,
Heled son of Baanah of Netophah,

11.6 2 Sam 8.16
11.9 2 Sam 3.1
11.10 2 Sam 23.8-39; v. 3
11.11 2 Sam 23.8
11.13 2 Sam 23.11, 12
11.15 2 Sam 23.13; 1 Chr 14.9
11.20 2 Sam 23.18
11.21 2 Sam 23.19
11.22 2 Sam 23.20
11.23 1 Sam 17.7
11.26 2 Sam 23.24

y Or *a Hachmonite* z Compare 2 Sam 23.8: Heb *Thirty* or *captains* a Gk Vg Tg Compare 2 Sam 23.18: Heb *Abshai* b Syr: Heb *Three* c Compare 2 Sam 23.19: Heb *more renowned among the two* d Syr: Heb *the son of a valiant man* e See 2 Sam 23.20: Heb lacks *sons of* f Compare 2 Sam 23.25: Heb *the Harorite*

31 Ithai son of Ribai of Gibeah of
the Benjaminites, Benaiah of Pirathon, 32 Hurai of the wadis of Gaash, Abiel the Arbathite, 33 Azmaveth of Baharum, Eliahba of
Shaalbon, 34 Hashem[g] the Gizo-
nite, Jonathan son of Shagee the
Hararite, 35 Ahiam son of Sachar
the Hararite, Eliphal son of Ur,
36 Hepher the Mecherathite, Ahijah
the Pelonite, 37 Hezro of Carmel,
Naarai son of Ezbai, 38 Joel the
brother of Nathan, Mibhar son of
Hagri, 39 Zelek the Ammonite, Naharai of Beeroth, the armor-bearer
of Joab son of Zeruiah, 40 Ira the
Ithrite, Gareb the Ithrite, 41 Uriah
the Hittite, Zabad son of Ahlai,
42 Adina son of Shiza the Reuben-
ite, a leader of the Reubenites, and
thirty with him, 43 Hanan son of
Maacah, and Joshaphat the Mith-
nite, 44 Uzzia the Ashterathite, Shama and Jeiel sons of Hotham the
Aroerite, 45 Jediael son of Shimri,
and his brother Joha the Tizite,
46 Eliel the Mahavite, and Jeribai
and Joshaviah sons of Elnaam, and
Ithmah the Moabite, 47 Eliel, and
Obed, and Jaasiel the Mezobaite.

David's Followers in the Wilderness

12 The following are those
who came to David at Zik-
lag, while he could not move about
freely because of Saul son of Kish;
they were among the mighty warriors who helped him in war. 2 They
were archers, and could shoot arrows and sling stones with either
the right hand or the left; they were
Benjaminites, Saul's kindred. 3 The
chief was Ahiezer, then Joash, both
sons of Shemaah of Gibeah; also
Jeziel and Pelet sons of Azmaveth;
Beracah, Jehu of Anathoth, 4 Ishmaiah of Gibeon, a warrior among
the Thirty and a leader over the
Thirty; Jeremiah,[h] Jahaziel, Johanan, Jozabad of Gederah, 5 Elu-
zai,[i] Jerimoth, Bealiah, Shemariah, Shephatiah the Haruphite;
6 Elkanah, Isshiah, Azarel, Joezer,
and Jashobeam, the Korahites;
7 and Joelah and Zebadiah, sons of
Jeroham of Gedor.

11.39 1 Chr 18.15
12.1 1 Sam 27.2-6
12.2 Judg 20.16
12.8 2 Sam 2.18
12.15 Josh 3.15
12.18 Judg 6.34; 2 Sam 17.25
12.19 1 Sam 29.2, 4

8 From the Gadites there went
over to David at the stronghold in
the wilderness mighty and experienced warriors, expert with shield
and spear, whose faces were like
the faces of lions, and who were
swift as gazelles on the mountains:
9 Ezer the chief, Obadiah second,
Eliab third, 10 Mishmannah fourth,
Jeremiah fifth, 11 Attai sixth, Eliel
seventh, 12 Johanan eighth, Elzabad ninth, 13 Jeremiah tenth,
Machbannai eleventh. 14 These
Gadites were officers of the army,
the least equal to a hundred and
the greatest to a thousand. 15 These
are the men who crossed the Jordan in the first month, when it was
overflowing all its banks, and put
to flight all those in the valleys, to
the east and to the west.

16 Some Benjaminites and
Judahites came to the stronghold
to David. 17 David went out to meet
them and said to them, "If you have
come to me in friendship, to help
me, then my heart will be knit to
you; but if you have come to betray
me to my adversaries, though my
hands have done no wrong, then
may the God of our ancestors see
and give judgment." 18 Then the
spirit came upon Amasai, chief of
the Thirty, and he said,

"We are yours, O David;
 and with you, O son of Jesse!
Peace, peace to you,
 and peace to the one who
 helps you!
For your God is the one
 who helps you."

Then David received them, and
made them officers of his troops.

19 Some of the Manassites deserted to David when he came with
the Philistines for the battle
against Saul. (Yet he did not help
them, for the rulers of the Philistines took counsel and sent him
away, saying, "He will desert to his
master Saul at the cost of our
heads.") 20 As he went to Ziklag

[g] Compare Gk and 2 Sam 23.32: Heb *the sons of Hashem* [h] Heb verse 5 [i] Heb verse 6

these Manassites deserted to him:
Adnah, Jozabad, Jediael, Michael,
Jozabad, Elihu, and Zillethai,
chiefs of the thousands in Manasseh. 21 They helped David against
the band of raiders,[j] for they were
all warriors and commanders in the
army. 22 Indeed from day to day
people kept coming to David to
help him, until there was a great
army, like an army of God.

David's Army at Hebron

23 These are the numbers of the
divisions of the armed troops who
came to David in Hebron to turn
the kingdom of Saul over to him,
according to the word of the LORD.
24 The people of Judah bearing
shield and spear numbered six
thousand eight hundred armed
troops. 25 Of the Simeonites,
mighty warriors, seven thousand
one hundred. 26 Of the Levites four
thousand six hundred. 27 Jehoiada,
leader of the house of Aaron, and
with him three thousand seven
hundred. 28 Zadok, a young warrior,
and twenty-two commanders from
his own ancestral house. 29 Of the
Benjaminites, the kindred of Saul,
three thousand, of whom the majority had continued to keep their
allegiance to the house of Saul.
30 Of the Ephraimites, twenty thousand eight hundred, mighty warriors, notables in their ancestral
houses. 31 Of the half-tribe of Manasseh, eighteen thousand, who
were expressly named to come and
make David king. 32 Of Issachar,
those who had understanding of
the times, to know what Israel
ought to do, two hundred chiefs,
and all their kindred under their
command. 33 Of Zebulun, fifty
thousand seasoned troops,
equipped for battle with all the
weapons of war, to help David[k]
with singleness of purpose. 34 Of
Naphtali, a thousand commanders, with whom there were thirty-
seven thousand armed with shield
and spear. 35 Of the Danites,
twenty-eight thousand six hundred
equipped for battle. 36 Of Asher,
forty thousand seasoned troops
ready for battle. 37 Of the Reubenites and Gadites and the half-tribe
of Manasseh from beyond the Jordan, one hundred twenty thousand
armed with all the weapons of war.

38 All these, warriors arrayed in
battle order, came to Hebron with
full intent to make David king over
all Israel; likewise all the rest of Israel were of a single mind to make
David king. 39 They were there with
David for three days, eating and
drinking, for their kindred had provided for them. 40 And also their
neighbors, from as far away as Issachar and Zebulun and Naphtali,
came bringing food on donkeys,
camels, mules, and oxen—
abundant provisions of meal, cakes
of figs, clusters of raisins, wine, oil,
oxen, and sheep, for there was joy
in Israel.

12.21 1 Sam 30.1, 9,10
12.23 2 Sam 2.3, 4; 1 Chr 11.1; 10.14; 1 Sam 16.1, 3
12.28 2 Sam 8.17
12.29 2 Sam 2.8, 9
12.32 Esther 1.13
12.33 Ps 12.2
12.38 2 Sam 5.1-3
12.40 1 Sam 25.18
13.2 1 Sam 31.1; Isa 37.4
13.3 1 Sam 7.1, 2
13.5 2 Sam 6.1; 1 Chr 15.3; 1 Sam 6.21; 7.1
13.6 Josh 15.9; 2 Kings 19.15
13.7 1 Sam 7.1

The Ark Brought from Kiriath-jearim

13 David consulted with the
commanders of the thou-
sands and of the hundreds, with every leader. 2 David said to the whole
assembly of Israel, "If it seems
good to you, and if it is the will of
the LORD our God, let us send
abroad to our kindred who remain
in all the land of Israel, including
the priests and Levites in the cities
that have pasture lands, that they
may come together to us. 3 Then let
us bring again the ark of our God to
us; for we did not turn to it in the
days of Saul." 4 The whole assembly agreed to do so, for the thing
pleased all the people.

5 So David assembled all Israel
from the Shihor of Egypt to Lebo-
hamath, to bring the ark of God
from Kiriath-jearim. 6 And David
and all Israel went up to Baalah,
that is, to Kiriath-jearim, which belongs to Judah, to bring up from
there the ark of God, the LORD, who
is enthroned on the cherubim,
which is called by his[l] name.
7 They carried the ark of God on a
new cart, from the house of Abina-

[j] Or *as officers of his troops* [k] Gk: Heb lacks *David* [l] Heb lacks *his*

dab, and Uzzah and Ahio[m] were
driving the cart. 8 David and all Israel were dancing before God with
all their might, with song and lyres
and harps and tambourines and
cymbals and trumpets.
9 When they came to the threshing floor of Chidon, Uzzah put out
his hand to hold the ark, for the
oxen shook it. 10 The anger of the
LORD was kindled against Uzzah; he
struck him down because he put
out his hand to the ark; and he died
there before God. 11 David was angry because the LORD had burst out
against Uzzah; so that place is
called Perez-uzzah[n] to this day.
12 David was afraid of God that day;
he said, "How can I bring the ark of
God into my care?" 13 So David did
not take the ark into his care into
the city of David; he took it instead
to the house of Obed-edom the
Gittite. 14 The ark of God remained
with the household of Obed-edom
in his house three months, and the
LORD blessed the household of
Obed-edom and all that he had.

David Established at Jerusalem

14 King Hiram of Tyre sent
messengers to David, along
with cedar logs, and masons and
carpenters to build a house for
him. 2 David then perceived that
the LORD had established him as
king over Israel, and that his kingdom was highly exalted for the
sake of his people Israel.
3 David took more wives in Jerusalem, and David became the father of more sons and daughters.
4 These are the names of the children whom he had in Jerusalem:
Shammua, Shobab, and Nathan;
Solomon, 5 Ibhar, Elishua, and El-
pelet; 6 Nogah, Nepheg, and Japhia; 7 Elishama, Beeliada, and
Eliphelet.

Defeat of the Philistines

8 When the Philistines heard
that David had been anointed king
over all Israel, all the Philistines
went up in search of David; and David heard of it and went out against
them. 9 Now the Philistines had
come and made a raid in the valley
of Rephaim. 10 David inquired of
God, "Shall I go up against the
Philistines? Will you give them into
my hand?" The LORD said to him,
"Go up, and I will give them into
your hand." 11 So he went up to
Baal-perazim, and David defeated
them there. David said, "God has
burst out[o] against my enemies by
my hand, like a bursting flood."
Therefore that place is called Baal-
perazim.[p] 12 They abandoned their
gods there, and at David's command they were burned.
13 Once again the Philistines
made a raid in the valley. 14 When
David again inquired of God, God
said to him, "You shall not go up
after them; go around and come on
them opposite the balsam trees.
15 When you hear the sound of
marching in the tops of the balsam
trees, then go out to battle; for God
has gone out before you to strike
down the army of the Philistines."
16 David did as God had commanded him, and they struck down the
Philistine army from Gibeon to Gezer. 17 The fame of David went out
into all lands, and the LORD brought
the fear of him on all nations.

The Ark Brought to Jerusalem

15 David[q] built houses for
himself in the city of David,
and he prepared a place for the ark
of God and pitched a tent for it.
2 Then David commanded that no
one but the Levites were to carry
the ark of God, for the LORD had
chosen them to carry the ark of the
LORD and to minister to him forever. 3 David assembled all Israel in
Jerusalem to bring up the ark of the
LORD to its place, which he had prepared for it. 4 Then David gathered
together the descendants of Aaron
and the Levites: 5 of the sons of Kohath, Uriel the chief, with one hundred twenty of his kindred; 6 of the
sons of Merari, Asaiah the chief,
with two hundred twenty of his kindred; 7 of the sons of Gershom, Joel

13.8 2 Sam 6.5
13.9 2 Sam 6.6
13.10 1 Chr 15.13, 15
13.14 1 Chr 26.4, 5
14.1 2 Sam 5.11
14.4 1 Chr 3.5
14.8 2 Sam 5.17
14.9 1 Chr 11.15
14.13 v. 9; 2 Sam 5.22
14.14 2 Sam 5.23
14.16 2 Sam 5.25
14.17 Josh 6.27; 2 Chr 26.8; Deut 2.25
15.1 1 Chr 16.1
15.2 Num 4.15; Deut 10.8; 31.9
15.3 1 Kings 8.1; 1 Chr 13.5

[m] Or *and his brother* [n] That is *Bursting Out Against Uzzah* [o] Heb *paraz* [p] That is *Lord of Bursting Out* [q] Heb *He*

the chief, with one hundred thirty
of his kindred; 8 of the sons of Eli-
zaphan, Shemaiah the chief, with
two hundred of his kindred; 9 of the
sons of Hebron, Eliel the chief,
with eighty of his kindred; 10 of the
sons of Uzziel, Amminadab the
chief, with one hundred twelve of
his kindred.
11 David summoned the priests
Zadok and Abiathar, and the Levites Uriel, Asaiah, Joel, Shemaiah,
Eliel, and Amminadab. 12 He said
to them, "You are the heads of families of the Levites; sanctify yourselves, you and your kindred, so
that you may bring up the ark of the
LORD, the God of Israel, to the place
that I have prepared for it. 13 Because you did not carry it the first
time,[r] the LORD our God burst out
against us, because we did not give
it proper care." 14 So the priests and
the Levites sanctified themselves
to bring up the ark of the LORD, the
God of Israel. 15 And the Levites
carried the ark of God on their
shoulders with the poles, as Moses
had commanded according to the
word of the LORD.
16 David also commanded the
chiefs of the Levites to appoint
their kindred as the singers to play
on musical instruments, on harps
and lyres and cymbals, to raise
loud sounds of joy. 17 So the Levites
appointed Heman son of Joel; and
of his kindred Asaph son of Berechiah; and of the sons of Merari,
their kindred, Ethan son of Kusha-
iah; 18 and with them their kindred
of the second order, Zechariah, Ja-
aziel, Shemiramoth, Jehiel, Unni,
Eliab, Benaiah, Maaseiah, Mattithiah, Eliphelehu, and Mikneiah,
and the gatekeepers Obed-edom
and Jeiel. 19 The singers Heman,
Asaph, and Ethan were to sound
bronze cymbals; 20 Zechariah, Aziel, Shemiramoth, Jehiel, Unni, Eliab, Maaseiah, and Benaiah were to
play harps according to Alamoth;
21 but Mattithiah, Eliphelehu, Mikneiah, Obed-edom, Jeiel, and Azaziah were to lead with lyres according to the Sheminith. 22 Chenaniah,
leader of the Levites in music, was
to direct the music, for he understood it. 23 Berechiah and Elkanah
were to be gatekeepers for the ark.
24 Shebaniah, Joshaphat, Nethanel, Amasai, Zechariah, Benaiah,
and Eliezer, the priests, were to
blow the trumpets before the ark of
God. Obed-edom and Jehiah also
were to be gatekeepers for the ark.
25 So David and the elders of Israel, and the commanders of the
thousands, went to bring up the ark
of the covenant of the LORD from
the house of Obed-edom with rejoicing. 26 And because God helped
the Levites who were carrying the
ark of the covenant of the LORD,
they sacrificed seven bulls and sev-
en rams. 27 David was clothed with
a robe of fine linen, as also were all
the Levites who were carrying the
ark, and the singers, and Chenaniah the leader of the music of the
singers; and David wore a linen
ephod. 28 So all Israel brought up
the ark of the covenant of the LORD
with shouting, to the sound of the
horn, trumpets, and cymbals, and
made loud music on harps and
lyres.
29 As the ark of the covenant of
the LORD came to the city of David,
Michal daughter of Saul looked out
of the window, and saw King David
leaping and dancing; and she despised him in her heart.

The Ark Placed in the Tent

16 They brought in the ark of
God, and set it inside the
tent that David had pitched for it;
and they offered burnt offerings
and offerings of well-being before
God. 2 When David had finished offering the burnt offerings and the
offerings of well-being, he blessed
the people in the name of the LORD;
3 and he distributed to every person
in Israel—man and woman alike—
to each a loaf of bread, a portion of
meat,[s] and a cake of raisins.
4 He appointed certain of the
Levites as ministers before the ark
of the LORD, to invoke, to thank,
and to praise the LORD, the God of

15.8 Ex 6.22
15.9 Ex 6.18
15.11 1 Chr 12.28; 1 Sam 22.20-23
15.12 Ex 19.14, 15; 2 Chr 35.6
15.13 2 Sam 6.3; 1 Chr 13.7, 10,11
15.14 v. 12
15.15 Ex 25.14; Num 4.5
15.16 1 Chr 25.1
15.17 1 Chr 6.33, 39,44
15.24 v. 28; 1 Chr 16.6
15.25 2 Sam 6.12, 15; 1 Chr 13.13
15.28 1 Chr 13.8
15.29 2 Sam 6.16
16.1 2 Sam 6.17-19

[r] Meaning of Heb uncertain [s] Compare Gk Syr Vg: Meaning of Heb uncertain

Israel. 5 Asaph was the chief, and
second to him Zechariah, Jeiel,
Shemiramoth, Jehiel, Mattithiah,
Eliab, Benaiah, Obed-edom, and
Jeiel, with harps and lyres; Asaph
was to sound the cymbals, 6 and the
priests Benaiah and Jahaziel were
to blow trumpets regularly, before
the ark of the covenant of God.

David's Psalm of Thanksgiving

7 Then on that day David first
appointed the singing of praises to
the LORD by Asaph and his kindred.

8 O give thanks to the LORD,
call on his name,
make known his deeds
among the peoples.
9 Sing to him, sing praises to
him,
tell of all his wonderful
works.
10 Glory in his holy name;
let the hearts of those who
seek the LORD rejoice.
11 Seek the LORD and his
strength,
seek his presence
continually.
12 Remember the wonderful
works he has done,
his miracles, and the
judgments he uttered,
13 O offspring of his servant
Israel,[t]
children of Jacob, his
chosen ones.

14 He is the LORD our God;
his judgments are in all the
earth.
15 Remember his covenant
forever,
the word that he
commanded, for a
thousand generations,
16 the covenant that he made
with Abraham,
his sworn promise to Isaac,
17 which he confirmed to Jacob
as a statute,
to Israel as an everlasting
covenant,
18 saying, "To you I will give
the land of Canaan
as your portion for an
inheritance."
19 When they were few in
number,
of little account, and
strangers in the land,[u]
20 wandering from nation to
nation,
from one kingdom to
another people,
21 he allowed no one to oppress
them;
he rebuked kings on their
account,
22 saying, "Do not touch my
anointed ones;
do my prophets no harm."

23 Sing to the LORD, all the
earth.
Tell of his salvation from
day to day.
24 Declare his glory among the
nations,
his marvelous works among
all the peoples.
25 For great is the LORD, and
greatly to be praised;
he is to be revered above
all gods.
26 For all the gods of the
peoples are idols,
but the LORD made the
heavens.
27 Honor and majesty are
before him;
strength and joy are in his
place.

28 Ascribe to the LORD,
O families of the
peoples,
ascribe to the LORD glory
and strength.
29 Ascribe to the LORD the glory
due his name;
bring an offering, and come
before him.
Worship the LORD in holy
splendor;
30 tremble before him, all the
earth.

16.5 Ps ch. 50; 73 **16.7** 2 Sam 23.1 **16.8** Ps 105.1-15 **16.11** Ps 24.6 **16.12** Ps 77.11; 78.43-68 **16.14** Isa 26.9 **16.16** Gen 17.2; 26.3; 28.13; 35.11 **16.17** Gen 35.11, 12 **16.19** Gen 34.30 **16.21** Gen 12.17; 20.3; Ex 7.15-18 **16.23** Ps 96.1-13 **16.25** Ps 48.1; 89.7 **16.26** Ps 96.5 **16.28** Ps 29.1,2

[t] Another reading is *Abraham* (compare Ps 105.6) [u] Heb *in it*

The world is firmly
established; it shall
never be moved.
31 Let the heavens be glad, and
let the earth rejoice,
and let them say among
the nations, "The LORD
is king!"
32 Let the sea roar, and all that
fills it;
let the field exult, and
everything in it.
33 Then shall the trees of the
forest sing for joy
before the LORD, for he
comes to judge the
earth.
34 O give thanks to the LORD,
for he is good;
for his steadfast love
endures forever.

35 Say also:
"Save us, O God of our
salvation,
and gather and rescue us
from among the nations,
that we may give thanks to
your holy name,
and glory in your praise.
36 Blessed be the LORD, the God
of Israel,
from everlasting to
everlasting."
Then all the people said "Amen!"
and praised the LORD.

Regular Worship Maintained

37 David left Asaph and his
kinsfolk there before the ark of the
covenant of the LORD to minister
regularly before the ark as each day
required, 38 and also Obed-edom
and his[v] sixty-eight kinsfolk; while
Obed-edom son of Jeduthun and
Hosah were to be gatekeepers.
39 And he left the priest Zadok and
his kindred the priests before the
tabernacle of the LORD in the high
place that was at Gibeon, 40 to offer
burnt offerings to the LORD on the
altar of burnt offering regularly,
morning and evening, according to
all that is written in the law of the
LORD that he commanded Israel.
41 With them were Heman and Jeduthun, and the rest of those chosen and expressly named to render
thanks to the LORD, for his steadfast
love endures forever. 42 Heman and
Jeduthun had with them trumpets
and cymbals for the music, and instruments for sacred song. The
sons of Jeduthun were appointed
to the gate.
43 Then all the people departed
to their homes, and David went
home to bless his household.

16.31 Isa 49.13; Ps 93.1 **16.32** Ps 98.7 **16.34** Ps 106.1 **16.35** Ps 106.47, 48 **16.36** 1 Kings 8.15; Deut 27.15 **16.37** vv. 4,5; 2 Chr 8.14 **16.38** 1 Chr 13.14; 26.10 **16.39** 1 Chr 15.11; 1 Kings 3.4 **16.40** Ex 29.38; Num 28.3 **16.41** 1 Chr 6.33; 25.1-6; 2 Chr 5.13

God's Covenant with David

17 Now when David settled in
his house, David said to the
prophet Nathan, "I am living in a
house of cedar, but the ark of the
covenant of the LORD is under a
tent." 2 Nathan said to David, "Do
all that you have in mind, for God
is with you."
3 But that same night the word
of the LORD came to Nathan, saying: 4 Go and tell my servant David:
Thus says the LORD: You shall not
build me a house to live in. 5 For I
have not lived in a house since the
day I brought out Israel to this very
day, but I have lived in a tent and
a tabernacle.[w] 6 Wherever I have
moved about among all Israel, did
I ever speak a word with any of the
judges of Israel, whom I commanded to shepherd my people, saying,
Why have you not built me a house
of cedar? 7 Now therefore thus you
shall say to my servant David: Thus
says the LORD of hosts: I took you
from the pasture, from following
the sheep, to be ruler over my people Israel; 8 and I have been with
you wherever you went, and have
cut off all your enemies before you;
and I will make for you a name, like
the name of the great ones of the
earth. 9 I will appoint a place for my
people Israel, and will plant them,
so that they may live in their own
place, and be disturbed no more;
and evildoers shall wear them
down no more, as they did formerly, 10 from the time that I appointed
judges over my people Israel; and I
will subdue all your enemies.

17.1 2 Sam 7.1-29 **17.4** 1 Chr 28.2, 3 **17.5** 2 Sam 7.6 **17.6** 2 Sam 7.7 **17.10** Judg 2.16

[v] Gk Syr Vg: Heb *their* [w] Gk 2 Sam 7.6: Heb *but I have been from tent to tent and from tabernacle*

Moreover I declare to you that
the LORD will build you a house.
11 When your days are fulfilled to go
to be with your ancestors, I will
raise up your offspring after you,
one of your own sons, and I will establish his kingdom. 12 He shall
build a house for me, and I will establish his throne forever. 13 I will
be a father to him, and he shall be
a son to me. I will not take my
steadfast love from him, as I took it
from him who was before you,
14 but I will confirm him in my
house and in my kingdom forever,
and his throne shall be established
forever. 15 In accordance with all
these words and all this vision, Nathan spoke to David.

David's Prayer

16 Then King David went in and
sat before the LORD, and said, "Who
am I, O LORD God, and what is my
house, that you have brought me
thus far? 17 And even this was a
small thing in your sight, O God;
you have also spoken of your servant's house for a great while to
come. You regard me as someone
of high rank,[x] O LORD God! 18 And
what more can David say to you for
honoring your servant? You know
your servant. 19 For your servant's
sake, O LORD, and according to
your own heart, you have done all
these great deeds, making known
all these great things. 20 There is no
one like you, O LORD, and there is
no God besides you, according to
all that we have heard with our
ears. 21 Who is like your people Israel, one nation on the earth whom
God went to redeem to be his people, making for yourself a name for
great and terrible things, in driving
out nations before your people
whom you redeemed from Egypt?
22 And you made your people Israel
to be your people forever; and you,
O LORD, became their God.
23 "And now, O LORD, as for the
word that you have spoken concerning your servant and concerning his house, let it be established
forever, and do as you have promised. 24 Thus your name will be established and magnified forever in
the saying, 'The LORD of hosts, the
God of Israel, is Israel's God'; and
the house of your servant David
will be established in your presence. 25 For you, my God, have revealed to your servant that you will
build a house for him; therefore
your servant has found it possible
to pray before you. 26 And now,
O LORD, you are God, and you have
promised this good thing to your
servant; 27 therefore may it please
you to bless the house of your servant, that it may continue forever
before you. For you, O LORD, have
blessed and are blessed[y] forever."

17.13 2 Sam 7.14, 15; Heb 1.5 **17.14** Lk 1.33 **17.16** 2 Sam 7.18 **17.19** Isa 37.35 **17.22** Ex 19.5,6 **17.24** Ps 46.7,11

David's Kingdom Established and Extended

18 Some time afterward, David attacked the Philistines
and subdued them; he took Gath
and its villages from the Philistines.
2 He defeated Moab, and the
Moabites became subject to David
and brought tribute.
3 David also struck down King
Hadadezer of Zobah, toward Hamath,[x] as he went to set up a monument at the river Euphrates. 4 David took from him one thousand
chariots, seven thousand cavalry,
and twenty thousand foot soldiers.
David hamstrung all the chariot
horses, but left one hundred of
them. 5 When the Arameans of Damascus came to help King Hadadezer of Zobah, David killed twenty-
two thousand Arameans. 6 Then
David put garrisons[z] in Aram of
Damascus; and the Arameans became subject to David, and
brought tribute. The LORD gave victory to David wherever he went.
7 David took the gold shields that
were carried by the servants of
Hadadezer, and brought them to
Jerusalem. 8 From Tibhath and
from Cun, cities of Hadadezer, David took a vast quantity of bronze;
with it Solomon made the bronze

18.1 2 Sam 8.1-18 **18.5** 1 Chr 19.6 **18.8** 1 Kings 7.15, 23; 2 Chr 4.12, 15,16

[x] Meaning of Heb uncertain [y] Or *and it is blessed* [z] Gk Vg 2 Sam 8.6 Compare Syr: Heb lacks *garrisons*

sea and the pillars and the vessels
of bronze.
9 When King Tou of Hamath
heard that David had defeated the
whole army of King Hadadezer of
Zobah, [10]he sent his son Hadoram
to King David, to greet him and to
congratulate him, because he had
fought against Hadadezer and defeated him. Now Hadadezer had often been at war with Tou. He sent
all sorts of articles of gold, of silver,
and of bronze; [11]these also King
David dedicated to the LORD, together with the silver and gold that
he had carried off from all the nations, from Edom, Moab, the Ammonites, the Philistines, and Amalek.
12 Abishai son of Zeruiah killed
eighteen thousand Edomites in the
Valley of Salt. [13]He put garrisons in
Edom; and all the Edomites became subject to David. And the
LORD gave victory to David wherever
he went.

David's Administration

14 So David reigned over all Israel; and he administered justice
and equity to all his people. [15]Joab
son of Zeruiah was over the army;
Jehoshaphat son of Ahilud was recorder; [16]Zadok son of Ahitub and
Ahimelech son of Abiathar were
priests; Shavsha was secretary;
[17]Benaiah son of Jehoiada was over
the Cherethites and the Pelethites;
and David's sons were the chief officials in the service of the king.

Defeat of the Ammonites and Arameans

19 Some time afterward, King
Nahash of the Ammonites
died, and his son succeeded him.
[2]David said, "I will deal loyally
with Hanun son of Nahash, for his
father dealt loyally with me." So
David sent messengers to console
him concerning his father. When
David's servants came to Hanun in
the land of the Ammonites, to console him, [3]the officials of the Ammonites said to Hanun, "Do you
think, because David has sent con-
solers to you, that he is honoring
your father? Have not his servants
come to you to search and to overthrow and to spy out the land?" [4]So
Hanun seized David's servants,
shaved them, cut off their garments in the middle at their hips,
and sent them away; [5]and they departed. When David was told about
the men, he sent messengers to
them, for they felt greatly humiliated. The king said, "Remain at Jericho until your beards have grown,
and then return."
6 When the Ammonites saw
that they had made themselves
odious to David, Hanun and the
Ammonites sent a thousand talents of silver to hire chariots and
cavalry from Mesopotamia, from
Aram-maacah and from Zobah.
[7]They hired thirty-two thousand
chariots and the king of Maacah
with his army, who came and
camped before Medeba. And the
Ammonites were mustered from
their cities and came to battle.
[8]When David heard of it, he sent
Joab and all the army of the warriors. [9]The Ammonites came out
and drew up in battle array at the
entrance of the city, and the kings
who had come were by themselves
in the open country.
10 When Joab saw that the line
of battle was set against him both
in front and in the rear, he chose
some of the picked men of Israel
and arrayed them against the Arameans; [11]the rest of his troops he
put in the charge of his brother
Abishai, and they were arrayed
against the Ammonites. [12]He said,
"If the Arameans are too strong for
me, then you shall help me; but if
the Ammonites are too strong for
you, then I will help you. [13]Be
strong, and let us be courageous for
our people and for the cities of our
God; and may the LORD do what
seems good to him." [14]So Joab and
the troops who were with him advanced toward the Arameans for
battle; and they fled before him.
[15]When the Ammonites saw that
the Arameans fled, they likewise
fled before Abishai, Joab's brother,

18.10 2 Sam 10.16
18.12 2 Sam 8.13
18.15 1 Chr 11.6
18.17 2 Sam 8.18
19.1 2 Sam 10.1
19.3 2 Sam 10.3
19.4 2 Sam 10.4
19.6 1 Chr 18.5, 9
19.7 Num 21.30; Josh 13.9, 16
19.8 2 Sam 10.7
19.11 2 Sam 10.10
19.12 2 Sam 10.11
19.14 2 Sam 10.13

and entered the city. Then Joab
came to Jerusalem.
16 But when the Arameans saw
that they had been defeated by Israel, they sent messengers and
brought out the Arameans who
were beyond the Euphrates, with
Shophach the commander of the
army of Hadadezer at their head.
17 When David was informed, he
gathered all Israel together,
crossed the Jordan, came to them,
and drew up his forces against
them. When David set the battle in
array against the Arameans, they
fought with him. 18 The Arameans
fled before Israel; and David killed
seven thousand Aramean charioteers and forty thousand foot soldiers, and also killed Shophach the
commander of their army. 19 When
the servants of Hadadezer saw that
they had been defeated by Israel,
they made peace with David, and
became subject to him. So the Arameans were not willing to help the
Ammonites any more.

Siege and Capture of Rabbah

20 In the spring of the year,
the time when kings go out
to battle, Joab led out the army,
ravaged the country of the Ammonites, and came and besieged Rabbah. But David remained at Jerusalem. Joab attacked Rabbah, and
overthrew it. 2 David took the
crown of Milcom[a] from his head;
he found that it weighed a talent of
gold, and in it was a precious stone;
and it was placed on David's head.
He also brought out the booty of
the city, a very great amount. 3 He
brought out the people who were in
it, and set them to work[b] with saws
and iron picks and axes.[c] Thus David did to all the cities of the Ammonites. Then David and all the
people returned to Jerusalem.

Exploits against the Philistines

4 After this, war broke out with
the Philistines at Gezer; then Sibbecai the Hushathite killed Sippai,
who was one of the descendants of
the giants; and the Philistines were
subdued. 5 Again there was war
with the Philistines; and Elhanan
son of Jair killed Lahmi the brother
of Goliath the Gittite, the shaft of
whose spear was like a weaver's
beam. 6 Again there was war at
Gath, where there was a man of
great size, who had six fingers on
each hand, and six toes on each
foot, twenty-four in number; he
also was descended from the
giants. 7 When he taunted Israel,
Jonathan son of Shimea, David's
brother, killed him. 8 These were
descended from the giants in Gath;
they fell by the hand of David and
his servants.

The Census and Plague

21 Satan stood up against Israel, and incited David to
count the people of Israel. 2 So David said to Joab and the commanders of the army, "Go, number Israel, from Beer-sheba to Dan, and
bring me a report, so that I may
know their number." 3 But Joab
said, "May the LORD increase the
number of his people a hundredfold! Are they not, my lord the king,
all of them my lord's servants? Why
then should my lord require this?
Why should he bring guilt on Israel?" 4 But the king's word prevailed
against Joab. So Joab departed and
went throughout all Israel, and
came back to Jerusalem. 5 Joab
gave the total count of the people
to David. In all Israel there were
one million one hundred thousand
men who drew the sword, and in
Judah four hundred seventy thousand who drew the sword. 6 But he
did not include Levi and Benjamin
in the numbering, for the king's
command was abhorrent to Joab.
7 But God was displeased with
this thing, and he struck Israel.
8 David said to God, "I have sinned
greatly in that I have done this
thing. But now, I pray you, take
away the guilt of your servant; for I
have done very foolishly." 9 The
LORD spoke to Gad, David's seer,
saying, 10 "Go and say to David,

19.16 2 Sam 10.15
19.17 2 Sam 10.17
19.18 2 Sam 10.18
19.19 2 Sam 10.19
20.1ff 2 Sam 11.1; 12.26
20.2 2 Sam 12.30, 31
20.3 2 Sam 12.31
20.4 2 Sam 21.18
20.5 2 Sam 21.19; 1 Sam 17.7
20.6 2 Sam 21.20
21.1 2 Sam 24.1-25
21.2 1 Chr 27.23
21.3 Deut 1.11
21.5 cf. 2 Sam 24.9
21.6 1 Chr 27.24
21.8 2 Sam 24.10; 12.13
21.10 1 Chr 29.29; 1 Sam 9.9

[a] Gk Vg See 1 Kings 11.5, 33: MT *of their king* [b] Compare 2 Sam 12.31: Heb *and he sawed* [c] Compare 2 Sam 12.31: Heb *saws*

'Thus says the LORD: Three things I
offer you; choose one of them, so
that I may do it to you.' " 11 So Gad
came to David and said to him,
"Thus says the LORD, 'Take your
choice: 12 either three years of famine; or three months of devastation
by your foes, while the sword of
your enemies overtakes you; or
three days of the sword of the LORD,
pestilence on the land, and the angel of the LORD destroying throughout all the territory of Israel.' Now
decide what answer I shall return
to the one who sent me." 13 Then
David said to Gad, "I am in great
distress; let me fall into the hand of
the LORD, for his mercy is very great;
but let me not fall into human
hands."

14 So the LORD sent a pestilence
on Israel; and seventy thousand
persons fell in Israel. 15 And God
sent an angel to Jerusalem to destroy it; but when he was about to
destroy it, the LORD took note and
relented concerning the calamity;
he said to the destroying angel,
"Enough! Stay your hand." The angel of the LORD was then standing
by the threshing floor of Ornan the
Jebusite. 16 David looked up and
saw the angel of the LORD standing
between earth and heaven, and in
his hand a drawn sword stretched
out over Jerusalem. Then David
and the elders, clothed in sackcloth, fell on their faces. 17 And David said to God, "Was it not I who
gave the command to count the
people? It is I who have sinned and
done very wickedly. But these
sheep, what have they done? Let
your hand, I pray, O LORD my God,
be against me and against my father's house; but do not let your
people be plagued!"

David's Altar and Sacrifice

18 Then the angel of the LORD
commanded Gad to tell David that
he should go up and erect an altar
to the LORD on the threshing floor
of Ornan the Jebusite. 19 So David
went up following Gad's instructions, which he had spoken in the
name of the LORD. 20 Ornan turned
and saw the angel; and while his
four sons who were with him hid
themselves, Ornan continued to
thresh wheat. 21 As David came to
Ornan, Ornan looked and saw David; he went out from the threshing
floor, and did obeisance to David
with his face to the ground. 22 David said to Ornan, "Give me the site
of the threshing floor that I may
build on it an altar to the LORD—
give it to me at its full price—so
that the plague may be averted
from the people." 23 Then Ornan
said to David, "Take it; and let my
lord the king do what seems good
to him; see, I present the oxen for
burnt offerings, and the threshing
sledges for the wood, and the
wheat for a grain offering. I give it
all." 24 But King David said to Ornan, "No; I will buy them for the
full price. I will not take for the
LORD what is yours, nor offer burnt
offerings that cost me nothing."
25 So David paid Ornan six hundred
shekels of gold by weight for the
site. 26 David built there an altar to
the LORD and presented burnt offerings and offerings of well-being. He
called upon the LORD, and he answered him with fire from heaven
on the altar of burnt offering.
27 Then the LORD commanded the
angel, and he put his sword back
into its sheath.

The Place Chosen for the Temple

28 At that time, when David saw
that the LORD had answered him at
the threshing floor of Ornan the
Jebusite, he made his sacrifices
there. 29 For the tabernacle of the
LORD, which Moses had made in
the wilderness, and the altar of
burnt offering were at that time in
the high place at Gibeon; 30 but David could not go before it to inquire
of God, for he was afraid of the
sword of the angel of the LORD.

22 1 Then David said, "Here
shall be the house of the
LORD God and here the altar of
burnt offering for Israel."

21.12 2 Sam 24.13
21.13 Ps 51.1; 130.4,7
21.14 1 Chr 27.24
21.15 2 Sam 24.16
21.16 2 Chr 3.1
21.17 2 Sam 7.8; Ps 74.1
21.18 2 Chr 3.1
21.21 2 Chr 3.1
21.25 2 Sam 24.24
21.26 Lev 9.24; Judg 6.21
21.29 1 Chr 16.39; 1 Kings 3.4
22.1 1 Chr 21.18-29; 2 Chr 3.1

David Prepares to Build the Temple

2 David gave orders to gather together the aliens who were residing
in the land of Israel, and he set
stonecutters to prepare dressed
stones for building the house of
God. 3 David also provided great
stores of iron for nails for the doors
of the gates and for clamps, as well
as bronze in quantities beyond
weighing, 4 and cedar logs without
number—for the Sidonians and
Tyrians brought great quantities of
cedar to David. 5 For David said,
"My son Solomon is young and inexperienced, and the house that is
to be built for the LORD must be exceedingly magnificent, famous and
glorified throughout all lands; I will
therefore make preparation for it."
So David provided materials in
great quantity before his death.

David's Charge to Solomon and the Leaders

6 Then he called for his son Solomon and charged him to build a
house for the LORD, the God of Israel. 7 David said to Solomon, "My
son, I had planned to build a house
to the name of the LORD my God.
8 But the word of the LORD came to
me, saying, 'You have shed much
blood and have waged great wars;
you shall not build a house to my
name, because you have shed so
much blood in my sight on the
earth. 9 See, a son shall be born to
you; he shall be a man of peace. I
will give him peace from all his enemies on every side; for his name
shall be Solomon,[d] and I will give
peace[e] and quiet to Israel in his
days. 10 He shall build a house for
my name. He shall be a son to me,
and I will be a father to him, and I
will establish his royal throne in Israel forever.' 11 Now, my son, the
LORD be with you, so that you may
succeed in building the house of
the LORD your God, as he has spoken concerning you. 12 Only, may
the LORD grant you discretion and
understanding, so that when he
gives you charge over Israel you
may keep the law of the LORD your
God. 13 Then you will prosper if you
are careful to observe the statutes
and the ordinances that the LORD
commanded Moses for Israel. Be
strong and of good courage. Do not
be afraid or dismayed. 14 With great
pains I have provided for the house
of the LORD one hundred thousand
talents of gold, one million talents
of silver, and bronze and iron beyond weighing, for there is so much
of it; timber and stone too I have
provided. To these you must add
more. 15 You have an abundance of
workers: stonecutters, masons,
carpenters, and all kinds of artisans without number, skilled in
working 16 gold, silver, bronze, and
iron. Now begin the work, and the
LORD be with you."

17 David also commanded all
the leaders of Israel to help his son
Solomon, saying, 18 "Is not the LORD
your God with you? Has he not giv-
en you peace on every side? For he
has delivered the inhabitants of the
land into my hand; and the land is
subdued before the LORD and his
people. 19 Now set your mind and
heart to seek the LORD your God.
Go and build the sanctuary of the
LORD God so that the ark of the covenant of the LORD and the holy vessels of God may be brought into a
house built for the name of the
LORD."

Families of the Levites and Their Functions

23 When David was old and
full of days, he made his
son Solomon king over Israel.

2 David assembled all the leaders of Israel and the priests and the
Levites. 3 The Levites, thirty years
old and upward, were counted, and
the total was thirty-eight thousand.
4 "Twenty-four thousand of these,"
David said, "shall have charge of
the work in the house of the LORD,
six thousand shall be officers and
judges, 5 four thousand gatekeepers, and four thousand shall offer
praises to the LORD with the instruments that I have made for praise."
6 And David organized them in divi-

22.2 1 Kings 9.21; 5.17,18
22.3 1 Chr 29.2, 7; v. 14
22.4 1 Kings 5.6
22.5 1 Chr 29.1
22.7 2 Sam 7.2; 1 Chr 17.1; Deut 12.5, 11
22.8 1 Kings 5.3; 1 Chr 28.3
22.9 1 Kings 4.20, 25; 2 Sam 12.24, 25
22.10 2 Sam 7.13; 1 Chr 17.12, 13
22.11 v. 16
22.12 1 Kings 3.9-12; 2 Chr 1.10
22.13 1 Chr 28.7; Josh 1.6-9; 1 Chr 28.20
22.14 v. 3
22.16 v. 11
22.17 1 Chr 28.1-6
22.18 2 Sam 7.1; 1 Chr 23.25
22.19 1 Chr 28.9; 1 Kings 8.6; 2 Chr 5.7; v. 7
23.1 1 Kings 1.33-39; 1 Chr 29.28; 28.5
23.3 Num 4.3-49; v. 24
23.4 2 Chr 19.8
23.5 1 Chr 15.16
23.6 2 Chr 8.14; 29.25

[d] Heb *Shelomoh* [e] Heb *shalom*

sions corresponding to the sons of
Levi: Gershon,[f] Kohath, and Merari.
7 The sons of Gershon[g] were
Ladan and Shimei. 8 The sons of
Ladan: Jehiel the chief, Zetham,
and Joel, three. 9 The sons of Shimei: Shelomoth, Haziel, and Haran,
three. These were the heads of
families of Ladan. 10 And the sons
of Shimei: Jahath, Zina, Jeush, and
Beriah. These four were the sons of
Shimei. 11 Jahath was the chief,
and Zizah the second; but Jeush
and Beriah did not have many sons,
so they were enrolled as a single
family.
12 The sons of Kohath: Amram,
Izhar, Hebron, and Uzziel, four.
13 The sons of Amram: Aaron and
Moses. Aaron was set apart to consecrate the most holy things, so
that he and his sons forever should
make offerings before the LORD,
and minister to him and pronounce
blessings in his name forever; 14 but
as for Moses the man of God, his
sons were to be reckoned among
the tribe of Levi. 15 The sons of Moses: Gershom and Eliezer. 16 The
sons of Gershom: Shebuel the
chief. 17 The sons of Eliezer: Rehabiah the chief; Eliezer had no other
sons, but the sons of Rehabiah
were very numerous. 18 The sons of
Izhar: Shelomith the chief. 19 The
sons of Hebron: Jeriah the chief,
Amariah the second, Jahaziel the
third, and Jekameam the fourth.
20 The sons of Uzziel: Micah the
chief and Isshiah the second.
21 The sons of Merari: Mahli
and Mushi. The sons of Mahli: Eleazar and Kish. 22 Eleazar died having no sons, but only daughters;
their kindred, the sons of Kish,
married them. 23 The sons of Mushi: Mahli, Eder, and Jeremoth,
three.
24 These were the sons of Levi
by their ancestral houses, the
heads of families as they were enrolled according to the number of
the names of the individuals from
twenty years old and upward who
were to do the work for the service
of the house of the LORD. 25 For David said, "The LORD, the God of Israel, has given rest to his people; and
he resides in Jerusalem forever.
26 And so the Levites no longer
need to carry the tabernacle or any
of the things for its service"— 27 for
according to the last words of David these were the number of the
Levites from twenty years old and
upward— 28 "but their duty shall
be to assist the descendants of Aaron for the service of the house of
the LORD, having the care of the
courts and the chambers, the
cleansing of all that is holy, and
any work for the service of the
house of God; 29 to assist also with
the rows of bread, the choice flour
for the grain offering, the wafers of
unleavened bread, the baked offering, the offering mixed with oil,
and all measures of quantity or
size. 30 And they shall stand every
morning, thanking and praising the
LORD, and likewise at evening,
31 and whenever burnt offerings are
offered to the LORD on sabbaths,
new moons, and appointed festivals, according to the number required of them, regularly before
the LORD. 32 Thus they shall keep
charge of the tent of meeting and
the sanctuary, and shall attend the
descendants of Aaron, their kindred, for the service of the house of
the LORD."

Divisions of the Priests

24 The divisions of the descendants of Aaron were
these. The sons of Aaron: Nadab,
Abihu, Eleazar, and Ithamar. 2 But
Nadab and Abihu died before their
father, and had no sons; so Eleazar
and Ithamar became the priests.
3 Along with Zadok of the sons of
Eleazar, and Ahimelech of the sons
of Ithamar, David organized them
according to the appointed duties
in their service. 4 Since more chief
men were found among the sons of
Eleazar than among the sons of Ithamar, they organized them under
sixteen heads of ancestral houses

23.12 Ex 6.18 **23.13** Ex 6.20; 28.1; 30.6-10; Deut 21.5 **23.16** 1 Chr 26.24ff **23.21** 1 Chr 24.26ff **23.24** Num 10.17, 21; v. 3 **23.25** 1 Chr 22.18 **23.26** Num 4.5 **23.29** Lev 23.5-9; Ex 25.30; Lev 6.20; 2.4-7; 19.35 **23.31** Isa 1.13,14; Lev 23.24 **23.32** Num 1.53; 1 Chr 9.27; Num 3.6 **24.1** Ex 6.23 **24.2** Lev 10.2; Num 3.4

[f] Or *Gershom*; See 1 Chr 6.1, note, and 23.15 [g] Vg Compare Gk Syr: Heb *to the Gershonite*

of the sons of Eleazar, and eight of
the sons of Ithamar. 5 They organized them by lot, all alike, for
there were officers of the sanctuary
and officers of God among both the
sons of Eleazar and the sons of Ithamar. 6 The scribe Shemaiah son of
Nethanel, a Levite, recorded them
in the presence of the king, and the
officers, and Zadok the priest, and
Ahimelech son of Abiathar, and the
heads of ancestral houses of the
priests and of the Levites; one ancestral house being chosen for Eleazar and one chosen for Ithamar.
7 The first lot fell to Jehoiarib,
the second to Jedaiah, 8 the third to
Harim, the fourth to Seorim, 9 the
fifth to Malchijah, the sixth to Mijamin, 10 the seventh to Hakkoz, the
eighth to Abijah, 11 the ninth to
Jeshua, the tenth to Shecaniah,
12 the eleventh to Eliashib, the
twelfth to Jakim, 13 the thirteenth
to Huppah, the fourteenth to Je-
shebeab, 14 the fifteenth to Bilgah,
the sixteenth to Immer, 15 the seventeenth to Hezir, the eighteenth
to Happizzez, 16 the nineteenth to
Pethahiah, the twentieth to Jehez-
kel, 17 the twenty-first to Jachin,
the twenty-second to Gamul, 18 the
twenty-third to Delaiah, the
twenty-fourth to Maaziah. 19 These
had as their appointed duty in their
service to enter the house of the
LORD according to the procedure
established for them by their ancestor Aaron, as the LORD God of
Israel had commanded him.

Other Levites

20 And of the rest of the sons of
Levi: of the sons of Amram, Shubael; of the sons of Shubael, Jehdeiah. 21 Of Rehabiah: of the sons of
Rehabiah, Isshiah the chief. 22 Of
the Izharites, Shelomoth; of the
sons of Shelomoth, Jahath. 23 The
sons of Hebron:[h] Jeriah the
chief,[i] Amariah the second, Jahaziel the third, Jekameam the
fourth. 24 The sons of Uzziel, Micah; of the sons of Micah, Shamir.
25 The brother of Micah, Isshiah; of
the sons of Isshiah, Zechariah.
26 The sons of Merari: Mahli and
Mushi. The sons of Jaaziah:
Beno.[j] 27 The sons of Merari: of Jaaziah, Beno,[j] Shoham, Zaccur,
and Ibri. 28 Of Mahli: Eleazar, who
had no sons. 29 Of Kish, the sons of
Kish: Jerahmeel. 30 The sons of
Mushi: Mahli, Eder, and Jerimoth.
These were the sons of the Levites
according to their ancestral
houses. 31 These also cast lots corresponding to their kindred, the
descendants of Aaron, in the presence of King David, Zadok, Ahimelech, and the heads of ancestral
houses of the priests and of the Levites, the chief as well as the youngest brother.

The Temple Musicians

25 David and the officers of
the army also set apart for
the service the sons of Asaph, and
of Heman, and of Jeduthun, who
should prophesy with lyres, harps,
and cymbals. The list of those who
did the work and of their duties
was: 2 Of the sons of Asaph: Zaccur,
Joseph, Nethaniah, and Asarelah,
sons of Asaph, under the direction
of Asaph, who prophesied under
the direction of the king. 3 Of Jeduthun, the sons of Jeduthun: Gedaliah, Zeri, Jeshaiah, Shimei,[k]
Hashabiah, and Mattithiah, six,
under the direction of their father
Jeduthun, who prophesied with
the lyre in thanksgiving and praise
to the LORD. 4 Of Heman, the sons
of Heman: Bukkiah, Mattaniah,
Uzziel, Shebuel, and Jerimoth,
Hananiah, Hanani, Eliathah, Giddalti, and Romamti-ezer, Joshbekashah, Mallothi, Hothir, Mahazioth. 5 All these were the sons of
Heman the king's seer, according
to the promise of God to exalt him;
for God had given Heman fourteen
sons and three daughters. 6 They
were all under the direction of their
father for the music in the house of
the LORD with cymbals, harps, and
lyres for the service of the house of
God. Asaph, Jeduthun, and Heman

24.5 v. 31
24.10 Neh 12.4, 17; Lk 1.5
24.19 1 Chr 9.25
24.21 1 Chr 23.17
24.23 1 Chr 23.19
24.26 1 Chr 23.21
24.31 vv. 5,6
25.1 1 Chr 6.33, 39; 15.16
25.3 1 Chr 16.41, 42
25.4 1 Chr 6.33; v. 25
25.6 1 Chr 15.16, 19

[h] See 23.19: Heb lacks *Hebron* [i] See 23.19: Heb lacks *the chief* [j] Or *his son*: Meaning of Heb uncertain [k] One Ms: Gk: MT lacks *Shimei*

were under the order of the king.
7 They and their kindred, who were
trained in singing to the LORD, all of
whom were skillful, numbered two
hundred eighty-eight. 8 And they
cast lots for their duties, small and
great, teacher and pupil alike.
9 The first lot fell for Asaph to
Joseph; the second to Gedaliah, to
him and his brothers and his sons,
twelve; 10 the third to Zaccur, his
sons and his brothers, twelve; 11 the
fourth to Izri, his sons and his
brothers, twelve; 12 the fifth to
Nethaniah, his sons and his brothers, twelve; 13 the sixth to Bukkiah,
his sons and his brothers, twelve;
14 the seventh to Jesarelah,[l] his
sons and his brothers, twelve; 15 the
eighth to Jeshaiah, his sons and his
brothers, twelve; 16 the ninth to
Mattaniah, his sons and his brothers, twelve; 17 the tenth to Shimei,
his sons and his brothers, twelve;
18 the eleventh to Azarel, his sons
and his brothers, twelve; 19 the
twelfth to Hashabiah, his sons and
his brothers, twelve; 20 to the thirteenth, Shubael, his sons and his
brothers, twelve; 21 to the fourteenth, Mattithiah, his sons and
his brothers, twelve; 22 to the fifteenth, to Jeremoth, his sons and
his brothers, twelve; 23 to the sixteenth, to Hananiah, his sons and
his brothers, twelve; 24 to the seventeenth, to Joshbekashah, his
sons and his brothers, twelve; 25 to
the eighteenth, to Hanani, his sons
and his brothers, twelve; 26 to the
nineteenth, to Mallothi, his sons
and his brothers, twelve; 27 to the
twentieth, to Eliathah, his sons
and his brothers, twelve; 28 to the
twenty-first, to Hothir, his sons and
his brothers, twelve; 29 to the
twenty-second, to Giddalti, his
sons and his brothers, twelve; 30 to
the twenty-third, to Mahazioth, his
sons and his brothers, twelve; 31 to
the twenty-fourth, to Romamti-
ezer, his sons and his brothers,
twelve.

The Gatekeepers

26 As for the divisions of the
gatekeepers: of the Korahites, Meshelemiah son of Kore, of
the sons of Asaph. 2 Meshelemiah
had sons: Zechariah the firstborn,
Jediael the second, Zebadiah the
third, Jathniel the fourth, 3 Elam
the fifth, Jehohanan the sixth, Eliehoenai the seventh. 4 Obed-edom
had sons: Shemaiah the firstborn,
Jehozabad the second, Joah the
third, Sachar the fourth, Nethanel
the fifth, 5 Ammiel the sixth, Issachar the seventh, Peullethai the
eighth; for God blessed him. 6 Also
to his son Shemaiah sons were
born who exercised authority in
their ancestral houses, for they
were men of great ability. 7 The
sons of Shemaiah: Othni, Rephael,
Obed, and Elzabad, whose brothers were able men, Elihu and Sem-
achiah. 8 All these, sons of Obed-
edom with their sons and brothers,
were able men qualified for the service; sixty-two of Obed-edom.
9 Meshelemiah had sons and brothers, able men, eighteen. 10 Hosah,
of the sons of Merari, had sons:
Shimri the chief (for though he was
not the firstborn, his father made
him chief), 11 Hilkiah the second,
Tebaliah the third, Zechariah the
fourth: all the sons and brothers of
Hosah totaled thirteen.
12 These divisions of the gatekeepers, corresponding to their
leaders, had duties, just as their
kindred did, ministering in the
house of the LORD; 13 and they cast
lots by ancestral houses, small and
great alike, for their gates. 14 The
lot for the east fell to Shelemiah.
They cast lots also for his son Zechariah, a prudent counselor, and his
lot came out for the north. 15 Obed-
edom's came out for the south, and
to his sons was allotted the storehouse. 16 For Shuppim and Hosah
it came out for the west, at the gate
of Shallecheth on the ascending
road. Guard corresponded to
guard. 17 On the east there were six
Levites each day,[m] on the north
four each day, on the south four
each day, as well as two and two at

25.8 1 Chr 26.13
25.9 1 Chr 6.39
25.16 v. 4
25.23 v. 4
25.25 v. 4
26.1 v. 19
26.4 1 Chr 15.18
26.10 1 Chr 16.38
26.12 v. 1
26.13 1 Chr 24.5, 31; 25.8

[l] Or *Asarelah*; see 25.2 [m] Gk: Heb lacks *each day*

the storehouse; [18]and for the colonnade[n] on the west there were four at the road and two at the colonnade.[n] [19]These were the divisions of the gatekeepers among the Korahites and the sons of Merari.

The Treasurers, Officers, and Judges

20 And of the Levites, Ahijah had charge of the treasuries of the house of God and the treasuries of the dedicated gifts. [21]The sons of Ladan, the sons of the Gershonites belonging to Ladan, the heads of families belonging to Ladan the Gershonite: Jehieli.[o]

22 The sons of Jehieli, Zetham and his brother Joel, were in charge of the treasuries of the house of the LORD. [23]Of the Amramites, the Izharites, the Hebronites, and the Uzzielites: [24]Shebuel son of Gershom, son of Moses, was chief officer in charge of the treasuries. [25]His brothers: from Eliezer were his son Rehabiah, his son Jeshaiah, his son Joram, his son Zichri, and his son Shelomoth. [26]This Shelomoth and his brothers were in charge of all the treasuries of the dedicated gifts that King David, and the heads of families, and the officers of the thousands and the hundreds, and the commanders of the army, had dedicated. [27]From booty won in battles they dedicated gifts for the maintenance of the house of the LORD. [28]Also all that Samuel the seer, and Saul son of Kish, and Abner son of Ner, and Joab son of Zeruiah had dedicated—all dedicated gifts were in the care of Shelomoth[p] and his brothers.

29 Of the Izharites, Chenaniah and his sons were appointed to outside duties for Israel, as officers and judges. [30]Of the Hebronites, Hashabiah and his brothers, one thousand seven hundred men of ability, had the oversight of Israel west of the Jordan for all the work of the LORD and for the service of the king. [31]Of the Hebronites, Jerijah was chief of the Hebronites. (In the fortieth year of David's reign search was made, of whatever genealogy or family, and men of great ability among them were found at Jazer in Gilead.) [32]King David appointed him and his brothers, two thousand seven hundred men of ability, heads of families, to have the oversight of the Reubenites, the Gadites, and the half-tribe of the Manassites for everything pertaining to God and for the affairs of the king.

26.20 1 Chr 28.12 **26.24** 1 Chr 23.16 **26.25** 1 Chr 23.18 **26.26** 2 Sam 8.11 **26.28** 1 Sam 9.9 **26.29** Neh 11.16; 1 Chr 23.4 **26.30** 1 Chr 27.17 **26.31** 1 Chr 23.19 **26.32** 2 Chr 19.11 **27.2** 2 Sam 23.8-30; 1 Chr 11.11-31 **27.6** 1 Chr 11.22ff **27.7** 1 Chr 11.26 **27.9** 1 Chr 11.28

The Military Divisions

27 This is the list of the people of Israel, the heads of families, the commanders of the thousands and the hundreds, and their officers who served the king in all matters concerning the divisions that came and went, month after month throughout the year, each division numbering twenty-four thousand:

2 Jashobeam son of Zabdiel was in charge of the first division in the first month; in his division were twenty-four thousand. [3]He was a descendant of Perez, and was chief of all the commanders of the army for the first month. [4]Dodai the Ahohite was in charge of the division of the second month; Mikloth was the chief officer of his division. In his division were twenty-four thousand. [5]The third commander, for the third month, was Benaiah son of the priest Jehoiada, as chief; in his division were twenty-four thousand. [6]This is the Benaiah who was a mighty man of the Thirty and in command of the Thirty; his son Ammizabad was in charge of his division.[q] [7]Asahel brother of Joab was fourth, for the fourth month, and his son Zebadiah after him; in his division were twenty-four thousand. [8]The fifth commander, for the fifth month, was Shamhuth, the Izrahite; in his division were twenty-four thousand. [9]Sixth, for the sixth month, was Ira son of Ikkesh the Tekoite; in his di-

n Heb *parbar*: meaning uncertain
o The Hebrew text of verse 21 is confused
p Gk Compare 26.28: Heb *Shelomith*
q Gk Vg: Heb *Ammizabad was his division*

vision were twenty-four thousand.
10 Seventh, for the seventh month,
was Helez the Pelonite, of the
Ephraimites; in his division were
twenty-four thousand. 11 Eighth,
for the eighth month, was Sibbecai
the Hushathite, of the Zerahites; in
his division were twenty-four thousand. 12 Ninth, for the ninth month,
was Abiezer of Anathoth, a Benjaminite; in his division were twenty-
four thousand. 13 Tenth, for the
tenth month, was Maharai of Netophah, of the Zerahites; in his division were twenty-four thousand.
14 Eleventh, for the eleventh
month, was Benaiah of Pirathon, of
the Ephraimites; in his division
were twenty-four thousand.
15 Twelfth, for the twelfth month,
was Heldai the Netophathite, of
Othniel; in his division were
twenty-four thousand.

Leaders of Tribes

16 Over the tribes of Israel, for
the Reubenites, Eliezer son of
Zichri was chief officer; for the
Simeonites, Shephatiah son of Maacah; 17 for Levi, Hashabiah son of
Kemuel; for Aaron, Zadok; 18 for Judah, Elihu, one of David's brothers;
for Issachar, Omri son of Michael;
19 for Zebulun, Ishmaiah son of
Obadiah; for Naphtali, Jerimoth
son of Azriel; 20 for the Ephraimites, Hoshea son of Azaziah; for the
half-tribe of Manasseh, Joel son of
Pedaiah; 21 for the half-tribe of Manasseh in Gilead, Iddo son of Zechariah; for Benjamin, Jaasiel son of
Abner; 22 for Dan, Azarel son of Jeroham. These were the leaders of
the tribes of Israel. 23 David did not
count those below twenty years of
age, for the LORD had promised to
make Israel as numerous as the
stars of heaven. 24 Joab son of Zeruiah began to count them, but did
not finish; yet wrath came upon Israel for this, and the number was
not entered into the account of the
Annals of King David.

Other Civic Officials

25 Over the king's treasuries
was Azmaveth son of Adiel. Over
the treasuries in the country, in the
cities, in the villages and in the
towers, was Jonathan son of Uzziah. 26 Over those who did the work
of the field, tilling the soil, was Ezri
son of Chelub. 27 Over the vineyards was Shimei the Ramathite.
Over the produce of the vineyards
for the wine cellars was Zabdi the
Shiphmite. 28 Over the olive and
sycamore trees in the Shephelah
was Baal-hanan the Gederite. Over
the stores of oil was Joash. 29 Over
the herds that pastured in Sharon
was Shitrai the Sharonite. Over the
herds in the valleys was Shaphat
son of Adlai. 30 Over the camels was
Obil the Ishmaelite. Over the donkeys was Jehdeiah the Meronothite. Over the flocks was Jaziz the
Hagrite. 31 All these were stewards
of King David's property.

32 Jonathan, David's uncle, was
a counselor, being a man of understanding and a scribe; Jehiel son of
Hachmoni attended the king's
sons. 33 Ahithophel was the king's
counselor, and Hushai the Archite
was the king's friend. 34 After
Ahithophel came Jehoiada son of
Benaiah, and Abiathar. Joab was
commander of the king's army.

Solomon Instructed to Build the Temple

28 David assembled at Jerusalem all the officials of Isra-
el, the officials of the tribes, the officers of the divisions that served
the king, the commanders of the
thousands, the commanders of the
hundreds, the stewards of all the
property and cattle of the king and
his sons, together with the palace
officials, the mighty warriors, and
all the warriors. 2 Then King David
rose to his feet and said: "Hear me,
my brothers and my people. I had
planned to build a house of rest for
the ark of the covenant of the LORD,
for the footstool of our God; and I
made preparations for building.
3 But God said to me, 'You shall not
build a house for my name, for you
are a warrior and have shed blood.'
4 Yet the LORD God of Israel chose
me from all my ancestral house to

27.10 1 Chr 11.27
27.11 1 Chr 11.29
27.12 1 Chr 11.28
27.13 1 Chr 11.30
27.14 1 Chr 11.31
27.22 1 Chr 28.1
27.23 Gen 15.5
27.24 2 Sam 24.15; 1 Chr 21.7
27.28 1 Kings 10.27; 2 Chr 1.15
27.33 2 Sam 15.12, 32,37
27.34 1 Kings 1.7; 1 Chr 11.6
28.1 1 Chr 27.1-31; 11.10-47
28.2 2 Sam 7.2; 1 Chr 17.1, 2; Ps 132.7
28.3 2 Sam 7.5, 13; 1 Chr 22.8
28.4 1 Sam 16.6-13; 1 Chr 17.23, 27; 5.2; Gen 49.8-10

be king over Israel forever; for he
chose Judah as leader, and in the
house of Judah my father's house,
and among my father's sons he
took delight in making me king
over all Israel. 5 And of all my sons,
for the LORD has given me many, he
has chosen my son Solomon to sit
upon the throne of the kingdom of
the LORD over Israel. 6 He said to
me, 'It is your son Solomon who
shall build my house and my
courts, for I have chosen him to be
a son to me, and I will be a father
to him. 7 I will establish his kingdom forever if he continues reso-
lute in keeping my commandments
and my ordinances, as he is today.'
8 Now therefore in the sight of all
Israel, the assembly of the LORD,
and in the hearing of our God, observe and search out all the commandments of the LORD your God;
that you may possess this good
land, and leave it for an inheritance
to your children after you forever.
9 "And you, my son Solomon,
know the God of your father, and
serve him with single mind and
willing heart; for the LORD searches
every mind, and understands every
plan and thought. If you seek him,
he will be found by you; but if you
forsake him, he will abandon you
forever. 10 Take heed now, for the
LORD has chosen you to build a
house as the sanctuary; be strong,
and act."
11 Then David gave his son Solomon the plan of the vestibule of
the temple, and of its houses, its
treasuries, its upper rooms, and its
inner chambers, and of the room
for the mercy seat;[r] 12 and the plan
of all that he had in mind: for the
courts of the house of the LORD, all
the surrounding chambers, the
treasuries of the house of God, and
the treasuries for dedicated gifts;
13 for the divisions of the priests
and of the Levites, and all the work
of the service in the house of the
LORD; for all the vessels for the service in the house of the LORD, 14 the
weight of gold for all golden vessels
for each service, the weight of silver
vessels for each service, 15 the

28.5 1 Chr 3.1-9; 22.9,10
28.6 2 Sam 7.13, 14; 1 Chr 22.9, 10
28.7 1 Chr 22.13
28.9 Jer 9.24; 1 Chr 29.17-19; 1 Sam 16.7; 2 Chr 15.2; Jer 29.13
28.10 1 Chr 22.13
28.11 vv. 12,19; Ex 25.40
28.12 1 Chr 26.20
28.13 1 Chr 24.1; 23.6
28.15 Ex 25.31-39
28.18 Ex 30.1-10; 25.18-22
28.19 vv. 11,12
28.20 Josh 1.6,7, 9; 1 Chr 22.13; Josh 1.5
28.21 v. 13; Ex 35.25-35; 36.1,2
29.1 1 Chr 22.5; v. 19
29.2 1 Chr 22.3-5

weight of the golden lampstands
and their lamps, the weight of gold
for each lampstand and its lamps,
the weight of silver for a lampstand
and its lamps, according to the use
of each in the service, 16 the weight
of gold for each table for the rows
of bread, the silver for the silver tables, 17 and pure gold for the forks,
the basins, and the cups; for the
golden bowls and the weight of
each; for the silver bowls and the
weight of each; 18 for the altar of incense made of refined gold, and its
weight; also his plan for the golden
chariot of the cherubim that spread
their wings and covered the ark of
the covenant of the LORD.
19 "All this, in writing at the
LORD's direction, he made clear to
me—the plan of all the works."
20 David said further to his son
Solomon, "Be strong and of good
courage, and act. Do not be afraid
or dismayed; for the LORD God, my
God, is with you. He will not fail
you or forsake you, until all the
work for the service of the house of
the LORD is finished. 21 Here are the
divisions of the priests and the Levites for all the service of the house
of God; and with you in all the work
will be every volunteer who has
skill for any kind of service; also
the officers and all the people will
be wholly at your command."

Offerings for Building the Temple

29 King David said to the
whole assembly, "My son
Solomon, whom alone God has
chosen, is young and inexperienced, and the work is great; for
the temple[s] will not be for mortals
but for the LORD God. 2 So I have
provided for the house of my God,
so far as I was able, the gold for the
things of gold, the silver for the
things of silver, and the bronze for
the things of bronze, the iron for
the things of iron, and wood for the
things of wood, besides great quantities of onyx and stones for setting, antimony, colored stones, all
sorts of precious stones, and mar-

[r] Or *the cover* [s] Heb *fortress*

ble in abundance. 3 Moreover, in
addition to all that I have provided
for the holy house, I have a treasure
of my own of gold and silver, and
because of my devotion to the
house of my God I give it to the
house of my God: 4 three thousand
talents of gold, of the gold of Ophir,
and seven thousand talents of refined silver, for overlaying the walls
of the house, 5 and for all the work
to be done by artisans, gold for the
things of gold and silver for the
things of silver. Who then will offer
willingly, consecrating themselves
today to the LORD?"
6 Then the leaders of ancestral
houses made their freewill offerings, as did also the leaders of the
tribes, the commanders of the
thousands and of the hundreds,
and the officers over the king's
work. 7 They gave for the service of
the house of God five thousand talents and ten thousand darics of
gold, ten thousand talents of silver,
eighteen thousand talents of
bronze, and one hundred thousand
talents of iron. 8 Whoever had precious stones gave them to the treasury of the house of the LORD, into
the care of Jehiel the Gershonite.
9 Then the people rejoiced because
these had given willingly, for with
single mind they had offered freely
to the LORD; King David also rejoiced greatly.

David's Praise to God

10 Then David blessed the LORD
in the presence of all the assembly;
David said: "Blessed are you,
O LORD, the God of our ancestor Israel, forever and ever. 11 Yours,
O LORD, are the greatness, the power, the glory, the victory, and the
majesty; for all that is in the heavens and on the earth is yours; yours
is the kingdom, O LORD, and you
are exalted as head above all.
12 Riches and honor come from
you, and you rule over all. In your
hand are power and might; and it is
in your hand to make great and to
give strength to all. 13 And now, our
God, we give thanks to you and
praise your glorious name.

29.4 1 Chr 22.14; 1 Kings 9.28
29.6 1 Chr 27.1; 28.1; 27.25ff
29.7 Ezra 2.69; Neh 7.70
29.8 1 Chr 26.21
29.9 1 Kings 8.61; 2 Cor 9.7
29.11 Mt 6.13; 1 Tim 1.17; Rev 5.13
29.12 2 Chr 1.12; Rom 11.36
29.15 Lev 25.23; Ps 39.12; Heb 11.13; 1 Pet 2.11; Job 14.2
29.17 1 Chr 28.9; Prov 11.20
29.19 1 Chr 28.9; Ps 72.1; v. 2; 1 Chr 22.14
29.21 1 Kings 8.62, 63
29.22 1 Chr 23.1; 1 Kings 1.33-39

14 "But who am I, and what is
my people, that we should be able
to make this freewill offering? For
all things come from you, and of
your own have we given you. 15 For
we are aliens and transients before
you, as were all our ancestors; our
days on the earth are like a shadow,
and there is no hope. 16 O LORD our
God, all this abundance that we
have provided for building you a
house for your holy name comes
from your hand and is all your own.
17 I know, my God, that you search
the heart, and take pleasure in uprightness; in the uprightness of my
heart I have freely offered all these
things, and now I have seen your
people, who are present here, offering freely and joyously to you.
18 O LORD, the God of Abraham,
Isaac, and Israel, our ancestors,
keep forever such purposes and
thoughts in the hearts of your people, and direct their hearts toward
you. 19 Grant to my son Solomon
that with single mind he may keep
your commandments, your decrees, and your statutes, performing all of them, and that he may
build the temple[t] for which I have
made provision."
20 Then David said to the whole
assembly, "Bless the LORD your
God." And all the assembly blessed
the LORD, the God of their ancestors, and bowed their heads and
prostrated themselves before the
LORD and the king. 21 On the next
day they offered sacrifices and
burnt offerings to the LORD, a thousand bulls, a thousand rams, and a
thousand lambs, with their libations, and sacrifices in abundance
for all Israel; 22 and they ate and
drank before the LORD on that day
with great joy.

Solomon Anointed King

They made David's son Solomon
king a second time; they anointed
him as the LORD's prince, and Zadok as priest. 23 Then Solomon sat
on the throne of the LORD, succeeding his father David as king; he
prospered, and all Israel obeyed

[t] Heb *fortress*

him. [24]All the leaders and the
mighty warriors, and also all the
sons of King David, pledged their
allegiance to King Solomon. [25]The
LORD highly exalted Solomon in the
sight of all Israel, and bestowed
upon him such royal majesty as
had not been on any king before
him in Israel.

Summary of David's Reign

26 Thus David son of Jesse
reigned over all Israel. [27]The period
that he reigned over Israel was forty
years; he reigned seven years in Hebron, and thirty-three years in Jerusalem. [28]He died in a good old
age, full of days, riches, and honor;
and his son Solomon succeeded
him. [29]Now the acts of King David,
from first to last, are written in the
records of the seer Samuel, and in
the records of the prophet Nathan,
and in the records of the seer Gad,
[30]with accounts of all his rule and
his might and of the events that befell him and Israel and all the kingdoms of the earth.

29.25 2 Chr 1.1, 12; 1 Kings 3.13
29.26 1 Chr 18.14
29.27 2 Sam 5.4, 5; 1 Kings 2.11
29.28 Gen 15.15; 25.8; 1 Chr 23.1
29.30 Dan 2.21; 4.23,25

2 Chronicles

Title and Background

See Introduction to 1 Chronicles.

Author and Date of Writing

See Introduction to 1 Chronicles.

Theme and Message

2 Chronicles continues the history of David's royal line. This book, like 1 Chronicles, shows that one's relationship to God was most important, for the author measured the kings of Judah on the basis of their faithfulness to God and his law. The reigns of evil kings receive only a brief account, while the reigns of good kings are described in more detail.

Outline

I. The Reign of Solomon (1.1–9.31)
II. The Kings of Judah (10.1–36.14)
III. The Destruction of Jerusalem (36.15-23)

Solomon Requests Wisdom

1 Solomon son of David established himself in his kingdom;
the LORD his God was with him and
made him exceedingly great.
2 Solomon summoned all Israel,
the commanders of the thousands
and of the hundreds, the judges,
and all the leaders of all Israel, the
heads of families. 3 Then Solomon,
and the whole assembly with him,
went to the high place that was at
Gibeon; for God's tent of meeting,
which Moses the servant of the
LORD had made in the wilderness,
was there. 4 (But David had brought
the ark of God up from Kiriath-
jearim to the place that David had
prepared for it; for he had pitched
a tent for it in Jerusalem.) 5 Moreover the bronze altar that Bezalel
son of Uri, son of Hur, had made,
was there in front of the tabernacle
of the LORD. And Solomon and the
assembly inquired at it. 6 Solomon
went up there to the bronze altar
before the LORD, which was at the
tent of meeting, and offered a thousand burnt offerings on it.
7 That night God appeared to
Solomon, and said to him, "Ask
what I should give you." 8 Solomon
said to God, "You have shown great
and steadfast love to my father David, and have made me succeed
him as king. 9 O LORD God, let your
promise to my father David now be
fulfilled, for you have made me
king over a people as numerous as
the dust of the earth. 10 Give me
now wisdom and knowledge to go
out and come in before this people,
for who can rule this great people
of yours?" 11 God answered Solomon, "Because this was in your
heart, and you have not asked for
possessions, wealth, honor, or the
life of those who hate you, and
have not even asked for long life,
but have asked for wisdom and
knowledge for yourself that you
may rule my people over whom I
have made you king, 12 wisdom and
knowledge are granted to you. I will
also give you riches, possessions,
and honor, such as none of the
kings had who were before you,
and none after you shall have the
like." 13 So Solomon came from[a]

1.1 1 Kings 2.12, 46; Gen 39.2; 1 Chr 29.25
1.2 1 Chr 28.1
1.3ff 1 Kings 3.4; Ex 36.8
1.4 2 Sam 6.2, 17; 1 Chr 15.1
1.5 Ex 38.1,2
1.6 1 Kings 3.4
1.7 1 Kings 3.5, 6
1.8 1 Chr 28.5
1.9 1 Kings 3.7, 8
1.10 1 Kings 3.9
1.11 1 Kings 3.11-13
1.12 1 Chr 29.25; 2 Chr 9.22

[a] Gk Vg: Heb *to*

the high place at Gibeon, from the
tent of meeting, to Jerusalem. And
he reigned over Israel.

Solomon's Military and Commercial Activity

14 Solomon gathered together
chariots and horses; he had fourteen hundred chariots and twelve
thousand horses, which he stationed in the chariot cities and
with the king in Jerusalem. 15 The
king made silver and gold as common in Jerusalem as stone, and he
made cedar as plentiful as the sycamore of the Shephelah. 16 Solomon's horses were imported from
Egypt and Kue; the king's traders
received them from Kue at the pre-
vailing price. 17 They imported from
Egypt, and then exported, a chariot
for six hundred shekels of silver,
and a horse for one hundred fifty;
so through them these were exported to all the kings of the Hittites and the kings of Aram.

Preparations for Building the Temple

2[b] Solomon decided to build a
temple for the name of the
LORD, and a royal palace for himself. 2[c] Solomon conscripted seventy thousand laborers and eighty
thousand stonecutters in the hill
country, with three thousand six
hundred to oversee them.

Alliance with Huram of Tyre

3 Solomon sent word to King
Huram of Tyre: "Once you dealt
with my father David and sent him
cedar to build himself a house to
live in. 4 I am now about to build a
house for the name of the LORD my
God and dedicate it to him for offering fragrant incense before him,
and for the regular offering of the
rows of bread, and for burnt offerings morning and evening, on the
sabbaths and the new moons and
the appointed festivals of the LORD
our God, as ordained forever for Israel. 5 The house that I am about to
build will be great, for our God is
greater than other gods. 6 But who
is able to build him a house, since
heaven, even highest heaven, cannot contain him? Who am I to build
a house for him, except as a place
to make offerings before him? 7 So
now send me an artisan skilled to
work in gold, silver, bronze, and
iron, and in purple, crimson, and
blue fabrics, trained also in engraving, to join the skilled workers who
are with me in Judah and Jerusalem, whom my father David provided. 8 Send me also cedar, cypress,
and algum timber from Lebanon,
for I know that your servants are
skilled in cutting Lebanon timber.
My servants will work with your
servants 9 to prepare timber for me
in abundance, for the house I am
about to build will be great and
wonderful. 10 I will provide for your
servants, those who cut the timber,
twenty thousand cors of crushed
wheat, twenty thousand cors of
barley, twenty thousand baths[d] of
wine, and twenty thousand baths
of oil."

11 Then King Huram of Tyre answered in a letter that he sent to
Solomon, "Because the LORD loves
his people he has made you king
over them." 12 Huram also said,
"Blessed be the LORD God of Israel,
who made heaven and earth, who
has given King David a wise son,
endowed with discretion and understanding, who will build a temple for the LORD, and a royal palace
for himself.

13 "I have dispatched Huram-
abi, a skilled artisan, endowed with
understanding, 14 the son of one of
the Danite women, his father a Tyrian. He is trained to work in gold,
silver, bronze, iron, stone, and
wood, and in purple, blue, and
crimson fabrics and fine linen, and
to do all sorts of engraving and execute any design that may be assigned him, with your artisans, the
artisans of my lord, your father David. 15 Now, as for the wheat, barley, oil, and wine, of which my lord
has spoken, let him send them to
his servants. 16 We will cut whatever timber you need from Lebanon,

1.14ff 1 Kings 4.26; 10.26-29; 2 Chr 9.25
1.15 1 Kings 10.27; 2 Chr 9.27
1.16 1 Kings 10.28, 29; 2 Chr 9.28
2.1 1 Kings 5.5
2.2 v. 18; 1 Kings 5.15, 16
2.3 1 Kings 5.2-11; 1 Chr 14.1
2.4 v. 1; Ex 30.7; 25.30; Num 28.9, 10
2.5 1 Chr 16.25; Ps 135.5
2.6 1 Kings 8.27; 2 Chr 6.18
2.7 vv. 13,14; 1 Chr 22.15
2.8 2 Chr 9.10, 11
2.10 1 Kings 5.11
2.11 1 Kings 10.9; 2 Chr 9.8
2.12 1 Kings 5.7; Ps 33.6; 102.25
2.14 1 Kings 7.13, 14
2.15 v. 10
2.16 1 Kings 5.8, 9

[b] Ch 1.18 in Heb [c] Ch 2.1 in Heb [d] A Hebrew measure of volume

and bring it to you as rafts by sea to
Joppa; you will take it up to Jerusalem."
17 Then Solomon took a census
of all the aliens who were residing
in the land of Israel, after the census that his father David had taken;
and there were found to be one
hundred fifty-three thousand six
hundred. 18 Seventy thousand of
them he assigned as laborers,
eighty thousand as stonecutters in
the hill country, and three thousand six hundred as overseers to
make the people work.

Solomon Builds the Temple

3 Solomon began to build the
house of the LORD in Jerusalem on Mount Moriah, where the
LORD had appeared to his father David, at the place that David had
designated, on the threshing floor
of Ornan the Jebusite. 2 He began
to build on the second day of the
second month of the fourth year of
his reign. 3 These are Solomon's
measurements[e] for building the
house of God: the length, in cubits
of the old standard, was sixty cubits, and the width twenty cubits.
4 The vestibule in front of the nave
of the house was twenty cubits
long, across the width of the
house;[f] and its height was one
hundred twenty cubits. He overlaid
it on the inside with pure gold.
5 The nave he lined with cypress,
covered it with fine gold, and made
palms and chains on it. 6 He
adorned the house with settings of
precious stones. The gold was gold
from Parvaim. 7 So he lined the
house with gold—its beams, its
thresholds, its walls, and its doors;
and he carved cherubim on the
walls.
8 He made the most holy place;
its length, corresponding to the
width of the house, was twenty cubits, and its width was twenty cubits; he overlaid it with six hundred
talents of fine gold. 9 The weight of
the nails was fifty shekels of gold.
He overlaid the upper chambers
with gold.
10 In the most holy place he
made two carved cherubim and
overlaid[g] them with gold. 11 The
wings of the cherubim together extended twenty cubits: one wing of
the one, five cubits long, touched
the wall of the house, and its other
wing, five cubits long, touched the
wing of the other cherub; 12 and of
this cherub, one wing, five cubits
long, touched the wall of the
house, and the other wing, also five
cubits long, was joined to the wing
of the first cherub. 13 The wings of
these cherubim extended twenty
cubits; the cherubim[h] stood on
their feet, facing the nave. 14 And
Solomon[i] made the curtain of
blue and purple and crimson fabrics and fine linen, and worked
cherubim into it.
15 In front of the house he made
two pillars thirty-five cubits high,
with a capital of five cubits on the
top of each. 16 He made encircling[j]
chains and put them on the tops of
the pillars; and he made one hundred pomegranates, and put them
on the chains. 17 He set up the pillars in front of the temple, one on
the right, the other on the left; the
one on the right he called Jachin,
and the one on the left, Boaz.

Furnishings of the Temple

4 He made an altar of bronze,
twenty cubits long, twenty cubits wide, and ten cubits high.
2 Then he made the molten sea; it
was round, ten cubits from rim to
rim, and five cubits high. A line of
thirty cubits would encircle it completely. 3 Under it were panels all
around, each of ten cubits, surrounding the sea; there were two
rows of panels, cast when it was
cast. 4 It stood on twelve oxen,
three facing north, three facing
west, three facing south, and three
facing east; the sea was set on
them. The hindquarters of each
were toward the inside. 5 Its thickness was a handbreadth; its rim
was made like the rim of a cup, like

2.17 1 Chr 22.2
2.18 v. 2
3.1 1 Kings 6.1ff; 1 Chr 21.18
3.5 1 Kings 6.17
3.7 1 Kings 6.20-22,29-35
3.8 1 Kings 6.16
3.10 1 Kings 6.23-28
3.14 Ex 26.31; Heb 9.3
3.15 1 Kings 7.15-20
3.17 1 Kings 7.21
4.1 Ex 27.1,2; 2 Kings 16.14
4.2 1 Kings 7.23
4.3 1 Kings 7.24-26
4.5 1 Kings 7.26

[e] Syr: Heb *foundations* [f] Compare 1 Kings 6.3: Meaning of Heb uncertain [g] Heb *they overlaid* [h] Heb *they* [i] Heb *he*
[j] Cn: Heb *in the inner sanctuary*

the flower of a lily; it held three
thousand baths.[k] 6 He also made
ten basins in which to wash, and
set five on the right side, and five
on the left. In these they were to
rinse what was used for the burnt
offering. The sea was for the priests
to wash in.
7 He made ten golden lampstands as prescribed, and set them
in the temple, five on the south
side and five on the north. 8 He also
made ten tables and placed them
in the temple, five on the right side
and five on the left. And he made
one hundred basins of gold. 9 He
made the court of the priests, and
the great court, and doors for the
court; he overlaid their doors with
bronze. 10 He set the sea at the
southeast corner of the house.
11 And Huram made the pots,
the shovels, and the basins. Thus
Huram finished the work that he
did for King Solomon on the house
of God: 12 the two pillars, the bowls,
and the two capitals on the top of
the pillars; and the two latticeworks to cover the two bowls of the
capitals that were on the top of the
pillars; 13 the four hundred pomegranates for the two latticeworks,
two rows of pomegranates for each
latticework, to cover the two bowls
of the capitals that were on the pillars. 14 He made the stands, the basins on the stands, 15 the one sea,
and the twelve oxen underneath it.
16 The pots, the shovels, the forks,
and all the equipment for these
Huram-abi made of burnished
bronze for King Solomon for the
house of the LORD. 17 In the plain of
the Jordan the king cast them, in
the clay ground between Succoth
and Zeredah. 18 Solomon made all
these things in great quantities, so
that the weight of the bronze was
not determined.
19 So Solomon made all the
things that were in the house of
God: the golden altar, the tables for
the bread of the Presence, 20 the
lampstands and their lamps of pure
gold to burn before the inner sanctuary, as prescribed; 21 the flowers,
the lamps, and the tongs, of purest
gold; 22 the snuffers, basins, ladles,
and firepans, of pure gold. As for
the entrance to the temple: the inner doors to the most holy place
and the doors of the nave of the
temple were of gold.

5 Thus all the work that Solomon did for the house of the
LORD was finished. Solomon
brought in the things that his father David had dedicated, and
stored the silver, the gold, and all
the vessels in the treasuries of the
house of God.

The Ark Brought into the Temple

2 Then Solomon assembled the
elders of Israel and all the heads of
the tribes, the leaders of the ancestral houses of the people of Israel,
in Jerusalem, to bring up the ark of
the covenant of the LORD out of the
city of David, which is Zion. 3 And
all the Israelites assembled before
the king at the festival that is in the
seventh month. 4 And all the elders
of Israel came, and the Levites carried the ark. 5 So they brought up
the ark, the tent of meeting, and all
the holy vessels that were in the
tent; the priests and the Levites
brought them up. 6 King Solomon
and all the congregation of Israel,
who had assembled before him,
were before the ark, sacrificing so
many sheep and oxen that they
could not be numbered or counted.
7 Then the priests brought the ark
of the covenant of the LORD to its
place, in the inner sanctuary of the
house, in the most holy place, underneath the wings of the cherubim. 8 For the cherubim spread out
their wings over the place of the
ark, so that the cherubim made a
covering above the ark and its
poles. 9 The poles were so long that
the ends of the poles were seen
from the holy place in front of the
inner sanctuary; but they could not
be seen from outside; they are
there to this day. 10 There was nothing in the ark except the two tablets that Moses put there at Horeb,

[k] A Hebrew measure of volume

4.6 1 Kings 7.38
4.7 1 Kings 7.49; Ex 25.31,40
4.8 1 Kings 7.48
4.9 1 Kings 6.36; 2 Kings 21.5
4.10 1 Kings 7.39
4.11 1 Kings 7.40
4.12 1 Kings 7.41
4.13 1 Kings 7.20
4.14 1 Kings 7.27
4.16 1 Kings 7.14
4.17 1 Kings 7.46
4.18 1 Kings 7.47
4.19 1 Kings 7.48-50; Ex 25.30
4.20 Ex 25.31-37
5.1 1 Kings 7.51
5.2 1 Kings 8.1-9; 2 Sam 6.12
5.4 v. 7
5.9 1 Kings 8.8, 9
5.10 Deut 10.2-5; Heb 9.4

where the LORD made a covenant[l]
with the people of Israel after they
came out of Egypt.
11 Now when the priests came
out of the holy place (for all the
priests who were present had sanctified themselves, without regard
to their divisions, 12 and all the levitical singers, Asaph, Heman, and
Jeduthun, their sons and kindred,
arrayed in fine linen, with cymbals,
harps, and lyres, stood east of the
altar with one hundred twenty
priests who were trumpeters). 13 It
was the duty of the trumpeters and
singers to make themselves heard
in unison in praise and thanksgiving to the LORD, and when the song
was raised, with trumpets and cymbals and other musical instruments, in praise to the LORD,
"For he is good,
for his steadfast love
endures forever,"
the house, the house of the LORD,
was filled with a cloud, 14 so that
the priests could not stand to minister because of the cloud; for the
glory of the LORD filled the house of
God.

Dedication of the Temple

6 Then Solomon said, "The
LORD has said that he would
reside in thick darkness. 2 I have
built you an exalted house, a place
for you to reside in forever."
3 Then the king turned around
and blessed all the assembly of Israel, while all the assembly of Israel stood. 4 And he said, "Blessed be
the LORD, the God of Israel, who
with his hand has fulfilled what he
promised with his mouth to my father David, saying, 5 'Since the day
that I brought my people out of the
land of Egypt, I have not chosen a
city from any of the tribes of Israel
in which to build a house, so that
my name might be there, and I
chose no one as ruler over my people Israel; 6 but I have chosen Jerusalem in order that my name may
be there, and I have chosen David
to be over my people Israel.' 7 My
father David had it in mind to build
a house for the name of the LORD,

5.11 1 Chr 24.1-5
5.12 1 Chr 25.1-4; 15.24
5.13 2 Chr 7.3; 1 Chr 16.34, 42
5.14 1 Kings 8.11; 2 Chr 7.2
6.1 1 Kings 8.12-50
6.6 2 Chr 12.13; 1 Chr 28.4
6.7 1 Chr 28.2
6.11 2 Chr 5.10
6.12 1 Kings 8.22
6.13 1 Kings 8.54
6.14 Ex 15.11; Deut 7.9
6.15 1 Chr 22.9, 10
6.16 2 Sam 7.12, 16; 1 Kings 2.4; 2 Chr 7.18
6.18 2 Chr 2.6

the God of Israel. 8 But the LORD
said to my father David, 'You did
well to consider building a house
for my name; 9 nevertheless you
shall not build the house, but your
son who shall be born to you shall
build the house for my name.'
10 Now the LORD has fulfilled his
promise that he made; for I have
succeeded my father David, and sit
on the throne of Israel, as the LORD
promised, and have built the house
for the name of the LORD, the God
of Israel. 11 There I have set the ark,
in which is the covenant of the
LORD that he made with the people
of Israel."

Solomon's Prayer of Dedication

12 Then Solomon[m] stood before the altar of the LORD in the
presence of the whole assembly of
Israel, and spread out his hands.
13 Solomon had made a bronze
platform five cubits long, five cubits wide, and three cubits high,
and had set it in the court; and he
stood on it. Then he knelt on his
knees in the presence of the whole
assembly of Israel, and spread out
his hands toward heaven. 14 He
said, "O LORD, God of Israel, there
is no God like you, in heaven or on
earth, keeping covenant in steadfast love with your servants who
walk before you with all their
heart— 15 you who have kept for
your servant, my father David, what
you promised to him. Indeed, you
promised with your mouth and this
day have fulfilled with your hand.
16 Therefore, O LORD, God of Israel,
keep for your servant, my father
David, that which you promised
him, saying, 'There shall never fail
you a successor before me to sit on
the throne of Israel, if only your
children keep to their way, to walk
in my law as you have walked before me.' 17 Therefore, O LORD, God
of Israel, let your word be confirmed, which you promised to
your servant David.
18 "But will God indeed reside
with mortals on earth? Even heav-
en and the highest heaven cannot

l Heb lacks *a covenant* m Heb *he*

contain you, how much less this
house that I have built! 19 Regard
your servant's prayer and his plea,
O LORD my God, heeding the cry
and the prayer that your servant
prays to you. 20 May your eyes be
open day and night toward this
house, the place where you promised to set your name, and may you
heed the prayer that your servant
prays toward this place. 21 And hear
the plea of your servant and of your
people Israel, when they pray toward this place; may you hear from
heaven your dwelling place; hear
and forgive.
22 "If someone sins against another and is required to take an
oath and comes and swears before
your altar in this house, 23 may you
hear from heaven, and act, and
judge your servants, repaying the
guilty by bringing their conduct on
their own head, and vindicating
those who are in the right by rewarding them in accordance with
their righteousness.
24 "When your people Israel,
having sinned against you, are defeated before an enemy but turn
again to you, confess your name,
pray and plead with you in this
house, 25 may you hear from heav-
en, and forgive the sin of your people Israel, and bring them again to
the land that you gave to them and
to their ancestors.
26 "When heaven is shut up and
there is no rain because they have
sinned against you, and then they
pray toward this place, confess
your name, and turn from their sin,
because you punish them, 27 may
you hear in heaven, forgive the sin
of your servants, your people Israel,
when you teach them the good way
in which they should walk; and
send down rain upon your land,
which you have given to your people as an inheritance.
28 "If there is famine in the
land, if there is plague, blight, mildew, locust, or caterpillar; if their
enemies besiege them in any of the
settlements of the lands; whatever
suffering, whatever sickness there
is; 29 whatever prayer, whatever

6.21 Mic 7.18
6.22 Mt 5.33
6.24 2 Chr 7.14
6.26 1 Kings 17.1
6.28 2 Chr 20.9
6.30 1 Sam 16.7; 1 Chr 28.9
6.32 Josh 12.20; Acts 8.27
6.33 2 Chr 7.14
6.36 Job 15.14-16; Jas 3.2; 1 Jn 1.8-10
6.37 2 Chr 7.14

plea from any individual or from all
your people Israel, all knowing
their own suffering and their own
sorrows so that they stretch out
their hands toward this house;
30 may you hear from heaven, your
dwelling place, forgive, and render
to all whose heart you know, according to all their ways, for only
you know the human heart. 31 Thus
may they fear you and walk in your
ways all the days that they live in
the land that you gave to our ancestors.
32 "Likewise when foreigners,
who are not of your people Israel,
come from a distant land because
of your great name, and your
mighty hand, and your outstretched arm, when they come
and pray toward this house, 33 may
you hear from heaven your dwelling place, and do whatever the foreigners ask of you, in order that all
the peoples of the earth may know
your name and fear you, as do your
people Israel, and that they may
know that your name has been invoked on this house that I have
built.
34 "If your people go out to battle against their enemies, by whatever way you shall send them, and
they pray to you toward this city
that you have chosen and the
house that I have built for your
name, 35 then hear from heaven
their prayer and their plea, and
maintain their cause.
36 "If they sin against you—for
there is no one who does not sin—
and you are angry with them and
give them to an enemy, so that they
are carried away captive to a land
far or near; 37 then if they come to
their senses in the land to which
they have been taken captive, and
repent, and plead with you in the
land of their captivity, saying, 'We
have sinned, and have done wrong;
we have acted wickedly'; 38 if they
repent with all their heart and soul
in the land of their captivity, to
which they were taken captive, and
pray toward their land, which you
gave to their ancestors, the city
that you have chosen, and the

house that I have built for your
name, 39 then hear from heaven
your dwelling place their prayer
and their pleas, maintain their
cause and forgive your people who
have sinned against you. 40 Now,
O my God, let your eyes be open
and your ears attentive to prayer
from this place.

41 "Now rise up, O LORD God,
and go to your resting
place,
you and the ark of your
might.
Let your priests, O LORD God,
be clothed with
salvation,
and let your faithful rejoice
in your goodness.
42 O LORD God, do not reject
your anointed one.
Remember your steadfast
love for your servant
David."

Solomon Dedicates the Temple

7 When Solomon had ended his
prayer, fire came down from
heaven and consumed the burnt
offering and the sacrifices; and the
glory of the LORD filled the temple.
2 The priests could not enter the
house of the LORD, because the glory of the LORD filled the LORD's
house. 3 When all the people of Israel saw the fire come down and
the glory of the LORD on the temple,
they bowed down on the pavement
with their faces to the ground, and
worshiped and gave thanks to the
LORD, saying,

"For he is good,
for his steadfast love
endures forever."

4 Then the king and all the people offered sacrifice before the
LORD. 5 King Solomon offered as a
sacrifice twenty-two thousand
oxen and one hundred twenty
thousand sheep. So the king and
all the people dedicated the house
of God. 6 The priests stood at their
posts; the Levites also, with the instruments for music to the LORD
that King David had made for giving thanks to the LORD—for his
steadfast love endures forever—

6.40 2 Chr 7.15; Ps 17.1
6.41 Ps 132.8-10; 1 Chr 28.2
7.1 1 Kings 8.54; 18.24,38; 2 Chr 5.13, 14
7.2 Deut 12.5, 11
7.3 2 Chr 5.13; Ps 136.1; 1 Chr 16.41
7.4 1 Kings 8.62, 63
7.6 1 Chr 15.16-21; 2 Chr 5.12
7.7 1 Kings 8.64-66
7.8 1 Kings 8.65
7.9 Lev 23.36
7.10 1 Kings 8.66
7.11 1 Kings 9.1-9
7.13 2 Chr 6.26-28
7.14 2 Chr 6.27, 30,37-39
7.15 2 Chr 6.40
7.16 1 Kings 9.3; 2 Chr 6.6; v. 12

whenever David offered praises by
their ministry. Opposite them the
priests sounded trumpets; and all
Israel stood.
7 Solomon consecrated the
middle of the court that was in
front of the house of the LORD; for
there he offered the burnt offerings
and the fat of the offerings of well-
being because the bronze altar Solomon had made could not hold the
burnt offering and the grain offering and the fat parts.
8 At that time Solomon held the
festival for seven days, and all Israel with him, a very great congregation, from Lebo-hamath to the
Wadi of Egypt. 9 On the eighth day
they held a solemn assembly; for
they had observed the dedication
of the altar seven days and the festival seven days. 10 On the twenty-
third day of the seventh month he
sent the people away to their
homes, joyful and in good spirits
because of the goodness that the
LORD had shown to David and to
Solomon and to his people Israel.
11 Thus Solomon finished the
house of the LORD and the king's
house; all that Solomon had
planned to do in the house of the
LORD and in his own house he successfully accomplished.

God's Second Appearance to Solomon

12 Then the LORD appeared to
Solomon in the night and said to
him: "I have heard your prayer, and
have chosen this place for myself
as a house of sacrifice. 13 When I
shut up the heavens so that there is
no rain, or command the locust to
devour the land, or send pestilence
among my people, 14 if my people
who are called by my name humble
themselves, pray, seek my face,
and turn from their wicked ways,
then I will hear from heaven, and
will forgive their sin and heal their
land. 15 Now my eyes will be open
and my ears attentive to the prayer
that is made in this place. 16 For
now I have chosen and consecrated
this house so that my name may be
there forever; my eyes and my heart

will be there for all time. 17 As for
you, if you walk before me, as your
father David walked, doing according to all that I have commanded
you and keeping my statutes and
my ordinances, 18 then I will establish your royal throne, as I made
covenant with your father David
saying, 'You shall never lack a successor to rule over Israel.'
19 "But if you[n] turn aside and
forsake my statutes and my commandments that I have set before
you, and go and serve other gods
and worship them, 20 then I will
pluck you[o] up from the land that I
have given you;[o] and this house,
which I have consecrated for my
name, I will cast out of my sight,
and will make it a proverb and a
byword among all peoples. 21 And
regarding this house, now exalted,
everyone passing by will be astonished, and say, 'Why has the LORD
done such a thing to this land and
to this house?' 22 Then they will
say, 'Because they abandoned the
LORD the God of their ancestors
who brought them out of the land
of Egypt, and they adopted other
gods, and worshiped them and
served them; therefore he has
brought all this calamity upon
them.' "

Various Activities of Solomon

8 At the end of twenty years,
during which Solomon had
built the house of the LORD and his
own house, 2 Solomon rebuilt the
cities that Huram had given to him,
and settled the people of Israel in
them.
3 Solomon went to Hamath-
zobah, and captured it. 4 He built
Tadmor in the wilderness and all
the storage towns that he built in
Hamath. 5 He also built Upper
Beth-horon and Lower Beth-horon,
fortified cities, with walls, gates,
and bars, 6 and Baalath, as well as
all Solomon's storage towns, and
all the towns for his chariots, the
towns for his cavalry, and whatever
Solomon desired to build, in Jerusalem, in Lebanon, and in all the
land of his dominion. 7 All the people who were left of the Hittites,
the Amorites, the Perizzites, the
Hivites, and the Jebusites, who
were not of Israel, 8 from their descendants who were still left in the
land, whom the people of Israel
had not destroyed—these Solomon conscripted for forced labor,
as is still the case today. 9 But of the
people of Israel Solomon made no
slaves for his work; they were soldiers, and his officers, the commanders of his chariotry and cavalry. 10 These were the chief officers
of King Solomon, two hundred fifty
of them, who exercised authority
over the people.
11 Solomon brought Pharaoh's
daughter from the city of David to
the house that he had built for her,
for he said, "My wife shall not live
in the house of King David of Israel, for the places to which the ark of
the LORD has come are holy."
12 Then Solomon offered up
burnt offerings to the LORD on the
altar of the LORD that he had built
in front of the vestibule, 13 as the
duty of each day required, offering
according to the commandment of
Moses for the sabbaths, the new
moons, and the three annual
festivals—the festival of unleavened bread, the festival of weeks,
and the festival of booths. 14 According to the ordinance of his father David, he appointed the divisions of the priests for their service,
and the Levites for their offices of
praise and ministry alongside the
priests as the duty of each day required, and the gatekeepers in
their divisions for the several gates;
for so David the man of God had
commanded. 15 They did not turn
away from what the king had commanded the priests and Levites regarding anything at all, or regarding the treasuries.
16 Thus all the work of Solomon
was accomplished from[p] the day
the foundation of the house of the
LORD was laid until the house of the
LORD was finished completely.

7.17 1 Kings 9.4ff
7.18 2 Chr 6.16
7.19 Lev 26.14, 33; Deut 28.15
7.20 Deut 29.28
7.21 Deut 29.24
8.1 1 Kings 9.1-28
8.5 1 Chr 7.24; 2 Chr 14.7
8.8 1 Kings 4.6; 9.21
8.11 1 Kings 3.1; 7.8
8.12 2 Chr 4.1
8.13 Ex 29.38; Num 28.3; Ex 23.14-17
8.14 1 Chr 24.1; 25.1; 26.1; Neh 12.24, 36

[n] The word *you* in this verse is plural
[o] Heb *them* [p] Gk Syr Vg: Heb *to*

17 Then Solomon went to
Ezion-geber and Eloth on the shore
of the sea, in the land of Edom.
18 Huram sent him, in the care of
his servants, ships and servants familiar with the sea. They went to
Ophir, together with the servants
of Solomon, and imported from
there four hundred fifty talents of
gold and brought it to King Solomon.

Visit of the Queen of Sheba

9 When the queen of Sheba
heard of the fame of Solomon,
she came to Jerusalem to test him
with hard questions, having a very
great retinue and camels bearing
spices and very much gold and precious stones. When she came to
Solomon, she discussed with him
all that was on her mind. 2 Solomon
answered all her questions; there
was nothing hidden from Solomon
that he could not explain to her.
3 When the queen of Sheba had observed the wisdom of Solomon, the
house that he had built, 4 the food
of his table, the seating of his officials, and the attendance of his servants, and their clothing, his valets, and their clothing, and his
burnt offerings[q] that he offered at
the house of the LORD, there was no
more spirit left in her.
5 So she said to the king, "The
report was true that I heard in my
own land of your accomplishments
and of your wisdom, 6 but I did not
believe the[r] reports until I came
and my own eyes saw it. Not even
half of the greatness of your wisdom had been told to me; you far
surpass the report that I had heard.
7 Happy are your people! Happy are
these your servants, who continually attend you and hear your wisdom! 8 Blessed be the LORD your
God, who has delighted in you and
set you on his throne as king for the
LORD your God. Because your God
loved Israel and would establish
them forever, he has made you king
over them, that you may execute
justice and righteousness." 9 Then
she gave the king one hundred
twenty talents of gold, a very great
quantity of spices, and precious
stones: there were no spices such
as those that the queen of Sheba
gave to King Solomon.
10 Moreover the servants of Huram and the servants of Solomon
who brought gold from Ophir
brought algum wood and precious
stones. 11 From the algum wood,
the king made steps[s] for the house
of the LORD and for the king's
house, lyres also and harps for the
singers; there never was seen the
like of them before in the land of
Judah.
12 Meanwhile King Solomon
granted the queen of Sheba every
desire that she expressed, well beyond what she had brought to the
king. Then she returned to her own
land, with her servants.

Solomon's Great Wealth

13 The weight of gold that came
to Solomon in one year was six
hundred sixty-six talents of gold,
14 besides that which the traders
and merchants brought; and all the
kings of Arabia and the governors
of the land brought gold and silver
to Solomon. 15 King Solomon made
two hundred large shields of beat-
en gold; six hundred shekels of
beaten gold went into each large
shield. 16 He made three hundred
shields of beaten gold; three hundred shekels of gold went into each
shield; and the king put them in
the House of the Forest of Lebanon. 17 The king also made a great
ivory throne, and overlaid it with
pure gold. 18 The throne had six
steps and a footstool of gold, which
were attached to the throne, and
on each side of the seat were arm
rests and two lions standing beside
the arm rests, 19 while twelve lions
were standing, one on each end of
a step on the six steps. The like of
it was never made in any kingdom.
20 All King Solomon's drinking vessels were of gold, and all the vessels of the House of the Forest of
Lebanon were of pure gold; silver

8.17 1 Kings 9.26 **8.18** 1 Kings 9.27; 2 Chr 9.10, 13 **9.1** 1 Kings 10.1-13; Mt 12.42; Lk 11.31 **9.3** 1 Kings 5.12 **9.5** 1 Kings 10.6 **9.8** 1 Chr 28.5; 29.23; 2 Chr 2.11 **9.9** 1 Kings 10.10 **9.10** 2 Chr 8.18 **9.13** 1 Kings 10.14-28 **9.18** 1 Kings 10.18 **9.19** 1 Kings 10.20

[q] Gk Syr Vg 1 Kings 10.5: Heb *ascent* [r] Heb *their* [s] Gk Vg: Meaning of Heb uncertain

was not considered as anything in
the days of Solomon. 21 For the
king's ships went to Tarshish with
the servants of Huram; once every
three years the ships of Tarshish
used to come bringing gold, silver,
ivory, apes, and peacocks.[t]
22 Thus King Solomon excelled
all the kings of the earth in riches
and in wisdom. 23 All the kings of
the earth sought the presence of
Solomon to hear his wisdom,
which God had put into his mind.
24 Every one of them brought a
present, objects of silver and gold,
garments, weaponry, spices,
horses, and mules, so much year by
year. 25 Solomon had four thousand
stalls for horses and chariots, and
twelve thousand horses, which he
stationed in the chariot cities and
with the king in Jerusalem. 26 He
ruled over all the kings from the
Euphrates to the land of the Philistines, and to the border of Egypt.
27 The king made silver as common
in Jerusalem as stone, and cedar as
plentiful as the sycamore of the
Shephelah. 28 Horses were imported for Solomon from Egypt and
from all lands.

Death of Solomon

29 Now the rest of the acts of
Solomon, from first to last, are they
not written in the history of the
prophet Nathan, and in the prophecy of Ahijah the Shilonite, and in
the visions of the seer Iddo concerning Jeroboam son of Nebat?
30 Solomon reigned in Jerusalem
over all Israel forty years. 31 Solomon slept with his ancestors and
was buried in the city of his father
David; and his son Rehoboam succeeded him.

The Revolt against Rehoboam

10 Rehoboam went to She-
chem, for all Israel had
come to Shechem to make him
king. 2 When Jeroboam son of Nebat heard of it (for he was in Egypt,
where he had fled from King Solomon), then Jeroboam returned
from Egypt. 3 They sent and called
him; and Jeroboam and all Israel
came and said to Rehoboam,
4 "Your father made our yoke
heavy. Now therefore lighten the
hard service of your father and his
heavy yoke that he placed on us,
and we will serve you." 5 He said to
them, "Come to me again in three
days." So the people went away.
6 Then King Rehoboam took
counsel with the older men who
had attended his father Solomon
while he was still alive, saying,
"How do you advise me to answer
this people?" 7 They answered him,
"If you will be kind to this people
and please them, and speak good
words to them, then they will be
your servants forever." 8 But he rejected the advice that the older
men gave him, and consulted the
young men who had grown up with
him and now attended him. 9 He
said to them, "What do you advise
that we answer this people who
have said to me, 'Lighten the yoke
that your father put on us'?" 10 The
young men who had grown up with
him said to him, "Thus should you
speak to the people who said to
you, 'Your father made our yoke
heavy, but you must lighten it for
us'; tell them, 'My little finger is
thicker than my father's loins.
11 Now, whereas my father laid on
you a heavy yoke, I will add to your
yoke. My father disciplined you
with whips, but I will discipline you
with scorpions.' "
12 So Jeroboam and all the people came to Rehoboam the third
day, as the king had said, "Come to
me again the third day." 13 The king
answered them harshly. King Rehoboam rejected the advice of the
older men; 14 he spoke to them in
accordance with the advice of the
young men, "My father made your
yoke heavy, but I will add to it; my
father disciplined you with whips,
but I will discipline you with scorpions." 15 So the king did not listen
to the people, because it was a turn
of affairs brought about by God so
that the LORD might fulfill his word,
which he had spoken by Ahijah the

9.21 2 Chr 20.36, 37
9.22 2 Chr 1.12; 1 Kings 3.13
9.25 1 Kings 4.26; 10.26; 2 Chr 1.14
9.26 1 Kings 4.21; Ps 72.8
9.27 1 Kings 10.27; 2 Chr 1.15
9.28 1 Kings 10.28; 2 Chr 1.16
9.29 1 Kings 11.41; 1 Chr 29.29
9.30 1 Kings 11.42, 43
9.31 1 Kings 2.10
10.1 1 Kings 12.1-20
10.2 1 Kings 11.40
10.6 1 Kings 12.6
10.9 1 Kings 12.9
10.12 v. 5
10.15 1 Kings 12.15, 24; 2 Chr 25.16-20; 1 Kings 11.29

t Or *baboons*

Shilonite to Jeroboam son of Nebat.
16 When all Israel saw that the
king would not listen to them, the
people answered the king,

"What share do we have in
David?
We have no inheritance in
the son of Jesse.
Each of you to your tents,
O Israel!
Look now to your own
house, O David."

So all Israel departed to their tents.
17 But Rehoboam reigned over the
people of Israel who were living in
the cities of Judah. 18 When King
Rehoboam sent Hadoram, who was
taskmaster over the forced labor,
the people of Israel stoned him to
death. King Rehoboam hurriedly
mounted his chariot to flee to Jerusalem. 19 So Israel has been in rebellion against the house of David
to this day.

Judah and Benjamin Fortified

11 When Rehoboam came to
Jerusalem, he assembled
one hundred eighty thousand chosen troops of the house of Judah
and Benjamin to fight against Israel, to restore the kingdom to Rehoboam. 2 But the word of the LORD
came to Shemaiah the man of God:
3 Say to King Rehoboam of Judah,
son of Solomon, and to all Israel in
Judah and Benjamin, 4 "Thus says
the LORD: You shall not go up or
fight against your kindred. Let everyone return home, for this thing
is from me." So they heeded the
word of the LORD and turned back
from the expedition against Jeroboam.
5 Rehoboam resided in Jerusalem, and he built cities for defense
in Judah. 6 He built up Bethlehem,
Etam, Tekoa, 7 Beth-zur, Soco,
Adullam, 8 Gath, Mareshah, Ziph,
9 Adoraim, Lachish, Azekah, 10 Zorah, Aijalon, and Hebron, fortified
cities that are in Judah and in Benjamin. 11 He made the fortresses
strong, and put commanders in
them, and stores of food, oil, and
wine. 12 He also put large shields
and spears in all the cities, and
made them very strong. So he held
Judah and Benjamin.

Priests and Levites Support Rehoboam

13 The priests and the Levites
who were in all Israel presented
themselves to him from all their
territories. 14 The Levites had left
their common lands and their
holdings and had come to Judah
and Jerusalem, because Jeroboam
and his sons had prevented them
from serving as priests of the LORD,
15 and had appointed his own
priests for the high places, and for
the goat-demons, and for the
calves that he had made. 16 Those
who had set their hearts to seek the
LORD God of Israel came after them
from all the tribes of Israel to Jerusalem to sacrifice to the LORD, the
God of their ancestors. 17 They
strengthened the kingdom of Judah, and for three years they made
Rehoboam son of Solomon secure,
for they walked for three years in
the way of David and Solomon.

Rehoboam's Marriages

18 Rehoboam took as his wife
Mahalath daughter of Jerimoth son
of David, and of Abihail daughter of
Eliab son of Jesse. 19 She bore him
sons: Jeush, Shemariah, and Za-
ham. 20 After her he took Maacah
daughter of Absalom, who bore
him Abijah, Attai, Ziza, and Shelomith. 21 Rehoboam loved Maacah
daughter of Absalom more than all
his other wives and concubines (he
took eighteen wives and sixty concubines, and became the father of
twenty-eight sons and sixty daughters). 22 Rehoboam appointed Abijah son of Maacah as chief prince
among his brothers, for he intended to make him king. 23 He dealt
wisely, and distributed some of his
sons through all the districts of Judah and Benjamin, in all the fortified cities; he gave them abundant
provisions, and found many wives
for them.

10;16 2 Sam 20.1; v. 19
10.19 1 Kings 12.19
11.1 1 Kings 12.21-24
11.2 2 Chr 12.15
11.4 2 Chr 10.15
11.14 Num 35.2-5; 2 Chr 13.9
11.15 1 Kings 12.28-33; 13.33; 2 Chr 13.9
11.16 2 Chr 15.9
11.17 2 Chr 12.1
11.18 1 Sam 16.6
11.21 Deut 17.17
11.22 Deut 21.15-17

Egypt Attacks Judah

12 When the rule of Rehoboam was established and he
grew strong, he abandoned the law
of the LORD, he and all Israel with
him. 2 In the fifth year of King Rehoboam, because they had been
unfaithful to the LORD, King Shishak of Egypt came up against Jerusalem 3 with twelve hundred
chariots and sixty thousand cavalry. A countless army came with
him from Egypt—Libyans, Sukki-
im, and Ethiopians.[u] 4 He took the
fortified cities of Judah and came
as far as Jerusalem. 5 Then the
prophet Shemaiah came to Rehoboam and to the officers of Judah,
who had gathered at Jerusalem because of Shishak, and said to them,
"Thus says the LORD: You abandoned me, so I have abandoned
you to the hand of Shishak." 6 Then
the officers of Israel and the king
humbled themselves and said,
"The LORD is in the right." 7 When
the LORD saw that they humbled
themselves, the word of the LORD
came to Shemaiah, saying: "They
have humbled themselves; I will
not destroy them, but I will grant
them some deliverance, and my
wrath shall not be poured out on
Jerusalem by the hand of Shishak.
8 Nevertheless they shall be his servants, so that they may know the
difference between serving me and
serving the kingdoms of other
lands."
9 So King Shishak of Egypt
came up against Jerusalem; he
took away the treasures of the
house of the LORD and the treasures
of the king's house; he took everything. He also took away the
shields of gold that Solomon had
made; 10 but King Rehoboam made
in place of them shields of bronze,
and committed them to the hands
of the officers of the guard, who
kept the door of the king's house.
11 Whenever the king went into the
house of the LORD, the guard would
come along bearing them, and
would then bring them back to the
guardroom. 12 Because he humbled
himself the wrath of the LORD
turned from him, so as not to destroy them completely; moreover,
conditions were good in Judah.

Death of Rehoboam

13 So King Rehoboam established himself in Jerusalem and
reigned. Rehoboam was forty-one
years old when he began to reign;
he reigned seventeen years in Jerusalem, the city that the LORD had
chosen out of all the tribes of Israel
to put his name there. His mother's
name was Naamah the Ammonite.
14 He did evil, for he did not set his
heart to seek the LORD.
15 Now the acts of Rehoboam,
from first to last, are they not written in the records of the prophet
Shemaiah and of the seer Iddo, recorded by genealogy? There were
continual wars between Rehoboam
and Jeroboam. 16 Rehoboam slept
with his ancestors and was buried
in the city of David; and his son
Abijah succeeded him.

Abijah Reigns over Judah

13 In the eighteenth year of
King Jeroboam, Abijah be-
gan to reign over Judah. 2 He
reigned for three years in Jerusalem. His mother's name was Micaiah daughter of Uriel of Gibeah.
Now there was war between Abijah and Jeroboam. 3 Abijah engaged in battle, having an army of
valiant warriors, four hundred
thousand picked men; and Jeroboam drew up his line of battle
against him with eight hundred
thousand picked mighty warriors.
4 Then Abijah stood on the slope of
Mount Zemaraim that is in the hill
country of Ephraim, and said, "Listen to me, Jeroboam and all Israel!
5 Do you not know that the LORD
God of Israel gave the kingship over
Israel forever to David and his sons
by a covenant of salt? 6 Yet Jeroboam son of Nebat, a servant of Solomon son of David, rose up and rebelled against his lord; 7 and
certain worthless scoundrels gathered around him and defied Reho-

12.1 2 Chr 11.17; 1 Kings 14.22-24
12.2 1 Kings 14.24, 25; 11.40
12.3 2 Chr 16.8
12.5 2 Chr 11.2; 15.2; Deut 28.15
12.6 Ex 9.27; Dan 9.14
12.7 1 Kings 21.29
12.8 Deut 28.47, 48
12.9 1 Kings 14.25, 26; 2 Chr 9.15, 16
12.12 2 Chr 19.3
12.13 1 Kings 14.21; 2 Chr 6.6
12.14 2 Chr 19.3
12.15 1 Kings 14.29, 30; 2 Chr 9.29
12.16 1 Kings 14.31; 2 Chr 11.20
13.1 1 Kings 15.1, 2
13.2 2 Chr 11.20; 1 Kings 15.7
13.4 Josh 18.22
13.5 2 Sam 7.12, 13,16; Num 18.19
13.6 1 Kings 11.26

[u] Or *Nubians*; Heb *Cushites*

boam son of Solomon, when Rehoboam was young and irresolute and
could not withstand them.
8 "And now you think that you
can withstand the kingdom of the
LORD in the hand of the sons of David, because you are a great multitude and have with you the golden
calves that Jeroboam made as gods
for you. 9 Have you not driven out
the priests of the LORD, the descendants of Aaron, and the Levites,
and made priests for yourselves
like the peoples of other lands?
Whoever comes to be consecrated
with a young bull or seven rams becomes a priest of what are no gods.
10 But as for us, the LORD is our God,
and we have not abandoned him.
We have priests ministering to the
LORD who are descendants of Aaron, and Levites for their service.
11 They offer to the LORD every
morning and every evening burnt
offerings and fragrant incense, set
out the rows of bread on the table
of pure gold, and care for the gold-
en lampstand so that its lamps may
burn every evening; for we keep the
charge of the LORD our God, but you
have abandoned him. 12 See, God is
with us at our head, and his priests
have their battle trumpets to sound
the call to battle against you.
O Israelites, do not fight against
the LORD, the God of your ancestors; for you cannot succeed."
13 Jeroboam had sent an ambush around to come on them from
behind; thus his troops[v] were in
front of Judah, and the ambush
was behind them. 14 When Judah
turned, the battle was in front of
them and behind them. They cried
out to the LORD, and the priests
blew the trumpets. 15 Then the people of Judah raised the battle
shout. And when the people of Judah shouted, God defeated Jeroboam and all Israel before Abijah and
Judah. 16 The Israelites fled before
Judah, and God gave them into
their hands. 17 Abijah and his army
defeated them with great slaughter; five hundred thousand picked
men of Israel fell slain. 18 Thus the
Israelites were subdued at that
time, and the people of Judah prevailed, because they relied on the
LORD, the God of their ancestors.
19 Abijah pursued Jeroboam, and
took cities from him: Bethel with
its villages and Jeshanah with its
villages and Ephron[w] with its villages. 20 Jeroboam did not recover
his power in the days of Abijah; the
LORD struck him down, and he died.
21 But Abijah grew strong. He took
fourteen wives, and became the father of twenty-two sons and sixteen daughters. 22 The rest of the
acts of Abijah, his behavior and his
deeds, are written in the story of
the prophet Iddo.

Asa Reigns

14 [x] So Abijah slept with his ancestors, and they buried
him in the city of David. His son
Asa succeeded him. In his days the
land had rest for ten years. 2 [y] Asa
did what was good and right in the
sight of the LORD his God. 3 He took
away the foreign altars and the
high places, broke down the pillars, hewed down the sacred
poles,[z] 4 and commanded Judah to
seek the LORD, the God of their ancestors, and to keep the law and
the commandment. 5 He also removed from all the cities of Judah
the high places and the incense altars. And the kingdom had rest under him. 6 He built fortified cities in
Judah while the land had rest. He
had no war in those years, for the
LORD gave him peace. 7 He said to
Judah, "Let us build these cities,
and surround them with walls and
towers, gates and bars; the land is
still ours because we have sought
the LORD our God; we have sought
him, and he has given us peace on
every side." So they built and prospered. 8 Asa had an army of three
hundred thousand from Judah,
armed with large shields and
spears, and two hundred eighty
thousand troops from Benjamin
who carried shields and drew bows;
all these were mighty warriors.

13.8 1 Kings 12.28; 2 Chr 11.15
13.9 2 Chr 11.14; Ex 29.35; Jer 2.11; 5.7
13.11 2 Chr 2.4; Lev 24.5-9
13.12 Num 10.8,9; Acts 5.39
13.14 2 Chr 14.11
13.15 2 Chr 14.12
13.16 2 Chr 16.8
13.18 1 Chr 5.20; 2 Chr 14.11; Ps 22.5
13.20 1 Sam 25.38; 1 Kings 14.20
13.22 2 Chr 12.15
14.1 1 Kings 15.8
14.3 Deut 7.5; 1 Kings 15.12-14; Ex 34.13
14.5 2 Chr 34.4, 7
14.6 2 Chr 15.15

[v] Heb *they* [w] Another reading is *Ephrain*
[x] Ch 13.23 in Heb [y] Ch 14.1 in Heb
[z] Heb *Asherim*

Ethiopian Invasion Repulsed

9 Zerah the Ethiopian[a] came
out against them with an army of a
million men and three hundred
chariots, and came as far as Mareshah. 10 Asa went out to meet him,
and they drew up their lines of battle in the valley of Zephathah at
Mareshah. 11 Asa cried to the LORD
his God, "O LORD, there is no difference for you between helping the
mighty and the weak. Help us,
O LORD our God, for we rely on you,
and in your name we have come
against this multitude. O LORD, you
are our God; let no mortal prevail
against you." 12 So the LORD defeated the Ethiopians[b] before Asa and
before Judah, and the Ethiopians[b]
fled. 13 Asa and the army with him
pursued them as far as Gerar, and
the Ethiopians[b] fell until no one
remained alive; for they were broken before the LORD and his army.
The people of Judah[c] carried away
a great quantity of booty. 14 They
defeated all the cities around Gerar, for the fear of the LORD was on
them. They plundered all the cities; for there was much plunder in
them. 15 They also attacked the
tents of those who had livestock,[d]
and carried away sheep and goats
in abundance, and camels. Then
they returned to Jerusalem.

15 The spirit of God came
upon Azariah son of Oded.
2 He went out to meet Asa and said
to him, "Hear me, Asa, and all Judah and Benjamin: The LORD is
with you, while you are with him. If
you seek him, he will be found by
you, but if you abandon him, he
will abandon you. 3 For a long time
Israel was without the true God,
and without a teaching priest, and
without law; 4 but when in their distress they turned to the LORD, the
God of Israel, and sought him, he
was found by them. 5 In those times
it was not safe for anyone to go or
come, for great disturbances afflicted all the inhabitants of the
lands. 6 They were broken in
pieces, nation against nation and
city against city, for God troubled
them with every sort of distress.
7 But you, take courage! Do not let
your hands be weak, for your work
shall be rewarded."

8 When Asa heard these words,
the prophecy of Azariah son of
Oded,[e] he took courage, and put
away the abominable idols from all
the land of Judah and Benjamin
and from the towns that he had
taken in the hill country of Ephraim. He repaired the altar of the
LORD that was in front of the vestibule of the house of the LORD.[f] 9 He
gathered all Judah and Benjamin,
and those from Ephraim, Manasseh, and Simeon who were residing
as aliens with them, for great numbers had deserted to him from Israel when they saw that the LORD his
God was with him. 10 They were
gathered at Jerusalem in the third
month of the fifteenth year of the
reign of Asa. 11 They sacrificed to
the LORD on that day, from the booty that they had brought, seven
hundred oxen and seven thousand
sheep. 12 They entered into a covenant to seek the LORD, the God of
their ancestors, with all their heart
and with all their soul. 13 Whoever
would not seek the LORD, the God
of Israel, should be put to death,
whether young or old, man or woman. 14 They took an oath to the LORD
with a loud voice, and with shouting, and with trumpets, and with
horns. 15 All Judah rejoiced over
the oath; for they had sworn with
all their heart, and had sought him
with their whole desire, and he was
found by them, and the LORD gave
them rest all around.

16 King Asa even removed his
mother Maacah from being queen
mother because she had made an
abominable image for Asherah.
Asa cut down her image, crushed
it, and burned it at the Wadi Kidron. 17 But the high places were not
taken out of Israel. Nevertheless
the heart of Asa was true all his

14.9 2 Chr 16.8; 11.8
14.11 2 Chr 13.14, 18; 1 Sam 14.6; 17.45
14.12 2 Chr 13.15
14.13 Gen 10.19
14.14 Gen 35.5; 2 Chr 17.10
15.1 Num 24.2; 2 Chr 20.14; 24.20
15.2 Jas 4.8; vv. 4,15; 2 Chr 24.20
15.3 Hos 3.4; Lev 10.11; 2 Chr 17.9
15.4 Deut 4.29
15.5 Judg 5.6
15.6 Mt 24.7
15.7 Josh 1.7,9
15.8 2 Chr 13.19
15.9 2 Chr 11.16
15.11 2 Chr 14.13-15
15.12 2 Chr 23.16; 34.31
15.13 Ex 22.20; Deut 13.5,9, 15
15.15 v. 2; 2 Chr 14.7
15.16 1 Kings 15.13-15; Ex 34.13; 2 Chr 14.2-5

[a] Or *Nubian*; Heb *Cushite* [b] Or *Nubians*; Heb *Cushites* [c] Heb *They* [d] Meaning of Heb uncertain [e] Compare Syr Vg: Heb *the prophecy, the prophet Obed* [f] Heb *the vestibule of the LORD*

days. 18He brought into the house
of God the votive gifts of his father
and his own votive gifts—silver,
gold, and utensils. 19And there was
no more war until the thirty-fifth
year of the reign of Asa.

Alliance with Aram Condemned

16 In the thirty-sixth year of
the reign of Asa, King Baasha of Israel went up against Judah, and built Ramah, to prevent
anyone from going out or coming
into the territory of[g] King Asa of
Judah. 2Then Asa took silver and
gold from the treasures of the
house of the LORD and the king's
house, and sent them to King Ben-
hadad of Aram, who resided in Damascus, saying, 3"Let there be an
alliance between me and you, like
that between my father and your
father; I am sending to you silver
and gold; go, break your alliance
with King Baasha of Israel, so that
he may withdraw from me." 4Ben-
hadad listened to King Asa, and
sent the commanders of his armies
against the cities of Israel. They
conquered Ijon, Dan, Abel-maim,
and all the store-cities of Naphtali.
5When Baasha heard of it, he
stopped building Ramah, and let
his work cease. 6Then King Asa
brought all Judah, and they carried
away the stones of Ramah and its
timber, with which Baasha had
been building, and with them he
built up Geba and Mizpah.
7 At that time the seer Hanani
came to King Asa of Judah, and
said to him, "Because you relied on
the king of Aram, and did not rely
on the LORD your God, the army of
the king of Aram has escaped you.
8Were not the Ethiopians[h] and the
Libyans a huge army with exceedingly many chariots and cavalry?
Yet because you relied on the LORD,
he gave them into your hand. 9For
the eyes of the LORD range throughout the entire earth, to strengthen
those whose heart is true to him.
You have done foolishly in this; for
from now on you will have wars."
10Then Asa was angry with the
seer, and put him in the stocks, in
prison, for he was in a rage with
him because of this. And Asa inflicted cruelties on some of the
people at the same time.

Asa's Disease and Death

11 The acts of Asa, from first to
last, are written in the Book of the
Kings of Judah and Israel. 12In the
thirty-ninth year of his reign Asa
was diseased in his feet, and his
disease became severe; yet even in
his disease he did not seek the
LORD, but sought help from physicians. 13Then Asa slept with his ancestors, dying in the forty-first year
of his reign. 14They buried him in
the tomb that he had hewn out for
himself in the city of David. They
laid him on a bier that had been
filled with various kinds of spices
prepared by the perfumer's art; and
they made a very great fire in his
honor.

Jehoshaphat's Reign

17 His son Jehoshaphat succeeded him, and strength-
ened himself against Israel. 2He
placed forces in all the fortified cities of Judah, and set garrisons in
the land of Judah, and in the cities
of Ephraim that his father Asa had
taken. 3The LORD was with Jehoshaphat, because he walked in the
earlier ways of his father;[i] he did
not seek the Baals, 4but sought the
God of his father and walked in his
commandments, and not according to the ways of Israel. 5Therefore
the LORD established the kingdom
in his hand. All Judah brought tribute to Jehoshaphat, and he had
great riches and honor. 6His heart
was courageous in the ways of the
LORD; and furthermore he removed
the high places and the sacred
poles[j] from Judah.
7 In the third year of his reign he
sent his officials, Ben-hail, Obadiah, Zechariah, Nethanel, and Micaiah, to teach in the cities of Judah. 8With them were the Levites,
Shemaiah, Nethaniah, Zebadiah,

16.1 1 Kings 15.17-22
16.4 1 Kings 15.18, 20
16.7 2 Chr 19.2; 14.11; 32.7,8
16.8 2 Chr 14.9; 12.3
16.9 Prov 15.3; Zech 4.10; 1 Sam 13.13
16.11 1 Kings 15.23
16.12 Jer 17.5
16.13 1 Kings 15.24
16.14 Gen 50.2; Jn 19.39,40; 2 Chr 21.19; Jer 34.5
17.1 1 Kings 15.24
17.2 2 Chr 15.8
17.4 1 Kings 12.28
17.5 2 Chr 18.1
17.6 2 Chr 15.17
17.7 2 Chr 15.3
17.8 2 Chr 19.8

[g] Heb lacks *the territory of* [h] Or *Nubians;* Heb *Cushites* [i] Another reading is *his father David* [j] Heb *Asherim*

Asahel, Shemiramoth, Jehonathan, Adonijah, Tobijah, and Tob-
adonijah; and with these Levites,
the priests Elishama and Jehoram.
9 They taught in Judah, having the
book of the law of the LORD with
them; they went around through all
the cities of Judah and taught
among the people.

10 The fear of the LORD fell on
all the kingdoms of the lands
around Judah, and they did not
make war against Jehoshaphat.
11 Some of the Philistines brought
Jehoshaphat presents, and silver
for tribute; and the Arabs also
brought him seven thousand seven
hundred rams and seven thousand
seven hundred male goats. 12 Jehoshaphat grew steadily greater.
He built fortresses and storage cities in Judah. 13 He carried out great
works in the cities of Judah. He
had soldiers, mighty warriors, in
Jerusalem. 14 This was the muster
of them by ancestral houses: Of Judah, the commanders of the thousands: Adnah the commander,
with three hundred thousand
mighty warriors, 15 and next to him
Jehohanan the commander, with
two hundred eighty thousand,
16 and next to him Amasiah son of
Zichri, a volunteer for the service of
the LORD, with two hundred thousand mighty warriors. 17 Of Benjamin: Eliada, a mighty warrior, with
two hundred thousand armed with
bow and shield, 18 and next to him
Jehozabad with one hundred
eighty thousand armed for war.
19 These were in the service of the
king, besides those whom the king
had placed in the fortified cities
throughout all Judah.

Micaiah Predicts Failure

18 Now Jehoshaphat had
great riches and honor; and
he made a marriage alliance with
Ahab. 2 After some years he went
down to Ahab in Samaria. Ahab
slaughtered an abundance of sheep
and oxen for him and for the people who were with him, and induced him to go up against
Ramoth-gilead. 3 King Ahab of Israel said to King Jehoshaphat of Judah, "Will you go with me to
Ramoth-gilead?" He answered
him, "I am with you, my people are
your people. We will be with you in
the war."

4 But Jehoshaphat also said to
the king of Israel, "Inquire first for
the word of the LORD." 5 Then the
king of Israel gathered the prophets together, four hundred of them,
and said to them, "Shall we go to
battle against Ramoth-gilead, or
shall I refrain?" They said, "Go up;
for God will give it into the hand of
the king." 6 But Jehoshaphat said,
"Is there no other prophet of the
LORD here of whom we may inquire?" 7 The king of Israel said to
Jehoshaphat, "There is still one
other by whom we may inquire of
the LORD, Micaiah son of Imlah; but
I hate him, for he never prophesies
anything favorable about me, but
only disaster." Jehoshaphat said,
"Let the king not say such a thing."
8 Then the king of Israel summoned
an officer and said, "Bring quickly
Micaiah son of Imlah." 9 Now the
king of Israel and King Jehoshaphat of Judah were sitting on their
thrones, arrayed in their robes; and
they were sitting at the threshing
floor at the entrance of the gate of
Samaria; and all the prophets were
prophesying before them. 10 Zedekiah son of Chenaanah made for
himself horns of iron, and he said,
"Thus says the LORD: With these
you shall gore the Arameans until
they are destroyed." 11 All the
prophets were prophesying the
same and saying, "Go up to
Ramoth-gilead and triumph; the
LORD will give it into the hand of the
king."

12 The messenger who had
gone to summon Micaiah said to
him, "Look, the words of the
prophets with one accord are favorable to the king; let your word be
like the word of one of them, and
speak favorably." 13 But Micaiah
said, "As the LORD lives, whatever
my God says, that I will speak."

14 When he had come to the
king, the king said to him, "Mica-

17.9 Deut 6.4-9
17.10 2 Chr 14.14
17.11 2 Chr 9.14; 26.8
17.16 Judg 5.2,9; 1 Chr 29.9
18.1 2 Chr 17.5
18.2 1 Kings 22.2-35
18.4 1 Sam 23.2, 4,9; 2 Sam 2.1
18.7 1 Kings 22.8
18.9 Ruth 4.1
18.11 2 Chr 22.5
18.13 Num 22.18-20, 35

iah, shall we go to Ramoth-gilead
to battle, or shall I refrain?" He answered, "Go up and triumph; they
will be given into your hand." 15 But
the king said to him, "How many
times must I make you swear to tell
me nothing but the truth in the
name of the LORD?" 16 Then Micaiah[k] said, "I saw all Israel scattered on the mountains, like sheep
without a shepherd; and the LORD
said, 'These have no master; let
each one go home in peace.' "
17 The king of Israel said to Jehoshaphat, "Did I not tell you that he
would not prophesy anything favorable about me, but only disaster?"
18 Then Micaiah[k] said, "Therefore hear the word of the LORD: I
saw the LORD sitting on his throne,
with all the host of heaven standing
to the right and to the left of him.
19 And the LORD said, 'Who will entice King Ahab of Israel, so that he
may go up and fall at Ramoth-
gilead?' Then one said one thing,
and another said another, 20 until a
spirit came forward and stood before the LORD, saying, 'I will entice
him.' The LORD asked him, 'How?'
21 He replied, 'I will go out and be a
lying spirit in the mouth of all his
prophets.' Then the LORD[k] said,
'You are to entice him, and you
shall succeed; go out and do it.'
22 So you see, the LORD has put a
lying spirit in the mouth of these
your prophets; the LORD has decreed disaster for you."
23 Then Zedekiah son of Chenaanah came up to Micaiah, slapped
him on the cheek, and said,
"Which way did the spirit of the
LORD pass from me to speak to
you?" 24 Micaiah replied, "You will
find out on that day when you go in
to hide in an inner chamber."
25 The king of Israel then ordered,
"Take Micaiah, and return him to
Amon the governor of the city and
to Joash the king's son; 26 and say,
'Thus says the king: Put this fellow
in prison, and feed him on reduced
rations of bread and water until I
return in peace.' " 27 Micaiah said,
"If you return in peace, the LORD
has not spoken by me." And he

18.16 Num 27.17; Ezek 34.5-8
18.20 Job 1.6
18.22 Job 12.16; Ezek 14.9
18.23 Jer 20.2; Mk 14.65; Acts 23.2
18.25 v. 8
18.26 2 Chr 16.10
18.27 Mic 1.9
18.31 2 Chr 13.14, 15
18.33 1 Kings 22.34
19.2 1 Kings 16.1; Ps 139.21; 2 Chr 32.25
19.3 2 Chr 12.12, 14; 17.6; Ezra 7.10
19.4 2 Chr 15.8-13

said, "Hear, you peoples, all of
you!"

Defeat and Death of Ahab

28 So the king of Israel and King
Jehoshaphat of Judah went up to
Ramoth-gilead. 29 The king of Israel
said to Jehoshaphat, "I will disguise myself and go into battle, but
you wear your robes." So the king
of Israel disguised himself, and
they went into battle. 30 Now the
king of Aram had commanded the
captains of his chariots, "Fight
with no one small or great, but only
with the king of Israel." 31 When the
captains of the chariots saw Jehoshaphat, they said, "It is the king
of Israel." So they turned to fight
against him; and Jehoshaphat
cried out, and the LORD helped him.
God drew them away from him,
32 for when the captains of the chariots saw that it was not the king of
Israel, they turned back from pursuing him. 33 But a certain man
drew his bow and unknowingly
struck the king of Israel between
the scale armor and the breastplate; so he said to the driver of his
chariot, "Turn around, and carry
me out of the battle, for I am
wounded." 34 The battle grew hot
that day, and the king of Israel
propped himself up in his chariot
facing the Arameans until evening;
then at sunset he died.

19 King Jehoshaphat of Judah
returned in safety to his
house in Jerusalem. 2 Jehu son of
Hanani the seer went out to meet
him and said to King Jehoshaphat,
"Should you help the wicked and
love those who hate the LORD? Because of this, wrath has gone out
against you from the LORD. 3 Nevertheless, some good is found in you,
for you destroyed the sacred
poles[l] out of the land, and have
set your heart to seek God."

The Reforms of Jehoshaphat

4 Jehoshaphat resided at Jerusalem; then he went out again
among the people, from Beer-
sheba to the hill country of Ephra-

[k] Heb *he* [l] Heb *Asheroth*

im, and brought them back to the
LORD, the God of their ancestors.
[5]He appointed judges in the land
in all the fortified cities of Judah,
city by city, [6]and said to the judges,
"Consider what you are doing, for
you judge not on behalf of human
beings but on the LORD's behalf; he
is with you in giving judgment.
[7]Now, let the fear of the LORD be
upon you; take care what you do,
for there is no perversion of justice
with the LORD our God, or partiality, or taking of bribes."
8 Moreover in Jerusalem Jehoshaphat appointed certain Levites and priests and heads of families of Israel, to give judgment for
the LORD and to decide disputed
cases. They had their seat at Jerusalem. [9]He charged them: "This is
how you shall act: in the fear of the
LORD, in faithfulness, and with your
whole heart; [10]whenever a case
comes to you from your kindred
who live in their cities, concerning
bloodshed, law or commandment,
statutes or ordinances, then you
shall instruct them, so that they
may not incur guilt before the LORD
and wrath may not come on you
and your kindred. Do so, and you
will not incur guilt. [11]See, Amariah
the chief priest is over you in all
matters of the LORD; and Zebadiah
son of Ishmael, the governor of the
house of Judah, in all the king's
matters; and the Levites will serve
you as officers. Deal courageously,
and may the LORD be with the
good!"

Invasion from the East

20 After this the Moabites and
Ammonites, and with them
some of the Meunites,[m] came
against Jehoshaphat for battle.
[2]Messengers[n] came and told Jehoshaphat, "A great multitude is
coming against you from Edom,[o]
from beyond the sea; already they
are at Hazazon-tamar" (that is, En-
gedi). [3]Jehoshaphat was afraid; he
set himself to seek the LORD, and
proclaimed a fast throughout all
Judah. [4]Judah assembled to seek
help from the LORD; from all the

19.6 Deut 1.17 **19.7** Gen 18.25; Deut 32.4; 10.17,18; Rom 2.11; Col 3.25 **19.8** 2 Chr 17.8, 9 **19.9** 2 Sam 23.3 **19.10** Deut 17.8; v. 2 **19.11** v. 8; 1 Chr 28.20 **20.2** Gen 14.7 **20.3** 2 Chr 19.3

20.6 Deut 4.39; Mt 6.9; 1 Chr 29.11, 12; Mt 6.13 **20.7** Isa 41.8 **20.9** 1 Kings 8.33, 37; 2 Chr 6.20, 28-30 **20.10** vv. 1,22; Deut 2.4,9, 19; Num 20.21 **20.11** Ps 83.12 **20.12** Judg 11.27; Ps 25.15; 121.1,2 **20.14** 2 Chr 15.1; 24.20 **20.15** Ex 14.13, 14; 2 Chr 32.7, 8; 1 Sam 17.47

towns of Judah they came to seek
the LORD.

Jehoshaphat's Prayer and Victory

5 Jehoshaphat stood in the assembly of Judah and Jerusalem, in
the house of the LORD, before the
new court, [6]and said, "O LORD, God
of our ancestors, are you not God in
heaven? Do you not rule over all
the kingdoms of the nations? In
your hand are power and might, so
that no one is able to withstand
you. [7]Did you not, O our God, drive
out the inhabitants of this land before your people Israel, and give it
forever to the descendants of your
friend Abraham? [8]They have lived
in it, and in it have built you a sanctuary for your name, saying, [9]'If disaster comes upon us, the sword,
judgment,[p] or pestilence, or famine, we will stand before this
house, and before you, for your
name is in this house, and cry to
you in our distress, and you will
hear and save.' [10]See now, the people of Ammon, Moab, and Mount
Seir, whom you would not let Israel
invade when they came from the
land of Egypt, and whom they
avoided and did not destroy—
[11]they reward us by coming to drive
us out of your possession that you
have given us to inherit. [12]O our
God, will you not execute judgment upon them? For we are powerless against this great multitude
that is coming against us. We do
not know what to do, but our eyes
are on you."
13 Meanwhile all Judah stood
before the LORD, with their little
ones, their wives, and their children. [14]Then the spirit of the LORD
came upon Jahaziel son of Zechariah, son of Benaiah, son of Jeiel,
son of Mattaniah, a Levite of the
sons of Asaph, in the middle of the
assembly. [15]He said, "Listen, all
Judah and inhabitants of Jerusalem, and King Jehoshaphat: Thus
says the LORD to you: 'Do not fear or

[m] Compare 26.7: Heb *Ammonites*
[n] Heb *They* [o] One Ms: MT *Aram*
[p] Or *the sword of judgment*

be dismayed at this great multitude; for the battle is not yours
but God's. 16 Tomorrow go down
against them; they will come up by
the ascent of Ziz; you will find them
at the end of the valley, before the
wilderness of Jeruel. 17 This battle
is not for you to fight; take your position, stand still, and see the victory of the LORD on your behalf,
O Judah and Jerusalem.' Do not
fear or be dismayed; tomorrow go
out against them, and the LORD will
be with you."

18 Then Jehoshaphat bowed
down with his face to the ground,
and all Judah and the inhabitants
of Jerusalem fell down before the
LORD, worshiping the LORD. 19 And
the Levites, of the Kohathites and
the Korahites, stood up to praise
the LORD, the God of Israel, with a
very loud voice.

20 They rose early in the morning and went out into the wilderness of Tekoa; and as they went
out, Jehoshaphat stood and said,
"Listen to me, O Judah and inhabitants of Jerusalem! Believe in the
LORD your God and you will be established; believe his prophets."
21 When he had taken counsel with
the people, he appointed those
who were to sing to the LORD and
praise him in holy splendor, as they
went before the army, saying,

"Give thanks to the LORD,
for his steadfast love
endures forever."

22 As they began to sing and praise,
the LORD set an ambush against the
Ammonites, Moab, and Mount
Seir, who had come against Judah,
so that they were routed. 23 For the
Ammonites and Moab attacked the
inhabitants of Mount Seir, destroying them utterly; and when they
had made an end of the inhabitants
of Seir, they all helped to destroy
one another.

24 When Judah came to the
watchtower of the wilderness, they
looked toward the multitude; they
were corpses lying on the ground;
no one had escaped. 25 When Jehoshaphat and his people came to
take the booty from them, they
found livestock[q] in great numbers,
goods, clothing, and precious
things, which they took for themselves until they could carry no
more. They spent three days taking
the booty, because of its abundance. 26 On the fourth day they assembled in the Valley of Beracah,
for there they blessed the LORD;
therefore that place has been
called the Valley of Beracah[r] to
this day. 27 Then all the people of
Judah and Jerusalem, with Jehoshaphat at their head, returned to Jerusalem with joy, for the LORD had
enabled them to rejoice over their
enemies. 28 They came to Jerusalem, with harps and lyres and trumpets, to the house of the LORD.
29 The fear of God came on all the
kingdoms of the countries when
they heard that the LORD had
fought against the enemies of Israel. 30 And the realm of Jehoshaphat
was quiet, for his God gave him rest
all around.

The End of Jehoshaphat's Reign

31 So Jehoshaphat reigned over
Judah. He was thirty-five years old
when he began to reign; he reigned
twenty-five years in Jerusalem. His
mother's name was Azubah daughter of Shilhi. 32 He walked in the
way of his father Asa and did not
turn aside from it, doing what was
right in the sight of the LORD. 33 Yet
the high places were not removed;
the people had not yet set their
hearts upon the God of their ancestors.

34 Now the rest of the acts of Jehoshaphat, from first to last, are
written in the Annals of Jehu son of
Hanani, which are recorded in the
Book of the Kings of Israel.

35 After this King Jehoshaphat
of Judah joined with King Ahaziah
of Israel, who did wickedly. 36 He
joined him in building ships to go
to Tarshish; they built the ships in
Ezion-geber. 37 Then Eliezer son of
Dodavahu of Mareshah prophesied
against Jehoshaphat, saying, "Because you have joined with Ahaziah, the LORD will destroy what you

20.17 Ex 14.13, 14; 2 Chr 15.2
20.18 Ex 4.31; 2 Chr 7.3
20.20 Isa 7.9
20.21 1 Chr 16.29, 34,41; Ps 29.2
20.22 Judg 7.22; 2 Chr 13.13
20.23 1 Sam 14.20
20.27 Neh 12.43
20.29 2 Chr 14.14; 17.10
20.30 2 Chr 14.6, 7; 15.15
20.31 1 Kings 22.41-43
20.33 2 Chr 17.6; 19.3
20.34 1 Kings 16.1, 7
20.35 1 Kings 22.48, 49
20.37 2 Chr 9.21

[q] Gk: Heb *among them* [r] That is *Blessing*

have made." And the ships were
wrecked and were not able to go to
Tarshish.

Jehoram's Reign

21 Jehoshaphat slept with his
ancestors and was buried
with his ancestors in the city of David; his son Jehoram succeeded
him. 2 He had brothers, the sons of
Jehoshaphat: Azariah, Jehiel,
Zechariah, Azariah, Michael, and
Shephatiah; all these were the sons
of King Jehoshaphat of Judah.[s]
3 Their father gave them many gifts,
of silver, gold, and valuable possessions, together with fortified cities
in Judah; but he gave the kingdom
to Jehoram, because he was the
firstborn. 4 When Jehoram had ascended the throne of his father and
was established, he put all his
brothers to the sword, and also
some of the officials of Israel. 5 Jehoram was thirty-two years old
when he began to reign; he reigned
eight years in Jerusalem. 6 He
walked in the way of the kings of
Israel, as the house of Ahab had
done; for the daughter of Ahab was
his wife. He did what was evil in the
sight of the LORD. 7 Yet the LORD
would not destroy the house of David because of the covenant that he
had made with David, and since he
had promised to give a lamp to him
and to his descendants forever.

Revolt of Edom

8 In his days Edom revolted
against the rule of Judah and set up
a king of their own. 9 Then Jehoram
crossed over with his commanders
and all his chariots. He set out by
night and attacked the Edomites,
who had surrounded him and his
chariot commanders. 10 So Edom
has been in revolt against the rule
of Judah to this day. At that time
Libnah also revolted against his
rule, because he had forsaken the
LORD, the God of his ancestors.

Elijah's Letter

11 Moreover he made high
places in the hill country of Judah,
and led the inhabitants of Jerusalem into unfaithfulness, and made

21.1 1 Kings 22.50 **21.3** 2 Chr 11.5 **21.5** 2 Kings 8.17-22 **21.7** 2 Sam 7.12, 13; 1 Kings 11.36 **21.8** 2 Kings 8.20-24 **21.11** Lev 20.5

21.12 2 Chr 17.3, 4; 14.2-5 **21.13** vv. 6,11; 1 Kings 16.31-33; v. 4 **21.15** vv. 18,19 **21.16** 2 Chr 33.11 **21.17** 2 Chr 25.23 **21.18** v. 15 **21.19** 2 Chr 16.14 **21.20** Jer 22.18, 28; 2 Chr 24.25; 28.27 **22.1** 2 Kings 8.24-29; 2 Chr 21.16, 17

Judah go astray. 12 A letter came to
him from the prophet Elijah, saying: "Thus says the LORD, the God
of your father David: Because you
have not walked in the ways of your
father Jehoshaphat or in the ways
of King Asa of Judah, 13 but have
walked in the way of the kings of
Israel, and have led Judah and the
inhabitants of Jerusalem into unfaithfulness, as the house of Ahab
led Israel into unfaithfulness, and
because you also have killed your
brothers, members of your father's
house, who were better than yourself, 14 see, the LORD will bring a
great plague on your people, your
children, your wives, and all your
possessions, 15 and you yourself
will have a severe sickness with a
disease of your bowels, until your
bowels come out, day after day, because of the disease."
16 The LORD aroused against Jehoram the anger of the Philistines
and of the Arabs who are near the
Ethiopians.[t] 17 They came up
against Judah, invaded it, and carried away all the possessions they
found that belonged to the king's
house, along with his sons and his
wives, so that no son was left to
him except Jehoahaz, his youngest
son.

Disease and Death of Jehoram

18 After all this the LORD struck
him in his bowels with an incurable
disease. 19 In course of time, at the
end of two years, his bowels came
out because of the disease, and he
died in great agony. His people
made no fire in his honor, like the
fires made for his ancestors. 20 He
was thirty-two years old when he
began to reign; he reigned eight
years in Jerusalem. He departed
with no one's regret. They buried
him in the city of David, but not in
the tombs of the kings.

Ahaziah's Reign

22 The inhabitants of Jerusalem made his youngest son
Ahaziah king as his successor; for

[s] Gk Syr: Heb *Israel* [t] Or *Nubians*; Heb *Cushites*

the troops who came with the
Arabs to the camp had killed all the
older sons. So Ahaziah son of Jehoram reigned as king of Judah.
2 Ahaziah was forty-two years old
when he began to reign; he reigned
one year in Jerusalem. His mother's name was Athaliah, a granddaughter of Omri. 3 He also walked
in the ways of the house of Ahab,
for his mother was his counselor in
doing wickedly. 4 He did what was
evil in the sight of the LORD, as the
house of Ahab had done; for after
the death of his father they were
his counselors, to his ruin. 5 He
even followed their advice, and
went with Jehoram son of King
Ahab of Israel to make war against
King Hazael of Aram at Ramoth-
gilead. The Arameans wounded Joram, 6 and he returned to be healed
in Jezreel of the wounds that he
had received at Ramah, when he
fought King Hazael of Aram. And
Ahaziah son of King Jehoram of Judah went down to see Joram son of
Ahab in Jezreel, because he was
sick.

7 But it was ordained by God
that the downfall of Ahaziah
should come about through his going to visit Joram. For when he
came there he went out with Jehoram to meet Jehu son of Nimshi,
whom the LORD had anointed to destroy the house of Ahab. 8 When
Jehu was executing judgment on
the house of Ahab, he met the officials of Judah and the sons of Ahaziah's brothers, who attended Ahaziah, and he killed them. 9 He
searched for Ahaziah, who was captured while hiding in Samaria and
was brought to Jehu, and put to
death. They buried him, for they
said, "He is the grandson of Jehoshaphat, who sought the LORD
with all his heart." And the house
of Ahaziah had no one able to rule
the kingdom.

Athaliah Seizes the Throne

10 Now when Athaliah, Ahaziah's mother, saw that her son was
dead, she set about to destroy all
the royal family of the house of Judah. 11 But Jehoshabeath, the
king's daughter, took Joash son of
Ahaziah, and stole him away from
among the king's children who
were about to be killed; she put
him and his nurse in a bedroom.
Thus Jehoshabeath, daughter of
King Jehoram and wife of the priest
Jehoiada—because she was a sister of Ahaziah—hid him from Athaliah, so that she did not kill him;
12 he remained with them six years,
hidden in the house of God, while
Athaliah reigned over the land.

23 But in the seventh year Jehoiada took courage, and
entered into a compact with the
commanders of the hundreds, Azariah son of Jeroham, Ishmael son of
Jehohanan, Azariah son of Obed,
Maaseiah son of Adaiah, and Elish-
aphat son of Zichri. 2 They went
around through Judah and gathered the Levites from all the towns
of Judah, and the heads of families
of Israel, and they came to Jerusalem. 3 Then the whole assembly
made a covenant with the king in
the house of God. Jehoiada[u] said
to them, "Here is the king's son!
Let him reign, as the LORD promised concerning the sons of David.
4 This is what you are to do: one
third of you, priests and Levites,
who come on duty on the sabbath,
shall be gatekeepers, 5 one third
shall be at the king's house, and
one third at the Gate of the Foundation; and all the people shall be
in the courts of the house of the
LORD. 6 Do not let anyone enter the
house of the LORD except the
priests and ministering Levites;
they may enter, for they are holy,
but all the other[v] people shall observe the instructions of the LORD.
7 The Levites shall surround the
king, each with his weapons in his
hand; and whoever enters the
house shall be killed. Stay with the
king in his comings and goings."

Joash Crowned King

8 The Levites and all Judah did
according to all that the priest Jehoiada commanded; each brought

22.2 2 Chr 21.6
22.5 2 Kings 8.28ff
22.6 2 Kings 9.15
22.7 2 Chr 10.15; 2 Kings 9.6, 7,21
22.8 2 Kings 10.10-14
22.9 2 Kings 9.27, 28; 2 Chr 17.4
22.10 2 Kings 11.1-3
23.1 2 Kings 11.4-20
23.3 2 Sam 7.12; 1 Kings 2.4; 2 Chr 6.16; 7.18; 21.7
23.4 1 Chr 9.25
23.7 1 Chr 23.28-32
23.8 1 Chr 24.1

[u] Heb *He* [v] Heb lacks *other*

his men, who were to come on duty
on the sabbath, with those who
were to go off duty on the sabbath;
for the priest Jehoiada did not dismiss the divisions. 9 The priest Jehoiada delivered to the captains
the spears and the large and small
shields that had been King David's,
which were in the house of God;
10 and he set all the people as a
guard for the king, everyone with
weapon in hand, from the south
side of the house to the north side
of the house, around the altar and
the house. 11 Then he brought out
the king's son, put the crown on
him, and gave him the covenant;[w]
they proclaimed him king, and Jehoiada and his sons anointed him;
and they shouted, "Long live the
king!"

Athaliah Murdered

12 When Athaliah heard the
noise of the people running and
praising the king, she went into the
house of the LORD to the people;
13 and when she looked, there was
the king standing by his pillar at
the entrance, and the captains and
the trumpeters beside the king,
and all the people of the land rejoicing and blowing trumpets, and
the singers with their musical instruments leading in the celebration. Athaliah tore her clothes, and
cried, "Treason! Treason!" 14 Then
the priest Jehoiada brought out the
captains who were set over the
army, saying to them, "Bring her
out between the ranks; anyone who
follows her is to be put to the
sword." For the priest said, "Do not
put her to death in the house of the
LORD." 15 So they laid hands on her;
she went into the entrance of the
Horse Gate of the king's house, and
there they put her to death.

16 Jehoiada made a covenant
between himself and all the people
and the king that they should be
the LORD's people. 17 Then all the
people went to the house of Baal,
and tore it down; his altars and his
images they broke in pieces, and
they killed Mattan, the priest of
Baal, in front of the altars. 18 Jehoi-

23.9 v. 1
23.11 Ex 25.16; 1 Sam 10.24
23.12 2 Kings 11.13
23.15 Neh 3.28; Jer 31.40
23.17 Deut 13.9
23.18 2 Chr 5.5; 1 Chr 23.6, 30,31; 25.1,2, 6
23.19 1 Chr 9.22
23.20 2 Kings 11.19
24.1 2 Kings 11.21; 12.1-15
24.2 2 Chr 26.5
24.4 v. 7
24.6 Ex 30.12-16
24.7 2 Chr 21.17

ada assigned the care of the house
of the LORD to the levitical priests
whom David had organized to be in
charge of the house of the LORD, to
offer burnt offerings to the LORD, as
it is written in the law of Moses,
with rejoicing and with singing, according to the order of David. 19 He
stationed the gatekeepers at the
gates of the house of the LORD so
that no one should enter who was
in any way unclean. 20 And he took
the captains, the nobles, the governors of the people, and all the people of the land, and they brought
the king down from the house of
the LORD, marching through the upper gate to the king's house. They
set the king on the royal throne.
21 So all the people of the land rejoiced, and the city was quiet after
Athaliah had been killed with the
sword.

Joash Repairs the Temple

24 Joash was seven years old
when he began to reign; he
reigned forty years in Jerusalem;
his mother's name was Zibiah of
Beer-sheba. 2 Joash did what was
right in the sight of the LORD all the
days of the priest Jehoiada. 3 Jehoiada got two wives for him, and he
became the father of sons and
daughters.

4 Some time afterward Joash
decided to restore the house of the
LORD. 5 He assembled the priests
and the Levites and said to them,
"Go out to the cities of Judah and
gather money from all Israel to repair the house of your God, year by
year; and see that you act quickly."
But the Levites did not act quickly.
6 So the king summoned Jehoiada
the chief, and said to him, "Why
have you not required the Levites
to bring in from Judah and Jerusalem the tax levied by Moses, the
servant of the LORD, on[x] the congregation of Israel for the tent of
the covenant?"[w] 7 For the children
of Athaliah, that wicked woman,
had broken into the house of God,
and had even used all the dedicat-

[w] Or *treaty*, or *testimony*; Heb *eduth*
[x] Compare Vg: Heb *and*

ed things of the house of the LORD
for the Baals.
8 So the king gave command,
and they made a chest, and set it
outside the gate of the house of the
LORD. 9 A proclamation was made
throughout Judah and Jerusalem
to bring in for the LORD the tax that
Moses the servant of God laid on
Israel in the wilderness. 10 All the
leaders and all the people rejoiced
and brought their tax and dropped
it into the chest until it was full.
11 Whenever the chest was brought
to the king's officers by the Levites,
when they saw that there was a
large amount of money in it, the
king's secretary and the officer of
the chief priest would come and
empty the chest and take it and return it to its place. So they did day
after day, and collected money in
abundance. 12 The king and Jehoiada gave it to those who had charge
of the work of the house of the
LORD, and they hired masons and
carpenters to restore the house of
the LORD, and also workers in iron
and bronze to repair the house of
the LORD. 13 So those who were engaged in the work labored, and the
repairing went forward at their
hands, and they restored the house
of God to its proper condition and
strengthened it. 14 When they had
finished, they brought the rest of
the money to the king and Jehoiada, and with it were made utensils
for the house of the LORD, utensils
for the service and for the burnt offerings, and ladles, and vessels of
gold and silver. They offered burnt
offerings in the house of the LORD
regularly all the days of Jehoiada.

Apostasy of Joash

15 But Jehoiada grew old and
full of days, and died; he was one
hundred thirty years old at his
death. 16 And they buried him in
the city of David among the kings,
because he had done good in Israel, and for God and his house.
17 Now after the death of Jehoiada the officials of Judah came and
did obeisance to the king; then the
king listened to them. 18 They

24.9 v. 6
24.11 2 Kings 12.10
24.13 Neh 10.39
24.16 2 Chr 21.2, 20
24.18 v. 4; Ex 34.12-14; 1 Kings 14.23; Josh 22.20; 2 Chr 19.2
24.19 Jer 7.25
24.20 2 Chr 20.14; Num 14.41; 2 Chr 15.2
24.21 Neh 9.26; Mt 23.35; Acts 7.58,59
24.22 Gen 9.5
24.23 2 Kings 12.17
24.24 Lev 26.25; Deut 28.25; 2 Chr 22.8; Isa 10.5
24.25 2 Kings 12.20; v. 21

abandoned the house of the LORD,
the God of their ancestors, and
served the sacred poles[y] and the
idols. And wrath came upon Judah
and Jerusalem for this guilt of
theirs. 19 Yet he sent prophets
among them to bring them back to
the LORD; they testified against
them, but they would not listen.
20 Then the spirit of God took
possession of[z] Zechariah son of
the priest Jehoiada; he stood above
the people and said to them, "Thus
says God: Why do you transgress
the commandments of the LORD, so
that you cannot prosper? Because
you have forsaken the LORD, he has
also forsaken you." 21 But they conspired against him, and by command of the king they stoned him
to death in the court of the house
of the LORD. 22 King Joash did not
remember the kindness that Jehoiada, Zechariah's father, had shown
him, but killed his son. As he was
dying, he said, "May the LORD see
and avenge!"

Death of Joash

23 At the end of the year the
army of Aram came up against Joash. They came to Judah and Jerusalem, and destroyed all the officials of the people from among
them, and sent all the booty they
took to the king of Damascus. 24 Although the army of Aram had come
with few men, the LORD delivered
into their hand a very great army,
because they had abandoned the
LORD, the God of their ancestors.
Thus they executed judgment on
Joash.
25 When they had withdrawn,
leaving him severely wounded, his
servants conspired against him because of the blood of the son[a] of
the priest Jehoiada, and they killed
him on his bed. So he died; and
they buried him in the city of David, but they did not bury him in
the tombs of the kings. 26 Those
who conspired against him were
Zabad son of Shimeath the Ammonite, and Jehozabad son of

[y] Heb *Asherim* [z] Heb *clothed itself with*
[a] Gk Vg: Heb *sons*

Shimrith the Moabite. 27 Accounts
of his sons, and of the many oracles
against him, and of the rebuilding[b]
of the house of God are written in
the Commentary on the Book of
the Kings. And his son Amaziah
succeeded him.

Reign of Amaziah

25 Amaziah was twenty-five
years old when he began to
reign, and he reigned twenty-nine
years in Jerusalem. His mother's
name was Jehoaddan of Jerusalem.
2 He did what was right in the sight
of the LORD, yet not with a true
heart. 3 As soon as the royal power
was firmly in his hand he killed his
servants who had murdered his father the king. 4 But he did not put
their children to death, according
to what is written in the law, in the
book of Moses, where the LORD
commanded, "The parents shall
not be put to death for the children, or the children be put to
death for the parents; but all shall
be put to death for their own sins."

Slaughter of the Edomites

5 Amaziah assembled the people of Judah, and set them by ancestral houses under commanders
of the thousands and of the hundreds for all Judah and Benjamin.
He mustered those twenty years
old and upward, and found that
they were three hundred thousand
picked troops fit for war, able to
handle spear and shield. 6 He also
hired one hundred thousand
mighty warriors from Israel for one
hundred talents of silver. 7 But a
man of God came to him and said,
"O king, do not let the army of Israel go with you, for the LORD is not
with Israel—all these Ephraimites.
8 Rather, go by yourself and act; be
strong in battle, or God will fling
you down before the enemy; for
God has power to help or to overthrow." 9 Amaziah said to the man
of God, "But what shall we do
about the hundred talents that I
have given to the army of Israel?"
The man of God answered, "The
LORD is able to give you much more

24.27 2 Kings 12.18, 21
25.1 2 Kings 14.1-6
25.2 v. 14
25.4 Deut 24.16; 2 Kings 14.6
25.5 Num 1.3
25.8 2 Chr 14.11; 20.6
25.11 2 Kings 14.7
25.14 2 Chr 28.23; Ex 20.3,5
25.15 Ps 96.5; vv. 11,12
25.17 2 Kings 14.8-14
25.18 Judg 9.8-15

than this." 10 Then Amaziah discharged the army that had come to
him from Ephraim, letting them go
home again. But they became very
angry with Judah, and returned
home in fierce anger.
11 Amaziah took courage, and
led out his people; he went to the
Valley of Salt, and struck down ten
thousand men of Seir. 12 The people of Judah captured another ten
thousand alive, took them to the
top of Sela, and threw them down
from the top of Sela, so that all of
them were dashed to pieces. 13 But
the men of the army whom Amaziah sent back, not letting them go
with him to battle, fell on the cities
of Judah from Samaria to Beth-
horon; they killed three thousand
people in them, and took much
booty.
14 Now after Amaziah came
from the slaughter of the Edomites, he brought the gods of the
people of Seir, set them up as his
gods, and worshiped them, making
offerings to them. 15 The LORD was
angry with Amaziah and sent to
him a prophet, who said to him,
"Why have you resorted to a people's gods who could not deliver
their own people from your hand?"
16 But as he was speaking the king[c]
said to him, "Have we made you a
royal counselor? Stop! Why should
you be put to death?" So the prophet stopped, but said, "I know that
God has determined to destroy
you, because you have done this
and have not listened to my advice."

Israel Defeats Judah

17 Then King Amaziah of Judah
took counsel and sent to King Joash son of Jehoahaz son of Jehu of
Israel, saying, "Come, let us look
one another in the face." 18 King
Joash of Israel sent word to King
Amaziah of Judah, "A thornbush
on Lebanon sent to a cedar on Lebanon, saying, 'Give your daughter
to my son for a wife'; but a wild animal of Lebanon passed by and
trampled down the thornbush.

[b] Heb *founding* [c] Heb *he*

19 You say, 'See, I have defeated
Edom,' and your heart has lifted
you up in boastfulness. Now stay at
home; why should you provoke
trouble so that you fall, you and Judah with you?"
20 But Amaziah would not
listen—it was God's doing, in order
to hand them over, because they
had sought the gods of Edom. 21 So
King Joash of Israel went up; he
and King Amaziah of Judah faced
one another in battle at Beth-
shemesh, which belongs to Judah.
22 Judah was defeated by Israel; everyone fled home. 23 King Joash of
Israel captured King Amaziah of
Judah, son of Joash, son of Ahaziah, at Beth-shemesh; he brought
him to Jerusalem, and broke down
the wall of Jerusalem from the
Ephraim Gate to the Corner Gate, a
distance of four hundred cubits.
24 He seized all the gold and silver,
and all the vessels that were found
in the house of God, and Obed-
edom with them; he seized also the
treasuries of the king's house, also
hostages; then he returned to Samaria.

Death of Amaziah

25 King Amaziah son of Joash of
Judah, lived fifteen years after the
death of King Joash son of Jehoahaz of Israel. 26 Now the rest of the
deeds of Amaziah, from first to last,
are they not written in the Book of
the Kings of Judah and Israel?
27 From the time that Amaziah
turned away from the LORD they
made a conspiracy against him in
Jerusalem, and he fled to Lachish.
But they sent after him to Lachish,
and killed him there. 28 They
brought him back on horses; he
was buried with his ancestors in
the city of David.

Reign of Uzziah

26 Then all the people of Judah took Uzziah, who was
sixteen years old, and made him
king to succeed his father Amaziah. 2 He rebuilt Eloth and restored
it to Judah, after the king slept
with his ancestors. 3 Uzziah was
sixteen years old when he began to
reign, and he reigned fifty-two
years in Jerusalem. His mother's
name was Jecoliah of Jerusalem.
4 He did what was right in the sight
of the LORD, just as his father Amaziah had done. 5 He set himself to
seek God in the days of Zechariah,
who instructed him in the fear of
God; and as long as he sought the
LORD, God made him prosper.
6 He went out and made war
against the Philistines, and broke
down the wall of Gath and the wall
of Jabneh and the wall of Ashdod;
he built cities in the territory of
Ashdod and elsewhere among the
Philistines. 7 God helped him
against the Philistines, against the
Arabs who lived in Gur-baal, and
against the Meunites. 8 The Ammonites paid tribute to Uzziah, and
his fame spread even to the border
of Egypt, for he became very
strong. 9 Moreover Uzziah built
towers in Jerusalem at the Corner
Gate, at the Valley Gate, and at the
Angle, and fortified them. 10 He
built towers in the wilderness and
hewed out many cisterns, for he
had large herds, both in the Shephelah and in the plain, and he had
farmers and vinedressers in the
hills and in the fertile lands, for he
loved the soil. 11 Moreover Uzziah
had an army of soldiers, fit for war,
in divisions according to the numbers in the muster made by the secretary Jeiel and the officer Maaseiah, under the direction of
Hananiah, one of the king's commanders. 12 The whole number of
the heads of ancestral houses of
mighty warriors was two thousand
six hundred. 13 Under their command was an army of three hundred seven thousand five hundred,
who could make war with mighty
power, to help the king against the
enemy. 14 Uzziah provided for all
the army the shields, spears, helmets, coats of mail, bows, and
stones for slinging. 15 In Jerusalem
he set up machines, invented by
skilled workers, on the towers and
the corners for shooting arrows and
large stones. And his fame spread

25.19 2 Chr 26.16; 32.25
25.20 1 Kings 12.15; 2 Chr 22.7
25.23 2 Chr 21.17; 22.1
25.25 2 Kings 14.17-22
26.1 2 Kings 14.21, 22; 15.2,3
26.5 2 Chr 24.2; Dan 1.17; 2.19; 2 Chr 15.2
26.6 Isa 14.29
26.7 2 Chr 21.16
26.8 2 Chr 17.11
26.9 2 Chr 25.23; Neh 3.13
26.13 2 Chr 25.5

far, for he was marvelously helped
until he became strong.

Pride and Apostasy

16 But when he had become
strong he grew proud, to his destruction. For he was false to the
LORD his God, and entered the temple of the LORD to make offering on
the altar of incense. 17But the
priest Azariah went in after him,
with eighty priests of the LORD who
were men of valor; 18they withstood King Uzziah, and said to him,
"It is not for you, Uzziah, to make
offering to the LORD, but for the
priests the descendants of Aaron,
who are consecrated to make offering. Go out of the sanctuary; for
you have done wrong, and it will
bring you no honor from the LORD
God." 19Then Uzziah was angry.
Now he had a censer in his hand to
make offering, and when he became angry with the priests a leprous[d] disease broke out on his
forehead, in the presence of the
priests in the house of the LORD, by
the altar of incense. 20When the
chief priest Azariah, and all the
priests, looked at him, he was leprous[d] in his forehead. They hurried
him out, and he himself hurried to
get out, because the LORD had
struck him. 21King Uzziah was leprous[d] to the day of his death, and
being leprous[d] lived in a separate
house, for he was excluded from
the house of the LORD. His son Jotham was in charge of the palace of
the king, governing the people of
the land.
22 Now the rest of the acts of
Uzziah, from first to last, the
prophet Isaiah son of Amoz wrote.
23Uzziah slept with his ancestors;
they buried him near his ancestors
in the burial field that belonged to
the kings, for they said, "He is leprous."[d] His son Jotham succeeded
him.

Reign of Jotham

27 Jotham was twenty-five
years old when he began to
reign; he reigned sixteen years in
Jerusalem. His mother's name was
Jerushah daughter of Zadok. 2He
did what was right in the sight of
the LORD just as his father Uzziah
had done—only he did not invade
the temple of the LORD. But the
people still followed corrupt practices. 3He built the upper gate of
the house of the LORD, and did extensive building on the wall of
Ophel. 4Moreover he built cities in
the hill country of Judah, and forts
and towers on the wooded hills.
5He fought with the king of the
Ammonites and prevailed against
them. The Ammonites gave him
that year one hundred talents of
silver, ten thousand cors of wheat
and ten thousand of barley. The
Ammonites paid him the same
amount in the second and the third
years. 6So Jotham became strong
because he ordered his ways before
the LORD his God. 7Now the rest of
the acts of Jotham, and all his wars
and his ways, are written in the
Book of the Kings of Israel and Judah. 8He was twenty-five years old
when he began to reign; he reigned
sixteen years in Jerusalem. 9Jo-
tham slept with his ancestors, and
they buried him in the city of David; and his son Ahaz succeeded
him.

Reign of Ahaz

28 Ahaz was twenty years old
when he began to reign; he
reigned sixteen years in Jerusalem.
He did not do what was right in the
sight of the LORD, as his ancestor
David had done, 2but he walked in
the ways of the kings of Israel. He
even made cast images for the Baals; 3and he made offerings in the
valley of the son of Hinnom, and
made his sons pass through fire,
according to the abominable practices of the nations whom the LORD
drove out before the people of Israel. 4He sacrificed and made offerings on the high places, on the
hills, and under every green tree.

Aram and Israel Defeat Judah

5 Therefore the LORD his God

26.16 Deut 32.15; 2 Chr 25.19; 2 Kings 16.12, 13
26.17 1 Chr 6.10
26.18 Num 16.39, 40; Ex 30.7, 8
26.19 2 Kings 5.25-27
26.21 2 Kings 15.5-7; Lev 13.46; Num 5.2
26.22 Isa 1.1
26.23 2 Kings 15.7; Isa 6.1
27.1 2 Kings 15.33-35
27.2 2 Chr 26.16
27.3 2 Chr 33.14; Neh 3.26
27.6 2 Chr 26.5
27.7 2 Kings 15.36
27.8 v. 1
28.1 2 Kings 16.2-4
28.2 2 Chr 22.3; Ex 34.17
28.3 2 Kings 23.10; Lev 18.21; 2 Kings 16.3; 2 Chr 33.6
28.4 v. 25
28.5 Isa 7.1; 2 Kings 16.5, 6

[d] A term for several skin diseases; precise meaning uncertain

gave him into the hand of the king
of Aram, who defeated him and
took captive a great number of his
people and brought them to Damascus. He was also given into the
hand of the king of Israel, who defeated him with great slaughter.
6 Pekah son of Remaliah killed one
hundred twenty thousand in Judah
in one day, all of them valiant warriors, because they had abandoned
the LORD, the God of their ancestors. 7 And Zichri, a mighty warrior
of Ephraim, killed the king's son
Maaseiah, Azrikam the commander of the palace, and Elkanah the
next in authority to the king.

Intervention of Oded

8 The people of Israel took captive two hundred thousand of their
kin, women, sons, and daughters;
they also took much booty from
them and brought the booty to Samaria. 9 But a prophet of the LORD
was there, whose name was Oded;
he went out to meet the army that
came to Samaria, and said to them,
"Because the LORD, the God of your
ancestors, was angry with Judah,
he gave them into your hand, but
you have killed them in a rage that
has reached up to heaven. 10 Now
you intend to subjugate the people
of Judah and Jerusalem, male and
female, as your slaves. But what
have you except sins against the
LORD your God? 11 Now hear me,
and send back the captives whom
you have taken from your kindred,
for the fierce wrath of the LORD is
upon you." 12 Moreover, certain
chiefs of the Ephraimites, Azariah
son of Johanan, Berechiah son of
Meshillemoth, Jehizkiah son of
Shallum, and Amasa son of Hadlai,
stood up against those who were
coming from the war, 13 and said to
them, "You shall not bring the captives in here, for you propose to
bring on us guilt against the LORD in
addition to our present sins and
guilt. For our guilt is already great,
and there is fierce wrath against Israel." 14 So the warriors left the captives and the booty before the officials and all the assembly. 15 Then
those who were mentioned by
name got up and took the captives,
and with the booty they clothed all
that were naked among them; they
clothed them, gave them sandals,
provided them with food and drink,
and anointed them; and carrying
all the feeble among them on donkeys, they brought them to their
kindred at Jericho, the city of palm
trees. Then they returned to Samaria.

Assyria Refuses to Help Judah

16 At that time King Ahaz sent
to the king[e] of Assyria for help.
17 For the Edomites had again invaded and defeated Judah, and carried away captives. 18 And the Philistines had made raids on the cities
in the Shephelah and the Negeb of
Judah, and had taken Beth-
shemesh, Aijalon, Gederoth, Soco
with its villages, Timnah with its
villages, and Gimzo with its villages; and they settled there. 19 For
the LORD brought Judah low because of King Ahaz of Israel, for he
had behaved without restraint in
Judah and had been faithless to
the LORD. 20 So King Tilgath-
pilneser of Assyria came against
him, and oppressed him instead of
strengthening him. 21 For Ahaz
plundered the house of the LORD
and the houses of the king and of
the officials, and gave tribute to the
king of Assyria; but it did not help
him.

Apostasy and Death of Ahaz

22 In the time of his distress he
became yet more faithless to the
LORD—this same King Ahaz. 23 For
he sacrificed to the gods of Damascus, which had defeated him, and
said, "Because the gods of the
kings of Aram helped them, I will
sacrifice to them so that they may
help me." But they were the ruin of
him, and of all Israel. 24 Ahaz gathered together the utensils of the
house of God, and cut in pieces the
utensils of the house of God. He
shut up the doors of the house of
the LORD and made himself altars

28.6 2 Kings 15.27
28.8 2 Chr 11.4
28.9 2 Chr 25.15; Isa 10.5; 47.6; Ezra 9.6; Rev 18.5
28.10 Lev 25.39, 42,43,46
28.11 v. 8
28.15 v. 12; 2 Kings 6.22; Prov 25.21, 22; Deut 34.3; Judg 1.16
28.16 2 Kings 16.7
28.18 Ezek 16.57
28.19 2 Chr 21.2
28.20 1 Chr 5.26; 2 Kings 16.8, 9
28.23 2 Chr 25.14; Jer 44.17,18
28.24 2 Kings 16.17; 2 Chr 29.7; 30.14; 33.3-5

[e] Gk Syr Vg Compare 2 Kings 16.7: Heb *kings*

in every corner of Jerusalem. 25 In
every city of Judah he made high
places to make offerings to other
gods, provoking to anger the LORD,
the God of his ancestors. 26 Now
the rest of his acts and all his ways,
from first to last, are written in the
Book of the Kings of Judah and Israel. 27 Ahaz slept with his ancestors, and they buried him in the
city, in Jerusalem; but they did not
bring him into the tombs of the
kings of Israel. His son Hezekiah
succeeded him.

Reign of Hezekiah

29 Hezekiah began to reign
when he was twenty-five
years old; he reigned twenty-nine
years in Jerusalem. His mother's
name was Abijah daughter of Zechariah. 2 He did what was right in the
sight of the LORD, just as his ancestor David had done.

The Temple Cleansed

3 In the first year of his reign, in
the first month, he opened the
doors of the house of the LORD and
repaired them. 4 He brought in the
priests and the Levites and assembled them in the square on the
east. 5 He said to them, "Listen to
me, Levites! Sanctify yourselves,
and sanctify the house of the LORD,
the God of your ancestors, and carry out the filth from the holy place.
6 For our ancestors have been unfaithful and have done what was
evil in the sight of the LORD our
God; they have forsaken him, and
have turned away their faces from
the dwelling of the LORD, and
turned their backs. 7 They also shut
the doors of the vestibule and put
out the lamps, and have not offered
incense or made burnt offerings in
the holy place to the God of Israel.
8 Therefore the wrath of the LORD
came upon Judah and Jerusalem,
and he has made them an object of
horror, of astonishment, and of
hissing, as you see with your own
eyes. 9 Our fathers have fallen by
the sword and our sons and our
daughters and our wives are in captivity for this. 10 Now it is in my
heart to make a covenant with the
LORD, the God of Israel, so that his
fierce anger may turn away from us.
11 My sons, do not now be negligent, for the LORD has chosen you
to stand in his presence to minister
to him, and to be his ministers and
make offerings to him."

12 Then the Levites arose, Mahath son of Amasai, and Joel son of
Azariah, of the sons of the Kohathites; and of the sons of Merari, Kish
son of Abdi, and Azariah son of Jehallelel; and of the Gershonites,
Joah son of Zimmah, and Eden son
of Joah; 13 and of the sons of Elizaphan, Shimri and Jeuel; and of the
sons of Asaph, Zechariah and Mattaniah; 14 and of the sons of Heman, Jehuel and Shimei; and of the
sons of Jeduthun, Shemaiah and
Uzziel. 15 They gathered their
brothers, sanctified themselves,
and went in as the king had commanded, by the words of the LORD,
to cleanse the house of the LORD.
16 The priests went into the inner
part of the house of the LORD to
cleanse it, and they brought out all
the unclean things that they found
in the temple of the LORD into the
court of the house of the LORD; and
the Levites took them and carried
them out to the Wadi Kidron.
17 They began to sanctify on the
first day of the first month, and on
the eighth day of the month they
came to the vestibule of the LORD;
then for eight days they sanctified
the house of the LORD, and on the
sixteenth day of the first month
they finished. 18 Then they went inside to King Hezekiah and said,
"We have cleansed all the house of
the LORD, the altar of burnt offering
and all its utensils, and the table
for the rows of bread and all its
utensils. 19 All the utensils that
King Ahaz repudiated during his
reign when he was faithless, we
have made ready and sanctified;
see, they are in front of the altar of
the LORD."

Temple Worship Restored

20 Then King Hezekiah rose
early, assembled the officials of the

28.26 2 Kings 16.19, 20
28.27 2 Chr 24.25
29.1 2 Kings 18.1-3
29.2 2 Chr 28.1
29.3 v. 7; 2 Chr 28.24
29.5 vv. 15,34; 2 Chr 35.6
29.6 Jer 2.27; Ezek 8.16
29.8 2 Chr 24.18; 28.5; Deut 28.25; Jer 25.9,18
29.9 2 Chr 28.5-8, 17
29.10 2 Chr 15.12; 23.16
29.11 Num 3.6; 8.14
29.15 v. 5; 2 Chr 30.12; 1 Chr 23.28
29.17 v. 3
29.19 2 Chr 28.24

city, and went up to the house of the LORD. 21 They brought seven bulls, seven rams, seven lambs, and seven male goats for a sin offering for the kingdom and for the sanctuary and for Judah. He commanded the priests the descendants of Aaron to offer them on the altar of the LORD. 22 So they slaughtered the bulls, and the priests received the blood and dashed it against the altar; they slaughtered the rams and their blood was dashed against the altar; they also slaughtered the lambs and their blood was dashed against the altar. 23 Then the male goats for the sin offering were brought to the king and the assembly; they laid their hands on them, 24 and the priests slaughtered them and made a sin offering with their blood at the altar, to make atonement for all Israel. For the king commanded that the burnt offering and the sin offering should be made for all Israel.

25 He stationed the Levites in the house of the LORD with cymbals, harps, and lyres, according to the commandment of David and of Gad the king's seer and of the prophet Nathan, for the commandment was from the LORD through his prophets. 26 The Levites stood with the instruments of David, and the priests with the trumpets. 27 Then Hezekiah commanded that the burnt offering be offered on the altar. When the burnt offering began, the song to the LORD began also, and the trumpets, accompanied by the instruments of King David of Israel. 28 The whole assembly worshiped, the singers sang, and the trumpeters sounded; all this continued until the burnt offering was finished. 29 When the offering was finished, the king and all who were present with him bowed down and worshiped. 30 King Hezekiah and the officials commanded the Levites to sing praises to the LORD with the words of David and of the seer Asaph. They sang praises with gladness, and they bowed down and worshiped.

31 Then Hezekiah said, "You have now consecrated yourselves to the LORD; come near, bring sacrifices and thank offerings to the house of the LORD." The assembly brought sacrifices and thank offerings; and all who were of a willing heart brought burnt offerings. 32 The number of the burnt offerings that the assembly brought was seventy bulls, one hundred rams, and two hundred lambs; all these were for a burnt offering to the LORD. 33 The consecrated offerings were six hundred bulls and three thousand sheep. 34 But the priests were too few and could not skin all the burnt offerings, so, until other priests had sanctified themselves, their kindred, the Levites, helped them until the work was finished—for the Levites were more conscientious[f] than the priests in sanctifying themselves. 35 Besides the great number of burnt offerings there was the fat of the offerings of well-being, and there were the drink offerings for the burnt offerings. Thus the service of the house of the LORD was restored. 36 And Hezekiah and all the people rejoiced because of what God had done for the people; for the thing had come about suddenly.

The Great Passover

30 Hezekiah sent word to all Israel and Judah, and wrote letters also to Ephraim and Manasseh, that they should come to the house of the LORD at Jerusalem, to keep the passover to the LORD the God of Israel. 2 For the king and his officials and all the assembly in Jerusalem had taken counsel to keep the passover in the second month 3 (for they could not keep it at its proper time because the priests had not sanctified themselves in sufficient number, nor had the people assembled in Jerusalem). 4 The plan seemed right to the king and all the assembly. 5 So they decreed to make a proclamation throughout all Israel, from Beer-sheba to Dan, that the

29.21 Lev 4.3-14
29.22 Lev 4.18; 8.14
29.23 Lev 4.15
29.24 Lev 4.26
29.25 1 Chr 25.6; 2 Chr 8.14; 2 Sam 24.11; 7.2
29.26 1 Chr 23.5; 2 Chr 5.12
29.27 2 Chr 23.18
29.29 2 Chr 20.18
29.31 2 Chr 13.9; Ex 35.5,22
29.34 2 Chr 35.11; 30.3
29.35 v. 32; Lev 3.16; Num 15.5-10
30.2 vv. 13,15; Num 9.10, 11
30.3 Ex 12.6,18; 2 Chr 29.34
30.5 Judg 20.1

[f] Heb *upright in heart*

people should come and keep the
passover to the LORD the God of Israel, at Jerusalem; for they had not
kept it in great numbers as prescribed. 6 So couriers went
throughout all Israel and Judah
with letters from the king and his
officials, as the king had commanded, saying, "O people of Israel, return to the LORD, the God of
Abraham, Isaac, and Israel, so that
he may turn again to the remnant
of you who have escaped from the
hand of the kings of Assyria. 7 Do
not be like your ancestors and your
kindred, who were faithless to the
LORD God of their ancestors, so that
he made them a desolation, as you
see. 8 Do not now be stiff-necked as
your ancestors were, but yield
yourselves to the LORD and come to
his sanctuary, which he has sanctified forever, and serve the LORD
your God, so that his fierce anger
may turn away from you. 9 For as
you return to the LORD, your kindred and your children will find
compassion with their captors, and
return to this land. For the LORD
your God is gracious and merciful,
and will not turn away his face from
you, if you return to him."

10 So the couriers went from
city to city through the country of
Ephraim and Manasseh, and as far
as Zebulun; but they laughed them
to scorn, and mocked them. 11 Only
a few from Asher, Manasseh, and
Zebulun humbled themselves and
came to Jerusalem. 12 The hand of
God was also on Judah to give
them one heart to do what the king
and the officials commanded by
the word of the LORD.

13 Many people came together
in Jerusalem to keep the festival of
unleavened bread in the second
month, a very large assembly.
14 They set to work and removed
the altars that were in Jerusalem,
and all the altars for offering incense they took away and threw
into the Wadi Kidron. 15 They
slaughtered the passover lamb on
the fourteenth day of the second
month. The priests and the Levites
were ashamed, and they sanctified

30.6 Esther 8.14; Job 9.25; Jer 51.31; 2 Chr 20.8
30.7 Ezek 20.18; 2 Chr 29.8
30.8 Ex 32.9; 2 Chr 29.10
30.9 Deut 30.2; Ex 34.6,7; Mic 7.18; Isa 55.7
30.10 2 Chr 36.16
30.11 vv. 18,21,25
30.13 v. 2
30.14 2 Chr 28.24
30.15 vv. 2,3; 2 Chr 29.34
30.16 2 Chr 35.10, 15
30.17 2 Chr 29.34
30.18 vv. 11,25; Ex 12.43-49
30.19 2 Chr 19.3
30.21 Ex 12.15; 13.6
30.22 2 Chr 32.6; Ezra 10.11
30.23 1 Kings 8.65
30.24 2 Chr 35.7, 8; 29.34

themselves and brought burnt offerings into the house of the LORD.
16 They took their accustomed
posts according to the law of Moses
the man of God; the priests dashed
the blood that they received[g] from
the hands of the Levites. 17 For
there were many in the assembly
who had not sanctified themselves;
therefore the Levites had to slaughter the passover lamb for everyone
who was not clean, to make it holy
to the LORD. 18 For a multitude of
the people, many of them from
Ephraim, Manasseh, Issachar, and
Zebulun, had not cleansed themselves, yet they ate the passover
otherwise than as prescribed. But
Hezekiah prayed for them, saying,
"The good LORD pardon all 19 who
set their hearts to seek God, the
LORD the God of their ancestors,
even though not in accordance
with the sanctuary's rules of cleanness." 20 The LORD heard Hezekiah,
and healed the people. 21 The people of Israel who were present at
Jerusalem kept the festival of unleavened bread seven days with
great gladness; and the Levites and
the priests praised the LORD day by
day, accompanied by loud instruments for the LORD. 22 Hezekiah
spoke encouragingly to all the Levites who showed good skill in the
service of the LORD. So the people
ate the food of the festival for seven
days, sacrificing offerings of well-
being and giving thanks to the LORD
the God of their ancestors.

23 Then the whole assembly
agreed together to keep the festival
for another seven days; so they
kept it for another seven days with
gladness. 24 For King Hezekiah of
Judah gave the assembly a thousand bulls and seven thousand
sheep for offerings, and the officials gave the assembly a thousand
bulls and ten thousand sheep. The
priests sanctified themselves in
great numbers. 25 The whole assembly of Judah, the priests and
the Levites, and the whole assembly that came out of Israel, and the

[g] Heb lacks *that they received*

resident aliens who came out of the
land of Israel, and the resident
aliens who lived in Judah, rejoiced.
26 There was great joy in Jerusalem,
for since the time of Solomon son
of King David of Israel there had
been nothing like this in Jerusalem. 27 Then the priests and the Levites stood up and blessed the people, and their voice was heard;
their prayer came to his holy dwelling in heaven.

Pagan Shrines Destroyed

31 Now when all this was finished, all Israel who were
present went out to the cities of Judah and broke down the pillars,
hewed down the sacred poles,[h]
and pulled down the high places
and the altars throughout all Judah
and Benjamin, and in Ephraim and
Manasseh, until they had destroyed them all. Then all the people of Israel returned to their cities,
all to their individual properties.

2 Hezekiah appointed the divisions of the priests and of the Levites, division by division, everyone
according to his service, the priests
and the Levites, for burnt offerings
and offerings of well-being, to minister in the gates of the camp of the
LORD and to give thanks and praise.
3 The contribution of the king from
his own possessions was for the
burnt offerings: the burnt offerings
of morning and evening, and the
burnt offerings for the sabbaths,
the new moons, and the appointed
festivals, as it is written in the law
of the LORD. 4 He commanded the
people who lived in Jerusalem to
give the portion due to the priests
and the Levites, so that they might
devote themselves to the law of the
LORD. 5 As soon as the word spread,
the people of Israel gave in abundance the first fruits of grain, wine,
oil, honey, and of all the produce of
the field; and they brought in abundantly the tithe of everything. 6 The
people of Israel and Judah who
lived in the cities of Judah also
brought in the tithe of cattle and
sheep, and the tithe of the dedicated things that had been consecrated to the LORD their God, and laid
them in heaps. 7 In the third month
they began to pile up the heaps,
and finished them in the seventh
month. 8 When Hezekiah and the
officials came and saw the heaps,
they blessed the LORD and his people Israel. 9 Hezekiah questioned
the priests and the Levites about
the heaps. 10 The chief priest Azariah, who was of the house of Zadok,
answered him, "Since they began
to bring the contributions into the
house of the LORD, we have had
enough to eat and have plenty to
spare; for the LORD has blessed his
people, so that we have this great
supply left over."

Reorganization of Priests and Levites

11 Then Hezekiah commanded
them to prepare store-chambers in
the house of the LORD; and they
prepared them. 12 Faithfully they
brought in the contributions, the
tithes and the dedicated things.
The chief officer in charge of them
was Conaniah the Levite, with his
brother Shimei as second; 13 while
Jehiel, Azaziah, Nahath, Asahel,
Jerimoth, Jozabad, Eliel, Ismachi-
ah, Mahath, and Benaiah were
overseers assisting Conaniah and
his brother Shimei, by the appointment of King Hezekiah and of Azariah the chief officer of the house of
God. 14 Kore son of Imnah the Levite, keeper of the east gate, was in
charge of the freewill offerings to
God, to apportion the contribution
reserved for the LORD and the most
holy offerings. 15 Eden, Miniamin,
Jeshua, Shemaiah, Amariah, and
Shecaniah were faithfully assisting
him in the cities of the priests, to
distribute the portions to their kindred, old and young alike, by divisions, 16 except those enrolled by
genealogy, males from three years
old and upwards, all who entered
the house of the LORD as the duty of
each day required, for their service
according to their offices, by their
divisions. 17 The enrollment of the
priests was according to their an-

30.27 2 Chr 23.18; Num 6.23; Deut 26.15; Ps 68.5
31.1 2 Kings 18.4
31.2 1 Chr 24.1; 23.28-31
31.3 Num 28.29
31.4 Num 18.8; Neh 13.10
31.5 Neh 13.12
31.6 Lev 27.30; Deut 14.28
31.10 Mal 3.10
31.13 2 Chr 35.9
31.15 2 Chr 29.12; Josh 21.9-19
31.16 Ezra 3.4
31.17 1 Chr 23.24

[h] Heb *Asherim*

cestral houses; that of the Levites
from twenty years old and upwards
was according to their offices, by
their divisions. 18 The priests were
enrolled with all their little children, their wives, their sons, and
their daughters, the whole multitude; for they were faithful in keeping themselves holy. 19 And for the
descendants of Aaron, the priests,
who were in the fields of common
land belonging to their towns, town
by town, the people designated by
name were to distribute portions to
every male among the priests and
to everyone among the Levites who
was enrolled.
20 Hezekiah did this throughout all Judah; he did what was good
and right and faithful before the
LORD his God. 21 And every work
that he undertook in the service of
the house of God, and in accordance with the law and the commandments, to seek his God, he
did with all his heart; and he prospered.

Sennacherib's Invasion

32 After these things and
these acts of faithfulness,
King Sennacherib of Assyria came
and invaded Judah and encamped
against the fortified cities, thinking
to win them for himself. 2 When
Hezekiah saw that Sennacherib
had come and intended to fight
against Jerusalem, 3 he planned
with his officers and his warriors to
stop the flow of the springs that
were outside the city; and they
helped him. 4 A great many people
were gathered, and they stopped
all the springs and the wadi that
flowed through the land, saying,
"Why should the Assyrian kings
come and find water in abundance?" 5 Hezekiah[i] set to work
resolutely and built up the entire
wall that was broken down, and
raised towers on it,[j] and outside it
he built another wall; he also
strengthened the Millo in the city
of David, and made weapons and
shields in abundance. 6 He appointed combat commanders over
the people, and gathered them together to him in the square at the
gate of the city and spoke encouragingly to them, saying, 7 "Be
strong and of good courage. Do not
be afraid or dismayed before the
king of Assyria and all the horde
that is with him; for there is one
greater with us than with him.
8 With him is an arm of flesh; but
with us is the LORD our God, to help
us and to fight our battles." The
people were encouraged by the
words of King Hezekiah of Judah.
9 After this, while King Sennacherib of Assyria was at Lachish
with all his forces, he sent his servants to Jerusalem to King Hezekiah of Judah and to all the people of
Judah that were in Jerusalem, saying, 10 "Thus says King Sennacherib of Assyria: On what are you relying, that you undergo the siege of
Jerusalem? 11 Is not Hezekiah misleading you, handing you over to
die by famine and by thirst, when
he tells you, 'The LORD our God will
save us from the hand of the king of
Assyria'? 12 Was it not this same
Hezekiah who took away his high
places and his altars and commanded Judah and Jerusalem, saying, 'Before one altar you shall worship, and upon it you shall make
your offerings'? 13 Do you not know
what I and my ancestors have done
to all the peoples of other lands?
Were the gods of the nations of
those lands at all able to save their
lands out of my hand? 14 Who
among all the gods of those nations
that my ancestors utterly destroyed
was able to save his people from my
hand, that your God should be able
to save you from my hand? 15 Now
therefore do not let Hezekiah deceive you or mislead you in this
fashion, and do not believe him, for
no god of any nation or kingdom
has been able to save his people
from my hand or from the hand of
my ancestors. How much less will
your God save you out of my hand!"
16 His servants said still more
against the Lord GOD and against

31.19 Lev 25.34; Num 35.2; vv. 12-15
31.20 2 Kings 20.3; 22.2
32.1 2 Kings 18.13-19; Isa 36.1ff
32.4 2 Kings 20.20; v. 30
32.5 2 Chr 25.23; 1 Kings 9.24
32.6 2 Chr 30.22
32.7 1 Chr 22.13; 2 Kings 6.16
32.8 Jer 17.5; 2 Chr 13.12; 20.17
32.11 2 Kings 18.30
32.12 2 Kings 18.22; 2 Chr 31.1
32.13 2 Kings 18.33-35
32.14 Isa 10.9-11
32.15 2 Kings 18.29

[i] Heb *He* [j] Vg: Heb *and raised on the towers*

his servant Hezekiah. 17 He also
wrote letters to throw contempt on
the LORD the God of Israel and to
speak against him, saying, "Just as
the gods of the nations in other
lands did not rescue their people
from my hands, so the God of Hezekiah will not rescue his people
from my hand." 18 They shouted it
with a loud voice in the language of
Judah to the people of Jerusalem
who were on the wall, to frighten
and terrify them, in order that they
might take the city. 19 They spoke
of the God of Jerusalem as if he
were like the gods of the peoples of
the earth, which are the work of human hands.

Sennacherib's Defeat and Death

20 Then King Hezekiah and the
prophet Isaiah son of Amoz prayed
because of this and cried to heav-
en. 21 And the LORD sent an angel
who cut off all the mighty warriors
and commanders and officers in
the camp of the king of Assyria. So
he returned in disgrace to his own
land. When he came into the house
of his god, some of his own sons
struck him down there with the
sword. 22 So the LORD saved Hezekiah and the inhabitants of Jerusalem from the hand of King Sennacherib of Assyria and from the
hand of all his enemies; he gave
them rest[k] on every side. 23 Many
brought gifts to the LORD in Jerusalem and precious things to King
Hezekiah of Judah, so that he was
exalted in the sight of all nations
from that time onward.

Hezekiah's Sickness

24 In those days Hezekiah became sick and was at the point of
death. He prayed to the LORD, and
he answered him and gave him a
sign. 25 But Hezekiah did not respond according to the benefit
done to him, for his heart was
proud. Therefore wrath came upon
him and upon Judah and Jerusalem. 26 Then Hezekiah humbled
himself for the pride of his heart,
both he and the inhabitants of Jerusalem, so that the wrath of the
LORD did not come upon them in
the days of Hezekiah.

Hezekiah's Prosperity and Achievements

27 Hezekiah had very great
riches and honor; and he made
for himself treasuries for silver, for
gold, for precious stones, for
spices, for shields, and for all kinds
of costly objects; 28 storehouses
also for the yield of grain, wine, and
oil; and stalls for all kinds of cattle,
and sheepfolds.[l] 29 He likewise
provided cities for himself, and
flocks and herds in abundance; for
God had given him very great possessions. 30 This same Hezekiah
closed the upper outlet of the waters of Gihon and directed them
down to the west side of the city of
David. Hezekiah prospered in all
his works. 31 So also in the matter
of the envoys of the officials of Babylon, who had been sent to him to
inquire about the sign that had
been done in the land, God left him
to himself, in order to test him and
to know all that was in his heart.
32 Now the rest of the acts of
Hezekiah, and his good deeds, are
written in the vision of the prophet
Isaiah son of Amoz in the Book of
the Kings of Judah and Israel.
33 Hezekiah slept with his ancestors, and they buried him on the ascent to the tombs of the descendants of David; and all Judah and
the inhabitants of Jerusalem did
him honor at his death. His son
Manasseh succeeded him.

Reign of Manasseh

33 Manasseh was twelve years
old when he began to reign;
he reigned fifty-five years in Jerusalem. 2 He did what was evil in the
sight of the LORD, according to the
abominable practices of the nations whom the LORD drove out before the people of Israel. 3 For he
rebuilt the high places that his father Hezekiah had pulled down,
and erected altars to the Baals,
made sacred poles,[m] worshiped all

32.17 2 Kings 19.9,12
32.18 2 Kings 18.26-28
32.19 2 Kings 19.18
32.20 2 Kings 19.2,4,15
32.21 2 Kings 19.35ff
32.23 2 Chr 17.5
32.24 2 Kings 20.1-11; Isa 38.1-8
32.25 Ps 116.12; 2 Chr 26.16; 24.18
32.26 Jer 26.18,19
32.29 1 Chr 29.12
32.30 2 Kings 20.20; 1 Kings 1.33
32.31 2 Kings 20.12; Isa 39.1; Deut 8.2,16
32.33 2 Kings 20.21; Prov 10.7
33.1 2 Kings 21.1-9
33.2 Deut 18.9; 2 Chr 28.3
33.3 2 Chr 31.1; Deut 16.21; 2 Kings 23.5,6; Deut 17.3

[k] Gk Vg: Heb *guided them* [l] Gk Vg: Heb *flocks for folds* [m] Heb *Asheroth*

the host of heaven, and served
them. 4 He built altars in the house
of the LORD, of which the LORD had
said, "In Jerusalem shall my name
be forever." 5 He built altars for all
the host of heaven in the two
courts of the house of the LORD.
6 He made his son pass through fire
in the valley of the son of Hinnom,
practiced soothsaying and augury
and sorcery, and dealt with mediums and with wizards. He did
much evil in the sight of the LORD,
provoking him to anger. 7 The
carved image of the idol that he
had made he set in the house of
God, of which God said to David
and to his son Solomon, "In this
house, and in Jerusalem, which I
have chosen out of all the tribes of
Israel, I will put my name forever;
8 I will never again remove the feet
of Israel from the land that I appointed for your ancestors, if only
they will be careful to do all that I
have commanded them, all the
law, the statutes, and the ordinances given through Moses."
9 Manasseh misled Judah and the
inhabitants of Jerusalem, so that
they did more evil than the nations
whom the LORD had destroyed before the people of Israel.

Manasseh Restored after Repentance

10 The LORD spoke to Manasseh
and to his people, but they gave no
heed. 11 Therefore the LORD brought
against them the commanders of
the army of the king of Assyria, who
took Manasseh captive in manacles, bound him with fetters, and
brought him to Babylon. 12 While
he was in distress he entreated the
favor of the LORD his God and humbled himself greatly before the God
of his ancestors. 13 He prayed to
him, and God received his entreaty, heard his plea, and restored
him again to Jerusalem and to his
kingdom. Then Manasseh knew
that the LORD indeed was God.
14 Afterward he built an outer
wall for the city of David west of
Gihon, in the valley, reaching the
entrance at the Fish Gate; he carried it around Ophel, and raised it
to a very great height. He also put
commanders of the army in all the
fortified cities in Judah. 15 He took
away the foreign gods and the idol
from the house of the LORD, and all
the altars that he had built on the
mountain of the house of the LORD
and in Jerusalem, and he threw
them out of the city. 16 He also restored the altar of the LORD and offered on it sacrifices of well-being
and of thanksgiving; and he commanded Judah to serve the LORD
the God of Israel. 17 The people,
however, still sacrificed at the high
places, but only to the LORD their
God.

Death of Manasseh

18 Now the rest of the acts of
Manasseh, his prayer to his God,
and the words of the seers who
spoke to him in the name of the
LORD God of Israel, these are in the
Annals of the Kings of Israel. 19 His
prayer, and how God received his
entreaty, all his sin and his faithlessness, the sites on which he
built high places and set up the sacred poles[n] and the images, before
he humbled himself, these are
written in the records of the
seers.[o] 20 So Manasseh slept with
his ancestors, and they buried him
in his house. His son Amon succeeded him.

Amon's Reign and Death

21 Amon was twenty-two years
old when he began to reign; he
reigned two years in Jerusalem.
22 He did what was evil in the sight
of the LORD, as his father Manasseh
had done. Amon sacrificed to all
the images that his father Manasseh had made, and served them.
23 He did not humble himself before the LORD, as his father Manasseh had humbled himself, but this
Amon incurred more and more
guilt. 24 His servants conspired
against him and killed him in his
house. 25 But the people of the land
killed all those who had conspired
against King Amon; and the people

33.4 2 Chr 28.24; 7.16
33.5 2 Chr 4.9
33.6 Lev 18.21; 2 Chr 28.3; Deut 18.10, 11; 2 Kings 21.6
33.7 2 Kings 21.7; vv. 4,15
33.8 2 Sam 7.10
33.11 Deut 28.36; Ps 107.10, 11
33.12 2 Chr 32.26; 1 Pet 5.6
33.13 1 Chr 5.20; Ezra 8.23; Dan 4.25,32
33.14 1 Kings 1.33; Neh 3.3; 2 Chr 27.3
33.15 vv. 3-7
33.17 2 Chr 32.12
33.18 vv. 10,12,18
33.19 vv. 3,13
33.20 2 Kings 21.18
33.21 2 Kings 21.19-24
33.22 vv. 2-7
33.23 v. 12
33.24 2 Chr 25.27

[n] Heb *Asherim* [o] One Ms Gk: MT *of Hozai*

of the land made his son Josiah
king to succeed him.

Reign of Josiah

34 Josiah was eight years old
when he began to reign; he
reigned thirty-one years in Jerusalem. 2 He did what was right in the
sight of the LORD, and walked in the
ways of his ancestor David; he did
not turn aside to the right or to the
left. 3 For in the eighth year of his
reign, while he was still a boy, he
began to seek the God of his ancestor David, and in the twelfth year
he began to purge Judah and Jerusalem of the high places, the sacred poles,[p] and the carved and
the cast images. 4 In his presence
they pulled down the altars of the
Baals; he demolished the incense
altars that stood above them. He
broke down the sacred poles[p] and
the carved and the cast images; he
made dust of them and scattered it
over the graves of those who had
sacrificed to them. 5 He also
burned the bones of the priests on
their altars, and purged Judah and
Jerusalem. 6 In the towns of Manasseh, Ephraim, and Simeon, and as
far as Naphtali, in their ruins[q] all
around, 7 he broke down the altars,
beat the sacred poles[p] and the images into powder, and demolished
all the incense altars throughout
all the land of Israel. Then he returned to Jerusalem.

Discovery of the Book of the Law

8 In the eighteenth year of his
reign, when he had purged the land
and the house, he sent Shaphan
son of Azaliah, Maaseiah the governor of the city, and Joah son of Joahaz, the recorder, to repair the
house of the LORD his God. 9 They
came to the high priest Hilkiah and
delivered the money that had been
brought into the house of God,
which the Levites, the keepers of
the threshold, had collected from
Manasseh and Ephraim and from
all the remnant of Israel and from
all Judah and Benjamin and from
the inhabitants of Jerusalem.
10 They delivered it to the workers
who had the oversight of the house
of the LORD, and the workers who
were working in the house of the
LORD gave it for repairing and restoring the house. 11 They gave it to
the carpenters and the builders to
buy quarried stone, and timber for
binders, and beams for the buildings that the kings of Judah had let
go to ruin. 12 The people did the
work faithfully. Over them were appointed the Levites Jahath and
Obadiah, of the sons of Merari,
along with Zechariah and Meshullam, of the sons of the Kohathites,
to have oversight. Other Levites, all
skillful with instruments of music,
13 were over the burden bearers and
directed all who did work in every
kind of service; and some of the Levites were scribes, and officials,
and gatekeepers.

14 While they were bringing out
the money that had been brought
into the house of the LORD, the
priest Hilkiah found the book of
the law of the LORD given through
Moses. 15 Hilkiah said to the secretary Shaphan, "I have found the
book of the law in the house of the
LORD"; and Hilkiah gave the book
to Shaphan. 16 Shaphan brought
the book to the king, and further
reported to the king, "All that was
committed to your servants they
are doing. 17 They have emptied out
the money that was found in the
house of the LORD and have delivered it into the hand of the overseers and the workers." 18 The secretary Shaphan informed the king,
"The priest Hilkiah has given me a
book." Shaphan then read it aloud
to the king.

19 When the king heard the
words of the law he tore his
clothes. 20 Then the king commanded Hilkiah, Ahikam son of
Shaphan, Abdon son of Micah, the
secretary Shaphan, and the king's
servant Asaiah: 21 "Go, inquire of
the LORD for me and for those who
are left in Israel and in Judah, con-

34.1 2 Kings 22.1, 2
34.3 2 Chr 15.2; 1 Kings 13.2; 2 Chr 33.17, 22
34.4 Lev 26.30; 2 Kings 23.4; Ex 32.20
34.5 1 Kings 13.2; 2 Kings 23.20
34.6 2 Kings 23.15, 19
34.7 2 Chr 31.1
34.8 2 Kings 22.3-20
34.9 2 Chr 35.8
34.11 2 Chr 33.4-7
34.12 1 Chr 25.1
34.13 1 Chr 23.4, 5
34.14 v. 9
34.16 v. 8
34.19 Josh 7.6
34.21 2 Chr 29.8

[p] Heb *Asherim* [q] Meaning of Heb uncertain

cerning the words of the book that
has been found; for the wrath of the
LORD that is poured out on us is
great, because our ancestors did
not keep the word of the LORD, to
act in accordance with all that is
written in this book."

The Prophet Huldah Consulted

22 So Hilkiah and those whom
the king had sent went to the
prophet Huldah, the wife of Shallum son of Tokhath son of Hasrah,
keeper of the wardrobe (who lived
in Jerusalem in the Second Quarter) and spoke to her to that effect.
23 She declared to them, "Thus says
the LORD, the God of Israel: Tell the
man who sent you to me, 24 Thus
says the LORD: I will indeed bring
disaster upon this place and upon
its inhabitants, all the curses that
are written in the book that was
read before the king of Judah.
25 Because they have forsaken me
and have made offerings to other
gods, so that they have provoked
me to anger with all the works of
their hands, my wrath will be
poured out on this place and will
not be quenched. 26 But as to the
king of Judah, who sent you to inquire of the LORD, thus shall you say
to him: Thus says the LORD, the
God of Israel: Regarding the words
that you have heard, 27 because
your heart was penitent and you
humbled yourself before God when
you heard his words against this
place and its inhabitants, and you
have humbled yourself before me,
and have torn your clothes and
wept before me, I also have heard
you, says the LORD. 28 I will gather
you to your ancestors and you shall
be gathered to your grave in peace;
your eyes shall not see all the disaster that I will bring on this place
and its inhabitants." They took the
message back to the king.

The Covenant Renewed

29 Then the king sent word and
gathered together all the elders of
Judah and Jerusalem. 30 The king
went up to the house of the LORD,
with all the people of Judah, the
inhabitants of Jerusalem, the
priests and the Levites, all the people both great and small; he read in
their hearing all the words of the
book of the covenant that had been
found in the house of the LORD.
31 The king stood in his place and
made a covenant before the LORD,
to follow the LORD, keeping his
commandments, his decrees, and
his statutes, with all his heart and
all his soul, to perform the words of
the covenant that were written in
this book. 32 Then he made all who
were present in Jerusalem and in
Benjamin pledge themselves to it.
And the inhabitants of Jerusalem
acted according to the covenant of
God, the God of their ancestors.
33 Josiah took away all the abominations from all the territory that
belonged to the people of Israel,
and made all who were in Israel
worship the LORD their God. All his
days they did not turn away from
following the LORD the God of their
ancestors.

Celebration of the Passover

35 Josiah kept a passover to
the LORD in Jerusalem; they
slaughtered the passover lamb on
the fourteenth day of the first
month. 2 He appointed the priests
to their offices and encouraged
them in the service of the house of
the LORD. 3 He said to the Levites
who taught all Israel and who were
holy to the LORD, "Put the holy ark
in the house that Solomon son of
David, king of Israel, built; you
need no longer carry it on your
shoulders. Now serve the LORD your
God and his people Israel. 4 Make
preparations by your ancestral
houses by your divisions, following
the written directions of King David of Israel and the written directions of his son Solomon. 5 Take
position in the holy place according to the groupings of the ancestral houses of your kindred the people, and let there be Levites for
each division of an ancestral
house.[r] 6 Slaughter the passover
lamb, sanctify yourselves, and on

34.22 2 Kings 22.14
34.24 2 Chr 36.14-20; Deut 28.15-68
34.25 2 Chr 33.3
34.27 2 Chr 12.7; 32.26
34.29 2 Kings 23.1-3
34.30 Neh 8.1-3
34.31 2 Kings 11.14; 23.3; 2 Chr 23.3, 16; 29.10
34.33 vv. 3-7; 2 Chr 33.2-7
35.1 2 Kings 23.21, 22; Ex 12.6; Num 9.3
35.2 2 Chr 23.18; 29.11
35.3 Deut 33.10; 2 Chr 5.7; 1 Chr 23.26
35.4 1 Chr 9.10-13; 2 Chr 8.14
35.5 Ps 134.1
35.6 v. 1; 2 Chr 29.5, 15; Ezra 6.20

[r] Meaning of Heb uncertain

behalf of your kindred make preparations, acting according to the
word of the LORD by Moses."
7 Then Josiah contributed to
the people, as passover offerings
for all that were present, lambs and
kids from the flock to the number
of thirty thousand, and three thousand bulls; these were from the
king's possessions. 8 His officials
contributed willingly to the people,
to the priests, and to the Levites.
Hilkiah, Zechariah, and Jehiel, the
chief officers of the house of God,
gave to the priests for the passover
offerings two thousand six hundred
lambs and kids and three hundred
bulls. 9 Conaniah also, and his
brothers Shemaiah and Nethanel,
and Hashabiah and Jeiel and Jozabad, the chiefs of the Levites, gave
to the Levites for the passover offerings five thousand lambs and
kids and five hundred bulls.
10 When the service had been
prepared for, the priests stood in
their place, and the Levites in their
divisions according to the king's
command. 11 They slaughtered the
passover lamb, and the priests
dashed the blood that they received[s] from them, while the Levites did the skinning. 12 They set
aside the burnt offerings so that
they might distribute them according to the groupings of the ancestral houses of the people, to offer to
the LORD, as it is written in the book
of Moses. And they did the same
with the bulls. 13 They roasted the
passover lamb with fire according
to the ordinance; and they boiled
the holy offerings in pots, in caldrons, and in pans, and carried
them quickly to all the people.
14 Afterward they made preparations for themselves and for the
priests, because the priests the descendants of Aaron were occupied
in offering the burnt offerings and
the fat parts until night; so the Levites made preparations for themselves and for the priests, the descendants of Aaron. 15 The singers,
the descendants of Asaph, were in
their place according to the command of David, and Asaph, and Heman, and the king's seer Jeduthun.
The gatekeepers were at each gate;
they did not need to interrupt their
service, for their kindred the Levites made preparations for them.
16 So all the service of the LORD
was prepared that day, to keep the
passover and to offer burnt offerings on the altar of the LORD, according to the command of King
Josiah. 17 The people of Israel who
were present kept the passover at
that time, and the festival of unleavened bread seven days. 18 No
passover like it had been kept in
Israel since the days of the prophet
Samuel; none of the kings of Israel
had kept such a passover as was
kept by Josiah, by the priests and
the Levites, by all Judah and Israel
who were present, and by the inhabitants of Jerusalem. 19 In the
eighteenth year of the reign of Josiah this passover was kept.

Defeat by Pharaoh Neco and Death of Josiah

20 After all this, when Josiah
had set the temple in order, King
Neco of Egypt went up to fight at
Carchemish on the Euphrates, and
Josiah went out against him. 21 But
Neco[t] sent envoys to him, saying,
"What have I to do with you, king of
Judah? I am not coming against
you today, but against the house
with which I am at war; and God
has commanded me to hurry.
Cease opposing God, who is with
me, so that he will not destroy
you." 22 But Josiah would not turn
away from him, but disguised himself in order to fight with him. He
did not listen to the words of Neco
from the mouth of God, but joined
battle in the plain of Megiddo.
23 The archers shot King Josiah;
and the king said to his servants,
"Take me away, for I am badly
wounded." 24 So his servants took
him out of the chariot and carried
him in his second chariot[u] and
brought him to Jerusalem. There
he died, and was buried in the
tombs of his ancestors. All Judah

35.7 2 Chr 30.24
35.9 2 Chr 31.12
35.10 v. 5; Ezra 6.18
35.11 vv. 1,6; 2 Chr 29.22, 34
35.13 Ex 12.8,9; Lev 6.25; 1 Sam 2.13-15
35.15 1 Chr 25.1; 26.12-19
35.17 Ex 12.15; 2 Chr 30.21
35.18 2 Kings 23.21-23
35.20 2 Kings 23.29, 30; Isa 10.9; Jer 46.2
35.22 2 Chr 18.29; Judg 5.19
35.24 2 Kings 23.30; Zech 12.11

[s] Heb lacks *that they received* [t] Heb *he*
[u] Or *the chariot of his deputy*

and Jerusalem mourned for Josiah. [25]Jeremiah also uttered a lament for Josiah, and all the singing men and singing women have spoken of Josiah in their laments to this day. They made these a custom in Israel; they are recorded in the Laments. [26]Now the rest of the acts of Josiah and his faithful deeds in accordance with what is written in the law of the LORD, [27]and his acts, first and last, are written in the Book of the Kings of Israel and Judah.

Reign of Jehoahaz

36 The people of the land took Jehoahaz son of Josiah and made him king to succeed his father in Jerusalem. [2]Jehoahaz was twenty-three years old when he began to reign; he reigned three months in Jerusalem. [3]Then the king of Egypt deposed him in Jerusalem and laid on the land a tribute of one hundred talents of silver and one talent of gold. [4]The king of Egypt made his brother Eliakim king over Judah and Jerusalem, and changed his name to Jehoiakim; but Neco took his brother Jehoahaz and carried him to Egypt.

Reign and Captivity of Jehoiakim

5 Jehoiakim was twenty-five years old when he began to reign; he reigned eleven years in Jerusalem. He did what was evil in the sight of the LORD his God. [6]Against him King Nebuchadnezzar of Babylon came up, and bound him with fetters to take him to Babylon. [7]Nebuchadnezzar also carried some of the vessels of the house of the LORD to Babylon and put them in his palace in Babylon. [8]Now the rest of the acts of Jehoiakim, and the abominations that he did, and what was found against him, are written in the Book of the Kings of Israel and Judah; and his son Jehoiachin succeeded him.

Reign and Captivity of Jehoiachin

9 Jehoiachin was eight years old when he began to reign; he reigned three months and ten days in Jerusalem. He did what was evil in the sight of the LORD. [10]In the spring of the year King Nebuchadnezzar sent and brought him to Babylon, along with the precious vessels of the house of the LORD, and made his brother Zedekiah king over Judah and Jerusalem.

Reign of Zedekiah

11 Zedekiah was twenty-one years old when he began to reign; he reigned eleven years in Jerusalem. [12]He did what was evil in the sight of the LORD his God. He did not humble himself before the prophet Jeremiah who spoke from the mouth of the LORD. [13]He also rebelled against King Nebuchadnezzar, who had made him swear by God; he stiffened his neck and hardened his heart against turning to the LORD, the God of Israel. [14]All the leading priests and the people also were exceedingly unfaithful, following all the abominations of the nations; and they polluted the house of the LORD that he had consecrated in Jerusalem.

The Fall of Jerusalem

15 The LORD, the God of their ancestors, sent persistently to them by his messengers, because he had compassion on his people and on his dwelling place; [16]but they kept mocking the messengers of God, despising his words, and scoffing at his prophets, until the wrath of the LORD against his people became so great that there was no remedy.

17 Therefore he brought up against them the king of the Chaldeans, who killed their youths with the sword in the house of their sanctuary, and had no compassion on young man or young woman, the aged or the feeble; he gave them all into his hand. [18]All the vessels of the house of God, large and small, and the treasures of the

35.25 Lam 4.20; Jer 22.20
36.1 2 Kings 23.30-34; Jer 22.11
36.5 2 Kings 23.36, 37
36.6 2 Kings 24.1; 2 Chr 33.11
36.7 2 Kings 24.13
36.8 2 Kings 24.5; 1 Chr 3.16
36.9 2 Kings 24.8-17
36.10 2 Sam 11.1; Jer 37.1
36.11 2 Kings 24.18-20; Jer 52.1
36.12 2 Chr 33.23; Jer 21.3-7
36.13 Jer 52.3; Ezek 17.15; 2 Kings 17.14; 2 Chr 30.8
36.15 Jer 25.3,4; 35.15; 44.4
36.16 2 Chr 30.10; Jer 5.12,13; Prov 1.25; Ezra 5.12
36.17 2 Kings 25.1-7
36.18 2 Kings 25.13ff

house of the LORD, and the treasures of the king and of his officials, all these he brought to Babylon. 19 They burned the house of
God, broke down the wall of Jerusalem, burned all its palaces with
fire, and destroyed all its precious
vessels. 20 He took into exile in
Babylon those who had escaped
from the sword, and they became
servants to him and to his sons until the establishment of the kingdom of Persia, 21 to fulfill the word
of the LORD by the mouth of Jeremiah, until the land had made up for
its sabbaths. All the days that it lay
desolate it kept sabbath, to fulfill
seventy years.

36.19 2 Kings 25.9; Jer 52.13
36.20 2 Kings 25.11; Jer 27.7
36.21 Jer 29.10; Lev 26.34; 25.4
36.22 Ezra 1.1; Jer 25.12; Isa 44.28
36.23 Ezra 1.2,3

Cyrus Proclaims Liberty for the Exiles

22 In the first year of King Cyrus
of Persia, in fulfillment of the word
of the LORD spoken by Jeremiah,
the LORD stirred up the spirit of
King Cyrus of Persia so that he sent
a herald throughout all his kingdom and also declared in a written
edict: 23 "Thus says King Cyrus of
Persia: The LORD, the God of heav-
en, has given me all the kingdoms
of the earth, and he has charged me
to build him a house at Jerusalem,
which is in Judah. Whoever is
among you of all his people, may
the LORD his God be with him! Let
him go up."

Ezra

Title and Background

The books of Ezra and Nehemiah were one in the earliest Hebrew manuscripts. The separation into two books first began among the church fathers in the third century A.D. Although they were regarded as one book, the caption to Nehemiah 1.1 indicates they were two separate compositions.

Author and Date of Writing

Many scholars have assumed that the author/compiler of Ezra-Nehemiah was also the author of 1,2 Chronicles. This viewpoint is based on certain characteristics common to both. The verses at the end of Chronicles and at the beginning of Ezra are virtually identical, and both of these books exhibit a fondness for lists. But there are also striking differences, so the name of the author cannot be known for certain. The book of Ezra can be dated about 440 B.C.

Theme and Message

Ezra tells about the return of the Jews from exile in Babylon and the rebuilding of the temple. The people completed and dedicated the temple in 516 B.C., after a delay of eighteen years instigated by their enemies from the north. Ezra led a second group of Jews back to the promised land, where he taught the people God's law and reformed their religious life so that the other nations around them could see they were God's chosen nation.

Outline

I. The First Exiles Return to the Land of Judah (1.1–2.70)
II. The Temple Is Rebuilt (3.1–6.22)
III. Ezra's Return and Ministry (7.1–10.44)

End of the Babylonian Captivity

1 In the first year of King Cyrus
of Persia, in order that the
word of the LORD by the mouth of
Jeremiah might be accomplished,
the LORD stirred up the spirit of
King Cyrus of Persia so that he sent
a herald throughout all his kingdom, and also in a written edict declared:
2 "Thus says King Cyrus of Persia: The LORD, the God of heaven,
has given me all the kingdoms of
the earth, and he has charged me
to build him a house at Jerusalem
in Judah. 3 Any of those among you
who are of his people—may their
God be with them!—are now permitted to go up to Jerusalem in Judah, and rebuild the house of the
LORD, the God of Israel—he is the

1.1ff 2 Chr 36.22,23; Jer 25.12; 29.10; Ezra 5.13,14
1.2 Isa 44.28; 45.1,12,13
1.3 Dan 6.26
1.5 Phil 2.13
1.7 Ezra 5.14; 6.5; 2 Kings 24.13; 2 Chr 36.7

God who is in Jerusalem; 4 and let
all survivors, in whatever place
they reside, be assisted by the people of their place with silver and
gold, with goods and with animals,
besides freewill offerings for the
house of God in Jerusalem."
5 The heads of the families of
Judah and Benjamin, and the
priests and the Levites—everyone
whose spirit God had stirred—got
ready to go up and rebuild the
house of the LORD in Jerusalem.
6 All their neighbors aided them
with silver vessels, with gold, with
goods, with animals, and with valuable gifts, besides all that was freely offered. 7 King Cyrus himself
brought out the vessels of the
house of the LORD that Nebuchadnezzar had carried away from Jerusalem and placed in the house of

his gods. 8 King Cyrus of Persia had them released into the charge of Mithredath the treasurer, who counted them out to Sheshbazzar the prince of Judah. 9 And this was the inventory: gold basins, thirty; silver basins, one thousand; knives,[a] twenty-nine; 10 gold bowls, thirty; other silver bowls, four hundred ten; other vessels, one thousand; 11 the total of the gold and silver vessels was five thousand four hundred. All these Sheshbazzar brought up, when the exiles were brought up from Babylonia to Jerusalem.

List of the Returned Exiles

2 Now these were the people of the province who came from those captive exiles whom King Nebuchadnezzar of Babylon had carried captive to Babylonia; they returned to Jerusalem and Judah, all to their own towns. 2 They came with Zerubbabel, Jeshua, Nehemiah, Seraiah, Reelaiah, Mordecai, Bilshan, Mispar, Bigvai, Rehum, and Baanah.

The number of the Israelite people: 3 the descendants of Parosh, two thousand one hundred seventy-two. 4 Of Shephatiah, three hundred seventy-two. 5 Of Arah, seven hundred seventy-five. 6 Of Pahath-moab, namely the descendants of Jeshua and Joab, two thousand eight hundred twelve. 7 Of Elam, one thousand two hundred fifty-four. 8 Of Zattu, nine hundred forty-five. 9 Of Zaccai, seven hundred sixty. 10 Of Bani, six hundred forty-two. 11 Of Bebai, six hundred twenty-three. 12 Of Azgad, one thousand two hundred twenty-two. 13 Of Adonikam, six hundred sixty-six. 14 Of Bigvai, two thousand fifty-six. 15 Of Adin, four hundred fifty-four. 16 Of Ater, namely of Hezekiah, ninety-eight. 17 Of Bezai, three hundred twenty-three. 18 Of Jorah, one hundred twelve. 19 Of Hashum, two hundred twenty-three. 20 Of Gibbar, ninety-five. 21 Of Bethlehem, one hundred twenty-three. 22 The people of Netophah, fifty-six. 23 Of Anathoth, one hundred twenty-eight. 24 The descendants of Azmaveth, forty-two. 25 Of Kiriatharim, Chephirah, and Beeroth, seven hundred forty-three. 26 Of Ramah and Geba, six hundred twenty-one. 27 The people of Michmas, one hundred twenty-two. 28 Of Bethel and Ai, two hundred twenty-three. 29 The descendants of Nebo, fifty-two. 30 Of Magbish, one hundred fifty-six. 31 Of the other Elam, one thousand two hundred fifty-four. 32 Of Harim, three hundred twenty. 33 Of Lod, Hadid, and Ono, seven hundred twenty-five. 34 Of Jericho, three hundred forty-five. 35 Of Senaah, three thousand six hundred thirty.

36 The priests: the descendants of Jedaiah, of the house of Jeshua, nine hundred seventy-three. 37 Of Immer, one thousand fifty-two. 38 Of Pashhur, one thousand two hundred forty-seven. 39 Of Harim, one thousand seventeen.

40 The Levites: the descendants of Jeshua and Kadmiel, of the descendants of Hodaviah, seventy-four. 41 The singers: the descendants of Asaph, one hundred twenty-eight. 42 The descendants of the gatekeepers: of Shallum, of Ater, of Talmon, of Akkub, of Hatita, and of Shobai, in all one hundred thirty-nine.

43 The temple servants: the descendants of Ziha, Hasupha, Tabbaoth, 44 Keros, Siaha, Padon, 45 Lebanah, Hagabah, Akkub, 46 Hagab, Shamlai, Hanan, 47 Giddel, Gahar, Reaiah, 48 Rezin, Nekoda, Gazzam, 49 Uzza, Paseah, Besai, 50 Asnah, Meunim, Nephisim, 51 Bakbuk, Hakupha, Harhur, 52 Bazluth, Mehida, Harsha, 53 Barkos, Sisera, Temah, 54 Neziah, and Hatipha.

55 The descendants of Solomon's servants: Sotai, Hassophereth, Peruda, 56 Jaalah, Darkon, Giddel, 57 Shephatiah, Hattil, Pochereth-hazzebaim, and Ami.

1.8 Ezra 5.14
2.1 Neh 7.6-73; 2 Kings 24.14-16; 25.11; 2 Chr 36.20
2.5 cf. Neh 7.10
2.6 cf. Neh 7.11
2.16 Neh 7.21
2.21 Neh 7.26
2.31 v. 7
2.36 1 Chr 24.7-18
2.38 1 Chr 9.12
2.39 1 Chr 24.8
2.43 1 Chr 9.2
2.48 Neh 7.50
2.55 Neh 7.57, 60; 11.3

[a] Vg: Meaning of Heb uncertain

RETURN FROM EXILE

1. RESTORATION of the exiles began under Cyrus (559-530 B.C.), who allowed them to return to Judah with the captured temple treasures.

2. THE TEMPLE was consecrated by official permission of Darius I (522-486 B.C.).

3. EZRA won the approval of Artaxerxes I (465-424 B.C.) to return with additional exiles; Nehemiah, to rebuild the walls of Jerusalem.

4. CLAY TABLETS from the Murashu archives at Nippur reveal the presence of Jews remaining a half century after Ezra.

58 All the temple servants and
the descendants of Solomon's servants were three hundred ninety-
two.
59 The following were those
who came up from Tel-melah, Tel-
harsha, Cherub, Addan, and Immer, though they could not prove
their families or their descent,
whether they belonged to Israel:
60 the descendants of Delaiah, Tobiah, and Nekoda, six hundred
fifty-two. 61 Also, of the descendants of the priests: the descendants of Habaiah, Hakkoz, and
Barzillai (who had married one of
the daughters of Barzillai the Gileadite, and was called by their
name). 62 These looked for their
entries in the genealogical records,
but they were not found there, and
so they were excluded from the
priesthood as unclean; 63 the governor told them that they were not to
partake of the most holy food, until
there should be a priest to consult
Urim and Thummim.
64 The whole assembly together
was forty-two thousand three hundred sixty, 65 besides their male
and female servants, of whom
there were seven thousand three
hundred thirty-seven; and they had
two hundred male and female singers. 66 They had seven hundred
thirty-six horses, two hundred
forty-five mules, 67 four hundred
thirty-five camels, and six thousand seven hundred twenty donkeys.
68 As soon as they came to the
house of the LORD in Jerusalem,
some of the heads of families made
freewill offerings for the house of
God, to erect it on its site. 69 According to their resources they gave
to the building fund sixty-one
thousand darics of gold, five thousand minas of silver, and one hundred priestly robes.
70 The priests, the Levites, and
some of the people lived in Jerusalem and its vicinity;[b] and the singers, the gatekeepers, and the temple servants lived in their towns,
and all Israel in their towns.

Worship Restored at Jerusalem

3 When the seventh month
came, and the Israelites were
in the towns, the people gathered
together in Jerusalem. 2 Then Jeshua son of Jozadak, with his fellow
priests, and Zerubbabel son of Shealtiel with his kin set out to build
the altar of the God of Israel, to offer burnt offerings on it, as prescribed in the law of Moses the
man of God. 3 They set up the altar
on its foundation, because they
were in dread of the neighboring
peoples, and they offered burnt offerings upon it to the LORD, morning and evening. 4 And they kept
the festival of booths,[c] as prescribed, and offered the daily burnt
offerings by number according to
the ordinance, as required for each
day, 5 and after that the regular
burnt offerings, the offerings at the
new moon and at all the sacred festivals of the LORD, and the offerings
of everyone who made a freewill offering to the LORD. 6 From the first
day of the seventh month they began to offer burnt offerings to the
LORD. But the foundation of the
temple of the LORD was not yet laid.
7 So they gave money to the masons
and the carpenters, and food,
drink, and oil to the Sidonians and
the Tyrians to bring cedar trees
from Lebanon to the sea, to Joppa,
according to the grant that they
had from King Cyrus of Persia.

Foundation Laid for the Temple

8 In the second year after their
arrival at the house of God at Jerusalem, in the second month, Zerubbabel son of Shealtiel and Jeshua son of Jozadak made a
beginning, together with the rest of
their people, the priests and the
Levites and all who had come to Jerusalem from the captivity. They
appointed the Levites, from twenty
years old and upward, to have the
oversight of the work on the house
of the LORD. 9 And Jeshua with his
sons and his kin, and Kadmiel and

2.58 v. 55
2.61 2 Sam 17.27
2.62 Num 3.10; 16.39,40
2.63 Lev 2.3,10; Ex 28.30
2.64 Neh 7.66ff
2.69 Ezra 8.25-34
3.1 Neh 7.73; 8.1
3.2 Neh 12.1,8; Ezra 2.2; 1 Chr 3.17; Deut 12.5,6
3.3 Ezra 4.4; Num 28.2-4
3.4 Neh 8.14; Ex 23.16; Num 29.12
3.5 Num 28.3, 11,19,26; 29.39
3.7 2 Chr 2.10, 16; Ezra 1.2; 6.3
3.8 v. 2; Ezra 4.3; 1 Chr 23.24, 27
3.9 Ezra 2.40

[b] 1 Esdras 5.46: Heb lacks *lived in Jerusalem and its vicinity* [c] Or *tabernacles*; Heb *succoth*

his sons, Binnui and Hodaviah[d]
along with the sons of Henadad,
the Levites, their sons and kin, together took charge of the workers
in the house of God.
10 When the builders laid the
foundation of the temple of the
LORD, the priests in their vestments
were stationed to praise the LORD
with trumpets, and the Levites, the
sons of Asaph, with cymbals, according to the directions of King
David of Israel; 11 and they sang re-
sponsively, praising and giving
thanks to the LORD,

"For he is good,
for his steadfast love endures
forever toward Israel."

And all the people responded with
a great shout when they praised the
LORD, because the foundation of
the house of the LORD was laid.
12 But many of the priests and Levites and heads of families, old
people who had seen the first
house on its foundations, wept
with a loud voice when they saw
this house, though many shouted
aloud for joy, 13 so that the people
could not distinguish the sound of
the joyful shout from the sound of
the people's weeping, for the people shouted so loudly that the
sound was heard far away.

Resistance to Rebuilding the Temple

4 When the adversaries of Judah
and Benjamin heard that the
returned exiles were building a
temple to the LORD, the God of Israel, 2 they approached Zerubbabel
and the heads of families and said
to them, "Let us build with you, for
we worship your God as you do,
and we have been sacrificing to
him ever since the days of King
Esar-haddon of Assyria who
brought us here." 3 But Zerubbabel,
Jeshua, and the rest of the heads of
families in Israel said to them,
"You shall have no part with us in
building a house to our God; but
we alone will build to the LORD, the
God of Israel, as King Cyrus of Persia has commanded us."
4 Then the people of the land
discouraged the people of Judah,
and made them afraid to build,
5 and they bribed officials to frustrate their plan throughout the
reign of King Cyrus of Persia and
until the reign of King Darius of
Persia.

Rebuilding of Jerusalem Opposed

6 In the reign of Ahasuerus, in
his accession year, they wrote an
accusation against the inhabitants
of Judah and Jerusalem.
7 And in the days of Artaxerxes,
Bishlam and Mithredath and Tabeel and the rest of their associates
wrote to King Artaxerxes of Persia;
the letter was written in Aramaic
and translated.[e] 8 Rehum the royal
deputy and Shimshai the scribe
wrote a letter against Jerusalem to
King Artaxerxes as follows 9 (then
Rehum the royal deputy, Shimshai
the scribe, and the rest of their associates, the judges, the envoys,
the officials, the Persians, the people of Erech, the Babylonians, the
people of Susa, that is, the Elamites, 10 and the rest of the nations
whom the great and noble Osnap-
par deported and settled in the cities of Samaria and in the rest of the
province Beyond the River wrote—
and now 11 this is a copy of the letter that they sent):
"To King Artaxerxes: Your servants, the people of the province
Beyond the River, send greeting.
And now 12 may it be known to the
king that the Jews who came up
from you to us have gone to Jerusalem. They are rebuilding that rebellious and wicked city; they are finishing the walls and repairing the
foundations. 13 Now may it be
known to the king that, if this city
is rebuilt and the walls finished,
they will not pay tribute, custom,
or toll, and the royal revenue will
be reduced. 14 Now because we
share the salt of the palace and it is

3.10 1 Chr 16.5, 6,42; 6.31; 25.1 **3.11** Ex 15.21; 2 Chr 7.3; Neh 12.24; 1 Chr 16.34, 41 **4.1** vv. 7-10 **4.2** 2 Kings 17.24, 32,33; 19.37 **4.3** Neh 2.20; Ezra 1.1-3 **4.4** Ezra 3.3 **4.6ff** Esther 1.1; Dan 9.1 **4.7** 2 Kings 18.26; Dan 2.4 **4.10** v. 1 **4.12** Ezra 5.3,9 **4.13** v. 20; Ezra 7.24

[d] Compare 2.40; Neh 7.43; 1 Esdras 5.58: Heb *sons of Judah* [e] Heb adds *in Aramaic,* indicating that 4.8-6.18 is in Aramaic. Another interpretation is *The letter was written in the Aramaic script and set forth in the Aramaic language*

not fitting for us to witness the
king's dishonor, therefore we send
and inform the king, 15 so that a
search may be made in the annals
of your ancestors. You will discover
in the annals that this is a rebellious city, hurtful to kings and
provinces, and that sedition was
stirred up in it from long ago. On
that account this city was laid
waste. 16 We make known to the
king that, if this city is rebuilt and
its walls finished, you will then
have no possession in the province
Beyond the River."
17 The king sent an answer: "To
Rehum the royal deputy and Shimshai the scribe and the rest of their
associates who live in Samaria and
in the rest of the province Beyond
the River, greeting. And now 18 the
letter that you sent to us has been
read in translation before me. 19 So
I made a decree, and someone
searched and discovered that this
city has risen against kings from
long ago, and that rebellion and sedition have been made in it. 20 Jerusalem has had mighty kings who
ruled over the whole province Beyond the River, to whom tribute,
custom, and toll were paid.
21 Therefore issue an order that
these people be made to cease, and
that this city not be rebuilt, until I
make a decree. 22 Moreover, take
care not to be slack in this matter;
why should damage grow to the
hurt of the king?"
23 Then when the copy of King
Artaxerxes' letter was read before
Rehum and the scribe Shimshai
and their associates, they hurried
to the Jews in Jerusalem and by
force and power made them cease.
24 At that time the work on the
house of God in Jerusalem stopped
and was discontinued until the
second year of the reign of King Darius of Persia.

Restoration of the Temple Resumed

5 Now the prophets, Haggai[f]
and Zechariah son of Iddo,
prophesied to the Jews who were in
Judah and Jerusalem, in the name
of the God of Israel who was over
them. 2 Then Zerubbabel son of
Shealtiel and Jeshua son of Jozadak set out to rebuild the house of
God in Jerusalem; and with them
were the prophets of God, helping
them.
3 At the same time Tattenai the
governor of the province Beyond
the River and Shethar-bozenai and
their associates came to them and
spoke to them thus, "Who gave you
a decree to build this house and to
finish this structure?" 4 They[g] also
asked them this, "What are the
names of the men who are building
this building?" 5 But the eye of
their God was upon the elders of
the Jews, and they did not stop
them until a report reached Darius
and then answer was returned by
letter in reply to it.
6 The copy of the letter that Tattenai the governor of the province
Beyond the River and Shethar-
bozenai and his associates the envoys who were in the province Beyond the River sent to King Darius;
7 they sent him a report, in which
was written as follows: "To Darius
the king, all peace! 8 May it be
known to the king that we went to
the province of Judah, to the house
of the great God. It is being built of
hewn stone, and timber is laid in
the walls; this work is being done
diligently and prospers in their
hands. 9 Then we spoke to those elders and asked them, 'Who gave
you a decree to build this house
and to finish this structure?' 10 We
also asked them their names, for
your information, so that we might
write down the names of the men
at their head. 11 This was their reply
to us: 'We are the servants of the
God of heaven and earth, and we
are rebuilding the house that was
built many years ago, which a great
king of Israel built and finished.
12 But because our ancestors had
angered the God of heaven, he gave
them into the hand of King Nebuchadnezzar of Babylon, the Chal-

4.18 Neh 8.8 **4.20** 1 Kings 4.21; Ps 72.8 **5.1** Hag 1.1; Zech 1.1 **5.2** Ezra 3.2 **5.3** Ezra 6.6; v. 9; Ezra 1.3 **5.4** v. 10 **5.5** Ezra 7.6,28; Ps 33.18 **5.6** Ezra 4.9 **5.9** vv. 3,4 **5.11** 1 Kings 6.1 **5.12** 2 Chr 36.16, 17; 2 Kings 24.2; 25.8,9,11

[f] Aram adds *the prophet* [g] Gk Syr: Aram *We*

dean, who destroyed this house
and carried away the people to
Babylonia. 13 However, King Cyrus
of Babylon, in the first year of his
reign, made a decree that this
house of God should be rebuilt.
14 Moreover, the gold and silver vessels of the house of God, which
Nebuchadnezzar had taken out of
the temple in Jerusalem and had
brought into the temple of Babylon, these King Cyrus took out of
the temple of Babylon, and they
were delivered to a man named
Sheshbazzar, whom he had made
governor. 15 He said to him, "Take
these vessels; go and put them in
the temple in Jerusalem, and let
the house of God be rebuilt on its
site." 16 Then this Sheshbazzar
came and laid the foundations of
the house of God in Jerusalem; and
from that time until now it has
been under construction, and it is
not yet finished.' 17 And now, if it
seems good to the king, have a
search made in the royal archives
there in Babylon, to see whether a
decree was issued by King Cyrus for
the rebuilding of this house of God
in Jerusalem. Let the king send us
his pleasure in this matter."

The Decree of Darius

6 Then King Darius made a decree, and they searched the archives where the documents were
stored in Babylon. 2 But it was in
Ecbatana, the capital in the province of Media, that a scroll was
found on which this was written:
"A record. 3 In the first year of his
reign, King Cyrus issued a decree:
Concerning the house of God at Jerusalem, let the house be rebuilt,
the place where sacrifices are offered and burnt offerings are
brought;[h] its height shall be sixty
cubits and its width sixty cubits,
4 with three courses of hewn stones
and one course of timber; let the
cost be paid from the royal treasury. 5 Moreover, let the gold and
silver vessels of the house of God,
which Nebuchadnezzar took out of
the temple in Jerusalem and
brought to Babylon, be restored
and brought back to the temple in
Jerusalem, each to its place; you
shall put them in the house of
God."

6 "Now you, Tattenai, governor
of the province Beyond the River,
Shethar-bozenai, and you, their associates, the envoys in the province
Beyond the River, keep away; 7 let
the work on this house of God
alone; let the governor of the Jews
and the elders of the Jews rebuild
this house of God on its site.
8 Moreover I make a decree regarding what you shall do for these elders of the Jews for the rebuilding
of this house of God: the cost is to
be paid to these people, in full and
without delay, from the royal revenue, the tribute of the province Beyond the River. 9 Whatever is
needed—young bulls, rams, or
sheep for burnt offerings to the
God of heaven, wheat, salt, wine, or
oil, as the priests in Jerusalem
require—let that be given to them
day by day without fail, 10 so that
they may offer pleasing sacrifices
to the God of heaven, and pray for
the life of the king and his children.
11 Furthermore I decree that if anyone alters this edict, a beam shall
be pulled out of the house of the
perpetrator, who then shall be impaled on it. The house shall be
made a dunghill. 12 May the God
who has established his name
there overthrow any king or people
that shall put forth a hand to alter
this, or to destroy this house of God
in Jerusalem. I, Darius, make a decree; let it be done with all diligence."

Completion and Dedication of the Temple

13 Then, according to the word
sent by King Darius, Tattenai, the
governor of the province Beyond
the River, Shethar-bozenai, and
their associates did with all diligence what King Darius had ordered. 14 So the elders of the Jews
built and prospered, through the
prophesying of the prophet Haggai
and Zechariah son of Iddo. They

5.13 Ezra 1.1
5.14 Ezra 1.7; 6.5; Dan 5.2; v. 16; Ezra 1.8
5.16 Ezra 3.8,10; 6.15
5.17 Ezra 6.1,2
6.1 Ezra 5.17
6.3 Ezra 1.1
6.4 1 Kings 6.36
6.5 Ezra 1.7,8; 5.14
6.6 v. 13; Ezra 5.3
6.10 Ezra 7.23
6.11 Ezra 7.26; Dan 2.5; 3.29
6.12 Deut 12.5; 11
6.13 v. 6
6.14 Ezra 5.1,2; 1.1; v. 12; Ezra 7.1

h Meaning of Aram uncertain

finished their building by command of the God of Israel and by
decree of Cyrus, Darius, and King
Artaxerxes of Persia; 15 and this
house was finished on the third day
of the month of Adar, in the sixth
year of the reign of King Darius.
16 The people of Israel, the
priests and the Levites, and the rest
of the returned exiles, celebrated
the dedication of this house of God
with joy. 17 They offered at the dedication of this house of God one
hundred bulls, two hundred rams,
four hundred lambs, and as a sin
offering for all Israel, twelve male
goats, according to the number of
the tribes of Israel. 18 Then they set
the priests in their divisions and
the Levites in their courses for the
service of God at Jerusalem, as it is
written in the book of Moses.

The Passover Celebrated

19 On the fourteenth day of the
first month the returned exiles
kept the passover. 20 For both the
priests and the Levites had purified
themselves; all of them were clean.
So they killed the passover lamb for
all the returned exiles, for their fellow priests, and for themselves.
21 It was eaten by the people of Israel who had returned from exile,
and also by all who had joined
them and separated themselves
from the pollutions of the nations
of the land to worship the LORD, the
God of Israel. 22 With joy they celebrated the festival of unleavened
bread seven days; for the LORD had
made them joyful, and had turned
the heart of the king of Assyria to
them, so that he aided them in the
work on the house of God, the God
of Israel.

The Coming and Work of Ezra

7 After this, in the reign of King
Artaxerxes of Persia, Ezra son
of Seraiah, son of Azariah, son of
Hilkiah, 2 son of Shallum, son of
Zadok, son of Ahitub, 3 son of Amariah, son of Azariah, son of Meraioth, 4 son of Zerahiah, son of Uzzi,
son of Bukki, 5 son of Abishua, son
of Phinehas, son of Eleazar, son of
the chief priest Aaron— 6 this Ezra
went up from Babylonia. He was a
scribe skilled in the law of Moses
that the LORD the God of Israel had
given; and the king granted him all
that he asked, for the hand of the
LORD his God was upon him.
7 Some of the people of Israel,
and some of the priests and Levites, the singers and gatekeepers,
and the temple servants also went
up to Jerusalem, in the seventh
year of King Artaxerxes. 8 They
came to Jerusalem in the fifth
month, which was in the seventh
year of the king. 9 On the first day of
the first month the journey up from
Babylon was begun, and on the
first day of the fifth month he came
to Jerusalem, for the gracious hand
of his God was upon him. 10 For
Ezra had set his heart to study the
law of the LORD, and to do it, and to
teach the statutes and ordinances
in Israel.

The Letter of Artaxerxes to Ezra

11 This is a copy of the letter
that King Artaxerxes gave to the
priest Ezra, the scribe, a scholar of
the text of the commandments of
the LORD and his statutes for Israel:
12 "Artaxerxes, king of kings, to the
priest Ezra, the scribe of the law of
the God of heaven: Peace.[i] And
now 13 I decree that any of the people of Israel or their priests or Levites in my kingdom who freely offers to go to Jerusalem may go with
you. 14 For you are sent by the king
and his seven counselors to make
inquiries about Judah and Jerusalem according to the law of your
God, which is in your hand, 15 and
also to convey the silver and gold
that the king and his counselors
have freely offered to the God of Israel, whose dwelling is in Jerusalem, 16 with all the silver and gold
that you shall find in the whole
province of Babylonia, and with the
freewill offerings of the people and
the priests, given willingly for the
house of their God in Jerusalem.
17 With this money, then, you shall
with all diligence buy bulls, rams,

6.16 1 Kings 8.63; 2 Chr 7.5
6.17 Ezra 8.35
6.18 2 Chr 35.5; 1 Chr 23.6; Num 3.6; 8.9
6.19 Ezra 1.11; Ex 12.6
6.20 2 Chr 29.34; 30.15; 35.11
6.21 Neh 9.2; 10.28; Ezra 9.11
6.22 Ex 12.15; Ezra 7.27; 1.1; 6.2
7.1 1 Chr 6.4-14; vv. 12,21; Neh 2.1
7.6 vv. 9,11,12, 21,28
7.7 Ezra 8.1-20
7.9 v. 6
7.10 Ps 119.45; v. 25; Neh 8.1-8
7.12 Ezek 26.7; Dan 2.37
7.14 Esther 1.14
7.15 2 Chr 6.2; Ezra 6.12
7.16 Ezra 8.25; 1 Chr 29.6, 9; Ezra 1.4, 6
7.17 Num 15.4-13; Deut 12.5-11

[i] Syr Vg 1 Esdras 8.9: Aram *Perfect*

and lambs, and their grain offerings and their drink offerings, and
you shall offer them on the altar of
the house of your God in Jerusalem. 18 Whatever seems good to you
and your colleagues to do with the
rest of the silver and gold, you may
do, according to the will of your
God. 19 The vessels that have been
given you for the service of the
house of your God, you shall deliver before the God of Jerusalem.
20 And whatever else is required for
the house of your God, which you
are responsible for providing, you
may provide out of the king's treasury.

21 "I, King Artaxerxes, decree
to all the treasurers in the province
Beyond the River: Whatever the
priest Ezra, the scribe of the law of
the God of heaven, requires of you,
let it be done with all diligence,
22 up to one hundred talents of silver, one hundred cors of wheat, one
hundred baths[j] of wine, one hundred baths[j] of oil, and unlimited
salt. 23 Whatever is commanded by
the God of heaven, let it be done
with zeal for the house of the God
of heaven, or wrath will come upon
the realm of the king and his heirs.
24 We also notify you that it shall
not be lawful to impose tribute,
custom, or toll on any of the
priests, the Levites, the singers, the
doorkeepers, the temple servants,
or other servants of this house of
God.

25 "And you, Ezra, according to
the God-given wisdom you possess,
appoint magistrates and judges
who may judge all the people in the
province Beyond the River who
know the laws of your God; and you
shall teach those who do not know
them. 26 All who will not obey the
law of your God and the law of the
king, let judgment be strictly executed on them, whether for death
or for banishment or for confiscation of their goods or for imprisonment."

27 Blessed be the LORD, the God
of our ancestors, who put such a
thing as this into the heart of the
king to glorify the house of the
LORD in Jerusalem, 28 and who extended to me steadfast love before
the king and his counselors, and
before all the king's mighty officers. I took courage, for the hand of
the LORD my God was upon me, and
I gathered leaders from Israel to go
up with me.

Heads of Families Who Returned with Ezra

8 These are their family heads,
and this is the genealogy of
those who went up with me from
Babylonia, in the reign of King Artaxerxes: 2 Of the descendants of
Phinehas, Gershom. Of Ithamar,
Daniel. Of David, Hattush, 3 of the
descendants of Shecaniah. Of Parosh, Zechariah, with whom were
registered one hundred fifty males.
4 Of the descendants of Pahath-
moab, Eliehoenai son of Zerahiah,
and with him two hundred males.
5 Of the descendants of Zattu,[k]
Shecaniah son of Jahaziel, and
with him three hundred males. 6 Of
the descendants of Adin, Ebed son
of Jonathan, and with him fifty
males. 7 Of the descendants of
Elam, Jeshaiah son of Athaliah,
and with him seventy males. 8 Of
the descendants of Shephatiah,
Zebadiah son of Michael, and with
him eighty males. 9 Of the descendants of Joab, Obadiah son of Jehiel, and with him two hundred eighteen males. 10 Of the descendants
of Bani,[l] Shelomith son of Josiphiah, and with him one hundred
sixty males. 11 Of the descendants
of Bebai, Zechariah son of Bebai,
and with him twenty-eight males.
12 Of the descendants of Azgad, Johanan son of Hakkatan, and with
him one hundred ten males. 13 Of
the descendants of Adonikam,
those who came later, their names
being Eliphelet, Jeuel, and Shemaiah, and with them sixty males.
14 Of the descendants of Bigvai,
Uthai and Zaccur, and with them
seventy males.

7.20 Ezra 6.4 **7.21** v. 6 **7.23** Ezra 6.10 **7.25** Ex 18.21; Deut 16.18; v. 10 **7.27** 1 Chr 29.10; Ezra 6.22 **7.28** Ezra 9.9; vv. 6,9 **8.2** 1 Chr 3.22 **8.3** Ezra 2.3

[j] A Heb measure of volume [k] Gk 1 Esdras 8.32: Heb lacks *of Zattu* [l] Gk 1 Esdras 8.36: Heb lacks *Bani*

Servants for the Temple

15 I gathered them by the river
that runs to Ahava, and there we
camped three days. As I reviewed
the people and the priests, I found
there none of the descendants of
Levi. 16 Then I sent for Eliezer, Ariel, Shemaiah, Elnathan, Jarib, Elnathan, Nathan, Zechariah, and
Meshullam, who were leaders, and
for Joiarib and Elnathan, who were
wise, 17 and sent them to Iddo, the
leader at the place called Casiphia,
telling them what to say to Iddo
and his colleagues the temple servants at Casiphia, namely, to send
us ministers for the house of our
God. 18 Since the gracious hand of
our God was upon us, they brought
us a man of discretion, of the descendants of Mahli son of Levi son
of Israel, namely Sherebiah, with
his sons and kin, eighteen; 19 also
Hashabiah and with him Jeshaiah
of the descendants of Merari, with
his kin and their sons, twenty;
20 besides two hundred twenty of
the temple servants, whom David
and his officials had set apart to attend the Levites. These were all
mentioned by name.

Fasting and Prayer for Protection

21 Then I proclaimed a fast
there, at the river Ahava, that we
might deny ourselves[m] before our
God, to seek from him a safe journey for ourselves, our children, and
all our possessions. 22 For I was
ashamed to ask the king for a band
of soldiers and cavalry to protect us
against the enemy on our way,
since we had told the king that the
hand of our God is gracious to all
who seek him, but his power and
his wrath are against all who forsake him. 23 So we fasted and petitioned our God for this, and he listened to our entreaty.

Gifts for the Temple

24 Then I set apart twelve of the
leading priests: Sherebiah, Hashabiah, and ten of their kin with
them. 25 And I weighed out to them
the silver and the gold and the vessels, the offering for the house of
our God that the king, his counselors, his lords, and all Israel there
present had offered; 26 I weighed
out into their hand six hundred fifty talents of silver, and one hundred silver vessels worth . . . talents,[n] and one hundred talents of
gold, 27 twenty gold bowls worth a
thousand darics, and two vessels of
fine polished bronze as precious as
gold. 28 And I said to them, "You are
holy to the LORD, and the vessels
are holy; and the silver and the gold
are a freewill offering to the LORD,
the God of your ancestors. 29 Guard
them and keep them until you
weigh them before the chief priests
and the Levites and the heads of
families in Israel at Jerusalem,
within the chambers of the house
of the LORD." 30 So the priests and
the Levites took over the silver, the
gold, and the vessels as they were
weighed out, to bring them to Jerusalem, to the house of our God.

The Return to Jerusalem

31 Then we left the river Ahava
on the twelfth day of the first
month, to go to Jerusalem; the
hand of our God was upon us, and
he delivered us from the hand of
the enemy and from ambushes
along the way. 32 We came to Jerusalem and remained there three
days. 33 On the fourth day, within
the house of our God, the silver,
the gold, and the vessels were
weighed into the hands of the
priest Meremoth son of Uriah, and
with him was Eleazar son of Phinehas, and with them were the Levites, Jozabad son of Jeshua and
Noadiah son of Binnui. 34 The total
was counted and weighed, and the
weight of everything was recorded.

35 At that time those who had
come from captivity, the returned
exiles, offered burnt offerings to
the God of Israel, twelve bulls for
all Israel, ninety-six rams, seventy-
seven lambs, and as a sin offering
twelve male goats; all this was a
burnt offering to the LORD. 36 They

8.15 vv. 21,31; Ezra 7.7
8.17 Ezra 2.43
8.18 Ezra 7.6
8.20 Ezra 2.43
8.21 2 Chr 20.3; Isa 58.3,5
8.22 Ezra 7.6,9, 28; Ps 33.18,19; 34.16; 2 Chr 15.2
8.23 2 Chr 33.13
8.25 Ezra 7.15,16
8.26 Ezra 1.9-11
8.28 Lev 21.6-8; 22.2,3
8.29 vv. 33,34
8.31 Ezra 7.6,9, 28
8.32 Neh 2.11
8.33 vv. 26,30
8.35 Ezra 2.1; 6.17
8.36 Ezra 7.21

m Or *might fast*
n The number of talents is lacking

also delivered the king's commis-
sions to the king's satraps and to
the governors of the province Beyond the River; and they supported
the people and the house of God.

Denunciation of Mixed Marriages

9 After these things had been
done, the officials approached
me and said, "The people of Israel,
the priests, and the Levites have
not separated themselves from the
peoples of the lands with their
abominations, from the Canaanites, the Hittites, the Perizzites, the
Jebusites, the Ammonites, the Moabites, the Egyptians, and the Amorites. 2 For they have taken some
of their daughters as wives for
themselves and for their sons. Thus
the holy seed has mixed itself with
the peoples of the lands, and in this
faithlessness the officials and leaders have led the way." 3 When I
heard this, I tore my garment and
my mantle, and pulled hair from
my head and beard, and sat appalled. 4 Then all who trembled at
the words of the God of Israel, because of the faithlessness of the returned exiles, gathered around me
while I sat appalled until the evening sacrifice.

Ezra's Prayer

5 At the evening sacrifice I got
up from my fasting, with my garments and my mantle torn, and fell
on my knees, spread out my hands
to the LORD my God, 6 and said,
"O my God, I am too ashamed
and embarrassed to lift my face to
you, my God, for our iniquities
have risen higher than our heads,
and our guilt has mounted up to
the heavens. 7 From the days of our
ancestors to this day we have been
deep in guilt, and for our iniquities
we, our kings, and our priests have
been handed over to the kings of
the lands, to the sword, to captivity, to plundering, and to utter
shame, as is now the case. 8 But
now for a brief moment favor has
been shown by the LORD our God,
who has left us a remnant, and giv-
en us a stake in his holy place, in
order that he[o] may brighten our
eyes and grant us a little sustenance in our slavery. 9 For we are
slaves; yet our God has not forsak-
en us in our slavery, but has extended to us his steadfast love before the kings of Persia, to give us
new life to set up the house of our
God, to repair its ruins, and to give
us a wall in Judea and Jerusalem.

10 "And now, our God, what
shall we say after this? For we have
forsaken your commandments,
11 which you commanded by your
servants the prophets, saying, 'The
land that you are entering to possess is a land unclean with the pollutions of the peoples of the lands,
with their abominations. They
have filled it from end to end with
their uncleanness. 12 Therefore do
not give your daughters to their
sons, neither take their daughters
for your sons, and never seek their
peace or prosperity, so that you
may be strong and eat the good of
the land and leave it for an inheritance to your children forever.'
13 After all that has come upon us
for our evil deeds and for our great
guilt, seeing that you, our God,
have punished us less than our iniquities deserved and have given us
such a remnant as this, 14 shall we
break your commandments again
and intermarry with the peoples
who practice these abominations?
Would you not be angry with us until you destroy us without remnant
or survivor? 15 O LORD, God of Israel, you are just, but we have escaped as a remnant, as is now the
case. Here we are before you in our
guilt, though no one can face you
because of this."

The People's Response

10 While Ezra prayed and
made confession, weeping
and throwing himself down before
the house of God, a very great assembly of men, women, and children gathered to him out of Israel;
the people also wept bitterly.
2 Shecaniah son of Jehiel, of the de-

9.1 Ezra 6.21; Neh 9.2; Lev 18.24-30
9.2 Ezra 10.2, 18; Ex 22.31; Neh 13.3
9.3 Job 1.20; Neh 1.4
9.4 Ezra 10.3; Ex 29.39
9.5 Ex 9.29,33
9.6 Dan 9.7,8; 2 Chr 28.9; Rev 18.5
9.7 Dan 9.5,6; Deut 28.36, 64; Dan 9.7, 8
9.8 Isa 22.23; Ps 13.3; 34.5
9.9 Neh 9.36; Ezra 7.28
9.11 Ezra 6.21
9.12 Deut 7.3; 23.6; Prov 13.22
9.13 vv. 6-8
9.14 v. 2; Neh 13.23, 27; Deut 9.8,14
9.15 Neh 9.33; Dan 9.14; v. 6; Ps 130.3
10.1 Dan 9.4,20; 2 Chr 20.9
10.2 Ezra 9.2; Neh 13.27

o Heb *our God*

scendants of Elam, addressed Ezra,
saying, "We have broken faith with
our God and have married foreign
women from the peoples of the
land, but even now there is hope
for Israel in spite of this. 3 So now
let us make a covenant with our
God to send away all these wives
and their children, according to the
counsel of my lord and of those
who tremble at the commandment
of our God; and let it be done according to the law. 4 Take action,
for it is your duty, and we are with
you; be strong, and do it." 5 Then
Ezra stood up and made the leading priests, the Levites, and all Israel swear that they would do as had
been said. So they swore.

Foreign Wives and Their Children Rejected

6 Then Ezra withdrew from before the house of God, and went to
the chamber of Jehohanan son of
Eliashib, where he spent the
night.[p] He did not eat bread or
drink water, for he was mourning
over the faithlessness of the exiles.
7 They made a proclamation
throughout Judah and Jerusalem
to all the returned exiles that they
should assemble at Jerusalem,
8 and that if any did not come within three days, by order of the officials and the elders all their property should be forfeited, and they
themselves banned from the congregation of the exiles.
9 Then all the people of Judah
and Benjamin assembled at Jerusalem within the three days; it was
the ninth month, on the twentieth
day of the month. All the people sat
in the open square before the
house of God, trembling because of
this matter and because of the
heavy rain. 10 Then Ezra the priest
stood up and said to them, "You
have trespassed and married foreign women, and so increased the
guilt of Israel. 11 Now make confession to the LORD the God of your
ancestors, and do his will; separate
yourselves from the peoples of the
land and from the foreign wives."
12 Then all the assembly answered
with a loud voice, "It is so; we must
do as you have said. 13 But the people are many, and it is a time of
heavy rain; we cannot stand in the
open. Nor is this a task for one day
or for two, for many of us have
transgressed in this matter. 14 Let
our officials represent the whole
assembly, and let all in our towns
who have taken foreign wives come
at appointed times, and with them
the elders and judges of every
town, until the fierce wrath of our
God on this account is averted
from us." 15 Only Jonathan son of
Asahel and Jahzeiah son of Tikvah
opposed this, and Meshullam and
Shabbethai the Levites supported
them.
16 Then the returned exiles did
so. Ezra the priest selected men,[q]
heads of families, according to
their families, each of them designated by name. On the first day of
the tenth month they sat down to
examine the matter. 17 By the first
day of the first month they had
come to the end of all the men who
had married foreign women.
18 There were found of the descendants of the priests who had
married foreign women, of the descendants of Jeshua son of Jozadak
and his brothers: Maaseiah, Eliezer, Jarib, and Gedaliah. 19 They
pledged themselves to send away
their wives, and their guilt offering
was a ram of the flock for their
guilt. 20 Of the descendants of Immer: Hanani and Zebadiah. 21 Of
the descendants of Harim: Maaseiah, Elijah, Shemaiah, Jehiel, and
Uzziah. 22 Of the descendants of
Pashhur: Elioenai, Maaseiah, Ishmael, Nethanel, Jozabad, and Elasah.
23 Of the Levites: Jozabad,
Shimei, Kelaiah (that is, Kelita),
Pethahiah, Judah, and Eliezer.
24 Of the singers: Eliashib. Of the
gatekeepers: Shallum, Telem, and
Uri.
25 And of Israel: of the descendants of Parosh: Ramiah, Izziah,

10.3 2 Chr 34.31; v. 44; Ezra 9.4; Deut 7.2,3
10.4 1 Chr 28.10
10.5 Neh 5.12
10.6 Deut 9.18
10.9 v. 3; Ezra 9.4
10.11 Lev 26.40; v. 3
10.14 2 Chr 29.10; 30.8
10.16 Ezra 4.1
10.19 2 Kings 10.15; 2 Chr 30.8; Lev 5.15; 6.6
10.23 Ex 6.25
10.25 v. 1

[p] 1 Esdras 9.2: Heb *where he went*
[q] 1 Esdras 9.16: Syr: Heb *And there were selected Ezra,*

Malchijah, Mijamin, Eleazar,
Hashabiah,[r] and Benaiah. 26 Of
the descendants of Elam: Mattaniah, Zechariah, Jehiel, Abdi, Jeremoth, and Elijah. 27 Of the descendants of Zattu: Elioenai, Eliashib,
Mattaniah, Jeremoth, Zabad, and
Aziza. 28 Of the descendants of Bebai: Jehohanan, Hananiah, Zabbai,
and Athlai. 29 Of the descendants of
Bani: Meshullam, Malluch, Adaiah, Jashub, Sheal, and Jeremoth.
30 Of the descendants of Pahath-
moab: Adna, Chelal, Benaiah, Maaseiah, Mattaniah, Bezalel, Binnui,
and Manasseh. 31 Of the descendants of Harim: Eliezer, Isshijah,
Malchijah, Shemaiah, Shimeon,
32 Benjamin, Malluch, and Shemariah. 33 Of the descendants of Hashum: Mattenai, Mattattah, Zabad,
Eliphelet, Jeremai, Manasseh, and
Shimei. 34 Of the descendants of
Bani: Maadai, Amram, Uel, 35 Benaiah, Bedeiah, Cheluhi, 36 Vaniah,
Meremoth, Eliashib, 37 Mattaniah,
Mattenai, and Jaasu. 38 Of the descendants of Binnui:[s] Shimei,
39 Shelemiah, Nathan, Adaiah,
40 Machnadebai, Shashai, Sharai,
41 Azarel, Shelemiah, Shemariah,
42 Shallum, Amariah, and Joseph.
43 Of the descendants of Nebo: Jeiel, Mattithiah, Zabad, Zebina, Jad-
dai, Joel, and Benaiah. 44 All these
had married foreign women, and
they sent them away with their
children.[t]

10.44 v. 3

[r] 1 Esdras 9.26 Gk: Heb *Malchijah*
[s] Gk: Heb *Bani, Binnui* [t] 1 Esdras 9.36; Meaning of Heb uncertain

Nehemiah

Title and Background

See Introduction to Ezra.

Author and Date of Writing

See Introduction to Ezra. The book of Nehemiah can be dated about 430 B.C.

Theme and Message

Nehemiah continues the history of the Jews after their return from exile in Babylon where Ezra leaves off. Nehemiah went to Jerusalem in 445 B.C. and inspired the people to repair the city walls. With Ezra he provided religious leadership for the people too. A recurring theme of this book is the importance of prayer to Nehemiah.

Outline

I. Nehemiah Rebuilds the Walls (1.1–7.3)
II. Changes Under Ezra (7.4–10.39)
III. Nehemiah's Plans (11.1–13.31)

Nehemiah Prays for His People

1 The words of Nehemiah son of
Hacaliah. In the month of
Chislev, in the twentieth year,
while I was in Susa the capital,
2 one of my brothers, Hanani, came
with certain men from Judah; and
I asked them about the Jews that
survived, those who had escaped
the captivity, and about Jerusalem.
3 They replied, "The survivors there
in the province who escaped captivity
are in great trouble and
shame; the wall of Jerusalem is
broken down, and its gates have
been destroyed by fire."
4 When I heard these words I sat
down and wept, and mourned for
days, fasting and praying before the
God of heaven. 5 I said, "O LORD
God of heaven, the great and awesome
God who keeps covenant and
steadfast love with those who love
him and keep his commandments;
6 let your ear be attentive and your
eyes open to hear the prayer of your
servant that I now pray before you
day and night for your servants, the
people of Israel, confessing the
sins of the people of Israel, which
we have sinned against you. Both I
and my family have sinned. 7 We
have offended you deeply, failing
to keep the commandments, the
statutes, and the ordinances that
you commanded your servant Moses.
8 Remember the word that you
commanded your servant Moses,
'If you are unfaithful, I will scatter
you among the peoples; 9 but if you
return to me and keep my commandments
and do them, though
your outcasts are under the farthest
skies, I will gather them from
there and bring them to the place
at which I have chosen to establish
my name.' 10 They are your servants
and your people, whom you redeemed
by your great power and
your strong hand. 11 O Lord, let
your ear be attentive to the prayer
of your servant, and to the prayer of
your servants who delight in revering
your name. Give success to
your servant today, and grant him
mercy in the sight of this man!"

At the time, I was cupbearer to the king.

1.1 Neh 10.1; 2.1; Esther 1.2; Dan 8.2
1.3 Neh 7.6; 2.17; 2.3
1.4 Ezra 9.3; 10.1; Neh 2.4
1.5 Neh 4.14; 9.32; Ex 20.6
1.6 Dan 9.17; Ezra 10.1; Dan 9.20; 2 Chr 29.6
1.7 Dan 9.5; Deut 28.14, 15
1.8 Lev 26.33
1.9 Deut 30.2-4; 12.5
1.10 Deut 9.29; Dan 9.15
1.11 v. 6

Nehemiah Sent to Judah

2 In the month of Nisan, in the twentieth year of King Artaxerxes, when wine was served him, I carried the wine and gave it to the king. Now, I had never been sad in his presence before. 2 So the king said to me, "Why is your face sad, since you are not sick? This can only be sadness of the heart." Then I was very much afraid. 3 I said to the king, "May the king live forever! Why should my face not be sad, when the city, the place of my ancestors' graves, lies waste, and its gates have been destroyed by fire?" 4 Then the king said to me, "What do you request?" So I prayed to the God of heaven. 5 Then I said to the king, "If it pleases the king, and if your servant has found favor with you, I ask that you send me to Judah, to the city of my ancestors' graves, so that I may rebuild it." 6 The king said to me (the queen also was sitting beside him), "How long will you be gone, and when will you return?" So it pleased the king to send me, and I set him a date. 7 Then I said to the king, "If it pleases the king, let letters be given me to the governors of the province Beyond the River, that they may grant me passage until I arrive in Judah; 8 and a letter to Asaph, the keeper of the king's forest, directing him to give me timber to make beams for the gates of the temple fortress, and for the wall of the city, and for the house that I shall occupy." And the king granted me what I asked, for the gracious hand of my God was upon me.

9 Then I came to the governors of the province Beyond the River, and gave them the king's letters. Now the king had sent officers of the army and cavalry with me. 10 When Sanballat the Horonite and Tobiah the Ammonite official heard this, it displeased them greatly that someone had come to seek the welfare of the people of Israel.

Nehemiah's Inspection of the Walls

11 So I came to Jerusalem and was there for three days. 12 Then I got up during the night, I and a few men with me; I told no one what my God had put into my heart to do for Jerusalem. The only animal I took was the animal I rode. 13 I went out by night by the Valley Gate past the Dragon's Spring and to the Dung Gate, and I inspected the walls of Jerusalem that had been broken down and its gates that had been destroyed by fire. 14 Then I went on to the Fountain Gate and to the King's Pool; but there was no place for the animal I was riding to continue. 15 So I went up by way of the valley by night and inspected the wall. Then I turned back and entered by the Valley Gate, and so returned. 16 The officials did not know where I had gone or what I was doing; I had not yet told the Jews, the priests, the nobles, the officials, and the rest that were to do the work.

Decision to Restore the Walls

17 Then I said to them, "You see the trouble we are in, how Jerusalem lies in ruins with its gates burned. Come, let us rebuild the wall of Jerusalem, so that we may no longer suffer disgrace." 18 I told them that the hand of my God had been gracious upon me, and also the words that the king had spoken to me. Then they said, "Let us start building!" So they committed themselves to the common good. 19 But when Sanballat the Horonite and Tobiah the Ammonite official, and Geshem the Arab heard of it, they mocked and ridiculed us, saying, "What is this that you are doing? Are you rebelling against the king?" 20 Then I replied to them, "The God of heaven is the one who will give us success, and we his servants are going to start building; but you have no share or claim or historic right in Jerusalem."

2.1 Neh 1.1; Ezra 7.1; Neh 1.11
2.2 Prov 15.13
2.3 Dan 2.4; Neh 1.3
2.4 Neh 1.4
2.6 Neh 5.14; 13.6
2.7 Ezra 7.21; 8.36
2.8 Neh 7.2; v. 18; Ezra 7.6
2.9 v. 7; Ezra 8.22
2.10 v. 19; Neh 4.1
2.13 Neh 3.13; vv. 3,17; Neh 1.3
2.14 Neh 3.15; 2 Kings 20.20
2.17 Neh 1.3
2.18 v. 8; 2 Sam 2.7
2.19 Ps 44.13; Neh 6.6
2.20 v. 4

Organization of the Work

3 Then the high priest Eliashib
set to work with his fellow
priests and rebuilt the Sheep Gate.
They consecrated it and set up its
doors; they consecrated it as far as
the Tower of the Hundred and as
far as the Tower of Hananel. 2 And
the men of Jericho built next to
him. And next to them[a] Zaccur
son of Imri built.

3 The sons of Hassenaah built
the Fish Gate; they laid its beams
and set up its doors, its bolts, and
its bars. 4 Next to them Meremoth
son of Uriah son of Hakkoz made
repairs. Next to them Meshullam
son of Berechiah son of Meshezabel made repairs. Next to them Zadok son of Baana made repairs.
5 Next to them the Tekoites made
repairs; but their nobles would not
put their shoulders to the work of
their Lord.[b]

6 Joiada son of Paseah and Meshullam son of Besodeiah repaired
the Old Gate; they laid its beams
and set up its doors, its bolts, and
its bars. 7 Next to them repairs were
made by Melatiah the Gibeonite
and Jadon the Meronothite—the
men of Gibeon and of Mizpah—
who were under the jurisdiction
of[c] the governor of the province
Beyond the River. 8 Next to them
Uzziel son of Harhaiah, one of the
goldsmiths, made repairs. Next to
him Hananiah, one of the perfumers, made repairs; and they restored Jerusalem as far as the
Broad Wall. 9 Next to them Rephaiah son of Hur, ruler of half the district of[d] Jerusalem, made repairs.
10 Next to them Jedaiah son of Harumaph made repairs opposite his
house; and next to him Hattush
son of Hashabneiah made repairs.
11 Malchijah son of Harim and Hasshub son of Pahath-moab repaired
another section and the Tower of
the Ovens. 12 Next to him Shallum
son of Hallohesh, ruler of half the
district of[d] Jerusalem, made repairs, he and his daughters.

13 Hanun and the inhabitants
of Zanoah repaired the Valley Gate;
they rebuilt it and set up its doors,
its bolts, and its bars, and repaired
a thousand cubits of the wall, as far
as the Dung Gate.

14 Malchijah son of Rechab,
ruler of the district of[e] Beth-haccherem, repaired the Dung
Gate; he rebuilt it and set up its
doors, its bolts, and its bars.

15 And Shallum son of Col-hozeh, ruler of the district of[e] Mizpah, repaired the Fountain Gate;
he rebuilt it and covered it and set
up its doors, its bolts, and its bars;
and he built the wall of the Pool of
Shelah of the king's garden, as far
as the stairs that go down from the
City of David. 16 After him Nehemiah son of Azbuk, ruler of half the
district of[d] Beth-zur, repaired from
a point opposite the graves of David, as far as the artificial pool and
the house of the warriors. 17 After
him the Levites made repairs: Rehum son of Bani; next to him Hashabiah, ruler of half the district of[d]
Keilah, made repairs for his district. 18 After him their kin made repairs: Binnui,[f] son of Henadad,
ruler of half the district of[d] Keilah;
19 next to him Ezer son of Jeshua,
ruler[g] of Mizpah, repaired another
section opposite the ascent to the
armory at the Angle. 20 After him
Baruch son of Zabbai repaired another section from the Angle to the
door of the house of the high priest
Eliashib. 21 After him Meremoth
son of Uriah son of Hakkoz repaired another section from the
door of the house of Eliashib to the
end of the house of Eliashib. 22 After him the priests, the men of the
surrounding area, made repairs.
23 After them Benjamin and Hasshub made repairs opposite their
house. After them Azariah son of
Maaseiah son of Ananiah made repairs beside his own house. 24 After
him Binnui son of Henadad repaired another section, from the
house of Azariah to the Angle and

3.1 vv. 20,32; Neh 6.1; 7.1; 12.39; Jer 31.38
3.2 Neh 7.36
3.3 Neh 12.39
3.6 Neh 12.39
3.7 Neh 2.7
3.8 vv. 31,32; Neh 12.38
3.9 vv. 12,17
3.11 Neh 12.38
3.12 v. 9
3.13 Neh 2.13
3.15 Neh 2.14; 2 Kings 25.4; Neh 12.37
3.16 vv. 9,12,17; 2 Kings 20.20
3.19 v. 15; 2 Chr 26.9
3.20 v. 1; Neh 13.7
3.22 Neh 12.28
3.24 v. 19

[a] Heb *him* [b] Or *lords* [c] Meaning of Heb uncertain [d] Or *supervisor of half the portion assigned to* [e] Or *supervisor of the portion assigned to* [f] Gk Syr Compare verse 24, 10.9: Heb *Bavvai* [g] Or *supervisor*

to the corner. 25 Palal son of Uzai
repaired opposite the Angle and
the tower projecting from the upper house of the king at the court of
the guard. After him Pedaiah son of
Parosh 26 and the temple servants
living[h] on Ophel made repairs up
to a point opposite the Water Gate
on the east and the projecting tower. 27 After him the Tekoites repaired another section opposite
the great projecting tower as far as
the wall of Ophel.
28 Above the Horse Gate the
priests made repairs, each one opposite his own house. 29 After them
Zadok son of Immer made repairs
opposite his own house. After him
Shemaiah son of Shecaniah, the
keeper of the East Gate, made repairs. 30 After him Hananiah son of
Shelemiah and Hanun sixth son of
Zalaph repaired another section.
After him Meshullam son of Berechiah made repairs opposite his
living quarters. 31 After him Malchijah, one of the goldsmiths, made
repairs as far as the house of the
temple servants and of the merchants, opposite the Muster
Gate,[i] and to the upper room of
the corner. 32 And between the upper room of the corner and the
Sheep Gate the goldsmiths and the
merchants made repairs.

Hostile Plots Thwarted

4[j] Now when Sanballat heard
that we were building the wall,
he was angry and greatly enraged,
and he mocked the Jews. 2 He said
in the presence of his associates
and of the army of Samaria, "What
are these feeble Jews doing? Will
they restore things? Will they sacrifice? Will they finish it in a day?
Will they revive the stones out of
the heaps of rubbish—and burned
ones at that?" 3 Tobiah the Ammonite was beside him, and he
said, "That stone wall they are
building—any fox going up on it
would break it down!" 4 Hear,
O our God, for we are despised;
turn their taunt back on their own
heads, and give them over as plunder in a land of captivity. 5 Do not
cover their guilt, and do not let
their sin be blotted out from your
sight; for they have hurled insults
in the face of the builders.
6 So we rebuilt the wall, and all
the wall was joined together to half
its height; for the people had a
mind to work.
7[k] But when Sanballat and Tobiah and the Arabs and the Ammonites and the Ashdodites heard that
the repairing of the walls of Jerusalem was going forward and the gaps
were beginning to be closed, they
were very angry, 8 and all plotted together to come and fight against
Jerusalem and to cause confusion
in it. 9 So we prayed to our God, and
set a guard as a protection against
them day and night.
10 But Judah said, "The
strength of the burden bearers is
failing, and there is too much rubbish so that we are unable to work
on the wall." 11 And our enemies
said, "They will not know or see
anything before we come upon
them and kill them and stop the
work." 12 When the Jews who lived
near them came, they said to us ten
times, "From all the places where
they live[l] they will come up
against us."[m] 13 So in the lowest
parts of the space behind the wall,
in open places, I stationed the people according to their families,[n]
with their swords, their spears, and
their bows. 14 After I looked these
things over, I stood up and said to
the nobles and the officials and the
rest of the people, "Do not be
afraid of them. Remember the
LORD, who is great and awesome,
and fight for your kin, your sons,
your daughters, your wives, and
your homes."
15 When our enemies heard
that their plot was known to us,
and that God had frustrated it, we
all returned to the wall, each to his
work. 16 From that day on, half of
my servants worked on construc-

3.25 Jer 32.2
3.26 Neh 7.46; 11.21; 8.1
3.28 2 Kings 11.16; 2 Chr 23.15; Jer 31.40
3.31 vv. 8,32
3.32 v. 1
4.1 Neh 2.10,19
4.2 v. 10
4.3 Neh 2.10,19
4.4 Ps 123.3,4; 79.12
4.5 Ps 69.27,28; Jer 18.23
4.7 v. 1
4.9 Ps 50.15
4.13 vv. 17,18
4.14 Num 14.9; Deut 1.29; 2 Sam 10.12
4.15 2 Sam 17.14; Job 5.12

[h] Cn: Heb *were living* [i] Or *Hammiphkad Gate* [j] Ch 3.33 in Heb [k] Ch 4.1 in Heb [l] Cn: Heb *you return* [m] Compare Gk Syr: Meaning of Heb uncertain [n] Meaning of Heb uncertain

tion, and half held the spears, shields, bows, and body-armor; and the leaders posted themselves behind the whole house of Judah, [17]who were building the wall. The burden bearers carried their loads in such a way that each labored on the work with one hand and with the other held a weapon. [18]And each of the builders had his sword strapped at his side while he built. The man who sounded the trumpet was beside me. [19]And I said to the nobles, the officials, and the rest of the people, "The work is great and widely spread out, and we are separated far from one another on the wall. [20]Rally to us wherever you hear the sound of the trumpet. Our God will fight for us."

21 So we labored at the work, and half of them held the spears from break of dawn until the stars came out. [22]I also said to the people at that time, "Let every man and his servant pass the night inside Jerusalem, so that they may be a guard for us by night and may labor by day." [23]So neither I nor my brothers nor my servants nor the men of the guard who followed me ever took off our clothes; each kept his weapon in his right hand.[o]

Nehemiah Deals with Oppression

5 Now there was a great outcry of the people and of their wives against their Jewish kin. [2]For there were those who said, "With our sons and our daughters, we are many; we must get grain, so that we may eat and stay alive." [3]There were also those who said, "We are having to pledge our fields, our vineyards, and our houses in order to get grain during the famine." [4]And there were those who said, "We are having to borrow money on our fields and vineyards to pay the king's tax. [5]Now our flesh is the same as that of our kindred; our children are the same as their children; and yet we are forcing our sons and daughters to be slaves, and some of our daughters have been ravished; we are powerless, and our fields and vineyards now belong to others."

6 I was very angry when I heard their outcry and these complaints. [7]After thinking it over, I brought charges against the nobles and the officials; I said to them, "You are all taking interest from your own people." And I called a great assembly to deal with them, [8]and said to them, "As far as we were able, we have bought back our Jewish kindred who had been sold to other nations; but now you are selling your own kin, who must then be bought back by us!" They were silent, and could not find a word to say. [9]So I said, "The thing that you are doing is not good. Should you not walk in the fear of our God, to prevent the taunts of the nations our enemies? [10]Moreover I and my brothers and my servants are lending them money and grain. Let us stop this taking of interest. [11]Restore to them, this very day, their fields, their vineyards, their olive orchards, and their houses, and the interest on money, grain, wine, and oil that you have been exacting from them." [12]Then they said, "We will restore everything and demand nothing more from them. We will do as you say." And I called the priests, and made them take an oath to do as they had promised. [13]I also shook out the fold of my garment and said, "So may God shake out everyone from house and from property who does not perform this promise. Thus may they be shaken out and emptied." And all the assembly said, "Amen," and praised the LORD. And the people did as they had promised.

The Generosity of Nehemiah

14 Moreover from the time that I was appointed to be their governor in the land of Judah, from the twentieth year to the thirty-second year of King Artaxerxes, twelve years, neither I nor my brothers ate the food allowance of the governor. [15]The former governors who were before me laid heavy burdens on

4.20 Ex 14.14; Deut 1.30; Josh 23.10
5.1 Lev 25.35; Deut 15.7
5.4 Ezra 4.13; 7.24
5.5 Gen 37.27; Lev 25.39
5.7 Ex 22.25; Lev 25.36
5.8 Lev 25.48
5.9 2 Sam 12.14; Neh 4.4; Rom 2.24
5.12 Ezra 10.5
5.13 Acts 18.6; Neh 8.6
5.14 Neh 13.6; Ezra 4.13,14
5.15 v. 9

[o] Cn: Heb *each his weapon the water*

the people, and took food and wine
from them, besides forty shekels of
silver. Even their servants lorded it
over the people. But I did not do so,
because of the fear of God. 16In-
deed, I devoted myself to the work
on this wall, and acquired no land;
and all my servants were gathered
there for the work. 17Moreover
there were at my table one hundred
fifty people, Jews and officials, besides those who came to us from
the nations around us. 18Now that
which was prepared for one day
was one ox and six choice sheep;
also fowls were prepared for me,
and every ten days skins of wine in
abundance; yet with all this I did
not demand the food allowance of
the governor, because of the heavy
burden of labor on the people.
19Remember for my good, O my
God, all that I have done for this
people.

Intrigues of Enemies Foiled

6 Now when it was reported to
Sanballat and Tobiah and to
Geshem the Arab and to the rest of
our enemies that I had built the
wall and that there was no gap left
in it (though up to that time I had
not set up the doors in the gates),
2Sanballat and Geshem sent to me,
saying, "Come and let us meet together in one of the villages in the
plain of Ono." But they intended to
do me harm. 3So I sent messengers
to them, saying, "I am doing a great
work and I cannot come down. Why
should the work stop while I leave
it to come down to you?" 4They
sent to me four times in this way,
and I answered them in the same
manner. 5In the same way Sanballat for the fifth time sent his servant to me with an open letter in
his hand. 6In it was written, "It is
reported among the nations—and
Geshem[p] also says it—that you
and the Jews intend to rebel; that
is why you are building the wall;
and according to this report you
wish to become their king. 7You
have also set up prophets to proclaim in Jerusalem concerning
you, 'There is a king in Judah!' And
now it will be reported to the king
according to these words. So come,
therefore, and let us confer together." 8Then I sent to him, saying,
"No such things as you say have
been done; you are inventing them
out of your own mind" 9—for they
all wanted to frighten us, thinking,
"Their hands will drop from the
work, and it will not be done." But
now, O God, strengthen my hands.
10 One day when I went into the
house of Shemaiah son of Delaiah
son of Mehetabel, who was confined to his house, he said, "Let us
meet together in the house of God,
within the temple, and let us close
the doors of the temple, for they
are coming to kill you; indeed, tonight they are coming to kill you."
11But I said, "Should a man like me
run away? Would a man like me go
into the temple to save his life? I
will not go in!" 12Then I perceived
and saw that God had not sent him
at all, but he had pronounced the
prophecy against me because Tobiah and Sanballat had hired him.
13He was hired for this purpose, to
intimidate me and make me sin by
acting in this way, and so they
could give me a bad name, in order
to taunt me. 14Remember Tobiah
and Sanballat, O my God, according to these things that they did,
and also the prophetess Noadiah
and the rest of the prophets who
wanted to make me afraid.

The Wall Completed

15 So the wall was finished on
the twenty-fifth day of the month
Elul, in fifty-two days. 16And when
all our enemies heard of it, all the
nations around us were afraid[q]
and fell greatly in their own esteem; for they perceived that this
work had been accomplished with
the help of our God. 17Moreover in
those days the nobles of Judah sent
many letters to Tobiah, and Tobiah's letters came to them. 18For
many in Judah were bound by oath
to him, because he was the son-in-
law of Shecaniah son of Arah: and
his son Jehohanan had married the

5.17 1 Kings 18.19
5.18 1 Kings 4.22, 23; 2 Thes 3.8
5.19 Neh 13.14, 22,31
6.1 Neh 2.10, 19; 4.1,7; 3.1, 3
6.2 1 Chr 8.12
6.6 Neh 2.19
6.10 Jer 36.5
6.12 Ezek 13.22
6.13 v. 6
6.14 Neh 13.29; Ezek 13.17
6.16 Neh 2.10; 4.1,7; Ex 14.25; Ps 126.2

[p] Heb *Gashmu* [q] Another reading is *saw*

daughter of Meshullam son of Berechiah. [19]Also they spoke of his
good deeds in my presence, and reported my words to him. And Tobiah sent letters to intimidate me.

7 Now when the wall had been
built and I had set up the
doors, and the gatekeepers, the
singers, and the Levites had been
appointed, [2]I gave my brother Hanani charge over Jerusalem, along
with Hananiah the commander of
the citadel—for he was a faithful
man and feared God more than
many. [3]And I said to them, "The
gates of Jerusalem are not to be
opened until the sun is hot; while
the gatekeepers[r] are still standing
guard, let them shut and bar the
doors. Appoint guards from among
the inhabitants of Jerusalem, some
at their watch posts, and others before their own houses." [4]The city
was wide and large, but the people
within it were few and no houses
had been built.

Lists of the Returned Exiles

5 Then my God put it into my
mind to assemble the nobles and
the officials and the people to be
enrolled by genealogy. And I found
the book of the genealogy of those
who were the first to come back,
and I found the following written in
it:

6 These are the people of the
province who came up out of the
captivity of those exiles whom
King Nebuchadnezzar of Babylon
had carried into exile; they returned to Jerusalem and Judah,
each to his town. [7]They came with
Zerubbabel, Jeshua, Nehemiah,
Azariah, Raamiah, Nahamani,
Mordecai, Bilshan, Mispereth, Bigvai, Nehum, Baanah.

The number of the Israelite people: [8]the descendants of Parosh,
two thousand one hundred
seventy-two. [9]Of Shephatiah, three
hundred seventy-two. [10]Of Arah,
six hundred fifty-two. [11]Of Pahath-
moab, namely the descendants of
Jeshua and Joab, two thousand
eight hundred eighteen. [12]Of
Elam, one thousand two hundred
fifty-four. [13]Of Zattu, eight hundred forty-five. [14]Of Zaccai, seven
hundred sixty. [15]Of Binnui, six
hundred forty-eight. [16]Of Bebai,
six hundred twenty-eight. [17]Of Azgad, two thousand three hundred
twenty-two. [18]Of Adonikam, six
hundred sixty-seven. [19]Of Bigvai,
two thousand sixty-seven. [20]Of
Adin, six hundred fifty-five. [21]Of
Ater, namely of Hezekiah, ninety-
eight. [22]Of Hashum, three hundred
twenty-eight. [23]Of Bezai, three
hundred twenty-four. [24]Of Hariph,
one hundred twelve. [25]Of Gibeon,
ninety-five. [26]The people of Bethlehem and Netophah, one hundred
eighty-eight. [27]Of Anathoth, one
hundred twenty-eight. [28]Of Beth-
azmaveth, forty-two. [29]Of Kiriath-
jearim, Chephirah, and Beeroth,
seven hundred forty-three. [30]Of
Ramah and Geba, six hundred
twenty-one. [31]Of Michmas, one
hundred twenty-two. [32]Of Bethel
and Ai, one hundred twenty-three.
[33]Of the other Nebo, fifty-two.
[34]The descendants of the other
Elam, one thousand two hundred
fifty-four. [35]Of Harim, three hundred twenty. [36]Of Jericho, three
hundred forty-five. [37]Of Lod, Hadid, and Ono, seven hundred
twenty-one. [38]Of Senaah, three
thousand nine hundred thirty.

39 The priests: the descendants
of Jedaiah, namely the house of
Jeshua, nine hundred seventy-
three. [40]Of Immer, one thousand
fifty-two. [41]Of Pashhur, one thousand two hundred forty-seven. [42]Of
Harim, one thousand seventeen.

43 The Levites: the descendants
of Jeshua, namely of Kadmiel of
the descendants of Hodevah,
seventy-four. [44]The singers: the descendants of Asaph, one hundred
forty-eight. [45]The gatekeepers: the
descendants of Shallum, of Ater, of
Talmon, of Akkub, of Hatita, of
Shobai, one hundred thirty-eight.

46 The temple servants: the descendants of Ziha, of Hasupha, of
Tabbaoth, [47]of Keros, of Sia, of Padon, [48]of Lebana, of Hagaba, of

7.1 Neh 6.1,15
7.2 Neh 2.8
7.6 Ezra 2.1-70
7.7 Ezra 2.2
7.12 Ezra 2.7
7.17 Ezra 2.12
7.23 Ezra 2.17
7.27 Ezra 2.23
7.34 Ezra 2.31
7.39 Ezra 2.36
7.43 Ezra 2.40
7.46 Ezra 2.43

[r] Heb *while they*

Shalmai, [49]of Hanan, of Giddel, of
Gahar, [50]of Reaiah, of Rezin, of Nekoda, [51]of Gazzam, of Uzza, of Paseah, [52]of Besai, of Meunim, of Ne-
phushesim, [53]of Bakbuk, of
Hakupha, of Harhur, [54]of Bazlith,
of Mehida, of Harsha, [55]of Barkos,
of Sisera, of Temah, [56]of Neziah, of
Hatipha.

57 The descendants of Solomon's servants: of Sotai, of Sophe-
reth, of Perida, [58]of Jaala, of Darkon, of Giddel, [59]of Shephatiah, of
Hattil, of Pochereth-hazzebaim, of
Amon.

60 All the temple servants and
the descendants of Solomon's servants were three hundred ninety-
two.

61 The following were those
who came up from Tel-melah, Tel-
harsha, Cherub, Addon, and Immer, but they could not prove their
ancestral houses or their descent,
whether they belonged to Israel:
[62]the descendants of Delaiah, of
Tobiah, of Nekoda, six hundred
forty-two. [63]Also, of the priests: the
descendants of Hobaiah, of Hakkoz, of Barzillai (who had married
one of the daughters of Barzillai
the Gileadite and was called by
their name). [64]These sought their
registration among those enrolled
in the genealogies, but it was not
found there, so they were excluded
from the priesthood as unclean;
[65]the governor told them that they
were not to partake of the most
holy food, until a priest with Urim
and Thummim should come.

66 The whole assembly together
was forty-two thousand three hundred sixty, [67]besides their male
and female slaves, of whom there
were seven thousand three hundred thirty-seven; and they had two
hundred forty-five singers, male
and female. [68]They had seven hundred thirty-six horses, two hundred
forty-five mules,[s] [69]four hundred
thirty-five camels, and six thousand seven hundred twenty donkeys.

70 Now some of the heads of ancestral houses contributed to the
work. The governor gave to the
treasury one thousand darics of
gold, fifty basins, and five hundred
thirty priestly robes. [71]And some of
the heads of ancestral houses gave
into the building fund twenty thousand darics of gold and two thousand two hundred minas of silver.
[72]And what the rest of the people
gave was twenty thousand darics of
gold, two thousand minas of silver,
and sixty-seven priestly robes.

73 So the priests, the Levites,
the gatekeepers, the singers, some
of the people, the temple servants,
and all Israel settled in their towns.

Ezra Summons the People to Obey the Law

When the seventh month
came—the people of Israel being
8 settled in their towns— [1]all
the people gathered together
into the square before the Water
Gate. They told the scribe Ezra to
bring the book of the law of Moses,
which the LORD had given to Israel.
[2]Accordingly, the priest Ezra
brought the law before the assembly, both men and women and all
who could hear with understanding. This was on the first day of the
seventh month. [3]He read from it
facing the square before the Water
Gate from early morning until midday, in the presence of the men and
the women and those who could
understand; and the ears of all the
people were attentive to the book
of the law. [4]The scribe Ezra stood
on a wooden platform that had
been made for the purpose; and beside him stood Mattithiah, Shema,
Anaiah, Uriah, Hilkiah, and Maaseiah on his right hand; and Pedaiah,
Mishael, Malchijah, Hashum,
Hash-baddanah, Zechariah, and
Meshullam on his left hand. [5]And
Ezra opened the book in the sight
of all the people, for he was standing above all the people; and when
he opened it, all the people stood
up. [6]Then Ezra blessed the LORD,
the great God, and all the people
answered, "Amen, Amen," lifting
up their hands. Then they bowed

7.57 Ezra 2.55
7.60 v. 46
7.63 Ezra 2.61
7.65 Neh 8.9; 10.1
7.70 Neh 8.9
7.71 Ezra 2.69
7.73 Ezra 3.1
8.1 Ezra 3.1; Neh 3.26; Ezra 7.6
8.2 Deut 31.11, 12; Lev 23.24
8.6 Neh 5.13; Gen 14.22; Ex 4.31

[s] Ezra 2.66 and the margins of some Hebrew Mss: MT lacks *They had . . . forty-five mules*

their heads and worshiped the LORD
with their faces to the ground.
7 Also Jeshua, Bani, Sherebiah, Jamin, Akkub, Shabbethai, Hodiah,
Maaseiah, Kelita, Azariah, Jozabad, Hanan, Pelaiah, the Levites,[t]
helped the people to understand
the law, while the people remained
in their places. 8 So they read from
the book, from the law of God, with
interpretation. They gave the
sense, so that the people understood the reading.
9 And Nehemiah, who was the
governor, and Ezra the priest and
scribe, and the Levites who taught
the people said to all the people,
"This day is holy to the LORD your
God; do not mourn or weep." For
all the people wept when they
heard the words of the law. 10 Then
he said to them, "Go your way, eat
the fat and drink sweet wine and
send portions of them to those for
whom nothing is prepared, for this
day is holy to our LORD; and do not
be grieved, for the joy of the LORD is
your strength." 11 So the Levites
stilled all the people, saying, "Be
quiet, for this day is holy; do not be
grieved." 12 And all the people went
their way to eat and drink and to
send portions and to make great rejoicing, because they had understood the words that were declared
to them.

The Festival of Booths Celebrated

13 On the second day the heads
of ancestral houses of all the people, with the priests and the Levites, came together to the scribe
Ezra in order to study the words of
the law. 14 And they found it written in the law, which the LORD had
commanded by Moses, that the
people of Israel should live in
booths[u] during the festival of the
seventh month, 15 and that they
should publish and proclaim in all
their towns and in Jerusalem as follows, "Go out to the hills and bring
branches of olive, wild olive, myrtle, palm, and other leafy trees to
make booths,[u] as it is written."
16 So the people went out and
brought them, and made booths[u]
for themselves, each on the roofs of
their houses, and in their courts
and in the courts of the house of
God, and in the square at the Water
Gate and in the square at the Gate
of Ephraim. 17 And all the assembly
of those who had returned from the
captivity made booths[u] and lived
in them; for from the days of Jeshua son of Nun to that day the people of Israel had not done so. And
there was very great rejoicing.
18 And day by day, from the first day
to the last day, he read from the
book of the law of God. They kept
the festival seven days; and on the
eighth day there was a solemn assembly, according to the ordinance.

National Confession

9 Now on the twenty-fourth day
of this month the people of Israel were assembled with fasting
and in sackcloth, and with earth on
their heads.[v] 2 Then those of Israelite descent separated themselves
from all foreigners, and stood and
confessed their sins and the iniquities of their ancestors. 3 They stood
up in their place and read from the
book of the law of the LORD their
God for a fourth part of the day,
and for another fourth they made
confession and worshiped the LORD
their God. 4 Then Jeshua, Bani,
Kadmiel, Shebaniah, Bunni, Sherebiah, Bani, and Chenani stood on
the stairs of the Levites and cried
out with a loud voice to the LORD
their God. 5 Then the Levites, Jeshua, Kadmiel, Bani, Hashabneiah,
Sherebiah, Hodiah, Shebaniah,
and Pethahiah, said, "Stand up and
bless the LORD your God from everlasting to everlasting. Blessed be
your glorious name, which is exalted above all blessing and praise."
6 And Ezra said:[w] "You are the
LORD, you alone; you have made
heaven, the heaven of heavens,
with all their host, the earth and all
that is on it, the seas and all that is

8.7 2 Chr 17.7-9 **8.9** Neh 7.65, 70; 12.26; Num 29.1; Deut 16.14, 15 **8.10** Deut 26.11, 13 **8.12** vv. 10,7,8 **8.13** Lev 23.34, 42 **8.15** Lev 23.4; Deut 16.16; Lev 23.40 **8.16** Jer 32.29; Neh 12.39; 2 Kings 14.13 **8.17** 2 Chr 30.21 **8.18** Deut 31.11; Lev 23.36; Num 29.35 **9.1** Neh 8.2; Ezra 8.23; 1 Sam 4.12 **9.2** Ezra 10.11; Neh 13.3,30 **9.3** Neh 8.4 **9.4** Neh 8.7 **9.5** 1 Chr 29.13 **9.6** 2 Kings 19.15; Gen 1.1; Ps 36.6; Col 1.17

t 1 Esdras 9.48 Vg: Heb *and the Levites*
u Or *tabernacles*; Heb *succoth* v Heb *on them* w Gk: Heb lacks *And Ezra said*

in them. To all of them you give
life, and the host of heaven worships you. [7]You are the LORD, the
God who chose Abram and brought
him out of Ur of the Chaldeans and
gave him the name Abraham; [8]and
you found his heart faithful before
you, and made with him a covenant
to give to his descendants the land
of the Canaanite, the Hittite, the
Amorite, the Perizzite, the Jebusite, and the Girgashite; and you
have fulfilled your promise, for you
are righteous.
9 "And you saw the distress of
our ancestors in Egypt and heard
their cry at the Red Sea.[x] [10]You
performed signs and wonders
against Pharaoh and all his servants and all the people of his land,
for you knew that they acted insolently against our ancestors. You
made a name for yourself, which
remains to this day. [11]And you divided the sea before them, so that
they passed through the sea on dry
land, but you threw their pursuers
into the depths, like a stone into
mighty waters. [12]Moreover, you led
them by day with a pillar of cloud,
and by night with a pillar of fire, to
give them light on the way in which
they should go. [13]You came down
also upon Mount Sinai, and spoke
with them from heaven, and gave
them right ordinances and true
laws, good statutes and commandments, [14]and you made known
your holy sabbath to them and gave
them commandments and statutes
and a law through your servant Moses. [15]For their hunger you gave
them bread from heaven, and for
their thirst you brought water for
them out of the rock, and you told
them to go in to possess the land
that you swore to give them.
16 "But they and our ancestors
acted presumptuously and stiffened their necks and did not obey
your commandments; [17]they refused to obey, and were not mindful of the wonders that you performed among them; but they
stiffened their necks and determined to return to their slavery in
Egypt. But you are a God ready to
forgive, gracious and merciful, slow
to anger and abounding in steadfast love, and you did not forsake
them. [18]Even when they had cast
an image of a calf for themselves
and said, 'This is your God who
brought you up out of Egypt,' and
had committed great blasphemies,
[19]you in your great mercies did not
forsake them in the wilderness; the
pillar of cloud that led them in the
way did not leave them by day, nor
the pillar of fire by night that gave
them light on the way by which
they should go. [20]You gave your
good spirit to instruct them, and
did not withhold your manna from
their mouths, and gave them water
for their thirst. [21]Forty years you
sustained them in the wilderness
so that they lacked nothing; their
clothes did not wear out and their
feet did not swell. [22]And you gave
them kingdoms and peoples, and
allotted to them every corner,[y] so
they took possession of the land of
King Sihon of Heshbon and the
land of King Og of Bashan. [23]You
multiplied their descendants like
the stars of heaven, and brought
them into the land that you had
told their ancestors to enter and
possess. [24]So the descendants
went in and possessed the land,
and you subdued before them the
inhabitants of the land, the Canaanites, and gave them into their
hands, with their kings and the
peoples of the land, to do with
them as they pleased. [25]And they
captured fortress cities and a rich
land, and took possession of
houses filled with all sorts of
goods, hewn cisterns, vineyards, olive orchards, and fruit trees in
abundance; so they ate, and were
filled and became fat, and delighted themselves in your great goodness.
26 "Nevertheless they were disobedient and rebelled against you
and cast your law behind their
backs and killed your prophets,
who had warned them in order to

9.7 Gen 11.31; 12.1; 17.5
9.8 Gen 15.6, 18-21; Josh 21.43-45
9.9 Ex 3.7; 14.10-12
9.10 Ex 5.2; 9.16
9.11 Ex 14.21; 15.5,10
9.12 Ex 13.21,22
9.13 Ex 19.20; 20.1; Ps 19.7-9
9.14 Gen 2.3; Ex 20.8,11
9.15 Ex 16.14; 17.6; Num 20.7-13; Deut 1.8
9.16 Ps 106.6; Deut 31.27
9.17 Ps 78.11; Num 14.4; Ex 34.6,7
9.18 Ex 32.4
9.19 vv. 27,31,12
9.20 Num 11.17; Isa 63.11-14; Ex 16.15; 17.6
9.21 Deut 2.7; 8.4; 29.5
9.22 Num 21.21-35
9.23 Gen 15.5
9.24 Josh 21.43; 18.1
9.25 Deut 3.9; Num 13.27; Deut 6.11; 32.15; 1 Kings 8.66
9.26 Judg 2.11; 1 Kings 14.9; 2 Chr 36.16; v. 30

[x] Or *Sea of Reeds* [y] Meaning of Heb uncertain

turn them back to you, and they committed great blasphemies. 27 Therefore you gave them into the hands of their enemies, who made them suffer. Then in the time of their suffering they cried out to you and you heard them from heaven, and according to your great mercies you gave them saviors who saved them from the hands of their enemies. 28 But after they had rest, they again did evil before you, and you abandoned them to the hands of their enemies, so that they had dominion over them; yet when they turned and cried to you, you heard from heaven, and many times you rescued them according to your mercies. 29 And you warned them in order to turn them back to your law. Yet they acted presumptuously and did not obey your commandments, but sinned against your ordinances, by the observance of which a person shall live. They turned a stubborn shoulder and stiffened their neck and would not obey. 30 Many years you were patient with them, and warned them by your spirit through your prophets; yet they would not listen. Therefore you handed them over to the peoples of the lands. 31 Nevertheless, in your great mercies you did not make an end of them or forsake them, for you are a gracious and merciful God.

32 "Now therefore, our God—the great and mighty and awesome God, keeping covenant and steadfast love—do not treat lightly all the hardship that has come upon us, upon our kings, our officials, our priests, our prophets, our ancestors, and all your people, since the time of the kings of Assyria until today. 33 You have been just in all that has come upon us, for you have dealt faithfully and we have acted wickedly; 34 our kings, our officials, our priests, and our ancestors have not kept your law or heeded the commandments and the warnings that you gave them. 35 Even in their own kingdom, and in the great goodness you bestowed on them, and in the large and rich land that you set before them, they did not serve you and did not turn from their wicked works. 36 Here we are, slaves to this day—slaves in the land that you gave to our ancestors to enjoy its fruit and its good gifts. 37 Its rich yield goes to the kings whom you have set over us because of our sins; they have power also over our bodies and over our livestock at their pleasure, and we are in great distress."

9.27 Judg 2.14; Deut 4.29; Judg 2.16, 18
9.28 Judg 3.11; Ps 106.43
9.29 vv. 26,30, 16; Lev 18.5; Zech 7.11
9.30 2 Kings 17.13; Acts 7.51,52
9.31 Jer 4.27
9.32 Neh 1.5; 2 Kings 15.19; 17.3
9.33 Jer 12.1; Dan 9.5,6,8
9.35 Deut 28.47
9.36 Deut 28.48
9.37 Deut 28.33
9.38 2 Chr 29.10; 34.31
10.1 Neh 9.38
10.28 Ezra 2.36-58; Neh 9.2

Those Who Signed the Covenant

38[z] Because of all this we make a firm agreement in writing, and on that sealed document are inscribed the names of our officials, our Levites, and our priests.

10 [a] Upon the sealed document are the names of Nehemiah the governor, son of Hacaliah, and Zedekiah; 2 Seraiah, Azariah, Jeremiah, 3 Pashhur, Amariah, Malchijah, 4 Hattush, Shebaniah, Malluch, 5 Harim, Meremoth, Obadiah, 6 Daniel, Ginnethon, Baruch, 7 Meshullam, Abijah, Mijamin, 8 Maaziah, Bilgai, Shemaiah; these are the priests. 9 And the Levites: Jeshua son of Azaniah, Binnui of the sons of Henadad, Kadmiel; 10 and their associates, Shebaniah, Hodiah, Kelita, Pelaiah, Hanan, 11 Mica, Rehob, Hashabiah, 12 Zaccur, Sherebiah, Shebaniah, 13 Hodiah, Bani, Beninu. 14 The leaders of the people: Parosh, Pahath-moab, Elam, Zattu, Bani, 15 Bunni, Azgad, Bebai, 16 Adonijah, Bigvai, Adin, 17 Ater, Hezekiah, Azzur, 18 Hodiah, Hashum, Bezai, 19 Hariph, Anathoth, Nebai, 20 Magpiash, Meshullam, Hezir, 21 Meshezabel, Zadok, Jaddua, 22 Pelatiah, Hanan, Anaiah, 23 Hoshea, Hananiah, Hasshub, 24 Hallohesh, Pilha, Shobek, 25 Rehum, Hashabnah, Maaseiah, 26 Ahiah, Hanan, Anan, 27 Malluch, Harim, and Baanah.

Summary of the Covenant

28 The rest of the people, the priests, the Levites, the gatekeepers, the singers, the temple servants, and all who have separated

[z] Ch 10.1 in Heb [a] Ch 10.2 in Heb

themselves from the peoples of the
lands to adhere to the law of God,
their wives, their sons, their daughters, all who have knowledge and
understanding, 29 join with their
kin, their nobles, and enter into a
curse and an oath to walk in God's
law, which was given by Moses the
servant of God, and to observe and
do all the commandments of the
LORD our Lord and his ordinances
and his statutes. 30 We will not give
our daughters to the peoples of the
land or take their daughters for our
sons; 31 and if the peoples of the
land bring in merchandise or any
grain on the sabbath day to sell, we
will not buy it from them on the
sabbath or on a holy day; and we
will forego the crops of the seventh
year and the exaction of every debt.
32 We also lay on ourselves the
obligation to charge ourselves yearly one-third of a shekel for the service of the house of our God: 33 for
the rows of bread, the regular grain
offering, the regular burnt offering,
the sabbaths, the new moons, the
appointed festivals, the sacred donations, and the sin offerings to
make atonement for Israel, and for
all the work of the house of our
God. 34 We have also cast lots
among the priests, the Levites, and
the people, for the wood offering,
to bring it into the house of our
God, by ancestral houses, at appointed times, year by year, to burn
on the altar of the LORD our God, as
it is written in the law. 35 We obli-
gate ourselves to bring the first
fruits of our soil and the first fruits
of all fruit of every tree, year by
year, to the house of the LORD;
36 also to bring to the house of our
God, to the priests who minister in
the house of our God, the firstborn
of our sons and of our livestock, as
it is written in the law, and the
firstlings of our herds and of our
flocks; 37 and to bring the first of
our dough, and our contributions,
the fruit of every tree, the wine and
the oil, to the priests, to the chambers of the house of our God; and to
bring to the Levites the tithes from
our soil, for it is the Levites who

10.29 Neh 5.12; 2 Chr 34.31
10.30 Ex 34.16; Deut 7.3
10.31 Neh 13.15-22; Ex 23.10, 11; Deut 15.1,2
10.32 Ex 30.11-16
10.34 Neh 11.1; 13.31
10.35 Ex 23.19; Deut 26.2
10.36 Ex 13.2; Num 18.15, 16
10.37 Lev 23.17; Neh 13.5,9; Lev 27.30
10.38 Num 18.26; Neh 13.12, 13
10.39 Deut 12.6; Neh 13.10, 11
11.1 Neh 10.34; v. 18; Isa 48.2
11.3 1 Chr 9.2, 3; v. 20; Ezra 2.43; Neh 7.57
11.4 1 Chr 9.3ff
11.7 v. 4

collect the tithes in all our rural
towns. 38 And the priest, the descendant of Aaron, shall be with
the Levites when the Levites receive the tithes; and the Levites
shall bring up a tithe of the tithes
to the house of our God, to the
chambers of the storehouse. 39 For
the people of Israel and the sons of
Levi shall bring the contribution of
grain, wine, and oil to the store-
rooms where the vessels of the
sanctuary are, and where the
priests that minister, and the gatekeepers and the singers are. We
will not neglect the house of our
God.

Population of the City Increased

11 Now the leaders of the people lived in Jerusalem; and
the rest of the people cast lots to
bring one out of ten to live in the
holy city Jerusalem, while nine-
tenths remained in the other
towns. 2 And the people blessed all
those who willingly offered to live
in Jerusalem.
3 These are the leaders of the
province who lived in Jerusalem;
but in the towns of Judah all lived
on their property in their towns: Israel, the priests, the Levites, the
temple servants, and the descendants of Solomon's servants. 4 And
in Jerusalem lived some of the
Judahites and of the Benjaminites.
Of the Judahites: Athaiah son of
Uzziah son of Zechariah son of Amariah son of Shephatiah son of Mahalalel, of the descendants of Perez; 5 and Maaseiah son of Baruch
son of Col-hozeh son of Hazaiah
son of Adaiah son of Joiarib son of
Zechariah son of the Shilonite. 6 All
the descendants of Perez who lived
in Jerusalem were four hundred
sixty-eight valiant warriors.
7 And these are the Benjaminites: Sallu son of Meshullam son of
Joed son of Pedaiah son of Kolaiah
son of Maaseiah son of Ithiel son of
Jeshaiah. 8 And his brothers[b] Gab-
bai, Sallai: nine hundred twenty-
eight. 9 Joel son of Zichri was their
overseer; and Judah son of Hasse-

[b] Gk Mss: Heb *And after him*

nuah was second in charge of the
city.
10 Of the priests: Jedaiah son of
Joiarib, Jachin, 11 Seraiah son of
Hilkiah son of Meshullam son of
Zadok son of Meraioth son of Ahitub, officer of the house of God,
12 and their associates who did the
work of the house, eight hundred
twenty-two; and Adaiah son of Jeroham son of Pelaliah son of Amzi
son of Zechariah son of Pashhur
son of Malchijah, 13 and his associates, heads of ancestral houses,
two hundred forty-two; and
Amashsai son of Azarel son of Ah-
zai son of Meshillemoth son of Immer, 14 and their associates, valiant
warriors, one hundred twenty-
eight; their overseer was Zabdiel
son of Haggedolim.
15 And of the Levites: Shemaiah
son of Hasshub son of Azrikam son
of Hashabiah son of Bunni; 16 and
Shabbethai and Jozabad, of the
leaders of the Levites, who were
over the outside work of the house
of God; 17 and Mattaniah son of
Mica son of Zabdi son of Asaph,
who was the leader to begin the
thanksgiving in prayer, and Bakbukiah, the second among his associates; and Abda son of Shammua
son of Galal son of Jeduthun. 18 All
the Levites in the holy city were
two hundred eighty-four.
19 The gatekeepers, Akkub,
Talmon and their associates, who
kept watch at the gates, were one
hundred seventy-two. 20 And the
rest of Israel, and of the priests and
the Levites, were in all the towns of
Judah, all of them in their inheritance. 21 But the temple servants
lived on Ophel; and Ziha and Gish-
pa were over the temple servants.
22 The overseer of the Levites in
Jerusalem was Uzzi son of Bani son
of Hashabiah son of Mattaniah son
of Mica, of the descendants of
Asaph, the singers, in charge of the
work of the house of God. 23 For
there was a command from the
king concerning them, and a settled provision for the singers, as
was required every day. 24 And
Pethahiah son of Meshezabel, of

11.10 1 Chr 9.10
11.16 1 Chr 26.29
11.18 v. 1
11.21 Neh 3.26
11.22 vv. 9,14
11.23 Ezra 6.8; 7.20; Neh 12.47
11.25 Josh 14.15; 13.9,17
12.1 Ezra 2.1,2; see Neh 10.2-8
12.7 Ezra 3.2
12.8 Neh 11.17

the descendants of Zerah son of Judah, was at the king's hand in all
matters concerning the people.

Villages outside Jerusalem

25 And as for the villages, with
their fields, some of the people of
Judah lived in Kiriath-arba and its
villages, and in Dibon and its villages, and in Jekabzeel and its villages, 26 and in Jeshua and in
Moladah and Beth-pelet, 27 in
Hazar-shual, in Beer-sheba and its
villages, 28 in Ziklag, in Meconah
and its villages, 29 in En-rimmon, in
Zorah, in Jarmuth, 30 Zanoah, Adullam, and their villages, Lachish and
its fields, and Azekah and its villages. So they camped from Beer-
sheba to the valley of Hinnom.
31 The people of Benjamin also
lived from Geba onward, at Michmash, Aija, Bethel and its villages,
32 Anathoth, Nob, Ananiah, 33 Hazor, Ramah, Gittaim, 34 Hadid, Zeboim, Neballat, 35 Lod, and Ono,
the valley of artisans. 36 And certain
divisions of the Levites in Judah
were joined to Benjamin.

A List of Priests and Levites

12 These are the priests and
the Levites who came up
with Zerubbabel son of Shealtiel,
and Jeshua: Seraiah, Jeremiah,
Ezra, 2 Amariah, Malluch, Hattush,
3 Shecaniah, Rehum, Meremoth,
4 Iddo, Ginnethoi, Abijah, 5 Mijamin, Maadiah, Bilgah, 6 Shemaiah,
Joiarib, Jedaiah, 7 Sallu, Amok,
Hilkiah, Jedaiah. These were the
leaders of the priests and of their
associates in the days of Jeshua.
8 And the Levites: Jeshua, Binnui, Kadmiel, Sherebiah, Judah,
and Mattaniah, who with his associates was in charge of the songs of
thanksgiving. 9 And Bakbukiah and
Unno their associates stood opposite them in the service. 10 Jeshua
was the father of Joiakim, Joiakim
the father of Eliashib, Eliashib the
father of Joiada, 11 Joiada the father of Jonathan, and Jonathan the
father of Jaddua.
12 In the days of Joiakim the
priests, heads of ancestral houses,

were: of Seraiah, Meraiah; of Jeremiah, Hananiah; 13 of Ezra, Meshullam; of Amariah, Jehohanan;
14 of Malluchi, Jonathan; of Shebaniah, Joseph; 15 of Harim, Adna; of
Meraioth, Helkai; 16 of Iddo, Zechariah; of Ginnethon, Meshullam;
17 of Abijah, Zichri; of Miniamin, of
Moadiah, Piltai; 18 of Bilgah, Shammua; of Shemaiah, Jehonathan;
19 of Joiarib, Mattenai; of Jedaiah,
Uzzi; 20 of Sallai, Kallai; of Amok,
Eber; 21 of Hilkiah, Hashabiah; of
Jedaiah, Nethanel.

22 As for the Levites, in the days
of Eliashib, Joiada, Johanan, and
Jaddua, there were recorded the
heads of ancestral houses; also the
priests until the reign of Darius the
Persian. 23 The Levites, heads of
ancestral houses, were recorded in
the Book of the Annals until the
days of Johanan son of Eliashib.
24 And the leaders of the Levites:
Hashabiah, Sherebiah, and Jeshua
son of Kadmiel, with their associates over against them, to praise
and to give thanks, according to
the commandment of David the
man of God, section opposite to
section. 25 Mattaniah, Bakbukiah,
Obadiah, Meshullam, Talmon, and
Akkub were gatekeepers standing
guard at the storehouses of the
gates. 26 These were in the days of
Joiakim son of Jeshua son of Jozadak, and in the days of the governor
Nehemiah and of the priest Ezra,
the scribe.

Dedication of the City Wall

27 Now at the dedication of the
wall of Jerusalem they sought out
the Levites in all their places, to
bring them to Jerusalem to celebrate the dedication with rejoicing,
with thanksgivings and with singing, with cymbals, harps, and lyres.
28 The companies of the singers
gathered together from the circuit
around Jerusalem and from the villages of the Netophathites; 29 also
from Beth-gilgal and from the region of Geba and Azmaveth; for the
singers had built for themselves villages around Jerusalem. 30 And the
priests and the Levites purified
themselves; and they purified the
people and the gates and the wall.

31 Then I brought the leaders of
Judah up onto the wall, and appointed two great companies that
gave thanks and went in procession. One went to the right on the
wall to the Dung Gate; 32 and after
them went Hoshaiah and half the
officials of Judah, 33 and Azariah,
Ezra, Meshullam, 34 Judah, Benjamin, Shemaiah, and Jeremiah,
35 and some of the young priests
with trumpets: Zechariah son of
Jonathan son of Shemaiah son of
Mattaniah son of Micaiah son of
Zaccur son of Asaph; 36 and his kindred, Shemaiah, Azarel, Milalai,
Gilalai, Maai, Nethanel, Judah,
and Hanani, with the musical instruments of David the man of
God; and the scribe Ezra went in
front of them. 37 At the Fountain
Gate, in front of them, they went
straight up by the stairs of the city
of David, at the ascent of the wall,
above the house of David, to the
Water Gate on the east.

38 The other company of those
who gave thanks went to the left,[c]
and I followed them with half of
the people on the wall, above the
Tower of the Ovens, to the Broad
Wall, 39 and above the Gate of
Ephraim, and by the Old Gate, and
by the Fish Gate and the Tower of
Hananel and the Tower of the Hundred, to the Sheep Gate; and they
came to a halt at the Gate of the
Guard. 40 So both companies of
those who gave thanks stood in the
house of God, and I and half of the
officials with me; 41 and the priests
Eliakim, Maaseiah, Miniamin, Micaiah, Elioenai, Zechariah, and
Hananiah, with trumpets; 42 and
Maaseiah, Shemaiah, Eleazar,
Uzzi, Jehohanan, Malchijah, Elam,
and Ezer. And the singers sang with
Jezrahiah as their leader. 43 They
offered great sacrifices that day
and rejoiced, for God had made
them rejoice with great joy; the
women and children also rejoiced.

[c] Cn: Heb *opposite*

12.23 1 Chr 9.14ff
12.24 Neh 11.17
12.25 1 Chr 26.15
12.26 Neh 8.9; Ezra 7.6,11
12.27 1 Chr 25.6
12.28 1 Chr 9.16
12.30 Neh 13.22, 30
12.31 v. 38; Neh 2.13; 3.13
12.35 Num 10.2,8
12.36 1 Chr 23.5
12.37 Neh 2.14; 3.15; 3.26
12.38 v. 31; Neh 3.11; 3.8
12.39 Neh 8.16; 3.6; 3.3; 3.1; 3.25

The joy of Jerusalem was heard far
away.

Temple Responsibilities

44 On that day men were appointed over the chambers for the
stores, the contributions, the first
fruits, and the tithes, to gather into
them the portions required by the
law for the priests and for the Levites from the fields belonging to
the towns; for Judah rejoiced over
the priests and the Levites who
ministered. 45 They performed the
service of their God and the service
of purification, as did the singers
and the gatekeepers, according to
the command of David and his son
Solomon. 46 For in the days of David and Asaph long ago there was a
leader of the singers, and there
were songs of praise and thanksgiving to God. 47 In the days of Zerubbabel and in the days of Nehemiah
all Israel gave the daily portions for
the singers and the gatekeepers.
They set apart that which was for
the Levites; and the Levites set
apart that which was for the descendants of Aaron.

Foreigners Separated from Israel

13 On that day they read from
the book of Moses in the
hearing of the people; and in it was
found written that no Ammonite or
Moabite should ever enter the assembly of God, 2 because they did
not meet the Israelites with bread
and water, but hired Balaam
against them to curse them—yet
our God turned the curse into a
blessing. 3 When the people heard
the law, they separated from Israel
all those of foreign descent.

The Reforms of Nehemiah

4 Now before this, the priest Eliashib, who was appointed over the
chambers of the house of our God,
and who was related to Tobiah,
5 prepared for Tobiah a large room
where they had previously put the
grain offering, the frankincense,
the vessels, and the tithes of grain,
wine, and oil, which were given by
commandment to the Levites,
singers, and gatekeepers, and the
contributions for the priests.
6 While this was taking place I was
not in Jerusalem, for in the thirty-
second year of King Artaxerxes of
Babylon I went to the king. After
some time I asked leave of the king
7 and returned to Jerusalem. I then
discovered the wrong that Eliashib
had done on behalf of Tobiah, preparing a room for him in the courts
of the house of God. 8 And I was
very angry, and I threw all the
household furniture of Tobiah out
of the room. 9 Then I gave orders
and they cleansed the chambers,
and I brought back the vessels of
the house of God, with the grain offering and the frankincense.

10 I also found out that the portions of the Levites had not been
given to them; so that the Levites
and the singers, who had conducted the service, had gone back to
their fields. 11 So I remonstrated
with the officials and said, "Why is
the house of God forsaken?" And I
gathered them together and set
them in their stations. 12 Then all
Judah brought the tithe of the
grain, wine, and oil into the storehouses. 13 And I appointed as treasurers over the storehouses the
priest Shelemiah, the scribe Zadok,
and Pedaiah of the Levites, and as
their assistant Hanan son of Zaccur
son of Mattaniah, for they were
considered faithful; and their duty
was to distribute to their associates. 14 Remember me, O my God,
concerning this, and do not wipe
out my good deeds that I have done
for the house of my God and for his
service.

Sabbath Reforms Begun

15 In those days I saw in Judah
people treading wine presses on
the sabbath, and bringing in heaps
of grain and loading them on donkeys; and also wine, grapes, figs,
and all kinds of burdens, which
they brought into Jerusalem on the
sabbath day; and I warned them at
that time against selling food.
16 Tyrians also, who lived in the
city, brought in fish and all kinds of
merchandise and sold them on the

12.44 Neh 13.5, 12,13
12.45 1 Chr 25.1; 26.1
12.46 2 Chr 29.30
12.47 Neh 11.23; Num 18.21
13.1 Neh 9.3; Deut 23.3-5
13.2 Num 22.3-11; 23.11
13.3 Neh 9.2; Ex 12.38
13.4 Neh 12.44; 2.10; 6.1,17, 18
13.5 Num 18.21
13.6 Neh 5.14; Ezra 6.22
13.7 v. 5
13.9 2 Chr 29.5, 15,16
13.10 Neh 10.37; 12.28,29
13.11 vv. 17,25; Neh 10.39
13.12 Neh 10.37-39; 12.44
13.13 Neh 12.44; 7.2
13.14 vv. 22,31; Neh 5.19
13.15 Ex 20.8,10; Neh 10.31

sabbath to the people of Judah,
and in Jerusalem. 17 Then I remonstrated with the nobles of Judah
and said to them, "What is this evil
thing that you are doing, profaning
the sabbath day? 18 Did not your
ancestors act in this way, and did
not our God bring all this disaster
on us and on this city? Yet you
bring more wrath on Israel by profaning the sabbath."

19 When it began to be dark at
the gates of Jerusalem before the
sabbath, I commanded that the
doors should be shut and gave orders that they should not be
opened until after the sabbath.
And I set some of my servants over
the gates, to prevent any burden
from being brought in on the sabbath day. 20 Then the merchants
and sellers of all kinds of merchandise spent the night outside Jerusalem once or twice. 21 But I
warned them and said to them,
"Why do you spend the night in
front of the wall? If you do so again,
I will lay hands on you." From that
time on they did not come on the
sabbath. 22 And I commanded the
Levites that they should purify
themselves and come and guard
the gates, to keep the sabbath day
holy. Remember this also in my favor, O my God, and spare me according to the greatness of your
steadfast love.

13.17 vv. 11,25
13.18 Jer 17.21-23
13.19 Lev 23.32; Jer 17.21
13.21 v. 15
13.22 Neh 12.30; vv. 14,31
13.23 Ezra 9.2
13.25 vv. 11,17; Deut 25.2; Ezra 10.29, 30
13.26 1 Kings 11.1; 3.13; 2 Chr 1.12; 1 Kings 11.4ff
13.27 v. 23; Ezra 10.2
13.28 Neh 12.10; 2.10,19
13.29 Neh 6.14; Num 25.13
13.30 Neh 10.30
13.31 Neh 10.34; vv. 14,22

Mixed Marriages Condemned

23 In those days also I saw Jews
who had married women of Ashdod, Ammon, and Moab; 24 and half
of their children spoke the language of Ashdod, and they could
not speak the language of Judah,
but spoke the language of various
peoples. 25 And I contended with
them and cursed them and beat
some of them and pulled out their
hair; and I made them take an oath
in the name of God, saying, "You
shall not give your daughters to
their sons, or take their daughters
for your sons or for yourselves.
26 Did not King Solomon of Israel
sin on account of such women?
Among the many nations there was
no king like him, and he was beloved by his God, and God made
him king over all Israel; nevertheless, foreign women made even
him to sin. 27 Shall we then listen to
you and do all this great evil and
act treacherously against our God
by marrying foreign women?"

28 And one of the sons of Jehoiada, son of the high priest Eliashib,
was the son-in-law of Sanballat the
Horonite; I chased him away from
me. 29 Remember them, O my God,
because they have defiled the
priesthood, the covenant of the
priests and the Levites.

30 Thus I cleansed them from
everything foreign, and I established the duties of the priests and
Levites, each in his work; 31 and I
provided for the wood offering, at
appointed times, and for the first
fruits. Remember me, O my God,
for good.

Esther

Title and Background

This book has the name of its leading character, a beautiful Jewish girl whom King Ahasuerus of Persia chose to be his queen. The setting is in Susa, the Persian capital at this time (486-465 B.C.).

Author and Date of Writing

We do not know who wrote the book, but it is clear that the author was a Jew, both from the purpose of the book in accounting for the origin of a Jewish festival and from the Jewish nationalism that permeates the story. Many things point to the fact that he was a resident of a Persian city. The earliest date for the book would be shortly after the events narrated, i.e., c. 450 B.C.; the latest date would be before the Persian empire fell to Greece in 331.

Theme and Message

The central purpose of the author was to record the institution of the annual feast of Purim and to keep alive for later generations the memory of the great deliverance of the Jewish people during the reign of Ahasuerus. Although the name of God does not appear in the book, his care for his chosen people is clearly shown. Feasting is a prominent theme in Esther (see Outline).

Outline

I. The Banquet of Ahasuerus (1.1–2.18)
II. The Banquets of Esther (2.19–7.10)
III. The Feast of Purim (8.1–10.3)

King Ahasuerus Deposes Queen Vashti

1 This happened in the days of
Ahasuerus, the same Ahasuerus who ruled over one hundred
twenty-seven provinces from India
to Ethiopia.[a] 2 In those days when
King Ahasuerus sat on his royal
throne in the citadel of Susa, 3 in
the third year of his reign, he gave
a banquet for all his officials and
ministers. The army of Persia and
Media and the nobles and governors of the provinces were present,
4 while he displayed the great
wealth of his kingdom and the
splendor and pomp of his majesty
for many days, one hundred eighty
days in all.
5 When these days were completed, the king gave for all the
people present in the citadel of
Susa, both great and small, a banquet lasting for seven days, in the
court of the garden of the king's
palace. 6 There were white cotton
curtains and blue hangings tied
with cords of fine linen and purple
to silver rings[b] and marble pillars.
There were couches of gold and silver on a mosaic pavement of por-
phyry, marble, mother-of-pearl,
and colored stones. 7 Drinks were
served in golden goblets, goblets of
different kinds, and the royal wine
was lavished according to the
bounty of the king. 8 Drinking was
by flagons, without restraint; for
the king had given orders to all the
officials of his palace to do as each
one desired. 9 Furthermore, Queen
Vashti gave a banquet for the wom-
en in the palace of King Ahasuerus.
10 On the seventh day, when
the king was merry with wine, he

1.1 Ezra 4.6; Dan 9.1; Esther 8.9; 9.30
1.2 Neh 1.1
1.3 Esther 2.18
1.5 Esther 7.7,8
1.6 Ezek 23.41; Am 6.4
1.7 Esther 2.18
1.10 Judg 16.25; Esther 7.9

[a] Or *Nubia*; Heb *Cush*
[b] Or *rods*

commanded Mehuman, Biztha,
Harbona, Bigtha and Abagtha, Ze-
thar and Carkas, the seven eunuchs
who attended him, 11 to bring
Queen Vashti before the king,
wearing the royal crown, in order to
show the peoples and the officials
her beauty; for she was fair to behold. 12 But Queen Vashti refused
to come at the king's command
conveyed by the eunuchs. At this
the king was enraged, and his anger
burned within him.
13 Then the king consulted the
sages who knew the laws[c] (for this
was the king's procedure toward all
who were versed in law and custom, 14 and those next to him were
Carshena, Shethar, Admatha, Tarshish, Meres, Marsena, and Memucan, the seven officials of Persia
and Media, who had access to the
king, and sat first in the kingdom):
15 "According to the law, what is to
be done to Queen Vashti because
she has not performed the command of King Ahasuerus conveyed
by the eunuchs?" 16 Then Memucan said in the presence of the king
and the officials, "Not only has
Queen Vashti done wrong to the
king, but also to all the officials
and all the peoples who are in all
the provinces of King Ahasuerus.
17 For this deed of the queen will be
made known to all women, causing
them to look with contempt on
their husbands, since they will say,
'King Ahasuerus commanded
Queen Vashti to be brought before
him, and she did not come.' 18 This
very day the noble ladies of Persia
and Media who have heard of the
queen's behavior will rebel
against[d] the king's officials, and
there will be no end of contempt
and wrath! 19 If it pleases the king,
let a royal order go out from him,
and let it be written among the
laws of the Persians and the Medes
so that it may not be altered, that
Vashti is never again to come before King Ahasuerus; and let the
king give her royal position to another who is better than she. 20 So
when the decree made by the king
is proclaimed throughout all his
kingdom, vast as it is, all women
will give honor to their husbands,
high and low alike."
21 This advice pleased the king
and the officials, and the king did
as Memucan proposed; 22 he sent
letters to all the royal provinces, to
every province in its own script and
to every people in its own language,
declaring that every man should be
master in his own house.[e]

1.13 Jer 10.7; Dan 2.12; 1 Chr 12.32 **1.14** 2 Kings 25.19 **1.17** Eph 5.33 **1.19** Esther 8.8; Dan 6.8 **1.20** Eph 5.22; Col 3.18 **1.22** Esther 8.9; Eph 5.22-24; 1 Tim 2.12 **2.1** Esther 7.10; 1.19,20 **2.3** vv. 8,15 **2.5** Esther 3.2 **2.6** 2 Kings 24.14, 15; 24.6 **2.7** v. 15 **2.8** vv. 3,15

Esther Becomes Queen

2 After these things, when the
anger of King Ahasuerus had
abated, he remembered Vashti and
what she had done and what had
been decreed against her. 2 Then
the king's servants who attended
him said, "Let beautiful young virgins be sought out for the king.
3 And let the king appoint commis-
sioners in all the provinces of his
kingdom to gather all the beautiful
young virgins to the harem in the
citadel of Susa under custody of
Hegai, the king's eunuch, who is in
charge of the women; let their cosmetic treatments be given them.
4 And let the girl who pleases the
king be queen instead of Vashti."
This pleased the king, and he did
so.
5 Now there was a Jew in the
citadel of Susa whose name was
Mordecai son of Jair son of Shimei
son of Kish, a Benjaminite. 6 Kish[f]
had been carried away from Jerusalem among the captives carried
away with King Jeconiah of Judah,
whom King Nebuchadnezzar of
Babylon had carried away. 7 Mordecai[g] had brought up Hadassah,
that is Esther, his cousin, for she
had neither father nor mother; the
girl was fair and beautiful, and
when her father and her mother
died, Mordecai adopted her as his
own daughter. 8 So when the king's
order and his edict were proclaimed, and when many young
women were gathered in the citadel of Susa in custody of Hegai, Es-

[c] Cn: Heb *times* [d] Cn: Heb *will tell* [e] Heb adds *and speak according to the language of his people* [f] Heb *a Benjamite* [6] *who* [g] Heb *He*

ther also was taken into the king's
palace and put in custody of Hegai,
who had charge of the women.
9 The girl pleased him and won his
favor, and he quickly provided her
with her cosmetic treatments and
her portion of food, and with seven
chosen maids from the king's palace, and advanced her and her
maids to the best place in the harem. 10 Esther did not reveal her
people or kindred, for Mordecai
had charged her not to tell. 11 Every
day Mordecai would walk around
in front of the court of the harem,
to learn how Esther was and how
she fared.

12 The turn came for each girl
to go in to King Ahasuerus, after
being twelve months under the regulations for the women, since this
was the regular period of their cosmetic treatment, six months with
oil of myrrh and six months with
perfumes and cosmetics for wom-
en. 13 When the girl went in to the
king she was given whatever she
asked for to take with her from the
harem to the king's palace. 14 In
the evening she went in; then in the
morning she came back to the second harem in custody of Shaash-
gaz, the king's eunuch, who was in
charge of the concubines; she did
not go in to the king again, unless
the king delighted in her and she
was summoned by name.

15 When the turn came for Esther daughter of Abihail the uncle
of Mordecai, who had adopted her
as his own daughter, to go in to the
king, she asked for nothing except
what Hegai the king's eunuch, who
had charge of the women, advised.
Now Esther was admired by all who
saw her. 16 When Esther was taken
to King Ahasuerus in his royal palace in the tenth month, which is
the month of Tebeth, in the seventh year of his reign, 17 the king
loved Esther more than all the other women; of all the virgins she won
his favor and devotion, so that he
set the royal crown on her head and
made her queen instead of Vashti.
18 Then the king gave a great banquet to all his officials and
ministers—"Esther's banquet."
He also granted a holiday[h] to the
provinces, and gave gifts with royal
liberality.

Mordecai Discovers a Plot

19 When the virgins were being
gathered together,[i] Mordecai was
sitting at the king's gate. 20 Now Esther had not revealed her kindred
or her people, as Mordecai had
charged her; for Esther obeyed
Mordecai just as when she was
brought up by him. 21 In those days,
while Mordecai was sitting at the
king's gate, Bigthan and Teresh,
two of the king's eunuchs, who
guarded the threshold, became angry and conspired to assassinate[j]
King Ahasuerus. 22 But the matter
came to the knowledge of Mordecai, and he told it to Queen Esther,
and Esther told the king in the
name of Mordecai. 23 When the affair was investigated and found to
be so, both the men were hanged
on the gallows. It was recorded in
the book of the annals in the presence of the king.

Haman Undertakes to Destroy the Jews

3 After these things King Ahasuerus promoted Haman son of
Hammedatha the Agagite, and advanced him and set his seat above
all the officials who were with him.
2 And all the king's servants who
were at the king's gate bowed down
and did obeisance to Haman; for
the king had so commanded concerning him. But Mordecai did not
bow down or do obeisance. 3 Then
the king's servants who were at the
king's gate said to Mordecai, "Why
do you disobey the king's command?" 4 When they spoke to him
day after day and he would not listen to them, they told Haman, in
order to see whether Mordecai's
words would avail; for he had told
them that he was a Jew. 5 When Haman saw that Mordecai did not
bow down or do obeisance to him,
Haman was infuriated. 6 But he

2.9 vv. 3,12
2.10 v. 20
2.15 v. 6; Esther 9.29
2.17 Esther 1.11
2.18 Esther 1.3; 1.7
2.20 v. 10
2.21 Esther 6.2
2.22 Esther 6.1,2
2.23 Esther 10.2
3.1 Esther 5.11; v. 10
3.2 Esther 2.19; v. 5
3.3 v. 2
3.5 v. 2; Esther 5.9
3.6 Ps 83.4

[h] Or *an amnesty* [i] Heb adds *a second time* [j] Heb *to lay hands on*

thought it beneath him to lay
hands on Mordecai alone. So, having been told who Mordecai's people were, Haman plotted to destroy
all the Jews, the people of Mordecai, throughout the whole kingdom
of Ahasuerus.
7 In the first month, which is
the month of Nisan, in the twelfth
year of King Ahasuerus, they cast
Pur—which means "the lot"—
before Haman for the day and for
the month, and the lot fell on the
thirteenth day[k] of the twelfth
month, which is the month of Adar.
[8]Then Haman said to King Ahasuerus, "There is a certain people scattered and separated among the
peoples in all the provinces of your
kingdom; their laws are different
from those of every other people,
and they do not keep the king's
laws, so that it is not appropriate
for the king to tolerate them. [9]If it
pleases the king, let a decree be issued for their destruction, and I
will pay ten thousand talents of silver into the hands of those who
have charge of the king's business,
so that they may put it into the
king's treasuries." [10]So the king
took his signet ring from his hand
and gave it to Haman son of Hammedatha the Agagite, the enemy of
the Jews. [11]The king said to Haman, "The money is given to you,
and the people as well, to do with
them as it seems good to you."
12 Then the king's secretaries
were summoned on the thirteenth
day of the first month, and an
edict, according to all that Haman
commanded, was written to the
king's satraps and to the governors
over all the provinces and to the officials of all the peoples, to every
province in its own script and every
people in its own language; it was
written in the name of King Ahasuerus and sealed with the king's
ring. [13]Letters were sent by couriers to all the king's provinces, giving orders to destroy, to kill, and to
annihilate all Jews, young and old,
women and children, in one day,
the thirteenth day of the twelfth
month, which is the month of Adar,

3.7 Esther 9.24; Ezra 6.15
3.8 Ezra 4.12-15; Acts 16.20
3.10 Esther 8.2; Gen 41.42; Esther 7.6
3.12 Esther 8.8-10; 1 Kings 21.8
3.13 Esther 8.10-14
3.14 Esther 8.13, 14
3.15 Esther 8.15
4.1ff Esther 3.8-10; Jon 3.5,6; Ezek 27.30
4.3 Isa 58.5
4.7 Esther 3.9
4.8 Esther 3.14, 15

and to plunder their goods. [14]A
copy of the document was to be issued as a decree in every province
by proclamation, calling on all the
peoples to be ready for that day.
[15]The couriers went quickly by order of the king, and the decree was
issued in the citadel of Susa. The
king and Haman sat down to drink;
but the city of Susa was thrown
into confusion.

Esther Agrees to Help the Jews

4 When Mordecai learned all
that had been done, Mordecai
tore his clothes and put on sackcloth and ashes, and went through
the city, wailing with a loud and
bitter cry; [2]he went up to the entrance of the king's gate, for no one
might enter the king's gate clothed
with sackcloth. [3]In every province,
wherever the king's command and
his decree came, there was great
mourning among the Jews, with
fasting and weeping and lamenting, and most of them lay in sackcloth and ashes.
4 When Esther's maids and her
eunuchs came and told her, the
queen was deeply distressed; she
sent garments to clothe Mordecai,
so that he might take off his sackcloth; but he would not accept
them. [5]Then Esther called for Hathach, one of the king's eunuchs,
who had been appointed to attend
her, and ordered him to go to Mordecai to learn what was happening
and why. [6]Hathach went out to
Mordecai in the open square of the
city in front of the king's gate, [7]and
Mordecai told him all that had happened to him, and the exact sum of
money that Haman had promised
to pay into the king's treasuries for
the destruction of the Jews. [8]Mor-
decai also gave him a copy of the
written decree issued in Susa for
their destruction, that he might
show it to Esther, explain it to her,
and charge her to go to the king to
make supplication to him and entreat him for her people.
9 Hathach went and told Esther

[k] Cn Compare Gk and verse 13 below: Heb *the twelfth month*

what Mordecai had said. [10]Then
Esther spoke to Hathach and gave
him a message for Mordecai, saying, [11]"All the king's servants and
the people of the king's provinces
know that if any man or woman
goes to the king inside the inner
court without being called, there is
but one law—all alike are to be put
to death. Only if the king holds out
the golden scepter to someone,
may that person live. I myself have
not been called to come in to the
king for thirty days." [12]When they
told Mordecai what Esther had
said, [13]Mordecai told them to reply
to Esther, "Do not think that in the
king's palace you will escape any
more than all the other Jews. [14]For
if you keep silence at such a time
as this, relief and deliverance will
rise for the Jews from another
quarter, but you and your father's
family will perish. Who knows?
Perhaps you have come to royal
dignity for just such a time as this."
[15]Then Esther said in reply to Mordecai, [16]"Go, gather all the Jews to
be found in Susa, and hold a fast on
my behalf, and neither eat nor
drink for three days, night or day. I
and my maids will also fast as you
do. After that I will go to the king,
though it is against the law; and if
I perish, I perish." [17]Mordecai then
went away and did everything as
Esther had ordered him.

Esther's Banquet

5 On the third day Esther put on
her royal robes and stood in
the inner court of the king's palace,
opposite the king's hall. The king
was sitting on his royal throne inside the palace opposite the entrance to the palace. [2]As soon as
the king saw Queen Esther standing in the court, she won his favor
and he held out to her the golden
scepter that was in his hand. Then
Esther approached and touched
the top of the scepter. [3]The king
said to her, "What is it, Queen Esther? What is your request? It shall
be given you, even to the half of my
kingdom." [4]Then Esther said, "If it
pleases the king, let the king and
Haman come today to a banquet
that I have prepared for the king."
[5]Then the king said, "Bring Haman
quickly, so that we may do as Esther desires." So the king and Haman came to the banquet that Esther had prepared. [6]While they
were drinking wine, the king said
to Esther, "What is your petition? It
shall be granted you. And what is
your request? Even to the half of
my kingdom, it shall be fulfilled."
[7]Then Esther said, "This is my petition and request: [8]If I have won
the king's favor, and if it pleases
the king to grant my petition and
fulfill my request, let the king and
Haman come tomorrow to the banquet that I will prepare for them,
and then I will do as the king has
said."

Haman Plans to Have Mordecai Hanged

9 Haman went out that day happy and in good spirits. But when
Haman saw Mordecai in the king's
gate, and observed that he neither
rose nor trembled before him, he
was infuriated with Mordecai;
[10]nevertheless Haman restrained
himself and went home. Then he
sent and called for his friends and
his wife Zeresh, [11]and Haman recounted to them the splendor of
his riches, the number of his sons,
all the promotions with which the
king had honored him, and how he
had advanced him above the officials and the ministers of the king.
[12]Haman added, "Even Queen Esther let no one but myself come
with the king to the banquet that
she prepared. Tomorrow also I am
invited by her, together with the
king. [13]Yet all this does me no good
so long as I see the Jew Mordecai
sitting at the king's gate." [14]Then
his wife Zeresh and all his friends
said to him, "Let a gallows fifty cubits high be made, and in the
morning tell the king to have Mordecai hanged on it; then go with
the king to the banquet in good
spirits." This advice pleased Haman, and he had the gallows made.

4.11 Esther 5.1; 6.4; Dan 2.9; Esther 5.2; 8.4
4.15 Esther 5.1
5.1 Esther 4.16; 4.11; 6.4
5.2 Prov 21.1; Esther 4.11; 8.4
5.3 Esther 7.2; Mk 6.23
5.5 Esther 6.14
5.6 Esther 7.2; v. 3
5.8 Esther 7.3; 8.5; 6.14
5.9 Esther 2.19; 3.5
5.10 Esther 6.13
5.11 Esther 9.7-10; 3.1
5.12 v. 8
5.13 v. 9
5.14 Esther 6.4; 7.9,10

The King Honors Mordecai

6 On that night the king could
not sleep, and he gave orders
to bring the book of records, the
annals, and they were read to the
king. 2 It was found written how
Mordecai had told about Bigthana
and Teresh, two of the king's eunuchs, who guarded the threshold,
and who had conspired to assassinate[l] King Ahasuerus. 3 Then the
king said, "What honor or distinction has been bestowed on Mordecai for this?" The king's servants
who attended him said, "Nothing
has been done for him." 4 The king
said, "Who is in the court?" Now
Haman had just entered the outer
court of the king's palace to speak
to the king about having Mordecai
hanged on the gallows that he had
prepared for him. 5 So the king's
servants told him, "Haman is
there, standing in the court." The
king said, "Let him come in." 6 So
Haman came in, and the king said
to him, "What shall be done for the
man whom the king wishes to hon-
or?" Haman said to himself,
"Whom would the king wish to
honor more than me?" 7 So Haman
said to the king, "For the man
whom the king wishes to honor,
8 let royal robes be brought, which
the king has worn, and a horse that
the king has ridden, with a royal
crown on its head. 9 Let the robes
and the horse be handed over to
one of the king's most noble officials; let him[m] robe the man whom
the king wishes to honor, and let
him[m] conduct the man on horseback through the open square of
the city, proclaiming before him:
'Thus shall it be done for the man
whom the king wishes to honor.' "
10 Then the king said to Haman,
"Quickly, take the robes and the
horse, as you have said, and do so
to the Jew Mordecai who sits at the
king's gate. Leave out nothing that
you have mentioned." 11 So Haman
took the robes and the horse and
robed Mordecai and led him riding
through the open square of the
city, proclaiming, "Thus shall it be
done for the man whom the king
wishes to honor."
12 Then Mordecai returned to
the king's gate, but Haman hurried
to his house, mourning and with
his head covered. 13 When Haman
told his wife Zeresh and all his
friends everything that had happened to him, his advisers and his
wife Zeresh said to him, "If Mordecai, before whom your downfall has
begun, is of the Jewish people, you
will not prevail against him, but
will surely fall before him."

Haman's Downfall and Mordecai's Advancement

14 While they were still talking
with him, the king's eunuchs arrived and hurried Haman off to the
banquet that Esther had prepared.
7 1 So the king and Haman went
in to feast with Queen Esther.
2 On the second day, as they were
drinking wine, the king again said
to Esther, "What is your petition,
Queen Esther? It shall be granted
you. And what is your request?
Even to the half of my kingdom, it
shall be fulfilled." 3 Then Queen
Esther answered, "If I have won
your favor, O king, and if it pleases
the king, let my life be given me—
that is my petition—and the lives
of my people—that is my request.
4 For we have been sold, I and my
people, to be destroyed, to be
killed, and to be annihilated. If we
had been sold merely as slaves,
men and women, I would have held
my peace; but no enemy can compensate for this damage to the
king."[n] 5 Then King Ahasuerus
said to Queen Esther, "Who is he,
and where is he, who has presumed
to do this?" 6 Esther said, "A foe
and enemy, this wicked Haman!"
Then Haman was terrified before
the king and the queen. 7 The king
rose from the feast in wrath and
went into the palace garden, but
Haman stayed to beg his life from
Queen Esther, for he saw that the
king had determined to destroy
him. 8 When the king returned from

6.1 Dan 6.18; Esther 2.23; 10.2
6.2 Esther 2.21, 22
6.4 Esther 4.11; 5.1; 5.14
6.6 vv. 7,9,11
6.8 1 Kings 1.33
6.9 Gen 41.43
6.12 2 Sam 15.30
6.13 Esther 5.10
6.14 Esther 5.8
7.2 Esther 5.6; 5.3
7.3 Esther 5.8; 8.5
7.4 Esther 3.9, 13
7.6 Esther 3.10
7.8 Esther 1.6

[l] Heb *to lay hands on* [m] Heb *them*
[n] Meaning of Heb uncertain

the palace garden to the banquet
hall, Haman had thrown himself on
the couch where Esther was reclining; and the king said, "Will he
even assault the queen in my presence, in my own house?" As the
words left the mouth of the king,
they covered Haman's face. 9 Then
Harbona, one of the eunuchs in attendance on the king, said, "Look,
the very gallows that Haman has
prepared for Mordecai, whose word
saved the king, stands at Haman's
house, fifty cubits high." And the
king said, "Hang him on that." 10 So
they hanged Haman on the gallows
that he had prepared for Mordecai.
Then the anger of the king abated.

Esther Saves the Jews

8 On that day King Ahasuerus
gave to Queen Esther the
house of Haman, the enemy of the
Jews; and Mordecai came before
the king, for Esther had told what
he was to her. 2 Then the king took
off his signet ring, which he had
taken from Haman, and gave it to
Mordecai. So Esther set Mordecai
over the house of Haman.

3 Then Esther spoke again to
the king; she fell at his feet, weeping and pleading with him to avert
the evil design of Haman the Agagite and the plot that he had devised
against the Jews. 4 The king held
out the golden scepter to Esther,
5 and Esther rose and stood before
the king. She said, "If it pleases the
king, and if I have won his favor,
and if the thing seems right before
the king, and I have his approval,
let an order be written to revoke
the letters devised by Haman son
of Hammedatha the Agagite, which
he wrote giving orders to destroy
the Jews who are in all the provinces of the king. 6 For how can I
bear to see the calamity that is
coming on my people? Or how can
I bear to see the destruction of my
kindred?" 7 Then King Ahasuerus
said to Queen Esther and to the
Jew Mordecai, "See, I have given
Esther the house of Haman, and
they have hanged him on the gallows, because he plotted to lay
hands on the Jews. 8 You may write
as you please with regard to the
Jews, in the name of the king, and
seal it with the king's ring; for an
edict written in the name of the
king and sealed with the king's ring
cannot be revoked."

9 The king's secretaries were
summoned at that time, in the
third month, which is the month of
Sivan, on the twenty-third day; and
an edict was written, according to
all that Mordecai commanded, to
the Jews and to the satraps and the
governors and the officials of the
provinces from India to Ethiopia,[o]
one hundred twenty-seven provinces, to every province in its own
script and to every people in its
own language, and also to the Jews
in their script and their language.
10 He wrote letters in the name of
King Ahasuerus, sealed them with
the king's ring, and sent them by
mounted couriers riding on fast
steeds bred from the royal herd.[p]
11 By these letters the king allowed
the Jews who were in every city to
assemble and defend their lives, to
destroy, to kill, and to annihilate
any armed force of any people or
province that might attack them,
with their children and women,
and to plunder their goods 12 on a
single day throughout all the provinces of King Ahasuerus, on the
thirteenth day of the twelfth
month, which is the month of Adar.
13 A copy of the writ was to be issued as a decree in every province
and published to all peoples, and
the Jews were to be ready on that
day to take revenge on their enemies. 14 So the couriers, mounted
on their swift royal steeds, hurried
out, urged by the king's command.
The decree was issued in the citadel of Susa.

15 Then Mordecai went out
from the presence of the king,
wearing royal robes of blue and
white, with a great golden crown
and a mantle of fine linen and purple, while the city of Susa shouted

7.9 Esther 1.10; 5.14; Ps 7.16; Prov 11.5,6
8.1 Esther 7.6; 2.7
8.2 Esther 3.10
8.4 Esther 4.11; 5.2
8.5 Esther 5.8; 7.3; 3.13
8.6 Esther 7.4; 9.1
8.7 v. 1
8.8 v. 10; Esther 3.12; 1.19
8.9 Esther 3.12; 1.1; 1.22
8.10 1 Kings 21.8; Esther 3.12, 13
8.11 Esther 9.2, 10,15,16; 3.13
8.13 Esther 3.14
8.15 Esther 3.15

[o] Or *Nubia*; Heb *Cush* [p] Meaning of Heb uncertain

and rejoiced. 16 For the Jews there was light and gladness, joy and honor. 17 In every province and in every city, wherever the king's command and his edict came, there was gladness and joy among the Jews, a festival and a holiday. Furthermore, many of the peoples of the country professed to be Jews, because the fear of the Jews had fallen upon them.

Destruction of the Enemies of the Jews

9 Now in the twelfth month, which is the month of Adar, on the thirteenth day, when the king's command and edict were about to be executed, on the very day when the enemies of the Jews hoped to gain power over them, but which had been changed to a day when the Jews would gain power over their foes, 2 the Jews gathered in their cities throughout all the provinces of King Ahasuerus to lay hands on those who had sought their ruin; and no one could withstand them, because the fear of them had fallen upon all peoples. 3 All the officials of the provinces, the satraps and the governors, and the royal officials were supporting the Jews, because the fear of Mordecai had fallen upon them. 4 For Mordecai was powerful in the king's house, and his fame spread throughout all the provinces as the man Mordecai grew more and more powerful. 5 So the Jews struck down all their enemies with the sword, slaughtering, and destroying them, and did as they pleased to those who hated them. 6 In the citadel of Susa the Jews killed and destroyed five hundred people. 7 They killed Parshandatha, Dalphon, Aspatha, 8 Poratha, Adalia, Aridatha, 9 Parmashta, Arisai, Aridai, Vaizatha, 10 the ten sons of Haman son of Hammedatha, the enemy of the Jews; but they did not touch the plunder.

11 That very day the number of those killed in the citadel of Susa was reported to the king. 12 The king said to Queen Esther, "In the citadel of Susa the Jews have killed five hundred people and also the ten sons of Haman. What have they done in the rest of the king's provinces? Now what is your petition? It shall be granted you. And what further is your request? It shall be fulfilled." 13 Esther said, "If it pleases the king, let the Jews who are in Susa be allowed tomorrow also to do according to this day's edict, and let the ten sons of Haman be hanged on the gallows." 14 So the king commanded this to be done; a decree was issued in Susa, and the ten sons of Haman were hanged. 15 The Jews who were in Susa gathered also on the fourteenth day of the month of Adar and they killed three hundred persons in Susa; but they did not touch the plunder.

16 Now the other Jews who were in the king's provinces also gathered to defend their lives, and gained relief from their enemies, and killed seventy-five thousand of those who hated them; but they laid no hands on the plunder. 17 This was on the thirteenth day of the month of Adar, and on the fourteenth day they rested and made that a day of feasting and gladness.

The Feast of Purim Inaugurated

18 But the Jews who were in Susa gathered on the thirteenth day and on the fourteenth, and rested on the fifteenth day, making that a day of feasting and gladness. 19 Therefore the Jews of the villages, who live in the open towns, hold the fourteenth day of the month of Adar as a day for gladness and feasting, a holiday on which they send gifts of food to one another.

20 Mordecai recorded these things, and sent letters to all the Jews who were in all the provinces of King Ahasuerus, both near and far, 21 enjoining them that they should keep the fourteenth day of the month Adar and also the fifteenth day of the same month, year by year, 22 as the days on which the Jews gained relief from their ene-

8.17 Esther 9.2, 19,27
9.1 Esther 8.12; v. 17; Esther 3.13
9.2 vv. 15-18; Esther 8.11; Ps 71.13,24; Esther 8.17
9.3 Ezra 8.36
9.5 2 Sam 3.1; Prov 4.18
9.10 Esther 5.11; 8.11
9.12 Esther 7.2
9.13 Esther 8.11
9.15 v. 10
9.16 vv. 2,10,15
9.17 vv. 1,21
9.18 vv. 2,21
9.19 Deut 16.11, 14; v. 22; Neh 8.10
9.22 v. 19

mies, and as the month that had
been turned for them from sorrow
into gladness and from mourning
into a holiday; that they should
make them days of feasting and
gladness, days for sending gifts of
food to one another and presents to
the poor. 23 So the Jews adopted as
a custom what they had begun to
do, as Mordecai had written to
them.
24 Haman son of Hammedatha
the Agagite, the enemy of all the
Jews, had plotted against the Jews
to destroy them, and had cast
Pur—that is "the lot"—to crush
and destroy them; 25 but when Esther came before the king, he gave
orders in writing that the wicked
plot that he had devised against
the Jews should come upon his
own head, and that he and his sons
should be hanged on the gallows.
26 Therefore these days are called
Purim, from the word Pur. Thus because of all that was written in this
letter, and of what they had faced
in this matter, and of what had
happened to them, 27 the Jews established and accepted as a custom for themselves and their descendants and all who joined them,
that without fail they would continue to observe these two days every year, as it was written and at the
time appointed. 28 These days
should be remembered and kept
throughout every generation, in every family, province, and city; and
these days of Purim should never
fall into disuse among the Jews,
nor should the commemoration of
these days cease among their descendants.
29 Queen Esther daughter of
Abihail, along with the Jew Mordecai, gave full written authority,
confirming this second letter about
Purim. 30 Letters were sent wishing
peace and security to all the Jews,
to the one hundred twenty-seven
provinces of the kingdom of Ahasuerus, 31 and giving orders that these
days of Purim should be observed
at their appointed seasons, as the
Jew Mordecai and Queen Esther
enjoined on the Jews, just as they
had laid down for themselves and
for their descendants regulations
concerning their fasts and their
lamentations. 32 The command of
Queen Esther fixed these practices
of Purim, and it was recorded in
writing.

10 King Ahasuerus laid tribute on the land and on the
islands of the sea. 2 All the acts of
his power and might, and the full
account of the high honor of Mordecai, to which the king advanced
him, are they not written in the annals of the kings of Media and Persia? 3 For Mordecai the Jew was
next in rank to King Ahasuerus,
and he was powerful among the
Jews and popular with his many
kindred, for he sought the good of
his people and interceded for the
welfare of all his descendants.

9.24 Esther 3.6,7
9.25 Esther 7.4-10; 3.6-15; Ps 7.16
9.26 v. 20
9.27 Esther 8.17; v. 20,21
9.29 Esther 2.15; vv. 20,21
9.30 Esther 1.1
9.31 Esther 4.3
9.32 v. 26
10.1 Isa 24.15
10.2 Esther 8.15; 9.4; 2.23
10.3 Gen 41.40; Neh 2.10

Job

Title and Background

The book of Job is named for its main character, an upright man who was very rich. Even after losing everything he owned and suffering from a terrible sickness, Job still confessed his trust in God.

Author and Date of Writing

Although most of the book consists of the words of Job and his friends, Job himself was not the author. Undoubtedly the author was an Israelite who probably had access to oral and/or written sources from which he composed the book.

Two dates are involved: (1) the date of the man Job and his historical setting, and (2) the date of the inspired writer of the book. The latter could be dated anytime from the reign of Solomon to the exile. The date of the actual events described in this book was most likely between 2000 and 1000 B.C., and probably late in that millennium.

Theme and Message

This book provides a profound statement on the justice of God in light of human suffering. How can the justice of an almighty God be defended in the face of evil, especially human suffering, and even more particularly, the suffering of the innocent? The final answer of this book is that God is in control and that the suffering of the righteous must be seen in the light of the cosmic struggle between God and Satan.

Outline

I. Prologue (1.1–2.13)
II. Dialogue-Dispute: Job and His Friends (3.1–27.23)
III. Interlude on Wisdom (28.1-28)
IV. Monologues: Job, Elihu, and God (29.1–42.6)
V. Epilogue (42.7-17)

Job and His Family

1 There was once a man in the
land of Uz whose name was
Job. That man was blameless and
upright, one who feared God and
turned away from evil. 2 There were
born to him seven sons and three
daughters. 3 He had seven thousand sheep, three thousand camels, five hundred yoke of oxen, five
hundred donkeys, and very many
servants; so that this man was the
greatest of all the people of the
east. 4 His sons used to go and hold
feasts in one another's houses in
turn; and they would send and invite their three sisters to eat and
drink with them. 5 And when the
feast days had run their course, Job
would send and sanctify them, and
he would rise early in the morning
and offer burnt offerings according
to the number of them all; for Job
said, "It may be that my children
have sinned, and cursed God in
their hearts." This is what Job always did.

Attack on Job's Character

6 One day the heavenly beings[a]
came to present themselves before
the LORD, and Satan[b] also came
among them. 7 The LORD said to Satan,[b] "Where have you come
from?" Satan[b] answered the LORD,

1.1 Jer 25.20; Ezek 14.14; Jas 5.11; Gen 6.9; 17.1; Ex 18.21
1.2 Job 42.13
1.3 Job 42.12
1.5 Ex 19.10; Gen 8.20; 1 Kings 21.10, 13
1.6 Job 38.7; 1 Chr 21.1
1.7 1 Pet 5.8

[a] Heb *sons of God* [b] Or *the Accuser*; Heb *ha-satan*

"From going to and fro on the
earth, and from walking up and
down on it." 8 The LORD said to Satan,[c] "Have you considered my
servant Job? There is no one like
him on the earth, a blameless and
upright man who fears God and
turns away from evil." 9 Then Satan[c] answered the LORD, "Does Job
fear God for nothing? 10 Have you
not put a fence around him and his
house and all that he has, on every
side? You have blessed the work of
his hands, and his possessions
have increased in the land. 11 But
stretch out your hand now, and
touch all that he has, and he will
curse you to your face." 12 The LORD
said to Satan,[c] "Very well, all that
he has is in your power; only do not
stretch out your hand against him!"
So Satan[c] went out from the presence of the LORD.

Job Loses Property and Children

13 One day when his sons and
daughters were eating and drinking
wine in the eldest brother's house,
14 a messenger came to Job and
said, "The oxen were plowing and
the donkeys were feeding beside
them, 15 and the Sabeans fell on
them and carried them off, and
killed the servants with the edge of
the sword; I alone have escaped to
tell you." 16 While he was still
speaking, another came and said,
"The fire of God fell from heaven
and burned up the sheep and the
servants, and consumed them; I
alone have escaped to tell you."
17 While he was still speaking, another came and said, "The Chaldeans formed three columns, made a
raid on the camels and carried
them off, and killed the servants
with the edge of the sword; I alone
have escaped to tell you." 18 While
he was still speaking, another
came and said, "Your sons and
daughters were eating and drinking
wine in their eldest brother's
house, 19 and suddenly a great wind
came across the desert, struck the
four corners of the house, and it fell
on the young people, and they are

1.8 Job 42.7,8; v. 1 **1.9** 1 Tim 6.5 **1.10** Job 29.2-6; Ps 128.1,2; Job 31.25 **1.11** Job 2.5; 19.21 **1.15** Job 6.19 **1.16** Gen 19.24; Lev 10.2; Num 11.1-3; 2 Kings 1.10 **1.17** Gen 11.28, 31 **1.18** vv. 4,13 **1.19** Jer 4.11; 13.24

1.20 Gen 37.29; 1 Pet 5.6 **1.21** Eccl 5.15; 1 Tim 6.7; Job 2.10; Eph 5.20; 1 Thes 5.18 **1.22** Job 2.10 **2.1** Job 1.6 **2.2** Job 1.7 **2.3** Job 1.1,8; 27.5,6; 9.17 **2.5** Job 1.11 **2.6** Job 1.12 **2.7** Job 7.5 **2.8** Job 42.6; Ezek 27.30; Mt 11.21 **2.10** Job 1.21,22; Ps 39.1

dead; I alone have escaped to tell
you."
20 Then Job arose, tore his
robe, shaved his head, and fell on
the ground and worshiped. 21 He
said, "Naked I came from my
mother's womb, and naked shall I
return there; the LORD gave, and the
LORD has taken away; blessed be
the name of the LORD."
22 In all this Job did not sin or
charge God with wrongdoing.

Attack on Job's Health

2 One day the heavenly beings[d]
came to present themselves
before the LORD, and Satan[c] also
came among them to present himself before the LORD. 2 The LORD said
to Satan,[c] "Where have you come
from?" Satan[e] answered the LORD,
"From going to and fro on the
earth, and from walking up and
down on it." 3 The LORD said to Satan,[c] "Have you considered my
servant Job? There is no one like
him on the earth, a blameless and
upright man who fears God and
turns away from evil. He still persists in his integrity, although you
incited me against him, to destroy
him for no reason." 4 Then Satan[c]
answered the LORD, "Skin for skin!
All that people have they will give
to save their lives.[f] 5 But stretch
out your hand now and touch his
bone and his flesh, and he will
curse you to your face." 6 The LORD
said to Satan,[c] "Very well, he is in
your power; only spare his life."
7 So Satan[c] went out from the
presence of the LORD, and inflicted
loathsome sores on Job from the
sole of his foot to the crown of his
head. 8 Job[g] took a potsherd with
which to scrape himself, and sat
among the ashes.
9 Then his wife said to him, "Do
you still persist in your integrity?
Curse[h] God, and die." 10 But he
said to her, "You speak as any foolish woman would speak. Shall we
receive the good at the hand of

[c] Or *the Accuser*; Heb *ha-satan*
[d] Heb *sons of God* [e] Or *The Accuser*; Heb *ha-satan* [f] Or *All that the man has he will give for his life* [g] Heb *He* [h] Heb *Bless*

God, and not receive the bad?" In
all this Job did not sin with his lips.

Job's Three Friends

11 Now when Job's three
friends heard of all these troubles
that had come upon him, each of
them set out from his home—
Eliphaz the Temanite, Bildad the
Shuhite, and Zophar the Naamathite. They met together to go and
console and comfort him. 12 When
they saw him from a distance, they
did not recognize him, and they
raised their voices and wept aloud;
they tore their robes and threw
dust in the air upon their heads.
13 They sat with him on the ground
seven days and seven nights, and
no one spoke a word to him, for
they saw that his suffering was very
great.

Job Curses the Day He Was Born

3 After this Job opened his
mouth and cursed the day of
his birth. 2 Job said:

3 "Let the day perish in which
I was born,
and the night that said,
'A man-child is conceived.'
4 Let that day be darkness!
May God above not seek it,
or light shine on it.
5 Let gloom and deep darkness
claim it.
Let clouds settle upon it;
let the blackness of the day
terrify it.
6 That night—let thick
darkness seize it!
let it not rejoice among the
days of the year;
let it not come into the
number of the months.
7 Yes, let that night be barren;
let no joyful cry be heard[i]
in it.
8 Let those curse it who curse
the Sea,[j]
those who are skilled to
rouse up Leviathan.
9 Let the stars of its dawn be
dark;
let it hope for light, but
have none;
may it not see the eyelids
of the morning—
10 because it did not shut the
doors of my mother's
womb,
and hide trouble from my
eyes.

11 "Why did I not die at birth,
come forth from the womb
and expire?
12 Why were there knees to
receive me,
or breasts for me to suck?
13 Now I would be lying down
and quiet;
I would be asleep; then I
would be at rest
14 with kings and counselors of
the earth
who rebuild ruins for
themselves,
15 or with princes who have
gold,
who fill their houses with
silver.
16 Or why was I not buried like
a stillborn child,
like an infant that never
sees the light?
17 There the wicked cease from
troubling,
and there the weary are at
rest.
18 There the prisoners are at
ease together;
they do not hear the voice
of the taskmaster.
19 The small and the great are
there,
and the slaves are free
from their masters.

20 "Why is light given to one in
misery,
and life to the bitter in
soul,
21 who long for death, but it
does not come,
and dig for it more than for
hidden treasures;
22 who rejoice exceedingly,
and are glad when they
find the grave?

2.11 1 Chr 1.45; Gen 25.2; Job 42.11 **2.12** Josh 7.6; Lam 2.10; Ezek 27.30 **2.13** Gen 50.10; Ezek 3.15 **3.3** Job 10.18; Jer 20.14 **3.5** Job 10.21; Ps 23.4; Jer 2.6 **3.6** Job 23.17 **3.8** Job 41.10 **3.9** Job 41.18

3.11 Job 10.18 **3.12** Gen 30.3; Isa 66.12 **3.14** Job 12.17, 18; 15.28 **3.16** Eccl 6.3 **3.17** Job 17.16 **3.20** 1 Sam 1.10; Prov 31.6; Isa 38.15; Ezek 27.31 **3.21** Rev 9.6

[i] Heb *come* [j] Cn: Heb *day*

23 Why is light given to one
who cannot see the
way,
whom God has fenced in?
24 For my sighing comes like[k]
my bread,
and my groanings are
poured out like water.
25 Truly the thing that I fear
comes upon me,
and what I dread befalls
me.
26 I am not at ease, nor am I
quiet;
I have no rest; but trouble
comes."

Eliphaz Speaks: Job Has Sinned

4 Then Eliphaz the Temanite answered:
2 "If one ventures a word with
you, will you be
offended?
But who can keep from
speaking?
3 See, you have instructed
many;
you have strengthened the
weak hands.
4 Your words have supported
those who were
stumbling,
and you have made firm
the feeble knees.
5 But now it has come to you,
and you are impatient;
it touches you, and you are
dismayed.
6 Is not your fear of God your
confidence,
and the integrity of your
ways your hope?

7 "Think now, who that was
innocent ever perished?
Or where were the upright
cut off?
8 As I have seen, those who
plow iniquity
and sow trouble reap the
same.
9 By the breath of God they
perish,
and by the blast of his
anger they are
consumed.
10 The roar of the lion, the
voice of the fierce lion,
and the teeth of the young
lions are broken.
11 The strong lion perishes for
lack of prey,
and the whelps of the
lioness are scattered.

12 "Now a word came stealing
to me,
my ear received the
whisper of it.
13 Amid thoughts from visions
of the night,
when deep sleep falls on
mortals,
14 dread came upon me, and
trembling,
which made all my bones
shake.
15 A spirit glided past my face;
the hair of my flesh
bristled.
16 It stood still,
but I could not discern its
appearance.
A form was before my eyes;
there was silence, then I
heard a voice:
17 'Can mortals be righteous
before[l] God?
Can human beings be pure
before[l] their Maker?
18 Even in his servants he puts
no trust,
and his angels he charges
with error;
19 how much more those who
live in houses of clay,
whose foundation is in the
dust,
who are crushed like a
moth.
20 Between morning and
evening they are
destroyed;
they perish forever without
any regarding it.
21 Their tent-cord is plucked up
within them,
and they die devoid of
wisdom.'

3.23 Job 19.6,8, 12; Lam 3.7
3.24 Ps 42.3,4
4.2 Job 32.18-20
4.3 Isa 35.3; Heb 12.12
4.4 Isa 35.3; Heb 12.12
4.5 Job 6.14; 19.21
4.6 Job 1.1
4.7 Ps 37.25
4.8 Prov 22.8; Hos 10.13; Gal 6.7,8
4.9 Job 15.30; Isa 30.33; Ps 59.13
4.10 Ps 58.6
4.11 Ps 34.10
4.12 Job 26.14
4.14 Jer 23.9
4.17 Job 9.2; 35.10
4.18 Job 15.15
4.19 Job 10.9; 22.16
4.20 Ps 90.5,6; Job 20.7
4.21 Job 36.12

[k] Heb *before* [l] Or *more than*

Job Is Corrected by God

5 "Call now; is there anyone
who will answer you?
To which of the holy ones
will you turn?
2 Surely vexation kills the fool,
and jealousy slays the
simple.
3 I have seen fools taking root,
but suddenly I cursed their
dwelling.
4 Their children are far from
safety,
they are crushed in the
gate,
and there is no one to
deliver them.
5 The hungry eat their harvest,
and they take it even out
of the thorns;[m]
and the thirsty[n] pant after
their wealth.
6 For misery does not come
from the earth,
nor does trouble sprout
from the ground;
7 but human beings are born
to trouble
just as sparks[o] fly upward.

8 "As for me, I would seek
God,
and to God I would commit
my cause.
9 He does great things and
unsearchable,
marvelous things without
number.
10 He gives rain on the earth
and sends waters on the
fields;
11 he sets on high those who
are lowly,
and those who mourn are
lifted to safety.
12 He frustrates the devices of
the crafty,
so that their hands achieve
no success.
13 He takes the wise in their
own craftiness;
and the schemes of the
wily are brought to a
quick end.
14 They meet with darkness in
the daytime,
and grope at noonday as in
the night.
15 But he saves the needy from
the sword of their
mouth,
from the hand of the
mighty.
16 So the poor have hope,
and injustice shuts its
mouth.

17 "How happy is the one
whom God reproves;
therefore do not despise
the discipline of the
Almighty.[p]
18 For he wounds, but he binds
up;
he strikes, but his hands
heal.
19 He will deliver you from six
troubles;
in seven no harm shall
touch you.
20 In famine he will redeem you
from death,
and in war from the power
of the sword.
21 You shall be hidden from the
scourge of the tongue,
and shall not fear
destruction when it
comes.
22 At destruction and famine
you shall laugh,
and shall not fear the wild
animals of the earth.
23 For you shall be in league
with the stones of the
field,
and the wild animals shall
be at peace with you.
24 You shall know that your
tent is safe,
you shall inspect your fold
and miss nothing.
25 You shall know that your
descendants will be
many,
and your offspring like the
grass of the earth.
26 You shall come to your grave
in ripe old age,

5.1 Job 15.15 **5.2** Prov 12.16 **5.3** Ps 37.35 **5.4** Am 5.12 **5.5** Job 18.8-10 **5.7** Job 14.1 **5.8** Ps 35.23 **5.9** Ps 40.5; 72.18 **5.10** Ps 65.9 **5.11** 1 Sam 2.7; Ps 113.7 **5.12** Neh 4.15; Ps 33.10; Isa 8.10 **5.14** Job 12.25; Deut 28.29 **5.15** Ps 35.10 **5.16** Ps 107.42 **5.17** Ps 94.12; Jas 1.12; Heb 12.5-11 **5.18** Isa 30.26 **5.19** Ps 34.19; 91.10 **5.20** Ps 33.19; 144.10 **5.21** Ps 31.20; 91.5,6 **5.22** Ps 91.13; Ezek 34.25 **5.23** Ps 91.12; Isa 11.6-9 **5.24** Job 8.6; 21.9 **5.25** Ps 72.16; 112.2 **5.26** Gen 15.15; Prov 9.11

[m] Meaning of Heb uncertain [n] Aquila Symmachus Syr Vg: Heb *snare* [o] Or *birds*; Heb *sons of Resheph* [p] Traditional rendering of Heb *Shaddai*

as a shock of grain comes
up to the threshing
floor in its season.
27 See, we have searched this
out; it is true.
Hear, and know it for
yourself."

Job Replies: My Complaint Is Just

6 Then Job answered:
2 "O that my vexation were
weighed,
and all my calamity laid in
the balances!
3 For then it would be heavier
than the sand of the
sea;
therefore my words have
been rash.
4 For the arrows of the
Almighty[q] are in me;
my spirit drinks their
poison;
the terrors of God are
arrayed against me.
5 Does the wild ass bray over
its grass,
or the ox low over its
fodder?
6 Can that which is tasteless
be eaten without salt,
or is there any flavor in the
juice of mallows?[r]
7 My appetite refuses to touch
them;
they are like food that is
loathsome to me.[r]

8 "O that I might have my
request,
and that God would grant
my desire;
9 that it would please God to
crush me,
that he would let loose his
hand and cut me off!
10 This would be my
consolation;
I would even exult[r] in
unrelenting pain;
for I have not denied the
words of the Holy One.
11 What is my strength, that I
should wait?
And what is my end, that I
should be patient?
12 Is my strength the strength
of stones,
or is my flesh bronze?
13 In truth I have no help in
me,
and any resource is driven
from me.

14 "Those who withhold[s]
kindness from a friend
forsake the fear of the
Almighty.[q]
15 My companions are
treacherous like a
torrent-bed,
like freshets that pass
away,
16 that run dark with ice,
turbid with melting snow.
17 In time of heat they
disappear;
when it is hot, they vanish
from their place.
18 The caravans turn aside from
their course;
they go up into the waste,
and perish.
19 The caravans of Tema look,
the travelers of Sheba
hope.
20 They are disappointed
because they were
confident;
they come there and are
confounded.
21 Such you have now become
to me;[t]
you see my calamity, and
are afraid.
22 Have I said, 'Make me a
gift'?
Or, 'From your wealth offer
a bribe for me'?
23 Or, 'Save me from an
opponent's hand'?
Or, 'Ransom me from the
hand of oppressors'?

24 "Teach me, and I will be
silent;

6.2 Job 31.6
6.3 Prov 27.3
6.4 Ps 38.2; Job 21.20; Ps 88.15
6.8 Job 14.13
6.9 1 Kings 19.4
6.10 Job 23.11, 12; Lev 19.2; Isa 57.15; Hos 11.9
6.11 Job 21.4
6.13 Job 26.2,3
6.15 Ps 38.11; Jer 15.18
6.17 Job 24.19
6.19 Gen 25.15; Isa 21.14; 1 Kings 10.1
6.20 Jer 14.3

[q] Traditional rendering of Heb *Shaddai*
[r] Meaning of Heb uncertain
[s] Syr Vg Compare Tg: Meaning of Heb uncertain
[t] Cn Compare Gk Syr: Meaning of Heb uncertain

make me understand how I have gone wrong.
25 How forceful are honest words!
But your reproof, what does it reprove?
26 Do you think that you can reprove words,
as if the speech of the desperate were wind?
27 You would even cast lots over the orphan,
and bargain over your friend.

28 "But now, be pleased to look at me;
for I will not lie to your face.
29 Turn, I pray, let no wrong be done.
Turn now, my vindication is at stake.
30 Is there any wrong on my tongue?
Cannot my taste discern calamity?

Job: My Suffering Is without End

7 "Do not human beings have a hard service on earth,
and are not their days like the days of a laborer?
2 Like a slave who longs for the shadow,
and like laborers who look for their wages,
3 so I am allotted months of emptiness,
and nights of misery are apportioned to me.
4 When I lie down I say, 'When shall I rise?'
But the night is long,
and I am full of tossing until dawn.
5 My flesh is clothed with worms and dirt;
my skin hardens, then breaks out again.
6 My days are swifter than a weaver's shuttle,
and come to their end without hope.[u]
7 "Remember that my life is a breath;
my eye will never again see good.
8 The eye that beholds me will see me no more;
while your eyes are upon me, I shall be gone.
9 As the cloud fades and vanishes,
so those who go down to Sheol do not come up;
10 they return no more to their houses,
nor do their places know them any more.

11 "Therefore I will not restrain my mouth;
I will speak in the anguish of my spirit;
I will complain in the bitterness of my soul.
12 Am I the Sea, or the Dragon, that you set a guard over me?
13 When I say, 'My bed will comfort me,
my couch will ease my complaint,'
14 then you scare me with dreams
and terrify me with visions,
15 so that I would choose strangling
and death rather than this body.
16 I loathe my life; I would not live forever.
Let me alone, for my days are a breath.
17 What are human beings, that you make so much of them,
that you set your mind on them,
18 visit them every morning,
test them every moment?
19 Will you not look away from me for a while,
let me alone until I swallow my spittle?
20 If I sin, what do I do to you, you watcher of humanity?

6.25 Eccl 12.10, 11 **6.26** Job 8.2 **6.27** Joel 3.3; 2 Pet 3.3 **6.28** Job 27.4 **6.30** Job 27.4; 12.11 **7.1** Job 10.17; 14.14; Isa 40.2; Job 14.6 **7.2** Lev 19.13 **7.3** Lam 1.7; Ps 6.6 **7.4** Deut 28.67 **7.6** Job 9.25; 13.15; 17.15, 16 **7.7** Ps 78.39; Job 9.25 **7.8** Job 20.9; v. 21 **7.9** Job 30.15; 11.8; 2 Sam 12.23 **7.10** Job 10.21; Ps 103.16 **7.11** Ps 40.9; 1 Sam 1.10 **7.12** Ezek 32.2,3 **7.13** Job 9.27 **7.14** Job 9.34 **7.15** 1 Kings 19.4 **7.16** Job 10.1; Eccl 7.15 **7.17** Ps 8.4; 144.3; Heb 2.6 **7.20** Job 35.3,6; v. 12; Job 16.12

[u] Or *as the thread runs out*

Why have you made me your target?
Why have I become a burden to you?
21 Why do you not pardon my transgression
and take away my iniquity?
For now I shall lie in the earth;
you will seek me, but I shall not be."

Bildad Speaks: Job Should Repent

8 Then Bildad the Shuhite answered:
2 "How long will you say these things,
and the words of your mouth be a great wind?
3 Does God pervert justice?
Or does the Almighty[v] pervert the right?
4 If your children sinned against him,
he delivered them into the power of their transgression.
5 If you will seek God
and make supplication to the Almighty,[v]
6 if you are pure and upright,
surely then he will rouse himself for you
and restore to you your rightful place.
7 Though your beginning was small,
your latter days will be very great.

8 "For inquire now of bygone generations,
and consider what their ancestors have found;
9 for we are but of yesterday, and we know nothing,
for our days on earth are but a shadow.
10 Will they not teach you and tell you
and utter words out of their understanding?

11 "Can papyrus grow where there is no marsh?

7.21 Job 10.14; Ps 104.29; v. 8
8.3 Gen 18.25; Deut 32.4; 2 Chr 19.7; Dan 9.14; Rom 3.5
8.4 Job 1.5,18, 19
8.5 Job 5.8; 11.13; 9.15
8.6 Ps 7.6
8.7 Job 42.12
8.8 Deut 4.32; 32.7; Job 15.18
8.9 Gen 47.9; 1 Chr 29.15; Job 7.5
8.12 Ps 129.6; Jer 17.6
8.13 Ps 9.17; Job 11.20; Prov 10.28
8.14 Isa 59.5,6
8.15 Job 27.18
8.16 Ps 37.35; 80.11
8.18 Job 7.10; Ps 37.36
8.19 Job 20.5; Eccl 1.4
8.20 Job 4.7; 21.30
8.21 Ps 126.2; 132.16
8.22 Ps 35.26; 109.29; v. 15
9.2 Ps 143.2; Rom 3.20

Can reeds flourish where there is no water?
12 While yet in flower and not cut down,
they wither before any other plant.
13 Such are the paths of all who forget God;
the hope of the godless shall perish.
14 Their confidence is gossamer,
a spider's house their trust.
15 If one leans against its house, it will not stand;
if one lays hold of it, it will not endure.
16 The wicked thrive[w] before the sun,
and their shoots spread over the garden.
17 Their roots twine around the stoneheap;
they live among the rocks.[x]
18 If they are destroyed from their place,
then it will deny them, saying, 'I have never seen you.'
19 See, these are their happy ways,[y]
and out of the earth still others will spring.

20 "See, God will not reject a blameless person,
nor take the hand of evildoers.
21 He will yet fill your mouth with laughter,
and your lips with shouts of joy.
22 Those who hate you will be clothed with shame,
and the tent of the wicked will be no more."

Job Replies: There Is No Mediator

9 Then Job answered:
2 "Indeed I know that this is so;

[v] Traditional rendering of Heb *Shaddai*
[w] Heb *He thrives* [x] Gk Vg: Meaning of Heb uncertain [y] Meaning of Heb uncertain

but how can a mortal be
just before God?
3 If one wished to contend
with him,
one could not answer him
once in a thousand.
4 He is wise in heart, and
mighty in strength
—who has resisted him, and
succeeded?—
5 he who removes mountains,
and they do not know
it,
when he overturns them in
his anger;
6 who shakes the earth out of
its place,
and its pillars tremble;
7 who commands the sun, and
it does not rise;
who seals up the stars;
8 who alone stretched out the
heavens
and trampled the waves of
the Sea;[z]
9 who made the Bear and
Orion,
the Pleiades and the
chambers of the south;
10 who does great things
beyond understanding,
and marvelous things
without number.
11 Look, he passes by me, and I
do not see him;
he moves on, but I do not
perceive him.
12 He snatches away; who can
stop him?
Who will say to him, 'What
are you doing?'

13 "God will not turn back his
anger;
the helpers of Rahab
bowed beneath him.
14 How then can I answer him,
choosing my words with
him?
15 Though I am innocent, I
cannot answer him;
I must appeal for mercy to
my accuser.[a]
16 If I summoned him and he
answered me,
I do not believe that he
would listen to my
voice.
17 For he crushes me with a
tempest,
and multiplies my wounds
without cause;
18 he will not let me get my
breath,
but fills me with bitterness.
19 If it is a contest of strength,
he is the strong one!
If it is a matter of justice,
who can summon him?[b]
20 Though I am innocent, my
own mouth would
condemn me;
though I am blameless, he
would prove me
perverse.
21 I am blameless; I do not
know myself;
I loathe my life.
22 It is all one; therefore I say,
he destroys both the
blameless and the
wicked.
23 When disaster brings sudden
death,
he mocks at the calamity[c]
of the innocent.
24 The earth is given into the
hand of the wicked;
he covers the eyes of its
judges—
if it is not he, who then is
it?

25 "My days are swifter than a
runner;
they flee away, they see no
good.
26 They go by like skiffs of
reed,
like an eagle swooping on
the prey.
27 If I say, 'I will forget my
complaint;
I will put off my sad
countenance and be of
good cheer,'
28 I become afraid of all my
suffering,

9.4 Job 36.5; 2 Chr 13.12 **9.5** Mic 1.4 **9.6** Isa 2.19,21; Hag 2.6; Heb 12.26; Job 26.11 **9.8** Gen 1.6; Ps 104.2,3 **9.9** Gen 1.16; Job 38.31; Am 5.8 **9.10** Ps 71.15 **9.11** Job 23.8,9; 35.14 **9.12** Isa 45.9; Rom 9.20; Job 11.10 **9.13** Job 26.12; Isa 30.7 **9.14** vv. 3,32 **9.15** Job 10.15; 8.5 **9.17** Job 16.12, 14; 2.3 **9.18** Job 27.2 **9.20** vv. 15,29 **9.21** Job 1.1; 7.16 **9.22** Eccl 9.2,3; Ezek 21.3 **9.23** Ps 64.4; Heb 11.36; 1 Pet 1.7 **9.24** Job 10.3; 12.6; 12.17 **9.25** Job 7.6,7 **9.26** Hab 1.8 **9.27** Job 7.13 **9.28** Ps 119.120; Job 7.21

[z] Or *trampled the back of the sea dragon*
[a] Or *for my right*
[b] Compare Gk: Heb *me*
[c] Meaning of Heb uncertain

for I know you will not
hold me innocent.
29 I shall be condemned;
why then do I labor in
vain?
30 If I wash myself with soap
and cleanse my hands with
lye,
31 yet you will plunge me into
filth,
and my own clothes will
abhor me.
32 For he is not a mortal, as I
am, that I might answer
him,
that we should come to
trial together.
33 There is no umpire[d]
between us,
who might lay his hand on
us both.
34 If he would take his rod
away from me,
and not let dread of him
terrify me,
35 then I would speak without
fear of him,
for I know I am not what I
am thought to be.[e]

Job: I Loathe My Life

10 "I loathe my life;
I will give free utterance
to my complaint;
I will speak in the
bitterness of my soul.
2 I will say to God, Do not
condemn me;
let me know why you
contend against me.
3 Does it seem good to you to
oppress,
to despise the work of your
hands
and favor the schemes of
the wicked?
4 Do you have eyes of flesh?
Do you see as humans
see?
5 Are your days like the days
of mortals,
or your years like human
years,
6 that you seek out my
iniquity
and search for my sin,
7 although you know that I am
not guilty,
and there is no one to
deliver out of your
hand?
8 Your hands fashioned and
made me;
and now you turn and
destroy me.[f]
9 Remember that you
fashioned me like clay;
and will you turn me to
dust again?
10 Did you not pour me out like
milk
and curdle me like
cheese?
11 You clothed me with skin
and flesh,
and knit me together with
bones and sinews.
12 You have granted me life and
steadfast love,
and your care has
preserved my spirit.
13 Yet these things you hid in
your heart;
I know that this was your
purpose.
14 If I sin, you watch me,
and do not acquit me of
my iniquity.
15 If I am wicked, woe to me!
If I am righteous, I cannot
lift up my head,
for I am filled with disgrace
and look upon my
affliction.
16 Bold as a lion you hunt me;
you repeat your exploits
against me.
17 You renew your witnesses
against me,
and increase your vexation
toward me;
you bring fresh troops
against me.[g]

18 "Why did you bring me forth
from the womb?

9.29 v. 20 **9.30** Jer 2.22 **9.32** Eccl 6.10; Rom 9.20; v. 3; Ps 143.2 **9.33** 1 Sam 2.25 **9.34** Job 13.21; Ps 39.10 **9.35** Job 13.22 **10.1** 1 Kings 19.4; Job 7.16; 7.11 **10.2** Job 9.29; Hos 4.1 **10.3** v. 8; Job 21.16; 22.18 **10.4** 1 Sam 16.7 **10.5** Ps 90.4; 2 Pet 3.8

10.7 Job 9.21; 9.12 **10.8** Ps 119.73 **10.9** Gen 2.7; 3.19; Isa 64.8 **10.10** Ps 139.14-16 **10.12** Job 33.4 **10.14** Job 13.27; 9.28 **10.15** Isa 3.11; Job 9.12,15; Ps 25.8 **10.16** Isa 38.13; Lam 3.10; Job 5.9 **10.17** Job 16.8; 7.1 **10.18** Job 3.11

[d] Another reading is *Would that there were an umpire* [e] Cn: Heb *for I am not so in myself* [f] Cn Compare Gk Syr: Heb *made me together all around, and you destroy me* [g] Cn Compare Gk: Heb *toward me; changes and a troop are with me*

Would that I had died
before any eye had seen
me,
19 and were as though I had not
been,
carried from the womb to
the grave.
20 Are not the days of my life
few?[h]
Let me alone, that I may
find a little comfort[i]
21 before I go, never to return,
to the land of gloom and
deep darkness,
22 the land of gloom[j] and
chaos,
where light is like
darkness."

Zophar Speaks: Job's Guilt Deserves Punishment

11 Then Zophar the Naamathite answered:
2 "Should a multitude of
words go unanswered,
and should one full of talk
be vindicated?
3 Should your babble put
others to silence,
and when you mock, shall
no one shame you?
4 For you say, 'My conduct[k] is
pure,
and I am clean in God's[l]
sight.'
5 But oh, that God would
speak,
and open his lips to you,
6 and that he would tell you
the secrets of wisdom!
For wisdom is
many-sided.[m]
Know then that God exacts
of you less than your
guilt deserves.

7 "Can you find out the deep
things of God?
Can you find out the limit
of the Almighty?[n]
8 It is higher than
heaven[o]—what can you
do?
Deeper than Sheol—what
can you know?
9 Its measure is longer than
the earth,
and broader than the sea.
10 If he passes through, and
imprisons,
and assembles for
judgment, who can
hinder him?
11 For he knows those who are
worthless;
when he sees iniquity, will
he not consider it?
12 But a stupid person will get
understanding,
when a wild ass is born
human.[m]

13 "If you direct your heart
rightly,
you will stretch out your
hands toward him.
14 If iniquity is in your hand,
put it far away,
and do not let wickedness
reside in your tents.
15 Surely then you will lift up
your face without
blemish;
you will be secure, and will
not fear.
16 You will forget your misery;
you will remember it as
waters that have passed
away.
17 And your life will be brighter
than the noonday;
its darkness will be like the
morning.
18 And you will have
confidence, because
there is hope;
you will be protected[p] and
take your rest in safety.
19 You will lie down, and no
one will make you
afraid;
many will entreat your
favor.
20 But the eyes of the wicked
will fail;
all way of escape will be
lost to them,

10.20 Job 14.1; 7.16,19; 9.27 **10.21** Ps 88.12; 23.4 **11.2** Job 8.2 **11.3** Jas 3.5; Job 17.2; 21.3 **11.4** Job 6.10; 10.7 **11.6** Job 28.21; Ezra 9.13 **11.7** Eccl 3.11; Rom 11.33 **11.8** Job 22.12; 17.16 **11.10** Job 9.12; Rev 3.7 **11.11** Job 34.21-25; Ps 10.14 **11.13** Ps 78.8; 88.9 **11.14** Job 22.23; Ps 101.3 **11.15** 1 Jn 3.21; Ps 27.3 **11.16** Isa 65.16; Job 22.11 **11.17** Ps 37.6; 112.4; Isa 58.8,10 **11.18** Ps 3.5; Prov 3.24 **11.19** v. 18 **11.20** Deut 28.65; Jer 15.9

[h] Cn Compare Gk Syr: Heb *Are not my days few? Let him cease!* [i] Heb *that I may brighten up a little* [j] Heb *gloom as darkness, deep darkness* [k] Gk: Heb *teaching* [l] Heb *your* [m] Meaning of Heb uncertain [n] Traditional rendering of Heb *Shaddai* [o] Heb *The heights of heaven* [p] Or *you will look around*

and their hope is to
breathe their last."

Job Replies: I Am a Laughingstock

12 Then Job answered:
2 "No doubt you are the
people,
and wisdom will die with
you.
3 But I have understanding as
well as you;
I am not inferior to
you.
Who does not know such
things as these?
4 I am a laughingstock to my
friends;
I, who called upon God
and he answered me,
a just and blameless man, I
am a laughingstock.
5 Those at ease have contempt
for misfortune,[q]
but it is ready for those
whose feet are unstable.
6 The tents of robbers are at
peace,
and those who provoke
God are secure,
who bring their god in their
hands.[r]

7 "But ask the animals, and
they will teach you;
the birds of the air, and
they will tell you;
8 ask the plants of the earth,[s]
and they will teach you;
and the fish of the sea will
declare to you.
9 Who among all these does
not know
that the hand of the LORD
has done this?
10 In his hand is the life of
every living thing
and the breath of every
human being.
11 Does not the ear test words
as the palate tastes food?
12 Is wisdom with the aged,
and understanding in
length of days?

13 "With God[t] are wisdom and
strength;
he has counsel and
understanding.
14 If he tears down, no one can
rebuild;
if he shuts someone in, no
one can open up.
15 If he withholds the waters,
they dry up;
if he sends them out, they
overwhelm the land.
16 With him are strength and
wisdom;
the deceived and the
deceiver are his.
17 He leads counselors away
stripped,
and makes fools of judges.
18 He looses the sash of kings,
and binds a waistcloth on
their loins.
19 He leads priests away
stripped,
and overthrows the mighty.
20 He deprives of speech those
who are trusted,
and takes away the
discernment of the
elders.
21 He pours contempt on
princes,
and looses the belt of the
strong.
22 He uncovers the deeps out of
darkness,
and brings deep darkness
to light.
23 He makes nations great, then
destroys them;
he enlarges nations, then
leads them away.
24 He strips understanding from
the leaders[u] of the
earth,
and makes them wander in
a pathless waste.
25 They grope in the dark
without light;
he makes them stagger like
a drunkard.

13 "Look, my eye has seen
all this,

12.3 Job 13.2 **12.4** Job 6.10,20; 21.3; Ps 91.15; Job 6.29 **12.5** Ps 123.4 **12.6** Job 9.24; 21.9; 22.18 **12.9** Isa 41.20 **12.10** Acts 17.28; Job 27.3; 33.4 **12.11** Job 34.3 **12.12** Job 32.7 **12.13** Job 9.4; 11.6 **12.14** Job 19.10; 37.7 **12.15** 1 Kings 8.35; Gen 7.11 **12.16** v. 13; Job 13.7,9 **12.17** Job 3.14; 19.9; 9.24 **12.18** Ps 116.16 **12.20** Job 32.9 **12.21** Ps 107.40; v. 18 **12.22** Dan 2.22; 1 Cor 4.5; Job 3.5 **12.23** Ps 107.38; Isa 9.3; Jer 25.9; Deut 12.20; Ps 78.61 **12.24** v. 20; Ps 107.40 **12.25** Job 5.14; Ps 107.27 **13.1** Job 12.9

[q] Meaning of Heb uncertain [r] Or *whom God brought forth by his hand*; Meaning of Heb uncertain [s] Or *speak to the earth* [t] Heb *him* [u] Heb adds *of the people*

my ear has heard and
understood it.
2 What you know, I also know;
I am not inferior to you.
3 But I would speak to the
Almighty,[v]
and I desire to argue my
case with God.
4 As for you, you whitewash
with lies;
all of you are worthless
physicians.
5 If you would only keep
silent,
that would be your
wisdom!
6 Hear now my reasoning,
and listen to the pleadings
of my lips.
7 Will you speak falsely for
God,
and speak deceitfully for
him?
8 Will you show partiality
toward him,
will you plead the case for
God?
9 Will it be well with you when
he searches you out?
Or can you deceive him, as
one person deceives
another?
10 He will surely rebuke you
if in secret you show
partiality.
11 Will not his majesty terrify
you,
and the dread of him fall
upon you?
12 Your maxims are proverbs of
ashes,
your defenses are defenses
of clay.

13 "Let me have silence, and I
will speak,
and let come on me what
may.
14 I will take my flesh in my
teeth,
and put my life in my
hand.[w]
15 See, he will kill me; I have
no hope;[x]
but I will defend my ways
to his face.
16 This will be my salvation,
that the godless shall not
come before him.
17 Listen carefully to my words,
and let my declaration be
in your ears.
18 I have indeed prepared my
case;
I know that I shall be
vindicated.
19 Who is there that will
contend with me?
For then I would be silent
and die.

Job's Despondent Prayer

20 Only grant two things to me,
then I will not hide myself
from your face:
21 withdraw your hand far from
me,
and do not let dread of you
terrify me.
22 Then call, and I will answer;
or let me speak, and you
reply to me.
23 How many are my iniquities
and my sins?
Make me know my
transgression and my
sin.
24 Why do you hide your face,
and count me as your
enemy?
25 Will you frighten a
windblown leaf
and pursue dry chaff?
26 For you write bitter things
against me,
and make me reap[y] the
iniquities of my youth.
27 You put my feet in the
stocks,
and watch all my paths;
you set a bound to the
soles of my feet.
28 One wastes away like a
rotten thing,
like a garment that is
moth-eaten.

14 "A mortal, born of
woman, few of days and
full of trouble,

13.2 Job 12.3
13.3 Job 23.3,4; v. 15
13.4 Ps 119.69; Jer 23.32
13.5 Prov 17.28
13.7 Job 36.4
13.9 Ps 44.21; Gal 6.7
13.10 v. 8
13.11 Job 31.23
13.12 Job 15.3
13.13 v. 5
13.14 1 Sam 19.5
13.15 Ps 23.4; Prov 14.32; Job 27.5
13.16 Ps 5.5
13.17 Job 21.2
13.18 Job 23.4; 9.2
13.19 Isa 50.8; Job 40.4
13.20 Job 9.34
13.21 Ps 39.10
13.22 Job 14.15
13.23 1 Sam 26.18
13.24 Deut 32.20; Ps 13.1; Job 19.11
13.25 Isa 42.3
13.26 Ps 25.7
13.27 Job 33.11
13.28 Isa 50.9; Jas 5.2
14.1 Job 5.7; Eccl 2.23

[v] Traditional rendering of Heb *Shaddai* [w] Gk: Heb *Why should I take . . . in my hand?* [x] Or *Though he kill me, yet I will trust in him* [y] Heb *inherit*

2 comes up like a flower and
withers,
flees like a shadow and
does not last.
3 Do you fix your eyes on such
a one?
Do you bring me into
judgment with you?
4 Who can bring a clean thing
out of an unclean?
No one can.
5 Since their days are
determined,
and the number of their
months is known to
you,
and you have appointed
the bounds that they
cannot pass,
6 look away from them, and
desist,[z]
that they may enjoy, like
laborers, their days.

7 "For there is hope for a tree,
if it is cut down, that it
will sprout again,
and that its shoots will not
cease.
8 Though its root grows old in
the earth,
and its stump dies in the
ground,
9 yet at the scent of water it
will bud
and put forth branches like
a young plant.
10 But mortals die, and are laid
low;
humans expire, and where
are they?
11 As waters fail from a lake,
and a river wastes away
and dries up,
12 so mortals lie down and do
not rise again;
until the heavens are no
more, they will not
awake
or be roused out of their
sleep.
13 Oh that you would hide me
in Sheol,
that you would conceal me
until your wrath is past,
that you would appoint me
a set time, and
remember me!
14 If mortals die, will they live
again?
All the days of my service I
would wait
until my release should
come.
15 You would call, and I would
answer you;
you would long for the
work of your hands.
16 For then you would not[a]
number my steps,
you would not keep watch
over my sin;
17 my transgression would be
sealed up in a bag,
and you would cover over
my iniquity.

18 "But the mountain falls and
crumbles away,
and the rock is removed
from its place;
19 the waters wear away the
stones;
the torrents wash away the
soil of the earth;
so you destroy the hope of
mortals.
20 You prevail forever against
them, and they pass
away;
you change their
countenance, and send
them away.
21 Their children come to
honor, and they do not
know it;
they are brought low, and
it goes unnoticed.
22 They feel only the pain of
their own bodies,
and mourn only for
themselves."

Eliphaz Speaks: Job Undermines Religion

15 Then Eliphaz the Temanite answered:
2 "Should the wise answer
with windy knowledge,

14.2 Ps 90.5,6; Jas 1.10; 1 Pet 1.24
14.3 Ps 144.3; 143.2
14.4 Ps 51.2,10; Jn 3.6; Rom 5.12; Eph 2.3
14.5 Ps 139.16; Job 21.21; Acts 17.26
14.6 Job 7.19; 7.1
14.9 Isa 55.10
14.10 Job 13.19
14.11 Isa 19.5
14.12 Ps 102.26; Acts 3.21; Rev 20.11; 21.1
14.13 Isa 26.20
14.14 Job 7.1
14.15 Job 13.22
14.16 Job 10.6; 31.4; 34.21; Prov 5.21; Jer 32.19
14.17 Deut 32.34; Hos 13.12
14.18 Job 18.4
14.19 Job 7.6
14.20 Job 34.20; Jas 1.10
14.21 Eccl 9.5; Isa 63.16
15.2 Job 6.26

z Cn: Heb *that they may desist* a Syr: Heb lacks *not*

and fill themselves with
the east wind?
3 Should they argue in
unprofitable talk,
or in words with which
they can do no good?
4 But you are doing away with
the fear of God,
and hindering meditation
before God.
5 For your iniquity teaches
your mouth,
and you choose the tongue
of the crafty.
6 Your own mouth condemns
you, and not I;
your own lips testify
against you.

7 "Are you the firstborn of the
human race?
Were you brought forth
before the hills?
8 Have you listened in the
council of God?
And do you limit wisdom
to yourself?
9 What do you know that we
do not know?
What do you understand
that is not clear to us?
10 The gray-haired and the aged
are on our side,
those older than your
father.
11 Are the consolations of God
too small for you,
or the word that deals
gently with you?
12 Why does your heart carry
you away,
and why do your eyes
flash,[b]
13 so that you turn your spirit
against God,
and let such words go out
of your mouth?
14 What are mortals, that they
can be clean?
Or those born of woman,
that they can be
righteous?
15 God puts no trust even in his
holy ones,
and the heavens are not
clean in his sight;

15.5 Ps 36.3; Prov 16.23; Job 5.12,13
15.6 Job 9.20; Lk 19.22
15.7 Job 38.4,21; Ps 90.2; Prov 8.25
15.8 Rom 11.34; Job 12.2
15.9 Job 13.2
15.10 Job 32.6,7
15.11 Job 36.15, 16; 2 Cor 1.3, 4; Zech 1.13
15.13 Job 33.13
15.14 Job 14.4; Prov 20.9; Eccl 7.20; Job 25.4; Ps 51.5
15.15 Job 4.18; 25.5
15.16 Ps 14.1,3; Job 34.7
15.18 Job 8.8
15.20 Job 27.13
15.21 Job 18.11; 20.25; 1 Thes 5.3
15.22 v. 30; Job 27.14
15.23 Ps 59.15; 109.10; Job 18.12
15.25 Job 36.9
15.27 Ps 17.10

16 how much less one who is
abominable and
corrupt,
one who drinks iniquity
like water!

17 "I will show you; listen to
me;
what I have seen I will
declare—
18 what sages have told,
and their ancestors have
not hidden,
19 to whom alone the land was
given,
and no stranger passed
among them.
20 The wicked writhe in pain all
their days,
through all the years that
are laid up for the
ruthless.
21 Terrifying sounds are in their
ears;
in prosperity the destroyer
will come upon them.
22 They despair of returning
from darkness,
and they are destined for
the sword.
23 They wander abroad for
bread, saying, 'Where is
it?'
They know that a day of
darkness is ready at
hand;
24 distress and anguish terrify
them;
they prevail against them,
like a king prepared for
battle.
25 Because they stretched out
their hands against
God,
and bid defiance to the
Almighty,[c]
26 running stubbornly against
him
with a thick-bossed shield;
27 because they have covered
their faces with their
fat,
and gathered fat upon their
loins,

[b] Meaning of Heb uncertain [c] Traditional rendering of Heb *Shaddai*

28 they will live in desolate cities,
in houses that no one should inhabit,
houses destined to become heaps of ruins;
29 they will not be rich, and their wealth will not endure,
nor will they strike root in the earth;[d]
30 they will not escape from darkness;
the flame will dry up their shoots,
and their blossom[e] will be swept away[f] by the wind.
31 Let them not trust in emptiness, deceiving themselves;
for emptiness will be their recompense.
32 It will be paid in full before their time,
and their branch will not be green.
33 They will shake off their unripe grape, like the vine,
and cast off their blossoms, like the olive tree.
34 For the company of the godless is barren,
and fire consumes the tents of bribery.
35 They conceive mischief and bring forth evil
and their heart prepares deceit."

Job Reaffirms His Innocence

16 Then Job answered:
2 "I have heard many such things;
miserable comforters are you all.
3 Have windy words no limit?
Or what provokes you that you keep on talking?
4 I also could talk as you do,
if you were in my place;
I could join words together against you,
and shake my head at you.
5 I could encourage you with my mouth,
and the solace of my lips would assuage your pain.

6 "If I speak, my pain is not assuaged,
and if I forbear, how much of it leaves me?
7 Surely now God has worn me out;
he has[g] made desolate all my company.
8 And he has[g] shriveled me up,
which is a witness against me;
my leanness has risen up against me,
and it testifies to my face.
9 He has torn me in his wrath, and hated me;
he has gnashed his teeth at me;
my adversary sharpens his eyes against me.
10 They have gaped at me with their mouths;
they have struck me insolently on the cheek;
they mass themselves together against me.
11 God gives me up to the ungodly,
and casts me into the hands of the wicked.
12 I was at ease, and he broke me in two;
he seized me by the neck and dashed me to pieces;
he set me up as his target;
13 his archers surround me.
He slashes open my kidneys, and shows no mercy;
he pours out my gall on the ground.
14 He bursts upon me again and again;
he rushes at me like a warrior.
15 I have sewed sackcloth upon my skin,

15.29 Job 27.16, 17 **15.30** Job 5.14; 22.20; 4.9 **15.31** Isa 59.4 **15.32** Job 22.16; Ps 55.23; Job 18.16 **15.33** Hab 3.17 **15.34** Job 16.7; 8.22 **15.35** Ps 7.14; Isa 59.4; Hos 10.13 **16.2** Job 13.4 **16.3** Job 6.26 **16.4** Ps 22.7; 109.25; Lam 2.15; Mt 27.39 **16.7** Job 7.3; v. 20 **16.8** Job 10.17; 19.20 **16.9** Ps 35.16; Job 13.24 **16.10** Ps 22.13; Lam 3.30; Mic 5.1; Ps 35.15 **16.11** Job 1.15,17 **16.12** Job 9.17 **16.13** Job 19.12; 27.22; 20.25 **16.14** Job 9.17; Joel 2.7 **16.15** Gen 37.34; Job 30.19

[d] Vg: Meaning of Heb uncertain [e] Gk: Heb *mouth* [f] Cn: Heb *will depart* [g] Heb *you have*

and have laid my strength
in the dust.
16 My face is red with weeping,
and deep darkness is on
my eyelids,
17 though there is no violence
in my hands,
and my prayer is pure.

18 "O earth, do not cover my
blood;
let my outcry find no
resting place.
19 Even now, in fact, my
witness is in heaven,
and he that vouches for me
is on high.
20 My friends scorn me;
my eye pours out tears to
God,
21 that he would maintain the
right of a mortal with
God,
as[h] one does for a
neighbor.
22 For when a few years have
come,
I shall go the way from
which I shall not
return.

Job Prays for Relief

17 My spirit is broken, my
days are extinct,
the grave is ready for me.
2 Surely there are mockers
around me,
and my eye dwells on their
provocation.

3 "Lay down a pledge for me
with yourself;
who is there that will give
surety for me?
4 Since you have closed their
minds to
understanding,
therefore you will not let
them triumph.
5 Those who denounce friends
for reward—
the eyes of their children
will fail.

6 "He has made me a byword
of the peoples,
and I am one before whom
people spit.
7 My eye has grown dim from
grief,
and all my members are
like a shadow.
8 The upright are appalled at
this,
and the innocent stir
themselves up against
the godless.
9 Yet the righteous hold to
their way,
and they that have clean
hands grow stronger
and stronger.
10 But you, come back now, all
of you,
and I shall not find a
sensible person among
you.
11 My days are past, my plans
are broken off,
the desires of my heart.
12 They make night into day;
'The light,' they say, 'is
near to the darkness.'[i]
13 If I look for Sheol as my
house,
if I spread my couch in
darkness,
14 if I say to the Pit, 'You are
my father,'
and to the worm, 'My
mother,' or 'My sister,'
15 where then is my hope?
Who will see my hope?
16 Will it go down to the bars of
Sheol?
Shall we descend together
into the dust?"

Bildad Speaks: God Punishes the Wicked

18 Then Bildad the Shuhite
answered:
2 "How long will you hunt for
words?
Consider, and then we
shall speak.
3 Why are we counted as
cattle?
Why are we stupid in your
sight?

16.16 v. 20
16.17 Job 27.4
16.18 Isa 26.21; Ps 66.18,19
16.19 Rom 1.9
16.20 v. 7; Lam 2.19
16.21 1 Kings 8.45; Ps 9.4
16.22 Eccl 12.5
17.1 Ps 88.3,4
17.2 v. 6; 1 Sam 1.6,7
17.3 Ps 119.122; Prov 6.1
17.4 Job 12.20
17.5 Lev 19.16; Job 11.20
17.6 Job 30.9,10
17.7 Job 16.16; 16.8
17.8 Job 22.19
17.9 Prov 4.18; Job 22.30
17.10 Job 12.2
17.11 Job 7.6
17.13 Job 3.13
17.14 Ps 16.10; Job 21.26; 24.20
17.15 Job 7.6
17.16 Jon 2.6; Job 3.17-19
18.3 Ps 73.22; Job 36.14

[h] Syr Vg Tg: Heb *and* [i] Meaning of Heb uncertain

4 You who tear yourself in your
anger—
shall the earth be forsaken
because of you,
or the rock be removed out
of its place?
5 "Surely the light of the
wicked is put out,
and the flame of their fire
does not shine.
6 The light is dark in their
tent,
and the lamp above them
is put out.
7 Their strong steps are
shortened,
and their own schemes
throw them down.
8 For they are thrust into a net
by their own feet,
and they walk into a pitfall.
9 A trap seizes them by the
heel;
a snare lays hold of them.
10 A rope is hid for them in the
ground,
a trap for them in the path.
11 Terrors frighten them on
every side,
and chase them at their
heels.
12 Their strength is consumed
by hunger,[j]
and calamity is ready for
their stumbling.
13 By disease their skin is
consumed,[k]
the firstborn of Death
consumes their limbs.
14 They are torn from the tent
in which they trusted,
and are brought to the king
of terrors.
15 In their tents nothing
remains;
sulfur is scattered upon
their habitations.
16 Their roots dry up beneath,
and their branches wither
above.
17 Their memory perishes from
the earth,
and they have no name in
the street.
18 They are thrust from light
into darkness,
and driven out of the
world.
19 They have no offspring or
descendant among their
people,
and no survivor where they
used to live.
20 They of the west are
appalled at their fate,
and horror seizes those of
the east.
21 Surely such are the dwellings
of the ungodly,
such is the place of those
who do not know God."

Job Replies: I Know That My Redeemer Lives

19 Then Job answered:
2 "How long will you
torment me,
and break me in pieces
with words?
3 These ten times you have
cast reproach upon me;
are you not ashamed to
wrong me?
4 And even if it is true that I
have erred,
my error remains with me.
5 If indeed you magnify
yourselves against me,
and make my humiliation
an argument against
me,
6 know then that God has put
me in the wrong,
and closed his net around
me.
7 Even when I cry out,
'Violence!' I am not
answered;
I call aloud, but there is no
justice.
8 He has walled up my way so
that I cannot pass,
and he has set darkness
upon my paths.
9 He has stripped my glory
from me,
and taken the crown from
my head.
10 He breaks me down on every
side, and I am gone,

18.4 Job 13.14; 14.18 **18.5** Prov 13.9; 20.20; 24.20 **18.7** Prov 4.12; Job 5.13 **18.8** Job 22.10; Ps 9.15; 35.8 **18.9** Ps 140.5; Job 5.5 **18.10** Ps 69.22 **18.11** Job 15.21; Jer 6.25; 20.3 **18.12** Isa 8.21 **18.14** Job 8.22; 15.21 **18.15** Ps 11.6 **18.16** Isa 5.24; Hos 9.1-16; Am 2.9; Mal 4.1; Job 15.30, 32 **18.17** Ps 34.16; Prov 2.22; 10.7 **18.18** Job 5.14; 27.21-23 **18.19** Isa 14.22; Jer 22.30 **18.21** Jer 9.3; 1 Thes 4.5 **19.4** Job 6.24 **19.5** Ps 35.26; 38.16 **19.6** Job 27.2; 18.8-10 **19.7** Job 30.20 **19.8** Job 3.23; 30.26 **19.9** Ps 89.44; 89.39 **19.10** Job 12.14; 7.6; 24.20

j Or *Disaster is hungry for them* k Cn: Heb *It consumes the limbs of his skin*

he has uprooted my hope
like a tree.
11 He has kindled his wrath
against me,
and counts me as his
adversary.
12 His troops come on together;
they have thrown up
siegeworks[l] against
me,
and encamp around my
tent.

13 "He has put my family far
from me,
and my acquaintances are
wholly estranged from
me.
14 My relatives and my close
friends have failed me;
15 the guests in my house
have forgotten me;
my serving girls count me as
a stranger;
I have become an alien in
their eyes.
16 I call to my servant, but he
gives me no answer;
I must myself plead with
him.
17 My breath is repulsive to my
wife;
I am loathsome to my own
family.
18 Even young children despise
me;
when I rise, they talk
against me.
19 All my intimate friends
abhor me,
and those whom I loved
have turned against me.
20 My bones cling to my skin
and to my flesh,
and I have escaped by the
skin of my teeth.
21 Have pity on me, have pity
on me, O you my
friends,
for the hand of God has
touched me!
22 Why do you, like God,
pursue me,
never satisfied with my
flesh?

23 "O that my words were
written down!
O that they were inscribed
in a book!
24 O that with an iron pen and
with lead
they were engraved on a
rock forever!
25 For I know that my
Redeemer[m] lives,
and that at the last he[n]
will stand upon the
earth;[o]
26 and after my skin has been
thus destroyed,
then in[p] my flesh I shall
see God,[q]
27 whom I shall see on my
side,[r]
and my eyes shall behold,
and not another.
My heart faints within
me!
28 If you say, 'How we will
persecute him!'
and, 'The root of the
matter is found in him';
29 be afraid of the sword,
for wrath brings the
punishment of the
sword,
so that you may know
there is a judgment."

19.11 Job 16.9; 13.24 **19.12** Job 30.12 **19.14** v. 19 **19.15** Gen 14.14; Eccl 2.7 **19.18** 2 Kings 2.23 **19.19** Ps 38.11; 55.13 **19.20** Job 33.21; Ps 102.5 **19.21** Job 6.14; Ps 38.2 **19.22** Job 16.11 **19.23** Isa 30.8 **19.24** Jer 17.1 **19.25** Job 16.19; Ps 78.35; Isa 43.14; Jer 50.34 **19.26** Mt 5.8; 1 Cor 13.12; 1 Jn 3.2 **19.27** Ps 73.26 **19.28** Ps 69.26 **19.29** Job 22.4 **20.3** Job 19.3 **20.4** Deut 4.32 **20.5** Ps 37.35; 73.19

Zophar Speaks: Wickedness Receives Just Retribution

20 Then Zophar the Naama-
thite answered:
2 "Pay attention! My thoughts
urge me to answer,
because of the agitation
within me.
3 I hear censure that insults
me,
and a spirit beyond my
understanding answers
me.
4 Do you not know this from
of old,
ever since mortals were
placed on earth,
5 that the exulting of the
wicked is short,

[l] Cn: Heb *their way* [m] Or *Vindicator* [n] Or *that he the Last* [o] Heb *dust* [p] Or *without* [q] Meaning of Heb of this verse uncertain [r] Or *for myself*

and the joy of the godless
is but for a moment?
6 Even though they mount up
high as the heavens,
and their head reaches to
the clouds,
7 they will perish forever like
their own dung;
those who have seen them
will say, 'Where are
they?'
8 They will fly away like a
dream, and not be
found;
they will be chased away
like a vision of the
night.
9 The eye that saw them will
see them no more,
nor will their place behold
them any longer.
10 Their children will seek the
favor of the poor,
and their hands will give
back their wealth.
11 Their bodies, once full of
youth,
will lie down in the dust
with them.

12 "Though wickedness is sweet
in their mouth,
though they hide it under
their tongues,
13 though they are loath to let
it go,
and hold it in their
mouths,
14 yet their food is turned in
their stomachs;
it is the venom of asps
within them.
15 They swallow down riches
and vomit them up
again;
God casts them out of their
bellies.
16 They will suck the poison of
asps;
the tongue of a viper will
kill them.
17 They will not look on the
rivers,
the streams flowing with
honey and curds.
18 They will give back the fruit
of their toil,
and will not swallow it
down;
from the profit of their
trading
they will get no enjoyment.
19 For they have crushed and
abandoned the poor,
they have seized a house
that they did not build.

20 "They knew no quiet in their
bellies;
in their greed they let
nothing escape.
21 There was nothing left after
they had eaten;
therefore their prosperity
will not endure.
22 In full sufficiency they will
be in distress;
all the force of misery will
come upon them.
23 To fill their belly to the full
God[s] will send his fierce
anger into them,
and rain it upon them as
their food.[t]
24 They will flee from an iron
weapon;
a bronze arrow will strike
them through.
25 It is drawn forth and comes
out of their body,
and the glittering point
comes out of their gall;
terrors come upon them.
26 Utter darkness is laid up for
their treasures;
a fire fanned by no one will
devour them;
what is left in their tent
will be consumed.
27 The heavens will reveal their
iniquity,
and the earth will rise up
against them.
28 The possessions of their
house will be carried
away,
dragged off in the day of
God's[u] wrath.
29 This is the portion of the
wicked from God,

20.6 Isa 14.13, 14; Ob 3,4
20.7 Job 4.20; 7.10; 8.18
20.8 Ps 73.20; 90.5; Job 18.18; 27.21-23
20.9 Job 7.8,10
20.10 Job 5.4; 27.16,17
20.11 Job 13.26; 21.26
20.12 Prov 20.17; Ps 10.7
20.16 Deut 32.24, 33
20.17 Job 29.6; Deut 32.13, 14
20.18 vv. 10,15
20.19 Job 24.2-4; 35.9
20.20 Eccl 5.13,14
20.21 Job 15.29
20.23 Ps 78.30,31
20.24 Isa 24.18; Jer 48.43; Am 5.19
20.25 Job 16.13; 18.11
20.26 Job 18.18; Ps 21.9
20.27 Deut 31.28
20.28 Deut 28.31; Job 21.30
20.29 Job 27.13

s Heb *he*
t Cn: Meaning of Heb uncertain
u Heb *his*

the heritage decreed for
them by God."

Job Replies: The Wicked Often Go Unpunished

21 Then Job answered:
2 "Listen carefully to
my words,
and let this be your
consolation.
3 Bear with me, and I will
speak;
then after I have spoken,
mock on.
4 As for me, is my complaint
addressed to mortals?
Why should I not be
impatient?
5 Look at me, and be appalled,
and lay your hand upon
your mouth.
6 When I think of it I am
dismayed,
and shuddering seizes my
flesh.
7 Why do the wicked live on,
reach old age, and grow
mighty in power?
8 Their children are
established in their
presence,
and their offspring before
their eyes.
9 Their houses are safe from
fear,
and no rod of God is upon
them.
10 Their bull breeds without
fail;
their cow calves and never
miscarries.
11 They send out their little
ones like a flock,
and their children dance
around.
12 They sing to the tambourine
and the lyre,
and rejoice to the sound of
the pipe.
13 They spend their days in
prosperity,
and in peace they go down
to Sheol.
14 They say to God, 'Leave us
alone!
We do not desire to know
your ways.
15 What is the Almighty,[v] that
we should serve him?
And what profit do we get
if we pray to him?'
16 Is not their prosperity indeed
their own
achievement?[w]
The plans of the wicked
are repugnant to me.
17 "How often is the lamp of
the wicked put out?
How often does calamity
come upon them?
How often does God[x]
distribute pains in his
anger?
18 How often are they like
straw before the wind,
and like chaff that the
storm carries away?
19 You say, 'God stores up their
iniquity for their
children.'
Let it be paid back to
them, so that they may
know it.
20 Let their own eyes see their
destruction,
and let them drink of the
wrath of the Almighty.[v]
21 For what do they care for
their household after
them,
when the number of their
months is cut off?
22 Will any teach God
knowledge,
seeing that he judges those
that are on high?
23 One dies in full prosperity,
being wholly at ease and
secure,
24 his loins full of milk
and the marrow of his
bones moist.
25 Another dies in bitterness of
soul,
never having tasted of
good.
26 They lie down alike in the
dust,

21.3 Job 16.10 **21.4** Job 6.11 **21.5** Judg 18.19; Job 29.9; 40.4 **21.7** Job 12.6; Ps 73.3,12; Jer 12.1 **21.8** Ps 17.14 **21.9** Ps 73.5 **21.10** Ex 23.26 **21.12** Ps 81.2; Job 30.31 **21.13** Job 36.11 **21.14** Job 22.17; Prov 1.29 **21.15** Ex 5.2; Job 34.9; Mal 3.14 **21.16** Job 22.18 **21.17** Job 18.5,6, 12 **21.18** Ps 1.4 **21.19** Ex 20.5 **21.20** Ps 75.8; Isa 51.17; Jer 25.15; Rev 14.10 **21.21** Job 14.5 **21.22** Isa 40.13, 14; Rom 11.34 **21.26** Eccl 9.2; Job 24.20

[v] Traditional rendering of Heb *Shaddai* [w] Heb *in their hand* [x] Heb *he*

and the worms cover them.

27 "Oh, I know your thoughts,
and your schemes to wrong me.
28 For you say, 'Where is the house of the prince?
Where is the tent in which the wicked lived?'
29 Have you not asked those who travel the roads,
and do you not accept their testimony,
30 that the wicked are spared in the day of calamity,
and are rescued in the day of wrath?
31 Who declares their way to their face,
and who repays them for what they have done?
32 When they are carried to the grave,
a watch is kept over their tomb.
33 The clods of the valley are sweet to them;
everyone will follow after,
and those who went before are innumerable.
34 How then will you comfort me with empty nothings?
There is nothing left of your answers but falsehood."

Eliphaz Speaks: Job's Wickedness Is Great

22 Then Eliphaz the Temanite answered:
2 "Can a mortal be of use to God?
Can even the wisest be of service to him?
3 Is it any pleasure to the Almighty[y] if you are righteous,
or is it gain to him if you make your ways blameless?
4 Is it for your piety that he reproves you,
and enters into judgment with you?
5 Is not your wickedness great?
There is no end to your iniquities.
6 For you have exacted pledges from your family for no reason,
and stripped the naked of their clothing.
7 You have given no water to the weary to drink,
and you have withheld bread from the hungry.
8 The powerful possess the land,
and the favored live in it.
9 You have sent widows away empty-handed,
and the arms of the orphans you have crushed.[z]
10 Therefore snares are around you,
and sudden terror overwhelms you,
11 or darkness so that you cannot see;
a flood of water covers you.

12 "Is not God high in the heavens?
See the highest stars, how lofty they are!
13 Therefore you say, 'What does God know?
Can he judge through the deep darkness?
14 Thick clouds enwrap him, so that he does not see,
and he walks on the dome of heaven.'
15 Will you keep to the old way that the wicked have trod?
16 They were snatched away before their time;
their foundation was washed away by a flood.
17 They said to God, 'Leave us alone,'
and 'What can the Almighty[y] do to us?'[a]
18 Yet he filled their houses with good things—
but the plans of the wicked are repugnant to me.

21.28 Job 12.21; 8.22 **21.30** Prov 16.4; 2 Pet 2.9; Job 20.28; Rom 2.5 **21.33** Job 3.22; 17.16; 3.19; 24.24 **21.34** Job 16.2 **22.2** Lk 17.10 **22.4** Job 14.3; Ps 143.2 **22.5** Job 11.6; 15.5

22.6 Ex 22.26; Deut 24.6, 17; Ezek 18.12, 16 **22.7** Mt 10.42; Job 31.31 **22.9** Job 24.3; Isa 10.2 **22.11** Job 5.14; Ps 69.2 **22.12** Job 11.7-9 **22.13** Ps 10.11 **22.14** Job 26.9 **22.16** Job 15.32; 14.19; Mt 7.26,27 **22.18** Job 12.6; 21.16

[y] Traditional rendering of Heb *Shaddai*
[z] Gk Syr Tg Vg: Heb *were crushed*
[a] Gk Syr: Heb *them*

19 The righteous see it and are glad;
the innocent laugh them to scorn,
20 saying, 'Surely our adversaries are cut off,
and what they left, the fire has consumed.'

21 "Agree with God,[b] and be at peace;
in this way good will come to you.
22 Receive instruction from his mouth,
and lay up his words in your heart.
23 If you return to the Almighty,[c] you will be restored,
if you remove unrighteousness from your tents,
24 if you treat gold like dust,
and gold of Ophir like the stones of the torrent-bed,
25 and if the Almighty[c] is your gold
and your precious silver,
26 then you will delight yourself in the Almighty,[c]
and lift up your face to God.
27 You will pray to him, and he will hear you,
and you will pay your vows.
28 You will decide on a matter, and it will be established for you,
and light will shine on your ways.
29 When others are humiliated, you say it is pride;
for he saves the humble.
30 He will deliver even those who are guilty;
they will escape because of the cleanness of your hands."[d]

Job Replies: My Complaint Is Bitter

23 Then Job answered:
2 "Today also my complaint is bitter;[e]
his[f] hand is heavy despite my groaning.
3 Oh, that I knew where I might find him,
that I might come even to his dwelling!
4 I would lay my case before him,
and fill my mouth with arguments.
5 I would learn what he would answer me,
and understand what he would say to me.
6 Would he contend with me in the greatness of his power?
No; but he would give heed to me.
7 There an upright person could reason with him,
and I should be acquitted forever by my judge.

8 "If I go forward, he is not there;
or backward, I cannot perceive him;
9 on the left he hides, and I cannot behold him;
I turn[g] to the right, but I cannot see him.
10 But he knows the way that I take;
when he has tested me, I shall come out like gold.
11 My foot has held fast to his steps;
I have kept his way and have not turned aside.
12 I have not departed from the commandment of his lips;
I have treasured in[h] my bosom the words of his mouth.
13 But he stands alone and who can dissuade him?
What he desires, that he does.

22.19 Ps 58.10; 107.42 **22.20** Ps 18.39; Job 15.30 **22.21** Jer 9.24; Gal 4.9 **22.22** Ps 138.4 **22.23** Job 8.5; Isa 19.22; Acts 20.32; Job 11.14 **22.24** Ps 19.10 **22.25** Isa 33.6; Mt 6.20 **22.26** Job 27.10; Isa 58.14 **22.27** Job 33.26; Isa 58.9; Job 34.28; Ps 22.25 **22.28** Ps 145.19 **22.29** Prov 29.23; Mt 23.12; 1 Pet 5.5 **22.30** Job 42.7,8; 2 Sam 22.21 **23.2** Job 7.11; 6.2,3 **23.3** Deut 4.29; Ps 9.4 **23.4** Job 13.18 **23.6** Job 9.4 **23.7** Job 13.3,16 **23.8** Job 9.11 **23.10** Ps 139.1-3 **23.11** Ps 44.18 **23.12** Jn 4.32,34 **23.13** Job 9.12; 12.14; Ps 115.3

[b] Heb *him* [c] Traditional rendering of Heb *Shaddai* [d] Meaning of Heb uncertain [e] Syr Vg Tg: Heb *rebellious* [f] Gk Syr: Heb *my* [g] Syr Vg: Heb *he turns* [h] Gk Vg: Heb *from*

14 For he will complete what he
appoints for me;
and many such things are
in his mind.
15 Therefore I am terrified at
his presence;
when I consider, I am in
dread of him.
16 God has made my heart
faint;
the Almighty[i] has terrified
me;
17 If only I could vanish in
darkness,
and thick darkness would
cover my face![j]

Job Complains of Violence on the Earth

24 "Why are times not kept
by the Almighty,[i]
and why do those who
know him never see his
days?
2 The wicked[k] remove
landmarks;
they seize flocks and
pasture them.
3 They drive away the donkey
of the orphan;
they take the widow's ox
for a pledge.
4 They thrust the needy off the
road;
the poor of the earth all
hide themselves.
5 Like wild asses in the desert
they go out to their toil,
scavenging in the wasteland
food for their young.
6 They reap in a field not their
own
and they glean in the
vineyard of the wicked.
7 They lie all night naked,
without clothing,
and have no covering in
the cold.
8 They are wet with the rain of
the mountains,
and cling to the rock for
want of shelter.

9 "There are those who snatch
the orphan child from
the breast,
and take as a pledge the
infant of the poor.
10 They go about naked,
without clothing;
though hungry, they carry
the sheaves;
11 between their terraces[l] they
press out oil;
they tread the wine
presses, but suffer
thirst.
12 From the city the dying
groan,
and the throat of the
wounded cries for help;
yet God pays no attention
to their prayer.

13 "There are those who rebel
against the light,
who are not acquainted
with its ways,
and do not stay in its
paths.
14 The murderer rises at dusk
to kill the poor and needy,
and in the night is like a
thief.
15 The eye of the adulterer also
waits for the twilight,
saying, 'No eye will see
me';
and he disguises his face.
16 In the dark they dig through
houses;
by day they shut
themselves up;
they do not know the light.
17 For deep darkness is
morning to all of them;
for they are friends with
the terrors of deep
darkness.

18 "Swift are they on the face of
the waters;
their portion in the land is
cursed;
no treader turns toward
their vineyards.
19 Drought and heat snatch
away the snow waters;

23.14 1 Thes 3.3
23.16 Ps 22.14; Jer 51.46
23.17 Job 10.18, 19; 19.8
24.1 Ps 31.15; Jer 46.10
24.2 Deut 19.14; 27.17; 28.31
24.3 Ex 22.26; Deut 24.6, 10,12,17; Job 22.6
24.4 Deut 24.14; Prov 28.28
24.5 Job 39.5-8; Ps 104.23
24.7 Ex 22.26; Job 22.6
24.8 Lam 4.5
24.9 Deut 24.17
24.12 Jer 51.52; Ezek 26.15; Job 9.23,24
24.13 Isa 5.20; Jn 3.19
24.14 Mic 2.1; Ps 10.8
24.15 Prov 7.9; Ps 10.11
24.16 Ex 22.2
24.17 Ps 91.5
24.18 Job 9.26; Ps 90.5
24.19 Job 6.16,17; 21.13

[i] Traditional rendering of Heb *Shaddai*
[j] Or *But I am not destroyed by the darkness; he has concealed the thick darkness from me*
[k] Gk: Heb *they*
[l] Meaning of Heb uncertain

so does Sheol those who
have sinned.
20 The womb forgets them;
the worm finds them
sweet;
they are no longer
remembered;
so wickedness is broken
like a tree.

21 "They harm[m] the childless
woman,
and do no good to the
widow.
22 Yet God[n] prolongs the life of
the mighty by his
power;
they rise up when they
despair of life.
23 He gives them security, and
they are supported;
his eyes are upon their
ways.
24 They are exalted a little
while, and then are
gone;
they wither and fade like
the mallow;[o]
they are cut off like the
heads of grain.
25 If it is not so, who will prove
me a liar,
and show that there is
nothing in what I say?"

Bildad Speaks: How Can a Mortal Be Righteous Before God?

25 Then Bildad the Shuhite
answered:
2 "Dominion and fear are with
God;[p]
he makes peace in his high
heaven.
3 Is there any number to his
armies?
Upon whom does his light
not arise?
4 How then can a mortal be
righteous before God?
How can one born of
woman be pure?
5 If even the moon is not
bright
and the stars are not pure
in his sight,
6 how much less a mortal, who
is a maggot,
and a human being, who is
a worm!"

Job Replies: God's Majesty Is Unsearchable

26 Then Job answered:
2 "How you have helped
one who has no power!
How you have assisted the
arm that has no
strength!
3 How you have counseled one
who has no wisdom,
and given much good
advice!
4 With whose help have you
uttered words,
and whose spirit has come
forth from you?
5 The shades below tremble,
the waters and their
inhabitants.
6 Sheol is naked before God,
and Abaddon has no
covering.
7 He stretches out Zaphon[q]
over the void,
and hangs the earth upon
nothing.
8 He binds up the waters in
his thick clouds,
and the cloud is not torn
open by them.
9 He covers the face of the full
moon,
and spreads over it his
cloud.
10 He has described a circle on
the face of the waters,
at the boundary between
light and darkness.
11 The pillars of heaven
tremble,
and are astounded at his
rebuke.
12 By his power he stilled the
Sea;
by his understanding he
struck down Rahab.
13 By his wind the heavens
were made fair;

24.20 Ps 31.12; Prov 10.7 **24.21** Job 22.9 **24.22** Deut 28.66 **24.23** Job 12.6; 11.11 **24.24** Ps 37.10; Job 14.21; Isa 17.5 **24.25** Job 6.28; 27.4 **25.2** Job 9.4; Rev 1.6; Job 22.12 **25.3** Jas 1.17 **25.4** Job 4.17; Ps 143.2; Job 14.4 **25.5** Job 31.26; 15.15 **25.6** Job 7.17; Ps 22.6 **26.2** Ps 71.9 **26.6** Ps 139.8,11; Heb 4.13 **26.7** Job 9.8 **26.8** Prov 30.4 **26.9** Ps 97.2 **26.10** Job 38.8-11; Prov 8.29; Job 38.19, 20,24 **26.12** Ex 14.21; Isa 51.15; Jer 31.35 **26.13** Job 9.8; Isa 27.1

[m] Gk Tg: Heb *feed on* or *associate with*
[n] Heb *he*
[o] Gk: Heb *like all others*
[p] Heb *him*
[q] Or *the North*

his hand pierced the fleeing serpent.
14 These are indeed but the outskirts of his ways;
and how small a whisper do we hear of him!
But the thunder of his power who can understand?"

Job Maintains His Integrity

27 Job again took up his discourse and said:
2 "As God lives, who has taken away my right,
and the Almighty,[r] who has made my soul bitter,
3 as long as my breath is in me
and the spirit of God is in my nostrils,
4 my lips will not speak falsehood,
and my tongue will not utter deceit.
5 Far be it from me to say that you are right;
until I die I will not put away my integrity from me.
6 I hold fast my righteousness, and will not let it go;
my heart does not reproach me for any of my days.

7 "May my enemy be like the wicked,
and may my opponent be like the unrighteous.
8 For what is the hope of the godless when God cuts them off,
when God takes away their lives?
9 Will God hear their cry
when trouble comes upon them?
10 Will they take delight in the Almighty?[r]
Will they call upon God at all times?
11 I will teach you concerning the hand of God;
that which is with the Almighty[r] I will not conceal.
12 All of you have seen it yourselves;
why then have you become altogether vain?

13 "This is the portion of the wicked with God,
and the heritage that oppressors receive from the Almighty:[r]
14 If their children are multiplied, it is for the sword;
and their offspring have not enough to eat.
15 Those who survive them the pestilence buries,
and their widows make no lamentation.
16 Though they heap up silver like dust,
and pile up clothing like clay—
17 they may pile it up, but the just will wear it,
and the innocent will divide the silver.
18 They build their houses like nests,
like booths made by sentinels of the vineyard.
19 They go to bed with wealth, but will do so no more;
they open their eyes, and it is gone.
20 Terrors overtake them like a flood;
in the night a whirlwind carries them off.
21 The east wind lifts them up and they are gone;
it sweeps them out of their place.
22 It[s] hurls at them without pity;
they flee from its[t] power in headlong flight.
23 It[s] claps its[t] hands at them,
and hisses at them from its[t] place.

26.14 Job 36.29 **27.1** Job 13.12; 29.1 **27.2** Job 34.5; 9.18 **27.3** Job 32.8; 33.4 **27.4** Job 6.28 **27.5** Job 2.9; 13.15 **27.6** Job 2.3; 13.18; Acts 23.1 **27.8** Job 8.13; 11.20 **27.9** Job 35.12; Prov 1.28; Isa 1.15; Jer 14.12; Mic 3.4 **27.10** Job 22.26, 27

27.13 Job 20.29; 15.20 **27.14** Deut 28.41; Hos 9.13; Job 20.10 **27.15** Ps 78.64 **27.16** Zech 9.3 **27.17** Prov 28.8; Eccl 2.26 **27.19** Ezek 29.5; Job 7.8,21 **27.20** Job 15.21; 20.8 **27.21** Job 21.18; 7.10 **27.22** Jer 13.14; Ezek 5.11; Job 11.20 **27.23** Lam 2.15; Job 18.18

[r] Traditional rendering of Heb *Shaddai*
[s] Or *He* (that is God) [t] Or *his*

Interlude: Where Wisdom Is Found

28 "Surely there is a mine for silver,
and a place for gold to be refined.
2 Iron is taken out of the earth,
and copper is smelted from ore.
3 Miners put[u] an end to darkness,
and search out to the farthest bound
the ore in gloom and deep darkness.
4 They open shafts in a valley away from human habitation;
they are forgotten by travelers,
they sway suspended, remote from people.
5 As for the earth, out of it comes bread;
but underneath it is turned up as by fire.
6 Its stones are the place of sapphires,[v]
and its dust contains gold.

7 "That path no bird of prey knows,
and the falcon's eye has not seen it.
8 The proud wild animals have not trodden it;
the lion has not passed over it.

9 "They put their hand to the flinty rock,
and overturn mountains by the roots.
10 They cut out channels in the rocks,
and their eyes see every precious thing.
11 The sources of the rivers they probe;[w]
hidden things they bring to light.

12 "But where shall wisdom be found?
And where is the place of understanding?
13 Mortals do not know the way to it,[x]
and it is not found in the land of the living.
14 The deep says, 'It is not in me,'
and the sea says, 'It is not with me.'
15 It cannot be gotten for gold,
and silver cannot be weighed out as its price.
16 It cannot be valued in the gold of Ophir,
in precious onyx or sapphire.[v]
17 Gold and glass cannot equal it,
nor can it be exchanged for jewels of fine gold.
18 No mention shall be made of coral or of crystal;
the price of wisdom is above pearls.
19 The chrysolite of Ethiopia[y] cannot compare with it,
nor can it be valued in pure gold.

20 "Where then does wisdom come from?
And where is the place of understanding?
21 It is hidden from the eyes of all living,
and concealed from the birds of the air.
22 Abaddon and Death say,
'We have heard a rumor of it with our ears.'

23 "God understands the way to it,
and he knows its place.
24 For he looks to the ends of the earth,
and sees everything under the heavens.
25 When he gave to the wind its weight,
and apportioned out the waters by measure;

28.2 Deut 8.9 **28.5** Ps 104.14 **28.9** Deut 8.15; 32.13 **28.12** vv. 23,28 **28.13** Prov 3.15 **28.17** Prov 8.10; 16.16 **28.18** Prov 3.15; 8.11 **28.19** Prov 8.19 **28.20** vv. 23,28 **28.22** Job 26.6 **28.23** vv. 23-28 **28.24** Ps 33.13; Prov 15.3 **28.25** Ps 135.7; Job 12.15

u Heb *He puts* v Or *lapis lazuli* w Gk Vg: Heb *bind* x Gk: Heb *its price* y Or *Nubia*; Heb *Cush*

26 when he made a decree for the rain,
and a way for the thunderbolt;
27 then he saw it and declared it;
he established it, and searched it out.
28 And he said to humankind,
'Truly, the fear of the Lord, that is wisdom;
and to depart from evil is understanding.' "

Job Finishes His Defense

29 Job again took up his discourse and said:
2 "Oh, that I were as in the months of old,
as in the days when God watched over me;
3 when his lamp shone over my head,
and by his light I walked through darkness;
4 when I was in my prime,
when the friendship of God was upon my tent;
5 when the Almighty[z] was still with me,
when my children were around me;
6 when my steps were washed with milk,
and the rock poured out for me streams of oil!
7 When I went out to the gate of the city,
when I took my seat in the square,
8 the young men saw me and withdrew,
and the aged rose up and stood;
9 the nobles refrained from talking,
and laid their hands on their mouths;
10 the voices of princes were hushed,
and their tongues stuck to the roof of their mouths.
11 When the ear heard, it commended me,
and when the eye saw, it approved;
12 because I delivered the poor who cried,
and the orphan who had no helper.
13 The blessing of the wretched came upon me,
and I caused the widow's heart to sing for joy.
14 I put on righteousness, and it clothed me;
my justice was like a robe and a turban.
15 I was eyes to the blind,
and feet to the lame.
16 I was a father to the needy,
and I championed the cause of the stranger.
17 I broke the fangs of the unrighteous,
and made them drop their prey from their teeth.
18 Then I thought, 'I shall die in my nest,
and I shall multiply my days like the phoenix;[a]
19 my roots spread out to the waters,
with the dew all night on my branches;
20 my glory was fresh with me,
and my bow ever new in my hand.'

21 "They listened to me, and waited,
and kept silence for my counsel.
22 After I spoke they did not speak again,
and my word dropped upon them like dew.[b]
23 They waited for me as for the rain;
they opened their mouths as for the spring rain.
24 I smiled on them when they had no confidence;
and the light of my countenance they did not extinguish.[c]
25 I chose their way, and sat as chief,

28.26 Job 37.6,11,12; 37.3; 38.25 **28.28** Deut 4.6; Ps 111.10; Prov 1.7; 9.10 **29.1** Job 13.12; 27.1 **29.2** Jer 31.28 **29.3** Job 11.17 **29.4** Ps 25.14 **29.6** Job 20.17; Deut 32.13,14 **29.9** v. 21; Job 21.5 **29.10** v. 22 **29.12** Job 31.16,17,21 **29.13** Job 31.19,20 **29.14** Ps 132.9; Isa 59.17; 61.10; Eph 6.14 **29.16** Prov 29.7 **29.17** Ps 3.7 **29.18** Ps 30.6 **29.19** Job 18.16; Jer 17.8 **29.20** Gen 49.24; Ps 18.34 **29.21** v. 9 **29.22** v. 10; Job 32.2 **29.25** Job 1.3; 31.37; 4.4

[z] Traditional rendering of Heb *Shaddai*
[a] Or *like sand* [b] Heb lacks *like dew*
[c] Meaning of Heb uncertain

and I lived like a king
among his troops,
like one who comforts
mourners.

30 "But now they make
sport of me,
those who are younger than
I,
whose fathers I would have
disdained
to set with the dogs of my
flock.
2 What could I gain from the
strength of their hands?
All their vigor is gone.
3 Through want and hard
hunger
they gnaw the dry and
desolate ground,
4 they pick mallow and the
leaves of bushes,
and to warm themselves
the roots of broom.
5 They are driven out from
society;
people shout after them as
after a thief.
6 In the gullies of wadis they
must live,
in holes in the ground, and
in the rocks.
7 Among the bushes they bray;
under the nettles they
huddle together.
8 A senseless, disreputable
brood,
they have been whipped
out of the land.

9 "And now they mock me in
song;
I am a byword to them.
10 They abhor me, they keep
aloof from me;
they do not hesitate to spit
at the sight of me.
11 Because God has loosed my
bowstring and humbled
me,
they have cast off restraint
in my presence.
12 On my right hand the rabble
rise up;
they send me sprawling,
and build roads for my
ruin.

30.1 Job 12.4 **30.9** Job 12.4; 17.6 **30.10** Num 12.14; Deut 25.9; Isa 50.6; Mt 26.67 **30.11** Ruth 1.21; Ps 88.7 **30.12** Ps 140.4,5; Job 19.12

13 They break up my path,
they promote my calamity;
no one restrains[d] them.
14 As through a wide breach
they come;
amid the crash they roll
on.
15 Terrors are turned upon me;
my honor is pursued as by
the wind,
and my prosperity has
passed away like a
cloud.

16 "And now my soul is poured
out within me;
days of affliction have
taken hold of me.
17 The night racks my bones,
and the pain that gnaws
me takes no rest.
18 With violence he seizes my
garment;[e]
he grasps me by[f] the
collar of my tunic.
19 He has cast me into the
mire,
and I have become like
dust and ashes.
20 I cry to you and you do not
answer me;
I stand, and you merely
look at me.
21 You have turned cruel to me;
with the might of your
hand you persecute me.
22 You lift me up on the wind,
you make me ride on it,
and you toss me about in
the roar of the storm.
23 I know that you will bring
me to death,
and to the house appointed
for all living.

24 "Surely one does not turn
against the needy,[g]
when in disaster they cry
for help.[h]
25 Did I not weep for those
whose day was hard?
Was not my soul grieved
for the poor?

30.15 Job 3.25; 31.23; Hos 13.3 **30.16** Ps 22.14; 42.4 **30.17** v. 30 **30.19** Ps 69.2,14 **30.20** Ps 19.7 **30.21** Job 10.3; 16.9,14; 19.6, 22 **30.22** Job 9.17; 27.21 **30.23** Job 9.22; 10.8; 3.19; 17.13 **30.24** Job 19.7 **30.25** Ps 35.13,14; Rom 12.15

[d] Cn: Heb *helps* [e] Gk: Heb *my garment is disfigured* [f] Heb *like* [g] Heb *ruin* [h] Cn: Meaning of Heb uncertain

26 But when I looked for good,
evil came;
and when I waited for light,
darkness came.
27 My inward parts are in
turmoil, and are never
still;
days of affliction come to
meet me.
28 I go about in sunless gloom;
I stand up in the assembly
and cry for help.
29 I am a brother of jackals,
and a companion of
ostriches.
30 My skin turns black and falls
from me,
and my bones burn with
heat.
31 My lyre is turned to
mourning,
and my pipe to the voice of
those who weep.

31 "I have made a covenant
with my eyes;
how then could I look
upon a virgin?
2 What would be my portion
from God above,
and my heritage from the
Almighty[i] on high?
3 Does not calamity befall the
unrighteous,
and disaster the workers of
iniquity?
4 Does he not see my ways,
and number all my steps?

5 "If I have walked with
falsehood,
and my foot has hurried to
deceit—
6 let me be weighed in a just
balance,
and let God know my
integrity!—
7 if my step has turned aside
from the way,
and my heart has followed
my eyes,
and if any spot has clung
to my hands;
8 then let me sow, and another
eat;
and let what grows for me
be rooted out.

9 "If my heart has been
enticed by a woman,
and I have lain in wait at
my neighbor's door;
10 then let my wife grind for
another,
and let other men kneel
over her.
11 For that would be a heinous
crime;
that would be a criminal
offense;
12 for that would be a fire
consuming down to
Abaddon,
and it would burn to the
root all my harvest.

13 "If I have rejected the cause
of my male or female
slaves,
when they brought a
complaint against me;
14 what then shall I do when
God rises up?
When he makes inquiry,
what shall I answer
him?
15 Did not he who made me in
the womb make them?
And did not one fashion us
in the womb?

16 "If I have withheld anything
that the poor desired,
or have caused the eyes of
the widow to fail,
17 or have eaten my morsel
alone,
and the orphan has not
eaten from it—
18 for from my youth I reared
the orphan[j] like a
father,
and from my mother's
womb I guided the
widow[k]—
19 if I have seen anyone perish
for lack of clothing,
or a poor person without
covering,
20 whose loins have not blessed
me,

30.26 Job 3.25,26; Jer 8.15; Job 19.8
30.28 Ps 38.6; 42.9; 43.2; Job 19.7
30.29 Mic 1.8
30.30 Ps 119.83; Lam 4.8; Ps 102.3
30.31 Ps 107.1,2
31.1 Mt 5.28
31.2 Job 20.29
31.3 Job 21.30; 34.22
31.4 2 Chr 16.9; Prov 5.21
31.5 Mic 2.11
31.6 Job 6.2,3; 27.5,6
31.7 Job 23.11; 9.30
31.8 Lev 26.16; Job 20.18
31.9 Job 24.15
31.10 Jer 8.10
31.11 Gen 38.24; Deut 22.22-24
31.12 Job 15.30; 26.6; 20.28
31.13 Deut 24.14, 15
31.15 Mal 2.10
31.16 Job 20.19; 22.7,9
31.17 Job 22.7; 29.12
31.19 Job 22.6; 29.13
31.20 Deut 31.20

[i] Traditional rendering of Heb *Shaddai*
[j] Heb *him* [k] Heb *her*

and who was not warmed
with the fleece of my
sheep;
21 if I have raised my hand
against the orphan,
because I saw I had
supporters at the gate;
22 then let my shoulder blade
fall from my shoulder,
and let my arm be broken
from its socket.
23 For I was in terror of
calamity from God,
and I could not have faced
his majesty.

24 "If I have made gold my
trust,
or called fine gold my
confidence;
25 if I have rejoiced because my
wealth was great,
or because my hand had
gotten much;
26 if I have looked at the sun[l]
when it shone,
or the moon moving in
splendor,
27 and my heart has been
secretly enticed,
and my mouth has kissed
my hand;
28 this also would be an
iniquity to be punished
by the judges,
for I should have been false
to God above.

29 "If I have rejoiced at the ruin
of those who hated me,
or exulted when evil
overtook them—
30 I have not let my mouth sin
by asking for their lives
with a curse—
31 if those of my tent ever said,
'O that we might be sated
with his flesh!'[m]—
32 the stranger has not lodged
in the street;
I have opened my doors to
the traveler—
33 if I have concealed my
transgressions as others
do,[n]
by hiding my iniquity in my
bosom,

31.21 Job 22.9
31.22 Job 38.15
31.23 v. 3; Job 13.11
31.24 Mk 10.24
31.25 Ps 62.10
31.26 Deut 4.19; Ezek 8.16
31.28 v. 11
31.29 Prov 17.5
31.30 Mt 5.44
31.31 Job 22.7
31.32 Gen 19.2,3; Rom 12.13
31.33 Gen 3.8; Prov 28.13
31.34 Ex 23.2
31.35 Job 19.7; 30.20,24,28; 35.14
31.37 v. 4; Job 1.3; 29.25
31.38 Gen 4.10,11
31.39 Lev 19.13; 1 Kings 21.19; Jas 5.4
31.40 Gen 3.18
32.1 Job 33.9
32.2 Gen 22.21; Jer 25.23
32.3 Job 11.6; 15.16; 22.5

34 because I stood in great fear
of the multitude,
and the contempt of
families terrified me,
so that I kept silence, and
did not go out of
doors—
35 Oh, that I had one to hear
me!
(Here is my signature! let
the Almighty[o] answer
me!)
Oh, that I had the
indictment written by
my adversary!
36 Surely I would carry it on my
shoulder;
I would bind it on me like
a crown;
37 I would give him an account
of all my steps;
like a prince I would
approach him.

38 "If my land has cried out
against me,
and its furrows have wept
together;
39 if I have eaten its yield
without payment,
and caused the death of its
owners;
40 let thorns grow instead of
wheat,
and foul weeds instead of
barley."

The words of Job are ended.

Elihu Rebukes Job's Friends

32 So these three men ceased
to answer Job, because he
was righteous in his own eyes.
2 Then Elihu son of Barachel the
Buzite, of the family of Ram, became angry. He was angry at Job
because he justified himself rather
than God; 3 he was angry also at
Job's three friends because they
had found no answer, though they
had declared Job to be in the
wrong.[p] 4 Now Elihu had waited to

[l] Heb *the light* [m] Meaning of Heb uncertain [n] Or *as Adam did*
[o] Traditional rendering of Heb *Shaddai*
[p] Another ancient tradition reads *answer, and had put God in the wrong*

speak to Job, because they were
older than he. 5 But when Elihu saw
that there was no answer in the
mouths of these three men, he became angry.
6 Elihu son of Barachel the Buzite answered:

"I am young in years,
and you are aged;
therefore I was timid and afraid
to declare my opinion to you.
7 I said, 'Let days speak,
and many years teach wisdom.'
8 But truly it is the spirit in a mortal,
the breath of the Almighty,[q] that makes for understanding.
9 It is not the old[r] that are wise,
nor the aged that understand what is right.
10 Therefore I say, 'Listen to me;
let me also declare my opinion.'

11 "See, I waited for your words,
I listened for your wise sayings,
while you searched out what to say.
12 I gave you my attention,
but there was in fact no one that confuted Job,
no one among you that answered his words.
13 Yet do not say, 'We have found wisdom;
God may vanquish him, not a human.'
14 He has not directed his words against me,
and I will not answer him with your speeches.

15 "They are dismayed, they answer no more;
they have not a word to say.
16 And am I to wait, because they do not speak,
because they stand there, and answer no more?
17 I also will give my answer;
I also will declare my opinion.
18 For I am full of words;
the spirit within me constrains me.
19 My heart is indeed like wine that has no vent;
like new wineskins, it is ready to burst.
20 I must speak, so that I may find relief;
I must open my lips and answer.
21 I will not show partiality to any person
or use flattery toward anyone.
22 For I do not know how to flatter—
or my Maker would soon put an end to me!

Elihu Rebukes Job

33 "But now, hear my speech, O Job,
and listen to all my words.
2 See, I open my mouth;
the tongue in my mouth speaks.
3 My words declare the uprightness of my heart,
and what my lips know they speak sincerely.
4 The spirit of God has made me,
and the breath of the Almighty[q] gives me life.
5 Answer me, if you can;
set your words in order before me; take your stand.
6 See, before God I am as you are;
I too was formed from a piece of clay.
7 No fear of me need terrify you;
my pressure will not be heavy on you.

32.6 Job 15.10 **32.8** Job 27.3; 33.4; 1 Kings 3.12; Prov 2.6 **32.9** 1 Cor 1.26 **32.11** Job 5.27 **32.13** Jer 9.23 **32.18** Acts 18.5 **32.19** Acts 9.17 **32.21** Lev 19.15; Mt 22.16 **32.22** 1 Thes 2.5 **33.3** Job 6.28; 27.4; 36.4 **33.4** Gen 2.7; Job 27.3 **33.5** v. 32; Job 13.18 **33.7** Job 9.34; 13.21; 2 Cor 2.5

q Traditional rendering of Heb *Shaddai*
r Gk Syr Vg: Heb *many*

8 "Surely, you have spoken in
my hearing,
and I have heard the sound
of your words.
9 You say, 'I am clean, without
transgression;
I am pure, and there is no
iniquity in me.
10 Look, he finds occasions
against me,
he counts me as his
enemy;
11 he puts my feet in the
stocks,
and watches all my paths.'

12 "But in this you are not
right. I will answer you:
God is greater than any
mortal.
13 Why do you contend against
him,
saying, 'He will answer
none of my[s] words'?
14 For God speaks in one way,
and in two, though people
do not perceive it.
15 In a dream, in a vision of the
night,
when deep sleep falls on
mortals,
while they slumber on their
beds,
16 then he opens their ears,
and terrifies them with
warnings,
17 that he may turn them aside
from their deeds,
and keep them from pride,
18 to spare their souls from the
Pit,
their lives from traversing
the River.
19 They are also chastened with
pain upon their beds,
and with continual strife in
their bones,
20 so that their lives loathe
bread,
and their appetites dainty
food.
21 Their flesh is so wasted away
that it cannot be seen;
and their bones, once
invisible, now stick out.
22 Their souls draw near the
Pit,
and their lives to those
who bring death.
23 Then, if there should be for
one of them an angel,
a mediator, one of a
thousand,
one who declares a person
upright,
24 and he is gracious to that
person, and says,
'Deliver him from going
down into the Pit;
I have found a ransom;
25 let his flesh become fresh
with youth;
let him return to the days
of his youthful vigor.'
26 Then he prays to God, and is
accepted by him,
he comes into his presence
with joy,
and God[t] repays him for his
righteousness.
27 That person sings to others
and says,
'I sinned, and perverted what
was right,
and it was not paid back to
me.
28 He has redeemed my soul
from going down to the
Pit,
and my life shall see the
light.'

29 "God indeed does all these
things,
twice, three times, with
mortals,
30 to bring back their souls
from the Pit,
so that they may see the
light of life.[u]
31 Pay heed, Job, listen to me;
be silent, and I will speak.
32 If you have anything to say,
answer me;
speak, for I desire to justify
you.
33 If not, listen to me;
be silent, and I will teach
you wisdom."

33.9 Job 10.7; 13.23; 16.17
33.10 Job 13.24
33.11 Job 13.27; 14.16
33.13 Job 15.25; Isa 45.9
33.14 Ps 62.11
33.15 Num 12.6; Job 4.13
33.16 Job 36.10, 15
33.18 vv. 24,28,30
33.19 Job 30.17
33.20 Ps 107.18
33.21 Job 16.8; 19.20
33.22 Ps 88.3
33.23 Mic 6.8
33.24 Isa 38.17
33.25 2 Kings 5.14
33.26 Job 22.27; 34.28; 22.26; Ps 51.12
33.27 Lk 15.21; Rom 6.21
33.28 Ps 103.14; Job 22.28
33.29 Eph 1.11; 1 Cor 12.6; Phil 2.13
33.30 Ps 56.13
33.33 Ps 34.11

[s] Compare Gk: Heb *his* [t] Heb *he*
[u] Syr: Heb *to be lighted with the light of life*

Elihu Proclaims God's Justice

34 Then Elihu continued and said:
2 "Hear my words, you wise men,
and give ear to me, you who know;
3 for the ear tests words
as the palate tastes food.
4 Let us choose what is right;
let us determine among ourselves what is good.
5 For Job has said, 'I am innocent,
and God has taken away my right;
6 in spite of being right I am counted a liar;
my wound is incurable, though I am without transgression.'
7 Who is there like Job,
who drinks up scoffing like water,
8 who goes in company with evildoers
and walks with the wicked?
9 For he has said, 'It profits one nothing
to take delight in God.'

10 "Therefore, hear me, you who have sense,
far be it from God that he should do wickedness,
and from the Almighty[v] that he should do wrong.
11 For according to their deeds he will repay them,
and according to their ways he will make it befall them.
12 Of a truth, God will not do wickedly,
and the Almighty[v] will not pervert justice.
13 Who gave him charge over the earth
and who laid on him[w] the whole world?
14 If he should take back his spirit[x] to himself,
and gather to himself his breath,
15 all flesh would perish together,
and all mortals return to dust.

16 "If you have understanding, hear this;
listen to what I say.
17 Shall one who hates justice govern?
Will you condemn one who is righteous and mighty,
18 who says to a king, 'You scoundrel!'
and to princes, 'You wicked men!';
19 who shows no partiality to nobles,
nor regards the rich more than the poor,
for they are all the work of his hands?
20 In a moment they die;
at midnight the people are shaken and pass away,
and the mighty are taken away by no human hand.

21 "For his eyes are upon the ways of mortals,
and he sees all their steps.
22 There is no gloom or deep darkness
where evildoers may hide themselves.
23 For he has not appointed a time[y] for anyone
to go before God in judgment.
24 He shatters the mighty without investigation,
and sets others in their place.
25 Thus, knowing their works,
he overturns them in the night, and they are crushed.
26 He strikes them for their wickedness
while others look on,
27 because they turned aside from following him,

34.3 Job 12.11 **34.4** 1 Thes 5.21 **34.5** Job 33.9; 27.2 **34.6** Jer 15.18; 30.12 **34.7** Job 15.16 **34.8** Ps 50.18 **34.9** Job 21.15; 35.3 **34.10** Job 8.3 **34.11** Ps 62.12; Mt 16.27; Rom 2.6; 2 Cor 5.10; Rev 22.12 **34.12** Job 8.3 **34.13** Job 38.5,6 **34.14** Ps 104.29 **34.15** Isa 40.6,7; Gen 3.19 **34.17** 2 Sam 23.3 **34.18** Ex 22.28 **34.19** Deut 10.17; Gal 2.6; Job 31.15 **34.20** Ex 12.29; Job 12.19 **34.21** Job 31.4 **34.22** Ps 139.12; Am 9.2,3 **34.24** Dan 2.21 **34.25** vv. 11,20 **34.26** Job 26.12 **34.27** 1 Sam 15.11; Ps 28.5; Isa 5.12

[v] Traditional rendering of Heb *Shaddai* [w] Heb lacks *on him* [x] Heb *his heart his spirit* [y] Cn: Heb *yet*

and had no regard for any
of his ways,
28 so that they caused the cry
of the poor to come to
him,
and he heard the cry of the
afflicted—
29 When he is quiet, who can
condemn?
When he hides his face,
who can behold him,
whether it be a nation or
an individual?—
30 so that the godless should
not reign,
or those who ensnare the
people.

31 "For has anyone said to God,
'I have endured
punishment; I will not
offend any more;
32 teach me what I do not see;
if I have done iniquity, I
will do it no more'?
33 Will he then pay back to suit
you,
because you reject it?
For you must choose, and
not I;
therefore declare what you
know.[z]
34 Those who have sense will
say to me,
and the wise who hear me
will say,
35 'Job speaks without
knowledge,
his words are without
insight.'
36 Would that Job were tried to
the limit,
because his answers are
those of the wicked.
37 For he adds rebellion to his
sin;
he claps his hands among
us,
and multiplies his words
against God."

Elihu Condemns Self-Righteousness

35 Elihu continued and said:
2 "Do you think this to
be just?
You say, 'I am in the right
before God.'
3 If you ask, 'What advantage
have I?
How am I better off than if
I had sinned?'
4 I will answer you
and your friends with you.
5 Look at the heavens and see;
observe the clouds, which
are higher than you.
6 If you have sinned, what do
you accomplish against
him?
And if your transgressions
are multiplied, what do
you do to him?
7 If you are righteous, what do
you give to him;
or what does he receive
from your hand?
8 Your wickedness affects
others like you,
and your righteousness,
other human beings.

9 "Because of the multitude of
oppressions people cry
out;
they call for help because
of the arm of the
mighty.
10 But no one says, 'Where is
God my Maker,
who gives strength in the
night,
11 who teaches us more than
the animals of the
earth,
and makes us wiser than
the birds of the air?'
12 There they cry out, but he
does not answer,
because of the pride of
evildoers.
13 Surely God does not hear an
empty cry,
nor does the Almighty[a]
regard it.
14 How much less when you say
that you do not see
him,

34.28 Job 35.9; Jas 5.4; Ex 22.23
34.29 1 Chr 22.9
34.30 v. 17
34.32 Job 35.11; Ps 25.4
34.35 Job 35.16
34.36 Job 23.10; 22.15
35.2 Job 32.2
35.3 Job 34.9; 9.30,31
35.5 Job 22.12
35.6 Prov 8.36; Jer 7.19
35.7 Job 22.2,3; Prov 9.12; Lk 17.10
35.9 Ex 2.23; Job 12.19
35.10 Job 27.10; Ps 42.8; 149.5; Acts 16.25
35.11 Ps 94.12; Lk 12.24
35.12 Prov 1.28
35.13 Job 27.9; Prov 15.29; Isa 1.15; Jer 11.11
35.14 Ps 37.5,6

[z] Meaning of Heb of verses 29-33 uncertain
[a] Traditional rendering of Heb *Shaddai*

that the case is before him,
and you are waiting for
him!
15 And now, because his anger
does not punish,
and he does not greatly
heed transgression,[b]
16 Job opens his mouth in
empty talk,
he multiplies words
without knowledge."

Elihu Exalts God's Goodness

36 Elihu continued and said:
2 "Bear with me a little,
and I will show you,
for I have yet something to
say on God's behalf.
3 I will bring my knowledge
from far away,
and ascribe righteousness
to my Maker.
4 For truly my words are not
false;
one who is perfect in
knowledge is with you.

5 "Surely God is mighty and
does not despise any;
he is mighty in strength of
understanding.
6 He does not keep the wicked
alive,
but gives the afflicted their
right.
7 He does not withdraw his
eyes from the righteous,
but with kings on the
throne
he sets them forever, and
they are exalted.
8 And if they are bound in
fetters
and caught in the cords of
affliction,
9 then he declares to them
their work
and their transgressions,
that they are behaving
arrogantly.
10 He opens their ears to
instruction,
and commands that they
return from iniquity.
11 If they listen, and serve him,
they complete their days in
prosperity,
and their years in
pleasantness.
12 But if they do not listen,
they shall perish by the
sword,
and die without knowledge.

13 "The godless in heart cherish
anger;
they do not cry for help
when he binds them.
14 They die in their youth,
and their life ends in
shame.[c]
15 He delivers the afflicted by
their affliction,
and opens their ear by
adversity.
16 He also allured you out of
distress
into a broad place where
there was no constraint,
and what was set on your
table was full of
fatness.

17 "But you are obsessed with
the case of the wicked;
judgment and justice seize
you.
18 Beware that wrath does not
entice you into scoffing,
and do not let the
greatness of the ransom
turn you aside.
19 Will your cry avail to keep
you from distress,
or will all the force of your
strength?
20 Do not long for the night,
when peoples are cut off in
their place.
21 Beware! Do not turn to
iniquity;
because of that you have
been tried by affliction.
22 See, God is exalted in his
power;
who is a teacher like
him?
23 Who has prescribed for him
his way,

35.15 Eccl 8.11 **35.16** Job 34.37, 35 **36.3** Job 8.3; 37.23 **36.4** Job 33.3; 37.16 **36.5** Ps 22.24; Job 12.13 **36.6** Job 8.22; 5.15 **36.7** Ps 33.18; 113.8 **36.8** Ps 107.10; vv. 15,21 **36.9** Job 15.25 **36.10** Job 33.16; 2 Kings 17.13 **36.11** Isa 1.19,20 **36.12** Job 15.22; 4.21 **36.13** Rom 2.5 **36.14** Job 15.32; 22.16 **36.15** Ps 119.67; v. 10 **36.16** Hos 2.14; Ps 118.5; 23.5 **36.18** Job 34.33; Jon 4.4,9; Job 33.24 **36.20** Job 34.20, 25 **36.21** Ps 66.18; Heb 11.25 **36.22** Isa 40.13; 1 Cor 2.16 **36.23** Job 34.13; Job 8.3

[b] Theodotion Symmachus Compare Vg: Meaning of Heb uncertain [c] Heb *ends among the temple prostitutes*

or who can say, 'You have
done wrong'?

Elihu Proclaims God's Majesty

24 "Remember to extol his
work,
of which mortals have
sung.
25 All people have looked on it;
everyone watches it from
far away.
26 Surely God is great, and we
do not know him;
the number of his years is
unsearchable.
27 For he draws up the drops of
water;
he distills[d] his mist in
rain,
28 which the skies pour down
and drop upon mortals
abundantly.
29 Can anyone understand the
spreading of the clouds,
the thunderings of his
pavilion?
30 See, he scatters his lightning
around him
and covers the roots of the
sea.
31 For by these he governs
peoples;
he gives food in
abundance.
32 He covers his hands with the
lightning,
and commands it to strike
the mark.
33 Its crashing[e] tells about
him;
he is jealous[e] with anger
against iniquity.

37 "At this also my heart
trembles,
and leaps out of its place.
2 Listen, listen to the thunder
of his voice
and the rumbling that
comes from his mouth.
3 Under the whole heaven he
lets it loose,
and his lightning to the
corners of the earth.
4 After it his voice roars;
he thunders with his
majestic voice
and he does not restrain
the lightnings[f] when
his voice is heard.
5 God thunders wondrously
with his voice;
he does great things that
we cannot comprehend.
6 For to the snow he says,
'Fall on the earth';
and the shower of rain, his
heavy shower of rain,
7 serves as a sign on
everyone's hand,
so that all whom he has
made may know it.[g]
8 Then the animals go into
their lairs
and remain in their dens.
9 From its chamber comes the
whirlwind,
and cold from the
scattering winds.
10 By the breath of God ice is
given,
and the broad waters are
frozen fast.
11 He loads the thick cloud
with moisture;
the clouds scatter his
lightning.
12 They turn round and round
by his guidance,
to accomplish all that he
commands them
on the face of the
habitable world.
13 Whether for correction, or for
his land,
or for love, he causes it to
happen.

14 "Hear this, O Job;
stop and consider the
wondrous works of God.
15 Do you know how God lays
his command upon
them,
and causes the lightning of
his cloud to shine?
16 Do you know the balancings
of the clouds,
the wondrous works of the
one whose knowledge is
perfect,

36.24 2 Sam 7.26; Ps 35.27; 59.16 **36.26** Ps 102.24 **36.27** Ps 147.8 **36.29** Job 37.11, 16; 26.14 **36.31** Job 37.13; Ps 136.25 **36.32** Job 37.15 **36.33** Job 37.2 **37.2** Job 36.33 **37.3** v. 12 **37.4** Ps 29.3
37.5 Job 5.9; 36.26 **37.6** Job 38.22; 36.27 **37.7** Job 12.14 **37.8** Ps 104.22 **37.9** Job 9.9; Ps 147.17 **37.10** Job 38.29; Ps 147.17 **37.11** Job 36.27, 29; v. 15 **37.12** Ps 148.8; Isa 14.21; 27.6; Prov 8.31 **37.13** Ex 9.18; 1 Sam 12.18; Job 38.26; 1 Kings 18.45 **37.14** Ps 111.2 **37.16** vv. 5,14,23; Job 36.4

[d] Cn: Heb *they distill* [e] Meaning of Heb uncertain [f] Heb *them* [g] Meaning of Heb of verse 7 uncertain

17 you whose garments are hot
when the earth is still
because of the south
wind?
18 Can you, like him, spread
out the skies,
hard as a molten mirror?
19 Teach us what we shall say
to him;
we cannot draw up our
case because of
darkness.
20 Should he be told that I
want to speak?
Did anyone ever wish to be
swallowed up?
21 Now, no one can look on the
light
when it is bright in the
skies,
when the wind has passed
and cleared them.
22 Out of the north comes
golden splendor;
around God is awesome
majesty.
23 The Almighty[h]—we cannot
find him;
he is great in power and
justice,
and abundant
righteousness he will
not violate.
24 Therefore mortals fear him;
he does not regard any who
are wise in their own
conceit."

The LORD Answers Job

38 Then the LORD answered
Job out of the whirlwind:
2 "Who is this that darkens
counsel by words
without knowledge?
3 Gird up your loins like a
man,
I will question you, and
you shall declare to me.

4 "Where were you when I laid
the foundation of the
earth?
Tell me, if you have
understanding.
5 Who determined its
measurements—surely
you know!
Or who stretched the line
upon it?
6 On what were its bases sunk,
or who laid its cornerstone
7 when the morning stars sang
together
and all the heavenly
beings[i] shouted for joy?

8 "Or who shut in the sea with
doors
when it burst out from the
womb?—
9 when I made the clouds its
garment,
and thick darkness its
swaddling band,
10 and prescribed bounds for it,
and set bars and doors,
11 and said, 'Thus far shall you
come, and no farther,
and here shall your proud
waves be stopped'?

12 "Have you commanded the
morning since your days
began,
and caused the dawn to
know its place,
13 so that it might take hold of
the skirts of the earth,
and the wicked be shaken
out of it?
14 It is changed like clay under
the seal,
and it is dyed[j] like a
garment.
15 Light is withheld from the
wicked,
and their uplifted arm is
broken.

16 "Have you entered into the
springs of the sea,
or walked in the recesses
of the deep?
17 Have the gates of death been
revealed to you,
or have you seen the gates
of deep darkness?

37.18 Job 9.8; Ps 104.2; Isa 44.24 **37.23** 1 Tim 6.16; Job 9.4; 8.3; Isa 63.9 **37.24** Mt 10.28; 11.25; 1 Cor 1.26 **38.1** Job 40.6 **38.2** Job 42.3; 35.16; 1 Tim 1.7 **38.3** Job 40.7 **38.4** Ps 104.5; Prov 8.29

38.6 Job 26.7 **38.7** Job 1.6 **38.8** Gen 1.9 **38.9** Prov 30.4 **38.10** Job 26.10 **38.11** Ps 89.9 **38.12** Ps 74.16 **38.13** Ps 104.35 **38.15** Job 18.5; Ps 10.15 **38.16** Ps 77.19 **38.17** Ps 9.13

[h] Traditional rendering of Heb *Shaddai*
[i] Heb *sons of God* [j] Cn: Heb *and they stand forth*

18 Have you comprehended the
expanse of the earth?
Declare, if you know all
this.

19 "Where is the way to the
dwelling of light,
and where is the place of
darkness,
20 that you may take it to its
territory
and that you may discern
the paths to its home?
21 Surely you know, for you
were born then,
and the number of your
days is great!

22 "Have you entered the
storehouses of the
snow,
or have you seen the
storehouses of the hail,
23 which I have reserved for the
time of trouble,
for the day of battle and
war?
24 What is the way to the place
where the light is
distributed,
or where the east wind is
scattered upon the
earth?

25 "Who has cut a channel for
the torrents of rain,
and a way for the
thunderbolt,
26 to bring rain on a land where
no one lives,
on the desert, which is
empty of human life,
27 to satisfy the waste and
desolate land,
and to make the ground
put forth grass?

28 "Has the rain a father,
or who has begotten the
drops of dew?
29 From whose womb did the
ice come forth,
and who has given birth to
the hoarfrost of heaven?
30 The waters become hard like
stone,
and the face of the deep is
frozen.

31 "Can you bind the chains of
the Pleiades,
or loose the cords of
Orion?
32 Can you lead forth the
Mazzaroth in their
season,
or can you guide the Bear
with its children?
33 Do you know the ordinances
of the heavens?
Can you establish their rule
on the earth?

34 "Can you lift up your voice
to the clouds,
so that a flood of waters
may cover you?
35 Can you send forth
lightnings, so that they
may go
and say to you, 'Here we
are'?
36 Who has put wisdom in the
inward parts,[k]
or given understanding to
the mind?[k]
37 Who has the wisdom to
number the clouds?
Or who can tilt the
waterskins of the
heavens,
38 when the dust runs into a
mass
and the clods cling
together?

39 "Can you hunt the prey for
the lion,
or satisfy the appetite of
the young lions,
40 when they crouch in their
dens,
or lie in wait in their
covert?
41 Who provides for the raven
its prey,
when its young ones cry to
God,
and wander about for lack
of food?

38.18 Job 28.24 **38.20** Job 26.10; 24.13 **38.21** Job 15.7 **38.22** Job 37.6 **38.23** Ex 9.18; Josh 10.11; Isa 30.30; Ezek 13.11, 13; Rev 16.21 **38.24** Job 26.10; 27.21 **38.25** Job 28.26 **38.26** Job 36.27; Ps 107.35 **38.27** Ps 104.13, 14 **38.28** Ps 147.8; Jer 14.22 **38.29** Ps 147.16, 17 **38.31** Job 9.9; Am 5.8 **38.33** Job 31.35 **38.34** v. 37; Job 22.11; 36.27,28 **38.35** Job 36.32; 37.3 **38.36** Job 32.8; Ps 51.6; Eccl 2.26; Job 32.8 **38.39** Ps 104.21 **38.40** Job 38.8; Ps 17.12 **38.41** Ps 147.9; Mt 6.26

[k] Meaning of Heb uncertain

39 "Do you know when the mountain goats give birth?
Do you observe the calving of the deer?
2 Can you number the months that they fulfill,
and do you know the time when they give birth,
3 when they crouch to give birth to their offspring,
and are delivered of their young?
4 Their young ones become strong, they grow up in the open;
they go forth, and do not return to them.

5 "Who has let the wild ass go free?
Who has loosed the bonds of the swift ass,
6 to which I have given the steppe for its home,
the salt land for its dwelling place?
7 It scorns the tumult of the city;
it does not hear the shouts of the driver.
8 It ranges the mountains as its pasture,
and it searches after every green thing.

9 "Is the wild ox willing to serve you?
Will it spend the night at your crib?
10 Can you tie it in the furrow with ropes,
or will it harrow the valleys after you?
11 Will you depend on it because its strength is great,
and will you hand over your labor to it?
12 Do you have faith in it that it will return,
and bring your grain to your threshing floor?[l]

13 "The ostrich's wings flap wildly,
though its pinions lack plumage.[m]
14 For it leaves its eggs to the earth,
and lets them be warmed on the ground,
15 forgetting that a foot may crush them,
and that a wild animal may trample them.
16 It deals cruelly with its young, as if they were not its own;
though its labor should be in vain, yet it has no fear;
17 because God has made it forget wisdom,
and given it no share in understanding.
18 When it spreads its plumes aloft,[m]
it laughs at the horse and its rider.

19 "Do you give the horse its might?
Do you clothe its neck with mane?
20 Do you make it leap like the locust?
Its majestic snorting is terrible.
21 It paws[n] violently, exults mightily;
it goes out to meet the weapons.
22 It laughs at fear, and is not dismayed;
it does not turn back from the sword.
23 Upon it rattle the quiver,
the flashing spear, and the javelin.
24 With fierceness and rage it swallows the ground;
it cannot stand still at the sound of the trumpet.
25 When the trumpet sounds, it says 'Aha!'
From a distance it smells the battle,

39.1 Ps 29.9 **39.3** 1 Sam 4.19 **39.5** Job 6.5; 11.12; 24.5 **39.6** Job 24.5; Jer 2.24; Hos 8.9; Ps 107.34 **39.9** Num 23.22; Deut 33.17 **39.16** Lam 4.3; v. 22 **39.17** Job 35.11 **39.19** Ps 147.10 **39.20** Joel 2.5; Jer 8.16 **39.21** Jer 8.6 **39.24** Jer 4.19; Ezek 7.14; Am 3.6 **39.25** Josh 6.5; Am 1.14; 2.2

[l] Heb *your grain and your threshing floor*
[m] Meaning of Heb uncertain
[n] Gk Syr Vg: Heb *they dig*

the thunder of the
captains, and the
shouting.

26 "Is it by your wisdom that
the hawk soars,
and spreads its wings
toward the south?
27 Is it at your command that
the eagle mounts up
and makes its nest on
high?
28 It lives on the rock and
makes its home
in the fastness of the rocky
crag.
29 From there it spies the prey;
its eyes see it from far
away.
30 Its young ones suck up
blood;
and where the slain are,
there it is."

40 And the LORD said to Job:
2 "Shall a faultfinder
contend with the
Almighty?[o]
Anyone who argues with
God must respond."

Job's Response to God

3 Then Job answered the LORD:
4 "See, I am of small account;
what shall I answer
you?
I lay my hand on my
mouth.
5 I have spoken once, and I
will not answer;
twice, but will proceed no
further."

God's Challenge to Job

6 Then the LORD answered Job
out of the whirlwind;
7 "Gird up your loins like a
man;
I will question you, and
you declare to me.
8 Will you even put me in the
wrong?
Will you condemn me that
you may be justified?
9 Have you an arm like God,
and can you thunder with a
voice like his?

39.27 Jer 46.16; Ob 4
39.30 Mt 24.28; Lk 17.37
40.1 Job 33.13; 13.3; 23.4; 31.35
40.4 Job 42.6; 29.9
40.5 Job 9.3,15
40.6 Job 38.1
40.7 Job 38.3; 42.4
40.8 Isa 14.27; Rom 3.4
40.9 2 Chr 32.8; Jer 17.5; Job 37.5
40.10 Ps 93.1; 104.1
40.11 Isa 42.25; 2.12; Dan 4.37
40.12 1 Sam 2.7; Isa 13.11; 63.3; Job 36.20
40.14 Ps 20.6; 60.5; 108.6
40.15 v. 19
40.19 Job 41.33; v. 15
40.20 Ps 104.26
40.22 Isa 44.4

10 "Deck yourself with majesty
and dignity;
clothe yourself with glory
and splendor.
11 Pour out the overflowings of
your anger,
and look on all who are
proud, and abase them.
12 Look on all who are proud,
and bring them low;
tread down the wicked
where they stand.
13 Hide them all in the dust
together;
bind their faces in the
world below.[p]
14 Then I will also acknowledge
to you
that your own right hand
can give you victory.

15 "Look at Behemoth,
which I made just as I
made you;
it eats grass like an ox.
16 Its strength is in its loins,
and its power in the
muscles of its belly.
17 It makes its tail stiff like a
cedar;
the sinews of its thighs are
knit together.
18 Its bones are tubes of
bronze,
its limbs like bars of iron.

19 "It is the first of the great
acts of God—
only its Maker can
approach it with the
sword.
20 For the mountains yield food
for it
where all the wild animals
play.
21 Under the lotus plants it lies,
in the covert of the reeds
and in the marsh.
22 The lotus trees cover it for
shade;
the willows of the wadi
surround it.
23 Even if the river is turbulent,
it is not frightened;

o Traditional rendering of Heb *Shaddai*
p Heb *the hidden place*

it is confident though
Jordan rushes against
its mouth.
24 Can one take it with hooks[q]
or pierce its nose with a
snare?

41 [r] "Can you draw out
Leviathan[s] with a
fishhook,
or press down its tongue
with a cord?
2 Can you put a rope in its
nose,
or pierce its jaw with a
hook?
3 Will it make many
supplications to you?
Will it speak soft words to
you?
4 Will it make a covenant with
you
to be taken as your servant
forever?
5 Will you play with it as with
a bird,
or will you put it on leash
for your girls?
6 Will traders bargain over it?
Will they divide it up
among the merchants?
7 Can you fill its skin with
harpoons,
or its head with fishing
spears?
8 Lay hands on it;
think of the battle; you will
not do it again!
9 [t]Any hope of capturing it[u]
will be disappointed;
were not even the gods[v]
overwhelmed at the
sight of it?
10 No one is so fierce as to dare
to stir it up.
Who can stand before it?[w]
11 Who can confront it[w] and be
safe?[x]
—under the whole heaven,
who?[y]

12 "I will not keep silence
concerning its limbs,
or its mighty strength, or
its splendid frame.
13 Who can strip off its outer
garment?
Who can penetrate its
double coat of mail?[z]
14 Who can open the doors of
its face?
There is terror all around
its teeth.
15 Its back[a] is made of shields
in rows,
shut up closely as with a
seal.
16 One is so near to another
that no air can come
between them.
17 They are joined one to
another;
they clasp each other and
cannot be separated.
18 Its sneezes flash forth light,
and its eyes are like the
eyelids of the dawn.
19 From its mouth go flaming
torches;
sparks of fire leap out.
20 Out of its nostrils comes
smoke,
as from a boiling pot and
burning rushes.
21 Its breath kindles coals,
and a flame comes out of
its mouth.
22 In its neck abides strength,
and terror dances before it.
23 The folds of its flesh cling
together;
it is firmly cast and
immovable.
24 Its heart is as hard as stone,
as hard as the lower
millstone.
25 When it raises itself up the
gods are afraid;
at the crashing they are
beside themselves.
26 Though the sword reaches it,
it does not avail,
nor does the spear, the
dart, or the javelin.
27 It counts iron as straw,
and bronze as rotten wood.
28 The arrow cannot make it
flee;

40.24 Prov 1.17
41.1 Ps 104.26; Isa 27.1
41.2 Isa 37.29
41.10 Job 3.8
41.11 Rom 11.35; Ex 19.5; Deut 10.14; Ps 24.1; 50.12; 1 Cor 10.26
41.18 Job 3.9

[q] Cn: Heb *in his eyes* [r] Ch 40.25 in Heb
[s] Or *the crocodile* [t] Ch 41.1 in Heb
[u] Heb *of it* [v] Cn Compare Symmachus Syr: Heb *one is* [w] Heb *me* [x] Gk: Heb *that I shall repay* [y] Heb *to me*
[z] Gk: Heb *bridle* [a] Cn Compare Gk Vg: Heb *pride*

slingstones, for it, are
turned to chaff.
29 Clubs are counted as chaff;
it laughs at the rattle of
javelins.
30 Its underparts are like sharp
potsherds;
it spreads itself like a
threshing sledge on the
mire.
31 It makes the deep boil like a
pot;
it makes the sea like a pot
of ointment.
32 It leaves a shining wake
behind it;
one would think the deep
to be white-haired.
33 On earth it has no equal,
a creature without fear.
34 It surveys everything that is
lofty;
it is king over all that are
proud."

Job Is Humbled and Satisfied

42 Then Job answered the
LORD:
2 "I know that you can do all
things,
and that no purpose of
yours can be thwarted.
3 'Who is this that hides
counsel without
knowledge?'
Therefore I have uttered
what I did not
understand,
things too wonderful for
me, which I did not
know.
4 'Hear, and I will speak;
I will question you, and
you declare to me.'
5 I had heard of you by the
hearing of the ear,
but now my eye sees you;
6 therefore I despise myself,
and repent in dust and
ashes."

Job's Friends Are Humiliated

7 After the LORD had spoken
these words to Job, the LORD said to
Eliphaz the Temanite: "My wrath is
kindled against you and against
your two friends; for you have not
spoken of me what is right, as my
servant Job has. 8 Now therefore
take seven bulls and seven rams,
and go to my servant Job, and offer
up for yourselves a burnt offering;
and my servant Job shall pray for
you, for I will accept his prayer not
to deal with you according to your
folly; for you have not spoken of me
what is right, as my servant Job has
done." 9 So Eliphaz the Temanite
and Bildad the Shuhite and Zophar
the Naamathite went and did what
the LORD had told them; and the
LORD accepted Job's prayer.

Job's Fortunes Are Restored Twofold

10 And the LORD restored the
fortunes of Job when he had prayed
for his friends; and the LORD gave
Job twice as much as he had before. 11 Then there came to him all
his brothers and sisters and all who
had known him before, and they
ate bread with him in his house;
they showed him sympathy and
comforted him for all the evil that
the LORD had brought upon him;
and each of them gave him a piece
of money[b] and a gold ring. 12 The
LORD blessed the latter days of Job
more than his beginning; and he
had fourteen thousand sheep, six
thousand camels, a thousand yoke
of oxen, and a thousand donkeys.
13 He also had seven sons and three
daughters. 14 He named the first Je-
mimah, the second Keziah, and the
third Keren-happuch. 15 In all the
land there were no women so beautiful as Job's daughters; and their
father gave them an inheritance
along with their brothers. 16 After
this Job lived one hundred and forty years, and saw his children, and
his children's children, four generations. 17 And Job died, old and full
of days.

41.33 Job 40.19
42.2 Gen 18.14; Mt 19.26; Mk 10.27; Lk 18.27; 2 Chr 20.6; Isa 14.27
42.3 Job 38.2; Ps 40.5; 131.1; 139.6
42.4 Job 38.3; 40.7
42.5 Job 26.14; Judg 13.22; Isa 6.5
42.6 Ezra 9.6; Job 40.4
42.7 Job 32.3; vv. 1-6; 40.3-5
42.8 Num 23.1; Job 1.5; Jas 5.15,16
42.10 Ps 14.7; 126.1
42.11 Job 19.13
42.12 Job 1.10; 8.7; 1.3
42.13 Job 1.2
42.16 Job 5.26; Prov 3.16
42.17 Gen 25.8

[b] Heb *a qesitah*

The Psalms

Title and Background

The names "Psalms" and "Psalter" come from the Septuagint (the Greek translation of the Old Testament). Both originally referred to stringed instruments (e.g., harp, lyre, lute), then to songs sung with their accompaniment. The traditional Hebrew title means "praises," even though many of the psalms are prayers.

Author and Date of Writing

Of the 150 Psalms, 100 of them are thought to be written by the following authors: David–73; Asaph–12; Sons of Korah–10; Solomon–2; Moses–1; Heman the Ezrahite–1; and Ethan the Ezrahite–1. The rest of the Psalms have no recorded author.

The final collection and arrangement of the Psalter was the work of postexilic temple personnel, completed probably in the third century B.C. By the first century A.D. it could be referred to as the "Book of Psalms" (Lk 20.42; Ac 1.20).

Theme and Message

For the most part, the Psalter is a book of prayer and praise, not a book of doctrine. The psalmists pour their hearts out to God in prayer; they go on to praise him and profess their faith and trust in him. The core teaching of the Psalter is the conviction that the gravitational center not only of life, but of all history and the whole creation, is God. He is the great King over all, and the One to whom all things are subject.

Outline

Book I: Psalms 1-41
Book II: Psalms 42-72
Book III: Psalms 73-89
Book IV: Psalms 90-106
Book V: Psalms 107-150

BOOK I

(Psalms 1–41)

Psalm 1

The Two Ways

1 Happy are those
who do not follow the
advice of the wicked,
or take the path that sinners
tread,
or sit in the seat of
scoffers;
2 but their delight is in the law
of the LORD,
and on his law they
meditate day and night.
3 They are like trees
planted by streams of
water,
which yield their fruit in its
season,
and their leaves do not
wither.
In all that they do, they
prosper.

4 The wicked are not so,
but are like chaff that the
wind drives away.
5 Therefore the wicked will not
stand in the judgment,
nor sinners in the
congregation of the
righteous;

1.1 Prov 4.14; Job 21.16; Ps 17.4; 26.5; Jer 15.17
1.2 Ps 119.35; Josh 1.8; Ps 119.1
1.3 Jer 17.8; Ezek 47.12; Gen 39.3; Ps 128.2
1.4 Job 21.18; Isa 17.13
1.5 Ps 5.5; 9.7; 8.16; 111.1; 149.1

6 for the LORD watches over the
way of the righteous,
but the way of the wicked
will perish.

Psalm 2

God's Promise to His Anointed

1 Why do the nations conspire,
and the peoples plot in
vain?
2 The kings of the earth set
themselves,
and the rulers take counsel
together,
against the LORD and his
anointed, saying,
3 "Let us burst their bonds
asunder,
and cast their cords from
us."

4 He who sits in the heavens
laughs;
the LORD has them in
derision.
5 Then he will speak to them
in his wrath,
and terrify them in his fury,
saying,
6 "I have set my king on Zion,
my holy hill."

7 I will tell of the decree of the
LORD:
He said to me, "You are my
son;
today I have begotten
you.
8 Ask of me, and I will make
the nations your
heritage,
and the ends of the earth
your possession.
9 You shall break them with a
rod of iron,
and dash them in pieces
like a potter's vessel."

10 Now therefore, O kings, be
wise;
be warned, O rulers of the
earth.
11 Serve the LORD with fear,
with trembling 12 kiss his
feet,[a]
or he will be angry, and you
will perish in the way;
for his wrath is quickly
kindled.

Happy are all who take
refuge in him.

Psalm 3

Trust in God under Adversity

A Psalm of David, when he fled
from his son Absalom.

1 O LORD, how many are my
foes!
Many are rising against
me;
2 many are saying to me,
"There is no help for you[b]
in God." *Selah*

3 But you, O LORD, are a shield
around me,
my glory, and the one who
lifts up my head.
4 I cry aloud to the LORD,
and he answers me from
his holy hill. *Selah*

5 I lie down and sleep;
I wake again, for the LORD
sustains me.
6 I am not afraid of ten
thousands of people
who have set themselves
against me all around.

7 Rise up, O LORD!
Deliver me, O my God!
For you strike all my
enemies on the cheek;
you break the teeth of the
wicked.

8 Deliverance belongs to the
LORD;
may your blessing be on
your people! *Selah*

1.6 Ps 37.18; 2 Tim 2.19; Ps 9.3-6
2.1ff Acts 4.25; Ps 21.11
2.2 Ps 48.4-6; 74.18,23; Jn 1.41
2.3 Jer 5.5
2.4 Ps 59.8; 37.13; Prov 1.26
2.5 Ps 21.8,9; 78.49,50
2.6 Ps 3.4
2.7 Acts 13.33; Heb 1.5
2.8 Ps 22.27
2.9 Ps 89.23; Rev 2.27; 12.5
2.11 Heb 12.28; Ps 119.119, 120
2.12 Jn 5.23; Rev 6.16; Ps 34.8; Rom 9.33
3.1 2 Sam 15.12
3.2 Ps 71.11
3.3 Ps 28.7; 27.6
3.4 Ps 34.4; 99.9
3.5 Lev 26.6; Ps 139.18
3.6 Ps 27.3
3.7 Ps 7.6; 6.4; Job 16.10; Ps 58.6
3.8 Isa 43.11; Jer 3.23; Num 6.23-27

[a] Cn: Meaning of Heb of verses 11b and 12a is uncertain [b] Syr: Heb *him*

Psalm 4

Confident Plea for Deliverance from Enemies

To the leader:
with stringed instruments.
A Psalm of David.

1 Answer me when I call,
O God of my right!
You gave me room when I
was in distress.
Be gracious to me, and
hear my prayer.

2 How long, you people, shall
my honor suffer
shame?
How long will you love vain
words, and seek after
lies? *Selah*
3 But know that the LORD has
set apart the faithful for
himself;
the LORD hears when I call
to him.

4 When you are disturbed,[c] do
not sin;
ponder it on your beds,
and be silent. *Selah*
5 Offer right sacrifices,
and put your trust in the
LORD.

6 There are many who say,
"O that we might see
some good!
Let the light of your face
shine on us, O LORD!"
7 You have put gladness in my
heart
more than when their grain
and wine abound.

8 I will both lie down and
sleep in peace;
for you alone, O LORD,
make me lie down in
safety.

4.1 Ps 27.7; 18.6; 24.5; 18.18; 25.16; 17.6
4.2 Ps 31.6,18
4.3 Ps 31.23; 6.8,9
4.4 Ps 33.8; Eph 4.26; Ps 77.6
4.5 Deut 33.19; Ps 50.14; 37.3
4.6 Num 6.26
4.7 Acts 14.17; Isa 9.3
4.8 Ps 3.5; Lev 25.18
5.1 Ps 54.2; 19.14
5.2 Ps 3.4; 84.3
5.3 Ps 88.13; Hab 2.1
5.4 Ps 11.5; 92.15
5.5 Ps 73.3; 1.5; 11.5
5.6 Rev 21.8; Ps 55.23
5.7 Ps 69.13; 28.2
5.8 Ps 27.11; 31.1
5.9 Deut 32.20; Lk 11.44; Rom 3.13; Ps 12.2
5.10 Ps 9.16; Lam 1.5; Ps 107.10, 11

Psalm 5

Trust in God for Deliverance from Enemies

To the leader: for the flutes. A
Psalm of David.

1 Give ear to my words,
O LORD;
give heed to my sighing.
2 Listen to the sound of my
cry,
my King and my God,
for to you I pray.
3 O LORD, in the morning you
hear my voice;
in the morning I plead my
case to you, and watch.

4 For you are not a God who
delights in wickedness;
evil will not sojourn with
you.
5 The boastful will not stand
before your eyes;
you hate all evildoers.
6 You destroy those who speak
lies;
the LORD abhors the
bloodthirsty and
deceitful.

7 But I, through the
abundance of your
steadfast love,
will enter your house,
I will bow down toward your
holy temple
in awe of you.
8 Lead me, O LORD, in your
righteousness
because of my enemies;
make your way straight
before me.

9 For there is no truth in their
mouths;
their hearts are
destruction;
their throats are open graves;
they flatter with their
tongues.
10 Make them bear their guilt,
O God;

[c] Or *are angry*

let them fall by their own counsels;
because of their many transgressions cast them out,
for they have rebelled against you.

11 But let all who take refuge in you rejoice;
let them ever sing for joy.
Spread your protection over them,
so that those who love your name may exult in you.
12 For you bless the righteous, O LORD;
you cover them with favor as with a shield.

Psalm 6

Prayer for Recovery from Grave Illness

To the leader: with stringed instruments; according to The Sheminith. A Psalm of David.

1 O LORD, do not rebuke me in your anger,
or discipline me in your wrath.
2 Be gracious to me, O LORD, for I am languishing;
O LORD, heal me, for my bones are shaking with terror.
3 My soul also is struck with terror,
while you, O LORD—how long?

4 Turn, O LORD, save my life;
deliver me for the sake of your steadfast love.
5 For in death there is no remembrance of you;
in Sheol who can give you praise?

6 I am weary with my moaning;
every night I flood my bed with tears;
I drench my couch with my weeping.

5.11 Ps 2.12; Isa 65.13; Zech 9.15; Ps 69.36
5.12 Ps 112.2; 32.7,10
6.1 Ps 38.1; 2.5
6.2 Ps 51.1; 102.4,11; 41.4; 22.14
6.3 Jn 12.27; Ps 90.13
6.4 Ps 17.13
6.5 Ps 30.9; Isa 38.18
6.6 Ps 69.3; 22.1; 42.3
6.7 Ps 31.9
6.8 Ps 119.115; Lk 13.27; Ps 5.5; 28.6
6.9 Ps 116.1; 66.19,20
6.10 Ps 71.24; 40.14; 73.19
7.1 Ps 11.1; 31.15
7.2 Ps 17.12; 50.22
7.3 2 Sam 16.7; 1 Sam 24.11
7.4 1 Sam 24.7
7.6 Ps 3.7; 94.2; 44.23

7 My eyes waste away because of grief;
they grow weak because of all my foes.

8 Depart from me, all you workers of evil,
for the LORD has heard the sound of my weeping.
9 The LORD has heard my supplication;
the LORD accepts my prayer.
10 All my enemies shall be ashamed and struck with terror;
they shall turn back, and in a moment be put to shame.

Psalm 7

Plea for Help against Persecutors

A Shiggaion of David, which he sang to the LORD concerning Cush, a Benjaminite.

1 O LORD my God, in you I take refuge;
save me from all my pursuers, and deliver me,
2 or like a lion they will tear me apart;
they will drag me away, with no one to rescue.

3 O LORD my God, if I have done this,
if there is wrong in my hands,
4 if I have repaid my ally with harm
or plundered my foe without cause,
5 then let the enemy pursue and overtake me,
trample my life to the ground,
and lay my soul in the dust. *Selah*

6 Rise up, O LORD, in your anger;
lift yourself up against the fury of my enemies;

awake, O my God;[d] you
have appointed a
judgment.
7 Let the assembly of the
peoples be gathered
around you,
and over it take your seat[e]
on high.
8 The LORD judges the peoples;
judge me, O LORD,
according to my
righteousness
and according to the
integrity that is in me.

9 O let the evil of the wicked
come to an end,
but establish the righteous,
you who test the minds and
hearts,
O righteous God.
10 God is my shield,
who saves the upright in
heart.
11 God is a righteous judge,
and a God who has
indignation every day.

12 If one does not repent, God[f]
will whet his sword;
he has bent and strung his
bow;
13 he has prepared his deadly
weapons,
making his arrows fiery
shafts.
14 See how they conceive evil,
and are pregnant with
mischief,
and bring forth lies.
15 They make a pit, digging it
out,
and fall into the hole that
they have made.
16 Their mischief returns upon
their own heads,
and on their own heads
their violence descends.

17 I will give to the LORD the
thanks due to his
righteousness,
and sing praise to the
name of the LORD, the
Most High.

7.7 Ps 68.18 **7.8** Ps 96.13; 18.20; 35.24 **7.9** Ps 34.21; Isa 54.14; 1 Chr 28.9; Jer 11.20; Rev 2.23 **7.10** Ps 18.2; 125.4 **7.11** Ps 50.6; Isa 34.2 **7.12** Ezek 3.19; 33.9; Deut 32.41; Ps 21.12 **7.13** Ps 64.7 **7.14** Isa 59.4; Jas 1.15 **7.15** Job 4.8; Ps 9.15; Eccl 10.8 **7.16** Ps 140.9; Esther 9.25 **7.17** Ps 71.15,16; 9.2

8.1 Ps 66.2; 148.13; 57.5, 11; 113.4 **8.2** Mt 21.16; Ps 44.16 **8.3** Ps 89.11; 102.5; 136.9 **8.4** Job 7.17; Ps 144.3; Heb 2.6 **8.5** Ps 103.4; 21.5; Heb 2.9 **8.6** Gen 1.26; Heb 2.8 **8.9** v. 1

Psalm 8

Divine Majesty and Human Dignity

To the leader: according to The Gittith. A Psalm of David.

1 O LORD, our Sovereign,
how majestic is your name
in all the earth!

You have set your glory
above the heavens.
2 Out of the mouths of babes
and infants
you have founded a bulwark
because of your foes,
to silence the enemy and
the avenger.

3 When I look at your heavens,
the work of your
fingers,
the moon and the stars
that you have
established;
4 what are human beings that
you are mindful of
them,
mortals[g] that you care for
them?

5 Yet you have made them a
little lower than God,[h]
and crowned them with
glory and honor.
6 You have given them
dominion over the
works of your hands;
you have put all things
under their feet,
7 all sheep and oxen,
and also the beasts of the
field,
8 the birds of the air, and the
fish of the sea,
whatever passes along the
paths of the seas.

9 O LORD, our Sovereign,
how majestic is your name
in all the earth!

[d] Or *awake for me* [e] Cn: Heb *return* [f] Heb *he* [g] Heb *ben adam*, lit. *son of man* [h] Or *than the divine beings* or *angels*: Heb *elohim*

Psalm 9

God's Power and Justice

To the leader: according to Muth-labben. A Psalm of David.

1 I will give thanks to the LORD
with my whole heart;
I will tell of all your
wonderful deeds.
2 I will be glad and exult in
you;
I will sing praise to your
name, O Most High.

3 When my enemies turned
back,
they stumbled and
perished before you.
4 For you have maintained my
just cause;
you have sat on the throne
giving righteous
judgment.

5 You have rebuked the
nations, you have
destroyed the wicked;
you have blotted out their
name forever and ever.
6 The enemies have vanished
in everlasting ruins;
their cities you have rooted
out;
the very memory of them
has perished.

7 But the LORD sits enthroned
forever,
he has established his
throne for judgment.
8 He judges the world with
righteousness;
he judges the peoples with
equity.

9 The LORD is a stronghold for
the oppressed,
a stronghold in times of
trouble.
10 And those who know your
name put their trust in
you,
for you, O LORD, have not
forsaken those who
seek you.
11 Sing praises to the LORD, who
dwells in Zion.
Declare his deeds among
the peoples.
12 For he who avenges blood is
mindful of them;
he does not forget the cry
of the afflicted.

13 Be gracious to me, O LORD.
See what I suffer from
those who hate me;
you are the one who lifts
me up from the gates of
death,
14 so that I may recount all
your praises,
and, in the gates of
daughter Zion,
rejoice in your deliverance.

15 The nations have sunk in the
pit that they made;
in the net that they hid has
their own foot been
caught.
16 The LORD has made himself
known, he has executed
judgment;
the wicked are snared in
the work of their own
hands. *Higgaion. Selah*

17 The wicked shall depart to
Sheol,
all the nations that forget
God.

18 For the needy shall not
always be forgotten,
nor the hope of the poor
perish forever.

19 Rise up, O LORD! Do not let
mortals prevail;
let the nations be judged
before you.
20 Put them in fear, O LORD;
let the nations know that
they are only human.
Selah

9.1 Ps 86.12; 26.7 **9.2** Ps 5.11; 83.18 **9.3** Ps 56.9; 27.2 **9.4** Ps 140.12; 47.8; 67.4; 1 Pet 2.23 **9.5** Deut 9.14 **9.6** Ps 40.15; 34.16 **9.7** Ps 29.10; 89.14 **9.8** Ps 96.13 **9.9** Ps 18.2; 32.7; 37.39 **9.10** Ps 91.14; 37.28 **9.11** Ps 76.2; 105.1 **9.12** Gen 9.5; v. 18 **9.13** Ps 30.10; 25.18; 38.19; 30.3 **9.14** Ps 106.2; 87.2; 13.5 **9.15** Ps 7.15; 35.8 **9.16** Isa 64.2; v. 4 **9.17** Ps 49.14; 50.22; Job 8.13 **9.18** v. 12; Ps 74.19 **9.19** Ps 3.7; 2 Chr 14.11; Ps 110.6 **9.20** Ps 83.15; Isa 31.3

Psalm 10

Prayer for Deliverance from Enemies

1 Why, O Lord, do you stand
far off?
Why do you hide yourself
in times of trouble?
2 In arrogance the wicked
persecute the poor—
let them be caught in the
schemes they have
devised.

3 For the wicked boast of the
desires of their heart,
those greedy for gain curse
and renounce the Lord.
4 In the pride of their
countenance the wicked
say, "God will not seek
it out";
all their thoughts are,
"There is no God."

5 Their ways prosper at all
times;
your judgments are on
high, out of their sight;
as for their foes, they scoff
at them.
6 They think in their heart,
"We shall not be
moved;
throughout all generations
we shall not meet
adversity."

7 Their mouths are filled with
cursing and deceit and
oppression;
under their tongues are
mischief and iniquity.
8 They sit in ambush in the
villages;
in hiding places they
murder the innocent.

Their eyes stealthily watch
for the helpless;
9 they lurk in secret like a
lion in its covert;
they lurk that they may seize
the poor;
they seize the poor and
drag them off in their
net.

10 They stoop, they crouch,
and the helpless fall by
their might.
11 They think in their heart,
"God has forgotten,
he has hidden his face, he
will never see it."

12 Rise up, O Lord; O God, lift
up your hand;
do not forget the
oppressed.
13 Why do the wicked renounce
God,
and say in their hearts,
"You will not call us to
account"?

14 But you do see! Indeed you
note trouble and grief,
that you may take it into
your hands;
the helpless commit
themselves to you;
you have been the helper
of the orphan.

15 Break the arm of the wicked
and evildoers;
seek out their wickedness
until you find none.
16 The Lord is king forever and
ever;
the nations shall perish
from his land.

17 O Lord, you will hear the
desire of the meek;
you will strengthen their
heart, you will incline
your ear
18 to do justice for the orphan
and the oppressed,
so that those from earth
may strike terror no
more.[i]

10.1 Ps 22.1; 13.1 **10.2** Ps 109.16; 7.15; 9.16 **10.3** Ps 94.4; Job 1.5,11; v. 13 **10.4** v. 13; Ps 14.1 **10.6** Ps 30.6; 49.11 **10.7** Rom 3.14; Ps 59.12; 73.8; 140.3 **10.8** Prov 1.11; Ps 94.6 **10.9** Ps 17.12; 59.3; v. 2; 140.5 **10.11** v. 4; Job 22.13; Ps 73.11 **10.12** Mic 5.9; Ps 9.12 **10.13** v. 3 **10.14** Job 11.11; Jer 51.56; Ps 37.5; 68.5; Hos 14.3 **10.15** Ps 37.17; 9.12 **10.16** Ps 29.10; Deut 8.20 **10.17** Ps 145.19; 1 Chr 29.18; Ps 34.15 **10.18** Ps 82.3; 9.9; Isa 29.20

[i] Meaning of Heb uncertain

Psalm 11

Song of Trust in God

To the leader. Of David.

1 In the LORD I take refuge;
how can you say to me,
"Flee like a bird to the
mountains;[j]
2 for look, the wicked bend
the bow,
they have fitted their arrow
to the string,
to shoot in the dark at the
upright in heart.
3 If the foundations are
destroyed,
what can the righteous
do?"

4 The LORD is in his holy
temple;
the LORD's throne is in
heaven.
His eyes behold, his gaze
examines humankind.
5 The LORD tests the righteous
and the wicked,
and his soul hates the lover
of violence.
6 On the wicked he will rain
coals of fire and sulfur;
a scorching wind shall be
the portion of their cup.
7 For the LORD is righteous;
he loves righteous deeds;
the upright shall behold his
face.

Psalm 12

Plea for Help in Evil Times

To the leader: according to The Sheminith. A Psalm of David.

1 Help, O LORD, for there is no
longer anyone who is
godly;
the faithful have
disappeared from
humankind.
2 They utter lies to each other;
with flattering lips and a
double heart they
speak.

11.1 Ps 56.11 **11.2** Ps 7.12; 64.3,4 **11.3** Ps 82.5 **11.4** Ps 18.6; 103.19; 33.13; 34.15, 16 **11.5** Gen 22.1; Jas 1.12; Ps 5.5 **11.6** Ezek 38.22; Jer 4.11,12; Ps 75.8 **11.7** Ps 7.9,11; 33.5; 17.15 **12.1** Isa 57.1 **12.2** Ps 41.6; 55.21; 1 Chr 12.33

12.3 Ps 73.8,9 **12.5** Ps 10.18; 3.7; 34.6 **12.6** Ps 18.30; Prov 30.5 **12.7** Ps 37.28 **12.8** Ps 55.10,11 **13.1** Job 13.24; Ps 44.24; 88.14 **13.2** Ps 42.4,9; 94.3 **13.3** Ps 5.1; Ezra 9.8; Jer 51.39

3 May the LORD cut off all
flattering lips,
the tongue that makes
great boasts,
4 those who say, "With our
tongues we will prevail;
our lips are our own—who
is our master?"

5 "Because the poor are
despoiled, because the
needy groan,
I will now rise up," says
the LORD;
"I will place them in the
safety for which they
long."
6 The promises of the LORD are
promises that are pure,
silver refined in a furnace
on the ground,
purified seven times.
7 You, O LORD, will protect us;
you will guard us from this
generation forever.
8 On every side the wicked
prowl,
as vileness is exalted
among humankind.

Psalm 13

Prayer for Deliverance from Enemies

To the leader. A Psalm of David.

1 How long, O LORD? Will you
forget me forever?
How long will you hide
your face from me?
2 How long must I bear pain[k]
in my soul,
and have sorrow in my
heart all day long?
How long shall my enemy be
exalted over me?

3 Consider and answer me,
O LORD my God!
Give light to my eyes, or I
will sleep the sleep of
death,

[j] Gk Syr Jerome Tg: Heb *flee to your mountain, O bird* [k] Syr: Heb *hold counsels*

4 and my enemy will say, "I
have prevailed";
my foes will rejoice
because I am shaken.

5 But I trusted in your
steadfast love;
my heart shall rejoice in
your salvation.
6 I will sing to the LORD,
because he has dealt
bountifully with me.

Psalm 14

Denunciation of Godlessness

To the leader. Of David.

1 Fools say in their hearts,
"There is no God."
They are corrupt, they do
abominable deeds;
there is no one who does
good.

2 The LORD looks down from
heaven on humankind
to see if there are any who
are wise,
who seek after God.

3 They have all gone astray,
they are all alike
perverse;
there is no one who does
good,
no, not one.

4 Have they no knowledge, all
the evildoers
who eat up my people as
they eat bread,
and do not call upon the
LORD?

5 There they shall be in great
terror,
for God is with the
company of the
righteous.
6 You would confound the
plans of the poor,
but the LORD is their
refuge.

7 O that deliverance for Israel
would come from Zion!
When the LORD restores the
fortunes of his people,
Jacob will rejoice; Israel
will be glad.

Psalm 15

Who Shall Abide in God's Sanctuary?

A Psalm of David.

1 O LORD, who may abide in
your tent?
Who may dwell on your
holy hill?

2 Those who walk blamelessly,
and do what is right,
and speak the truth from
their heart;
3 who do not slander with
their tongue,
and do no evil to their
friends,
nor take up a reproach
against their neighbors;
4 in whose eyes the wicked are
despised,
but who honor those who
fear the LORD;
who stand by their oath even
to their hurt;
5 who do not lend money at
interest,
and do not take a bribe
against the innocent.

Those who do these things
shall never be moved.

Psalm 16

Song of Trust and Security in God

A Miktam of David.

1 Protect me, O God, for in
you I take refuge.
2 I say to the LORD, "You are
my Lord;
I have no good apart from
you."[1]

13.4 Jer 20.10; Ps 25.2 **13.5** Ps 52.8; 9.14 **13.6** Ps 59.16; 116.7 **14.1** Ps 10.4; 53.1-6; 73.8; Rom 3.10-12 **14.2** Ps 33.13; 92.6; Ezra 6.21 **14.3** Ps 58.3; 2 Pet 2.7; Rev 22.11; Ps 143.2 **14.4** Ps 82.5; 27.2; 79.6; Isa 64.7 **14.5** Ps 73.15 **14.6** Ps 9.9; 40.17 **14.7** Ps 53.6; Job 42.10

15.1 Ps 24.3-5; 27.5,6; 2.6 **15.2** Ps 24.4; 51.6; Eph 4.25 **15.3** Lev 19.16; Ex 23.1 **15.4** 2 Tim 3.8; Acts 28.10; Judg 11.35 **15.5** Ex 22.25; 23.8; Deut 16.19; Ps 112.6 **16.1** Ps 17.8; 7.1 **16.2** Ps 73.25

[1] Jerome Tg: Meaning of Heb uncertain

3 As for the holy ones in the
land, they are the noble,
in whom is all my delight.

4 Those who choose another
god multiply their
sorrows;[m]
their drink offerings of
blood I will not pour
out
or take their names upon
my lips.

5 The LORD is my chosen
portion and my cup;
you hold my lot.
6 The boundary lines have
fallen for me in
pleasant places;
I have a goodly heritage.

7 I bless the LORD who gives
me counsel;
in the night also my heart
instructs me.
8 I keep the LORD always
before me;
because he is at my right
hand, I shall not be
moved.

9 Therefore my heart is glad,
and my soul rejoices;
my body also rests secure.
10 For you do not give me up to
Sheol,
or let your faithful one see
the Pit.

11 You show me the path of
life.
In your presence there is
fullness of joy;
in your right hand are
pleasures forevermore.

Psalm 17

Prayer for Deliverance from Persecutors

A Prayer of David.

1 Hear a just cause, O LORD;
attend to my cry;
give ear to my prayer from
lips free of deceit.

2 From you let my vindication
come;
let your eyes see the right.

3 If you try my heart, if you
visit me by night,
if you test me, you will find
no wickedness in me;
my mouth does not
transgress.
4 As for what others do, by the
word of your lips
I have avoided the ways of
the violent.
5 My steps have held fast to
your paths;
my feet have not slipped.

6 I call upon you, for you will
answer me, O God;
incline your ear to me,
hear my words.
7 Wondrously show your
steadfast love,
O savior of those who seek
refuge
from their adversaries at
your right hand.

8 Guard me as the apple of the
eye;
hide me in the shadow of
your wings,
9 from the wicked who despoil
me,
my deadly enemies who
surround me.
10 They close their hearts to
pity;
with their mouths they
speak arrogantly.
11 They track me down;[n] now
they surround me;
they set their eyes to cast
me to the ground.
12 They are like a lion eager to
tear,
like a young lion lurking in
ambush.

13 Rise up, O LORD, confront
them, overthrow them!
By your sword deliver my
life from the wicked,

16.3 Deut 33.3; Ps 101.6
16.4 Ps 32.10; 106.37,38; Ex 23.13
16.5 Ps 73.26; 23.5; 125.3
16.6 Ps 78.55; Jer 3.19
16.7 Ps 73.24; 77.6
16.8 Ps 54.3; 73.23; 62.2
16.9 Ps 4.7; 30.12; 4.8
16.10 Acts 2.27; 13.35; Ps 49.9
16.11 Mt 7.14; Ps 17.15; 36.7,8
17.1 Ps 9.4; 61.1; 55.1; Isa 29.13
17.2 1 Chr 29.17
17.3 Ps 26.2; 66.10; Job 23.10; Jer 50.20; Ps 39.1
17.4 Prov 1.15
17.5 Ps 44.18; 18.36
17.6 Ps 86.7; 88.2
17.7 Ps 31.21; 20.6
17.8 Deut 32.10; Ps 36.7
17.9 Ps 31.20; 38.12; 109.3
17.10 Ps 73.7; 1 Sam 2.3; Ps 31.18
17.11 Ps 88.17; 37.14
17.12 Ps 7.2; 10.9
17.13 Ps 73.18; 22.20; 7.12

[m] Cn: Meaning of Heb uncertain [n] One Ms Compare Syr: MT *Our steps*

14 from mortals—by your hand,
O LORD—
from mortals whose portion
in life is in this world.
May their bellies be filled
with what you have
stored up for them;
may their children have
more than enough;
may they leave something
over to their little ones.

15 As for me, I shall behold
your face in
righteousness;
when I awake I shall be
satisfied, beholding
your likeness.

Psalm 18

Royal Thanksgiving for Victory

To the leader. A Psalm of David the servant of the LORD, who addressed the words of this song to the LORD on the day when the LORD delivered him from the hand of all his enemies, and from the hand of Saul. He said:

1 I love you, O LORD, my
strength.
2 The LORD is my rock, my
fortress, and my
deliverer,
my God, my rock in whom
I take refuge,
my shield, and the horn of
my salvation, my
stronghold.
3 I call upon the LORD, who is
worthy to be praised,
so I shall be saved from my
enemies.

4 The cords of death
encompassed me;
the torrents of perdition
assailed me;
5 the cords of Sheol entangled
me;
the snares of death
confronted me.

6 In my distress I called upon
the LORD;
to my God I cried for help.
From his temple he heard
my voice,
and my cry to him reached
his ears.

7 Then the earth reeled and
rocked;
the foundations also of the
mountains trembled
and quaked, because he
was angry.
8 Smoke went up from his
nostrils,
and devouring fire from his
mouth;
glowing coals flamed forth
from him.
9 He bowed the heavens, and
came down;
thick darkness was under
his feet.
10 He rode on a cherub, and
flew;
he came swiftly upon the
wings of the wind.
11 He made darkness his
covering around him,
his canopy thick clouds
dark with water.
12 Out of the brightness before
him
there broke through his
clouds
hailstones and coals of fire.
13 The LORD also thundered in
the heavens,
and the Most High uttered
his voice.[o]
14 And he sent out his arrows,
and scattered them;
he flashed forth lightnings,
and routed them.
15 Then the channels of the sea
were seen,
and the foundations of the
world were laid bare
at your rebuke, O LORD,
at the blast of the breath of
your nostrils.

16 He reached down from on
high, he took me;
he drew me out of mighty
waters.

17.14 Lk 16.8; Ps 73.3-7; Isa 2.7; Job 21.11 **17.15** 1 Jn 3.2; Ps 4.6,7; 16.11 **18.1** Ps 27.1 **18.2** Ps 19.14; 91.2; 40.17; 11.1; 59.11; 75.10; 9.9 **18.3** Ps 48.1; Num 10.9 **18.4** Ps 116.3; 124.3,4 **18.5** Ps 116.3; Prov 14.27 **18.6** Ps 86.7; 11.4; 34.15 **18.7** Ps 68.7,8; 114.4,6 **18.8** Deut 29.20; Hab 3.5 **18.9** Ps 144.5; Ex 20.21 **18.10** Ps 80.1; 104.3 **18.11** Ps 97.2 **18.12** Ps 104.2; Isa 30.30; Ps 140.10 **18.13** Ps 29.3; 104.7 **18.14** Ps 7.13; 144.6; Ex 14.24; Judg 4.15 **18.15** Ps 106.9; 76.6; Ex 15.8 **18.16** Ps 144.7

o Gk See 2 Sam 22.14: Heb adds *hailstones and coals of fire*

17 He delivered me from my
strong enemy,
and from those who hated
me;
for they were too mighty
for me.
18 They confronted me in the
day of my calamity;
but the LORD was my
support.
19 He brought me out into a
broad place;
he delivered me, because
he delighted in me.

20 The LORD rewarded me
according to my
righteousness;
according to the cleanness
of my hands he
recompensed me.
21 For I have kept the ways of
the LORD,
and have not wickedly
departed from my God.
22 For all his ordinances were
before me,
and his statutes I did not
put away from me.
23 I was blameless before him,
and I kept myself from
guilt.
24 Therefore the LORD has
recompensed me
according to my
righteousness,
according to the cleanness
of my hands in his
sight.

25 With the loyal you show
yourself loyal;
with the blameless you
show yourself
blameless;
26 with the pure you show
yourself pure;
and with the crooked you
show yourself perverse.
27 For you deliver a humble
people,
but the haughty eyes you
bring down.
28 It is you who light my lamp;
the LORD, my God, lights up
my darkness.
29 By you I can crush a troop,
and by my God I can leap
over a wall.
30 This God—his way is
perfect;
the promise of the LORD
proves true;
he is a shield for all who
take refuge in him.

31 For who is God except the
LORD?
And who is a rock besides
our God?—
32 the God who girded me with
strength,
and made my way safe.
33 He made my feet like the
feet of a deer,
and set me secure on the
heights.
34 He trains my hands for war,
so that my arms can bend
a bow of bronze.
35 You have given me the shield
of your salvation,
and your right hand has
supported me;
your help[p] has made me
great.
36 You gave me a wide place for
my steps under me,
and my feet did not slip.
37 I pursued my enemies and
overtook them;
and did not turn back until
they were consumed.
38 I struck them down, so that
they were not able to
rise;
they fell under my feet.
39 For you girded me with
strength for the battle;
you made my assailants
sink under me.
40 You made my enemies turn
their backs to me,
and those who hated me I
destroyed.
41 They cried for help, but
there was no one to
save them;
they cried to the LORD, but
he did not answer
them.

18.17 v. 48; Ps 35.10 **18.18** Ps 59.16; Isa 10.20 **18.19** Ps 31.8; 118.5; 37.23 **18.20** Ps 7.8; 1 Kings 8.32; Ps 24.4 **18.21** Ps 119.33; 2 Chr 34.33; Ps 119.102 **18.22** Ps 119.30, 83 **18.24** 1 Sam 26.23 **18.25** Ps 62.12; Mt 5.7 **18.26** Job 25.5; Prov 3.34 **18.27** Ps 72.12; Prov 6.17 **18.28** Job 18.6; Ps 27.1; Job 29.3 **18.29** 2 Cor 12.9; Heb 11.34 **18.30** Deut 32.4; Ps 12.6; 17.7 **18.31** Deut 32.31, 39; Ps 86.8-10; Isa 45.5 **18.32** Isa 45.5; Heb 13.21; 1 Pet 5.10 **18.33** Hab 3.19; Deut 32.13 **18.34** Ps 144.1; Job 20.24 **18.35** Deut 33.29; Ps 119.117; 138.6 **18.36** Ps 31.8; 71.5 **18.37** Ps 44.5; 37.20 **18.38** Ps 110.6; 36.12; 47.3 **18.39** vv. 32,47 **18.40** Ps 21.21; 94.23 **18.41** Ps 50.22; Prov 1.28

p Or *gentleness*

42 I beat them fine, like dust
before the wind;
I cast them out like the
mire of the streets.

43 You delivered me from strife
with the peoples;[q]
you made me head of the
nations;
people whom I had not
known served me.
44 As soon as they heard of me
they obeyed me;
foreigners came cringing to
me.
45 Foreigners lost heart,
and came trembling out of
their strongholds.

46 The LORD lives! Blessed be
my rock,
and exalted be the God of
my salvation,
47 the God who gave me
vengeance
and subdued peoples under
me;
48 who delivered me from my
enemies;
indeed, you exalted me
above my adversaries;
you delivered me from the
violent.

49 For this I will extol you,
O LORD, among the
nations,
and sing praises to your
name.
50 Great triumphs he gives to
his king,
and shows steadfast love to
his anointed,
to David and his
descendants forever.

Psalm 19

God's Glory in Creation and the Law

To the leader. A Psalm of David.

1 The heavens are telling the
glory of God;
and the firmament[r]
proclaims his
handiwork.
2 Day to day pours forth
speech,
and night to night declares
knowledge.
3 There is no speech, nor are
there words;
their voice is not heard;
4 yet their voice[s] goes out
through all the earth,
and their words to the end
of the world.

In the heavens[t] he has set a
tent for the sun,
5 which comes out like a
bridegroom from his
wedding canopy,
and like a strong man runs
its course with joy.
6 Its rising is from the end of
the heavens,
and its circuit to the end of
them;
and nothing is hid from its
heat.

7 The law of the LORD is
perfect,
reviving the soul;
the decrees of the LORD are
sure,
making wise the simple;
8 the precepts of the LORD are
right,
rejoicing the heart;
the commandment of the
LORD is clear,
enlightening the eyes;
9 the fear of the LORD is pure,
enduring forever;
the ordinances of the LORD
are true
and righteous altogether.
10 More to be desired are they
than gold,
even much fine gold;
sweeter also than honey,
and drippings of the
honeycomb.

11 Moreover by them is your
servant warned;
in keeping them there is
great reward.

18.42 Ps 83.13 **18.43** Ps 35.1; Isa 52.15; 55.5 **18.44** Ps 66.3 **18.46** Ps 42.2; 51.14 **18.47** Ps 94.1; 47.3 **18.48** Ps 143.9; 27.6; 140.1,4 **18.49** Rom 15.9; Ps 108.1 **18.50** Ps 144.10; 28.8; 89.4,29 **19.1** Gen 1.6; Isa 40.22; Rom 1.19, 20 **19.2** Ps 74.16 **19.4** Rom 10.18 **19.5** Eccl 1.5 **19.6** Ps 113.3; Deut 30.4 **19.7** Ps 119.142; 23.3; 93.5; 111.7; 119.98-100 **19.8** Ps 119.128; 12.6; 119.30 **19.9** Ps 119.42 **19.10** Prov 8.10; 16.24 **19.11** Ps 17.4; Prov 29.18

q Gk Tg: Heb *people* r Or *dome*
s Gk Jerome Compare Syr: Heb *line*
t Heb *In them*

12 But who can detect their
errors?
Clear me from hidden
faults.
13 Keep back your servant also
from the insolent;[u]
do not let them have
dominion over me.
Then I shall be blameless,
and innocent of great
transgression.

14 Let the words of my mouth
and the meditation of
my heart
be acceptable to you,
O LORD, my rock and my
redeemer.

Psalm 20

Prayer for Victory

To the leader. A Psalm of David.

1 The LORD answer you in the
day of trouble!
The name of the God of
Jacob protect you!
2 May he send you help from
the sanctuary,
and give you support from
Zion.
3 May he remember all your
offerings,
and regard with favor your
burnt sacrifices. *Selah*

4 May he grant you your
heart's desire,
and fulfill all your plans.
5 May we shout for joy over
your victory,
and in the name of our
God set up our banners.
May the LORD fulfill all your
petitions.

6 Now I know that the LORD
will help his anointed;
he will answer him from
his holy heaven
with mighty victories by his
right hand.
7 Some take pride in chariots,
and some in horses,

19.12 Ps 139.6; 51.1,2; 90.8 **19.13** Ps 119.33; 32.2; 25.11 **19.14** Ps 104.34; 18.2; Isa 41.14; 43.14 **20.01** Ps 102.2; 91.14; 36.7, 11; 59.1 **20.2** Ps 3.4; 119.28 **20.3** Ps 51.19 **20.4** Ps 21.2; 145.19 **20.5** Ps 9.14; 1 Sam 1.17 **20.6** Ps 41.11; Isa 58.9; Ps 28.8 **20.7** Isa 36.9; 31.1; 2 Chr 32.8

20.8 Ps 37.24 **20.9** Ps 3.7 **21.1** Ps 59.16,17; 9.14 **21.2** Ps 37.4 **21.3** Ps 59.10 **21.4** Ps 133.3; 91.16 **21.5** Ps 18.50; 45.3,4 **21.6** 1 Chr 17.27; Ps 16.11 **21.7** 2 Kings 18.5; Ps 16.8 **21.8** Isa 10.10 **21.9** Mal 4.1; Lam 2.2

but our pride is in the
name of the LORD our God.
8 They will collapse and fall,
but we shall rise and stand
upright.

9 Give victory to the king,
O LORD;
answer us when we call.[v]

Psalm 21

Thanksgiving for Victory

To the leader. A Psalm of David.

1 In your strength the king
rejoices, O LORD,
and in your help how
greatly he exults!
2 You have given him his
heart's desire,
and have not withheld the
request of his lips.
Selah
3 For you meet him with rich
blessings;
you set a crown of fine
gold on his head.
4 He asked you for life; you
gave it to him—
length of days forever and
ever.
5 His glory is great through
your help;
splendor and majesty you
bestow on him.
6 You bestow on him blessings
forever;
you make him glad with
the joy of your
presence.
7 For the king trusts in the
LORD,
and through the steadfast
love of the Most High
he shall not be moved.

8 Your hand will find out all
your enemies;
your right hand will find
out those who hate you.
9 You will make them like a
fiery furnace
when you appear.

[u] Or *from proud thoughts* [v] Gk: Heb *give victory, O LORD; let the King answer us when we call*

9 The LORD will swallow them up in his wrath,
and fire will consume them.
10 You will destroy their offspring from the earth,
and their children from among humankind.
11 If they plan evil against you,
if they devise mischief,
they will not succeed.
12 For you will put them to flight;
you will aim at their faces with your bows.

13 Be exalted, O LORD, in your strength!
We will sing and praise your power.

Psalm 22

Plea for Deliverance from Suffering and Hostility

To the leader: according to The Deer of the Dawn. A Psalm of David.

1 My God, my God, why have you forsaken me?
Why are you so far from helping me, from the words of my groaning?
2 O my God, I cry by day, but you do not answer;
and by night, but find no rest.

3 Yet you are holy,
enthroned on the praises of Israel.
4 In you our ancestors trusted;
they trusted, and you delivered them.
5 To you they cried, and were saved;
in you they trusted, and were not put to shame.

6 But I am a worm, and not human;
scorned by others, and despised by the people.
7 All who see me mock at me;
they make mouths at me,
they shake their heads;
8 "Commit your cause to the LORD; let him deliver—
let him rescue the one in whom he delights!"

9 Yet it was you who took me from the womb;
you kept me safe on my mother's breast.
10 On you I was cast from my birth,
and since my mother bore me you have been my God.
11 Do not be far from me,
for trouble is near
and there is no one to help.

12 Many bulls encircle me,
strong bulls of Bashan surround me;
13 they open wide their mouths at me,
like a ravening and roaring lion.

14 I am poured out like water,
and all my bones are out of joint;
my heart is like wax;
it is melted within my breast;
15 my mouth[w] is dried up like a potsherd,
and my tongue sticks to my jaws;
you lay me in the dust of death.

16 For dogs are all around me;
a company of evildoers encircles me.
My hands and feet have shriveled;[x]
17 I can count all my bones.
They stare and gloat over me;
18 they divide my clothes among themselves,
and for my clothing they cast lots.

21.10 Deut 28.18; Ps 37.28 **21.11** Ps 2.1-3; 10.2 **21.12** Ps 18.40; 7.12,13 **21.13** Ps 57.5; 81.1 **22.1** Mt 27.46; Ps 10.1 **22.2** Ps 42.3 **22.3** Ps 99.9; 35.8 **22.5** Ps 107.6; 25.2,3; Rom 9.33 **22.6** Job 25.6; Isa 41.14; Ps 31.11; Isa 49.7 **22.7** Mt 27.39; Mk 15.29 **22.8** Mt 27.43; Mk 1.11 **22.9** Ps 71.6 **22.10** Isa 46.3 **22.11** Ps 72.12 **22.12** Ps 68.30; Deut 32.14 **22.13** Ps 35.21; 17.12 **22.14** Job 30.16; Ps 31.10; 107.26 **22.15** Ps 38.10; 137.6; 104.29 **22.16** Ps 59.6; Mt 27.35 **22.18** Mt 27.35

[w] Cn: Heb *strength* [x] Meaning of Heb uncertain

19 But you, O LORD, do not be far away!
O my help, come quickly to my aid!
20 Deliver my soul from the sword,
my life[y] from the power of the dog!
21 Save me from the mouth of the lion!

From the horns of the wild oxen you have rescued[z] me.
22 I will tell of your name to my brothers and sisters;[a]
in the midst of the congregation I will praise you:
23 You who fear the LORD, praise him!
All you offspring of Jacob, glorify him;
stand in awe of him, all you offspring of Israel!
24 For he did not despise or abhor
the affliction of the afflicted;
he did not hide his face from me,[b]
but heard when I[c] cried to him.

25 From you comes my praise in the great congregation;
my vows I will pay before those who fear him.
26 The poor[d] shall eat and be satisfied;
those who seek him shall praise the LORD.
May your hearts live forever!

27 All the ends of the earth shall remember
and turn to the LORD;
and all the families of the nations
shall worship before him.[e]
28 For dominion belongs to the LORD,
and he rules over the nations.
29 To him,[f] indeed, shall all who sleep in[g] the earth bow down;
before him shall bow all who go down to the dust,
and I shall live for him.[h]
30 Posterity will serve him;
future generations will be told about the Lord,
31 and[i] proclaim his deliverance to a people yet unborn,
saying that he has done it.

Psalm 23

The Divine Shepherd

A Psalm of David.

1 The LORD is my shepherd, I shall not want.
2 He makes me lie down in green pastures;
he leads me beside still waters;[j]
3 he restores my soul.[k]
He leads me in right paths[l]
for his name's sake.

4 Even though I walk through the darkest valley,[m]
I fear no evil;
for you are with me;
your rod and your staff—
they comfort me.

5 You prepare a table before me
in the presence of my enemies;
you anoint my head with oil;
my cup overflows.
6 Surely[n] goodness and mercy[o] shall follow me
all the days of my life,

[y] Heb *my only one* [z] Heb *answered*
[a] Or *kindred* [b] Heb *him* [c] Heb *he*
[d] Or *afflicted* [e] Gk Syr Jerome: Heb *you*
[f] Cn: Heb *They have eaten and* [g] Cn: Heb *all the fat ones* [h] Compare Gk Syr Vg: Heb *and he who cannot keep himself alive*
[i] Compare Gk: Heb *it will be told about the Lord to the generation, [31]they will come and*
[j] Heb *waters of rest* [k] Or *life*
[l] Or *paths of righteousness* [m] Or *the valley of the shadow of death* [n] Or *Only*
[o] Or *kindness*

22.19 v. 11; Ps 70.5 **22.20** Ps 35.17 **22.21** v. 13; Ps 34.4 **22.22** Heb 2.12 **22.23** Ps 135.19. 86.12; 33.8 **22.24** Ps 102.17; 69.17; Heb 5.7 **22.25** Ps 35.18; 66.13 **22.26** Ps 107.9; 40.16; 69.32 **22.27** Ps 2.8; 86.9 **22.28** Ps 47.7,8; Mt 6.13 **22.29** Ps 47.7; Isa 27.13; Ps 95.6 **22.30** Ps 102.28; 71.18 **22.31** Ps 78.6 **23.1** Isa 40.11; Jer 23.4; Jn 10.11; 1 Pet 2.25; Phil 4.19 **23.2** Ezek 34.14; Rev 7.17 **23.3** Ps 19.7; 5.8; 85.13; 143.11 **23.4** Ps 138.7; Job 3.5; Ps 27.1; Isa 43.2 **23.5** Ps 78.19; 31.19; 92.10; 16.5 **23.6** Ps 25.7,10; 27.4-6

and I shall dwell in the
house of the LORD
my whole life long.[p]

Psalm 24

Entrance into the Temple

Of David. A Psalm.

1 The earth is the LORD's and
all that is in it,
the world, and those who
live in it;
2 for he has founded it on the
seas,
and established it on the
rivers.

3 Who shall ascend the hill of
the LORD?
And who shall stand in his
holy place?
4 Those who have clean hands
and pure hearts,
who do not lift up their
souls to what is false,
and do not swear
deceitfully.
5 They will receive blessing
from the LORD,
and vindication from the
God of their salvation.
6 Such is the company of
those who seek him,
who seek the face of the
God of Jacob.[q] *Selah*

7 Lift up your heads, O gates!
and be lifted up, O ancient
doors!
that the King of glory may
come in.
8 Who is the King of glory?
The LORD, strong and
mighty,
the LORD, mighty in battle.
9 Lift up your heads, O gates!
and be lifted up, O ancient
doors!
that the King of glory may
come in.
10 Who is this King of glory?
The LORD of hosts,
he is the King of glory.
Selah

24.1 Ex 9.29; Job 41.11; 1 Cor 10.26; Ps 89.11 **24.3** Ps 15.1; 2.6; 65.4 **24.4** Job 17.9; Mt 5.8; Ps 15.4 **24.5** Deut 11.26, 27; Isa 46.13; Ps 25.5 **24.6** Ps 27.8 **24.7** Isa 26.2; 1 Cor 2.8 **24.8** Ps 89.13; 76.3-6 **24.9** Zech 9.9; Mt 21.5

25.1 Ps 86.4 **25.2** Ps 31.6; 41.11 **25.3** Isa 49.23; 33.1 **25.4** Ps 5.8; 86.11 **25.5** Jn 16.13; Ps 24.5; 40.1 **25.6** Ps 103.17; Isa 63.15 **25.7** Job 13.26; Jer 3.25; Ps 51.1 **25.8** Ps 106.1; 92.15; 32.8 **25.9** Ps 23.3; 27.11 **25.10** Ps 40.11; 103.18

Psalm 25

Prayer for Guidance and for Deliverance

Of David.

1 To you, O LORD, I lift up my
soul.
2 O my God, in you I trust;
do not let me be put to
shame;
do not let my enemies
exult over me.
3 Do not let those who wait for
you be put to shame;
let them be ashamed who
are wantonly
treacherous.

4 Make me to know your ways,
O LORD;
teach me your paths.
5 Lead me in your truth, and
teach me,
for you are the God of my
salvation;
for you I wait all day long.

6 Be mindful of your mercy,
O LORD, and of your
steadfast love,
for they have been from of
old.
7 Do not remember the sins of
my youth or my
transgressions;
according to your steadfast
love remember me,
for your goodness' sake,
O LORD!

8 Good and upright is the
LORD;
therefore he instructs
sinners in the way.
9 He leads the humble in what
is right,
and teaches the humble his
way.
10 All the paths of the LORD are
steadfast love and
faithfulness,

[p] Heb *for length of days* [q] Gk Syr: Heb *your face, O Jacob*

for those who keep his
covenant and his
decrees.

11 For your name's sake,
O LORD,
pardon my guilt, for it is
great.
12 Who are they that fear the
LORD?
He will teach them the way
that they should
choose.

13 They will abide in prosperity,
and their children shall
possess the land.
14 The friendship of the LORD is
for those who fear him,
and he makes his covenant
known to them.
15 My eyes are ever toward the
LORD,
for he will pluck my feet
out of the net.

16 Turn to me and be gracious
to me,
for I am lonely and
afflicted.
17 Relieve the troubles of my
heart,
and bring me[r] out of my
distress.
18 Consider my affliction and
my trouble,
and forgive all my sins.

19 Consider how many are my
foes,
and with what violent
hatred they hate me.
20 O guard my life, and deliver
me;
do not let me be put to
shame, for I take refuge
in you.
21 May integrity and
uprightness preserve
me,
for I wait for you.

22 Redeem Israel, O God,
out of all its troubles.

25.11 Ps 31.1; Rom 5.20
25.13 Prov 19.23; Ps 37.11
25.14 Prov 3.32; Jn 7.17
25.15 Ps 141.8
25.16 Ps 69.16
25.17 Ps 88.3; 107.6
25.18 2 Sam 16.12
25.19 Ps 3.1; 27.12
25.20 Ps 86.2
25.21 Ps 41.12; v. 3
25.22 Ps 130.8
26.1 Ps 7.8; Prov 20.7; Ps 25.2; Heb 10.23
26.2 Ps 7.9; 66.10
26.3 2 Kings 20.3
26.4 Ps 1.1
26.5 Ps 139.21; 1.1
26.6 Ps 73.13
26.7 Ps 35.18; 9.1
26.8 Ps 27.4
26.9 Ps 28.3
26.10 1 Sam 8.3
26.11 v. 1; Ps 69.18

Psalm 26

Plea for Justice and Declaration of Righteousness

Of David.

1 Vindicate me, O LORD,
for I have walked in my
integrity,
and I have trusted in the
LORD without wavering.
2 Prove me, O LORD, and try
me;
test my heart and mind.
3 For your steadfast love is
before my eyes,
and I walk in faithfulness
to you.[s]

4 I do not sit with the
worthless,
nor do I consort with
hypocrites;
5 I hate the company of
evildoers,
and will not sit with the
wicked.

6 I wash my hands in
innocence,
and go around your altar,
O LORD,
7 singing aloud a song of
thanksgiving,
and telling all your
wondrous deeds.

8 O LORD, I love the house in
which you dwell,
and the place where your
glory abides.
9 Do not sweep me away with
sinners,
nor my life with the
bloodthirsty,
10 those in whose hands are
evil devices,
and whose right hands are
full of bribes.

11 But as for me, I walk in my
integrity;
redeem me, and be
gracious to me.

[r] Or *The troubles of my heart are enlarged; bring me* [s] Or *in your faithfulness*

12 My foot stands on level ground;
in the great congregation I will bless the LORD.

Psalm 27

Triumphant Song of Confidence

Of David.

1 The LORD is my light and my salvation;
whom shall I fear?
The LORD is the stronghold[t] of my life;
of whom shall I be afraid?

2 When evildoers assail me
to devour my flesh—
my adversaries and foes—
they shall stumble and fall.

3 Though an army encamp against me,
my heart shall not fear;
though war rise up against me,
yet I will be confident.

4 One thing I asked of the LORD,
that will I seek after:
to live in the house of the LORD
all the days of my life,
to behold the beauty of the LORD,
and to inquire in his temple.

5 For he will hide me in his shelter
in the day of trouble;
he will conceal me under the cover of his tent;
he will set me high on a rock.

6 Now my head is lifted up
above my enemies all around me,
and I will offer in his tent
sacrifices with shouts of joy;
I will sing and make melody to the LORD.

7 Hear, O LORD, when I cry aloud,
be gracious to me and answer me!
8 "Come," my heart says, "seek his face!"
Your face, LORD, do I seek.
9 Do not hide your face from me.

Do not turn your servant away in anger,
you who have been my help.
Do not cast me off, do not forsake me,
O God of my salvation!
10 If my father and mother forsake me,
the LORD will take me up.

11 Teach me your way, O LORD,
and lead me on a level path
because of my enemies.
12 Do not give me up to the will of my adversaries,
for false witnesses have risen against me,
and they are breathing out violence.

13 I believe that I shall see the goodness of the LORD
in the land of the living.
14 Wait for the LORD;
be strong, and let your heart take courage;
wait for the LORD!

Psalm 28

Prayer for Help and Thanksgiving for It

Of David.

1 To you, O LORD, I call;
my rock, do not refuse to hear me,
for if you are silent to me,
I shall be like those who go down to the Pit.
2 Hear the voice of my supplication,
as I cry to you for help,

26.12 Ps 40.2; 27.11; 22.22 **27.1** Isa 60.19; Ex 15.2; Ps 62.2 **27.2** Ps 14.4 **27.3** Ps 3.6 **27.4** Ps 26.8 **27.5** Ps 31.20; 40.2 **27.6** Ps 3.3 **27.7** Ps 39.12; 13.3 **27.8** Ps 24.6 **27.9** Ps 69.17 **27.10** Isa 49.15; 40.11 **27.11** Ps 25.4; 86.11; 5.8 **27.12** Ps 41.2; 35.11; Mt 26.60; Acts 9.1 **27.13** Ps 31.19; Jer 11.19 **27.14** Ps 40.1; Josh 1.6 **28.1** Ps 83.1; 88.4 **28.2** Ps 140.6; 5.7; 138.2

[t] Or *refuge*

as I lift up my hands
toward your most holy
sanctuary.[u]

3 Do not drag me away with
the wicked,
with those who are workers
of evil,
who speak peace with their
neighbors,
while mischief is in their
hearts.
4 Repay them according to
their work,
and according to the evil of
their deeds;
repay them according to the
work of their hands;
render them their due
reward.
5 Because they do not regard
the works of the LORD,
or the work of his
hands,
he will break them down and
build them up no more.

6 Blessed be the LORD,
for he has heard the sound
of my pleadings.
7 The LORD is my strength and
my shield;
in him my heart trusts;
so I am helped, and my heart
exults,
and with my song I give
thanks to him.

8 The LORD is the strength of
his people;
he is the saving refuge of
his anointed.
9 O save your people, and
bless your heritage;
be their shepherd, and
carry them forever.

Psalm 29

The Voice of God in a Great Storm

A Psalm of David.

1 Ascribe to the LORD,
O heavenly beings,[v]
ascribe to the LORD glory
and strength.
2 Ascribe to the LORD the glory
of his name;
worship the LORD in holy
splendor.

3 The voice of the LORD is over
the waters;
the God of glory thunders,
the LORD, over mighty
waters.
4 The voice of the LORD is
powerful;
the voice of the LORD is full
of majesty.

5 The voice of the LORD breaks
the cedars;
the LORD breaks the cedars
of Lebanon.
6 He makes Lebanon skip like
a calf,
and Sirion like a young
wild ox.

7 The voice of the LORD flashes
forth flames of fire.
8 The voice of the LORD shakes
the wilderness;
the LORD shakes the
wilderness of Kadesh.

9 The voice of the LORD causes
the oaks to whirl,[w]
and strips the forest
bare;
and in his temple all say,
"Glory!"

10 The LORD sits enthroned over
the flood;
the LORD sits enthroned as
king forever.
11 May the LORD give strength
to his people!
May the LORD bless his
people with peace!

28.3 Ps 26.9; 12.2; Jer 9.8
28.4 Rev 18.6
28.5 Isa 5.12
28.6 Ps 116.1
28.7 Ps 18.2; 13.5
28.8 Ps 20.6
28.9 Deut 9.29; Ezra 1.4
29.1 1 Chr 16.28, 29; Ps 96.7-9
29.2 2 Chr 20.21
29.3 Job 37.4,5
29.4 Ps 68.33
29.5 Isa 2.13
29.6 Ps 114.4; Deut 3.9
29.8 Num 13.26
29.9 Ps 26.8
29.10 Ps 10.16
29.11 Ps 28.8; 37.11

[u] Heb *your innermost sanctuary*
[v] Heb *sons of gods*
[w] Or *causes the deer to calve*

Psalm 30

Thanksgiving for Recovery from Grave Illness

A Psalm. A Song at the dedication of the temple. Of David.

1 I will extol you, O LORD, for
you have drawn me up,
and did not let my foes
rejoice over me.
2 O LORD my God, I cried to
you for help,
and you have healed me.
3 O LORD, you brought up my
soul from Sheol,
restored me to life from
among those gone down
to the Pit.[x]

4 Sing praises to the LORD,
O you his faithful ones,
and give thanks to his holy
name.
5 For his anger is but for a
moment;
his favor is for a lifetime.
Weeping may linger for the
night,
but joy comes with the
morning.

6 As for me, I said in my
prosperity,
"I shall never be moved."
7 By your favor, O LORD,
you had established me as
a strong mountain;
you hid your face;
I was dismayed.

8 To you, O LORD, I cried,
and to the LORD I made
supplication:
9 "What profit is there in my
death,
if I go down to the Pit?
Will the dust praise you?
Will it tell of your
faithfulness?
10 Hear, O LORD, and be
gracious to me!
O LORD, be my helper!"

11 You have turned my
mourning into dancing;
you have taken off my
sackcloth
and clothed me with joy,
12 so that my soul[y] may praise
you and not be silent.
O LORD my God, I will give
thanks to you forever.

Psalm 31

Prayer and Praise for Deliverance from Enemies

To the leader. A Psalm of David.

1 In you, O LORD, I seek refuge;
do not let me ever be put
to shame;
in your righteousness
deliver me.
2 Incline your ear to me;
rescue me speedily.
Be a rock of refuge for me,
a strong fortress to save
me.

3 You are indeed my rock and
my fortress;
for your name's sake lead
me and guide me,
4 take me out of the net that
is hidden for me,
for you are my refuge.
5 Into your hand I commit my
spirit;
you have redeemed me,
O LORD, faithful God.

6 You hate[z] those who pay
regard to worthless
idols,
but I trust in the LORD.
7 I will exult and rejoice in
your steadfast love,
because you have seen my
affliction;
you have taken heed of my
adversities,
8 and have not delivered me
into the hand of the
enemy;
you have set my feet in a
broad place.

30.1 Ps 28.9; 25.2 **30.2** Ps 88.13; 6.2 **30.3** Ps 86.13; 28.1 **30.4** Ps 149.1; 50.5; 97.12 **30.5** Ps 103.9; 63.3 **30.7** Ps 104.29 **30.9** Ps 6.5 **30.11** Ps 6.8; Jer 31.4,13; Ps 4.7

30.12 Ps 16.9; 44.8 **31.1** Ps 22.5; Isa 49.23 **31.2** Ps 71.2 **31.3** Ps 18.2; 23.3 **31.4** Ps 25.15; 28.8 **31.5** Lk 23.46; Acts 7.59 **31.6** Jon 2.8 **31.7** Ps 90.14; 10.14; Jn 10.27 **31.8** Deut 32.30; Ps 4.1

[x] Or *that I should not go down to the Pit*
[y] Heb *that glory*
[z] One Heb Ms Gk Syr Jerome: MT *I hate*

9 Be gracious to me, O LORD,
for I am in distress;
my eye wastes away from grief,
my soul and body also.
10 For my life is spent with sorrow,
and my years with sighing;
my strength fails because of my misery,[a]
and my bones waste away.

11 I am the scorn of all my adversaries,
a horror[b] to my neighbors,
an object of dread to my acquaintances;
those who see me in the street flee from me.
12 I have passed out of mind like one who is dead;
I have become like a broken vessel.
13 For I hear the whispering of many—
terror all around!—
as they scheme together against me,
as they plot to take my life.

14 But I trust in you, O LORD;
I say, "You are my God."
15 My times are in your hand;
deliver me from the hand of my enemies and persecutors.
16 Let your face shine upon your servant;
save me in your steadfast love.
17 Do not let me be put to shame, O LORD,
for I call on you;
let the wicked be put to shame;
let them go dumbfounded to Sheol.
18 Let the lying lips be stilled
that speak insolently against the righteous
with pride and contempt.

19 O how abundant is your goodness
that you have laid up for those who fear you,
and accomplished for those who take refuge in you,
in the sight of everyone!
20 In the shelter of your presence you hide them
from human plots;
you hold them safe under your shelter
from contentious tongues.

21 Blessed be the LORD,
for he has wondrously shown his steadfast love to me
when I was beset as a city under siege.
22 I had said in my alarm,
"I am driven far[c] from your sight."
But you heard my supplications
when I cried out to you for help.

23 Love the LORD, all you his saints.
The LORD preserves the faithful,
but abundantly repays the one who acts haughtily.
24 Be strong, and let your heart take courage,
all you who wait for the LORD.

Psalm 32

The Joy of Forgiveness

Of David. A Maskil.

1 Happy are those whose transgression is forgiven,
whose sin is covered.
2 Happy are those to whom the LORD imputes no iniquity,
and in whose spirit there is no deceit.

3 While I kept silence, my body wasted away

31.9 Ps 6.7 **31.10** Ps 13.2; 39.11; 38.3 **31.11** Isa 53.4; Ps 38.11; 64.8 **31.12** Ps 88.4,5 **31.13** Jer 20.10; Lam 2.20; Mt 27.1 **31.14** Ps 140.6 **31.15** Job 24.1; Ps 143.9 **31.16** Num 6.25; Ps 4.6 **31.17** Ps 25.2,3 **31.18** Ps 120.2; 94.4 **31.19** Isa 64.4; Rom 11.22; Ps 5.11

31.20 Ps 27.5; Job 5.21 **31.21** Ps 17.7; 1 Sam 23.7 **31.22** Ps 116.11; Lam 3.54 **31.23** Ps 34.9; 145.20; 94.2 **31.24** Ps 27.14 **32.1** Ps 85.2 **32.2** 2 Cor 5.19; Jn 1.47 **32.3** Ps 39.2,3; 31.10; 38.8

[a] Gk Syr: Heb *my iniquity* [b] Cn: Heb *exceedingly* [c] Another reading is *cut off*

through my groaning all
day long.
4 For day and night your hand
was heavy upon me;
my strength was dried up[d]
as by the heat of
summer. *Selah*

5 Then I acknowledged my sin
to you,
and I did not hide my
iniquity;
I said, "I will confess my
transgressions to the
LORD,"
and you forgave the guilt of
my sin. *Selah*

6 Therefore let all who are
faithful
offer prayer to you;
at a time of distress,[e] the
rush of mighty waters
shall not reach them.
7 You are a hiding place for
me;
you preserve me from
trouble;
you surround me with glad
cries of deliverance.
Selah

8 I will instruct you and teach
you the way you should
go;
I will counsel you with my
eye upon you.
9 Do not be like a horse or a
mule, without
understanding,
whose temper must be
curbed with bit and
bridle,
else it will not stay near
you.

10 Many are the torments of the
wicked,
but steadfast love
surrounds those who
trust in the LORD.
11 Be glad in the LORD and
rejoice, O righteous,
and shout for joy, all you
upright in heart.

32.4 Job 33.7 **32.5** Lev 26.40; Job 31.33; Prov 28.13; Ps 103.12 **32.6** Ps 69.13; 144.7; Isa 43.2 **32.7** Ps 31.20; 121.7; Ex 15.1 **32.8** Ps 25.8; 33.18 **32.9** Jas 3.3 **32.10** Rom 2.9; Prov 16.20 **32.11** Ps 64.10

33.1 Ps 32.11; 147.1 **33.2** Ps 92.3 **33.3** Ps 96.1; 98.4 **33.4** Ps 19.8; 119.90 **33.5** Ps 11.7; 119.64 **33.6** Gen 11.3; Job 23.13 **33.7** Ps 78.13 **33.8** Ps 67.7; 96.9 **33.9** Gen 1.3; Ps 148.5 **33.10** Isa 8.10; 19.3 **33.11** Job 23.13; Prov 19.21; Ps 40.5

Psalm 33

The Greatness and Goodness of God

1 Rejoice in the LORD, O you
righteous.
Praise befits the upright.
2 Praise the LORD with the lyre;
make melody to him with
the harp of ten strings.
3 Sing to him a new song;
play skillfully on the
strings, with loud
shouts.

4 For the word of the LORD is
upright,
and all his work is done in
faithfulness.
5 He loves righteousness and
justice;
the earth is full of the
steadfast love of the
LORD.

6 By the word of the LORD the
heavens were made,
and all their host by the
breath of his mouth.
7 He gathered the waters of
the sea as in a bottle;
he put the deeps in
storehouses.

8 Let all the earth fear the
LORD;
let all the inhabitants of
the world stand in awe
of him.
9 For he spoke, and it came to
be;
he commanded, and it
stood firm.

10 The LORD brings the counsel
of the nations to
nothing;
he frustrates the plans of
the peoples.
11 The counsel of the LORD
stands forever,
the thoughts of his heart to
all generations.

[d] Meaning of Heb uncertain [e] Cn: Heb *at a time of finding only*

12 Happy is the nation whose
God is the LORD,
the people whom he has
chosen as his heritage.
13 The LORD looks down from
heaven;
he sees all humankind.
14 From where he sits
enthroned he watches
all the inhabitants of the
earth—
15 he who fashions the hearts
of them all,
and observes all their
deeds.
16 A king is not saved by his
great army;
a warrior is not delivered
by his great strength.
17 The war horse is a vain hope
for victory,
and by its great might it
cannot save.

18 Truly the eye of the LORD is
on those who fear him,
on those who hope in his
steadfast love,
19 to deliver their soul from
death,
and to keep them alive in
famine.

20 Our soul waits for the LORD;
he is our help and shield.
21 Our heart is glad in him,
because we trust in his
holy name.
22 Let your steadfast love,
O LORD, be upon us,
even as we hope in you.

Psalm 34

Praise for Deliverance from Trouble

Of David, when he feigned madness before Abimelech, so that he drove him out, and he went away.

1 I will bless the LORD at all
times;
his praise shall continually
be in my mouth.
2 My soul makes its boast in
the LORD;
let the humble hear and be
glad.
3 O magnify the LORD with me,
and let us exalt his name
together.

4 I sought the LORD, and he
answered me,
and delivered me from all
my fears.
5 Look to him, and be radiant;
so your[f] faces shall never
be ashamed.
6 This poor soul cried, and was
heard by the LORD,
and was saved from every
trouble.
7 The angel of the LORD
encamps
around those who fear him,
and delivers them.
8 O taste and see that the
LORD is good;
happy are those who take
refuge in him.
9 O fear the LORD, you his holy
ones,
for those who fear him
have no want.
10 The young lions suffer want
and hunger,
but those who seek the
LORD lack no good
thing.

11 Come, O children, listen to
me;
I will teach you the fear of
the LORD.
12 Which of you desires life,
and covets many days to
enjoy good?
13 Keep your tongue from evil,
and your lips from
speaking deceit.
14 Depart from evil, and do
good;
seek peace, and pursue it.

15 The eyes of the LORD are on
the righteous,
and his ears are open to
their cry.

33.12 Ps 144.15; Ex 19.5; Deut 7.6
33.13 Job 28.24; Ps 11.4
33.15 Jer 32.19
33.16 Ps 44.6
33.17 Ps 20.7; Prov 21.31
33.18 Job 36.7; Ps 34.15; 147.11
33.19 Ps 37.19
33.20 Ps 130.6; 115.9
33.21 Zech 10.7; Jn 16.22
34.1 Eph 5.20; Ps 71.6
34.2 Jer 9.24; Ps 119.74
34.3 Lk 1.46
34.4 Mt 7.7; vv. 6,17,19
34.5 Ps 36.9; 25.3
34.6 vv. 4,17,19
34.7 Dan 6.22; 2 Kings 6.17
34.8 1 Pet 2.3; Ps 2.12
34.9 Ps 23.1
34.10 Ps 84.11
34.11 Ps 111.10
34.12 1 Pet 3.10
34.13 1 Pet 2.22
34.14 Ps 37.27; Heb 12.14
34.15 Job 36.7; Ps 33.18

f Gk Syr Jerome: Heb *their*

16 The face of the Lord is
against evildoers,
to cut off the remembrance
of them from the earth.
17 When the righteous cry for
help, the Lord hears,
and rescues them from all
their troubles.
18 The Lord is near to the
brokenhearted,
and saves the crushed in
spirit.

19 Many are the afflictions of
the righteous,
but the Lord rescues them
from them all.
20 He keeps all their bones;
not one of them will be
broken.
21 Evil brings death to the
wicked,
and those who hate the
righteous will be
condemned.
22 The Lord redeems the life of
his servants;
none of those who take
refuge in him will be
condemned.

Psalm 35

Prayer for Deliverance from Enemies

Of David.

1 Contend, O Lord, with those
who contend with me;
fight against those who
fight against me!
2 Take hold of shield and
buckler,
and rise up to help me!
3 Draw the spear and javelin
against my pursuers;
say to my soul,
"I am your salvation."

4 Let them be put to shame
and dishonor
who seek after my life.
Let them be turned back and
confounded
who devise evil against me.
5 Let them be like chaff before
the wind,
with the angel of the Lord
driving them on.
6 Let their way be dark and
slippery,
with the angel of the Lord
pursuing them.

7 For without cause they hid
their net[g] for me;
without cause they dug a
pit[h] for my life.
8 Let ruin come on them
unawares.
And let the net that they hid
ensnare them;
let them fall in it—to their
ruin.

9 Then my soul shall rejoice in
the Lord,
exulting in his deliverance.
10 All my bones shall say,
"O Lord, who is like you?
You deliver the weak
from those too strong for
them,
the weak and needy from
those who despoil
them."

11 Malicious witnesses rise up;
they ask me about things I
do not know.
12 They repay me evil for good;
my soul is forlorn.
13 But as for me, when they
were sick,
I wore sackcloth;
I afflicted myself with
fasting.
I prayed with head bowed[i]
on my bosom,
14 as though I grieved for a
friend or a brother;
I went about as one who
laments for a mother,
bowed down and in
mourning.

15 But at my stumbling they
gathered in glee,
they gathered together
against me;

34.16 Jer 44.11; Prov 10.7
34.17 Ps 145.19; v. 19
34.18 Ps 145.18; Isa 57.15
34.19 Prov 24.16; vv. 4,6,17
34.20 Jn 19.36
34.21 Ps 94.23
34.22 1 Kings 1.29; Ps 71.23
35.1 Ps 43.1
35.3 Ps 62.2
35.4 Ps 70.2,3
35.5 Job 21.18; Ps 1.4; Isa 29.5
35.6 Ps 73.18; Jer 23.12
35.7 Ps 9.15
35.8 1 Thes 5.3
35.9 Isa 61.10; Lk 1.47
35.10 Ex 15.11; Ps 18.17; 37.14
35.11 Ps 27.12
35.12 Jn 10.32
35.13 Job 30.25; Ps 69.10
35.15 Job 30.1,8

[g] Heb *a pit, their net* [h] The word *pit* is transposed from the preceding line
[i] Or *My prayer turned back*

ruffians whom I did not
know
tore at me without ceasing;
16 they impiously mocked more
and more,[j]
gnashing at me with their
teeth.

17 How long, O LORD, will you
look on?
Rescue me from their
ravages,
my life from the lions!
18 Then I will thank you in the
great congregation;
in the mighty throng I will
praise you.

19 Do not let my treacherous
enemies rejoice over
me,
or those who hate me
without cause wink the
eye.
20 For they do not speak peace,
but they conceive deceitful
words
against those who are quiet
in the land.
21 They open wide their mouths
against me;
they say, "Aha, Aha,
our eyes have seen it."

22 You have seen, O LORD; do
not be silent!
O Lord, do not be far from
me!
23 Wake up! Bestir yourself for
my defense,
for my cause, my God and
my Lord!
24 Vindicate me, O LORD, my
God,
according to your
righteousness,
and do not let them rejoice
over me.
25 Do not let them say to
themselves,
"Aha, we have our heart's
desire."
Do not let them say, "We
have swallowed you[k] up."

26 Let all those who rejoice at
my calamity
be put to shame and
confusion;
let those who exalt
themselves against me
be clothed with shame and
dishonor.

27 Let those who desire my
vindication
shout for joy and be glad,
and say evermore,
"Great is the LORD,
who delights in the welfare
of his servant."
28 Then my tongue shall tell of
your righteousness
and of your praise all day
long.

Psalm 36
Human Wickedness and Divine Goodness

To the leader. Of David, the servant of the LORD.

1 Transgression speaks to the
wicked
deep in their hearts;
there is no fear of God
before their eyes.
2 For they flatter themselves in
their own eyes
that their iniquity cannot
be found out and hated.
3 The words of their mouths
are mischief and deceit;
they have ceased to act
wisely and do good.
4 They plot mischief while on
their beds;
they are set on a way that
is not good;
they do not reject evil.

5 Your steadfast love, O LORD,
extends to the heavens,
your faithfulness to the
clouds.
6 Your righteousness is like
the mighty mountains,
your judgments are like the
great deep;

35.16 Lam 2.16 **35.17** Hab 1.13; Ps 22.20 **35.18** Ps 22.22,25 **35.19** Ps 13.4; 38.19; Prov 6.13; Ps 69.4; Jn 15.25 **35.21** Ps 22.13; 40.15 **35.22** Ex 3.7; Ps 28.1; 10.1 **35.23** Ps 44.23 **35.24** Ps 9.4; v. 19 **35.25** Lam 2.16 **35.26** Ps 40.14; 38.16 **35.27** Ps 32.11; 9.4; 40.16; 147.11 **35.28** Ps 51.14 **36.1** Rom 3.18 **36.3** Jer 4.22 **36.4** Prov 4.16; Mic 2.1; Isa 65.2 **36.6** Job 11.8; Ps 77.19; Rom 11.33

[j] Cn Compare Gk: Heb *like the profanest of mockers of a cake* [k] Heb *him*

you save humans and
animals alike, O LORD.

7 How precious is your
steadfast love, O God!
All people may take refuge
in the shadow of your
wings.
8 They feast on the abundance
of your house,
and you give them drink
from the river of your
delights.
9 For with you is the fountain
of life;
in your light we see light.

10 O continue your steadfast
love to those who know
you,
and your salvation to the
upright of heart!
11 Do not let the foot of the
arrogant tread on me,
or the hand of the wicked
drive me away.
12 There the evildoers lie
prostrate;
they are thrust down,
unable to rise.

Psalm 37

Exhortation to Patience and Trust

Of David.

1 Do not fret because of the
wicked;
do not be envious of
wrongdoers,
2 for they will soon fade like
the grass,
and wither like the green
herb.

3 Trust in the LORD, and do
good;
so you will live in the land,
and enjoy security.
4 Take delight in the LORD,
and he will give you the
desires of your heart.

5 Commit your way to the
LORD;
trust in him, and he will
act.
6 He will make your
vindication shine like
the light,
and the justice of your
cause like the noonday.

7 Be still before the LORD, and
wait patiently for him;
do not fret over those who
prosper in their way,
over those who carry out
evil devices.

8 Refrain from anger, and
forsake wrath.
Do not fret—it leads only
to evil.
9 For the wicked shall be cut
off,
but those who wait for the
LORD shall inherit the
land.

10 Yet a little while, and the
wicked will be no more;
though you look diligently
for their place, they will
not be there.
11 But the meek shall inherit
the land,
and delight themselves in
abundant prosperity.

12 The wicked plot against the
righteous,
and gnash their teeth at
them;
13 but the LORD laughs at the
wicked,
for he sees that their day is
coming.

14 The wicked draw the sword
and bend their bows
to bring down the poor and
needy,
to kill those who walk
uprightly;
15 their sword shall enter their
own heart,
and their bows shall be
broken.

16 Better is a little that the
righteous person has

36.7 Ruth 2.12 **36.8** Ps 65.4; Job 20.17; Rev 22.1 **36.9** Jer 2.13; 1 Pet 2.9 **36.12** Ps 140.10 **37.1** Ps 73.3; Prov 23.17 **37.2** Ps 90.5,6 **37.3** Ps 62.8; Deut 30.20; Isa 40.11 **37.4** Isa 58.14 **37.5** Ps 55.22; Prov 16.3; 1 Pet 5.7 **37.6** Job 11.17; Mic 7.9 **37.7** Ps 62.5; 40.1; vv. 1,8 **37.8** Ps 73.3; Eph 4.26 **37.9** Isa 60.21 **37.10** Job 24.24; 7.10 **37.11** Mt 5.5 **37.12** Ps 35.16 **37.13** Ps 2.4; 1 Sam 26.10 **37.14** Ps 11.2; 35.10 **37.15** Ps 9.16 **37.16** Prov 15.16

than the abundance of
many wicked.
17 For the arms of the wicked
shall be broken,
but the LORD upholds the
righteous.

18 The LORD knows the days of
the blameless,
and their heritage will
abide forever;
19 they are not put to shame in
evil times,
in the days of famine they
have abundance.

20 But the wicked perish,
and the enemies of the
LORD are like the glory
of the pastures;
they vanish—like smoke
they vanish away.

21 The wicked borrow, and do
not pay back,
but the righteous are
generous and keep
giving;
22 for those blessed by the LORD
shall inherit the land,
but those cursed by him
shall be cut off.

23 Our steps[l] are made firm by
the LORD,
when he delights in our[m]
way;
24 though we stumble,[n] we[o]
shall not fall headlong,
for the LORD holds us[p] by
the hand.

25 I have been young, and now
am old,
yet I have not seen the
righteous forsaken
or their children begging
bread.
26 They are ever giving liberally
and lending,
and their children become
a blessing.

27 Depart from evil, and do
good;
so you shall abide forever.
28 For the LORD loves justice;
he will not forsake his
faithful ones.

The righteous shall be kept
safe forever,
but the children of the
wicked shall be cut off.
29 The righteous shall inherit
the land,
and live in it forever.

30 The mouths of the righteous
utter wisdom,
and their tongues speak
justice.
31 The law of their God is in
their hearts;
their steps do not slip.

32 The wicked watch for the
righteous,
and seek to kill them.
33 The LORD will not abandon
them to their power,
or let them be condemned
when they are brought
to trial.

34 Wait for the LORD, and keep
to his way,
and he will exalt you to
inherit the land;
you will look on the
destruction of the
wicked.

35 I have seen the wicked
oppressing,
and towering like a cedar
of Lebanon.[q]
36 Again I[r] passed by, and they
were no more;
though I sought them, they
could not be found.

37 Mark the blameless, and
behold the upright,
for there is posterity for the
peaceable.
38 But transgressors shall be
altogether destroyed;
the posterity of the wicked
shall be cut off.

37.17 Job 38.15; Ps 10.15
37.18 Ps 1.6
37.19 Job 5.20; Ps 33.19
37.20 Ps 72.27; 102.3
37.21 Ps 112.5,9
37.22 Prov 3.33; Job 5.3
37.23 1 Sam 2.9; Ps 147.11
37.24 Prov 24.16; Ps 147.6
37.25 Heb 13.5; Job 15.23
37.26 v. 21; Ps 147.13
37.27 Ps 34.14; v. 18
37.28 Ps 11.7; 21.10; Isa 14.20
37.29 vv. 9,18
37.30 Mt 12.35
37.31 Ps 40.8; Isa 51.7; v. 23
37.32 Ps 10.8
37.33 2 Pet 2.9; Ps 109.31
37.34 Ps 27.14; 52.5,6
37.35 Job 5.3
37.36 Job 20.5
37.37 Isa 57.1,2
37.38 Ps 1.4; vv. 9,20,28

[l] Heb *a man's steps* [m] Heb *his* [n] Heb *he stumbles* [o] Heb *he* [p] Heb *him* [q] Gk: Meaning of Heb uncertain [r] Gk Syr Jerome: Heb *he*

39 The salvation of the righteous is from the LORD;
he is their refuge in the time of trouble.
40 The LORD helps them and rescues them;
he rescues them from the wicked, and saves them,
because they take refuge in him.

Psalm 38

A Penitent Sufferer's Plea for Healing

A Psalm of David, for the memorial offering.

1 O LORD, do not rebuke me in your anger,
or discipline me in your wrath.
2 For your arrows have sunk into me,
and your hand has come down on me.

3 There is no soundness in my flesh
because of your indignation;
there is no health in my bones
because of my sin.
4 For my iniquities have gone over my head;
they weigh like a burden too heavy for me.

5 My wounds grow foul and fester
because of my foolishness;
6 I am utterly bowed down and prostrate;
all day long I go around mourning.
7 For my loins are filled with burning,
and there is no soundness in my flesh.
8 I am utterly spent and crushed;
I groan because of the tumult of my heart.

37.39 Ps 3.8; 9.9 **37.40** Isa 31.5; 1 Chr 5.20 **38.1** Ps 6.1 **38.2** Job 6.4; Ps 32.4 **38.3** Isa 1.6; Ps 6.2 **38.4** Ezra 9.6 **38.5** Ps 69.5 **38.6** Ps 35.14; 42.9 **38.7** Ps 102.3; v. 3 **38.8** Job 3.24; Ps 22.1

38.9 Ps 10.17; 6.6 **38.10** Ps 31.10; 6.7 **38.11** Ps 31.11; Lk 23.49 **38.12** Ps 54.3; 140.5; 35.4, 20 **38.13** Ps 39.2,9 **38.15** Ps 39.7; 17.6 **38.16** Ps 13.4; 35.26 **38.17** Ps 13.2 **38.18** Ps 32.5; 2 Cor 7.9 **38.19** Ps 18.17; 35.19 **38.20** Ps 35.12; 1 Jn 3.12

9 O Lord, all my longing is known to you;
my sighing is not hidden from you.
10 My heart throbs, my strength fails me;
as for the light of my eyes—it also has gone from me.
11 My friends and companions stand aloof from my affliction,
and my neighbors stand far off.

12 Those who seek my life lay their snares;
those who seek to hurt me speak of ruin,
and meditate treachery all day long.

13 But I am like the deaf, I do not hear;
like the mute, who cannot speak.
14 Truly, I am like one who does not hear,
and in whose mouth is no retort.

15 But it is for you, O LORD, that I wait;
it is you, O LORD my God, who will answer.
16 For I pray, "Only do not let them rejoice over me,
those who boast against me when my foot slips."

17 For I am ready to fall,
and my pain is ever with me.
18 I confess my iniquity;
I am sorry for my sin.
19 Those who are my foes without cause[s] are mighty,
and many are those who hate me wrongfully.
20 Those who render me evil for good
are my adversaries because I follow after good.

[s] Q Ms: MT *my living foes*

21 Do not forsake me, O LORD;
O my God, do not be far from me;
22 make haste to help me,
O Lord, my salvation.

Psalm 39

Prayer for Wisdom and Forgiveness

To the leader: to Jeduthun. A Psalm of David.

1 I said, "I will guard my ways
that I may not sin with my tongue;
I will keep a muzzle on my mouth
as long as the wicked are in my presence."
2 I was silent and still;
I held my peace to no avail;
my distress grew worse,
3 my heart became hot within me.
While I mused, the fire burned;
then I spoke with my tongue:

4 "LORD, let me know my end,
and what is the measure of my days;
let me know how fleeting my life is.
5 You have made my days a few handbreadths,
and my lifetime is as nothing in your sight.
Surely everyone stands as a mere breath. *Selah*
6 Surely everyone goes about like a shadow.
Surely for nothing they are in turmoil;
they heap up, and do not know who will gather.

7 "And now, O Lord, what do I wait for?
My hope is in you.
8 Deliver me from all my transgressions.
Do not make me the scorn of the fool.
9 I am silent; I do not open my mouth,
for it is you who have done it.
10 Remove your stroke from me;
I am worn down by the blows[t] of your hand.

11 "You chastise mortals
in punishment for sin,
consuming like a moth what is dear to them;
surely everyone is a mere breath. *Selah*

12 "Hear my prayer, O LORD,
and give ear to my cry;
do not hold your peace at my tears.
For I am your passing guest,
an alien, like all my forebears.
13 Turn your gaze away from me, that I may smile again,
before I depart and am no more."

Psalm 40

Thanksgiving for Deliverance and Prayer for Help

To the leader. Of David. A Psalm.

1 I waited patiently for the LORD;
he inclined to me and heard my cry.
2 He drew me up from the desolate pit,[u]
out of the miry bog,
and set my feet upon a rock,
making my steps secure.
3 He put a new song in my mouth,
a song of praise to our God.
Many will see and fear,
and put their trust in the LORD.

4 Happy are those who make the LORD their trust,
who do not turn to the proud,

38.21 Ps 35.22 **38.22** Ps 40.13,17; 27.1 **39.1** 1 Kings 2.4; Job 2.10; Jas 3.2 **39.2** Ps 38.13 **39.4** Ps 90.12; 103.14 **39.5** Ps 89.47; 144.4; 62.9 **39.6** 1 Pet 1.24; Ps 127.2; Job 27.17; Lk 12.20 **39.7** Ps 38.15 **39.8** Ps 51.9; 44.13 **39.9** v. 2; Job 2.10 **39.10** Job 9.34; Ps 32.4 **39.11** 2 Pet 2.16; Job 13.28; v. 5 **39.12** Ps 102.1; 56.8; Heb 11.13; 1 Pet 2.11 **39.13** Job 10.20; 14.10 **40.1** Ps 27.14; 34.15 **40.2** Ps 69.2; 27.5 **40.3** Ps 33.3 **40.4** Ps 84.12

[t] Heb *hostility* [u] Cn: Heb *pit of tumult*

to those who go astray
after false gods.
5 You have multiplied, O LORD my God,
your wondrous deeds and your thoughts toward us;
none can compare with you.
Were I to proclaim and tell of them,
they would be more than can be counted.

6 Sacrifice and offering you do not desire,
but you have given me an open ear.[v]
Burnt offering and sin offering
you have not required.
7 Then I said, "Here I am;
in the scroll of the book it is written of me.[w]
8 I delight to do your will, O my God;
your law is within my heart."

9 I have told the glad news of deliverance
in the great congregation;
see, I have not restrained my lips,
as you know, O LORD.
10 I have not hidden your saving help within my heart,
I have spoken of your faithfulness and your salvation;
I have not concealed your steadfast love and your faithfulness
from the great congregation.

11 Do not, O LORD, withhold your mercy from me;
let your steadfast love and your faithfulness
keep me safe forever.
12 For evils have encompassed me
without number;
my iniquities have overtaken me,
until I cannot see;
they are more than the hairs of my head,
and my heart fails me.

13 Be pleased, O LORD, to deliver me;
O LORD, make haste to help me.
14 Let all those be put to shame and confusion
who seek to snatch away my life;
let those be turned back and brought to dishonor
who desire my hurt.
15 Let those be appalled because of their shame
who say to me, "Aha, Aha!"

16 But may all who seek you rejoice and be glad in you;
may those who love your salvation
say continually, "Great is the LORD!"
17 As for me, I am poor and needy,
but the Lord takes thought for me.
You are my help and my deliverer;
do not delay, O my God.

Psalm 41

Assurance of God's Help and a Plea for Healing

To the leader. A Psalm of David.

1 Happy are those who consider the poor;[x]
the LORD delivers them in the day of trouble.
2 The LORD protects them and keeps them alive;
they are called happy in the land.
You do not give them up to the will of their enemies.

40.5 Ps 136.4; Isa 55.8; Ps 139.18
40.6 1 Sam 15.22
40.8 Jn 4.34; Rom 7.22; Ps 37.31
40.9 Ps 22.22; 119.13
40.10 Acts 20.20; Ps 89.1
40.11 Ps 43.3
40.12 Ps 116.3; 38.4; 69.4; 73.26
40.13 Ps 70.1
40.14 Ps 35.4; 63.9
40.15 Ps 70.3
40.16 Ps 70.4; 35.27
40.17 Ps 70.5
41.1 Ps 82.3,4; Prov 14.21
41.2 Ps 37.22,28; 27.12

[v] Heb *ears you have dug for me* [w] Meaning of Heb uncertain [x] Or *weak*

[3] The LORD sustains them on
their sickbed;
in their illness you heal all
their infirmities.[y]

[4] As for me, I said, "O LORD,
be gracious to me;
heal me, for I have sinned
against you."
[5] My enemies wonder in
malice
when I will die, and my
name perish.
[6] And when they come to see
me, they utter empty
words,
while their hearts gather
mischief;
when they go out, they tell
it abroad.
[7] All who hate me whisper
together about me;
they imagine the worst for
me.

[8] They think that a deadly
thing has fastened on
me,
that I will not rise again
from where I lie.
[9] Even my bosom friend in
whom I trusted,
who ate of my bread, has
lifted the heel against
me.
[10] But you, O LORD, be gracious
to me,
and raise me up, that I
may repay them.

[11] By this I know that you are
pleased with me;
because my enemy has not
triumphed over me.
[12] But you have upheld me
because of my integrity,
and set me in your
presence forever.

[13] Blessed be the LORD, the God
of Israel,
from everlasting to
everlasting.
Amen and Amen.

41.3 Ps 6.6 **41.4** Ps 6.2; 51.4 **41.5** Ps 38.12 **41.6** Ps 12.2 **41.7** Ps 56.5 **41.8** Ps 71.10,11 **41.9** Job 19.19; Ps 55.12; Jn 13.18 **41.10** Ps 3.3 **41.11** Ps 147.11; 25.2 **41.12** Ps 37.17; Job 36.7 **41.13** Ps 106.48

BOOK II

(Psalms 42–72)

Psalm 42

Longing for God and His Help in Distress

To the leader. A Maskil of the Korahites.

[1] As a deer longs for flowing
streams,
so my soul longs for you,
O God.
[2] My soul thirsts for God,
for the living God.
When shall I come and
behold
the face of God?
[3] My tears have been my food
day and night,
while people say to me
continually,
"Where is your God?"

[4] These things I remember,
as I pour out my soul:
how I went with the throng,[z]
and led them in procession
to the house of God,
with glad shouts and songs
of thanksgiving,
a multitude keeping
festival.
[5] Why are you cast down,
O my soul,
and why are you disquieted
within me?
Hope in God; for I shall
again praise him,
my help [6] and my God.

My soul is cast down within
me;
therefore I remember you
from the land of Jordan and
of Hermon,
from Mount Mizar.
[7] Deep calls to deep
at the thunder of your
cataracts;
all your waves and your
billows

42.1 Ps 119.131 **42.2** Ps 63.1; Jer 10.10; Ps 43.4 **42.3** Ps 80.5; 79.10 **42.4** Ps 62.8; Isa 30.29; Ps 100.4 **42.5** Ps 38.6; 77.3; Lam 3.24; Ps 44.3 **42.7** Ps 88.7; Jon 2.3

[y] Heb *you change all his bed* [z] Meaning of Heb uncertain

have gone over me.
8 By day the LORD commands
his steadfast love,
and at night his song is
with me,
a prayer to the God of my
life.

9 I say to God, my rock,
"Why have you forgotten
me?
Why must I walk about
mournfully
because the enemy
oppresses me?"
10 As with a deadly wound in
my body,
my adversaries taunt me,
while they say to me
continually,
"Where is your God?"

11 Why are you cast down,
O my soul,
and why are you disquieted
within me?
Hope in God; for I shall
again praise him,
my help and my God.

Psalm 43

Prayer to God in Time of Trouble

1 Vindicate me, O God, and
defend my cause
against an ungodly people;
from those who are deceitful
and unjust
deliver me!
2 For you are the God in
whom I take refuge;
why have you cast me off?
Why must I walk about
mournfully
because of the oppression
of the enemy?

3 O send out your light and
your truth;
let them lead me;
let them bring me to your
holy hill
and to your dwelling.
4 Then I will go to the altar of
God,
to God my exceeding joy;
and I will praise you with the
harp,
O God, my God.

5 Why are you cast down,
O my soul,
and why are you disquieted
within me?
Hope in God; for I shall
again praise him,
my help and my God.

Psalm 44

National Lament and Prayer for Help

To the leader. Of the Korahites.
A Maskil.

1 We have heard with our ears,
O God,
our ancestors have told us,
what deeds you performed in
their days,
in the days of old:
2 you with your own hand
drove out the nations,
but them you planted;
you afflicted the peoples,
but them you set free;
3 for not by their own sword
did they win the land,
nor did their own arm give
them victory;
but your right hand, and
your arm,
and the light of your
countenance,
for you delighted in them.

4 You are my King and my
God;
you command[a] victories
for Jacob.
5 Through you we push down
our foes;
through your name we
tread down our
assailants.
6 For not in my bow do I trust,
nor can my sword save me.
7 But you have saved us from
our foes,

42.8 Ps 57.3; Job 35.10; Ps 63.6; 149.5
42.9 Ps 38.6
42.10 v. 3
42.11 v. 5
43.1 Ps 26.1; 1 Sam 24.15; Ps 5.6
43.2 Ps 18.1; 44.9; 42.9
43.3 Ps 36.9; 42.4; 84.1
43.4 Ps 26.6; 33.2
43.5 Ps 42.5,11
44.1 Ex 12.26; Ps 78.3,12
44.2 Ex 15.17; Ps 78.55; 80.8
44.3 Josh 24.12; Ps 77.15; Deut 4.37; 7.7,8
44.4 Ps 74.12; 79.9
44.5 Dan 8.4; Ps 108.13
44.6 Ps 33.16
44.7 Ps 136.24; 53.5

[a] Gk Syr: Heb *You are my King, O God; command*

and have put to confusion
those who hate us.
8 In God we have boasted
continually,
and we will give thanks to
your name forever. *Selah*

9 Yet you have rejected us and
abased us,
and have not gone out with
our armies.
10 You made us turn back from
the foe,
and our enemies have
gotten spoil.
11 You have made us like sheep
for slaughter,
and have scattered us
among the nations.
12 You have sold your people
for a trifle,
demanding no high price
for them.

13 You have made us the taunt
of our neighbors,
the derision and scorn of
those around us.
14 You have made us a byword
among the nations,
a laughingstock[b] among
the peoples.
15 All day long my disgrace is
before me,
and shame has covered my
face
16 at the words of the taunters
and revilers,
at the sight of the enemy
and the avenger.

17 All this has come upon
us,
yet we have not forgotten
you,
or been false to your
covenant.
18 Our heart has not turned
back,
nor have our steps
departed from your way,
19 yet you have broken us in
the haunt of jackals,
and covered us with deep
darkness.

44.8 Ps 34.2; 30.12 **44.9** Ps 60.1,10; 74.1 **44.10** Lev 26.17; Josh 7.8; Ps 89.41 **44.11** v. 22; Deut 4.27; 28.64; Ps 106.27 **44.12** Isa 52.3,4; Jer 15.13 **44.13** Ps 79.4; 80.6 **44.14** Jer 24.9; Ps 109.25 **44.16** Ps 74.10; 8.2 **44.17** Dan 9.13; Ps 78.7,57 **44.18** Ps 78.57; Job 23.11 **44.19** Ps 51.8; Job 3.5

44.20 Ps 78.11; 68.31; 81.9 **44.21** Ps 139.1,2; Jer 17.10 **44.22** Rom 8.36; Isa 53.7 **44.23** Ps 7.6; 78.65; 77.7 **44.24** Job 13.24; Ps 42.9 **44.25** Ps 119.25 **44.26** Ps 35.2; 25.22 **45.1** Ezra 7.6 **45.2** Lk 4.22 **45.3** Isa 9.6 **45.4** Rev 6.2

20 If we had forgotten the name
of our God,
or spread out our hands to
a strange god,
21 would not God discover this?
For he knows the secrets of
the heart.
22 Because of you we are being
killed all day long,
and accounted as sheep for
the slaughter.

23 Rouse yourself! Why do you
sleep, O Lord?
Awake, do not cast us off
forever!
24 Why do you hide your face?
Why do you forget our
affliction and
oppression?
25 For we sink down to the
dust;
our bodies cling to the
ground.
26 Rise up, come to our help.
Redeem us for the sake of
your steadfast love.

Psalm 45

Ode for a Royal Wedding

To the leader: according to Lilies. Of the Korahites. A Maskil. A love song.

1 My heart overflows with a
goodly theme;
I address my verses to the
king;
my tongue is like the pen
of a ready scribe.

2 You are the most handsome
of men;
grace is poured upon your
lips;
therefore God has blessed
you forever.
3 Gird your sword on your
thigh, O mighty one,
in your glory and majesty.

4 In your majesty ride on
victoriously

[b] Heb *a shaking of the head*

for the cause of truth and
to defend[c] the right;
let your right hand teach
you dread deeds.
5 Your arrows are sharp
in the heart of the king's
enemies;
the peoples fall under you.

6 Your throne, O God,[d]
endures forever and
ever.
Your royal scepter is a
scepter of equity;
7 you love righteousness and
hate wickedness.
Therefore God, your God,
has anointed you
with the oil of gladness
beyond your
companions;
8 your robes are all fragrant
with myrrh and aloes
and cassia.
From ivory palaces stringed
instruments make you
glad;
9 daughters of kings are
among your ladies of
honor;
at your right hand stands
the queen in gold of
Ophir.

10 Hear, O daughter, consider
and incline your ear;
forget your people and your
father's house,
11 and the king will desire
your beauty.
Since he is your lord, bow to
him;
12 the people[e] of Tyre will
seek your favor with
gifts,
the richest of the people
13 with all kinds of
wealth.

The princess is decked in her
chamber with
gold-woven robes;[f]
14 in many-colored robes she
is led to the king;
behind her the virgins, her
companions, follow.

15 With joy and gladness they
are led along
as they enter the palace of
the king.

16 In the place of ancestors
you, O king,[g] shall
have sons;
you will make them princes
in all the earth.
17 I will cause your name to be
celebrated in all
generations;
therefore the peoples will
praise you forever and
ever.

Psalm 46

God's Defense of His City and People

To the leader. Of the Korahites. According to Alamoth. A Song.

1 God is our refuge and
strength,
a very present[h] help in
trouble.
2 Therefore we will not fear,
though the earth should
change,
though the mountains
shake in the heart of
the sea;
3 though its waters roar and
foam,
though the mountains
tremble with its tumult.
Selah

4 There is a river whose
streams make glad the
city of God,
the holy habitation of the
Most High.
5 God is in the midst of the
city;[i] it shall not be
moved;
God will help it when the
morning dawns.
6 The nations are in an uproar,
the kingdoms totter;

45.6 Ps 93.2; Heb 1.8,9; Ps 98.9
45.7 Ps 33.5; Isa 61.1; Ps 79.4; 21.6
45.8 Song 1.3
45.9 Song 6.8; 1 Kings 2.19
45.10 Deut 21.13
45.11 Ps 95.6; Isa 54.5
45.12 Ps 22.29
45.13 Isa 61.10
45.14 Song 1.4; v. 9
45.16 1 Pet 2.9; Rev 1.6; 20.6
45.17 Mal 1.11; Ps 138.4
46.1 Ps 14.6; Deut 4.7; Ps 9.9
46.2 Ps 23.4; 82.5; 18.7
46.3 Ps 93.3,4
46.4 Isa 8.7; Ps 48.1,8; Isa 60.14
46.5 Isa 12.6; Ps 37.40
46.6 Ps 2.1; 68.33; Mic 1.4

[c] Cn: Heb *and the meekness of* [d] Or *Your throne is a throne of God, it* [e] Heb *daughter* [f] Or *people.* [13]*All glorious is the princess within, gold embroidery is her clothing* [g] Heb lacks *O king* [h] Or *well proved* [i] Heb *of it*

he utters his voice, the
earth melts.
7 The LORD of hosts is with us;
the God of Jacob is our
refuge.[j] *Selah*

8 Come, behold the works of
the LORD;
see what desolations he
has brought on the
earth.
9 He makes wars cease to the
end of the earth;
he breaks the bow, and
shatters the spear;
he burns the shields with
fire.
10 "Be still, and know that I am
God!
I am exalted among the
nations,
I am exalted in the earth."
11 The LORD of hosts is with us;
the God of Jacob is our
refuge.[j] *Selah*

Psalm 47

God's Rule over the Nations

To the leader. Of the Korahites.
A Psalm.

1 Clap your hands, all you
peoples;
shout to God with loud
songs of joy.
2 For the LORD, the Most High,
is awesome,
a great king over all the
earth.
3 He subdued peoples under
us,
and nations under our feet.
4 He chose our heritage for us,
the pride of Jacob whom
he loves. *Selah*

5 God has gone up with a
shout,
the LORD with the sound of
a trumpet.
6 Sing praises to God, sing
praises;
sing praises to our King,
sing praises.
7 For God is the king of all the
earth;

46.7 2 Chr 13.12; Ps 9.9
46.8 Ps 66.5; Isa 61.4
46.9 Isa 2.4; Ps 76.3; Ezek 39.9
46.10 Ps 100.3; Isa 2.11,17
47.1 Ps 98.8; Isa 55.12; Ps 106.47
47.2 Deut 7.21
47.3 Ps 18.47
47.4 1 Pet 1.4
47.5 Ps 68.33; 98.6
47.6 Ps 68.4; 89.18
47.7 1 Cor 14.15
47.8 1 Chr 16.31
47.9 Ps 72.11; Rom 4.11, 12; Ps 89.18; 97.9
48.1 Ps 96.4; Zech 8.3
48.2 Ps 50.2; Lam 2.15; Mt 5.35
48.3 Ps 46.7
48.4 2 Sam 10.6-19
48.5 Ex 15.15
48.7 Jer 18.17
48.8 Ps 87.5
48.9 Ps 26.3

sing praises with a psalm.[k]
8 God is king over the nations;
God sits on his holy
throne.
9 The princes of the peoples
gather
as the people of the God of
Abraham.
For the shields of the earth
belong to God;
he is highly exalted.

Psalm 48

The Glory and Strength of Zion

A Song. A Psalm of the
Korahites.

1 Great is the LORD and greatly
to be praised
in the city of our God.
His holy mountain,
2 beautiful in elevation,
is the joy of all the earth,
Mount Zion, in the far north,
the city of the great King.
3 Within its citadels God
has shown himself a sure
defense.

4 Then the kings assembled,
they came on together.
5 As soon as they saw it, they
were astounded;
they were in panic, they
took to flight;
6 trembling took hold of them
there,
pains as of a woman in
labor,
7 as when an east wind
shatters
the ships of Tarshish.
8 As we have heard, so have
we seen
in the city of the LORD of
hosts,
in the city of our God,
which God establishes
forever. *Selah*

9 We ponder your steadfast
love, O God,

[j] Or *fortress* [k] Heb *Maskil*

in the midst of your
temple.
10 Your name, O God, like your
praise,
reaches to the ends of the
earth.
Your right hand is filled with
victory.
11 Let Mount Zion be glad,
let the towns[l] of Judah
rejoice
because of your judgments.

12 Walk about Zion, go all
around it,
count its towers,
13 consider well its ramparts;
go through its citadels,
that you may tell the next
generation
14 that this is God,
our God forever and ever.
He will be our guide
forever.

Psalm 49

The Folly of Trust in Riches

To the leader. Of the Korahites.
A Psalm.

1 Hear this, all you peoples;
give ear, all inhabitants of
the world,
2 both low and high,
rich and poor together.
3 My mouth shall speak
wisdom;
the meditation of my heart
shall be understanding.
4 I will incline my ear to a
proverb;
I will solve my riddle to the
music of the harp.

5 Why should I fear in times of
trouble,
when the iniquity of my
persecutors surrounds
me,
6 those who trust in their
wealth
and boast of the
abundance of their
riches?
7 Truly, no ransom avails for
one's life,[m]
there is no price one can
give to God for it.
8 For the ransom of life is
costly,
and can never suffice
9 that one should live on
forever
and never see the grave.[n]

10 When we look at the wise,
they die;
fool and dolt perish
together
and leave their wealth to
others.
11 Their graves[o] are their
homes forever,
their dwelling places to all
generations,
though they named lands
their own.
12 Mortals cannot abide in their
pomp;
they are like the animals
that perish.

13 Such is the fate of the
foolhardy,
the end of those[p] who are
pleased with their lot.
Selah
14 Like sheep they are
appointed for Sheol;
Death shall be their
shepherd;
straight to the grave they
descend,[q]
and their form shall waste
away;
Sheol shall be their
home.[r]
15 But God will ransom my soul
from the power of
Sheol,
for he will receive me.
Selah

16 Do not be afraid when some
become rich,
when the wealth of their
houses increases.

48.10 Josh 7.9; Isa 41.10 **48.11** Ps 97.8 **48.13** Ps 122.7; 78.5-7 **48.14** Ps 23.4 **49.1** Ps 78.1; 33.8 **49.3** Ps 37.30; 119.130 **49.4** Ps 78.2; Num 12.8 **49.5** Ps 23.4 **49.6** Job 31.24 **49.7** Mt 25.8,9; Job 36.18

49.8 Mt 16.26 **49.9** Ps 22.29; 89.48 **49.10** Eccl 2.16,18 **49.11** Ps 64.6; 10.6; Deut 3.14 **49.12** v. 20 **49.13** Lk 12.20 **49.14** Ps 9.17; Dan 7.18; Mal 4.3; 1 Cor 6.2; Rev 2.26; Job 24.19 **49.15** Ps 56.13; 73.24 **49.16** Ps 37.7

[l] Heb *daughters* [m] Another reading is *no one can ransom a brother* [n] Heb *the pit* [o] Gk Syr Compare Tg: Heb *their inward (thought)* [p] Tg: Heb *after them* [q] Cn: Heb *the upright shall have dominion over them in the morning* [r] Meaning of Heb uncertain

17 For when they die they will
carry nothing away;
their wealth will not go
down after them.
18 Though in their lifetime they
count themselves happy
—for you are praised when
you do well for
yourself—
19 they[s] will go to the company
of their ancestors,
who will never again see
the light.
20 Mortals cannot abide in their
pomp;
they are like the animals
that perish.

Psalm 50

The Acceptable Sacrifice

A Psalm of Asaph.

1 The mighty one, God the
LORD,
speaks and summons the
earth
from the rising of the sun
to its setting.
2 Out of Zion, the perfection
of beauty,
God shines forth.

3 Our God comes and does not
keep silence,
before him is a devouring
fire,
and a mighty tempest all
around him.
4 He calls to the heavens
above
and to the earth, that he
may judge his people:
5 "Gather to me my faithful
ones,
who made a covenant with
me by sacrifice!"
6 The heavens declare his
righteousness,
for God himself is judge.
Selah

7 "Hear, O my people, and I
will speak,
O Israel, I will testify
against you.
I am God, your God.

49.17 Ps 17.14 **49.18** Lk 12.19 **49.19** Gen 15.15; Job 33.30 **49.20** v. 12 **50.1** Josh 22.22; Ps 113.3 **50.2** Ps 48.2; Deut 33.2 **50.3** Ps 96.13; 97.3; Dan 7.10 **50.4** Deut 4.26; Isa 1.2 **50.5** Ps 30.4; Ex 24.7; v. 8 **50.6** Ps 89.5; 75.7 **50.7** Ps 81.8; Ex 20.2

50.8 Ps 40.6; Hos 6.6 **50.9** Ps 69.31 **50.10** Ps 104.24 **50.12** Ex 19.5 **50.14** Heb 13.15; Deut 23.21 **50.15** Ps 91.15; 81.7; 22.23 **50.16** Isa 29.13 **50.17** Rom 2.21, 22; Neh 9.26 **50.18** Rom 1.32; 1 Tim 5.22 **50.19** Ps 10.7; 52.2 **50.20** Mt 10.21 **50.21** Eccl 8.11; Isa 42.14; Ps 90.8

8 Not for your sacrifices do I
rebuke you;
your burnt offerings are
continually before me.
9 I will not accept a bull from
your house,
or goats from your folds.
10 For every wild animal of the
forest is mine,
the cattle on a thousand
hills.
11 I know all the birds of the
air,[t]
and all that moves in the
field is mine.

12 "If I were hungry, I would
not tell you,
for the world and all that is
in it is mine.
13 Do I eat the flesh of bulls,
or drink the blood of goats?
14 Offer to God a sacrifice of
thanksgiving,[u]
and pay your vows to the
Most High.
15 Call on me in the day of
trouble;
I will deliver you, and you
shall glorify me."

16 But to the wicked God says:
"What right have you to
recite my statutes,
or take my covenant on
your lips?
17 For you hate discipline,
and you cast my words
behind you.
18 You make friends with a
thief when you see one,
and you keep company
with adulterers.

19 "You give your mouth free
rein for evil,
and your tongue frames
deceit.
20 You sit and speak against
your kin;
you slander your own
mother's child.
21 These things you have done
and I have been silent;

[s] Cn: Heb *you* [t] Gk Syr Tg: Heb *mountains* [u] Or *make thanksgiving your sacrifice to God*

you thought that I was one
just like yourself.
But now I rebuke you, and
lay the charge before
you.

22 "Mark this, then, you who
forget God,
or I will tear you apart, and
there will be no one to
deliver.
23 Those who bring
thanksgiving as their
sacrifice honor me;
to those who go the right
way[v]
I will show the salvation of
God."

Psalm 51

Prayer for Cleansing and Pardon

To the leader. A Psalm of David, when the prophet Nathan came to him, after he had gone in to Bathsheba.

1 Have mercy on me, O God,
according to your steadfast
love;
according to your abundant
mercy
blot out my transgressions.
2 Wash me thoroughly from
my iniquity,
and cleanse me from my
sin.

3 For I know my
transgressions,
and my sin is ever before
me.
4 Against you, you alone, have
I sinned,
and done what is evil in
your sight,
so that you are justified in
your sentence
and blameless when you
pass judgment.
5 Indeed, I was born guilty,
a sinner when my mother
conceived me.

6 You desire truth in the
inward being;[w]

50.22 Job 8.13; Ps 9.17; 7.2
50.23 v. 14; Ps 85.13; 91.16
51.1 Ps 4.1; 106.45; Isa 43.25; Acts 3.19
51.2 Heb 9.14; 1 Jn 1.7
51.3 Isa 59.12
51.4 Gen 20.6; Lk 15.21; Rom 3.4
51.5 Ps 58.3; Job 14.4
51.6 Ps 15.2; Prov 2.6
51.7 Lev 14.4; Heb 9.19; Isa 1.18
51.8 Ps 35.10
51.9 Jer 16.17
51.10 Acts 15.9; Eph 2.10; Ps 78.37
51.11 2 Kings 13.23; Eph 4.30
51.12 Ps 13.5; 2 Cor 3.17
51.13 Acts 9.21, 22; Ps 22.27
51.14 2 Sam 12.9; Ps 25.5; 35.28
51.15 Ps 9.14
51.16 1 Sam 15.22; Ps 40.6
51.17 Ps 34.18
51.18 Isa 51.3; Ps 102.16

therefore teach me wisdom
in my secret heart.
7 Purge me with hyssop, and I
shall be clean;
wash me, and I shall be
whiter than snow.
8 Let me hear joy and
gladness;
let the bones that you have
crushed rejoice.
9 Hide your face from my sins,
and blot out all my
iniquities.

10 Create in me a clean heart,
O God,
and put a new and right[x]
spirit within me.
11 Do not cast me away from
your presence,
and do not take your holy
spirit from me.
12 Restore to me the joy of your
salvation,
and sustain in me a
willing[y] spirit.

13 Then I will teach
transgressors your ways,
and sinners will return to
you.
14 Deliver me from bloodshed,
O God,
O God of my salvation,
and my tongue will sing
aloud of your
deliverance.

15 O Lord, open my lips,
and my mouth will declare
your praise.
16 For you have no delight in
sacrifice;
if I were to give a burnt
offering, you would not
be pleased.
17 The sacrifice acceptable to
God[z] is a broken spirit;
a broken and contrite
heart, O God, you will
not despise.

18 Do good to Zion in your good
pleasure;

[v] Heb *who set a way* [w] Meaning of Heb uncertain [x] Or *steadfast* [y] Or *generous* [z] Or *My sacrifice, O God,*

rebuild the walls of
Jerusalem,
19 then you will delight in right
sacrifices,
in burnt offerings and
whole burnt offerings;
then bulls will be offered
on your altar.

Psalm 52

Judgment on the Deceitful

To the leader. A Maskil of David, when Doeg the Edomite came to Saul and said to him, "David has come to the house of Ahimelech."

1 Why do you boast, O mighty
one,
of mischief done against
the godly?[a]
All day long 2 you are
plotting destruction.
Your tongue is like a sharp
razor,
you worker of treachery.
3 You love evil more than
good,
and lying more than
speaking the truth.
Selah
4 You love all words that
devour,
O deceitful tongue.
5 But God will break you down
forever;
he will snatch and tear you
from your tent;
he will uproot you from the
land of the living. *Selah*
6 The righteous will see, and
fear,
and will laugh at the
evildoer,[b] saying,
7 "See the one who would not
take
refuge in God,
but trusted in abundant
riches,
and sought refuge in
wealth!"[c]
8 But I am like a green olive
tree
in the house of God.

51.19 Ps 4.5; 66.13,15
52.1 1 Sam 22.9; Ps 94.4
52.2 Ps 50.19; 57.4; 59.7
52.3 Jer 9.4,5
52.4 Ps 120.3
52.5 Prov 2.22; Ps 27.13
52.6 Job 22.19; Ps 37.34; 40.3
52.7 Ps 49.6
52.8 Jer 11.16; Ps 13.5
52.9 Ps 30.12; 54.6
53.1 Ps 14.1-7; Rom 3.10
53.2 Ps 33.13
53.3 Rom 3.12
53.4 Jer 4.22
53.5 Lev 26.17, 36; Ezek 6.5

I trust in the steadfast love
of God
forever and ever.
9 I will thank you forever,
because of what you have
done.
In the presence of the
faithful
I will proclaim[d] your
name, for it is good.

Psalm 53

Denunciation of Godlessness

To the leader: according to Mahalath. A Maskil of David.

1 Fools say in their hearts,
"There is no God."
They are corrupt, they
commit abominable
acts;
there is no one who does
good.
2 God looks down from heaven
on humankind
to see if there are any who
are wise,
who seek after God.
3 They have all fallen away,
they are all alike
perverse;
there is no one who does
good,
no, not one.
4 Have they no knowledge,
those evildoers,
who eat up my people as
they eat bread,
and do not call upon God?
5 There they shall be in great
terror,
in terror such as has not
been.
For God will scatter the
bones of the ungodly;[e]

[a] Cn Compare Syr: Heb *the kindness of God*
[b] Heb *him* [c] Syr Tg: Heb *in his destruction*
[d] Cn: Heb *wait for* [e] Cn Compare Gk Syr: Heb *him who encamps against you*

they will be put to
shame,[f] for God has
rejected them.

6 O that deliverance for Israel
would come from Zion!
When God restores the
fortunes of his people,
Jacob will rejoice; Israel
will be glad.

Psalm 54

Prayer for Vindication

To the leader:
with stringed instruments.
A Maskil of David
when the Ziphites went
and told Saul, "David is in
hiding among us."

1 Save me, O God, by your
name,
and vindicate me by your
might.
2 Hear my prayer, O God;
give ear to the words of my
mouth.

3 For the insolent have risen
against me,
the ruthless seek my
life;
they do not set God before
them. *Selah*

4 But surely, God is my
helper;
the Lord is the upholder
of[g] my life.
5 He will repay my enemies for
their evil.
In your faithfulness, put an
end to them.

6 With a freewill offering I will
sacrifice to you;
I will give thanks to your
name, O LORD, for it is
good.
7 For he has delivered me from
every trouble,
and my eye has looked in
triumph on my
enemies.

53.6 Ps 14.7 **54.1** Ps 20.1; 2 Chr 20.6 **54.2** Ps 55.1; 5.1 **54.3** Ps 86.14; 40.14; 36.1 **54.4** Ps 118.7; 41.12 **54.5** Ps 94.23; 143.12; 89.49 **54.6** Ps 50.14; 52.9 **54.7** Ps 34.6; 59.10

55.1 Ps 61.1; 27.9 **55.2** Ps 66.19; 77.3; Isa 38.14 **55.3** Ps 17.9; 2 Sam 16.7, 8; Ps 71.11 **55.4** Ps 116.3 **55.5** Ps 119.120; Job 21.6 **55.6** Job 3.13 **55.8** Isa 4.6 **55.9** Jer 6.7 **55.11** Ps 5.9; 10.7

Psalm 55

Complaint about a Friend's Treachery

To the leader: with stringed
instruments. A Maskil of David.

1 Give ear to my prayer,
O God;
do not hide yourself from
my supplication.
2 Attend to me, and answer
me;
I am troubled in my
complaint.
I am distraught 3 by the noise
of the enemy,
because of the clamor of
the wicked.
For they bring[h] trouble upon
me,
and in anger they cherish
enmity against me.

4 My heart is in anguish within
me,
the terrors of death have
fallen upon me.
5 Fear and trembling come
upon me,
and horror overwhelms me.
6 And I say, "O that I had
wings like a dove!
I would fly away and be at
rest;
7 truly, I would flee far away;
I would lodge in the
wilderness; *Selah*
8 I would hurry to find a
shelter for myself
from the raging wind and
tempest."

9 Confuse, O Lord, confound
their speech;
for I see violence and strife
in the city.
10 Day and night they go
around it
on its walls,
and iniquity and trouble are
within it;
11 ruin is in its midst;

[f] Gk: Heb *you will put to shame* [g] Gk Syr Jerome: Heb *is of those who uphold* or *is with those who uphold* [h] Cn Compare Gk: Heb *they cause to totter*

oppression and fraud
do not depart from its
marketplace.

12 It is not enemies who taunt
me —
I could bear that;
it is not adversaries who deal
insolently with me —
I could hide from them.
13 But it is you, my equal,
my companion, my familiar
friend,
14 with whom I kept pleasant
company;
we walked in the house of
God with the throng.
15 Let death come upon them;
let them go down alive to
Sheol;
for evil is in their homes
and in their hearts.

16 But I call upon God,
and the LORD will save me.
17 Evening and morning and at
noon
I utter my complaint and
moan,
and he will hear my voice.
18 He will redeem me
unharmed
from the battle that I wage,
for many are arrayed
against me.
19 God, who is enthroned from
of old, *Selah*
will hear, and will humble
them —
because they do not change,
and do not fear God.

20 My companion laid hands on
a friend
and violated a covenant
with me[i]
21 with speech smoother than
butter,
but with a heart set on
war;
with words that were softer
than oil,
but in fact were drawn
swords.

22 Cast your burden[j] on the
LORD,

55.12 Ps 41.9 **55.13** 2 Sam 15.12; Ps 41.9; Jer 9.4 **55.14** Ps 42.4 **55.15** Ps 64.7; Num 16.30, 33 **55.16** Ps 57.2,3 **55.17** Ps 141.2; Dan 6.10; Acts 3.1; Ps 5.3 **55.18** Ps 103.4; 2 Chr 32.7,8 **55.19** Ps 78.59; Deut 33.27 **55.20** Ps 7.4; 89.34 **55.21** Ps 28.3; 57.4; Prov 5.3; Ps 59.7 **55.22** Ps 37.5; Mt 6.25; 1 Pet 5.7; Ps 37.24

55.23 Ps 73.18; 5.6; Job 15.32; Prov 10.27; Ps 25.2 **56.1** Ps 57.1,3 **56.2** Ps 57.3; 35.1 **56.3** Ps 55.4,5; 11.1 **56.4** Ps 118.6; Heb 13.6 **56.5** Ps 41.7 **56.6** Ps 59.3; 140.2; 19.10, 11 **56.7** Ps 36.12; 55.23 **56.8** Ps 139.3; 39.12; Mal 3.16

and he will sustain you;
he will never permit
the righteous to be moved.

23 But you, O God, will cast
them down
into the lowest pit;
the bloodthirsty and
treacherous
shall not live out half their
days.
But I will trust in you.

Psalm 56

Trust in God under Persecution

To the leader: according to The Dove on Far-off Terebinths. Of David. A Miktam, when the Philistines seized him in Gath.

1 Be gracious to me, O God,
for people trample on
me;
all day long foes oppress
me;
2 my enemies trample on me
all day long,
for many fight against me.
O Most High, [3] when I am
afraid,
I put my trust in you.
4 In God, whose word I praise,
in God I trust; I am not
afraid;
what can flesh do to me?
5 All day long they seek to
injure my cause;
all their thoughts are
against me for evil.
6 They stir up strife, they lurk,
they watch my steps.
As they hoped to have my
life,
7 so repay[k] them for their
crime;
in wrath cast down the
peoples, O God!

8 You have kept count of my
tossings;
put my tears in your bottle.
Are they not in your
record?

[i] Heb lacks *with me* [j] Or *Cast what he has given you* [k] Cn: Heb *rescue*

9 Then my enemies will retreat
in the day when I call.
This I know, that[l] God is
for me.
10 In God, whose word I praise,
in the LORD, whose word I
praise,
11 in God I trust; I am not
afraid.
What can a mere mortal do
to me?

12 My vows to you I must
perform, O God;
I will render thank
offerings to you.
13 For you have delivered my
soul from death,
and my feet from falling,
so that I may walk before
God
in the light of life.

Psalm 57
Praise and Assurance under Persecution

To the leader: Do Not Destroy. Of David. A Miktam, when he fled from Saul, in the cave.

1 Be merciful to me, O God,
be merciful to me,
for in you my soul takes
refuge;
in the shadow of your wings
I will take refuge,
until the destroying storms
pass by.
2 I cry to God Most High,
to God who fulfills his
purpose for me.
3 He will send from heaven
and save me,
he will put to shame those
who trample on me.
Selah
God will send forth his
steadfast love and his
faithfulness.

4 I lie down among lions
that greedily devour[m]
human prey;
their teeth are spears and
arrows,
their tongues sharp swords.

56.9 Ps 9.3; 102.2; Rom 8.31 **56.12** Ps 50.14 **56.13** Ps 116.8; Job 33.30 **57.1** Ps 2.12; 17.8; Isa 26.20 **57.2** Ps 138.8 **57.3** Ps 18.16; 56.2; 40.11 **57.4** Ps 35.17; Prov 30.14; Ps 55.21

57.5 Ps 108.5 **57.6** Ps 35.7; 145.14; 7.15; Prov 28.10 **57.7** Ps 108.1 **57.8** Ps 16.9; 30.12; 150.3 **57.9** Ps 108.3 **57.10** Ps 36.5 **57.11** v. 5 **58.1** Ps 82.2 **58.2** Mal 3.15; Ps 94.20 **58.3** Ps 51.5; Isa 48.8; Ps 53.3 **58.4** Ps 140.3; Eccl 10.11 **58.5** Ps 81.11

5 Be exalted, O God, above the
heavens.
Let your glory be over all
the earth.

6 They set a net for my steps;
my soul was bowed down.
They dug a pit in my path,
but they have fallen into it
themselves. *Selah*
7 My heart is steadfast, O God,
my heart is steadfast.
I will sing and make melody.
8 Awake, my soul!
Awake, O harp and lyre!
I will awake the dawn.
9 I will give thanks to you,
O Lord, among the
peoples;
I will sing praises to you
among the nations.
10 For your steadfast love is as
high as the heavens;
your faithfulness extends
to the clouds.

11 Be exalted, O God, above the
heavens.
Let your glory be over all
the earth.

Psalm 58
Prayer for Vengeance

To the leader: Do Not Destroy. Of David. A Miktam.

1 Do you indeed decree what
is right, you gods?[n]
Do you judge people fairly?
2 No, in your hearts you devise
wrongs;
your hands deal out
violence on earth.

3 The wicked go astray from
the womb;
they err from their birth,
speaking lies.
4 They have venom like the
venom of a serpent,
like the deaf adder that
stops its ear,
5 so that it does not hear the
voice of charmers

[l] Or *because* [m] Cn: Heb *are aflame for* [n] Or *mighty lords*

or of the cunning
enchanter.

6 O God, break the teeth in
their mouths;
tear out the fangs of the
young lions, O LORD!
7 Let them vanish like water
that runs away;
like grass let them be
trodden down[o] and
wither.
8 Let them be like the snail
that dissolves into
slime;
like the untimely birth that
never sees the sun.
9 Sooner than your pots can
feel the heat of thorns,
whether green or ablaze,
may he sweep them
away!

10 The righteous will rejoice
when they see
vengeance done;
they will bathe their feet in
the blood of the
wicked.
11 People will say, "Surely there
is a reward for the
righteous;
surely there is a God who
judges on earth."

Psalm 59

Prayer for Deliverance from Enemies

To the leader: Do Not Destroy. Of David. A Miktam, when Saul ordered his house to be watched in order to kill him.

1 Deliver me from my enemies,
O my God;
protect me from those who
rise up against me.
2 Deliver me from those who
work evil;
from the bloodthirsty save
me.

3 Even now they lie in wait for
my life;
the mighty stir up strife
against me.
For no transgression or sin of
mine, O LORD,
4 for no fault of mine, they
run and make ready.

Rouse yourself, come to my
help and see!
5 You, LORD God of hosts, are
God of Israel.
Awake to punish all the
nations;
spare none of those who
treacherously plot evil.
Selah

6 Each evening they come
back,
howling like dogs
and prowling about the
city.
7 There they are, bellowing
with their mouths,
with sharp words[p] on their
lips—
for "Who," they think,[q]
"will hear us?"

8 But you laugh at them,
O LORD;
you hold all the nations in
derision.
9 O my strength, I will watch
for you;
for you, O God, are my
fortress.
10 My God in his steadfast love
will meet me;
my God will let me look in
triumph on my
enemies.

11 Do not kill them, or my
people may forget;
make them totter by your
power, and bring them
down,
O Lord, our shield.
12 For the sin of their mouths,
the words of their lips,
let them be trapped in
their pride.
For the cursing and lies that
they utter,
13 consume them in wrath;

58.6 Job 4.10; Ps 3.7 **58.7** Josh 7.5; Ps 112.10; 64.3 **58.8** Job 3.16 **58.9** Ps 118.12; Prov 10.25 **58.10** Ps 64.10; 91.8; 68.23 **58.11** Ps 18.20; 9.8 **59.1** Ps 143.9 **59.2** Ps 28.3; 139.19 **59.3** Ps 56.6

59.4 Ps 35.19,23 **59.5** Ps 9.5; Jer 18.23 **59.6** v. 14 **59.7** Ps 57.4; 10.11 **59.8** Ps 37.13; 2.4 **59.9** Ps 9.9 **59.10** Ps 21.3; 54.7 **59.11** Deut 4.9; Ps 106.27; 84.9 **59.12** Prov 12.13; Zeph 3.11; Ps 10.7 **59.13** Ps 104.35; 83.18

[o] Cn: Meaning of Heb uncertain
[p] Heb *with swords*
[q] Heb lacks *they think*

consume them until they
are no more.
Then it will be known to the
ends of the earth
that God rules over Jacob.
Selah

14 Each evening they come
back,
howling like dogs
and prowling about the
city.
15 They roam about for food,
and growl if they do not
get their fill.

16 But I will sing of your might;
I will sing aloud of your
steadfast love in the
morning.
For you have been a fortress
for me
and a refuge in the day of
my distress.
17 O my strength, I will sing
praises to you,
for you, O God, are my
fortress,
the God who shows me
steadfast love.

Psalm 60

Prayer for National Victory after Defeat

To the leader: according to the Lily of the Covenant. A Miktam of David; for instruction; when he struggled with Aram-naharaim and with Aram-zobah, and when Joab on his return killed twelve thousand Edomites in the Valley of Salt.

1 O God, you have rejected us,
broken our defenses;
you have been angry; now
restore us!
2 You have caused the land to
quake; you have torn it
open;
repair the cracks in it, for
it is tottering.
3 You have made your people
suffer hard things;
you have given us wine to
drink that made us reel.

59.14 v. 6 **59.16** Ps 21.13; 101.1; 88.13; v. 9; Ps 46.1 **59.17** vv. 9,10 **60.1** Ps 44.9; 2 Sam 5.20; Ps 79.5; 80.3 **60.2** Ps 18.7; 2 Chr 7.14 **60.03** Ps 71.20; Isa 51.17,22 **60.4** Ps 20.5 **60.5** Ps 108.6; 127.2; 17.7 **60.6** Ps 89.35; Josh 1.6; Gen 12.6 **60.7** Josh 13.31; Deut 33.17; Gen 49.10 **60.8** 2 Sam 8.1 **60.10** v. 1; Ps 44.9 **60.11** Ps 146.3 **60.12** Num 24.18; Ps 44.5 **61.1** Ps 64.1; 86.6 **61.2** Ps 77.3; 18.2 **61.3** Ps 62.7; Prov 18.10

4 You have set up a banner for
those who fear you,
to rally to it out of
bowshot.[r] *Selah*
5 Give victory with your right
hand, and answer us,[s]
so that those whom you
love may be rescued.

6 God has promised in his
sanctuary:[t]
"With exultation I will
divide up Shechem,
and portion out the Vale of
Succoth.
7 Gilead is mine, and
Manasseh is mine;
Ephraim is my helmet;
Judah is my scepter.
8 Moab is my washbasin;
on Edom I hurl my shoe;
over Philistia I shout in
triumph."

9 Who will bring me to the
fortified city?
Who will lead me to Edom?
10 Have you not rejected us,
O God?
You do not go out, O God,
with our armies.
11 O grant us help against the
foe,
for human help is
worthless.
12 With God we shall do
valiantly;
it is he who will tread
down our foes.

Psalm 61

Assurance of God's Protection

To the leader: with stringed instruments. Of David.

1 Hear my cry, O God;
listen to my prayer.
2 From the end of the earth I
call to you,
when my heart is faint.

Lead me to the rock
that is higher than I;
3 for you are my refuge,

[r] Gk Syr Jerome: Heb *because of the truth*
[s] Another reading is *me* [t] Or *by his holiness*

a strong tower against the
enemy.
4 Let me abide in your tent
forever,
find refuge under the
shelter of your wings.
Selah
5 For you, O God, have heard
my vows;
you have given me the
heritage of those who
fear your name.

6 Prolong the life of the king;
may his years endure to all
generations!
7 May he be enthroned forever
before God;
appoint steadfast love and
faithfulness to watch
over him!

8 So I will always sing praises
to your name,
as I pay my vows day after
day.

Psalm 62

Song of Trust in God Alone

To the leader: according to
Jeduthun. A Psalm of David.

1 For God alone my soul waits
in silence;
from him comes my
salvation.
2 He alone is my rock and my
salvation,
my fortress; I shall never be
shaken.

3 How long will you assail a
person,
will you batter your victim,
all of you,
as you would a leaning
wall, a tottering fence?
4 Their only plan is to bring
down a person of
prominence.
They take pleasure in
falsehood;
they bless with their mouths,
but inwardly they curse.
Selah

5 For God alone my soul waits
in silence,
for my hope is from him.
6 He alone is my rock and my
salvation,
my fortress; I shall not be
shaken.
7 On God rests my deliverance
and my honor;
my mighty rock, my refuge
is in God.

8 Trust in him at all times,
O people;
pour out your heart before
him;
God is a refuge for us.
Selah

9 Those of low estate are but a
breath,
those of high estate are a
delusion;
in the balances they go up;
they are together lighter
than a breath.
10 Put no confidence in
extortion,
and set no vain hopes on
robbery;
if riches increase, do not
set your heart on them.

11 Once God has spoken;
twice have I heard this:
that power belongs to God,
12 and steadfast love belongs
to you, O Lord.
For you repay to all
according to their work.

Psalm 63

Comfort and Assurance in God's Presence

A Psalm of David, when he was
in the Wilderness of Judah.

1 O God, you are my God, I
seek you,
my soul thirsts for you;
my flesh faints for you,
as in a dry and weary land
where there is no water.
2 So I have looked upon you in
the sanctuary,

61.4 Ps 23.6; 91.4
61.5 Ps 56.12; 86.11
61.6 Ps 21.4
61.7 Ps 41.12; 40.11
61.8 Ps 71.22; 65.1
62.1 Ps 33.20
62.2 Ps 89.26; v. 6
62.3 Isa 30.13
62.4 Ps 4.2; 28.3
62.6 v. 2
62.7 Ps 85.9; 46.1
62.8 Ps 37.3; 1 Sam 1.15; Ps 42.4; Lam 2.19
62.9 Ps 39.5,11; Isa 40.15, 17; Rom 3.4
62.10 Isa 30.12; 61.8; Job 31.25; Ps 52.7; 1 Tim 6.7
62.11 Job 33.14; 1 Chr 29.11
62.12 Job 34.11; Mt 16.27; Col 3.25
63.1 Ps 42.2; 84.2
63.2 Ps 27.4

beholding your power and
glory.
3 Because your steadfast love
is better than life,
my lips will praise you.
4 So I will bless you as long as
I live;
I will lift up my hands and
call on your name.

5 My soul is satisfied as with a
rich feast,[u]
and my mouth praises you
with joyful lips
6 when I think of you on my
bed,
and meditate on you in the
watches of the night;
7 for you have been my help,
and in the shadow of your
wings I sing for joy.
8 My soul clings to you;
your right hand upholds
me.

9 But those who seek to
destroy my life
shall go down into the
depths of the earth;
10 they shall be given over to
the power of the sword,
they shall be prey for
jackals.
11 But the king shall rejoice in
God;
all who swear by him shall
exult,
for the mouths of liars will
be stopped.

Psalm 64

Prayer for Protection from Enemies

To the leader. A Psalm of David.

1 Hear my voice, O God, in my
complaint;
preserve my life from the
dread enemy.
2 Hide me from the secret
plots of the wicked,
from the scheming of
evildoers,
3 who whet their tongues like
swords,
who aim bitter words like
arrows,
4 shooting from ambush at the
blameless;
they shoot suddenly and
without fear.
5 They hold fast to their evil
purpose;
they talk of laying snares
secretly,
thinking, "Who can see us?[v]
6 Who can search out our
crimes?[w]
We have thought out a
cunningly conceived
plot."
For the human heart and
mind are deep.

7 But God will shoot his arrow
at them;
they will be wounded
suddenly.
8 Because of their tongue he
will bring them to
ruin;[x]
all who see them will
shake with horror.
9 Then everyone will fear;
they will tell what God has
brought about,
and ponder what he has
done.

10 Let the righteous rejoice in
the LORD
and take refuge in him.
Let all the upright in heart
glory.

Psalm 65

Thanksgiving for Earth's Bounty

To the leader. A Psalm of David.
A Song.

1 Praise is due to you,
O God, in Zion;
and to you shall vows be
performed,
2 O you who answer prayer!
To you all flesh shall come.

63.3 Ps 69.16 **63.4** Ps 104.33; 28.2 **63.5** Ps 36.8; 71.23 **63.6** Ps 42.8 **63.7** Ps 27.9 **63.8** Ps 18.35 **63.9ff** Ps 40.14; 55.15 **63.11** Ps 21.1; Deut 6.13; Isa 45.23 **64.1** Ps 55.2; 140.1 **64.2** Ps 56.6; 59.2 **64.3** Ps 58.7 **64.4** Ps 11.2; 55.19 **64.5** Ps 10.11 **64.6** Ps 49.11 **64.8** Ps 9.3; Prov 18.7; Ps 22.7 **64.9** Jer 50.28 **64.10** Ps 32.11; 25.20 **65.1** Ps 116.18 **65.2** Isa 66.23

[u] Heb *with fat and fatness* [v] Syr: Heb *them* [w] Cn: Heb *They search out crimes* [x] Cn: Heb *They will bring him to ruin, their tongue being against them*

3 When deeds of iniquity
overwhelm us,
you forgive our
transgressions.
4 Happy are those whom you
choose and bring near
to live in your courts.
We shall be satisfied with
the goodness of your
house,
your holy temple.

5 By awesome deeds you
answer us with
deliverance,
O God of our salvation;
you are the hope of all the
ends of the earth
and of the farthest seas.
6 By your[y] strength you
established the
mountains;
you are girded with might.
7 You silence the roaring of
the seas,
the roaring of their waves,
the tumult of the peoples.
8 Those who live at earth's
farthest bounds are
awed by your signs;
you make the gateways of
the morning and the
evening shout for joy.

9 You visit the earth and water
it,
you greatly enrich it;
the river of God is full of
water;
you provide the people
with grain,
for so you have prepared it.
10 You water its furrows
abundantly,
settling its ridges,
softening it with showers,
and blessing its growth.
11 You crown the year with your
bounty;
your wagon tracks overflow
with richness.
12 The pastures of the
wilderness overflow,
the hills gird themselves
with joy,
13 the meadows clothe
themselves with flocks,
the valleys deck themselves
with grain,
they shout and sing
together for joy.

Psalm 66

Praise for God's Goodness to Israel

To the leader. A Song. A Psalm.

1 Make a joyful noise to God,
all the earth;
2 sing the glory of his name;
give to him glorious praise.
3 Say to God, "How awesome
are your deeds!
Because of your great
power, your enemies
cringe before you.
4 All the earth worships you;
they sing praises to you,
sing praises to your name."
Selah

5 Come and see what God has
done:
he is awesome in his deeds
among mortals.
6 He turned the sea into dry
land;
they passed through the
river on foot.
There we rejoiced in him,
7 who rules by his might
forever,
whose eyes keep watch on
the nations—
let the rebellious not exalt
themselves. *Selah*

8 Bless our God, O peoples,
let the sound of his praise
be heard,
9 who has kept us among the
living,
and has not let our feet
slip.
10 For you, O God, have tested
us;
you have tried us as silver
is tried.
11 You brought us into the net;
you laid burdens on our
backs;

65.3 Ps 38.4; Heb 9.14
65.4 Ps 33.12; 4.3; 36.8
65.5 Ps 66.3; 85.4; 22.27; 107.23
65.6 Ps 93.1
65.7 Mt 8.26; Isa 17.12
65.9 Ps 68.9,10; 46.4; 104.14
65.12 Job 38.26, 27; Ps 98.8
65.13 Ps 144.13; 72.16; 98.8
66.1 Ps 100.1
66.2 Ps 81.1; 79.9
66.3 Ps 65.5; 18.44
66.4 Ps 22.27; 67.3,4
66.5 Ps 46.8; 106.22
66.6 Ex 14.21; Josh 3.6; Ps 105.43
66.7 Ps 145.13; 11.4; 140.8
66.8 Ps 98.4
66.9 Ps 121.3
66.10 Ps 17.3; Isa 48.10; Zech 13.9; 1 Pet 1.6,7
66.11 Lam 1.13

[y] Gk Jerome: Heb *his*

12 you let people ride over our
heads;
we went through fire and
through water;
yet you have brought us out
to a spacious place.[z]

13 I will come into your house
with burnt offerings;
I will pay you my vows,
14 those that my lips uttered
and my mouth promised
when I was in trouble.
15 I will offer to you burnt
offerings of fatlings,
with the smoke of the
sacrifice of rams;
I will make an offering of
bulls and goats. *Selah*

16 Come and hear, all you who
fear God,
and I will tell what he has
done for me.
17 I cried aloud to him,
and he was extolled with
my tongue.
18 If I had cherished iniquity in
my heart,
the Lord would not have
listened.
19 But truly God has listened;
he has given heed to the
words of my prayer.

20 Blessed be God,
because he has not
rejected my prayer
or removed his steadfast
love from me.

Psalm 67

The Nations Called to Praise God

To the leader: with stringed instruments. A Psalm. A Song.

1 May God be gracious to us
and bless us
and make his face to shine
upon us, *Selah*
2 that your way may be known
upon earth,
your saving power among
all nations.
3 Let the peoples praise you,
O God;
let all the peoples praise
you.

4 Let the nations be glad and
sing for joy,
for you judge the peoples
with equity
and guide the nations upon
earth. *Selah*
5 Let the peoples praise you,
O God;
let all the peoples praise
you.

6 The earth has yielded its
increase;
God, our God, has blessed
us.
7 May God continue to bless
us;
let all the ends of the earth
revere him.

Psalm 68

Praise and Thanksgiving

To the leader. Of David. A Psalm. A Song.

1 Let God rise up, let his
enemies be scattered;
let those who hate him flee
before him.
2 As smoke is driven away, so
drive them away;
as wax melts before the
fire,
let the wicked perish
before God.
3 But let the righteous be
joyful;
let them exult before God;
let them be jubilant with
joy.

4 Sing to God, sing praises to
his name;
lift up a song to him who
rides upon the
clouds[a]—
his name is the LORD—
be exultant before him.

66.12 Isa 51.23; 43.2 **66.13** Eccl 5.4 **66.14** Ps 18.6 **66.15** Ps 51.19; Num 6.14 **66.16** Ps 34.11; 71.15,24 **66.18** Job 36.21; Isa 1.15; Jas 4.3 **66.19** Ps 116.1,2 **66.20** Ps 68.35; 22.24 **67.1** Num 6.25; Ps 4.6 **67.2** Acts 18.25; Titus 2.11 **67.4** Ps 96.10; 98.9 **67.5** v. 3 **67.6** Lev 26.4; Ps 85.12; Ezek 34.27 **67.7** Ps 33.8 **68.1** Num 10.35; Isa 33.3 **68.2** Isa 9.18; Hos 13.3; Ps 97.5; Mic 1.4 **68.3** Ps 32.11 **68.4** Ps 66.2; Isa 57.14; 40.3; Ps 83.18

[z] Cn Compare Gk Syr Jerome Tg: Heb *to a saturation* [a] Or *cast up a highway for him who rides through the deserts*

5 Father of orphans and
protector of widows
is God in his holy
habitation.
6 God gives the desolate a
home to live in;
he leads out the prisoners
to prosperity,
but the rebellious live in a
parched land.

7 O God, when you went out
before your people,
when you marched through
the wilderness, *Selah*
8 the earth quaked, the
heavens poured down
rain
at the presence of God, the
God of Sinai,
at the presence of God, the
God of Israel.
9 Rain in abundance, O God,
you showered abroad;
you restored your heritage
when it languished;
10 your flock found a dwelling
in it;
in your goodness, O God,
you provided for the
needy.

11 The Lord gives the
command;
great is the company of
those[b] who bore the
tidings:
12 "The kings of the armies,
they flee, they flee!"
The women at home divide
the spoil,
13 though they stay among
the sheepfolds—
the wings of a dove covered
with silver,
its pinions with green gold.
14 When the Almighty[c]
scattered kings there,
snow fell on Zalmon.

15 O mighty mountain,
mountain of Bashan;
O many-peaked mountain,
mountain of Bashan!
16 Why do you look with envy,
O many-peaked
mountain,
at the mount that God
desired for his abode,
where the LORD will reside
forever?

17 With mighty chariotry, twice
ten thousand,
thousands upon thousands,
the Lord came from Sinai
into the holy place.[d]
18 You ascended the high
mount,
leading captives in your
train
and receiving gifts from
people,
even from those who rebel
against the LORD God's
abiding there.
19 Blessed be the Lord,
who daily bears us up;
God is our salvation. *Selah*
20 Our God is a God of
salvation,
and to GOD, the Lord,
belongs escape from
death.

21 But God will shatter the
heads of his enemies,
the hairy crown of those
who walk in their guilty
ways.
22 The Lord said,
"I will bring them back
from Bashan,
I will bring them back from
the depths of the sea,
23 so that you may bathe[e] your
feet in blood,
so that the tongues of your
dogs may have their
share from the foe."

24 Your solemn processions are
seen,[f] O God,
the processions of my God,
my King, into the
sanctuary—
25 the singers in front, the
musicians last,

68.5 Ps 146.9; Deut 10.18; 26.15
68.6 Ps 113.9; Acts 21.6; Ps 107.34
68.7 Ex 13.21; Judg 4.14
68.8 Ex 19.16, 18; Judg 5.4
68.9 Deut 11.11
68.10 Deut 26.5; Ps 74.19
68.12 Ps 135.11; 1 Sam 30.24
68.13 Gen 49.14
68.14 Josh 10.10
68.16 Deut 12.5; Ps 87.1,2
68.17 Deut 33.2; Dan 7.10
68.18 Acts 1.9; Eph 4.8; Judg 5.12; 1 Tim 1.13
68.19 Ps 55.22; 65.5
68.20 Ps 49.15; 56.13
68.21 Ps 110.6; 55.23
68.22 Num 21.33; Ex 14.22
68.23 Ps 58.10; 1 Kings 21.19
68.24 Ps 77.13; 63.2
68.25 1 Chr 13.8; Judg 11.34

[b] Or *company of the women* [c] Traditional rendering of Heb *Shaddai* [d] Cn: Heb *The Lord among them Sinai in the holy* (place) [e] Gk Syr Tg: Heb *shatter* [f] Or *have been seen*

between them girls playing tambourines:
26 "Bless God in the great congregation,
the LORD, O you who are of Israel's fountain!"
27 There is Benjamin, the least of them, in the lead,
the princes of Judah in a body,
the princes of Zebulun, the princes of Naphtali.

28 Summon your might, O God;
show your strength, O God, as you have done for us before.
29 Because of your temple at Jerusalem
kings bear gifts to you.
30 Rebuke the wild animals that live among the reeds,
the herd of bulls with the calves of the peoples.
Trample[g] under foot those who lust after tribute;
scatter the peoples who delight in war.[h]
31 Let bronze be brought from Egypt;
let Ethiopia[i] hasten to stretch out its hands to God.

32 Sing to God, O kingdoms of the earth;
sing praises to the Lord, *Selah*
33 O rider in the heavens, the ancient heavens;
listen, he sends out his voice, his mighty voice.
34 Ascribe power to God,
whose majesty is over Israel;
and whose power is in the skies.
35 Awesome is God in his[j] sanctuary,
the God of Israel;
he gives power and strength to his people.

Blessed be God!

68.26 Ps 26.12; Deut 33.28; Isa 48.1
68.27 1 Sam 9.21
68.29 Ps 72.10
68.30 Ps 22.12; 89.10
68.31 Isa 19.19; 45.14
68.33 Ps 18.10; Deut 10.14; Ps 44.6; 29.4
68.34 Ps 29.1
68.35 Ps 47.2; 29.11; 66.20

69.1 vv. 14,15
69.2 Ps 40.2; Jon 2.3
69.3 Ps 6.6; 119.82; Isa 38.14
69.4 Ps 35.19; Jn 15.25; Ps 38.19; 35.11
69.5 Ps 38.5; 44.21
69.6 2 Sam 12.14
69.7 Jer 15.15; Ps 44.15
69.8 Ps 31.11; Isa 53.3
69.9 Jn 2.17; Ps 89.50

Psalm 69

Prayer for Deliverance from Persecution

To the leader: according to Lilies. Of David.

1 Save me, O God,
for the waters have come up to my neck.
2 I sink in deep mire,
where there is no foothold;
I have come into deep waters,
and the flood sweeps over me.
3 I am weary with my crying;
my throat is parched.
My eyes grow dim
with waiting for my God.

4 More in number than the hairs of my head
are those who hate me without cause;
many are those who would destroy me,
my enemies who accuse me falsely.
What I did not steal
must I now restore?
5 O God, you know my folly;
the wrongs I have done are not hidden from you.

6 Do not let those who hope in you be put to shame because of me,
O Lord GOD of hosts;
do not let those who seek you be dishonored because of me,
O God of Israel.
7 It is for your sake that I have borne reproach,
that shame has covered my face.
8 I have become a stranger to my kindred,
an alien to my mother's children.

9 It is zeal for your house that has consumed me;

[g] Cn: Heb *Trampling* [h] Meaning of Heb of verse 30 is uncertain [i] Or *Nubia*; Heb *Cush* [j] Gk: Heb *from your*

the insults of those who
insult you have fallen
on me.
10 When I humbled my soul
with fasting,[k]
they insulted me for doing
so.
11 When I made sackcloth my
clothing,
I became a byword to
them.
12 I am the subject of gossip for
those who sit in the
gate,
and the drunkards make
songs about me.

13 But as for me, my prayer is
to you, O LORD.
At an acceptable time,
O God,
in the abundance of your
steadfast love, answer
me.
With your faithful help
14 rescue me
from sinking in the mire;
let me be delivered from my
enemies
and from the deep waters.
15 Do not let the flood sweep
over me,
or the deep swallow me up,
or the Pit close its mouth
over me.

16 Answer me, O LORD, for your
steadfast love is good;
according to your abundant
mercy, turn to me.
17 Do not hide your face from
your servant,
for I am in distress—make
haste to answer me.
18 Draw near to me, redeem
me,
set me free because of my
enemies.

19 You know the insults I
receive,
and my shame and
dishonor;
my foes are all known to
you.
20 Insults have broken my
heart,
so that I am in despair.
I looked for pity, but there
was none;
and for comforters, but I
found none.
21 They gave me poison for
food,
and for my thirst they gave
me vinegar to drink.

22 Let their table be a trap for
them,
a snare for their allies.
23 Let their eyes be darkened
so that they cannot see,
and make their loins
tremble continually.
24 Pour out your indignation
upon them,
and let your burning anger
overtake them.
25 May their camp be a
desolation;
let no one live in their
tents.
26 For they persecute those
whom you have struck
down,
and those whom you have
wounded, they attack
still more.[l]
27 Add guilt to their guilt;
may they have no acquittal
from you.
28 Let them be blotted out of
the book of the living;
let them not be enrolled
among the righteous.
29 But I am lowly and in pain;
let your salvation, O God,
protect me.

30 I will praise the name of God
with a song;
I will magnify him with
thanksgiving.
31 This will please the LORD
more than an ox
or a bull with horns and
hoofs.
32 Let the oppressed see it and
be glad;

69.10 Ps 35.13
69.11 Ps 35.13; Jer 24.9
69.12 Job 30.9
69.13 Isa 49.8; 2 Cor 6.2; Ps 51.1
69.14 v. 2; Ps 144.7
69.15 Ps 124.4,5; Num 16.33
69.16 Ps 63.3; 51.1; 25.16
69.17 Ps 27.9; 66.14
69.18 Ps 49.15
69.19 Ps 22.6,7; Isa 53.3
69.20 Jer 23.9; Isa 63.5; Job 16.2
69.21 Mt 27.34; Jn 19.29
69.22 Rom 11.9,10
69.23 Isa 6.9,10; Dan 5.6
69.24 Ps 79.6
69.25 Mt 23.38; Acts 1.20
69.26 Isa 53.4
69.28 Ex 32.32; Phil 4.3; Lk 10.20
69.29 Ps 70.5; 59.1
69.30 Ps 28.7; 34.3; 50.14
69.31 Ps 50.13,14
69.32 Ps 34.2; 22.26

k Gk Syr: Heb *I wept, with fasting my soul*, or *I made my soul mourn with fasting*
l Gk Syr: Heb *recount the pain of*

you who seek God, let your
hearts revive.
33 For the LORD hears the
needy,
and does not despise his
own that are in bonds.

34 Let heaven and earth praise
him,
the seas and everything
that moves in them.
35 For God will save Zion
and rebuild the cities of
Judah;
and his servants shall live[m]
there and possess it;
36 the children of his servants
shall inherit it,
and those who love his
name shall live in it.

Psalm 70

Prayer for Deliverance from Enemies

To the leader. Of David, for the memorial offering.

1 Be pleased, O God, to deliver
me.
O LORD, make haste to help
me!
2 Let those be put to shame
and confusion
who seek my life.
Let those be turned back
and brought to dishonor
who desire to hurt me.
3 Let those who say, "Aha,
Aha!"
turn back because of their
shame.

4 Let all who seek you
rejoice and be glad in you.
Let those who love your
salvation
say evermore, "God is
great!"
5 But I am poor and needy;
hasten to me, O God!
You are my help and my
deliverer;
O LORD, do not delay!

69.33 Ps 12.9; 68.6 **69.34** Ps 96.11; 148.1; Isa 44.23; 49.13 **69.35** Ps 51.18; Isa 44.26 **69.36** Ps 102.28; 37.29 **70.1** Ps 40.13 **70.2** Ps 35.4,26 **70.3** Ps 40.15 **70.5** Ps 40.17; 141.1

71.1 Ps 25.2,3 **71.2** Ps 31.1; 17.6 **71.3** Ps 31.2,3; 44.4 **71.4** Ps 140.1,4 **71.5** Jer 17.7 **71.6** Ps 22.9,10; Isa 46.3; Ps 34.1 **71.7** 1 Cor 4.9; Ps 61.3 **71.8** Ps 35.28 **71.9** v. 18 **71.10** Ps 56.6; Mt 27.1 **71.11** Ps 3.2; 7.2

Psalm 71

Prayer for Lifelong Protection and Help

1 In you, O LORD, I take refuge;
let me never be put to
shame.
2 In your righteousness deliver
me and rescue me;
incline your ear to me and
save me.
3 Be to me a rock of refuge,
a strong fortress,[n] to save
me,
for you are my rock and my
fortress.

4 Rescue me, O my God, from
the hand of the wicked,
from the grasp of the
unjust and cruel.
5 For you, O Lord, are my
hope,
my trust, O LORD, from my
youth.
6 Upon you I have leaned from
my birth;
it was you who took me
from my mother's
womb.
My praise is continually of
you.

7 I have been like a portent to
many,
but you are my strong
refuge.
8 My mouth is filled with your
praise,
and with your glory all day
long.
9 Do not cast me off in the
time of old age;
do not forsake me when
my strength is spent.
10 For my enemies speak
concerning me,
and those who watch for
my life consult
together.
11 They say, "Pursue and seize
that person

[m] Syr: Heb *and they shall live*
[n] Gk Compare 31.3: Heb *to come continually you have commanded*

whom God has forsaken,
for there is no one to
deliver."
12 O God, do not be far from
me;
O my God, make haste to
help me!
13 Let my accusers be put to
shame and consumed;
let those who seek to hurt
me
be covered with scorn and
disgrace.
14 But I will hope continually,
and will praise you yet
more and more.
15 My mouth will tell of your
righteous acts,
of your deeds of salvation
all day long,
though their number is
past my knowledge.
16 I will come praising the
mighty deeds of the
Lord GOD,
I will praise your
righteousness, yours
alone.
17 O God, from my youth you
have taught me,
and I still proclaim your
wondrous deeds.
18 So even to old age and gray
hairs,
O God, do not forsake
me,
until I proclaim your might
to all the generations to
come.[o]
Your power 19 and your
righteousness, O God,
reach the high heavens.
You who have done great
things,
O God, who is like you?
20 You who have made me see
many troubles and
calamities
will revive me again;
from the depths of the earth
you will bring me up again.
21 You will increase my honor,
and comfort me once
again.
22 I will also praise you with
the harp
for your faithfulness, O my
God;
I will sing praises to you with
the lyre,
O Holy One of Israel.
23 My lips will shout for joy
when I sing praises to you;
my soul also, which you
have rescued.
24 All day long my tongue will
talk of your righteous
help,
for those who tried to do me
harm
have been put to shame,
and disgraced.

Psalm 72

Prayer for Guidance and Support for the King

Of Solomon.

1 Give the king your justice,
O God,
and your righteousness to a
king's son.
2 May he judge your people
with righteousness,
and your poor with justice.
3 May the mountains yield
prosperity for the
people,
and the hills, in
righteousness.
4 May he defend the cause of
the poor of the people,
give deliverance to the
needy,
and crush the oppressor.
5 May he live[p] while the sun
endures,
and as long as the moon,
throughout all
generations.
6 May he be like rain that falls
on the mown grass,
like showers that water the
earth.
7 In his days may
righteousness flourish

71.12 Ps 35.22; 70.1 **71.13** Ps 35.4; 109.29; v. 24 **71.15** Ps 35.28; 40.5 **71.16** Ps 106.2; 51.14 **71.17** Deut 4.5; 6.7; Ps 26.7 **71.18** v. 9 **71.19** Ps 57.10; 35.10 **71.20** Ps 60.3; Hos 6.1,2 **71.22** Ps 33.2; 78.41 **71.23** Ps 5.11; 103.4 **71.24** Ps 35.28; v. 13 **72.1** Ps 24.5 **72.2** Isa 9.7; Ps 82.3 **72.3** Ps 85.10; Isa 32.17 **72.4** Isa 11.4 **72.5** Ps 89.36 **72.6** 2 Sam 23.4; Hos 6.3 **72.7** Ps 92.12

[o] Gk Compare Syr: Heb *to a generation, to all that come* [p] Gk: Heb *may they fear you*

and peace abound, until
the moon is no more.

8 May he have dominion from
sea to sea,
and from the River to the
ends of the earth.
9 May his foes[q] bow down
before him,
and his enemies lick the
dust.
10 May the kings of Tarshish
and of the isles
render him tribute,
may the kings of Sheba and
Seba
bring gifts.
11 May all kings fall down
before him,
all nations give him
service.

12 For he delivers the needy
when they call,
the poor and those who
have no helper.
13 He has pity on the weak and
the needy,
and saves the lives of the
needy.
14 From oppression and
violence he redeems
their life;
and precious is their blood
in his sight.

15 Long may he live!
May gold of Sheba be given
to him.
May prayer be made for him
continually,
and blessings invoked for
him all day long.
16 May there be abundance of
grain in the land;
may it wave on the tops of
the mountains;
may its fruit be like
Lebanon;
and may people blossom in
the cities
like the grass of the field.
17 May his name endure
forever,
his fame continue as long
as the sun.
May all nations be blessed in
him;[r]
may they pronounce him
happy.

18 Blessed be the LORD, the God
of Israel,
who alone does wondrous
things.
19 Blessed be his glorious name
forever;
may his glory fill the whole
earth.
Amen and Amen.

20 The prayers of David son of
Jesse are ended.

BOOK III

(Psalms 73–89)

Psalm 73

Plea for Relief from Oppressors

A Psalm of Asaph.

1 Truly God is good to the
upright,[s]
to those who are pure in
heart.
2 But as for me, my feet had
almost stumbled;
my steps had nearly
slipped.
3 For I was envious of the
arrogant;
I saw the prosperity of the
wicked.

4 For they have no pain;
their bodies are sound and
sleek.
5 They are not in trouble as
others are;
they are not plagued like
other people.
6 Therefore pride is their
necklace;
violence covers them like a
garment.
7 Their eyes swell out with
fatness;

72.8 Ex 23.31; Zech 9.10 **72.9** Ps 74.14; Isa 49.23; Mic 7.17 **72.10** 2 Chr 9.21; Ps 68.29 **72.11** Ps 49.23 **72.12** Job 29.12 **72.14** Ps 116.15 **72.15** Isa 60.6 **72.16** Ps 104.16; Job 5.25 **72.17** Ps 89.36; Gen 12.3; 22.18; Lk 1.48 **72.18** Ps 41.13; 106.48; 77.14 **72.19** Neh 9.5; Zech 14.9 **73.1** Ps 86.5; 51.10 **73.2** Ps 94.18 **73.3** Ps 37.1; Jer 12.1 **73.5** Job 21.9 **73.6** Ps 109.18 **73.7** Job 15.27; Ps 17.10

[q] Cn: Heb *those who live in the wilderness*
[r] Or *bless themselves by him*
[s] Or *good to Israel*

their hearts overflow with follies.
8 They scoff and speak with malice;
loftily they threaten oppression.
9 They set their mouths against heaven,
and their tongues range over the earth.

10 Therefore the people turn and praise them,[t]
and find no fault in them.[u]
11 And they say, "How can God know?
Is there knowledge in the Most High?"
12 Such are the wicked;
always at ease, they increase in riches.
13 All in vain I have kept my heart clean
and washed my hands in innocence.
14 For all day long I have been plagued,
and am punished every morning.

15 If I had said, "I will talk on in this way,"
I would have been untrue to the circle of your children.
16 But when I thought how to understand this,
it seemed to me a wearisome task,
17 until I went into the sanctuary of God;
then I perceived their end.
18 Truly you set them in slippery places;
you make them fall to ruin.
19 How they are destroyed in a moment,
swept away utterly by terrors!
20 They are[v] like a dream when one awakes;
on awaking you despise their phantoms.

21 When my soul was embittered,
when I was pricked in heart,
22 I was stupid and ignorant;
I was like a brute beast toward you.
23 Nevertheless I am continually with you;
you hold my right hand.
24 You guide me with your counsel,
and afterward you will receive me with honor.[w]
25 Whom have I in heaven but you?
And there is nothing on earth that I desire other than you.
26 My flesh and my heart may fail,
but God is the strength[x] of my heart and my portion forever.

27 Indeed, those who are far from you will perish;
you put an end to those who are false to you.
28 But for me it is good to be near God;
I have made the Lord GOD my refuge,
to tell of all your works.

Psalm 74

Plea for Help in Time of National Humiliation

A Maskil of Asaph.

1 O God, why do you cast us off forever?
Why does your anger smoke against the sheep of your pasture?
2 Remember your congregation, which you acquired long ago,
which you redeemed to be the tribe of your heritage.

73.8 Ps 53.1; Jude 16
73.11 Job 22.13
73.12 Ps 49.6; Jer 49.31
73.13 Job 21.15; 34.9; 36.3; Ps 26.6
73.14 Ps 38.6; 118.18
73.16 Eccl 8.17
73.17 Ps 77.13; 37.38
73.18 Ps 35.6,8
73.19 Num 16.21; Job 18.11
73.20 Job 20.8; Ps 78.65; 1 Sam 2.30
73.22 Ps 49.10; Job 18.3
73.24 Ps 32.8; 48.14
73.25 Phil 3.8
73.26 Ps 84.2; 16.5
73.27 Ps 37.20; 119.155
73.28 Heb 10.22; Ps 71.7; 40.5
74.1 Ps 44.9,23; Deut 29.20; Ps 95.7
74.2 Deut 34.6; Ps 77.15; 68.16

[t] Cn: Heb *his people return here*
[u] Cn: Heb *abundant waters are drained by them*
[v] Cn: Heb *Lord*
[w] Or *to glory*
[x] Heb *rock*

Remember Mount Zion,
where you came to
dwell.
3 Direct your steps to the
perpetual ruins;
the enemy has destroyed
everything in the
sanctuary.

4 Your foes have roared within
your holy place;
they set up their emblems
there.
5 At the upper entrance they
hacked
the wooden trellis with
axes.[y]
6 And then, with hatchets and
hammers,
they smashed all its carved
work.
7 They set your sanctuary on
fire;
they desecrated the
dwelling place of your
name,
bringing it to the ground.
8 They said to themselves, "We
will utterly subdue
them";
they burned all the
meeting places of God
in the land.

9 We do not see our emblems;
there is no longer any
prophet,
and there is no one among
us who knows how
long.
10 How long, O God, is the foe
to scoff?
Is the enemy to revile your
name forever?
11 Why do you hold back your
hand;
why do you keep your hand
in[z] your bosom?

12 Yet God my King is from of
old,
working salvation in the
earth.
13 You divided the sea by your
might;
you broke the heads of the
dragons in the waters.
14 You crushed the heads of
Leviathan;
you gave him as food[a] for
the creatures of the
wilderness.
15 You cut openings for springs
and torrents;
you dried up ever-flowing
streams.
16 Yours is the day, yours also
the night;
you established the
luminaries[b] and the
sun.
17 You have fixed all the
bounds of the earth;
you made summer and
winter.

18 Remember this, O LORD, how
the enemy scoffs,
and an impious people
reviles your name.
19 Do not deliver the soul of
your dove to the wild
animals;
do not forget the life of
your poor forever.

20 Have regard for your[c]
covenant,
for the dark places of the
land are full of the
haunts of violence.
21 Do not let the downtrodden
be put to shame;
let the poor and needy
praise your name.
22 Rise up, O God, plead your
cause;
remember how the impious
scoff at you all day
long.
23 Do not forget the clamor of
your foes,
the uproar of your
adversaries that goes up
continually.

74.3 Isa 61.4; Ps 79.1
74.4 Lam 2.7; Num 2.2
74.5 Jer 46.22
74.7 2 Kings 25.9
74.8 Ps 83.4
74.9 Ps 78.43; 1 Sam 3.1; Ps 79.5
74.10 Ps 44.16; Lev 24.16
74.11 Lam 2.3; Ps 59.13
74.12 Ps 44.4
74.13 Ex 14.21; Isa 51.9
74.15 Ex 17.5,6; Num 20.11; Josh 3.13
74.16 Ps 104.19
74.17 Gen 8.22
74.18 v. 10; Ps 39.8
74.19 Song 2.14; Ps 9.18
74.20 Gen 17.7; Ps 106.45; 88.6
74.21 Ps 103.6; 35.10
74.22 Ps 43.1; v. 18
74.23 v. 10; Ps 65.7

[y] Cn Compare Gk Syr: Meaning of Heb uncertain [z] Cn: Heb *do you consume your right hand from* [a] Heb *food for the people* [b] Or *moon*; Heb *light* [c] Gk Syr: Heb *the*

Psalm 75

Thanksgiving for God's Wondrous Deeds

To the leader: Do Not Destroy. A Psalm of Asaph. A Song.

1 We give thanks to you,
O God;
we give thanks; your name
is near.
People tell of your wondrous
deeds.

2 At the set time that I
appoint
I will judge with equity.
3 When the earth totters, with
all its inhabitants,
it is I who keep its pillars
steady. *Selah*
4 I say to the boastful, "Do not
boast,"
and to the wicked, "Do not
lift up your horn;
5 do not lift up your horn on
high,
or speak with insolent
neck."

6 For not from the east or
from the west
and not from the
wilderness comes lifting
up;
7 but it is God who executes
judgment,
putting down one and
lifting up another.
8 For in the hand of the LORD
there is a cup
with foaming wine, well
mixed;
he will pour a draught from
it,
and all the wicked of the
earth
shall drain it down to the
dregs.
9 But I will rejoice[d] forever;
I will sing praises to the
God of Jacob.

10 All the horns of the wicked I
will cut off,

75.1 Ps 79.13; 145.18; 44.1
75.3 Ps 46.6; 1 Sam 2.8
75.4 Zech 1.21
75.5 Ps 94.4
75.6 Ps 3.3
75.7 Ps 50.6; 1 Sam 2.7; Dan 2.21
75.8 Job 21.20; Ps 60.3; Jer 26.15; Prov 23.30; Ps 73.10
75.9 Ps 40.10
75.10 Ps 89.17; 148.14
76.1 Ps 48.3
76.2 Ps 27.5; 9.11
76.3 Ps 46.9
76.5 Isa 46.12; Ps 13.3
76.6 Ex 15.1,21; Ps 78.53
76.7 Ps 96.4; Nah 1.6
76.8 Ezek 38.20; 2 Chr 20.29, 30
76.9 Ps 9.7-9; 72.4
76.10 Ex 9.16; Rom 9.17

but the horns of the
righteous shall be
exalted.

Psalm 76

Israel's God—Judge of All the Earth

To the leader: with stringed instruments. A Psalm of Asaph. A Song.

1 In Judah God is known,
his name is great in Israel.
2 His abode has been
established in Salem,
his dwelling place in Zion.
3 There he broke the flashing
arrows,
the shield, the sword, and
the weapons of war.
Selah

4 Glorious are you, more
majestic
than the everlasting
mountains.[e]
5 The stouthearted were
stripped of their spoil;
they sank into sleep;
none of the troops
was able to lift a hand.
6 At your rebuke, O God of
Jacob,
both rider and horse lay
stunned.

7 But you indeed are awesome!
Who can stand before
you
when once your anger is
roused?
8 From the heavens you
uttered judgment;
the earth feared and was
still
9 when God rose up to
establish judgment,
to save all the oppressed of
the earth. *Selah*

10 Human wrath serves only to
praise you,

[d] Gk: Heb *declare* [e] Gk: Heb *the mountains of prey*

when you bind the last bit
of your[f] wrath around
you.
11 Make vows to the LORD your
God, and perform them;
let all who are around him
bring gifts
to the one who is
awesome,
12 who cuts off the spirit of
princes,
who inspires fear in the
kings of the earth.

Psalm 77

God's Mighty Deeds Recalled

To the leader: according to Jeduthun. Of Asaph. A Psalm.

1 I cry aloud to God,
aloud to God, that he may
hear me.
2 In the day of my trouble I
seek the Lord;
in the night my hand is
stretched out without
wearying;
my soul refuses to be
comforted.
3 I think of God, and I moan;
I meditate, and my spirit
faints. *Selah*

4 You keep my eyelids from
closing;
I am so troubled that I
cannot speak.
5 I consider the days of old,
and remember the years of
long ago.
6 I commune[g] with my heart
in the night;
I meditate and search my
spirit:[h]
7 "Will the Lord spurn forever,
and never again be
favorable?
8 Has his steadfast love ceased
forever?
Are his promises at an end
for all time?
9 Has God forgotten to be
gracious?
Has he in anger shut up
his compassion?" *Selah*

10 And I say, "It is my grief
that the right hand of the
Most High has
changed."

11 I will call to mind the deeds
of the LORD;
I will remember your
wonders of old.
12 I will meditate on all your
work,
and muse on your mighty
deeds.
13 Your way, O God, is holy.
What god is so great as our
God?
14 You are the God who works
wonders;
you have displayed your
might among the
peoples.
15 With your strong arm you
redeemed your people,
the descendants of Jacob
and Joseph. *Selah*

16 When the waters saw you,
O God,
when the waters saw you,
they were afraid;
the very deep trembled.
17 The clouds poured out
water;
the skies thundered;
your arrows flashed on
every side.
18 The crash of your thunder
was in the whirlwind;
your lightnings lit up the
world;
the earth trembled and
shook.
19 Your way was through the
sea,
your path, through the
mighty waters;
yet your footprints were
unseen.
20 You led your people like a
flock
by the hand of Moses and
Aaron.

76.11 Ps 50.14; 68.29 **76.12** Ps 68.35 **77.1** Ps 3.4 **77.2** Ps 50.15; Isa 26.9,16 **77.3** Ps 142.3; 143.4 **77.5** Deut 32.7; Ps 143.5; Isa 51.9 **77.6** Ps 42.8; 4.4 **77.7** Ps 74.1; 85.1 **77.8** Ps 89.49; 2 Pet 3.9 **77.9** Isa 49.15; Ps 25.6

77.10 Ps 31.22; 44.2,3 **77.11** Ps 143.5 **77.13** Ps 73.17; Ex 15.11 **77.15** Ex 6.6; Deut 9.29 **77.16** Ex 14.21 **77.17** Judg 5.4; Ps 68.33; 2 Sam 22.15 **77.18** 2 Sam 22.8 **77.19** Hab 3.15; Ex 14.28 **77.20** Ex 13.21; Isa 63.11-13; Ex 6.26

f Heb lacks *your* g Gk Syr: Heb *My music* h Syr Jerome: Heb *my spirit searches*

Psalm 78

God's Goodness and Israel's Ingratitude

A Maskil of Asaph.

1 Give ear, O my people, to my
teaching;
incline your ears to the
words of my mouth.
2 I will open my mouth in a
parable;
I will utter dark sayings
from of old,
3 things that we have heard
and known,
that our ancestors have
told us.
4 We will not hide them from
their children;
we will tell to the coming
generation
the glorious deeds of the
Lord, and his might,
and the wonders that he
has done.

5 He established a decree in
Jacob,
and appointed a law in
Israel,
which he commanded our
ancestors
to teach to their children;
6 that the next generation
might know them,
the children yet unborn,
and rise up and tell them to
their children,
7 so that they should set
their hope in God,
and not forget the works of
God,
but keep his
commandments;
8 and that they should not be
like their ancestors,
a stubborn and rebellious
generation,
a generation whose heart was
not steadfast,
whose spirit was not
faithful to God.

9 The Ephraimites, armed
with[i] the bow,
turned back on the day of
battle.
10 They did not keep God's
covenant,
but refused to walk
according to his law.
11 They forgot what he had
done,
and the miracles that he
had shown them.
12 In the sight of their
ancestors he worked
marvels
in the land of Egypt, in the
fields of Zoan.
13 He divided the sea and let
them pass through it,
and made the waters stand
like a heap.
14 In the daytime he led them
with a cloud,
and all night long with a
fiery light.
15 He split rocks open in the
wilderness,
and gave them drink
abundantly as from the
deep.
16 He made streams come out
of the rock,
and caused waters to flow
down like rivers.

17 Yet they sinned still more
against him,
rebelling against the Most
High in the desert.
18 They tested God in their
heart
by demanding the food
they craved.
19 They spoke against God,
saying,
"Can God spread a table in
the wilderness?
20 Even though he struck the
rock so that water
gushed out
and torrents overflowed,
can he also give bread,
or provide meat for his
people?"

78.1 Isa 51.4
78.2 Mt 13.35
78.3 Ps 44.1
78.4 Ex 12.26; Ps 22.30; 71.17
78.5 Ps 147.19; Deut 4.9
78.6 Ps 102.18
78.7 Deut 6.12; 27.1
78.8 Ezek 20.18; Ex 32.9; v. 37
78.9 1 Chr 12.2; Judg 20.39
78.10 2 Kings 18.12; Ps 119.1
78.11 Ps 106.13
78.12 Ex 7-12; Num 13.22; Isa 19.11, 13; Ezek 30.14
78.13 Ex 14.21; 15.8
78.14 Ex 13.21
78.15 Num 20.11; 1 Cor 10.4
78.17 Deut 9.22; Heb 3.16
78.18 Ex 16.2; 1 Cor 10.9
78.19 Num 11.4
78.20 Num 20.11

[i] Heb *armed with shooting*

21 Therefore, when the LORD heard, he was full of rage;
a fire was kindled against Jacob,
his anger mounted against Israel,
22 because they had no faith in God,
and did not trust his saving power.
23 Yet he commanded the skies above,
and opened the doors of heaven;
24 he rained down on them manna to eat,
and gave them the grain of heaven.
25 Mortals ate of the bread of angels;
he sent them food in abundance.
26 He caused the east wind to blow in the heavens,
and by his power he led out the south wind;
27 he rained flesh upon them like dust,
winged birds like the sand of the seas;
28 he let them fall within their camp,
all around their dwellings.
29 And they ate and were well filled,
for he gave them what they craved.
30 But before they had satisfied their craving,
while the food was still in their mouths,
31 the anger of God rose against them
and he killed the strongest of them,
and laid low the flower of Israel.

32 In spite of all this they still sinned;
they did not believe in his wonders.
33 So he made their days vanish like a breath,
and their years in terror.
34 When he killed them, they sought for him;
they repented and sought God earnestly.
35 They remembered that God was their rock,
the Most High God their redeemer.
36 But they flattered him with their mouths;
they lied to him with their tongues.
37 Their heart was not steadfast toward him;
they were not true to his covenant.
38 Yet he, being compassionate, forgave their iniquity,
and did not destroy them;
often he restrained his anger,
and did not stir up all his wrath.
39 He remembered that they were but flesh,
a wind that passes and does not come again.
40 How often they rebelled against him in the wilderness
and grieved him in the desert!
41 They tested God again and again,
and provoked the Holy One of Israel.
42 They did not keep in mind his power,
or the day when he redeemed them from the foe;
43 when he displayed his signs in Egypt,
and his miracles in the fields of Zoan.
44 He turned their rivers to blood,
so that they could not drink of their streams.
45 He sent among them swarms of flies, which devoured them,
and frogs, which destroyed them.
46 He gave their crops to the caterpillar,
and the fruit of their labor to the locust.
47 He destroyed their vines with hail,

78.21 Num 11.1
78.22 Heb 3.18
78.23 Mal 3.10
78.24 Jn 6.31
78.26 Num 11.31
78.27 Ps 105.40
78.29 Num 11.20
78.31 Num 11.33
78.32 Num 14,16, 17; v. 22
78.33 Num 14.29, 35
78.34 Hos 5.15
78.35 Deut 32.4; Isa 41.14
78.36 Ezek 33.31; Ex 32.7,8
78.38 Num 14.18; Isa 48.9; 1 Kings 21.29
78.39 Ps 103.14; Gen 6.3; Job 7.7,16
78.40 Ps 95.8-10; Heb 3.16
78.41 Num 14.22; Ps 89.18
78.44 Ex 7.20
78.45 Ex 8.24; Ps 105.31; Ex 8.6
78.47 Ex 9.25

and their sycamores with
frost.
48 He gave over their cattle to
the hail,
and their flocks to
thunderbolts.
49 He let loose on them his
fierce anger,
wrath, indignation, and
distress,
a company of destroying
angels.
50 He made a path for his
anger;
he did not spare them from
death,
but gave their lives over to
the plague.
51 He struck all the firstborn in
Egypt,
the first issue of their
strength in the tents of
Ham.
52 Then he led out his people
like sheep,
and guided them in the
wilderness like a flock.
53 He led them in safety, so
that they were not
afraid;
but the sea overwhelmed
their enemies.
54 And he brought them to his
holy hill,
to the mountain that his
right hand had won.
55 He drove out nations before
them;
he apportioned them for a
possession
and settled the tribes of
Israel in their tents.

56 Yet they tested the Most
High God,
and rebelled against
him.
They did not observe his
decrees,
57 but turned away and were
faithless like their
ancestors;
they twisted like a
treacherous bow.
58 For they provoked him to
anger with their high
places;

78.48 Ex 9.23
78.49 Ex 15.7
78.51 Ex 12.29; Ps 106.22
78.52 Ps 77.20
78.53 Ex 14.19,27
78.54 Ex 15.17; Ps 44.3
78.55 Ps 44.2; 105.11
78.56 vv. 18,40
78.57 Ezek 20.27, 28; Hos 7.16
78.58 Deut 32.16, 21; 12.2; 1 Kings 11.7
78.60 1 Sam 4.11
78.61 Judg 18.30
78.62 1 Sam 4.10
78.63 Jer 7.34
78.64 1 Sam 22.18; Job 27.15
78.65 Isa 42.13
78.66 1 Sam 5.6
78.68 Ps 87.2
78.69 1 Sam 6.1-38
78.70 1 Sam 16.11, 12
78.71 2 Sam 7.8; Gen 33.13; 2 Sam 5.2; 1 Chr 11.2
78.72 1 Kings 9.4

they moved him to jealousy
with their idols.
59 When God heard, he was full
of wrath,
and he utterly rejected
Israel.
60 He abandoned his dwelling
at Shiloh,
the tent where he dwelt
among mortals,
61 and delivered his power to
captivity,
his glory to the hand of the
foe.
62 He gave his people to the
sword,
and vented his wrath on
his heritage.
63 Fire devoured their young
men,
and their girls had no
marriage song.
64 Their priests fell by the
sword,
and their widows made no
lamentation.
65 Then the Lord awoke as
from sleep,
like a warrior shouting
because of wine.
66 He put his adversaries to
rout;
he put them to everlasting
disgrace.
67 He rejected the tent of
Joseph,
he did not choose the tribe
of Ephraim;
68 but he chose the tribe of
Judah,
Mount Zion, which he
loves.
69 He built his sanctuary like
the high heavens,
like the earth, which he
has founded forever.
70 He chose his servant David,
and took him from the
sheepfolds;
71 from tending the nursing
ewes he brought him
to be the shepherd of his
people Jacob,
of Israel, his inheritance.
72 With upright heart he tended
them,

and guided them with
skillful hand.

Psalm 79

Plea for Mercy for Jerusalem

A Psalm of Asaph.

1 O God, the nations have
come into your
inheritance;
they have defiled your holy
temple;
they have laid Jerusalem in
ruins.
2 They have given the bodies
of your servants
to the birds of the air for
food,
the flesh of your faithful to
the wild animals of the
earth.
3 They have poured out their
blood like water
all around Jerusalem,
and there was no one to
bury them.
4 We have become a taunt to
our neighbors,
mocked and derided by
those around us.

5 How long, O LORD? Will you
be angry forever?
Will your jealous wrath
burn like fire?
6 Pour out your anger on the
nations
that do not know you,
and on the kingdoms
that do not call on your
name.
7 For they have devoured
Jacob
and laid waste his
habitation.

8 Do not remember against us
the iniquities of our
ancestors;
let your compassion come
speedily to meet us,
for we are brought very
low.
9 Help us, O God of our
salvation,
for the glory of your name;
deliver us, and forgive our
sins,
for your name's sake.
10 Why should the nations say,
"Where is their God?"
Let the avenging of the
outpoured blood of your
servants
be known among the
nations before our eyes.

11 Let the groans of the
prisoners come before
you;
according to your great
power preserve those
doomed to die.
12 Return sevenfold into the
bosom of our neighbors
the taunts with which they
taunted you, O Lord!
13 Then we your people, the
flock of your pasture,
will give thanks to you
forever;
from generation to
generation we will
recount your praise.

Psalm 80

Prayer for Israel's Restoration

To the leader: on Lilies, a
Covenant. Of Asaph. A Psalm.

1 Give ear, O Shepherd of
Israel,
you who lead Joseph like a
flock!
You who are enthroned upon
the cherubim, shine
forth
2 before Ephraim and
Benjamin and
Manasseh.
Stir up your might,
and come to save us!

3 Restore us, O God;
let your face shine, that we
may be saved.

4 O LORD God of hosts,
how long will you be angry
with your people's
prayers?

79.1 Ex 15.17; Ps 74.2; 2 Kings 25.9; Mic 3.12
79.2 Jer 7.33
79.3 Jer 14.16
79.4 Ps 44.13
79.5 Ps 74.1,9; Zeph 3.8
79.6 Jer 10.25; Rev 16.1; Isa 45.4,5; 2 Thes 1.8
79.8 Isa 64.9
79.9 2 Chr 14.11; Jer 14.7
79.10 Ps 42.10; 94.1,2
79.11 Ps 102.20
79.12 Isa 65.6,7; Jer 32.18; Lk 6.38; Ps 74.18,22
79.13 Ps 74.1; 95.7; Isa 43.21
80.1 Ps 23.1; 77.20; 99.1
80.2 Ps 35.23
80.3 Lam 5.21; Num 6.25
80.4 Ps 85.5

5 You have fed them with the
bread of tears,
and given them tears to
drink in full measure.
6 You make us the scorn[j] of
our neighbors;
our enemies laugh among
themselves.

7 Restore us, O God of
hosts;
let your face shine, that we
may be saved.

8 You brought a vine out of
Egypt;
you drove out the nations
and planted it.
9 You cleared the ground for
it;
it took deep root and filled
the land.
10 The mountains were covered
with its shade,
the mighty cedars with its
branches;
11 it sent out its branches to
the sea,
and its shoots to the River.
12 Why then have you broken
down its walls,
so that all who pass along
the way pluck its fruit?
13 The boar from the forest
ravages it,
and all that move in the
field feed on it.

14 Turn again, O God of hosts;
look down from heaven,
and see;
have regard for this vine,
15 the stock that your right
hand planted.[k]
16 They have burned it with
fire, they have cut it
down;[l]
may they perish at the
rebuke of your
countenance.
17 But let your hand be upon
the one at your right
hand,
the one whom you made
strong for yourself.
18 Then we will never turn back
from you;
give us life, and we will
call on your name.

19 Restore us, O LORD God of
hosts;
let your face shine, that we
may be saved.

Psalm 81

God's Appeal to Stubborn Israel

To the leader: according to The
Gittith. Of Asaph.

1 Sing aloud to God our
strength;
shout for joy to the God of
Jacob.
2 Raise a song, sound the
tambourine,
the sweet lyre with the
harp.
3 Blow the trumpet at the new
moon,
at the full moon, on our
festal day.
4 For it is a statute for Israel,
an ordinance of the God of
Jacob.
5 He made it a decree in
Joseph,
when he went out over[m]
the land of Egypt.

I hear a voice I had not
known:
6 "I relieved your[n] shoulder of
the burden;
your[n] hands were freed
from the basket.
7 In distress you called, and I
rescued you;
I answered you in the
secret place of thunder;
I tested you at the waters
of Meribah. *Selah*
8 Hear, O my people, while I
admonish you;
O Israel, if you would but
listen to me!
9 There shall be no strange
god among you;

80.5 Ps 42.3; 102.9
80.6 Ps 44.13; 79.4
80.8 Isa 5.1,7; Jer 2.21; Ezek 15.6; Ps 44.2
80.9 Hos 14.5
80.12 Ps 89.40; Nah 2.2
80.13 Jer 5.6
80.14 Isa 63.15
80.16 Ps 39.11; 76.6
80.17 Ps 89.21
80.18 Isa 50.5; Ps 71.20
81.1 Ps 59.16; 66.1
81.3 Num 10.10; Lev 23.24
81.5 Ex 11.4
81.6 Isa 9.4; 10.27
81.7 Ex 2.23; Ps 50.15; Ex 19.19; 17.6,7
81.8 Ps 50.7
81.9 Deut 32.12; Isa 43.12

[j] Syr: Heb *strife* [k] Heb adds from verse 17 *and upon the one whom you made strong for yourself* [l] Cn: Heb *it is cut down* [m] Or *against* [n] Heb *his*

you shall not bow down to
a foreign god.
10 I am the LORD your God,
who brought you up out of
the land of Egypt.
Open your mouth wide and
I will fill it.

11 "But my people did not
listen to my voice;
Israel would not submit to
me.
12 So I gave them over to their
stubborn hearts,
to follow their own
counsels.
13 O that my people would
listen to me,
that Israel would walk in
my ways!
14 Then I would quickly subdue
their enemies,
and turn my hand against
their foes.
15 Those who hate the LORD
would cringe before
him,
and their doom would last
forever.
16 I would feed you[o] with the
finest of the wheat,
and with honey from the
rock I would satisfy
you."

Psalm 82

A Plea for Justice

A Psalm of Asaph.

1 God has taken his place in
the divine council;
in the midst of the gods he
holds judgment:
2 "How long will you judge
unjustly
and show partiality to the
wicked? *Selah*
3 Give justice to the weak and
the orphan;
maintain the right of the
lowly and the destitute.
4 Rescue the weak and the
needy;
deliver them from the hand
of the wicked."

5 They have neither knowledge
nor understanding,
they walk around in
darkness;
all the foundations of the
earth are shaken.

6 I say, "You are gods,
children of the Most High,
all of you;
7 nevertheless, you shall die
like mortals,
and fall like any prince."[p]

8 Rise up, O God, judge the
earth;
for all the nations belong
to you!

Psalm 83

Prayer for Judgment on Israel's Foes

A Song. A Psalm of Asaph.

1 O God, do not keep silence;
do not hold your peace or
be still, O God!
2 Even now your enemies are
in tumult;
those who hate you have
raised their heads.
3 They lay crafty plans against
your people;
they consult together
against those you
protect.
4 They say, "Come, let us wipe
them out as a nation;
let the name of Israel be
remembered no more."
5 They conspire with one
accord;
against you they make a
covenant—
6 the tents of Edom and the
Ishmaelites,
Moab and the Hagrites,
7 Gebal and Ammon and
Amalek,
Philistia with the
inhabitants of Tyre;
8 Assyria also has joined them;

81.10 Ex 20.2; Ps 103.5
81.11 Ex 32.1
81.12 Acts 7.42; Rom 1.24
81.13 Deut 5.29; Isa 48.18; Ps 128.1
81.14 Ps 47.3; Am 1.8
81.16 Deut 32.13; Ps 147.14
82.1 Isa 3.13; Ex 21.6
82.2 Ps 58.1; Deut 1.17; Prov 18.5
82.3 Deut 24.17
82.4 Job 29.12
82.5 Mic 3.1; Ps 11.3
82.6 Jn 10.34; Ps 89.26
82.7 Ps 49.12; Ezek 31.14
82.8 Ps 12.5; Mic 7.2,7; Ps 2.8; Rev 11.15
83.1 Ps 28.1; 109.1
83.2 Ps 2.1; 81.15
83.3 Ps 27.5
83.4 Esther 3.6
83.5 Ps 2.2
83.6 2 Chr 20.1, 10,11

[o] Cn Compare verse 16b: Heb *he would feed him* [p] Or *fall as one man, O princes*

they are the strong arm of
the children of Lot. *Selah*

9 Do to them as you did to Midian,
as to Sisera and Jabin at the Wadi Kishon,
10 who were destroyed at En-dor,
who became dung for the ground.
11 Make their nobles like Oreb and Zeeb,
all their princes like Zebah and Zalmunna,
12 who said, "Let us take the pastures of God
for our own possession."

13 O my God, make them like whirling dust,[q]
like chaff before the wind.
14 As fire consumes the forest,
as the flame sets the mountains ablaze,
15 so pursue them with your tempest
and terrify them with your hurricane.
16 Fill their faces with shame,
so that they may seek your name, O LORD.
17 Let them be put to shame and dismayed forever;
let them perish in disgrace.
18 Let them know that you alone,
whose name is the LORD,
are the Most High over all the earth.

Psalm 84

The Joy of Worship in the Temple

To the leader: according to The Gittith. Of the Korahites. A Psalm.

1 How lovely is your dwelling place,
O LORD of hosts!
2 My soul longs, indeed it faints
for the courts of the LORD;
my heart and my flesh sing for joy
to the living God.

3 Even the sparrow finds a home,
and the swallow a nest for herself,
where she may lay her young,
at your altars, O LORD of hosts,
my King and my God.
4 Happy are those who live in your house,
ever singing your praise. *Selah*

5 Happy are those whose strength is in you,
in whose heart are the highways to Zion.[r]
6 As they go through the valley of Baca
they make it a place of springs;
the early rain also covers it with pools.
7 They go from strength to strength;
the God of gods will be seen in Zion.

8 O LORD God of hosts, hear my prayer;
give ear, O God of Jacob! *Selah*
9 Behold our shield, O God;
look on the face of your anointed.

10 For a day in your courts is better
than a thousand elsewhere.
I would rather be a doorkeeper in the house of my God
than live in the tents of wickedness.
11 For the LORD God is a sun and shield;
he bestows favor and honor.
No good thing does the LORD withhold
from those who walk uprightly.

83.9 Judg 4.22, 23 **83.11** Judg 8.12, 21 **83.12** 2 Chr 20.11; Ps 132.13 **83.13** Isa 17.13; Ps 35.5 **83.14** Deut 32.22 **83.15** Job 9.17 **83.17** Ps 70.2 **83.18** Ps 59.13; Ex 6.3; Ps 92.8 **84.1** Ps 27.4 **84.2** Ps 42.1,2 **84.3** Ps 43.4; 5.2 **84.4** Ps 65.4 **84.5** Ps 81.1 **84.6** 2 Sam 4.23; Ps 107.35 **84.7** Prov 4.18; 2 Cor 3.18; Deut 16.16; Ps 42.2 **84.9** Gen 15.1; Ps 2.2 **84.10** 1 Chr 23.5 **84.11** Isa 60.19; Rev 21.23; Ps 34.10

q Or *a tumbleweed* r Heb lacks *to Zion*

12 O LORD of hosts,
happy is everyone who trusts in you.

Psalm 85

Prayer for the Restoration of God's Favor

To the leader. Of the Korahites. A Psalm.

1 LORD, you were favorable to your land;
you restored the fortunes of Jacob.
2 You forgave the iniquity of your people;
you pardoned all their sin. *Selah*
3 You withdrew all your wrath;
you turned from your hot anger.

4 Restore us again, O God of our salvation,
and put away your indignation toward us.
5 Will you be angry with us forever?
Will you prolong your anger to all generations?
6 Will you not revive us again,
so that your people may rejoice in you?
7 Show us your steadfast love, O LORD,
and grant us your salvation.

8 Let me hear what God the LORD will speak,
for he will speak peace to his people,
to his faithful, to those who turn to him in their hearts.[s]
9 Surely his salvation is at hand for those who fear him,
that his glory may dwell in our land.

10 Steadfast love and faithfulness will meet;
righteousness and peace will kiss each other.
11 Faithfulness will spring up from the ground,
and righteousness will look down from the sky.
12 The LORD will give what is good,
and our land will yield its increase.
13 Righteousness will go before him,
and will make a path for his steps.

Psalm 86

Supplication for Help against Enemies

A Prayer of David.

1 Incline your ear, O LORD, and answer me,
for I am poor and needy.
2 Preserve my life, for I am devoted to you;
save your servant who trusts in you.
You are my God; 3 be gracious to me, O Lord,
for to you do I cry all day long.
4 Gladden the soul of your servant,
for to you, O Lord, I lift up my soul.
5 For you, O Lord, are good and forgiving,
abounding in steadfast love to all who call on you.
6 Give ear, O LORD, to my prayer;
listen to my cry of supplication.
7 In the day of my trouble I call on you,
for you will answer me.

8 There is none like you among the gods, O Lord,
nor are there any works like yours.
9 All the nations you have made shall come
and bow down before you, O Lord,
and shall glorify your name.

84.12 Ps 2.12
85.1 Ezra 1.11; Jer 30.18; Ezek 39.25
85.2 Ps 103.3; 32.1
85.3 Ps 78.38; Deut 13.17
85.4 Ps 80.3,7
85.5 Ps 74.1; 79.5; 80.4
85.6 Hab 3.2
85.7 Ps 106.4
85.8 Hab 2.1; Zech 9.10
85.9 Isa 46.13; Zech 2.5; Jn 1.14
85.10 Ps 72.3; Isa 32.17; Lk 2.14
85.12 Ps 84.11; Jas 1.17
85.13 Ps 89.14
86.1 Ps 17.6; 40.17
86.2 Ps 25.20; 4.3; 31.14
86.3 Ps 57.1; 88.9
86.4 Ps 25.1; 143.8
86.5 Ps 130.7; 145.9; Joel 2.13
86.6 Ps 55.1
86.7 Ps 50.15; 17.6
86.8 Ex 15.11; Ps 89.6; Deut 3.24
86.9 Ps 22.31; Isa 43.7; Rev 15.4

[s] Gk: Heb *but let them not turn back to folly*

10 For you are great and do
wondrous things;
you alone are God.
11 Teach me your way, O LORD,
that I may walk in your
truth;
give me an undivided heart
to revere your name.
12 I give thanks to you, O Lord
my God, with my whole
heart,
and I will glorify your name
forever.
13 For great is your steadfast
love toward me;
you have delivered my soul
from the depths of
Sheol.

14 O God, the insolent rise up
against me;
a band of ruffians seeks my
life,
and they do not set you
before them.
15 But you, O Lord, are a God
merciful and gracious,
slow to anger and
abounding in steadfast
love and faithfulness.
16 Turn to me and be gracious
to me;
give your strength to your
servant;
save the child of your
serving girl.
17 Show me a sign of your
favor,
so that those who hate me
may see it and be put
to shame,
because you, LORD, have
helped me and
comforted me.

Psalm 87

The Joy of Living in Zion

Of the Korahites. A Psalm.
A Song.

1 On the holy mount stands
the city he founded;
2 the LORD loves the gates of
Zion
more than all the dwellings
of Jacob.

86.10 Ex 15.11; Ps 72.18; Deut 6.4; Mk 12.29
86.11 Ps 25.4
86.12 Ps 111.1
86.13 Ps 30.3
86.14 Ps 54.3
86.15 Ex 34.6; Neh 9.17; Ps 103.8; Joel 2.13
86.16 Ps 25.16; 68.35; 116.16
86.17 Ps 112.10; 118.13
87.2 Ps 78.67
87.3 Isa 60.1
87.5 Ps 48.8
87.6 Ezek 13.9
87.7 Ps 36.9
88.1 Ps 27.9; 51.14
88.2 Ps 18.6; 86.1
88.3 Ps 107.18, 26
88.4 Ps 28.1
88.5 Isa 53.8

3 Glorious things are spoken of
you,
O city of God. *Selah*

4 Among those who know me I
mention Rahab and
Babylon;
Philistia too, and Tyre,
with Ethiopia[t]—
"This one was born there,"
they say.

5 And of Zion it shall be said,
"This one and that one
were born in it";
for the Most High himself
will establish it.
6 The LORD records, as he
registers the peoples,
"This one was born there."
Selah

7 Singers and dancers alike
say,
"All my springs are in you."

Psalm 88

Prayer for Help in Despondency

A Song. A Psalm of the
Korahites. To the leader:
according to Mahalath Leannoth.
A Maskil of Heman the Ezrahite.

1 O LORD, God of my salvation,
when, at night, I cry out in
your presence,
2 let my prayer come before
you;
incline your ear to my cry.

3 For my soul is full of
troubles,
and my life draws near to
Sheol.
4 I am counted among those
who go down to the Pit;
I am like those who have
no help,
5 like those forsaken among
the dead,
like the slain that lie in the
grave,
like those whom you
remember no more,

[t] Or *Nubia*; Heb *Cush*

for they are cut off from
your hand.
6 You have put me in the
depths of the Pit,
in the regions dark and
deep.
7 Your wrath lies heavy upon
me,
and you overwhelm me
with all your waves.
Selah

8 You have caused my
companions to shun
me;
you have made me a thing
of horror to them.
I am shut in so that I cannot
escape;
9 my eye grows dim through
sorrow.
Every day I call on you,
O LORD;
I spread out my hands to
you.
10 Do you work wonders for the
dead?
Do the shades rise up to
praise you? *Selah*
11 Is your steadfast love
declared in the grave,
or your faithfulness in
Abaddon?
12 Are your wonders known in
the darkness,
or your saving help in the
land of forgetfulness?

13 But I, O LORD, cry out to you;
in the morning my prayer
comes before you.
14 O LORD, why do you cast me
off?
Why do you hide your face
from me?
15 Wretched and close to death
from my youth up,
I suffer your terrors; I am
desperate.[u]
16 Your wrath has swept over
me;
your dread assaults destroy
me.
17 They surround me like a
flood all day long;
from all sides they close in
on me.

88.6 Ps 86.13; 143.3; 69.15 **88.7** Ps 42.7 **88.8** Job 19.13; Ps 31.11; 142.4; Lam 3.7 **88.9** Ps 38.10; 86.3; Job 11.13; Ps 143.6 **88.10** Ps 6.5; Isa 38.18 **88.12** Job 10.21 **88.13** Ps 5.3; 119.147 **88.14** Job 13.24; Ps 13.1 **88.15** Job 6.4 **88.17** Ps 22.16

88.18 Job 19.13; Ps 31.11; 38.11 **89.1** Ps 101.1 **89.2** Ps 103.17; 36.5 **89.3** 1 Kings 8.16; Ps 132.11 **89.4** 2 Sam 7.16; Isa 9.7; Lk 1.33 **89.5** Ps 19.1; 149.1 **89.6** Mic 7.18; Ps 29.1 **89.7** Ps 47.2; 96.4 **89.8** Ps 71.19 **89.9** Ps 65.7

18 You have caused friend and
neighbor to shun me;
my companions are in
darkness.

Psalm 89

God's Covenant with David

A Maskil of Ethan the Ezrahite.

1 I will sing of your steadfast
love, O LORD,[v] forever;
with my mouth I will
proclaim your
faithfulness to all
generations.
2 I declare that your steadfast
love is established
forever;
your faithfulness is as firm
as the heavens.

3 You said, "I have made a
covenant with my
chosen one,
I have sworn to my servant
David:
4 'I will establish your
descendants forever,
and build your throne for
all generations.'" *Selah*

5 Let the heavens praise your
wonders, O LORD,
your faithfulness in the
assembly of the holy
ones.
6 For who in the skies can be
compared to the LORD?
Who among the heavenly
beings is like the LORD,
7 a God feared in the council
of the holy ones,
great and awesome[w] above
all that are around him?
8 O LORD God of hosts,
who is as mighty as you,
O LORD?
Your faithfulness surrounds
you.
9 You rule the raging of the
sea;
when its waves rise, you
still them.

[u] Meaning of Heb uncertain [v] Gk: Heb *the steadfast love of the LORD* [w] Gk Syr: Heb *greatly awesome*

10 You crushed Rahab like a carcass;
you scattered your enemies with your mighty arm.
11 The heavens are yours, the earth also is yours;
the world and all that is in it—you have founded them.
12 The north and the south[x]—you created them;
Tabor and Hermon joyously praise your name.
13 You have a mighty arm;
strong is your hand, high your right hand.
14 Righteousness and justice are the foundation of your throne;
steadfast love and faithfulness go before you.
15 Happy are the people who know the festal shout,
who walk, O LORD, in the light of your countenance;
16 they exult in your name all day long,
and extol[y] your righteousness.
17 For you are the glory of their strength;
by your favor our horn is exalted.
18 For our shield belongs to the LORD,
our king to the Holy One of Israel.

19 Then you spoke in a vision to your faithful one,
and said:
"I have set the crown[z] on one who is mighty,
I have exalted one chosen from the people.
20 I have found my servant David;
with my holy oil I have anointed him;
21 my hand shall always remain with him;
my arm also shall strengthen him.
22 The enemy shall not outwit him,
the wicked shall not humble him.
23 I will crush his foes before him
and strike down those who hate him.
24 My faithfulness and steadfast love shall be with him;
and in my name his horn shall be exalted.
25 I will set his hand on the sea
and his right hand on the rivers.
26 He shall cry to me, 'You are my Father,
my God, and the Rock of my salvation!'
27 I will make him the firstborn,
the highest of the kings of the earth.
28 Forever I will keep my steadfast love for him,
and my covenant with him will stand firm.
29 I will establish his line forever,
and his throne as long as the heavens endure.
30 If his children forsake my law
and do not walk according to my ordinances,
31 if they violate my statutes
and do not keep my commandments,
32 then I will punish their transgression with the rod
and their iniquity with scourges;
33 but I will not remove from him my steadfast love,
or be false to my faithfulness.
34 I will not violate my covenant,
or alter the word that went forth from my lips.
35 Once and for all I have sworn by my holiness;
I will not lie to David.

89.10 Ps 87.4; Isa 51.9; Ps 68.1 **89.11** 1 Chr 29.11; Ps 24.1,2 **89.12** Josh 19.22; 12.1 **89.13** Ps 98.1 **89.14** Ps 97.2; 85.13 **89.15** Num 10.10 **89.17** Ps 28.8; 75.10 **89.18** Ps 47.9; 71.22 **89.19** 1 Kings 11.34 **89.20** Acts 13.22; 1 Sam 16.1, 12

89.22 2 Sam 7.10 **89.23** 2 Sam 7.9 **89.24** 2 Sam 7.15 **89.26** 2 Sam 7.14; 22.47 **89.27** Col 1.15; Num 24.7; Rev 1.5 **89.28** Isa 55.3 **89.29** Isa 9.7; Jer 33.17; Deut 11.21 **89.30** 2 Sam 7.14 **89.32** 2 Sam 7.14 **89.33** 2 Sam 7.15 **89.34** Deut 7.9; Num 23.19 **89.35** Am 4.2

x Or *Zaphon and Yamin* y Cn: Heb *are exalted in* z Cn: Heb *help*

36 His line shall continue
forever,
and his throne endure
before me like the sun.
37 It shall be established
forever like the moon,
an enduring witness in the
skies." *Selah*

38 But now you have spurned
and rejected him;
you are full of wrath
against your anointed.
39 You have renounced the
covenant with your
servant;
you have defiled his crown
in the dust.
40 You have broken through all
his walls;
you have laid his
strongholds in ruins.
41 All who pass by plunder
him;
he has become the scorn of
his neighbors.
42 You have exalted the right
hand of his foes;
you have made all his
enemies rejoice.
43 Moreover, you have turned
back the edge of his
sword,
and you have not
supported him in
battle.
44 You have removed the
scepter from his hand,[a]
and hurled his throne to
the ground.
45 You have cut short the days
of his youth;
you have covered him with
shame. *Selah*

46 How long, O LORD? Will you
hide yourself forever?
How long will your wrath
burn like fire?
47 Remember how short my
time is —[b]
for what vanity you have
created all mortals!
48 Who can live and never see
death?
Who can escape the power
of Sheol? *Selah*

89.36 Ps 72.5 **89.38** 1 Chr 28.9; Deut 32.19 **89.39** Lam 5.16 **89.40** Ps 80.12; Lam 2.2,5 **89.41** Ps 44.13 **89.42** Ps 13.2; 80.6 **89.43** Ps 44.10 **89.44** Ezek 28.7 **89.45** Ps 102.23; 44.15 **89.46** Ps 79.5 **89.47** Job 7.7; 10.9; 14.1; Ps 39.5 **89.48** Ps 49.9; Heb 11.5 **89.49** 2 Sam 7.15; Ps 54.5 **89.50** Ps 69.9,19 **89.51** Ps 74.10 **89.52** Ps 41.13 **90.1** Deut 33.27; Ezek 11.16 **90.2** Prov 8.25; Ps 102.25; 93.2 **90.3** Gen 3.19 **90.4** 2 Pet 3.8; Ps 39.5 **90.5** Job 27.20; Ps 73.20; 103.15; Isa 40.6

49 Lord, where is your steadfast
love of old,
which by your faithfulness
you swore to David?
50 Remember, O Lord, how
your servant is taunted;
how I bear in my bosom
the insults of the
peoples,[c]
51 with which your enemies
taunt, O LORD,
with which they taunted
the footsteps of your
anointed.

52 Blessed be the LORD forever.
Amen and Amen.

BOOK IV

(Psalms 90–106)

Psalm 90

God's Eternity and Human Frailty

A Prayer of Moses, the man of God.

1 Lord, you have been our
dwelling place[d]
in all generations.
2 Before the mountains were
brought forth,
or ever you had formed the
earth and the world,
from everlasting to
everlasting you are God.

3 You turn us[e] back to dust,
and say, "Turn back, you
mortals."
4 For a thousand years in your
sight
are like yesterday when it
is past,
or like a watch in the
night.

5 You sweep them away; they
are like a dream,

[a] Cn: Heb *removed his cleanness* [b] Meaning of Heb uncertain [c] Cn: Heb *bosom all of many peoples* [d] Another reading is *our refuge* [e] Heb *humankind*

like grass that is renewed
in the morning;
6 in the morning it flourishes
and is renewed;
in the evening it fades and
withers.

7 For we are consumed by
your anger;
by your wrath we are
overwhelmed.
8 You have set our iniquities
before you,
our secret sins in the light
of your countenance.

9 For all our days pass away
under your wrath;
our years come to an end[f]
like a sigh.
10 The days of our life are
seventy years,
or perhaps eighty, if we are
strong;
even then their span[g] is only
toil and trouble;
they are soon gone, and we
fly away.

11 Who considers the power of
your anger?
Your wrath is as great as
the fear that is due you.
12 So teach us to count our
days
that we may gain a wise
heart.

13 Turn, O LORD! How long?
Have compassion on your
servants!
14 Satisfy us in the morning
with your steadfast
love,
so that we may rejoice and
be glad all our days.
15 Make us glad as many days
as you have afflicted us,
and as many years as we
have seen evil.
16 Let your work be manifest to
your servants,
and your glorious power to
their children.
17 Let the favor of the Lord our
God be upon us,
and prosper for us the work
of our hands—
O prosper the work of our
hands!

Psalm 91

Assurance of God's Protection

1 You who live in the shelter
of the Most High,
who abide in the shadow of
the Almighty,[h]
2 will say to the LORD, "My
refuge and my fortress;
my God, in whom I trust."
3 For he will deliver you from
the snare of the fowler
and from the deadly
pestilence;
4 he will cover you with his
pinions,
and under his wings you
will find refuge;
his faithfulness is a shield
and buckler.
5 You will not fear the terror of
the night,
or the arrow that flies by
day,
6 or the pestilence that stalks
in darkness,
or the destruction that
wastes at noonday.

7 A thousand may fall at your
side,
ten thousand at your right
hand,
but it will not come near
you.
8 You will only look with your
eyes
and see the punishment of
the wicked.

9 Because you have made the
LORD your refuge,[i]
the Most High your
dwelling place,
10 no evil shall befall you,
no scourge come near your
tent.

90.6 Job 14.2; Ps 92.7 **90.8** Ps 50.21; Jer 16.17; Ps 19.12 **90.9** Ps 78.33 **90.10** Eccl 12.2-7 **90.11** Ps 76.7 **90.12** Ps 39.4 **90.13** Deut 32.26; Ps 135.14 **90.14** Ps 65.4; 85.6 **90.16** Hab 3.2; 1 Kings 8.11 **90.17** Ps 27.4; Isa 26.12

91.1 Ps 27.5; 31.20; 17.8 **91.2** Ps 142.5 **91.3** Ps 124.7 **91.4** Isa 51.16; Ps 57.1; 40.11; 35.2 **91.5** Ps 23.4; Song 3.8; Ps 64.4 **91.6** v. 10; Job 5.22 **91.8** Ps 37.34; Mal 1.5 **91.10** Prov 12.21

[f] Syr: Heb *we bring our years to an end*
[g] Cn Compare Gk Syr Jerome Tg: Heb *pride*
[h] Traditional rendering of Heb *Shaddai*
[i] Cn: Heb *Because you, LORD, are my refuge; you have made*

11 For he will command his angels concerning you
to guard you in all your ways.
12 On their hands they will bear you up,
so that you will not dash your foot against a stone.
13 You will tread on the lion and the adder,
the young lion and the serpent you will trample under foot.

14 Those who love me, I will deliver;
I will protect those who know my name.
15 When they call to me, I will answer them;
I will be with them in trouble,
I will rescue them and honor them.
16 With long life I will satisfy them,
and show them my salvation.

Psalm 92

Thanksgiving for Vindication

A Psalm. A Song for the Sabbath Day.

1 It is good to give thanks to the LORD,
to sing praises to your name, O Most High;
2 to declare your steadfast love in the morning,
and your faithfulness by night,
3 to the music of the lute and the harp,
to the melody of the lyre.
4 For you, O LORD, have made me glad by your work;
at the works of your hands I sing for joy.

5 How great are your works, O LORD!
Your thoughts are very deep!
6 The dullard cannot know,
the stupid cannot understand this:
7 though the wicked sprout like grass
and all evildoers flourish,
they are doomed to destruction forever,
8 but you, O LORD, are on high forever.
9 For your enemies, O LORD,
for your enemies shall perish;
all evildoers shall be scattered.

10 But you have exalted my horn like that of the wild ox;
you have poured over me[j] fresh oil.
11 My eyes have seen the downfall of my enemies;
my ears have heard the doom of my evil assailants.

12 The righteous flourish like the palm tree,
and grow like a cedar in Lebanon.
13 They are planted in the house of the LORD;
they flourish in the courts of our God.
14 In old age they still produce fruit;
they are always green and full of sap,
15 showing that the LORD is upright;
he is my rock, and there is no unrighteousness in him.

Psalm 93

The Majesty of God's Rule

1 The LORD is king, he is robed in majesty;
the LORD is robed, he is girded with strength.
He has established the world; it shall never be moved;

91.11 Ps 34.7; Mt 4.6; Lk 4.10; Heb 1.14
91.13 Lk 10.19
91.14 Ps 145.20; 59.1; 9.10
91.15 Ps 50.15; 1 Sam 2.30; Jn 12.26
91.16 Ps 21.4; 50.23
92.1 Ps 157.1
92.2 Ps 89.1
92.3 1 Chr 23.5; Ps 33.2
92.5 Ps 40.5; Isa 28.29; Rom 11.33
92.6 Ps 73.22
92.7 Ps 90.5; 94.4; 37.38; 93.4
92.8 Ps 83.18
92.9 Ps 68.1; 89.10
92.10 Ps 89.17; 23.5
92.11 Ps 54.7; 59.10
92.12 Ps 52.8; Isa 65.22; Hos 14.5,6; Ps 104.16
92.13 Ps 80.15; 100.4
92.14 Isa 37.31
92.15 Ps 25.8; Deut 32.4; Rom 9.14
93.1 Ps 96.10; 97.1; 99.1; 104.1; 65.6

[j] Syr: Meaning of Heb uncertain

2 your throne is established
from of old;
you are from everlasting.

3 The floods have lifted up,
O LORD,
the floods have lifted up
their voice;
the floods lift up their
roaring.
4 More majestic than the
thunders of mighty
waters,
more majestic than the
waves[k] of the sea,
majestic on high is the
LORD!

5 Your decrees are very sure;
holiness befits your house,
O LORD, forevermore.

Psalm 94

God the Avenger of the Righteous

1 O LORD, you God of
vengeance,
you God of vengeance,
shine forth!
2 Rise up, O judge of the
earth;
give to the proud what they
deserve!
3 O LORD, how long shall the
wicked,
how long shall the wicked
exult?

4 They pour out their arrogant
words;
all the evildoers boast.
5 They crush your people,
O LORD,
and afflict your heritage.
6 They kill the widow and the
stranger,
they murder the orphan,
7 and they say, "The LORD does
not see;
the God of Jacob does not
perceive."

8 Understand, O dullest of the
people;

93.2 Ps 45.6; 90.2 **93.3** Ps 98.7,8 **93.4** Ps 65.7; 89.9 **93.5** Ps 19.7; 1 Cor 3.17 **94.1** Deut 32.35; Nah 1.2; Ps 50.2 **94.2** Ps 7.6; Gen 18.25; Ps 31.23 **94.3** Job 20.5 **94.4** Ps 31.18; 10.3 **94.6** Isa 10.2 **94.7** Ps 10.11 **94.8** Ps 92.6

94.9 Ex 4.11; Prov 20.12 **94.10** Ps 44.2; Job 35.11; Isa 28.26 **94.11** 1 Cor 3.20 **94.12** Job 5.17; Heb 12.5 **94.13** Ps 49.5; 9.15 **94.14** 1 Sam 12.22; Rom 11.1,2 **94.16** Isa 28.21; Ps 59.2 **94.17** Ps 124.1 **94.18** Ps 38.16 **94.19** Isa 66.13 **94.20** Am 6.3; Isa 10.1

fools, when will you be
wise?
9 He who planted the ear, does
he not hear?
He who formed the eye, does
he not see?
10 He who disciplines the
nations,
he who teaches knowledge to
humankind,
does he not chastise?
11 The LORD knows our
thoughts,[l]
that they are but an empty
breath.

12 Happy are those whom you
discipline, O LORD,
and whom you teach out of
your law,
13 giving them respite from
days of trouble,
until a pit is dug for the
wicked.
14 For the LORD will not forsake
his people;
he will not abandon his
heritage;
15 for justice will return to the
righteous,
and all the upright in heart
will follow it.

16 Who rises up for me against
the wicked?
Who stands up for me
against evildoers?
17 If the LORD had not been my
help,
my soul would soon have
lived in the land of
silence.
18 When I thought, "My foot is
slipping,"
your steadfast love, O LORD,
held me up.
19 When the cares of my heart
are many,
your consolations cheer my
soul.
20 Can wicked rulers be allied
with you,
those who contrive
mischief by statute?

[k] Cn: Heb *majestic are the waves*
[l] Heb *the thoughts of humankind*

21 They band together against
the life of the righteous,
and condemn the innocent
to death.
22 But the LORD has become my
stronghold,
and my God the rock of my
refuge.
23 He will repay them for their
iniquity
and wipe them out for their
wickedness;
the LORD our God will wipe
them out.

Psalm 95

A Call to Worship and Obedience

1 O come, let us sing to the
LORD;
let us make a joyful noise
to the rock of our
salvation!
2 Let us come into his
presence with
thanksgiving;
let us make a joyful noise
to him with songs of
praise!
3 For the LORD is a great God,
and a great King above all
gods.
4 In his hand are the depths of
the earth;
the heights of the
mountains are his also.
5 The sea is his, for he made
it,
and the dry land, which his
hands have formed.

6 O come, let us worship and
bow down,
let us kneel before the
LORD, our Maker!
7 For he is our God,
and we are the people of
his pasture,
and the sheep of his hand.

O that today you would
listen to his voice!
8 Do not harden your hearts,
as at Meribah,
as on the day at Massah in
the wilderness,
9 when your ancestors tested
me,
and put me to the proof,
though they had seen
my work.
10 For forty years I loathed that
generation
and said, "They are a
people whose hearts go
astray,
and they do not regard my
ways."
11 Therefore in my anger I
swore,
"They shall not enter my
rest."

Psalm 96

Praise to God Who Comes in Judgment

1 O sing to the LORD a new
song;
sing to the LORD, all the
earth.
2 Sing to the LORD, bless his
name;
tell of his salvation from
day to day.
3 Declare his glory among the
nations,
his marvelous works among
all the peoples.
4 For great is the LORD, and
greatly to be praised;
he is to be revered above
all gods.
5 For all the gods of the
peoples are idols,
but the LORD made the
heavens.
6 Honor and majesty are
before him;
strength and beauty are in
his sanctuary.

7 Ascribe to the LORD,
O families of the
peoples,
ascribe to the LORD glory
and strength.
8 Ascribe to the LORD the glory
due his name;

94.21 Ps 56.6; Mt 27.1; Prov 17.15
94.22 Ps 59.9; 71.7
94.23 Ps 7.16
95.1 Ps 100.1; Deut 32.15; 2 Sam 22.47
95.2 Mic 6.6; Ps 100.4; 81.2
95.3 Ps 96.4; 97.9; 135.5
95.5 Gen 1.9,10
95.6 Ps 99.5,9; 2 Chr 6.13; Ps 100.3
95.7 Ps 79.13; 100.3; Heb 3.7-11
95.8 Ex 17.2,7; Deut 6.16
95.9 Ps 78.18; 1 Cor 10.9
95.10 Heb 3.10,17
95.11 Heb 4.3,5
96.1 1 Chr 16.23-33
96.2 Ps 71.15
96.3 Ps 145.12
96.4 Ps 145.3; 18.3; 95.3
96.5 1 Chr 16.26; Ps 115.15
96.6 Ps 104.1
96.7 Ps 29.1,2
96.8 Ps 79.9

bring an offering, and come
into his courts.
9 Worship the LORD in holy
splendor;
tremble before him, all the
earth.
10 Say among the nations, "The
LORD is king!
The world is firmly
established; it shall
never be moved.
He will judge the peoples
with equity."
11 Let the heavens be glad, and
let the earth rejoice;
let the sea roar, and all
that fills it;
12 let the field exult, and
everything in it.
Then shall all the trees of
the forest sing for joy
13 before the LORD; for he is
coming,
for he is coming to judge
the earth.
He will judge the world with
righteousness,
and the peoples with his
truth.

Psalm 97

The Glory of God's Reign

1 The LORD is king! Let the
earth rejoice;
let the many coastlands be
glad!
2 Clouds and thick darkness
are all around him;
righteousness and justice
are the foundation of
his throne.
3 Fire goes before him,
and consumes his
adversaries on every
side.
4 His lightnings light up the
world;
the earth sees and
trembles.
5 The mountains melt like wax
before the LORD,
before the Lord of all the
earth.
6 The heavens proclaim his
righteousness;
and all the peoples behold
his glory.
7 All worshipers of images are
put to shame,
those who make their boast
in worthless idols;
all gods bow down before
him.
8 Zion hears and is glad,
and the towns[m] of Judah
rejoice,
because of your judgments,
O God.
9 For you, O LORD, are most
high over all the earth;
you are exalted far above
all gods.

10 The LORD loves those who
hate[n] evil;
he guards the lives of his
faithful;
he rescues them from the
hand of the wicked.
11 Light dawns[o] for the
righteous,
and joy for the upright in
heart.
12 Rejoice in the LORD, O you
righteous,
and give thanks to his holy
name!

Psalm 98

Praise the Judge of the World

A Psalm.

1 O sing to the LORD a new
song,
for he has done marvelous
things.
His right hand and his holy
arm
have gotten him victory.
2 The LORD has made known
his victory;
he has revealed his
vindication in the sight
of the nations.

96.9 Ps 29.2
96.10 Ps 93.1; 67.4
96.11 Ps 97.1; 98.7
96.13 Ps 67.4; Rev 19.11
97.1 Ps 96.10,11
97.2 1 Kings 8.12; Ps 18.11; 89.14
97.3 Ps 18.8; Dan 7.10; Hab 3.5; Heb 12.29
97.4 Ps 77.18
97.5 Mic 1.4; Josh 3.11
97.6 Ps 50.6
97.7 Ex 20.4; Lev 26.1; Heb 1.6
97.8 Ps 48.11
97.9 Ps 83.18; Ex 18.11; Ps 95.3
97.10 Ps 34.14; Am 5.15; Prov 2.8; Ps 37.39; Dan 3.28
97.11 Job 22.28; Ps 112.4
97.12 Ps 32.11; 30.4
98.1 Ps 33.3; 40.5; Ex 15.6; Isa 52.10
98.2 Rom 3.25

m Heb *daughters* n Cn: Heb *You who love the LORD hate* o Gk Syr Jerome: Heb *is sown*

[3] He has remembered his steadfast love and faithfulness
to the house of Israel.
All the ends of the earth have seen
the victory of our God.

[4] Make a joyful noise to the LORD, all the earth;
break forth into joyous song and sing praises.
[5] Sing praises to the LORD with the lyre,
with the lyre and the sound of melody.
[6] With trumpets and the sound of the horn
make a joyful noise before the King, the LORD.

[7] Let the sea roar, and all that fills it;
the world and those who live in it.
[8] Let the floods clap their hands;
let the hills sing together for joy
[9] at the presence of the LORD,
for he is coming
to judge the earth.
He will judge the world with righteousness,
and the peoples with equity.

Psalm 99

Praise to God for His Holiness

[1] The LORD is king; let the peoples tremble!
He sits enthroned upon the cherubim; let the earth quake!
[2] The LORD is great in Zion;
he is exalted over all the peoples.
[3] Let them praise your great and awesome name.
Holy is he!
[4] Mighty King,[p] lover of justice,
you have established equity;
you have executed justice and righteousness in Jacob.

98.3 Lk 1.54; Isa 49.6
98.4 Ps 100.1
98.6 Num 10.10
98.7 Ps 96.11; 24.1
98.8 Ps 93.3; 65.12
98.9 Ps 96.10,13
99.1 Ex 25.22
99.2 Ps 97.9
99.4 Ps 11.7; 17.2; 103.6
99.5 Ps 132.7; Lev 19.2
99.6 Jer 15.1; Ex 14.15; 1 Sam 7.9
99.7 Ex 33.9
99.8 Ps 106.44; Num 14.20; Deut 9.20
99.9 Ps 34.3
100.1 Ps 98.4
100.3 Ps 46.10; 95.6,7
100.4 Ps 95.2; 96.2

[5] Extol the LORD our God;
worship at his footstool.
Holy is he!

[6] Moses and Aaron were among his priests,
Samuel also was among those who called on his name.
They cried to the LORD, and he answered them.
[7] He spoke to them in the pillar of cloud;
they kept his decrees,
and the statutes that he gave them.

[8] O LORD our God, you answered them;
you were a forgiving God to them,
but an avenger of their wrongdoings.
[9] Extol the LORD our God,
and worship at his holy mountain;
for the LORD our God is holy.

Psalm 100

All Lands Summoned to Praise God

A Psalm of thanksgiving.

[1] Make a joyful noise to the LORD, all the earth.
[2] Worship the LORD with gladness;
come into his presence with singing.

[3] Know that the LORD is God.
It is he that made us, and we are his;[q]
we are his people, and the sheep of his pasture.

[4] Enter his gates with thanksgiving,
and his courts with praise.
Give thanks to him, bless his name.

[p] Cn: Heb *And a king's strength* [q] Another reading is *and not we ourselves*

5 For the LORD is good;
his steadfast love endures forever,
and his faithfulness to all generations.

Psalm 101

A Sovereign's Pledge of Integrity and Justice

Of David. A Psalm.

1 I will sing of loyalty and of justice;
to you, O LORD, I will sing.
2 I will study the way that is blameless.
When shall I attain it?

I will walk with integrity of heart
within my house;
3 I will not set before my eyes
anything that is base.

I hate the work of those who fall away;
it shall not cling to me.
4 Perverseness of heart shall be far from me;
I will know nothing of evil.

5 One who secretly slanders a neighbor
I will destroy.
A haughty look and an arrogant heart
I will not tolerate.

6 I will look with favor on the faithful in the land,
so that they may live with me;
whoever walks in the way that is blameless
shall minister to me.

7 No one who practices deceit
shall remain in my house;
no one who utters lies
shall continue in my presence.

8 Morning by morning I will destroy
all the wicked in the land,
cutting off all evildoers
from the city of the LORD.

Psalm 102

Prayer to the Eternal King for Help

A prayer of one afflicted, when faint and pleading before the LORD.

1 Hear my prayer, O LORD;
let my cry come to you.
2 Do not hide your face from me
in the day of my distress.
Incline your ear to me;
answer me speedily in the day when I call.

3 For my days pass away like smoke,
and my bones burn like a furnace.
4 My heart is stricken and withered like grass;
I am too wasted to eat my bread.
5 Because of my loud groaning
my bones cling to my skin.
6 I am like an owl of the wilderness,
like a little owl of the waste places.
7 I lie awake;
I am like a lonely bird on the housetop.
8 All day long my enemies taunt me;
those who deride me use my name for a curse.
9 For I eat ashes like bread,
and mingle tears with my drink,
10 because of your indignation and anger;
for you have lifted me up and thrown me aside.
11 My days are like an evening shadow;
I wither away like grass.

12 But you, O LORD, are enthroned forever;
your name endures to all generations.
13 You will rise up and have compassion on Zion,

100.5 Ps 25.8; 119.90
101.1 Ps 89.1
101.2 1 Sam 18.14; 1 Kings 9.4
101.3 Deut 15.9; Ps 40.4
101.4 Prov 11.20
101.5 Ps 50.20; Prov 6.17
101.6 Ps 119.1
101.8 Ps 75.10; 118.10-12
102.1 Ex 2.23; 1 Sam 9.16
102.2 Ps 69.17; 71.2
102.3 Jas 4.14; Job 30.30; Ps 31.10
102.4 Ps 37.2
102.5 Lam 4.8
102.6 Isa 34.11
102.7 Ps 77.4; 38.11
102.8 Acts 26.11; 23;12
102.9 Ps 42.3
102.10 Ps 38.3; Job 30.22
102.11 Job 14.2; v. 4
102.12 Ps 9.7; Lam 5.19; Ps 135.13
102.13 Isa 60.10; Zech 1.12; Ps 75.2

for it is time to favor it;
the appointed time has come.
14 For your servants hold its stones dear,
and have pity on its dust.
15 The nations will fear the name of the LORD,
and all the kings of the earth your glory.
16 For the LORD will build up Zion;
he will appear in his glory.
17 He will regard the prayer of the destitute,
and will not despise their prayer.

18 Let this be recorded for a generation to come,
so that a people yet unborn may praise the LORD:
19 that he looked down from his holy height,
from heaven the LORD looked at the earth,
20 to hear the groans of the prisoners,
to set free those who were doomed to die;
21 so that the name of the LORD may be declared in Zion,
and his praise in Jerusalem,
22 when peoples gather together,
and kingdoms, to worship the LORD.

23 He has broken my strength in midcourse;
he has shortened my days.
24 "O my God," I say, "do not take me away
at the mid-point of my life,
you whose years endure throughout all generations."

25 Long ago you laid the foundation of the earth,
and the heavens are the work of your hands.
26 They will perish, but you endure;
they will all wear out like a garment.
You change them like clothing, and they pass away;
27 but you are the same, and your years have no end.
28 The children of your servants shall live secure;
their offspring shall be established in your presence.

Psalm 103

Thanksgiving for God's Goodness

Of David.

1 Bless the LORD, O my soul,
and all that is within me, bless his holy name.
2 Bless the LORD, O my soul,
and do not forget all his benefits—
3 who forgives all your iniquity,
who heals all your diseases,
4 who redeems your life from the Pit,
who crowns you with steadfast love and mercy,
5 who satisfies you with good as long as you live[r]
so that your youth is renewed like the eagle's.

6 The LORD works vindication
and justice for all who are oppressed.
7 He made known his ways to Moses,
his acts to the people of Israel.
8 The LORD is merciful and gracious,
slow to anger and abounding in steadfast love.
9 He will not always accuse,
nor will he keep his anger forever.

102.15 1 Kings 8.43; Ps 138.4 **102.16** Isa 60.1,2 **102.17** Neh 1.6 **102.18** Rom 15.4; Ps 22.31 **102.19** Deut 26.15; Ps 33.13 **102.20** Ps 79.11 **102.21** Ps 22.22 **102.22** Ps 86.9 **102.23** Job 21.21 **102.24** Isa 38.10; Ps 90.2; Hab 1.12 **102.25** Gen 1.1; Heb 1.10; Ps 96.5 **102.26** Isa 34.4; Mt 24.35; 2 Pet 3.7, 10; Rev 20.11 **102.27** Mal 3.6; Heb 13.8; Jas 1.17 **102.28** Ps 69.36; 89.4 **103.1** Ps 104.1; 33.21 **103.3** Ps 130.8; Isa 43.25; Ex 15.26 **103.4** Ps 49.15; 5.12 **103.5** Isa 40.31 **103.8** Ex 34.6; Neh 9.17; Ps 145.8 **103.9** Ps 30.5; Isa 57.16; Jer 3.5

[r] Meaning of Heb uncertain

10 He does not deal with us according to our sins,
nor repay us according to our iniquities.
11 For as the heavens are high above the earth,
so great is his steadfast love toward those who fear him;
12 as far as the east is from the west,
so far he removes our transgressions from us.
13 As a father has compassion for his children,
so the LORD has compassion for those who fear him.
14 For he knows how we were made;
he remembers that we are dust.

15 As for mortals, their days are like grass;
they flourish like a flower of the field;
16 for the wind passes over it, and it is gone,
and its place knows it no more.
17 But the steadfast love of the LORD is from everlasting to everlasting
on those who fear him,
and his righteousness to children's children,
18 to those who keep his covenant
and remember to do his commandments.

19 The LORD has established his throne in the heavens,
and his kingdom rules over all.
20 Bless the LORD, O you his angels,
you mighty ones who do his bidding,
obedient to his spoken word.
21 Bless the LORD, all his hosts,
his ministers that do his will.
22 Bless the LORD, all his works,
in all places of his dominion.
Bless the LORD, O my soul.

Psalm 104

God the Creator and Provider

1 Bless the LORD, O my soul.
O LORD my God, you are very great.
You are clothed with honor and majesty,
2 wrapped in light as with a garment.
You stretch out the heavens like a tent,
3 you set the beams of your[s] chambers on the waters,
you make the clouds your[s] chariot,
you ride on the wings of the wind,
4 you make the winds your[s] messengers,
fire and flame your[s] ministers.

5 You set the earth on its foundations,
so that it shall never be shaken.
6 You cover it with the deep as with a garment;
the waters stood above the mountains.
7 At your rebuke they flee;
at the sound of your thunder they take to flight.
8 They rose up to the mountains, ran down to the valleys
to the place that you appointed for them.
9 You set a boundary that they may not pass,
so that they might not again cover the earth.

10 You make springs gush forth in the valleys;
they flow between the hills,
11 giving drink to every wild animal;

103.10 Ezra 9.13
103.11 Ps 36.5
103.12 2 Sam 12.13; Isa 38.17; Heb 9.26
103.13 Mal 3.17
103.14 Isa 29.16; Gen 3.19
103.15 1 Pet 1.24; Job 14.1,2
103.16 Job 7.10
103.18 Deut 7.9
103.19 Ps 11.4; 47.2
103.20 Ps 148.2; Mt 6.10; Heb 1.14
103.21 Ps 148.2
104.1 Ps 103.1
104.2 Dan 7.9; Isa 40.22
104.3 Am 9.6; Isa 19.1; Ps 18.10
104.4 Heb 1.7
104.5 Job 26.7; Ps 24.2
104.6 Gen 7.19
104.8 Ps 33.7
104.9 Job 38.10, 11; Jer 5.22
104.10 Ps 107.35
104.11 Job 39.5

[s] Heb *his*

the wild asses quench their
thirst.
12 By the streams[t] the birds of
the air have their
habitation;
they sing among the
branches.
13 From your lofty abode you
water the mountains;
the earth is satisfied with
the fruit of your work.

14 You cause the grass to grow
for the cattle,
and plants for people to
use,[u]
to bring forth food from the
earth,
15 and wine to gladden the
human heart,
oil to make the face shine,
and bread to strengthen
the human heart.
16 The trees of the LORD are
watered abundantly,
the cedars of Lebanon that
he planted.
17 In them the birds build their
nests;
the stork has its home in
the fir trees.
18 The high mountains are for
the wild goats;
the rocks are a refuge for
the coneys.
19 You have made the moon to
mark the seasons;
the sun knows its time for
setting.
20 You make darkness, and it is
night,
when all the animals of the
forest come creeping
out.
21 The young lions roar for their
prey,
seeking their food from
God.
22 When the sun rises, they
withdraw
and lie down in their dens.
23 People go out to their work
and to their labor until the
evening.

24 O LORD, how manifold are
your works!
In wisdom you have made
them all;
the earth is full of your
creatures.
25 Yonder is the sea, great and
wide,
creeping things
innumerable are there,
living things both small
and great.
26 There go the ships,
and Leviathan that you
formed to sport in it.

27 These all look to you
to give them their food in
due season;
28 when you give to them, they
gather it up;
when you open your hand,
they are filled with
good things.
29 When you hide your face,
they are dismayed;
when you take away their
breath, they die
and return to their dust.
30 When you send forth your
spirit,[v] they are
created;
and you renew the face of
the ground.

31 May the glory of the LORD
endure forever;
may the LORD rejoice in his
works—
32 who looks on the earth and
it trembles,
who touches the mountains
and they smoke.
33 I will sing to the LORD as
long as I live;
I will sing praise to my God
while I have being.
34 May my meditation be
pleasing to him,
for I rejoice in the LORD.
35 Let sinners be consumed
from the earth,
and let the wicked be no
more.
Bless the LORD, O my soul.
Praise the LORD!

104.12 Mt 8.20
104.13 Ps 65.9; 147.8
104.14 Ps 147.8; Job 38.27; Gen 1.29; Job 28.5
104.15 Judg 9.13; Ps 23.5
104.18 Prov 30.26
104.19 Gen 1.14
104.20 Isa 45.7
104.21 Job 38.39
104.23 Gen 3.19
104.24 Ps 40.5; Prov 3.19; Ps 65.9
104.26 Ps 107.23; Job 41.1
104.27 Ps 136.25; 145.14
104.29 Job 34.14; Ps 146.4; Eccl 12.7
104.30 Isa 32.15; Ezek 37.9
104.31 Gen 1.31
104.32 Ps 97.4,5; 144.5
104.33 Ps 63.4; 146.2
104.35 Ps 59.13; 37.10; v. 1

[t] Heb *By them* [u] Or *to cultivate*
[v] Or *your breath*

Psalm 105

God's Faithfulness to Israel

1 O give thanks to the LORD,
call on his name,
make known his deeds
among the peoples.
2 Sing to him, sing praises to
him;
tell of all his wonderful
works.
3 Glory in his holy name;
let the hearts of those who
seek the LORD rejoice.
4 Seek the LORD and his
strength;
seek his presence
continually.
5 Remember the wonderful
works he has done,
his miracles, and the
judgments he uttered,
6 O offspring of his servant
Abraham,[w]
children of Jacob, his
chosen ones.

7 He is the LORD our God;
his judgments are in all the
earth.
8 He is mindful of his
covenant forever,
of the word that he
commanded, for a
thousand generations,
9 the covenant that he made
with Abraham,
his sworn promise to Isaac,
10 which he confirmed to Jacob
as a statute,
to Israel as an everlasting
covenant,
11 saying, "To you I will give
the land of Canaan
as your portion for an
inheritance."

12 When they were few in
number,
of little account, and
strangers in it,
13 wandering from nation to
nation,
from one kingdom to
another people,
14 he allowed no one to oppress
them;
he rebuked kings on their
account,
15 saying, "Do not touch my
anointed ones;
do my prophets no harm."

16 When he summoned famine
against the land,
and broke every staff of
bread,
17 he had sent a man ahead of
them,
Joseph, who was sold as a
slave.
18 His feet were hurt with
fetters,
his neck was put in a collar
of iron;
19 until what he had said came
to pass,
the word of the LORD kept
testing him.
20 The king sent and released
him;
the ruler of the peoples set
him free.
21 He made him lord of his
house,
and ruler of all his
possessions,
22 to instruct[x] his officials at
his pleasure,
and to teach his elders
wisdom.

23 Then Israel came to Egypt;
Jacob lived as an alien in
the land of Ham.
24 And the LORD made his
people very fruitful,
and made them stronger
than their foes,
25 whose hearts he then turned
to hate his people,
to deal craftily with his
servants.

26 He sent his servant Moses,
and Aaron whom he had
chosen.
27 They performed his signs
among them,

105.1 1 Chr 16.8; Ps 145.12
105.2 Ps 77.12
105.3 Ps 33.21
105.4 Ps 27.8
105.5 Ps 77.11
105.7 Isa 26.9
105.8 Lk 1.72
105.9 Gen 17.2; 22.16; 26.3
105.10 Gen 28.13-15
105.11 Gen 13.15; 15.18
105.12 Gen 34.30; Deut 7.7; Heb 11.9
105.14 Gen 35.5; 12.17
105.16 Gen 41.54; Lev 26.26; Isa 3.1; Ezek 4.16
105.17 Gen 45.5; 37.28,36
105.18 Gen 39.20
105.19 Gen 40.20, 21; Ps 66.10
105.20 Gen 41.14
105.21 Gen 41.40
105.23 Gen 46.6; Acts 13.17
105.24 Ex 1.7
105.25 Ex 1.8,10
105.26 Ex 3.10; Num 16.5
105.27 Ex 7-12; Ps 78.43

[w] Another reading is *Israel* (compare 1 Chr 16.13) [x] Gk Syr Jerome: Heb *to bind*

and miracles in the land of
Ham.
28 He sent darkness, and made
the land dark;
they rebelled[y] against his
words.
29 He turned their waters into
blood,
and caused their fish to
die.
30 Their land swarmed with
frogs,
even in the chambers of
their kings.
31 He spoke, and there came
swarms of flies,
and gnats throughout their
country.
32 He gave them hail for rain,
and lightning that flashed
through their land.
33 He struck their vines and fig
trees,
and shattered the trees of
their country.
34 He spoke, and the locusts
came,
and young locusts without
number;
35 they devoured all the
vegetation in their land,
and ate up the fruit of their
ground.
36 He struck down all the
firstborn in their land,
the first issue of all their
strength.

37 Then he brought Israel[z] out
with silver and gold,
and there was no one
among their tribes who
stumbled.
38 Egypt was glad when they
departed,
for dread of them had
fallen upon it.
39 He spread a cloud for a
covering,
and fire to give light by
night.
40 They asked, and he brought
quails,
and gave them food from
heaven in abundance.
41 He opened the rock, and
water gushed out;
it flowed through the
desert like a river.
42 For he remembered his holy
promise,
and Abraham, his servant.

43 So he brought his people out
with joy,
his chosen ones with
singing.
44 He gave them the lands of
the nations,
and they took possession of
the wealth of the
peoples,
45 that they might keep his
statutes
and observe his laws.
Praise the LORD!

105.28 Ex 10.22; Ps 99.7 **105.29** Ex 7.20 **105.30** Ex 8.6 **105.31** Ex 8.16,21 **105.32** Ex 9.23 **105.34** Ex 10.4; Ps 73.46 **105.36** Ex 12.29; Ps 78.51 **105.37** Ex 12.35 **105.38** Ex 12.33 **105.39** Ex 13.21; Neh 9.12 **105.40** Ex 16.12ff; Ps 78.24ff **105.41** Ex 17.6; Ps 78.15,16; 1 Cor 10.4 **105.42** v. 8 **105.44** Deut 6-10; Josh 13.7 **105.45** Deut 6.21-25 **106.1** Ps 105.1; 100.5; 1 Chr 16.34 **106.2** Ps 145.4,12 **106.3** Ps 15.2 **106.4** Ps 119.132 **106.5** Ps 1.3; 118.15; 105.3 **106.6** Dan 9.5

Psalm 106

A Confession of Israel's Sins

1 Praise the LORD!
O give thanks to the LORD,
for he is good;
for his steadfast love
endures forever.
2 Who can utter the mighty
doings of the LORD,
or declare all his praise?
3 Happy are those who observe
justice,
who do righteousness at all
times.

4 Remember me, O LORD, when
you show favor to your
people;
help me when you deliver
them;
5 that I may see the prosperity
of your chosen ones,
that I may rejoice in the
gladness of your nation,
that I may glory in your
heritage.

6 Both we and our ancestors
have sinned;
we have committed
iniquity, have done
wickedly.

[y] Cn Compare Gk Syr: Heb *they did not rebel*
[z] Heb *them*

7 Our ancestors, when they
were in Egypt,
did not consider your
wonderful works;
they did not remember the
abundance of your
steadfast love,
but rebelled against the
Most High[a] at the Red
Sea.[b]
8 Yet he saved them for his
name's sake,
so that he might make
known his mighty
power.
9 He rebuked the Red Sea,[b]
and it became dry;
he led them through the
deep as through a
desert.
10 So he saved them from the
hand of the foe,
and delivered them from
the hand of the enemy.
11 The waters covered their
adversaries;
not one of them was left.
12 Then they believed his
words;
they sang his praise.

13 But they soon forgot his
works;
they did not wait for his
counsel.
14 But they had a wanton
craving in the
wilderness,
and put God to the test in
the desert;
15 he gave them what they
asked,
but sent a wasting disease
among them.

16 They were jealous of Moses
in the camp,
and of Aaron, the holy one
of the LORD.
17 The earth opened and
swallowed up Dathan,
and covered the faction of
Abiram.
18 Fire also broke out in their
company;
the flame burned up the
wicked.

19 They made a calf at Horeb
and worshiped a cast
image.
20 They exchanged the glory of
God[c]
for the image of an ox that
eats grass.
21 They forgot God, their
Savior,
who had done great things
in Egypt,
22 wondrous works in the land
of Ham,
and awesome deeds by the
Red Sea.[b]
23 Therefore he said he would
destroy them—
had not Moses, his chosen
one,
stood in the breach before
him,
to turn away his wrath
from destroying them.

24 Then they despised the
pleasant land,
having no faith in his
promise.
25 They grumbled in their tents,
and did not obey the voice
of the LORD.
26 Therefore he raised his hand
and swore to them
that he would make them
fall in the wilderness,
27 and would disperse[d] their
descendants among the
nations,
scattering them over the
lands.

28 Then they attached
themselves to the Baal
of Peor,
and ate sacrifices offered to
the dead;
29 they provoked the LORD to
anger with their deeds,
and a plague broke out
among them.
30 Then Phinehas stood up and
interceded,

106.7 Ps 78.11,42; Ex 14.11
106.8 Ex 9.16
106.9 Ex 14.21; Ps 18.15; 78.11,42; Isa 63.11-14
106.10 Ex 14.30; Ps 107.2
106.11 Ex 14.28; 15.5
106.12 Ex 14.31; 15.1-21
106.13 Ex 15.24
106.14 1 Cor 10.6,9
106.15 Num 11.31; Isa 10.16
106.16 Num 16.1-3
106.17 Deut 11.6
106.18 Num 16.35
106.19 Ex 32.14
106.20 Jer 2.11; Rom 1.23
106.21 Ps 78.11; Deut 10.21
106.22 Ps 105.27
106.23 Ex 32.10; 32.11-14
106.24 Deut 8.7; Heb 3.18,19
106.25 Num 14.2
106.26 Num 14.28-35; Heb 11.3
106.27 Ps 44.11
106.28 Num 25.2,3
106.30 Num 25.7

[a] Cn Compare 78.17, 56: Heb *rebelled at the sea* [b] Or *Sea of Reeds* [c] Compare Gk Mss: Heb *exchanged their glory* [d] Syr Compare Ezek 20.23: Heb *cause to fall*

and the plague was
stopped.
31 And that has been reckoned
to him as righteousness
from generation to
generation forever.

32 They angered the LORD[e] at
the waters of Meribah,
and it went ill with Moses
on their account;
33 for they made his spirit
bitter,
and he spoke words that
were rash.

34 They did not destroy the
peoples,
as the LORD commanded
them,
35 but they mingled with the
nations
and learned to do as they
did.
36 They served their idols,
which became a snare to
them.
37 They sacrificed their sons
and their daughters to the
demons;
38 they poured out innocent
blood,
the blood of their sons and
daughters,
whom they sacrificed to the
idols of Canaan;
and the land was polluted
with blood.
39 Thus they became unclean
by their acts,
and prostituted themselves
in their doings.

40 Then the anger of the LORD
was kindled against his
people,
and he abhorred his
heritage;
41 he gave them into the hand
of the nations,
so that those who hated
them ruled over them.
42 Their enemies oppressed
them,
and they were brought into
subjection under their
power.

43 Many times he delivered
them,
but they were rebellious in
their purposes,
and were brought low
through their iniquity.
44 Nevertheless he regarded
their distress
when he heard their cry.
45 For their sake he
remembered his
covenant,
and showed compassion
according to the
abundance of his
steadfast love.
46 He caused them to be pitied
by all who held them
captive.

47 Save us, O LORD our God,
and gather us from among
the nations,
that we may give thanks to
your holy name
and glory in your praise.

48 Blessed be the LORD, the God
of Israel,
from everlasting to
everlasting.
And let all the people say,
"Amen."
Praise the LORD!

BOOK V

(Psalms 107–150)

Psalm 107

Thanksgiving for Deliverance from Many Troubles

1 O give thanks to the LORD,
for he is good;
for his steadfast love
endures forever.
2 Let the redeemed of the
LORD say so,
those he redeemed from
trouble
3 and gathered in from the
lands,

106.31 Num 25.11-13 **106.32** Num 20.3, 13; Ps 81.7 **106.33** Num 20.10 **106.34** Judg 1.21; Deut 7.2,16 **106.35** Judg 3.5,6 **106.36** Judg 2.12 **106.37** 2 Kings 17.7 **106.38** Ps 94.21; Num 35.33 **106.39** Ezek 20.18; Lev 17.7; Num 15.39 **106.40** Ps 78.59 **106.41** Judg 2.14; Neh 9.27 **106.43** Judg 2.16-18 **106.44** Judg 3.9; 10.10 **106.45** Ps 105.8; Judg 2.18 **106.46** Ezra 9.9; Jer 42.12 **106.47** 1 Chr 16.35, 36; Ps 147.2 **106.48** Ps 41.13 **107.1** Ps 106.1 **107.2** Ps 106.10 **107.3** Ps 106.47; Isa 43.5,6

e Heb *him*

from the east and from the
west,
from the north and from
the south.[f]

4 Some wandered in desert
wastes,
finding no way to an
inhabited town;
5 hungry and thirsty,
their soul fainted within
them.
6 Then they cried to the LORD
in their trouble,
and he delivered them from
their distress;
7 he led them by a straight
way,
until they reached an
inhabited town.
8 Let them thank the LORD for
his steadfast love,
for his wonderful works to
humankind.
9 For he satisfies the thirsty,
and the hungry he fills with
good things.

10 Some sat in darkness and in
gloom,
prisoners in misery and in
irons,
11 for they had rebelled against
the words of God,
and spurned the counsel of
the Most High.
12 Their hearts were bowed
down with hard labor;
they fell down, with no one
to help.
13 Then they cried to the LORD
in their trouble,
and he saved them from
their distress;
14 he brought them out of
darkness and gloom,
and broke their bonds
asunder.
15 Let them thank the LORD for
his steadfast love,
for his wonderful works to
humankind.
16 For he shatters the doors of
bronze,
and cuts in two the bars of
iron.

17 Some were sick[g] through
their sinful ways,
and because of their
iniquities endured
affliction;
18 they loathed any kind of
food,
and they drew near to the
gates of death.
19 Then they cried to the LORD
in their trouble,
and he saved them from
their distress;
20 he sent out his word and
healed them,
and delivered them from
destruction.
21 Let them thank the LORD for
his steadfast love,
for his wonderful works to
humankind.
22 And let them offer
thanksgiving sacrifices,
and tell of his deeds with
songs of joy.

23 Some went down to the sea
in ships,
doing business on the
mighty waters;
24 they saw the deeds of the
LORD,
his wondrous works in the
deep.
25 For he commanded and
raised the stormy wind,
which lifted up the waves
of the sea.
26 They mounted up to heaven,
they went down to the
depths;
their courage melted away
in their calamity;
27 they reeled and staggered
like drunkards,
and were at their wits' end.
28 Then they cried to the LORD
in their trouble,
and he brought them out
from their distress;
29 he made the storm be still,
and the waves of the sea
were hushed.
30 Then they were glad because
they had quiet,

107.4 Num 14.33; 32.13
107.6 Ps 50.15
107.7 Ezra 8.21
107.8 vv. 15,21,31
107.9 Ps 22.26; Lk 1.53
107.10 Lk 1.79; Job 36.8
107.11 Ps 106.7; 2 Chr 36.16
107.12 Ps 22.11
107.13 v. 6
107.14 Ps 116.16; Lk 13.16; Acts 12.7
107.15 vv. 8,21,31
107.16 Isa 45.2
107.17 Isa 65.6,7
107.18 Job 33.20, 22; Ps 9.13; 88.3
107.20 Mt 8.8; Ps 30.2; 103.3
107.22 Lev 7.12; Ps 50.14; 9.11; 73.28; 118.17
107.25 Ps 105.31, 34; Jon 1.4; Ps 93.3,4
107.26 Ps 22.14; 119.28
107.27 Job 12.25
107.28 vv. 6,13,19
107.29 Ps 89.9; Mt 8.26

[f] Cn: Heb *sea* [g] Cn: Heb *fools*

and he brought them to
their desired haven.
31 Let them thank the LORD for
his steadfast love,
for his wonderful works to
humankind.
32 Let them extol him in the
congregation of the
people,
and praise him in the
assembly of the elders.

33 He turns rivers into a
desert,
springs of water into thirsty
ground,
34 a fruitful land into a salty
waste,
because of the wickedness
of its inhabitants.
35 He turns a desert into pools
of water,
a parched land into springs
of water.
36 And there he lets the hungry
live,
and they establish a town
to live in;
37 they sow fields, and plant
vineyards,
and get a fruitful yield.
38 By his blessing they multiply
greatly,
and he does not let their
cattle decrease.

39 When they are diminished
and brought low
through oppression,
trouble, and sorrow,
40 he pours contempt on
princes
and makes them wander in
trackless wastes;
41 but he raises up the needy
out of distress,
and makes their families
like flocks.
42 The upright see it and are
glad;
and all wickedness stops
its mouth.
43 Let those who are wise give
heed to these things,
and consider the steadfast
love of the LORD.

107.31 vv. 8,15,21
107.32 Ps 22.22,25; 35.18
107.33 Ps 74.15
107.34 Gen 13.10; 14.3; 19.25
107.35 Ps 114.8; Isa 41.18
107.37 Isa 65.21
107.38 Gen 12.2; 17.16,20; Ex 1.7
107.39 Ezek 5.11; Ps 57.6
107.40 Job 12.21, 24
107.41 1 Sam 2.8; Ps 113.7-9
107.42 Job 22.19; Ps 52.6; Job 5.16; Ps 63.11; Rom 3.19
107.43 Ps 64.9; Jer 9.12; Hos 14.9

108.1 Ps 57.7
108.2 Ps 57.8-11
108.4 Ps 113.4
108.6 Ps 60.5-12
108.8 Ps 60.7
108.11 Ps 44.9

Psalm 108

Praise and Prayer for Victory

A Song. A Psalm of David.

1 My heart is steadfast, O God,
my heart is steadfast;[h]
I will sing and make
melody.
Awake, my soul![i]
2 Awake, O harp and lyre!
I will awake the dawn.
3 I will give thanks to you,
O LORD, among the
peoples,
and I will sing praises to
you among the nations.
4 For your steadfast love is
higher than the
heavens,
and your faithfulness
reaches to the clouds.

5 Be exalted, O God, above the
heavens,
and let your glory be over
all the earth.
6 Give victory with your right
hand, and answer me,
so that those whom you
love may be rescued.

7 God has promised in his
sanctuary:[j]
"With exultation I will
divide up Shechem,
and portion out the Vale of
Succoth.
8 Gilead is mine; Manasseh is
mine;
Ephraim is my helmet;
Judah is my scepter.
9 Moab is my washbasin;
on Edom I hurl my shoe;
over Philistia I shout in
triumph."

10 Who will bring me to the
fortified city?
Who will lead me to Edom?
11 Have you not rejected us,
O God?
You do not go out, O God,
with our armies.

[h] Heb Mss Gk Syr: MT lacks *my heart is steadfast* [i] Compare 57.8: Heb *also my soul*
[j] Or *by his holiness*

12 O grant us help against the foe,
for human help is worthless.
13 With God we shall do valiantly;
it is he who will tread down our foes.

Psalm 109

Prayer for Vindication and Vengeance

To the leader. Of David. A Psalm.

1 Do not be silent, O God of my praise.
2 For wicked and deceitful mouths are opened against me,
speaking against me with lying tongues.
3 They beset me with words of hate,
and attack me without cause.
4 In return for my love they accuse me,
even while I make prayer for them.[k]
5 So they reward me evil for good,
and hatred for my love.

6 They say,[l] "Appoint a wicked man against him;
let an accuser stand on his right.
7 When he is tried, let him be found guilty;
let his prayer be counted as sin.
8 May his days be few;
may another seize his position.
9 May his children be orphans,
and his wife a widow.
10 May his children wander about and beg;
may they be driven out of[m] the ruins they inhabit.
11 May the creditor seize all that he has;
may strangers plunder the fruits of his toil.
12 May there be no one to do him a kindness,
nor anyone to pity his orphaned children.
13 May his posterity be cut off;
may his name be blotted out in the second generation.
14 May the iniquity of his father[n] be remembered before the LORD,
and do not let the sin of his mother be blotted out.
15 Let them be before the LORD continually,
and may his[o] memory be cut off from the earth.
16 For he did not remember to show kindness,
but pursued the poor and needy
and the brokenhearted to their death.
17 He loved to curse; let curses come on him.
He did not like blessing; may it be far from him.
18 He clothed himself with cursing as his coat,
may it soak into his body like water,
like oil into his bones.
19 May it be like a garment that he wraps around himself,
like a belt that he wears every day."

20 May that be the reward of my accusers from the LORD,
of those who speak evil against my life.
21 But you, O LORD my Lord,
act on my behalf for your name's sake;
because your steadfast love is good, deliver me.
22 For I am poor and needy,
and my heart is pierced within me.
23 I am gone like a shadow at evening;

109.1 Ps 83.1 **109.2** Ps 52.4; 120.2 **109.3** Ps 69.4 **109.4** Ps 38.20; 69.13 **109.5** Ps 35.12; 38.20 **109.6** Zech 3.1 **109.7** Prov 28.9 **109.8** Acts 1.20 **109.9** Ex 22.24 **109.11** Job 5.5; 18.9

109.12 Isa 9.17 **109.13** Ps 37.28; Prov 10.7 **109.14** Ex 20.5; Neh 4.5; Jer 18.23 **109.15** Ps 34.16 **109.16** Ps 37.14,32 **109.17** Prov 14.14; Ezek 35.6 **109.18** Ps 73.6; Num 5.22 **109.20** Ps 94.23; 2 Tim 4.14; Ps 71.10 **109.21** Ps 79.9; 69.16 **109.22** Ps 40.17; 143.4 **109.23** Ps 102.11

[k] Syr: Heb *I prayer* [l] Heb lacks *They say* [m] Gk: Heb *and seek* [n] Cn: Heb *fathers* [o] Gk: Heb *their*

I am shaken off like a locust.
24 My knees are weak through fasting;
my body has become gaunt.
25 I am an object of scorn to my accusers;
when they see me, they shake their heads.

26 Help me, O LORD my God!
Save me according to your steadfast love.
27 Let them know that this is your hand;
you, O LORD, have done it.
28 Let them curse, but you will bless.
Let my assailants be put to shame;[p] may your servant be glad.
29 May my accusers be clothed with dishonor;
may they be wrapped in their own shame as in a mantle.
30 With my mouth I will give great thanks to the LORD;
I will praise him in the midst of the throng.
31 For he stands at the right hand of the needy,
to save them from those who would condemn them to death.

Psalm 110

Assurance of Victory for God's Priest-King

Of David. A Psalm.

1 The LORD says to my lord,
"Sit at my right hand
until I make your enemies your footstool."

2 The LORD sends out from Zion
your mighty scepter.
Rule in the midst of your foes.
3 Your people will offer themselves willingly
on the day you lead your forces
on the holy mountains.[q]
From the womb of the morning,
like dew, your youth[r] will come to you.
4 The LORD has sworn and will not change his mind,
"You are a priest forever according to the order of Melchizedek."[s]

5 The Lord is at your right hand;
he will shatter kings on the day of his wrath.
6 He will execute judgment among the nations,
filling them with corpses;
he will shatter heads
over the wide earth.
7 He will drink from the stream by the path;
therefore he will lift up his head.

Psalm 111

Praise for God's Wonderful Works

1 Praise the LORD!
I will give thanks to the LORD with my whole heart,
in the company of the upright, in the congregation.
2 Great are the works of the LORD,
studied by all who delight in them.
3 Full of honor and majesty is his work,
and his righteousness endures forever.
4 He has gained renown by his wonderful deeds;
the LORD is gracious and merciful.
5 He provides food for those who fear him;
he is ever mindful of his covenant.

109.24 Heb 12.12
109.25 Ps 22.6,7; Mt 27.39; Mk 15.29
109.26 Ps 119.86
109.27 Job 37.7
109.28 2 Sam 16.11, 12; Isa 65.14
109.29 Ps 35.26; 132.18
109.30 Ps 35.18
109.31 Ps 16.8; 121.5
110.1 Mt 22.44; Mk 12.36; Lk 20.42; Acts 2.34; 1 Cor 15.25
110.2 Ps 45.6; 2.9
110.3 Judg 5.2; Ps 96.9
110.4 Heb 5.6,10; 6.20; 7.11,15, 21
110.5 Ps 16.8; 2.5, 12; Rom 2.5; Rev 11.18
110.6 Isa 2.4; 66.24; Ps 68.21
110.7 Ps 27.6
111.1 Ps 138.1; 149.1
111.2 Ps 92.5
111.3 Ps 145.5
111.4 Ps 86.5; 103.8
111.5 Mt 6.26,33

[p] Gk: Heb *They have risen up and have been put to shame* [q] Another reading is *in holy splendor* [r] Cn: Heb *the dew of your youth* [s] Or *forever, a rightful king by my edict*

6 He has shown his people the
power of his works,
in giving them the heritage
of the nations.
7 The works of his hands are
faithful and just;
all his precepts are
trustworthy.
8 They are established forever
and ever,
to be performed with
faithfulness and
uprightness.
9 He sent redemption to his
people;
he has commanded his
covenant forever.
Holy and awesome is his
name.
10 The fear of the LORD is the
beginning of wisdom;
all those who practice it[t]
have a good
understanding.
His praise endures forever.

Psalm 112

Blessings of the Righteous

1 Praise the LORD!
Happy are those who fear
the LORD,
who greatly delight in his
commandments.
2 Their descendants will be
mighty in the land;
the generation of the
upright will be blessed.
3 Wealth and riches are in
their houses,
and their righteousness
endures forever.
4 They rise in the darkness as
a light for the upright;
they are gracious, merciful,
and righteous.
5 It is well with those who
deal generously and
lend,
who conduct their affairs
with justice.
6 For the righteous will never
be moved;
they will be remembered
forever.
7 They are not afraid of evil
tidings;
their hearts are firm,
secure in the LORD.
8 Their hearts are steady, they
will not be afraid;
in the end they will look in
triumph on their foes.
9 They have distributed freely,
they have given to the
poor;
their righteousness endures
forever;
their horn is exalted in
honor.
10 The wicked see it and are
angry;
they gnash their teeth and
melt away;
the desire of the wicked
comes to nothing.

Psalm 113

God the Helper of the Needy

1 Praise the LORD!
Praise, O servants of the
LORD;
praise the name of the
LORD.

2 Blessed be the name of the
LORD
from this time on and
forevermore.
3 From the rising of the sun to
its setting
the name of the LORD is to
be praised.
4 The LORD is high above all
nations,
and his glory above the
heavens.

5 Who is like the LORD our
God,
who is seated on high,
6 who looks far down
on the heavens and the
earth?
7 He raises the poor from the
dust,
and lifts the needy from
the ash heap,

111.7 Rev 15.3; Ps 19.7
111.8 Mt 5.18; Ps 19.9
111.9 Lk 1.68; Ps 99.3
111.10 Prov 9.10; 3.4; Ps 145.2
112.1 Ps 128.1; 119.16
112.2 Ps 25.13
112.3 Prov 3.16; 8.18
112.4 Job 11.17; Ps 97.11
112.5 Ps 37.26
112.6 Prov 10.7
112.7 Prov 1.33; Ps 57.7
112.8 Ps 59.10; 118.7
112.9 2 Cor 9.9; Deut 24.13; Ps 75.10
112.10 Ps 86.17; 37.12; 58.7,8; Prov 10.28; 11.7
113.1 Ps 135.1
113.2 Dan 2.20
113.3 Ps 50.1
113.4 Ps 97.9; 99.2; 8.1
113.5 Ps 89.6; 103.19
113.6 Ps 11.4; 138.6; Isa 57.15
113.7 1 Sam 2.8; Ps 107.41

[t] Gk Syr: Heb *them*

8 to make them sit with princes,
with the princes of his people.
9 He gives the barren woman a home,
making her the joyous mother of children.
Praise the LORD!

Psalm 114

God's Wonders at the Exodus

1 When Israel went out from Egypt,
the house of Jacob from a people of strange language,
2 Judah became God's[u] sanctuary,
Israel his dominion.

3 The sea looked and fled;
Jordan turned back.
4 The mountains skipped like rams,
the hills like lambs.

5 Why is it, O sea, that you flee?
O Jordan, that you turn back?
6 O mountains, that you skip like rams?
O hills, like lambs?

7 Tremble, O earth, at the presence of the LORD,
at the presence of the God of Jacob,
8 who turns the rock into a pool of water,
the flint into a spring of water.

Psalm 115

The Impotence of Idols and the Greatness of God

1 Not to us, O LORD, not to us,
but to your name give glory,
for the sake of your steadfast love and your faithfulness.
2 Why should the nations say,
"Where is their God?"
3 Our God is in the heavens;
he does whatever he pleases.
4 Their idols are silver and gold,
the work of human hands.
5 They have mouths, but do not speak;
eyes, but do not see.
6 They have ears, but do not hear;
noses, but do not smell.
7 They have hands, but do not feel;
feet, but do not walk;
they make no sound in their throats.
8 Those who make them are like them;
so are all who trust in them.

9 O Israel, trust in the LORD!
He is their help and their shield.
10 O house of Aaron, trust in the LORD!
He is their help and their shield.
11 You who fear the LORD, trust in the LORD!
He is their help and their shield.

12 The LORD has been mindful of us; he will bless us;
he will bless the house of Israel;
he will bless the house of Aaron;
13 he will bless those who fear the LORD,
both small and great.

14 May the LORD give you increase,
both you and your children.
15 May you be blessed by the LORD,
who made heaven and earth.

113.8 Job 36.7 **113.9** 1 Sam 2.5; Ps 68.6; Isa 54.1 **114.1** Ex 13.3 **114.2** Ex 19.6; 29.45,46 **114.3** Ex 14.21; Josh 3.13, 16 **114.4** Ps 29.6; Hab 3.6 **114.5** Hab 3.6 **114.7** Ps 96.9 **114.8** Ex 17.6; Num 20.11; Ps 107.35; Deut 8.15 **115.1** Isa 48.11; Ezek 36.32; Ps 96.8 **115.2** Ps 42.3; 79.10

115.3 Ps 103.19; 135.6; Dan 4.35 **115.4** Deut 4.28; Ps 135.15-17; Jer 10.3ff **115.5** Jer 10.5 **115.8** Ps 135.18 **115.9** Ps 118.2-4; 33.20 **115.11** Ps 135.20 **115.13** Ps 128.1,4 **115.14** Deut 1.11 **115.15** Gen 14.19; 1.1; Ps 96.5

[u] Heb *his*

16 The heavens are the LORD's
heavens,
but the earth he has given
to human beings.
17 The dead do not praise the
LORD,
nor do any that go down
into silence.
18 But we will bless the LORD
from this time on and
forevermore.
Praise the LORD!

Psalm 116

Thanksgiving for Recovery from Illness

1 I love the LORD, because he
has heard
my voice and my
supplications.
2 Because he inclined his ear
to me,
therefore I will call on him
as long as I live.
3 The snares of death
encompassed me;
the pangs of Sheol laid
hold on me;
I suffered distress and
anguish.
4 Then I called on the name of
the LORD:
"O LORD, I pray, save my
life!"

5 Gracious is the LORD, and
righteous;
our God is merciful.
6 The LORD protects the
simple;
when I was brought low, he
saved me.
7 Return, O my soul, to your
rest,
for the LORD has dealt
bountifully with you.

8 For you have delivered my
soul from death,
my eyes from tears,
my feet from stumbling.
9 I walk before the LORD
in the land of the living.
10 I kept my faith, even when I
said,
"I am greatly afflicted";
11 I said in my consternation,
"Everyone is a liar."

12 What shall I return to the
LORD
for all his bounty to me?
13 I will lift up the cup of
salvation
and call on the name of
the LORD,
14 I will pay my vows to the
LORD
in the presence of all his
people.
15 Precious in the sight of the
LORD
is the death of his faithful
ones.
16 O LORD, I am your servant;
I am your servant, the child
of your serving girl.
You have loosed my bonds.
17 I will offer to you a
thanksgiving sacrifice
and call on the name of
the LORD.
18 I will pay my vows to the
LORD
in the presence of all his
people,
19 in the courts of the house of
the LORD,
in your midst,
O Jerusalem.
Praise the LORD!

Psalm 117

Universal Call to Worship

1 Praise the LORD, all you
nations!
Extol him, all you peoples!
2 For great is his steadfast love
toward us,
and the faithfulness of the
LORD endures forever.
Praise the LORD!

Psalm 118

A Song of Victory

1 O give thanks to the LORD,
for he is good;
his steadfast love endures
forever!

115.16 Ps 89.11; 8.6
115.17 Ps 6.5; 31.17
115.18 Ps 113.2
116.1 Ps 18.1; 66.19
116.2 Ps 40.1
116.3 Ps 18.4-6
116.4 Ps 118.5; 22.20
116.5 Ps 103.8; Ezra 9.15; Neh 9.8; Ps 145.17; Ex 34.6
116.6 Ps 19.7; 79.8
116.7 Jer 6.16; Mt 11.29; Ps 13.6
116.8 Ps 56.13
116.9 Ps 27.13
116.10 2 Cor 4.13
116.11 Ps 31.22; Rom 3.4
116.13 Ps 16.5; 80.18
116.14 Ps 22.25; Jon 2.9
116.15 Ps 72.14
116.16 Ps 119.125; 143.12; 86.16
116.17 Ps 50.14; v. 13
116.18 v. 14
116.19 Ps 96.8; 135.2
117.1 Rom 15.11
117.2 Ps 100.5
118.1 Ps 106.1; 136.1

2 Let Israel say,
"His steadfast love endures forever."
3 Let the house of Aaron say,
"His steadfast love endures forever."
4 Let those who fear the LORD say,
"His steadfast love endures forever."

5 Out of my distress I called on the LORD;
the LORD answered me and set me in a broad place.
6 With the LORD on my side I do not fear.
What can mortals do to me?
7 The LORD is on my side to help me;
I shall look in triumph on those who hate me.
8 It is better to take refuge in the LORD
than to put confidence in mortals.
9 It is better to take refuge in the LORD
than to put confidence in princes.

10 All nations surrounded me;
in the name of the LORD I cut them off!
11 They surrounded me, surrounded me on every side;
in the name of the LORD I cut them off!
12 They surrounded me like bees;
they blazed[v] like a fire of thorns;
in the name of the LORD I cut them off!
13 I was pushed hard,[w] so that I was falling,
but the LORD helped me.
14 The LORD is my strength and my might;
he has become my salvation.

15 There are glad songs of victory in the tents of the righteous:
"The right hand of the LORD does valiantly;
16 the right hand of the LORD is exalted;
the right hand of the LORD does valiantly."
17 I shall not die, but I shall live,
and recount the deeds of the LORD.
18 The LORD has punished me severely,
but he did not give me over to death.

19 Open to me the gates of righteousness,
that I may enter through them
and give thanks to the LORD.

20 This is the gate of the LORD;
the righteous shall enter through it.

21 I thank you that you have answered me
and have become my salvation.
22 The stone that the builders rejected
has become the chief cornerstone.
23 This is the LORD's doing;
it is marvelous in our eyes.
24 This is the day that the LORD has made;
let us rejoice and be glad in it.[x]
25 Save us, we beseech you, O LORD!
O LORD, we beseech you, give us success!

26 Blessed is the one who comes in the name of the LORD.[y]
We bless you from the house of the LORD.
27 The LORD is God,
and he has given us light.

118.2 Ps 115.9 **118.5** Ps 120.1; 18.19 **118.6** Ps 27.1; Heb 13.6; Ps 56.4,11 **118.7** Ps 54.4; 59.10 **118.8** Ps 40.4; Jer 17.5 **118.9** Ps 146.3 **118.10** Ps 3.6; 18.40 **118.12** Deut 1.44; Ps 58.9 **118.13** Ps 140.4; 86.17 **118.14** Ex 15.2; Isa 12.2 **118.15** Ps 68.3; 89.13 **118.16** Ex 15.6 **118.17** Hab 1.12; Ps 73.28 **118.18** 2 Cor 6.9 **118.19** Isa 26.2 **118.20** Ps 24.7; Isa 35.8; Rev 22.14 **118.21** Ps 116.1; v. 14 **118.22** Mt 21.42; Mk 12.10; Lk 20.17; Acts 4.11; Eph 2.20; 1 Pet 2.4,7 **118.26** Mt 21.9; Mk 11.9; Lk 13.35; 19.38; Jn 12.13 **118.27** 1 Kings 18.39; Esther 8.16; 1 Pet 2.9

[v] Gk: Heb *were extinguished* [w] Gk Syr Jerome: Heb *You pushed me hard* [x] Or *in him* [y] Or *Blessed in the name of the LORD is the one who comes*

Bind the festal procession
with branches,
up to the horns of the
altar.[z]

28 You are my God, and I will
give thanks to you;
you are my God, I will
extol you.

29 O give thanks to the LORD,
for he is good,
for his steadfast love
endures forever.

Psalm 119

The Glories of God's Law

1 Happy are those whose way
is blameless,
who walk in the law of the
LORD.
2 Happy are those who keep
his decrees,
who seek him with their
whole heart,
3 who also do no wrong,
but walk in his ways.
4 You have commanded your
precepts
to be kept diligently.
5 O that my ways may be
steadfast
in keeping your statutes!
6 Then I shall not be put to
shame,
having my eyes fixed on all
your commandments.
7 I will praise you with an
upright heart,
when I learn your righteous
ordinances.
8 I will observe your statutes;
do not utterly forsake me.

9 How can young people keep
their way pure?
By guarding it according to
your word.
10 With my whole heart I seek
you;
do not let me stray from
your commandments.
11 I treasure your word in my
heart,
so that I may not sin
against you.
12 Blessed are you, O LORD;
teach me your statutes.
13 With my lips I declare
all the ordinances of your
mouth.
14 I delight in the way of your
decrees
as much as in all riches.
15 I will meditate on your
precepts,
and fix my eyes on your
ways.
16 I will delight in your
statutes;
I will not forget your word.

17 Deal bountifully with your
servant,
so that I may live and
observe your word.
18 Open my eyes, so that I may
behold
wondrous things out of
your law.
19 I live as an alien in the land;
do not hide your
commandments from
me.
20 My soul is consumed with
longing
for your ordinances at all
times.
21 You rebuke the insolent,
accursed ones,
who wander from your
commandments;
22 take away from me their
scorn and contempt,
for I have kept your
decrees.
23 Even though princes sit
plotting against me,
your servant will meditate
on your statutes.
24 Your decrees are my delight,
they are my counselors.

25 My soul clings to the dust;
revive me according to your
word.
26 When I told of my ways, you
answered me;
teach me your statutes.

118.28 Ex 15.2; Isa 25.1
118.29 v. 1
119.1 Ps 101.2,6; 128.1
119.2 vv. 22,10; Deut 6.5
119.3 1 Jn 3.9; 5.18
119.6 v. 80
119.7 v. 62
119.9 2 Chr 6.16
119.10 2 Chr 15.15; vv. 21,118
119.11 Ps 37.31; Lk 2.19,51
119.12 vv. 26,64, 68,108,124, 135,171
119.13 Ps 40.9; v. 72
119.15 vv. 23,48, 78; Ps 1.2
119.16 Ps 1.2
119.17 Ps 13.6
119.19 Gen 47.9; 1 Chr 29.15; Ps 39.12; 2 Cor 5.6; Heb 11.13
119.20 Ps 42.1,2
119.21 vv. 10,118
119.22 Ps 39.8
119.23 v. 15
119.24 v. 16
119.25 Ps 44.25; v. 37
119.26 v. 12

[z] Meaning of Heb uncertain

27 Make me understand the way of your precepts,
and I will meditate on your wondrous works.
28 My soul melts away for sorrow;
strengthen me according to your word.
29 Put false ways far from me;
and graciously teach me your law.
30 I have chosen the way of faithfulness;
I set your ordinances before me.
31 I cling to your decrees, O LORD;
let me not be put to shame.
32 I run the way of your commandments,
for you enlarge my understanding.

33 Teach me, O LORD, the way of your statutes,
and I will observe it to the end.
34 Give me understanding, that I may keep your law
and observe it with my whole heart.
35 Lead me in the path of your commandments,
for I delight in it.
36 Turn my heart to your decrees,
and not to selfish gain.
37 Turn my eyes from looking at vanities;
give me life in your ways.
38 Confirm to your servant your promise,
which is for those who fear you.
39 Turn away the disgrace that I dread,
for your ordinances are good.
40 See, I have longed for your precepts;
in your righteousness give me life.

41 Let your steadfast love come to me, O LORD,

119.27 Ps 145.5 **119.28** Ps 107.26; 20.2; 1 Pet 5.10 **119.31** Deut 11.22 **119.32** 1 Kings 4.29; Isa 60.5; 2 Cor 6.11 **119.33** vv. 5,12 **119.34** v. 73; Prov 2.6; Jas 1.5 **119.35** v. 16 **119.36** 1 Kings 8.58; Lk 12.15 **119.37** Isa 33.15; Ps 71.20 **119.38** 2 Sam 7.25 **119.40** vv. 20,25 **119.41** vv. 77,116

119.42 Prov 27.11 **119.46** Mt 10.18; Acts 26.1,2 **119.47** v. 16 **119.48** v. 15 **119.50** Rom 15.4 **119.51** Jer 20.7; v. 157; Job 23.11; Ps 44.18 **119.52** Ps 103.18 **119.53** Ezra 9.3; Ps 89.30 **119.55** Ps 63.6

your salvation according to your promise.
42 Then I shall have an answer for those who taunt me,
for I trust in your word.
43 Do not take the word of truth utterly out of my mouth,
for my hope is in your ordinances.
44 I will keep your law continually,
forever and ever.
45 I shall walk at liberty,
for I have sought your precepts.
46 I will also speak of your decrees before kings,
and shall not be put to shame;
47 I find my delight in your commandments,
because I love them.
48 I revere your commandments, which I love,
and I will meditate on your statutes.

49 Remember your word to your servant,
in which you have made me hope.
50 This is my comfort in my distress,
that your promise gives me life.
51 The arrogant utterly deride me,
but I do not turn away from your law.
52 When I think of your ordinances from of old,
I take comfort, O LORD.
53 Hot indignation seizes me because of the wicked,
those who forsake your law.
54 Your statutes have been my songs
wherever I make my home.
55 I remember your name in the night, O LORD,
and keep your law.
56 This blessing has fallen to me,

for I have kept your
precepts.

57 The LORD is my portion;
I promise to keep your
words.
58 I implore your favor with all
my heart;
be gracious to me
according to your
promise.
59 When I think of your ways,
I turn my feet to your
decrees;
60 I hurry and do not delay
to keep your
commandments.
61 Though the cords of the
wicked ensnare me,
I do not forget your law.
62 At midnight I rise to praise
you,
because of your righteous
ordinances.
63 I am a companion of all who
fear you,
of those who keep your
precepts.
64 The earth, O LORD, is full of
your steadfast love;
teach me your statutes.

65 You have dealt well with
your servant,
O LORD, according to your
word.
66 Teach me good judgment
and knowledge,
for I believe in your
commandments.
67 Before I was humbled I went
astray,
but now I keep your word.
68 You are good and do
good;
teach me your statutes.
69 The arrogant smear me with
lies,
but with my whole heart I
keep your precepts.
70 Their hearts are fat and
gross,
but I delight in your law.
71 It is good for me that I was
humbled,
so that I might learn your
statutes.

119.57 Ps 16.5; Deut 33.9
119.58 1 Kings 13.6; v. 41
119.59 Lk 15.17,18
119.61 Ps 140.5; v. 83
119.62 Acts 16.25
119.63 Ps 101.6
119.64 Ps 33.5; v. 12
119.67 v. 71; Jer 31.18, 19; Heb 12.11
119.68 Ps 106.1; Deut 8.16; v. 12
119.69 Job 13.4; v. 56
119.70 Ps 17.10; Isa 6.10; v. 16

119.72 v. 127; Ps 19.10; Prov 8.10, 11,19
119.73 Job 10.8; Ps 138.8; v. 34
119.74 Ps 34.2; v. 43
119.75 Heb 12.10
119.77 vv. 41,47
119.78 Jer 50.32; vv. 86,15
119.80 vv. 1,46
119.81 Ps 84.2
119.82 Ps 69.3
119.83 Job 30.30
119.84 Ps 39.4; Rev 6.10

72 The law of your mouth is
better to me
than thousands of gold and
silver pieces.

73 Your hands have made and
fashioned me;
give me understanding that
I may learn your
commandments.
74 Those who fear you shall see
me and rejoice,
because I have hoped in
your word.
75 I know, O LORD, that your
judgments are right,
and that in faithfulness you
have humbled me.
76 Let your steadfast love
become my comfort
according to your promise
to your servant.
77 Let your mercy come to me,
that I may live;
for your law is my delight.
78 Let the arrogant be put to
shame,
because they have
subverted me with
guile;
as for me, I will meditate
on your precepts.
79 Let those who fear you turn
to me,
so that they may know
your decrees.
80 May my heart be blameless
in your statutes,
so that I may not be put to
shame.

81 My soul languishes for your
salvation;
I hope in your word.
82 My eyes fail with watching
for your promise;
I ask, "When will you
comfort me?"
83 For I have become like a
wineskin in the smoke,
yet I have not forgotten
your statutes.
84 How long must your servant
endure?
When will you judge those
who persecute me?

85 The arrogant have dug
pitfalls for me;
they flout your law.
86 All your commandments are
enduring;
I am persecuted without
cause; help me!
87 They have almost made an
end of me on earth;
but I have not forsaken
your precepts.
88 In your steadfast love spare
my life,
so that I may keep the
decrees of your mouth.

89 The LORD exists forever;
your word is firmly fixed in
heaven.
90 Your faithfulness endures to
all generations;
you have established the
earth, and it stands
fast.
91 By your appointment they
stand today,
for all things are your
servants.
92 If your law had not been my
delight,
I would have perished in
my misery.
93 I will never forget your
precepts,
for by them you have given
me life.
94 I am yours; save me,
for I have sought your
precepts.
95 The wicked lie in wait to
destroy me,
but I consider your
decrees.
96 I have seen a limit to all
perfection,
but your commandment is
exceedingly broad.

97 Oh, how I love your law!
It is my meditation all day
long.
98 Your commandment makes
me wiser than my
enemies,
for it is always with me.
99 I have more understanding
than all my teachers,

119.85 Ps 35.7 **119.86** v. 78; Ps 35.19; 109.26 **119.87** Isa 58.2 **119.89** Mt 24.34, 35; 1 Pet 1.25 **119.90** Ps 36.5; 148.6; Eccl 1.4 **119.91** Jer 33.25 **119.92** vv. 16,50 **119.93** vv. 16,25 **119.94** vv. 146,45 **119.97** Ps 1.2 **119.98** v. 130; Deut 4.6 **119.99** v. 15

119.100 Job 32.7-9 **119.101** Prov 1.15 **119.103** Ps 19.10 **119.104** vv. 128,130 **119.105** Prov 6.23 **119.106** Neh 10.29 **119.107** v. 25 **119.108** Hos 14.2; Heb 13.15; v. 12 **119.109** Job 13.14; v. 16 **119.110** Ps 140.5; 141.9; v. 10 **119.111** Deut 33.4; vv. 14.162 **119.112** v. 33 **119.113** Jas 1.8; v. 47 **119.114** Ps 32.7; 91.1; v. 74 **119.115** Ps 6.8; 139.19; Mt 7.23

for your decrees are my
meditation.
100 I understand more than the
aged,
for I keep your precepts.
101 I hold back my feet from
every evil way,
in order to keep your word.
102 I do not turn away from
your ordinances,
for you have taught me.
103 How sweet are your words
to my taste,
sweeter than honey to my
mouth!
104 Through your precepts I get
understanding;
therefore I hate every false
way.

105 Your word is a lamp to my
feet
and a light to my path.
106 I have sworn an oath and
confirmed it,
to observe your righteous
ordinances.
107 I am severely afflicted;
give me life, O LORD,
according to your word.
108 Accept my offerings of
praise, O LORD,
and teach me your
ordinances.
109 I hold my life in my hand
continually,
but I do not forget your
law.
110 The wicked have laid a
snare for me,
but I do not stray from
your precepts.
111 Your decrees are my
heritage forever;
they are the joy of my
heart.
112 I incline my heart to
perform your statutes
forever, to the end.

113 I hate the double-minded,
but I love your law.
114 You are my hiding place and
my shield;
I hope in your word.
115 Go away from me, you
evildoers,

that I may keep the
commandments of my
God.
116 Uphold me according to
your promise, that I
may live,
and let me not be put to
shame in my hope.
117 Hold me up, that I may be
safe
and have regard for your
statutes continually.
118 You spurn all who go astray
from your statutes;
for their cunning is in
vain.
119 All the wicked of the earth
you count as dross;
therefore I love your
decrees.
120 My flesh trembles for fear of
you,
and I am afraid of your
judgments.

121 I have done what is just and
right;
do not leave me to my
oppressors.
122 Guarantee your servant's
well-being;
do not let the godless
oppress me.
123 My eyes fail from watching
for your salvation,
and for the fulfillment of
your righteous promise.
124 Deal with your servant
according to your
steadfast love,
and teach me your
statutes.
125 I am your servant; give me
understanding,
so that I may know your
decrees.
126 It is time for the LORD to
act,
for your law has been
broken.
127 Truly I love your
commandments
more than gold, more than
fine gold.
128 Truly I direct my steps by
all your precepts;[a]
I hate every false way.

129 Your decrees are wonderful;
therefore my soul keeps
them.
130 The unfolding of your words
gives light;
it imparts understanding to
the simple.
131 With open mouth I pant,
because I long for your
commandments.
132 Turn to me and be gracious
to me,
as is your custom toward
those who love your
name.
133 Keep my steps steady
according to your
promise,
and never let iniquity have
dominion over me.
134 Redeem me from human
oppression,
that I may keep your
precepts.
135 Make your face shine upon
your servant,
and teach me your
statutes.
136 My eyes shed streams of
tears
because your law is not
kept.

137 You are righteous, O LORD,
and your judgments are
right.
138 You have appointed your
decrees in
righteousness
and in all faithfulness.
139 My zeal consumes me
because my foes forget
your words.
140 Your promise is well tried,
and your servant loves it.
141 I am small and despised,
yet I do not forget your
precepts.
142 Your righteousness is an
everlasting
righteousness,
and your law is the truth.
143 Trouble and anguish have
come upon me,

119.116 Ps 54.4; 25.2; Rom 5.5; 9.33
119.118 v. 21
119.119 Ezek 22.18
119.120 Hab 3.16
119.122 Job 17.3
119.123 vv. 81,82
119.124 v. 12
119.125 Ps 116.16
119.127 Ps 19.10
119.128 v. 104
119.129 vv. 18,22
119.130 Prov 6.23; Ps 19.7
119.131 Ps 42.1; v. 20
119.132 Ps 25.16
119.133 Ps 17.15; 19.13
119.134 Ps 142.6
119.135 Ps 4.6; v. 12
119.136 Jer 9.1; Ezek 9.4
119.137 Ezra 9.15; Neh 9.13; Jer 12.1
119.138 Ps 19.7-9
119.139 Ps 69.9
119.140 Ps 12.6
119.142 Ps 19.9; vv. 151,160
119.143 vv. 24,77

[a] Gk Jerome: Meaning of Heb uncertain

but your commandments
are my delight.
144 Your decrees are righteous
forever;
give me understanding that
I may live.

145 With my whole heart I cry;
answer me, O LORD.
I will keep your statutes.
146 I cry to you; save me,
that I may observe your
decrees.
147 I rise before dawn and cry
for help;
I put my hope in your
words.
148 My eyes are awake before
each watch of the
night,
that I may meditate on
your promise.
149 In your steadfast love hear
my voice;
O LORD, in your justice
preserve my life.
150 Those who persecute me
with evil purpose draw
near;
they are far from your
law.
151 Yet you are near, O LORD,
and all your
commandments are
true.
152 Long ago I learned from
your decrees
that you have established
them forever.

153 Look on my misery and
rescue me,
for I do not forget your law.
154 Plead my cause and redeem
me;
give me life according to
your promise.
155 Salvation is far from the
wicked,
for they do not seek your
statutes.
156 Great is your mercy, O LORD;
give me life according to
your justice.
157 Many are my persecutors
and my adversaries,
yet I do not swerve from
your decrees.
158 I look at the faithless with
disgust,
because they do not keep
your commands.
159 Consider how I love your
precepts;
preserve my life according
to your steadfast love.
160 The sum of your word is
truth;
and every one of your
righteous ordinances
endures forever.

161 Princes persecute me
without cause,
but my heart stands in awe
of your words.
162 I rejoice at your word
like one who finds great
spoil.
163 I hate and abhor falsehood,
but I love your law.
164 Seven times a day I praise
you
for your righteous
ordinances.
165 Great peace have those who
love your law;
nothing can make them
stumble.
166 I hope for your salvation,
O LORD,
and I fulfill your
commandments.
167 My soul keeps your
decrees;
I love them exceedingly.
168 I keep your precepts and
decrees,
for all my ways are before
you.

169 Let my cry come before you,
O LORD;
give me understanding
according to your word.
170 Let my supplication come
before you;
deliver me according to
your promise.
171 My lips will pour forth
praise,
because you teach me your
statutes.

119.144 Ps 19.9; vv. 34,73
119.145 vv. 10,22,55
119.148 Ps 5.3
119.149 vv. 40,154
119.151 Ps 145.18; v. 142
119.152 Lk 21.33
119.153 v. 50; Prov 3.1
119.154 1 Sam 24.15; v. 134
119.155 Job 5.4
119.156 2 Sam 24.14
119.157 Ps 7.1; v. 51
119.158 Ps 139.21
119.159 vv. 47,88
119.160 Ps 139.17; v. 142
119.161 1 Sam 24.11
119.162 1 Sam 30.16
119.164 vv. 7,160
119.165 Prov 3.2; Isa 26.3; 32.17
119.166 v. 174; Gen 49.18
119.168 v. 22; Prov 5.21
119.169 Ps 18.6; vv. 27,65
119.170 Ps 28.2; 31.2
119.171 Ps 51.15; 94.12

172 My tongue will sing of your
promise,
for all your commandments
are right.
173 Let your hand be ready to
help me,
for I have chosen your
precepts.
174 I long for your salvation,
O LORD,
and your law is my
delight.
175 Let me live that I may
praise you,
and let your ordinances
help me.
176 I have gone astray like a
lost sheep; seek out
your servant,
for I do not forget your
commandments.

Psalm 120

Prayer for Deliverance from Slanderers

A Song of Ascents.

1 In my distress I cry to the
LORD,
that he may answer me:
2 "Deliver me, O LORD,
from lying lips,
from a deceitful tongue."

3 What shall be given to
you?
And what more shall be
done to you,
you deceitful tongue?
4 A warrior's sharp arrows,
with glowing coals of the
broom tree!

5 Woe is me, that I am an
alien in Meshech,
that I must live among the
tents of Kedar.
6 Too long have I had my
dwelling
among those who hate
peace.
7 I am for peace;
but when I speak,
they are for war.

119.173 Ps 37.24
119.174 vv. 166,24
119.175 Isa 55.3
119.176 Isa 53.6; v. 16
120.1 Ps 102.2; Jon 2.2
120.2 Prov 12.22; Ps 52.4
120.4 Ps 45.5; 140.10
120.5 Gen 10.2; Ezek 27.13; Gen 25.13; Jer 49.28
120.7 Ps 55.21
121.2 Ps 124.8; 115.15
121.3 Ps 66.9; 127.1
121.5 Isa 25.4; Ps 16.8
121.6 Ps 91.5; Isa 49.10; Rev 7.16
121.7 Ps 91.10-12
121.8 Deut 28.6
122.1 Isa 2.3; Zech 8.21
122.3 Ps 48.13

Psalm 121

Assurance of God's Protection

A Song of Ascents.

1 I lift up my eyes to the
hills—
from where will my help
come?
2 My help comes from the
LORD,
who made heaven and
earth.

3 He will not let your foot be
moved;
he who keeps you will not
slumber.
4 He who keeps Israel
will neither slumber nor
sleep.

5 The LORD is your keeper;
the LORD is your shade at
your right hand.
6 The sun shall not strike you
by day,
nor the moon by night.

7 The LORD will keep you from
all evil;
he will keep your life.
8 The LORD will keep
your going out and your
coming in
from this time on and
forevermore.

Psalm 122

Song of Praise and Prayer for Jerusalem

A Song of Ascents. Of David.

1 I was glad when they said to
me,
"Let us go to the house of
the LORD!"
2 Our feet are standing
within your gates,
O Jerusalem.

3 Jerusalem—built as a city
that is bound firmly
together.

4 To it the tribes go up,
the tribes of the LORD,
as was decreed for Israel,
to give thanks to the name
of the LORD.
5 For there the thrones for
judgment were set up,
the thrones of the house of
David.

6 Pray for the peace of
Jerusalem:
"May they prosper who
love you.
7 Peace be within your walls,
and security within your
towers."
8 For the sake of my relatives
and friends
I will say, "Peace be within
you."
9 For the sake of the house of
the LORD our God,
I will seek your good.

Psalm 123

Supplication for Mercy

A Song of Ascents.

1 To you I lift up my eyes,
O you who are enthroned
in the heavens!
2 As the eyes of servants
look to the hand of their
master,
as the eyes of a maid
to the hand of her
mistress,
so our eyes look to the LORD
our God,
until he has mercy upon
us.

3 Have mercy upon us, O LORD,
have mercy upon us,
for we have had more than
enough of contempt.
4 Our soul has had more than
its fill
of the scorn of those who
are at ease,
of the contempt of the
proud.

122.4 Deut 16.16; Ex 16.34
122.5 Deut 17.8; 2 Chr 19.8
122.6 Ps 51.18
122.9 Neh 2.10
123.1 Ps 121.1; 141.8; 2.4; 11.4
123.2 Prov 27.18; Ps 25.15
123.3 Ps 4.1; 51.1
123.4 Ps 79.4

124.1 Ps 94.17; 129.1
124.3 Ps 56.1; 57.3; Prov 1.12
124.5 Ps 69.2
124.6 Ps 27.2
124.7 Prov 6.5; Ps 91.3
124.8 Ps 121.2; Gen 1.1
125.1 Ps 46.5
125.2 Zech 2.5; Ps 121.8
125.3 Prov 22.8; Isa 14.5; Ps 55.20

Psalm 124

Thanksgiving for Israel's Deliverance

A Song of Ascents. Of David.

1 If it had not been the LORD
who was on our side
—let Israel now say—
2 if it had not been the LORD
who was on our side,
when our enemies attacked
us,
3 then they would have
swallowed us up alive,
when their anger was
kindled against us;
4 then the flood would have
swept us away,
the torrent would have
gone over us;
5 then over us would have
gone
the raging waters.

6 Blessed be the LORD,
who has not given us
as prey to their teeth.
7 We have escaped like a bird
from the snare of the
fowlers;
the snare is broken,
and we have escaped.

8 Our help is in the name of
the LORD,
who made heaven and
earth.

Psalm 125

The Security of God's People

A Song of Ascents.

1 Those who trust in the LORD
are like Mount Zion,
which cannot be moved,
but abides forever.
2 As the mountains surround
Jerusalem,
so the LORD surrounds his
people,
from this time on and
forevermore.
3 For the scepter of
wickedness shall not
rest

on the land allotted to the righteous,
so that the righteous might not stretch out
their hands to do wrong.
4 Do good, O LORD, to those who are good,
and to those who are upright in their hearts.
5 But those who turn aside to their own crooked ways
the LORD will lead away with evildoers.
Peace be upon Israel!

Psalm 126

A Harvest of Joy

A Song of Ascents.

1 When the LORD restored the fortunes of Zion,[b]
we were like those who dream.
2 Then our mouth was filled with laughter,
and our tongue with shouts of joy;
then it was said among the nations,
"The LORD has done great things for them."
3 The LORD has done great things for us,
and we rejoiced.

4 Restore our fortunes, O LORD,
like the watercourses in the Negeb.
5 May those who sow in tears
reap with shouts of joy.
6 Those who go out weeping,
bearing the seed for sowing,
shall come home with shouts of joy,
carrying their sheaves.

Psalm 127

God's Blessings in the Home

A Song of Ascents. Of Solomon.

1 Unless the LORD builds the house,
those who build it labor in vain.
Unless the LORD guards the city,
the guard keeps watch in vain.
2 It is in vain that you rise up early
and go late to rest,
eating the bread of anxious toil;
for he gives sleep to his beloved.[c]

3 Sons are indeed a heritage from the LORD,
the fruit of the womb a reward.
4 Like arrows in the hand of a warrior
are the sons of one's youth.
5 Happy is the man who has his quiver full of them.
He shall not be put to shame
when he speaks with his enemies in the gate.

Psalm 128

The Happy Home of the Faithful

A Song of Ascents.

1 Happy is everyone who fears the LORD,
who walks in his ways.
2 You shall eat the fruit of the labor of your hands;
you shall be happy, and it shall go well with you.

3 Your wife will be like a fruitful vine
within your house;
your children will be like olive shoots
around your table.
4 Thus shall the man be blessed
who fears the LORD.

5 The LORD bless you from Zion.
May you see the prosperity of Jerusalem
all the days of your life.

125.4 Ps 119.68; 7.10; 94.15
125.5 Prov 2.15; Ps 128.6
126.1 Ps 85.1; Acts 12.9
126.2 Job 8.21; Ps 51.14; 71.19
126.3 Isa 25.9
126.4 Isa 35.6; 43.19
126.5 Jer 31.16; Isa 35.10
127.1 Ps 78.69; 121.4
127.2 Gen 3.17; Job 11.18, 19
127.3 Gen 33.5; Josh 24.3,4; Deut 28.4
127.5 Job 5.4; Prov 27.11
128.1 Ps 112.1; 119.3
128.2 Isa 3.10; Ezek 23.29; Eccl 8.12
128.3 Ezek 19.10; Ps 52.8; 144.12
128.5 Ps 134.3; 20.2; 122.9

[b] Or *brought back those who returned to Zion*
[c] Or *for he provides for his beloved during sleep*

6 May you see your children's
children.
Peace be upon Israel!

Psalm 129

Prayer for the Downfall of Israel's Enemies

A Song of Ascents.

1 "Often have they attacked
me from my youth"
—let Israel now say—
2 "often have they attacked me
from my youth,
yet they have not prevailed
against me.
3 The plowers plowed on my
back;
they made their furrows
long."
4 The LORD is righteous;
he has cut the cords of the
wicked.
5 May all who hate Zion
be put to shame and
turned backward.
6 Let them be like the grass on
the housetops
that withers before it grows
up,
7 with which reapers do not
fill their hands
or binders of sheaves their
arms,
8 while those who pass by do
not say,
"The blessing of the LORD
be upon you!
We bless you in the name
of the LORD!"

Psalm 130

Waiting for Divine Redemption

A Song of Ascents.

1 Out of the depths I cry to
you, O LORD.
2 Lord, hear my voice!
Let your ears be attentive
to the voice of my
supplications!
3 If you, O LORD, should mark
iniquities,
Lord, who could stand?

128.6 Gen 50.23; Job 42.16; Ps 125.5
129.1 Ps 88.15; Hos 2.15; Ps 124.1
129.2 Mt 16.18
129.4 Ps 119.137
129.5 Mic 4.11; Ps 71.13
129.6 Ps 37.2
129.8 Ruth 2.4; Ps 118.26
130.1 Ps 42.7; 69.2
130.2 Ps 64.1; 2 Chr 6.40; Ps 28.2
130.3 Ps 76.7
130.4 Ex 34.7; Isa 55.7; 1 Kings 8.40; Jer 33.8
130.5 Ps 33.20; Isa 8.17; Ps 119.81
130.6 Ps 63.6; 119.147
130.7 Ps 131.3; Isa 55.7
130.8 Lk 1.68
131.1 Ps 101.5; Isa 5.15; Rom 12.16
131.2 Ps 62.1; Mt 18.3; 1 Cor 14.20
131.3 Ps 130.7

4 But there is forgiveness with
you,
so that you may be revered.

5 I wait for the LORD, my soul
waits,
and in his word I hope;
6 my soul waits for the Lord
more than those who
watch for the morning,
more than those who
watch for the morning.

7 O Israel, hope in the LORD!
For with the LORD there is
steadfast love,
and with him is great
power to redeem.
8 It is he who will redeem
Israel
from all its iniquities.

Psalm 131

Song of Quiet Trust

A Song of Ascents. Of David.

1 O LORD, my heart is not
lifted up,
my eyes are not raised too
high;
I do not occupy myself with
things
too great and too
marvelous for me.
2 But I have calmed and
quieted my soul,
like a weaned child with its
mother;
my soul is like the weaned
child that is with me.[d]

3 O Israel, hope in the LORD
from this time on and
forevermore.

Psalm 132

The Eternal Dwelling of God in Zion

A Song of Ascents.

1 O LORD, remember in David's
favor

[d] Or *my soul within me is like a weaned child*

all the hardships he
endured;
2 how he swore to the LORD
and vowed to the Mighty
One of Jacob,
3 "I will not enter my house
or get into my bed;
4 I will not give sleep to my
eyes
or slumber to my eyelids,
5 until I find a place for the
LORD,
a dwelling place for the
Mighty One of Jacob."
6 We heard of it in Ephrathah;
we found it in the fields of
Jaar.
7 "Let us go to his dwelling
place;
let us worship at his
footstool."

8 Rise up, O LORD, and go to
your resting place,
you and the ark of your
might.
9 Let your priests be clothed
with righteousness,
and let your faithful shout
for joy.
10 For your servant David's sake
do not turn away the face
of your anointed one.

11 The LORD swore to David a
sure oath
from which he will not turn
back:
"One of the sons of your
body
I will set on your throne.
12 If your sons keep my
covenant
and my decrees that I shall
teach them,
their sons also, forevermore,
shall sit on your throne."

13 For the LORD has chosen
Zion;
he has desired it for his
habitation:
14 "This is my resting place
forever;
here I will reside, for I have
desired it.

132.2 Gen 49.24 **132.4** Prov 6.4 **132.5** Acts 7.46 **132.6** 1 Sam 17.12; 7.1; 1 Chr 13.5 **132.7** Ps 4.7; 99.5 **132.8** Num 10.35; 2 Chr 6.41; Ps 78.61 **132.9** v. 16; Job 29.14; Isa 61.10 **132.11** Ps 89.3,4; 2 Sam 7.12; 2 Chr 6.16 **132.12** Lk 1.32; Acts 2.30 **132.13** Ps 48.1,2; 68.16 **132.14** v. 8 **132.15** Ps 147.14; 107.9 **132.16** v. 9 **132.17** Ezek 29.21; Lk 1.69; 1 Kings 11.36; 15.4; 2 Chr 21.7 **132.18** Ps 35.26; 109.29 **133.1** Gen 13.8; Heb 13.1 **133.2** Ex 30.25; 39.24 **133.3** Deut 4.48; Lev 25.21; Deut 28.8; Ps 42.8 **134.1** Ps 103.21; 135.1,2; 1 Chr 9.33 **134.2** Ps 28.2; 1 Tim 2.8 **134.3** Ps 124.8; 128.5

15 I will abundantly bless its
provisions;
I will satisfy its poor with
bread.
16 Its priests I will clothe with
salvation,
and its faithful will shout
for joy.
17 There I will cause a horn to
sprout up for David;
I have prepared a lamp for
my anointed one.
18 His enemies I will clothe
with disgrace,
but on him, his crown will
gleam."

Psalm 133

The Blessedness of Unity

A Song of Ascents.

1 How very good and pleasant
it is
when kindred live together
in unity!
2 It is like the precious oil on
the head,
running down upon the
beard,
on the beard of Aaron,
running down over the
collar of his robes.
3 It is like the dew of Hermon,
which falls on the
mountains of Zion.
For there the LORD ordained
his blessing,
life forevermore.

Psalm 134

Praise in the Night

A Song of Ascents.

1 Come, bless the LORD, all you
servants of the LORD,
who stand by night in the
house of the LORD!
2 Lift up your hands to the
holy place,
and bless the LORD.

3 May the LORD, maker of
heaven and earth,
bless you from Zion.

Psalm 135

Praise for God's Goodness and Might

1 Praise the LORD!
Praise the name of the LORD;
give praise, O servants of the LORD,
2 you that stand in the house of the LORD,
in the courts of the house of our God.
3 Praise the LORD, for the LORD is good;
sing to his name, for he is gracious.
4 For the LORD has chosen Jacob for himself,
Israel as his own possession.

5 For I know that the LORD is great;
our Lord is above all gods.
6 Whatever the LORD pleases he does,
in heaven and on earth,
in the seas and all deeps.
7 He it is who makes the clouds rise at the end of the earth;
he makes lightnings for the rain
and brings out the wind from his storehouses.

8 He it was who struck down the firstborn of Egypt,
both human beings and animals;
9 he sent signs and wonders into your midst, O Egypt,
against Pharaoh and all his servants.
10 He struck down many nations
and killed mighty kings—
11 Sihon, king of the Amorites,
and Og, king of Bashan,
and all the kingdoms of Canaan—
12 and gave their land as a heritage,
a heritage to his people Israel.

135.1 Ps 113.1; 134.1 **135.2** Lk 2.37; Ps 92.13 **135.3** Ps 119.68; 147.1 **135.4** Deut 7.6,7; 10.15; Ex 19.5; 1 Pet 2.9 **135.5** Ps 48.1; 97.9 **135.6** Ps 115.3 **135.7** Jer 10.13; Job 28.25; Zech 10.1; Job 38.22 **135.8** Ex 12.12; Ps 78.51 **135.9** Ps 78.43; 136.15 **135.10** Num 21.24; Ps 136.17 **135.11** Num 21.21-26, 33-35; Josh 12.7 **135.12** Ps 78.55

135.13 Ex 3.15; Ps 102.12 **135.14** Deut 32.36; Ps 106.45 **135.15** Ps 115.4-8 **135.19** Ps 115.9 **135.20** Ps 118.4 **135.21** Ps 134.3; 132.14 **136.1** Ps 106.1; 107.1; 118.1; 1 Chr 16.34; 2 Chr 20.21 **136.2** Deut 10.17

13 Your name, O LORD, endures forever,
your renown, O LORD, throughout all ages.
14 For the LORD will vindicate his people,
and have compassion on his servants.

15 The idols of the nations are silver and gold,
the work of human hands.
16 They have mouths, but they do not speak;
they have eyes, but they do not see;
17 they have ears, but they do not hear,
and there is no breath in their mouths.
18 Those who make them
and all who trust them
shall become like them.

19 O house of Israel, bless the LORD!
O house of Aaron, bless the LORD!
20 O house of Levi, bless the LORD!
You that fear the LORD, bless the LORD!
21 Blessed be the LORD from Zion,
he who resides in Jerusalem.
Praise the LORD!

Psalm 136

God's Work in Creation and in History

1 O give thanks to the LORD, for he is good,
for his steadfast love endures forever.
2 O give thanks to the God of gods,
for his steadfast love endures forever.
3 O give thanks to the Lord of lords,
for his steadfast love endures forever;

4 who alone does great
wonders,
for his steadfast love
endures forever;
5 who by understanding made
the heavens,
for his steadfast love
endures forever;
6 who spread out the earth on
the waters,
for his steadfast love
endures forever;
7 who made the great lights,
for his steadfast love
endures forever;
8 the sun to rule over the day,
for his steadfast love
endures forever;
9 the moon and stars to rule
over the night,
for his steadfast love
endures forever;

10 who struck Egypt through
their firstborn,
for his steadfast love
endures forever;
11 and brought Israel out from
among them,
for his steadfast love
endures forever;
12 with a strong hand and an
outstretched arm,
for his steadfast love
endures forever;
13 who divided the Red Sea[e] in
two,
for his steadfast love
endures forever;
14 and made Israel pass through
the midst of it,
for his steadfast love
endures forever;
15 but overthrew Pharaoh and
his army in the Red
Sea,[e]
for his steadfast love
endures forever;
16 who led his people through
the wilderness,
for his steadfast love
endures forever;
17 who struck down great kings,
for his steadfast love
endures forever;
18 and killed famous kings,
for his steadfast love
endures forever;
19 Sihon, king of the Amorites,
for his steadfast love
endures forever;
20 and Og, king of Bashan,
for his steadfast love
endures forever;
21 and gave their land as a
heritage,
for his steadfast love
endures forever;
22 a heritage to his servant
Israel,
for his steadfast love
endures forever.

23 It is he who remembered us
in our low estate,
for his steadfast love
endures forever;
24 and rescued us from our
foes,
for his steadfast love
endures forever;
25 who gives food to all flesh,
for his steadfast love
endures forever.

26 O give thanks to the God of
heaven,
for his steadfast love
endures forever.

Psalm 137

Lament over the Destruction of Jerusalem

1 By the rivers of Babylon—
there we sat down and
there we wept
when we remembered Zion.
2 On the willows[f] there
we hung up our harps.
3 For there our captors
asked us for songs,
and our tormentors asked for
mirth, saying,
"Sing us one of the songs
of Zion!"

4 How could we sing the
LORD's song
in a foreign land?
5 If I forget you, O Jerusalem,

136.4 Ps 72.18
136.5 Gen 1.1; Prov 3.19; Jer 51.15
136.6 Gen 1.9; Ps 24.2; Jer 10.12
136.7 Gen 1.14,16
136.8 Gen 1.16
136.10 Ex 12.29; Ps 135.8
136.11 Ex 12.51
136.12 Ex 6.6; Ps 44.3; Deut 4.34
136.13 Ex 14.21; Ps 78.13
136.14 Ex 14.22
136.15 Ex 14.27; Ps 135.9
136.16 Ex 13.18; 15.22; Deut 8.15
136.17 Ps 135.10-12
136.21 Josh 12.1
136.23 Ps 113.7
136.24 Ps 107.2
136.25 Ps 104.27; 145.15
137.1 Ezek 1.1,3; Neh 1.4
137.3 Ps 80.6

[e] Or *Sea of Reeds* [f] Or *poplars*

let my right hand wither!
6 Let my tongue cling to the
roof of my mouth,
if I do not remember you,
if I do not set Jerusalem
above my highest joy.

7 Remember, O LORD, against
the Edomites
the day of Jerusalem's fall,
how they said, "Tear it down!
Tear it down!
Down to its foundations!"
8 O daughter Babylon, you
devastator![g]
Happy shall they be who
pay you back
what you have done to us!
9 Happy shall they be who
take your little ones
and dash them against the
rock!

Psalm 138

Thanksgiving and Praise

Of David.

1 I give you thanks, O LORD,
with my whole heart;
before the gods I sing your
praise;
2 I bow down toward your holy
temple
and give thanks to your
name for your steadfast
love and your
faithfulness;
for you have exalted your
name and your word
above everything.[h]
3 On the day I called, you
answered me,
you increased my strength
of soul.[i]

4 All the kings of the earth
shall praise you,
O LORD,
for they have heard the
words of your mouth.
5 They shall sing of the ways
of the LORD,
for great is the glory of the
LORD.
6 For though the LORD is high,
he regards the lowly;
but the haughty he
perceives from far away.

7 Though I walk in the midst
of trouble,
you preserve me against
the wrath of my
enemies;
you stretch out your hand,
and your right hand
delivers me.
8 The LORD will fulfill his
purpose for me;
your steadfast love, O LORD,
endures forever.
Do not forsake the work of
your hands.

Psalm 139

The Inescapable God

To the leader. Of David. A Psalm.

1 O LORD, you have searched
me and known me.
2 You know when I sit down
and when I rise up;
you discern my thoughts
from far away.
3 You search out my path and
my lying down,
and are acquainted with all
my ways.
4 Even before a word is on my
tongue,
O LORD, you know it
completely.
5 You hem me in, behind and
before,
and lay your hand upon
me.
6 Such knowledge is too
wonderful for me;
it is so high that I cannot
attain it.

7 Where can I go from your
spirit?
Or where can I flee from
your presence?
8 If I ascend to heaven, you
are there;

137.6 Ezek 3.26 **137.7** Jer 49.7; Lam 4.22; Ezek 25.12; Ob 10-14 **137.8** Isa 13.1,6; Jer 25.12; 50.15; Rev 18.6 **137.9** 2 Kings 8.12; Isa 13.16 **138.1** Ps 111.1; 95.3; 96.4 **138.2** Ps 28.2; 1 Kings 8.29, 30; Isa 42.21 **138.3** Ps 118.5; 28.7; 46.1 **138.4** Ps 102.15 **138.6** Ps 113.5,6; Isa 57.15; Prov 3.34; Jas 4.6 **138.7** Ps 23.3,4; 71.20; Jer 41.25; Ps 20.6 **138.8** Ps 57.2; Phil 1.6; Ps 136.1; 27.9; Job 10.3,8; 14.15 **139.1** Ps 17.3; Jer 12.3 **139.2** 2 Kings 19.27; Mt 9.4; Jn 2.24 **139.3** Job 31.4 **139.4** Heb 4.13 **139.5** Ps 34.7; Job 9.33 **139.6** Rom 11.33; Job 42.3 **139.7** Jer 23.24; Jon 1.3 **139.8ff** Am 9.2-4; Job 26.6; Prov 15.11

[g] Or *you who are devastated* [h] Cn: Heb *you have exalted your word above all your name* [i] Syr Compare Gk Tg: Heb *you made me arrogant in my soul with strength*

if I make my bed in Sheol,
you are there.
9 If I take the wings of the morning
and settle at the farthest limits of the sea,
10 even there your hand shall lead me,
and your right hand shall hold me fast.
11 If I say, "Surely the darkness shall cover me,
and the light around me become night,"
12 even the darkness is not dark to you;
the night is as bright as the day,
for darkness is as light to you.

13 For it was you who formed my inward parts;
you knit me together in my mother's womb.
14 I praise you, for I am fearfully and wonderfully made.
Wonderful are your works;
that I know very well.
15 My frame was not hidden from you,
when I was being made in secret,
intricately woven in the depths of the earth.
16 Your eyes beheld my unformed substance.
In your book were written
all the days that were formed for me,
when none of them as yet existed.
17 How weighty to me are your thoughts, O God!
How vast is the sum of them!
18 I try to count them—they are more than the sand;
I come to the end[j]—I am still with you.

19 O that you would kill the wicked, O God,
and that the bloodthirsty would depart from me—
20 those who speak of you maliciously,
and lift themselves up against you for evil![k]
21 Do I not hate those who hate you, O LORD?
And do I not loathe those who rise up against you?
22 I hate them with perfect hatred;
I count them my enemies.
23 Search me, O God, and know my heart;
test me and know my thoughts.
24 See if there is any wicked[l] way in me,
and lead me in the way everlasting.[m]

Psalm 140

Prayer for Deliverance from Enemies

To the leader. A Psalm of David.

1 Deliver me, O LORD, from evildoers;
protect me from those who are violent,
2 who plan evil things in their minds
and stir up wars continually.
3 They make their tongue sharp as a snake's,
and under their lips is the venom of vipers. *Selah*

4 Guard me, O LORD, from the hands of the wicked;
protect me from the violent who have planned my downfall.
5 The arrogant have hidden a trap for me,
and with cords they have spread a net,[n]

139.10 Ps 23.2,3 **139.11** Job 22.13 **139.12** Job 34.22; Dan 2.22; Heb 4.13 **139.13ff** Ps 119.73; Job 10.11 **139.14** Ps 40.5 **139.17** Ps 40.5 **139.19** Isa 11.4; Ps 119.115

139.20 Jude 15 **139.21** Ps 119.158 **139.23** Job 31.6; Ps 26.2; Jer 11.20 **139.24** Prov 15.9; Ps 5.8; 143.10 **140.1** Ps 17.13; 18.48 **140.2** Ps 36.4; 56.6 **140.3** Ps 57.4; 68.4; Jas 3.8 **140.4** Ps 71.4 **140.5** Ps 35.7; 31.4; 141.9

j Or *I awake* k Cn: Meaning of Heb uncertain l Heb *hurtful* m Or *the ancient way.* Compare Jer 6.16 n Or *they have spread cords as a net*

along the road they have
set snares for me. *Selah*
6 I say to the LORD, "You are
my God;
give ear, O LORD, to the
voice of my
supplications."
7 O LORD, my Lord, my strong
deliverer,
you have covered my head
in the day of battle.
8 Do not grant, O LORD, the
desires of the wicked;
do not further their evil
plot.[o] *Selah*
9 Those who surround me lift
up their heads;[p]
let the mischief of their
lips overwhelm them!
10 Let burning coals fall on
them!
Let them be flung into pits,
no more to rise!
11 Do not let the slanderer be
established in the land;
let evil speedily hunt down
the violent!

12 I know that the LORD
maintains the cause of
the needy,
and executes justice for the
poor.
13 Surely the righteous shall
give thanks to your
name;
the upright shall live in
your presence.

Psalm 141
Prayer for Preservation from Evil

A Psalm of David.

1 I call upon you, O LORD;
come quickly to me;
give ear to my voice when I
call to you.
2 Let my prayer be counted as
incense before you,
and the lifting up of my
hands as an evening
sacrifice.
3 Set a guard over my mouth,
O LORD;
keep watch over the door
of my lips.
4 Do not turn my heart to any
evil,
to busy myself with wicked
deeds
in company with those who
work iniquity;
do not let me eat of their
delicacies.

5 Let the righteous strike
me;
let the faithful correct
me.
Never let the oil of the
wicked anoint my
head,[q]
for my prayer is
continually[r] against
their wicked deeds.
6 When they are given over to
those who shall
condemn them,
then they shall learn that
my words were
pleasant.
7 Like a rock that one breaks
apart and shatters on
the land,
so shall their bones be
strewn at the mouth of
Sheol.[s]

8 But my eyes are turned
toward you, O GOD, my
Lord;
in you I seek refuge; do not
leave me defenseless.
9 Keep me from the trap that
they have laid for me,
and from the snares of
evildoers.
10 Let the wicked fall into their
own nets,
while I alone escape.

140.6 Ps 16.2; 143.1; 116.1 **140.7** Ps 28.8; 144.10 **140.8** Ps 112.10; 10.2 **140.9** Ps 7.16 **140.10** Ps 11.6; 21.9; 36.12 **140.11** Ps 34.21 **140.12** Ps 9.4; 35.10 **140.13** Ps 97.12; 11.7 **141.1** Ps 22.19; 70.5; 143.1 **141.2** Rev 5.8; 8.3; Ps 134.2; Ex 29.39 **141.4** Ps 119.36; Prov 23.6 **141.5** Prov 9.8; Ps 23.5; 35.14 **141.7** Ps 53.5 **141.8** Ps 25.15; 2.12; 27.9 **141.9** Ps 38.12; 140.5 **141.10** Ps 35.8

o Heb adds *they are exalted*
p Cn Compare Gk: Heb *those who surround me are uplifted in head*; Heb divides verses 8 and 9 differently
q Gk: Meaning of Heb uncertain
r Cn: Heb *for continually and my prayer*
s Meaning of Heb of verses 5-7 is uncertain

Psalm 142

Prayer for Deliverance from Persecutors

A Maskil of David. When he was in the cave. A Prayer.

1 With my voice I cry to the LORD;
with my voice I make supplication to the LORD.
2 I pour out my complaint before him;
I tell my trouble before him.
3 When my spirit is faint,
you know my way.

In the path where I walk
they have hidden a trap for me.
4 Look on my right hand and see—
there is no one who takes notice of me;
no refuge remains to me;
no one cares for me.

5 I cry to you, O LORD;
I say, "You are my refuge,
my portion in the land of the living."
6 Give heed to my cry,
for I am brought very low.

Save me from my persecutors,
for they are too strong for me.
7 Bring me out of prison,
so that I may give thanks to your name.
The righteous will surround me,
for you will deal bountifully with me.

Psalm 143

Prayer for Deliverance from Enemies

A Psalm of David.

1 Hear my prayer, O LORD;
give ear to my supplications in your faithfulness;
answer me in your righteousness.
2 Do not enter into judgment with your servant,
for no one living is righteous before you.

3 For the enemy has pursued me,
crushing my life to the ground,
making me sit in darkness like those long dead.
4 Therefore my spirit faints within me;
my heart within me is appalled.

5 I remember the days of old,
I think about all your deeds,
I meditate on the works of your hands.
6 I stretch out my hands to you;
my soul thirsts for you like a parched land. *Selah*

7 Answer me quickly, O LORD;
my spirit fails.
Do not hide your face from me,
or I shall be like those who go down to the Pit.
8 Let me hear of your steadfast love in the morning,
for in you I put my trust.
Teach me the way I should go,
for to you I lift up my soul.

9 Save me, O LORD, from my enemies;
I have fled to you for refuge.[t]
10 Teach me to do your will,
for you are my God.
Let your good spirit lead me on a level path.

11 For your name's sake,
O LORD, preserve my life.

142.1 Ps 77.1; 30.8
142.2 Isa 26.16
142.3 Ps 143.4; 140.5
142.4 Ps 31.11; Job 11.20; Jer 30.17
142.5 Ps 46.1; 16.5; 27.13
142.6 Ps 17.1; 79.8; 116.6
142.7 Ps 146.7; 13.6
143.1 Ps 140.6; 89.1,2; 71.2
143.2 Job 14.3; 4.17; Ps 130.3; Eccl 7.20; Rom 3.20
143.4 Ps 142.3; Lam 3.11
143.5 Ps 77.5; 77.12; 105.2
143.6 Ps 88.9; 63.1
143.7 Ps 69.17; 27.9; 28.1
143.8 Ps 90.14; 25.2; 27.11; 25.1
143.9 Ps 31.15
143.10 Ps 25.4,5; Neh 9.20; Ps 23.3
143.11 Ps 119.25; 31.1

[t] One Heb Ms Gk: MT *to you I have hidden*

In your righteousness bring
me out of trouble.
12 In your steadfast love cut off
my enemies,
and destroy all my
adversaries,
for I am your servant.

Psalm 144

Prayer for National Deliverance and Security

Of David.

1 Blessed be the LORD, my
rock,
who trains my hands for
war, and my fingers for
battle;
2 my rock[u] and my fortress,
my stronghold and my
deliverer,
my shield, in whom I take
refuge,
who subdues the peoples[v]
under me.

3 O LORD, what are human
beings that you regard
them,
or mortals that you think
of them?
4 They are like a breath;
their days are like a
passing shadow.

5 Bow your heavens, O LORD,
and come down;
touch the mountains so
that they smoke.
6 Make the lightning flash and
scatter them;
send out your arrows and
rout them.
7 Stretch out your hand from
on high;
set me free and rescue me
from the mighty waters,
from the hand of aliens,
8 whose mouths speak lies,
and whose right hands are
false.

9 I will sing a new song to you,
O God;
upon a ten-stringed harp I
will play to you,
10 the one who gives victory to
kings,
who rescues his servant
David.
11 Rescue me from the cruel
sword,
and deliver me from the
hand of aliens,
whose mouths speak lies,
and whose right hands are
false.

12 May our sons in their youth
be like plants full grown,
our daughters like corner
pillars,
cut for the building of a
palace.
13 May our barns be filled,
with produce of every kind;
may our sheep increase by
thousands,
by tens of thousands in our
fields,
14 and may our cattle be
heavy with young.
May there be no breach in
the walls,[w] no exile,
and no cry of distress in
our streets.

15 Happy are the people to
whom such blessings
fall;
happy are the people
whose God is the LORD.

Psalm 145

The Greatness and the Goodness of God

Praise. Of David.

1 I will extol you, my God and
King,
and bless your name
forever and ever.
2 Every day I will bless you,
and praise your name
forever and ever.
3 Great is the LORD, and greatly
to be praised;
his greatness is
unsearchable.

143.12 Ps 54.5; 52.5; 116.16
144.1 Ps 18.2,34
144.2 Ps 91.2; 59.9; 84.9; 18.39
144.3 Ps 8.4; Heb 2.6
144.4 Ps 39.11; 102.11
144.5 Ps 18.9; Isa 64.1; Ps 104.32
144.6 Ps 18.13,14; 7.13
144.7 Ps 69.1,14; 18.44
144.8 Ps 12.2; Isa 44.20
144.9 Ps 33.2,3
144.10 Ps 18.50; 140.7
144.11 Ps 12.2; Isa 44.20
144.12 Ps 128.3
144.15 Ps 33.12
145.1 Ps 30.1; 5.2; 34.1
145.2 Ps 71.6
145.3 Ps 96.4; Job 5.9; Rom 11.33

[u] With 18.2 and 2 Sam 22.2: Heb *my steadfast love* [v] Heb Mss Syr Aquila Jerome: MT *my people* [w] Heb lacks *in the walls*

4 One generation shall laud
your works to another,
and shall declare your
mighty acts.
5 On the glorious splendor of
your majesty,
and on your wondrous
works, I will meditate.
6 The might of your awesome
deeds shall be
proclaimed,
and I will declare your
greatness.
7 They shall celebrate the
fame of your abundant
goodness,
and shall sing aloud of
your righteousness.

8 The LORD is gracious and
merciful,
slow to anger and
abounding in steadfast
love.
9 The LORD is good to all,
and his compassion is over
all that he has made.

10 All your works shall give
thanks to you, O LORD,
and all your faithful shall
bless you.
11 They shall speak of the glory
of your kingdom,
and tell of your power,
12 to make known to all people
your[x] mighty deeds,
and the glorious splendor
of your[y] kingdom.
13 Your kingdom is an
everlasting kingdom,
and your dominion endures
throughout all
generations.

The LORD is faithful in all his
words,
and gracious in all his
deeds.[z]
14 The LORD upholds all who
are falling,
and raises up all who are
bowed down.
15 The eyes of all look to you,
and you give them their
food in due season.
16 You open your hand,

145.4 Isa 38.19
145.5 v. 12; Ps 119.27
145.6 Ps 66.3; Deut 32.3
145.7 Isa 63.7; Ps 51.14
145.8 Ex 34.6; Ps 86.5,15
145.9 Ps 100.5; Nah 1.7
145.10 Ps 19.1; 68.26
145.12 Ps 105.1; v. 54
145.13 Ps 146.10; 2 Pet 1.11
145.14 Ps 37.24; 146.8
145.15 Ps 104.27
145.16 Ps 124.28
145.18 Deut 4.7; Jn 4.24
145.19 Ps 37.4; Prov 15.29
145.20 Ps 31.23; 97.10; 9.5
145.21 Ps 71.8; 65.2; v. 1,2
146.1 Ps 103.1
146.2 Ps 104.33
146.3 Ps 118.8; Isa 2.22
146.4 Ps 104.29; Eccl 12.7; Ps 33.10
146.5 Ps 144.15; 71.5
146.6 Ps 115.15; Acts 14.15; Ps 117.2
146.7 Ps 103.6; 107.9; 68.6

satisfying the desire of
every living thing.
17 The LORD is just in all his
ways,
and kind in all his doings.
18 The LORD is near to all who
call on him,
to all who call on him in
truth.
19 He fulfills the desire of all
who fear him;
he also hears their cry, and
saves them.
20 The LORD watches over all
who love him,
but all the wicked he will
destroy.

21 My mouth will speak the
praise of the LORD,
and all flesh will bless his
holy name forever and
ever.

Psalm 146

Praise for God's Help

1 Praise the LORD!
Praise the LORD, O my soul!
2 I will praise the LORD as long
as I live;
I will sing praises to my
God all my life long.

3 Do not put your trust in
princes,
in mortals, in whom there
is no help.
4 When their breath departs,
they return to the earth;
on that very day their plans
perish.

5 Happy are those whose help
is the God of Jacob,
whose hope is in the LORD
their God,
6 who made heaven and earth,
the sea, and all that is in
them;
who keeps faith forever;
7 who executes justice for
the oppressed;

[x] Gk Jerome Syr: Heb *his* [y] Heb *his*
[z] These two lines supplied by Q Ms Gk Syr

who gives food to the hungry.

The LORD sets the prisoners free;
8 the LORD opens the eyes of the blind.
The LORD lifts up those who are bowed down;
the LORD loves the righteous.
9 The LORD watches over the strangers;
he upholds the orphan and the widow,
but the way of the wicked he brings to ruin.

10 The LORD will reign forever,
your God, O Zion, for all generations.
Praise the LORD!

Psalm 147

Praise for God's Care for Jerusalem

1 Praise the LORD!
How good it is to sing praises to our God;
for he is gracious, and a song of praise is fitting.
2 The LORD builds up Jerusalem;
he gathers the outcasts of Israel.
3 He heals the brokenhearted,
and binds up their wounds.
4 He determines the number of the stars;
he gives to all of them their names.
5 Great is our Lord, and abundant in power;
his understanding is beyond measure.
6 The LORD lifts up the downtrodden;
he casts the wicked to the ground.

7 Sing to the LORD with thanksgiving;
make melody to our God on the lyre.
8 He covers the heavens with clouds,
prepares rain for the earth,
makes grass grow on the hills.
9 He gives to the animals their food,
and to the young ravens when they cry.
10 His delight is not in the strength of the horse,
nor his pleasure in the speed of a runner;[a]
11 but the LORD takes pleasure in those who fear him,
in those who hope in his steadfast love.

12 Praise the LORD, O Jerusalem!
Praise your God, O Zion!
13 For he strengthens the bars of your gates;
he blesses your children within you.
14 He grants peace[b] within your borders;
he fills you with the finest of wheat.
15 He sends out his command to the earth;
his word runs swiftly.
16 He gives snow like wool;
he scatters frost like ashes.
17 He hurls down hail like crumbs—
who can stand before his cold?
18 He sends out his word, and melts them;
he makes his wind blow, and the waters flow.
19 He declares his word to Jacob,
his statutes and ordinances to Israel.
20 He has not dealt thus with any other nation;
they do not know his ordinances.
Praise the LORD!

146.8 Mt 9.30; Jn 9.7; Ps 145.14; 11.7
146.9 Ex 22.21; Deut 10.18; Ps 68.5; 147.6
146.10 Ex 15.18; Ps 10.16; Rev 11.15
147.1 Ps 135.3; 33.1
147.2 Ps 102.16; Deut 30.3
147.3 Isa 61.1; 30.26
147.4 Isa 40.26
147.5 Ps 48.1; Isa 40.28
147.6 Ps 146.8,9
147.7 Ps 33.2
147.8 Job 38.26; Ps 104.13
147.9 Ps 104.27; Job 38.41
147.10 Ps 33.16,17; 1 Sam 16.7
147.11 Ps 102.15
147.13 Ps 37.26
147.14 Isa 60.17; Ps 132.15
147.15 Job 37.12; Ps 104.4
147.16 Job 37.6; 38.29
147.18 Ps 33.9; 107.25
147.19 Deut 33.2; Mal 4.4
147.20 Deut 4.32

[a] Heb *legs of a person* [b] Or *prosperity*

Psalm 148

Praise for God's Universal Glory

1 Praise the LORD!
Praise the LORD from the heavens;
praise him in the heights!
2 Praise him, all his angels;
praise him, all his host!

3 Praise him, sun and moon;
praise him, all you shining stars!
4 Praise him, you highest heavens,
and you waters above the heavens!

5 Let them praise the name of the LORD,
for he commanded and they were created.
6 He established them forever and ever;
he fixed their bounds, which cannot be passed.[c]

7 Praise the LORD from the earth,
you sea monsters and all deeps,
8 fire and hail, snow and frost,
stormy wind fulfilling his command!

9 Mountains and all hills,
fruit trees and all cedars!
10 Wild animals and all cattle,
creeping things and flying birds!

11 Kings of the earth and all peoples,
princes and all rulers of the earth!
12 Young men and women alike,
old and young together!

13 Let them praise the name of the LORD,
for his name alone is exalted;
his glory is above earth and heaven.
14 He has raised up a horn for his people,
praise for all his faithful,
for the people of Israel who are close to him.
Praise the LORD!

Psalm 149

Praise for God's Goodness to Israel

1 Praise the LORD!
Sing to the LORD a new song,
his praise in the assembly of the faithful.
2 Let Israel be glad in its Maker;
let the children of Zion rejoice in their King.
3 Let them praise his name with dancing,
making melody to him with tambourine and lyre.
4 For the LORD takes pleasure in his people;
he adorns the humble with victory.
5 Let the faithful exult in glory;
let them sing for joy on their couches.
6 Let the high praises of God be in their throats
and two-edged swords in their hands,
7 to execute vengeance on the nations
and punishment on the peoples,
8 to bind their kings with fetters
and their nobles with chains of iron,
9 to execute on them the judgment decreed.
This is glory for all his faithful ones.
Praise the LORD!

Psalm 150

Praise for God's Surpassing Greatness

1 Praise the LORD!
Praise God in his sanctuary;

148.2 Ps 103.20, 21
148.4 1 Kings 8.27; Gen 1.7
148.5 Gen 1.1; Ps 33.6,9
148.6 Ps 89.37; Jer 33.25; Job 38.33
148.7 Ps 74.13
148.8 Ps 147.15-18
148.9 Isa 44.23; 49.13; 55.12
148.13 Ps 8.1; Isa 12.4; Ps 113.4
148.14 Ps 75.10; Deut 10.21; Eph 2.17
149.1 Ps 33.3; 35.18
149.2 Ps 95.6; 47.6
149.3 Ps 150.4; 81.2
149.4 Ps 35.27; 132.16
149.5 Ps 132.16; Job 35.10
149.6 Ps 66.17; Heb 4.12; Rev 1.16
149.9 Ezek 28.26; Ps 148.14
150.1 Ps 102.19; 19.1

[c] Or *he set a law that cannot pass away*

praise him in his mighty firmament![d]

2 Praise him for his mighty deeds;
praise him according to his surpassing greatness!

3 Praise him with trumpet sound;
praise him with lute and harp!

4 Praise him with tambourine and dance;
praise him with strings and pipe!

5 Praise him with clanging cymbals;
praise him with loud clashing cymbals!

6 Let everything that breathes praise the LORD!
Praise the LORD!

150.2 Ps 145.5,6; Deut 3.24 **150.3** Ps 149.3 **150.4** Ex 15.20; Isa 38.20 **150.5** 1 Chr 13.8; 15.16 **150.6** Ps 145.21

[d] Or *dome*

Proverbs

Title and Background

The Hebrew word translated "proverb" is also translated "taunt" (Isa 14.4), "oracle" (Nu 23.7,18) and "allegory" (Eze 17.2), so its meaning is considerably broader than the English term. Most proverbs are short, compact statements that express a truth about human behavior. A common feature of the proverbs is the use of figurative language.

Author and Date of Writing

Although this book begins with a title ascribing the proverbs to Solomon, it is clear from later chapters that he was not the only author of the book (see Outline). Since Solomon had a prominent role in the book, most of Proverbs stem from the tenth century B.C., from the time of Israel's united kingdom. The compliation of these sayings of Solomon began during the reign of Hezekiah (see 25.1), though it may not have been completed until later.

Theme and Message

According to the prologue (1.1-7), Proverbs was written to give "shrewdness to the simple, knowledge and prudence to the young" (1.4), and to make wise men wiser (1.5). Acquiring wisdom and knowing how to avoid the pitfalls of folly lead to health and success. Although Proverbs is a practical book dealing with the art of living, it bases wisdom solidly on the fear of the Lord (1.7).

Outline

I. Prologue: Purpose and Theme (1.1-7)
II. The Superiority of the Way of Wisdom (1.8–9.18)
III. Wise Sayings of Solomon (10.1–22.16)
IV. Sayings of the Wise (22.17–24.34)
V. More Wise Sayings of Solomon (25.1–29.27)
VI. The Words of Agur and Lemuel (30.1–31.9)
VII. Epilogue: The Capable Wife (31.10-31)

---

1 The proverbs of Solomon son of David, king of Israel:

Prologue

2 For learning about wisdom
and instruction,
for understanding words of
insight,
3 for gaining instruction in
wise dealing,
righteousness, justice, and
equity;
4 to teach shrewdness to the
simple,
knowledge and prudence to
the young—
5 Let the wise also hear and
gain in learning,
and the discerning acquire
skill,
6 to understand a proverb and
a figure,
the words of the wise and
their riddles.

7 The fear of the LORD is the
beginning of knowledge;
fools despise wisdom and
instruction.

1.1 1 Kings 4.32; Eccl 12.9
1.3 Prov 19.20; 2.9
1.4 Prov 8.5,12; 2.10,11
1.5 Prov 9.9; 14.6
1.6 Ps 78.2
1.7 Job 28.28; Ps 111.10; Eccl 12.13

Warnings against Evil Companions

8 Hear, my child, your father's instruction,
and do not reject your mother's teaching;
9 for they are a fair garland for your head,
and pendants for your neck.
10 My child, if sinners entice you,
do not consent.
11 If they say, "Come with us,
let us lie in wait for blood;
let us wantonly ambush the innocent;
12 like Sheol let us swallow them alive
and whole, like those who go down to the Pit.
13 We shall find all kinds of costly things;
we shall fill our houses with booty.
14 Throw in your lot among us;
we will all have one purse"—
15 my child, do not walk in their way,
keep your foot from their paths;
16 for their feet run to evil,
and they hurry to shed blood.
17 For in vain is the net baited
while the bird is looking on;
18 yet they lie in wait—to kill themselves!
and set an ambush—for their own lives!
19 Such is the end[a] of all who are greedy for gain;
it takes away the life of its possessors.

The Call of Wisdom

20 Wisdom cries out in the street;
in the squares she raises her voice.
21 At the busiest corner she cries out;
at the entrance of the city gates she speaks:
22 "How long, O simple ones, will you love being simple?
How long will scoffers delight in their scoffing
and fools hate knowledge?
23 Give heed to my reproof;
I will pour out my thoughts to you;
I will make my words known to you.
24 Because I have called and you refused,
have stretched out my hand and no one heeded,
25 and because you have ignored all my counsel
and would have none of my reproof,
26 I also will laugh at your calamity;
I will mock when panic strikes you,
27 when panic strikes you like a storm,
and your calamity comes like a whirlwind,
when distress and anguish come upon you.
28 Then they will call upon me, but I will not answer;
they will seek me diligently, but will not find me.
29 Because they hated knowledge
and did not choose the fear of the LORD,
30 would have none of my counsel,
and despised all my reproof,
31 therefore they shall eat the fruit of their way
and be sated with their own devices.
32 For waywardness kills the simple,
and the complacency of fools destroys them;
33 but those who listen to me will be secure

1.8 Prov 4.1; 6.20
1.9 Prov 4.9; Gen 41.42
1.10 Deut 13.8; Eph 5.11
1.11 Prov 12.6; v. 18
1.12 Ps 124.3; 28.1
1.15 Ps 1.1; 119.101
1.16 Isa 59.7
1.19 Prov 15.27
1.20 Prov 8.1
1.22 vv. 4,32; Ps 1.1; v. 29
1.23 Joel 2.28
1.24 Isa 65.12; Zech 7.11; Rom 10.21
1.25 Ps 107.11; Lk 7.30; Prov 15.10
1.26 Ps 2.4; Prov 6.15; 10.24
1.28 Isa 1.15; Ezek 8.18; Mic 3.4; Zech 7.13
1.30 Ps 81.11
1.31 Job 4.8; Prov 14.14; Isa 3.11; Jer 6.19
1.32 Jer 2.19
1.33 Ps 25.12

[a] Gk: Heb *ways*

and will live at ease,
without dread of
disaster."

The Value of Wisdom

2 My child, if you accept my
words
and treasure up my
commandments within
you,
2 making your ear attentive to
wisdom
and inclining your heart to
understanding;
3 if you indeed cry out for
insight,
and raise your voice for
understanding;
4 if you seek it like silver,
and search for it as for
hidden treasures—
5 then you will understand the
fear of the LORD
and find the knowledge of
God.
6 For the LORD gives wisdom;
from his mouth come
knowledge and
understanding;
7 he stores up sound wisdom
for the upright;
he is a shield to those who
walk blamelessly,
8 guarding the paths of justice
and preserving the way of
his faithful ones.
9 Then you will understand
righteousness and
justice
and equity, every good
path;
10 for wisdom will come into
your heart,
and knowledge will be
pleasant to your soul;
11 prudence will watch over
you;
and understanding will
guard you.
12 It will save you from the way
of evil,
from those who speak
perversely,
13 who forsake the paths of
uprightness
to walk in the ways of
darkness,
14 who rejoice in doing evil
and delight in the
perverseness of evil;
15 those whose paths are
crooked,
and who are devious in
their ways.

16 You will be saved from the
loose[b] woman,
from the adulteress with
her smooth words,
17 who forsakes the partner of
her youth
and forgets her sacred
covenant;
18 for her way[c] leads down to
death,
and her paths to the
shades;
19 those who go to her never
come back,
nor do they regain the
paths of life.

20 Therefore walk in the way of
the good,
and keep to the paths of
the just.
21 For the upright will abide in
the land,
and the innocent will
remain in it;
22 but the wicked will be cut
off from the land,
and the treacherous will be
rooted out of it.

Admonition to Trust and Honor God

3 My child, do not forget my
teaching,
but let your heart keep my
commandments;
2 for length of days and years
of life
and abundant welfare they
will give you.

3 Do not let loyalty and
faithfulness forsake
you;
bind them around your
neck,

2.1 Prov 4.10
2.2 Prov 3.1
2.4 Prov 3.14; Mt 13.44
2.5 Prov 1.7
2.6 1 Kings 3.9, 12; Jas 1.5
2.7 Ps 84.11
2.8 1 Sam 2.9; Ps 66.9
2.9 Prov 8.20; 4.18
2.10 Prov 14.33; 22.18
2.11 Prov 6.22
2.13 Jn 3.19
2.14 Prov 10.23; Jer 11.15
2.15 Ps 125.5
2.16 Prov 6.24; 23.27
2.17 Mal 2.14,15
2.18 Prov 7.27
2.21 Ps 37.29; 28.10
2.22 Ps 37.38; Deut 28.63
3.1 Prov 4.5; Ex 20.6; Deut 30.16
3.2 Prov 4.10; Ps 119.165
3.3 2 Sam 15.20; Prov 1.9; 7.3

[b] Heb *strange* [c] Cn: Heb *house*

write them on the tablet of
your heart.
4 So you will find favor and
good repute
in the sight of God and of
people.

5 Trust in the LORD with all
your heart,
and do not rely on your
own insight.
6 In all your ways acknowledge
him,
and he will make straight
your paths.
7 Do not be wise in your own
eyes;
fear the LORD, and turn
away from evil.
8 It will be a healing for your
flesh
and a refreshment for your
body.

9 Honor the LORD with your
substance
and with the first fruits of
all your produce;
10 then your barns will be filled
with plenty,
and your vats will be
bursting with wine.

11 My child, do not despise the
LORD's discipline
or be weary of his reproof,
12 for the LORD reproves the one
he loves,
as a father the son in
whom he delights.

The True Wealth

13 Happy are those who find
wisdom,
and those who get
understanding,
14 for her income is better than
silver,
and her revenue better
than gold.
15 She is more precious than
jewels,
and nothing you desire can
compare with her.
16 Long life is in her right
hand;
in her left hand are riches
and honor.
17 Her ways are ways of
pleasantness,
and all her paths are
peace.
18 She is a tree of life to those
who lay hold of her;
those who hold her fast are
called happy.

God's Wisdom in Creation

19 The LORD by wisdom founded
the earth;
by understanding he
established the
heavens;
20 by his knowledge the deeps
broke open,
and the clouds drop down
the dew.

The True Security

21 My child, do not let these
escape from your sight:
keep sound wisdom and
prudence,
22 and they will be life for your
soul
and adornment for your
neck.
23 Then you will walk on your
way securely
and your foot will not
stumble.
24 If you sit down,[d] you will
not be afraid;
when you lie down, your
sleep will be sweet.
25 Do not be afraid of sudden
panic,
or of the storm that strikes
the wicked;
26 for the LORD will be your
confidence
and will keep your foot
from being caught.

27 Do not withhold good from
those to whom it is
due,[e]
when it is in your power to
do it.
28 Do not say to your neighbor,
"Go, and come again,

3.4 Prov 8.5; Ps 111.10
3.5 Ps 37.3,5; Jer 9.23
3.6 1 Chr 28.9; Isa 45.13
3.7 Rom 12.16; Prov 16.6
3.8 Job 21.24
3.9 Isa 43.23; Ex 23.19
3.10 Deut 28.8
3.11 Heb 12.5,6
3.12 Deut 8.5
3.13 Prov 8.32,34
3.14 Job 28.13; Prov 8.10,19
3.15 Job 28.18; Prov 8.11
3.16 Prov 8.18
3.17 Prov 16.7
3.18 Prov 11.30; Gen 2.9
3.19 Ps 104.24
3.20 Gen 7.11; Job 36.28
3.22 Prov 4.22; 1.9
3.23 Prov 4.12
3.24 Ps 3.5
3.25 Ps 91.5; Job 5.21
3.27 Rom 13.7; Gal 6.10
3.28 Lev 19.13

d Gk: Heb *lie down* e Heb *from its owners*

tomorrow I will give
it"—when you have it
with you.
29 Do not plan harm against
your neighbor
who lives trustingly beside
you.
30 Do not quarrel with anyone
without cause,
when no harm has been
done to you.
31 Do not envy the violent
and do not choose any of
their ways;
32 for the perverse are an
abomination to the
LORD,
but the upright are in his
confidence.
33 The LORD's curse is on the
house of the wicked,
but he blesses the abode of
the righteous.
34 Toward the scorners he is
scornful,
but to the humble he
shows favor.
35 The wise will inherit honor,
but stubborn fools,
disgrace.

Parental Advice

4 Listen, children, to a
father's instruction,
and be attentive, that you
may gain[f] insight;
2 for I give you good precepts:
do not forsake my
teaching.
3 When I was a son with my
father,
tender, and my mother's
favorite,
4 he taught me, and said to
me,
"Let your heart hold fast my
words;
keep my commandments,
and live.
5 Get wisdom; get insight: do
not forget, nor turn
away
from the words of my
mouth.
6 Do not forsake her, and she
will keep you;
love her, and she will guard
you.
7 The beginning of wisdom is
this: Get wisdom,
and whatever else you get,
get insight.
8 Prize her highly, and she will
exalt you;
she will honor you if you
embrace her.
9 She will place on your head
a fair garland;
she will bestow on you a
beautiful crown."

Admonition to Keep to the Right Path

10 Hear, my child, and accept
my words,
that the years of your life
may be many.
11 I have taught you the way of
wisdom;
I have led you in the paths
of uprightness.
12 When you walk, your step
will not be hampered;
and if you run, you will not
stumble.
13 Keep hold of instruction; do
not let go;
guard her, for she is your
life.
14 Do not enter the path of the
wicked,
and do not walk in the way
of evildoers.
15 Avoid it; do not go on it;
turn away from it and pass
on.
16 For they cannot sleep unless
they have done wrong;
they are robbed of sleep
unless they have made
someone stumble.
17 For they eat the bread of
wickedness
and drink the wine of
violence.
18 But the path of the righteous
is like the light of
dawn,
which shines brighter and
brighter until full day.

3.29 Prov 14.22 **3.30** Rom 12.18 **3.31** Ps 37.1; Prov 24.1 **3.32** Prov 11.20; Ps 25.14 **3.33** Deut 11.28; Mal 2.2; Job 8.6 **3.34** Jas 4.6; 1 Pet 5.5 **4.1** Prov 1.8; 2.2 **4.3** 1 Chr 22.5 **4.4** 1 Chr 28.9; Prov 7.2 **4.5** v. 7; Prov 16.16 **4.6** 2 Thes 2.10 **4.7** Prov 23.23 **4.8** 1 Sam 2.30 **4.9** Prov 1.9 **4.10** Prov 2.1; 3.2 **4.11** 1 Sam 12.23 **4.12** Ps 18.36; Prov 3.23 **4.14** Ps 1.1; Prov 1.15 **4.16** Ps 36.4; Mic 2.1 **4.18** Isa 26.7; 2 Sam 23.4; Dan 12.3

[f] Heb *know*

19 The way of the wicked is like
deep darkness;
they do not know what
they stumble over.
20 My child, be attentive to my
words;
incline your ear to my
sayings.
21 Do not let them escape from
your sight;
keep them within your
heart.
22 For they are life to those
who find them,
and healing to all their
flesh.
23 Keep your heart with all
vigilance,
for from it flow the springs
of life.
24 Put away from you crooked
speech,
and put devious talk far
from you.
25 Let your eyes look directly
forward,
and your gaze be straight
before you.
26 Keep straight the path of
your feet,
and all your ways will be
sure.
27 Do not swerve to the right or
to the left;
turn your foot away from
evil.

Warning against Impurity and Infidelity

5 My child, be attentive to my
wisdom;
incline your ear to my
understanding,
2 so that you may hold on to
prudence,
and your lips may guard
knowledge.
3 For the lips of a loose[g]
woman drip honey,
and her speech is smoother
than oil;
4 but in the end she is bitter
as wormwood,
sharp as a two-edged
sword.
5 Her feet go down to death;
her steps follow the path to
Sheol.
6 She does not keep straight to
the path of life;
her ways wander, and she
does not know it.

7 And now, my child,[h] listen
to me,
and do not depart from the
words of my mouth.
8 Keep your way far from her,
and do not go near the
door of her house;
9 or you will give your honor
to others,
and your years to the
merciless,
10 and strangers will take their
fill of your wealth,
and your labors will go to
the house of an alien;
11 and at the end of your life
you will groan,
when your flesh and body
are consumed,
12 and you say, "Oh, how I
hated discipline,
and my heart despised
reproof!
13 I did not listen to the voice
of my teachers
or incline my ear to my
instructors.
14 Now I am at the point of
utter ruin
in the public assembly."

15 Drink water from your own
cistern,
flowing water from your
own well.
16 Should your springs be
scattered abroad,
streams of water in the
streets?
17 Let them be for yourself
alone,
and not for sharing with
strangers.
18 Let your fountain be blessed,
and rejoice in the wife of
your youth,
19 a lovely deer, a graceful
doe.

4.19 Job 18.5; Isa 59.9,10; Jer 23.12; Jn 12.35
4.21 Prov 3.21; 7.1,2
4.22 Prov 3.8; 12.18
4.23 Mt 12.34; Mk 7.21; Lk 6.45
4.24 Prov 6.12; 19.1
4.26 Heb 12.13; Ps 119.5
4.27 Deut 5.32; 28.14; Prov 1.15
5.1 Prov 4.20; 22.17
5.2 Mal 2.7
5.3 Prov 2.16; Ps 55.21
5.4 Eccl 7.26; Ps 57.4
5.5 Prov 7.27
5.7 Prov 7.24; Ps 119.102
5.8 Prov 7.25; 9.14
5.12 Prov 1.29; 12.1
5.16 Prov 9.17
5.18 Eccl 9.9; Mal 2.14
5.19 Song 2.9; 4.5; 7.3

g Heb *strange*
h Gk Vg: Heb *children*

May her breasts satisfy you
at all times;
may you be intoxicated
always by her love.
20 Why should you be
intoxicated, my son, by
another woman
and embrace the bosom of
an adulteress?
21 For human ways are under
the eyes of the LORD,
and he examines all their
paths.
22 The iniquities of the wicked
ensnare them,
and they are caught in the
toils of their sin.
23 They die for lack of
discipline,
and because of their great
folly they are lost.

Practical Admonitions

6 My child, if you have given
your pledge to your
neighbor,
if you have bound yourself
to another,[i]
2 you are snared by the
utterance of your lips,[j]
caught by the words of
your mouth.
3 So do this, my child, and
save yourself,
for you have come into
your neighbor's power:
go, hurry,[k] and plead with
your neighbor.
4 Give your eyes no sleep
and your eyelids no
slumber;
5 save yourself like a gazelle
from the hunter,[l]
like a bird from the hand
of the fowler.

6 Go to the ant, you lazybones;
consider its ways, and be
wise.
7 Without having any chief
or officer or ruler,
8 it prepares its food in
summer,
and gathers its sustenance
in harvest.
9 How long will you lie there,
O lazybones?
When will you rise from
your sleep?
10 A little sleep, a little
slumber,
a little folding of the hands
to rest,
11 and poverty will come upon
you like a robber,
and want, like an armed
warrior.

12 A scoundrel and a villain
goes around with crooked
speech,
13 winking the eyes, shuffling
the feet,
pointing the fingers,
14 with perverted mind devising
evil,
continually sowing discord;
15 on such a one calamity will
descend suddenly;
in a moment, damage
beyond repair.

16 There are six things that the
LORD hates,
seven that are an
abomination to him:
17 haughty eyes, a lying tongue,
and hands that shed
innocent blood,
18 a heart that devises wicked
plans,
feet that hurry to run to
evil,
19 a lying witness who testifies
falsely,
and one who sows discord
in a family.

20 My child, keep your father's
commandment,
and do not forsake your
mother's teaching.
21 Bind them upon your heart
always;
tie them around your neck.
22 When you walk, they[m] will
lead you;
when you lie down, they[m]
will watch over you;

5.20 Prov 2.16; 7.5 **5.21** Job 31.4; 34.21; Prov 15.3; Jer 16.17; 32.19; Hos 7.2; Heb 4.13 **5.22** Ps 9.15 **5.23** Job 4.21; 36.12 **6.1** Prov 11.15; 17.18; 20.16; 22.26; 27.13 **6.4** Ps 132.4 **6.5** Ps 91.3 **6.6** Prov 30.24, 25 **6.8** Prov 10.5 **6.9** Prov 24.33 **6.11** Prov 10.4; 13.4; 20.4 **6.12** Prov 16.27; 10.32 **6.13** Ps 35.19; Prov 10.10 **6.14** Mic 2.1; v. 19 **6.15** Prov 24.22; Jer 19.11; 2 Chr 36.16 **6.17** Ps 18.27; 120.2; Isa 1.15 **6.18** Gen 6.5; Prov 1.16 **6.19** Ps 27.12; v. 4 **6.20** Prov 7.1; 1.8 **6.21** Prov 3.3 **6.22** Prov 3.23,24

[i] Or *a stranger* [j] Cn Compare Gk Syr: Heb *the words of your mouth* [k] Or *humble yourself* [l] Cn: Heb *from the hand* [m] Heb *it*

and when you awake,
they[n] will talk with
you.
23 For the commandment is a
lamp and the teaching
a light,
and the reproofs of
discipline are the way
of life,
24 to preserve you from the wife
of another,[o]
from the smooth tongue of
the adulteress.
25 Do not desire her beauty in
your heart,
and do not let her capture
you with her eyelashes;
26 for a prostitute's fee is only a
loaf of bread,[p]
but the wife of another
stalks a man's very life.
27 Can fire be carried in the
bosom
without burning one's
clothes?
28 Or can one walk on hot
coals
without scorching the feet?
29 So is he who sleeps with his
neighbor's wife;
no one who touches her
will go unpunished.
30 Thieves are not despised who
steal only
to satisfy their appetite
when they are hungry.
31 Yet if they are caught, they
will pay sevenfold;
they will forfeit all the
goods of their house.
32 But he who commits
adultery has no sense;
he who does it destroys
himself.
33 He will get wounds and
dishonor,
and his disgrace will not be
wiped away.
34 For jealousy arouses a
husband's fury,
and he shows no restraint
when he takes revenge.
35 He will accept no
compensation,
and refuses a bribe no
matter how great.

6.23 Ps 19.8 **6.24** Prov 2.16; 5.3 **6.25** Mt 5.28 **6.26** Prov 29.3; 7.23; Ezek 13.18 **6.29** Ezek 18.6; 33.26 **6.31** Ex 22.1-4 **6.32** Prov 7.7 **6.34** Prov 27.4; 11.4

7.1 Prov 2.1 **7.2** Prov 4.4; Deut 32.10 **7.3** Deut 6.8; Prov 3.3 **7.5** Prov 2.16; 5.3; 6.24 **7.7** Prov 1.22; 6.32 **7.8** vv. 12,27 **7.9** Job 24.15 **7.11** Prov 9.13; 1 Tim 5.13 **7.12** Prov 23.28

The False Attractions of Adultery

7 My child, keep my words
and store up my
commandments with
you;
2 keep my commandments and
live,
keep my teachings as the
apple of your eye;
3 bind them on your fingers,
write them on the tablet of
your heart.
4 Say to wisdom, "You are my
sister,"
and call insight your
intimate friend,
5 that they may keep you from
the loose[q] woman,
from the adulteress with
her smooth words.

6 For at the window of my
house
I looked out through my
lattice,
7 and I saw among the simple
ones,
I observed among the
youths,
a young man without
sense,
8 passing along the street near
her corner,
taking the road to her
house
9 in the twilight, in the
evening,
at the time of night and
darkness.

10 Then a woman comes toward
him,
decked out like a
prostitute, wily of
heart.[r]
11 She is loud and wayward;
her feet do not stay at
home;
12 now in the street, now in the
squares,
and at every corner she lies
in wait.

[n] Heb *it* [o] Gk: MT *the evil woman*
[p] Cn Compare Gk Syr Vg Tg: Heb *for because of a harlot to a piece of bread*
[q] Heb *strange* [r] Meaning of Heb uncertain

13 She seizes him and kisses
him,
and with impudent face
she says to him:
14 "I had to offer sacrifices,
and today I have paid my
vows;
15 so now I have come out to
meet you,
to seek you eagerly, and I
have found you!
16 I have decked my couch with
coverings,
colored spreads of Egyptian
linen;
17 I have perfumed my bed with
myrrh,
aloes, and cinnamon.
18 Come, let us take our fill of
love until morning;
let us delight ourselves
with love.
19 For my husband is not at
home;
he has gone on a long
journey.
20 He took a bag of money with
him;
he will not come home
until full moon."

21 With much seductive speech
she persuades him;
with her smooth talk she
compels him.
22 Right away he follows her,
and goes like an ox to the
slaughter,
or bounds like a stag toward
the trap[s]
23 until an arrow pierces its
entrails.
He is like a bird rushing into
a snare,
not knowing that it will
cost him his life.

24 And now, my children, listen
to me,
and be attentive to the
words of my mouth.
25 Do not let your hearts turn
aside to her ways;
do not stray into her
paths.
26 for many are those she has
laid low,
and numerous are her
victims.
27 Her house is the way to
Sheol,
going down to the
chambers of death.

7.14 Prov 7.11,16 **7.16** Prov 31.22; Isa 19.9 **7.21** Prov 5.3 **7.23** Eccl 9.12 **7.24** Prov 5.7 **7.25** Prov 5.8 **7.26** Prov 9.18 **7.27** Prov 2.18; 5.5; 9.18 **8.1** Prov 1.20; 9.3 **8.3** Job 29.7 **8.5** Prov 1.4,22, 32 **8.6** Prov 22.20; 23.16 **8.7** Ps 37.30 **8.9** Prov 14.6; 3.13 **8.10** Prov 3.14,15 **8.11** Job 28.18; Prov 3.15 **8.12** v. 5; Prov 1.4

The Gifts of Wisdom

8 Does not wisdom call,
and does not
understanding raise her
voice?
2 On the heights, beside the
way,
at the crossroads she takes
her stand;
3 beside the gates in front of
the town,
at the entrance of the
portals she cries out:
4 "To you, O people, I call,
and my cry is to all that
live.
5 O simple ones, learn
prudence;
acquire intelligence, you
who lack it.
6 Hear, for I will speak noble
things,
and from my lips will come
what is right;
7 for my mouth will utter
truth;
wickedness is an
abomination to my lips.
8 All the words of my mouth
are righteous;
there is nothing twisted or
crooked in them.
9 They are all straight to one
who understands
and right to those who find
knowledge.
10 Take my instruction instead
of silver,
and knowledge rather than
choice gold;
11 for wisdom is better than
jewels,
and all that you may desire
cannot compare with
her.
12 I, wisdom, live with
prudence,[t]

[s] Cn Compare Gk: Meaning of Heb uncertain
[t] Meaning of Heb uncertain

and I attain knowledge and discretion.
13 The fear of the LORD is hatred of evil.
Pride and arrogance and the way of evil
and perverted speech I hate.
14 I have good advice and sound wisdom;
I have insight, I have strength.
15 By me kings reign,
and rulers decree what is just;
16 by me rulers rule,
and nobles, all who govern rightly.
17 I love those who love me,
and those who seek me diligently find me.
18 Riches and honor are with me,
enduring wealth and prosperity.
19 My fruit is better than gold, even fine gold,
and my yield than choice silver.
20 I walk in the way of righteousness,
along the paths of justice,
21 endowing with wealth those who love me,
and filling their treasuries.

Wisdom's Part in Creation

22 The LORD created me at the beginning[u] of his work,[v]
the first of his acts of long ago.
23 Ages ago I was set up,
at the first, before the beginning of the earth.
24 When there were no depths I was brought forth,
when there were no springs abounding with water.
25 Before the mountains had been shaped,
before the hills, I was brought forth—
26 when he had not yet made earth and fields,[w]
or the world's first bits of soil.
27 When he established the heavens, I was there,
when he drew a circle on the face of the deep,
28 when he made firm the skies above,
when he established the fountains of the deep,
29 when he assigned to the sea its limit,
so that the waters might not transgress his command,
when he marked out the foundations of the earth,
30 then I was beside him, like a master worker;[x]
and I was daily his[y] delight,
rejoicing before him always,
31 rejoicing in his inhabited world
and delighting in the human race.

32 And now, my children, listen to me:
happy are those who keep my ways.
33 Hear instruction and be wise,
and do not neglect it.
34 Happy is the one who listens to me,
watching daily at my gates,
waiting beside my doors.
35 For whoever finds me finds life
and obtains favor from the LORD;
36 but those who miss me injure themselves;
all who hate me love death."

Wisdom's Feast

9 Wisdom has built her house,
she has hewn her seven pillars.
2 She has slaughtered her animals, she has mixed her wine,

8.13 Prov 16.6; 16.18; 15.9; 6.12 **8.14** Prov 1.25; 2.7; Eccl 7.19 **8.15** Dan 2.21; Rom 13.1 **8.17** 1 Sam 2.30; Ps 91.14; Jn 14.21; Jas 1.5 **8.18** Prov 3.16; Mt 6.33 **8.19** Prov 3.14; 10.20 **8.21** Prov 24.4 **8.22** Prov 3.19 **8.23** Jn 17.5 **8.25** Ps 90.2 **8.27** Prov 3.19; Job 26.10 **8.29** Job 38.10; Ps 104.9; Job 38.6 **8.30** Jn 1.1-3 **8.31** Ps 16.3 **8.32** Prov 5.7; Ps 119.1,2; Lk 11.28 **8.33** Prov 4.1 **8.34** Prov 3.13,18 **8.35** Prov 4.22; 12.2 **8.36** Prov 20.2 **9.1** Mt 16.18; Eph 2.20, 22; 1 Pet 2.5 **9.2** Mt 22.4; Lk 14.16,17

[u] Or *me as the beginning* [v] Heb *way* [w] Meaning of Heb uncertain [x] Another reading is *little child* [y] Gk: Heb lacks *his*

she has also set her table.
3 She has sent out her
servant-girls, she calls
from the highest places in
the town,
4 "You that are simple, turn in
here!"
To those without sense she
says,
5 "Come, eat of my bread
and drink of the wine I
have mixed.
6 Lay aside immaturity,[z] and
live,
and walk in the way of
insight."

General Maxims

7 Whoever corrects a scoffer
wins abuse;
whoever rebukes the
wicked gets hurt.
8 A scoffer who is rebuked will
only hate you;
the wise, when rebuked,
will love you.
9 Give instruction[a] to the
wise, and they will
become wiser still;
teach the righteous and
they will gain in
learning.
10 The fear of the LORD is the
beginning of wisdom,
and the knowledge of the
Holy One is insight.
11 For by me your days will be
multiplied,
and years will be added to
your life.
12 If you are wise, you are wise
for yourself;
if you scoff, you alone will
bear it.

Folly's Invitation and Promise

13 The foolish woman is loud;
she is ignorant and knows
nothing.
14 She sits at the door of her
house,
on a seat at the high places
of the town,
15 calling to those who pass by,
who are going straight on
their way,
16 "You who are simple, turn in
here!"
And to those without sense
she says,
17 "Stolen water is sweet,
and bread eaten in secret
is pleasant."
18 But they do not know that
the dead[b] are there,
that her guests are in the
depths of Sheol.

Wise Sayings of Solomon

10 The proverbs of Solomon.

A wise child makes a glad
father,
but a foolish child is a
mother's grief.
2 Treasures gained by
wickedness do not
profit,
but righteousness delivers
from death.
3 The LORD does not let the
righteous go hungry,
but he thwarts the craving
of the wicked.
4 A slack hand causes poverty,
but the hand of the
diligent makes rich.
5 A child who gathers in
summer is prudent,
but a child who sleeps in
harvest brings shame.
6 Blessings are on the head of
the righteous,
but the mouth of the
wicked conceals
violence.
7 The memory of the righteous
is a blessing,
but the name of the wicked
will rot.
8 The wise of heart will heed
commandments,
but a babbling fool will
come to ruin.
9 Whoever walks in integrity
walks securely,
but whoever follows
perverse ways will be
found out.

9.3 Ps 68.11; Mt 22.3; Prov 8.1,2
9.4 Prov 8.5; 6.32
9.5 Song 5.1; Isa 55.1; Jn 6.27
9.6 Ezek 11.20; 37.24
9.7 Prov 23.9
9.8 Mt 7.6; Ps 141.5
9.9 Prov 1.5
9.10 Job 28.28; Prov 1.7
9.11 Prov 3.16; 10.27
9.12 Prov 19.29
9.13 Prov 7.11; 5.6
9.14 v. 3
9.16 v. 4
9.17 Prov 20.17
9.18 Prov 7.27
10.1 Prov 1.1; 15.20; 29.3, 15
10.2 Ps 49.6; Prov 11.4; Lk 12.19,20; Prov 11.4,6
10.3 Ps 34.9,10; Mt 6.33; Ps 112.10
10.4 Prov 12.24; 13.4
10.5 Prov 6.8; 17.2
10.6 Esther 7.8
10.7 Ps 9.5,6; Eccl 8.10
10.8 Prov 13.3
10.9 Ps 23.4; Prov 28.18; Isa 33.15; Prov 26.26

[z] Or *simpleness* [a] Heb lacks *instruction*
[b] Heb *shades*

10 Whoever winks the eye
causes trouble,
but the one who rebukes
boldly makes peace.[c]
11 The mouth of the righteous
is a fountain of life,
but the mouth of the
wicked conceals
violence.
12 Hatred stirs up strife,
but love covers all offenses.
13 On the lips of one who has
understanding wisdom
is found,
but a rod is for the back of
one who lacks sense.
14 The wise lay up knowledge,
but the babbling of a fool
brings ruin near.
15 The wealth of the rich is
their fortress;
the poverty of the poor is
their ruin.
16 The wage of the righteous
leads to life,
the gain of the wicked to
sin.
17 Whoever heeds instruction is
on the path to life,
but one who rejects a
rebuke goes astray.
18 Lying lips conceal hatred,
and whoever utters slander
is a fool.
19 When words are many,
transgression is not
lacking,
but the prudent are
restrained in speech.
20 The tongue of the righteous
is choice silver;
the mind of the wicked is
of little worth.
21 The lips of the righteous
feed many,
but fools die for lack of
sense.
22 The blessing of the LORD
makes rich,
and he adds no sorrow with
it.[d]
23 Doing wrong is like sport to
a fool,
but wise conduct is
pleasure to a person of
understanding.

10.10 Prov 6.13
10.11 Ps 37.30
10.12 1 Pet 4.8
10.13 Prov 26.3
10.14 Prov 9.9; 18.7
10.15 Job 31.24; Ps 52.7; Prov 18.11; 19.7
10.17 Prov 6.23
10.18 Prov 26.24; Ps 15.3
10.19 Prov 18.21; Eccl 5.3; Jas 3.2
10.20 Prov 8.19
10.21 v. 11; Prov 5.23
10.22 Gen 24.35; Ps 37.22
10.23 Prov 15.21
10.24 Ps 145.19; Mt 5.6; 1 Jn 5.14, 15
10.25 Prov 12.7; Ps 15.5; Mt 7.24; 16.18
10.26 Prov 26.6
10.27 Prov 9.11; Ps 55.23
10.29 Ps 28.8; Prov 21.15
10.30 Ps 37.29
10.31 Ps 37.30; Prov 17.20
11.1 Lev 19.35; Deut 25.13-16
11.2 Prov 16.18
11.3 Prov 13.6

24 What the wicked dread will
come upon them,
but the desire of the
righteous will be
granted.
25 When the tempest passes,
the wicked are no more,
but the righteous are
established forever.
26 Like vinegar to the teeth,
and smoke to the eyes,
so are the lazy to their
employers.
27 The fear of the LORD prolongs
life,
but the years of the wicked
will be short.
28 The hope of the righteous
ends in gladness,
but the expectation of the
wicked comes to
nothing.
29 The way of the LORD is a
stronghold for the
upright,
but destruction for
evildoers.
30 The righteous will never be
removed,
but the wicked will not
remain in the land.
31 The mouth of the righteous
brings forth wisdom,
but the perverse tongue
will be cut off.
32 The lips of the righteous
know what is
acceptable,
but the mouth of the
wicked what is
perverse.

11 A false balance is an
abomination to the
LORD,
but an accurate weight is
his delight.
2 When pride comes, then
comes disgrace;
but wisdom is with the
humble.
3 The integrity of the upright
guides them,

[c] Gk: Heb *but a babbling fool will come to ruin* [d] Or *and toil adds nothing to it*

but the crookedness of the
treacherous destroys
them.
4 Riches do not profit in the
day of wrath,
but righteousness delivers
from death.
5 The righteousness of the
blameless keeps their
ways straight,
but the wicked fall by their
own wickedness.
6 The righteousness of the
upright saves them,
but the treacherous are
taken captive by their
schemes.
7 When the wicked die, their
hope perishes,
and the expectation of the
godless comes to
nothing.
8 The righteous are delivered
from trouble,
and the wicked get into it
instead.
9 With their mouths the
godless would destroy
their neighbors,
but by knowledge the
righteous are delivered.
10 When it goes well with the
righteous, the city
rejoices;
and when the wicked
perish, there is
jubilation.
11 By the blessing of the
upright a city is
exalted,
but it is overthrown by the
mouth of the wicked.
12 Whoever belittles another
lacks sense,
but an intelligent person
remains silent.
13 A gossip goes about telling
secrets,
but one who is trustworthy
in spirit keeps a
confidence.
14 Where there is no guidance,
a nation[e] falls,
but in an abundance of
counselors there is
safety.

11.4 Ezek 7.19; Zeph 1.18; Gen 7.1
11.6 Eccl 10.8
11.7 Prov 10.28
11.8 Prov 21.18
11.10 Prov 28.12
11.11 Prov 29.8
11.12 Prov 14.21; 10.19
11.13 Lev 19.16; Prov 20.19; 1 Tim 5.13; Prov 19.11
11.14 Prov 15.22; 20.18; 24.6
11.16 Prov 31.30
11.17 Mt 5.7; 25.34-36
11.18 Hos 10.12; Gal 6.8,9
11.20 Prov 12.22; Ps 119.1
11.21 Prov 16.5; Ps 112.2
11.23 Rom 2.8,9
11.24 Prov 13.7; 19.17
11.25 2 Cor 9.6-10; Mt 5.7
11.26 Am 8.5,6; Job 29.13

15 To guarantee loans for a
stranger brings trouble,
but there is safety in
refusing to do so.
16 A gracious woman gets honor.
but she who hates virtue is
covered with shame.[f]
The timid become
destitute,[g]
but the aggressive gain
riches.
17 Those who are kind reward
themselves,
but the cruel do
themselves harm.
18 The wicked earn no real
gain,
but those who sow
righteousness get a true
reward.
19 Whoever is steadfast in
righteousness will live,
but whoever pursues evil
will die.
20 Crooked minds are an
abomination to the
LORD,
but those of blameless
ways are his delight.
21 Be assured, the wicked will
not go unpunished,
but those who are
righteous will escape.
22 Like a gold ring in a pig's
snout
is a beautiful woman
without good sense.
23 The desire of the righteous
ends only in good;
the expectation of the
wicked in wrath.
24 Some give freely, yet grow all
the richer;
others withhold what is
due, and only suffer
want.
25 A generous person will be
enriched,
and one who gives water
will get water.
26 The people curse those who
hold back grain,
but a blessing is on the
head of those who sell it.

[e] Or *an army* [f] Compare Gk Syr: Heb lacks *but she . . . shame* [g] Gk: Heb lacks *The timid . . . destitute*

27 Whoever diligently seeks good seeks favor,
but evil comes to the one who searches for it.
28 Those who trust in their riches will wither,[h]
but the righteous will flourish like green leaves.
29 Those who trouble their households will inherit wind,
and the fool will be servant to the wise.
30 The fruit of the righteous is a tree of life,
but violence[i] takes lives away.
31 If the righteous are repaid on earth,
how much more the wicked and the sinner!

12 Whoever loves discipline loves knowledge,
but those who hate to be rebuked are stupid.
2 The good obtain favor from the LORD,
but those who devise evil he condemns.
3 No one finds security by wickedness,
but the root of the righteous will never be moved.
4 A good wife is the crown of her husband,
but she who brings shame is like rottenness in his bones.
5 The thoughts of the righteous are just;
the advice of the wicked is treacherous.
6 The words of the wicked are a deadly ambush,
but the speech of the upright delivers them.
7 The wicked are overthrown and are no more,
but the house of the righteous will stand.
8 One is commended for good sense,
but a perverse mind is despised.
9 Better to be despised and have a servant,
than to be self-important and lack food.
10 The righteous know the needs of their animals,
but the mercy of the wicked is cruel.
11 Those who till their land will have plenty of food,
but those who follow worthless pursuits have no sense.
12 The wicked covet the proceeds of wickedness,[j]
but the root of the righteous bears fruit.
13 The evil are ensnared by the transgression of their lips,
but the righteous escape from trouble.
14 From the fruit of the mouth one is filled with good things,
and manual labor has its reward.
15 Fools think their own way is right,
but the wise listen to advice.
16 Fools show their anger at once,
but the prudent ignore an insult.
17 Whoever speaks the truth gives honest evidence,
but a false witness speaks deceitfully.
18 Rash words are like sword thrusts,
but the tongue of the wise brings healing.
19 Truthful lips endure forever,
but a lying tongue lasts only a moment.
20 Deceit is in the mind of those who plan evil,
but those who counsel peace have joy.
21 No harm happens to the righteous,

11.27 Esther 7.10; Ps 7.15; 10.2
11.28 Ps 52.7; Mk 10.24; 1 Tim 6.17; Ps 1.3; Jer 17.8
11.30 1 Cor 9.19; Jas 5.20
11.31 Prov 13.21; 2 Sam 22.21, 25
12.1 Prov 9.8; 15.10
12.2 Prov 8.35
12.3 Prov 10.25
12.4 Prov 31.23; 1 Cor 11.7; Prov 14.30
12.6 Prov 1.11; 14.3
12.7 Ps 37.36; Mt 7.24
12.10 Deut 25.4
12.11 Prov 28.19; Judg 9.4
12.13 Prov 18.7; 2 Pet 2.9
12.14 Prov 13.2; Job 34.11; Isa 3.10,11
12.15 Prov 14.12; Lk 18.11
12.16 Prov 29.11
12.17 Prov 14.5
12.18 Ps 57.4
12.19 Ps 52.5
12.20 v. 5
12.21 Ps 91.10; 1 Pet 3.13; Prov 14.14

h Cn: Heb *fall*
i Cn Compare Gk Syr: Heb *a wise man*
j Or *covet the catch of the wicked*

but the wicked are filled
with trouble.
22 Lying lips are an
abomination to the
LORD,
but those who act faithfully
are his delight.
23 One who is clever conceals
knowledge,
but the mind of a fool[k]
broadcasts folly.
24 The hand of the diligent will
rule,
while the lazy will be put
to forced labor.
25 Anxiety weighs down the
human heart,
but a good word cheers it
up.
26 The righteous gives good
advice to friends,[l]
but the way of the wicked
leads astray.
27 The lazy do not roast[m] their
game,
but the diligent obtain
precious wealth.[m]
28 In the path of righteousness
there is life,
in walking its path there is
no death.

13 A wise child loves
discipline,[n]
but a scoffer does not
listen to rebuke.
2 From the fruit of their words
good persons eat good
things,
but the desire of the
treacherous is for
wrongdoing.
3 Those who guard their
mouths preserve their
lives;
those who open wide their
lips come to ruin.
4 The appetite of the lazy
craves, and gets
nothing,
while the appetite of the
diligent is richly
supplied.
5 The righteous hate
falsehood,
but the wicked act
shamefully and
disgracefully.

12.22 Prov 6.17; 11.20; Rev 22.15 **12.23** Prov 13.16; 15.2 **12.25** Prov 15.13; Isa 50.4 **12.28** Prov 11.19 **13.1** Prov 10.1; 15.12 **13.2** Prov 12.14 **13.3** Ps 39.1; Jas 3.2 **13.4** Prov 10.4

13.6 Prov 11.3,5 **13.7** Prov 11.24; Lk 12.20,21, 33; 2 Cor 6.10 **13.9** Job 18.5; Prov 24.20 **13.10** Prov 11.14 **13.11** Prov 10.2; 14.23 **13.12** v. 19 **13.13** 2 Chr 36.16 **13.14** Prov 10.11; Ps 18.5 **13.15** Prov 3.4; 21.8 **13.16** Prov 12.23; 15.2 **13.17** Prov 25.13 **13.18** Prov 15.5, 31,32

6 Righteousness guards one
whose way is upright,
but sin overthrows the
wicked.
7 Some pretend to be rich, yet
have nothing;
others pretend to be poor,
yet have great wealth.
8 Wealth is a ransom for a
person's life,
but the poor get no threats.
9 The light of the righteous
rejoices,
but the lamp of the wicked
goes out.
10 By insolence the heedless
make strife,
but wisdom is with those
who take advice.
11 Wealth hastily gotten[o] will
dwindle,
but those who gather little
by little will increase it.
12 Hope deferred makes the
heart sick,
but a desire fulfilled is a
tree of life.
13 Those who despise the word
bring destruction on
themselves,
but those who respect the
commandment will be
rewarded.
14 The teaching of the wise is a
fountain of life,
so that one may avoid the
snares of death.
15 Good sense wins favor,
but the way of the faithless
is their ruin.[p]
16 The clever do all things
intelligently,
but the fool displays folly.
17 A bad messenger brings
trouble,
but a faithful envoy,
healing.
18 Poverty and disgrace are for
the one who ignores
instruction,
but one who heeds reproof
is honored.

[k] Heb *the heart of fools* [l] Syr: Meaning of Heb uncertain [m] Meaning of Heb uncertain [n] Cn: Heb *A wise child the discipline of his father* [o] Gk Vg: Heb *from vanity* [p] Cn Compare Gk Syr Vg Tg: Heb *is enduring*

19 A desire realized is sweet to the soul,
but to turn away from evil is an abomination to fools.
20 Whoever walks with the wise becomes wise,
but the companion of fools suffers harm.
21 Misfortune pursues sinners,
but prosperity rewards the righteous.
22 The good leave an inheritance to their children's children,
but the sinner's wealth is laid up for the righteous.
23 The field of the poor may yield much food,
but it is swept away through injustice.
24 Those who spare the rod hate their children,
but those who love them are diligent to discipline them.
25 The righteous have enough to satisfy their appetite,
but the belly of the wicked is empty.

14 The wise woman[q] builds her house,
but the foolish tears it down with her own hands.
2 Those who walk uprightly fear the LORD,
but one who is devious in conduct despises him.
3 The talk of fools is a rod for their backs,[r]
but the lips of the wise preserve them.
4 Where there are no oxen, there is no grain;
abundant crops come by the strength of the ox.
5 A faithful witness does not lie,
but a false witness breathes out lies.
6 A scoffer seeks wisdom in vain,
but knowledge is easy for one who understands.
7 Leave the presence of a fool,
for there you do not find words of knowledge.
8 It is the wisdom of the clever to understand where they go,
but the folly of fools misleads.
9 Fools mock at the guilt offering,[s]
but the upright enjoy God's favor.
10 The heart knows its own bitterness,
and no stranger shares its joy.
11 The house of the wicked is destroyed,
but the tent of the upright flourishes.
12 There is a way that seems right to a person,
but its end is the way to death.[t]
13 Even in laughter the heart is sad,
and the end of joy is grief.
14 The perverse get what their ways deserve,
and the good, what their deeds deserve.[u]
15 The simple believe everything,
but the clever consider their steps.
16 The wise are cautious and turn away from evil,
but the fool throws off restraint and is careless.
17 One who is quick-tempered acts foolishly,
and the schemer is hated.
18 The simple are adorned with[v] folly,
but the clever are crowned with knowledge.
19 The evil bow down before the good,
the wicked at the gates of the righteous.
20 The poor are disliked even by their neighbors,
but the rich have many friends.

13.20 Prov 15.31; 28.19
13.21 Ps 32.10
13.22 Job 27.16, 17; Prov 28.8; Eccl 2.26
13.23 Prov 12.11
13.24 Prov 19.18; 22.15; 29.15, 17
13.25 Ps 34.10; 37.3
14.1 Prov 24.3
14.2 Prov 19.1; Rom 2.4
14.3 Prov 12.6
14.5 Ex 20.16; Prov 6.19; 12.17
14.6 Prov 24.7; 8.9; 17.24
14.8 Prov 15.21; v. 24
14.11 Prov 3.33; 12.7; 15.25
14.12 Prov 16.25; Rom 6.21
14.13 Prov 5.4; Eccl 2.2
14.14 Prov 1.31; 12.14
14.16 Prov 22.3
14.17 v. 29
14.18 Prov 18.15
14.19 Prov 11.29
14.20 Prov 19.7

[q] Heb *Wisdom of women* [r] Cn: Heb *a rod of pride* [s] Meaning of Heb uncertain [t] Heb *ways of death* [u] Cn: Heb *from upon him* [v] Or *inherit*

21 Those who despise their
neighbors are sinners,
but happy are those who
are kind to the poor.
22 Do they not err that plan
evil?
Those who plan good find
loyalty and faithfulness.
23 In all toil there is profit,
but mere talk leads only to
poverty.
24 The crown of the wise is
their wisdom,[w]
but folly is the garland[x] of
fools.
25 A truthful witness saves
lives,
but one who utters lies is a
betrayer.
26 In the fear of the LORD one
has strong confidence,
and one's children will
have a refuge.
27 The fear of the LORD is a
fountain of life,
so that one may avoid the
snares of death.
28 The glory of a king is a
multitude of people;
without people a prince is
ruined.
29 Whoever is slow to anger has
great understanding,
but one who has a hasty
temper exalts folly.
30 A tranquil mind gives life to
the flesh,
but passion makes the
bones rot.
31 Those who oppress the poor
insult their Maker,
but those who are kind to
the needy honor him.
32 The wicked are overthrown
by their evildoing,
but the righteous find a
refuge in their
integrity.[y]
33 Wisdom is at home in the
mind of one who has
understanding,
but it is not[z] known in the
heart of fools.
34 Righteousness exalts a
nation,
but sin is a reproach to any
people.
35 A servant who deals wisely
has the king's favor,
but his wrath falls on one
who acts shamefully.

15 A soft answer turns away
wrath,
but a harsh word stirs up
anger.
2 The tongue of the wise
dispenses knowledge,[a]
but the mouths of fools
pour out folly.
3 The eyes of the LORD are in
every place,
keeping watch on the evil
and the good.
4 A gentle tongue is a tree of
life,
but perverseness in it
breaks the spirit.
5 A fool despises a parent's
instruction,
but the one who heeds
admonition is prudent.
6 In the house of the righteous
there is much treasure,
but trouble befalls the
income of the wicked.
7 The lips of the wise spread
knowledge;
not so the minds of fools.
8 The sacrifice of the wicked is
an abomination to the
LORD,
but the prayer of the
upright is his delight.
9 The way of the wicked is an
abomination to the
LORD,
but he loves the one who
pursues righteousness.
10 There is severe discipline for
one who forsakes the
way,
but one who hates a
rebuke will die.
11 Sheol and Abaddon lie open
before the LORD,
how much more human
hearts!
12 Scoffers do not like to be
rebuked;

14.21 Prov 11.12; Ps 41.1
14.25 v. 5
14.26 Prov 19.23; Isa 33.6
14.27 Prov 13.14
14.29 Prov 16.32; Jas 1.19; Prov 29.20
14.30 Prov 12.4
14.31 Prov 17.5; v. 21
14.32 Job 13.15; Ps 23.4; 2 Cor 1.9; 2 Tim 4.18
14.33 Prov 2.10; 12.16
14.34 Prov 11.11
14.35 Mt 24.45
15.1 Judg 8.1-3; 1 Sam 25.10-13
15.2 Prov 12.23; 13.16
15.3 Job 34.21; Heb 4.13
15.5 Prov 13.1,18
15.8 Isa 1.11; Jer 6.20; Mic 6.7
15.9 Prov 21.21; 1 Tim 6.11
15.10 Prov 1.29-32; 5.12
15.11 Job 26.6; Ps 139.8; 2 Chr 6.30
15.12 Prov 13.1; Am 5.10

[w] Cn Compare Gk: Heb *riches* [x] Cn: Heb *is the folly* [y] Gk Syr: Heb *in their death* [z] Gk Syr: Heb lacks *not* [a] Cn: Heb *makes knowledge good*

they will not go to the
wise.
13 A glad heart makes a
cheerful countenance,
but by sorrow of heart the
spirit is broken.
14 The mind of one who has
understanding seeks
knowledge,
but the mouths of fools
feed on folly.
15 All the days of the poor are
hard,
but a cheerful heart has a
continual feast.
16 Better is a little with the fear
of the LORD
than great treasure and
trouble with it.
17 Better is a dinner of
vegetables where love is
than a fatted ox and hatred
with it.
18 Those who are hot-tempered
stir up strife,
but those who are slow to
anger calm contention.
19 The way of the lazy is
overgrown with thorns,
but the path of the upright
is a level highway.
20 A wise child makes a glad
father,
but the foolish despise
their mothers.
21 Folly is a joy to one who has
no sense,
but a person of
understanding walks
straight ahead.
22 Without counsel, plans go
wrong,
but with many advisers
they succeed.
23 To make an apt answer is a
joy to anyone,
and a word in season, how
good it is!
24 For the wise the path of life
leads upward,
in order to avoid Sheol
below.
25 The LORD tears down the
house of the proud,
but maintains the widow's
boundaries.

15.13 Prov 17.22; 12.25
15.15 v. 13
15.16 Ps 37.16; Prov 16.8; 1 Tim 6.6
15.17 Prov 17.1
15.18 Prov 26.21; 29.22; 14.29
15.19 Prov 22.5
15.20 Prov 10.1; 30.17
15.21 Prov 10.23; Eph 5.15
15.22 Prov 11.14; 20.18
15.23 Prov 25.11
15.24 Prov 4.18
15.25 Prov 12.7; Ps 68.5,6
15.26 Prov 6.16-19; 16.24
15.27 Prov 28.25; 1 Tim 6.10; Isa 33.15
15.28 1 Pet 3.15
15.29 Ps 34.16; 145.18
15.31 v. 5
15.32 Prov 1.7; 8.36; 15.5
15.33 Prov 1.7; 18.12
16.1 Prov 19.21
16.2 Prov 21.2
16.3 Ps 37.5
16.4 Isa 43.7; Job 21.30
16.5 Prov 6.17; 11.21

26 Evil plans are an
abomination to the
LORD,
but gracious words are
pure.
27 Those who are greedy for
unjust gain make
trouble for their
households,
but those who hate bribes
will live.
28 The mind of the righteous
ponders how to answer,
but the mouth of the
wicked pours out evil.
29 The LORD is far from the
wicked,
but he hears the prayer of
the righteous.
30 The light of the eyes rejoices
the heart,
and good news refreshes
the body.
31 The ear that heeds
wholesome admonition
will lodge among the wise.
32 Those who ignore instruction
despise themselves,
but those who heed
admonition gain
understanding.
33 The fear of the LORD is
instruction in wisdom,
and humility goes before
honor.

16 The plans of the mind
belong to mortals,
but the answer of the
tongue is from the
LORD.
2 All one's ways may be pure
in one's own eyes,
but the LORD weighs the
spirit.
3 Commit your work to the
LORD,
and your plans will be
established.
4 The LORD has made
everything for its
purpose,
even the wicked for the day
of trouble.
5 All those who are arrogant
are an abomination to
the LORD;

be assured, they will not go
unpunished.
6 By loyalty and faithfulness
iniquity is atoned for,
and by the fear of the LORD
one avoids evil.
7 When the ways of people
please the LORD,
he causes even their
enemies to be at peace
with them.
8 Better is a little with
righteousness
than large income with
injustice.
9 The human mind plans the
way,
but the LORD directs the
steps.
10 Inspired decisions are on the
lips of a king;
his mouth does not sin in
judgment.
11 Honest balances and scales
are the LORD's;
all the weights in the bag
are his work.
12 It is an abomination to kings
to do evil,
for the throne is
established by
righteousness.
13 Righteous lips are the delight
of a king,
and he loves those who
speak what is right.
14 A king's wrath is a
messenger of death,
and whoever is wise will
appease it.
15 In the light of a king's face
there is life,
and his favor is like the
clouds that bring the
spring rain.
16 How much better to get
wisdom than gold!
To get understanding is to
be chosen rather than
silver.
17 The highway of the upright
avoids evil;
those who guard their way
preserve their lives.
18 Pride goes before
destruction,
and a haughty spirit before
a fall.
19 It is better to be of a lowly
spirit among the poor
than to divide the spoil
with the proud.
20 Those who are attentive to a
matter will prosper,
and happy are those who
trust in the LORD.
21 The wise of heart is called
perceptive,
and pleasant speech
increases
persuasiveness.
22 Wisdom is a fountain of life
to one who has it,
but folly is the punishment
of fools.
23 The mind of the wise makes
their speech judicious,
and adds persuasiveness to
their lips.
24 Pleasant words are like a
honeycomb,
sweetness to the soul and
health to the body.
25 Sometimes there is a way
that seems to be right,
but in the end it is the way
to death.
26 The appetite of workers
works for them;
their hunger urges them
on.
27 Scoundrels concoct evil,
and their speech is like a
scorching fire.
28 A perverse person spreads
strife,
and a whisperer separates
close friends.
29 The violent entice their
neighbors,
and lead them in a way
that is not good.
30 One who winks the eyes
plans[b] perverse things;
one who compresses the
lips brings evil to pass.
31 Gray hair is a crown of glory;
it is gained in a righteous
life.
32 One who is slow to anger is
better than the mighty,

16.6 Dan 4.27; Prov 14.16 **16.7** 2 Chr 17.10 **16.9** Ps 37.23; Prov 20.24; Jer 10.23 **16.11** Prov 11.1 **16.12** Prov 25.5 **16.13** Prov 14.35 **16.14** Prov 19.12 **16.15** Job 29.23 **16.16** Prov 8.10,19 **16.18** Prov 11.2

16.20 Ps 2.12; 34.8; Jer 17.7 **16.22** Prov 13.14; 7.22 **16.23** Prov 37.30 **16.25** Prov 14.12 **16.27** Prov 6.12, 14,18; Jas 3.6 **16.28** Prov 15.18; 17.9 **16.29** Prov 1.10 **16.31** Prov 20.29 **16.32** Prov 19.11

b Gk Syr Vg Tg: Heb *to plan*

and one whose temper is
controlled than one
who captures a city.
33 The lot is cast into the lap,
but the decision is the
LORD's alone.

17

Better is a dry morsel
with quiet
than a house full of
feasting with strife.
2 A slave who deals wisely will
rule over a child who
acts shamefully,
and will share the
inheritance as one of
the family.
3 The crucible is for silver, and
the furnace is for gold,
but the LORD tests the
heart.
4 An evildoer listens to wicked
lips;
and a liar gives heed to a
mischievous tongue.
5 Those who mock the poor
insult their Maker;
those who are glad at
calamity will not go
unpunished.
6 Grandchildren are the crown
of the aged,
and the glory of children is
their parents.
7 Fine speech is not becoming
to a fool;
still less is false speech to
a ruler.[c]
8 A bribe is like a magic stone
in the eyes of those
who give it;
wherever they turn they
prosper.
9 One who forgives an affront
fosters friendship,
but one who dwells on
disputes will alienate a
friend.
10 A rebuke strikes deeper into
a discerning person
than a hundred blows into
a fool.
11 Evil people seek only
rebellion,
but a cruel messenger will
be sent against them.
12 Better to meet a she-bear
robbed of its cubs

17.1 Prov 15.17
17.2 Prov 10.5
17.3 Prov 27.21; Ps 26.2
17.5 Prov 14.31; Job 31.29
17.6 Prov 13.22
17.8 Prov 21.14; Isa 1.23; Am 5.12
17.9 Prov 10.12; Jas 5.20; 1 Pet 4.8; Prov 16.28
17.12 Hos 13.8
17.13 Ps 109.4,5; Jer 18.20
17.14 Prov 20.3
17.15 Ex 23.7; Isa 5.23
17.17 Ruth 1.16; Prov 18.24
17.18 Prov 6.1
17.19 Prov 29.22; 16.18
17.20 Jas 3.8
17.21 Prov 10.1; 19.13
17.22 Prov 15.13; Ps 22.15
17.23 Ex 23.8
17.24 Eccl 2.14
17.25 Prov 10.1

than to confront a fool
immersed in folly.
13 Evil will not depart from the
house
of one who returns evil for
good.
14 The beginning of strife is like
letting out water;
so stop before the quarrel
breaks out.
15 One who justifies the wicked
and one who condemns
the righteous
are both alike an
abomination to the
LORD.
16 Why should fools have a
price in hand
to buy wisdom, when they
have no mind to learn?
17 A friend loves at all times,
and kinsfolk are born to
share adversity.
18 It is senseless to give a
pledge,
to become surety for a
neighbor.
19 One who loves transgression
loves strife;
one who builds a high
threshold invites broken
bones.
20 The crooked of mind do not
prosper,
and the perverse of tongue
fall into calamity.
21 The one who begets a fool
gets trouble;
the parent of a fool has no
joy.
22 A cheerful heart is a good
medicine,
but a downcast spirit dries
up the bones.
23 The wicked accept a
concealed bribe
to pervert the ways of
justice.
24 The discerning person looks
to wisdom,
but the eyes of a fool to
the ends of the earth.
25 Foolish children are a grief
to their father

[c] Or *a noble person*

and bitterness to her who
bore them.
26 To impose a fine on the
innocent is not right,
or to flog the noble for
their integrity.
27 One who spares words is
knowledgeable;
one who is cool in spirit
has understanding.
28 Even fools who keep silent
are considered wise;
when they close their lips,
they are deemed
intelligent.

18 The one who lives alone
is self-indulgent,
showing contempt for all
who have sound
judgment.[d]
2 A fool takes no pleasure in
understanding,
but only in expressing
personal opinion.
3 When wickedness comes,
contempt comes also;
and with dishonor comes
disgrace.
4 The words of the mouth are
deep waters;
the fountain of wisdom is a
gushing stream.
5 It is not right to be partial to
the guilty,
or to subvert the innocent
in judgment.
6 A fool's lips bring strife,
and a fool's mouth invites
a flogging.
7 The mouths of fools are their
ruin,
and their lips a snare to
themselves.
8 The words of a whisperer are
like delicious morsels;
they go down into the
inner parts of the body.
9 One who is slack in work
is close kin to a vandal.
10 The name of the LORD is a
strong tower;
the righteous run into it
and are safe.
11 The wealth of the rich is
their strong city;
in their imagination it is
like a high wall.

17.26 Prov 18.5 **17.27** Jas 1.19 **17.28** Job 13.5 **18.2** Prov 12.23 **18.4** Prov 20.5; 10.11 **18.5** Lev 19.15; Deut 1.17; Prov 24.23 **18.7** Prov 10.14; Eccl 10.12 **18.8** Prov 26.22 **18.9** Prov 28.24 **18.10** 2 Sam 22.3; Ps 18.2 **18.11** Prov 10.15 **18.12** Prov 11.2 **18.13** Jn 7.51 **18.16** Gen 32.20; 1 Sam 25.27 **18.18** Prov 16.33 **18.20** Prov 12.14 **18.21** Mt 12.37 **18.22** Prov 19.14; 8.35 **18.23** Jas 2.3 **18.24** Prov 17.17 **19.1** Prov 28.6

12 Before destruction one's
heart is haughty,
but humility goes before
honor.
13 If one gives answer before
hearing,
it is folly and shame.
14 The human spirit will endure
sickness;
but a broken spirit—who
can bear?
15 An intelligent mind acquires
knowledge,
and the ear of the wise
seeks knowledge.
16 A gift opens doors;
it gives access to the great.
17 The one who first states a
case seems right,
until the other comes and
cross-examines.
18 Casting the lot puts an end
to disputes
and decides between
powerful contenders.
19 An ally offended is stronger
than a city;[e]
such quarreling is like the
bars of a castle.
20 From the fruit of the mouth
one's stomach is
satisfied;
the yield of the lips brings
satisfaction.
21 Death and life are in the
power of the tongue,
and those who love it will
eat its fruits.
22 He who finds a wife finds a
good thing,
and obtains favor from the
LORD.
23 The poor use entreaties,
but the rich answer
roughly.
24 Some[f] friends play at
friendship[g]
but a true friend sticks
closer than one's
nearest kin.

19 Better the poor walking in
integrity

[d] Meaning of Heb uncertain [e] Gk Syr Vg Tg: Meaning of Heb uncertain [f] Syr Tg: Heb *A man of* [g] Cn Compare Syr Vg Tg: Meaning of Heb uncertain

than one perverse of
speech who is a fool.
2 Desire without knowledge is
not good,
and one who moves too
hurriedly misses the
way.
3 One's own folly leads to
ruin,
yet the heart rages against
the LORD.
4 Wealth brings many friends,
but the poor are left
friendless.
5 A false witness will not go
unpunished,
and a liar will not escape.
6 Many seek the favor of the
generous,
and everyone is a friend to
a giver of gifts.
7 If the poor are hated even by
their kin,
how much more are they
shunned by their
friends!
When they call after them,
they are not there.[h]
8 To get wisdom is to love
oneself;
to keep understanding is to
prosper.
9 A false witness will not go
unpunished,
and the liar will perish.
10 It is not fitting for a fool to
live in luxury,
much less for a slave to
rule over princes.
11 Those with good sense are
slow to anger,
and it is their glory to
overlook an offense.
12 A king's anger is like the
growling of a lion,
but his favor is like dew on
the grass.
13 A stupid child is ruin to a
father,
and a wife's quarreling is a
continual dripping of
rain.
14 House and wealth are
inherited from parents,
but a prudent wife is from
the LORD.
15 Laziness brings on deep
sleep;
an idle person will suffer
hunger.
16 Those who keep the
commandment will live;
those who are heedless of
their ways will die.
17 Whoever is kind to the poor
lends to the LORD,
and will be repaid in full.
18 Discipline your children
while there is hope;
do not set your heart on
their destruction.
19 A violent tempered person
will pay the penalty;
if you effect a rescue, you
will only have to do it
again.[h]
20 Listen to advice and accept
instruction,
that you may gain wisdom
for the future.
21 The human mind may devise
many plans,
but it is the purpose of the
LORD that will be
established.
22 What is desirable in a person
is loyalty,
and it is better to be poor
than a liar.
23 The fear of the LORD is life
indeed;
filled with it one rests
secure
and suffers no harm.
24 The lazy person buries a
hand in the dish,
and will not even bring it
back to the mouth.
25 Strike a scoffer, and the
simple will learn
prudence;
reprove the intelligent, and
they will gain
knowledge.
26 Those who do violence to
their father and chase
away their mother
are children who cause
shame and bring
reproach.

19.3 Prov 11.3; Ps 37.7
19.4 Prov 14.20
19.5 Ex 23.1; Prov 6.19
19.6 Prov 29.26; 17.8
19.7 v. 4; Ps 38.11
19.8 Prov 16.20
19.9 v. 5
19.10 Eccl 10.6,7
19.11 Jas 1.19; Prov 16.32
19.12 Prov 16.14; Hos 14.5
19.13 Prov 10.1; 21.9
19.14 2 Cor 12.14; Prov 18.22
19.15 Prov 6.9; 10.4
19.16 Lk 10.28
19.17 Eccl 11.1; Mt 10.42; 2 Cor 9.6-8; Heb 6.10
19.18 Prov 13.24
19.20 Prov 8.33
19.21 Prov 16.1,9; Ps 33.10,11
19.23 1 Tim 4.8; Ps 25.13; Prov 12.21
19.24 Prov 26.15
19.25 Prov 21.11; 9.8
19.26 Prov 28.24; 17.2

h Meaning of Heb uncertain

27 Cease straying, my child,
from the words of
knowledge,
in order that you may hear
instruction.
28 A worthless witness mocks at
justice,
and the mouth of the
wicked devours iniquity.
29 Condemnation is ready for
scoffers,
and flogging for the backs
of fools.

20 Wine is a mocker, strong
drink a brawler,
and whoever is led astray
by it is not wise.
2 The dread anger of a king is
like the growling of a
lion;
anyone who provokes him
to anger forfeits life
itself.
3 It is honorable to refrain
from strife,
but every fool is quick to
quarrel.
4 The lazy person does not
plow in season;
harvest comes, and there is
nothing to be found.
5 The purposes in the human
mind are like deep
water,
but the intelligent will
draw them out.
6 Many proclaim themselves
loyal,
but who can find one
worthy of trust?
7 The righteous walk in
integrity—
happy are the children who
follow them!
8 A king who sits on the
throne of judgment
winnows all evil with his
eyes.
9 Who can say, "I have made
my heart clean;
I am pure from my
sin"?
10 Diverse weights and diverse
measures
are both alike an
abomination to the
LORD.

19.28 Job 15.16
19.29 Prov 10.13; 26.3
20.1 Gen 9.21; Isa 5.22
20.2 Prov 19.12; 8.36; 1 Kings 2.23
20.3 Prov 17.14
20.4 Prov 10.4; 19.15,24
20.5 Prov 18.4
20.6 Prov 25.14; Mt 6.2; Lk 18.11; Ps 12.1; Lk 18.8
20.7 2 Cor 1.12; Ps 37.26
20.8 v. 26
20.9 1 Kings 8.46; 1 Jn 1.8
20.10 Deut 25.13; v. 23
20.11 Mt 7.16
20.12 Ex 4.11
20.13 Prov 6.9,10; Rom 12.11
20.16 Prov 27.13
20.17 Prov 9.17
20.18 Prov 15.22; 24.6; Lk 14.31
20.19 Prov 11.13; Rom 16.18
20.20 Mt 15.4; Job 18.5
20.21 Prov 28.20
20.22 Rom 12.17; 1 Pet 3.9; Ps 27.14
20.24 Ps 37.23; Prov 16.9; Jer 10.23

11 Even children make
themselves known by
their acts,
by whether what they do is
pure and right.
12 The hearing ear and the
seeing eye—
the LORD has made them
both.
13 Do not love sleep, or else
you will come to
poverty;
open your eyes, and you
will have plenty of
bread.
14 "Bad, bad," says the buyer,
then goes away and boasts.
15 There is gold, and
abundance of costly
stones;
but the lips informed by
knowledge are a
precious jewel.
16 Take the garment of one who
has given surety for a
stranger;
seize the pledge given as
surety for foreigners.
17 Bread gained by deceit is
sweet,
but afterward the mouth
will be full of gravel.
18 Plans are established by
taking advice;
wage war by following wise
guidance.
19 A gossip reveals secrets;
therefore do not associate
with a babbler.
20 If you curse father or
mother,
your lamp will go out in
utter darkness.
21 An estate quickly acquired in
the beginning
will not be blessed in the
end.
22 Do not say, "I will repay
evil";
wait for the LORD, and he
will help you.
23 Differing weights are an
abomination to the LORD,
and false scales are not
good.
24 All our steps are ordered by
the LORD;

how then can we
understand our own
ways?
25 It is a snare for one to say
rashly, "It is holy,"
and begin to reflect only
after making a vow.
26 A wise king winnows the
wicked,
and drives the wheel over
them.
27 The human spirit is the lamp
of the LORD,
searching every inmost
part.
28 Loyalty and faithfulness
preserve the king,
and his throne is upheld by
righteousness.[i]
29 The glory of youths is their
strength,
but the beauty of the aged
is their gray hair.
30 Blows that wound cleanse
away evil;
beatings make clean the
innermost parts.

21 The king's heart is a
stream of water in the
hand of the LORD;
he turns it wherever he
will.
2 All deeds are right in the
sight of the doer,
but the LORD weighs the
heart.
3 To do righteousness and
justice
is more acceptable to the
LORD than sacrifice.
4 Haughty eyes and a proud
heart—
the lamp of the
wicked—are sin.
5 The plans of the diligent
lead surely to
abundance,
but everyone who is hasty
comes only to want.
6 The getting of treasures by a
lying tongue
is a fleeting vapor and a
snare[j] of death.
7 The violence of the wicked
will sweep them away,
because they refuse to do
what is just.

20.25 Eccl 5.4,5 **20.26** v. 8 **20.27** 1 Cor 2.11 **20.28** Prov 29.14 **20.29** Prov 16.31 **21.2** Prov 16.2; 24.12; Lk 16.15 **21.3** 1 Sam 15.22; Prov 15.8; Isa 1.11-17; Hos 6.6; Mic 6.7,8 **21.4** Prov 6.17 **21.5** Prov 10.4; 28.22 **21.6** 2 Pet 2.3 **21.7** Prov 10.25

21.9 Prov 25.24 **21.10** Prov 2.14; 14.21 **21.11** Prov 19.25 **21.12** Prov 14.11 **21.13** Mt 18.30-34; 1 Jn 3.17; Jas 2.13 **21.14** Prov 18.16; 19.6 **21.16** Ps 49.14 **21.18** Prov 11.8 **21.19** v. 9 **21.20** Prov 22.4; Job 20.15, 18

8 The way of the guilty is
crooked,
but the conduct of the
pure is right.
9 It is better to live in a corner
of the housetop
than in a house shared
with a contentious wife.
10 The souls of the wicked
desire evil;
their neighbors find no
mercy in their eyes.
11 When a scoffer is punished,
the simple become
wiser;
when the wise are
instructed, they
increase in knowledge.
12 The Righteous One observes
the house of the
wicked;
he casts the wicked down
to ruin.
13 If you close your ear to the
cry of the poor,
you will cry out and not be
heard.
14 A gift in secret averts anger;
and a concealed bribe in
the bosom, strong
wrath.
15 When justice is done, it is a
joy to the righteous,
but dismay to evildoers.
16 Whoever wanders from the
way of understanding
will rest in the assembly of
the dead.
17 Whoever loves pleasure will
suffer want;
whoever loves wine and oil
will not be rich.
18 The wicked is a ransom for
the righteous,
and the faithless for the
upright.
19 It is better to live in a desert
land
than with a contentious
and fretful wife.
20 Precious treasure remains[k]
in the house of the
wise,
but the fool devours it.

[i] Gk: Heb *loyalty* [j] Gk: Heb *seekers*
[k] Gk: Heb *and oil*

21 Whoever pursues
righteousness and
kindness
will find life[l] and honor.
22 One wise person went up
against a city of
warriors
and brought down the
stronghold in which
they trusted.
23 To watch over mouth and
tongue
is to keep out of trouble.
24 The proud, haughty person,
named "Scoffer,"
acts with arrogant pride.
25 The craving of the lazy
person is fatal,
for lazy hands refuse to
labor.
26 All day long the wicked
covet,[m]
but the righteous give and
do not hold back.
27 The sacrifice of the wicked is
an abomination;
how much more when
brought with evil intent.
28 A false witness will perish,
but a good listener will
testify successfully.
29 The wicked put on a bold
face,
but the upright give
thought to[n] their ways.
30 No wisdom, no
understanding, no
counsel,
can avail against the LORD.
31 The horse is made ready for
the day of battle,
but the victory belongs to
the LORD.

22 A good name is to be
chosen rather than
great riches,
and favor is better than
silver or gold.
2 The rich and the poor have
this in common:
the LORD is the maker of
them all.
3 The clever see danger and
hide;
but the simple go on, and
suffer for it.
4 The reward for humility and
fear of the LORD
is riches and honor and
life.
5 Thorns and snares are in the
way of the perverse;
the cautious will keep far
from them.
6 Train children in the right
way,
and when old, they will not
stray.
7 The rich rules over the poor,
and the borrower is the
slave of the lender.
8 Whoever sows injustice will
reap calamity,
and the rod of anger will
fail.
9 Those who are generous are
blessed,
for they share their bread
with the poor.
10 Drive out a scoffer, and strife
goes out;
quarreling and abuse will
cease.
11 Those who love a pure heart
and are gracious in
speech
will have the king as a
friend.
12 The eyes of the LORD keep
watch over knowledge,
but he overthrows the
words of the faithless.
13 The lazy person says, "There
is a lion outside!
I shall be killed in the
streets!"
14 The mouth of a loose[o]
woman is a deep pit;
he with whom the LORD is
angry falls into it.
15 Folly is bound up in the
heart of a boy,
but the rod of discipline
drives it far away.
16 Oppressing the poor in order
to enrich oneself,
and giving to the rich, will
lead only to loss.

21.21 Mt 5.6
21.22 Eccl 9.15,16
21.23 Prov 12.13; Jas 3.2
21.24 Ps 1.1; Prov 1.22; Isa 16.6; Jer 48.29
21.25 Prov 13.4; 20.4
21.26 Ps 37.26; Mt 5.42; Eph 4.28
21.27 Isa 66.3; Jer 6.20; Am 5.22
21.28 Prov 19.5,9
21.29 Eccl 8.1
21.30 Isa 8.9,10; Jer 9.23; Acts 5.39
21.31 Isa 31.1; Ps 3.8; 1 Cor 15.28
22.1 Eccl 7.1
22.3 Prov 14.16; 27.12
22.5 Prov 15.19
22.6 Eph 6.4
22.7 Prov 18.23; Jas 2.6
22.8 Prov 24.16; Ps 125.3
22.9 2 Cor 9.6
22.10 Prov 18.6; 26.20
22.11 Mt 5.8; Prov 16.13
22.12 Prov 21.12
22.13 Prov 26.13
22.14 Prov 2.16; 5.3; 23.27; Eccl 7.26
22.15 Prov 13.24; 23.14

l Gk: Heb *life and righteousness*
m Gk: Heb *all day long one covets covetously*
n Another reading is *establish*
o Heb *strange*

Sayings of the Wise

17 The words of the wise:

Incline your ear and hear my
words,[p]
and apply your mind to my
teaching;
18 for it will be pleasant if you
keep them within you,
if all of them are ready on
your lips.
19 So that your trust may be in
the LORD,
I have made them known
to you today—yes, to
you.
20 Have I not written for you
thirty sayings
of admonition and
knowledge,
21 to show you what is right
and true,
so that you may give a true
answer to those who
sent you?

22 Do not rob the poor because
they are poor,
or crush the afflicted at the
gate;
23 for the LORD pleads their
cause
and despoils of life those
who despoil them.
24 Make no friends with those
given to anger,
and do not associate with
hotheads,
25 or you may learn their ways
and entangle yourself in a
snare.
26 Do not be one of those who
give pledges,
who become surety for
debts.
27 If you have nothing with
which to pay,
why should your bed be
taken from under you?
28 Do not remove the ancient
landmark
that your ancestors set
up.
29 Do you see those who are
skillful in their work?
they will serve kings;
they will not serve common
people.

23 When you sit down to eat
with a ruler,
observe carefully what[q] is
before you,
2 and put a knife to your
throat
if you have a big appetite.
3 Do not desire the ruler's[r]
delicacies,
for they are deceptive food.
4 Do not wear yourself out to
get rich;
be wise enough to desist.
5 When your eyes light upon
it, it is gone;
for suddenly it takes wings
to itself,
flying like an eagle toward
heaven.
6 Do not eat the bread of the
stingy;
do not desire their
delicacies;
7 for like a hair in the throat,
so are they.[s]
"Eat and drink!" they say
to you;
but they do not mean it.
8 You will vomit up the little
you have eaten,
and you will waste your
pleasant words.
9 Do not speak in the hearing
of a fool,
who will only despise the
wisdom of your words.
10 Do not remove an ancient
landmark
or encroach on the fields of
orphans,
11 for their redeemer is strong;
he will plead their cause
against you.
12 Apply your mind to
instruction
and your ear to words of
knowledge.
13 Do not withhold discipline
from your children;
if you beat them with a
rod, they will not die.

22.17 Prov 5.1; 23.12 **22.18** Prov 2.10 **22.19** Prov 3.5 **22.20** Prov 8.6,10 **22.21** Lk 1.3,4 **22.22** Zech 7.10; Mal 3.5 **22.23** 1 Sam 25.39; Ps 12.5; 35.10; Prov 23.11 **22.26** Prov 11.15 **22.28** Prov 23.10 **22.29** Rom 12.11; 1 Kings 10.8
23.2 v. 20 **23.3** v. 6; Ps 141.4 **23.4** Prov 28.20; 1 Tim 6.9, 10; Rom 12.16 **23.5** Prov 27.24 **23.6** Ps 141.4 **23.7** Prov 26.24, 25 **23.9** Mt 7.6; Prov 1.7 **23.10** Prov 22.28; Jer 22.3; Zech 7.10 **23.11** Prov 22.23 **23.12** Prov 22.17 **23.13** Prov 13.24; 19.18; 22.15

[p] Cn Compare Gk: Heb *Incline your ear, and hear the words of the wise* [q] Or *who* [r] Heb *his* [s] Meaning of Heb uncertain

14 If you beat them with the
rod,
you will save their lives
from Sheol.
15 My child, if your heart is
wise,
my heart too will be glad.
16 My soul will rejoice
when your lips speak what
is right.
17 Do not let your heart envy
sinners,
but always continue in the
fear of the LORD.
18 Surely there is a future,
and your hope will not be
cut off.

19 Hear, my child, and be wise,
and direct your mind in the
way.
20 Do not be among
winebibbers,
or among gluttonous eaters
of meat;
21 for the drunkard and the
glutton will come to
poverty,
and drowsiness will clothe
them with rags.

22 Listen to your father who
begot you,
and do not despise your
mother when she is old.
23 Buy truth, and do not sell it;
buy wisdom, instruction,
and understanding.
24 The father of the righteous
will greatly rejoice;
he who begets a wise son
will be glad in him.
25 Let your father and mother
be glad;
let her who bore you
rejoice.

26 My child, give me your heart,
and let your eyes observe[t]
my ways.
27 For a prostitute is a deep pit;
an adulteress[u] is a narrow
well.
28 She lies in wait like a robber
and increases the number
of the faithless.

23.16 vv. 24,25; Prov 27.11 **23.17** Ps 37.1; Prov 28.14 **23.20** Isa 5.22; Mt 24.49; Lk 21.34; Rom 13.13; Eph 5.18 **23.21** Prov 21.17; 6.10,11 **23.22** Prov 1.8; 30.17; Eph 6.1 **23.23** Prov 4.5,7; Mt 13.44 **23.24** Prov 10.1; 15.20 **23.26** Prov 3.1; 4.4; Ps 1.2 **23.27** Prov 22.14 **23.28** Prov 7.12; Eccl 7.26

29 Who has woe? Who has
sorrow?
Who has strife? Who has
complaining?
Who has wounds without
cause?
Who has redness of eyes?
30 Those who linger late over
wine,
those who keep trying
mixed wines.
31 Do not look at wine when it
is red,
when it sparkles in the cup
and goes down smoothly.
32 At the last it bites like a
serpent,
and stings like an adder.
33 Your eyes will see strange
things,
and your mind utter
perverse things.
34 You will be like one who lies
down in the midst of
the sea,
like one who lies on the
top of a mast.[v]
35 "They struck me," you will
say,[w] "but I was not
hurt;
they beat me, but I did not
feel it.
When shall I awake?
I will seek another drink."

24 Do not envy the wicked,
nor desire to be with
them;
2 for their minds devise
violence,
and their lips talk of
mischief.

3 By wisdom a house is built,
and by understanding it is
established;
4 by knowledge the rooms are
filled
with all precious and
pleasant riches.
5 Wise warriors are mightier
than strong ones,[x]

23.29 Isa 5.11,22 **23.30** Eph 5.18; Ps 75.8 **23.33** Prov 2.12 **23.35** Jer 5.3 **24.1** Ps 37.1; 73.3; Prov 3.31 **24.2** Jer 22.17; Job 15.35 **24.3** Prov 9.1 **24.5** Prov 21.22

[t] Another reading is *delight in* [u] Heb *an alien woman* [v] Meaning of Heb uncertain [w] Gk Syr Vg Tg: Heb lacks *you will say* [x] Gk Compare Syr Tg: Heb *A wise man is strength*

and those who have
knowledge than those
who have strength;
6 for by wise guidance you can
wage your war,
and in abundance of
counselors there is
victory.
7 Wisdom is too high for
fools;
in the gate they do not
open their mouths.

8 Whoever plans to do evil
will be called a
mischief-maker.
9 The devising of folly is sin,
and the scoffer is an
abomination to all.

10 If you faint in the day of
adversity,
your strength being small;
11 if you hold back from
rescuing those taken
away to death,
those who go staggering to
the slaughter;
12 if you say, "Look, we did not
know this" —
does not he who weighs
the heart perceive it?
Does not he who keeps
watch over your soul
know it?
And will he not repay all
according to their
deeds?

13 My child, eat honey, for it is
good,
and the drippings of the
honeycomb are sweet to
your taste.
14 Know that wisdom is such to
your soul;
if you find it, you will find
a future,
and your hope will not be
cut off.

15 Do not lie in wait like an
outlaw against the
home of the righteous;
do no violence to the place
where the righteous
live;
16 for though they fall seven
times, they will rise
again;
but the wicked are
overthrown by calamity.

17 Do not rejoice when your
enemies fall,
and do not let your heart
be glad when they
stumble,
18 or else the LORD will see it
and be displeased,
and turn away his anger
from them.

19 Do not fret because of
evildoers.
Do not envy the wicked;
20 for the evil have no future;
the lamp of the wicked will
go out.

21 My child, fear the LORD and
the king,
and do not disobey either
of them;[y]
22 for disaster comes from them
suddenly,
and who knows the ruin
that both can bring?

Further Sayings of the Wise

23 These also are sayings of
the wise:

Partiality in judging is not
good.
24 Whoever says to the wicked,
"You are innocent,"
will be cursed by peoples,
abhorred by nations;
25 but those who rebuke the
wicked will have
delight,
and a good blessing will
come upon them.
26 One who gives an honest
answer
gives a kiss on the lips.

27 Prepare your work outside,
get everything ready for you
in the field;

24.6 Lk 14.31 **24.7** Ps 10.5 **24.8** Prov 6.14; Rom 1.30 **24.10** Jer 51.46; Heb 12.3 **24.11** Ps 82.4; Isa 58.6,7 **24.12** Prov 21.2; Eccl 5.8; Ps 121.3-8; 94.9-11; Prov 12.14 **24.13** Song 5.1 **24.14** Prov 2.10 **24.15** Ps 10.9,10 **24.16** Ps 34.19; Mic 7.8; v. 22 **24.17** Job 31.29; Ob 12 **24.19** Ps 37.1 **24.20** Prov 13.9 **24.21** Rom 13.1-7; 1 Pet 2.17 **24.23** Prov 1.6; 18.5; Lev 19.15; Deut 1.17 **24.24** Prov 17.15 **24.25** Prov 28.23

[y] Gk: Heb *do not associate with those who change*

and after that build your
house.
28 Do not be a witness against
your neighbor without
cause,
and do not deceive with
your lips.
29 Do not say, "I will do to
others as they have
done to me;
I will pay them back for
what they have done."

30 I passed by the field of one
who was lazy,
by the vineyard of a stupid
person;
31 and see, it was all overgrown
with thorns;
the ground was covered
with nettles,
and its stone wall was
broken down.
32 Then I saw and considered
it;
I looked and received
instruction.
33 A little sleep, a little
slumber,
a little folding of the hands
to rest,
34 and poverty will come upon
you like a robber,
and want, like an armed
warrior.

Further Wise Sayings of Solomon

25 These are other proverbs of Solomon that the officials of King Hezekiah of Judah copied.

2 It is the glory of God to
conceal things,
but the glory of kings is to
search things out.
3 Like the heavens for height,
like the earth for depth,
so the mind of kings is
unsearchable.
4 Take away the dross from
the silver,
and the smith has material
for a vessel;
5 take away the wicked from
the presence of the
king,
and his throne will be
established in
righteousness.
6 Do not put yourself forward
in the king's presence
or stand in the place of the
great;
7 for it is better to be told,
"Come up here,"
than to be put lower in the
presence of a noble.

What your eyes have seen
8 do not hastily bring into
court;
for[z] what will you do in the
end,
when your neighbor puts
you to shame?
9 Argue your case with your
neighbor directly,
and do not disclose
another's secret;
10 or else someone who hears
you will bring shame
upon you,
and your ill repute will
have no end.

11 A word fitly spoken
is like apples of gold in a
setting of silver.
12 Like a gold ring or an
ornament of gold
is a wise rebuke to a
listening ear.
13 Like the cold of snow in the
time of harvest
are faithful messengers to
those who send them;
they refresh the spirit of
their masters.
14 Like clouds and wind
without rain
is one who boasts of a gift
never given.
15 With patience a ruler may be
persuaded,
and a soft tongue can
break bones.
16 If you have found honey, eat
only enough for you,

24.28 Prov 25.18; Eph 4.25
24.29 Prov 20.22; Mt 5.39; Rom 12.17
24.30 Prov 6.6-11
24.33 Prov 6.9; 20.13
25.1 Prov 1.1
25.2 Deut 29.29; Ezra 6.1
25.4 2 Tim 2.21
25.5 Prov 20.8; 16.12
25.7 Lk 14.7-11
25.8 Mt 5.25
25.9 Mt 18.15; Prov 11.13
25.11 Prov 15.23
25.12 Prov 15.31; 20.12
25.13 v. 25; Prov 13.17
25.14 Prov 20.6; Jude 12
25.15 Gen 32.4; 1 Sam 25.24; Prov 15.1; 16.14
25.16 v. 27

[z] Cn: Heb *or else*

or else, having too much,
you will vomit it.
17 Let your foot be seldom in
your neighbor's house,
otherwise the neighbor will
become weary of you
and hate you.
18 Like a war club, a sword, or
a sharp arrow
is one who bears false
witness against a
neighbor.
19 Like a bad tooth or a lame
foot
is trust in a faithless
person in time of
trouble.
20 Like vinegar on a wound[a]
is one who sings songs to a
heavy heart.
Like a moth in clothing or a
worm in wood,
sorrow gnaws at the human
heart.[b]
21 If your enemies are hungry,
give them bread to eat;
and if they are thirsty, give
them water to drink;
22 for you will heap coals of fire
on their heads,
and the LORD will reward
you.
23 The north wind produces
rain,
and a backbiting tongue,
angry looks.
24 It is better to live in a corner
of the housetop
than in a house shared
with a contentious wife.
25 Like cold water to a thirsty
soul,
so is good news from a far
country.
26 Like a muddied spring or a
polluted fountain
are the righteous who give
way before the wicked.
27 It is not good to eat much
honey,
or to seek honor on top of
honor.
28 Like a city breached, without
walls,
is one who lacks
self-control.

25.18 Ps 57.4; Prov 12.18 **25.21** Ex 23.4,5; Mt 5.44; Rom 12.20 **25.22** 2 Sam 16.12 **25.23** Ps 101.5 **25.24** Prov 21.9 **25.25** v. 13; Prov 15.30 **25.26** Ezek 32.2; 34.18,19 **25.27** v. 16; Prov 27.2 **25.28** Prov 16.32

26.1 1 Sam 12.17 **26.2** Num 23.8; Deut 23.5 **26.3** Ps 32.9 **26.4** Prov 23.9; 29.9 **26.5** Mt 16.1-4; 21.24-27 **26.7** v. 9 **26.8** v. 1 **26.9** v. 7 **26.11** 2 Pet 2.22; Ex 8.15 **26.12** v. 5; Prov 3.7; 29.20 **26.13** Prov 22.13

26

Like snow in summer or
rain in harvest,
so honor is not fitting for a
fool.
2 Like a sparrow in its flitting,
like a swallow in its
flying,
an undeserved curse goes
nowhere.
3 A whip for the horse, a bridle
for the donkey,
and a rod for the back of
fools.
4 Do not answer fools
according to their folly,
or you will be a fool
yourself.
5 Answer fools according to
their folly,
or they will be wise in their
own eyes.
6 It is like cutting off one's
foot and drinking down
violence,
to send a message by a
fool.
7 The legs of a disabled person
hang limp;
so does a proverb in the
mouth of a fool.
8 It is like binding a stone in a
sling
to give honor to a fool.
9 Like a thornbush brandished
by the hand of a
drunkard
is a proverb in the mouth
of a fool.
10 Like an archer who wounds
everybody
is one who hires a passing
fool or drunkard.[c]
11 Like a dog that returns to its
vomit
is a fool who reverts to his
folly.
12 Do you see persons wise in
their own eyes?
There is more hope for
fools than for them.
13 The lazy person says, "There
is a lion in the road!

[a] Gk: Heb *Like one who takes off a garment on a cold day, like vinegar on lye* [b] Gk Syr Tg: Heb lacks *Like a moth . . . human heart* [c] Meaning of Heb uncertain

There is a lion in the streets!"
14 As a door turns on its hinges,
so does a lazy person in bed.
15 The lazy person buries a hand in the dish,
and is too tired to bring it back to the mouth.
16 The lazy person is wiser in self-esteem
than seven who can answer discreetly.
17 Like somebody who takes a passing dog by the ears
is one who meddles in the quarrel of another.
18 Like a maniac who shoots deadly firebrands and arrows,
19 so is one who deceives a neighbor
and says, "I am only joking!"
20 For lack of wood the fire goes out,
and where there is no whisperer, quarreling ceases.
21 As charcoal is to hot embers and wood to fire,
so is a quarrelsome person for kindling strife.
22 The words of a whisperer are like delicious morsels;
they go down into the inner parts of the body.
23 Like the glaze[d] covering an earthen vessel
are smooth[e] lips with an evil heart.
24 An enemy dissembles in speaking
while harboring deceit within;
25 when an enemy speaks graciously, do not believe it,
for there are seven abominations concealed within;
26 though hatred is covered with guile,
the enemy's wickedness will be exposed in the assembly.
27 Whoever digs a pit will fall into it,
and a stone will come back on the one who starts it rolling.
28 A lying tongue hates its victims,
and a flattering mouth works ruin.

27 Do not boast about tomorrow,
for you do not know what a day may bring.
2 Let another praise you, and not your own mouth—
a stranger, and not your own lips.
3 A stone is heavy, and sand is weighty,
but a fool's provocation is heavier than both.
4 Wrath is cruel, anger is overwhelming,
but who is able to stand before jealousy?
5 Better is open rebuke
than hidden love.
6 Well meant are the wounds a friend inflicts,
but profuse are the kisses of an enemy.
7 The sated appetite spurns honey,
but to a ravenous appetite even the bitter is sweet.
8 Like a bird that strays from its nest
is one who strays from home.
9 Perfume and incense make the heart glad,
but the soul is torn by trouble.[f]
10 Do not forsake your friend or the friend of your parent;
do not go to the house of your kindred in the day of your calamity.
Better is a neighbor who is nearby
than kindred who are far away.

26.15 Prov 19.24 **26.17** Prov 3.30 **26.18** Isa 50.11 **26.19** Prov 24.28 **26.20** Prov 16.28; 22.10 **26.21** Prov 15.18 **26.22** Prov 18.8 **26.24** Prov 10.18; 12.20 **26.25** Ps 28.3; Jer 9.8 **26.26** Mt 23.28; Lk 8.17 **26.27** Ps 7.15; Prov 28.10; Eccl 10.8 **26.28** Prov 29.5 **27.1** Lk 12.19,20; Jas 4.14 **27.2** Prov 25.27; 2 Cor 10.12, 18 **27.3** Prov 12.16 **27.5** Prov 28.23 **27.7** Prov 25.16 **27.10** 2 Chr 10.6-8; Prov 17.17; 18.24

[d] Cn: Heb *silver of dross* [e] Gk: Heb *burning* [f] Gk: Heb *the sweetness of a friend is better than one's own counsel*

11 Be wise, my child, and make
my heart glad,
so that I may answer
whoever reproaches me.
12 The clever see danger and
hide;
but the simple go on, and
suffer for it.
13 Take the garment of one who
has given surety for a
stranger;
seize the pledge given as
surety for foreigners.[g]
14 Whoever blesses a neighbor
with a loud voice,
rising early in the morning,
will be counted as cursing.
15 A continual dripping on a
rainy day
and a contentious wife are
alike;
16 to restrain her is to restrain
the wind
or to grasp oil in the right
hand.[h]
17 Iron sharpens iron,
and one person sharpens
the wits[i] of another.
18 Anyone who tends a fig tree
will eat its fruit,
and anyone who takes care
of a master will be
honored.
19 Just as water reflects the
face,
so one human heart
reflects another.
20 Sheol and Abaddon are never
satisfied,
and human eyes are never
satisfied.
21 The crucible is for silver, and
the furnace is for gold,
so a person is tested[j] by
being praised.
22 Crush a fool in a mortar with
a pestle
along with crushed grain,
but the folly will not be
driven out.
23 Know well the condition of
your flocks,
and give attention to your
herds;
24 for riches do not last forever,
nor a crown for all
generations.
25 When the grass is gone, and
new growth appears,
and the herbage of the
mountains is gathered,
26 the lambs will provide your
clothing,
and the goats the price of a
field;
27 there will be enough goats'
milk for your food,
for the food of your
household
and nourishment for your
servant-girls.

28 The wicked flee when no
one pursues,
but the righteous are as
bold as a lion.
2 When a land rebels
it has many rulers;
but with an intelligent ruler
there is lasting order.[h]
3 A ruler[k] who oppresses the
poor
is a beating rain that leaves
no food.
4 Those who forsake the law
praise the wicked,
but those who keep the law
struggle against them.
5 The evil do not understand
justice,
but those who seek the
LORD understand it
completely.
6 Better to be poor and walk
in integrity
than to be crooked in one's
ways even though rich.
7 Those who keep the law are
wise children,
but companions of gluttons
shame their parents.
8 One who augments wealth
by exorbitant interest
gathers it for another who
is kind to the poor.
9 When one will not listen to
the law,
even one's prayers are an
abomination.

27.11 Prov 10.1; 23.15; Ps 119.42
27.12 Prov 22.3
27.13 Prov 20.16
27.15 Prov 19.13
27.18 1 Cor 9.7; Lk 12.42-44; 19.17
27.20 Hab 2.5; Eccl 1.8
27.21 Lk 6.26
27.22 Prov 23.35; Jer 5.3
27.24 Prov 23.5; Job 19.9
27.25 Ps 104.14
28.1 Lev 26.17; Ps 53.5
28.2 Prov 11.11
28.3 Mt 18.28
28.4 Rom 1.32; 1 Kings 18.18
28.5 Ps 92.6; Jn 7.17; 1 Cor 2.15
28.6 Prov 19.1; v. 18
28.7 Prov 23.20
28.8 Lev 25.36; Prov 13.22; 14.31
28.9 Ps 66.18; Prov 15.8

[g] Vg and 20.16: Heb *for a foreign woman*
[h] Meaning of Heb uncertain
[i] Heb *face*
[j] Heb lacks *is tested*
[k] Cn: Heb *A poor person*

10 Those who mislead the
upright into evil ways
will fall into pits of their
own making,
but the blameless will have
a goodly inheritance.
11 The rich is wise in
self-esteem,
but an intelligent poor
person sees through the
pose.
12 When the righteous triumph,
there is great glory,
but when the wicked
prevail, people go into
hiding.
13 No one who conceals
transgressions will
prosper,
but one who confesses and
forsakes them will
obtain mercy.
14 Happy is the one who is
never without fear,
but one who is
hard-hearted will fall
into calamity.
15 Like a roaring lion or a
charging bear
is a wicked ruler over a
poor people.
16 A ruler who lacks
understanding is a cruel
oppressor;
but one who hates unjust
gain will enjoy a long
life.
17 If someone is burdened with
the blood of another,
let that killer be a fugitive
until death;
let no one offer assistance.
18 One who walks in integrity
will be safe,
but whoever follows
crooked ways will fall
into the Pit.[1]
19 Anyone who tills the land
will have plenty of
bread,
but one who follows
worthless pursuits will
have plenty of poverty.
20 The faithful will abound with
blessings,

28.10 Prov 26.27; Mt 6.33; Heb 6.12
28.11 Prov 26.5, 12; 18.17
28.12 Prov 11.10; Eccl 10.5,6
28.13 Ps 32.3,5
28.14 Ps 16.8; Rom 2.5
28.15 1 Pet 5.8; Mt 2.16
28.17 Gen 9.6; Ex 21.14
28.18 Prov 10.9, 25; v. 6
28.19 Prov 12.11
28.20 Prov 10.6; v. 22; 1 Tim 6.9
28.21 Prov 18.5; Ezek 13.19
28.22 Prov 23.6; v. 20
28.23 Prov 27.5,6
28.24 Prov 19.26; 18.9
28.25 Prov 15.27; 29.25
28.26 Prov 3.5; v. 18
28.27 Deut 15.7; Prov 19.17; 21.13
28.28 v. 12
29.1 1 Sam 2.25; 2 Chr 36.16; Prov 6.15
29.2 Esther 8.15; Prov 28.15
29.3 Prov 10.1; 5.9,10; Lk 15.13

but one who is in a hurry
to be rich will not go
unpunished.
21 To show partiality is not
good—
yet for a piece of bread a
person may do wrong.
22 The miser is in a hurry to get
rich
and does not know that
loss is sure to come.
23 Whoever rebukes a person
will afterward find more
favor
than one who flatters with
the tongue.
24 Anyone who robs father or
mother
and says, "That is no
crime,"
is partner to a thug.
25 The greedy person stirs up
strife,
but whoever trusts in the
LORD will be enriched.
26 Those who trust in their own
wits are fools;
but those who walk in
wisdom come through
safely.
27 Whoever gives to the poor
will lack nothing,
but one who turns a blind
eye will get many a
curse.
28 When the wicked prevail,
people go into hiding;
but when they perish, the
righteous increase.

29 One who is often
reproved, yet remains
stubborn,
will suddenly be broken
beyond healing.
2 When the righteous are in
authority, the people
rejoice;
but when the wicked rule,
the people groan.
3 A child who loves wisdom
makes a parent glad,
but to keep company with
prostitutes is to
squander one's
substance.

[1] Syr: Heb *fall all at once*

4 By justice a king gives
stability to the land,
but one who makes heavy
exactions ruins it.
5 Whoever flatters a neighbor
is spreading a net for the
neighbor's feet.
6 In the transgression of the
evil there is a snare,
but the righteous sing and
rejoice.
7 The righteous know the
rights of the poor;
the wicked have no such
understanding.
8 Scoffers set a city aflame,
but the wise turn away
wrath.
9 If the wise go to law with
fools,
there is ranting and
ridicule without relief.
10 The bloodthirsty hate the
blameless,
and they seek the life of
the upright.
11 A fool gives full vent to
anger,
but the wise quietly holds
it back.
12 If a ruler listens to
falsehood,
all his officials will be
wicked.
13 The poor and the oppressor
have this in common:
the LORD gives light to the
eyes of both.
14 If a king judges the poor
with equity,
his throne will be
established forever.
15 The rod and reproof give
wisdom,
but a mother is disgraced
by a neglected child.
16 When the wicked are in
authority, transgression
increases,
but the righteous will look
upon their downfall.
17 Discipline your children, and
they will give you rest;
they will give delight to
your heart.
18 Where there is no prophecy,
the people cast off
restraint,
but happy are those who
keep the law.
19 By mere words servants are
not disciplined,
for though they
understand, they will
not give heed.
20 Do you see someone who is
hasty in speech?
There is more hope for a
fool than for anyone
like that.
21 A slave pampered from
childhood
will come to a bad end.[m]
22 One given to anger stirs up
strife,
and the hothead causes
much transgression.
23 A person's pride will bring
humiliation,
but one who is lowly in
spirit will obtain honor.
24 To be a partner of a thief is
to hate one's own life;
one hears the victim's
curse, but discloses
nothing.[n]
25 The fear of others[o] lays a
snare,
but one who trusts in the
LORD is secure.
26 Many seek the favor of a
ruler,
but it is from the LORD that
one gets justice.
27 The unjust are an
abomination to the
righteous,
but the upright are an
abomination to the
wicked.

Sayings of Agur

30 The words of Agur son of Jakeh. An oracle.

Thus says the man: I am
weary, O God,
I am weary, O God. How
can I prevail?[p]

29.5 Ps 5.9 **29.6** Prov 22.5; Ex 15.1 **29.7** Job 29.16; Ps 41.1 **29.8** Prov 11.11; 16.14 **29.10** 1 Jn 3.12 **29.11** Prov 12.16; 19.11 **29.13** Ps 13.3 **29.14** Ps 72.4; Isa 11.4; Prov 16.12; 25.5 **29.15** Prov 13.24; 10.1 **29.16** Ps 37.36; 58.10; 91.8; 92.11 **29.17** v. 15; Prov 10.1 **29.18** 1 Sam 3.1; Am 8.11,12; Jn 13.17 **29.20** Jas 1.19; Prov 26.12 **29.22** Prov 15.18; 17.19 **29.23** Job 22.29; Isa 66.2; Dan 4.30; Mt 23.12 **29.24** Lev 5.1 **29.25** Gen 12.12; Ps 91.1-16 **29.26** Isa 49.4 **30.1** Prov 31.1

m Vg: Meaning of Heb uncertain n Meaning of Heb uncertain o Or *human fear* p Or *I am spent.* Meaning of Heb uncertain

2 Surely I am too stupid to be
human;
I do not have human
understanding.
3 I have not learned wisdom,
nor have I knowledge of
the holy ones.[q]
4 Who has ascended to heaven
and come down?
Who has gathered the wind
in the hollow of the
hand?
Who has wrapped up the
waters in a garment?
Who has established all the
ends of the earth?
What is the person's name?
And what is the name of
the person's child?
Surely you know!

5 Every word of God proves
true;
he is a shield to those who
take refuge in him.
6 Do not add to his words,
or else he will rebuke you,
and you will be found a
liar.

7 Two things I ask of you;
do not deny them to me
before I die:
8 Remove far from me
falsehood and lying;
give me neither poverty nor
riches;
feed me with the food that
I need,
9 or I shall be full, and deny
you,
and say, "Who is the
LORD?"
or I shall be poor, and steal,
and profane the name of
my God.

10 Do not slander a servant to a
master,
or the servant will curse
you, and you will be
held guilty.

11 There are those who curse
their fathers
and do not bless their
mothers.

30.2 Ps 73.22
30.3 Prov 9.10
30.4 Jn 3.13; Ps 104.3; Isa 40.12; Job 38.8,9; Isa 45.18
30.5 Ps 12.6; 18.30; 84.11
30.6 Deut 4.2; 12.32; Rev 22.18
30.8 Mt 6.11
30.9 Deut 8.12; Neh 9.25; Job 31.24; Hos 13.6
30.10 Eccl 7.21
30.11 Prov 20.20
30.12 Lk 18.11
30.13 Ps 131.1; Prov 6.17
30.14 Job 29.17; Ps 52.2; 14.4; Am 8.4
30.16 Prov 27.20
30.17 Gen 9.22; Prov 23.22; Deut 28.26
30.20 Prov 5.6

12 There are those who are pure
in their own eyes
yet are not cleansed of
their filthiness.
13 There are those—how lofty
are their eyes,
how high their eyelids lift!
14 There are those whose teeth
are swords,
whose teeth are knives,
to devour the poor from off
the earth,
the needy from among
mortals.

15 The leech[r] has two
daughters;
"Give, give," they cry.
Three things are never
satisfied;
four never say, "Enough":
16 Sheol, the barren womb,
the earth ever thirsty for
water,
and the fire that never
says, "Enough."[r]

17 The eye that mocks a father
and scorns to obey a
mother
will be pecked out by the
ravens of the valley
and eaten by the vultures.

18 Three things are too
wonderful for me;
four I do not understand:
19 the way of an eagle in the
sky,
the way of a snake on a
rock,
the way of a ship on the high
seas,
and the way of a man with
a girl.

20 This is the way of an
adulteress:
she eats, and wipes her
mouth,
and says, "I have done no
wrong."

21 Under three things the earth
trembles;

[q] Or *Holy One* [r] Meaning of Heb uncertain

under four it cannot bear
up:
22 a slave when he becomes
king,
and a fool when glutted
with food;
23 an unloved woman when she
gets a husband,
and a maid when she
succeeds her mistress.

24 Four things on earth are
small,
yet they are exceedingly
wise:
25 the ants are a people without
strength,
yet they provide their food
in the summer;
26 the badgers are a people
without power,
yet they make their homes
in the rocks;
27 the locusts have no king,
yet all of them march in
rank;
28 the lizard[s] can be grasped in
the hand,
yet it is found in kings'
palaces.

29 Three things are stately in
their stride;
four are stately in their
gait:
30 the lion, which is mightiest
among wild animals
and does not turn back
before any;
31 the strutting rooster,[t] the
he-goat,
and a king striding before[u]
his people.

32 If you have been foolish,
exalting yourself,
or if you have been
devising evil,
put your hand on your
mouth.
33 For as pressing milk
produces curds,
and pressing the nose
produces blood,
so pressing anger produces
strife.

30.22 Prov 19.10 **30.25** Prov 6.6-8 **30.26** Ps 104.18 **30.30** Judg 14.18; Mic 5.8 **30.32** Job 21.5; 40.4; Mic 7.16 **30.33** Prov 10.12; 29.22

31.1 Prov 30.1 **31.2** Isa 49.15 **31.3** Prov 5.9; Deut 17.17; 1 Kings 11.1; Neh 13.26 **31.4** Eccl 10.17; Prov 20.1 **31.5** Hos 4.11 **31.8** Job 29.12-17 **31.9** Lev 19.15; Deut 1.16 **31.10** Prov 12.4; 19.14 **31.13** vv. 21-24

The Teaching of King Lemuel's Mother

31 The words of King Lemuel. An oracle that his mother taught him:

2 No, my son! No, son of my
womb!
No, son of my vows!
3 Do not give your strength to
women,
your ways to those who
destroy kings.
4 It is not for kings, O Lemuel,
it is not for kings to drink
wine,
or for rulers to desire[v]
strong drink;
5 or else they will drink and
forget what has been
decreed,
and will pervert the rights
of all the afflicted.
6 Give strong drink to one who
is perishing,
and wine to those in bitter
distress;
7 let them drink and forget
their poverty,
and remember their misery
no more.
8 Speak out for those who
cannot speak,
for the rights of all the
destitute.[w]
9 Speak out, judge righteously,
defend the rights of the
poor and needy.

Ode to a Capable Wife

10 A capable wife who can find?
She is far more precious
than jewels.
11 The heart of her husband
trusts in her,
and he will have no lack of
gain.
12 She does him good, and not
harm,
all the days of her life.
13 She seeks wool and flax,

[s] Or *spider* [t] Gk Syr Tg Compare Vg: Meaning of Heb uncertain [u] Meaning of Heb uncertain [v] Cn: Heb *where* [w] Heb *all children of passing away*

and works with willing
hands.
14 She is like the ships of the
merchant,
she brings her food from
far away.
15 She rises while it is still
night
and provides food for her
household
and tasks for her
servant-girls.
16 She considers a field and
buys it;
with the fruit of her hands
she plants a vineyard.
17 She girds herself with
strength,
and makes her arms strong.
18 She perceives that her
merchandise is
profitable.
Her lamp does not go out
at night.
19 She puts her hands to the
distaff,
and her hands hold the
spindle.
20 She opens her hand to the
poor,
and reaches out her hands
to the needy.
21 She is not afraid for her
household when it
snows,
for all her household are
clothed in crimson.
22 She makes herself coverings;
her clothing is fine linen
and purple.
23 Her husband is known in the
city gates,
taking his seat among the
elders of the land.
24 She makes linen garments
and sells them;
she supplies the merchant
with sashes.
25 Strength and dignity are her
clothing,
and she laughs at the time
to come.
26 She opens her mouth with
wisdom,
and the teaching of
kindness is on her
tongue.
27 She looks well to the ways of
her household,
and does not eat the bread
of idleness.
28 Her children rise up and call
her happy;
her husband too, and he
praises her:
29 "Many women have done
excellently,
but you surpass them all."
30 Charm is deceitful, and
beauty is vain,
but a woman who fears the
LORD is to be praised.
31 Give her a share in the fruit
of her hands,
and let her works praise
her in the city gates.

31.15 Rom 12.11; Lk 12.42
31.20 Eph 4.28; Heb 13.16
31.21 1 Sam 1.24
31.23 Ruth 4.1,11; Prov 12.4
31.25 v. 17
31.26 Prov 10.31
31.27 Prov 19.15
31.29 Prov 12.4
31.30 Prov 6.25; 22.4

Ecclesiastes

Title and Background

The writer's title ("Teacher") comes from a Hebrew root word related to "assembly" or "congregation." Perhaps the Teacher also held an office in the assembly. The Septuagint word for "Teacher" is *ecclesiastes*, from which most English titles of the book are taken.

Author and Date of Writing

No time period or writer's name is mentioned in the book, but several passages suggest the possibility that Solomon is the author; this would demand a date in the tenth century B.C. Others, however, date the book as late as the third century B.C.

Theme and Message

Life not centered on God is purposeless and meaningless. Without him, nothing can satisfy (2.25). With him, all of life and his other good gifts are to be gratefully received and used and enjoyed to the full (2.26; 11.8). The book contains the philosophical and theological reflections of an old man, most of whose life was meaningless because he had not himself relied on God.

Outline

I. Introduction: The Vanity of Life (1.1-11)
II. Life to Be Enjoyed as a Gift From God (1.12–11.6)
III. Youth as the Time to Begin Enjoying Life (11.7–12.8)
IV. Conclusion: Reverently Trust in and Obey God (12.9-14)

Reflections of a Royal Philosopher

1 The words of the Teacher,[a] the son of David, king in Jerusalem.
2 Vanity of vanities, says the
Teacher,[a]
vanity of vanities! All is
vanity.
3 What do people gain from all
the toil
at which they toil under
the sun?
4 A generation goes, and a
generation comes,
but the earth remains
forever.
5 The sun rises and the sun
goes down,
and hurries to the place
where it rises.
6 The wind blows to the south,
and goes around to the
north;
round and round goes the
wind,
and on its circuits the wind
returns.
7 All streams run to the sea,
but the sea is not full;
to the place where the
streams flow,
there they continue to
flow.
8 All things[b] are wearisome;
more than one can express;
the eye is not satisfied with
seeing,
or the ear filled with
hearing.
9 What has been is what will
be,

1.1 v. 12; Eccl 7.27; 12.8-10 **1.2** Ps 39.5,6; 62.9; 144.4; Eccl 12.8 **1.3** Eccl 2.22; 3.9 **1.4** Ps 104.5; 119.90 **1.5** Ps 19.5,6 **1.6** Eccl 11.5; Jn 3.8 **1.8** Prov 27.20 **1.9** Eccl 2.12; 3.15

[a] Heb *Qoheleth*, traditionally rendered *Preacher* [b] Or *words*

and what has been done is
what will be done;
there is nothing new under
the sun.
10 Is there a thing of which it is
said,
"See, this is new"?
It has already been,
in the ages before us.
11 The people of long ago are
not remembered,
nor will there be any
remembrance
of people yet to come
by those who come after
them.

The Futility of Seeking Wisdom

12 I, the Teacher,[c] when king
over Israel in Jerusalem, 13 applied
my mind to seek and to search out
by wisdom all that is done under
heaven; it is an unhappy business
that God has given to human beings to be busy with. 14 I saw all the
deeds that are done under the sun;
and see, all is vanity and a chasing
after wind.[d]
15 What is crooked cannot be
made straight,
and what is lacking cannot
be counted.
16 I said to myself, "I have acquired great wisdom, surpassing all
who were over Jerusalem before
me; and my mind has had great experience of wisdom and knowledge." 17 And I applied my mind to
know wisdom and to know madness and folly. I perceived that this
also is but a chasing after wind.[d]
18 For in much wisdom is much
vexation,
and those who increase
knowledge increase
sorrow.

The Futility of Self-Indulgence

2 I said to myself, "Come now, I
will make a test of pleasure;
enjoy yourself." But again, this also
was vanity. 2 I said of laughter, "It is
mad," and of pleasure, "What use
is it?" 3 I searched with my mind
how to cheer my body with wine—
my mind still guiding me with
wisdom—and how to lay hold on
folly, until I might see what was
good for mortals to do under heav-
en during the few days of their life.
4 I made great works; I built houses
and planted vineyards for myself; 5 I
made myself gardens and parks,
and planted in them all kinds of
fruit trees. 6 I made myself pools
from which to water the forest of
growing trees. 7 I bought male and
female slaves, and had slaves who
were born in my house; I also had
great possessions of herds and
flocks, more than any who had
been before me in Jerusalem. 8 I
also gathered for myself silver and
gold and the treasure of kings and
of the provinces; I got singers, both
men and women, and delights of
the flesh, and many concubines.[e]
9 So I became great and surpassed all who were before me in
Jerusalem; also my wisdom remained with me. 10 Whatever my
eyes desired I did not keep from
them; I kept my heart from no pleasure, for my heart found pleasure
in all my toil, and this was my reward for all my toil. 11 Then I considered all that my hands had done
and the toil I had spent in doing it,
and again, all was vanity and a
chasing after wind,[d] and there was
nothing to be gained under the
sun.

Wisdom and Joy Given to One Who Pleases God

12 So I turned to consider wisdom and madness and folly; for
what can the one do who comes after the king? Only what has already
been done. 13 Then I saw that wisdom excels folly as light excels
darkness.
14 The wise have eyes in their
head,
but fools walk in darkness.
Yet I perceived that the same
fate befalls all of them. 15 Then I
said to myself, "What happens to
the fool will happen to me also;
why then have I been so very wise?"

1.11 Eccl 2.16; 9.5
1.12 v. 1
1.13 v. 17; Eccl 3.10
1.14 Eccl 2.11,17
1.15 Eccl 7.13
1.16 1 Kings 3.12, 13; 4.30; 10.23; Eccl 2.9
1.17 Eccl 2.3,12; 7.23,25
1.18 Eccl 12.12
2.1 Lk 12.19; Eccl 1.2
2.2 Prov 14.13; Eccl 7.6
2.4 1 Kings 7.1-12; Song 8.10, 11
2.5 Song 4.16; 5.1; Neh 2.8
2.8 1 Kings 9.28; 10.10,14,21; 4.21; 20.14; 2 Sam 19.35
2.9 Eccl 1.16
2.10 Eccl 3.22; 5.18; 9.9
2.11 Eccl 1.3,14
2.12 Eccl 1.17; 7.25
2.13 Eccl 7.11,12
2.14 Prov 17.24; Ps 49.10; Eccl 9.2,3, 11
2.15 Eccl 6.8,11

[c] Heb *Qoheleth*, traditionally rendered *Preacher* [d] Or *a feeding on wind.* See Hos 12.1 [e] Meaning of Heb uncertain

And I said to myself that this also is
vanity. 16 For there is no enduring
remembrance of the wise or of
fools, seeing that in the days to
come all will have been long forgotten. How can the wise die just like
fools? 17 So I hated life, because
what is done under the sun was
grievous to me; for all is vanity and
a chasing after wind.[f]
18 I hated all my toil in which I
had toiled under the sun, seeing
that I must leave it to those who
come after me 19 —and who knows
whether they will be wise or foolish? Yet they will be master of all
for which I toiled and used my wisdom under the sun. This also is
vanity. 20 So I turned and gave my
heart up to despair concerning all
the toil of my labors under the sun,
21 because sometimes one who has
toiled with wisdom and knowledge
and skill must leave all to be enjoyed by another who did not toil
for it. This also is vanity and a great
evil. 22 What do mortals get from all
the toil and strain with which they
toil under the sun? 23 For all their
days are full of pain, and their work
is a vexation; even at night their
minds do not rest. This also is vanity.
24 There is nothing better for
mortals than to eat and drink, and
find enjoyment in their toil. This
also, I saw, is from the hand of God;
25 for apart from him[g] who can eat
or who can have enjoyment? 26 For
to the one who pleases him God
gives wisdom and knowledge and
joy; but to the sinner he gives the
work of gathering and heaping,
only to give to one who pleases
God. This also is vanity and a chasing after wind.[f]

Everything Has Its Time

3 For everything there is a season, and a time for every matter under heaven:

2 a time to be born, and a
time to die;
a time to plant, and a time
to pluck up what is
planted;
3 a time to kill, and a time to
heal;
a time to break down, and a
time to build up;
4 a time to weep, and a time
to laugh;
a time to mourn, and a time
to dance;
5 a time to throw away stones,
and a time to gather
stones together;
a time to embrace, and a time
to refrain from
embracing;
6 a time to seek, and a time to
lose;
a time to keep, and a time to
throw away;
7 a time to tear, and a time to
sew;
a time to keep silence, and a
time to speak;
8 a time to love, and a time to
hate;
a time for war, and a time
for peace.

The God-Given Task

9 What gain have the workers
from their toil? 10 I have seen the
business that God has given to everyone to be busy with. 11 He has
made everything suitable for its
time; moreover he has put a sense
of past and future into their minds,
yet they cannot find out what God
has done from the beginning to the
end. 12 I know that there is nothing
better for them than to be happy
and enjoy themselves as long as
they live; 13 moreover, it is God's
gift that all should eat and drink
and take pleasure in all their toil.
14 I know that whatever God does
endures forever; nothing can be
added to it, nor anything taken
from it; God has done this, so that
all should stand in awe before him.
15 That which is, already has been;
that which is to be, already is; and
God seeks out what has gone by.[h]

2.16 Eccl 1.11; 9.5; v. 14 **2.17** Eccl 4.2; vv. 22,23 **2.18** v. 11; Ps 39.6; 49.10 **2.20** v. 11 **2.21** Eccl 4.4; v. 18 **2.22** Eccl 1.3; 3.9 **2.23** Job 5.7; 14.1; Eccl 1.18; Ps 127.2 **2.24** Eccl 3.12, 13,22; 5.18; 8.15 **2.26** Job 32.8; 27.16,17; Eccl 1.14 **3.1** v. 17; Eccl 8.6 **3.2** Heb 9.27 **3.4** Rom 12.15; Ps 126.2; Ex 15.20 **3.5** 1 Cor 7.5 **3.7** Am 5.13 **3.8** Lk 14.26 **3.9** Eccl 1.3 **3.10** Eccl 1.13 **3.11** Gen 1.31; Eccl 8.17; Rom 11.33 **3.13** Eccl 2.24; 5.19 **3.14** Jas 1.17; Eccl 5.7; 1.3; 3.9 **3.15** Eccl 1.9; 6.10

f Or *a feeding on wind.* See Hos 12.1
g Gk Syr: Heb *apart from me*
h Heb *what is pursued*

Judgment and the Future Belong to God

16 Moreover I saw under the
sun that in the place of justice,
wickedness was there, and in the
place of righteousness, wickedness
was there as well. 17 I said in my
heart, God will judge the righteous
and the wicked, for he has appointed a time for every matter, and for
every work. 18 I said in my heart
with regard to human beings that
God is testing them to show that
they are but animals. 19 For the fate
of humans and the fate of animals
is the same; as one dies, so dies the
other. They all have the same
breath, and humans have no advantage over the animals; for all is
vanity. 20 All go to one place; all are
from the dust, and all turn to dust
again. 21 Who knows whether the
human spirit goes upward and the
spirit of animals goes downward to
the earth? 22 So I saw that there is
nothing better than that all should
enjoy their work, for that is their
lot; who can bring them to see what
will be after them?

4 Again I saw all the oppressions
that are practiced under the
sun. Look, the tears of the
oppressed—with no one to comfort them! On the side of their oppressors there was power—with no
one to comfort them. 2 And I
thought the dead, who have already died, more fortunate than
the living, who are still alive; 3 but
better than both is the one who has
not yet been, and has not seen the
evil deeds that are done under the
sun.

4 Then I saw that all toil and all
skill in work come from one person's envy of another. This also is
vanity and a chasing after wind.[i]

5 Fools fold their hands
and consume their own
flesh.
6 Better is a handful with
quiet
than two handfuls with
toil,
and a chasing after wind.[i]

7 Again, I saw vanity under the
sun: 8 the case of solitary individuals, without sons or brothers; yet
there is no end to all their toil, and
their eyes are never satisfied with
riches. "For whom am I toiling,"
they ask, "and depriving myself of
pleasure?" This also is vanity and
an unhappy business.

The Value of a Friend

9 Two are better than one, because they have a good reward for
their toil. 10 For if they fall, one will
lift up the other; but woe to one
who is alone and falls and does not
have another to help. 11 Again, if
two lie together, they keep warm;
but how can one keep warm alone?
12 And though one might prevail
against another, two will withstand
one. A threefold cord is not quickly
broken.

13 Better is a poor but wise
youth than an old but foolish king,
who will no longer take advice.
14 One can indeed come out of prison to reign, even though born poor
in the kingdom. 15 I saw all the living who, moving about under the
sun, follow that[j] youth who replaced the king;[k] 16 there was no
end to all those people whom he
led. Yet those who come later will
not rejoice in him. Surely this also
is vanity and a chasing after wind.[i]

Reverence, Humility, and Contentment

5 1[l] Guard your steps when you go
to the house of God; to draw
near to listen is better than the sacrifice offered by fools; for they do
not know how to keep from doing
evil.[m] 2[n] Never be rash with your
mouth, nor let your heart be quick
to utter a word before God, for God
is in heaven, and you upon earth;
therefore let your words be few.

3 For dreams come with many
cares, and a fool's voice with many
words.

4 When you make a vow to God,
do not delay fulfilling it; for he has
no pleasure in fools. Fulfill what

3.17 Mt 16.27; Rom 2.6-8; 2 Cor 5.10; 2 Thes 1.6, 7; v. 1
3.19 Ps 73.22; Eccl 9.12
3.20 Gen 3.19; Eccl 12.7
3.21 Eccl 12.7
3.22 Eccl 2.24; 5.18; 6.12; 8.7; 10.14
4.1 Eccl 3.16; 5.8; Isa 5.7; Lam 1.9
4.2 Job 3.11-26; Eccl 2.17
4.3 Eccl 6.3
4.4 Eccl 2.21; 1.14
4.5 Prov 6.10; Isa 9.20
4.6 Prov 15.16, 17; 16.8
4.8 Prov 27.20; 1 Jn 2.16
4.11 1 Kings 1.1
4.13 Eccl 9.15
4.14 Gen 41.14, 41-43
4.16 Eccl 1.14
5.1 Ex 3.5; Isa 1.12; 1 Sam 15.22; Prov 15.8; 21-27; Hos 6.6
5.2 Prov 20.25; 10.19; Mt 6.7
5.4 Deut 23.21-23; Ps 50.14; 76.11; 66.13, 14

[i] Or *a feeding on wind.* See Hos 12.1
[j] Heb *the second*
[k] Heb *him*
[l] Ch 4.17 in Heb
[m] Cn: Heb *they do not know how to do evil*
[n] Ch 5.1 in Heb

you vow. 5 It is better that you
should not vow than that you
should vow and not fulfill it. 6 Do
not let your mouth lead you into
sin, and do not say before the messenger that it was a mistake; why
should God be angry at your words,
and destroy the work of your
hands?
7 With many dreams come vanities and a multitude of words;[o] but
fear God.
8 If you see in a province the oppression of the poor and the violation of justice and right, do not be
amazed at the matter; for the high
official is watched by a higher, and
there are yet higher ones over
them. 9 But all things considered,
this is an advantage for a land: a
king for a plowed field.[o]
10 The lover of money will not
be satisfied with money; nor the
lover of wealth, with gain. This also
is vanity.
11 When goods increase, those
who eat them increase; and what
gain has their owner but to see
them with his eyes?
12 Sweet is the sleep of laborers, whether they eat little or
much; but the surfeit of the rich
will not let them sleep.
13 There is a grievous ill that I
have seen under the sun: riches
were kept by their owners to their
hurt, 14 and those riches were lost
in a bad venture; though they are
parents of children, they have
nothing in their hands. 15 As they
came from their mother's womb, so
they shall go again, naked as they
came; they shall take nothing for
their toil, which they may carry
away with their hands. 16 This also
is a grievous ill: just as they came,
so shall they go; and what gain do
they have from toiling for the wind?
17 Besides, all their days they eat in
darkness, in much vexation and
sickness and resentment.
18 This is what I have seen to be
good: it is fitting to eat and drink
and find enjoyment in all the toil
with which one toils under the sun
the few days of the life God gives
us; for this is our lot. 19 Likewise all

5.5 Prov 20.25; Acts 5.4 **5.7** Eccl 3.14; 12.13 **5.8** Eccl 4.1; Ps 12.5; 58.11; 82.1 **5.10** Eccl 2.10,11 **5.11** Eccl 2.9 **5.12** Prov 3.24 **5.13** Eccl 6.1,2 **5.15** Job 1.21; Ps 49.17; 1 Tim 6.7 **5.16** Eccl 1.3; Prov 11.29 **5.17** Eccl 2.23 **5.18** Eccl 2.10, 24; 3.22 **5.19** 2 Chr 1.12; Eccl 2.24; 3.13; 6.2

6.1 Eccl 5.13 **6.2** 1 Kings 3.13; Ps 17.14; 73.7 **6.3** 2 Kings 9.35; Isa 14.19, 20; Jer 22.19; Eccl 4.3 **6.7** Prov 16.26 **6.8** Eccl 2.15 **6.9** Eccl 11.9; 1.14 **6.10** Eccl 1.9; Job 9.32; Isa 45.9; Jer 49.19 **6.12** Jas 4.14; Ps 39.6; Eccl 8.7

to whom God gives wealth and possessions and whom he enables to
enjoy them, and to accept their lot
and find enjoyment in their toil—
this is the gift of God. 20 For they
will scarcely brood over the days of
their lives, because God keeps
them occupied with the joy of their
hearts.

The Frustration of Desires

6 There is an evil that I have
seen under the sun, and it lies
heavy upon humankind: 2 those to
whom God gives wealth, possessions, and honor, so that they lack
nothing of all that they desire, yet
God does not enable them to enjoy
these things, but a stranger enjoys
them. This is vanity; it is a grievous
ill. 3 A man may beget a hundred
children, and live many years; but
however many are the days of his
years, if he does not enjoy life's
good things, or has no burial, I say
that a stillborn child is better off
than he. 4 For it comes into vanity
and goes into darkness, and in
darkness its name is covered;
5 moreover it has not seen the sun
or known anything; yet it finds rest
rather than he. 6 Even though he
should live a thousand years twice
over, yet enjoy no good—do not all
go to one place?
7 All human toil is for the
mouth, yet the appetite is not satisfied. 8 For what advantage have the
wise over fools? And what do the
poor have who know how to conduct themselves before the living?
9 Better is the sight of the eyes than
the wandering of desire; this also is
vanity and a chasing after wind.[p]
10 Whatever has come to be has
already been named, and it is
known what human beings are, and
that they are not able to dispute
with those who are stronger. 11 The
more words, the more vanity, so
how is one the better? 12 For who
knows what is good for mortals
while they live the few days of their
vain life, which they pass like a
shadow? For who can tell them

[o] Meaning of Heb uncertain [p] Or *a feeding on wind.* See Hos 12.1

what will be after them under the
sun?

A Disillusioned View of Life

7 A good name is better than
precious ointment,
and the day of death, than
the day of birth.
2 It is better to go to the
house of mourning
than to go to the house of
feasting;
for this is the end of
everyone,
and the living will lay it to
heart.
3 Sorrow is better than
laughter,
for by sadness of
countenance the heart
is made glad.
4 The heart of the wise is in
the house of mourning;
but the heart of fools is in
the house of mirth.
5 It is better to hear the
rebuke of the wise
than to hear the song of
fools.
6 For like the crackling of
thorns under a pot,
so is the laughter of fools;
this also is vanity.
7 Surely oppression makes the
wise foolish,
and a bribe corrupts the
heart.
8 Better is the end of a thing
than its beginning;
the patient in spirit are
better than the proud in
spirit.
9 Do not be quick to anger,
for anger lodges in the
bosom of fools.
10 Do not say, "Why were the
former days better than
these?"
For it is not from wisdom
that you ask this.
11 Wisdom is as good as an
inheritance,
an advantage to those who
see the sun.
12 For the protection of wisdom
is like the protection of
money,
and the advantage of
knowledge is that
wisdom gives life to the
one who possesses it.
13 Consider the work of God;
who can make straight
what he has made
crooked?
14 In the day of prosperity be
joyful, and in the day of adversity
consider; God has made the one as
well as the other, so that mortals
may not find out anything that will
come after them.

The Riddles of Life

15 In my vain life I have seen everything; there are righteous people who perish in their righteousness, and there are wicked people
who prolong their life in their evildoing. 16 Do not be too righteous,
and do not act too wise; why should
you destroy yourself? 17 Do not be
too wicked, and do not be a fool;
why should you die before your
time? 18 It is good that you should
take hold of the one, without letting go of the other; for the one who
fears God shall succeed with both.
19 Wisdom gives strength to the
wise more than ten rulers that are
in a city.
20 Surely there is no one on
earth so righteous as to do good
without ever sinning.
21 Do not give heed to everything that people say, or you may
hear your servant cursing you;
22 your heart knows that many
times you have yourself cursed others.
23 All this I have tested by wisdom; I said, "I will be wise," but it
was far from me. 24 That which is, is
far off, and deep, very deep; who
can find it out? 25 I turned my mind
to know and to search out and to
seek wisdom and the sum of
things, and to know that wickedness is folly and that foolishness is
madness. 26 I found more bitter
than death the woman who is a
trap, whose heart is snares and
nets, whose hands are fetters; one
who pleases God escapes her, but
the sinner is taken by her. 27 See,

7.1 Prov 15.30; 22.1; Eccl 4.2
7.2 Eccl 2.16; Ps 90.12
7.3 2 Cor 7.10
7.5 Ps 141.5; Prov 13.18; 15.31,32
7.6 Ps 118.12; Eccl 2.2
7.7 Ex 23.8; Deut 16.19
7.8 v. 1; Prov 14.29; Gal 5.22; Eph 4.2
7.9 Prov 14.17; Jas 1.19
7.11 Prov 8.10,11
7.12 Eccl 9.18; Prov 3.18; 8.35
7.13 Eccl 3.11; 8.17; 1.15; Isa 14.27
7.14 Eccl 3.4; Deut 8.5
7.15 Eccl 6.12; 8.14
7.16 Rom 12.3
7.17 Job 15.32; Ps 55.23; Prov 10.27
7.19 Eccl 9.13-18
7.20 1 Kings 8.46; 2 Chr 6.36; Prov 20.9; Rom 3.23
7.23 Rom 1.22
7.24 Job 28.12; Rom 11.33
7.25 Eccl 1.17; 2.12
7.26 Prov 5.3,4; 22.14
7.27 Eccl 1.1,2

this is what I found, says the Teacher,[q] adding one thing to another to find the sum, 28 which my mind has sought repeatedly, but I have not found. One man among a thousand I found, but a woman among all these I have not found. 29 See, this alone I found, that God made human beings straightforward, but they have devised many schemes.

Obey the King and Enjoy Yourself

8 Who is like the wise man?
And who knows the
interpretation of a
thing?
Wisdom makes one's face
shine,
and the hardness of one's
countenance is
changed.

2 Keep[r] the king's command because of your sacred oath. 3 Do not be terrified; go from his presence, do not delay when the matter is unpleasant, for he does whatever he pleases. 4 For the word of the king is powerful, and who can say to him, "What are you doing?" 5 Whoever obeys a command will meet no harm, and the wise mind will know the time and way. 6 For every matter has its time and way, although the troubles of mortals lie heavy upon them. 7 Indeed, they do not know what is to be, for who can tell them how it will be? 8 No one has power over the wind[s] to restrain the wind,[s] or power over the day of death; there is no discharge from the battle, nor does wickedness deliver those who practice it. 9 All this I observed, applying my mind to all that is done under the sun, while one person exercises authority over another to the other's hurt.

God's Ways Are Inscrutable

10 Then I saw the wicked buried; they used to go in and out of the holy place, and were praised in the city where they had done such things.[t] This also is vanity. 11 Because sentence against an evil deed is not executed speedily, the human heart is fully set to do evil. 12 Though sinners do evil a hundred times and prolong their lives, yet I know that it will be well with those who fear God, because they stand in fear before him, 13 but it will not be well with the wicked, neither will they prolong their days like a shadow, because they do not stand in fear before God.

14 There is a vanity that takes place on earth, that there are righteous people who are treated according to the conduct of the wicked, and there are wicked people who are treated according to the conduct of the righteous. I said that this also is vanity. 15 So I commend enjoyment, for there is nothing better for people under the sun than to eat, and drink, and enjoy themselves, for this will go with them in their toil through the days of life that God gives them under the sun.

16 When I applied my mind to know wisdom, and to see the business that is done on earth, how one's eyes see sleep neither day nor night, 17 then I saw all the work of God, that no one can find out what is happening under the sun. However much they may toil in seeking, they will not find it out; even though those who are wise claim to know, they cannot find it out.

Take Life as It Comes

9 All this I laid to heart, examining it all, how the righteous and the wise and their deeds are in the hand of God; whether it is love or hate one does not know. Everything that confronts them 2 is vanity,[u] since the same fate comes to all, to the righteous and the wicked, to the good and the evil,[v] to the clean and the unclean, to those who sacrifice and those who do not sacrifice. As are the good, so are the sinners; those who swear are like those who shun an oath. 3 This

7.29 Gen 1.27; 3.6,7
8.1 Prov 4.8,9; Deut 28.50
8.2 Ezek 17.18
8.4 Job 9.12; Dan 4.35
8.6 Eccl 3.1,17
8.7 Prov 24.22; Eccl 6.12; 9.12; 10.14
8.8 Ps 49.6,7; Deut 20.5-8; v. 13
8.9 Eccl 4.1; 5.8
8.12 Isa 65.20; Ps 37.11,18, 19; Prov 1.32, 33; Isa 3.10, 11
8.13 v. 8; Isa 3.11; Eccl 6.12
8.14 Ps 73.14; Eccl 7.15; Job 21.7; Mal 3.15
8.15 Eccl 2.24; 3.12,13; 5.18; 9.7
8.16 Eccl 1.13, 14; 2.23
8.17 Job 5.9; Eccl 3.11; Rom 11.33; Eccl 8.7; Ps 73.16
9.1 Deut 33.3; Job 12.10; Ps 119.109; v. 6; Eccl 10.14
9.2 Job 9.22; Eccl 6.6; 7.2
9.3 v. 2; Eccl 8.11; 1.17

[q] *Qoheleth*, traditionally rendered *Preacher*
[r] Heb *I keep* [s] Or *breath* [t] Meaning of Heb uncertain [u] Syr Compare Gk: Heb *Everything that confronts them* [2]*is everything*
[v] Gk Syr Vg: Heb lacks *and the evil*

is an evil in all that happens under
the sun, that the same fate comes
to everyone. Moreover, the hearts
of all are full of evil; madness is in
their hearts while they live, and after that they go to the dead. 4 But
whoever is joined with all the living
has hope, for a living dog is better
than a dead lion. 5 The living know
that they will die, but the dead
know nothing; they have no more
reward, and even the memory of
them is lost. 6 Their love and their
hate and their envy have already
perished; never again will they
have any share in all that happens
under the sun.
7 Go, eat your bread with enjoyment, and drink your wine with a
merry heart; for God has long ago
approved what you do. 8 Let your
garments always be white; do not
let oil be lacking on your head.
9 Enjoy life with the wife whom you
love, all the days of your vain life
that are given you under the sun,
because that is your portion in life
and in your toil at which you toil
under the sun. 10 Whatever your
hand finds to do, do with your
might; for there is no work or
thought or knowledge or wisdom in
Sheol, to which you are going.
11 Again I saw that under the
sun the race is not to the swift, nor
the battle to the strong, nor bread
to the wise, nor riches to the intelligent, nor favor to the skillful; but
time and chance happen to them
all. 12 For no one can anticipate the
time of disaster. Like fish taken in
a cruel net, and like birds caught in
a snare, so mortals are snared at a
time of calamity, when it suddenly
falls upon them.

Wisdom Superior to Folly

13 I have also seen this example
of wisdom under the sun, and it
seemed great to me. 14 There was a
little city with few people in it. A
great king came against it and besieged it, building great siegeworks
against it. 15 Now there was found
in it a poor wise man, and he by his
wisdom delivered the city. Yet no
one remembered that poor man.
16 So I said, "Wisdom is better than
might; yet the poor man's wisdom
is despised, and his words are not
heeded."

17 The quiet words of the wise
are more to be heeded
than the shouting of a ruler
among fools.
18 Wisdom is better than
weapons of war,
but one bungler destroys
much good.

Miscellaneous Observations

10 Dead flies make the
perfumer's ointment
give off a foul odor;
so a little folly outweighs
wisdom and honor.
2 The heart of the wise
inclines to the right,
but the heart of a fool to
the left.
3 Even when fools walk on the
road, they lack sense,
and show to everyone that
they are fools.
4 If the anger of the ruler rises
against you, do not
leave your post,
for calmness will undo
great offenses.

5 There is an evil that I have
seen under the sun, as great an error as if it proceeded from the ruler:
6 folly is set in many high places,
and the rich sit in a low place. 7 I
have seen slaves on horseback, and
princes walking on foot like slaves.

8 Whoever digs a pit will fall
into it;
and whoever breaks
through a wall will be
bitten by a snake.
9 Whoever quarries stones will
be hurt by them;
and whoever splits logs will
be endangered by them.
10 If the iron is blunt, and one
does not whet the edge,
then more strength must
be exerted;
but wisdom helps one to
succeed.
11 If the snake bites before it is
charmed,

9.5 Job 14.21; Eccl 1.11; 2.16; Ps 88.12; Isa 26.14
9.6 Eccl 3.22
9.7 Eccl 8.15
9.8 Rev 3.4; Ps 23.5
9.9 Eccl 6.12; 7.15
9.10 Rom 12.11; Col 3.23; Isa 38.10
9.11 Am 2.14,15; Deut 8.17, 18; 1 Sam 6.9
9.12 Eccl 8.7; Prov 29.6; Isa 24.18; Lk 21.34,35
9.15 Eccl 4.13; 2.16; 8.10
9.16 Prov 21.22; Eccl 7.19
9.17 Eccl 7.5; 10.12
9.18 v. 16; Josh 7.1,11, 12
10.3 Prov 13.16; 18.2
10.4 Eccl 8.3; 1 Sam 25.24-33; Prov 25.15
10.5 Eccl 5.6
10.6 Esther 3.1
10.7 Prov 19.10; Esther 6.8
10.8 Ps 7.15; Prov 26.27
10.11 Ps 58.4,5; Jer 8.17

there is no advantage in a
charmer.

12 Words spoken by the wise
bring them favor,
but the lips of fools
consume them.
13 The words of their mouths
begin in foolishness,
and their talk ends in
wicked madness;
14 yet fools talk on and on.
No one knows what is to
happen,
and who can tell anyone
what the future holds?
15 The toil of fools wears them
out,
for they do not even know
the way to town.

16 Alas for you, O land, when
your king is a servant,[w]
and your princes feast in
the morning!
17 Happy are you, O land, when
your king is a
nobleman,
and your princes feast at
the proper time—
for strength, and not for
drunkenness!
18 Through sloth the roof sinks
in,
and through indolence the
house leaks.
19 Feasts are made for laughter;
wine gladdens life,
and money meets every
need.
20 Do not curse the king, even
in your thoughts,
or curse the rich, even in
your bedroom;
for a bird of the air may
carry your voice,
or some winged creature
tell the matter.

The Value of Diligence

11 Send out your bread
upon the waters,
for after many days you
will get it back.
2 Divide your means seven
ways, or even eight,
for you do not know what
disaster may happen on
earth.
3 When clouds are full,
they empty rain on the earth;
whether a tree falls to the
south or to the north,
in the place where the tree
falls, there it will lie.
4 Whoever observes the wind
will not sow;
and whoever regards the
clouds will not reap.
5 Just as you do not know how
the breath comes to the bones in
the mother's womb, so you do not
know the work of God, who makes
everything.
6 In the morning sow your seed,
and at evening do not let your
hands be idle; for you do not know
which will prosper, this or that, or
whether both alike will be good.

Youth and Old Age

7 Light is sweet, and it is pleasant for the eyes to see the sun.
8 Even those who live many
years should rejoice in them all; yet
let them remember that the days of
darkness will be many. All that
comes is vanity.
9 Rejoice, young man, while you
are young, and let your heart cheer
you in the days of your youth. Follow the inclination of your heart
and the desire of your eyes, but
know that for all these things God
will bring you into judgment.
10 Banish anxiety from your
mind, and put away pain from your
body; for youth and the dawn of life
are vanity.

12 Remember your creator in
the days of your youth, before the days of trouble come, and
the years draw near when you will
say, "I have no pleasure in them";
2 before the sun and the light and
the moon and the stars are darkened and the clouds return with[x]
the rain; 3 in the day when the
guards of the house tremble, and
the strong men are bent, and the
women who grind cease working
because they are few, and those

10.12 Prov 10.32; Lk 4.22; Prov 10.14; 18.7
10.13 Eccl 7.25
10.14 Prov 15.2; Eccl 3.22; 6.12; 8.7
10.16 Isa 3.4,5,12; 5.11
10.17 Prov 31.4; Isa 5.11
10.18 Prov 24.30-34
10.19 Ps 104.15; Eccl 7.12
10.20 Ex 22.28; Acts 23.5; 2 Kings 6.12; Lk 12.3
11.1 Isa 32.20; Deut 15.10; Prov 19.17; Mt 10.42; 2 Cor 9.8; Gal 6.9,10; Heb 6.10
11.2 Ps 112.9; Lk 6.30; 1 Tim 6.18, 19; Eccl 12.1
11.5 Jn 3.8; Ps 139.14, 15
11.6 Eccl 9.10
11.7 Eccl 7.11
11.8 Eccl 9.7; 12.1
11.9 Eccl 2.10; Num 15.39; Eccl 3.17; 12.14; Rom 14.10
11.10 2 Cor 7.1; 2 Tim 2.22
12.1ff Ps 63.6; 119.55; Eccl 11.8; 2 Sam 19.35

w Or *a child* x Or *after*; Heb *'ahar*

who look through the windows see
dimly; 4 when the doors on the
street are shut, and the sound of
the grinding is low, and one rises
up at the sound of a bird, and all
the daughters of song are brought
low; 5 when one is afraid of heights,
and terrors are in the road; the almond tree blossoms, the grasshopper drags itself along[y] and desire
fails; because all must go to their
eternal home, and the mourners
will go about the streets; 6 before
the silver cord is snapped,[z] and
the golden bowl is broken, and the
pitcher is broken at the fountain,
and the wheel broken at the cistern, 7 and the dust returns to the
earth as it was, and the breath[a] returns to God who gave it. 8 Vanity of
vanities, says the Teacher;[b] all is
vanity.

Epilogue

9 Besides being wise, the
Teacher[b] also taught the people
knowledge, weighing and studying
and arranging many proverbs.
10 The Teacher[b] sought to find
pleasing words, and he wrote words
of truth plainly.

11 The sayings of the wise are
like goads, and like nails firmly
fixed are the collected sayings that
are given by one shepherd.[c] 12 Of
anything beyond these, my child,
beware. Of making many books
there is no end, and much study is
a weariness of the flesh.

13 The end of the matter; all has
been heard. Fear God, and keep his
commandments; for that is the
whole duty of everyone. 14 For God
will bring every deed into judgment, including[d] every secret
thing, whether good or evil.

12.4 Jer 25.10; 2 Sam 19.35
12.5 Job 17.13; Jer 9.17
12.7 Gen 3.19; Job 34.15; Ps 90.3; Job 34.14; Isa 57.16; Zech 12.1
12.8 Eccl 1.2
12.9 1 Kings 4.32
12.10 Prov 10.32; 22.20,21
12.11 Eccl 7.5; Acts 2.37; Ezra 9.8; Isa 22.23
12.13 Deut 4.2; Eccl 8.5; Mic 6.8
12.14 Mt 10.26; 12.36; 1 Cor 4.5

[y] Or *is a burden* [z] Syr Vg Compare Gk: Heb *is removed* [a] Or *the spirit* [b] *Qoheleth,* traditionally rendered *Preacher* [c] Meaning of Heb uncertain [d] Or *into the judgment on*

THE
Song of Solomon

Title and Background

The title in the Hebrew text is "Solomon's Song of Songs," meaning by, for, or about Solomon. The phrase "Song of Songs" means the greatest of songs.

Author and Date of Writing

Verse 1 seems to ascribe authorship to Solomon, and he is referred to seven times in the book. But whether he was the author remains an open question. Consistency of language, style, tone, perspective, and recurring refrains seems to argue for a single author.

If Solomon is the author, the Song must be dated in the tenth century B.C. If he was not the author, it could have been written any time between the tenth and third centuries.

Theme and Message

In ancient Israel everything human came to expression in words. In the Song, love finds words–inspired words that disclose its exquisite charm and beauty as one of God's choicest gifts. The woman's voice of love in the Song suggests that love and wisdom draw men powerfully with the subtlety and mystery of a woman's allurements. God intends that such love be a normal part of marital life in his good creation.

Outline

I. Courtship (1.1–3.5)
II. Wedding Procession (3.6-11)
III. Expressions of Love (4.1–8.4)
IV. Homecoming (8.5-14)

---

1 The Song of Songs, which is Solomon's.

Colloquy of Bride and Friends

2 Let him kiss me with the
kisses of his mouth!
For your love is better than
wine,
3 your anointing oils are
fragrant,
your name is perfume poured
out;
therefore the maidens love
you.
4 Draw me after you, let us
make haste.
The king has brought me
into his chambers.
We will exult and rejoice in
you;
we will extol your love
more than wine;
rightly do they love you.

5 I am black and beautiful,
O daughters of Jerusalem,
like the tents of Kedar,
like the curtains of
Solomon.
6 Do not gaze at me because I
am dark,
because the sun has gazed
on me.
My mother's sons were angry
with me;
they made me keeper of
the vineyards,
but my own vineyard I have
not kept!
7 Tell me, you whom my soul
loves,

1.1 1 Kings 4.32
1.2 Song 4.10
1.3 Song 4.10; Eccl 7.1
1.4 Ps 45.14,15
1.5 Song 2.14; 4.3; 2.7; 5.8
1.6 Ps 69.8; Song 8.11
1.7 Song 3.1-4; 2.16; 8.13

where you pasture your
flock,
where you make it lie down
at noon;
for why should I be like one
who is veiled
beside the flocks of your
companions?

8 If you do not know,
O fairest among women,
follow the tracks of the flock,
and pasture your kids
beside the shepherds'
tents.

Colloquy of Bridegroom, Friends, and Bride

9 I compare you, my love,
to a mare among Pharaoh's
chariots.
10 Your cheeks are comely with
ornaments,
your neck with strings of
jewels.
11 We will make you ornaments
of gold,
studded with silver.

12 While the king was on his
couch,
my nard gave forth its
fragrance.
13 My beloved is to me a bag of
myrrh
that lies between my
breasts.
14 My beloved is to me a
cluster of henna
blossoms
in the vineyards of En-gedi.

15 Ah, you are beautiful, my
love;
ah, you are beautiful;
your eyes are doves.
16 Ah, you are beautiful, my
beloved,
truly lovely.
Our couch is green;
17 the beams of our house are
cedar,
our rafters[a] are pine.

2 I am a rose[b] of Sharon,
a lily of the valleys.

1.8 Song 5.9; 6.1
1.9 Song 2.2,10, 13; 2 Chr 1.16
1.10 5.13
1.14 Song 4.13
1.15 Song 4.1; 5.12
1.17 1 Kings 6.9, 10; 2 Chr 3.5
2.1 Isa 35.1,2; Song 5.13; 7.2

2 As a lily among brambles,
so is my love among
maidens.

3 As an apple tree among the
trees of the wood,
so is my beloved among
young men.
With great delight I sat in his
shadow,
and his fruit was sweet to
my taste.
4 He brought me to the
banqueting house,
and his intention toward
me was love.
5 Sustain me with raisins,
refresh me with apples;
for I am faint with love.
6 O that his left hand were
under my head,
and that his right hand
embraced me!
7 I adjure you, O daughters of
Jerusalem,
by the gazelles or the wild
does:
do not stir up or awaken love
until it is ready!

Springtime Rhapsody

8 The voice of my beloved!
Look, he comes,
leaping upon the mountains,
bounding over the hills.
9 My beloved is like a gazelle
or a young stag.
Look, there he stands
behind our wall,
gazing in at the windows,
looking through the lattice.
10 My beloved speaks and says
to me:
"Arise, my love, my fair one,
and come away;
11 for now the winter is past,
the rain is over and gone.
12 The flowers appear on the
earth;
the time of singing has
come,
and the voice of the
turtledove
is heard in our land.

2.3 Song 8.5; 4.13
2.4 Ps 20.5
2.5 Song 7.8; 5.8
2.6 Song 8.3
2.7 Song 3.5; 8.4
2.8 v. 17
2.9 v. 17
2.10 v. 13
2.12 Ps 74.19

[a] Meaning of Heb uncertain [b] Heb *crocus*

13 The fig tree puts forth its figs,
and the vines are in blossom;
they give forth fragrance.
Arise, my love, my fair one,
and come away.
14 O my dove, in the clefts of the rock,
in the covert of the cliff,
let me see your face,
let me hear your voice;
for your voice is sweet,
and your face is lovely.
15 Catch us the foxes,
the little foxes,
that ruin the vineyards—
for our vineyards are in blossom."

16 My beloved is mine and I am his;
he pastures his flock
among the lilies.
17 Until the day breathes
and the shadows flee,
turn, my beloved, be like a gazelle
or a young stag on the cleft mountains.[c]

Love's Dream

3 Upon my bed at night
I sought him whom my soul loves;
I sought him, but found him not;
I called him, but he gave no answer.[d]
2 "I will rise now and go about the city,
in the streets and in the squares;
I will seek him whom my soul loves."
I sought him, but found him not.
3 The sentinels found me,
as they went about in the city.
"Have you seen him whom my soul loves?"
4 Scarcely had I passed them,
when I found him whom my soul loves.
I held him, and would not let him go
until I brought him into my mother's house,
and into the chamber of her that conceived me.
5 I adjure you, O daughters of Jerusalem,
by the gazelles or the wild does:
do not stir up or awaken love
until it is ready!

The Groom and His Party Approach

6 What is that coming up from the wilderness,
like a column of smoke,
perfumed with myrrh and frankincense,
with all the fragrant powders of the merchant?
7 Look, it is the litter of Solomon!
Around it are sixty mighty men
of the mighty men of Israel,
8 all equipped with swords
and expert in war,
each with his sword at his thigh
because of alarms by night.
9 King Solomon made himself a palanquin
from the wood of Lebanon.
10 He made its posts of silver,
its back of gold, its seat of purple;
its interior was inlaid with love.[e]
Daughters of Jerusalem,
11 come out.
Look, O daughters of Zion,
at King Solomon,
at the crown with which his mother crowned him
on the day of his wedding,
on the day of the gladness of his heart.

2.13 Mt 24.32; Song 7.12; v. 10 **2.14** Song 5.2; Jer 48.28; Song 8.13; 1.5 **2.15** Ezek 13.4 **2.16** Song 6.3; 7.10 **2.17** Song 4.6; vv. 8,9 **3.1** Isa 26.9; Song 1.7; 5.6 **3.2** Jer 5.1 **3.3** Song 5.7 **3.4** Song 8.2 **3.5** Song 2.7; 8.4 **3.6** Song 8.5; 1.13; 4.6,14 **3.8** Jer 50.9; Ps 45.3; 91.5 **3.10** Song 1.5 **3.11** Song 3.16, 17

[c] Or *on the mountains of Bether*: meaning of Heb uncertain [d] Gk: Heb lacks this line [e] Meaning of Heb uncertain

The Bride's Beauty Extolled

4 How beautiful you are, my love,
how very beautiful!
Your eyes are doves
behind your veil.
Your hair is like a flock of goats,
moving down the slopes of Gilead.
2 Your teeth are like a flock of shorn ewes
that have come up from the washing,
all of which bear twins,
and not one among them is bereaved.
3 Your lips are like a crimson thread,
and your mouth is lovely.
Your cheeks are like halves of a pomegranate
behind your veil.
4 Your neck is like the tower of David,
built in courses;
on it hang a thousand bucklers,
all of them shields of warriors.
5 Your two breasts are like two fawns,
twins of a gazelle,
that feed among the lilies.
6 Until the day breathes
and the shadows flee,
I will hasten to the mountain of myrrh
and the hill of frankincense.
7 You are altogether beautiful, my love;
there is no flaw in you.
8 Come with me from Lebanon, my bride;
come with me from Lebanon.
Depart[f] from the peak of Amana,
from the peak of Senir and Hermon,
from the dens of lions,
from the mountains of leopards.

9 You have ravished my heart, my sister, my bride,
you have ravished my heart with a glance of your eyes,
with one jewel of your necklace.
10 How sweet is your love, my sister, my bride!
how much better is your love than wine,
and the fragrance of your oils than any spice!
11 Your lips distill nectar, my bride;
honey and milk are under your tongue;
the scent of your garments is like the scent of Lebanon.
12 A garden locked is my sister, my bride,
a garden locked, a fountain sealed.
13 Your channel[g] is an orchard of pomegranates
with all choicest fruits,
henna with nard,
14 nard and saffron, calamus and cinnamon,
with all trees of frankincense,
myrrh and aloes,
with all chief spices—
15 a garden fountain, a well of living water,
and flowing streams from Lebanon.

16 Awake, O north wind,
and come, O south wind!
Blow upon my garden
that its fragrance may be wafted abroad.
Let my beloved come to his garden,
and eat its choicest fruits.

5 I come to my garden, my sister, my bride;
I gather my myrrh with my spice,
I eat my honeycomb with my honey,

4.1 Song 1.15; 5.12; 6.5,7 **4.2** Song 6.6 **4.3** Song 6.7 **4.4** Song 7.4; Neh 3.19 **4.5** Song 7.3; 2.16; 6.2,3 **4.6** Song 2.17; v. 14 **4.7** Song 1.15 **4.8** Song 5.1; Deut 3.9 **4.9** vv. 10,12; Prov 1.9; Ezek 16.11 **4.10** Song 1.2-4 **4.11** Prov 5.3; 24.13; Gen 27.27; Hos 14.6 **4.12** Prov 5.15-18; Gen 29.3 **4.13** Eccl 2.5; Song 6.11; 7.12; v. 16; Song 1.14 **4.14** Song 1.12; Ex 30.23; v. 6; Song 3.6; Jn 19.39 **4.15** Jn 4.10; 7.38 **4.16** Song 5.1; 6.2 **5.1** Song 6.2; 4.9,11,14; Lk 15.7,10; Jn 3.29

[f] Or *Look* [g] Meaning of Heb uncertain

I drink my wine with my
milk.

Eat, friends, drink,
and be drunk with love.

Another Dream

2 I slept, but my heart was
awake.
Listen! my beloved is
knocking.
"Open to me, my sister, my
love,
my dove, my perfect one;
for my head is wet with dew,
my locks with the drops of
the night."
3 I had put off my garment;
how could I put it on
again?
I had bathed my feet;
how could I soil them?
4 My beloved thrust his hand
into the opening,
and my inmost being
yearned for him.
5 I arose to open to my
beloved,
and my hands dripped with
myrrh,
my fingers with liquid myrrh,
upon the handles of the
bolt.
6 I opened to my beloved,
but my beloved had turned
and was gone.
My soul failed me when he
spoke.
I sought him, but did not
find him;
I called him, but he gave
no answer.
7 Making their rounds in the
city
the sentinels found me;
they beat me, they wounded
me,
they took away my mantle,
those sentinels of the
walls.
8 I adjure you, O daughters of
Jerusalem,
if you find my beloved,
tell him this:
I am faint with love.

5.2 Song 4.9; 6.9; v. 11
5.3 Lk 11.7; Gen 19.2
5.5 v. 13
5.6 Song 6.1; 3.1; Prov 1.28
5.7 Song 3.3
5.8 Song 2.7; 3.5; 2.5
5.9 Song 1.8; 6.1
5.12 Song 1.15; 4.1
5.13 Song 6.2; 2.1
5.16 Song 7.9; 2 Sam 1.23
6.1 Song 5.6; 1.8
6.2 Song 4.16; 5.1,13; 1.7; 2.1

Colloquy of Friends and Bride

9 What is your beloved more
than another beloved,
O fairest among women?
What is your beloved more
than another beloved,
that you thus adjure us?

10 My beloved is all radiant and
ruddy,
distinguished among ten
thousand.
11 His head is the finest gold;
his locks are wavy,
black as a raven.
12 His eyes are like doves
beside springs of water,
bathed in milk,
fitly set.[h]
13 His cheeks are like beds of
spices,
yielding fragrance.
His lips are lilies,
distilling liquid myrrh.
14 His arms are rounded gold,
set with jewels.
His body is ivory work,[h]
encrusted with sapphires.[i]
15 His legs are alabaster
columns,
set upon bases of gold.
His appearance is like
Lebanon,
choice as the cedars.
16 His speech is most sweet,
and he is altogether
desirable.
This is my beloved and this
is my friend,
O daughters of Jerusalem.

6 Where has your beloved
gone,
O fairest among women?
Which way has your beloved
turned,
that we may seek him with
you?

2 My beloved has gone down
to his garden,
to the beds of spices,
to pasture his flock in the
gardens,

[h] Meaning of Heb uncertain [i] Heb *lapis lazuli*

and to gather lilies.
3 I am my beloved's and my
beloved is mine;
he pastures his flock
among the lilies.

The Bride's Matchless Beauty

4 You are beautiful as Tirzah,
my love,
comely as Jerusalem,
terrible as an army with
banners.
5 Turn away your eyes from
me,
for they overwhelm me!
Your hair is like a flock of
goats,
moving down the slopes of
Gilead.
6 Your teeth are like a flock of
ewes,
that have come up from
the washing;
all of them bear twins,
and not one among them is
bereaved.
7 Your cheeks are like halves
of a pomegranate
behind your veil.
8 There are sixty queens and
eighty concubines,
and maidens without
number.
9 My dove, my perfect one, is
the only one,
the darling of her mother,
flawless to her that bore
her.
The maidens saw her and
called her happy;
the queens and concubines
also, and they praised
her.
10 "Who is this that looks forth
like the dawn,
fair as the moon, bright as
the sun,
terrible as an army with
banners?"

11 I went down to the nut
orchard,
to look at the blossoms of
the valley,
to see whether the vines had
budded,
whether the pomegranates
were in bloom.
12 Before I was aware, my fancy
set me
in a chariot beside my
prince.[j]

13 [k]Return, return,
O Shulammite!
Return, return, that we
may look upon you.

Why should you look upon
the Shulammite,
as upon a dance before two
armies?[l]

Expressions of Praise

7 How graceful are your feet in
sandals,
O queenly maiden!
Your rounded thighs are like
jewels,
the work of a master hand.
2 Your navel is a rounded bowl
that never lacks mixed
wine.
Your belly is a heap of
wheat,
encircled with lilies.
3 Your two breasts are like two
fawns,
twins of a gazelle.
4 Your neck is like an ivory
tower.
Your eyes are pools in
Heshbon,
by the gate of Bath-rabbim.
Your nose is like a tower of
Lebanon,
overlooking Damascus.
5 Your head crowns you like
Carmel,
and your flowing locks are
like purple;
a king is held captive in
the tresses.[m]

6 How fair and pleasant you
are,
O loved one, delectable
maiden![n]

6.3 Song 2.16; 7.10 **6.4** Song 1.15; v. 10 **6.5** Song 4.1 **6.6** Song 4.2 **6.7** Song 4.3 **6.8** 1 Kings 11.3; Song 1.3 **6.9** Song 2.14; 5.2; Gen 30.13 **6.10** v. 4 **6.11** Song 7.12

6.13 Judg 21.21; Gen 32.2 **7.1** Ps 45.13 **7.3** Song 4.5 **7.4** Song 4.4 **7.5** Isa 35.2 **7.6** Song 1.15, 16

[j] Cn: Meaning of Heb uncertain [k] Ch 7.1 in Heb [l] Or *dance of Mahanaim* [m] Meaning of Heb uncertain [n] Syr: Heb *in delights*

7 You are stately[o] as a palm
tree,
and your breasts are like
its clusters.
8 I say I will climb the palm
tree
and lay hold of its
branches.
Oh, may your breasts be like
clusters of the vine,
and the scent of your
breath like apples,
9 and your kisses[p] like the
best wine
that goes down[q] smoothly,
gliding over lips and
teeth.[r]

10 I am my beloved's,
and his desire is for me.
11 Come, my beloved,
let us go forth into the
fields,
and lodge in the villages;
12 let us go out early to the
vineyards,
and see whether the vines
have budded,
whether the grape blossoms
have opened
and the pomegranates are
in bloom.
There I will give you my love.
13 The mandrakes give forth
fragrance,
and over our doors are all
choice fruits,
new as well as old,
which I have laid up for
you, O my beloved.

8 O that you were like a
brother to me,
who nursed at my mother's
breast!
If I met you outside, I would
kiss you,
and no one would despise
me.
2 I would lead you and bring
you
into the house of my
mother,
and into the chamber of
the one who bore me.[s]
I would give you spiced wine
to drink,
the juice of my
pomegranates.
3 O that his left hand were
under my head,
and that his right hand
embraced me!
4 I adjure you, O daughters of
Jerusalem,
do not stir up or awaken
love
until it is ready!

Homecoming

5 Who is that coming up from
the wilderness,
leaning upon her beloved?

Under the apple tree I
awakened you.
There your mother was in
labor with you;
there she who bore you
was in labor.

6 Set me as a seal upon your
heart,
as a seal upon your arm;
for love is strong as death,
passion fierce as the grave.
Its flashes are flashes of fire,
a raging flame.
7 Many waters cannot quench
love,
neither can floods drown it.
If one offered for love
all the wealth of his house,
it would be utterly scorned.

8 We have a little sister,
and she has no breasts.
What shall we do for our
sister,
on the day when she is
spoken for?
9 If she is a wall,
we will build upon her a
battlement of silver;
but if she is a door,
we will enclose her with
boards of cedar.
10 I was a wall,
and my breasts were like
towers;

7.8 Song 2.5 **7.10** Song 2.16; 6.3; Ps 45.11 **7.12** Song 6.11 **7.13** Gen 30.14; Song 2.3; 4.13,16 **8.2** Song 3.4 **8.3** Song 2.6 **8.4** Song 2.7; 3.5 **8.5** Song 3.6; 2.3 **8.6** Isa 49.16; Jer 22.24; Hag 2.23; Prov 6.34 **8.8** Ezek 16.7

[o] Heb *This your stature is* [p] Heb *palate* [q] Heb *down for my lover* [r] Gk Syr Vg: Heb *lips of sleepers* [s] Gk Syr: Heb *my mother; she (or you) will teach me*

then I was in his eyes
as one who brings[t] peace.
11 Solomon had a vineyard at Baal-hamon;
he entrusted the vineyard to keepers;
each one was to bring for its fruit a thousand pieces of silver.
12 My vineyard, my very own, is for myself;
you, O Solomon, may have the thousand,
and the keepers of the fruit two hundred!
13 O you who dwell in the gardens,
my companions are listening for your voice;
let me hear it.

14 Make haste, my beloved,
and be like a gazelle
or a young stag
upon the mountains of spices!

8.11 Eccl 2.4; Mt 21.33; Song 1.6; 2.3; Isa 7.23

8.13 Song 1.7; 2.14

8.14 Song 2.17; 4.6

[t] Or *finds*

Isaiah

Title and Background

This book is named after the prophet whose message it records. Isaiah wrote during the stormy period marking the expansion of the Assyrian empire and the decline of Israel. He warned the people of Judah that their sin would bring captivity at the hands of Babylon. Although the fall of Jerusalem would not take place until 586 B.C., Isaiah assumed its demise and proceeded to predict the restoration of the people from captivity. A decree of Cyrus would allow the Jews to return home, a deliverance that prefigured the greater salvation from sin through Jesus Christ. Significantly, Isaiah's name means "The LORD saves."

Author and Date of Writing

Isaiah son of Amoz was the greatest of the writing prophets and a contemporary of Amos, Hosea, and Micah. Most of the events discussed in chapters 1-39 occurred during Isaiah's ministry, so it is likely they were completed around 700 B.C. He lived until at least 681 and may have written chapters 40-66 during his later years. Some scholars, however, think that these latter chapters were written by a later devoted disciple of Isaiah, rather than by the prophet himself.

Theme and Message

Isaiah unveils the full dimensions of God's judgment and salvation. The awful judgment unleashed on Israel and all who defy God is called "the day of the LORD." The Lord's kingdom on earth, with its righteous Ruler and his righteous subjects, is the goal toward which the book of Isaiah steadily moves. The restored earth and the restored people will then conform to the divine ideal, and all will result in the praise and glory of the Holy God of Israel.

Outline

I. Rebuke and Promise (1.1–6.13)
II. Immanuel and His Kingdom (7.1–12.6)
III. Judgment Against the Nations (13.1–23.18)
IV. Judgment and Promise (24.1–27.13)
V. Six Woes on Israel and Assyria (28.1–33.24)
VI. Judgment and Promise (34.1–35.10)
VII. From the Assyrian Threat to the Babylonian Exile (36.1–39.8)
VIII. Deliverance and Restoration of Israel (40.1–48.22)
IX. The Servant's Ministry and Israel's Restoration (49.1–57.21)
X. Everlasting Deliverance and Judgment (58.1–66.24)

---

1 The vision of Isaiah son of Amoz, which he saw concerning Judah and Jerusalem in the days of Uzziah, Jotham, Ahaz, and Hezekiah, kings of Judah.

The Wickedness of Judah

2 Hear, O heavens, and listen,
O earth;
for the LORD has spoken:
I reared children and brought
them up,
but they have rebelled
against me.
3 The ox knows its owner,
and the donkey its master's
crib;
but Israel does not know,
my people do not
understand.

1.1 Num 12.6; Isa 2.1; 2 Kings 15.1, 13,32; 16.1; 18.1
1.2 Deut 23.1
1.3 Jer 8.7; 9.3, 6

4 Ah, sinful nation,
people laden with iniquity,
offspring who do evil,
children who deal
corruptly,
who have forsaken the LORD,
who have despised the
Holy One of Israel,
who are utterly estranged!

5 Why do you seek further
beatings?
Why do you continue to
rebel?
The whole head is sick,
and the whole heart faint.
6 From the sole of the foot
even to the head,
there is no soundness in it,
but bruises and sores
and bleeding wounds;
they have not been drained,
or bound up,
or softened with oil.

7 Your country lies desolate,
your cities are burned with
fire;
in your very presence
aliens devour your land;
it is desolate, as
overthrown by
foreigners.
8 And daughter Zion is left
like a booth in a vineyard,
like a shelter in a cucumber
field,
like a besieged city.
9 If the LORD of hosts
had not left us a few
survivors,
we would have been like
Sodom,
and become like
Gomorrah.

10 Hear the word of the LORD,
you rulers of Sodom!
Listen to the teaching of our
God,
you people of Gomorrah!
11 What to me is the multitude
of your sacrifices?
says the LORD;
I have had enough of burnt
offerings of rams
and the fat of fed beasts;
I do not delight in the blood
of bulls,
or of lambs, or of goats.

12 When you come to appear
before me,[a]
who asked this from your
hand?
Trample my courts no
more;
13 bringing offerings is futile;
incense is an abomination
to me.
New moon and sabbath and
calling of
convocation—
I cannot endure solemn
assemblies with
iniquity.
14 Your new moons and your
appointed festivals
my soul hates;
they have become a burden
to me,
I am weary of bearing
them.
15 When you stretch out your
hands,
I will hide my eyes from
you;
even though you make many
prayers,
I will not listen;
your hands are full of
blood.
16 Wash yourselves; make
yourselves clean;
remove the evil of your
doings
from before my eyes;
cease to do evil,
17 learn to do good;
seek justice,
rescue the oppressed,
defend the orphan,
plead for the widow.

18 Come now, let us argue it
out,
says the LORD:
though your sins are like
scarlet,
they shall be like snow;
though they are red like
crimson,

1.4 Isa 14.20; v. 28; Isa 5.24
1.5 Isa 31.6; 33.24
1.6 Job 2.7; Ps 38.3; Isa 30.26; Lk 10.34
1.7 Isa 6.11; Jer 44.6
1.8 Job 27.18
1.9 Rom 9.29; Isa 10.20-22
1.10 Isa 28.14; 3.9; Ezek 16.46; Rev 11.8
1.11 1 Sam 15.22; Jer 6.20; Mic 6.7
1.12 Ex 23.17
1.13 Isa 66.3; 1 Chr 23.31; Ex 12.16; Jer 7.9,10
1.14 Num 28.11; Lev 23.2; Isa 7.13; 43.24
1.15 1 Kings 8.22; Isa 8.17; 59.2; Mic 3.4; Isa 59.3
1.16 Jer 4.14; Isa 52.11; 55.7; Jer 25.5
1.17 Jer 22.3; Isa 58.6; Ps 82.3
1.18 Isa 43.26; Ps 51.7; Rev 7.14

[a] Or *see my face*

they shall become like wool.
19 If you are willing and obedient,
you shall eat the good of the land;
20 but if you refuse and rebel,
you shall be devoured by the sword;
for the mouth of the LORD has spoken.

The Degenerate City

21 How the faithful city
has become a whore!
She that was full of justice,
righteousness lodged in her—
but now murderers!
22 Your silver has become dross,
your wine is mixed with water.
23 Your princes are rebels
and companions of thieves.
Everyone loves a bribe
and runs after gifts.
They do not defend the orphan,
and the widow's cause does not come before them.

24 Therefore says the Sovereign, the LORD of hosts, the Mighty One of Israel:
Ah, I will pour out my wrath on my enemies,
and avenge myself on my foes!
25 I will turn my hand against you;
I will smelt away your dross as with lye
and remove all your alloy.
26 And I will restore your judges as at the first,
and your counselors as at the beginning.
Afterward you shall be called the city of righteousness,
the faithful city.

27 Zion shall be redeemed by justice,
and those in her who repent, by righteousness.
28 But rebels and sinners shall be destroyed together,
and those who forsake the LORD shall be consumed.
29 For you shall be ashamed of the oaks
in which you delighted;
and you shall blush for the gardens
that you have chosen.
30 For you shall be like an oak
whose leaf withers,
and like a garden without water.
31 The strong shall become like tinder,
and their work[b] like a spark;
they and their work shall burn together,
with no one to quench them.

The Future House of God

2 The word that Isaiah son of Amoz saw concerning Judah and Jerusalem.

2 In days to come
the mountain of the LORD's house
shall be established as the highest of the mountains,
and shall be raised above the hills;
all the nations shall stream to it.
3 Many peoples shall come and say,
"Come, let us go up to the mountain of the LORD,
to the house of the God of Jacob;
that he may teach us his ways
and that we may walk in his paths."
For out of Zion shall go forth instruction,

1.19 Deut 30.15, 16
1.20 Isa 3.25; 34.16
1.21 Jer 2.20; Isa 59.7
1.22 Ezek 22.18
1.23 Hos 9.15; Ex 23.8; Mic 7.3; Jer 5.28; Zech 7.10
1.24 Isa 49.26; 35.4
1.25 Mal 3.3
1.26 Jer 33.7; Zech 8.3
1.28 Isa 24.20; Ps 9.5; 2 Thes 1.8, 9
1.29 Isa 57.5; 65.3
1.31 Isa 5.24; 66.24; Mt 3.12
2.1ff Isa 1.1
2.2 Mic 4.1-3; Isa 27.13; 66.20; 56.7
2.3 Isa 55.5; 66.18; Zech 8.20-23; Lk 24.47

[b] Or *its makers*

and the word of the LORD
from Jerusalem.
4 He shall judge between the
nations,
and shall arbitrate for
many peoples;
they shall beat their swords
into plowshares,
and their spears into
pruning hooks;
nation shall not lift up sword
against nation,
neither shall they learn war
any more.

Judgment Pronounced on Arrogance

5 O house of Jacob,
come, let us walk
in the light of the LORD!
6 For you have forsaken the
ways of[c] your people,
O house of Jacob.
Indeed they are full of
diviners[d] from the east
and of soothsayers like the
Philistines,
and they clasp hands with
foreigners.
7 Their land is filled with silver
and gold,
and there is no end to their
treasures;
their land is filled with
horses,
and there is no end to their
chariots.
8 Their land is filled with
idols;
they bow down to the work
of their hands,
to what their own fingers
have made.
9 And so people are humbled,
and everyone is brought
low—
do not forgive them!
10 Enter into the rock,
and hide in the dust
from the terror of the LORD,
and from the glory of his
majesty.
11 The haughty eyes of people
shall be brought low,
and the pride of everyone
shall be humbled;
and the LORD alone will be
exalted
in that day.
12 For the LORD of hosts has a
day
against all that is proud
and lofty,
against all that is lifted up
and high;[e]
13 against all the cedars of
Lebanon,
lofty and lifted up;
and against all the oaks of
Bashan;
14 against all the high
mountains,
and against all the lofty
hills;
15 against every high tower,
and against every fortified
wall;
16 against all the ships of
Tarshish,
and against all the
beautiful craft.[f]
17 The haughtiness of people
shall be humbled,
and the pride of everyone
shall be brought low;
and the LORD alone will be
exalted on that day.
18 The idols shall utterly pass
away.
19 Enter the caves of the rocks
and the holes of the
ground,
from the terror of the LORD,
and from the glory of his
majesty,
when he rises to terrify the
earth.
20 On that day people will
throw away
to the moles and to the
bats
their idols of silver and their
idols of gold,
which they made for
themselves to worship,
21 to enter the caverns of the
rocks
and the clefts in the crags,
from the terror of the LORD,

2.4 Isa 32.17, 18; Hos 2.18
2.5 Isa 58.1; 60.1,2,19; 18.14
2.6 Deut 31.17; 2 Kings 16.7, 8
2.7 Deut 17.16
2.8 Isa 10.11; 17.8
2.9 Isa 5.15; Neh 4.5
2.10 Rev 6.15; 2 Thes 1.9
2.11 Isa 13.11; Zech 9.16
2.12 Isa 24.4,21
2.13 Isa 10.33, 34; Zech 11.2
2.14 Isa 30.25
2.16 1 Kings 10.22
2.17 v. 11
2.18 Isa 21.9
2.19 Hos 10.8; Rev 9.6; 2 Thes 1.9; Heb 12.26
2.20 Isa 30.22
2.21 vv. 10,19

[c] Heb lacks *the ways of* [d] Cn: Heb lacks *of diviners* [e] Cn Compare Gk: Heb *low* [f] Compare Gk: Meaning of Heb uncertain

and from the glory of his
majesty,
when he rises to terrify the
earth.
22 Turn away from mortals,
who have only breath in
their nostrils,
for of what account are
they?

3 For now the Sovereign, the
LORD of hosts,
is taking away from
Jerusalem and from
Judah
support and staff—
all support of bread,
and all support of water—
2 warrior and soldier,
judge and prophet,
diviner and elder,
3 captain of fifty
and dignitary,
counselor and skillful
magician
and expert enchanter.
4 And I will make boys their
princes,
and babes shall rule over
them.
5 The people will be
oppressed,
everyone by another
and everyone by a
neighbor;
the youth will be insolent to
the elder,
and the base to the
honorable.

6 Someone will even seize a
relative,
a member of the clan,
saying,
"You have a cloak;
you shall be our leader,
and this heap of ruins
shall be under your rule."
7 But the other will cry out on
that day, saying,
"I will not be a healer;
in my house there is
neither bread nor cloak;
you shall not make me
leader of the people."
8 For Jerusalem has stumbled
and Judah has fallen,

2.22 Ps 146.3; Job 27.3; Jas 4.14
3.1 Jer 37.21; Lev 26.26
3.2 2 Kings 24.14
3.4 Eccl 10.16
3.5 Mic 7.3-6; Isa 9.19
3.6 Isa 4.1
3.7 Ezek 34.4
3.8 Isa 1.7; 6.11; 9.17; 65.3,5
3.9 Isa 1.10; Gen 13.13
3.10 Deut 28.1-14
3.11 Isa 65.6,7
3.12 v. 4; Isa 9.16
3.13 Isa 66.16; Mic 6.2
3.14 Ezek 20.35, 36; Isa 10.1, 2; Jas 2.6
3.15 Ps 94.5
3.16 Isa 4.4

because their speech and
their deeds are against
the LORD,
defying his glorious presence.
9 The look on their faces bears
witness against them;
they proclaim their sin like
Sodom,
they do not hide it.
Woe to them!
For they have brought evil
on themselves.
10 Tell the innocent how
fortunate they are,
for they shall eat the fruit
of their labors.
11 Woe to the guilty! How
unfortunate they are,
for what their hands have
done shall be done to
them.
12 My people—children are
their oppressors,
and women rule over them.
O my people, your leaders
mislead you,
and confuse the course of
your paths.

13 The LORD rises to argue his
case;
he stands to judge the
peoples.
14 The LORD enters into
judgment
with the elders and princes
of his people:
It is you who have devoured
the vineyard;
the spoil of the poor is in
your houses.
15 What do you mean by
crushing my people,
by grinding the face of the
poor? says the Lord GOD
of hosts.

16 The LORD said:
Because the daughters of
Zion are haughty
and walk with outstretched
necks,
glancing wantonly with
their eyes,
mincing along as they go,
tinkling with their feet;

17 the Lord will afflict with
scabs
the heads of the daughters
of Zion,
and the LORD will lay bare
their secret parts.

18 In that day the Lord will take
away the finery of the anklets, the
headbands, and the crescents;
19 the pendants, the bracelets, and
the scarfs; 20 the headdresses, the
armlets, the sashes, the perfume
boxes, and the amulets; 21 the signet rings and nose rings; 22 the festal robes, the mantles, the cloaks,
and the handbags; 23 the garments
of gauze, the linen garments, the
turbans, and the veils.

24 Instead of perfume there will
be a stench;
and instead of a sash, a
rope;
and instead of well-set hair,
baldness;
and instead of a rich robe,
a binding of sackcloth;
instead of beauty, shame.[g]
25 Your men shall fall by the
sword
and your warriors in battle.
26 And her gates shall lament
and mourn;
ravaged, she shall sit upon
the ground.

4 Seven women shall take hold
of one man in that day, saying,
"We will eat our own bread
and wear our own
clothes;
just let us be called by your
name;
take away our disgrace."

The Future Glory of the Survivors in Zion

2 On that day the branch of the
LORD shall be beautiful and glorious, and the fruit of the land shall
be the pride and glory of the survivors of Israel. 3 Whoever is left in
Zion and remains in Jerusalem will
be called holy, everyone who has
been recorded for life in Jerusalem,
4 once the Lord has washed away
the filth of the daughters of Zion

3.17 Isa 47.3 **3.18** Judg 8.21 **3.20** Ex 39.28 **3.21** Ezek 16.12 **3.24** Prov 31.24; Isa 22.12; 15.3 **3.25** Isa 1.20; 65.12 **3.26** Jer 14.2; Lam 2.10 **4.1** Isa 13.12; 2 Thes 3.12; Isa 54.4 **4.2** Isa 11.1; Zech 3.8; 6.12; Ps 72.16; Isa 10.20 **4.3** Isa 28.5; 60.21; 52.1; Lk 10.20 **4.4** Isa 3.16,24; 1.15; 28.6; Mal 3.2,3

4.5 Ex 13.21; Isa 60.1,2 **4.6** Isa 25.4 **5.1** Ps 80.8; Mt 21.33; Mk 12.1; Lk 20.9 **5.2** Jer 2.21; Mt 21.19; Mk 11.13; Lk 13.6 **5.3** Mt 21.40 **5.4** Mt 23.37 **5.5** Ps 89.40; Isa 6.13; Ps 80.12; Isa 10.6; Lk 21.24; Rev 11.2 **5.6** Isa 24.1,3; Heb 6.8; 1 Kings 8.35

and cleansed the bloodstains of Jerusalem from its midst by a spirit of
judgment and by a spirit of burning. 5 Then the LORD will create over
the whole site of Mount Zion and
over its places of assembly a cloud
by day and smoke and the shining
of a flaming fire by night. Indeed
over all the glory there will be a
canopy. 6 It will serve as a pavilion,
a shade by day from the heat, and
a refuge and a shelter from the
storm and rain.

The Song of the Unfruitful Vineyard

5 Let me sing for my beloved
my love-song concerning
his vineyard:
My beloved had a vineyard
on a very fertile hill.
2 He dug it and cleared it of
stones,
and planted it with choice
vines;
he built a watchtower in the
midst of it,
and hewed out a wine vat
in it;
he expected it to yield
grapes,
but it yielded wild grapes.

3 And now, inhabitants of
Jerusalem
and people of Judah,
judge between me
and my vineyard.
4 What more was there to do
for my vineyard
that I have not done in it?
When I expected it to yield
grapes,
why did it yield wild
grapes?

5 And now I will tell you
what I will do to my
vineyard.
I will remove its hedge,
and it shall be devoured;
I will break down its wall,
and it shall be trampled
down.
6 I will make it a waste;

g Q Ms: MT lacks *shame*

it shall not be pruned or hoed,
and it shall be overgrown with briers and thorns;
I will also command the clouds
that they rain no rain upon it.

7 For the vineyard of the LORD of hosts
is the house of Israel,
and the people of Judah
are his pleasant planting;
he expected justice,
but saw bloodshed;
righteousness,
but heard a cry!

Social Injustice Denounced

8 Ah, you who join house to house,
who add field to field,
until there is room for no one but you,
and you are left to live alone
in the midst of the land!
9 The LORD of hosts has sworn in my hearing:
Surely many houses shall be desolate,
large and beautiful houses, without inhabitant.
10 For ten acres of vineyard shall yield but one bath,
and a homer of seed shall yield a mere ephah.[h]

11 Ah, you who rise early in the morning
in pursuit of strong drink,
who linger in the evening
to be inflamed by wine,
12 whose feasts consist of lyre and harp,
tambourine and flute and wine,
but who do not regard the deeds of the LORD,
or see the work of his hands!
13 Therefore my people go into exile without knowledge;
their nobles are dying of hunger,
and their multitude is parched with thirst.
14 Therefore Sheol has enlarged its appetite
and opened its mouth beyond measure;
the nobility of Jerusalem[i] and her multitude go down,
her throng and all who exult in her.
15 People are bowed down, everyone is brought low,
and the eyes of the haughty are humbled.
16 But the LORD of hosts is exalted by justice,
and the Holy God shows himself holy by righteousness.
17 Then the lambs shall graze as in their pasture,
fatlings and kids[j] shall feed among the ruins.

18 Ah, you who drag iniquity along with cords of falsehood,
who drag sin along as with cart ropes,
19 who say, "Let him make haste,
let him speed his work that we may see it;
let the plan of the Holy One of Israel hasten to fulfillment,
that we may know it!"
20 Ah, you who call evil good
and good evil,
who put darkness for light
and light for darkness,
who put bitter for sweet
and sweet for bitter!
21 Ah, you who are wise in your own eyes,
and shrewd in your own sight!
22 Ah, you who are heroes in drinking wine

5.7 Ps 80.8-11; Isa 3.14,15
5.8 Mic 2.2
5.9 Isa 22.14; 6.11,12
5.10 Isa 7.23; Ezek 45.11
5.11 Prov 23.29, 30; Eccl 10.16
5.12 Am 6.5,6; Job 34.27; Ps 28.5
5.13 Hos 4.6; Isa 1.3; 3.3; 9.14,15
5.14 Prov 30.16; Num 16.30-34; Ps 141.7
5.15 Isa 2.9,11
5.16 Isa 2.11,17; 8.13; 29.23
5.18 Isa 59.4-8
5.19 Ezek 12.22; 2 Pet 3.3,4
5.20 Prov 17.15; Mt 6.22,23; Lk 11.34,35
5.21 Rom 12.16
5.22 v. 11

[h] The Heb *bath, homer,* and *ephah* are measures of quantity [i] Heb *her nobility*
[j] Cn Compare Gk: Heb *aliens*

and valiant at mixing
drink,
23 who acquit the guilty for a
bribe,
and deprive the innocent of
their rights!

Foreign Invasion Predicted

24 Therefore, as the tongue of
fire devours the stubble,
and as dry grass sinks
down in the flame,
so their root will become
rotten,
and their blossom go up
like dust;
for they have rejected the
instruction of the LORD
of hosts,
and have despised the word
of the Holy One of
Israel.

25 Therefore the anger of the
LORD was kindled
against his people,
and he stretched out his
hand against them and
struck them;
the mountains quaked,
and their corpses were like
refuse
in the streets.
For all this his anger has not
turned away,
and his hand is stretched
out still.

26 He will raise a signal for a
nation far away,
and whistle for a people at
the ends of the earth;
Here they come, swiftly,
speedily!
27 None of them is weary, none
stumbles,
none slumbers or sleeps,
not a loincloth is loose,
not a sandal-thong broken;
28 their arrows are sharp,
all their bows bent,
their horses' hoofs seem like
flint,
and their wheels like the
whirlwind.
29 Their roaring is like a lion,
like young lions they roar;

5.23 Isa 10.1,2; Ps 94.21
5.24 Isa 9.18,19; Job 18.16; Hos 5.12; Acts 13.41
5.25 2 Kings 22.13; Jer 4.24; Isa 14.19; 9.12,17,21; 23.11
5.26 Isa 13.2,3; 7.18; Deut 28.49; Isa 13.4,5
5.27 Joel 2.7,8; Dan 5.6
5.28 Ps 7.12,13; Jer 4.13
5.29 Jer 51.38; Isa 10.6; 42.22
5.30 Isa 17.12; 8.22
6.1 Isa 1.1; 2 Kings 15.7; 1 Kings 22.19
6.2 Rev 4.8; Ezek 1.11
6.3 Rev 4.8; Ps 72.19
6.5 Ex 33.20; Jer 9.3-8; 51.57
6.7 Jer 1.9; Isa 40.2; 1 Jn 1.7
6.8 Ezek 10.5; Acts 9.4; 26.19
6.9 Ezek 3.11; Mt 13.14, 15; Mk 4.12; Lk 8.10; Jn 12.40; Rom 11.8
6.10 Ps 119.70; Jer 5.21

they growl and seize their
prey,
they carry it off, and no
one can rescue.
30 They will roar over it on that
day,
like the roaring of the sea.
And if one look to the
land—
only darkness and distress;
and the light grows dark with
clouds.

A Vision of God in the Temple

6 In the year that King Uzziah
died, I saw the Lord sitting on
a throne, high and lofty; and the
hem of his robe filled the temple.
2 Seraphs were in attendance above
him; each had six wings: with two
they covered their faces, and with
two they covered their feet, and
with two they flew. 3 And one called
to another and said:
"Holy, holy, holy is the LORD
of hosts;
the whole earth is full of his
glory."
4 The pivots[k] on the thresholds
shook at the voices of those who
called, and the house filled with
smoke. 5 And I said: "Woe is me! I
am lost, for I am a man of unclean
lips, and I live among a people of
unclean lips; yet my eyes have seen
the King, the LORD of hosts!"
6 Then one of the seraphs flew
to me, holding a live coal that had
been taken from the altar with a
pair of tongs. 7 The seraph[l]
touched my mouth with it and said:
"Now that this has touched your
lips, your guilt has departed and
your sin is blotted out." 8 Then I
heard the voice of the Lord saying,
"Whom shall I send, and who will
go for us?" And I said, "Here am I;
send me!" 9 And he said, "Go and
say to this people:
'Keep listening, but do not
comprehend;
keep looking, but do not
understand.'
10 Make the mind of this
people dull,

[k] Meaning of Heb uncertain [l] Heb *He*

and stop their ears,
and shut their eyes,
so that they may not look
with their eyes,
and listen with their ears,
and comprehend with their
minds,
and turn and be healed."
11 Then I said, "How long,
O Lord?" And he said:
"Until cities lie waste
without inhabitant,
and houses without people,
and the land is utterly
desolate;
12 until the LORD sends
everyone far away,
and vast is the emptiness
in the midst of the
land.
13 Even if a tenth part remain
in it,
it will be burned again,
like a terebinth or an oak
whose stump remains
standing
when it is felled."[m]
The holy seed is its stump.

Isaiah Reassures King Ahaz

7 In the days of Ahaz son of Jotham son of Uzziah, king of Judah, King Rezin of Aram and King
Pekah son of Remaliah of Israel
went up to attack Jerusalem, but
could not mount an attack against
it. 2 When the house of David heard
that Aram had allied itself with
Ephraim, the heart of Ahaz[n] and
the heart of his people shook as the
trees of the forest shake before the
wind.
3 Then the LORD said to Isaiah,
Go out to meet Ahaz, you and your
son Shear-jashub,[o] at the end of
the conduit of the upper pool on
the highway to the Fuller's Field,
4 and say to him, Take heed, be quiet, do not fear, and do not let your
heart be faint because of these two
smoldering stumps of firebrands,
because of the fierce anger of Rezin
and Aram and the son of Remaliah.
5 Because Aram—with Ephraim
and the son of Remaliah—has
plotted evil against you, saying,
6 Let us go up against Judah and
cut off Jerusalem[p] and conquer it
for ourselves and make the son of
Tabeel king in it; 7 therefore thus
says the Lord GOD:
It shall not stand,
and it shall not come to
pass.
8 For the head of Aram is
Damascus,
and the head of Damascus
is Rezin.
(Within sixty-five years Ephraim
will be shattered, no longer a people.)
9 The head of Ephraim is
Samaria,
and the head of Samaria is
the son of Remaliah.
If you do not stand firm in
faith,
you shall not stand at all.

Isaiah Gives Ahaz the Sign of Immanuel

10 Again the LORD spoke to
Ahaz, saying, 11 Ask a sign of the
LORD your God; let it be deep as
Sheol or high as heaven. 12 But
Ahaz said, I will not ask, and I will
not put the LORD to the test. 13 Then
Isaiah[q] said: "Hear then, O house
of David! Is it too little for you to
weary mortals, that you weary my
God also? 14 Therefore the Lord
himself will give you a sign. Look,
the young woman[r] is with child
and shall bear a son, and shall
name him Immanuel.[s] 15 He shall
eat curds and honey by the time he
knows how to refuse the evil and
choose the good. 16 For before the
child knows how to refuse the evil
and choose the good, the land before whose two kings you are in
dread will be deserted. 17 The LORD
will bring on you and on your people and on your ancestral house
such days as have not come since
the day that Ephraim departed
from Judah—the king of Assyria."
18 On that day the LORD will
whistle for the fly that is at the

6.11 Mic 3.12 **6.12** Jer 4.29 **6.13** Isa 1.9; Job 14.7; Ezra 9.2 **7.1** 2 Kings 16.1; 15.37; 15.25 **7.2** v. 13; Isa 8.12 **7.3** Isa 10.21; 2 Kings 18.17 **7.4** Isa 30.15; 10.24; 35.4 **7.7** Isa 8.10 **7.8** Isa 17.1-3 **7.9** 2 Chr 20.20 **7.11** Isa 37.30; 38.7,8; 2 Kings 19.29 **7.14** Mt 1.23; Lk 1.31; Isa 9.6; 8.8 **7.15** v. 22 **7.16** Isa 8.4 **7.17** 2 Chr 28.19; 1 Kings 12.16 **7.18** Isa 5.26

m Meaning of Heb uncertain n Heb *his heart* o That is *A remnant shall return* p Heb *cut it off* q Heb *he* r Gk *the virgin* s That is *God is with us*

sources of the streams of Egypt,
and for the bee that is in the land
of Assyria. 19 And they will all come
and settle in the steep ravines, and
in the clefts of the rocks, and on all
the thornbushes, and on all the
pastures.
20 On that day the Lord will
shave with a razor hired beyond the
River—with the king of Assyria—
the head and the hair of the feet,
and it will take off the beard as
well.
21 On that day one will keep
alive a young cow and two sheep,
22 and will eat curds because of the
abundance of milk that they give;
for everyone that is left in the land
shall eat curds and honey.
23 On that day every place
where there used to be a thousand
vines, worth a thousand shekels of
silver, will become briers and
thorns. 24 With bow and arrows one
will go there, for all the land will be
briers and thorns; 25 and as for all
the hills that used to be hoed with
a hoe, you will not go there for fear
of briers and thorns; but they will
become a place where cattle are let
loose and where sheep tread.

Isaiah's Son a Sign of the Assyrian Invasion

8 Then the LORD said to me,
Take a large tablet and write
on it in common characters, "Belonging to Maher-shalal-hash-
baz,"[t] 2 and have it attested[u] for
me by reliable witnesses, the priest
Uriah and Zechariah son of Jebere-
chiah. 3 And I went to the prophetess, and she conceived and bore a
son. Then the LORD said to me,
Name him Maher-shalal-hash-baz;
4 for before the child knows how to
call "My father" or "My mother,"
the wealth of Damascus and the
spoil of Samaria will be carried
away by the king of Assyria.
5 The LORD spoke to me again:
6 Because this people has refused
the waters of Shiloah that flow
gently, and melt in fear before[v] Rezin and the son of Remaliah;
7 therefore, the Lord is bringing up
against it the mighty flood waters
of the River, the king of Assyria and
all his glory; it will rise above all its
channels and overflow all its
banks; 8 it will sweep on into Judah
as a flood, and, pouring over, it will
reach up to the neck; and its out-
spread wings will fill the breadth of
your land, O Immanuel.

9 Band together, you peoples,
and be dismayed;
listen, all you far countries;
gird yourselves and be
dismayed;
gird yourselves and be
dismayed!
10 Take counsel together, but it
shall be brought to
naught;
speak a word, but it will
not stand,
for God is with us.[w]

11 For the LORD spoke thus to
me while his hand was strong upon
me, and warned me not to walk in
the way of this people, saying: 12 Do
not call conspiracy all that this
people calls conspiracy, and do not
fear what it fears, or be in dread.
13 But the LORD of hosts, him you
shall regard as holy; let him be your
fear, and let him be your dread.
14 He will become a sanctuary, a
stone one strikes against; for both
houses of Israel he will become a
rock one stumbles over—a trap
and a snare for the inhabitants of
Jerusalem. 15 And many among
them shall stumble; they shall fall
and be broken; they shall be snared
and taken.

Disciples of Isaiah

16 Bind up the testimony, seal
the teaching among my disciples.
17 I will wait for the LORD, who is
hiding his face from the house of
Jacob, and I will hope in him.
18 See, I and the children whom the
LORD has given me are signs and
portents in Israel from the LORD of
hosts, who dwells on Mount Zion.

7.19 Isa 2.19; Jer 16.16
7.20 Isa 24.1; Ezek 5.1-4; Isa 10.5,15; 8.7
7.23 Isa 5.6
7.25 Isa 5.17
8.1 Isa 30.8; Hab 2.2
8.2 2 Kings 16.10
8.4 Isa 7.16; 7.8,9
8.6 Neh 3.15; Jn 9.7; Isa 7.1,2,6
8.7 Isa 17.12, 13; 7.20; 10.5,6
8.8 Isa 10.6; 30.28; 7.14
8.10 Job 5.12; Isa 7.7; Rom 8.31
8.11 Ezek 3.14; 2.8
8.12 Isa 7.2; 1 Pet 3.14, 15
8.13 Isa 5.16; 29.23; Num 20.12
8.14 Ezek 11.16; Lk 2.34; Rom 9.33; 1 Pet 2.8
8.15 Isa 28.13; Mt 21.44; Lk 20.18; Rom 9.32
8.16 vv. 1,2; Dan 12.4
8.17 Isa 54.8; Hab 2.3
8.18 Heb 2.13; Ps 71.7; Zech 3.8

[t] That is *The spoil speeds, the prey hastens*
[u] Q Ms Gk Syr: MT *and I caused to be attested*
[v] Cn: Meaning of Heb uncertain
[w] Heb *immanu el*

19 Now if people say to you, "Consult the ghosts and the familiar
spirits that chirp and mutter;
should not a people consult their
gods, the dead on behalf of the living, 20 for teaching and for instruction?" Surely, those who speak like
this will have no dawn! 21 They will
pass through the land,[x] greatly distressed and hungry; when they are
hungry, they will be enraged and
will curse[y] their king and their
gods. They will turn their faces upward, 22 or they will look to the
earth, but will see only distress and
darkness, the gloom of anguish;
and they will be thrust into thick
darkness.[z]

The Righteous Reign of the Coming King

9[a] But there will be no gloom for
those who were in anguish. In
the former time he brought into
contempt the land of Zebulun and
the land of Naphtali, but in the latter time he will make glorious the
way of the sea, the land beyond the
Jordan, Galilee of the nations.

2[b] The people who walked in
    darkness
  have seen a great light;
those who lived in a land of
    deep darkness—
  on them light has shined.
3 You have multiplied the
    nation,
  you have increased its joy;
they rejoice before you
  as with joy at the harvest,
  as people exult when
    dividing plunder.
4 For the yoke of their burden,
  and the bar across their
    shoulders,
  the rod of their oppressor,
  you have broken as on the
    day of Midian.
5 For all the boots of the
    tramping warriors
  and all the garments rolled
    in blood
  shall be burned as fuel for
    the fire.
6 For a child has been born for
    us,
  a son given to us;
authority rests upon his
    shoulders;
  and he is named
Wonderful Counselor, Mighty
    God,
  Everlasting Father, Prince
    of Peace.
7 His authority shall grow
    continually,
  and there shall be endless
    peace
for the throne of David and
    his kingdom.
  He will establish and
    uphold it
with justice and with
    righteousness
  from this time onward and
    forevermore.
The zeal of the LORD of hosts
    will do this.

Judgment on Arrogance and Oppression

8 The Lord sent a word against
    Jacob,
  and it fell on Israel;
9 and all the people knew it—
  Ephraim and the
    inhabitants of
    Samaria—
  but in pride and arrogance
    of heart they said:
10 "The bricks have fallen,
  but we will build with
    dressed stones;
the sycamores have been cut
    down,
  but we will put cedars in
    their place."
11 So the LORD raised
    adversaries[c] against
    them,
  and stirred up their
    enemies,
12 the Arameans on the east
    and the Philistines on
    the west,
  and they devoured Israel
    with open mouth.
For all this his anger has not
    turned away;

8.19 1 Sam 28.8; Isa 19.3; 30.2; 45.11
8.20 Lk 16.29; Mic 3.6
8.21 Isa 9.20,21; Rev 16.11
8.22 Isa 5.30; 9.1
9.1 2 Kings 15.29; 2 Chr 16.4
9.2 Mt 4.15,16
9.3 Isa 26.15; 35.10; 1 Sam 30.16
9.4 Isa 10.27; 14.4; 10.26
9.5 Isa 2.4
9.6 Isa 7.14; Lk 2.11; Jn 3.16; Mt 28.18; 1 Cor 15.25; Isa 28.29; 10.21; 63.16; Eph 2.14
9.7 Dan 2.44; Lk 1.32,33; Isa 16.15; 11.4,5; 37.32
9.9 Isa 7.8,9; 46.12
9.11 Isa 7.1,8
9.12 2 Kings 16.6; 2 Chr 28.18; Ps 79.7; Isa 5.25

[x] Heb *it* [y] Or *curse by* [z] Meaning of Heb uncertain [a] Ch 8.23 in Heb [b] Ch 9.1 in Heb [c] Cn: Heb *the adversaries of Rezin*

his hand is stretched out
still.

13 The people did not turn to
him who struck them,
or seek the LORD of hosts.
14 So the LORD cut off from
Israel head and tail,
palm branch and reed in
one day—
15 elders and dignitaries are the
head,
and prophets who teach
lies are the tail;
16 for those who led this people
led them astray,
and those who were led by
them were left in
confusion.
17 That is why the Lord did not
have pity on[d] their
young people,
or compassion on their
orphans and widows;
for everyone was godless and
an evildoer,
and every mouth spoke
folly.
For all this his anger has not
turned away,
his hand is stretched out
still.

18 For wickedness burned like a
fire,
consuming briers and
thorns;
it kindled the thickets of the
forest,
and they swirled upward in
a column of smoke.
19 Through the wrath of the
LORD of hosts
the land was burned,
and the people became like
fuel for the fire;
no one spared another.
20 They gorged on the right, but
still were hungry,
and they devoured on the
left, but were not
satisfied;
they devoured the flesh of
their own kindred;[e]
21 Manasseh devoured Ephraim,
and Ephraim Manasseh,
and together they were
against Judah.
For all this his anger has not
turned away;
his hand is stretched out
still.

10 Ah, you who make
iniquitous decrees,
who write oppressive
statutes,
2 to turn aside the needy from
justice
and to rob the poor of my
people of their right,
that widows may be your
spoil,
and that you may make the
orphans your prey!
3 What will you do on the day
of punishment,
in the calamity that will
come from far away?
To whom will you flee for
help,
and where will you leave
your wealth,
4 so as not to crouch among
the prisoners
or fall among the slain?
For all this his anger has not
turned away;
his hand is stretched out
still.

Arrogant Assyria Also Judged

5 Ah, Assyria, the rod of my
anger—
the club in their hands is
my fury!
6 Against a godless nation I
send him,
and against the people of
my wrath I command
him,
to take spoil and seize
plunder,
and to tread them down
like the mire of the
streets.
7 But this is not what he
intends,
nor does he have this in
mind;

9.13 Jer 5.3; Hos 7.10; Isa 31.1 **9.14** Isa 19.15; Rev 18.8 **9.15** Isa 3.2,3; 28.15 **9.16** Isa 3.12 **9.17** Jer 18.21; Isa 27.11; 10.6; Mic 7.2; Isa 5.25 **9.18** Isa 10.17; Mal 4.1 **9.19** Isa 10.6; Joel 2.3; Isa 1.31; 24.6; Mic 7.2,6 **9.20** Isa 8.21,22; 49.26 **9.21** Isa 5.25

10.1 Ps 94.20 **10.2** Isa 5.23; 1.23 **10.3** Job 31.14; Hos 9.7; Lk 19.44; Isa 5.26; 20.6 **10.4** Isa 24.22; 22.2; 5.25 **10.5** Jer 51.20 **10.6** Isa 9.17,19; Jer 34.22; Isa 5.25,29 **10.7** Gen 50.20

[d] Q Ms: MT *rejoice over* [e] Or *arm*

but it is in his heart to
destroy,
and to cut off nations not a
few.
8 For he says:
"Are not my commanders all
kings?
9 Is not Calno like
Carchemish?
Is not Hamath like Arpad?
Is not Samaria like
Damascus?
10 As my hand has reached to
the kingdoms of the
idols
whose images were greater
than those of Jerusalem
and Samaria,
11 shall I not do to Jerusalem
and her idols
what I have done to
Samaria and her
images?"

12 When the Lord has finished
all his work on Mount Zion and on
Jerusalem, he[f] will punish the arrogant boasting of the king of Assyria and his haughty pride. 13 For
he says:
"By the strength of my hand
I have done it,
and by my wisdom, for I
have understanding;
I have removed the
boundaries of peoples,
and have plundered their
treasures;
like a bull I have brought
down those who sat on
thrones.
14 My hand has found, like a
nest,
the wealth of the
peoples;
and as one gathers eggs that
have been forsaken,
so I have gathered all the
earth;
and there was none that
moved a wing,
or opened its mouth, or
chirped."

15 Shall the ax vaunt itself over
the one who wields it,
or the saw magnify itself
against the one who
handles it?
As if a rod should raise the
one who lifts it up,
or as if a staff should lift
the one who is not
wood!
16 Therefore the Sovereign, the
LORD of hosts,
will send wasting sickness
among his stout
warriors,
and under his glory a
burning will be kindled,
like the burning of fire.
17 The light of Israel will
become a fire,
and his Holy One a flame;
and it will burn and devour
his thorns and briers in one
day.
18 The glory of his forest and
his fruitful land
the LORD will destroy, both
soul and body,
and it will be as when an
invalid wastes away.
19 The remnant of the trees of
his forest will be so few
that a child can write them
down.

The Repentant Remnant of Israel

20 On that day the remnant of
Israel and the survivors of the
house of Jacob will no more lean
on the one who struck them, but
will lean on the LORD, the Holy One
of Israel, in truth. 21 A remnant will
return, the remnant of Jacob, to
the mighty God. 22 For though your
people Israel were like the sand of
the sea, only a remnant of them
will return. Destruction is decreed,
overflowing with righteousness.
23 For the Lord GOD of hosts will
make a full end, as decreed, in all
the earth.[g]

24 Therefore thus says the Lord
GOD of hosts: O my people, who
live in Zion, do not be afraid of the

10.8 2 Kings 18.24, 34; 19.10ff **10.9** Am 6.2; 2 Chr 35.20; 2 Kings 16.9 **10.10** 2 Kings 19.17, 18 **10.12** 2 Kings 19.31; Jer 50.18; Isa 37.23 **10.13** Isa 37.24; Ezek 28.4; Dan 4.30 **10.14** Job 31.25 **10.15** Jer 51.20; Rom 9.20, 21; v. 5 **10.16** Isa 17.4; Ps 106.15; v. 18 **10.17** Isa 30.33; 37.23; 27.4 **10.18** Jer 21.14 **10.19** Isa 21.17 **10.20** 2 Kings 16.7; 2 Chr 28.20; Isa 17.7,8 **10.21** Isa 6.13; 9.6 **10.22** Rom 9.27, 28; Isa 28.22 **10.23** Dan 9.27 **10.24** Ps 87.5,6; Isa 37.6; Ex 5.14-16

[f] Heb *I* [g] Or *land*

Assyrians when they beat you with
a rod and lift up their staff against
you as the Egyptians did. 25 For in
a very little while my indignation
will come to an end, and my anger
will be directed to their destruction.
26 The LORD of hosts will wield a
whip against them, as when he
struck Midian at the rock of Oreb;
his staff will be over the sea, and he
will lift it as he did in Egypt. 27 On
that day his burden will be removed from your shoulder, and his
yoke will be destroyed from your
neck.

He has gone up from
Rimmon,[h]
28 he has come to Aiath;
he has passed through
Migron,
at Michmash he stores his
baggage;
29 they have crossed over the
pass,
at Geba they lodge for the
night;
Ramah trembles,
Gibeah of Saul has fled.
30 Cry aloud, O daughter
Gallim!
Listen, O Laishah!
Answer her, O Anathoth!
31 Madmenah is in flight,
the inhabitants of Gebim
flee for safety.
32 This very day he will halt at
Nob,
he will shake his fist
at the mount of daughter
Zion,
the hill of Jerusalem.

33 Look, the Sovereign, the
LORD of hosts,
will lop the boughs with
terrifying power;
the tallest trees will be cut
down,
and the lofty will be
brought low.
34 He will hack down the
thickets of the forest
with an ax,
and Lebanon with its
majestic trees[i] will fall.

10.25 Isa 17.14; v. 5
10.26 Isa 37.36-38; Judg 7.25; Ex 14.16,27
10.27 Isa 9.4; 30.23
10.28 1 Sam 14.2; 13.2,5; 17.22
10.29 Josh 21.17; 18.25; 1 Sam 10.26
10.30 1 Sam 25.44; Josh 21.18
10.31 Josh 15.31
10.32 1 Sam 21.1; Neh 11.32; Isa 13.2; 37.22
10.33 Am 2.9

11.1 Zech 6.12; Rev 5.5; Acts 13.23; Isa 4.2
11.2 Isa 61.1; Mt 3.16; Jn 1.32
11.3 Jn 2.25; 7.24
11.4 Isa 9.7; 3.14; 29.19; Mal 4.6; Job 4.9; 2 Thes 2.8
11.5 Eph 6.14; Isa 25.1
11.6 Isa 65.25
11.7 Isa 65.25

The Peaceful Kingdom

11 A shoot shall come out
from the stump of
Jesse,
and a branch shall grow
out of his roots.
2 The spirit of the LORD shall
rest on him,
the spirit of wisdom and
understanding,
the spirit of counsel and
might,
the spirit of knowledge and
the fear of the LORD.
3 His delight shall be in the
fear of the LORD.

He shall not judge by what
his eyes see,
or decide by what his ears
hear;
4 but with righteousness he
shall judge the poor,
and decide with equity for
the meek of the earth;
he shall strike the earth with
the rod of his mouth,
and with the breath of his
lips he shall kill the
wicked.
5 Righteousness shall be the
belt around his waist,
and faithfulness the belt
around his loins.

6 The wolf shall live with the
lamb,
the leopard shall lie down
with the kid,
the calf and the lion and the
fatling together,
and a little child shall lead
them.
7 The cow and the bear shall
graze,
their young shall lie down
together;
and the lion shall eat straw
like the ox.
8 The nursing child shall play
over the hole of the
asp,

[h] Cn: Heb *and his yoke from your neck, and a yoke will be destroyed because of fatness*
[i] Cn Compare Gk Vg: Heb *with a majestic one*

and the weaned child shall
put its hand on the
adder's den.
9 They will not hurt or destroy
on all my holy mountain;
for the earth will be full of
the knowledge of the
LORD
as the waters cover the sea.

Return of the Remnant of Israel and Judah

10 On that day the root of Jesse
shall stand as a signal to the peoples; the nations shall inquire of
him, and his dwelling shall be glorious.
11 On that day the Lord will extend his hand yet a second time to
recover the remnant that is left of
his people, from Assyria, from
Egypt, from Pathros, from Ethiopia,[j] from Elam, from Shinar, from
Hamath, and from the coastlands
of the sea.
12 He will raise a signal for the
nations,
and will assemble the
outcasts of Israel,
and gather the dispersed of
Judah
from the four corners of
the earth.
13 The jealousy of Ephraim
shall depart,
the hostility of Judah shall
be cut off;
Ephraim shall not be jealous
of Judah,
and Judah shall not be
hostile towards
Ephraim.
14 But they shall swoop down
on the backs of the
Philistines in the west,
together they shall plunder
the people of the east.
They shall put forth their
hand against Edom and
Moab,
and the Ammonites shall
obey them.
15 And the LORD will utterly
destroy
the tongue of the sea of
Egypt;
and will wave his hand over
the River
with his scorching wind;
and will split it into seven
channels,
and make a way to cross
on foot;
16 so there shall be a highway
from Assyria
for the remnant that is left
of his people,
as there was for Israel
when they came up from
the land of Egypt.

Thanksgiving and Praise

12 You will say in that day:
I will give thanks to
you, O LORD,
for though you were angry
with me,
your anger turned away,
and you comforted me.

2 Surely God is my salvation;
I will trust, and will not be
afraid,
for the LORD GOD[k] is my
strength and my might;
he has become my
salvation.

3 With joy you will draw water
from the wells of salvation. 4 And
you will say in that day:
Give thanks to the LORD,
call on his name;
make known his deeds
among the nations;
proclaim that his name is
exalted.

5 Sing praises to the LORD, for
he has done gloriously;
let this be known[l] in all
the earth.
6 Shout aloud and sing for joy,
O royal[m] Zion,
for great in your midst is
the Holy One of Israel.

11.9 Job 5.23; Hab 2.14 **11.10** Rom 15.12; Jn 3.14,15; Lk 2.32; Isa 14.3 **11.11** Zech 10.10; Mic 7.12; Isa 66.19 **11.12** v. 10; Zech 10.6; Isa 24.16 **11.13** Jer 3.18; Ezek 37.16, 17,22; Hos 1.11 **11.14** Dan 11.41; Joel 3.19; Isa 16.14; 25.10 **11.15** Isa 43.16; 19.16; 7.20; 8.7

11.16 Isa 19.23; 62.10; Ex 14.26-29; Isa 51.10; 63.12,13 **12.1** Isa 26.1; 25.1; 40.1,2 **12.2** Isa 33.2; 26.3; Ex 15.2; Ps 118.14 **12.3** Jn 4.10; 7.37,38; Isa 41.18 **12.5** Isa 24.14; Ex 15.1; Ps 98.1 **12.6** Zeph 3.14; Isa 49.26

[j] Or *Nubia*; Heb *Cush* [k] Heb *for Yah, the* LORD [l] Or *this is made known* [m] Or *O inhabitant of*

Proclamation against Babylon

13 The oracle concerning Babylon that Isaiah son of Amoz saw.

2 On a bare hill raise a signal,
cry aloud to them;
wave the hand for them to enter
the gates of the nobles.
3 I myself have commanded my consecrated ones,
have summoned my warriors, my proudly exulting ones,
to execute my anger.

4 Listen, a tumult on the mountains
as of a great multitude!
Listen, an uproar of kingdoms,
of nations gathering together!
The LORD of hosts is mustering
an army for battle.
5 They come from a distant land,
from the end of the heavens,
the LORD and the weapons of his indignation,
to destroy the whole earth.

6 Wail, for the day of the LORD is near;
it will come like destruction from the Almighty![n]
7 Therefore all hands will be feeble,
and every human heart will melt,
8 and they will be dismayed.
Pangs and agony will seize them;
they will be in anguish like a woman in labor.
They will look aghast at one another;
their faces will be aflame.
9 See, the day of the LORD comes,
cruel, with wrath and fierce anger,
to make the earth a desolation,
and to destroy its sinners from it.
10 For the stars of the heavens and their constellations
will not give their light;
the sun will be dark at its rising,
and the moon will not shed its light.
11 I will punish the world for its evil,
and the wicked for their iniquity;
I will put an end to the pride of the arrogant,
and lay low the insolence of tyrants.
12 I will make mortals more rare than fine gold,
and humans than the gold of Ophir.
13 Therefore I will make the heavens tremble,
and the earth will be shaken out of its place,
at the wrath of the LORD of hosts
in the day of his fierce anger.
14 Like a hunted gazelle,
or like sheep with no one to gather them,
all will turn to their own people,
and all will flee to their own lands.
15 Whoever is found will be thrust through,
and whoever is caught will fall by the sword.
16 Their infants will be dashed to pieces
before their eyes;
their houses will be plundered,
and their wives ravished.
17 See, I am stirring up the Medes against them,
who have no regard for silver
and do not delight in gold.
18 Their bows will slaughter the young men;

13.1 Jer chs. 50, 51 **13.2** Jer 50.2; 51.25; Isa 10.32 **13.3** Joel 3.11; Ps 149.2 **13.4** Isa 5.30 **13.5** Isa 5.26; 42.13; 10.5; 24.1 **13.6** Zeph 1.7; Isa 10.25; Joel 1.15 **13.7** Ezek 7.17; 21.7 **13.8** Isa 21.3; 26.17 **13.9** Isa 66.15,16
13.10 Isa 5.30; Joel 2.10; Mt 24.29; Mk 13.24; Lk 21.25 **13.11** Isa 26.21; 11.4; 2.11; Jer 48.29 **13.12** Isa 4.1; 6.11,12 **13.13** Isa 34.4; 51.6; Jer 10.10; Am 8.8; Hag 2.6 **13.14** 1 Kings 22.17; Jer 50.16; 51.9 **13.15** Isa 14.19 **13.16** Ps 137.9; Nah 3.10; Zech 14.2 **13.17** Isa 21.2; Jer 51.11; Dan 5.28 **13.18** 2 Kings 8.12; Ezek 9.5,10

[n] Traditional rendering of Heb *Shaddai*

they will have no mercy on
the fruit of the womb;
their eyes will not pity
children.
19 And Babylon, the glory of
kingdoms,
the splendor and pride of
the Chaldeans,
will be like Sodom and
Gomorrah
when God overthrew them.
20 It will never be inhabited
or lived in for all
generations;
Arabs will not pitch their
tents there,
shepherds will not make
their flocks lie down
there.
21 But wild animals will lie
down there,
and its houses will be full
of howling creatures;
there ostriches will live,
and there goat-demons will
dance.
22 Hyenas will cry in its towers,
and jackals in the pleasant
palaces;
its time is close at hand,
and its days will not be
prolonged.

Restoration of Judah

14 But the LORD will have
compassion on Jacob and
will again choose Israel, and will
set them in their own land; and
aliens will join them and attach
themselves to the house of Jacob.
2 And the nations will take them
and bring them to their place, and
the house of Israel will possess the
nations[o] as male and female slaves
in the LORD's land; they will take
captive those who were their captors, and rule over those who oppressed them.

Downfall of the King of Babylon

3 When the LORD has given you
rest from your pain and turmoil
and the hard service with which
you were made to serve, 4 you will
take up this taunt against the king
of Babylon:

13.19 Isa 21.9; Dan 4.30; Gen 19.24; Deut 29.23; Jer 49.18
13.20 Jer 51.37-43
13.21 Isa 34.11-15
13.22 Jer 51.33
14.1 Ps 102.13; Zech 1.17; 2.12; Isa 60.4,5, 10; Eph 2.12-19
14.2 Isa 49.22; 60.9,10; 66.20; 60.14
14.3 Isa 40.2
14.4 Isa 13.19; Hab 2.6; Rev 18.6
14.6 Isa 10.14; 47.6
14.8 Isa 55.12
14.9 Ezek 32.21
14.11 Isa 5.14; Ezek 28.13; Isa 51.8
14.12 Isa 34.4; Lk 10.18

How the oppressor has
ceased!
How his insolence[p] has
ceased!
5 The LORD has broken the
staff of the wicked,
the scepter of rulers,
6 that struck down the peoples
in wrath
with unceasing blows,
that ruled the nations in
anger
with unrelenting
persecution.
7 The whole earth is at rest
and quiet;
they break forth into
singing.
8 The cypresses exult over you,
the cedars of Lebanon,
saying,
"Since you were laid low,
no one comes to cut us
down."
9 Sheol beneath is stirred up
to meet you when you
come;
it rouses the shades to greet
you,
all who were leaders of the
earth;
it raises from their thrones
all who were kings of the
nations.
10 All of them will speak
and say to you:
"You too have become as
weak as we!
You have become like us!"
11 Your pomp is brought down
to Sheol,
and the sound of your
harps;
maggots are the bed beneath
you,
and worms are your
covering.
12 How you are fallen from
heaven,
O Day Star, son of Dawn!
How you are cut down to the
ground,

[o] Heb *them* [p] Q Ms Compare Gk Syr Vg: Meaning of MT uncertain

you who laid the nations
low!
13 You said in your heart,
"I will ascend to heaven;
I will raise my throne
above the stars of God;
I will sit on the mount of
assembly
on the heights of Zaphon;[q]
14 I will ascend to the tops of
the clouds,
I will make myself like the
Most High."
15 But you are brought down to
Sheol,
to the depths of the Pit.
16 Those who see you will stare
at you,
and ponder over you:
"Is this the man who made
the earth tremble,
who shook kingdoms,
17 who made the world like a
desert
and overthrew its cities,
who would not let his
prisoners go home?"
18 All the kings of the nations
lie in glory,
each in his own tomb;
19 but you are cast out, away
from your grave,
like loathsome carrion,[r]
clothed with the dead, those
pierced by the sword,
who go down to the stones
of the Pit,
like a corpse trampled
underfoot.
20 You will not be joined with
them in burial,
because you have destroyed
your land,
you have killed your
people.

May the descendants of
evildoers
nevermore be named!
21 Prepare slaughter for his
sons
because of the guilt of
their father.[s]
Let them never rise to
possess the earth
or cover the face of the
world with cities.

22 I will rise up against them,
says the LORD of hosts, and will cut
off from Babylon name and remnant, offspring and posterity, says
the LORD. 23 And I will make it a
possession of the hedgehog, and
pools of water, and I will sweep it
with the broom of destruction, says
the LORD of hosts.

An Oracle concerning Assyria

24 The LORD of hosts has sworn:
As I have designed,
so shall it be;
and as I have planned,
so shall it come to pass:
25 I will break the Assyrian in
my land,
and on my mountains
trample him under foot;
his yoke shall be removed
from them,
and his burden from their
shoulders.
26 This is the plan that is
planned
concerning the whole
earth;
and this is the hand that is
stretched out
over all the nations.
27 For the LORD of hosts has
planned,
and who will annul it?
His hand is stretched out,
and who will turn it back?

An Oracle concerning Philistia

28 In the year that King Ahaz died
this oracle came:

29 Do not rejoice, all you
Philistines,
that the rod that struck
you is broken,
for from the root of the
snake will come forth
an adder,
and its fruit will be a flying
fiery serpent.
30 The firstborn of the poor will
graze,

14.13 Ezek 28.2; Dan 8.10 **14.14** Isa 47.8; 2 Thes 2.4 **14.15** Mt 11.23 **14.16** Jer 50.23 **14.17** Joel 2.3; Isa 45.13 **14.19** Isa 22.16-18; Jer 41.7,9; Isa 5.25 **14.20** Job 18.19; Ps 21.10; 37.28; Isa 31.2 **14.21** Ex 20.5; Isa 13.16; Mt 23.35; Isa 27.6 **14.22** Isa 26.14; Prov 10.7; Isa 47.9 **14.23** Isa 34.11-15; Zeph 2.14; Isa 13.6 **14.24** Isa 45.23; 55.8,9; Acts 4.28 **14.25** Isa 10.12,27 **14.26** Isa 23.9; Ex 15.12 **14.27** 2 Chr 20.6; Isa 43.13; Dan 4.31,35 **14.28** 2 Kings 16.20 **14.29** Jer 47.1-7; 2 Chr 26.6 **14.30** Isa 3.14,15; 7.21; 8.21; Jer 25.16,20

q Or *assembly in the far north*
r Cn Compare Gk: Heb *like a loathed branch*
s Syr Compare Gk: Heb *fathers*

and the needy lie down in safety;
but I will make your root die of famine,
and your remnant I[t] will kill.
31 Wail, O gate; cry, O city;
melt in fear, O Philistia, all of you!
For smoke comes out of the north,
and there is no straggler in its ranks.

32 What will one answer the messengers of the nation?
"The LORD has founded Zion,
and the needy among his people
will find refuge in her."

An Oracle concerning Moab

15 An oracle concerning Moab.

Because Ar is laid waste in a night,
Moab is undone;
because Kir is laid waste in a night,
Moab is undone.
2 Dibon[u] has gone up to the temple,
to the high places to weep;
over Nebo and over Medeba
Moab wails.
On every head is baldness,
every beard is shorn;
3 in the streets they bind on sackcloth;
on the housetops and in the squares
everyone wails and melts in tears.
4 Heshbon and Elealeh cry out,
their voices are heard as far as Jahaz;
therefore the loins of Moab quiver;[v]
his soul trembles.
5 My heart cries out for Moab;
his fugitives flee to Zoar,
to Eglath-shelishiyah.
For at the ascent of Luhith
they go up weeping;
on the road to Horonaim
they raise a cry of destruction;
6 the waters of Nimrim
are a desolation;
the grass is withered, the new growth fails,
the verdure is no more.
7 Therefore the abundance they have gained
and what they have laid up
they carry away
over the Wadi of the Willows.
8 For a cry has gone
around the land of Moab;
the wailing reaches to Eglaim,
the wailing reaches to Beer-elim.
9 For the waters of Dibon[w] are full of blood;
yet I will bring upon Dibon[w] even more—
a lion for those of Moab who escape,
for the remnant of the land.

16 Send lambs
to the ruler of the land,
from Sela, by way of the desert,
to the mount of daughter Zion.
2 Like fluttering birds,
like scattered nestlings,
so are the daughters of Moab
at the fords of the Arnon.
3 "Give counsel,
grant justice;
make your shade like night
at the height of noon;
hide the outcasts,
do not betray the fugitive;
4 let the outcasts of Moab
settle among you;
be a refuge to them
from the destroyer."

When the oppressor is no more,
and destruction has ceased,

14.31 Isa 3.26; v. 29; Jer 1.14; Isa 34.16
14.32 Isa 37.9; Ps 87.1,5; Zeph 3.12; Zech 11.11
15.1 Isa 11.14; Jer 48; Ezek 25.8-11; Jer 48.41
15.2 Lev 21.5
15.3 Jon 3.6-8; Jer 48.38; Isa 22.4
15.5 Jer 48.5,31, 34; Isa 59.7
15.6 Isa 19.5-7; Joel 1.10-12
15.7 Isa 30.6
15.9 2 Kings 17.25; Jer 50.17
16.1 2 Kings 3.4; 14.7; Isa 10.32
16.2 Num 21.13, 14
16.3 Isa 25.4
16.4 Isa 9.4; 54.14

[t] Q Ms Vg: MT *he* [u] Cn: Heb *the house and Dibon* [v] Cn Compare Gk Syr: Heb *the armed men of Moab cry aloud* [w] Q Ms Vg Compare Syr: MT *Dimon*

and marauders have vanished
from the land,
5 then a throne shall be
established in steadfast
love
in the tent of David,
and on it shall sit in
faithfulness
a ruler who seeks justice
and is swift to do what is
right.

6 We have heard of the pride
of Moab
—how proud he is!—
of his arrogance, his pride,
and his insolence;
his boasts are false.
7 Therefore let Moab wail,
let everyone wail for Moab.
Mourn, utterly stricken,
for the raisin cakes of
Kir-hareseth.

8 For the fields of Heshbon
languish,
and the vines of Sibmah,
whose clusters once made
drunk
the lords of the nations,
reached to Jazer
and strayed to the desert;
their shoots once spread
abroad
and crossed over the sea.
9 Therefore I weep with the
weeping of Jazer
for the vines of Sibmah;
I drench you with my tears,
O Heshbon and Elealeh;
for the shout over your fruit
harvest
and your grain harvest has
ceased.
10 Joy and gladness are taken
away
from the fruitful field;
and in the vineyards no
songs are sung,
no shouts are raised;
no treader treads out wine in
the presses;
the vintage-shout is
hushed.[x]
11 Therefore my heart throbs
like a harp for Moab,
and my very soul for
Kir-heres.

12 When Moab presents himself, when he wearies himself upon
the high place, when he comes to
his sanctuary to pray, he will not
prevail.
13 This was the word that the
LORD spoke concerning Moab in the
past. 14 But now the LORD says, In
three years, like the years of a hired
worker, the glory of Moab will be
brought into contempt, in spite of
all its great multitude; and those
who survive will be very few and
feeble.

16.5 Dan 7.14; Mic 4.7; Lk 1.33; Isa 9.7
16.6 Jer 48.29, 30; Zeph 2.8,10
16.7 1 Chr 16.3; 2 Kings 3.25; Jer 48.31
16.8 Isa 15.4; Num 32.38; Jer 48.32
16.9 Jer 48.32; Isa 15.4; Jer 40.10,12
16.10 Isa 24.7,8; Jer 48.33; Job 24.11
16.11 Isa 15.5; 63.15; Jer 48.36
16.12 Jer 48.35; 1 Kings 18.29; Isa 15.2; 2 Kings 19.12
16.14 Isa 21.16; 25.10
17.1 2 Kings 16.9; Jer 49.23; Am 1.3; Zech 9.1; Isa 8.4; 10.9
17.2 Jer 7.33
17.3 Isa 7.16; 8.4
17.4 Isa 10.3,16
17.5 Jer 51.33; 2 Sam 5.18, 22

An Oracle concerning Damascus

17 An oracle concerning Damascus.

See, Damascus will cease to
be a city,
and will become a heap of
ruins.
2 Her towns will be deserted
forever;[y]
they will be places for
flocks,
which will lie down, and no
one will make them
afraid.
3 The fortress will disappear
from Ephraim,
and the kingdom from
Damascus;
and the remnant of Aram
will be
like the glory of the
children of Israel,
says the LORD of hosts.

4 On that day
the glory of Jacob will be
brought low,
and the fat of his flesh will
grow lean.
5 And it shall be as when
reapers gather standing
grain
and their arms harvest the
ears,
and as when one gleans the
ears of grain

[x] Gk: Heb *I have hushed* [y] Cn Compare Gk: Heb *the cities of Aroer are deserted*

in the Valley of Rephaim.
6 Gleanings will be left in it,
as when an olive tree is
beaten —
two or three berries
in the top of the highest
bough,
four or five
on the branches of a fruit
tree,
says the LORD God
of Israel.

7 On that day people will regard
their Maker, and their eyes will
look to the Holy One of Israel;
8 they will not have regard for the
altars, the work of their hands, and
they will not look to what their own
fingers have made, either the sacred poles[z] or the altars of incense.
9 On that day their strong cities
will be like the deserted places of
the Hivites and the Amorites,[a]
which they deserted because of the
children of Israel, and there will be
desolation.

10 For you have forgotten the
God of your salvation,
and have not remembered
the Rock of your refuge;
therefore, though you plant
pleasant plants
and set out slips of an
alien god,
11 though you make them grow
on the day that you
plant them,
and make them blossom in
the morning that you
sow;
yet the harvest will flee away
in a day of grief and
incurable pain.

12 Ah, the thunder of many
peoples,
they thunder like the
thundering of the sea!
Ah, the roar of nations,
they roar like the roaring of
mighty waters!
13 The nations roar like the
roaring of many waters,
but he will rebuke them,
and they will flee far
away,
chased like chaff on the
mountains before the
wind
and whirling dust before
the storm.
14 At evening time, lo, terror!
Before morning, they are
no more.
This is the fate of those who
despoil us,
and the lot of those who
plunder us.

An Oracle concerning Ethiopia

18 Ah, land of whirring wings
beyond the rivers of
Ethiopia,[b]
2 sending ambassadors by the
Nile
in vessels of papyrus on the
waters!
Go, you swift messengers,
to a nation tall and
smooth,
to a people feared near and
far,
a nation mighty and
conquering,
whose land the rivers
divide.

3 All you inhabitants of the
world,
you who live on the earth,
when a signal is raised on
the mountains, look!
When a trumpet is blown,
listen!
4 For thus the LORD said to me:
I will quietly look from my
dwelling
like clear heat in sunshine,
like a cloud of dew in the
heat of harvest.
5 For before the harvest, when
the blossom is over
and the flower becomes a
ripening grape,
he will cut off the shoots
with pruning hooks,

17.6 Isa 24.13; 27.12 **17.7** Isa 10.20; Mic 7.7 **17.8** Isa 27.9; 30.22; 31.7; Ex 34.13; Deut 7.5 **17.9** Isa 7.25 **17.10** Isa 51.13; Ps 68.19; Isa 26.4; 30.29 **17.11** Ps 90.6; Job 4.8 **17.12** Jer 6.23; Ezek 43.2; Ps 18.4 **17.13** Isa 33.3; Ps 9.5; Isa 13.14; 29.5; 41.15, 16

17.14 Isa 41.12; 2 Kings 19.35 **18.1** Isa 20.3-5; Ezek 30.4,5, 9; Zeph 2.12; 3.10 **18.2** Ex 2.3; v. 7; 2 Chr 12.2-4 **18.3** Ps 49.1; Isa 5.26; 26.11 **18.4** Isa 26.21; 2 Sam 23.4; Isa 26.19 **18.5** Ezek 17.6-10; Isa 27.11

z Heb *Asherim* a Cn Compare Gk: Heb *places of the wood and the highest bough* b Or *Nubia*; Heb *Cush*

and the spreading branches
he will hew away.
6 They shall all be left
to the birds of prey of the mountains
and to the animals of the earth.
And the birds of prey will summer on them,
and all the animals of the earth will winter on them.

7 At that time gifts will be
brought to the LORD of hosts from[c]
a people tall and smooth, from a
people feared near and far, a nation
mighty and conquering, whose
land the rivers divide, to Mount
Zion, the place of the name of the
LORD of hosts.

An Oracle concerning Egypt

19 An oracle concerning Egypt.

See, the LORD is riding on a swift cloud
and comes to Egypt;
the idols of Egypt will tremble at his presence,
and the heart of the Egyptians will melt within them.
2 I will stir up Egyptians against Egyptians,
and they will fight, one against the other,
neighbor against neighbor,
city against city, kingdom against kingdom;
3 the spirit of the Egyptians within them will be emptied out,
and I will confound their plans;
they will consult the idols and the spirits of the dead
and the ghosts and the familiar spirits;
4 I will deliver the Egyptians into the hand of a hard master;
a fierce king will rule over them,
says the Sovereign, the LORD of hosts.

5 The waters of the Nile will be dried up,
and the river will be parched and dry;
6 its canals will become foul,
and the branches of Egypt's Nile will diminish and dry up,
reeds and rushes will rot away.
7 There will be bare places by the Nile,
on the brink of the Nile;
and all that is sown by the Nile will dry up,
be driven away, and be no more.
8 Those who fish will mourn;
all who cast hooks in the Nile will lament,
and those who spread nets on the water will languish.
9 The workers in flax will be in despair,
and the carders and those at the loom will grow pale.
10 Its weavers will be dismayed,
and all who work for wages will be grieved.

11 The princes of Zoan are utterly foolish;
the wise counselors of Pharaoh give stupid counsel.
How can you say to Pharaoh,
"I am one of the sages,
a descendant of ancient kings"?
12 Where now are your sages?
Let them tell you and make known
what the LORD of hosts has planned against Egypt.
13 The princes of Zoan have become fools,
and the princes of Memphis are deluded;

18.6 Isa 46.11; 56.9; Jer 7.33
18.7 Ps 68.31; Isa 45.14; Zeph 3.10; Zech 14.16, 17
19.1 Isa 13.1; Jer 46.13-26; Ezek chs. 29,30; Ps 18.10; 104.3; Ex 12.12; Jer 43.12
19.2 Judg 7.22; 1 Sam 14.16, 20; 2 Chr 20.23; Mt 10.21,36
19.3 vv. 11-14; Isa 8.19
19.4 Isa 20.4; Jer 46.26; Ezek 29.19
19.5 Jer 51.36; Ezek 30.12
19.6 Ex 7.18; Isa 37.25; 15.6
19.7 Isa 23.3,10
19.9 Prov 7.16; Ezek 27.7
19.10 Ps 11.3
19.11 Num 13.22; 1 Kings 4.30; Acts 7.22
19.12 1 Cor 1.20; Isa 14.24; Rom 9.17
19.13 Jer 2.16; Ezek 30.13; Zech 10.4

c Q Ms Gk Vg: MT *of*

those who are the
cornerstones of its tribes
have led Egypt astray.
14 The LORD has poured into
them[d]
a spirit of confusion;
and they have made Egypt
stagger in all its doings
as a drunkard staggers
around in vomit.
15 Neither head nor tail, palm
branch or reed,
will be able to do anything
for Egypt.

16 On that day the Egyptians
will be like women, and tremble
with fear before the hand that the
LORD of hosts raises against them.
17 And the land of Judah will become a terror to the Egyptians; everyone to whom it is mentioned
will fear because of the plan that
the LORD of hosts is planning
against them.

Egypt, Assyria, and Israel Blessed

18 On that day there will be five
cities in the land of Egypt that
speak the language of Canaan and
swear allegiance to the LORD of
hosts. One of these will be called
the City of the Sun.
19 On that day there will be an
altar to the LORD in the center of
the land of Egypt, and a pillar to
the LORD at its border. 20 It will be a
sign and a witness to the LORD of
hosts in the land of Egypt; when
they cry to the LORD because of oppressors, he will send them a savior, and will defend and deliver
them. 21 The LORD will make himself known to the Egyptians; and
the Egyptians will know the LORD
on that day, and will worship with
sacrifice and burnt offering, and
they will make vows to the LORD
and perform them. 22 The LORD will
strike Egypt, striking and healing;
they will return to the LORD, and he
will listen to their supplications
and heal them.
23 On that day there will be a
highway from Egypt to Assyria, and
the Assyrian will come into Egypt,
and the Egyptian into Assyria, and
the Egyptians will worship with the
Assyrians.
24 On that day Israel will be the
third with Egypt and Assyria, a
blessing in the midst of the earth,
25 whom the LORD of hosts has
blessed, saying, "Blessed be Egypt
my people, and Assyria the work of
my hands, and Israel my heritage."

Isaiah Dramatizes the Conquest of Egypt and Ethiopia

20 In the year that the
commander-in-chief, who
was sent by King Sargon of Assyria,
came to Ashdod and fought against
it and took it— 2 at that time the
LORD had spoken to Isaiah son of
Amoz, saying, "Go, and loose the
sackcloth from your loins and take
your sandals off your feet," and he
had done so, walking naked and
barefoot. 3 Then the LORD said,
"Just as my servant Isaiah has
walked naked and barefoot for
three years as a sign and a portent
against Egypt and Ethiopia,[e] 4 so
shall the king of Assyria lead away
the Egyptians as captives and the
Ethiopians[f] as exiles, both the
young and the old, naked and barefoot, with buttocks uncovered, to
the shame of Egypt. 5 And they
shall be dismayed and confounded
because of Ethiopia[e] their hope
and of Egypt their boast. 6 In that
day the inhabitants of this coastland will say, 'See, this is what has
happened to those in whom we
hoped and to whom we fled for
help and deliverance from the king
of Assyria! And we, how shall we
escape?' "

Oracles concerning Babylon, Edom, and Arabia

21 The oracle concerning the
wilderness of the sea.

As whirlwinds in the Negeb
sweep on,
it comes from the desert,
from a terrible land.

19.14 Isa 29.10; Mt 17.17; Isa 3.12; 9.16; 28.7
19.15 Isa 9.14,15
19.16 Jer 51.30; Isa 2.19; 11.15; 30.32
19.17 Isa 14.24
19.18 Isa 45.23; 65.16
19.19 Isa 56.7; Gen 28.18; Ex 24.4; Josh 22.10, 26,27
19.20 Isa 43.3,11; 49.25
19.21 Isa 11.9; Mal 1.11; Isa 44.5
19.22 Isa 30.26; 27.13; 45.14
19.23 Isa 11.16; 27.13
19.25 Isa 45.14; Hos 2.23; Eph 2.10
20.1 2 Kings 18.17; 1 Sam 5.1
20.2 Zech 13.4; Ezek 24.17, 23; 1 Sam 19.24; Mic 1.8
20.3 Isa 8.18; 37.9; 43.3
20.4 Isa 19.4; 3.17; Jer 13.22,26
20.5 2 Kings 18.21; Isa 30.3,5,7; Ezek 29.6,7
20.6 Isa 10.3; 30.7; Mt 23.33; Heb 2.3
21.1 Isa 31.1; Jer 51.42; Zech 9.14

[d] Gk Compare Tg: Heb *it* [e] Or *Nubia*; Heb *Cush* [f] Or *Nubians*; Heb *Cushites*

2 A stern vision is told to me;
the betrayer betrays,
and the destroyer destroys.
Go up, O Elam,
lay siege, O Media;
all the sighing she has
caused
I bring to an end.
3 Therefore my loins are filled
with anguish;
pangs have seized me,
like the pangs of a woman
in labor;
I am bowed down so that I
cannot hear,
I am dismayed so that I
cannot see.
4 My mind reels, horror has
appalled me;
the twilight I longed for
has been turned for me
into trembling.
5 They prepare the table,
they spread the rugs,
they eat, they drink.
Rise up, commanders,
oil the shield!
6 For thus the Lord said to
me:
"Go, post a lookout,
let him announce what he
sees.
7 When he sees riders,
horsemen in pairs,
riders on donkeys, riders
on camels,
let him listen diligently,
very diligently."
8 Then the watcher[g] called
out:
"Upon a watchtower I stand,
O Lord,
continually by day,
and at my post I am
stationed
throughout the night.
9 Look, there they come,
riders,
horsemen in pairs!"
Then he responded,
"Fallen, fallen is Babylon;
and all the images of her
gods
lie shattered on the
ground."
10 O my threshed and
winnowed one,

21.2 Isa 33.1; 13.17; Jer 49.34 **21.3** Isa 15.5; 16.11; 13.8 **21.4** Deut 28.67 **21.5** Jer 51.39, 57; Dan 5.1-4 **21.7** v. 9 **21.8** Hab 2.1 **21.9** Jer 51.8; Rev 14.8; 18.2; Isa 46.1; Jer 50.2; 51.44 **21.10** Jer 51.33

what I have heard from the
LORD of hosts,
the God of Israel, I
announce to you.

11 The oracle concerning
Dumah.

One is calling to me from
Seir,
"Sentinel, what of the
night?
Sentinel, what of the
night?"
12 The sentinel says:
"Morning comes, and also
the night.
If you will inquire, inquire;
come back again."

13 The oracle concerning the
desert plain.

In the scrub of the desert
plain you will lodge,
O caravans of Dedanites.
14 Bring water to the thirsty,
meet the fugitive with
bread,
O inhabitants of the land
of Tema.
15 For they have fled from the
swords,
from the drawn sword,
from the bent bow,
and from the stress of
battle.

16 For thus the Lord said to me:
Within a year, according to the
years of a hired worker, all the glory
of Kedar will come to an end; 17 and
the remaining bows of Kedar's warriors will be few; for the LORD, the
God of Israel, has spoken.

21.11 Gen 25.14; 32.3 **21.13** Isa 13.1; Jer 49.28; 1 Chr 1.9, 32 **21.14** Gen 25.15; Job 6.19 **21.15** Isa 13.14, 15; 17.13 **21.16** Isa 16.14; 17.4; Ps 120.5; Isa 60.7 **21.17** Isa 10.19; Num 23.19; Zech 1.6 **22.1** Isa 13.1; Joel 3.12, 14; Isa 15.3

A Warning of Destruction of Jerusalem

22 The oracle concerning the valley of vision.

What do you mean that you
have gone up,
all of you, to the
housetops,

g Q Ms: MT *a lion*

2 you that are full of
shoutings,
tumultuous city, exultant
town?
Your slain are not slain by
the sword,
nor are they dead in
battle.
3 Your rulers have all fled
together;
they were captured without
the use of a bow.[h]
All of you who were found
were captured,
though they had fled far
away.[i]
4 Therefore I said:
Look away from me,
let me weep bitter tears;
do not try to comfort me
for the destruction of my
beloved people.

5 For the Lord GOD of hosts
has a day
of tumult and trampling
and confusion
in the valley of vision,
a battering down of walls
and a cry for help to the
mountains.
6 Elam bore the quiver
with chariots and cavalry,[j]
and Kir uncovered the
shield.
7 Your choicest valleys were
full of chariots,
and the cavalry took their
stand at the gates.
8 He has taken away the
covering of Judah.

On that day you looked to the
weapons of the House of the Forest, 9 and you saw that there were
many breaches in the city of David,
and you collected the waters of the
lower pool. 10 You counted the
houses of Jerusalem, and you
broke down the houses to fortify
the wall. 11 You made a reservoir
between the two walls for the water
of the old pool. But you did not
look to him who did it, or have regard for him who planned it long
ago.

22.2 Isa 32.13; Jer 14.18; Lam 2.20
22.3 Isa 21.15
22.4 Isa 15.3; Jer 4.19; 9.1
22.5 Isa 37.3; 63.3; Lam 1.5; 2.2; v. 1
22.6 Jer 49.35; 2 Kings 16.9
22.7 2 Chr 32.1
22.8 2 Chr 32.3-5, 30; 1 Kings 7.2; 10.17
22.9 Neh 3.16
22.11 2 Kings 25.4; 20.20; 2 Chr 32.3, 4; Isa 37.26
22.12 Joel 1.13; Isa 15.2; Mic 1.16
22.13 Isa 5.11,22; 56.12; 1 Cor 15.32
22.14 Isa 5.9; 65.7,20
22.15 2 Kings 18.37; Isa 36.3
22.16 2 Sam 18.18; 2 Chr 16.14; Mt 27.60
22.18 Isa 17.13; Job 18.18
22.19 Job 40.11, 12; Ezek 17.24
22.20 2 Kings 18.18; Isa 36.3
22.22 Rev 3.7; Isa 7.2,13; Job 12.14

12 In that day the Lord GOD of
hosts
called to weeping and
mourning,
to baldness and putting on
sackcloth;
13 but instead there was joy
and festivity,
killing oxen and
slaughtering sheep,
eating meat and drinking
wine.
"Let us eat and drink,
for tomorrow we die."
14 The LORD of hosts has
revealed himself in my
ears:
Surely this iniquity will not
be forgiven you until
you die,
says the Lord GOD of hosts.

Denunciation of Self-Seeking Officials

15 Thus says the Lord GOD of
hosts: Come, go to this steward, to
Shebna, who is master of the
household, and say to him: 16 What
right do you have here? Who are
your relatives here, that you have
cut out a tomb here for yourself,
cutting a tomb on the height, and
carving a habitation for yourself in
the rock? 17 The LORD is about to
hurl you away violently, my fellow.
He will seize firm hold on you,
18 whirl you round and round, and
throw you like a ball into a wide
land; there you shall die, and there
your splendid chariots shall lie,
O you disgrace to your master's
house! 19 I will thrust you from your
office, and you will be pulled down
from your post.
20 On that day I will call my servant Eliakim son of Hilkiah, 21 and
will clothe him with your robe and
bind your sash on him. I will commit your authority to his hand, and
he shall be a father to the inhabitants of Jerusalem and to the
house of Judah. 22 I will place on
his shoulder the key of the house of
David; he shall open, and no one

[h] Or *without their bows* [i] Gk Syr Vg: Heb *fled from far away* [j] Meaning of Heb uncertain

shall shut; he shall shut, and no
one shall open. [23]I will fasten him
like a peg in a secure place, and he
will become a throne of honor to
his ancestral house. [24]And they
will hang on him the whole weight
of his ancestral house, the offspring and issue, every small vessel, from the cups to all the flagons.
[25]On that day, says the LORD of
hosts, the peg that was fastened in
a secure place will give way; it will
be cut down and fall, and the load
that was on it will perish, for the
LORD has spoken.

An Oracle concerning Tyre

23 The oracle concerning Tyre.

Wail, O ships of Tarshish,
for your fortress is
destroyed.[k]
When they came in from
Cyprus
they learned of it.
2 Be still, O inhabitants of the
coast,
O merchants of Sidon,
your messengers crossed over
the sea[l]
3 and were on the mighty
waters;
your revenue was the grain of
Shihor,
the harvest of the Nile;
you were the merchant of
the nations.
4 Be ashamed, O Sidon, for
the sea has spoken,
the fortress of the sea,
saying:
"I have neither labored nor
given birth,
I have neither reared young
men
nor brought up young
women."
5 When the report comes to
Egypt,
they will be in anguish over
the report about Tyre.
6 Cross over to Tarshish—
wail, O inhabitants of the
coast!
7 Is this your exultant city
whose origin is from days
of old,
whose feet carried her
to settle far away?
8 Who has planned this
against Tyre, the bestower
of crowns,
whose merchants were
princes,
whose traders were the
honored of the earth?
9 The LORD of hosts has
planned it—
to defile the pride of all
glory,
to shame all the honored
of the earth.
10 Cross over to your own land,
O ships of[m] Tarshish;
this is a harbor[n] no more.
11 He has stretched out his
hand over the sea,
he has shaken the
kingdoms;
the LORD has given command
concerning Canaan
to destroy its fortresses.
12 He said:
You will exult no longer,
O oppressed virgin
daughter Sidon;
rise, cross over to Cyprus—
even there you will have no
rest.

13 Look at the land of the Chaldeans! This is the people; it was not
Assyria. They destined Tyre for
wild animals. They erected their
siege towers, they tore down her
palaces, they made her a ruin.[o]
14 Wail, O ships of Tarshish,
for your fortress is
destroyed.
[15]From that day Tyre will be forgotten for seventy years, the lifetime
of one king. At the end of seventy
years, it will happen to Tyre as in
the song about the prostitute:
16 Take a harp,
go about the city,

22.23 Ezra 9.8; Job 36.7 **22.25** v. 23; Isa 46.11; Mic 4.4 **23.1** Jer 25.22; 47.4; Ezek chs. 26,27,28; v. 12 **23.2** Isa 47.5 **23.3** Jer 2.18; Ezek 27.3-23 **23.4** Ezek 28.21, 22 **23.7** Isa 22.2; 32.13

23.9 Isa 2.11; 13.11; Job 40.11, 12; Isa 5.13; 9.15 **23.11** Isa 14.26; 50.2; 25.2 **23.12** Rev 18.22; Isa 47.1; v. 1 **23.13** Isa 10.5,7 **23.14** v. 1 **23.15** Jer 25.11,22

[k] Cn Compare verse 14: Heb *for it is destroyed, without houses* [l] Q Ms: MT *crossing over the sea, they replenished you* [m] Cn Compare Gk: Heb *like the Nile, daughter* [n] Cn: Heb *restraint* [o] Meaning of Heb uncertain

you forgotten prostitute!
Make sweet melody,
sing many songs,
that you may be
remembered.

17 At the end of seventy years, the
LORD will visit Tyre, and she will return to her trade, and will prostitute herself with all the kingdoms
of the world on the face of the
earth. 18 Her merchandise and her
wages will be dedicated to the
LORD; her profits[p] will not be
stored or hoarded, but her merchandise will supply abundant
food and fine clothing for those
who live in the presence of the
LORD.

Impending Judgment on the Earth

24 Now the LORD is about
to lay waste the earth
and make it desolate,
and he will twist its surface
and scatter its
inhabitants.
2 And it shall be, as with the
people, so with the
priest;
as with the slave, so with
his master;
as with the maid, so with
her mistress;
as with the buyer, so with
the seller;
as with the lender, so with
the borrower;
as with the creditor, so
with the debtor.
3 The earth shall be utterly
laid waste and utterly
despoiled;
for the LORD has spoken
this word.
4 The earth dries up and
withers,
the world languishes and
withers;
the heavens languish
together with the earth.
5 The earth lies polluted
under its inhabitants;
for they have transgressed
laws,
violated the statutes,
broken the everlasting
covenant.
6 Therefore a curse devours
the earth,
and its inhabitants suffer
for their guilt;
therefore the inhabitants of
the earth dwindled,
and few people are left.
7 The wine dries up,
the vine languishes,
all the merry-hearted sigh.
8 The mirth of the timbrels is
stilled,
the noise of the jubilant
has ceased,
the mirth of the lyre is
stilled.
9 No longer do they drink wine
with singing;
strong drink is bitter to
those who drink it.
10 The city of chaos is broken
down,
every house is shut up so
that no one can enter.
11 There is an outcry in the
streets for lack of wine;
all joy has reached its
eventide;
the gladness of the earth is
banished.
12 Desolation is left in the city,
the gates are battered into
ruins.
13 For thus it shall be on the
earth
and among the nations,
as when an olive tree is
beaten,
as at the gleaning when the
grape harvest is ended.
14 They lift up their voices, they
sing for joy;
they shout from the west
over the majesty of the
LORD.
15 Therefore in the east give
glory to the LORD;
in the coastlands of the sea
glorify the name of the
LORD, the God of Israel.

23.17 Rev 17.2
23.18 Isa 60.5-9; Zech 14.20
24.1 vv. 19,20; Isa 13.13,14
24.2 Hos 4.9; Lev 25.36, 37; Deut 23.19, 20
24.3 Isa 6.11,12
24.4 Isa 33.9; 2.12
24.5 Gen 3.17; Num 35.33; Isa 59.12
24.6 Isa 34.5; Mal 4.6; Isa 5.24; 9.19
24.7 Isa 16.8-10; Joel 1.10-12
24.8 Jer 7.34; 16.9; 25.10; Ezek 26.13; Hos 2.11; Rev 18.22
24.9 Isa 5.11,20, 22
24.10 Isa 23.1
24.11 Jer 14.2; 46.12; Isa 16.10; 32.13
24.12 Isa 14.31; 45.2
24.13 Isa 17.5,6
24.14 Isa 12.6; 42.10
24.15 Isa 25.3; Mal 1.11; Isa 66.19

p Heb *it*

16 From the ends of the earth
we hear songs of praise,
of glory to the Righteous
One.
But I say, I pine away,
I pine away. Woe is me!
For the treacherous deal
treacherously,
the treacherous deal very
treacherously.

17 Terror, and the pit, and the
snare
are upon you, O inhabitant
of the earth!
18 Whoever flees at the sound
of the terror
shall fall into the pit;
and whoever climbs out of
the pit
shall be caught in the
snare.
For the windows of heaven
are opened,
and the foundations of the
earth tremble.
19 The earth is utterly broken,
the earth is torn asunder,
the earth is violently
shaken.
20 The earth staggers like a
drunkard,
it sways like a hut;
its transgression lies heavy
upon it,
and it falls, and will not
rise again.

21 On that day the LORD will
punish
the host of heaven in
heaven,
and on earth the kings of
the earth.
22 They will be gathered
together
like prisoners in a pit;
they will be shut up in a
prison,
and after many days they
will be punished.
23 Then the moon will be
abashed,
and the sun ashamed;
for the LORD of hosts will
reign
on Mount Zion and in
Jerusalem,
and before his elders he will
manifest his glory.

24.16 Isa 11.12; 28.5; Jer 5.11
24.17 1 Kings 19.17
24.18 Jer 48.43, 44; Gen 7.11; Ps 18.7
24.19 v. 1; Jer 4.23
24.20 Isa 19.14; 66.24; Dan 11.19; Am 8.14
24.21 Isa 10.12; v. 4; Ps 76.12
24.22 Isa 10.4; 42.22; Ezek 38.8; Zech 9.11, 12
24.23 Isa 13.10; 60.19; Zech 14.6,7; Mic 4.7; Heb 12.22

Praise for Deliverance from Oppression

25 O LORD, you are my God;
I will exalt you, I will
praise your name;
for you have done wonderful
things,
plans formed of old,
faithful and sure.
2 For you have made the city a
heap,
the fortified city a ruin;
the palace of aliens is a city
no more,
it will never be rebuilt.
3 Therefore strong peoples will
glorify you;
cities of ruthless nations
will fear you.
4 For you have been a refuge
to the poor,
a refuge to the needy in
their distress,
a shelter from the
rainstorm and a shade
from the heat.
When the blast of the
ruthless was like a
winter rainstorm,
5 the noise of aliens like
heat in a dry place,
you subdued the heat with
the shade of clouds;
the song of the ruthless
was stilled.

6 On this mountain the LORD
of hosts will make for
all peoples
a feast of rich food, a feast
of well-aged wines,
of rich food filled with
marrow, of well-aged
wines strained clear.
7 And he will destroy on this
mountain
the shroud that is cast over
all peoples,
the sheet that is spread
over all nations;

25.1 Ps 118.28; 98.1; Num 23.19
25.2 Isa 17.1; 13.22; 32.14
25.4 Isa 14.32; 11.4; 32.2; 49.25
25.5 Jer 51.54-56
25.6 Isa 2.2-4; Prov 9.2; Mt 22.4; Dan 7.14; Mt 8.11

he will swallow up death
forever.
8 Then the Lord GOD will wipe
away the tears from all
faces,
and the disgrace of his
people he will take
away from all the earth,
for the LORD has spoken.
9 It will be said on that day,
Lo, this is our God; we
have waited for him, so
that he might save us.
This is the LORD for whom
we have waited;
let us be glad and rejoice
in his salvation.
10 For the hand of the LORD will
rest on this mountain.

The Moabites shall be
trodden down in their
place
as straw is trodden down in
a dung-pit.
11 Though they spread out their
hands in the midst of
it,
as swimmers spread out
their hands to swim,
their pride will be laid low
despite the struggle[q] of
their hands.
12 The high fortifications of his
walls will be brought
down,
laid low, cast to the
ground, even to the
dust.

Judah's Song of Victory

26 On that day this song will be sung in the land of Judah:
We have a strong city;
he sets up victory
like walls and bulwarks.
2 Open the gates,
so that the righteous
nation that keeps faith
may enter in.
3 Those of steadfast mind you
keep in peace—
in peace because they trust
in you.
4 Trust in the LORD forever,
for in the LORD GOD[r]
you have an everlasting
rock.
5 For he has brought low
the inhabitants of the
height;
the lofty city he lays low.
He lays it low to the ground,
casts it to the dust.
6 The foot tramples it,
the feet of the poor,
the steps of the needy.

7 The way of the righteous is
level;
O Just One, you make
smooth the path of the
righteous.
8 In the path of your
judgments,
O LORD, we wait for you;
your name and your renown
are the soul's desire.
9 My soul yearns for you in the
night,
my spirit within me
earnestly seeks you.
For when your judgments are
in the earth,
the inhabitants of the
world learn
righteousness.
10 If favor is shown to the
wicked,
they do not learn
righteousness;
in the land of uprightness
they deal perversely
and do not see the majesty
of the LORD.
11 O LORD, your hand is lifted
up,
but they do not see it.
Let them see your zeal for
your people, and be
ashamed.
Let the fire for your
adversaries consume
them.
12 O LORD, you will ordain
peace for us,
for indeed, all that we have
done, you have done for
us.

25.8 Hos 13.14; 1 Cor 15.54; Rev 7.17; 21.4; Isa 54.4
25.9 Isa 40.9; 30.18; 33.22; 66.10; Ps 20.5
25.10 Isa 16.14
26.1 Isa 4.2; 12.1; 14.31; 60.18
26.2 Isa 60.11, 18; 61.3; 62.1,2
26.4 Isa 12.2; 17.10
26.5 Isa 25.12; Job 40.11-13
26.6 Isa 28.3; 3.14,15
26.7 Isa 57.2; 42.16
26.8 Isa 51.4; 56.1; v. 13; Ex 3.15
26.9 Ps 63.6; Isa 55.6; Hos 5.15
26.10 Rom 2.4; Isa 22.12, 13; Hos 11.7; Jn 5.37,38
26.11 Isa 5.12; 9.7; 10.17; 66.15,24
26.12 v. 3; Isa 64.8

[q] Meaning of Heb uncertain [r] Heb *in Yah, the LORD*

13 O LORD our God,
other lords besides you
have ruled over us,
but we acknowledge your
name alone.
14 The dead do not live;
shades do not rise—
because you have punished
and destroyed them,
and wiped out all memory
of them.
15 But you have increased the
nation, O LORD,
you have increased the
nation; you are
glorified;
you have enlarged all the
borders of the land.

16 O LORD, in distress they
sought you,
they poured out a prayer[s]
when your chastening was
on them.
17 Like a woman with child,
who writhes and cries out
in her pangs
when she is near her time,
so were we because of you,
O LORD;
18 we were with child, we
writhed,
but we gave birth only to
wind.
We have won no victories on
earth,
and no one is born to
inhabit the world.
19 Your dead shall live, their
corpses[t] shall rise.
O dwellers in the dust,
awake and sing for joy!
For your dew is a radiant
dew,
and the earth will give
birth to those long
dead.[u]

20 Come, my people, enter your
chambers,
and shut your doors behind
you;
hide yourselves for a little
while
until the wrath is past.
21 For the LORD comes out from
his place

26.13 Isa 2.8; 10.11; 63.7
26.14 Isa 8.19; Hab 2.19; Isa 10.3
26.15 Isa 9.3; 33.17
26.16 Hos 5.15
26.17 Isa 13.8; Jn 16.21
26.18 Isa 33.11; Ps 17.14
26.19 Ezek 37.1-14; Dan 12.2
26.20 Ex 12.22, 23; Ps 30.5; Isa 54.7,8; 2 Cor 4.17
26.21 Mic 1.3; Jude 14; Isa 13.11; Job 16.18
27.1 Isa 34.5,6; Job 3.8; Ps 74.14; Isa 51.9
27.2 Ps 5.7; 80.8; Jer 2.21
27.3 Isa 58.11; 31.5; 1 Sam 2.9
27.4 2 Sam 23.6; Isa 33.12
27.5 Isa 25.4; Job 22.21
27.6 Isa 37.31; Hos 14.5,6
27.7 Isa 10.12,17
27.8 Job 23.6; Jer 10.23; Ps 78.38
27.9 Isa 1.25; Rom 11.27; Isa 17.8

to punish the inhabitants
of the earth for their
iniquity;
the earth will disclose the
blood shed on it,
and will no longer cover its
slain.

Israel's Redemption

27 On that day the LORD with
his cruel and great and
strong sword will punish Leviathan
the fleeing serpent, Leviathan the
twisting serpent, and he will kill
the dragon that is in the sea.

2 On that day:
A pleasant vineyard, sing
about it!
3 I, the LORD, am its keeper;
every moment I water it.
I guard it night and day
so that no one can harm it;
4 I have no wrath.
If it gives me thorns and
briers,
I will march to battle
against it.
I will burn it up.
5 Or else let it cling to me for
protection,
let it make peace with me,
let it make peace with me.

6 In days to come[v] Jacob shall
take root,
Israel shall blossom and
put forth shoots,
and fill the whole world
with fruit.

7 Has he struck them down as
he struck down those
who struck them?
Or have they been killed as
their killers were killed?
8 By expulsion,[s] by exile you
struggled against them;
with his fierce blast he
removed them in the
day of the east wind.
9 Therefore by this the guilt of
Jacob will be expiated,

[s] Meaning of Heb uncertain [t] Cn Compare Syr Tg: Heb *my corpse* [u] Heb *to the shades* [v] Heb *Those to come*

and this will be the full
fruit of the removal of
his sin:
when he makes all the
stones of the altars
like chalkstones crushed to
pieces,
no sacred poles[w] or
incense altars will
remain standing.
10 For the fortified city is
solitary,
a habitation deserted and
forsaken, like the
wilderness;
the calves graze there,
there they lie down, and
strip its branches.
11 When its boughs are dry,
they are broken;
women come and make a
fire of them.
For this is a people without
understanding;
therefore he that made
them will not have
compassion on them,
he that formed them will
show them no favor.

12 On that day the LORD will
thresh from the channel of the Euphrates to the Wadi of Egypt, and
you will be gathered one by one,
O people of Israel. 13 And on that
day a great trumpet will be blown,
and those who were lost in the land
of Assyria and those who were driv-
en out to the land of Egypt will
come and worship the LORD on the
holy mountain at Jerusalem.

Judgment on Corrupt Rulers, Priests, and Prophets

28 Ah, the proud garland of
the drunkards of
Ephraim,
and the fading flower of its
glorious beauty,
which is on the head of
those bloated with rich
food, of those overcome
with wine!
2 See, the Lord has one who is
mighty and strong;
like a storm of hail, a
destroying tempest,
like a storm of mighty,
overflowing waters;
with his hand he will hurl
them down to the
earth.
3 Trampled under foot will be
the proud garland of the
drunkards of Ephraim.
4 And the fading flower of its
glorious beauty,
which is on the head of
those bloated with rich
food,
will be like a first-ripe fig
before the summer;
whoever sees it, eats it up
as soon as it comes to
hand.

5 In that day the LORD of hosts
will be a garland of
glory,
and a diadem of beauty, to
the remnant of his
people;
6 and a spirit of justice to the
one who sits in
judgment,
and strength to those who
turn back the battle at
the gate.

7 These also reel with wine
and stagger with strong
drink;
the priest and the prophet
reel with strong drink,
they are confused with
wine,
they stagger with strong
drink;
they err in vision,
they stumble in giving
judgment.
8 All tables are covered with
filthy vomit;
no place is clean.

9 "Whom will he teach
knowledge,
and to whom will he
explain the message?

27.10 Isa 32.13, 14; Jer 26.6, 18
27.11 Deut 32.28; Isa 1.3; Jer 8.7; Deut 32.18; Isa 43.1,7; 44.2,21,24
27.12 Isa 11.11; Gen 15.18; Deut 30.3,4
27.13 Lev 25.9; Mt 24.31; Rev 11.15; Isa 19.23-25
28.1 vv. 3,4,7
28.2 Isa 40.10; 30.30; Ezek 13.11; Isa 29.6; 30.28
28.3 vv. 1,18
28.4 Hos 9.10; Mic 7.1; Nah 3.12
28.5 Isa 41.16; 62.3; 4.2
28.6 Isa 11.2; 32.15; 25.4
28.7 Prov 20.1; Hos 4.11; Isa 56.10,12
28.8 Jer 48.26
28.9 v. 26; Ps 131.2; Heb 5.12,13

[w] Heb *Asherim*

Those who are weaned from milk,
those taken from the breast?
10 For it is precept upon precept, precept upon precept,
line upon line, line upon line,
here a little, there a little."[x]

11 Truly, with stammering lip
and with alien tongue
he will speak to this people,
12 to whom he has said,
"This is rest;
give rest to the weary;
and this is repose";
yet they would not hear.
13 Therefore the word of the LORD will be to them,
"Precept upon precept,
precept upon precept,
line upon line, line upon line,
here a little, there a little;"[x]
in order that they may go,
and fall backward,
and be broken, and snared,
and taken.

14 Therefore hear the word of the LORD, you scoffers
who rule this people in Jerusalem.
15 Because you have said, "We have made a covenant with death,
and with Sheol we have an agreement;
when the overwhelming scourge passes through
it will not come to us;
for we have made lies our refuge,
and in falsehood we have taken shelter";
16 therefore thus says the Lord GOD,
See, I am laying in Zion a foundation stone,
a tested stone,
a precious cornerstone, a sure foundation:
"One who trusts will not panic."
17 And I will make justice the line,
and righteousness the plummet;
hail will sweep away the refuge of lies,
and waters will overwhelm the shelter.
18 Then your covenant with death will be annulled,
and your agreement with Sheol will not stand;
when the overwhelming scourge passes through
you will be beaten down by it.
19 As often as it passes through, it will take you;
for morning by morning it will pass through,
by day and by night;
and it will be sheer terror to understand the message.
20 For the bed is too short to stretch oneself on it,
and the covering too narrow to wrap oneself in it.
21 For the LORD will rise up as on Mount Perazim,
he will rage as in the valley of Gibeon;
to do his deed—strange is his deed!
and to work his work—alien is his work!
22 Now therefore do not scoff,
or your bonds will be made stronger;
for I have heard a decree of destruction
from the Lord GOD of hosts upon the whole land.

23 Listen, and hear my voice;
Pay attention, and hear my speech.
24 Do those who plow for sowing plow continually?

28.10 Neh 9.30 **28.11** 1 Cor 14.21 **28.12** Jer 6.16; Mt 11.28,29 **28.13** Mt 21.44 **28.14** v. 22; Isa 29.20 **28.15** vv. 18,2; Isa 59.3,4; 29.15 **28.16** Ps 118.22; Mt 21.42; Acts 4.11; Rom 9.33; 10.11; Eph 2.20; 1 Pet 2.4-6 **28.17** Isa 5.16; v. 2 **28.18** v. 15 **28.19** Isa 50.4; Ps 88.15; Jer 15.8 **28.21** 2 Sam 5.20; 1 Chr 14.11; Josh 10.10, 12; 2 Sam 5.25; 1 Chr 14.16; Lam 3.33 **28.22** v. 14; Isa 10.22,23

[x] Meaning of Heb of this verse uncertain

Do they continually open
and harrow their
ground?
25 When they have leveled its
surface,
do they not scatter dill,
sow cummin,
and plant wheat in rows
and barley in its proper
place,
and spelt as the border?
26 For they are well instructed;
their God teaches them.

27 Dill is not threshed with a
threshing sledge,
nor is a cart wheel rolled
over cummin;
but dill is beaten out with a
stick,
and cummin with a rod.
28 Grain is crushed for bread,
but one does not thresh it
forever;
one drives the cart wheel
and horses over it,
but does not pulverize it.
29 This also comes from the
LORD of hosts;
he is wonderful in counsel,
and excellent in wisdom.

The Siege of Jerusalem

29 Ah, Ariel, Ariel,
the city where David
encamped!
Add year to year;
let the festivals run their
round.
2 Yet I will distress Ariel,
and there shall be moaning
and lamentation,
and Jerusalem[y] shall be to
me like an Ariel.[z]
3 And like David[a] I will
encamp against you;
I will besiege you with
towers
and raise siegeworks
against you.
4 Then deep from the earth
you shall speak,
from low in the dust your
words shall come;
your voice shall come from
the ground like the
voice of a ghost,
and your speech shall
whisper out of the dust.

5 But the multitude of your
foes[b] shall be like
small dust,
and the multitude of
tyrants like flying chaff.
And in an instant, suddenly,
6 you will be visited by the
LORD of hosts
with thunder and earthquake
and great noise,
with whirlwind and
tempest, and the flame
of a devouring fire.
7 And the multitude of all the
nations that fight
against Ariel,
all that fight against her
and her stronghold, and
who distress her,
shall be like a dream, a
vision of the night.
8 Just as when a hungry
person dreams of eating
and wakes up still hungry,
or a thirsty person dreams of
drinking
and wakes up faint, still
thirsty,
so shall the multitude of all
the nations be
that fight against Mount
Zion.

9 Stupefy yourselves and be in
a stupor,
blind yourselves and be
blind!
Be drunk, but not from wine;
stagger, but not from
strong drink!
10 For the LORD has poured out
upon you
a spirit of deep sleep;
he has closed your eyes, you
prophets,
and covered your heads,
you seers.
11 The vision of all this has be-

28.27 Am 1.3 **28.29** Isa 9.6; 31.2; Rom 11.33 **29.1** 2 Sam 5.9; vv. 9,13 **29.2** Isa 3.26; Lam 2.5 **29.3** Lk 19.43,44 **29.4** Isa 8.19; Lev 20.6; Deut 18.10, 11; 1 Sam 28.8, 15; 2 Chr 33.6

29.5 Isa 17.13, 14; 25.3-5; 30.13; 1 Thes 5.3 **29.6** Isa 28.2; Mt 24.7; Mk 13.8; Lk 21.11; Rev 11.13, 19; 16.18 **29.7** Mic 4.11,12; Zech 12.9; Job 20.8; Ps 73.20 **29.8** Isa 54.17 **29.9** Isa 51.17, 21,22 **29.10** Rom 11.8; Ps 69.23; Isa 6.9,10; Mic 3.6 **29.11** Isa 27.7; 8.16; Dan 12.4,9; Mt 13.11

y Heb *she* z Probable meaning, *altar hearth*; compare Ezek 43.15
a Gk: Meaning of Heb uncertain
b Cn: Heb *strangers*

come for you like the words of a
sealed document. If it is given to
those who can read, with the command, "Read this," they say, "We
cannot, for it is sealed." 12 And if it
is given to those who cannot read,
saying, "Read this," they say, "We
cannot read."

13 The Lord said:
Because these people draw
near with their mouths
and honor me with their
lips,
while their hearts are far
from me,
and their worship of me is a
human commandment
learned by rote;
14 so I will again do
amazing things with this
people,
shocking and amazing.
The wisdom of their wise
shall perish,
and the discernment of the
discerning shall be
hidden.

15 Ha! You who hide a plan too
deep for the LORD,
whose deeds are in the
dark,
and who say, "Who sees
us? Who knows us?"
16 You turn things upside down!
Shall the potter be
regarded as the clay?
Shall the thing made say of
its maker,
"He did not make me";
or the thing formed say of
the one who formed it,
"He has no
understanding"?

Hope for the Future

17 Shall not Lebanon in a very
little while
become a fruitful field,
and the fruitful field be
regarded as a forest?
18 On that day the deaf shall
hear
the words of a scroll,

29.13 Ezek 33.31; Mt 15.8,9; Mk 7.6,7
29.14 Hab 1.5; Jer 8.9; 49.7; 1 Cor 1.19
29.15 Isa 30.1; 57.12; Ps 94.7
29.16 Isa 45.9; Jer 18.1-6; Rom 9.19-21
29.17 Isa 32.15
29.18 Isa 35.5; v. 11
29.19 Isa 61.1; Mt 11.5; Jas 2.5
29.20 v. 5; Isa 28.14, 22; 59.4
29.21 Am 5.10,12; Prov 28.21
29.22 Isa 41.8; 45.17; 54.4
29.23 Isa 49.20-26; 45.11; 5.16; 8.13
29.24 Isa 28.7
30.1 v. 9; Isa 29.15; 8.11,12
30.2 Isa 31.1; Num 27.21; Josh 9.14; 1 Kings 22.7; Jer 21.2

and out of their gloom and
darkness
the eyes of the blind shall
see.
19 The meek shall obtain fresh
joy in the LORD,
and the neediest people
shall exult in the
Holy One of Israel.
20 For the tyrant shall be no
more,
and the scoffer shall cease
to be;
all those alert to do evil
shall be cut off—
21 those who cause a person to
lose a lawsuit,
who set a trap for the
arbiter in the gate,
and without grounds deny
justice to the one in the
right.

22 Therefore thus says the LORD,
who redeemed Abraham, concerning the house of Jacob:
No longer shall Jacob be
ashamed,
no longer shall his face
grow pale.
23 For when he sees his
children,
the work of my hands, in
his midst,
they will sanctify my name;
they will sanctify the Holy
One of Jacob,
and will stand in awe of
the God of Israel.
24 And those who err in spirit
will come to
understanding,
and those who grumble will
accept instruction.

The Futility of Reliance on Egypt

30 Oh, rebellious children,
says the LORD,
who carry out a plan, but not
mine;
who make an alliance, but
against my will,
adding sin to sin;
2 who set out to go down to
Egypt

without asking for my
counsel,
to take refuge in the
protection of Pharaoh,
and to seek shelter in the
shadow of Egypt;
3 Therefore the protection of
Pharaoh shall become
your shame,
and the shelter in the
shadow of Egypt your
humiliation.
4 For though his officials are
at Zoan
and his envoys reach
Hanes,
5 everyone comes to shame
through a people that
cannot profit them,
that brings neither help nor
profit,
but shame and disgrace.

6 An oracle concerning the animals of the Negeb.
Through a land of trouble
and distress,
of lioness and roaring[c] lion,
of viper and flying serpent,
they carry their riches on the
backs of donkeys,
and their treasures on the
humps of camels,
to a people that cannot
profit them.
7 For Egypt's help is worthless
and empty,
therefore I have called her,
"Rahab who sits still."[d]

A Rebellious People

8 Go now, write it before them
on a tablet,
and inscribe it in a book,
so that it may be for the
time to come
as a witness forever.
9 For they are a rebellious
people,
faithless children,
children who will not hear
the instruction of the LORD;
10 who say to the seers, "Do
not see";
and to the prophets, "Do
not prophesy to us what
is right;
speak to us smooth things,
prophesy illusions,
11 leave the way, turn aside
from the path,
let us hear no more about
the Holy One of Israel."
12 Therefore thus says the Holy
One of Israel:
Because you reject this word,
and put your trust in
oppression and deceit,
and rely on them;
13 therefore this iniquity shall
become for you
like a break in a high wall,
bulging out, and about
to collapse,
whose crash comes
suddenly, in an instant;
14 its breaking is like that of a
potter's vessel
that is smashed so
ruthlessly
that among its fragments not
a sherd is found
for taking fire from the
hearth,
or dipping water out of the
cistern.

15 For thus said the Lord GOD,
the Holy One of Israel:
In returning and rest you
shall be saved;
in quietness and in trust
shall be your strength.
But you refused 16 and said,
"No! We will flee upon
horses"—
therefore you shall flee!
and, "We will ride upon swift
steeds"—
therefore your pursuers
shall be swift!
17 A thousand shall flee at the
threat of one,
at the threat of five you
shall flee,
until you are left
like a flagstaff on the top
of a mountain,
like a signal on a hill.

30.3 Isa 20.5; Jer 37.3,5
30.4 Isa 19.11
30.5 Jer 2.36; v. 7
30.6 Isa 46.1,2; 8.22; 14.29; 15.7
30.7 Jer 37.7; v. 15
30.8 Isa 8.1; Hab 2.2
30.9 v. 1; Isa 28.15; 24.5
30.10 Isa 29.10; 5.20; 1 Kings 22.8, 13
30.11 Job 21.14
30.12 Isa 5.24; 59.13
30.13 Isa 26.21; Ps 62.3; Isa 29.5
30.14 Ps 2.9; Jer 19.10,11
30.15 Isa 7.4; 28.12; 32.17
30.16 Isa 31.1,3
30.17 Lev 26.8; Deut 28.25; 32.30; Josh 23.10

[c] Cn: Heb *from them* [d] Meaning of Heb uncertain

God's Promise to Zion

18 Therefore the LORD waits to
be gracious to you;
therefore he will rise up to
show mercy to you.
For the LORD is a God of
justice;
blessed are all those who
wait for him.

19 Truly, O people in Zion, inhabitants of Jerusalem, you shall
weep no more. He will surely be
gracious to you at the sound of your
cry; when he hears it, he will answer you. 20 Though the Lord may
give you the bread of adversity and
the water of affliction, yet your
Teacher will not hide himself any
more, but your eyes shall see your
Teacher. 21 And when you turn to
the right or when you turn to the
left, your ears shall hear a word behind you, saying, "This is the way;
walk in it." 22 Then you will defile
your silver-covered idols and your
gold-plated images. You will scatter them like filthy rags; you will
say to them, "Away with you!"
23 He will give rain for the seed
with which you sow the ground,
and grain, the produce of the
ground, which will be rich and
plenteous. On that day your cattle
will graze in broad pastures; 24 and
the oxen and donkeys that till the
ground will eat silage, which has
been winnowed with shovel and
fork. 25 On every lofty mountain
and every high hill there will be
brooks running with water—on a
day of the great slaughter, when
the towers fall. 26 Moreover the
light of the moon will be like the
light of the sun, and the light of the
sun will be sevenfold, like the light
of seven days, on the day when the
LORD binds up the injuries of his
people, and heals the wounds inflicted by his blow.

Judgment on Assyria

27 See, the name of the LORD
comes from far away,
burning with his anger, and
in thick rising smoke;[e]
his lips are full of
indignation,
and his tongue is like a
devouring fire;
28 his breath is like an
overflowing stream
that reaches up to the
neck—
to sift the nations with the
sieve of destruction,
and to place on the jaws of
the peoples a bridle
that leads them astray.

29 You shall have a song as in
the night when a holy festival is
kept; and gladness of heart, as
when one sets out to the sound of
the flute to go to the mountain of
the LORD, to the Rock of Israel.
30 And the LORD will cause his majestic voice to be heard and the descending blow of his arm to be
seen, in furious anger and a flame
of devouring fire, with a cloudburst
and tempest and hailstones. 31 The
Assyrian will be terror-stricken at
the voice of the LORD, when he
strikes with his rod. 32 And every
stroke of the staff of punishment
that the LORD lays upon him will be
to the sound of timbrels and lyres;
battling with brandished arm he
will fight with him. 33 For his burning place[f] has long been prepared;
truly it is made ready for the king,[g]
its pyre made deep and wide, with
fire and wood in abundance; the
breath of the LORD, like a stream of
sulfur, kindles it.

Alliance with Egypt Is Futile

31 Alas for those who go
down to Egypt for help
and who rely on horses,
who trust in chariots because
they are many
and in horsemen because
they are very strong,
but do not look to the Holy
One of Israel
or consult the LORD!
2 Yet he too is wise and brings
disaster;

30.18 Isa 42.14; 33.5; 5.16; 25.9 **30.19** Isa 65.9; 60.20; 61.1-3; Mt 7.7-11 **30.20** 1 Kings 22.27; Ps 80.5; 74.9; Am 8.11 **30.21** Isa 35.8,9; Prov 3.6; Isa 29.24 **30.22** Isa 2.20; 31.7; 46.6; Mt 4.10 **30.23** Ps 65.9-13; Isa 65.21, 22; 32.20 **30.26** Isa 60.19, 20; Rev 21.23; 22.5; Isa 61.1; 1.6; Jer 33.6 **30.27** Isa 59.19; 10.5,13,17; 66.15 **30.28** Isa 11.4; 2 Thes 2.8; Isa 8.8; 37.29 **30.29** Ps 42.4; Isa 2.3; 17.10 **30.30** Isa 28.2; 32.19 **30.31** Isa 31.8 **30.32** Isa 10.24; Jer 31.4; Ezek 32.10 **30.33** Jer 7.3; 19.6; vv. 27, 28; Isa 34.9 **31.1** Isa 30.2; Ezek 17.15; Isa 2.7; Ps 20.7; Dan 9.13; Isa 10.17 **31.2** Isa 28.29; Rom 16.27; Isa 45.7; Num 23.19; Isa 14.20; 22.14

e Meaning of Heb uncertain f Or *Topheth* g Or *Molech*

he does not call back his words,
but will rise against the house of the evildoers,
and against the helpers of those who work iniquity.
3 The Egyptians are human, and not God;
their horses are flesh, and not spirit.
When the LORD stretches out his hand,
the helper will stumble, and the one helped will fall,
and they will all perish together.

4 For thus the LORD said to me,
As a lion or a young lion growls over its prey,
and—when a band of shepherds is called out against it—
is not terrified by their shouting
or daunted at their noise,
so the LORD of hosts will come down
to fight upon Mount Zion and upon its hill.
5 Like birds hovering overhead, so the LORD of hosts
will protect Jerusalem;
he will protect and deliver it,
he will spare and rescue it.

6 Turn back to him whom you[h]
have deeply betrayed, O people of
Israel. 7 For on that day all of you
shall throw away your idols of silver
and idols of gold, which your hands
have sinfully made for you.
8 "Then the Assyrian shall fall by a sword, not of mortals;
and a sword, not of humans, shall devour him;
he shall flee from the sword,
and his young men shall be put to forced labor.
9 His rock shall pass away in terror,
and his officers desert the standard in panic,"
says the LORD, whose fire is in Zion,
and whose furnace is in Jerusalem.

Government with Justice Predicted

32 See, a king will reign in righteousness,
and princes will rule with justice.
2 Each will be like a hiding place from the wind,
a covert from the tempest,
like streams of water in a dry place,
like the shade of a great rock in a weary land.
3 Then the eyes of those who have sight will not be closed,
and the ears of those who have hearing will listen.
4 The minds of the rash will have good judgment,
and the tongues of stammerers will speak readily and distinctly.
5 A fool will no longer be called noble,
nor a villain said to be honorable.
6 For fools speak folly,
and their minds plot iniquity:
to practice ungodliness,
to utter error concerning the LORD,
to leave the craving of the hungry unsatisfied,
and to deprive the thirsty of drink.
7 The villainies of villains are evil;
they devise wicked devices
to ruin the poor with lying words,
even when the plea of the needy is right.
8 But those who are noble plan noble things,
and by noble things they stand.

31.3 Ezek 28.9; Isa 36.9; 9.17; 30.5,7
31.4 Hos 11.10; Am 3.8; Isa 42.13
31.5 Ps 91.4; Isa 17.13
31.6 Isa 44.22; 1.2,5
31.7 Isa 2.20
31.8 Isa 10.12; 66.16; 21.15; 14.2
31.9 Deut 32.31, 37; Isa 5.26; 10.16
32.1 Isa 9.6,7; Jer 23.5; Zech 9.9
32.2 Isa 4.6; 35.6; 41.18; 43.19,20
32.3 Isa 29.18
32.4 Isa 29.24
32.5 1 Sam 25.25
32.6 Isa 59.7,13; 10.6; 9.15,16; 3.15
32.7 Jer 5.26-28; Isa 11.4; 5.23
32.8 2 Cor 9.6-11

[h] Heb *they*

Complacent Women Warned of Disaster

9 Rise up, you women who are
at ease, hear my voice;
you complacent daughters,
listen to my speech.
10 In little more than a year
you will shudder, you
complacent ones;
for the vintage will fail,
the fruit harvest will not
come.
11 Tremble, you women who
are at ease,
shudder, you complacent
ones;
strip, and make yourselves
bare,
and put sackcloth on your
loins.
12 Beat your breasts for the
pleasant fields,
for the fruitful vine,
13 for the soil of my people
growing up in thorns and
briers;
yes, for all the joyous houses
in the jubilant city.
14 For the palace will be
forsaken,
the populous city deserted;
the hill and the watchtower
will become dens forever,
the joy of wild asses,
a pasture for flocks;
15 until a spirit from on high is
poured out on us,
and the wilderness
becomes a fruitful field,
and the fruitful field is
deemed a forest.

The Peace of God's Reign

16 Then justice will dwell in the
wilderness,
and righteousness abide in
the fruitful field.
17 The effect of righteousness
will be peace,
and the result of
righteousness,
quietness and trust
forever.
18 My people will abide in a
peaceful habitation,
in secure dwellings, and in
quiet resting places.

32.9 Isa 47.8; 28.23
32.10 Isa 5.5,6
32.11 Isa 22.12; 47.2
32.12 Nah 2.7
32.13 Isa 34.13; 22.2
32.14 Isa 13.22; 6.11; 13.21
32.15 Isa 11.2; Ezek 39.29; Joel 2.28; Isa 29.17; 35.2
32.16 Isa 33.5
32.17 Rom 14.17; Jas 3.18; Isa 30.15
32.19 Isa 30.30; Zech 11.2
32.20 Isa 30.24
33.1 Isa 21.2; Hab 2.8; Isa 24.16; Jer 25.12-14; Mt 7.2
33.2 Isa 25.9
33.3 Isa 17.13; Jer 25.30,31
33.5 Ps 97.9
33.6 v. 20; Isa 45.17; 11.9; Mt 6.33
33.7 2 Kings 18.18, 37

19 The forest will disappear
completely,[i]
and the city will be utterly
laid low.
20 Happy will you be who sow
beside every stream,
who let the ox and the
donkey range freely.

A Prophecy of Deliverance from Foes

33 Ah, you destroyer,
who yourself have not
been destroyed;
you treacherous one,
with whom no one has
dealt treacherously!
When you have ceased to
destroy,
you will be destroyed;
and when you have stopped
dealing treacherously,
you will be dealt with
treacherously.

2 O LORD, be gracious to us; we
wait for you.
Be our arm every morning,
our salvation in the time of
trouble.
3 At the sound of tumult,
peoples fled;
before your majesty,
nations scattered.
4 Spoil was gathered as the
caterpillar gathers;
as locusts leap, they
leaped[j] upon it.
5 The LORD is exalted, he
dwells on high;
he filled Zion with justice
and righteousness;
6 he will be the stability of
your times,
abundance of salvation,
wisdom, and
knowledge;
the fear of the LORD is
Zion's treasure.[k]

7 Listen! the valiant[j] cry in
the streets;

[i] Cn: Heb *And it will hail when the forest comes down* [j] Meaning of Heb uncertain
[k] Heb *his treasure*; meaning of Heb uncertain

the envoys of peace weep
bitterly.
8 The highways are deserted,
travelers have quit the
road.
The treaty is broken,
its oaths[l] are despised,
its obligation[m] is
disregarded.
9 The land mourns and
languishes;
Lebanon is confounded
and withers away;
Sharon is like a desert;
and Bashan and Carmel
shake off their leaves.

10 "Now I will arise," says the
LORD,
"now I will lift myself up;
now I will be exalted.
11 You conceive chaff, you bring
forth stubble;
your breath is a fire that
will consume you.
12 And the peoples will be as if
burned to lime,
like thorns cut down, that
are burned in the fire."

13 Hear, you who are far away,
what I have done;
and you who are near,
acknowledge my might.
14 The sinners in Zion are
afraid;
trembling has seized the
godless:
"Who among us can live with
the devouring fire?
Who among us can live
with everlasting
flames?"
15 Those who walk righteously
and speak uprightly,
who despise the gain of
oppression,
who wave away a bribe
instead of accepting it,
who stop their ears from
hearing of bloodshed
and shut their eyes from
looking on evil,
16 they will live on the heights;
their refuge will be the
fortresses of rocks;
their food will be supplied,
their water assured.

The Land of the Majestic King

17 Your eyes will see the king in
his beauty;
they will behold a land that
stretches far away.
18 Your mind will muse on the
terror:
"Where is the one who
counted?
Where is the one who
weighed the tribute?
Where is the one who
counted the towers?"
19 No longer will you see the
insolent people,
the people of an obscure
speech that you cannot
comprehend,
stammering in a language
that you cannot
understand.
20 Look on Zion, the city of our
appointed festivals!
Your eyes will see
Jerusalem,
a quiet habitation, an
immovable tent,
whose stakes will never be
pulled up,
and none of whose ropes
will be broken.
21 But there the LORD in
majesty will be for us
a place of broad rivers and
streams,
where no galley with oars
can go,
nor stately ship can pass.
22 For the LORD is our judge,
the LORD is our ruler,
the LORD is our king; he
will save us.

23 Your rigging hangs loose;
it cannot hold the mast
firm in its place,
or keep the sail spread out.

Then prey and spoil in
abundance will be
divided;

33.8 Isa 35.8; 24.5 **33.9** Isa 24.4; 2.13; 35.2 **33.10** Ps 12.5 **33.11** Ps 7.14; Isa 59.4 **33.12** Isa 9.18; 10.17 **33.13** Isa 49.1 **33.14** Isa 32.11; 30.27,30; 9.18,19 **33.15** Ps 15.2; 24.4; 119.37 **33.16** Isa 25.4; 26.1; 49.10

33.17 vv. 21,22; Isa 26.15 **33.18** Isa 17.14; 1 Cor 1.20 **33.19** 2 Kings 19.32; Deut 28.49, 50; Jer 5.15 **33.20** Ps 48.12; 46.5; 125.1,2; Isa 37.33; 54.2 **33.21** Isa 41.18 **33.22** Isa 2.4; Jas 4.12; v. 17; Zech 9.9; Isa 35.4 **33.23** 2 Kings 7.8, 16

[l] Q Ms: MT *cities* [m] Or *everyone*

even the lame will fall to
plundering.
24 And no inhabitant will say,
"I am sick";
the people who live there
will be forgiven their
iniquity.

Judgment on the Nations

34 Draw near, O nations, to
hear;
O peoples, give heed!
Let the earth hear, and all
that fills it;
the world, and all that
comes from it.
2 For the LORD is enraged
against all the nations,
and furious against all their
hoards;
he has doomed them, has
given them over for
slaughter.
3 Their slain shall be cast out,
and the stench of their
corpses shall rise;
the mountains shall flow
with their blood.
4 All the host of heaven shall
rot away,
and the skies roll up like a
scroll.
All their host shall wither
like a leaf withering on a
vine,
or fruit withering on a fig
tree.

5 When my sword has drunk
its fill in the heavens,
lo, it will descend upon
Edom,
upon the people I have
doomed to judgment.
6 The LORD has a sword; it is
sated with blood,
it is gorged with fat,
with the blood of lambs
and goats,
with the fat of the kidneys
of rams.
For the LORD has a sacrifice
in Bozrah,
a great slaughter in the
land of Edom.
7 Wild oxen shall fall with
them,
and young steers with the
mighty bulls.
Their land shall be soaked
with blood,
and their soil made rich
with fat.

8 For the LORD has a day of
vengeance,
a year of vindication by
Zion's cause.[n]
9 And the streams of Edom[o]
shall be turned into
pitch,
and her soil into sulfur;
her land shall become
burning pitch.
10 Night and day it shall not be
quenched;
its smoke shall go up
forever.
From generation to
generation it shall lie
waste;
no one shall pass through
it forever and ever.
11 But the hawk[p] and the
hedgehog[p] shall
possess it;
the owl[p] and the raven
shall live in it.
He shall stretch the line of
confusion over it,
and the plummet of chaos
over[q] its nobles.
12 They shall name it No
Kingdom There,
and all its princes shall be
nothing.
13 Thorns shall grow over its
strongholds,
nettles and thistles in its
fortresses.
It shall be the haunt of
jackals,
an abode for ostriches.
14 Wildcats shall meet with
hyenas,
goat-demons shall call to
each other;
there too Lilith shall repose,
and find a place to rest.
15 There shall the owl nest

33.24 Jer 30.17; 50.20
34.1 Ps 49.1; Deut 32.1
34.2 Isa 26.20, 21; 13.5; 30.25
34.3 Joel 2.20; Ezek 14.19
34.4 Ezek 32.7,8; Joel 2.31; Mt 24.29; 2 Pet 3.10; Rev 6.13,14
34.5 Jer 46.10; 49.7; Mal 1.4
34.6 Jer 49.13; Isa 63.1
34.7 Ps 22.21; 68.30; Isa 29.9; 49.26
34.8 Isa 63.4
34.9 Deut 29.23
34.10 Isa 66.24; Rev 14.11; 19.3; Mal 1.4; Ezek 29.11
34.11 Isa 14.23; Zeph 2.14; Rev 18.2; 2 Kings 21.13; Lam 2.8
34.13 Isa 13.22; 32.13; Jer 9.11; 10.22
34.14 Isa 13.21
34.15 Deut 14.13

n Or *of recompense by Zion's defender*
o Heb *her streams*
p Identification uncertain
q Heb lacks *over*

and lay and hatch and
brood in its shadow;
there too the buzzards shall
gather,
each one with its mate.
16 Seek and read from the book
of the LORD:
Not one of these shall be
missing;
none shall be without its
mate.
For the mouth of the LORD
has commanded,
and his spirit has gathered
them.
17 He has cast the lot for
them,
his hand has portioned it
out to them with the
line;
they shall possess it forever,
from generation to
generation they shall
live in it.

The Return of the Redeemed to Zion

35 The wilderness and the
dry land shall be glad,
the desert shall rejoice and
blossom;
like the crocus 2 it shall
blossom abundantly,
and rejoice with joy and
singing.
The glory of Lebanon shall
be given to it,
the majesty of Carmel and
Sharon.
They shall see the glory of
the LORD,
the majesty of our God.

3 Strengthen the weak
hands,
and make firm the feeble
knees.
4 Say to those who are of a
fearful heart,
"Be strong, do not fear!
Here is your God.
He will come with
vengeance,
with terrible recompense.
He will come and save
you."

34.16 Isa 30.8; 40.5 **34.17** Jer 13.25; vv. 10,11 **35.1f** Isa 55.12; 51.3 **35.2** Isa 32.15; v. 10; Isa 60.13; 25.9 **35.3** Job 4.3,4; Heb 12.12 **35.4** Isa 1.24; 34.8; Ps 145.19

35.5 Isa 29.18; Mt 11.5; Jn 9.6,7 **35.6** Mt 15.30; Jn 5.8,9; Acts 3.8; Mt 9.32; Isa 41.18; 43.19; Jn 7.38 **35.7** Isa 49.10; 34.13 **35.8** Isa 62.10; Mt 7.13,14; Jer 14.8 **35.9** Isa 30.6; 34.14; 62.12 **35.10** Isa 51.11; 25.8; 65.19; Rev 7.17; 21.4 **36.1** 2 Kings 18.13; Isa 1.1

5 Then the eyes of the blind
shall be opened,
and the ears of the deaf
unstopped;
6 then the lame shall leap like
a deer,
and the tongue of the
speechless sing for joy.
For waters shall break forth
in the wilderness,
and streams in the desert;
7 the burning sand shall
become a pool,
and the thirsty ground
springs of water;
the haunt of jackals shall
become a swamp,[r]
the grass shall become
reeds and rushes.

8 A highway shall be there,
and it shall be called the
Holy Way;
the unclean shall not travel
on it,[s]
but it shall be for God's
people;[t]
no traveler, not even fools,
shall go astray.
9 No lion shall be there,
nor shall any ravenous
beast come up on it;
they shall not be found
there,
but the redeemed shall
walk there.
10 And the ransomed of the
LORD shall return,
and come to Zion with
singing;
everlasting joy shall be upon
their heads;
they shall obtain joy and
gladness,
and sorrow and sighing
shall flee away.

Sennacherib Threatens Jerusalem

36 In the fourteenth year of
King Hezekiah, King Sen-
nacherib of Assyria came up
against all the fortified cities of Ju-

[r] Cn: Heb *in the haunt of jackals is her resting place* [s] Or *pass it by* [t] Cn: Heb *for them*

dah and captured them. [2]The king
of Assyria sent the Rabshakeh from
Lachish to King Hezekiah at Jerusalem, with a great army. He stood
by the conduit of the upper pool on
the highway to the Fuller's Field.
[3]And there came out to him Eliakim son of Hilkiah, who was in
charge of the palace, and Shebna
the secretary, and Joah son of
Asaph, the recorder.
4 The Rabshakeh said to them,
"Say to Hezekiah: Thus says the
great king, the king of Assyria: On
what do you base this confidence
of yours? [5]Do you think that mere
words are strategy and power for
war? On whom do you now rely,
that you have rebelled against me?
[6]See, you are relying on Egypt, that
broken reed of a staff, which will
pierce the hand of anyone who
leans on it. Such is Pharaoh king of
Egypt to all who rely on him. [7]But
if you say to me, 'We rely on the
LORD our God,' is it not he whose
high places and altars Hezekiah
has removed, saying to Judah and
to Jerusalem, 'You shall worship
before this altar'? [8]Come now,
make a wager with my master the
king of Assyria: I will give you two
thousand horses, if you are able on
your part to set riders on them.
[9]How then can you repulse a single
captain among the least of my master's servants, when you rely on
Egypt for chariots and for horsemen? [10]Moreover, is it without the
LORD that I have come up against
this land to destroy it? The LORD
said to me, Go up against this land,
and destroy it."
11 Then Eliakim, Shebna, and
Joah said to the Rabshakeh,
"Please speak to your servants in
Aramaic, for we understand it; do
not speak to us in the language of
Judah within the hearing of the
people who are on the wall." [12]But
the Rabshakeh said, "Has my master sent me to speak these words to
your master and to you, and not to
the people sitting on the wall, who
are doomed with you to eat their
own dung and drink their own
urine?"

36.2 2 Kings 18.17-20; Isa 7.3
36.3 Isa 22.15,20
36.4 2 Kings 18.19
36.5 2 Kings 18.7
36.6 Ezek 29.6,7; Isa 30.3,5,7
36.7 2 Kings 18.4, 5
36.9 Isa 37.29; 20.5
36.11 Ezra 4.7; v. 13
36.13 2 Chr 32.18
36.14 Isa 37.10
36.15 v. 18
36.16 Zech 3.10; Prov 5.15
36.18 v. 15
36.19 Isa 37.11-13; 2 Kings 17.6
36.20 1 Kings 20.23, 28; v. 15
36.22 v. 3; Isa 22.15,20
37.1 2 Kings 19.1-37
37.2 Isa 22.15,20
37.3 Isa 26.16-18

13 Then the Rabshakeh stood
and called out in a loud voice in the
language of Judah, "Hear the
words of the great king, the king of
Assyria! [14]Thus says the king: 'Do
not let Hezekiah deceive you, for
he will not be able to deliver you.
[15]Do not let Hezekiah make you
rely on the LORD by saying, The
LORD will surely deliver us; this city
will not be given into the hand of
the king of Assyria.' [16]Do not listen
to Hezekiah; for thus says the king
of Assyria: 'Make your peace with
me and come out to me; then everyone of you will eat from your
own vine and your own fig tree and
drink water from your own cistern,
[17]until I come and take you away to
a land like your own land, a land of
grain and wine, a land of bread and
vineyards. [18]Do not let Hezekiah
mislead you by saying, The LORD
will save us. Has any of the gods of
the nations saved their land out of
the hand of the king of Assyria?
[19]Where are the gods of Hamath
and Arpad? Where are the gods of
Sepharvaim? Have they delivered
Samaria out of my hand? [20]Who
among all the gods of these countries have saved their countries out
of my hand, that the LORD should
save Jerusalem out of my hand?' "
21 But they were silent and answered him not a word, for the
king's command was, "Do not answer him." [22]Then Eliakim son of
Hilkiah, who was in charge of the
palace, and Shebna the secretary,
and Joah son of Asaph, the recorder, came to Hezekiah with their
clothes torn, and told him the
words of the Rabshakeh.

Hezekiah Consults Isaiah

37 When King Hezekiah heard
it, he tore his clothes, covered himself with sackcloth, and
went into the house of the LORD.
[2]And he sent Eliakim, who was in
charge of the palace, and Shebna
the secretary, and the senior
priests, covered with sackcloth, to
the prophet Isaiah son of Amoz.
[3]They said to him, "Thus says Hezekiah, This day is a day of distress,

of rebuke, and of disgrace; children
have come to the birth, and there is
no strength to bring them forth. 4 It
may be that the LORD your God
heard the words of the Rabshakeh,
whom his master the king of Assyria has sent to mock the living God,
and will rebuke the words that the
LORD your God has heard; therefore
lift up your prayer for the remnant
that is left."
5 When the servants of King
Hezekiah came to Isaiah, 6 Isaiah
said to them, "Say to your master,
'Thus says the LORD: Do not be
afraid because of the words that
you have heard, with which the servants of the king of Assyria have reviled me. 7 I myself will put a spirit
in him, so that he shall hear a rumor, and return to his own land; I
will cause him to fall by the sword
in his own land.' "
8 The Rabshakeh returned, and
found the king of Assyria fighting
against Libnah; for he had heard
that the king had left Lachish.
9 Now the king[u] heard concerning
King Tirhakah of Ethiopia,[v] "He
has set out to fight against you."
When he heard it, he sent messengers to Hezekiah, saying, 10 "Thus
shall you speak to King Hezekiah
of Judah: Do not let your God on
whom you rely deceive you by
promising that Jerusalem will not
be given into the hand of the king
of Assyria. 11 See, you have heard
what the kings of Assyria have done
to all lands, destroying them utterly. Shall you be delivered? 12 Have
the gods of the nations delivered
them, the nations that my predecessors destroyed, Gozan, Haran,
Rezeph, and the people of Eden
who were in Telassar? 13 Where is
the king of Hamath, the king of Arpad, the king of the city of Sepharvaim, the king of Hena, or the king
of Ivvah?"

Hezekiah's Prayer

14 Hezekiah received the letter
from the hand of the messengers
and read it; then Hezekiah went up
to the house of the LORD and spread
it before the LORD. 15 And Hezekiah
prayed to the LORD, saying:
16 "O LORD of hosts, God of Israel,
who are enthroned above the cherubim, you are God, you alone, of all
the kingdoms of the earth; you
have made heaven and earth. 17 Incline your ear, O LORD, and hear;
open your eyes, O LORD, and see;
hear all the words of Sennacherib,
which he has sent to mock the living God. 18 Truly, O LORD, the kings
of Assyria have laid waste all the
nations and their lands, 19 and have
hurled their gods into the fire,
though they were no gods, but the
work of human hands—wood and
stone—and so they were destroyed. 20 So now, O LORD our God,
save us from his hand, so that all
the kingdoms of the earth may
know that you alone are the LORD."
21 Then Isaiah son of Amoz sent
to Hezekiah, saying: "Thus says the
LORD, the God of Israel: Because
you have prayed to me concerning
King Sennacherib of Assyria, 22 this
is the word that the LORD has spoken concerning him:

She despises you, she scorns
you—
virgin daughter Zion;
she tosses her head—behind
your back,
daughter Jerusalem.

23 Whom have you mocked and
reviled?
Against whom have you
raised your voice
and haughtily lifted your
eyes?
Against the Holy One of
Israel!
24 By your servants you have
mocked the Lord,
and you have said, 'With
my many chariots
I have gone up the heights of
the mountains,
to the far recesses of
Lebanon;
I felled its tallest cedars,
its choicest cypresses;
I came to its remotest
height,

37.4 Isa 36.15, 18,20 **37.6** Isa 7.4; 35.4 **37.7** vv. 9,37,38 **37.9** v. 7; Isa 18.1; 20.5 **37.10** Isa 36.15 **37.11** Isa 10.9-11; 36.18-20 **37.12** 2 Kings 17.6; 18.11; Gen 11.31; 12.1-4; Acts 7.2

37.16 Ex 25.22; Deut 10.17; Isa 42.5; 45.12 **37.17** Dan 9.18; Ps 74.22; v. 4 **37.18** 2 Kings 15.29; 1 Chr 5.26; Nah 2.11,12 **37.19** Isa 2.8; 26.14 **37.20** Isa 25.9; Ps 46.10; Ezek 36.23 **37.21** v. 2 **37.22** Jer 14.17; Lam 2.13; Zech 2.10; Job 16.4 **37.23** v. 4; Isa 2.11; 5.15,21; Ezek 39.7; Hab 1.12 **37.24** Isa 8.7,8; 10.18,33,34; 14.8

[u] Heb *he* [v] Or *Nubia*; Heb *Cush*

its densest forest.
25 I dug wells
and drank waters,
I dried up with the sole of
my foot
all the streams of Egypt.'

26 Have you not heard
that I determined it long
ago?
I planned from days of old
what now I bring to pass,
that you should make
fortified cities
crash into heaps of ruins,
27 while their inhabitants,
shorn of strength,
are dismayed and
confounded;
they have become like plants
of the field
and like tender grass,
like grass on the housetops,
blighted[w] before it is
grown.

28 I know your rising up[x] and
your sitting down,
your going out and coming
in,
and your raging against me.
29 Because you have raged
against me
and your arrogance has
come to my ears,
I will put my hook in your
nose
and my bit in your mouth;
I will turn you back on the
way
by which you came.

30 "And this shall be the sign
for you: This year eat what grows of
itself, and in the second year what
springs from that; then in the third
year sow, reap, plant vineyards,
and eat their fruit. 31 The surviving
remnant of the house of Judah
shall again take root downward,
and bear fruit upward; 32 for from
Jerusalem a remnant shall go out,
and from Mount Zion a band of survivors. The zeal of the LORD of hosts
will do this.
33 "Therefore thus says the
LORD concerning the king of Assyria: He shall not come into this city,
shoot an arrow there, come before
it with a shield, or cast up a siege
ramp against it. 34 By the way that
he came, by the same he shall return; he shall not come into this
city, says the LORD. 35 For I will defend this city to save it, for my own
sake and for the sake of my servant
David."

Sennacherib's Defeat and Death

36 Then the angel of the LORD
set out and struck down one hundred eighty-five thousand in the
camp of the Assyrians; when morning dawned, they were all dead
bodies. 37 Then King Sennacherib
of Assyria left, went home, and
lived at Nineveh. 38 As he was worshiping in the house of his god Nisroch, his sons Adrammelech and
Sharezer killed him with the sword,
and they escaped into the land of
Ararat. His son Esar-haddon succeeded him.

Hezekiah's Illness

38 In those days Hezekiah became sick and was at the
point of death. The prophet Isaiah
son of Amoz came to him, and said
to him, "Thus says the LORD: Set
your house in order, for you shall
die; you shall not recover." 2 Then
Hezekiah turned his face to the
wall, and prayed to the LORD: 3 "Remember now, O LORD, I implore
you, how I have walked before you
in faithfulness with a whole heart,
and have done what is good in your
sight." And Hezekiah wept bitterly.
4 Then the word of the LORD
came to Isaiah: 5 "Go and say to
Hezekiah, Thus says the LORD, the
God of your ancestor David: I have
heard your prayer, I have seen your
tears; I will add fifteen years to your
life. 6 I will deliver you and this city
out of the hand of the king of Assyria, and defend this city.
7 "This is the sign to you from
the LORD, that the LORD will do this
thing that he has promised: 8 See, I

37.26 Isa 40.21, 28; Acts 2.23; 4.27,28; Isa 46.11; 10.6; 17.1
37.27 Isa 40.7; Ps 129.6
37.28 Ps 139.1
37.29 Isa 10.12; 30.28; Ezek 38.4; v. 34
37.30 Lev 25.5,11
37.31 v. 4; Isa 4.2; 10.20; 27.6
37.32 v. 4; 2 Kings 19.31; Isa 9.7; Zech 1.14
37.33 Jer 6.6; 32.24
37.35 2 Kings 20.6; Isa 38.6; 48.9,11
37.36 2 Kings 19.35; Isa 10.12, 33,34
37.38 Jer 51.27; Ezra 4.2
38.1 2 Kings 20.1-6,9-11; 2 Chr 32.24; 2 Sam 17.23
38.3 Neh 13.14; 2 Kings 18.5, 6; 1 Chr 28.9; 29.19; Deut 6.18
38.5 2 Kings 18.2, 13
38.6 Isa 37.35
38.7 Isa 7.11
38.8 2 Kings 20.9-11; Josh 10.12-14

w With 2 Kings 19.26: Heb *field* x Q Ms Gk: MT lacks *your rising up*

will make the shadow cast by the
declining sun on the dial of Ahaz
turn back ten steps." So the sun
turned back on the dial the ten
steps by which it had declined.[y]

9 A writing of King Hezekiah of
Judah, after he had been sick and
had recovered from his sickness:

10 I said: In the noontide of my
days
I must depart;
I am consigned to the gates
of Sheol
for the rest of my years.
11 I said, I shall not see the
LORD
in the land of the living;
I shall look upon mortals no
more
among the inhabitants of
the world.
12 My dwelling is plucked up
and removed from me
like a shepherd's tent;
like a weaver I have rolled up
my life;
he cuts me off from the
loom;
from day to night you bring
me to an end;[y]
13 I cry for help[z] until
morning;
like a lion he breaks all my
bones;
from day to night you bring
me to an end.[y]

14 Like a swallow or a crane[y] I
clamor,
I moan like a dove.
My eyes are weary with
looking upward.
O Lord, I am oppressed; be
my security!
15 But what can I say? For he
has spoken to me,
and he himself has done it.
All my sleep has fled[a]
because of the bitterness of
my soul.

16 O Lord, by these things
people live,
and in all these is the life
of my spirit.[y]
Oh, restore me to health
and make me live!
17 Surely it was for my welfare
that I had great bitterness;
but you have held back[b] my
life
from the pit of destruction,
for you have cast all my sins
behind your back.
18 For Sheol cannot thank you,
death cannot praise you;
those who go down to the Pit
cannot hope
for your faithfulness.
19 The living, the living, they
thank you,
as I do this day;
fathers make known to
children
your faithfulness.

20 The LORD will save me,
and we will sing to stringed
instruments[c]
all the days of our lives,
at the house of the LORD.

21 Now Isaiah had said, "Let
them take a lump of figs, and apply
it to the boil, so that he may recover." 22 Hezekiah also had said,
"What is the sign that I shall go up
to the house of the LORD?"

Envoys from Babylon Welcomed

39 At that time King
Merodach-baladan son of
Baladan of Babylon sent envoys
with letters and a present to Hezekiah, for he heard that he had been
sick and had recovered. 2 Hezekiah
welcomed them; he showed them
his treasure house, the silver, the
gold, the spices, the precious oil,
his whole armory, all that was
found in his storehouses. There
was nothing in his house or in all
his realm that Hezekiah did not
show them. 3 Then the prophet Isaiah came to King Hezekiah and
said to him, "What did these men
say? From where did they come to
you?" Hezekiah answered, "They

38.10 Ps 102.24; 107.18; Job 17.11, 15; 2 Cor 1.9
38.11 Ps 27.13; 116.9
38.12 2 Cor 5.1, 4; Heb 1.12; Job 7.6; 6.9; Ps 73.14
38.13 Job 10.16; 16.12; Ps 51.8; 32.4
38.14 Isa 59.11; Ps 119.122, 123
38.15 Ps 39.9; 1 Kings 21.27; Job 7.11; 10.1
38.16 Ps 119.71, 75; 39.13
38.17 Ps 30.3; Isa 43.25; Jer 31.34; Mic 7.19
38.18 Ps 6.5; 88.11; 115.17; Eccl 9.10; Ps 28.1
38.19 Ps 118.17; Deut 6.7; Ps 78.5-7
38.20 Ps 86.5; 33.1-3; 104.33; 116.17-19
38.21 2 Kings 20.7, 8
39.1 2 Kings 20.12-19; 2 Chr 32.31
39.2 2 Chr 32.25, 31; 2 Kings 18.15, 16
39.3 2 Sam 12.1; 2 Chr 16.7; Jer 5.15

[y] Meaning of Heb uncertain [z] Cn: Meaning of Heb uncertain [a] Cn Compare Syr: Heb *I will walk slowly all my years* [b] Cn Compare Gk Vg: Heb *loved* [c] Heb *my stringed instruments*

have come to me from a far country, from Babylon." 4 He said,
"What have they seen in your
house?" Hezekiah answered,
"They have seen all that is in my
house; there is nothing in my storehouses that I did not show them."
5 Then Isaiah said to Hezekiah,
"Hear the word of the LORD of
hosts: 6 Days are coming when all
that is in your house, and that
which your ancestors have stored
up until this day, shall be carried to
Babylon; nothing shall be left, says
the LORD. 7 Some of your own sons
who are born to you shall be taken
away; they shall be eunuchs in the
palace of the king of Babylon."
8 Then Hezekiah said to Isaiah,
"The word of the LORD that you
have spoken is good." For he
thought, "There will be peace and
security in my days."

God's People Are Comforted

40 Comfort, O comfort my
 people,
 says your God.
2 Speak tenderly to Jerusalem,
 and cry to her
that she has served her
 term,
 that her penalty is paid,
that she has received from
 the LORD's hand
 double for all her sins.

3 A voice cries out:
"In the wilderness prepare
 the way of the LORD,
 make straight in the desert
 a highway for our God.
4 Every valley shall be lifted
 up,
 and every mountain and
 hill be made low;
the uneven ground shall
 become level,
 and the rough places a
 plain.
5 Then the glory of the LORD
 shall be revealed,
 and all people shall see it
 together,
 for the mouth of the LORD
 has spoken."

6 A voice says, "Cry out!"
 And I said, "What shall I
 cry?"
All people are grass,
 their constancy is like the
 flower of the field.
7 The grass withers, the flower
 fades,
 when the breath of the
 LORD blows upon it;
 surely the people are grass.
8 The grass withers, the flower
 fades;
 but the word of our God
 will stand forever.
9 Get you up to a high
 mountain,
 O Zion, herald of good
 tidings;[d]
lift up your voice with
 strength,
 O Jerusalem, herald of
 good tidings,[e]
 lift it up, do not fear;
say to the cities of Judah,
 "Here is your God!"
10 See, the Lord GOD comes
 with might,
 and his arm rules for him;
his reward is with him,
 and his recompense before
 him.
11 He will feed his flock like a
 shepherd;
 he will gather the lambs in
 his arms,
and carry them in his bosom,
 and gently lead the mother
 sheep.
12 Who has measured the
 waters in the hollow of
 his hand
 and marked off the heavens
 with a span,
enclosed the dust of the
 earth in a measure,
 and weighed the mountains
 in scales
 and the hills in a balance?
13 Who has directed the spirit
 of the LORD,
 or as his counselor has
 instructed him?

39.5 1 Sam 13.13, 14; 15.16
39.6 Jer 20.5
39.7 Dan 1.2-7
39.8 2 Chr 32.26; 1 Sam 3.18; 2 Chr 34.28
40.1 Isa 12.1
40.2 Isa 35.4; 41.11-13; 33.24; Jer 16.18
40.3 Mt 3.3; Mk 1.3; Lk 3.4-6; Jn 1.23; Mal 3.1
40.4 Isa 45.2
40.5 Isa 6.3; 52.10
40.6 Job 14.2; Ps 102.11; 103.15; 1 Pet 1.24, 25
40.7 Ps 90.5,6; v. 24
40.8 Isa 55.11; Mt 5.18; 1 Pet 1.24, 25
40.9 Isa 60.1; 52.7; Acts 10.36; Rom 10.15
40.10 Isa 59.16, 18; 62.11; Rev 22.7,12
40.11 Ezek 34.23; Mic 5.4; Jn 10.11; Heb 13.20
40.12 Isa 48.13; Job 38.8-11; Heb 1.10-12
40.13 Rom 11.34; 1 Cor 2.16

[d] Or *O herald of good tidings to Zion*
[e] Or *O herald of good tidings to Jerusalem*

14 Whom did he consult for his
enlightenment,
and who taught him the
path of justice?
Who taught him knowledge,
and showed him the way of
understanding?
15 Even the nations are like a
drop from a bucket,
and are accounted as dust
on the scales;
see, he takes up the isles
like fine dust.
16 Lebanon would not provide
fuel enough,
nor are its animals enough
for a burnt offering.
17 All the nations are as
nothing before him;
they are accounted by him
as less than nothing
and emptiness.

18 To whom then will you liken
God,
or what likeness compare
with him?
19 An idol? —A workman casts
it,
and a goldsmith overlays it
with gold,
and casts for it silver
chains.
20 As a gift one chooses
mulberry wood[f]
—wood that will not rot—
then seeks out a skilled
artisan
to set up an image that will
not topple.

21 Have you not known? Have
you not heard?
Has it not been told you
from the beginning?
Have you not understood
from the foundations of
the earth?
22 It is he who sits above the
circle of the earth,
and its inhabitants are like
grasshoppers;
who stretches out the
heavens like a curtain,
and spreads them like a
tent to live in;

40.14 Job 38.4; 21.22
40.15 Jer 10.10; Isa 17.13; 29.5
40.17 Isa 29.7; 30.28
40.18 v. 25; Isa 46.5; Mic 7.18; Acts 17.29
40.19 Isa 41.6,7; 44.12; Jer 10.3
40.20 Isa 41.7; Jer 10.3-5
40.21 Ps 19.1; Acts 14.17; Rom 1.19
40.22 Job 22.14; Num 13.33; Isa 42.5; 44.24; Ps 104.2
40.23 Job 12.21; Ps 107.40; Isa 5.21
40.24 Isa 17.10, 11; v. 7; Isa 17.13; 41.16
40.25 v. 18
40.26 Isa 51.6; 42.5; Ps 147.4; 89.11-13; Isa 34.16
40.27 Isa 49.4,14; 54.8; Lk 18.7,8; Isa 25.1
40.28 Ps 90.2; 147.5; Rom 11.33
40.29 Isa 50.4; Jer 31.25; Isa 41.10
40.30 Jer 6.11; Isa 9.17
40.31 Ps 103.5; 2 Cor 4.8-10, 16; Deut 32.11; 2 Cor 4.1; Heb 12.3

23 who brings princes to
naught,
and makes the rulers of the
earth as nothing.
24 Scarcely are they planted,
scarcely sown,
scarcely has their stem
taken root in the earth,
when he blows upon them,
and they wither,
and the tempest carries
them off like stubble.

25 To whom then will you
compare me,
or who is my equal? says
the Holy One.
26 Lift up your eyes on high
and see:
Who created these?
He who brings out their host
and numbers them,
calling them all by name;
because he is great in
strength,
mighty in power,
not one is missing.

27 Why do you say, O Jacob,
and speak, O Israel,
"My way is hidden from the
Lord,
and my right is disregarded
by my God"?
28 Have you not known? Have
you not heard?
The Lord is the everlasting
God,
the Creator of the ends of
the earth.
He does not faint or grow
weary;
his understanding is
unsearchable.
29 He gives power to the faint,
and strengthens the
powerless.
30 Even youths will faint and be
weary,
and the young will fall
exhausted;
31 but those who wait for the
Lord shall renew their
strength,

[f] Meaning of Heb uncertain

they shall mount up with
wings like eagles,
they shall run and not be
weary,
they shall walk and not
faint.

Israel Assured of God's Help

41 Listen to me in silence,
O coastlands;
let the peoples renew their
strength;
let them approach, then let
them speak;
let us together draw near
for judgment.

2 Who has roused a victor from
the east,
summoned him to his
service?
He delivers up nations to
him,
and tramples kings under
foot;
he makes them like dust
with his sword,
like driven stubble with his
bow.
3 He pursues them and passes
on safely,
scarcely touching the path
with his feet.
4 Who has performed and done
this,
calling the generations
from the beginning?
I, the LORD, am first,
and will be with the last.
5 The coastlands have seen
and are afraid,
the ends of the earth
tremble;
they have drawn near and
come.
6 Each one helps the other,
saying to one another,
"Take courage!"
7 The artisan encourages the
goldsmith,
and the one who smooths
with the hammer
encourages the one who
strikes the anvil,
saying of the soldering, "It is
good";
and they fasten it with
nails so that it cannot
be moved.
8 But you, Israel, my servant,
Jacob, whom I have
chosen,
the offspring of Abraham,
my friend;
9 you whom I took from the
ends of the earth,
and called from its farthest
corners,
saying to you, "You are my
servant,
I have chosen you and not
cast you off";
10 do not fear, for I am with
you,
do not be afraid, for I am
your God;
I will strengthen you, I will
help you,
I will uphold you with my
victorious right hand.

11 Yes, all who are incensed
against you
shall be ashamed and
disgraced;
those who strive against you
shall be as nothing and
shall perish.
12 You shall seek those who
contend with you,
but you shall not find
them;
those who war against you
shall be as nothing at all.
13 For I, the LORD your God,
hold your right hand;
it is I who say to you, "Do
not fear,
I will help you."

14 Do not fear, you worm
Jacob,
you insect[g] Israel!
I will help you, says the
LORD;
your Redeemer is the Holy
One of Israel.
15 Now, I will make of you a
threshing sledge,
sharp, new, and having
teeth;

41.1 Zech 2.13; Isa 40.31; 34.1; 43.26 **41.2** Isa 45.1-3; 46.11; 42.6; 2 Chr 36.23; Isa 29.5; 40.24 **41.4** Isa 44.7; 46.10; 43.10; 44.6; Rev 1.17; 22.13 **41.5** Ps 67.7 **41.6** Isa 40.19 **41.7** Isa 40.19,20

41.8 Isa 44.1; 2 Chr 20.7; Jas 2.23 **41.9** Isa 11.11; 43.5-7; 42.1; Ps 135.4 **41.10** Isa 43.5; Rom 8.31; Isa 44.2 **41.11** Isa 45.24; 17.13 **41.12** Isa 17.14; 29.20 **41.13** Isa 42.6; v. 10 **41.14** Job 25.6; Isa 43.14 **41.15** Mic 4.13

g Syr: Heb *men of*

you shall thresh the
mountains and crush
them,
and you shall make the
hills like chaff.
16 You shall winnow them and
the wind shall carry
them away,
and the tempest shall
scatter them.
Then you shall rejoice in the
LORD;
in the Holy One of Israel
you shall glory.

17 When the poor and needy
seek water,
and there is none,
and their tongue is parched
with thirst,
I the LORD will answer them,
I the God of Israel will not
forsake them.
18 I will open rivers on the bare
heights,[h]
and fountains in the midst
of the valleys;
I will make the wilderness a
pool of water,
and the dry land springs of
water.
19 I will put in the wilderness
the cedar,
the acacia, the myrtle, and
the olive;
I will set in the desert the
cypress,
the plane and the pine
together,
20 so that all may see and
know,
all may consider and
understand,
that the hand of the LORD
has done this,
the Holy One of Israel has
created it.

The Futility of Idols

21 Set forth your case, says the
LORD;
bring your proofs, says the
King of Jacob.
22 Let them bring them, and
tell us
what is to happen.
Tell us the former things,
what they are,
so that we may consider
them,
and that we may know their
outcome;
or declare to us the things
to come.
23 Tell us what is to come
hereafter,
that we may know that you
are gods;
do good, or do harm,
that we may be afraid and
terrified.
24 You, indeed, are nothing
and your work is nothing at
all;
whoever chooses you is an
abomination.

25 I stirred up one from the
north, and he has
come,
from the rising of the sun
he was summoned by
name.[i]
He shall trample[j] on rulers
as on mortar,
as the potter treads clay.
26 Who declared it from the
beginning, so that we
might know,
and beforehand, so that we
might say, "He is
right"?
There was no one who
declared it, none who
proclaimed,
none who heard your
words.
27 I first have declared it to
Zion,[k]
and I give to Jerusalem a
herald of good tidings.
28 But when I look there is no
one;
among these there is no
counselor
who, when I ask, gives an
answer.
29 No, they are all a delusion;
their works are nothing;

41.16 Jer 51.2; Isa 45.25 **41.17** Isa 43.20; 30.19; 42.16 **41.18** Isa 35.6,7; 43.19 **41.20** Isa 40.5; Job 12.9 **41.21** v. 1; Isa 43.15 **41.22** Isa 45.21; 43.9

41.23 Isa 42.9; 44.7,8; 45.3; Jn 13.19; Jer 10.5 **41.24** Ps 115.8; Isa 44.9; 1 Cor 8.4; v. 29 **41.25** v. 2; Isa 10.6 **41.26** Isa 44.7; 45.21; Hab 2.18,19 **41.27** v. 4; Isa 40.9 **41.28** Isa 63.5; 40.13,14; 46.7 **41.29** v. 24; Isa 44.9; Jer 5.13

[h] Or *trails* [i] Cn Compare Q Ms Gk: MT *and he shall call on my name* [j] Cn: Heb *come* [k] Cn: Heb *First to Zion—Behold, behold them*

their images are empty
wind.

The Servant, a Light to the Nations

42 Here is my servant,
whom I uphold,
my chosen, in whom my
soul delights;
I have put my spirit upon
him;
he will bring forth justice
to the nations.
2 He will not cry or lift up his
voice,
or make it heard in the
street;
3 a bruised reed he will not
break,
and a dimly burning wick
he will not quench;
he will faithfully bring forth
justice.
4 He will not grow faint or be
crushed
until he has established
justice in the earth;
and the coastlands wait for
his teaching.

5 Thus says God, the LORD,
who created the heavens
and stretched them out,
who spread out the earth
and what comes from
it,
who gives breath to the
people upon it
and spirit to those who
walk in it:
6 I am the LORD, I have called
you in righteousness,
I have taken you by the
hand and kept you;
I have given you as a
covenant to the
people,[l]
a light to the nations,
7 to open the eyes that are
blind,
to bring out the prisoners
from the dungeon,
from the prison those who
sit in darkness.
8 I am the LORD, that is my
name;
my glory I give to no other,
nor my praise to idols.
9 See, the former things have
come to pass,
and new things I now
declare;
before they spring forth,
I tell you of them.

A Hymn of Praise

10 Sing to the LORD a new song,
his praise from the end of
the earth!
Let the sea roar[m] and all
that fills it,
the coastlands and their
inhabitants.
11 Let the desert and its towns
lift up their voice,
the villages that Kedar
inhabits;
let the inhabitants of Sela
sing for joy,
let them shout from the
tops of the mountains.
12 Let them give glory to the
LORD,
and declare his praise in
the coastlands.
13 The LORD goes forth like a
soldier,
like a warrior he stirs up
his fury;
he cries out, he shouts
aloud,
he shows himself mighty
against his foes.

14 For a long time I have held
my peace,
I have kept still and
restrained myself;
now I will cry out like a
woman in labor,
I will gasp and pant.
15 I will lay waste mountains
and hills,
and dry up all their
herbage;
I will turn the rivers into
islands,
and dry up the pools.
16 I will lead the blind

42.1 Isa 43.10; 53.11; Mt 12.18-20; 3.16,17; 17.5; Isa 2.4
42.3 Isa 57.15; Ps 72.2
42.4 Isa 40.28; vv. 10,12
42.5 Isa 44.24; Zech 12.1; Acts 17.25
42.6 Isa 43.1; 49.6,8; Lk 2.32; Acts 13.47
42.7 Isa 35.5; 61.1; Lk 4.18; 2 Tim 2.26; Heb 2.14
42.8 Isa 48.11
42.9 Isa 48.3,6
42.10 Isa 33.3; 40.3; 98.1; 107.23
42.12 Isa 24.15; v. 4
42.13 Isa 9.7; Ex 15.3; Hos 11.10; Isa 66.14-16
42.14 Isa 57.11
42.15 Isa 2.12-16; 44.27
42.16 Isa 29.18; Lk 1.78,79; 3.5; Isa 41.17

[l] Meaning of Heb uncertain [m] Cn Compare Ps 96.11; 98.7: Heb *Those who go down to the sea*

by a road they do not
know,
by paths they have not
known
I will guide them.
I will turn the darkness
before them into light,
the rough places into level
ground.
These are the things I will
do,
and I will not forsake
them.
17 They shall be turned back
and utterly put to
shame—
those who trust in carved
images,
who say to cast images,
"You are our gods."

18 Listen, you that are deaf;
and you that are blind,
look up and see!
19 Who is blind but my servant,
or deaf like my messenger
whom I send?
Who is blind like my
dedicated one,
or blind like the servant of
the LORD?
20 He sees many things, but
does[n] not observe
them;
his ears are open, but he
does not hear.

Israel's Disobedience

21 The LORD was pleased, for
the sake of his
righteousness,
to magnify his teaching
and make it glorious.
22 But this is a people robbed
and plundered,
all of them are trapped in
holes
and hidden in prisons;
they have become a prey
with no one to rescue,
a spoil with no one to say,
"Restore!"
23 Who among you will give
heed to this,
who will attend and listen
for the time to come?

42.17 Ps 97.7; Isa 1.29; 44.11; 45.16
42.19 Isa 43.8; Ezek 12.2
42.20 Jer 6.10
42.21 Isa 58.13
42.22 Isa 24.18, 22; 10.6
42.24 Isa 30.15; 48.18
42.25 Isa 5.25; 2 Kings 25.9; Hos 7.9
43.1 vv. 7,15,21; Isa 44.2,6, 21
43.2 Ps 66.12; Deut 31.6,8; Dan 3.25,27
43.3 Ex 20.2; v. 11; Prov 11.8; 21.18
43.4 Isa 63.9

24 Who gave up Jacob to the
spoiler,
and Israel to the robbers?
Was it not the LORD, against
whom we have sinned,
in whose ways they would
not walk,
and whose law they would
not obey?
25 So he poured upon him the
heat of his anger
and the fury of war;
it set him on fire all around,
but he did not
understand;
it burned him, but he did
not take it to heart.

Restoration and Protection Promised

43 But now thus says the
LORD,
he who created you,
O Jacob,
he who formed you,
O Israel:
Do not fear, for I have
redeemed you;
I have called you by name,
you are mine.
2 When you pass through the
waters, I will be with
you;
and through the rivers, they
shall not overwhelm
you;
when you walk through fire
you shall not be
burned,
and the flame shall not
consume you.
3 For I am the LORD your God,
the Holy One of Israel,
your Savior.
I give Egypt as your ransom,
Ethiopia[o] and Seba in
exchange for you.
4 Because you are precious in
my sight,
and honored, and I love
you,
I give people in return for
you,

[n] Heb *You see many things but do*
[o] Or *Nubia*; Heb *Cush*

nations in exchange for your life.
5 Do not fear, for I am with you;
I will bring your offspring from the east,
and from the west I will gather you;
6 I will say to the north, "Give them up,"
and to the south, "Do not withhold;
bring my sons from far away
and my daughters from the end of the earth—
7 everyone who is called by my name,
whom I created for my glory,
whom I formed and made."

8 Bring forth the people who are blind, yet have eyes,
who are deaf, yet have ears!
9 Let all the nations gather together,
and let the peoples assemble.
Who among them declared this,
and foretold to us the former things?
Let them bring their witnesses to justify them,
and let them hear and say, "It is true."
10 You are my witnesses, says the LORD,
and my servant whom I have chosen,
so that you may know and believe me
and understand that I am he.
Before me no god was formed,
nor shall there be any after me.
11 I, I am the LORD,
and besides me there is no savior.
12 I declared and saved and proclaimed,
when there was no strange god among you;

43.5 Isa 41.10, 14; 44.2; Jer 30.10, 11; 46.27,28
43.6 Ps 107.3; Isa 14.2
43.7 Ps 100.3; Isa 29.23; Eph 2.10; v. 1
43.8 Isa 6.9; 42.19; Ezek 12.2
43.9 Isa 41.21, 22,26
43.10 Isa 44.8; 42.1; 41.4; 44.6
43.11 Isa 45.21
43.12 Deut 32.16; Ps 81.9; v. 10; Isa 44.8
43.13 Ps 90.2; Job 9.12; Isa 14.27
43.14 Isa 41.14; 13.14,15
43.16 Ex 14.16; Ps 77.19; Isa 51.10; Josh 3.13
43.17 Ex 14.4-9, 25
43.18 Jer 16.14
43.19 2 Cor 5.17; Rev 21.5; Ex 17.6; Num 20.11; Isa 35.6
43.20 Isa 48.21

and you are my witnesses, says the LORD.
13 I am God, and also henceforth I am He;
there is no one who can deliver from my hand;
I work and who can hinder it?

14 Thus says the LORD,
your Redeemer, the Holy One of Israel:
For your sake I will send to Babylon
and break down all the bars,
and the shouting of the Chaldeans will be turned to lamentation.[p]
15 I am the LORD, your Holy One,
the Creator of Israel, your King.
16 Thus says the LORD,
who makes a way in the sea,
a path in the mighty waters,
17 who brings out chariot and horse,
army and warrior;
they lie down, they cannot rise,
they are extinguished, quenched like a wick:
18 Do not remember the former things,
or consider the things of old.
19 I am about to do a new thing;
now it springs forth, do you not perceive it?
I will make a way in the wilderness
and rivers in the desert.
20 The wild animals will honor me,
the jackals and the ostriches;
for I give water in the wilderness,
rivers in the desert,
to give drink to my chosen people,

[p] Meaning of Heb uncertain

[21] the people whom I formed
for myself
so that they might declare
my praise.

[22] Yet you did not call upon
me, O Jacob;
but you have been weary of
me, O Israel!
[23] You have not brought me
your sheep for burnt
offerings,
or honored me with your
sacrifices.
I have not burdened you with
offerings,
or wearied you with
frankincense.
[24] You have not bought me
sweet cane with money,
or satisfied me with the fat
of your sacrifices.
But you have burdened me
with your sins;
you have wearied me with
your iniquities.

[25] I, I am He
who blots out your
transgressions for my
own sake,
and I will not remember
your sins.
[26] Accuse me, let us go to trial;
set forth your case, so that
you may be proved
right.
[27] Your first ancestor sinned,
and your interpreters
transgressed against
me.
[28] Therefore I profaned the
princes of the
sanctuary,
I delivered Jacob to utter
destruction,
and Israel to reviling.

God's Blessing on Israel

44 But now hear, O Jacob
my servant,
Israel whom I have chosen!
[2] Thus says the Lord who
made you,

43.21 v. 1; Ps 102.18; Lk 1.74,75 **43.22** Isa 30.9-11; Mal 1.13 **43.23** Am 5.25; Mal 1.6-8 **43.24** Ex 30.23; Isa 1.14; Mal 2.17 **43.25** Isa 44.23; Ezek 36.22; Jer 31.34 **43.26** Isa 1.18; v. 9 **43.28** Isa 47.6; Lam 2.2,6; Zech 8.13 **44.1** Isa 41.8; Jer 30.10; 46.27,28 **44.2** Isa 43.1,7; Deut 32.15

44.3 Isa 35.7; Joel 2.28; Jn 7.38; Acts 2.18 **44.5** Isa 19.21; Zech 8.20-22 **44.6** Isa 43.1,14; 41.4; 48.12; Rev 1.8,17; 22.13 **44.7** Isa 41.4,22 **44.8** Isa 41.22; 43.10; Deut 4.35; 1 Sam 2.2; Isa 26.4 **44.9** Isa 41.24; 66.3; 43.9; 42.17

who formed you in the
womb and will help
you:
Do not fear, O Jacob my
servant,
Jeshurun whom I have
chosen.
[3] For I will pour water on the
thirsty land,
and streams on the dry
ground;
I will pour my spirit upon
your descendants,
and my blessing on your
offspring.
[4] They shall spring up like a
green tamarisk,
like willows by flowing
streams.
[5] This one will say, "I am the
Lord's,"
another will be called by
the name of Jacob,
yet another will write on the
hand, "The Lord's,"
and adopt the name of
Israel.

[6] Thus says the Lord, the King
of Israel,
and his Redeemer, the
Lord of hosts:
I am the first and I am the
last;
besides me there is no god.
[7] Who is like me? Let them
proclaim it,
let them declare and set it
forth before me.
Who has announced from of
old the things to
come?[q]
Let them tell us[r] what is
yet to be.
[8] Do not fear, or be afraid;
have I not told you from of
old and declared it?
You are my witnesses!
Is there any god besides me?
There is no other rock; I
know not one.

The Absurdity of Idol Worship

9 All who make idols are nothing, and the things they delight in

[q] Cn: Heb *from my placing an eternal people and things to come* [r] Tg: Heb *them*

do not profit; their witnesses neither see nor know. And so they will
be put to shame. [10]Who would
fashion a god or cast an image that
can do no good? [11]Look, all its dev-
otees shall be put to shame; the artisans too are merely human. Let
them all assemble, let them stand
up; they shall be terrified, they
shall all be put to shame.

12 The ironsmith fashions it[s]
and works it over the coals, shaping
it with hammers, and forging it
with his strong arm; he becomes
hungry and his strength fails, he
drinks no water and is faint. [13]The
carpenter stretches a line, marks it
out with a stylus, fashions it with
planes, and marks it with a com-
pass; he makes it in human form,
with human beauty, to be set up in
a shrine. [14]He cuts down cedars or
chooses a holm tree or an oak and
lets it grow strong among the trees
of the forest. He plants a cedar and
the rain nourishes it. [15]Then it can
be used as fuel. Part of it he takes
and warms himself; he kindles a
fire and bakes bread. Then he
makes a god and worships it,
makes it a carved image and bows
down before it. [16]Half of it he burns
in the fire; over this half he roasts
meat, eats it and is satisfied. He
also warms himself and says, "Ah,
I am warm, I can feel the fire!"
[17]The rest of it he makes into a god,
his idol, bows down to it and worships it; he prays to it and says,
"Save me, for you are my god!"

18 They do not know, nor do
they comprehend; for their eyes are
shut, so that they cannot see, and
their minds as well, so that they
cannot understand. [19]No one considers, nor is there knowledge or
discernment to say, "Half of it I
burned in the fire; I also baked
bread on its coals, I roasted meat
and have eaten. Now shall I make
the rest of it an abomination? Shall
I fall down before a block of
wood?" [20]He feeds on ashes; a deluded mind has led him astray, and
he cannot save himself or say, "Is
not this thing in my right hand a
fraud?"

44.10 Jer 10.5; Hab 2.18
44.11 Isa 1.29; 42.17
44.12 Isa 40.19; 41.6; Jer 10.3-5
44.13 Isa 41.7; Ps 115.5-7
44.15 vv. 17,19; 2 Chr 25.14
44.17 v. 15; Isa 45.20; 1 Kings 18.26, 28
44.18 Isa 1.3; 6.9, 10
44.19 Isa 5.13; 45.20; 27.11; Deut 27.15
44.20 Ps 102.9; Job 15.31; Isa 57.11
44.21 Isa 46.8; vv. 1,2; Isa 49.15
44.22 Isa 43.25; 55.7; 43.1; 1 Pet 1.18, 19
44.23 Isa 42.10; 55.12; 43.1; 61.3
44.24 Isa 43.14; v. 2; Isa 40.14,22
44.25 Isa 40.14; 29.14; 1 Cor 1.20, 27
44.26 Isa 55.11; 49.7-20; Jer 32.15,44

Israel Is Not Forgotten

21 Remember these things,
O Jacob,
and Israel, for you are my
servant;
I formed you, you are my
servant;
O Israel, you will not be
forgotten by me.
22 I have swept away your
transgressions like a
cloud,
and your sins like mist;
return to me, for I have
redeemed you.

23 Sing, O heavens, for the LORD
has done it;
shout, O depths of the
earth;
break forth into singing,
O mountains,
O forest, and every tree in
it!
For the LORD has redeemed
Jacob,
and will be glorified in
Israel.

24 Thus says the LORD, your
Redeemer,
who formed you in the
womb:
I am the LORD, who made all
things,
who alone stretched out
the heavens,
who by myself spread out
the earth;
25 who frustrates the omens of
liars,
and makes fools of
diviners;
who turns back the wise,
and makes their knowledge
foolish;
26 who confirms the word of his
servant,
and fulfills the prediction
of his messengers;
who says of Jerusalem, "It
shall be inhabited,"
and of the cities of Judah,
"They shall be rebuilt,

[s] Cn: Heb *an ax*

and I will raise up their
ruins";
27 who says to the deep, "Be
dry—
I will dry up your rivers";
28 who says of Cyrus, "He is my
shepherd,
and he shall carry out all
my purpose";
and who says of Jerusalem,
"It shall be rebuilt,"
and of the temple, "Your
foundation shall be
laid."

Cyrus, God's Instrument

45 Thus says the LORD to
his anointed, to Cyrus,
whose right hand I have
grasped
to subdue nations before
him
and strip kings of their
robes,
to open doors before him—
and the gates shall not be
closed:
2 I will go before you
and level the mountains,[t]
I will break in pieces the
doors of bronze
and cut through the bars of
iron,
3 I will give you the treasures
of darkness
and riches hidden in secret
places,
so that you may know that it
is I, the LORD,
the God of Israel, who call
you by your name.
4 For the sake of my servant
Jacob,
and Israel my chosen,
I call you by your name,
I surname you, though you
do not know me.
5 I am the LORD, and there is
no other;
besides me there is no
god.
I arm you, though you do
not know me,
6 so that they may know, from
the rising of the sun
and from the west, that
there is no one besides
me;
I am the LORD, and there is
no other.
7 I form light and create
darkness,
I make weal and create
woe;
I the LORD do all these
things.

8 Shower, O heavens, from
above,
and let the skies rain down
righteousness;
let the earth open, that
salvation may spring
up,[u]
and let it cause
righteousness to sprout
up also;
I the LORD have created it.

9 Woe to you who strive with
your Maker,
earthen vessels with the
potter![v]
Does the clay say to the one
who fashions it, "What
are you making"?
or "Your work has no
handles"?
10 Woe to anyone who says to a
father, "What are you
begetting?"
or to a woman, "With what
are you in labor?"
11 Thus says the LORD,
the Holy One of Israel, and
its Maker:
Will you question me[w] about
my children,
or command me
concerning the work of
my hands?
12 I made the earth,
and created humankind
upon it;
it was my hands that
stretched out the
heavens,

44.27 Isa 43.16; 42.15 **44.28** Isa 45.1; 14.32; 45.13 **45.1** Isa 44.28; 41.13; Jer 50.3,35; v. 5 **45.2** Isa 40.4; Ps 107.16; Jer 51.30 **45.3** Jer 41.8; Isa 43.1 **45.4** Isa 41.8; 43.1; Acts 17.23 **45.5** v. 6; Isa 44.6,8; Ps 18.39 **45.6** Mal 1.11; Isa 43.5; v. 5 **45.7** Isa 42.16; Ps 104.20; Am 3.6 **45.8** Ps 72.6; 85.11; Isa 12.3; 60.21 **45.9** Isa 29.16; Rom 9.20, 21 **45.11** Isa 43.15; 54.5; 8.19; Jer 31.9; 60.21 **45.12** v. 18; Isa 42.5; Neh 9.6

[t] Q Ms Gk: MT *the swellings* [u] Q Ms: MT *that they may bring forth salvation* [v] Cn: Heb *with the potsherds*, or *with the potters* [w] Cn: Heb *Ask me of things to come*

and I commanded all their
host.
13 I have aroused Cyrus[x] in
righteousness,
and I will make all his
paths straight;
he shall build my city
and set my exiles free,
not for price or reward,
says the LORD of hosts.
14 Thus says the LORD:
The wealth of Egypt and the
merchandise of
Ethiopia,[y]
and the Sabeans, tall of
stature,
shall come over to you and
be yours,
they shall follow you;
they shall come over in
chains and bow down
to you.
They will make supplication
to you, saying,
"God is with you alone,
and there is no other;
there is no god besides
him."
15 Truly, you are a God who
hides himself,
O God of Israel, the Savior.
16 All of them are put to shame
and confounded,
the makers of idols go in
confusion together.
17 But Israel is saved by the
LORD
with everlasting salvation;
you shall not be put to
shame or confounded
to all eternity.

18 For thus says the LORD,
who created the heavens
(he is God!),
who formed the earth and
made it
(he established it;
he did not create it a chaos,
he formed it to be
inhabited!):
I am the LORD, and there is
no other.
19 I did not speak in secret,
in a land of darkness;
I did not say to the offspring
of Jacob,
"Seek me in chaos."
I the LORD speak the truth,
I declare what is right.

Idols Cannot Save Babylon

20 Assemble yourselves and
come together,
draw near, you survivors of
the nations!
They have no knowledge—
those who carry about their
wooden idols,
and keep on praying to a god
that cannot save.
21 Declare and present your
case;
let them take counsel
together!
Who told this long ago?
Who declared it of old?
Was it not I, the LORD?
There is no other god
besides me,
a righteous God and a
Savior;
there is no one besides me.

22 Turn to me and be saved,
all the ends of the earth!
For I am God, and there is
no other.
23 By myself I have sworn,
from my mouth has gone
forth in righteousness
a word that shall not
return:
"To me every knee shall
bow,
every tongue shall swear."

24 Only in the LORD, it shall be
said of me,
are righteousness and
strength;
all who were incensed
against him
shall come to him and be
ashamed.
25 In the LORD all the offspring
of Israel
shall triumph and glory.

46 Bel bows down, Nebo
stoops,

45.13 Isa 41.2; v. 2; Isa 44.28; 52.3 **45.14** Isa 14.1,2; Ps 149.8; Isa 49.23; Jer 16.19; 1 Cor 14.25; v. 5 **45.15** Isa 8.17; 43.3 **45.16** Isa 44.9,11 **45.17** Isa 26.4; Rom 11.26; Isa 49.23 **45.18** Isa 42.5; v. 12; Gen 1.2,26; v. 5 **45.19** Isa 48.16; 41.8; Jer 29.13, 14; Isa 63.1; 44.8

45.20 Isa 43.9; 44.18,19; Jer 10.5; Isa 46.6,7 **45.21** Isa 41.23, 26; v. 5; Isa 43.3,11 **45.22** Num 21.8,9; Isa 30.15; 49.6,12 **45.23** Isa 62.8; Rom 14.11; Isa 55.11; 65.16 **45.24** Isa 54.17; 41.11 **45.25** Isa 53.11; 60.19 **46.1** Jer 50.2-4; Isa 45.20

[x] Heb *him* [y] Or *Nubia*; Heb *Cush*

their idols are on beasts
and cattle;
these things you carry are
loaded
as burdens on weary
animals.
2 They stoop, they bow down
together;
they cannot save the
burden,
but themselves go into
captivity.

3 Listen to me, O house of
Jacob,
all the remnant of the
house of Israel,
who have been borne by me
from your birth,
carried from the womb;
4 even to your old age I am he,
even when you turn gray I
will carry you.
I have made, and I will bear;
I will carry and will save.

5 To whom will you liken me
and make me equal,
and compare me, as
though we were alike?
6 Those who lavish gold from
the purse,
and weigh out silver in the
scales—
they hire a goldsmith, who
makes it into a god;
then they fall down and
worship!
7 They lift it to their
shoulders, they carry it,
they set it in its place, and
it stands there;
it cannot move from its
place.
If one cries out to it, it does
not answer
or save anyone from
trouble.

8 Remember this and
consider,[z]
recall it to mind, you
transgressors,
9 remember the former
things of old;
for I am God, and there is no
other;
I am God, and there is no
one like me,
10 declaring the end from the
beginning
and from ancient times
things not yet done,
saying, "My purpose shall
stand,
and I will fulfill my
intention,"
11 calling a bird of prey from
the east,
the man for my purpose
from a far country.
I have spoken, and I will
bring it to pass;
I have planned, and I will
do it.

12 Listen to me, you stubborn
of heart,
you who are far from
deliverance:
13 I bring near my deliverance,
it is not far off,
and my salvation will not
tarry;
I will put salvation in Zion,
for Israel my glory.

The Humiliation of Babylon

47 Come down and sit in
the dust,
virgin daughter Babylon!
Sit on the ground without a
throne,
daughter Chaldea!
For you shall no more be
called
tender and delicate.
2 Take the millstones and
grind meal,
remove your veil,
strip off your robe, uncover
your legs,
pass through the rivers.
3 Your nakedness shall be
uncovered,
and your shame shall be
seen.
I will take vengeance,
and I will spare no one.
4 Our Redeemer—the LORD of
hosts is his name—
is the Holy One of Israel.

46.2 Jer 43.12,13 **46.3** v. 12; Isa 45.19; 10.21,22; 63.9 **46.4** Isa 43.13; Ps 71.18 **46.5** Isa 40.18,25 **46.6** Isa 40.19; 44.15,17 **46.7** v. 1; Isa 40.20; 44.17; 41.26, 28; 45.20 **46.8** Isa 44.19, 21; 48.8 **46.9** Isa 45.5,21; 41.26,27 **46.10** Isa 45.21; 14.24; Acts 5.39 **46.11** Isa 18.6; 41.2,25; 37.26 **46.12** v. 3; Isa 48.4; Jer 2.5 **46.13** Isa 61.11; 43.7; 44.23 **47.1** Jer 48.18; 46.11; 51.33 **47.3** Ezek 16.37; Isa 34.8; 63.4 **47.4** Isa 41.14

[z] Meaning of Heb uncertain

[5] Sit in silence, and go into
darkness,
daughter Chaldea!
For you shall no more be
called
the mistress of kingdoms.
[6] I was angry with my people,
I profaned my heritage;
I gave them into your hand,
you showed them no
mercy;
on the aged you made your
yoke
exceedingly heavy.
[7] You said, "I shall be mistress
forever,"
so that you did not lay
these things to heart
or remember their end.

[8] Now therefore hear this, you
lover of pleasures,
who sit securely,
who say in your heart,
"I am, and there is no one
besides me;
I shall not sit as a widow
or know the loss of
children"—
[9] both these things shall come
upon you
in a moment, in one day:
the loss of children and
widowhood
shall come upon you in full
measure,
in spite of your many
sorceries
and the great power of your
enchantments.

[10] You felt secure in your
wickedness;
you said, "No one sees
me."
Your wisdom and your
knowledge
led you astray,
and you said in your heart,
"I am, and there is no one
besides me."
[11] But evil shall come upon
you,
which you cannot charm
away;
disaster shall fall upon you,
which you will not be able
to ward off;
and ruin shall come on you
suddenly,
of which you know
nothing.

[12] Stand fast in your
enchantments
and your many sorceries,
with which you have
labored from your
youth;
perhaps you may be able to
succeed,
perhaps you may inspire
terror.
[13] You are wearied with your
many consultations;
let those who study[a] the
heavens
stand up and save you,
those who gaze at the
stars,
and at each new moon
predict
what[b] shall befall you.

[14] See, they are like stubble,
the fire consumes them;
they cannot deliver
themselves
from the power of the
flame.
No coal for warming oneself
is this,
no fire to sit before!
[15] Such to you are those with
whom you have
labored,
who have trafficked with
you from your youth;
they all wander about in
their own paths;
there is no one to save you.

47.5 Isa 23.2; 13.10; Isa 13.19; Dan 2.37 **47.6** Zech 1.15; Isa 43.28; 10.14; Deut 28.50 **47.7** v. 5; Isa 42.25; 45.21 **47.8** Isa 32.9,11; Zeph 2.15; Rev 18.7 **47.9** Isa 13.16, 18; 1 Thes 5.3; Nah 3.4 **47.10** Ps 52.7; Isa 29.15; 44.20; v. 8 **47.11** Isa 57.1; 1 Thes 5.3; v. 9 **47.12** v. 9 **47.13** Isa 57.10; Dan 2.2 **47.14** Nah 1.10; Mal 4.1 **47.15** Rev 18.11; Isa 43.13; 46.7 **48.1** Isa 46.12; Num 24.7; Ps 68.26; Isa 45.23

God the Creator and Redeemer

48 Hear this, O house of
Jacob,
who are called by the name
of Israel,
and who came forth from
the loins[c] of Judah;

[a] Meaning of Heb uncertain [b] Gk Syr Compare Vg: Heb *from what* [c] Cn: Heb *waters*

who swear by the name of
the LORD,
and invoke the God of
Israel,
but not in truth or right.
2 For they call themselves
after the holy city,
and lean on the God of
Israel;
the LORD of hosts is his
name.

3 The former things I declared
long ago,
they went out from my
mouth and I made
them known;
then suddenly I did them
and they came to pass.
4 Because I know that you are
obstinate,
and your neck is an iron
sinew
and your forehead brass,
5 I declared them to you from
long ago,
before they came to pass I
announced them to
you,
so that you would not say,
"My idol did them,
my carved image and my
cast image commanded
them."

6 You have heard; now see all
this;
and will you not declare it?
From this time forward I
make you hear new
things,
hidden things that you
have not known.
7 They are created now, not
long ago;
before today you have
never heard of them,
so that you could not say,
"I already knew them."
8 You have never heard, you
have never known,
from of old your ear has
not been opened.
For I knew that you would
deal very treacherously,
and that from birth you
were called a rebel.

9 For my name's sake I defer
my anger,
for the sake of my praise I
restrain it for you,
so that I may not cut you
off.
10 See, I have refined you, but
not like[d] silver;
I have tested you in the
furnace of adversity.
11 For my own sake, for my
own sake, I do it,
for why should my name[e]
be profaned?
My glory I will not give to
another.

12 Listen to me, O Jacob,
and Israel, whom I called:
I am He; I am the first,
and I am the last.
13 My hand laid the foundation
of the earth,
and my right hand spread
out the heavens;
when I summon them,
they stand at attention.

14 Assemble, all of you, and
hear!
Who among them has
declared these things?
The LORD loves him;
he shall perform his
purpose on Babylon,
and his arm shall be
against the Chaldeans.
15 I, even I, have spoken and
called him,
I have brought him, and he
will prosper in his way.
16 Draw near to me, hear this!
From the beginning I have
not spoken in secret,
from the time it came to
be I have been there.
And now the Lord GOD has
sent me and his spirit.

17 Thus says the LORD,
your Redeemer, the Holy
One of Israel:
I am the LORD your God,

48.2 Isa 52.1; Mic 3.11; Rom 2.17
48.3 Isa 41.22; 42.9; 43.9; 44.7,8; 45.21; Josh 21.45
48.4 Ezek 2.4; Ex 32.9; Deut 31.27; Ezek 3.7-9
48.5 Ezek 2.4; 3.7
48.6 Isa 42.9; 43.19
48.8 Isa 42.25; 46.8; Ps 58.3
48.9 v. 11; Ps 78.38; Isa 30.18
48.10 Jer 9.7; Ezek 22.18-22; Jer 11.4
48.11 v. 9; Deut 32.26; Ezek 20.9; Isa 42.8
48.12 Deut 32.39; Isa 41.4; Rev 1.17; 22.13
48.13 Ps 102.25; Isa 40.26
48.14 Isa 43.9; 45.21; 46.10, 11; Jer 50.21-29
48.15 Isa 41.2; 45.1,2
48.16 Isa 41.1; 45.19; 43.13; Zech 2.9,11
48.17 Isa 43.14; Ps 32.8

[d] Cn: Heb *with*
[e] Gk Old Latin: Heb *for why should it*

who teaches you for your own good,
who leads you in the way you should go.
18 O that you had paid attention to my commandments!
Then your prosperity would have been like a river,
and your success like the waves of the sea;
19 your offspring would have been like the sand,
and your descendants like its grains;
their name would never be cut off
or destroyed from before me.

20 Go out from Babylon, flee from Chaldea,
declare this with a shout of joy, proclaim it,
send it forth to the end of the earth;
say, "The LORD has redeemed his servant Jacob!"
21 They did not thirst when he led them through the deserts;
he made water flow for them from the rock;
he split open the rock and the water gushed out.

22 "There is no peace," says the LORD, "for the wicked."

The Servant's Mission

49 Listen to me, O coastlands,
pay attention, you peoples from far away!
The LORD called me before I was born,
while I was in my mother's womb he named me.
2 He made my mouth like a sharp sword,
in the shadow of his hand he hid me;
he made me a polished arrow,
in his quiver he hid me away.
3 And he said to me, "You are my servant,
Israel, in whom I will be glorified."
4 But I said, "I have labored in vain,
I have spent my strength for nothing and vanity;
yet surely my cause is with the LORD,
and my reward with my God."

5 And now the LORD says,
who formed me in the womb to be his servant,
to bring Jacob back to him,
and that Israel might be gathered to him,
for I am honored in the sight of the LORD,
and my God has become my strength—
6 he says,
"It is too light a thing that you should be my servant
to raise up the tribes of Jacob
and to restore the survivors of Israel;
I will give you as a light to the nations,
that my salvation may reach to the end of the earth."

7 Thus says the LORD,
the Redeemer of Israel and his Holy One,
to one deeply despised, abhorred by the nations,
the slave of rulers,
"Kings shall see and stand up,
princes, and they shall prostrate themselves,
because of the LORD, who is faithful,
the Holy One of Israel, who has chosen you."

48.18 Deut 32.29; Ps 119.165; Isa 61.10,11
48.19 Gen 22.17; Jer 33.22; Isa 56.5; 66.22
48.20 Jer 50.8; Isa 42.10; 62.11; 43.1
48.21 Isa 41.17; Ex 17.6; Ps 105.41
48.22 Isa 57.21
49.1 Isa 42.4; 66.19; 44.2, 24; Isa 7.14; 9.6; Mt 1.20; Gal 1.15
49.2 Isa 11.4; Heb 4.12; Isa 51.16; Hab 3.11
49.3 Isa 42.1; 44.23
49.4 Isa 65.23
49.5 Isa 44.2,23; 27.12; 43.4; 12.2
49.6 Isa 42.6; Lk 2.32; Acts 13.47; 26.23
49.7 Isa 48.17; 53.3; Ps 22.6-8; Isa 52.15; 66.23

Zion's Children to Be Brought Home

8 Thus says the LORD:
In a time of favor I have
answered you,
on a day of salvation I have
helped you;
I have kept you and given
you
as a covenant to the
people,[f]
to establish the land,
to apportion the desolate
heritages;
9 saying to the prisoners,
"Come out,"
to those who are in
darkness, "Show
yourselves."
They shall feed along the
ways,
on all the bare heights[g]
shall be their pasture;
10 they shall not hunger or
thirst,
neither scorching wind nor
sun shall strike them
down,
for he who has pity on them
will lead them,
and by springs of water will
guide them.
11 And I will turn all my
mountains into a road,
and my highways shall be
raised up.
12 Lo, these shall come from far
away,
and lo, these from the
north and from the
west,
and these from the land of
Syene.[h]

13 Sing for joy, O heavens, and
exult, O earth;
break forth, O mountains,
into singing!
For the LORD has comforted
his people,
and will have compassion
on his suffering ones.

14 But Zion said, "The LORD has
forsaken me,
my Lord has forgotten me."
15 Can a woman forget her
nursing child,
or show no compassion for
the child of her womb?
Even these may forget,
yet I will not forget you.
16 See, I have inscribed you on
the palms of my hands;
your walls are continually
before me.
17 Your builders outdo your
destroyers,[i]
and those who laid you
waste go away from
you.
18 Lift up your eyes all around
and see;
they all gather, they come
to you.
As I live, says the LORD,
you shall put all of them
on like an ornament,
and like a bride you shall
bind them on.

19 Surely your waste and your
desolate places
and your devastated land—
surely now you will be too
crowded for your
inhabitants,
and those who swallowed
you up will be far away.
20 The children born in the
time of your
bereavement
will yet say in your hearing:
"The place is too crowded
for me;
make room for me to
settle."
21 Then you will say in your
heart,
"Who has borne me these?
I was bereaved and barren,
exiled and put away—
so who has reared these?
I was left all alone—
where then have these
come from?"

22 Thus says the Lord GOD:
I will soon lift up my hand to
the nations,

49.8 Ps 69.13; 2 Cor 6.2; Isa 42.6; 44.26
49.9 Isa 42.7; Lk 4.18; Isa 41.18
49.10 Rev 7.16; Ps 121.6; Isa 14.1; 40.11; 41.17
49.11 Isa 40.4; 62.10
49.12 Isa 43.5,6
49.13 Isa 44.23; 40.1; 54.7,8, 10; Rev 12.12; 18.20
49.14 Isa 40.27
49.15 Isa 44.21
49.16 Song 8.6; Isa 62.6,7
49.17 v. 19
49.18 Isa 60.4; 43.5; 45.23; 52.1
49.19 Isa 51.3; 54.1,2; Zech 10.10; Ps 56.1,2
49.20 Isa 54.1-3
49.21 Isa 54.6,7; 27.10; 5.13; 1.8
49.22 Isa 62.10; 60.4; 66.20

[f] Meaning of Heb uncertain [g] Or *the trails* [h] Q Ms: MT *Sinim* [i] Or *Your children come swiftly; your destroyers*

and raise my signal to the
peoples;
and they shall bring your
sons in their bosom,
and your daughters shall be
carried on their
shoulders.
23 Kings shall be your foster
fathers,
and their queens your
nursing mothers.
With their faces to the
ground they shall bow
down to you,
and lick the dust of your
feet.
Then you will know that I
am the LORD;
those who wait for me shall
not be put to shame.

24 Can the prey be taken from
the mighty,
or the captives of a tyrant[j]
be rescued?
25 But thus says the LORD:
Even the captives of the
mighty shall be taken,
and the prey of the tyrant
be rescued;
for I will contend with those
who contend with you,
and I will save your
children.
26 I will make your oppressors
eat their own flesh,
and they shall be drunk
with their own blood as
with wine.
Then all flesh shall know
that I am the LORD your
Savior,
and your Redeemer, the
Mighty One of Jacob.

50 Thus says the LORD:
Where is your mother's
bill of divorce
with which I put her away?
Or which of my creditors is it
to whom I have sold you?
No, because of your sins you
were sold,
and for your transgressions
your mother was put
away.

49.23 Isa 60.16; 45.14; Ps 72.9; Mic 7.17; Isa 43.10; 25.9; Ps 25.3
49.25 Isa 14.1,2; 25.9
49.26 Isa 9.4,20; 45.6; 43.3; v. 7
50.1 Deut 24.1,3; Jer 3.8; Isa 54.6,7; Deut 32.30; Isa 52.3; 48.8
50.2 Isa 65.12; 66.4; Num 11.23; Isa 59.1; Ex 14.21; Josh 3.16
50.3 Isa 13.10; Rev 6.12
50.4 Isa 54.13; Jer 31.25; Ps 143.8
50.5 Ps 40.6; Mt 26.39; Jn 8.29; 14.31; Phil 2.8
50.6 Isa 53.5; Mt 26.67; Lk 22.63
50.7 Isa 49.8; 54.4; Ezek 3.8,9
50.8 Rom 8.32-34

2 Why was no one there when
I came?
Why did no one answer
when I called?
Is my hand shortened, that it
cannot redeem?
Or have I no power to
deliver?
By my rebuke I dry up the
sea,
I make the rivers a desert;
their fish stink for lack of
water,
and die of thirst.[k]
3 I clothe the heavens with
blackness,
and make sackcloth their
covering.

The Servant's Humiliation and Vindication

4 The Lord GOD has given me
the tongue of a teacher,[l]
that I may know how to
sustain
the weary with a word.
Morning by morning he
wakens—
wakens my ear
to listen as those who are
taught.
5 The Lord GOD has opened my
ear,
and I was not rebellious,
I did not turn backward.
6 I gave my back to those who
struck me,
and my cheeks to those
who pulled out the
beard;
I did not hide my face
from insult and spitting.

7 The Lord GOD helps me;
therefore I have not been
disgraced;
therefore I have set my face
like flint,
and I know that I shall not
be put to shame;
8 he who vindicates me is
near.
Who will contend with me?

[j] Q Ms Syr Vg: MT *of a righteous person*
[k] Or *die on the thirsty ground*
[l] Cn: Heb *of those who are taught*

Let us stand up together.
Who are my adversaries?
Let them confront me.
9 It is the Lord GOD who helps
me;
who will declare me guilty?
All of them will wear out like
a garment;
the moth will eat them up.

10 Who among you fears the
LORD
and obeys the voice of his
servant,
who walks in darkness
and has no light,
yet trusts in the name of the
LORD
and relies upon his God?
11 But all of you are kindlers of
fire,
lighters of firebrands.[m]
Walk in the flame of your
fire,
and among the brands that
you have kindled!
This is what you shall have
from my hand:
you shall lie down in
torment.

Blessings in Store for God's People

51 Listen to me, you that
pursue righteousness,
you that seek the LORD.
Look to the rock from which
you were hewn,
and to the quarry from
which you were dug.
2 Look to Abraham your father
and to Sarah who bore you;
for he was but one when I
called him,
but I blessed him and
made him many.
3 For the LORD will comfort
Zion;
he will comfort all her
waste places,
and will make her wilderness
like Eden,
her desert like the garden
of the LORD;
joy and gladness will be
found in her,
thanksgiving and the voice
of song.

4 Listen to me, my people,
and give heed to me, my
nation;
for a teaching will go out
from me,
and my justice for a light
to the peoples.
5 I will bring near my
deliverance swiftly,
my salvation has gone out
and my arms will rule the
peoples;
the coastlands wait for me,
and for my arm they hope.
6 Lift up your eyes to the
heavens,
and look at the earth
beneath;
for the heavens will vanish
like smoke,
the earth will wear out like
a garment,
and those who live on it
will die like gnats;[n]
but my salvation will be
forever,
and my deliverance will
never be ended.

7 Listen to me, you who know
righteousness,
you people who have my
teaching in your hearts;
do not fear the reproach of
others,
and do not be dismayed
when they revile you.
8 For the moth will eat them
up like a garment,
and the worm will eat
them like wool;
but my deliverance will be
forever,
and my salvation to all
generations.

9 Awake, awake, put on
strength,
O arm of the LORD!
Awake, as in days of old,

50.9 Isa 41.10; 54.17; 5.18
50.10 Isa 49.2,3; 9.2; Eph 5.8; Isa 12.2
50.11 Ps 35.8; Isa 65.13-15
51.1 v. 7; Ps 94.15
51.2 Rom 4.16; Heb 11.11, 12; Gen 12.1; 24.35
51.3 Isa 40.1; 52.9; Joel 2.3; Gen 13.10; Isa 66.10
51.4 Ps 50.7; Isa 2.3; 42.4,6
51.5 Isa 46.13; 40.10; 42.4; 63.5
51.6 Isa 40.26; Ps 102.26; Mt 24.35; 2 Pet 3.10; Isa 45.17
51.7 v. 1; Ps 37.31; Mt 5.11; Acts 5.41
51.8 Isa 50.9; v. 6
51.9 Isa 52.1; Deut 4.34; Ps 89.10; 74.13; Ezek 29.3

[m] Syr: Heb *you gird yourselves with firebrands*
[n] Or *in like manner*

the generations of long
ago!
Was it not you who cut
Rahab in pieces,
who pierced the dragon?
10 Was it not you who dried up
the sea,
the waters of the great
deep;
who made the depths of the
sea a way
for the redeemed to cross
over?
11 So the ransomed of the LORD
shall return,
and come to Zion with
singing;
everlasting joy shall be upon
their heads;
they shall obtain joy and
gladness,
and sorrow and sighing
shall flee away.

12 I, I am he who comforts you;
why then are you afraid of
a mere mortal who
must die,
a human being who fades
like grass?
13 You have forgotten the LORD,
your Maker,
who stretched out the
heavens
and laid the foundations of
the earth.
You fear continually all day
long
because of the fury of the
oppressor,
who is bent on destruction.
But where is the fury of the
oppressor?
14 The oppressed shall speedily
be released;
they shall not die and go
down to the Pit,
nor shall they lack bread.
15 For I am the LORD your God,
who stirs up the sea so
that its waves roar—
the LORD of hosts is his
name.
16 I have put my words in your
mouth,
and hidden you in the
shadow of my hand,
stretching out[o] the heavens
and laying the foundations
of the earth,
and saying to Zion, "You
are my people."

17 Rouse yourself, rouse
yourself!
Stand up, O Jerusalem,
you who have drunk at the
hand of the LORD
the cup of his wrath,
who have drunk to the dregs
the bowl of staggering.
18 There is no one to guide her
among all the children she
has borne;
there is no one to take her
by the hand
among all the children she
has brought up.
19 These two things have
befallen you
—who will grieve with
you?—
devastation and destruction,
famine and sword—
who will comfort you?[p]
20 Your children have fainted,
they lie at the head of
every street
like an antelope in a net;
they are full of the wrath of
the LORD,
the rebuke of your God.

21 Therefore hear this, you who
are wounded,[q]
who are drunk, but not
with wine:
22 Thus says your Sovereign,
the LORD,
your God who pleads the
cause of his people:
See, I have taken from your
hand the cup of
staggering;
you shall drink no more
from the bowl of my wrath.
23 And I will put it into the
hand of your
tormentors,
who have said to you,

51.10 Ex 14.21; Isa 43.16; 63.9,16
51.11 Isa 35.10; 60.19; Rev 7.17; 22.3
51.12 v. 3; 2 Cor 1.3; Ps 118.6; Isa 40.6,7; 1 Pet 1.24
51.13 Isa 17.10; Job 9.8; Ps 104.2; Isa 40.22; 7.4; 49.26
51.14 Isa 52.2; 38.18; 49.10
51.16 Deut 18.18; Isa 59.21; 49.2; 65.17
51.17 Isa 52.1; Job 21.20; Jer 25.15
51.18 Isa 59.21
51.19 Isa 9.20
51.20 Isa 5.25; 42.25; 66.15
51.21 Isa 54.11; 29.9
51.22 Jer 50.34; v. 17
51.23 Jer 25.15-17, 26,28; Zech 12.2; Josh 10.24

[o] Syr: Heb *planting* [p] Q Ms Gk Syr Vg: MT *how may I comfort you?* [q] Or *humbled*

"Bow down, that we may
walk on you";
and you have made your
back like the ground
and like the street for them
to walk on.

Let Zion Rejoice

52 Awake, awake,
put on your strength,
O Zion!
Put on your beautiful
garments,
O Jerusalem, the holy city;
for the uncircumcised and
the unclean
shall enter you no more.
2 Shake yourself from the dust,
rise up,
O captive[r] Jerusalem;
loose the bonds from your
neck,
O captive daughter Zion!

3 For thus says the LORD: You
were sold for nothing, and you shall
be redeemed without money. 4For
thus says the Lord GOD: Long ago,
my people went down into Egypt to
reside there as aliens; the Assyrian,
too, has oppressed them without
cause. 5Now therefore what am I
doing here, says the LORD, seeing
that my people are taken away
without cause? Their rulers howl,
says the LORD, and continually, all
day long, my name is despised.
6Therefore my people shall know
my name; therefore in that day
they shall know that it is I who
speak; here am I.

7 How beautiful upon the
mountains
are the feet of the
messenger who
announces peace,
who brings good news,
who announces salvation,
who says to Zion, "Your
God reigns."
8 Listen! Your sentinels lift up
their voices,
together they sing for joy;
for in plain sight they see
the return of the LORD to
Zion.
9 Break forth together into
singing,
you ruins of Jerusalem;
for the LORD has comforted
his people,
he has redeemed
Jerusalem.
10 The LORD has bared his holy
arm
before the eyes of all the
nations;
and all the ends of the earth
shall see
the salvation of our God.

11 Depart, depart, go out from
there!
Touch no unclean thing;
go out from the midst of it,
purify yourselves,
you who carry the vessels
of the LORD.
12 For you shall not go out in
haste,
and you shall not go in
flight;
for the LORD will go before
you,
and the God of Israel will
be your rear guard.

The Suffering Servant

13 See, my servant shall
prosper;
he shall be exalted and
lifted up,
and shall be very high.
14 Just as there were many who
were astonished at
him[s]
—so marred was his
appearance, beyond
human semblance,
and his form beyond that
of mortals—
15 so he shall startle[t] many
nations;
kings shall shut their
mouths because of him;
for that which had not been
told them they shall
see,

52.1 Isa 51.9,17; Neh 11.1; Mt 4.5; Rev 21.2,27
52.2 Isa 29.4; 9.4; 51.14
52.3 Ps 44.12; Isa 63.4; 45.13
52.4 Gen 46.6
52.5 Ezek 36.20; Rom 2.24
52.6 Isa 49.23
52.7 Nah 1.15; Rom 10.15; Ps 93.1
52.8 Isa 62.6
52.9 Isa 44.23, 26; 48.20
52.10 Ps 98.2,3; Isa 45.22; 48.20; Lk 3.6
52.11 Jer 50.8; 2 Cor 6.17; 2 Tim 2.19; Isa 1.16
52.12 Ex 12.33; Isa 42.16; 58.8
52.13 Isa 42.1; Phil 2.9
52.14 Ps 22.6,7; Isa 53.2,3
52.15 Ezek 36.25; Rom 15.21

[r] Cn: Heb *rise up, sit* [s] Syr Tg: Heb *you* [t] Meaning of Heb uncertain

and that which they had
not heard they shall
contemplate.

53 Who has believed what
we have heard?
And to whom has the arm
of the LORD been
revealed?
2 For he grew up before him
like a young plant,
and like a root out of dry
ground;
he had no form or majesty
that we should look at
him,
nothing in his appearance
that we should desire
him.
3 He was despised and
rejected by others;
a man of suffering[u] and
acquainted with
infirmity;
and as one from whom
others hide their faces[v]
he was despised, and we
held him of no account.

4 Surely he has borne our
infirmities
and carried our diseases;
yet we accounted him
stricken,
struck down by God, and
afflicted.
5 But he was wounded for our
transgressions,
crushed for our iniquities;
upon him was the
punishment that made
us whole,
and by his bruises we are
healed.
6 All we like sheep have gone
astray;
we have all turned to our
own way,
and the LORD has laid on him
the iniquity of us all.

7 He was oppressed, and he
was afflicted,
yet he did not open his
mouth;
like a lamb that is led to the
slaughter,
and like a sheep that
before its shearers is
silent,
so he did not open his
mouth.
8 By a perversion of justice he
was taken away.
Who could have imagined
his future?
For he was cut off from the
land of the living,
stricken for the
transgression of my
people.
9 They made his grave with the
wicked
and his tomb[w] with the
rich,[x]
although he had done no
violence,
and there was no deceit in
his mouth.

10 Yet it was the will of the
LORD to crush him with
pain.[y]
When you make his life an
offering for sin,[z]
he shall see his offspring,
and shall prolong his
days;
through him the will of the
LORD shall prosper.
11 Out of his anguish he shall
see light;[a]
he shall find satisfaction
through his knowledge.
The righteous one,[b] my
servant, shall make
many righteous,
and he shall bear their
iniquities.
12 Therefore I will allot him a
portion with the great,
and he shall divide the
spoil with the strong;
because he poured out
himself to death,
and was numbered with
the transgressors;

53.1 Jn 12.38; Rom 10.16
53.2 Isa 11.1; 52.14
53.3 Ps 22.6; v. 10; Jn 1.10,11
53.4 Mt 8.17; Heb 9.28; 1 Pet 2.24
53.5 Rom 4.25; 1 Cor 15.3; 1 Pet 2.24
53.6 v. 11
53.7 Mt 26.63; Acts 8.32
53.8 vv. 5,12
53.9 Mt 27.57; 1 Pet 2.22
53.10 vv. 3-6; Isa 54.3; 46.10
53.11 Jn 10.14-18; Rom 5.18, 19; vv. 5,6
53.12 Isa 52.13; Mt 26.38, 39,42; Lk 22.37; 2 Cor 5.21

[u] Or *a man of sorrows* [v] Or *as one who hides his face from us* [w] Q Ms: MT *and in his death* [x] Cn: Heb *with a rich person* [y] Or *by disease*; meaning of Heb uncertain [z] Meaning of Heb uncertain [a] Q Mss: MT lacks *light* [b] Or *and he shall find satisfaction. Through his knowledge, the righteous one*

yet he bore the sin of many,
and made intercession for
the transgressors.

The Eternal Covenant of Peace

54 Sing, O barren one who
did not bear;
burst into song and shout,
you who have not been in
labor!
For the children of the
desolate woman will be
more
than the children of her
that is married, says the
LORD.
2 Enlarge the site of your tent,
and let the curtains of your
habitations be stretched
out;
do not hold back; lengthen
your cords
and strengthen your stakes.
3 For you will spread out to
the right and to the
left,
and your descendants will
possess the nations
and will settle the desolate
towns.

4 Do not fear, for you will not
be ashamed;
do not be discouraged, for
you will not suffer
disgrace;
for you will forget the shame
of your youth,
and the disgrace of your
widowhood you will
remember no more.
5 For your Maker is your
husband,
the LORD of hosts is his
name;
the Holy One of Israel is
your Redeemer,
the God of the whole earth
he is called.
6 For the LORD has called you
like a wife forsaken and
grieved in spirit,
like the wife of a man's
youth when she is cast
off,
says your God.

54.1 Gal 4.27; 1 Sam 2.5; Isa 62.4
54.2 Isa 49.19,20
54.3 Isa 43.5,6; 49.19,23
54.4 Isa 45.17; Jer 31.19; Isa 4.1; 25.8
54.5 Jer 3.14; Isa 43.14; 48.17; 6.3
54.6 Isa 62.4
54.7 Isa 26.20; 43.5
54.8 Isa 60.10; v. 10; Isa 49.10, 13; v. 5
54.9 Gen 9.11; Isa 12.1
54.10 Isa 51.6; Ps 89.33,34; v. 8
54.11 1 Chr 29.2; Rev 21.18
54.13 Jer 31.34; Jn 6.45; Ps 119.165
54.14 Isa 62.1; 9.4; 14.4; v. 4

7 For a brief moment I
abandoned you,
but with great compassion
I will gather you.
8 In overflowing wrath for a
moment
I hid my face from you,
but with everlasting love I
will have compassion
on you,
says the LORD, your
Redeemer.

9 This is like the days of Noah
to me:
Just as I swore that the
waters of Noah
would never again go over
the earth,
so I have sworn that I will
not be angry with you
and will not rebuke you.
10 For the mountains may
depart
and the hills be removed,
but my steadfast love shall
not depart from you,
and my covenant of peace
shall not be removed,
says the LORD, who has
compassion on you.

11 O afflicted one,
storm-tossed, and not
comforted,
I am about to set your
stones in antimony,
and lay your foundations
with sapphires.[c]
12 I will make your pinnacles of
rubies,
your gates of jewels,
and all your wall of
precious stones.
13 All your children shall be
taught by the LORD,
and great shall be the
prosperity of your
children.
14 In righteousness you shall be
established;
you shall be far from
oppression, for you
shall not fear;

[c] Or *lapis lazuli*

and from terror, for it shall
not come near you.
15 If anyone stirs up strife,
it is not from me;
whoever stirs up strife with
you
shall fall because of you.
16 See it is I who have created
the smith
who blows the fire of coals,
and produces a weapon fit
for its purpose;
I have also created the
ravager to destroy.
17 No weapon that is
fashioned against you
shall prosper,
and you shall confute every
tongue that rises
against you in
judgment.
This is the heritage of the
servants of the LORD
and their vindication from
me, says the LORD.

An Invitation to Abundant Life

55 Ho, everyone who thirsts,
come to the waters;
and you that have no money,
come, buy and eat!
Come, buy wine and milk
without money and without
price.
2 Why do you spend your
money for that which is
not bread,
and your labor for that
which does not satisfy?
Listen carefully to me, and
eat what is good,
and delight yourselves in
rich food.
3 Incline your ear, and come
to me;
listen, so that you may live.
I will make with you an
everlasting covenant,
my steadfast, sure love for
David.
4 See, I made him a witness to
the peoples,
a leader and commander
for the peoples.
5 See, you shall call nations
that you do not know,
and nations that do not
know you shall run to
you,
because of the LORD your
God, the Holy One of
Israel,
for he has glorified you.

6 Seek the LORD while he may
be found,
call upon him while he is
near;
7 let the wicked forsake their
way,
and the unrighteous their
thoughts;
let them return to the LORD,
that he may have mercy
on them,
and to our God, for he will
abundantly pardon.
8 For my thoughts are not your
thoughts,
nor are your ways my ways,
says the LORD.
9 For as the heavens are
higher than the earth,
so are my ways higher than
your ways
and my thoughts than your
thoughts.

10 For as the rain and the snow
come down from
heaven,
and do not return there
until they have watered
the earth,
making it bring forth and
sprout,
giving seed to the sower
and bread to the eater,
11 so shall my word be that
goes out from my
mouth;
it shall not return to me
empty,
but it shall accomplish that
which I purpose,
and succeed in the thing
for which I sent it.

12 For you shall go out in joy,
and be led back in peace;
the mountains and the hills
before you
shall burst into song,

54.15 Isa 41.11-16
54.17 Isa 29.8; 50.8,9; 45.24
55.1 Isa 41.17; Jn 4.14; 7.37; Mt 13.44; Rev 3.18
55.2 Hos 8.7; Isa 62.8,9; 25.6
55.3 Isa 51.4; Rom 10.5; Isa 61.8; Acts 13.34
55.4 Jer 30.9; Ezek 34.23, 24; Dan 9.25
55.5 Isa 49.6,12, 23; Zech 8.22; Isa 60.9
55.6 Ps 32.6; Isa 49.8; 2 Cor 6.1, 2
55.7 Isa 1.16; 59.7; 31.6; 54.8,10; 44.22
55.9 Ps 103.11
55.10 Isa 30.23; 2 Cor 9.10
55.11 Isa 45.23; 59.21; 46.10
55.12 Isa 51.11; 54.10,13; 44.23; 1 Chr 16.33

and all the trees of the field shall clap their hands.
13 Instead of the thorn shall come up the cypress;
instead of the brier shall come up the myrtle;
and it shall be to the LORD for a memorial,
for an everlasting sign that shall not be cut off.

The Covenant Extended to All Who Obey

56 Thus says the LORD:
Maintain justice, and do what is right,
for soon my salvation will come,
and my deliverance be revealed.

2 Happy is the mortal who does this,
the one who holds it fast,
who keeps the sabbath, not profaning it,
and refrains from doing any evil.

3 Do not let the foreigner joined to the LORD say,
"The LORD will surely separate me from his people";
and do not let the eunuch say,
"I am just a dry tree."
4 For thus says the LORD:
To the eunuchs who keep my sabbaths,
who choose the things that please me
and hold fast my covenant,
5 I will give, in my house and within my walls,
a monument and a name better than sons and daughters;
I will give them an everlasting name
that shall not be cut off.

6 And the foreigners who join themselves to the LORD,
to minister to him, to love the name of the LORD,
and to be his servants,
all who keep the sabbath, and do not profane it,
and hold fast my covenant—
7 these I will bring to my holy mountain,
and make them joyful in my house of prayer;
their burnt offerings and their sacrifices
will be accepted on my altar;
for my house shall be called a house of prayer
for all peoples.
8 Thus says the Lord GOD,
who gathers the outcasts of Israel,
I will gather others to them
besides those already gathered.[d]

The Corruption of Israel's Rulers

9 All you wild animals,
all you wild animals in the forest, come to devour!
10 Israel's[e] sentinels are blind,
they are all without knowledge;
they are all silent dogs
that cannot bark;
dreaming, lying down,
loving to slumber.
11 The dogs have a mighty appetite;
they never have enough.
The shepherds also have no understanding;
they have all turned to their own way,
to their own gain, one and all.
12 "Come," they say, "let us[f] get wine;
let us fill ourselves with strong drink.
And tomorrow will be like today,
great beyond measure."

55.13 Isa 41.19; 32.13; 63.12, 14; 19.20
56.1 Isa 61.8; 46.13
56.2 Isa 58.13
56.3 v. 6; Acts 8.27
56.4 vv. 2,6
56.5 v. 7; Isa 66.20; 26.1; 62.2; 48.19
56.6 Isa 60.10; 61.5; vv. 2,4
56.7 Isa 11.9; 65.25; Rom 12.1; Heb 13.15; Mt 21.13; Mk 11.17; Lk 19.46
56.8 Isa 11.12; 60.3-11; Jn 10.16
56.9 Jer 12.9
56.10 Isa 29.9-14; Nah 3.18

d Heb *besides his gathered ones*
e Heb *His*
f Q Ms Syr Vg Tg: MT *me*

Israel's Futile Idolatry

57 The righteous perish,
and no one takes it to heart;
the devout are taken away,
while no one understands.
For the righteous are taken away from calamity,
2 and they enter into peace;
those who walk uprightly
will rest on their couches.
3 But as for you, come here,
you children of a sorceress,
you offspring of an adulterer and a whore.[g]
4 Whom are you mocking?
Against whom do you open your mouth wide
and stick out your tongue?
Are you not children of transgression,
the offspring of deceit—
5 you that burn with lust among the oaks,
under every green tree;
you that slaughter your children in the valleys,
under the clefts of the rocks?
6 Among the smooth stones of the valley is your portion;
they, they, are your lot;
to them you have poured out a drink offering,
you have brought a grain offering.
Shall I be appeased for these things?
7 Upon a high and lofty mountain
you have set your bed,
and there you went up to offer sacrifice.
8 Behind the door and the doorpost
you have set up your symbol;
for, in deserting me,[h] you have uncovered your bed,
you have gone up to it,
you have made it wide;
and you have made a bargain for yourself with them,
you have loved their bed,
you have gazed on their nakedness.[i]
9 You journeyed to Molech[j] with oil,
and multiplied your perfumes;
you sent your envoys far away,
and sent down even to Sheol.
10 You grew weary from your many wanderings,
but you did not say, "It is useless."
You found your desire rekindled,
and so you did not weaken.

11 Whom did you dread and fear
so that you lied,
and did not remember me
or give me a thought?
Have I not kept silent and closed my eyes,[k]
and so you do not fear me?
12 I will concede your righteousness and your works,
but they will not help you.
13 When you cry out, let your collection of idols deliver you!
The wind will carry them off,
a breath will take them away.
But whoever takes refuge in me shall possess the land
and inherit my holy mountain.

A Promise of Help and Healing

14 It shall be said,
"Build up, build up, prepare the way,
remove every obstruction from my people's way."
15 For thus says the high and lofty one
who inhabits eternity,
whose name is Holy:

57.1 Ps 12.1; Isa 42.25; 47.7,11 **57.2** Isa 26.7 **57.3** Mt 16.4; Isa 1.21 **57.4** Isa 48.8 **57.5** 2 Kings 16.4; Lev 18.21; 2 Kings 16.3; Jer 7.31 **57.6** Jer 3.9; 7.18; 5.9,29 **57.7** Ezek 16.16; 23.41 **57.8** Ezek 23.7, 18; 16.26,28 **57.9** Ezek 23.16, 40 **57.10** Isa 47.13; Jer 2.25 **57.11** Isa 51.12; Jer 2.32; v. 1; Ps 50.21 **57.13** Jer 22.20; Isa 25.4; 60.21; 65.9 **57.14** Isa 62.10; Jer 18.15 **57.15** Isa 52.13; 40.28; 66.1; Ps 34.18; 51.17; 14.2,3; Isa 61.1

[g] Heb *an adulterer and she plays the whore* [h] Meaning of Heb uncertain [i] Or *their phallus*; Heb *the hand* [j] Or *the king* [k] Gk Vg: Heb *silent even for a long time*

I dwell in the high and holy place,
and also with those who are contrite and humble in spirit,
to revive the spirit of the humble,
and to revive the heart of the contrite.
16 For I will not continually accuse,
nor will I always be angry;
for then the spirits would grow faint before me,
even the souls that I have made.
17 Because of their wicked covetousness I was angry;
I struck them, I hid and was angry;
but they kept turning back to their own ways.
18 I have seen their ways, but I will heal them;
I will lead them and repay them with comfort,
creating for their mourners the fruit of the lips.[1]
19 Peace, peace, to the far and the near, says the LORD;
and I will heal them.
20 But the wicked are like the tossing sea
that cannot keep still;
its waters toss up mire and mud.
21 There is no peace, says my God, for the wicked.

False and True Worship

58 Shout out, do not hold back!
Lift up your voice like a trumpet!
Announce to my people their rebellion,
to the house of Jacob their sins.
2 Yet day after day they seek me
and delight to know my ways,
as if they were a nation that practiced righteousness

57.16 Gen 6.3; Ps 85.5; 103.9; Mic 7.18; Job 34.14; Isa 42.5
57.17 Jer 6.13; Isa 1.4
57.18 Isa 53.5; 52.12; 61.1-3
57.19 Heb 13.15; Acts 2.39; Eph 2.17
57.20 Job 18.5-14
57.21 Isa 48.22
58.1 Isa 48.8; 50.1; 59.12
58.2 Isa 1.11; 48.1; 59.13; 29.13
58.3 Mal 3.14; Isa 22.12,13
58.4 1 Kings 21.9, 12,13; Isa 59.2
58.5 Zech 7.5; Esther 4.3; Job 2.8
58.6 Neh 5.10-12; Jer 34.9
58.7 Ezek 18.7, 16; Mt 25.35; Job 31.19; Gen 29.14; Neh 5.5
58.8 v. 10; Isa 30.26; 62.1; Ex 14.19; Isa 52.12

and did not forsake the ordinance of their God;
they ask of me righteous judgments,
they delight to draw near to God.
3 "Why do we fast, but you do not see?
Why humble ourselves, but you do not notice?"
Look, you serve your own interest on your fast day,
and oppress all your workers.
4 Look, you fast only to quarrel and to fight
and to strike with a wicked fist.
Such fasting as you do today
will not make your voice heard on high.
5 Is such the fast that I choose,
a day to humble oneself?
Is it to bow down the head like a bulrush,
and to lie in sackcloth and ashes?
Will you call this a fast,
a day acceptable to the LORD?

6 Is not this the fast that I choose:
to loose the bonds of injustice,
to undo the thongs of the yoke,
to let the oppressed go free,
and to break every yoke?
7 Is it not to share your bread with the hungry,
and bring the homeless poor into your house;
when you see the naked, to cover them,
and not to hide yourself from your own kin?
8 Then your light shall break forth like the dawn,
and your healing shall spring up quickly;

[1] Meaning of Heb uncertain

your vindicator[m] shall go
before you,
the glory of the LORD shall
be your rear guard.
9 Then you shall call, and the
LORD will answer;
you shall cry for help, and
he will say, Here I am.

If you remove the yoke from
among you,
the pointing of the finger,
the speaking of evil,
10 if you offer your food to the
hungry
and satisfy the needs of the
afflicted,
then your light shall rise in
the darkness
and your gloom be like the
noonday.
11 The LORD will guide you
continually,
and satisfy your needs in
parched places,
and make your bones
strong;
and you shall be like a
watered garden,
like a spring of water,
whose waters never fail.
12 Your ancient ruins shall be
rebuilt;
you shall raise up the
foundations of many
generations;
you shall be called the
repairer of the breach,
the restorer of streets to
live in.

13 If you refrain from trampling
the sabbath,
from pursuing your own
interests on my holy
day;
if you call the sabbath a
delight
and the holy day of the
LORD honorable;
if you honor it, not going
your own ways,
serving your own interests,
or pursuing your own
affairs;[n]
14 then you shall take delight
in the LORD,

58.9 Isa 55.6; v. 6; Ps 12.2
58.10 v. 7; Ps 37.6
58.11 Isa 49.10; 41.17; 66.14; Jn 4.14; 7.38
58.12 Isa 49.8; 44.28; 30.13; Am 9.11
58.13 Isa 56.2; Ps 84.2,10; Isa 55.8; 59.13
58.14 Isa 61.10; Deut 32.13; Isa 1.19,20

59.1 Num 11.23; Isa 50.2; 58.9
59.2 Isa 1.15; 58.4
59.3 Isa 1.15; Jer 2.30; v. 13; Isa 28.15
59.4 vv. 14,15; Isa 30.12; Job 15.35; Ps 7.14
59.5 Isa 14.29; Job 8.14
59.6 Isa 28.20; 57.12; 58.4
59.7 Rom 3.15-17; Isa 65.2

and I will make you ride
upon the heights of the
earth;
I will feed you with the
heritage of your
ancestor Jacob,
for the mouth of the LORD
has spoken.

Injustice and Oppression to Be Punished

59 See, the LORD's hand is
not too short to save,
nor his ear too dull to hear.
2 Rather, your iniquities have
been barriers
between you and your God,
and your sins have hidden
his face from you
so that he does not hear.
3 For your hands are defiled
with blood,
and your fingers with
iniquity;
your lips have spoken lies,
your tongue mutters
wickedness.
4 No one brings suit justly,
no one goes to law
honestly;
they rely on empty pleas,
they speak lies,
conceiving mischief and
begetting iniquity.
5 They hatch adders' eggs,
and weave the spider's
web;
whoever eats their eggs dies,
and the crushed egg
hatches out a viper.
6 Their webs cannot serve as
clothing;
they cannot cover
themselves with what
they make.
Their works are works of
iniquity,
and deeds of violence are
in their hands.
7 Their feet run to evil,
and they rush to shed
innocent blood;
their thoughts are thoughts
of iniquity,

m Or *vindication* n Heb *or speaking words*

desolation and destruction
are in their highways.
8 The way of peace they do
not know,
and there is no justice in
their paths.
Their roads they have made
crooked;
no one who walks in them
knows peace.

9 Therefore justice is far from
us,
and righteousness does not
reach us;
we wait for light, and lo!
there is darkness;
and for brightness, but we
walk in gloom.
10 We grope like the blind
along a wall,
groping like those who
have no eyes;
we stumble at noon as in the
twilight,
among the vigorous[o] as
though we were dead.
11 We all growl like bears;
like doves we moan
mournfully.
We wait for justice, but there
is none;
for salvation, but it is far
from us.
12 For our transgressions before
you are many,
and our sins testify against
us.
Our transgressions indeed
are with us,
and we know our
iniquities:
13 transgressing, and denying
the LORD,
and turning away from
following our God,
talking oppression and
revolt,
conceiving lying words and
uttering them from the
heart.
14 Justice is turned back,
and righteousness stands at
a distance;
for truth stumbles in the
public square,

59.8 vv. 9,11; Ps 125.5; v. 14
59.9 v. 14; Isa 5.30; 8.21,22
59.10 Deut 28.29; Job 5.14; Am 8.9; Isa 8.14,15
59.11 Isa 38.14; Ezek 7.16; vv. 9,14
59.12 Isa 58.1; Jer 14.7
59.13 Josh 24.27; Titus 1.16; Isa 30.12; vv. 3,4
59.14 Isa 1.21; 46.12; 48.1
59.15 Isa 5.23; 1.21-23
59.16 Isa 63.5; Ezek 22.30; Ps 98.1
59.17 Eph 6.14; 1 Thes 5.8; Isa 63.2,3
59.18 Isa 65.6,7; 66.6
59.19 Ps 113.3; Isa 66.12
59.20 Rom 11.26, 27; Ezek 18.30, 31; Acts 2.38,39
59.21 Jer 31.31-34; Isa 44.3,26; 54.10; Jer 32.40

and uprightness cannot
enter.
15 Truth is lacking,
and whoever turns from
evil is despoiled.

The LORD saw it, and it
displeased him
that there was no justice.
16 He saw that there was no
one,
and was appalled that
there was no one to
intervene;
so his own arm brought him
victory,
and his righteousness
upheld him.
17 He put on righteousness like
a breastplate,
and a helmet of salvation
on his head;
he put on garments of
vengeance for clothing,
and wrapped himself in
fury as in a mantle.
18 According to their deeds, so
will he repay;
wrath to his adversaries,
requital to his enemies;
to the coastlands he will
render requital.
19 So those in the west shall
fear the name of the
LORD,
and those in the east, his
glory;
for he will come like a
pent-up stream
that the wind of the LORD
drives on.

20 And he will come to Zion as
Redeemer,
to those in Jacob who turn
from transgression, says
the LORD.

21 And as for me, this is my covenant with them, says the LORD: my
spirit that is upon you, and my
words that I have put in your
mouth, shall not depart out of your
mouth, or out of the mouths of
your children, or out of the mouths

[o] Meaning of Heb uncertain

of your children's children, says the LORD, from now on and forever.

The Ingathering of the Dispersed

60 Arise, shine; for your light has come,
and the glory of the LORD has risen upon you.
2 For darkness shall cover the earth,
and thick darkness the peoples;
but the LORD will arise upon you,
and his glory will appear over you.
3 Nations shall come to your light,
and kings to the brightness of your dawn.

4 Lift up your eyes and look around;
they all gather together, they come to you;
your sons shall come from far away,
and your daughters shall be carried on their nurses' arms.
5 Then you shall see and be radiant;
your heart shall thrill and rejoice,[p]
because the abundance of the sea shall be brought to you,
the wealth of the nations shall come to you.
6 A multitude of camels shall cover you,
the young camels of Midian and Ephah;
all those from Sheba shall come.
They shall bring gold and frankincense,
and shall proclaim the praise of the LORD.
7 All the flocks of Kedar shall be gathered to you,
the rams of Nebaioth shall minister to you;
they shall be acceptable on my altar,
and I will glorify my glorious house.
8 Who are these that fly like a cloud,
and like doves to their windows?
9 For the coastlands shall wait for me,
the ships of Tarshish first,
to bring your children from far away,
their silver and gold with them,
for the name of the LORD your God,
and for the Holy One of Israel,
because he has glorified you.
10 Foreigners shall build up your walls,
and their kings shall minister to you;
for in my wrath I struck you down,
but in my favor I have had mercy on you.
11 Your gates shall always be open;
day and night they shall not be shut,
so that nations shall bring you their wealth,
with their kings led in procession.
12 For the nation and kingdom that will not serve you shall perish;
those nations shall be utterly laid waste.
13 The glory of Lebanon shall come to you,
the cypress, the plane, and the pine,
to beautify the place of my sanctuary;
and I will glorify where my feet rest.
14 The descendants of those who oppressed you
shall come bending low to you,
and all who despised you

60.1 Eph 5.14; Mal 4.2 **60.2** Col 1.13; Isa 4.5 **60.3** Isa 49.6,23; v. 11 **60.4** Isa 49.18, 20-22 **60.5** Ps 34.5; Isa 23.18; 24.14; 61.6 **60.6** Gen 25.4; Ps 72.10; Isa 43.23; 42.10 **60.7** Gen 25.13; Isa 56.7; Hag 2.7,9

60.9 Isa 66.19; 2.16; 49.22; 55.5 **60.10** Zech 6.15; Isa 49.23; 54.8 **60.11** vv. 18,5; Ps 149.8 **60.12** Zech 14.17 **60.13** Isa 35.2; 41.19; 1 Chr 28.2; Ps 132.7 **60.14** Isa 49.23; Heb 12.22; Rev 3.9

p Heb *be enlarged*

shall bow down at your feet;
they shall call you the City of the LORD,
the Zion of the Holy One of Israel.
15 Whereas you have been forsaken and hated,
with no one passing through,
I will make you majestic forever,
a joy from age to age.
16 You shall suck the milk of nations,
you shall suck the breasts of kings;
and you shall know that I, the LORD, am your Savior
and your Redeemer, the Mighty One of Jacob.

17 Instead of bronze I will bring gold,
instead of iron I will bring silver;
instead of wood, bronze,
instead of stones, iron.
I will appoint Peace as your overseer
and Righteousness as your taskmaster.
18 Violence shall no more be heard in your land,
devastation or destruction within your borders;
you shall call your walls Salvation,
and your gates Praise.

God the Glory of Zion

19 The sun shall no longer be your light by day,
nor for brightness shall the moon
give light to you by night;[q]
but the LORD will be your everlasting light,
and your God will be your glory.
20 Your sun shall no more go down,
or your moon withdraw itself;
for the LORD will be your everlasting light,
and your days of mourning shall be ended.
21 Your people shall all be righteous;
they shall possess the land forever.
They are the shoot that I planted, the work of my hands,
so that I might be glorified.
22 The least of them shall become a clan,
and the smallest one a mighty nation;
I am the LORD;
in its time I will accomplish it quickly.

The Good News of Deliverance

61 The spirit of the Lord GOD is upon me,
because the LORD has anointed me;
he has sent me to bring good news to the oppressed,
to bind up the brokenhearted,
to proclaim liberty to the captives,
and release to the prisoners;
2 to proclaim the year of the LORD's favor,
and the day of vengeance of our God;
to comfort all who mourn;
3 to provide for those who mourn in Zion—
to give them a garland instead of ashes,
the oil of gladness instead of mourning,
the mantle of praise instead of a faint spirit.
They will be called oaks of righteousness,
the planting of the LORD, to display his glory.
4 They shall build up the ancient ruins,
they shall raise up the former devastations;
they shall repair the ruined cities,

60.15 Jer 30.17; Isa 66.5; 33.8,9; 65.18 **60.16** Isa 49.23; 66.11; 63.8, 16 **60.18** Isa 54.14; 51.19; 26.1; v. 11 **60.19** Rev 21.23; 22.5; Isa 9.2; Zech 2.5 **60.20** Isa 30.26; 65.19 **60.21** Isa 52.1; Ps 37.11,22; Isa 29.23; 45.11 **60.22** Isa 51.2 **61.1f** Isa 11.2; Lk 4.18; Ps 45.7; Isa 57.15; 42.7 **61.2** Isa 49.8; 34.8; 57.18; Mt 5.4 **61.3** Isa 60.20; Ps 45.7; Isa 60.21 **61.4** Isa 49.8; Ezek 36.33

[q] Q Ms Gk Old Latin Tg: MT lacks *by night*

the devastations of many
generations.
5 Strangers shall stand and
feed your flocks,
foreigners shall till your
land and dress your
vines;
6 but you shall be called
priests of the LORD,
you shall be named
ministers of our God;
you shall enjoy the wealth of
the nations,
and in their riches you
shall glory.
7 Because their[r] shame was
double,
and dishonor was
proclaimed as their lot,
therefore they shall possess a
double portion;
everlasting joy shall be
theirs.

8 For I the LORD love justice,
I hate robbery and
wrongdoing;[s]
I will faithfully give them
their recompense,
and I will make an
everlasting covenant
with them.
9 Their descendants shall be
known among the
nations,
and their offspring among
the peoples;
all who see them shall
acknowledge
that they are a people
whom the LORD has
blessed.
10 I will greatly rejoice in the
LORD,
my whole being shall exult
in my God;
for he has clothed me with
the garments of
salvation,
he has covered me with the
robe of righteousness,
as a bridegroom decks
himself with a garland,
and as a bride adorns
herself with her jewels.

61.5 Isa 60.10 **61.6** Isa 66.21; 60.5,11 **61.7** Isa 54.4; 40.2; Zech 9.12; Isa 60.15; Ps 16.11 **61.8** Isa 30.18; 55.3 **61.9** Isa 54.3; 44.3 **61.10** Isa 12.1,2; 49.4,18; Rev 21.2

61.11 Isa 55.10; 45.23,24; Ps 72.3; 85.11; Isa 60.18 **62.1** Isa 61.11; 52.10 **62.2** Isa 60.3; vv. 4,12; Isa 65.15 **62.3** Zech 9.16 **62.4** Hos 1.10; Isa 54.6,7; Jer 32.41; 3.14 **62.5** Isa 65.19

11 For as the earth brings forth
its shoots,
and as a garden causes
what is sown in it to
spring up,
so the Lord GOD will cause
righteousness and
praise
to spring up before all the
nations.

The Vindication and Salvation of Zion

62 For Zion's sake I will not
keep silent,
and for Jerusalem's sake I
will not rest,
until her vindication shines
out like the dawn,
and her salvation like a
burning torch.
2 The nations shall see your
vindication,
and all the kings your
glory;
and you shall be called by a
new name
that the mouth of the LORD
will give.
3 You shall be a crown of
beauty in the hand of
the LORD,
and a royal diadem in the
hand of your God.
4 You shall no more be termed
Forsaken,[t]
and your land shall no
more be termed
Desolate;[u]
but you shall be called My
Delight Is in Her,[v]
and your land Married;[w]
for the LORD delights in you,
and your land shall be
married.
5 For as a young man marries
a young woman,
so shall your builder[x]
marry you,
and as the bridegroom
rejoices over the bride,
so shall your God rejoice
over you.

[r] Heb *your offering* [s] Or *robbery with a burnt offering* [t] Heb *Azubah* [u] Heb *Shemamah* [v] Heb *Hephzibah* [w] Heb *Beulah* [x] Cn: Heb *your sons*

6 Upon your walls,
O Jerusalem,
I have posted sentinels;
all day and all night
they shall never be silent.
You who remind the LORD,
take no rest,
7 and give him no rest
until he establishes
Jerusalem
and makes it renowned
throughout the earth.
8 The LORD has sworn by his
right hand
and by his mighty arm:
I will not again give your
grain
to be food for your
enemies,
and foreigners shall not
drink the wine
for which you have labored;
9 but those who garner it shall
eat it
and praise the LORD,
and those who gather it shall
drink it
in my holy courts.

10 Go through, go through the
gates,
prepare the way for the
people;
build up, build up the
highway,
clear it of stones,
lift up an ensign over the
peoples.
11 The LORD has proclaimed
to the end of the earth:
Say to daughter Zion,
"See, your salvation comes;
his reward is with him,
and his recompense before
him."
12 They shall be called, "The
Holy People,
The Redeemed of the
LORD";
and you shall be called,
"Sought Out,
A City Not Forsaken."

Vengeance on Edom

63 "Who is this that comes
from Edom,

62.6 Isa 52.8; Jer 6.17; Ezek 3.17; Ps 74.2
62.7 Mt 15.21-28; Lk 18.1-8; Jer 33.9
62.8 Isa 45.23; Deut 28.31, 33; Jer 5.17
62.9 Isa 65.13, 21-23
62.10 Isa 57.14; 49.11; 11.10, 12
62.11 Isa 49.6; Zech 9.9; Mt 21.5; Isa 51.1; 40.10
62.12 Isa 4.3; 51.10; v. 4
63.1 Isa 34.5,6; Am 1.12; Zeph 3.17
63.2 Rev 19.13, 15
63.3 Isa 22.5; 28.3; Mic 7.10; Rev 19.15
63.4 Isa 34.8; 61.2
63.5 Isa 59.16; Ps 98.1; Isa 52.10
63.6 Isa 65.12; 51.17,21,22; 34.3
63.7 Isa 54.8,10; 1 Kings 8.66; Ps 51.1

from Bozrah in garments
stained crimson?
Who is this so splendidly
robed,
marching in his great
might?"

"It is I, announcing
vindication,
mighty to save."

2 "Why are your robes red,
and your garments like
theirs who tread the
wine press?"

3 "I have trodden the
wine press alone,
and from the peoples no
one was with me;
I trod them in my anger
and trampled them in my
wrath;
their juice spattered on my
garments,
and stained all my robes.
4 For the day of vengeance was
in my heart,
and the year for my
redeeming work had
come.
5 I looked, but there was no
helper;
I stared, but there was no
one to sustain me;
so my own arm brought me
victory,
and my wrath sustained
me.
6 I trampled down peoples in
my anger,
I crushed them in my
wrath,
and I poured out their
lifeblood on the earth."

God's Mercy Remembered

7 I will recount the gracious
deeds of the LORD,
the praiseworthy acts of
the LORD,
because of all that the LORD
has done for us,
and the great favor to the
house of Israel

that he has shown them
according to his mercy,
according to the
abundance of his
steadfast love.
8 For he said, "Surely they are
my people,
children who will not deal
falsely";
and he became their savior
9 in all their distress.
It was no messenger[y] or
angel
but his presence that saved
them;[z]
in his love and in his pity he
redeemed them;
he lifted them up and
carried them all the
days of old.

10 But they rebelled
and grieved his holy spirit;
therefore he became their
enemy;
he himself fought against
them.
11 Then they[a] remembered the
days of old,
of Moses his servant.[b]
Where is the one who
brought them up out of
the sea
with the shepherds of his
flock?
Where is the one who put
within them
his holy spirit,
12 who caused his glorious arm
to march at the right hand
of Moses,
who divided the waters
before them
to make for himself an
everlasting name,
13 who led them through the
depths?
Like a horse in the desert,
they did not stumble.
14 Like cattle that go down into
the valley,
the spirit of the LORD gave
them rest.
Thus you led your people,
to make for yourself a
glorious name.

63.9 Judg 10.16; Ex 23.20-23; Deut 7.7,8; Ex 19.4; Deut 1.31
63.10 Ps 78.40; Acts 7.51; Eph 4.30; Ps 106.40
63.11 Ps 106.44, 45; Ex 14.30; Isa 51.9,10; Num 11.17
63.12 Ex 15.6; 14.21; Isa 50.10,11
63.13 Ps 106.9
63.14 Deut 32.12
63.15 Deut 26.15; Ps 80.14; Jer 31.20; Hos 11.8
63.16 Isa 64.8; 51.2; 44.6; 60.16
63.17 Ezek 14.7-9; Isa 29.13, 14; Num 10.36
63.18 Deut 7.6; Ps 74.3-7
63.19 Lam 3.43-45
64.1 Ps 144.5; Judg 5.5
64.2 Jer 5.22

A Prayer of Penitence

15 Look down from heaven and
see,
from your holy and glorious
habitation.
Where are your zeal and your
might?
The yearning of your heart
and your compassion?
They are withheld from me.
16 For you are our father,
though Abraham does not
know us
and Israel does not
acknowledge us;
you, O LORD, are our father;
our Redeemer from of old
is your name.
17 Why, O LORD, do you make
us stray from your ways
and harden our heart, so
that we do not fear
you?
Turn back for the sake of
your servants,
for the sake of the tribes
that are your heritage.
18 Your holy people took
possession for a little
while;
but now our adversaries
have trampled down
your sanctuary.
19 We have long been like those
whom you do not rule,
like those not called by
your name.

64 O that you would tear
open the heavens and
come down,
so that the mountains
would quake at your
presence—
2 [c]as when fire kindles
brushwood
and the fire causes water
to boil—
to make your name known to
your adversaries,
so that the nations might
tremble at your
presence!

[y] Gk: Heb *anguish* [z] Or *savior. In all their distress he was distressed; the angel of his presence saved them;* [a] Heb *he* [b] Cn: Heb *his people* [c] Ch 64.1 in Heb

3 When you did awesome
deeds that we did not
expect,
you came down, the
mountains quaked at
your presence.
4 From ages past no one has
heard,
no ear has perceived,
no eye has seen any God
besides you,
who works for those who
wait for him.
5 You meet those who gladly
do right,
those who remember you
in your ways.
But you were angry, and we
sinned;
because you hid yourself
we transgressed.[d]
6 We have all become like one
who is unclean,
and all our righteous deeds
are like a filthy cloth.
We all fade like a leaf,
and our iniquities, like the
wind, take us away.
7 There is no one who calls on
your name,
or attempts to take hold of
you;
for you have hidden your
face from us,
and have delivered[e] us
into the hand of our
iniquity.
8 Yet, O LORD, you are our
Father;
we are the clay, and you
are our potter;
we are all the work of your
hand.
9 Do not be exceedingly angry,
O LORD,
and do not remember
iniquity forever.
Now consider, we are all
your people.
10 Your holy cities have become
a wilderness,
Zion has become a
wilderness,
Jerusalem a desolation.
11 Our holy and beautiful
house,
where our ancestors
praised you,
has been burned by fire,
and all our pleasant places
have become ruins.
12 After all this, will you
restrain yourself,
O LORD?
Will you keep silent, and
punish us so severely?

64.3 Ps 65.5; 66.3,5; 106.22 **64.4** 1 Cor 2.9; Isa 40.31 **64.5** Ex 20.24; Isa 56.1; 63.7,10 **64.6** Isa 6.5; 46.12; Ps 90.5,6; Isa 50.1 **64.7** Isa 59.4; 27.5; 54.8; 9.18 **64.8** Isa 63.16; 29.16; 60.21 **64.9** Isa 60.10; 43.25; 63.8 **64.10** Isa 6.11 **64.11** Isa 63.18; Ps 74.5-7; Isa 7.23 **64.12** Isa 42.14; Ps 83.1 **65.1** Rom 10.20; Hos 1.10 **65.2** Rom 10.21; Isa 30.1,9; 59.7 **65.3** Isa 3.8; 66.3,17 **65.4** Lev 11.7; Isa 66.3,17 **65.5** Mt 9.11; Lk 18.9-12 **65.6** Ps 50.3; 79.12; Jer 16.18

The Righteousness of God's Judgment

65 I was ready to be sought
out by those who did
not ask,
to be found by those who
did not seek me.
I said, "Here I am, here I
am,"
to a nation that did not
call on my name.
2 I held out my hands all day
long
to a rebellious people,
who walk in a way that is
not good,
following their own
devices;
3 a people who provoke me
to my face continually,
sacrificing in gardens
and offering incense on
bricks;
4 who sit inside tombs,
and spend the night in
secret places;
who eat swine's flesh,
with broth of abominable
things in their vessels;
5 who say, "Keep to yourself,
do not come near me, for I
am too holy for you."
These are a smoke in my
nostrils,
a fire that burns all day
long.
6 See, it is written before me:
I will not keep silent, but I
will repay;
I will indeed repay into their
laps

[d] Meaning of Heb uncertain [e] Gk Syr Old Latin Tg: Heb *melted*

7 their[f] iniquities and their[f]
ancestors' iniquities
together,
says the LORD;
because they offered incense
on the mountains
and reviled me on the hills,
I will measure into their laps
full payment for their
actions.
8 Thus says the LORD:
As the wine is found in the
cluster,
and they say, "Do not
destroy it,
for there is a blessing in
it,"
so I will do for my servants'
sake,
and not destroy them all.
9 I will bring forth
descendants[g] from
Jacob,
and from Judah inheritors[h]
of my mountains;
my chosen shall inherit it,
and my servants shall settle
there.
10 Sharon shall become a
pasture for flocks,
and the Valley of Achor a
place for herds to lie
down,
for my people who have
sought me.
11 But you who forsake the
LORD,
who forget my holy
mountain,
who set a table for Fortune
and fill cups of mixed wine
for Destiny;
12 I will destine you to the
sword,
and all of you shall bow
down to the slaughter;
because, when I called, you
did not answer,
when I spoke, you did not
listen,
but you did what was evil in
my sight,
and chose what I did not
delight in.
13 Therefore thus says the Lord
GOD:
My servants shall eat,

65.7 Isa 30.13, 14; 57.7; Ezek 20.27, 28; Jer 5.29 **65.9f** Isa 45.19, 25; 49.8; 57.13; 32.18 **65.10** Isa 33.9; Josh 7.24; Hos 2.15 **65.11** Deut 29.24, 25; Isa 56.7 **65.12** Isa 34.5,6; 63.6; 2 Chr 36.15, 16; Prov 1.24; Jer 7.13 **65.13** Isa 1.19; 8.21; 41.17, 18; 5.13; 66.5,14

65.14 Mt 8.12; Lk 13.28 **65.15** Zech 8.13; Isa 62.2 **65.16** Ps 72.17; 31.5; Isa 45.23; Jer 31.12 **65.17** 2 Pet 3.13; Isa 43.18 **65.18** Isa 61.10 **65.19** Isa 62.5; 35.10; Rev 7.17 **65.20** Deut 4.40; Eccl 8.12,13

but you shall be hungry;
my servants shall drink,
but you shall be thirsty;
my servants shall rejoice,
but you shall be put to
shame;
14 my servants shall sing for
gladness of heart,
but you shall cry out for
pain of heart,
and shall wail for anguish
of spirit.
15 You shall leave your name to
my chosen to use as a
curse,
and the Lord GOD will put
you to death;
but to his servants he will
give a different name.
16 Then whoever invokes a
blessing in the land
shall bless by the God of
faithfulness,
and whoever takes an oath in
the land
shall swear by the God of
faithfulness;
because the former troubles
are forgotten
and are hidden from my
sight.

The Glorious New Creation

17 For I am about to create new
heavens
and a new earth;
the former things shall not
be remembered
or come to mind.
18 But be glad and rejoice
forever
in what I am creating;
for I am about to create
Jerusalem as a joy,
and its people as a delight.
19 I will rejoice in Jerusalem,
and delight in my people;
no more shall the sound of
weeping be heard in it,
or the cry of distress.
20 No more shall there be in it
an infant that lives but a
few days,
or an old person who does
not live out a lifetime;

[f] Gk Syr: Heb *your* [g] Or *a descendant* [h] Or *an inheritor*

for one who dies at a
hundred years will be
considered a youth,
and one who falls short of
a hundred will be
considered accursed.
21 They shall build houses and
inhabit them;
they shall plant vineyards
and eat their fruit.
22 They shall not build and
another inhabit;
they shall not plant and
another eat;
for like the days of a tree
shall the days of my
people be,
and my chosen shall long
enjoy the work of their
hands.
23 They shall not labor in vain,
or bear children for
calamity;[i]
for they shall be offspring
blessed by the LORD—
and their descendants as
well.
24 Before they call I will
answer,
while they are yet speaking
I will hear.
25 The wolf and the lamb shall
feed together,
the lion shall eat straw like
the ox;
but the serpent—its food
shall be dust!
They shall not hurt or
destroy
on all my holy mountain,
says the LORD.

The Worship God Demands

66 Thus says the LORD:
Heaven is my throne
and the earth is my
footstool;
what is the house that you
would build for me,
and what is my resting
place?
2 All these things my hand has
made,
and so all these things are
mine,[j]
says the LORD.

65.21 Am 9.14; Isa 37.30
65.22 Isa 62.8,9; Ps 92.12-14; Deut 32.46, 47
65.23 Isa 55.2; 61.9
65.24 Dan 9.27
65.25 Isa 11.6,7,9; Gen 3.14
66.1 1 Kings 8.27; 2 Chr 6.18; Mt 5.34,35; Jer 7.4; Acts 7.49,50
66.2 Isa 40.26; 57.15; Mt 5.3,4; v. 5
66.3 Isa 1.11,13; 65.2,4
66.4 Prov 1.24; Isa 65.12; Jer 7.13
66.5 v. 2; Isa 60.15; Mt 5.10-12; Lk 13.17
66.6 Isa 6.1,8; 65.6

But this is the one to whom
I will look,
to the humble and contrite
in spirit,
who trembles at my word.

3 Whoever slaughters an ox is
like one who kills a
human being;
whoever sacrifices a lamb,
like one who breaks a
dog's neck;
whoever presents a grain
offering, like one who
offers swine's blood;[k]
whoever makes a memorial
offering of frankincense,
like one who blesses an
idol.
These have chosen their own
ways,
and in their abominations
they take delight;
4 I also will choose to mock[l]
them,
and bring upon them what
they fear;
because, when I called, no
one answered,
when I spoke, they did not
listen;
but they did what was evil in
my sight,
and chose what did not
please me.

The LORD Vindicates Zion

5 Hear the word of the LORD,
you who tremble at his
word:
Your own people who hate
you
and reject you for my
name's sake
have said, "Let the LORD be
glorified,
so that we may see your
joy";
but it is they who shall be
put to shame.

6 Listen, an uproar from the
city!

[i] Or *sudden terror*
[j] Gk Syr: Heb *these things came to be*
[k] Meaning of Heb uncertain
[l] Or *to punish*

A voice from the temple!
The voice of the LORD,
dealing retribution to his enemies!

7 Before she was in labor
she gave birth;
before her pain came upon her
she delivered a son.
8 Who has heard of such a thing?
Who has seen such things?
Shall a land be born in one day?
Shall a nation be delivered in one moment?
Yet as soon as Zion was in labor
she delivered her children.
9 Shall I open the womb and not deliver?
says the LORD;
shall I, the one who delivers, shut the womb?
says your God.

10 Rejoice with Jerusalem, and be glad for her,
all you who love her;
rejoice with her in joy,
all you who mourn over her—
11 that you may nurse and be satisfied
from her consoling breast;
that you may drink deeply with delight
from her glorious bosom.

12 For thus says the LORD:
I will extend prosperity to her like a river,
and the wealth of the nations like an overflowing stream;
and you shall nurse and be carried on her arm,
and dandled on her knees.
13 As a mother comforts her child,
so I will comfort you;
you shall be comforted in Jerusalem.

66.7 Isa 37.3 **66.8** Isa 64.4 **66.10** Isa 65.18; Ps 26.8; 137.6 **66.11** Isa 60.16 **66.12** Isa 48.18; 60.4,5 **66.13** 2 Cor 1.3, 4

66.14 Isa 33.20; Zech 10.7; Isa 58.11; Ezra 7.9; Isa 34.2 **66.15** Isa 31.9; 2 Thes 1.8; Ps 78.16 **66.16** Isa 30.30; 65.12; 34.3 **66.17** Isa 65.3,4; Ps 37.20 **66.18** Isa 59.7; 45.22-25 **66.19** Isa 62.10; 42.12 **66.20** Isa 60.4; 65.11,25; 52.11

The Reign and Indignation of God

14 You shall see, and your heart shall rejoice;
your bodies[m] shall flourish like the grass;
and it shall be known that the hand of the LORD is with his servants,
and his indignation is against his enemies.
15 For the LORD will come in fire,
and his chariots like the whirlwind,
to pay back his anger in fury,
and his rebuke in flames of fire.
16 For by fire will the LORD execute judgment,
and by his sword, on all flesh;
and those slain by the LORD shall be many.

17 Those who sanctify and purify themselves to go into the gardens, following the one in the center, eating the flesh of pigs, vermin, and rodents, shall come to an end together, says the LORD.

18 For I know[n] their works and
their thoughts, and I am[o] coming
to gather all nations and tongues;
and they shall come and shall see
my glory, 19 and I will set a sign
among them. From them I will
send survivors to the nations, to
Tarshish, Put,[p] and Lud—which
draw the bow—to Tubal and Javan, to the coastlands far away that
have not heard of my fame or seen
my glory; and they shall declare my
glory among the nations. 20 They
shall bring all your kindred from all
the nations as an offering to the
LORD, on horses, and in chariots,
and in litters, and on mules, and on
dromedaries, to my holy mountain
Jerusalem, says the LORD, just as
the Israelites bring a grain offering
in a clean vessel to the house of the

[m] Heb *bones* [n] Gk Syr: Heb lacks *know* [o] Gk Syr Vg Tg: Heb *it is* [p] Gk: Heb *Pul*

LORD. [21]And I will also take some of
them as priests and as Levites, says
the LORD.

22 For as the new heavens and
the new earth,
which I will make,
shall remain before me, says
the LORD;
so shall your descendants
and your name remain.
23 From new moon to new
moon,
and from sabbath to
sabbath,
all flesh shall come to
worship before me,
says the LORD.

24 And they shall go out and
look at the dead bodies of the people who have rebelled against me;
for their worm shall not die, their
fire shall not be quenched, and
they shall be an abhorrence to all
flesh.

66.21 Isa 61.6; 1 Pet 2.5,9
66.22 Isa 65.17; 2 Pet 3.13; Rev 21.1; Isa 65.22, 23; 56.5
66.23 Isa 1.13,14; 49.7
66.24 Isa 5.25; 24.20; Mk 9.48; Isa 1.31; Dan 12.2

Jeremiah

Title and Background

This book is named after the prophet whose ministry it records. Jeremiah prophesied in Judah during the reigns of Josiah and succeeding kings, living to see the destruction of Jerusalem and the Babylonian exile. It was a period of storm and stress throughout the entire world. After Josiah's reign, Jeremiah was often in danger from political and religious leaders in Judah who were angry because of his messages. Through all this, God protected Jeremiah so he could continue to warn the wicked and comfort those who trusted in God.

Author and Date of Writing

This book preserves an account of the prophetic ministry of Jeremiah, whose personal life and struggles are known to us in greater depth and detail than those of any other Old Testament prophet. His prophetic ministry began in 626 B.C. and ended sometime after 586.

Theme and Message

Jeremiah was always conscious of his call from the Lord to be a prophet, and as such proclaimed words that were spoken first by God himself and were therefore certain of fulfillment. Judgment is one of his all-pervasive themes. He was careful to point out, however, that repentance, if sincere, would postpone the inevitable.

For Jeremiah God was ultimate. He conceived of God as the Creator of all that exists, and as the all-powerful and everywhere present Lord. At the same time he emphasized that God was very much concerned about individual people who were accountable to God.

Outline

I. The Call of Jeremiah (1.1-19)
II. Warnings and Exhortations to Judah (2.1–29.32)
III. Promises of Restoration (30.1–33.26)
IV. Historical Insertion (34.1–35.19)
V. The Sufferings of Jeremiah (36.1–38.28)
VI. The Fall of Jerusalem and Its Aftermath (39.1–45.5)
VII. Judgment Against the Nations (46.1–51.64)
VIII. Historical Appendix (52.1-34)

---

1 The words of Jeremiah son of
Hilkiah, of the priests who
were in Anathoth in the land of
Benjamin, 2 to whom the word of
the LORD came in the days of King
Josiah son of Amon of Judah, in
the thirteenth year of his reign. 3 It
came also in the days of King Jehoiakim son of Josiah of Judah,
and until the end of the eleventh
year of King Zedekiah son of Josiah
of Judah, until the captivity of Jerusalem in the fifth month.

1.1 2 Chr 35.25; 1 Chr 6.60; Isa 32.7-9
1.2 1 Kings 13.2; 2 Kings 21.18, 24
1.3 Jer 25.1; 39.2; 52.12
1.5 Ps 139.15, 16; Isa 49.1, 5
1.6 Ex 4.10; Isa 6.5

Jeremiah's Call and Commission

4 Now the word of the LORD
came to me saying,
5 "Before I formed you in the
womb I knew you,
and before you were born I
consecrated you;
I appointed you a prophet to
the nations."
6 Then I said, "Ah, Lord GOD! Truly
I do not know how to speak, for I
am only a boy." 7 But the LORD said
to me,

"Do not say, 'I am only a
boy';
for you shall go to all to
whom I send you,
and you shall speak whatever
I command you,
8 Do not be afraid of them,
for I am with you to deliver
you,
says the LORD."
9 Then the LORD put out his hand
and touched my mouth; and the
LORD said to me,
"Now I have put my words in
your mouth.
10 See, today I appoint you over
nations and over
kingdoms,
to pluck up and to pull
down,
to destroy and to overthrow,
to build and to plant."
11 The word of the LORD came to
me, saying, "Jeremiah, what do you
see?" And I said, "I see a branch of
an almond tree."[a] 12 Then the LORD
said to me, "You have seen well, for
I am watching[b] over my word to
perform it." 13 The word of the LORD
came to me a second time, saying,
"What do you see?" And I said, "I
see a boiling pot, tilted away from
the north."
14 Then the LORD said to me:
Out of the north disaster shall
break out on all the inhabitants of
the land. 15 For now I am calling all
the tribes of the kingdoms of the
north, says the LORD; and they shall
come and all of them shall set their
thrones at the entrance of the gates
of Jerusalem, against all its surrounding walls and against all the
cities of Judah. 16 And I will utter
my judgments against them, for all
their wickedness in forsaking me;
they have made offerings to other
gods, and worshiped the works of
their own hands. 17 But you, gird up
your loins; stand up and tell them
everything that I command you. Do
not break down before them, or I
will break you before them. 18 And
I for my part have made you today
a fortified city, an iron pillar, and a
bronze wall, against the whole
land—against the kings of Judah,
its princes, its priests, and the people of the land. 19 They will fight
against you; but they shall not prevail against you, for I am with you,
says the LORD, to deliver you.

1.8 Ezek 2.6; Jer 15.20
1.9 Isa 6.7; Ex 4.11-16
1.10 Jer 18.7; 2 Cor 10.4, 5
1.11 Jer 24.3
1.13 Zech 4.2; Ezek 11.3,7; 24.3
1.14 Jer 4.6; 6.1
1.15 Isa 22.7; Jer 9.11
1.16 Deut 28.20; Jer 17.13; 7.9; 10.3-5
1.17 1 Kings 18.46; Ex 3.12; Ezek 2.6
1.18 Isa 50.7; Jer 6.27; 15.20
1.19 Jer 11.19; 15.10,11; v. 8
2.1 Jer 1.2,11
2.2 Jer 7.2; 11.6; Ezek 16.8; Deut 2.7
2.3 Ex 19.5,6; Jer 30.16; 50.7
2.5 Isa 5.4; Mic 6.3; Jer 8.19; 2 Kings 17.15
2.6 Ex 20.2; Isa 63.11; Hos 13.4; Deut 8.15; 32.10
2.7 Num 13.27; Lev 18.25; Ps 78.58

God Pleads with Israel to Repent

2 The word of the LORD came to
me, saying: 2 Go and proclaim
in the hearing of Jerusalem, Thus
says the LORD:
I remember the devotion of
your youth,
your love as a bride,
how you followed me in the
wilderness,
in a land not sown.
3 Israel was holy to the LORD,
the first fruits of his
harvest.
All who ate of it were held
guilty;
disaster came upon them,
says the LORD.

4 Hear the word of the LORD,
O house of Jacob, and all the families of the house of Israel. 5 Thus
says the LORD:
What wrong did your
ancestors find in me
that they went far from me,
and went after worthless
things, and became
worthless themselves?
6 They did not say, "Where is
the LORD
who brought us up from
the land of Egypt,
who led us in the wilderness,
in a land of deserts and
pits,
in a land of drought and
deep darkness,
in a land that no one
passes through,
where no one lives?"
7 I brought you into a plentiful
land
to eat its fruits and its
good things.
But when you entered you
defiled my land,

[a] Heb *shaqed* [b] Heb *shoqed*

and made my heritage an
abomination.
8 The priests did not say,
"Where is the LORD?"
Those who handle the law
did not know me;
the rulers[c] transgressed
against me;
the prophets prophesied by
Baal,
and went after things that
do not profit.

9 Therefore once more I
accuse you,
says the LORD,
and I accuse your
children's children.
10 Cross to the coasts of Cyprus
and look,
send to Kedar and examine
with care;
see if there has ever been
such a thing.
11 Has a nation changed its
gods,
even though they are no
gods?
But my people have changed
their glory
for something that does
not profit.
12 Be appalled, O heavens, at
this,
be shocked, be utterly
desolate,
says the LORD,
13 for my people have
committed two evils:
they have forsaken me,
the fountain of living water,
and dug out cisterns for
themselves,
cracked cisterns
that can hold no water.

14 Is Israel a slave? Is he a
homeborn servant?
Why then has he become
plunder?
15 The lions have roared against
him,
they have roared loudly.
They have made his land a
waste;
his cities are in ruins,
without inhabitant.
16 Moreover, the people of
Memphis and
Tahpanhes
have broken the crown of
your head.
17 Have you not brought this
upon yourself
by forsaking the LORD your
God,
while he led you in the
way?
18 What then do you gain by
going to Egypt,
to drink the waters of the
Nile?
Or what do you gain by
going to Assyria,
to drink the waters of the
Euphrates?
19 Your wickedness will punish
you,
and your apostasies will
convict you.
Know and see that it is evil
and bitter
for you to forsake the LORD
your God;
the fear of me is not in
you,
says the Lord GOD
of hosts.

20 For long ago you broke your
yoke
and burst your bonds,
and you said, "I will not
serve!"
On every high hill
and under every green tree
you sprawled and played
the whore.
21 Yet I planted you as a choice
vine,
from the purest stock.
How then did you turn
degenerate
and become a wild vine?
22 Though you wash yourself
with lye
and use much soap,
the stain of your guilt is
still before me,
says the Lord GOD.
23 How can you say, "I am not
defiled,

2.8 Jer 10.21; Mal 2.6,7; Rom 2.20; Jer 23.13; 16.19
2.9 Ezek 20.35, 36; Mic 6.2
2.10 Isa 23.12; Jer 49.28
2.11 Mic 4.5; Ps 106.20; Rom 1.23
2.13 Ps 36.9; Jer 17.13; Jn 4.14; Jer 14.3
2.14 Ex 4.22; Jer 5.19
2.15 Jer 50.17; 4.7
2.16 Jer 44.1; 43.7-9; 48.45
2.17 Jer 4.18; Deut 32.10
2.18 Isa 30.1,2; Josh 13.3; Jer 50.17
2.19 Isa 3.9; Hos 5.5; 11.7; Jer 5.24; Ps 36.1
2.20 Lev 26.13; v. 25; Deut 12.2; Isa 57.5,7
2.21 Ex 15.17; Isa 5.4
2.22 Jer 4.14
2.23 Prov 30.12; Jer 9.14; 7.31

[c] Heb *shepherds*

I have not gone after the
Baals"?
Look at your way in the
valley;
know what you have
done—
a restive young camel
interlacing her tracks,
24 a wild ass at home in the
wilderness,
in her heat sniffing the wind!
Who can restrain her lust?
None who seek her need
weary themselves;
in her month they will find
her.
25 Keep your feet from going
unshod
and your throat from thirst.
But you said, "It is hopeless,
for I have loved strangers,
and after them I will go."

26 As a thief is shamed when
caught,
so the house of Israel shall
be shamed—
they, their kings, their
officials,
their priests, and their
prophets,
27 who say to a tree, "You are
my father,"
and to a stone, "You gave
me birth."
For they have turned their
backs to me,
and not their faces.
But in the time of their
trouble they say,
"Come and save us!"
28 But where are your gods
that you made for yourself?
Let them come, if they can
save you,
in your time of trouble;
for you have as many gods
as you have towns,
O Judah.

29 Why do you complain against
me?
You have all rebelled
against me,
says the LORD.
30 In vain I have struck down
your children;
they accepted no
correction.
Your own sword devoured
your prophets
like a ravening lion.
31 And you, O generation,
behold the word of the
LORD![d]
Have I been a wilderness to
Israel,
or a land of thick
darkness?
Why then do my people say,
"We are free,
we will come to you no
more"?
32 Can a girl forget her
ornaments,
or a bride her attire?
Yet my people have forgotten
me,
days without number.

33 How well you direct your
course
to seek lovers!
So that even to wicked
women
you have taught your ways.
34 Also on your skirts is found
the lifeblood of the
innocent poor,
though you did not catch
them breaking in.
Yet in spite of all these
things[d]
35 you say, "I am innocent;
surely his anger has turned
from me."
Now I am bringing you to
judgment
for saying, "I have not
sinned."
36 How lightly you gad about,
changing your ways!
You shall be put to shame by
Egypt
as you were put to shame
by Assyria.
37 From there also you will
come away
with your hands on your
head;

2.24 Jer 14.6
2.25 Jer 18.12; 14.10; Deut 32.16
2.26 Jer 48.27
2.27 Jer 3.9; 18.17; 22.23; Isa 26.16
2.28 Deut 32.37; Isa 45.20; Jer 11.13
2.29 Jer 5.1; 6.13
2.30 Isa 1.5; Jer 26.20-24
2.31 Isa 45.19; Deut 32.15
2.32 Isa 17.10; Hos 8.14
2.34 Jer 19.4; Ex 22.2
2.35 v. 23; Jer 25.31; 1 Jn 1.8, 10
2.36 v. 23; Hos 12.1; Isa 30.3; 2 Chr 28.16, 20,21
2.37 2 Sam 13.19; Jer 37.7-10

d Meaning of Heb uncertain

for the LORD has rejected
those in whom you
trust,
and you will not prosper
through them.

Unfaithful Israel

3 If[e] a man divorces his wife
and she goes from him
and becomes another man's
wife,
will he return to her?
Would not such a land be
greatly polluted?
You have played the whore
with many lovers;
and would you return to
me? says the LORD.
2 Look up to the bare
heights,[f] and see!
Where have you not been
lain with?
By the waysides you have sat
waiting for lovers,
like a nomad in the
wilderness.
You have polluted the land
with your whoring and
wickedness.
3 Therefore the showers have
been withheld,
and the spring rain has not
come;
yet you have the forehead of
a whore,
you refuse to be ashamed.
4 Have you not just now called
to me,
"My Father, you are the
friend of my youth—
5 will he be angry forever,
will he be indignant to the
end?"
This is how you have spoken,
but you have done all the
evil that you could.

A Call to Repentance

6 The LORD said to me in the
days of King Josiah: Have you seen
what she did, that faithless one, Israel, how she went up on every high
hill and under every green tree, and
played the whore there? 7 And I
thought, "After she has done all
this she will return to me"; but she
did not return, and her false sister
Judah saw it. 8 She[g] saw that for all
the adulteries of that faithless one,
Israel, I had sent her away with a
decree of divorce; yet her false sister Judah did not fear, but she too
went and played the whore. 9 Because she took her whoredom so
lightly, she polluted the land, committing adultery with stone and
tree. 10 Yet for all this her false sister Judah did not return to me with
her whole heart, but only in pretense, says the LORD.

11 Then the LORD said to me:
Faithless Israel has shown herself
less guilty than false Judah. 12 Go,
and proclaim these words toward
the north, and say:

Return, faithless Israel,
says the LORD.
I will not look on you in
anger,
for I am merciful,
says the LORD;
I will not be angry forever.
13 Only acknowledge your guilt,
that you have rebelled
against the LORD your
God,
and scattered your favors
among strangers under
every green tree,
and have not obeyed my
voice,
says the LORD.
14 Return, O faithless children,
says the LORD,
for I am your master;
I will take you, one from a
city and two from a
family,
and I will bring you to
Zion.

15 I will give you shepherds after my own heart, who will feed you
with knowledge and understanding. 16 And when you have multiplied and increased in the land, in
those days, says the LORD, they
shall no longer say, "The ark of the
covenant of the LORD." It shall not
come to mind, or be remembered,

3.1 Deut 24.4; Jer 2.20; Ezek 16.26, 28,29; Zech 1.3
3.2 Deut 12.2; Jer 2.20; Prov 23.28; Jer 2.7
3.3 Lev 26.19; Jer 6.15; Ezek 3.7
3.4 v. 19; Ps 71.17
3.5 v. 12; Isa 57.16
3.6 Jer 7.24; 17.2
3.7 Ezek 16.46, 47
3.8 2 Kings 17.6; Isa 50.1; Ezek 23.11
3.9 Jer 2.7,27
3.10 Hos 7.14
3.11 Ezek 16.51; v. 7
3.12 2 Kings 17.6; Ps 86.15
3.13 Deut 30.1-3; Jer 2.20,25; Deut 12.2
3.14 Hos 2.19; Jer 50.4,5
3.15 Jer 23.4; Acts 20.28
3.16 Isa 65.17

[e] Q Ms Gk Syr: MT *Saying, If* [f] Or *the trails* [g] Q Ms Gk Mss Syr: MT *I*

or missed; nor shall another one be
made. 17 At that time Jerusalem
shall be called the throne of the
LORD, and all nations shall gather to
it, to the presence of the LORD in
Jerusalem, and they shall no longer
stubbornly follow their own evil
will. 18 In those days the house of
Judah shall join the house of Israel,
and together they shall come from
the land of the north to the land
that I gave your ancestors for a heritage.

19 I thought
how I would set you among
my children,
and give you a pleasant land,
the most beautiful heritage
of all the nations.
And I thought you would call
me, My Father,
and would not turn from
following me.
20 Instead, as a faithless wife
leaves her husband,
so you have been faithless
to me, O house of
Israel,
says the LORD.

21 A voice on the bare heights[h]
is heard,
the plaintive weeping of
Israel's children,
because they have perverted
their way,
they have forgotten the
LORD their God:
22 Return, O faithless children,
I will heal your
faithlessness.

"Here we come to you;
for you are the LORD our
God.
23 Truly the hills are[i] a
delusion,
the orgies on the
mountains.
Truly in the LORD our God
is the salvation of Israel.
24 "But from our youth the
shameful thing has devoured all for
which our ancestors had labored,
their flocks and their herds, their
sons and their daughters. 25 Let us
lie down in our shame, and let our
dishonor cover us; for we have
sinned against the LORD our God,
we and our ancestors, from our
youth even to this day; and we have
not obeyed the voice of the LORD
our God."

4 If you return, O Israel,
says the LORD,
if you return to me,
if you remove your
abominations from my
presence,
and do not waver,
2 and if you swear, "As the
LORD lives!"
in truth, in justice, and in
uprightness,
then nations shall be
blessed[j] by him,
and by him they shall
boast.
3 For thus says the LORD to the
people of Judah and to the inhabitants of Jerusalem:
Break up your fallow ground,
and do not sow among
thorns.
4 Circumcise yourselves to the
LORD,
remove the foreskin of your
hearts,
O people of Judah and
inhabitants of
Jerusalem,
or else my wrath will go forth
like fire,
and burn with no one to
quench it,
because of the evil of your
doings.

Invasion and Desolation of Judah Threatened

5 Declare in Judah, and proclaim in Jerusalem, and say:
Blow the trumpet through
the land;
shout aloud[k] and say,
"Gather together, and let us
go

3.17 Jer 17.12; v. 19; Isa 60.9; Jer 11.8 **3.18** Isa 11.13; Hos 1.11; Jer 31.8; Am 9.15 **3.19** Dan 8.9; Ps 16.6; Isa 63.16 **3.20** vv. 6,7; Isa 48.8 **3.21** Isa 15.2; Jer 2.32 **3.22** v. 14; Hos 6.1; 14.4; Jer 31.6 **3.23** Ps 121.1,2; 3.8 **3.24** Jer 8.16 **3.25** Ezra 9.7; Jer 22.21

4.1 Jer 3.1,22; Joel 2.12; Jer 7.3,7 **4.2** Deut 10.20; Gen 22.18; Gal 3.8; Isa 45.25; 1 Cor 1.31 **4.3** Hos 10.12; Mt 13.7,22 **4.4** Deut 10.16; 30.6; Jer 9.26; Rom 2.28, 29; Jer 21.12; Mk 9.43,48 **4.5** Jer 6.1; 8.14

[h] Or *the trails* [i] Gk Syr Vg: Heb *Truly from the hills is* [j] Or *shall bless themselves* [k] Or *shout, take your weapons*: Heb *shout, fill (your hand)*

into the fortified cities!"
6 Raise a standard toward
Zion,
flee for safety, do not
delay,
for I am bringing evil from
the north,
and a great destruction.
7 A lion has gone up from its
thicket,
a destroyer of nations has
set out;
he has gone out from his
place
to make your land a waste;
your cities will be ruins
without inhabitant.
8 Because of this put on
sackcloth,
lament and wail:
"The fierce anger of the LORD
has not turned away from
us."

9 On that day, says the LORD, courage shall fail the king and the officials; the priests shall be appalled
and the prophets astounded.
10 Then I said, "Ah, Lord GOD, how
utterly you have deceived this people and Jerusalem, saying, 'It shall
be well with you,' even while the
sword is at the throat!"

11 At that time it will be said to
this people and to Jerusalem: A hot
wind comes from me out of the
bare heights[l] in the desert toward
my poor people, not to winnow or
cleanse— 12 a wind too strong for
that. Now it is I who speak in judgment against them.
13 Look! He comes up like
clouds,
his chariots like the
whirlwind;
his horses are swifter than
eagles—
woe to us, for we are
ruined!
14 O Jerusalem, wash your
heart clean of
wickedness
so that you may be saved.
How long shall your evil
schemes
lodge within you?

4.6 Jer 1.13-15; 6.1,22
4.7 2 Kings 24.1; Jer 5.6; Dan 7.4; Jer 25.9; Isa 1.7; Jer 2.15
4.8 Isa 22.12; Jer 6.26; 30.24
4.9 Isa 22.3-5; 29.9,10
4.10 Ezek 14.9; 2 Thes 2.11; Jer 5.12; 14.13
4.11 Jer 51.1; Ezek 17.10; Hos 13.15
4.12 Jer 1.16
4.13 Isa 19.1; 5.28; Deut 28.49; Lam 4.19; Isa 3.8
4.14 Isa 1.16; Jas 4.8; Jer 6.19; 13.27
4.15 Jer 8.16
4.16 Jer 5.6,15; Isa 39.3; Ezek 21.22
4.17 2 Kings 25.1, 4; Jer 5.23
4.18 Ps 107.17; Isa 50.1; Jer 2.17,19
4.19 Isa 15.5; 16.11; 21.3; 22.4; Jer 9.1,10
4.20 Ps 42.7; Ezek 7.26; Jer 10.20
4.22 Jer 10.8; 2.8; Rom 16.19

15 For a voice declares from
Dan
and proclaims disaster
from Mount Ephraim.
16 Tell the nations, "Here they
are!"
Proclaim against
Jerusalem,
"Besiegers come from a
distant land;
they shout against the
cities of Judah.
17 They have closed in around
her like watchers of a
field,
because she has rebelled
against me,
says the LORD.
18 Your ways and your doings
have brought this upon
you.
This is your doom; how
bitter it is!
It has reached your very
heart."

Sorrow for a Doomed Nation

19 My anguish, my anguish! I
writhe in pain!
Oh, the walls of my heart!
My heart is beating wildly;
I cannot keep silent;
for I[m] hear the sound of the
trumpet,
the alarm of war.
20 Disaster overtakes disaster,
the whole land is laid
waste.
Suddenly my tents are
destroyed,
my curtains in a moment.
21 How long must I see the
standard,
and hear the sound of the
trumpet?
22 "For my people are foolish,
they do not know me;
they are stupid children,
they have no
understanding.
They are skilled in doing
evil,
but do not know how to do
good."

[l] Or *the trails* [m] Another reading is *for you, O my soul,*

23 I looked on the earth, and lo,
it was waste and void;
and to the heavens, and
they had no light.
24 I looked on the mountains,
and lo, they were
quaking,
and all the hills moved to
and fro.
25 I looked, and lo, there was
no one at all,
and all the birds of the air
had fled.
26 I looked, and lo, the fruitful
land was a desert,
and all its cities were laid
in ruins
before the LORD, before his
fierce anger.

27 For thus says the LORD: The
whole land shall be a desolation;
yet I will not make a full end.

28 Because of this the earth
shall mourn,
and the heavens above
grow black;
for I have spoken, I have
purposed;
I have not relented nor will
I turn back.

29 At the noise of horseman
and archer
every town takes to flight;
they enter thickets; they
climb among rocks;
all the towns are forsaken,
and no one lives in them.
30 And you, O desolate one,
what do you mean that you
dress in crimson,
that you deck yourself with
ornaments of gold,
that you enlarge your eyes
with paint?
In vain you beautify yourself.
Your lovers despise you;
they seek your life.
31 For I heard a cry as of a
woman in labor,
anguish as of one bringing
forth her first child,
the cry of daughter Zion
gasping for breath,
stretching out her hands,
"Woe is me! I am fainting
before killers!"

4.23 Gen 1.2; Isa 24.19
4.24 Isa 5.25; Ezek 38.20
4.25 Zeph 1.3
4.26 Jer 9.10
4.27 Jer 12.11, 12; 5.10,18; 30.11; 46.28
4.28 Hos 4.3; Isa 5.30; 50.3; Num 23.19; Jer 7.16
4.29 Jer 6.23; 16.16
4.30 Jer 13.21; 2 Kings 9.30; Ezek 23.40; Jer 22.20,22
4.31 Jer 13.21; Isa 42.14; 1.15; Lam 1.17
5.1 2 Chr 16.9; Ezek 22.30; Gen 18.23, 26,32
5.2 Titus 1.16; Jer 4.2; 7.9
5.3 Isa 1.5; 9.13; Jer 2.30; Zeph 3.2; Jer 7.26; 19.15
5.4 Jer 4.22; 8.7
5.5 Mic 3.1; Ps 2.3
5.6 Hab 1.8; Zeph 3.3; Hos 13.7; Jer 30.14,15
5.7 Josh 23.7; Zeph 1.5; Deut 32.21; Gal 4.8; Jer 7.9; Num 25.1-3

The Utter Corruption of God's People

5 Run to and fro through the
streets of Jerusalem,
look around and take note!
Search its squares and see
if you can find one person
who acts justly
and seeks truth—
so that I may pardon
Jerusalem.[n]
2 Although they say, "As the
LORD lives,"
yet they swear falsely.
3 O LORD, do your eyes not
look for truth?
You have struck them,
but they felt no anguish;
you have consumed them,
but they refused to take
correction.
They have made their faces
harder than rock;
they have refused to turn
back.

4 Then I said, "These are only
the poor,
they have no sense;
for they do not know the way
of the LORD,
the law of their God.
5 Let me go to the rich[o]
and speak to them;
surely they know the way of
the LORD,
the law of their God."
But they all alike had broken
the yoke,
they had burst the bonds.

6 Therefore a lion from the
forest shall kill them,
a wolf from the desert shall
destroy them.
A leopard is watching against
their cities;
everyone who goes out of
them shall be torn in
pieces—
because their transgressions
are many,
their apostasies are great.

7 How can I pardon you?

[n] Heb *it* [o] Or *the great*

Your children have
forsaken me,
and have sworn by those
who are no gods.
When I fed them to the full,
they committed adultery
and trooped to the houses
of prostitutes.
8 They were well-fed lusty
stallions,
each neighing for his
neighbor's wife.
9 Shall I not punish them for
these things?
says the LORD;
and shall I not bring
retribution
on a nation such as this?

10 Go up through her vine-rows
and destroy,
but do not make a full end;
strip away her branches,
for they are not the LORD's.
11 For the house of Israel and
the house of Judah
have been utterly faithless
to me,
says the LORD.
12 They have spoken falsely of
the LORD,
and have said, "He will do
nothing.
No evil will come upon us,
and we shall not see sword
or famine."
13 The prophets are nothing but
wind,
for the word is not in
them.
Thus shall it be done to
them!

14 Therefore thus says the LORD,
the God of hosts:
Because they[p] have spoken
this word,
I am now making my words
in your mouth a fire,
and this people wood, and
the fire shall devour
them.
15 I am going to bring upon you
a nation from far away,
O house of Israel,
says the LORD.
It is an enduring nation,
it is an ancient nation,
a nation whose language you
do not know,
nor can you understand
what they say.
16 Their quiver is like an open
tomb;
all of them are mighty
warriors.
17 They shall eat up your
harvest and your food;
they shall eat up your sons
and your daughters;
they shall eat up your flocks
and your herds;
they shall eat up your vines
and your fig trees;
they shall destroy with the
sword
your fortified cities in
which you trust.

18 But even in those days, says
the LORD, I will not make a full end
of you. 19 And when your people
say, "Why has the LORD our God
done all these things to us?" you
shall say to them, "As you have forsaken me and served foreign gods
in your land, so you shall serve
strangers in a land that is not
yours."

20 Declare this in the house of
Jacob,
proclaim it in Judah:
21 Hear this, O foolish and
senseless people,
who have eyes, but do not
see,
who have ears, but do not
hear.
22 Do you not fear me? says the
LORD;
Do you not tremble before
me?
I placed the sand as a
boundary for the sea,
a perpetual barrier that it
cannot pass;
though the waves toss, they
cannot prevail,
though they roar, they
cannot pass over it.

5.8 Ezek 22.11; Jer 13.27
5.9 Jer 9.9; 44.22
5.10 Jer 39.8; v. 18; Jer 4.27
5.11 Jer 3.20
5.12 2 Chr 36.16; Isa 28.15; Jer 23.17; 14.13
5.13 Jer 14.13,15
5.14 Jer 1.9; 23.29
5.15 Deut 28.49; Isa 5.26; Jer 1.15; 6.22; 4.16; Isa 39.3
5.16 Isa 5.28; 13.18
5.17 Lev 26.16; Deut 28.31, 33; Jer 8.13; Hos 8.14
5.18 Jer 4.27
5.19 Deut 29.24-26; 1 Kings 9.8, 9; Jer 16.10-13; Deut 28.48
5.21 v. 4; Isa 6.9; Ezek 12.2; Mt 13.14; Jer 6.10
5.22 Jer 2.19; Job 26.10; Ps 104.9

p Heb *you*

23 But this people has a
stubborn and rebellious
heart;
they have turned aside and
gone away.
24 They do not say in their
hearts,
"Let us fear the LORD our
God,
who gives the rain in its
season,
the autumn rain and the
spring rain,
and keeps for us
the weeks appointed for
the harvest."
25 Your iniquities have turned
these away,
and your sins have
deprived you of good.
26 For scoundrels are found
among my people;
they take over the goods of
others.
Like fowlers they set a trap;[q]
they catch human beings.
27 Like a cage full of birds,
their houses are full of
treachery;
therefore they have become
great and rich,
28 they have grown fat and
sleek.
They know no limits in
deeds of wickedness;
they do not judge with
justice
the cause of the orphan, to
make it prosper,
and they do not defend the
rights of the needy.
29 Shall I not punish them for
these things?
says the LORD,
and shall I not bring
retribution
on a nation such as this?

30 An appalling and horrible
thing
has happened in the land:
31 the prophets prophesy falsely,
and the priests rule as the
prophets direct;[r]
my people love to have it so,
but what will you do when
the end comes?

5.23 Jer 4.17; 6.28 **5.24** Ps 147.8; Mt 5.45; Joel 2.23; Gen 8.22 **5.25** Jer 2.17; 4.18 **5.26** Ps 10.9; Prov 1.11; Hab 1.15 **5.27** Jer 9.6; 12.1 **5.28** Deut 32.15; Isa 1.23; Zech 7.10; Jer 2.34 **5.29** Mal 3.5 **5.30** Hos 6.10 **5.31** Jer 14.14; Ezek 13.6; Mic 2.11

6.1 2 Chr 11.6; Neh 3.14; Jer 1.14; 4.6 **6.2** Deut 28.56; Jer 4.31 **6.3** Jer 12.10; 2 Kings 25.1; Jer 4.17 **6.4** Joel 3.9; Jer 15.8 **6.5** Jer 52.13 **6.6** Deut 20.19, 20; Jer 32.24; 22.17 **6.7** Isa 57.20; Ps 55.9-11; Jer 20.8; Ezek 7.11, 23 **6.8** Jer 7.28; Ezek 23.18; Hos 9.12

The Imminence and Horror of the Invasion

6 Flee for safety, O children of
Benjamin,
from the midst of
Jerusalem!
Blow the trumpet in Tekoa,
and raise a signal on
Beth-haccherem;
for evil looms out of the
north,
and great destruction.
2 I have likened daughter Zion
to the loveliest pasture.[s]
3 Shepherds with their flocks
shall come against her.
They shall pitch their tents
around her;
they shall pasture, all in
their places.
4 "Prepare war against her;
up, and let us attack at
noon!"
"Woe to us, for the day
declines,
the shadows of evening
lengthen!"
5 "Up, and let us attack by
night,
and destroy her palaces!"
6 For thus says the LORD of
hosts:
Cut down her trees;
cast up a siege ramp
against Jerusalem.
This is the city that must be
punished;[t]
there is nothing but
oppression within her.
7 As a well keeps its water
fresh,
so she keeps fresh her
wickedness;
violence and destruction are
heard within her;
sickness and wounds are
ever before me.
8 Take warning, O Jerusalem,
or I shall turn from you in
disgust,
and make you a desolation,
an uninhabited land.

[q] Meaning of Heb uncertain [r] Or *rule by their own authority* [s] Or *I will destroy daughter Zion, the loveliest pasture* [t] Or *the city of license*

9 Thus says the LORD of hosts:
Glean[u] thoroughly as a vine the remnant of Israel;
like a grape-gatherer, pass your hand again
over its branches.

10 To whom shall I speak and give warning,
that they may hear?
See, their ears are closed,[v]
they cannot listen.
The word of the LORD is to them an object of scorn;
they take no pleasure in it.
11 But I am full of the wrath of the LORD;
I am weary of holding it in.

Pour it out on the children in the street,
and on the gatherings of young men as well;
both husband and wife shall be taken,
the old folk and the very aged.
12 Their houses shall be turned over to others,
their fields and wives together;
for I will stretch out my hand
against the inhabitants of the land,
says the LORD.

13 For from the least to the greatest of them,
everyone is greedy for unjust gain;
and from prophet to priest,
everyone deals falsely.
14 They have treated the wound of my people carelessly,
saying, "Peace, peace,"
when there is no peace.
15 They acted shamefully, they committed abomination;
yet they were not ashamed,
they did not know how to blush.
Therefore they shall fall among those who fall;
at the time that I punish them, they shall be overthrown,
says the LORD.

16 Thus says the LORD:
Stand at the crossroads, and look,
and ask for the ancient paths,
where the good way lies; and walk in it,
and find rest for your souls.
But they said, "We will not walk in it."
17 Also I raised up sentinels for you:
"Give heed to the sound of the trumpet!"
But they said, "We will not give heed."
18 Therefore hear, O nations,
and know, O congregation, what will happen to them.
19 Hear, O earth; I am going to bring disaster on this people,
the fruit of their schemes,
because they have not given heed to my words;
and as for my teaching, they have rejected it.
20 Of what use to me is frankincense that comes from Sheba,
or sweet cane from a distant land?
Your burnt offerings are not acceptable,
nor are your sacrifices pleasing to me.
21 Therefore thus says the LORD:
See, I am laying before this people
stumbling blocks against which they shall stumble;
parents and children together,
neighbor and friend shall perish.

22 Thus says the LORD:
See, a people is coming from the land of the north,

6.9 Jer 49.9; 8.3 **6.10** Jer 7.26; Acts 7.51; Jer 20.8 **6.11** Job 32.18, 19; Jer 20.9; 9.21 **6.12** Deut 28.30; Jer 8.10; 15.6 **6.13** Isa 56.11; Jer 8.10; 22.17; Mic 3.5,11 **6.14** Jer 8.11; Ezek 13.10; Jer 4.10; 23.17 **6.15** Isa 8.20; Jer 3.3; 8.12 **6.16** Jer 18.15; Mal 4.4; Lk 16.29; Mt 11.29 **6.17** Isa 21.11; 58.1; Jer 25.4; Ezek 3.17; Hab 2.1 **6.19** Isa 1.2; Jer 19.3,15; Prov 1.31; Jer 8.9 **6.20** Isa 1.11; Am 5.21; Mic 6.6; Isa 60.6; Jer 7.21 **6.21** Isa 8.14; Jer 13.16; 9.21,22 **6.22** Jer 1.15; 5.15; 10.22; 50.41-43; Neh 1.9

[u] Cn: Heb *They shall glean* [v] Heb *are uncircumcised*

a great nation is stirring
from the farthest parts
of the earth.
23 They grasp the bow and the
javelin,
they are cruel and have no
mercy,
their sound is like the
roaring sea;
they ride on horses,
equipped like a warrior for
battle,
against you, O daughter
Zion!

24 "We have heard news of
them,
our hands fall helpless;
anguish has taken hold of us,
pain as of a woman in
labor.
25 Do not go out into the
field,
or walk on the road;
for the enemy has a sword,
terror is on every side."

26 O my poor people, put on
sackcloth,
and roll in ashes;
make mourning as for an
only child,
most bitter lamentation:
for suddenly the destroyer
will come upon us.

27 I have made you a tester and
a refiner[w] among my
people
so that you may know and
test their ways.
28 They are all stubbornly
rebellious,
going about with slanders;
they are bronze and iron,
all of them act corruptly.
29 The bellows blow fiercely,
the lead is consumed by
the fire;
in vain the refining goes on,
for the wicked are not
removed.
30 They are called "rejected
silver,"
for the LORD has rejected
them.

6.23 Jer 4.29; 50.42; Isa 5.30
6.24 Jer 4.31; 13.21; 49.24; 50.43
6.25 Jer 14.18; 12.12; 20.10
6.26 Jer 4.8; 25.34; Mic 1.10; Zech 12.10
6.27 Jer 1.18; 15.20; 9.7
6.28 Jer 5.23; 9.4; Ezek 22.18
6.29 Jer 15.19
6.30 Jer 7.29
7.1f Jer 26.1,2
7.2 Jer 17.19; 2.4
7.3 Jer 18.11; 26.13
7.4 Mic 3.11
7.5 Jer 4.1,2; 22.3
7.6 Deut 6.14, 15; 8.19; Jer 13.10
7.8 Jer 13.25
7.9 Ex 20.3; Jer 11.13, 17; 19.4
7.10 Ezek 23.39; Jer 32.34; 2.23,35
7.11 Mt 21.13; Mk 11.17; Lk 19.46
7.12 Jer 26.6; 1 Sam 4.10, 11
7.13 2 Chr 36.15; Jer 35.17; Isa 65.12
7.14 1 Kings 9.7; vv. 4,12

Jeremiah Proclaims God's Judgment on the Nation

7 The word that came to Jeremiah from the LORD: 2 Stand in
the gate of the LORD's house, and
proclaim there this word, and say,
Hear the word of the LORD, all you
people of Judah, you that enter
these gates to worship the LORD.
3 Thus says the LORD of hosts, the
God of Israel: Amend your ways
and your doings, and let me dwell
with you[x] in this place. 4 Do not
trust in these deceptive words:
"This is[y] the temple of the LORD,
the temple of the LORD, the temple
of the LORD."
5 For if you truly amend your
ways and your doings, if you truly
act justly one with another, 6 if you
do not oppress the alien, the orphan, and the widow, or shed innocent blood in this place, and if you
do not go after other gods to your
own hurt, 7 then I will dwell with
you in this place, in the land that I
gave of old to your ancestors forever and ever.
8 Here you are, trusting in deceptive words to no avail. 9 Will you
steal, murder, commit adultery,
swear falsely, make offerings to
Baal, and go after other gods that
you have not known, 10 and then
come and stand before me in this
house, which is called by my name,
and say, "We are safe!"—only to go
on doing all these abominations?
11 Has this house, which is called
by my name, become a den of robbers in your sight? You know, I too
am watching, says the LORD. 12 Go
now to my place that was in Shiloh,
where I made my name dwell at
first, and see what I did to it for the
wickedness of my people Israel.
13 And now, because you have done
all these things, says the LORD, and
when I spoke to you persistently,
you did not listen, and when I
called you, you did not answer,
14 therefore I will do to the house
that is called by my name, in which
you trust, and to the place that I

[w] Or *a fortress* [x] Or *and I will let you dwell* [y] Heb *They are*

gave to you and to your ancestors,
just what I did to Shiloh. 15 And I
will cast you out of my sight, just as
I cast out all your kinsfolk, all the
offspring of Ephraim.

The People's Disobedience

16 As for you, do not pray for
this people, do not raise a cry or
prayer on their behalf, and do not
intercede with me, for I will not
hear you. 17 Do you not see what
they are doing in the towns of Judah and in the streets of Jerusalem? 18 The children gather wood,
the fathers kindle fire, and the
women knead dough, to make
cakes for the queen of heaven; and
they pour out drink offerings to
other gods, to provoke me to anger.
19 Is it I whom they provoke? says
the LORD. Is it not themselves, to
their own hurt? 20 Therefore thus
says the Lord GOD: My anger and
my wrath shall be poured out on
this place, on human beings and
animals, on the trees of the field
and the fruit of the ground; it will
burn and not be quenched.

21 Thus says the LORD of hosts,
the God of Israel: Add your burnt
offerings to your sacrifices, and eat
the flesh. 22 For in the day that I
brought your ancestors out of the
land of Egypt, I did not speak to
them or command them concerning burnt offerings and sacrifices.
23 But this command I gave them,
"Obey my voice, and I will be your
God, and you shall be my people;
and walk only in the way that I
command you, so that it may be
well with you." 24 Yet they did not
obey or incline their ear, but, in the
stubbornness of their evil will, they
walked in their own counsels, and
looked backward rather than forward. 25 From the day that your ancestors came out of the land of
Egypt until this day, I have persistently sent all my servants the
prophets to them, day after day;
26 yet they did not listen to me, or
pay attention, but they stiffened
their necks. They did worse than
their ancestors did.

27 So you shall speak all these
words to them, but they will not listen to you. You shall call to them,
but they will not answer you. 28 You
shall say to them: This is the nation
that did not obey the voice of the
LORD their God, and did not accept
discipline; truth has perished; it is
cut off from their lips.

29 Cut off your hair and throw
    it away;
  raise a lamentation on the
    bare heights,[z]
for the LORD has rejected and
    forsaken
  the generation that
    provoked his wrath.

30 For the people of Judah have
done evil in my sight, says the LORD;
they have set their abominations in
the house that is called by my
name, defiling it. 31 And they go on
building the high place[a] of Topheth, which is in the valley of the
son of Hinnom, to burn their sons
and their daughters in the fire—
which I did not command, nor did
it come into my mind. 32 Therefore,
the days are surely coming, says
the LORD, when it will no more be
called Topheth, or the valley of the
son of Hinnom, but the valley of
Slaughter: for they will bury in Topheth until there is no more room.
33 The corpses of this people will be
food for the birds of the air, and for
the animals of the earth; and no
one will frighten them away. 34 And
I will bring to an end the sound of
mirth and gladness, the voice of
the bride and bridegroom in the
cities of Judah and in the streets of
Jerusalem; for the land shall become a waste.

8 At that time, says the LORD,
the bones of the kings of Judah, the bones of its officials, the
bones of the priests, the bones of
the prophets, and the bones of the
inhabitants of Jerusalem shall be
brought out of their tombs; 2 and
they shall be spread before the sun
and the moon and all the host of
heaven, which they have loved and
served, which they have followed,

7.15 Jer 15.1; 2 Kings 17.23; Ps 78.67
7.16 Ex 32.10; Jer 11.14; 15.1
7.18 Jer 44.17; 19.13; 11.17
7.19 Deut 32.16, 21
7.20 Jer 6.11,12; 8.13; 11.16
7.21 Isa 1.11; Am 5.21; Hos 8.13
7.22 1 Sam 15.22; Ps 51.16; Hos 6.6
7.23 Ex 15.26; Lev 26.12; Isa 3.10
7.24 Ps 81.11,12; Jer 15.6
7.25 Jer 25.4; Lk 11.49
7.26 Jer 19.15; 16.12
7.27 Ezek 2.7; 3.7; Isa 50.2
7.28 Jer 6.17; 5.3; 9.5
7.29 Job 1.20; Isa 15.2; Jer 16.6; Mic 1.16; Jer 3.21; 14.19
7.30 2 Kings 21.4; 2 Chr 33.4, 5,7; Jer 23.11; Ezek 7.20; Dan 9.27
7.31 2 Kings 23.10; Jer 19.5; Ps 106.38; Deut 17.3
7.32 Jer 19.5,7, 11; 2 Kings 23.10
7.34 Isa 24.7,8; Ezek 26.13; Hos 2.11; Rev 18.23; Isa 1.7
8.1 Ezek 6.5
8.2 Acts 7.42; Jer 22.19

[z] Or *the trails*   [a] Gk Tg: Heb *high places*

and which they have inquired of and worshiped; and they shall not be gathered or buried; they shall be like dung on the surface of the ground. [3]Death shall be preferred to life by all the remnant that remains of this evil family in all the places where I have driven them, says the LORD of hosts.

The Blind Perversity of the Whole Nation

4 You shall say to them, Thus
says the LORD:
When people fall, do they
not get up again?
If they go astray, do they
not turn back?
5 Why then has this people[b]
turned away
in perpetual backsliding?
They have held fast to
deceit,
they have refused to return.
6 I have given heed and
listened,
but they do not speak
honestly;
no one repents of
wickedness,
saying, "What have I done!"
All of them turn to their own
course,
like a horse plunging
headlong into battle.
7 Even the stork in the
heavens
knows its times;
and the turtledove, swallow,
and crane[c]
observe the time of their
coming;
but my people do not know
the ordinance of the LORD.

8 How can you say, "We are
wise,
and the law of the LORD is
with us,"
when, in fact, the false pen
of the scribes
has made it into a lie?
9 The wise shall be put to
shame,
they shall be dismayed and
taken;
since they have rejected the
word of the LORD,
what wisdom is in them?
10 Therefore I will give their
wives to others
and their fields to
conquerors,
because from the least to the
greatest
everyone is greedy for
unjust gain;
from prophet to priest
everyone deals falsely.
11 They have treated the wound
of my people carelessly,
saying, "Peace, peace,"
when there is no peace.
12 They acted shamefully, they
committed
abomination;
yet they were not at all
ashamed,
they did not know how to
blush.
Therefore they shall fall
among those who fall;
at the time when I punish
them, they shall be
overthrown,
says the LORD.
13 When I wanted to gather
them, says the LORD,
there are[d] no grapes on
the vine,
nor figs on the fig tree;
even the leaves are withered,
and what I gave them has
passed away from
them.[c]
14 Why do we sit still?
Gather together, let us go
into the fortified cities
and perish there;
for the LORD our God has
doomed us to perish,
and has given us poisoned
water to drink,
because we have sinned
against the LORD.
15 We look for peace, but find
no good,
for a time of healing, but
there is terror instead.

8.3 Job 3.21; 7.15,16; Rev 9.6; Jer 23.3,8 **8.4** Prov 24.16 **8.5** Jer 5.6; 7.24; 5.27; 9.6 **8.6** Ps 14.2; Ezek 22.30; Rev 9.20; Job 39.21-25 **8.7** Isa 1.3; Song 2.12; Jer 5.4,5 **8.8** Jer 4.22; Rom 2.17 **8.9** Jer 6.15,19 **8.10** Deut 28.30; Isa 56.11 **8.11** Jer 6.14; Ezek 13.10 **8.12** Jer 3.3; 6.21; 10.15 **8.13** Jer 14.12; Ezek 22.20, 21; Isa 5.2; Joel 1.7; Mt 21.19 **8.14** Jer 4.5; 35.11; 9.15; Mt 27.34; Jer 3.25; 14.20 **8.15** Jer 14.19

[b] One Ms Gk: MT *this people, Jerusalem,* [c] Meaning of Heb uncertain [d] Or *I will make an end of them, says the LORD. There are*

16 The snorting of their horses
is heard from Dan;
at the sound of the
neighing of their
stallions
the whole land quakes.
They come and devour the
land and all that fills it,
the city and those who live
in it.
17 See, I am letting snakes
loose among you,
adders that cannot be
charmed,
and they shall bite you,
says the LORD.

The Prophet Mourns for the People

18 My joy is gone, grief is upon
me,
my heart is sick.
19 Hark, the cry of my poor
people
from far and wide in the
land:
"Is the LORD not in Zion?
Is her King not in her?"
("Why have they provoked
me to anger with their
images,
with their foreign idols?")
20 "The harvest is past, the
summer is ended,
and we are not saved."
21 For the hurt of my poor
people I am hurt,
I mourn, and dismay has
taken hold of me.

22 Is there no balm in Gilead?
Is there no physician there?
Why then has the health of
my poor people
not been restored?
9 [e] O that my head were a
spring of water,
and my eyes a fountain of
tears,
so that I might weep day and
night
for the slain of my poor
people!
2 [f] O that I had in the desert
a traveler's lodging place,
that I might leave my people
and go away from them!
For they are all adulterers,
a band of traitors.
3 They bend their tongues like
bows;
they have grown strong in
the land for falsehood,
and not for truth;
for they proceed from evil to
evil,
and they do not know me,
says the LORD.

4 Beware of your neighbors,
and put no trust in any of
your kin;[g]
for all your kin[h] are
supplanters,
and every neighbor goes
around like a slanderer.
5 They all deceive their
neighbors,
and no one speaks the
truth;
they have taught their
tongues to speak lies;
they commit iniquity and
are too weary to
repent.[i]
6 Oppression upon oppression,
deceit[j] upon deceit!
They refuse to know me,
says the LORD.

7 Therefore thus says the LORD
of hosts:
I will now refine and test
them,
for what else can I do with
my sinful people?[k]
8 Their tongue is a deadly
arrow;
it speaks deceit through
the mouth.
They all speak friendly words
to their neighbors,
but inwardly are planning
to lay an ambush.
9 Shall I not punish them for
these things? says the
LORD;

8.16 Jer 4.15; Judg 5.22; Jer 3.24; 10.25
8.17 Num 21.6; Ps 58.4,5
8.19 Jer 4.16; Isa 39.3; Jer 14.9; Deut 32.21; Ps 31.6
8.21 Jer 14.17; Joel 2.6; Nah 2.10
8.22 Gen 37.25; Jer 14.19; 30.13
9.1 Isa 22.4; Lam 2.11; Jer 6.26; 8.21,22
9.2 Isa 55.6,7; Jer 5,7,8,11; 12.1,6
9.3 Ps 64.3; Isa 59.4; Jer 4.22; 1 Sam 2.12; Hos 4.1
9.4 v. 8; Jer 12.6; Gen 27.35; Jer 6.28
9.5 Mic 6.12; Jer 12.13; 51.58,64
9.6 Jer 5.27; 11.10; Jn 3.19,20
9.7 Isa 1.25; Mal 3.3; Hos 11.8
9.8 Ps 12.2; 28.3; Jer 5.26
9.9 Jer 5.9,29

e Ch 8.23 in Heb f Ch 9.1 in Heb
g Heb *in a brother* h Heb *for every brother*
i Cn Compare Gk: Heb *they weary themselves with iniquity.* 6*Your dwelling* j Cn: Heb *Your dwelling in the midst of deceit*
k Or *my poor people*

and shall I not bring
retribution
on a nation such as this?

10 Take up[1] weeping and
wailing for the
mountains,
and a lamentation for the
pastures of the
wilderness,
because they are laid waste
so that no one passes
through,
and the lowing of cattle is
not heard;
both the birds of the air and
the animals
have fled and are gone.
11 I will make Jerusalem a heap
of ruins,
a lair of jackals;
and I will make the towns of
Judah a desolation,
without inhabitant.

12 Who is wise enough to understand this? To whom has the
mouth of the LORD spoken, so that
they may declare it? Why is the
land ruined and laid waste like a
wilderness, so that no one passes
through? 13 And the LORD says: Because they have forsaken my law
that I set before them, and have not
obeyed my voice, or walked in accordance with it, 14 but have stubbornly followed their own hearts
and have gone after the Baals, as
their ancestors taught them.
15 Therefore thus says the LORD of
hosts, the God of Israel: I am feeding this people with wormwood,
and giving them poisonous water
to drink. 16 I will scatter them
among nations that neither they
nor their ancestors have known;
and I will send the sword after
them, until I have consumed them.

The People Mourn in Judgment

17 Thus says the LORD of hosts:
Consider, and call for the
mourning women to
come;
send for the skilled women
to come;
18 let them quickly raise a dirge
over us,
so that our eyes may run
down with tears,
and our eyelids flow with
water.
19 For a sound of wailing is
heard from Zion:
"How we are ruined!
We are utterly shamed,
because we have left the
land,
because they have cast
down our dwellings."

20 Hear, O women, the word of
the LORD,
and let your ears receive
the word of his mouth;
teach to your daughters a
dirge,
and each to her neighbor a
lament.
21 "Death has come up into our
windows,
it has entered our palaces,
to cut off the children from
the streets
and the young men from
the squares."
22 Speak! Thus says the LORD:
"Human corpses shall fall
like dung upon the open
field,
like sheaves behind the
reaper,
and no one shall gather
them."

23 Thus says the LORD: Do not
let the wise boast in their wisdom,
do not let the mighty boast in their
might, do not let the wealthy boast
in their wealth; 24 but let those who
boast boast in this, that they understand and know me, that I am
the LORD; I act with steadfast love,
justice, and righteousness in the
earth, for in these things I delight,
says the LORD.

25 The days are surely coming,
says the LORD, when I will attend to
all those who are circumcised only
in the foreskin: 26 Egypt, Judah,
Edom, the Ammonites, Moab, and

9.10 Jer 4.24-26; Hos 4.3; Ezek 14.15
9.11 Isa 25.2; 13.22; 34.13; Jer 4.27; 26.9
9.12 Ps 107.43; Hos 14.9; Jer 23.10,16
9.13 Jer 5.19; Ps 89.30
9.14 Rom 1.21-24; Gal 1.14; 1 Pet 1.18
9.15 Jer 8.14; 23.15
9.16 Lev 26.33; Deut 28.64; Jer 44.27; Ezek 5.2
9.17 2 Chr 35.25; Eccl 12.5; Am 5.16
9.18 Jer 14.17
9.19 Jer 4.13; 7.15; 15.1
9.20 Isa 32.9
9.21 Jer 15.7; 18.21; 6.11
9.22 Jer 8.2; 16.4
9.23 Eccl 9.11; Isa 10.8-12; Ps 49.6-9
9.24 1 Cor 1.31; 2 Cor 10.17; Gal 6.14; Ps 36.5,7; Mic 7.18
9.25 Rom 2.8,9
9.26 Jer 25.23; Lev 26.41; Ezek 44.7; Rom 2.28

[1] Gk Syr: Heb *I will take up*

all those with shaven temples who live in the desert. For all these nations are uncircumcised, and all the house of Israel is uncircumcised in heart.

Idolatry Has Brought Ruin on Israel

10 Hear the word that the LORD speaks to you,
O house of Israel. 2 Thus says the
LORD:

Do not learn the way of the nations,
or be dismayed at the signs of the heavens;
for the nations are dismayed at them.
3 For the customs of the peoples are false:
a tree from the forest is cut down,
and worked with an ax by the hands of an artisan;
4 people deck it with silver and gold;
they fasten it with hammer and nails
so that it cannot move.
5 Their idols[m] are like scarecrows in a cucumber field,
and they cannot speak;
they have to be carried,
for they cannot walk.
Do not be afraid of them,
for they cannot do evil,
nor is it in them to do good.

6 There is none like you, O LORD;
you are great, and your name is great in might.
7 Who would not fear you, O King of the nations?
For that is your due;
among all the wise ones of the nations
and in all their kingdoms
there is no one like you.
8 They are both stupid and foolish;
the instruction given by idols
is no better than wood![n]
9 Beaten silver is brought from Tarshish,
and gold from Uphaz.
They are the work of the artisan and of the hands of the goldsmith;
their clothing is blue and purple;
they are all the product of skilled workers.
10 But the LORD is the true God;
he is the living God and the everlasting King.
At his wrath the earth quakes,
and the nations cannot endure his indignation.

11 Thus shall you say to them:
The gods who did not make the
heavens and the earth shall perish
from the earth and from under the
heavens.[o]

12 It is he who made the earth by his power,
who established the world by his wisdom,
and by his understanding stretched out the heavens.
13 When he utters his voice, there is a tumult of waters in the heavens,
and he makes the mist rise from the ends of the earth.
He makes lightnings for the rain,
and he brings out the wind from his storehouses.
14 Everyone is stupid and without knowledge;
goldsmiths are all put to shame by their idols;
for their images are false,
and there is no breath in them.
15 They are worthless, a work of delusion;
at the time of their punishment they shall perish.

10.2 Lev 18.3; Isa 47.12-14 **10.3** Isa 40.19; 45.20 **10.4** v. 14; Isa 41.7 **10.5** Ps 115.5; 1 Cor 12.2; Isa 46.1,7; 41.23 **10.6** Deut 33.26; Isa 12.6; Jer 32.18 **10.7** Ps 22.28; Dan 2.27, 28; 1 Cor 1.19, 20 **10.8** v. 14; Jer 4.22; 2.27 **10.9** Isa 40.19; Ps 72.10; Dan 10.5; Ps 115.4 **10.10** Isa 65.16; Jer 4.2; 50.46; Ps 76.7 **10.11** Ps 96.5; Isa 2.18; Zeph 2.11 **10.12** Jer 51.15-19; Ps 78.69; Job 9.8; Isa 40.22 **10.13** Ps 29.3-9; Job 36.27-29; Ps 135.7 **10.14** Jer 51.17; Isa 42.17; Hab 2.18 **10.15** Jer 8.19; 51.18

m Heb *They* n Meaning of Heb uncertain
o This verse is in Aramaic

16 Not like these is the LORD,[p]
the portion of Jacob,
for he is the one who
formed all things,
and Israel is the tribe of his
inheritance;
the LORD of hosts is his
name.

The Coming Exile

17 Gather up your bundle from
the ground,
O you who live under
siege!
18 For thus says the LORD:
I am going to sling out the
inhabitants of the land
at this time,
and I will bring distress on
them,
so that they shall feel it.

19 Woe is me because of my
hurt!
My wound is severe.
But I said, "Truly this is my
punishment,
and I must bear it."
20 My tent is destroyed,
and all my cords are
broken;
my children have gone from
me,
and they are no more;
there is no one to spread my
tent again,
and to set up my curtains.
21 For the shepherds are stupid,
and do not inquire of the
LORD;
therefore they have not
prospered,
and all their flock is
scattered.

22 Hear, a noise! Listen, it is
coming—
a great commotion from
the land of the north
to make the cities of Judah a
desolation,
a lair of jackals.

23 I know, O LORD, that the way
of human beings is not
in their control,
that mortals as they walk
cannot direct their
steps.
24 Correct me, O LORD, but in
just measure;
not in your anger, or you
will bring me to
nothing.

25 Pour out your wrath on the
nations that do not
know you,
and on the peoples that do
not call on your name;
for they have devoured
Jacob;
they have devoured him
and consumed him,
and have laid waste his
habitation.

Israel and Judah Have Broken the Covenant

11 The word that came to Jeremiah from the LORD:
2 Hear the words of this covenant,
and speak to the people of Judah
and the inhabitants of Jerusalem.
3 You shall say to them, Thus says
the LORD, the God of Israel: Cursed
be anyone who does not heed the
words of this covenant, 4 which I
commanded your ancestors when I
brought them out of the land of
Egypt, from the iron-smelter, saying, Listen to my voice, and do all
that I command you. So shall you
be my people, and I will be your
God, 5 that I may perform the oath
that I swore to your ancestors, to
give them a land flowing with milk
and honey, as at this day. Then I
answered, "So be it, LORD."
6 And the LORD said to me: Proclaim all these words in the cities
of Judah, and in the streets of Jerusalem: Hear the words of this covenant and do them. 7 For I solemnly
warned your ancestors when I
brought them up out of the land of
Egypt, warning them persistently,
even to this day, saying, Obey my
voice. 8 Yet they did not obey or incline their ear, but everyone
walked in the stubbornness of an

10.16 Ps 73.26; Jer 51.19; Isa 45.7; Deut 32.9; Jer 31.35 **10.17** Ezek 12.3-12 **10.18** 1 Sam 25.29; Ezek 6.10 **10.19** Jer 4.19,31; 14.17; Mic 7.9 **10.20** Jer 4.20; 31.15; Isa 51.18 **10.21** Jer 2.8; 23.2 **10.22** Jer 4.15; 1.14; 9.11 **10.23** Prov 20.24; Isa 26.7 **10.24** Ps 6.1 **10.25** Ps 79.6,7; Job 18.21; Jer 8.16; 50.7,17 **11.3** Deut 27.26; Gal 3.10 **11.4** Ex 24.3-8; Deut 4.20; 1 Kings 8.51; Jer 7.23; 24.7 **11.5** Ex 13.5; Deut 7.12; Jer 32.22; 28.6 **11.6** Jer 3.12; v. 2; Rom 2.13 **11.7** 1 Sam 8.9; Jer 7.13,25 **11.8** Jer 7.26; Mic 7.9; Lev 26.14-43

[p] Heb lacks *the LORD*

evil will. So I brought upon them
all the words of this covenant,
which I commanded them to do,
but they did not.
9 And the LORD said to me: Conspiracy exists among the people of
Judah and the inhabitants of Jerusalem. 10 They have turned back to
the iniquities of their ancestors of
old, who refused to heed my words;
they have gone after other gods to
serve them; the house of Israel and
the house of Judah have broken
the covenant that I made with their
ancestors. 11 Therefore, thus says
the LORD, assuredly I am going to
bring disaster upon them that they
cannot escape; though they cry out
to me, I will not listen to them.
12 Then the cities of Judah and the
inhabitants of Jerusalem will go
and cry out to the gods to whom
they make offerings, but they will
never save them in the time of their
trouble. 13 For your gods have become as many as your towns,
O Judah; and as many as the
streets of Jerusalem are the altars
you have set up to shame, altars to
make offerings to Baal.
14 As for you, do not pray for
this people, or lift up a cry or prayer
on their behalf, for I will not listen
when they call to me in the time of
their trouble. 15 What right has my
beloved in my house, when she has
done vile deeds? Can vows[q] and
sacrificial flesh avert your doom?
Can you then exult? 16 The LORD
once called you, "A green olive
tree, fair with goodly fruit"; but
with the roar of a great tempest he
will set fire to it, and its branches
will be consumed. 17 The LORD of
hosts, who planted you, has pronounced evil against you, because
of the evil that the house of Israel
and the house of Judah have done,
provoking me to anger by making
offerings to Baal.

Jeremiah's Life Threatened

18 It was the LORD who made it
known to me, and I
knew;
then you showed me their
evil deeds.
19 But I was like a gentle lamb
led to the slaughter.
And I did not know it was
against me
that they devised schemes,
saying,
"Let us destroy the tree with
its fruit,
let us cut him off from the
land of the living,
so that his name will no
longer be remembered!"
20 But you, O LORD of hosts,
who judge righteously,
who try the heart and the
mind,
let me see your retribution
upon them,
for to you I have
committed my cause.
21 Therefore thus says the LORD
concerning the people of Anathoth, who seek your life, and say,
"You shall not prophesy in the
name of the LORD, or you will die by
our hand" — 22 therefore thus says
the LORD of hosts: I am going to
punish them; the young men shall
die by the sword; their sons and
their daughters shall die by famine;
23 and not even a remnant shall be
left of them. For I will bring disaster upon the people of Anathoth,
the year of their punishment.

Jeremiah Complains to God

12 You will be in the right,
O LORD,
when I lay charges against
you;
but let me put my case to
you.
Why does the way of the
guilty prosper?
Why do all who are
treacherous thrive?
2 You plant them, and they
take root;
they grow and bring forth
fruit;
you are near in their mouths
yet far from their hearts.
3 But you, O LORD, know me;

11.9 Ezek 22.25; Hos 6.9
11.10 1 Sam 15.11; Jer 13.10; Judg 2.11-13; Jer 3.6-11
11.11 v. 17; Jer 25.35; v. 14; Jer 14.12
11.12 Deut 32.37; Jer 44.17
11.13 Jer 2.28; 3.24; 7.9
11.14 Ex 32.10; v. 11; Ps 66.18
11.15 Jer 12.7; 13.27; 4.22
11.16 Ps 52.8; 83.2; Jer 21.14
11.17 Jer 12.2; 16.10,11; 32.27
11.18 1 Sam 23.11, 12
11.19 Isa 53.7; Jer 18.18; Ps 83.4; 52.5; 109.13
11.20 Jer 20.12; Ps 7.9
11.21 Jer 12.5,6; Am 2.12; Jer 26.8; 38.4
11.22 Jer 21.14; 18.21
11.23 Jer 6.9; 23.12; 48.44
12.1 Jer 11.20; Job 13.3; Jer 5.27,28; 20.5,11
12.2 Jer 11.17; Isa 29.13; Ezek 33.31
12.3 Ps 139.1-4; Jer 11.20; 17.18

[q] Gk: Heb *Can many*

You see me and test
me — my heart is with
you.
Pull them out like sheep for
the slaughter,
and set them apart for the
day of slaughter.
4 How long will the land
mourn,
and the grass of every field
wither?
For the wickedness of those
who live in it
the animals and the birds
are swept away,
and because people said,
"He is blind to our
ways."[r]

God Replies to Jeremiah

5 If you have raced with
foot-runners and they
have wearied you,
how will you compete with
horses?
And if in a safe land you fall
down,
how will you fare in the
thickets of the Jordan?
6 For even your kinsfolk and
your own family,
even they have dealt
treacherously with you;
they are in full cry after
you;
do not believe them,
though they speak friendly
words to you.

7 I have forsaken my house,
I have abandoned my
heritage;
I have given the beloved of
my heart
into the hands of her
enemies.
8 My heritage has become to
me
like a lion in the forest;
she has lifted up her voice
against me —
therefore I hate her.
9 Is the hyena greedy[s] for my
heritage at my
command?
Are the birds of prey all
around her?
Go, assemble all the wild
animals;
bring them to devour her.
10 Many shepherds have
destroyed my vineyard,
they have trampled down
my portion,
they have made my pleasant
portion
a desolate wilderness.
11 They have made it a
desolation;
desolate, it mourns to me.
The whole land is made
desolate,
but no one lays it to heart.
12 Upon all the bare heights[t]
in the desert
spoilers have come;
for the sword of the LORD
devours
from one end of the land
to the other;
no one shall be safe.
13 They have sown wheat and
have reaped thorns,
they have tired themselves
out but profit nothing.
They shall be ashamed of
their[u] harvests
because of the fierce anger
of the LORD.

14 Thus says the LORD concerning all my evil neighbors who touch
the heritage that I have given my
people Israel to inherit: I am about
to pluck them up from their land,
and I will pluck up the house of Judah from among them. 15 And after
I have plucked them up, I will again
have compassion on them, and I
will bring them again to their heritage and to their land, everyone of
them. 16 And then, if they will diligently learn the ways of my people,
to swear by my name, "As the LORD
lives," as they taught my people to
swear by Baal, then they shall be
built up in the midst of my people.
17 But if any nation will not listen,

12.4 Jer 9.10; Joel 1.10-17; Hos 4.3; Jer 4.25 **12.5** Jer 26.8; 38.4-6; 49.19; 50.44 **12.6** Jer 9.4; Ps 12.2; Prov 26.25 **12.7** Jer 7.29; 11.15; Lam 2.1 **12.8** Isa 59.13; Hos 9.15 **12.9** 2 Kings 24.2; Isa 56.9 **12.10** Jer 23.1; Isa 5.1-7; 63.18; Jer 3.19 **12.11** Jer 4.20,27; Isa 42.25 **12.12** Jer 3.2,21; Isa 34.6; Jer 16.5; 30.5 **12.13** Lev 26.16; Deut 28.38; Mic 6.15; Hag 1.6; Jer 9.5; 17.10 **12.14** Zech 2.8-10; Deut 30.3; Isa 11.11-16 **12.15** Ezek 28.25; Jer 48.47; 49.6,39; Am 9.14 **12.16** Isa 42.6; Jer 4.2; 5.7; Eph 2.20,21 **12.17** Isa 60.12

[r] Gk: Heb *to our future*
[s] Cn: Heb *Is the hyena, the bird of prey*
[t] Or *the trails*
[u] Heb *your*

then I will completely uproot it and
destroy it, says the LORD.

The Linen Loincloth

13 Thus said the LORD to me,
"Go and buy yourself a lin-
en loincloth, and put it on your
loins, but do not dip it in water."
2 So I bought a loincloth according
to the word of the LORD, and put it
on my loins. 3 And the word of the
LORD came to me a second time,
saying, 4 "Take the loincloth that
you bought and are wearing, and go
now to the Euphrates,[v] and hide it
there in a cleft of the rock." 5 So I
went, and hid it by the Euphrates,[w]
as the LORD commanded me. 6 And
after many days the LORD said to
me, "Go now to the Euphrates,[v]
and take from there the loincloth
that I commanded you to hide
there." 7 Then I went to the Euphrates,[v] and dug, and I took the
loincloth from the place where I
had hidden it. But now the loincloth was ruined; it was good for
nothing.
8 Then the word of the LORD
came to me: 9 Thus says the LORD:
Just so I will ruin the pride of Judah and the great pride of Jerusalem. 10 This evil people, who refuse
to hear my words, who stubbornly
follow their own will and have gone
after other gods to serve them and
worship them, shall be like this
loincloth, which is good for nothing. 11 For as the loincloth clings to
one's loins, so I made the whole
house of Israel and the whole
house of Judah cling to me, says
the LORD, in order that they might
be for me a people, a name, a
praise, and a glory. But they would
not listen.

Symbol of the Wine-Jars

12 You shall speak to them this
word: Thus says the LORD, the God
of Israel: Every wine-jar should be
filled with wine. And they will say
to you, "Do you think we do not
know that every wine-jar should be
filled with wine?" 13 Then you shall
say to them: Thus says the LORD: I
am about to fill all the inhabitants
of this land—the kings who sit on
David's throne, the priests, the
prophets, and all the inhabitants of
Jerusalem—with drunkenness.
14 And I will dash them one against
another, parents and children together, says the LORD. I will not pity
or spare or have compassion when
I destroy them.

Exile Threatened

15 Hear and give ear; do not be haughty,
for the LORD has spoken.
16 Give glory to the LORD your God
before he brings darkness,
and before your feet stumble
on the mountains at twilight;
while you look for light,
he turns it into gloom
and makes it deep darkness.
17 But if you will not listen,
my soul will weep in secret
for your pride;
my eyes will weep bitterly
and run down with tears,
because the LORD's flock
has been taken captive.

18 Say to the king and the queen mother;
"Take a lowly seat,
for your beautiful crown
has come down from your head."[x]
19 The towns of the Negeb are shut up
with no one to open them;
all Judah is taken into exile,
wholly taken into exile.

20 Lift up your eyes and see
those who come from the north.
Where is the flock that was given you,
your beautiful flock?

13.1 v. 11 **13.2** Isa 20.2 **13.4** Jer 51.63 **13.5** Ex 39.42, 43; 40.16 **13.9** Lev 26.19; vv. 15-17 **13.10** Jer 9.14; 11.8; 16.12 **13.11** Ex 19.5,6; Jer 7.23; 32.20; 33.9 **13.13** Isa 51.17, 21; 63.6; Jer 25.27; 51.7 **13.14** Jer 19.9-11; 6.21; 16.5; Isa 27.11 **13.15** Prov 16.5 **13.16** Ps 96.8; Isa 59.9; Jer 23.12; 2.6 **13.17** Mal 2.2; Jer 9.1; 14.17; 23.1,2 **13.18** 2 Chr 33.12, 19; Isa 3.20; Ezek 24.17, 23 **13.19** Jer 32.44; 20.4; 52.27-30 **13.20** Jer 6.22; v. 17

[v] Or *to Parah*; Heb *perath* [w] Or *by Parah*; Heb *perath* [x] Gk Syr Vg: Meaning of Heb uncertain

21 What will you say when they
set as head over you
those whom you have
trained
to be your allies?
Will not pangs take hold of
you,
like those of a woman in
labor?
22 And if you say in your heart,
"Why have these things
come upon me?"
it is for the greatness of your
iniquity
that your skirts are lifted
up,
and you are violated.
23 Can Ethiopians[y] change
their skin
or leopards their spots?
Then also you can do good
who are accustomed to do
evil.
24 I will scatter you[z] like chaff
driven by the wind from
the desert.
25 This is your lot,
the portion I have
measured out to you,
says the LORD,
because you have forgotten
me
and trusted in lies.
26 I myself will lift up your
skirts over your face,
and your shame will be
seen.
27 I have seen your
abominations,
your adulteries and
neighings, your
shameless prostitutions
on the hills of the
countryside.
Woe to you, O Jerusalem!
How long will it be
before you are made clean?

The Great Drought

14 The word of the LORD that came to Jeremiah concerning the drought:

2 Judah mourns
and her gates languish;
they lie in gloom on the
ground,
and the cry of Jerusalem
goes up.
3 Her nobles send their
servants for water;
they come to the cisterns,
they find no water,
they return with their
vessels empty.
They are ashamed and
dismayed
and cover their heads,
4 because the ground is
cracked.
Because there has been no
rain on the land
the farmers are dismayed;
they cover their heads.
5 Even the doe in the field
forsakes her newborn
fawn
because there is no grass.
6 The wild asses stand on the
bare heights,[a]
they pant for air like
jackals;
their eyes fail
because there is no
herbage.

7 Although our iniquities
testify against us,
act, O LORD, for your
name's sake;
our apostasies indeed are
many,
and we have sinned against
you.
8 O hope of Israel,
its savior in time of
trouble,
why should you be like a
stranger in the land,
like a traveler turning aside
for the night?
9 Why should you be like
someone confused,
like a mighty warrior who
cannot give help?
Yet you, O LORD, are in the
midst of us,
and we are called by your
name;
do not forsake us!

13.21 Jer 5.31; 2.25; 4.31 **13.22** Deut 7.17; Jer 5.19; 16.10 **13.23** Prov 27.22; Jer 4.22 **13.24** Jer 9.16; 4.11; 18.17 **13.25** Ps 11.6; Jer 2.32; 3.21 **13.26** Ezek 16.37; Hos 2.10 **13.27** Jer 5.7,8; 11.15; 2.20; 4.14; Hos 8.5 **14.1** Jer 17.8 **14.2** Isa 3.26; Jer 8.21; 11.11; 46.12 **14.3** 1 Kings 18.5; 2 Kings 18.31; 2 Sam 15.30 **14.4** Joel 1.19, 20; Jer 3.3; Joel 1.11 **14.5** Isa 15.6 **14.6** Jer 2.24; Joel 1.18 **14.7** Isa 59.12; Jer 5.6; 8.5 **14.8** Jer 17.13; Isa 43.3; 63.8; Ps 50.15 **14.9** Isa 50.2; Jer 8.19; 15.16; Isa 63.19

y Or *Nubians*; Heb *Cushites* z Heb *them*
a Or *the trails*

10 Thus says the LORD
concerning this people:
Truly they have loved to
wander,
they have not restrained
their feet;
therefore the LORD does not
accept them,
now he will remember their
iniquity
and punish their sins.

11 The LORD said to me: Do not
pray for the welfare of this people.
12 Although they fast, I do not hear
their cry, and although they offer
burnt offering and grain offering, I
do not accept them; but by the
sword, by famine, and by pestilence I consume them.

Denunciation of Lying Prophets

13 Then I said: "Ah, Lord GOD!
Here are the prophets saying to
them, 'You shall not see the sword,
nor shall you have famine, but I
will give you true peace in this
place.' " 14 And the LORD said to me:
The prophets are prophesying lies
in my name; I did not send them,
nor did I command them or speak
to them. They are prophesying to
you a lying vision, worthless divination, and the deceit of their own
minds. 15 Therefore thus says the
LORD concerning the prophets who
prophesy in my name though I did
not send them, and who say,
"Sword and famine shall not come
on this land": By sword and famine
those prophets shall be consumed.
16 And the people to whom they
prophesy shall be thrown out into
the streets of Jerusalem, victims of
famine and sword. There shall be
no one to bury them—themselves,
their wives, their sons, and their
daughters. For I will pour out their
wickedness upon them.

17 You shall say to them this
word:
Let my eyes run down with
tears night and day,
and let them not cease,

14.10 Jer 2.25; 6.20; Hos 8.13
14.11 Ex 32.10; Jer 7.16
14.12 Isa 1.15; Jer 11.11; 6.20; 7.21; 9.16; 21.9
14.13 Jer 5.12; 23.17; 6.14
14.14 Jer 5.31; 27.15; 23.16, 26; Ezek 12.24
14.15 Jer 5.12,13; Ezek 14.10
14.16 Isa 9.16; Jer 7.33; 8.1,2; 13.22-25
14.17 Jer 9.1; Lam 1.15, 16; Jer 10.19; 30.14,15
14.18 Jer 6.25; Ezek 7.15; Jer 6.13; 2.8; 5.5
14.19 Jer 6.30; 30.13; 8.15; 1 Thes 5.3
14.20 Jer 3.25; 8.14
14.21 v. 7; Jer 3.17; 17.12
14.22 Isa 41.29; Jer 10.3; 5.24; Isa 41.4; 43.10; Lam 3.26
15.1 Ezek 14.14, 20; Ex 32.11, 12; 1 Sam 7.9; 12.23; 2 Kings 17.20; Jer 7.15; 10.20

for the virgin daughter—my
people—is struck down
with a crushing blow,
with a very grievous wound.
18 If I go out into the field,
look—those killed by the
sword!
And if I enter the city,
look—those sick with[b]
famine!
For both prophet and priest
ply their trade
throughout the land,
and have no knowledge.

The People Plead for Mercy

19 Have you completely rejected
Judah?
Does your heart loathe
Zion?
Why have you struck us
down
so that there is no healing
for us?
We look for peace, but find
no good;
for a time of healing, but
there is terror instead.
20 We acknowledge our
wickedness, O LORD,
the iniquity of our
ancestors,
for we have sinned against
you.
21 Do not spurn us, for your
name's sake;
do not dishonor your
glorious throne;
remember and do not
break your covenant
with us.
22 Can any idols of the nations
bring rain?
Or can the heavens give
showers?
Is it not you, O LORD our
God?
We set our hope on you,
for it is you who do all this.

Punishment Is Inevitable

15 Then the LORD said to me:
Though Moses and Samuel
stood before me, yet my heart
would not turn toward this people.

[b] Heb *look—the sicknesses of*

Send them out of my sight, and let
them go! 2 And when they say to
you, "Where shall we go?" you shall
say to them: Thus says the LORD:
Those destined for
pestilence, to
pestilence,
and those destined for the
sword, to the sword;
those destined for famine, to
famine,
and those destined for
captivity, to captivity.
3 And I will appoint over them four
kinds of destroyers, says the LORD:
the sword to kill, the dogs to drag
away, and the birds of the air and
the wild animals of the earth to devour and destroy. 4 I will make
them a horror to all the kingdoms
of the earth because of what King
Manasseh son of Hezekiah of Judah did in Jerusalem.

5 Who will have pity on you,
O Jerusalem,
or who will bemoan you?
Who will turn aside
to ask about your welfare?
6 You have rejected me, says
the LORD,
you are going backward;
so I have stretched out my
hand against you and
destroyed you —
I am weary of relenting.
7 I have winnowed them with
a winnowing fork
in the gates of the land;
I have bereaved them, I have
destroyed my people;
they did not turn from
their ways.
8 Their widows became more
numerous
than the sand of the seas;
I have brought against the
mothers of youths
a destroyer at noonday;
I have made anguish and
terror
fall upon her suddenly.
9 She who bore seven has
languished;
she has swooned away;
her sun went down while it
was yet day;
she has been shamed and
disgraced.
And the rest of them I will
give to the sword
before their enemies,
says the LORD.

Jeremiah Complains Again and Is Reassured

10 Woe is me, my mother, that
you ever bore me, a man of strife
and contention to the whole land!
I have not lent, nor have I borrowed, yet all of them curse me.
11 The LORD said: Surely I have intervened in your life[c] for good,
surely I have imposed enemies on
you in a time of trouble and in a
time of distress.[d] 12 Can iron and
bronze break iron from the north?
13 Your wealth and your treasures I will give as plunder, without
price, for all your sins, throughout
all your territory. 14 I will make you
serve your enemies in a land that
you do not know, for in my anger a
fire is kindled that shall burn forever.
15 O LORD, you know;
remember me and visit me,
and bring down retribution
for me on my
persecutors.
In your forbearance do not
take me away;
know that on your account
I suffer insult.
16 Your words were found, and I
ate them,
and your words became to
me a joy
and the delight of my
heart;
for I am called by your
name,
O LORD, God of hosts.
17 I did not sit in the company
of merrymakers,
nor did I rejoice;
under the weight of your
hand I sat alone,
for you had filled me with
indignation.
18 Why is my pain unceasing,

15.2 Jer 43.11; Ezek 5.2,12; Zech 11.9
15.3 Lev 26.16; 1 Kings 21.23, 24; Deut 28.26; Jer 7.33
15.4 Deut 28.25; 2 Kings 21.11ff; 23.26
15.5 Ps 69.20; Isa 51.19; Jer 16.5
15.6 Jer 6.19; 7.24; 6.11,12; 7.16
15.7 Jer 51.2; 18.21; 5.3
15.8 Isa 3.25,26; Jer 22.7; 6.4
15.9 1 Sam 2.5; Isa 47.9; Jer 6.4; Am 8.9; Jer 50.12; 21.7
15.10 Job 3.1; Jer 20.14; Deut 23.19
15.11 Isa 41.10; Jer 39.11, 12; 40.4,5
15.12 Jer 28.14
15.13 Ps 44.12; Jer 17.3; Isa 52.3,5
15.14 Jer 16.13; 17.4; Deut 32.22
15.15 Jer 12.3; 20.11; Ps 69.7-9
15.16 Ezek 3.1-3; Ps 119.72; Jer 14.9
15.17 Jer 16.8; Ezek 3.24, 25
15.18 Jer 30.15; Mic 1.9; Jer 14.3

[c] Heb *intervened with you* [d] Meaning of Heb uncertain

my wound incurable,
refusing to be healed?
Truly, you are to me like a
deceitful brook,
like waters that fail.

19 Therefore thus says the LORD:
If you turn back, I will take
you back,
and you shall stand before
me.
If you utter what is precious,
and not what is
worthless,
you shall serve as my
mouth.
It is they who will turn to
you,
not you who will turn to
them.
20 And I will make you to this
people
a fortified wall of bronze;
they will fight against you,
but they shall not prevail
over you,
for I am with you
to save you and deliver
you,
says the LORD.
21 I will deliver you out of the
hand of the wicked,
and redeem you from the
grasp of the ruthless.

Jeremiah's Celibacy and Message

16 The word of the LORD came
to me: [2]You shall not take
a wife, nor shall you have sons or
daughters in this place. [3]For thus
says the LORD concerning the sons
and daughters who are born in this
place, and concerning the mothers
who bear them and the fathers who
beget them in this land: [4]They
shall die of deadly diseases. They
shall not be lamented, nor shall
they be buried; they shall become
like dung on the surface of the
ground. They shall perish by the
sword and by famine, and their
dead bodies shall become food for
the birds of the air and for the wild
animals of the earth.
5 For thus says the LORD: Do not
enter the house of mourning, or go
to lament, or bemoan them; for I
have taken away my peace from
this people, says the LORD, my
steadfast love and mercy. [6]Both
great and small shall die in this
land; they shall not be buried, and
no one shall lament for them; there
shall be no gashing, no shaving of
the head for them. [7]No one shall
break bread[e] for the mourner, to
offer comfort for the dead; nor shall
anyone give them the cup of consolation to drink for their fathers or
their mothers. [8]You shall not go
into the house of feasting to sit
with them, to eat and drink. [9]For
thus says the LORD of hosts, the
God of Israel: I am going to banish
from this place, in your days and
before your eyes, the voice of mirth
and the voice of gladness, the voice
of the bridegroom and the voice of
the bride.
10 And when you tell this people all these words, and they say to
you, "Why has the LORD pronounced all this great evil against
us? What is our iniquity? What is
the sin that we have committed
against the LORD our God?" [11]then
you shall say to them: It is because
your ancestors have forsaken me,
says the LORD, and have gone after
other gods and have served and
worshiped them, and have forsak-
en me and have not kept my law;
[12]and because you have behaved
worse than your ancestors, for here
you are, every one of you, following
your stubborn evil will, refusing to
listen to me. [13]Therefore I will hurl
you out of this land into a land that
neither you nor your ancestors
have known, and there you shall
serve other gods day and night, for
I will show you no favor.

God Will Restore Israel

14 Therefore, the days are surely coming, says the LORD, when it
shall no longer be said, "As the
LORD lives who brought the people
of Israel up out of the land of
Egypt," [15]but "As the LORD lives
who brought the people of Israel up
out of the land of the north and out

15.19 Jer 4.1; Ezek 22.26
15.20 Jer 1.18,19; 20.11; Isa 41.10
15.21 Jer 20.13; 31.11
16.1 Jer 1.2,4
16.2 1 Cor 7.26
16.3 Jer 6.11; 15.8; 6.21
16.4 Ps 83.10; Jer 9.22; 15.3; 34.20
16.5 Ezek 24.16-23; Jer 12.12; 13.14
16.6 Ezek 9.6; Jer 41.5; 47.5
16.7 Ezek 24.17; Hos 9.4
16.8 Jer 15.17
16.9 Jer 7.34; 25.10; Hos 2.11; Rev 18.23
16.10 Deut 29.24; 1 Kings 9.8, 9; Jer 5.19
16.11 Jer 22.9; Ezek 11.21; 1 Pet 4.3
16.12 Jer 7.26; 13.10; Eccl 9.3
16.13 Deut 4.26-28; 28.36; Jer 15.4; 5.19
16.14 Isa 43.18; Jer 23.7,8; Ex 20.2
16.15 Ps 106.47; Isa 11.11-16; Jer 24.6

[e] Two Mss Gk: MT *break for them*

of all the lands where he had driven them." For I will bring them back to their own land that I gave to their ancestors.

16 I am now sending for many fishermen, says the LORD, and they shall catch them; and afterward I will send for many hunters, and they shall hunt them from every mountain and every hill, and out of the clefts of the rocks. 17 For my eyes are on all their ways; they are not hidden from my presence, nor is their iniquity concealed from my sight. 18 And[f] I will doubly repay their iniquity and their sin, because they have polluted my land with the carcasses of their detestable idols, and have filled my inheritance with their abominations.

19 O LORD, my strength and my
 stronghold,
my refuge in the day of
 trouble,
to you shall the nations
 come
from the ends of the earth
 and say:
Our ancestors have inherited
 nothing but lies,
worthless things in which
 there is no profit.
20 Can mortals make for
 themselves gods?
Such are no gods!

21 "Therefore I am surely going to teach them, this time I am going to teach them my power and my might, and they shall know that my name is the LORD."

Judah's Sin and Punishment

17 The sin of Judah is written with an iron pen; with a diamond point it is engraved on the tablet of their hearts, and on the horns of their altars, 2 while their children remember their altars and their sacred poles,[g] beside every green tree, and on the high hills, 3 on the mountains in the open country. Your wealth and all your treasures I will give for spoil as the price of your sin[h] throughout all your territory. 4 By your own act you shall lose the heritage that I gave you, and I will make you serve your enemies in a land that you do not know, for in my anger a fire is kindled[i] that shall burn forever.

5 Thus says the LORD:
Cursed are those who trust
 in mere mortals
and make mere flesh their
 strength,
whose hearts turn away
 from the LORD.
6 They shall be like a shrub in
 the desert,
and shall not see when
 relief comes.
They shall live in the
 parched places of the
 wilderness,
in an uninhabited salt
 land.

7 Blessed are those who trust
 in the LORD,
whose trust is the LORD.
8 They shall be like a tree
 planted by water,
sending out its roots by the
 stream.
It shall not fear when heat
 comes,
and its leaves shall stay
 green;
in the year of drought it is
 not anxious,
and it does not cease to
 bear fruit.

9 The heart is devious above
 all else;
it is perverse—
who can understand it?
10 I the LORD test the mind
 and search the heart,
to give to all according to
 their ways,
according to the fruit of
 their doings.

11 Like the partridge hatching
 what it did not lay,

16.16 Am 4.2; Hab 1.14, 15; Mic 7.2; Isa 2.21 **16.17** Ps 90.8; 1 Cor 4.5; Heb 4.13; Jer 2.22 **16.18** Rev 18.6; Ezek 11.18, 21 **16.19** Jer 15.11; Ps 14.6; Hab 2.18,19 **16.20** Isa 37.19; Jer 2.11; Gal 4.8 **16.21** Ps 9.16; Jer 33.2; Am 5.8 **17.1** Jer 2.22; Job 19.24; Prov 3.3; 2 Cor 3.3 **17.2** Jer 7.18; Ex 34.13; Jer 3.6 **17.3** Jer 26.18; 15.13 **17.4** Jer 12.7; 15.14; 7.20 **17.5** Isa 30.1-3; 2 Chr 32.8 **17.6** Jer 48.6; Deut 29.23 **17.7** Ps 34.8; 84.12; 40.4; Prov 16.20 **17.8** Ps 1.3; Jer 14.1-6 **17.9** Mk 7.21,22; Rom 7.11; Eph 4.22 **17.10** 1 Sam 16.7; Jer 11.20; 20.12; Rom 8.27; Jer 32.19; Rom 2.6 **17.11** Jer 6.13; 8.10; 22.13, 17

[f] Gk: Heb *And first* [g] Heb *Asherim*
[h] Cn: Heb *spoil your high places for sin*
[i] Two Mss Theodotion: *you kindled*

so are all who amass
wealth unjustly;
in mid-life it will leave them,
and at their end they will
prove to be fools.

12 O glorious throne, exalted
from the beginning,
shrine of our sanctuary!
13 O hope of Israel! O LORD!
All who forsake you shall
be put to shame;
those who turn away from
you[j] shall be recorded
in the underworld,[k]
for they have forsaken the
fountain of living water,
the LORD.

Jeremiah Prays for Vindication

14 Heal me, O LORD, and I shall
be healed;
save me, and I shall be
saved;
for you are my praise.
15 See how they say to me,
"Where is the word of the
LORD?
Let it come!"
16 But I have not run away from
being a shepherd[l] in
your service,
nor have I desired the fatal
day.
You know what came from
my lips;
it was before your face.
17 Do not become a terror to
me;
you are my refuge in the
day of disaster;
18 Let my persecutors be
shamed,
but do not let me be
shamed;
let them be dismayed,
but do not let me be
dismayed;
bring on them the day of
disaster;
destroy them with double
destruction!

Hallow the Sabbath Day

19 Thus said the LORD to me: Go
and stand in the People's Gate, by
which the kings of Judah enter and
by which they go out, and in all the
gates of Jerusalem, 20 and say to
them: Hear the word of the LORD,
you kings of Judah, and all Judah,
and all the inhabitants of Jerusalem, who enter by these gates.
21 Thus says the LORD: For the sake
of your lives, take care that you do
not bear a burden on the sabbath
day or bring it in by the gates of
Jerusalem. 22 And do not carry a
burden out of your houses on the
sabbath or do any work, but keep
the sabbath day holy, as I commanded your ancestors. 23 Yet they
did not listen or incline their ear;
they stiffened their necks and
would not hear or receive instruction.

24 But if you listen to me, says
the LORD, and bring in no burden by
the gates of this city on the sabbath
day, but keep the sabbath day holy
and do no work on it, 25 then there
shall enter by the gates of this city
kings[m] who sit on the throne of David, riding in chariots and on
horses, they and their officials, the
people of Judah and the inhabitants of Jerusalem; and this city
shall be inhabited forever. 26 And
people shall come from the towns
of Judah and the places around Jerusalem, from the land of Benjamin, from the Shephelah, from the
hill country, and from the Negeb,
bringing burnt offerings and sacrifices, grain offerings and frankincense, and bringing thank offerings
to the house of the LORD. 27 But if
you do not listen to me, to keep the
sabbath day holy, and to carry in no
burden through the gates of Jerusalem on the sabbath day, then I
will kindle a fire in its gates; it shall
devour the palaces of Jerusalem
and shall not be quenched.

The Potter and the Clay

18 The word that came to Jeremiah from the LORD:
2 "Come, go down to the potter's

17.12 Jer 3.17; 14.21 **17.13** Jer 14.8; Ps 73.27; Isa 1.28; Jer 2.13,17 **17.14** Jer 30.17; Ps 54.1; Deut 10.21; Ps 109.1 **17.15** Isa 5.19; Am 5.18 **17.16** Jer 1.6; 12.3 **17.17** Ps 88.15; Jer 16.19 **17.18** Ps 35.4,26; 35.8; Jer 16.18 **17.19** Jer 7.2; 26.2

17.20 Jer 19.3; 22.2; Hos 5.1 **17.21** Deut 4.9,15, 23; Num 15.32-36; Neh 13.15-21 **17.22** Ex 20.8; 23.12; 31.13; Ezek 20.12 **17.23** Jer 7.24,26; 11.10; 19.15 **17.24** Deut 11.13; Ex 20.8-11; Ezek 20.20 **17.25** Jer 22.4; Isa 9.7; Lk 1.32; Heb 12.22 **17.26** Zech 7.7; Ps 107.22 **17.27** Jer 22.5; Isa 9.18,19; Jer 11.16; Am 2.5; 7.20 **18.2** Jer 19.1,2; 23.22

j Heb *me* k Or *in the earth* l Meaning of Heb uncertain m Cn: Heb *kings and officials*

house, and there I will let you hear
my words." 3 So I went down to the
potter's house, and there he was
working at his wheel. 4 The vessel
he was making of clay was spoiled
in the potter's hand, and he re-
worked it into another vessel, as
seemed good to him.
5 Then the word of the LORD
came to me: 6 Can I not do with
you, O house of Israel, just as this
potter has done? says the LORD.
Just like the clay in the potter's
hand, so are you in my hand,
O house of Israel. 7 At one moment
I may declare concerning a nation
or a kingdom, that I will pluck up
and break down and destroy it,
8 but if that nation, concerning
which I have spoken, turns from its
evil, I will change my mind about
the disaster that I intended to bring
on it. 9 And at another moment I
may declare concerning a nation or
a kingdom that I will build and
plant it, 10 but if it does evil in my
sight, not listening to my voice,
then I will change my mind about
the good that I had intended to do
to it. 11 Now, therefore, say to the
people of Judah and the inhabitants of Jerusalem: Thus says the
LORD: Look, I am a potter shaping
evil against you and devising a plan
against you. Turn now, all of you
from your evil way, and amend your
ways and your doings.

Israel's Stubborn Idolatry

12 But they say, "It is no use!
We will follow our own plans, and
each of us will act according to the
stubbornness of our evil will."

13 Therefore thus says the LORD:
Ask among the nations:
Who has heard the like of
this?
The virgin Israel has done
a most horrible thing.
14 Does the snow of Lebanon
leave
the crags of Sirion?[n]
Do the mountain[o] waters
run dry,[p]
the cold flowing streams?
15 But my people have
forgotten me,
they burn offerings to a
delusion;
they have stumbled[q] in their
ways,
in the ancient roads,
and have gone into bypaths,
not the highway,
16 making their land a horror,
a thing to be hissed at
forever.
All who pass by it are
horrified
and shake their heads.
17 Like the wind from the east,
I will scatter them before
the enemy.
I will show them my back,
not my face,
in the day of their
calamity.

A Plot against Jeremiah

18 Then they said, "Come, let
us make plots against Jeremiah—
for instruction shall not perish
from the priest, nor counsel from
the wise, nor the word from the
prophet. Come, let us bring
charges against him,[r] and let us
not heed any of his words."

19 Give heed to me, O LORD,
and listen to what my
adversaries say!
20 Is evil a recompense for
good?
Yet they have dug a pit for
my life.
Remember how I stood
before you
to speak good for them,
to turn away your wrath
from them.
21 Therefore give their children
over to famine;
hurl them out to the power
of the sword,
let their wives become
childless and widowed.
May their men meet death
by pestilence,

18.6 Isa 45.9; Mt 20.15; Rom 9.20, 21
18.7 Jer 1.10
18.8 Ezek 18.21; Jer 26.3; Jon 3.10
18.9 Jer 1.10; 31.28
18.10 Jer 7.24-28; Ezek 33.18
18.11 Jer 4.6; 2 Kings 17.13; Isa 1.16-19; Acts 26.20
18.12 Jer 2.25; 7.24; 16.12
18.13 Jer 2.10,11; 14.17; 5.30; 23.14
18.15 Isa 65.7; Jer 7.9; 6.16; Isa 57.14; 62.10
18.16 Jer 25.9; 50.13; 48.27
18.17 Job 27.21; Jer 13.24; 2.27; 46.21
18.18 Jer 11.19; Mal 2.7; Jer 8.8; 5.13; 20.10; 43.2
18.20 Ps 35.7; 57.6; 106.23
18.21 Ps 109.9,10; Isa 13.18; Jer 15.8; Ezek 22.25; Jer 9.21; 11.22

[n] Cn: Heb *of the field* [o] Cn: Heb *foreign* [p] Cn: Heb *Are . . . plucked up?* [q] Gk Syr Vg: Heb *they made them stumble* [r] Heb *strike him with the tongue*

their youths be slain by the
sword in battle.
22 May a cry be heard from
their houses,
when you bring the
marauder suddenly
upon them!
For they have dug a pit to
catch me,
and laid snares for my feet.
23 Yet you, O LORD, know
all their plotting to kill me.
Do not forgive their iniquity,
do not blot out their sin
from your sight.
Let them be tripped up
before you;
deal with them while you
are angry.

The Broken Earthenware Jug

19 Thus said the LORD: Go and
buy a potter's earthenware
jug. Take with you[s] some of the elders of the people and some of the
senior priests, 2 and go out to the
valley of the son of Hinnom at
the entry of the Potsherd Gate, and
proclaim there the words that I tell
you. 3 You shall say: Hear the word
of the LORD, O kings of Judah and
inhabitants of Jerusalem. Thus
says the LORD of hosts, the God of
Israel: I am going to bring such disaster upon this place that the ears
of everyone who hears of it will tingle. 4 Because the people have forsaken me, and have profaned this
place by making offerings in it to
other gods whom neither they nor
their ancestors nor the kings of Judah have known; and because they
have filled this place with the
blood of the innocent, 5 and gone
on building the high places of Baal
to burn their children in the fire as
burnt offerings to Baal, which I did
not command or decree, nor did it
enter my mind. 6 Therefore the
days are surely coming, says the
LORD, when this place shall no
more be called Topheth, or the valley of the son of Hinnom, but the
valley of Slaughter. 7 And in this
place I will make void the plans of
Judah and Jerusalem, and will
make them fall by the sword before
their enemies, and by the hand of
those who seek their life. I will give
their dead bodies for food to the
birds of the air and to the wild animals of the earth. 8 And I will make
this city a horror, a thing to be
hissed at; everyone who passes by
it will be horrified and will hiss because of all its disasters. 9 And I will
make them eat the flesh of their
sons and the flesh of their daughters, and all shall eat the flesh of
their neighbors in the siege, and in
the distress with which their enemies and those who seek their life
afflict them.
10 Then you shall break the jug
in the sight of those who go with
you, 11 and shall say to them: Thus
says the LORD of hosts: So will I
break this people and this city, as
one breaks a potter's vessel, so that
it can never be mended. In Topheth they shall bury until there is
no more room to bury. 12 Thus will
I do to this place, says the LORD,
and to its inhabitants, making this
city like Topheth. 13 And the
houses of Jerusalem and the
houses of the kings of Judah shall
be defiled like the place of
Topheth—all the houses upon
whose roofs offerings have been
made to the whole host of heaven,
and libations have been poured out
to other gods.
14 When Jeremiah came from
Topheth, where the LORD had sent
him to prophesy, he stood in the
court of the LORD's house and said
to all the people: 15 Thus says the
LORD of hosts, the God of Israel: I
am now bringing upon this city and
upon all its towns all the disaster
that I have pronounced against it,
because they have stiffened their
necks, refusing to hear my words.

Jeremiah Persecuted by Pashhur

20 Now the priest Pashhur
son of Immer, who was
chief officer in the house of the
LORD, heard Jeremiah prophesying
these things. 2 Then Pashhur struck
the prophet Jeremiah, and put him
in the stocks that were in the upper

18.22 Jer 6.26; Ps 140.5
18.23 Ps 109.14; Isa 2.9; Jer 6.15,21; 7.20
19.1 Jer 18.2; v. 10; Num 11.16; 2 Kings 19.2
19.2 Josh 15.8; Jer 7.31
19.3 Jer 17.20; 1 Sam 3.11; 4.18
19.4 Deut 28.20; Isa 65.11; 2 Kings 21.16; Jer 2.34
19.5 Jer 32.35; 2 Kings 17.17; Lev 18.21
19.6 Jer 7.32; Josh 15.8
19.7 Jer 15.2,9; Ps 79.2; Jer 16.4
19.8 Jer 18.16; 49.13; 1 Kings 9.8; 2 Chr 7.21
19.9 Deut 28.53, 55; Isa 9.20; Lam 4.10
19.10 v. 1
19.11 Ps 2.9; Isa 30.14; Rev 2.27; Jer 7.32
19.13 Jer 52.13; 7.18; Ezek 20.28; Acts 7.42
19.14 Jer 26.2
19.15 Jer 7.26; 17.23; Ps 58.4
20.1 1 Chr 24.14; 2 Kings 25.18
20.2 Jer 1.19; Job 13.27; Jer 37.13; 38.7

[s] Syr Tg Compare Gk: Heb lacks *take with you*

Benjamin Gate of the house of the
LORD. 3 The next morning when
Pashhur released Jeremiah from
the stocks, Jeremiah said to him,
The LORD has named you not Pashhur but "Terror-all-around." 4 For
thus says the LORD: I am making
you a terror to yourself and to all
your friends; and they shall fall by
the sword of their enemies while
you look on. And I will give all Judah into the hand of the king of
Babylon; he shall carry them captive to Babylon, and shall kill them
with the sword. 5 I will give all the
wealth of this city, all its gains, all
its prized belongings, and all the
treasures of the kings of Judah into
the hand of their enemies, who
shall plunder them, and seize
them, and carry them to Babylon.
6 And you, Pashhur, and all who
live in your house, shall go into
captivity, and to Babylon you shall
go; there you shall die, and there
you shall be buried, you and all
your friends, to whom you have
prophesied falsely.

Jeremiah Denounces His Persecutors

7 O LORD, you have enticed
me,
and I was enticed;
you have overpowered me,
and you have prevailed.
I have become a
laughingstock all day
long;
everyone mocks me.
8 For whenever I speak, I must
cry out,
I must shout, "Violence
and destruction!"
For the word of the LORD has
become for me
a reproach and derision all
day long.
9 If I say, "I will not mention
him,
or speak any more in his
name,"
then within me there is
something like a
burning fire
shut up in my bones;
I am weary with holding it
in,
and I cannot.
10 For I hear many whispering:
"Terror is all around!
Denounce him! Let us
denounce him!"
All my close friends
are watching for me to
stumble.
"Perhaps he can be enticed,
and we can prevail against
him,
and take our revenge on
him."
11 But the LORD is with me like
a dread warrior;
therefore my persecutors
will stumble,
and they will not prevail.
They will be greatly shamed,
for they will not succeed.
Their eternal dishonor
will never be forgotten.
12 O LORD of hosts, you test the
righteous,
you see the heart and the
mind;
let me see your retribution
upon them,
for to you I have
committed my cause.

13 Sing to the LORD;
praise the LORD!
For he has delivered the life
of the needy
from the hands of
evildoers.

14 Cursed be the day
on which I was born!
The day when my mother
bore me,
let it not be blessed!
15 Cursed be the man
who brought the news to
my father, saying,
"A child is born to you, a
son,"
making him very glad.
16 Let that man be like the
cities
that the LORD overthrew
without pity;
let him hear a cry in the
morning

20.3 v. 10
20.4 Job 18.11-21; Jer 29.21; 21.4-10; 52.27
20.5 Jer 15.13; 17.3; 2 Kings 20.17; 2 Chr 36.10; Jer 3.24
20.6 v. 1; Jer 28.15-17; 14.13-15; 29.21
20.7 Jer 1.6-8; Mic 3.8; Jer 38.19
20.8 Jer 6.7,10; 2 Chr 36.16
20.9 1 Kings 19.3, 4; Ps 39.3; Job 32.18-20; Acts 4.20
20.10 Ps 31.13; 41.9; Lk 11.53,54
20.11 Jer 1.8,19; 15.20; 17.18; 23.40
20.12 Jer 11.20; 17.10; Ps 54.7; 59.10
20.13 Jer 31.7; Ps 35.9,10; Jer 15.21
20.14 Job 3.3; Jer 15.10
20.15 Gen 21.6,7
20.16 Gen 19.25; Jer 18.22

and an alarm at noon,
17 because he did not kill me in
the womb;
so my mother would have
been my grave,
and her womb forever
great.
18 Why did I come forth from
the womb
to see toil and sorrow,
and spend my days in
shame?

Jerusalem Will Fall to Nebuchadrezzar

21 This is the word that came
to Jeremiah from the LORD,
when King Zedekiah sent to him
Pashhur son of Malchiah and the
priest Zephaniah son of Maaseiah,
saying, 2 "Please inquire of the
LORD on our behalf, for King Nebuchadrezzar of Babylon is making
war against us; perhaps the LORD
will perform a wonderful deed for
us, as he has often done, and will
make him withdraw from us."
3 Then Jeremiah said to them:
4 Thus you shall say to Zedekiah:
Thus says the LORD, the God of Israel: I am going to turn back the
weapons of war that are in your
hands and with which you are
fighting against the king of Babylon and against the Chaldeans
who are besieging you outside the
walls; and I will bring them together into the center of this city. 5 I myself will fight against you with outstretched hand and mighty arm, in
anger, in fury, and in great wrath.
6 And I will strike down the inhabitants of this city, both human beings and animals; they shall die of
a great pestilence. 7 Afterward, says
the LORD, I will give King Zedekiah
of Judah, and his servants, and the
people in this city—those who survive the pestilence, sword, and
famine—into the hands of King
Nebuchadrezzar of Babylon, into
the hands of their enemies, into
the hands of those who seek their
lives. He shall strike them down
with the edge of the sword; he shall
not pity them, or spare them, or
have compassion.
8 And to this people you shall
say: Thus says the LORD: See, I am
setting before you the way of life
and the way of death. 9 Those who
stay in this city shall die by the
sword, by famine, and by pestilence; but those who go out and
surrender to the Chaldeans who
are besieging you shall live and
shall have their lives as a prize of
war. 10 For I have set my face
against this city for evil and not for
good, says the LORD: it shall be giv-
en into the hands of the king of
Babylon, and he shall burn it with
fire.

Message to the House of David

11 To the house of the king of
Judah say: Hear the word of the
LORD, 12 O house of David! Thus
says the LORD:
Execute justice in the
morning,
and deliver from the hand
of the oppressor
anyone who has been
robbed,
or else my wrath will go forth
like fire,
and burn, with no one to
quench it,
because of your evil doings.

13 See, I am against you,
O inhabitant of the
valley,
O rock of the plain,
says the LORD;
you who say, "Who can come
down against us,
or who can enter our
places of refuge?"
14 I will punish you according
to the fruit of your
doings,
says the LORD;
I will kindle a fire in its
forest,
and it shall devour all that
is around it.

Exhortation to Repent

22 Thus says the LORD: Go
down to the house of the

20.17 Job 3.10,11; 10.18,19 **20.18** Job 3.20; Ps 90.9; Jer 3.25 **21.1** 2 Kings 24.17, 18; Jer 38.1; 2 Kings 25.18; Jer 29.25; 37.3 **21.2** Jer 37.3,7 **21.4** Zech 14.2 **21.5** Isa 63.10; Jer 32.37 **21.6** Jer 7.20; 14.12 **21.7** Jer 37.17; 39.5; 52.9; 13.14 **21.8** Deut 30.15, 19 **21.9** Jer 38.2,17, 18; 14.12; 39.18; 45.5 **21.10** Jer 44.11, 27; 39.16; 32.28,29; 38.18,23; 52.13 **21.11** Jer 13.18; 17.20 **21.12** Isa 7.2,13; Jer 22.3; Zech 7.9; Jer 7.20 **21.13** Ezek 13.8; Jer 49.4 **21.14** Isa 3.10,11; Ezek 20.46, 48; 2 Chr 36.19; Jer 52.13 **22.1** Jer 21.11; 2 Chr 25.15, 16

king of Judah, and speak there this
word, 2 and say: Hear the word of
the LORD, O King of Judah sitting
on the throne of David—you, and
your servants, and your people who
enter these gates. 3 Thus says the
LORD: Act with justice and righteousness, and deliver from the
hand of the oppressor anyone who
has been robbed. And do no wrong
or violence to the alien, the orphan, and the widow, or shed innocent blood in this place. 4 For if you
will indeed obey this word, then
through the gates of this house
shall enter kings who sit on the
throne of David, riding in chariots
and on horses, they, and their servants, and their people. 5 But if you
will not heed these words, I swear
by myself, says the LORD, that this
house shall become a desolation.
6 For thus says the LORD concerning
the house of the king of Judah:

You are like Gilead to me,
like the summit of
Lebanon;
but I swear that I will make
you a desert,
an uninhabited city.[t]

7 I will prepare destroyers
against you,
all with their weapons;
they shall cut down your
choicest cedars
and cast them into the fire.

8 And many nations will pass by
this city, and all of them will say
one to another, "Why has the LORD
dealt in this way with that great
city?" 9 And they will answer, "Because they abandoned the covenant of the LORD their God, and
worshiped other gods and served
them."

10 Do not weep for him who is
dead,
nor bemoan him;
weep rather for him who
goes away,
for he shall return no more
to see his native land.

Message to the Sons of Josiah

11 For thus says the LORD concerning Shallum son of King Josiah
of Judah, who succeeded his father
Josiah, and who went away from
this place: He shall return here no
more, 12 but in the place where they
have carried him captive he shall
die, and he shall never see this land
again.

13 Woe to him who builds his
house by
unrighteousness,
and his upper rooms by
injustice;
who makes his neighbors
work for nothing,
and does not give them
their wages;

14 who says, "I will build myself
a spacious house
with large upper rooms,"
and who cuts out windows
for it,
paneling it with cedar,
and painting it with
vermilion.

15 Are you a king
because you compete in
cedar?
Did not your father eat and
drink
and do justice and
righteousness?
Then it was well with him.

16 He judged the cause of the
poor and needy;
then it was well.
Is not this to know me?
says the LORD.

17 But your eyes and heart
are only on your dishonest
gain,
for shedding innocent blood,
and for practicing
oppression and
violence.

18 Therefore thus says the LORD
concerning King Jehoiakim son of
Josiah of Judah:

They shall not lament for
him, saying,
"Alas, my brother!" or
"Alas, sister!"
They shall not lament for
him, saying,

22.2 Jer 19.3; 29.20 **22.3** Jer 21.12; Ps 72.4; Ex 22.21-24 **22.4** Jer 17.25 **22.5** Jer 17.27; 26.4; Heb 6.13; Jer 7.14; 26.6,9 **22.6** Jer 7.34 **22.7** Isa 10.3-6; Jer 4.6,7; Isa 10.33,34 **22.8** Deut 29.24, 25; 1 Kings 9.8, 9; Jer 16.10 **22.9** 2 Kings 22.17; 2 Chr 34.25 **22.10** 2 Kings 22.20; v. 18; Jer 16.7; 44.14 **22.11** 2 Kings 23.30, 34

22.13 Mic 3.10; Hab 2.9; Jas 5.4 **22.14** Isa 5.8,9; 2 Sam 7.2 **22.15** 2 Kings 23.25; Jer 7.5; 42.6 **22.16** Ps 72.1-4, 12,13; 1 Chr 28.9; Jer 9.24 **22.17** Jer 6.13; 8.10; 6.6 **22.18** 1 Kings 13.30; Jer 34.5

[t] Cn: Heb *uninhabited cities*

"Alas, lord!" or "Alas, his
majesty!"
19 With the burial of a donkey
he shall be buried—
dragged off and thrown out
beyond the gates of
Jerusalem.

20 Go up to Lebanon, and cry
out,
and lift up your voice in
Bashan;
cry out from Abarim,
for all your lovers are
crushed.
21 I spoke to you in your
prosperity,
but you said, "I will not
listen."
This has been your way from
your youth,
for you have not obeyed my
voice.
22 The wind shall shepherd all
your shepherds,
and your lovers shall go
into captivity;
then you will be ashamed
and dismayed
because of all your
wickedness.
23 O inhabitant of Lebanon,
nested among the cedars,
how you will groan[u] when
pangs come upon you,
pain as of a woman in
labor!

Judgment on Coniah (Jehoiachin)

24 As I live, says the LORD, even
if King Coniah son of Jehoiakim of
Judah were the signet ring on my
right hand, even from there I would
tear you off 25 and give you into the
hands of those who seek your life,
into the hands of those of whom
you are afraid, even into the hands
of King Nebuchadrezzar of Babylon
and into the hands of the Chaldeans. 26 I will hurl you and the mother who bore you into another country, where you were not born, and
there you shall die. 27 But they shall
not return to the land to which they
long to return.

22.19 Jer 36.30
22.20 Deut 32.49; Jer 2.25; 3.1
22.21 Jer 13.10; 19.15; 3.24, 25; 32.30
22.22 Jer 5.13; 30.14; Isa 65.13; Jer 20.11
22.23 Jer 4.31; 6.24
22.24 Jer 37.1; Song 8.6; Hag 2.23
22.25 2 Kings 24.15, 16; Jer 34.20
22.26 2 Kings 24.15; 2 Chr 36.10; 2 Kings 24.8
22.28 Ps 31.12; Jer 48.38; Hos 8.8; Jer 15.1; 17.4
22.29 Deut 32.1; Jer 6.19; Mic 1.2
22.30 1 Chr 3.16, 17; Mt 1.12
23.1 Ezek 13.3; Jer 10.21; 50.6; Ezek 34.31
23.3 Isa 11.11-16; Jer 32.37; Ezek 34.13-16
23.4 Jer 3.15; Ezek 34.23; Jer 30.10; Jn 6.39; 10.28
23.5 Isa 4.2; 11.1; 53.2; Jer 33.14-16; Zech 3.8; 6.12; Isa 9.7; Lk 1.32,33
23.6 Deut 33.28; Zech 14.11; Isa 7.14; 9.6; Mt 1.21-23; Jer 33.16; Rom 3.22; 1 Cor 1.30

28 Is this man Coniah a
despised broken pot,
a vessel no one wants?
Why are he and his offspring
hurled out
and cast away in a land
that they do not know?
29 O land, land, land,
hear the word of the LORD!
30 Thus says the LORD:
Record this man as childless,
a man who shall not
succeed in his days;
for none of his offspring shall
succeed
in sitting on the throne of
David,
and ruling again in Judah.

Restoration after Exile

23 Woe to the shepherds who
destroy and scatter the
sheep of my pasture! says the LORD.
2 Therefore thus says the LORD, the
God of Israel, concerning the shepherds who shepherd my people: It
is you who have scattered my flock,
and have driven them away, and
you have not attended to them. So
I will attend to you for your evil doings, says the LORD. 3 Then I myself
will gather the remnant of my flock
out of all the lands where I have
driven them, and I will bring them
back to their fold, and they shall be
fruitful and multiply. 4 I will raise
up shepherds over them who will
shepherd them, and they shall not
fear any longer, or be dismayed,
nor shall any be missing, says the
LORD.

The Righteous Branch of David

5 The days are surely coming,
says the LORD, when I will raise up
for David a righteous Branch, and
he shall reign as king and deal
wisely, and shall execute justice
and righteousness in the land. 6 In
his days Judah will be saved and
Israel will live in safety. And this is
the name by which he will be
called: "The LORD is our righteousness."

[u] Gk Vg Syr: Heb *will be pitied*

7 Therefore, the days are surely
coming, says the LORD, when it
shall no longer be said, "As the
LORD lives who brought the people
of Israel up out of the land of
Egypt," 8 but "As the LORD lives who
brought out and led the offspring of
the house of Israel out of the land
of the north and out of all the lands
where he[v] had driven them." Then
they shall live in their own land.

False Prophets of Hope Denounced

9 Concerning the prophets:
My heart is crushed within me,
all my bones shake;
I have become like a drunkard,
like one overcome by wine,
because of the LORD
and because of his holy words.
10 For the land is full of adulterers;
because of the curse the land mourns,
and the pastures of the wilderness are dried up.
Their course has been evil,
and their might is not right.
11 Both prophet and priest are ungodly;
even in my house I have found their wickedness,
says the LORD.
12 Therefore their way shall be to them
like slippery paths in the darkness,
into which they shall be driven and fall;
for I will bring disaster upon them
in the year of their punishment,
says the LORD.
13 In the prophets of Samaria
I saw a disgusting thing:
they prophesied by Baal
and led my people Israel astray.
14 But in the prophets of Jerusalem
I have seen a more shocking thing:
they commit adultery and walk in lies;
they strengthen the hands of evildoers,
so that no one turns from wickedness;
all of them have become like Sodom to me,
and its inhabitants like Gomorrah.
15 Therefore thus says the LORD of hosts concerning the prophets:
"I am going to make them eat wormwood,
and give them poisoned water to drink;
for from the prophets of Jerusalem
ungodliness has spread throughout the land."

16 Thus says the LORD of hosts:
Do not listen to the words of the
prophets who prophesy to you;
they are deluding you. They speak
visions of their own minds, not
from the mouth of the LORD. 17 They
keep saying to those who despise
the word of the LORD, "It shall be
well with you"; and to all who stubbornly follow their own stubborn
hearts, they say, "No calamity shall
come upon you."

18 For who has stood in the council of the LORD
so as to see and to hear his word?
Who has given heed to his word so as to proclaim it?
19 Look, the storm of the LORD!
Wrath has gone forth,
a whirling tempest;
it will burst upon the head of the wicked.
20 The anger of the LORD will not turn back
until he has executed and accomplished
the intents of his mind.

23.7 Isa 43.18, 19; Jer 16.14,15 **23.9** Hab 3.16; Jer 20.8,9 **23.10** Jer 5.7,8; Hos 4.2,3; Jer 9.10; 12.4 **23.11** Jer 6.13; 8.10; 7.9,10; 32.34 **23.12** Ps 35.6; Jn 12.35; Jer 11.23 **23.13** Hos 9.7,8; Jer 2.8 **23.14** Jer 5.30; 29.23; Ezek 13.22; Isa 1.9,10; Jer 20.16 **23.15** Jer 8.14; 9.15 **23.16** Jer 27.9,10; 14.14; 9.12, 20 **23.17** Jer 8.11; 13.10; 18.12; 5.12; Mic 3.11 **23.18** Job 15.8; 33.31 **23.19** Jer 25.32; 30.23 **23.20** Jer 30.24; Gen 49.1

[v] Gk: Heb *I*

In the latter days you will
understand it clearly.

21 I did not send the prophets,
yet they ran;
I did not speak to them,
yet they prophesied.
22 But if they had stood in my
council,
then they would have
proclaimed my words to
my people,
and they would have turned
them from their evil
way,
and from the evil of their
doings.

23 Am I a God near by, says the
LORD, and not a God far off? 24 Who
can hide in secret places so that I
cannot see them? says the LORD. Do
I not fill heaven and earth? says the
LORD. 25 I have heard what the
prophets have said who prophesy
lies in my name, saying, "I have
dreamed, I have dreamed!" 26 How
long? Will the hearts of the prophets ever turn back—those who
prophesy lies, and who prophesy
the deceit of their own heart?
27 They plan to make my people forget my name by their dreams that
they tell one another, just as their
ancestors forgot my name for Baal.
28 Let the prophet who has a dream
tell the dream, but let the one who
has my word speak my word faithfully. What has straw in common
with wheat? says the LORD. 29 Is not
my word like fire, says the LORD,
and like a hammer that breaks a
rock in pieces? 30 See, therefore, I
am against the prophets, says the
LORD, who steal my words from one
another. 31 See, I am against the
prophets, says the LORD, who use
their own tongues and say, "Says
the LORD." 32 See, I am against
those who prophesy lying dreams,
says the LORD, and who tell them,
and who lead my people astray by
their lies and their recklessness,
when I did not send them or appoint them; so they do not profit
this people at all, says the LORD.
33 When this people, or a
prophet, or a priest asks you,
"What is the burden of the LORD?"
you shall say to them, "You are the
burden,[w] and I will cast you off,
says the LORD." 34 And as for the
prophet, priest, or the people who
say, "The burden of the LORD," I
will punish them and their households. 35 Thus shall you say to one
another, among yourselves, "What
has the LORD answered?" or "What
has the LORD spoken?" 36 But "the
burden of the LORD" you shall mention no more, for the burden is everyone's own word, and so you pervert the words of the living God, the
LORD of hosts, our God. 37 Thus you
shall ask the prophet, "What has
the LORD answered you?" or "What
has the LORD spoken?" 38 But if you
say, "the burden of the LORD," thus
says the LORD: Because you have
said these words, "the burden of
the LORD," when I sent to you, saying, You shall not say, "the burden
of the LORD," 39 therefore, I will
surely lift you up[x] and cast you
away from my presence, you and
the city that I gave to you and your
ancestors. 40 And I will bring upon
you everlasting disgrace and perpetual shame, which shall not be
forgotten.

23.21 Jer 14.14; 27.15; 29.9 **23.22** Jer 9.12; 35.15; 1 Thes 1.9, 10 **23.23** Ps 139.1-10; Jer 50.51 **23.24** Ps 139.7-12; Isa 29.15; Am 9.2; 1 Kings 8.27 **23.25** Jer 8.6; 14.14; 29.8 **23.27** Judg 3.7; 8.33,34 **23.28** Jer 9.12,20 **23.29** Jer 5.14; 20.9; 2 Cor 10.4, 5 **23.30** Ezek 13.8 **23.31** v. 17 **23.32** vv. 25,28 **23.33** Isa 13.1; Hab 1.1; Mal 1.1; v. 39 **23.34** Lam 2.14; Zech 13.3 **23.35** Jer 33.3; 42.4 **23.36** Jer 10.10 **23.38** v. 36 **23.39** Jer 7.14,15; Ezek 8.18 **23.40** Jer 20.11 **24.1** Am 8.1; 2 Kings 24.10-16; 2 Chr 36.10; Jer 22.24; 29.2 **24.2** Nah 3.12; Jer 27.19 **24.3** Jer 1.11,13

The Good and the Bad Figs

24 The LORD showed me two
baskets of figs placed before the temple of the LORD. This
was after King Nebuchadrezzar of
Babylon had taken into exile from
Jerusalem King Jeconiah son of Jehoiakim of Judah, together with
the officials of Judah, the artisans,
and the smiths, and had brought
them to Babylon. 2 One basket had
very good figs, like first-ripe figs,
but the other basket had very bad
figs, so bad that they could not be
eaten. 3 And the LORD said to me,
"What do you see, Jeremiah?" I
said, "Figs, the good figs very good,
and the bad figs very bad, so bad
that they cannot be eaten."
4 Then the word of the LORD

[w] Gk Vg: Heb *What burden* [x] Heb Mss Gk Vg: MT *forget you*

came to me: [5]Thus says the LORD, the God of Israel: Like these good figs, so I will regard as good the exiles from Judah, whom I have sent away from this place to the land of the Chaldeans. [6]I will set my eyes upon them for good, and I will bring them back to this land. I will build them up, and not tear them down; I will plant them, and not pluck them up. [7]I will give them a heart to know that I am the LORD; and they shall be my people and I will be their God, for they shall return to me with their whole heart.

8 But thus says the LORD: Like the bad figs that are so bad they cannot be eaten, so will I treat King Zedekiah of Judah, his officials, the remnant of Jerusalem who remain in this land, and those who live in the land of Egypt. [9]I will make them a horror, an evil thing, to all the kingdoms of the earth—a disgrace, a byword, a taunt, and a curse in all the places where I shall drive them. [10]And I will send sword, famine, and pestilence upon them, until they are utterly destroyed from the land that I gave to them and their ancestors.

The Babylonian Captivity Foretold

25 The word that came to Jeremiah concerning all the people of Judah, in the fourth year of King Jehoiakim son of Josiah of Judah (that was the first year of King Nebuchadrezzar of Babylon), [2]which the prophet Jeremiah spoke to all the people of Judah and all the inhabitants of Jerusalem: [3]For twenty-three years, from the thirteenth year of King Josiah son of Amon of Judah, to this day, the word of the LORD has come to me, and I have spoken persistently to you, but you have not listened. [4]And though the LORD persistently sent you all his servants the prophets, you have neither listened nor inclined your ears to hear [5]when they said, "Turn now, everyone of you, from your evil way and wicked doings, and you will remain upon the land that the LORD has given to you and your ancestors from of old and forever; [6]do not go after other gods to serve and worship them, and do not provoke me to anger with the work of your hands. Then I will do you no harm." [7]Yet you did not listen to me, says the LORD, and so you have provoked me to anger with the work of your hands to your own harm.

8 Therefore thus says the LORD of hosts: Because you have not obeyed my words, [9]I am going to send for all the tribes of the north, says the LORD, even for King Nebuchadrezzar of Babylon, my servant, and I will bring them against this land and its inhabitants, and against all these nations around; I will utterly destroy them, and make them an object of horror and of hissing, and an everlasting disgrace.[y] [10]And I will banish from them the sound of mirth and the sound of gladness, the voice of the bridegroom and the voice of the bride, the sound of the millstones and the light of the lamp. [11]This whole land shall become a ruin and a waste, and these nations shall serve the king of Babylon seventy years. [12]Then after seventy years are completed, I will punish the king of Babylon and that nation, the land of the Chaldeans, for their iniquity, says the LORD, making the land an everlasting waste. [13]I will bring upon that land all the words that I have uttered against it, everything written in this book, which Jeremiah prophesied against all the nations. [14]For many nations and great kings shall make slaves of them also; and I will repay them according to their deeds and the work of their hands.

The Cup of God's Wrath

15 For thus the LORD, the God of Israel, said to me: Take from my hand this cup of the wine of wrath, and make all the nations to whom I send you drink it. [16]They shall

24.5 Nah 1.7; Zech 13.9
24.6 Jer 29.10; Ezek 11.17; Jer 33.7; 42.10
24.7 Jer 31.33; 32.40; Zech 8.8; Heb 8.10; Jer 29.13
24.8 Jer 29.17; 39.5,9; 44.26-30
24.9 Jer 15.4; 29.18; 34.17; 1 Kings 9.7; Ps 44.13,14; Isa 65.15
24.10 Isa 51.19; Jer 21.9; 27.8
25.1 Jer 36.1; 2 Kings 24.1, 2
25.2 Jer 18.11
25.3 Jer 1.2; 2 Chr 34.1-3, 8; Jer 36.2; 7.13; 22.21
25.4 Jer 7.13,25; 26.5
25.5 Isa 55.6,7; Jer 4.1; 7.7
25.6 Deut 6.14; 8.19; Jer 35.15
25.7 Deut 32.21; 2 Kings 17.17; 21.15; Jer 7.19
25.9 Jer 1.15; 27.6; 18.16
25.10 Isa 24.7; Ezek 26.13; Eccl 12.4; Isa 47.2
25.11 Jer 4.27; 12.11,12; Dan 9.2
25.12 Ezra 1.1; Jer 29.10; Isa 13.14; 13.19; 14.23
25.14 Jer 50.9; 51.27,28; 50.41; 51.6, 24

25.15 Ps 75.8; Isa 51.17 **25.16** Jer 51.7; Nah 3.11

y Gk Compare Syr: Heb *and everlasting desolations*

drink and stagger and go out of
their minds because of the sword
that I am sending among them.
17 So I took the cup from the
LORD's hand, and made all the nations to whom the LORD sent me
drink it: 18 Jerusalem and the towns
of Judah, its kings and officials, to
make them a desolation and a
waste, an object of hissing and of
cursing, as they are today; 19 Pharaoh king of Egypt, his servants, his
officials, and all his people; 20 all
the mixed people;[z] all the kings of
the land of Uz; all the kings of the
land of the Philistines—Ashkelon,
Gaza, Ekron, and the remnant of
Ashdod; 21 Edom, Moab, and the
Ammonites; 22 all the kings of Tyre,
all the kings of Sidon, and the kings
of the coastland across the sea;
23 Dedan, Tema, Buz, and all who
have shaven temples; 24 all the
kings of Arabia and all the kings of
the mixed peoples[z] that live in the
desert; 25 all the kings of Zimri, all
the kings of Elam, and all the kings
of Media; 26 all the kings of the
north, far and near, one after another, and all the kingdoms of the
world that are on the face of the
earth. And after them the king of
Sheshach[a] shall drink.
27 Then you shall say to them,
Thus says the LORD of hosts, the
God of Israel: Drink, get drunk and
vomit, fall and rise no more, because of the sword that I am sending among you.
28 And if they refuse to accept
the cup from your hand to drink,
then you shall say to them: Thus
says the LORD of hosts: You must
drink! 29 See, I am beginning to
bring disaster on the city that is
called by my name, and how can
you possibly avoid punishment?
You shall not go unpunished, for I
am summoning a sword against all
the inhabitants of the earth, says
the LORD of hosts.
30 You, therefore, shall prophesy against them all these words,
and say to them:

The LORD will roar from on
high,
and from his holy
habitation utter his voice;
he will roar mightily against
his fold,
and shout, like those who
tread grapes,
against all the inhabitants
of the earth.
31 The clamor will resound to
the ends of the earth,
for the LORD has an
indictment against the
nations;
he is entering into judgment
with all flesh,
and the guilty he will put
to the sword,
says the LORD.

32 Thus says the LORD of hosts:
See, disaster is spreading
from nation to nation,
and a great tempest is
stirring
from the farthest parts of
the earth!

33 Those slain by the LORD on
that day shall extend from one end
of the earth to the other. They shall
not be lamented, or gathered, or
buried; they shall become dung on
the surface of the ground.

34 Wail, you shepherds, and cry
out;
roll in ashes, you lords of
the flock,
for the days of your slaughter
have come—and your
dispersions,[z]
and you shall fall like a
choice vessel.
35 Flight shall fail the
shepherds,
and there shall be no
escape for the lords of
the flock.
36 Hark! the cry of the
shepherds,
and the wail of the lords of
the flock!
For the LORD is despoiling
their pasture,
37 and the peaceful folds are
devastated,

25.17 v. 28; Ezek 43.3
25.18 Isa 51.17; Jer 24.9; 44.22
25.19 Jer 46.2-28
25.20 Job 1.1; Jer 47.1-7; Isa 20.1
25.21 Jer 49.1-22; 48.1-47
25.22 Jer 47.4; 49.23
25.23 Jer 49.7,8; 9.26; 49.32
25.24 2 Chr 9.14
25.26 Jer 50.9
25.27 Hab 2.16; Ezek 21.4,5
25.29 Ezek 9.6; 1 Pet 4.17; 1 Kings 8.43; v. 31
25.30 Isa 42.13; Joel 3.16; Am 1.2; Isa 16.9
25.31 Hos 4.1; Mic 6.2; Joel 3.2
25.32 Isa 34.2; Jer 29.19; 30.23
25.33 Isa 66.16; Ps 79.3; Jer 16.4; Isa 5.25
25.34 Jer 6.26; Ezek 27.30; Isa 34.7; Jer 50.27
25.35 Jer 11.11
25.36 v. 34
25.37 Isa 27.10, 11; Jer 5.17; 13.10

[z] Meaning of Heb uncertain [a] *Sheshach* is a cryptogram for *Babel*, Babylon

because of the fierce anger
of the LORD.
38 Like a lion he has left his
covert;
for their land has become a
waste
because of the cruel sword,
and because of his fierce
anger.

Jeremiah's Prophecies in the Temple

26 At the beginning of the
reign of King Jehoiakim
son of Josiah of Judah, this word
came from the LORD: 2 Thus says the
LORD: Stand in the court of the
LORD's house, and speak to all the
cities of Judah that come to worship in the house of the LORD;
speak to them all the words that I
command you; do not hold back a
word. 3 It may be that they will listen, all of them, and will turn from
their evil way, that I may change
my mind about the disaster that I
intend to bring on them because of
their evil doings. 4 You shall say to
them: Thus says the LORD: If you
will not listen to me, to walk in my
law that I have set before you, 5 and
to heed the words of my servants
the prophets whom I send to you
urgently—though you have not
heeded— 6 then I will make this
house like Shiloh, and I will make
this city a curse for all the nations
of the earth.

7 The priests and the prophets
and all the people heard Jeremiah
speaking these words in the house
of the LORD. 8 And when Jeremiah
had finished speaking all that the
LORD had commanded him to speak
to all the people, then the priests
and the prophets and all the people
laid hold of him, saying, "You shall
die! 9 Why have you prophesied in
the name of the LORD, saying, 'This
house shall be like Shiloh, and this
city shall be desolate, without inhabitant'?" And all the people
gathered around Jeremiah in the
house of the LORD.

10 When the officials of Judah
heard these things, they came up
from the king's house to the house
of the LORD and took their seat in
the entry of the New Gate of the
house of the LORD. 11 Then the
priests and the prophets said to the
officials and to all the people,
"This man deserves the sentence of
death because he has prophesied
against this city, as you have heard
with your own ears."

12 Then Jeremiah spoke to all
the officials and all the people, saying, "It is the LORD who sent me to
prophesy against this house and
this city all the words you have
heard. 13 Now therefore amend
your ways and your doings, and
obey the voice of the LORD your
God, and the LORD will change his
mind about the disaster that he has
pronounced against you. 14 But as
for me, here I am in your hands. Do
with me as seems good and right to
you. 15 Only know for certain that if
you put me to death, you will be
bringing innocent blood upon
yourselves and upon this city and
its inhabitants, for in truth the
LORD sent me to you to speak all
these words in your ears."

16 Then the officials and all the
people said to the priests and the
prophets, "This man does not deserve the sentence of death, for he
has spoken to us in the name of the
LORD our God." 17 And some of the
elders of the land arose and said to
all the assembled people, 18 "Micah
of Moresheth, who prophesied during the days of King Hezekiah of
Judah, said to all the people of Judah: 'Thus says the LORD of hosts,
Zion shall be plowed as a
field;
Jerusalem shall become a
heap of ruins,
and the mountain of the
house a wooded
height.'
19 Did King Hezekiah of Judah and
all Judah actually put him to
death? Did he not fear the LORD and
entreat the favor of the LORD, and
did not the LORD change his mind
about the disaster that he had pronounced against them? But we are

25.38 Jer 4.7
26.1 2 Kings 23.36; 2 Chr 36.4, 5; Jer 7.1,2
26.2 Jer 19.14; Lk 19.47,48; Jer 1.17; Acts 20.20, 27; Deut 4.2
26.3 Jer 36.3-7; 18.8
26.4 Lev 26.14; Deut 28.15; Jer 17.27; 32.23; 44.10, 23
26.5 2 Kings 9.7; Jer 25.3,4
26.6 1 Sam 4.10, 11; Isa 65.15; Jer 24.9
26.8 Jer 20.1,2; 11.19; 18.23
26.9 Jer 9.11; 33.10
26.10 Jer 36.10
26.11 Jer 18.23; Deut 18.20; Mt 26.66; Jer 38.4; Acts 6.11-14
26.12 Jer 1.17,18; 5.6; 46.16
26.13 Jer 7.3,5; 18.11; Joel 2.14; Jon 3.9; 4.2
26.14 Jer 38.5
26.15 Prov 6.16, 17; Jer 7.6
26.16 v. 11; Acts 5.34-39; 23.9,29; 25.25; 26.31
26.18 Mic 1.1; Ps 79.1; Mic 3.12; Zech 8.3
26.19 2 Chr 29.6-11; 32.26; 2 Sam 24.16; Acts 5.39

about to bring great disaster on ourselves!"

20 There was another man prophesying in the name of the Lord, Uriah son of Shemaiah from Kiriath-jearim. He prophesied against this city and against this land in words exactly like those of Jeremiah. 21 And when King Jehoiakim, with all his warriors and all the officials, heard his words, the king sought to put him to death; but when Uriah heard of it, he was afraid and fled and escaped to Egypt. 22 Then King Jehoiakim sent[b] Elnathan son of Achbor and men with him to Egypt, 23 and they took Uriah from Egypt and brought him to King Jehoiakim, who struck him down with the sword and threw his dead body into the burial place of the common people.

24 But the hand of Ahikam son of Shaphan was with Jeremiah so that he was not given over into the hands of the people to be put to death.

The Sign of the Yoke

27 In the beginning of the reign of King Zedekiah[c] son of Josiah of Judah, this word came to Jeremiah from the Lord. 2 Thus the Lord said to me: Make yourself a yoke of straps and bars, and put them on your neck. 3 Send word[d] to the king of Edom, the king of Moab, the king of the Ammonites, the king of Tyre, and the king of Sidon by the hand of the envoys who have come to Jerusalem to King Zedekiah of Judah. 4 Give them this charge for their masters: Thus says the Lord of hosts, the God of Israel: This is what you shall say to your masters: 5 It is I who by my great power and my outstretched arm have made the earth, with the people and animals that are on the earth, and I give it to whomever I please. 6 Now I have given all these lands into the hand of King Nebuchadnezzar of Babylon, my servant, and I have given him even the wild animals of the field to serve him. 7 All the nations shall serve him and his son and his grandson, until the time of his own land comes; then many nations and great kings shall make him their slave.

8 But if any nation or kingdom will not serve this king, Nebuchadnezzar of Babylon, and put its neck under the yoke of the king of Babylon, then I will punish that nation with the sword, with famine, and with pestilence, says the Lord, until I have completed its[e] destruction by his hand. 9 You, therefore, must not listen to your prophets, your diviners, your dreamers,[f] your soothsayers, or your sorcerers, who are saying to you, 'You shall not serve the king of Babylon.' 10 For they are prophesying a lie to you, with the result that you will be removed far from your land; I will drive you out, and you will perish. 11 But any nation that will bring its neck under the yoke of the king of Babylon and serve him, I will leave on its own land, says the Lord, to till it and live there.

12 I spoke to King Zedekiah of Judah in the same way: Bring your necks under the yoke of the king of Babylon, and serve him and his people, and live. 13 Why should you and your people die by the sword, by famine, and by pestilence, as the Lord has spoken concerning any nation that will not serve the king of Babylon? 14 Do not listen to the words of the prophets who are telling you not to serve the king of Babylon, for they are prophesying a lie to you. 15 I have not sent them, says the Lord, but they are prophesying falsely in my name, with the result that I will drive you out and you will perish, you and the prophets who are prophesying to you.

16 Then I spoke to the priests and to all this people, saying, Thus says the Lord: Do not listen to the words of your prophets who are prophesying to you, saying, "The vessels of the Lord's house will soon be brought back from Bab-

26.20 Josh 9.17; 1 Sam 6.21; 7.2
26.21 1 Kings 19.2-4; Mt 10.23,28
26.22 Jer 36.12
26.23 Jer 2.30
26.24 2 Kings 22.12-14; Jer 39.14
27.1 Jer 26.1
27.2 Jer 28.10,13
27.3 Jer 25.21,22
27.5 Jer 10.12; 51.15; Ps 115.15, 16; Acts 17.26
27.6 Ezek 29.18-20; Jer 25.9; 28.14
27.7 Jer 44.30; 46.13; 25.12; Isa 14.4-6
27.8 Jer 38.17-19; Ezek 17.19-21; Jer 29.17, 18; Ezek 14.21
27.9 Ex 22.18; Deut 18.10; Isa 8.19; Mal 3.5
27.10 Jer 23.25; 8.19; 32.31
27.11 Jer 21.9
27.12 Jer 28.1
27.13 Ezek 18.31
27.14 Jer 14.14; Ezek 13.22
27.15 Jer 23.21, 25; 6.13-15; 14.15,16
27.16 2 Chr 36.7, 10; Jer 28.3; Dan 1.2; v. 10

[b] Heb adds *men to Egypt* [c] Another reading is *Jehoiakim* [d] Cn: Heb *send them* [e] Heb *their* [f] Gk Syr Vg: Heb *dreams*

ylon," for they are prophesying a lie to you. 17 Do not listen to them; serve the king of Babylon and live. Why should this city become a desolation? 18 If indeed they are prophets, and if the word of the LORD is with them, then let them intercede with the LORD of hosts, that the vessels left in the house of the LORD, in the house of the king of Judah, and in Jerusalem may not go to Babylon. 19 For thus says the LORD of hosts concerning the pillars, the sea, the stands, and the rest of the vessels that are left in this city, 20 which King Nebuchadnezzar of Babylon did not take away when he took into exile from Jerusalem to Babylon King Jeconiah son of Jehoiakim of Judah, and all the nobles of Judah and Jerusalem— 21 thus says the LORD of hosts, the God of Israel, concerning the vessels left in the house of the LORD, in the house of the king of Judah, and in Jerusalem: 22 They shall be carried to Babylon, and there they shall stay, until the day when I give attention to them, says the LORD. Then I will bring them up and restore them to this place.

Hananiah Opposes Jeremiah and Dies

28 In that same year, at the beginning of the reign of King Zedekiah of Judah, in the fifth month of the fourth year, the prophet Hananiah son of Azzur, from Gibeon, spoke to me in the house of the LORD, in the presence of the priests and all the people, saying, 2 "Thus says the LORD of hosts, the God of Israel: I have broken the yoke of the king of Babylon. 3 Within two years I will bring back to this place all the vessels of the LORD's house, which King Nebuchadnezzar of Babylon took away from this place and carried to Babylon. 4 I will also bring back to this place King Jeconiah son of Jehoiakim of Judah, and all the exiles from Judah who went to Babylon, says the LORD, for I will break the yoke of the king of Babylon."

5 Then the prophet Jeremiah spoke to the prophet Hananiah in the presence of the priests and all the people who were standing in the house of the LORD; 6 and the prophet Jeremiah said, "Amen! May the LORD do so; may the LORD fulfill the words that you have prophesied, and bring back to this place from Babylon the vessels of the house of the LORD, and all the exiles. 7 But listen now to this word that I speak in your hearing and in the hearing of all the people. 8 The prophets who preceded you and me from ancient times prophesied war, famine, and pestilence against many countries and great kingdoms. 9 As for the prophet who prophesies peace, when the word of that prophet comes true, then it will be known that the LORD has truly sent the prophet."

10 Then the prophet Hananiah took the yoke from the neck of the prophet Jeremiah, and broke it. 11 And Hananiah spoke in the presence of all the people, saying, "Thus says the LORD: This is how I will break the yoke of King Nebuchadnezzar of Babylon from the neck of all the nations within two years." At this, the prophet Jeremiah went his way.

12 Sometime after the prophet Hananiah had broken the yoke from the neck of the prophet Jeremiah, the word of the LORD came to Jeremiah: 13 Go, tell Hananiah, Thus says the LORD: You have broken wooden bars only to forge iron bars in place of them! 14 For thus says the LORD of hosts, the God of Israel: I have put an iron yoke on the neck of all these nations so that they may serve King Nebuchadnezzar of Babylon, and they shall indeed serve him; I have even given him the wild animals. 15 And the prophet Jeremiah said to the prophet Hananiah, "Listen, Hananiah, the LORD has not sent you, and you made this people trust in a lie. 16 Therefore thus says the LORD: I am going to send you off the face of the earth. Within this year you will be dead, because you have spoken rebellion against the LORD."

27.17 v. 13
27.18 1 Sam 7.8; 12.19,23
27.19 2 Kings 25.13, 17; Jer 52.17-23
27.20 2 Kings 24.14-16; Jer 24.1
27.22 2 Kings 25.13; 2 Chr 36.18; Jer 29.10; 32.5; Ezra 1.7; 7.19
28.1 Jer 27.1,3, 12; Josh 9.3; 10.12
28.3 2 Kings 24.13; 2 Chr 36.10; Jer 27.12
28.4 Jer 22.24, 26,27; 27.8
28.5 v. 1
28.6 1 Kings 1.36; Jer 11.5
28.7 1 Kings 22.28
28.8 1 Kings 14.15; Isa 5.5-7; Joel 1.20; Am 1.2; Nah 1.2
28.9 Deut 18.22
28.10 Jer 27.2
28.11 Jer 14.14; 27.10
28.12 Jer 1.2
28.13 Ps 107.16; Isa 45.2
28.14 Deut 28.48; Jer 27.6-8; 25.11
28.15 Jer 29.31; Ezek 13.22
28.16 Deut 6.15; 13.5; Jer 29.32

17 In that same year, in the seventh month, the prophet Hananiah
died.

Jeremiah's Letter to the Exiles in Babylon

29 These are the words of the
letter that the prophet Jeremiah sent from Jerusalem to the
remaining elders among the exiles,
and to the priests, the prophets,
and all the people, whom Nebuchadnezzar had taken into exile
from Jerusalem to Babylon. 2 This
was after King Jeconiah, and the
queen mother, the court officials,
the leaders of Judah and Jerusalem, the artisans, and the smiths
had departed from Jerusalem.
3 The letter was sent by the hand of
Elasah son of Shaphan and Gemariah son of Hilkiah, whom King
Zedekiah of Judah sent to Babylon
to King Nebuchadnezzar of Babylon. It said: 4 Thus says the LORD of
hosts, the God of Israel, to all the
exiles whom I have sent into exile
from Jerusalem to Babylon: 5 Build
houses and live in them; plant gardens and eat what they produce.
6 Take wives and have sons and
daughters; take wives for your sons,
and give your daughters in marriage, that they may bear sons and
daughters; multiply there, and do
not decrease. 7 But seek the welfare
of the city where I have sent you
into exile, and pray to the LORD on
its behalf, for in its welfare you will
find your welfare. 8 For thus says
the LORD of hosts, the God of Israel:
Do not let the prophets and the diviners who are among you deceive
you, and do not listen to the
dreams that they dream,[g] 9 for it is
a lie that they are prophesying to
you in my name; I did not send
them, says the LORD.

10 For thus says the LORD: Only
when Babylon's seventy years are
completed will I visit you, and I will
fulfill to you my promise and bring
you back to this place. 11 For surely
I know the plans I have for you,
says the LORD, plans for your welfare and not for harm, to give you a
future with hope. 12 Then when you
call upon me and come and pray to
me, I will hear you. 13 When you
search for me, you will find me; if
you seek me with all your heart, 14 I
will let you find me, says the LORD,
and I will restore your fortunes and
gather you from all the nations and
all the places where I have driven
you, says the LORD, and I will bring
you back to the place from which I
sent you into exile.

15 Because you have said, "The
LORD has raised up prophets for us
in Babylon,"— 16 Thus says the
LORD concerning the king who sits
on the throne of David, and concerning all the people who live in
this city, your kinsfolk who did not
go out with you into exile: 17 Thus
says the LORD of hosts, I am going to
let loose on them sword, famine,
and pestilence, and I will make
them like rotten figs that are so bad
they cannot be eaten. 18 I will pursue them with the sword, with famine, and with pestilence, and will
make them a horror to all the kingdoms of the earth, to be an object
of cursing, and horror, and hissing,
and a derision among all the nations where I have driven them,
19 because they did not heed my
words, says the LORD, when I persistently sent to you my servants the
prophets, but they[h] would not listen, says the LORD. 20 But now, all
you exiles whom I sent away from
Jerusalem to Babylon, hear the
word of the LORD: 21 Thus says the
LORD of hosts, the God of Israel,
concerning Ahab son of Kolaiah
and Zedekiah son of Maaseiah,
who are prophesying a lie to you in
my name: I am going to deliver
them into the hand of King Nebuchadrezzar of Babylon, and he shall
kill them before your eyes. 22 And
on account of them this curse shall
be used by all the exiles from Judah in Babylon: "The LORD make
you like Zedekiah and Ahab, whom
the king of Babylon roasted in the
fire," 23 because they have perpetrated outrage in Israel and have

29.1 vv. 25,29
29.2 2 Kings 24.12-16; Jer 22.24-28; 24.1; 28.4
29.4ff Isa 10.5,6; Jer 24.5
29.6 Jer 16.2-4
29.7 Ezra 6.10; Dan 4.19; 1 Tim 2.2
29.8 Jer 27.9; 14.14; 23.21, 25,27
29.9 Jer 27.15; v. 31
29.10 2 Chr 36.21, 22; Jer 25.12; 27.22; Dan 9.2
29.11 Isa 40.9-11; Jer 30.18-22; 31.17
29.12 Ps 50.15; Jer 33.3; Ps 145.19
29.13 1 Chr 22.19; 2 Chr 22.9; Jer 24.7
29.14 Deut 30.1-10; Jer 30.3; Isa 43.5,6; Jer 3.14
29.16 Jer 38.2,3, 17-23
29.17 Jer 27.8; 32.24; 24.3, 8-10
29.18 Isa 65.15; Jer 42.18; 25.9
29.19 Jer 6.19; 25.4; 26.5
29.20 Jer 24.5
29.21 vv. 8,9
29.22 Isa 65.15; Dan 3.6
29.23 2 Sam 13.12; Prov 5.21; Jer 16.17

[g] Cn: Heb *your dreams that you cause to dream* [h] Syr: Heb *you*

committed adultery with their
neighbors' wives, and have spoken
in my name lying words that I did
not command them; I am the one
who knows and bears witness, says
the LORD.

The Letter of Shemaiah

24 To Shemaiah of Nehelam
you shall say: 25 Thus says the LORD
of hosts, the God of Israel: In your
own name you sent a letter to all
the people who are in Jerusalem,
and to the priest Zephaniah son of
Maaseiah, and to all the priests,
saying, 26 The LORD himself has
made you priest instead of the
priest Jehoiada, so that there may
be officers in the house of the LORD
to control any madman who plays
the prophet, to put him in the
stocks and the collar. 27 So now
why have you not rebuked Jeremiah of Anathoth who plays the
prophet for you? 28 For he has actually sent to us in Babylon, saying,
"It will be a long time; build houses
and live in them, and plant gardens
and eat what they produce."
29 The priest Zephaniah read
this letter in the hearing of the
prophet Jeremiah. 30 Then the
word of the LORD came to Jeremiah:
31 Send to all the exiles, saying,
Thus says the LORD concerning
Shemaiah of Nehelam: Because
Shemaiah has prophesied to you,
though I did not send him, and has
led you to trust in a lie, 32 therefore
thus says the LORD: I am going to
punish Shemaiah of Nehelam and
his descendants; he shall not have
anyone living among this people to
see[i] the good that I am going to do
to my people, says the LORD, for he
has spoken rebellion against the
LORD.

Restoration Promised for Israel and Judah

30 The word that came to Jeremiah from the LORD:
2 Thus says the LORD, the God of Israel: Write in a book all the words
that I have spoken to you. 3 For the
days are surely coming, says the
LORD, when I will restore the fortunes of my people, Israel and Judah, says the LORD, and I will bring
them back to the land that I gave to
their ancestors and they shall take
possession of it.
4 These are the words that the
LORD spoke concerning Israel and
Judah:
5 Thus says the LORD:
We have heard a cry of
panic,
of terror, and no peace.
6 Ask now, and see,
can a man bear a child?
Why then do I see every man
with his hands on his loins
like a woman in labor?
Why has every face turned
pale?
7 Alas! that day is so great
there is none like it;
it is a time of distress for
Jacob;
yet he shall be rescued
from it.
8 On that day, says the LORD of
hosts, I will break the yoke from off
his[j] neck, and I will burst his[j]
bonds, and strangers shall no more
make a servant of him. 9 But they
shall serve the LORD their God and
David their king, whom I will raise
up for them.

10 But as for you, have no fear,
my servant Jacob, says
the LORD,
and do not be dismayed,
O Israel;
for I am going to save you
from far away,
and your offspring from the
land of their captivity.
Jacob shall return and have
quiet and ease,
and no one shall make him
afraid.
11 For I am with you, says the
LORD, to save you;
I will make an end of all the
nations
among which I scattered
you,

29.24 vv. 31,32
29.25 vv. 1,29; 2 Kings 25.18; Jer 21.1
29.26 Jer 20.1; 2 Kings 9.11; Acts 26.24; Jer 20.2
29.28 vv. 1,5,10
29.29 v. 25
29.31 vv. 20,24; Jer 14.14, 15; 28.15
29.32 Jer 36.31; 22.30; 17.6; 28.16
30.2 Jer 25.13; Hab 2.2
30.3 Jer 29.10; Ps 53.6; Zeph 3.20; Jer 16.15; Ezek 20.42
30.5 Isa 5.30; Am 5.16-18
30.6 Jer 4.31; 6.24
30.7 Isa 2.12; Joel 2.11; Lam 1.12; Jer 2.27,28; v. 10
30.8 Isa 9.4; Jer 27.2; Ezek 34.27
30.9 Isa 55.3,4; Ezek 34.23; 37.24; Hos 3.5; Lk 1.69; Acts 2.30; 13.23
30.10 Isa 43.5; 44.2; Jer 46.27, 28; Isa 60.4; Jer 33.16; Mic 4.4
30.11 Jer 46.28; 4.27; 10.24

[i] Gk: Heb *and he shall not see* [j] Cn: Heb *your*

but of you I will not make
an end.
I will chastise you in just
measure,
and I will by no means
leave you unpunished.

12 For thus says the LORD:
Your hurt is incurable,
your wound is grievous.
13 There is no one to uphold
your cause,
no medicine for your
wound,
no healing for you.
14 All your lovers have forgotten
you;
they care nothing for you;
for I have dealt you the blow
of an enemy,
the punishment of a
merciless foe,
because your guilt is great,
because your sins are so
numerous.
15 Why do you cry out over your
hurt?
Your pain is incurable.
Because your guilt is great,
because your sins are so
numerous,
I have done these things to
you.
16 Therefore all who devour you
shall be devoured,
and all your foes, everyone
of them, shall go into
captivity;
those who plunder you shall
be plundered,
and all who prey on you I
will make a prey.
17 For I will restore health to
you,
and your wounds I will
heal,
says the LORD,
because they have called you
an outcast:
"It is Zion; no one cares for
her!"

18 Thus says the LORD:
I am going to restore the
fortunes of the tents of
Jacob,
and have compassion on
his dwellings;
the city shall be rebuilt upon
its mound,
and the citadel set on its
rightful site.
19 Out of them shall come
thanksgiving,
and the sound of
merrymakers.
I will make them many, and
they shall not be few;
I will make them honored,
and they shall not be
disdained.
20 Their children shall be as of
old,
their congregation shall be
established before me;
and I will punish all who
oppress them.
21 Their prince shall be one of
their own,
their ruler shall come from
their midst;
I will bring him near, and he
shall approach me,
for who would otherwise
dare to approach me?
says the LORD.
22 And you shall be my people,
and I will be your God.

23 Look, the storm of the LORD!
Wrath has gone forth,
a whirling[k] tempest;
it will burst upon the head
of the wicked.
24 The fierce anger of the LORD
will not turn back
until he has executed and
accomplished
the intents of his mind.
In the latter days you will
understand this.

The Joyful Return of the Exiles

31 At that time, says the LORD,
I will be the God of all the
families of Israel, and they shall be
my people.
2 Thus says the LORD:
The people who survived the
sword
found grace in the
wilderness;

30.12 v. 15; Jer 15.18 **30.13** Jer 14.19; 46.11 **30.14** Lam 1.2; 2.4,5; Jer 5.6; 32.30-35 **30.16** Isa 33.1; 41.11; Jer 10.25; 50.10 **30.17** Jer 8.22; 22.33; 33.24 **30.18** Jer 31.23; Ps 102.13; Jer 31.4, 38-40 **30.19** Isa 35.10; Jer 31.4,12, 13; 33.10,11, 22 **30.20** Isa 54.13; Jer 31.17; Isa 54.14 **30.21** Num 16.5; Jer 50.44 **30.22** Jer 32.38; Ezek 11.20; 36.28; Zech 13.9 **30.23f** Jer 23.19, 20; 25.32 **30.24** Jer 4.8; 23.20 **31.1** Jer 30.22, 24; Isa 41.10; Rom 11.26-28 **31.2** Num 14.20; Josh 1.13; Isa 63.14

[k] One Ms: Meaning of MT uncertain

when Israel sought for rest,
3 the LORD appeared to him[l]
from far away.[m]
I have loved you with an
everlasting love;
therefore I have continued
my faithfulness to you.
4 Again I will build you, and
you shall be built,
O virgin Israel!
Again you shall take[n] your
tambourines,
and go forth in the dance
of the merrymakers.
5 Again you shall plant
vineyards
on the mountains of
Samaria;
the planters shall plant,
and shall enjoy the fruit.
6 For there shall be a day
when sentinels will call
in the hill country of
Ephraim:
"Come, let us go up to Zion,
to the LORD our God."

7 For thus says the LORD:
Sing aloud with gladness for
Jacob,
and raise shouts for the
chief of the nations;
proclaim, give praise, and
say,
"Save, O LORD, your people,
the remnant of Israel."
8 See, I am going to bring
them from the land of
the north,
and gather them from the
farthest parts of the
earth,
among them the blind and
the lame,
those with child and those
in labor, together;
a great company, they shall
return here.
9 With weeping they shall
come,
and with consolations[o] I
will lead them back,
I will let them walk by
brooks of water,
in a straight path in which
they shall not stumble;
for I have become a father to
Israel,
and Ephraim is my
firstborn.

10 Hear the word of the LORD,
O nations,
and declare it in the
coastlands far away;
say, "He who scattered Israel
will gather him,
and will keep him as a
shepherd a flock."
11 For the LORD has ransomed
Jacob,
and has redeemed him
from hands too strong
for him.
12 They shall come and sing
aloud on the height of
Zion,
and they shall be radiant
over the goodness of
the LORD,
over the grain, the wine, and
the oil,
and over the young of the
flock and the herd;
their life shall become like a
watered garden,
and they shall never
languish again.
13 Then shall the young women
rejoice in the dance,
and the young men and the
old shall be merry.
I will turn their mourning
into joy,
I will comfort them, and
give them gladness for
sorrow.
14 I will give the priests their
fill of fatness,
and my people shall be
satisfied with my
bounty,
says the LORD.

15 Thus says the LORD:
A voice is heard in Ramah,
lamentation and bitter
weeping.
Rachel is weeping for her
children;

31.3 Deut 7.8; Ps 25.6; Hos 11.4
31.4 Jer 30.19
31.5 Isa 65.21; Jer 50.19
31.6 Isa 2.3; Mic 4.2
31.7 Ps 14.7; Deut 28.13; Isa 61.9; Ps 28.9; Isa 37.31
31.8 Jer 3.18; 23.8; Isa 43.6; Ezek 20.34, 41; Isa 42.16; 40.11
31.9 Isa 43.19; 49.10,11; 64.8; Jer 3.4,19
31.10 Isa 66.19; Jer 50.19; Isa 40.11
31.11 Isa 44.23; 48.20; Jer 50.34; Isa 49.24,25
31.12 Ezek 17.23; Hos 3.5; Isa 58.11; 35.10; 65.19; Rev 21.4
31.13 Ps 30.11; Zech 8.4,5; Isa 61.3; 51.11
31.14 v. 25; Jer 50.19
31.15 Mt 2.17,18; Gen 37.35; Ps 77.2; Jer 10.20

[l] Gk: Heb *me* [m] Or *to him long ago* [n] Or *adorn yourself with* [o] Gk Compare Vg Tg: Heb *supplications*

she refuses to be comforted
for her children,
because they are no more.
16 Thus says the LORD:
Keep your voice from
weeping,
and your eyes from tears;
for there is a reward for your
work,
says the LORD:
they shall come back from
the land of the enemy;
17 there is hope for your future,
says the LORD:
your children shall come
back to their own
country.

18 Indeed I heard Ephraim
pleading:
"You disciplined me, and I
took the discipline;
I was like a calf untrained.
Bring me back, let me come
back,
for you are the LORD my
God.
19 For after I had turned away I
repented;
and after I was discovered,
I struck my thigh;
I was ashamed, and I was
dismayed
because I bore the disgrace
of my youth."
20 Is Ephraim my dear son?
Is he the child I delight in?
As often as I speak against
him,
I still remember him.
Therefore I am deeply moved
for him;
I will surely have mercy on
him,
says the LORD.

21 Set up road markers for
yourself,
make yourself guideposts;
consider well the highway,
the road by which you
went.
Return, O virgin Israel,
return to these your cities.
22 How long will you waver,
O faithless daughter?
For the LORD has created a
new thing on the earth:
a woman encompasses[p] a
man.

23 Thus says the LORD of hosts,
the God of Israel: Once more they
shall use these words in the land of
Judah and in its towns when I restore their fortunes:
"The LORD bless you,
O abode of
righteousness,
O holy hill!"
24 And Judah and all its towns shall
live there together, and the farmers
and those who wander[q] with their
flocks.
25 I will satisfy the weary,
and all who are faint I will
replenish.
26 Thereupon I awoke and
looked, and my sleep was pleasant
to me.

Individual Retribution

27 The days are surely coming,
says the LORD, when I will sow the
house of Israel and the house of Judah with the seed of humans and
the seed of animals. 28 And just as
I have watched over them to pluck
up and break down, to overthrow,
destroy, and bring evil, so I will
watch over them to build and to
plant, says the LORD. 29 In those
days they shall no longer say:
"The parents have eaten sour
grapes,
and the children's teeth are
set on edge."
30 But all shall die for their own
sins; the teeth of everyone who eats
sour grapes shall be set on edge.

A New Covenant

31 The days are surely coming,
says the LORD, when I will make a
new covenant with the house of Israel and the house of Judah. 32 It
will not be like the covenant that I
made with their ancestors when I
took them by the hand to bring
them out of the land of Egypt—a
covenant that they broke, though I

31.16 Isa 25.8; 30.19; Heb 6.10; vv. 4,5; Jer 30.3; Ezek 11.17
31.17 Jer 29.11
31.18 Job 5.17; Ps 94.12; Hos 4.16; Ps 80.3,7, 19; Jer 17.14; Acts 3.26
31.19 Ezek 36.31; Zech 12.10; Ezek 21.12; Jer 3.25; Ps 25.7; Jer 22.21
31.20 Hos 11.8; Gen 43.30; Isa 63.15; 55.7; Hos 14.4
31.21 Jer 6.16; 50.5; Isa 48.20; v. 4
31.22 Jer 2.18,23, 36; 49.4
31.23 Jer 30.18; 32.44; Isa 1.26; Jer 50.7; Zech 8.3
31.24 Jer 33.12,13
31.25 Mt 5.6
31.27 Ezek 36.9-11; Hos 2.23
31.28 Jer 44.27; 1.10
31.29 Ezek 18.2
31.30 Deut 24.16; Ezek 18.4, 20; Gal 6.5, 7
31.31 Jer 32.40; Ezek 37.26; Heb 8.8-12
31.32 Ex 19.5; 24.6-8; Deut 1.31; Jer 11.7,8; 3.14

[p] Meaning of Heb uncertain [q] Cn Compare Syr Vg Tg: Heb *and they shall wander*

was their husband,[r] says the LORD.
33 But this is the covenant that I
will make with the house of Israel
after those days, says the LORD: I
will put my law within them, and
I will write it on their hearts; and I
will be their God, and they shall be
my people. 34 No longer shall they
teach one another, or say to each
other, "Know the LORD," for they
shall all know me, from the least of
them to the greatest, says the LORD;
for I will forgive their iniquity, and
remember their sin no more.

35 Thus says the LORD,
who gives the sun for light
by day
and the fixed order of the
moon and the stars for
light by night,
who stirs up the sea so that
its waves roar—
the LORD of hosts is his
name:
36 If this fixed order were ever
to cease
from my presence, says the
LORD,
then also the offspring of
Israel would cease
to be a nation before me
forever.

37 Thus says the LORD:
If the heavens above can be
measured,
and the foundations of the
earth below can be
explored,
then I will reject all the
offspring of Israel
because of all they have
done,
says the LORD.

Jerusalem to Be Enlarged

38 The days are surely coming,
says the LORD, when the city shall
be rebuilt for the LORD from the
tower of Hananel to the Corner
Gate. 39 And the measuring line
shall go out farther, straight to the
hill Gareb, and shall then turn to
Goah. 40 The whole valley of the
dead bodies and the ashes, and all
the fields as far as the Wadi Kidron,
to the corner of the Horse Gate toward the east, shall be sacred to
the LORD. It shall never again be uprooted or overthrown.

Jeremiah Buys a Field During the Siege

32 The word that came to Jeremiah from the LORD in the
tenth year of King Zedekiah of Judah, which was the eighteenth year
of Nebuchadrezzar. 2 At that time
the army of the king of Babylon was
besieging Jerusalem, and the
prophet Jeremiah was confined in
the court of the guard that was in
the palace of the king of Judah,
3 where King Zedekiah of Judah
had confined him. Zedekiah had
said, "Why do you prophesy and
say: Thus says the LORD: I am going
to give this city into the hand of the
king of Babylon, and he shall take
it; 4 King Zedekiah of Judah shall
not escape out of the hands of the
Chaldeans, but shall surely be given into the hands of the king of
Babylon, and shall speak with him
face to face and see him eye to eye;
5 and he shall take Zedekiah to
Babylon, and there he shall remain
until I attend to him, says the LORD;
though you fight against the Chaldeans, you shall not succeed?"
6 Jeremiah said, The word of
the LORD came to me: 7 Hanamel
son of your uncle Shallum is going
to come to you and say, "Buy my
field that is at Anathoth, for the
right of redemption by purchase is
yours." 8 Then my cousin Hanamel
came to me in the court of the
guard, in accordance with the word
of the LORD, and said to me, "Buy
my field that is at Anathoth in the
land of Benjamin, for the right of
possession and redemption is
yours; buy it for yourself." Then I
knew that this was the word of the
LORD.
9 And I bought the field at Anathoth from my cousin Hanamel,
and weighed out the money to him,
seventeen shekels of silver. 10 I

31.33 Jer 32.40; 24.7; 32.38
31.34 1 Thes 4.9; Isa 54.13; Jn 6.45; Mic 7.18; Rom 11.27
31.35 Gen 1.16; Ps 19.1-6; Jer 10.16
31.36 Isa 54.9,10; Jer 33.20; Am 9.8,9
31.37 Jer 33.22-26
31.38 Neh 3.1; Zech 14.10; 2 Kings 14.13
31.40 Jer 7.32; 2 Sam 15.23; 2 Kings 23.6; Joel 3.17
32.1 2 Kings 25.1, 2; Jer 39.1; 25.1
32.2 Neh 3.25; Jer 37.21; 39.14
32.3 2 Kings 6.31, 32; Jer 26.8, 9; 34.2,3
32.4 Jer 38.18, 23; 39.5
32.5 Jer 39.7; 27.22; 34.4,5; 21.4
32.7 Jer 1.1; Lev 25.25; Ruth 4.4
32.8 vv. 2,7,25
32.9 Gen 23.16; 24.22; Ex 21.32
32.10 Ruth 4.1,9

[r] Or *master*

signed the deed, sealed it, got witnesses, and weighed the money on scales. 11 Then I took the sealed deed of purchase, containing the terms and conditions, and the open copy; 12 and I gave the deed of purchase to Baruch son of Neriah son of Mahseiah, in the presence of my cousin Hanamel, in the presence of the witnesses who signed the deed of purchase, and in the presence of all the Judeans who were sitting in the court of the guard. 13 In their presence I charged Baruch, saying, 14 Thus says the LORD of hosts, the God of Israel: Take these deeds, both this sealed deed of purchase and this open deed, and put them in an earthenware jar, in order that they may last for a long time. 15 For thus says the LORD of hosts, the God of Israel: Houses and fields and vineyards shall again be bought in this land.

Jeremiah Prays for Understanding

16 After I had given the deed of purchase to Baruch son of Neriah, I prayed to the LORD, saying: 17 Ah Lord GOD! It is you who made the heavens and the earth by your great power and by your outstretched arm! Nothing is too hard for you. 18 You show steadfast love to the thousandth generation,[s] but repay the guilt of parents into the laps of their children after them, O great and mighty God whose name is the LORD of hosts, 19 great in counsel and mighty in deed; whose eyes are open to all the ways of mortals, rewarding all according to their ways and according to the fruit of their doings. 20 You showed signs and wonders in the land of Egypt, and to this day in Israel and among all humankind, and have made yourself a name that continues to this very day. 21 You brought your people Israel out of the land of Egypt with signs and wonders, with a strong hand and outstretched arm, and with great terror; 22 and you gave them this land, which you swore to their ancestors to give them, a land flowing with milk and honey; 23 and they entered and took possession of it. But they did not obey your voice or follow your law; of all you commanded them to do, they did nothing. Therefore you have made all these disasters come upon them. 24 See, the siege ramps have been cast up against the city to take it, and the city, faced with sword, famine, and pestilence, has been given into the hands of the Chaldeans who are fighting against it. What you spoke has happened, as you yourself can see. 25 Yet you, O Lord GOD, have said to me, "Buy the field for money and get witnesses"—though the city has been given into the hands of the Chaldeans.

God's Assurance of the People's Return

26 The word of the LORD came to Jeremiah: 27 See, I am the LORD, the God of all flesh; is anything too hard for me? 28 Therefore, thus says the LORD: I am going to give this city into the hands of the Chaldeans and into the hand of King Nebuchadrezzar of Babylon, and he shall take it. 29 The Chaldeans who are fighting against this city shall come, set it on fire, and burn it, with the houses on whose roofs offerings have been made to Baal and libations have been poured out to other gods, to provoke me to anger. 30 For the people of Israel and the people of Judah have done nothing but evil in my sight from their youth; the people of Israel have done nothing but provoke me to anger by the work of their hands, says the LORD. 31 This city has aroused my anger and wrath, from the day it was built until this day, so that I will remove it from my sight 32 because of all the evil of the people of Israel and the people of Judah that they did to provoke me to anger—they, their kings and their officials, their priests and their prophets, the citizens of Judah and the inhabitants of Jerusalem. 33 They have turned their

32.11 Lk 2.27
32.12 Jer 36.4; 51.59
32.14 vv. 10-12
32.15 Jer 33.12, 13; Zech 3.10
32.17 Jer 1.6; 4.10; 2 Kings 19.15; Isa 40.26-28
32.18 Ex 34.7; Jer 20.11; 10.16
32.19 Isa 28.29; Jer 16.17; 17.10
32.20 Ex 9.16; Dan 9.15
32.21 Ex 6.6; 1 Chr 17.21
32.22 Ex 3.8,17; Jer 11.5
32.23 Jer 2.7; 26.4; 44.10; Neh 9.26; Jer 11.8; Dan 9.10-14
32.24 Jer 33.4; Ezek 14.21; Deut 4.26; Zech 1.6
32.25 vv. 8,24
32.27 Num 16.22
32.28 Jer 34.2,3
32.29 Jer 21.10; 37.8,10; 52.13; 19.13
32.30 Jer 2.7; 22.21; 25.7
32.31 2 Kings 23.27; 24.3
32.32 Isa 1.4-6; Dan 9.8
32.33 Jer 2.27; Ezek 8.16; Jer 35.15

[s] Or *to thousands*

backs to me, not their faces;
though I have taught them persistently, they would not listen and
accept correction. 34 They set up
their abominations in the house
that bears my name, and defiled it.
35 They built the high places of Baal
in the valley of the son of Hinnom,
to offer up their sons and daughters to Molech, though I did not
command them, nor did it enter my mind that they should do
this abomination, causing Judah
to sin.
36 Now therefore thus says the
LORD, the God of Israel, concerning
this city of which you say, "It is being given into the hand of the king
of Babylon by the sword, by famine, and by pestilence": 37 See, I am
going to gather them from all the
lands to which I drove them in my
anger and my wrath and in great indignation; I will bring them back to
this place, and I will settle them in
safety. 38 They shall be my people,
and I will be their God. 39 I will give
them one heart and one way, that
they may fear me for all time, for
their own good and the good of
their children after them. 40 I will
make an everlasting covenant with
them, never to draw back from doing good to them; and I will put the
fear of me in their hearts, so that
they may not turn from me. 41 I will
rejoice in doing good to them, and
I will plant them in this land in
faithfulness, with all my heart and
all my soul.
42 For thus says the LORD: Just
as I have brought all this great disaster upon this people, so I will
bring upon them all the good fortune that I now promise them.
43 Fields shall be bought in this
land of which you are saying, It is a
desolation, without human beings
or animals; it has been given into
the hands of the Chaldeans.
44 Fields shall be bought for money,
and deeds shall be signed and
sealed and witnessed, in the land
of Benjamin, in the places around
Jerusalem, and in the cities of Judah, of the hill country, of the
Shephelah, and of the Negeb; for I

32.34 Jer 7.30,31; Ezek 8.5,6
32.35 Jer 7.31; 19.5; Lev 18.21; 1 Kings 11.33
32.37 Deut 30.3; Jer 23.3,6; Zech 14.11
32.38 Jer 30.22; 31.33
32.39 Jer 24.7; Ezek 11.19, 20; 37.25
32.40 Isa 55.3; 31.31,33; Ezek 39.29
32.41 Deut 30.9; Zeph 3.17; Am 9.15
32.42 Jer 31.28; Zech 8.14, 15; Jer 33.14
32.43 vv. 15,25
32.44 Jer 17.26; 33.7,11,26

33.1 Jer 32.2,3
33.2 Jer 10.16; 51.19; Ex 15.3
33.3 Ps 50.15; Jer 29.12; 32.17,27; Isa 48.6
33.4 Jer 32.13, 14,24
33.5 Isa 8.17; Jer 21.10
33.6 Isa 66.12; Gal 5.22,23
33.7 Jer 32.44; Am 9.14,15
33.8 Mic 7.18; Zech 13.1; Heb 9.13,14
33.9 Isa 62.7; Jer 13.11; Isa 60.5
33.10 Jer 32.43; 26.9; 34.22
33.11 Isa 35.10; 51.3,11; 1 Chr 16.8, 34;

will restore their fortunes, says the
LORD.

Healing after Punishment

33 The word of the LORD came
to Jeremiah a second time,
while he was still confined in the
court of the guard: 2 Thus says the
LORD who made the earth,[t] the
LORD who formed it to establish
it—the LORD is his name: 3 Call to
me and I will answer you, and will
tell you great and hidden things
that you have not known. 4 For thus
says the LORD, the God of Israel,
concerning the houses of this city
and the houses of the kings of Judah that were torn down to make a
defense against the siege ramps
and before the sword:[u] 5 The Chaldeans are coming in to fight[v] and
to fill them with the dead bodies of
those whom I shall strike down in
my anger and my wrath, for I have
hidden my face from this city because of all their wickedness. 6 I am
going to bring it recovery and healing; I will heal them and reveal to
them abundance[u] of prosperity
and security. 7 I will restore the fortunes of Judah and the fortunes of
Israel, and rebuild them as they
were at first. 8 I will cleanse them
from all the guilt of their sin
against me, and I will forgive all the
guilt of their sin and rebellion
against me. 9 And this city[w] shall
be to me a name of joy, a praise and
a glory before all the nations of the
earth who shall hear of all the good
that I do for them; they shall fear
and tremble because of all the
good and all the prosperity I provide for it.
10 Thus says the LORD: In this
place of which you say, "It is a
waste without human beings or animals," in the towns of Judah and
the streets of Jerusalem that are
desolate, without inhabitants, human or animal, there shall once
more be heard 11 the voice of mirth
and the voice of gladness, the voice

2 Chr 5.13; Lev 7.12

[t] Gk: Heb *it* [u] Meaning of Heb uncertain
[v] Cn: Heb *They are coming in to fight against the Chaldeans* [w] Heb *And it*

of the bridegroom and the voice of the bride, the voices of those who sing, as they bring thank offerings to the house of the LORD:

"Give thanks to the LORD of
    hosts,
  for the LORD is good,
  for his steadfast love
    endures forever!"

For I will restore the fortunes of the land as at first, says the LORD.

12 Thus says the LORD of hosts: In this place that is waste, without human beings or animals, and in all its towns there shall again be pasture for shepherds resting their flocks. [13]In the towns of the hill country, of the Shephelah, and of the Negeb, in the land of Benjamin, the places around Jerusalem, and in the towns of Judah, flocks shall again pass under the hands of the one who counts them, says the LORD.

The Righteous Branch and the Covenant with David

14 The days are surely coming, says the LORD, when I will fulfill the promise I made to the house of Israel and the house of Judah. [15]In those days and at that time I will cause a righteous Branch to spring up for David; and he shall execute justice and righteousness in the land. [16]In those days Judah will be saved and Jerusalem will live in safety. And this is the name by which it will be called: "The LORD is our righteousness."

17 For thus says the LORD: David shall never lack a man to sit on the throne of the house of Israel, [18]and the levitical priests shall never lack a man in my presence to offer burnt offerings, to make grain offerings, and to make sacrifices for all time.

19 The word of the LORD came to Jeremiah: [20]Thus says the LORD: If any of you could break my covenant with the day and my covenant with the night, so that day and night would not come at their appointed time, [21]only then could my covenant with my servant David be broken, so that he would not have a son to reign on his throne, and my

33.12 Isa 65.10; Ezek 34.12-14
33.13 Jer 17.26; Lev 27.32; Lk 15.4
33.14 Jer 23.5; Ezek 34.23-25
33.15 Isa 4.2; 11.1; Zech 3.8; Ps 72.1-5
33.16 Jer 23.6; Isa 45.24, 25; Phil 3.9
33.17 2 Sam 7.16; 1 Kings 2.4; Lk 1.32,33
33.18 Deut 18.1; 24.8; Heb 13.15
33.20 Ps 89.37; Isa 54.9; Jer 31.36
33.21 Ps 89.34
33.22 Gen 15.5; 22.17; Jer 30.19
33.24 Neh 4.2-4; Ezek 36.2
33.25 Ps 74.16,17; Jer 31.35,36
33.26 Jer 31.37; Isa 14.1; Hos 1.7; 2.23
34.1 2 Kings 25.1ff; Jer 39.1; 1.15; Dan 2.37,38
34.2 Jer 22.1,2; 37.1-4; Jer 32.29
34.3 Jer 32.4; 2 Kings 25.6, 7; Jer 39.6,7
34.5 2 Chr 16.14; 21.19; Jer 22.18

covenant with my ministers the Levites. [22]Just as the host of heaven cannot be numbered and the sands of the sea cannot be measured, so I will increase the offspring of my servant David, and the Levites who minister to me.

23 The word of the LORD came to Jeremiah: [24]Have you not observed how these people say, "The two families that the LORD chose have been rejected by him," and how they hold my people in such contempt that they no longer regard them as a nation? [25]Thus says the LORD: Only if I had not established my covenant with day and night and the ordinances of heaven and earth, [26]would I reject the offspring of Jacob and of my servant David and not choose any of his descendants as rulers over the offspring of Abraham, Isaac, and Jacob. For I will restore their fortunes, and will have mercy upon them.

Death in Captivity Predicted for Zedekiah

34 The word that came to Jeremiah from the LORD, when King Nebuchadrezzar of Babylon and all his army and all the kingdoms of the earth and all the peoples under his dominion were fighting against Jerusalem and all its cities: [2]"Thus says the LORD, the God of Israel: Go and speak to King Zedekiah of Judah and say to him: Thus says the LORD: I am going to give this city into the hand of the king of Babylon, and he shall burn it with fire. [3]And you yourself shall not escape from his hand, but shall surely be captured and handed over to him; you shall see the king of Babylon eye to eye and speak with him face to face; and you shall go to Babylon. [4]Yet hear the word of the LORD, O King Zedekiah of Judah! Thus says the LORD concerning you: You shall not die by the sword; [5]you shall die in peace. And as spices were burned[x] for your ancestors, the earlier kings who preceded you, so they shall burn

[x] Heb *as there was burning*

spices[y] for you and lament for you,
saying, "Alas, lord!" For I have spoken the word, says the LORD.
6 Then the prophet Jeremiah
spoke all these words to Zedekiah
king of Judah, in Jerusalem, 7 when
the army of the king of Babylon was
fighting against Jerusalem and
against all the cities of Judah that
were left, Lachish and Azekah; for
these were the only fortified cities
of Judah that remained.

Treacherous Treatment of Slaves

8 The word that came to Jeremiah from the LORD, after King Zedekiah had made a covenant with all
the people in Jerusalem to make a
proclamation of liberty to them,
9 that all should set free their Hebrew slaves, male and female, so
that no one should hold another
Judean in slavery. 10 And they
obeyed, all the officials and all the
people who had entered into the
covenant that all would set free
their slaves, male or female, so that
they would not be enslaved again;
they obeyed and set them free.
11 But afterward they turned
around and took back the male and
female slaves they had set free, and
brought them again into subjection
as slaves. 12 The word of the LORD
came to Jeremiah from the LORD:
13 Thus says the LORD, the God of
Israel: I myself made a covenant
with your ancestors when I brought
them out of the land of Egypt, out
of the house of slavery, saying,
14 "Every seventh year each of you
must set free any Hebrews who
have been sold to you and have
served you six years; you must set
them free from your service." But
your ancestors did not listen to me
or incline their ears to me. 15 You
yourselves recently repented and
did what was right in my sight by
proclaiming liberty to one another,
and you made a covenant before
me in the house that is called by
my name; 16 but then you turned
around and profaned my name
when each of you took back your
male and female slaves, whom you
had set free according to their desire, and you brought them again
into subjection to be your slaves.
17 Therefore, thus says the LORD:
You have not obeyed me by granting a release to your neighbors and
friends; I am going to grant a release to you, says the LORD—a release to the sword, to pestilence,
and to famine. I will make you a
horror to all the kingdoms of the
earth. 18 And those who transgressed my covenant and did not
keep the terms of the covenant that
they made before me, I will make
like[z] the calf when they cut it in
two and passed between its parts:
19 the officials of Judah, the officials of Jerusalem, the eunuchs,
the priests, and all the people of
the land who passed between the
parts of the calf 20 shall be handed
over to their enemies and to those
who seek their lives. Their corpses
shall become food for the birds of
the air and the wild animals of the
earth. 21 And as for King Zedekiah
of Judah and his officials, I will
hand them over to their enemies
and to those who seek their lives,
to the army of the king of Babylon,
which has withdrawn from you. 22 I
am going to command, says the
LORD, and will bring them back to
this city; and they will fight against
it, and take it, and burn it with fire.
The towns of Judah I will make a
desolation without inhabitant.

The Rechabites Commended

35 The word that came to Jeremiah from the LORD in the
days of King Jehoiakim son of Josiah of Judah: 2 Go to the house of
the Rechabites, and speak with
them, and bring them to the house
of the LORD, into one of the chambers; then offer them wine to drink.
3 So I took Jaazaniah son of Jeremiah son of Habazziniah, and his
brothers, and all his sons, and the
whole house of the Rechabites. 4 I
brought them to the house of the
LORD into the chamber of the sons
of Hanan son of Igdaliah, the man
of God, which was near the cham-

34.7 2 Chr 11.9; 2 Kings 18.13; 19.8
34.8 Ex 21.2; Lev 25.10
34.9 Neh 5.11; Lev 25.39-46
34.11 v. 21; Jer 37.5; Hos 6.4
34.13 Ex 24.3,7,8; Deut 15.22
34.14 Ex 21.2; 23.10; Deut 15.12; 1 Sam 8.7, 8; 2 Kings 17.13, 14
34.15 2 Kings 23.3; Neh 10.29; Jer 7.10,11; 32.34
34.16 Ex 20.7; Lev 19.12
34.17 Mt 7.2; Gal 6.7; Deut 28.25, 64
34.18 Deut 17.2; Hos 6.7; Gen 15.10, 17
34.19 v. 10
34.20 Jer 11.21; 7.33; 19.7
34.21 Jer 37.5,11
34.22 Jer 37.8,10; 4.7; 33.10; 44.22
35.1 2 Kings 24.1; Jer 1.3; 27.20
35.2 2 Kings 10.15; 1 Chr 2.55; 1 Kings 6.5
35.4 Deut 33.1; 1 Kings 12.22; 2 Kings 12.9; 25.18; 1 Chr 9.18, 19

[y] Heb *shall burn* [z] Cn: Heb lacks *like*

ber of the officials, above the
chamber of Maaseiah son of Shallum, keeper of the threshold.
5 Then I set before the Rechabites
pitchers full of wine, and cups; and
I said to them, "Have some wine."
6 But they answered, "We will drink
no wine, for our ancestor Jonadab
son of Rechab commanded us,
'You shall never drink wine, neither you nor your children; 7 nor
shall you ever build a house, or sow
seed; nor shall you plant a vineyard, or even own one; but you
shall live in tents all your days, that
you may live many days in the land
where you reside.' 8 We have
obeyed the charge of our ancestor
Jonadab son of Rechab in all that
he commanded us, to drink no
wine all our days, ourselves, our
wives, our sons, or our daughters,
9 and not to build houses to live in.
We have no vineyard or field or
seed; 10 but we have lived in tents,
and have obeyed and done all that
our ancestor Jonadab commanded
us. 11 But when King Nebuchadrezzar of Babylon came up against the
land, we said, 'Come, and let us go
to Jerusalem for fear of the army of
the Chaldeans and the army of the
Arameans.' That is why we are living in Jerusalem."
12 Then the word of the LORD
came to Jeremiah: 13 Thus says the
LORD of hosts, the God of Israel: Go
and say to the people of Judah and
the inhabitants of Jerusalem, Can
you not learn a lesson and obey my
words? says the LORD. 14 The command has been carried out that
Jonadab son of Rechab gave to his
descendants to drink no wine; and
they drink none to this day, for they
have obeyed their ancestor's command. But I myself have spoken to
you persistently, and you have not
obeyed me. 15 I have sent to you all
my servants the prophets, sending
them persistently, saying, 'Turn
now everyone of you from your evil
way, and amend your doings, and
do not go after other gods to serve
them, and then you shall live in the
land that I gave to you and your ancestors.' But you did not incline
your ear or obey me. 16 The descendants of Jonadab son of Rechab
have carried out the command that
their ancestor gave them, but this
people has not obeyed me.
17 Therefore, thus says the LORD,
the God of hosts, the God of Israel:
I am going to bring on Judah and
on all the inhabitants of Jerusalem
every disaster that I have pronounced against them; because I
have spoken to them and they have
not listened, I have called to them
and they have not answered.
18 But to the house of the Rechabites Jeremiah said: Thus says the
LORD of hosts, the God of Israel: Because you have obeyed the command of your ancestor Jonadab,
and kept all his precepts, and done
all that he commanded you,
19 therefore thus says the LORD of
hosts, the God of Israel: Jonadab
son of Rechab shall not lack a descendant to stand before me for all
time.

The Scroll Read in the Temple

36 In the fourth year of King
Jehoiakim son of Josiah of
Judah, this word came to Jeremiah
from the LORD: 2 Take a scroll and
write on it all the words that I have
spoken to you against Israel and
Judah and all the nations, from the
day I spoke to you, from the days of
Josiah until today. 3 It may be that
when the house of Judah hears of
all the disasters that I intend to do
to them, all of them may turn from
their evil ways, so that I may forgive
their iniquity and their sin.
4 Then Jeremiah called Baruch
son of Neriah, and Baruch wrote on
a scroll at Jeremiah's dictation all
the words of the LORD that he had
spoken to him. 5 And Jeremiah ordered Baruch, saying, "I am prevented from entering the house of
the LORD; 6 so you go yourself, and
on a fast day in the hearing of the
people in the LORD's house you
shall read the words of the LORD
from the scroll that you have written at my dictation. You shall read

35.5 Am 2.12
35.6 2 Kings 10.15; 1 Chr 2.55; Lev 10.9; Lk 1.15
35.7 Gen 25.27; Heb 11.9; Ex 20.12; Eph 6.2,3
35.8 Prov 1.8,9; Eph 6.1; Col 3.20
35.9 v. 7
35.10 vv. 6,7
35.11 2 Kings 24.1, 2; Jer 4.5-7; 8.14
35.13 Isa 28.9-12; Jer 32.33
35.14 2 Chr 36.15; Jer 7.13; 25.3; Isa 30.9; 50.2
35.15 Jer 26.5; 32.33; Isa 1.16,17; Jer 4.1; 18.11; 7.6; 13.10; 22.4; 34.14
35.16 v. 14
35.17 Jer 19.3,15; Mic 3.12; Prov 1.24; Isa 65.12; 66.4; Jer 7.13
35.19 Jer 33.17; 15.19
36.1 2 Kings 24.1; Jer 25.1,3
36.2 vv. 6,23,28; Zech 5.1; Jer 1.9,10; 25.9-29; 25.3
36.3 v. 7; Jer 26.3; Isa 55.7; Jer 18.8; Jon 3.8; Mk 4.12; Acts 3.19
36.4 v. 18; Jer 32.12; v. 14; Ezek 2.9
36.5 Jer 32.2; 33.1

them also in the hearing of all the people of Judah who come up from their towns. 7 It may be that their plea will come before the LORD, and that all of them will turn from their evil ways, for great is the anger and wrath that the LORD has pronounced against this people." 8 And Baruch son of Neriah did all that the prophet Jeremiah ordered him about reading from the scroll the words of the LORD in the LORD's house.

9 In the fifth year of King Jehoiakim son of Josiah of Judah, in the ninth month, all the people in Jerusalem and all the people who came from the towns of Judah to Jerusalem proclaimed a fast before the LORD. 10 Then, in the hearing of all the people, Baruch read the words of Jeremiah from the scroll, in the house of the LORD, in the chamber of Gemariah son of Shaphan the secretary, which was in the upper court, at the entry of the New Gate of the LORD's house.

The Scroll Read in the Palace

11 When Micaiah son of Gemariah son of Shaphan heard all the words of the LORD from the scroll, 12 he went down to the king's house, into the secretary's chamber; and all the officials were sitting there: Elishama the secretary, Delaiah son of Shemaiah, Elnathan son of Achbor, Gemariah son of Shaphan, Zedekiah son of Hananiah, and all the officials. 13 And Micaiah told them all the words that he had heard, when Baruch read the scroll in the hearing of the people. 14 Then all the officials sent Jehudi son of Nethaniah son of Shelemiah son of Cushi to say to Baruch, "Bring the scroll that you read in the hearing of the people, and come." So Baruch son of Neriah took the scroll in his hand and came to them. 15 And they said to him, "Sit down and read it to us." So Baruch read it to them. 16 When they heard all the words, they turned to one another in alarm, and said to Baruch, "We certainly must report all these words to the king." 17 Then they questioned Baruch, "Tell us now, how did you write all these words? Was it at his dictation?" 18 Baruch answered them, "He dictated all these words to me, and I wrote them with ink on the scroll." 19 Then the officials said to Baruch, "Go and hide, you and Jeremiah, and let no one know where you are."

Jehoiakim Burns the Scroll

20 Leaving the scroll in the chamber of Elishama the secretary, they went to the court of the king; and they reported all the words to the king. 21 Then the king sent Jehudi to get the scroll, and he took it from the chamber of Elishama the secretary; and Jehudi read it to the king and all the officials who stood beside the king. 22 Now the king was sitting in his winter apartment (it was the ninth month), and there was a fire burning in the brazier before him. 23 As Jehudi read three or four columns, the king[a] would cut them off with a penknife and throw them into the fire in the brazier, until the entire scroll was consumed in the fire that was in the brazier. 24 Yet neither the king, nor any of his servants who heard all these words, was alarmed, nor did they tear their garments. 25 Even when Elnathan and Delaiah and Gemariah urged the king not to burn the scroll, he would not listen to them. 26 And the king commanded Jerahmeel the king's son and Seraiah son of Azriel and Shelemiah son of Abdeel to arrest the secretary Baruch and the prophet Jeremiah. But the LORD hid them.

Jeremiah Dictates Another

27 Now, after the king had burned the scroll with the words that Baruch wrote at Jeremiah's dictation, the word of the LORD came to Jeremiah: 28 Take another scroll and write on it all the former words that were in the first scroll, which King Jehoiakim of Judah has burned. 29 And concerning King Jehoiakim of Judah you shall

36.7 2 Kings 22.13; Jer 4.4; 21.5
36.8 v. 6
36.9 v. 6; Esther 4.16; Jon 3.5
36.10 Jer 26.10
36.11 v. 13
36.12 vv. 20,25; Jer 26.22
36.13 2 Kings 22.10; 36.14; v. 21
36.15 v. 21
36.16 v. 24; Acts 24.25; Jer 13.18; Am 7.10,11
36.18 v. 4
36.19 v. 26; Jer 26.20-24
36.20 v. 12
36.21 v. 14; 2 Chr 34.18
36.22 Am 3.15
36.23 v. 29
36.24 2 Kings 19.1, 2; 22.11; Isa 36.22; 37.1
36.25 Acts 5.34-39
36.26 1 Kings 19.1ff; Jer 15.20,21
36.27 vv. 23,4,18
36.28 Jer 28.13,14
36.29 Job 15.24, 25; Isa 45.9; 30.10; Jer 26.9; 32.3; 25.9-11

a Heb *he*

say: Thus says the LORD, You have
dared to burn this scroll, saying,
Why have you written in it that the
king of Babylon will certainly come
and destroy this land, and will cut
off from it human beings and animals? 30 Therefore thus says the
LORD concerning King Jehoiakim of
Judah: He shall have no one to sit
upon the throne of David, and his
dead body shall be cast out to the
heat by day and the frost by night.
31 And I will punish him and his offspring and his servants for their iniquity; I will bring on them, and on
the inhabitants of Jerusalem, and
on the people of Judah, all the disasters with which I have threatened them—but they would not
listen.
32 Then Jeremiah took another
scroll and gave it to the secretary
Baruch son of Neriah, who wrote
on it at Jeremiah's dictation all the
words of the scroll that King Jehoiakim of Judah had burned in the
fire; and many similar words were
added to them.

Zedekiah's Vain Hope

37 Zedekiah son of Josiah,
whom King Nebuchadrez-
zar of Babylon made king in the
land of Judah, succeeded Coniah
son of Jehoiakim. 2 But neither he
nor his servants nor the people of
the land listened to the words of
the LORD that he spoke through the
prophet Jeremiah.
3 King Zedekiah sent Jehucal
son of Shelemiah and the priest
Zephaniah son of Maaseiah to the
prophet Jeremiah saying, "Please
pray for us to the LORD our God."
4 Now Jeremiah was still going in
and out among the people, for he
had not yet been put in prison.
5 Meanwhile, the army of Pharaoh
had come out of Egypt; and when
the Chaldeans who were besieging
Jerusalem heard news of them,
they withdrew from Jerusalem.
6 Then the word of the LORD
came to the prophet Jeremiah:
7 Thus says the LORD, God of Israel:
This is what the two of you shall
say to the king of Judah, who sent
you to me to inquire of me, Pharaoh's army, which set out to help
you, is going to return to its own
land, to Egypt. 8 And the Chaldeans
shall return and fight against this
city; they shall take it and burn it
with fire. 9 Thus says the LORD: Do
not deceive yourselves, saying,
"The Chaldeans will surely go away
from us," for they will not go away.
10 Even if you defeated the whole
army of Chaldeans who are fighting
against you, and there remained of
them only wounded men in their
tents, they would rise up and burn
this city with fire.

Jeremiah Is Imprisoned

11 Now when the Chaldean
army had withdrawn from Jerusalem at the approach of Pharaoh's
army, 12 Jeremiah set out from Jerusalem to go to the land of Benjamin to receive his share of property[b] among the people there.
13 When he reached the Benjamin
Gate, a sentinel there named Irijah
son of Shelemiah son of Hananiah
arrested the prophet Jeremiah saying, "You are deserting to the Chaldeans." 14 And Jeremiah said,
"That is a lie; I am not deserting to
the Chaldeans." But Irijah would
not listen to him, and arrested Jeremiah and brought him to the officials. 15 The officials were enraged
at Jeremiah, and they beat him and
imprisoned him in the house of the
secretary Jonathan, for it had been
made a prison. 16 Thus Jeremiah
was put in the cistern house, in the
cells, and remained there many
days.
17 Then King Zedekiah sent for
him, and received him. The king
questioned him secretly in his
house, and said, "Is there any word
from the LORD?" Jeremiah said,
"There is!" Then he said, "You
shall be handed over to the king of
Babylon." 18 Jeremiah also said to
King Zedekiah, "What wrong have I
done to you or your servants or this
people, that you have put me in
prison? 19 Where are your prophets

36.30 2 Kings 24.12-15; Jer 22.30; 22.19
36.31 Jer 23.34; Deut 28.15; Jer 19.15
36.32 vv. 28,4,23
37.1 2 Kings 24.17; 2 Chr 36.10; Jer 22.24; Ezek 17.12-21
37.2 2 Chr 36.12, 14
37.3 Jer 21.1,2; 29.25; 52.24; 1 Kings 13.6; Acts 8.24
37.4 v. 15
37.5 2 Kings 24.7; Ezek 17.15; Jer 34.21
37.7 Jer 21.2; Isa 30.1-3; 31.1-3; Ezek 17.17
37.8 Jer 34.22
37.9 Jer 29.8
37.10 Jer 21.4,5; Joel 2.11
37.11 v. 5
37.13 Jer 38.7; Zech 14.10; Jer 18.18; 20.10; Lk 23.2; Acts 24.5-9, 13
37.14 Jer 40.4-6; Mt 5.11,12
37.15 Jer 18.23; 2 Chr 16.10; 18.26
37.16 Jer 38.6
37.17 Jer 38.5, 14-16,24-27
37.18 Dan 6.22; Jn 10.32; Acts 25.8, 11,25
37.19 Jer 2.28; 6.14; 29.31

[b] Meaning of Heb uncertain

who prophesied to you, saying,
'The king of Babylon will not come
against you and against this land'?
20 Now please hear me, my lord
king: be good enough to listen to
my plea, and do not send me back
to the house of the secretary Jonathan to die there." 21 So King Zedekiah gave orders, and they committed Jeremiah to the court of the
guard; and a loaf of bread was given
him daily from the bakers' street,
until all the bread of the city was
gone. So Jeremiah remained in the
court of the guard.

Jeremiah in the Cistern

38 Now Shephatiah son of
Mattan, Gedaliah son of
Pashhur, Jucal son of Shelemiah,
and Pashhur son of Malchiah heard
the words that Jeremiah was saying
to all the people, 2 Thus says the
LORD, Those who stay in this city
shall die by the sword, by famine,
and by pestilence; but those who
go out to the Chaldeans shall live;
they shall have their lives as a prize
of war, and live. 3 Thus says the
LORD, This city shall surely be
handed over to the army of the king
of Babylon and be taken. 4 Then the
officials said to the king, "This man
ought to be put to death, because
he is discouraging the soldiers who
are left in this city, and all the people, by speaking such words to
them. For this man is not seeking
the welfare of this people, but their
harm." 5 King Zedekiah said, "Here
he is; he is in your hands; for the
king is powerless against you." 6 So
they took Jeremiah and threw him
into the cistern of Malchiah, the
king's son, which was in the court
of the guard, letting Jeremiah
down by ropes. Now there was no
water in the cistern, but only mud,
and Jeremiah sank in the mud.

Jeremiah Is Rescued by Ebed-melech

7 Ebed-melech the Ethiopian,[c]
a eunuch in the king's house, heard
that they had put Jeremiah into the
cistern. The king happened to be
sitting at the Benjamin Gate, 8 So
Ebed-melech left the king's house
and spoke to the king, 9 "My lord
king, these men have acted wickedly in all they did to the prophet
Jeremiah by throwing him into the
cistern to die there of hunger, for
there is no bread left in the city."
10 Then the king commanded
Ebed-melech the Ethiopian,[c]
"Take three men with you from
here, and pull the prophet Jeremiah up from the cistern before he
dies." 11 So Ebed-melech took the
men with him and went to the
house of the king, to a wardrobe
of[d] the storehouse, and took from
there old rags and worn-out
clothes, which he let down to Jeremiah in the cistern by ropes.
12 Then Ebed-melech the Ethiopian[c] said to Jeremiah, "Just put the
rags and clothes between your arm-
pits and the ropes." Jeremiah did
so. 13 Then they drew Jeremiah up
by the ropes and pulled him out of
the cistern. And Jeremiah remained in the court of the guard.

Zedekiah Consults Jeremiah Again

14 King Zedekiah sent for the
prophet Jeremiah and received
him at the third entrance of the
temple of the LORD. The king said
to Jeremiah, "I have something to
ask you; do not hide anything from
me." 15 Jeremiah said to Zedekiah,
"If I tell you, you will put me to
death, will you not? And if I give
you advice, you will not listen to
me." 16 So King Zedekiah swore an
oath in secret to Jeremiah, "As the
LORD lives, who gave us our lives, I
will not put you to death or hand
you over to these men who seek
your life."
17 Then Jeremiah said to Zedekiah, "Thus says the LORD, the God
of hosts, the God of Israel, If you
will only surrender to the officials
of the king of Babylon, then your
life shall be spared, and this city
shall not be burned with fire, and
you and your house shall live.

37.20 Jer 36.7; 38.26; 18.23 **37.21** Jer 32.3; 38.13,28; Isa 33.16; Jer 38.9; 52.6; 39.14, 15 **38.1** Jer 37.3; 21.1,8 **38.2** Jer 21.9; 42.17; 45.5 **38.3** Jer 21.10; 32.3 **38.4** Jer 18.23; 26.11; 1 Kings 18.17, 18; 21.20; Am 7.10; Acts 16.20; Jer 29.7 **38.5** 2 Sam 3.39 **38.6** Jer 37.21; Acts 16.24; Zech 9.11 **38.7** Jer 39.16; 37.13; Am 5.10 **38.9** Jer 37.21; 52.6 **38.11** v. 6 **38.13** Jer 37.21; 39.14,15 **38.14** Jer 21.1,2; 37.17; 15.11; 42.2-5,20 **38.15** Lk 22.67,68 **38.16** Jer 37.17; Isa 57.16; Zech 12.1; vv. 4-6 **38.17** Ps 80.7,14; 1 Chr 17.24; Ezek 8.4; 2 Kings 24.12; 26.27-30

[c] Or *Nubian*; Heb *Cushite* [d] Cn: Heb *to under*

18 But if you do not surrender to the
officials of the king of Babylon,
then this city shall be handed over
to the Chaldeans, and they shall
burn it with fire, and you yourself
shall not escape from their hand."
19 King Zedekiah said to Jeremiah,
"I am afraid of the Judeans who
have deserted to the Chaldeans, for
I might be handed over to them and
they would abuse me." 20 Jeremiah
said, "That will not happen. Just
obey the voice of the LORD in what
I say to you, and it shall go well
with you, and your life shall be
spared. 21 But if you are determined
not to surrender, this is what the
LORD has shown me— 22 a vision of
all the women remaining in the
house of the king of Judah being
led out to the officials of the king of
Babylon and saying,

'Your trusted friends have
    seduced you
  and have overcome you;
Now that your feet are stuck
    in the mud,
  they desert you.'

23 All your wives and your children
shall be led out to the Chaldeans,
and you yourself shall not escape
from their hand, but shall be seized
by the king of Babylon; and this
city shall be burned with fire."
24 Then Zedekiah said to Jeremiah, "Do not let anyone else
know of this conversation, or you
will die. 25 If the officials should
hear that I have spoken with you,
and they should come and say to
you, 'Just tell us what you said to
the king; do not conceal it from us,
or we will put you to death. What
did the king say to you?' 26 then you
shall say to them, 'I was presenting
my plea to the king not to send me
back to the house of Jonathan to
die there.' " 27 All the officials did
come to Jeremiah and questioned
him; and he answered them in the
very words the king had commanded. So they stopped questioning
him, for the conversation had not
been overheard. 28 And Jeremiah
remained in the court of the guard
until the day that Jerusalem was
taken.

The Fall of Jerusalem

39 In the ninth year of King
Zedekiah of Judah, in the
tenth month, King Nebuchadrezzar of Babylon and all his army
came against Jerusalem and besieged it; 2 in the eleventh year of
Zedekiah, in the fourth month, on
the ninth day of the month, a
breach was made in the city.
3 When Jerusalem was taken,[e] all
the officials of the king of Babylon
came and sat in the middle gate:
Nergal-sharezer, Samgar-nebo,
Sarsechim the Rabsaris, Nergal-
sharezer the Rabmag, with all the
rest of the officials of the king of
Babylon. 4 When King Zedekiah of
Judah and all the soldiers saw
them, they fled, going out of the
city at night by way of the king's
garden through the gate between
the two walls; and they went toward the Arabah. 5 But the army of
the Chaldeans pursued them, and
overtook Zedekiah in the plains of
Jericho; and when they had taken
him, they brought him up to King
Nebuchadrezzar of Babylon, at
Riblah, in the land of Hamath; and
he passed sentence on him. 6 The
king of Babylon slaughtered the
sons of Zedekiah at Riblah before
his eyes; also the king of Babylon
slaughtered all the nobles of Judah. 7 He put out the eyes of Zedekiah, and bound him in fetters to
take him to Babylon. 8 The Chaldeans burned the king's house and
the houses of the people, and
broke down the walls of Jerusalem.
9 Then Nebuzaradan the captain of
the guard exiled to Babylon the
rest of the people who were left in
the city, those who had deserted to
him, and the people who remained.
10 Nebuzaradan the captain of the
guard left in the land of Judah
some of the poor people who
owned nothing, and gave them
vineyards and fields at the same
time.

[e] This clause has been transposed from 38.28

38.18 Jer 27.8; 32.4; 34.3 **38.19** Isa 51.12, 13; Jn 12.42; 19.12,13; Jer 39.9; 2 Chr 30.10; Neh 4.1 **38.20** Jer 11.4,8; 7.23; Isa 55.3 **38.22** Jer 6.12; 8.10; 43.6 **38.23** Jer 39.6; 41.10 **38.25** vv. 4-6,27 **38.26** Jer 37.15,20 **38.27** 1 Sam 10.15, 16; 16.2-5 **38.28** Jer 37.21; 39.14
39.1 2 Kings 25.1-4; Jer 52.4-7; Ezek 24.1,2 **39.2** 2 Kings 25.4; Jer 52.7 **39.3** Jer 38.17 **39.4** 2 Kings 25.4; Jer 52.7; Am 2.14; 2 Chr 32.5 **39.5** Jer 32.4; 38.18,23; Josh 4.13; 2 Kings 23.33 **39.6** 2 Kings 25.7; Jer 34.19-21 **39.7** 2 Kings 25.7; Jer 52.11; Ezek 12.13; Jer 32.5 **39.8** 2 Kings 25.9, 10; Jer 38.18; 52.13 **39.9** 2 Kings 25.11, 20; Jer 52.12-16; 24.8; 38.19 **39.10** 2 Kings 25.12; Jer 52.16

Jeremiah, Set Free, Remembers Ebed-melech

11 King Nebuchadrezzar of
Babylon gave command concerning Jeremiah through Nebuzaradan, the captain of the guard, saying, 12 "Take him, look after him
well and do him no harm, but deal
with him as he may ask you." 13 So
Nebuzaradan the captain of the
guard, Nebushazban the Rabsaris,
Nergal-sharezer the Rabmag, and
all the chief officers of the king of
Babylon sent 14 and took Jeremiah
from the court of the guard. They
entrusted him to Gedaliah son of
Ahikam son of Shaphan to be
brought home. So he stayed with
his own people.
15 The word of the LORD came to
Jeremiah while he was confined in
the court of the guard: 16 Go and
say to Ebed-melech the Ethiopian:[f] Thus says the LORD of hosts,
the God of Israel: I am going to fulfill my words against this city for
evil and not for good, and they shall
be accomplished in your presence
on that day. 17 But I will save you on
that day, says the LORD, and you
shall not be handed over to those
whom you dread. 18 For I will surely
save you, and you shall not fall by
the sword; but you shall have your
life as a prize of war, because you
have trusted in me, says the LORD.

Jeremiah with Gedaliah the Governor

40 The word that came to Jeremiah from the LORD after
Nebuzaradan the captain of the
guard had let him go from Ramah,
when he took him bound in fetters
along with all the captives of Jerusalem and Judah who were being
exiled to Babylon. 2 The captain of
the guard took Jeremiah and said
to him, "The LORD your God threatened this place with this disaster;
3 and now the LORD has brought it
about, and has done as he said, because all of you sinned against the
LORD and did not obey his voice.
Therefore this thing has come
upon you. 4 Now look, I have just
released you today from the fetters
on your hands. If you wish to come
with me to Babylon, come, and I
will take good care of you; but if
you do not wish to come with me to
Babylon, you need not come. See,
the whole land is before you; go
wherever you think it good and
right to go. 5 If you remain,[g] then
return to Gedaliah son of Ahikam
son of Shaphan, whom the king of
Babylon appointed governor of the
towns of Judah, and stay with him
among the people; or go wherever
you think it right to go." So the captain of the guard gave him an allowance of food and a present, and let
him go. 6 Then Jeremiah went to
Gedaliah son of Ahikam at Mizpah,
and stayed with him among the
people who were left in the land.
7 When all the leaders of the
forces in the open country and
their troops heard that the king of
Babylon had appointed Gedaliah
son of Ahikam governor in the
land, and had committed to him
men, women, and children, those
of the poorest of the land who had
not been taken into exile to Babylon, 8 they went to Gedaliah at
Mizpah—Ishmael son of Nethaniah, Johanan son of Kareah, Seraiah
son of Tanhumeth, the sons of
Ephai the Netophathite, Jezaniah
son of the Maacathite, they and
their troops. 9 Gedaliah son of Ahikam son of Shaphan swore to them
and their troops, saying, "Do not be
afraid to serve the Chaldeans. Stay
in the land and serve the king of
Babylon, and it shall go well with
you. 10 As for me, I am staying at
Mizpah to represent you before the
Chaldeans who come to us; but as
for you, gather wine and summer
fruits and oil, and store them in
your vessels, and live in the towns
that you have taken over." 11 Likewise, when all the Judeans who
were in Moab and among the Ammonites and in Edom and in other
lands heard that the king of Babylon had left a remnant in Judah

39.11 Jer 1.8; 15.20,21; Acts 24.23
39.14 Jer 38.28; 40.1-6; 2 Kings 22.12, 14; 2 Chr 34.20
39.16 Jer 38.7,12; 21.10; Dan 9.12; Zech 1.6
39.17 Ps 41.1,2; 50.15
39.18 Jer 21.9; 45.5; Ps 34.22; Jer 17.7,8
40.1 Jer 39.9,11, 14; 31.15; Eph 6.20
40.2 Jer 22.8,9; 50.7
40.3 Deut 29.24, 25; Dan 9.11
40.4 Jer 39.11, 12; Gen 20.15
40.5 Jer 39.14; 2 Kings 25.23; v. 4; Jer 52.34
40.6 Jer 39.14; Judg 20.1
40.7 2 Kings 25.23, 24; Jer 39.10; 52.16
40.8 Jer 41.1
40.9 2 Kings 25.24; Jer 27.11; 38.17-20
40.10 v. 6; Jer 35.19; 39.10; v. 12; Jer 48.32
40.11 Isa 16.4; 1 Sam 11.1; 12.12; Isa 11.14

[f] Or *Nubian*; Heb *Cushite* [g] Syr: Meaning of Heb uncertain

and had appointed Gedaliah son of Ahikam son of Shaphan as governor over them, 12 then all the Judeans returned from all the places to which they had been scattered and came to the land of Judah, to Gedaliah at Mizpah; and they gathered wine and summer fruits in great abundance.

13 Now Johanan son of Kareah and all the leaders of the forces in the open country came to Gedaliah at Mizpah 14 and said to him, "Are you at all aware that Baalis king of the Ammonites has sent Ishmael son of Nethaniah to take your life?" But Gedaliah son of Ahikam would not believe them. 15 Then Johanan son of Kareah spoke secretly to Gedaliah at Mizpah, "Please let me go and kill Ishmael son of Nethaniah, and no one else will know. Why should he take your life, so that all the Judeans who are gathered around you would be scattered, and the remnant of Judah would perish?" 16 But Gedaliah son of Ahikam said to Johanan son of Kareah, "Do not do such a thing, for you are telling a lie about Ishmael."

Insurrection against Gedaliah

41 In the seventh month, Ishmael son of Nethaniah son of Elishama, of the royal family, one of the chief officers of the king, came with ten men to Gedaliah son of Ahikam, at Mizpah. As they ate bread together there at Mizpah, 2 Ishmael son of Nethaniah and the ten men with him got up and struck down Gedaliah son of Ahikam son of Shaphan with the sword and killed him, because the king of Babylon had appointed him governor in the land. 3 Ishmael also killed all the Judeans who were with Gedaliah at Mizpah, and the Chaldean soldiers who happened to be there.

4 On the day after the murder of Gedaliah, before anyone knew of it, 5 eighty men arrived from Shechem and Shiloh and Samaria, with their beards shaved and their clothes torn, and their bodies gashed, bringing grain offerings and incense to present at the temple of the LORD. 6 And Ishmael son of Nethaniah came out from Mizpah to meet them, weeping as he came. As he met them, he said to them, "Come to Gedaliah son of Ahikam." 7 When they reached the middle of the city, Ishmael son of Nethaniah and the men with him slaughtered them, and threw them[h] into a cistern. 8 But there were ten men among them who said to Ishmael, "Do not kill us, for we have stores of wheat, barley, oil, and honey hidden in the fields." So he refrained, and did not kill them along with their companions.

9 Now the cistern into which Ishmael had thrown all the bodies of the men whom he had struck down was the large cistern[i] that King Asa had made for defense against King Baasha of Israel; Ishmael son of Nethaniah filled that cistern with those whom he had killed. 10 Then Ishmael took captive all the rest of the people who were in Mizpah, the king's daughters and all the people who were left at Mizpah, whom Nebuzaradan, the captain of the guard, had committed to Gedaliah son of Ahikam. Ishmael son of Nethaniah took them captive and set out to cross over to the Ammonites.

11 But when Johanan son of Kareah and all the leaders of the forces with him heard of all the crimes that Ishmael son of Nethaniah had done, 12 they took all their men and went to fight against Ishmael son of Nethaniah. They came upon him at the great pool that is in Gibeon. 13 And when all the people who were with Ishmael saw Johanan son of Kareah and all the leaders of the forces with him, they were glad. 14 So all the people whom Ishmael had carried away captive from Mizpah turned around and came back, and went to Johanan son of Kareah. 15 But Ishmael son of Nethaniah escaped from Johanan with eight men, and

40.12 Jer 43.5; v. 10
40.13 v. 8
40.14 Jer 41.10
40.15 1 Sam 26.8; 2 Sam 21.17; Jer 42.2
40.16 Mt 10.16
41.1 2 Kings 25.25; Jer 40.6,8, 14
41.2 2 Kings 25.25; Jer 40.5
41.5 Gen 33.18; Josh 18.1; 1 Kings 16.24, 29; Jer 16.6; 2 Kings 25.9
41.6 Jer 50.4
41.7 Isa 59.7; Ezek 22.27
41.9 1 Kings 15.22; 2 Chr 16.6
41.10 Jer 40.11, 12; 43.6; 40.7,14
41.11 Jer 40.7,8, 13-16
41.12 2 Sam 2.13
41.13 vv. 10,14
41.15 v. 2

[h] Syr: Heb lacks *and threw them*; compare verse 9 [i] Gk: Heb *whom he had killed by the hand of Gedaliah*

went to the Ammonites. 16 Then Johanan son of Kareah and all the
leaders of the forces with him took
all the rest of the people whom Ishmael son of Nethaniah had carried
away captive[j] from Mizpah after
he had slain Gedaliah son of
Ahikam — soldiers, women, children, and eunuchs, whom Johanan
brought back from Gibeon.[k] 17 And
they set out, and stopped at Geruth
Chimham near Bethlehem, intending to go to Egypt 18 because of the
Chaldeans; for they were afraid of
them, because Ishmael son of
Nethaniah had killed Gedaliah son
of Ahikam, whom the king of Babylon had made governor over the
land.

Jeremiah Advises Survivors Not to Migrate

42 Then all the commanders
of the forces, and Johanan
son of Kareah and Azariah[l] son of
Hoshaiah, and all the people from
the least to the greatest, approached 2 the prophet Jeremiah
and said, "Be good enough to listen
to our plea, and pray to the LORD
your God for us — for all this remnant. For there are only a few of us
left out of many, as your eyes can
see. 3 Let the LORD your God show
us where we should go and what we
should do." 4 The prophet Jeremiah said to them, "Very well: I am
going to pray to the LORD your God
as you request, and whatever the
LORD answers you I will tell you; I
will keep nothing back from you."
5 They in their turn said to Jeremiah, "May the LORD be a true and
faithful witness against us if we do
not act according to everything
that the LORD your God sends us
through you. 6 Whether it is good or
bad, we will obey the voice of the
LORD our God to whom we are sending you, in order that it may go well
with us when we obey the voice of
the LORD our God."
7 At the end of ten days the
word of the LORD came to Jeremiah.
8 Then he summoned Johanan son
of Kareah and all the commanders
of the forces who were with him,
and all the people from the least to
the greatest, 9 and said to them,
"Thus says the LORD, the God of Israel, to whom you sent me to
present your plea before him: 10 If
you will only remain in this land,
then I will build you up and not
pull you down; I will plant you, and
not pluck you up; for I am sorry for
the disaster that I have brought
upon you. 11 Do not be afraid of the
king of Babylon, as you have been;
do not be afraid of him, says the
LORD, for I am with you, to save you
and to rescue you from his hand.
12 I will grant you mercy, and he will
have mercy on you and restore you
to your native soil. 13 But if you continue to say, 'We will not stay in
this land,' thus disobeying the
voice of the LORD your God 14 and
saying, 'No, we will go to the land
of Egypt, where we shall not see
war, or hear the sound of the trumpet, or be hungry for bread, and
there we will stay,' 15 then hear the
word of the LORD, O remnant of Judah. Thus says the LORD of hosts,
the God of Israel: If you are determined to enter Egypt and go to settle there, 16 then the sword that you
fear shall overtake you there, in the
land of Egypt; and the famine that
you dread shall follow close after
you into Egypt; and there you shall
die. 17 All the people who have determined to go to Egypt to settle
there shall die by the sword, by
famine, and by pestilence; they
shall have no remnant or survivor
from the disaster that I am bringing
upon them.
18 "For thus says the LORD of
hosts, the God of Israel: Just as my
anger and my wrath were poured
out on the inhabitants of Jerusalem, so my wrath will be poured
out on you when you go to Egypt.
You shall become an object of execration and horror, of cursing and
ridicule. You shall see this place no
more. 19 The LORD has said to you,

41.16 Jer 42.8; 43.4-7 **41.17** 2 Sam 19.37, 38; Jer 42.14 **41.18** Jer 42.11, 16; Lk 12.4, 5; Jer 40.5 **42.1** Jer 40.8,13; 41.11 **42.2** Jer 36.7; 37.20; v. 20; 1 Kings 13.6; Acts 8.24; Deut 28.62; Lam 1.1 **42.3** Ps 86.11; Mic 4.2 **42.4** 1 Sam 12.23; 1 Kings 22.14; Jer 23.28; 1 Sam 3.17, 18; Ps 40.10 **42.5** Gen 31.50; Mic 1.2 **42.6** Deut 6.3; Jer 7.23 **42.8** v. 1 **42.9** 2 Kings 19.4, 6,20; 22.15 **42.10** Jer 24.6; 31.28; Ezek 36.36; Jon 3.10; 4.2 **42.11** Jer 41.18; Isa 43.5; Rom 8.31 **42.12** Ps 106.45, 46 **42.13** Jer 44.16 **42.14** Jer 41.17; 4.19,21 **42.15** Jer 44.12-14 **42.16** Jer 44.13, 27; Ezek 11.8 **42.17** Jer 44.13, 14,28 **42.18** Jer 7.20; 33.5; Isa 65.15; Jer 29.18; 22.10,27 **42.19** Deut 17.16; Isa 30.1-7; Neh 9.26,29,30

[j] Cn: Heb *whom he recovered from Ishmael son of Nethaniah* [k] Meaning of Heb uncertain [l] Gk: Heb *Jezaniah*

O remnant of Judah, Do not go to
Egypt. Be well aware that I have
warned you today 20 that you have
made a fatal mistake. For you yourselves sent me to the LORD your
God, saying, 'Pray for us to the LORD
our God, and whatever the LORD our
God says, tell us and we will do it.'
21 So I have told you today, but you
have not obeyed the voice of the
LORD your God in anything that he
sent me to tell you. 22 Be well
aware, then, that you shall die by
the sword, by famine, and by pestilence in the place where you desire
to go and settle."

Taken to Egypt, Jeremiah Warns of Judgment

43 When Jeremiah finished
speaking to all the people
all these words of the LORD their
God, with which the LORD their God
had sent him to them, 2 Azariah son
of Hoshaiah and Johanan son of
Kareah and all the other insolent
men said to Jeremiah, "You are
telling a lie. The LORD our God did
not send you to say, 'Do not go to
Egypt to settle there'; 3 but Baruch
son of Neriah is inciting you
against us, to hand us over to the
Chaldeans, in order that they may
kill us or take us into exile in Babylon." 4 So Johanan son of Kareah
and all the commanders of the
forces and all the people did not
obey the voice of the LORD, to stay
in the land of Judah. 5 But Johanan
son of Kareah and all the commanders of the forces took all the
remnant of Judah who had returned to settle in the land of Judah from all the nations to which
they had been driven— 6 the men,
the women, the children, the princesses, and everyone whom Nebuzaradan the captain of the guard
had left with Gedaliah son of Ahikam son of Shaphan; also the
prophet Jeremiah and Baruch son
of Neriah. 7 And they came into the
land of Egypt, for they did not obey
the voice of the LORD. And they arrived at Tahpanhes.

8 Then the word of the LORD
came to Jeremiah in Tahpanhes:
9 Take some large stones in your
hands, and bury them in the clay
pavement[m] that is at the entrance
to Pharaoh's palace in Tahpanhes.
Let the Judeans see you do it,
10 and say to them, Thus says the
LORD of hosts, the God of Israel: I
am going to send and take my servant King Nebuchadrezzar of Babylon, and he[n] will set his throne
above these stones that I have buried, and he will spread his royal
canopy over them. 11 He shall come
and ravage the land of Egypt, giving

those who are destined for
pestilence, to
pestilence,
and those who are destined
for captivity, to
captivity,
and those who are destined
for the sword, to the
sword.

12 He[o] shall kindle a fire in the
temples of the gods of Egypt; and
he shall burn them and carry them
away captive; and he shall pick
clean the land of Egypt, as a shepherd picks his cloak clean of vermin; and he shall depart from there
safely. 13 He shall break the obe-
lisks of Heliopolis, which is in the
land of Egypt; and the temples of
the gods of Egypt he shall burn
with fire.

Denunciation of Persistent Idolatry

44 The word that came to Jeremiah for all the Judeans
living in the land of Egypt, at Migdol, at Tahpanhes, at Memphis,
and in the land of Pathros, 2 Thus
says the LORD of hosts, the God of
Israel: You yourselves have seen all
the disaster that I have brought on
Jerusalem and on all the towns of
Judah. Look at them; today they
are a desolation, without an inhabitant in them, 3 because of the
wickedness that they committed,
provoking me to anger, in that they
went to make offerings and serve
other gods that they had not

42.20 v. 2
42.21 Jer 43.1; Ezek 2.7; Jer 43.4
42.22 Jer 43.11; Hos 9.6
43.1 Jer 26.8; 51.63; 42.10-18
43.2 Jer 42.1; 2 Chr 36.13; Jer 42.5
43.3 Jer 38.4
43.4 Jer 42.5,6, 10-12
43.5 Jer 40.11,12
43.6 Jer 41.10; 39.10; 40.7
43.7 Jer 44.1
43.8 Jer 2.16; 44.1; 46.14
43.10 Jer 25.9,11; 27.5,6; 31.20
43.11 Isa 19.1-25; Jer 44.13; 46.13; Ezek 29.19, 20; Jer 15.2
43.12 Isa 19.1; Jer 46.25; Ezek 30.13
44.1 Jer 46.14; 43.7; Isa 19.13
44.2 Jer 9.11; 34.22; Mic 3.12
44.3 Ezek 8.17, 18; Dan 9.5; Isa 3.8; Jer 19.4; Deut 13.6; 32.17

[m] Meaning of Heb uncertain [n] Gk Syr: Heb *I* [o] Gk Syr Vg: Heb *I*

known, neither they, nor you, nor
your ancestors. [4]Yet I persistently
sent to you all my servants the
prophets, saying, "I beg you not to
do this abominable thing that I
hate!" [5]But they did not listen or
incline their ear, to turn from their
wickedness and make no offerings
to other gods. [6]So my wrath and my
anger were poured out and kindled
in the towns of Judah and in the
streets of Jerusalem; and they became a waste and a desolation, as
they still are today. [7]And now thus
says the LORD God of hosts, the God
of Israel: Why are you doing such
great harm to yourselves, to cut off
man and woman, child and infant,
from the midst of Judah, leaving
yourselves without a remnant?
[8]Why do you provoke me to anger
with the works of your hands, making offerings to other gods in the
land of Egypt where you have come
to settle? Will you be cut off and
become an object of cursing and
ridicule among all the nations of
the earth? [9]Have you forgotten the
crimes of your ancestors, of the
kings of Judah, of their[p] wives,
your own crimes and those of your
wives, which they committed in
the land of Judah and in the streets
of Jerusalem? [10]They have shown
no contrition or fear to this day, nor
have they walked in my law and my
statutes that I set before you and
before your ancestors.

11 Therefore thus says the LORD
of hosts, the God of Israel: I am determined to bring disaster on you,
to bring all Judah to an end. [12]I will
take the remnant of Judah who are
determined to come to the land of
Egypt to settle, and they shall perish, everyone; in the land of Egypt
they shall fall; by the sword and by
famine they shall perish; from the
least to the greatest, they shall die
by the sword and by famine; and
they shall become an object of execration and horror, of cursing and
ridicule. [13]I will punish those who
live in the land of Egypt, as I have
punished Jerusalem, with the
sword, with famine, and with pestilence, [14]so that none of the remnant of Judah who have come to
settle in the land of Egypt shall escape or survive or return to the land
of Judah. Although they long to go
back to live there, they shall not go
back, except some fugitives.

15 Then all the men who were
aware that their wives had been
making offerings to other gods, and
all the women who stood by, a
great assembly, all the people who
lived in Pathros in the land of
Egypt, answered Jeremiah: [16]"As
for the word that you have spoken
to us in the name of the LORD, we
are not going to listen to you. [17]In-
stead, we will do everything that we
have vowed, make offerings to the
queen of heaven and pour out libations to her, just as we and our ancestors, our kings and our officials,
used to do in the towns of Judah
and in the streets of Jerusalem. We
used to have plenty of food, and
prospered, and saw no misfortune.
[18]But from the time we stopped
making offerings to the queen of
heaven and pouring out libations
to her, we have lacked everything
and have perished by the sword
and by famine." [19]And the women
said,[q] "Indeed we will go on making offerings to the queen of heav-
en and pouring out libations to her;
do you think that we made cakes
for her, marked with her image,
and poured out libations to her
without our husbands' being involved?"

20 Then Jeremiah said to all the
people, men and women, all the
people who were giving him this
answer: [21]"As for the offerings that
you made in the towns of Judah
and in the streets of Jerusalem, you
and your ancestors, your kings and
your officials, and the people of the
land, did not the LORD remember
them? Did it not come into his
mind? [22]The LORD could no longer
bear the sight of your evil doings,
the abominations that you com-

44.4 2 Chr 36.15; Jer 7.25; 25.4; 26.5; Ezek 8.10
44.5 Jer 11.8,10; 13.10
44.6 Jer 42.18
44.7 Jer 26.19; Ezek 33.11; Jer 9.21; 51.22
44.8 2 Kings 17.15-17; Jer 25.6,7; 42.18
44.9 Jer 7.9,10, 17,18
44.10 Jer 6.15; 8.12; 26.4; 32.23
44.11 Lev 26.17; Jer 21.10; Am 9.4
44.12 Jer 42.15-18, 22
44.13 Jer 11.22; 21.9; 24.10; 42.17,22
44.14 Jer 22.26, 27; Isa 4.2; 10.20; v. 28; Rom 9.27
44.15 Jer 5.1-5
44.16 Jer 8.6,12; 13.10
44.17 2 Kings 17.16; Jer 7.18; Hos 2.5-9; Phil 3.19
44.18 Jer 40.12
44.19 Jer 7.18; Num 30.6,7
44.21 Ezek 8.10, 11; 16.24; Isa 64.9; Jer 14.10; Hos 7.2
44.22 Isa 7.13; Jer 4.4; 21.12; 25.11, 18,38

[p] Heb *his* [q] Compare Syr: Heb lacks *And the women said*

mitted; therefore your land became
a desolation and a waste and a
curse, without inhabitant, as it is to
this day. 23 It is because you burned
offerings, and because you sinned
against the LORD and did not obey
the voice of the LORD or walk in his
law and in his statutes and in his
decrees, that this disaster has befallen you, as is still evident today."
24 Jeremiah said to all the people and all the women, "Hear the
word of the LORD, all you Judeans
who are in the land of Egypt,
25 Thus says the LORD of hosts, the
God of Israel: You and your wives
have accomplished in deeds what
you declared in words, saying, 'We
are determined to perform the
vows that we have made, to make
offerings to the queen of heaven
and to pour out libations to her.' By
all means, keep your vows and
make your libations! 26 Therefore
hear the word of the LORD, all you
Judeans who live in the land of
Egypt: Lo, I swear by my great
name, says the LORD, that my name
shall no longer be pronounced on
the lips of any of the people of Judah in all the land of Egypt, saying,
'As the Lord GOD lives.' 27 I am going to watch over them for harm
and not for good; all the people of
Judah who are in the land of Egypt
shall perish by the sword and by
famine, until not one is left. 28 And
those who escape the sword shall
return from the land of Egypt to the
land of Judah, few in number; and
all the remnant of Judah, who have
come to the land of Egypt to settle,
shall know whose words will stand,
mine or theirs! 29 This shall be the
sign to you, says the LORD, that I am
going to punish you in this place, in
order that you may know that my
words against you will surely be
carried out: 30 Thus says the LORD, I
am going to give Pharaoh Hophra,
king of Egypt, into the hands of his
enemies, those who seek his life,
just as I gave King Zedekiah of Judah into the hand of King Nebuchadrezzar of Babylon, his enemy
who sought his life."

44.23 Jer 40.3; vv. 10,2; Dan 9.11,12
44.24 Jer 42.15; v. 15; Jer 43.7
44.25 Mt 14.9; Acts 23.12
44.26 Gen 22.16; Am 6.8; Heb 6.13, 18; Ezek 20.39; Jer 5.2
44.27 Jer 1.10; 31.28; Ezek 7.6
44.28 Isa 27.13; vv. 17,25,26
44.29 Isa 7.11,14; 8.18; Prov 19.21; Isa 40.8
44.30 Jer 46.25, 26; Ezek 29.3; 2 Kings 25.4-7; Jer 39.5

45.1 Jer 36.1,4, 18,32
45.3 Ps 6.6; 2 Cor 4.1, 16
45.4 Isa 5.5; Jer 11.17; 18.7-10
45.5 1 Kings 3.9, 11; Mt 6.25, 32,33; Rom 12.16; Jer 25.31; 21.9; 38.2; 39.18
46.1 Jer 25.15-38
46.2 2 Kings 23.29; 2 Chr 35.20; Jer 45.1
46.3 Jer 51.11, 12; Nah 2.1; 3.14
46.4 Ezek 21.9-11; Jer 51.3
46.5 Isa 42.17; Ezek 39.18; Jer 6.25; 49.29
46.6 Isa 30.16; Dan 11.19

A Word of Comfort to Baruch

45 The word that the prophet
Jeremiah spoke to Baruch
son of Neriah, when he wrote these
words in a scroll at the dictation of
Jeremiah, in the fourth year of King
Jehoiakim son of Josiah of Judah:
2 Thus says the LORD, the God of Israel, to you, O Baruch: 3 You said,
"Woe is me! The LORD has added
sorrow to my pain; I am weary with
my groaning, and I find no rest."
4 Thus you shall say to him, "Thus
says the LORD: I am going to break
down what I have built, and pluck
up what I have planted—that is,
the whole land. 5 And you, do you
seek great things for yourself? Do
not seek them; for I am going to
bring disaster upon all flesh, says
the LORD; but I will give you your
life as a prize of war in every place
to which you may go."

Judgment on Egypt

46 The word of the LORD that
came to the prophet Jere-
miah concerning the nations.
2 Concerning Egypt, about the
army of Pharaoh Neco, king of
Egypt, which was by the river Euphrates at Carchemish and which
King Nebuchadrezzar of Babylon
defeated in the fourth year of King
Jehoiakim son of Josiah of Judah:

3 Prepare buckler and shield,
  and advance for battle!
4 Harness the horses;
  mount the steeds!
Take your stations with your
  helmets,
  whet your lances,
  put on your coats of mail!
5 Why do I see them terrified?
  They have fallen back;
their warriors are beaten
  down,
  and have fled in haste.
They do not look back—
  terror is all around!
    says the LORD.
6 The swift cannot flee away,
  nor can the warrior escape;
in the north by the river
  Euphrates

they have stumbled and
fallen.

7 Who is this, rising like the
Nile,
like rivers whose waters
surge?
8 Egypt rises like the Nile,
like rivers whose waters
surge.
It said, Let me rise, let me
cover the earth,
let me destroy cities and
their inhabitants.
9 Advance, O horses,
and dash madly,
O chariots!
Let the warriors go forth:
Ethiopia[r] and Put who
carry the shield,
the Ludim, who draw[s] the
bow.
10 That day is the day of the
Lord GOD of hosts,
a day of retribution,
to gain vindication from his
foes.
The sword shall devour and
be sated,
and drink its fill of their
blood.
For the Lord GOD of hosts
holds a sacrifice
in the land of the north by
the river Euphrates.
11 Go up to Gilead, and take
balm,
O virgin daughter Egypt!
In vain you have used many
medicines;
there is no healing for you.
12 The nations have heard of
your shame,
and the earth is full of your
cry;
for warrior has stumbled
against warrior;
both have fallen together.

Babylonia Will Strike Egypt

13 The word that the LORD
spoke to the prophet Jeremiah
about the coming of King Nebuchadrezzar of Babylon to attack the
land of Egypt:

14 Declare in Egypt, and
proclaim in Migdol;
proclaim in Memphis and
Tahpanhes;
Say, "Take your stations and
be ready,
for the sword shall devour
those around you."
15 Why has Apis fled?[t]
Why did your bull not
stand?
—because the LORD thrust
him down.
16 Your multitude stumbled[u]
and fell,
and one said to another,[v]
"Come, let us go back to our
own people
and to the land of our
birth,
because of the destroying
sword."
17 Give Pharaoh, king of Egypt,
the name
"Braggart who missed his
chance."

18 As I live, says the King,
whose name is the LORD of
hosts,
one is coming
like Tabor among the
mountains,
and like Carmel by the sea.
19 Pack your bags for exile,
sheltered daughter Egypt!
For Memphis shall become a
waste,
a ruin, without inhabitant.

20 A beautiful heifer is Egypt—
a gadfly from the north
lights upon her.
21 Even her mercenaries in her
midst
are like fatted calves;
they too have turned and
fled together,
they did not stand;
for the day of their calamity
has come upon them,

46.7 Jer 47.2
46.8 Isa 37.24; 10.13
46.9 Jer 47.3; Nah 2.4; 3.9; Isa 66.19
46.10 Isa 13.6; Joel 1.15; 2.1; Jer 50.15, 28; Isa 34.6; Zeph 1.7
46.11 Jer 8.22; 51.8; Isa 47.1; Jer 31.4,21; 30.13; Ezek 30.21
46.12 Jer 2.36; Nah 3.8-10; Jer 14.2
46.13 Isa 19.1; Jer 43.10,11
46.14 Jer 44.1; 43.8; Nah 2.13
46.16 Lev 26.36, 37; Jer 51.9; 50.16
46.17 Isa 19.11-16
46.18 Jer 48.15; Ps 89.12; 1 Kings 18.42
46.19 Jer 48.18; Isa 20.4; v. 4; Ezek 30.13
46.20 Jer 50.11; v. 24
46.21 v. 5; Ps 37.13; Jer 50.27

[r] Or *Nubia*; Heb *Cush* [s] Cn: Heb *who grasp, who draw* [t] Gk: Heb *Why was it swept away* [u] Gk: Meaning of Heb uncertain [v] Gk: Heb *and fell one to another and they said*

the time of their
punishment.

22 She makes a sound like a
snake gliding away;
for her enemies march in
force,
and come against her with
axes,
like those who fell trees.

23 They shall cut down her
forest,
says the LORD,
though it is impenetrable,
because they are more
numerous
than locusts;
they are without number.

24 Daughter Egypt shall be put
to shame;
she shall be handed over to
a people from the
north.

25 The LORD of hosts, the God of
Israel, said: See, I am bringing punishment upon Amon of Thebes,
and Pharaoh, and Egypt and her
gods and her kings, upon Pharaoh
and those who trust in him. 26 I will
hand them over to those who seek
their life, to King Nebuchadrezzar
of Babylon and his officers. Afterward Egypt shall be inhabited as in
the days of old, says the LORD.

God Will Save Israel

27 But as for you, have no fear,
my servant Jacob,
and do not be dismayed,
O Israel;
for I am going to save you
from far away,
and your offspring from the
land of their captivity.
Jacob shall return and have
quiet and ease,
and no one shall make him
afraid.

28 As for you, have no fear, my
servant Jacob,
says the LORD,
for I am with you.
I will make an end of all the
nations
among which I have
banished you,
but I will not make an end
of you!
I will chastise you in just
measure,
and I will by no means
leave you unpunished.

Judgment on the Philistines

47 The word of the LORD that
came to the prophet Jere-
miah concerning the Philistines,
before Pharaoh attacked Gaza:

2 Thus says the LORD:
See, waters are rising out of
the north
and shall become an
overflowing torrent;
they shall overflow the land
and all that fills it,
the city and those who live
in it.
People shall cry out,
and all the inhabitants of
the land shall wail.

3 At the noise of the stamping
of the hoofs of his
stallions,
at the clatter of his
chariots, at the
rumbling of their
wheels,
parents do not turn back for
children,
so feeble are their hands,

4 because of the day that is
coming
to destroy all the
Philistines,
to cut off from Tyre and
Sidon
every helper that remains.
For the LORD is destroying
the Philistines,
the remnant of the
coastland of Caphtor.

5 Baldness has come upon
Gaza,
Ashkelon is silenced.
O remnant of their power![w]
How long will you gash
yourselves?

6 Ah, sword of the LORD!

46.22 Isa 29.4 **46.23** Isa 10.34; Jer 21.14; Judg 6.5; Joel 2.25 **46.24** v. 19; Jer 1.15 **46.25** Jer 43.12; Ezek 30.14-16; Jer 44.30; Ezek 30.13; Isa 20.5 **46.26** Jer 44.30; Ezek 32.11; 29.11-14 **46.27** Isa 41.13; 43.5; Jer 30.10, 11; 23.3,4,6; 50.19 **46.28** Isa 8.9,10; Jer 1.19; 4.27; Am 9.8,9; Jer 10.24; 30.11

47.1 Jer 25.17, 20; Am 1.6; Zeph 2.4 **47.2** Isa 14.31; Jer 46.20, 24; Isa 8.7; 15.2-5; Jer 46.12 **47.3** Jer 8.16; Nah 3.2 **47.4** Isa 14.31; 23.5,6,11; Joel 3.4; Zech 9.2-4; Gen 10.14 **47.5** Mic 1.16; Jer 25.20; 16.6; 41.5 **47.6** Jer 12.12; 4.21

[w] Gk: Heb *their valley*

How long until you are
quiet?
Put yourself into your
scabbard,
rest and be still!
7 How can it[x] be quiet,
when the LORD has given it
an order?
Against Ashkelon and against
the seashore—
there he has appointed it.

Judgment on Moab

48 Concerning Moab.
Thus says the LORD of hosts, the God of Israel:
Alas for Nebo, it is laid
waste!
Kiriathaim is put to shame,
it is taken;
the fortress is put to shame
and broken down;
2 the renown of Moab is no
more.
In Heshbon they planned evil
against her:
"Come, let us cut her off
from being a nation!"
You also, O Madmen, shall
be brought to silence;[y]
the sword shall pursue you.

3 Hark! a cry from Horonaim,
"Desolation and great
destruction!"
4 "Moab is destroyed!"
her little ones cry out.
5 For at the ascent of Luhith
they go[z] up weeping
bitterly;
for at the descent of
Horonaim
they have heard the
distressing cry of
anguish.
6 Flee! Save yourselves!
Be like a wild ass[a] in the
desert!

7 Surely, because you trusted
in your strongholds[b]
and your treasures,
you also shall be taken;
Chemosh shall go out into
exile,
with his priests and his
attendants.
8 The destroyer shall come
upon every town,
and no town shall escape;
the valley shall perish,
and the plain shall be
destroyed,
as the LORD has spoken.

9 Set aside salt for Moab,
for she will surely fall;
her towns shall become a
desolation,
with no inhabitant in them.

10 Accursed is the one who is
slack in doing the work of the LORD;
and accursed is the one who keeps
back the sword from bloodshed.

11 Moab has been at ease from
his youth,
settled like wine[c] on its
dregs;
he has not been emptied
from vessel to vessel,
nor has he gone into exile;
therefore his flavor has
remained
and his aroma is unspoiled.
12 Therefore, the time is surely
coming, says the LORD, when I shall
send to him decanters to decant
him, and empty his vessels, and
break his[d] jars in pieces. 13 Then
Moab shall be ashamed of Chemosh, as the house of Israel was
ashamed of Bethel, their confidence.

14 How can you say, "We are
heroes
and mighty warriors"?
15 The destroyer of Moab and
his towns has come up,
and the choicest of his
young men have gone
down to slaughter,
says the King, whose name
is the LORD of hosts.

47.7 Ezek 14.17; Mic 6.9 **48.1** Isa 15.2; vv. 22,23; Num 32.37 **48.2** Isa 16.14; 15.4; Jer 49.3 **48.3** Isa 15.5; vv. 5,34 **48.5** Isa 15.5 **48.6** Jer 51.6; 17.6 **48.7** Jer 9.23; Num 21.29; 1 Kings 11.33; Jer 49.3 **48.8** Jer 6.26 **48.9** Isa 16.2; Jer 44.22 **48.10** Jer 11.3; 1 Sam 15.3, 9; 1 Kings 20.42; Jer 47.6,7 **48.11** Jer 22.21; Zech 1.15; Zeph 1.12; Nah 2.2 **48.13** Isa 45.16; v. 39; Hos 10.6; 1 Kings 12.29 **48.14** Isa 10.13-16 **48.15** Jer 50.27; 46.18

[x] Gk Vg: Heb *you* [y] The place-name *Madmen* sounds like the Hebrew verb *to be silent* [z] Cn: Heb *he goes* [a] Gk Aquila: Heb *like Aroer* [b] Gk: Heb *works* [c] Heb lacks *like wine* [d] Gk Aquila: Heb *their*

16 The calamity of Moab is near
at hand
and his doom approaches
swiftly.
17 Mourn over him, all you his
neighbors,
and all who know his
name;
say, "How the mighty scepter
is broken,
the glorious staff!"

18 Come down from glory,
and sit on the parched
ground,
enthroned daughter Dibon!
For the destroyer of Moab
has come up against
you;
he has destroyed your
strongholds.
19 Stand by the road and watch,
you inhabitant of Aroer!
Ask the man fleeing and the
woman escaping;
say, "What has happened?"
20 Moab is put to shame, for it
is broken down;
wail and cry!
Tell it by the Arnon,
that Moab is laid waste.

21 Judgment has come upon
the tableland, upon Holon, and
Jahzah, and Mephaath, 22 and Dibon, and Nebo, and Beth-
diblathaim, 23 and Kiriathaim, and
Beth-gamul, and Beth-meon,
24 and Kerioth, and Bozrah, and all
the towns of the land of Moab, far
and near. 25 The horn of Moab is
cut off, and his arm is broken, says
the LORD.
26 Make him drunk, because he
magnified himself against the
LORD; let Moab wallow in his vomit;
he too shall become a laughingstock. 27 Israel was a laughingstock
for you, though he was not caught
among thieves; but whenever you
spoke of him you shook your head!

28 Leave the towns, and live on
the rock,
O inhabitants of Moab!
Be like the dove that nests
on the sides of the mouth
of a gorge.
29 We have heard of the pride
of Moab—
he is very proud—
of his loftiness, his pride,
and his arrogance,
and the haughtiness of his
heart.
30 I myself know his insolence,
says the LORD;
his boasts are false,
his deeds are false.
31 Therefore I wail for Moab;
I cry out for all Moab;
for the people of Kir-heres
I mourn.
32 More than for Jazer I weep
for you,
O vine of Sibmah!
Your branches crossed over
the sea,
reached as far as Jazer;[e]
upon your summer fruits and
your vintage
the destroyer has fallen.
33 Gladness and joy have been
taken away
from the fruitful land of
Moab;
I have stopped the wine from
the wine presses;
no one treads them with
shouts of joy;
the shouting is not the
shout of joy.

34 Heshbon and Elealeh cry
out;[f] as far as Jahaz they utter
their voice, from Zoar to Horonaim
and Eglath-shelishiyah. For even
the waters of Nimrim have become
desolate. 35 And I will bring to an
end in Moab, says the LORD, those
who offer sacrifice at a high place
and make offerings to their gods.
36 Therefore my heart moans for
Moab like a flute, and my heart
moans like a flute for the people of
Kir-heres; for the riches they
gained have perished.
37 For every head is shaved and
every beard cut off; on all the hands
there are gashes, and on the loins

48.16 Isa 13.22 **48.17** Jer 9.17-20; Isa 14.5 **48.18** Isa 47.1; Jer 46.19; v. 8 **48.19** Deut 2.36; 1 Sam 4.13, 16 **48.20** Isa 16.7; Num 21.13 **48.21** vv. 8,34; Josh 13.18 **48.24** Am 2.2 **48.25** Ps 75.10; Ezek 30.21 **48.26** Jer 25.15,27 **48.27** Zeph 2.8; Jer 2.26; 18.16 **48.28** Jer 49.16; Ps 55.6,7; Song 2.14

48.29 Isa 16.6; Zeph 2.8; Ps 138.6 **48.30** Isa 37.28; 16.6 **48.31** Isa 15.5; 16.7,11 **48.32** Isa 16.8,9; Num 21.32 **48.33** Isa 16.10; Joel 1.12; Isa 5.10; Hag 2.16 **48.34** Isa 15.4-6 **48.35** Isa 15.2; 16.12; Jer 7.9; 11.13 **48.36** Isa 16.11; 15.7 **48.37** Isa 15.2,3; Jer 47.5

[e] Two Mss and Isa 16.8: MT *the sea of Jazer*
[f] Cn: Heb *From the cry of Heshbon to Elealeh*

sackcloth. 38 On all the housetops
of Moab and in the squares there is
nothing but lamentation; for I have
broken Moab like a vessel that no
one wants, says the LORD. 39 How it
is broken! How they wail! How
Moab has turned his back in
shame! So Moab has become a derision and a horror to all his neighbors.

40 For thus says the LORD:
Look, he shall swoop down
like an eagle,
and spread his wings
against Moab;
41 the towns[g] shall be taken
and the strongholds seized.
The hearts of the warriors of
Moab, on that day,
shall be like the heart of a
woman in labor.
42 Moab shall be destroyed as a
people,
because he magnified
himself against the
LORD.
43 Terror, pit, and trap
are before you,
O inhabitants of Moab!
says the LORD.
44 Everyone who flees from the
terror
shall fall into the pit,
and everyone who climbs out
of the pit
shall be caught in the trap.
For I will bring these things[h]
upon Moab
in the year of their
punishment,
says the LORD.

45 In the shadow of Heshbon
fugitives stop exhausted;
for a fire has gone out from
Heshbon,
a flame from the house of
Sihon;
it has destroyed the forehead
of Moab,
the scalp of the people of
tumult.[i]
46 Woe to you, O Moab!
The people of Chemosh
have perished,
for your sons have been
taken captive,
and your daughters into
captivity.
47 Yet I will restore the fortunes
of Moab
in the latter days, says the
LORD.
Thus far is the judgment on
Moab.

Judgment on the Ammonites

49 Concerning the Ammon-
ites.

Thus says the LORD:
Has Israel no sons?
Has he no heir?
Why then has Milcom
dispossessed Gad,
and his people settled in
its towns?
2 Therefore, the time is surely
coming,
says the LORD,
when I will sound the battle
alarm
against Rabbah of the
Ammonites;
it shall become a desolate
mound,
and its villages shall be
burned with fire;
then Israel shall dispossess
those who dispossessed
him,
says the LORD.

3 Wail, O Heshbon, for Ai is
laid waste!
Cry out, O daughters[j] of
Rabbah!
Put on sackcloth,
lament, and slash
yourselves with whips![k]
For Milcom shall go into
exile,
with his priests and his
attendants.
4 Why do you boast in your
strength?
Your strength is ebbing,
O faithless daughter.
You trusted in your
treasures, saying,

48.38 Jer 22.28; 25.34 **48.39** Ezek 26.16 **48.40** Jer 49.22; Dan 7.4; Hos 8.1; Isa 8.8 **48.41** Isa 21.3; Jer 30.6; 49.22,24; Mic 4.9 **48.42** v. 2; Ps 83.4; v. 26; Isa 37.23 **48.43** Isa 24.17, 18; Lam 3.47 **48.44** 1 Kings 19.17; Jer 11.23; 46.21 **48.45** v. 2; Num 21.21, 26,28,29; 24.17 **48.46** Num 21.29; v. 7

48.47 Jer 49.6,39 **49.1** Ezek 21.28; 25.2; Am 1.13; Zeph 2.8,9 **49.2** Jer 4.19; Ezek 21.20; Isa 14.2 **49.3** Jer 48.2; Josh 7.2-5; 8.1-29; Isa 32.11; Jer 4.8; 48.7 **49.4** Jer 9.23; 31.22; Ps 62.10; Ezek 28.4,5

[g] Or *Kerioth* [h] Gk Syr: Heb *bring upon it* [i] Or *of Shaon* [j] Or *villages* [k] Cn: Meaning of Heb uncertain

"Who will attack me?"
5 I am going to bring terror
upon you,
says the Lord GOD of hosts,
from all your neighbors,
and you will be scattered,
each headlong,
with no one to gather the
fugitives.
6 But afterward I will restore the
fortunes of the Ammonites, says
the LORD.

Judgment on Edom

7 Concerning Edom.

Thus says the LORD of hosts:
Is there no longer wisdom in
Teman?
Has counsel perished from
the prudent?
Has their wisdom
vanished?
8 Flee, turn back, get down
low,
inhabitants of Dedan!
For I will bring the calamity
of Esau upon him,
the time when I punish
him.
9 If grape-gatherers came to
you,
would they not leave
gleanings?
If thieves came by night,
even they would pillage
only what they wanted.
10 But as for me, I have
stripped Esau bare,
I have uncovered his hiding
places,
and he is not able to
conceal himself.
His offspring are destroyed,
his kinsfolk
and his neighbors; and he
is no more.
11 Leave your orphans, I will
keep them alive;
and let your widows trust
in me.
12 For thus says the LORD: If
those who do not deserve to drink
the cup still have to drink it, shall
you be the one to go unpunished?
You shall not go unpunished; you
must drink it. 13For by myself I
have sworn, says the LORD, that
Bozrah shall become an object of
horror and ridicule, a waste, and an
object of cursing; and all her towns
shall be perpetual wastes.
14 I have heard tidings from the
LORD,
and a messenger has been
sent among the nations:
"Gather yourselves together
and come against her,
and rise up for battle!"
15 For I will make you least
among the nations,
despised by humankind.
16 The terror you inspire
and the pride of your heart
have deceived you,
you who live in the clefts of
the rock,[l]
who hold the height of the
hill.
Although you make your nest
as high as the eagle's,
from there I will bring you
down,
says the LORD.
17 Edom shall become an object of horror; everyone who passes
by it will be horrified and will hiss
because of all its disasters. 18As
when Sodom and Gomorrah and
their neighbors were overthrown,
says the LORD, no one shall live
there, nor shall anyone settle in it.
19Like a lion coming up from the
thickets of the Jordan against a perennial pasture, I will suddenly
chase Edom[m] away from it; and I
will appoint over it whomever I
choose.[n] For who is like me? Who
can summon me? Who is the shepherd who can stand before me?
20Therefore hear the plan that the
LORD has made against Edom and
the purposes that he has formed
against the inhabitants of Teman:
Surely the little ones of the flock
shall be dragged away; surely their
fold shall be appalled at their fate.
21At the sound of their fall the
earth shall tremble; the sound of
their cry shall be heard at the Red

49.5 Jer 48.43, 44; 16.16; 46.5; Lam 4.15
49.6 v. 39; Jer 48.47
49.7 Isa 34.5,6; Ezek 25.12; Am 1.11,12; Jer 8.9; v. 20
49.8 v. 30; Jer 25.23; 46.21
49.9 Ob 5
49.10 Jer 13.26; Mal 1.3; Isa 17.14
49.11 Ps 68.5
49.12 Jer 25.28, 29; 1 Pet 4.17
49.13 Jer 44.26; Isa 34.6; 34.9-15
49.14 Ob 1-4; Isa 18.2; 30.4; Jer 50.14
49.16 Isa 25.5; 14.13-15; Am 9.2
49.17 Jer 50.13; 1 Kings 9.8; Jer 51.37
49.18 Gen 19.25; Deut 29.23; Am 4.11
49.19 Jer 50.44; 12.5; Isa 46.9
49.20 Jer 50.45; Mal 1.3,4
49.21 Jer 50.46; Ezek 26.15, 18

[l] Or *of Sela* [m] Heb *him* [n] Or *and I will single out the choicest of his rams:* Meaning of Heb uncertain

Sea.[o] 22 Look, he shall mount up
and swoop down like an eagle, and
spread his wings against Bozrah,
and the heart of the warriors of
Edom in that day shall be like the
heart of a woman in labor.

Judgment on Damascus

23 Concerning Damascus.

Hamath and Arpad are
confounded,
for they have heard bad
news;
they melt in fear, they are
troubled like the sea[p]
that cannot be quiet.
24 Damascus has become
feeble, she turned to
flee,
and panic seized her;
anguish and sorrows have
taken hold of her,
as of a woman in labor.
25 How the famous city is
forsaken,[q]
the joyful town![r]
26 Therefore her young men
shall fall in her squares,
and all her soldiers shall be
destroyed in that day,
says the LORD of hosts.
27 And I will kindle a fire at the
wall of Damascus,
and it shall devour the
strongholds of
Ben-hadad.

Judgment on Kedar and Hazor

28 Concerning Kedar and the
kingdoms of Hazor that King Nebuchadrezzar of Babylon defeated.

Thus says the LORD:
Rise up, advance against
Kedar!
Destroy the people of the
east!
29 Take their tents and their
flocks,
their curtains and all their
goods;
carry off their camels for
yourselves,
and a cry shall go up:
"Terror is all around!"
30 Flee, wander far away, hide
in deep places,
O inhabitants of Hazor!
says the LORD.
For King Nebuchadrezzar of
Babylon
has made a plan against
you
and formed a purpose
against you.
31 Rise up, advance against a
nation at ease,
that lives secure,
says the LORD,
that has no gates or bars,
that lives alone.
32 Their camels shall become
booty,
their herds of cattle a spoil.
I will scatter to every wind
those who have shaven
temples,
and I will bring calamity
against them from every
side,
says the LORD.
33 Hazor shall become a lair of
jackals,
an everlasting waste;
no one shall live there,
nor shall anyone settle in
it.

Judgment on Elam

34 The word of the LORD that
came to the prophet Jeremiah concerning Elam, at the beginning of
the reign of King Zedekiah of Judah.
35 Thus says the LORD of hosts:
I am going to break the bow of
Elam, the mainstay of their might;
36 and I will bring upon Elam the
four winds from the four quarters
of heaven; and I will scatter them
to all these winds, and there shall
be no nation to which the exiles
from Elam shall not come. 37 I will
terrify Elam before their enemies,
and before those who seek their
life; I will bring disaster upon

49.22 Jer 4.13; 48.40,41 **49.23** 2 Chr 16.2; Jer 39.5; Isa 10.9; 57.20 **49.24** v. 22; Jer 6.24; 30.6; 48.41 **49.25** Jer 33.9; 51.41 **49.26** Jer 50.30; 51.4; Am 4.10 **49.27** Jer 43.12; Am 1.3-5; 1 Kings 15.18-20 **49.28** Isa 21.16, 17; Jer 2.10; Ezek 27.21; Isa 11.14 **49.29** Jer 6.25; 20.3,10; 46.5 **49.30** Jer 25.9 **49.31** Isa 47.8; Ezek 38.11; Deut 33.28 **49.32** Ezek 12.14, 15; Jer 9.26; 25.23 **49.33** Jer 10.22; Zeph 2.9, 13-15 **49.34** Ezek 32.24; 2 Kings 24.17, 18; Jer 28.1 **49.35** Isa 22.6; Jer 51.56 **49.36** Rev 7.1; Ezek 5.10; Am 9.9 **49.37** Jer 8.9; 17.18; 6.19; 30.24; 9.16

o Or *Sea of Reeds* p Cn: Heb *there is trouble in the sea* q Vg: Heb *is not forsaken* r Syr Vg Tg: Heb *the town of my joy*

them, my fierce anger, says the
LORD. I will send the sword after
them, until I have consumed them;
38 and I will set my throne in Elam,
and destroy their king and officials,
says the LORD.
39 But in the latter days I will
restore the fortunes of Elam, says
the LORD.

Judgment on Babylon

50 The word that the LORD
spoke concerning Babylon,
concerning the land of the Chaldeans, by the prophet Jeremiah:

2 Declare among the nations
and proclaim,
set up a banner and
proclaim,
do not conceal it, say:
Babylon is taken,
Bel is put to shame,
Merodach is dismayed.
Her images are put to
shame,
her idols are dismayed.

3 For out of the north a nation
has come up against her; it shall
make her land a desolation, and no
one shall live in it; both human beings and animals shall flee away.

4 In those days and in that time,
says the LORD, the people of Israel
shall come, they and the people of
Judah together; they shall come
weeping as they seek the LORD their
God. 5 They shall ask the way to
Zion, with faces turned toward it,
and they shall come and join[s]
themselves to the LORD by an everlasting covenant that will never be
forgotten.

6 My people have been lost
sheep; their shepherds have led
them astray, turning them away on
the mountains; from mountain to
hill they have gone, they have forgotten their fold. 7 All who found
them have devoured them, and
their enemies have said, "We are
not guilty, because they have
sinned against the LORD, the true
pasture, the LORD, the hope of their
ancestors."

49.39 Jer 48.47
50.1 Isa 13.1; Rev 14.8
50.2 Jer 51.27, 31; Isa 46.1; Jer 51.44,47
50.3 Jer 51.48; 9.10; Zeph 1.3
50.4 Hos 1.11; Ezra 3.12, 13; Jer 31.9; Zech 12.10; Hos 3.5
50.6 Isa 53.6; Ezek 34.15, 16; Jer 23.11-14; 2.20; 3.6,23; 33.12
50.7 Jer 40.2,3; 31.23; 14.8; 17.13
50.8 Jer 51.6,45; Rev 18.4
50.9 Jer 51.1,2
50.10 Jer 51.24, 35; Rev 17.16
50.11 Jer 12.14; 46.20
50.12 Jer 22.6; 51.43
50.13 Jer 25.12; 49.17
50.14 Jer 49.35; Hab 2.8,17
50.15 Jer 51.14; 1 Chr 29.24; Ezek 17.18; Jer 51.44, 58; 46.10

8 Flee from Babylon, and go out
of the land of the Chaldeans, and
be like male goats leading the
flock. 9 For I am going to stir up and
bring against Babylon a company
of great nations from the land of
the north; and they shall array
themselves against her; from there
she shall be taken. Their arrows are
like the arrows of a skilled warrior
who does not return empty-
handed. 10 Chaldea shall be plundered; all who plunder her shall be
sated, says the LORD.

11 Though you rejoice, though
you exult,
O plunderers of my
heritage,
though you frisk about like a
heifer on the grass,
and neigh like stallions,
12 your mother shall be utterly
shamed,
and she who bore you shall
be disgraced.
Lo, she shall be the last of
the nations,
a wilderness, dry land, and
a desert.
13 Because of the wrath of the
LORD she shall not be
inhabited,
but shall be an utter
desolation;
everyone who passes by
Babylon shall be
appalled
and hiss because of all her
wounds.
14 Take up your positions
around Babylon,
all you that bend the bow;
shoot at her, spare no
arrows,
for she has sinned against
the LORD.
15 Raise a shout against her
from all sides,
"She has surrendered;
her bulwarks have fallen,
her walls are thrown
down."
For this is the vengeance of
the LORD:

[s] Gk: Heb *toward it. Come! They shall join*

take vengeance on her,
do to her as she has done.
16 Cut off from Babylon the
sower,
and the wielder of the
sickle in time of
harvest;
because of the destroying
sword
all of them shall return to
their own people,
and all of them shall flee
to their own land.

17 Israel is a hunted sheep driv-
en away by lions. First the king of
Assyria devoured it, and now at the
end King Nebuchadrezzar of Babylon has gnawed its bones.
18 Therefore, thus says the LORD of
hosts, the God of Israel: I am going
to punish the king of Babylon and
his land, as I punished the king of
Assyria. 19 I will restore Israel to its
pasture, and it shall feed on Carmel
and in Bashan, and on the hills of
Ephraim and in Gilead its hunger
shall be satisfied. 20 In those days
and at that time, says the LORD, the
iniquity of Israel shall be sought,
and there shall be none; and the
sins of Judah, and none shall be
found; for I will pardon the remnant that I have spared.

21 Go up to the land of
Merathaim;[t]
go up against her,
and attack the inhabitants of
Pekod[u]
and utterly destroy the last
of them,[v] says the LORD;
do all that I have
commanded you.
22 The noise of battle is in the
land,
and great destruction!
23 How the hammer of the
whole earth
is cut down and broken!
How Babylon has become
a horror among the
nations!
24 You set a snare for yourself
and you were caught,
O Babylon,

50.16 Joel 1.11; Jer 51.9 **50.17** Jer 2.15; 2 Kings 17.6; 24.10,14 **50.18** Isa 10.12; Ezek 31.3, 11,12 **50.19** Jer 31.10; 33.12; 31.5 **50.20** Jer 31.34; Mic 7.19; Isa 1.9; Jer 33.8 **50.21** Ezek 23.23; Isa 10.6; 44.28; 48.14; Jer 34.22 **50.22** Jer 51.54-56 **50.23** Isa 14.6; Jer 51.20-24 **50.24** Jer 48.43, 44; 51.8,31, 39,57; Dan 5.30,31

50.25 Isa 13.5; Jer 51.12, 25,55 **50.26** v. 41; Isa 14.23 **50.27** Isa 34.7; Ezek 7.7; Jer 48.44 **50.28** Isa 48.20; Jer 51.6; 51.10,11 **50.29** Jer 51.56; Rev 18.6; Isa 47.10 **50.30** Isa 13.17, 18; Jer 49.26; 51.56,57 **50.31** Jer 21.13; Nah 2.13 **50.32** Isa 10.12-15; Jer 21.14; 49.27

but you did not know it;
you were discovered and
seized,
because you challenged the
LORD.
25 The LORD has opened his
armory,
and brought out the
weapons of his wrath,
for the Lord GOD of hosts has
a task to do
in the land of the
Chaldeans.
26 Come against her from every
quarter;
open her granaries;
pile her up like heaps of
grain, and destroy her
utterly;
let nothing be left of her.
27 Kill all her bulls,
let them go down to the
slaughter.
Alas for them, their day has
come,
the time of their
punishment!

28 Listen! Fugitives and refu-
gees from the land of Babylon are
coming to declare in Zion the vengeance of the LORD our God, vengeance for his temple.

29 Summon archers against
Babylon, all who bend the bow. Encamp all around her; let no one escape. Repay her according to her
deeds; just as she has done, do to
her—for she has arrogantly defied
the LORD, the Holy One of Israel.
30 Therefore her young men shall
fall in her squares, and all her soldiers shall be destroyed on that
day, says the LORD.

31 I am against you, O arrogant
one,
says the Lord GOD of hosts;
for your day has come,
the time when I will punish
you.
32 The arrogant one shall
stumble and fall,

[t] Or *of Double Rebellion* [u] Or *of Punishment* [v] Tg: Heb *destroy after them*

with no one to raise him
up,
and I will kindle a fire in his
cities,
and it will devour
everything around him.

33 Thus says the LORD of hosts:
The people of Israel are oppressed,
and so too are the people of Judah;
all their captors have held them
fast and refuse to let them go.
34 Their Redeemer is strong; the
LORD of hosts is his name. He will
surely plead their cause, that he
may give rest to the earth, but unrest to the inhabitants of Babylon.

35 A sword against the
Chaldeans, says the
LORD,
and against the inhabitants
of Babylon,
and against her officials
and her sages!
36 A sword against the diviners,
so that they may become
fools!
A sword against her warriors,
so that they may be
destroyed!
37 A sword against her[w] horses
and against her[w]
chariots,
and against all the foreign
troops in her midst,
so that they may become
women!
A sword against all her
treasures,
that they may be
plundered!
38 A drought[x] against her
waters,
that they may be dried up!
For it is a land of images,
and they go mad over idols.

39 Therefore wild animals shall
live with hyenas in Babylon,[y] and
ostriches shall inhabit her; she
shall never again be peopled, or inhabited for all generations. 40 As
when God overthrew Sodom and
Gomorrah and their neighbors,
says the LORD, so no one shall live
there, nor shall anyone settle in
her.

41 Look, a people is coming
from the north;
a mighty nation and many
kings
are stirring from the
farthest parts of the
earth.
42 They wield bow and spear,
they are cruel and have no
mercy.
The sound of them is like
the roaring sea;
they ride upon horses,
set in array as a warrior for
battle,
against you, O daughter
Babylon!

43 The king of Babylon heard
news of them,
and his hands fell helpless;
anguish seized him,
pain like that of a woman
in labor.

44 Like a lion coming up from
the thickets of the Jordan against a
perennial pasture, I will suddenly
chase them away from her; and I
will appoint over her whomever I
choose.[z] For who is like me? Who
can summon me? Who is the shepherd who can stand before me?
45 Therefore hear the plan that the
LORD has made against Babylon,
and the purposes that he has
formed against the land of the
Chaldeans: Surely the little ones of
the flock shall be dragged away;
surely their[a] fold shall be appalled
at their fate. 46 At the sound of the
capture of Babylon the earth shall
tremble, and her cry shall be heard
among the nations.

51 Thus says the LORD:
I am going to stir up a
destructive wind[b]

50.33 Isa 14.17; 58.6
50.34 Isa 43.14; Jer 15.21; 31.11; 32.18; 51.19,36; Isa 14.3-7
50.35 Dan 5.1,2,7, 8,30
50.36 Isa 44.25; Jer 49.22
50.37 Jer 51.21, 22; 25.30; Ezek 30.5; Jer 51.30; Nah 3.13
50.38 Jer 51.32, 36,42,47,52
50.39 Isa 13.21, 22; Jer 51.37; Isa 13.20
50.40 Gen 19.25; Jer 49.18; Lk 17.28-30
50.41 cf. v. 3; Jer 6.22; Rev 17.16
50.42 Jer 6.23; Isa 13.18; 5.30
50.43 Jer 51.31; 49.24
50.44 Jer 49.19-21; Isa 46.9; Job 41.10; Jer 49.19
50.45 Isa 14.24; Jer 51.11; 49.20
50.46 Rev 18.9; Ezek 27.28
51.1 Jer 4.11; Hos 13.15

[w] Cn: Heb *his* [x] Another reading is *A sword* [y] Heb lacks *in Babylon* [z] Or *and I will single out the choicest of her rams*: Meaning of Heb uncertain [a] Syr Gk Tg Compare 49.20: Heb lacks *their* [b] Or *stir up the spirit of a destroyer*

against Babylon
and against the inhabitants of Leb-qamai;[c]
2 and I will send winnowers to Babylon,
and they shall winnow her.
They shall empty her land
when they come against her from every side
on the day of trouble.
3 Let not the archer bend his bow,
and let him not array himself in his coat of mail.
Do not spare her young men;
utterly destroy her entire army.
4 They shall fall down slain in the land of the Chaldeans,
and wounded in her streets.
5 Israel and Judah have not been forsaken
by their God, the LORD of hosts,
though their land is full of guilt
before the Holy One of Israel.

6 Flee from the midst of Babylon,
save your lives, each of you!
Do not perish because of her guilt,
for this is the time of the LORD's vengeance;
he is repaying her what is due.
7 Babylon was a golden cup in the LORD's hand,
making all the earth drunken;
the nations drank of her wine,
and so the nations went mad.
8 Suddenly Babylon has fallen and is shattered;
wail for her!
Bring balm for her wound;
perhaps she may be healed.
9 We tried to heal Babylon,
but she could not be healed.
Forsake her, and let each of us go
to our own country;
for her judgment has reached up to heaven
and has been lifted up even to the skies.
10 The LORD has brought forth our vindication;
come, let us declare in Zion
the work of the LORD our God.

11 Sharpen the arrows!
Fill the quivers!

The LORD has stirred up the spirit of
the kings of the Medes, because his
purpose concerning Babylon is to
destroy it, for that is the vengeance
of the LORD, vengeance for his temple.
12 Raise a standard against the walls of Babylon;
make the watch strong;
post sentinels;
prepare the ambushes;
for the LORD has both planned and done
what he spoke concerning the inhabitants of Babylon.
13 You who live by mighty waters,
rich in treasures,
your end has come,
the thread of your life is cut.
14 The LORD of hosts has sworn by himself:
Surely I will fill you with troops like a swarm of locusts,
and they shall raise a shout of victory over you.

15 It is he who made the earth by his power,
who established the world by his wisdom,

51.2 Isa 41.16; Jer 15.7; Mt 3.12
51.3 Jer 50.14; 46.4; 50.21
51.4 Jer 49.26; 50.30,37
51.5 Isa 54.7,8; Jer 33.24-26
51.6 Jer 50.8; Rev 18.4; Num 16.26; Jer 50.15; 25.14
51.7 Rev 17.4; Jer 25.15; Rev 14.8; 18.3; Jer 25.16
51.8 Isa 21.9; Rev 14.8; 18.2; Jer 48.20; Rev 18.9,11, 19
51.9 Isa 13.14; Jer 50.16; Rev 18.5
51.10 Ps 37.6; Mic 7.9; Isa 40.2; Jer 50.28
51.11 Jer 46.4; Joel 3.9,10; Jer 50.3,9, 28
51.12 Isa 13.2; Jer 50.2
51.13 Rev 17.1,15
51.14 Jer 49.13; Am 6.8; Nah 3.15; Jer 50.15
51.15ff Gen 1.1,6; Jer 10.12-16; Acts 14.15; Rom 1.20; Job 9.8; Ps 104.2; Isa 40.22

[c] *Leb-qamai* is a cryptogram for *Kasdim*, Chaldea

and by his understanding
stretched out the
heavens.
16 When he utters his voice
there is a tumult of
waters in the heavens,
and he makes the mist rise
from the ends of the
earth.
He makes lightnings for the
rain,
and he brings out the wind
from his storehouses.
17 Everyone is stupid and
without knowledge;
goldsmiths are all put to
shame by their idols;
for their images are false,
and there is no breath in
them.
18 They are worthless, a work of
delusion;
at the time of their
punishment they shall
perish.
19 Not like these is the LORD,[d]
the portion of Jacob,
for he is the one who
formed all things,
and Israel is the tribe of his
inheritance;
the LORD of hosts is his
name.

Israel the Creator's Instrument

20 You are my war club, my
weapon of battle:
with you I smash nations;
with you I destroy
kingdoms;
21 with you I smash the horse
and its rider;
with you I smash the
chariot and the
charioteer;
22 with you I smash man and
woman;
with you I smash the old
man and the boy;
with you I smash the young
man and the girl;
23 with you I smash
shepherds and their
flocks;
with you I smash farmers
and their teams;
with you I smash governors
and deputies.

The Doom of Babylon

24 I will repay Babylon and all
the inhabitants of Chaldea before
your very eyes for all the wrong that
they have done in Zion, says the
LORD.

25 I am against you,
O destroying mountain,
says the LORD,
that destroys the whole
earth;
I will stretch out my hand
against you,
and roll you down from the
crags,
and make you a burned-out
mountain.
26 No stone shall be taken from
you for a corner
and no stone for a
foundation,
but you shall be a perpetual
waste,
says the LORD.

27 Raise a standard in the land,
blow the trumpet among
the nations;
prepare the nations for war
against her,
summon against her the
kingdoms,
Ararat, Minni, and
Ashkenaz;
appoint a marshal against
her,
bring up horses like
bristling locusts.
28 Prepare the nations for war
against her,
the kings of the Medes,
with their governors
and deputies,
and every land under their
dominion.
29 The land trembles and
writhes,
for the LORD's purposes
against Babylon stand,
to make the land of Babylon
a desolation,

51.16 Ps 18.13; Jer 10.13; Ps 135.7
51.17 Jer 10.14; 50.2; Hab 2.18,19
51.18 Jer 10.15
51.19 Jer 10.16; 50.34
51.20 Isa 10.5,15; Jer 50.23; Isa 41.15, 16; Mic 4.12,13
51.22 2 Chr 36.17
51.23 v. 57
51.24 Jer 50.10, 15,29
51.25 Jer 50.31; Zech 4.7; Rev 8.8
51.26 v. 29; Jer 50.13
51.27 Isa 13.2; Jer 50.2; 25.14; 50.41, 42
51.28 v. 11
51.29 Jer 8.16; 10.10; 50.46; Am 8.8; Isa 13.19, 20; 47.11

[d] Heb lacks *the LORD*

without inhabitant.
30 The warriors of Babylon have
given up fighting,
they remain in their
strongholds;
their strength has failed,
they have become women;
her buildings are set on fire,
her bars are broken.
31 One runner runs to meet
another,
and one messenger to meet
another,
to tell the king of Babylon
that his city is taken from
end to end:
32 the fords have been seized,
the marshes have been
burned with fire,
and the soldiers are in
panic.
33 For thus says the LORD of
hosts, the God of Israel:
Daughter Babylon is like a
threshing floor
at the time when it is
trodden;
yet a little while
and the time of her harvest
will come.

34 "King Nebuchadrezzar of
Babylon has devoured
me,
he has crushed me;
he has made me an empty
vessel,
he has swallowed me like a
monster;
he has filled his belly with
my delicacies,
he has spewed me out.
35 May my torn flesh be
avenged on Babylon,"
the inhabitants of Zion
shall say.
"May my blood be avenged
on the inhabitants of
Chaldea,"
Jerusalem shall say.
36 Therefore thus says the LORD:
I am going to defend your
cause
and take vengeance for
you.
I will dry up her sea
and make her fountain dry;
37 and Babylon shall become a
heap of ruins,
a den of jackals,
an object of horror and of
hissing,
without inhabitant.
38 Like lions they shall roar
together;
they shall growl like lions'
whelps.
39 When they are inflamed, I
will set out their drink
and make them drunk,
until they become
merry
and then sleep a perpetual
sleep
and never wake, says the
LORD.
40 I will bring them down like
lambs to the slaughter,
like rams and goats.

41 How Sheshach[e] is taken,
the pride of the whole
earth seized!
How Babylon has become
an object of horror among
the nations!
42 The sea has risen over
Babylon;
she has been covered by its
tumultuous waves.
43 Her cities have become an
object of horror,
a land of drought and a
desert,
a land in which no one lives,
and through which no
mortal passes.
44 I will punish Bel in Babylon,
and make him disgorge
what he has swallowed.
The nations shall no longer
stream to him;
the wall of Babylon has
fallen.

45 Come out of her, my people!
Save your lives, each of
you,
from the fierce anger of the
LORD!

51.30 Ps 76.5; Jer 50.36, 37; Isa 13.7, 8; Lam 2.9; Am 1.5; Nah 3.13
51.31 2 Chr 30.6; 2 Sam 18.19-31; Jer 50.24
51.32 Jer 50.37,38
51.33 Isa 21.10; 41.15; Hab 3.12; Isa 17.5-7; Hos 6.11; Joel 3.13
51.34 Jer 50.17; Isa 24.1-3; Am 8.4
51.35 Ps 137.8; v. 24
51.36 Ps 140.12; Jer 50.34; Rom 12.19; Jer 50.38
51.37 Isa 13.22; Jer 50.39; Rev 18.2 Jer 49.33; 50.13
51.39 Jer 25.27
51.40 Jer 50.27
51.41 Jer 25.26; Isa 13.19; Jer 49.25
51.42 Isa 8.7,8; Dan 9.26
51.43 Jer 50.12; Isa 13.20
51.44 Isa 46.1; Jer 50.2; vv. 34,58
51.45 v. 6; Jer 50.8; Rev 18.4; Acts 2.40

[e] *Sheshach* is a cryptogram for *Babel*, Babylon

46 Do not be fainthearted or
fearful
at the rumors heard in the
land—
one year one rumor comes,
the next year another,
rumors of violence in the
land
and of ruler against ruler.

47 Assuredly, the days are
coming
when I will punish the
images of Babylon;
her whole land shall be put
to shame,
and all her slain shall fall
in her midst.
48 Then the heavens and the
earth,
and all that is in them,
shall shout for joy over
Babylon;
for the destroyers shall
come against them out
of the north,
says the LORD.
49 Babylon must fall for the
slain of Israel,
as the slain of all the earth
have fallen because of
Babylon.

50 You survivors of the sword,
go, do not linger!
Remember the LORD in a
distant land,
and let Jerusalem come
into your mind:
51 We are put to shame, for we
have heard insults;
dishonor has covered our
face,
for aliens have come
into the holy places of the
LORD's house.

52 Therefore the time is surely
coming, says the LORD,
when I will punish her
idols,
and through all her land
the wounded shall groan.
53 Though Babylon should
mount up to heaven,

51.46 Jer 46.27, 28; 2 Kings 19.7; Isa 13.3-5; 19.2
51.47 Isa 46.1,2; v. 52; Jer 50.2; 50.12,35-37
51.48 Isa 44.23; 49.13; Rev 12.12; 18.20; vv. 11,27
51.49 Jer 50.29
51.50 v. 45; Ps 137.6
51.51 Ps 79.4
51.52 v. 47; Jer 50.38
51.53 Isa 14.12, 13; Jer 49.16; Isa 13.3
51.54 Jer 50.46
51.55 v. 42
51.56 v. 48; Hab 2.8; Ps 94.1,2; vv. 6,24
51.57 v. 39; Ps 76.5,6; Jer 46.18; 48.15
51.58 v. 44; Jer 50.15; Hab 2.13; v. 64
51.59 Jer 32.12; 28.1

and though she should
fortify her strong height,
from me destroyers would
come upon her,
says the LORD.

54 Listen!—a cry from Babylon!
A great crashing from the
land of the Chaldeans!
55 For the LORD is laying
Babylon waste,
and stilling her loud
clamor.
Their waves roar like mighty
waters,
the sound of their clamor
resounds;
56 for a destroyer has come
against her,
against Babylon;
her warriors are taken,
their bows are broken;
for the LORD is a God of
recompense,
he will repay in full.
57 I will make her officials and
her sages drunk,
also her governors, her
deputies, and her
warriors;
they shall sleep a perpetual
sleep and never wake,
says the King, whose name
is the LORD of hosts.

58 Thus says the LORD of hosts:
The broad wall of Babylon
shall be leveled to the
ground,
and her high gates
shall be burned with fire.
The peoples exhaust
themselves for nothing,
and the nations weary
themselves only for
fire.[f]

Jeremiah's Command to Seraiah

59 The word that the prophet
Jeremiah commanded Seraiah son
of Neriah son of Mahseiah, when
he went with King Zedekiah of Judah to Babylon, in the fourth year
of his reign. Seraiah was the quar-

[f] Gk Syr Compare Hab 2.13: Heb *and the nations for fire, and they are weary*

termaster. 60 Jeremiah wrote in a[g] scroll all the disasters that would come on Babylon, all these words that are written concerning Babylon. 61 And Jeremiah said to Seraiah: "When you come to Babylon, see that you read all these words, 62 and say, 'O LORD, you yourself threatened to destroy this place so that neither human beings nor animals shall live in it, and it shall be desolate forever.' 63 When you finish reading this scroll, tie a stone to it, and throw it into the middle of the Euphrates, 64 and say, 'Thus shall Babylon sink, to rise no more, because of the disasters that I am bringing on her.' "[h]

Thus far are the words of Jeremiah.

The Destruction of Jerusalem Reviewed

52 Zedekiah was twenty-one years old when he began to reign; he reigned eleven years in Jerusalem. His mother's name was Hamutal daughter of Jeremiah of Libnah. 2 He did what was evil in the sight of the LORD, just as Jehoiakim had done. 3 Indeed, Jerusalem and Judah so angered the LORD that he expelled them from his presence.

Zedekiah rebelled against the king of Babylon. 4 And in the ninth year of his reign, in the tenth month, on the tenth day of the month, King Nebuchadrezzar of Babylon came with all his army against Jerusalem, and they laid siege to it; they built siegeworks against it all around. 5 So the city was besieged until the eleventh year of King Zedekiah. 6 On the ninth day of the fourth month the famine became so severe in the city that there was no food for the people of the land. 7 Then a breach was made in the city wall;[i] and all the soldiers fled and went out from the city by night by the way of the gate between the two walls, by the king's garden, though the Chaldeans were all around the city. They went in the direction of the Arabah. 8 But the army of the Chaldeans pursued the king, and overtook Zedekiah in the plains of Jericho; and all his army was scattered, deserting him. 9 Then they captured the king, and brought him up to the king of Babylon at Riblah in the land of Hamath, and he passed sentence on him. 10 The king of Babylon killed the sons of Zedekiah before his eyes, and also killed all the officers of Judah at Riblah. 11 He put out the eyes of Zedekiah, and bound him in fetters, and the king of Babylon took him to Babylon, and put him in prison until the day of his death.

12 In the fifth month, on the tenth day of the month—which was the nineteenth year of King Nebuchadrezzar, king of Babylon—Nebuzaradan the captain of the bodyguard who served the king of Babylon, entered Jerusalem. 13 He burned the house of the LORD, the king's house, and all the houses of Jerusalem; every great house he burned down. 14 All the army of the Chaldeans, who were with the captain of the guard, broke down all the walls around Jerusalem. 15 Nebuzaradan the captain of the guard carried into exile some of the poorest of the people and the rest of the people who were left in the city and the deserters who had defected to the king of Babylon, together with the rest of the artisans. 16 But Nebuzaradan the captain of the guard left some of the poorest people of the land to be vinedressers and tillers of the soil.

17 The pillars of bronze that were in the house of the LORD, and the stands and the bronze sea that were in the house of the LORD, the Chaldeans broke in pieces, and carried all the bronze to Babylon. 18 They took away the pots, the shovels, the snuffers, the basins, the ladles, and all the vessels of bronze used in the temple service. 19 The captain of the guard took

51.60 Jer 30.2,3; 36.2,4,32
51.62 Jer 25.12; 50.3,39; v. 43; Ezek 35.9
51.63 Rev 18.21
51.64 Nah 1.8,9; v. 58
52.1 2 Kings 24.18; 2 Chr 36.11-13
52.2 Jer 36.30,31
52.3 Isa 3.1,4,5; 2 Chr 36.13
52.4 2 Kings 25.1-7; Jer 39.1; Ezek 24.1,2; Jer 32.24
52.6 Jer 38.9
52.7 Jer 39.2; 39.4-7
52.8 Jer 21.7; 32.4; 34.21; 37.17; 38.23
52.9 Jer 32.4; 2 Kings 25.6; Jer 39.5
52.10 Jer 39.6
52.11 Jer 39.7; Ezek 12.13
52.12 2 Kings 25.8-21; Jer 39.9
52.13 2 Chr 36.19; Lam 2.7; Mic 3.12; Jer 39.8
52.14 2 Kings 25.10
52.15 2 Kings 25.11; Jer 39.9
52.16 2 Kings 25.12; Jer 39.10; 40.2-6
52.17 1 Kings 7.15-36; Jer 27.19-22
52.18 1 Kings 7.40, 45
52.19 1 Kings 7.49, 50

[g] Or *one* [h] Gk: Heb *on her. And they shall weary themselves* [i] Heb lacks *wall*

away the small bowls also, the firepans, the basins, the pots, the
lampstands, the ladles, and the
bowls for libation, both those of
gold and those of silver. 20 As for
the two pillars, the one sea, the
twelve bronze bulls that were under the sea, and the stands,[j] which
King Solomon had made for the
house of the LORD, the bronze of all
these vessels was beyond weighing.
21 As for the pillars, the height of
the one pillar was eighteen cubits,
its circumference was twelve cubits; it was hollow and its thickness
was four fingers. 22 Upon it was a
capital of bronze; the height of the
one capital was five cubits; latticework and pomegranates, all of
bronze, encircled the top of the
capital. And the second pillar had
the same, with pomegranates.
23 There were ninety-six pomegranates on the sides; all the pomegranates encircling the latticework
numbered one hundred.

24 The captain of the guard
took the chief priest Seraiah, the
second priest Zephaniah, and the
three guardians of the threshold;
25 and from the city he took an officer who had been in command of
the soldiers, and seven men of the
king's council who were found in
the city; the secretary of the commander of the army who mustered
the people of the land; and sixty
men of the people of the land who
were found inside the city. 26 Then
Nebuzaradan the captain of the
guard took them, and brought
them to the king of Babylon at Riblah. 27 And the king of Babylon
struck them down, and put them to
death at Riblah in the land of Hamath. So Judah went into exile out
of its land.

28 This is the number of the
people whom Nebuchadrezzar
took into exile: in the seventh year,
three thousand twenty-three Judeans; 29 in the eighteenth year of
Nebuchadrezzar he took into exile
from Jerusalem eight hundred
thirty-two persons; 30 in the twenty-
third year of Nebuchadrezzar, Nebuzaradan the captain of the guard
took into exile of the Judeans sev-
en hundred forty-five persons; all
the persons were four thousand six
hundred.

Jehoiachin Favored in Captivity

31 In the thirty-seventh year of
the exile of King Jehoiachin of Judah, in the twelfth month, on the
twenty-fifth day of the month, King
Evil-merodach of Babylon, in the
year he began to reign, showed favor to King Jehoiachin of Judah
and brought him out of prison; 32 he
spoke kindly to him, and gave him
a seat above the seats of the other
kings who were with him in Babylon. 33 So Jehoiachin put aside his
prison clothes, and every day of his
life he dined regularly at the king's
table. 34 For his allowance, a regular daily allowance was given him
by the king of Babylon, as long as
he lived, up to the day of his death.

52.20 1 Kings 7.47
52.21 1 Kings 7.15
52.22 1 Kings 7.16, 20,42
52.24 2 Kings 25.18; Jer 21.1; 29.25; 37.3; 35.4
52.26 vv. 12,15, 16; 2 Kings 25.20, 21; v. 9
52.27 Isa 6.11,12; Jer 13.19; Ezek 33.28; Mic 4.10
52.28 2 Kings 24.2, 3,12-16; Neh 7.6; Dan 1.1-3
52.30 2 Kings 25.11; Jer 39.9
52.31 2 Kings 25.27-30; Gen 40.13
52.33 Gen 41.14, 42; 2 Sam 9.13; 1 Kings 2.7
52.34 2 Sam 9.10

j Cn: Heb *that were under the stands*

Lamentations

Title and Background

Because of its subject matter, this book is referred to in Jewish tradition as "Lamentations." It was written as an expression of the people's feelings after Jerusalem was destroyed and the temple burned to the ground.

Author and Date of Writing

Although the writer of Lamentations is anonymous, ancient Jewish and Christian tradition ascribes it to Jeremiah. Since he was an eyewitness to the divine judgment on Jerusalem in 586 B.C., it is reasonable to assume he was the author. The book was probably written shortly after 586.

Theme and Message

Lamentations is the only Old Testament book that consists solely of laments. Jeremiah recognizes that the judgment on Jerusalem and the temple is the judgment of a righteous God. The book that begins with a lament (1.1-2) rightly ends in repentance (5.21-22). Knowing that God is merciful, he appeals for mercy in prayer to God. In the middle of the book, the theology of Lamentations reaches its apex as it focuses on the goodness of God. In spite of all evidence to the contrary, "his mercies never come to an end" (3.22).

Outline

I. Jerusalem's Misery and Desolation (1.1-22)
II. The Lord's Anger Against His People (2.1-22)
III. Judah's Complaint and the Basis for Consolation (3.1-66)
IV. The Contrast Between Zion's Past and Present (4.1-22)
V. Judah's Appeal for God's Forgiveness (5.1-22)

The Deserted City

1 How lonely sits the city
that once was full of
people!
How like a widow she has
become,
she that was great among
the nations!
She that was a princess
among the provinces
has become a vassal.

2 She weeps bitterly in the
night,
with tears on her cheeks;
among all her lovers
she has no one to comfort
her;
all her friends have dealt
treacherously with her,
they have become her
enemies.

3 Judah has gone into exile
with suffering
and hard servitude;
she lives now among the
nations,
and finds no resting place;
her pursuers have all
overtaken her
in the midst of her distress.

4 The roads to Zion mourn,
for no one comes to the
festivals;
all her gates are desolate,
her priests groan;
her young girls grieve,[a]
and her lot is bitter.

1.1 Isa 3.26; 54.4; Ezra 4.20; Jer 40.9
1.2 Ps 6.6; Jer 2.25; 4.30
1.3 Jer 13.19; Deut 28.64, 65; 2 Kings 25.4, 5
1.4 Jer 9.11; 10.22; Joel 1.8-13

[a] Meaning of Heb uncertain

5 Her foes have become the masters,
her enemies prosper,
because the LORD has made her suffer
for the multitude of her transgressions;
her children have gone away,
captives before the foe.

6 From daughter Zion has departed
all her majesty.
Her princes have become like stags
that find no pasture;
they fled without strength
before the pursuer.

7 Jerusalem remembers,
in the days of her affliction and wandering,
all the precious things
that were hers in days of old.
When her people fell into the hand of the foe,
and there was no one to help her,
the foe looked on mocking
over her downfall.

8 Jerusalem sinned grievously,
so she has become a mockery;
all who honored her despise her,
for they have seen her nakedness;
she herself groans,
and turns her face away.

9 Her uncleanness was in her skirts;
she took no thought of her future;
her downfall was appalling,
with none to comfort her.
"O LORD, look at my affliction,
for the enemy has triumphed!"

10 Enemies have stretched out their hands
over all her precious things;
she has even seen the nations
invade her sanctuary,
those whom you forbade
to enter your congregation.

11 All her people groan
as they search for bread;
they trade their treasures for food
to revive their strength.
Look, O LORD, and see
how worthless I have become.

12 Is it nothing to you,[b] all you who pass by?
Look and see
if there is any sorrow like my sorrow,
which was brought upon me,
which the LORD inflicted
on the day of his fierce anger.

13 From on high he sent fire;
it went deep into my bones;
he spread a net for my feet;
he turned me back;
he has left me stunned,
faint all day long.

14 My transgressions were bound[b] into a yoke;
by his hand they were fastened together;
they weigh on my neck,
sapping my strength;
the Lord handed me over
to those whom I cannot withstand.

15 The LORD has rejected
all my warriors in the midst of me;
he proclaimed a time against me
to crush my young men;
the Lord has trodden as in a wine press
the virgin daughter Judah.

1.5 Deut 28.43, 44; Jer 30.14, 15; 39.9; 52.28
1.6 Jer 13.18; 2 Kings 25.4, 5
1.7 Ps 42.4; Isa 5.1-4; Jer 37.7; Lam 4.17; Jer 48.27
1.8 1 Kings 8.46; vv. 5,20,17; Jer 13.22, 26; vv. 4,11, 21,22
1.9 Ezek 24.13; Deut 32.29; Isa 47.7; Jer 13.17, 18; 16.7
1.10 Isa 64.10, 11; Jer 51.51; Deut 23.3
1.11 Jer 38.9; 52.6; 1 Sam 30.12
1.12 Jer 18.16; 48.27; v. 18; Jer 30.23, 24; 4.8
1.13 Job 30.30; Hab 3.16; Job 19.6; Jer 44.6
1.14 Deut 28.48; Isa 47.6; Jer 28.13, 14; 32.3,5; Ezek 25.4,7
1.15 Isa 41.2; Jer 13.24; 18.21; Isa 28.18; Mic 7.10; Rev 14.19

[b] Meaning of Heb uncertain

16 For these things I weep;
my eyes flow with tears;
for a comforter is far from
me,
one to revive my courage;
my children are desolate,
for the enemy has
prevailed.

17 Zion stretches out her hands,
but there is no one to
comfort her;
the LORD has commanded
against Jacob
that his neighbors should
become his foes;
Jerusalem has become
a filthy thing among them.

18 The LORD is in the right,
for I have rebelled against
his word;
but hear, all you peoples,
and behold my suffering;
my young women and young
men
have gone into captivity.

19 I called to my lovers
but they deceived me;
my priests and elders
perished in the city
while seeking food
to revive their strength.

20 See, O LORD, how distressed I
am;
my stomach churns,
my heart is wrung within me,
because I have been very
rebellious.
In the street the sword
bereaves;
in the house it is like
death.

21 They heard how I was
groaning,
with no one to comfort me.
All my enemies heard of my
trouble;
they are glad that you have
done it.
Bring on the day you have
announced,
and let them be as I am.

1.16 Jer 13.17; 14.17; Lam 2.18; vv. 2,9
1.17 Jer 4.31; 2 Kings 24.2-4; v. 8
1.18 Jer 12.1; 1 Sam 12.14; v. 12; Deut 28.32, 41
1.19 Jer 30.14; 14.15; Lam 2.20
1.20 Isa 16.11; Jer 4.19; Lam 2.11; Deut 32.29; Ezek 7.15
1.21 Lam 2.15; Isa 14.5,6; Jer 30.16
1.22 Neh 4.4,5; Ps 137.7,8
2.1 Lam 3.43, 44; Ezek 28.14-16; Isa 64.11; Ps 99.5; 132.7
2.2 Ps 21.9; Lam 3.43; Mic 5.11,14; Isa 25.12; Ps 89.39
2.3 Ps 75.5,10; 74.11; Jer 21.4,5; 21.14
2.4 Lam 3.12, 13; Ezek 24.25; Isa 42.25; Jer 7.20
2.5 Jer 30.14; 6.26; 9.17-20

22 Let all their evil doing come
before you;
and deal with them
as you have dealt with me
because of all my
transgressions;
for my groans are many
and my heart is faint.

God's Warnings Fulfilled

2 How the Lord in his anger
has humiliated[c] daughter
Zion!
He has thrown down from
heaven to earth
the splendor of Israel;
he has not remembered his
footstool
in the day of his anger.

2 The Lord has destroyed
without mercy
all the dwellings of Jacob;
in his wrath he has broken
down
the strongholds of daughter
Judah;
he has brought down to the
ground in dishonor
the kingdom and its rulers.

3 He has cut down in fierce
anger
all the might of Israel;
he has withdrawn his right
hand from them
in the face of the enemy;
he has burned like a flaming
fire in Jacob,
consuming all around.

4 He has bent his bow like an
enemy,
with his right hand set like
a foe;
he has killed all in whom we
took pride
in the tent of daughter
Zion;
he has poured out his fury
like fire.

5 The Lord has become like an
enemy;
he has destroyed Israel;

c Meaning of Heb uncertain

He has destroyed all its palaces,
laid in ruins its strongholds,
and multiplied in daughter Judah
mourning and lamentation.

6 He has broken down his booth like a garden,
he has destroyed his tabernacle;
the LORD has abolished in Zion
festival and sabbath,
and in his fierce indignation has spurned
king and priest.

7 The Lord has scorned his altar,
disowned his sanctuary;
he has delivered into the hand of the enemy
the walls of her palaces;
a clamor was raised in the house of the LORD
as on a day of festival.

8 The LORD determined to lay in ruins
the wall of daughter Zion;
he stretched the line;
he did not withhold his hand from destroying;
he caused rampart and wall to lament;
they languish together.

9 Her gates have sunk into the ground;
he has ruined and broken her bars;
her king and princes are among the nations;
guidance is no more,
and her prophets obtain
no vision from the LORD.

10 The elders of daughter Zion
sit on the ground in silence;
they have thrown dust on their heads
and put on sackcloth;
the young girls of Jerusalem
have bowed their heads to the ground.

11 My eyes are spent with weeping;
my stomach churns;
my bile is poured out on the ground
because of the destruction of my people,
because infants and babes faint
in the streets of the city.

12 They cry to their mothers,
"Where is bread and wine?"
as they faint like the wounded
in the streets of the city,
as their life is poured out
on their mothers' bosom.

13 What can I say for you, to what compare you,
O daughter Jerusalem?
To what can I liken you, that I may comfort you,
O virgin daughter Zion?
For vast as the sea is your ruin;
who can heal you?

14 Your prophets have seen for you
false and deceptive visions;
they have not exposed your iniquity
to restore your fortunes,
but have seen oracles for you
that are false and misleading.

15 All who pass along the way
clap their hands at you;
they hiss and wag their heads
at daughter Jerusalem;
"Is this the city that was called
the perfection of beauty,
the joy of all the earth?"

16 All your enemies
open their mouths against you;

2.6 Jer 7.14; 52.13; Lam 1.4; Zeph 3.18; Lam 4.16, 20; 5.12
2.7 Isa 64.11; Ezek 7.20-22; Jer 33.4,5; Ps 74.4
2.8 Jer 5.10; 2 Kings 21.13; Isa 34.11; 3.26; Jer 14.2
2.9 Neh 1.3; Jer 51.30; Deut 28.36; 2 Kings 24.15; 2 Chr 15.3; Jer 14.14; 23.16; Ezek 7.26
2.10 Job 2.13; Isa 3.26; Am 8.3; Job 2.12; Ezek 27.30, 31; Isa 15.3; Lam 1.4
2.11 Ps 6.7; Lam 3.48; 1.20; Job 16.13; Ps 22.14; Lam 4.4
2.12 Jer 5.17; Lam 4.4; Job 30.16
2.13 Lam 1.12; Isa 37.22; Jer 14.17; 8.22; 30.12-15
2.14 Jer 2.8; 29.8,9; Isa 58.1; Jer 23.36; Ezek 22.25, 28
2.15 Jer 19.8; Zeph 2.15; Isa 37.22; Ps 48.2; 50.2
2.16 Ps 22.13; Lam 3.46; Ps 37.12; 56.2; Ob 12-15

they hiss, they gnash their teeth,
they cry: "We have devoured her!
Ah, this is the day we longed for;
at last we have seen it!"

17 The LORD has done what he purposed,
he has carried out his threat;
as he ordained long ago,
he has demolished without pity;
he has made the enemy rejoice over you,
and exalted the might of your foes.

18 Cry aloud[d] to the Lord!
O wall of daughter Zion!
Let tears stream down like a torrent
day and night!
Give yourself no rest,
your eyes no respite!

19 Arise, cry out in the night,
at the beginning of the watches!
Pour out your heart like water
before the presence of the Lord!
Lift your hands to him
for the lives of your children,
who faint for hunger
at the head of every street.

20 Look, O LORD, and consider!
To whom have you done this?
Should women eat their offspring,
the children they have borne?
Should priest and prophet be killed
in the sanctuary of the Lord?

21 The young and the old are lying
on the ground in the streets;
my young women and my young men
have fallen by the sword;
in the day of your anger you have killed them,
slaughtering without mercy.

22 You invited my enemies from all around
as if for a day of festival;
and on the day of the anger of the LORD
no one escaped or survived;
those whom I bore and reared
my enemy has destroyed.

God's Steadfast Love Endures

3 I am one who has seen affliction
under the rod of God's[e] wrath;
2 he has driven and brought me
into darkness without any light;
3 against me alone he turns his hand,
again and again, all day long.

4 He has made my flesh and my skin waste away,
and broken my bones;
5 he has besieged and enveloped me
with bitterness and tribulation;
6 he has made me sit in darkness
like the dead of long ago.

7 He has walled me about so that I cannot escape;
he has put heavy chains on me;
8 though I call and cry for help,
he shuts out my prayer;
9 he has blocked my ways with hewn stones,
he has made my paths crooked.

2.17 Deut 28.15; Jer 18.11; vv. 1,2; Ps 35.24,26; Lam 1.5 **2.18** Hos 7.14; Jer 9.1; Lam 1.2,16 **2.19** Ps 42.3; Isa 26.9; Ps 62.8; Isa 51.20 **2.20** Jer 19.9; 14.15; Lam 4.13,16 **2.21** 2 Chr 36.17; Jer 6.11; Ps 78.62,63; Jer 13.14; Zech 11.6 **2.22** Ps 31.13; Jer 6.25; Hos 9.12,13 **3.1** Job 19.21; Jer 15.17,18 **3.2** Isa 59.9; Jer 4.23 **3.3** Isa 5.25 **3.4** Job 16.8; Ps 51.8; Isa 38.13; Jer 50.17 **3.5** Job 19.8; Jer 23.15 **3.6** Ps 88.5,6 **3.7** Job 3.23; Jer 40.4 **3.8** Job 30.20; Ps 22.2 **3.9** Hos 2.6; Isa 63.17

[d] Cn: Heb *Their heart cried* [e] Heb *his*

10 He is a bear lying in wait for me,
a lion in hiding;
11 he led me off my way and tore me to pieces;
he has made me desolate;
12 he bent his bow and set me as a mark for his arrow.

13 He shot into my vitals
the arrows of his quiver;
14 I have become the laughingstock of all my people,
the object of their taunt-songs all day long.
15 He has filled me with bitterness,
he has sated me with wormwood.

16 He has made my teeth grind on gravel,
and made me cower in ashes;
17 my soul is bereft of peace;
I have forgotten what happiness is;
18 so I say, "Gone is my glory,
and all that I had hoped for from the LORD."

19 The thought of my affliction and my homelessness
is wormwood and gall!
20 My soul continually thinks of it
and is bowed down within me.
21 But this I call to mind,
and therefore I have hope:

22 The steadfast love of the LORD never ceases,[f]
his mercies never come to an end;
23 they are new every morning;
great is your faithfulness.
24 "The LORD is my portion,"
says my soul,
"therefore I will hope in him."

25 The LORD is good to those who wait for him,
to the soul that seeks him.

26 It is good that one should wait quietly
for the salvation of the LORD.
27 It is good for one to bear
the yoke in youth,
28 to sit alone in silence
when the Lord has imposed it,
29 to put one's mouth to the dust
(there may yet be hope),
30 to give one's cheek to the smiter,
and be filled with insults.

31 For the Lord will not
reject forever.
32 Although he causes grief, he will have compassion
according to the abundance of his steadfast love;
33 for he does not willingly afflict
or grieve anyone.

34 When all the prisoners of the land
are crushed under foot,
35 when human rights are perverted
in the presence of the Most High,
36 when one's case is subverted
—does the Lord not see it?

37 Who can command and have it done,
if the Lord has not ordained it?
38 Is it not from the mouth of the Most High
that good and bad come?
39 Why should any who draw breath complain
about the punishment of their sins?

40 Let us test and examine our ways,
and return to the LORD.
41 Let us lift up our hearts as well as our hands

3.10 Job 10.16; Isa 38.13 **3.11** Hos 6.1 **3.12** Ps 7.12,13; Job 7.20 **3.13** Job 6.4 **3.14** Jer 20.7; Job 30.9 **3.15** Jer 9.15 **3.16** Prov 20.17; Jer 6.26 **3.17** Jer 12.12 **3.18** Ps 31.22 **3.19** Jer 9.15 **3.20** Ps 42.5,6,11 **3.21** Ps 130.7 **3.22** Mal 3.6 **3.23** Zeph 3.5 **3.24** Ps 16.5; 33.18 **3.25** Isa 25.9; 30.18; 26.9 **3.26** Ps 37.7; 40.1; Isa 30.15 **3.27** Ps 94.12 **3.28** Jer 15.17 **3.29** Job 16.15; Jer 31.17 **3.30** Isa 50.6; Mt 5.39 **3.31** Ps 94.14 **3.32** Ps 78.38; Hos 11.8 **3.33** Ezek 33.11; Heb 12.10 **3.35** Ps 140.12 **3.36** Hab 1.13 **3.37** Ps 33.9 **3.38** Job 2.10; Isa 45.7; Jer 32.42 **3.39** Mic 7.9; Heb 12.5,6 **3.40** Ps 119.59; 2 Cor 13.5 **3.41** Ps 25.1; 28.2

[f] Syr Tg: Heb *LORD, we are not cut off*

to God in heaven.
42 We have transgressed and
rebelled,
and you have not forgiven.

43 You have wrapped yourself
with anger and pursued
us,
killing without pity;
44 you have wrapped yourself
with a cloud
so that no prayer can pass
through.
45 You have made us filth and
rubbish
among the peoples.

46 All our enemies
have opened their mouths
against us;
47 panic and pitfall have come
upon us,
devastation and
destruction.
48 My eyes flow with rivers of
tears
because of the destruction
of my people.

49 My eyes will flow without
ceasing,
without respite,
50 until the LORD from heaven
looks down and sees.
51 My eyes cause me grief
at the fate of all the young
women in my city.

52 Those who were my enemies
without cause
have hunted me like a bird;
53 they flung me alive into a pit
and hurled stones on me;
54 water closed over my head;
I said, "I am lost."

55 I called on your name,
O LORD,
from the depths of the pit;
56 you heard my plea, "Do not
close your ear
to my cry for help, but give
me relief!"
57 You came near when I called
on you;
you said, "Do not fear!"

3.42 Dan 9.5; Jer 5.7,9
3.43 Lam 2.21; Ps 83.15
3.44 Ps 97.2; v. 8
3.45 1 Cor 4.13
3.46 Lam 2.16
3.47 Isa 24.17; Jer 48.43; Isa 51.19
3.48 Lam 1.16; 2.11,18
3.49 Ps 77.2
3.50 Isa 63.15
3.52 Ps 35.7
3.53 Jer 37.16
3.54 Ps 69.2; Isa 38.10
3.55 Jon 2.2
3.56 Ps 116.1,2
3.57 Ps 145.18; Isa 41.10,14
3.58 Jer 51.36; Ps 71.23
3.59 Jer 18.19, 20; Ps 35.23
3.60 Jer 11.19, 20; 18.18
3.61 Lam 5.1
3.62 Ezek 36.3
3.63 Ps 139.2
3.64 Ps 28.4
3.65 Isa 6.10
3.66 Ps 8.3
4.1 Ezek 7.19-22; Jer 52.13,14
4.2 Isa 51.18; 30.14; Jer 19.11
4.3 Isa 34.13; 49.15; Job 39.14, 16

58 You have taken up my cause,
O Lord,
you have redeemed my life.
59 You have seen the wrong
done to me, O LORD;
judge my cause.
60 You have seen all their
malice,
all their plots against me.

61 You have heard their taunts,
O LORD,
all their plots against me.
62 The whispers and murmurs
of my assailants
are against me all day long.
63 Whether they sit or
rise—see,
I am the object of their
taunt-songs.

64 Pay them back for their
deeds, O LORD,
according to the work of
their hands!
65 Give them anguish of heart;
your curse be on them!
66 Pursue them in anger and
destroy them
from under the LORD's
heavens.

The Punishment of Zion

4 How the gold has grown dim,
how the pure gold is
changed!
The sacred stones lie
scattered
at the head of every street.

2 The precious children of
Zion,
worth their weight in fine
gold—
how they are reckoned as
earthen pots,
the work of a potter's
hands!

3 Even the jackals offer the
breast
and nurse their young,
but my people has become
cruel,
like the ostriches in the
wilderness.

4 The tongue of the infant sticks
to the roof of its mouth for thirst;
the children beg for food,
but no one gives them anything.

5 Those who feasted on delicacies
perish in the streets;
those who were brought up in purple
cling to ash heaps.

6 For the chastisement[g] of my people has been greater
than the punishment[h] of Sodom,
which was overthrown in a moment,
though no hand was laid on it.[i]

7 Her princes were purer than snow,
whiter than milk;
their bodies were more ruddy than coral,
their hair[i] like sapphire.[j]

8 Now their visage is blacker than soot;
they are not recognized in the streets.
Their skin has shriveled on their bones;
it has become as dry as wood.

9 Happier were those pierced by the sword
than those pierced by hunger,
whose life drains away, deprived
of the produce of the field.

10 The hands of compassionate women
have boiled their own children;
they became their food
in the destruction of my people.

11 The LORD gave full vent to his wrath;
he poured out his hot anger,
and kindled a fire in Zion
that consumed its foundations.

12 The kings of the earth did not believe,
nor did any of the inhabitants of the world,
that foe or enemy could enter
the gates of Jerusalem.

13 It was for the sins of her prophets
and the iniquities of her priests,
who shed the blood of the righteous
in the midst of her.

14 Blindly they wandered through the streets,
so defiled with blood
that no one was able
to touch their garments.

15 "Away! Unclean!" people shouted at them;
"Away! Away! Do not touch!"
So they became fugitives and wanderers;
it was said among the nations,
"They shall stay here no longer."

16 The LORD himself has scattered them,
he will regard them no more;
no honor was shown to the priests,
no favor to the elders.

17 Our eyes failed, ever watching
vainly for help;
we were watching eagerly

4.4 Jer 14.3; Lam 2.12 **4.5** Jer 6.2; Am 6.3-7; Ps 113.7 **4.6** Ezek 16.48; Gen 19.23; Jer 20.16 **4.7** Ps 51.7 **4.8** Job 30.30; Lam 5.10; Ps 102.5 **4.9** Jer 15.2; Ezek 24.23 **4.10** Lam 2.20; 2 Kings 6.29; Deut 28.57 **4.11** Jer 7.20; v. 22; Deut 32.22; Jer 21.14 **4.12** 1 Kings 9.8, 9; Jer 21.13 **4.13** Jer 5.31; 6.13; Ezek 22.26; Mic 3.11,12; Mt 23.31 **4.14** Isa 56.10; 59.9,10; Jer 19.4; 2.34 **4.15** Lev 13.45; Jer 49.5 **4.16** Lam 5.12 **4.17** 2 Kings 24.7; Isa 20.5; Jer 37.7; Ezek 29.16

g Or *iniquity* h Or *sin* i Meaning of Heb uncertain j Or *lapis lazuli*

for a nation that could not
save.
18 They dogged our steps
so that we could not walk
in our streets;
our end drew near; our days
were numbered;
for our end had come.
19 Our pursuers were swifter
than the eagles in the
heavens;
they chased us on the
mountains,
they lay in wait for us in
the wilderness.
20 The LORD's anointed, the
breath of our life,
was taken in their pits—
the one of whom we said,
"Under his shadow
we shall live among the
nations."
21 Rejoice and be glad,
O daughter Edom,
you that live in the land of
Uz;
but to you also the cup shall
pass;
you shall become drunk
and strip yourself bare.
22 The punishment of your
iniquity, O daughter
Zion, is accomplished,
he will keep you in exile
no longer;
but your iniquity, O daughter
Edom, he will punish,
he will uncover your sins.

A Plea for Mercy

5 Remember, O LORD, what
has befallen us;
look, and see our disgrace!
2 Our inheritance has been
turned over to
strangers,
our homes to aliens.
3 We have become orphans,
fatherless;
our mothers are like
widows.
4 We must pay for the water
we drink;
the wood we get must be
bought.
5 With a yoke[k] on our necks
we are hard driven;
we are weary, we are given
no rest.
6 We have made a pact with[l]
Egypt and Assyria,
to get enough bread.
7 Our ancestors sinned; they
are no more,
and we bear their
iniquities.
8 Slaves rule over us;
there is no one to deliver
us from their hand.
9 We get our bread at the peril
of our lives,
because of the sword in the
wilderness.
10 Our skin is black as an oven
from the scorching heat of
famine.
11 Women are raped in Zion,
virgins in the towns of
Judah.
12 Princes are hung up by their
hands;
no respect is shown to the
elders.
13 Young men are compelled to
grind,
and boys stagger under
loads of wood.
14 The old men have left the
city gate,
the young men their music.
15 The joy of our hearts has
ceased;
our dancing has been
turned to mourning.
16 The crown has fallen from
our head;
woe to us, for we have
sinned!
17 Because of this our hearts
are sick,
because of these things our
eyes have grown dim:
18 because of Mount Zion,
which lies desolate;
jackals prowl over it.

4.18 2 Kings 25.4; Ezek 7.2,3; Am 8.2
4.19 Deut 28.49; Jer 4.13; Hab 1.8
4.20 2 Sam 1.14; 19.21; Ezek 12.13; 19.4,8
4.21 Isa 34.7; Am 1.11,12; Ob 1,16
4.22 Isa 40.2; Mal 1.3,4
5.1 Ps 89.50; 44.13-16
5.2 Ps 79.1; Zeph 1.13
5.3 Jer 15.8; 18.21
5.4 Isa 3.1
5.5 Jer 28.14; Neh 9.36,37
5.6 Jer 2.36; Hos 5.13; 7.11; 9.3
5.7 Jer 14.20; 16.12
5.8 Neh 5.15; Zech 11.6
5.10 Lam 4.8
5.11 Isa 13.16; Zech 14.2
5.12 Lam 4.16
5.13 Jer 7.18
5.14 Lam 4.8; Jer 7.34
5.15 Jer 25.10
5.16 Ps 89.39; Isa 3.9-11
5.17 Isa 1.5; Ps 6.7
5.18 Ps 74.2,3; Neh 4.3

k Symmachus: Heb lacks *With a yoke*
l Heb *have given the hand to*

19 But you, O LORD, reign
forever;
your throne endures to all
generations.
20 Why have you forgotten us
completely?
Why have you forsaken us
these many days?
21 Restore us to yourself,
O LORD, that we may be
restored;
renew our days as of old—
22 unless you have utterly
rejected us,
and are angry with us
beyond measure.

5.19 Ps 9.7; 102.12,25-27; 45.6
5.20 Ps 13.1
5.21 Jer 31.18
5.22 Jer 7.29; Isa 64.9

Ezekiel

Title and Background

This book is named after the prophet Ezekiel, whose name means "God is strong." The Babylonians laid siege to Jerusalem in 588 B.C., and in 586 the city and temple were burned. Israel's monarchy was ended; the City of David and the Lord's temple were no more.

Author and Date of Writing

Ezekiel was among the more than 3,000 Jews exiled to Babylon by Nebuchadnezzar in 597 B.C., and there among the exiles he received his call to become a prophet. As a priest-prophet called to minister to the exiles, his message had much to do with the temple and its ritual.

Since the book of Ezekiel contains many dates, its prophecies can be dated with considerable precision. Ezekiel's period of activity coincides with Jerusalem's darkest hour. His messages are to be dated between 593 and 571 B.C.

Theme and Message

Nowhere in the Bible are God's initiative and control over all creation expressed more clearly and pervasively than in Ezekiel. This sovereign God must be known and acknowledged by everyone, for at least 65 times we read the clause (or variations): "Then they will know that I am the LORD."

God's total sovereignty is also evident in his mobility. He is not limited to the temple or even to the city of Jerusalem; he can respond to his people anywhere and under any circumstance.

Outline

I. Ezekiel's Call and Commission (1.1–3.27)
II. Judgment Against Judah and Jerusalem (4.1–24.27)
III. Judgment Against the Nations (25.1–32.32)
IV. Preparation for Restoration (33.1–39.29)
V. Renewed Worship (40.1–48.35)

The Vision of the Chariot

1 In the thirtieth year, in the
fourth month, on the fifth day
of the month, as I was among the
exiles by the river Chebar, the
heavens were opened, and I saw visions of God. 2 On the fifth day of
the month (it was the fifth year of
the exile of King Jehoiachin), 3 the
word of the LORD came to the priest
Ezekiel son of Buzi, in the land of
the Chaldeans by the river Chebar;
and the hand of the LORD was on
him there.
4 As I looked, a stormy wind
came out of the north: a great
cloud with brightness around it
and fire flashing forth continually,
and in the middle of the fire, something like gleaming amber. 5 In the
middle of it was something like
four living creatures. This was their
appearance: they were of human
form. 6 Each had four faces, and
each of them had four wings.
7 Their legs were straight, and the
soles of their feet were like the sole
of a calf's foot; and they sparkled
like burnished bronze. 8 Under
their wings on their four sides they
had human hands. And the four

1.1 Ezek 3.15, 23; Mt 3.16; Acts 7.56 **1.2** 2 Kings 24.12 **1.3** 1 Kings 18.46; 2 Kings 3.15 **1.4** Isa 21.1 **1.5** Rev 4.6; Ezek 10.8, 14 **1.6** vv. 10,23 **1.7** Rev 1.15; 2.18

1.8 Ezek 10.8,21

had their faces and their wings thus: 9 their wings touched one another; each of them moved straight ahead, without turning as they moved. 10 As for the appearance of their faces: the four had the face of a human being, the face of a lion on the right side, the face of an ox on the left side, and the face of an eagle; 11 such were their faces. Their wings were spread out above; each creature had two wings, each of which touched the wing of another, while two covered their bodies. 12 Each moved straight ahead; wherever the spirit would go, they went, without turning as they went. 13 In the middle of[a] the living creatures there was something that looked like burning coals of fire, like torches moving to and fro among the living creatures; the fire was bright, and lightning issued from the fire. 14 The living creatures darted to and fro, like a flash of lightning.

15 As I looked at the living creatures, I saw a wheel on the earth beside the living creatures, one for each of the four of them.[b] 16 As for the appearance of the wheels and their construction: their appearance was like the gleaming of beryl; and the four had the same form, their construction being something like a wheel within a wheel. 17 When they moved, they moved in any of the four directions without veering as they moved. 18 Their rims were tall and awesome, for the rims of all four were full of eyes all around. 19 When the living creatures moved, the wheels moved beside them; and when the living creatures rose from the earth, the wheels rose. 20 Wherever the spirit would go, they went, and the wheels rose along with them; for the spirit of the living creatures was in the wheels. 21 When they moved, the others moved; when they stopped, the others stopped; and when they rose from the earth, the wheels rose along with them; for the spirit of the living creatures was in the wheels.

22 Over the heads of the living creatures there was something like a dome, shining like crystal,[c] spread out above their heads. 23 Under the dome their wings were stretched out straight, one toward another; and each of the creatures had two wings covering its body. 24 When they moved, I heard the sound of their wings like the sound of mighty waters, like the thunder of the Almighty,[d] a sound of tumult like the sound of an army; when they stopped, they let down their wings. 25 And there came a voice from above the dome over their heads; when they stopped, they let down their wings.

26 And above the dome over their heads there was something like a throne, in appearance like sapphire;[e] and seated above the likeness of a throne was something that seemed like a human form. 27 Upward from what appeared like the loins I saw something like gleaming amber, something that looked like fire enclosed all around; and downward from what looked like the loins I saw something that looked like fire, and there was a splendor all around. 28 Like the bow in a cloud on a rainy day, such was the appearance of the splendor all around. This was the appearance of the likeness of the glory of the LORD.

When I saw it, I fell on my face, and I heard the voice of someone speaking.

The Vision of the Scroll

2 He said to me: O mortal,[f] stand up on your feet, and I will speak with you. 2 And when he spoke to me, a spirit entered into me and set me on my feet; and I heard him speaking to me. 3 He said to me, Mortal, I am sending you to the people of Israel, to a nation[g] of rebels who have rebelled against me; they and their ances-

1.9 vv. 17,12
1.10 Rev 4.7; Ezek 10.14
1.11 Ezek 10.16, 19; Isa 6.2
1.12 vv. 9,20
1.13 Ps 104.4; Rev 4.5
1.14 Mt 24.27
1.15 vv. 19-21
1.16 Ezek 10.9-11; Dan 10.6
1.17 v. 12
1.18 Ezek 10.12; Rev 4.6,8
1.19 Ezek 10.16, 17,19
1.20 v. 12; Ezek 10.17
1.21 Ezek 10.17
1.22 Ezek 10.1
1.23 vv. 6,4
1.24 Ezek 10.5; 43.2; Rev 1.15; 19.6; 2 Kings 7.6
1.25 v. 22
1.26 Ezek 10.1; Ex 24.10; Ezek 43.6,7; Rev 1.13
1.27 v. 4; Ezek 8.2
1.28 Rev 4.3; 10.1; Ezek 3.23; 8.4; Dan 8.17; Rev 1.17
2.1 Dan 10.11
2.2 Dan 8.18; Ezek 3.24
2.3 Jer 3.25; Ezek 20.18, 30

[a] Gk OL: Heb *And the appearance of*
[b] Heb *of their faces*
[c] Gk: Heb *like the awesome crystal*
[d] Traditional rendering of Heb *Shaddai*
[e] Or *lapis lazuli*
[f] Or *son of man*; Heb *ben adam* (and so throughout the book when Ezekiel is addressed)
[g] Syr: Heb *to nations*

tors have transgressed against me
to this very day. 4 The descendants
are impudent and stubborn. I am
sending you to them, and you shall
say to them, "Thus says the Lord
GOD." 5 Whether they hear or refuse
to hear (for they are a rebellious
house), they shall know that there
has been a prophet among them.
6 And you, O mortal, do not be
afraid of them, and do not be afraid
of their words, though briers and
thorns surround you and you live
among scorpions; do not be afraid
of their words, and do not be dismayed at their looks, for they are a
rebellious house. 7 You shall speak
my words to them, whether they
hear or refuse to hear; for they are
a rebellious house.
8 But you, mortal, hear what I
say to you; do not be rebellious like
that rebellious house; open your
mouth and eat what I give you. 9 I
looked, and a hand was stretched
out to me, and a written scroll was
in it. 10 He spread it before me; it
had writing on the front and on the
back, and written on it were words
of lamentation and mourning and
woe.

3 He said to me, O mortal, eat
what is offered to you; eat this
scroll, and go, speak to the house
of Israel. 2 So I opened my mouth,
and he gave me the scroll to eat.
3 He said to me, Mortal, eat this
scroll that I give you and fill your
stomach with it. Then I ate it; and
in my mouth it was as sweet as
honey.
4 He said to me: Mortal, go to
the house of Israel and speak my
very words to them. 5 For you are
not sent to a people of obscure
speech and difficult language, but
to the house of Israel— 6 not to
many peoples of obscure speech
and difficult language, whose
words you cannot understand.
Surely, if I sent you to them, they
would listen to you. 7 But the house
of Israel will not listen to you, for
they are not willing to listen to me;
because all the house of Israel have
a hard forehead and a stubborn
heart. 8 See, I have made your face
hard against their faces, and your
forehead hard against their foreheads. 9 Like the hardest stone,
harder than flint, I have made your
forehead; do not fear them or be
dismayed at their looks, for they
are a rebellious house. 10 He said to
me: Mortal, all my words that I
shall speak to you receive in your
heart and hear with your ears;
11 then go to the exiles, to your people, and speak to them. Say to
them, "Thus says the Lord GOD";
whether they hear or refuse to hear.

Ezekiel at the River Chebar

12 Then the spirit lifted me up,
and as the glory of the LORD rose[h]
from its place, I heard behind me
the sound of loud rumbling; 13 it
was the sound of the wings of the
living creatures brushing against
one another, and the sound of the
wheels beside them, that sounded
like a loud rumbling. 14 The spirit
lifted me up and bore me away; I
went in bitterness in the heat of my
spirit, the hand of the LORD being
strong upon me. 15 I came to the exiles at Tel-abib, who lived by the
river Chebar.[i] And I sat there
among them, stunned, for seven
days.
16 At the end of seven days, the
word of the LORD came to me:
17 Mortal, I have made you a sentinel for the house of Israel; whenever you hear a word from my mouth,
you shall give them warning from
me. 18 If I say to the wicked, "You
shall surely die," and you give them
no warning, or speak to warn the
wicked from their wicked way, in
order to save their life, those wicked persons shall die for their iniquity; but their blood I will require
at your hand. 19 But if you warn the
wicked, and they do not turn from
their wickedness, or from their
wicked way, they shall die for their
iniquity; but you will have saved

2.4 Jer 5.3; Ezek 3.7 **2.5** Ezek 3.11, 26,27; 33.33 **2.6** Jer 1.8,17; Isa 9.18; Mic 7.4; Ezek 3.9 **2.7** Jer 1.7,17 **2.8** Isa 50.5; Rev 10.9 **2.9** Ezek 8.3; 3.1 **2.10** Rev 8.13 **3.1** Ezek 2.8,9 **3.3** Rev 10.9,10; Jer 15.16; Ps 19.10; 119.103 **3.4** v. 11 **3.5** Jon 1.2; Isa 28.11; 33.19 **3.6** Mt 11.21, 23; Acts 13.46-48 **3.7** Jn 15.20; Ezek 2.4 **3.8** Jer 1.18; 15.20 **3.9** Isa 50.7; Mic 3.8; Ezek 2.6 **3.10** vv. 1-3 **3.11** Ezek 2.5,7 **3.12** Ezek 8.3; Acts 8.39; 2.2 **3.13** Ezek 1.24; 10.5,16,17 **3.14** Jer 6.11; Ezek 1.3; 8.1 **3.15** Ezek 1.1; Job 2.13 **3.17** Ezek 33.7-9; Isa 52.8; 56.10; Jer 6.17 **3.18** Gen 2.17; Ezek 33.6; Jn 8.21,24 **3.19** Ezek 33.3,9; Acts 18.6; 20.26

[h] Cn: Heb *and blessed be the glory of the* LORD
[i] Two Mss Syr: Heb *Chebar, and to where they lived.* Another reading is *Chebar, and I sat where they sat*

your life. 20 Again, if the righteous
turn from their righteousness and
commit iniquity, and I lay a stumbling block before them, they shall
die; because you have not warned
them, they shall die for their sin,
and their righteous deeds that they
have done shall not be remembered; but their blood I will require
at your hand. 21 If, however, you
warn the righteous not to sin, and
they do not sin, they shall surely
live, because they took warning;
and you will have saved your life.

Ezekiel Isolated and Silenced

22 Then the hand of the LORD
was upon me there; and he said to
me, Rise up, go out into the valley,
and there I will speak with you.
23 So I rose up and went out into the
valley; and the glory of the LORD
stood there, like the glory that I
had seen by the river Chebar; and I
fell on my face. 24 The spirit entered into me, and set me on my
feet; and he spoke with me and
said to me: Go, shut yourself inside
your house. 25 As for you, mortal,
cords shall be placed on you, and
you shall be bound with them, so
that you cannot go out among the
people; 26 and I will make your
tongue cling to the roof of your
mouth, so that you shall be speechless and unable to reprove them;
for they are a rebellious house.
27 But when I speak with you, I will
open your mouth, and you shall say
to them, "Thus says the Lord GOD";
let those who will hear, hear; and
let those who refuse to hear, refuse; for they are a rebellious
house.

The Siege of Jerusalem Portrayed

4 And you, O mortal, take a
brick and set it before you. On
it portray a city, Jerusalem; 2 and
put siegeworks against it, and build
a siege wall against it, and cast up
a ramp against it; set camps also
against it, and plant battering rams
against it all around. 3 Then take an
iron plate and place it as an iron
wall between you and the city; set
your face toward it, and let it be in
a state of siege, and press the siege
against it. This is a sign for the
house of Israel.
4 Then lie on your left side, and
place the punishment of the house
of Israel upon it; you shall bear
their punishment for the number
of the days that you lie there. 5 For
I assign to you a number of days,
three hundred ninety days, equal
to the number of the years of their
punishment; and so you shall bear
the punishment of the house of Israel. 6 When you have completed
these, you shall lie down a second
time, but on your right side, and
bear the punishment of the house
of Judah; forty days I assign you,
one day for each year. 7 You shall
set your face toward the siege of Jerusalem, and with your arm bared
you shall prophesy against it. 8 See,
I am putting cords on you so that
you cannot turn from one side to
the other until you have completed
the days of your siege.
9 And you, take wheat and barley, beans and lentils, millet and
spelt; put them into one vessel, and
make bread for yourself. During the
number of days that you lie on your
side, three hundred ninety days,
you shall eat it. 10 The food that you
eat shall be twenty shekels a day by
weight; at fixed times you shall eat
it. 11 And you shall drink water by
measure, one-sixth of a hin; at
fixed times you shall drink. 12 You
shall eat it as a barley-cake, baking
it in their sight on human dung.
13 The LORD said, "Thus shall the
people of Israel eat their bread, unclean, among the nations to which
I will drive them." 14 Then I said,
"Ah Lord GOD! I have never defiled
myself; from my youth up until now
I have never eaten what died of itself or was torn by animals, nor has
carrion flesh come into my
mouth." 15 Then he said to me,
"See, I will let you have cow's dung
instead of human dung, on which
you may prepare your bread."
16 Then he said to me, Mortal, I
am going to break the staff of bread
in Jerusalem; they shall eat bread

3.20 Ezek 18.24; 33.12,13; Jer 6.21
3.21 Acts 20.31; v. 19
3.22 v. 14; Ezek 8.4; Acts 9.6
3.23 Ezek 1.28; 1.1
3.24 Ezek 2.2
3.25 Ezek 4.8
3.26 Ezek 24.27; Lk 1.20,22; Ezek 2.5-7
3.27 Ezek 24.27; 33.22; vv. 11,9,26
4.1 Isa 20.2; Ezek 5.1
4.2 Ezek 21.22
4.3 Ezek 5.2; 12.6,11; 24.24,27
4.4 Lev 10.17; Num 18.1
4.5 Num 14.34
4.7 v. 3; Ezek 21.2
4.8 Ezek 3.25
4.9 v. 5
4.10 v. 16
4.12 Isa 36.12
4.13 Hos 9.3
4.14 Ezek 9.8; Acts 10.14; Ex 22.31; Lev 17.15; Deut 14.3; Isa 65.4
4.16 Lev 26.26; Isa 3.1; Ezek 5.16; 14.13; vv. 10,11; Ezek 12.19

by weight and with fearfulness; and they shall drink water by measure and in dismay. 17 Lacking bread and water, they will look at one another in dismay, and waste away under their punishment.

A Sword against Jerusalem

5 And you, O mortal, take a sharp sword; use it as a barber's razor and run it over your head and your beard; then take balances for weighing, and divide the hair. 2 One third of the hair you shall burn in the fire inside the city, when the days of the siege are completed; one third you shall take and strike with the sword all around the city;[j] and one third you shall scatter to the wind, and I will unsheathe the sword after them. 3 Then you shall take from these a small number, and bind them in the skirts of your robe. 4 From these, again, you shall take some, throw them into the fire and burn them up; from there a fire will come out against all the house of Israel.

5 Thus says the Lord GOD: This is Jerusalem; I have set her in the center of the nations, with countries all around her. 6 But she has rebelled against my ordinances and my statutes, becoming more wicked than the nations and the countries all around her, rejecting my ordinances and not following my statutes. 7 Therefore thus says the Lord GOD: Because you are more turbulent than the nations that are all around you, and have not followed my statutes or kept my ordinances, but have acted according to the ordinances of the nations that are all around you; 8 therefore thus says the Lord GOD: I, I myself, am coming against you; I will execute judgments among you in the sight of the nations. 9 And because of all your abominations, I will do to you what I have never yet done, and the like of which I will never do again. 10 Surely, parents shall eat their children in your midst, and children shall eat their parents; I will execute judgments on you, and any of you who survive I will scatter to every wind. 11 Therefore, as I live, says the Lord GOD, surely, because you have defiled my sanctuary with all your detestable things and with all your abominations—therefore I will cut you down;[k] my eye will not spare, and I will have no pity. 12 One third of you shall die of pestilence or be consumed by famine among you; one third shall fall by the sword around you; and one third I will scatter to every wind and will unsheathe the sword after them.

13 My anger shall spend itself, and I will vent my fury on them and satisfy myself; and they shall know that I, the LORD, have spoken in my jealousy, when I spend my fury on them. 14 Moreover I will make you a desolation and an object of mocking among the nations around you, in the sight of all that pass by. 15 You shall be[l] a mockery and a taunt, a warning and a horror, to the nations around you, when I execute judgments on you in anger and fury, and with furious punishments—I, the LORD, have spoken— 16 when I loose against you[m] my deadly arrows of famine, arrows for destruction, which I will let loose to destroy you, and when I bring more and more famine upon you, and break your staff of bread. 17 I will send famine and wild animals against you, and they will rob you of your children; pestilence and bloodshed shall pass through you; and I will bring the sword upon you. I, the LORD, have spoken.

Judgment on Idolatrous Israel

6 The word of the LORD came to me: 2 O mortal, set your face toward the mountains of Israel, and prophesy against them, 3 and say, You mountains of Israel, hear the word of the Lord GOD! Thus says the Lord GOD to the mountains and the hills, to the ravines and the valleys: I, I myself will bring a

4.17 Lev 26.39; Ezek 24.23
5.1 Lev 21.5; Isa 7.20; Ezek 44.20
5.2 v. 12; Ezek 4.2-8; Lev 26.33
5.3 Jer 39.10
5.4 Jer 41.1,2; 44.14
5.5 Ezek 4.1; Lam 1.1
5.6 Ezek 16.47, 48,51; Jer 11.10; Zech 7.11
5.7 2 Chr 33.9; Ezek 16.47
5.8 Ezek 15.7
5.9 Dan 9.12; Mt 24.21
5.10 Lev 26.29; Ezek 12.14; Zech 2.6
5.11 2 Chr 36.14; Ezek 7.4,9; 8.18
5.12 Jer 43.10, 11; Ezek 12.14
5.13 Lam 4.11; Ezek 21.17; 36.6
5.14 Lev 26.31, 32; Neh 2.17
5.15 Deut 28.37; 1 Kings 9.7; Jer 24.9; Ezek 25.17
5.16 Deut 32.23, 24; Ezek 4.16
5.17 Ezek 14.21; 28.23
6.2 Ezek 36.1
6.3 Ezek 36.4,6

[j] Heb *it withdraw* [k] Another reading is *I will* [l] Gk Syr Vg Tg: Heb *It shall be* [m] Heb *them*

sword upon you, and I will destroy
your high places. 4 Your altars shall
become desolate, and your incense
stands shall be broken; and I will
throw down your slain in front of
your idols. 5 I will lay the corpses of
the people of Israel in front of their
idols; and I will scatter your bones
around your altars. 6 Wherever you
live, your towns shall be waste and
your high places ruined, so that
your altars will be waste and ruined,[n] your idols broken and destroyed, your incense stands cut
down, and your works wiped out.
7 The slain shall fall in your midst;
then you shall know that I am the
LORD.
8 But I will spare some. Some of
you shall escape the sword among
the nations and be scattered
through the countries. 9 Those of
you who escape shall remember
me among the nations where they
are carried captive, how I was
crushed by their wanton heart that
turned away from me, and their
wanton eyes that turned after their
idols. Then they will be loathsome
in their own sight for the evils that
they have committed, for all their
abominations. 10 And they shall
know that I am the LORD; I did not
threaten in vain to bring this disaster upon them.
11 Thus says the Lord GOD: Clap
your hands and stamp your foot,
and say, Alas for all the vile abominations of the house of Israel! For
they shall fall by the sword, by famine, and by pestilence. 12 Those far
off shall die of pestilence; those
nearby shall fall by the sword; and
any who are left and are spared
shall die of famine. Thus I will
spend my fury upon them. 13 And
you shall know that I am the LORD,
when their slain lie among their
idols around their altars, on every
high hill, on all the mountain tops,
under every green tree, and under
every leafy oak, wherever they offered pleasing odor to all their
idols. 14 I will stretch out my hand
against them, and make the land
desolate and waste, throughout all
their settlements, from the wilderness to Riblah.[o] Then they shall
know that I am the LORD.

6.4 Lev 26.30 **6.5** Jer 8.1,2 **6.6** Lev 26.31; Zech 13.2 **6.7** Ezek 11.10, 12 **6.8** Jer 44.28; Ezek 5.2,12; 12.16; 14.22 **6.9** Jer 51.50; Ps 78.40; Isa 7.13; Ezek 43.24; 20.7,24; 20.43 **6.10** v. 7 **6.11** Ezek 21.14; 25.6; 5.12; 7.15 **6.12** Dan 9.7; Ezek 5.13 **6.13** v. 7; Jer 2.20; Hos 4.13; Isa 57.5 **6.14** Isa 5.25; Ezek 14.13; Num 33.46

7.2 Am 8.2; Ezek 11.13; Rev 7.1; 20.8 **7.3** vv. 8,9,27 **7.4** Ezek 5.11; 8.18; 11.21; 6.7 **7.5** 2 Kings 21.12, 13 **7.6** vv. 2,10 **7.7** v. 12; Isa 22.5 **7.8** Ezek 20.8, 21; 6.12; v. 3

Impending Disaster

7 The word of the LORD came to
me: 2 You, O mortal, thus says
the Lord GOD to the land of Israel:
An end! The end has come
upon the four corners of
the land.
3 Now the end is upon you,
I will let loose my anger
upon you;
I will judge you according to
your ways,
I will punish you for all
your abominations.
4 My eye will not spare you, I
will have no pity.
I will punish you for your
ways,
while your abominations
are among you.
Then you shall know that I am the
LORD.
5 Thus says the Lord GOD:
Disaster after disaster! See, it
comes.
6 An end has come, the end
has come.
It has awakened against you;
see, it comes!
7 Your doom[p] has come to
you,
O inhabitant of the land.
The time has come, the day
is near—
of tumult, not of reveling
on the mountains.
8 Soon now I will pour out my
wrath upon you;
I will spend my anger
against you.
I will judge you according to
your ways,
and punish you for all your
abominations.
9 My eye will not spare; I will
have no pity.
I will punish you according
to your ways,
while your abominations
are among you.

[n] Syr Vg Tg: Heb *and be made guilty*
[o] Another reading is *Diblah* [p] Meaning of Heb uncertain

Then you shall know that it is I the
LORD who strike.

10 See, the day! See, it comes!
Your doom[q] has gone out.
The rod has blossomed,
pride has budded.
11 Violence has grown into a
rod of wickedness.
None of them shall remain,
not their abundance, not
their wealth;
no pre-eminence among
them.[q]
12 The time has come, the day
draws near;
let not the buyer rejoice,
nor the seller mourn,
for wrath is upon all their
multitude.

13 For the sellers shall not return to
what has been sold as long as they
remain alive. For the vision concerns all their multitude; it shall
not be revoked. Because of their iniquity, they cannot maintain their
lives.[q]

14 They have blown the horn
and made everything
ready;
but no one goes to battle,
for my wrath is upon all
their multitude.
15 The sword is outside,
pestilence and famine
are inside;
those in the field die by
the sword;
those in the city—famine
and pestilence devour
them.
16 If any survivors escape,
they shall be found on the
mountains
like doves of the valleys,
all of them moaning over
their iniquity.
17 All hands shall grow feeble,
all knees turn to water.
18 They shall put on sackcloth,
horror shall cover them.
Shame shall be on all faces,
baldness on all their heads.
19 They shall fling their silver
into the streets,
their gold shall be treated
as unclean.
Their silver and gold cannot save
them on the day of the wrath of the
LORD. They shall not satisfy their
hunger or fill their stomachs with
it. For it was the stumbling block of
their iniquity. 20 From their[r] beautiful ornament, in which they took
pride, they made their abominable
images, their detestable things;
therefore I will make of it an unclean thing to them.

21 I will hand it over to
strangers as booty,
to the wicked of the earth
as plunder;
they shall profane it.
22 I will avert my face from
them,
so that they may profane
my treasured[s] place;
the violent shall enter it,
they shall profane it.
23 Make a chain![q]
For the land is full of bloody
crimes;
the city is full of violence.
24 I will bring the worst of the
nations
to take possession of their
houses.
I will put an end to the
arrogance of the strong,
and their holy places shall
be profaned.
25 When anguish comes, they
will seek peace,
but there shall be
none.
26 Disaster comes upon
disaster,
rumor follows rumor;
they shall keep seeking a
vision from the prophet;
instruction shall perish
from the priest,
and counsel from the
elders.
27 The king shall mourn,
the prince shall be
wrapped in despair,
and the hands of the
people of the land shall
tremble.
According to their way I will
deal with them;

7.10 v. 7; Isa 10.5 **7.11** Jer 6.7; 16.5,6; Ezek 24.16, 22 **7.12** vv. 5-7,10; 1 Cor 7.30; v. 14 **7.14** Jer 4.5; v. 12 **7.15** Deut 32.25; Ezek 5.12 **7.16** Ezek 6.8; 14.22; Isa 38.14; 59.11 **7.17** Isa 13.7; Ezek 21.7; Heb 12.12 **7.18** Isa 15.2,3; Am 8.10; Ezek 27.31 **7.19** Isa 30.22; Prov 11.4; Zeph 1.18; Ezek 13.5; 14.3,4 **7.20** Jer 7.30 **7.21** Ps 74.2-8 **7.22** Ezek 39.23, 24 **7.23** 2 Kings 21.16; Ezek 9.9; 8.17 **7.24** Ezek 21.31; 33.28; 24.21 **7.25** Ezek 13.10, 16 **7.26** Deut 32.23; Jer 4.20; Ezek 21.7; Ps 74.9; Ezek 20.1,3 **7.27** Ps 35.26; Ezek 26.16; vv. 3,4,8; Ezek 18.20

q Meaning of Heb uncertain r Syr Symmachus: Heb *its* s Or *secret*

according to their own
judgments I will judge
them.
And they shall know that I am the
LORD.

Abominations in the Temple

8 In the sixth year, in the sixth
month, on the fifth day of the
month, as I sat in my house, with
the elders of Judah sitting before
me, the hand of the Lord GOD fell
upon me there. 2 I looked, and
there was a figure that looked like
a human being;[t] below what appeared to be its loins it was fire,
and above the loins it was like the
appearance of brightness, like
gleaming amber. 3 It stretched out
the form of a hand, and took me by
a lock of my head; and the spirit
lifted me up between earth and
heaven, and brought me in visions
of God to Jerusalem, to the entrance of the gateway of the inner
court that faces north, to the seat
of the image of jealousy, which provokes to jealousy. 4 And the glory of
the God of Israel was there, like the
vision that I had seen in the valley.
5 Then God[u] said to me,
"O mortal, lift up your eyes now in
the direction of the north." So I lifted up my eyes toward the north,
and there, north of the altar gate, in
the entrance, was this image of
jealousy. 6 He said to me, "Mortal,
do you see what they are doing, the
great abominations that the house
of Israel are committing here, to
drive me far from my sanctuary?
Yet you will see still greater abominations."
7 And he brought me to the entrance of the court; I looked, and
there was a hole in the wall. 8 Then
he said to me, "Mortal, dig through
the wall"; and when I dug through
the wall, there was an entrance.
9 He said to me, "Go in, and see the
vile abominations that they are
committing here." 10 So I went in
and looked; there, portrayed on the
wall all around, were all kinds of
creeping things, and loathsome animals, and all the idols of the house
of Israel. 11 Before them stood seventy of the elders of the house of
Israel, with Jaazaniah son of Shaphan standing among them. Each
had his censer in his hand, and the
fragrant cloud of incense was ascending. 12 Then he said to me,
"Mortal, have you seen what the elders of the house of Israel are doing
in the dark, each in his room of images? For they say, 'The LORD does
not see us, the LORD has forsaken
the land.' " 13 He said also to me,
"You will see still greater abominations that they are committing."
14 Then he brought me to the
entrance of the north gate of the
house of the LORD; women were sitting there weeping for Tammuz.
15 Then he said to me, "Have you
seen this, O mortal? You will see
still greater abominations than
these."
16 And he brought me into the
inner court of the house of the
LORD; there, at the entrance of the
temple of the LORD, between the
porch and the altar, were about
twenty-five men, with their backs
to the temple of the LORD, and their
faces toward the east, prostrating
themselves to the sun toward the
east. 17 Then he said to me, "Have
you seen this, O mortal? Is it not
bad enough that the house of Judah commits the abominations
done here? Must they fill the land
with violence, and provoke my anger still further? See, they are putting the branch to their nose!
18 Therefore I will act in wrath; my
eye will not spare, nor will I have
pity; and though they cry in my
hearing with a loud voice, I will not
listen to them."

The Slaughter of the Idolaters

9 Then he cried in my hearing
with a loud voice, saying,
"Draw near, you executioners of
the city, each with his destroying
weapon in his hand." 2 And six men
came from the direction of the upper gate, which faces north, each
with his weapon for slaughter in his
hand; among them was a man
clothed in linen, with a writing

8.1 Ezek 14.1; 20.1; 33.31; 1.3; 3.22
8.2 Ezek 1.4,27
8.3 Dan 5.5; Ezek 3.12, 14; 11.1; Jer 32.34; Ezek 5.11
8.4 Ezek 1.28
8.5 Zech 5.5; v. 3
8.6 vv. 9,17; Ezek 5.11; 7.22,24; vv. 11,14,16
8.10 Ex 20.4; Ezek 14.3
8.11 Jer 19.1; Num 16.17, 35; Ezek 16.18; 23.41
8.12 Ezek 9.9
8.13 Ezek 9.3
8.14 Ezek 44.4; 46.9
8.16 Ezek 11.1; Jer 2.27; Deut 4.19; Job 31.26; Jer 44.17
8.17 Ezek 9.9; Mic 2.2; Jer 7.18,19; Ezek 16.26
8.18 Ezek 5.13; 7.4; 9.5,10; Isa 1.15; Jer 11.11; Mic 3.4; Zech 7.13
9.2 Ezek 10.2; Rev 15.6

[t] Gk: Heb *like fire* [u] Heb *he*

case at his side. They went in and stood beside the bronze altar.

3 Now the glory of the God of Israel had gone up from the cherub on which it rested to the threshold of the house. The LORD called to the man clothed in linen, who had the writing case at his side; 4 and said to him, "Go through the city, through Jerusalem, and put a mark on the foreheads of those who sigh and groan over all the abominations that are committed in it." 5 To the others he said in my hearing, "Pass through the city after him, and kill; your eye shall not spare, and you shall show no pity. 6 Cut down old men, young men and young women, little children and women, but touch no one who has the mark. And begin at my sanctuary." So they began with the elders who were in front of the house. 7 Then he said to them, "Defile the house, and fill the courts with the slain. Go!" So they went out and killed in the city. 8 While they were killing, and I was left alone, I fell prostrate on my face and cried out, "Ah Lord GOD! will you destroy all who remain of Israel as you pour out your wrath upon Jerusalem?" 9 He said to me, "The guilt of the house of Israel and Judah is exceedingly great; the land is full of bloodshed and the city full of perversity; for they say, 'The LORD has forsaken the land, and the LORD does not see.' 10 As for me, my eye will not spare, nor will I have pity, but I will bring down their deeds upon their heads."

11 Then the man clothed in linen, with the writing case at his side, brought back word, saying, "I have done as you commanded me."

God's Glory Leaves Jerusalem

10 Then I looked, and above the dome that was over the heads of the cherubim there appeared above them something like a sapphire,[v] in form resembling a throne. 2 He said to the man clothed in linen, "Go within the wheelwork underneath the cherubim; fill your hands with burning coals from among the cherubim, and scatter them over the city." He went in as I looked on. 3 Now the cherubim were standing on the south side of the house when the man went in; and a cloud filled the inner court. 4 Then the glory of the LORD rose up from the cherub to the threshold of the house; the house was filled with the cloud, and the court was full of the brightness of the glory of the LORD. 5 The sound of the wings of the cherubim was heard as far as the outer court, like the voice of God Almighty[w] when he speaks.

6 When he commanded the man clothed in linen, "Take fire from within the wheelwork, from among the cherubim," he went in and stood beside a wheel. 7 And a cherub stretched out his hand from among the cherubim to the fire that was among the cherubim, took some of it and put it into the hands of the man clothed in linen, who took it and went out. 8 The cherubim appeared to have the form of a human hand under their wings.

9 I looked, and there were four wheels beside the cherubim, one beside each cherub; and the appearance of the wheels was like gleaming beryl. 10 And as for their appearance, the four looked alike, something like a wheel within a wheel. 11 When they moved, they moved in any of the four directions without veering as they moved; but in whatever direction the front wheel faced, the others followed without veering as they moved. 12 Their entire body, their rims, their spokes, their wings, and the wheels—the wheels of the four of them—were full of eyes all around. 13 As for the wheels, they were called in my hearing "the wheelwork." 14 Each one had four faces: the first face was that of the cherub, the second face was that of a human being, the third that of a lion, and the fourth that of an eagle.

9.3 Ezek 8.4; 10.4,18; 11.22,23
9.4 Ex 12.7; 1 Pet 4.17; Rev 7.3; 9.4; Ps 119.53, 136; Jer 13.17
9.5 Ezek 5.11; 7.4,9
9.6 2 Chr 36.17; Rev 9.4; Jer 25.29; Am 3.2; Ezek 8.11, 12,16
9.7 2 Chr 36.17; Ezek 7.20-22; 6.4
9.8 1 Chr 21.16; Josh 7.6; Ezek 11.13
9.9 Ezek 7.23; 22.29; 8.12
9.10 Isa 65.6; Ezek 8.18; 7.4; 11.21
10.1 Ezek 1.22, 26; Rev 4.2
10.2 Ezek 9.2,3; v. 13; Isa 6.6; Rev 8.5
10.3 Ezek 8.3,16
10.4 Ezek 1.28; 9.3; Ex 40.34, 35; 1 Kings 8.10, 11
10.5 Ezek 1.24
10.6 v. 2
10.7 Ezek 1.13
10.8 Ezek 1.8
10.9 Ezek 1.15, 16
10.11 Ezek 1.17; v. 22
10.12 Rev 4.6,8; Ezek 1.18
10.13 v. 2
10.14 Ezek 1.6,10; Rev 4.7

[v] Or *lapis lazuli* [w] Traditional rendering of Heb *El Shaddai*

15 The cherubim rose up. These
were the living creatures that I saw
by the river Chebar. 16 When the
cherubim moved, the wheels
moved beside them; and when the
cherubim lifted up their wings to
rise up from the earth, the wheels
at their side did not veer. 17 When
they stopped, the others stopped,
and when they rose up, the others
rose up with them; for the spirit of
the living creatures was in them.
18 Then the glory of the LORD
went out from the threshold of the
house and stopped above the cherubim. 19 The cherubim lifted up
their wings and rose up from the
earth in my sight as they went out
with the wheels beside them. They
stopped at the entrance of the east
gate of the house of the LORD; and
the glory of the God of Israel was
above them.
20 These were the living creatures that I saw underneath the
God of Israel by the river Chebar;
and I knew that they were cherubim. 21 Each had four faces, each
four wings, and underneath their
wings something like human
hands. 22 As for what their faces
were like, they were the same faces
whose appearance I had seen by
the river Chebar. Each one moved
straight ahead.

Judgment on Wicked Counselors

11 The spirit lifted me up and
brought me to the east gate
of the house of the LORD, which
faces east. There, at the entrance
of the gateway, were twenty-five
men; among them I saw Jaazaniah
son of Azzur, and Pelatiah son of
Benaiah, officials of the people.
2 He said to me, "Mortal, these are
the men who devise iniquity and
who give wicked counsel in this
city; 3 they say, 'The time is not
near to build houses; this city is the
pot, and we are the meat.' 4 Therefore prophesy against them; prophesy, O mortal."
5 Then the spirit of the LORD fell
upon me, and he said to me, "Say,
Thus says the LORD: This is what
you think, O house of Israel; I

10.15 Ezek 1.3,5
10.16 Ezek 1.19
10.17 Ezek 1.12, 20,21
10.18 v. 4
10.19 11.1,22
10.20 v. 15; Ezek 1.22; 1.1
10.21 Ezek 1.6,8
10.22 Ezek 1.10, 12
11.1 Ezek 3.12, 14; 8.3; 10.19; 8.16
11.2 Isa 30.1; Mic 2.1
11.3 Ezek 12.22, 27; 2 Pet 3.4; Jer 1.13; Ezek 24.3,6
11.4 Ezek 3.4,17
11.5 Ezek 2.2; 3.24; Jer 11.20; Ezek 38.10
11.6 Ezek 7.23; 22.3,4
11.7 Ezek 24.3,6, 10,11; Mic 3.3; v. 9
11.9 Ps 106.41; Ezek 5.8
11.10 2 Kings 25.19-21; Jer 52.10; 2 Kings 14.25; Ezek 6.7
11.11 v. 3
11.12 v. 10; Ezek 18.8,9; 8.10,14,16
11.13 v. 1; Ezek 9.8
11.15 Ezek 33.24
11.16 Isa 8.14
11.17 Jer 24.5; Ezek 28.25; 34.13
11.18 Ezek 37.23; 5.11

know the things that come into
your mind. 6 You have killed many
in this city, and have filled its
streets with the slain. 7 Therefore
thus says the Lord GOD: The slain
whom you have placed within it are
the meat, and this city is the pot;
but you shall be taken out of it.
8 You have feared the sword; and I
will bring the sword upon you, says
the Lord GOD. 9 I will take you out of
it and give you over to the hands of
foreigners, and execute judgments
upon you. 10 You shall fall by the
sword; I will judge you at the border of Israel. And you shall know
that I am the LORD. 11 This city shall
not be your pot, and you shall not
be the meat inside it; I will judge
you at the border of Israel. 12 Then
you shall know that I am the LORD,
whose statutes you have not followed, and whose ordinances you
have not kept, but you have acted
according to the ordinances of the
nations that are around you."
13 Now, while I was prophesying, Pelatiah son of Benaiah died.
Then I fell down on my face, cried
with a loud voice, and said, "Ah
Lord GOD! will you make a full end
of the remnant of Israel?"

God Will Restore Israel

14 Then the word of the LORD
came to me: 15 Mortal, your kinsfolk, your own kin, your fellow exiles,[x] the whole house of Israel, all
of them, are those of whom the inhabitants of Jerusalem have said,
"They have gone far from the LORD;
to us this land is given for a possession." 16 Therefore say: Thus says
the Lord GOD: Though I removed
them far away among the nations,
and though I scattered them
among the countries, yet I have
been a sanctuary to them for a little
while[y] in the countries where they
have gone. 17 Therefore say: Thus
says the Lord GOD: I will gather you
from the peoples, and assemble
you out of the countries where you
have been scattered, and I will give
you the land of Israel. 18 When they

[x] Gk Syr: Heb *people of your kindred*
[y] Or *to some extent*

come there, they will remove from it all its detestable things and all its abominations. 19 I will give them one[z] heart, and put a new spirit within them; I will remove the heart of stone from their flesh and give them a heart of flesh, 20 so that they may follow my statutes and keep my ordinances and obey them. Then they shall be my people, and I will be their God. 21 But as for those whose heart goes after their detestable things and their abominations,[a] I will bring their deeds upon their own heads, says the Lord GOD.

22 Then the cherubim lifted up their wings, with the wheels beside them; and the glory of the God of Israel was above them. 23 And the glory of the LORD ascended from the middle of the city, and stopped on the mountain east of the city. 24 The spirit lifted me up and brought me in a vision by the spirit of God into Chaldea, to the exiles. Then the vision that I had seen left me. 25 And I told the exiles all the things that the LORD had shown me.

Judah's Captivity Portrayed

12 The word of the LORD came to me: 2 Mortal, you are living in the midst of a rebellious house, who have eyes to see but do not see, who have ears to hear but do not hear; 3 for they are a rebellious house. Therefore, mortal, prepare for yourself an exile's baggage, and go into exile by day in their sight; you shall go like an exile from your place to another place in their sight. Perhaps they will understand, though they are a rebellious house. 4 You shall bring out your baggage by day in their sight, as baggage for exile; and you shall go out yourself at evening in their sight, as those do who go into exile. 5 Dig through the wall in their sight, and carry the baggage through it. 6 In their sight you shall lift the baggage on your shoulder, and carry it out in the dark; you shall cover your face, so that you may not see the land; for I have made you a sign for the house of Israel.

7 I did just as I was commanded. I brought out my baggage by day, as baggage for exile, and in the evening I dug through the wall with my own hands; I brought it out in the dark, carrying it on my shoulder in their sight.

8 In the morning the word of the LORD came to me: 9 Mortal, has not the house of Israel, the rebellious house, said to you, "What are you doing?" 10 Say to them, "Thus says the Lord GOD: This oracle concerns the prince in Jerusalem and all the house of Israel in it." 11 Say, "I am a sign for you: as I have done, so shall it be done to them; they shall go into exile, into captivity." 12 And the prince who is among them shall lift his baggage on his shoulder in the dark, and shall go out; he[b] shall dig through the wall and carry it through; he shall cover his face, so that he may not see the land with his eyes. 13 I will spread my net over him, and he shall be caught in my snare; and I will bring him to Babylon, the land of the Chaldeans, yet he shall not see it; and he shall die there. 14 I will scatter to every wind all who are around him, his helpers and all his troops; and I will unsheathe the sword behind them. 15 And they shall know that I am the LORD, when I disperse them among the nations and scatter them through the countries. 16 But I will let a few of them escape from the sword, from famine and pestilence, so that they may tell of all their abominations among the nations where they go; then they shall know that I am the LORD.

Judgment Not Postponed

17 The word of the LORD came to me: 18 Mortal, eat your bread with quaking, and drink your water with trembling and with fearfulness; 19 and say to the people of the land, Thus says the Lord GOD concerning

11.19 Jer 32.39; Ezek 36.26, 27; 18.31; Zech 7.12; 2 Cor 3.3
11.20 Ps 105.45; Ezek 14.11
11.21 Ezek 9.10
11.22 Ezek 1.19; 10.19
11.23 Ezek 8.4; 9.3; Zech 14.4
11.24 Ezek 8.3; 1.1,3
11.25 Ezek 2.7
12.2 Ezek 2.6-8; Jer 5.21; Mt 13.13,14
12.3 Jer 26.3; 36.3,7; 2 Tim 2.25
12.4 Jer 39.4; v. 12
12.6 vv. 12,13; Isa 8.18; Ezek 4.3; 24.24
12.7 Ezek 24.18; vv. 3-6
12.9 Ezek 2.5; 17.12; 24.19
12.10 Mal 1.1
12.11 v. 6; 2 Kings 25.4-7
12.12 Jer 39.4
12.13 Isa 24.17, 18; Hos 7.12; Jer 52.11; Ezek 17.16
12.14 2 Kings 25.4, 5; Ezek 5.2, 12
12.15 Ezek 6.7,14
12.16 Ezek 6.8-10; 14.22; Jer 22.8,9
12.18 Ezek 4.16
12.19 Ezek 4.16; 23.33; Zech 7.14

[z] Another reading is *a new* [a] Cn: Heb *And to the heart of their detestable things and their abominations their heart goes* [b] Gk Syr: Heb *they*

the inhabitants of Jerusalem in the
land of Israel: They shall eat their
bread with fearfulness, and drink
their water in dismay, because
their land shall be stripped of all it
contains, on account of the violence of all those who live in it.
20 The inhabited cities shall be laid
waste, and the land shall become a
desolation; and you shall know
that I am the LORD.
21 The word of the LORD came to
me: 22 Mortal, what is this proverb
of yours about the land of Israel,
which says, "The days are prolonged, and every vision comes to
nothing"? 23 Tell them therefore,
"Thus says the Lord GOD: I will put
an end to this proverb, and they
shall use it no more as a proverb in
Israel." But say to them, The days
are near, and the fulfillment of every vision. 24 For there shall no longer be any false vision or flattering
divination within the house of Israel. 25 But I the LORD will speak the
word that I speak, and it will be fulfilled. It will no longer be delayed;
but in your days, O rebellious
house, I will speak the word and
fulfill it, says the Lord GOD.
26 The word of the LORD came to
me: 27 Mortal, the house of Israel is
saying, "The vision that he sees is
for many years ahead; he prophesies for distant times." 28 Therefore
say to them, Thus says the Lord
GOD: None of my words will be delayed any longer, but the word that
I speak will be fulfilled, says the
Lord GOD.

False Prophets Condemned

13 The word of the LORD came
to me: 2 Mortal, prophesy
against the prophets of Israel who
are prophesying; say to those who
prophesy out of their own imagination: "Hear the word of the LORD!"
3 Thus says the Lord GOD, Alas for
the senseless prophets who follow
their own spirit, and have seen
nothing! 4 Your prophets have been
like jackals among ruins, O Israel.
5 You have not gone up into the
breaches, or repaired a wall for the
house of Israel, so that it might
stand in battle on the day of the
LORD. 6 They have envisioned falsehood and lying divination; they say,
"Says the LORD," when the LORD has
not sent them, and yet they wait for
the fulfillment of their word! 7 Have
you not seen a false vision or uttered a lying divination, when you
have said, "Says the LORD," even
though I did not speak?
8 Therefore thus says the Lord
GOD: Because you have uttered
falsehood and envisioned lies, I am
against you, says the Lord GOD.
9 My hand will be against the
prophets who see false visions and
utter lying divinations; they shall
not be in the council of my people,
nor be enrolled in the register of
the house of Israel, nor shall they
enter the land of Israel; and you
shall know that I am the Lord GOD.
10 Because, in truth, because they
have misled my people, saying,
"Peace," when there is no peace;
and because, when the people
build a wall, these prophets[c]
smear whitewash on it. 11 Say to
those who smear whitewash on it
that it shall fall. There will be a deluge of rain,[d] great hailstones will
fall, and a stormy wind will break
out. 12 When the wall falls, will it
not be said to you, "Where is the
whitewash you smeared on it?"
13 Therefore thus says the Lord
GOD: In my wrath I will make a
stormy wind break out, and in my
anger there shall be a deluge of
rain, and hailstones in wrath to destroy it. 14 I will break down the
wall that you have smeared with
whitewash, and bring it to the
ground, so that its foundation will
be laid bare; when it falls, you shall
perish within it; and you shall
know that I am the LORD. 15 Thus I
will spend my wrath upon the wall,
and upon those who have smeared
it with whitewash; and I will say to
you, The wall is no more, nor those
who smeared it— 16 the prophets
of Israel who prophesied concerning Jerusalem and saw visions of

12.20 Ezek 5.14; 36.3
12.22 Ezek 16.44; 11.3; v. 27; Am 6.3; 2 Pet 3.4
12.23 Joel 2.1; Zeph 1.14
12.24 Ezek 13.23; Zech 13.2-4
12.25 v. 28; Isa 55.11; Dan 9.12; Hab 1.5; v. 2
12.27 v. 22; Dan 10.14; 2 Pet 3.4
12.28 v. 25; Mt 24.48-50
13.2 Jer 37.19; v. 17; Jer 14.14; 23.16,26; Am 7.16
13.3 Lam 2.14; Jer 23.28-32
13.5 Ps 106.23, 30; Ezek 22.30; Isa 58.12; Ezek 7.19
13.6 v. 22; Ezek 22.28; Jer 28.15
13.7 Ezek 22.28
13.8 Ezek 21.29; 5.8
13.9 Ezra 2.59, 62; Neh 7.5; Ps 69.28; Ezek 11.10, 12
13.10 Jer 50.6; 8.11; v. 16; Ezek 22.28
13.11 Ezek 38.22
13.13 v. 11; Isa 30.30; Rev 11.19; 16.21
13.14 Mic 1.6; v. 9; Ezek 14.8
13.16 Ezek 6.14; Isa 57.21

[c] Heb *they* [d] Heb *rain and you*

peace for it, when there was no
peace, says the Lord GOD.
17 As for you, mortal, set your
face against the daughters of your
people, who prophesy out of their
own imagination; prophesy against
them 18 and say, Thus says the Lord
GOD: Woe to the women who sew
bands on all wrists, and make veils
for the heads of persons of every
height, in the hunt for human lives!
Will you hunt down lives among my
people, and maintain your own
lives? 19 You have profaned me
among my people for handfuls of
barley and for pieces of bread, putting to death persons who should
not die and keeping alive persons
who should not live, by your lies to
my people, who listen to lies.
20 Therefore thus says the Lord
GOD: I am against your bands with
which you hunt lives;[e] I will tear
them from your arms, and let the
lives go free, the lives that you hunt
down like birds. 21 I will tear off
your veils, and save my people from
your hands; they shall no longer be
prey in your hands; and you shall
know that I am the LORD. 22 Because
you have disheartened the righteous falsely, although I have not
disheartened them, and you have
encouraged the wicked not to turn
from their wicked way and save
their lives; 23 therefore you shall no
longer see false visions or practice
divination; I will save my people
from your hand. Then you will
know that I am the LORD.

God's Judgments Justified

14 Certain elders of Israel
came to me and sat down
before me. 2 And the word of the
LORD came to me: 3 Mortal, these
men have taken their idols into
their hearts, and placed their iniquity as a stumbling block before
them; shall I let myself be consulted by them? 4 Therefore speak to
them, and say to them, Thus says
the Lord GOD: Any of those of the
house of Israel who take their idols
into their hearts and place their iniquity as a stumbling block before
them, and yet come to the
prophet—I the LORD will answer
those who come with the multitude of their idols, 5 in order that I
may take hold of the hearts of the
house of Israel, all of whom are estranged from me through their
idols.
6 Therefore say to the house of
Israel, Thus says the Lord GOD: Repent and turn away from your idols;
and turn away your faces from all
your abominations. 7 For any of
those of the house of Israel, or of
the aliens who reside in Israel, who
separate themselves from me, taking their idols into their hearts and
placing their iniquity as a stumbling block before them, and yet
come to a prophet to inquire of me
by him, I the LORD will answer them
myself. 8 I will set my face against
them; I will make them a sign and
a byword and cut them off from the
midst of my people; and you shall
know that I am the LORD.
9 If a prophet is deceived and
speaks a word, I, the LORD, have deceived that prophet, and I will
stretch out my hand against him,
and will destroy him from the
midst of my people Israel. 10 And
they shall bear their punishment—
the punishment of the inquirer and
the punishment of the prophet
shall be the same— 11 so that the
house of Israel may no longer go
astray from me, nor defile themselves any more with all their transgressions. Then they shall be my
people, and I will be their God, says
the Lord GOD.
12 The word of the LORD came to
me: 13 Mortal, when a land sins
against me by acting faithlessly,
and I stretch out my hand against
it, and break its staff of bread and
send famine upon it, and cut off
from it human beings and animals,
14 even if Noah, Daniel,[f] and Job,
these three, were in it, they would
save only their own lives by their
righteousness, says the Lord GOD.
15 If I send wild animals through

13.17 Ezek 20.46; 21.2; v. 2
13.18 Ezek 22.25; 2 Pet 2.14
13.19 Ezek 20.39; Prov 28.21; Mic 3.5; Jer 23.14,17
13.20 v. 17
13.21 Ps 124.7; v. 9
13.22 Am 5.12; Jer 23.14; Ezek 33.14-16
13.23 v. 6; Ezek 12.24; Mic 3.6; v. 9; Ezek 14.8
14.1 Ezek 8.1; 20.1; 33.31
14.3 Ezek 20.16; 7.19; Jer 11.11; Ezek 20.3, 31
14.4 v. 7
14.5 Isa 1.4; Jer 2.11; Zech 11.8
14.6 Isa 2.20; 30.22; Ezek 18.30; 8.6
14.7 Ex 12.48; 20.10; v. 4
14.8 Jer 44.11; Ezek 15.7; Isa 65.15; Ezek 5.15; 6.7
14.9 1 Kings 22.23; Job 12.16; Jer 4.10; 2 Thes 2.11; Jer 14.15
14.11 Ezek 44.10, 15; 11.20; 37.27
14.13 Ezek 15.8; 6.14; 5.16; vv. 17,19,21
14.14 Jer 15.1; Gen 6.8; Dan 1.6; Job 1.1,5; vv. 16,18,20
14.15 Ezek 5.17

[e] Gk Syr: Heb *lives for birds* [f] Or, as otherwise read, *Danel*

the land to ravage it, so that it is
made desolate, and no one may
pass through because of the animals; [16]even if these three men
were in it, as I live, says the Lord
GOD, they would save neither sons
nor daughters; they alone would be
saved, but the land would be desolate. [17]Or if I bring a sword upon
that land and say, 'Let a sword pass
through the land,' and I cut off human beings and animals from it;
[18]though these three men were in
it, as I live, says the Lord GOD, they
would save neither sons nor daughters, but they alone would be
saved. [19]Or if I send a pestilence
into that land, and pour out my
wrath upon it with blood, to cut off
humans and animals from it;
[20]even if Noah, Daniel,[g] and Job
were in it, as I live, says the Lord
GOD, they would save neither son
nor daughter; they would save only
their own lives by their righteousness.

21 For thus says the Lord GOD:
How much more when I send upon
Jerusalem my four deadly acts of
judgment, sword, famine, wild animals, and pestilence, to cut off humans and animals from it! [22]Yet,
survivors shall be left in it, sons and
daughters who will be brought out;
they will come out to you. When
you see their ways and their deeds,
you will be consoled for the evil
that I have brought upon Jerusalem, for all that I have brought
upon it. [23]They shall console you,
when you see their ways and their
deeds; and you shall know that it
was not without cause that I did all
that I have done in it, says the Lord
GOD.

The Useless Vine

15 The word of the LORD came to me:

[2] O mortal, how does the
wood of the vine
surpass all other
wood—
the vine branch that is
among the trees of the
forest?

[3] Is wood taken from it to
make anything?
Does one take a peg from
it on which to hang any
object?
[4] It is put in the fire for fuel;
when the fire has
consumed both ends of
it
and the middle of it is
charred,
is it useful for anything?
[5] When it was whole it was
used for nothing;
how much less—when the
fire has consumed it,
and it is charred—
can it ever be used for
anything!

6 Therefore thus says the Lord
GOD: Like the wood of the vine
among the trees of the forest,
which I have given to the fire for
fuel, so I will give up the inhabitants of Jerusalem. [7]I will set my
face against them; although they
escape from the fire, the fire shall
still consume them; and you shall
know that I am the LORD, when I set
my face against them. [8]And I will
make the land desolate, because
they have acted faithlessly, says
the Lord GOD.

God's Faithless Bride

16 The word of the LORD came
to me: [2]Mortal, make
known to Jerusalem her abominations, [3]and say, Thus says the Lord
GOD to Jerusalem: Your origin and
your birth were in the land of the
Canaanites; your father was an Amorite, and your mother a Hittite.
[4]As for your birth, on the day you
were born your navel cord was not
cut, nor were you washed with water to cleanse you, nor rubbed with
salt, nor wrapped in cloths. [5]No
eye pitied you, to do any of these
things for you out of compassion
for you; but you were thrown out in
the open field, for you were abhorred on the day you were born.
6 I passed by you, and saw you
flailing about in your blood. As you
lay in your blood, I said to you,

14.16 vv. 14,18, 20; Ezek 18.20
14.17 Ezek 5.12; 21.3,4; 25.13; Zeph 1.3
14.18 v. 14
14.19 v. 21; Ezek 38.22; 7.8
14.20 v. 14
14.21 Ezek 5.17; Jer 15.2,3; Rev 6.8
14.22 Ezek 12.16; 7.16; 20.43; 16.54
14.23 Jer 22.8,9
15.2 Isa 5.1-7; Jer 2.21; Hos 10.1
15.4 v. 6; Ezek 19.14; Jn 15.6
15.6 v. 2; Ezek 17.3-10
15.7 Lev 17.10; Ezek 14.8; Isa 24.18; Ezek 6.7; 7.4; 14.8
15.8 Ezek 14.13
16.2 Ezek 20.4; 22.2; 8.9-17
16.3 Ezek 21.30; v. 45
16.4 Hos 2.3
16.5 Deut 32.10
16.6 v. 22; Ex 19.4

[g] Or, as otherwise read, *Danel*

"Live! 7 and grow up[h] like a plant of
the field." You grew up and became
tall and arrived at full womanhood;[i] your breasts were formed,
and your hair had grown; yet you
were naked and bare.
8 I passed by you again and
looked on you; you were at the age
for love. I spread the edge of my
cloak over you, and covered your
nakedness: I pledged myself to you
and entered into a covenant with
you, says the Lord GOD, and you became mine. 9 Then I bathed you
with water and washed off the
blood from you, and anointed you
with oil. 10 I clothed you with embroidered cloth and with sandals of
fine leather; I bound you in fine lin-
en and covered you with rich fabric.[j] 11 I adorned you with ornaments: I put bracelets on your
arms, a chain on your neck, 12 a ring
on your nose, earrings in your ears,
and a beautiful crown upon your
head. 13 You were adorned with
gold and silver, while your clothing
was of fine linen, rich fabric,[j] and
embroidered cloth. You had choice
flour and honey and oil for food.
You grew exceedingly beautiful, fit
to be a queen. 14 Your fame spread
among the nations on account of
your beauty, for it was perfect because of my splendor that I had bestowed on you, says the Lord GOD.
15 But you trusted in your beauty, and played the whore because
of your fame, and lavished your
whorings on any passer-by.[k] 16 You
took some of your garments, and
made for yourself colorful shrines,
and on them played the whore;
nothing like this has ever been or
ever shall be.[j] 17 You also took
your beautiful jewels of my gold
and my silver that I had given you,
and made for yourself male images,
and with them played the whore;
18 and you took your embroidered
garments to cover them, and set my
oil and my incense before them.
19 Also my bread that I gave you—I
fed you with choice flour and oil
and honey—you set it before them
as a pleasing odor; and so it was,
says the Lord GOD. 20 You took your
sons and your daughters, whom
you had borne to me, and these you
sacrificed to them to be devoured.
As if your whorings were not
enough! 21 You slaughtered my
children and delivered them up as
an offering to them. 22 And in all
your abominations and your whorings you did not remember the
days of your youth, when you were
naked and bare, flailing about in
your blood.
23 After all your wickedness
(woe, woe to you! says the Lord
GOD), 24 you built yourself a platform and made yourself a lofty
place in every square; 25 at the head
of every street you built your lofty
place and prostituted your beauty,
offering yourself to every passer-by,
and multiplying your whoring.
26 You played the whore with the
Egyptians, your lustful neighbors,
multiplying your whoring, to provoke me to anger. 27 Therefore I
stretched out my hand against you,
reduced your rations, and gave you
up to the will of your enemies, the
daughters of the Philistines, who
were ashamed of your lewd behavior. 28 You played the whore with
the Assyrians, because you were insatiable; you played the whore with
them, and still you were not satisfied. 29 You multiplied your whoring with Chaldea, the land of merchants; and even with this you were
not satisfied.
30 How sick is your heart, says
the Lord GOD, that you did all these
things, the deeds of a brazen
whore; 31 building your platform at
the head of every street, and making your lofty place in every square!
Yet you were not like a whore, because you scorned payment.
32 Adulterous wife, who receives
strangers instead of her husband!
33 Gifts are given to all whores; but
you gave your gifts to all your lovers, bribing them to come to you
from all around for your whorings.
34 So you were different from other

16.7 Ex 1.7; v. 22
16.8 Ruth 3.9; Gen 22.16-18; Ex 24.7,8; 19.5; Jer 2.2
16.10 v. 13
16.11 Ezek 23.40; Gen 24.22, 47; Prov 1.9
16.13 Deut 32.13, 14; 1 Sam 10.1
16.14 Ps 50.2; Lam 2.15
16.15 Isa 57.8; Jer 2.20; Ezek 23.3,8, 11,12
16.16 v. 10; Ezek 6.3,6; Hos 2.8
16.17 Ezek 7.20
16.18 v. 10
16.19 Hos 2.8
16.20 2 Kings 16.3; Isa 57.5
16.21 2 Kings 17.17; Jer 19.5
16.22 Hos 11.1; vv. 4-6
16.24 Isa 57.5,7; Jer 2.20; 3.2
16.25 Prov 9.14; v. 15
16.26 Ezek 8.17; 20.7,8; 23.19-21
16.27 Ezek 14.13; 20.33,34; 2 Chr 28.18, 19
16.28 2 Kings 16.7, 10; 2 Chr 28.23
16.29 Ezek 23.14-17
16.30 Jer 3.3
16.31 v. 24; Isa 52.3
16.33 Isa 30.6; Hos 8.9,10

[h] Gk Syr: Heb *Live! I made you a myriad*
[i] Cn: Heb *ornament of ornaments*
[j] Meaning of Heb uncertain [k] Heb adds *let it be his*

women in your whorings: no one
solicited you to play the whore; and
you gave payment, while no payment was given to you; you were
different.
35 Therefore, O whore, hear the
word of the LORD: [36]Thus says the
Lord GOD, Because your lust was
poured out and your nakedness uncovered in your whoring with your
lovers, and because of all your
abominable idols, and because of
the blood of your children that you
gave to them, [37]therefore, I will
gather all your lovers, with whom
you took pleasure, all those you
loved and all those you hated; I will
gather them against you from all
around, and will uncover your nakedness to them, so that they may
see all your nakedness. [38]I will
judge you as women who commit
adultery and shed blood are
judged, and bring blood upon you
in wrath and jealousy. [39]I will deliver you into their hands, and they
shall throw down your platform
and break down your lofty places;
they shall strip you of your clothes
and take your beautiful objects and
leave you naked and bare. [40]They
shall bring up a mob against you,
and they shall stone you and cut
you to pieces with their swords.
[41]They shall burn your houses and
execute judgments on you in the
sight of many women; I will stop
you from playing the whore, and
you shall also make no more payments. [42]So I will satisfy my fury on
you, and my jealousy shall turn
away from you; I will be calm, and
will be angry no longer. [43]Because
you have not remembered the days
of your youth, but have enraged me
with all these things; therefore, I
have returned your deeds upon
your head, says the Lord GOD.
Have you not committed lewdness beyond all your abominations? [44]See, everyone who uses
proverbs will use this proverb
about you, "Like mother, like
daughter." [45]You are the daughter
of your mother, who loathed her
husband and her children; and you
are the sister of your sisters, who
loathed their husbands and their
children. Your mother was a Hittite
and your father an Amorite. [46]Your
elder sister is Samaria, who lived
with her daughters to the north of
you; and your younger sister, who
lived to the south of you, is Sodom
with her daughters. [47]You not only
followed their ways, and acted according to their abominations;
within a very little time you were
more corrupt than they in all your
ways. [48]As I live, says the Lord GOD,
your sister Sodom and her daughters have not done as you and your
daughters have done. [49]This was
the guilt of your sister Sodom: she
and her daughters had pride, excess of food, and prosperous ease,
but did not aid the poor and needy.
[50]They were haughty, and did
abominable things before me;
therefore I removed them when I
saw it. [51]Samaria has not committed half your sins; you have committed more abominations than
they, and have made your sisters
appear righteous by all the abominations that you have committed.
[52]Bear your disgrace, you also, for
you have brought about for your
sisters a more favorable judgment;
because of your sins in which you
acted more abominably than they,
they are more in the right than you.
So be ashamed, you also, and bear
your disgrace, for you have made
your sisters appear righteous.
53 I will restore their fortunes,
the fortunes of Sodom and her
daughters and the fortunes of Samaria and her daughters, and I will
restore your own fortunes along
with theirs, [54]in order that you may
bear your disgrace and be ashamed
of all that you have done, becoming
a consolation to them. [55]As for
your sisters, Sodom and her daughters shall return to their former
state, Samaria and her daughters
shall return to their former state,
and you and your daughters shall
return to your former state. [56]Was
not your sister Sodom a byword in
your mouth in the day of your

16.36 v. 15; Ezek 23.10, 18,29; Jer 19.5
16.37 Jer 13.22, 26; Hos 2.10; Nah 3.5; Isa 47.3
16.38 Lev 20.10; Ezek 23.45; Jer 18.21
16.39 Ezek 21.31; vv. 24,31; Ezek 23.26
16.40 Ezek 23.46, 47; Jn 8.5,7
16.41 Deut 13.16; 2 Kings 25.9; Jer 52.13; Ezek 23.10, 27
16.42 Ezek 5.13; Isa 54.9,10; Ezek 39.29
16.43 Ps 78.42; v. 22; Ezek 6.9; 11.21; 22.31
16.44 Ezek 12.22, 23
16.46 Gen 13.11-13; Isa 1.10
16.47 2 Kings 21.9; Ezek 5.6,7
16.48 Mt 10.15; 11.24
16.49 Isa 3.9; Gen 13.10; Lk 12.16-20; Ezek 18.7, 12,16
16.50 Ezek 7.10
16.51 Ezek 5.6; Jer 3.11; Mt 12.41,42
16.52 vv. 54,61, 47,48,51
16.53 vv. 60,61; Isa 19.24,25
16.54 Ezek 14.22, 23
16.55 v. 53; Ezek 36.11; Mal 3.4

pride, 57 before your wickedness
was uncovered? Now you are a
mockery to the daughters of
Aram[1] and all her neighbors, and
to the daughters of the Philistines,
those all around who despise you.
58 You must bear the penalty of
your lewdness and your abominations, says the LORD.

An Everlasting Covenant

59 Yes, thus says the Lord GOD:
I will deal with you as you have
done, you who have despised the
oath, breaking the covenant; 60 yet
I will remember my covenant with
you in the days of your youth, and
I will establish with you an everlasting covenant. 61 Then you will
remember your ways, and be
ashamed when I[m] take your sisters,
both your elder and your younger,
and give them to you as daughters,
but not on account of my[n] covenant with you. 62 I will establish my
covenant with you, and you shall
know that I am the LORD, 63 in order
that you may remember and be
confounded, and never open your
mouth again because of your
shame, when I forgive you all that
you have done, says the Lord GOD.

The Two Eagles and the Vine

17 The word of the LORD came
to me: 2 O mortal, pro-
pound a riddle, and speak an allegory to the house of Israel. 3 Say:
Thus says the Lord GOD:

A great eagle, with great
wings and long pinions,
rich in plumage of many
colors,
came to the Lebanon.
He took the top of the cedar,
4 broke off its topmost shoot;
He carried it to a land of
trade,
set it in a city of
merchants.
5 Then he took a seed from
the land,
placed it in fertile soil;
A plant[o] by abundant
waters,
he set it like a willow twig.
6 It sprouted and became a
vine
spreading out, but low;
Its branches turned toward
him,
its roots remained where it
stood.
So it became a vine;
it brought forth branches,
put forth foliage.
7 There was another great
eagle,
with great wings and much
plumage.
And see! This vine stretched
out
its roots toward him;
It shot out its branches
toward him,
so that he might water it.
From the bed where it was
planted
8 it was transplanted
to good soil by abundant
waters,
so that it might produce
branches
and bear fruit
and become a noble vine.
9 Say: Thus says the Lord GOD:
Will it prosper?
Will he not pull up its roots,
cause its fruit to rot[o] and
wither,
its fresh sprouting leaves to
fade?
No strong arm or mighty
army will be needed
to pull it from its roots.
10 When it is transplanted, will
it thrive?
When the east wind strikes
it,
will it not utterly wither,
wither on the bed where it
grew?

11 Then the word of the LORD
came to me: 12 Say now to the rebellious house: Do you not know
what these things mean? Tell
them: The king of Babylon came to
Jerusalem, took its king and its officials, and brought them back with

16.57 2 Kings 16.5; 2 Chr 28.18; Ezek 5.14
16.58 Ezek 23.49
16.59 Ezek 17.13; Deut 29.12
16.60 Jer 2.2; Hos 2.15; Jer 32.40; Ezek 37.26
16.61 Ezek 20.43; Isa 54.1; 60.4; Jer 31.31
16.62 Ezek 20.37; Hos 2.19, 20; Ezek 20.43, 44
16.63 v. 61; Rom 3.19
17.2 Ezek 20.49; 24.3
17.3 Jer 22.23
17.5 Deut 8.7-9; Isa 44.4
17.6 v. 14
17.7 v. 15
17.8 v. 5
17.9 vv. 10,15-21
17.10 v. 15; Ezek 19.14; Hos 13.15
17.12 Ezek 2.5; 12.9; v. 3; 2 Kings 24.11-16

[1] Another reading is *Edom* [m] Syr: Heb *you* [n] Heb lacks *my* [o] Meaning of Heb uncertain

him to Babylon. 13 He took one of
the royal offspring and made a covenant with him, putting him under
oath (he had taken away the chief
men of the land), 14 so that the
kingdom might be humble and not
lift itself up, and that by keeping
his covenant it might stand. 15 But
he rebelled against him by sending
ambassadors to Egypt, in order
that they might give him horses
and a large army. Will he succeed?
Can one escape who does such
things? Can he break the covenant
and yet escape? 16 As I live, says the
Lord GOD, surely in the place where
the king resides who made him
king, whose oath he despised, and
whose covenant with him he
broke—in Babylon he shall die.
17 Pharaoh with his mighty army
and great company will not help
him in war, when ramps are cast up
and siege walls built to cut off
many lives. 18 Because he despised
the oath and broke the covenant,
because he gave his hand and yet
did all these things, he shall not escape. 19 Therefore thus says the
Lord GOD: As I live, I will surely return upon his head my oath that he
despised, and my covenant that he
broke. 20 I will spread my net over
him, and he shall be caught in my
snare; I will bring him to Babylon
and enter into judgment with him
there for the treason he has committed against me. 21 All the pick[p]
of his troops shall fall by the sword,
and the survivors shall be scattered
to every wind; and you shall know
that I, the LORD, have spoken.

Israel Exalted at Last

22 Thus says the Lord GOD:
I myself will take a sprig
from the lofty top of a
cedar;
I will set it out.
I will break off a tender one
from the topmost of its
young twigs;
I myself will plant it
on a high and lofty
mountain.
23 On the mountain height of
Israel
I will plant it,
in order that it may produce
boughs and bear fruit,
and become a noble cedar.
Under it every kind of bird
will live;
in the shade of its
branches will nest
winged creatures of every
kind.
24 All the trees of the field shall
know
that I am the LORD.
I bring low the high tree,
I make high the low tree;
I dry up the green tree
and make the dry tree
flourish.
I the LORD have spoken;
I will accomplish it.

Individual Retribution

18 The word of the LORD came
to me: 2 What do you mean
by repeating this proverb concerning the land of Israel, "The parents
have eaten sour grapes, and the
children's teeth are set on edge"?
3 As I live, says the Lord GOD, this
proverb shall no more be used by
you in Israel. 4 Know that all lives
are mine; the life of the parent as
well as the life of the child is mine:
it is only the person who sins that
shall die.
5 If a man is righteous and does
what is lawful and right— 6 if he
does not eat upon the mountains
or lift up his eyes to the idols of the
house of Israel, does not defile his
neighbor's wife or approach a
woman during her menstrual period, 7 does not oppress anyone, but
restores to the debtor his pledge,
commits no robbery, gives his
bread to the hungry and covers the
naked with a garment, 8 does not
take advance or accrued interest,
withholds his hand from iniquity,
executes true justice between contending parties, 9 follows my statutes, and is careful to observe my
ordinances, acting faithfully—

17.13 2 Kings 24.15-17; 2 Chr 36.13
17.14 v. 6; Ezek 29.14
17.15 2 Kings 24.20; 2 Chr 36.13
17.16 vv. 13,18, 19; Jer 52.11; Ezek 12.13
17.17 Jer 37.7; Ezek 29.6,7; 4.2
17.18 Lam 5.6
17.19 Ezek 16.59
17.20 Ezek 12.13; 32.3; 20.36
17.21 2 Kings 25.5, 11; Ezek 12.14; 6.7,10
17.22 Isa 11.1; Jer 23.5; Zech 3.8; Ezek 36.36; 20.40
17.23 Isa 2.2,3; Ezek 20.40; Hos 14.5-7; Mt 13.31,32
17.24 Ps 96.12; Ezek 21.26; 19.12; 22.14; 24.14
18.2 Jer 31.29; Lam 5.7
18.3 vv. 11,20,30
18.4 Isa 42.5; v. 20; Rom 6.23
18.6 Ezek 22.9; vv. 12,15; Lev 18.19; 20.18; Ezek 22.10
18.7 Ex 22.21; Lev 19.15; Deut 24.12, 13; Lev 19.13
18.8 Ex 22.25; Lev 25.36, 37; Deut 23.19; 1.16; Zech 8.16
18.9 Ezek 20.11; Am 5.4

[p] Another reading is *fugitives*

such a one is righteous; he shall
surely live, says the Lord God.
10 If he has a son who is violent,
a shedder of blood, 11 who does any
of these things (though his father[q]
does none of them), who eats upon
the mountains, defiles his neighbor's wife, 12 oppresses the poor
and needy, commits robbery, does
not restore the pledge, lifts up his
eyes to the idols, commits abomination, 13 takes advance or accrued
interest; shall he then live? He
shall not. He has done all these
abominable things; he shall surely
die; his blood shall be upon himself.
14 But if this man has a son who
sees all the sins that his father has
done, considers, and does not do
likewise, 15 who does not eat upon
the mountains or lift up his eyes to
the idols of the house of Israel,
does not defile his neighbor's wife,
16 does not wrong anyone, exacts
no pledge, commits no robbery,
but gives his bread to the hungry
and covers the naked with a garment, 17 withholds his hand from
iniquity,[r] takes no advance or accrued interest, observes my ordinances, and follows my statutes; he
shall not die for his father's iniquity; he shall surely live. 18 As for his
father, because he practiced extortion, robbed his brother, and did
what is not good among his people,
he dies for his iniquity.
19 Yet you say, "Why should not
the son suffer for the iniquity of the
father?" When the son has done
what is lawful and right, and has
been careful to observe all my statutes, he shall surely live. 20 The person who sins shall die. A child shall
not suffer for the iniquity of a parent, nor a parent suffer for the iniquity of a child; the righteousness of
the righteous shall be his own, and
the wickedness of the wicked shall
be his own.
21 But if the wicked turn away
from all their sins that they have
committed and keep all my statutes and do what is lawful and
right, they shall surely live; they
shall not die. 22 None of the transgressions that they have committed shall be remembered against
them; for the righteousness that
they have done they shall live.
23 Have I any pleasure in the death
of the wicked, says the Lord God,
and not rather that they should
turn from their ways and live?
24 But when the righteous turn
away from their righteousness and
commit iniquity and do the same
abominable things that the wicked
do, shall they live? None of the
righteous deeds that they have
done shall be remembered; for the
treachery of which they are guilty
and the sin they have committed,
they shall die.
25 Yet you say, "The way of the
Lord is unfair." Hear now, O house
of Israel: Is my way unfair? Is it not
your ways that are unfair? 26 When
the righteous turn away from their
righteousness and commit iniquity, they shall die for it; for the iniquity that they have committed they
shall die. 27 Again, when the wicked
turn away from the wickedness
they have committed and do what
is lawful and right, they shall save
their life. 28 Because they considered and turned away from all the
transgressions that they had committed, they shall surely live; they
shall not die. 29 Yet the house of Israel says, "The way of the Lord is
unfair." O house of Israel, are my
ways unfair? Is it not your ways that
are unfair?
30 Therefore I will judge you,
O house of Israel, all of you according to your ways, says the Lord God.
Repent and turn from all your
transgressions; otherwise iniquity
will be your ruin.[s] 31 Cast away
from you all the transgressions that
you have committed against me,
and get yourselves a new heart and
a new spirit! Why will you die,
O house of Israel? 32 For I have no
pleasure in the death of anyone,
says the Lord God. Turn, then, and
live.

18.10 Ex 21.12; Num 35.31
18.11 vv. 6,15
18.12 Am 4.1; Isa 59.6,7; Ezek 8.6,17
18.13 vv. 8,17; Ezek 33.4,5
18.14 Prov 23.24
18.15 vv. 6,11,12
18.16 Ps 41.1
18.17 vv. 8,9,13, 19,20
18.18 vv. 10-13; Ezek 3.18
18.19 Ex 20.5; Deut 5.9; 2 Kings 23.26
18.20 Deut 24.16; Isa 3.10,11; Rom 2.9
18.21 Ezek 33.12, 19; 3.21
18.22 Ezek 33.16; Mic 7.19; Ps 18.20-24
18.23 Ezek 33.11; 1 Tim 2.4; 2 Pet 3.9
18.24 Ezek 3.20; 33.12,13,18; 2 Pet 2.20
18.25 v. 29; Ezek 33.17, 20; Zeph 3.5
18.26 v. 24
18.27 v. 21
18.28 vv. 22,30,31
18.29 v. 25
18.30 Ezek 7.3; 33.20; Mt 3.2; Rev 2.5
18.31 Isa 1.16,17; 55.7; Ezek 11.19; 36.26
18.32 Ezek 33.11; 2 Pet 3.9

q Heb *he* r Gk: Heb *the poor* s Or *so that they shall not be a stumbling block of iniquity to you*

Israel Degraded

19 As for you, raise up a lamentation for the princes of Israel, 2 and say:

What a lioness was your mother
among lions!
She lay down among young lions,
rearing her cubs.
3 She raised up one of her cubs;
he became a young lion,
and he learned to catch prey;
he devoured humans.
4 The nations sounded an alarm against him;
he was caught in their pit;
and they brought him with hooks
to the land of Egypt.
5 When she saw that she was thwarted,
that her hope was lost,
she took another of her cubs
and made him a young lion.
6 He prowled among the lions;
he became a young lion,
and he learned to catch prey;
he devoured people.
7 And he ravaged their strongholds,[t]
and laid waste their towns;
the land was appalled, and all in it,
at the sound of his roaring.
8 The nations set upon him
from the provinces all around;
they spread their net over him;
he was caught in their pit.
9 With hooks they put him in a cage,
and brought him to the king of Babylon;
they brought him into custody,
so that his voice should be heard no more
on the mountains of Israel.
10 Your mother was like a vine in a vineyard[u]
transplanted by the water,
fruitful and full of branches
from abundant water.
11 Its strongest stem became a ruler's scepter;[v]
it towered aloft
among the thick boughs;
it stood out in its height
with its mass of branches.
12 But it was plucked up in fury,
cast down to the ground;
the east wind dried it up;
its fruit was stripped off,
its strong stem was withered;
the fire consumed it.
13 Now it is transplanted into the wilderness,
into a dry and thirsty land.
14 And fire has gone out from its stem,
has consumed its branches and fruit,
so that there remains in it no strong stem,
no scepter for ruling.

This is a lamentation, and it is used as a lamentation.

Israel's Continuing Rebellion

20 In the seventh year, in the fifth month, on the tenth
day of the month, certain elders of
Israel came to consult the LORD,
and sat down before me. 2 And the
word of the LORD came to me:
3 Mortal, speak to the elders of Israel, and say to them: Thus says the
Lord GOD: Why are you coming? To
consult me? As I live, says the Lord
GOD, I will not be consulted by you.
4 Will you judge them, mortal, will
you judge them? Then let them
know the abominations of their ancestors, 5 and say to them: Thus
says the Lord GOD: On the day
when I chose Israel, I swore to the
offspring of the house of Jacob—
making myself known to them in
the land of Egypt—I swore to
them, saying, I am the LORD your
God. 6 On that day I swore to them
that I would bring them out of the
land of Egypt into a land that I had
searched out for them, a land flow-

19.1 Ezek 26.17; 27.2
19.2 Nah 2.11, 12; Isa 5.29; Zech 11.3
19.3 2 Kings 23.31, 32; v. 6
19.4 2 Kings 23.33; 2 Chr 36.4
19.5 2 Kings 23.34
19.6 2 Kings 24.9; v. 3
19.7 Ezek 12.19; 30.12
19.8 2 Kings 24.2; v. 4
19.9 2 Chr 36.6; Jer 22.18; Ezek 6.2
19.10 Ps 80.8-11
19.11 Ezek 31.3; Dan 4.11
19.12 Jer 31.28; Ezek 28.17; 17.10; Hos 13.15
19.13 Hos 2.3
19.14 Ezek 15.4; Lam 4.20
20.1 Ezek 8.1,11, 12; 9.6
20.3 v. 31; Ezek 14.3; Mic 3.7
20.4 Ezek 16.2; 22.2
20.5 Ex 6.7; Deut 7.6; Ex 6.2,3; 20.2
20.6 Ex 3.8,17; Deut 8.7-9; Jer 32.22; Ps 48.2; Dan 8.9

[t] Heb *his widows* [u] Cn: Heb *in your blood*
[v] Heb *Its strongest stems became rulers' scepters*

ing with milk and honey, the most
glorious of all lands. 7 And I said to
them, Cast away the detestable
things your eyes feast on, every one
of you, and do not defile yourselves
with the idols of Egypt; I am the
LORD your God. 8 But they rebelled
against me and would not listen to
me; not one of them cast away the
detestable things their eyes feasted
on, nor did they forsake the idols of
Egypt.

Then I thought I would pour out
my wrath upon them and spend my
anger against them in the midst of
the land of Egypt. 9 But I acted for
the sake of my name, that it should
not be profaned in the sight of the
nations among whom they lived, in
whose sight I made myself known
to them in bringing them out of the
land of Egypt. 10 So I led them out
of the land of Egypt and brought
them into the wilderness. 11 I gave
them my statutes and showed
them my ordinances, by whose observance everyone shall live.
12 Moreover I gave them my sabbaths, as a sign between me and
them, so that they might know that
I the LORD sanctify them. 13 But the
house of Israel rebelled against me
in the wilderness; they did not observe my statutes but rejected my
ordinances, by whose observance
everyone shall live; and my sabbaths they greatly profaned.

Then I thought I would pour out
my wrath upon them in the wilderness, to make an end of them.
14 But I acted for the sake of my
name, so that it should not be profaned in the sight of the nations, in
whose sight I had brought them
out. 15 Moreover I swore to them in
the wilderness that I would not
bring them into the land that I had
given them, a land flowing with
milk and honey, the most glorious
of all lands, 16 because they rejected my ordinances and did not observe my statutes, and profaned my
sabbaths; for their heart went after
their idols. 17 Nevertheless my eye
spared them, and I did not destroy
them or make an end of them in
the wilderness.

18 I said to their children in the
wilderness, Do not follow the statutes of your parents, nor observe
their ordinances, nor defile yourselves with their idols. 19 I the LORD
am your God; follow my statutes,
and be careful to observe my ordinances, 20 and hallow my sabbaths
that they may be a sign between me
and you, so that you may know that
I the LORD am your God. 21 But the
children rebelled against me; they
did not follow my statutes, and
were not careful to observe my ordinances, by whose observance everyone shall live; they profaned my
sabbaths.

Then I thought I would pour out
my wrath upon them and spend my
anger against them in the wilderness. 22 But I withheld my hand,
and acted for the sake of my name,
so that it should not be profaned in
the sight of the nations, in whose
sight I had brought them out.
23 Moreover I swore to them in the
wilderness that I would scatter
them among the nations and disperse them through the countries,
24 because they had not executed
my ordinances, but had rejected
my statutes and profaned my sabbaths, and their eyes were set on
their ancestors' idols. 25 Moreover I
gave them statutes that were not
good and ordinances by which they
could not live. 26 I defiled them
through their very gifts, in their offering up all their firstborn, in order
that I might horrify them, so that
they might know that I am the
LORD.

27 Therefore, mortal, speak to
the house of Israel and say to them,
Thus says the Lord GOD: In this
again your ancestors blasphemed
me, by dealing treacherously with
me. 28 For when I had brought them
into the land that I swore to give
them, then wherever they saw any
high hill or any leafy tree, there
they offered their sacrifices and
presented the provocation of their
offering; there they sent up their

20.7 Ezek 18.31; Deut 29.16, 18; Ex 20.2 **20.8** Isa 63.10; Ezek 7.8 **20.9** Ex 32.12; Num 14.13ff; Ezek 36.21; 39.7 **20.10** Ex 13.18 **20.11** Deut 4.8; Lev 18.5; Rom 10.5; Gal 3.12 **20.12** Ex 31.13, 17; v. 20 **20.13** Num 14.22; Ps 78.40; 95.8-10; Prov 1.25; Num 14.29; Ps 106.23 **20.14** vv. 9,22; Ezek 36.22, 23 **20.15** Num 14.28; Ps 95.11; v. 6 **20.16** Num 15.39; Ps 78.37; Am 5.25 **20.18** Deut 4.3-6; Zech 1.4; v. 7 **20.19** Ex 6.7; 20.2; Deut 5.32 **20.20** v. 12 **20.21** Num 25.1; vv. 8,13,16 **20.22** v. 17; Ps 78.38; vv. 9,14 **20.23** Lev 26.33; Deut 28.64; Ps 106.27; Jer 15.4 **20.24** vv. 13,16; Ezek 6.9 **20.25** Ps 81.12; Rom 1.24; 2 Thes 2.11 **20.26** v. 30; 2 Kings 17.17; 2 Chr 28.3; Ezek 16.20, 21; 6.7

20.27 Ezek 2.7; Rom 2.24; Ezek 18.24; 39.23,26 **20.28** Isa 57.5-7; Ezek 6.13; 16.19

pleasing odors, and there they
poured out their drink offerings.
29 (I said to them, What is the high
place to which you go? So it is
called Bamah[w] to this day.)
30 Therefore say to the house of Israel, Thus says the Lord GOD: Will
you defile yourselves after the
manner of your ancestors and go
astray after their detestable things?
31 When you offer your gifts and
make your children pass through
the fire, you defile yourselves with
all your idols to this day. And shall
I be consulted by you, O house of
Israel? As I live, says the Lord GOD,
I will not be consulted by you.

32 What is in your mind shall
never happen—the thought, "Let
us be like the nations, like the
tribes of the countries, and worship
wood and stone."

God Will Restore Israel

33 As I live, says the Lord GOD,
surely with a mighty hand and an
outstretched arm, and with wrath
poured out, I will be king over you.
34 I will bring you out from the peoples and gather you out of the
countries where you are scattered,
with a mighty hand and an outstretched arm, and with wrath
poured out; 35 and I will bring you
into the wilderness of the peoples,
and there I will enter into judgment
with you face to face. 36 As I entered
into judgment with your ancestors
in the wilderness of the land of
Egypt, so I will enter into judgment
with you, says the Lord GOD. 37 I will
make you pass under the staff, and
will bring you within the bond of
the covenant. 38 I will purge out the
rebels among you, and those who
transgress against me; I will bring
them out of the land where they reside as aliens, but they shall not
enter the land of Israel. Then you
shall know that I am the LORD.

39 As for you, O house of Israel,
thus says the Lord GOD: Go serve
your idols, everyone of you now
and hereafter, if you will not listen
to me; but my holy name you shall
no more profane with your gifts and
your idols.

40 For on my holy mountain,
the mountain height of Israel, says
the Lord GOD, there all the house of
Israel, all of them, shall serve me in
the land; there I will accept them,
and there I will require your contributions and the choicest of your
gifts, with all your sacred things.
41 As a pleasing odor I will accept
you, when I bring you out from the
peoples, and gather you out of the
countries where you have been
scattered; and I will manifest my
holiness among you in the sight of
the nations. 42 You shall know that
I am the LORD, when I bring you
into the land of Israel, the country
that I swore to give to your ancestors. 43 There you shall remember
your ways and all the deeds by
which you have polluted yourselves; and you shall loathe yourselves for all the evils that you have
committed. 44 And you shall know
that I am the LORD, when I deal with
you for my name's sake, not according to your evil ways, or corrupt deeds, O house of Israel, says
the Lord GOD.

A Prophecy against the Negeb

45 [x]The word of the LORD came
to me: 46 Mortal, set your face toward the south, preach against the
south, and prophesy against the
forest land in the Negeb; 47 say to
the forest of the Negeb, Hear the
word of the LORD: Thus says the
Lord GOD, I will kindle a fire in you,
and it shall devour every green tree
in you and every dry tree; the blazing flame shall not be quenched,
and all faces from south to north
shall be scorched by it. 48 All flesh
shall see that I the LORD have kindled it; it shall not be quenched.
49 Then I said, "Ah Lord GOD! they
are saying of me, 'Is he not a maker
of allegories?' "

The Drawn Sword of God

21 [y] The word of the LORD came
to me: 2 Mortal, set your
face toward Jerusalem and preach

20.30 v. 43; Jer 7.26; 16.12 **20.31** Ps 106.37-39; Jer 7.31; Ezek 16.20 **20.32** Ezek 11.5; 16.16; Jer 2.25; 44.17 **20.33** Jer 21.5 **20.34** v. 38; Jer 42.18; 44.6; Lam 2.4 **20.35** Ezek 17.20 **20.36** vv. 13,21; 1 Cor 10.5-10; Deut 32.10 **20.37** Lam 27.32; Jer 33.13; Ezek 16.60, 62 **20.38** Ezek 34.17, 20; Am 9.9, 10; Jer 44.14; Ezek 6.7 **20.39** Jer 44.25, 26; Am 4.4; Isa 1.13; Ezek 23.38, 39 **20.40** Ezek 17.23; Mic 4.1; Ezek 37.22, 24; Isa 56.7; 60.7; Mal 3.4 **20.41** Eph 5.2; Phil 4.18 **20.42** Ezek 34.13; 36.24 **20.43** Ezek 16.61; Hos 5.15; Ezek 36.31; Zech 12.10 **20.44** Ezek 24.44; 36.22 **20.46** Ezek 6.2; 21.2 **20.47** Jer 21.14; 17.24; 21.4 **20.48** Jer 7.20; 17.27 **20.49** Ezek 17.2; Mt 13.13,14

21.2 Ezek 20.46; Am 7.16

[w] That is *High Place* [x] Ch 21.1 in Heb
[y] Ch 21.6 in Heb

against the sanctuaries; prophesy
against the land of Israel 3 and say
to the land of Israel, Thus says the
LORD: I am coming against you, and
will draw my sword out of its
sheath, and will cut off from you
both righteous and wicked. 4 Because I will cut off from you both
righteous and wicked, therefore my
sword shall go out of its sheath
against all flesh from south to
north; 5 and all flesh shall know
that I the LORD have drawn my
sword out of its sheath; it shall not
be sheathed again. 6 Moan therefore, mortal; moan with breaking
heart and bitter grief before their
eyes. 7 And when they say to you,
"Why do you moan?" you shall say,
"Because of the news that has
come. Every heart will melt and all
hands will be feeble, every spirit
will faint and all knees will turn to
water. See, it comes and it will be
fulfilled," says the Lord GOD.
8 And the word of the LORD
came to me: 9 Mortal, prophesy and
say: Thus says the Lord; Say:

A sword, a sword is
sharpened,
it is also polished;
10 It is sharpened for slaughter,
honed to flash like
lightning!
How can we make merry?
You have despised the rod,
and all discipline.[z]
11 The sword[a] is given to be
polished,
to be grasped in the hand;
It is sharpened, the sword is
polished,
to be placed in the slayer's
hand.
12 Cry and wail, O mortal,
for it is against my people;
it is against all Israel's
princes;
they are thrown to the
sword,
together with my people.
Ah! Strike the thigh!

13 For consider: What! If you despise the rod, will it not happen?[z]
says the Lord GOD.

14 And you, mortal, prophesy;
Strike hand to hand.
Let the sword fall twice,
thrice;
it is a sword for killing.
A sword for great slaughter—
it surrounds them;
15 therefore hearts melt
and many stumble.
At all their gates I have
set
the point[z] of the sword.
Ah! It is made for flashing,
it is polished[b] for
slaughter.
16 Attack to the right!
Engage to the left!
Wherever your edge is
directed.
17 I too will strike hand to
hand,
I will satisfy my fury;
I the LORD have spoken.

18 The word of the LORD came to
me: 19 Mortal, mark out two roads
for the sword of the king of Babylon
to come; both of them shall issue
from the same land. And make a
signpost, make it for a fork in the
road leading to a city; 20 mark out
the road for the sword to come to
Rabbah of the Ammonites or to Judah and to[c] Jerusalem the fortified. 21 For the king of Babylon
stands at the parting of the way, at
the fork in the two roads, to use
divination; he shakes the arrows,
he consults the teraphim,[d] he in-
spects the liver. 22 Into his right
hand comes the lot for Jerusalem,
to set battering rams, to call out for
slaughter, for raising the battle cry,
to set battering rams against the
gates, to cast up ramps, to build
siege towers. 23 But to them it will
seem like a false divination; they
have sworn solemn oaths; but he
brings their guilt to remembrance,
bringing about their capture.
24 Therefore thus says the Lord
GOD: Because you have brought
your guilt to remembrance, in that
your transgressions are uncovered,
so that in all your deeds your sins

21.3 Jer 21.13; Ezek 5.8; vv. 9-11,19; Job 9.22 **21.4** Ezek 20.47 **21.5** Ezek 20.48; Jer 23.20; Nah 1.9 **21.6** Isa 22.4 **21.7** Ezek 7.26; Isa 13.7; Ezek 7.17; 22.14 **21.9** Deut 32.41 **21.10** Isa 34.5,6; v. 15 **21.11** vv. 15,19 **21.12** Jer 31.19 **21.14** Num 24.10; Ezek 6.11; Lev 26.21, 24; Ezek 30.24 **21.15** vv. 7,10 **21.17** v. 14; Ezek 22.13; 5.13 **21.19** Ezek 4.1-3; v. 15 **21.20** Jer 49.2; Ezek 25.5; Am 1.14 **21.21** Num 23.23; Prov 16.33; Judg 17.5 **21.22** Jer 51.14; Ezek 4.2 **21.23** Ezek 17.13, 15,16,18; 29.16

[z] Meaning of Heb uncertain [a] Heb *It* [b] Tg: Heb *wrapped up* [c] Gk Syr: Heb *Judah in* [d] Or *the household gods*

appear—because you have come
to remembrance, you shall be tak-
en in hand.[e]

25 As for you, vile, wicked
prince of Israel,
you whose day has come,
the time of final
punishment,
26 thus says the Lord GOD:
Remove the turban, take off
the crown;
things shall not remain as
they are.
Exalt that which is low,
abase that which is
high.
27 A ruin, a ruin, a ruin—
I will make it!
(Such has never occurred.)
Until he comes whose right
it is;
to him I will give it.

28 As for you, mortal, prophesy,
and say, Thus says the Lord GOD
concerning the Ammonites, and
concerning their reproach; say:

A sword, a sword! Drawn for
slaughter
Polished to consume,[f] to
flash like lightning.
29 Offering false visions for you,
divining lies for you,
they place you over the
necks
of the vile, wicked ones—
those whose day has come,
the time of final
punishment.
30 Return it to its sheath!
In the place where you were
created,
in the land of your origin,
I will judge you.
31 I will pour out my
indignation upon you,
with the fire of my wrath
I will blow upon you.
I will deliver you into brutish
hands,
those skillful to destroy.
32 You shall be fuel for the fire,
your blood shall enter the
earth;
You shall be remembered no
more,
for I the LORD have spoken.

The Bloody City

22 The word of the LORD came
to me: 2 You, mortal, will
you judge, will you judge the
bloody city? Then declare to it all
its abominable deeds. 3 You shall
say, Thus says the Lord GOD: A city!
Shedding blood within itself; its
time has come; making its idols,
defiling itself. 4 You have become
guilty by the blood that you have
shed, and defiled by the idols that
you have made; you have brought
your day near, the appointed time
of your years has come. Therefore I
have made you a disgrace before
the nations, and a mockery to all
the countries. 5 Those who are near
and those who are far from you will
mock you, you infamous one, full
of tumult.
6 The princes of Israel in you,
everyone according to his power,
have been bent on shedding blood.
7 Father and mother are treated
with contempt in you; the alien residing within you suffers extortion;
the orphan and the widow are
wronged in you. 8 You have despised my holy things, and profaned my sabbaths. 9 In you are
those who slander to shed blood,
those in you who eat upon the
mountains, who commit lewdness
in your midst. 10 In you they uncover their fathers' nakedness; in you
they violate women in their menstrual periods. 11 One commits
abomination with his neighbor's
wife; another lewdly defiles his
daughter-in-law; another in you
defiles his sister, his father's
daughter. 12 In you, they take
bribes to shed blood; you take both
advance interest and accrued interest, and make gain of your neighbors by extortion; and you have forgotten me, says the Lord GOD.
13 See, I strike my hands together at the dishonest gain you
have made, and at the blood that
has been shed within you. 14 Can

21.25 Ezek 7.2,3, 7; 35.5 **21.26** Jer 13.18; Ezek 16.12; 17.24; Lk 1.52 **21.27** Hag 2.21, 22; Ps 2.6; Jer 23.5,6; Ezek 34.24; 37.24 **21.28** Jer 49.1; Ezek 25.2,3; Zeph 2.8; Isa 31.8; Jer 12.12 **21.29** Ezek 13.6-9; 22.28; v. 25; Ezek 35.5 **21.30** Jer 47.6,7; Ezek 16.3 **21.31** Ezek 7.8; 14.19; 22.20, 21; Jer 6.22, 23; 51.20,21 **21.32** Mal 4.1; Ezek 25.10

22.2 Ezek 20.4; 24.6-9; Nah 3.1; Ezek 16.2; 20.4 **22.3** vv. 6,27; Ezek 23.37, 45 **22.4** 2 Kings 21.16; Ezek 24.7,8; 21.25; 5.14, 15; 16.57 **22.5** Isa 22.5 **22.6** Isa 1.23 **22.7** Deut 27.16; Ex 22.21,22 **22.8** v. 26; Lev 19.30; Ezek 23.38, 39 **22.9** Ezek 18.6, 11,15 **22.10** Lev 18.8,19; Ezek 18.6 **22.11** Ezek 18.11; Lev 18.15; 18.9 **22.12** Mic 7.2,3; Lev 25.36; 19.13; Jer 3.21 **22.13** Ezek 21.17; Isa 33.15; v. 3 **22.14** Ezek 21.7; 24.14

[e] Or *be taken captive* [f] Cn: Heb *to contain*

your courage endure, or can your
hands remain strong in the days
when I shall deal with you? I the
LORD have spoken, and I will do it.
15 I will scatter you among the nations and disperse you through the
countries, and I will purge your
filthiness out of you. 16 And I[g] shall
be profaned through you in the
sight of the nations; and you shall
know that I am the LORD.
17 The word of the LORD came to
me: 18 Mortal, the house of Israel
has become dross to me; all of
them, silver,[h] bronze, tin, iron, and
lead. In the smelter they have become dross. 19 Therefore thus says
the Lord GOD: Because you have all
become dross, I will gather you into
the midst of Jerusalem. 20 As one
gathers silver, bronze, iron, lead,
and tin into a smelter, to blow the
fire upon them in order to melt
them; so I will gather you in my anger and in my wrath, and I will put
you in and melt you. 21 I will gather
you and blow upon you with the
fire of my wrath, and you shall be
melted within it. 22 As silver is
melted in a smelter, so you shall be
melted in it; and you shall know
that I the LORD have poured out my
wrath upon you.
23 The word of the LORD came to
me: 24 Mortal, say to it: You are a
land that is not cleansed, not
rained upon in the day of indignation. 25 Its princes[i] within it are
like a roaring lion tearing the prey;
they have devoured human lives;
they have taken treasure and precious things; they have made many
widows within it. 26 Its priests have
done violence to my teaching and
have profaned my holy things; they
have made no distinction between
the holy and the common, neither
have they taught the difference between the unclean and the clean,
and they have disregarded my sabbaths, so that I am profaned among
them. 27 Its officials within it are
like wolves tearing the prey, shedding blood, destroying lives to get
dishonest gain. 28 Its prophets have
smeared whitewash on their behalf, seeing false visions and divining lies for them, saying, "Thus
says the Lord GOD," when the LORD
has not spoken. 29 The people of
the land have practiced extortion
and committed robbery; they have
oppressed the poor and needy, and
have extorted from the alien without redress. 30 And I sought for anyone among them who would repair
the wall and stand in the breach
before me on behalf of the land, so
that I would not destroy it; but I
found no one. 31 Therefore I have
poured out my indignation upon
them; I have consumed them with
the fire of my wrath; I have returned their conduct upon their
heads, says the Lord GOD.

Oholah and Oholibah

23 The word of the LORD came
to me: 2 Mortal, there were
two women, the daughters of one
mother; 3 they played the whore in
Egypt; they played the whore in
their youth; their breasts were caressed there, and their virgin bo-
soms were fondled. 4 Oholah was
the name of the elder and Oholibah the name of her sister. They
became mine, and they bore sons
and daughters. As for their names,
Oholah is Samaria, and Oholibah
is Jerusalem.
5 Oholah played the whore
while she was mine; she lusted after her lovers the Assyrians, warriors[j] 6 clothed in blue, governors
and commanders, all of them
handsome young men, mounted
horsemen. 7 She bestowed her favors upon them, the choicest men
of Assyria all of them; and she defiled herself with all the idols of everyone for whom she lusted. 8 She
did not give up her whorings that
she had practiced since Egypt; for
in her youth men had lain with her
and fondled her virgin bosom and
poured out their lust upon her.
9 Therefore I delivered her into the
hands of her lovers, into the hands

22.15 Deut 4.27; Zech 4.17; Ezek 23.27
22.18 Isa 1.22; Jer 6.28
22.20 v. 21; Mal 3.2
22.22 Ezek 21.7; 20.8,33
22.24 Ezek 24.13; v. 31
22.25 Hos 6.9; Ps 10.9; Jer 15.8
22.26 Mal 2.8; Lev 10.10; Ezek 44.23; Hag 2.11-14; Ezek 20.12, 13; 36.20
22.27 Isa 1.23
22.28 Ezek 13.10-16; 13.6,7
22.29 Isa 5.7; Am 3.10; Ex 22.21; 23.9
22.30 Jer 5.1; Ezek 13.5; Ps 106.23
22.31 Isa 13.5; Ezek 9.10; 11.21; 16.43
23.2 Jer 3.7,8; Ezek 16.44, 46; 16.3,45
23.3 Josh 24.14; Ezek 20.8; 16.22
23.4 Ezek 16.8, 20
23.5 1 Kings 12.28-30; Ezek 16.28; Hos 8.9,10
23.6 vv. 12,23
23.7 v. 30; Ezek 16.15; 20.7; Hos 5.3; 6.10
23.8 Ex 32.4; v. 3; Ezek 16.15
23.9 v. 22; Ezek 16.37; 2 Kings 18.9-11; Hos 11.5

[g] Gk Syr Vg: Heb *you* [h] Transposed from the end of the verse; compare verse 20
[i] Gk: Heb *indignation.* 25*A conspiracy of its prophets* [j] Meaning of Heb uncertain

of the Assyrians, for whom she lusted. 10 These uncovered her nakedness; they seized her sons and her
daughters; and they killed her with
the sword. Judgment was executed
upon her, and she became a byword among women.

11 Her sister Oholibah saw this,
yet she was more corrupt than she
in her lusting and in her whorings,
which were worse than those of her
sister. 12 She lusted after the Assyrians, governors and commanders,
warriors[k] clothed in full armor,
mounted horsemen, all of them
handsome young men. 13 And I saw
that she was defiled; they both
took the same way. 14 But she carried her whorings further; she saw
male figures carved on the wall, images of the Chaldeans portrayed in
vermilion, 15 with belts around
their waists, with flowing turbans
on their heads, all of them looking
like officers—a picture of Babylonians whose native land was Chaldea. 16 When she saw them she
lusted after them, and sent messengers to them in Chaldea. 17 And
the Babylonians came to her into
the bed of love, and they defiled
her with their lust; and after she
defiled herself with them, she
turned from them in disgust.
18 When she carried on her whorings so openly and flaunted her nakedness, I turned in disgust from
her, as I had turned from her sister.
19 Yet she increased her whorings,
remembering the days of her
youth, when she played the whore
in the land of Egypt 20 and lusted
after her paramours there, whose
members were like those of donkeys, and whose emission was like
that of stallions. 21 Thus you longed
for the lewdness of your youth,
when the Egyptians[l] fondled your
bosom and caressed[m] your young
breasts.

22 Therefore, O Oholibah, thus
says the Lord GOD: I will rouse
against you your lovers from whom
you turned in disgust, and I will
bring them against you from every
side: 23 the Babylonians and all the
Chaldeans, Pekod and Shoa and
Koa, and all the Assyrians with
them, handsome young men, governors and commanders all of
them, officers and warriors,[n] all of
them riding on horses. 24 They shall
come against you from the north[o]
with chariots and wagons and a
host of peoples; they shall set
themselves against you on every
side with buckler, shield, and helmet, and I will commit the judgment to them, and they shall judge
you according to their ordinances.
25 I will direct my indignation
against you, in order that they may
deal with you in fury. They shall cut
off your nose and your ears, and
your survivors shall fall by the
sword. They shall seize your sons
and your daughters, and your survivors shall be devoured by fire.
26 They shall also strip you of your
clothes and take away your fine
jewels. 27 So I will put an end to
your lewdness and your whoring
brought from the land of Egypt; you
shall not long for them, or remember Egypt any more. 28 For thus
says the Lord GOD: I will deliver you
into the hands of those whom you
hate, into the hands of those from
whom you turned in disgust; 29 and
they shall deal with you in hatred,
and take away all the fruit of your
labor, and leave you naked and
bare, and the nakedness of your
whorings shall be exposed. Your
lewdness and your whorings 30 have
brought this upon you, because
you played the whore with the nations, and polluted yourself with
their idols. 31 You have gone the
way of your sister; therefore I will
give her cup into your hand. 32 Thus
says the Lord GOD:

You shall drink your sister's
cup,
deep and wide;
you shall be scorned and
derided,
it holds so much.

23.10 Ezek 16.37; Hos 2.10; v. 47; Ezek 16.57
23.11 Jer 3.8-11; Ezek 16.47
23.12 2 Kings 16.7-10; 2 Chr 28.16-23; v. 6,23
23.14 Ezek 8.10; 16.29; Jer 22.14
23.15 Isa 22.21
23.16 v. 20
23.17 vv. 28,30
23.18 v. 10; Jer 6.8
23.19 vv. 14,3
23.20 Ezek 16.26
23.21 v. 3
23.22 v. 28; Ezek 16.37
23.23 Ezek 21.19; 2 Kings 24.2; Jer 50.21; vv. 6,12
23.24 Ezek 21.15, 19; Jer 47.3; Ezek 16.40; Jer 39.5,6
23.25 Ezek 8.17, 18; Zeph 1.18; v. 47; Ezek 20.47, 48; 22.20,21
23.26 Ezek 16.39
23.27 Ezek 16.41; 22.15; vv. 3, 19
23.28 Ezek 16.37
23.29 v. 26; Ezek 16.39
23.30 vv. 7,17; Jer 2.18-20; Ezek 6.9
23.32 Isa 51.17; Jer 25.15; Ezek 22.4,5

[k] Meaning of Heb uncertain [l] Two Mss: MT *from Egypt* [m] Cn: Heb *for the sake of*
[n] Compare verses 6 and 12: Heb *officers and called ones* [o] Gk: Meaning of Heb uncertain

[33] You shall be filled with
drunkenness and
sorrow.
A cup of horror and
desolation
is the cup of your sister
Samaria;
[34] you shall drink it and drain
it out,
and gnaw its sherds,
and tear out your breasts;

for I have spoken, says the Lord GOD. [35] Therefore thus says the Lord GOD: Because you have forgotten me and cast me behind your back, therefore bear the consequences of your lewdness and whorings.

36 The LORD said to me: Mortal, will you judge Oholah and Oholibah? Then declare to them their abominable deeds. [37] For they have committed adultery, and blood is on their hands; with their idols they have committed adultery; and they have even offered up to them for food the children whom they had borne to me. [38] Moreover this they have done to me: they have defiled my sanctuary on the same day and profaned my sabbaths. [39] For when they had slaughtered their children for their idols, on the same day they came into my sanctuary to profane it. This is what they did in my house.

40 They even sent for men to come from far away, to whom a messenger was sent, and they came. For them you bathed yourself, painted your eyes, and decked yourself with ornaments; [41] you sat on a stately couch, with a table spread before it on which you had placed my incense and my oil. [42] The sound of a raucous multitude was around her, with many of the rabble brought in drunken from the wilderness; and they put bracelets on the arms[p] of the women, and beautiful crowns upon their heads.

43 Then I said, Ah, she is worn out with adulteries, but they carry on their sexual acts with her. [44] For they have gone in to her, as one goes in to a whore. Thus they went in to Oholah and to Oholibah, wanton women. [45] But righteous judges shall declare them guilty of adultery and of bloodshed; because they are adulteresses and blood is on their hands.

46 For thus says the Lord GOD: Bring up an assembly against them, and make them an object of terror and of plunder. [47] The assembly shall stone them and with their swords they shall cut them down; they shall kill their sons and their daughters, and burn up their houses. [48] Thus will I put an end to lewdness in the land, so that all women may take warning and not commit lewdness as you have done. [49] They shall repay you for your lewdness, and you shall bear the penalty for your sinful idolatry; and you shall know that I am the Lord GOD.

The Boiling Pot

24 In the ninth year, in the tenth month, on the tenth day of the month, the word of the LORD came to me: [2] Mortal, write down the name of this day, this very day. The king of Babylon has laid siege to Jerusalem this very day. [3] And utter an allegory to the rebellious house and say to them, Thus says the Lord GOD:

Set on the pot, set it on,
pour in water also;
[4] put in it the pieces,
all the good pieces, the
thigh and the shoulder;
fill it with choice bones.
[5] Take the choicest one of the
flock,
pile the logs[q] under it;
boil its pieces,[r]
seethe[s] also its bones in
it.

6 Therefore thus says the Lord GOD:

Woe to the bloody city,
the pot whose rust is in it,

23.33 Jer 25.15, 16,27; Ezek 4.16 **23.34** Ps 75.8; Isa 51.17 **23.35** Jer 3.21; Hos 8.14; 1 Kings 14.9; Neh 9.26 **23.36** Ezek 20.4; 22.2; Isa 58.1 **23.37** vv. 3,45; Ezek 16.20, 21,36,45 **23.38** Ezek 5.11; 7.20; 22.8 **23.39** 2 Kings 21.4 **23.40** Isa 57.9; 2 Kings 9.30; Jer 4.30; Ezek 16.13-16 **23.41** Esther 1.6; Am 6.4; Prov 7.17; Hos 2.8 **23.42** Ezek 16.49; Jer 51.7; Ezek 16.11, 12 **23.45** Ezek 16.38; Hos 6.5; Lev 20.10 **23.46** v. 24; Ezek 16.40; Jer 15.4; 24.9; 29.18 **23.47** Ezek 16.40; 2 Chr 36.17, 19; Ezek 24.21; Jer 39.8 **23.48** v. 27; Ezek 22.15; 2 Pet 2.6 **23.49** v. 35; Ezek 6.7; 20.38,42,44 **24.1** Ezek 1.2; 8.1; 20.1; 26.1 **24.2** Isa 8.1; 2 Kings 25.1; Jer 39.1; 52.4 **24.3** Ezek 17.2; Jer 1.13; Ezek 11.3

24.4 Ezek 22.19-22; Mic 3.2,3 **24.5** v. 10 **24.6** v. 9; Ezek 22.3; Mic 7.2; Joel 3.3; Nah 3.10

[p] Heb *hands* [q] Compare verse 10: Heb *the bones* [r] Two Mss: Heb *its boilings*
[s] Cn: Heb *its bones seethe*

whose rust has not gone
out of it!
Empty it piece by piece,
making no choice at all.[t]
7 For the blood she shed is
inside it;
she placed it on a bare
rock;
she did not pour it out on
the ground,
to cover it with earth.
8 To rouse my wrath, to take
vengeance,
I have placed the blood she
shed
on a bare rock,
so that it may not be
covered.
9 Therefore thus says the Lord God:
Woe to the bloody city!
I will even make the pile
great.
10 Heap up the logs, kindle the
fire;
boil the meat well, mix in
the spices,
let the bones be burned.
11 Stand it empty upon the
coals,
so that it may become hot,
its copper glow,
its filth melt in it, its rust
be consumed.
12 In vain I have wearied
myself;[u]
its thick rust does not
depart.
To the fire with its rust![v]
13 Yet, when I cleansed you in
your filthy lewdness,
you did not become clean
from your filth;
you shall not again be
cleansed
until I have satisfied my
fury upon you.
14 I the Lord have spoken; the time
is coming, I will act. I will not refrain, I will not spare, I will not relent. According to your ways and
your doings I will judge you, says
the Lord God.

Ezekiel's Bereavement

15 The word of the Lord came to
me: 16 Mortal, with one blow I am
about to take away from you the
delight of your eyes; yet you shall
not mourn or weep, nor shall your
tears run down. 17 Sigh, but not
aloud; make no mourning for the
dead. Bind on your turban, and put
your sandals on your feet; do not
cover your upper lip or eat the
bread of mourners.[w] 18 So I spoke
to the people in the morning, and
at evening my wife died. And on the
next morning I did as I was commanded.

19 Then the people said to me,
"Will you not tell us what these
things mean for us, that you are
acting this way?" 20 Then I said to
them: The word of the Lord came
to me: 21 Say to the house of Israel,
Thus says the Lord God: I will profane my sanctuary, the pride of
your power, the delight of your
eyes, and your heart's desire; and
your sons and your daughters
whom you left behind shall fall by
the sword. 22 And you shall do as I
have done; you shall not cover your
upper lip or eat the bread of
mourners.[w] 23 Your turbans shall
be on your heads and your sandals
on your feet; you shall not mourn
or weep, but you shall pine away in
your iniquities and groan to one
another. 24 Thus Ezekiel shall be a
sign to you; you shall do just as he
has done. When this comes, then
you shall know that I am the Lord
God.

25 And you, mortal, on the day
when I take from them their stronghold, their joy and glory, the delight of their eyes and their heart's
affection, and also[x] their sons and
their daughters, 26 on that day, one
who has escaped will come to you
to report to you the news. 27 On
that day your mouth shall be
opened to the one who has escaped, and you shall speak and no
longer be silent. So you shall be a
sign to them; and they shall know
that I am the Lord.

24.7 Ezek 23.37, 45; Lev 17.13; Deut 12.16
24.8 Mt 7.2
24.9 v. 6; Nah 3.1; Hab 2.12
24.10 v. 5
24.11 Ezek 21.10; 22.15
24.13 Jer 6.28-30; Ezek 22.24; 5.13; 8.18; 16.42
24.14 1 Sam 15.29; Isa 55.11; Ezek 9.10; 18.30; 36.19
24.16 Job 23.2; Jer 16.5; 22.10; 13.17
24.17 Jer 16.5-7; 2 Sam 15.30; Mic 3.7
24.19 Ezek 12.9; 37.18
24.21 Jer 7.14; Ps 27.4; Jer 6.11; Ezek 23.47
24.22 Jer 16.6,7; v. 17
24.23 Job 27.15; Ps 78.64; Ezek 33.10
24.24 Ezek 4.3; 12.6,11; Jer 17.15; Ezek 6.7; 25.5
24.25 Jer 11.22
24.26 Ezek 33.21f
24.27 Ezek 3.26, 27; 33.22; v. 24

[t] Heb *piece, no lot has fallen on it*
[u] Cn: Meaning of Heb uncertain
[v] Meaning of Heb uncertain
[w] Vg Tg: Heb *of men*
[x] Heb lacks *and also*

Proclamation against Ammon

25 The word of the LORD came
to me: 2Mortal, set your
face toward the Ammonites and
prophesy against them. 3Say to the
Ammonites, Hear the word of the
Lord GOD: Thus says the Lord GOD,
Because you said, "Aha!" over my
sanctuary when it was profaned,
and over the land of Israel when it
was made desolate, and over the
house of Judah when it went into
exile; 4therefore I am handing you
over to the people of the east for a
possession. They shall set their encampments among you and pitch
their tents in your midst; they shall
eat your fruit, and they shall drink
your milk. 5I will make Rabbah a
pasture for camels and Ammon a
fold for flocks. Then you shall
know that I am the LORD. 6For thus
says the Lord GOD: Because you
have clapped your hands and
stamped your feet and rejoiced
with all the malice within you
against the land of Israel, 7there-
fore I have stretched out my hand
against you, and will hand you over
as plunder to the nations. I will cut
you off from the peoples and will
make you perish out of the countries; I will destroy you. Then you
shall know that I am the LORD.

Proclamation against Moab

8 Thus says the Lord GOD: Because Moab[y] said, The house of
Judah is like all the other nations,
9therefore I will lay open the flank
of Moab from the towns[z] on its
frontier, the glory of the country,
Beth-jeshimoth, Baal-meon, and
Kiriathaim. 10I will give it along
with Ammon to the people of the
east as a possession. Thus Ammon
shall be remembered no more
among the nations, 11and I will execute judgments upon Moab. Then
they shall know that I am the LORD.

Proclamation against Edom

12 Thus says the Lord GOD: Because Edom acted revengefully
against the house of Judah and has
grievously offended in taking vengeance upon them, 13therefore
thus says the Lord GOD, I will
stretch out my hand against Edom,
and cut off from it humans and animals, and I will make it desolate;
from Teman even to Dedan they
shall fall by the sword. 14I will lay
my vengeance upon Edom by the
hand of my people Israel; and they
shall act in Edom according to my
anger and according to my wrath;
and they shall know my vengeance,
says the Lord GOD.

Proclamation against Philistia

15 Thus says the Lord GOD: Because with unending hostilities the
Philistines acted in vengeance, and
with malice of heart took revenge
in destruction; 16therefore thus
says the Lord GOD, I will stretch out
my hand against the Philistines,
cut off the Cherethites, and destroy
the rest of the seacoast. 17I will execute great vengeance on them
with wrathful punishments. Then
they shall know that I am the LORD,
when I lay my vengeance on them.

Proclamation against Tyre

26 In the eleventh year, on the
first day of the month, the
word of the LORD came to me:
2Mortal, because Tyre said concerning Jerusalem,
"Aha, broken is the gateway
of the peoples;
it has swung open to me;
I shall be replenished,
now that it is wasted."
3Therefore, thus says the Lord GOD:
See, I am against you,
O Tyre!
I will hurl many nations
against you,
as the sea hurls its waves.
4 They shall destroy the walls
of Tyre
and break down its towers.
I will scrape its soil from it
and make it a bare rock.
5 It shall become, in the midst
of the sea,
a place for spreading nets.
I have spoken, says the Lord GOD.

25.2 Jer 27.3; Ezek 21.28; Am 1.13; Zeph 2.8,9
25.3 Prov 17.5; Ezek 26.2
25.4 Ezek 21.31
25.5 Ezek 21.20; Isa 17.2; Zeph 2.14
25.6 Job 27.23; Lam 2.15; Zeph 2.8,10
25.7 Ezek 26.5; Am 1.14,15; Ezek 6.14
25.8 Isa chs. 15, 16; Jer 48.1; Am 2.1; Ezek 35.2,5
25.9 Num 33.49; 32.3,38; 32.37
25.10 v. 4; Ezek 21.32
25.11 Ezek 5.15; 11.9
25.12 Lam 4.21, 22; Ezek 35.2; Am 1.11; Ob 10-16
25.13 Am 1.12; Jer 25.23
25.14 Isa 11.14; Jer 49.2
25.15 Jer 25.20; Isa 14.29-31; Joel 3.4; 2 Chr 28.18
25.16 Zeph 2.4,5; 1 Sam 30.14; Jer 47.1-7
25.17 Ezek 5.15; Ps 9.16
26.2 Isa ch. 23; Jer 25.22; Ezek 25.3; 36.2
26.3 Mic 4.11; Isa 5.30; Jer 50.42
26.4 Am 1.10
26.5 Ezek 27.32; 29.19

[y] Gk Old Latin: Heb *Moab and Seir*
[z] Heb *towns from its towns*

It shall become plunder for
the nations,
6 and its daughter-towns in
the country
shall be killed by the
sword.
Then they shall know that I am the
LORD.
7 For thus says the Lord GOD: I
will bring against Tyre from the
north King Nebuchadrezzar of Babylon, king of kings, together with
horses, chariots, cavalry, and a
great and powerful army.
8 Your daughter-towns in the
country
he shall put to the sword.
He shall set up a siege wall
against you,
cast up a ramp against you,
and raise a roof of shields
against you.
9 He shall direct the shock of
his battering rams
against your walls
and break down your
towers with his axes.
10 His horses shall be so many
that their dust shall cover
you.
At the noise of cavalry,
wheels, and chariots
your very walls shall shake,
when he enters your gates
like those entering a
breached city.
11 With the hoofs of his horses
he shall trample all your
streets.
He shall put your people to
the sword,
and your strong pillars
shall fall to the ground.
12 They will plunder your riches
and loot your merchandise;
they shall break down your
walls
and destroy your fine
houses.
Your stones and timber and
soil
they shall cast into the
water.
13 I will silence the music of
your songs;
the sound of your lyres
shall be heard no more.

26.6 Ezek 25.5 **26.7** Jer 27.3-6; Ezra 7.12; Dan 2.37; Ezek 23.24 **26.8** v. 6; Ezek 21.22; Jer 6.6; 32.24 **26.9** Ezek 21.22 **26.10** Jer 4.13; 39.3; Ezek 27.28 **26.11** Hab 1.8; Isa 26.5; Jer 43.13 **26.12** v. 5 **26.13** Isa 14.11; 25.10; Isa 23.16; Rev 18.22

26.14 vv. 4,5; Mal 1.4; Isa 14.27 **26.15** v. 18; Ezek 31.16 **26.16** Ezek 27.35; Jon 3.6; Job 2.13 **26.17** Ezek 27.32; Rev 18.9; Isa 23.4; Ezek 28.2 **26.18** v. 15 **26.20** Ezek 32.18, 24; Am 9.2; Jer 33.9 **26.21** Ezek 27.36; 28.19; v. 14

14 I will make you a bare rock;
you shall be a place for
spreading nets.
You shall never again be
rebuilt,
for I the LORD have spoken,
says the Lord GOD.
15 Thus says the Lord GOD to
Tyre: Shall not the coastlands
shake at the sound of your fall,
when the wounded groan, when
slaughter goes on within you?
16 Then all the princes of the sea
shall step down from their thrones;
they shall remove their robes and
strip off their embroidered garments. They shall clothe themselves with trembling, and shall sit
on the ground; they shall tremble
every moment, and be appalled at
you. 17 And they shall raise a lamentation over you, and say to you:
How you have vanished[a]
from the seas,
O city renowned,
once mighty on the sea,
you and your inhabitants,[b]
who imposed your[c] terror
on all the mainland![d]
18 Now the coastlands tremble
on the day of your fall;
the coastlands by the sea
are dismayed at your
passing.
19 For thus says the Lord GOD:
When I make you a city laid waste,
like cities that are not inhabited,
when I bring up the deep over you,
and the great waters cover you,
20 then I will thrust you down with
those who descend into the Pit, to
the people of long ago, and I will
make you live in the world below,
among primeval ruins, with those
who go down to the Pit, so that you
will not be inhabited or have a
place[e] in the land of the living. 21 I
will bring you to a dreadful end,
and you shall be no more; though
sought for, you will never be found
again, says the Lord GOD.

[a] Gk OL Aquila: Heb *have vanished, O inhabited one,* [b] Heb *it and its inhabitants* [c] Heb *their* [d] Cn: Heb *its inhabitants* [e] Gk: Heb *I will give beauty*

Lamentation over Tyre

27 The word of the LORD came
to me: 2 Now you, mortal,
raise a lamentation over Tyre, 3 and
say to Tyre, which sits at the entrance to the sea, merchant of the
peoples on many coastlands, Thus
says the Lord GOD:

O Tyre, you have said,
"I am perfect in beauty."
4 Your borders are in the heart
of the seas;
your builders made perfect
your beauty.
5 They made all your planks
of fir trees from Senir;
they took a cedar from
Lebanon
to make a mast for you.
6 From oaks of Bashan
they made your oars;
they made your deck of
pines[f]
from the coasts of Cyprus,
inlaid with ivory.
7 Of fine embroidered linen
from Egypt
was your sail,
serving as your ensign;
blue and purple from the
coasts of Elishah
was your awning.
8 The inhabitants of Sidon and
Arvad
were your rowers;
skilled men of Zemer[g] were
within you,
they were your pilots.
9 The elders of Gebal and its
artisans were within
you,
caulking your seams;
all the ships of the sea with
their mariners were
within you,
to barter for your wares.
10 Paras[h] and Lud and Put
were in your army,
your mighty warriors;
they hung shield and helmet
in you;
they gave you splendor.
11 Men of Arvad and Helech[i]
were on your walls all
around;
men of Gamad were at
your towers.
They hung their quivers all
around your walls;
they made perfect your
beauty.

12 Tarshish did business with
you out of the abundance of your
great wealth; silver, iron, tin, and
lead they exchanged for your
wares. 13 Javan, Tubal, and Meshech traded with you; they exchanged human beings and vessels
of bronze for your merchandise.
14 Beth-togarmah exchanged for
your wares horses, war horses, and
mules. 15 The Rhodians[j] traded
with you; many coastlands were
your own special markets; they
brought you in payment ivory tusks
and ebony. 16 Edom[k] did business
with you because of your abundant
goods; they exchanged for your
wares turquoise, purple, embroidered work, fine linen, coral, and
rubies. 17 Judah and the land of Israel traded with you; they exchanged for your merchandise
wheat from Minnith, millet,[l] honey, oil, and balm. 18 Damascus traded with you for your abundant
goods—because of your great
wealth of every kind—wine of Hel-
bon, and white wool. 19 Vedan and
Javan from Uzal[l] entered into
trade for your wares; wrought iron,
cassia, and sweet cane were bar-
tered for your merchandise. 20 Dedan traded with you in saddle-
cloths for riding. 21 Arabia and all
the princes of Kedar were your favored dealers in lambs, rams, and
goats; in these they did business
with you. 22 The merchants of Sheba and Raamah traded with you;
they exchanged for your wares the
best of all kinds of spices, and all
precious stones, and gold. 23 Haran,
Canneh, Eden, the merchants of
Sheba, Asshur, and Chilmad traded
with you. 24 These traded with you
in choice garments, in clothes of

27.2 Ezek 28.12
27.3 Ezek 28.2; v. 33; Ezek 28.12
27.4 vv. 25-27
27.5 Deut 3.9
27.6 Zech 11.2; Isa 2.13; Jer 2.10
27.8 1 Kings 9.27
27.9 1 Kings 5.18; v. 27
27.10 Ezek 30.5; 38.5; v. 11
27.11 vv. 3,8,10
27.12 2 Chr 20.36; Isa 23.6,10; vv. 18,33
27.13 Gen 10.2; Isa 66.19; Ezek 38.2; Joel 3.3; Rev 18.13
27.14 Gen 10.3; Ezek 38.6
27.15 Gen 10.7; Rev 18.12
27.16 Ezek 28.13; 16.13,18
27.17 Judg 11.33; Jer 8.22
27.18 Jer 49.23; Ezek 47.16-18; vv. 12,33
27.20 v. 15
27.21 Jer 25.24; 49.28; Isa 60.7
27.22 Gen 10.7; 1 Kings 10.1, 2; Isa 60.6
27.23 Gen 11.31; 2 Kings 19.12; Am 1.5

[f] Or *boxwood* [g] Cn Compare Gen 10.18: Heb *your skilled men, O Tyre* [h] Or *Persia* [i] Or *and your army* [j] Gk: Heb *The Dedanites* [k] Another reading is *Aram* [l] Meaning of Heb uncertain

blue and embroidered work, and in
carpets of colored material, bound
with cords and made secure; in
these they traded with you.[m] 25 The
ships of Tarshish traveled for you in
your trade.

So you were filled and
heavily laden
in the heart of the seas.

26 Your rowers have brought
you
into the high seas.
The east wind has wrecked
you
in the heart of the seas.

27 Your riches, your wares, your
merchandise,
your mariners and your
pilots,
your caulkers, your dealers in
merchandise,
and all your warriors within
you,
with all the company
that is with you,
sink into the heart of the
seas
on the day of your ruin.

28 At the sound of the cry of
your pilots
the countryside shakes,

29 and down from their ships
come all that handle the
oar.
The mariners and all the
pilots of the sea
stand on the shore

30 and wail aloud over you,
and cry bitterly.
They throw dust on their
heads
and wallow in ashes;

31 they make themselves bald
for you,
and put on sackcloth,
and they weep over you in
bitterness of soul,
with bitter mourning.

32 In their wailing they raise a
lamentation for you,
and lament over you:
"Who was ever destroyed[n]
like Tyre
in the midst of the sea?

33 When your wares came from
the seas,
you satisfied many peoples;
with your abundant wealth
and merchandise
you enriched the kings of
the earth.

34 Now you are wrecked by the
seas,
in the depths of the waters;
your merchandise and all
your crew
have sunk with you.

35 All the inhabitants of the
coastlands
are appalled at you;
and their kings are horribly
afraid,
their faces are convulsed.

36 The merchants among the
peoples hiss at you;
you have come to a
dreadful end
and shall be no more
forever."

Proclamation against the King of Tyre

28 The word of the LORD came
to me: 2 Mortal, say to the
prince of Tyre, Thus says the Lord
GOD:

Because your heart is proud
and you have said, "I am a
god;
I sit in the seat of the gods,
in the heart of the seas,"
yet you are but a mortal, and
no god,
though you compare your
mind
with the mind of a god.

3 You are indeed wiser than
Daniel;[o]
no secret is hidden from
you;

4 by your wisdom and your
understanding
you have amassed wealth
for yourself,
and have gathered gold and
silver
into your treasuries.

5 By your great wisdom in
trade
you have increased your
wealth,

27.25 Isa 2.16; 23.14; v. 4 **27.26** Ezek 26.19; Ps 48.7; vv. 4,25,27 **27.27** Prov 11.4; Rev 18.9-19 **27.28** Ezek 26.15 **27.29** Rev 18.17-19 **27.30** Job 2.12; Rev 18.19; Esther 4.1, 3; Jer 6.26 **27.31** Jer 16.6; Ezek 29.18; Isa 22.12; 16.9 **27.32** v. 2; Ezek 26.17; Rev 18.18 **27.33** Rev 18.19 **27.34** vv. 26,27; Ezek 26.19; Zech 9.3,4 **27.35** Ezek 26.15, 16; 32.10 **27.36** Jer 18.16; Zeph 2.15; Ezek 26.21; Ps 37.10,36 **28.2** Ezek 27.25-27; Isa 31.3; v. 6 **28.3** Dan 1.20 **28.4** Ezek 27.33 **28.5** Ps 62.10; Zech 9.3; Hos 13.6

[m] Cn: Heb *in your market* [n] Tg Vg: Heb *like silence* [o] Or, as otherwise read, *Danel*

and your heart has become
proud in your wealth.
6 Therefore thus says the Lord
GOD:
Because you compare your
mind
with the mind of a god,
7 therefore, I will bring
strangers against you,
the most terrible of the
nations;
they shall draw their swords
against the beauty of
your wisdom
and defile your splendor.
8 They shall thrust you down
to the Pit,
and you shall die a violent
death
in the heart of the seas.
9 Will you still say, "I am a
god,"
in the presence of those
who kill you,
though you are but a mortal,
and no god,
in the hands of those who
wound you?
10 You shall die the death of
the uncircumcised
by the hand of foreigners;
for I have spoken, says the
Lord GOD.

Lamentation over the King of Tyre

11 Moreover the word of the
LORD came to me: 12 Mortal, raise a
lamentation over the king of Tyre,
and say to him, Thus says the Lord
GOD:

You were the signet of
perfection,[p]
full of wisdom and perfect
in beauty.
13 You were in Eden, the
garden of God;
every precious stone was
your covering,
carnelian, chrysolite, and
moonstone,
beryl, onyx, and jasper,
sapphire,[q] turquoise, and
emerald;
and worked in gold were
your settings
and your engravings.[p]

28.6 v. 2
28.7 Ezek 26.7; 30.11; 31.12; 32.12; v. 17
28.8 Ezek 32.30; 27.26,27,34
28.9 v. 2
28.10 Ezek 31.18; 32.19,21,25, 27
28.12 Ezek 27.2; v. 3; Ezek 27.3
28.13 Ezek 31.8,9; 36.35
28.14 Ex 25.20; v. 16; Ezek 20.40; Rev 18.16
28.15 Ezek 27.3,4; Isa 14.12; vv. 17,18
28.16 Ezek 27.12ff; 8.17; Gen 3.24; v. 14
28.17 vv. 2,5; Ezek 31.10; 27.3,4; 26.16
28.18 v. 16; Am 1.9,10; Mal 4.3
28.19 Ezek 26.21; 27.36; Jer 51.64

On the day that you were
created
they were prepared.
14 With an anointed cherub as
guardian I placed you;[p]
you were on the holy
mountain of God;
you walked among the
stones of fire.
15 You were blameless in your
ways
from the day that you were
created,
until iniquity was found in
you.
16 In the abundance of your
trade
you were filled with
violence, and you
sinned;
so I cast you as a profane
thing from the
mountain of God,
and the guardian cherub
drove you out
from among the stones of
fire.
17 Your heart was proud
because of your beauty;
you corrupted your wisdom
for the sake of your
splendor.
I cast you to the ground;
I exposed you before kings,
to feast their eyes on
you.
18 By the multitude of your
iniquities,
in the unrighteousness of
your trade,
you profaned your
sanctuaries.
So I brought out fire from
within you;
it consumed you,
and I turned you to ashes on
the earth
in the sight of all who saw
you.
19 All who know you among the
peoples
are appalled at you;
you have come to a dreadful
end

[p] Meaning of Heb uncertain [q] Or *lapis lazuli*

and shall be no more
forever.

Proclamation against Sidon

20 The word of the LORD came to
me: 21 Mortal, set your face toward
Sidon, and prophesy against it,
22 and say, Thus says the Lord GOD:
I am against you, O Sidon,
and I will gain glory in your
midst.
They shall know that I am
the LORD
when I execute judgments
in it,
and manifest my holiness
in it;
23 for I will send pestilence into
it,
and bloodshed into its
streets;
and the dead shall fall in its
midst,
by the sword that is against
it on every side.
And they shall know that I
am the LORD.
24 The house of Israel shall no
longer find a pricking brier or a
piercing thorn among all their
neighbors who have treated them
with contempt. And they shall
know that I am the Lord GOD.

Future Blessing for Israel

25 Thus says the Lord GOD:
When I gather the house of Israel
from the peoples among whom
they are scattered, and manifest
my holiness in them in the sight of
the nations, then they shall settle
on their own soil that I gave to my
servant Jacob. 26 They shall live in
safety in it, and shall build houses
and plant vineyards. They shall live
in safety, when I execute judgments upon all their neighbors who
have treated them with contempt.
And they shall know that I am the
LORD their God.

Proclamation against Egypt

29 In the tenth year, in the
tenth month, on the
twelfth day of the month, the word
of the LORD came to me: 2 Mortal,
set your face against Pharaoh king
of Egypt, and prophesy against him
and against all Egypt; 3 speak, and
say, Thus says the Lord GOD:
I am against you,
Pharaoh king of Egypt,
the great dragon sprawling
in the midst of its
channels,
saying, "My Nile is my own;
I made it for myself."
4 I will put hooks in your jaws,
and make the fish of your
channels stick to your
scales.
I will draw you up from your
channels,
with all the fish of your
channels
sticking to your scales.
5 I will fling you into the
wilderness,
you and all the fish of your
channels;
you shall fall in the open
field,
and not be gathered and
buried.
To the animals of the earth
and to the birds of the
air
I have given you as food.
6 Then all the inhabitants of
Egypt shall know
that I am the LORD
because you[r] were a staff of
reed
to the house of Israel;
7 when they grasped you with
the hand, you broke,
and tore all their
shoulders;
and when they leaned on
you, you broke,
and made all their legs
unsteady.[s]
8 Therefore, thus says the Lord
GOD: I will bring a sword upon you,
and will cut off from you human
being and animal; 9 and the land of
Egypt shall be a desolation and a
waste. Then they shall know that I
am the LORD.
Because you[t] said, "The Nile is
mine, and I made it," 10 therefore, I
am against you, and against your

28.21 Ezek 6.2; 25.2; Isa 23.4,12; Ezek 32.30
28.22 Ezek 26.3; 39.13; Ps 9.16; v. 26; Ezek 38.16
28.23 Ezek 38.22; Jer 51.52; vv. 24,26
28.24 Num 33.55; Josh 23.13; Isa 55.13; Ezek 25.6; 36.5
28.25 Isa 11.12; Jer 32.37; Ezek 20.41; Jer 23.8; 27.11; Ezek 37.25
28.26 Jer 23.6; Isa 65.21; Am 9.13,14
29.2 Ezek 28.21; Jer 44.30; Isa 19.1; Jer 25.19; 46.2,25
29.3 Jer 44.30; Ezek 28.22; Isa 27.1; 51.9; Ezek 32.2
29.4 2 Kings 19.28; Isa 37.29; Ezek 38.4
29.5 Ezek 32.4-6; Jer 7.33; 34.20; Ezek 39.4
29.6 Isa 36.6
29.7 Jer 37.5-11; Ezek 17.17
29.8 Ezek 14.17; 32.11-13
29.9 vv. 10-12,6, 3
29.10 Ezek 30.12, 6

[r] Gk Syr Vg: Heb *they* [s] Syr: Heb *stand*
[t] Gk Syr Vg: Heb *he*

channels, and I will make the land
of Egypt an utter waste and desolation, from Migdol to Syene, as far
as the border of Ethiopia.[u] 11 No
human foot shall pass through it,
and no animal foot shall pass
through it; it shall be uninhabited
forty years. 12 I will make the land
of Egypt a desolation among desolated countries; and her cities shall
be a desolation forty years among
cities that are laid waste. I will
scatter the Egyptians among the
nations, and disperse them among
the countries.

13 Further, thus says the Lord
GOD: At the end of forty years I will
gather the Egyptians from the peoples among whom they were scattered; 14 and I will restore the fortunes of Egypt, and bring them
back to the land of Pathros, the
land of their origin; and there they
shall be a lowly kingdom. 15 It shall
be the most lowly of the kingdoms,
and never again exalt itself above
the nations; and I will make them
so small that they will never again
rule over the nations. 16 The Egyptians[v] shall never again be the reli-
ance of the house of Israel; they
will recall their iniquity, when they
turned to them for aid. Then they
shall know that I am the Lord GOD.

Babylonia Will Plunder Egypt

17 In the twenty-seventh year,
in the first month, on the first day
of the month, the word of the LORD
came to me: 18 Mortal, King Nebuchadrezzar of Babylon made his
army labor hard against Tyre; every
head was made bald and every
shoulder was rubbed bare; yet neither he nor his army got anything
from Tyre to pay for the labor that
he had expended against it.
19 Therefore thus says the Lord
GOD: I will give the land of Egypt to
King Nebuchadrezzar of Babylon;
and he shall carry off its wealth and
despoil it and plunder it; and it
shall be the wages for his army. 20 I
have given him the land of Egypt as
his payment for which he labored,
because they worked for me, says
the Lord GOD.

29.11 Jer 43.11, 12; Ezek 32.13
29.12 Ezek 30.7, 26
29.13 Isa 19.22, 23; Jer 46.26
29.14 Ezek 30.14; 17.6,14
29.15 v. 14; Zech 10.11
29.16 Isa 30.2,3; 36.4,6; Jer 14.10; Hos 8.13; vv. 6,9,21
29.18 Jer 27.6; Ezek 26.7,8; 27.31
29.19 Ezek 30.10; Jer 43.10-13; Ezek 30.4
29.20 Isa 45.1-3; Jer 25.9
29.21 Ps 132.17; Ezek 24.27; 33.22; Lk 21.15; Ezek 6.7; v. 6
30.2 Isa 13.6; Ezek 21.12; Joel 1.5,11, 13
30.3 Ezek 7.7,12; Joel 2.1; Ob 15; Zeph 1.7; v. 18
30.4 vv. 11,5,9; Ezek 29.19
30.5 Jer 25.20,24
30.6 Isa 20.3-6; Ezek 29.10
30.7 Ezek 29.12
30.8 Ezek 29.6; 9.16; vv. 14, 16,5,6
30.9 Isa 18.1,2; Ezek 38.11; 32.9,10

21 On that day I will cause a
horn to sprout up for the house of
Israel, and I will open your lips
among them. Then they shall know
that I am the LORD.

Lamentation for Egypt

30 The word of the LORD came
to me: 2 Mortal, prophesy,
and say, Thus says the Lord GOD:
Wail, "Alas for the day!"
3 For a day is near,
the day of the LORD is near;
it will be a day of clouds,
a time of doom[w] for the
nations.
4 A sword shall come upon
Egypt,
and anguish shall be in
Ethiopia,[u]
when the slain fall in Egypt,
and its wealth is carried
away,
and its foundations are
torn down.

5 Ethiopia,[u] and Put, and Lud, and
all Arabia, and Libya,[x] and the
people of the allied land[y] shall fall
with them by the sword.

6 Thus says the LORD:
Those who support Egypt
shall fall,
and its proud might shall
come down;
from Migdol to Syene
they shall fall within it by
the sword,
says the Lord GOD.
7 They shall be desolated
among other desolated
countries,
and their cities shall lie
among cities laid waste.
8 Then they shall know that I
am the LORD,
when I have set fire to
Egypt,
and all who help it are
broken.

9 On that day, messengers shall
go out from me in ships to terrify
the unsuspecting Ethiopians;[z] and

[u] Or *Nubia*; Heb *Cush* [v] Heb *It*
[w] Heb lacks *of doom* [x] Compare Gk Syr Vg: Heb *Cub* [y] Meaning of Heb uncertain
[z] Or *Nubians*; Heb *Cush*

anguish shall come upon them on
the day of Egypt's doom;[a] for it is
coming!

10 Thus says the Lord GOD:
I will put an end to the
hordes of Egypt,
by the hand of King
Nebuchadrezzar of
Babylon.
11 He and his people with him,
the most terrible of the
nations,
shall be brought in to
destroy the land;
and they shall draw their
swords against Egypt,
and fill the land with the
slain.
12 I will dry up the channels,
and will sell the land into
the hand of evildoers;
I will bring desolation upon
the land and everything
in it
by the hand of foreigners;
I the LORD have spoken.

13 Thus says the Lord GOD:
I will destroy the idols
and put an end to the
images in Memphis;
there shall no longer be a
prince in the land of
Egypt;
so I will put fear in the
land of Egypt.
14 I will make Pathros a
desolation,
and will set fire to Zoan,
and will execute acts of
judgment on Thebes.
15 I will pour my wrath upon
Pelusium,
the stronghold of Egypt,
and cut off the hordes of
Thebes.
16 I will set fire to Egypt;
Pelusium shall be in great
agony;
Thebes shall be breached,
and Memphis face
adversaries by day.
17 The young men of On and of
Pi-beseth shall fall by
the sword;
and the cities themselves[b]
shall go into captivity.
18 At Tehaphnehes the day
shall be dark,
when I break there the
dominion of Egypt,
and its proud might shall
come to an end;
the city[c] shall be covered
by a cloud,
and its daughter-towns
shall go into captivity.
19 Thus I will execute acts of
judgment on Egypt.
Then they shall know that I
am the LORD.

Proclamation against Pharaoh

20 In the eleventh year, in the
first month, on the seventh day of
the month, the word of the LORD
came to me: 21 Mortal, I have broken the arm of Pharaoh king of
Egypt; it has not been bound up for
healing or wrapped with a bandage,
so that it may become strong to
wield the sword. 22 Therefore thus
says the Lord GOD: I am against
Pharaoh king of Egypt, and will
break his arms, both the strong arm
and the one that was broken; and I
will make the sword fall from his
hand. 23 I will scatter the Egyptians
among the nations, and disperse
them throughout the lands. 24 I will
strengthen the arms of the king of
Babylon, and put my sword in his
hand; but I will break the arms of
Pharaoh, and he will groan before
him with the groans of one mortally wounded. 25 I will strengthen the
arms of the king of Babylon, but
the arms of Pharaoh shall fall. And
they shall know that I am the LORD,
when I put my sword into the hand
of the king of Babylon. He shall
stretch it out against the land of
Egypt, 26 and I will scatter the
Egyptians among the nations and
disperse them throughout the
countries. Then they shall know
that I am the LORD.

30.10 Ezek 29.19
30.11 Ezek 28.7; v. 4
30.12 Isa 19.5,6; Ezek 29.3,9
30.13 Isa 19.1; Zech 13.2; v. 16; Zech 10.11; Isa 19.16
30.14 Ezek 29.14; Ps 78.12,43; vv. 15,16
30.15 Jer 46.25; v. 16
30.16 vv. 8,13-15
30.18 Jer 43.8-13; Ezek 34.27; v. 3
30.19 vv. 14,25,26
30.21 Ps 10.15; Jer 46.11
30.22 Ezek 29.3; Ps 37.17
30.23 Ezek 29.12; v. 26
30.24 vv. 10,25; Zech 10.12; Zeph 2.12; Ezek 26.15; 21.14,25
30.25 vv. 24,22, 11; Isa 5.25
30.26 Ezek 29.12

[a] Heb *the day of Egypt* [b] Heb *and they* [c] Heb *she*

The Lofty Cedar

31 In the eleventh year, in the third month, on the first day of the month, the word of the LORD came to me: [2] Mortal, say to Pharaoh king of Egypt and to his hordes:

Whom are you like in your
greatness?
3 Consider Assyria, a cedar of
Lebanon,
with fair branches and forest
shade,
and of great height,
its top among the clouds.[d]
4 The waters nourished it,
the deep made it grow tall,
making its rivers flow[e]
around the place it was
planted,
sending forth its streams
to all the trees of the field.
5 So it towered high
above all the trees of the
field;
its boughs grew large
and its branches long,
from abundant water in its
shoots.
6 All the birds of the air
made their nests in its
boughs;
under its branches all the
animals of the field
gave birth to their young;
and in its shade
all great nations lived.
7 It was beautiful in its
greatness,
in the length of its
branches;
for its roots went down
to abundant water.
8 The cedars in the garden of
God could not rival it,
nor the fir trees equal its
boughs;
the plane trees were as
nothing
compared with its
branches;
no tree in the garden of God
was like it in beauty.
9 I made it beautiful
with its mass of branches,
the envy of all the trees of
Eden
that were in the garden of
God.

10 Therefore thus says the Lord
GOD: Because it[f] towered high and
set its top among the clouds,[d] and
its heart was proud of its height, [11] I
gave it into the hand of the prince
of the nations; he has dealt with it
as its wickedness deserves. I have
cast it out. [12] Foreigners from the
most terrible of the nations have
cut it down and left it. On the
mountains and in all the valleys its
branches have fallen, and its
boughs lie broken in all the watercourses of the land; and all the peoples of the earth went away from its
shade and left it.

13 On its fallen trunk settle
all the birds of the air,
and among its boughs lodge
all the wild animals.

14 All this is in order that no trees by
the waters may grow to lofty height
or set their tops among the
clouds,[d] and that no trees that
drink water may reach up to them
in height.

For all of them are handed
over to death,
to the world below;
along with all mortals,
with those who go down to
the Pit.

15 Thus says the Lord GOD: On
the day it went down to Sheol I
closed the deep over it and covered
it; I restrained its rivers, and its
mighty waters were checked. I
clothed Lebanon in gloom for it,
and all the trees of the field fainted
because of it. [16] I made the nations
quake at the sound of its fall, when
I cast it down to Sheol with those
who go down to the Pit; and all the
trees of Eden, the choice and best
of Lebanon, all that were well watered, were consoled in the world
below. [17] They also went down to
Sheol with it, to those killed by the
sword, along with its allies,[g] those

31.2 Ezek 29.19; 30.10; v. 18 **31.3** Nah 3.1ff; Ezek 17.23; vv. 5,10 **31.4** Ezek 17.5,8; Rev 17.1,15 **31.5** Ps 37.35; Ezek 17.5 **31.6** Ezek 17.23; Dan 4.12; Mt 13.32; Mk 4.32; Lk 13.19 **31.7** vv. 2,9 **31.8** Gen 2.8; 13.10; Ezek 28.13; vv. 16,18 **31.9** Ezek 16.14 **31.10** Isa 14.13, 14; Ezek 28.17; Dan 5.20 **31.11** Ezek 30.10, 11; Nah 3.18 **31.12** Ezek 28.7; Hab 1.6; Ezek 32.5; 35.8; Nah 3.17,18 **31.13** Isa 18.6; Ezek 32.4 **31.14** vv. 16,17; Ps 63.9; v. 18; Ezek 32.24 **31.15** Ezek 32.7; Nah 2.10 **31.16** Ezek 26.15; Isa 14.15; Ezek 32.18; Isa 14.8; Ezek 32.31 **31.17** Ps 9.17; Ezek 32.18-20

[d] Gk: Heb *thick boughs* [e] Gk: Heb *rivers going* [f] Syr Vg: Heb *you* [g] Heb *its arms*

who lived in its shade among the nations.

18 Which among the trees of Eden was like you in glory and in greatness? Now you shall be brought down with the trees of Eden to the world below; you shall lie among the uncircumcised, with those who are killed by the sword. This is Pharaoh and all his horde, says the Lord GOD.

Lamentation over Pharaoh and Egypt

32 In the twelfth year, in the twelfth month, on the first day of the month, the word of the LORD came to me: 2 Mortal, raise a lamentation over Pharaoh king of Egypt, and say to him:

You consider yourself a lion
among the nations,
but you are like a dragon
in the seas;
you thrash about in your
streams,
trouble the water with your
feet,
and foul your[h] streams.
3 Thus says the Lord GOD:
In an assembly of many
peoples
I will throw my net over
you;
and I[i] will haul you up in
my dragnet.
4 I will throw you on the
ground,
on the open field I will
fling you,
and will cause all the birds
of the air to settle on
you,
and I will let the wild
animals of the whole
earth gorge themselves
with you.
5 I will strew your flesh on the
mountains,
and fill the valleys with
your carcass.[j]
6 I will drench the land with
your flowing blood
up to the mountains,
and the watercourses will
be filled with you.
7 When I blot you out, I will
cover the heavens,
and make their stars dark;
I will cover the sun with a
cloud,
and the moon shall not
give its light.
8 All the shining lights of the
heavens
I will darken above you,
and put darkness on your
land,
says the Lord GOD.
9 I will trouble the hearts of
many peoples,
as I carry you captive[k]
among the nations,
into countries you have not
known.
10 I will make many peoples
appalled at you;
their kings shall shudder
because of you.
When I brandish my sword
before them,
they shall tremble every
moment
for their lives, each one of
them,
on the day of your
downfall.
11 For thus says the Lord GOD:
The sword of the king of
Babylon shall come
against you.
12 I will cause your hordes to
fall
by the swords of mighty
ones,
all of them most terrible
among the nations.
They shall bring to ruin the
pride of Egypt,
and all its hordes shall
perish.
13 I will destroy all its livestock
from beside abundant
waters;
and no human foot shall
trouble them any more,
nor shall the hoofs of cattle
trouble them.
14 Then I will make their
waters clear,

31.18 Ezek 32.19; vv. 8,9,14; Ezek 28.10; 32.19,21
32.2 Ezek 27.2; 19.3,6; 38.13; 34.18
32.3 Ezek 12.13; 17.20; Hos 7.12
32.4 Ezek 29.5; 31.13; Isa 18.6
32.5 Ezek 35.8
32.6 Ezek 35.6; Rev 14.20
32.7 Prov 13.9; Isa 34.4; 13.10; Joel 2.31; 3.15; Am 8.9; Mt 24.29; Rev 6.12,13
32.9 Ezek 28.19; Rev 18.10-15; Ex 15.14-16
32.10 Ezek 27.35; 26.16; Jer 46.10
32.11 Jer 46.26; Ezek 30.4
32.12 Ezek 28.7; 31.12; 30.18
32.13 Ezek 29.8, 11

[h] Heb *their* [i] Gk Vg: Heb *they*
[j] Symmachus Syr Vg: Heb *your height*
[k] Gk: Heb *bring your destruction*

and cause their streams to
run like oil, says the
Lord GOD.
15 When I make the land of
Egypt desolate
and when the land is
stripped of all that fills
it,
when I strike down all who
live in it,
then they shall know that I
am the LORD.
16 This is a lamentation; it
shall be chanted.
The women of the nations
shall chant it.
Over Egypt and all its hordes
they shall chant it,
says the Lord GOD.

Dirge over Egypt

17 In the twelfth year, in the
first month,[l] on the fifteenth day
of the month, the word of the LORD
came to me:
18 Mortal, wail over the hordes
of Egypt,
and send them down,
with Egypt[m] and the
daughters of majestic
nations,
to the world below,
with those who go down to
the Pit.
19 "Whom do you surpass in
beauty?
Go down! Be laid to rest
with the
uncircumcised!"
20 They shall fall among those who
are killed by the sword. Egypt[n] has
been handed over to the sword;
carry away both it and its hordes.
21 The mighty chiefs shall speak of
them, with their helpers, out of the
midst of Sheol: "They have come
down, they lie still, the uncircumcised, killed by the sword."
22 Assyria is there, and all its
company, their graves all around it,
all of them killed, fallen by the
sword. 23 Their graves are set in the
uttermost parts of the Pit. Its company is all around its grave, all of
them killed, fallen by the sword,
who spread terror in the land of the
living.

32.15 Ezek 29.12, 19,20; Ps 9.16; Ezek 6.7 **32.16** 2 Sam 1.17; 2 Chr 35.25; Ezek 26.17 **32.18** vv. 2,16; Mic 1.8; Ezek 26.20; 31.14; v. 24 **32.19** Ezek 31.2, 18; 28.10; vv. 21,24,29 **32.21** Isa 1.31; 14.9,10; vv. 27,31,32 **32.22** Ezek 31.3, 16 **32.23** Isa 14.15; vv. 24-27,32 **32.24** Jer 49.34-39; Ps 27.13; Isa 38.11; Jer 11.19; vv. 25,30 **32.25** Ps 139.8; vv. 19,23,24 **32.26** Gen 10.2; Ezek 27.13; 38.2; vv. 19, 32 **32.27** Isa 14.18, 19,21,23 **32.28** v. 19 **32.29** Isa 34.5-15; Jer 49.7-22; Ezek 25.13 **32.30** Ezek 38.6, 15; 39.2; 28.21 **32.31** vv. 18,21; Ezek 31.16 **32.32** vv. 19-24

24 Elam is there, and all its
hordes around its grave; all of them
killed, fallen by the sword, who
went down uncircumcised into the
world below, who spread terror in
the land of the living. They bear
their shame with those who go
down to the Pit. 25 They have made
Elam[m] a bed among the slain with
all its hordes, their graves all
around it, all of them uncircumcised, killed by the sword; for terror
of them was spread in the land of
the living, and they bear their
shame with those who go down to
the Pit; they are placed among the
slain.
26 Meshech and Tubal are
there, and all their multitude, their
graves all around them, all of them
uncircumcised, killed by the
sword; for they spread terror in the
land of the living. 27 And they do
not lie with the fallen warriors of
long ago[o] who went down to Sheol
with their weapons of war, whose
swords were laid under their heads,
and whose shields[p] are upon their
bones; for the terror of the warriors
was in the land of the living. 28 So
you shall be broken and lie among
the uncircumcised, with those who
are killed by the sword.
29 Edom is there, its kings and
all its princes, who for all their
might are laid with those who are
killed by the sword; they lie with
the uncircumcised, with those who
go down to the Pit.
30 The princes of the north are
there, all of them, and all the Sidonians, who have gone down in
shame with the slain, for all the terror that they caused by their might;
they lie uncircumcised with those
who are killed by the sword, and
bear their shame with those who go
down to the Pit.
31 When Pharaoh sees them, he
will be consoled for all his
hordes—Pharaoh and all his army,
killed by the sword, says the Lord
GOD. 32 For he[q] spread terror in the

[l] Gk: Heb lacks *in the first month* [m] Heb *it* [n] Heb *It* [o] Gk Old Latin: Heb *of the uncircumcised* [p] Cn: Heb *iniquities* [q] Cn: Heb *I*

land of the living; therefore he shall
be laid to rest among the uncircumcised, with those who are slain
by the sword — Pharaoh and all his
multitude, says the Lord GOD.

Ezekiel Israel's Sentry

33 The word of the LORD came
to me: 2 O Mortal, speak to
your people and say to them, If I
bring the sword upon a land, and
the people of the land take one of
their number as their sentinel;
3 and if the sentinel sees the sword
coming upon the land and blows
the trumpet and warns the people;
4 then if any who hear the sound of
the trumpet do not take warning,
and the sword comes and takes
them away, their blood shall be
upon their own heads. 5 They heard
the sound of the trumpet and did
not take warning; their blood shall
be upon themselves. But if they
had taken warning, they would
have saved their lives. 6 But if the
sentinel sees the sword coming and
does not blow the trumpet, so that
the people are not warned, and the
sword comes and takes any of
them, they are taken away in their
iniquity, but their blood I will require at the sentinel's hand.

7 So you, mortal, I have made a
sentinel for the house of Israel;
whenever you hear a word from my
mouth, you shall give them warning from me. 8 If I say to the wicked,
"O wicked ones, you shall surely
die," and you do not speak to warn
the wicked to turn from their ways,
the wicked shall die in their iniquity, but their blood I will require at
your hand. 9 But if you warn the
wicked to turn from their ways, and
they do not turn from their ways,
the wicked shall die in their iniquity, but you will have saved your life.

God's Justice and Mercy

10 Now you, mortal, say to the
house of Israel, Thus you have said:
"Our transgressions and our sins
weigh upon us, and we waste away
because of them; how then can we
live?" 11 Say to them, As I live, says
the Lord GOD, I have no pleasure in
the death of the wicked, but that
the wicked turn from their ways
and live; turn back, turn back from
your evil ways; for why will you die,
O house of Israel? 12 And you, mortal, say to your people, The righteousness of the righteous shall
not save them when they transgress; and as for the wickedness of
the wicked, it shall not make them
stumble when they turn from their
wickedness; and the righteous
shall not be able to live by their
righteousness[r] when they sin.
13 Though I say to the righteous
that they shall surely live, yet if
they trust in their righteousness
and commit iniquity, none of their
righteous deeds shall be remembered; but in the iniquity that they
have committed they shall die.
14 Again, though I say to the wicked, "You shall surely die," yet if
they turn from their sin and do
what is lawful and right — 15 if the
wicked restore the pledge, give
back what they have taken by robbery, and walk in the statutes of
life, committing no iniquity — they
shall surely live, they shall not die.
16 None of the sins that they have
committed shall be remembered
against them; they have done what
is lawful and right, they shall surely
live.

17 Yet your people say, "The
way of the Lord is not just," when
it is their own way that is not just.
18 When the righteous turn from
their righteousness, and commit
iniquity, they shall die for it.[s]
19 And when the wicked turn from
their wickedness, and do what is
lawful and right, they shall live by
it.[s] 20 Yet you say, "The way of the
Lord is not just." O house of Israel,
I will judge all of you according to
your ways!

The Fall of Jerusalem

21 In the twelfth year of our exile, in the tenth month, on the fifth
day of the month, someone who
had escaped from Jerusalem came
to me and said, "The city has fall-

33.2 Ezek 3.11; Jer 12.12; Zech 13.7; 2 Sam 18.24, 25; 2 Kings 9.17
33.3 Hos 8.1; Joel 2.1
33.4 Jer 6.17; Zech 1.4; Ezek 18.13; Acts 18.6
33.5 Heb 11.7
33.6 Isa 56.10, 11; v. 8; Ezek 3.18, 20
33.7 Ezek 3.17-21; Jer 26.2; Acts 5.20
33.8 vv. 14,6
33.9 Acts 13.40, 41,46; Ezek 3.19, 21
33.10 Ezek 18.2; 24.23; 37.11
33.11 2 Sam 14.14; Ezek 18.23, 32; 2 Pet 3.9; Ezek 18.30, 31
33.12 Ezek 3.20; 2 Chr 7.14
33.13 Ezek 3.20; 18.24; 2 Pet 2.20, 21
33.14 Ezek 3.18, 19; 18.27
33.15 Lev 6.2,4,5; Num 5.6,7; Lk 19.8; Ezek 20.11
33.16 Ezek 18.22
33.17 Ezek 18.25, 29; v. 20
33.18 Ezek 18.26
33.19 vv. 12,14
33.20 Ezek 18.25; v. 17
33.21 Ezek 1.2; 24.26; 2 Kings 25.4

[r] Heb *by it* [s] Heb *them*

en." 22 Now the hand of the LORD had been upon me the evening before the fugitive came; but he had opened my mouth by the time the fugitive came to me in the morning; so my mouth was opened, and I was no longer unable to speak.

The Survivors in Judah

23 The word of the LORD came to me: 24 Mortal, the inhabitants of these waste places in the land of Israel keep saying, "Abraham was only one man, yet he got possession of the land; but we are many; the land is surely given us to possess." 25 Therefore say to them, Thus says the Lord GOD: You eat flesh with the blood, and lift up your eyes to your idols, and shed blood; shall you then possess the land? 26 You depend on your swords, you commit abominations, and each of you defiles his neighbor's wife; shall you then possess the land? 27 Say this to them, Thus says the Lord GOD: As I live, surely those who are in the waste places shall fall by the sword; and those who are in the open field I will give to the wild animals to be devoured; and those who are in strongholds and in caves shall die by pestilence. 28 I will make the land a desolation and a waste, and its proud might shall come to an end; and the mountains of Israel shall be so desolate that no one will pass through. 29 Then they shall know that I am the LORD, when I have made the land a desolation and a waste because of all their abominations that they have committed.

30 As for you, mortal, your people who talk together about you by the walls, and at the doors of the houses, say to one another, each to a neighbor, "Come and hear what the word is that comes from the LORD." 31 They come to you as people come, and they sit before you as my people, and they hear your words, but they will not obey them. For flattery is on their lips, but their heart is set on their gain. 32 To them you are like a singer of love songs,[t] one who has a beautiful voice and plays well on an instrument; they hear what you say, but they will not do it. 33 When this comes—and come it will!—then they shall know that a prophet has been among them.

Israel's False Shepherds

34 The word of the LORD came to me: 2 Mortal, prophesy against the shepherds of Israel: prophesy, and say to them—to the shepherds: Thus says the Lord GOD: Ah, you shepherds of Israel who have been feeding yourselves! Should not shepherds feed the sheep? 3 You eat the fat, you clothe yourselves with the wool, you slaughter the fatlings; but you do not feed the sheep. 4 You have not strengthened the weak, you have not healed the sick, you have not bound up the injured, you have not brought back the strayed, you have not sought the lost, but with force and harshness you have ruled them. 5 So they were scattered, because there was no shepherd; and scattered, they became food for all the wild animals. 6 My sheep were scattered, they wandered over all the mountains and on every high hill; my sheep were scattered over all the face of the earth, with no one to search or seek for them.

7 Therefore, you shepherds, hear the word of the LORD: 8 As I live, says the Lord GOD, because my sheep have become a prey, and my sheep have become food for all the wild animals, since there was no shepherd; and because my shepherds have not searched for my sheep, but the shepherds have fed themselves, and have not fed my sheep; 9 therefore, you shepherds, hear the word of the LORD: 10 Thus says the Lord GOD, I am against the shepherds; and I will demand my sheep at their hand, and put a stop to their feeding the sheep; no longer shall the shepherds feed themselves. I will rescue my sheep from their mouths, so that they may not be food for them.

33.22 Ezek 1.3; 24.27; Lk 1.64
33.24 Ezek 36.4; Isa 51.2; Acts 7.5
33.25 Deut 12.16; Ezek 20.24; 22.6,9
33.26 Ezek 18.6; 22.11
33.27 Ezek 39.4; 1 Sam 13.6; Isa 2.19
33.28 Jer 44.2,6, 22; Ezek 7.24; 36.34,35
33.29 Ezek 23.33, 35
33.30 vv. 2,17; Isa 29.13; 58.2
33.31 Ezek 14.1; 20.1; 8.1; Ps 78.36,37; Isa 29.13; Mt 13.22
33.33 1 Sam 3.20; Ezek 2.5
34.2 Jer 10.21; vv. 8-10,14, 15; Jn 10.11; 21.15-17
34.3 Isa 56.11; Zech 11.16; Ezek 22.25, 27
34.4 Zech 11.16; Mt 9.36; Lk 15.4; 1 Pet 5.3
34.5 Jer 10.21; 50.6,7; Jer 23.2; Mt 9.36
34.8 Acts 20.29; vv. 5,6,2
34.10 Ezek 3.18; Heb 13.17; vv. 2,8

[t] Cn: Heb *like a love song*

God, the True Shepherd

11 For thus says the Lord GOD: I
myself will search for my sheep,
and will seek them out. [12]As shepherds seek out their flocks when
they are among their scattered
sheep, so I will seek out my sheep.
I will rescue them from all the
places to which they have been
scattered on a day of clouds and
thick darkness. [13]I will bring them
out from the peoples and gather
them from the countries, and will
bring them into their own land; and
I will feed them on the mountains
of Israel, by the watercourses, and
in all the inhabited parts of the
land. [14]I will feed them with good
pasture, and the mountain heights
of Israel shall be their pasture;
there they shall lie down in good
grazing land, and they shall feed on
rich pasture on the mountains of
Israel. [15]I myself will be the shepherd of my sheep, and I will make
them lie down, says the Lord GOD.
[16]I will seek the lost, and I will
bring back the strayed, and I will
bind up the injured, and I will
strengthen the weak, but the fat
and the strong I will destroy. I will
feed them with justice.

17 As for you, my flock, thus
says the Lord GOD: I shall judge between sheep and sheep, between
rams and goats: [18]Is it not enough
for you to feed on the good pasture,
but you must tread down with your
feet the rest of your pasture? When
you drink of clear water, must you
foul the rest with your feet? [19]And
must my sheep eat what you have
trodden with your feet, and drink
what you have fouled with your
feet?

20 Therefore, thus says the Lord
GOD to them: I myself will judge between the fat sheep and the lean
sheep. [21]Because you pushed with
flank and shoulder, and butted at
all the weak animals with your
horns until you scattered them far
and wide, [22]I will save my flock,
and they shall no longer be ravaged; and I will judge between
sheep and sheep.

23 I will set up over them one
shepherd, my servant David, and
he shall feed them: he shall feed
them and be their shepherd. [24]And
I, the LORD, will be their God, and
my servant David shall be prince
among them; I, the LORD, have spoken.

25 I will make with them a covenant of peace and banish wild animals from the land, so that they
may live in the wild and sleep in
the woods securely. [26]I will make
them and the region around my hill
a blessing; and I will send down the
showers in their season; they shall
be showers of blessing. [27]The trees
of the field shall yield their fruit,
and the earth shall yield its increase. They shall be secure on
their soil; and they shall know that
I am the LORD, when I break the
bars of their yoke, and save them
from the hands of those who enslaved them. [28]They shall no more
be plunder for the nations, nor
shall the animals of the land devour them; they shall live in safety,
and no one shall make them afraid.
[29]I will provide for them a splendid
vegetation so that they shall no
more be consumed with hunger in
the land, and no longer suffer the
insults of the nations. [30]They shall
know that I, the LORD their God, am
with them, and that they, the
house of Israel, are my people, says
the Lord GOD. [31]You are my sheep,
the sheep of my pasture[u] and I am
your God, says the Lord GOD.

Judgment on Mount Seir

35 The word of the LORD came
to me: [2]Mortal, set your
face against Mount Seir, and
prophesy against it, [3]and say to it,
Thus says the Lord GOD:

I am against you, Mount
Seir;
I stretch out my hand
against you
to make you a desolation
and a waste.

34.11 Ezek 11.17; 20.41 **34.12** Jn 10.16; Ezek 30.3; Joel 2.2 **34.13** Isa 65.9,10; Jer 23.3; Ezek 37.22; Isa 30.25 **34.14** Ps 23.1,2; Ezek 20.40; 28.25,26 **34.16** Mt 18.11; Lk 5.32; Isa 49.26 **34.17** Ezek 20.37, 38; Zech 10.3; Mt 25.32,33 **34.18** 2 Sam 7.19 **34.20** v. 17 **34.21** Deut 33.17; Dan 8.4 **34.22** vv. 5,8,10, 17 **34.23** Isa 40.11; Jer 23.4,5; 30.9; Hos 3.5 **34.24** Ezek 36.28; 37.27; 37.24, 25; Hos 3.5 **34.25** Isa 11.6-9; Hos 2.18; Jer 23.6 **34.26** Isa 56.7; Zech 8.13 **34.27** Ps 85.12; Isa 4.2; Jer 2.20 **34.28** Jer 30.10 **34.29** Isa 60.21; Ezek 36.29, 3,6 **34.30** Ezek 36.28; 37.27 **34.31** Ps 100.3; Jn 10.11 **35.2** Jer 49.7,8 **35.3** Ezek 21.3; Jer 6.12; 15.6; Ezek 25.13; v. 7

[u] Gk OL: Heb *pasture, you are people*

4 I lay your towns in ruins;
you shall become a
desolation,
and you shall know that I
am the LORD.
5 Because you cherished an ancient
enmity, and gave over the people of
Israel to the power of the sword at
the time of their calamity, at the
time of their final punishment;
6 therefore, as I live, says the Lord
GOD, I will prepare you for blood,
and blood shall pursue you; since
you did not hate bloodshed, bloodshed shall pursue you. 7 I will make
Mount Seir a waste and a desolation; and I will cut off from it all
who come and go. 8 I will fill its
mountains with the slain; on your
hills and in your valleys and in all
your watercourses those killed
with the sword shall fall. 9 I will
make you a perpetual desolation,
and your cities shall never be inhabited. Then you shall know that
I am the LORD.
10 Because you said, "These
two nations and these two countries shall be mine, and we will
take possession of them,"—
although the LORD was there—
11 therefore, as I live, says the Lord
GOD, I will deal with you according
to the anger and envy that you
showed because of your hatred
against them; and I will make myself known among you,[v] when I
judge you. 12 You shall know that I,
the LORD, have heard all the abusive speech that you uttered
against the mountains of Israel,
saying, "They are laid desolate,
they are given us to devour." 13 And
you magnified yourselves against
me with your mouth, and multiplied your words against me; I
heard it. 14 Thus says the Lord GOD:
As the whole earth rejoices, I will
make you desolate. 15 As you rejoiced over the inheritance of the
house of Israel, because it was desolate, so I will deal with you; you
shall be desolate, Mount Seir, and
all Edom, all of it. Then they shall
know that I am the LORD.

35.4 v. 9; Mal 1.3,4
35.5 Ezek 25.12; Ob 10; Ezek 7.2; 21.25,29
35.6 Ezek 16.38; 32.6
35.7 Ezek 25.13; 29.11
35.8 Isa 34.5,6; Ezek 31.12; 32.4,5
35.9 Jer 49.13; Ezek 6.7; 36.11
35.10 Ezek 36.2,5; Ps 48.1,3; Ezek 48.35
35.11 Am 1.11; Mt 7.2; Ps 9.16
35.13 Ezek 36.3; Jer 7.11; 29.23
35.14 Isa 49.13; Jer 51.48
35.15 Jer 50.11; Ob 4,21; Ezek 6.7

36.1 Ezek 6.2,3
36.2 Ezek 25.3; Hab 3.19; Ezek 35.10
36.3 Jer 2.15; 51.34; 18.16; Ezek 35.13
36.4 Ezek 6.3; 34.28; Ps 79.4; Jer 48.27
36.5 Ezek 38.19; 25.12-14; 35.10,12; Jer 50.11; Mic 7.8
36.6 Ps 123.3,4; Ezek 34.29
36.7 Ezek 20.6, 15,23; Jer 25.9,15, 29
36.8 v. 4; Isa 27.6; Ezek 17.23

Blessing on Israel

36 And you, mortal, prophesy
to the mountains of Israel,
and say: O mountains of Israel,
hear the word of the LORD. 2 Thus
says the Lord GOD: Because the enemy said of you, "Aha!" and, "The
ancient heights have become our
possession," 3 therefore prophesy,
and say: Thus says the Lord GOD:
Because they made you desolate
indeed, and crushed you from all
sides, so that you became the possession of the rest of the nations,
and you became an object of gossip
and slander among the people;
4 therefore, O mountains of Israel,
hear the word of the Lord GOD:
Thus says the Lord GOD to the
mountains and the hills, the watercourses and the valleys, the desolate wastes and the deserted towns,
which have become a source of
plunder and an object of derision
to the rest of the nations all
around; 5 therefore thus says the
Lord GOD: I am speaking in my hot
jealousy against the rest of the nations, and against all Edom, who,
with wholehearted joy and utter
contempt, took my land as their
possession, because of its pasture,
to plunder it. 6 Therefore prophesy
concerning the land of Israel, and
say to the mountains and hills, to
the watercourses and valleys, Thus
says the Lord GOD: I am speaking in
my jealous wrath, because you
have suffered the insults of the nations; 7 therefore thus says the Lord
GOD: I swear that the nations that
are all around you shall themselves
suffer insults.
8 But you, O mountains of Israel, shall shoot out your branches,
and yield your fruit to my people
Israel; for they shall soon come
home. 9 See now, I am for you; I will
turn to you, and you shall be tilled
and sown; 10 and I will multiply
your population, the whole house
of Israel, all of it; the towns shall be
inhabited and the waste places re-

36.10 Isa 27.6; Ezek 37.21, 22; v. 33

[v] Gk: Heb *them*

built; 11 and I will multiply human beings and animals upon you. They shall increase and be fruitful; and I will cause you to be inhabited as in your former times, and will do more good to you than ever before. Then you shall know that I am the LORD. 12 I will lead people upon you—my people Israel—and they shall possess you, and you shall be their inheritance. No longer shall you bereave them of children.

13 Thus says the Lord GOD: Because they say to you, "You devour people, and you bereave your nation of children," 14 therefore you shall no longer devour people and no longer bereave your nation of children, says the Lord GOD; 15 and no longer will I let you hear the insults of the nations, no longer shall you bear the disgrace of the peoples; and no longer shall you cause your nation to stumble, says the Lord GOD.

The Renewal of Israel

16 The word of the LORD came to me: 17 Mortal, when the house of Israel lived on their own soil, they defiled it with their ways and their deeds; their conduct in my sight was like the uncleanness of a woman in her menstrual period. 18 So I poured out my wrath upon them for the blood that they had shed upon the land, and for the idols with which they had defiled it. 19 I scattered them among the nations, and they were dispersed through the countries; in accordance with their conduct and their deeds I judged them. 20 But when they came to the nations, wherever they came, they profaned my holy name, in that it was said of them, "These are the people of the LORD, and yet they had to go out of his land." 21 But I had concern for my holy name, which the house of Israel had profaned among the nations to which they came.

22 Therefore say to the house of Israel, Thus says the Lord GOD: It is not for your sake, O house of Israel, that I am about to act, but for the sake of my holy name, which you have profaned among the nations to which you came. 23 I will sanctify my great name, which has been profaned among the nations, and which you have profaned among them; and the nations shall know that I am the LORD, says the Lord GOD, when through you I display my holiness before their eyes. 24 I will take you from the nations, and gather you from all the countries, and bring you into your own land. 25 I will sprinkle clean water upon you, and you shall be clean from all your uncleannesses, and from all your idols I will cleanse you. 26 A new heart I will give you, and a new spirit I will put within you; and I will remove from your body the heart of stone and give you a heart of flesh. 27 I will put my spirit within you, and make you follow my statutes and be careful to observe my ordinances. 28 Then you shall live in the land that I gave to your ancestors; and you shall be my people, and I will be your God. 29 I will save you from all your uncleannesses, and I will summon the grain and make it abundant and lay no famine upon you. 30 I will make the fruit of the tree and the produce of the field abundant, so that you may never again suffer the disgrace of famine among the nations. 31 Then you shall remember your evil ways, and your dealings that were not good; and you shall loathe yourselves for your iniquities and your abominable deeds. 32 It is not for your sake that I will act, says the Lord GOD; let that be known to you. Be ashamed and dismayed for your ways, O house of Israel.

33 Thus says the Lord GOD: On the day that I cleanse you from all your iniquities, I will cause the towns to be inhabited, and the waste places shall be rebuilt. 34 The land that was desolate shall be tilled, instead of being the desolation that it was in the sight of all who passed by. 35 And they will say, "This land that was desolate has become like the garden of Eden;

36.11 Jer 30.18; Ezek 16.55; 35.9
36.13 Num 13.32
36.15 Ezek 34.29; 22.4; Jer 13.16; 18.15
36.17 Lev 18.25, 27,28; Jer 2.7
36.18 Ezek 22.20; 16.36,38; 23.37
36.19 Am 9.9; Ezek 39.24; Rom 2.6
36.20 Isa 52.5; Rom 2.24; Jer 33.24
36.21 Ps 74.18; Isa 48.9; Ezek 20.44
36.22 Ps 106.8
36.23 Ezek 20.41; Ps 126.2; Ezek 28.25; 39.27
36.24 Ezek 34.13; 37.21
36.25 Isa 52.15; Heb 10.22; Zech 13.1
36.26 Ps 51.10; Ezek 11.19
36.27 Ezek 11.19; 37.14
36.28 Jer 30.22; Ezek 11.20; 37.27
36.29 Zech 13.1
36.30 Ezek 34.27, 29; Hos 2.21-23
36.31 Ezek 16.61-63; 20.43; 6.9
36.32 Ezek 20.44; v. 22
36.33 v. 25; Zech 8.7,8; Isa 58.12; v. 10
36.34 v. 9
36.35 Isa 51.3; Ezek 31.9; Joel 2.3

and the waste and desolate and ruined towns are now inhabited and
fortified." 36 Then the nations that
are left all around you shall know
that I, the LORD, have rebuilt the ruined places, and replanted that
which was desolate; I, the LORD,
have spoken, and I will do it.
37 Thus says the Lord GOD: I will
also let the house of Israel ask me
to do this for them: to increase
their population like a flock. 38 Like
the flock for sacrifices,[w] like the
flock at Jerusalem during her appointed festivals, so shall the ruined towns be filled with flocks of
people. Then they shall know that
I am the LORD.

The Valley of Dry Bones

37 The hand of the LORD came
upon me, and he brought
me out by the spirit of the LORD and
set me down in the middle of a valley; it was full of bones. 2 He led me
all around them; there were very
many lying in the valley, and they
were very dry. 3 He said to me,
"Mortal, can these bones live?" I
answered, "O Lord GOD, you
know." 4 Then he said to me,
"Prophesy to these bones, and say
to them: O dry bones, hear the
word of the LORD. 5 Thus says the
Lord GOD to these bones: I will
cause breath[x] to enter you, and
you shall live. 6 I will lay sinews on
you, and will cause flesh to come
upon you, and cover you with skin,
and put breath[x] in you, and you
shall live; and you shall know that
I am the LORD."
7 So I prophesied as I had been
commanded; and as I prophesied,
suddenly there was a noise, a rattling, and the bones came together,
bone to its bone. 8 I looked, and
there were sinews on them, and
flesh had come upon them, and
skin had covered them; but there
was no breath in them. 9 Then he
said to me, "Prophesy to the
breath, prophesy, mortal, and say
to the breath:[y] Thus says the Lord
GOD: Come from the four winds,
O breath,[y] and breathe upon
these slain, that they may live." 10 I
prophesied as he commanded me,
and the breath came into them,
and they lived, and stood on their
feet, a vast multitude.
11 Then he said to me, "Mortal,
these bones are the whole house of
Israel. They say, 'Our bones are
dried up, and our hope is lost; we
are cut off completely.' 12 Therefore
prophesy, and say to them, Thus
says the Lord GOD: I am going to
open your graves, and bring you up
from your graves, O my people; and
I will bring you back to the land of
Israel. 13 And you shall know that I
am the LORD, when I open your
graves, and bring you up from your
graves, O my people. 14 I will put
my spirit within you, and you shall
live, and I will place you on your
own soil; then you shall know that
I, the LORD, have spoken and will
act," says the LORD.

The Two Sticks

15 The word of the LORD came to
me: 16 Mortal, take a stick and write
on it, "For Judah, and the Israelites
associated with it"; then take another stick and write on it, "For Joseph (the stick of Ephraim) and all
the house of Israel associated with
it"; 17 and join them together into
one stick, so that they may become
one in your hand. 18 And when your
people say to you, "Will you not
show us what you mean by these?"
19 say to them, Thus says the Lord
GOD: I am about to take the stick of
Joseph (which is in the hand of
Ephraim) and the tribes of Israel
associated with it; and I will put
the stick of Judah upon it,[z] and
make them one stick, in order that
they may be one in my hand.
20 When the sticks on which you
write are in your hand before their
eyes, 21 then say to them, Thus says
the Lord GOD: I will take the people
of Israel from the nations among
which they have gone, and will
gather them from every quarter,
and bring them to their own land.

36.36 Ezek 39.27, 28; 22.14; 37.14
36.38 1 Kings 8.63; vv. 33-35; Zech 11.17
37.1 Ezek 1.3; 8.3; 11.24; Lk 4.1; Acts 8.39
37.2 v. 11
37.3 Isa 26.19; Deut 32.39; 1 Sam 2.6
37.4 vv. 9,12; Isa 42.18; Ezek 36.1
37.5 Ps 104.29, 30; vv. 9,10
37.6 vv. 8-10; Ezek 6.7; 35.12; Joel 2.27; 3.17
37.7 Jer 13.5-7; Ezek 38.19
37.9 Ps 104.30; v. 5; Hos 13.14
37.10 vv. 5,6; Rev 11.11
37.11 Ezek 36.10; 39.25; Ps 141.7; Isa 49.14
37.12 Isa 26.19; Hos 13.14; v. 25; Ezek 36.24; Am 9.14,15
37.13 Ezek 6.7; vv. 6,12
37.14 Ezek 36.27; 39.29; 36.36
37.16 Num 17.2; 2 Chr 11.11-17; 15.9
37.17 vv. 22-24
37.18 Ezek 12.9; 24.19
37.19 Zech 10.6; vv. 16,17
37.21 Ezek 36.24; 39.27

[w] Heb *flock of holy things* [x] Or *spirit*
[y] Or *wind* or *spirit* [z] Heb *I will put them upon it*

22 I will make them one nation in
the land, on the mountains of Israel; and one king shall be king over
them all. Never again shall they be
two nations, and never again shall
they be divided into two kingdoms.
23 They shall never again defile
themselves with their idols and
their detestable things, or with any
of their transgressions. I will save
them from all the apostasies into
which they have fallen,[a] and will
cleanse them. Then they shall be
my people, and I will be their GOD.
24 My servant David shall be
king over them; and they shall all
have one shepherd. They shall follow my ordinances and be careful
to observe my statutes. 25 They
shall live in the land that I gave to
my servant Jacob, in which your
ancestors lived; they and their children and their children's children
shall live there forever; and my servant David shall be their prince forever. 26 I will make a covenant of
peace with them; it shall be an everlasting covenant with them; and
I will bless[b] them and multiply
them, and will set my sanctuary
among them forevermore. 27 My
dwelling place shall be with them;
and I will be their God, and they
shall be my people. 28 Then the nations shall know that I the LORD
sanctify Israel, when my sanctuary
is among them forevermore.

Invasion by Gog

38 The word of the LORD came
to me: 2 Mortal, set your
face toward Gog, of the land of Magog, the chief prince of Meshech
and Tubal. Prophesy against him
3 and say: Thus says the Lord GOD:
I am against you, O Gog, chief
prince of Meshech and Tubal; 4 I
will turn you around and put hooks
into your jaws, and I will lead you
out with all your army, horses and
horsemen, all of them clothed in
full armor, a great company, all of
them with shield and buckler,
wielding swords. 5 Persia, Ethiopia,[c] and Put are with them, all of
them with buckler and helmet;
6 Gomer and all its troops; Beth-
togarmah from the remotest parts
of the north with all its troops—
many peoples are with you.
7 Be ready and keep ready, you
and all the companies that are assembled around you, and hold
yourselves in reserve for them. 8 After many days you shall be mustered; in the latter years you shall
go against a land restored from war,
a land where people were gathered
from many nations on the mountains of Israel, which had long lain
waste; its people were brought out
from the nations and now are living
in safety, all of them. 9 You shall advance, coming on like a storm; you
shall be like a cloud covering the
land, you and all your troops, and
many peoples with you.
10 Thus says the Lord GOD: On
that day thoughts will come into
your mind, and you will devise an
evil scheme. 11 You will say, "I will
go up against the land of unwalled
villages; I will fall upon the quiet
people who live in safety, all of
them living without walls, and having no bars or gates"; 12 to seize
spoil and carry off plunder; to assail the waste places that are now
inhabited, and the people who
were gathered from the nations,
who are acquiring cattle and goods,
who live at the center[d] of the
earth. 13 Sheba and Dedan and the
merchants of Tarshish and all its
young warriors[e] will say to you,
"Have you come to seize spoil?
Have you assembled your horde to
carry off plunder, to carry away silver and gold, to take away cattle
and goods, to seize a great amount
of booty?"
14 Therefore, mortal, prophesy,
and say to Gog: Thus says the Lord
GOD: On that day when my people
Israel are living securely, you will
rouse yourself[f] 15 and come from
your place out of the remotest
parts of the north, you and many
peoples with you, all of them riding

37.22 Isa 11.13; Jer 3.18; Hos 1.11; Ezek 34.23
37.23 Ezek 11.18; 43.7; 36.25; 36.28
37.24 Jer 30.9; Isa 40.11; Hos 3.5; Ezek 36.27
37.25 Ezek 28.25; 36.28; Zech 6.12
37.26 Isa 55.3; Ezek 36.10; 20.40; 43.7
37.27 Lev 26.11; Jn 1.14
37.28 Ezek 36.23; 20.12
38.2 Ezek 39.1; Rev 20.8
38.3 Ezek 39.1
38.4 2 Kings 19.28; Ezek 39.2
38.5 Ezek 27.10; 30.4,5
38.6 Gen 10.2; Ezek 27.14
38.7 Jer 46.3; 51.12
38.8 Isa 24.22; Ezek 36.24
38.9 Isa 28.2; Joel 2.2
38.10 Mic 2.1
38.11 Zech 2.4; Jer 49.31; v. 8
38.12 Isa 10.6; Ezek 29.19; v. 8
38.13 Ezek 27.22; 27.15; Nah 2.11-13
38.14 Jer 23.6; Zech 2.5,8
38.15 v. 6; Ezek 39.2

[a] Another reading is *from all the settlements in which they have sinned* [b] Tg: Heb *give*
[c] Or *Nubia*; Heb *Cush* [d] Heb *navel*
[e] Heb *young lions* [f] Gk: Heb *will you not know?*

on horses, a great horde, a mighty army; [16]you will come up against my people Israel, like a cloud covering the earth. In the latter days I will bring you against my land, so that the nations may know me, when through you, O Gog, I display my holiness before their eyes.

Judgment on Gog

17 Thus says the Lord GOD: Are you he of whom I spoke in former days by my servants the prophets of Israel, who in those days prophesied for years that I would bring you against them? [18]On that day, when Gog comes against the land of Israel, says the Lord GOD, my wrath shall be aroused. [19]For in my jealousy and in my blazing wrath I declare: On that day there shall be a great shaking in the land of Israel; [20]the fish of the sea, and the birds of the air, and the animals of the field, and all creeping things that creep on the ground, and all human beings that are on the face of the earth, shall quake at my presence, and the mountains shall be thrown down, and the cliffs shall fall, and every wall shall tumble to the ground. [21]I will summon the sword against Gog[g] in[h] all my mountains, says the Lord GOD; the swords of all will be against their comrades. [22]With pestilence and bloodshed I will enter into judgment with him; and I will pour down torrential rains and hailstones, fire and sulfur, upon him and his troops and the many peoples that are with him. [23]So I will display my greatness and my holiness and make myself known in the eyes of many nations. Then they shall know that I am the LORD.

Gog's Armies Destroyed

39 And you, mortal, prophesy against Gog, and say: Thus says the Lord GOD: I am against you, O Gog, chief prince of Meshech and Tubal! [2]I will turn you around and drive you forward, and bring you up from the remotest parts of the north, and lead you against the mountains of Israel. [3]I will strike your bow from your left hand, and will make your arrows drop out of your right hand. [4]You shall fall upon the mountains of Israel, you and all your troops and the peoples that are with you; I will give you to birds of prey of every kind and to the wild animals to be devoured. [5]You shall fall in the open field; for I have spoken, says the Lord GOD. [6]I will send fire on Magog and on those who live securely in the coastlands; and they shall know that I am the LORD.

7 My holy name I will make known among my people Israel; and I will not let my holy name be profaned any more; and the nations shall know that I am the LORD, the Holy One in Israel. [8]It has come! It has happened, says the Lord GOD. This is the day of which I have spoken.

9 Then those who live in the towns of Israel will go out and make fires of the weapons and burn them—bucklers and shields, bows and arrows, handpikes and spears—and they will make fires of them for seven years. [10]They will not need to take wood out of the field or cut down any trees in the forests, for they will make their fires of the weapons; they will despoil those who despoiled them, and plunder those who plundered them, says the Lord GOD.

The Burial of Gog

11 On that day I will give to Gog a place for burial in Israel, the Valley of the Travelers[i] east of the sea; it shall block the path of the travelers, for there Gog and all his horde will be buried; it shall be called the Valley of Hamon-gog.[j] [12]Seven months the house of Israel shall spend burying them, in order to cleanse the land. [13]All the people of the land shall bury them; and it will bring them honor on the day that I show my glory, says the Lord GOD. [14]They will set apart men to pass through the land regularly and

38.16 Ezek 36.23; 39.21
38.17 Isa 34.1-6
38.18 v. 2; Ps 18.8,15
38.19 Ezek 36.5,6; Nah 1.2; Hag 2.6,7; Rev 16.18
38.20 Jer 4.24; Hos 4.3; Nah 1.5,6; Zech 14.4
38.21 Ezek 14.17; Judg 7.22; 1 Sam 14.20; 2 Chr 20.23
38.22 Isa 66.16; Jer 25.31; Rev 16.21; Ps 11.6
38.23 Ezek 36.23; Ps 9.16; Ezek 37.28
39.1 Ezek 38.2-4
39.2 Ezek 38.15
39.3 Ezek 30.21-24; Hos 1.5
39.4 Ezek 38.21; 33.37
39.6 Ezek 38.22; Am 1.4; Ps 72.10; Jer 25.22
39.7 Ezek 36.20-22; v. 25; Ezek 20.39; 38.16; Isa 60.9,14
39.8 Ezek 38.17
39.9 Ps 46.9
39.10 Isa 14.2; Hab 2.8
39.11 Ezek 38.2; vv. 1,15
39.12 vv. 14,16
39.13 Jer 33.9; Ezek 28.22
39.14 Jer 14.16; v. 12

g Heb *him* h Heb *to* or *for* i Or *of the Abarim* j That is, *the Horde of Gog*

bury any invaders[k] who remain on
the face of the land, so as to
cleanse it; for seven months they
shall make their search. 15 As the
searchers[k] pass through the land,
anyone who sees a human bone
shall set up a sign by it, until the
buriers have buried it in the Valley
of Hamon-gog.[l] 16 (A city Hamo-
nah[m] is there also.) Thus they shall
cleanse the land.
17 As for you, mortal, thus says
the Lord GOD: Speak to the birds of
every kind and to all the wild animals: Assemble and come, gather
from all around to the sacrificial
feast that I am preparing for you, a
great sacrificial feast on the mountains of Israel, and you shall eat
flesh and drink blood. 18 You shall
eat the flesh of the mighty, and
drink the blood of the princes of
the earth—of rams, of lambs, and
of goats, of bulls, all of them fatlings of Bashan. 19 You shall eat fat
until you are filled, and drink blood
until you are drunk, at the sacrificial feast that I am preparing for
you. 20 And you shall be filled at my
table with horses and charioteers,[n]
with warriors and all kinds of soldiers, says the Lord GOD.

Israel Restored to the Land

21 I will display my glory among
the nations; and all the nations
shall see my judgment that I have
executed, and my hand that I have
laid on them. 22 The house of Israel
shall know that I am the LORD their
God, from that day forward. 23 And
the nations shall know that the
house of Israel went into captivity
for their iniquity, because they
dealt treacherously with me. So I
hid my face from them and gave
them into the hand of their adversaries, and they all fell by the
sword. 24 I dealt with them according to their uncleanness and their
transgressions, and hid my face
from them.
25 Therefore thus says the Lord
GOD: Now I will restore the fortunes
of Jacob, and have mercy on the
whole house of Israel; and I will be
jealous for my holy name. 26 They
shall forget[o] their shame, and all
the treachery they have practiced
against me, when they live securely
in their land with no one to make
them afraid, 27 when I have brought
them back from the peoples and
gathered them from their enemies'
lands, and through them have displayed my holiness in the sight of
many nations. 28 Then they shall
know that I am the LORD their God
because I sent them into exile
among the nations, and then gathered them into their own land. I
will leave none of them behind;
29 and I will never again hide my
face from them, when I pour out
my spirit upon the house of Israel,
says the Lord GOD.

The Vision of the New Temple

40 In the twenty-fifth year of
our exile, at the beginning
of the year, on the tenth day of the
month, in the fourteenth year after
the city was struck down, on that
very day, the hand of the LORD was
upon me, and he brought me there.
2 He brought me, in visions of God,
to the land of Israel, and set me
down upon a very high mountain,
on which was a structure like a city
to the south. 3 When he brought me
there, a man was there, whose appearance shone like bronze, with a
linen cord and a measuring reed in
his hand; and he was standing in
the gateway. 4 The man said to me,
"Mortal, look closely and listen attentively, and set your mind upon
all that I shall show you, for you
were brought here in order that I
might show it to you; declare all
that you see to the house of Israel."
5 Now there was a wall all
around the outside of the temple
area. The length of the measuring
reed in the man's hand was six long
cubits, each being a cubit and a
handbreadth in length; so he measured the thickness of the wall, one
reed; and the height, one reed.

39.15 v. 11
39.16 v. 12
39.17 v. 4; Rev 19.17; Isa 34.6,7; Jer 46.10; Zeph 1.7
39.18 Rev 19.18; Deut 32.14; Ps 22.12; Am 4.1
39.20 Ps 76.6; Ezek 38.4; Rev 19.18
39.21 Ezek 38.16, 23; v. 13
39.22 vv. 7,28
39.23 Ezek 36.18-20, 23; 20.27; v. 26; Isa 59.2; v. 29
39.24 Ezek 36.19; v. 23
39.25 Jer 30.3,18; Ezek 34.13; 36.24; 20.40; Hos 1.11
39.26 Ezek 34.25-28; Isa 17.2; Mic 4.4
39.27 Ezek 28.25, 26; 36.23,24; 38.16
39.28 Ezek 34.30; v. 22
39.29 Isa 32.15; Ezek 36.27; 37.14; Joel 2.28; Acts 2.17
40.1 Ezek 33.21; 1.2,3
40.2 Ezek 8.3; Dan 7.1,7; Ezek 17.23; Rev 21.10
40.3 Ezek 1.7; Dan 10.6; Ezek 47.3; Rev 11.1; 21.15
40.4 Ezek 44.5; 43.10; Jer 26.2; Acts 20.27
40.5 Ezek 42.20; v. 3

k Heb *travelers* l That is, *the Horde of Gog*
m That is *The Horde* n Heb *chariots*
o Another reading is *They shall bear*

6 Then he went into the gateway
facing east, going up its steps, and
measured the threshold of the
gate, one reed deep.[p] There were
7 recesses, and each recess was one
reed wide and one reed deep; and
the space between the recesses,
five cubits; and the threshold of the
gate by the vestibule of the gate at
the inner end was one reed deep.
8 Then he measured the inner vestibule of the gateway, one cubit.
9 Then he measured the vestibule
of the gateway, eight cubits; and its
pilasters, two cubits; and the vestibule of the gate was at the inner
end. 10 There were three recesses
on either side of the east gate; the
three were of the same size; and
the pilasters on either side were of
the same size. 11 Then he measured
the width of the opening of the
gateway, ten cubits; and the width
of the gateway, thirteen cubits.
12 There was a barrier before the recesses, one cubit on either side;
and the recesses were six cubits on
either side. 13 Then he measured
the gate from the back[q] of the one
recess to the back[q] of the other, a
width of twenty-five cubits, from
wall to wall.[r] 14 He measured[s]
also the vestibule, twenty cubits;
and the gate next to the pilaster on
every side of the court.[t] 15 From
the front of the gate at the entrance
to the end of the inner vestibule of
the gate was fifty cubits. 16 The recesses and their pilasters had windows, with shutters[t] on the inside
of the gateway all around, and the
vestibules also had windows on the
inside all around; and on the pilasters were palm trees.

17 Then he brought me into the
outer court; there were chambers
there, and a pavement, all around
the court; thirty chambers fronted
on the pavement. 18 The pavement
ran along the side of the gates, corresponding to the length of the
gates; this was the lower pavement.
19 Then he measured the distance
from the inner front of[u] the lower
gate to the outer front of the inner
court, one hundred cubits.[v]

20 Then he measured the gate
of the outer court that faced
north—its depth and width. 21 Its
recesses, three on either side, and
its pilasters and its vestibule were
of the same size as those of the first
gate; its depth was fifty cubits, and
its width twenty-five cubits. 22 Its
windows, its vestibule, and its
palm trees were of the same size as
those of the gate that faced toward
the east. Seven steps led up to it;
and its vestibule was on the inside.[w] 23 Opposite the gate on the
north, as on the east, was a gate to
the inner court; he measured from
gate to gate, one hundred cubits.

24 Then he led me toward the
south, and there was a gate on the
south; and he measured its pilasters and its vestibule; they had the
same dimensions as the others.
25 There were windows all around
in it and in its vestibule, like the
windows of the others; its depth
was fifty cubits, and its width
twenty-five cubits. 26 There were
seven steps leading up to it; its vestibule was on the inside.[w] It had
palm trees on its pilasters, one on
either side. 27 There was a gate on
the south of the inner court; and he
measured from gate to gate toward
the south, one hundred cubits.

28 Then he brought me to the
inner court by the south gate, and
he measured the south gate; it was
of the same dimensions as the others. 29 Its recesses, its pilasters, and
its vestibule were of the same size
as the others; and there were windows all around in it and in its vestibule; its depth was fifty cubits,
and its width twenty-five cubits.
30 There were vestibules all around,
twenty-five cubits deep and five cubits wide. 31 Its vestibule faced the
outer court, and palm trees were on
its pilasters, and its stairway had
eight steps.

32 Then he brought me to the
inner court on the east side, and he

40.6 vv. 20,26
40.7 vv. 10-16, 21,29,33,36
40.10 v. 7
40.14 vv. 9,16; 1 Chr 28.6; Isa 62.9; Ezek 42.1
40.16 1 Kings 6.4; vv. 21,22, 26,31,34,37
40.17 Rev 11.2; 1 Chr 9.26; 2 Chr 31.11; Ezek 41.6; 45.5
40.19 vv. 23,27
40.20 v. 6
40.21 vv. 7,16,30, 15,13
40.22 vv. 16,6,26, 31,34,37,49
40.23 vv. 19,27
40.24 v. 21
40.25 vv. 16,22, 21,33
40.26 vv. 6,22,16
40.27 vv. 23,32,19
40.28 vv. 32,35
40.29 vv. 7,10,21, 16,22,25
40.30 vv. 16,21,25
40.31 vv. 16,22, 26,34,37
40.32 vv. 28-31,35

[p] Heb *deep, and one threshold, one reed deep*
[q] Gk: Heb *roof*
[r] Heb *opening facing opening*
[s] Heb *made*
[t] Meaning of Heb uncertain
[u] Compare Gk: Heb *from before*
[v] Heb adds *the east and the north*
[w] Gk: Heb *before them*

measured the gate; it was of the
same size as the others. 33 Its recesses, its pilasters, and its vestibule were of the same dimensions
as the others; and there were windows all around in it and in its vestibule; its depth was fifty cubits,
and its width twenty-five cubits.
34 Its vestibule faced the outer
court, and it had palm trees on its
pilasters, on either side; and its
stairway had eight steps.
35 Then he brought me to the
north gate, and he measured it; it
had the same dimensions as the
others. 36 Its recesses, its pilasters,
and its vestibule were of the same
size as the others;[x] and it had windows all around. Its depth was fifty
cubits, and its width twenty-five
cubits. 37 Its vestibule[y] faced the
outer court, and it had palm trees
on its pilasters, on either side; and
its stairway had eight steps.
38 There was a chamber with its
door in the vestibule of the gate,[z]
where the burnt offering was to be
washed. 39 And in the vestibule of
the gate were two tables on either
side, on which the burnt offering
and the sin offering and the guilt
offering were to be slaughtered.
40 On the outside of the vestibule[a]
at the entrance of the north gate
were two tables; and on the other
side of the vestibule of the gate
were two tables. 41 Four tables were
on the inside, and four tables on
the outside of the side of the gate,
eight tables, on which the sacrifices were to be slaughtered.
42 There were also four tables of
hewn stone for the burnt offering, a
cubit and a half long, and one cubit
and a half wide, and one cubit high,
on which the instruments were to
be laid with which the burnt offerings and the sacrifices were slaughtered. 43 There were pegs, one
handbreadth long, fastened all
around the inside. And on the tables the flesh of the offering was to
be laid.
44 On the outside of the inner
gateway there were chambers for
the singers in the inner court, one[b]
at the side of the north gate facing
south, the other at the side of the
east gate facing north. 45 He said to
me, "This chamber that faces
south is for the priests who have
charge of the temple, 46 and the
chamber that faces north is for the
priests who have charge of the altar; these are the descendants of
Zadok, who alone among the descendants of Levi may come near
to the LORD to minister to him."
47 He measured the court, one hundred cubits deep, and one hundred
cubits wide, a square; and the altar
was in front of the temple.

The Temple

48 Then he brought me to the
vestibule of the temple and measured the pilasters of the vestibule,
five cubits on either side; and the
width of the gate was fourteen cubits; and the sidewalls of the gate
were three cubits[c] on either side.
49 The depth of the vestibule was
twenty cubits, and the width
twelve[d] cubits; ten steps led up[e]
to it; and there were pillars beside
the pilasters on either side.

41 Then he brought me to the
nave, and measured the pilasters; on each side six cubits was
the width of the pilasters.[f] 2 The
width of the entrance was ten cubits; and the sidewalls of the entrance were five cubits on either
side. He measured the length of
the nave, forty cubits, and its
width, twenty cubits. 3 Then he
went into the inner room and measured the pilasters of the entrance,
two cubits; and the width of the entrance, six cubits; and the sidewalls[g] of the entrance, seven cubits. 4 He measured the depth of
the room, twenty cubits, and its
width, twenty cubits, beyond the
nave. And he said to me, This is the
most holy place.
5 Then he measured the wall of

40.33 vv. 29,16,21 **40.34** vv. 16,22,37 **40.35** Ezek 44.4; 47.2 **40.36** vv. 7,29,16, 21 **40.37** vv. 16,35 **40.38** Ezek 41.10; 42.13; 2 Chr 4.6 **40.39** Lev 4.2,3; 5.6; 6.6; 7.1 **40.41** vv. 39,40 **40.42** v. 39; Ex 20.25 **40.44** vv. 23,27, 17,38; 1 Chr 6.31; 25.1-7 **40.45** vv. 17,38; Lev 8.35; 1 Chr 9.23; 2 Chr 13.11 **40.46** vv. 17,38; Num 18.5; Ezek 44.15; 43.19; 1 Kings 2.35 **40.47** vv. 19,23,27 **40.49** 1 Kings 6.3; 2 Kings 7.21; Jer 52.17-23; Rev 3.12 **41.1** Ezek 40.2,3, 17; vv. 21, 23; Ezek 40.9 **41.2** 1 Kings 6.2, 17; 2 Chr 3.3 **41.3** Ezek 40.16; v. 1 **41.4** 1 Kings 6.20; 2 Chr 3.8 **41.5** vv. 6-11

[x] One Ms: Compare verses 29 and 33: MT lacks *were of the same size as the others* [y] Gk Vg Compare verses 26, 31, 34: Heb *pilasters* [z] Cn: Heb *at the pilasters of the gates* [a] Cn: Heb *to him who goes up* [b] Heb lacks *one* [c] Gk: Heb *and the width of the gate was three cubits* [d] Gk: Heb *eleven* [e] Gk: Heb *and by steps that went up* [f] Compare Gk: Heb *tent* [g] Gk: Heb *width*

the temple, six cubits thick; and
the width of the side chambers,
four cubits, all around the temple.
6 The side chambers were in three
stories, one over another, thirty in
each story. There were offsets[h] all
around the wall of the temple to
serve as supports for the side
chambers, so that they should not
be supported by the wall of the
temple. 7 The passageway[i] of the
side chambers widened from story
to story; for the structure was supplied with a stairway all around the
temple. For this reason the structure became wider from story to
story. One ascended from the bottom story to the uppermost story by
way of the middle one. 8 I saw also
that the temple had a raised platform all around; the foundations of
the side chambers measured a full
reed of six long cubits. 9 The thickness of the outer wall of the side
chambers was five cubits; and the
free space between the side chambers of the temple 10 and the chambers of the court was a width of
twenty cubits all around the temple on every side. 11 The side chambers opened onto the area left free,
one door toward the north, and another door toward the south; and
the width of the part that was left
free was five cubits all around.
12 The building that was facing
the temple yard on the west side
was seventy cubits wide; and the
wall of the building was five cubits
thick all around, and its depth
ninety cubits.
13 Then he measured the temple, one hundred cubits deep; and
the yard and the building with its
walls, one hundred cubits deep;
14 also the width of the east front of
the temple and the yard, one hundred cubits.
15 Then he measured the depth
of the building facing the yard at
the west, together with its galleries[j] on either side, one hundred
cubits.
The nave of the temple and the
inner room and the outer[k] vestibule 16 were paneled,[l] and, all
around, all three had windows with
recessed[m] frames. Facing the
threshold the temple was paneled
with wood all around, from the
floor up to the windows (now
the windows were covered), 17 to the
space above the door, even to the
inner room, and on the outside.
And on all the walls all around in
the inner room and the nave there
was a pattern.[n] 18 It was formed of
cherubim and palm trees, a palm
tree between cherub and cherub.
Each cherub had two faces: 19 a human face turned toward the palm
tree on the one side, and the face of
a young lion turned toward the
palm tree on the other side. They
were carved on the whole temple
all around; 20 from the floor to the
area above the door, cherubim and
palm trees were carved on the
wall.[o]
21 The doorposts of the nave
were square. In front of the holy
place was something resembling
22 an altar of wood, three cubits
high, two cubits long, and two cubits wide;[p] its corners, its base,[q]
and its walls were of wood. He said
to me, "This is the table that stands
before the LORD." 23 The nave and
the holy place had each a double
door. 24 The doors had two leaves
apiece, two swinging leaves for
each door. 25 On the doors of the
nave were carved cherubim and
palm trees, such as were carved on
the walls; and there was a canopy
of wood in front of the vestibule
outside. 26 And there were recessed
windows and palm trees on either
side, on the sidewalls of the vestibule.[r]

The Holy Chambers and the Outer Wall

42 Then he led me out into
the outer court, toward the

41.6 1 Kings 6.5, 6 **41.7** 1 Kings 6.8 **41.8** Ezek 40.5 **41.9** v. 11 **41.10** Ezek 40.17 **41.11** v. 9 **41.12** vv. 13-15; Ezek 42.1 **41.13** Ezek 40.47; vv. 13-15 **41.14** Ezek 40.47 **41.15** Ezek 42.1, 10,13; 40.6; v. 25 **41.16** vv. 25,26; Ezek 40.16; v. 15; Ezek 42.3; 1 Kings 6.15
41.18 1 Kings 6.29; 7.36; Ezek 40.16; 2 Chr 3.5 **41.19** Ezek 1.10; 10.14 **41.20** v. 18 **41.21** v. 1; 1 Kings 6.33; Ezek 40.9, 14,16 **41.22** Ex 30.1; Rev 8.3; Ezek 44.16; Mal 1.7,12; Ex 30.8 **41.23** 1 Kings 6.31-35; vv. 1,4 **41.25** v. 16 **41.26** v. 16; Ezek 40.9, 16,48 **42.1** Ezek 40.17, 28; 41.1,12; vv. 10,13

h Gk Compare 1 Kings 6.6: Heb *they entered*
i Cn: Heb *it was surrounded*
j Cn: Meaning of Heb uncertain
k Gk: Heb *of the court* l Gk: Heb *the thresholds* m Cn Compare Gk 1 Kings 6.4: Meaning of Heb uncertain n Heb *measures*
o Cn Compare verse 25: Heb *and the wall*
p Gk: Heb lacks *two cubits wide*
q Gk: Heb *length* r Cn: Heb *vestibule. And the side chambers of the temple and the canopies*

north, and he brought me to
the chambers that were opposite
the temple yard and opposite the
building on the north. 2 The length
of the building that was on the
north side[s] was[t] one hundred cubits, and the width fifty cubits.
3 Across the twenty cubits that belonged to the inner court, and facing the pavement that belonged to
the outer court, the chambers
rose[u] gallery[v] by gallery[v] in three
stories. 4 In front of the chambers
was a passage on the inner side, ten
cubits wide and one hundred cubits deep,[w] and its[x] entrances
were on the north. 5 Now the upper
chambers were narrower, for the
galleries[v] took more away from
them than from the lower and middle chambers in the building. 6 For
they were in three stories, and they
had no pillars like the pillars of the
outer[y] court; for this reason the
upper chambers were set back
from the ground more than the
lower and the middle ones. 7 There
was a wall outside parallel to the
chambers, toward the outer court,
opposite the chambers, fifty cubits
long. 8 For the chambers on the
outer court were fifty cubits long,
while those opposite the temple
were one hundred cubits long. 9 At
the foot of these chambers ran a
passage that one entered from the
east in order to enter them from
the outer court. 10 The width of the
passage[z] is fixed by the wall of the
court.

On the south[a] also, opposite the
vacant area and opposite the building, there were chambers 11 with a
passage in front of them; they were
similar to the chambers on the
north, of the same length and
width, with the same exits[b] and ar-
rangements and doors. 12 So the entrances of the chambers to the
south were entered through the entrance at the head of the corresponding passage, from the east,
along the matching wall.[v]

13 Then he said to me, "The
north chambers and the south
chambers opposite the vacant area
are the holy chambers, where the
priests who approach the LORD
shall eat the most holy offerings;
there they shall deposit the most
holy offerings—the grain offering,
the sin offering, and the guilt offering, for the place is holy. 14 When
the priests enter the holy place,
they shall not go out of it into the
outer court without laying there
the vestments in which they minister, for these are holy; they shall
put on other garments before they
go near to the area open to the people."

15 When he had finished measuring the interior of the temple
area, he led me out by the gate that
faces east, and measured the temple area all around. 16 He measured
the east side with the measuring
reed, five hundred cubits by the
measuring reed. 17 Then he turned
and measured[c] the north side, five
hundred cubits by the measuring
reed. 18 Then he turned and measured[c] the south side, five hundred cubits by the measuring reed.
19 Then he turned to the west side
and measured, five hundred cubits
by the measuring reed. 20 He measured it on the four sides. It had a
wall around it, five hundred cubits
long and five hundred cubits wide,
to make a separation between the
holy and the common.

The Divine Glory Returns to the Temple

43 Then he brought me to the
gate, the gate facing east.
2 And there, the glory of the God of
Israel was coming from the east;
the sound was like the sound of
mighty waters; and the earth shone
with his glory. 3 The[d] vision I saw
was like the vision that I had seen
when he came to destroy the city,
and[e] like the vision that I had seen
by the river Chebar; and I fell upon
my face. 4 As the glory of the LORD

42.2 Ezek 41.13
42.3 Ezek 41.10, 16
42.4 Ezek 46.19
42.5 v. 3
42.6 Ezek 41.6
42.7 vv. 10,12
42.8 Ezek 41.13, 14
42.9 Ezek 44.5; 46.19
42.10 vv. 7,1,13; Ezek 40.17
42.11 v. 4
42.13 Lev 7.6; 10.13,14,17; Lev 6.25,29; Num 18.9, 10
42.14 Ezek 44.19; Ex 29.4-9; Zech 3.4,5
42.15 Ezek 40.6; 43.1
42.16 Ezek 40.3
42.20 Ezek 40.5; Zech 2.5; Ezek 45.2
43.1 Ezek 10.19; 44.1; 46.1
43.2 Ezek 11.23; 1.24; Rev 1.15; 18.1; Ezek 10.4
43.3 Ezek 1.4,28; Jer 1.10; Ezek 1.3; 3.23
43.4 Ezek 10.19; 44.2

[s] Gk: Heb *door* [t] Gk: Heb *before the length* [u] Heb lacks *the chambers rose* [v] Meaning of Heb uncertain [w] Gk Syr: Heb *a way of one cubit* [x] Heb *their* [y] Gk: Heb lacks *outer* [z] Heb lacks *of the passage* [a] Gk: Heb *east* [b] Heb *and all their exits* [c] Gk: Heb *measuring reed all around. He measured* [d] Gk: Heb *Like the vision* [e] Syr: Heb *and the visions*

entered the temple by the gate facing east, 5 the spirit lifted me up,
and brought me into the inner
court; and the glory of the LORD
filled the temple.
6 While the man was standing
beside me, I heard someone speaking to me out of the temple. 7 He
said to me: Mortal, this is the place
of my throne and the place for the
soles of my feet, where I will reside
among the people of Israel forever.
The house of Israel shall no more
defile my holy name, neither they
nor their kings, by their whoring,
and by the corpses of their kings at
their death.[f] 8 When they placed
their threshold by my threshold
and their doorposts beside my
doorposts, with only a wall between me and them, they were defiling my holy name by their abominations that they committed;
therefore I have consumed them in
my anger. 9 Now let them put away
their idolatry and the corpses of
their kings far from me, and I will
reside among them forever.
10 As for you, mortal, describe
the temple to the house of Israel,
and let them measure the pattern;
and let them be ashamed of their
iniquities. 11 When they are
ashamed of all that they have done,
make known to them the plan of
the temple, its arrangement, its exits and its entrances, and its whole
form—all its ordinances and its
entire plan and all its laws; and
write it down in their sight, so that
they may observe and follow the
entire plan and all its ordinances.
12 This is the law of the temple: the
whole territory on the top of the
mountain all around shall be most
holy. This is the law of the temple.

The Altar

13 These are the dimensions of
the altar by cubits (the cubit being
one cubit and a handbreadth): its
base shall be one cubit high,[g] and
one cubit wide, with a rim of one
span around its edge. This shall be
the height of the altar: 14 From the
base on the ground to the lower
ledge, two cubits, with a width of
one cubit; and from the smaller
ledge to the larger ledge, four cubits, with a width of one cubit;
15 and the altar hearth, four cubits;
and from the altar hearth projecting upward, four horns. 16 The altar
hearth shall be square, twelve cubits long by twelve wide. 17 The
ledge also shall be square, fourteen
cubits long by fourteen wide, with
a rim around it half a cubit wide,
and its surrounding base, one cubit. Its steps shall face east.
18 Then he said to me: Mortal,
thus says the Lord GOD: These are
the ordinances for the altar: On the
day when it is erected for offering
burnt offerings upon it and for
dashing blood against it, 19 you
shall give to the levitical priests of
the family of Zadok, who draw near
to me to minister to me, says the
Lord GOD, a bull for a sin offering.
20 And you shall take some of its
blood, and put it on the four horns
of the altar, and on the four corners
of the ledge, and upon the rim all
around; thus you shall purify it and
make atonement for it. 21 You shall
also take the bull of the sin offering, and it shall be burnt in the appointed place belonging to the
temple, outside the sacred area.
22 On the second day you shall
offer a male goat without blemish
for a sin offering; and the altar shall
be purified, as it was purified with
the bull. 23 When you have finished
purifying it, you shall offer a bull
without blemish and a ram from
the flock without blemish. 24 You
shall present them before the LORD,
and the priests shall throw salt on
them and offer them up as a burnt
offering to the LORD. 25 For seven
days you shall provide daily a goat
for a sin offering; also a bull and a
ram from the flock, without blemish, shall be provided. 26 Seven days
shall they make atonement for the
altar and cleanse it, and so consecrate it. 27 When these days are
over, then from the eighth day onward the priests shall offer upon

43.5 Ezek 3.14; 8.3; 1 Kings 8.10, 11; Ezek 44.4
43.6 Ezek 1.26; 40.3
43.7 Ps 47.8; Ezek 1.26; 37.26,28; Jer 16.18; Ezek 6.5,13
43.8 Ezek 8.3; 23.39; 44.7
43.9 Ezek 18.30, 31
43.10 Ezek 40.4; v. 11
43.11 Ezek 44.5; 12.3; 11.20; 36.27
43.12 Ezek 40.2
43.13 Ezek 40.5; 41.8
43.14 vv. 17,20; Ezek 45.19
43.15 Ex 27.2; Lev 9.9; 1 Kings 1.50
43.16 Ex 27.1
43.17 Ex 20.26; Ezek 40.6
43.18 Ezek 2.1; Ex 40.29; Lev 1.5
43.19 1 Kings 2.35; Ezek 44.15; Num 16.5, 40; v. 23; Ezek 45.18, 19
43.21 Ex 29.14; Heb 13.11
43.22 vv. 25,20,26
43.23 Ex 29.1
43.24 Lev 2.13; Mk 9.49,50; Col 4.6
43.25 Ex 29.35, 36; Lev 8.33
43.27 Lev 9.1; 3.1; 17.5; Ezek 20.40

[f] Or *on their high places* [g] Gk: Heb lacks *high*

the altar your burnt offerings and
your offerings of well-being; and I
will accept you, says the Lord GOD.

The Closed Gate

44 Then he brought me back
to the outer gate of the
sanctuary, which faces east; and it
was shut. 2 The LORD said to me:
This gate shall remain shut; it shall
not be opened, and no one shall
enter by it; for the LORD, the God of
Israel, has entered by it; therefore
it shall remain shut. 3 Only the
prince, because he is a prince, may
sit in it to eat food before the LORD;
he shall enter by way of the vestibule of the gate, and shall go out by
the same way.

Admission to the Temple

4 Then he brought me by way of
the north gate to the front of the
temple; and I looked, and lo! the
glory of the LORD filled the temple
of the LORD; and I fell upon my face.
5 The LORD said to me: Mortal, mark
well, look closely, and listen attentively to all that I shall tell you concerning all the ordinances of the
temple of the LORD and all its laws;
and mark well those who may be
admitted to[h] the temple and all
those who are to be excluded from
the sanctuary. 6 Say to the rebellious house,[i] to the house of Israel, Thus says the Lord GOD:
O house of Israel, let there be an
end to all your abominations 7 in
admitting foreigners, uncircumcised in heart and flesh, to be in my
sanctuary, profaning my temple
when you offer to me my food, the
fat and the blood. You[j] have broken my covenant with all your
abominations. 8 And you have not
kept charge of my sacred offerings;
but you have appointed foreigners[k] to act for you in keeping my
charge in my sanctuary.
9 Thus says the Lord GOD: No
foreigner, uncircumcised in heart
and flesh, of all the foreigners who
are among the people of Israel,
shall enter my sanctuary. 10 But the
Levites who went far from me, going astray from me after their idols
when Israel went astray, shall bear
their punishment. 11 They shall be
ministers in my sanctuary, having
oversight at the gates of the temple, and serving in the temple; they
shall slaughter the burnt offering
and the sacrifice for the people,
and they shall attend on them and
serve them. 12 Because they ministered to them before their idols and
made the house of Israel stumble
into iniquity, therefore I have
sworn concerning them, says the
Lord GOD, that they shall bear their
punishment. 13 They shall not
come near to me, to serve me as
priest, nor come near any of my sacred offerings, the things that are
most sacred; but they shall bear
their shame, and the consequences
of the abominations that they have
committed. 14 Yet I will appoint
them to keep charge of the temple,
to do all its chores, all that is to be
done in it.

The Levitical Priests

15 But the levitical priests, the
descendants of Zadok, who kept
the charge of my sanctuary when
the people of Israel went astray
from me, shall come near to me to
minister to me; and they shall attend me to offer me the fat and the
blood, says the Lord GOD. 16 It is
they who shall enter my sanctuary,
it is they who shall approach my table, to minister to me, and they
shall keep my charge. 17 When they
enter the gates of the inner court,
they shall wear linen vestments;
they shall have nothing of wool on
them, while they minister at the
gates of the inner court, and within. 18 They shall have linen turbans
on their heads, and linen undergarments on their loins; they shall not
bind themselves with anything that
causes sweat. 19 When they go out
into the outer court to the people,
they shall remove the vestments in
which they have been ministering,
and lay them in the holy chambers;
and they shall put on other gar-

44.1 Ezek 42.14; 43.1
44.2 Ezek 43.4
44.3 Ezek 37.25; Gen 31.54; 1 Cor 10.18; Ezek 46.2,8
44.4 Ezek 40.20, 40; 3.23; 43.5; 1.28; Rev 15.8
44.5 Ezek 40.4; 43.10,11
44.6 Ezek 2.5; 3.9; 45.9; 1 Pet 4.3
44.7 Ex 12.43-49; Lev 26.41; Deut 10.16; Jer 4.4; 9.26; Lev 22.25; Gen 17.14
44.8 Num 18.7
44.9 v. 7; Zech 14.21
44.10 2 Kings 23.8, 9; Ezek 22.26; Num 18.23
44.11 1 Chr 26.1; 2 Chr 29.34; Num 16.9
44.12 2 Kings 16.10-16; Ezek 14.3,4; Ps 106.26
44.13 Num 18.3; 2 Kings 23.9; Ezek 32.30; 39.26
44.14 Num 18.4; v. 11
44.15 Ezek 40.46; 48.11; Deut 10.8
44.16 Ezek 41.22; Mal 1.7,12
44.17 Ex 28.39, 40,43; 39.27, 28
44.18 Ex 28.40, 42; Isa 3.20
44.19 Ezek 42.14; 46.20

[h] Cn: Heb *the entrance of* [i] Gk: Heb lacks *house* [j] Gk Syr Vg: Heb *They* [k] Heb lacks *foreigners*

ments, so that they may not communicate holiness to the people
with their vestments. 20 They shall
not shave their heads or let their
locks grow long; they shall only
trim the hair of their heads. 21 No
priest shall drink wine when he enters the inner court. 22 They shall
not marry a widow, or a divorced
woman, but only a virgin of the
stock of the house of Israel, or a
widow who is the widow of a priest.
23 They shall teach my people the
difference between the holy and
the common, and show them how
to distinguish between the unclean
and the clean. 24 In a controversy
they shall act as judges, and they
shall decide it according to my
judgments. They shall keep my
laws and my statutes regarding all
my appointed festivals, and they
shall keep my sabbaths holy.
25 They shall not defile themselves
by going near to a dead person; for
father or mother, however, and for
son or daughter, and for brother or
unmarried sister they may defile
themselves. 26 After he has become
clean, they shall count seven days
for him. 27 On the day that he goes
into the holy place, into the inner
court, to minister in the holy place,
he shall offer his sin offering, says
the Lord GOD.

28 This shall be their inheritance: I am their inheritance; and
you shall give them no holding in
Israel; I am their holding. 29 They
shall eat the grain offering, the sin
offering, and the guilt offering; and
every devoted thing in Israel shall
be theirs. 30 The first of all the first
fruits of all kinds, and every offering of all kinds from all your offerings, shall belong to the priests;
you shall also give to the priests the
first of your dough, in order that a
blessing may rest on your house.
31 The priests shall not eat of anything, whether bird or animal, that
died of itself or was torn by animals.

The Holy District

45 When you allot the land as
an inheritance, you shall
set aside for the LORD a portion of
the land as a holy district, twenty-
five thousand cubits long and
twenty[l] thousand cubits wide; it
shall be holy throughout its entire
extent. 2 Of this, a square plot of
five hundred by five hundred cubits
shall be for the sanctuary, with fifty
cubits for an open space around it.
3 In the holy district you shall measure off a section twenty-five thousand cubits long and ten thousand
wide, in which shall be the sanctuary, the most holy place. 4 It shall
be a holy portion of the land; it
shall be for the priests, who minister in the sanctuary and approach
the LORD to minister to him; and it
shall be both a place for their
houses and a holy place for the
sanctuary. 5 Another section,
twenty-five thousand cubits long
and ten thousand cubits wide,
shall be for the Levites who minister at the temple, as their holding
for cities to live in.[m]

6 Alongside the portion set
apart as the holy district you shall
assign as a holding for the city an
area five thousand cubits wide, and
twenty-five thousand cubits long;
it shall belong to the whole house
of Israel.

7 And to the prince shall belong
the land on both sides of the holy
district and the holding of the city,
alongside the holy district and the
holding of the city, on the west and
on the east, corresponding in
length to one of the tribal portions,
and extending from the western to
the eastern boundary 8 of the land.
It is to be his property in Israel. And
my princes shall no longer oppress
my people; but they shall let the
house of Israel have the land according to their tribes.

9 Thus says the Lord GOD:
Enough, O princes of Israel! Put
away violence and oppression, and
do what is just and right. Cease
your evictions of my people, says
the Lord GOD.

44.20 Lev 21.5; Num 6.5
44.21 Lev 10.9
44.22 Lev 21.7,13, 14
44.23 Lev 10.10; Mal 2.7
44.24 Deut 17.8,9; Ezek 20.12, 20
44.25 Lev 21.1-3
44.26 Num 19.13-19
44.28 Num 18.20; Deut 10.9; Josh 13.14, 33
44.29 Num 18.9, 14; Lev 27.21, 28
44.30 Ex 29.19; Num 3.13; 15.20; Neh 10.37; Mal 3.10
44.31 Ex 22.31; Lev 22.8
45.1 Ezek 47.21, 22; 48.8
45.2 Ezek 42.20
45.3 Ezek 48.10
45.4 v. 1; Ezek 48.10, 11
45.5 Ezek 48.13
45.6 Ezek 48.15
45.7 Ezek 46.16-18; 48.21
45.8 Isa 11.3-5; Jer 23.5; Ezek 22.27; 46.18; Josh 11.23
45.9 Ezek 44.6; Jer 6.7; 22.3; Neh 5.1-5

[l] Gk: Heb *ten*
[m] Gk: Heb *as their holding, twenty chambers*

Weights and Measures

10 You shall have honest balances, an honest ephah, and an
honest bath.[n] 11 The ephah and the
bath shall be of the same measure,
the bath containing one-tenth of a
homer, and the ephah one-tenth of
a homer; the homer shall be the
standard measure. 12 The shekel
shall be twenty gerahs. Twenty
shekels, twenty-five shekels, and
fifteen shekels shall make a mina
for you.

Offerings

13 This is the offering that you
shall make: one-sixth of an ephah
from each homer of wheat, and
one-sixth of an ephah from each
homer of barley, 14 and as the fixed
portion of oil,[o] one-tenth of a bath
from each cor (the cor,[p] like the
homer, contains ten baths); 15 and
one sheep from every flock of two
hundred, from the pastures of Israel. This is the offering for grain offerings, burnt offerings, and offerings of well-being, to make
atonement for them, says the Lord
God. 16 All the people of the land
shall join with the prince in Israel
in making this offering. 17 But this
shall be the obligation of the prince
regarding the burnt offerings, grain
offerings, and drink offerings, at
the festivals, the new moons, and
the sabbaths, all the appointed festivals of the house of Israel: he
shall provide the sin offerings,
grain offerings, the burnt offerings,
and the offerings of well-being, to
make atonement for the house of
Israel.

Festivals

18 Thus says the Lord God: In
the first month, on the first day of
the month, you shall take a young
bull without blemish, and purify
the sanctuary. 19 The priest shall
take some of the blood of the sin
offering and put it on the doorposts
of the temple, the four corners of
the ledge of the altar, and the posts
of the gate of the inner court. 20 You
shall do the same on the seventh
day of the month for anyone who
has sinned through error or ignorance; so you shall make atonement for the temple.

21 In the first month, on the
fourteenth day of the month, you
shall celebrate the festival of the
passover, and for seven days unleavened bread shall be eaten.
22 On that day the prince shall provide for himself and all the people
of the land a young bull for a sin
offering. 23 And during the seven
days of the festival he shall provide
as a burnt offering to the Lord sev-
en young bulls and seven rams
without blemish, on each of the
seven days; and a male goat daily
for a sin offering. 24 He shall provide as a grain offering an ephah for
each bull, an ephah for each ram,
and a hin of oil to each ephah. 25 In
the seventh month, on the fifteenth day of the month and for the
seven days of the festival, he shall
make the same provision for sin offerings, burnt offerings, and grain
offerings, and for the oil.

Miscellaneous Regulations

46 Thus says the Lord God:
The gate of the inner court
that faces east shall remain closed
on the six working days; but on the
sabbath day it shall be opened and
on the day of the new moon it shall
be opened. 2 The prince shall enter
by the vestibule of the gate from
outside, and shall take his stand by
the post of the gate. The priests
shall offer his burnt offering and
his offerings of well-being, and he
shall bow down at the threshold of
the gate. Then he shall go out, but
the gate shall not be closed until
evening. 3 The people of the land
shall bow down at the entrance of
that gate before the Lord on the
sabbaths and on the new moons.
4 The burnt offering that the prince
offers to the Lord on the sabbath
day shall be six lambs without
blemish and a ram without blemish; 5 and the grain offering with the
ram shall be an ephah, and the
grain offering with the lambs shall

45.10 Lev 19.35, 36; Prov 11.1 **45.11** Isa 5.10 **45.12** Ex 30.13; Lev 27.25; Num 3.47 **45.15** v. 17; Lev 1.4; 6.30 **45.17** Ezek 46.4-12; 1 Kings 8.64; 2 Chr 31.3; Lev 23.1-44; Ezek 43.27 **45.18** Ezek 46.1,3, 6; Lev 16.16 **45.19** Ezek 43.20 **45.20** Lev 4.27; 16.20; vv. 15,18

45.21 Ex 12.18; Lev 23.5,6; Num 9.2,3; 28.16,17 **45.22** Lev 4.14 **45.23** Lev 23.8; Num 28.16-25; Job 42.8 **45.25** Lev 23.34; Num 29.12; Deut 16.13 **46.1** Ezek 45.17-19 **46.2** v. 8; Ezek 44.3; 45.9; v. 12 **46.3** Lk 1.10; v. 1 **46.4** Ezek 45.17 **46.5** Ezek 45.24; vv. 7,11

[n] A Heb measure of volume [o] Cn: Heb *oil, the bath the oil* [p] Vg: Heb *homer*

be as much as he wishes to give,
together with a hin of oil to each
ephah. 6 On the day of the new
moon he shall offer a young bull
without blemish, and six lambs
and a ram, which shall be without
blemish; 7 as a grain offering he
shall provide an ephah with the
bull and an ephah with the ram,
and with the lambs as much as he
wishes, together with a hin of oil to
each ephah. 8 When the prince enters, he shall come in by the vestibule of the gate, and he shall go out
by the same way.
9 When the people of the land
come before the LORD at the appointed festivals, whoever enters
by the north gate to worship shall
go out by the south gate; and whoever enters by the south gate shall
go out by the north gate: they shall
not return by way of the gate by
which they entered, but shall go
out straight ahead. 10 When they
come in, the prince shall come in
with them; and when they go out,
he shall go out.
11 At the festivals and the appointed seasons the grain offering
with a young bull shall be an
ephah, and with a ram an ephah,
and with the lambs as much as one
wishes to give, together with a hin
of oil to an ephah. 12 When the
prince provides a freewill offering,
either a burnt offering or offerings
of well-being as a freewill offering
to the LORD, the gate facing east
shall be opened for him; and he
shall offer his burnt offering or his
offerings of well-being as he does
on the sabbath day. Then he shall
go out, and after he has gone out
the gate shall be closed.
13 He shall provide a lamb, a
yearling, without blemish, for a
burnt offering to the LORD daily;
morning by morning he shall provide it. 14 And he shall provide a
grain offering with it morning by
morning regularly, one-sixth of an
ephah, and one-third of a hin of oil
to moisten the choice flour, as a
grain offering to the LORD; this is
the ordinance for all time. 15 Thus
the lamb and the grain offering and
the oil shall be provided, morning
by morning, as a regular burnt offering.
16 Thus says the Lord GOD: If
the prince makes a gift to any of his
sons out of his inheritance,[q] it
shall belong to his sons, it is their
holding by inheritance. 17 But if he
makes a gift out of his inheritance
to one of his servants, it shall be his
to the year of liberty; then it shall
revert to the prince; only his sons
may keep a gift from his inheritance. 18 The prince shall not take
any of the inheritance of the people, thrusting them out of their
holding; he shall give his sons their
inheritance out of his own holding,
so that none of my people shall be
dispossessed of their holding.
19 Then he brought me through
the entrance, which was at the side
of the gate, to the north row of the
holy chambers for the priests; and
there I saw a place at the extreme
western end of them. 20 He said to
me, "This is the place where the
priests shall boil the guilt offering
and the sin offering, and where
they shall bake the grain offering,
in order not to bring them out into
the outer court and so communicate holiness to the people."
21 Then he brought me out to
the outer court, and led me past
the four corners of the court; and in
each corner of the court there was
a court— 22 in the four corners of
the court were small[r] courts, forty
cubits long and thirty wide; the
four were of the same size. 23 On
the inside, around each of the four
courts[s] was a row of masonry, with
hearths made at the bottom of the
rows all around. 24 Then he said to
me, "These are the kitchens where
those who serve at the temple shall
boil the sacrifices of the people."

Water Flowing from the Temple

47 Then he brought me back
to the entrance of the temple; there, water was flowing from

46.6 v. 1 **46.7** v. 5 **46.8** Ezek 44.3; v. 2 **46.9** Ex 23.14-17; Deut 16.16 **46.11** Ezek 45.17; vv. 5,7 **46.12** 2 Chr 29.31; Ezek 44.3; v. 2; Ezek 45.17 **46.13** Ex 29.38; Num 28.3; Isa 50.4 **46.14** Num 28.5 **46.15** Ex 29.42; Num 28.6

46.16 2 Chr 21.3 **46.17** Lev 27.10 **46.18** Ezek 45.8; Mic 2.1,2; Ezek 34.3-6, 21 **46.19** Ezek 42.9, 13 **46.20** 2 Chr 35.13; Lev 2.4,5,7; Ezek 44.19 **46.24** Ezek 44.11; v. 20 **47.1** Jer 2.13; Joel 3.18; Zech 13.1; 14.8; Rev 22.1

[q] Gk: Heb *it is his inheritance*
[r] Gk Syr Vg: Meaning of Heb uncertain
[s] Heb *the four of them*

below the threshold of the temple
toward the east (for the temple
faced east); and the water was flowing down from below the south end
of the threshold of the temple,
south of the altar. 2 Then he
brought me out by way of the north
gate, and led me around on the
outside to the outer gate that faces
toward the east;[t] and the water
was coming out on the south side.
3 Going on eastward with a cord
in his hand, the man measured one
thousand cubits, and then led me
through the water; and it was
ankle-deep. 4 Again he measured
one thousand, and led me through
the water; and it was knee-deep.
Again he measured one thousand,
and led me through the water; and
it was up to the waist. 5 Again he
measured one thousand, and it was
a river that I could not cross, for the
water had risen; it was deep
enough to swim in, a river that
could not be crossed. 6 He said to
me, "Mortal, have you seen this?"
Then he led me back along the
bank of the river. 7 As I came back,
I saw on the bank of the river a
great many trees on the one side
and on the other. 8 He said to me,
"This water flows toward the eastern region and goes down into the
Arabah; and when it enters the sea,
the sea of stagnant waters, the water will become fresh. 9 Wherever
the river goes,[u] every living creature that swarms will live, and
there will be very many fish, once
these waters reach there. It will become fresh; and everything will live
where the river goes. 10 People will
stand fishing beside the sea[v] from
En-gedi to En-eglaim; it will be a
place for the spreading of nets; its
fish will be of a great many kinds,
like the fish of the Great Sea. 11 But
its swamps and marshes will not
become fresh; they are to be left for
salt. 12 On the banks, on both sides
of the river, there will grow all
kinds of trees for food. Their leaves
will not wither nor their fruit fail,
but they will bear fresh fruit every
month, because the water for them
flows from the sanctuary. Their
fruit will be for food, and their
leaves for healing."

The New Boundaries of the Land

13 Thus says the Lord GOD:
These are the boundaries by which
you shall divide the land for inheritance among the twelve tribes of Israel. Joseph shall have two portions. 14 You shall divide it equally;
I swore to give it to your ancestors,
and this land shall fall to you as
your inheritance.
15 This shall be the boundary of
the land: On the north side, from
the Great Sea by way of Hethlon to
Lebo-hamath, and on to Zedad,[w]
16 Berothah, Sibraim (which lies
between the border of Damascus
and the border of Hamath), as far
as Hazer-hatticon, which is on the
border of Hauran. 17 So the boundary shall run from the sea to Hazar-
enon, which is north of the border
of Damascus, with the border of
Hamath to the north.[t] This shall
be the north side.
18 On the east side, between
Hauran and Damascus; along the
Jordan between Gilead and the
land of Israel; to the eastern sea
and as far as Tamar.[x] This shall be
the east side.
19 On the south side, it shall
run from Tamar as far as the waters
of Meribath-kadesh, from there
along the Wadi of Egypt[y] to the
Great Sea. This shall be the south
side.
20 On the west side, the Great
Sea shall be the boundary to a
point opposite Lebo-hamath. This
shall be the west side.
21 So you shall divide this land
among you according to the tribes
of Israel. 22 You shall allot it as an
inheritance for yourselves and for
the aliens who reside among you
and have begotten children among
you. They shall be to you as citi-

47.2 Ezek 44.1,2, 4
47.3 Ezek 40.3
47.5 Isa 11.9; Hab 2.14
47.6 Ezek 2.1; 8.6; 40.4; 44.5
47.7 v. 12; Rev 22.2
47.8 Deut 3.17; Isa 35.6,7; Josh 3.16
47.9 Jn 4.14; 7.37,38; Rev 21.7
47.10 Gen 14.7; 2 Chr 20.2; Ezek 26.5, 14; Num 34.6; Josh 23.4; Ezek 48.28
47.12 v. 7; Job 8.16; Ps 1.3; Jer 17.8; Rev 22.2
47.13 Num 34.2-12; Gen 48.5; 1 Chr 5.1; Ezek 48.4
47.14 Gen 12.7; Deut 1.8; Ezek 20.5,6
47.15 Num 34.8; Ezek 48.1
47.16 vv. 17,20; Ezek 48.1; v. 18
47.17 Num 34.9; Ezek 48.1; v. 16
47.18 v. 16; Jer 50.19; Gen 13.10, 11
47.19 Ezek 48.28; Deut 32.51; Isa 27.12
47.20 Num 34.6; vv. 10,15; Ezek 48.1; Am 6.14
47.22 Num 26.55, 56; Isa 56.6, 7; Rom 10.12; Eph 2.12-14; 3.6; Col 3.11

[t] Meaning of Heb uncertain [u] Gk Syr Vg Tg: Heb *the two rivers go* [v] Heb *it* [w] Gk: Heb *Lebo-zedad, 16Hamath* [x] Compare Syr: Heb *you shall measure* [y] Heb lacks *of Egypt*

zens of Israel; with you they shall be allotted an inheritance among the tribes of Israel. 23 In whatever tribe aliens reside, there you shall assign them their inheritance, says the Lord GOD.

The Tribal Portions

48 These are the names of the tribes: Beginning at the northern border, on the Hethlon road,[z] from Lebo-hamath, as far as Hazar-enon (which is on the border of Damascus, with Hamath to the north), and[a] extending from the east side to the west,[b] Dan, one portion. 2 Adjoining the territory of Dan, from the east side to the west, Asher, one portion. 3 Adjoining the territory of Asher, from the east side to the west, Naphtali, one portion. 4 Adjoining the territory of Naphtali, from the east side to the west, Manasseh, one portion. 5 Adjoining the territory of Manasseh, from the east side to the west, Ephraim, one portion. 6 Adjoining the territory of Ephraim, from the east side to the west, Reuben, one portion. 7 Adjoining the territory of Reuben, from the east side to the west, Judah, one portion.

8 Adjoining the territory of Judah, from the east side to the west, shall be the portion that you shall set apart, twenty-five thousand cubits in width, and in length equal to one of the tribal portions, from the east side to the west, with the sanctuary in the middle of it. 9 The portion that you shall set apart for the LORD shall be twenty-five thousand cubits in length, and twenty[c] thousand in width. 10 These shall be the allotments of the holy portion: the priests shall have an allotment measuring twenty-five thousand cubits on the northern side, ten thousand cubits in width on the western side, ten thousand in width on the eastern side, and twenty-five thousand in length on the southern side, with the sanctuary of the LORD in the middle of it. 11 This shall be for the consecrated priests, the descendants[d] of Zadok, who kept my charge, who did not go astray when the people of Israel went astray, as the Levites did. 12 It shall belong to them as a special portion from the holy portion of the land, a most holy place, adjoining the territory of the Levites. 13 Alongside the territory of the priests, the Levites shall have an allotment twenty-five thousand cubits in length and ten thousand in width. The whole length shall be twenty-five thousand cubits and the width twenty[e] thousand. 14 They shall not sell or exchange any of it; they shall not transfer this choice portion of the land, for it is holy to the LORD.

15 The remainder, five thousand cubits in width and twenty-five thousand in length, shall be for ordinary use for the city, for dwellings and for open country. In the middle of it shall be the city; 16 and these shall be its dimensions: the north side four thousand five hundred cubits, the south side four thousand five hundred, the east side four thousand five hundred, and the west side four thousand and five hundred. 17 The city shall have open land: on the north two hundred fifty cubits, on the south two hundred fifty, on the east two hundred fifty, on the west two hundred fifty. 18 The remainder of the length alongside the holy portion shall be ten thousand cubits to the east, and ten thousand to the west, and it shall be alongside the holy portion. Its produce shall be food for the workers of the city. 19 The workers of the city, from all the tribes of Israel, shall cultivate it. 20 The whole portion that you shall set apart shall be twenty-five thousand cubits square, that is, the holy portion together with the property of the city.

21 What remains on both sides of the holy portion and of the property of the city shall belong to the

48.1 Ezek 47.15-17, 20; Josh 19.40-48
48.2 Josh 19.24-31
48.3 Josh 19.32-39
48.4 Josh 13.29-31; 17.1-11
48.5 Josh 16.5-9; 17.8-10,14-18
48.6 Josh 13.15-21
48.7 Josh 15.1-63
48.8 Ezek 45.1-6
48.10 Ezek 44.28; 45.4; v. 8
48.11 Ezek 44.15, 10,12
48.12 Ezek 45.4
48.13 Ezek 45.3
48.14 Lev 25.32-34
48.15 Ezek 42.20; 45.6
48.16 Rev 21.16
48.17 Ezek 45.2
48.18 v. 8
48.19 Ezek 45.6
48.20 v. 16
48.21 Ezek 34.24; 45.7; vv. 22, 8,10

[z] Compare 47.15: Heb *by the side of the way* [a] Cn: Heb *and they shall be his* [b] Gk Compare verses 2-8: Heb *the east side the west* [c] Compare 45.1: Heb *ten* [d] One Ms Gk: Heb *of the descendants* [e] Gk: Heb *ten*

prince. Extending from the twenty-
five thousand cubits of the holy
portion to the east border, and
westward from the twenty-five
thousand cubits to the west border,
parallel to the tribal portions, it
shall belong to the prince. The holy
portion with the sanctuary of the
temple in the middle of it, 22 and
the property of the Levites and of
the city, shall be in the middle of
that which belongs to the prince.
The portion of the prince shall lie
between the territory of Judah and
the territory of Benjamin.

23 As for the rest of the tribes:
from the east side to the west, Benjamin, one portion. 24 Adjoining the
territory of Benjamin, from the east
side to the west, Simeon, one portion. 25 Adjoining the territory of
Simeon, from the east side to the
west, Issachar, one portion. 26 Adjoining the territory of Issachar,
from the east side to the west, Zebulun, one portion. 27 Adjoining the
territory of Zebulun, from the east
side to the west, Gad, one portion.
28 And adjoining the territory of
Gad to the south, the boundary
shall run from Tamar to the waters
of Meribath-kadesh, from there
along the Wadi of Egypt[f] to the
Great Sea. 29 This is the land that
you shall allot as an inheritance
among the tribes of Israel, and
these are their portions, says the
Lord GOD.

30 These shall be the exits of
the city: On the north side, which is
to be four thousand five hundred
cubits by measure, 31 three gates,
the gate of Reuben, the gate of Judah, and the gate of Levi, the gates
of the city being named after the
tribes of Israel. 32 On the east side,
which is to be four thousand five
hundred cubits, three gates, the
gate of Joseph, the gate of Benjamin, and the gate of Dan. 33 On the
south side, which is to be four
thousand five hundred cubits by
measure, three gates, the gate of
Simeon, the gate of Issachar, and
the gate of Zebulun. 34 On the west
side, which is to be four thousand
five hundred cubits, three gates,[g]
the gate of Gad, the gate of Asher,
and the gate of Naphtali. 35 The circumference of the city shall be
eighteen thousand cubits. And the
name of the city from that time on
shall be, The LORD is There.

48.23 vv. 1-7; Josh 18.21-28
48.24 Josh 19.1-9
48.25 Josh 19.17-23
48.26 Josh 19.10-16
48.27 Josh 13.24-28
48.28 Ezek 47.19, 20
48.29 Ezek 47.13-20
48.30 vv. 31-34
48.31 Rev 21.12, 13
48.35 Jer 23.6; 33.16; 3.17; Joel 3.21; Zech 2.10; Rev 21.3; 22.3

[f] Heb lacks *of Egypt* [g] One Ms Gk Syr: MT *their gates three*

Daniel

Title and Background

This book is named after the prophet whose ministry it records. Daniel recounts events that took place during Israel's captivity in Babylon.

Author and Date of Writing

In several passages, such as 9.2 and 10.2, the book itself mentions Daniel as the author. Jesus himself referred to Daniel as the author (Mt 24.15). This would indicate that the book was written about 530 B.C., shortly after the capture of Babylon by Cyrus in 539. Not all scholars agree with this date, however.

Theme and Message

The theological theme of the book is God's sovereignty: "the Most High God has sovereignty over the kingdom of mortals" (5.21). Daniel's visions always show God as triumphant. The prophet encourages the people to trust in the God who controls all history; by depending on him they would experience victory over their enemies.

Outline

I. Introduction: The Setting (1.1-21)
II. The Destinies of the Nations (2.1–7.28)
  A. Nebuchadnezzar's Dreams (2.1–4.37)
  B. Belshazzar's and Babylon's Downfall (5.1-31)
  C. Daniel's Deliverance and Dream (6.1–7.28)
III. The Destiny of Israel (8.1–12.13)
  A. Daniel's Vision of a Ram and a Goat (8.1-27)
  B. Daniel's Prayer and the Seventy "Sevens" (9.1-27)
  C. Daniel's Vision of Israel's Future (10.1–12.13)

Four Young Israelites at the Babylonian Court

1 In the third year of the reign of
King Jehoiakim of Judah,
King Nebuchadnezzar of Babylon
came to Jerusalem and besieged it.
2 The Lord let King Jehoiakim of
Judah fall into his power, as well as
some of the vessels of the house of
God. These he brought to the land
of Shinar,[a] and placed the vessels
in the treasury of his gods.
3 Then the king commanded his
palace master Ashpenaz to bring
some of the Israelites of the royal
family and of the nobility, 4 young
men without physical defect and
handsome, versed in every branch
of wisdom, endowed with knowledge
and insight, and competent to
serve in the king's palace; they
were to be taught the literature and
language of the Chaldeans. 5 The
king assigned them a daily portion
of the royal rations of food and
wine. They were to be educated for
three years, so that at the end of
that time they could be stationed
in the king's court. 6 Among them
were Daniel, Hananiah, Mishael,
and Azariah, from the tribe of Judah.
7 The palace master gave them
other names: Daniel he called Belteshazzar,
Hananiah he called Shadrach,
Mishael he called Meshach,
and Azariah he called Abednego.
8 But Daniel resolved that he
would not defile himself with the

1.1 2 Kings 24.1; 2 Chr 36.6
1.2 Jer 27.19, 20; Isa 11.11; Zech 5.11
1.3 2 Kings 20.17, 18; Isa 39.7
1.4 2 Sam 14.25; Dan 2.4
1.5ff vv. 8,18; 1 Kings 10.8; v. 19
1.6 Ezek 14.14, 20; 28.3
1.7 Dan 4.8; 5.12; 2.49; 3.12
1.8 Deut 32.38; Ezek 4.13; Hos 9.3

[a] Gk Theodotion: Heb adds *to the house of his own gods*

royal rations of food and wine; so
he asked the palace master to allow him not to defile himself.
9 Now God allowed Daniel to receive favor and compassion from
the palace master. 10 The palace
master said to Daniel, "I am afraid
of my lord the king; he has appointed your food and your drink. If he
should see you in poorer condition
than the other young men of your
own age, you would endanger my
head with the king." 11 Then Daniel
asked the guard whom the palace
master had appointed over Daniel,
Hananiah, Mishael, and Azariah:
12 "Please test your servants for ten
days. Let us be given vegetables to
eat and water to drink. 13 You can
then compare our appearance with
the appearance of the young men
who eat the royal rations, and deal
with your servants according to
what you observe." 14 So he agreed
to this proposal and tested them
for ten days. 15 At the end of ten
days it was observed that they appeared better and fatter than all
the young men who had been eating the royal rations. 16 So the
guard continued to withdraw their
royal rations and the wine they
were to drink, and gave them vegetables. 17 To these four young men
God gave knowledge and skill in
every aspect of literature and wisdom; Daniel also had insight into
all visions and dreams.

18 At the end of the time that
the king had set for them to be
brought in, the palace master
brought them into the presence of
Nebuchadnezzar, 19 and the king
spoke with them. And among them
all, no one was found to compare
with Daniel, Hananiah, Mishael,
and Azariah; therefore they were
stationed in the king's court. 20 In
every matter of wisdom and understanding concerning which the
king inquired of them, he found
them ten times better than all the
magicians and enchanters in his
whole kingdom. 21 And Daniel continued there until the first year of
King Cyrus.

1.9 Job 5.15,16; Ps 106.46; Prov 16.7
1.10 v. 7
1.12 v. 16
1.15 Ex 23.25; Prov 10.22
1.16 v. 12
1.17 1 Kings 3.12; Jas 1.5,17; Dan 2.19; 7.1; 8.1
1.18 vv. 5,3,7
1.19 Gen 41.46; 1 Kings 10.8; Jer 15.1
1.20 Dan 2.27, 28,46,48; 2.2
1.21 Dan 6.28; 10.1
2.1 Gen 41.8; Dan 4.5; Esther 6.1; Dan 6.18
2.2 Gen 41.8; Ex 7.11; vv. 10,27; Dan 5.7
2.3 Gen 40.8; 41.15; Dan 4.5
2.4 Isa 36.11; 1 Kings 1.31; Dan 3.9; 5.10; 6.6,21
2.5 Ezra 6.11; v. 12; Dan 3.29
2.6 Dan 5.7,16, 29
2.7 v. 4
2.9 Esther 4.11; Isa 41.23
2.10 v. 27
2.11 Dan 5.11; Isa 57.15
2.12 v. 5

Nebuchadnezzar's Dream

2 In the second year of Nebuchadnezzar's reign, Nebu-
chadnezzar dreamed such dreams
that his spirit was troubled and his
sleep left him. 2 So the king commanded that the magicians, the
enchanters, the sorcerers, and the
Chaldeans be summoned to tell
the king his dreams. When they
came in and stood before the king,
3 he said to them, "I have had such
a dream that my spirit is troubled
by the desire to understand it."
4 The Chaldeans said to the king (in
Aramaic),[b] "O king, live forever!
Tell your servants the dream, and
we will reveal the interpretation."
5 The king answered the Chaldeans, "This is a public decree: if you
do not tell me both the dream and
its interpretation, you shall be torn
limb from limb, and your houses
shall be laid in ruins. 6 But if you do
tell me the dream and its interpretation, you shall receive from me
gifts and rewards and great honor.
Therefore tell me the dream and its
interpretation." 7 They answered a
second time, "Let the king first tell
his servants the dream, then we
can give its interpretation." 8 The
king answered, "I know with certainty that you are trying to gain
time, because you see I have firmly
decreed: 9 if you do not tell me the
dream, there is but one verdict for
you. You have agreed to speak lying
and misleading words to me until
things take a turn. Therefore, tell
me the dream, and I shall know
that you can give me its interpretation." 10 The Chaldeans answered
the king, "There is no one on earth
who can reveal what the king demands! In fact no king, however
great and powerful, has ever asked
such a thing of any magician or enchanter or Chaldean. 11 The thing
that the king is asking is too difficult, and no one can reveal it to the
king except the gods, whose dwelling is not with mortals."

12 Because of this the king flew

[b] The text from this point to the end of chapter 7 is in Aramaic

into a violent rage and commanded
that all the wise men of Babylon be
destroyed. 13 The decree was issued, and the wise men were about
to be executed; and they looked for
Daniel and his companions, to execute them. 14 Then Daniel responded with prudence and discretion to
Arioch, the king's chief executioner, who had gone out to execute
the wise men of Babylon; 15 he
asked Arioch, the royal official,
"Why is the decree of the king so
urgent?" Arioch then explained the
matter to Daniel. 16 So Daniel went
in and requested that the king give
him time and he would tell the king
the interpretation.

God Reveals Nebuchadnezzar's Dream

17 Then Daniel went to his
home and informed his companions, Hananiah, Mishael, and Azariah, 18 and told them to seek mercy
from the God of heaven concerning
this mystery, so that Daniel and his
companions with the rest of the
wise men of Babylon might not perish. 19 Then the mystery was revealed to Daniel in a vision of the
night, and Daniel blessed the God
of heaven.

20 Daniel said:

"Blessed be the name of God
    from age to age,
  for wisdom and power are
    his.
21 He changes times and
    seasons,
  deposes kings and sets up
    kings;
  he gives wisdom to the wise
    and knowledge to those
    who have
    understanding.
22 He reveals deep and hidden
    things;
  he knows what is in the
    darkness,
  and light dwells with him.
23 To you, O God of my
    ancestors,
  I give thanks and praise,
  for you have given me
    wisdom and power,
  and have now revealed to
    me what we asked of you,
  for you have revealed to us
    what the king ordered."

Daniel Interprets the Dream

24 Therefore Daniel went to Arioch, whom the king had appointed
to destroy the wise men of Babylon, and said to him, "Do not destroy the wise men of Babylon;
bring me in before the king, and I
will give the king the interpretation."

25 Then Arioch quickly brought
Daniel before the king and said to
him: "I have found among the exiles from Judah a man who can tell
the king the interpretation." 26 The
king said to Daniel, whose name
was Belteshazzar, "Are you able to
tell me the dream that I have seen
and its interpretation?" 27 Daniel
answered the king, "No wise men,
enchanters, magicians, or diviners
can show to the king the mystery
that the king is asking, 28 but there
is a God in heaven who reveals
mysteries, and he has disclosed to
King Nebuchadnezzar what will
happen at the end of days. Your
dream and the visions of your head
as you lay in bed were these: 29 To
you, O king, as you lay in bed,
came thoughts of what would be
hereafter, and the revealer of mysteries disclosed to you what is to
be. 30 But as for me, this mystery
has not been revealed to me because of any wisdom that I have
more than any other living being,
but in order that the interpretation
may be known to the king and that
you may understand the thoughts
of your mind.

31 "You were looking, O king,
and lo! there was a great statue.
This statue was huge, its brilliance
extraordinary; it was standing before you, and its appearance was
frightening. 32 The head of that
statue was of fine gold, its chest
and arms of silver, its middle and
thighs of bronze, 33 its legs of iron,
its feet partly of iron and partly of
clay. 34 As you looked on, a stone

2.13 Dan 1.19,20
2.14 v. 24; Jer 52.12,14
2.15 Dan 3.22; vv. 1-12
2.16 Dan 1.19
2.18 Isa 37.4; Jer 33.3; Dan 9.9
2.19 vv. 22, 27-29; Num 12.6; Job 33.15, 16
2.20 Ps 113.2; Jer 32.19; vv. 21-23
2.21 Esther 1.13; Dan 7.25; Job 12.18; Ps 75.6,7; Jas 1.5
2.22 Job 12.22; Ps 25.14; 139.11,12; Isa 45.7; Jer 23.24; Dan 5.11, 14; Jas 1.17
2.23 Gen 31.42; v. 21; Dan 1.17; vv. 18,29,30
2.24 vv. 12-14
2.25 Gen 41.14; Dan 1.6; 5.13; 6.13
2.26 Dan 1.7; vv. 3-7
2.27 vv. 2,10
2.28 Gen 40.8; 41.16; 49.1; Isa 2.2; Mic 4.1; Dan 4.5
2.29 vv. 22,28
2.30 Gen 41.16; Isa 45.3; Ps 139.2
2.31 Dan 7.7; Hab 1.7
2.32 vv. 38,39
2.33 vv. 40-43
2.34 Dan 8.25; Zech 4.6; Isa 2.9; 60.12

was cut out, not by human hands,
and it struck the statue on its feet
of iron and clay and broke them in
pieces. 35 Then the iron, the clay,
the bronze, the silver, and the gold,
were all broken in pieces and became like the chaff of the summer
threshing floors; and the wind carried them away, so that not a trace
of them could be found. But the
stone that struck the statue became a great mountain and filled
the whole earth.
36 "This was the dream; now we
will tell the king its interpretation.
37 You, O king, the king of kings—
to whom the God of heaven has giv-
en the kingdom, the power, the
might, and the glory, 38 into whose
hand he has given human beings,
wherever they live, the wild animals of the field, and the birds of
the air, and whom he has established as ruler over them all—you
are the head of gold. 39 After you
shall arise another kingdom inferi-
or to yours, and yet a third kingdom
of bronze, which shall rule over the
whole earth. 40 And there shall be a
fourth kingdom, strong as iron; just
as iron crushes and smashes everything,[c] it shall crush and shatter
all these. 41 As you saw the feet and
toes partly of potter's clay and partly of iron, it shall be a divided kingdom; but some of the strength of
iron shall be in it, as you saw the
iron mixed with the clay. 42 As the
toes of the feet were part iron and
part clay, so the kingdom shall be
partly strong and partly brittle.
43 As you saw the iron mixed with
clay, so will they mix with one another in marriage,[d] but they will
not hold together, just as iron does
not mix with clay. 44 And in the
days of those kings the God of
heaven will set up a kingdom that
shall never be destroyed, nor shall
this kingdom be left to another
people. It shall crush all these
kingdoms and bring them to an
end, and it shall stand forever;
45 just as you saw that a stone was
cut from the mountain not by
hands, and that it crushed the iron,
the bronze, the clay, the silver, and

2.35 Ps 1.4; Hos 13.3; Ps 37.10,36; Isa 2.2,3
2.36 v. 24
2.37 Isa 47.5; Jer 27.6,7; Ezek 26.7; Ezra 1.2; Ps 62.11
2.38 Jer 27.6; Dan 4.21, 22; v. 32
2.39 v. 32
2.40 Dan 7.7,23
2.41 v. 33
2.44 Ps 2.9; Isa 60.12; 1 Cor 15.24
2.45 Isa 28.16; v. 35; Dan 8.25; v. 29; Mal 1.11; Gen 41.28, 32
2.46 Dan 8.17; Acts 10.25; 14.13; 28.6; Rev 19.10
2.47 Dan 11.36; vv. 22,28
2.48 v. 6; Dan 4.9; 5.11
2.49 Dan 3.12; Esther 2.19, 21; Dan 3.2
3.1 Isa 46.6; Hab 2.19; v. 30; Dan 2.48
3.2 vv. 3,27
3.4 Isa 40.9; 58.1; Rev 18.2; Dan 4.1; 6.25
3.5 vv. 7,10,15

the gold. The great God has informed the king what shall be hereafter. The dream is certain, and its
interpretation trustworthy."

Daniel and His Friends Promoted

46 Then King Nebuchadnezzar
fell on his face, worshiped Daniel,
and commanded that a grain offering and incense be offered to him.
47 The king said to Daniel, "Truly,
your God is God of gods and Lord of
kings and a revealer of mysteries,
for you have been able to reveal
this mystery!" 48 Then the king promoted Daniel, gave him many great
gifts, and made him ruler over the
whole province of Babylon and
chief prefect over all the wise men
of Babylon. 49 Daniel made a request of the king, and he appointed
Shadrach, Meshach, and Abednego
over the affairs of the province of
Babylon. But Daniel remained at
the king's court.

The Golden Image

3 King Nebuchadnezzar made a
golden statue whose height
was sixty cubits and whose width
was six cubits; he set it up on the
plain of Dura in the province of
Babylon. 2 Then King Nebuchadnezzar sent for the satraps, the prefects, and the governors, the counselors, the treasurers, the justices,
the magistrates, and all the officials of the provinces to assemble
and come to the dedication of the
statue that King Nebuchadnezzar
had set up. 3 So the satraps, the
prefects, and the governors, the
counselors, the treasurers, the justices, the magistrates, and all the
officials of the provinces, assembled for the dedication of the statue that King Nebuchadnezzar had
set up. When they were standing
before the statue that Nebuchadnezzar had set up, 4 the herald proclaimed aloud, "You are commanded, O peoples, nations, and
languages, 5 that when you hear the
sound of the horn, pipe, lyre, tri-

[c] Gk Theodotion Syr Vg: Aram adds *and like iron that crushes* [d] Aram *by human seed*

gon, harp, drum, and entire musical ensemble, you are to fall down
and worship the golden statue that
King Nebuchadnezzar has set up.
6 Whoever does not fall down and
worship shall immediately be
thrown into a furnace of blazing
fire." 7 Therefore, as soon as all the
peoples heard the sound of the
horn, pipe, lyre, trigon, harp, drum,
and entire musical ensemble, all
the peoples, nations, and languages fell down and worshiped
the golden statue that King Nebuchadnezzar had set up.
8 Accordingly, at this time certain Chaldeans came forward and
denounced the Jews. 9 They said to
King Nebuchadnezzar, "O king,
live forever! 10 You, O king, have
made a decree, that everyone who
hears the sound of the horn, pipe,
lyre, trigon, harp, drum, and entire
musical ensemble, shall fall down
and worship the golden statue,
11 and whoever does not fall down
and worship shall be thrown into a
furnace of blazing fire. 12 There are
certain Jews whom you have appointed over the affairs of the province of Babylon: Shadrach, Meshach, and Abednego. These pay
no heed to you, O King. They do
not serve your gods and they do not
worship the golden statue that you
have set up."
13 Then Nebuchadnezzar in furious rage commanded that Shadrach, Meshach, and Abednego be
brought in; so they brought those
men before the king. 14 Nebuchadnezzar said to them, "Is it true,
O Shadrach, Meshach, and Abednego, that you do not serve my gods
and you do not worship the golden
statue that I have set up? 15 Now if
you are ready when you hear the
sound of the horn, pipe, lyre, trigon, harp, drum, and entire musical ensemble to fall down and worship the statue that I have made,
well and good.[e] But if you do not
worship, you shall immediately be
thrown into a furnace of blazing
fire, and who is the god that will
deliver you out of my hands?"
16 Shadrach, Meshach, and
Abednego answered the king,
"O Nebuchadnezzar, we have no
need to present a defense to you in
this matter. 17 If our God whom we
serve is able to deliver us from the
furnace of blazing fire and out of
your hand, O king, let him deliver
us.[f] 18 But if not, be it known to
you, O king, that we will not serve
your gods and we will not worship
the golden statue that you have set
up."

The Fiery Furnace

19 Then Nebuchadnezzar was
so filled with rage against Shadrach, Meshach, and Abednego
that his face was distorted. He ordered the furnace heated up seven
times more than was customary,
20 and ordered some of the strongest guards in his army to bind Shadrach, Meshach, and Abednego
and to throw them into the furnace
of blazing fire. 21 So the men were
bound, still wearing their tunics,[g]
their trousers,[g] their hats, and
their other garments, and they
were thrown into the furnace of
blazing fire. 22 Because the king's
command was urgent and the furnace was so overheated, the raging
flames killed the men who lifted
Shadrach, Meshach, and Abednego. 23 But the three men, Shadrach,
Meshach, and Abednego, fell
down, bound, into the furnace of
blazing fire.
24 Then King Nebuchadnezzar
was astonished and rose up quickly. He said to his counselors, "Was
it not three men that we threw
bound into the fire?" They answered the king, "True, O king."
25 He replied, "But I see four men
unbound, walking in the middle of
the fire, and they are not hurt; and
the fourth has the appearance of a
god."[h] 26 Nebuchadnezzar then approached the door of the furnace of
blazing fire and said, "Shadrach,
Meshach, and Abednego, servants

3.6 vv. 11,15, 21; Jer 29.22; Rev 14.11 **3.7** vv. 4,5 **3.8** Dan 4.7; 6.12 **3.9** Dan 2.4; 5.10 **3.10** vv. 4-6; Dan 6.2; vv. 5,7,15 **3.12** Dan 2.49; 1.7; 6.13 **3.13** Dan 2.12; v. 19 **3.14** Isa 46.1; Jer 50.2; v. 1 **3.15** vv. 5,6; Ex 5.2; Isa 36.18-20; Dan 2.47 **3.16** v. 12 **3.17** Ps 27.1,2; Isa 26.3,4; Jer 15.20,21 **3.18** v. 28 **3.19** v. 13; Dan 5.6; v. 12 **3.20** vv. 23-25 **3.21** v. 27 **3.22** Ex 12.33; Dan 2.15 **3.23** v. 21 **3.25** Isa 43.2; v. 28 **3.26** v. 17; Dan 4.2

[e] Aram lacks *well and good* [f] Or *If our God whom we serve is able to deliver us, he will deliver us from the furnace of blazing fire and out of your hand, O king.* [g] Meaning of Aram word uncertain [h] Aram *a son of the gods*

of the Most High God, come out!
Come here!" So Shadrach, Meshach, and Abednego came out
from the fire. 27 And the satraps,
the prefects, the governors, and the
king's counselors gathered together and saw that the fire had not had
any power over the bodies of those
men; the hair of their heads was
not singed, their tunics[i] were not
harmed, and not even the smell of
fire came from them. 28 Nebuchadnezzar said, "Blessed be the God of
Shadrach, Meshach, and Abednego, who has sent his angel and delivered his servants who trusted in
him. They disobeyed the king's
command and yielded up their
bodies rather than serve and worship any god except their own God.
29 Therefore I make a decree: Any
people, nation, or language that utters blasphemy against the God of
Shadrach, Meshach, and Abednego
shall be torn limb from limb, and
their houses laid in ruins; for there
is no other god who is able to deliver in this way." 30 Then the king
promoted Shadrach, Meshach, and
Abednego in the province of Babylon.

Nebuchadnezzar's Second Dream

4 [j] King Nebuchadnezzar to all
peoples, nations, and languages that live throughout the
earth: May you have abundant
prosperity! 2 The signs and wonders
that the Most High God has worked
for me I am pleased to recount.

3 How great are his signs,
how mighty his wonders!
His kingdom is an
everlasting kingdom,
and his sovereignty is from
generation to
generation.

4 [k]I, Nebuchadnezzar, was living
at ease in my home and prospering
in my palace. 5 I saw a dream that
frightened me; my fantasies in bed
and the visions of my head terrified
me. 6 So I made a decree that all the
wise men of Babylon should be
brought before me, in order that
they might tell me the interpretation of the dream. 7 Then the magicians, the enchanters, the Chaldeans, and the diviners came in, and
I told them the dream, but they
could not tell me its interpretation.
8 At last Daniel came in before
me—he who was named Belteshazzar after the name of my god,
and who is endowed with a spirit of
the holy gods[l]—and I told him the
dream: 9 "O Belteshazzar, chief of
the magicians, I know that you are
endowed with a spirit of the holy
gods[l] and that no mystery is too
difficult for you. Hear[m] the dream
that I saw; tell me its interpretation.

10 [n]Upon my bed this is what I
saw;
there was a tree at the
center of the earth,
and its height was great.
11 The tree grew great and
strong,
its top reached to heaven,
and it was visible to the
ends of the whole
earth.
12 Its foliage was beautiful,
its fruit abundant,
and it provided food for all.
The animals of the field
found shade under it,
the birds of the air nested
in its branches,
and from it all living beings
were fed.

13 I continued looking, in the visions of my head as I lay in bed, and
there was a holy watcher, coming
down from heaven. 14 He cried
aloud and said:
'Cut down the tree and chop
off its branches,
strip off its foliage and
scatter its fruit.
Let the animals flee from
beneath it
and the birds from its
branches.

3.27 v. 2; Isa 43.2; Heb 11.34; v. 21
3.28 vv. 15,25; Acts 5.19; 12.7; Ps 34.7,8; Jer 17.7; v. 18
3.29 Dan 6.26; v. 12; Dan 2.5; 2.47; 6.27
3.30 Dan 2.49
4.1 Dan 6.25
4.2 Dan 3.26
4.3 Dan 6.27; v. 34; Dan 2.44; 6.26
4.4 Isa 47.7,8
4.5 Dan 2.28, 29; 2.1
4.6 Dan 2.2
4.7 Dan 2.2
4.8 Dan 1.7; 2.26; Dan 5.11,14
4.9 Dan 2.48; 5.11; 2.47; 2.4,5
4.10 vv. 5,20; Ezek 31.3-6
4.11 vv. 20,22
4.12 Ezek 31.6,7; Lam 4.20; Mt 13.32; Lk 13.19
4.13 Dan 7.1; vv. 17,23; Dan 8.13; Zech 14.5
4.14 Ezek 31.10-14; Mt 3.10; Ezek 31.12, 13

[i] Meaning of Aram word uncertain [j] Ch 3.31 in Aram [k] Ch 4.1 in Aram [l] Or *a holy, divine spirit* [m] Theodotion: Aram *The visions of* [n] Theodotion Syr Compare Gk: Aram adds *The visions of my head*

15 But leave its stump and
roots in the ground,
with a band of iron and
bronze,
in the tender grass of the
field.
Let him be bathed with the
dew of heaven,
and let his lot be with the
animals of the field
in the grass of the earth.
16 Let his mind be changed
from that of a human,
and let the mind of an
animal be given to him.
And let seven times pass
over him.
17 The sentence is rendered by
decree of the watchers,
the decision is given by
order of the holy ones,
in order that all who live
may know
that the Most High is
sovereign over the
kingdom of mortals;
he gives it to whom he will
and sets over it the lowliest
of human beings.'

18 This is the dream that I, King
Nebuchadnezzar, saw. Now you,
Belteshazzar, declare the interpretation, since all the wise men of my
kingdom are unable to tell me the
interpretation. You are able, however, for you are endowed with a
spirit of the holy gods."[o]

Daniel Interprets the Second Dream

19 Then Daniel, who was called
Belteshazzar, was severely distressed for a while. His thoughts
terrified him. The king said, "Belteshazzar, do not let the dream or
the interpretation terrify you." Belteshazzar answered, "My lord, may
the dream be for those who hate
you, and its interpretation for your
enemies! 20 The tree that you saw,
which grew great and strong, so
that its top reached to heaven and
was visible to the end of the whole
earth, 21 whose foliage was beautiful and its fruit abundant, and
which provided food for all, under
which animals of the field lived,
and in whose branches the birds of
the air had nests— 22 it is you,
O king! You have grown great and
strong. Your greatness has increased and reaches to heaven, and
your sovereignty to the ends of the
earth. 23 And whereas the king saw
a holy watcher coming down from
heaven and saying, 'Cut down the
tree and destroy it, but leave its
stump and roots in the ground,
with a band of iron and bronze, in
the grass of the field; and let him
be bathed with the dew of heaven,
and let his lot be with the animals
of the field, until seven times pass
over him'— 24 this is the interpretation, O king, and it is a decree of
the Most High that has come upon
my lord the king: 25 You shall be
driven away from human society,
and your dwelling shall be with the
wild animals. You shall be made to
eat grass like oxen, you shall be
bathed with the dew of heaven, and
seven times shall pass over you, until you have learned that the Most
High has sovereignty over the kingdom of mortals, and gives it to
whom he will. 26 As it was commanded to leave the stump and
roots of the tree, your kingdom
shall be re-established for you
from the time that you learn that
Heaven is sovereign. 27 Therefore,
O king, may my counsel be acceptable to you: atone for[p] your sins
with righteousness, and your iniquities with mercy to the oppressed,
so that your prosperity may be prolonged."

Nebuchadnezzar's Humiliation

28 All this came upon King
Nebuchadnezzar. 29 At the end of
twelve months he was walking on
the roof of the royal palace of Babylon, 30 and the king said, "Is this
not magnificent Babylon, which I
have built as a royal capital by my
mighty power and for my glorious
majesty?" 31 While the words were
still in the king's mouth, a voice
came from heaven: "O King Nebuchadnezzar, to you it is declared:

[o] Or *a holy, divine spirit* [p] Aram *break off*

4.15 Job 14.7-9; v. 32
4.16 Dan 7.25; 11.13; 12.7
4.17 Ps 9.16; vv. 2,25; Dan 5.18, 19; Dan 11.21
4.18 Gen 41.8, 15; Dan 5.8, 15; vv. 7-9
4.19 Dan 7.15, 28; 2 Sam 18.32; Jer 29.7
4.20 vv. 10-12
4.21 see v. 12
4.22 2 Sam 12.7; Dan 2.37, 38; 5.18,19; Jer 27.6-8
4.23 vv. 13-17; Dan 5.21
4.24 vv. 17,2; Job 40.11, 12; Ps 107.40
4.25 Dan 5.21; Ps 83.18; Jer 27.5
4.26 Mt 21.25; Lk 15.18
4.27 Isa 55.6,7; Ezek 18.21, 22; Ps 41.1-3; 1 Kings 21.29
4.28ff Zech 1.6
4.30 Hab 2.4; v. 25; Dan 5.20, 21; Isa 37.24,25
4.31 Dan 5.5; vv. 13,14,23

THE NEO-BABYLONIAN EMPIRE 626-539 B.C.

MEDIAN EMPIRE
Caspian Sea
Khorsabad
Tigris R.
ASSYRIA
Nineveh
Carchemish
Haran
Euphrates R.
Babylon boasted one of the world's seven wonders, the famed Hanging Gardens, as well as a staged temple-tower 295 feet high and, according to Herodotus, several colossal gold statues weighing many tons.
Hamath
Route of Judahite Exiles
Great Sea
ARAM
Sidon
Tyre
Damascus
Tigris R.
ELAM
Arabian Desert
Babylon
Susa
Nippur
Jerusalem
BABYLONIA
Ur
Euphrates R.
Miles 0 100 200 300
Kms 0 100 200 300 400 500
Lower Sea

The kingdom has departed from
you! 32 You shall be driven away
from human society, and your
dwelling shall be with the animals
of the field. You shall be made to
eat grass like oxen, and seven
times shall pass over you, until you
have learned that the Most High
has sovereignty over the kingdom
of mortals and gives it to whom he
will." 33 Immediately the sentence
was fulfilled against Nebuchadnezzar. He was driven away from human society, ate grass like oxen,
and his body was bathed with the
dew of heaven, until his hair grew
as long as eagles' feathers and his
nails became like birds' claws.

Nebuchadnezzar Praises God

34 When that period was over, I,
Nebuchadnezzar, lifted my eyes to
heaven, and my reason returned to
me.

I blessed the Most High,
and praised and honored
the one who lives
forever.
For his sovereignty is an
everlasting sovereignty,
and his kingdom endures
from generation to
generation.
35 All the inhabitants of the
earth are accounted as
nothing,
and he does what he wills
with the host of heaven
and the inhabitants of the
earth.
There is no one who can stay
his hand
or say to him, "What are
you doing?"

36 At that time my reason returned
to me; and my majesty and splendor were restored to me for the glory of my kingdom. My counselors
and my lords sought me out, I was
re-established over my kingdom,
and still more greatness was added
to me. 37 Now I, Nebuchadnezzar,
praise and extol and honor the
King of heaven,

for all his works are truth,
and his ways are justice;
and he is able to bring low
those who walk in pride.

4.32 v. 25
4.33 Dan 5.21
4.34 vv. 16,25, 32,36,2; Dan 5.18, 21; 12.7; Rev 4.10; Lk 1.33
4.35 Isa 40.15, 17; Ps 135.6; Isa 43.13; 45.9; Rom 9.20
4.36 vv. 34,30; Dan 2.31; v. 26
4.37 Ps 33.4,5; Ex 18.11; Dan 5.20
5.1 Esther 1.3
5.2 Dan 1.2; Jer 52.19; v.23
5.4 v. 23; Rev 9.20
5.5 Dan 4.31; v. 24
5.6 Dan 4.5,19; Nah 2.10; Ezek 7.17; 21.7
5.7 Isa 47.13; Dan 2.6; Ezek 16.11; Dan 6.2,3
5.8 Dan 2.10, 27; 4.7
5.9 Isa 21.2-4; Jer 6.24; v. 6
5.10 Dan 2.4; 3.9

Belshazzar's Feast

5 King Belshazzar made a great
festival for a thousand of his
lords, and he was drinking wine in
the presence of the thousand.
2 Under the influence of the
wine, Belshazzar commanded that
they bring in the vessels of gold and
silver that his father Nebuchadnezzar had taken out of the temple in
Jerusalem, so that the king and his
lords, his wives, and his concubines might drink from them. 3 So
they brought in the vessels of gold
and silver[q] that had been taken
out of the temple, the house of God
in Jerusalem, and the king and his
lords, his wives, and his concubines drank from them. 4 They
drank the wine and praised the
gods of gold and silver, bronze,
iron, wood, and stone.

The Writing on the Wall

5 Immediately the fingers of a
human hand appeared and began
writing on the plaster of the wall of
the royal palace, next to the lampstand. The king was watching the
hand as it wrote. 6 Then the king's
face turned pale, and his thoughts
terrified him. His limbs gave way,
and his knees knocked together.
7 The king cried aloud to bring in
the enchanters, the Chaldeans,
and the diviners; and the king said
to the wise men of Babylon, "Whoever can read this writing and tell
me its interpretation shall be
clothed in purple, have a chain of
gold around his neck, and rank
third in the kingdom." 8 Then all
the king's wise men came in, but
they could not read the writing or
tell the king the interpretation.
9 Then King Belshazzar became
greatly terrified and his face turned
pale, and his lords were perplexed.
10 The queen, when she heard
the discussion of the king and his
lords, came into the banqueting
hall. The queen said, "O king, live
forever! Do not let your thoughts

[q] Theodotion Vg: Aram lacks *and silver*

terrify you or your face grow pale.
11 There is a man in your kingdom
who is endowed with a spirit of the
holy gods.[r] In the days of your father he was found to have enlightenment, understanding, and wisdom like the wisdom of the gods.
Your father, King Nebuchadnezzar,
made him chief of the magicians,
enchanters, Chaldeans, and diviners,[s] 12 because an excellent spirit,
knowledge, and understanding to
interpret dreams, explain riddles,
and solve problems were found in
this Daniel, whom the king named
Belteshazzar. Now let Daniel be
called, and he will give the interpretation."

The Writing on the Wall Interpreted

13 Then Daniel was brought in
before the king. The king said to
Daniel, "So you are Daniel, one of
the exiles of Judah, whom my father the king brought from Judah?
14 I have heard of you that a spirit of
the gods[t] is in you, and that enlightenment, understanding, and
excellent wisdom are found in you.
15 Now the wise men, the enchanters, have been brought in before
me to read this writing and tell me
its interpretation, but they were
not able to give the interpretation
of the matter. 16 But I have heard
that you can give interpretations
and solve problems. Now if you are
able to read the writing and tell me
its interpretation, you shall be
clothed in purple, have a chain of
gold around your neck, and rank
third in the kingdom."
17 Then Daniel answered in the
presence of the king, "Let your gifts
be for yourself, or give your rewards
to someone else! Nevertheless I
will read the writing to the king and
let him know the interpretation.
18 O king, the Most High God gave
your father Nebuchadnezzar kingship, greatness, glory, and majesty.
19 And because of the greatness
that he gave him, all peoples, nations, and languages trembled and
feared before him. He killed those
he wanted to kill, kept alive those
he wanted to keep alive, honored
those he wanted to honor, and degraded those he wanted to degrade.
20 But when his heart was lifted up
and his spirit was hardened so that
he acted proudly, he was deposed
from his kingly throne, and his glory was stripped from him. 21 He was
driven from human society, and his
mind was made like that of an animal. His dwelling was with the wild
asses, he was fed grass like oxen,
and his body was bathed with the
dew of heaven, until he learned
that the Most High God has sovereignty over the kingdom of mortals,
and sets over it whomever he will.
22 And you, Belshazzar his son,
have not humbled your heart, even
though you knew all this! 23 You
have exalted yourself against the
Lord of heaven! The vessels of his
temple have been brought in before you, and you and your lords,
your wives and your concubines
have been drinking wine from
them. You have praised the gods of
silver and gold, of bronze, iron,
wood, and stone, which do not see
or hear or know; but the God in
whose power is your very breath,
and to whom belong all your ways,
you have not honored.
24 "So from his presence the
hand was sent and this writing was
inscribed. 25 And this is the writing
that was inscribed: MENE, MENE, TE-
KEL, and PARSIN. 26 This is the interpretation of the matter: MENE, God
has numbered the days of[u] your
kingdom and brought it to an end;
27 TEKEL, you have been weighed on
the scales and found wanting; 28 PE-
RES,[v] your kingdom is divided and
given to the Medes and Persians."
29 Then Belshazzar gave the
command, and Daniel was clothed
in purple, a chain of gold was put
around his neck, and a proclamation was made concerning him that
he should rank third in the kingdom.
30 That very night Belshazzar,

5.11 Dan 2.47, 48; 4.8,9,18; 1.17
5.12 Dan 6.3; 1.7
5.13 Dan 2.25; 6.13; 1.1,2
5.14 vv. 11,12
5.16 Gen 40.8; vv.7,29
5.17 2 Kings 5.16
5.18 v. 21; Dan 2.37, 38; 4.17; Jer 27.5-7
5.19 Dan 3.4; 2.12,13
5.20 Dan 4.30, 37; 2 Kings 17.14; 2 Chr 36.13; Jer 13.18
5.21 Dan 4.32-34; 4.16; Ezek 17.24; Dan 4.34,35
5.22 2 Chr 33.23; 36.12
5.23 Jer 50.29; vv. 3,4; Ps 115.5,6; Hab 2.18, 19; Job 12.10; 31.4; Jer 10.23
5.24 v. 5
5.26 Isa 13.6,17; Jer 27.7; 50.41-43
5.27 Job 31.6; Ps 62.9
5.29 vv. 7,16
5.30 Isa 21.4-9; Jer 51.31, 39,57

[r] Or *a holy, divine spirit* [s] Aram adds *the king your father* [t] Or *a divine spirit* [u] Aram lacks *the days of* [v] The singular of *Parsin*

the Chaldean king, was killed.
31 [w]And Darius the Mede received
the kingdom, being about sixty-
two years old.

The Plot against Daniel

6 It pleased Darius to set over
the kingdom one hundred
twenty satraps, stationed throughout the whole kingdom, 2 and over
them three presidents, including
Daniel; to these the satraps gave
account, so that the king might suffer no loss. 3 Soon Daniel distinguished himself above all the other
presidents and satraps because an
excellent spirit was in him, and the
king planned to appoint him over
the whole kingdom. 4 So the presidents and the satraps tried to find
grounds for complaint against Daniel in connection with the kingdom. But they could find no
grounds for complaint or any corruption, because he was faithful,
and no negligence or corruption
could be found in him. 5 The men
said, "We shall not find any ground
for complaint against this Daniel
unless we find it in connection
with the law of his God."

6 So the presidents and satraps
conspired and came to the king
and said to him, "O King Darius,
live forever! 7 All the presidents of
the kingdom, the prefects and the
satraps, the counselors and the
governors are agreed that the king
should establish an ordinance and
enforce an interdict, that whoever
prays to anyone, divine or human,
for thirty days, except to you,
O king, shall be thrown into a den
of lions. 8 Now, O king, establish
the interdict and sign the document, so that it cannot be changed,
according to the law of the Medes
and the Persians, which cannot be
revoked." 9 Therefore King Darius
signed the document and interdict.

Daniel in the Lions' Den

10 Although Daniel knew that
the document had been signed, he
continued to go to his house,
which had windows in its upper
room open toward Jerusalem, and
to get down on his knees three
times a day to pray to his God and
praise him, just as he had done previously. 11 The conspirators came
and found Daniel praying and seeking mercy before his God. 12 Then
they approached the king and said
concerning the interdict, "O king!
Did you not sign an interdict, that
anyone who prays to anyone, divine or human, within thirty days
except to you, O king, shall be
thrown into a den of lions?" The
king answered, "The thing stands
fast, according to the law of the
Medes and Persians, which cannot
be revoked." 13 Then they responded to the king, "Daniel, one of the
exiles from Judah, pays no attention to you, O king, or to the interdict you have signed, but he is saying his prayers three times a day."

14 When the king heard the
charge, he was very much distressed. He was determined to save
Daniel, and until the sun went
down he made every effort to rescue him. 15 Then the conspirators
came to the king and said to him,
"Know, O king, that it is a law of
the Medes and Persians that no interdict or ordinance that the king
establishes can be changed."

16 Then the king gave the command, and Daniel was brought and
thrown into the den of lions. The
king said to Daniel, "May your
God, whom you faithfully serve, deliver you!" 17 A stone was brought
and laid on the mouth of the den,
and the king sealed it with his own
signet and with the signet of his
lords, so that nothing might be
changed concerning Daniel.
18 Then the king went to his palace
and spent the night fasting; no food
was brought to him, and sleep fled
from him.

Daniel Saved from the Lions

19 Then, at break of day, the
king got up and hurried to the den
of lions. 20 When he came near the
den where Daniel was, he cried out
anxiously to Daniel, "O Daniel,
servant of the living God, has your

5.31 Dan 6.1; 9.1
6.1 Esther 1.1; Dan 5.31
6.2 Dan 2.48, 49; Ezra 4.22
6.3 Dan 1.20; 5.12,14; Esther 10.3
6.4 Gen 43.18; v.22
6.6 v. 21; Neh 2.3; Dan 2.4
6.7 Dan 3.2,27; Ps 59.3; Dan 3.6; v. 16
6.8 vv. 12,15; Esther 1.19; 8.8
6.9 Ps 118.9; 146.3
6.10 1 Kings 8.48, 49; Ps 95.6; 55.17; 1 Thes 5.17, 18
6.11 v.6
6.12 Dan 3.8; Acts 16.19-21
6.13 Dan 1.6; 5.13; Esther 3.8; Dan 3.12; Acts 5.29
6.14 Mk 6.26
6.15 Esther 8.8; v.8
6.16 Jer 38.5; vv. 7,20; Ps 37.39,40
6.17 Lam 3.55; Mt 27.66
6.18 2 Sam 12.16, 17; Esther 6.1; Dan 2.1
6.20 vv. 26,27; Jer 32.17; Dan 3.17

[w] Ch 6.1 in Aram

God whom you faithfully serve
been able to deliver you from the
lions?" 21 Daniel then said to the
king, "O king, live forever! 22 My
God sent his angel and shut the lions' mouths so that they would not
hurt me, because I was found
blameless before him; and also before you, O king, I have done no
wrong." 23 Then the king was exceedingly glad and commanded
that Daniel be taken up out of the
den. So Daniel was taken up out of
the den, and no kind of harm was
found on him, because he had
trusted in his God. 24 The king gave
a command, and those who had accused Daniel were brought and
thrown into the den of lions—they,
their children, and their wives. Before they reached the bottom of the
den the lions overpowered them
and broke all their bones in pieces.
25 Then King Darius wrote to all
peoples and nations of every language throughout the whole world:
"May you have abundant prosperity! 26 I make a decree, that in all my
royal dominion people should
tremble and fear before the God of
Daniel:

For he is the living God,
    enduring forever.
His kingdom shall never be
        destroyed,
    and his dominion has no
        end.
27 He delivers and rescues,
    he works signs and
        wonders in heaven and
        on earth;
for he has saved Daniel
    from the power of the
        lions."

28 So this Daniel prospered during
the reign of Darius and the reign of
Cyrus the Persian.

Visions of the Four Beasts

7 In the first year of King Belshazzar of Babylon, Daniel
had a dream and visions of his head
as he lay in bed. Then he wrote
down the dream:[x] 2 I,[y] Daniel, saw
in my vision by night the four winds
of heaven stirring up the great sea,
3 and four great beasts came up out
of the sea, different from one another. 4 The first was like a lion and
had eagles' wings. Then, as I
watched, its wings were plucked
off, and it was lifted up from the
ground and made to stand on two
feet like a human being; and a human mind was given to it. 5 Another
beast appeared, a second one, that
looked like a bear. It was raised up
on one side, had three tusks[z] in its
mouth among its teeth and was
told, "Arise, devour many bodies!"
6 After this, as I watched, another
appeared, like a leopard. The beast
had four wings of a bird on its back
and four heads; and dominion was
given to it. 7 After this I saw in the
visions by night a fourth beast, terrifying and dreadful and exceedingly strong. It had great iron teeth
and was devouring, breaking in
pieces, and stamping what was left
with its feet. It was different from
all the beasts that preceded it, and
it had ten horns. 8 I was considering
the horns, when another horn appeared, a little one coming up
among them; to make room for it,
three of the earlier horns were
plucked up by the roots. There
were eyes like human eyes in this
horn, and a mouth speaking arrogantly.

Judgment before the Ancient One

9 As I watched,
    thrones were set in place,
        and an Ancient One[a] took
            his throne,
    his clothing was white as
            snow,
        and the hair of his head
            like pure wool;
    his throne was fiery flames,
        and its wheels were
            burning fire.
10 A stream of fire issued
        and flowed out from his
            presence.
    A thousand thousands served
            him,

6.21 Dan 2.4; v. 6
6.22 Acts 12.11; 2 Tim 4.17; Heb 11.33; 1 Sam 24.10
6.23 vv. 14,18; Dan 3.25, 27; Isa 26.3; Heb 11.33
6.24 2 Kings 14.6; Ps 54.5; Isa 38.13
6.25 Ezra 1.1,2; Esther 3.12; 8.9; Dan 4.1; 1 Pet 1.2
6.26 Dan 3.29; Ps 99.1; Dan 4.34; Ps 93.1,2; Dan 4.3; 7.14,27
6.27 v. 22; Dan 4.3
6.28 Ezra 1.1,2; Dan 1.21; 10.1
7.1 Dan 5.1,22, 30; 1.17; vv. 7,13,15; Jer 36.4,32
7.3 v. 17; Rev 13.1
7.4 Jer 48.40; Ezek 17.3; Hab 1.8
7.5 Dan 2.39
7.6 v. 12
7.7 Rev 12.3; 13.1; 17.3
7.8 vv. 20,21; Rev 9.7; vv. 11,25
7.9 Mk 9.3; Rev 1.14; Ezek 1.13, 26; 10.2,6
7.10 Ps 50.3; 97.3; Isa 30.33; Rev 5.11; 20.12

[x] Q Ms Theodotion: MT adds *the beginning of the words; he said* [y] Theodotion: Aram *Daniel answered and said, "I* [z] Or *ribs* [a] Aram *an Ancient of Days*

and ten thousand times ten
thousand stood
attending him.
The court sat in judgment,
and the books were
opened.

11 I watched then because of the
noise of the arrogant words that the
horn was speaking. And as I
watched, the beast was put to
death, and its body destroyed and
given over to be burned with fire.
12 As for the rest of the beasts, their
dominion was taken away, but
their lives were prolonged for a season and a time. 13 As I watched in
the night visions,

I saw one like a human
being[b]
coming with the clouds of
heaven.
And he came to the Ancient
One[c]
and was presented before
him.
14 To him was given dominion
and glory and kingship,
that all peoples, nations, and
languages
should serve him.
His dominion is an
everlasting dominion
that shall not pass away,
and his kingship is one
that shall never be
destroyed.

Daniel's Visions Interpreted

15 As for me, Daniel, my spirit
was troubled within me,[d] and the
visions of my head terrified me. 16 I
approached one of the attendants
to ask him the truth concerning all
this. So he said that he would disclose to me the interpretation of
the matter: 17 "As for these four
great beasts, four kings shall arise
out of the earth. 18 But the holy
ones of the Most High shall receive
the kingdom and possess the kingdom forever—forever and ever."

19 Then I desired to know the
truth concerning the fourth beast,
which was different from all the
rest, exceedingly terrifying, with its
teeth of iron and claws of bronze,
and which devoured and broke in
pieces, and stamped what was left
with its feet; 20 and concerning the
ten horns that were on its head,
and concerning the other horn,
which came up and to make room
for which three of them fell out—
the horn that had eyes and a mouth
that spoke arrogantly, and that
seemed greater than the others.
21 As I looked, this horn made war
with the holy ones and was prevail-
ing over them, 22 until the Ancient
One[c] came; then judgment was
given for the holy ones of the Most
High, and the time arrived when
the holy ones gained possession of
the kingdom.

23 This is what he said: "As for
the fourth beast,
there shall be a fourth
kingdom on earth
that shall be different from
all the other kingdoms;
it shall devour the whole
earth,
and trample it down, and
break it to pieces.
24 As for the ten horns,
out of this kingdom ten
kings shall arise,
and another shall arise
after them.
This one shall be different
from the former ones,
and shall put down three
kings.
25 He shall speak words against
the Most High,
shall wear out the holy
ones of the Most High,
and shall attempt to
change the sacred
seasons and the law;
and they shall be given into
his power
for a time, two times,[e] and
half a time.
26 Then the court shall sit in
judgment,
and his dominion shall be
taken away,
to be consumed and totally
destroyed.
27 The kingship and dominion

7.11 vv. 7,8; Rev 19.20 **7.12** vv. 3-6 **7.13** Ezek 1.26; Mt 24.30; 26.64; Mk 13.26; Lk 21.27; Rev 1.7,13 **7.14** Ps 2.6-8; 1 Cor 15.27; Eph 1.22; Phil 2.9-11; Ps 72.11; 102.22; Dan 2.44; Mic 4.7; Heb 12.28 **7.15** vv. 1,28 **7.16** Rev 5.5; 7.13,14; Dan 8.16,17 **7.17** v. 3 **7.18** Isa 60.12-14; Rev 2.26; 20.4 **7.19** vv. 7,8 **7.21** Rev 13.7 **7.22** vv. 9,13; 1 Cor 6.2, 3; v. 18 **7.23** vv. 7,19 **7.24** vv. 7,8; Rev 17.12 **7.25** Isa 37.23; Dan 8.24, 25; Rev 13.5; 17.6; 18.24; Dan 2.21; 12.7; Rev 12.14 **7.26** vv. 10,22 **7.27** vv. 14,18, 22; Lk 1.33; Jn 12.34; Rev 11.15; Ps 2.6-12; Isa 60.12

b Aram *one like a son of man* c Aram *the Ancient of Days* d Aram *troubled in its sheath* e Aram *a time, times*

and the greatness of the
kingdoms under the
whole heaven
shall be given to the people
of the holy ones of the
Most High;
their kingdom shall be an
everlasting kingdom,
and all dominions shall
serve and obey them."

28 Here the account ends. As
for me, Daniel, my thoughts greatly
terrified me, and my face turned
pale; but I kept the matter in my
mind.

Vision of a Ram and a Goat

8 In the third year of the reign of
King Belshazzar a vision appeared to me, Daniel, after the one
that had appeared to me at first.
2 In the vision I was looking and
saw myself in Susa the capital, in
the province of Elam,[f] and I was
by the river Ulai.[g] 3 I looked up and
saw a ram standing beside the river.[h] It had two horns. Both horns
were long, but one was longer than
the other, and the longer one came
up second. 4 I saw the ram charging
westward and northward and
southward. All beasts were powerless to withstand it, and no one
could rescue from its power; it did
as it pleased and became strong.
5 As I was watching, a male goat
appeared from the west, coming
across the face of the whole earth
without touching the ground. The
goat had a horn[i] between its eyes.
6 It came toward the ram with the
two horns that I had seen standing
beside the river,[h] and it ran at it
with savage force. 7 I saw it approaching the ram. It was enraged
against it and struck the ram,
breaking its two horns. The ram did
not have power to withstand it; it
threw the ram down to the ground
and trampled upon it, and there
was no one who could rescue the
ram from its power. 8 Then the
male goat grew exceedingly great;
but at the height of its power, the
great horn was broken, and in its
place there came up four prominent horns toward the four winds
of heaven.
9 Out of one of them came another[j] horn, a little one, which
grew exceedingly great toward the
south, toward the east, and toward
the beautiful land. 10 It grew as high
as the host of heaven. It threw
down to the earth some of the host
and some of the stars, and trampled on them. 11 Even against the
prince of the host it acted arrogantly; it took the regular burnt offering
away from him and overthrew the
place of his sanctuary. 12 Because
of wickedness, the host was given
over to it together with the regular
burnt offering;[k] it cast truth to the
ground, and kept prospering in
what it did. 13 Then I heard a holy
one speaking, and another holy
one said to the one that spoke,
"For how long is this vision concerning the regular burnt offering,
the transgression that makes desolate, and the giving over of the
sanctuary and host to be trampled?"[k] 14 And he answered him,[l]
"For two thousand three hundred
evenings and mornings; then the
sanctuary shall be restored to its
rightful state."

Gabriel Interprets the Vision

15 When I, Daniel, had seen the
vision, I tried to understand it.
Then someone appeared standing
before me, having the appearance
of a man, 16 and I heard a human
voice by the Ulai, calling, "Gabriel,
help this man understand the vision." 17 So he came near where I
stood; and when he came, I became frightened and fell prostrate.
But he said to me, "Understand,
O mortal,[m] that the vision is for
the time of the end."
18 As he was speaking to me, I
fell into a trance, face to the
ground; then he touched me and
set me on my feet. 19 He said, "Lis-

7.28 v. 15; Dan 8.27; Lk 2.19
8.1 Dan 7.1,15, 28
8.2 Dan 7.2,15; Esther 1.2; Ezek 32.24; v. 16
8.3 Dan 10.5; v. 20
8.4 v. 7
8.5 v. 21
8.6 v. 3
8.7 Dan 11.11; 7.7
8.8 2 Chr 26.16; Dan 5.20; v. 22; Dan 7.2; Rev 7.1
8.9 v. 23; Dan 11.16, 41
8.10 Rev 12.4
8.11 Dan 11.36, 37; Josh 5.14; Dan 11.31; 12.11; Ezek 46.13, 14
8.13 Dan 4.13, 23; 12.6,8; Rev 11.2
8.15 v. 1; Dan 7.13
8.16 Dan 9.21; Lk 1.19,26
8.17 Ezek 1.28; Rev 1.17
8.18 Dan 10.9, 16,18; Ezek 2.2
8.19 Hab 2.3

[f] Gk Theodotion: MT Q Ms repeat *in the vision I was looking* [g] Or *the Ulai Gate* [h] Or *gate* [i] Theodotion: Gk *one horn*; Heb *a horn of vision* [j] Cn Compare 7.8: Heb *one* [k] Meaning of Heb uncertain [l] Gk Theodotion Syr Vg: Heb *me* [m] Heb *son of man*

ten, and I will tell you what will
take place later in the period of
wrath; for it refers to the appointed
time of the end. 20 As for the ram
that you saw with the two horns,
these are the kings of Media and
Persia. 21 The male goat[n] is the
king of Greece, and the great horn
between its eyes is the first king.
22 As for the horn that was broken,
in place of which four others arose,
four kingdoms shall arise from
his[o] nation, but not with his power.

23 At the end of their rule,
 when the transgressions
  have reached their full
  measure,
 a king of bold countenance
  shall arise,
 skilled in intrigue.
24 He shall grow strong in
  power,[p]
 shall cause fearful
  destruction,
 and shall succeed in what
  he does.
 He shall destroy the powerful
 and the people of the holy
  ones.
25 By his cunning
 he shall make deceit
  prosper under his hand,
 and in his own mind he
  shall be great.
 Without warning he shall
  destroy many
 and shall even rise up
  against the Prince of
  princes.
 But he shall be broken, and
  not by human hands.

26 The vision of the evenings and
the mornings that has been told is
true. As for you, seal up the vision,
for it refers to many days from
now."

27 So I, Daniel, was overcome
and lay sick for some days; then I
arose and went about the king's
business. But I was dismayed by
the vision and did not understand
it.

Daniel's Prayer for the People

9 In the first year of Darius son
of Ahasuerus, by birth a Mede,
who became king over the realm of
the Chaldeans— 2 in the first year
of his reign, I, Daniel, perceived in
the books the number of years that,
according to the word of the LORD
to the prophet Jeremiah, must be
fulfilled for the devastation of Jerusalem, namely, seventy years.

3 Then I turned to the Lord God,
to seek an answer by prayer and
supplication with fasting and sackcloth and ashes. 4 I prayed to the
LORD my God and made confession,
saying,

"Ah, Lord, great and awesome
God, keeping covenant and steadfast love with those who love you
and keep your commandments,
5 we have sinned and done wrong,
acted wickedly and rebelled, turning aside from your commandments and ordinances. 6 We have
not listened to your servants the
prophets, who spoke in your name
to our kings, our princes, and our
ancestors, and to all the people of
the land.

7 "Righteousness is on your
side, O Lord, but open shame, as at
this day, falls on us, the people of
Judah, the inhabitants of Jerusalem, and all Israel, those who are
near and those who are far away, in
all the lands to which you have
driven them, because of the treachery that they have committed
against you. 8 Open shame, O LORD,
falls on us, our kings, our officials,
and our ancestors, because we
have sinned against you. 9 To the
Lord our God belong mercy and
forgiveness, for we have rebelled
against him, 10 and have not obeyed
the voice of the LORD our God by
following his laws, which he set before us by his servants the prophets.

11 "All Israel has transgressed
your law and turned aside, refusing
to obey your voice. So the curse
and the oath written in the law of
Moses, the servant of God, have
been poured out upon us, because
we have sinned against you. 12 He

8.21 v. 5; Dan 10.20 **8.22** v. 8 **8.24** Dan 11.36 **8.25** Dan 11.21; v. 11; Dan 2.34,45 **8.26** Dan 10.1; 12.4,9; 10.14 **8.27** Dan 7.28; Hab 3.16 **9.1** Dan 5.31; 11.1

9.2 2 Chr 36.21; Jer 29.10; Zech 7.5 **9.3** Neh 1.4; Jer 29.12; Jas 4.8 **9.4** Deut 7.21; Neh 9.32; Deut 7.9 **9.5** Ps 106.6; Lam 1.18, 20; v. 11 **9.6** 2 Chr 36.15, 16; v. 8 **9.7** Jer 23.6; 33.16; Am 9.9 **9.8** vv. 6,5 **9.9** Neh 9.17; Ps 130.4 **9.10** 2 Kings 17.13-15; 18.12 **9.11** Isa 1.4-6; Jer 8.5,10; Deut 27.15 **9.12** Isa 44.26; Zech 1.6; Ezek 5.9

[n] Or *shaggy male goat* [o] Gk Theodotion Vg: Heb *the* [p] Theodotion and one Gk Ms: Heb repeats (from 8.22) *but not with his power*

has confirmed his words, which he
spoke against us and against our
rulers, by bringing upon us a calamity so great that what has been
done against Jerusalem has never
before been done under the whole
heaven. 13 Just as it is written in the
law of Moses, all this calamity has
come upon us. We did not entreat
the favor of the LORD our God, turning from our iniquities and reflecting on his[q] fidelity. 14 So the LORD
kept watch over this calamity until
he brought it upon us. Indeed, the
LORD our God is right in all that he
has done; for we have disobeyed
his voice.
15 "And now, O Lord our God,
who brought your people out of the
land of Egypt with a mighty hand
and made your name renowned
even to this day—we have sinned,
we have done wickedly. 16 O Lord,
in view of all your righteous acts,
let your anger and wrath, we pray,
turn away from your city Jerusalem, your holy mountain; because
of our sins and the iniquities of our
ancestors, Jerusalem and your people have become a disgrace among
all our neighbors. 17 Now therefore,
O our God, listen to the prayer of
your servant and to his supplication, and for your own sake, Lord,[r]
let your face shine upon your desolated sanctuary. 18 Incline your ear,
O my God, and hear. Open your
eyes and look at our desolation and
the city that bears your name. We
do not present our supplication before you on the ground of our righteousness, but on the ground of
your great mercies. 19 O Lord, hear;
O Lord, forgive; O Lord, listen and
act and do not delay! For your own
sake, O my God, because your city
and your people bear your name!"

The Seventy Weeks

20 While I was speaking, and
was praying and confessing my sin
and the sin of my people Israel, and
presenting my supplication before
the LORD my God on behalf of the
holy mountain of my God—
21 while I was speaking in prayer,
the man Gabriel, whom I had seen
before in a vision, came to me in
swift flight at the time of the evening sacrifice. 22 He came[s] and
said to me, "Daniel, I have now
come out to give you wisdom and
understanding. 23 At the beginning
of your supplications a word went
out, and I have come to declare it,
for you are greatly beloved. So consider the word and understand the
vision:
24 "Seventy weeks are decreed
for your people and your holy city:
to finish the transgression, to put
an end to sin, and to atone for iniquity, to bring in everlasting righteousness, to seal both vision and
prophet, and to anoint a most holy
place.[t] 25 Know therefore and understand: from the time that the
word went out to restore and rebuild Jerusalem until the time of
an anointed prince, there shall be
seven weeks; and for sixty-two
weeks it shall be built again with
streets and moat, but in a troubled
time. 26 After the sixty-two weeks,
an anointed one shall be cut off
and shall have nothing, and the
troops of the prince who is to come
shall destroy the city and the sanctuary. Its[u] end shall come with a
flood, and to the end there shall be
war. Desolations are decreed. 27 He
shall make a strong covenant with
many for one week, and for half of
the week he shall make sacrifice
and offering cease; and in their
place[v] shall be an abomination
that desolates, until the decreed
end is poured out upon the desola-
tor."

Conflict of Nations and Heavenly Powers

10 In the third year of King Cyrus of Persia a word was revealed to Daniel, who was named
Belteshazzar. The word was true,
and it concerned a great conflict.
He understood the word, having received understanding in the vision.
2 At that time I, Daniel, had

9.13 Isa 9.13; Jer 2.30
9.14 Jer 31.28; 44.27; vv. 7, 10
9.15 Ex 6.1,6; Jer 32.21; Neh 9.10; Jer 32.20
9.16 1 Sam 12.7; Ps 31.1; Zech 8.3
9.17 Num 6.25; Lam 5.18
9.18 Isa 37.17; Jer 25.29; 36.7
9.19 Ps 44.23; 74.10,11
9.20 v. 3; Isa 58.9; 6.5
9.21 Dan 8.16; Isa 6.2; Dan 8.18; 10.10,16,18
9.23 Dan 10.12; Lk 1.28; Mt 24.15
9.24 Isa 55.10; Rom 5.10; Acts 3.14
9.25 Ezra 4.24; Neh 2.1-8; 3.1; Jn 1.41; 4.25; Isa 9.6
9.26 Isa 53.8; Mk 9.12; Lk 19.43,44; Nah 1.8
9.27 Dan 11.31; Mt 24.15; Lk 21.20; Isa 10.23
10.1 Dan 6.28; 1.7; 8.26; 2.21
10.2 Ezra 9.4,5; Neh 1.4

q Heb *your* r Theodotion Vg Compare Syr: Heb *for the Lord's sake* s Gk Syr: Heb *He made to understand* t Or *thing* or *one* u Or *His* v Cn: Meaning of Heb uncertain

been mourning for three weeks. [3]I
had eaten no rich food, no meat or
wine had entered my mouth, and I
had not anointed myself at all, for
the full three weeks. [4]On the
twenty-fourth day of the first
month, as I was standing on the
bank of the great river (that is, the
Tigris), [5]I looked up and saw a man
clothed in linen, with a belt of gold
from Uphaz around his waist. [6]His
body was like beryl, his face like
lightning, his eyes like flaming
torches, his arms and legs like the
gleam of burnished bronze, and the
sound of his words like the roar of
a multitude. [7]I, Daniel, alone saw
the vision; the people who were
with me did not see the vision,
though a great trembling fell upon
them, and they fled and hid themselves. [8]So I was left alone to see
this great vision. My strength left
me, and my complexion grew
deathly pale, and I retained no
strength. [9]Then I heard the sound
of his words; and when I heard the
sound of his words, I fell into a
trance, face to the ground.

10 But then a hand touched me
and roused me to my hands and
knees. [11]He said to me, "Daniel,
greatly beloved, pay attention to
the words that I am going to speak
to you. Stand on your feet, for I
have now been sent to you." So
while he was speaking this word to
me, I stood up trembling. [12]He said
to me, "Do not fear, Daniel, for
from the first day that you set your
mind to gain understanding and to
humble yourself before your God,
your words have been heard, and I
have come because of your words.
[13]But the prince of the kingdom of
Persia opposed me twenty-one
days. So Michael, one of the chief
princes, came to help me, and I left
him there with the prince of the
kingdom of Persia,[w] [14]and have
come to help you understand what
is to happen to your people at the
end of days. For there is a further
vision for those days."

15 While he was speaking these
words to me, I turned my face toward the ground and was speechless. [16]Then one in human form
touched my lips, and I opened my
mouth to speak, and said to the
one who stood before me, "My
lord, because of the vision such
pains have come upon me that I retain no strength. [17]How can my
lord's servant talk with my lord?
For I am shaking,[x] no strength remains in me, and no breath is left
in me."

18 Again one in human form
touched me and strengthened me.
[19]He said, "Do not fear, greatly beloved, you are safe. Be strong and
courageous!" When he spoke to
me, I was strengthened and said,
"Let my lord speak, for you have
strengthened me." [20]Then he said,
"Do you know why I have come to
you? Now I must return to fight
against the prince of Persia, and
when I am through with him, the
prince of Greece will come. [21]But I
am to tell you what is inscribed in
the book of truth. There is no one
with me who contends against
these princes except Michael, your

11 prince. [1]As for me, in the
first year of Darius the
Mede, I stood up to support and
strengthen him.

2 "Now I will announce the
truth to you. Three more kings
shall arise in Persia. The fourth
shall be far richer than all of them,
and when he has become strong
through his riches, he shall stir up
all against the kingdom of Greece.
[3]Then a warrior king shall arise,
who shall rule with great dominion
and take action as he pleases. [4]And
while still rising in power, his kingdom shall be broken and divided
toward the four winds of heaven,
but not to his posterity, nor according to the dominion with which he
ruled; for his kingdom shall be uprooted and go to others besides
these.

5 "Then the king of the south
shall grow strong, but one of his officers shall grow stronger than he

10.4 Dan 8.2; Gen 2.14 **10.5** Dan 12.6,7; Rev 1.13; Jer 10.9 **10.6** Mt 17.2; Rev 1.16,14; 1.15; 2.18 **10.7** 2 Kings 6.17; Acts 9.7; Ezek 12.18 **10.8** Gen 32.24; Dan 7.28; 8.27 **10.9** Dan 8.18 **10.10** Jer 1.9; Dan 9.21; Rev 1.17 **10.11** Dan 9.23 **10.12** Rev 1.17; Dan 9.3, 20-23 **10.13** vv. 20,21; Dan 12.1; Jude 9; Rev 12.7 **10.14** Dan 2.28; 8.26; Hab 2.3 **10.15** Ezek 24.27; Lk 1.20 **10.16** Dan 8.15; v. 10; Jer 1.9; v. 8 **10.17** Isa 6.1-5; v. 8 **10.18** v. 16; Isa 35.3,4 **10.19** vv. 11,12; Judg 6.23 **10.20** v. 13; Dan 8.21; 11.2 **10.21** Dan 11.2; v. 13 **11.1ff** Dan 9.1; 5.31 **11.2** Dan 8.26; 8.21 **11.3** Dan 8.4,5, 21 **11.4** Dan 8.8,22; Ezek 37.9; Zech 2.6; Rev 7.1 **11.5** vv. 9,11,14,25,40

[w] Gk Theodotion: Heb *I was left there with the kings of Persia* [x] Gk: Heb *from now*

and shall rule a realm greater than
his own realm. 6 After some years
they shall make an alliance, and
the daughter of the king of the
south shall come to the king of the
north to ratify the agreement. But
she shall not retain her power, and
his offspring shall not endure. She
shall be given up, she and her attendants and her child and the one
who supported her.

"In those times 7 a branch from
her roots shall rise up in his place.
He shall come against the army
and enter the fortress of the king of
the north, and he shall take action
against them and prevail. 8 Even
their gods, with their idols and with
their precious vessels of silver and
gold, he shall carry off to Egypt as
spoils of war. For some years he
shall refrain from attacking the
king of the north; 9 then the latter
shall invade the realm of the king
of the south, but will return to his
own land.

10 "His sons shall wage war and
assemble a multitude of great
forces, which shall advance like a
flood and pass through, and again
shall carry the war as far as his fortress. 11 Moved with rage, the king
of the south shall go out and do
battle against the king of the north,
who shall muster a great multitude, which shall, however, be defeated by his enemy. 12 When the
multitude has been carried off, his
heart shall be exalted, and he shall
overthrow tens of thousands, but
he shall not prevail. 13 For the king
of the north shall again raise a multitude, larger than the former, and
after some years[y] he shall advance
with a great army and abundant
supplies.

14 "In those times many shall
rise against the king of the south.
The lawless among your own people shall lift themselves up in order
to fulfill the vision, but they shall
fail. 15 Then the king of the north
shall come and throw up siegeworks, and take a well-fortified
city. And the forces of the south
shall not stand, not even his picked
troops, for there shall be no
strength to resist. 16 But he who
comes against him shall take the
actions he pleases, and no one
shall withstand him. He shall take
a position in the beautiful land,
and all of it shall be in his power.
17 He shall set his mind to come
with the strength of his whole kingdom, and he shall bring terms of
peace[z] and perform them. In order
to destroy the kingdom,[a] he shall
give him a woman in marriage; but
it shall not succeed or be to his advantage. 18 Afterward he shall turn
to the coastlands, and shall capture many. But a commander shall
put an end to his insolence; indeed,[b] he shall turn his insolence
back upon him. 19 Then he shall
turn back toward the fortresses of
his own land, but he shall stumble
and fall, and shall not be found.

20 "Then shall arise in his place
one who shall send an official for
the glory of the kingdom; but within a few days he shall be broken,
though not in anger or in battle.
21 In his place shall arise a contemptible person on whom royal
majesty had not been conferred; he
shall come in without warning and
obtain the kingdom through intrigue. 22 Armies shall be utterly
swept away and broken before him,
and the prince of the covenant as
well. 23 And after an alliance is
made with him, he shall act deceitfully and become strong with a
small party. 24 Without warning he
shall come into the richest parts[c]
of the province and do what none
of his predecessors had ever done,
lavishing plunder, spoil, and
wealth on them. He shall devise
plans against strongholds, but only
for a time. 25 He shall stir up his
power and determination against
the king of the south with a great
army, and the king of the south
shall wage war with a much greater
and stronger army. But he shall not
succeed, for plots shall be devised
against him 26 by those who eat of

11.6 vv. 13,15,40
11.7 vv. 19,38,39
11.8 Isa 37.19; 46.1,2; Jer 43.12,13
11.10 Isa 8.8; Jer 46.7,8; Dan 9.26; v. 7
11.11 v. 5; Dan 8.7; vv. 13,10
11.13 Dan 4.16; 12.7
11.15 Jer 6.6; Ezek 4.2; 17.17
11.16 Dan 8.4,7; vv. 3,36; Josh 1.5; vv. 41,45
11.17 2 Kings 12.17; Ezek 4.3,7
11.18 Isa 66.19; Jer 31.10; Hos 12.14
11.19 Ps 27.2; Job 20.8; Ezek 26.21
11.20 Isa 60.17
11.21 vv. 24,32,34
11.22 v. 10; Dan 8.10,11
11.23 Dan 8.25
11.24 v. 21; Ezek 34,14
11.26 vv. 10,40

[y] Heb *and at the end of the times years*
[z] Gk: Heb *kingdom, and upright ones with him*
[a] Heb *it* [b] Meaning of Heb uncertain
[c] Or *among the richest men*

the royal rations. They shall break him, his army shall be swept away, and many shall fall slain. 27 The two kings, their minds bent on evil, shall sit at one table and exchange lies. But it shall not succeed, for there remains an end at the time appointed. 28 He shall return to his land with great wealth, but his heart shall be set against the holy covenant. He shall work his will, and return to his own land.

29 "At the time appointed he shall return and come into the south, but this time it shall not be as it was before. 30 For ships of Kittim shall come against him, and he shall lose heart and withdraw. He shall be enraged and take action against the holy covenant. He shall turn back and pay heed to those who forsake the holy covenant. 31 Forces sent by him shall occupy and profane the temple and fortress. They shall abolish the regular burnt offering and set up the abomination that makes desolate. 32 He shall seduce with intrigue those who violate the covenant; but the people who are loyal to their God shall stand firm and take action. 33 The wise among the people shall give understanding to many; for some days, however, they shall fall by sword and flame, and suffer captivity and plunder. 34 When they fall victim, they shall receive a little help, and many shall join them insincerely. 35 Some of the wise shall fall, so that they may be refined, purified, and cleansed,[d] until the time of the end, for there is still an interval until the time appointed.

36 "The king shall act as he pleases. He shall exalt himself and consider himself greater than any god, and shall speak horrendous things against the God of gods. He shall prosper until the period of wrath is completed, for what is determined shall be done. 37 He shall pay no respect to the gods of his ancestors, or to the one beloved by women; he shall pay no respect to any other god, for he shall consider himself greater than all. 38 He shall honor the god of fortresses instead of these; a god whom his ancestors did not know he shall honor with gold and silver, with precious stones and costly gifts. 39 He shall deal with the strongest fortresses by the help of a foreign god. Those who acknowledge him he shall make more wealthy, and shall appoint them as rulers over many, and shall distribute the land for a price.

The Time of the End

40 "At the time of the end the king of the south shall attack him. But the king of the north shall rush upon him like a whirlwind, with chariots and horsemen, and with many ships. He shall advance against countries and pass through like a flood. 41 He shall come into the beautiful land, and tens of thousands shall fall victim, but Edom and Moab and the main part of the Ammonites shall escape from his power. 42 He shall stretch out his hand against the countries, and the land of Egypt shall not escape. 43 He shall become ruler of the treasures of gold and of silver, and all the riches of Egypt; and the Libyans and the Ethiopians[e] shall follow in his train. 44 But reports from the east and the north shall alarm him, and he shall go out with great fury to bring ruin and complete destruction to many. 45 He shall pitch his palatial tents between the sea and the beautiful holy mountain. Yet he shall come to his end, with no one to help him.

The Resurrection of the Dead

12 "At that time Michael, the great prince, the protector of your people, shall arise. There shall be a time of anguish, such as has never occurred since nations first came into existence. But at that time your people shall be delivered, everyone who is found written in the book. 2 Many of those who sleep in the dust of the earth[f] shall awake, some to everlasting

11.27 Ps 52.1; 64.6; Jer 9.3-5; vv. 35,40; Hab 2.3
11.30 Gen 10.4; Num 24.24; Jer 2.10
11.31 Dan 8.11; 9.27; Mt 24.15; Mk 13.14
11.32 vv. 21,34; Mic 5.7-9
11.33 Mt 24.9; Jn 16.2; Heb 11.36-38
11.34 Mt 7.15; Rom 16.18
11.35 Zech 13.9; Jn 15.2; vv. 27,40
11.36 2 Thes 2.4; Rev 13.5,6; Dan 2.47; 8.12; 8.19; 9.27
11.37 v. 36
11.40 vv. 10,13, 15,26; Isa 5.28
11.41 Jer 48.47; 49.6
11.43 2 Chr 12.3; Ezek 30.4,5; Nah 3.9
11.45 vv. 16,41; Isa 65.25; 66.20; Dan 9.16,20
12.1 Dan 10.13, 21; 9.12; Mt 24.21; Rev 16.18; v. 4
12.2 Isa 26.19; Mt 25.46; Jn 5.28; Acts 24.15

[d] Heb *made them white* [e] Or *Nubians*; Heb *Cushites* [f] Or *the land of dust*

life, and some to shame and everlasting contempt. 3 Those who are
wise shall shine like the brightness
of the sky,[g] and those who lead
many to righteousness, like the
stars forever and ever. 4 But you,
Daniel, keep the words secret and
the book sealed until the time of
the end. Many shall be running
back and forth, and evil[h] shall increase."
5 Then I, Daniel, looked, and
two others appeared, one standing
on this bank of the stream and one
on the other. 6 One of them said to
the man clothed in linen, who was
upstream, "How long shall it be until the end of these wonders?" 7 The
man clothed in linen, who was upstream, raised his right hand and
his left hand toward heaven. And I
heard him swear by the one who
lives forever that it would be for a
time, two times, and half a time,[i]
and that when the shattering of the
power of the holy people comes to
an end, all these things would be
accomplished. 8 I heard but could
not understand; so I said, "My lord,
what shall be the outcome of these
things?" 9 He said, "Go your way,
Daniel, for the words are to remain
secret and sealed until the time of
the end. 10 Many shall be purified,
cleansed, and refined, but the
wicked shall continue to act wickedly. None of the wicked shall understand, but those who are wise
shall understand. 11 From the time
that the regular burnt offering is
taken away and the abomination
that desolates is set up, there shall
be one thousand two hundred
ninety days. 12 Happy are those who
persevere and attain the thousand
three hundred thirty-five days.
13 But you, go your way,[j] and rest;
you shall rise for your reward at the
end of the days."

12.3 Mt 13.43; Dan 11.33
12.4 Rev 22.10; Dan 11.33
12.5 Dan 10.4ff
12.7 Rev 10.5,6; Dan 4.34; 7.25; Rev 12.14; Lk 21.24; Rev 10.7
12.8 v. 6
12.9 vv. 13,4
12.10 Dan 11.35; Isa 32.6,7
12.11f Dan 8.11-14; 9.27; 11.31; Mt 24.15
12.12 Isa 30.18; Rev 11.2; 12.6; 13.5
12.13 vv. 9,4; Rev 14.13

g Or *dome*
h Cn Compare Gk: Heb *knowledge*
i Heb *a time, times, and a half*
j Gk Theodotion: Heb adds *to the end*

Hosea

Title and Background

This book is named after the prophet whose message it preserves. Hosea lived during the tragic last days of the northern kingdom, when six kings reigned in twenty-five years. Assyria was expanding westward and in about 733 B.C. they dismembered Israel. Twelve years later, in 722-721 B.C., Samaria was captured and its people exiled. The northern kingdom was at an end.

Author and Date of Writing

Hosea prophesied about the middle of the eighth century B.C., shortly after the ministry of Amos. Amos had threatened God's judgment on Israel at the hands of an unnamed enemy; Hosea identified that enemy as Assyria. Hosea stands first in the division of the Bible called the Minor Prophets (Hosea through Malachi).

Theme and Message

In the first half of the book Hosea's family life is made a symbolic action to convey God's message for his people. The Lord loved his covenant people and would take them back, however often they would wander. The second half of the book gives the details of Israel's involvement in Canaanite religion. Like other prophetic books, Hosea is a call to repentance. The alternative to futility is to forsake idols and return to the Lord.

Outline

- I. The Unfaithful Wife and the Faithful Husband (1.1–3.5)
- II. The Unfaithful Nation and the Faithful God (4.1–14.9)
  - A. Israel's Unfaithfulness (4.1–6.3)
  - B. Israel's Punishment (6.4–10.15)
  - C. The Lord's Compassion and Faithful Love (11.1–14.9)

---

1 The word of the LORD that
came to Hosea son of Beeri, in
the days of Kings Uzziah, Jotham,
Ahaz, and Hezekiah of Judah, and
in the days of King Jeroboam son of
Joash of Israel.

The Family of Hosea

2 When the LORD first spoke
through Hosea, the LORD said to
Hosea, "Go, take for yourself a wife
of whoredom and have children of
whoredom, for the land commits
great whoredom by forsaking the
LORD." 3 So he went and took Gomer daughter of Diblaim, and she
conceived and bore him a son.
4 And the LORD said to him,
"Name him Jezreel;[a] for in a little
while I will punish the house of
Jehu for the blood of Jezreel, and I
will put an end to the kingdom of
the house of Israel. 5 On that day I
will break the bow of Israel in the
valley of Jezreel."
6 She conceived again and bore
a daughter. Then the LORD said to
him, "Name her Lo-ruhamah,[b] for
I will no longer have pity on the
house of Israel or forgive them.
7 But I will have pity on the house of
Judah, and I will save them by the
LORD their God; I will not save them
by bow, or by sword, or by war, or
by horses, or by horsemen."
8 When she had weaned Lo-
ruhamah, she conceived and bore a
son. 9 Then the LORD said, "Name

1.1 Rom 9.25; 2 Kings 5.1-7; 2 Chr 27.1-9; 2 Kings 16.1-20; 2 Chr 28.1-27; 2 Kings 18.1-20; 2 Chr 29.1-32; 2 Kings 13.13; 14.23-29
1.2 Hos 3.1; Jer 3.1,12, 14; Hos 2.5; 3.5
1.4 2 Kings 10.1-14; 15.10
1.5 2 Kings 15.29
1.6 vv. 3,9; Hos 2.4
1.7 Isa 30.18; Jer 25.5,6; Zech 9.9,10 **1.9** v. 6

[a] That is *God sows* [b] That is *Not pitied*

him Lo-ammi,[c] for you are not my
people and I am not your God."[d]

The Restoration of Israel

10[e] Yet the number of the people of Israel shall be like the sand
of the sea, which can be neither
measured nor numbered; and in
the place where it was said to
them, "You are not my people," it
shall be said to them, "Children of
the living God." 11 The people of
Judah and the people of Israel shall
be gathered together, and they
shall appoint for themselves one
head; and they shall take possession of[f] the land, for great shall be
the day of Jezreel.

2 [g] Say to your brother,[h] Ammi,[i]
and to your sister,[j] Ruha-
mah.[k]

Israel's Infidelity, Punishment, and Redemption

2 Plead with your mother,
plead—
for she is not my wife,
and I am not her
husband—
that she put away her
whoring from her face,
and her adultery from
between her breasts,
3 or I will strip her naked
and expose her as in the
day she was born,
and make her like a
wilderness,
and turn her into a parched
land,
and kill her with thirst.
4 Upon her children also I will
have no pity,
because they are children
of whoredom.
5 For their mother has played
the whore;
she who conceived them
has acted shamefully.
For she said, "I will go after
my lovers;
they give me my bread and
my water,
my wool and my flax, my
oil and my drink."
6 Therefore I will hedge up
her[l] way with thorns;
and I will build a wall
against her,
so that she cannot find her
paths.
7 She shall pursue her lovers,
but not overtake them;
and she shall seek them,
but shall not find them.
Then she shall say, "I will go
and return to my first
husband,
for it was better with me
then than now."
8 She did not know
that it was I who gave her
the grain, the wine, and
the oil,
and who lavished upon her
silver
and gold that they used for
Baal.
9 Therefore I will take back
my grain in its time,
and my wine in its season;
and I will take away my wool
and my flax,
which were to cover her
nakedness.
10 Now I will uncover her
shame
in the sight of her lovers,
and no one shall rescue her
out of my hand.
11 I will put an end to all her
mirth,
her festivals, her new
moons, her sabbaths,
and all her appointed
festivals.
12 I will lay waste her vines and
her fig trees,
of which she said,
"These are my pay,
which my lovers have given
me."
I will make them a forest,
and the wild animals shall
devour them.
13 I will punish her for the
festival days of the
Baals,

1.10 Gen 32.12; Jer 33.22; Rom 9.25-27; v. 9; Isa 63.16; 64.8
1.11 Isa 11.12; Jer 23.5,6; Ezek 37.21-24; Hos 3.5
2.1 v. 23
2.2 v. 5; Hos 4.5; Isa 50.1; Hos 1.2
2.3 Ezek 16.7, 22,39; Isa 32.13, 14; Am 8.11
2.4 Jer 13.14; Ezek 8.18
2.5 Isa 1.21; Jer 3.1,2,6; 44.17,18
2.6 Job 3.23; 19.8; Hos 9.6; 10.8
2.7 Jer 2.2; 3.1; Ezek 16.8; Hos 13.6
2.8 Isa 1.3; Ezek 16.19; Hos 8.4
2.9 Hos 8.7; 9.2
2.10 Ezek 16.37
2.11 Jer 7.34; 16.9; Am 8.10; Isa 1.13,14
2.12 v. 5; Isa 5.5; Hos 13.8
2.13 Ezek 16.12, 17; Hos 4.6; 8.14; 13.6

[c] That is *Not my people* [d] Heb *I am not yours* [e] Ch 2.1 in Heb [f] Heb *rise up from* [g] Ch 2.3 in Heb [h] Gk: Heb *brothers* [i] That is *My People* [j] Gk Vg: Heb *sisters* [k] That is *Pitied* [l] Gk Syr: Heb *your*

when she offered incense
to them
and decked herself with her
ring and jewelry,
and went after her lovers,
and forgot me, says the
LORD.

14 Therefore, I will now allure
her,
and bring her into the
wilderness,
and speak tenderly to her.
15 From there I will give her
her vineyards,
and make the Valley of
Achor a door of hope.
There she shall respond as in
the days of her youth,
as at the time when she
came out of the land of
Egypt.

16 On that day, says the LORD, you
will call me, "My husband," and no
longer will you call me, "My
Baal."[m] 17 For I will remove the
names of the Baals from her
mouth, and they shall be mentioned by name no more. 18 I will
make for you[n] a covenant on that
day with the wild animals, the
birds of the air, and the creeping
things of the ground; and I will
abolish[o] the bow, the sword, and
war from the land; and I will make
you lie down in safety. 19 And I will
take you for my wife forever; I will
take you for my wife in righteousness and in justice, in steadfast
love, and in mercy. 20 I will take you
for my wife in faithfulness; and you
shall know the LORD.

21 On that day I will answer,
says the LORD,
I will answer the heavens
and they shall answer the
earth;
22 and the earth shall answer
the grain, the wine, and
the oil,
and they shall answer
Jezreel;[p]
23 and I will sow him[q] for
myself in the land.
And I will have pity on
Lo-ruhamah,[r]
and I will say to
Lo-ammi,[s] "You are my
people";
and he shall say, "You are
my God."

Further Assurances of God's Redeeming Love

3 The LORD said to me again,
"Go, love a woman who has a
lover and is an adulteress, just as
the LORD loves the people of Israel,
though they turn to other gods and
love raisin cakes." 2 So I bought her
for fifteen shekels of silver and a
homer of barley and a measure of
wine.[t] 3 And I said to her, "You
must remain as mine for many
days; you shall not play the whore,
you shall not have intercourse with
a man, nor I with you." 4 For the Israelites shall remain many days
without king or prince, without
sacrifice or pillar, without ephod or
teraphim. 5 Afterward the Israelites
shall return and seek the LORD their
God, and David their king; they
shall come in awe to the LORD and
to his goodness in the latter days.

God Accuses Israel

4 Hear the word of the LORD,
O people of Israel;
for the LORD has an
indictment against the
inhabitants of the land.
There is no faithfulness or
loyalty,
and no knowledge of God
in the land.
2 Swearing, lying, and murder,
and stealing and adultery
break out;
bloodshed follows
bloodshed.
3 Therefore the land mourns,
and all who live in it
languish;
together with the wild
animals
and the birds of the air,
even the fish of the sea are
perishing.

2.14 Ezek 20.33-38 **2.15** Ezek 28.25, 26; Josh 7.26; Jer 2.2; Ex 15.1,2; Hos 11.1 **2.17** Ex 23.13; Josh 23.7; Ps 16.4; Zech 13.2; v. 13 **2.18** Job 5.23; Isa 11.6-9; Ps 46.9; Ezek 34.25 **2.19** Isa 62.4,5; Jer 3.14; Isa 1.27 **2.20** Hos 6.6; 13.4 **2.21** Isa 55.10; Zech 8.12 **2.22** Jer 31.12; Joel 2.19 **2.23** Jer 31.27; Hos 1.6; 1.9,10; Zech 13.9; Rom 9.25, 26

3.1 Hos 1.2; 2 Sam 6.19; 1 Chr 16.3 **3.2** Ruth 4.10 **3.4** Hos 13.10, 11; 2.11; Ex 28.6; Judg 17.5; Zech 10.2 **3.5** Jer 50.4,5; Ezek 34.23, 24; Jer 31.9; Mic 4.1 **4.1** Hos 5.1; 12.2; Mic 6.2; Isa 59.4; Jer 7.28; Hos 6.6; 5.4 **4.2** Hos 10.4; 7.3; 6.9; 7.1, 4; 6.8 **4.3** Jer 4.28; Zeph 1.3; Jer 4.25

m That is, *"My master"* n Heb *them*
o Heb *break* p That is *God sows*
q Cn: Heb *her* r That is *Not pitied*
s That is *Not my people* t Gk: Heb *a homer of barley and a lethech of barley*

4 Yet let no one contend,
and let none accuse,
for with you is my
contention, O priest.[u]
5 You shall stumble by day;
the prophet also shall
stumble with you by
night,
and I will destroy your
mother.
6 My people are destroyed for
lack of knowledge;
because you have rejected
knowledge,
I reject you from being a
priest to me.
And since you have forgotten
the law of your God,
I also will forget your
children.

7 The more they increased,
the more they sinned
against me;
they changed[v] their glory
into shame.
8 They feed on the sin of my
people;
they are greedy for their
iniquity.
9 And it shall be like people,
like priest;
I will punish them for their
ways,
and repay them for their
deeds.
10 They shall eat, but not be
satisfied;
they shall play the whore,
but not multiply;
because they have forsaken
the LORD
to devote themselves to
11 whoredom.

The Idolatry of Israel

Wine and new wine
take away the
understanding.
12 My people consult a piece of
wood,
and their divining rod gives
them oracles.
For a spirit of whoredom has
led them astray,
and they have played the
whore, forsaking their
God.
13 They sacrifice on the tops of
the mountains,
and make offerings upon
the hills,
under oak, poplar, and
terebinth,
because their shade is
good.

Therefore your daughters
play the whore,
and your daughters-in-law
commit adultery.
14 I will not punish your
daughters when they
play the whore,
nor your daughters-in-law
when they commit
adultery;
for the men themselves go
aside with whores,
and sacrifice with temple
prostitutes;
thus a people without
understanding comes to
ruin.

15 Though you play the whore,
O Israel,
do not let Judah become
guilty.
Do not enter into Gilgal,
or go up to Beth-aven,
and do not swear, "As the
LORD lives."
16 Like a stubborn heifer,
Israel is stubborn;
can the LORD now feed them
like a lamb in a broad
pasture?

17 Ephraim is joined to idols—
let him alone.
18 When their drinking is
ended, they indulge in
sexual orgies;
they love lewdness more
than their glory.[w]
19 A wind has wrapped them[x]
in its wings,

4.4 Ezek 3.26; Deut 17.12 **4.5** Hos 5.5; Ezek 14.3,7; Hos 2.2,5 **4.6** v. 1; Mal 2.7,8; Hos 2.13; 8.1,12 **4.7** Hos 10.1; 13.6; Hab 2.16; Mal 2.9 **4.8** Hos 10.13; Isa 56.11 **4.9** Isa 24.2; Jer 5.31; Hos 9.9 **4.10** Lev 26.26; Mic 6.14; Hos 7.14; 9.17 **4.11** Hos 5.4; Isa 28.7 **4.12** Jer 2.27; Hab 2.19; Hos 5.4; 9.1 **4.13** Jer 3.6; Ezek 6.13; Hos 2.13; 11.2; Am 7.17; Rom 1.28 **4.14** v. 18; Deut 23.17; vv. 6,11 **4.15** Am 4.4; 1 Kings 12.28, 29 **4.16** Ps 78.8; Isa 5.17; 7.25 **4.17** Ps 81.12; v. 4 **4.18** vv. 14,7 **4.19** Hos 12.1; 13.15; Isa 1.29

[u] Cn: Meaning of Heb uncertain [v] Ancient Heb tradition: MT *I will change* [w] Cn Compare Gk: Meaning of Heb uncertain [x] Heb *her*

and they shall be ashamed
because of their
altars.[y]

Impending Judgment on Israel and Judah

5 Hear this, O priests!
Give heed, O house of
Israel!
Listen, O house of the king!
For the judgment pertains
to you;
for you have been a snare at
Mizpah,
and a net spread upon
Tabor,
2 and a pit dug deep in
Shittim;[z]
but I will punish all of
them.

3 I know Ephraim,
and Israel is not hidden
from me;
for now, O Ephraim, you
have played the whore;
Israel is defiled.
4 Their deeds do not permit
them
to return to their God.
For the spirit of whoredom is
within them,
and they do not know the
LORD.

5 Israel's pride testifies against
him;
Ephraim[a] stumbles in his
guilt;
Judah also stumbles with
them.
6 With their flocks and herds
they shall go
to seek the LORD,
but they will not find him;
he has withdrawn from
them.
7 They have dealt faithlessly
with the LORD;
for they have borne
illegitimate children.
Now the new moon shall
devour them along with
their fields.

8 Blow the horn in Gibeah,
the trumpet in Ramah.
Sound the alarm at
Beth-aven;
look behind you, Benjamin!
9 Ephraim shall become a
desolation
in the day of punishment;
among the tribes of Israel
I declare what is sure.
10 The princes of Judah have
become
like those who remove the
landmark;
on them I will pour out
my wrath like water.
11 Ephraim is oppressed,
crushed in judgment,
because he was determined
to go after vanity.[b]
12 Therefore I am like maggots
to Ephraim,
and like rottenness to the
house of Judah.
13 When Ephraim saw his
sickness,
and Judah his wound,
then Ephraim went to
Assyria,
and sent to the great
king.[c]
But he is not able to cure
you
or heal your wound.
14 For I will be like a lion to
Ephraim,
and like a young lion to
the house of Judah.
I myself will tear and go
away;
I will carry off, and no one
shall rescue.
15 I will return again to my
place
until they acknowledge
their guilt and seek my
face.
In their distress they will
beg my favor:

A Call to Repentance

6 "Come, let us return to the
LORD;
for it is he who has torn,
and he will heal us;

5.1 Hos 4.1; 6.9 **5.3** Am 3.2; Hos 6.10 **5.4** Hos 4.11,12 **5.5** Hos 7.10; 4.5; Ezek 23.31-35 **5.6** Mic 6.6,7; Isa 1.15; Ezek 8.6 **5.7** Isa 48.8; Hos 6.7; 2.4,11,12 **5.8** Hos 9.9; 10.9; Isa 10.29, 30; Hos 4.15
5.9 Isa 37.3; 46.10; Zech 1.6 **5.10** Deut 19.14; Ezek 7.8; Ps 93.3,4 **5.11** Hos 9.16 **5.12** Ps 39.11; Prov 12.4 **5.13** Jer 30.12; Hos 7.11; 8.9; 10.6; 14.3 **5.14** Hos 13.7,8; Ps 50.22; Mic 5.8 **5.15** Isa 64.7-9; Jer 2.27; Hos 3.5 **6.1** Jer 50.4,5; Hos 5.14; 14.4; Isa 30.26

[y] Gk Syr: Heb *sacrifices* [z] Cn: Meaning of Heb uncertain [a] Heb *Israel and Ephraim* [b] Gk: Meaning of Heb uncertain [c] Cn: Heb *to a king who will contend*

he has struck down, and he
will bind us up.
2 After two days he will revive
us;
on the third day he will
raise us up,
that we may live before
him.
3 Let us know, let us press on
to know the LORD;
his appearing is as sure as
the dawn;
he will come to us like the
showers,
like the spring rains that
water the earth."

Impenitence of Israel and Judah

4 What shall I do with you,
O Ephraim?
What shall I do with you,
O Judah?
Your love is like a morning
cloud,
like the dew that goes away
early.
5 Therefore I have hewn them
by the prophets,
I have killed them by the
words of my mouth,
and my[d] judgment goes
forth as the light.
6 For I desire steadfast love
and not sacrifice,
the knowledge of God
rather than burnt
offerings.

7 But at[e] Adam they
transgressed the
covenant;
there they dealt faithlessly
with me.
8 Gilead is a city of evildoers,
tracked with blood.
9 As robbers lie in wait[f] for
someone,
so the priests are banded
together;[g]
they murder on the road to
Shechem,
they commit a monstrous
crime.
10 In the house of Israel I have
seen a horrible thing;
Ephraim's whoredom is
there, Israel is defiled.

6.2 Ps 30.5 **6.3** Isa 2.3; Mic 4.2; Ps 19.6; Mic 5.2; Joel 2.23 **6.4** Hos 7.1; 11.8; 13.3 **6.5** Jer 1.10,18; Heb 4.12; v. 3 **6.6** Mt 9.13; Ps 50.8,9; Hos 2.20 **6.7** Hos 8.1; 5.7 **6.8** Hos 4.2 **6.9** Hos 7.1; Jer 7.9,10; Ezek 22.9; 23.27 **6.10** Jer 5.30,31; Hos 5.3 **6.11** Joel 3.13; Zeph 2.7 **7.1** v. 13; Hos 6.4; 11.8; 4.2; 6.9 **7.2** Hos 8.13; 9.9; Am 8.7; Jer 2.19; Hos 4.9 **7.3** v. 5; Mic 7.3; Hos 4.2; 11.12; Rom 1.32 **7.4** Jer 9.2; 23.10 **7.5** Isa 28.1,7,8 **7.7** Ps 21.9; v. 16; Isa 64.7

11 For you also, O Judah, a
harvest is appointed.

When I would restore the
fortunes of my people,

7

1 when I would heal Israel,
the corruption of Ephraim
is revealed,
and the wicked deeds of
Samaria;
for they deal falsely,
the thief breaks in,
and the bandits raid
outside.
2 But they do not consider
that I remember all their
wickedness.
Now their deeds surround
them,
they are before my face.
3 By their wickedness they
make the king glad,
and the officials by their
treachery.
4 They are all adulterers;
they are like a heated oven,
whose baker does not need
to stir the fire,
from the kneading of the
dough until it is
leavened.
5 On the day of our king the
officials
became sick with the heat
of wine;
he stretched out his hand
with mockers.
6 For they are kindled[h] like an
oven, their heart burns
within them;
all night their anger
smolders;
in the morning it blazes
like a flaming fire.
7 All of them are hot as an
oven,
and they devour their
rulers.
All their kings have fallen;
none of them calls upon
me.

[d] Gk Syr: Heb *your* [e] Cn: Heb *like*
[f] Cn: Meaning of Heb uncertain
[g] Syr: Heb *are a company* [h] Gk Syr: Heb *brought near*

8 Ephraim mixes himself with
the peoples;
Ephraim is a cake not
turned.
9 Foreigners devour his
strength,
but he does not know it;
gray hairs are sprinkled upon
him,
but he does not know it.
10 Israel's pride testifies
against[i] him;
yet they do not return to
the LORD their God,
or seek him, for all this.

Futile Reliance on the Nations

11 Ephraim has become like a
dove,
silly and without sense;
they call upon Egypt, they
go to Assyria.
12 As they go, I will cast my net
over them;
I will bring them down like
birds of the air;
I will discipline them
according to the report
made to their
assembly.[j]
13 Woe to them, for they have
strayed from me!
Destruction to them, for
they have rebelled
against me!
I would redeem them,
but they speak lies against
me.
14 They do not cry to me from
the heart,
but they wail upon their
beds;
they gash themselves for
grain and wine;
they rebel against me.
15 It was I who trained and
strengthened their
arms,
yet they plot evil against
me.
16 They turn to that which does
not profit;[k]
they have become like a
defective bow;
their officials shall fall by the
sword
because of the rage of their
tongue.
So much for their babbling
in the land of Egypt.

Israel's Apostasy

8 Set the trumpet to your lips!
One like a vulture[j] is over
the house of the LORD,
because they have broken my
covenant,
and transgressed my law.
2 Israel cries to me,
"My God,
we — Israel — know
you!"
3 Israel has spurned the good;
the enemy shall pursue
him.
4 They made kings, but not
through me;
they set up princes, but
without my knowledge.
With their silver and gold
they made idols
for their own destruction.
5 Your calf is rejected,
O Samaria.
My anger burns against
them.
How long will they be
incapable of innocence?
6 For it is from Israel,
an artisan made it;
it is not God.
The calf of Samaria
shall be broken to pieces.[l]
7 For they sow the wind,
and they shall reap the
whirlwind.
The standing grain has no
heads,
it shall yield no meal;
if it were to yield,
foreigners would devour it.
8 Israel is swallowed up;
now they are among the
nations
as a useless vessel.

7.8 Ps 106.35; v. 11; Hos 5.13 **7.9** Isa 1.7; Hos 4.6 **7.10** Hos 5.5; vv. 7,14; Hos 5.4 **7.11** Hos 11.11; 4.6,11,14; v. 16; Hos 5.13; 8.9; 12.1 **7.12** Ezek 12.13 **7.13** Hos 9.12, 17; Jer 14.10; Ezek 34.6; v. 1; Mt 23.37 **7.14** Jer 3.10; Am 2.8; Mic 2.11; Hos 13.16 **7.15** Hos 11.13; Nah 1.9 **7.16** Ps 78.57; v. 7; Ezek 23.32

8.1 Hos 5.8; Hab 1.8; Hos 6.7; 4.6 **8.2** Hos 7.14 **8.4** Hos 13.10, 11; 2.8 **8.5** v. 6; Hos 10.5; 13.2; Jer 13.27 **8.6** Hos 13.2 **8.7** Hos 10.12, 13; Isa 66.15; Nah 1.3 **8.8** Jer 51.34; Hos 13.15

[i] Or *humbles* [j] Meaning of Heb uncertain
[k] Cn: Meaning of Heb uncertain
[l] Or *shall go up in flames*

[9] For they have gone up to
Assyria,
a wild ass wandering alone;
Ephraim has bargained for
lovers.
[10] Though they bargain with
the nations,
I will now gather them up.
They shall soon writhe
under the burden of kings
and princes.

[11] When Ephraim multiplied
altars to expiate sin,
they became to him altars
for sinning.
[12] Though I write for him the
multitude of my
instructions,
they are regarded as a
strange thing.
[13] Though they offer choice
sacrifices,[m]
though they eat flesh,
the LORD does not accept
them.
Now he will remember their
iniquity,
and punish their sins;
they shall return to Egypt.
[14] Israel has forgotten his
Maker,
and built palaces;
and Judah has multiplied
fortified cities;
but I will send a fire upon
his cities,
and it shall devour his
strongholds.

Punishment for Israel's Sin

9 Do not rejoice, O Israel!
Do not exult[n] as other
nations do;
for you have played the
whore, departing from
your God.
You have loved a
prostitute's pay
on all threshing floors.
[2] Threshing floor and wine vat
shall not feed them,
and the new wine shall fail
them.
[3] They shall not remain in the
land of the LORD;
but Ephraim shall return to
Egypt,
and in Assyria they shall
eat unclean food.

[4] They shall not pour drink
offerings of wine to the
LORD,
and their sacrifices shall
not please him.
Such sacrifices shall be like
mourners' bread;
all who eat of it shall be
defiled;
for their bread shall be for
their hunger only;
it shall not come to the
house of the LORD.

[5] What will you do on the day
of appointed festival,
and on the day of the
festival of the LORD?
[6] For even if they escape
destruction,
Egypt shall gather them,
Memphis shall bury them.
Nettles shall possess their
precious things of
silver;[o]
thorns shall be in their
tents.

[7] The days of punishment have
come,
the days of recompense
have come;
Israel cries,[p]
"The prophet is a fool,
the man of the spirit is
mad!"
Because of your great
iniquity,
your hostility is great.
[8] The prophet is a sentinel for
my God over Ephraim,
yet a fowler's snare is on all
his ways,
and hostility in the house
of his God.
[9] They have deeply corrupted
themselves
as in the days of Gibeah;

8.9 Hos 7.11; Jer 2.24; Ezek 16.3
8.10 Ezek 16.37; 22.40; Jer 42.2
8.11 Hos 10.1; 12.11
8.12 v. 1; Hos 4.6
8.13 Jer 7.21; Hos 7.2; 1 Cor 4.5; Hos 4.9; 9.7; 9.3,6
8.14 Hos 2.13; 13.6; Jer 17.27
9.1 Isa 22.12, 13; Hos 10.5; 4.12; Jer 44.17
9.2 Hos 2.9
9.3 Jer 2.7; Hos 8.13; Ezek 4.13; Hos 7.11
9.4 Jer 6.20; Hos 5.6; 8.13; Hag 2.14
9.5 Isa 10.3; Jer 5.31; Joel 1.13
9.6 v. 3; Jer 2.16; Ezek 30.13, 16; Isa 5.6; Hos 10.8
9.7 Jer 10.15; Mic 7.4; Isa 34.8; Jer 16.18; Ezek 14.9, 10
9.8 Hos 5.1
9.9 Isa 31.6; Judg 19.12; Hos 5.8; 10.9; 7.2; 8.13

m Cn: Meaning of Heb uncertain
n Gk: Heb *To exultation*
o Meaning of Heb uncertain
p Cn Compare Gk: Heb *shall know*

he will remember their
iniquity,
he will punish their sins.

10 Like grapes in the
wilderness,
I found Israel.
Like the first fruit on the fig
tree,
in its first season,
I saw your ancestors.
But they came to Baal-peor,
and consecrated
themselves to a thing of
shame,
and became detestable like
the thing they loved.
11 Ephraim's glory shall fly
away like a bird—
no birth, no pregnancy, no
conception!
12 Even if they bring up
children,
I will bereave them until
no one is left.
Woe to them indeed
when I depart from them!
13 Once I saw Ephraim as a
young palm planted in
a lovely meadow,[q]
but now Ephraim must
lead out his children for
slaughter.
14 Give them, O LORD—
what will you give?
Give them a miscarrying
womb
and dry breasts.

15 Every evil of theirs began at
Gilgal;
there I came to hate them.
Because of the wickedness of
their deeds
I will drive them out of my
house.
I will love them no more;
all their officials are rebels.

16 Ephraim is stricken,
their root is dried up,
they shall bear no fruit.
Even though they give birth,
I will kill the cherished
offspring of their womb.
17 Because they have not
listened to him,
my God will reject them;
they shall become
wanderers among the
nations.

Israel's Sin and Captivity

10 Israel is a luxuriant vine
that yields its fruit.
The more his fruit increased
the more altars he built;
as his country improved,
he improved his pillars.
2 Their heart is false;
now they must bear their
guilt.
The LORD[r] will break down
their altars,
and destroy their pillars.

3 For now they will say:
"We have no king,
for we do not fear the LORD,
and a king—what could he
do for us?"
4 They utter mere words;
with empty oaths they
make covenants;
so litigation springs up like
poisonous weeds
in the furrows of the field.
5 The inhabitants of Samaria
tremble
for the calf[s] of Beth-aven.
Its people shall mourn for it,
and its idolatrous priests
shall wail[t] over it,
over its glory that has
departed from it.
6 The thing itself shall be
carried to Assyria
as tribute to the great
king.[u]
Ephraim shall be put to
shame,
and Israel shall be
ashamed of his idol.[v]

7 Samaria's king shall perish
like a chip on the face of
the waters.
8 The high places of Aven, the
sin of Israel,
shall be destroyed.

9.10 Mic 7.1; Jer 24.2; Num 25.3; Hos 4.14; Jer 11.13 **9.11** Hos 4.7; 10.5; v. 14 **9.12** v. 16; Hos 7.13 **9.13** Ezek 27.3,4 **9.14** v. 11; Lk 23.29 **9.15** Hos 4.9; 7.2; 12.2; Isa 1.23 **9.16** Hos 5.11; 8.7; v. 12 **9.17** Hos 4.10; Deut 28.65

10.1 Ezek 15.1-5; Hos 8.11; 3.4 **10.2** 1 Kings 18.21; Mt 6.24; Hos 13.16; v. 8 **10.3** Ps 12.4 **10.4** Ezek 17.13-19; Hos 4.2; Deut 31.16, 17 **10.5** Hos 8.5,6; 9.11 **10.6** Hos 11.5; 5.13; 4.7; Isa 30.3; Jer 7.24 **10.7** Hos 13.11 **10.8** v. 5; 1 Kings 12.30; v. 2; Hos 9.6; Lk 23.30; Rev 6.16

[q] Meaning of Heb uncertain [r] Heb *he* [s] Gk Syr: Heb *calves* [t] Cn: Heb *exult* [u] Cn: Heb *to a king who will contend* [v] Cn: Heb *counsel*

Thorn and thistle shall grow
up
on their altars.
They shall say to the
mountains, Cover us,
and to the hills, Fall on us.

9 Since the days of Gibeah you
have sinned, O Israel;
there they have continued.
Shall not war overtake
them in Gibeah?
10 I will come[w] against the
wayward people to
punish them;
and nations shall be
gathered against them
when they are punished[x]
for their double
iniquity.

11 Ephraim was a trained heifer
that loved to thresh,
and I spared her fair neck;
but I will make Ephraim
break the ground;
Judah must plow;
Jacob must harrow for
himself.
12 Sow for yourselves
righteousness;
reap steadfast love;
break up your fallow
ground;
for it is time to seek the
LORD,
that he may come and rain
righteousness upon you.

13 You have plowed wickedness,
you have reaped injustice,
you have eaten the fruit of
lies.
Because you have trusted in
your power
and in the multitude of
your warriors,
14 therefore the tumult of war
shall rise against your
people,
and all your fortresses shall
be destroyed,
as Shalman destroyed
Beth-arbel on the day
of battle
when mothers were dashed
in pieces with their
children.
15 Thus it shall be done to you,
O Bethel,
because of your great
wickedness.
At dawn the king of Israel
shall be utterly cut off.

God's Compassion Despite Israel's Ingratitude

11 When Israel was a child, I
loved him,
and out of Egypt I called
my son.
2 The more I[y] called them,
the more they went from
me;[z]
they kept sacrificing to the
Baals,
and offering incense to
idols.

3 Yet it was I who taught
Ephraim to walk,
I took them up in my[a]
arms;
but they did not know that
I healed them.
4 I led them with cords of
human kindness,
with bands of love.
I was to them like those
who lift infants to their
cheeks.[b]
I bent down to them and
fed them.

5 They shall return to the land
of Egypt,
and Assyria shall be their
king,
because they have refused
to return to me.
6 The sword rages in their
cities,
it consumes their
oracle-priests,
and devours because of
their schemes.
7 My people are bent on
turning away from me.

10.9 Hos 5.8; 9.9
10.10 Ezek 5.13; Hos 4.9
10.11 Jer 50.11; Hos 4.16; Jer 28.14; Ps 66.12
10.12 Prov 11.18; Jer 4.3; Hos 12.6; 6.3; Isa 44.3; 45.8
10.13 Job 4.8; Gal 6.7,8; Hos 4.2; 7.3
10.14 Isa 17.3; Hos 13.16
10.15 v. 7
11.1 Hos 2.15; 12.9,13; 13.4; Mt 2.15
11.2 2 Kings 17.13-15; Hos 2.13; Isa 65.7; Jer 18.15
11.3 Hos 7.15; Deut 1.31; Jer 30.17
11.4 Jer 31.2,3; Lev 26.13; Ex 16.32; Ps 78.25
11.5 Hos 10.6; 7.16
11.6 Hos 13.16; 4.16,17
11.7 Jer 8.5; v. 2

w Cn Compare Gk: Heb *In my desire*
x Gk: Heb *bound*
y Gk: Heb *they*
z Gk: Heb *them*
a Gk Syr Vg: Heb *his*
b Or *who ease the yoke on their jaws*

To the Most High they call,
but he does not raise them
up at all.[c]

8 How can I give you up,
Ephraim?
How can I hand you over,
O Israel?
How can I make you like
Admah?
How can I treat you like
Zeboiim?
My heart recoils within
me;
my compassion grows
warm and tender.
9 I will not execute my fierce
anger;
I will not again destroy
Ephraim;
for I am God and no mortal,
the Holy One in your
midst,
and I will not come in
wrath.[c]

10 They shall go after the LORD,
who roars like a lion;
when he roars,
his children shall come
trembling from the
west.
11 They shall come trembling
like birds from Egypt,
and like doves from the
land of Assyria;
and I will return them to
their homes, says the
LORD.

12 [d]Ephraim has surrounded me
with lies,
and the house of Israel
with deceit;
but Judah still walks[e] with
God,
and is faithful to the Holy
One.

12

Ephraim herds the wind,
and pursues the east
wind all day long;
they multiply falsehood and
violence;
they make a treaty with
Assyria,
and oil is carried to Egypt.

11.8 Hos 6.4; Gen 14.8; Isa 63.15
11.9 Deut 13.17; Jer 26.3; Isa 41.14, 16; 55.8,9; Mal 3.6
11.10 Hos 6.1-3; Joel 3.16; Isa 66.2,5
11.11 Isa 11.11; 60.8; Ezek 28.25, 26
11.12 Hos 4.2; 7.3
12.1 2 Kings 17.4; Isa 30.6
12.2 Mic 6.2; Hos 4.9
12.3 Gen 25.26; 32.24,28
12.4 Gen 32.26; 28.12-15
12.5 Ex 3.15
12.6 Mic 6.8; Hos 6.6; Mic 7.7
12.7 Am 8.5; Mic 6.11
12.8 Hos 13.6; Rev 3.17; Hos 4.8; 14.1
12.9 Hos 11.1; 13.4; Lev 23.42; Neh 8.17
12.10 2 Kings 17.13; Jer 7.25; Ezek 17.2; 20.49
12.11 Hos 6.8; 4.15; 9.15; 10.1,2

The Long History of Rebellion

2 The LORD has an indictment
against Judah,
and will punish Jacob
according to his ways,
and repay him according to
his deeds.
3 In the womb he tried to
supplant his brother,
and in his manhood he
strove with God.
4 He strove with the angel and
prevailed,
he wept and sought his
favor;
he met him at Bethel,
and there he spoke with
him.[f]
5 The LORD the God of hosts,
the LORD is his name!
6 But as for you, return to your
God,
hold fast to love and
justice,
and wait continually for
your God.

7 A trader, in whose hands are
false balances,
he loves to oppress.
8 Ephraim has said, "Ah, I am
rich,
I have gained wealth for
myself;
in all of my gain
no offense has been found
in me
that would be sin."[c]
9 I am the LORD your God
from the land of Egypt;
I will make you live in tents
again,
as in the days of the
appointed festival.

10 I spoke to the prophets;
it was I who multiplied
visions,
and through the prophets I
will bring destruction.
11 In Gilead[g] there is iniquity,
they shall surely come to
nothing.

[c] Meaning of Heb uncertain [d] Ch 12.1 in Heb [e] Heb *roams* or *rules* [f] Gk Syr: Heb *us* [g] Compare Syr: Heb *Gilead*

In Gilgal they sacrifice bulls,
so their altars shall be like stone heaps
on the furrows of the field.
12 Jacob fled to the land of Aram,
there Israel served for a wife,
and for a wife he guarded sheep.[h]
13 By a prophet the LORD brought Israel up from Egypt,
and by a prophet he was guarded.
14 Ephraim has given bitter offense,
so his Lord will bring his crimes down on him
and pay him back for his insults.

Relentless Judgment on Israel

13 When Ephraim spoke, there was trembling;
he was exalted in Israel;
but he incurred guilt through Baal and died.
2 And now they keep on sinning
and make a cast image for themselves,
idols of silver made according to their understanding,
all of them the work of artisans.
"Sacrifice to these," they say.[i]
People are kissing calves!
3 Therefore they shall be like the morning mist
or like the dew that goes away early,
like chaff that swirls from the threshing floor
or like smoke from a window.

4 Yet I have been the LORD your God
ever since the land of Egypt;
you know no God but me,
and besides me there is no savior.
5 It was I who fed[j] you in the wilderness,
in the land of drought.
6 When I fed[k] them, they were satisfied;
they were satisfied, and their heart was proud;
therefore they forgot me.
7 So I will become like a lion to them,
like a leopard I will lurk beside the way.
8 I will fall upon them like a bear robbed of her cubs,
and will tear open the covering of their heart;
there I will devour them like a lion,
as a wild animal would mangle them.

9 I will destroy you, O Israel;
who can help you?[l]
10 Where now is[m] your king, that he may save you?
Where in all your cities are your rulers,
of whom you said,
"Give me a king and rulers"?
11 I gave you a king in my anger,
and I took him away in my wrath.

12 Ephraim's iniquity is bound up;
his sin is kept in store.
13 The pangs of childbirth come for him,
but he is an unwise son;
for at the proper time he does not present himself
at the mouth of the womb.

14 Shall I ransom them from the power of Sheol?
Shall I redeem them from Death?

12.12 Gen 28.5; 29.20 **12.13** Ex 13.3 **12.14** Ezek 18.10-13; Dan 11.18; Mic 6.16 **13.1** Judg 8.1; 12.1; Hos 2.8-17 **13.2** Isa 46.6; Hos 8.6 **13.3** Hos 6.4; Dan 2.35; Ps 68.2 **13.4** Hos 12.9; Isa 43.11 **13.5** Deut 2.7; 8.15; 32.10 **13.6** Deut 8.12, 14; 32.15; Hos 2.13; 4.6; 8.14 **13.7** Lam 3.10; Jer 5.6 **13.8** 2 Sam 17.8; Ps 50.22 **13.10** 2 Kings 17.4; Hos 8.4 **13.11** 1 Sam 8.7; 1 Kings 14.7-10 **13.12** Deut 32.34; Rom 2.5 **13.13** Mic 4.9,10; Isa 37.3; 66.9 **13.14** Ezek 37.12, 13; 1 Cor 15.54, 55; Rom 11.29

[h] Heb lacks *sheep* [i] Cn Compare Gk: Heb *To these they say sacrifices of people* [j] Gk Syr: Heb *knew* [k] Cn: Heb *according to their pasture* [l] Gk Syr: Heb *for in me is your help* [m] Gk Syr Vg: Heb *I will be*

O Death, where are[n] your
plagues?
O Sheol, where is[n] your
destruction?
Compassion is hidden from
my eyes.

15 Although he may flourish
among rushes,[o]
the east wind shall come, a
blast from the LORD,
rising from the wilderness;
and his fountain shall dry
up,
his spring shall be parched.
It shall strip his treasury
of every precious thing.
16[p] Samaria shall bear her guilt,
because she has rebelled
against her God;
they shall fall by the sword,
their little ones shall be
dashed in pieces,
and their pregnant women
ripped open.

A Plea for Repentance

14 Return, O Israel, to the
LORD your God,
for you have stumbled
because of your
iniquity.
2 Take words with you
and return to the LORD;
say to him,
"Take away all guilt;
accept that which is good,
and we will offer
the fruit[q] of our lips.
3 Assyria shall not save us;
we will not ride upon
horses;
we will say no more, 'Our
God,'
to the work of our hands.
In you the orphan finds
mercy."

Assurance of Forgiveness

4 I will heal their disloyalty;
I will love them freely,
for my anger has turned
from them.
5 I will be like the dew to
Israel;
he shall blossom like the
lily,
he shall strike root like the
forests of Lebanon.[r]
6 His shoots shall spread out;
his beauty shall be like the
olive tree,
and his fragrance like that
of Lebanon.
7 They shall again live beneath
my[s] shadow,
they shall flourish as a
garden;[t]
they shall blossom like the
vine,
their fragrance shall be like
the wine of Lebanon.
8 O Ephraim, what have I[u] to
do with idols?
It is I who answer and look
after you.[v]
I am like an evergreen
cypress;
your faithfulness[w] comes
from me.
9 Those who are wise
understand these
things;
those who are discerning
know them.
For the ways of the LORD are
right,
and the upright walk in
them,
but transgressors stumble
in them.

13.15 Hos 10.1; Ezek 17.10; 19.12; Jer 51.36; 20.5 **13.16** Hos 10.2; 7.14; Isa 13.16; Hos 10.14; 2 Kings 15.16 **14.1** Hos 10.12; 14.6; Joel 2.13 **14.2** Mic 7.18,19; Heb 13.15 **14.3** Hos 5.13; Isa 31.1; Hos 8.6; 13.2; Ps 10.14 **14.4** Zeph 3.17; Isa 12.1 **14.5** Job 29.19; Mt 6.28; Isa 35.2 **14.6** Ps 52.8; Song 4.11 **14.7** Ps 91.4; Ezek 17.23; Hos 2.21,22 **14.8** v. 3; Isa 41.19; Ezek 17.23 **14.9** Ps 107.43; Acts 13.10; Isa 26.7; 1.28

[n] Gk Syr: Heb *I will be* [o] Or *among brothers* [p] Ch 14.1 in Heb [q] Gk Syr: Heb *bulls* [r] Cn: Heb *like Lebanon* [s] Heb *his* [t] Cn: Heb *they shall grow grain* [u] Or *What more has Ephraim* [v] Heb *him* [w] Heb *your fruit*

Joel

Title and Background

Joel was a common Old Testament name, meaning "The LORD is God." This prophet ministered during a time of a severe plague of locusts. Such plagues occur frequently in the Near East; Joel sees this one as a judgment from God on the nation of Israel.

Author and Date of Writing

This book contains no references to datable historical events, but a good case can be made for its being written about 830 B.C. during the reign of King Joash, when Jehoiada the high priest was regent in Judah.

Theme and Message

Joel sees in the massive locust plague and severe drought devastating Judah a harbinger of "the great and terrible day of the LORD" (2.31). Confronted with this crisis, he calls on everyone to repent. He sees this day as a day of punishment for the unfaithful Israelites as well as their neighbors. Restoration and blessing will come only after judgment and repentance.

Outline

I. A Foretaste of the Day of the Lord (1.1–2.17)
- A. A Call to Lament and Prayer (1.2-14)
- B. The Announcement of the Day of the Lord (1.15–2.11)
- C. A Call to Repentance (2.12-17)

II. Salvation in the Day of the Lord (2.18–3.21)
- A. The Lord's Restoration of Judah (2.18-27)
- B. The Lord's Renewal of His People (2.28-32)
- C. The Coming of the Day of the Lord (3.1-21)

---

1 The word of the LORD that came to Joel son of Pethuel:

Lament over the Ruin of the Country

2 Hear this, O elders,
give ear, all inhabitants of the land!
Has such a thing happened in your days,
or in the days of your ancestors?
3 Tell your children of it,
and let your children tell their children,
and their children another generation.
4 What the cutting locust left,
the swarming locust has eaten.
What the swarming locust left,
the hopping locust has eaten,
and what the hopping locust left,
the destroying locust has eaten.

5 Wake up, you drunkards, and weep;
and wail, all you wine-drinkers,
over the sweet wine,
for it is cut off from your mouth.
6 For a nation has invaded my land,
powerful and innumerable;

1.1 Jer 1.2; Ezek 1.3; Hos 1.1; Acts 2.16
1.2 Hos 4.1; 5.1; v. 14; Joel 2.2
1.3 Ps 78.4
1.4 Deut 28.38; Joel 2.25; Nah 3.15, 16; Isa 33.4
1.5 Joel 3.3; Isa 32.10
1.6 Joel 2.2,11; Rev 9.8

its teeth are lions' teeth,
and it has the fangs of a lioness.
7 It has laid waste my vines,
and splintered my fig trees;
it has stripped off their bark
and thrown it down;
their branches have turned white.

8 Lament like a virgin dressed in sackcloth
for the husband of her youth.
9 The grain offering and the drink offering are cut off
from the house of the LORD.
The priests mourn,
the ministers of the LORD.
10 The fields are devastated,
the ground mourns;
for the grain is destroyed,
the wine dries up,
the oil fails.

11 Be dismayed, you farmers,
wail, you vinedressers,
over the wheat and the barley;
for the crops of the field are ruined.
12 The vine withers,
the fig tree droops.
Pomegranate, palm, and apple—
all the trees of the field are dried up;
surely, joy withers away
among the people.

A Call to Repentance and Prayer

13 Put on sackcloth and lament, you priests;
wail, you ministers of the altar.
Come, pass the night in sackcloth,
you ministers of my God!
Grain offering and drink offering
are withheld from the house of your God.

14 Sanctify a fast,
call a solemn assembly.
Gather the elders
and all the inhabitants of the land
to the house of the LORD your God,
and cry out to the LORD.

15 Alas for the day!
For the day of the LORD is near,
and as destruction from the Almighty[a] it comes.
16 Is not the food cut off
before our eyes,
joy and gladness
from the house of our God?

17 The seed shrivels under the clods,[b]
the storehouses are desolate;
the granaries are ruined
because the grain has failed.
18 How the animals groan!
The herds of cattle wander about
because there is no pasture for them;
even the flocks of sheep are dazed.[c]

19 To you, O LORD, I cry.
For fire has devoured
the pastures of the wilderness,
and flames have burned
all the trees of the field.
20 Even the wild animals cry to you
because the watercourses are dried up,
and fire has devoured
the pastures of the wilderness.

2 Blow the trumpet in Zion;
sound the alarm on my holy mountain!
Let all the inhabitants of the land tremble,
for the day of the LORD is coming, it is near—
2 a day of darkness and gloom,

1.7 Isa 5.6; Am 4.9 **1.8** v. 13; Am 8.10 **1.9** Joel 2.14,17 **1.10** Isa 24.4,7; Hos 9.2 **1.11** Jer 14.3,4; Isa 17.11; Jer 9.12 **1.12** Hab 3.17, 18; Isa 16.10; 24.11; Jer 48.33 **1.13** v. 8; Jer 4.8; v. 9; Joel 2.17; 1 Kings 21.27 **1.14** 2 Chr 20.3, 4; Joel 2.15, 16; v. 2; Jon 3.8 **1.15** Jer 30.7; Isa 13.6,9; Joel 2.1,11, 31 **1.16** Isa 3.7; Deut 12.6,7; Ps 43.4 **1.17** Isa 17.10,11 **1.18** 1 Kings 18.5; Jer 14.5,6; Hos 4.3 **1.19** Ps 50.15; Jer 9.10; Joel 2.3 **1.20** Job 38.41; Ps 104.21; 1 Kings 17.7; 18.5 **2.1** Jer 4.5; Num 10.9; Zeph 1.14-16; vv. 11,31; Joel 1.15 **2.2** Am 5.18; Joel 1.6; Lam 1.12; Joel 1.2

[a] Traditional rendering of Heb *Shaddai* [b] Meaning of Heb uncertain [c] Compare Gk Syr Vg: Meaning of Heb uncertain

a day of clouds and thick
darkness!
Like blackness spread upon
the mountains
a great and powerful army
comes;
their like has never been
from of old,
nor will be again after
them
in ages to come.

3 Fire devours in front of
them,
and behind them a flame
burns.
Before them the land is like
the garden of Eden,
but after them a desolate
wilderness,
and nothing escapes them.

4 They have the appearance of
horses,
and like war-horses they
charge.
5 As with the rumbling of
chariots,
they leap on the tops of
the mountains,
like the crackling of a flame
of fire
devouring the stubble,
like a powerful army
drawn up for battle.

6 Before them peoples are in
anguish,
all faces grow pale.[d]
7 Like warriors they charge,
like soldiers they scale the
wall.
Each keeps to its own
course,
they do not swerve from[e]
their paths.
8 They do not jostle one
another,
each keeps to its own
track;
they burst through the
weapons
and are not halted.
9 They leap upon the city,
they run upon the walls;
they climb up into the
houses,
they enter through the
windows like a thief.

10 The earth quakes before
them,
the heavens tremble.
The sun and the moon are
darkened,
and the stars withdraw
their shining.
11 The LORD utters his voice
at the head of his army;
how vast is his host!
Numberless are those who
obey his command.
Truly the day of the LORD is
great;
terrible indeed—who can
endure it?

12 Yet even now, says the LORD,
return to me with all your
heart,
with fasting, with weeping,
and with mourning;
13 rend your hearts and not
your clothing.
Return to the LORD, your
God,
for he is gracious and
merciful,
slow to anger, and abounding
in steadfast love,
and relents from punishing.
14 Who knows whether he will
not turn and relent,
and leave a blessing behind
him,
a grain offering and a drink
offering
for the LORD, your God?

15 Blow the trumpet in Zion;
sanctify a fast;
call a solemn assembly;
16 gather the people.
Sanctify the congregation;
assemble the aged;
gather the children,
even infants at the breast.
Let the bridegroom leave his
room,
and the bride her canopy.

2.3 Joel 1.19, 20; Gen 2.8; Isa 51.3; Ps 105.34, 35
2.4 Rev 9.7
2.5 Rev 9.9; Isa 5.24; 30.30
2.6 Isa 13.8; Nah 2.10; Jer 30.6
2.7 Isa 5.26,27; v. 9
2.9 v. 7; Jer 9.21; Jn 10.1
2.10 Ps 18.7; Isa 13.10; Joel 3.15; Mt 24.29
2.11 Joel 3.16; Am 1.2; vv. 2,25; Jer 50.34; Rev 18.8; Joel 3.14; Ezek 22.14
2.12 Jer 4.1; Hos 12.6
2.13 Ps 34.18; Isa 57.15; 2 Sam 1.11; Jon 4.2; Jer 18.8; 42.10
2.14 Jer 26.3; Hag 2.19; Joel 1.9,13
2.15 Num 10.3; v. 1; Jer 36.9; Joel 1.14
2.16 Ex 19.10, 22; Ps 19.5

[d] Meaning of Heb uncertain [e] Gk Syr Vg: Heb *they do not take a pledge along*

17 Between the vestibule and
the altar
let the priests, the
ministers of the LORD,
weep.
Let them say, "Spare your
people, O LORD,
and do not make your
heritage a mockery,
a byword among the
nations.
Why should it be said among
the peoples,
'Where is their God?' "

God's Response and Promise

18 Then the LORD became
jealous for his land,
and had pity on his people.
19 In response to his people the
LORD said:
I am sending you
grain, wine, and oil,
and you will be satisfied;
and I will no more make you
a mockery among the
nations.

20 I will remove the northern
army far from you,
and drive it into a parched
and desolate land,
its front into the eastern sea,
and its rear into the
western sea;
its stench and foul smell will
rise up.
Surely he has done great
things!

21 Do not fear, O soil;
be glad and rejoice,
for the LORD has done great
things!
22 Do not fear, you animals of
the field,
for the pastures of the
wilderness are green;
the tree bears its fruit,
the fig tree and vine give
their full yield.

23 O children of Zion, be glad
and rejoice in the LORD
your God;

2.17 Ezek 8.16; Mt 23.35; Joel 1.9; Deut 9.26-29; Isa 37.20; Ps 44.13; 42.10
2.18 Zech 1.14; Isa 60.10
2.19 Hos 2.21, 22; Ezek 34.29; 36.15
2.20 Jer 1.14,15; Zech 14.8; Deut 11.24; Isa 34.3; Am 4.10
2.21 Jer 30.10; v. 26
2.22 Ps 65.12,13
2.23 Ps 149.2; Isa 41.16; Deut 11.14; Jer 5.24; Hos 6.3
2.24 Am 9.13; Mal 3.10
2.25 Joel 1.4
2.26 Isa 62.9; Ps 67.5-7; Isa 25.1; 45.17
2.27 Joel 3.17, 21; Isa 45.1, 21; 49.23
2.28 Acts 2.17-21; Ezek 39.29; Isa 40.5
2.29 1 Cor 12.13; Gal 3.28
2.30 Mt 24.29; Lk 21.11,25; Acts 2.19
2.31 Isa 13.9,10; Mt 24.29; Mal 4.1,5; Rev 6.12

for he has given the early
rain[f] for your vindication,
he has poured down for
you abundant rain,
the early and the later rain,
as before.
24 The threshing floors shall be
full of grain,
the vats shall overflow with
wine and oil.

25 I will repay you for the years
that the swarming locust
has eaten,
the hopper, the destroyer,
and the cutter,
my great army, which I
sent against you.

26 You shall eat in plenty and
be satisfied,
and praise the name of the
LORD your God,
who has dealt wondrously
with you.
And my people shall never
again be put to shame.
27 You shall know that I am in
the midst of Israel,
and that I, the LORD, am
your God and there is
no other.
And my people shall never
again
be put to shame.

God's Spirit Poured Out

28 [g]Then afterward
I will pour out my spirit on
all flesh;
your sons and your daughters
shall prophesy,
your old men shall dream
dreams,
and your young men shall
see visions.
29 Even on the male and female
slaves,
in those days, I will pour
out my spirit.

30 I will show portents in the
heavens and on the earth, blood
and fire and columns of smoke.
31 The sun shall be turned to dark-

[f] Meaning of Heb uncertain [g] Ch 3.1 in Heb

ness, and the moon to blood, before the great and terrible day of
the LORD comes. 32 Then everyone
who calls on the name of the LORD
shall be saved; for in Mount Zion
and in Jerusalem there shall be
those who escape, as the LORD has
said, and among the survivors shall
be those whom the LORD calls.

3[h] For then, in those days and at
that time, when I restore the
fortunes of Judah and Jerusalem,
2 I will gather all the nations and
bring them down to the valley of
Jehoshaphat, and I will enter into
judgment with them there, on account of my people and my heritage Israel, because they have scattered them among the nations.
They have divided my land, 3 and
cast lots for my people, and traded
boys for prostitutes, and sold girls
for wine, and drunk it down.

4 What are you to me, O Tyre
and Sidon, and all the regions of
Philistia? Are you paying me back
for something? If you are paying me
back, I will turn your deeds back
upon your own heads swiftly and
speedily. 5 For you have taken my
silver and my gold, and have carried my rich treasures into your
temples.[i] 6 You have sold the people of Judah and Jerusalem to the
Greeks, removing them far from
their own border. 7 But now I will
rouse them to leave the places to
which you have sold them, and I
will turn your deeds back upon
your own heads. 8 I will sell your
sons and your daughters into the
hand of the people of Judah, and
they will sell them to the Sabeans,
to a nation far away; for the LORD
has spoken.

Judgment in the Valley of Jehoshaphat

9 Proclaim this among the
nations:
Prepare war,[j]
stir up the warriors.
Let all the soldiers draw
near,
let them come up.

10 Beat your plowshares into
swords,
and your pruning hooks
into spears;
let the weakling say, "I am
a warrior."

11 Come quickly,[k]
all you nations all around,
gather yourselves there.
Bring down your warriors,
O LORD.

12 Let the nations rouse
themselves,
and come up to the valley
of Jehoshaphat;
for there I will sit to judge
all the neighboring nations.

13 Put in the sickle,
for the harvest is ripe.
Go in, tread,
for the wine press is full.
The vats overflow,
for their wickedness is
great.

14 Multitudes, multitudes,
in the valley of decision!
For the day of the LORD is
near
in the valley of decision.

15 The sun and the moon are
darkened,
and the stars withdraw
their shining.

16 The LORD roars from Zion,
and utters his voice from
Jerusalem,
and the heavens and the
earth shake.
But the LORD is a refuge for
his people,
a stronghold for the people
of Israel.

The Glorious Future of Judah

17 So you shall know that I, the
LORD your God,
dwell in Zion, my holy
mountain.

2.32 Isa 46.13; Mic 4.7; Rom 9.27
3.1 Jer 30.3; Ezek 38.14
3.2 Isa 66.16; Ezek 34.6; 35.10; 36.1-5
3.3 Ob 11; Nah 3.10
3.4 Am 1.9,10; Ezek 25.12, 17
3.5 2 Kings 12.18; 2 Chr 21.16, 17
3.7 Isa 43.5,6; Jer 23.8
3.8 Isa 14.2; 60.14; Ezek 23.42; Jer 6.20
3.9 Isa 8.9,10; Jer 51.27, 28; 6.4; 46.3, 4; Zech 14.2,3
3.10 Isa 2.4; Mic 4.3; Zech 12.8
3.11 Ezek 38.15, 16; Isa 13.3
3.12 Isa 2.4; 3.13
3.13 Mt 13.39; Rev 14.15; Isa 63.3; Rev 14.19
3.14 Isa 34.2-8; Joel 1.15; 2.1
3.15 Joel 2.10,31
3.16 Am 1.2; Joel 2.11; Hag 2.6; Jer 17.17
3.17 v. 21; Ezek 20.40; Ob 17; Isa 52.1; Nah 1.15

h Ch 4.1 in Heb
i Or *palaces*
j Heb *sanctify war*
k Meaning of Heb uncertain

And Jerusalem shall be holy,
and strangers shall never
again pass through it.

18 In that day
the mountains shall drip
sweet wine,
the hills shall flow with
milk,
and all the stream beds of
Judah
shall flow with water;
a fountain shall come forth
from the house of the
LORD
and water the Wadi
Shittim.

19 Egypt shall become a
desolation
and Edom a desolate
wilderness,
because of the violence done
to the people of Judah,
in whose land they have
shed innocent blood.
20 But Judah shall be inhabited
forever,
and Jerusalem to all
generations.
21 I will avenge their blood, and
I will not clear the
guilty,[1]
for the LORD dwells in Zion.

[1] Gk Syr: Heb *I will hold innocent their blood that I have not held innocent*

3.18 Am 9.13; Isa 30.25; 35.6; Ezek 47.1-12; Rev 22.1
3.19 Ob 10
3.20 Ezek 37.25; Am 9.15
3.21 Ezek 36.25; v. 17

Amos

Title and Background

The concurrent reigns of Uzziah of Judah and Jeroboam II of Israel were marked by a period of peace and prosperity. But such prosperity was accompanied by an almost unprecedented degree of social corruption, and it is to this that the book of Amos is addressed.

Author and Date of Writing

Amos was a herdsman from the small town of Tekoa; he was not a man of the court like Isaiah or a priest like Jeremiah. Though he lived in Judah, God sent him to announce judgment on the northern kingdom (Israel). The main part of his ministry was probably carried out about 760-750 B.C., and this book can be dated during that time.

Theme and Message

The dominant theme is clearly stated in 5.24, which calls for social justice as the indispensable expression of true piety. In other words, Amos was a vigorous spokesman for God's justice and righteousness. He condemns all who make themselves powerful or rich at the expense of others.

Outline

I. Judgments on Israel's Neighbors (1.1–2.5)
II. Judgment on Israel (2.6-16)
III. Oracles Against Israel (3.1–5.17)
IV. Announcements of Exile (5.18–6.14)
V. Visions of Divine Retribution (7.1–9.10)
VI. Restoration of Israel (9.11-15)

---

1 The words of Amos, who was
among the shepherds of Tekoa, which he saw concerning Israel in the days of King Uzziah of Judah and in the days of King
Jeroboam son of Joash of Israel,
two years[a] before the earthquake.

Judgment on Israel's Neighbors

2 And he said:
The LORD roars from Zion,
and utters his voice from
Jerusalem;
the pastures of the
shepherds wither,
and the top of Carmel dries
up.

3 Thus says the LORD:
For three transgressions of
Damascus,
and for four, I will not
revoke the
punishment;[b]
because they have threshed
Gilead
with threshing sledges of
iron.
4 So I will send a fire on the
house of Hazael,
and it shall devour the
strongholds of
Ben-hadad.
5 I will break the gate bars of
Damascus,
and cut off the inhabitants
from the Valley of Aven,
and the one who holds the
scepter from Beth-eden;

1.1 2 Sam 14.2; 2 Kings 14.23-29; Zech 14.5
1.2 Jer 25.30; Joel 3.16; 1.18,19; Am 9.3
1.3 Isa 7.8; 8.4; v. 13
1.4 Jer 49.27; 1 Kings 20.1; 2 Kings 6.24
1.5 Jer 51.30; 2 Kings 16.9; Am 9.7

[a] Or *during two years* [b] Heb *cause it to return*

and the people of Aram
shall go into exile to
Kir,
says the LORD.

6 Thus says the LORD:
For three transgressions of
Gaza,
and for four, I will not
revoke the
punishment;[c]
because they carried into
exile entire
communities,
to hand them over to
Edom.
7 So I will send a fire on the
wall of Gaza,
fire that shall devour its
strongholds.
8 I will cut off the inhabitants
from Ashdod,
and the one who holds the
scepter from Ashkelon;
I will turn my hand against
Ekron,
and the remnant of the
Philistines shall perish,
says the Lord GOD.

9 Thus says the LORD:
For three transgressions of
Tyre,
and for four, I will not
revoke the
punishment;[c]
because they delivered entire
communities over to
Edom,
and did not remember the
covenant of kinship.
10 So I will send a fire on the
wall of Tyre,
fire that shall devour its
strongholds.

11 Thus says the LORD:
For three transgressions of
Edom,
and for four, I will not
revoke the
punishment;[c]
because he pursued his
brother with the sword
and cast off all pity;
he maintained his anger
perpetually,[d]
and kept his wrath[e]
forever.
12 So I will send a fire on
Teman,
and it shall devour the
strongholds of Bozrah.

13 Thus says the LORD:
For three transgressions of
the Ammonites,
and for four, I will not
revoke the
punishment;[c]
because they have ripped
open pregnant women
in Gilead
in order to enlarge their
territory.
14 So I will kindle a fire against
the wall of Rabbah,
fire that shall devour its
strongholds,
with shouting on the day of
battle,
with a storm on the day of
the whirlwind;
15 then their king shall go into
exile,
he and his officials
together,
says the LORD.

2 Thus says the LORD:
For three transgressions of
Moab,
and for four, I will not
revoke the
punishment;[c]
because he burned to lime
the bones of the king of
Edom.
2 So I will send a fire on
Moab,
and it shall devour the
strongholds of Kerioth,
and Moab shall die amid
uproar,
amid shouting and the
sound of the trumpet;
3 I will cut off the ruler from
its midst,
and will kill all its officials
with him,
says the LORD.

1.6 1 Sam 6.17; Jer 47.1,5; v. 9; Ob 11 **1.7** Jer 47.1; v. 6 **1.8** Zeph 2.4; Zech 9.6; Ps 81.14; Ezek 25.16 **1.9** Isa 23.1-18; Ezek 26.2-4; 1 Kings 5.1; 9.11-14 **1.10** Zech 9.4 **1.11** Isa 34.5,6; 63.1-6; Jer 49.7-22; Ob 10-12; Isa 57.16; Mic 7.18 **1.12** Jer 49.7,20; Ob 9,10 **1.13** Jer 49.1-6; Ezek 25.2-7; 2 Kings 15.16 **1.14** Jer 49.2; Am 2.2; Ezek 21.22; Isa 29.6; 30.30 **1.15** Jer 49.3 **2.1** Isa chs. 15, 16; Jer ch. 48; Zeph 2.8,9 **2.2** Jer 48.41,45 **2.3** Am 5.7,12; 6.12; Ps 2.10; Isa 40.23; Jer 48.7

[c] Heb *cause it to return* [d] Syr Vg: Heb *and his anger tore perpetually* [e] Gk Syr Vg: Heb *and his wrath kept*

Judgment on Judah

4 Thus says the LORD:
For three transgressions of
Judah,
and for four, I will not
revoke the
punishment;[f]
because they have rejected
the law of the LORD,
and have not kept his
statutes,
but they have been led astray
by the same lies
after which their ancestors
walked.
5 So I will send a fire on
Judah,
and it shall devour the
strongholds of
Jerusalem.

Judgment on Israel

6 Thus says the LORD:
For three transgressions of
Israel,
and for four, I will not
revoke the
punishment;[f]
because they sell the
righteous for silver,
and the needy for a pair of
sandals—
7 they who trample the head
of the poor into the
dust of the earth,
and push the afflicted out
of the way;
father and son go in to the
same girl,
so that my holy name is
profaned;
8 they lay themselves down
beside every altar
on garments taken in
pledge;
and in the house of their
God they drink
wine bought with fines
they imposed.

9 Yet I destroyed the Amorite
before them,
whose height was like the
height of cedars,
and who was as strong as
oaks;
I destroyed his fruit above,
and his roots beneath.
10 Also I brought you up out of
the land of Egypt,
and led you forty years in
the wilderness,
to possess the land of the
Amorite.
11 And I raised up some of your
children to be prophets
and some of your youths to
be nazirites.[g]
Is it not indeed so,
O people of Israel?
says the LORD.
12 But you made the nazirites[g]
drink wine,
and commanded the
prophets,
saying, "You shall not
prophesy."
13 So, I will press you down in
your place,
just as a cart presses down
when it is full of sheaves.[h]
14 Flight shall perish from the
swift,
and the strong shall not
retain their strength,
nor shall the mighty save
their lives;
15 those who handle the bow
shall not stand,
and those who are swift of
foot shall not save
themselves,
nor shall those who ride
horses save their lives;
16 and those who are stout of
heart among the mighty
shall flee away naked in
that day,
says the LORD.

Israel's Guilt and Punishment

3 Hear this word that the LORD
has spoken against you,
O people of Israel, against the
whole family that I brought up out
of the land of Egypt:
2 You only have I known

2.4 2 Kings 17.19; Joel 3.2; Jer 6.19; 8.9; Dan 9.11; Isa 28.15; Jer 16.19; Ezek 20.13, 16,18
2.5 Jer 17.27; Hos 8.14
2.6 2 Kings 18.12; Joel 3.3; Am 5.11,12; 8.6
2.7 Am 8.4; 5.12; Lev 20.3; Hos 4.14
2.8 1 Cor 8.10; Ex 22.26; Am 4.1; 6.6
2.9 Deut 2.31; Num 13.33; Isa 5.24; Mal 4.1
2.10 Ex 12.51; Deut 2.7; Ex 3.8
2.11 Jer 7.25; Num 6.2,3
2.12 Isa 30.10; Jer 11.21; Am 7.12,13; Mic 2.6
2.13 Joel 3.13
2.14 Isa 30.16, 17; Jer 9.23; Ps 33.16
2.15 Jer 51.56; Ezek 39.3; Isa 31.3
2.16 Jer 48.41
3.1 Jer 8.3; 13.11; Am 2.10; 9.7
3.2 Deut 7.6; Jer 14.20; Ezek 20.36; Lk 12.47; Rom 2.9

[f] Heb *cause it to return* [g] That is, *those separated* or *those consecrated* [h] Meaning of Heb uncertain

of all the families of the
earth;
therefore I will punish you
for all your iniquities.

3 Do two walk together
unless they have made an
appointment?
4 Does a lion roar in the
forest,
when it has no prey?
Does a young lion cry out
from its den,
if it has caught nothing?
5 Does a bird fall into a snare
on the earth,
when there is no trap for
it?
Does a snare spring up from
the ground,
when it has taken nothing?
6 Is a trumpet blown in a city,
and the people are not
afraid?
Does disaster befall a city,
unless the LORD has done
it?
7 Surely the Lord GOD does
nothing,
without revealing his secret
to his servants the
prophets.
8 The lion has roared;
who will not fear?
The Lord GOD has spoken;
who can but prophesy?

9 Proclaim to the strongholds
in Ashdod,
and to the strongholds in
the land of Egypt,
and say, "Assemble
yourselves on Mount[i]
Samaria,
and see what great tumults
are within it,
and what oppressions are
in its midst."
10 They do not know how to do
right, says the LORD,
those who store up
violence and robbery in
their strongholds.
11 Therefore thus says the Lord
GOD:
An adversary shall surround
the land,
and strip you of your
defense;
and your strongholds shall
be plundered.

12 Thus says the LORD: As the
shepherd rescues from the mouth
of the lion two legs, or a piece of an
ear, so shall the people of Israel
who live in Samaria be rescued,
with the corner of a couch and
part[j] of a bed.

13 Hear, and testify against the
house of Jacob,
says the Lord GOD, the God
of hosts:
14 On the day I punish Israel
for its transgressions,
I will punish the altars of
Bethel,
and the horns of the altar
shall be cut off
and fall to the ground.
15 I will tear down the winter
house as well as the
summer house;
and the houses of ivory
shall perish,
and the great houses[k] shall
come to an end,
says the LORD.

4 Hear this word, you cows of
Bashan
who are on Mount Samaria,
who oppress the poor, who
crush the needy,
who say to their husbands,
"Bring something to
drink!"
2 The Lord GOD has sworn by
his holiness:
The time is surely coming
upon you,
when they shall take you
away with hooks,
even the last of you with
fishhooks.
3 Through breaches in the wall
you shall leave,
each one straight ahead;

3.3 Lev 26.23, 24 **3.4** Hos 11.10 **3.6** Jer 6.1; Hos 5.8; Isa 14.24-27; 45.7 **3.7** Gen 18.17; Jn 15.15; Rev 10.7 **3.8** Am 1.2; Jon 1.1; 3.1; Jer 20.9; Acts 4.20 **3.9** Am 1.8; 4.1; 6.1; 8.6 **3.10** Jer 4.22; Am 5.7; 6.12; Hab 2.8-11; Zeph 1.9; Zech 5.3,4 **3.11** Am 6.14; 2.14; 2.5
3.12 1 Sam 17.34-37; Am 6.4; Ps 132.3 **3.13** Ezek 2.7 **3.14** v.2; Am 4.4; 5.5,6 **3.15** Jer 36.22; Judg 3.20; 1 Kings 22.39 **4.1** Ps 22.12; Ezek 39.18; Am 3.9; 6.1; 5.11; 8.6; 2.8; 6.6 **4.2** Ps 89.25; Am 6.8; 8.7; Isa 37.29; Ezek 38.4; 29.4 **4.3** Jer 52.7; Ezek 12.5

[i] Gk Syr: Heb *the mountains of* [j] Meaning of Heb uncertain [k] Or *many houses*

and you shall be flung out
into Harmon,[l]
says the LORD.

4 Come to Bethel — and
transgress;
to Gilgal — and multiply
transgression;
bring your sacrifices every
morning,
your tithes every three
days;
5 bring a thank offering of
leavened bread,
and proclaim freewill
offerings, publish them;
for so you love to do,
O people of Israel!
says the Lord GOD.

Israel Rejects Correction

6 I gave you cleanness of teeth
in all your cities,
and lack of bread in all
your places,
yet you did not return to me,
says the LORD.

7 And I also withheld the rain
from you
when there were still three
months to the harvest;
I would send rain on one
city,
and send no rain on
another city;
one field would be rained
upon,
and the field on which it
did not rain withered;
8 so two or three towns
wandered to one town
to drink water, and were
not satisfied;
yet you did not return to me,
says the LORD.

9 I struck you with blight and
mildew;
I laid waste[m] your gardens
and your vineyards;
the locust devoured your
fig trees and your olive
trees;
yet you did not return to me,
says the LORD.

4.4 Am 3.14; 5.5; Hos 4.15; Num 28.3,4; Deut 14.28
4.5 Lev 7.13; 22.18,21; Hos 9.1,10
4.6 Isa 3.1; Jer 14.18; 5.3; Hag 2.17
4.7 Deut 11.17; 2 Chr 7.13; Ex 9.4,26; 10.22,23
4.8 Jer 14.4; Ezek 4.16; Jer 3.7
4.9 Deut 28.22; Hag 2.17; Joel 1.4; 2.25; Jer 3.10
4.10 Ex 9.3,6; Deut 28.27, 60; Jer 11.22; 18.21; 48.15; Joel 2.20; Isa 9.13
4.11 Isa 13.19; Zech 3.2; Jer 23.14
4.12 v. 2; Ezek 13.5
4.13 Jer 10.13; Ps 139.2; Dan 2.28; Jer 13.16; Mic 1.3; Am 5.8,27; 9.6
5.1 Ezek 19.1
5.2 Jer 14.17; Am 8.14; Isa 51.18; Jer 50.32
5.3 Isa 6.13; Am 6.9

10 I sent among you a
pestilence after the
manner of Egypt;
I killed your young men
with the sword;
I carried away your horses;[n]
and I made the stench of
your camp go up into
your nostrils;
yet you did not return to me,
says the LORD.

11 I overthrew some of you,
as when God overthrew
Sodom and Gomorrah,
and you were like a brand
snatched from the fire;
yet you did not return to me,
says the LORD.

12 Therefore thus I will do to
you, O Israel;
because I will do this to
you,
prepare to meet your God,
O Israel!

13 For lo, the one who forms
the mountains, creates
the wind,
reveals his thoughts to
mortals,
makes the morning darkness,
and treads on the heights
of the earth —
the LORD, the God of hosts,
is his name!

A Lament for Israel's Sin

5 Hear this word that I take up
over you in lamentation,
O house of Israel:
2 Fallen, no more to rise,
is maiden Israel;
forsaken on her land,
with no one to raise her
up.

3 For thus says the Lord GOD:
The city that marched out a
thousand
shall have a hundred left,
and that which marched out
a hundred

[l] Meaning of Heb uncertain [m] Cn: Heb *the multitude of* [n] Heb *with the captivity of your horses*

shall have ten left.[o]

4 For thus says the LORD to the
house of Israel:
Seek me and live;
5 but do not seek Bethel,
and do not enter into Gilgal
or cross over to Beer-sheba;
for Gilgal shall surely go into
exile,
and Bethel shall come to
nothing.

6 Seek the LORD and live,
or he will break out against
the house of Joseph
like fire,
and it will devour Bethel,
with no one to quench
it.
7 Ah, you that turn justice to
wormwood,
and bring righteousness to
the ground!

8 The one who made the
Pleiades and Orion,
and turns deep darkness
into the morning,
and darkens the day into
night,
who calls for the waters of
the sea,
and pours them out on the
surface of the earth,
the LORD is his name,
9 who makes destruction flash
out against the strong,
so that destruction comes
upon the fortress.

10 They hate the one who
reproves in the gate,
and they abhor the one
who speaks the truth.
11 Therefore because you
trample on the poor
and take from them levies
of grain,
you have built houses of
hewn stone,
but you shall not live in
them;
you have planted pleasant
vineyards,
but you shall not drink
their wine.

5.4 Jer 29.3; Isa 55.3
5.5 Am 4.4; 1 Sam 7.16; 11.14; Am 8.14
5.6 Isa 55.3,6,7; v. 14; Deut 4.24; Am 3.14
5.7 Am 6.12
5.8 Job 9.9; 12.22; Isa 42.16; Am 8.9; Ps 104.6-9; Am 9.6; 4.13
5.9 Isa 29.5; Mic 5.11
5.10 Isa 29.21; 1 Kings 22.8; Isa 59.15
5.11 Am 3.9; 8.6; 3.15; 6.11; Mic 6.15
5.12 Am 2.6,7; Isa 29.21
5.13 Eccl 3.7
5.14 v. 6; Mic 3.11
5.15 Ps 97.10; Rom 12.9; Joel 2.14; Mic 5.3,7,8
5.16 Jer 9.17; Joel 1.11; 2 Chr 35.25
5.17 Isa 16.10; Jer 48.33; Nah 1.2
5.18 Isa 5.19; Joel 1.15; 2.1,11,31; 2 Pet 3.4; Jer 30.7
5.19 Jer 48.44

12 For I know how many are
your transgressions,
and how great are your
sins—
you who afflict the righteous,
who take a bribe,
and push aside the needy
in the gate.
13 Therefore the prudent will
keep silent in such a
time;
for it is an evil time.

14 Seek good and not evil,
that you may live;
and so the LORD, the God of
hosts, will be with you,
just as you have said.
15 Hate evil and love good,
and establish justice in the
gate;
it may be that the LORD, the
God of hosts,
will be gracious to the
remnant of Joseph.

16 Therefore thus says the LORD,
the God of hosts, the
Lord:
In all the squares there shall
be wailing;
and in all the streets they
shall say, "Alas! alas!"
They shall call the farmers to
mourning,
and those skilled in
lamentation, to wailing;
17 in all the vineyards there
shall be wailing,
for I will pass through the
midst of you,
says the LORD.

The Day of the LORD a Dark Day

18 Alas for you who desire the
day of the LORD!
Why do you want the day
of the LORD?
It is darkness, not light;
19 as if someone fled from a
lion,
and was met by a bear;
or went into the house and
rested a hand against
the wall,

[o] Heb adds *to the house of Israel*

and was bitten by a snake.
20 Is not the day of the LORD
darkness, not light,
and gloom with no
brightness in it?

21 I hate, I despise your
festivals,
and I take no delight in
your solemn
assemblies.
22 Even though you offer me
your burnt offerings and
grain offerings,
I will not accept them;
and the offerings of
well-being of your
fatted animals
I will not look upon.
23 Take away from me the
noise of your songs;
I will not listen to the
melody of your harps.
24 But let justice roll down like
waters,
and righteousness like an
ever-flowing stream.

25 Did you bring to me sacrifices and offerings the forty years in
the wilderness, O house of Israel?
26 You shall take up Sakkuth your
king, and Kaiwan your star-god,
your images,[p] which you made for
yourselves; 27 therefore I will take
you into exile beyond Damascus,
says the LORD, whose name is the
God of hosts.

Complacent Self-Indulgence Will Be Punished

6 Alas for those who are at
ease in Zion,
and for those who feel
secure on Mount
Samaria,
the notables of the first of
the nations,
to whom the house of
Israel resorts!
2 Cross over to Calneh, and
see;
from there go to Hamath
the great;
then go down to Gath of
the Philistines.
Are you better[q] than these
kingdoms?
Or is your[r] territory greater
than their[s] territory,
3 O you that put far away the
evil day,
and bring near a reign of
violence?

4 Alas for those who lie on
beds of ivory,
and lounge on their
couches,
and eat lambs from the
flock,
and calves from the stall;
5 who sing idle songs to the
sound of the harp,
and like David improvise
on instruments of
music;
6 who drink wine from bowls,
and anoint themselves with
the finest oils,
but are not grieved over the
ruin of Joseph!
7 Therefore they shall now be
the first to go into
exile,
and the revelry of the
loungers shall pass
away.

8 The Lord GOD has sworn by
himself
(says the LORD, the God of
hosts):
I abhor the pride of Jacob
and hate his strongholds;
and I will deliver up the
city and all that is in it.

9 If ten people remain in one
house, they shall die. 10 And if a relative, one who burns the dead,[t]
shall take up the body to bring it
out of the house, and shall say to
someone in the innermost parts of
the house, "Is anyone else with
you?" the answer will come, "No."
Then the relative[u] shall say,
"Hush! We must not mention the
name of the LORD."

5.20 Isa 13.10; Zeph 1.15 **5.21** Isa 1.11-16; Lev 26.31 **5.22** Isa 66.3; Mic 6.6,7; Am 4.5 **5.23** Am 6.4,5; 8.10 **5.24** Jer 22.3; Ezek 45.9; Mic 6.8 **5.25** Deut 32.17; Ezek 20.8, 16,24; Acts 7.42 **5.27** 2 Kings 17.6; Am 4.13 **6.1** Isa 32.9-11; Lk 6.24; Ex 19.5; Am 3.2 **6.2** Jer 2.10; Isa 10.9; 2 Kings 18.34; 2 Chr 26.6; Nah 3.8 **6.3** Isa 56.12; Am 9.10 **6.4** Am 3.15; 3.12; Ezek 34.2,3 **6.5** Isa 5.12; Am 5.23; 1 Chr 23.5 **6.6** Am 2.8; 4.1; Gen 37.25; Ezek 9.4 **6.7** Am 7.11,17; Dan 5.4-6, 30; v. 4 **6.8** Jer 51.14; Heb 6.13; Deut 32.19; Ps 106.40; Am 3.10,11; Hos 11.6 **6.9** Am 5.3 **6.10** Am 5.13; 8.3

p Heb *your images, your star-god* q Or *Are they better* r Heb *their* s Heb *your*
t Or *who makes a burning for him*
u Heb *he*

11 See, the LORD commands,
and the great house shall be shattered to bits,
and the little house to pieces.
12 Do horses run on rocks?
Does one plow the sea with oxen?[v]
But you have turned justice into poison
and the fruit of righteousness into wormwood—
13 you who rejoice in Lo-debar,[w]
who say, "Have we not by our own strength
taken Karnaim[x] for ourselves?"
14 Indeed, I am raising up against you a nation,
O house of Israel, says the LORD, the God of hosts,
and they shall oppress you from Lebo-hamath
to the Wadi Arabah.

Locusts, Fire, and a Plumb Line

7 This is what the Lord GOD
showed me: he was forming
locusts at the time the latter
growth began to sprout (it was the
latter growth after the king's mow-
ings). 2 When they had finished eating the grass of the land, I said,
"O Lord GOD, forgive, I beg you!
How can Jacob stand?
He is so small!"
3 The LORD relented concerning this;
"It shall not be," said the LORD.

4 This is what the Lord GOD
showed me: the Lord GOD was calling for a shower of fire,[y] and it devoured the great deep and was eating up the land. 5 Then I said,
"O Lord GOD, cease, I beg you!
How can Jacob stand?
He is so small!"
6 The LORD relented concerning this;
"This also shall not be,"
said the Lord GOD.

7 This is what he showed me:
the Lord was standing beside a wall
built with a plumb line, with a
plumb line in his hand. 8 And the
LORD said to me, "Amos, what do
you see?" And I said, "A plumb
line." Then the Lord said,
"See, I am setting a plumb line
in the midst of my people Israel;
I will never again pass them by;
9 the high places of Isaac shall be made desolate,
and the sanctuaries of Israel shall be laid waste,
and I will rise against the house of Jeroboam with the sword."

Amaziah Complains to the King

10 Then Amaziah, the priest of
Bethel, sent to King Jeroboam of
Israel, saying, "Amos has conspired
against you in the very center of the
house of Israel; the land is not able
to bear all his words. 11 For thus
Amos has said,
'Jeroboam shall die by the sword,
and Israel must go into exile
away from his land.' "
12 And Amaziah said to Amos,
"O seer, go, flee away to the land of
Judah, earn your bread there, and
prophesy there; 13 but never again
prophesy at Bethel, for it is the
king's sanctuary, and it is a temple
of the kingdom."
14 Then Amos answered Amaziah, "I am[z] no prophet, nor a
prophet's son; but I am[z] a herdsman, and a dresser of sycamore
trees, 15 and the LORD took me from
following the flock, and the LORD
said to me, 'Go, prophesy to my
people Israel.'

6.11 Isa 55.11; Am 3.15 **6.12** Isa 59.13, 14; Hos 10.4; Am 5.7 **6.13** Ps 75.4,5 **6.14** Jer 5.15; Am 3.11; Num 34.8; 1 Kings 8.65 **7.1** vv. 4,7; Am 8.1; Joel 1.4; Am 4.9; Nah 3.15 **7.2** Ex 10.14, 15; Ezek 9.8; 11.13; Isa 37.4; Jer 42.2 **7.3** Deut 32.36; Jer 26.19; Jon 3.10 **7.4** Isa 66.15, 16; Am 2.5 **7.5** v. 2 **7.6** v. 3 **7.8** Am 8.2; Isa 28.17; 34.11; Lam 2.8; Mic 7.18 **7.9** Hos 10.8; Mic 1.5; Isa 63.18; 2 Kings 15.10 **7.10** 1 Kings 12.32; 2 Kings 14.23; Jer 26.8-11 **7.11** vv. 9,17 **7.13** Am 2.12; 1 Kings 12.32; 13.1 **7.14** 1 Kings 20.35; 2 Kings 2.5; 4.38; 2 Chr 19.2; Am 1.1 **7.15** 2 Sam 7.8; Am 3.8; Jer 7.1; Ezek 2.3,4

[v] Or *Does one plow them with oxen*
[w] Or *in a thing of nothingness* [x] Or *horns*
[y] Or *for a judgment by fire* [z] Or *was*

16 "Now therefore hear the
word of the LORD.
You say, 'Do not prophesy
against Israel,
and do not preach against
the house of Isaac.'
17 Therefore thus says the LORD:
'Your wife shall become a
prostitute in the city,
and your sons and your
daughters shall fall by
the sword,
and your land shall be
parceled out by line;
you yourself shall die in an
unclean land,
and Israel shall surely go
into exile away from its
land.'"

The Basket of Fruit

8 This is what the Lord GOD
showed me—a basket of sum-
mer fruit.[a] 2 He said, "Amos, what
do you see?" And I said, "A basket
of summer fruit."[a] Then the LORD
said to me,
"The end[b] has come upon my
people Israel;
I will never again pass
them by.
3 The songs of the temple[c]
shall become wailings
in that day,"
says the Lord GOD;
"the dead bodies shall be
many,
cast out in every place. Be
silent!"

4 Hear this, you that trample
on the needy,
and bring to ruin the poor
of the land,
5 saying, "When will the new
moon be over
so that we may sell grain;
and the sabbath,
so that we may offer wheat
for sale?
We will make the ephah
small and the shekel
great,
and practice deceit with
false balances,
6 buying the poor for silver
and the needy for a pair of
sandals,
and selling the sweepings
of the wheat."

7 The LORD has sworn by the
pride of Jacob:
Surely I will never forget any
of their deeds.
8 Shall not the land tremble
on this account,
and everyone mourn who
lives in it,
and all of it rise like the
Nile,
and be tossed about and
sink again, like the Nile
of Egypt?

9 On that day, says the Lord
GOD,
I will make the sun go
down at noon,
and darken the earth in
broad daylight.
10 I will turn your feasts into
mourning,
and all your songs into
lamentation;
I will bring sackcloth on all
loins,
and baldness on every
head;
I will make it like the
mourning for an only
son,
and the end of it like a
bitter day.

11 The time is surely coming,
says the Lord GOD,
when I will send a famine
on the land;
not a famine of bread, or a
thirst for water,
but of hearing the words of
the LORD.
12 They shall wander from sea
to sea,
and from north to east;
they shall run to and fro,
seeking the word of the
LORD,
but they shall not find it.

7.16 Am 2.12; Ezek 21.2; Mic 2.6 **7.17** Jer 29.21; Hos 4.13, 14; Jer 14.16; Ezek 4.13; Hos 9.3 **8.2** Am 7.8; Jer 24.3; Ezek 7.2 **8.3** Am 5.23; 6.9,10 **8.4** Ps 14.4; Am 5.11,12 **8.5** 2 Kings 4.23; Neh 13.15, 16; Mic 6.10,11 **8.6** Am 2.6

8.7 Am 6.8; Deut 33.26, 29; Hos 8.13; 9.9 **8.8** Isa 5.25; Hos 4.3; Am 9.5 **8.9** Isa 13.10; Jer 15.9; Mic 3.6; Am 4.13; 5.8 **8.10** Am 5.21; 6.4,5; Jer 48.37; Ezek 7.18; Jer 6.26; Zech 12.10 **8.11** 1 Sam 3.1; 2 Chr 15.3; Ezek 7.26; Mic 3.6 **8.12** Ezek 20.3, 31

a Heb *qayits* b Heb *qets* c Or *palace*

13 In that day the beautiful
young women and the
young men
shall faint for thirst.
14 Those who swear by
Ashimah of Samaria,
and say, "As your god lives,
O Dan,"
and, "As the way of
Beer-sheba lives"—
they shall fall, and never
rise again.

The Destruction of Israel

9 I saw the LORD standing beside[d] the altar, and he said:
Strike the capitals until the
thresholds shake,
and shatter them on the
heads of all the
people;[e]
and those who are left I will
kill with the sword;
not one of them shall flee
away,
not one of them shall
escape.

2 Though they dig into Sheol,
from there shall my hand
take them;
though they climb up to
heaven,
from there I will bring
them down.
3 Though they hide themselves
on the top of Carmel,
from there I will search out
and take them;
and though they hide from
my sight at the bottom
of the sea,
there I will command the
sea-serpent, and it shall
bite them.
4 And though they go into
captivity in front of
their enemies,
there I will command the
sword, and it shall kill
them;
and I will fix my eyes on
them
for harm and not for good.

5 The Lord, GOD of hosts,
he who touches the earth
and it melts,
and all who live in it
mourn,
and all of it rises like the
Nile,
and sinks again, like the
Nile of Egypt;
6 who builds his upper
chambers in the
heavens,
and founds his vault upon
the earth;
who calls for the waters of
the sea,
and pours them out upon
the surface of the
earth—
the LORD is his name.

7 Are you not like the
Ethiopians[f] to me,
O people of Israel? says the
LORD.
Did I not bring Israel up
from the land of Egypt,
and the Philistines from
Caphtor and the
Arameans from Kir?
8 The eyes of the Lord GOD are
upon the sinful
kingdom,
and I will destroy it from
the face of the earth
—except that I will not
utterly destroy the
house of Jacob,
says the LORD.

9 For lo, I will command,
and shake the house of
Israel among all the
nations
as one shakes with a sieve,
but no pebble shall fall to
the ground.
10 All the sinners of my people
shall die by the sword,
who say, "Evil shall not
overtake or meet us."

The Restoration of David's Kingdom

11 On that day I will raise up

8.13 Lam 1.18; Isa 41.17; Hos 2.3
8.14 Hos 4.15; 1 Kings 12.28, 29; Am 5.5
9.1 Am 3.14; Zeph 2.14; Hab 3.13; v. 4; Am 2.14
9.2 Ps 139.8; Jer 51.53; Ob 4
9.3 Am 1.2; Jer 16.16, 17; Isa 27.1
9.4 Lev 26.33; Ezek 5.12; Jer 44.11
9.5 Mic 1.4; Am 8.8
9.6 Ps 104.3; Am 5.8; 4.13
9.7 Isa 43.3; Am 2.10; 3.1; Deut 2.23; Jer 47.4; Am 1.5
9.8 Jer 44.27; vv. 4,10; Jer 30.11; Joel 2.32
9.9 Isa 30.28
9.10 Am 8.14; 6.3
9.11 Acts 15.16, 17; Ps 80.12; Isa 63.11; Jer 46.26

[d] Or *on* [e] Heb *all of them*
[f] Or *Nubians*; Heb *Cushites*

the booth of David that is
fallen,
and repair its[g] breaches,
and raise up its[h] ruins,
and rebuild it as in the
days of old;
12 in order that they may
possess the remnant of
Edom
and all the nations who are
called by my name,
says the LORD who does
this.

13 The time is surely coming,
says the LORD,
when the one who plows
shall overtake the one
who reaps,
and the treader of grapes
the one who sows the
seed;

9.12 Ob 19; Isa 11.14; 43.7
9.13 Lev 26.5; Joel 3.18
9.14 Isa 60.4; Jer 30.18; Isa 61.4; Ezek 36.35; 28.26
9.15 Jer 24.6; 31.28; Isa 60.21; Jer 32.41; Ezek 34.28

the mountains shall drip
sweet wine,
and all the hills shall flow
with it.
14 I will restore the fortunes of
my people Israel,
and they shall rebuild the
ruined cities and
inhabit them;
they shall plant vineyards
and drink their wine,
and they shall make
gardens and eat their
fruit.
15 I will plant them upon their
land,
and they shall never again
be plucked up
out of the land that I have
given them,
says the LORD your God.

[g] Gk: Heb *their* [h] Gk: Heb *his*

Obadiah

Title and Background

Obadiah's name means "servant of the LORD." His prophecy centers around an ancient feud between Edom and Israel. The Edomites were descendants of Esau, and had always held a grudge against Israel because Jacob had cheated their ancestor out of his birthright.

Author and Date of Writing

The author is Obadiah. The date and place of composition are uncertain. A date between 853 and 841 B.C. is suggested by relating verses 11-14 to the invasion of Jerusalem by Philistines and Arabians during Jehoram's reign (2 Kings 8.20-22). An exilic date is also possible by relating those verses to the Babylonian attacks on Jerusalem.

Theme and Message

Obadiah's theme is that Edomites are proud of their own security and have gloated when Israel was devastated by foreign powers. But their participation in that disaster will bring on God's wrath; the Edomites themselves will be destroyed, while Mount Zion and Israel will be delivered and God's kingdom will triumph.

Outline

I. The Doom of Edom (1-14)
II. Edom in the Day of the Lord (15-21)

Proud Edom Will Be Brought Low

1 The vision of Obadiah.

Thus says the Lord GOD
concerning Edom:
We have heard a report from
the LORD,
and a messenger has been
sent among the nations:
"Rise up! Let us rise against
it for battle!"
2 I will surely make you least
among the nations;
you shall be utterly
despised.
3 Your proud heart has
deceived you,
you that live in the clefts
of the rock,[a]
whose dwelling is in the
heights.
You say in your heart,
"Who will bring me down
to the ground?"

1 Isa 34.5; Ezek 25.12; Joel 3.19; Jer 49.14; Isa 30.4; Jer 6.4,5
3 Isa 16.6; Jer 49.16; 2 Kings 14.7; Isa 14.13-15; Rev 18.7
4 Job 20.6; Hab 2.9; Isa 14.13-15
5 Jer 49.9; vv. 9,10; Isa 17.6
6 Jer 49.10
7 Jer 30.14; 38.22; Ps 41.9; Jer 49.7

4 Though you soar aloft like
the eagle,
though your nest is set
among the stars,
from there I will bring you
down,
says the LORD.

Pillage and Slaughter Will Repay Edom's Cruelty

5 If thieves came to you,
if plunderers by night
—how you have been
destroyed!—
would they not steal only
what they wanted?
If grape-gatherers came to
you,
would they not leave
gleanings?
6 How Esau has been pillaged,
his treasures searched out!
7 All your allies have deceived
you,

[a] Or *clefts of Sela*

they have driven you to the
border;
your confederates have
prevailed against you;
those who ate[b] your bread
have set a trap for
you—
there is no understanding
of it.
8 On that day, says the LORD,
I will destroy the wise out
of Edom,
and understanding out of
Mount Esau.
9 Your warriors shall be
shattered, O Teman,
so that everyone from
Mount Esau will be cut
off.

Edom Mistreated His Brother

10 For the slaughter and
violence done to your
brother Jacob,
shame shall cover you,
and you shall be cut off
forever.
11 On the day that you stood
aside,
on the day that strangers
carried off his wealth,
and foreigners entered his
gates
and cast lots for Jerusalem,
you too were like one of
them.
12 But you should not have
gloated[c] over[d] your
brother
on the day of his
misfortune;
you should not have rejoiced
over the people of
Judah
on the day of their ruin;
you should not have boasted
on the day of distress.
13 You should not have entered
the gate of my people
on the day of their
calamity;
you should not have joined
in the gloating over
Judah's[e] disaster
on the day of his calamity;
you should not have looted
his goods

8 Job 5.12; Isa 29.14
9 Jer 49.22; Am 1.12; Hab 3.3; v. 5
10 Ps 137.7; Joel 3.19; Am 1.11
11 Ps 137.7; Joel 3.3; Nah 3.10
12 Mic 4.11; Ezek 35.15; 36.5; Ps 31.18
13 Ezek 35.5, 10; 36.2,3
15 Ezek 30.3; Joel 1.15; Jer 50.29; Hab 2.8; Ezek 35.11
16 Jer 49.12, 13; 25.15,16
17 Isa 4.2,3; Am 9.11-15
18 Isa 10.17; Jer 11.23; Am 1.8
19 Am 9.12; Isa 11.14; Zeph 2.7; Jer 31.5; 32.44

on the day of his calamity.
14 You should not have stood at
the crossings
to cut off his fugitives;
you should not have handed
over his survivors
on the day of distress.

15 For the day of the LORD is
near against all the
nations.
As you have done, it shall be
done to you;
your deeds shall return on
your own head.
16 For as you have drunk on my
holy mountain,
all the nations around you
shall drink;
they shall drink and gulp
down,[f]
and shall be as though they
had never been.

Israel's Final Triumph

17 But on Mount Zion there
shall be those that
escape,
and it shall be holy;
and the house of Jacob shall
take possession of
those who dispossessed
them.
18 The house of Jacob shall be
a fire,
the house of Joseph a
flame,
and the house of Esau
stubble;
they shall burn them and
consume them,
and there shall be no
survivor of the house of
Esau;
for the LORD has
spoken.
19 Those of the Negeb shall
possess Mount Esau,
and those of the Shephelah
the land of the
Philistines;

[b] Cn: Heb lacks *those who ate* [c] Heb *But do not gloat* (and similarly through verse 14) [d] Heb *on the day of* [e] Heb *his* [f] Meaning of Heb uncertain

they shall possess the land of
Ephraim and the land
of Samaria,
and Benjamin shall possess
Gilead.
20 The exiles of the Israelites
who are in Halah[g]
shall possess[h] Phoenicia as
far as Zarephath;
and the exiles of Jerusalem
who are in Sepharad
shall possess the towns of
the Negeb.
21 Those who have been saved[i]
shall go up to Mount
Zion
to rule Mount Esau;
and the kingdom shall be
the LORD's.

20 1 Kings 17.9; Jer 32.44; 33.13
21 Neh 9.27; Ps 22.28; 67.4; Dan 2.44; Zech 14.9

[g] Cn: Heb *in this army* [h] Cn: Meaning of Heb uncertain [i] Or *Saviors*

Jonah

Title and Background

The book is named after its principal character, whose name means "dove." The events in the book probably took place during the eighth century, when the Assyrians were a feared and despised enemy.

Author and Date of Writing

Traditionally, the book has been ascribed to Jonah son of Amittai (see 2 Kings 14.25), though nowhere in the book is that plainly stated. Acceptance of the book's authorship by Jonah would necessitate a date no later than the third quarter of the eighth century B.C.

Theme and Message

The theme that runs throughout the four chapters of this book is that God's great mercy extends equally to Gentile nations if they repent. In addition, the book depicts the larger scope of God's purpose for his people: they must rediscover God's concern for the whole creation and understand their own role in carrying out that concern.

Outline

- I. Jonah Flees His Mission (1.1–2.10)
  - A. Jonah's Commission and Flight (1.1-3)
  - B. The Endangered Sailors' Cry to Their Gods (1.4-6)
  - C. Jonah's Disobedience Exposed (1.7-10)
  - D. Jonah's Punishment, Deliverance, and Thanks (1.11–2.10)
- II. Jonah Reluctantly Fulfills His Mission (3.1–4.11)
  - A. Jonah's Renewed Commission and Obedience (3.1-4)
  - B. The Ninevites' Repentance (3.5–4.4)
  - D. Jonah's Deliverance and Reproof (4.5-11)

Jonah Tries to Run Away from God

1 Now the word of the LORD
came to Jonah son of Amittai,
saying, 2"Go at once to Nineveh,
that great city, and cry out against
it; for their wickedness has come
up before me." 3But Jonah set out
to flee to Tarshish from the presence of the LORD. He went down to
Joppa and found a ship going to
Tarshish; so he paid his fare and
went on board, to go with them to
Tarshish, away from the presence
of the LORD.
4 But the LORD hurled a great
wind upon the sea, and such a
mighty storm came upon the sea
that the ship threatened to break

1.1 2 Kings 14.25; Mt 12.39
1.2 Jon 3.2,3; 4.1; Ezra 9.6
1.3 Ps 139.7,9, 10; Acts 9.36
1.4 Ps 107.25
1.5 Acts 27.18; 1 Sam 24.3
1.6 Ps 107.28; Jon 3.9
1.7 Josh 7.14; 1 Sam 10.20; 14.41,42; Acts 1.26

up. 5Then the mariners were
afraid, and each cried to his god.
They threw the cargo that was in
the ship into the sea, to lighten it
for them. Jonah, meanwhile, had
gone down into the hold of the ship
and had lain down, and was fast
asleep. 6The captain came and said
to him, "What are you doing sound
asleep? Get up, call on your god!
Perhaps the god will spare us a
thought so that we do not perish."
7 The sailors[a] said to one another, "Come, let us cast lots, so
that we may know on whose account this calamity has come upon
us." So they cast lots, and the lot

[a] Heb *They*

fell on Jonah. 8 Then they said to
him, "Tell us why this calamity has
come upon us. What is your occupation? Where do you come from?
What is your country? And of what
people are you?" 9 "I am a Hebrew,"
he replied. "I worship the LORD, the
God of heaven, who made the sea
and the dry land." 10 Then the men
were even more afraid, and said to
him, "What is this that you have
done!" For the men knew that he
was fleeing from the presence of
the LORD, because he had told them
so.

11 Then they said to him, "What
shall we do to you, that the sea may
quiet down for us?" For the sea was
growing more and more tempestuous. 12 He said to them, "Pick me
up and throw me into the sea; then
the sea will quiet down for you; for
I know it is because of me that this
great storm has come upon you."
13 Nevertheless the men rowed
hard to bring the ship back to land,
but they could not, for the sea grew
more and more stormy against
them. 14 Then they cried out to the
LORD, "Please, O LORD, we pray, do
not let us perish on account of this
man's life. Do not make us guilty of
innocent blood; for you, O LORD,
have done as it pleased you." 15 So
they picked Jonah up and threw
him into the sea; and the sea
ceased from its raging. 16 Then the
men feared the LORD even more,
and they offered a sacrifice to the
LORD and made vows.

17 [b]But the LORD provided a
large fish to swallow up Jonah; and
Jonah was in the belly of the fish
three days and three nights.

A Psalm of Thanksgiving

2 Then Jonah prayed to the LORD
his God from the belly of the
fish, 2 saying,

"I called to the LORD out of
my distress,
and he answered me;
out of the belly of Sheol I
cried,
and you heard my voice.
3 You cast me into the deep,
into the heart of the seas,
and the flood surrounded
me;
all your waves and your
billows
passed over me.
4 Then I said, 'I am driven
away
from your sight;
how[c] shall I look again
upon your holy temple?'
5 The waters closed in over
me;
the deep surrounded me;
weeds were wrapped around
my head
6 at the roots of the
mountains.
I went down to the land
whose bars closed upon me
forever;
yet you brought up my life
from the Pit,
O LORD my God.
7 As my life was ebbing away,
I remembered the LORD;
and my prayer came to you,
into your holy temple.
8 Those who worship vain
idols
forsake their true loyalty.
9 But I with the voice of
thanksgiving
will sacrifice to you;
what I have vowed I will pay.
Deliverance belongs to the
LORD!"

10 Then the LORD spoke to the fish,
and it spewed Jonah out upon the
dry land.

Conversion of Nineveh

3 The word of the LORD came to
Jonah a second time, saying,
2 "Get up, go to Nineveh, that great
city, and proclaim to it the message
that I tell you." 3 So Jonah set out
and went to Nineveh, according to
the word of the LORD. Now Nineveh
was an exceedingly large city, a
three days' walk across. 4 Jonah began to go into the city, going a day's
walk. And he cried out, "Forty days
more, and Nineveh shall be overthrown!" 5 And the people of Nineveh believed God; they proclaimed

1.8 Josh 7.19; 1 Sam 14.43
1.9 Ps 146.6; Acts 17.24
1.10 Job 27.22
1.12 2 Sam 24.17; Jn 11.50; 1 Chr 21.17
1.13 Prov 21.30
1.14 v. 16; Deut 21.8; Ps 115.3
1.15 Ps 89.9; 107.29; Lk 8.24
1.16 1 Sam 6.2-5; Mk 4.41
1.17 Jon 4.6; Mt 12.40; 16.4; Lk 11.30
2.1 Ps 130.1
2.2 Ps 18.4-6
2.3 Ps 88.6; 42.7
2.4 Ps 31.22; 1 Kings 8.38
2.5 Ps 69.1; Lam 3.54
2.6 Ps 16.10
2.7 Ps 142.3; 77.10,11; 18.6
2.8 2 Kings 17.15; Ps 31;6; Jer 10.8; 16.19
2.9 Ps 50.14; Hos 14.2; Heb 13.15; Job 22.27; Ps 3.8
2.10 Jon 1.17
3.1 Jon 1.1,2
3.5 Dan 9.3; Joel 1.14; Jer 31.34

[b] Ch 2.1 in Heb [c] Theodotion: Heb *surely*

a fast, and everyone, great and
small, put on sackcloth.
6 When the news reached the
king of Nineveh, he rose from his
throne, removed his robe, covered
himself with sackcloth, and sat in
ashes. 7 Then he had a proclamation made in Nineveh: "By the decree of the king and his nobles: No
human being or animal, no herd or
flock, shall taste anything. They
shall not feed, nor shall they drink
water. 8 Human beings and animals
shall be covered with sackcloth,
and they shall cry mightily to God.
All shall turn from their evil ways
and from the violence that is in
their hands. 9 Who knows? God
may relent and change his mind;
he may turn from his fierce anger,
so that we do not perish."
10 When God saw what they
did, how they turned from their evil
ways, God changed his mind about
the calamity that he had said he
would bring upon them; and he did
not do it.

Jonah's Anger

4 But this was very displeasing
to Jonah, and he became angry. 2 He prayed to the LORD and
said, "O LORD! Is not this what I
said while I was still in my own
country? That is why I fled to Tarshish at the beginning; for I knew
that you are a gracious God and
merciful, slow to anger, and
abounding in steadfast love, and
ready to relent from punishing.
3 And now, O LORD, please take my
life from me, for it is better for me
to die than to live." 4 And the LORD
said, "Is it right for you to be angry?" 5 Then Jonah went out of the
city and sat down east of the city,
and made a booth for himself
there. He sat under it in the shade,
waiting to see what would become
of the city.
6 The LORD God appointed a
bush,[d] and made it come up over
Jonah, to give shade over his head,
to save him from his discomfort; so
Jonah was very happy about the
bush. 7 But when dawn came up the
next day, God appointed a worm
that attacked the bush, so that it
withered. 8 When the sun rose, God
prepared a sultry east wind, and
the sun beat down on the head of
Jonah so that he was faint and
asked that he might die. He said,
"It is better for me to die than to
live."

Jonah Is Reproved

9 But God said to Jonah, "Is it
right for you to be angry about the
bush?" And he said, "Yes, angry
enough to die." 10 Then the LORD
said, "You are concerned about the
bush, for which you did not labor
and which you did not grow; it
came into being in a night and perished in a night. 11 And should I not
be concerned about Nineveh, that
great city, in which there are more
than a hundred and twenty thousand persons who do not know
their right hand from their left, and
also many animals?"

3.6 Job 2.8; Jer 6.25; Dan 9.3
3.7 v. 5; 2 Chr 20.3
3.8 Ps 130.1; Jon 1.6,14; Isa 55.6,7; Jer 18.11
3.9 2 Sam 12.22; Joel 2.14
3.10 Jer 31.18; Ex 32.14; Jer 18.8; Am 7.3,6
4.1 vv. 4,9; Mt 20.15; Lk 15.28
4.2 Jon 1.3; Ex 34.6; Ps 86.5; Joel 2.13
4.3 1 Kings 19.4; v. 8; Job 7.15,16
4.4 v. 9; Mt 20.11,15
4.5 1 Kings 19.9, 13
4.7 Joel 1.12
4.9 v. 4
4.11 Jon 1.2; 3.2, 3; Deut 1.39; Ps 36.6

[d] Heb *qiqayon*, possibly *the castor bean plant*

Micah

Title and Background

The book is named after Micah, a shortened form of Micaiah, meaning "Who is like the LORD?" Judah had enjoyed comparative economic prosperity when Micah came on the scene. This prosperity placed wealth and power in the hands of a few and brought with it social injustice.

Author and Date of Writing

Little is known about Micah beyond what can be learned from the book itself. He was deeply sensitive to the social ills of his day, especially as they affected the small towns and villages of his homeland. Micah prophesied sometime after 750 B.C. and prior to 686 B.C..

Theme and Message

Micah's message alternated between oracles of doom and oracles of hope. The theme is judgment and deliverance by God. Micah also stressed that God hates idolatry, injustice, rebellion, and empty ritualism, but he delights in pardoning the penitent.

Outline

I. Judgment Against Israel and Judah (1.1–3.12)
II. Hope for Israel and Judah (4.1–5.15)
III. The Lord's Case Against Israel (6.1-16)
IV. Gloom Turns to Triumph (7.1-20)

---

1 The word of the LORD that came to Micah of Moresheth in the days of Kings Jotham, Ahaz, and Hezekiah of Judah, which he saw concerning Samaria and Jerusalem.

Judgment Pronounced against Samaria

2 Hear, you peoples, all of you;
listen, O earth, and all that is in it;
and let the Lord GOD be a witness against you,
the Lord from his holy temple.
3 For lo, the LORD is coming out of his place,
and will come down and tread upon the high places of the earth.
4 Then the mountains will melt under him
and the valleys will burst open,
like wax near the fire,
like waters poured down a steep place.
5 All this is for the transgression of Jacob
and for the sins of the house of Israel.
What is the transgression of Jacob?
Is it not Samaria?
And what is the high place[a] of Judah?
Is it not Jerusalem?
6 Therefore I will make Samaria a heap in the open country,
a place for planting vineyards.
I will pour down her stones into the valley,

1.1 Jer 26.18; 2 Kings 15.5, 7,32-38; 16.1-20; 18.1-21
1.2 Jer 6.19; 22.29; Ps 50.7; 11.4
1.3 Isa 26.21; Am 4.13
1.4 Isa 64.1,2; Nah 1.5
1.5 Isa 28.1; Am 8.14; 2 Chr 34.3, 4
1.6 Jer 31.5; Am 5.11; Ezek 13.14

[a] Heb *what are the high places*

and uncover her
foundations.
7 All her images shall be
beaten to pieces,
all her wages shall be
burned with fire,
and all her idols I will lay
waste;
for as the wages of a
prostitute she gathered
them,
and as the wages of a
prostitute they shall
again be used.

The Doom of the Cities of Judah

8 For this I will lament and
wail;
I will go barefoot and
naked;
I will make lamentation like
the jackals,
and mourning like the
ostriches.
9 For her wound[b] is incurable.
It has come to Judah;
it has reached to the gate of
my people,
to Jerusalem.

10 Tell it not in Gath,
weep not at all;
in Beth-leaphrah
roll yourselves in the dust.
11 Pass on your way,
inhabitants of Shaphir,
in nakedness and shame;
the inhabitants of Zaanan
do not come forth;
Beth-ezel is wailing
and shall remove its
support from you.
12 For the inhabitants of
Maroth
wait anxiously for good,
yet disaster has come down
from the LORD
to the gate of Jerusalem.
13 Harness the steeds to the
chariots,
inhabitants of Lachish;
it was the beginning of sin
to daughter Zion,
for in you were found
the transgressions of Israel.

1.7 Deut 9.21; 2 Chr 34.7; Isa 23.17
1.8 Isa 22.4; 32.11; 13.21, 22
1.9 Jer 30.12, 15; 2 Kings 18.13; v. 12
1.10 2 Sam 1.20
1.11 Ezek 23.29
1.12 Isa 59.9-11; Jer 14.19
1.13 2 Kings 14.19; Isa 36.2
1.14 2 Kings 16.8; Josh 15.44; Jer 15.18
1.15 Josh 15.44; Mic 5.2; Josh 12.15; 2 Sam 23.13
1.16 Isa 15.2; 22.12; Lam 4.5; Am 7.11,17
2.1 Isa 32.7; Nah 1.11; Hos 7.6,7; Prov 3.27
2.2 Am 8.4; Isa 5.8; 1 Kings 21.1-15
2.3 Am 3.1,2; Deut 28.48; Jer 18.11; Isa 2.11,12; Am 5.13
2.4 Hab 2.6; Mic 1.8; Isa 24.3; Jer 4.13; 6.12; 8.10

14 Therefore you shall give
parting gifts
to Moresheth-gath;
the houses of Achzib shall be
a deception
to the kings of Israel.
15 I will again bring a
conqueror upon you,
inhabitants of Mareshah;
the glory of Israel
shall come to Adullam.
16 Make yourselves bald and
cut off your hair
for your pampered
children;
make yourselves as bald as
the eagle,
for they have gone from
you into exile.

Social Evils Denounced

2 Alas for those who devise
wickedness
and evil deeds[c] on their
beds!
When the morning dawns,
they perform it,
because it is in their
power.
2 They covet fields, and seize
them;
houses, and take them
away;
they oppress householder
and house,
people and their
inheritance.
3 Therefore thus says the LORD:
Now, I am devising against
this family an evil
from which you cannot
remove your necks;
and you shall not walk
haughtily,
for it will be an evil time.
4 On that day they shall take
up a taunt song against
you,
and wail with bitter
lamentation,
and say, "We are utterly
ruined;

[b] Gk Syr Vg: Heb *wounds* [c] Cn: Heb *work evil*

the LORD[d] alters the inheritance of my people;
how he removes it from me!
Among our captors[e] he parcels out our fields."
5 Therefore you will have no one to cast the line by lot
in the assembly of the LORD.

6 "Do not preach"—thus they preach—
"one should not preach of such things;
disgrace will not overtake us."
7 Should this be said, O house of Jacob?
Is the LORD's patience exhausted?
Are these his doings?
Do not my words do good to one who walks uprightly?
8 But you rise up against my people[f] as an enemy;
you strip the robe from the peaceful,[g]
from those who pass by trustingly
with no thought of war.
9 The women of my people you drive out
from their pleasant houses;
from their young children you take away
my glory forever.
10 Arise and go;
for this is no place to rest,
because of uncleanness that destroys
with a grievous destruction.[h]
11 If someone were to go about uttering empty falsehoods,
saying, "I will preach to you of wine and strong drink,"
such a one would be the preacher for this people!

2.5 Josh 18.4, 10 **2.6** Isa 30.10; Am 2.12; 7.16; Mic 3.6; 6.16 **2.7** Isa 50.2; 59.1; Jer 15.16; Ps 15.2; 84.11 **2.8** Jer 12.8; Mic 3.2,3; 7.2,3; Ps 120.6,7 **2.9** Jer 10.20 **2.10** Lev 18.25, 28,29; Deut 12.9; Ps 106.38 **2.11** Jer 5.13,31; Isa 28.7; 30.10,11

2.12 Mic 4.6,7; 5.7,8; 7.18; Jer 33.22 **2.13** Hos 3.5; Isa 52.12 **3.1** Jer 5.4,5 **3.2** Mic 2.8; 7.2,3; Ezek 22.27 **3.3** Ps 14.4; Zeph 3.3; Ezek 34.2,3; 11.3 **3.4** Ps 18.41; Prov 1.28; Isa 1.15; Zech 7.13; Isa 59.2; Mic 7.13 **3.5** Isa 56.10; Ezek 13.10; Jer 14.14, 15; Mic 2.11; Jer 6.14; Ezek 13.18, 19

A Promise for the Remnant of Israel

12 I will surely gather all of you, O Jacob,
I will gather the survivors of Israel;
I will set them together like sheep in a fold,
like a flock in its pasture;
it will resound with people.
13 The one who breaks out will go up before them;
they will break through and pass the gate,
going out by it.
Their king will pass on before them,
the LORD at their head.

Wicked Rulers and Prophets

3 And I said:
Listen, you heads of Jacob
and rulers of the house of Israel!
Should you not know justice?—
2 you who hate the good and love the evil,
who tear the skin off my people,[i]
and the flesh off their bones;
3 who eat the flesh of my people,
flay their skin off them,
break their bones in pieces,
and chop them up like meat[j] in a kettle,
like flesh in a caldron.

4 Then they will cry to the LORD,
but he will not answer them;
he will hide his face from them at that time,
because they have acted wickedly.

5 Thus says the LORD concerning the prophets

[d] Heb *he* [e] Cn: Heb *the rebellious*
[f] Cn: Heb *But yesterday my people rose*
[g] Cn: Heb *from before a garment* [h] Meaning of Heb uncertain [i] Heb *from them*
[j] Gk: Heb *as*

who lead my people astray,
who cry "Peace"
when they have something to eat,
but declare war against those
who put nothing into their mouths.
6 Therefore it shall be night to you, without vision,
and darkness to you, without revelation.
The sun shall go down upon the prophets,
and the day shall be black over them;
7 the seers shall be disgraced,
and the diviners put to shame;
they shall all cover their lips,
for there is no answer from God.
8 But as for me, I am filled with power,
with the spirit of the LORD,
and with justice and might,
to declare to Jacob his transgression
and to Israel his sin.

9 Hear this, you rulers of the house of Jacob
and chiefs of the house of Israel,
who abhor justice
and pervert all equity,
10 who build Zion with blood
and Jerusalem with wrong!
11 Its rulers give judgment for a bribe,
its priests teach for a price,
its prophets give oracles for money;
yet they lean upon the LORD and say,
"Surely the LORD is with us!
No harm shall come upon us."
12 Therefore because of you
Zion shall be plowed as a field;
Jerusalem shall become a heap of ruins,
and the mountain of the house a wooded height.

3.6 Isa 8.20,22; Ezek 13.23; Am 8.9 **3.7** Zech 13.4; Isa 44.25; Mic 7.16; 1 Sam 28.6; v. 4 **3.8** Isa 61.1,2; 58.1 **3.9** v. 1; Isa 1.23 **3.10** Jer 22.13; Ezek 22.27; Hab 2.12 **3.11** Isa 1.23; Hos 4.18; Jer 6.13; Isa 48.2; Jer 7.4 **3.12** Jer 26.18; Mic 4.1,2

4.1 Isa 2.2-4; Ezek 17.22; 43.12; Jer 3.17 **4.2** Zech 2.11; 14.16; Jer 31.6; Isa 54.13; 42.1-4; Zech 14.8,9 **4.3** Isa 2.4; Joel 3.10; Ps 72.7 **4.4** 1 Kings 4.25; Zech 3.10; Isa 1.20; 40.5 **4.5** 2 Kings 17.29; Isa 26.8,13; Zech 10.12 **4.6** Ezek 34.16; Zeph 3.19; Ps 147.2; Ezek 34.13

Peace and Security through Obedience

4 In days to come
the mountain of the LORD's house
shall be established as the highest of the mountains,
and shall be raised up above the hills.
Peoples shall stream to it,
2 and many nations shall come and say:
"Come, let us go up to the mountain of the LORD,
to the house of the God of Jacob;
that he may teach us his ways
and that we may walk in his paths."
For out of Zion shall go forth instruction,
and the word of the LORD from Jerusalem.
3 He shall judge between many peoples,
and shall arbitrate between strong nations far away;
they shall beat their swords into plowshares,
and their spears into pruning hooks;
nation shall not lift up sword against nation,
neither shall they learn war any more;
4 but they shall all sit under their own vines and under their own fig trees,
and no one shall make them afraid;
for the mouth of the LORD of hosts has spoken.

5 For all the peoples walk,
each in the name of its god,
but we will walk in the name of the LORD our God
forever and ever.

Restoration Promised after Exile

6 In that day, says the LORD,
I will assemble the lame

and gather those who have
been driven away,
and those whom I have
afflicted.
7 The lame I will make the
remnant,
and those who were cast
off, a strong nation;
and the LORD will reign over
them in Mount Zion
now and forevermore.

8 And you, O tower of the
flock,
hill of daughter Zion,
to you it shall come,
the former dominion shall
come,
the sovereignty of daughter
Jerusalem.

9 Now why do you cry aloud?
Is there no king in you?
Has your counselor perished,
that pangs have seized you
like a woman in labor?
10 Writhe and groan,[k]
O daughter Zion,
like a woman in labor;
for now you shall go forth
from the city
and camp in the open
country;
you shall go to Babylon.
There you shall be rescued,
there the LORD will redeem
you
from the hands of your
enemies.

11 Now many nations
are assembled against you,
saying, "Let her be profaned,
and let our eyes gaze upon
Zion."
12 But they do not know
the thoughts of the LORD;
they do not understand his
plan,
that he has gathered them
as sheaves to the
threshing floor.
13 Arise and thresh,
O daughter Zion,
for I will make your horn
iron
and your hoofs bronze;
you shall beat in pieces
many peoples,
and shall[l] devote their
gain to the LORD,
their wealth to the Lord of
the whole earth.

5 [m]Now you are walled
around with a wall;[n]
siege is laid against us;
with a rod they strike the
ruler of Israel
upon the cheek.

The Ruler from Bethlehem

2 [o]But you, O Bethlehem of
Ephrathah,
who are one of the little
clans of Judah,
from you shall come forth for
me
one who is to rule in Israel,
whose origin is from of old,
from ancient days.
3 Therefore he shall give them
up until the time
when she who is in labor
has brought forth;
then the rest of his kindred
shall return
to the people of Israel.
4 And he shall stand and feed
his flock in the strength
of the LORD,
in the majesty of the name
of the LORD his God.
And they shall live secure,
for now he shall be
great
to the ends of the earth;
5 and he shall be the one of
peace.

If the Assyrians come into
our land
and tread upon our soil,[p]
we will raise against them
seven shepherds
and eight installed as
rulers.
6 They shall rule the land of
Assyria with the sword,

4.7 Mic 2.12; 5.7,8; 7.18; Isa 9.6; Dan 7.14; Lk 1.33; Rev 11.15
4.8 Mic 2.12; Isa 1.26; Zech 9.10
4.9 Jer 8.19; Isa 13.8; Jer 30.6
4.10 Hos 2.14; Isa 45.13; Mic 7.8-12; Isa 48.20; 52.9-12
4.11 Lam 2.16; Ob 12; Mic 7.10
4.12 Isa 55.8; Rom 11.33; Isa 21.10
4.13 Isa 41.15; Dan 2.44; Zech 4.14
5.1 Jer 5.7; 1 Kings 22.24; Lam 3.30
5.2 Mt 2.6; 1 Sam 17.12; 23.23; Lk 2.4; Isa 9.6
5.3 Mic 4.10; Hos 11.8; Isa 10.20-22
5.4 Isa 40.11; Ezek 34.23; Isa 52.13; Lk 1.32
5.5 Isa 9.6; Rev 11.15; Isa 8.7,8
5.6 Nah 2.11-13; Zeph 2.13; Gen 10.8; Isa 37.36,37

[k] Meaning of Heb uncertain [l] Gk Syr Tg: Heb *and I will* [m] Ch 4.14 in Heb
[n] Cn Compare Gk: Meaning of Heb uncertain
[o] Ch 5.1 in Heb [p] Gk: Heb *in our palaces*

and the land of Nimrod
with the drawn sword;[q]
they[r] shall rescue us from
the Assyrians
if they come into our land
or tread within our border.

The Future Role of the Remnant

7 Then the remnant of Jacob,
surrounded by many
peoples,
shall be like dew from the
LORD,
like showers on the grass,
which do not depend upon
people
or wait for any mortal.
8 And among the nations the
remnant of Jacob,
surrounded by many
peoples,
shall be like a lion among
the animals of the
forest,
like a young lion among
the flocks of sheep,
which, when it goes through,
treads down
and tears in pieces, with no
one to deliver.
9 Your hand shall be lifted up
over your adversaries,
and all your enemies shall
be cut off.

10 In that day, says the LORD,
I will cut off your horses
from among you
and will destroy your
chariots;
11 and I will cut off the cities of
your land
and throw down all your
strongholds;
12 and I will cut off sorceries
from your hand,
and you shall have no more
soothsayers;
13 and I will cut off your images
and your pillars from
among you,
and you shall bow down no
more
to the work of your hands;
14 and I will uproot your sacred
poles[s] from among you
and destroy your towns.
15 And in anger and wrath I will
execute vengeance
on the nations that did not
obey.

God Challenges Israel

6 Hear what the LORD says:
Rise, plead your case
before the mountains,
and let the hills hear your
voice.
2 Hear, you mountains, the
controversy of the LORD,
and you enduring
foundations of the
earth;
for the LORD has a
controversy with his
people,
and he will contend with
Israel.

3 "O my people, what have I
done to you?
In what have I wearied
you? Answer me!
4 For I brought you up from
the land of Egypt,
and redeemed you from the
house of slavery;
and I sent before you Moses,
Aaron, and Miriam.
5 O my people, remember now
what King Balak of
Moab devised,
what Balaam son of Beor
answered him,
and what happened from
Shittim to Gilgal,
that you may know the
saving acts of the
LORD."

What God Requires

6 "With what shall I come
before the LORD,
and bow myself before God
on high?
Shall I come before him with
burnt offerings,
with calves a year old?
7 Will the LORD be pleased
with thousands of rams,

5.7 Mic 2.12; Deut 32.2; Hos 14.5 **5.8** Mic 4.13; Zech 10.5; Hos 5.14; Ps 50.22 **5.9** Ps 10.12; 21.8; Isa 26.11 **5.10** Isa 2.7; Hos 14.3; Zech 9.10 **5.11** Isa 1.7; Hos 10.14; Am 5.9 **5.12** Deut 18.10-12; Isa 2.6 **5.13** Zech 13.2; Isa 2.8 **5.14** Ex 34.13; Isa 17.8; 27.9 **5.15** Ps 149.7; Isa 65.12 **6.1** Ps 50.1; Ezek 6.2,3 **6.2** Deut 32.1; Hos 12.2; Isa 1.8; Hos 4.1 **6.3** Ps 50.7; Jer 2.5; Isa 43.22,23 **6.4** Ex 12.51; Deut 4.20; 7.8; Ps 77.20; Ex 15.20 **6.5** Num 22.5,6; Rev 2.14; Num 25.1; Josh 4.19; 5.9,10; Judg 5.11; 1 Sam 12.7 **6.6** Ps 40.6-8; 51.16,17 **6.7** 2 Kings 16.3; 21.6; Jer 7.31

[q] Cn: Heb *in its entrances* [r] Heb *he*
[s] Heb *Asherim*

with ten thousands of
rivers of oil?
Shall I give my firstborn for
my transgression,
the fruit of my body for the
sin of my soul?"
8 He has told you, O mortal,
what is good;
and what does the LORD
require of you
but to do justice, and to love
kindness,
and to walk humbly with
your God?

Cheating and Violence to Be Punished

9 The voice of the LORD cries
to the city
(it is sound wisdom to fear
your name):
Hear, O tribe and assembly
of the city![t]
10 Can I forget[u] the treasures
of wickedness in the
house of the wicked,
and the scant measure that
is accursed?
11 Can I tolerate wicked scales
and a bag of dishonest
weights?
12 Your[v] wealthy are full of
violence;
your[w] inhabitants speak
lies,
with tongues of deceit in
their mouths.
13 Therefore I have begun[x] to
strike you down,
making you desolate
because of your sins.
14 You shall eat, but not be
satisfied,
and there shall be a
gnawing hunger within
you;
you shall put away, but not
save,
and what you save, I will
hand over to the sword.
15 You shall sow, but not reap;
you shall tread olives, but
not anoint yourselves
with oil;
you shall tread grapes, but
not drink wine.
16 For you have kept the
statutes of Omri[y]
and all the works of the
house of Ahab,
and you have followed their
counsels.
Therefore I will make you a
desolation, and your[z]
inhabitants an object of
hissing;
so you shall bear the scorn
of my people.

The Total Corruption of the People

7 Woe is me! For I have
become like one who,
after the summer fruit has
been gathered,
after the vintage has been
gleaned,
finds no cluster to eat;
there is no first-ripe fig for
which I hunger.
2 The faithful have
disappeared from the
land,
and there is no one left
who is upright;
they all lie in wait for blood,
and they hunt each other
with nets.
3 Their hands are skilled to do
evil;
the official and the judge
ask for a bribe,
and the powerful dictate
what they desire;
thus they pervert justice.[a]
4 The best of them is like a
brier,
the most upright of them a
thorn hedge.
The day of their[b] sentinels,
of their[b] punishment,
has come;
now their confusion is at
hand.
5 Put no trust in a friend,

6.8 Deut 10.12; 1 Sam 15.22; Hos 6.6; 12.6; Isa 56.1; 57.15; 66.2
6.10 Jer 5.26,27; Am 3.10; 8.5
6.11 Hos 12.7
6.12 Am 6.3,4; Mic 2.1,2; Jer 9.3,5; Hos 7.13; Am 2.4; Isa 3.8
6.13 Mic 1.9; Isa 1.7; 6.11
6.14 Lev 26.26; Isa 9.20; 30.6
6.15 Deut 28.38; Jer 12.13; Am 5.11; Zeph 1.13
6.16 1 Kings 16.25-33; Jer 7.24; 19.8; 29.18; 51.51
7.1 Isa 24.13; 28.4; Hos 9.10
7.2 Ps 12.1; Isa 57.1; 59.7; Jer 5.26; Hos 5.1
7.3 Prov 4.16, 17; Am 5.12; Mic 3.11
7.4 Ezek 2.6; 28.24; Nah 1.10; Isa 10.3; Hos 9.7; Isa 22.5
7.5 Jer 9.4

[t] Cn Compare Gk: Heb *tribe, and who has appointed it yet?* [u] Cn: Meaning of Heb uncertain [v] Heb *Whose* [w] Heb *whose* [x] Gk Syr Vg: Heb *have made sick* [y] Gk Syr Vg Tg: Heb *the statutes of Omri are kept* [z] Heb *its* [a] Cn: Heb *they weave it* [b] Heb *your*

have no confidence in a loved one;
guard the doors of your mouth
from her who lies in your embrace;
6 for the son treats the father with contempt,
the daughter rises up against her mother,
the daughter-in-law against her mother-in-law;
your enemies are members of your own household.
7 But as for me, I will look to the LORD,
I will wait for the God of my salvation;
my God will hear me.

Penitence and Trust in God

8 Do not rejoice over me, O my enemy;
when I fall, I shall rise;
when I sit in darkness,
the LORD will be a light to me.
9 I must bear the indignation of the LORD,
because I have sinned against him,
until he takes my side
and executes judgment for me.
He will bring me out to the light;
I shall see his vindication.
10 Then my enemy will see,
and shame will cover her who said to me,
"Where is the LORD your God?"
My eyes will see her downfall;[c]
now she will be trodden down
like the mire of the streets.

A Prophecy of Restoration

11 A day for the building of your walls!
In that day the boundary shall be far extended.
12 In that day they will come to you
from Assyria to[d] Egypt,
and from Egypt to the River,
from sea to sea and from mountain to mountain.
13 But the earth will be desolate
because of its inhabitants,
for the fruit of their doings.

14 Shepherd your people with your staff,
the flock that belongs to you,
which lives alone in a forest
in the midst of a garden land;
let them feed in Bashan and Gilead
as in the days of old.
15 As in the days when you came out of the land of Egypt,
show us[e] marvelous things.
16 The nations shall see and be ashamed
of all their might;
they shall lay their hands on their mouths;
their ears shall be deaf;
17 they shall lick dust like a snake,
like the crawling things of the earth;
they shall come trembling out of their fortresses;
they shall turn in dread to the LORD our God,
and they shall stand in fear of you.

God's Compassion and Steadfast Love

18 Who is a God like you,
pardoning iniquity
and passing over the transgression
of the remnant of your[f] possession?
He does not retain his anger forever,
because he delights in showing clemency.

7.6 Ezek 22.7; Mt 10.21, 35,36; Lk 12.53 **7.7** Hab 2.1; Ps 130.5; 4.3 **7.8** Prov 24.17; Lam 4.21; Ps 37.24; Isa 9.2 **7.9** Lam 3.29, 40; Isa 42.7, 16; 56.1 **7.10** Ps 35.26; Isa 51.23; Zech 10.5 **7.11** Isa 54.11; Zeph 2.2 **7.12** Isa 11.16; 19.23-25 **7.13** Jer 25.11; Mic 6.13; Isa 3.10,11; Mic 3.4 **7.14** Mic 5.4; Ps 23.4; Jer 50.19; Am 9.11 **7.15** Ex 3.20; 20.34; Ps 78.12 **7.16** Job 21.5; Mic 3.7 **7.17** Ps 72.9; Isa 49.23; Deut 32.24; Ps 18.45; Isa 59.19 **7.18** Ex 34.7,9; Isa 43.25; Jer 32.41

[c] Heb lacks *downfall* [d] One Ms: MT *Assyria and cities of* [e] Cn: Heb *I will show him* [f] Heb *his*

19 He will again have
compassion upon us;
he will tread our iniquities
under foot.
You will cast all our[g] sins
into the depths of the sea.
20 You will show faithfulness to
Jacob
and unswerving loyalty to
Abraham,
as you have sworn to our
ancestors
from the days of old.

7.19 Jer 50.20; Isa 38.17; 43.25; Jer 31.34
7.20 Lk 1.55,72; Deut 7.8,12

[g] Gk Syr Vg Tg: Heb *their*

Nahum

Title and Background

The name Nahum means "comfort" or "consolation." During Jonah's time Nineveh repented and their destruction was temporarily averted. Not long after that, however, Nineveh reverted to its extreme wickedness, brutality, and pride.

Author and Date of Writing

Nothing is known about Nahum except his hometown (Elkosh), but even its precise location is uncertain. In all three chapters Nahum prophesied Nineveh's fall, which was fulfilled in 612 B.C. Nahum therefore uttered this oracle between 663 and 612, perhaps near the middle of this period.

Theme and Message

The focal point of this whole book is the Lord's judgment on the Ninevites for their oppression, cruelty, idolatry, and wickedness. God's righteous and just kingdom will ultimately triumph, while kingdoms built on wickedness and tyranny must eventually fall. In addition, Nahum declares the universal sovereignty of God. God is Lord of history and all nations; as such he controls their destinies.

Outline

I. The Lord's Anger Against Nineveh (1.1-15)
II. Nineveh's Fall (2.1-13)
III. Woe to Nineveh (3.1-19)

---

1 An oracle concerning Nineveh. The book of the vision of Nahum of Elkosh.

The Consuming Wrath of God

2 A jealous and avenging God
is the LORD,
the LORD is avenging and
wrathful;
the LORD takes vengeance on
his adversaries
and rages against his
enemies.
3 The LORD is slow to anger
but great in power,
and the LORD will by no
means clear the guilty.

His way is in whirlwind and
storm,
and the clouds are the dust
of his feet.
4 He rebukes the sea and
makes it dry,
and he dries up all the
rivers;
Bashan and Carmel wither,
and the bloom of Lebanon
fades.
5 The mountains quake before
him,
and the hills melt;
the earth heaves before him,
the world and all who live
in it.

6 Who can stand before his
indignation?
Who can endure the heat
of his anger?
His wrath is poured out like
fire,
and by him the rocks are
broken in pieces.
7 The LORD is good,
a stronghold in a day of
trouble;
he protects those who take
refuge in him,
8 even in a rushing flood.

1.1 Isa 13.1; Hab 1.1; Nah 2.8; 3.7; Zeph 2.13
1.2 Ex 20.5; Deut 4.24; 32.35,41; Ps 94.1
1.3 Ex 34.6,7; Ps 103.8; Isa 29.6; Ps 104.3
1.4 Ps 106.9; Isa 33.9
1.5 Ex 19.18; Mic 1.4; Isa 24.1,20
1.6 Jer 10.10; Mal 3.2; Isa 66.15; 1 Kings 19.11
1.7 1 Chr 16.34; Ps 28.8
1.8 Isa 28.2,18; 13.9,10

He will make a full end of his adversaries,[a]
and will pursue his enemies into darkness.
9 Why do you plot against the LORD?
He will make an end;
no adversary will rise up twice.
10 Like thorns they are entangled,
like drunkards they are drunk;
they are consumed like dry straw.
11 From you one has gone out
who plots evil against the LORD,
who counsels wickedness.

Good News for Judah

12 Thus says the LORD,
"Though they are at full strength and many,[b]
they will be cut off and pass away.
Though I have afflicted you,
I will afflict you no more.
13 And now I will break off his yoke from you
and snap the bonds that bind you."

14 The LORD has commanded concerning you:
"Your name shall be perpetuated no longer;
from the house of your gods I will cut off
the carved image and the cast image.
I will make your grave, for you are worthless."

15[c] Look! On the mountains the feet of one
who brings good tidings,
who proclaims peace!
Celebrate your festivals, O Judah,
fulfill your vows,
for never again shall the wicked invade you;
they are utterly cut off.

1.9 Ps 2.1; Isa 28.22
1.10 2 Sam 23.6; Mal 4.1
1.11 v. 9; Ezek 11.2
1.12 Isa 10.16-19, 33,34; 54.7,8
1.13 Isa 9.4; Jer 2.20
1.14 Isa 46.1,2; Mic 5.13,14; Ezek 32.22, 23
1.15 Isa 40.9; Ps 52.7; Rom 10.15; Lev 23.2,4; Isa 52.1; Joel 3.17; Isa 29.7,8
2.1 Jer 51.20-23; Nah 3.12,14
2.2 Isa 60.15; Ezek 37.21-23
2.3 Ezek 23.14, 15; Job 39.23
2.4 Ezek 26.10; Jer 4.13
2.5 Nah 3.18; Jer 46.12
2.6 Nah 3.18
2.7 Isa 59.11; 32.12
2.8 Nah 3.7; Jer 46.5; 47.3

The Destruction of the Wicked City

2 A shatterer[d] has come up against you.
Guard the ramparts;
watch the road;
gird your loins;
collect all your strength.

2 (For the LORD is restoring the majesty of Jacob,
as well as the majesty of Israel,
though ravagers have ravaged them
and ruined their branches.)

3 The shields of his warriors are red;
his soldiers are clothed in crimson.
The metal on the chariots flashes
on the day when he musters them;
the chargers[e] prance.
4 The chariots race madly through the streets,
they rush to and fro through the squares;
their appearance is like torches,
they dart like lightning.
5 He calls his officers;
they stumble as they come forward;
they hasten to the wall,
and the mantelet[b] is set up.
6 The river gates are opened,
the palace trembles.
7 It is decreed[b] that the city[f] be exiled,
its slave women led away,
moaning like doves
and beating their breasts.
8 Nineveh is like a pool
whose waters[g] run away.
"Halt! Halt!"—
but no one turns back.
9 "Plunder the silver,

[a] Gk: Heb *of her place* [b] Meaning of Heb uncertain [c] Ch 2.1 in Heb [d] Cn: Heb *scatterer* [e] Cn Compare Gk Syr: Heb *cypresses* [f] Heb *it* [g] Cn Compare Gk: Heb *a pool; from the days that she has become, and they*

plunder the gold!
There is no end of treasure!
An abundance of every
precious thing!"

10 Devastation, desolation, and
destruction!
Hearts faint and knees
tremble,
all loins quake,
all faces grow pale!
11 What became of the lions'
den,
the cave[h] of the young
lions,
where the lion goes,
and the lion's cubs, with
no one to disturb them?
12 The lion has torn enough for
his whelps
and strangled prey for his
lionesses;
he has filled his caves with
prey
and his dens with torn
flesh.

13 See, I am against you, says
the LORD of hosts, and I will burn
your[i] chariots in smoke, and the
sword shall devour your young lions; I will cut off your prey from the
earth, and the voice of your messengers shall be heard no more.

Ruin Imminent and Inevitable

3 Ah! City of bloodshed,
utterly deceitful, full of
booty—
no end to the plunder!
2 The crack of whip and
rumble of wheel,
galloping horse and
bounding chariot!
3 Horsemen charging,
flashing sword and
glittering spear,
piles of dead,
heaps of corpses,
dead bodies without end—
they stumble over the
bodies!
4 Because of the countless
debaucheries of the
prostitute,
gracefully alluring, mistress
of sorcery,
who enslaves[j] nations
through her
debaucheries,
and peoples through her
sorcery,
5 I am against you,
says the LORD of hosts,
and will lift up your skirts
over your face;
and I will let nations look on
your nakedness
and kingdoms on your
shame.
6 I will throw filth at you
and treat you with
contempt,
and make you a spectacle.
7 Then all who see you will
shrink from you and
say,
"Nineveh is devastated; who
will bemoan her?"
Where shall I seek
comforters for you?

8 Are you better than Thebes[k]
that sat by the Nile,
with water around her,
her rampart a sea,
water her wall?
9 Ethiopia[l] was her strength,
Egypt too, and that without
limit;
Put and the Libyans were
her[m] helpers.

10 Yet she became an exile,
she went into captivity;
even her infants were dashed
in pieces
at the head of every street;
lots were cast for her nobles,
all her dignitaries were
bound in fetters.
11 You also will be drunken,
you will go into hiding;[n]
you will seek
a refuge from the enemy.
12 All your fortresses are like fig
trees
with first-ripe figs—
if shaken they fall

2.10 Ps 22.14; Isa 13.7,8; Joel 2.6
2.11 Isa 5.29; Jer 4.7; Nah 3.1
2.12 Isa 10.6-14; Jer 51.34
2.13 Nah 3.5; Ps 46.9; Isa 49.24,25
3.1 Ezek 24.6,9
3.2 Nah 2.3,4; Jer 47.3
3.3 Hab 3.11; Isa 34.3; 66.16; 2 Kings 19.35
3.4 Isa 23.17; Rev 17.1,2; Isa 47.9; Rev 18.3
3.5 Nah 2.13; Isa 47.2,3; Jer 13.22; Ezek 16.37
3.6 Job 9.31; Mal 2.9; Isa 14.16; Jer 51.37
3.7 Jer 51.9; Nah 2.8; Zeph 2.13; Isa 51.19; Jer 15.5
3.8 Jer 46.25; Ezek 30.14-16; Isa 19.6-8
3.9 Isa 20.5; Ezek 27.10; 30.5; 38.5; 2 Chr 12.3; 16.8
3.10 Isa 20.4; 13.16; Hos 13.16; Lam 2.19; Joel 3.3; Ob 11
3.11 Jer 25.27; Isa 2.10,19
3.12 Isa 28.4; Rev 6.13

h Cn: Heb *pasture* i Heb *her*
j Heb *sells* k Heb *No-amon*
l Or *Nubia*; Heb *Cush* m Gk: Heb *your*
n Meaning of Heb uncertain

into the mouth of the
eater.
13 Look at your troops:
they are women in your
midst.
The gates of your land
are wide open to your foes;
fire has devoured the bars
of your gates.

14 Draw water for the siege,
strengthen your forts;
trample the clay,
tread the mortar,
take hold of the brick
mold!
15 There the fire will devour
you,
the sword will cut you off.
It will devour you like the
locust.

Multiply yourselves like the
locust,
multiply like the
grasshopper!
16 You increased your
merchants
more than the stars of the
heavens.
The locust sheds its skin
and flies away.
17 Your guards are like
grasshoppers,
your scribes like swarms[o]
of locusts
settling on the fences
on a cold day—
when the sun rises, they fly
away;
no one knows where they
have gone.

18 Your shepherds are asleep,
O king of Assyria;
your nobles slumber.
Your people are scattered on
the mountains
with no one to gather
them.
19 There is no assuaging your
hurt,
your wound is mortal.
All who hear the news about
you
clap their hands over you.
For who has ever escaped
your endless cruelty?

3.13 Jer 50.37; 51.30; Ps 147.13 **3.14** 2 Chr 32.3, 4,11; Nah 2.1 **3.15** v. 13; Joel 1.4 **3.16** Isa 23.8 **3.17** Jer 51.27; Rev 9.7 **3.18** Ps 76.5,6; Isa 56.10; Jer 51.57; Nah 2.5; 1 Kings 22.17 **3.19** Mic 1.9; Lam 2.15; Zeph 2.15

[o] Meaning of Heb uncertain

Habakkuk

Title and Background

The title of this book is the author's name and apparently comes from a Hebrew root meaning "to clasp" or "to embrace." Habakkuk prayed and prophesied in a time of impending crisis. Externally the nation of Babylon was increasing in power and influence. Internally the people of God were caught up in religious and moral bewilderment.

Author and Date of Writing

Little is known about the author except his name and that he was a contemporary of Jeremiah. He was a man of vigorous faith, a faith rooted deeply in the religious traditions of Israel. The prophecy is generally dated a little before or after the battle of Carchemish (605 B.C.).

Theme and Message

Habakkuk was written as a dialogue or conversation between God and the prophet. Habakkuk saw that the leaders were oppressing the poor, so he asked why God allowed the wicked to prosper. After God replied to him, Habakkuk responds with a beautiful confession of faith. His confession appears to have been used as a psalm.

Outline

I. Habakkuk's First Question and God's Answer (1.1-11)
II. Habakkuk's Second Question and God's Answer (1.12–2.20)
III. Habakkuk's Prayer (3.1-19)

---

1 The oracle that the prophet Habakkuk saw.

The Prophet's Complaint

2 O LORD, how long shall I cry
for help,
and you will not listen?
Or cry to you "Violence!"
and you will not save?
3 Why do you make me see
wrongdoing
and look at trouble?
Destruction and violence are
before me;
strife and contention arise.
4 So the law becomes slack
and justice never prevails.
The wicked surround the
righteous —
therefore judgment comes
forth perverted.

5 Look at the nations, and see!
Be astonished! Be
astounded!
For a work is being done in
your days
that you would not believe
if you were told.
6 For I am rousing the
Chaldeans,
that fierce and impetuous
nation,
who march through the
breadth of the earth
to seize dwellings not their
own.
7 Dread and fearsome are they;
their justice and dignity
proceed from
themselves.
8 Their horses are swifter than
leopards,
more menacing than
wolves at dusk;
their horses charge.
Their horsemen come from
far away;
they fly like an eagle swift
to devour.
9 They all come for violence,

1.1 Isa 13.1; Nah 1.1
1.2 Ps 13.1,2; 22.1,2
1.3 v. 13; Jer 20.8
1.4 Ps 119.126; 22.12; Isa 5.20
1.5 Acts 13.41; Isa 29.9,14
1.6 2 Kings 24.2; Jer 4.11-13; 5.15; 8.10
1.7 Isa 18.2,7; Jer 39.5-9
1.8 Jer 4.13; 5.6; Ezek 17.3; Hos 8.1
1.9 Hab 2.5

with faces pressing[a] forward;
they gather captives like sand.
10 At kings they scoff,
and of rulers they make sport.
They laugh at every fortress,
and heap up earth to take it.
11 Then they sweep by like the wind;
they transgress and become guilty;
their own might is their god!

12 Are you not from of old,
O LORD my God, my Holy One?
You[b] shall not die.
O LORD, you have marked them for judgment;
and you, O Rock, have established them for punishment.
13 Your eyes are too pure to behold evil,
and you cannot look on wrongdoing;
why do you look on the treacherous,
and are silent when the wicked swallow
those more righteous than they?
14 You have made people like the fish of the sea,
like crawling things that have no ruler.
15 The enemy[c] brings all of them up with a hook;
he drags them out with his net,
he gathers them in his seine;
so he rejoices and exults.
16 Therefore he sacrifices to his net
and makes offerings to his seine;
for by them his portion is lavish,
and his food is rich.
17 Is he then to keep on emptying his net,
and destroying nations without mercy?

God's Reply to the Prophet's Complaint

2 I will stand at my watchpost,
and station myself on the rampart;
I will keep watch to see what he will say to me,
and what he[d] will answer concerning my complaint.
2 Then the LORD answered me and said:
Write the vision;
make it plain on tablets,
so that a runner may read it.
3 For there is still a vision for the appointed time;
it speaks of the end, and does not lie.
If it seems to tarry, wait for it;
it will surely come, it will not delay.
4 Look at the proud!
Their spirit is not right in them,
but the righteous live by their faith.[e]
5 Moreover, wealth[f] is treacherous;
the arrogant do not endure.
They open their throats wide as Sheol;
like Death they never have enough.
They gather all nations for themselves,
and collect all peoples as their own.

The Woes of the Wicked

6 Shall not everyone taunt such
people and, with mocking riddles,
say about them,
"Alas for you who heap up what is not your own!"

1.10 2 Chr 36.6, 10; Isa 10.9; 14.16; Jer 32.24; Ezek 26.8 **1.11** Jer 4.11,12; 2.3; Dan 4.30 **1.12** Deut 33.27; Ps 90.2; Isa 10.5-7; Deut 32.4 **1.13** Jer 12.1,2; Isa 24.16; Ps 50.21; 56.1,2 **1.14** Eccl 9.12 **1.15** Jer 16.16; Am 4.2; Ps 10.9 **1.17** Isa 19.8; 14.5,6
2.1 Isa 21.8,11; Ps 5.3; 85.8 **2.2** Deut 27.8; Isa 8.1; Rev 1.19 **2.3** Dan 8.17, 19; 10.14; Ezek 12.25; Heb 10.37, 38 **2.4** Rom 1.17; Gal 3.11; Heb 10.38, 39 **2.5** Prov 20.1; 21.24; 2 Kings 14.10; Jer 25.9 **2.6ff** Jer 50.13; v. 12; Ezek 18.12; Am 2.8

[a] Meaning of Heb uncertain [b] Ancient Heb tradition: MT *We* [c] Heb *He* [d] Syr: Heb *I* [e] Or *faithfulness* [f] Other Heb Mss read *wine*

How long will you load
yourselves with goods
taken in pledge?
7 Will not your own creditors
suddenly rise,
and those who make you
tremble wake up?
Then you will be booty for
them.
8 Because you have plundered
many nations,
all that survive of the
peoples shall plunder
you—
because of human
bloodshed, and violence
to the earth,
to cities and all who live in
them.

9 "Alas for you who get evil
gain for your houses,
setting your nest on high
to be safe from the reach
of harm!"
10 You have devised shame for
your house
by cutting off many
peoples;
you have forfeited your life.
11 The very stones will cry out
from the wall,
and the plaster[g] will
respond from the
woodwork.

12 "Alas for you who build a
town by bloodshed,
and found a city on
iniquity!"
13 Is it not from the LORD of
hosts
that peoples labor only to
feed the flames,
and nations weary
themselves for nothing?
14 But the earth will be filled
with the knowledge of the
glory of the LORD,
as the waters cover the sea.

15 "Alas for you who make your
neighbors drink,
pouring out your wrath[h]
until they are drunk,
in order to gaze on their
nakedness!"

2.7 Prov 29.1
2.8 Isa 33.1; Zech 2.8; v. 17
2.9 Jer 22.13; Ezek 22.27; Jer 49.16
2.10 2 Kings 9.26; v. 16; Prov 1.18; Jer 26.29
2.11 Josh 24.27; Lk 19.40
2.12 Mic 3.10; Nah 3.1
2.13 Isa 50.11; Jer 51.58
2.14 Isa 11.9; Zech 14.8,9
2.15 Isa 28.7,8; Hos 7.5
2.16 v. 10; Lam 4.21; Jer 25.15, 27; Nah 3.6
2.17 Zech 11.1; v. 8; Jer 51.35
2.18 Isa 42.17; Jer 2.27,28; 10.8,14; Zech 10.2; Ps 115.4,8
2.19 Jer 2.27,28; 1 Kings 18.26-29; Jer 10.9,14; Ps 135.17
2.20 Mic 1.2; Zeph 1.7; Zech 2.13
3.2 Job 42.5,6; Ps 119.120; Jer 10.7; Ps 85.6; Isa 54.8

16 You will be sated with
contempt instead of
glory.
Drink, you yourself, and
stagger![i]
The cup in the LORD's right
hand
will come around to you,
and shame will come upon
your glory!
17 For the violence done to
Lebanon will
overwhelm you;
the destruction of the
animals will terrify
you—[j]
because of human bloodshed
and violence to the
earth,
to cities and all who live in
them.

18 What use is an idol
once its maker has shaped
it—
a cast image, a teacher of
lies?
For its maker trusts in what
has been made,
though the product is only
an idol that cannot
speak!
19 Alas for you who say to the
wood, "Wake up!"
to silent stone, "Rouse
yourself!"
Can it teach?
See, it is gold and silver
plated,
and there is no breath in it
at all.

20 But the LORD is in his holy
temple;
let all the earth keep
silence before him!

3 A prayer of the prophet Habakkuk according to Shigionoth.

The Prophet's Prayer

2 O LORD, I have heard of your
renown,

[g] Or *beam* [h] Or *poison* [i] Q Ms Gk: MT *be uncircumcised* [j] Gk Syr: Meaning of Heb uncertain

and I stand in awe, O LORD,
of your work.
In our own time revive it;
in our own time make it
known;
in wrath may you
remember mercy.
3 God came from Teman,
the Holy One from Mount
Paran. *Selah*
His glory covered the
heavens,
and the earth was full of
his praise.
4 The brightness was like the
sun;
rays came forth from his
hand,
where his power lay
hidden.
5 Before him went pestilence,
and plague followed close
behind.
6 He stopped and shook the
earth;
he looked and made the
nations tremble.
The eternal mountains were
shattered;
along his ancient pathways
the everlasting hills sank
low.
7 I saw the tents of Cushan
under affliction;
the tent-curtains of the
land of Midian
trembled.
8 Was your wrath against the
rivers,[k] O LORD?
Or your anger against the
rivers,[k]
or your rage against the
sea,[l]
when you drove your horses,
your chariots to victory?
9 You brandished your naked
bow,
sated[m] were the arrows at
your command.[n] *Selah*
You split the earth with
rivers.
10 The mountains saw you, and
writhed;
a torrent of water swept by;
the deep gave forth its voice.
The sun[o] raised high its
hands;
11 the moon[p] stood still in its
exalted place,
at the light of your arrows
speeding by,
at the gleam of your
flashing spear.
12 In fury you trod the earth,
in anger you trampled
nations.
13 You came forth to save your
people,
to save your anointed.
You crushed the head of the
wicked house,
laying it bare from
foundation to roof.[n]
Selah
14 You pierced with his own
arrows the head[q] of his
warriors,[r]
who came like a whirlwind
to scatter us,[s]
gloating as if ready to
devour the poor who
were in hiding.
15 You trampled the sea with
your horses,
churning the mighty
waters.

16 I hear, and I tremble within;
my lips quiver at the
sound.
Rottenness enters into my
bones,
and my steps tremble[t]
beneath me.
I wait quietly for the day of
calamity
to come upon the people
who attack us.

Trust and Joy in the Midst of Trouble

17 Though the fig tree does not
blossom,
and no fruit is on the
vines;
though the produce of the
olive fails

3.3 Am 1.12; Deut 33.2; Ps 113.4; 48.10 **3.4** Ps 18.12; Job 26.14 **3.5** Ex 12.29, 30; Num 16.46-49 **3.6** Ps 35.5; 114.1-6; Mic 5.2 **3.7** Ex 15.14-16; Judg 7.24, 25 **3.8** Ex 7.19,20; 14.16,21; Deut 33.26; Ps 68.17 **3.9** Gen 26.3; Deut 7.8; Ps 78.16; 105.41 **3.10** Ps 114.1-6; 98.7,8; Ex 14.22 **3.11** Josh 10.12-14; Ps 18.9,11, 14 **3.12** Ps 68.7; Isa 41.15; Jer 51.33 **3.13** Ex 15.2; Ps 68.19,20; 110.6; Ezek 13.14 **3.14** Judg 7.22; Dan 11.40; Zech 9.14; Ps 10.8; 64.2-5 **3.15** Ps 77.19; Ex 15.8 **3.16** Jer 23.9; 5.15 **3.17ff** Joel 1.18; Jer 5.17

k Or *against River* l Or *against Sea* m Cn: Heb *oaths* n Meaning of Heb uncertain o Heb *It* p Heb *sun, moon* q Or *leader* r Vg Compare Gk Syr: Meaning of Heb uncertain s Heb *me* t Cn Compare Gk: Meaning of Heb uncertain

and the fields yield no
food;
though the flock is cut off
from the fold
and there is no herd in the
stalls,
18 yet I will rejoice in the
LORD;
I will exult in the God of
my salvation.

19 GOD, the Lord, is my
strength;
he makes my feet like the
feet of a deer,
and makes me tread upon
the heights.[u]

To the leader: with
stringed[v] instruments.

3.18 Isa 61.10; Ps 46.1-5; Isa 12.2

3.19 2 Sam 22.34; Ps 18.33; Deut 33.29

[u] Heb *my heights* [v] Heb *my stringed*

Zephaniah

Title and Background

The name Zephaniah means "The LORD hides (or protects)." The religious state of Judah declined markedly following the death of Hezekiah, but Josiah launched a sweeping reform. He was backed by Jeremiah and Nahum, but their calls for repentance fell on deaf ears. Judah became ripe for judgment.

Author and Date of Writing

Zephaniah, a fourth generation descendant of King Hezekiah, was evidently a person of considerable social standing in Judah. The prophet shows great familiarity with court circles and current political issues. According to 1.1, he prophesied during the reign of King Josiah (640-609 B.C.), so this prophecy could have been written about 630.

Theme and Message

The intent of the author was to announce to Judah God's approaching judgment. His main theme was the coming of the day of the Lord when God would severely punish the nations. He portrayed the stark horror of that ordeal, but also made it clear that God would yet be merciful toward his people.

Outline

I. Introduction (1.1-3)
II. The Day of the Lord Coming on Judah and the Nations (1.4-18)
III. God's Judgment on the Nations (2.1–3.8)
IV. Redemption of the Remnant (3.9-20)

---

1 The word of the LORD that came to Zephaniah son of Cushi son of Gedaliah son of Amariah son of Hezekiah, in the days of King Josiah son of Amon of Judah.

The Coming Judgment on Judah

2 I will utterly sweep away everything
from the face of the earth,
says the LORD.
3 I will sweep away humans and animals;
I will sweep away the birds of the air
and the fish of the sea.
I will make the wicked stumble.[a]
I will cut off humanity
from the face of the earth,
says the LORD.
4 I will stretch out my hand against Judah,
and against all the inhabitants of Jerusalem;
and I will cut off from this place every remnant of Baal
and the name of the idolatrous priests;[b]
5 those who bow down on the roofs
to the host of the heavens;
those who bow down and swear to the LORD,
but also swear by Milcom;[c]
6 those who have turned back from following the LORD,

1.1 2 Kings 22.1-23, 34; 21.18-26
1.2 Ezek 33.27
1.3 Isa 6.11,12; Jer 9.10; Ezek 7.19
1.4 Ezek 6.14; Mic 5.13; Hos 10.5
1.5 Jer 19.13; 5.2,7; 49.1
1.6 Isa 1.4; Jer 2.13; Isa 9.13; Hos 7.7

[a] Cn: Heb *sea, and those who cause the wicked to stumble* [b] Compare Gk: Heb *the idolatrous priests with the priests* [c] Gk Mss Syr Vg: Heb *Malcam* (or, *their king*)

who have not sought the
LORD or inquired of him.

7 Be silent before the Lord GOD!
For the day of the LORD is
at hand;
the LORD has prepared a
sacrifice,
he has consecrated his
guests.
8 And on the day of the LORD's
sacrifice
I will punish the officials and
the king's sons
and all who dress
themselves in foreign
attire.
9 On that day I will punish
all who leap over the
threshold,
who fill their master's
house
with violence and fraud.

10 On that day, says the LORD,
a cry will be heard from
the Fish Gate,
a wail from the Second
Quarter,
a loud crash from the
hills.
11 The inhabitants of the
Mortar wail,
for all the traders have
perished;
all who weigh out silver are
cut off.
12 At that time I will search
Jerusalem with lamps,
and I will punish the
people
who rest complacently[d] on
their dregs,
those who say in their
hearts,
"The LORD will not do good,
nor will he do harm."
13 Their wealth shall be
plundered,
and their houses laid
waste.
Though they build houses,
they shall not inhabit
them;
though they plant vineyards,
they shall not drink wine
from them.

The Great Day of the LORD

14 The great day of the LORD is
near,
near and hastening fast;
the sound of the day of the
LORD is bitter,
the warrior cries aloud
there.
15 That day will be a day of
wrath,
a day of distress and
anguish,
a day of ruin and
devastation,
a day of darkness and
gloom,
a day of clouds and thick
darkness,
16 a day of trumpet blast and
battle cry
against the fortified cities
and against the lofty
battlements.

17 I will bring such distress
upon people
that they shall walk like
the blind;
because they have sinned
against the LORD,
their blood shall be poured
out like dust,
and their flesh like dung.
18 Neither their silver nor their
gold
will be able to save them
on the day of the LORD's
wrath;
in the fire of his passion
the whole earth shall be
consumed;
for a full, a terrible end
he will make of all the
inhabitants of the
earth.

Judgment on Israel's Enemies

2 Gather together, gather,
O shameless nation,
2 before you are driven away
like the drifting chaff,[e]
before there comes upon you

1.7 Hab 2.20; Zech 2.13; Isa 13.6; v. 14; Isa 34.6; Jer 46.10
1.8 Isa 24.21; Jer 39.6; Isa 2.6
1.9 Jer 5.27; Am 3.10
1.10 Am 8.3; 2 Chr 33.14; 34.22; Ezek 6.13
1.11 Jas 5.1; Zeph 2.5; Hos 9.6
1.12 Jer 16.16, 17; Jer 48.11; Am 6.1; Ezek 8.12; 9.9
1.13 Deut 28.30, 39; Am 5.11; Mic 6.15
1.14 Joel 2.1,11
1.15 Isa 22.5; Jer 30.7; Am 5.18-20
1.16 Jer 4.19; Isa 2.12-15
1.17 Jer 10.18; Isa 59.10; Ps 79.3; Jer 9.22
1.18 Prov 11.4; Zeph 3.8; vv. 2,3
2.1 Joel 1.14; Jer 3.3; 6.15
2.2 Isa 17.13; Hos 13.3; Nah 1.6; Zeph 1.18

[d] Heb *who thicken* [e] Cn Compare Gk Syr: Heb *before a decree is born; like chaff a day has passed away*

the fierce anger of the LORD,
before there comes upon you
the day of the LORD's wrath.
3 Seek the LORD, all you humble of the land,
who do his commands;
seek righteousness, seek humility;
perhaps you may be hidden
on the day of the LORD's wrath.
4 For Gaza shall be deserted,
and Ashkelon shall become a desolation;
Ashdod's people shall be driven out at noon,
and Ekron shall be uprooted.

5 Ah, inhabitants of the seacoast,
you nation of the Cherethites!
The word of the LORD is against you,
O Canaan, land of the Philistines;
and I will destroy you until no inhabitant is left.
6 And you, O seacoast, shall be pastures,
meadows for shepherds
and folds for flocks.
7 The seacoast shall become the possession
of the remnant of the house of Judah,
on which they shall pasture,
and in the houses of Ashkelon
they shall lie down at evening.
For the LORD their God will be mindful of them
and restore their fortunes.

8 I have heard the taunts of Moab
and the revilings of the Ammonites,
how they have taunted my people
and made boasts against their territory.
9 Therefore, as I live, says the LORD of hosts,
the God of Israel,
Moab shall become like Sodom
and the Ammonites like Gomorrah,
a land possessed by nettles and salt pits,
and a waste forever.
The remnant of my people shall plunder them,
and the survivors of my nation shall possess them.
10 This shall be their lot in return for their pride,
because they scoffed and boasted
against the people of the LORD of hosts.
11 The LORD will be terrible against them;
he will shrivel all the gods of the earth,
and to him shall bow down,
each in its place,
all the coasts and islands of the nations.

12 You also, O Ethiopians,[f]
shall be killed by my sword.

13 And he will stretch out his hand against the north,
and destroy Assyria;
and he will make Nineveh a desolation,
a dry waste like the desert.
14 Herds shall lie down in it,
every wild animal;[g]
the desert owl[h] and the screech owl[h]
shall lodge on its capitals;
the owl[i] shall hoot at the window,
the raven[j] croak on the threshold;
for its cedar work will be laid bare.
15 Is this the exultant city
that lived secure,
that said to itself,

2.3 Am 5.6; Ps 76.9; Am 5.14,15; Ps 57.1 **2.4** Am 1.7,8; Zech 9.5-7 **2.5** Ezek 25.16; Am 3.1; Isa 14.29-31; Zeph 3.6 **2.6** Isa 17.2 **2.7** Mic 4.7; Isa 32.14; Ps 80.14; Lk 1.68; Ps 126.1,4 **2.8** Ezek 25.3,6, 8; Jer 49.1 **2.9** Isa 15.1-16, 14; Am 1.13; Deut 29.23; Isa 11.14 **2.10** Isa 16.6; Jer 48.29; v. 8 **2.11** Joel 2.11; Zeph 1;4; 3.9; Mal 1.11; Isa 24.15 **2.12** Isa 18.1 **2.13** Isa 14.26; 10.12; Nah 3.7 **2.14** v. 6; Isa 13.21; 34.11,14; Jer 22.14 **2.15** Isa 22.2; 47.8; 32.14; Jer 18.16; 19.8

[f] Or *Nubians*; Heb *Cushites* [g] Tg Compare Gk: Heb *nation* [h] Meaning of Heb uncertain [i] Cn: Heb *a voice* [j] Gk Vg: Heb *desolation*

"I am, and there is no one
else"?
What a desolation it has
become,
a lair for wild animals!
Everyone who passes by it
hisses and shakes the fist.

The Wickedness of Jerusalem

3 Ah, soiled, defiled,
oppressing city!
2 It has listened to no voice;
it has accepted no
correction.
It has not trusted in the
LORD;
it has not drawn near to its
God.

3 The officials within it
are roaring lions;
its judges are evening wolves
that leave nothing until the
morning.
4 Its prophets are reckless,
faithless persons;
its priests have profaned
what is sacred,
they have done violence to
the law.
5 The LORD within it is
righteous;
he does no wrong.
Every morning he renders his
judgment,
each dawn without fail;
but the unjust knows no
shame.

6 I have cut off nations;
their battlements are in
ruins;
I have laid waste their streets
so that no one walks in
them;
their cities have been made
desolate,
without people, without
inhabitants.
7 I said, "Surely the city[k] will
fear me,
it will accept correction;
it will not lose sight[l]
of all that I have brought
upon it."

3.1 Jer 5.23; Ezek 23.30; Jer 6.6 **3.2** Jer 22.21; 5.3; Ps 78.22; 73.28 **3.3** Ezek 22.27; Hab 1.8 **3.4** Hos 9.7; Ezek 22.26 **3.5** vv. 15,17; Deut 32.4; Jer 3.3 **3.6** Zeph 1.16; Isa 6.11; Zeph 2.5 **3.7** v. 2; Jer 7.7; Hos 9.9 **3.8** Ps 27.14; Zeph 2.2; Joel 3.2; Zeph 1.18 **3.9** Isa 19.18; Ps 22.27; Zeph 2.11 **3.10** Ps 68.31; Isa 18.1,7; 60.6,7 **3.11** Isa 45.17; Joel 2.26, 27; Isa 2.12; 5.15; Ezek 20.40 **3.12** Isa 14.32; Nah 1.7 **3.13** Mic 4.7; Isa 60.21; Zech 8.3,16; Rev 14.5; Ezek 34.28; Mic 4.4

But they were the more
eager
to make all their deeds
corrupt.

Punishment and Conversion of the Nations

8 Therefore wait for me, says
the LORD,
for the day when I arise as
a witness.
For my decision is to gather
nations,
to assemble kingdoms,
to pour out upon them my
indignation,
all the heat of my anger;
for in the fire of my passion
all the earth shall be
consumed.

9 At that time I will change
the speech of the
peoples
to a pure speech,
that all of them may call on
the name of the LORD
and serve him with one
accord.
10 From beyond the rivers of
Ethiopia[m]
my suppliants, my
scattered ones,
shall bring my offering.

11 On that day you shall not be
put to shame
because of all the deeds by
which you have rebelled
against me;
for then I will remove from
your midst
your proudly exultant ones,
and you shall no longer be
haughty
in my holy mountain.
12 For I will leave in the midst
of you
a people humble and lowly.
They shall seek refuge in the
name of the LORD—
13 the remnant of Israel;
they shall do no wrong
and utter no lies,

[k] Heb *it* [l] Gk Syr: Heb *its dwelling will not be cut off* [m] Or *Nubia*; Heb *Cush*

nor shall a deceitful tongue
be found in their mouths.
Then they will pasture and
lie down,
and no one shall make
them afraid.

A Song of Joy

14 Sing aloud, O daughter Zion;
shout, O Israel!
Rejoice and exult with all
your heart,
O daughter Jerusalem!
15 The LORD has taken away the
judgments against you,
he has turned away your
enemies.
The king of Israel, the LORD,
is in your midst;
you shall fear disaster no
more.
16 On that day it shall be said
to Jerusalem:
Do not fear, O Zion;
do not let your hands grow
weak.
17 The LORD, your God, is in
your midst,
a warrior who gives victory;
he will rejoice over you with
gladness,

3.14 Isa 12.6; Zech 2.10 **3.15** Ezek 37.26-28; v. 5; Isa 54.14 **3.16** Isa 35.3,4; Heb 12.12 **3.17** vv. 5,15; Isa 63.1; 62.5 **3.19** Isa 60.14; Ezek 34.16; Mic 4.6,7 **3.20** Ezek 37.12, 21; Isa 56.5; 66.22; Zeph 2.7

he will renew you[n] in his
love;
he will exult over you with
loud singing
18 as on a day of festival.[o]
I will remove disaster from
you,[p]
so that you will not bear
reproach for it.
19 I will deal with all your
oppressors
at that time.
And I will save the lame
and gather the outcast,
and I will change their
shame into praise
and renown in all the
earth.
20 At that time I will bring you
home,
at the time when I gather
you;
for I will make you renowned
and praised
among all the peoples of
the earth,
when I restore your fortunes
before your eyes, says the
LORD.

[n] Gk Syr: Heb *he will be silent* [o] Gk Syr: Meaning of Heb uncertain [p] Cn: Heb *I will remove from you; they were*

Haggai

Title and Background

This book is named for its author, and the name means "festal" or "festival." In 538 B.C. Cyrus issued a decree allowing the Jews to return to Jerusalem and rebuild the temple. Samaritans and other neighbors opposed the project vigorously and managed to halt work until Darius the Great became king. Haggai began to preach in Darius's second year.

Author and Date of Writing

Haggai was a prophet who, along with Zechariah, encouraged the returned exiles to rebuild the temple. Based on 2.3, Haggai may have witnessed the destruction of Solomon's temple. If so, he was about 80 years old during his ministry recorded in this book. The messages of Haggai were given during a four-month period in 520 B.C.

Theme and Message

Haggai clearly shows the consequences of disobedience and the blessings of obedience. When the people give priority to God and his house, they will be blessed. Obedience brings the encouragement and strength of the Spirit of God.

Outline

I. First Message: The Call to Rebuild the Temple (1.1-11)
II. The Response of Zerubbabel and the People (1.12-15)
III. Second Message: The Temple to Be Filled With Glory (2.1-9)
IV. Third Message: A Defiled People Purified and Blessed (2.10-19)
V. Fourth Message: The Promise to Zerubbabel (2.20-23)

The Command to Rebuild the Temple

1 In the second year of King Darius, in the sixth month, on the first day of the month, the word of the LORD came by the prophet Haggai to Zerubbabel son of Shealtiel, governor of Judah, and to Joshua son of Jehozadak, the high priest: 2 Thus says the LORD of hosts: These people say the time has not yet come to rebuild the LORD's house. 3 Then the word of the LORD came by the prophet Haggai, saying: 4 Is it a time for you yourselves to live in your paneled houses, while this house lies in ruins? 5 Now therefore thus says the LORD of hosts: Consider how you have fared. 6 You have sown much, and harvested little; you eat, but you never have enough; you drink, but you never have your fill; you clothe yourselves, but no one is warm; and you that earn wages earn wages to put them into a bag with holes.

7 Thus says the LORD of hosts: Consider how you have fared. 8 Go up to the hills and bring wood and build the house, so that I may take pleasure in it and be honored, says the LORD. 9 You have looked for much, and, lo, it came to little; and when you brought it home, I blew it away. Why? says the LORD of hosts. Because my house lies in ruins, while all of you hurry off to your own houses. 10 Therefore the heavens above you have withheld the dew, and the earth has withheld its produce. 11 And I have called for a drought on the land and the hills,

1.1 Zech 1.1; 1 Chr 3.17; Ezra 3.2; Zech 6.11 **1.2** v. 15 **1.4** 2 Sam 7.2; v. 9 **1.5** Lam 3.40 **1.6** Deut 28.38; Mic 6.14; Zech 8.10 **1.7** v. 1 **1.8** Ezra 3.7; Ps 132.13, 14; Hag 2.7, 9 **1.9** v. 6; Isa 40.7 **1.10** Lev 26.19; Deut 28.23; 1 Kings 8.35

1.11 Mal 3.9-11; Deut 28.22; Hag 2.17

on the grain, the new wine, the oil,
on what the soil produces, on human beings and animals, and on all
their labors.

12 Then Zerubbabel son of Shealtiel, and Joshua son of Jehozadak, the high priest, with all the
remnant of the people, obeyed the
voice of the LORD their God, and the
words of the prophet Haggai, as
the LORD their God had sent him; and
the people feared the LORD. 13 Then
Haggai, the messenger of the LORD,
spoke to the people with the LORD's
message, saying, I am with you,
says the LORD. 14 And the LORD
stirred up the spirit of Zerubbabel
son of Shealtiel, governor of Judah,
and the spirit of Joshua son of Jehozadak, the high priest, and the
spirit of all the remnant of the people; and they came and worked on
the house of the LORD of hosts,
their God, 15 on the twenty-fourth
day of the month, in the sixth
month.

The Future Glory of the Temple

2 In the second year of King Darius, 1 in the seventh month,
on the twenty-first day of the
month, the word of the LORD came
by the prophet Haggai, saying:
2 Speak now to Zerubbabel son of
Shealtiel, governor of Judah, and
to Joshua son of Jehozadak, the
high priest, and to the remnant of
the people, and say, 3 Who is left
among you that saw this house in
its former glory? How does it look
to you now? Is it not in your sight
as nothing? 4 Yet now take courage,
O Zerubbabel, says the LORD; take
courage, O Joshua, son of Jehozadak, the high priest; take courage,
all you people of the land, says the
LORD; work, for I am with you, says
the LORD of hosts, 5 according to the
promise that I made you when you
came out of Egypt. My spirit abides
among you; do not fear. 6 For thus
says the LORD of hosts: Once again,
in a little while, I will shake the
heavens and the earth and the sea
and the dry land; 7 and I will shake
all the nations, so that the treasure
of all nations shall come, and I will
fill this house with splendor, says
the LORD of hosts. 8 The silver is
mine, and the gold is mine, says
the LORD of hosts. 9 The latter
splendor of this house shall be
greater than the former, says the
LORD of hosts; and in this place I
will give prosperity, says the LORD
of hosts.

A Rebuke and a Promise

10 On the twenty-fourth day of
the ninth month, in the second
year of Darius, the word of the LORD
came by the prophet Haggai, saying: 11 Thus says the LORD of hosts:
Ask the priests for a ruling: 12 If one
carries consecrated meat in the
fold of one's garment, and with the
fold touches bread, or stew, or
wine, or oil, or any kind of food,
does it become holy? The priests
answered, "No." 13 Then Haggai
said, "If one who is unclean by contact with a dead body touches any
of these, does it become unclean?"
The priests answered, "Yes, it becomes unclean." 14 Haggai then
said, So is it with this people, and
with this nation before me, says the
LORD; and so with every work of
their hands; and what they offer
there is unclean. 15 But now, consider what will come to pass from
this day on. Before a stone was
placed upon a stone in the LORD's
temple, 16 how did you fare?[a]
When one came to a heap of twenty
measures, there were but ten;
when one came to the winevat to
draw fifty measures, there were but
twenty. 17 I struck you and all the
products of your toil with blight
and mildew and hail; yet you did
not return to me, says the LORD.
18 Consider from this day on, from
the twenty-fourth day of the ninth
month. Since the day that the
foundation of the LORD's temple
was laid, consider: 19 Is there any
seed left in the barn? Do the vine,
the fig tree, the pomegranate, and
the olive tree still yield nothing?
From this day on I will bless you.

1.12 Hag 2.2; Isa 1.19; 50.10
1.13 Mal 2.7; 3.1; Mt 28.30; Rom 8.31
1.14 2 Chr 36.22; Ezra 1.1; 5.2,8
2.3 Ezra 3.12; Zech 4.10
2.4 Zech 8.9; Acts 7.9
2.5 Ex 29.45, 46; Neh 9.20; Isa 63.11,14
2.6 Heb 12.26; Isa 10.25; 29.17; v. 21
2.7 Dan 2.44; Isa 60.4-9
2.9 Isa 66.12; Zech 2.5
2.10 vv. 1,20
2.11 Lev 10.10; Deut 33.10; Mal 2.7
2.12 Ezek 44.19; Mt 23.19
2.13 Num 19.11, 22
2.14 Prov 15.8; Isa 1.11-15
2.15 Hag 1.5; Ezra 3.10; 4.24
2.16 Hag 1.6,9; Zech 8.10
2.17 1 Kings 8.37; Am 4.9; Isa 9.13
2.18 Zech 8.9
2.19 Zech 8.12

a Gk: Heb *since they were*

God's Promise to Zerubbabel

20 The word of the LORD came a
second time to Haggai on the
twenty-fourth day of the month:
21 Speak to Zerubbabel, governor of
Judah, saying, I am about to shake
the heavens and the earth, 22 and to
overthrow the throne of kingdoms;
I am about to destroy the strength
of the kingdoms of the nations, and
overthrow the chariots and their
riders; and the horses and their riders shall fall, every one by the
sword of a comrade. 23 On that day,
says the LORD of hosts, I will take
you, O Zerubbabel my servant, son
of Shealtiel, says the LORD, and
make you like a signet ring; for I
have chosen you, says the LORD of
hosts.

2.20ff v. 10
2.21 Hag 1.14; Zech 4.6-10; Heb 12.26
2.22 Dan 2.44; Mic 5.10; Zech 4.6; 2 Chr 20.23
2.23 Song 8.6; Jer 22.24; Isa 42.1; 43.10

Zechariah

Title and Background

The book is named after its author, and the title means "The LORD remembers." Zechariah's prophetic ministry took place in the postexilic period, the time when the Jews returned from Babylon to the land of Judah. His prophecies began two months after Haggai's first message.

Author and Date of Writing

Zechariah was not only a prophet but also a priest. He was among those who returned to Judah in 538 B.C. He was a contemporary of Haggai but continued his ministry long after him. The book of Zechariah was probably written sometime before 480 B.C.

Theme and Message

Zechariah was concerned about the rebuilding of the temple, and in his first message he warned the people they ought to listen to God's message through the prophets. He was also interested in their spiritual renewal.

Zechariah contains many Messianic passages: he predicted Christ's coming in lowliness (9.9), his humanity (6.12; 13.7), his rejection and betrayal for thirty shekels of silver (11.12-13), his being struck by the sword of the Lord (13.7), his priesthood (6.13), his kingship (6.13; 9.9; 14.9,16), his coming in power (14.4), his building of the Lord's temple (6.12-13), his reign (9.10,14) and his establishment of enduring peace and prosperity (3.10; 9.9-10).

Outline

I. A Call to Repentance (1.1-6)
II. Eight Visions (1.7–6.8)
III. The Coronation of Joshua the High Priest (6.9-15)
IV. Fasting and the Future (7.1–8.23)
V. The Advent and Rejection of the Messiah (9.1–11.17)
VI. The Advent and Redemption of the Messiah (12.1–14.21)

Israel Urged to Repent

1 In the eighth month, in the
second year of Darius, the
word of the LORD came to the
prophet Zechariah son of Berechiah son of Iddo, saying: 2 The LORD
was very angry with your ancestors.
3 Therefore say to them, Thus says
the LORD of hosts: Return to me,
says the LORD of hosts, and I will
return to you, says the LORD of
hosts. 4 Do not be like your ancestors, to whom the former prophets
proclaimed, "Thus says the LORD of
hosts, Return from your evil ways
and from your evil deeds." But they
did not hear or heed me, says the
LORD. 5 Your ancestors, where are
they? And the prophets, do they
live forever? 6 But my words and my
statutes, which I commanded my
servants the prophets, did they not
overtake your ancestors? So they
repented and said, "The LORD of
hosts has dealt with us according
to our ways and deeds, just as he
planned to do."

1.1 Ezra 4.24; Hag 1.1; Neh 12.4,16
1.3 Isa 31.6; Mal 3.7; Jas 4.8
1.4 2 Chr 36.15; Hos 14.1; Jer 6.17; 11.7,8
1.6 Jer 12.16, 17; Lam 2.17

First Vision: The Horsemen

7 On the twenty-fourth day of
the eleventh month, the month of
Shebat, in the second year of Darius, the word of the LORD came to
the prophet Zechariah son of Bere-

chiah son of Iddo; and Zechariah[a]
said, 8 In the night I saw a man riding on a red horse! He was standing
among the myrtle trees in the glen;
and behind him were red, sorrel,
and white horses. 9 Then I said,
"What are these, my lord?" The angel who talked with me said to me,
"I will show you what they are."
10 So the man who was standing
among the myrtle trees answered,
"They are those whom the LORD has
sent to patrol the earth." 11 Then
they spoke to the angel of the LORD
who was standing among the myrtle trees, "We have patrolled the
earth, and lo, the whole earth remains at peace." 12 Then the angel
of the LORD said, "O LORD of hosts,
how long will you withhold mercy
from Jerusalem and the cities of
Judah, with which you have been
angry these seventy years?" 13 Then
the LORD replied with gracious and
comforting words to the angel who
talked with me. 14 So the angel who
talked with me said to me, Proclaim this message: Thus says the
LORD of hosts; I am very jealous for
Jerusalem and for Zion. 15 And I am
extremely angry with the nations
that are at ease; for while I was only
a little angry, they made the disaster worse. 16 Therefore, thus says
the LORD, I have returned to Jerusalem with compassion; my house
shall be built in it, says the LORD of
hosts, and the measuring line shall
be stretched out over Jerusalem.
17 Proclaim further: Thus says the
LORD of hosts: My cities shall again
overflow with prosperity; the LORD
will again comfort Zion and again
choose Jerusalem.

Second Vision: The Horns and the Smiths

18 [b]And I looked up and saw four
horns. 19 I asked the angel who
talked with me, "What are these?"
And he answered me, "These are
the horns that have scattered Judah, Israel, and Jerusalem."
20 Then the LORD showed me four
blacksmiths. 21 And I asked, "What
are they coming to do?" He answered, "These are the horns that
scattered Judah, so that no head
could be raised; but these have
come to terrify them, to strike
down the horns of the nations that
lifted up their horns against the
land of Judah to scatter its people."[c]

Third Vision: The Man with a Measuring Line

2 [d]I looked up and saw a man
with a measuring line in his
hand. 2 Then I asked, "Where are
you going?" He answered me, "To
measure Jerusalem, to see what is
its width and what is its length."
3 Then the angel who talked with
me came forward, and another angel came forward to meet him,
4 and said to him, "Run, say to that
young man: Jerusalem shall be inhabited like villages without walls,
because of the multitude of people
and animals in it. 5 For I will be a
wall of fire all around it, says the
LORD, and I will be the glory within
it."

Interlude: An Appeal to the Exiles

6 Up, up! Flee from the land of
the north, says the LORD; for I have
spread you abroad like the four
winds of heaven, says the LORD.
7 Up! Escape to Zion, you that live
with daughter Babylon. 8 For thus
said the LORD of hosts (after his glory[e] sent me) regarding the nations
that plundered you: Truly, one who
touches you touches the apple of
my eye.[f] 9 See now, I am going to
raise[g] my hand against them, and
they shall become plunder for their
own slaves. Then you will know
that the LORD of hosts has sent me.
10 Sing and rejoice, O daughter
Zion! For lo, I will come and dwell
in your midst, says the LORD.
11 Many nations shall join themselves to the LORD on that day, and
shall be my people; and I will dwell
in your midst. And you shall know
that the LORD of hosts has sent me
to you. 12 The LORD will inherit Ju-

1.8 Josh 5.13; Rev 6.4; Zech 6.2-7
1.9 Zech 2.3; 4.5
1.10 Heb 1.14
1.11 Isa 14.7
1.12 Hab 1.2; Dan 9.2
1.13 Zech 4.1; Isa 40.1,2
1.14 Zech 8.2
1.15 Ps 123.4; Am 1.11
1.16 Isa 54.8; Zech 2.1,2, 10
1.17 Isa 44.26; 51.3; Zech 2.12; 3.2
1.20 Isa 44.12; 54.16
1.21 Ps 75.10
2.1 Zech 1.18; Ezek 40.3
2.2 Ezek 40.3; Rev 21.15-17
2.4 Ezek 38.11; Jer 30.19
2.5 Isa 26.1; Zech 9.8; Rev 21.23
2.6 Isa 48.20; Jer 1.14; Ezek 17.21
2.8 Isa 60.7-9; Deut 32.10
2.9 Isa 11.15; Zech 4.9
2.10 Isa 12.6; Zeph 3.14; Lev 26.12; Ezek 37.27
2.12 Deut 32.9; Zech 1.17

[a] Heb *and he* [b] Ch 2.1 in Heb [c] Heb *it* [d] Ch 2.5 in Heb [e] Cn: Heb *after glory he* [f] Heb *his eye* [g] Or *wave*

dah as his portion in the holy land,
and will again choose Jerusalem.
13 Be silent, all people, before
the LORD; for he has roused himself
from his holy dwelling.

Fourth Vision: Joshua and Satan

3 Then he showed me the high
priest Joshua standing before
the angel of the LORD, and Satan[h]
standing at his right hand to accuse
him. 2 And the LORD said to Satan,[h]
"The LORD rebuke you, O Satan![h]
The LORD who has chosen Jerusalem rebuke you! Is not this man a
brand plucked from the fire?"
3 Now Joshua was dressed with
filthy clothes as he stood before
the angel. 4 The angel said to those
who were standing before him,
"Take off his filthy clothes." And to
him he said, "See, I have taken
your guilt away from you, and I will
clothe you with festal apparel."
5 And I said, "Let them put a clean
turban on his head." So they put a
clean turban on his head and
clothed him with the apparel; and
the angel of the LORD was standing
by.
6 Then the angel of the LORD assured Joshua, saying 7 "Thus says
the LORD of hosts: If you will walk in
my ways and keep my requirements, then you shall rule my
house and have charge of my
courts, and I will give you the right
of access among those who are
standing here. 8 Now listen, Joshua, high priest, you and your colleagues who sit before you! For
they are an omen of things to
come: I am going to bring my servant the Branch. 9 For on the stone
that I have set before Joshua, on a
single stone with seven facets, I
will engrave its inscription, says
the LORD of hosts, and I will remove
the guilt of this land in a single day.
10 On that day, says the LORD of
hosts, you shall invite each other to
come under your vine and fig tree."

Fifth Vision: The Lampstand and Olive Trees

4 The angel who talked with me
came again, and wakened me,
as one is wakened from sleep. 2 He
said to me, "What do you see?" And
I said, "I see a lampstand all of
gold, with a bowl on the top of it;
there are seven lamps on it, with
seven lips on each of the lamps
that are on the top of it. 3 And by it
there are two olive trees, one on the
right of the bowl and the other on
its left." 4 I said to the angel who
talked with me, "What are these,
my lord?" 5 Then the angel who
talked with me answered me, "Do
you not know what these are?" I
said, "No, my lord." 6 He said to
me, "This is the word of the LORD to
Zerubbabel: Not by might, nor by
power, but by my spirit, says the
LORD of hosts. 7 What are you,
O great mountain? Before Zerubbabel you shall become a plain;
and he shall bring out the top stone
amid shouts of 'Grace, grace to
it!' "
8 Moreover the word of the LORD
came to me, saying, 9 "The hands of
Zerubbabel have laid the foundation of this house; his hands shall
also complete it. Then you will
know that the LORD of hosts has
sent me to you. 10 For whoever has
despised the day of small things
shall rejoice, and shall see the
plummet in the hand of Zerubbabel.
"These seven are the eyes of the
LORD, which range through the
whole earth." 11 Then I said to him,
"What are these two olive trees on
the right and the left of the lampstand?" 12 And a second time I said
to him, "What are these two
branches of the olive trees, which
pour out the oil[i] through the two
golden pipes?" 13 He said to me,
"Do you not know what these are?"
I said, "No, my lord." 14 Then he
said, "These are the two anointed
ones who stand by the Lord of the
whole earth."

Sixth Vision: The Flying Scroll

5 Again I looked up and saw a
flying scroll. 2 And he said to
me, "What do you see?" I an-

2.13 Hab 2.20; Ps 78.65; Isa 51.9
3.1 Hag 1.1; Ps 109.6
3.2 Jude 9,23; Am 4.11
3.4 Isa 43.25; Rev 19.8
3.5 Ex 29.6
3.7 1 Kings 3.14; Ezek 44.16; Deut 17.9; Zech 4.14
3.8 Isa 20.3; Ezek 12.11; Isa 4.2; 53.2; Jer 33.15
3.9 Isa 28.16; Zech 4.10; Jer 31.34; Mic 7.18
3.10 1 Kings 4.25; Isa 36.16
4.1 Zech 1.9; 2.3; Dan 8.18
4.2 Ex 25.31; Rev 1.12; Ex 25.37; Rev 4.5
4.3 Rev 11.4
4.5 Zech 1.9
4.6 Hag 2.4,5; Hos 1.7; Eph 6.17
4.7 Jer 51.25; Ps 118.22; Ezra 3.10,11
4.9 Ezra 3.10; 6.15; Zech 2.9,11; 6.15; Isa 48.16; Zech 2.8
4.10 Hag 2.3; Zech 3.9; Rev 8.2; Zech 1.10
4.11 v. 3
4.14 Rev 11.4; Zech 3.1-7; Mic 4.13
5.1 Ezek 2.9

[h] Or *the Accuser*; Heb *the Adversary*
[i] Cn: Heb *gold*

swered, "I see a flying scroll; its length is twenty cubits, and its width ten cubits." 3 Then he said to me, "This is the curse that goes out over the face of the whole land; for everyone who steals shall be cut off according to the writing on one side, and everyone who swears falsely[j] shall be cut off according to the writing on the other side. 4 I have sent it out, says the LORD of hosts, and it shall enter the house of the thief, and the house of anyone who swears falsely by my name; and it shall abide in that house and consume it, both timber and stones."

Seventh Vision: The Woman in a Basket

5 Then the angel who talked with me came forward and said to me, "Look up and see what this is that is coming out." 6 I said, "What is it?" He said, "This is a basket[k] coming out." And he said, "This is their iniquity[l] in all the land." 7 Then a leaden cover was lifted, and there was a woman sitting in the basket![k] 8 And he said, "This is Wickedness." So he thrust her back into the basket,[k] and pressed the leaden weight down on its mouth. 9 Then I looked up and saw two women coming forward. The wind was in their wings; they had wings like the wings of a stork, and they lifted up the basket[k] between earth and sky. 10 Then I said to the angel who talked with me, "Where are they taking the basket?"[k] 11 He said to me, "To the land of Shinar, to build a house for it; and when this is prepared, they will set the basket[k] down there on its base."

Eighth Vision: Four Chariots

6 And again I looked up and saw four chariots coming out from between two mountains—mountains of bronze. 2 The first chariot had red horses, the second chariot black horses, 3 the third chariot white horses, and the fourth chariot dappled gray[m] horses. 4 Then I said to the angel who talked with me, "What are these, my lord?" 5 The angel answered me, "These are the four winds[n] of heaven going out, after presenting themselves before the LORD of all the earth. 6 The chariot with the black horses goes toward the north country, the white ones go toward the west country,[o] and the dappled ones go toward the south country." 7 When the steeds came out, they were impatient to get off and patrol the earth. And he said, "Go, patrol the earth." So they patrolled the earth. 8 Then he cried out to me, "Lo, those who go toward the north country have set my spirit at rest in the north country."

The Coronation of the Branch

9 The word of the LORD came to me: 10 Collect silver and gold[p] from the exiles—from Heldai, Tobijah, and Jedaiah—who have arrived from Babylon; and go the same day to the house of Josiah son of Zephaniah. 11 Take the silver and gold and make a crown,[q] and set it on the head of the high priest Joshua son of Jehozadak; 12 say to him: Thus says the LORD of hosts: Here is a man whose name is Branch: for he shall branch out in his place, and he shall build the temple of the LORD. 13 It is he that shall build the temple of the LORD; he shall bear royal honor, and shall sit and rule on his throne. There shall be a priest by his throne, with peaceful understanding between the two of them. 14 And the crown[r] shall be in the care of Heldai,[s] Tobijah, Jedaiah, and Josiah[t] son of Zephaniah, as a memorial in the temple of the LORD.

15 Those who are far off shall come and help to build the temple of the LORD; and you shall know that the LORD of hosts has sent me to you. This will happen if you dili-

5.3 Jer 26.6; Ex 20.15; Mal 3.8,9; v. 4 **5.4** Mal 3.5; Hos 4.2,3; Lev 14.45; Hab 2.9-11 **5.5** Zech 1.9,18 **5.6** Lev 19.36; Am 8.5 **5.8** Hos 12.7; Am 8.5; Mic 6.11 **5.9** v. 5; Jer 8.7 **5.11** Jer 29.5,28; Gen 10.10 **6.1** Zech 1.18; 5.9; v. 5 **6.2** Rev 6.4,5 **6.3** Rev 6.2 **6.4** Zech 5.10 **6.5** Jer 49.36; Ezek 37.9; Mt 24.31; Rev 7.1 **6.6** Jer 1.14; Ezek 1.4; Dan 11.5 **6.7** Zech 1.10 **6.8** Ezek 5.13 **6.9** Zech 1.1; 7.1; 8.1 **6.10** Jer 28.6 **6.11** Ezra 3.2; Hag 1.1 **6.12** Isa 11.1; Zech 3.8; Isa 53.2 **6.13** Isa 9.6; 22.24; 9.7; Ps 110.1,4 **6.14** v. 11 **6.15** Isa 57.19; 60.10; Zech 4.9; 3.7

[j] The word *falsely* added from verse 4
[k] Heb *ephah*
[l] Gk Compare Syr: Heb *their eye*
[m] Compare Gk: Meaning of Heb uncertain
[n] Or *spirits*
[o] Cn: Heb *go after them*
[p] Cn Compare verse 11: Heb lacks *silver and gold*
[q] Gk Mss Syr Tg: Heb *crowns*
[r] Gk Syr: Heb *crowns*
[s] Syr Compare verse 10: Heb *Helem*
[t] Syr Compare verse 10: Heb *Hen*

gently obey the voice of the LORD your God.

Hypocritical Fasting Condemned

7 In the fourth year of King Darius, the word of the LORD came to Zechariah on the fourth day of the ninth month, which is Chislev. 2 Now the people of Bethel had sent Sharezer and Regem-melech and their men, to entreat the favor of the LORD, 3 and to ask the priests of the house of the LORD of hosts and the prophets, "Should I mourn and practice abstinence in the fifth month, as I have done for so many years?" 4 Then the word of the LORD of hosts came to me: 5 Say to all the people of the land and the priests: When you fasted and lamented in the fifth month and in the seventh, for these seventy years, was it for me that you fasted? 6 And when you eat and when you drink, do you not eat and drink only for yourselves? 7 Were not these the words that the LORD proclaimed by the former prophets, when Jerusalem was inhabited and in prosperity, along with the towns around it, and when the Negeb and the Shephelah were inhabited?

Punishment for Rejecting God's Demands

8 The word of the LORD came to Zechariah, saying: 9 Thus says the LORD of hosts: Render true judgments, show kindness and mercy to one another; 10 do not oppress the widow, the orphan, the alien, or the poor; and do not devise evil in your hearts against one another. 11 But they refused to listen, and turned a stubborn shoulder, and stopped their ears in order not to hear. 12 They made their hearts adamant in order not to hear the law and the words that the LORD of hosts had sent by his spirit through the former prophets. Therefore great wrath came from the LORD of hosts. 13 Just as, when I[u] called, they would not hear, so, when they called, I would not hear, says the LORD of hosts, 14 and I scattered them with a whirlwind among all the nations that they had not known. Thus the land they left was desolate, so that no one went to and fro, and a pleasant land was made desolate.

God's Promises to Zion

8 The word of the LORD of hosts came to me, saying: 2 Thus says the LORD of hosts: I am jealous for Zion with great jealousy, and I am jealous for her with great wrath. 3 Thus says the LORD: I will return to Zion, and will dwell in the midst of Jerusalem; Jerusalem shall be called the faithful city, and the mountain of the LORD of hosts shall be called the holy mountain. 4 Thus says the LORD of hosts: Old men and old women shall again sit in the streets of Jerusalem, each with staff in hand because of their great age. 5 And the streets of the city shall be full of boys and girls playing in its streets. 6 Thus says the LORD of hosts: Even though it seems impossible to the remnant of this people in these days, should it also seem impossible to me, says the LORD of hosts? 7 Thus says the LORD of hosts: I will save my people from the east country and from the west country; 8 and I will bring them to live in Jerusalem. They shall be my people and I will be their God, in faithfulness and in righteousness.

9 Thus says the LORD of hosts: Let your hands be strong—you that have recently been hearing these words from the mouths of the prophets who were present when the foundation was laid for the rebuilding of the temple, the house of the LORD of hosts. 10 For before those days there were no wages for people or for animals, nor was there any safety from the foe for those who went out or came in, and I set them all against one other. 11 But now I will not deal with the remnant of this people as in the former days, says the LORD of hosts. 12 For there shall be a sowing of

7.1 Zech 1.1,7; Neh 1.1
7.2 Jer 26.19; Zech 8.21
7.3 Jer 52.12; Zech 8.19; 12.12-14
7.5 Isa 58.5; Zech 8.19; Jer 41.1; Rom 14.6
7.7 Zech 1.4; Jer 22.21; 17.26
7.9 Ezek 18.8; Zech 8.16; Mic 6.8
7.10 Deut 24.17; Jer 7.6; Mic 2.1
7.11 Jer 11.10; 17.23; 5.21; Acts 7.57
7.12 Ezek 11.19; 36.26; Neh 9.29, 30; Dan 9.11
7.13 Prov 1.24; Isa 1.15; Mic 3.4
7.14 Deut 4.27; Jer 23.19; 44.6; Isa 60.15
8.2 Zech 1.14
8.3 Zech 1.16; 2.10,11; Jer 31.23
8.4 Isa 65.20
8.5 Jer 30.19,20
8.6 Ps 118.23; Jer 32.17,27
8.7 Isa 11.11; 43.5,6; Am 9.14
8.8 Zech 10.10; Ezek 37.25; Zech 2.11
8.9 Hag 2.4; Ezra 5.1
8.10 Hag 1.6
8.11 Ps 103.9; Isa 12.1
8.12 Joel 2.22; Hag 1.10; Isa 61.7

[u] Heb *he*

peace; the vine shall yield its fruit,
the ground shall give its produce,
and the skies shall give their dew;
and I will cause the remnant of this
people to possess all these things.
13 Just as you have been a cursing
among the nations, O house of Judah and house of Israel, so I will
save you and you shall be a blessing. Do not be afraid, but let your
hands be strong.
14 For thus says the LORD of
hosts: Just as I purposed to bring
disaster upon you, when your ancestors provoked me to wrath, and
I did not relent, says the LORD of
hosts, 15 so again I have purposed in
these days to do good to Jerusalem
and to the house of Judah; do not
be afraid. 16 These are the things
that you shall do: Speak the truth
to one another, render in your
gates judgments that are true and
make for peace, 17 do not devise
evil in your hearts against one another, and love no false oath; for all
these are things that I hate, says
the LORD.

Joyful Fasting

18 The word of the LORD of hosts
came to me, saying: 19 Thus says
the LORD of hosts: The fast of the
fourth month, and the fast of the
fifth, and the fast of the seventh,
and the fast of the tenth, shall be
seasons of joy and gladness, and
cheerful festivals for the house of
Judah: therefore love truth and
peace.

Many Peoples Drawn to Jerusalem

20 Thus says the LORD of hosts:
Peoples shall yet come, the inhabitants of many cities; 21 the inhabitants of one city shall go to another, saying, "Come, let us go to
entreat the favor of the LORD, and to
seek the LORD of hosts; I myself am
going." 22 Many peoples and strong
nations shall come to seek the LORD
of hosts in Jerusalem, and to entreat the favor of the LORD. 23 Thus
says the LORD of hosts: In those
days ten men from nations of every
language shall take hold of a Jew,
grasping his garment and saying,
"Let us go with you, for we have
heard that God is with you."

8.13 Jer 42.18; Gen 12.2; Ruth 4.11
8.14 Jer 31.28; Ezek 24.14
8.15 Jer 29.11; v. 13
8.16 Zech 7.9; Eph 4.25
8.17 Prov 3.29; Zech 7.10; 5.4; Hab 1.13
8.19 Zech 7.3,5; Jer 39.2; 52.4; Isa 12.1; v. 16
8.21 Mic 4.1,2
8.22 Isa 60.3; 66.23; v. 21
8.23 Isa 45.14, 24; 60.14; 1 Cor 14.25; 2 Chr 15.5; Isa 19.2

Judgment on Israel's Enemies

9 An Oracle.

The word of the LORD is
against the land of
Hadrach
and will rest upon
Damascus.
For to the LORD belongs the
capital[v] of Aram,[w]
as do all the tribes of
Israel;
2 Hamath also, which borders
on it,
Tyre and Sidon, though
they are very wise.
3 Tyre has built itself a
rampart,
and heaped up silver like
dust,
and gold like the dirt of
the streets.
4 But now, the Lord will strip
it of its possessions
and hurl its wealth into the
sea,
and it shall be devoured by
fire.

5 Ashkelon shall see it and be
afraid;
Gaza too, and shall writhe
in anguish;
Ekron also, because its
hopes are withered.
The king shall perish from
Gaza;
Ashkelon shall be
uninhabited;
6 a mongrel people shall settle
in Ashdod,
and I will make an end of
the pride of Philistia.
7 I will take away its blood
from its mouth,
and its abominations from
between its teeth;
it too shall be a remnant for
our God;

9.2 Jer 49.23; Ezek 28.3-5, 12,21
9.3 2 Sam 24.7; Ezek 27.33; 1 Kings 10.21, 27
9.4 Isa 23.1; Ezek 28.18
9.5 Am 1.6-8
9.6 Am 1.6-8
9.7 Ezek 25.15-17

[v] Heb *eye* [w] Cn: Heb *of Adam* (or *of humankind*)

it shall be like a clan in
Judah,
and Ekron shall be like the
Jebusites.
8 Then I will encamp at my
house as a guard,
so that no one shall march
to and fro;
no oppressor shall again
overrun them,
for now I have seen with
my own eyes.

The Coming Ruler of God's People

9 Rejoice greatly, O daughter
Zion!
Shout aloud, O daughter
Jerusalem!
Lo, your king comes to you;
triumphant and victorious
is he,
humble and riding on a
donkey,
on a colt, the foal of a
donkey.
10 He[x] will cut off the chariot
from Ephraim
and the war horse from
Jerusalem;
and the battle bow shall be
cut off,
and he shall command
peace to the nations;
his dominion shall be from
sea to sea,
and from the River to the
ends of the earth.

11 As for you also, because of
the blood of my
covenant with you,
I will set your prisoners
free from the waterless
pit.
12 Return to your stronghold,
O prisoners of hope;
today I declare that I will
restore to you double.
13 For I have bent Judah as my
bow;
I have made Ephraim its
arrow.
I will arouse your sons,
O Zion,

9.8 Zech 2.5; Isa 52.1; 54.14; 60.18
9.9 Zeph 3.14, 15; Isa 9.6, 7; Mt 21.5; Jn 12.15; Isa 43.3,11; 57.15
9.10 Hos 1.7; 2.18; Hag 2.22; Isa 57.19; Ps 72.8; Isa 60.12
9.11 Ex 24.8; Heb 10.29; Isa 51.14
9.12 Jer 16.19; 17.13; Isa 61.7
9.13 Jer 51.20; Joel 3.6; Ps 45.3; Isa 49.2
9.14 Isa 31.5; Ps 18.14; Isa 27.13; 21.1; 66.15
9.15 Isa 37.35; Zech 12.6; Job 41.28; Ps 78.65; Ex 27.2
9.16 Jer 31.10, 11; Isa 62.3
9.17 Jer 31.12,14
10.1 Jer 14.22; 10.13; Isa 30.23
10.2 Ezek 21.21; Hos 3.4; Jer 27.9; Job 13.4; Ezek 34.5

against your sons,
O Greece,
and wield you like a
warrior's sword.
14 Then the LORD will appear
over them,
and his arrow go forth like
lightning;
the Lord GOD will sound the
trumpet
and march forth in the
whirlwinds of the south.
15 The LORD of hosts will
protect them,
and they shall devour and
tread down the
slingers;[y]
they shall drink their blood[z]
like wine,
and be full like a bowl,
drenched like the corners
of the altar.
16 On that day the LORD their
God will save them
for they are the flock of his
people;
for like the jewels of a crown
they shall shine on his
land.
17 For what goodness and
beauty are his!
Grain shall make the young
men flourish,
and new wine the young
women.

Restoration of Judah and Israel

10 Ask rain from the LORD
in the season of the
spring rain,
from the LORD who makes
the storm clouds,
who gives showers of rain
to you,[a]
the vegetation in the field
to everyone.
2 For the teraphim[b] utter
nonsense,
and the diviners see lies;
the dreamers tell false
dreams,

[x] Gk: Heb *I* [y] Cn: Heb *the slingstones* [z] Gk: Heb *shall drink* [a] Heb *them* [b] Or *household gods*

and give empty
consolation.
Therefore the people wander
like sheep;
they suffer for lack of a
shepherd.

3 My anger is hot against the
shepherds,
and I will punish the
leaders;[c]
for the LORD of hosts cares
for his flock, the house
of Judah,
and will make them like
his proud war horse.
4 Out of them shall come the
cornerstone,
out of them the tent peg,
out of them the battle bow,
out of them every
commander.
5 Together they shall be like
warriors in battle,
trampling the foe in the
mud of the streets;
they shall fight, for the LORD
is with them,
and they shall put to
shame the riders on
horses.

6 I will strengthen the house
of Judah,
and I will save the house of
Joseph.
I will bring them back
because I have
compassion on them,
and they shall be as though
I had not rejected
them;
for I am the LORD their God
and I will answer them.
7 Then the people of Ephraim
shall become like
warriors,
and their hearts shall be
glad as with wine.
Their children shall see it
and rejoice,
their hearts shall exult in
the LORD.

8 I will signal for them and
gather them in,
for I have redeemed them,
and they shall be as
numerous as they were
before.
9 Though I scattered them
among the nations,
yet in far countries they
shall remember me,
and they shall rear their
children and return.
10 I will bring them home from
the land of Egypt,
and gather them from
Assyria;
I will bring them to the land
of Gilead and to
Lebanon,
until there is no room for
them.
11 They[d] shall pass through the
sea of distress,
and the waves of the sea
shall be struck down,
and all the depths of the
Nile dried up.
The pride of Assyria shall be
laid low,
and the scepter of Egypt
shall depart.
12 I will make them strong in
the LORD,
and they shall walk in his
name,
says the LORD.

11 Open your doors,
O Lebanon,
so that fire may devour
your cedars!
2 Wail, O cypress, for the
cedar has fallen,
for the glorious trees are
ruined!
Wail, oaks of Bashan,
for the thick forest has
been felled!
3 Listen, the wail of the
shepherds,
for their glory is despoiled!
Listen, the roar of the lions,
for the thickets of the
Jordan are destroyed!

Two Kinds of Shepherds

4 Thus said the LORD my God: Be
a shepherd of the flock doomed to

10.3 Jer 25.34-36; Ezek 34.12, 17
10.4 Zech 9.10
10.5 2 Sam 22.43; Hag 2.22
10.6 v. 12; Zech 9.16; 8.8; 1.1,6; 13.9
10.7 Zech 9.13, 15; Isa 54.13
10.8 Isa 5.26; Jer 33.22; Ezek 36.11
10.9 Ezek 6.9
10.10 Isa 11.11; Jer 50.19; Isa 49.19,20
10.11 Isa 51.9,10; 19.5-7; Zeph 2.13; Ezek 30.13
10.12 Mic 4.5
11.1 Jer 22.6,7; Ezek 31.3
11.2 Isa 32.19
11.3 Jer 25.34-36; 50.44
11.4 v. 7

c Or *male goats* d Gk: Heb *He*

slaughter. 5 Those who buy them
kill them and go unpunished; and
those who sell them say, "Blessed
be the LORD, for I have become
rich"; and their own shepherds
have no pity on them. 6 For I will no
longer have pity on the inhabitants
of the earth, says the LORD. I will
cause them, every one, to fall each
into the hand of a neighbor, and
each into the hand of the king; and
they shall devastate the earth, and
I will deliver no one from their
hand.
7 So, on behalf of the sheep
merchants, I became the shepherd
of the flock doomed to slaughter. I
took two staffs; one I named Favor,
the other I named Unity, and I
tended the sheep. 8 In one month I
disposed of the three shepherds,
for I had become impatient with
them, and they also detested me.
9 So I said, "I will not be your shepherd. What is to die, let it die; what
is to be destroyed, let it be destroyed; and let those that are left
devour the flesh of one another!"
10 I took my staff Favor and broke it,
annulling the covenant that I had
made with all the peoples. 11 So it
was annulled on that day, and the
sheep merchants, who were watching me, knew that it was the word
of the LORD. 12 I then said to them,
"If it seems right to you, give me my
wages; but if not, keep them." So
they weighed out as my wages thirty shekels of silver. 13 Then the
LORD said to me, "Throw it into the
treasury"[e]—this lordly price at
which I was valued by them. So I
took the thirty shekels of silver and
threw them into the treasury[e] in
the house of the LORD. 14 Then I
broke my second staff Unity, annulling the family ties between Judah and Israel.
15 Then the LORD said to me:
Take once more the implements of
a worthless shepherd. 16 For I am
now raising up in the land a shepherd who does not care for the perishing, or seek the wandering,[f] or
heal the maimed, or nourish the
healthy,[g] but devours the flesh of
the fat ones, tearing off even their
hoofs.

17 Oh, my worthless shepherd,
who deserts the flock!
May the sword strike his arm
and his right eye!
Let his arm be completely
withered,
his right eye utterly
blinded!

Jerusalem's Victory

12 An Oracle.

The word of the LORD concerning
Israel: Thus says the LORD, who
stretched out the heavens and
founded the earth and formed the
human spirit within: 2 See, I am
about to make Jerusalem a cup of
reeling for all the surrounding peoples; it will be against Judah also in
the siege against Jerusalem. 3 On
that day I will make Jerusalem a
heavy stone for all the peoples; all
who lift it shall grievously hurt
themselves. And all the nations of
the earth shall come together
against it. 4 On that day, says the
LORD, I will strike every horse with
panic, and its rider with madness.
But on the house of Judah I will
keep a watchful eye, when I strike
every horse of the peoples with
blindness. 5 Then the clans of Judah shall say to themselves, "The
inhabitants of Jerusalem have
strength through the LORD of hosts,
their God."
6 On that day I will make the
clans of Judah like a blazing pot on
a pile of wood, like a flaming torch
among sheaves; and they shall devour to the right and to the left all
the surrounding peoples, while Jerusalem shall again be inhabited in
its place, in Jerusalem.
7 And the LORD will give victory
to the tents of Judah first, that the
glory of the house of David and the
glory of the inhabitants of Jerusalem may not be exalted over that of

11.5 Jer 50.7; Hos 12.8
11.6 Jer 13.14; Zech 14.13; Mic 5.8
11.7 Zeph 3.12; Ezek 37.16; vv. 10,14
11.8 Hos 5.7
11.9 Jer 15.2; 43.11
11.10 v. 7; Jer 14.21
11.11 Zeph 3.12
11.12 1 Kings 5.6; Gen 37.28; Ex 21.32; Mt 26.15; 27.9,10
11.13 Mt 27.9
11.15 Ezek 34.2-4
11.16 Jer 23.2; Ezek 34.2-6
11.17 Jer 23.1; Jn 10.12; Ezek 30.21, 22; Mic 3.6, 7
12.1 Isa 42.5; 57.16; Heb 12.9
12.2 Isa 51.22, 23; Zech 14.14
12.3 Dan 2.34, 35,44,45; Mt 21.44; Zech 14.2
12.4 Ps 76.6; Ezek 38.4; Zech 9.10
12.5 Zech 10.6, 12
12.6 Isa 10.17, 18; Ob 18; Zech 2.4; 8.3-5
12.7 Jer 30.18; Am 9.11

[e] Syr: Heb *it to the potter* [f] Syr Compare Gk Vg: Heb *the youth* [g] Meaning of Heb uncertain

Judah. 8 On that day the LORD will
shield the inhabitants of Jerusalem
so that the feeblest among them on
that day shall be like David, and
the house of David shall be like
God, like the angel of the LORD, at
their head. 9 And on that day I will
seek to destroy all the nations that
come against Jerusalem.

Mourning for the Pierced One

10 And I will pour out a spirit of
compassion and supplication on
the house of David and the inhabitants of Jerusalem, so that, when
they look on the one[h] whom they
have pierced, they shall mourn for
him, as one mourns for an only
child, and weep bitterly over him,
as one weeps over a firstborn. 11 On
that day the mourning in Jerusalem will be as great as the mourning for Hadad-rimmon in the plain
of Megiddo. 12 The land shall
mourn, each family by itself; the
family of the house of David by itself, and their wives by themselves;
the family of the house of Nathan
by itself, and their wives by themselves; 13 the family of the house of
Levi by itself, and their wives by
themselves; the family of the Shimeites by itself, and their wives by
themselves; 14 and all the families
that are left, each by itself, and
their wives by themselves.

13 On that day a fountain
shall be opened for the
house of David and the inhabitants
of Jerusalem, to cleanse them from
sin and impurity.

Idolatry Cut Off

2 On that day, says the LORD of
hosts, I will cut off the names of the
idols from the land, so that they
shall be remembered no more; and
also I will remove from the land the
prophets and the unclean spirit.
3 And if any prophets appear again,
their fathers and mothers who bore
them will say to them, "You shall
not live, for you speak lies in the
name of the LORD"; and their fathers and their mothers who bore
them shall pierce them through
when they prophesy. 4 On that day
the prophets will be ashamed, every one, of their visions when they
prophesy; they will not put on a
hairy mantle in order to deceive,
5 but each of them will say, "I am no
prophet, I am a tiller of the soil; for
the land has been my possession[i]
since my youth." 6 And if anyone
asks them, "What are these
wounds on your chest?"[j] the answer will be "The wounds I received in the house of my friends."

The Shepherd Struck, the Flock Scattered

7 "Awake, O sword, against my
shepherd,
against the man who is my
associate,"
says the LORD of hosts.
Strike the shepherd, that the
sheep may be scattered;
I will turn my hand against
the little ones.
8 In the whole land, says the
LORD,
two-thirds shall be cut off
and perish,
and one-third shall be left
alive.
9 And I will put this third into
the fire,
refine them as one refines
silver,
and test them as gold is
tested.
They will call on my name,
and I will answer them.
I will say, "They are my
people";
and they will say, "The
LORD is our God."

Future Warfare and Final Victory

14 See, a day is coming for the
LORD, when the plunder
taken from you will be divided in
your midst. 2 For I will gather all
the nations against Jerusalem to
battle, and the city shall be taken
and the houses looted and the
women raped; half the city shall go
into exile, but the rest of the peo-

12.8 Zech 9.14, 15; Mic 7.8; Ps 8.5; 82.6
12.9 v. 3; Zech 14.2,3
12.10 Isa 44.3; Ezek 39.29; Joel 2.28; Jn 19.34; Rev 1.7; Jer 6.26; Am 8.10
12.11 2 Kings 23.29
12.12 Mt 24.30; Rev 1.7
13.1 Jer 2.13; Heb 9.14; Ps 51.2,7; Ezek 36.25
13.2 Ex 23.13; Hos 2.17; Jer 23.14, 15; Ezek 36.25, 29
13.3 Jer 23.34; Deut 18.20; 13.6-11
13.4 Mic 3.6,7; 2 Kings 1.8; Mt 3.4
13.5 Am 7.14
13.6 2 Kings 9.24
13.7 Jer 47.6; Mic 5.2,4; Jer 23.5,6; Isa 53.4,5, 10; Mt 26.31; Isa 1.25
13.8 Isa 6.13
13.9 Isa 48.10; 1 Pet 1.6; Zech 10.6; Jer 30.22; Hos 2.23
14.1 Isa 13.9; Joel 2.1; Mal 4.1; v. 14
14.2 Zech 12.2,3; Isa 13.6; Zech 13.8

[h] Heb *on me* [i] Cn: Heb *for humankind has caused me to possess* [j] Heb *wounds between your hands*

ple shall not be cut off from the city. 3 Then the LORD will go forth and fight against those nations as when he fights on a day of battle. 4 On that day his feet shall stand on the Mount of Olives, which lies before Jerusalem on the east; and the Mount of Olives shall be split in two from east to west by a very wide valley; so that one half of the Mount shall withdraw northward, and the other half southward. 5 And you shall flee by the valley of the LORD's mountain,[k] for the valley between the mountains shall reach to Azal;[l] and you shall flee as you fled from the earthquake in the days of King Uzziah of Judah. Then the LORD my God will come, and all the holy ones with him.

6 On that day there shall not be[m] either cold or frost.[n] 7 And there shall be continuous day (it is known to the LORD), not day and not night, for at evening time there shall be light.

8 On that day living waters shall flow out from Jerusalem, half of them to the eastern sea and half of them to the western sea; it shall continue in summer as in winter.

9 And the LORD will become king over all the earth; on that day the LORD will be one and his name one.

10 The whole land shall be turned into a plain from Geba to Rimmon south of Jerusalem. But Jerusalem shall remain aloft on its site from the Gate of Benjamin to the place of the former gate, to the Corner Gate, and from the Tower of Hananel to the king's wine presses. 11 And it shall be inhabited, for never again shall it be doomed to destruction; Jerusalem shall abide in security.

12 This shall be the plague with which the LORD will strike all the peoples that wage war against Jerusalem: their flesh shall rot while they are still on their feet; their eyes shall rot in their sockets, and their tongues shall rot in their mouths. 13 On that day a great panic from the LORD shall fall on them, so that each will seize the hand of a neighbor, and the hand of the one will be raised against the hand of the other; 14 even Judah will fight at Jerusalem. And the wealth of all the surrounding nations shall be collected — gold, silver, and garments in great abundance. 15 And a plague like this plague shall fall on the horses, the mules, the camels, the donkeys, and whatever animals may be in those camps.

16 Then all who survive of the nations that have come against Jerusalem shall go up year after year to worship the King, the LORD of hosts, and to keep the festival of booths.[o] 17 If any of the families of the earth do not go up to Jerusalem to worship the King, the LORD of hosts, there will be no rain upon them. 18 And if the family of Egypt do not go up and present themselves, then on them shall[p] come the plague that the LORD inflicts on the nations that do not go up to keep the festival of booths.[o] 19 Such shall be the punishment of Egypt and the punishment of all the nations that do not go up to keep the festival of booths.[o]

20 On that day there shall be inscribed on the bells of the horses, "Holy to the LORD." And the cooking pots in the house of the LORD shall be as holy as[q] the bowls in front of the altar; 21 and every cooking pot in Jerusalem and Judah shall be sacred to the LORD of hosts, so that all who sacrifice may come and use them to boil the flesh of the sacrifice. And there shall no longer be traders[r] in the house of the LORD of hosts on that day.

14.3 Zech 9.14, 15
14.4 Ezek 11.23; Mic 1.3,4; Hab 3.6
14.5 Am 1.1; Isa 66.15, 16; Mt 25.31; Jude 14
14.7 Isa 30.26; Rev 21.23
14.8 Ezek 47.1; Joel 3.18; Rev 22.1
14.9 Rev 11.15; Isa 45.21-24; Eph 4.5,6
14.10 Am 9.11; Zech 12.6; Jer 37.13; 38.7; 31.38
14.11 Zech 2.4; Rev 22.3; Jer 23.5,6
14.12 Deut 28.21, 22
14.13 1 Sam 14.15, 20; Zech 11.6; Ezek 38.21
14.14 Zech 12.2,5; Isa 23.18
14.15 v. 12
14.16 Isa 60.6,7,9; 66.23; v. 9
14.17 vv. 9,16; Am 4.7
14.18 v. 12
14.19 v. 12
14.20 Ex 28.36-38; Zech 9.15
14.21 Neh 8.10; 1 Cor 10.31; Ezek 44.9; Zech 9.8

[k] Heb *my mountains* [l] Meaning of Heb uncertain [m] Cn: Heb *there shall not be light* [n] Compare Gk Syr Vg Tg: Meaning of Heb uncertain [o] Or *tabernacles*; Heb *succoth* [p] Gk Syr: Heb *shall not* [q] Heb *shall be like* [r] Or *Canaanites*

Malachi

Title and Background

The temple had been rebuilt, but times of prosperity had not come. The people were suffering drought, famine, and blighted crops, and they met these conditions with indifference and spiritual lethargy. They had forgotten God and treated him with dishonor. They had also married foreign women. Against such a background Malachi (meaning "my messenger") was written.

Author and Date of Writing

Since the term "my messenger" occurs in 3.1, and since both prophets and priests were called messengers of the Lord, some have thought "Malachi" is only a title. There is no certainty about this, however, and it seems probable that Malachi was in fact the author's name. The book was probably written 433-430 B.C.

Theme and Message

Malachi's message was filled with indictments and warnings. He rebuked the Jews for doubting God's love (1.2-5) and for the faithlessness of both priests (1.6–2.9) and people (2.10-16). How quickly the nation had forgotten! Only through repentance and reformation would the people again experience God's blessing (3.6-12). That "great and terrible day of the LORD" (4.5) was coming, and Malachi both reassured and warned his people.

Outline

I. God's Covenant Love for Israel (1.1-5)
II. Israel's Unfaithfulness (1.6–2.16)
  A. The Unfaithfulness of the Priests (1.6–2.9)
  B. The Unfaithfulness of the People (2.10-16)
III. The Lord's Coming (2.17–4.6)

---

1 An oracle. The word of the
LORD to Israel by Malachi.[a]

Israel Preferred to Edom

2 I have loved you, says the
LORD. But you say, "How have you
loved us?" Is not Esau Jacob's
brother? says the LORD. Yet I have
loved Jacob [3]but I have hated
Esau; I have made his hill country
a desolation and his heritage a
desert for jackals. [4]If Edom says,
"We are shattered but we will rebuild the ruins," the LORD of hosts
says: They may build, but I will tear
down, until they are called the
wicked country, the people with
whom the LORD is angry forever.
[5]Your own eyes shall see this, and
you shall say, "Great is the LORD beyond the borders of Israel!"

Corruption of the Priesthood

6 A son honors his father, and
servants their master. If then I am
a father, where is the honor due
me? And if I am a master, where is
the respect due me? says the LORD
of hosts to you, O priests, who despise my name. You say, "How
have we despised your name?" [7]By
offering polluted food on my altar.
And you say, "How have we polluted it?"[b] By thinking that the LORD's
table may be despised. [8]When you
offer blind animals in sacrifice, is
that not wrong? And when you offer those that are lame or sick, is
that not wrong? Try presenting that

1.1 Nah 1.1; Hab 1.1
1.2 Isa 41.8,9; Jer 31.3; Rom 9.13
1.3 Jer 49.18; Ezek 35.3-9
1.5 Ps 35.27; Job 42.8
1.6 Ex 20.12; Mal 2.10; Lk 6.46; Mal 3.5; 2.1-9
1.7 Lev 21.6,8; v. 12
1.8 Lev 22.22

[a] Or *by my messenger* [b] Gk: Heb *you*

to your governor; will he be pleased
with you or show you favor? says
the LORD of hosts. 9 And now implore the favor of God, that he may
be gracious to us. The fault is
yours. Will he show favor to any of
you? says the LORD of hosts. 10 Oh,
that someone among you would
shut the temple[c] doors, so that
you would not kindle fire on my altar in vain! I have no pleasure in
you, says the LORD of hosts, and I
will not accept an offering from
your hands. 11 For from the rising of
the sun to its setting my name is
great among the nations, and in every place incense is offered to my
name, and a pure offering; for my
name is great among the nations,
says the LORD of hosts. 12 But you
profane it when you say that the
Lord's table is polluted, and the
food for it[d] may be despised.
13 "What a weariness this is," you
say, and you sniff at me,[e] says the
LORD of hosts. You bring what has
been taken by violence or is lame
or sick, and this you bring as your
offering! Shall I accept that from
your hand? says the LORD. 14 Cursed
be the cheat who has a male in the
flock and vows to give it, and yet
sacrifices to the Lord what is blemished; for I am a great King, says
the LORD of hosts, and my name is
reverenced among the nations.

2 And now, O priests, this command is for you. 2 If you will
not listen, if you will not lay it to
heart to give glory to my name, says
the LORD of hosts, then I will send
the curse on you and I will curse
your blessings; indeed I have already cursed them,[f] because you
do not lay it to heart. 3 I will rebuke
your offspring, and spread dung on
your faces, the dung of your offerings, and I will put you out of my
presence.[g]

4 Know, then, that I have sent
this command to you, that my covenant with Levi may hold, says the
LORD of hosts. 5 My covenant with
him was a covenant of life and well-
being, which I gave him; this called
for reverence, and he revered me
and stood in awe of my name.
6 True instruction was in his
mouth, and no wrong was found on
his lips. He walked with me in integrity and uprightness, and he
turned many from iniquity. 7 For
the lips of a priest should guard
knowledge, and people should
seek instruction from his mouth,
for he is the messenger of the LORD
of hosts. 8 But you have turned
aside from the way; you have
caused many to stumble by your instruction; you have corrupted the
covenant of Levi, says the LORD of
hosts, 9 and so I make you despised
and abased before all the people,
inasmuch as you have not kept my
ways but have shown partiality in
your instruction.

The Covenant Profaned by Judah

10 Have we not all one father?
Has not one God created us? Why
then are we faithless to one another, profaning the covenant of our
ancestors? 11 Judah has been faithless, and abomination has been
committed in Israel and in Jerusalem; for Judah has profaned the
sanctuary of the LORD, which he
loves, and has married the daughter of a foreign god. 12 May the LORD
cut off from the tents of Jacob anyone who does this—any to witness[h] or answer, or to bring an offering to the LORD of hosts.

13 And this you do as well: You
cover the LORD's altar with tears,
with weeping and groaning because he no longer regards the offering or accepts it with favor at
your hand. 14 You ask, "Why does
he not?" Because the LORD was a
witness between you and the wife
of your youth, to whom you have
been faithless, though she is your
companion and your wife by covenant. 15 Did not one God make
her?[i] Both flesh and spirit are

1.9 Am 5.22; Lev 23.34-44
1.10 Isa 1.13; Jer 14.10-12; Hos 5.6
1.11 Isa 45.6; 60.3,5,6; Rev 8.3; Jer 10.6,7
1.12 Deut 28.15; v. 7
1.13 Isa 43.22; 61.8; Lev 22.20
1.14 Lev 22.18-20; Zech 14.9; Zeph 2.11
2.1 vv. 7,8
2.2 Lev 26.14; Deut 28.15-20
2.3 Nah 3.6; Ex 29.14
2.4 Num 3.45; 18.21
2.5 Num 25.12; Ezek 34.25; Deut 33.9
2.6 Deut 33.8-10; Jer 23.22; Jas 5.20
2.7 Lev 10.11; Jer 18.18; Num 27.21
2.8 Mal 3.7; Jer 18.15; Ezek 44.10
2.9 1 Sam 2.30; Deut 1.17; Mic 3.11
2.10 Isa 63.16; 1 Cor 8.6; Jer 9.4,5; Ex 19.4-6
2.11 Jer 3.7-9; Ezra 9.1; Neh 13.23
2.12 Hos 9.12; Mal 1.10,13
2.13 Jer 11.14; 14.12
2.14 Prov 5.18; 2.17
2.15 Gen 2.24; Mt 19.4; Ex 20.14; Lev 20.10

[c] Heb lacks *temple* [d] Compare Syr Tg: Heb *its fruit, its food* [e] Another reading is *at it* [f] Heb *it* [g] Cn Compare Gk Syr: Heb *and he shall bear you to it* [h] Cn Compare Gk: Heb *arouse* [i] Or *Has he not made one?*

his.[j] And what does the one God[k] desire? Godly offspring. So look to yourselves, and do not let anyone be faithless to the wife of his youth. 16 For I hate[l] divorce, says the LORD, the God of Israel, and covering one's garment with violence, says the LORD of hosts. So take heed to yourselves and do not be faithless.

17 You have wearied the LORD with your words. Yet you say, "How have we wearied him?" By saying, "All who do evil are good in the sight of the LORD, and he delights in them." Or by asking, "Where is the God of justice?"

The Coming Messenger

3 See, I am sending my messenger to prepare the way before me, and the Lord whom you seek will suddenly come to his temple. The messenger of the covenant in whom you delight—indeed, he is coming, says the LORD of hosts. 2 But who can endure the day of his coming, and who can stand when he appears?

For he is like a refiner's fire and like fullers' soap; 3 he will sit as a refiner and purifier of silver, and he will purify the descendants of Levi and refine them like gold and silver, until they present offerings to the LORD in righteousness.[m] 4 Then the offering of Judah and Jerusalem will be pleasing to the LORD as in the days of old and as in former years.

5 Then I will draw near to you for judgment; I will be swift to bear witness against the sorcerers, against the adulterers, against those who swear falsely, against those who oppress the hired workers in their wages, the widow and the orphan, against those who thrust aside the alien, and do not fear me, says the LORD of hosts.

6 For I the LORD do not change; therefore you, O children of Jacob, have not perished. 7 Ever since the days of your ancestors you have turned aside from my statutes and have not kept them. Return to me, and I will return to you, says the LORD of hosts. But you say, "How shall we return?"

2.16 Deut 24.1; Mt 5.31,32; Ps 73.6; Isa 59.6
2.17 Isa 43.24; 5.19,20
3.1 Mt 11.10; Mk 1.2; Lk 1.76; 7.27
3.2 Ezek 22.14; Zech 13.9; Mt 3.10-12; 1 Cor 3.13-15
3.3 Isa 1.25; Zech 13.9
3.4 Mal 1.11
3.5 Deut 18.10; Ezek 22.9-11; Zech 5.4; Lev 19.13
3.6 Num 23.19; Jas 1.17
3.7 Acts 7.51; Zech 1.3
3.8 Neh 13.10-12
3.9 Mal 2.2
3.10 Prov 3.9,10; Ps 78.23-29; 2 Chr 31.10
3.11 Joel 1.4; 2.25
3.12 Isa 61.9; 62.4
3.13 Mal 2.17
3.14 Ps 73.13; Jer 2.25; 18.12; Isa 58.3
3.15 Mal 4.1; Jer 7.10
3.16 Ps 34.15; 56.8; Rev 20.12
3.17 1 Pet 2.9; Isa 26.20
3.18 Gen 18.25; Am 5.15

Do Not Rob God

8 Will anyone rob God? Yet you are robbing me! But you say, "How are we robbing you?" In your tithes and offerings! 9 You are cursed with a curse, for you are robbing me—the whole nation of you! 10 Bring the full tithe into the storehouse, so that there may be food in my house, and thus put me to the test, says the LORD of hosts; see if I will not open the windows of heaven for you and pour down for you an overflowing blessing. 11 I will rebuke the locust[n] for you, so that it will not destroy the produce of your soil; and your vine in the field shall not be barren, says the LORD of hosts. 12 Then all nations will count you happy, for you will be a land of delight, says the LORD of hosts.

13 You have spoken harsh words against me, says the LORD. Yet you say, "How have we spoken against you?" 14 You have said, "It is vain to serve God. What do we profit by keeping his command or by going about as mourners before the LORD of hosts? 15 Now we count the arrogant happy; evildoers not only prosper, but when they put God to the test they escape."

The Reward of the Faithful

16 Then those who revered the LORD spoke with one another. The LORD took note and listened, and a book of remembrance was written before him of those who revered the LORD and thought on his name. 17 They shall be mine, says the LORD of hosts, my special possession on the day when I act, and I will spare them as parents spare their children who serve them. 18 Then once more you shall see the difference between the righteous and the wicked, between one who serves God and one who does not serve him.

[j] Cn: Heb *and a remnant of spirit was his*
[k] Heb *he* [l] Cn: Heb *he hates*
[m] Or *right offerings to the LORD*
[n] Heb *devourer*

The Great Day of the LORD

4[o] See, the day is coming, burning like an oven, when all the
arrogant and all evildoers will be
stubble; the day that comes shall
burn them up, says the LORD of
hosts, so that it will leave them neither root nor branch. 2 But for you
who revere my name the sun of
righteousness shall rise, with healing in its wings. You shall go out
leaping like calves from the stall.
3 And you shall tread down the
wicked, for they will be ashes under the soles of your feet, on the
day when I act, says the LORD of
hosts.
4 Remember the teaching of my
servant Moses, the statutes and ordinances that I commanded him at
Horeb for all Israel.
5 Lo, I will send you the prophet
Elijah before the great and terrible
day of the LORD comes. 6 He will
turn the hearts of parents to their
children and the hearts of children
to their parents, so that I will not
come and strike the land with a
curse.[p]

4.1 Joel 2.31; Ob 18; Am 2.9
4.2 Mal 3.16; Lk 1.78; Eph 5.14
4.3 Mic 7.10; Zech 10.5
4.4 Ex 20.3
4.5 Mt 11.14; Mk 9.11; Lk 1.17

[o] Ch 4.1-6 are Ch 3.19-24 in Heb [p] Or *a ban of utter destruction*

FROM MALACHI TO CHRIST

THE PERSIAN PERIOD 450-330 B.C.

For about 200 years after Nehemiah's time the Persians controlled Judah, but the Jews were allowed to carry on their religious observances and were not interfered with. During this time Judah was ruled by high priests who were responsible to the Jewish government.

THE HELLENISTIC PERIOD 330-166 B.C.

In 333 B.C. the Persian armies stationed in Macedonia were defeated by Alexander the Great. He was convinced that Greek culture was the one force that could unify the world. Alexander permitted the Jews to observe their laws and even granted them exemption from tribute or tax during their sabbath years. The Greek conquest prepared the way for the translation of the OT into Greek (Septuagint version) c. 250 B.C.

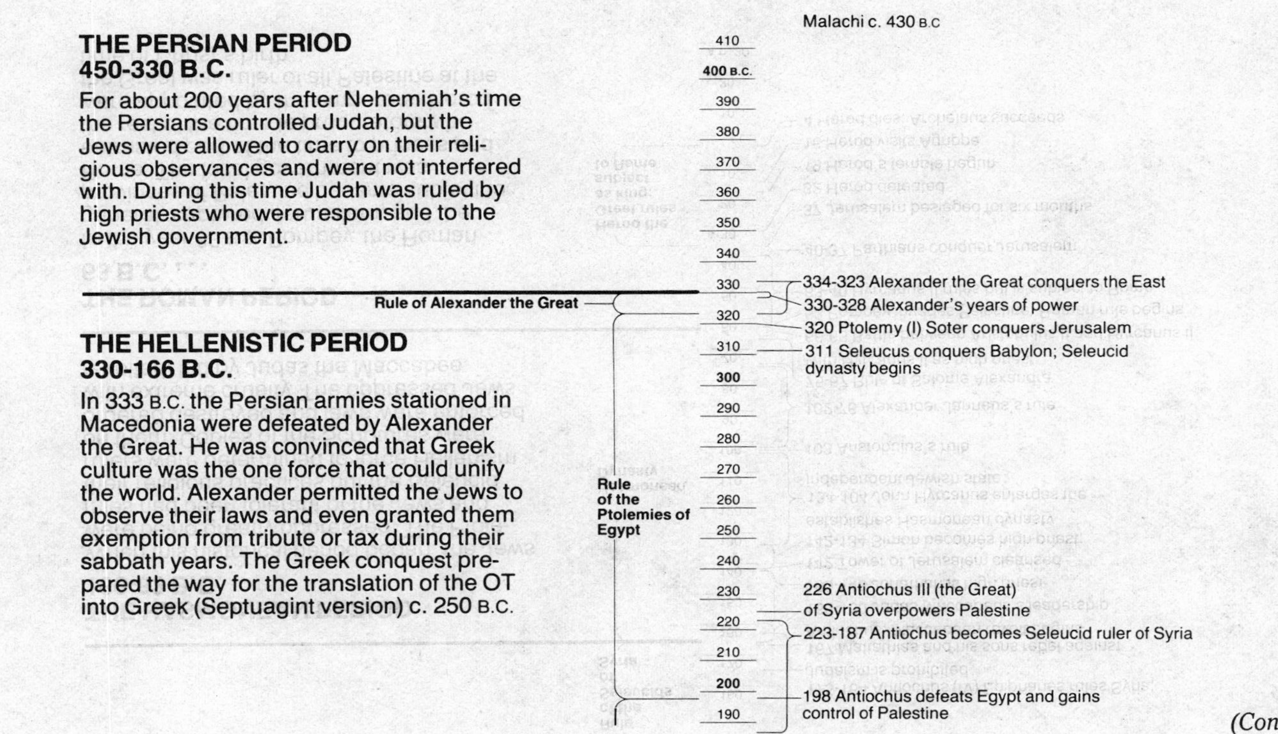

(Continued)

THE HASMONEAN PERIOD 166-63 B.C.

When this historical period began, the Jews were being greatly oppressed. The Ptolemies had been tolerant of the Jews and their religious practices but the Seleucid rulers were determined to force Hellenism on them. Copies of the Scriptures were ordered destroyed and laws were enforced with extreme cruelty. The oppressed Jews revolted, led by Judas the Maccabee.

THE ROMAN PERIOD 63 B.C. . . .

In the year 63 B.C. Pompey, the Roman general, captured Jerusalem, and the provinces of Palestine became subject to Rome. The local government was entrusted part of the time to princes and the rest of the time to procurators who were appointed by the emperors. Herod the Great was ruler of all Palestine at the time of Christ's birth.

Rule of the Seleucids of Syria

Hasmonean Dynasty

Herod the Great rules as king; subject to Rome

180
170
160
150
140
130
120
110
100
90
80
70
60
50
40
30
20
10
10
20
A.D. 30

175-164 Antiochus (IV) Epiphanes rules Syria; Judaism is prohibited
167 Mattathias and his sons rebel against Antiochus; Maccabean revolt begins
166-160 Judas Maccabeus's leadership
160-143 Jonathan is high priest
142 Tower of Jerusalem cleansed
142-134 Simon becomes high priest; establishes Hasmonean dynasty
134-104 John Hyrcanus enlarges the independent Jewish state
103 Aristobulus's rule
102-76 Alexander Janneus's rule
75-67 Rule of Salome Alexandra with Hyrcanus II as high priest
66-63 Battle between Aristobulus II and Hyrcanus II
63 Pompey invades Palestine; Roman rule begins
63-40 Hyrcanus II rules but is subject to Rome
40-37 Parthians conquer Jerusalem
37 Jerusalem besieged for six months
32 Herod defeated
19 Herod's temple begun
16 Herod visits Agrippa
4 Herod dies; Archelaus succeeds

The Apocryphal / Deuterocanonical Books

of the Old Testament

(a) The following books and parts of books from Tobit through 2 Maccabees are recognized as Deuterocanonical Scripture by the Roman Catholic, Greek, and Russian Orthodox Churches.

Tobit

Title and Background

This book is named after its main character, Tobit son of Tobiel. It tells the story of several God-fearing exiles from the northern kingdom of Israel who had been taken to Assyria by King Shalmaneser.

Author and Date of Writing

Tobit has traditionally been dated in the seventh century B.C., but most scholars now place it much later. Fragments of a Hebrew copy of Tobit have been found at Qumran, suggesting it was written by a pious Jew around 200 B.C.

Theme and Message

The book of Tobit teaches that the righteous are eventually rewarded for their good deeds while the wicked are punished. In parallel stories, Tobit and Sarah–both virtuous and God-fearing–experience intense suffering. But their stories come together and both are miraculously delivered through the intervention of an angel.

Outline

I. Tobit's Virtuous Life and Suffering (1.1–2.14)
II. Tobit's Prayer (3.1-6)
III. Sarah's Suffering and Prayer (3.7-17)
IV. Tobias' Search for a Bride (4.1–11.18)
  A. Instructions from his Father Tobit (4.1-20)
  B. Raphael's Guidance of Tobias to the House of Raguel (5.1–7.8)
  C. Marriage of Tobias and Sarah (7.9–9.6)
  D. Return to Nineveh (10.1–11.18)
V. Raphael Discloses His Identity (12.1-22)
VI. Tobit's Song and Final Counsel (13.1–14.15)

---

1 This book tells the story of Tobit son of Tobiel son of Hananiel son of Aduel son of Gabael son
of Raphael[a] of the descendants of
Asiel, of the tribe of Naphtali,
2 who in the days of King Shalmaneser[b] of the Assyrians was taken
into captivity from Thisbe, which
is to the south of Kedesh Naphtali
in Upper Galilee, above Asher toward the west, and north of Pho-
gor.

Tobit's Youth and Virtuous Life

3 I, Tobit, walked in the ways of
truth and righteousness all the
days of my life. I performed many
acts of charity for my kindred and
my people who had gone with me
in exile to Nineveh in the land of
the Assyrians. 4 When I was in my
own country, in the land of Israel,
while I was still a young man, the
whole tribe of my ancestor Naphtali deserted the house of David
and Jerusalem. This city had been
chosen from among all the tribes
of Israel, where all the tribes of Israel should offer sacrifice and
where the temple, the dwelling of
God, had been consecrated and es-

1.2 2 Kings 17.3-4;15.29
1.3 Gen 6.7; Job 29.12-16; 2 Kings 17.6
1.4 1 Kings 11.13; 8.1-64

[a] Other ancient authorities lack *son of Raphael son of Raguel* [b] Gk *Enemessaros*

tablished for all generations forever.
5 All my kindred and our ancestral house of Naphtali sacrificed to
the calf[c] that King Jeroboam of Israel had erected in Dan and on all
the mountains of Galilee. 6 But I
alone went often to Jerusalem for
the festivals, as it is prescribed for
all Israel by an everlasting decree. I
would hurry off to Jerusalem with
the first fruits of the crops and the
firstlings of the flock, the tithes of
the cattle, and the first shearings
of the sheep. 7 I would give these to
the priests, the sons of Aaron, at
the altar; likewise the tenth of the
grain, wine, olive oil, pomegranates, figs, and the rest of the fruits
to the sons of Levi who ministered
at Jerusalem. Also for six years I
would save up a second tenth in
money and go and distribute it in
Jerusalem. 8 A third tenth[d] I would
give to the orphans and widows
and to the converts who had attached themselves to Israel. I
would bring it and give it to them
in the third year, and we would eat
it according to the ordinance decreed concerning it in the law of
Moses and according to the instructions of Deborah, the mother
of my father Tobiel,[e] for my father
had died and left me an orphan.
9 When I became a man I married a
woman,[f] a member of our own
family, and by her I became the father of a son whom I named Tobias.

Taken Captive to Nineveh

10 After I was carried away captive to Assyria and came as a captive to Nineveh, everyone of my
kindred and my people ate the
food of the Gentiles, 11 but I kept
myself from eating the food of the
Gentiles. 12 Because I was mindful
of God with all my heart, 13 the
Most High gave me favor and good
standing with Shalmaneser,[g] and I
used to buy everything he needed.
14 Until his death I used to go into
Media, and buy for him there.
While in the country of Media I left
bags of silver worth ten talents in
trust with Gabael, the brother of
Gabri. 15 But when Shalmaneser[g]
died, and his son Sennacherib
reigned in his place, the highways
into Media became unsafe and I
could no longer go there.

Courage in Burying the Dead

16 In the days of Shalmaneser[g]
I performed many acts of charity to
my kindred, those of my tribe. 17 I
would give my food to the hungry
and my clothing to the naked; and
if I saw the dead body of any of my
people thrown out behind the wall
of Nineveh, I would bury it. 18 I also
buried any whom King Sennacherib put to death when he came
fleeing from Judea in those days of
judgment that the king of heaven
executed upon him because of his
blasphemies. For in his anger he
put to death many Israelites; but I
would secretly remove the bodies
and bury them. So when Sennacherib looked for them he could not
find them. 19 Then one of the Ninevites went and informed the king
about me, that I was burying them;
so I hid myself. But when I realized
that the king knew about me and
that I was being searched for to be
put to death, I was afraid and ran
away. 20 Then all my property was
confiscated; nothing was left to me
that was not taken into the royal
treasury except my wife Anna and
my son Tobias.
21 But not forty[h] days passed
before two of Sennacherib's[i] sons
killed him, and they fled to the
mountains of Ararat, and his son
Esar-haddon[j] reigned after him.
He appointed Ahikar, the son of
my brother Hanael[k] over all the
accounts of his kingdom, and he
had authority over the entire administration. 22 Ahikar interceded
for me, and I returned to Nineveh.
Now Ahikar was chief cupbearer,
keeper of the signet, and in charge

1.5 1 Kings 12.28-29
1.6 Ex 23.14-17; Deut 12.11-14; 16.16-17; Lev 23.9-14
1.7 Lev 27.30; Deut 14.23; Num 18.26
1.8 Deut 14.28-29
1.10 2 Kings 17.6
1.11 Dan 1.8-15
1.12 Deut 6.5
1.14 Ezra 6.2; Tob 5.6; 4.20
1.15 2 Kings 18.13
1.17 Mt 25.35
1.18 2 Kings 19.35-36; 2 Chr 32.1-22; 1 Sam 31.8-13; 1 Macc 7.17; Wis 18.12; Sir 38.16
1.19 1 Kings 19.1-4
1.20 Heb 10.34
1.21 2 Kings 19.37; Tob 14.10
1.22 Neh 1.11

c Other ancient authorities read *heifer*
d *A third tenth* added from other ancient authorities
e Lat: Gk *Hananiel*
f Other ancient authorities add *Anna*
g Gk *Enemessaros*
h Other ancient authorities read either *forty-five* or *fifty*
i Gk *his*
j Gk *Sacherdonos*
k Other authorities read *Hananael*

of administrations of the accounts
under King Sennacherib of Assyria;
so Esar-haddon[l] reappointed him.
He was my nephew and so a close
relative.

2 Then during the reign of Esar-
haddon[l] I returned home,
and my wife Anna and my son Tobias were restored to me. At our
festival of Pentecost, which is the
sacred festival of weeks, a good
dinner was prepared for me and I
reclined to eat. 2 When the table
was set for me and an abundance
of food placed before me, I said to
my son Tobias, "Go, my child, and
bring whatever poor person you
may find of our people among the
exiles in Nineveh, who is wholeheartedly mindful of God,[m] and he
shall eat together with me. I will
wait for you, until you come back."
3 So Tobias went to look for some
poor person of our people. When
he had returned he said, "Father!"
And I replied, "Here I am, my
child." Then he went on to say,
"Look, father, one of our own people has been murdered and thrown
into the market place, and now he
lies there strangled." 4 Then I
sprang up, left the dinner before
even tasting it, and removed the
body[n] from the square[o] and laid
it[n] in one of the rooms until sunset when I might bury it.[n] 5 When I
returned, I washed myself and ate
my food in sorrow. 6 Then I remembered the prophecy of Amos, how
he said against Bethel,[p]

"Your festivals shall be
turned into mourning,
and all your songs into
lamentation."

And I wept.

Tobit Becomes Blind

7 When the sun had set, I went
and dug a grave and buried him.
8 And my neighbors laughed and
said, "Is he still not afraid? He has
already been hunted down to be
put to death for doing this, and he
ran away; yet here he is again burying the dead!" 9 That same night I
washed myself and went into my
courtyard and slept by the wall of
the courtyard; and my face was uncovered because of the heat. 10 I
did not know that there were sparrows on the wall; their fresh drop-
pings fell into my eyes and produced white films. I went to
physicians to be healed, but the
more they treated me with ointments the more my vision was obscured by the white films, until I
became completely blind. For four
years I remained unable to see. All
my kindred were sorry for me, and
Ahikar took care of me for two
years before he went to Elymais.

Tobit's Wife Earns Their Livelihood

11 At that time, also, my wife
Anna earned money at women's
work. 12 She used to send what she
made to the owners and they
would pay wages to her. One day,
the seventh of Dystrus, when she
cut off a piece she had woven and
sent it to the owners, they paid her
full wages and also gave her a
young goat for a meal. 13 When she
returned to me, the goat began to
bleat. So I called her and said,
"Where did you get this goat? It is
surely not stolen, is it? Return it to
the owners; for we have no right to
eat anything stolen." 14 But she
said to me, "It was given to me as
a gift in addition to my wages." But
I did not believe her, and told her
to return it to the owners. I became
flushed with anger against her over
this. Then she replied to me,
"Where are your acts of charity?
Where are your righteous deeds?
These things are known about
you!"[q]

Tobit's Prayer

3 Then with much grief and anguish of heart I wept, and with
groaning began to pray:

2 "You are righteous, O Lord,
and all your deeds are just;
all your ways are mercy and
truth;

2.1 Lev 23.15-21; Deut 16.9-11; Acts 2.1 **2.2** Tob 4.7-11; Lk 14.13,21 **2.3** 1 Sam 3.4-5 **2.4** Tob 1.18 **2.6** Am 8.10 **2.8** Job 12.4; Eccl 7.3,6 **2.9** Lev 22.4-6; Num 5.1-4 **2.10** Mk 5.26; Tob 1.21; 1 Macc 6.1 **2.11** Acts 9.39; 16.14 **2.12** Deut 24.14-15 **2.13** Ex 20.15 **3.2** Ps 116.15; 145.17; 96.13

[l] Gk *Sacherdonos* [m] Lat: Gk *wholeheartedly mindful* [n] Gk *him* [o] Other ancient authorities lack *from the square* [p] Other ancient authorities read *against Bethlehem* [q] Or *to you*; Gk *with you*

you judge the world.[r]
3 And now, O Lord, remember
me
and look favorably upon
me.
Do not punish me for my
sins
and for my unwitting
offenses
and those that my
ancestors committed
before you.
They sinned against you,
4 and disobeyed your
commandments.
So you gave us over to
plunder, exile, and
death,
to become the talk, the
byword, and an object
of reproach
among all the nations
among whom you have
dispersed us.
5 And now your many
judgments are true
in exacting penalty from
me for my sins.
For we have not kept your
commandments
and have not walked in
accordance with truth
before you.
6 So now deal with me as you
will;
command my spirit to be
taken from me,
so that I may be released
from the face of the
earth and become dust.
For it is better for me to die
than to live,
because I have had to
listen to undeserved
insults,
and great is the sorrow
within me.
Command, O Lord, that I be
released from this
distress;
release me to go to the
eternal home,
and do not, O Lord, turn
your face away from me.
For it is better for me to die
than to see so much
distress in my life
and to listen to insults."

Sarah Falsely Accused

7 On the same day, at Ecbatana
in Media, it also happened that
Sarah, the daughter of Raguel, was
reproached by one of her father's
maids. 8 For she had been married
to seven husbands, and the wicked
demon Asmodeus had killed each
of them before they had been with
her as is customary for wives. So
the maid said to her, "You are the
one who kills[s] your husbands!
See, you have already been married
to seven husbands and have not
borne the name of[t] a single one of
them. 9 Why do you beat us? Because your husbands are dead? Go
with them! May we never see a son
or daughter of yours!"

Sarah's Prayer for Death

10 On that day she was grieved
in spirit and wept. When she had
gone up to her father's upper
room, she intended to hang herself. But she thought it over and
said, "Never shall they reproach
my father, saying to him, 'You had
only one beloved daughter but she
hanged herself because of her distress.' And I shall bring my father
in his old age down in sorrow to
Hades. It is better for me not to
hang myself, but to pray the Lord
that I may die and not listen to
these reproaches anymore." 11 At
that same time, with hands outstretched toward the window, she
prayed and said,

"Blessed are you, merciful
God!
Blessed is your name
forever;
let all your works praise
you forever.
12 And now, Lord,[u] I turn my
face to you,
and raise my eyes toward
you.
13 Command that I be released
from the earth

3.3 Neh 13.14, 22,29,31; Num 15.22-29 **3.4** Neh 9.32-36, 26-30; Deut 28.37; Ps 44.9-16 **3.5** Ps 119.75; Song of Thr 1.4; Tob 1.3 **3.6** Ps 104.29; Eccl 12.7; Phil 1.23; Lam 1.12; Ps 27.9; 143.7

3.7 Ezra 6.2; Jdt 1.1-4; Tob 10.7-10 **3.8** Mk 12.19-23; Tob 3.17 **3.10** Gen 37.35; 44.29; 1 Kings 19.4; Job 3.11-22 **3.11** Ps 68.19; 72.19; 145.10 **3.12** Ps 25.15

[r] Other ancient authorities read *you render true and righteous judgment forever* [s] Other ancient authorities read *strangles* [t] Other ancient authorities read *have had no benefit from* [u] Other ancient authorities lack *Lord*

and not listen to such
reproaches any more.
14 You know, O Master, that I
am innocent
of any defilement with a
man,
15 and that I have not disgraced
my name
or the name of my father in
the land of my exile.
I am my father's only child;
he has no other child to be
his heir;
and he has no close relative
or other kindred
for whom I should keep
myself as wife.
Already seven husbands of
mine have died.
Why should I still live?
But if it is not pleasing to
you, O Lord, to take my
life,
hear me in my disgrace."

An Answer to Prayer

16 At that very moment, the
prayers of both of them were heard
in the glorious presence of God.
17 So Raphael was sent to heal both
of them: Tobit, by removing the
white films from his eyes, so that
he might see God's light with his
eyes; and Sarah, daughter of Raguel, by giving her in marriage to
Tobias son of Tobit, and by setting
her free from the wicked demon
Asmodeus. For Tobias was entitled
to have her before all others who
had desired to marry her. At the
same time that Tobit returned
from the courtyard into his house,
Sarah daughter of Raguel came
down from her upper room.

Tobit Gives Instructions to His Son

4 That same day Tobit remembered the money that he had
left in trust with Gabael at Rages in
Media, 2 and he said to himself,
"Now I have asked for death. Why
do I not call my son Tobias and explain to him about the money before I die?" 3 Then he called his son
Tobias, and when he came to him
he said, "My son, when I die,[v] give
me a proper burial. Honor your
mother and do not abandon her all
the days of her life. Do whatever
pleases her, and do not grieve her
in anything. 4 Remember her, my
son, because she faced many dangers for you while you were in
her womb. And when she dies,
bury her beside me in the same
grave.

5 "Revere the Lord all your
days, my son, and refuse to sin or
to transgress his commandments.
Live uprightly all the days of your
life, and do not walk in the ways of
wrongdoing; 6 for those who act in
accordance with truth will prosper
in all their activities. To all those
who practice righteousness[w] 7 give
alms from your possessions, and
do not let your eye begrudge the
gift when you make it. Do not turn
your face away from anyone who is
poor, and the face of God will not
be turned away from you. 8 If you
have many possessions, make your
gift from them in proportion; if
few, do not be afraid to give according to the little you have. 9 So
you will be laying up a good treasure for yourself against the day of
necessity. 10 For almsgiving delivers from death and keeps you from
going into the Darkness. 11 Indeed,
almsgiving, for all who practice it,
is an excellent offering in the presence of the Most High.

12 "Beware, my son, of every
kind of fornication. First of all,
marry a woman from among the
descendants of your ancestors; do
not marry a foreign woman, who is
not of your father's tribe; for we are
the descendants of the prophets.
Remember, my son, that Noah,
Abraham, Isaac, and Jacob, our ancestors of old, all took wives from
among their kindred. They were
blessed in their children, and their
posterity will inherit the land. 13 So
now, my son, love your kindred,
and in your heart do not disdain
your kindred, the sons and daugh-

3.14 Ps 73.13 **3.15** Num 27.1-8; Job 1.21 **3.17** Tob 5.4; 2.10; 7.13; 1.9; 3.8; 7.10 **4.1** Tob 1.14 **4.3** Mt 8.21; Ex 20.12; Prov 23.22 **4.4** Gen 25.10 **4.5** Josh 24.14; Prov 14.2 **4.6** Jn 3.21 **4.7** Lk 12.33; Sir 4.4 **4.8** 1 Cor 16.2; 2 Cor 8.1-4 **4.10** Jas 2.13 **4.11** Sir 3.30 **4.12** Prov 5.7-11; 1 Cor 6.18; Ex 34.15-16; Deut 7.3-4; Gen 24.1-4; 28.1-5 **4.13** Prov 16.18; 6.9-11

[v] Lat [w] The text of codex Sinaiticus goes directly from verse 6 to verse 19, reading *To those who practice righteousness 19the Lord will give good counsel.* In order to fill the lacuna verses 7 to 18 are derived from other ancient authorities

ters of your people, by refusing to
take a wife for yourself from among
them. For in pride there is ruin and
great confusion. And in idleness
there is loss and dire poverty, because idleness is the mother of
famine.
14 "Do not keep over until the
next day the wages of those who
work for you, but pay them at once.
If you serve God you will receive
payment. "Watch yourself, my son,
in everything you do, and discipline yourself in all your conduct.
15 And what you hate, do not do to
anyone. Do not drink wine to excess or let drunkenness go with
you on your way. 16 Give some of
your food to the hungry, and some
of your clothing to the naked. Give
all your surplus as alms, and do not
let your eye begrudge your giving of
alms. 17 Place your bread on the
grave of the righteous, but give
none to sinners. 18 Seek advice
from every wise person and do not
despise any useful counsel. 19 At all
times bless the Lord God, and ask
him that your ways may be made
straight and that all your paths and
plans may prosper. For none of the
nations has understanding, but the
Lord himself will give them good
counsel; but if he chooses otherwise, he casts down to deepest Hades. So now, my child, remember
these commandments, and do not
let them be erased from your heart.

Money Left in Trust with Gabael

20 "And now, my son, let me explain to you that I left ten talents
of silver in trust with Gabael son of
Gabrias, at Rages in Media. 21 Do
not be afraid, my son, because we
have become poor. You have great
wealth if you fear God and flee
from every sin and do what is good
in the sight of the Lord your God."

The Angel Raphael

5 Then Tobias answered his father Tobit, "I will do everything that you have commanded
me, father; 2 but how can I obtain
the money[x] from him, since he
does not know me and I do not
know him? What evidence[y] am I
to give him so that he will recognize and trust me, and give me the
money? Also, I do not know the
roads to Media, or how to get
there." 3 Then Tobit answered his
son Tobias, "He gave me his bond
and I gave him my bond. I[z] divided
his in two; we each took one part,
and I put one with the money. And
now twenty years have passed
since I left this money in trust. So
now, my son, find yourself a trustworthy man to go with you, and we
will pay him wages until you return. But get back the money from
Gabael."[a]
4 So Tobias went out to look for
a man to go with him to Media,
someone who was acquainted with
the way. He went out and found
the angel Raphael standing in front
of him; but he did not perceive that
he was an angel of God. 5 Tobias[b]
said to him, "Where do you come
from, young man?" "From your
kindred, the Israelites," he replied,
"and I have come here to work."
Then Tobias[c] said to him, "Do you
know the way to go to Media?"
6 "Yes," he replied, "I have been
there many times; I am acquainted
with it and know all the roads. I
have often traveled to Media, and
would stay with our kinsman
Gabael who lives in Rages of Media. It is a journey of two days from
Ecbatana to Rages; for it lies in a
mountainous area, while Ecbatana
is in the middle of the plain."
7 Then Tobias said to him, "Wait
for me, young man, until I go in
and tell my father; for I do need
you to travel with me, and I will pay
you your wages." 8 He replied, "All
right, I will wait; but do not take
too long."
9 So Tobias[c] went in to tell his
father Tobit and said to him, "I
have just found a man who is one
of our own Israelite kindred!" He
replied, "Call the man in, my son,
so that I may learn about his family
and to what tribe he belongs, and
whether he is trustworthy enough
to go with you."
10 Then Tobias went out and

4.14 Lev 19.13; Deut 24.15; Jas 5.4
4.15 Mt 7.12; 1 Tim 3.3; Prov 20.1; 23.29-35
4.16 Mt 25.35-36
4.17 Deut 26.14
4.18 2 Chr 10.6-15
4.19 Ps 103.1-2; 1.3; Num 15.39-40
4.20 Tob 1.14
4.21 Ps 25.12-13
5.2 2 Cor 8.17-23
5.4 Tob 3.17; Gen 18.1-22; Heb 13.2
5.6 Tob 4.1
5.9 Prov 25.13
5.10 Job 19.20-21; Josh 1.9

x Gk *it* y Gk *sign* z Other authorities read *He* a Gk *from him* b Gk *He* c Gk *he*

called him, and said, "Young man,
my father is calling for you." So he
went in to him, and Tobit greeted
him first. He replied, "Joyous
greetings to you!" But Tobit re-
torted, "What joy is left for me any
more? I am a man without eyesight; I cannot see the light of
heaven, but I lie in darkness like
the dead who no longer see the
light. Although still alive, I am
among the dead. I hear people but
I cannot see them." But the young
man[d] said, "Take courage; the
time is near for God to heal you;
take courage." Then Tobit said to
him, "My son Tobias wishes to go
to Media. Can you accompany him
and guide him? I will pay your
wages, brother." He answered, "I
can go with him and I know all the
roads, for I have often gone to Media and have crossed all its plains,
and I am familiar with its mountains and all of its roads."
11 Then Tobit[d] said to him,
"Brother, of what family are you
and from what tribe? Tell me,
brother." 12 He replied, "Why do
you need to know my tribe?" But
Tobit[d] said, "I want to be sure,
brother, whose son you are and
what your name is." 13 He replied,
"I am Azariah, the son of the great
Hananiah, one of your relatives."
14 Then Tobit said to him, "Welcome! God save you, brother. Do
not feel bitter toward me, brother,
because I wanted to be sure about
your ancestry. It turns out that you
are a kinsman, and of good and noble lineage. For I knew Hananiah
and Nathan,[e] the two sons of
Shemeliah,[f] and they used to go
with me to Jerusalem and worshiped with me there, and were not
led astray. Your kindred are good
people; you come of good stock.
Hearty welcome!"
15 Then he added, "I will pay
you a drachma a day as wages, as
well as expenses for yourself and
my son. So go with my son, 16 and[g]
I will add something to your
wages." Raphael[h] answered, "I
will go with him; so do not fear. We
shall leave in good health and return to you in good health, because
the way is safe." 17 So Tobit[d] said
to him, "Blessings be upon you,
brother."
Then he called his son and said
to him, "Son, prepare supplies for
the journey and set out with your
brother. May God in heaven bring
you safely there and return you in
good health to me; and may his angel, my son, accompany you both
for your safety."
Before he went out to start his
journey, he kissed his father and
mother. Tobit then said to him,
"Have a safe journey."
18 But his mother[i] began to
weep, and said to Tobit, "Why is it
that you have sent my child away?
Is he not the staff of our hand as he
goes in and out before us? 19 Do not
heap money upon money, but let it
be a ransom for our child. 20 For
the life that is given to us by the
Lord is enough for us." 21 Tobit[h]
said to her, "Do not worry; our
child will leave in good health and
return to us in good health. Your
eyes will see him on the day when
he returns to you in good health.
Say no more! Do not fear for them,
my sister. 22 For a good angel will
accompany him; his journey will
be successful, and he will come
6 back in good health." 1 So she
stopped weeping.

Journey to Rages

The young man went out and the
angel went with him; 2 and the dog
came out with him and went along
with them. So they both journeyed
along, and when the first night
overtook them they camped by the
Tigris river. 3 Then the young man
went down to wash his feet in the
Tigris river. Suddenly a large fish
leaped up from the water and tried
to swallow the young man's foot,
and he cried out. 4 But the angel
said to the young man, "Catch hold
of the fish and hang on to it!" So
the young man grasped the fish

5.13 Tob 7.8
5.14 Phil 3.5; 1 Esd 9.21, 34; Lk 2.41
5.15 Mt 20.2
5.17 Ezra 8.21-23, 31; Ps 91.11-12; Dan 6.22; Acts 27.23-25; Gen 31.55
5.19 Mt 6.19-21
5.21 Phil 4.6
5.22 1 Chr 22.13; 2 Chr 20.20
6.2 Dan 10.4
6.3 Judg 19.21; Jn 13.5; Jon 1.17

[d] Gk *he* [e] Other ancient authorities read *Jathan* or *Nathamiah*
[f] Other ancient authorities read *Shemaiah*
[g] Other ancient authorities add *when you return safely* [h] Gk *He*
[i] Other ancient authorities add *Anna*

and drew it up on the land. 5 Then
the angel said to him, "Cut open
the fish and take out its gall, heart,
and liver. Keep them with you, but
throw away the intestines. For its
gall, heart, and liver are useful as
medicine." 6 So after cutting open
the fish the young man gathered
together the gall, heart, and liver;
then he roasted and ate some of
the fish, and kept some to be
salted.
The two continued on their way
together until they were near Media.[j] 7 Then the young man questioned the angel and said to him,
"Brother Azariah, what medicinal
value is there in the fish's heart
and liver, and in the gall?" 8 He replied, "As for the fish's heart and
liver, you must burn them to make
a smoke in the presence of a man
or woman afflicted by a demon or
evil spirit, and every affliction will
flee away and never remain with
that person any longer. 9 And as for
the gall, anoint a person's eyes
where white films have appeared
on them; blow upon them, upon
the white films, and the eyes[k] will
be healed."

Raphael's Instructions

10 When he entered Media and
already was approaching Ecbatana,[l] 11 Raphael said to the young
man, "Brother Tobias." "Here I
am," he answered. Then Raphael[m]
said to him, "We must stay this
night in the home of Raguel. He is
your relative, and he has a daughter named Sarah. 12 He has no male
heir and no daughter except Sarah
only, and you, as next of kin to her,
have before all other men a heredi-
tary claim on her. Also it is right for
you to inherit her father's possessions. Moreover, the girl is sensible, brave, and very beautiful, and
her father is a good man." 13 He
continued, "You have every right to
take her in marriage. So listen to
me, brother; tonight I will speak to
her father about the girl, so that we
may take her to be your bride.
When we return from Rages we will
celebrate her marriage. For I know
that Raguel can by no means keep
her from you or promise her to another man without incurring the
penalty of death according to the
decree of the book of Moses. Indeed he knows that you, rather
than any other man, are entitled to
marry his daughter. So now listen
to me, brother, and tonight we
shall speak concerning the girl and
arrange her engagement to you.
And when we return from Rages we
will take her and bring her back
with us to your house."
14 Then Tobias said in answer
to Raphael, "Brother Azariah, I
have heard that she already has
been married to seven husbands
and that they died in the bridal
chamber. On the night when they
went in to her, they would die. I
have heard people saying that it
was a demon that killed them. 15 It
does not harm her, but it kills anyone who desires to approach her.
So now, since I am the only son my
father has, I am afraid that I may
die and bring my father's and
mother's life down to their grave,
grieving for me—and they have no
other son to bury them."
16 But Raphael[m] said to him,
"Do you not remember your father's orders when he commanded
you to take a wife from your father's house? Now listen to me,
brother, and say no more about
this demon. Take her. I know that
this very night she will be given to
you in marriage. 17 When you enter
the bridal chamber, take some of
the fish's liver and heart, and put
them on the embers of the incense.
An odor will be given off; 18 the demon will smell it and flee, and will
never be seen near her any more.
Now when you are about to go to
bed with her, both of you must first
stand up and pray, imploring the
Lord of heaven that mercy and
safety may be granted to you. Do
not be afraid, for she was set apart
for you before the world was made.
You will save her, and she will go
with you. I presume that you will
have children by her, and they will

6.6 Jn 21.9
6.8 Tob 8.1-3
6.9 Rev 3.18; Tob 11.7-14
6.11 Tob 3.7
6.12 Tob 3.15; Deut 25.5-10; Ruth 3.8-13
6.13 Num 36.6-8; Gen 24.50-59
6.14 Tob 5.12; 3.8
6.15 Tob 3.15; Gen 37.35; 44.27-29; Tob 1.17; 4.3-4
6.16 Tob 4.12
6.18 Tob 8.1-3; Mk 9.29; Ezra 8.21; Gen 29.18

[j] Other ancient authorities read *Ecbatana*
[k] Gk *they* [l] Other ancient authorities read *Rages* [m] Gk *he*

be as brothers to you. Now say no
more!" When Tobias heard the
words of Raphael and learned that
she was his kinswoman,[n] related
through his father's lineage, he
loved her very much, and his heart
was drawn to her.

Arrival at Home of Raguel

7 Now when they[o] entered Ecbatana, Tobias[p] said to him,
"Brother Azariah, take me straight
to our brother Raguel." So he took
him to Raguel's house, where they
found him sitting beside the courtyard door. They greeted him first,
and he replied, "Joyous greetings,
brothers; welcome and good
health!" Then he brought them
into his house. 2 He said to his wife
Edna, "How much the young man
resembles my kinsman Tobit!"
3 Then Edna questioned them, saying, "Where are you from, brothers?" They answered, "We belong
to the descendants of Naphtali
who are exiles in Nineveh." 4 She
said to them, "Do you know our
kinsman Tobit?" And they replied,
"Yes, we know him." Then she
asked them, "Is he[q] in good
health?" 5 They replied, "He is
alive and in good health." And Tobias added, "He is my father!" 6 At
that Raguel jumped up and kissed
him and wept. 7 He also spoke to
him as follows, "Blessings on you,
my child, son of a good and noble
father!"[r] "O most miserable of calamities that such an upright and
beneficent man has become
blind!" He then embraced his kinsman Tobias and wept. 8 His wife
Edna also wept for him, and their
daughter Sarah likewise wept.
9 Then Raguel[p] slaughtered a ram
from the flock and received them
very warmly.

Marriage of Tobias and Sarah

When they had bathed and
washed themselves and had reclined to dine, Tobias said to Raphael, "Brother Azariah, ask Raguel to give me my kinswoman[n]
Sarah." 10 But Raguel overheard it
and said to the lad, "Eat and drink,
and be merry tonight. For no one
except you, brother, has the right
to marry my daughter Sarah. Likewise I am not at liberty to give her
to any other man than yourself, because you are my nearest relative.
But let me explain to you the true
situation more fully, my child. 11 I
have given her to seven men of our
kinsmen, and all died on the night
when they went in to her. But now,
my child, eat and drink, and the
Lord will act on behalf of you
both." But Tobias said, "I will neither eat nor drink anything until
you settle the things that pertain to
me." So Raguel said, "I will do so.
She is given to you in accordance
with the decree in the book of Moses, and it has been decreed from
heaven that she be given to you.
Take your kinswoman;[n] from now
on you are her brother and she is
your sister. She is given to you from
today and forever. May the Lord of
heaven, my child, guide and prosper you both this night and grant
you mercy and peace." 12 Then Raguel summoned his daughter
Sarah. When she came to him he
took her by the hand and gave her
to Tobias,[s] saying, "Take her to be
your wife in accordance with the
law and decree written in the book
of Moses. Take her and bring her
safely to your father. And may the
God of heaven prosper your journey with his peace." 13 Then he
called her mother and told her to
bring writing material; and he
wrote out a copy of a marriage con-
tract, to the effect that he gave her
to him as wife according to the decree of the law of Moses. 14 Then
they began to eat and drink.
15 Raguel called his wife Edna
and said to her, "Sister, get the
other room ready, and take her
there." 16 So she went and made
the bed in the room as he had told
her, and brought Sarah[t] there.
She wept for her daughter.[t] Then,

7.1 Tob 5.12; Gen 18.1
7.3 Tob 1.1-5; Gen 29.11-14
7.7 Tob 2.10
7.8 Gen 18.7-8; Lk 15.23
7.9 Lk 7.36,44
7.10 Lk 12.19; 1 Cor 15.32; Deut 25.5-10
7.11 Tob 3.8; Gen 24.33; Num 36.6-8; Deut 25.5-10; Gen 20.1-5, 12; 2.24; 2 Pet 1.2
7.12 Gen 24.60-61; 31.55
7.14 Mt 22.4; Jn 2.1-2,10

[n] Gk *sister* [o] Other ancient authorities read *he* [p] Gk *he* [q] Other ancient authorities add *alive and* [r] Other ancient authorities add *When he heard that Tobit had lost his sight, he was stricken with grief and wept. Then he said,* [s] Gk *him* [t] Gk *her*

wiping away the tears,[u] she said to
her, "Take courage, my daughter;
the Lord of heaven grant you joy[v]
in place of your sorrow. Take courage, my daughter." Then she went
out.

Tobias Routs the Demon

8 When they had finished eating
and drinking they wanted to
retire; so they took the young man
and brought him into the bedroom. 2 Then Tobias remembered
the words of Raphael, and he took
the fish's liver and heart out of the
bag where he had them and put
them on the embers of the incense.
3 The odor of the fish so repelled
the demon that he fled to the remotest parts[w] of Egypt. But Raphael followed him, and at once
bound him there hand and foot.
4 When the parents[x] had gone
out and shut the door of the room,
Tobias got out of bed and said to
Sarah,[y] "Sister, get up, and let us
pray and implore our Lord that he
grant us mercy and safety." 5 So she
got up, and they began to pray and
implore that they might be kept
safe. Tobias[z] began by saying,

"Blessed are you, O God of
our ancestors,
and blessed is your name
in all generations
forever.
Let the heavens and the
whole creation bless
you forever.
6 You made Adam, and for
him you made his wife
Eve
as a helper and support.
From the two of them the
human race has sprung.
You said, 'It is not good that
the man should be
alone;
let us make a helper for
him like himself.'
7 I now am taking this
kinswoman of mine,
not because of lust,
but with sincerity.
Grant that she and I may
find mercy
and that we may grow old
together."

8 And they both said, "Amen,
Amen." 9 Then they went to sleep
for the night.
But Raguel arose and called his
servants to him, and they went and
dug a grave, 10 for he said, "It is
possible that he will die and we
will become an object of ridicule
and derision." 11 When they had
finished digging the grave, Raguel
went into his house and called his
wife, 12 saying, "Send one of the
maids and have her go in to see if
he is alive. But if he is dead, let us
bury him without anyone knowing
it." 13 So they sent the maid, lit a
lamp, and opened the door; and
she went in and found them sound
asleep together. 14 Then the maid
came out and informed them that
he was alive and that nothing was
wrong. 15 So they blessed the God
of heaven, and Raguel[x] said,

"Blessed are you, O God,
with every pure
blessing;
let all your chosen ones
bless you.[a]
Let them bless you forever.
16 Blessed are you because you
have made me glad.
It has not turned out as I
expected,
but you have dealt with us
according to your great
mercy.
17 Blessed are you because you
had compassion
on two only children.
Be merciful to them,
O Master, and keep
them safe;
bring their lives to
fulfillment
in happiness and mercy."

18 Then he ordered his servants to
fill in the grave before daybreak.

Wedding Feast

19 After this he asked his wife
to bake many loaves of bread; and
he went out to the herd and
brought two steers and four rams

8.3 Tob 3.8; 6.8; Rev 20.2 **8.4** Ezra 8.21 **8.5** Ps 72.18-19; Jdt 13.17; Ps 148.1-13 **8.6** Gen 2.7, 18-23; 3.20; 5.1-5; Acts 17.26

8.8 Ps 72.19 **8.10** Tob 3.15 **8.12** Tob 3.8 **8.15** Ps 105.1-2,6 **8.16** Neh 9.31 **8.17** Ps 27.7; 86.15-16; 128 **8.19** Gen 18.6; Mt 22.2-4

u Other ancient authorities read *the tears of her daughter* v Other ancient authorities read *favor* w Or *fled through the air to the parts* x Gk *they* y Gk *her* z Gk *He*
a Other ancient authorities lack this line

and ordered them to be slaughtered. So they began to make preparations. 20 Then he called for Tobias and swore on oath to him in
these words:[b] "You shall not leave
here for fourteen days, but shall
stay here eating and drinking with
me; and you shall cheer up my
daughter, who has been depressed.
21 Take at once half of what I own
and return in safety to your father;
the other half will be yours when
my wife and I die. Take courage,
my child. I am your father and
Edna is your mother, and we belong to you as well as to your wife[c]
now and forever. Take courage, my
child."

The Money Recovered

9 Then Tobias called Raphael
and said to him, 2 "Brother Azariah, take four servants and two
camels with you and travel to
Rages. Go to the home of Gabael,
give him the bond, get the money,
and then bring him with you to the
wedding celebration. 4 For you
know that my father must be
counting the days, and if I delay
even one day I will upset him very
much. 3 You are witness to the oath
Raguel has sworn, and I cannot violate his oath."[d] 5 So Raphael with
the four servants and two camels
went to Rages in Media and stayed
with Gabael. Raphael[e] gave him
the bond and informed him that
Tobit's son Tobias had married
and was inviting him to the wedding celebration. So Gabael[f] got
up and counted out to him the
money bags, with their seals in-
tact; then they loaded them on the
camels.[g] 6 In the morning they
both got up early and went to the
wedding celebration. When they
came into Raguel's house they
found Tobias reclining at table. He
sprang up and greeted Gabael,[h]
who wept and blessed him with the
words, "Good and noble son of a
father good and noble, upright and
generous! May the Lord grant the
blessing of heaven to you and your
wife, and to your wife's father and
mother. Blessed be God, for I see
in Tobias the very image of my
cousin Tobit."

Anxiety of the Parents

10 Now, day by day, Tobit
kept counting how many
days Tobias[f] would need for going
and for returning. And when the
days had passed and his son did
not appear, 2 he said, "Is it possible
that he has been detained? Or that
Gabael has died, and there is no
one to give him the money?" 3 And
he began to worry. 4 His wife Anna
said, "My child has perished and is
no longer among the living." And
she began to weep and mourn for
her son, saying, 5 "Woe to me, my
child, the light of my eyes, that I let
you make the journey." 6 But Tobit
kept saying to her, "Be quiet and
stop worrying, my dear;[c] he is all
right. Probably something unexpected has happened there. The
man who went with him is trustworthy and is one of our own kin.
Do not grieve for him, my dear;[c]
he will soon be here." 7 She answered him, "Be quiet yourself!
Stop trying to deceive me! My child
has perished." She would rush out
every day and watch the road her
son had taken, and would heed no
one.[i] When the sun had set she
would go in and mourn and weep
all night long, getting no sleep at
all.

Tobias and Sarah Start for Home

Now when the fourteen days of
the wedding celebration had
ended that Raguel had sworn to
observe for his daughter, Tobias
came to him and said, "Send me
back, for I know that my father and
mother do not believe that they
will see me again. So I beg of you,
father, to let me go so that I may
return to my own father. I have already explained to you how I left
him." 8 But Raguel said to Tobias,
"Stay, my child, stay with me; I will

[b] Other ancient authorities read *Tobias and said to him* [c] Gk *sister* [d] In other ancient authorities verse 3 precedes verse 4 [e] Gk *He* [f] Gk *he* [g] Other ancient authorities lack *on the camels* [h] Gk *him*
[i] Other ancient authorities read *and she would eat nothing*

8.20 Judg 14.12; Tob 11.19; 3.10
8.21 Lk 15.12
9.2 Tob 5.13; 4.20; 5.3
9.4 Tob 10.1
9.3 Tob 8.20
9.5 Gen 24.10; 37.25
9.6 Tob 8.19; Ps 128.5; Gen 5.3
10.1 Tob 9.4
10.4 Gen 37.35
10.5 Gen 43.1-14
10.6 Mt 6.25; Phil 4.6; Tob 5.13-14
10.7 Lk 15.20; Ps 6.6; Tob 8.20; Lk 15.18

send messengers to your father Tobit and they will inform him about you." 9 But he said, "No! I beg you to send me back to my father." 10 So Raguel promptly gave Tobias his wife Sarah, as well as half of all his property: male and female slaves, oxen and sheep, donkeys and camels, clothing, money, and household goods. 11 Then he saw them safely off; he embraced Tobias[j] and said, "Farewell, my child; have a safe journey. The Lord of heaven prosper you and your wife Sarah, and may I see children of yours before I die." 12 Then he kissed his daughter Sarah and said to her, "My daughter, honor your father-in-law and your mother-in-law,[k] since from now on they are as much your parents as those who gave you birth. Go in peace, daughter, and may I hear a good report about you as long as I live." Then he bade them farewell and let them go. Then Edna said to Tobias, "My child and dear brother, the Lord of heaven bring you back safely, and may I live long enough to see children of you and of my daughter Sarah before I die. In the sight of the Lord I entrust my daughter to you; do nothing to grieve her all the days of your life. Go in peace, my child. From now on I am your mother and Sarah is your beloved wife.[l] May we all prosper together all the days of our lives." Then she kissed them both and saw them safely off. 13 Tobias parted from Raguel with happiness and joy, praising the Lord of heaven and earth, King over all, because he had made his journey a success. Finally, he blessed Raguel and his wife Edna, and said, "I have been commanded by the Lord to honor you all the days of my life."[m]

Homeward Journey

11 When they came near to Kaserin, which is opposite Nineveh, Raphael said, 2 "You are aware of how we left your father. 3 Let us run ahead of your wife and prepare the house while they are still on the way." 4 As they went on together Raphael[n] said to him, "Have the gall ready." And the dog[o] went along behind them.

5 Meanwhile Anna sat looking intently down the road by which her son would come. 6 When she caught sight of him coming, she said to his father, "Look, your son is coming, and the man who went with him!"

Tobit's Sight Restored

7 Raphael said to Tobias, before he had approached his father, "I know that his eyes will be opened. 8 Smear the gall of the fish on his eyes; the medicine will make the white films shrink and peel off from his eyes, and your father will regain his sight and see the light."

9 Then Anna ran up to her son and threw her arms around him, saying, "Now that I have seen you, my child, I am ready to die." And she wept. 10 Then Tobit got up and came stumbling out through the courtyard door. Tobias went up to him, 11 with the gall of the fish in his hand, and holding him firmly, he blew into his eyes, saying, "Take courage, father." With this he applied the medicine on his eyes, 12 and it made them smart.[m] 13 Next, with both his hands he peeled off the white films from the corners of his eyes. Then Tobit[n] saw his son and[p] threw his arms around him, 14 and he wept and said to him, "I see you, my son, the light of my eyes!" Then he said,

"Blessed be God,
and blessed be his great name,
and blessed be all his holy angels.
May his holy name be blessed[q]
throughout all the ages.
15 Though he afflicted me,

10.10 Gen 24.59 **10.11** Tob 5.17; Ezra 1.2; Jdt 5.8; Ps 128.6; Prov 17.6 **10.12** Ex 20.12; 1 Sam 20.42; Mk 5.34; Eph 5.25,28; Col 3.19; Gen 31.55 **10.13** Jdt 9.12; 1 Tim 1.17; Tob 5.22; Ex 20.12

11.4 Tob 6.5-6, 2 **11.6** Lk 15.20 **11.7** Tob 2.10; 3.17 **11.8** Tob 6.9 **11.9** Lk 2.28-32 **11.14** Ps 72.18-19; Lk 9.26 **11.15** Job 34.28; Ps 9.12-13; Tob 5.22; 9.5

[j] Gk *him* [k] Other ancient authorities lack parts of *Then . . . mother-in-law* [l] Gk *sister* [m] Lat: Meaning of Gk uncertain [n] Gk *he* [o] Codex Sinaiticus reads *And the Lord* [p] Other ancient authorities lack *saw his son and* [q] Codex Sinaiticus reads *May his great name be upon us and blessed be all the angels*

he has had mercy upon
me.[r]
Now I see my son Tobias!"
So Tobit went in rejoicing and
praising God at the top of his voice.
Tobias reported to his father that
his journey had been successful,
that he had brought the money,
that he had married Raguel's
daughter Sarah, and that she was,
indeed, on her way there, very near
to the gate of Nineveh.
16 Then Tobit, rejoicing and
praising God, went out to meet his
daughter-in-law at the gate of Nineveh. When the people of Nineveh
saw him coming, walking along in
full vigor and with no one leading
him, they were amazed. 17 Before
them all, Tobit acknowledged that
God had been merciful to him and
had restored his sight. When Tobit
met Sarah the wife of his son Tobias, he blessed her saying, "Come
in, my daughter, and welcome.
Blessed be your God who has
brought you to us, my daughter.
Blessed be your father and your
mother, blessed be my son Tobias,
and blessed be you, my daughter.
Come in now to your home, and
welcome, with blessing and joy.
Come in, my daughter." So on that
day there was rejoicing among all
the Jews who were in Nineveh.
18 Ahikar and his nephew Nadab
were also present to share Tobit's
joy. With merriment they celebrated Tobias's wedding feast for
seven days, and many gifts were
given to him.[s]

Raphael's Wages

12 When the wedding celebration was ended, Tobit
called his son Tobias and said to
him, "My child, see to paying the
wages of the man who went with
you, and give him a bonus as well."
2 He replied, "Father, how much
shall I pay him? It would do no
harm to give him half of the possessions brought back with me.
3 For he has led me back to you
safely, he cured my wife, he
brought the money back with me,
and he healed you. How much extra shall I give him as a bonus?"
4 Tobit said, "He deserves, my
child, to receive half of all that he
brought back." 5 So Tobias[t] called
him and said, "Take for your wages
half of all that you brought back,
and farewell."

Raphael's Exhortation

6 Then Raphael[t] called the two
of them privately and said to them,
"Bless God and acknowledge him
in the presence of all the living for
the good things he has done for
you. Bless and sing praise to his
name. With fitting honor declare to
all people the deeds[u] of God. Do
not be slow to acknowledge him.
7 It is good to conceal the secret of
a king, but to acknowledge and reveal the works of God, and with fitting honor to acknowledge him. Do
good and evil will not overtake you.
8 Prayer with fasting[v] is good, but
better than both is almsgiving with
righteousness. A little with righteousness is better than wealth
with wrongdoing.[w] It is better to
give alms than to lay up gold. 9 For
almsgiving saves from death and
purges away every sin. Those who
give alms will enjoy a full life,
10 but those who commit sin and
do wrong are their own worst enemies.

Raphael Discloses His Identity

11 "I will now declare the whole
truth to you and will conceal nothing from you. Already I have declared it to you when I said, 'It is
good to conceal the secret of a
king, but to reveal with due honor
the works of God.' 12 So now when
you and Sarah prayed, it was I who
brought and read[x] the record of
your prayer before the glory of the
Lord, and likewise whenever you
would bury the dead. 13 And that
time when you did not hesitate to
get up and leave your dinner to go
and bury the dead, 14 I was sent to
you to test you. And at the same

11.16 Acts 3.8,10
11.17 Mk 10.47-48; 1 Sam 25.32; 1 Kings 10.9
11.18 Tob 1.21-22; 8.20; 14.10
12.1 Tob 5.15-16
12.6 Tob 5.4; Ps 52.9; 68.4; 9.11
12.8 Ezra 8.23; Mt 6.1-18; Acts 10.2; Prov 15.16
12.9 Sir 3.30
12.11 Tob 12.7
12.12 Tob 3.1-6, 11-15; Rev 8.3
12.14 Gen 22.1; Tob 3.17

r Lat: Gk lacks this line
s Other ancient authorities lack parts of this sentence
t Gk *he*
u Gk *words*; other ancient authorities read *words of the deeds*
v Codex Sinaiticus *with sincerity*
w Lat
x Lat: Gk lacks *and read*

time God sent me to heal you and
Sarah your daughter-in-law. 15 I am
Raphael, one of the seven angels
who stand ready and enter before
the glory of the Lord."
16 The two of them were
shaken; they fell face down, for
they were afraid. 17 But he said to
them, "Do not be afraid; peace be
with you. Bless God forevermore.
18 As for me, when I was with you,
I was not acting on my own will,
but by the will of God. Bless him
each and every day; sing his
praises. 19 Although you were
watching me, I really did not eat or
drink anything—but what you saw
was a vision. 20 So now get up from
the ground,[y] and acknowledge
God. See, I am ascending to him
who sent me. Write down all these
things that have happened to you."
And he ascended. 21 Then they
stood up, and could see him no
more. 22 They kept blessing God
and singing his praises, and they
acknowledged God for these marvelous deeds of his, when an angel
of God had appeared to them.

Tobit's Thanksgiving to God

13 Then Tobit[z] said:
"Blessed be God who
lives forever,
because his kingdom[a]
lasts throughout all
ages.
2 For he afflicts, and he shows
mercy;
he leads down to Hades in
the lowest regions of
the earth,
and he brings up from the
great abyss,[b]
and there is nothing that
can escape his hand.
3 Acknowledge him before the
nations, O children of
Israel;
for he has scattered you
among them.
4 He has shown you his
greatness even there.
Exalt him in the presence of
every living being,
because he is our Lord and
he is our God;
he is our Father and he is
God forever.
5 He will afflict[c] you for your
iniquities,
but he will again show
mercy on all of you.
He will gather you from all
the nations
among whom you have
been scattered.
6 If you turn to him with all
your heart and with all
your soul,
to do what is true before
him,
then he will turn to you
and will no longer hide his
face from you.
So now see what he has
done for you;
acknowledge him at the
top of your voice.
Bless the Lord of
righteousness,
and exalt the King of the
ages.[d]
In the land of my exile I
acknowledge him,
and show his power and
majesty to a nation of
sinners:
'Turn back, you sinners, and
do what is right before
him;
perhaps he may look with
favor upon you and
show you mercy.'
7 As for me, I exalt my God,
and my soul rejoices in the
King of heaven.
8 Let all people speak of his
majesty,
and acknowledge him in
Jerusalem.
9 O Jerusalem, the holy city,
he afflicted[e] you for the
deeds of your hands,[f]
but will again have mercy
on the children of the
righteous.

12.15 Mt 18.10; Rev 8.2 **12.16** Lk 2.9 **12.17** Mt 28.5,10 **12.18** Jn 5.30; 6.38 **12.20** Rev 19.10; 22.9; Jn 20.17; Rev 1.11 **12.21** Acts 1.9 **13.1** Ps 89.52; Rev 11.15 **13.2** 1 Sam 2.6-8; Lk 1.52-53 **13.3** Ps 96.3,10; Ezek 36.19 **13.4** Deut 6.4; Isa 63.16; 64.8; Mt 6.9 **13.5** Ezek 28.25; 34.10; Zech 10.9-10 **13.6** Isa 45.22; Deut 6.5; Mt 22.37; Ps 86.16; 22.24; Sir 36.22; Ezek 18.30-32; 2 Chr 6.38-39 **13.7** Isa 25.1; 1 Tim 1.17 **13.8** Ps 68.34 **13.9** Neh 11.1; Isa 48.2; Deut 29.22

y Other ancient authorities read *now bless the Lord on earth* z Gk *he*
a Other ancient authorities read *forever, and his kingdom* b Gk *from destruction*
c Other ancient authorities read *He afflicted*
d The lacuna in codex Sinaiticus, verses 6b to 10a, is filled in from other ancient authorities
e Other ancient authorities read *will afflict*
f Other ancient authorities read *your children*

10 Acknowledge the Lord, for
he is good,[g]
and bless the King of the
ages,
so that his tent[h] may be
rebuilt in you in joy.
May he cheer all those
within you who are
captives,
and love all those within
you who are distressed,
to all generations forever.
11 A bright light will shine to
all the ends of the
earth;
many nations will come to
you from far away,
the inhabitants of the
remotest parts of the
earth to your holy
name,
bearing gifts in their hands
for the King of heaven.
Generation after generation
will give joyful praise in
you,
the name of the chosen
city will endure forever.
12 Cursed are all who speak a
harsh word against you;
cursed are all who conquer
you
and pull down your walls,
all who overthrow your
towers
and set your homes on fire.
But blessed forever will be
all who revere you.[i]
13 Go, then, and rejoice over
the children of the
righteous,
for they will be gathered
together
and will praise the Lord of
the ages.
14 Happy are those who love
you,
and happy are those who
rejoice in your
prosperity.
Happy also are all people
who grieve with you
because of your afflictions;
for they will rejoice with you
and witness all your glory
forever.
15 My soul blesses[j] the Lord,
the great King!

13.10 Ps 106.1; 118.1; Tob 13.6 **13.11** Isa 60.1-3; Ps 68.29; Isa 60.4-9; 1 Kings 11.13,32,36 **13.12** Gen 12.3; Num 24.9; 2 Chr 36.19; Ps 128.4 **13.13** 2 Esd 8.39; Jer 31.7-8 **13.14** Rom 12.15 **13.15** Ps 103.1

13.16 Isa 10.20-22; Tob 13.7,11; Isa 54.11-12; Rev 21.18-21 **13.17** Ps 147.1-2; Rev 19.1; Ps 72.18-19 **14.2** Tob 1.3; 13.8 **14.4** Nah 2.1-13; Zeph 2.13-15; Isa 55.10-11; Mt 5.17-18; Eph 1.10; Jer 25.11; Lk 13.35; Mt 23.28; 2 Kings 25.9; Mk 13.2

16 For Jerusalem will be
built[k] as his house for
all ages.
How happy I will be if a
remnant of my
descendants should
survive
to see your glory and
acknowledge the King
of heaven.
The gates of Jerusalem will
be built with sapphire
and emerald,
and all your walls with
precious stones.
The towers of Jerusalem will
be built with gold,
and their battlements with
pure gold.
The streets of Jerusalem will
be paved
with ruby and with stones
of Ophir.
17 The gates of Jerusalem will
sing hymns of joy,
and all her houses will cry,
'Hallelujah!
Blessed be the God of Israel!'
and the blessed will bless
the holy name forever
and ever."

Tobit's Final Counsel

14 So ended Tobit's words of
praise.
2 Tobit[l] died in peace when he
was one hundred twelve years old,
and was buried with great honor in
Nineveh. He was sixty-two[m] years
old when he lost his eyesight, and
after regaining it he lived in prosperity, giving alms and continually
blessing God and acknowledging
God's majesty.
3 When he was about to die, he
called his son Tobias and the seven
sons of Tobias[n] and gave this command: "My son, take your children
4 and hurry off to Media, for I believe the word of God that Nahum
spoke about Nineveh, that all
these things will take place and

[g] Other ancient authorities read *Lord worthily*
[h] Or *tabernacle* [i] Other ancient authorities read *who build you up* [j] Or *O my soul, bless*
[k] Other ancient authorities add *for a city*
[l] Gk *He* [m] Other ancient authorities read *fifty-eight* [n] Lat: Gk lacks *and the seven sons of Tobias*

overtake Assyria and Nineveh. Indeed, everything that was spoken by the prophets of Israel, whom God sent, will occur. None of all their words will fail, but all will come true at their appointed times. So it will be safer in Media than in Assyria and Babylon. For I know and believe that whatever God has said will be fulfilled and will come true; not a single word of the prophecies will fail. All of our kindred, inhabitants of the land of Israel, will be scattered and taken as captives from the good land; and the whole land of Israel will be desolate, even Samaria and Jerusalem will be desolate. And the temple of God in it will be burned to the ground, and it will be desolate for a while.[o]

5 "But God will again have mercy on them, and God will bring them back into the land of Israel; and they will rebuild the temple of God, but not like the first one until the period when the times of fulfillment shall come. After this they all will return from their exile and will rebuild Jerusalem in splendor; and in it the temple of God will be rebuilt, just as the prophets of Israel have said concerning it. 6 Then the nations in the whole world will all be converted and worship God in truth. They will all abandon their idols, which deceitfully have led them into their error; 7 and in righteousness they will praise the eternal God. All the Israelites who are saved in those days and are truly mindful of God will be gathered together; they will go to Jerusalem and live in safety forever in the land of Abraham, and it will be given over to them. Those who sincerely love God will rejoice, but those who commit sin and injustice will vanish from all the earth. 8,9 So now, my children, I command you, serve God faithfully and do what is pleasing in his sight. Your children are also to be commanded to do what is right and to give alms, and to be mindful of God and to bless his name at all times with sincerity and with all their strength. So now, my son, leave Nineveh; do not remain here. 10 On whatever day you bury your mother beside me, do not stay overnight within the confines of the city. For I see that there is much wickedness within it, and that much deceit is practiced within it, while the people are without shame. See, my son, what Nadab did to Ahikar who had reared him. Was he not, while still alive, brought down into the earth? For God repaid him to his face for this shameful treatment. Ahikar came out into the light, but Nadab went into the eternal darkness, because he tried to kill Ahikar. Because he gave alms, Ahikar[p] escaped the fatal trap that Nadab had set for him, but Nadab fell into it himself, and was destroyed. 11 So now, my children, see what almsgiving accomplishes, and what injustice does — it brings death! But now my breath fails me."

Death of Tobit and Anna

Then they laid him on his bed, and he died; and he received an honorable funeral. 12 When Tobias's mother died, he buried her beside his father. Then he and his wife and children[q] returned to Media and settled in Ecbatana with Raguel his father-in-law. 13 He treated his parents-in-law[r] with great respect in their old age, and buried them in Ecbatana of Media. He inherited both the property of Raguel and that of his father Tobit. 14 He died highly respected at the age of one hundred seventeen[s] years. 15 Before he died he heard[t] of the destruction of Nineveh, and he saw its prisoners being led into

14.5 Jer 29.10; Ezra 3.8-13; 6.13-15; Jer 27.22 **14.6** Jer 29.10-14; Zech 8.20-23 **14.7** Ps 90.1-2; Sus 1.42; Gen 13, 14-17; 17.8; Ps 37.20 **14.8,9** Josh 24.14-15; Tob 14.4 **14.10** Jon 1.2; Zeph 3.5; Rom 1.27; Tob 1.21; Mt 8.12; Jude 13; Tob 4.7-11 **14.11** Rom 6.23; 1 Jn 5.16 **14.12** Tob 14.10; 3.7; 7.6 **14.13** Prov 23.22

[o] Lat: Other ancient authorities read *of God will be in distress and will be burned for a while* [p] Gk *he*; other ancient authorities read *Manasses* [q] Codex Sinaiticus lacks *and children* [r] Gk *them*
[s] Other authorities read other numbers
[t] Codex Sinaiticus reads *saw and heard*

Media, those whom King Cyaxares[u] of Media had taken captive. Tobias[v] praised God for all he had done to the people of Nineveh and Assyria; before he died he rejoiced over Nineveh, and he blessed the Lord God forever and ever. Amen.[w]

14.15 Tob 14.4; Ps 72.18-19

[u]Cn: Codex Sinaiticus *Ahikar*; other ancient authorities read *Nebuchadnezzar and Ahasuerus* [v]Gk *He* [w]Other ancient authorities lack *Amen*

Judith

Title and Background

The title of this book comes from the main character, Judith, who reportedly killed Holofernes, the commander of the "Assyrian" (actually Babylonian) army. The book tells of events around the time of the Babylonian Captivity, though its historical accuracy is highly questionable.

Author and Date of Writing

The author of Judith is unknown, but was most likely a Jew, as the book probably was written in Hebrew. Scholarly consensus dates the writing of Judith in the middle of the second century B.C.

Theme and Message

Judith is a folktale about a godly, law-abiding Israelite widow who takes it upon herself to save her city. Holofernes and his army besiege the possibly fictitious city of Bethulia, where Judith lives. Through various deceptive measures, Judith rescues her people. The book teaches that God watches over, protects, and delivers those who are obedient to him.

Outline

I. The Campaign of Nebuchadnezzar against Arphaxad (1.1–16)
II. The Campaign of Nebuchadnezzar against the West (2.1—3.9)
III. The Campaign of Nebuchadnezzar against Judea (4.1—7.32)
  A. Prayer of the Israelites (4.1–15)
  B. Advice of Achior to Holofernes (5.1—6.20)
  C. Siege of Bethulia (7.1–32)
IV. Deliverance of the Israelites by Judith (8.1—16.25)
  A. Her Preparations (8.1—9.14)
  B. Her Deception and Killing of Holofernes (10.1—15.7)
  C. The Celebration of Victory (15.8—16.25)

Arphaxad Fortifies Ecbatana

1 It was the twelfth year of the
reign of Nebuchadnezzar, who
ruled over the Assyrians in the
great city of Nineveh. In those days
Arphaxad ruled over the Medes in
Ecbatana. 2 He built walls around
Ecbatana with hewn stones three
cubits thick and six cubits long; he
made the walls seventy cubits high
and fifty cubits wide. 3 At its gates
he raised towers one hundred cubits high and sixty cubits wide at
the foundations. 4 He made its
gates seventy cubits high and forty
cubits wide to allow his armies to
march out in force and his infantry
to form their ranks. 5 Then King
Nebuchadnezzar made war against
King Arphaxad in the great plain
that is on the borders of Ragau.
6 There rallied to him all the people
of the hill country and all those
who lived along the Euphrates, the
Tigris, and the Hydaspes, and, on
the plain, Arioch, king of the Ely-
means. Thus, many nations joined
the forces of the Chaldeans.[a]

Nebuchadnezzar Issues Ultimatum

7 Then Nebuchadnezzar, king
of the Assyrians, sent messengers
to all who lived in Persia and to all
who lived in the west, those who
lived in Cilicia and Damascus,
Lebanon and Antilebanon, and all
who lived along the seacoast, 8 and
those among the nations of Carmel

1.1 2 Kings 24.11-12; Jdt 1.13,15; Ezra 6.2; Tob 3.7
1.5 Jdt 1.15
1.6 Gen 1.14; 2 Kings 24.7
1.7 1 Macc 11.14; Acts 15.23; 2 Sam 8.5-6; Jer 49.23-24; Acts 9.2-3; Deut 1.7; Ps 29.5-6
1.8 1 Sam 25.2; 1 Kings 18.19-20; Jer 46.18; Gen 31.21-25

[a] Syr: Gk *Cheleoudites*

and Gilead, and Upper Galilee and
the great plain of Esdraelon, 9 and
all who were in Samaria and its
towns, and beyond the Jordan as
far as Jerusalem and Bethany and
Chelous and Kadesh and the river
of Egypt, and Tahpanhes and Ra-
amses and the whole land of Goshen, 10 even beyond Tanis and
Memphis, and all who lived in
Egypt as far as the borders of Ethiopia. 11 But all who lived in the
whole region disregarded the summons of Nebuchadnezzar, king of
the Assyrians, and refused to join
him in the war; for they were not
afraid of him, but regarded him as
only one man.[b] So they sent back
his messengers empty-handed and
in disgrace.
12 Then Nebuchadnezzar became very angry with this whole region, and swore by his throne and
kingdom that he would take revenge on the whole territory of Cilicia and Damascus and Syria, that
he would kill with his sword also
all the inhabitants of the land of
Moab, and the people of Ammon,
and all Judea, and every one in
Egypt, as far as the coasts of the
two seas.

Arphaxad Is Defeated

13 In the seventeenth year he
led his forces against King Arphaxad and defeated him in battle,
overthrowing the whole army of Arphaxad and all his cavalry and all
his chariots. 14 Thus he took possession of his towns and came to
Ecbatana, captured its towers,
plundered its markets, and turned
its glory into disgrace. 15 He captured Arphaxad in the mountains
of Ragau and struck him down
with his spears, thus destroying
him once and for all. 16 Then he returned to Nineveh, he and all his
combined forces, a vast body of
troops; and there he and his forces
rested and feasted for one hundred
twenty days.

The Expedition against the West

2 In the eighteenth year, on the
twenty-second day of the first
month, there was talk in the palace
of Nebuchadnezzar, king of the Assyrians, about carrying out his revenge on the whole region, just as
he had said. 2 He summoned all his
ministers and all his nobles and set
before them his secret plan and recounted fully, with his own lips, all
the wickedness of the region.[c]
3 They decided that every one who
had not obeyed his command
should be destroyed.
4 When he had completed his
plan, Nebuchadnezzar, king of the
Assyrians, called Holofernes, the
chief general of his army, second
only to himself, and said to him,
5 "Thus says the Great King, the
lord of the whole earth: Leave my
presence and take with you men
confident in their strength, one
hundred twenty thousand foot soldiers and twelve thousand cavalry.
6 March out against all the land to
the west, because they disobeyed
my orders. 7 Tell them to prepare
earth and water, for I am coming
against them in my anger, and will
cover the whole face of the earth
with the feet of my troops, to
whom I will hand them over to be
plundered. 8 Their wounded shall
fill their ravines and gullies, and
the swelling river shall be filled
with their dead. 9 I will lead them
away captive to the ends of the
whole earth. 10 You shall go and
seize all their territory for me in advance. They must yield themselves
to you, and you shall hold them for
me until the day of their punishment. 11 But to those who resist
show no mercy, but hand them
over to slaughter and plunder
throughout your whole region.
12 For as I live, and by the power of
my kingdom, what I have spoken I
will accomplish by my own hand.
13 And you—take care not to transgress any of your lord's commands,
but carry them out exactly as I
have ordered you; do it without delay."

Campaign of Holofernes

14 So Holofernes left the presence of his lord, and summoned all

1.9 Mk 11.1, 11-12; Jn 11.1; Jer 43.7-9; Gen 47.11; Ex 1.11; Gen 46.28-29
1.10 Jer 2.16; 44.1
1.11 Mk 12.3
1.12 Dan 3.19
1.13 Jdt 1.1
1.14 Jdt 1.1
1.16 2 Kings 19.36; Esth 1.4
2.1 Jdt 1.12
2.3 Dan 3.4-6
2.4 Jdt 4.1; 5.1
2.5 Jdt 11.7; 2 Chr 12.3; Jdt 7.2
2.6 2 Chr 20.1-2
2.7 Gen 1.29; Ezek 38.20, 11-13
2.9 2 Kings 7.6; 25.11
2.11 Deut 7.2; Isa 47.6
2.13 Jer 4.6; 3 Macc 5.42

[b] Or *a man* [c] Meaning of Gk uncertain

the commanders, generals, and officers of the Assyrian army. 15 He
mustered the picked troops by divisions as his lord had ordered him
to do, one hundred twenty thousand of them, together with twelve
thousand archers on horseback,
16 and he organized them as a great
army is marshaled for a campaign.
17 He took along a vast number of
camels and donkeys and mules for
transport, and innumerable sheep
and oxen and goats for food; 18 also
ample rations for everyone, and a
huge amount of gold and silver
from the royal palace.
19 Then he set out with his
whole army, to go ahead of King
Nebuchadnezzar and to cover the
whole face of the earth to the west
with their chariots and cavalry and
picked foot soldiers. 20 Along with
them went a mixed crowd like a
swarm of locusts, like the dust[d] of
the earth—a multitude that could
not be counted.
21 They marched for three days
from Nineveh to the plain of Bec-
tileth, and camped opposite Bec-
tileth near the mountain that is to
the north of Upper Cilicia. 22 From
there Holofernes[e] took his whole
army, the infantry, cavalry, and
chariots, and went up into the hill
country. 23 He ravaged Put and
Lud, and plundered all the Rassi-
sites and the Ishmaelites on the
border of the desert, south of the
country of the Chelleans. 24 Then
he followed[f] the Euphrates and
passed through Mesopotamia and
destroyed all the fortified towns
along the brook Abron, as far as
the sea. 25 He also seized the territory of Cilicia, and killed everyone
who resisted him. Then he came to
the southern borders of Japheth,
facing Arabia. 26 He surrounded all
the Midianites, and burned their
tents and plundered their sheepfolds. 27 Then he went down into
the plain of Damascus during the
wheat harvest, and burned all their
fields and destroyed their flocks
and herds and sacked their towns
and ravaged their lands and put all
their young men to the sword.
28 So fear and dread of him fell
upon all the people who lived
along the seacoast, at Sidon and
Tyre, and those who lived in Sur
and Ocina and all who lived in
Jamnia. Those who lived in Azotus
and Ascalon feared him greatly.

Entreaties for Peace

3 They therefore sent messengers to him to sue for peace in
these words: 2 "We, the servants of
Nebuchadnezzar, the Great King,
lie prostrate before you. Do with us
whatever you will. 3 See, our buildings and all our land and all our
wheat fields and our flocks and
herds and all our encampments[g]
lie before you; do with them as you
please. 4 Our towns and their inhabitants are also your slaves;
come and deal with them as you
see fit."
5 The men came to Holofernes
and told him all this. 6 Then he
went down to the seacoast with his
army and stationed garrisons in the
fortified towns and took picked
men from them as auxiliaries.
7 These people and all in the countryside welcomed him with garlands and dances and tambourines. 8 Yet he demolished all their
shrines[h] and cut down their sacred groves; for he had been commissioned to destroy all the gods of
the land, so that all nations should
worship Nebuchadnezzar alone,
and that all their dialects and
tribes should call upon him as a
god.
9 Then he came toward Esdraelon, near Dothan, facing the great
ridge of Judea; 10 he camped between Geba and Scythopolis, and
remained for a whole month in order to collect all the supplies for
his army.

Judea on the Alert

4 When the Israelites living in
Judea heard of everything that
Holofernes, the general of Nebuchadnezzar, the king of the Assyrians, had done to the nations, and
how he had plundered and de-

2.15 Jdt 2.5 **2.17** Gen 37.25; 1 Kings 10.2; Ex 9.5; 1 Chr 12.40; Zech 14.15 **2.20** Judg 6.5; Joel 1.4; 2.4-5; Nah 3.15-16; Gen 13.16 **2.21** Jdt 1.7 **2.23** Isa 66.19; Ezek 30.5; Gen 25.12-17; 37.25-28 **2.25** Gen 10.1-5; Jer 25.24; Ezek 30.5 **2.26** Judg 6.1-3 **2.27** Judg 6.4-5; 2 Kings 8.12; Jer 11.22 **2.28** Gen 10.15, 19; Jer 25.22; Isa 23.1-17; Ezek 26.2-15; 1 Macc 4.15; 5.58,56; 11.4; Josh 13.3; Jer 47.5,7 **3.2** Dan 3.1-7 **3.5** Jdt 2.4 **3.6** Num 13.28; Josh 10.20 **3.7** Ex 15.20; 1 Sam 18.6 **3.8** Dan 3.1-7; 6.6-9 **3.9** Jdt 1.8; Gen 37.17; Jdt 4.6 **4.1** 2 Kings 25.9

[d] Gk *sand* [e] Gk *he* [f] Or *crossed*
[g] Gk *all the sheepfolds of our tents*
[h] Syr: Gk *borders*

stroyed all their temples, 2 they
were therefore greatly terrified at
his approach; they were alarmed
both for Jerusalem and for the
temple of the Lord their God. 3 For
they had only recently returned
from exile, and all the people of
Judea had just now gathered together, and the sacred vessels and
the altar and the temple had been
consecrated after their profanation. 4 So they sent word to every
district of Samaria, and to Kona,
Beth-horon, Belmain, and Jericho,
and to Choba and Aesora, and the
valley of Salem. 5 They immediately seized all the high hilltops
and fortified the villages on them
and stored up food in preparation
for war—since their fields had recently been harvested.
6 The high priest, Joakim, who
was in Jerusalem at the time,
wrote to the people of Bethulia
and Betomesthaim, which faces
Esdraelon opposite the plain near
Dothan, 7 ordering them to seize
the mountain passes, since by
them Judea could be invaded; and
it would be easy to stop any who
tried to enter, for the approach was
narrow, wide enough for only two
at a time to pass.

Prayer and Penance

8 So the Israelites did as they
had been ordered by the high
priest Joakim and the senate of the
whole people of Israel, in session
at Jerusalem. 9 And every man of
Israel cried out to God with great
fervor, and they humbled themselves with much fasting. 10 They
and their wives and their children
and their cattle and every resident
alien and hired laborer and purchased slave—they all put sackcloth around their waists. 11 And all
the Israelite men, women, and
children living at Jerusalem prostrated themselves before the temple and put ashes on their heads
and spread out their sackcloth before the Lord. 12 They even draped
the altar with sackcloth and cried
out in unison, praying fervently to
the God of Israel not to allow their
infants to be carried off and their
wives to be taken as booty, and the
towns they had inherited to be destroyed, and the sanctuary to be
profaned and desecrated to the
malicious joy of the Gentiles.
13 The Lord heard their prayers
and had regard for their distress;
for the people fasted many days
throughout Judea and in Jerusalem before the sanctuary of the
Lord Almighty. 14 The high priest
Joakim and all the priests who
stood before the Lord and ministered to the Lord, with sackcloth
around their loins, offered the
daily burnt offerings, the votive
offerings, and freewill offerings of
the people. 15 With ashes on their
turbans, they cried out to the Lord
with all their might to look with favor on the whole house of Israel.

Council against the Israelites

5 It was reported to Holofernes,
the general of the Assyrian
army, that the people of Israel had
prepared for war and had closed
the mountain passes and fortified
all the high hilltops and set up bar-
ricades in the plains. 2 In great anger he called together all the
princes of Moab and the commanders of Ammon and all the
governors of the coastland, 3 and
said to them, "Tell me, you Canaanites, what people is this that
lives in the hill country? What
towns do they inhabit? How large
is their army, and in what does
their power and strength consist?
Who rules over them as king and
leads their army? 4 And why have
they alone, of all who live in the
west, refused to come out and
meet me?"

Achior's Report

5 Then Achior, the leader of all
the Ammonites, said to him, "May
my lord please listen to a report
from the mouth of your servant,
and I will tell you the truth about
this people that lives in the mountain district near you. No falsehood shall come from your servant's mouth. 6 These people are
descended from the Chaldeans.
7 At one time they lived in Mesopo-

4.3 Ezra 1.1-3,7; 6.14-16
4.4 Josh 10.10-11; 2 Chr 8.5; Josh 6.1-21; 1 Kings 16.34; Jdt 15.4-5
4.6 Neh 12.26; Jdt 15.8; 2 Esd 5.5; Jdt 3.9
4.8 1 Macc 12.6
4.9 2 Chr 20.1-12; 32.20; Neh 9.1-2; Ps 69.10; 2 Macc 13.12
4.10 2 Kings 19.1-2; Esth 4.1-4
4.11 Isa 58.5; Jer 6.26
4.12 Gen 14.14-16; 1 Sam 30.1-3
4.13 Ps 40.1
4.14 Deut 10.8; 18.5,7; Ex 29.38-42; Lev 7.16; 22.18-30; Num 29.39
4.15 Lev 8.9
5.1 Jdt 4.2
5.3 Josh 10.40; 11.16,21; Ps 62.11; 68.34-35; 28.7-8; 46.1; 29.10; 47.6-8
5.5 Jdt 14.5-6,10; Gen 19.38; 2 Chr 20.1
5.6 Gen 11.27-31
5.7 Gen 11.31; Acts 7.2; Josh 24.2

tamia, because they did not wish to follow the gods of their ancestors who were in Chaldea. 8 Since they had abandoned the ways of their ancestors, and worshiped the God of heaven, the God they had come to know, their ancestors[i] drove them out from the presence of their gods. So they fled to Mesopotamia, and lived there for a long time. 9 Then their God commanded them to leave the place where they were living and go to the land of Canaan. There they settled, and grew very prosperous in gold and silver and very much livestock. 10 When a famine spread over the land of Canaan they went down to Egypt and lived there as long as they had food. There they became so great a multitude that their race could not be counted. 11 So the king of Egypt became hostile to them; he exploited them and forced them to make bricks. 12 They cried out to their God, and he afflicted the whole land of Egypt with incurable plagues. So the Egyptians drove them out of their sight. 13 Then God dried up the Red Sea before them, 14 and he led them by the way of Sinai and Kadesh-barnea. They drove out all the people of the desert, 15 and took up residence in the land of the Amorites, and by their might destroyed all the inhabitants of Heshbon; and crossing over the Jordan they took possession of all the hill country. 16 They drove out before them the Canaanites, the Perizzites, the Jebusites, the Shechemites, and all the Gergesites, and lived there a long time.

17 "As long as they did not sin against their God they prospered, for the God who hates iniquity is with them. 18 But when they departed from the way he had prescribed for them, they were utterly defeated in many battles and were led away captive to a foreign land. The temple of their God was razed to the ground, and their towns were occupied by their enemies. 19 But now they have returned to their God, and have come back from the places where they were scattered, and have occupied Jerusalem, where their sanctuary is, and have settled in the hill country, because it was uninhabited.

20 "So now, my master and lord, if there is any oversight in this people and they sin against their God and we find out their offense, then we can go up and defeat them. 21 But if they are not a guilty nation, then let my lord pass them by; for their Lord and God will defend them, and we shall become the laughingstock of the whole world."

22 When Achior had finished saying these things, all the people standing around the tent began to complain; Holofernes' officers and all the inhabitants of the seacoast and Moab insisted that he should be cut to pieces. 23 They said, "We are not afraid of the Israelites; they are a people with no strength or power for making war. 24 Therefore let us go ahead, Lord Holofernes, and your vast army will swallow them up."

Achior Handed over to the Israelites

6 When the disturbance made by the people outside the council had died down, Holofernes, the commander of the Assyrian army, said to Achior[j] in the presence of all the foreign contingents:

2 "Who are you, Achior and you mercenaries of Ephraim, to prophesy among us as you have done today and tell us not to make war against the people of Israel because their God will defend them? What god is there except Nebuchadnezzar? He will send his forces and destroy them from the face of the earth. Their God will not save them; 3 we the king's[k] servants will destroy them as one man. They cannot resist the might of our cavalry. 4 We will overwhelm them;[l] their mountains will be drunk with their blood, and their fields will be full of their dead. Not

5.8 Ezra 1.2; Tob 10.11
5.9 Gen 12.1-3; Josh 24.3; Acts 7.3-4; Gen 24.34-35; 26.12-14
5.10 Gen 46.1-7; Ex 1.7
5.11 Ex 1.8-14
5.12 Ex 3.7; 7.14-10.29; 12.29-33
5.13 Ex 14.21-22
5.14 Ex 19.1-2; Num 13.26; Deut 1.2
5.15 Num 21.21-31; 21.27; Josh 3.14-17; 10.40; 11.16, 21
5.16 Josh 3.10; 9.1
5.17 Deut 28.1-14
5.18 2 Kings 24.14-16; 25.11,9
5.19 Ezra 1.1-5,11; 6.15
5.20 Lev 26.14-17; Deut 28.25
5.21 Lev 26.7-9; Deut 28.7; Ps 2.4; Sir 6.4
5.22 1 Kings 22.24-27
5.23 2 Chr 32.9-15
6.2 Dan 3.1-7; Jdt 2.7; 2 Chr 32.9-15; Ps 55.16-18
6.3 Ps 33.17; Jdt 2.5-6
6.4 Rev 17.6; Isa 46.9-10; 55.11

[i] Gk *they* [j] Other ancient authorities add *and to all the Moabites* [k] Gk *his*
[l] Other ancient authorities add *with it*

even their footprints will survive
our attack; they will utterly perish.
So says King Nebuchadnezzar, lord
of the whole earth. For he has spoken; none of his words shall be in
vain.
5 "As for you, Achior, you Ammonite mercenary, you have said
these words in a moment of perversity; you shall not see my face
again from this day until I take revenge on this race that came out of
Egypt. 6 Then at my return the
sword of my army and the spear[m]
of my servants shall pierce your
sides, and you shall fall among
their wounded. 7 Now my slaves are
going to take you back into the hill
country and put you in one of the
towns beside the passes. 8 You will
not die until you perish along with
them. 9 If you really hope in your
heart that they will not be taken,
then do not look downcast! I have
spoken, and none of my words
shall fail to come true."
10 Then Holofernes ordered his
slaves, who waited on him in his
tent, to seize Achior and take him
away to Bethulia and hand him
over to the Israelites. 11 So the
slaves took him and led him out of
the camp into the plain, and from
the plain they went up into the hill
country and came to the springs
below Bethulia. 12 When the men
of the town saw them,[n] they
seized their weapons and ran out
of the town to the top of the hill,
and all the slingers kept them from
coming up by throwing stones at
them. 13 So having taken shelter
below the hill, they bound Achior
and left him lying at the foot of the
hill, and returned to their master.
14 Then the Israelites came
down from their town and found
him; they untied him and brought
him into Bethulia and placed him
before the magistrates of their
town, 15 who in those days were Uzziah son of Micah, of the tribe of
Simeon, and Chabris son of Go-
thoniel, and Charmis son of Mel-
chiel. 16 They called together all
the elders of the town, and all their
young men and women ran to the
assembly. They set Achior in the
midst of all their people, and Uzziah questioned him about what
had happened. 17 He answered and
told them what had taken place at
the council of Holofernes, and all
that he had said in the presence of
the Assyrian leaders, and all that
Holofernes had boasted he would
do against the house of Israel.
18 Then the people fell down and
worshiped God, and cried out:
19 "O Lord God of heaven, see
their arrogance, and have pity on
our people in their humiliation,
and look kindly today on the faces
of those who are consecrated to
you."
20 Then they reassured Achior,
and praised him highly. 21 Uzziah
took him from the assembly to his
own house and gave a banquet for
the elders; and all that night they
called on the God of Israel for help.

The Campaign against Bethulia

7 The next day Holofernes ordered his whole army, and all
the allies who had joined him, to
break camp and move against Bethulia, and to seize the passes up
into the hill country and make war
on the Israelites. 2 So all their warriors marched off that day; their
fighting forces numbered one hundred seventy thousand infantry
and twelve thousand cavalry, not
counting the baggage and the foot
soldiers handling it, a very great
multitude. 3 They encamped in the
valley near Bethulia, beside the
spring, and they spread out in
breadth over Dothan as far as Bal-
baim and in length from Bethulia
to Cyamon, which faces Esdraelon.
4 When the Israelites saw their
vast numbers, they were greatly
terrified and said to one another,
"They will now strip clean the
whole land; neither the high
mountains nor the valleys nor the
hills will bear their weight." 5 Yet
they all seized their weapons, and
when they had kindled fires on
their towers, they remained on
guard all that night.

6.5 Jdt 14.6; Ps 81.5,10; Hos 11.1 **6.6** Isa 14.19 **6.9** Isa 46.9-10; 55.11 **6.10** Jdt 4.6 **6.12** Jdt 7.5; 14.11; 2 Kings 3.25; 1 Macc 9.11 **6.15** Jdt 7.23; 8.10; 10.6 **6.17** Jdt 6.2-4 **6.19** Neh 1.5; Tob 7.11-12; Isa 37.29; 63.9; Ezek 7.24 **6.21** 2 Kings 19.15-19; 2 Chr 20.5-12 **7.2** Jdt 2.5; 2 Chr 20.12 **7.3** Jdt 3.9 **7.4** 2 Chr 20.3 **7.5** Neh 4.22

[m] Lat Syr: Gk *people*
[n] Other ancient authorities add *on the top of the hill*

6 On the second day Holofernes
led out all his cavalry in full view of
the Israelites in Bethulia. 7 He re-
connoitered the approaches to
their town, and visited the springs
that supplied their water; he seized
them and set guards of soldiers
over them, and then returned to
his army.
8 Then all the chieftains of the
Edomites and all the leaders of the
Moabites and the commanders of
the coastland came to him and
said, 9 "Listen to what we have to
say, my lord, and your army will
suffer no losses. 10 This people, the
Israelites, do not rely on their
spears but on the height of the
mountains where they live, for it is
not easy to reach the tops of their
mountains. 11 Therefore, my lord,
do not fight against them in regular
formation, and not a man of your
army will fall. 12 Remain in your
camp, and keep all the men in your
forces with you; let your servants
take possession of the spring of
water that flows from the foot of
the mountain, 13 for this is where
all the people of Bethulia get their
water. So thirst will destroy them,
and they will surrender their town.
Meanwhile, we and our people will
go up to the tops of the nearby
mountains and camp there to keep
watch to see that no one gets out of
the town. 14 They and their wives
and children will waste away with
famine, and before the sword
reaches them they will be strewn
about in the streets where they
live. 15 Thus you will pay them back
with evil, because they rebelled
and did not receive you peaceably."
16 These words pleased Holofernes and all his attendants, and
he gave orders to do as they had
said. 17 So the army of the Ammonites moved forward, together with
five thousand Assyrians, and they
encamped in the valley and seized
the water supply and the springs of
the Israelites. 18 And the Edomites
and Ammonites went up and encamped in the hill country opposite Dothan; and they sent some of
their men toward the south and

7.8 Gen 36.9; 1 Sam 14.47; Isa 34.4-7; Gen 19.37
7.10 1 Kings 20.23-24
7.12 Jdt 7.3
7.13 2 Chr 32.11; Lam 4.4
7.14 2 Kings 6.25; Lam 2.12,19
7.15 Jdt 5.1-4
7.17 Gen 19.38; Jdt 5.5
7.18 Jdt 7.8; 2 Chr 20.2, 13; Jdt 7.2
7.19 2 Chr 20.4; Ps 50.15; 107.6
7.21 Jer 14.3
7.22 Lam 4.4; Num 11.6; Ps 38.10
7.23 Jdt 6.15
7.24 Gen 16.5; 1 Sam 24.12; Jdt 3.1-4
7.26 Jer 38.17-18; Jdt 7.13
7.27 Ex 16.3; 17.3; Lam 2.21; 4.5
7.28 Ex 32.34; Lev 26.28; Neh 9.26-30; Dan 9.7-10

the east, toward Egrebeh, which is
near Chusi beside the Wadi Moch-
mur. The rest of the Assyrian army
encamped in the plain, and covered the whole face of the land.
Their tents and supply trains
spread out in great number, and
they formed a vast multitude.

The Distress of the Israelites

19 The Israelites then cried out
to the Lord their God, for their
courage failed, because all their
enemies had surrounded them,
and there was no way of escape
from them. 20 The whole Assyrian
army, their infantry, chariots, and
cavalry, surrounded them for
thirty-four days, until all the water
containers of every inhabitant of
Bethulia were empty; 21 their cisterns were going dry, and on no day
did they have enough water to
drink, for their drinking water was
rationed. 22 Their children were
listless, and the women and young
men fainted from thirst and were
collapsing in the streets of the
town and in the gateways; they no
longer had any strength.
23 Then all the people, the
young men, the women, and the
children, gathered around Uzziah
and the rulers of the town and
cried out with a loud voice, and
said before all the elders, 24 "Let
God judge between you and us!
You have done us a great injury in
not making peace with the Assyrians. 25 For now we have no one to
help us; God has sold us into their
hands, to be strewn before them in
thirst and exhaustion. 26 Now summon them and surrender the whole
town as booty to the army of Holofernes and to all his forces. 27 For it
would be better for us to be captured by them.[o] We shall indeed
become slaves, but our lives will be
spared, and we shall not witness
our little ones dying before our
eyes, and our wives and children
drawing their last breath. 28 We call
to witness against you heaven and
earth and our God, the Lord of our
ancestors, who punishes us for our

[o] Other ancient authorities add *than to die of thirst*

sins and the sins of our ancestors;
do today the things that we have
described!"
29 Then great and general lamentation arose throughout the assembly, and they cried out to the
Lord God with a loud voice. 30 But
Uzziah said to them, "Courage, my
brothers and sisters![p] Let us hold
out for five days more; by that time
the Lord our God will turn his
mercy to us again, for he will not
forsake us utterly. 31 But if these
days pass by, and no help comes
for us, I will do as you say."
32 Then he dismissed the people to their various posts, and they
went up on the walls and towers of
their town. The women and children he sent home. In the town
they were in great misery.

The Character of Judith

8 Now in those days Judith
heard about these things: she
was the daughter of Merari son of
Ox son of Joseph son of Oziel son
of Elkiah son of Ananias son of
Gideon son of Raphain son of Ahitub son of Elijah son of Hilkiah son
of Eliab son of Nathanael son of
Salamiel son of Sarasadai son of Israel. 2 Her husband Manasseh, who
belonged to her tribe and family,
had died during the barley harvest.
3 For as he stood overseeing those
who were binding sheaves in the
field, he was overcome by the
burning heat, and took to his bed
and died in his town Bethulia. So
they buried him with his ancestors
in the field between Dothan and
Balamon. 4 Judith remained as a
widow for three years and four
months 5 at home where she set up
a tent for herself on the roof of her
house. She put sackcloth around
her waist and dressed in widow's
clothing. 6 She fasted all the days
of her widowhood, except the day
before the sabbath and the sabbath itself, the day before the new
moon and the day of the new
moon, and the festivals and days of
rejoicing of the house of Israel.
7 She was beautiful in appearance,
and was very lovely to behold. Her
husband Manasseh had left her
gold and silver, men and women
slaves, livestock, and fields; and
she maintained this estate. 8 No
one spoke ill of her, for she feared
God with great devotion.

Judith and the Elders

9 When Judith heard the harsh
words spoken by the people
against the ruler, because they
were faint for lack of water, and
when she heard all that Uzziah said
to them, and how he promised
them under oath to surrender the
town to the Assyrians after five
days, 10 she sent her maid, who was
in charge of all she possessed, to
summon Uzziah and[q] Chabris and
Charmis, the elders of her town.
11 They came to her, and she said to
them,
"Listen to me, rulers of the people of Bethulia! What you have said
to the people today is not right;
you have even sworn and pronounced this oath between God
and you, promising to surrender
the town to our enemies unless the
Lord turns and helps us within so
many days. 12 Who are you to put
God to the test today, and to set
yourselves up in the place of[r] God
in human affairs? 13 You are putting the Lord Almighty to the test,
but you will never learn anything!
14 You cannot plumb the depths of
the human heart or understand the
workings of the human mind; how
do you expect to search out God,
who made all these things, and
find out his mind or comprehend
his thought? No, my brothers, do
not anger the Lord our God. 15 For
if he does not choose to help us
within these five days, he has
power to protect us within any
time he pleases, or even to destroy
us in the presence of our enemies.
16 Do not try to bind the purposes
of the Lord our God; for God is not
like a human being, to be threatened, or like a mere mortal, to be
won over by pleading. 17 Therefore,
while we wait for his deliverance,
let us call upon him to help us, and

7.29 Isa 29.2; Jer 31.15
7.30 Josh 1.6-7; 2 Chr 32.7; Ps 106.44-46; 123.3-4; Josh 1.5; Ps 94.14
7.32 Bar 2.25; 2 Esd 15.15
8.1 Jdt 16.6
8.3 2 Kings 4.18-20; Gen 49.29; 2 Kings 12.21; Jdt 4.6
8.4 Lk 2.36-37
8.6 Gen 38.14; Jdt 10.3; Num 29.6; Isa 1.13
8.7 Gen 12.11; 1 Sam 25.3; Sus 1.2
8.8 Acts 11.23
8.9 Jdt 6.15; 7.30-31
8.12 Deut 6.16; Ps 95.8-9; Dan 3.1-6; Acts 12.21-22
8.14 Job 11.7; Eccl 8.17; Rom 11.33-34; Gen 1.1; Ex 20.11; 1 Kings 16.2, 7,13; Jer 25.6
8.15 Neh 1.10; Ps 130.7; Jdt 9.14; Isa 10.17-18; Jer 25.9
8.16 Num 23.19; 1 Sam 15.29
8.17 Ps 27.14; Hos 12.6; Ex 2.23-25; Deut 26.7

[p] Gk *Courage, brothers*
[q] Other ancient authorities lack *Uzziah and* (see verses 28 and 35)
[r] Or *above*

he will hear our voice, if it pleases
him.
18 "For never in our generation,
nor in these present days, has
there been any tribe or family or
people or town of ours that worships gods made with hands, as
was done in days gone by. 19 That
was why our ancestors were
handed over to the sword and to
pillage, and so they suffered a great
catastrophe before our enemies.
20 But we know no other god but
him, and so we hope that he will
not disdain us or any of our nation.
21 For if we are captured, all Judea
will be captured and our sanctuary
will be plundered; and he will
make us pay for its desecration
with our blood. 22 The slaughter of
our kindred and the captivity of the
land and the desolation of our
inheritance—all this he will bring
on our heads among the Gentiles,
wherever we serve as slaves; and
we shall be an offense and a disgrace in the eyes of those who acquire us. 23 For our slavery will not
bring us into favor, but the Lord
our God will turn it to dishonor.
24 "Therefore, my brothers, let
us set an example for our kindred,
for their lives depend upon us, and
the sanctuary—both the temple
and the altar—rests upon us. 25 In
spite of everything let us give
thanks to the Lord our God, who is
putting us to the test as he did our
ancestors. 26 Remember what he
did with Abraham, and how he
tested Isaac, and what happened
to Jacob in Syrian Mesopotamia,
while he was tending the sheep of
Laban, his mother's brother. 27 For
he has not tried us with fire, as he
did them, to search their hearts,
nor has he taken vengeance on us;
but the Lord scourges those who
are close to him in order to admonish them."
28 Then Uzziah said to her, "All
that you have said was spoken out
of a true heart, and there is no one
who can deny your words. 29 Today
is not the first time your wisdom
has been shown, but from the beginning of your life all the people
have recognized your understanding, for your heart's disposition is
right. 30 But the people were so
thirsty that they compelled us to
do for them what we have promised, and made us take an oath
that we cannot break. 31 Now since
you are a God-fearing woman, pray
for us, so that the Lord may send
us rain to fill our cisterns. Then we
will no longer feel faint from
thirst."
32 Then Judith said to them,
"Listen to me. I am about to do
something that will go down
through all generations of our descendants. 33 Stand at the town
gate tonight so that I may go out
with my maid; and within the days
after which you have promised to
surrender the town to our enemies,
the Lord will deliver Israel by my
hand. 34 Only, do not try to find out
what I am doing; for I will not tell
you until I have finished what I am
about to do."
35 Uzziah and the rulers said to
her, "Go in peace, and may the
Lord God go before you, to take
vengeance on our enemies." 36 So
they returned from the tent and
went to their posts.

The Prayer of Judith

9 Then Judith prostrated herself, put ashes on her head,
and uncovered the sackcloth she
was wearing. At the very time when
the evening incense was being offered in the house of God in Jerusalem, Judith cried out to the Lord
with a loud voice, and said,
2 "O Lord God of my ancestor
Simeon, to whom you gave a sword
to take revenge on those strangers
who had torn off a virgin's cloth-
ings[s] to defile her, and exposed her
thighs to put her to shame, and
polluted her womb to disgrace her;
for you said, 'It shall not be done'
—yet they did it. 3 So you gave up
their rulers to be killed, and their
bed, which was ashamed of the deceit they had practiced, was
stained with blood, and you struck
down slaves along with princes,
and princes on their thrones. 4 You

8.18 Ps 115.4; Isa 2.8; 1 Kings 16.31-33; 2 Kings 21.3-9
8.19 2 Kings 21.10-15; Jer 19.3-9
8.20 Isa 44.8; 45.21-22
8.21 Ezek 8.1-18
8.22 Neh 9.36; Jer 25.14; 23.40; 24.9; Ezek 22.4
8.24 Jn 13.15; 1 Tim 4.16
8.25 1 Chr 16.34-35; Ps 97.12; Jdt 8.13
8.26 Gen 22.1-14; 30.25-43
8.27 Ezek 22.18-22; Wis 3.6; Prov 3.11-12; Heb 12.5-6
8.30 Jdt 7.13
8.31 Gen 20.7; 1 Sam 7.5; Job 42.8; 1 Kings 18.41-46; Jas 5.17-18
8.33 Jdt 7.30; Judg 6.36-37
8.35 Ex 4.18; Mk 5.34; Josh 22.23; Ps 149.5-7
9.1 Ex 30.8; Ps 141.2
9.2 Gen 34.25-26, 1-3; Deut 22.25-27
9.4 Gen 34.28-29; Deut 10.18; Ps 146.9

[s] Cn: Gk *loosed her womb*

gave up their wives for booty and
their daughters to captivity, and all
their booty to be divided among
your beloved children who burned
with zeal for you and abhorred the
pollution of their blood and called
on you for help — O God, my God,
hear me also — a widow.

5 "For you have done these
things and those that went before
and those that followed. You have
designed the things that are now,
and those that are to come. What
you had in mind has happened;
6 the things you decided on presented themselves and said, 'Here
we are!' For all your ways are prepared in advance, and your judgment is with foreknowledge.

7 "Here now are the Assyrians, a
greatly increased force, priding
themselves in their horses and riders, boasting in the strength of
their foot soldiers, and trusting in
shield and spear, in bow and sling.
They do not know that you are the
Lord who crushes wars; the Lord is
your name. 8 Break their strength
by your might, and bring down
their power in your anger; for they
intend to defile your sanctuary,
and to pollute the tabernacle
where your glorious name resides,
and to break off the horns[t] of your
altar with the sword. 9 Look at their
pride, and send your wrath upon
their heads. Give to me, a widow,
the strong hand to do what I plan.
10 By the deceit of my lips strike
down the slave with the prince and
the prince with his servant; crush
their arrogance by the hand of a
woman.

11 "For your strength does not
depend on numbers, nor your
might on the powerful. But you are
the God of the lowly, helper of the
oppressed, upholder of the weak,
protector of the forsaken, savior of
those without hope. 12 Please,
please, God of my father, God of
the heritage of Israel, Lord of
heaven and earth, Creator of the
waters, King of all your creation,
hear my prayer! 13 Make my deceitful words bring wound and bruise
on those who have planned cruel
things against your covenant, and
against your sacred house, and
against Mount Zion, and against
the house your children possess.
14 Let your whole nation and every
tribe know and understand that
you are God, the God of all power
and might, and that there is no
other who protects the people of
Israel but you alone!"

Judith Prepares to Go to Holofernes

10 When Judith[u] had stopped
crying out to the God of
Israel, and had ended all these
words, 2 she rose from where
she lay prostrate. She called her
maid and went down into the
house where she lived on sabbaths
and on her festal days. 3 She removed the sackcloth she had been
wearing, took off her widow's garments, bathed her body with water, and anointed herself with precious ointment. She combed her
hair, put on a tiara, and dressed
herself in the festive attire that she
used to wear while her husband
Manasseh was living. 4 She put sandals on her feet, and put on her anklets, bracelets, rings, earrings,
and all her other jewelry. Thus she
made herself very beautiful, to entice the eyes of all the men who
might see her. 5 She gave her maid
a skin of wine and a flask of oil,
and filled a bag with roasted grain,
dried fig cakes, and fine bread;[v]
then she wrapped up all her dishes
and gave them to her to carry.

6 Then they went out to the
town gate of Bethulia and found
Uzziah standing there with the elders of the town, Chabris and
Charmis. 7 When they saw her
transformed in appearance and
dressed differently, they were very
greatly astounded at her beauty
and said to her, 8 "May the God of
our ancestors grant you favor and
fulfill your plans, so that the people of Israel may glory and Jerusalem may be exalted." She bowed
down to God.

9 Then she said to them, "Order
the gate of the town to be opened

9.6 Isa 44.7; Jer 1.5; Eph 1.11; Acts 2.23
9.7 Jdt 1.1; 7.1-3; Ps 20.7; 33.16; Isa 36.9; Ps 44.6; 46.8-9
9.8 Ps 10.15; Ezek 30.22; Deut 28.58; 2 Chr 6.34; Ex 27.2; Ps 118.27
9.10 Judg 4.21; 9.54
9.11 Judg 7.2; Ps 138.6; Lk 1.52; Ps 9.9; 146.7
9.12 Ezra 5.11; Acts 4.24
9.13 Jdt 10.12-13
9.14 Ezek 6.13-14; 29.6,9,16,21; Jdt 8.15; Ps 91.14; Isa 31.5
10.2 Deut 9.18; Ezek 9.8
10.3 Gen 38.14; Jdt 8.3,2
10.4 Hos 2.13; Jdt 12.15
10.6 Jdt 8.33
10.8 Ps 90.17; Zech 8.21-22; Prov 11.11; Jdt 13.4; Gen 24.26; Ex 4.31; Jdt 13.17
10.9 Jdt 13.11

[t] Syr: Gk *horn* [u] Gk *she*
[v] Other ancient authorities add *and cheese*

for me so that I may go out and accomplish the things you have just
said to me." So they ordered the
young men to open the gate for
her, as she requested. 10 When they
had done this, Judith went out, accompanied by her maid. The men
of the town watched her until she
had gone down the mountain and
passed through the valley, where
they lost sight of her.

Judith Is Captured

11 As the women[w] were going
straight on through the valley, an
Assyrian patrol met her 12 and took
her into custody. They asked her,
"To what people do you belong,
and where are you coming from,
and where are you going?" She replied, "I am a daughter of the Hebrews, but I am fleeing from them,
for they are about to be handed
over to you to be devoured. 13 I am
on my way to see Holofernes the
commander of your army, to give
him a true report; I will show him
a way by which he can go and capture all the hill country without
losing one of his men, captured or
slain."

14 When the men heard her
words, and observed her face—she
was in their eyes marvelously
beautiful—they said to her, 15 "You
have saved your life by hurrying
down to see our lord. Go at once to
his tent; some of us will escort you
and hand you over to him. 16 When
you stand before him, have no fear
in your heart, but tell him what you
have just said, and he will treat you
well."

17 They chose from their number a hundred men to accompany
her and her maid, and they brought
them to the tent of Holofernes.
18 There was great excitement in
the whole camp, for her arrival was
reported from tent to tent. They
came and gathered around her as
she stood outside the tent of Holofernes, waiting until they told him
about her. 19 They marveled at her
beauty and admired the Israelites,
judging them by her. They said to
one another, "Who can despise
these people, who have women
like this among them? It is not
wise to leave one of their men
alive, for if we let them go they will
be able to beguile the whole
world!"

Judith Is Brought before Holofernes

20 Then the guards of Holofernes and all his servants came out
and led her into the tent. 21 Holofernes was resting on his bed under
a canopy that was woven with purple and gold, emeralds and other
precious stones. 22 When they told
him of her, he came to the front of
the tent, with silver lamps carried
before him. 23 When Judith came
into the presence of Holofernes[x]
and his servants, they all marveled
at the beauty of her face. She prostrated herself and did obeisance to
him, but his slaves raised her up.

11 Then Holofernes said to
her, "Take courage,
woman, and do not be afraid in
your heart, for I have never hurt
anyone who chose to serve Nebuchadnezzar, king of all the earth.
2 Even now, if your people who live
in the hill country had not slighted
me, I would never have lifted my
spear against them. They have
brought this on themselves. 3 But
now tell me why you have fled from
them and have come over to us. In
any event, you have come to safety.
Take courage! You will live tonight
and ever after. 4 No one will hurt
you. Rather, all will treat you well,
as they do the servants of my lord
King Nebuchadnezzar."

Judith Explains Her Presence

5 Judith answered him, "Accept
the words of your slave, and let
your servant speak in your presence. I will say nothing false to my
lord this night. 6 If you follow out
the words of your servant, God will
accomplish something through
you, and my lord will not fail to
achieve his purposes. 7 By the life
of Nebuchadnezzar, king of the
whole earth, and by the power of
him who has sent you to direct ev-

10.10 Jdt 7.3
10.12 Gen 32.17; Judg 19.17; Ex 3.18
10.13 Jdt 2.4; 7.1; 5.3
10.14 Jdt 10.4
10.16 Jdt 11.1
10.19 Jdt 11.21
10.21 Jdt 13.9,15; 16.19; Am 6.4
10.23 2 Sam 14.22; 24.20
11.1 Jdt 10.16; 2 Sam 16.16-19; Dan 4.1
11.2 Jdt 5.1-4
11.5 Ex 20.16
11.6 Isa 10.5; 44.28; Jer 25.9
11.7 Jdt 2.5; Dan 2.37-38

[w] Gk *they* [x] Gk *him*

ery living being! Not only do human beings serve him because of
you, but also the animals of the
field and the cattle and the birds of
the air will live, because of your
power, under Nebuchadnezzar and
all his house. 8 For we have heard
of your wisdom and skill, and it is
reported throughout the whole
world that you alone are the best in
the whole kingdom, the most informed and the most astounding in
military strategy.
9 "Now as for Achior's speech
in your council, we have heard his
words, for the people of Bethulia
spared him and he told them all he
had said to you. 10 Therefore, lord
and master, do not disregard what
he said, but keep it in your mind,
for it is true. Indeed our nation
cannot be punished, nor can the
sword prevail against them, unless
they sin against their God.
11 "But now, in order that my
lord may not be defeated and his
purpose frustrated, death will fall
upon them, for a sin has overtaken
them by which they are about to
provoke their God to anger when
they do what is wrong. 12 Since
their food supply is exhausted and
their water has almost given out,
they have planned to kill their livestock and have determined to use
all that God by his laws has forbidden them to eat. 13 They have decided to consume the first fruits of
the grain and the tithes of the wine
and oil, which they had consecrated and set aside for the priests
who minister in the presence of
our God in Jerusalem—things it is
not lawful for any of the people
even to touch with their hands.
14 Since even the people in Jerusalem have been doing this, they
have sent messengers there in order to bring back permission from
the council of the elders. 15 When
the response reaches them and
they act upon it, on that very day
they will be handed over to you to
be destroyed.
16 "So when I, your slave,
learned all this, I fled from them.
God has sent me to accomplish
with you things that will astonish
the whole world wherever people
shall hear about them. 17 Your servant is indeed God-fearing and
serves the God of heaven night and
day. So, my lord, I will remain with
you; but every night your servant
will go out into the valley and pray
to God. He will tell me when they
have committed their sins. 18 Then
I will come and tell you, so that you
may go out with your whole army,
and not one of them will be able to
withstand you. 19 Then I will lead
you through Judea, until you come
to Jerusalem; there I will set your
throne.[y] You will drive them like
sheep that have no shepherd, and
no dog will so much as growl at
you. For this was told me to give
me foreknowledge; it was announced to me, and I was sent to
tell you."
20 Her words pleased Holofernes and all his servants. They marveled at her wisdom and said,
21 "No other woman from one end
of the earth to the other looks so
beautiful or speaks so wisely!"
22 Then Holofernes said to her,
"God has done well to send you
ahead of the people, to strengthen
our hands and bring destruction on
those who have despised my lord.
23 You are not only beautiful in appearance, but wise in speech. If
you do as you have said, your God
shall be my God, and you shall live
in the palace of King Nebuchadnezzar and be renowned throughout the whole world."

Judith as a Guest of Holofernes

12 Then he commanded them
to bring her in where his
silver dinnerware was kept, and ordered them to set a table for her
with some of his own delicacies,
and with some of his own wine to
drink. 2 But Judith said, "I cannot
partake of them, or it will be an offense; but I will have enough with
the things I brought with me."
3 Holofernes said to her, "If your
supply runs out, where can we get
you more of the same? For none of
your people are here with us." 4 Ju-

11.8 Jdt 2.6-13
11.9 Jdt 5.5-21
11.10 Deut 28.20-37; Jdt 5.17-18
11.11 Jer 25.6; Jdt 8.14
11.12 2 Kings 6.24-25; Lam 2.11-12
11.13 Ex 22.29; 23.19; Lev 27.30; Mal 3.8; Ex 29.32-33; Lev 24.5-9; 1 Sam 21.1-6
11.16 2 Kings 21.12; Jer 19.3
11.17 Jdt 8.5-8; 5.8; 12.7; 13.10
11.18 Judg 2.4; 1 Macc 10.73
11.19 Ezek 34.5; Mt 9.36
11.21 Jdt 10.14,19
11.23 Ruth 1.16; Dan 4.34-37; 1 Macc 3.9
12.1 Ps 141.4; Prov 23.3
12.2 Dan 1.8; Jdt 10.5
12.4 Jdt 13.6-10; Jer 44.11; Dan 11.36

[y] Or *chariot*

dith replied, "As surely as you live, my lord, your servant will not use up the supplies I have with me before the Lord carries out by my hand what he has determined."

5 Then the servants of Holofernes brought her into the tent, and she slept until midnight. Toward the morning watch she got up 6 and sent this message to Holofernes: "Let my lord now give orders to allow your servant to go out and pray." 7 So Holofernes commanded his guards not to hinder her. She remained in the camp three days. She went out each night to the valley of Bethulia, and bathed at the spring in the camp.[z] 8 After bathing, she prayed the Lord God of Israel to direct her way for the triumph of his[a] people. 9 Then she returned purified and stayed in the tent until she ate her food toward evening.

Judith Attends Holofernes' Banquet

10 On the fourth day Holofernes held a banquet for his personal attendants only, and did not invite any of his officers. 11 He said to Bagoas, the eunuch who had charge of his personal affairs, "Go and persuade the Hebrew woman who is in your care to join us and to eat and drink with us. 12 For it would be a disgrace if we let such a woman go without having intercourse with her. If we do not seduce her, she will laugh at us."

13 So Bagoas left the presence of Holofernes, and approached her and said, "Let this pretty girl not hesitate to come to my lord to be honored in his presence, and to enjoy drinking wine with us, and to become today like one of the Assyrian women who serve in the palace of Nebuchadnezzar." 14 Judith replied, "Who am I to refuse my lord? Whatever pleases him I will do at once, and it will be a joy to me until the day of my death." 15 So she proceeded to dress herself in all her woman's finery. Her maid went ahead and spread for her on the ground before Holofernes the lambskins she had received from Bagoas for her daily use in reclining.

16 Then Judith came in and lay down. Holofernes' heart was ravished with her and his passion was aroused, for he had been waiting for an opportunity to seduce her from the day he first saw her. 17 So Holofernes said to her, "Have a drink and be merry with us!" 18 Judith said, "I will gladly drink, my lord, because today is the greatest day in my whole life." 19 Then she took what her maid had prepared and ate and drank before him. 20 Holofernes was greatly pleased with her, and drank a great quantity of wine, much more than he had ever drunk in any one day since he was born.

Judith Beheads Holofernes

13 When evening came, his slaves quickly withdrew. Bagoas closed the tent from outside and shut out the attendants from his master's presence. They went to bed, for they all were weary because the banquet had lasted so long. 2 But Judith was left alone in the tent, with Holofernes stretched out on his bed, for he was dead drunk.

3 Now Judith had told her maid to stand outside the bedchamber and to wait for her to come out, as she did on the other days; for she said she would be going out for her prayers. She had said the same thing to Bagoas. 4 So everyone went out, and no one, either small or great, was left in the bedchamber. Then Judith, standing beside his bed, said in her heart, "O Lord God of all might, look in this hour on the work of my hands for the exaltation of Jerusalem. 5 Now indeed is the time to help your heritage and to carry out my design to destroy the enemies who have risen up against us."

6 She went up to the bedpost near Holofernes' head, and took down his sword that hung there. 7 She came close to his bed, took hold of the hair of his head, and

12.5 Ex 14.24; 1 Sam 11.11
12.6 Jdt 11.17
12.7 Jdt 11.17
12.8 Sir 37.15; 1 Thess 3.11; Ps 54.7; 59.10
12.11 Esth 2.15; Acts 8.27; Esth 5.4-6; 6.14-7.2
12.12 Sus 1.11
12.15 Jdt 10.4
12.16 Neh 5.5; Jdt 16.9
12.17 Gen 43.34; Esth 1.10; Lk 12.19
12.19 Jdt 12.2
12.20 Gen 9.21; Esth 1.7-8
13.1 Jdt 12.11
13.2 Jdt 10.21; 1 King 16.9-10; 1 Macc 16.16
13.3 Jdt 11.17; 12.7
13.4 Judg 3.19-22; Prov 11.11; Jdt 10.8
13.5 Jer 47.4; 51.11
13.6 1 Sam 17.51
13.7 Judg 16.28

[z] Other ancient authorities lack *in the camp*
[a] Other ancient authorities read *her*

said, "Give me strength today,
O Lord God of Israel!" 8 Then she
struck his neck twice with all her
might, and cut off his head. 9 Next
she rolled his body off the bed and
pulled down the canopy from the
posts. Soon afterward she went out
and gave Holofernes' head to her
maid, 10 who placed it in her food
bag.

Judith Returns to Bethulia

Then the two of them went out
together, as they were accustomed
to do for prayer. They passed
through the camp, circled around
the valley, and went up the mountain to Bethulia, and came to its
gates. 11 From a distance Judith
called out to the sentries at the
gates, "Open, open the gate! God,
our God, is with us, still showing
his power in Israel and his strength
against our enemies, as he has
done today!"
12 When the people of her town
heard her voice, they hurried down
to the town gate and summoned
the elders of the town. 13 They all
ran together, both small and great,
for it seemed unbelievable that she
had returned. They opened the
gate and welcomed them. Then
they lit a fire to give light, and
gathered around them. 14 Then she
said to them with a loud voice,
"Praise God, O praise him! Praise
God, who has not withdrawn his
mercy from the house of Israel, but
has destroyed our enemies by my
hand this very night!"
15 Then she pulled the head
out of the bag and showed it to
them, and said, "See here, the
head of Holofernes, the commander of the Assyrian army, and
here is the canopy beneath which
he lay in his drunken stupor. The
Lord has struck him down by the
hand of a woman. 16 As the Lord
lives, who has protected me in the
way I went, I swear that it was my
face that seduced him to his destruction, and that he committed
no sin with me, to defile and
shame me."
17 All the people were greatly
astonished. They bowed down and
worshiped God, and said with one
accord, "Blessed are you our God,
who have this day humiliated the
enemies of your people."
18 Then Uzziah said to her,
"O daughter, you are blessed by
the Most High God above all other
women on earth; and blessed be
the Lord God, who created the
heavens and the earth, who has
guided you to cut off the head of
the leader of our enemies. 19 Your
praise[b] will never depart from the
hearts of those who remember the
power of God. 20 May God grant
this to be a perpetual honor to you,
and may he reward you with blessings, because you risked your own
life when our nation was brought
low, and you averted our ruin,
walking in the straight path before
our God." And all the people said,
"Amen. Amen."

Judith's Counsel

14 Then Judith said to them,
"Listen to me, my friends.
Take this head and hang it upon
the parapet of your wall. 2 As soon
as day breaks and the sun rises on
the earth, each of you take up your
weapons, and let every able-bodied
man go out of the town; set a captain over them, as if you were going
down to the plain against the Assyrian outpost; only do not go
down. 3 Then they will seize their
arms and go into the camp and
rouse the officers of the Assyrian
army. They will rush into the tent
of Holofernes and will not find
him. Then panic will come over
them, and they will flee before you.
4 Then you and all who live within
the borders of Israel will pursue
them and cut them down in their
tracks. 5 But before you do all this,
bring Achior the Ammonite to me
so that he may see and recognize
the man who despised the house of
Israel and sent him to us as if to his
death."
6 So they summoned Achior
from the house of Uzziah. When he
came and saw the head of Holofernes in the hand of one of the men

13.8 Judg 4.21; 5.26-27
13.9 Jdt 10.21
13.10 Jdt 10.5; 11.17
13.11 Jdt 10.9; 2 Chr 13.12; Ps 46.7,11; 62.11; 68.34-35; 130.7; Neh 1.11
13.14 Ps 106.1-2; 113.1; 40.11-14; 103.4; 18.48; 54.7; 89.10
13.15 Judg 5.26-27
13.16 Josh 24.17; 2 Macc 13.17
13.17 Ex 12.27; Jdt 10.8; 15.9; Ps 72.18-19; Tob 3.11
13.18 Judg 5.24; Lk 1.42; Gen 1.1; Isa 42.5; 44.24; Ex 15.13
13.19 Jdt 15.9
13.20 Ruth 2.12; 1 Sam 24.19; Ps 58.10-11; Judg 9.17; 2 Macc 14.38; Ps 5.8; Prov 4.25-26; Sir 51.15; Ps 72.19; Jdt 15.10
14.2 Jdt 6.12
14.3 Josh 10.10; Ps 48.4-6
14.4 1 Kings 20.20; 2 Chr 14.13
14.5 Jdt 5.5
14.6 Jdt 6.5

[b] Other ancient authorities read *hope*

in the assembly of the people, he
fell down on his face in a faint.
7When they raised him up he threw
himself at Judith's feet, and did
obeisance to her, and said,
"Blessed are you in every tent of
Judah! In every nation those who
hear your name will be alarmed.
8Now tell me what you have done
during these days."
So Judith told him in the presence of the people all that she had
done, from the day she left until
the moment she began speaking to
them. 9When she had finished, the
people raised a great shout and
made a joyful noise in their town.
10When Achior saw all that the
God of Israel had done, he believed
firmly in God. So he was circumcised, and joined the house of Israel, remaining so to this day.

Holofernes' Death Is Discovered

11 As soon as it was dawn they
hung the head of Holofernes on
the wall. Then they all took their
weapons, and they went out in
companies to the mountain
passes. 12When the Assyrians saw
them they sent word to their commanders, who then went to the
generals and the captains and to
all their other officers. 13They
came to Holofernes' tent and said
to the steward in charge of all his
personal affairs, "Wake up our
lord, for the slaves have been so
bold as to come down against us to
give battle, to their utter destruction."
14 So Bagoas went in and
knocked at the entry of the tent,
for he supposed that he was sleeping with Judith. 15But when no one
answered, he opened it and went
into the bedchamber and found
him sprawled on the floor dead,
with his head missing. 16He cried
out with a loud voice and wept and
groaned and shouted, and tore his
clothes. 17Then he went to the tent
where Judith had stayed, and when
he did not find her, he rushed out
to the people and shouted, 18"The
slaves have tricked us! One Hebrew woman has brought disgrace
on the house of King Nebuchadnezzar. Look, Holofernes is lying
on the ground, and his head is
missing!"
19 When the leaders of the Assyrian army heard this, they tore
their tunics and were greatly dismayed, and their loud cries and
shouts rose up throughout the
camp.

The Assyrians Flee in Panic

15 When the men in the tents
heard it, they were amazed
at what had happened. 2Overcome
with fear and trembling, they did
not wait for one another, but with
one impulse all rushed out and
fled by every path across the plain
and through the hill country.
3Those who had camped in the
hills around Bethulia also took to
flight. Then the Israelites, everyone that was a soldier, rushed out
upon them. 4Uzziah sent men to
Betomasthaim[c] and Choba and
Kola, and to all the frontiers of Israel, to tell what had taken place
and to urge all to rush out upon the
enemy to destroy them. 5When the
Israelites heard it, with one accord
they fell upon the enemy,[d] and cut
them down as far as Choba. Those
in Jerusalem and all the hill country also came, for they were told
what had happened in the camp of
the enemy. The men in Gilead and
in Galilee outflanked them with
great slaughter, even beyond Damascus and its borders. 6The rest
of the people of Bethulia fell upon
the Assyrian camp and plundered
it, acquiring great riches. 7And the
Israelites, when they returned from
the slaughter, took possession of
what remained. Even the villages
and towns in the hill country and
in the plain got a great amount of
booty, since there was a vast quantity of it.

The Israelites Celebrate Their Victory

8 Then the high priest Joakim
and the elders of the Israelites who
lived in Jerusalem came to witness
the good things that the Lord had

14.7 Jdt 13.18
14.9 Josh 6.5,20; 2 Chr 13.15; Ps 20.5; 66.1; 95.1-2; 100.1
14.10 Deut 23.3
14.12 Jdt 14.3
14.14 Jdt 12.11
14.15 Judg 3.24-25; Jdt 13.6-10
14.16 Josh 7.6; 2 Kings 11.14; Acts 14.14
15.2 Judg 7.21-22; 2 Kings 7.6-7; 2 Chr 14.9-13
15.3 Jdt 7.18
15.4 Jdt 4.6; 4.4; Judg 3.27-28; 7.24
15.5 Gen 31.21, 23; Josh 17.5-6; 20.7; 2 Kings 15.29; Jdt 1.8
15.6 1 Sam 17.53; 2 Kings 7.16; 2 Chr 14.14-15
15.8 Jdt 4.6,8,14

c Other ancient authorities add *and Bebai*
d Gk *them*

done for Israel, and to see Judith
and to wish her well. 9 When they
met her, they all blessed her with
one accord and said to her, "You
are the glory of Jerusalem, you are
the great boast of Israel, you are
the great pride of our nation! 10 You
have done all this with your own
hand; you have done great good to
Israel, and God is well pleased with
it. May the Almighty Lord bless
you forever!" And all the people
said, "Amen."

11 All the people plundered the
camp for thirty days. They gave Judith the tent of Holofernes and all
his silver dinnerware, his beds, his
bowls, and all his furniture. She
took them and loaded her mules
and hitched up her carts and piled
the things on them.

12 All the women of Israel gathered to see her, and blessed her,
and some of them performed a
dance in her honor. She took ivy-
wreathed wands in her hands and
distributed them to the women
who were with her; 13 and she and
those who were with her crowned
themselves with olive wreaths. She
went before all the people in the
dance, leading all the women,
while all the men of Israel followed, bearing their arms and
wearing garlands and singing
hymns.

Judith Offers Her Hymn of Praise

14 Judith began this thanksgiving before all Israel, and all the
people loudly sang this song of
16 praise. 1 And Judith said,
Begin a song to my God
with tambourines,
sing to my Lord with
cymbals.
Raise to him a new psalm;[e]
exalt him, and call upon
his name.
2 For the Lord is a God who
crushes wars;
he sets up his camp among
his people;
he delivered me from the
hands of my pursuers.

3 The Assyrian came down
from the mountains of
the north;
he came with myriads of
his warriors;
their numbers blocked up
the wadis,
and their cavalry covered
the hills.
4 He boasted that he would
burn up my territory,
and kill my young men
with the sword,
and dash my infants to the
ground,
and seize my children as
booty,
and take my virgins as
spoil.

5 But the Lord Almighty has
foiled them
by the hand of a woman.[f]
6 For their mighty one did not
fall by the hands of the
young men,
nor did the sons of the
Titans strike him down,
nor did tall giants set upon
him;
but Judith daughter of
Merari
with the beauty of her
countenance undid
him.

7 For she put away her
widow's clothing
to exalt the oppressed in
Israel.
She anointed her face with
perfume;
8 she fastened her hair with
a tiara
and put on a linen gown to
beguile him.
9 Her sandal ravished his eyes,
her beauty captivated his
mind,
and the sword severed his
neck!
10 The Persians trembled at her
boldness,
the Medes were daunted at
her daring.

15.9 Jdt 13.17-18; 13.19
15.10 Ps 41.11; 147.11; Gen 28.3; 49.25; Ps 72.19; Jdt 13.20
15.11 Jdt 10.20-21
15.12 Ex 15.20-21; 1 Sam 18.6; 1 Macc 13.51; 2 Macc 10.7
15.13 Sir 32.2
15.14 Ex 15.21; Judg 5.2
16.1 Ex 15.20; Ps 81.2; Jdt 3.7; 1 Chr 25.6; Ps 150.5; 96.1; 98.1; 149.1; 34.3; Isa 25.1
16.2 Ps 46.8-9; Jdt 9.7; Ps 18.17,48; 118.10-14
16.3 2 Kings 19.13,35; Jdt 7.2
16.4 Jer 11.22; Lam 2.21; Isa 13.16; Nah 3.10; Lam 5.11; 2 Esd 10.22
16.5 Judg 4.21; 9.54; Jdt 13.15
16.6 Jdt 10.4,19; 11.21
16.7 Jdt 10.3; 9.11
16.9 Jdt 12.16; 10.14,19; 11.21; 13.8

[e] Other ancient authorities read *a psalm and praise* [f] Other ancient authorities add *he has confounded them*

11 Then my oppressed people
shouted;
my weak people cried
out,[g] and the enemy[h]
trembled;
they lifted up their voices,
and the enemy[h] were
turned back.
12 Sons of slave-girls pierced
them through
and wounded them like the
children of fugitives;
they perished before the
army of my Lord.

13 I will sing to my God a new
song:
O Lord, you are great and
glorious,
wonderful in strength,
invincible.
14 Let all your creatures serve
you,
for you spoke, and they
were made.
You sent forth your spirit,[i]
and it formed them;[j]
there is none that can
resist your voice.
15 For the mountains shall be
shaken to their
foundations with the
waters;
before your glance the
rocks shall melt like
wax.
But to those who fear you
you show mercy.
16 For every sacrifice as a
fragrant offering is a
small thing,
and the fat of all whole
burnt offerings to you is
a very little thing;
but whoever fears the Lord is
great forever.

17 Woe to the nations that rise
up against my people!
The Lord Almighty will
take vengeance on
them in the day of
judgment;
he will send fire and worms
into their flesh;
they shall weep in pain
forever.

18 When they arrived at Jerusalem, they worshiped God. As soon
as the people were purified, they
offered their burnt offerings, their
freewill offerings, and their gifts.
19 Judith also dedicated to God all
the possessions of Holofernes,
which the people had given her;
and the canopy that she had taken
for herself from his bedchamber
she gave as a votive offering. 20 For
three months the people continued feasting in Jerusalem before
the sanctuary, and Judith remained with them.

The Renown and Death of Judith

21 After this they all returned
home to their own inheritances.
Judith went to Bethulia, and remained on her estate. For the rest
of her life she was honored
throughout the whole country.
22 Many desired to marry her, but
she gave herself to no man all the
days of her life after her husband
Manasseh died and was gathered
to his people. 23 She became more
and more famous, and grew old in
her husband's house, reaching the
age of one hundred five. She set
her maid free. She died in Bethulia, and they buried her in the cave
of her husband Manasseh; 24 and
the house of Israel mourned her for
seven days. Before she died she
distributed her property to all
those who were next of kin to her
husband Manasseh, and to her
own nearest kindred. 25 No one
ever again spread terror among the
Israelites during the lifetime of Judith, or for a long time after her
death.

[g] Other ancient authorities read *feared*
[h] Gk *they* [i] Or *breath*
[j] Other ancient authorities read *they were created*

16.11 Jdt 14.19; 15.5 **16.12** 2 Sam 1.12 **16.13** Ps 144.9; Ex 15.6; Ps 76.4 **16.14** Gen 1.24-25; Ps 33.6,9; 104.30 **16.15** Judg 5.5; Isa 64.1,3; Ps 97.5; Mic 1.4; Ps 103.8,11 **16.16** 1 Sam 15.22; Isa 1.11; Mic 6.6-7; Ps 40.6-8; 51.16-17; Hos 6.6 **16.17** Num 21.29; Jer 48.46; Deut 32.35; Rom 12.19; Heb 10.30-31; Isa 66.24; Mk 9.48; Acts 12.23; Dan 12.2; Mt 25.46 **16.18** Num 31.50-54; Deut 13.16 **16.19** Jdt 15.11; Deut 12.5-6, 11 **16.21** Josh 24.28; Judg 2.6 **16.22** Lk 2.36-37 **16.23** Jdt 10.2,5; Gen 23.19; 49.31 **16.24** 1 Sam 25.1; 2 Chr 35.24; Num 27.11

Esther

(THE GREEK VERSION CONTAINING THE ADDITIONAL CHAPTERS)

NOTE. The deuterocanonical portions of the Book of Esther are several additional passages found in the Greek translation of the Hebrew Book of Esther, a translation that differs also in other respects from the Hebrew text (the latter is translated in the NRSV Old Testament). The disordered chapter numbers come from the displacement of the additions to the end of the canonical Book of Esther by Jerome in his Latin translation and from the subsequent division of the Bible into chapters by Stephen Langton, who numbered the additions consecutively as though they formed a direct continuation of the Hebrew text. So that the additions may be read in their proper context, the whole of the Greek version is here translated, though certain familiar names are given according to their Hebrew rather than their Greek form; for example, Mordecai and Vashti instead of Mardocheus and Astin. The order followed is that of the Greek text, but the chapter and verse numbers conform to those of the King James or Authorized Version. The additions, conveniently indicated by the letters A–F, are located as follows: A, before 1.1; B, after 3.13; C and D, after 4.17; E, after 8.12; F, after 10.3.

Title and Background

This book takes its name from its leading character, the beautiful Jewish girl whom king Artaxerxes (486-465 B.C.) took as his queen. The Hebrew book of Esther never mentions "God" or "Lord." However, the Greek Septuagint version contains additional sections, and in that version the names "God" and "Lord" appear more than fifty times. The entire Septuagint version of Esther is included here.

Author and Date of Writing

The additions to the original Hebrew Esther (see the introduction to Esther) were probably written by a Jew. They were most likely put down in writing about the end of the second century B.C.

Theme and Message

The additions to Esther make explicit what is only implicit in the original Esther–that God watched over his covenant people while they were in exile and delivered them from the threat of extinction.

Outline

I. Mordecai's Dream (11.2–12.6)
II. The Feasts of Artaxerxes (1.1–22)
III. Esther Made Queen (2.1-23)
IV. The Plot of Haman (3.1-16; 13.1-7)
V. Deliverance through Esther (4.1–7.10; 13.8–15.15)
VI. The Feast of Purim (8.1–11.1; 16.1-24)

ADDITION A

Mordecai's Dream

11 [a] 2 In the second year of the
reign of Artaxerxes the
Great, on the first day of Nisan,
Mordecai son of Jair son of
Shimei[b] son of Kish, of the tribe of
Benjamin, had a dream. 3 He was a
Jew living in the city of Susa, a
great man, serving in the court of
the king. 4 He was one of the cap-
tives whom King Nebuchadnezzar

11.2 Ezra 4.7; 7.1; Esth 1.1; Dan 9.1; Neh 1.1; Esth 3.7; 1 Sam 9.1,3; Esth 2.5; Add Esth 10.7
11.3 Esth 2.19; 8.2

[a] Chapters 11.2–12.6 correspond to chapter A 1-17 in some translations. [b] Gk *Semeios*

of Babylon had brought from Jerusalem with King Jeconiah of Judea. And this was his dream:
5 Noises[c] and confusion, thunders
and earthquake, tumult on the
earth! 6 Then two great dragons
came forward, both ready to fight,
and they roared terribly. 7 At their
roaring every nation prepared for
war, to fight against the righteous
nation. 8 It was a day of darkness
and gloom, of tribulation and distress, affliction and great tumult
on the earth! 9 And the whole righteous nation was troubled; they
feared the evils that threatened
them,[d] and were ready to perish.
10 Then they cried out to God; and
at their outcry, as though from a
tiny spring, there came a great
river, with abundant water; 11 light
came, and the sun rose, and the
lowly were exalted and devoured
those held in honor.
12 Mordecai saw in this dream
what God had determined to do,
and after he awoke he had it on his
mind, seeking all day to understand it in every detail.

A Plot against the King

12 Now Mordecai took his
rest in the courtyard with
Gabatha and Tharra, the two eunuchs of the king who kept watch
in the courtyard. 2 He overheard
their conversation and inquired
into their purposes, and learned
that they were preparing to lay
hands on King Artaxerxes; and he
informed the king concerning
them. 3 Then the king examined
the two eunuchs, and after they
had confessed it, they were led
away to execution. 4 The king made
a permanent record of these
things, and Mordecai wrote an account of them. 5 And the king ordered Mordecai to serve in the
court, and rewarded him for these
things. 6 But Haman son of Hammedatha, a Bougean, who was in
great honor with the king, determined to injure Mordecai and his
people because of the two eunuchs
of the king.

END OF ADDITION A

11.4 2 Kings 24.15; Esth 2.6; Jer 22.24-30 **11.7** Isa 26.2 **11.8** Isa 29.18; Joel 2.2; Am 5.20 **11.9** Esth 3.8-13 **11.10** Ex 2.23-25; Ps 107.6,13, 19; Add Esth 10.6 **11.11** Lk 14.11; 18.14 **12.2** Esth 2.19-23 **12.4** Esth 6.1-3 **12.6** Esth 3.1-2

1.1 Esth 1.1; Add Esth 11.2; Esth 8.9; 9.30 **1.2** Ezra 4.9; Neh 1.1 **1.3** 1 Kings 3.15; Esth 2.18; Jdt 1.16 **1.5** Dan 1.5; 2 Kings 21.18; Esth 7.7 **1.6** Ezek 23.41; Am 3.12; 6.4 **1.7** Esth 2.18 **1.10** Judg 16.25; Prov 31.1-4; Dan 5.1; Add Esth 12.1

Artaxerxes' Banquet

1 It was after this that the following things happened in
the days of Artaxerxes, the same
Artaxerxes who ruled over one
hundred twenty-seven provinces
from India to Ethiopia.[e] 2 In those
days, when King Artaxerxes was
enthroned in the city of Susa, 3 in
the third year of his reign, he gave
a banquet for his Friends and other
persons of various nations, the Persians and Median nobles, and the
governors of the provinces. 4 After
this, when he had displayed to
them the riches of his kingdom
and the splendor of his bountiful
celebration during the course of
one hundred eighty days, 5 at the
end of the festivity[f] the king gave
a drinking party for the people of
various nations who lived in the
city. This was held for six days in
the courtyard of the royal palace,
6 which was adorned with curtains
of fine linen and cotton, held by
cords of purple linen attached to
gold and silver blocks on pillars of
marble and other stones. Gold and
silver couches were placed on a
mosaic floor of emerald, mother-
of-pearl, and marble. There were
coverings of gauze, embroidered in
various colors, with roses arranged
around them. 7 The cups were of
gold and silver, and a miniature
cup was displayed, made of ruby,
worth thirty thousand talents.
There was abundant sweet wine,
such as the king himself drank.
8 The drinking was not according to
a fixed rule; but the king wished to
have it so, and he commanded his
stewards to comply with his pleasure and with that of the guests.
9 Meanwhile, Queen Vashti[g]
gave a drinking party for the
women in the palace where King
Artaxerxes was.

Dismissal of Queen Vashti

10 On the seventh day, when
the king was in good humor, he

c Or *Voices* d Gk *their own evils*
e Other ancient authorities lack *to Ethiopia*
f Gk *marriage feast* g Gk *Astin*

told Haman, Bazan, Tharra,
Boraze, Zatholtha, Abataza, and
Tharaba, the seven eunuchs who
served King Artaxerxes, 11 to escort
the queen to him in order to proclaim her as queen and to place
the diadem on her head, and to
have her display her beauty to all
the governors and the people of
various nations, for she was indeed
a beautiful woman. 12 But Queen
Vashti[h] refused to obey him and
would not come with the eunuchs.
This offended the king and he became furious. 13 He said to his
Friends, "This is how Vashti[h] has
answered me.[i] Give therefore your
ruling and judgment on this matter." 14 Arkesaeus, Sarsathaeus,
and Malesear, then the governors
of the Persians and Medes who
were closest to the king—
Arkesaeus, Sarsathaeus, and Malesear, who sat beside him in the
chief seats—came to him 15 and
told him what must be done to
Queen Vashti[h] for not obeying the
order that the king had sent her by
the eunuchs. 16 Then Muchaeus
said to the king and the governors,
"Queen Vashti[h] has insulted not
only the king but also all the king's
governors and officials" 17 (for he
had reported to them what the
queen had said and how she had
defied the king). "And just as she
defied King Artaxerxes, 18 so now
the other ladies who are wives of
the Persian and Median governors,
on hearing what she has said to the
king, will likewise dare to insult
their husbands. 19 If therefore it
pleases the king, let him issue a
royal decree, inscribed in accordance with the laws of the Medes
and Persians so that it may not be
altered, that the queen may no longer come into his presence; but let
the king give her royal rank to a
woman better than she. 20 Let
whatever law the king enacts be
proclaimed in his kingdom, and
thus all women will give honor to
their husbands, rich and poor
alike." 21 This speech pleased the
king and the governors, and the
king did as Muchaeus had rec-
ommended. 22 The king sent
the decree into all his kingdom,
to every province in its own
language, so that in every house
respect would be shown to every
husband.

1.11 Song 2.4; Ps 45.11; Ezek 16.14 **1.12** Gen 39.19; Esth 2.21; 7.7; Prov 19.12 **1.13** Ezra 7.14; Dan 2.12; 1 Macc 2.18 **1.18** Prov 19.13; 27.15 **1.19** Eccl 8.3-4; Esth 8.8; Dan 6.8,12 **1.20** Eph 5.22; Col 3.18 **1.22** Neh 13.24; Esth 8.9 **2.1** Esth 1.19-20; 7.10 **2.3** Esth 2.8,15, 12 **2.5** Add Esth 11.2 **2.6** 2 Kings 24.14-15; Dan 1.1-5 **2.7** Gen 39.6; Song 1.5 **2.8** Neh 1.1; Esth 1.2; 2.3 **2.9** Gen 39.21; Esth 2.3; Gen 37.3; Ezek 16.9-13

Esther Becomes Queen

2 After these things, the king's
anger abated, and he no longer was concerned about Vashti[h]
or remembered what he had said
and how he had condemned her.
2 Then the king's servants said,
"Let beautiful and virtuous girls be
sought out for the king. 3 The king
shall appoint officers in all the
provinces of his kingdom, and they
shall select beautiful young virgins
to be brought to the harem in Susa,
the capital. Let them be entrusted
to the king's eunuch who is in
charge of the women, and let ointments and whatever else they need
be given them. 4 And the woman
who pleases the king shall
be queen instead of Vashti.[h]
This pleased the king, and he
did so.
5 Now there was a Jew in Susa
the capital whose name was Mordecai son of Jair son of Shimei[j]
son of Kish, of the tribe of Benjamin; 6 he had been taken captive
from Jerusalem among those
whom King Nebuchadnezzar of
Babylon had captured. 7 And he
had a foster child, the daughter of
his father's brother, Aminadab,
and her name was Esther. When
her parents died, he brought her
up to womanhood as his own. The
girl was beautiful in appearance.
8 So, when the decree of the king
was proclaimed, and many girls
were gathered in Susa the capital
in custody of Gai, Esther also was
brought to Gai, who had custody of
the women. 9 The girl pleased him
and won his favor, and he quickly
provided her with ointments and
her portion of food,[k] as well as
seven maids chosen from the pal-

[h] Gk *Astin* [i] Gk *Astin has said thus and so*
[j] Gk *Semeios* [k] Gk lacks *of food*

ace; he treated her and her maids
with special favor in the harem.
10 Now Esther had not disclosed
her people or country, for Mordecai had commanded her not to
make it known. 11 And every day
Mordecai walked in the courtyard
of the harem, to see what would
happen to Esther.
12 Now the period after which a
girl was to go to the king was
twelve months. During this time
the days of beautification are
completed—six months while
they are anointing themselves with
oil of myrrh, and six months with
spices and ointments for women.
13 Then she goes in to the king; she
is handed to the person appointed,
and goes with him from the harem
to the king's palace. 14 In the evening she enters and in the morning
she departs to the second harem,
where Gai the king's eunuch is in
charge of the women; and she does
not go in to the king again unless
she is summoned by name.
15 When the time was fulfilled
for Esther daughter of Aminadab,
the brother of Mordecai's father, to
go in to the king, she neglected
none of the things that Gai, the eunuch in charge of the women, had
commanded. Now Esther found favor in the eyes of all who saw her.
16 So Esther went in to King Artaxerxes in the twelfth month, which
is Adar, in the seventh year of his
reign. 17 And the king loved Esther
and she found favor beyond all the
other virgins, so he put on her the
queen's diadem. 18 Then the king
gave a banquet lasting seven days
for all his Friends and the officers
to celebrate his marriage to Esther;
and he granted a remission of
taxes to those who were under his
rule.

The Plot Discovered

19 Meanwhile Mordecai was
serving in the courtyard. 20 Esther
had not disclosed her country—
such were the instructions of Mordecai; but she was to fear God and
keep his laws, just as she had done
when she was with him. So Esther
did not change her mode of life.
21 Now the king's eunuchs,
who were chief bodyguards, were
angry because of Mordecai's ad-
vancement, and they plotted to kill
King Artaxerxes. 22 The matter became known to Mordecai, and he
warned Esther, who in turn revealed the plot to the king. 23 He
investigated the two eunuchs and
hanged them. Then the king ordered a memorandum to be deposited in the royal library in praise of
the goodwill shown by Mordecai.

Mordecai Refuses to Do Obeisance

3 After these events King Artaxerxes promoted Haman son
of Hammedatha, a Bougean, advancing him and granting him precedence over all the king's[l]
Friends. 2 So all who were at court
used to do obeisance to Haman,[m]
for so the king had commanded to
be done. Mordecai, however, did
not do obeisance. 3 Then the king's
courtiers said to Mordecai, "Mordecai, why do you disobey the
king's command?" 4 Day after day
they spoke to him, but he would
not listen to them. Then they informed Haman that Mordecai was
resisting the king's command.
Mordecai had told them that he
was a Jew. 5 So when Haman
learned that Mordecai was not doing obeisance to him, he became
furiously angry, 6 and plotted to destroy all the Jews under Artaxerxes' rule.
7 In the twelfth year of King
Artaxerxes Haman[n] came to a decision by casting lots, taking the
days and the months one by one, to
fix on one day to destroy the whole
race of Mordecai. The lot fell on
the fourteenth[o] day of the month
of Adar.

Decree against the Jews

8 Then Haman[n] said to King
Artaxerxes, "There is a certain nation scattered among the other nations in all your kingdom; their
laws are different from those of ev-

2.10 Esth 2.20 **2.12** Prov 27.9; Song 1.3; Isa 3.24 **2.14** 1 Kings 11.3; Song 6.8; Dan 5.2; Esth 4.11 **2.15** Esth 9.29; Ps 45.14; Esth 2.9 **2.17** Esth 1.11; Ezek 16.9-13 **2.18** 1 Kings 3.15; Esth 1.3 **2.19** Esth 3.2; 4.2; Add Esth 11.3 **2.20** Esth 2.10; Deut 10.12-13; Eccl 12.13 **2.21** Add Esth 12.1-4 **2.22** Gen 40.2; Esth 6.1-2 **2.23** Gen 40.19; Ps 7.14-16; Prov 26.27; Esth 7.10; 6.1; 10.2 **3.1** Add Esth 12.6; Esth 5.11 **3.3** Dan 3.12 **3.4** Gen 39.10 **3.5** Esth 3.2; 2.21; 5.9 **3.6** Ps 74.8; 83.4 **3.7** Lev 16.8; 1 Sam 10.21; Esth 9.24,26; Ezra 6.15; Esth 3.13; 9.19 **3.8** Ezra 4.15; Dan 6.13; Acts 16.20,21

[l] Gk *all his* [m] Gk *him* [n] Gk *he*
[o] Other ancient witnesses read *thirteenth;* see 8.12

ery other nation, and they do not
keep the laws of the king. It is not
expedient for the king to tolerate
them. 9 If it pleases the king, let it
be decreed that they are to be destroyed, and I will pay ten thousand talents of silver into the
king's treasury." 10 So the king took
off his signet ring and gave it to Haman to seal the decree[p] that was
to be written against the Jews.
11 The king told Haman, "Keep the
money, and do whatever you want
with that nation."
12 So on the thirteenth day of
the first month the king's secretaries were summoned, and in accordance with Haman's instructions
they wrote in the name of King
Artaxerxes to the magistrates and
the governors in every province
from India to Ethiopia. There were
one hundred twenty-seven provinces in all, and the governors were
addressed each in his own language. 13 Instructions were sent by
couriers throughout all the empire
of Artaxerxes to destroy the Jewish
people on a given day of the
twelfth month, which is Adar, and
to plunder their goods.

Addition B

The King's Letter

13 [q] This is a copy of the letter:
"The Great King, Arta-
xerxes, writes the following to the
governors of the hundred twenty-
seven provinces from India to Ethiopia and to the officials under
them:
2 "Having become ruler of
many nations and master of the
whole world (not elated with presumption of authority but always
acting reasonably and with kindness), I have determined to settle
the lives of my subjects in lasting
tranquility and, in order to make
my kingdom peaceable and open
to travel throughout all its extent,
to restore the peace desired by all
people.
3 "When I asked my counselors how this might be accomplished, Haman—who excels

3.9 Esth 7.4 **3.10** Gen 41.42; Esth 7.6; 8.2; Hag 2.23 **3.12** 1 Kings 21.8; Esth 1.1; Neh 13.14; Esth 1.22 **3.13** Esth 8.8-10; 2.7; 8.11; 9.10 **13.1** Ezra 4.11; 5.6; 1 Macc 8.22; 12.5,19; Add Esth 11.2 **13.2** Dan 4.1; Add Esth 16.8 **13.3** Esth 3.1; 5.11; Add Esth 16.11 **13.4** Esth 3.8; Jer 30.11; 36.19; Ezra 4.12,15; Dan 3.12; 6.13 **13.5** Esth 3.8; Acts 16.20-21; 17.6 **13.6** Esth 3.1; Add Esth 13.3; Esth 3.13; 8.12; 9.1; Add Esth 16.20 **13.7** Add Esth 13.2 **13.14** Esth 8.13-14; 9.1 **13.15** Esth 1.10; 8.15 **4.1** Gen 37.34; Num 14.6; Josh 7.6; 2 Sam 13.19; Ezek 27.30-31; Jon 3.5-6; Jdt 4.12

among us in sound judgment, and
is distinguished for his unchanging
goodwill and steadfast fidelity, and
has attained the second place in
the kingdom— 4 pointed out to us
that among all the nations in the
world there is scattered a certain
hostile people, who have laws contrary to those of every nation and
continually disregard the ordinances of kings, so that the unifying of the kingdom that we honorably intend cannot be brought
about. 5 We understand that this
people, and it alone, stands constantly in opposition to every nation, perversely following a strange
manner of life and laws, and is ill-
disposed to our government, doing
all the harm they can so that our
kingdom may not attain stability.
6 "Therefore we have decreed
that those indicated to you in the
letters written by Haman, who is in
charge of affairs and is our second
father, shall all—wives and children included—be utterly destroyed by the swords of their enemies, without pity or restraint, on
the fourteenth day of the twelfth
month, Adar, of this present year,
7 so that those who have long been
hostile and remain so may in a single day go down in violence to Hades, and leave our government
completely secure and untroubled
hereafter."

End of Addition B

3 14 Copies of the document
were posted in every province, and all the nations were ordered to be prepared for that day.
15 The matter was expedited also in
Susa. And while the king and Haman caroused together, the city of
Susa[r] was thrown into confusion.

Mordecai Seeks Esther's Aid

4 When Mordecai learned of all
that had been done, he tore
his clothes, put on sackcloth, and
sprinkled himself with ashes; then

[p] Gk lacks *the decree*
[q] Chapter 13.1-7 corresponds to chapter B 1-7 in some translations. [r] Gk *the city*

he rushed through the street of the
city, shouting loudly: "An innocent
nation is being destroyed!" 2 He got
as far as the king's gate, and there
he stopped, because no one was allowed to enter the courtyard
clothed in sackcloth and ashes.
3 And in every province where the
king's proclamation had been
posted there was a loud cry of
mourning and lamentation among
the Jews, and they put on sackcloth and ashes. 4 When the
queen's[s] maids and eunuchs
came and told her, she was deeply
troubled by what she heard had
happened, and sent some clothes
to Mordecai to put on instead of
sackcloth; but he would not consent. 5 Then Esther summoned
Hachratheus, the eunuch who attended her, and ordered him to get
accurate information for her from
Mordecai.[t]
7 So Mordecai told him what
had happened and how Haman
had promised to pay ten thousand
talents into the royal treasury to
bring about the destruction of the
Jews. 8 He also gave him a copy of
what had been posted in Susa for
their destruction, to show to Esther; and he told him to charge her
to go in to the king and plead for
his favor in behalf of the people.
"Remember," he said, "the days
when you were an ordinary person,
being brought up under my care—
for Haman, who stands next to the
king, has spoken against us and
demands our death. Call upon the
Lord; then speak to the king in our
behalf, and save us from death."
9 Hachratheus went in and told
Esther all these things. 10 And she
said to him, "Go to Mordecai and
say, 11 'All nations of the empire
know that if any man or woman
goes to the king inside the inner
court without being called, there is
no escape for that person. Only the
one to whom the king stretches out
the golden scepter is safe—and it
is now thirty days since I was called
to go to the king.' "
12 When Hachratheus delivered
her entire message to Mordecai,
13 Mordecai told him to go back
and say to her, "Esther, do not say
to yourself that you alone among
all the Jews will escape alive. 14 For
if you keep quiet at such a time as
this, help and protection will come
to the Jews from another quarter,
but you and your father's family
will perish. Yet, who knows
whether it was not for such a time
as this that you were made
queen?" 15 Then Esther gave the
messenger this answer to take
back to Mordecai: 16 "Go and
gather all the Jews who are in Susa
and fast on my behalf; for three
days and nights do not eat or drink,
and my maids and I will also go
without food. After that I will go to
the king, contrary to the law, even
if I must die." 17 So Mordecai went
away and did what Esther had told
him to do.

ADDITION C

Mordecai's Prayer

13 8[u] Then Mordecai[v] prayed
to the Lord, calling to remembrance all the works of the
Lord.
9 He said, "O Lord, Lord, you
rule as King over all things, for the
universe is in your power and there
is no one who can oppose you
when it is your will to save Israel,
10 for you have made heaven and
earth and every wonderful thing
under heaven. 11 You are Lord of
all, and there is no one who can resist you, the Lord. 12 You know all
things; you know, O Lord, that it
was not in insolence or pride or for
any love of glory that I did this, and
refused to bow down to this proud
Haman; 13 for I would have been
willing to kiss the soles of his feet
to save Israel! 14 But I did this so
that I might not set human glory
above the glory of God, and I will
not bow down to anyone but you,

4.2 Esth 2.19 **4.3** Esth 3.14; Add Esth 13.1 **4.4** Esth 2.15 **4.7** Esth 3.9; 7.4 **4.8** Add Esth 13.1; Esth 5.1-2; 2.7; Ps 18.3; 50.15; 55.16 **4.11** Esth 2.14; Dan 2.9; Esth 5.2; 8.4; Add Esth 15.11 **4.14** Eccl 3.7; Isa 62.1; Am 5.13; Deut 28.29; Esth 9.16,22; Gen 45.7; 50.20 **4.16** 2 Chr 20.3; Esth 9.31; Joel 1.14; 2.15; Esth 4.11 **13.8** Ps 77.11; 105.5; 143.5 **13.9** Ps 10.16; 24.7-10; 47.6-8; 2 Kings 19.19,34; Ps 28.9; 69.35; **13.10** Gen 1.1; Ex 20.11; Ps 33.6 **13.11** Jdt 16.14; Rom 9.19 **13.12** Ps 139.1-6; Esth 3.2; 5.9 **13.14** Ps 81.9; 95.6; Jdt 10.8; Rev 19.10 **13.15** 1 Kings 18.36; 1 Chr 29.18; Ps 47.9; Esth 3.9,11; 1 Kings 8.51, 53 **13.16** Deut 32.9; Jer 12.10 **13.17** Ps 25.6; 123.2-3; Rom 9.15-18; Ps 30.11; Jer 31.4,13

[s] Gk *When her* [t] Other ancient witnesses add 6 *So Hachratheus went out to Mordecai in the street of the city opposite the city gate.*
[u] Chapters 13.8—15.16 correspond to chapters C 1-30 and D 1-16 in some translations.
[v] Gk *he*

who are my Lord; and I will not do
these things in pride. 15And now,
O Lord God and King, God of
Abraham, spare your people; for
the eyes of our foes are upon us[w]
to annihilate us, and they desire to
destroy the inheritance that has
been yours from the beginning.
16Do not neglect your portion,
which you redeemed for yourself
out of the land of Egypt. 17Hear my
prayer, and have mercy upon your
inheritance; turn our mourning
into feasting that we may live and
sing praise to your name, O Lord;
do not destroy the lips[x] of those
who praise you."

18 And all Israel cried out
mightily, for their death was before
their eyes.

Esther's Prayer

14 Then Queen Esther, seized
with deadly anxiety, fled
to the Lord. 2She took off her
splendid apparel and put on the
garments of distress and mourning, and instead of costly perfumes
she covered her head with ashes
and dung, and she utterly humbled
her body; every part that she loved
to adorn she covered with her tan-
gled hair. 3She prayed to the Lord
God of Israel, and said: "O my
Lord, you only are our king; help
me, who am alone and have no
helper but you, 4for my danger is in
my hand. 5Ever since I was born I
have heard in the tribe of my family
that you, O Lord, took Israel out of
all the nations, and our ancestors
from among all their forebears, for
an everlasting inheritance, and
that you did for them all that you
promised. 6And now we have
sinned before you, and you have
handed us over to our enemies
7because we glorified their gods.
You are righteous, O Lord! 8And
now they are not satisfied that we
are in bitter slavery, but they have
covenanted with their idols 9to
abolish what your mouth has ordained, and to destroy your inheritance, to stop the mouths of those
who praise you and to quench your
altar and the glory of your house,
10to open the mouths of the nations for the praise of vain idols,
and to magnify forever a mortal
king.

11 "O Lord, do not surrender
your scepter to what has no being;
and do not let them laugh at our
downfall; but turn their plan
against them, and make an example of him who began this against
us. 12Remember, O Lord; make
yourself known in this time of our
affliction, and give me courage,
O King of the gods and Master of
all dominion! 13Put eloquent
speech in my mouth before the
lion, and turn his heart to hate the
man who is fighting against us, so
that there may be an end of him
and those who agree with him.
14But save us by your hand, and
help me, who am alone and have
no helper but you, O Lord. 15You
have knowledge of all things, and
you know that I hate the splendor
of the wicked and abhor the bed of
the uncircumcised and of any
alien. 16You know my necessity—
that I abhor the sign of my proud
position, which is upon my head
on days when I appear in public. I
abhor it like a filthy rag, and I do
not wear it on the days when I am
at leisure. 17And your servant has
not eaten at Haman's table, and I
have not honored the king's feast
or drunk the wine of libations.
18Your servant has had no joy since
the day that I was brought here until now, except in you, O Lord God
of Abraham. 19O God, whose
might is over all, hear the voice of
the despairing, and save us from
the hands of evildoers. And save
me from my fear!"

End of Addition C

Addition D

Esther Is Received by the King

15 On the third day, when she
ended her prayer, she
took off the garments in which she
had worshiped, and arrayed herself
in splendid attire. 2Then, majesti-

13.18 Add Esth 10.9
14.2 Gen 38.14; 2 Sam 14.2; Esth 2.12; 4.1
14.3 Add Esth 13.9; Ps 46.1; 54.4; Heb 13.6
14.4 Esth 4.16
14.5 Gen 12.1-3; Am 3.2; Deut 7.6; Ps 78.71; Ezek 44.28
14.6 Ezra 9.6-7; Neh 9.16, 26-30; Dan 9.11-13
14.7 2 Chr 25.14; 28.25; Jer 5.19; 11.10-13
14.9 Esth 3.9; Add Esth 13.6
14.11 Isa 44.9-20; Jer 10.3-5; 1 Cor 8.4; Ps 80.6
14.12 Ps 74.18; Isa 38.3
14.13 Ps 7.2; 22.13, 21; Esth 7.10
14.14 Add Esth 14.3
14.16 Esth 1.11; 2.17; Isa 30.22; 64.6
14.17 Esth 2.18; 5.5; 7.1
14.19 Ps 28.9; Add Esth 13.9; 15.5
15.1 Add Esth 14.2
15.2 2 Macc 9.5

[w] Gk *for they are eying us* [x] Gk *mouth*

cally adorned, after invoking the
aid of the all-seeing God and Savior, she took two maids with her;
3on one she leaned gently for support, 4while the other followed,
carrying her train. 5She was radiant with perfect beauty, and she
looked happy, as if beloved, but
her heart was frozen with fear.
6When she had gone through all
the doors, she stood before the
king. He was seated on his royal
throne, clothed in the full array of
his majesty, all covered with gold
and precious stones. He was most
terrifying.
7 Lifting his face, flushed with
splendor, he looked at her in fierce
anger. The queen faltered, and
turned pale and faint, and collapsed on the head of the maid
who went in front of her. 8Then
God changed the spirit of the king
to gentleness, and in alarm he
sprang from his throne and took
her in his arms until she came to
herself. He comforted her with
soothing words, and said to her,
9"What is it, Esther? I am your husband.[y] Take courage; 10You shall
not die, for our law applies only to
our subjects.[z] Come near."
11 Then he raised the golden
scepter and touched her neck with
it; 12he embraced her, and said,
"Speak to me." 13She said to him,
"I saw you, my lord, like an angel of
God, and my heart was shaken
with fear at your glory. 14For you
are wonderful, my lord, and your
countenance is full of grace."
15And while she was speaking, she
fainted and fell. 16Then the king
was agitated, and all his servants
tried to comfort her.

End of Addition D

5[a] 3The king said to her, "What
do you wish, Esther? What is
your request? It shall be given you,
even to half of my kingdom." 4And
Esther said, "Today is a special day
for me. If it pleases the king, let
him and Haman come to the dinner that I shall prepare today."
5Then the king said, "Bring Haman

15.5 Esth 2.7; Add Esth 14.19
15.6 1 Kings 9.5; 2 Chr 23.20; Esth 5.1
15.8 Prov 21.1; 1 Cor 4.21; Eph 4.2
15.10 Esth 4.11
15.11 Esth 5.2
15.13 Add Esth 15.5
5.3 Esth 7.2; Dan 5.16; Mk 6.23
5.6 Esth 1.10; 7.2; 9.12
5.8 Esth 7.3; 8.5; 6.14
5.9 Esth 2.19,21; 3.5; Prov 14.17
5.10 Esth 6.13
5.11 Esth 3.1
5.12 Esth 5.8; 6.14
5.13 Esth 2.19,21
5.14 Esth 6.4; 7.9-10
6.1 Dan 2.1; 6.18; Esth 2.23; 10.2
6.2 Esth 2.21; Add Esth 12.2

quickly, so that we may do as Esther desires." So they both came to
the dinner that Esther had spoken
about. 6While they were drinking
wine, the king said to Esther,
"What is it, Queen Esther? It shall
be granted you." 7She said, "My
petition and request is: 8if I have
found favor in the sight of the king,
let the king and Haman come to
the dinner that I shall prepare
them, and tomorrow I will do as I
have done today."

Haman's Plot against Mordecai

9 So Haman went out from the
king joyful and glad of heart. But
when he saw Mordecai the Jew in
the courtyard, he was filled with
anger. 10Nevertheless, he went
home and summoned his friends
and his wife Zosara. 11And he told
them about his riches and the
honor that the king had bestowed
on him, and how he had advanced
him to be the first in the kingdom.
12And Haman said, "The queen
did not invite anyone to the dinner
with the king except me; and I am
invited again tomorrow. 13But
these things give me no pleasure as
long as I see Mordecai the Jew in
the courtyard." 14His wife Zosara
and his friends said to him, "Let a
gallows be made, fifty cubits high,
and in the morning tell the king to
have Mordecai hanged on it. Then,
go merrily with the king to the dinner." This advice pleased Haman,
and so the gallows was prepared.

Mordecai's Reward from the King

6 That night the Lord took sleep
from the king, so he gave orders to his secretary to bring the
book of daily records, and to read
to him. 2He found the words written about Mordecai, how he had
told the king about the two royal
eunuchs who were on guard and
sought to lay hands on King Artaxerxes. 3The king said, "What
honor or dignity did we bestow on
Mordecai?" The king's servants

[y] Gk *brother* [z] Meaning of Gk uncertain
[a] In Greek, Chapter D replaces verses 1 and 2 in Hebrew.

said, "You have not done anything
for him." 4 While the king was inquiring about the goodwill shown
by Mordecai, Haman was in the
courtyard. The king asked, "Who is
in the courtyard?" Now Haman
had come to speak to the king
about hanging Mordecai on the
gallows that he had prepared. 5 The
servants of the king answered,
"Haman is standing in the courtyard." And the king said, "Summon him." 6 Then the king said to
Haman, "What shall I do for the
person whom I wish to honor?"
And Haman said to himself,
"Whom would the king wish to
honor more than me?" 7 So he said
to the king, "For a person whom
the king wishes to honor, 8 let the
king's servants bring out the fine
linen robe that the king has worn,
and the horse on which the king
rides, 9 and let both be given to one
of the king's honored Friends, and
let him robe the person whom the
king loves and mount him on the
horse, and let it be proclaimed
through the open square of the
city, saying, 'Thus shall it be done
to everyone whom the king honors.' " 10 Then the king said to Haman, "You have made an excellent
suggestion! Do just as you have
said for Mordecai the Jew, who is
on duty in the courtyard. And let
nothing be omitted from what you
have proposed." 11 So Haman got
the robe and the horse; he put the
robe on Mordecai and made him
ride through the open square of
the city, proclaiming, "Thus shall
it be done to everyone whom the
king wishes to honor." 12 Then
Mordecai returned to the courtyard, and Haman hurried back to
his house, mourning and with his
head covered. 13 Haman told his
wife Zosara and his friends what
had befallen him. His friends and
his wife said to him, "If Mordecai
is of the Jewish people, and you
have begun to be humiliated before him, you will surely fall. You
will not be able to defend yourself,
because the living God is with
him."

6.4 Eccl 9.13-16; Add Esth 12.5
6.5 Esth 5.14
6.8 Gen 41.42; Isa 52.1; Dan 5.29; 1 Kings 1.33
6.9 Gen 41.43
6.11 Gen 41.42
6.12 2 Sam 15.30; Jer 14.3-4; Mic 3.7
6.13 Esth 5.10; Prov 16.18; 26.27; 28.18; Deut 5.26; 1 Sam 17.26, 36; Ps 42.2
6.14 Esth 5.4,8
7.2 Esth 1.10; 5.6; 5.3; Dan 5.16; Mk 6.23
7.3 Esth 8.5
7.4 Esth 3.9; Add Esth 13.16
7.6 Esth 3.8-10; Add Esth 15.5,13
7.7 2 Kings 21.18
7.8 Esth 1.6; Gen 34.7
7.9 Esth 1.10,12, 15; 4.4-5; 5.14; Ps 7.14-16; Prov 11.5-6; 26.27; Mt 7.2
7.10 Prov 10.28; Dan 6.24; Esth 2.1

Haman at Esther's Banquet

14 While they were still talking,
the eunuchs arrived and hurriedly
brought Haman to the banquet
7 that Esther had prepared. 1 So
the king and Haman went in
to drink with the queen. 2 And the
second day, as they were drinking
wine, the king said, "What is it,
Queen Esther? What is your petition and what is your request? It
shall be granted to you, even to
half of my kingdom." 3 She answered and said, "If I have found
favor with the king, let my life be
granted me at my petition, and my
people at my request. 4 For we have
been sold, I and my people, to be
destroyed, plundered, and made
slaves—we and our children—
male and female slaves. This has
come to my knowledge. Our antagonist brings shame on[b] the king's
court." 5 Then the king said, "Who
is the person that would dare to do
this thing?" 6 Esther said, "Our enemy is this evil man Haman!" At
this, Haman was terrified in the
presence of the king and queen.

Punishment of Haman

7 The king rose from the banquet and went into the garden, and
Haman began to beg for his life
from the queen, for he saw that he
was in serious trouble. 8 When the
king returned from the garden, Haman had thrown himself on the
couch, pleading with the queen.
The king said, "Will he dare even
assault my wife in my own house?"
Haman, when he heard, turned
away his face. 9 Then Bugathan,
one of the eunuchs, said to the
king, "Look, Haman has even prepared a gallows for Mordecai, who
gave information of concern to the
king; it is standing at Haman's
house, a gallows fifty cubits high."
So the king said, "Let Haman be
hanged on that." 10 So Haman was
hanged on the gallows he had prepared for Mordecai. With that the
anger of the king abated.

[b] Gk *is not worthy of*

Royal Favor Shown the Jews

8 On that very day King Artaxerxes granted to Esther all the property of the persecutor[c] Haman. Mordecai was summoned by the king, for Esther had told the king[d] that he was related to her. 2 The king took the ring that had been taken from Haman, and gave it to Mordecai; and Esther set Mordecai over everything that had been Haman's.

3 Then she spoke once again to the king and, falling at his feet, she asked him to avert all the evil that Haman had planned against the Jews. 4 The king extended his golden scepter to Esther, and she rose and stood before the king. 5 Esther said, "If it pleases you, and if I have found favor, let an order be sent rescinding the letters that Haman wrote and sent to destroy the Jews in your kingdom. 6 How can I look on the ruin of my people? How can I be safe if my ancestral nation[e] is destroyed?" 7 The king said to Esther, "Now that I[f] have granted all of Haman's property to you and have hanged him on a tree because he acted against the Jews, what else do you request? 8 Write in my name what you think best and seal it with my ring; for whatever is written at the king's command and sealed with my ring cannot be contravened."

9 The secretaries were summoned on the twenty-third day of the first month, that is, Nisan, in the same year; and all that he commanded with respect to the Jews was given in writing to the administrators and governors of the provinces from India to Ethiopia, one hundred twenty-seven provinces, to each province in its own language. 10 The edict was written[g] with the king's authority and sealed with his ring, and sent out by couriers. 11 He ordered the Jews in every city to observe their own laws, to defend themselves, and to act as they wished against their opponents and enemies 12 on a certain day, the thirteenth of the twelfth month, which is Adar, throughout all the kingdom of Artaxerxes.

ADDITION E

The Decree of Artaxerxes

16[h] The following is a copy of this letter:

"The Great King, Artaxerxes, to the governors of the provinces from India to Ethiopia, one hundred twenty-seven provinces, and to those who are loyal to our government, greetings.

2 "Many people, the more they are honored with the most generous kindness of their benefactors, the more proud do they become, 3 and not only seek to injure our subjects, but in their inability to stand prosperity, they even undertake to scheme against their own benefactors. 4 They not only take away thankfulness from others, but, carried away by the boasts of those who know nothing of goodness, they even assume that they will escape the evil-hating justice of God, who always sees everything. 5 And often many of those who are set in places of authority have been made in part responsible for the shedding of innocent blood, and have been involved in irremediable calamities, by the persuasion of friends who have been entrusted with the administration of public affairs, 6 when these persons by the false trickery of their evil natures beguile the sincere goodwill of their sovereigns.

7 "What has been wickedly accomplished through the pestilent behavior of those who exercise authority unworthily can be seen, not so much from the more ancient records that we hand on, as from investigation of matters close at hand.[i] 8 In the future we will take care to render our kingdom quiet and peaceable for all, 9 by changing

8.1 Esth 7.6; Prov 11.6; 22.22-23; Esth 2.7 **8.2** Gen 41.42; Esth 3.10; Prov 13.22; Dan 2.48-49 **8.3** Esth 5.4; 3.8-10 **8.4** Esth 4.11; 5.2 **8.5** Esth 5.8; 7.3; 3.12-13; Add Esth 13.1-7 **8.6** Esth 3.9; 7.4; Add Esth 13.6 **8.7** Esth 8.2 **8.8** Esth 3.10,12; Gen 41.42; Esth 1.19; Dan 6.15 **8.9** Esth 1.1; 9.30; 1.22 **8.11** Ezra 6.9; Esth 9.10, 15-16 **8.12** Esth 3.13; 9.1

16.1 Ezra 4.11; 5.6; Add Esth 13.1; 11.2; Esth 1.1; Add Esth 8.9 **16.3** Prov 13.10 **16.4** Ps 33.5; 103.6; Isa 30.18; Ps 139.7-12; Add Esth 15.2 **16.5** 2 Kings 21.16; 24.4; Prov 6.16-17 **16.8** Add Esth 13.2

[c] Gk *slanderer* [d] Gk *him* [e] Gk *country* [f] Gk *If I* [g] Gk *It was written* [h] Chapter 16.1-24 corresponds to chapter E 1-24 in some translations. [i] Gk *matters beside* (your) *feet*

our methods and always judging
what comes before our eyes with
more equitable consideration.
10 For Haman son of Hammedatha,
a Macedonian (really an alien to
the Persian blood, and quite devoid of our kindliness), having become our guest, 11 enjoyed so fully
the goodwill that we have for every
nation that he was called our father and was continually bowed
down to by all as the person second to the royal throne. 12 But, unable to restrain his arrogance, he
undertook to deprive us of our
kingdom and our life,[j] 13 and with
intricate craft and deceit asked for
the destruction of Mordecai, our
savior and perpetual benefactor,
and of Esther, the blameless partner of our kingdom, together with
their whole nation. 14 He thought
that by these methods he would
catch us undefended and would
transfer the kingdom of the Persians to the Macedonians.

15 "But we find that the Jews,
who were consigned to annihilation by this thrice-accursed man,
are not evildoers, but are governed
by most righteous laws 16 and are
children of the living God, most
high, most mighty,[k] who has directed the kingdom both for us and
for our ancestors in the most excellent order.

17 "You will therefore do well
not to put in execution the letters
sent by Haman son of Hammedatha, 18 since he, the one who did
these things, has been hanged at
the gate of Susa with all his
household—for God, who rules
over all things, has speedily inflicted on him the punishment that
he deserved.

19 "Therefore post a copy of
this letter publicly in every place,
and permit the Jews to live under
their own laws. 20 And give them re-
inforcements, so that on the thirteenth day of the twelfth month,
Adar, on that very day, they may
defend themselves against those
who attack them at the time of oppression. 21 For God, who rules
over all things, has made this day
to be a joy for his chosen people
instead of a day of destruction for
them.

22 "Therefore you shall observe this with all good cheer as a
notable day among your commem-
orative festivals, 23 so that both
now and hereafter it may represent
deliverance for you[l] and the loyal
Persians, but that it may be a reminder of destruction for those
who plot against us.

24 "Every city and country,
without exception, that does not
act accordingly shall be destroyed
in wrath with spear and fire. It
shall be made not only impassable
for human beings, but also most
hateful to wild animals and birds
for all time.

End of Addition E

8 13 "Let copies of the decree be
posted conspicuously in all
the kingdom, and let all the Jews
be ready on that day to fight
against their enemies."

14 So the messengers on horseback set out with all speed to perform what the king had commanded; and the decree was
published also in Susa. 15 Mordecai
went out dressed in the royal robe
and wearing a gold crown and a
turban of purple linen. The people
in Susa rejoiced on seeing him.
16 And the Jews had light and gladness 17 in every city and province
wherever the decree was published; wherever the proclamation
was made, the Jews had joy and
gladness, a banquet and a holiday.
And many of the Gentiles were circumcised and became Jews out of
fear of the Jews.

Victory of the Jews

9 Now on the thirteenth day of
the twelfth month, which is
Adar, the decree written by the
king arrived. 2 On that same day
the enemies of the Jews perished;
no one resisted, because they
feared them. 3 The chief provincial
governors, the princes, and the

16.10 Add Esth 12.6 **16.11** Esth 3.1; Add Esth 13.3,6 **16.13** Esth 3.9; Add Esth 13.6; Esth 2.21-22; Add Esth 12.1-3 **16.15** Neh 9.13; Ps 19.7 **16.16** Deut 5.26; 1 Sam 17.26, 36; Ps 42.2 **16.17** Esth 3.13 **16.18** Esth 7.10; Ps 22.28; 103.19; 3 Macc 5.28 **16.20** Esth 3.13; 8.12; 8.11; 9.10,15-16 **16.21** Esth 9.17-18 **16.22** Esth 9.19 **16.24** Dan 3.6 **8.13** Esth 3.14; 9.2,5 **8.14** Esth 3.15 **8.15** Esth 9.4; Gen 41.42; Dan 5.7 **8.16** Ps 112.1,4; Esth 9.18; Ps 35.27; 97.10-12 **8.17** Ex 15.14,16; Deut 11.25 **9.1** Esth 3.13; 8.12 **9.2** Esth 8.17 **9.3** Ezra 8.36

[j] Gk *our spirit* [k] Gk *greatest*
[l] Other ancient authorities read *for us*

royal secretaries were paying honor
to the Jews, because fear of Mordecai weighed upon them. 4The
king's decree required that Mordecai's name be held in honor
throughout the kingdom.[m] 6Now
in the city of Susa the Jews killed
five hundred people, 7including
Pharsannestain, Delphon, Phasga,
8Pharadatha, Barea, Sarbacha,
9Marmasima, Aruphaeus, Arsaeus,
Zabutheus, 10the ten sons of Haman son of Hammedatha, the Bougean, the enemy of the Jews—and
they indulged[n] themselves in
plunder.
11 That very day the number of
those killed in Susa was reported
to the king. 12The king said to Esther, "In Susa, the capital, the
Jews have destroyed five hundred
people. What do you suppose they
have done in the surrounding
countryside? Whatever more you
ask will be done for you." 13And
Esther said to the king, "Let the
Jews be allowed to do the same tomorrow. Also, hang up the bodies
of Haman's ten sons." 14So he permitted this to be done, and handed
over to the Jews of the city the bodies of Haman's sons to hang up.
15The Jews who were in Susa gathered on the fourteenth and killed
three hundred people, but took no
plunder.
16 Now the other Jews in the
kingdom gathered to defend themselves, and got relief from their enemies. They destroyed fifteen
thousand of them, but did not engage in plunder. 17On the fourteenth day they rested and made
that same day a day of rest, celebrating it with joy and gladness.
18The Jews who were in Susa, the
capital, came together also on the
fourteenth, but did not rest. They
celebrated the fifteenth with joy
and gladness. 19On this account
then the Jews who are scattered
around the country outside Susa
keep the fourteenth of Adar as a
joyful holiday, and send presents
of food to one another, while those
who live in the large cities keep the
fifteenth day of Adar as their joyful
holiday, also sending presents to
one another.

The Festival of Purim

20 Mordecai recorded these
things in a book, and sent it to the
Jews in the kingdom of Artaxerxes
both near and far, 21telling them
that they should keep the fourteenth and fifteenth days of Adar,
22for on these days the Jews got relief from their enemies. The whole
month (namely, Adar), in which
their condition had been changed
from sorrow into gladness and
from a time of distress to a holiday,
was to be celebrated as a time for
feasting[o] and gladness and for
sending presents of food to their
friends and to the poor.
23 So the Jews accepted what
Mordecai had written to them
24—how Haman son of Hammedatha, the Macedonian,[p] fought
against them, how he made a decree and cast lots[q] to destroy
them, 25and how he went in to the
king, telling him to hang Mordecai;
but the wicked plot he had devised
against the Jews came back upon
himself, and he and his sons were
hanged. 26Therefore these days
were called "Purim," because of
the lots (for in their language this
is the word that means "lots"). And
so, because of what was written in
this letter, and because of what
they had experienced in this affair
and what had befallen them, Mordecai established this festival,[r]
27and the Jews took upon themselves, upon their descendants,
and upon all who would join them,
to observe it without fail.[s] These
days of Purim should be a memorial and kept from generation to
generation, in every city, family,
and country. 28These days of Purim were to be observed for all
time, and the commemoration of

9.4 Esth 10.3
9.10 Esth 5.11; Gen 14.23; 1 Sam 14.32; Esth 8.11; Jdt 15.6-7
9.12 Esth 5.6; 7.2
9.13 Esth 5.11; 9.7-10
9.14 Deut 21.22-23
9.15 Esth 8.11; 9.10
9.16 Esth 4.14
9.17 1 Kings 3.15; Esth 8.16
9.19 Esth 3.15; Deut 16.14; Neh 8.10,12; Rev 11.10
9.22 Esth 4.14; 9.16; 9.19; Deut 15.11; Ps 41.1; Mt 25.34-35; Gal 2.10
9.24 Esth 3.7-10
9.25 Esth 5.14; 6.4; 7.10; 9.7-10
9.26 Esth 3.7; 8.17; 9.18-19
9.27 Add Esth 10.13

[m] Meaning of Gk uncertain. Some ancient authorities add verse 5, *So the Jews struck down all their enemies with the sword, killing and destroying them, and they did as they pleased to those who hated them.*
[n] Other ancient authorities read *did not indulge*
[o] Gk *of weddings*
[p] Other ancient witnesses read *the Bougean*
[q] Gk *a lot*
[r] Gk *he established* (it)
[s] Meaning of Gk uncertain

them was never to cease among
their descendants.
29 Then Queen Esther daughter
of Aminadab along with Mordecai
the Jew wrote down what they had
done, and gave full authority to the
letter about Purim.[t] 31 And Mordecai and Queen Esther established this decision on their own
responsibility, pledging their own
well-being to the plan.[u] 32 Esther
established it by a decree forever,
and it was written for a memorial.

10 The king levied a tax upon
his kingdom both by land
and sea. 2 And as for his power and
bravery, and the wealth and glory
of his kingdom, they were recorded
in the annals of the kings of the
Persians and the Medes. 3 Mordecai acted with authority on behalf
of King Artaxerxes and was great in
the kingdom, as well as honored by
the Jews. His way of life was such
as to make him beloved to his
whole nation.

Addition F

Mordecai's Dream Fulfilled

4[v] And Mordecai said, "These
things have come from God; 5 for I
remember the dream that I had
concerning these matters, and
none of them has failed to be fulfilled. 6 There was the little spring
that became a river, and there was
light and sun and abundant water
—the river is Esther, whom the
king married and made queen.
7 The two dragons are Haman and
myself. 8 The nations are those that
gathered to destroy the name of
the Jews. 9 And my nation, this is
Israel, who cried out to God and
were saved. The Lord has saved his
people; the Lord has rescued us
from all these evils; God has done
great signs and wonders, wonders
that have never happened among
the nations. 10 For this purpose he
made two lots, one for the people
of God and one for all the nations,
11 and these two lots came to the
hour and moment and day of decision before God and among all the
nations. 12 And God remembered
his people and vindicated his inheritance. 13 So they will observe
these days in the month of Adar,
on the fourteenth and fifteenth[w]
of that month, with an assembly
and joy and gladness before God,
from generation to generation forever among his people Israel."

Postscript

11 1 In the fourth year of the
reign of Ptolemy and Cleopatra, Dositheus, who said that he
was a priest and a Levite,[x] and his
son Ptolemy brought to Egypt[y] the
preceding Letter about Purim,
which they said was authentic and
had been translated by Lysimachus son of Ptolemy, one of the
residents of Jerusalem.

End of Addition F

9.29 Esth 2.15 **9.32** Esth 1.19; 8.8; Dan 6.15 **10.1** Ps 72.10; 97.1; Isa 24.15 **10.2** Esth 2.23; 6.1 **10.3** Gen 41.40-41; Dan 2.48; 6.3; Neh 2.10; Jer 29.7 **10.5** Add Esth 11.5-11 **10.6** Add Esth 11.10 **10.7** Add Esth 11.6 **10.8** Esth 3.9; Add Esth 13.6 **10.9** Add Esth 13.8,18; 14.3; Ps 28.9; Add Esth 13.9; 14.19; Ex 7.3; Deut 4.34; Ps 78.4; 136.4; Jer 32.20 **10.12** 2 Sam 18.31; Ps 43.1; 135.14; Deut 7.6; Add Esth 14.5 **10.13** Esth 9.20-22, 27 **11.1** 1 Macc 10.51, 55-57; Esth 9.24-26

---

t Verse 30 in Heb is lacking in Gk: *Letters were sent to all the Jews, to the one hundred twenty-seven provinces of the kingdom of Ahasuerus, in words of peace and truth.*
u Meaning of Gk uncertain
v Chapter 10.4-13 and 11.1 correspond to chapter F 1-11 in some translations.
w Other ancient authorities lack *and fifteenth*
x Or *priest, and Levitas*
y Cn: Gk *brought in*

Wisdom of Solomon

Title and Background

This book gets its name from Israel's wisest king, though Solomon didn't write it himself. The book combines traditional Hebrew wisdom with prevalent speculations on wisdom and life from Greek and Hellenistic philosophy.

Author and Date of Writing

The author of this book thoroughly knew both the Old Testament and contemporary Greek culture. The book was probably written in Greek during the first century B.C. by a Hellenistic Jew in Alexandria, Egypt.

Theme and Message

All wisdom comes from God, who created the world by wisdom and continues to rule it by wisdom. True wisdom lives within the righteous; it guides them throughout their lives and assures them of immortality. Those who despise wisdom and disobey the law of God will, like the Egyptians at the time of the Exodus, be punished.

Outline

I. Wisdom and Immortality (1.1—5.23)
II. Wisdom and King Solomon (6.1—9.18)
III. Wisdom and Israel's History (10.1—19.22)

Exhortation to Uprightness

1 Love righteousness, you
rulers of the earth,
think of the Lord in
goodness
and seek him with sincerity
of heart;
2 because he is found by those
who do not put him to
the test,
and manifests himself to
those who do not
distrust him.
3 For perverse thoughts
separate people from
God,
and when his power is
tested, it exposes the
foolish;
4 because wisdom will not
enter a deceitful soul,
or dwell in a body enslaved
to sin.
5 For a holy and disciplined
spirit will flee from
deceit,
and will leave foolish
thoughts behind,
and will be ashamed at the
approach of
unrighteousness.

6 For wisdom is a kindly spirit,
but will not free blasphemers
from the guilt of their
words;
because God is witness of
their inmost feelings,
and a true observer of their
hearts, and a hearer of
their tongues.
7 Because the spirit of the
Lord has filled the
world,
and that which holds all
things together knows
what is said,
8 therefore those who utter
unrighteous things will
not escape notice,
and justice, when it
punishes, will not pass
them by.
9 For inquiry will be made into
the counsels of the
ungodly,

1.1 Ps 2.10; Wis 6.1; 1 Chr 29.17; Ps 101.2
1.2 Num 14.22; 1 Cor 10.9; 1 Chr 28.9; 2 Chr 15.2
1.3 Isa 1.15; 52.2
1.4 Sir 15.7-9; Rom 6.16, 19-20; 7.14
1.5 Ps 34.12-13; Prov 12.22; 1 Pet 3.10
1.6 Ex 20.7; 1 Sam 16.7; 1 Kings 8.39; 1 Chr 28.9
1.7 Wis 12.1; Col 1.17
1.8 Prov 19.5
1.9 Ps 1.1

and a report of their words
will come to the Lord,
to convict them of their
lawless deeds;
10 because a jealous ear hears
all things,
and the sound of grumbling
does not go unheard.
11 Beware then of useless
grumbling,
and keep your tongue from
slander;
because no secret word is
without result,[a]
and a lying mouth destroys
the soul.

12 Do not invite death by the
error of your life,
or bring on destruction by
the works of your
hands;
13 because God did not make
death,
and he does not delight in
the death of the living.
14 For he created all things so
that they might exist;
the generative forces[b] of the
world are wholesome,
and there is no destructive
poison in them,
and the dominion[c] of Hades
is not on earth.
15 For righteousness is
immortal.

Life as the Ungodly See It

16 But the ungodly by their
words and deeds
summoned death;[d]
considering him a friend,
they pined away
and made a covenant with
him,
because they are fit to
belong to his company.

2 For they reasoned
unsoundly, saying to
themselves,
"Short and sorrowful is our
life,
and there is no remedy when
a life comes to its end,
and no one has been known
to return from Hades.
2 For we were born by mere
chance,
and hereafter we shall be as
though we had never
been,
for the breath in our nostrils
is smoke,
and reason is a spark kindled
by the beating of our
hearts;
3 when it is extinguished, the
body will turn to ashes,
and the spirit will dissolve
like empty air.
4 Our name will be forgotten
in time,
and no one will remember
our works;
our life will pass away like
the traces of a cloud,
and be scattered like mist
that is chased by the rays of
the sun
and overcome by its heat.
5 For our allotted time is the
passing of a shadow,
and there is no return from
our death,
because it is sealed up and
no one turns back.

6 "Come, therefore, let us
enjoy the good things
that exist,
and make use of the creation
to the full as in youth.
7 Let us take our fill of costly
wine and perfumes,
and let no flower of spring
pass us by.
8 Let us crown ourselves with
rosebuds before they
wither.
9 Let none of us fail to share
in our revelry;
everywhere let us leave signs
of enjoyment,
because this is our portion,
and this our lot.
10 Let us oppress the righteous
poor man;
let us not spare the widow
or regard the gray hairs of
the aged.
11 But let our might be our law
of right,

1.10 Num 14.27-28 **1.11** 1 Cor 10.10; Phil 2.14; Jas 4.11 **1.13** Ezek 18.32; 33.11; 2 Pet 3.9 **1.14** Gen 1.1; Jn 1.2-3; Rev 4.11; Wis 2.1; Bar 3.19; 2 Esd 4.7-8; Lk 16.23 **1.15** Isa 51.6 **1.16** Isa 28.15,18 **2.1** Job 14.1; 5.7; Eccl 2.23; 2 Esd 4.7-8; Lk 16.23-26 **2.2** Gen 2.7 **2.3** Eccl 12.7 **2.4** Job 7.10; Ps 103.15-16; Job 7.9; Ps 102.3; Jas 4.14 **2.5** Ps 102.11; 144.4; Job 7.9; 14.14 **2.6** Eccl 11.9 **2.9** Isa 22.13; Lk 12.19; 1 Cor 15.32; Jer 13.25 **2.10** Jas 5.6; Ex 22.22; Lk 20.47; Lev 19.32 **2.11** Rom 9.31

[a] Or *will go unpunished* [b] Or *the creatures* [c] Or *palace* [d] Gk *him*

for what is weak proves itself
to be useless.

12 "Let us lie in wait for the
righteous man,
because he is inconvenient
to us and opposes our
actions;
he reproaches us for sins
against the law,
and accuses us of sins
against our training.
13 He professes to have
knowledge of God,
and calls himself a child[e] of
the Lord.
14 He became to us a reproof of
our thoughts;
15 the very sight of him is a
burden to us,
because his manner of life is
unlike that of others,
and his ways are strange.
16 We are considered by him as
something base,
and he avoids our ways as
unclean;
he calls the last end of the
righteous happy,
and boasts that God is his
father.
17 Let us see if his words are
true,
and let us test what will
happen at the end of
his life;
18 for if the righteous man is
God's child, he will
help him,
and will deliver him from the
hand of his adversaries.
19 Let us test him with insult
and torture,
so that we may find out how
gentle he is,
and make trial of his
forbearance.
20 Let us condemn him to a
shameful death,
for, according to what he
says, he will be
protected."

Error of the Wicked

21 Thus they reasoned, but they
were led astray,
for their wickedness blinded
them,
22 and they did not know the
secret purposes of God,
nor hoped for the wages of
holiness,
nor discerned the prize for
blameless souls;
23 for God created us for
incorruption,
and made us in the image of
his own eternity,[f]
24 but through the devil's envy
death entered the
world,
and those who belong to his
company experience it.

The Destiny of the Righteous

3 But the souls of the
righteous are in the
hand of God,
and no torment will ever
touch them.
2 In the eyes of the foolish
they seemed to have
died,
and their departure was
thought to be a
disaster,
3 and their going from us to be
their destruction;
but they are at peace.
4 For though in the sight of
others they were
punished,
their hope is full of
immortality.
5 Having been disciplined a
little, they will receive
great good,
because God tested them
and found them worthy
of himself;
6 like gold in the furnace he
tried them,
and like a sacrificial burnt
offering he accepted
them.
7 In the time of their visitation
they will shine forth,
and will run like sparks
through the stubble.
8 They will govern nations and
rule over peoples,

2.12 Ps 59.3-4; Hos 6.7; 8.1 **2.13** Mt 27.43 **2.15** Hos 8.12 **2.16** Ps 1.1; Mt 27.43 **2.17** Gen 37.20 **2.18** Ps 22.8; Mk 15.29 **2.19** Ps 69.19-20; Mt 27.27-31; 11.29 **2.20** Mt 26.66; 27.23 **2.21** Rom 1.21

2.22 Isa 6.9; Mk 4.11-12; Ps 22.24-25; Prov 11.18 **2.23** Gen 1.26-27 **2.24** Gen 3.1-19; Jn 8.44; Rom 5.12 **3.1** Job 12.10; Acts 17.28 **3.3** Isa 57.1-2; Rom 5.1 **3.5** 2 Cor 4.7; Jas 1.2-4; 1 Pet 1.6-7 **3.6** Prov 17.3; Isa 48.10; Mal 3.3; Ps 51.19 **3.7** Lk 19.44; Dan 12.3; Mt 13.43 **3.8** Wis 8.14; 1 Cor 6.2; Rev 20.4; 19.6

[e] Or *servant*

[f] Other ancient authorities read *nature*

and the Lord will reign over
them forever.
9 Those who trust in him will
understand truth,
and the faithful will abide
with him in love,
because grace and mercy are
upon his holy ones,
and he watches over his
elect.[g]

The Destiny of the Ungodly

10 But the ungodly will be
punished as their
reasoning deserves,
those who disregarded the
righteous[h]
and rebelled against the
Lord;
11 for those who despise
wisdom and instruction
are miserable.
Their hope is vain, their
labors are unprofitable,
and their works are useless.
12 Their wives are foolish, and
their children evil;
13 their offspring are accursed.

On Childlessness

For blessed is the barren
woman who is
undefiled,
who has not entered into a
sinful union;
she will have fruit when God
examines souls.
14 Blessed also is the eunuch
whose hands have done
no lawless deed,
and who has not devised
wicked things against
the Lord;
for special favor will be
shown him for his
faithfulness,
and a place of great delight
in the temple of the
Lord.
15 For the fruit of good labors
is renowned,
and the root of
understanding does not
fail.
16 But children of adulterers
will not come to
maturity,
and the offspring of an
unlawful union will
perish.
17 Even if they live long they
will be held of no
account,
and finally their old age will
be without honor.
18 If they die young, they will
have no hope
and no consolation on the
day of judgment.
19 For the end of an
unrighteous generation
is grievous.

4 Better than this is
childlessness with
virtue,
for in the memory of virtue[i]
is immortality,
because it is known both by
God and by mortals.
2 When it is present, people
imitate[j] it,
and they long for it when it
has gone;
throughout all time it
marches, crowned in
triumph,
victor in the contest for
prizes that are
undefiled.
3 But the prolific brood of the
ungodly will be of no
use,
and none of their illegitimate
seedlings will strike a
deep root
or take a firm hold.
4 For even if they put forth
boughs for a while,
standing insecurely they will
be shaken by the wind,
and by the violence of the
winds they will be
uprooted.
5 The branches will be broken
off before they come to
maturity,
and their fruit will be
useless,
not ripe enough to eat, and
good for nothing.

3.9 Jn 15.9-10; Wis 4.15
3.10 Ps 73.17-20
3.11 Prov 1.7; Eccl 1.2-3; 2.22
3.12 Sir 41.5-6
3.13 Deut 28.15, 18; Lk 22.29; Rev 20.12
3.14 Isa 56.3-5
3.15 Sir 1.18
3.16 2 Sam 12.14
3.17 Sir 16.1-3
3.19 Ps 34.21; 73.18-20; 94.23
4.1 Sir 16.3
4.2 1 Cor 11.1; Eph 5.1; 1 Thess 1.6; 2 Cor 2.14; 1 Cor 9.24-25
4.3 Sir 23.25
4.4 Sir 40.15; Mt 13.5-6
4.5 Isa 5.2; Heb 6.7-8

[g] Text of this line uncertain; omitted by some ancient authorities. Compare 4.15
[h] Or *what is right*
[i] Gk *it*
[j] Other ancient authorities read *honor*

6 For children born of unlawful unions
are witnesses of evil against their parents when God examines them.[k]
7 But the righteous, though they die early, will be at rest.
8 For old age is not honored for length of time,
or measured by number of years;
9 but understanding is gray hair for anyone,
and a blameless life is ripe old age.

10 There were some who pleased God and were loved by him,
and while living among sinners were taken up.
11 They were caught up so that evil might not change their understanding
or guile deceive their souls.
12 For the fascination of wickedness obscures what is good,
and roving desire perverts the innocent mind.
13 Being perfected in a short time, they fulfilled long years;
14 for their souls were pleasing to the Lord,
therefore he took them quickly from the midst of wickedness.
15 Yet the peoples saw and did not understand,
or take such a thing to heart,
that God's grace and mercy are with his elect,
and that he watches over his holy ones.

The Triumph of the Righteous

16 The righteous who have died will condemn the ungodly who are living,
and youth that is quickly perfected[l] will condemn the prolonged old age of the unrighteous.
17 For they will see the end of the wise,
and will not understand what the Lord purposed for them,
and for what he kept them safe.
18 The unrighteous[m] will see, and will have contempt for them,
but the Lord will laugh them to scorn.
After this they will become dishonored corpses,
and an outrage among the dead forever;
19 because he will dash them speechless to the ground,
and shake them from the foundations;
they will be left utterly dry and barren,
and they will suffer anguish,
and the memory of them will perish.

The Final Judgment

20 They will come with dread when their sins are reckoned up,
and their lawless deeds will convict them to their face.

5 Then the righteous will stand with great confidence
in the presence of those who have oppressed them
and those who make light of their labors.
2 When the unrighteous[n] see them, they will be shaken with dreadful fear,
and they will be amazed at the unexpected salvation of the righteous.
3 They will speak to one another in repentance,
and in anguish of spirit they will groan, and say,
4 "These are persons whom we once held in derision

4.6 Wis 3.13, 16-18 **4.7** Isa 57.1-2; Wis 3.3-4 **4.8** Job 32.9 **4.9** Job 12.12; Sir 25.4-5 **4.10** Gen 5.24; 2 Kings 2.11; Heb 11.5 **4.11** Isa 57.1-2 **4.12** Prov 6.14; Mic 2.1 **4.14** Heb 11.6; Gen 5.24; 19.22,29; 2 Pet 2.7 **4.15** Wis 3.9 **4.16** Mt 12.41-42 **4.18** Ps 2.4; 37.13; Isa 14.19; Acts 1.18 **4.19** 2 Macc 3.29-30; Ps 9.6; 34.16; 109.15 **4.20** Jer 2.19; Hos 5.5 **5.1** Col 2.15 **5.2** Lk 19.22-23; Ps 37.39; 50.23; Mt 25.31-46 **5.4** Job 30.9; Ps 44.14; 69.11

[k] Gk *at their examination* [l] Or *ended* [m] Gk *They* [n] Gk *they*

and made a byword of
reproach—fools that we
were!
We thought that their lives
were madness
and that their end was
without honor.
5 Why have they been
numbered among the
children of God?
And why is their lot among
the saints?
6 So it was we who strayed
from the way of truth,
and the light of
righteousness did not
shine on us,
and the sun did not rise
upon us.
7 We took our fill of the paths
of lawlessness and
destruction,
and we journeyed through
trackless deserts,
but the way of the Lord we
have not known.
8 What has our arrogance
profited us?
And what good has our
boasted wealth brought
us?

9 "All those things have
vanished like a shadow,
and like a rumor that passes
by;
10 like a ship that sails through
the billowy water,
and when it has passed no
trace can be found,
no track of its keel in the
waves;
11 or as, when a bird flies
through the air,
no evidence of its passage is
found;
the light air, lashed by the
beat of its pinions
and pierced by the force of
its rushing flight,
is traversed by the movement
of its wings,
and afterward no sign of its
coming is found there;
12 or as, when an arrow is shot
at a target,
the air, thus divided, comes
together at once,

5.5 Acts 26.18; Col 1.12
5.6 Prov 4.18-19; 2 Pet 2.2
5.7 Isa 59.6-8; Rom 3.15-17; Ps 27.15; 44.18; Prov 10.29
5.8 Ps 47.5-6; Prov 10.2
5.9 1 Chr 29.15; Ps 102.11; Wis 2.9
5.10 Prov 30.18-19
5.11 Jn 3.8
5.12 2 Esd 16.16
5.13 Ps 90.7; Ezek 33.10
5.14 Job 21.18; Ps 1.4; 147.16-18; 37.20; 102.3; 73.20; 90.5-6
5.15 Ezek 18.9; Jn 6.51,58; Isa 40.10; 62.11
5.16 2 Tim 4.8; 1 Pet 5.4; Isa 62.3; Ps 5.12; 91.4; 2 Sam 22.31; Ps 18.30; 115.9-11
5.17 Eph 6.13
5.18 Isa 59.17; Eph 6.14,17
5.19 Eph 6.16
5.20 Ps 7.12; Rev 19.15
5.21 2 Sam 22.15; Zech 9.14

so that no one knows its
pathway.
13 So we also, as soon as we
were born, ceased to
be,
and we had no sign of virtue
to show,
but were consumed in our
wickedness."
14 Because the hope of the
ungodly is like
thistledown[o] carried by
the wind,
and like a light frost[p] driven
away by a storm;
it is dispersed like smoke
before the wind,
and it passes like the
remembrance of a guest
who stays but a day.

The Reward of the Righteous

15 But the righteous live
forever,
and their reward is with the
Lord;
the Most High takes care of
them.
16 Therefore they will receive a
glorious crown
and a beautiful diadem from
the hand of the Lord,
because with his right hand
he will cover them,
and with his arm he will
shield them.
17 The Lord[q] will take his zeal
as his whole armor,
and will arm all creation to
repel[r] his enemies;
18 he will put on righteousness
as a breastplate,
and wear impartial justice as
a helmet;
19 he will take holiness as an
invincible shield,
20 and sharpen stern wrath for
a sword,
and creation will join with
him to fight against his
frenzied foes.
21 Shafts of lightning will fly
with true aim,

[o] Other ancient authorities read *dust*
[p] Other ancient authorities read *spider's web*
[q] Gk *He* [r] Or *punish*

and will leap from the clouds
to the target, as from a
well-drawn bow,
22 and hailstones full of wrath
will be hurled as from a
catapult;
the water of the sea will rage
against them,
and rivers will relentlessly
overwhelm them;
23 a mighty wind will rise
against them,
and like a tempest it will
winnow them away.
Lawlessness will lay waste
the whole earth,
and evildoing will overturn
the thrones of rulers.

Kings Should Seek Wisdom

6 Listen therefore, O kings,
and understand;
learn, O judges of the ends
of the earth.
2 Give ear, you that rule over
multitudes,
and boast of many nations.
3 For your dominion was given
you from the Lord,
and your sovereignty from
the Most High;
he will search out your works
and inquire into your
plans.
4 Because as servants of his
kingdom you did not
rule rightly,
or keep the law,
or walk according to the
purpose of God,
5 he will come upon you
terribly and swiftly,
because severe judgment
falls on those in high
places.
6 For the lowliest may be
pardoned in mercy,
but the mighty will be
mightily tested.
7 For the Lord of all will not
stand in awe of anyone,
or show deference to
greatness;
because he himself made
both small and great,
and he takes thought for all
alike.

5.22 Ps 18.12; Ezek 13.11, 13; Sir 46.5; Lk 21.25 **5.23** Ps 83.15; Isa 28.2; 29.6 **6.1** Mic 3.1,9; Sir 33.19 **6.3** Dan 2.21; Jn 19.11; Rom 13.1; Job 31.4; Ps 139.3,23; Prov 16.1,9; 19.21 **6.4** Jer 16.11; Ezek 11.12; Am 2.4 **6.5** Jer 1.14-16; Ezek 17.1-9 **6.6** Mt 5.7 **6.7** Mt 22.16; Sir 4.22; Deut 10.17; Acts 10.34-35; Rom 2.11

6.9 Ps 2.10; Wis 1.1; 6.21; Prov 8.15-16 **6.11** Prov 5.7; 22.17; 21.11; Wis 6.25 **6.12** Wis 7.10; Prov 8.17; Wis 7.10; Jer 29.13 **6.13** Prov 8.3-11 **6.15** Prov 2.2; 3.13; 10.13 **6.17** Prov 1.3; 8.10; 9.9 **6.18** Prov 4.4-9; Sir 2.15-16; Jn 14.15; 1 Jn 5.3; Wis 8.13

8 But a strict inquiry is in
store for the mighty.
9 To you then, O monarchs,
my words are directed,
so that you may learn
wisdom and not
transgress.
10 For they will be made holy
who observe holy things
in holiness,
and those who have been
taught them will find a
defense.
11 Therefore set your desire on
my words;
long for them, and you will
be instructed.

Description of Wisdom

12 Wisdom is radiant and
unfading,
and she is easily discerned
by those who love her,
and is found by those who
seek her.
13 She hastens to make herself
known to those who
desire her.
14 One who rises early to seek
her will have no
difficulty,
for she will be found sitting
at the gate.
15 To fix one's thought on her
is perfect
understanding,
and one who is vigilant on
her account will soon
be free from care,
16 because she goes about
seeking those worthy of
her,
and she graciously appears to
them in their paths,
and meets them in every
thought.
17 The beginning of wisdom[s] is
the most sincere desire
for instruction,
and concern for instruction
is love of her,
18 and love of her is the
keeping of her laws,

[s]Gk *Her beginning*

and giving heed to her laws
is assurance of
immortality,
19 and immortality brings one
near to God;
20 so the desire for wisdom
leads to a kingdom.

21 Therefore if you delight in
thrones and scepters,
O monarchs over the
peoples,
honor wisdom, so that you
may reign forever.
22 I will tell you what wisdom
is and how she came to
be,
and I will hide no secrets
from you,
but I will trace her course
from the beginning of
creation,
and make knowledge of her
clear,
and I will not pass by the
truth;
23 nor will I travel in the
company of sickly envy,
for envy[t] does not associate
with wisdom.
24 The multitude of the wise is
the salvation of the
world,
and a sensible king is the
stability of any people.
25 Therefore be instructed by
my words, and you will
profit.

Solomon Like Other Mortals

7 I also am mortal, like
everyone else,
a descendant of the
first-formed child of
earth;
and in the womb of a mother
I was molded into flesh,
2 within the period of ten
months, compacted
with blood,
from the seed of a man and
the pleasure of
marriage.
3 And when I was born, I
began to breathe the
common air,

6.21 Wis 6.9; 1 Kings 3.9-14 **6.22** Tob 12.7,11; Mt 13.11; 1 Cor 2.6-7; Prov 8.22-31; Sir 1.4-8 **6.23** Ps 1.1; Prov 23.17; 24.1,19; Sir 9.11 **6.24** Prov 24.6; 29.4; Sir 10.1; Prov 21.11; Wis 6.11 **7.1** Acts 10.26; Gen 1.26-27; 2.7; Wis 10.1; 1 Kings 12.24-25

7.4 Lk 2.7 **7.6** Job 1.21; 1 Tim 6.7 **7.7** 1 Kings 3.1-14; 2 Chr 1.7-12 **7.8** Prov 2.1-15 **7.9** Job 28.12-19; Prov 3.13-15; 8.10-11; Wis 8.5; Prov 8.18-19 **7.10** Wis 6.12 **7.11** Mt 6.33; Lk 18.29-30; Prov 8.21 **7.14** Prov 8.35; 12.2; Jn 15.14-15; Jas 2.23

and fell upon the kindred
earth;
my first sound was a cry, as
is true of all.
4 I was nursed with care in
swaddling cloths.
5 For no king has had a
different beginning of
existence;
6 there is for all one entrance
into life, and one way
out.

Solomon's Respect for Wisdom

7 Therefore I prayed, and
understanding was
given me;
I called on God, and the
spirit of wisdom came
to me.
8 I preferred her to scepters
and thrones,
and I accounted wealth as
nothing in comparison
with her.
9 Neither did I liken to her any
priceless gem,
because all gold is but a
little sand in her sight,
and silver will be accounted
as clay before her.
10 I loved her more than health
and beauty,
and I chose to have her
rather than light,
because her radiance never
ceases.
11 All good things came to me
along with her,
and in her hands uncounted
wealth.
12 I rejoiced in them all,
because wisdom leads
them;
but I did not know that she
was their mother.
13 I learned without guile and I
impart without
grudging;
I do not hide her wealth,
14 for it is an unfailing treasure
for mortals;
those who get it obtain
friendship with God,
commended for the gifts that
come from instruction.

[t] Gk *this*

Solomon Prays for Wisdom

15 May God grant me to speak with judgment,
and to have thoughts worthy of what I have received;
for he is the guide even of wisdom
and the corrector of the wise.
16 For both we and our words are in his hand,
as are all understanding and skill in crafts.
17 For it is he who gave me unerring knowledge of what exists,
to know the structure of the world and the activity of the elements;
18 the beginning and end and middle of times,
the alternations of the solstices and the changes of the seasons,
19 the cycles of the year and the constellations of the stars,
20 the natures of animals and the tempers of wild animals,
the powers of spirits[u] and the thoughts of human beings,
the varieties of plants and the virtues of roots;
21 I learned both what is secret and what is manifest,
22 for wisdom, the fashioner of all things, taught me.

The Nature of Wisdom

There is in her a spirit that is intelligent, holy,
unique, manifold, subtle,
mobile, clear, unpolluted,
distinct, invulnerable, loving the good, keen,
irresistible, 23 beneficent, humane,
steadfast, sure, free from anxiety,
all-powerful, overseeing all,
and penetrating through all spirits
that are intelligent, pure, and altogether subtle.
24 For wisdom is more mobile than any motion;
because of her pureness she pervades and penetrates all things.
25 For she is a breath of the power of God,
and a pure emanation of the glory of the Almighty;
therefore nothing defiled gains entrance into her.
26 For she is a reflection of eternal light,
a spotless mirror of the working of God,
and an image of his goodness.
27 Although she is but one, she can do all things,
and while remaining in herself, she renews all things;
in every generation she passes into holy souls
and makes them friends of God, and prophets;
28 for God loves nothing so much as the person who lives with wisdom.
29 She is more beautiful than the sun,
and excels every constellation of the stars.
Compared with the light she is found to be superior,
30 for it is succeeded by the night,
but against wisdom evil does not prevail.

8 She reaches mightily from one end of the earth to the other,
and she orders all things well.

Solomon's Love for Wisdom

2 I loved her and sought her from my youth;
I desired to take her for my bride,
and became enamored of her beauty.
3 She glorifies her noble birth by living with God,
and the Lord of all loves her.

7.15 1 Kings 3.9; Sir 1.1; Jas 1.5 **7.16** Job 12.10; Wis 3.1; Ex 31.1-6; 35.30-36.1 **7.17** 1 Kings 4.29-33 **7.18** Eccl 3.1-8; Gen 8.22 **7.19** Job 9.9; 38.31; Am 5.8 **7.22** Prov 8.30; Wis 8.6; 14.2; 1.6; Jas 3.17 **7.23** Heb 4.12 **7.24** Wis 8.1; 1 Cor 1.24-25 **7.25** Jn 1.14; Heb 1.3 **7.26** Jn 1.3-5; 2 Cor 4.4; Col 1.15 **7.27** Job 42.2; Phil 4.13; Ps 104.30; Rev 21.5; Ex 33.11; 2 Chr 20.7; Jas 2.23 **7.29** Song 6.10 **8.1** Wis 7.24; 15.1 **8.2** 1 Kings 3.3-14; Sir 15.2; Ps 45.12

[u] Or *winds*

4 For she is an initiate in the
knowledge of God,
and an associate in his
works.
5 If riches are a desirable
possession in life,
what is richer than wisdom,
the active cause of all
things?
6 And if understanding is
effective,
who more than she is
fashioner of what
exists?
7 And if anyone loves
righteousness,
her labors are virtues;
for she teaches self-control
and prudence,
justice and courage;
nothing in life is more
profitable for mortals
than these.
8 And if anyone longs for wide
experience,
she knows the things of old,
and infers the things to
come;
she understands turns of
speech and the
solutions of riddles;
she has foreknowledge of
signs and wonders
and of the outcome of
seasons and times.

Wisdom Indispensible to Rulers

9 Therefore I determined to
take her to live with
me,
knowing that she would give
me good counsel
and encouragement in cares
and grief.
10 Because of her I shall have
glory among the
multitudes
and honor in the presence of
the elders, though I am
young.
11 I shall be found keen in
judgment,
and in the sight of rulers I
shall be admired.
12 When I am silent they will
wait for me,
and when I speak they will
give heed;
if I speak at greater length,
they will put their hands on
their mouths.
13 Because of her I shall have
immortality,
and leave an everlasting
remembrance to those
who come after me.
14 I shall govern peoples,
and nations will be subject
to me;
15 dread monarchs will be
afraid of me when they
hear of me;
among the people I shall
show myself capable,
and courageous in war.
16 When I enter my house, I
shall find rest with her;
for companionship with her
has no bitterness,
and life with her has no
pain, but gladness and
joy.
17 When I considered these
things inwardly,
and pondered in my heart
that in kinship with wisdom
there is immortality,
18 and in friendship with her,
pure delight,
and in the labors of her
hands, unfailing wealth,
and in the experience of her
company,
understanding,
and renown in sharing her
words,
I went about seeking how to
get her for myself.
19 As a child I was naturally
gifted,
and a good soul fell to my
lot;
20 or rather, being good, I
entered an undefiled
body.
21 But I perceived that I would
not possess wisdom
unless God gave her to
me—
and it was a mark of insight
to know whose gift she
was—
so I appealed to the Lord
and implored him,
and with my whole heart I
said:

8.4 Prov 8.22-30
8.5 Prov 8.18-19; Wis 7.8-9
8.6 Wis 7.22; Jn 1.3; Col 1.16; Heb 1.2
8.7 Prov 1.2-6
8.8 Prov 1.6; Sir 39.1-3; 42.19; Acts 2.22; Dan 2.21; 1 Thess 5.1
8.9 Prov 8.14-16
8.10 1 Kings 3.28; 4.34; 10.1-7; Job 29.7-11
8.11 1 Kings 3.16-27; 2 Chr 9.1-8
8.13 Wis 6.18-19; Isa 56.5; Sir 15.6; 41.12-13
8.14 Wis 3.8; Ps 18.47; 47.3
8.16 Prov 3.18; Sir 15.6
8.17 Sir 14.21; Wis 8.13
8.18 1 Kings 10.14-29; 3.9; Prov 1.2; Eccl 1.12-17; 2.3,12
8.21 Prov 2.6; Wis 7.15; Sir 1.1; Jas 1.5; 1 Kings 3.6-9

Solomon's Prayer for Wisdom

9 "O God of my ancestors and Lord of mercy,
who have made all things by your word,
2 and by your wisdom have formed humankind
to have dominion over the creatures you have made,
3 and rule the world in holiness and righteousness,
and pronounce judgment in uprightness of soul,
4 give me the wisdom that sits by your throne,
and do not reject me from among your servants.
5 For I am your servant[v] the son of your serving girl,
a man who is weak and short-lived,
with little understanding of judgment and laws;
6 for even one who is perfect among human beings
will be regarded as nothing without the wisdom that comes from you.
7 You have chosen me to be king of your people
and to be judge over your sons and daughters.
8 You have given command to build a temple on your holy mountain,
and an altar in the city of your habitation,
a copy of the holy tent that you prepared from the beginning.
9 With you is wisdom, she who knows your works
and was present when you made the world;
she understands what is pleasing in your sight
and what is right according to your commandments.
10 Send her forth from the holy heavens,
and from the throne of your glory send her,
that she may labor at my side,
and that I may learn what is pleasing to you.
11 For she knows and understands all things,
and she will guide me wisely in my actions
and guard me with her glory.
12 Then my works will be acceptable,
and I shall judge your people justly,
and shall be worthy of the throne[w] of my father.
13 For who can learn the counsel of God?
Or who can discern what the Lord wills?
14 For the reasoning of mortals is worthless,
and our designs are likely to fail;
15 for a perishable body weighs down the soul,
and this earthy tent burdens the thoughtful[x] mind.
16 We can hardly guess at what is on earth,
and what is at hand we find with labor;
but who has traced out what is in the heavens?
17 Who has learned your counsel,
unless you have given wisdom
and sent your holy spirit from on high?
18 And thus the paths of those on earth were set right,
and people were taught what pleases you,
and were saved by wisdom."

The Work of Wisdom from Adam to Moses

10 Wisdom[y] protected the first-formed father of the world, when he alone had been created;
she delivered him from his transgression,
2 and gave him strength to rule all things.

9.1 Wis 4.15; Sir 17.29; Ps 33.6; Jn 1.3; Heb 1.2-3
9.2 Prov 3.19; 8.22-31; Jer 10.12; Gen 1.28; Ps 8.6-8; Sir 17.3-4
9.4 1 Kings 3.9; 2 Chr 1.10
9.5 Ps 116.16; 119.125; 1 Kings 3.7
9.6 1 Cor 2.6-11; 3.18-20
9.7 1 Chr 22.9; 28.5
9.8 2 Sam 7.13; 1 Chr 22.10; 28.6; Ex 25.8-9,40; Heb 8.5
9.9 Prov 8.22-31; Wis 8.3-4; Sir 24.9; Deut 4.40; 6.17-18
9.10 Ps 47.8; 97.2; Wis 18.15; Mt 5.34
9.11 Prov 1.26; 2.6; 3.13
9.12 1 Kings 3.16-28; 10.9
9.13 Isa 40.13; 1 Cor 2.13
9.15 1 Cor 15.42, 53-54; Job 4.19; 2 Cor 5.1,4
9.16 Sir 1.3; Jn 3.12
9.17 Jn 14.26; 15.26; 1 Cor 2.7-12
9.18 Prov 28.26; Wis 10.9
10.1 Gen 2.7
10.2 Gen 1.28; Ps 8.6-8; Wis 9.2

[v] Gk *slave* [w] Gk *thrones* [x] Or *anxious*
[y] Gk *She*

3 But when an unrighteous
man departed from her
in his anger,
he perished because in rage
he killed his brother.
4 When the earth was flooded
because of him, wisdom
again saved it,
steering the righteous man
by a paltry piece of
wood.

5 Wisdom[z] also, when the
nations in wicked
agreement had been
put to confusion,
recognized the righteous
man and preserved him
blameless before God,
and kept him strong in the
face of his compassion
for his child.

6 Wisdom[z] rescued a
righteous man when the
ungodly were perishing;
he escaped the fire that
descended on the Five
Cities.[a]
7 Evidence of their wickedness
still remains:
a continually smoking
wasteland,
plants bearing fruit that does
not ripen,
and a pillar of salt standing
as a monument to an
unbelieving soul.
8 For because they passed
wisdom by,
they not only were hindered
from recognizing the
good,
but also left for humankind a
reminder of their folly,
so that their failures could
never go unnoticed.

9 Wisdom rescued from
troubles those who
served her.
10 When a righteous man fled
from his brother's
wrath,
she guided him on straight
paths;
she showed him the kingdom
of God,
and gave him knowledge of
holy things;
she prospered him in his
labors,
and increased the fruit of his
toil.
11 When his oppressors were
covetous,
she stood by him and made
him rich.
12 She protected him from his
enemies,
and kept him safe from
those who lay in wait
for him;
in his arduous contest she
gave him the victory,
so that he might learn that
godliness is more
powerful than anything
else.

13 When a righteous man was
sold, wisdom[b] did not
desert him,
but delivered him from sin.
She descended with him into
the dungeon,
14 and when he was in prison
she did not leave him,
until she brought him the
scepter of a kingdom
and authority over his
masters.
Those who accused him she
showed to be false,
and she gave him everlasting
honor.

Wisdom Led the Israelites out of Egypt

15 A holy people and blameless
race
wisdom delivered from a
nation of oppressors.
16 She entered the soul of a
servant of the Lord,
and withstood dread kings
with wonders and signs.
17 She gave to holy people the
reward of their labors;
she guided them along a
marvelous way,
and became a shelter to
them by day,

10.3 1 Jn 3.11-12; Gen 4.1-6
10.4 Gen 6.8-9; Sir 44.17; 1 Pet 2.5; Gen 6.14-22
10.5 Gen 11.1-9; 15.6; Rom 4.3,9,22; Gen 22.1-14; Heb 11.17-19
10.6 2 Pet 2.7; Gen 19.15-29
10.7 Gen 19.26; Lk 17.32
10.10 Gen 27.41-45; 28.1-5, 10-17; 30.37-43
10.11 Gen 31.1
10.12 Gen 31.22-55; 33.1-11; 32.22-30
10.13 Gen 37.25-28; 39.7-12, 20-23
10.14 Gen 41.37-45
10.15 Ex19.6; 3.9; 12.33-42
10.16 Ex 3.1-4.9; Wis 1.4; Ps 76.12; Ex 3.3; Deut 6.22; Ps 135.9; 2 Cor 12.12
10.17 Heb 11.6; Ex 13.21-22

[z] Gk *She* [a] Or *on Pentapolis* [b] Gk *she*

and a starry flame through
the night.
18 She brought them over the
Red Sea,
and led them through deep
waters;
19 but she drowned their
enemies,
and cast them up from the
depth of the sea.
20 Therefore the righteous
plundered the ungodly;
they sang hymns, O Lord, to
your holy name,
and praised with one accord
your defending hand;
21 for wisdom opened the
mouths of those who
were mute,
and made the tongues of
infants speak clearly.

Wisdom Led the Israelites through the Desert

11 Wisdom[c] prospered their
works by the hand of a
holy prophet.
2 They journeyed through an
uninhabited wilderness,
and pitched their tents in
untrodden places.
3 They withstood their
enemies and fought off
their foes.
4 When they were thirsty, they
called upon you,
and water was given them
out of flinty rock,
and from hard stone a
remedy for their thirst.
5 For through the very things
by which their enemies
were punished,
they themselves received
benefit in their need.
6 Instead of the fountain of an
ever-flowing river,
stirred up and defiled with
blood
7 in rebuke for the decree to
kill the infants,
you gave them abundant
water unexpectedly,
8 showing by their thirst at
that time
how you punished their
enemies.
9 For when they were tried,
though they were being
disciplined in mercy,
they learned how the
ungodly were tormented
when judged in wrath.
10 For you tested them as a
parent[d] does in
warning,
but you examined the
ungodly[e] as a stern
king does in
condemnation.
11 Whether absent or present,
they were equally
distressed,
12 for a twofold grief possessed
them,
and a groaning at the
memory of what had
occurred.
13 For when they heard that
through their own
punishments
the righteous[f] had received
benefit, they perceived
it was the Lord's doing.
14 For though they had
mockingly rejected him
who long before had
been cast out and
exposed,
at the end of the events they
marveled at him,
when they felt thirst in a
different way from the
righteous.

Punishment of the Wicked

15 In return for their foolish
and wicked thoughts,
which led them astray to
worship irrational
serpents and worthless
animals,
you sent upon them a
multitude of irrational
creatures to punish
them,
16 so that they might learn that
one is punished by the
very things by which
one sins.
17 For your all-powerful hand,

10.18 Ex 14.15-22
10.19 Ex 14.23-30
10.20 Ex 12.35-36; 15.1-21
10.21 Isa 35.6; Mt 9.32-33; Ps 8.3; Mt 21.16
11.1 Deut 18.15,18
11.2 Ex 15.22; 16.1
11.3 Ex 17.8-15; Num 21.21-26
11.4 Ex 17.5-6; Num 20.6-11; 1 Cor 10.4
11.6 Ex 1.22; 7.14-24
11.7 Ex 1.15-16; Wis 18.5
11.9 Prov 3.11-12; Wis 3.5; Heb 12.3-11; Ex 12.29-30; Wis 16.4
11.10 Deut 8.2-3; 1 Cor 4.14-15
11.13 Ex 14.18; Ps 118.23
11.14 Ex 5.21; Num 14.4; Ex 2.3; 14.31; Lk 16.24
11.15 Jer 10.14; Rom 1.23; Wis 15.18; Ex 8.1-30; 10.13-19
11.16 Ps 7.15-16; Prov 26.27; Wis 12.23-24
11.17 Gen 1.1-2; Heb 11.3; Hos 13.7-8; Wis 12.9

c Gk *She* d Gk *a father* e Gk *those*
f Gk *they*

which created the world out
of formless matter,
did not lack the means to
send upon them a
multitude of bears, or
bold lions,
18 or newly-created unknown
beasts full of rage,
or such as breathe out fiery
breath,
or belch forth a thick pall of
smoke,
or flash terrible sparks from
their eyes;
19 not only could the harm they
did destroy people,[g]
but the mere sight of them
could kill by fright.
20 Even apart from these,
people[h] could fall at a
single breath
when pursued by justice
and scattered by the breath
of your power.
But you have arranged all
things by measure and
number and weight.

God Is Powerful and Merciful

21 For it is always in your
power to show great
strength,
and who can withstand the
might of your arm?
22 Because the whole world
before you is like a
speck that tips the
scales,
and like a drop of morning
dew that falls on the
ground.
23 But you are merciful to all,
for you can do all
things,
and you overlook people's
sins, so that they may
repent.
24 For you love all things that
exist,
and detest none of the
things that you have
made,
for you would not have made
anything if you had
hated it.
25 How would anything have
endured if you had not
willed it?
Or how would anything not
called forth by you have
been preserved?
26 You spare all things, for they
are yours, O Lord, you
who love the living.

12 For your immortal spirit
is in all things.
2 Therefore you correct little
by little those who
trespass,
and you remind and warn
them of the things
through which they sin,
so that they may be freed
from wickedness and
put their trust in you,
O Lord.

The Sins of the Canaanites

3 Those who lived long ago in
your holy land
4 you hated for their
detestable practices,
their works of sorcery and
unholy rites,
5 their merciless slaughter[i] of
children,
and their sacrificial feasting
on human flesh and
blood.
These initiates from the
midst of a heathen
cult,[j]
6 these parents who murder
helpless lives,
you willed to destroy by the
hands of our ancestors,
7 so that the land most
precious of all to you
might receive a worthy
colony of the servants[k]
of God.
8 But even these you spared,
since they were but
mortals,
and sent wasps[l] as
forerunners of your
army
to destroy them little by
little,

11.18 Job 41.19-21, 18 **11.19** Job 41.9-10, 33 **11.20** Job 4.9; Isa 30.33 **11.21** Job 12.13,16; Ps 65.6; Wis 12.16-18; Jdt 16.13; 2 Chr 20.6; Wis 12.12 **11.22** Hos 13.3 **11.23** Rom 11.32; Titus 2.11; 2 Pet 3.9; Gen 18.14; Jer 32.17; Lk 1.37; 18.27; Acts 17.30-31; Rom 2.4 **11.24** Ps 145.8-9

11.25 Ps 115.3; Dan 4.35; Rev 4.11 **11.26** Ps 104.27-30; Wis 12.16 **12.1** Wis 1.7 **12.2** Deut 4.36; Sir 4.17; 32.14; Deut 8.19; 2 Kings 17.13; Ps 22.4-5; 107.6 **12.4** Deut 18.9-12 **12.5** Deut 12.31; Ps 106.35-38; Wis 14.23 **12.6** Num 33.51-53; Deut 20.16-17; Josh 6.17 **12.8** Ex 23.29-30; Deut 7.22

[g] Gk *them* [h] Gk *they* [i] Gk *slaughterers* [j] Meaning of Gk uncertain [k] Or *children* [l] Or *hornets*

9 though you were not unable
to give the ungodly into
the hands of the
righteous in battle,
or to destroy them at one
blow by dread wild
animals or your stern
word.
10 But judging them little by
little you gave them an
opportunity to repent,
though you were not
unaware that their
origin[m] was evil
and their wickedness inborn,
and that their way of
thinking would never
change.
11 For they were an accursed
race from the
beginning,
and it was not through fear
of anyone that you left
them unpunished for
their sins.

God Is Sovereign

12 For who will say, "What have
you done?"
Or will resist your judgment?
Who will accuse you for the
destruction of nations
that you made?
Or who will come before you
to plead as an advocate
for the unrighteous?
13 For neither is there any god
besides you, whose care
is for all people,[n]
to whom you should prove
that you have not
judged unjustly;
14 nor can any king or monarch
confront you about
those whom you have
punished.
15 You are righteous and you
rule all things
righteously,
deeming it alien to your
power
to condemn anyone who
does not deserve to be
punished.
16 For your strength is the
source of righteousness,
and your sovereignty over all
causes you to spare all.
17 For you show your strength
when people doubt the
completeness of your
power,
and you rebuke any
insolence among those
who know it.[o]
18 Although you are sovereign
in strength, you judge
with mildness,
and with great forbearance
you govern us;
for you have power to act
whenever you choose.

God's Lessons for Israel

19 Through such works you
have taught your people
that the righteous must be
kind,
and you have filled your
children with good
hope,
because you give repentance
for sins.
20 For if you punished with
such great care and
indulgence[p]
the enemies of your
servants[q] and those
deserving of death,
granting them time and
opportunity to give up
their wickedness,
21 with what strictness you
have judged your
children,
to whose ancestors you gave
oaths and covenants
full of good promises!
22 So while chastening us you
scourge our enemies
ten thousand times
more,
so that, when we judge, we
may meditate upon
your goodness,
and when we are judged, we
may expect mercy.

12.9 Josh 10.9-14 **12.10** Wis 11.23; 2 Esd 9.11; 2 Pet 3.9; Ps 51.5; 55.19 **12.11** Gen 9.25; Wis 3.13 **12.12** Eccl 8.4; Dan 4.35; Rom 9.19; Add Esth 13.11; Wis 11.21; Gen 18.22-33 **12.13** Deut 6.4; Isa 44.6; 1 Cor 8.3; 1 Tim 2.5; 2.4; 1 Pet 5.7 **12.14** Jer 49.19 **12.15** Gen 18.25; Deut 32.4; Jer 11.20 **12.16** Wis 11.21,26 **12.17** 3 Macc 2.3, 21; 6.9 **12.18** Rom 3.25; 2 Pet 3.9 **12.19** Prov 14.21, 31; Mic 6.8; Eph 4.32; Acts 11.18; 2 Cor 7.10 **12.20** Wis 12.10; Acts 17.30; 2 Pet 3.9 **12.21** Gen 12.1-3; 28.13-15; Deut 28.1-14; 2 Sam 7.9-16 **12.22** Prov 3.11-12; Heb 12.5-11; 2 Macc 6.12, 16; Ps 77.12; 143.5; 145.5

m Or *nature* n Or *all things*
o Meaning of Gk uncertain
p Other ancient authorities lack *and indulgence*; others read *and entreaty*
q Or *children*

The Punishment of the Egyptians

23 Therefore those who lived
unrighteously, in a life
of folly,
you tormented through their
own abominations.
24 For they went far astray on
the paths of error,
accepting as gods those
animals that even their
enemies[r] despised;
they were deceived like
foolish infants.
25 Therefore, as though to
children who cannot
reason,
you sent your judgment to
mock them.
26 But those who have not
heeded the warning of
mild rebukes
will experience the deserved
judgment of God.
27 For when in their suffering
they became incensed
at those creatures that they
had thought to be gods,
being punished by
means of them,
they saw and recognized as
the true God the one
whom they had before
refused to know.
Therefore the utmost
condemnation came
upon them.

The Foolishness of Nature Worship

13 For all people who were
ignorant of God were
foolish by nature;
and they were unable from
the good things that are
seen to know the one
who exists,
nor did they recognize the
artisan while paying
heed to his works;
2 but they supposed that
either fire or wind or
swift air,
or the circle of the stars, or
turbulent water,

12.23 Ps 7.15-16; Wis 11.16 **12.24** Rom 1.23 **12.25** Jer 4.22; 10.8 **12.26** Mt 12.41-42; Rom 2.5; 1 Cor 11.30-32 **12.27** Ex 8.1-6; 10.12-15; 9.27-30; 10.7; 12.29; 14.23-30 **13.1** Ps 8.3; 19.1; Rom 1.20-21; Acts 14.17 **13.2** Deut 4.19; 17.3; 2 Kings 17.16; 21.3,5

13.3 Gen 1.1, 14-19; Ps 8.3; Isa 44.24 **13.4** 1 Chr 29.11; Ps 29.3-5; 62.11 **13.5** Ps 19.1; Acts 14.17; Rom 1.19-20 **13.6** Acts 17.27 **13.8** Rom 1.20-21 **13.9** 1 Kings 4.33; Eccl 1.12 **13.10** Acts 17.29; Let Jer 6.51; Isa 46.6-7; Wis 15.9; Let Jer 6.24-25; Ps 135.15; Jer 10.9; Rom 1.23

or the luminaries of heaven
were the gods that rule
the world.
3 If through delight in the
beauty of these things
people assumed them
to be gods,
let them know how much
better than these is
their Lord,
for the author of beauty
created them.
4 And if people[r] were amazed
at their power and
working,
let them perceive from them
how much more powerful is
the one who formed
them.
5 For from the greatness and
beauty of created things
comes a corresponding
perception of their
Creator.
6 Yet these people are little to
be blamed,
for perhaps they go astray
while seeking God and
desiring to find him.
7 For while they live among
his works, they keep
searching,
and they trust in what they
see, because the things
that are seen are
beautiful.
8 Yet again, not even they are
to be excused;
9 for if they had the power to
know so much
that they could investigate
the world,
how did they fail to find
sooner the Lord of
these things?

The Foolishness of Idolatry

10 But miserable, with their
hopes set on dead
things, are those
who give the name "gods" to
the works of human
hands,
gold and silver fashioned
with skill,
and likenesses of animals,

r Gk *they*

or a useless stone, the work
of an ancient hand.
11 A skilled woodcutter may
saw down a tree easy to
handle
and skillfully strip off all its
bark,
and then with pleasing
workmanship
make a useful vessel that
serves life's needs,
12 and burn the cast-off pieces
of his work
to prepare his food, and eat
his fill.
13 But a cast-off piece from
among them, useful for
nothing,
a stick crooked and full of
knots,
he takes and carves with
care in his leisure,
and shapes it with skill
gained in idleness;[s]
he forms it in the likeness of
a human being,
14 or makes it like some
worthless animal,
giving it a coat of red paint
and coloring its surface
red
and covering every blemish
in it with paint;
15 then he makes a suitable
niche for it,
and sets it in the wall, and
fastens it there with
iron.
16 He takes thought for it, so
that it may not fall,
because he knows that it
cannot help itself,
for it is only an image and
has need of help.
17 When he prays about
possessions and his
marriage and children,
he is not ashamed to address
a lifeless thing.
18 For health he appeals to a
thing that is weak;
for life he prays to a thing
that is dead;
for aid he entreats a thing
that is utterly
inexperienced;

13.11 Isa 44.13-14; Jer 10.3; Wis 15.7
13.12 Isa 44.15-16
13.13 Isa 44.17-18
13.14 Ex 20.4-5; Deut 4.16-18; Jer 10.9
13.15 Isa 41.7
13.16 1 Sam 5.3-4; Isa 40.20; Let Jer 6.12; Judg 6.28-32; Isa 45.20; 46.1-7
13.17 Ps 115.4-7; 135.15-17; Isa 44.18; Jer 10.5

14.1 Jude 13; Ps 135.17; Isa 46.7
14.3 Ps 77.19; Isa 43.16; Ps 107.23-30
14.4 Ps 107.6-7, 13-14,19-20; Wis 16.8
14.5 Wis 10.4
14.6 Gen 6.4; 7.11-24; 9.1,7
14.7 1 Pet 3.20

for a prosperous journey, a
thing that cannot take a
step;
19 for money-making and work
and success with his
hands
he asks strength of a thing
whose hands have no
strength.

Folly of a Navigator Praying to an Idol

14 Again, one preparing to
sail and about to voyage
over raging waves
calls upon a piece of wood
more fragile than the
ship that carries him.
2 For it was desire for gain
that planned that
vessel,
and wisdom was the artisan
who built it;
3 but it is your providence,
O Father, that steers its
course,
because you have given it a
path in the sea,
and a safe way through the
waves,
4 showing that you can save
from every danger,
so that even a person who
lacks skill may put to
sea.
5 It is your will that works of
your wisdom should not
be without effect;
therefore people trust their
lives even to the
smallest piece of wood,
and passing through the
billows on a raft they
come safely to land.
6 For even in the beginning,
when arrogant giants
were perishing,
the hope of the world took
refuge on a raft,
and guided by your hand left
to the world the seed of
a new generation.
7 For blessed is the wood by
which righteousness
comes.

[s] Other ancient authorities read *with intelligent skill*

8 But the idol made with
hands is accursed, and
so is the one who made
it—
he for having made it, and
the perishable thing
because it was named a
god.
9 For equally hateful to God
are the ungodly and
their ungodliness;
10 for what was done will be
punished together with
the one who did it.
11 Therefore there will be a
visitation also upon the
heathen idols,
because, though part of what
God created, they
became an
abomination,
snares for human souls
and a trap for the feet of the
foolish.

The Origin and Evils of Idolatry

12 For the idea of making idols
was the beginning of
fornication,
and the invention of them
was the corruption of
life;
13 for they did not exist from
the beginning,
nor will they last forever.
14 For through human vanity
they entered the world,
and therefore their speedy
end has been planned.

15 For a father, consumed with
grief at an untimely
bereavement,
made an image of his child,
who had been suddenly
taken from him;
he now honored as a god
what was once a dead
human being,
and handed on to his
dependents secret rites
and initiations.
16 Then the ungodly custom,
grown strong with time,
was kept as a law,
and at the command of
monarchs carved
images were worshiped.
17 When people could not
honor monarchs[t] in
their presence, since
they lived at a distance,
they imagined their
appearance far away,
and made a visible image of
the king whom they
honored,
so that by their zeal they
might flatter the absent
one as though present.

18 Then the ambition of the
artisan impelled
even those who did not know
the king to intensify
their worship.
19 For he, perhaps wishing to
please his ruler,
skillfully forced the likeness
to take more beautiful
form,
20 and the multitude, attracted
by the charm of his
work,
now regarded as an object of
worship the one whom
shortly before they had
honored as a human
being.
21 And this became a hidden
trap for humankind,
because people, in bondage
to misfortune or to
royal authority,
bestowed on objects of stone
or wood the name that
ought not to be shared.

22 Then it was not enough for
them to err about the
knowledge of God,
but though living in great
strife due to ignorance,
they call such great evils
peace.
23 For whether they kill
children in their
initiations, or celebrate
secret mysteries,
or hold frenzied revels with
strange customs,

14.8 Wis 14.10; Rom 1.23 **14.9** Ps 5.5; 11.5 **14.10** Isa 13.11; 24.21-23; 46.1-3; Jer 2.9,29 **14.11** Wis 3.7; Num 33.4; Jer 10.15; 46.25; Josh 23.14; Judg 2.3 **14.12** Rom 1.23-31 **14.13** Ps 90.1-2; Isa 2.18; 21.9 **14.16** Dan 3.1-7; 1 Macc 1.47-50

14.18 Wis 13.11-15; 15.4 **14.20** Acts 17.20 **14.21** Josh 23.14; Judg 2.3; Wis 14.11 **14.22** Jer 6.14; Ezek 13.10 **14.23** Deut 12.31; Ps 106.35-38; Isa 57.5; Wis 12.5; 1 Kings 18.28-29

t Gk *them*

24 they no longer keep either
their lives or their
marriages pure,
but they either treacherously
kill one another, or
grieve one another by
adultery,
25 and all is a raging riot of
blood and murder, theft
and deceit, corruption,
faithlessness, tumult,
perjury,
26 confusion over what is good,
forgetfulness of favors,
defiling of souls, sexual
perversion,
disorder in marriages,
adultery, and
debauchery.
27 For the worship of idols not
to be named
is the beginning and cause
and end of every evil.
28 For their worshipers[u] either
rave in exultation,
or prophesy lies, or live
unrighteously, or readily
commit perjury;
29 for because they trust in
lifeless idols
they swear wicked oaths and
expect to suffer no
harm.
30 But just penalties will
overtake them on two
counts:
because they thought
wrongly about God in
devoting themselves to
idols,
and because in deceit they
swore unrighteously
through contempt for
holiness.
31 For it is not the power of the
things by which people
swear,[v]
but the just penalty for those
who sin,
that always pursues the
transgression of the
unrighteous.

Benefits of Worshiping the True God

15 But you, our God, are
kind and true,
patient, and ruling all
things[w] in mercy.
2 For even if we sin we are
yours, knowing your
power;
but we will not sin, because
we know that you
acknowledge us as
yours.
3 For to know you is complete
righteousness,
and to know your power is
the root of immortality.
4 For neither has the evil
intent of human art
misled us,
nor the fruitless toil of
painters,
a figure stained with varied
colors,
5 whose appearance arouses
yearning in fools,
so that they desire[x] the
lifeless form of a dead
image.
6 Lovers of evil things and fit
for such objects of
hope[y]
are those who either make or
desire or worship them.

The Foolishness of Worshiping Clay Idols

7 A potter kneads the soft
earth
and laboriously molds each
vessel for our service,
fashioning out of the same
clay
both the vessels that serve
clean uses
and those for contrary uses,
making all alike;
but which shall be the use of
each of them
the worker in clay decides.
8 With misspent toil, these
workers form a futile
god from the same
clay—
these mortals who were
made of earth a short
time before

14.24 Jer 2.20; Hos 7.4; Am 2.7; Jas 4.4
14.25 Hos 4.1-2; Rom 1.28-31
14.26 Rom 1.24-27; Gal 5.19-21; 1 Cor 6.9-10
14.28 1 Kings 18.26-29; Jer 5.31; 14.14
14.29 Isa 33.8; Ezek 16.59; Hos 10.4
14.30 Jer 2.13
15.1 Ps 145.17; Jn 14.6; 17.3; Ex 34.6-7; Isa 30.18; 2 Pet 3.9; Wis 8.1; Lk 6.35
15.2 1 Jn 3.9; 5.18; Tob 4.5
15.3 Jn 17.3
15.4 Wis 13.14; 14.19-20
15.6 Ps 115.8; 135.18
15.7 Isa 29.16; 64.8; Jer 18.1-11; Rom 9.21-23; 2 Tim 2.20-21
15.8 Wis 13.10-19; Gen 2.7; 3.19; Eccl 3.19-21; 12.7; Lk 12.20

[u] Gk *they* [v] Or *of the oaths people swear*
[w] Or *ruling the universe* [x] Gk *and he desires*
[y] Gk *such hopes*

and after a little while go to
the earth from which
all mortals are taken,
when the time comes to
return the souls that
were borrowed.
9 But the workers are not
concerned that mortals
are destined to die
or that their life is brief,
but they compete with
workers in gold and
silver,
and imitate workers in
copper;
and they count it a glorious
thing to mold
counterfeit gods.
10 Their heart is ashes, their
hope is cheaper than
dirt,
and their lives are of less
worth than clay,
11 because they failed to know
the one who formed
them
and inspired them with
active souls
and breathed a living spirit
into them.
12 But they considered our
existence an idle game,
and life a festival held for
profit,
for they say one must get
money however one
can, even by base
means.
13 For these persons, more than
all others, know that
they sin
when they make from earthy
matter fragile vessels
and carved images.
14 But most foolish, and more
miserable than an
infant,
are all the enemies who
oppressed your people.
15 For they thought that all
their heathen idols
were gods,
though these have neither
the use of their eyes to
see with,
nor nostrils with which to
draw breath,

15.9 Let Jer 6.46; Isa 46.6-7; Jer 10.9; Wis 13.10 **15.11** Gen 2.7; Ps 103.14; Zech 12.1; Gen 21.7; Job 33.4; Jn 20.22 **15.12** Jer 7.9; Jas 4.13-14; 5.1-5 **15.14** Ex 1.8-14; 5.5-9; Ps 106.42 **15.15** Ps 115.4-7; 135.15-17; Jer 10.5, 14-15; Wis 13.17

15.16 Wis 13.10-14; Gen 2.7; Ps 104.29-30; Wis 15.11 **15.17** Gen 3.19; Job 9.32; Eccl 12.7; Acts 17.23 **15.18** Jer 10.14; Wis 11.15; Rom 1.23 **15.19** Gen 1.25 **16.1** Ex 8.1-30; 10.13-19; Wis 12.23-24 **16.2** Wis 11.13-14; Ex 16.11-13; Num 11.31-34; Wis 19.11 **16.3** Deut 8.7-9

nor ears with which to hear,
nor fingers to feel with,
and their feet are of no use
for walking.
16 For a human being made
them,
and one whose spirit is
borrowed formed them;
for none can form gods that
are like themselves.
17 People are mortal, and what
they make with lawless
hands is dead;
for they are better than the
objects they worship,
since[z] they have life, but
the idols[a] never had.

Serpents in the Desert

18 Moreover, they worship even
the most hateful
animals,
which are worse than all
others when judged by
their lack of
intelligence;
19 and even as animals they are
not so beautiful in
appearance that one
would desire them,
but they have escaped both
the praise of God and
his blessing.

16 Therefore those people[b]
were deservedly
punished through such
creatures,
and were tormented by a
multitude of animals.
2 Instead of this punishment
you showed kindness to
your people,
and you prepared quails to
eat,
a delicacy to satisfy the
desire of appetite;
3 in order that those people,
when they desired food,
might lose the least remnant
of appetite[c]
because of the odious
creatures sent to them,
while your people,[b] after
suffering want a short
time,

[z] Other ancient authorities read *of which*
[a] Gk *but they* [b] Gk *they* [c] Gk *loathed the necessary appetite*

might partake of delicacies.
4 For it was necessary that
upon those oppressors
inescapable want
should come,
while to these others it was
merely shown how their
enemies were being
tormented.

5 For when the terrible rage of
wild animals came
upon your people[d]
and they were being
destroyed by the bites
of writhing serpents,
your wrath did not continue
to the end;
6 they were troubled for a little
while as a warning,
and received a symbol of
deliverance to remind
them of your law's
command.

7 For the one who turned
toward it was saved, not
by the thing that was
beheld,
but by you, the Savior of all.
8 And by this also you
convinced our enemies
that it is you who deliver
from every evil.
9 For they were killed by the
bites of locusts and
flies,
and no healing was found for
them,
because they deserved to be
punished by such
things.
10 But your children were not
conquered even by the
fangs of venomous
serpents,
for your mercy came to their
help and healed them.
11 To remind them of your
oracles they were
bitten,
and then were quickly
delivered,
so that they would not fall
into deep forgetfulness
and become unresponsive[e]
to your kindness.

16.4 Wis 15.14; 11.9 **16.5** Num 21.6-9; Deut 32.24 **16.6** Deut 8.2-3; Ex 12.14-27; 1 Cor 11.24-26 **16.7** 1 Tim 2.4; 4.10 **16.8** Wis 14.4; 2 Macc 1.25 **16.9** Ex 10.2-15; Rev 9.3; Ex 8.21-24 **16.10** Num 21.9 **16.11** Wis 15.1

16.12 Deut 32.27; Ps 103.3 **16.13** Deut 32.39; 1 Sam 2.6; Ps 9.13; Tob 13.2; Rev 1.18 **16.15** Wis 11.21 **16.16** Wis 12.27; Rom 1.19-21; Ex 9.22-25 **16.17** 1 Kings 18.30-38; Wis 19.20 **16.19** Ex 9.29-32 **16.20** Ps 78.24-25; Ex 16.14-19; Neh 9.15; Ps 78.24-25; Jn 6.31

12 For neither herb nor poultice
cured them,
but it was your word,
O Lord, that heals all
people.
13 For you have power over life
and death;
you lead mortals down to the
gates of Hades and
back again.
14 A person in wickedness kills
another,
but cannot bring back the
departed spirit,
or set free the imprisoned
soul.

Disastrous Storms Strike Egypt

15 To escape from your hand is
impossible;
16 for the ungodly, refusing to
know you,
were flogged by the strength
of your arm,
pursued by unusual rains
and hail and relentless
storms,
and utterly consumed by fire.
17 For—most incredible of all
—in water, which
quenches all things,
the fire had still greater
effect,
for the universe defends the
righteous.
18 At one time the flame was
restrained,
so that it might not consume
the creatures sent
against the ungodly,
but that seeing this they
might know
that they were being pursued
by the judgment of
God;
19 and at another time even in
the midst of water it
burned more intensely
than fire,
to destroy the crops of the
unrighteous land.

The Israelites Receive Manna

20 Instead of these things you
gave your people food
of angels,

[d] Gk *them* [e] Meaning of Gk uncertain

and without their toil you
supplied them from
heaven with bread
ready to eat,
providing every pleasure and
suited to every taste.
21 For your sustenance
manifested your
sweetness toward your
children;
and the bread, ministering[f]
to the desire of the one
who took it,
was changed to suit
everyone's liking.
22 Snow and ice withstood fire
without melting,
so that they might know that
the crops of their
enemies
were being destroyed by the
fire that blazed in the
hail
and flashed in the showers of
rain;
23 whereas the fire,[g] in order
that the righteous
might be fed,
even forgot its native power.

24 For creation, serving you
who made it,
exerts itself to punish the
unrighteous,
and in kindness relaxes on
behalf of those who
trust in you.
25 Therefore at that time also,
changed into all forms,
it served your all-nourishing
bounty,
according to the desire of
those who had need,[h]
26 so that your children, whom
you loved, O Lord,
might learn
that it is not the production
of crops that feeds
humankind
but that your word sustains
those who trust in you.
27 For what was not destroyed
by fire
was melted when simply
warmed by a fleeting
ray of the sun,

16.22 Wis 19.21; Ex 9.22-32; Rev 8.7
16.23 Ps 148.8
16.24 Gen 1.1; Isa 45.18; Josh 10.10-14; Wis 5.17-20; Sir 39.27- 31; Ex 9.6-7,26
16.26 Deut 8.3; Mt 4.4
16.27 Ex 16.21

16.28 Ps 57.8-9; 92.1-2
16.29 Wis 5.14
17.1 Ps 92.5; Rom 11.33
17.2 Ex 10.21-23; Ps 107.10-12; Mt 22.13
17.3 Prov 7.6-9; Wis 1.7-8
17.5 Ex 13.21-22; 14.19-20; Wis 10.17
17.6 Ex 9.23-24; Wis 16.15-19

28 to make it known that one
must rise before the
sun to give you thanks,
and must pray to you at the
dawning of the light;
29 for the hope of an ungrateful
person will melt like
wintry frost,
and flow away like waste
water.

Terror Strikes the Egyptians at Night

17 Great are your judgments
and hard to describe;
therefore uninstructed souls
have gone astray.
2 For when lawless people
supposed that they held
the holy nation in their
power,
they themselves lay as
captives of darkness
and prisoners of long
night,
shut in under their roofs,
exiles from eternal
providence.
3 For thinking that in their
secret sins they were
unobserved
behind a dark curtain of
forgetfulness,
they were scattered, terribly[i]
alarmed,
and appalled by specters.
4 For not even the inner
chamber that held them
protected them from
fear,
but terrifying sounds rang
out around them,
and dismal phantoms with
gloomy faces appeared.
5 And no power of fire was
able to give light,
nor did the brilliant flames
of the stars
avail to illumine that hateful
night.
6 Nothing was shining through
to them

[f] Gk *and it, ministering* [g] Gk *this*
[h] Or *who made supplication*
[i] Other ancient authorities read *unobserved, they were darkened behind a dark curtain of forgetfulness, terribly*

except a dreadful,
self-kindled fire,
and in terror they deemed
the things that they saw
to be worse than that unseen
appearance.
7 The delusions of their magic
art lay humbled,
and their boasted wisdom
was scornfully rebuked.
8 For those who promised to
drive off the fears and
disorders of a sick soul
were sick themselves with
ridiculous fear.
9 For even if nothing
disturbing frightened
them,
yet, scared by the passing of
wild animals and the
hissing of snakes
10 they perished in trembling
fear,
refusing to look even at the
air, though it nowhere
could be avoided.
11 For wickedness is a cowardly
thing, condemned by its
own testimony;[j]
distressed by conscience, it
has always
exaggerated[k] the
difficulties.
12 For fear is nothing but a
giving up of the helps
that come from reason;
13 and hope, defeated by this
inward weakness,
prefers ignorance of what
causes the torment.
14 But throughout the night,
which was really
powerless
and which came upon them
from the recesses of
powerless Hades,
they all slept the same sleep,
15 and now were driven by
monstrous specters,
and now were paralyzed by
their souls' surrender;
for sudden and unexpected
fear overwhelmed them.
16 And whoever was there fell
down,
and thus was kept shut up in
a prison not made of
iron;

17.7 Ex 8.18-19 **17.8** Ex 9.11 **17.10** Wis 16.1 **17.11** Rom 2.15; 1 Cor 8.7 **17.13** Wis 3.11,18; 16.29 **17.14** Mt 16.18; Rev 1.18 **17.15** Wis 18.17-19; Mk 6.49

17 for whether they were
farmers or shepherds
or workers who toiled in the
wilderness,
they were seized, and
endured the
inescapable fate;
for with one chain of
darkness they all were
bound.
18 Whether there came a
whistling wind,
or a melodious sound of
birds in wide-spreading
branches,
or the rhythm of violently
rushing water,
19 or the harsh crash of rocks
hurled down,
or the unseen running of
leaping animals,
or the sound of the most
savage roaring beasts,
or an echo thrown back from
a hollow of the
mountains,
it paralyzed them with
terror.
20 For the whole world was
illumined with brilliant
light,
and went about its work
unhindered,
21 while over those people
alone heavy night was
spread,
an image of the darkness
that was destined to
receive them;
but still heavier than
darkness were they to
themselves.

Light Shines on the Israelites

18 But for your holy ones
there was very great
light.
Their enemies[l] heard their
voices but did not see
their forms,
and counted them happy for
not having suffered,

17.17 Wis 18.4; 2 Pet 2.4; Jude 6 **17.19** Lev 26.36-37 **17.20** Gen 1.3; Ex 10.23; Isa 9.2; Ps 104.22-23 **17.21** 2 Pet 2.17; Jude 13 **18.1** Ex 10.23; Wis 17.20; Acts 9.7; 22.9

[j] Meaning of Gk uncertain
[k] Other ancient authorities read *anticipated*
[l] Gk *They*

2 and were thankful that your holy ones,[m] though previously wronged,
were doing them no injury;
and they begged their pardon for having been at variance with them.[m]
3 Therefore you provided a flaming pillar of fire
as a guide for your people's[n] unknown journey,
and a harmless sun for their glorious wandering.
4 For their enemies[o] deserved to be deprived of light and imprisoned in darkness,
those who had kept your children imprisoned,
through whom the imperishable light of the law was to be given to the world.

The Death of the Egyptian Firstborn

5 When they had resolved to kill the infants of your holy ones,
and one child had been abandoned and rescued,
you in punishment took away a multitude of their children;
and you destroyed them all together by a mighty flood.
6 That night was made known beforehand to our ancestors,
so that they might rejoice in sure knowledge of the oaths in which they trusted.
7 The deliverance of the righteous and the destruction of their enemies
were expected by your people.
8 For by the same means by which you punished our enemies
you called us to yourself and glorified us.
9 For in secret the holy children of good people offered sacrifices,
and with one accord agreed to the divine law,
so that the saints would share alike the same things,
both blessings and dangers;
and already they were singing the praises of the ancestors.[p]
10 But the discordant cry of their enemies echoed back,
and their piteous lament for their children was spread abroad.
11 The slave was punished with the same penalty as the master,
and the commoner suffered the same loss as the king;
12 and they all together, by the one form[q] of death,
had corpses too many to count.
For the living were not sufficient even to bury them,
since in one instant their most valued children had been destroyed.
13 For though they had disbelieved everything because of their magic arts,
yet, when their firstborn were destroyed, they acknowledged your people to be God's child.
14 For while gentle silence enveloped all things,
and night in its swift course was now half gone,
15 your all-powerful word leaped from heaven, from the royal throne,
into the midst of the land that was doomed,
a stern warrior

18.3 Ex 13.21-22; Ps 78.14; 105.39 **18.4** Ex 14.19-20; Wis 17.16-17; Ex 1.9-14; 20.1-17; 24.13; Ps 119.105; Rom 9.4 **18.5** Ex 1.15-23; 2.1-10; 12.29-30; 14.23-30 **18.6** Ex 11.4-8; 15.1-21; 6.8; 13.5; Wis 12.21 **18.7** Ex 14.13 **18.8** Ex 14.21-31; Wis 19.22 **18.9** Ex 24.1-4; Josh 24.16-18; Sir 44-50 **18.10** Ex 11.6; 12.30; Ps 105.38 **18.11** Ex 11.5; 12.12,29 **18.12** Num 33.4 **18.13** Ex 7.11-13,22 **18.14** Rev 8.1 **18.15** Heb 4.12; Rev 19.13; Ps 47.8; Wis 9.10; Ex 15.3; Ps 24.8

[m] Meaning of Gk uncertain [n] Gk *their* [o] Gk *those persons* [p] Other ancient authorities read *dangers, the ancestors already leading the songs of praise* [q] Gk *name*

16 carrying the sharp sword of
your authentic
command,
and stood and filled all
things with death,
and touched heaven while
standing on the earth.
17 Then at once apparitions in
dreadful dreams greatly
troubled them,
and unexpected fears
assailed them;
18 and one here and another
there, hurled down half
dead,
made known why they were
dying;
19 for the dreams that disturbed
them forewarned them
of this,
so that they might not perish
without knowing why
they suffered.

Threat of Annihilation in the Desert

20 The experience of death
touched also the
righteous,
and a plague came upon the
multitude in the desert,
but the wrath did not long
continue.
21 For a blameless man was
quick to act as their
champion;
he brought forward the
shield of his ministry,
prayer and propitiation by
incense;
he withstood the anger and
put an end to the
disaster,
showing that he was your
servant.
22 He conquered the wrath[r]
not by strength of body,
not by force of arms,
but by his word he subdued
the avenger,
appealing to the oaths and
covenants given to our
ancestors.
23 For when the dead had
already fallen on one
another in heaps,
he intervened and held back
the wrath,
and cut off its way to the
living.
24 For on his long robe the
whole world was
depicted,
and the glories of the
ancestors were engraved
on the four rows of
stones,
and your majesty was on the
diadem upon his head.
25 To these the destroyer
yielded, these he[s]
feared;
for merely to test the wrath
was enough.

The Red Sea

19 But the ungodly were
assailed to the end by
pitiless anger,
for God[t] knew in advance
even their future
actions:
2 how, though they themselves
had permitted[u] your
people to depart
and hastily sent them out,
they would change their
minds and pursue
them.
3 For while they were still
engaged in mourning,
and were lamenting at the
graves of their dead,
they reached another foolish
decision,
and pursued as fugitives
those whom they had
begged and compelled
to leave.
4 For the fate they deserved
drew them on to this
end,
and made them forget what
had happened,
in order that they might fill
up the punishment that
their torments still
lacked,

18.16 Heb 4.12; Rev 1.16; 2.12 **18.17** Wis 17.14-15 **18.19** Gen 40.1-22; Dan 4.9-33 **18.20** Num 16.41-50; 26.1-5 **18.21** Num 21.4-9; 24.46-47; 26.6-18; Ex 32.11-14; Num 14.13-20; 12.7-8; Deut 34.5; Ps 105.26 **18.22** Ex 32.13; Wis 12.21 **18.23** Num 14.29; 16.48-49
18.24 Ex 28.15-21; 39.8-14; Sir 45.8-12 **18.25** 1 Chr 21.15; Heb 11.28 **19.1** Ex 3.19; 7.1-4; 11.4-8; 14.4 **19.2** Ex 12.31-33; 14.5-12 **19.4** Rom 2.5-8; Ex 14.21-22, 26-30

[r] Cn: Gk *multitude*
[s] Other ancient authorities read *they* [t] Gk *he*
[u] Other ancient authorities read *had changed their minds to permit*

5 and that your people might
experience[v] an
incredible journey,
but they themselves might
meet a strange death.

God Guides and Protects His People

6 For the whole creation in its
nature was fashioned
anew,
complying with your
commands,
so that your children[w] might
be kept unharmed.
7 The cloud was seen
overshadowing the
camp,
and dry land emerging where
water had stood before,
an unhindered way out of
the Red Sea,
and a grassy plain out of the
raging waves,
8 where those protected by
your hand passed
through as one nation,
after gazing on marvelous
wonders.
9 For they ranged like horses,
and leaped like lambs,
praising you, O Lord, who
delivered them.
10 For they still recalled the
events of their sojourn,
how instead of producing
animals the earth
brought forth gnats,
and instead of fish the river
spewed out vast
numbers of frogs.
11 Afterward they saw also a
new kind[x] of birds,
when desire led them to ask
for luxurious food;
12 for, to give them relief,
quails came up from
the sea.

The Punishment of the Egyptians

13 The punishments did not
come upon the sinners
without prior signs in the
violence of thunder,
for they justly suffered
because of their wicked
acts;
for they practiced a more
bitter hatred of
strangers.
14 Others had refused to receive
strangers when they
came to them,
but these made slaves of
guests who were their
benefactors.
15 And not only so — but, while
punishment of some
sort will come upon the
former
for having received strangers
with hostility,
16 the latter, having first
received them with
festal celebrations,
afterward afflicted with
terrible sufferings
those who had already
shared the same rights.
17 They were stricken also with
loss of sight —
just as were those at the
door of the righteous
man —
when, surrounded by
yawning darkness,
all of them tried to find the
way through their own
doors.

A New Harmony in Nature

18 For the elements changed[y]
places with one
another,
as on a harp the notes vary
the nature of the
rhythm,
while each note remains the
same.[z]
This may be clearly inferred
from the sight of what
took place.
19 For land animals were
transformed into water
creatures,
and creatures that swim
moved over to the land.
20 Fire even in water retained
its normal power,

19.6 Ps 148.8; Wis 16.15-24 **19.7** Ex 13.21-22; 14.19-20; 1 Cor 10.1; Ex 14.21-22; Ps 18.15 **19.8** Ps 106.9; Isa 63.12-14 **19.9** Ps 114.4-6; Ex 15.1-21 **19.10** Ex 8.16-17, 5-7; Ps 105.30 **19.12** Ex 16.13; Num 11.4,20; Wis 16.2 **19.13** Add Esth 16.18; 2 Macc 4.38; Rom 2.5-9 **19.14** Gen 19.1-11; 45.16-20; 47.13-25 **19.16** Ex 1.9-14; Wis 17.2 **19.17** Ex 10.21-23; 2 Kings 6.18-19; Gen 19.11 **19.19** Ex 8.1-7 **19.20** Wis 16.17-19, 22-23

[v] Other ancient authorities read *accomplish* [w] Or *servants* [x] Or *production*
[y] Gk *changing* [z] Meaning of Gk uncertain

and water forgot its
fire-quenching nature.
21 Flames, on the contrary,
failed to consume
the flesh of perishable
creatures that walked
among them,
nor did they melt[a] the
crystalline,
quick-melting kind of
heavenly food.

19.21 Ex 16.21; Ps 78.24-25; Wis 16.20-21

19.22 Wis 18.8; Ps 28.6-7; 126.3; Heb 4.16; 13.6

Conclusion

22 For in everything, O Lord,
you have exalted and
glorified your people,
and you have not neglected
to help them at all
times and in all
places.

[a]Cn: Gk *nor could be melted*

ECCLESIASTICUS, OR THE WISDOM OF JESUS SON OF

Sirach

Title and Background

The title of this work comes from the surname of its author, Jesus ben Sirach, a sage and scribe. Sirach was likely living in Jerusalem around 200 B.C. when Antiochus III granted the Jews permission to live according to their ancestral laws. The author sought to communicate to his generation the wisdom of God contained in the Law and the Prophets. The other name of the book, Ecclesiasticus, indicates its wide use in early Christian communities for practical advice on daily living.

Author and Date of Writing

This collection of wisdom sayings was written down in Hebrew at the beginning of the second century B.C. by Jesus son of Eleazar son of Sirach (50.27). The only complete manuscript of the work, however, is from the Greek translation done by his grandson in 132 B.C. (see the prologue) and found in the Septuagint. Hebrew fragments have been found at Qumran, Cairo, and Masada.

Theme and Message

The theme of Sirach is similar to that of Proverbs: following true wisdom (as exemplified in the Israelites of old) allows one to live a successful and happy life. Such wisdom can only be obtained from the Lord (1.1). In general, the author's practical advice takes the shape of longer poems rather than the pithy sayings that characterize the book of Proverbs.

Outline

I. The Earlier Wisdom Sayings of Jesus ben Sirach (1.12–23.27)
   A. Hymn of Wisdom (1.1–2.17)
   B. Practical Advice of Wisdom (3.1–23.27)
II. The Later Wisdom Sayings of Jesus ben Sirach (24.1–50.24)
   A. Hymn of Wisdom (24.1-32)
   B. Practical Advice of Wisdom (25.1–42.14)
   C. Hymn of Praise to God (42.15–43.33)
   D. Hymn in Honor of the Ancestors (44.1–50.24)
III. Epilogue (50.25–51.30)

The Prologue

Many great teachings have been given to us through the Law and the Prophets and the others[a] that followed them, and for these we should praise Israel for instruction and wisdom. Now, those who read the scriptures must not only themselves understand them, but must also as lovers of learning be able through the spoken and written word to help the outsiders. So my grandfather Jesus, who had devoted himself especially to the reading of the Law and the Prophets and the other books of our ancestors, and had acquired considerable proficiency in them, was himself also led to write something pertaining to instruction and wisdom, so that by becoming familiar also with his book[b] those who love learning might make even greater progress in living according to the law.

You are invited therefore to read it with goodwill and attention, and to be indulgent in cases where, despite our diligent labor in translating, we may seem to have rendered

Prologue Lk 16.16,29; 24.27,44; Isa 34.16; Jn 5.39; Acts 17.11; Sir 50.27; 2 Chr 7.17; Ezra 10.3; 4.7; Neh 8.8

[a] Or *other books* [b] Gk *with these things*

some phrases imperfectly. For what was originally expressed in Hebrew does not have exactly the same sense when translated into another language. Not only this book, but even the Law itself, the Prophecies, and the rest of the books differ not a little when read in the original.

When I came to Egypt in the thirty-eighth year of the reign of Euergetes and stayed for some time, I found opportunity for no little instruction.[c] It seemed highly necessary that I should myself devote some diligence and labor to the translation of this book. During that time I have applied my skill day and night to complete and publish the book for those living abroad who wished to gain learning and are disposed to live according to the law.

In Praise of Wisdom

1 All wisdom is from the Lord,
and with him it remains forever.
2 The sand of the sea, the drops of rain,
and the days of eternity—who can count them?
3 The height of heaven, the breadth of the earth,
the abyss, and wisdom[d]—who can search them out?
4 Wisdom was created before all other things,
and prudent understanding from eternity.[e]
6 The root of wisdom—to whom has it been revealed?
Her subtleties—who knows them?[f]
8 There is but one who is wise, greatly to be feared,
seated upon his throne—the Lord.
9 It is he who created her;
he saw her and took her measure;
he poured her out upon all his works,
10 upon all the living according to his gift;
he lavished her upon those who love him.[g]

1.1 Ps 111.10; Prov 1.7; Wis 7.7; Jas 1.5
1.2 Gen 22.17
1.3 Job 28.14; Sir 24.5; 18.4-7; Rom 11.33
1.4 Job 28.23-28; Prov 8.22-26; Sir 24.9
1.6 Job 28.20
1.8 4 Macc 1.12; Rom 16.7; Rev 5.7
1.9 Prov 8.30-31
1.10 1 Cor 2.9
1.11 Deut 10.20-21; Ps 22.23
1.12 Prov 3.16; 10.27; 14.27; 19.23
1.14 Job 28.28; Ps 111.10; Prov 1.7; 9.10
1.18 Prov 14.24; Sir 6.31

Fear of the Lord Is True Wisdom

11 The fear of the Lord is glory and exultation,
and gladness and a crown of rejoicing.
12 The fear of the Lord delights the heart,
and gives gladness and joy and long life.[h]
13 Those who fear the Lord will have a happy end;
on the day of their death they will be blessed.

14 To fear the Lord is the beginning of wisdom;
she is created with the faithful in the womb.
15 She made[i] among human beings an eternal foundation,
and among their descendants she will abide faithfully.
16 To fear the Lord is fullness of wisdom;
she inebriates mortals with her fruits;
17 she fills their[j] whole house with desirable goods,
and their[j] storehouses with her produce.
18 The fear of the Lord is the crown of wisdom,
making peace and perfect health to flourish.[k]

[c] Other ancient authorities read *I found a copy affording no little instruction*
[d] Other ancient authorities read *the depth of the abyss*
[e] Other ancient authorities add as verse 5, *The source of wisdom is God's word in the highest heaven, and her ways are the eternal commandments.*
[f] Other ancient authorities add as verse 7, *The knowledge of wisdom—to whom was it manifested? And her abundant experience—who has understood it?*
[g] Other ancient authorities add *Love of the Lord is glorious wisdom; to those to whom he appears he apportions her, that they may see him.*
[h] Other ancient authorities add *The fear of the Lord is a gift from the Lord; also for love he makes firm paths.*
[i] Gk *made as a nest*
[j] Other ancient authorities read *her*
[k] Other ancient authorities add *Both are gifts of God for peace; glory opens out for those who love him. He saw her and took her measure.*

19 She rained down knowledge
and discerning
comprehension,
and she heightened the
glory of those who held
her fast.
20 To fear the Lord is the root
of wisdom,
and her branches are long
life.[1]

22 Unjust anger cannot be
justified,
for anger tips the scale to
one's ruin.
23 Those who are patient stay
calm until the right
moment,
and then cheerfulness
comes back to them.
24 They hold back their words
until the right moment;
then the lips of many tell
of their good sense.

25 In the treasuries of wisdom
are wise sayings,
but godliness is an
abomination to a
sinner.
26 If you desire wisdom, keep
the commandments,
and the Lord will lavish her
upon you.
27 For the fear of the Lord is
wisdom and discipline,
fidelity and humility are his
delight.

28 Do not disobey the fear of
the Lord;
do not approach him with
a divided mind.
29 Do not be a hypocrite before
others,
and keep watch over your
lips.
30 Do not exalt yourself, or you
may fall
and bring dishonor upon
yourself.
The Lord will reveal your
secrets
and overthrow you before
the whole congregation,
because you did not come in
the fear of the Lord,

1.19 Prov 1.2-6; 8.12 **1.20** Sir 1.6 **1.22** Prov 16.32; 27.4; Sir 30.24 **1.23** Eccl 7.8; Rom 12.12; Jas 5.7-8 **1.24** Prov 15.23; 25.11 **1.25** Col 2.3 **1.26** Deut 4.5-6; Prov 2.1-2; 10.8 **1.27** Ps 111.10; Prov 1.7; Sir 6.18; 32.14 **1.28** Ps 119.113; Jas 1.7-8 **1.29** Mt 6.2,5,16; Jas 1.19; 3.2 **1.30** Prov 11.2; 16.18; Sir 3.28; Rom 2.16; Acts 13.10

2.1 Gen 22.1; Jas 1.2-4 **2.3** Ps 37.5; Prov 3.5-6; Josh 1.8 **2.4** Sir 1.23; Jas 5.7-8 **2.5** 1 Pet 1.7 **2.6** Prov 3.5-6; Ps 130.7 **2.7** Ps 37.7 **2.8** Sir 36.21; 51.30; Heb 10.35 **2.10** Ps 22.4-5; 37.28; 94.14; Isa 42.16-17

and your heart was full of
deceit.

Duties toward God

2 My child, when you come to
serve the Lord,
prepare yourself for
testing.[m]
2 Set your heart right and be
steadfast,
and do not be impetuous
in time of calamity.
3 Cling to him and do not
depart,
so that your last days may
be prosperous.
4 Accept whatever befalls you,
and in times of humiliation
be patient.
5 For gold is tested in the fire,
and those found
acceptable, in the
furnace of
humiliation.[n]
6 Trust in him, and he will
help you;
make your ways straight,
and hope in him.

7 You who fear the Lord, wait
for his mercy;
do not stray, or else you
may fall.
8 You who fear the Lord, trust
in him,
and your reward will not be
lost.
9 You who fear the Lord, hope
for good things,
for lasting joy and mercy.[o]
10 Consider the generations of
old and see:
has anyone trusted in the
Lord and been
disappointed?
Or has anyone persevered in
the fear of the Lord[p]
and been forsaken?
Or has anyone called upon
him and been
neglected?

[1]Other ancient authorities add as verse 21, *The fear of the Lord drives away sins; and where it abides, it will turn away all anger.*
[m]Or *trials* [n]Other ancient authorities add *in sickness and poverty put your trust in him* [o]Other ancient authorities add *For his reward is an everlasting gift with joy.* [p]Gk *of him*

11 For the Lord is
compassionate and
merciful;
he forgives sins and saves
in time of distress.

12 Woe to timid hearts and to
slack hands,
and to the sinner who
walks a double path!
13 Woe to the fainthearted who
have no trust!
Therefore they will have no
shelter.
14 Woe to you who have lost
your nerve!
What will you do when the
Lord's reckoning
comes?

15 Those who fear the Lord do
not disobey his words,
and those who love him
keep his ways.
16 Those who fear the Lord
seek to please him,
and those who love him are
filled with his law.
17 Those who fear the Lord
prepare their hearts,
and humble themselves
before him.
Let us fall into the hands of
the Lord,
but not into the hands of
mortals;
for equal to his majesty is
his mercy,
and equal to his name are
his works.[q]

Duties toward Parents

3 Listen to me your father,
O children;
act accordingly, that you
may be kept in safety.
2 For the Lord honors a father
above his children,
and he confirms a mother's
right over her children.
3 Those who honor their father
atone for sins,
4 and those who respect
their mother are like
those who lay up
treasure.

2.11 Ex 34.6-7; Ps 103.8-9; Jon 4.2; Ps 37.40; 145.19
2.12 Prov 10.4; 18.9; Mt 6.24
2.13 Jer 51.45-46
2.15 Prov 8.13; 16.6; Deut 10.12-13; 11.1,13
2.16 Prov 16.7
2.17 Lk 14.11; Jas 4.6,10; 2 Sam 24.14; 1 Chr 21.13; Sir 2.11
3.1 Prov 1.8; 4.1
3.2 Ex 20.12; Eph 6.1-3; Prov 1.8; 6.20
3.4 Mt 6.19-20
3.6 Deut 5.16; Eph 6.1
3.8 Ex 20.12; Deut 5.16; Eph 6.1-3
3.9 Gen 27.1-29; 48.8-16; Tob 11.17
3.10 Gen 9.20-27
3.12 Prov 23.22
3.15 Sir 16.14
3.16 Prov 30.17; Ex 21.17; Lev 20.9

5 Those who honor their father
will have joy in their
own children,
and when they pray they
will be heard.
6 Those who respect their
father will have long
life,
and those who honor[r]
their mother obey the
Lord;
7 they will serve their parents
as their masters.[s]
8 Honor your father by word
and deed,
that his blessing may come
upon you.
9 For a father's blessing
strengthens the houses
of the children,
but a mother's curse
uproots their
foundations.
10 Do not glorify yourself by
dishonoring your father,
for your father's dishonor is
no glory to you.
11 The glory of one's father is
one's own glory,
and it is a disgrace for
children not to respect
their mother.

12 My child, help your father in
his old age,
and do not grieve him as
long as he lives;
13 even if his mind fails, be
patient with him;
because you have all your
faculties do not despise
him.
14 For kindness to a father will
not be forgotten,
and will be credited to you
against your sins;
15 in the day of your distress it
will be remembered in
your favor;
like frost in fair weather,
your sins will melt
away.
16 Whoever forsakes a father is
like a blasphemer,

[q] Syr: Gk lacks this line [r] Heb: Other ancient authorities read *comfort* [s] In other ancient authorities this line is preceded by *Those who fear the Lord honor their father,*

and whoever angers a mother is cursed by the Lord.

Humility

17 My child, perform your tasks with humility;[t]
then you will be loved by those whom God accepts.
18 The greater you are, the more you must humble yourself;
so you will find favor in the sight of the Lord.[u]
20 For great is the might of the Lord;
but by the humble he is glorified.
21 Neither seek what is too difficult for you,
nor investigate what is beyond your power.
22 Reflect upon what you have been commanded,
for what is hidden is not your concern.
23 Do not meddle in matters that are beyond you,
for more than you can understand has been shown you.
24 For their conceit has led many astray,
and wrong opinion has impaired their judgment.

25 Without eyes there is no light;
without knowledge there is no wisdom.[v]
26 A stubborn mind will fare badly at the end,
and whoever loves danger will perish in it.
27 A stubborn mind will be burdened by troubles,
and the sinner adds sin to sins.
28 When calamity befalls the proud, there is no healing,
for an evil plant has taken root in him.
29 The mind of the intelligent appreciates proverbs,

3.17 Prov 11.2; Sir 10.28; Phil 2.3; 1 Pet 5.5
3.18 Lk 14.11; 18.14; 1 Sam 2.26; Lk 2.40,52
3.21 Job 42.3-6; Ps 131.1; Eccl 7.24
3.22 Job 28.11-22; Mt 11.25
3.23 Isa 55.8-9
3.25 Mt 6.22-23; Lk 11.34-35; Prov 1.2-6
3.26 Deut 21.18-21; Ps 81.11-14
3.27 Rom 1.21-32; 7.8-11
3.28 Prov 16.18; Sir 1.30; 21.4
3.29 1 Kings 4.32; Eccl 12.9; Sir 6.35
3.30 Tob 14.10-11; Sir 7.10; 29.8-13
4.1 Am 5.11-13; Mk 10.19; Lk 3.14
4.2 Prov 14.31; 17.5
4.3 Mt 25.34-36; Lk 14.12-13; Acts 4.32-35
4.4 Deut 15.11; Gal 2.10; Jas 2.2-6
4.6 Ex 22.22-23
4.9 Ps 82.3-4; Isa 1.17; 58.6
4.10 Ps 10.18; 2 Esd 2.20; Jas 1.27; Ps 10.14; 146.9; Hos 14.3

and an attentive ear is the desire of the wise.

Alms for the Poor

30 As water extinguishes a blazing fire,
so almsgiving atones for sin.
31 Those who repay favors give thought to the future;
when they fall they will find support.

Duties toward the Poor and the Oppressed

4 My child, do not cheat the poor of their living,
and do not keep needy eyes waiting.
2 Do not grieve the hungry,
or anger one in need.
3 Do not add to the troubles of the desperate,
or delay giving to the needy.
4 Do not reject a suppliant in distress,
or turn your face away from the poor.
5 Do not avert your eye from the needy,
and give no one reason to curse you;
6 for if in bitterness of soul some should curse you,
their Creator will hear their prayer.

7 Endear yourself to the congregation;
bow your head low to the great.
8 Give a hearing to the poor,
and return their greeting politely.
9 Rescue the oppressed from the oppressor;
and do not be hesitant in giving a verdict.
10 Be a father to orphans,
and be like a husband to their mother;

[t] Heb: Gk *meekness*
[u] Other ancient authorities add as verse 19, *Many are lofty and renowned, but to the humble he reveals his secrets.*
[v] Heb: Other ancient authorities lack verse 25

you will then be like a son of
the Most High,
and he will love you more
than does your mother.

The Rewards of Wisdom

11 Wisdom teaches[w] her
children
and gives help to those
who seek her.
12 Whoever loves her loves life,
and those who seek her
from early morning are
filled with joy.
13 Whoever holds her fast
inherits glory,
and the Lord blesses the
place she[x] enters.
14 Those who serve her minister
to the Holy One;
the Lord loves those who
love her.
15 Those who obey her will
judge the nations,
and all who listen to her
will live secure.
16 If they remain faithful, they
will inherit her;
their descendants will also
obtain her.
17 For at first she will walk
with them on tortuous
paths;
she will bring fear and
dread upon them,
and will torment them by her
discipline
until she trusts them,[y]
and she will test them with
her ordinances.
18 Then she will come straight
back to them again and
gladden them,
and will reveal her secrets
to them.
19 If they go astray she will
forsake them,
and hand them over to
their ruin.

20 Watch for the opportune
time, and beware of
evil,
and do not be ashamed to
be yourself.
21 For there is a shame that
leads to sin,
and there is a shame that
is glory and favor.
22 Do not show partiality, to
your own harm,
or deference, to your
downfall.
23 Do not refrain from speaking
at the proper moment,[z]
and do not hide your
wisdom.[a]
24 For wisdom becomes known
through speech,
and education through the
words of the tongue.
25 Never speak against the
truth,
but be ashamed of your
ignorance.
26 Do not be ashamed to
confess your sins,
and do not try to stop the
current of a river.
27 Do not subject yourself to a
fool,
or show partiality to a
ruler.
28 Fight to the death for truth,
and the Lord God will fight
for you.

29 Do not be reckless in your
speech,
or sluggish and remiss in
your deeds.
30 Do not be like a lion in your
home,
or suspicious of your
servants.
31 Do not let your hand be
stretched out to receive
and closed when it is time
to give.

Precepts for Everyday Living

5 Do not rely on your wealth,
or say, "I have enough."
2 Do not follow your
inclination and strength
in pursuing the desires of
your heart.
3 Do not say, "Who can have
power over me?"

4.12 Prov 3.13-18; 8.17-18; 16.22; Prov 3.32-34
4.13 Wis 8.10; Prov 3.35
4.14 Prov 8.17
4.15 1 Cor 6.2; Prov 1.33
4.17 Prov 3.11-12; Heb 12.5-6
4.19 Prov 4.5-6
4.20 Eph 5.16; Col 4.5
4.21 2 Cor 7.10
4.22 Deut 16.19; Prov 28.21; 1 Tim 5.21; Jas 2.2-4
4.23 Prov 15.23; Sir 1.24
4.24 Wis 8.8-9
4.25 Col 3.9; Jas 3.14
4.26 Ps 32.5; 51.1-4; Jas 5.16
4.27 Rom 13.1
4.28 Prov 23.23; Eph 4.25; 2 Chr 20.17
4.29 Prov 5.1-2; 10.19; Jas 1.19
4.31 Deut 15.7-8; Mt 6.3; Acts 20.35
5.1 Ps 62.10; Prov 23.4; Mt 6.19-21; 1 Tim 6.9-10; Lk 12.19

[w] Heb Syr: Gk *exalts* [x] Or *he*
[y] Or *until they remain faithful in their heart*
[z] Heb: Gk *at a time of salvation*
[a] So some Gk Mss and Heb Syr Lat: Other Gk Mss lack *and do not hide your wisdom*

for the Lord will surely
punish you.
4 Do not say, "I sinned, yet
what has happened to
me?"
for the Lord is slow to
anger.
5 Do not be so confident of
forgiveness[b]
that you add sin to sin.
6 Do not say, "His mercy is
great,
he will forgive[c] the
multitude of my sins,"
for both mercy and wrath are
with him,
and his anger will rest on
sinners.
7 Do not delay to turn back to
the Lord,
and do not postpone it
from day to day;
for suddenly the wrath of the
Lord will come upon
you,
and at the time of
punishment you will
perish.
8 Do not depend on dishonest
wealth,
for it will not benefit you
on the day of calamity.

9 Do not winnow in every
wind,
or follow every path.[d]
10 Stand firm for what you
know,
and let your speech be
consistent.
11 Be quick to hear,
but deliberate in
answering.
12 If you know what to say,
answer your neighbor;
but if not, put your hand
over your mouth.

13 Honor and dishonor come
from speaking,
and the tongue of mortals
may be their downfall.
14 Do not be called
double-tongued[e]
and do not lay traps with
your tongue;

5.4 Ex 34.6; Neh 9.17; Ps 103.8 **5.5** Rom 3.8; 6.1 **5.6** Ps 30.5; Sir 16.11; 2 Chr 34.25; Rom 1.18; Heb 10.30-31 **5.7** 1 Thess 5.2-3; Rev 3.3; 2 Thess 1.6-9; Jude 14; Rev 20.15 **5.8** Ps 49.5-13; Ezek 28.5-8; Lk 16.11-13 **5.9** Eph 4.14 **5.11** Prov 5.1-2; Jas 1.19 **5.13** Sir 22.27; Jas 3.6 **5.14** Sir 28.13; Jas 3.9-12

6.1 Prov 16.28; 19.26 **6.2** Sir 18.30; 23.16 **6.3** Ps 1.3; 37.2 **6.4** Prov 5.3-6; 7.22-27; 9.18; Sir 18.31 **6.5** Prov 16.21; 21.11 **6.6** Prov 12.26 **6.8** Prov 18.24; Sir 12.8 **6.9** Sir 22.20; 37.4

for shame comes to the
thief,
and severe condemnation
to the double-tongued.
15 In great and small matters
cause no harm,[f]

6 1 and do not become an
enemy instead of a
friend;
for a bad name incurs shame
and reproach;
so it is with the
double-tongued sinner.

2 Do not fall into the grip of
passion,[g]
or you may be torn apart as
by a bull.[h]
3 Your leaves will be devoured
and your fruit
destroyed,
and you will be left like a
withered tree.
4 Evil passion destroys those
who have it,
and makes them the
laughingstock of their
enemies.

Friendship, False and True

5 Pleasant speech multiplies
friends,
and a gracious tongue
multiplies courtesies.
6 Let those who are friendly
with you be many,
but let your advisers be
one in a thousand.
7 When you gain friends, gain
them through testing,
and do not trust them
hastily.
8 For there are friends who are
such when it suits
them,
but they will not stand by
you in time of trouble.
9 And there are friends who
change into enemies,
and tell of the quarrel to
your disgrace.

[b] Heb: Gk *atonement* [c] Heb: Gk *he* (or *it*) *will atone for* [d] Gk adds *so it is with the double-tongued sinner* (see 6.1) [e] Heb: Gk *a slanderer* [f] Heb Syr: Gk *be ignorant* [g] Heb: Meaning of Gk uncertain [h] Meaning of Gk uncertain

10 And there are friends who sit
at your table,
but they will not stand by
you in time of trouble.
11 When you are prosperous,
they become your
second self,
and lord it over your
servants;
12 but if you are brought low,
they turn against you,
and hide themselves from
you.
13 Keep away from your
enemies,
and be on guard with your
friends.

14 Faithful friends are a sturdy
shelter:
whoever finds one has
found a treasure.
15 Faithful friends are beyond
price;
no amount can balance
their worth.
16 Faithful friends are
life-saving medicine;
and those who fear the
Lord will find them.
17 Those who fear the Lord
direct their friendship
aright,
for as they are, so are their
neighbors also.

Blessings of Wisdom

18 My child, from your youth
choose discipline,
and when you have gray
hair you will still find
wisdom.
19 Come to her like one who
plows and sows,
and wait for her good
harvest.
For when you cultivate her
you will toil but little,
and soon you will eat of
her produce.
20 She seems very harsh to the
undisciplined;
fools cannot remain with
her.
21 She will be like a heavy
stone to test them,
and they will not delay in
casting her aside.
22 For wisdom is like her name;
she is not readily perceived
by many.

23 Listen, my child, and accept
my judgment;
do not reject my counsel.
24 Put your feet into her fetters,
and your neck into her
collar.
25 Bend your shoulders and
carry her,
and do not fret under her
bonds.
26 Come to her with all your
soul,
and keep her ways with all
your might.
27 Search out and seek, and she
will become known to
you;
and when you get hold of
her, do not let her go.
28 For at last you will find the
rest she gives,
and she will be changed
into joy for you.
29 Then her fetters will become
for you a strong
defense,
and her collar a glorious
robe.
30 Her yoke[i] is a golden
ornament,
and her bonds a purple
cord.
31 You will wear her like a
glorious robe,
and put her on like a
splendid crown.[j]

32 If you are willing, my child,
you can be disciplined,
and if you apply yourself
you will become clever.
33 If you love to listen you will
gain knowledge,
and if you pay attention
you will become wise.
34 Stand in the company of the
elders.
Who is wise? Attach
yourself to such a one.

6.10 Ps 41.9; Sir 12.9; Jn 13.18 **6.11** Prov 14.20; 19.4 **6.12** Ps 38.11; Prov 19.7 **6.13** Sir 37.6 **6.14** 1 Sam 20.1-42; Job 2.11-13; Prov 17.7; Sir 9.10 **6.16** Prov 17.17; Eccl 4.9-12 **6.18** Prov 3.11; 12.1; Sir 1.27; 22.6; 32.14; Prov 22.6 **6.19** Prov 11.18; Gal 6.7-8; Jas 3.18; 1 Cor 9.10 **6.20** Prov 1.7,22; 15.7,14

6.23 Prov 2.1; 4.10; 3.1 **6.24** Mt 11.29 **6.26** Deut 6.5 **6.27** Prov 2.4-5; Eccl 1.13; Wis 6.12 **6.29** Sir 6.24 **6.30** Sir 51.26 **6.31** Prov 4.9; Sir 1.18 **6.32** Sir 6.18 **6.34** Ps 1.1; 1 Pet 5.5

[i] Heb: Gk *Upon her* [j] Heb: Gk *crown of gladness*

35 Be ready to listen to every
godly discourse,
and let no wise proverbs
escape you.
36 If you see an intelligent
person, rise early to
visit him;
let your foot wear out his
doorstep.
37 Reflect on the statutes of the
Lord,
and meditate at all times
on his commandments.
It is he who will give insight
to[k] your mind,
and your desire for wisdom
will be granted.

Miscellaneous Advice

7 Do no evil, and evil will
never overtake you.
2 Stay away from wrong, and it
will turn away from
you.
3 Do[l] not sow in the furrows
of injustice,
and you will not reap a
sevenfold crop.

4 Do not seek from the Lord
high office,
or the seat of honor from
the king.
5 Do not assert your
righteousness before
the Lord,
or display your wisdom
before the king.
6 Do not seek to become a
judge,
or you may be unable to
root out injustice;
you may be partial to the
powerful,
and so mar your integrity.
7 Commit no offense against
the public,
and do not disgrace
yourself among the
people.
8 Do not commit a sin twice;
not even for one will you
go unpunished.
9 Do not say, "He will consider
the great number of my
gifts,
and when I make an
offering to the Most
High God, he will
accept it."
10 Do not grow weary when you
pray;
do not neglect to give
alms.
11 Do not ridicule a person who
is embittered in spirit,
for there is One who
humbles and exalts.
12 Do not devise[m] a lie against
your brother,
or do the same to a friend.
13 Refuse to utter any lie,
for it is a habit that results
in no good.
14 Do not babble in the
assembly of the elders,
and do not repeat yourself
when you pray.

15 Do not hate hard labor
or farm work, which was
created by the Most
High.
16 Do not enroll in the ranks of
sinners;
remember that retribution
does not delay.
17 Humble yourself to the
utmost,
for the punishment of the
ungodly is fire and
worms.[n]

Relations with Others

18 Do not exchange a friend for
money,
or a real brother for the
gold of Ophir.
19 Do not dismiss[o] a wise and
good wife,
for her charm is worth
more than gold.
20 Do not abuse slaves who
work faithfully,
or hired laborers who
devote themselves to
their task.
21 Let your soul love intelligent
slaves;[p]

6.35 Prov 5.1-2; Sir 5.11; 3.29
6.37 Josh 1.8; Ps 1.2; 119.15-16; Prov 2.6; Jas 1.5; Sir 1.26; 15.1; 19.20
7.2 Ps 1.1; Prov 4.14-15
7.3 Sir 10.7-8; Hos 8.7; 10.13
7.4 Mt 20.20-28; Lk 14.8
7.5 Sir 10.26
7.6 Deut 16.19; Prov 18.5; Sir 4.27
7.7 Prov 11.2; 13.18
7.9 1 Sam 15.22; Ps 50.8-14; Isa 1.11-15
7.10 Gal 6.9; Tob 14.10-11; Sir 29.8
7.11 1 Sam 2.7-8; Lk 1.52
7.12 Ex 20.16; Lev 19.11; Eph 4.25
7.13 Sir 20.24-26
7.14 Sir 32.7-9; Eccl 5.2; Mt 6.7
7.15 Prov 6.6-11; 12.11; 27.23-27
7.16 Ps 1.1
7.17 Sir 2.17; Jas 4.6,10; Isa 66.24; Mk 9.48
7.18 1 Kings 9.28
7.19 Prov 5.18; Eccl 9.9; Sir 36.29
7.20 Lev 25.43; Eph 6.9; Col 4.1
7.21 Ex 21.2; Lev 25.9-43

[k]Heb: Gk *will confirm* [l]Gk *My child, do* [m]Heb: Gk *plow* [n]Heb *for the expectation of mortals is worms* [o]Heb: Gk *deprive yourself of* [p]Heb *Love a wise slave as yourself*

do not withhold from them
their freedom.

22 Do you have cattle? Look
after them;
if they are profitable to
you, keep them.
23 Do you have children?
Discipline them,
and make them obedient[q]
from their youth.
24 Do you have daughters? Be
concerned for their
chastity,[r]
and do not show yourself
too indulgent with
them.
25 Give a daughter in marriage,
and you complete a
great task;
but give her to a sensible
man.
26 Do you have a wife who
pleases you?[s] Do not
divorce her;
but do not trust yourself to
one whom you detest.

27 With all your heart honor
your father,
and do not forget the birth
pangs of your mother.
28 Remember that it was of
your parents[t] you were
born;
how can you repay what
they have given to you?

29 With all your soul fear the
Lord,
and revere his priests.
30 With all your might love your
Maker,
and do not neglect his
ministers.
31 Fear the Lord and honor the
priest,
and give him his portion,
as you have been
commanded:
the first fruits, the guilt
offering, the gift of the
shoulders,
the sacrifice of
sanctification, and the
first fruits of the holy
things.

7.22 Deut 25.4; Prov 12.10
7.23 Prov 22.15; 23.13-14
7.24 Sir 42.10
7.25 Sir 36.26
7.26 Mal 2.15-16; Sir 7.19; Mt 19.3-6; Deut 24.1-4; Mt 19.8
7.27 Ex 20.12; Eph 6.2
7.29 Deut 6.5,13; 10.12,20; Heb 13.7,17; 1 Pet 5.5
7.30 Deut 6.5; 11.1,13
7.31 Ex 29.27; Lev 7.31-34; Num 18.9-20; Deut 18.3
7.32 Prov 4.21; 19.17; Mt 25.35; Gal 2.10
7.33 Tob 1.17-18
7.34 Rom 12.15
7.35 Mt 25.36
7.36 Ps 73.16-26; Sir 11.27-28
8.2 Prov 15.27; 1 Tim 6.9-10; 1 Kings 10.23-11.8
8.3 Sir 9.18
8.5 Gal 6.1
8.6 Prov 23.22; Lam 5.12

32 Stretch out your hand to the
poor,
so that your blessing may
be complete.
33 Give graciously to all the
living;
do not withhold kindness
even from the dead.
34 Do not avoid those who
weep,
but mourn with those who
mourn.
35 Do not hesitate to visit the
sick,
because for such deeds you
will be loved.
36 In all you do, remember the
end of your life,
and then you will never
sin.

Prudence and Common Sense

8 Do not contend with the
powerful,
or you may fall into their
hands.
2 Do not quarrel with the rich,
in case their resources
outweigh yours;
for gold has ruined many,
and has perverted the
minds of kings.
3 Do not argue with the loud
of mouth,
and do not heap wood on
their fire.

4 Do not make fun of one who
is ill-bred,
or your ancestors may be
insulted.
5 Do not reproach one who is
turning away from sin;
remember that we all
deserve punishment.
6 Do not disdain one who is
old,
for some of us are also
growing old.
7 Do not rejoice over any one's
death;
remember that we must all
die.

q Gk *bend their necks* r Gk *body*
s Heb Syr lack *who pleases you* t Gk *them*

8 Do not slight the discourse of the sages,
but busy yourself with their maxims;
because from them you will learn discipline
and how to serve princes.
9 Do not ignore the discourse of the aged,
for they themselves learned from their parents;[u]
from them you learn how to understand
and to give an answer when the need arises.

10 Do not kindle the coals of sinners,
or you may be burned in their flaming fire.
11 Do not let the insolent bring you to your feet,
or they may lie in ambush against your words.
12 Do not lend to one who is stronger than you;
but if you do lend anything, count it as a loss.
13 Do not give surety beyond your means;
but if you give surety, be prepared to pay.

14 Do not go to law against a judge,
for the decision will favor him because of his standing.
15 Do not go traveling with the reckless,
or they will be burdensome to you;
for they will act as they please,
and through their folly you will perish with them.
16 Do not pick a fight with the quick-tempered,
and do not journey with them through lonely country,
because bloodshed means nothing to them,
and where no help is at hand, they will strike you down.
17 Do not consult with fools,
for they cannot keep a secret.
18 In the presence of strangers do nothing that is to be kept secret,
for you do not know what they will divulge.[v]
19 Do not reveal your thoughts to anyone,
or you may drive away your happiness.[w]

8.8 Job 5.17; Prov 1.7; 5.7-14; Ps 94.12; Prov 3.11 **8.9** Sir 25.4-6; Prov 15.23, 28; 24.26; Sir 11.8 **8.12** Prov 22.7; Sir 29.2,7 **8.13** Prov 6.1-3; 11.15; 22.26 **8.16** Prov 14.17, 29; 22.24 **8.17** Prov 11.13; 20.19; 25.9

Advice Concerning Women

9 Do not be jealous of the wife of your bosom,
or you will teach her an evil lesson to your own hurt.
2 Do not give yourself to a woman
and let her trample down your strength.
3 Do not go near a loose woman,
or you will fall into her snares.
4 Do not dally with a singing girl,
or you will be caught by her tricks.
5 Do not look intently at a virgin,
or you may stumble and incur penalties for her.
6 Do not give yourself to prostitutes,
or you may lose your inheritance.
7 Do not look around in the streets of a city,
or wander about in its deserted sections.
8 Turn away your eyes from a shapely woman,
and do not gaze at beauty belonging to another;
many have been seduced by a woman's beauty,
and by it passion is kindled like a fire.
9 Never dine with another man's wife,
or revel with her at wine;
or your heart may turn aside to her,

9.1 Sir 26.6 **9.3** Prov 5.3-8; 7.6-23 **9.5** Mt 5.28 **9.6** 1 Cor 6.13-18 **9.8** Prov 6.25; Mt 5.28; Jdt 12.13-16

[u] Or *ancestors* [v] Or *it will bring forth* [w] Heb: Gk *and let him not return a favor to you*

and in blood[x] you may be
plunged into
destruction.

Choice of Friends

10 Do not abandon old friends,
for new ones cannot equal
them.
A new friend is like new
wine;
when it has aged, you can
drink it with pleasure.

11 Do not envy the success of
sinners,
for you do not know what
their end will be like.
12 Do not delight in what
pleases the ungodly;
remember that they will
not be held guiltless all
their lives.

13 Keep far from those who
have power to kill,
and you will not be
haunted by the fear of
death.
But if you approach them,
make no misstep,
or they may rob you of your
life.
Know that you are stepping
among snares,
and that you are walking
on the city battlements.

14 As much as you can, aim to
know your neighbors,
and consult with the wise.
15 Let your conversation be
with intelligent people,
and let all your discussion
be about the law of the
Most High.
16 Let the righteous be your
dinner companions,
and let your glory be in the
fear of the Lord.

Concerning Rulers

17 A work is praised for the
skill of the artisan;
so a people's leader is
proved wise by his
words.

9.10 Prov 17.17; 18.24; Sir 25.9; 27.17; 6.14-15 **9.11** Ps 37.1; 73.3; 37.38; 73.16-20 **9.12** Ex 20.7; 23.7 **9.13** Ps 141.8-10; Rom 13.3-4; Prov 22.25 **9.14** Sir 25.1 **9.15** Sir 27.11 **9.16** Ps 30.30; Prov 10.11, 20-21,31; Sir 10.22; Prov 14.2,26; 15.16,33 **9.17** Ex 31.1-6; 35.30-36.1

9.18 Sir 8.3 **10.2** 2 Chr 30.23-31.1; 33.1-9 **10.3** 2 Chr 10.1-19 **10.4** Dan 2.21; Jn 19.11; Rom 13.1 **10.5** Deut 8.17-18; 2 Chr 26.5; Prov 10.22 **10.6** Sir 28.7; Eph 4.26; Rom 12.19; Eph 4.31; Col 3.8 **10.7** 1 Sam 2.3; Prov 8.13; Jas 4.16; Tob 14.11; Sir 7.3

18 The loud of mouth are
feared in their city,
and the one who is
reckless in speech is
hated.

10 A wise magistrate
educates his people,
and the rule of an
intelligent person is
well ordered.
2 As the people's judge is, so
are his officials;
as the ruler of the city is,
so are all its
inhabitants.
3 An undisciplined king ruins
his people,
but a city becomes fit to
live in through the
understanding of its
rulers.
4 The government of the earth
is in the hand of the
Lord,
and over it he will raise up
the right leader for the
time.
5 Human success is in the
hand of the Lord,
and it is he who confers
honor upon the
lawgiver.[y]

The Sin of Pride

6 Do not get angry with your
neighbor for every
injury,
and do not resort to acts of
insolence.
7 Arrogance is hateful to the
Lord and to mortals,
and injustice is outrageous
to both.
8 Sovereignty passes from
nation to nation
on account of injustice and
insolence and wealth.[z]
9 How can dust and ashes be
proud?
Even in life the human
body decays.[a]

[x]Heb: Gk *by your spirit* [y]Heb: Gk *scribe* [z]Other ancient authorities add here or after verse 9a, *Nothing is more wicked than one who loves money, for such a person puts his own soul up for sale.* [a]Heb: Meaning of Gk uncertain

10 A long illness baffles the physician;[b]
the king of today will die tomorrow.
11 For when one is dead
he inherits maggots and vermin[c] and worms.
12 The beginning of human pride is to forsake the Lord;
the heart has withdrawn from its Maker.
13 For the beginning of pride is sin,
and the one who clings to it pours out abominations.
Therefore the Lord brings upon them unheard-of calamities,
and destroys them completely.
14 The Lord overthrows the thrones of rulers,
and enthrones the lowly in their place.
15 The Lord plucks up the roots of the nations,[d]
and plants the humble in their place.
16 The Lord lays waste the lands of the nations,
and destroys them to the foundations of the earth.
17 He removes some of them and destroys them,
and erases the memory of them from the earth.
18 Pride was not created for human beings,
or violent anger for those born of women.

Persons Deserving Honor

19 Whose offspring are worthy of honor?
Human offspring.
Whose offspring are worthy of honor?
Those who fear the Lord.
Whose offspring are unworthy of honor?
Human offspring.
Whose offspring are unworthy of honor?
Those who break the commandments.
20 Among family members their leader is worthy of honor,
but those who fear the Lord are worthy of honor in his eyes.[e]
22 The rich, and the eminent, and the poor—
their glory is the fear of the Lord.
23 It is not right to despise one who is intelligent but poor,
and it is not proper to honor one who is sinful.
24 The prince and the judge and the ruler are honored,
but none of them is greater than the one who fears the Lord.
25 Free citizens will serve a wise servant,
and an intelligent person will not complain.

Concerning Humility

26 Do not make a display of your wisdom when you do your work,
and do not boast when you are in need.
27 Better is the worker who has goods in plenty
than the boaster who lacks bread.
28 My child, honor yourself with humility,
and give yourself the esteem you deserve.
29 Who will acquit those who condemn[f] themselves?
And who will honor those who dishonor themselves?[g]
30 The poor are honored for their knowledge,

10.10 Mk 5.26; Lk 8.43 **10.11** Job 26.5 **10.12** Lk 12.19-21 **10.13** Prov 11.2; 16.18 **10.14** 1 Sam 2.7-8; Lk 1.52 **10.15** 2 Chr 7.20; Jer 12.14; 24.6; 42.10 **10.16** Isa 26.21; 34.1-2; Mic 1.2-3 **10.17** Ps 9.5-6; Isa 26.14 **10.19** Ps 15.4; 84.11; Sir 16.1-2

10.22 Sir 9.16 **10.23** Eccl 9.15-16; 8.11 **10.25** 1 Cor 10.10; Phil 2.14 **10.26** Sir 7.5 **10.28** Prov 11.2; Sir 3.17; Phil 2.3 **10.30** Prov 26.8; Eccl 9.15; Prov 14.20; 18.11

[b] Heb Lat: Meaning of Gk uncertain
[c] Heb: Gk *wild animals*
[d] Other ancient authorities read *proud nations*
[e] Other ancient authorities add as verse 21, *The fear of the Lord is the beginning of acceptance; obduracy and pride are the beginning of rejection.*
[f] Heb: Gk *sin against*
[g] Heb Lat: Gk *their own life*

while the rich are honored
for their wealth.
31 One who is honored in
poverty, how much
more in wealth!
And one dishonored in
wealth, how much more
in poverty!

The Deceptiveness of Appearances

11 The wisdom of the
humble lifts their heads
high,
and seats them among the
great.
2 Do not praise individuals for
their good looks,
or loathe anyone because
of appearance alone.
3 The bee is small among
flying creatures,
but what it produces is the
best of sweet things.
4 Do not boast about wearing
fine clothes,
and do not exalt yourself
when you are honored;
for the works of the Lord are
wonderful,
and his works are
concealed from
humankind.
5 Many kings have had to sit
on the ground,
but one who was never
thought of has worn a
crown.
6 Many rulers have been
utterly disgraced,
and the honored have been
handed over to others.

Deliberation and Caution

7 Do not find fault before you
investigate;
examine first, and then
criticize.
8 Do not answer before you
listen,
and do not interrupt when
another is speaking.
9 Do not argue about a matter
that does not concern
you,
and do not sit with sinners
when they judge a case.

10.31 Sir 22.23; 13.4-7 **11.2** 1 Sam 16.6-7 **11.3** Judg 14.8-9, 14 **11.4** Jas 2.2-4; Ps 105.2,5; 139.14 **11.5** Gen 41.37-43; Eccl 4.14 **11.7** Sir 13.22 **11.8** Sir 8.9; Jas 1.19 **11.9** Ps 1.1; 26.5

11.10 Ps 131.1 **11.12** Ps 145.17; Prov 14.21, 31; Hos 11.1-4; Ps 107.41; 113.7 **11.14** Isa 45.7; Am 3.6; Jas 1.17; 1 Sam 2.6; Job 1.21; 1 Sam 2.7; Lk 1.53 **11.19** Eccl 6.1-2; Lk 12.19 **11.20** Eccl 5.4-6

10 My child, do not busy
yourself with many
matters;
if you multiply activities,
you will not be held
blameless.
If you pursue, you will not
overtake,
and by fleeing you will not
escape.
11 There are those who work
and struggle and hurry,
but are so much the more
in want.
12 There are others who are
slow and need help,
who lack strength and
abound in poverty;
but the eyes of the Lord look
kindly upon them;
he lifts them out of their
lowly condition
13 and raises up their heads
to the amazement of the
many.

14 Good things and bad, life
and death,
poverty and wealth, come
from the Lord.[h]
17 The Lord's gift remains with
the devout,
and his favor brings lasting
success.
18 One becomes rich through
diligence and
self-denial,
and the reward allotted to
him is this:
19 when he says, "I have found
rest,
and now I shall feast on
my goods!"
he does not know how long
it will be
until he leaves them to
others and dies.

20 Stand by your agreement and
attend to it,
and grow old in your work.

[h] Other ancient authorities add as verses 15 and 16, *15Wisdom, understanding, and knowledge of the law come from the Lord; affection and the ways of good works come from him. 16Error and darkness were created with sinners; evil grows old with those who take pride in malice.*

21 Do not wonder at the works
of a sinner,
but trust in the Lord and
keep at your job;
for it is easy in the sight of
the Lord
to make the poor rich
suddenly, in an instant.
22 The blessing of the Lord is[i]
the reward of the pious,
and quickly God causes his
blessing to flourish.
23 Do not say, "What do I need,
and what further benefit
can be mine?"
24 Do not say, "I have enough,
and what harm can come
to me now?"
25 In the day of prosperity,
adversity is forgotten,
and in the day of adversity,
prosperity is not
remembered.
26 For it is easy for the Lord on
the day of death
to reward individuals
according to their
conduct.
27 An hour's misery makes one
forget past delights,
and at the close of one's
life one's deeds are
revealed.
28 Call no one happy before his
death;
by how he ends, a person
becomes known.[j]

Care in Choosing Friends

29 Do not invite everyone into
your home,
for many are the tricks of
the crafty.
30 Like a decoy partridge in a
cage, so is the mind of
the proud,
and like spies they observe
your weakness;[k]
31 for they lie in wait, turning
good into evil,
and to worthy actions they
attach blame.
32 From a spark many coals are
kindled,
and a sinner lies in wait to
shed blood.
33 Beware of scoundrels, for
they devise evil,
and they may ruin your
reputation forever.
34 Receive strangers into your
home and they will stir
up trouble for you,
and will make you a
stranger to your own
family.

12 If you do good, know to
whom you do it,
and you will be thanked for
your good deeds.
2 Do good to the devout, and
you will be repaid—
if not by them, certainly by
the Most High.
3 No good comes to one who
persists in evil
or to one who does not
give alms.
4 Give to the devout, but do
not help the sinner.
5 Do good to the humble,
but do not give to the
ungodly;
hold back their bread, and
do not give it to them,
for by means of it they
might subdue you;
then you will receive twice
as much evil
for all the good you have
done to them.
6 For the Most High also hates
sinners
and will inflict punishment
on the ungodly.[l]
7 Give to the one who is good,
but do not help the
sinner.
8 A friend is not known[m] in
prosperity,
nor is an enemy hidden in
adversity.
9 One's enemies are friendly[n]
when one prospers,
but in adversity even one's
friend disappears.
10 Never trust your enemy,

11.21 Ps 37.3,5; Prov 3.5; 16.3; 18.9 **11.22** Ps 24.5; 129.8; Prov 10.22 **11.24** Lk 12.9 **11.26** Eccl 12.14; Sir 16.12-14; 2 Cor 5.10 **11.27** 1 Cor 3.13-15; 4.5; Rev 20.12 **11.28** Sir 7.36 **11.29** Sir 11.34; Ps 83.3 **11.32** Jas 3.5; Prov 1.16; Isa 59.7 **11.33** Ps 21.11; Prov 12.2; Isa 32.7 **11.34** Sir 11.29 **12.2** Mt 6.3-4; Col 3.23-24 **12.3** Prov 11.24; Tob 4.16; 12.8-9 **12.5** Rom 12.21; 13.3; 1 Pet 3.11 **12.6** Ps 5.5-6; 11.5-6 **12.7** Sir 12.4 **12.8** Sir 6.8-10 **12.9** Prov 14.20; 19.7; Sir 6.10

[i] Heb: Gk *is in* [j] Heb: Gk *and through his children a person becomes known* [k] Heb: Gk *downfall* [l] Other ancient authorities add *and he is keeping them for the day of their punishment* [m] Other ancient authorities read *punished* [n] Heb: Gk *grieved*

for like corrosion in
copper, so is his
wickedness.
11 Even if he humbles himself
and walks bowed down,
take care to be on your
guard against him.
Be to him like one who
polishes a mirror,
to be sure it does not
become completely
tarnished.
12 Do not put him next to you,
or he may overthrow you
and take your place.
Do not let him sit at your
right hand,
or else he may try to take
your own seat,
and at last you will realize
the truth of my words,
and be stung by what I
have said.

13 Who pities a snake charmer
when he is bitten,
or all those who go near
wild animals?
14 So no one pities a person
who associates with a
sinner
and becomes involved in
the other's sins.
15 He stands by you for a while,
but if you falter, he will
not be there.
16 An enemy speaks sweetly
with his lips,
but in his heart he plans to
throw you into a pit;
an enemy may have tears in
his eyes,
but if he finds an
opportunity he will
never have enough of
your blood.
17 If evil comes upon you, you
will find him there
ahead of you;
pretending to help, he will
trip you up.
18 Then he will shake his head,
and clap his hands,
and whisper much, and
show his true face.

12.11 Sir 13.13 **12.13** Eccl 10.11; Jer 8.17 **12.16** Ps 140.4; Prov 3.28-29; 6.18; Sir 19.28 **12.17** Sir 27.23; Job 34.37; Lam 2.15; Nah 3.19

13.2 Sir 9.13 **13.3** Prov 18.23 **13.4** Neh 5.1-7; Prov 22.16; Isa 3.14-15; Am 2.6-8; Jas 2.6; Prov 14.20; 19.4 **13.7** Ps 141.4; Prov 23.3,6; Sir 11.31 **13.8** Prov 20.1; Sir 31.5

Caution Regarding Associates

13 Whoever touches pitch
gets dirty,
and whoever associates
with a proud person
becomes like him.
2 Do not lift a weight too
heavy for you,
or associate with one
mightier and richer
than you.
How can the clay pot
associate with the iron
kettle?
The pot will strike against
it and be smashed.
3 A rich person does wrong,
and even adds insults;
a poor person suffers
wrong, and must add
apologies.
4 A rich person[o] will exploit
you if you can be of use
to him,
but if you are in need he
will abandon you.
5 If you own something, he
will live with you;
he will drain your resources
without a qualm.
6 When he needs you he will
deceive you,
and will smile at you and
encourage you;
he will speak to you kindly
and say, "What do you
need?"
7 He will embarrass you with
his delicacies,
until he has drained you
two or three times,
and finally he will laugh at
you.
Should he see you
afterwards, he will pass
you by
and shake his head at you.

8 Take care not to be led
astray
and humiliated when you
are enjoying yourself.[p]
9 When an influential person
invites you, be reserved,

[o] Gk *He* [p] Other ancient authorities read *in your folly*

and he will invite you more
insistently.
10 Do not be forward, or you
may be rebuffed;
do not stand aloof, or you
will be forgotten.
11 Do not try to treat him as an
equal,
or trust his lengthy
conversations;
for he will test you by
prolonged talk,
and while he smiles he will
be examining you.
12 Cruel are those who do not
keep your secrets;
they will not spare you
harm or imprisonment.
13 Be on your guard and very
careful,
for you are walking about
with your own
downfall.[q]

15 Every creature loves its like,
and every person the
neighbor.
16 All living beings associate
with their own kind,
and people stick close to
those like themselves.
17 What does a wolf have in
common with a lamb?
No more has a sinner with
the devout.
18 What peace is there between
a hyena and a dog?
And what peace between
the rich and the poor?
19 Wild asses in the wilderness
are the prey of lions;
likewise the poor are
feeding grounds for the
rich.
20 Humility is an abomination
to the proud;
likewise the poor are an
abomination to the
rich.
21 When the rich person totters,
he is supported by
friends,
but when the humble[r]
falls, he is pushed away
even by friends.
22 If the rich person slips, many
come to the rescue;

13.10 Prov 25.6-7; Lk 14.8-9 **13.11** Sir 13.6 **13.12** Prov 20.19; Sir 27.16-17 **13.13** Sir 12.11; Lk 12.15 **13.16** Gen 1.21, 24-25; 2.18-24; Prov 18.24 **13.17** 2 Cor 6.14-15; Gal 5.16-23; Eph 5.7-8 **13.19** Isa 3.14-15; Jer 2.34; Mic 3.1-3; Sir 13.3 **13.21** Prov 14.20; Sir 6.8-10; 12.8-9 **13.22** Sir 11.7

13.24 Sir 31.8 **13.25** Gen 4.5-6 **13.26** Prov 15.13; 17.22; Jas 3.2 **14.2** 1 Jn 3.20 **14.3** Eccl 5.13; Mt 6.19; Lk 12.16-19; Jas 5.1-3 **14.4** Eccl 2.18; 6.1-2

he speaks unseemly words,
but they justify him.
If the humble person slips,
they even criticize him;
he talks sense, but is not
given a hearing.
23 The rich person speaks and
all are silent;
they extol to the clouds
what he says.
The poor person speaks and
they say, "Who is this
fellow?"
And should he stumble,
they even push him
down.
24 Riches are good if they are
free from sin;
poverty is evil only in the
opinion of the ungodly.

25 The heart changes the
countenance,
either for good or for evil.[s]
26 The sign of a happy heart is
a cheerful face,
but to devise proverbs
requires painful
thinking.

14 Happy are those who do
not blunder with their
lips,
and need not suffer
remorse for sin.
2 Happy are those whose
hearts do not condemn
them,
and who have not given up
their hope.

Responsible Use of Wealth

3 Riches are inappropriate for
a small-minded person;
and of what use is wealth
to a miser?
4 What he denies himself he
collects for others;
and others will live in
luxury on his goods.

[q]Other ancient authorities add as verse 14, *When you hear these things in your sleep, wake up! During all your life love the Lord, and call on him for your salvation.*
[r]Other ancient authorities read *poor*
[s]Other ancient authorities add *and a glad heart makes a cheerful countenance*

5 If one is mean to himself, to
whom will he be
generous?
He will not enjoy his own
riches.
6 No one is worse than one
who is grudging to
himself;
this is the punishment for
his meanness.
7 If ever he does good, it is by
mistake;
and in the end he reveals
his meanness.
8 The miser is an evil person;
he turns away and
disregards people.
9 The eye of the greedy person
is not satisfied with his
share;
greedy injustice withers the
soul.
10 A miser begrudges bread,
and it is lacking at his
table.

11 My child, treat yourself well,
according to your
means,
and present worthy
offerings to the Lord.
12 Remember that death does
not tarry,
and the decree[t] of Hades
has not been shown to
you.
13 Do good to friends before
you die,
and reach out and give to
them as much as you
can.
14 Do not deprive yourself of a
day's enjoyment;
do not let your share of
desired good pass by
you.
15 Will you not leave the fruit
of your labors to
another,
and what you acquired by
toil to be divided by
lot?
16 Give, and take, and indulge
yourself,
because in Hades one
cannot look for luxury.
17 All living beings become old
like a garment,
for the decree[u] from of old
is, "You must die!"
18 Like abundant leaves on a
spreading tree
that sheds some and puts
forth others,
so are the generations of
flesh and blood:
one dies and another is
born.
19 Every work decays and
ceases to exist,
and the one who made it
will pass away with it.

The Happiness of Seeking Wisdom

20 Happy is the person who
meditates on[v] wisdom
and reasons intelligently,
21 who[w] reflects in his heart on
her ways
and ponders her secrets,
22 pursuing her like a hunter,
and lying in wait on her
paths;
23 who peers through her
windows
and listens at her doors;
24 who camps near her house
and fastens his tent peg to
her walls;
25 who pitches his tent near
her,
and so occupies an
excellent lodging place;
26 who places his children
under her shelter,
and lodges under her
boughs;
27 who is sheltered by her from
the heat,
and dwells in the midst of
her glory.

15 Whoever fears the Lord
will do this,
and whoever holds to the
law will obtain
wisdom.[x]
2 She will come to meet him
like a mother,
and like a young bride she
will welcome him.

14.9 Sir 31.13 **14.10** Prov 23.6; Sir 31.24; Prov 28.20,22 **14.11** Ex 25.1-7; Lev 23.8,36; Prov 3.9 **14.12** Ps 89.48; Eccl 8.8; Heb 9.27 **14.14** Eccl 2.24; 3.12-13; 5.18; 11.9 **14.15** Eccl 6.1-2; Sir 14.4 **14.17** Ps 102.26; Isa 50.9; Gen 3.19; Sir 41.4 **14.18** Eccl 1.4 **14.20** Prov 3.13; Sir 50.28; Prov 3.1-8 **14.21** Eccl 1.12-13, 17; Wis 8.17 **14.22** Sir 51.13-20; Prov 3.12-13, 20 **14.26** Sir 24.16 **15.1** Prov 4.10-13; Sir 1.26; 6.37 **15.2** Prov 3.16-19; 6.23-24

t Heb Syr: Gk *covenant* u Heb: Gk *covenant* v Other ancient authorities read *dies in* w The structure adopted in verses 21-27 follows the Heb x Gk *her*

[3] She will feed him with the bread of learning,
and give him the water of wisdom to drink.
[4] He will lean on her and not fall,
and he will rely on her and not be put to shame.
[5] She will exalt him above his neighbors,
and will open his mouth in the midst of the assembly.
[6] He will find gladness and a crown of rejoicing,
and will inherit an everlasting name.
[7] The foolish will not obtain her,
and sinners will not see her.
[8] She is far from arrogance,
and liars will never think of her.
[9] Praise is unseemly on the lips of a sinner,
for it has not been sent from the Lord.
[10] For in wisdom must praise be uttered,
and the Lord will make it prosper.

Freedom of Choice

[11] Do not say, "It was the Lord's doing that I fell away";
for he does not do[y] what he hates.
[12] Do not say, "It was he who led me astray";
for he has no need of the sinful.
[13] The Lord hates all abominations;
such things are not loved by those who fear him.
[14] It was he who created humankind in the beginning,
and he left them in the power of their own free choice.
[15] If you choose, you can keep the commandments,
and to act faithfully is a matter of your own choice.
[16] He has placed before you fire and water;
stretch out your hand for whichever you choose.
[17] Before each person are life and death,
and whichever one chooses will be given.
[18] For great is the wisdom of the Lord;
he is mighty in power and sees everything;
[19] his eyes are on those who fear him,
and he knows every human action.
[20] He has not commanded anyone to be wicked,
and he has not given anyone permission to sin.

God's Punishment of Sinners

16 Do not desire a multitude of worthless[z] children,
and do not rejoice in ungodly offspring.
[2] If they multiply, do not rejoice in them,
unless the fear of the Lord is in them.
[3] Do not trust in their survival,
or rely on their numbers;[a]
for one can be better than a thousand,
and to die childless better than to have ungodly children.
[4] For through one intelligent person a city can be filled with people,
but through a clan of outlaws it becomes desolate.

[5] Many such things my eye has seen,
and my ear has heard things more striking than these.

15.4 Prov 4.5-7; Ps 22.4-5; 25.2 **15.6** Prov 3.13; 23.15,24; Eccl 2.26; Wis 8.13 **15.7** Prov 1.20-33 **15.8** Prov 8.13 **15.10** Sir 51.22; Gen 39.23; 1 Chr 22.13; 2 Chr 26.5 **15.11** Jas 1.13 **15.13** Deut 16.22; Ps 5.5; Prov 6.16-19 **15.14** Gen 1.26-27; 2.7,16-17 **15.15** Josh 24.15-24; Prov 7.1-4 **15.17** Deut 30.15-20; Jer 21.8 **15.18** Ps 24.8; 89.8-10; Jer 32.18-19; Ps 139.7-12; Prov 15.3; Add Esth 15.2 **15.19** Ps 33.18; 34.15; Sir 34.19 **15.20** Jas 1.13 **16.1** Sir 10.19 **16.3** Sir 41.9; Eccl 6.3; Wis 4.1-3 **16.4** Eccl 9.14-16

[y] Heb: Gk *you ought not do*
[z] Heb: Gk *unprofitable*
[a] Other ancient authorities add *For you will groan in untimely mourning, and will know of their sudden end.*

6 In an assembly of sinners a
fire is kindled,
and in a disobedient nation
wrath blazes up.
7 He did not forgive the
ancient giants
who revolted in their
might.
8 He did not spare the
neighbors of Lot,
whom he loathed on
account of their
arrogance.
9 He showed no pity on the
doomed nation,
on those dispossessed
because of their sins;[b]
10 or on the six hundred
thousand foot soldiers
who assembled in their
stubbornness.[c]
11 Even if there were only one
stiff-necked person,
it would be a wonder if he
remained unpunished.
For mercy and wrath are
with the Lord;[d]
he is mighty to forgive—
but he also pours out
wrath.
12 Great as his mercy, so also is
his chastisement;
he judges a person
according to one's
deeds.
13 The sinner will not escape
with plunder,
and the patience of the
godly will not be
frustrated.
14 He makes room for every act
of mercy;
everyone receives in
accordance with one's
deeds.[e]

17 Do not say, "I am hidden
from the Lord,
and who from on high has
me in mind?
Among so many people I am
unknown,
for what am I in a
boundless creation?
18 Lo, heaven and the highest
heaven,
the abyss and the earth,
tremble at his
visitation![f]
19 The very mountains and the
foundations of the earth
quiver and quake when he
looks upon them.
20 But no human mind can
grasp this,
and who can comprehend
his ways?
21 Like a tempest that no one
can see,
so most of his works are
concealed.[g]
22 Who is to announce his acts
of justice?
Or who can await them?
For his decree[h] is far
off."[i]
23 Such are the thoughts of one
devoid of
understanding;
a senseless and misguided
person thinks foolishly.

God's Wisdom Seen in Creation

24 Listen to me, my child, and
acquire knowledge,
and pay close attention to
my words.
25 I will impart discipline
precisely[j]
and declare knowledge
accurately.

26 When the Lord created[k] his
works from the
beginning,
and, in making them,
determined their
boundaries,

16.6 Num 16.31-35 **16.7** Gen 6.4 **16.8** Gen 19.23-29; Ezek 16.49-50; 2 Pet 2.8 **16.9** Num 33.51-53; Deut 20.16-17 **16.10** Num 1.44-46; Sir 46.8; Num 14.1-10 **16.11** Ps 30.5; Sir 5.6; Ex 34.6; Neh 9.17; Ps 103.8-12; Mic 7.18-19; Num 16.46; 2 Kings 22.13; Rom 1.18; Rev 14.10 **16.12** Sir 17.29; 1 Pet 1.3 **16.14** Eccl 12.14; 2 Cor 5.10; Rev 20.12; Sir 3.14-15 **16.17** Ps 139.7-12 **16.18** Hag 2.21; Heb 12.26 **16.19** Isa 64.1,3; Ezek 38.20; Nah 1.5 **16.20** Isa 40.12-14; Rom 11.33 **16.21** Jn 3.8; 1 Cor 2.9-11 **16.24** Prov 2.1-5; 4.1,10; 5.1 **16.25** Prov 12.1; 23.13; Sir 6.18 **16.26** Gen 1.1; Ps 8.3; Isa 44.24; Deut 32.8; Ps 104.9; Acts 17.26

[b] Other ancient authorities add *All these things he did to the hard-hearted nations, and by the multitude of his holy ones he was not appeased.* [c] Other ancient authorities add *Chastising, showing mercy, striking, healing, the Lord persisted in mercy and discipline.* [d] Gk *him* [e] Other ancient authorities add *15The Lord hardened Pharaoh so that he did not recognize him, in order that his works might be known under heaven. 16His mercy is manifest to the whole of creation, and he divided his light and darkness with a plumb line.* [f] Other ancient authorities add *The whole world past and present is in his will.* [g] Meaning of Gk uncertain: Heb Syr *If I sin, no eye can see me, and if I am disloyal all in secret, who is to know?* [h] Heb *the decree*: Gk *the covenant* [i] Other ancient authorities add *and a scrutiny for all comes at the end* [j] Gk *by weight* [k] Heb: Gk *judged*

27 he arranged his works in an
eternal order,
and their dominion[l] for all
generations.
They neither hunger nor
grow weary,
and they do not abandon
their tasks.
28 They do not crowd one
another,
and they never disobey his
word.
29 Then the Lord looked upon
the earth,
and filled it with his good
things.
30 With all kinds of living
beings he covered its
surface,
and into it they must
return.

17 The Lord created human
beings out of earth,
and makes them return to
it again.
2 He gave them a fixed
number of days,
but granted them authority
over everything on the
earth.[m]
3 He endowed them with
strength like his own,[n]
and made them in his own
image.
4 He put the fear of them[o] in
all living beings,
and gave them dominion
over beasts and birds.[p]
6 Discretion and tongue and
eyes,
ears and a mind for
thinking he gave them.
7 He filled them with
knowledge and
understanding,
and showed them good and
evil.
8 He put the fear of him into[q]
their hearts
to show them the majesty
of his works.[r]
10 And they will praise his holy
name,
9 to proclaim the grandeur of
his works.
11 He bestowed knowledge
upon them,
and allotted to them the
law of life.[s]
12 He established with them an
eternal covenant,
and revealed to them his
decrees.
13 Their eyes saw his glorious
majesty,
and their ears heard the
glory of his voice.
14 He said to them, "Beware of
all evil."
And he gave
commandment to each
of them concerning the
neighbor.
15 Their ways are always known
to him;
they will not be hid from
his eyes.[t]
17 He appointed a ruler for
every nation,
but Israel is the Lord's own
portion.[u]
19 All their works are as clear
as the sun before him,
and his eyes are ever upon
their ways.
20 Their iniquities are not
hidden from him,
and all their sins are before
the Lord.[v]
22 One's almsgiving is like a
signet ring with the
Lord,[w]

16.27 Gen 1.3-31 **16.28** Ps 33.6; Jn 1.1-3 **16.29** Gen 1.31 **16.30** Gen 1.20-27; Ps 104.29; Eccl 12.7; Sir 40.11 **17.1** Gen 2.7; 3.19; Eccl 12.7; Sir 16.30 **17.2** Ps 39.4; 90.12; Gen 1.28; Ps 8.6 **17.3** Gen 1.26-27; 5.1 **17.4** Gen 9.2; 1.28; Ps 8.6 **17.7** Prov 2.6; Sir 1.1; Jas 1.5; Gen 2.16-17 **17.10** Ps 7.17; 9.2; 30.4 **17.9** Ps 71.17-18; Sir 18.4 **17.12** Gen 17.7; 1 Chr 16.17; Jer 32.40 **17.13** Ex 16.7; 19.16-19; 33.18-22; Isa 40.5 **17.14** Lev 19.18; Mt 22.39; Rom 13.9 **17.15** Sir 15.19 **17.17** Heb 2.5; Deut 32.9; Zech 2.12 **17.20** Ps 44.21; 69.5; Isa 40.27-28; Ps 51.3; Isa 59.12 **17.22** Tob 4.10-11; Sir 40.17,24; Mt 6.2-4; Ps 17.8; Zech 2.8

[l] Or *elements* [m] Lat: Gk *it* [n] Lat: Gk *proper to them* [o] Syr: Gk *him*
[p] Other ancient authorities add as verse 5, *They obtained the use of the five faculties of the Lord; as sixth he distributed to them the gift of mind, and as seventh, reason, the interpreter of one's faculties.*
[q] Other ancient authorities read *He set his eye upon* [r] Other ancient authorities add *and he gave them to boast of his marvels forever*
[s] Other ancient authorities add *so that they may know that they who are alive now are mortal* [t] Other ancient authorities add *16Their ways from youth tend toward evil, and they are unable to make for themselves hearts of flesh in place of their stony hearts. 17For in the division of the nations of the whole earth, he appointed* [u] Other ancient authorities add as verse 18, *whom, being his firstborn, he brings up with discipline, and allotting to him the light of his love, he does not neglect him.*
[v] Other ancient authorities add as verse 21, *But the Lord, who is gracious and knows how they are formed, has neither left them nor abandoned them, but has spared them.*
[w] Gk *him*

and he will keep a person's kindness like the apple of his eye.[x]

23 Afterward he will rise up and repay them,
and he will bring their recompense on their heads.

24 Yet to those who repent he grants a return,
and he encourages those who are losing hope.

A Call to Repentance

25 Turn back to the Lord and forsake your sins;
pray in his presence and lessen your offense.

26 Return to the Most High and turn away from iniquity,[y]
and hate intensely what he abhors.

27 Who will sing praises to the Most High in Hades
in place of the living who give thanks?

28 From the dead, as from one who does not exist, thanksgiving has ceased;
those who are alive and well sing the Lord's praises.

29 How great is the mercy of the Lord,
and his forgiveness for those who return to him!

30 For not everything is within human capability,
since human beings are not immortal.

31 What is brighter than the sun? Yet it can be eclipsed.
So flesh and blood devise evil.

32 He marshals the host of the height of heaven;
but all human beings are dust and ashes.

The Majesty of God

18 He who lives forever created the whole universe;

2 the Lord alone is just.[z]

4 To none has he given power to proclaim his works;
and who can search out his mighty deeds?

5 Who can measure his majestic power?
And who can fully recount his mercies?

6 It is not possible to diminish or increase them,
nor is it possible to fathom the wonders of the Lord.

7 When human beings have finished, they are just beginning,
and when they stop, they are still perplexed.

8 What are human beings, and of what use are they?
What is good in them, and what is evil?

9 The number of days in their life is great if they reach one hundred years.[a]

10 Like a drop of water from the sea and a grain of sand,
so are a few years among the days of eternity.

11 That is why the Lord is patient with them
and pours out his mercy upon them.

12 He sees and recognizes that their end is miserable;
therefore he grants them forgiveness all the more.

13 The compassion of human beings is for their neighbors,
but the compassion of the Lord is for every living thing.

17.23 Mt 25.34-40; 1 Cor 3.11-13 **17.24** 1 Kings 8.47-48; Acts 3.19 **17.25** Isa 31.6; Jer 15.19; Ezek 33.11 **17.26** 2 Tim 2.19; Ps 5.5; 26.5; 139.21 **17.27** Ps 6.5; 30.9; 115.17; Bar 2.17 **17.28** Ps 115.18; Isa 38.19 **17.29** Ps 51.1; 119.156; Sir 16.12 **17.30** Lk 18.27 **17.32** Gen 2.7; 18.27; Job 30.19 **18.1** Ps 90.1-2; Rev 1.18; Gen 1.1; Rev 4.11

18.4 Sir 17.9-10; Job 38.4-11; Isa 40.12; Rom 11.34 **18.6** Ps 145.3; Isa 40.28; Rom 11.33 **18.8** Job 7.17; Ps 8.4; 144.31; Heb 2.6 **18.9** Ps 90.10 **18.10** Ps 90.4; 2 Pet 3.8 **18.11** 2 Pet 3.9; Sir 17.29; Rom 5.5 **18.13** Ps 103.13; 145.9; 90.13; Ps 23.1; 80.1; Isa 40.11; Ezek 34.15, 23

[x] Other ancient authorities add *apportioning repentance to his sons and daughters*
[y] Other ancient authorities add *for he will lead you out of darkness to the light of health.*
[z] Other ancient authorities add *and there is no other beside him; [3]he steers the world with the span of his hand, and all things obey his will; for he is king of all things by his power, separating among them the holy things from the profane.*
[a] Other ancient authorities add *but the death of each one is beyond the calculation of all*

He rebukes and trains and teaches them,
and turns them back, as a shepherd his flock.
14 He has compassion on those who accept his discipline
and who are eager for his precepts.

The Right Spirit in Giving Alms

15 My child, do not mix reproach with your good deeds,
or spoil your gift by harsh words.
16 Does not the dew give relief from the scorching heat?
So a word is better than a gift.
17 Indeed, does not a word surpass a good gift?
Both are to be found in a gracious person.
18 A fool is ungracious and abusive,
and the gift of a grudging giver makes the eyes dim.

The Need of Reflection and Self-control

19 Before you speak, learn;
and before you fall ill, take care of your health.
20 Before judgment comes, examine yourself;
and at the time of scrutiny you will find forgiveness.
21 Before falling ill, humble yourself;
and when you have sinned, repent.
22 Let nothing hinder you from paying a vow promptly,
and do not wait until death to be released from it.
23 Before making a vow, prepare yourself;
do not be like one who puts the Lord to the test.
24 Think of his wrath on the day of death,
and of the moment of vengeance when he turns away his face.
25 In the time of plenty think of the time of hunger;
in days of wealth think of poverty and need.
26 From morning to evening conditions change;
all things move swiftly before the Lord.

27 One who is wise is cautious in everything;
when sin is all around, one guards against wrongdoing.
28 Every intelligent person knows wisdom,
and praises the one who finds her.
29 Those who are skilled in words become wise themselves,
and pour forth apt proverbs.[b]

SELF-CONTROL[c]

30 Do not follow your base desires,
but restrain your appetites.
31 If you allow your soul to take pleasure in base desire,
it will make you the laughingstock of your enemies.
32 Do not revel in great luxury,
or you may become impoverished by its expense.
33 Do not become a beggar by feasting with borrowed money,
when you have nothing in your purse.[d]

19 The one who does this[e] will not become rich;
one who despises small things will fail little by little.
2 Wine and women lead intelligent men astray,

18.14 Jer 31.18; Heb 12.5-12 **18.15** Prov 15.1; Tob 13.12 **18.16** Sir 43.22; Prov 15.23; 25.11 **18.18** Rom 12.8; 2 Cor 9.7 **18.19** Prov 10.19; Jas 1.19 **18.20** Lam 3.40; 1 Cor 11.28; 2 Cor 13.5 **18.21** Ezek 18.30; Sir 17.24; Acts 2.37-38 **18.22** Deut 23.21-23; Eccl 5.4-5 **18.23** Deut 6.16; Ps 106.14 **18.25** Deut 8.12-19; Prov 30.8-9 **18.27** Prov 16.17; Eccl 5.1 **18.28** Prov 18.15; Sir 21.15-16 **18.29** 1 Kings 4.32; Sir 3.29 **18.30** Sir 6.2; 1 Thess 4.4 **18.31** Sir 6.4 **18.32** Lk 15.13-14 **19.2** Prov 20.1; 23.29-30, 27-28; 29.3

[b] Other ancient authorities add *Better is confidence in the one Lord than clinging with a dead heart to a dead one.* [c] This heading is included in the Gk text.
[d] Other ancient authorities add *for you will be plotting against your own life* [e] Heb: Gk *A worker who is a drunkard*

and the man who consorts
with prostitutes is
reckless.
3 Decay and worms will take
possession of him,
and the reckless person
will be snatched away.

Against Loose Talk

4 One who trusts others too
quickly has a shallow
mind,
and one who sins does
wrong to oneself.
5 One who rejoices in
wickedness[f] will be
condemned,[g]
6 but one who hates gossip
has less evil.
7 Never repeat a conversation,
and you will lose nothing
at all.
8 With friend or foe do not
report it,
and unless it would be a
sin for you, do not
reveal it;
9 for someone may have heard
you and watched you,
and in time will hate you.
10 Have you heard something?
Let it die with you.
Be brave, it will not make
you burst!
11 Having heard something, the
fool suffers birth pangs
like a woman in labor with
a child.
12 Like an arrow stuck in a
person's thigh,
so is gossip inside a fool.

13 Question a friend; perhaps
he did not do it;
or if he did, so that he may
not do it again.
14 Question a neighbor;
perhaps he did not say
it;
or if he said it, so that he
may not repeat it.
15 Question a friend, for often
it is slander;
so do not believe
everything you hear.
16 A person may make a slip
without intending it.

19.6 Prov 11.13; 20.19
19.8 Esth 4.9-16
19.9 Prov 16.28
19.13 Prov 17.17; 18.24; 27.6; Sir 7.12
19.14 Ex 20.16; Lev 19.18; Prov 3.29
19.15 Prov 10.18; Sir 28.14-16
19.16 Sir 5.13-14; Jas 3.3-12
19.20 Ps 111.10; Prov 1.7; Wis 7.7; Sir 1.1; Prov 4.10-13; Sir 15.1
19.22 Ps 1.1; Prov 12.5; Sir 37.11
19.25 Prov 17.8,23; Eccl 7.7; Mic 3.11
19.26 Prov 12.20; 20.17; Wis 14.25
19.28 Sir 12.16

Who has not sinned with
his tongue?
17 Question your neighbor
before you threaten
him;
and let the law of the Most
High take its course.[h]

True and False Wisdom

20 The whole of wisdom is fear
of the Lord,
and in all wisdom there is
the fulfillment of the
law.[i]
22 The knowledge of
wickedness is not
wisdom,
nor is there prudence in
the counsel of sinners.
23 There is a cleverness that is
detestable,
and there is a fool who
merely lacks wisdom.
24 Better are the God-fearing
who lack understanding
than the highly intelligent
who transgress the law.
25 There is a cleverness that is
exact but unjust,
and there are people who
abuse favors to gain a
verdict.
26 There is the villain bowed
down in mourning,
but inwardly he is full of
deceit.
27 He hides his face and
pretends not to hear,
but when no one notices,
he will take advantage
of you.
28 Even if lack of strength
keeps him from sinning,

[f] Other ancient authorities read *heart*
[g] Other ancient authorities add *but one who withstands pleasures crowns his life.* *6One who controls the tongue will live without strife,*
[h] Other ancient authorities add *and do not be angry.* *18The fear of the Lord is the beginning of acceptance, and wisdom obtains his love.* *19The knowledge of the Lord's commandments is life-giving discipline; and those who do what is pleasing to him enjoy the fruit of the tree of immortality.*
[i] Other ancient authorities add *and the knowledge of his omnipotence.* *21When a slave says to his master, "I will not act as you wish," even if later he does it, he angers the one who supports him.*

he will nevertheless do evil when he finds the opportunity.
29 A person is known by his appearance,
and a sensible person is known when first met, face to face.
30 A person's attire and hearty laughter,
and the way he walks, show what he is.

Silence and Speech

20 There is a rebuke that is untimely,
and there is the person who is wise enough to keep silent.
2 How much better it is to rebuke than to fume!
3 And the one who admits his fault will be kept from failure.
4 Like a eunuch lusting to violate a girl
is the person who does right under compulsion.
5 Some people keep silent and are thought to be wise,
while others are detested for being talkative.
6 Some people keep silent because they have nothing to say,
while others keep silent because they know when to speak.
7 The wise remain silent until the right moment,
but a boasting fool misses the right moment.
8 Whoever talks too much is detested,
and whoever pretends to authority is hated.[j]

Paradoxes

9 There may be good fortune for a person in adversity,
and a windfall may result in a loss.
10 There is the gift that profits you nothing,
and the gift to be paid back double.
11 There are losses for the sake of glory,
and there are some who have raised their heads from humble circumstances.
12 Some buy much for little,
but pay for it seven times over.
13 The wise make themselves beloved by only few words,[k]
but the courtesies of fools are wasted.
14 A fool's gift will profit you nothing,[l]
for he looks for recompense sevenfold.[m]
15 He gives little and upbraids much;
he opens his mouth like a town crier.
Today he lends and tomorrow he asks it back;
such a one is hateful to God and humans.[n]
16 The fool says, "I have no friends,
and I get no thanks for my good deeds.
Those who eat my bread are evil-tongued."
17 How many will ridicule him, and how often![o]

Inappropriate Speech

18 A slip on the pavement is better than a slip of the tongue;
the downfall of the wicked will occur just as speedily.
19 A coarse person is like an inappropriate story,
continually on the lips of the ignorant.

20.1 1 Sam 25.10-13; Prov 15.1; 11.12; 17.28; Sir 20.6-7 **20.2** Prov 25.12; 27.5 **20.3** Sir 38.10 **20.5** Prov 17.28 **20.6** Prov 15.23; 25.11 **20.7** Prov 15.23; 25.11; 29.20 **20.8** Prov 15.2; Eccl 10.12-14 **20.9** Job 42.10; Lk 12.16-21 **20.10** Sir 20.14 **20.11** Gen 41.1-45 **20.14** Sir 20.10 **20.16** Prov 14.7; 18.7 **20.18** Sir 5.13 **20.19** Sir 19.11-12

j Other ancient authorities add *How good it is to show repentance when you are reproved, for so you will escape deliberate sin!*
k Heb: Gk *by words*
l Other ancient authorities add *so it is with the envious who give under compulsion*
m Syr: Gk *he has many eyes instead of one*
n Other ancient authorities lack *to God and humans*
o Other ancient authorities add *for he has not honestly received what he has, and what he does not have is unimportant to him*

20 A proverb from a fool's lips
will be rejected,
for he does not tell it at
the proper time.

21 One may be prevented from
sinning by poverty;
so when he rests he feels
no remorse.
22 One may lose his life
through shame,
or lose it because of
human respect.[p]
23 Another out of shame makes
promises to a friend,
and so makes an enemy for
nothing.

Lying

24 A lie is an ugly blot on a
person;
it is continually on the lips
of the ignorant.
25 A thief is preferable to a
habitual liar,
but the lot of both is ruin.
26 A liar's way leads to
disgrace,
and his shame is ever with
him.

Proverbial Sayings[q]

27 The wise person advances
himself by his words,
and one who is sensible
pleases the great.
28 Those who cultivate the soil
heap up their harvest,
and those who please the
great atone for
injustice.
29 Favors and gifts blind the
eyes of the wise;
like a muzzle on the mouth
they stop reproofs.
30 Hidden wisdom and unseen
treasure,
of what value is either?
31 Better are those who hide
their folly
than those who hide their
wisdom.[r]

Various Sins

21 Have you sinned, my
child? Do so no more,
but ask forgiveness for your
past sins.
2 Flee from sin as from a
snake;
for if you approach sin, it
will bite you.
Its teeth are lion's teeth,
and can destroy human
lives.
3 All lawlessness is like a
two-edged sword;
there is no healing for the
wound it inflicts.

4 Panic and insolence will
waste away riches;
thus the house of the
proud will be laid
waste.[s]
5 The prayer of the poor goes
from their lips to the
ears of God,[t]
and his judgment comes
speedily.
6 Those who hate reproof walk
in the sinner's steps,
but those who fear the
Lord repent in their
heart.
7 The mighty in speech are
widely known;
when they slip, the
sensible person knows
it.

8 Whoever builds his house
with other people's
money
is like one who gathers
stones for his burial
mound.[u]
9 An assembly of the wicked is
like a bundle of tow,
and their end is a blazing
fire.
10 The way of sinners is paved
with smooth stones,
but at its end is the pit of
Hades.

20.20 Prov 26.7,9 **20.22** Sir 5.20-26 **20.23** Sir 41.18-19 **20.24** Prov 6.16-17; 12.22; Sir 19.11-12 **20.25** Prov 19.5,9 **20.26** Sir 7.13 **20.27** Prov 13.2 **20.29** Sir 19.25 **20.30** Prov 2.4; Mt 13.44-46 **20.31** Sir 4.23-24; 41.15 **21.1** Jn 5.14; 8.11; Ps 32.1-5; 130.4; Prov 28.13 **21.2** Wis 1.5; 1 Cor 6.18; 10.14; 1 Pet 5.8 **21.3** Prov 5.3-4 **21.4** Prov 11.2; 16.18; Sir 1.30 **21.5** Ps 34.6; 40.17; Sir 35.17-22; Lk 18.1-7 **21.6** Prov 1.25,30; 5.12-14; Sir 32.17; 1 Kings 8.47-48; Job 42.6 **21.9** Isa 66.24; Mt 5.22; Rev 18.17-18 **21.10** Mt 7.13; Prov 14.12; 16.25

[p] Other ancient authorities read *his foolish look*
[q] This heading is included in the Gk text.
[r] Other ancient authorities add [32]*Unwearied endurance in seeking the Lord is better than a masterless charioteer of one's own life.*
[s] Other ancient authorities read *uprooted*
[t] Gk *his ears*
[u] Other ancient authorities read *for the winter*

Wisdom and Foolishness

11 Whoever keeps the law
controls his thoughts,
and the fulfillment of the
fear of the Lord is
wisdom.
12 The one who is not clever
cannot be taught,
but there is a cleverness
that increases
bitterness.
13 The knowledge of the wise
will increase like a
flood,
and their counsel like a
life-giving spring.
14 The mind[v] of a fool is like a
broken jar;
it can hold no knowledge.

15 When an intelligent person
hears a wise saying,
he praises it and adds to it;
when a fool[w] hears it, he
laughs at[x] it
and throws it behind his
back.
16 A fool's chatter is like a
burden on a journey,
but delight is found in the
speech of the
intelligent.
17 The utterance of a sensible
person is sought in the
assembly,
and they ponder his words
in their minds.

18 Like a house in ruins is
wisdom to a fool,
and to the ignorant,
knowledge is talk that
has no meaning.
19 To a senseless person
education is fetters on
his feet,
and like manacles on his
right hand.
20 A fool raises his voice when
he laughs,
but the wise[y] smile
quietly.
21 To the sensible person
education is like a
golden ornament,
and like a bracelet on the
right arm.

21.11 Ps 111.10; Prov 1.7; Sir 19.20 **21.13** Prov 21.11 **21.14** Prov 12.23; Sir 22.18; Jer 2.13 **21.15** Sir 18.28; 21.20 **21.16** Sir 22.14-15 **21.18** Prov 1.7,22; 10.14; 15.2 **21.19** Sir 16.23 **21.20** Sir 21.16; 27.13 **21.21** Sir 4.24

21.25 Prov 10.8,14; 20.19; 10.19; Job 31.6 **21.27** Gen 12.3; Ps 109.17; Prov 14.14 **21.28** Prov 16.28; 18.8; 26.22 **22.1** Sir 33.29 **22.3** Prov 10.1; 15.20; 19.13 **22.4** Sir 7.25

22 The foot of a fool rushes into
a house,
but an experienced person
waits respectfully
outside.
23 A boor peers into the house
from the door,
but a cultivated person
remains outside.
24 It is ill-mannered for a
person to listen at a
door;
the discreet would be
grieved by the disgrace.

25 The lips of babblers speak of
what is not their
concern.[z]
but the words of the
prudent are weighed in
the balance.
26 The mind of fools is in their
mouth,
but the mouth of the wise
is in[a] their mind.
27 When an ungodly person
curses an adversary,[b]
he curses himself.
28 A whisperer degrades himself
and is hated in his
neighborhood.

The Idler

22 The idler is like a filthy
stone,
and every one hisses at his
disgrace.
2 The idler is like the filth of
dunghills;
anyone that picks it up will
shake it off his hand.

Degenerate Children

3 It is a disgrace to be the
father of an
undisciplined son,
and the birth of a daughter
is a loss.
4 A sensible daughter obtains
a husband of her own,

[v] Syr Lat: Gk *entrails* [w] Syr: Gk *reveler* [x] Syr: Gk *dislikes* [y] Syr Lat: Gk *clever* [z] Other ancient authorities read *of strangers speak of these things* [a] Other ancient authorities omit *in* [b] Or *curses Satan*

but one who acts
shamefully is a grief to
her father.
5 An impudent daughter
disgraces father and
husband,
and is despised by both.
6 Like music in time of
mourning is ill-timed
conversation,
but a thrashing and
discipline are at all
times wisdom.[c]

Wisdom and Folly

9 Whoever teaches a fool is
like one who glues
potsherds together,
or who rouses a sleeper
from deep slumber.
10 Whoever tells a story to a
fool tells it to a drowsy
man;
and at the end he will say,
"What is it?"
11 Weep for the dead, for he
has left the light
behind;
and weep for the fool, for
he has left intelligence
behind.
Weep less bitterly for the
dead, for he is at rest;
but the life of the fool is
worse than death.
12 Mourning for the dead lasts
seven days,
but for the foolish or the
ungodly it lasts all the
days of their lives.

13 Do not talk much with a
senseless person
or visit an unintelligent
person.[d]
Stay clear of him, or you may
have trouble,
and be spattered when he
shakes himself off.
Avoid him and you will find
rest,
and you will never be
wearied by his lack of
sense.
14 What is heavier than lead?
And what is its name
except "Fool"?

22.5 Sir 26.10; 42.11; Prov 3.11-12; Sir 1.27; 6.18 **22.10** Prov 26.14; Sir 33.5 **22.11** 2 Sam 18.33; Sir 38.16; Jn 11.33-35 **22.12** Gen 50.10; 1 Sam 31.13 **22.13** Sir 16.23; 21.19

22.15 Sir 21.16; Prov 19.13; Sir 27.12 **22.16** Ps 56.3,4,11; Prov 3.21-26 **22.18** Sir 21.14,26 **22.20** Sir 6.9; 37.4 **22.22** Prov 18.24; Sir 13.12; 27.16-17

15 Sand, salt, and a piece of
iron
are easier to bear than a
stupid person.

16 A wooden beam firmly
bonded into a building
is not loosened by an
earthquake;
so the mind firmly resolved
after due reflection
will not be afraid in a
crisis.
17 A mind settled on an
intelligent thought
is like stucco decoration
that makes a wall
smooth.
18 Fences[e] set on a high place
will not stand firm against
the wind;
so a timid mind with a fool's
resolve
will not stand firm against
any fear.

The Preservation of Friendship

19 One who pricks the eye
brings tears,
and one who pricks the
heart makes clear its
feelings.
20 One who throws a stone at
birds scares them away,
and one who reviles a
friend destroys a
friendship.
21 Even if you draw your sword
against a friend,
do not despair, for there is
a way back.
22 If you open your mouth
against your friend,
do not worry, for
reconciliation is
possible.
But as for reviling, arrogance,
disclosure of secrets, or
a treacherous blow—
in these cases any friend
will take to flight.

[c] Other ancient authorities add *7Children who are brought up in a good life, conceal the lowly birth of their parents. 8Children who are disdainfully and boorishly haughty stain the nobility of their kindred.*
[d] Other ancient authorities add *For being without sense he will despise everything about you*
[e] Other ancient authorities read *Pebbles*

23 Gain the trust of your
neighbor in his poverty,
so that you may rejoice
with him in his
prosperity.
Stand by him in time of
distress,
so that you may share with
him in his
inheritance.[f]
24 The vapor and smoke of the
furnace precede the
fire;
so insults precede
bloodshed.
25 I am not ashamed to shelter
a friend,
and I will not hide from
him.
26 But if harm should come to
me because of him,
whoever hears of it will
beware of him.

A Prayer for Help against Sinning

27 Who will set a guard over my
mouth,
and an effective seal upon
my lips,
so that I may not fall
because of them,
and my tongue may not
destroy me?

23 O Lord, Father and
Master of my life,
do not abandon me to their
designs,
and do not let me fall
because of them!
2 Who will set whips over my
thoughts,
and the discipline of
wisdom over my mind,
so as not to spare me in my
errors,
and not overlook my[g] sins?
3 Otherwise my mistakes may
be multiplied,
and my sins may abound,
and I may fall before my
adversaries,
and my enemy may rejoice
over me.[h]
4 O Lord, Father and God of
my life,

22.23 Sir 10.31; Job 2.11-13; Sir 4.4 **22.24** 1 Sam 25.10-13 **22.27** Sir 28.24-26; 5.13-14; Jas 3.6 **23.1** Isa 63.16; Jer 31.9; Mt 6.9 **23.2** Prov 3.11-12; Sir 22.6; Ps 19.12; 90.8 **23.3** Hos 12.1; Sir 23.16; Pr Man 1.9; Ps 25.2; 41.11 **23.4** Ps 18.27; Prov 6.17; 21.4 **23.5** Prov 21.10; 1 Cor 10.6; Col 3.5 **23.6** Prov 23.21; Sir 37.30-31; 4 Macc 1.3; Eph 4.22; 1 Thess 4.5; 1 Jn 2.15-16 **23.8** Prov 18.6-7; Sir 1.29; 14.1 **23.9** Mt 5.34-37; Jas 5.12; Lev 19.12 **23.10** Ex 20.7; Deut 5.11 **23.11** Prov 17.20; Sir 10.13; 40.9; Jas 3.6 **23.12** Lev 24.11-16

do not give me haughty
eyes,
5 and remove evil desire
from me.
6 Let neither gluttony nor lust
overcome me,
and do not give me over to
shameless passion.

Discipline of the Tongue[i]

7 Listen, my children, to
instruction concerning
the mouth;
the one who observes it
will never be caught.
8 Sinners are overtaken
through their lips;
by them the reviler and the
arrogant are tripped up.
9 Do not accustom your mouth
to oaths,
nor habitually utter the
name of the Holy One;
10 for as a servant who is
constantly under
scrutiny
will not lack bruises,
so also the person who
always swears and
utters the Name
will never be cleansed[j]
from sin.
11 The one who swears many
oaths is full of iniquity,
and the scourge will not
leave his house.
If he swears in error, his sin
remains on him,
and if he disregards it, he
sins doubly;
if he swears a false oath, he
will not be justified,
for his house will be filled
with calamities.

Foul Language

12 There is a manner of
speaking comparable to
death;[k]

[f] Other ancient authorities add *For one should not always despise restricted circumstances, or admire a rich person who is stupid.*
[g] Gk *their*
[h] Other ancient authorities add *From them the hope of your mercy is remote*
[i] This heading is included in the Gk text.
[j] Syr *be free*
[k] Other ancient authorities read *clothed about with death*

may it never be found in
the inheritance of
Jacob!
Such conduct will be far
from the godly,
and they will not wallow in
sins.
13 Do not accustom your mouth
to coarse, foul
language,
for it involves sinful
speech.
14 Remember your father and
mother
when you sit among the
great,
or you may forget yourself in
their presence,
and behave like a fool
through bad habit;
then you will wish that you
had never been born,
and you will curse the day
of your birth.
15 Those who are accustomed
to using abusive
language
will never become
disciplined as long as
they live.

Concerning Sexual Sins

16 Two kinds of individuals
multiply sins,
and a third incurs
wrath.
Hot passion that blazes like
a fire
will not be quenched until
it burns itself out;
one who commits fornication
with his near of kin
will never cease until the
fire burns him up.
17 To a fornicator all bread is
sweet;
he will never weary until
he dies.
18 The one who sins against his
marriage bed
says to himself, "Who can
see me?
Darkness surrounds me, the
walls hide me,
and no one sees me. Why
should I worry?
The Most High will not
remember sins."
19 His fear is confined to
human eyes
and he does not realize
that the eyes of the
Lord
are ten thousand times
brighter than the sun;
they look upon every aspect
of human behavior
and see into hidden
corners.
20 Before the universe was
created, it was known
to him,
and so it is since its
completion.
21 This man will be punished in
the streets of the city,
and where he least
suspects it, he will be
seized.

22 So it is with a woman who
leaves her husband
and presents him with an
heir by another man.
23 For first of all, she has
disobeyed the law of
the Most High;
second, she has committed
an offense against her
husband;
and third, through her
fornication she has
committed adultery
and brought forth children
by another man.
24 She herself will be brought
before the assembly,
and her punishment will
extend to her
children.
25 Her children will not take
root,
and her branches will not
bear fruit.
26 She will leave behind an
accursed memory
and her disgrace will never
be blotted out.
27 Those who survive her will
recognize
that nothing is better than
the fear of the Lord,

23.13 Eph 5.4 **23.14** Job 3.11-16; 10.18; 3.1 **23.16** Hos 12.1; Sir 23.3; Prov 14.30; Sir 6.2-4; 1 Cor 7.9; Lev 18.6-18; 20.11-12 **23.17** Prov 9.17; 20.17 **3.18** Heb 13.4; Prov 7.7-9; 1 Thess 5.7; Hos 7.2 **23.19** Job 34.21; Ps 139.16; Prov 15.3 **23.20** Eph 1.3; Ps 139.15-16; Jer 1.5 **23.21** Prov 5.3-6; 7.22-27; Sir 6.4 **23.22** Prov 7.10-2 **23.23** Ex 20.14; Mt 19.9,18; 1 Cor 6.13-16 **23.24** Lev 20.10-12; Jn 8.3-4 **23.25** Wis 4.3 **23.26** Prov 6.32-33 **23.27** Sir 1.26; 15.1

and nothing sweeter than to heed the commandments of the Lord.[l]

THE PRAISE OF WISDOM[m]

24 Wisdom praises herself,
and tells of her glory in the midst of her people.
2 In the assembly of the Most High she opens her mouth,
and in the presence of his hosts she tells of her glory:
3 "I came forth from the mouth of the Most High,
and covered the earth like a mist.
4 I dwelt in the highest heavens,
and my throne was in a pillar of cloud.
5 Alone I compassed the vault of heaven
and traversed the depths of the abyss.
6 Over waves of the sea, over all the earth,
and over every people and nation I have held sway.[n]
7 Among all these I sought a resting place;
in whose territory should I abide?

8 "Then the Creator of all things gave me a command,
and my Creator chose the place for my tent.
He said, 'Make your dwelling in Jacob,
and in Israel receive your inheritance.'
9 Before the ages, in the beginning, he created me,
and for all the ages I shall not cease to be.
10 In the holy tent I ministered before him,
and so I was established in Zion.
11 Thus in the beloved city he gave me a resting place,
and in Jerusalem was my domain.
12 I took root in an honored people,
in the portion of the Lord, his heritage.

13 "I grew tall like a cedar in Lebanon,
and like a cypress on the heights of Hermon.
14 I grew tall like a palm tree in En-gedi,[o]
and like rosebushes in Jericho;
like a fair olive tree in the field,
and like a plane tree beside water[p] I grew tall.
15 Like cassia and camel's thorn I gave forth perfume,
and like choice myrrh I spread my fragrance,
like galbanum, onycha, and stacte,
and like the odor of incense in the tent.
16 Like a terebinth I spread out my branches,
and my branches are glorious and graceful.
17 Like the vine I bud forth delights,
and my blossoms become glorious and abundant fruit.[q]

19 "Come to me, you who desire me,
and eat your fill of my fruits.
20 For the memory of me is sweeter than honey,

24.1 Sir 15.10; 7.25; Wis 14.27 **24.3** Gen 1.2 **24.4** Wis 8.3; 9.4, 10; Sir 1.8 **24.5** Sir 1.3 **24.7** Sir 24.11 **24.8** Isa 40.26; Wis 1.14; Sir 18.1; Rev 4.11; Ps 78.71; Isa 51.19 **24.9** Prov 8.22-29; Wis 6.22; 8.13 **24.11** 2 Chr 6.41; Ps 132.14 **24.12** 1 Kings 8.51; Ps 28.9; 33.12; Isa 19.25 **24.13** 1 Kings 4.33; Ps 37.35; 92.12; Isa 60.13; Hos 14.8 **24.14** 2 Chr 28.15; Ps 92.12; Song 1.14; Ps 52.8; Hos 14.6; Isa 41.19; 60.13 **24.15** Song 1.3; 2 Esd 2.12; Ps 45.8; Song 3.6; 5.1, 5 **24.16** Sir 14.26 **24.17** Song 1.14; Sir 39.14 **24.19** Mt 11.28; Jn 7.37; Prov 9.5; Song 5.1; Isa 55.1 **24.20** Ps 19.10; Rev 10.9-10; Prov 24.13

[l] Other ancient authorities add as verse 28, *It is a great honor to follow God, and to be received by him is long life.*
[m] This heading is included in the Gk text.
[n] Other ancient authorities read *I have acquired a possession*
[o] Other ancient authorities read *on the beaches*
[p] Other ancient authorities omit *beside water*
[q] Other ancient authorities add as verse 18, *I am the mother of beautiful love, of fear, of knowledge, and of holy hope; being eternal, I am given to all my children, to those who are named by him.*

and the possession of me
sweeter than the
honeycomb.
21 Those who eat of me will
hunger for more,
and those who drink of me
will thirst for more.
22 Whoever obeys me will not
be put to shame,
and those who work with
me will not sin."

Wisdom and the Law

23 All this is the book of the
covenant of the Most
High God,
the law that Moses
commanded us
as an inheritance for the
congregations of
Jacob.[r]
25 It overflows, like the Pishon,
with wisdom,
and like the Tigris at the
time of the first fruits.
26 It runs over, like the
Euphrates, with
understanding,
and like the Jordan at
harvest time.
27 It pours forth instruction like
the Nile,[s]
like the Gihon at the time
of vintage.
28 The first man did not know
wisdom[t] fully,
nor will the last one
fathom her,
29 For her thoughts are more
abundant than the sea,
and her counsel deeper
than the great abyss.

30 As for me, I was like a canal
from a river,
like a water channel into a
garden.
31 I said, "I will water my
garden
and drench my
flower-beds."
And lo, my canal became a
river,
and my river a sea.
32 I will again make instruction
shine forth like the
dawn,

24.21 Mt 5.6; Jn 6.35; 4.13-14; 7.38
24.22 Isa 28.16; Rom 9.33; 10.11
24.23 Deut 29.21; 31.26; 2 Chr 34.30
24.25 Gen 2.11, 14
24.26 Gen 2.14; 15.18
24.27 Gen 41.1; Sir 47.14; Gen 2.13
24.28 Gen 3.1-7
24.29 Isa 55.8-9
24.30 Jn 7.38
24.31 Song 4.15-16; Isa 58.11; Ezek 47.1-6
24.32 Prov 4.18; Song 6.10; Isa 62.1
24.33 Prov 6.23; 13.14
24.34 Sir 6.27
25.1 Ps 133.1-2; Acts 2.44; Sir 9.14; Eph 5.21-33; Col 3.18-19
25.4 Prov 16.31; 20.29; Wis 4.9
25.5 Job 12.12-13; 15.10; Sir 8.8-9
25.6 2 Macc 7.16

and I will make it clear
from far away.
33 I will again pour out
teaching like prophecy,
and leave it to all future
generations.
34 Observe that I have not
labored for myself
alone,
but for all who seek
wisdom.[t]

Those Who Are Worthy of Praise

25

I take pleasure in three
things,
and they are beautiful in
the sight of God and of
mortals:[u]
agreement among brothers
and sisters, friendship
among neighbors,
and a wife and a husband
who live in harmony.
2 I hate three kinds of people,
and I loathe their manner
of life:
a pauper who boasts, a rich
person who lies,
and an old fool who
commits adultery.

3 If you gathered nothing in
your youth,
how can you find anything
in your old age?
4 How attractive is sound
judgment in the
gray-haired,
and for the aged to possess
good counsel!
5 How attractive is wisdom in
the aged,
and understanding and
counsel in the
venerable!
6 Rich experience is the crown
of the aged,
and their boast is the fear
of the Lord.

[r] Other ancient authorities add as verse 24, *"Do not cease to be strong in the Lord, cling to him so that he may strengthen you; the Lord Almighty alone is God, and besides him there is no savior."* [s] Syr: Gk *It makes instruction shine forth like light* [t] Gk *her*
[u] Syr Lat: Gk *In three things I was beautiful and I stood in beauty before the Lord and mortals.*

[7] I can think of nine whom I would call blessed,
and a tenth my tongue proclaims:
a man who can rejoice in his children;
a man who lives to see the downfall of his foes.
[8] Happy the man who lives with a sensible wife,
and the one who does not plow with ox and ass together.[v]
Happy is the one who does not sin with the tongue,
and the one who has not served an inferior.
[9] Happy is the one who finds a friend,[w]
and the one who speaks to attentive listeners.
[10] How great is the one who finds wisdom!
But none is superior to the one who fears the Lord.
[11] Fear of the Lord surpasses everything;
to whom can we compare the one who has it?[x]

Some Extreme Forms of Evil

[13] Any wound, but not a wound of the heart!
Any wickedness, but not the wickedness of a woman!
[14] Any suffering, but not suffering from those who hate!
And any vengeance, but not the vengeance of enemies!
[15] There is no venom[y] worse than a snake's venom,[y]
and no anger worse than a woman's[z] wrath.

The Evil of a Wicked Woman

[16] I would rather live with a lion and a dragon
than live with an evil woman.
[17] A woman's wickedness changes her appearance,
and darkens her face like that of a bear.
[18] Her husband sits[a] among the neighbors,
and he cannot help sighing[b] bitterly.
[19] Any iniquity is small compared to a woman's iniquity;
may a sinner's lot befall her!
[20] A sandy ascent for the feet of the aged—
such is a garrulous wife to a quiet husband.
[21] Do not be ensnared by a woman's beauty,
and do not desire a woman for her possessions.[c]
[22] There is wrath and impudence and great disgrace
when a wife supports her husband.
[23] Dejected mind, gloomy face,
and wounded heart come from an evil wife.
Drooping hands and weak knees
come from the wife who does not make her husband happy.
[24] From a woman sin had its beginning,
and because of her we all die.
[25] Allow no outlet to water,
and no boldness of speech to an evil wife.
[26] If she does not go as you direct,
separate her from yourself.

The Joy of a Good Wife

26 Happy is the husband of a good wife;
the number of his days will be doubled.
[2] A loyal wife brings joy to her husband,

25.7 Mt 5.2-12; Ps 127.3-5; Ps 9.1-4; 137.8-9 **25.8** Prov 12.4; 18.22; 19.14; Sir 26.1; Deut 22.10; Prov 15.4; Sir 6.5; 28.26 **25.9** Prov 17.17; Eccl 4.9-12; Sir 9.10 **25.10** Prov 3.13; 8.32-35; Sir 40.19 **25.11** Ps 112.1; Prov 19.23; Sir 1.12-20 **25.13** Prov 12.25; 14.10; 25.20 **25.14** Ps 9.13; 41.7; 109.2-5 **25.15** Prov 21.9,19; 25.24; Sir 26.6-8 **25.16** Prov 5.3-4; Eccl 7.26 **25.20** Prov 22.14; Sir 26.27 **25.21** Prov 11.22; Sir 9.8 **25.23** Sir 25.18; Isa 35.3; Heb 12.12 **25.24** Gen 3.1-5; 1 Tim 2.13-14; Gen 3.19; Rom 5.12 **25.26** Deut 24.1; Mt 19.3-9 **26.1** Prov 18.22; Eccl 9.9; Sir 25.8 **26.2** Prov 5.18; 12.4; Eccl 9.9; Sir 26.26

[v] Heb Syr: Gk lacks *and the one who does not plow with ox and ass together* [w] Lat Syr: Gk *good sense* [x] Other ancient authorities add as verse 12, *The fear of the Lord is the beginning of love for him, and faith is the beginning of clinging to him.* [y] Syr: Gk *head* [z] Other ancient authorities read *an enemy's* [a] Heb Syr: Gk *loses heart* [b] Other ancient authorities read *and listening he sighs* [c] Heb Syr: Other Gk authorities read *for her beauty*

and he will complete his years in peace.
3 A good wife is a great blessing;
she will be granted among the blessings of the man who fears the Lord.
4 Whether rich or poor, his heart is content,
and at all times his face is cheerful.

The Worst of Evils: A Wicked Wife

5 Of three things my heart is frightened,
and of a fourth I am in great fear:[d]
Slander in the city, the gathering of a mob,
and false accusation—all these are worse than death.
6 But it is heartache and sorrow when a wife is jealous of a rival,
and a tongue-lashing makes it known to all.
7 A bad wife is a chafing yoke;
taking hold of her is like grasping a scorpion.
8 A drunken wife arouses great anger;
she cannot hide her shame.
9 The haughty stare betrays an unchaste wife;
her eyelids give her away.

10 Keep strict watch over a headstrong daughter,
or else, when she finds liberty, she will make use of it.
11 Be on guard against her impudent eye,
and do not be surprised if she sins against you.
12 As a thirsty traveler opens his mouth
and drinks from any water near him,
so she will sit in front of every tent peg
and open her quiver to the arrow.

The Blessing of a Good Wife

13 A wife's charm delights her husband,
and her skill puts flesh on his bones.
14 A silent wife is a gift from the Lord,
and nothing is so precious as her self-discipline.
15 A modest wife adds charm to charm,
and no scales can weigh the value of her chastity.
16 Like the sun rising in the heights of the Lord,
so is the beauty of a good wife in her well-ordered home.
17 Like the shining lamp on the holy lampstand,
so is a beautiful face on a stately figure.
18 Like golden pillars on silver bases,
so are shapely legs and steadfast feet.

Other ancient authorities add verses 19–27:

19 *My child, keep sound the bloom of your youth,*
and do not give your strength to strangers.
20 *Seek a fertile field within the whole plain,*
and sow it with your own seed, trusting in your fine stock.
21 *So your offspring will prosper,*
and, having confidence in their good descent, will grow great.
22 *A prostitute is regarded as spittle,*
and a married woman as a tower of death to her lovers.
23 *A godless wife is given as a portion to a lawless man,*
but a pious wife is given to the man who fears the Lord.

26.3 Prov 31.28-31; Ps 128.3-4
26.5 Prov 10.18; Sir 28.14-15
26.6 Sir 9.1; 25.25
26.7 Prov 21.9,19; 25.24
26.8 Sir 25.15
26.9 Prov 6.17; 21.4; Sir 23.4
26.10 Sir 22.5; 42.11
26.12 Prov 5.3-5; 7.6-23
26.13 Prov 31.28-31
26.14 Ps 128.3-4; Prov 12.4; 21.9,19; Titus 2.4-5
26.15 Prov 31.10-27; Sir 7.24; 2 Cor 11.2; Titus 2.5
26.16 Song 1.5, 15-16; 4.1,7
26.18 Ps 144.12; Song 5.15; 7.1
26.19 Eccl 11.9-12.1
26.20 Prov 2.16-19; 6.24; Sir 9.9
26.21 Ps 128.3; 144.12
26.22 Prov 23.27; 2 Esd 16.49; Prov 2.18-19; 7.21-27

[d] Syr: Meaning of Gk uncertain

24 *A shameless woman*
constantly acts
disgracefully,
but a modest daughter will
even be embarrassed
before her husband.
25 *A headstrong wife is regarded*
as a dog,
but one who has a sense of
shame will fear the
Lord.
26 *A wife honoring her husband*
will seem wise to all,
but if she dishonors him in
her pride she will be
known to all as ungodly.
Happy is the husband of a
good wife;
for the number of his years
will be doubled.
27 *A loud-voiced and garrulous*
wife is like a trumpet
sounding the charge,
and every person like this
lives in the anarchy of
war.

Three Depressing Things

28 At two things my heart is
grieved,
and because of a third
anger comes over me:
a warrior in want through
poverty,
intelligent men who are
treated contemptuously,
and a man who turns back
from righteousness to
sin—
the Lord will prepare him
for the sword!

The Temptations of Commerce

29 A merchant can hardly keep
from wrongdoing,
nor is a tradesman
innocent of sin.

27 Many have committed sin
for gain,[e]
and those who seek to get
rich will avert their
eyes.
2 As a stake is driven firmly
into a fissure between
stones,
so sin is wedged in
between selling and
buying.
3 If a person is not steadfast in
the fear of the Lord,
his house will be quickly
overthrown.

Tests in Life

4 When a sieve is shaken, the
refuse appears;
so do a person's faults
when he speaks.
5 The kiln tests the potter's
vessels;
so the test of a person is in
his conversation.
6 Its fruit discloses the
cultivation of a tree;
so a person's speech
discloses the cultivation
of his mind.
7 Do not praise anyone before
he speaks,
for this is the way people
are tested.

Reward and Retribution

8 If you pursue justice, you
will attain it
and wear it like a glorious
robe.
9 Birds roost with their own
kind,
so honesty comes home to
those who practice it.
10 A lion lies in wait for prey;
so does sin for evildoers.

Varieties of Speech

11 The conversation of the
godly is always wise,
but the fool changes like
the moon.
12 Among stupid people limit
your time,
but among thoughtful
people linger on.
13 The talk of fools is offensive,
and their laughter is
wantonly sinful.
14 Their cursing and swearing
make one's hair stand
on end,

26.24 3 Macc 1.19; 1 Tim 2.9,15
26.26 Eph 5.22-24; Col 3.18; Titus 2.4-5; 1 Pet 3.1-6; Ps 128.3-4; Sir 26.1
26.27 Sir 25.20
26.28 Ezek 3.20; 18.24; 33.13
27.1 Prov 28.21; Ezek 13.19; Am 4.1; 5.12
27.3 Sir 10.19-20; 23.27; 25.11
27.4 Prov 12.17; 14.5
27.6 Mt 7.16; 12.33; Jas 3.2
27.7 Prov 23.16
27.8 Prov 21.3,15; Isa 16.5; Mic 6.8
27.9 Prov 12.17; 24.26; Sir 29.3
27.10 Jas 5.8
27.11 Sir 9.15
27.12 Sir 22.15
27.13 Eccl 7.3,6; Sir 21.14,20

[e] Other ancient authorities read *a trifle*

and their quarrels make
others stop their ears.
15 The strife of the proud leads
to bloodshed,
and their abuse is grievous
to hear.

Betraying Secrets

16 Whoever betrays secrets
destroys confidence,
and will never find a
congenial friend.
17 Love your friend and keep
faith with him;
but if you betray his
secrets, do not follow
after him.
18 For as a person destroys his
enemy,
so you have destroyed the
friendship of your
neighbor.
19 And as you allow a bird to
escape from your hand,
so you have let your
neighbor go, and will
not catch him again.
20 Do not go after him, for he is
too far off,
and has escaped like a
gazelle from a snare.
21 For a wound may be
bandaged,
and there is reconciliation
after abuse,
but whoever has betrayed
secrets is without hope.

Hypocrisy and Retribution

22 Whoever winks the eye plots
mischief,
and those who know him
will keep their distance.
23 In your presence his mouth
is all sweetness,
and he admires your words;
but later he will twist his
speech
and with your own words
he will trip you up.
24 I have hated many things,
but him above all;
even the Lord hates him.
25 Whoever throws a stone
straight up throws it on
his own head,
and a treacherous blow
opens up many wounds.
26 Whoever digs a pit will fall
into it,
and whoever sets a snare
will be caught in it.
27 If a person does evil, it will
roll back upon him,
and he will not know
where it came from.
28 Mockery and abuse issue
from the proud,
but vengeance lies in wait
for them like a lion.
29 Those who rejoice in the fall
of the godly will be
caught in a snare,
and pain will consume
them before their
death.

Anger and Vengeance

30 Anger and wrath, these also
are abominations,
yet a sinner holds on to
them.

28 The vengeful will face the
Lord's vengeance,
for he keeps a strict
account of[f] their sins.
2 Forgive your neighbor the
wrong he has done,
and then your sins will be
pardoned when you
pray.
3 Does anyone harbor anger
against another,
and expect healing from
the Lord?
4 If one has no mercy toward
another like himself,
can he then seek pardon
for his own sins?
5 If a mere mortal harbors
wrath,
who will make an atoning
sacrifice for his sins?
6 Remember the end of your
life, and set enmity
aside;
remember corruption and
death, and be true to
the commandments.

[f]Other ancient authorities read *for he firmly establishes*

27.15 Prov 10.12; 13.10; 15.18; 29.22; Sir 27.28
27.16 Prov 20.19; 25.9-10; Sir 13.12; 22.22
27.17 Prov 17.17; 18.24; Sir 9.10
27.18 Prov 16.28; Sir 6.9; 37.2
27.21 Prov 17.9; Sir 22.22
27.22 Prov 6.13; 10.10
27.23 2 Pet 3.16; Sir 12.16-17
27.24 Ps 5.5-6; 11.5-6; Sir 12.6
27.26 Ps 7.15; 9.15; Prov 26.27; Eccl 10.8; Ps 9.16
27.27 Ps 7.16; Prov 26.27
27.28 Prov 21.24; Isa 16.6; Sir 27.15
27.29 Ps 35.19-26
27.30 Ps 37.18; Prov 16.32; Eph 4.32
28.1 Deut 32.35; Rom 12.19; Heb 10.30
28.2 Col 3.13; Mt 6.12, 14-15; Mk 11.25
28.3 Mt 5.22-26; Eph 4.26-27
28.5 1 Jn 1.8-2.2

7 Remember the commandments, and do not be angry with your neighbor;
remember the covenant of the Most High, and overlook faults.

8 Refrain from strife, and your sins will be fewer;
for the hot-tempered kindle strife,
9 and the sinner disrupts friendships
and sows discord among those who are at peace.
10 In proportion to the fuel, so will the fire burn,
and in proportion to the obstinacy, so will strife increase;[g]
in proportion to a person's strength will be his anger,
and in proportion to his wealth he will increase his wrath.
11 A hasty quarrel kindles a fire,
and a hasty dispute sheds blood.

The Evil Tongue

12 If you blow on a spark, it will glow;
if you spit on it, it will be put out;
yet both come out of your mouth.

13 Curse the gossips and the double-tongued,
for they destroy the peace of many.
14 Slander[h] has shaken many,
and scattered them from nation to nation;
it has destroyed strong cities,
and overturned the houses of the great.
15 Slander[i] has driven virtuous women from their homes,
and deprived them of the fruit of their toil.
16 Those who pay heed to slander[j] will not find rest,
nor will they settle down in peace.
17 The blow of a whip raises a welt,
but a blow of the tongue crushes the bones.
18 Many have fallen by the edge of the sword,
but not as many as have fallen because of the tongue.
19 Happy is the one who is protected from it,
who has not been exposed to its anger,
who has not borne its yoke,
and has not been bound with its fetters.
20 For its yoke is a yoke of iron,
and its fetters are fetters of bronze;
21 its death is an evil death,
and Hades is preferable to it.
22 It has no power over the godly;
they will not be burned in its flame.
23 Those who forsake the Lord will fall into its power;
it will burn among them and will not be put out.
It will be sent out against them like a lion;
like a leopard it will mangle them.
24a As you fence in your property with thorns,
25b so make a door and a bolt for your mouth.
24b As you lock up your silver and gold,
25a so make balances and scales for your words.
26 Take care not to err with your tongue,[k]
and fall victim to one lying in wait.

On Lending and Borrowing

29 The merciful lend to their neighbors;
by holding out a helping hand they keep the commandments.

28.7 Sir 10.6; Eph 4.32; Acts 17.30; Rom 3.25 **28.8** Prov 15.18; 26.21; 29.22 **28.9** Sir 6.9; 22.20; Prov 6.14,19 **28.11** Prov 17.14; 20.3; Sir 6.9 **28.12** Prov 15.1; Jas 3.9-10 **28.13** Prov 11.13; 20.19; Sir 19.12; 5.14; 6.1 **28.14** Sir 26.5; Ps 140.9-11 **28.16** Prov 10.18; Sir 19.15 **28.17** Prov 25.15 **28.18** Lam 2.21; Lk 21.24; Jas 3.6 **28.23** Ps 101.5 **28.25** Sir 22.27 **28.26** Prov 6.17; Sir 35.8; Jas 3.5-12 **29.1** Ps 37.26; Prov 19.17; Ex 22.25; Lev 25.37; Deut 15.8

[g] Other ancient authorities read *burn*
[h] Gk *A third tongue* [i] Gk *a third tongue*
[j] Gk *it* [k] Gk *with it*

2 Lend to your neighbor in his
time of need;
repay your neighbor when a
loan falls due.
3 Keep your promise and be
honest with him,
and on every occasion you
will find what you need.
4 Many regard a loan as a
windfall,
and cause trouble to those
who help them.
5 One kisses another's hands
until he gets a loan,
and is deferential in
speaking of his
neighbor's money;
but at the time for
repayment he delays,
and pays back with empty
promises,
and finds fault with the
time.
6 If he can pay, his creditor[l]
will hardly get back
half,
and will regard that as a
windfall.
If he cannot pay, the
borrower[l] has robbed
the other of his money,
and he has needlessly
made him an enemy;
he will repay him with curses
and reproaches,
and instead of glory will
repay him with
dishonor.
7 Many refuse to lend, not
because of meanness,
but from fear[m] of being
defrauded needlessly.

8 Nevertheless, be patient with
someone in humble
circumstances,
and do not keep him
waiting for your alms.
9 Help the poor for the
commandment's sake,
and in their need do not
send them away
empty-handed.
10 Lose your silver for the sake
of a brother or a friend,
and do not let it rust under
a stone and be lost.

29.2 Sir 8.12 **29.3** Sir 27.9 **29.7** Prov 6.1-3; Sir 8.12-13 **29.8** Sir 1.23; 2.4; 2 Tim 2.24; Tob 1.16-17; Sir 7.10 **29.9** Deut 15.7-11; 24.19; Ps 112.9 **29.10** Jas 5.3

29.11 Mt 6.19-21 **29.12** Sir 17.22; Mt 6.2-4; Sir 16.12-14 **29.13** Eph 6.16-17 **29.14** Prov 11.15 **29.18** Prov 6.1-3; 17.18; 22.26 **29.20** Sir 8.13; 1 Cor 10.12 **29.21** Sir 39.26; Mt 6.11; 1 Tim 6.8

11 Lay up your treasure
according to the
commandments of the
Most High,
and it will profit you more
than gold.
12 Store up almsgiving in your
treasury,
and it will rescue you from
every disaster;
13 better than a stout shield
and a sturdy spear,
it will fight for you against
the enemy.

On Guaranteeing Debts

14 A good person will be surety
for his neighbor,
but the one who has lost
all sense of shame will
fail him.
15 Do not forget the kindness of
your guarantor,
for he has given his life for
you.
16 A sinner wastes the property
of his guarantor,
17 and the ungrateful person
abandons his rescuer.
18 Being surety has ruined
many who were
prosperous,
and has tossed them about
like waves of the sea;
it has driven the influential
into exile,
and they have wandered
among foreign nations.
19 The sinner comes to grief
through surety;
his pursuit of gain involves
him in lawsuits.
20 Assist your neighbor to the
best of your ability,
but be careful not to fall
yourself.

Home and Hospitality

21 The necessities of life are
water, bread, and
clothing,
and also a house to assure
privacy.

[l] Gk *he* [m] Other ancient authorities read *many refuse to lend, therefore, because of such meanness; they are afraid*

22 Better is the life of the poor
under their own crude
roof
than sumptuous food in
the house of others.
23 Be content with little or
much,
and you will hear no
reproach for being a
guest.[n]
24 It is a miserable life to go
from house to house;
as a guest you should not
open your mouth;
25 you will play the host and
provide drink without
being thanked,
and besides this you will
hear rude words like
these:
26 "Come here, stranger,
prepare the table;
let me eat what you have
there."
27 "Be off, stranger, for an
honored guest is here;
my brother has come for a
visit, and I need the
guest-room."
28 It is hard for a sensible
person to bear
scolding about lodging[o]
and the insults of the
moneylender.

CONCERNING CHILDREN[p]

30 He who loves his son will
whip him often,
so that he may rejoice at
the way he turns out.
2 He who disciplines his son
will profit by him,
and will boast of him
among acquaintances.
3 He who teaches his son will
make his enemies
envious,
and will glory in him
among his friends.
4 When the father dies he will
not seem to be dead,
for he has left behind him
one like himself,
5 whom in his life he looked
upon with joy
and at death, without grief.
6 He has left behind him an
avenger against his
enemies,
and one to repay the
kindness of his friends.

7 Whoever spoils his son will
bind up his wounds,
and will suffer heartache at
every cry.
8 An unbroken horse turns out
stubborn,
and an unchecked son
turns out headstrong.
9 Pamper a child, and he will
terrorize you;
play with him, and he will
grieve you.
10 Do not laugh with him, or
you will have sorrow
with him,
and in the end you will
gnash your teeth.
11 Give him no freedom in his
youth,
and do not ignore his
errors.
12 Bow down his neck in his
youth,[q]
and beat his sides while he
is young,
or else he will become
stubborn and disobey
you,
and you will have sorrow of
soul from him.[r]
13 Discipline your son and
make his yoke heavy,[s]
so that you may not be
offended by his
shamelessness.

14 Better off poor, healthy, and
fit
than rich and afflicted in
body.
15 Health and fitness are better
than any gold,
and a robust body than
countless riches.

29.22 Prov 15.17; 17.1 **29.23** Prov 30.8-9; Phil 4.11-12; Heb 13.5 **29.24** 2 Thess 3.6-15 **30.1** Prov 13.24; 22.15; 23.13-14; Eph 6.4; Prov 19.18 **30.2** Prov 29.15 **30.4** Tob 9.6 **30.5** Prov 10.1; 23.15,24-25; 27.11

30.6 Ps 127.5 **30.8** 1 Kings 12.1-11 **30.9** Prov 29.21 **30.10** Job 16.9; Ps 112.10 **30.12** Sir 30.1; Deut 21.18-21 **30.15** Sir 18.19

n Lat: Gk *reproach from your family*; other ancient authorities lack this line
o Or *scolding from the household*
p This heading is included in the Gk text.
q Other ancient authorities lack this line and the preceding line
r Other ancient authorities lack this line
s Heb: Gk *take pains with him*

16 There is no wealth better
than health of body,
and no gladness above joy
of heart.
17 Death is better than a life of
misery,
and eternal sleep[t] than
chronic sickness.

CONCERNING FOODS[u]

18 Good things poured out
upon a mouth that is
closed
are like offerings of food
placed upon a grave.
19 Of what use to an idol is a
sacrifice?
For it can neither eat nor
smell.
So is the one punished by
the Lord;
20 he sees with his eyes and
groans
as a eunuch groans when
embracing a girl.[v]

21 Do not give yourself over to
sorrow,
and do not distress yourself
deliberately.
22 A joyful heart is life itself,
and rejoicing lengthens
one's life span.
23 Indulge yourself[w] and take
comfort,
and remove sorrow far from
you,
for sorrow has destroyed
many,
and no advantage ever
comes from it.
24 Jealousy and anger shorten
life,
and anxiety brings on
premature old age.
25 Those who are cheerful and
merry at table
will benefit from their
food.

Right Attitude toward Riches

31 Wakefulness over wealth
wastes away one's flesh,
and anxiety about it drives
away sleep.
2 Wakeful anxiety prevents
slumber,
and a severe illness carries
off sleep.[x]
3 The rich person toils to
amass a fortune,
and when he rests he fills
himself with his
dainties.
4 The poor person toils to
make a meager living,
and if ever he rests he
becomes needy.

5 One who loves gold will not
be justified;
one who pursues money
will be led astray[y] by
it.
6 Many have come to ruin
because of gold,
and their destruction has
met them face to face.
7 It is a stumbling block to
those who are avid for
it,
and every fool will be taken
captive by it.
8 Blessed is the rich person
who is found blameless,
and who does not go after
gold.
9 Who is he, that we may
praise him?
For he has done wonders
among his people.
10 Who has been tested by it
and been found
perfect?
Let it be for him a ground
for boasting.
Who has had the power to
transgress and did not
transgress,
and to do evil and did not
do it?
11 His prosperity will be
established,[z]
and the assembly will
proclaim his acts of
charity.

30.16 Prov 15.30; 16.24 **30.17** Job 3.11-13; Tob 3.6,13; Sir 47.19 **30.19** Ps 115.4-6; Isa 44.18; Bel 3 **30.20** Prov 5.11; Jer 22.23; Lam 1.4,11 **30.21** Sir 38.20; Mt 6.25; Phil 4.6 **30.22** Prov 15.13, 15,30; 17.22; Mt 6.27 **30.23** Ps 23.4; 119.50; Isa 51.3; Mt 5.4; Prov 15.13; 25.20; Lam 1.12 **30.24** Ps 106.16-18; Prov 27.4; Gal 5.19-21; 16.32; Sir 1.22 **31.1** Mt 6.25-31; Lk 12.22-26 **31.3** Lk 12.16-19 **31.5** Sir 13.8 **31.6** Prov 15.27; 1 Tim 6.10; Jas 5.1-5 **31.8** Gen 17.1; 24.34-35; 26.12-14; Job 1.1-5; Sir 13.24; Gen 14.21-23; 1 Tim 6.17-19 **31.10** Job 42.7-9; 1.22 **31.11** Gen 17.1-8; Job 42.10-17

[t] Other ancient authorities lack *eternal sleep* [u] This heading is included in the Gk text; other ancient authorities place the heading before verse 16 [v] Other ancient authorities add *So is the person who does right under compulsion* [w] Other ancient authorities read *Beguile yourself* [x] Other ancient authorities read *sleep carries off a severe illness* [y] Heb Syr: Gk *pursues destruction will be filled* [z] Other ancient authorities add *because of this*

Table Etiquette

12 Are you seated at the table
of the great?[a]
Do not be greedy at it,
and do not say, "How
much food there is
here!"
13 Remember that a greedy eye
is a bad thing.
What has been created
more greedy than the
eye?
Therefore it sheds tears for
any reason.
14 Do not reach out your hand
for everything you see,
and do not crowd your
neighbor[b] at the dish.
15 Judge your neighbor's
feelings by your own,
and in every matter be
thoughtful.
16 Eat what is set before you
like a well brought-up
person,[c]
and do not chew greedily,
or you will give offense.
17 Be the first to stop, as befits
good manners,
and do not be insatiable,
or you will give offense.
18 If you are seated among
many persons,
do not help yourself[d]
before they do.

19 How ample a little is for a
well-disciplined person!
He does not breathe
heavily when in bed.
20 Healthy sleep depends on
moderate eating;
he rises early, and feels fit.
The distress of sleeplessness
and of nausea
and colic are with the
glutton.
21 If you are overstuffed with
food,
get up to vomit, and you
will have relief.
22 Listen to me, my child, and
do not disregard me,
and in the end you will
appreciate my words.
In everything you do be
moderate,[e]
and no sickness will
overtake you.
23 People bless the one who is
liberal with food,
and their testimony to his
generosity is
trustworthy.
24 The city complains of the
one who is stingy with
food,
and their testimony to his
stinginess is accurate.

Temperance in Drinking Wine

25 Do not try to prove your
strength by
wine-drinking,
for wine has destroyed
many.
26 As the furnace tests the work
of the smith,[f]
so wine tests hearts when
the insolent quarrel.
27 Wine is very life to human
beings
if taken in moderation.
What is life to one who is
without wine?
It has been created to
make people happy.
28 Wine drunk at the proper
time and in moderation
is rejoicing of heart and
gladness of soul.
29 Wine drunk to excess leads
to bitterness of spirit,
to quarrels and stumbling.
30 Drunkenness increases the
anger of a fool to his
own hurt,
reducing his strength and
adding wounds.
31 Do not reprove your neighbor
at a banquet of wine,
and do not despise him in
his merrymaking;
speak no word of reproach to
him,
and do not distress him by
making demands of
him.

31.12 Sir 37.29 **31.13** 1 Sam 2.29, 32; Sir 14.9 **31.14** 1 Tim 3.8; Titus 1.7 **31.15** Mt 7.12; Lk 6.31; Gal 5.14 **31.16** 1 Cor 10.27; Sir 37.29 **31.17** Prov 23.20-21; Sir 23.6; 37.30-31 **31.18** Lk 14.7-11 **31.20** Prov 30.21-24; Sir 37.30 **31.22** Prov 4.1; 7.24; 23.22; 1 Cor 6.12 **31.23** Prov 11.25; 22.9; 1 Tim 6.18 **31.24** Prov 23.6; Sir 14.10 **31.25** Gen9.20-27; Prov 20.1; 23.29-34 **31.27** 1 Tim 3.8; 5.23; Ps 104.15; Eccl 10.19; Zech 9.17 **31.29** Prov 31.4-5; 23.29-30 **31.30** Prov 20.1; Isa 5.11-12

[a]Heb Syr: Gk *at a great table* [b]Gk *him* [c]Heb: Gk *like a human being* [d]Gk *reach out your hand* [e]Heb Syr: Gk *industrious* [f]Heb: Gk *tests the hardening of steel by dipping*

Etiquette at a Banquet

32 If they make you master of the feast, do not exalt yourself;
be among them as one of their number.
Take care of them first and then sit down;
2 when you have fulfilled all your duties, take your place,
so that you may be merry along with them
and receive a wreath for your excellent leadership.

3 Speak, you who are older, for it is your right,
but with accurate knowledge, and do not interrupt the music.
4 Where there is entertainment, do not pour out talk;
do not display your cleverness at the wrong time.
5 A ruby seal in a setting of gold
is a concert of music at a banquet of wine.
6 A seal of emerald in a rich setting of gold
is the melody of music with good wine.

7 Speak, you who are young, if you are obliged to,
but no more than twice, and only if asked.
8 Be brief; say much in few words;
be as one who knows and can still hold his tongue.
9 Among the great do not act as their equal;
and when another is speaking, do not babble.

10 Lightning travels ahead of the thunder,
and approval goes before one who is modest.

32.1 Lk 14.7-11 **32.2** Lk 17.7-10; 1 Cor 9.25 **32.6** Sir 40.20; 49.1 **32.7** Job 32.4-10 **32.8** Prov 10.19; Eccl 5.2 **32.9** Sir 7.14 **32.10** Job 36.29-33; Sir 26.15 **32.13** Ps 103.1-2, 22; 104.1-4; Tob 12.6, 17-18; Mal 3.10; Rom 12.6; Jas 1.17 **32.14** Prov 3.11-12; Sir 1.27; 6.8; Heb 12.5-11; Sir 39.5 **32.15** Sir 1.29; Mt 7.1-5 **32.17** Prov 5.12-14; Sir 21.6 **32.18** Sir 21.7,17, 21; 33.3; Prov 13.10; 2 Macc 1.28 **32.19** Prov 15.22; 20.18; Sir 37.16 **32.21** Mt 7.13 **32.22** Prov 2.20; 4.26

11 Leave in good time and do not be the last;
go home quickly and do not linger.
12 Amuse yourself there to your heart's content,
but do not sin through proud speech.
13 But above all bless your Maker,
who fills you with his good gifts.

The Providence of God

14 The one who seeks God[g] will accept his discipline,
and those who rise early to seek him[h] will find favor.
15 The one who seeks the law will be filled with it,
but the hypocrite will stumble at it.
16 Those who fear the Lord will form true judgments,
and they will kindle righteous deeds like a light.
17 The sinner will shun reproof,
and will find a decision according to his liking.

18 A sensible person will not overlook a thoughtful suggestion;
an insolent[i] and proud person will not be deterred by fear.[j]
19 Do nothing without deliberation,
but when you have acted, do not regret it.
20 Do not go on a path full of hazards,
and do not stumble at an obstacle twice.[k]
21 Do not be overconfident on a smooth[l] road,
22 and give good heed to your paths.[m]

[g] Heb: Gk *who fears the Lord*
[h] Other ancient authorities lack *to seek him*
[i] Heb: Gk *alien*
[j] Meaning of Gk uncertain. Other ancient authorities add *and after acting, with him, without deliberation*
[k] Heb: Gk *stumble on stony ground*
[l] Or *an unexplored*
[m] Heb Syr: Gk *and beware of your children*

23 Guard[n] yourself in every act,
for this is the keeping of the commandments.
24 The one who keeps the law preserves himself,[o]
and the one who trusts the Lord will not suffer loss.

33 No evil will befall the one who fears the Lord,
but in trials such a one will be rescued again and again.
2 The wise will not hate the law,
but the one who is hypocritical about it is like a boat in a storm.
3 The sensible person will trust in the law;
for such a one the law is as dependable as a divine oracle.

4 Prepare what to say, and then you will be listened to;
draw upon your training, and give your answer.
5 The heart of a fool is like a cart wheel,
and his thoughts like a turning axle.
6 A mocking friend is like a stallion
that neighs no matter who the rider is.

Differences in Nature and in Humankind

7 Why is one day more important than another,
when all the daylight in the year is from the sun?
8 By the Lord's wisdom they were distinguished,
and he appointed the different seasons and festivals.
9 Some days he exalted and hallowed,
and some he made ordinary days.
10 All human beings come from the ground,
and humankind[p] was created out of the dust.
11 In the fullness of his knowledge the Lord distinguished them
and appointed their different ways.
12 Some he blessed and exalted,
and some he made holy and brought near to himself;
but some he cursed and brought low,
and turned them out of their place.
13 Like clay in the hand of the potter,
to be molded as he pleases,
so all are in the hand of their Maker,
to be given whatever he decides.

14 Good is the opposite of evil,
and life the opposite of death;
so the sinner is the opposite of the godly.
15 Look at all the works of the Most High;
they come in pairs, one the opposite of the other.

16 Now I was the last to keep vigil;
I was like a gleaner following the grape-pickers;
17 by the blessing of the Lord I arrived first,
and like a grape-picker I filled my wine press.
18 Consider that I have not labored for myself alone,
but for all who seek instruction.
19 Hear me, you who are great among the people,
and you leaders of the congregation, pay heed!

32.23 Deut 4.2,40; 6.17; 1 Cor 7.19 **32.24** 1 Chr 28.9; Prov 4.4; 7.1-2 **33.1** Ps 91.9-14; Prov 12.21 **33.2** Eph 4.14; Jas 1.5-8 **33.3** Sir 32.18; Rom 3.2 **33.4** 1 Tim 2.14-15; 5.2-5 **33.5** Prov 26.14; Sir 22.9-10 **33.8** Gen 1.14; Ps 104.19; Ex 23.14-17; Lev 23.4-36; Deut 16.1- 15 **33.9** Ex 20.8-11; Lev 23.3 **33.10** Gen 2.7; Ps 103.14; Sir 17.32 **33.12** 1 Sam 2.7-8; Ps 75.7; Lk 1.51-53 **33.13** Isa 29.16; 45.8; Jer 18.4-6; Wis 15.7-8; Prov 16.1,9 **33.14** Deut 30.15, 19; Ps 1.6 **33.15** Gen 1.27; 7.3,9; Sir 42.24 **33.16** Lev 19.10; Deut 24.21 **33.19** Heb 13.7,17

[n] Heb Syr: Gk *Trust* [o] Heb: Gk *who believes the law heeds the commandments*
[p] Heb: Gk *Adam*

The Advantage of Independence

20 To son or wife, to brother or friend,
do not give power over yourself, as long as you live;
and do not give your property to another,
in case you change your mind and must ask for it.
21 While you are still alive and have breath in you,
do not let anyone take your place.
22 For it is better that your children should ask from you
than that you should look to the hand of your children.
23 Excel in all that you do;
bring no stain upon your honor.
24 At the time when you end the days of your life,
in the hour of death, distribute your inheritance.

The Treatment of Slaves

25 Fodder and a stick and burdens for a donkey;
bread and discipline and work for a slave.
26 Set your slave to work, and you will find rest;
leave his hands idle, and he will seek liberty.
27 Yoke and thong will bow the neck,
and for a wicked slave there are racks and tortures.
28 Put him to work, in order that he may not be idle,
29 for idleness teaches much evil.
30 Set him to work, as is fitting for him,
and if he does not obey, make his fetters heavy.
Do not be overbearing toward anyone,
and do nothing unjust.
31 If you have but one slave, treat him like yourself,
because you have bought him with blood.
If you have but one slave, treat him like a brother,
for you will need him as you need your life.
32 If you ill-treat him, and he leaves you and runs away,
33 which way will you go to seek him?

Dreams Mean Nothing

34 The senseless have vain and false hopes,
and dreams give wings to fools.
2 As one who catches at a shadow and pursues the wind,
so is anyone who believes in[q] dreams.
3 What is seen in dreams is but a reflection,
the likeness of a face looking at itself.
4 From an unclean thing what can be clean?
And from something false what can be true?
5 Divinations and omens and dreams are unreal,
and like a woman in labor, the mind has fantasies.
6 Unless they are sent by intervention from the Most High,
pay no attention to them.
7 For dreams have deceived many,
and those who put their hope in them have perished.
8 Without such deceptions the law will be fulfilled,
and wisdom is complete in the mouth of the faithful.

Experience as a Teacher

9 An educated[r] person knows many things,

33.21 Ezek 37.5-10; Acts 17.25 **33.22** Prov 19.14; 2 Cor 12.14 **33.24** Prov 13.22; Lk 15.12 **33.25** Lk 7.8; 17.7-9; Eph 6.5-6 **33.28** Sir 37.11; Mt 20.3,6 **33.29** Prov 6.6-11; 26.13-15; Sir 22.1-2

33.31 Ex 21.2; Deut 15.12; Lev 25.43,46, 53; Eph 6.9; Col 4.1 **33.32** Philem 11-16 **34.2** Eccl 1.14; Hos 12.1; Deut 13.1-3; Eccl 5.7; Jer 29.8 **34.4** Job 14.4 **34.5** Deut 18,9-14; Rev 18.23 **34.6** Gen 37.5-9; 41.1-32; Dan 2.27-45 **34.7** Jer 23.25-28; 29.8; 2 Esd 10.36 **34.8** Mt 5.17 **34.9** Eccl 1.12-17; Sir 4.24; 21.21

q Syr: Gk *pays heed to*
r Other ancient authorities read *A traveled*

and one with much
experience knows what
he is talking about.
10 An inexperienced person
knows few things,
11 but he that has traveled
acquires much
cleverness.
12 I have seen many things in
my travels,
and I understand more
than I can express.
13 I have often been in danger
of death,
but have escaped because
of these experiences.

Fear the Lord

14 The spirit of those who fear
the Lord will live,
15 for their hope is in him
who saves them.
16 Those who fear the Lord will
not be timid,
or play the coward, for he
is their hope.
17 Happy is the soul that fears
the Lord!
18 To whom does he look?
And who is his support?
19 The eyes of the Lord are on
those who love him,
a mighty shield and strong
support,
a shelter from scorching
wind and a shade from
noonday sun,
a guard against stumbling
and a help against
falling.
20 He lifts up the soul and
makes the eyes sparkle;
he gives health and life and
blessing.

Offering Sacrifices

21 If one sacrifices ill-gotten
goods, the offering is
blemished;[s]
22 the gifts[t] of the lawless
are not acceptable.
23 The Most High is not
pleased with the
offerings of the
ungodly,

34.12 Eccl 3.10; 7.15
34.13 2 Cor 4.8-10; 11.23,26-27
34.15 Ps 33.18-19; 119.166; 130.7
34.17 Sir 51.29
34.19 Ps 33.18; 34.15; Sir 15.19; Gen 15.1; Deut 33.29; Ps 115.9-11; 61.4; 91.1; Isa 25.4; Ps 121.5-6
34.20 Ps 40.1-3; 42.5,11; 103.2-5; Acts 17.25; Jas 1.17
34.23 1 Sam 5.22; Ps 51.16-19; Prov 15.8; Jer 6.20; Isa 1.11- 14; Mic 6.7
34.24 Am 5.21-24
34.25 Ex 22.26-27; Deut 24.12-15
34.28 Eccl 3.3
34.30 Num 9.6,10; 19.11-22
34.31 1 Kings 21.27; Neh 9.1; Jon 3.6-9; Ps 66.18-19; Isa 1.15; 59.2-3; Jn 9.31
35.1 Ex 20.22-24; Deut 12.6-12
35.3 Num 15.4,6, 9; 28.5,9

nor for a multitude of
sacrifices does he
forgive sins.
24 Like one who kills a son
before his father's eyes
is the person who offers a
sacrifice from the
property of the poor.
25 The bread of the needy is
the life of the poor;
whoever deprives them of it
is a murderer.
26 To take away a neighbor's
living is to commit
murder;
27 to deprive an employee of
wages is to shed blood.

28 When one builds and
another tears down,
what do they gain but hard
work?
29 When one prays and another
curses,
to whose voice will the
Lord listen?
30 If one washes after touching
a corpse, and touches it
again,
what has been gained by
washing?
31 So if one fasts for his sins,
and goes again and does
the same things,
who will listen to his prayer?
And what has he gained by
humbling himself?

The Law and Sacrifices

35 The one who keeps the
law makes many
offerings;
2 one who heeds the
commandments makes
an offering of
well-being.
3 The one who returns a
kindness offers choice
flour,
4 and one who gives alms
sacrifices a thank
offering.
5 To keep from wickedness is
pleasing to the Lord,

[s] Other ancient authorities read *is made in mockery* [t] Other ancient authorities read *mockeries*

and to forsake
unrighteousness is an
atonement.
6 Do not appear before the
Lord empty-handed,
7 for all that you offer is in
fulfillment of the
commandment.
8 The offering of the righteous
enriches the altar,
and its pleasing odor rises
before the Most High.
9 The sacrifice of the righteous
is acceptable,
and it will never be
forgotten.
10 Be generous when you
worship the Lord,
and do not stint the first
fruits of your hands.
11 With every gift show a
cheerful face,
and dedicate your tithe
with gladness.
12 Give to the Most High as he
has given to you,
and as generously as you
can afford.
13 For the Lord is the one who
repays,
and he will repay you
sevenfold.

Divine Justice

14 Do not offer him a bribe, for
he will not accept it;
15 and do not rely on a
dishonest sacrifice;
for the Lord is the judge,
and with him there is no
partiality.
16 He will not show partiality to
the poor;
but he will listen to the
prayer of one who is
wronged.
17 He will not ignore the
supplication of the
orphan,
or the widow when she
pours out her
complaint.
18 Do not the tears of the
widow run down her
cheek
19 as she cries out against the
one who causes them
to fall?

35.6 Ex 23.15; 34.20; Deut 16.16; 1 Cor 16.2 **35.8** Lev 1.9,13, 17; 23.13,18; Num 15.3,7, 10 **35.9** Ps 51.17; Prov 21.3; Jer 6.19-20 **35.10** Deut 15.7,10; Prov 3.9; Rom 12.8 **35.11** Ex 35.21-22; 2 Cor 9.7 **35.12** 1 Cor 16.2 **35.13** Deut 15.4; Mal 3.8-10; 2 Cor 9.10 **35.14** Ex 23.8; Deut 10.17; Eccl 7.7 **35.15** Deut 10.17; Job 34.19; Acts 10.34; Gal 2.6 **35.16** Ex 23.3; Lev 19.15; Ps 34.6; 40.17; Sir 21.5 **35.17** Ex 22.22; Deut 10.18; Ps 146.9 **35.19** Lk 18.1-5

35.20 Ps 66.18-19; Isa 1.15-16; Jn 9.31 **35.22** Mt 16.27; Lk 18.7; Deut 7.10; Dan 9.19 **35.23** Deut 32.35, 41,43; Ps 94.1; 149.7; 2.9; Isa 14.5; Jer 48.17 **35.24** Ps 62.12; Mt 16.27; 2 Cor 5.10; 2 Tim 4.14 **35.25** Ps 67.4; 96.13; Rev 19.11 **35.26** Ps 103.8; 119.156;

20 The one whose service is
pleasing to the Lord
will be accepted,
and his prayer will reach to
the clouds.
21 The prayer of the humble
pierces the clouds,
and it will not rest until it
reaches its goal;
it will not desist until the
Most High responds
22 and does justice for the
righteous, and executes
judgment.
Indeed, the Lord will not
delay,
and like a warrior[u] will not
be patient
until he crushes the loins of
the unmerciful
23 and repays vengeance on
the nations;
until he destroys the
multitude of the
insolent,
and breaks the scepters of
the unrighteous;
24 until he repays mortals
according to their
deeds,
and the works of all
according to their
thoughts;
25 until he judges the case of
his people
and makes them rejoice in
his mercy.
26 His mercy is as welcome in
time of distress
as clouds of rain in time of
drought.

A Prayer for God's People

36 Have mercy upon us,
O God[v] of all,
2 and put all the nations in
fear of you.
3 Lift up your hand against
foreign nations
and let them see your
might.

Isa 55.7; Lk 1.50,54 **36.1** Ps 25.6; 51.1; Add Esth 13.17 **36.3** Ps 7.6; 77.14; 145.6; Jer 16.21

[u] Heb: Gk *and with them*
[v] Heb: Gk *O Master, the God*

4 As you have used us to show
your holiness to them,
so use them to show your
glory to us.
5 Then they will know,[w] as we
have known
that there is no God but
you, O Lord.
6 Give new signs, and work
other wonders;
7 make your hand and right
arm glorious.
8 Rouse your anger and pour
out your wrath;
9 destroy the adversary and
wipe out the enemy.
10 Hasten the day, and
remember the
appointed time,[x]
and let people recount your
mighty deeds.
11 Let survivors be consumed in
the fiery wrath,
and may those who harm
your people meet
destruction.
12 Crush the heads of hostile
rulers
who say, "There is no one
but ourselves."
13 Gather all the tribes of
Jacob,[y]
16 and give them their
inheritance, as at the
beginning.
17 Have mercy, O Lord, on the
people called by your
name,
on Israel, whom you have
named[z] your firstborn,
18 Have pity on the city of your
sanctuary,[a]
Jerusalem, the place of
your dwelling.[b]
19 Fill Zion with your majesty,[c]
and your temple[d] with
your glory.
20 Bear witness to those whom
you created in the
beginning,
and fulfill the prophecies
spoken in your name.
21 Reward those who wait for
you
and let your prophets be
found trustworthy.
22 Hear, O Lord, the prayer of
your servants, according
to your goodwill
toward[e] your people,
and all who are on the earth
will know
that you are the Lord, the
God of the ages.

Concerning Discrimination

23 The stomach will take any
food,
yet one food is better than
another.
24 As the palate tastes the
kinds of game,
so an intelligent mind
detects false words.
25 A perverse mind will cause
grief,
but a person with
experience will pay him
back.
26 A woman will accept any
man as a husband,
but one girl is preferable to
another.
27 A woman's beauty lights up
a man's face,
and there is nothing he
desires more.
28 If kindness and humility
mark her speech,
her husband is more
fortunate than other
men.
29 He who acquires a wife gets
his best possession,[f]
a helper fit for him and a
pillar of support.[g]
30 Where there is no fence, the
property will be
plundered;

36.4 Ezek 20.41; 28.25 **36.5** Isa 44.6; 45.14,22; 1 Cor 8.4 **36.6** Deut 4.34; 26.8; Ps 135.9; Acts 2.22,43 **36.8** Ps 7.6; 79.6; Jer 7.20 **36.10** Ps 7.6; Ezek 22.4; Dan 8.19 **36.11** Ps 9.3-6; 71.24; 143.12 **36.13** Jer 23.3; 29.14; 31.10 **36.16** Ps 78.71; Wis 24.8; Sir 44.21 **36.17** Sir 36.1; Jer 31.9; 2 Esd 6.58 **36.18** Deut 16.2,6, 11; Ezra 7.15; Ps 76.2; Joel 3.17 **36.19** Ex 40.30; 2 Chr 7.1 **36.20** Gen 1.1; Isa 43.1,7; 45.12; 2 Chr 36.21; Acts 3.18; Rom 15.8 **36.21** Sir 2.7-8; 1 Cor 4.2; Sir 46.15 **36.22** Ps 83.18; Ezek 36.23, 36; 39.7 **36.23** 1 Cor 6.13 **36.25** Prov 10.1; 17.25; Sir 22.4 **36.26** Sir 7.25; Prov 21.9,19; 25.24 **36.27** Song 1.5, 15-16; 4.1,7; Sir 26.16 **36.28** Prov 31.28-30 **36.29** Sir 7.19; Gen 2.18; 1 Cor 11.9

[w] Heb: Gk *And let them know you*
[x] Other ancient authorities read *remember your oath*
[y] Owing to a dislocation in the Greek Mss of Sirach, the verse numbers 14 and 15 are not used in chapter 36, though no text is missing.
[z] Other ancient authorities read *you have likened to*
[a] Or *on your holy city*
[b] Heb: Gk *your rest*
[c] Heb Syr: Gk *the celebration of your wondrous deeds*
[d] Heb Syr: Gk Lat *people*
[e] Heb and two Gk witnesses: Lat and most Gk witnesses read *according to the blessing of Aaron for*
[f] Heb: Gk *enters upon a possession*
[g] Heb: Gk *rest*

and where there is no wife,
a man will become a
fugitive and a
wanderer.[h]
31 For who will trust a nimble
robber
that skips from city to city?
So who will trust a man that
has no nest,
but lodges wherever night
overtakes him?

False Friends

37 Every friend says, "I too
am a friend";
but some friends are
friends only in name.
2 Is it not a sorrow like that
for death itself
when a dear friend turns
into an enemy?
3 O inclination to evil, why
were you formed
to cover the land with
deceit?
4 Some companions rejoice in
the happiness of a
friend,
but in time of trouble they
are against him.
5 Some companions help a
friend for their
stomachs' sake,
yet in battle they will carry
his shield.
6 Do not forget a friend during
the battle,[i]
and do not be unmindful
of him when you
distribute your spoils.[j]

Caution in Taking Advice

7 All counselors praise the
counsel they give,
but some give counsel in
their own interest.
8 Be wary of a counselor,
and learn first what is his
interest,
for he will take thought for
himself.
He may cast the lot against
you
9 and tell you, "Your way is
good,"
and then stand aside to see
what happens to you.

37.1 Sir 6.8-12 **37.2** Ps 41.8-9; Sir 27.16-21; Lk 22.48; Jn 13.21-26 **37.4** Sir 6.9; 12.9; 20.22 **37.6** Sir 6.13 **37.7** Prov 1.25,30; Dan 4.27; Sir 6.23

37.10 Prov 6.34; 27.24-25; 27.4 **37.11** Sir 22.1-2; Prov 12.5; Sir 19.22 **37.12** Sir 6.35; 27.11; 43.33 **37.13** Rom 2.14-15 **37.15** Ps 57.2; Dan 4.34; Sir 39.5; Prov 3.5-6; 2 Thess 3.5; Jdt 12.8 **37.16** Prov 15.22; 20.18; Sir 32.19

10 Do not consult the one who
regards you with
suspicion;
hide your intentions from
those who are jealous
of you.
11 Do not consult with a
woman about her rival
or with a coward about
war,
with a merchant about
business
or with a buyer about
selling,
with a miser about
generosity[k]
or with the merciless about
kindness,
with an idler about any work
or with a seasonal laborer
about completing his
work,
with a lazy servant about a
big task—
pay no attention to any
advice they give.
12 But associate with a godly
person
whom you know to be a
keeper of the
commandments,
who is like-minded with
yourself,
and who will grieve with
you if you fail.
13 And heed[l] the counsel of
your own heart,
for no one is more faithful
to you than it is.
14 For our own mind
sometimes keeps us
better informed
than seven sentinels sitting
high on a watchtower.
15 But above all pray to the
Most High
that he may direct your
way in truth.

True and False Wisdom

16 Discussion is the beginning
of every work,
and counsel precedes every
undertaking.

[h]Heb: Gk *wander about and sigh*
[i]Heb: Gk *in your heart* [j]Heb: Gk *him in your wealth* [k]Heb: Gk *gratitude*
[l]Heb: Gk *establish*

17 The mind is the root of all
conduct;
18 it sprouts four branches,[m]
good and evil, life and death;
and it is the tongue that
continually rules them.
19 Some people may be clever
enough to teach many,
and yet be useless to
themselves.
20 A skillful speaker may be
hated;
he will be destitute of all
food,
21 for the Lord has withheld the
gift of charm,
since he is lacking in all
wisdom.
22 If a person is wise to his own
advantage,
the fruits of his good sense
will be praiseworthy.[n]
23 A wise person instructs his
own people,
and the fruits of his good
sense will endure.
24 A wise person will have
praise heaped upon
him,
and all who see him will
call him happy.
25 The days of a person's life
are numbered,
but the days of Israel are
without number.
26 One who is wise among his
people will inherit
honor,[o]
and his name will live
forever.

Concerning Moderation

27 My child, test yourself while
you live;
see what is bad for you and
do not give in to it.
28 For not everything is good
for everyone,
and no one enjoys
everything.
29 Do not be greedy for every
delicacy,
and do not eat without
restraint;
30 for overeating brings
sickness,
and gluttony leads to
nausea.
31 Many have died of gluttony,
but the one who guards
against it prolongs his
life.

37.17 Prov 4.23 **37.18** Sir 23.7; 28.26; Jas 3.5-12 **37.19** Jas 3.1-2 **37.22** 2 Esd 8.48 **37.23** Ps 32.8; Prov 1.2-6; 8.33 **37.24** Prov 31.30; Sir 39.9; 44.15 **37.25** Ps 90.10; Eccl 12.2-7; Sir 41.13; Gen 17.7 **37.26** Sir 15.6; 41.13 **37.28** 1 Cor 6.12; 10.23 **37.29** Sir 31.12 **37.30** Prov 23.21; Sir 23.6; 31.17,20; 4 Macc 1.3

Concerning Physicians and Health

38 Honor physicians for their
services,
for the Lord created them;
2 for their gift of healing
comes from the Most
High,
and they are rewarded by
the king.
3 The skill of physicians makes
them distinguished,
and in the presence of the
great they are admired.
4 The Lord created medicines
out of the earth,
and the sensible will not
despise them.
5 Was not water made sweet
with a tree
in order that its[p] power
might be known?
6 And he gave skill to human
beings
that he[q] might be glorified
in his marvelous works.
7 By them the physician[r]
heals and takes away
pain;
8 the pharmacist makes a
mixture from them.
God's[s] works will never be
finished;
and from him health[t]
spreads over all the
earth.
9 My child, when you are ill,
do not delay,
but pray to the Lord, and
he will heal you.
10 Give up your faults and
direct your hands
rightly,

38.1 Sir 38.12 **38.2** Mt 10.8; Mk 16.18; Acts 3.16; 1 Cor 12.9,28 **38.5** Ex 15.25 **38.6** Ex 31.1-6; 35.30-36.1 **38.8** Jn 5.17; 14.10 **38.9** Ps 6.2; 41.4; Jas 5.14-16 **38.10** Sir 20.3; Ps 51.2; Acts 22.16; 2 Cor 7.1; 1 Jn 1.9

[m] Heb: Gk *As a clue to changes of heart four kinds of destiny appear*
[n] Other ancient witnesses read *trustworthy*
[o] Other ancient authorities read *confidence*
[p] Or *his* [q] Or *they* [r] Heb: Gk *he*
[s] Gk *His* [t] Or *peace*

and cleanse your heart
from all sin.
11 Offer a sweet-smelling
sacrifice, and a
memorial portion of
choice flour,
and pour oil on your
offering, as much as
you can afford.[u]
12 Then give the physician his
place, for the Lord
created him;
do not let him leave you,
for you need him.
13 There may come a time
when recovery lies in
the hands of
physicians,[v]
14 for they too pray to the
Lord
that he grant them success
in diagnosis[w]
and in healing, for the sake
of preserving life.
15 He who sins against his
Maker,
will be defiant toward the
physician.[x]

On Mourning for the Dead

16 My child, let your tears fall
for the dead,
and as one in great pain
begin the lament.
Lay out the body with due
ceremony,
and do not neglect the
burial.
17 Let your weeping be bitter
and your wailing
fervent;
make your mourning
worthy of the departed,
for one day, or two, to avoid
criticism;
then be comforted for your
grief.
18 For grief may result in death,
and a sorrowful heart saps
one's strength.
19 When a person is taken
away, sorrow is over;
but the life of the poor
weighs down the heart.
20 Do not give your heart to
grief;
drive it away, and
remember your own
end.
21 Do not forget, there is no
coming back;
you do the dead[y] no good,
and you injure yourself.
22 Remember his[z] fate, for
yours is like it;
yesterday it was his,[a] and
today it is yours.
23 When the dead is at rest, let
his remembrance rest
too,
and be comforted for him
when his spirit has
departed.

Trades and Crafts

24 The wisdom of the scribe
depends on the
opportunity of leisure;
only the one who has little
business can become
wise.
25 How can one become wise
who handles the plow,
and who glories in the
shaft of a goad,
who drives oxen and is
occupied with their
work,
and whose talk is about
bulls?
26 He sets his heart on plowing
furrows,
and he is careful about
fodder for the heifers.
27 So too is every artisan and
master artisan
who labors by night as well
as by day;
those who cut the signets of
seals,
each is diligent in making
a great variety;
they set their heart on
painting a lifelike
image,
and they are careful to
finish their work.
28 So too is the smith, sitting
by the anvil,

38.11 Lev 2.1-7; 14.10,21-22 **38.12** Sir 38.1 **38.13** Mt 9.12; Lk 10.34; Col 4.14 **38.16** 2 Sam 1.11-12; Sir 22.11; Jn 11.33-35; 1 Sam 31.13; Eccl 6.3; Tob 1.17-18; 12.12-13 **38.17** Jer 13.17; Lam 1.2; Gen 24.67; Ps 86.17; Isa 49.13; Mt 5.4 **38.18** Prov 15.13; 17.22 **38.20** Sir 30.21 **38.21** 2 Sam 12.22-33; Eccl 12.7; Lk 16.27-31 **38.22** Eccl 3.19-20; 6.6,12 **38.24** Prov 1.20-23; Eccl 1.13,17; 3.10-13 **38.25** 1 Kings 19.19-21; Lk 9.61-62 **38.27** Ex 31.1-6; 35.30-36.1; 2 Chr 2.7-8; Sir 9.17; Ex 28.36; 39.6; Hag 2.23 **38.28** Prov 25.4; Isa 54.16

[u]Heb: Lat lacks *as much as you can afford*; Meaning of Gk uncertain [v]Gk *in their hands* [w]Heb: Gk *rest* [x]Heb: Gk *may he fall into the hands of the physician* [y]Gk *him* [z]Heb: Gk *my* [a]Heb: Gk *mine*

intent on his iron-work;
the breath of the fire melts his flesh,
and he struggles with the heat of the furnace;
the sound of the hammer deafens his ears,[b]
and his eyes are on the pattern of the object.
He sets his heart on finishing his handiwork,
and he is careful to complete its decoration.

29 So too is the potter sitting at his work
and turning the wheel with his feet;
he is always deeply concerned over his products,
and he produces them in quantity.
30 He molds the clay with his arm
and makes it pliable with his feet;
he sets his heart to finish the glazing,
and he takes care in firing[c] the kiln.

31 All these rely on their hands,
and all are skillful in their own work.
32 Without them no city can be inhabited,
and wherever they live, they will not go hungry.[d]
Yet they are not sought out for the council of the people,[e]
33 nor do they attain eminence in the public assembly.
They do not sit in the judge's seat,
nor do they understand the decisions of the courts;
they cannot expound discipline or judgment,
and they are not found among the rulers.[f]
34 But they maintain the fabric of the world,
and their concern is for[g] the exercise of their trade.

38.29 Isa 45.9; Jer 18.1-6; Sir 33.13
38.31 Prov 22.29
38.32 Mt 10.10; 2 Thess 3.6-12; 1 Tim 5.18
38.34 1 Kings 7.13; 2 Chr 2.13-14; 4.11-18
39.1 Ezra 7.12; Neh 8.13; Isa 34.17; Acts 17.11
39.2 Prov 25.1
39.3 Eccl 12.9; Wis 8.8; Mk 4.11
39.4 Prov 8.14-16; Dan 2.17-47; Eccl 1.14; 2.9-11
39.5 Ps 92.1-2; Wis 6.14; Sir 32.14; 37.15; Ps 51.1-7; Mt 6.12
39.6 1 Kings 3.6-14; Isa 11.1-3; 1 Kings 4.29; Prov 1.1-6
39.7 Wis 7.7; Sir 1.1; Jas 1.5; Ps 1.2; 119.15,48
39.9 Sir 37.24; Prov 10.7; Sir 45.1; 49.13

The Activity of the Scribe

How different the one who devotes himself
to the study of the law of the Most High!

39 He seeks out the wisdom of all the ancients,
and is concerned with prophecies;
2 he preserves the sayings of the famous
and penetrates the subtleties of parables;
3 he seeks out the hidden meanings of proverbs
and is at home with the obscurities of parables.
4 He serves among the great
and appears before rulers;
he travels in foreign lands
and learns what is good and evil in the human lot.
5 He sets his heart to rise early
to seek the Lord who made him,
and to petition the Most High;
he opens his mouth in prayer
and asks pardon for his sins.

6 If the great Lord is willing,
he will be filled with the spirit of understanding;
he will pour forth words of wisdom of his own
and give thanks to the Lord in prayer.
7 The Lord[h] will direct his counsel and knowledge,
as he meditates on his mysteries.
8 He will show the wisdom of what he has learned,
and will glory in the law of the Lord's covenant.
9 Many will praise his understanding;
it will never be blotted out.
His memory will not disappear,

[b] Cn: Gk *renews his ear* [c] Cn: Gk *cleaning* [d] Syr: Gk *and people can neither live nor walk there* [e] Most ancient authorities lack this line [f] Cn: Gk *among parables* [g] Syr: Gk *prayer is in* [h] Gk *He himself*

and his name will live
through all generations.
10 Nations will speak of his
wisdom,
and the congregation will
proclaim his praise.
11 If he lives long, he will leave
a name greater than a
thousand,
and if he goes to rest, it is
enough[i] for him.

A Hymn of Praise to God

12 I have more on my mind to
express;
I am full like the full
moon.
13 Listen to me, my faithful
children, and blossom
like a rose growing by a
stream of water.
14 Send out fragrance like
incense,
and put forth blossoms like
a lily.
Scatter the fragrance, and
sing a hymn of praise;
bless the Lord for all his
works.
15 Ascribe majesty to his name
and give thanks to him
with praise,
with songs on your lips, and
with harps;
this is what you shall say
in thanksgiving:

16 "All the works of the Lord
are very good,
and whatever he
commands will be done
at the appointed time.
17 No one can say, 'What is
this?' or 'Why is
that?'—
for at the appointed time
all such questions will
be answered.
At his word the waters stood
in a heap,
and the reservoirs of water
at the word of his
mouth.
18 When he commands, his
every purpose is
fulfilled,

and none can limit his
saving power.
19 The works of all are before
him,
and nothing can be hidden
from his eyes.
20 From the beginning to the
end of time he can see
everything,
and nothing is too
marvelous for him.
21 No one can say, 'What is
this?' or 'Why is
that?'—
for everything has been
created for its own
purpose.

22 "His blessing covers the dry
land like a river,
and drenches it like a
flood.
23 But his wrath drives out the
nations,
as when he turned a
watered land into salt.
24 To the faithful his ways are
straight,
but full of pitfalls for the
wicked.
25 From the beginning good
things were created for
the good,
but for sinners good things
and bad.[j]
26 The basic necessities of
human life
are water and fire and iron
and salt
and wheat flour and milk
and honey,
the blood of the grape and
oil and clothing.
27 All these are good for the
godly,
but for sinners they turn
into evils.

28 "There are winds created for
vengeance,
and in their anger they can
dislodge mountains;[k]
on the day of reckoning they
will pour out their
strength

39.10 1 Kings 4.31, 34; 10.1,6-7
39.14 Sir 24.15-18; Ps 92.1; 96.1; 98.1; 103.1-5; Tob 8.15-17; 12.6; 13.17
39.15 Ps 68.34; 93.1; 104.1; Tob 13.8;2 Sam 6.5; 1 Chr 15.16, 20; Neh 12.27
39.16 Gen 1.31; Ps 104.24; Job 42.2; Prov 19.21; Eccl 3.11
39.17 Gen 1.6-10; Ex 14.21-22; Josh 3.16
39.18 Ps 33.9; 148.5; Eph 1.11
39.19 Ps 33.18; Sir 15.19; 42.20
39.21 Sir 39.17; Ps 138.8; Prov 16.4; Eccl 3.1
39.22 Ezek 34.26
39.23 Ex 23.27-31; 34.11-14; Deut 11.23; Gen 19.24-28; Jer 48.9
39.25 Gen 1.31; 2.16-17
39.26 Sir 29.21
39.28 Ps 18.7; Jer 4.23-26; Ezek 38.19-20; Rev 6.14-17

[i] Cn: Meaning of Gk uncertain [j] Heb Lat: Gk *sinners bad things* [k] Heb Syr: Gk *can scourge mightily*

and calm the anger of their
Maker.

29 Fire and hail and famine and
pestilence,
all these have been created
for vengeance;

30 the fangs of wild animals
and scorpions and
vipers,
and the sword that
punishes the ungodly
with destruction.

31 They take delight in doing
his bidding,
always ready for his service
on earth;
and when their time comes
they never disobey his
command."

32 So from the beginning I have
been convinced of all
this
and have thought it out
and left it in writing:

33 All the works of the Lord are
good,
and he will supply every
need in its time.

34 No one can say, "This is not
as good as that,"
for everything proves good
in its appointed time.

35 So now sing praise with all
your heart and voice,
and bless the name of the
Lord.

Human Wretchedness

40 Hard work was created for
everyone,
and a heavy yoke is laid on
the children of Adam,
from the day they come forth
from their mother's
womb
until the day they return
to[l] the mother of all
the living.[m]

2 Perplexities and fear of heart
are theirs,
and anxious thought of the
day of their death.

3 From the one who sits on a
splendid throne
to the one who grovels in
dust and ashes,

39.29 2 Sam 24.10-17; Rev 8.7
39.30 Num 21.4-6; Deut 8.15; Rev 9.7-10
39.31 Ps 147.15-18; 148.7-10
39.33 Gen 1.31; Sir 39.16; Job 42.2; Prov 19.21; Eccl 3.11
39.35 Ps 86.12; 111.1
40.1 Gen 3.17; Job 7.1; Eccl 2.23; Gen 3.19; Eccl 12.7
40.2 Eccl 2.20-21; 8.7-8; 12.1-6
40.4 Eccl 3.19-21; 8.8
40.5 Ps 6.5-7; Isa 38.15
40.9 Sir 39.28-31
40.10 Gen 6.1-7, 11-13
40.11 Gen 3.19; Eccl 12.7; Sir 16.30
40.12 Prov 22.8; Tob 14.7,11
40.13 Ps 73.18-20

4 from the one who wears
purple and a crown
to the one who is clothed
in burlap,

5 there is anger and envy and
trouble and unrest,
and fear of death, and fury
and strife.
And when one rests upon his
bed,
his sleep at night confuses
his mind.

6 He gets little or no rest;
he struggles in his sleep as
he did by day.[n]
He is troubled by the visions
of his mind
like one who has escaped
from the battlefield.

7 At the moment he reaches
safety he wakes up,
astonished that his fears
were groundless.

8 To all creatures, human and
animal,
but to sinners seven times
more,

9 come death and bloodshed
and strife and sword,
calamities and famine and
ruin and plague.

10 All these were created for
the wicked,
and on their account the
flood came.

11 All that is of earth returns to
earth,
and what is from above
returns above.[o]

Injustice Will Not Prosper

12 All bribery and injustice will
be blotted out,
but good faith will last
forever.

13 The wealth of the unjust will
dry up like a river,
and crash like a loud clap
of thunder in a storm.

14 As a generous person has
cause to rejoice,
so lawbreakers will utterly
fail.

[l] Other Gk and Lat authorities read *are buried in* [m] Heb: Gk *of all* [n] Arm: Meaning of Gk uncertain [o] Heb Syr: Gk Lat *from the waters returns to the sea*

15 The children of the ungodly
put out few branches;
they are unhealthy roots on
sheer rock.
16 The reeds by any water or
river bank
are plucked up before any
grass;
17 but kindness is like a garden
of blessings,
and almsgiving endures
forever.

The Joys of Life

18 Wealth and wages make life
sweet,[p]
but better than either is
finding a treasure.
19 Children and the building of
a city establish one's
name,
but better than either is
the one who finds
wisdom.
Cattle and orchards make
one prosperous;[q]
but a blameless wife is
accounted better than
either.
20 Wine and music gladden the
heart,
but the love of friends[r] is
better than either.
21 The flute and the harp make
sweet melody,
but a pleasant voice is
better than either.
22 The eye desires grace and
beauty,
but the green shoots of
grain more than either.
23 A friend or companion is
always welcome,
but a sensible wife[s] is
better than either.
24 Kindred and helpers are for a
time of trouble,
but almsgiving rescues
better than either.
25 Gold and silver make one
stand firm,
but good counsel is
esteemed more than
either.
26 Riches and strength build up
confidence,
but the fear of the Lord is
better than either.
There is no want in the fear
of the Lord,
and with it there is no
need to seek for help.
27 The fear of the Lord is like a
garden of blessing,
and covers a person better
than any glory.

The Disgrace of Begging

28 My child, do not lead the life
of a beggar;
it is better to die than to
beg.
29 When one looks to the table
of another,
one's way of life cannot be
considered a life.
One loses self-respect with
another person's food,
but one who is intelligent
and well instructed
guards against that.
30 In the mouth of the
shameless begging is
sweet,
but it kindles a fire inside
him.

Concerning Death

41 O death, how bitter is the
thought of you
to the one at peace among
possessions,
who has nothing to worry
about and is prosperous
in everything,
and still is vigorous enough
to enjoy food!
2 O death, how welcome is
your sentence
to one who is needy and
failing in strength,
worn down by age and
anxious about
everything;
to one who is contrary, and
has lost all patience!
3 Do not fear death's decree
for you;

40.15 Wis 4.4; Sir 41.5-10; Mt 13.5; Mk 4.5
40.17 Tob 4.10-11; Sir 17.22; 40.24
40.18 Mt 13.44-46
40.19 Prov 3.13; Sir 25.10; Prov 19.14
40.20 Ps 104.15; Sir 31.27-28; 32.5-6; 49.1; Prov 18.24; Sir 6.14-16
40.22 Mt 6.28-29
40.23 Prov 18.22; 19.14
40.24 Sir 40.17
40.25 Prov 15.22; Sir 21.13
40.26 Ps 33.18-19; 34.9; 103.13, 17
40.28 Sir 18.33
40.29 Sir 29.23-24
41.1 Lk 12.13-21
41.2 Job 3.11-13; Sir 30.17; 1 Kings 19.4
41.3 Sir 38.20-23

[p]Heb: Gk *Life is sweet for the self-reliant worker* [q]Heb Syr: Gk lacks *but better . . . prosperous* [r]Heb: Gk *wisdom* [s]Heb Compare Syr: Gk *wife with her husband*

remember those who went
before you and those
who will come after.
4 This is the Lord's decree for
all flesh;
why then should you reject
the will of the Most
High?
Whether life lasts for ten
years or a hundred or a
thousand,
there are no questions
asked in Hades.

The Fate of the Wicked

5 The children of sinners are
abominable children,
and they frequent the
haunts of the ungodly.
6 The inheritance of the
children of sinners will
perish,
and on their offspring will
be a perpetual disgrace.
7 Children will blame an
ungodly father,
for they suffer disgrace
because of him.
8 Woe to you, the ungodly,
who have forsaken the law
of the Most High God!
9 If you have children,
calamity will be theirs;
you will beget them only
for groaning.
When you stumble, there is
lasting joy;[t]
and when you die, a curse
is your lot.
10 Whatever comes from earth
returns to earth;
so the ungodly go from
curse to destruction.

11 The human body is a fleeting
thing,
but a virtuous name will
never be blotted out.[u]
12 Have regard for your name,
since it will outlive you
longer than a thousand
hoards of gold.
13 The days of a good life are
numbered,
but a good name lasts
forever.

41.4 Gen 3.19; Sir 14.17; Ps 90.10; 6.5; Sir 17.27 **41.5** Wis 3.12; Sir 40.15 **41.7** Ex 20.5; Jer 32.18; Sir 3.9-10 **41.8** Sir 16.3 **41.10** Gen 3.19; Eccl 3.20; Sir 40.11 **41.11** Ps 103.15-16; Isa 40.6-8; 1 Pet 1.24-25 **41.12** Prov 22.1; Eccl 7.1 **41.13** Ps 90.10; Sir 37.25; Wis 8.13; Sir 15.6; 37.26 **41.15** Sir 4.23-24; 20.31 **41.16** Prov 4.10,20; 22.17 **41.17** 1 Cor 6.9-10, 18; 1 Thess 4.3-5; Ex 20.16; Sir 20.24; Col 3.9 **41.18** Sir 20.23 **41.19** Ex 20.15; Eph 4.28; Eccl 5.4-5; Ezek 16.59 **41.20** Prov 23.27; Sir 9.6; 1 Cor 6.15-17 **41.21** Sir 9.8; Mt 5.28

14 My children, be true to your
training and be at
peace;
hidden wisdom and unseen
treasure—
of what value is either?

A Series of Contrasts

15 Better are those who hide
their folly
than those who hide their
wisdom.
16 Therefore show respect for
my words;
for it is not good to feel
shame in every
circumstance,
nor is every kind of
abashment to be
approved.[v]

17 Be ashamed of sexual
immorality, before your
father or mother;
and of a lie, before a
prince or a ruler;
18 of a crime, before a judge or
magistrate;
and of a breach of the law,
before the congregation
and the people;
of unjust dealing, before your
partner or your friend;
19 and of theft, in the place
where you live.
Be ashamed of breaking an
oath or agreement,[w]
and of leaning on your
elbow at meals;
of surliness in receiving or
giving,
20 and of silence, before those
who greet you;
of looking at a prostitute,
21 and of rejecting the appeal
of a relative;
of taking away someone's
portion or gift,
and of gazing at another
man's wife;
22 of meddling with his servant-
girl—

[t]Heb: Meaning of Gk uncertain
[u]Heb: Gk *People grieve over the death of the body, but the bad name of sinners will be blotted out* [v]Heb: Gk *and not everything is confidently esteemed by everyone*
[w]Heb: Gk *before the truth of God and the covenant*

and do not approach her
bed;
of abusive words, before
friends—
and do not be insulting
after making a gift.

42 Be ashamed of repeating
what you hear,
and of betraying secrets.
Then you will show proper
shame,
and will find favor with
everyone.

Of the following things do
not be ashamed,
and do not sin to save face:
2 Do not be ashamed of the
law of the Most High
and his covenant,
and of rendering judgment
to acquit the ungodly;
3 of keeping accounts with a
partner or with traveling
companions,
and of dividing the
inheritance of friends;
4 of accuracy with scales and
weights,
and of acquiring much or
little;
5 of profit from dealing with
merchants,
and of frequent disciplining
of children,
and of drawing blood from
the back of a wicked
slave.
6 Where there is an
untrustworthy wife, a
seal is a good thing;
and where there are many
hands, lock things up.
7 When you make a deposit,
be sure it is counted
and weighed,
and when you give or
receive, put it all in
writing.
8 Do not be ashamed to
correct the stupid or
foolish
or the aged who are guilty
of sexual immorality.
Then you will show your
sound training,
and will be approved by all.

42.1 Prov 20.19; 25.9-10; Sir 27.16 **42.4** Deut 25.13-16; Prov 11.1; 30.8-9 **42.5** Prov 22.15; 23.13-14; Sir 30.1-13; 33.25,33 **42.8** 1 Tim 4.11-16; 2 Tim 2.15

42.10 Sir 7.24-25 **42.11** Sir 22.5; 26.10 **42.12** Sir 9.8; 36.26 **42.14** 2 Cor 11.3; 1 Tim 2.13-14 **42.15** Ps 77.11-12; Sir 11.4; 16.26-27; 39.16-21,33; Gen 1.3; Ps 33.6,9

Daughters and Fathers

9 A daughter is a secret
anxiety to her father,
and worry over her robs
him of sleep;
when she is young, for fear
she may not marry,
or if married, for fear she
may be disliked;
10 while a virgin, for fear she
may be seduced
and become pregnant in
her father's house;
or having a husband, for fear
she may go astray,
or, though married, for fear
she may be barren.
11 Keep strict watch over a
headstrong daughter,
or she may make you a
laughingstock to your
enemies,
a byword in the city and the
assembly of[x] the
people,
and put you to shame in
public gatherings.[y]
See that there is no lattice in
her room,
no spot that overlooks the
approaches to the
house.[z]
12 Do not let her parade her
beauty before any man,
or spend her time among
married women;[x]
13 for from garments comes the
moth,
and from a woman comes
woman's wickedness.
14 Better is the wickedness of a
man than a woman who
does good;
it is woman who brings
shame and disgrace.

The Works of God in Nature

15 I will now call to mind the
works of the Lord,
and will declare what I
have seen.
By the word of the Lord his
works are made;

x Heb: Meaning of Gk uncertain
y Heb: Gk *to shame before the great multitude*
z Heb: Gk lacks *See . . . house*

and all his creatures do his
will.[a]
16 The sun looks down on
everything with its light,
and the work of the Lord is
full of his glory.
17 The Lord has not empowered
even his holy ones
to recount all his
marvelous works,
which the Lord the Almighty
has established
so that the universe may
stand firm in his glory.
18 He searches out the abyss
and the human heart;
he understands their
innermost secrets.
For the Most High knows all
that may be known;
he sees from of old the
things that are to
come.[b]
19 He discloses what has been
and what is to be,
and he reveals the traces of
hidden things.
20 No thought escapes him,
and nothing is hidden from
him.
21 He has set in order the
splendors of his
wisdom;
he is from all eternity one
and the same.
Nothing can be added or
taken away,
and he needs no one to be
his counselor.
22 How desirable are all his
works,
and how sparkling they are
to see![c]
23 All these things live and
remain forever;
each creature is preserved
to meet a particular
need.[d]
24 All things come in pairs, one
opposite the other,
and he has made nothing
incomplete.
25 Each supplements the
virtues of the other.
Who could ever tire of
seeing his glory?

42.16 Ps 19.4-6; Eccl 1.5; Sir 43.2; Ps 19.1 **42.17** Job 5.1; Ps 89.7 **42.18** Ps 139.23; Prov 15.11; Wis 1.6; Ps 139.1-6; Jer 1.5; Rev 1.19 **42.19** Wis 8.8 **42.20** Sir 15.19; 39.19 **42.21** Ps 90.2; Mal 3.6; Jas 1.17; Isa 40.13; Rom 11.34 **42.24** Gen 1.27; Sir 33.15

43.1 Gen 1.6-8, 14-18 **43.2** Sir 42.16 **43.3** Jas 1.11 **43.5** Ps 19.4-6; Eccl 1.5 **43.6** Gen 1.14; Ps 104.19 **43.7** Ps 81.3; Isa 1.13; Sir 50.6 **43.9** Job 22.12; Ps 8.3

The Splendor of the Sun

43 The pride of the higher
realms is the clear vault
of the sky,
as glorious to behold as the
sight of the heavens.
2 The sun, when it appears,
proclaims as it rises
what a marvelous
instrument it is, the
work of the Most High.
3 At noon it parches the land,
and who can withstand its
burning heat?
4 A man tending[e] a furnace
works in burning heat,
but three times as hot is
the sun scorching the
mountains;
it breathes out fiery vapors,
and its bright rays blind
the eyes.
5 Great is the Lord who made
it;
at his orders it hurries on
its course.

The Splendor of the Moon

6 It is the moon that marks
the changing seasons,[f]
governing the times, their
everlasting sign.
7 From the moon comes the
sign for festal days,
a light that wanes when it
completes its course.
8 The new moon, as its name
suggests, renews
itself;[g]
how marvelous it is in this
change,
a beacon to the hosts on
high,
shining in the vault of the
heavens!

The Glory of the Stars and the Rainbow

9 The glory of the stars is the
beauty of heaven,

[a] Syr Compare Heb: most Gk witnesses lack *and all . . . will* [b] Heb: Gk *he sees the sign(s) of the age* [c] Meaning of Gk uncertain [d] Heb: Gk *forever for every need, and all are obedient* [e] Other ancient authorities read *blowing upon* [f] Heb: Meaning of Gk uncertain [g] Heb: Gk *The month is named after the moon*

a glittering array in the heights of the Lord.
10 On the orders of the Holy One they stand in their appointed places;
they never relax in their watches.
11 Look at the rainbow, and praise him who made it;
it is exceedingly beautiful in its brightness.
12 It encircles the sky with its glorious arc;
the hands of the Most High have stretched it out.

The Marvels of Nature

13 By his command he sends the driving snow
and speeds the lightnings of his judgment.
14 Therefore the storehouses are opened,
and the clouds fly out like birds.
15 In his majesty he gives the clouds their strength,
and the hailstones are broken in pieces.
17a The voice of his thunder rebukes the earth;
16 when he appears, the mountains shake.
At his will the south wind blows;
17b so do the storm from the north and the whirlwind.
He scatters the snow like birds flying down,
and its descent is like locusts alighting.
18 The eye is dazzled by the beauty of its whiteness,
and the mind is amazed as it falls.
19 He pours frost over the earth like salt,
and icicles form like pointed thorns.
20 The cold north wind blows,
and ice freezes on the water;
it settles on every pool of water,
and the water puts it on like a breastplate.
21 He consumes the mountains and burns up the wilderness,
and withers the tender grass like fire.
22 A mist quickly heals all things;
the falling dew gives refreshment from the heat.

23 By his plan he stilled the deep
and planted islands in it.
24 Those who sail the sea tell of its dangers,
and we marvel at what we hear.
25 In it are strange and marvelous creatures,
all kinds of living things,
and huge sea-monsters.
26 Because of him each of his messengers succeeds,
and by his word all things hold together.

27 We could say more but could never say enough;
let the final word be: "He is the all."
28 Where can we find the strength to praise him?
For he is greater than all his works.
29 Awesome is the Lord and very great,
and marvelous is his power.
30 Glorify the Lord and exalt him as much as you can,
for he surpasses even that.
When you exalt him, summon all your strength,
and do not grow weary, for you cannot praise him enough.
31 Who has seen him and can describe him?
Or who can extol him as he is?
32 Many things greater than these lie hidden,

43.10 Job 9.9; 38.31; Am 5.8; Wis 7.19
43.11 Gen 9.13-16; Sir 50.7
43.13 Job 38.22; Ps 148.8; Wis 16.22; Job 36.30; 37.3,11,15; Ps 144.6
43.15 Job 38.22; Ps 18.12; Ezek 38.22
43.17 Ex 19.16,19; Job 40.9; Ps 29.3-4; 147.16
43.19 Ps 147.16
43.21 Isa 40.6-8; Sir 43.3; Jas 1.11
43.22 Job 38.28; Ps 133.3; Sir 18.16
43.23 Gen 1.9-10
43.24 Ps 107.23-30
43.25 Job 41.1-34; Ps 104.24-26
43.26 Col 1.17; Heb 1.3
43.27 Eph 1.23; 4.6; Col 3.11
43.29 Deut 10.17; Neh 4.14; Ps 47.2; 66.3-5
43.30 Ps 34.3; 86.12; Isa 25.1; Song of Thr 1.35-66
43.31 Isa 64.4; 1 Cor 2.9; Ps 106.2

for I[h] have seen but few of
his works.
33 For the Lord has made all
things,
and to the godly he has
given wisdom.

Hymn in Honor of Our Ancestors[i]

44 Let us now sing the
praises of famous men,
our ancestors in their
generations.
2 The Lord apportioned to
them[j] great glory,
his majesty from the
beginning.
3 There were those who ruled
in their kingdoms,
and made a name for
themselves by their
valor;
those who gave counsel
because they were
intelligent;
those who spoke in
prophetic oracles;
4 those who led the people by
their counsels
and by their knowledge of
the people's lore;
they were wise in their
words of instruction;
5 those who composed musical
tunes,
or put verses in writing;
6 rich men endowed with
resources,
living peacefully in their
homes—
7 all these were honored in
their generations,
and were the pride of their
times.
8 Some of them have left
behind a name,
so that others declare their
praise.
9 But of others there is no
memory;
they have perished as
though they had never
existed;
they have become as though
they had never been
born,
they and their children
after them.

43.33 Gen 1.1; Ex 20.11; Rev 4.11; Sir 27.11 **44.3** 1 Sam 17.41-51; 2 Sam 8.1-14; 1 Kings 3.16-28; 10.1-9; Isa 1.1; 61.1-3; Jer 1.1-3 **44.5** 2 Sam 22.1-51; 1 Kings 4.32

44.10 Heb 11.33-36 **44.12** Rom 9.4 **44.13** Ps 147.13 **44.15** Sir 37.24; 39.9 **44.16** Gen 5.22-24; Heb 11.5 **44.17** Gen 6.8-9, 5-7; 8.15-18 **44.18** Gen 9.8-17 **44.19** Gen 17.5-6; Jn 8.53; Rom 4.16-17

10 But these also were godly
men,
whose righteous deeds
have not been
forgotten;
11 their wealth will remain with
their descendants,
and their inheritance with
their children's
children.[k]
12 Their descendants stand by
the covenants;
their children also, for their
sake.
13 Their offspring will continue
forever,
and their glory will never
be blotted out.
14 Their bodies are buried in
peace,
but their name lives on
generation after
generation.
15 The assembly declares[l] their
wisdom,
and the congregation
proclaims their praise.

Enoch

16 Enoch pleased the Lord and
was taken up,
an example of repentance
to all generations.

Noah

17 Noah was found perfect and
righteous;
in the time of wrath he
kept the race alive;[m]
therefore a remnant was left
on the earth
when the flood came.
18 Everlasting covenants were
made with him
that all flesh should never
again be blotted out by
a flood.

Abraham

19 Abraham was the great
father of a multitude of
nations,

[h] Heb: Gk *we* [i] This title is included in the Gk text. [j] Heb: Gk *created* [k] Heb Compare Lat Syr: Meaning of Gk uncertain [l] Heb: Gk *Peoples declare* [m] Heb: Gk *was taken in exchange*

and no one has been found
like him in glory.
20 He kept the law of the Most
High,
and entered into a
covenant with him;
he certified the covenant in
his flesh,
and when he was tested he
proved faithful.
21 Therefore the Lord[n] assured
him with an oath
that the nations would be
blessed through his
offspring;
that he would make him as
numerous as the dust
of the earth,
and exalt his offspring like
the stars,
and give them an inheritance
from sea to sea
and from the Euphrates[o]
to the ends of the
earth.

Isaac and Jacob

22 To Isaac also he gave the
same assurance
for the sake of his father
Abraham.
The blessing of all people
and the covenant
23 he made to rest on the
head of Jacob;
he acknowledged him with
his blessings,
and gave him his
inheritance;
he divided his portions,
and distributed them
among twelve tribes.

Moses

From his descendants the
Lord[n] brought forth a
godly man,
who found favor in the
sight of all
45 1 and was beloved by
God and people,
Moses, whose memory is
blessed.
2 He made him equal in glory
to the holy ones,
and made him great, to the
terror of his enemies.
3 By his words he performed
swift miracles;[p]
the Lord[n] glorified him in
the presence of kings.
He gave him commandments
for his people,
and revealed to him his
glory.
4 For his faithfulness and
meekness he
consecrated him,
choosing him out of all
humankind.
5 He allowed him to hear his
voice,
and led him into the dark
cloud,
and gave him the
commandments face to
face,
the law of life and
knowledge,
so that he might teach Jacob
the covenant,
and Israel his decrees.

Aaron

6 He exalted Aaron, a holy
man like Moses[q]
who was his brother, of the
tribe of Levi.
7 He made an everlasting
covenant with him,
and gave him the
priesthood of the
people.
He blessed him with
stateliness,
and put a glorious robe on
him.
8 He clothed him in perfect
splendor,
and strengthened him with
the symbols of
authority,
the linen undergarments,
the long robe, and the
ephod.
9 And he encircled him with
pomegranates,
with many golden bells all
around,
to send forth a sound as he
walked,

44.20 Gen 17.4-8, 10-14; 22.1-18; Heb 11.17
44.21 Gen 12.2-3; 17.5; 22.16-18; Gal 3.16; Gen 13.16; 28.14; 15.5; 22.17; 26.4; Deut 10.22; Ex 22.31; Ps 72.8; Deut 1.7-8; 11.24; Josh 1.4-5
44.22 Gen 26.2-5
44.23 Gen 25.23; 28.13-15; 35.11-12; 27.27-29; 49.1-28; Ex 14.31
45.1 Ex 33.11; Sir 46.11
45.2 Ex 12.29-33; 17.8-13
45.3 Ex 15.23-25; 17.3-6; 24.12-18; 34.1-29; 33.18-23; 34.29-35
45.4 Num 12.7; Heb 3.2,5; Num 12.3
45.5 Num 12.8; Ex 24.15-18, 3-8
45.6 Ex 4.14; 6.20; 2.1
45.7 Ex 27.21; 28.43, 31-35
45.8 Ex 28.39,6-14
45.9 Ex 28.33-35

[n] Gk *he* [o] Syr: Heb Gk *River*
[p] Heb: Gk *caused signs to cease* [q] Gk *him*

to make their ringing heard
in the temple
as a reminder to his
people;
10 with the sacred vestment, of
gold and violet
and purple, the work of an
embroiderer;
with the oracle of judgment,
Urim and Thummim;
11 with twisted crimson, the
work of an artisan;
with precious stones
engraved like seals,
in a setting of gold, the
work of a jeweler,
to commemorate in engraved
letters
each of the tribes of Israel;
12 with a gold crown upon his
turban,
inscribed like a seal with
"Holiness,"
a distinction to be prized,
the work of an expert,
a delight to the eyes, richly
adorned.
13 Before him such beautiful
things did not exist.
No outsider ever put them
on,
but only his sons
and his descendants in
perpetuity.
14 His sacrifices shall be wholly
burned
twice every day continually.
15 Moses ordained him,
and anointed him with holy
oil;
it was an everlasting
covenant for him
and for his descendants as
long as the heavens
endure,
to minister to the Lord[r] and
serve as priest
and bless his people in his
name.
16 He chose him out of all the
living
to offer sacrifice to the
Lord,
incense and a pleasing odor
as a memorial portion,
to make atonement for
the[s] people.

45.10 Ex 28.39,30; Lev 8.8; Deut 33.8
45.11 Ex 28.17-21
45.12 Ex 28.36-38; Lev 8.9
45.13 Ex 27.21; 28.43
45.14 Ex 29.38-42; Num 28.1-8
45.15 Lev 8.10; Num 6.24-26
45.16 Ex 30.1-10; Deut 33.10; Lev 1.9,13,17; 2.2,9; 16.1-34
45.17 Deut 4.5; 6.1
45.18 Num 16.1-19; Jude 11
45.19 Num 16.31-35
45.20 Lev 23.9-14; Deut 18.3-5
45.21 Lev 6.16; 8.31
45.22 Deut 10.9; 18.1-2; Josh 13.4,33
45.23 Ex 6.25; 1 Chr 6.4; Num 25.6-8; Ps 106.30

17 In his commandments he
gave him
authority and statutes
and[t] judgments,
to teach Jacob the
testimonies,
and to enlighten Israel with
his law.
18 Outsiders conspired against
him,
and envied him in the
wilderness,
Dathan and Abiram and their
followers
and the company of Korah,
in wrath and anger.
19 The Lord saw it and was not
pleased,
and in the heat of his
anger they were
destroyed;
he performed wonders
against them
to consume them in
flaming fire.
20 He added glory to Aaron
and gave him a heritage;
he allotted to him the best
of the first fruits,
and prepared bread of first
fruits in abundance;
21 for they eat the sacrifices of
the Lord,
which he gave to him and
his descendants.
22 But in the land of the people
he has no inheritance,
and he has no portion
among the people;
for the Lord[u] himself is
his[v] portion and
inheritance.

Phinehas

23 Phinehas son of Eleazar
ranks third in glory
for being zealous in the
fear of the Lord,
and standing firm, when the
people turned away,
in the noble courage of his
soul;
and he made atonement
for Israel.

[r] Gk *him* or *your* [s] Other ancient authorities read *his* [t] Heb: Gk *authority in covenants of* [u] Gk *he* [v] Other ancient authorities read *your*

24 Therefore a covenant of friendship was established with him,
that he should be leader of the sanctuary and of his people,
that he and his descendants should have
the dignity of the priesthood forever.
25 Just as a covenant was established with David
son of Jesse of the tribe of Judah,
that the king's heritage passes only from son to son,
so the heritage of Aaron is for his descendants alone.

26 And now bless the Lord
who has crowned you with glory.[w]
May the Lord[x] grant you wisdom of mind
to judge his people with justice,
so that their prosperity may not vanish,
and that their glory may endure through all their generations.

Joshua and Caleb

46 Joshua son of Nun was mighty in war,
and was the successor of Moses in the prophetic office.
He became, as his name implies,
a great savior of God's[y] elect,
to take vengeance on the enemies that rose against them,
so that he might give Israel its inheritance.
2 How glorious he was when he lifted his hands
and brandished his sword against the cities!
3 Who before him ever stood so firm?
For he waged the wars of the Lord.
4 Was it not through him that the sun stood still
and one day become as long as two?
5 He called upon the Most High, the Mighty One,
when enemies pressed him on every side,
and the great Lord answered him
with hailstones of mighty power.
6 He overwhelmed that nation in battle,
and on the slope he destroyed his opponents,
so that the nations might know his armament,
that he was fighting in the sight of the Lord;
for he was a devoted follower of the Mighty One.
7 And in the days of Moses he proved his loyalty,
he and Caleb son of Jephunneh:
they opposed the congregation,[z]
restrained the people from sin,
and stilled their wicked grumbling.
8 And these two alone were spared
out of six hundred thousand infantry,
to lead the people[a] into their inheritance,
the land flowing with milk and honey.
9 The Lord gave Caleb strength,
which remained with him in his old age,
so that he went up to the hill country,
and his children obtained it for an inheritance,
10 so that all the Israelites might see
how good it is to follow the Lord.

45.24 Num 25.10-13; 2 Macc 2.54 **45.25** 2 Sam 7.4-17; 1 Chr 17.3-15 **45.26** Ps 103.1-2, 20-22; 8.5; Heb 2.7; Ps 72.1-2; 96.13; 98.9; 72.5-7,17; 89.36 **46.1** Ex 17.9-14; Josh 6.1-25; 10.1-28; Num 27.12-23; Deut 31.1-8; Rom 8.33; Titus 1.1; Josh 14-19 **46.2** Josh 10.29-12.24 **46.3** Josh 1.10-16 **46.4** Josh 10.12-14 **46.5** Gen 14.18-22; Deut 32.8; 33.12; 1 Tim 6.15; Josh 10.11; Wis 5.22 **46.6** Josh 10.28; 24.15 **46.7** Num 13.6; Josh 14.6; Num 13.30; 14.5-9 **46.8** Num 14.28-38; 26.65; 1.44-46; Ex 3.8,17; Deut 26.9,15; Josh 5.6 **46.9** Josh 14.10-11,9, 12-13; Judg 1.20 **46.10** Num 32.12; Deut 1.36

[w] Heb: Gk lacks *who . . . glory* [x] Gk *he* [y] Gk *his enemy* [z] Other ancient authorities read *the* [a] Gk *them*

The Judges

11 The judges also, with their
respective names,
whose hearts did not fall
into idolatry
and who did not turn away
from the Lord—
may their memory be
blessed!
12 May their bones send forth
new life from where
they lie,
and may the names of
those who have been
honored
live again in their children!

13 Samuel was beloved by his
Lord;
a prophet of the Lord, he
established the
kingdom
and anointed rulers over
his people.
14 By the law of the Lord he
judged the
congregation,
and the Lord watched over
Jacob.
15 By his faithfulness he was
proved to be a prophet,
and by his words he
became known as a
trustworthy seer.
16 He called upon the Lord, the
Mighty One,
when his enemies pressed
him on every side,
and he offered in sacrifice
a suckling lamb.
17 Then the Lord thundered
from heaven,
and made his voice heard
with a mighty sound;
18 he subdued the leaders of
the enemy[b]
and all the rulers of the
Philistines.
19 Before the time of his
eternal sleep,
Samuel[c] bore witness
before the Lord and his
anointed:
"No property, not so much
as a pair of shoes,
have I taken from anyone!"
And no one accused him.
20 Even after he had fallen
asleep, he prophesied
and made known to the
king his death,
and lifted up his voice from
the ground
in prophecy, to blot out the
wickedness of the
people.

Nathan

47 After him Nathan rose up
to prophesy in the days
of David.

David

2 As the fat is set apart from
the offering of
well-being,
so David was set apart
from the Israelites.
3 He played with lions as
though they were young
goats,
and with bears as though
they were lambs of the
flock.
4 In his youth did he not kill a
giant,
and take away the people's
disgrace,
when he whirled the stone in
the sling
and struck down the
boasting Goliath?
5 For he called on the Lord,
the Most High,
and he gave strength to his
right arm
to strike down a mighty
warrior,
and to exalt the power[d] of
his people.
6 So they glorified him for the
tens of thousands he
conquered,
and praised him for the
blessings bestowed by
the Lord,
when the glorious diadem
was given to him.
7 For he wiped out his
enemies on every side,

46.11 Judg 3.10; 4.4-6; 6.11-14; Sir 45.1; 1 Macc 3.7
46.12 Ezek 37.1-10; Sir 49.10
46.13 1 Sam 1.20; 2.18-20; 3.19-21; 10.1; 16.11-13
46.14 1 Sam 7.6, 15-16
46.15 1 Sam 3.19-21; 9.9, 18-19; 1 Chr 9.22
46.16 1 Sam 7.8; Sir 46.5-6; 1 Sam 7.9
46.17 1 Sam 7.10
46.18 1 Sam 7.11
46.19 Jer 51.39,57; Sir 30.17; 1 Sam 12.3,4
46.20 1 Sam 28.18-19
47.1 2 Sam 7.2-4; 12.1-15
47.2 Lev 3.1-11; 7.11-37; Deut 27.7
47.3 1 Sam 17.34-36
47.4 1 Sam 17.41-51
47.5 1 Sam 17.45; Ps 18.32-34, 39
47.6 1 Sam 18.7; 2 Sam 2.4; 5.1-3; 1 Chr 11.1-3
47.7 2 Sam 8.1-14; Ps 18.38-42; 1 Sam 18.24-27; 19.8; 2 Sam 8.1; 2 Chr 14.8-17

b Heb: Gk *leaders of the people of Tyre*
c Gk *he*
d Gk *horn*

and annihilated his adversaries the Philistines;
he crushed their power[e] to our own day.
8 In all that he did he gave thanks
to the Holy One, the Most High, proclaiming his glory;
he sang praise with all his heart,
and he loved his Maker.
9 He placed singers before the altar,
to make sweet melody with their voices.[f]
10 He gave beauty to the festivals,
and arranged their times throughout the year,[g]
while they praised God's[h] holy name,
and the sanctuary resounded from early morning.
11 The Lord took away his sins,
and exalted his power[e] forever;
he gave him a covenant of kingship
and a glorious throne in Israel.

Solomon

12 After him a wise son rose up
who because of him lived in security:[i]
13 Solomon reigned in an age of peace,
because God made all his borders tranquil,
so that he might build a house in his name
and provide a sanctuary to stand forever.
14 How wise you were when you were young!
You overflowed like the Nile[j] with understanding.
15 Your influence spread throughout the earth,
and you filled it with proverbs having deep meaning.

47.8 1 Chr 16.7-36; Ps 105.1-15; 96.1-13; 9.1; 86.12; 138.1
47.9 1 Chr 16.4-6; 25.1-7
47.10 1 Chr 23-24
47.11 2 Sam 12.13; Ps 32.1-5; 2 Sam 7.1-17; 1 Chr 17.1-15; 2 Sam 7.16; 8.15
47.12 2 Sam 7.10-12
47.13 1 Kings 4.20-21; 6.1-38; 2 Chr 3.1-5.1
47.14 1 Kings 3.1-28; 2 Chr 1.2-13; Sir 24.27
47.15 1 Kings 4.29-31; Mt 12.42; 1 Kings 4.32; Prov 1.1; 25.1
47.17 1 Kings 4.32; Song 1.1; 1 Kings 4.33; 10.1,6-7; 1 Chr 9.1,5-6
47.18 1 Kings 9.11, 28; 2 Chr 1.15; 9.13-21
47.19 1 Kings 11.1-8
47.20 1 Kings 11.9
47.21 1 Kings 11.26-39; 12.16-19; 2 Chr 10.16-19
47.22 2 Sam 7.16; Ps 89.29-37; 2 Kings 19.30-31; Isa 11.10; 53.2; Rom 15.12
47.23 1 Kings 11.43; 12.1-15; 2 Chr 10.1-15;

16 Your fame reached to far-off islands,
and you were loved for your peaceful reign.
17 Your songs, proverbs, and parables,
and the answers you gave astounded the nations.
18 In the name of the Lord God,
who is called the God of Israel,
you gathered gold like tin
and amassed silver like lead.
19 But you brought in women to lie at your side,
and through your body you were brought into subjection.
20 You stained your honor,
and defiled your family line,
so that you brought wrath upon your children,
and they were grieved[k] at your folly,
21 because the sovereignty was divided
and a rebel kingdom arose out of Ephraim.
22 But the Lord will never give up his mercy,
or cause any of his works to perish;
he will never blot out the descendants of his chosen one,
or destroy the family line of him who loved him.
So he gave a remnant to Jacob,
and to David a root from his own family.

Rehoboam and Jeroboam

23 Solomon rested with his ancestors,
and left behind him one of his sons,

1 Kings 12.25-33

[e] Gk *horn* [f] Other ancient authorities add *and daily they sing his praises* [g] Gk *to completion* [h] Gk *his* [i] Heb: Gk *in a broad place* [j] Heb: Gk *a river* [k] Other ancient authorities read *I was grieved*

broad in[l] folly and lacking
in sense,
Rehoboam, whose policy
drove the people to
revolt.
Then Jeroboam son of Nebat
led Israel into sin
and started Ephraim on its
sinful ways.
24 Their sins increased more
and more,
until they were exiled from
their land.
25 For they sought out every
kind of wickedness,
until vengeance came upon
them.

Elijah

48 Then Elijah arose, a
prophet like fire,
and his word burned like a
torch.
2 He brought a famine upon
them,
and by his zeal he made
them few in number.
3 By the word of the Lord he
shut up the heavens,
and also three times
brought down fire.
4 How glorious you were,
Elijah, in your
wondrous deeds!
Whose glory is equal to
yours?
5 You raised a corpse from
death
and from Hades, by the
word of the Most High.
6 You sent kings down to
destruction,
and famous men, from
their sickbeds.
7 You heard rebuke at Sinai
and judgments of
vengeance at Horeb.
8 You anointed kings to inflict
retribution,
and prophets to succeed
you.[m]
9 You were taken up by a
whirlwind of fire,
in a chariot with horses of
fire.
10 At the appointed time, it is
written, you are
destined[n]
to calm the wrath of God
before it breaks out in
fury,
to turn the hearts of parents
to their children,
and to restore the tribes of
Jacob.
11 Happy are those who saw
you
and were adorned[o] with
your love!
For we also shall surely
live.[p]

Elisha

12 When Elijah was enveloped
in the whirlwind,
Elisha was filled with his
spirit.
He performed twice as many
signs,
and marvels with every
utterance of his
mouth.[q]
Never in his lifetime did he
tremble before any
ruler,
nor could anyone
intimidate him at all.
13 Nothing was too hard for
him,
and when he was dead, his
body prophesied.
14 In his life he did wonders,
and in death his deeds
were marvelous.
15 Despite all this the people
did not repent,
nor did they forsake their
sins,
until they were carried off as
plunder from their land,
and were scattered over all
the earth.
The people were left very few
in number,
but with a ruler from the
house of David.

47.24 2 Kings 17.5-23
48.1 1 Kings 17.1
48.2 1 Kings 17.1; Jas 5.17
48.3 1 Kings 18.36-38; 2 Kings 1.10-12
48.5 1 Kings 17.17-24
48.6 2 Kings 1.15-16
48.7 1 Kings 19.11-18
48.8 1 Kings 19.15-16, 19-21
48.9 2 Kings 2.11-12
48.10 Mal 4.5-6; Lk 1.17; Mt 17.11
48.12 2 Kings 2.9, 13; 3.19-25; 4.1-6.7; 6.11-23
48.13 2 Kings 13.20-21
48.15 2 Kings 8.16-19, 25-27; 17.21-23; 25.11

[l]Heb (with a play on the name Rehoboam) Syr: Gk *the people's* [m]Heb: Gk *him*
[n]Heb: Gk *are for reproofs*
[o]Other ancient authorities read *and have died*
[p]Text and meaning of Gk uncertain
[q]Heb: Gk lacks *He performed . . . mouth*

16 Some of them did what was right,
but others sinned more and more.

Hezekiah

17 Hezekiah fortified his city,
and brought water into its midst;
he tunneled the rock with iron tools,
and built cisterns for the water.
18 In his days Sennacherib invaded the country;
he sent his commander[r] and departed;
he shook his fist against Zion,
and made great boasts in his arrogance.
19 Then their hearts were shaken and their hands trembled,
and they were in anguish, like women in labor.
20 But they called upon the Lord who is merciful,
spreading out their hands toward him.
The Holy One quickly heard them from heaven,
and delivered them through Isaiah.
21 The Lord[s] struck down the camp of the Assyrians,
and his angel wiped them out.
22 For Hezekiah did what was pleasing to the Lord,
and he kept firmly to the ways of his ancestor David,
as he was commanded by the prophet Isaiah,
who was great and trustworthy in his visions.

Isaiah

23 In Isaiah's[t] days the sun went backward,
and he prolonged the life of the king.
24 By his dauntless spirit he saw the future,
and comforted the mourners in Zion.
25 He revealed what was to occur to the end of time,
and the hidden things before they happened.

Josiah and Other Worthies

49 The name[u] of Josiah is like blended incense
prepared by the skill of the perfumer;
his memory[v] is as sweet as honey to every mouth,
and like music at a banquet of wine.
2 He did what was right by reforming the people,
and removing the wicked abominations.
3 He kept his heart fixed on the Lord;
in lawless times he made godliness prevail.

4 Except for David and Hezekiah and Josiah,
all of them were great sinners,
for they abandoned the law of the Most High;
the kings of Judah came to an end.
5 They[w] gave their power to others,
and their glory to a foreign nation,
6 who set fire to the chosen city of the sanctuary,
and made its streets desolate,
as Jeremiah had foretold.[x]
7 For they had mistreated him,
who even in the womb had been consecrated a prophet,
to pluck up and ruin and destroy,
and likewise to build and to plant.

48.16 2 Kings 15.3, 32; 18.3; 22.2; 16.2; 21.2,20; 23.32; 24.9, 19
48.17 2 Chr 32.5; 2 Kings 20.20; 2 Chr 32.3-4, 27-32
48.18 2 Kings 18.13-17; 2 Chr 32.1,9
48.19 2 Kings 19.1-2
48.20 2 Kings 19.1, 15-19; 2 Chr 32.20; 2 Kings 19.2, 20-34
48.21 2 Kings 19.35; 2 Chr 32.21; Acts 12.23
48.22 2 Kings 18.3; 2 Chr 29.2
48.23 2 Kings 20.8-11; Isa 38.7-8; 2 Kings 20.6; Isa 38.5
48.24 Isa 40.1-2; 61.2-3; Mt 5.4
48.25 Isa 65.17-25; 66.14-24
49.1 2 Kings 22.1; 2 Chr 34.1; Ps 19.10; Ezek 3.3; Rev 10.9; Sir 32.5-6
49.2 2 Kings 2.22; 2 Chr 34.2; 2 Kings 23.4-15; 2 Chr 34.4-7
49.3 2 Kings 23.21-25; 2 Chr 34.8-35.19
49.4 2 Kings 23.32; 24.9, 19; 25.6-7
49.6 2 Kings 25.9; 2 Chr 36.19; Jer 15.1-9; 16.5-9; 21.1-10
49.7 Jer 18.18; 20.1-6; 37.11-38.6; 1.5-10

[r] Other ancient authorities add *from Lachish*
[s] Gk *He*
[t] Gk *his*
[u] Heb: Gk *memory*
[v] Heb: Gk *it*
[w] Heb *He*
[x] Gk *by the hand of Jeremiah*

8 It was Ezekiel who saw the
vision of glory,
which God[y] showed him
above the chariot of the
cherubim.
9 For God[z] also mentioned
Job
who held fast to all the
ways of justice.[a]
10 May the bones of the Twelve
Prophets
send forth new life from
where they lie,
for they comforted the
people of Jacob
and delivered them with
confident hope.

11 How shall we magnify
Zerubbabel?
He was like a signet ring
on the right hand,
12 and so was Jeshua son of
Jozadak;
in their days they built the
house
and raised a temple[b] holy
to the Lord,
destined for everlasting
glory.
13 The memory of Nehemiah
also is lasting;
he raised our fallen walls,
and set up gates and bars,
and rebuilt our ruined
houses.

Retrospect

14 Few have[c] ever been created
on earth like Enoch,
for he was taken up from
the earth.
15 Nor was anyone ever born
like Joseph;[d]
even his bones were cared
for.
16 Shem and Seth and Enosh
were honored,[e]
but above every other
created living being was
Adam.

Simon Son of Onias

50 The leader of his brothers
and the pride of his
people[f]
was the high priest, Simon
son of Onias,
who in his life repaired the
house,
and in his time fortified
the temple.
2 He laid the foundations for
the high double walls,
the high retaining walls for
the temple enclosure.
3 In his days a water cistern
was dug,[g]
a reservoir like the sea in
circumference.
4 He considered how to save
his people from ruin,
and fortified the city
against siege.
5 How glorious he was,
surrounded by the
people,
as he came out of the
house of the curtain.
6 Like the morning star among
the clouds,
like the full moon at the
festal season;[g]
7 like the sun shining on the
temple of the Most
High,
like the rainbow gleaming
in splendid clouds;
8 like roses in the days of first
fruits,
like lilies by a spring of
water,
like a green shoot on
Lebanon on a summer
day;
9 like fire and incense in the
censer,
like a vessel of hammered
gold
studded with all kinds of
precious stones;
10 like an olive tree laden with
fruit,
and like a cypress towering
in the clouds.

49.8 Ezek 1.3-15; 10.1-19 **49.9** Ezek 14.14, 20 **49.10** Ezek 37.1-10; Sir 46.12; Hos 14.4-9; Joel 3.17-21; Am 6.11-15 **49.11** Ezra 2.2; 3.8; Hag 2.23 **49.12** Ezra 3.2; Hag 1.12; Zech 3.1; Ezra 3.8-10; 6.13-15 **49.13** Neh 1.1; 2.17-4.23; 6.15; 7.4; 11.1 **49.14** Gen 5.21-24; Heb 11.5 **49.15** Gen 30.24; 37.1-36; 50.25; Josh 24.32 **49.16** Gen 9.26-27; 4.25; 5.3; 4.26; 5.6

50.5 1 Kings 3.1; 2 Chr 3.14 **50.7** Ps 46.4; Gen 9.12-16; Rev 10.1 **50.8** 2 Esd 2.19 **50.9** Lev 16.12; Num 16.17; Ex 25.36; Num 8.4; 1 Kings 10.2, 10-11; 2 Chr 3.6 **50.10** Isa 41.19; 60.13

y Gk *He* z Gk *he* a Heb Compare Syr: Meaning of Gk uncertain b Other ancient authorities read *people* c Heb Syr: Gk *No one has* d Heb Syr: Gk adds *the leader of his brothers, the support of the people* e Heb: Gk *Shem and Seth were honored by people* f Heb Syr: Gk lacks this line. Compare 49.15 g Heb: Meaning of Gk uncertain

11 When he put on his glorious
robe
and clothed himself in
perfect splendor,
when he went up to the holy
altar,
he made the court of the
sanctuary glorious.

12 When he received the
portions from the hands
of the priests,
as he stood by the hearth
of the altar
with a garland of brothers
around him,
he was like a young cedar
on Lebanon
surrounded by the trunks
of palm trees.
13 All the sons of Aaron in their
splendor
held the Lord's offering in
their hands
before the whole
congregation of Israel.
14 Finishing the service at the
altars,[h]
and arranging the offering
to the Most High, the
Almighty,
15 he held out his hand for the
cup
and poured a drink offering
of the blood of the
grape;
he poured it out at the foot
of the altar,
a pleasing odor to the Most
High, the king of all.
16 Then the sons of Aaron
shouted;
they blew their trumpets of
hammered metal;
they sounded a mighty
fanfare
as a reminder before the
Most High.
17 Then all the people together
quickly
fell to the ground on their
faces
to worship their Lord,
the Almighty, God Most
High.

18 Then the singers praised him
with their voices
in sweet and full-toned
melody.[i]
19 And the people of the Lord
Most High offered
their prayers before the
Merciful One,
until the order of worship of
the Lord was ended,
and they completed his
ritual.
20 Then Simon[j] came down
and raised his hands
over the whole
congregation of
Israelites,
to pronounce the blessing of
the Lord with his lips,
and to glory in his name;
21 and they bowed down in
worship a second time,
to receive the blessing from
the Most High.

A Benediction

22 And now bless the God of
all,
who everywhere works
great wonders,
who fosters our growth from
birth,
and deals with us
according to his mercy.
23 May he give us[k] gladness of
heart,
and may there be peace in
our[l] days
in Israel, as in the days of
old.
24 May he entrust to us his
mercy,
and may he deliver us in
our[m] days!

Epilogue

25 Two nations my soul detests,
and the third is not even a
people:
26 Those who live in Seir,[n] and
the Philistines,

50.11 Ex 28.1-38; Lev 1.5-17; 16.18,20 **50.12** Lev 24.9; 1 Kings 4.33; Ps 37.35 **50.13** Lev 9.1-9 **50.15** Ex 25.29; 29.40-41; Num 15.5,7; Lev 6.15,21; Num 15.10, 13-14 **50.16** Num 10.2; 31.6 **50.17** Judg 13.20; 2 Chr 7.3; Gen 17.1
50.19 Ps 32.6; 2 Macc 1.23; Heb 5.7 **50.20** 2 Chr 6.12-13; Lk 24.50; Num 6.24-27 **50.21** Ex 12.27; Neh 8.6; Ps 95.6 **50.22** Ps 104.1; 77.14; 136.4; Dan 4.2-3; Ps 103.8-11 **50.23** Deut 28.47; Ps 4.7; Isa 65.14; Ps 29.11; 128.5-6 **50.24** Ps 40.13; 70.1 **50.26** Gen 36.8-9; Mal 1.3; Gen 10.14; Jer 47.4; 1 Kings 12.25; Ps 60.6; Jn 4.9

[h] Other ancient authorities read *altar*
[i] Other ancient authorities read *in sweet melody throughout the house*
[j] Gk *he*
[k] Other ancient authorities read *you*
[l] Other ancient authorities read *your*
[m] Other ancient authorities read *his*
[n] Heb Compare Lat: Gk *on the mountain of Samaria*

and the foolish people that
live in Shechem.

27 Instruction in understanding
and knowledge
I have written in this book,
Jesus son of Eleazar son of
Sirach[o] of Jerusalem,
whose mind poured forth
wisdom.
28 Happy are those who
concern themselves
with these things,
and those who lay them to
heart will become wise.
29 For if they put them into
practice, they will be
equal to anything,
for the fear[p] of the Lord is
their path.

PRAYER OF JESUS SON OF SIRACH[q]

51 I give you thanks, O Lord
and King,
and praise you, O God my
Savior.
I give thanks to your name,
2 for you have been my
protector and helper
and have delivered me from
destruction
and from the trap laid by a
slanderous tongue,
from lips that fabricate
lies.
In the face of my adversaries
you have been my helper
3 and delivered me,
in the greatness of your
mercy and of your
name,
from grinding teeth about to
devour me,
from the hand of those
seeking my life,
from the many troubles I
endured,
4 from choking fire on every
side,
and from the midst of fire
that I had not kindled,
5 from the deep belly of
Hades,
from an unclean tongue
and lying words—
6 the slander of an
unrighteous tongue to
the king.

50.27 Prov 1.2-4; Sir Pr 1 **50.28** Prov 3.13; 8.34; Sir 14.20 **50.29** Jn 13.17; Ps 111.10; Prov 1.7 **51.1** Mt 11.25; Isa 45.15; Lk 1.47; Ps 30.4 **51.2** Ps 54.4; Heb 13.6; Ps 5.6 **51.3** Ps 18.48; 118.5-6; 27.1-2 **51.5** Jon 2.6,9 **51.6** Ps 52.4-6; 120.2-3

51.7 Ps 118.10-12; Isa 63.5 **51.8** Ps 77.11-12; 106.4; 25.5; 55.16; 143 **51.10** Isa 63.19; Mt 6.9; Ps 27.9; 38.21-22 **51.11** Ps 34.1; 71.14; 2 Macc 10.7, 38; 1 Esd 5.61 **51.12** Ps 22.20-22; 81.7; 34.1; 136.1; 47.6-7; 149.6

My soul drew near to death,
and my life was on the
brink of Hades below.
7 They surrounded me on
every side,
and there was no one to
help me;
I looked for human
assistance,
and there was none.
8 Then I remembered your
mercy, O Lord,
and your kindness[r] from
of old,
for you rescue those who
wait for you
and save them from the
hand of their enemies.
9 And I sent up my prayer
from the earth,
and begged for rescue from
death.
10 I cried out, "Lord, you are
my Father;[s]
do not forsake me in the
days of trouble,
when there is no help
against the proud.
11 I will praise your name
continually,
and will sing hymns of
thanksgiving."
My prayer was heard,
12 for you saved me from
destruction
and rescued me in time of
trouble.
For this reason I thank you
and praise you,
and I bless the name of the
Lord.

Heb adds:
*Give thanks to the LORD, for
he is good,
for his mercy endures
forever;*

*Give thanks to the God of
praises,
for his mercy endures
forever;*

[o] Heb: Meaning of Gk uncertain
[p] Heb: Other ancient authorities read *light*
[q] This title is included in the Gk text.
[r] Other ancient authorities read *work*
[s] Heb: Gk *the Father of my lord*

Give thanks to the guardian
of Israel,
for his mercy endures
forever;

Give thanks to him who
formed all things,
for his mercy endures
forever;

Give thanks to the redeemer
of Israel,
for his mercy endures
forever;

Give thanks to him who
gathers the dispersed of
Israel,
for his mercy endures
forever;

Give thanks to him who
rebuilt his city and his
sanctuary,
for his mercy endures
forever;

Give thanks to him who
makes a horn to sprout
for the house of David,
for his mercy endures
forever;

Give thanks to him who has
chosen the sons of
Zadok to be priests,
for his mercy endures
forever;

Give thanks to the shield of
Abraham,
for his mercy endures
forever;

Give thanks to the rock of
Isaac,
for his mercy endures
forever;

Give thanks to the mighty one
of Jacob,
for his mercy endures
forever;

Give thanks to him who has
chosen Zion,
for his mercy endures
forever;

51.12 Ps 121.4; 1 Pet 2.25; Gen 1.1; Ps 33.6; Isa 49.7; 54.5; 11.12; Jer 31.8,10; Ps 69.35; Ezra 6.14-15; Ps 132.17; Isa 11.1; Ezek 29.21; 1 Chr 16.39; Ezek 40.46; Gen 15.1; 49.24; Ps 18.31,46; 50.1; 48.1-2; 132.13; 47.2; Rev 17.4; 19.16; Ps 148.18; 146.1; 150.1,6
51.13 Prov 3.13; Eccl 1.13; Sir 24.34; Jas 1.5
51.14 1 Kings 3.9; 2 Chr 1.10
51.15 Prov 8.30; Wis 8.18; P[illegible]v 3.6; 4[illegible]6; W[illegible] 10.10; Ps 119.9; Prov 1.4
51.16 Prov 1.2-3; Wis 6.17
51.17 Prov 2.6; Eccl 2.26; Jas 1.5
51.18 Ps 49.3; Prov 4.3-13
51.19 1 Kings 8.22; Ps 88.9

Give thanks to the King of the
kings of kings,
for his mercy endures
forever;

He has raised up a horn for
his people,
praise for all his loyal ones.

For the children of Israel, the
people close to him.
Praise the L*ORD!*

Autobiographical Poem on Wisdom

13 While I was still young,
before I went on my
travels,
I sought wisdom openly in
my prayer.
14 Before the temple I asked for
her,
and I will search for her
until the end.

15 From the first blossom to
the ripening grape
my heart delighted in her;
my foot walked on the
straight path;
from my youth I followed
her steps.

16 I inclined my ear a little and
received her,
and I found for myself
much instruction.
17 I made progress in her;
to him who gives wisdom I
will give glory.

18 For I resolved to live
according to wisdom,[t]
and I was zealous for the
good,
and I shall never be
disappointed.
19 My soul grappled with
wisdom,[t]
and in my conduct I was
strict;[u]

I spread out my hands to the
heavens,

[t] Gk *her* [u] Meaning of Gk uncertain

and lamented my ignorance
of her.
20 I directed my soul to her,
and in purity I found her.

With her I gained
understanding from the
first;
therefore I will never be
forsaken.
21 My heart was stirred to seek
her;
therefore I have gained a
prize possession.
22 The Lord gave me my tongue
as a reward,
and I will praise him with
it.

23 Draw near to me, you who
are uneducated,
and lodge in the house of
instruction.
24 Why do you say you are
lacking in these
things,[v]
and why do you endure
such great thirst?
25 I opened my mouth and said,
Acquire wisdom[w] for
yourselves without
money.
26 Put your neck under her[x]
yoke,
and let your souls receive
instruction;
it is to be found close by.

27 See with your own eyes that
I have labored but
little
and found for myself much
serenity.
28 Hear but a little of my
instruction,
and through me you will
acquire silver and
gold.[y]

29 May your soul rejoice in
God's[z] mercy,
and may you never be
ashamed to praise
him.
30 Do your work in good time,
and in his own time God[a]
will give you your
reward.

51.20 Prov 10.13; Wis 6.12; Prov 2.2-3,6; 14.33 **51.21** Prov 4.8; Phil 3.13-14 **51.23** Isa 48.16; Mt 11.28; Prov 1.2-3; 4.1,13 **51.25** Prov 4.5,7; 23.23 **51.26** Sir 6.30; Mt 11.29; Deut 30.11-14 **51.28** Prov 8.10,19; Wis 7.9 **51.29** Ps 16.9; Sir 34.17; Ps 34.5; Rom 1.16 **51.30** Eccl 12.13-14; Jer 32.19; Sir 2.8; Eph 6.5-8

[v]Cn Compare Heb Syr: Meaning of Gk uncertain [w]Heb: Gk lacks *wisdom* [x]Heb: other ancient authorities read *the* [y]Syr Compare Heb: Gk *Get instruction with a large sum of silver, and you will gain by it much gold.* [z]Gk *his* [a]Gk *he*

Baruch

Title and Background

This work gets its name from Baruch son of Neriah, Jeremiah's trusted secretary (see Jer 32.12; 36.4). Set at the time of the Babylonian exile, the book of Baruch was intended to instruct and encourage the Jews in a time of persecution.

Author and Date of Writing

Few scholars accept the historical Baruch as the author. The book was more likely written by a God-fearing Jew around the end of the second century B.C. Its many quotes from–and allusions to–earlier Old Testament passages confirm that the author was writing to a Jewish audience.

Theme and Message

The author calls God's people to confess the sins that had led to suffering and to seek forgiveness from the Lord. The book goes on to praise the wisdom of God as revealed through his Law and encourages the people to find their strength in the Lord.

Outline

I. Prayer of Penitence (1.1–3.8)
II. Praise of Wisdom (3.9–4.4)
III. Encouragement for Israel (4.5–5.9)

Baruch and the Jews in Babylon

1 These are the words of the
book that Baruch son of Neriah son of Mahseiah son of Zedekiah son of Hasadiah son of Hilkiah wrote in Babylon, [2]in the fifth
year, on the seventh day of the
month, at the time when the Chaldeans took Jerusalem and burned
it with fire.
3 Baruch read the words of this
book to Jeconiah son of Jehoiakim, king of Judah, and to all the
people who came to hear the book,
[4]and to the nobles and the princes,
and to the elders, and to all the
people, small and great, all who
lived in Babylon by the river Sud.
5 Then they wept, and fasted,
and prayed before the Lord; [6]they
collected as much money as each
could give, [7]and sent it to Jerusalem to the high priest[a] Jehoiakim
son of Hilkiah son of Shallum, and
to the priests, and to all the people
who were present with him in Jerusalem. [8]At the same time, on the
tenth day of Sivan, Baruch[b] took
the vessels of the house of the
Lord, which had been carried away
from the temple, to return them to
the land of Judah — the silver vessels that Zedekiah son of Josiah,
king of Judah, had made, [9]after
King Nebuchadnezzar of Babylon
had carried away from Jerusalem
Jeconiah and the princes and the
prisoners and the nobles and the
people of the land, and brought
them to Babylon.

A Letter to Jerusalem

10 They said: Here we send you
money; so buy with the money
burnt offerings and sin offerings
and incense, and prepare a grain
offering, and offer them on the altar of the Lord our God; [11]and pray
for the life of King Nebuchadnezzar of Babylon, and for the life of
his son Belshazzar, so that their
days on earth may be like the days

1.1 Jer 32.12; 36.4 **1.2** 2 Kings 25.8-9; 2 Chr 36.18-19; Jer 52.12-13 **1.3** 2 Kings 24.8-17; 2 Chr 36.9-10; Jer 22.24-30 **1.4** 2 Kings 24.10-17; 2 Chr 36.10 **1.5** Ezra 9.5; Neh 1.4; Esth 4.16-17 **1.6** Deut 16.17 **1.8** 2 Kings 24.13; 2 Chr 36.7, 10,18; Jer 52.18-23 **1.10** Lev 1.1-17; 4.1-5,13; 2.1-16; Jer 17.16 **1.11** Ezra 6.10; Jer 29.7; 1 Tim 2.1-2; Dan 5.1-4

[a] Gk *the priest* [b] Gk *he*

of heaven. 12 The Lord will give us strength, and light to our eyes; we shall live under the protection[c] of King Nebuchadnezzar of Babylon, and under the protection of his son Belshazzar, and we shall serve them many days and find favor in their sight. 13 Pray also for us to the Lord our God, for we have sinned against the Lord our God, and to this day the anger of the Lord and his wrath have not turned away from us. 14 And you shall read aloud this scroll that we are sending you, to make your confession in the house of the Lord on the days of the festivals and at appointed seasons.

Confession of Sins

15 And you shall say: The Lord our God is in the right, but there is open shame on us today, on the people of Judah, on the inhabitants of Jerusalem, 16 and on our kings, our rulers, our priests, our prophets, and our ancestors, 17 because we have sinned before the Lord. 18 We have disobeyed him, and have not heeded the voice of the Lord our God, to walk in the statutes of the Lord that he set before us. 19 From the time when the Lord brought our ancestors out of the land of Egypt until today, we have been disobedient to the Lord our God, and we have been negligent, in not heeding his voice. 20 So to this day there have clung to us the calamities and the curse that the Lord declared through his servant Moses at the time when he brought our ancestors out of the land of Egypt to give to us a land flowing with milk and honey. 21 We did not listen to the voice of the Lord our God in all the words of the prophets whom he sent to us, 22 but all of us followed the intent of our own wicked hearts by serving other gods and doing what is evil in the sight of the Lord our God.

2 So the Lord carried out the threat he spoke against us: against our judges who ruled Israel, and against our kings and our rulers and the people of Israel and Judah. 2 Under the whole heaven there has not been done the like of what he has done in Jerusalem, in accordance with the threats that were[d] written in the law of Moses. 3 Some of us ate the flesh of their sons and others the flesh of their daughters. 4 He made them subject to all the kingdoms around us, to be an object of scorn and a desolation among all the surrounding peoples, where the Lord has scattered them. 5 They were brought down and not raised up, because our nation[e] sinned against the Lord our God, in not heeding his voice.

6 The Lord our God is in the right, but there is open shame on us and our ancestors this very day. 7 All those calamities with which the Lord threatened us have come upon us. 8 Yet we have not entreated the favor of the Lord by turning away, each of us, from the thoughts of our wicked hearts. 9 And the Lord has kept the calamities ready, and the Lord has brought them upon us, for the Lord is just in all the works that he has commanded us to do. 10 Yet we have not obeyed his voice, to walk in the statutes of the Lord that he set before us.

Prayer for Deliverance

11 And now, O Lord God of Israel, who brought your people out of the land of Egypt with a mighty hand and with signs and wonders and with great power and outstretched arm, and made yourself a name that continues to this day, 12 we have sinned, we have been ungodly, we have done wrong, O Lord our God, against all your ordinances. 13 Let your anger turn away from us, for we are left, few in number, among the nations where you have scattered us. 14 Hear, O Lord, our prayer and our supplication, and for your own sake de-

1.12 Ps 28.8; 29.11; Isa 49.5; Jer 16.19; 25.11; 29.4-10 **1.13** Num 21.7; Ezra 9.10-11; Ps 106.6; Dan 9.5-6; Isa 51.17; Jer 25.15-16; Bar 2.20 **1.14** Deut 31.11; Neh 8.3; Jer 36.6; Lev 23.1-43; Num 28.16-29,39; Deut 16.1-17 **1.15** Neh 9.33; Dan 9.7; Bar 2.6 **1.17** Bar 1.13 **1.18** Lev 18.4-5; Deut 10.12-13; Ps 78.10; Bar 2.10 **1.19** Ex 12.29-39; Ps 78.17-41 **1.20** Deut 28.15-68; 2 Kings 17.5-7; 25.1-21; Ex 3.8,17; Num 13.27; Deut 8.7-10 **1.21** 2 Chr 36.16; Neh 9.30; Acts 7.51-52 **2.1** Judg 2.2-3; 1 Kings 10.11; 2 Kings 21.11-15 **2.2** Deut 28.15-68; Bar 1.20 **2.3** Jer 19.9; Lam 4.10; Ezek 5.10 **2.4** Jer 6.10; 20.8; Ezek 23.32 **2.6** Bar 1.15 **2.7** Bar 1.20; 3.4 **2.8** Gen 6.5; Jer 17.9

2.10 Bar 1.18 **2.11** Ex 12.29-39; Bar 1.19; Deut 4.34; 5.15; Ps 105.27 **2.12** Bar 1.13 **2.13** Ps 90.11,13; Dan 9.16; Deut 4.27; Jer 9.16; Ezek 11.16

[c] Gk *in the shadow* [d] Gk *in accordance with what is* [e] Gk *because we*

liver us, and grant us favor in the
sight of those who have carried us
into exile; 15 so that all the earth
may know that you are the Lord
our God, for Israel and his descendants are called by your name.
16 O Lord, look down from your
holy dwelling, and consider us. Incline your ear, O Lord, and hear;
17 open your eyes, O Lord, and see,
for the dead who are in Hades,
whose spirit has been taken from
their bodies, will not ascribe glory
or justice to the Lord; 18 but the
person who is deeply grieved, who
walks bowed and feeble, with failing eyes and famished soul, will
declare your glory and righteousness, O Lord.
19 For it is not because of any
righteous deeds of our ancestors or
our kings that we bring before you
our prayer for mercy, O Lord our
God. 20 For you have sent your anger and your wrath upon us, as you
declared by your servants the
prophets, saying: 21 Thus says the
Lord: Bend your shoulders and
serve the king of Babylon, and you
will remain in the land that I gave
to your ancestors. 22 But if you will
not obey the voice of the Lord and
will not serve the king of Babylon,
23 I will make to cease from the
towns of Judah and from the region around Jerusalem the voice of
mirth and the voice of gladness,
the voice of the bridegroom and
the voice of the bride, and the
whole land will be a desolation
without inhabitants.
24 But we did not obey your
voice, to serve the king of Babylon;
and you have carried out your
threats, which you spoke by your
servants the prophets, that the
bones of our kings and the bones
of our ancestors would be brought
out of their resting place; 25 and indeed they have been thrown out to
the heat of day and the frost of
night. They perished in great misery, by famine and sword and pestilence. 26 And the house that is
called by your name you have
made as it is today, because of the
wickedness of the house of Israel
and the house of Judah.

God's Promise Recalled

27 Yet you have dealt with us,
O Lord our God, in all your kindness and in all your great compassion, 28 as you spoke by your servant Moses on the day when you
commanded him to write your law
in the presence of the people of Israel, saying, 29 "If you will not obey
my voice, this very great multitude
will surely turn into a small number among the nations, where I will
scatter them. 30 For I know that
they will not obey me, for they are
a stiff-necked people. But in the
land of their exile they will come to
themselves 31 and know that I am
the Lord their God. I will give them
a heart that obeys and ears that
hear; 32 they will praise me in the
land of their exile, and will remember my name 33 and turn from their
stubbornness and their wicked
deeds; for they will remember the
ways of their ancestors, who
sinned before the Lord. 34 I will
bring them again into the land that
I swore to give to their ancestors,
to Abraham, Isaac, and Jacob, and
they will rule over it; and I will increase them, and they will not be
diminished. 35 I will make an everlasting covenant with them to be
their God and they shall be my
people; and I will never again remove my people Israel from the
land that I have given them."

3 O Lord Almighty, God of Israel, the soul in anguish and
the wearied spirit cry out to you.
2 Hear, O Lord, and have mercy, for
we have sinned before you. 3 For
you are enthroned forever, and we
are perishing forever. 4 O Lord Almighty, God of Israel, hear now the
prayer of the people[f] of Israel, the
children of those who sinned before you, who did not heed the
voice of the Lord their God, so that
calamities have clung to us. 5 Do
not remember the iniquities of our
ancestors, but in this crisis remember your power and your name.

2.15 Ezek 35.4,9; 38.23; 39.28; Deut 28.10; 2 Chr 7.14; Jer 14.9 **2.16** Deut 26.15; 2 Chr 6.21; Ps 33.13-14 **2.17** Ps 6.5; 30.9; Isa 38.18 **2.18** Ps 51.15; 96.3; Isa 66.19 **2.20** Ps 90.9; Zeph 1.18-2.3; Bar 1.13 **2.21** Jer 25.11; 27.12; Bar 1.12 **2.23** Isa 24.7-8; Ezek 26.13; Jer 7.34 **2.24** Bar 1.18; 2.2; Jer 8.1-2 **2.25** Jdt 7.32; Jer 14.12-13; 21.9 **2.26** 1 Kings 8.18-20; 1 Chr 22.10; Jer 7.11 **2.27** Deut 13.17; Ps 103.13; Isa 54.7-10 **2.28** Deut 4.25-28; 28.58-65; 29.28 **2.30** Ex 32.9; 33.3,5; 2 Chr 30.8 **2.31** Deut 4.30; 30.1-5,6; Jer 32.39; Ezek 36.26 **2.32** Jer 33.9; Tob 13.7; Ps 119.55 **2.33** Neh 9.16-31; Dan 9.7-14 **2.34** Gen 13.14-17; 26.3; 28.13-14; 50.24 **2.35** Gen 17.7; Jer 31.31-34; 32.40; Ezek 39.25-29; Jer 30.22; Ezek 36.28; Zech 13.9 **3.3** 2 Kings 19.15; Ps 9.7; 29.10 **3.4** Bar 1.20; 2.7,9 **3.5** Ps 74.2; Add Esth 14.12

[f] Gk *dead*

[6]For you are the Lord our God, and
it is you, O Lord, whom we will
praise. [7]For you have put the fear
of you in our hearts so that we
would call upon your name; and
we will praise you in our exile, for
we have put away from our hearts
all the iniquity of our ancestors
who sinned against you. [8]See, we
are today in our exile where you
have scattered us, to be reproached and cursed and punished
for all the iniquities of our ancestors, who forsook the Lord our
God.

In Praise of Wisdom

9 Hear the commandments of life, O Israel;
give ear, and learn wisdom!
10 Why is it, O Israel, why is it
that you are in the land of your enemies,
that you are growing old in a foreign country,
that you are defiled with the dead,
11 that you are counted among those in Hades?
12 You have forsaken the fountain of wisdom.
13 If you had walked in the way of God,
you would be living in peace forever.
14 Learn where there is wisdom,
where there is strength,
where there is understanding,
so that you may at the same time discern
where there is length of days, and life,
where there is light for the eyes, and peace.
15 Who has found her place?
And who has entered her storehouses?
16 Where are the rulers of the nations,
and those who lorded it over the animals on earth;
17 those who made sport of the birds of the air,
and who hoarded up silver and gold
in which people trust,
and there is no end to their getting;
18 those who schemed to get silver, and were anxious,
but there is no trace of their works?
19 They have vanished and gone down to Hades,
and others have arisen in their place.
20 Later generations have seen the light of day,
and have lived upon the earth;
but they have not learned the way to knowledge,
nor understood her paths,
nor laid hold of her.
21 Their descendants have strayed far from her[g] way.
22 She has not been heard of in Canaan,
or seen in Teman;
23 the descendants of Hagar, who seek for understanding on the earth,
the merchants of Merran and Teman,
the story-tellers and the seekers for understanding,
have not learned the way to wisdom,
or given thought to her paths.
24 O Israel, how great is the house of God,
how vast the territory that he possesses!
25 It is great and has no bounds;
it is high and immeasurable.
26 The giants were born there, who were famous of old,
great in stature, expert in war.

3.7 Jer 13.19; 52.27-30; Tob 3.4; Bar 2.32 **3.8** Bar 4.8 **3.9** Prov 4.5,7,20; Wis 6.9; Sir 1.1 **3.11** Ps 28.1; 88.4; Bar 2.17 **3.12** Prov 14.27; 16.22; Jer 2.13; 17.13 **13.3** Ps 119.165; Prov 3.1-2; Isa 26.3; 48.18 **3.14** Deut 31.12-13; Prov 8.5-21; Wis 6.1-11; Deut 30.20; Ps 21.4; Prov 3.2 **3.15** Job 28.12-28 **3.16** Jer 27.6 **3.17** Job 31.24-28; Ps 49.5-6; 1 Tim 6.17 **3.18** Lk 12.16-22 **3.19** Ps 73.18-20; Lk 16.23 **3.20** 1 Cor 2.8 **3.22** Jer 49.7,20; Am 1.12 **3.23** Gen 25.12-18 **3.25** 3 Macc 2.9 **3.26** Gen 6.4; Num 13.33; Wis 14.6; Sir 16.7; 1 Sam 17.4-11

[g] Other ancient authorities read *their*

[27] God did not choose them,
or give them the way to knowledge;
[28] so they perished because they had no wisdom,
they perished through their folly.

[29] Who has gone up into heaven, and taken her,
and brought her down from the clouds?
[30] Who has gone over the sea, and found her,
and will buy her for pure gold?
[31] No one knows the way to her,
or is concerned about the path to her.
[32] But the one who knows all things knows her,
he found her by his understanding.
The one who prepared the earth for all time
filled it with four-footed creatures;
[33] the one who sends forth the light, and it goes;
he called it, and it obeyed him, trembling;
[34] the stars shone in their watches, and were glad;
he called them, and they said, "Here we are!"
They shone with gladness for him who made them.
[35] This is our God;
no other can be compared to him.
[36] He found the whole way to knowledge,
and gave her to his servant Jacob
and to Israel, whom he loved.
[37] Afterward she appeared on earth
and lived with humankind.

4 She is the book of the commandments of God,
the law that endures forever.
All who hold her fast will live,
and those who forsake her will die.
[2] Turn, O Jacob, and take her;
walk toward the shining of her light.
[3] Do not give your glory to another,
or your advantages to an alien people.
[4] Happy are we, O Israel,
for we know what is pleasing to God.

Encouragement for Israel

[5] Take courage, my people,
who perpetuate Israel's name!
[6] It was not for destruction
that you were sold to the nations,
but you were handed over to your enemies
because you angered God.
[7] For you provoked the one who made you
by sacrificing to demons and not to God.
[8] You forgot the everlasting God, who brought you up,
and you grieved Jerusalem, who reared you.
[9] For she saw the wrath that came upon you from God,
and she said:
Listen, you neighbors of Zion,
God has brought great sorrow upon me;
[10] for I have seen the exile of my sons and daughters,
which the Everlasting brought upon them.
[11] With joy I nurtured them,
but I sent them away with weeping and sorrow.
[12] Let no one rejoice over me, a widow
and bereaved of many;
I was left desolate because of the sins of my children,
because they turned away from the law of God.
[13] They had no regard for his statutes;

3.28 1 Sam 17.48-51 **3.29** Deut 30.12-13; Rom 10.6-7 **3.30** Job 28.15-19; Prov 8.10,19; 16.16 **3.32** Ps 139.1-6; Rom 11.33; Gen 1.24-25; Jer 27.5 **3.33** Gen 1.3-5; Ps 104.1-2 **3.34** Job 38.7; Gen 1.16; Ps 147.4; Isa 40.26 **3.35** Ps 40.5; 89.8; Isa 40.18,25 **3.36** Ps 147.19; Sir 24.8-12 **3.37** Jn 1.14 **4.1** Ps 119.89; Mt 5.18; Deut 30.15-20 **4.2** Prov 4.18; Sir 24.32 **4.3** Isa 48.11; Deut 4.32-38; Rom 9.4-5 **4.5** 1 Chr 28.20; 2 Chr 32.7; Ps 27.14 **4.6** Jer 34.17-22; 2 Esd 3.27; Acts 7.42 **4.7** Deut 32.17; Ps 106.36-38; 1 Cor 10.20 **4.8** Bar 3.8; Isa 1.2; 63.16; Hos 11.1 **4.9** Jer 45.3; Lam 1.2-5,12 **4.10** Gen 21.33; 1 Chr 16.36; Ps 90.2; 93.2 **4.12** Lam 1.1 **4.13** Bar 2.19-26

they did not walk in the
ways of God's
commandments,
or tread the paths his
righteousness showed
them.
14 Let the neighbors of Zion
come;
remember the capture of
my sons and daughters,
which the Everlasting
brought upon them.
15 For he brought a distant
nation against them,
a nation ruthless and of a
strange language,
which had no respect for the
aged
and no pity for a child.
16 They led away the widow's
beloved sons,
and bereaved the lonely
woman of her
daughters.

17 But I, how can I help you?
18 For he who brought these
calamities upon you
will deliver you from the
hand of your enemies.
19 Go, my children, go;
for I have been left
desolate.
20 I have taken off the robe of
peace
and put on sackcloth for
my supplication;
I will cry to the Everlasting
all my days.

21 Take courage, my children,
cry to God,
and he will deliver you
from the power and
hand of the enemy.
22 For I have put my hope in
the Everlasting to save
you,
and joy has come to me
from the Holy One,
because of the mercy that
will soon come to you
from your everlasting
savior.[h]
23 For I sent you out with
sorrow and weeping,

4.15 Jer 4.16; 6.22; 5.15; Deut 28.49-50 **4.18** Bar 1.20; 3.4; Jer 15.21; 29.21; Bar 2.14 **4.20** Gen 37.34; 2 Kings 19.1; Isa 3.24; Jer 6.26; Bar 4.10 **4.21** Bar 4.5 **4.22** Isa 43.3,11; 49.26; Jer 14.8; Hos 13.4 **4.23** Ps 30.5; 126.5-6; Isa 35.10; Jer 31.13,16

4.24 Isa 45.17; 49.6,8; 52.10; Jer 3.23; Isa 60.1-3 **4.25** Sir 16.13; Jas 5.10; Deut 33.29; Mal 4.3 **4.26** Jer 13.17; 23.2 **4.27** Jer 31.20; Ezek 16.60 **4.28** Ps 27.8; Isa 55.6; Jer 29.13 **4.29** Isa 35.10; 51.11; 61.7 **4.30** Ps 46.1; Isa 40.1; 51.3; Jer 31.13 **4.31** Ezek 25.6-7; Ob 10-14 **4.32** Isa 13.19-22; Jer 51.24-26, 41-44

but God will give you back
to me with joy and
gladness forever.
24 For as the neighbors of Zion
have now seen your
capture,
so they soon will see your
salvation by God,
which will come to you with
great glory
and with the splendor of
the Everlasting.
25 My children, endure with
patience the wrath that
has come upon you
from God.
Your enemy has overtaken
you,
but you will soon see their
destruction
and will tread upon their
necks.
26 My pampered children have
traveled rough roads;
they were taken away like a
flock carried off by the
enemy.

27 Take courage, my children,
and cry to God,
for you will be remembered
by the one who brought
this upon you.
28 For just as you were
disposed to go astray
from God,
return with tenfold zeal to
seek him.
29 For the one who brought
these calamities upon
you
will bring you everlasting
joy with your salvation.

Jerusalem Is Assured of Help

30 Take courage, O Jerusalem,
for the one who named you
will comfort you.
31 Wretched will be those who
mistreated you
and who rejoiced at your
fall.
32 Wretched will be the cities
that your children
served as slaves;

[h] Or *from the Everlasting, your savior*

wretched will be the city
that received your
offspring.
33 For just as she rejoiced at
your fall
and was glad for your ruin,
so she will be grieved at
her own desolation.
34 I will take away her pride in
her great population,
and her insolence will be
turned to grief.
35 For fire will come upon her
from the Everlasting for
many days,
and for a long time she will
be inhabited by
demons.

36 Look toward the east,
O Jerusalem,
and see the joy that is
coming to you from
God.
37 Look, your children are
coming, whom you sent
away;
they are coming, gathered
from east and west,
at the word of the Holy One,
rejoicing in the glory of
God.

5 Take off the garment of your
sorrow and affliction,
O Jerusalem,
and put on forever the
beauty of the glory from
God.
2 Put on the robe of the
righteousness that
comes from God;
put on your head the
diadem of the glory of
the Everlasting;
3 for God will show your
splendor everywhere
under heaven.
4 For God will give you
evermore the name,
"Righteous Peace, Godly
Glory."

5 Arise, O Jerusalem, stand
upon the height;
look toward the east,
and see your children
gathered from west and
east
at the word of the Holy
One,
rejoicing that God has
remembered them.
6 For they went out from you
on foot,
led away by their enemies;
but God will bring them
back to you,
carried in glory, as on a
royal throne.
7 For God has ordered that
every high mountain
and the everlasting hills
be made low
and the valleys filled up, to
make level ground,
so that Israel may walk
safely in the glory of
God.
8 The woods and every fragrant
tree
have shaded Israel at God's
command.
9 For God will lead Israel with
joy,
in the light of his glory,
with the mercy and
righteousness that
come from him.

4.34 Isa 10.12; 13.11; Jer 51.41; Zech 10.11
4.35 Isa 34.8-10; Rev 14.11; Isa 13.21-22; Rev 18.2
4.37 Isa 59.19; Mt 8.11; Lk 13.29
5.1 Isa 52.1
5.2 Isa 61.10; Zech 3.4; Eph 4.24; Ex 39.30; Isa 62.3
5.4 Isa 1.26; 32.17; Jer 33.16
5.5 Bar 4.37
5.6 2 Kings 24.14-16; 25.11; 2 Chr 36.20; Isa 49.22; 60.4
5.7 Isa 40.4; 45.2; Lk 3.5
5.9 Bar 4.29

Letter of Jeremiah

Title and Background

The book of Jeremiah (29.1-23) records a letter written by the prophet to the Jews who had been taken into exile in Babylon. This book claims to be another similar letter by Jeremiah. More likely, however, it was written much later as a Jewish tirade against Jews who were assimilating pagan Hellenistic culture.

Author and Date of Writing

The author and even the original language of this book are unknown. It may have been written as early as the end of the third century B.C. or as late as the middle of the first century A.D. It starts with chapter 6 because in some manuscripts it appears as the sixth chapter of Baruch, though it is clearly not part of that book.

Theme and Message

This letter hurls harsh criticism at idols and demonstrates the foolishness of worshiping gods made by human hands. "It is you, O Lord, whom we must worship" (6.6).

Outline

I. Captivity Because of Human Sins (6.1-7)
II. The Helplessness of Idols (6.8-40)
III. The Foolishness of Worshiping Idols (6.41-73)

---

6 [a] A copy of a letter that Jeremiah sent to those who were to be taken to Babylon as exiles by the king of the Babylonians, to give them the message that God had commanded him.

The People Face a Long Captivity

2 Because of the sins that you have committed before God, you will be taken to Babylon as exiles by Nebuchadnezzar, king of the Babylonians. 3 Therefore when you have come to Babylon you will remain there for many years, for a long time, up to seven generations; after that I will bring you away from there in peace. 4 Now in Babylon you will see gods made of silver and gold and wood, which people carry on their shoulders, and which cause the heathen to fear. 5 So beware of becoming at all like the foreigners or of letting fear for these gods[b] possess you 6 when you see the multitude before and behind them worshiping them. But say in your heart, "It is you, O Lord, whom we must worship." 7 For my angel is with you, and he is watching over your lives.

6.1 Jer 29.1 **6.2** Jer 3.25; 40.2-3; 44.23; Bar 1.17 **6.3** 2 Chr 36.21; Jer 29.10 **6.4** Isa 44.11-17; 46.6-7; Jer 10.9; Wis 13.10-19 **6.5** Jer 10.1-2 **6.6** Deut 6.13; 10.20; 1 Chr 16.29; Ps 99.5,9; Mt 4.10 **6.7** Ex 23.20; Ps 91.11-12
6.8 Ps 135.16; Jer 10.5 **6.11** 2 Macc 6.4 **6.12** 1 Sam 5.3-4; Wis 13.16

The Helplessness of Idols

8 Their tongues are smoothed by the carpenter, and they themselves are overlaid with gold and silver; but they are false and cannot speak. 9 People[c] take gold and make crowns for the heads of their gods, as they might for a girl who loves ornaments. 10 Sometimes the priests secretly take gold and silver from their gods and spend it on themselves, 11 or even give some of it to the prostitutes on the terrace. They deck their gods[d] out with garments like human beings—these gods of silver and gold and wood 12 that cannot save themselves from rust and corrosion. When they have been dressed in purple robes, 13 their faces are wiped because of the dust from the temple, which is thick upon them. 14 One of them holds a scepter, like a district judge, but is unable to destroy anyone who offends it.

[a] The King James Version (like the Latin Vulgate) prints The Letter of Jeremiah as Chapter 6 of the Book of Baruch, and the chapter and verse numbers are here retained. In the Greek Septuagint, the Letter is separated from Baruch by the Book of Lamentations. [b] Gk *for them* [c] Gk *They* [d] Gk *them*

15 Another has a dagger in its right
hand, and an ax, but cannot defend itself from war and robbers.
16 From this it is evident that they
are not gods; so do not fear them.
17 For just as someone's dish is
useless when it is broken, 18 so are
their gods when they have been set
up in the temples. Their eyes are
full of the dust raised by the feet of
those who enter. And just as the
gates are shut on every side against
anyone who has offended a king, as
though under sentence of death,
so the priests make their temples
secure with doors and locks and
bars, in order that they may not be
plundered by robbers. 19 They light
more lamps for them than they
light for themselves, though their
gods[e] can see none of them.
20 They are[f] just like a beam of the
temple, but their hearts, it is said,
are eaten away when crawling
creatures from the earth devour
them and their robes. They do not
notice 21 when their faces have
been blackened by the smoke of
the temple. 22 Bats, swallows, and
birds alight on their bodies and
heads; and so do cats. 23 From this
you will know that they are not
gods; so do not fear them.
24 As for the gold that they wear
for beauty—it[g] will not shine unless someone wipes off the tarnish;
for even when they were being
cast, they did not feel it. 25 They are
bought without regard to cost, but
there is no breath in them. 26 Having no feet, they are carried on the
shoulders of others, revealing to
humankind their worthlessness.
And those who serve them are put
to shame 27 because, if any of these
gods falls[h] to the ground, they
themselves must pick it up. If anyone sets it upright, it cannot move
itself; and if it is tipped over, it
cannot straighten itself. Gifts are
placed before them just as before
the dead. 28 The priests sell the
sacrifices that are offered to these
gods[i] and use the money themselves. Likewise their wives preserve some of the meat[j] with salt,
but give none to the poor or helpless. 29 Sacrifices to them may even

6.16 Judg 6.25-32; Isa 36.18-21
6.18 Let Jer 6.57
6.19 Ps 135.16; Isa 44.18
6.24 Isa 46.6; Wis 13.10; 15.9
6.26 Isa 46.7; Jer 10.5
6.27 1 Sam 5.3-4; Isa 40.20; Let Jer 6.12
6.28 Deut 14.28-29
6.29 Lev 12.4; 15.19
6.31 Lev 10.6; 21.5; 1 Cor 11.5-6
6.32 1 Kings 18.27-28
6.34 Job 12.16-19; Dan 2.21; 4.35-37
6.36 Isa 44.20; 46.7; Jer 10.5
6.37 Isa 35.5; 42.7; Mt 11.5
6.39 Jer 50.2
6.40 Isa 46.1; Jer 51.44; Bel 3
6.43 Prov 7.10-14; Jer 3.2

be touched by women in their periods or at childbirth. Since you
know by these things that they are
not gods, do not fear them.
30 For how can they be called
gods? Women serve meals for gods
of silver and gold and wood; 31 and
in their temples the priests sit with
their clothes torn, their heads and
beards shaved, and their heads uncovered. 32 They howl and shout
before their gods as some do at a
funeral banquet. 33 The priests
take some of the clothing of their
gods[k] to clothe their wives and
children. 34 Whether one does evil
to them or good, they will not be
able to repay it. They cannot set up
a king or depose one. 35 Likewise
they are not able to give either
wealth or money; if one makes a
vow to them and does not keep it,
they will not require it. 36 They cannot save anyone from death or rescue the weak from the strong.
37 They cannot restore sight to the
blind; they cannot rescue one who
is in distress. 38 They cannot take
pity on a widow or do good to an
orphan. 39 These things that are
made of wood and overlaid with
gold and silver are like stones from
the mountain, and those who serve
them will be put to shame. 40 Why
then must anyone think that they
are gods, or call them gods?

The Foolishness of Worshiping Idols

Besides, even the Chaldeans
themselves dishonor them; for
when they see someone who cannot speak, they bring Bel and pray
that the mute may speak, as
though Bel[l] were able to understand! 41 Yet they themselves cannot perceive this and abandon
them, for they have no sense.
42 And the women, with cords
around them, sit along the pas-
sageways, burning bran for incense. 43 When one of them is led
off by one of the passers-by and is
taken to bed by him, she derides
the woman next to her, because

[e] Gk *they* [f] Gk *It is* [g] Lat Syr: Gk *they*
[h] Gk *if they fall* [i] Gk *to them* [j] Gk *of them*
[k] Gk *some of their clothing* [l] Gk *he*

she was not as attractive as herself
and her cord was not broken.
44 Whatever is done for these
idols[m] is false. Why then must anyone think that they are gods, or call
them gods?
45 They are made by carpenters
and goldsmiths; they can be nothing but what the artisans wish
them to be. 46 Those who make
them will certainly not live very
long themselves; 47 how then can
the things that are made by them
be gods? They have left only lies
and reproach for those who come
after. 48 For when war or calamity
comes upon them, the priests consult together as to where they can
hide themselves and their gods.[m]
49 How then can one fail to see that
these are not gods, for they cannot
save themselves from war or calamity? 50 Since they are made of
wood and overlaid with gold and
silver, it will afterward be known
that they are false. 51 It will be
manifest to all the nations and
kings that they are not gods but the
work of human hands, and that
there is no work of God in them.
52 Who then can fail to know that
they are not gods?[n]
53 For they cannot set up a king
over a country or give rain to people. 54 They cannot judge their own
cause or deliver one who is
wronged, for they have no power;
55 they are like crows between
heaven and earth. When fire
breaks out in a temple of wooden
gods overlaid with gold or silver,
their priests will flee and escape,
but the gods[o] will be burned up
like timbers. 56 Besides, they can
offer no resistance to king or enemy. Why then must anyone admit
or think that they are gods?
57 Gods made of wood and
overlaid with silver and gold are
unable to save themselves from
thieves or robbers. 58 Anyone who
can will strip them of their gold
and silver and of the robes they
wear, and go off with this booty,
and they will not be able to help
themselves. 59 So it is better to be a
king who shows his courage, or a
household utensil that serves its
owner's need, than to be these
false gods; better even the door of
a house that protects its contents,
than these false gods; better also a
wooden pillar in a palace, than
these false gods.
60 For sun and moon and stars
are bright, and when sent to do a
service, they are obedient. 61 So
also the lightning, when it flashes,
is widely seen; and the wind likewise blows in every land. 62 When
God commands the clouds to go
over the whole world, they carry
out his command. 63 And the fire
sent from above to consume
mountains and woods does what it
is ordered. But these idols[p] are
not to be compared with them in
appearance or power. 64 Therefore
one must not think that they are
gods, nor call them gods, for they
are not able either to decide a case
or to do good to anyone. 65 Since
you know then that they are not
gods, do not fear them.
66 They can neither curse nor
bless kings; 67 they cannot show
signs in the heavens for the nations, or shine like the sun or give
light like the moon. 68 The wild animals are better than they are, for
they can flee to shelter and help
themselves. 69 So we have no evidence whatever that they are gods;
therefore do not fear them.
70 Like a scarecrow in a cucumber bed, which guards nothing, so
are their gods of wood, overlaid
with gold and silver. 71 In the same
way, their gods of wood, overlaid
with gold and silver, are like a
thornbush in a garden on which every bird perches; or like a corpse
thrown out in the darkness.
72 From the purple and linen[q] that
rot upon them you will know that
they are not gods; and they will finally be consumed themselves,
and be a reproach in the land.
73 Better, therefore, is someone upright who has no idols; such a person will be far above reproach.

6.45 Isa 44.13-17; Wis 13.11-15; Isa 46.7
6.46 Wis 15.9
6.50 Let Jer 6.8
6.51 Bel 5; Acts 17.29
6.53 1 Kings 17.1; 18.1-6,41-46
6.57 Let Jer 6.18; 2 Macc 9.2
6.58 Wis 13.16; Let Jer 6.27
6.62 Ps 147.15-18; 148.8; Sir 43.13-17
6.63 1 Kings 18.38; 2 Kings 1.9-12
6.64 Let Jer 6.16, 29,40,54
6.66 Jer 10.2; Dan 6.27; Lk 21.11,25; Acts 2.19
6.70 Jer 10.5
6.73 1 Cor 10.14; 1 Jn 5.21

[m] Gk *them* [n] Meaning of Gk uncertain
[o] Gk *they* [p] Gk *these things*
[q] Cn: Gk *marble*, Syr *silk*

THE PRAYER OF

Azariah

AND THE SONG OF THE THREE JEWS

Title and Background

This prayer appears after Dan 3.23 in the Septuagint. As the title indicates, it is a prayer of Azariah, one of the three friends of Daniel. The text purports that Azariah prayed this prayer as the young men stood in the flames of Nebuchadnezzar's fiery furnace. This addition to Daniel also includes a song reportedly sung by the three friends during their deliverance from the furnace.

Author and Date of Writing

The author of this brief addition to the Hebrew book of Daniel is unknown. Many claim it was originally written in Hebrew about the middle of the second century B.C., though equally as many claim it had a Greek origin.

Theme and Message

Azariah confesses the sins of God's people that had led to Israel's exile into Babylon and concludes with a prayer for deliverance. After their deliverance, the three young men call upon all creation to praise the Lord for his many blessings.

Outline

I. The Prayer of Azariah (1-22)
II. Deliverance by the Angel of the Lord (23-27)
III. The Song of Praise (28-68)

(Additions to Daniel, inserted between 3.23 and 3.24)

The Prayer of Azariah in the Furnace

1 They[a] walked around in the
midst of the flames, singing hymns
to God and blessing the Lord.
2 Then Azariah stood still in the fire
and prayed aloud:

3 "Blessed are you, O Lord,
God of our ancestors,
and worthy of praise;
and glorious is your name
forever!
4 For you are just in all you
have done;
all your works are true and
your ways right,
and all your judgments are
true.
5 You have executed true
judgments in all you
have brought upon us
and upon Jerusalem, the
holy city of our
ancestors;
by a true judgment you
have brought all this
upon us because of our
sins.
6 For we have sinned and
broken your law in
turning away from you;
in all matters we have
sinned grievously.
7 We have not obeyed your
commandments,
we have not kept them or
done what you have
commanded us for our
own good.
8 So all that you have brought
upon us,
and all that you have done
to us,

1 Dan 3.24-25
2 Dan 1.6
3 Ps 41.13; 72.18-19; Tob 13.1; Jdt 13.17-18; Deut 28.58; Tob 11.14; 13.17
4 Deut 32.4; Ps 92.15; Sir 18.2; Bar 2.9; Ps 119.75, 137; Tob 3.5
5 Neh 11.1,18; Isa 48.2; 52.1; Rev 21.2,10
6 Dan 9.5-6; Bar 1.13,17; Let Jer 6.2
7 Ps 78.17-41; Bar 1.19

[a] That is, Hananiah, Mishael, and Azariah (Dan 2.17), the original names of Shadrach, Meshach, and Abednego (Dan 1.6-7)

you have done by a true
judgment.
9 You have handed us over to
our enemies, lawless
and hateful rebels,
and to an unjust king, the
most wicked in all the
world.
10 And now we cannot open our
mouths;
we, your servants who
worship you, have
become a shame and a
reproach.
11 For your name's sake do not
give us up forever,
and do not annul your
covenant.
12 Do not withdraw your
mercy from us,
for the sake of Abraham your
beloved
and for the sake of your
servant Isaac
and Israel your holy one,
13 to whom you promised
to multiply their
descendants like the
stars of heaven
and like the sand on the
shore of the sea.
14 For we, O Lord, have
become fewer than any
other nation,
and are brought low this
day in all the world
because of our sins.
15 In our day we have no ruler,
or prophet, or leader,
no burnt offering, or
sacrifice, or oblation, or
incense,
no place to make an
offering before you and
to find mercy.
16 Yet with a contrite heart and
a humble spirit may we
be accepted,
17 as though it were with
burnt offerings of rams
and bulls,
or with tens of thousands
of fat lambs;
such may our sacrifice be
in your sight today,
and may we unreservedly
follow you,[b]

9 Jer 32.17-22; Jdt 8.19; Bar 4.6; 1 Kings 25.1; Jer 27.6; 51.24-25 **10** Ps 44.13-16; Tob 3.4 **11** Ps 25.11; 79.9; 106.8; Isa 48.11; Jer 14.7,21 **12** Ps 105.7-11; 106.45; Isa 45.4 **13** Gen 15.5; 26.4; Sir 44.21; Gen 22.17; 32.12; 1 Kings 4.20; Hos 1.10 **15** Jer 18.18; Am 8.11-12; Ezek 34.5-6; Zech 10.2; Mt 9.36 **16** Ps 51.17; Jas 4.10 **17** 1 Sam 15.22; Isa 1.11; Mic 6.7-8; Ps 22.5; 25.2 **18** Deut 6.5; 10.12; Tob 1.12 **19** Wis 15.1; Sir 18.11; 2 Pet 3.9; Ex 34.6; Jer 31.20; Wis 15.1 **20** Ps. 29.2; 66.2; 79.9; 96.8 **21** Ps 31.17; 83.16-17 **22** Deut 6.4; Neh 9.6; Ps 83.18; Ezek 39.7 **23** Dan 3.19 **25** Dan 3.22 **26** Dan 3.25,28 **27** Dan 3.27 **29** 2 Chr 30.19, 22; Dan 2.23;

for no shame will come to
those who trust in you.
18 And now with all our heart
we follow you;
we fear you and seek your
presence.
19 Do not put us to shame,
but deal with us in your
patience
and in your abundant
mercy.
20 Deliver us in accordance
with your marvelous
works,
and bring glory to your
name, O Lord.
21 Let all who do harm to your
servants be put to
shame;
let them be disgraced and
deprived of all power,
and let their strength be
broken.
22 Let them know that you
alone are the Lord God,
glorious over the whole
world."

The Song of the Three Jews

23 Now the king's servants who
threw them in kept stoking the furnace with naphtha, pitch, tow, and
brushwood. 24 And the flames
poured out above the furnace
forty-nine cubits, 25 and spread out
and burned those Chaldeans who
were caught near the furnace.
26 But the angel of the Lord came
down into the furnace to be with
Azariah and his companions, and
drove the fiery flame out of the furnace, 27 and made the inside of the
furnace as though a moist wind
were whistling through it. The fire
did not touch them at all and
caused them no pain or distress.
28 Then the three with one
voice praised and glorified and
blessed God in the furnace:
29 "Blessed are you, O Lord,
God of our ancestors,
and to be praised and
highly exalted forever;
30 And blessed is your glorious,
holy name,

Tob 8.5 **1.30** Song of Thr 1.3

[b]Meaning of Gk uncertain

and to be highly praised
and highly exalted
forever.
31 Blessed are you in the
temple of your holy
glory,
and to be extolled and
highly glorified forever.
32 Blessed are you who look
into the depths from
your throne on the
cherubim,
and to be praised and
highly exalted forever.
33 Blessed are you on the
throne of your kingdom,
and to be extolled and
highly exalted forever.
34 Blessed are you in the
firmament of heaven,
and to be sung and
glorified forever.

35 "Bless the Lord, all you
works of the Lord;
sing praise to him and
highly exalt him
forever.
36 Bless the Lord, you heavens;
sing praise to him and
highly exalt him
forever.
37 Bless the Lord, you angels of
the Lord;
sing praise to him and
highly exalt him
forever.
38 Bless the Lord, all you
waters above the
heavens;
sing praise to him and
highly exalt him
forever.
39 Bless the Lord, all you
powers of the Lord;
sing praise to him and
highly exalt him
forever.
40 Bless the Lord, sun and
moon;
sing praise to him and
highly exalt him
forever.
41 Bless the Lord, stars of
heaven;
sing praise to him and
highly exalt him
forever.

32 1 Sam 4.4; 2 Sam 6.2; Ps 80.1; Isa 37.16
33 Ps 11.4; 47.8; 103.19; Isa 6.1; Sir 1.8
34 Ps 150.1
35 Ps 103.22
36 Ps 148.1
37 Ps 103.20; 148.2
38 Ps 148.4
40 Ps 148.3
41 Ps 148.3
43 Ps 148.8
44 Ps 148.8
45 Gen 8.22
46 Ps 148.8
50 Ps 148.8
53 Ps 148.9

42 "Bless the Lord, all rain and
dew;
sing praise to him and
highly exalt him
forever.
43 Bless the Lord, all you
winds;
sing praise to him and
highly exalt him
forever.
44 Bless the Lord, fire and heat;
sing praise to him and
highly exalt him
forever.
45 Bless the Lord, winter cold
and summer heat;
sing praise to him and
highly exalt him
forever.
46 Bless the Lord, dews and
falling snow;
sing praise to him and
highly exalt him
forever.
47 Bless the Lord, nights and
days;
sing praise to him and
highly exalt him
forever.
48 Bless the Lord, light and
darkness;
sing praise to him and
highly exalt him
forever.
49 Bless the Lord, ice and cold;
sing praise to him and
highly exalt him
forever.
50 Bless the Lord, frosts and
snows;
sing praise to him and
highly exalt him
forever.
51 Bless the Lord, lightnings
and clouds;
sing praise to him and
highly exalt him
forever.

52 "Let the earth bless the
Lord;
let it sing praise to him
and highly exalt him
forever.
53 Bless the Lord, mountains
and hills;

sing praise to him and
highly exalt him
forever.

54 Bless the Lord, all that grows
in the ground;
sing praise to him and
highly exalt him
forever.

55 Bless the Lord, seas and
rivers;
sing praise to him and
highly exalt him
forever.

56 Bless the Lord, you springs;
sing praise to him and
highly exalt him
forever.

57 Bless the Lord, you whales
and all that swim in the
waters;
sing praise to him and
highly exalt him
forever.

58 Bless the Lord, all birds of
the air;
sing praise to him and
highly exalt him
forever.

59 Bless the Lord, all wild
animals and cattle;
sing praise to him and
highly exalt him
forever.

60 "Bless the Lord, all people
on earth;
sing praise to him and
highly exalt him
forever.

61 Bless the Lord, O Israel;
sing praise to him and
highly exalt him
forever.

62 Bless the Lord, you priests of
the Lord;
sing praise to him and
highly exalt him
forever.

63 Bless the Lord, you servants
of the Lord;
sing praise to him and
highly exalt him
forever.

64 Bless the Lord, spirits and
souls of the righteous;
sing praise to him and
highly exalt him
forever.

65 Bless the Lord, you who are
holy and humble in
heart;
sing praise to him and
highly exalt him
forever.

66 "Bless the Lord, Hananiah,
Azariah, and Mishael;
sing praise to him and
highly exalt him
forever.
For he has rescued us from
Hades and saved us
from the power[c] of
death,
and delivered us from the
midst of the burning
fiery furnace;
from the midst of the fire
he has delivered us.

67 Give thanks to the Lord, for
he is good,
for his mercy endures
forever.

68 All who worship the Lord,
bless the God of gods,
sing praise to him and give
thanks to him,
for his mercy endures
forever."

54 Ps 148.9
58 Ps 148.10
59 Ps 148.10
60 Ps 117.1; 148.11
61 Ps 118.2; 135.19
62 Ps 118.3; 135.19-20
63 Ps 134.1
66 Dan 1.6; 3.25-28; Ps 107.13,19; Joel 2.32; Sir 51.12
67 1 Chr 16.34; Ps 107.1; 136.1
68 1 Chr 16.29; Ps 29.2; 100.2

[c] Gk *hand*

Susanna

(CHAPTER 13 OF THE GREEK VERSION OF DANIEL)

Title and Background

This book appears as chapter 13 in the Septuagint version of Daniel and gets its name from the young woman who was unjustly convicted of adultery. Daniel, still a young man, was already an important official in the court of the king of Babylon.

Author and Date of Writing

We don't know who wrote this legendary tale about Daniel, nor whether it was originally written in Hebrew, Aramaic, or Greek. It was probably composed about the middle of the second century B.C.

Theme and Message

Exposing the dishonesty of two lecherous Jewish elders making accusations against a faithful Jewish wife, Daniel stands out as a man in whom the spirit of the Lord lives. Like the accounts in the canonical Daniel, this story demonstrates that God vindicates those who obey his law and live virtuous lives.

Outline

I. The Elders' Attempted Seduction of Susanna (1-27)
II. Susanna's Trial and Conviction (28-46)
III. Daniel's Rescue of Susanna (47-64)

Susanna's Beauty Attracts Two Elders

1 There was a man living in
Babylon whose name was Joakim.
2 He married the daughter of Hilkiah, named Susanna, a very beautiful woman and one who feared
the Lord. 3 Her parents were righteous, and had trained their
daughter according to the law of
Moses. 4 Joakim was very rich, and
had a fine garden adjoining his
house; the Jews used to come to
him because he was the most honored of them all.
5 That year two elders from the
people were appointed as judges.
Concerning them the Lord had
said: "Wickedness came forth from
Babylon, from elders who were
judges, who were supposed to govern the people." 6 These men were
frequently at Joakim's house, and
all who had a case to be tried came
to them there.

2 Gen 12.11; Jdt 8.7
5 1 Sam 2.12-17; 3.13; 8.1-2
8 Ezek 23.8; Mt 5.28
9 Dan 4.26; 1 Macc 4.10, 40
11 Jdg 12.12,16

7 When the people left at noon,
Susanna would go into her husband's garden to walk. 8 Every day
the two elders used to see her, going in and walking about, and they
began to lust for her. 9 They sup-
pressed their consciences and
turned away their eyes from looking to Heaven or remembering
their duty to administer justice.
10 Both were overwhelmed with
passion for her, but they did not
tell each other of their distress,
11 for they were ashamed to disclose their lustful desire to seduce
her. 12 Day after day they watched
eagerly to see her.
13 One day they said to each
other, "Let us go home, for it is
time for lunch." So they both left
and parted from each other. 14 But
turning back, they met again; and
when each pressed the other for
the reason, they confessed their
lust. Then together they arranged
for a time when they could find her
alone.

The Elders Attempt to Seduce Susanna

15 Once, while they were
watching for an opportune day, she
went in as before with only two
maids, and wished to bathe in the
garden, for it was a hot day. 16 No
one was there except the two elders, who had hidden themselves
and were watching her. 17 She said
to her maids, "Bring me olive oil
and ointments, and shut the garden doors so that I can bathe."
18 They did as she told them: they
shut the doors of the garden and
went out by the side doors to bring
what they had been commanded;
they did not see the elders, because they were hiding.

19 When the maids had gone
out, the two elders got up and ran
to her. 20 They said, "Look, the garden doors are shut, and no one can
see us. We are burning with desire
for you; so give your consent, and
lie with us. 21 If you refuse, we will
testify against you that a young
man was with you, and this was
why you sent your maids away."

22 Susanna groaned and said, "I
am completely trapped. For if I do
this, it will mean death for me; if I
do not, I cannot escape your
hands. 23 I choose not to do it; I will
fall into your hands, rather than sin
in the sight of the Lord."

24 Then Susanna cried out with
a loud voice, and the two elders
shouted against her. 25 And one of
them ran and opened the garden
doors. 26 When the people in the
house heard the shouting in the
garden, they rushed in at the side
door to see what had happened to
her. 27 And when the elders told
their story, the servants felt very
much ashamed, for nothing like
this had ever been said about Susanna.

The Elders Testify against Susanna

28 The next day, when the people gathered at the house of her
husband Joakim, the two elders
came, full of their wicked plot to
have Susanna put to death. In the

15 2 Sam 11.2 **17** Add Esth 2.3, 9,12 **20** Gen 39.11-12; Prov 7.13-25 **22** Lev 20.10; Deut 22.22; Jn 8.3-5 **23** Gen 39.12; Ex 20.14 **28** Sus 22

31 Sus 2 **35** Sus 9 **36** Sus 21 **41** Num 35.30; Deut 17.6-7; Mt 18.16; Jn 8.17 **42** Tob 14.7; Rom 16.26; Ps 44.21; Jn 2.25; 13.11; Ps 139.1-4; Jer 1.4-5; Sir 17.19 **45** Dan 1.3-7

presence of the people they said,
29 "Send for Susanna daughter of
Hilkiah, the wife of Joakim." 30 So
they sent for her. And she came
with her parents, her children, and
all her relatives.

31 Now Susanna was a woman
of great refinement and beautiful
in appearance. 32 As she was veiled,
the scoundrels ordered her to be
unveiled, so that they might feast
their eyes on her beauty. 33 Those
who were with her and all who saw
her were weeping.

34 Then the two elders stood up
before the people and laid their
hands on her head. 35 Through her
tears she looked up toward
Heaven, for her heart trusted in the
Lord. 36 The elders said, "While we
were walking in the garden alone,
this woman came in with two
maids, shut the garden doors, and
dismissed the maids. 37 Then a
young man, who was hiding there,
came to her and lay with her. 38 We
were in a corner of the garden, and
when we saw this wickedness we
ran to them. 39 Although we saw
them embracing, we could not
hold the man, because he was
stronger than we, and he opened
the doors and got away. 40 We did,
however, seize this woman and
asked who the young man was,
41 but she would not tell us. These
things we testify."

Because they were elders of the
people and judges, the assembly
believed them and condemned her
to death.

42 Then Susanna cried out with
a loud voice, and said, "O eternal
God, you know what is secret and
are aware of all things before they
come to be; 43 you know that these
men have given false evidence
against me. And now I am to die,
though I have done none of the
wicked things that they have
charged against me!"

44 The Lord heard her cry.
45 Just as she was being led off to
execution, God stirred up the holy
spirit of a young lad named Daniel,
46 and he shouted with a loud
voice, "I want no part in shedding
this woman's blood!"

Daniel Rescues Susanna

47 All the people turned to him
and asked, "What is this you are
saying?" 48 Taking his stand among
them he said, "Are you such fools,
O Israelites, as to condemn a
daughter of Israel without examination and without learning the
facts? 49 Return to court, for these
men have given false evidence
against her."

50 So all the people hurried
back. And the rest of the[a] elders
said to him, "Come, sit among us
and inform us, for God has given
you the standing of an elder."
51 Daniel said to them, "Separate
them far from each other, and I will
examine them."

52 When they were separated
from each other, he summoned
one of them and said to him, "You
old relic of wicked days, your sins
have now come home, which you
have committed in the past, 53 pro-
nouncing unjust judgments, condemning the innocent and acquit-
ting the guilty, though the Lord
said, 'You shall not put an innocent and righteous person to
death.' 54 Now then, if you really
saw this woman, tell me this: Under what tree did you see them being intimate with each other?" He
answered, "Under a mastic tree."[b]
55 And Daniel said, "Very well! This
lie has cost you your head, for the
angel of God has received the sentence from God and will immediately cut[b] you in two."

56 Then, putting him to one
side, he ordered them to bring the
other. And he said to him, "You
offspring of Canaan and not of Judah, beauty has beguiled you and
lust has perverted your heart.
57 This is how you have been treating the daughters of Israel, and
they were intimate with you
through fear; but a daughter of Judah would not tolerate your wickedness. 58 Now then, tell me: Under what tree did you catch them
being intimate with each other?"
He answered, "Under an evergreen
oak."[c] 59 Daniel said to him, "Very
well! This lie has cost you also your
head, for the angel of God is waiting with his sword to split[c] you in
two, so as to destroy you both."

60 Then the whole assembly
raised a great shout and blessed
God, who saves those who hope in
him. 61 And they took action
against the two elders, because out
of their own mouths Daniel had
convicted them of bearing false
witness; they did to them as they
had wickedly planned to do to
their neighbor. 62 Acting in accordance with the law of Moses, they
put them to death. Thus innocent
blood was spared that day.

63 Hilkiah and his wife praised
God for their daughter Susanna,
and so did her husband Joakim
and all her relatives, because she
was found innocent of a shameful
deed. 64 And from that day onward
Daniel had a great reputation
among the people.

49 Ex 20.16
51 1 Kings 3.16-28
53 Ex 23.7
55 2 Sam 24.16; 1 Chr 21.15; Ps 78.49; Acts 5.3-5
56 Sus 8-11
59 Acts 5.7-10
60 Ps 7.10; 37.39-40; Sir 34.14-16
62 Deut 19.18-19; Prov 19.5,9
64 Dan 1.20; 2.48; 5.29; Bel 2

[a] Gk lacks *rest of the* [b] The Greek words for *mastic tree* and *cut* are similar, thus forming an ironic wordplay [c] The Greek words for *evergreen oak* and *split* are similar, thus forming an ironic wordplay

Bel and the Dragon

(CHAPTER 14 OF THE GREEK VERSION OF DANIEL)

Title and Background

This book gets its name from the stories it tells about Daniel. It appears as Chapter 14 of Daniel in the Septuagint.

Author and Date of Writing

We don't know who wrote these legendary tales, nor whether they were originally written in Hebrew, Aramaic, or Greek. The stories were probably composed about the middle of the second century B.C.

Theme and Message

Like the canonical story of Daniel in the lions' den, the three stories recorded in this brief chapter demonstrate the power of God over the gods of the pagan nations. Daniel himself receives his wisdom from God, and God protects him from those who would do him evil.

Outline

I. Daniel Exposes the Priests of Bel (1-22)
II. Daniel Kills the Dragon (23-27)
III. Daniel Survives Six Days in the Lions' Den (28–42)

Daniel and the Priests of Bel

1 When King Astyages was laid
to rest with his ancestors, Cyrus
the Persian succeeded to his kingdom. 2 Daniel was a companion of
the king, and was the most honored of all his friends.
3 Now the Babylonians had an
idol called Bel, and every day they
provided for it twelve bushels of
choice flour and forty sheep and
six measures[a] of wine. 4 The king
revered it and went every day to
worship it. But Daniel worshiped
his own God.
So the king said to him, "Why do
you not worship Bel?" 5 He answered, "Because I do not revere
idols made with hands, but the living God, who created heaven and
earth and has dominion over all
living creatures."
6 The king said to him, "Do you
not think that Bel is a living god?
Do you not see how much he eats
and drinks every day?" 7 And Daniel laughed, and said, "Do not be
deceived, O king, for this thing is
only clay inside and bronze outside, and it never ate or drank anything."
8 Then the king was angry and
called the priests of Bel[b] and said
to them, "If you do not tell me who
is eating these provisions, you
shall die. 9 But if you prove that Bel
is eating them, Daniel shall die,
because he has spoken blasphemy
against Bel." Daniel said to the
king, "Let it be done as you have
said."
10 Now there were seventy
priests of Bel, besides their wives
and children. So the king went
with Daniel into the temple of Bel.
11 The priests of Bel said, "See, we
are now going outside; you yourself, O king, set out the food and
prepare the wine, and shut the
door and seal it with your signet.
12 When you return in the morning,
if you do not find that Bel has
eaten it all, we will die; otherwise
Daniel will, who is telling lies
about us." 13 They were uncon-

2 Dan 6.1-3; Sus 64
3 Isa 46.1; Jer 50.2; Let Jer 6.40
4 Dan 6.10-11
5 Let Jer 6.8-73; Acts 17.29; Dan 6.20,26; 2 Cor 3.3; 1 Thess 1.9; Heb 9.14; 12.22; Gen 1.1; Isa 45.18; Sir 18.1
11 Let Jer 6.27-28; Dan 6.17; Mt 27.66

[a] A little more than fifty gallons
[b] Gk *his priests*

cerned, for beneath the table they had made a hidden entrance, through which they used to go in regularly and consume the provisions. 14 After they had gone out, the king set out the food for Bel. Then Daniel ordered his servants to bring ashes, and they scattered them throughout the whole temple in the presence of the king alone. Then they went out, shut the door and sealed it with the king's signet, and departed. 15 During the night the priests came as usual, with their wives and children, and they ate and drank everything.

16 Early in the morning the king rose and came, and Daniel with him. 17 The king said, "Are the seals unbroken, Daniel?" He answered, "They are unbroken, O king." 18 As soon as the doors were opened, the king looked at the table, and shouted in a loud voice, "You are great, O Bel, and in you there is no deceit at all!"

19 But Daniel laughed and restrained the king from going in. "Look at the floor," he said, "and notice whose footprints these are." 20 The king said, "I see the footprints of men and women and children."

21 Then the king was enraged, and he arrested the priests and their wives and children. They showed him the secret doors through which they used to enter to consume what was on the table. 22 Therefore the king put them to death, and gave Bel over to Daniel, who destroyed it and its temple.

Daniel Kills the Dragon

23 Now in that place[c] there was a great dragon, which the Babylonians revered. 24 The king said to Daniel, "You cannot deny that this is a living god; so worship him." 25 Daniel said, "I worship the Lord my God, for he is the living God. 26 But give me permission, O king, and I will kill the dragon without sword or club." The king said, "I give you permission."

27 Then Daniel took pitch, fat, and hair, and boiled them together and made cakes, which he fed to the dragon. The dragon ate them, and burst open. Then Daniel said, "See what you have been worshiping!"

28 When the Babylonians heard about it, they were very indignant and conspired against the king, saying, "The king has become a Jew; he has destroyed Bel, and killed the dragon, and slaughtered the priests." 29 Going to the king, they said, "Hand Daniel over to us, or else we will kill you and your household." 30 The king saw that they were pressing him hard, and under compulsion he handed Daniel over to them.

Daniel in the Lions' Den

31 They threw Daniel into the lions' den, and he was there for six days. 32 There were seven lions in the den, and every day they had been given two human bodies and two sheep; but now they were given nothing, so that they would devour Daniel.

33 Now the prophet Habakkuk was in Judea; he had made a stew and had broken bread into a bowl, and was going into the field to take it to the reapers. 34 But the angel of the Lord said to Habakkuk, "Take the food that you have to Babylon, to Daniel, in the lions' den." 35 Habakkuk said, "Sir, I have never seen Babylon, and I know nothing about the den." 36 Then the angel of the Lord took him by the crown of his head and carried him by his hair; with the speed of the wind[d] he set him down in Babylon, right over the den.

37 Then Habakkuk shouted, "Daniel, Daniel! Take the food that God has sent you." 38 Daniel said, "You have remembered me, O God, and have not forsaken those who love you." 39 So Daniel got up and ate. And the angel of God immediately returned Habakkuk to his own place.

40 On the seventh day the king came to mourn for Daniel. When

16 Dan 6.19
18 Acts 19.28
21 Bel 13
22 1 Kings 18.40
25 Bel 5
29 1 Kings 19.1-2
30 Dan 6.13-15
31 Dan 6.16
33 Hab 1.1; 3.1
34 Dan 6.22
36 Ezek 8.3
37 1 Kings 17.6; 19.5-8
38 Ps 98.3; 136.23; Add Esth 10.12; Ps 18.1-3; 31.23; 145.20
40 Dan 6.20-22

[c] Other ancient authorities lack *in that place*
[d] Or *by the power of his spirit*

he came to the den he looked in,
and there sat Daniel! 41 The king
shouted with a loud voice, "You
are great, O Lord, the God of Daniel, and there is no other besides
you!" 42 Then he pulled Daniel[e]
out, and threw into the den those
who had attempted his destruction, and they were instantly eaten
before his eyes.

41 Dan 2.47; Isa 44.6; Dan 4.34-35; Sir 12.13
42 Dan 6.24

[e] Gk *him*

1 Maccabees

Title and Background

This book gets its name from Judas Maccabeus, the leader of a group of Jews who sought to purify their people from the influences of the Hellenistic Greek culture. This group sought to free their nation from the Seleucid rulers (notably Antiochus IV Epiphanes), who wanted to destroy the Jewish faith. The book recounts the exploits of Judas and his four brothers.

Author and Date of Writing

The author of this book was undoubtedly a God-fearing Jew who wrote this history of the Maccabean period in Hebrew. Since the last event recorded in this book occurred in 135 B.C., it was probably written near the end of the second century B.C.

Theme and Message

The main theme of this book is that God does not want his people to distort the religion of the Holy Scriptures to fit the ways of the pagan world. Those who stand up for authentic Judaism will receive help from the Lord and will achieve great victory in his name.

Outline

I. The Policies of Antiochus IV Epiphanes (1.1-64)
II. The Life of Mattathais (2.1-70)
III. The Exploits of Judas Maccabeus (3.1–9.22)
IV. The Exploits of Jonathan, Brother of Judas (9.23–12.53)
V. The Exploits of Simon, Brother of Judas (12.1–16.24)

Alexander the Great

1 After Alexander son of Philip,
the Macedonian, who came
from the land of Kittim, had defeated[a] King Darius of the Persians and the Medes, he succeeded
him as king. (He had previously become king of Greece.)
2 He fought
many battles, conquered strongholds, and put to death the kings
of the earth.
3 He advanced to the
ends of the earth, and plundered
many nations. When the earth became quiet before him, he was exalted, and his heart was lifted up.
4 He gathered a very strong army
and ruled over countries, nations,
and princes, and they became trib-
utary to him.
5 After this he fell sick and perceived that he was dying.
6 So he
summoned his most honored officers, who had been brought up
with him from youth, and divided
his kingdom among them while he
was still alive.
7 And after Alexan-
der had reigned twelve years, he
died.
8 Then his officers began to
rule, each in his own place.
9 They
all put on crowns after his death,
and so did their descendants after
them for many years; and they
caused many evils on the earth.

Antiochus Epiphanes and Renegade Jews

10 From them came forth a sinful root, Antiochus Epiphanes, son
of King Antiochus; he had been a
hostage in Rome. He began to
reign in the one hundred thirty-
seventh year of the kingdom of the
Greeks.[b]
11 In those days certain renegades came out from Israel and
misled many, saying, "Let us go
and make a covenant with the
Gentiles around us, for since we

1.1 Dan 8.5-9; 11.2-4; 1 Macc 6.2
1.3 Dan 4.28-30
1.5 Dan 8.8
1.6 Dan 8.8
1.10 Dan 8.9; 11.21; 1 Macc 3.27; 6.1; 2 Macc 2.20; 4.7

[a] Gk adds *and he defeated* [b] 175 B.C.

separated from them many disasters have come upon us." 12 This
proposal pleased them, 13 and
some of the people eagerly went to
the king, who authorized them to
observe the ordinances of the Gentiles. 14 So they built a gymnasium
in Jerusalem, according to Gentile
custom, 15 and removed the marks
of circumcision, and abandoned
the holy covenant. They joined
with the Gentiles and sold themselves to do evil.

Antiochus in Egypt

16 When Antiochus saw that his
kingdom was established, he determined to become king of the
land of Egypt, in order that he
might reign over both kingdoms.
17 So he invaded Egypt with a
strong force, with chariots and elephants and cavalry and with a large
fleet. 18 He engaged King Ptolemy
of Egypt in battle, and Ptolemy
turned and fled before him, and
many were wounded and fell.
19 They captured the fortified cities
in the land of Egypt, and he plundered the land of Egypt.

Persecution of the Jews

20 After subduing Egypt, Antiochus returned in the one hundred
forty-third year.[c] He went up
against Israel and came to Jerusalem with a strong force. 21 He arrogantly entered the sanctuary and
took the golden altar, the lampstand for the light, and all its utensils. 22 He took also the table for
the bread of the Presence, the cups
for drink offerings, the bowls, the
golden censers, the curtain, the
crowns, and the gold decoration on
the front of the temple; he stripped
it all off. 23 He took the silver and
the gold, and the costly vessels; he
took also the hidden treasures that
he found. 24 Taking them all, he
went into his own land.

He shed much blood,
and spoke with great
arrogance.
25 Israel mourned deeply in
every community,
26 rulers and elders groaned,
young women and young
men became faint,
the beauty of the women
faded.
27 Every bridegroom took up
the lament;
she who sat in the bridal
chamber was mourning.
28 Even the land trembled for
its inhabitants,
and all the house of Jacob
was clothed with
shame.

The Occupation of Jerusalem

29 Two years later the king sent
to the cities of Judah a chief collector of tribute, and he came to
Jerusalem with a large force. 30 Deceitfully he spoke peaceable words
to them, and they believed him;
but he suddenly fell upon the city,
dealt it a severe blow, and destroyed many people of Israel.
31 He plundered the city, burned it
with fire, and tore down its houses
and its surrounding walls. 32 They
took captive the women and children, and seized the livestock.
33 Then they fortified the city of David with a great strong wall and
strong towers, and it became their
citadel. 34 They stationed there a
sinful people, men who were renegades. These strengthened their
position; 35 they stored up arms
and food, and collecting the spoils
of Jerusalem they stored them
there, and became a great menace,
36 for the citadel[d] became an
ambush against the
sanctuary,
an evil adversary of Israel
at all times.
37 On every side of the
sanctuary they shed
innocent blood;
they even defiled the
sanctuary.
38 Because of them the
residents of Jerusalem
fled;
she became a dwelling of
strangers;
she became strange to her
offspring,

1.13 2 Macc 4.13-15
1.14 2 Macc 4.12
1.15 1 Cor 7.18; 1 Macc 6.23
1.17 Dan 11.25, 29; 2 Macc 5.1; 4 Macc 4.22; 1 Macc 3.34; 6.30; 2 Macc 11.4; 13.2
1.18 1 Macc 10.51
1.20 2 Kings 25.1,8; 2 Macc 5.11
1.21 2 Macc 5.15; 2 Kings 25.13-17; 2 Macc 5.16
1.24 2 Macc 5.21; 9.8
1.25 Lam 1.4
1.26 Lam 1.18; 2.21
1.27 Jer 7.34; 16.9; 25.10
1.29 2 Macc 5.22-24
1.30 2 Macc 5.25, 24
1.31 2 Kings 25.9; 2 Chr 36.19
1.32 2 Kings 25.11; 2 Chr 36.20
1.33 1 Macc 6.18; 13.49; 2 Macc 15.31
1.34 Isa 1.4; 1 Macc 14.14
1.37 Ps 79.1; Jer 32.34; 1 Macc 4.45
1.38 Lam 5.2; Zeph 1.13

[c] 169 B.C. [d] Gk *it*

and her children forsook
her.
39 Her sanctuary became
desolate like a desert;
her feasts were turned into
mourning,
her sabbaths into a reproach,
her honor into contempt.
40 Her dishonor now grew as
great as her glory;
her exaltation was turned
into mourning.

Installation of Gentile Cults

41 Then the king wrote to his whole kingdom that all should be one people, 42 and that all should give up their particular customs. 43 All the Gentiles accepted the command of the king. Many even from Israel gladly adopted his religion; they sacrificed to idols and profaned the sabbath. 44 And the king sent letters by messengers to Jerusalem and the towns of Judah; he directed them to follow customs strange to the land, 45 to forbid burnt offerings and sacrifices and drink offerings in the sanctuary, to profane sabbaths and festivals, 46 to defile the sanctuary and the priests, 47 to build altars and sacred precincts and shrines for idols, to sacrifice swine and other unclean animals, 48 and to leave their sons uncircumcised. They were to make themselves abominable by everything unclean and profane, 49 so that they would forget the law and change all the ordinances. 50 He added,[e] "And whoever does not obey the command of the king shall die."

51 In such words he wrote to his whole kingdom. He appointed inspectors over all the people and commanded the towns of Judah to offer sacrifice, town by town. 52 Many of the people, everyone who forsook the law, joined them, and they did evil in the land; 53 they drove Israel into hiding in every place of refuge they had.

54 Now on the fifteenth day of Chislev, in the one hundred forty-fifth year,[f] they erected a desolating sacrilege on the altar of burnt offering. They also built altars in the surrounding towns of Judah, 55 and offered incense at the doors of the houses and in the streets. 56 The books of the law that they found they tore to pieces and burned with fire. 57 Anyone found possessing the book of the covenant, or anyone who adhered to the law, was condemned to death by decree of the king. 58 They kept using violence against Israel, against those who were found month after month in the towns. 59 On the twenty-fifth day of the month they offered sacrifice on the altar that was on top of the altar of burnt offering. 60 According to the decree, they put to death the women who had their children circumcised, 61 and their families and those who circumcised them; and they hung the infants from their mothers' necks.

62 But many in Israel stood firm and were resolved in their hearts not to eat unclean food. 63 They chose to die rather than to be defiled by food or to profane the holy covenant; and they did die. 64 Very great wrath came upon Israel.

Mattathias and His Sons

2 In those days Mattathias son of John son of Simeon, a priest of the family of Joarib, moved from Jerusalem and settled in Modein. 2 He had five sons, John surnamed Gaddi, 3 Simon called Thassi, 4 Judas called Maccabeus, 5 Eleazar called Avaran, and Jonathan called Apphus. 6 He saw the blasphemies being committed in Judah and Jerusalem, 7 and said,

"Alas! Why was I born to see
this,
the ruin of my people, the
ruin of the holy city,
and to live there when it was
given over to the
enemy,
the sanctuary given over to
aliens?
8 Her temple has become like
a person without
honor;[g]

1.39 Am 8.10; Tob 2.6
1.42 2 Macc 6.1
1.43 1 Macc 2.18; Ezek 22.8; 23.38
1.45 Dan 9.27; 11.31
1.46 Dan 11.31; 2 Macc 6.2; Dan 4.1-7; Wis 14.16; 2 Macc 6.18; 7.1
1.48 2 Macc 6.10
1.50 2 Macc 6.9-11,31; 7.1-20
1.54 1 Macc 4.52; Dan 9.27; 11.31; 1 Macc 6.7; Mt 24.15
1.56 2 Macc 2.14
1.57 2 Macc 6.18-7.41
1.59 2 Macc 6.4-5
1.60 2 Macc 6.10
1.63 2 Macc 6.18-31; 4 Macc 6.1-30
2.1 1 Chr 24.7; Neh 11.10
2.3 1 Macc 14.29
2.5 1 Macc 6.43
2.7 1 Macc 1.20-40; Ps 74.4-8

[e] Gk lacks *He added* [f] 167 B.C.
[g] Meaning of Gk uncertain

[9] her glorious vessels have
been carried into exile.
Her infants have been killed
in her streets,
her youths by the sword of
the foe.
[10] What nation has not
inherited her palaces[h]
and has not seized her
spoils?
[11] All her adornment has been
taken away;
no longer free, she has
become a slave.
[12] And see, our holy place, our
beauty,
and our glory have been
laid waste;
the Gentiles have profaned
them.
[13] Why should we live any
longer?"

14 Then Mattathias and his sons tore their clothes, put on sackcloth, and mourned greatly.

Pagan Worship Refused

15 The king's officers who were enforcing the apostasy came to the town of Modein to make them offer sacrifice. [16]Many from Israel
came to them; and Mattathias and
his sons were assembled. [17]Then
the king's officers spoke to Mattathias as follows: "You are a leader, honored and great in this town, and supported by sons and brothers. [18]Now be the first to come and
do what the king commands, as all the Gentiles and the people of Judah and those that are left in Jerusalem have done. Then you and your sons will be numbered among the Friends of the king, and you and your sons will be honored with silver and gold and many gifts."

19 But Mattathias answered and said in a loud voice: "Even if all the nations that live under the rule of the king obey him, and have chosen to obey his commandments, everyone of them abandoning the religion of their ancestors,
[20]I and my sons and my brothers
will continue to live by the covenant of our ancestors. [21]Far be it
from us to desert the law and the
ordinances. [22]We will not obey the
king's words by turning aside from our religion to the right hand or to the left."

23 When he had finished speaking these words, a Jew came forward in the sight of all to offer sacrifice on the altar in Modein, according to the king's command.
[24]When Mattathias saw it, he
burned with zeal and his heart was stirred. He gave vent to righteous anger; he ran and killed him on the
altar. [25]At the same time he killed
the king's officer who was forcing them to sacrifice, and he tore down
the altar. [26]Thus he burned with
zeal for the law, just as Phinehas did against Zimri son of Salu.

27 Then Mattathias cried out in the town with a loud voice, saying: "Let every one who is zealous for the law and supports the covenant
come out with me!" [28]Then he and
his sons fled to the hills and left all that they had in the town.

29 At that time many who were seeking righteousness and justice went down to the wilderness to live
there, [30]they, their sons, their
wives, and their livestock, because troubles pressed heavily upon
them. [31]And it was reported to the
king's officers, and to the troops in Jerusalem the city of David, that those who had rejected the king's command had gone down to the hiding places in the wilderness.
[32]Many pursued them, and over-
took them; they encamped opposite them and prepared for battle against them on the sabbath day.
[33]They said to them, "Enough of
this! Come out and do what the king commands, and you will live."
[34]But they said, "We will not come
out, nor will we do what the king commands and so profane the sabbath day." [35]Then the enemy[i]
quickly attacked them. [36]But they
did not answer them or hurl a stone at them or block up their
hiding places, [37]for they said, "Let
us all die in our innocence; heaven and earth testify for us that you are
killing us unjustly." [38]So they at-
tacked them on the sabbath, and

2.9 1 Macc 1.21-23; Lam 2.11,21; 1 Macc 1.26 **2.10** Ps 44.10 **2.11** Ps 44.12 **2.12** 1 Macc 1.45-49 **2.14** Gen 37.34 **2.15** 1 Macc 1.44-50 **2.18** 1 Macc 1.43; 6.10; 10.65; 14.39; 2 Macc 10.13 **2.20** Dan 1.8-16 **2.22** Dan 3.16-18; Acts 4.19; 5.28 **2.26** Num 25.6-14; 1 Macc 2.54 **2.28** 2 Macc 5.27; Mt 24.16 **2.34** 1 Macc 1.43, 45 **2.38** 2 Macc 5.25; 6.10

[h] Other ancient authorities read *has not had a part in her kingdom* [i] Gk *they*

they died, with their wives and
children and livestock, to the number of a thousand persons.
39 When Mattathias and his
friends learned of it, they mourned
for them deeply. 40 And all said to
their neighbors: "If we all do as our
kindred have done and refuse to
fight with the Gentiles for our lives
and for our ordinances, they will
quickly destroy us from the earth."
41 So they made this decision that
day: "Let us fight against anyone
who comes to attack us on the sabbath day; let us not all die as our
kindred died in their hiding
places."

Counter-Attack

42 Then there united with them
a company of Hasideans, mighty
warriors of Israel, all who offered
themselves willingly for the law.
43 And all who became fugitives to
escape their troubles joined them
and reinforced them. 44 They organized an army, and struck down
sinners in their anger and renegades in their wrath; the survivors
fled to the Gentiles for safety.
45 And Mattathias and his friends
went around and tore down the altars; 46 they forcibly circumcised all
the uncircumcised boys that they
found within the borders of Israel.
47 They hunted down the arrogant,
and the work prospered in their
hands. 48 They rescued the law out
of the hands of the Gentiles and
kings, and they never let the sinner
gain the upper hand.

The Last Words of Mattathias

49 Now the days drew near for
Mattathias to die, and he said to
his sons: "Arrogance and scorn
have now become strong; it is a
time of ruin and furious anger.
50 Now, my children, show zeal for
the law, and give your lives for the
covenant of our ancestors.
51 "Remember the deeds of the
ancestors, which they did in their
generations; and you will receive
great honor and an everlasting
name. 52 Was not Abraham found
faithful when tested, and it was
reckoned to him as righteousness?
53 Joseph in the time of his distress
kept the commandment, and became lord of Egypt. 54 Phinehas our
ancestor, because he was deeply
zealous, received the covenant of
everlasting priesthood. 55 Joshua,
because he fulfilled the command,
became a judge in Israel. 56 Caleb,
because he testified in the assembly, received an inheritance in the
land. 57 David, because he was
merciful, inherited the throne of
the kingdom forever. 58 Elijah, because of great zeal for the law, was
taken up into heaven. 59 Hananiah,
Azariah, and Mishael believed and
were saved from the flame. 60 Daniel, because of his innocence, was
delivered from the mouth of the lions.
61 "And so observe, from generation to generation, that none of
those who put their trust in him
will lack strength. 62 Do not fear
the words of sinners, for their
splendor will turn into dung and
worms. 63 Today they will be exalted, but tomorrow they will not
be found, because they will have
returned to the dust, and their
plans will have perished. 64 My
children, be courageous and grow
strong in the law, for by it you will
gain honor.
65 "Here is your brother Simeon who, I know, is wise in counsel; always listen to him; he shall
be your father. 66 Judas Maccabeus
has been a mighty warrior from his
youth; he shall command the army
for you and fight the battle against
the peoples.[j] 67 You shall rally
around you all who observe the
law, and avenge the wrong done to
your people. 68 Pay back the Gentiles in full, and obey the commands of the law."
69 Then he blessed them, and
was gathered to his ancestors.
70 He died in the one hundred
forty-sixth year[k] and was buried in
the tomb of his ancestors at Modein. And all Israel mourned for
him with great lamentation.

2.42 1 Macc 7.13; 2 Macc 14.6
2.44 Isa 63.3; Rev 19.15
2.49 1 Macc 2.1; 1.24
2.50 Acts 21.20; Gal 1.14; Phil 3.6
2.52 Gen 22.1-18; Heb 11.17; Gen 15.6; Jas 2.21-23
2.53 Gen 39.7-10; 41.39-43
2.54 Num 25.6-14; Sir 45.23-26; 1 Macc 2.26
2.55 Num 14.37-38; Josh 1.1-5; 14.6
2.56 Num 13.30; 14.6-9; Josh 14.14
2.57 1 Sam 16.12-13; 2 Sam 2.4; 5.1-5
2.58 2 Kings 2.11-12
2.59 Dan 3.24-27
2.60 Dan 6.19-23; Bel 31-32
2.61 Ps 22.4-5; Sir 2.10; Song of Thr 1.17
2.63 Ps 146.3-4; Eccl 12.7
2.64 Deut 31.6-8; Josh 1.7,9
2.66 1 Macc 2.4; 3.1; 4.10; 5.28; 6.42
2.67 1 Macc 13.6
2.69 Gen 49.1-27; Deut 33.1-29; Judg 2.10

[j] Or *of the people* [k] 166 B.C.

The Early Victories of Judas

3 Then his son Judas, who was
called Maccabeus, took command in his place. 2 All his brothers and all who had joined his father helped him; they gladly fought
for Israel.

3 He extended the glory of his
  people.
Like a giant he put on his
  breastplate;
he bound on his armor of
  war and waged battles,
protecting the camp by his
  sword.
4 He was like a lion in his
  deeds,
like a lion's cub roaring for
  prey.
5 He searched out and pursued
  those who broke the
  law;
he burned those who
  troubled his people.
6 Lawbreakers shrank back for
  fear of him;
all the evildoers were
  confounded;
and deliverance prospered
  by his hand.
7 He embittered many kings,
but he made Jacob glad by
  his deeds,
and his memory is blessed
  forever.
8 He went through the cities of
  Judah;
he destroyed the ungodly
  out of the land;[l]
thus he turned away wrath
  from Israel.
9 He was renowned to the
  ends of the earth;
he gathered in those who
  were perishing.

10 Apollonius now gathered together Gentiles and a large force
from Samaria to fight against Israel. 11 When Judas learned of it,
he went out to meet him, and he
defeated and killed him. Many
were wounded and fell, and the
rest fled. 12 Then they seized their
spoils; and Judas took the sword of
Apollonius, and used it in battle
the rest of his life.

13 When Seron, the com-
mander of the Syrian army, heard
that Judas had gathered a large
company, including a body of
faithful soldiers who stayed with
him and went out to battle, 14 he
said, "I will make a name for myself and win honor in the kingdom.
I will make war on Judas and his
companions, who scorn the king's
command." 15 Once again a strong
army of godless men went up with
him to help him, to take vengeance
on the Israelites.

16 When he approached the ascent of Beth-horon, Judas went
out to meet him with a small company. 17 But when they saw the
army coming to meet them, they
said to Judas, "How can we, few as
we are, fight against so great and
so strong a multitude? And we are
faint, for we have eaten nothing today." 18 Judas replied, "It is easy for
many to be hemmed in by few, for
in the sight of Heaven there is no
difference between saving by many
or by few. 19 It is not on the size of
the army that victory in battle depends, but strength comes from
Heaven. 20 They come against us in
great insolence and lawlessness to
destroy us and our wives and our
children, and to despoil us; 21 but
we fight for our lives and our laws.
22 He himself will crush them before us; as for you, do not be afraid
of them."

23 When he finished speaking,
he rushed suddenly against Seron
and his army, and they were
crushed before him. 24 They pursued them[m] down the descent of
Beth-horon to the plain; eight hundred of them fell, and the rest fled
into the land of the Philistines.
25 Then Judas and his brothers began to be feared, and terror fell on
the Gentiles all around them.
26 His fame reached the king, and
the Gentiles talked of the battles
of Judas.

The Policy of Antiochus

27 When King Antiochus heard
these reports, he was greatly angered; and he sent and gathered all

3.1 1 Macc 2.66
3.3 2 Macc 8.5-7
3.4 Gen 49.9; Num 23.24; Hos 13.7-8; 2 Macc 11.11
3.7 Sir 45.1; 46.11
3.8 Ps 53.5; Wis 20.10; 2 Macc 7.38
3.9 Jdt 11.23
3.10 1 Macc 1.29; 2 Macc 5.24
3.12 1 Macc 5.28; 6.6; 7.47; 1 Sam 17.51; 21.9
3.14 1 Macc 5.57
3.16 1 Macc 9.50
3.18 Sus 9; 1 Macc 4.10, 24,40; 2 Macc 7.11; 1 Sam 14.6
3.19 Judg 7.2; 1 Sam 14.45-47; Ps 18.29; 33.16-19
3.24 Josh 10.10
3.27 1 Macc 1.10

[l] Gk *it* [m] Other ancient authorities read *him*

the forces of his kingdom, a very
strong army. 28 He opened his cof-
fers and gave a year's pay to his
forces, and ordered them to be
ready for any need. 29 Then he saw
that the money in the treasury was
exhausted, and that the revenues
from the country were small because of the dissension and disaster that he had caused in the land
by abolishing the laws that had existed from the earliest days. 30 He
feared that he might not have such
funds as he had before for his expenses and for the gifts that he
used to give more lavishly than
preceding kings. 31 He was greatly
perplexed in mind; then he determined to go to Persia and collect
the revenues from those regions
and raise a large fund.

32 He left Lysias, a distinguished man of royal lineage, in
charge of the king's affairs from
the river Euphrates to the borders
of Egypt. 33 Lysias was also to take
care of his son Antiochus until he
returned. 34 And he turned over to
Lysias[n] half of his forces and the
elephants, and gave him orders
about all that he wanted done. As
for the residents of Judea and Jerusalem, 35 Lysias was to send a force
against them to wipe out and destroy the strength of Israel and the
remnant of Jerusalem; he was to
banish the memory of them from
the place, 36 settle aliens in all
their territory, and distribute their
land by lot. 37 Then the king took
the remaining half of his forces
and left Antioch his capital in the
one hundred and forty-seventh
year.[o] He crossed the Euphrates
river and went through the upper
provinces.

Preparations for Battle

38 Lysias chose Ptolemy son of
Dorymenes, and Nicanor and Gorgias, able men among the Friends
of the king, 39 and sent with them
forty thousand infantry and seven
thousand cavalry to go into the
land of Judah and destroy it, as the
king had commanded. 40 So they
set out with their entire force, and
when they arrived they encamped
near Emmaus in the plain. 41 When
the traders of the region heard
what was said to them, they took
silver and gold in immense
amounts, and fetters,[p] and went
to the camp to get the Israelites for
slaves. And forces from Syria and
the land of the Philistines joined
with them.

42 Now Judas and his brothers
saw that misfortunes had increased and that the forces were
encamped in their territory. They
also learned what the king had
commanded to do to the people to
cause their final destruction. 43 But
they said to one another, "Let us
restore the ruins of our people, and
fight for our people and the sanctuary." 44 So the congregation assembled to be ready for battle, and
to pray and ask for mercy and compassion.

45 Jerusalem was uninhabited
like a wilderness;
not one of her children
went in or out.
The sanctuary was trampled
down,
and aliens held the citadel;
it was a lodging place for
the Gentiles.
Joy was taken from Jacob;
the flute and the harp
ceased to play.

46 Then they gathered together
and went to Mizpah, opposite Jerusalem, because Israel formerly
had a place of prayer in Mizpah.
47 They fasted that day, put on
sackcloth and sprinkled ashes on
their heads, and tore their clothes.
48 And they opened the book of the
law to inquire into those matters
about which the Gentiles consulted the likenesses of their gods.
49 They also brought the vestments
of the priesthood and the first
fruits and the tithes, and they
stirred up the nazirites[q] who had
completed their days; 50 and they
cried aloud to Heaven, saying,
"What shall we do with
these?
Where shall we take them?

3.31 1 Macc 6.1-3 **3.32** 1 Macc 6.17 **3.33** 2 Macc 10.10-11 **3.34** 1 Macc 1.17; 6.30; 8.6; 2 Macc 11.4 **3.36** 2 Kings 17.24 **3.37** 1 Macc 11.13; Acts 11.19-20,26; 1 Macc 6.1; 2 Macc 9.23 **3.38** 2 Macc 4.45; 10.12; 1 Macc 7.26-43; 2 Macc 8.9-10; 1 Macc 4.1; 2 Macc 8.9; 10.14 **3.40** 1 Macc 9.50 **3.41** 2 Macc 8.10, 34 **3.43** 1 Macc 2.66; 3.21; 5.32 **3.45** Isa 27.10; 64.10; Ps 74.4-8; Isa 24.8 **3.46** 1 Sam 7.5-11 **3.47** Ezra 8.23; Esth 4.16 **3.49** Ex 23.19; Deut 26.2; Neh 10.35-38; Lev 27.30; Mal 3.8-10; Num 6.1-21; Acts 21.26

n Gk *him* o 165 B.C. p Syr: Gk Mss, Vg *slaves* q That is *those separated* or *those consecrated*

51 Your sanctuary is trampled
down and profaned,
and your priests mourn in
humiliation.
52 Here the Gentiles are
assembled against us to
destroy us;
you know what they plot
against us.
53 How will we be able to
withstand them,
if you do not help us?"
54 Then they sounded the
trumpets and gave a loud shout.
55 After this Judas appointed leaders of the people, in charge of
thousands and hundreds and fifties and tens. 56 Those who were
building houses, or were about to
be married, or were planting a
vineyard, or were fainthearted, he
told to go home again, according to
the law. 57 Then the army marched
out and encamped to the south of
Emmaus.
58 And Judas said, "Arm yourselves and be courageous. Be ready
early in the morning to fight with
these Gentiles who have assembled against us to destroy us and
our sanctuary. 59 It is better for us
to die in battle than to see the misfortunes of our nation and of the
sanctuary. 60 But as his will in
heaven may be, so shall he do."

The Battle at Emmaus

4 Now Gorgias took five thousand infantry and one thousand picked cavalry, and this division moved out by night 2 to fall
upon the camp of the Jews and attack them suddenly. Men from the
citadel were his guides. 3 But Judas
heard of it, and he and his warriors
moved out to attack the king's
force in Emmaus 4 while the division was still absent from the
camp. 5 When Gorgias entered the
camp of Judas by night, he found
no one there, so he looked for
them in the hills, because he said,
"These men are running away from
us."
6 At daybreak Judas appeared
in the plain with three thousand
men, but they did not have armor
and swords such as they desired.
7 And they saw the camp of the
Gentiles, strong and fortified, with
cavalry all around it; and these
men were trained in war. 8 But Judas said to those who were with
him, "Do not fear their numbers or
be afraid when they charge. 9 Remember how our ancestors were
saved at the Red Sea, when Pharaoh with his forces pursued them.
10 And now, let us cry to Heaven, to
see whether he will favor us and remember his covenant with our ancestors and crush this army before
us today. 11 Then all the Gentiles
will know that there is one who redeems and saves Israel."
12 When the foreigners looked
up and saw them coming against
them, 13 they went out from their
camp to battle. Then the men with
Judas blew their trumpets 14 and
engaged in battle. The Gentiles
were crushed, and fled into the
plain, 15 and all those in the rear
fell by the sword. They pursued
them to Gazara, and to the plains
of Idumea, and to Azotus and Jamnia; and three thousand of them
fell. 16 Then Judas and his force
turned back from pursuing them,
17 and he said to the people, "Do
not be greedy for plunder, for there
is a battle before us; 18 Gorgias and
his force are near us in the hills.
But stand now against our enemies
and fight them, and afterward seize
the plunder boldly."
19 Just as Judas was finishing
this speech, a detachment appeared, coming out of the hills.
20 They saw that their army[r] had
been put to flight, and that the
Jews[r] were burning the camp, for
the smoke that was seen showed
what had happened. 21 When they
perceived this, they were greatly
frightened, and when they also saw
the army of Judas drawn up in the
plain for battle, 22 they all fled into
the land of the Philistines. 23 Then
Judas returned to plunder the
camp, and they seized a great
amount of gold and silver, and
cloth dyed blue and sea purple,
and great riches. 24 On their return

3.51 1 Macc 3.45 **3.52** Acts 4.27 **3.53** 1 Macc 3.18-22 **3.54** Num 10.1-10 **3.55** Ex 18,.25; 2 Macc 8.22-23 **3.56** 2 Macc 8.13; Deut 20.5-8; Judg 7.3 **3.58** Josh 1.6-9; 10.25 **3.59** 1 Macc 9.10 **3.60** Mt 6.10; 1 Macc 2.20-21; Acts 4.28 **4.1** 1 Macc 3.38 **4.3** 1 Macc 2.66; 3.40 **4.9** Ex 14.21-29 **4.10** 1 Macc 3.19, 50 **4.11** Ezek 36.23, 36; 39.7,28; Isa 33.22; 60.16 **4.13** 1 Macc 3.54 **4.15** Josh 21.21; 1 Kings 9.17; 1 Macc 7.45; 9.52; 5.58; 10.69 **4.16** 2 Macc 8.26 **4.20** Josh 8.20-21 **4.23** 1 Macc 7.47; 2 Macc 8.27, 30 **4.24** 1 Macc 3.18-19; Ezra 3.11; Ps 118.1; 136.1

r Gk *they*

they sang hymns and praises to
Heaven—"For he is good, for his
mercy endures forever." 25 Thus Israel had a great deliverance that
day.

First Campaign of Lysias

26 Those of the foreigners who
escaped went and reported to Lysias all that had happened. 27 When
he heard it, he was perplexed and
discouraged, for things had not
happened to Israel as he had intended, nor had they turned out as
the king had ordered. 28 But the
next year he mustered sixty thousand picked infantry and five thousand cavalry to subdue them.
29 They came into Idumea and encamped at Beth-zur, and Judas
met them with ten thousand men.
30 When he saw that their army
was strong, he prayed, saying,
"Blessed are you, O Savior of Israel, who crushed the attack of the
mighty warrior by the hand of your
servant David, and gave the camp
of the Philistines into the hands of
Jonathan son of Saul, and of the
man who carried his armor. 31 Hem
in this army by the hand of your
people Israel, and let them be
ashamed of their troops and their
cavalry. 32 Fill them with cowardice; melt the boldness of their
strength; let them tremble in their
destruction. 33 Strike them down
with the sword of those who love
you, and let all who know your
name praise you with hymns."
34 Then both sides attacked,
and there fell of the army of Lysias
five thousand men; they fell in action.[s] 35 When Lysias saw the rout
of his troops and observed the
boldness that inspired those of Judas, and how ready they were either to live or to die nobly, he withdrew to Antioch and enlisted
mercenaries in order to invade Judea again with an even larger army.

Cleansing and Dedication of the Temple

36 Then Judas and his brothers
said, "See, our enemies are
crushed; let us go up to cleanse the
sanctuary and dedicate it." 37 So all
the army assembled and went up
to Mount Zion. 38 There they saw
the sanctuary desolate, the altar
profaned, and the gates burned. In
the courts they saw bushes sprung
up as in a thicket, or as on one of
the mountains. They saw also the
chambers of the priests in ruins.
39 Then they tore their clothes and
mourned with great lamentation;
they sprinkled themselves with
ashes 40 and fell face down on the
ground. And when the signal was
given with the trumpets, they cried
out to Heaven.
41 Then Judas detailed men to
fight against those in the citadel
until he had cleansed the sanctuary. 42 He chose blameless priests
devoted to the law, 43 and they
cleansed the sanctuary and removed the defiled stones to an unclean place. 44 They deliberated
what to do about the altar of burnt
offering, which had been profaned.
45 And they thought it best to tear it
down, so that it would not be a
lasting shame to them that the
Gentiles had defiled it. So they
tore down the altar, 46 and stored
the stones in a convenient place on
the temple hill until a prophet
should come to tell what to do with
them. 47 Then they took unhewn[t]
stones, as the law directs, and built
a new altar like the former one.
48 They also rebuilt the sanctuary
and the interior of the temple, and
consecrated the courts. 49 They
made new holy vessels, and
brought the lampstand, the altar of
incense, and the table into the
temple. 50 Then they offered incense on the altar and lit the lamps
on the lampstand, and these gave
light in the temple. 51 They placed
the bread on the table and hung up
the curtains. Thus they finished all
the work they had undertaken.
52 Early in the morning on the
twenty-fifth day of the ninth
month, which is the month of
Chislev, in the one hundred forty-
eighth year,[u] 53 they rose and offered sacrifice, as the law directs,
on the new altar of burnt offering

4.26 2 Macc 11.1
4.29 1 Macc 6.31; 9.52; 2 Macc 11.4
4.30 1 Sam 17.41-51; 14.1-15
4.33 Ps 99.3; 104.33; 147.1
4.35 2 Macc 11.10-11; 10.14,24
4.36 2 Macc 10.3
4.37 1 Macc 14.27
4.38 Ps 74.4-8; 1 Macc 1.46-47
4.39 1 Macc 3.47
4.40 2 Macc 3.15; 13.12; 1 Macc 3.50; 2 Macc 10.4
4.41 1 Macc 1.33-35
4.44 1 Kings 8.64; 1 Macc 1.37
4.45 1 Macc 6.7
4.46 1 Macc 9.27; 14.41
4.47 Ex 20.25; Deut 27.5-6
4.49 1 Macc 1.21-22; Ex 25.23-39; 30.1-6
4.50 Ex 30.7-8
4.51 Ex 25.30
4.52 1 Macc 1.54
4.53 Ex 30.10; Ezek 43.18-27

[s] Or *and some fell on the opposite side*
[t] Gk *whole*
[u] 164 B.C.

that they had built. 54 At the very
season and on the very day that the
Gentiles had profaned it, it was
dedicated with songs and harps
and lutes and cymbals. 55 All the
people fell on their faces and worshiped and blessed Heaven, who
had prospered them. 56 So they celebrated the dedication of the altar
for eight days, and joyfully offered
burnt offerings; they offered a sacrifice of well-being and a thanksgiving offering. 57 They decorated
the front of the temple with golden
crowns and small shields; they restored the gates and the chambers
for the priests, and fitted them
with doors. 58 There was very great
joy among the people, and the disgrace brought by the Gentiles was
removed.

59 Then Judas and his brothers
and all the assembly of Israel determined that every year at that
season the days of dedication of
the altar should be observed with
joy and gladness for eight days, beginning with the twenty-fifth day of
the month of Chislev.

60 At that time they fortified
Mount Zion with high walls and
strong towers all around, to keep
the Gentiles from coming and
trampling them down as they had
done before. 61 Judas[v] stationed a
garrison there to guard it; he also
fortified Beth-zur to guard it, so
that the people might have a
stronghold that faced Idumea.

Wars with Neighboring Peoples

5 When the Gentiles all around
heard that the altar had been
rebuilt and the sanctuary dedicated as it was before, they became
very angry, 2 and they determined
to destroy the descendants of Jacob who lived among them. So
they began to kill and destroy
among the people. 3 But Judas
made war on the descendants of
Esau in Idumea, at Akrabattene,
because they kept lying in wait for
Israel. He dealt them a heavy blow
and humbled them and despoiled
them. 4 He also remembered the
wickedness of the sons of Baean,
who were a trap and a snare to the
people and ambushed them on the
highways. 5 They were shut up by
him in their[w] towers; and he encamped against them, vowed their
complete destruction, and burned
with fire their towers and all who
were in them. 6 Then he crossed
over to attack the Ammonites,
where he found a strong band and
many people, with Timothy as
their leader. 7 He engaged in many
battles with them, and they were
crushed before him; he struck
them down. 8 He also took Jazer
and its villages; then he returned
to Judea.

Liberation of Galilean Jews

9 Now the Gentiles in Gilead
gathered together against the Israelites who lived in their territory,
and planned to destroy them. But
they fled to the stronghold of Dathema, 10 and sent to Judas and his
brothers a letter that said, "The
Gentiles around us have gathered
together to destroy us. 11 They are
preparing to come and capture the
stronghold to which we have fled,
and Timothy is leading their
forces. 12 Now then, come and rescue us from their hands, for many
of us have fallen, 13 and all our kindred who were in the land of Tob
have been killed; the enemy[x] have
captured their wives and children
and goods, and have destroyed
about a thousand persons there."

14 While the letter was still being read, other messengers, with
their garments torn, came from
Galilee and made a similar report;
15 they said that the people of Ptolemais and Tyre and Sidon, and all
Galilee of the Gentiles,[y] had gathered together against them "to annihilate us." 16 When Judas and the
people heard these messages, a
great assembly was called to determine what they should do for their
kindred who were in distress and
were being attacked by enemies.[z]
17 Then Judas said to his brother
Simon, "Choose your men and go
and rescue your kindred in Galilee;
Jonathan my brother and I will go

4.54 Ezra 6.16-18
4.56 Lev 3.1-17
4.59 2 Macc 1.9; 10.5-6; Jn 10.22
4.60 1 Macc 5.54; 6.48,62; 10.11
4.61 1 Macc 4.29; 6.26
5.3 1 Macc 4.61; 2 Macc 10.15-23
5.4 Num 32.3
5.6 Gen 19.38; Jdt 7.17-18; 2 Macc 8.30; 9.3
5.8 Num 32.3
5.9 Josh 22.9; 1 Macc 13.22
5.13 Josh 11.3; 2 Macc 12.17; Gen 14.12, 16; 1 Sam 30.1-3
5.15 Isa 9.1; Mt 4.15
5.17 1 Macc 2.3-4

v Gk *He* w Gk *her* x Gk *they* y Gk *aliens*
z Gk *them*

to Gilead." 18 But he left Joseph,
son of Zechariah, and Azariah, a
leader of the people, with the rest
of the forces, in Judea to guard it;
19 and he gave them this command,
"Take charge of this people, but do
not engage in battle with the Gentiles until we return." 20 Then three
thousand men were assigned to Simon to go to Galilee, and eight
thousand to Judas for Gilead.

21 So Simon went to Galilee
and fought many battles against
the Gentiles, and the Gentiles
were crushed before him. 22 He
pursued them to the gate of Ptolemais; as many as three thousand of
the Gentiles fell, and he despoiled
them. 23 Then he took the Jews[a] of
Galilee and Arbatta, with their
wives and children, and all they
possessed, and led them to Judea
with great rejoicing.

Judas and Jonathan in Gilead

24 Judas Maccabeus and his
brother Jonathan crossed the Jordan and made three days' journey
into the wilderness. 25 They encountered the Nabateans, who met
them peaceably and told them all
that had happened to their kindred
in Gilead: 26 "Many of them have
been shut up in Bozrah and Bosor,
in Alema and Chaspho, Maked and
Carnaim"—all these towns were
strong and large— 27 "and some
have been shut up in the other
towns of Gilead; the enemy[b] are
getting ready to attack the strongholds tomorrow and capture and
destroy all these people in a single
day."

28 Then Judas and his army
quickly turned back by the wilderness road to Bozrah; and he took
the town, and killed every male by
the edge of the sword; then he
seized all its spoils and burned it
with fire. 29 He left the place at
night, and they went all the way to
the stronghold of Dathema.[c] 30 At
dawn they looked out and saw a
large company, which could not be
counted, carrying ladders and engines of war to capture the stronghold, and attacking the Jews
within.[d] 31 So Judas saw that the

5.19 1 Macc 5.57-60
5.21 1 Macc 3.11, 24; 4.10,13
5.25 Gen 25.13; 1 Macc 9.35
5.26 Isa 63.1; Jer 48.24; Deut 4.43; Gen 14.5; Am 6.13; 2 Macc 12.21, 26
5.28 Gen 34.25; 1 Macc 3.12
5.29 1 Macc 5.9
5.30 1 Macc 6.20, 31,51; 11.20; 15.25
5.31 1 Macc 3.18, 50
5.32 1 Macc 3.43
5.34 1 Macc 6.6, 11; 2 Macc 8.32
5.37 2 Macc 10.24
5.39 2 Chr 21.16; 22.1; 2 Macc 12.10
5.40 1 Sam 14.9-10
5.43 2 Macc 12.26

battle had begun and that the cry
of the town went up to Heaven,
with trumpets and loud shouts,
32 and he said to the men of his
forces, "Fight today for your kindred!" 33 Then he came up behind
them in three companies, who
sounded their trumpets and cried
aloud in prayer. 34 And when the
army of Timothy realized that it
was Maccabeus, they fled before
him, and he dealt them a heavy
blow. As many as eight thousand of
them fell that day.

35 Next he turned aside to Maa-
pha,[e] and fought against it and
took it; and he killed every male in
it, plundered it, and burned it with
fire. 36 From there he marched on
and took Chaspho, Maked, and Bosor, and the other towns of Gilead.

37 After these things Timothy
gathered another army and encamped opposite Raphon, on the
other side of the stream. 38 Judas
sent men to spy out the camp, and
they reported to him, "All the Gentiles around us have gathered to
him; it is a very large force. 39 They
also have hired Arabs to help them,
and they are encamped across the
stream, ready to come and fight
against you." And Judas went to
meet them.

40 Now as Judas and his army
drew near to the stream of water,
Timothy said to the officers of his
forces, "If he crosses over to us
first, we will not be able to resist
him, for he will surely defeat us.
41 But if he shows fear and camps
on the other side of the river, we
will cross over to him and defeat
him." 42 When Judas approached
the stream of water, he stationed
the officers[f] of the army at the
stream and gave them this command, "Permit no one to encamp,
but make them all enter the battle." 43 Then he crossed over
against them first, and the whole
army followed him. All the Gentiles were defeated before him, and
they threw away their arms and

[a] Gk *those* [b] Gk *they* [c] Gk lacks *of Dathema.* See verse 9 [d] Gk *and they were attacking them* [e] Other ancient authorities read *Alema* [f] Or *scribes*

fled into the sacred precincts at
Carnaim. 44 But he took the town
and burned the sacred precincts
with fire, together with all who
were in them. Thus Carnaim was
conquered; they could stand before Judas no longer.

The Return to Jerusalem

45 Then Judas gathered together all the Israelites in Gilead,
the small and the great, with their
wives and children and goods, a
very large company, to go to the
land of Judah. 46 So they came to
Ephron. This was a large and very
strong town on the road, and they
could not go around it to the right
or to the left; they had to go
through it. 47 But the people of the
town shut them out and blocked
up the gates with stones.
48 Judas sent them this friendly
message, "Let us pass through
your land to get to our land. No
one will do you harm; we will simply pass by on foot." But they refused to open to him. 49 Then Judas ordered proclamation to be
made to the army that all should
encamp where they were. 50 So the
men of the forces encamped, and
he fought against the town all that
day and all the night, and the town
was delivered into his hands. 51 He
destroyed every male by the edge
of the sword, and razed and plundered the town. Then he passed
through the town over the bodies
of the dead.
52 Then they crossed the Jordan into the large plain before
Beth-shan. 53 Judas kept rallying
the laggards and encouraging the
people all the way until he came to
the land of Judah. 54 So they went
up to Mount Zion with joy and
gladness, and offered burnt offerings, because they had returned in
safety; not one of them had fallen.

Joseph and Azariah Defeated

55 Now while Judas and Jonathan were in Gilead and their[g]
brother Simon was in Galilee before Ptolemais, 56 Joseph son of
Zechariah, and Azariah, the commanders of the forces, heard of
their brave deeds and of the heroic
war they had fought. 57 So they
said, "Let us also make a name for
ourselves; let us go and make war
on the Gentiles around us." 58 So
they issued orders to the men of
the forces that were with them and
marched against Jamnia. 59 Gorgias and his men came out of the
town to meet them in battle.
60 Then Joseph and Azariah were
routed, and were pursued to the
borders of Judea; as many as two
thousand of the people of Israel
fell that day. 61 Thus the people
suffered a great rout because,
thinking to do a brave deed, they
did not listen to Judas and his
brothers. 62 But they did not belong
to the family of those men through
whom deliverance was given to Israel.
63 The man Judas and his
brothers were greatly honored in
all Israel and among all the Gentiles, wherever their name was
heard. 64 People gathered to them
and praised them.

Success at Hebron and Philistia

65 Then Judas and his brothers
went out and fought the descendants of Esau in the land to the
south. He struck Hebron and its
villages and tore down its strongholds and burned its towers on all
sides. 66 Then he marched off to go
into the land of the Philistines,
and passed through Marisa.[h] 67 On
that day some priests, who wished
to do a brave deed, fell in battle,
for they went out to battle un-
wisely. 68 But Judas turned aside to
Azotus in the land of the Philistines; he tore down their altars,
and the carved images of their gods
he burned with fire; he plundered
the towns and returned to the land
of Judah.

The Last Days of Antiochus Epiphanes

6 King Antiochus was going
through the upper provinces
when he heard that Elymais in Persia was a city famed for its wealth

5.46 2 Macc 12.27; Num 20.17
5.48 Num 21.21-24
5.51 1 Macc 5.28
5.52 Judg 1.27; 1 Kings 4.12; 1 Macc 12.40
5.54 1 Macc 4.37, 60,53-56
5.56 1 Macc 5.18
5.57 1 Macc 3.14
5.58 1 Macc 4.15
5.59 1 Macc 4.1
5.61 1 Macc 5.19
5.65 Gen 23.2; 1 Sam 2.21
5.66 Josh 15.44; 2 Macc 12.35
5.68 1 Macc 4.15; 10.77; Acts 8.40; 1 Macc 5.35, 51; 10.84
6.1 1 Macc 3.37, 31

[g] Gk *his*
[h] Other ancient authorities read *Samaria*

in silver and gold. 2 Its temple was
very rich, containing golden
shields, breastplates, and weapons
left there by Alexander son of
Philip, the Macedonian king who
first reigned over the Greeks. 3 So
he came and tried to take the city
and plunder it, but he could not
because his plan had become
known to the citizens 4 and they
withstood him in battle. So he fled
and in great disappointment left
there to return to Babylon.
5 Then someone came to him in
Persia and reported that the armies that had gone into the land of
Judah had been routed; 6 that Lysias had gone first with a strong
force, but had turned and fled before the Jews;[i] that the Jews[j] had
grown strong from the arms, supplies, and abundant spoils that
they had taken from the armies
they had cut down; 7 that they had
torn down the abomination that he
had erected on the altar in Jerusalem; and that they had surrounded
the sanctuary with high walls as
before, and also Beth-zur, his
town.
8 When the king heard this
news, he was astounded and badly
shaken. He took to his bed and became sick from disappointment,
because things had not turned out
for him as he had planned. 9 He
lay there for many days, because
deep disappointment continually
gripped him, and he realized that
he was dying. 10 So he called all his
Friends and said to them, "Sleep
has departed from my eyes and I
am downhearted with worry. 11 I
said to myself, 'To what distress I
have come! And into what a great
flood I now am plunged! For I was
kind and beloved in my power.'
12 But now I remember the wrong I
did in Jerusalem. I seized all its
vessels of silver and gold, and I
sent to destroy the inhabitants of
Judah without good reason. 13 I
know that it is because of this that
these misfortunes have come upon
me; here I am, perishing of bitter
disappointment in a strange land."
14 Then he called for Philip,
one of his Friends, and made him

6.2 2 Macc 1.15; Dan 8.5-8; 1 Macc 1.1
6.4 2 Macc 9.2
6.5 2 Macc 9.3
6.6 1 Macc 4.34-35; 3.12; 4.23; 5.28,35, 68
6.7 1 Macc 1.54; 4.45,29,61
6.9 2 Macc 9.3
6.10 1 Macc 2.18; 10.65
6.12 2 Chr 36.18; Dan 5.2; 1 Macc 1.21-24
6.13 2 Macc 9.18
6.14 2 Macc 9.29
6.15 1 Macc 6.55
6.16 2 Macc 9.28
6.17 1 Macc 3.32; 7.2; 2 Macc 2.20; 10.10
6.18 1 Macc 1.33
6.20 1 Macc 6.51; 13.43-44; 5.30
6.21 1 Macc 1.11-15
6.26 1 Macc 4.61

ruler over all his kingdom. 15 He
gave him the crown and his robe
and the signet, so that he might
guide his son Antiochus and bring
him up to be king. 16 Thus King Antiochus died there in the one hundred forty-ninth year.[k] 17 When
Lysias learned that the king was
dead, he set up Antiochus the
king's[l] son to reign. Lysias[m] had
brought him up from boyhood; he
named him Eupator.

Renewed Attacks from Syria

18 Meanwhile the garrison in
the citadel kept hemming Israel in
around the sanctuary. They were
trying in every way to harm them
and strengthen the Gentiles. 19 Judas therefore resolved to destroy
them, and assembled all the people to besiege them. 20 They gathered together and besieged the citadel[n] in the one hundred fiftieth
year;[o] and he built siege towers
and other engines of war. 21 But
some of the garrison escaped from
the siege and some of the ungodly
Israelites joined them. 22 They
went to the king and said, "How
long will you fail to do justice and
to avenge our kindred? 23 We were
happy to serve your father, to live
by what he said, and to follow his
commands. 24 For this reason the
sons of our people besieged the
citadel[p] and became hostile to us;
moreover, they have put to death
as many of us as they have caught,
and they have seized our inheritances. 25 It is not against us alone
that they have stretched out their
hands; they have also attacked all
the lands on their borders. 26 And
see, today they have encamped
against the citadel in Jerusalem to
take it; they have fortified both the
sanctuary and Beth-zur; 27 unless
you quickly prevent them, they will
do still greater things, and you will
not be able to stop them."
28 The king was enraged when
he heard this. He assembled all his
Friends, the commanders of his

[i] Gk *them* [j] Gk *they* [k] 163 B.C. [l] Gk *his* [m] Gk *He* [n] Gk *it* [o] 162 B.C. [p] Meaning of Gk uncertain

forces and those in authority.[q]
29 Mercenary forces also came to
him from other kingdoms and from
islands of the seas. 30 The number
of his forces was one hundred
thousand foot soldiers, twenty
thousand horsemen, and thirty-
two elephants accustomed to war.
31 They came through Idumea and
encamped against Beth-zur, and
for many days they fought and built
engines of war; but the Jews[r] sal-
lied out and burned these with fire,
and fought courageously.

The Battle at Beth-zechariah

32 Then Judas marched away
from the citadel and encamped at
Beth-zechariah, opposite the camp
of the king. 33 Early in the morning
the king set out and took his army
by a forced march along the road to
Beth-zechariah, and his troops
made ready for battle and sounded
their trumpets. 34 They offered the
elephants the juice of grapes and
mulberries, to arouse them for battle. 35 They distributed the animals
among the phalanxes; with each
elephant they stationed a thousand men armed with coats of
mail, and with brass helmets on
their heads; and five hundred
picked horsemen were assigned to
each beast. 36 These took their position beforehand wherever the animal was; wherever it went, they
went with it, and they never left it.
37 On the elephants[s] were wooden
towers, strong and covered; they
were fastened on each animal by
special harness, and on each were
four[t] armed men who fought from
there, and also its Indian driver.
38 The rest of the cavalry were stationed on either side, on the two
flanks of the army, to harass the
enemy while being themselves protected by the phalanxes. 39 When
the sun shone on the shields of
gold and brass, the hills were
ablaze with them and gleamed like
flaming torches.

40 Now a part of the king's army
was spread out on the high hills,
and some troops were on the plain,
and they advanced steadily and in
good order. 41 All who heard the
noise made by their multitude, by
the marching of the multitude and
the clanking of their arms, trembled, for the army was very large
and strong. 42 But Judas and his
army advanced to the battle, and
six hundred of the king's army fell.
43 Now Eleazar, called Avaran, saw
that one of the animals was
equipped with royal armor. It was
taller than all the others, and he
supposed that the king was on it.
44 So he gave his life to save his
people and to win for himself an
everlasting name. 45 He courageously ran into the midst of the
phalanx to reach it; he killed men
right and left, and they parted before him on both sides. 46 He got
under the elephant, stabbed it
from beneath, and killed it; but it
fell to the ground upon him and he
died. 47 When the Jews[r] saw the
royal might and the fierce attack of
the forces, they turned away in
flight.

The Siege of the Temple

48 The soldiers of the king's
army went up to Jerusalem against
them, and the king encamped in
Judea and at Mount Zion. 49 He
made peace with the people of
Beth-zur, and they evacuated the
town because they had no provisions there to withstand a siege,
since it was a sabbatical year for
the land. 50 So the king took Beth-
zur and stationed a guard there to
hold it. 51 Then he encamped before the sanctuary for many days.
He set up siege towers, engines of
war to throw fire and stones, machines to shoot arrows, and catapults. 52 The Jews[r] also made engines of war to match theirs, and
fought for many days. 53 But they
had no food in storage,[u] because it
was the seventh year; those who
had found safety in Judea from the
Gentiles had consumed the last of
the stores. 54 Only a few men were
left in the sanctuary; the rest scattered to their own homes, for the
famine proved too much for them.

6.29 1 Macc 4.35; 2 Macc 10.14, 24
6.31 1 Macc 4.29; 9.52; 2 Macc 14.19; 13.1-2
6.34 1 Macc 1.17; 3.34
6.38 1 Macc 9.12; 10.82
6.43 1 Macc 2.5
6.44 1 Macc 2.51; 3.14; 5.57
6.46 2 Macc 13.15
6.48 1 Macc 1.33
6.49 2 Macc 13.22; 1 Macc 4.29, 61; 6.26; Ex 23.11; Lev 25.3-7
6.51 1 Macc 6.20-21; 13.43-44

[q] Gk *those over the reins* [r] Gk *they*
[s] Gk *them* [t] Cn: Some authorities read *thirty*; others *thirty-two* [u] Other ancient authorities read *in the sanctuary*

Syria Offers Terms

55 Then Lysias heard that Philip, whom King Antiochus while still living had appointed to bring up his son Antiochus to be king, 56 had returned from Persia and Media with the forces that had gone with the king, and that he was trying to seize control of the government. 57 So he quickly gave orders to withdraw, and said to the king, to the commanders of the forces, and to the troops, men, "Daily we grow weaker, our food supply is scant, the place against which we are fighting is strong, and the affairs of the kingdom press urgently on us. 58 Now then let us come to terms with these people, and make peace with them and with all their nation. 59 Let us agree to let them live by their laws as they did before; for it was on account of their laws that we abolished that they became angry and did all these things."

60 The speech pleased the king and the commanders, and he sent to the Jews[v] an offer of peace, and they accepted it. 61 So the king and the commanders gave them their oath. On these conditions the Jews[w] evacuated the stronghold. 62 But when the king entered Mount Zion and saw what a strong fortress the place was, he broke the oath he had sworn and gave orders to tear down the wall all around. 63 Then he set off in haste and returned to Antioch. He found Philip in control of the city, but he fought against him, and took the city by force.

Expedition of Bacchides and Alcimus

7 In the one hundred fifty-first year[x] Demetrius son of Seleucus set out from Rome, sailed with a few men to a town by the sea, and there began to reign. 2 As he was entering the royal palace of his ancestors, the army seized Antiochus and Lysias to bring them to him. 3 But when this act became known to him, he said, "Do not let me see their faces!" 4 So the army killed them, and Demetrius took his seat on the throne of his kingdom.

5 Then there came to him all the renegade and godless men of Israel; they were led by Alcimus, who wanted to be high priest. 6 They brought to the king this accusation against the people: "Judas and his brothers have destroyed all your Friends, and have driven us out of our land. 7 Now then send a man whom you trust; let him go and see all the ruin that Judas[y] has brought on us and on the land of the king, and let him punish them and all who help them."

8 So the king chose Bacchides, one of the king's Friends, governor of the province Beyond the River; he was a great man in the kingdom and was faithful to the king. 9 He sent him, and with him he sent the ungodly Alcimus, whom he made high priest; and he commanded him to take vengeance on the Israelites. 10 So they marched away and came with a large force into the land of Judah; and he sent messengers to Judas and his brothers with peaceable but treacherous words. 11 But they paid no attention to their words, for they saw that they had come with a large force.

12 Then a group of scribes appeared in a body before Alcimus and Bacchides to ask for just terms. 13 The Hasideans were first among the Israelites to seek peace from them, 14 for they said, "A priest of the line of Aaron has come with the army, and he will not harm us." 15 Alcimus[z] spoke peaceable words to them and swore this oath to them, "We will not seek to injure you or your Friends." 16 So they trusted him; but he seized sixty of them and killed them in one day, in accordance with the word that was written,

17 "The flesh of your faithful
ones and their blood
they poured out all around
Jerusalem,

6.55 1 Macc 3.22, 33-38; 4.34-35; 6.15
6.56 2 Macc 13.23
6.58 2 Macc 11.13-19; 13.23
6.59 1 Macc 2.1-28
6.62 1 Macc 4.60; 5.54
6.63 2 Macc 13.26
7.1 2 Macc 14.1
7.2 1 Macc 6.17; 2 Macc 14.2
7.5 1 Macc 1.11-15,34; 9.23; 10.61; 9.1; 2 Macc 14.3
7.8 1 Macc 9.1; 2 Macc 8.30; Ezra 4.11
7.9 2 Macc 14.13
7.13 1 Macc 2.42; 2 Macc 14.6
7.14 Ex 28.4,43; 2 Chr 29.21
7.15 1 Macc 6.61-62
7.16 1 Macc 12.46-48; Ps 79.2-3
7.17 Jer 14.16; Tob 1.18; 2 Macc 5.10

v Gk *them* w Gk *they* x 161 B.C. y Gk *he* z Gk *He*

and there was no one to
bury them."

18 Then the fear and dread of them fell on all the people, for they said, "There is no truth or justice in them, for they have violated the agreement and the oath that they swore."

19 Then Bacchides withdrew from Jerusalem and encamped in Beth-zaith. And he sent and seized many of the men who had deserted to him,[a] and some of the people, and killed them and threw them into a great pit. 20 He placed Alcimus in charge of the country and left with him a force to help him; then Bacchides went back to the king.

21 Alcimus struggled to maintain his high priesthood, 22 and all who were troubling their people joined him. They gained control of the land of Judah and did great damage in Israel. 23 And Judas saw all the wrongs that Alcimus and those with him had done among the Israelites; it was more than the Gentiles had done. 24 So Judas[b] went out into all the surrounding parts of Judea, taking vengeance on those who had deserted and preventing those in the city[c] from going out into the country. 25 When Alcimus saw that Judas and those with him had grown strong, and realized that he could not withstand them, he returned to the king and brought malicious charges against them.

Nicanor in Judea

26 Then the king sent Nicanor, one of his honored princes, who hated and detested Israel, and he commanded him to destroy the people. 27 So Nicanor came to Jerusalem with a large force, and treacherously sent to Judas and his brothers this peaceable message, 28 "Let there be no fighting between you and me; I shall come with a few men to see you face to face in peace."

29 So he came to Judas, and they greeted one another peaceably; but the enemy were preparing to kidnap Judas. 30 It became known to Judas that Nicanor[b] had come to him with treacherous intent, and he was afraid of him and would not meet him again. 31 When Nicanor learned that his plan had been disclosed, he went out to meet Judas in battle near Capharsalama. 32 About five hundred of the army of Nicanor fell, and the rest[d] fled into the city of David.

Nicanor Threatens the Temple

33 After these events Nicanor went up to Mount Zion. Some of the priests from the sanctuary and some of the elders of the people came out to greet him peaceably and to show him the burnt offering that was being offered for the king. 34 But he mocked them and derided them and defiled them and spoke arrogantly, 35 and in anger he swore this oath, "Unless Judas and his army are delivered into my hands this time, then if I return safely I will burn up this house." And he went out in great anger. 36 At this the priests went in and stood before the altar and the temple; they wept and said,

37 "You chose this house to be
called by your name,
and to be for your people a
house of prayer and
supplication.
38 Take vengeance on this man
and on his army,
and let them fall by the
sword;
remember their blasphemies,
and let them live no
longer."

The Death of Nicanor

39 Now Nicanor went out from Jerusalem and encamped in Beth-horon, and the Syrian army joined him. 40 Judas encamped in Adasa with three thousand men. Then Judas prayed and said, 41 "When the messengers from the king spoke blasphemy, your angel went out and struck down one hundred eighty-five thousand of the Assyrians.[e] 42 So also crush this army

7.23 1 Macc 9.54-55
7.26 1 Macc 3.38; 2 Macc 8.9; 12.2; 14.12
7.27 2 Macc 14.19
7.28 1 Macc 6.58; 7.15
7.29 2 Macc 14.29
7.30 1 Macc 7.16-18; 2 Macc 14.30
7.32 2 Sam 6.12, 16; 1 Kings 2.10
7.34 1 Macc 1.24
7.35 2 Macc 14.27, 33
7.36 Joel 2.17
7.37 1 Kings 8.29, 43; Isa 56.7; Mk 11.17
7.38 Deut 32.35, 41; Ps 94.1; Heb 10.30; 1 Macc 2.6
7.39 Josh 10.10; 1 Macc 3.16, 24
7.41 1 Sam 25.38; Acts 12.23; 2 Kings 19.35; 2 Macc 8.19; 15.8

[a] Or *many of his men who had deserted*
[b] Gk *he*
[c] Gk *and they were prevented*
[d] Gk *they*
[e] Gk *of them*

before us today; let the rest learn that Nicanor[f] has spoken wickedly against the sanctuary, and judge him according to this wickedness."

43 So the armies met in battle on the thirteenth day of the month of Adar. The army of Nicanor was crushed, and he himself was the first to fall in the battle. 44 When his army saw that Nicanor had fallen, they threw down their arms and fled. 45 The Jews[g] pursued them a day's journey, from Adasa as far as Gazara, and as they followed they kept sounding the battle call on the trumpets. 46 People came out of all the surrounding villages of Judea, and they outflanked the enemy[h] and drove them back to their pursuers,[i] so that they all fell by the sword; not even one of them was left. 47 Then the Jews[g] seized the spoils and the plunder; they cut off Nicanor's head and the right hand that he had so arrogantly stretched out, and brought them and displayed them just outside Jerusalem. 48 The people rejoiced greatly and celebrated that day as a day of great gladness. 49 They decreed that this day should be celebrated each year on the thirteenth day of Adar. 50 So the land of Judah had rest for a few days.

A Eulogy of the Romans

8 Now Judas heard of the fame of the Romans, that they were very strong and were well-disposed toward all who made an alliance with them, that they pledged friendship to those who came to them, 2 and that they were very strong. He had been told of their wars and of the brave deeds that they were doing among the Gauls, how they had defeated them and forced them to pay tribute, 3 and what they had done in the land of Spain to get control of the silver and gold mines there, 4 and how they had gained control of the whole region by their planning and patience, even though the place was far distant from them. They also subdued the kings who came against them from the ends of the earth, until they crushed them and inflicted great disaster on them; the rest paid them tribute every year. 5 They had crushed in battle and conquered Philip, and King Perseus of the Macedonians,[j] and the others who rose up against them. 6 They also had defeated Antiochus the Great, king of Asia, who went to fight against them with one hundred twenty elephants and with cavalry and chariots and a very large army. He was crushed by them; 7 they took him alive and decreed that he and those who would reign after him should pay a heavy tribute and give hostages and surrender some of their best provinces, 8 the countries of India, Media, and Lydia. These they took from him and gave to King Eumenes. 9 The Greeks planned to come and destroy them, 10 but this became known to them, and they sent a general against the Greeks[h] and attacked them. Many of them were wounded and fell, and the Romans[g] took captive their wives and children; they plundered them, conquered the land, tore down their strongholds, and enslaved them to this day. 11 The remaining kingdoms and islands, as many as ever opposed them, they destroyed and enslaved; 12 but with their friends and those who rely on them they have kept friendship. They have subdued kings far and near, and as many as have heard of their fame have feared them. 13 Those whom they wish to help and to make kings, they make kings, and those whom they wish they depose; and they have been greatly exalted. 14 Yet for all this not one of them has put on a crown or worn purple as a mark of pride, 15 but they have built for themselves a senate chamber, and every day three hundred twenty senators constantly deliberate concerning the people, to govern them well. 16 They trust one man each year to rule over them and to control all

7.43 2 Macc 15.27
7.45 1 Macc 4.15; 3.54; 4.13,40
7.47 1 Macc 3.12; 5.28; 1 Sam 17.54; 2 Macc 15.30; 2 Sam 31.9; Jdt 14.1
7.49 2 Macc 15.36; 1 Macc 13.52
8.1 Lk 2.1; 3.1
8.3 Rom 15.24,28
8.6 1 Macc 1.10
8.8 Esth 1.1; 8.9; Ezra 6.2; Esth 1.3; 1 Macc 6.56
8.14 1 Macc 10.20, 62; 14.43-44

f Gk *he* g Gk *they* h Gk *them* i Gk *these* j Or *Kittim*

their land; they all heed the one man, and there is no envy or jealousy among them.

An Alliance with Rome

17 So Judas chose Eupolemus son of John son of Accos, and Jason son of Eleazar, and sent them to Rome to establish friendship and alliance, 18 and to free themselves from the yoke; for they saw that the kingdom of the Greeks was enslaving Israel completely. 19 They went to Rome, a very long journey; and they entered the senate chamber and spoke as follows: 20 "Judas, who is also called Maccabeus, and his brothers and the people of the Jews have sent us to you to establish alliance and peace with you, so that we may be enrolled as your allies and friends." 21 The proposal pleased them, 22 and this is a copy of the letter that they wrote in reply, on bronze tablets, and sent to Jerusalem to remain with them there as a memorial of peace and alliance:

23 "May all go well with the Romans and with the nation of the Jews at sea and on land forever, and may sword and enemy be far from them. 24 If war comes first to Rome or to any of their allies in all their dominion, 25 the nation of the Jews shall act as their allies wholeheartedly, as the occasion may indicate to them. 26 To the enemy that makes war they shall not give or supply grain, arms, money, or ships, just as Rome has decided; and they shall keep their obligations without receiving any return. 27 In the same way, if war comes first to the nation of the Jews, the Romans shall willingly act as their allies, as the occasion may indicate to them. 28 And to their enemies there shall not be given grain, arms, money, or ships, just as Rome has decided; and they shall keep these obligations and do so without deceit. 29 Thus on these terms the Romans make a treaty with the Jewish people. 30 If after these terms are in effect both parties shall determine to add or delete anything, they shall do so at

8.17 2 Macc 4.11; Ezra 2.61
8.18 1 Macc 3.41; 2 Macc 5.24
8.19 1 Macc 8.15
8.20 1 Macc 2.4
8.22 1 Macc 14.17, 27; 2 Sam 9.15-16; 1 Macc 12.1; 15.15-22
8.27 Josh 10.6-11
8.31 1 Macc 7.1-4
9.1 1 Macc 7.43-44,8,5; 2 Macc 14.3
9.2 Deut 11.30; Josh 4.19-20
9.6 Judg 7.3
9.7 Ps 34.18
9.10 1 Macc 3.58-59

their discretion, and any addition or deletion that they may make shall be valid.

31 "Concerning the wrongs that King Demetrius is doing to them, we have written to him as follows, 'Why have you made your yoke heavy on our friends and allies the Jews? 32 If now they appeal again for help against you, we will defend their rights and fight you on sea and on land.' "

Bacchides Returns to Judea

9 When Demetrius heard that Nicanor and his army had fallen in battle, he sent Bacchides and Alcimus into the land of Judah a second time, and with them the right wing of the army. 2 They went by the road that leads to Gilgal and encamped against Mesaloth in Arbela, and they took it and killed many people. 3 In the first month of the one hundred fifty-second year[k] they encamped against Jerusalem; 4 then they marched off and went to Berea with twenty thousand foot soldiers and two thousand cavalry.

5 Now Judas was encamped in Elasa, and with him were three thousand picked men. 6 When they saw the huge number of the enemy forces, they were greatly frightened, and many slipped away from the camp, until no more than eight hundred of them were left.

7 When Judas saw that his army had slipped away and the battle was imminent, he was crushed in spirit, for he had no time to assemble them. 8 He became faint, but he said to those who were left, "Let us get up and go against our enemies. We may have the strength to fight them." 9 But they tried to dissuade him, saying, "We do not have the strength. Let us rather save our own lives now, and let us come back with our kindred and fight them; we are too few." 10 But Judas said, "Far be it from us to do such a thing as to flee from them. If our time has come, let us die bravely

[k] 160 B.C.

for our kindred, and leave no cause
to question our honor."

The Last Battle of Judas

11 Then the army of Bacchides[l] marched out from the camp
and took its stand for the encounter. The cavalry was divided into
two companies, and the slingers
and the archers went ahead of the
army, as did all the chief warriors.
12 Bacchides was on the right wing.
Flanked by the two companies, the
phalanx advanced to the sound of
the trumpets; and the men with
Judas also blew their trumpets.
13 The earth was shaken by the
noise of the armies, and the battle
raged from morning until evening.
14 Judas saw that Bacchides
and the strength of his army were
on the right; then all the stouthearted men went with him, 15 and
they crushed the right wing, and he
pursued them as far as Mount Azotus. 16 When those on the left wing
saw that the right wing was
crushed, they turned and followed
close behind Judas and his men.
17 The battle became desperate,
and many on both sides were
wounded and fell. 18 Judas also
fell, and the rest fled.
19 Then Jonathan and Simon
took their brother Judas and buried him in the tomb of their ancestors at Modein, 20 and wept for
him. All Israel made great lamentation for him; they mourned many
days and said,
21 "How is the mighty fallen,
the savior of Israel!"
22 Now the rest of the acts of Judas,
and his wars and the brave deeds
that he did, and his greatness, have
not been recorded, but they were
very many.

Jonathan Succeeds Judas

23 After the death of Judas, the
renegades emerged in all parts of
Israel; all the wrongdoers reap-
peared. 24 In those days a very great
famine occurred, and the country
went over to their side. 25 Bacchides chose the godless and put
them in charge of the country.
26 They made inquiry and searched
for the friends of Judas, and
brought them to Bacchides, who
took vengeance on them and made
sport of them. 27 So there was great
distress in Israel, such as had not
been since the time that prophets
ceased to appear among them.
28 Then all the friends of Judas
assembled and said to Jonathan,
29 "Since the death of your brother
Judas there has been no one like
him to go against our enemies and
Bacchides, and to deal with those
of our nation who hate us. 30 Now
therefore we have chosen you today to take his place as our ruler
and leader, to fight our battle."
31 So Jonathan accepted the leadership at that time in place of his
brother Judas.

The Campaigns of Jonathan

32 When Bacchides learned of
this, he tried to kill him. 33 But Jonathan and his brother Simon and
all who were with him heard of it,
and they fled into the wilderness of
Tekoa and camped by the water of
the pool of Asphar. 34 Bacchides
found this out on the sabbath day,
and he with all his army crossed
the Jordan.
35 So Jonathan[m] sent his
brother as leader of the multitude
and begged the Nabateans, who
were his friends, for permission to
store with them the great amount
of baggage that they had. 36 But the
family of Jambri from Medeba
came out and seized John and all
that he had, and left with it.
37 After these things it was reported to Jonathan and his brother
Simon, "The family of Jambri are
celebrating a great wedding, and
are conducting the bride, a daughter of one of the great nobles of Canaan, from Nadabath with a large
escort." 38 Remembering how their
brother John had been killed, they
went up and hid under cover of the
mountain. 39 They looked out and
saw a tumultuous procession with
a great amount of baggage; and the
bridegroom came out with his
friends and his brothers to meet

9.12 1 Macc 6.35-38; 3.54; 4.13,40 **9.15** 1 Macc 4.14, 36; 5.7,21; 7.43 **9.19** 1 Macc 2.1, 70; 13.27-30 **9.21** 2 Sam 1.19, 27 **9.22** 1 Kings 11.41; 14.29; 15.23 **9.23** 1 Macc 1.11-15; 7.5 **9.25** 1 Macc 9.1; 1.12; 2 Macc 4.13-15 **9.27** 1 Macc 4.46 **9.28** 1 Macc 2.5 **9.30** 1 Macc 13.8-9 **9.33** 2 Chr 20.20; Am 1.1 **9.35** 1 Macc 2.2; 5.25 **9.38** 1 Macc 9.36 **9.39** Mt 25.1; Jn 3.29

[l] Gk *the army* [m] Gk *he*

them with tambourines and musicians and many weapons. 40 Then they rushed on them from the ambush and began killing them. Many were wounded and fell, and the rest fled to the mountain; and the Jews[n] took all their goods. 41 So the wedding was turned into mourning and the voice of their musicians into a funeral dirge. 42 After they had fully avenged the blood of their brother, they returned to the marshes of the Jordan.

43 When Bacchides heard of this, he came with a large force on the sabbath day to the banks of the Jordan. 44 And Jonathan said to those with him, "Let us get up now and fight for our lives, for today things are not as they were before. 45 For look! the battle is in front of us and behind us; the water of the Jordan is on this side and on that, with marsh and thicket; there is no place to turn. 46 Cry out now to Heaven that you may be delivered from the hands of our enemies." 47 So the battle began, and Jonathan stretched out his hand to strike Bacchides, but he eluded him and went to the rear. 48 Then Jonathan and the men with him leaped into the Jordan and swam across to the other side, and the enemy[n] did not cross the Jordan to attack them. 49 And about one thousand of Bacchides' men fell that day.

Bacchides Builds Fortifications

50 Then Bacchides[o] returned to Jerusalem and built strong cities in Judea: the fortress in Jericho, and Emmaus, and Beth-horon, and Bethel, and Timnath, and[p] Pharathon, and Tephon, with high walls and gates and bars. 51 And he placed garrisons in them to harass Israel. 52 He also fortified the town of Beth-zur, and Gazara, and the citadel, and in them he put troops and stores of food. 53 And he took the sons of the leading men of the land as hostages and put them under guard in the citadel at Jerusalem.

54 In the one hundred and fifty-third year,[q] in the second month, Alcimus gave orders to tear down the wall of the inner court of the sanctuary. He tore down the work of the prophets! 55 But he only began to tear it down, for at that time Alcimus was stricken and his work was hindered; his mouth was stopped and he was paralyzed, so that he could no longer say a word or give commands concerning his house. 56 And Alcimus died at that time in great agony. 57 When Bacchides saw that Alcimus was dead, he returned to the king, and the land of Judah had rest for two years.

The End of the War

58 Then all the lawless plotted and said, "See! Jonathan and his men are living in quiet and confidence. So now let us bring Bacchides back, and he will capture them all in one night." 59 And they went and consulted with him. 60 He started to come with a large force, and secretly sent letters to all his allies in Judea, telling them to seize Jonathan and his men; but they were unable to do it, because their plan became known. 61 And Jonathan's men[n] seized about fifty of the men of the country who were leaders in this treachery, and killed them.

62 Then Jonathan with his men, and Simon, withdrew to Bethbasi in the wilderness; he rebuilt the parts of it that had been demolished, and they fortified it. 63 When Bacchides learned of this, he assembled all his forces, and sent orders to the men of Judea. 64 Then he came and encamped against Bethbasi; he fought against it for many days and made machines of war.

65 But Jonathan left his brother Simon in the town, while he went out into the country; and he went with only a few men. 66 He struck down Odomera and his kindred and the people of Phasiron in their tents. 67 Then he[r] began to attack

9.40 1 Macc 5.28; 7.47
9.41 Lam 5.15; Bar 2.23
9.43 1 Macc 2.32-41
9.46 1 Macc 3.19, 50; 4.10,40; 5.31
9.50 Josh 5.15-20; 1 Kings 16.34; 1 Macc 3.40, 16; Gen 12.8; 28.19; Josh 8.9
9.52 1 Macc 4.29; 6.31; 4.15
9.53 1 Macc 10.6-9
9.54 1 Macc 7.5,9, 21-25; Ezra 5.1; 6.14; Hag 1.1; Zech 1.1
9.57 Josh 11.23; 1 Macc 7.50; 14.4
9.58 1 Macc 1.12; 9.25; 2 Macc 4.13-15
9.61 1 Macc 9.25
9.64 2 Chr 26.15; 1 Macc 6.51

[n] Gk *they* [o] Gk *he* [p] Some authorities omit *and* [q] 159 B.C. [r] Other ancient authorities read *they*

and went into battle with his
forces; and Simon and his men sal-
lied out from the town and set fire
to the machines of war. 68 They
fought with Bacchides, and he was
crushed by them. They pressed
him very hard, for his plan and his
expedition had been in vain. 69 So
he was very angry at the renegades
who had counseled him to come
into the country, and he killed
many of them. Then he decided to
go back to his own land.
70 When Jonathan learned of
this, he sent ambassadors to him
to make peace with him and obtain
release of the captives. 71 He
agreed, and did as he said; and he
swore to Jonathan[s] that he would
not try to harm him as long as he
lived. 72 He restored to him the
captives whom he had taken previously from the land of Judah; then
he turned and went back to his
own land, and did not come again
into their territory. 73 Thus the
sword ceased from Israel. Jonathan settled in Michmash and began to judge the people; and he destroyed the godless out of Israel.

Revolt of Alexander Epiphanes

10 In the one hundred sixtieth
year[t] Alexander Epipha-
nes, son of Antiochus, landed and
occupied Ptolemais. They welcomed him, and there he began to
reign. 2 When King Demetrius
heard of it, he assembled a very
large army and marched out to
meet him in battle. 3 Demetrius
sent Jonathan a letter in peaceable
words to honor him; 4 for he said to
himself, "Let us act first to make
peace with him[u] before he makes
peace with Alexander against us,
5 for he will remember all the
wrongs that we did to him and to
his brothers and his nation." 6 So
Demetrius[v] gave him authority to
recruit troops, to equip them with
arms, and to become his ally; and
he commanded that the hostages
in the citadel should be released to
him.
7 Then Jonathan came to Jerusalem and read the letter in the
hearing of all the people and of
those in the citadel. 8 They were
greatly alarmed when they heard
that the king had given him authority to recruit troops. 9 But
those in the citadel released the
hostages to Jonathan, and he returned them to their parents.
10 And Jonathan took up residence in Jerusalem and began to
rebuild and restore the city. 11 He
directed those who were doing the
work to build the walls and encircle Mount Zion with squared
stones, for better fortification; and
they did so.
12 Then the foreigners who
were in the strongholds that Bacchides had built fled; 13 all of them
left their places and went back to
their own lands. 14 Only in Beth-zur
did some remain who had forsaken
the law and the commandments,
for it served as a place of refuge.
15 Now King Alexander heard
of all the promises that Demetrius
had sent to Jonathan, and he heard
of the battles that Jonathan[v] and
his brothers had fought, of the
brave deeds that they had done,
and of the troubles that they had
endured. 16 So he said, "Shall we
find another such man? Come
now, we will make him our friend
and ally." 17 And he wrote a letter
and sent it to him, in the following
words:

Jonathan Becomes High Priest

18 "King Alexander to his
brother Jonathan, greetings. 19 We
have heard about you, that you are
a mighty warrior and worthy to be
our friend. 20 And so we have appointed you today to be the high
priest of your nation; you are to be
called the king's Friend and you
are to take our side and keep
friendship with us." He also sent
him a purple robe and a golden
crown.
21 So Jonathan put on the sacred vestments in the seventh
month of the one hundred sixtieth
year,[t] at the festival of booths,[w]
and he recruited troops and
equipped them with arms in abun-

9.68 1 Macc 9.15
9.69 1 Macc 9.23, 58-59
9.73 1 Sam 14.5-23; Judg 10.2-3, 12.7-8,11; 1 Sam 7.15-17; 1 Macc 9.23-27
10.1 1 Macc 10.39
10.2 1 Macc 7.1,4; 9.1
10.4 1 Macc 10.58
10.5 1 Macc 9.1-69
10.6 1 Macc 9.53
10.11 Neh 3.1-4,23; 6.15; 1 Macc 6.62
10.12 1 Macc 9.50-52
10.14 1 Macc 4.29, 61; 6.7,26; 1.12; 9.25; 2 Macc 4.13-15
10.15 1 Macc 10.1
10.20 1 Macc 11.27, 57; 2.18; 6.10; 8.14; 10.62,64
10.21 Ex 28.1-39; 39.1-6; Lev 23.33-43; Zech 14.16-19; 1 Macc 10.6

[s] Gk *him* [t] 152 B.C. [u] Gk *them* [v] Gk *he* [w] Or *tabernacles*

dance. 22 When Demetrius heard of
these things he was distressed and
said, 23 "What is this that we have
done? Alexander has gotten ahead
of us in forming a friendship with
the Jews to strengthen himself. 24 I
also will write them words of encouragement and promise them
honor and gifts, so that I may have
their help." 25 So he sent a message
to them in the following words:

A Letter from Demetrius to Jonathan

"King Demetrius to the nation of
the Jews, greetings. 26 Since you
have kept your agreement with us
and have continued your friendship with us, and have not sided
with our enemies, we have heard of
it and rejoiced. 27 Now continue
still to keep faith with us, and we
will repay you with good for what
you do for us. 28 We will grant you
many immunities and give you
gifts.

29 "I now free you and exempt
all the Jews from payment of tribute and salt tax and crown levies,
30 and instead of collecting the
third of the grain and the half of
the fruit of the trees that I should
receive, I release them from this
day and henceforth. I will not collect them from the land of Judah
or from the three districts added to
it from Samaria and Galilee, from
this day and for all time. 31 Jerusalem and its environs, its tithes and
its revenues, shall be holy and free
from tax. 32 I release also my control of the citadel in Jerusalem and
give it to the high priest, so that he
may station in it men of his own
choice to guard it. 33 And everyone
of the Jews taken as a captive from
the land of Judah into any part of
my kingdom, I set free without payment; and let all officials cancel
also the taxes on their livestock.

34 "All the festivals and sabbaths and new moons and appointed days, and the three days
before a festival and the three after
a festival—let them all be days of
immunity and release for all the
Jews who are in my kingdom. 35 No
one shall have authority to exact
anything from them or annoy any
of them about any matter.

36 "Let Jews be enrolled in the
king's forces to the number of
thirty thousand men, and let the
maintenance be given them that is
due to all the forces of the king.
37 Let some of them be stationed in
the great strongholds of the king,
and let some of them be put in positions of trust in the kingdom. Let
their officers and leaders be of
their own number, and let them
live by their own laws, just as the
king has commanded in the land of
Judah.

38 "As for the three districts
that have been added to Judea
from the country of Samaria, let
them be annexed to Judea so that
they may be considered to be under one ruler and obey no other authority than the high priest. 39 Ptolemais and the land adjoining it I
have given as a gift to the sanctuary
in Jerusalem, to meet the necessary expenses of the sanctuary. 40 I
also grant fifteen thousand shekels
of silver yearly out of the king's revenues from appropriate places.
41 And all the additional funds that
the government officials have not
paid as they did in the first years,[x]
they shall give from now on for the
service of the temple.[y] 42 Moreover, the five thousand shekels of
silver that my officials[z] have received every year from the income
of the services of the temple, this
too is canceled, because it belongs
to the priests who minister there.
43 And all who take refuge at the
temple in Jerusalem, or in any of
its precincts, because they owe
money to the king or are in debt,
let them be released and receive
back all their property in my kingdom.

44 "Let the cost of rebuilding
and restoring the structures of the
sanctuary be paid from the revenues of the king. 45 And let the cost
of rebuilding the walls of Jerusalem and fortifying it all around,
and the cost of rebuilding the walls

10.24 3 Macc 1.7
10.25 1 Macc 11.30-37, 20; Acts 15.23
10.29 1 Macc 11.28-29
10.30 1 Macc 11.34
10.31 1 Macc 11.34
10.32 1 Macc 1.33; 11.20; 10.20
10.34 Lev 23.1-43
10.37 Ezra 7.25; Add Esth 16.19
10.38 1 Macc 10.30; 11.34
10.39 1 Macc 10.1
10.42 Ex 30.12-16
10.44 Ezra 6.8; 7.20
10.45 Neh 2.8

[x] Meaning of Gk uncertain [y] Gk *house*
[z] Gk *they*

in Judea, also be paid from the revenues of the king."

Death of Demetrius

46 When Jonathan and the people heard these words, they did not
believe or accept them, because
they remembered the great wrongs
that Demetrius[a] had done in Israel and how much he had oppressed them. 47 They favored Alexander, because he had been the
first to speak peaceable words to
them, and they remained his allies
all his days.
48 Now King Alexander assembled large forces and encamped
opposite Demetrius. 49 The two
kings met in battle, and the army
of Demetrius fled, and Alexander[b]
pursued him and defeated them.
50 He pressed the battle strongly
until the sun set, and on that day
Demetrius fell.

Treaty of Ptolemy and Alexander

51 Then Alexander sent ambassadors to Ptolemy king of Egypt
with the following message:
52 "Since I have returned to my
kingdom and have taken my seat
on the throne of my ancestors, and
established my rule—for I crushed
Demetrius and gained control of
our country; 53 I met him in battle,
and he and his army were crushed
by us, and we have taken our seat
on the throne of his kingdom—
54 now therefore let us establish
friendship with one another; give
me now your daughter as my wife,
and I will become your son-in-law,
and will make gifts to you and to
her in keeping with your position."
55 Ptolemy the king replied and
said, "Happy was the day on which
you returned to the land of your
ancestors and took your seat on
the throne of their kingdom. 56 And
now I will do for you as you wrote,
but meet me at Ptolemais, so that
we may see one another, and I will
become your father-in-law, as you
have said."
57 So Ptolemy set out from
Egypt, he and his daughter Cleopatra, and came to Ptolemais in the
one hundred sixty-second year.[c]

10.46 1 Macc 9.1-69; 10.4
10.47 1 Macc 10.4, 15-20
10.51 1 Macc 1.18; 2 Macc 8.8-9
10.54 1 Kings 3.1; 7.8
10.56 1 Macc 5.15, 22; 10.1
10.57 1 Macc 11.9
10.58 Ps 45
10.60 1 Macc 2.18
10.61 1 Macc 1.11-15; 7.5; 9.23
10.62 Gen 41.42; 1 Macc 11.58
10.63 Esth 6.6-9
10.65 1 Macc 2.18
10.67 1 Macc 10.2, 50
10.69 2 Macc 3.5; 1 Macc 4.15; 5.58; 10.20-21

58 King Alexander met him, and
Ptolemy[a] gave him his daughter
Cleopatra in marriage, and celebrated her wedding at Ptolemais
with great pomp, as kings do.
59 Then King Alexander wrote
to Jonathan to come and meet
him. 60 So he went with pomp to
Ptolemais and met the two kings;
he gave them and their Friends silver and gold and many gifts, and
found favor with them. 61 A group
of malcontents from Israel, renegades, gathered together against
him to accuse him; but the king
paid no attention to them. 62 The
king gave orders to take off Jonathan's garments and to clothe him
in purple, and they did so. 63 The
king also seated him at his side;
and he said to his officers, "Go out
with him into the middle of the
city and proclaim that no one is to
bring charges against him about
any matter, and let no one annoy
him for any reason." 64 When his
accusers saw the honor that was
paid him, in accord with the proclamation, and saw him clothed in
purple, they all fled. 65 Thus the
king honored him and enrolled
him among his chief[d] Friends, and
made him general and governor of
the province. 66 And Jonathan returned to Jerusalem in peace and
gladness.

Apollonius Is Defeated by Jonathan

67 In the one hundred sixty-
fifth year[e] Demetrius son of Demetrius came from Crete to the
land of his ancestors. 68 When King
Alexander heard of it, he was
greatly distressed and returned to
Antioch. 69 And Demetrius appointed Apollonius the governor of
Coelesyria, and he assembled a
large force and encamped against
Jamnia. Then he sent the following
message to the high priest Jonathan:
70 "You are the only one to rise
up against us, and I have fallen
into ridicule and disgrace because

[a] Gk *he* [b] Other ancient authorities read *Alexander fled, and Demetrius* [c] 150 B.C.
[d] Gk *first* [e] 147 B.C.

of you. Why do you assume authority against us in the hill country?
71 If you now have confidence in
your forces, come down to the
plain to meet us, and let us match
strength with each other there, for
I have with me the power of the cities. 72 Ask and learn who I am and
who the others are that are helping
us. People will tell you that you
cannot stand before us, for your
ancestors were twice put to flight
in their own land. 73 And now you
will not be able to withstand my
cavalry and such an army in the
plain, where there is no stone or
pebble, or place to flee."
74 When Jonathan heard the
words of Apollonius, his spirit was
aroused. He chose ten thousand
men and set out from Jerusalem,
and his brother Simon met him to
help him. 75 He encamped before
Joppa, but the people of the city
closed its gates, for Apollonius had
a garrison in Joppa. 76 So they
fought against it, and the people of
the city became afraid and opened
the gates, and Jonathan gained
possession of Joppa.
77 When Apollonius heard of it,
he mustered three thousand cavalry and a large army, and went to
Azotus as though he were going
farther. At the same time he advanced into the plain, for he had a
large troop of cavalry and put confidence in it. 78 Jonathan[f] pursued
him to Azotus, and the armies engaged in battle. 79 Now Apollonius
had secretly left a thousand cavalry
behind them. 80 Jonathan learned
that there was an ambush behind
him, for they surrounded his army
and shot arrows at his men from
early morning until late afternoon.
81 But his men stood fast, as Jonathan had commanded, and the enemy's[g] horses grew tired.
82 Then Simon brought forward
his force and engaged the phalanx
in battle (for the cavalry was exhausted); they were overwhelmed
by him and fled, 83 and the cavalry
was dispersed in the plain. They
fled to Azotus and entered Beth-
dagon, the temple of their idol, for
safety. 84 But Jonathan burned
Azotus and the surrounding towns
and plundered them; and the temple of Dagon, and those who had
taken refuge in it, he burned with
fire. 85 The number of those who
fell by the sword, with those
burned alive, came to eight thousand.
86 Then Jonathan left there and
encamped against Askalon, and
the people of the city came out to
meet him with great pomp.
87 He and those with him then
returned to Jerusalem with a large
amount of booty. 88 When King Alexander heard of these things, he
honored Jonathan still more;
89 and he sent to him a golden
buckle, such as it is the custom to
give to the King's Kinsmen. He
also gave him Ekron and all its environs as his possession.

Ptolemy Invades Syria

11 Then the king of Egypt
gathered great forces, like
the sand by the seashore, and
many ships; and he tried to get
possession of Alexander's kingdom by trickery and add it to his
own kingdom. 2 He set out for Syria
with peaceable words, and the
people of the towns opened their
gates to him and went to meet
him, for King Alexander had commanded them to meet him, since
he was Alexander's[h] father-in-law.
3 But when Ptolemy entered the
towns he stationed forces as a garrison in each town.
4 When he[i] approached Azotus, they showed him the burnt-
out temple of Dagon, and Azotus
and its suburbs destroyed, and the
corpses lying about, and the
charred bodies of those whom Jonathan[f] had burned in the war, for
they had piled them in heaps along
his route. 5 They also told the king
what Jonathan had done, to throw
blame on him; but the king kept silent. 6 Jonathan met the king at
Joppa with pomp, and they greeted
one another and spent the night
there. 7 And Jonathan went with
the king as far as the river called

10.71 1 Kings 20.23-25 **10.72** 1 Macc 6.54; 9.18 **10.74** 1 Macc 2.3; 5.20-21; 9.65-67 **10.75** Josh 19.46; 2 Chr 2.16; Acts 9.36 **10.77** 1 Macc 4.15; 5.68; Acts 8.40 **10.82** 1 Macc 6.35-38 **10.83** Judg 16.23 **10.84** 1 Macc 3.12; 7.47; 1 Sam 5.2-5; 1 Macc 5.68; 11.4

10.86 Josh 13.3; 1 Sam 6.17 **10.89** 1 Macc 11.58; 1 Esd 4.12; 1 Sam 27.6 **11.1** Gen 22.17; Josh 11.4; Judg 7.12 **11.2** 1 Macc 10.57-58 **11.4** 1 Macc 10.84 **11.6** 1 Macc 10.75 **11.7** 1 Macc 12.30

[f] Gk *he* [g] Gk *their* [h] Gk *his*
[i] Other ancient authorities read *they*

Eleutherus; then he returned to Jerusalem.
8 So King Ptolemy gained control of the coastal cities as far as
Seleucia by the sea, and he kept
devising wicked designs against Alexander. 9 He sent envoys to King
Demetrius, saying, "Come, let us
make a covenant with each other,
and I will give you in marriage my
daughter who was Alexander's
wife, and you shall reign over your
father's kingdom. 10 I now regret
that I gave him my daughter, for he
has tried to kill me." 11 He threw
blame on Alexander[j] because he
coveted his kingdom. 12 So he took
his daughter away from him and
gave her to Demetrius. He was estranged from Alexander, and their
enmity became manifest.
13 Then Ptolemy entered Antioch and put on the crown of Asia.
Thus he put two crowns on his
head, the crown of Egypt and that
of Asia. 14 Now King Alexander was
in Cilicia at that time, because the
people of that region were in revolt. 15 When Alexander heard of it,
he came against him in battle.
Ptolemy marched out and met him
with a strong force, and put him to
flight. 16 So Alexander fled into
Arabia to find protection there,
and King Ptolemy was triumphant.
17 Zabdiel the Arab cut off the head
of Alexander and sent it to Ptolemy. 18 But King Ptolemy died
three days later, and his troops in
the strongholds were killed by the
inhabitants of the strongholds.
19 So Demetrius became king in the
one hundred sixty-seventh year.[k]

Jonathan's Diplomacy

20 In those days Jonathan assembled the Judeans to attack the
citadel in Jerusalem, and he built
many engines of war to use against
it. 21 But certain renegades who
hated their nation went to the king
and reported to him that Jonathan
was besieging the citadel. 22 When
he heard this he was angry, and as
soon as he heard it he set out and
came to Ptolemais; and he wrote
Jonathan not to continue the
siege, but to meet him for a confer-
ence at Ptolemais as quickly as
possible.
23 When Jonathan heard this,
he gave orders to continue the
siege. He chose some of the elders
of Israel and some of the priests,
and put himself in danger, 24 for he
went to the king at Ptolemais, taking silver and gold and clothing
and numerous other gifts. And he
won his favor. 25 Although certain
renegades of his nation kept making complaints against him, 26 the
king treated him as his predecessors had treated him; he exalted
him in the presence of all his
Friends. 27 He confirmed him in
the high priesthood and in as many
other honors as he had formerly
had, and caused him to be reckoned among his chief[l] Friends.
28 Then Jonathan asked the king to
free Judea and the three districts
of Samaria[m] from tribute, and
promised him three hundred talents. 29 The king consented, and
wrote a letter to Jonathan about all
these things; its contents were as
follows:
30 "King Demetrius to his
brother Jonathan and to the nation
of the Jews, greetings. 31 This copy
of the letter that we wrote concerning you to our kinsman Lasthenes
we have written to you also, so that
you may know what it says. 32 'King
Demetrius to his father Lasthenes,
greetings. 33 We have determined
to do good to the nation of the
Jews, who are our friends and fulfill their obligations to us, because
of the goodwill they show toward
us. 34 We have confirmed as their
possession both the territory of Judea and the three districts of
Aphairema and Lydda and Ratha-
min; the latter, with all the region
bordering them, were added to Judea from Samaria. To all those who
offer sacrifice in Jerusalem we
have granted release from[n] the
royal taxes that the king formerly
received from them each year,
from the crops of the land and the

11.8 Acts 13.4
11.9 1 Macc 10.67, 57
11.11 Ex 20.17; Josh 7.21; Prov 21.26
11.13 1 Macc 3.37; Acts 11.19-20,26; 13.1
11.14 2 Macc 4.36; Acts 22.3
11.16 1 Kings 10.15; Ezek 30.5; Gal 1.17
11.19 1 Macc 10.67
11.20 1 Macc 10.32; 5.20
11.21 1 Macc 1.11-15; 7.5; 10.61
11.22 1 Macc 10.56
11.26 1 Macc 10.18-20,32, 59-63
11.27 1 Macc 10.20, 89
11.28 1 Macc 10.29
11.29 1 Macc 10.25-45
11.33 1 Macc 8.23, 27; Acts 10.22
11.34 1 Macc 10.30; 1 Sam 1.1; 1 Macc 10.31

[j] Gk *him* [k] 145 B.C. [l] Gk *first*
[m] Cn: Gk *the three districts and Samaria*
[n] Or *Samaria, for all those who offer sacrifice in Jerusalem, in place of*

fruit of the trees. [35]And the other
payments henceforth due to us of
the tithes, and the taxes due to us,
and the salt pits and the crown
taxes due to us—from all these we
shall grant them release. [36]And not
one of these grants shall be canceled from this time on forever.
[37]Now therefore take care to make
a copy of this, and let it be given to
Jonathan and put up in a conspicuous place on the holy mountain.' "

The Intrigue of Trypho

38 When King Demetrius saw
that the land was quiet before him
and that there was no opposition
to him, he dismissed all his troops,
all of them to their own homes, except the foreign troops that he had
recruited from the islands of the
nations. So all the troops who had
served under his predecessors
hated him. [39]A certain Trypho had
formerly been one of Alexander's
supporters; he saw that all the
troops were grumbling against Demetrius. So he went to Imalkue the
Arab, who was bringing up Antiochus, the young son of Alexander,
[40]and insistently urged him to
hand Antiochus[o] over to him, to
become king in place of his father.
He also reported to Imalkue[o] what
Demetrius had done and told of
the hatred that the troops of Demetrius[p] had for him; and he
stayed there many days.

41 Now Jonathan sent to King
Demetrius the request that he remove the troops of the citadel from
Jerusalem, and the troops in the
strongholds; for they kept fighting
against Israel. [42]And Demetrius
sent this message back to Jonathan: "Not only will I do these
things for you and your nation, but
I will confer great honor on you
and your nation, if I find an opportunity. [43]Now then you will do well
to send me men who will help me,
for all my troops have revolted."
[44]So Jonathan sent three thousand
stalwart men to him at Antioch,
and when they came to the king,
the king rejoiced at their arrival.

45 Then the people of the city
assembled within the city, to the
number of a hundred and twenty
thousand, and they wanted to kill
the king. [46]But the king fled into
the palace. Then the people of the
city seized the main streets of the
city and began to fight. [47]So the
king called the Jews to his aid, and
they all rallied around him and
then spread out through the city;
and they killed on that day about
one hundred thousand. [48]They set
fire to the city and seized a large
amount of spoil on that day, and
saved the king. [49]When the people
of the city saw that the Jews had
gained control of the city as they
pleased, their courage failed and
they cried out to the king with this
entreaty: [50]"Grant us peace, and
make the Jews stop fighting
against us and our city." [51]And
they threw down their arms and
made peace. So the Jews gained
glory in the sight of the king and of
all the people in his kingdom, and
they returned to Jerusalem with a
large amount of spoil.

52 So King Demetrius sat on
the throne of his kingdom, and the
land was quiet before him. [53]But
he broke his word about all that he
had promised; he became estranged from Jonathan and did not
repay the favors that Jonathan[q]
had done him, but treated him very
harshly.

Trypho Seizes Power

54 After this Trypho returned,
and with him the young boy Antiochus who began to reign and put
on the crown. [55]All the troops that
Demetrius had discharged gathered around him; they fought
against Demetrius,[o] and he fled
and was routed. [56]Trypho captured
the elephants[r] and gained control
of Antioch. [57]Then the young Antiochus wrote to Jonathan, saying, "I
confirm you in the high priesthood
and set you over the four districts
and make you one of the king's
Friends." [58]He also sent him gold
plate and a table service, and
granted him the right to drink from

11.35 1 Macc 10.29
11.37 1 Macc 11.31; Ps 48.11; Isa 27.13; Dan 9.16; Wis 9.8
11.39 1 Macc 10.48; 11.54; 12.39
11.41 1 Macc 11.20
11.42 1 Macc 15.9
11.44 1 Macc 11.13
11.48 2 Kings 25.9; 1 Macc 1.31; 5.28,35
11.51 1 Macc 3.12; 7.47; 11.84
11.53 1 Macc 11.42-43
11.54 1 Macc 11.39; 12.39; 13.31
11.55 1 Macc 11.38
11.57 1 Macc 10.20; 11.27; 10.89; 11.34; 2.18
11.58 Esth 1.7; 1 Macc 10.62, 59

[o]Gk *him* [p]Gk *his troops* [q]Gk *he* [r]Gk *animals*

gold cups and dress in purple and
wear a gold buckle. 59 He appointed Jonathan's[s] brother Simon governor from the Ladder of
Tyre to the borders of Egypt.

Campaigns of Jonathan and Simon

60 Then Jonathan set out and
traveled beyond the river and
among the towns, and all the army
of Syria gathered to him as allies.
When he came to Askalon, the
people of the city met him and
paid him honor. 61 From there he
went to Gaza, but the people of
Gaza shut him out. So he besieged
it and burned its suburbs with fire
and plundered them. 62 Then the
people of Gaza pleaded with Jonathan, and he made peace with
them, and took the sons of their
rulers as hostages and sent them to
Jerusalem. And he passed through
the country as far as Damascus.
63 Then Jonathan heard that
the officers of Demetrius had come
to Kadesh in Galilee with a large
army, intending to remove him
from office. 64 He went to meet
them, but left his brother Simon in
the country. 65 Simon encamped
before Beth-zur and fought against
it for many days and hemmed it in.
66 Then they asked him to grant
them terms of peace, and he did
so. He removed them from there,
took possession of the town, and
set a garrison over it.
67 Jonathan and his army encamped by the waters of Gennesaret. Early in the morning they
marched to the plain of Hazor,
68 and there in the plain the army of
the foreigners met him; they had
set an ambush against him in the
mountains, but they themselves
met him face to face. 69 Then the
men in ambush emerged from
their places and joined battle.
70 All the men with Jonathan fled;
not one of them was left except
Mattathias son of Absalom and Judas son of Chalphi, commanders of
the forces of the army. 71 Jonathan
tore his clothes, put dust on his
head, and prayed. 72 Then he
turned back to the battle against
the enemy[t] and routed them, and
they fled. 73 When his men who
were fleeing saw this, they returned to him and joined him in
the pursuit as far as Kadesh, to
their camp, and there they encamped. 74 As many as three thousand of the foreigners fell that day.
And Jonathan returned to Jerusalem.

Alliances with Rome and Sparta

12 Now when Jonathan saw
that the time was favorable
for him, he chose men and sent
them to Rome to confirm and renew the friendship with them. 2 He
also sent letters to the same effect
to the Spartans and to other
places. 3 So they went to Rome and
entered the senate chamber and
said, "The high priest Jonathan
and the Jewish nation have sent us
to renew the former friendship and
alliance with them." 4 And the Romans[u] gave them letters to the
people in every place, asking them
to provide for the envoys[t] safe
conduct to the land of Judah.
5 This is a copy of the letter that
Jonathan wrote to the Spartans:
6 "The high priest Jonathan, the
senate of the nation, the priests,
and the rest of the Jewish people
to their brothers the Spartans,
greetings. 7 Already in time past a
letter was sent to the high priest
Onias from Arius,[v] who was king
among you, stating that you are our
brothers, as the appended copy
shows. 8 Onias welcomed the envoy with honor, and received the
letter, which contained a clear
declaration of alliance and friendship. 9 Therefore, though we have
no need of these things, since we
have as encouragement the holy
books that are in our hands, 10 we
have undertaken to send to renew
our family ties and friendship with
you, so that we may not become
estranged from you, for considerable time has passed since you
sent your letter to us. 11 We therefore remember you constantly on
every occasion, both at our festi-

11.59 1 Macc 2.3
11.60 1 Macc 10.86
11.61 Gen 10.19; Judg 16.1; 1 Sam 6.17
11.62 1 Macc 9.53; 10.6,9
11.63 Judg 4.9
11.65 1 Macc 4.29, 61
11.67 Mt 14.34; Lk 5.1; Josh 11.1
11.68 Josh 8.2-19; 2 Chr 13.13; 1 Macc 9.40
11.70 1 Macc 13.11
11.71 1 Macc 2.14; 3.47; 4.39; 3.50; 4.10-11
12.1 1 Macc 8.17-32
12.2 1 Macc 14.20
12.6 Jdt 4.8; 2 Macc 1.10; Mk 14.55
12.7 2 Macc 3.1,5; 15.12; 1 Macc 12.20-23
12.9 Rom 15.4; 2 Tim 3.16-17
12.11 Rom 1.9; 2 Tim 1.3; Lev 23.2-4; 1 Macc 10.34

[s] Gk *his* [t] Gk *them* [u] Gk *they*
[v] Vg Compare verse 20: Gk *Darius*

vals and on other appropriate days,
at the sacrifices that we offer and
in our prayers, as it is right and
proper to remember brothers.
12 And we rejoice in your glory.
13 But as for ourselves, many trials
and many wars have encircled us;
the kings around us have waged
war against us. 14 We were unwilling to annoy you and our other allies and friends with these wars,
15 for we have the help that comes
from Heaven for our aid, and so we
were delivered from our enemies,
and our enemies were humbled.
16 We therefore have chosen Numenius son of Antiochus and Antipater son of Jason, and have sent
them to Rome to renew our former
friendship and alliance with them.
17 We have commanded them to go
also to you and greet you and deliver to you this letter from us concerning the renewal of our family
ties. 18 And now please send us a
reply to this."

19 This is a copy of the letter
that they sent to Onias: 20 "King
Arius of the Spartans, to the high
priest Onias, greetings. 21 It has
been found in writing concerning
the Spartans and the Jews that
they are brothers and are of the
family of Abraham. 22 And now that
we have learned this, please write
us concerning your welfare; 23 we
on our part write to you that your
livestock and your property belong
to us, and ours belong to you. We
therefore command that our envoys[w] report to you accordingly."

Further Campaigns of Jonathan and Simon

24 Now Jonathan heard that
the commanders of Demetrius had
returned, with a larger force than
before, to wage war against him.
25 So he marched away from Jerusalem and met them in the region
of Hamath, for he gave them no opportunity to invade his own country. 26 He sent spies to their camp,
and they returned and reported to
him that the enemy[w] were being
drawn up in formation to attack
the Jews[x] by night. 27 So when the
sun had set, Jonathan commanded
his troops to be alert and to keep
their arms at hand so as to be ready
all night for battle, and he stationed outposts around the camp.
28 When the enemy heard that Jonathan and his troops were prepared
for battle, they were afraid and
were terrified at heart; so they kindled fires in their camp and withdrew.[y] 29 But Jonathan and his
troops did not know it until morning, for they saw the fires burning.
30 Then Jonathan pursued them,
but he did not overtake them, for
they had crossed the Eleutherus
river. 31 So Jonathan turned aside
against the Arabs who are called
Zabadeans, and he crushed them
and plundered them. 32 Then he
broke camp and went to Damascus, and marched through all that
region.

33 Simon also went out and
marched through the country as far
as Askalon and the neighboring
strongholds. He turned aside to
Joppa and took it by surprise, 34 for
he had heard that they were ready
to hand over the stronghold to
those whom Demetrius had sent.
And he stationed a garrison there
to guard it.

35 When Jonathan returned he
convened the elders of the people
and planned with them to build
strongholds in Judea, 36 to build
the walls of Jerusalem still higher,
and to erect a high barrier between
the citadel and the city to separate
it from the city, in order to isolate
it so that its garrison[w] could neither buy nor sell. 37 So they gathered together to rebuild the city;
part of the wall on the valley to the
east had fallen, and he repaired the
section called Chaphenatha. 38 Simon also built Adida in the Shephelah; he fortified it and installed
gates with bolts.

Trypho Captures Jonathan

39 Then Trypho attempted to
become king in Asia and put on the
crown, and to raise his hand
against King Antiochus. 40 He
feared that Jonathan might not

12.15 1 Macc 3.19; 4.24,55; 16.3
12.16 1 Macc 14.22; 15.15; 11.39
12.19 1 Macc 12.7; 2 Macc 3.1,5
12.21 Gen 25.1-4, 12-18
12.23 2 Sam 10.2; 2 Kings 20.12; 1 Macc 11.9
12.24 1 Macc 10.67; 11.9,63
12.25 2 Kings 14.28; Ezek 47.16-17
12.26 Josh 2.1; Judg 7.11-14, 19
12.28 2 Kings 7.6-7
12.30 1 Macc 11.7
12.31 1 Macc 4.14; 5.21; 10.52
12.33 1 Macc 2.3; 11.64; 10.75
12.36 1 Macc 11.20-21, 41-42,53
12.37 1 Kings 2.37; Neh 3.26-29
12.38 Deut 1.7; 2 Chr 28.18
12.39 1 Macc 11.39-40,54
12.40 Judg 1.27; 1 Kings 4.12; 1 Macc 5.52

[w] Gk *they* [x] Gk *them*
[y] Other ancient authorities omit *and withdrew*

permit him to do so, but might make war on him, so he kept seeking to seize and kill him, and he marched out and came to Beth-shan. 41 Jonathan went out to meet him with forty thousand picked warriors, and he came to Beth-shan. 42 When Trypho saw that he had come with a large army, he was afraid to raise his hand against him. 43 So he received him with honor and commended him to all his Friends, and he gave him gifts and commanded his Friends and his troops to obey him as they would himself. 44 Then he said to Jonathan, "Why have you put all these people to so much trouble when we are not at war? 45 Dismiss them now to their homes and choose for yourself a few men to stay with you, and come with me to Ptolemais. I will hand it over to you as well as the other strongholds and the remaining troops and all the officials, and will turn around and go home. For that is why I am here."

46 Jonathan[z] trusted him and did as he said; he sent away the troops, and they returned to the land of Judah. 47 He kept with himself three thousand men, two thousand of whom he left in Galilee, while one thousand accompanied him. 48 But when Jonathan entered Ptolemais, the people of Ptolemais closed the gates and seized him, and they killed with the sword all who had entered with him.

49 Then Trypho sent troops and cavalry into Galilee and the Great Plain to destroy all Jonathan's soldiers. 50 But they realized that Jonathan had been seized and had perished along with his men, and they encouraged one another and kept marching in close formation, ready for battle. 51 When their pursuers saw that they would fight for their lives, they turned back. 52 So they all reached the land of Judah safely, and they mourned for Jonathan and his companions and were in great fear; and all Israel mourned deeply. 53 All the nations around them tried to destroy them, for they said, "They have no leader or helper. Now therefore let us make war on them and blot out the memory of them from humankind."

Simon Takes Command

13 Simon heard that Trypho had assembled a large army to invade the land of Judah and destroy it, 2 and he saw that the people were trembling with fear. So he went up to Jerusalem, and gathering the people together 3 he encouraged them, saying to them, "You yourselves know what great things my brothers and I and the house of my father have done for the laws and the sanctuary; you know also the wars and the difficulties that my brothers and I have seen. 4 By reason of this all my brothers have perished for the sake of Israel, and I alone am left. 5 And now, far be it from me to spare my life in any time of distress, for I am not better than my brothers. 6 But I will avenge my nation and the sanctuary and your wives and children, for all the nations have gathered together out of hatred to destroy us."

7 The spirit of the people was rekindled when they heard these words, 8 and they answered in a loud voice, "You are our leader in place of Judas and your brother Jonathan. 9 Fight our battles, and all that you say to us we will do." 10 So he assembled all the warriors and hurried to complete the walls of Jerusalem, and he fortified it on every side. 11 He sent Jonathan son of Absalom to Joppa, and with him a considerable army; he drove out its occupants and remained there.

Deceit and Treachery of Trypho

12 Then Trypho left Ptolemais with a large army to invade the land of Judah, and Jonathan was with him under guard. 13 Simon encamped in Adida, facing the plain. 14 Trypho learned that Simon had risen up in place of his brother Jonathan, and that he was about to join battle with him, so he sent en-

12.43 1 Macc 11.57
12.45 1 Macc 11.22
12.46 1 Macc 7.16-18
12.52 1 Macc 2.70; 9.19-21
12.53 Deut 32.26; 1 Macc 5.2; 13.6
13.1 1 Macc 2.3; 11.59
13.2 2 Chr 20.1-3
13.3 1 Macc 4.36-51
13.4 1 Macc 6.46; 9.18,36-38; 12.46-48; 13.23
13.6 1 Macc 2.67; 5.2; 12.53
13.8 1 Macc 9.30-31
13.10 1 Macc 12.35-37
13.11 1 Macc 11.70; 12.33
13.12 1 Macc 12.39, 45
13.13 1 Macc 12.38

[z] Gk *he*

voys to him and said, 15 "It is for the
money that your brother Jonathan
owed the royal treasury, in connection with the offices he held, that
we are detaining him. 16 Send now
one hundred talents of silver and
two of his sons as hostages, so that
when released he will not revolt
against us, and we will release
him."

17 Simon knew that they were
speaking deceitfully to him, but he
sent to get the money and the sons,
so that he would not arouse great
hostility among the people, who
might say, 18 "It was because Simon[a] did not send him the money
and the sons, that Jonathan[b] perished." 19 So he sent the sons and
the hundred talents, but Trypho[b]
broke his word and did not release
Jonathan.

20 After this Trypho came to invade the country and destroy it,
and he circled around by the way
to Adora. But Simon and his army
kept marching along opposite him
to every place he went. 21 Now the
men in the citadel kept sending
envoys to Trypho urging him to
come to them by way of the wilderness and to send them food. 22 So
Trypho got all his cavalry ready to
go, but that night a very heavy
snow fell, and he did not go because of the snow. He marched off
and went into the land of Gilead.
23 When he approached Baskama,
he killed Jonathan, and he was
buried there. 24 Then Trypho
turned and went back to his own
land.

Jonathan's Tomb

25 Simon sent and took the
bones of his brother Jonathan, and
buried him in Modein, the city of
his ancestors. 26 All Israel bewailed
him with great lamentation, and
mourned for him many days. 27 And
Simon built a monument over the
tomb of his father and his brothers;
he made it high so that it might be
seen, with polished stone at the
front and back. 28 He also erected
seven pyramids, opposite one another, for his father and mother
and four brothers. 29 For the pyramids[c] he devised an elaborate setting, erecting about them great
columns, and on the columns he
put suits of armor for a permanent
memorial, and beside the suits of
armor he carved ships, so that they
could be seen by all who sail the
sea. 30 This is the tomb that he
built in Modein; it remains to this
day.

Judea Gains Independence

31 Trypho dealt treacherously
with the young King Antiochus; he
killed him 32 and became king in
his place, putting on the crown of
Asia; and he brought great calamity on the land. 33 But Simon built
up the strongholds of Judea and
walled them all around, with high
towers and great walls and gates
and bolts, and he stored food in
the strongholds. 34 Simon also
chose emissaries and sent them to
King Demetrius with a request to
grant relief to the country, for all
that Trypho did was to plunder.
35 King Demetrius sent him a favorable reply to this request, and
wrote him a letter as follows,
36 "King Demetrius to Simon, the
high priest and friend of kings, and
to the elders and nation of the
Jews, greetings. 37 We have received the gold crown and the
palm branch that you[d] sent, and
we are ready to make a general
peace with you and to write to our
officials to grant you release from
tribute. 38 All the grants that we
have made to you remain valid,
and let the strongholds that you
have built be your possession.
39 We pardon any errors and offenses committed to this day, and
cancel the crown tax that you owe;
and whatever other tax has been
collected in Jerusalem shall be
collected no longer. 40 And if any of
you are qualified to be enrolled in
our bodyguard,[e] let them be enrolled, and let there be peace between us."

41 In the one hundred seventi-
eth year[f] the yoke of the Gentiles

13.15 1 Macc 11.57; 12.50
13.19 1 Macc 12.46-48
13.20 2 Chr 11.9
13.21 1 Macc 12.36
13.22 Josh 22.9; 1 Macc 5.9,17
13.25 1 Macc 2.1, 70; 9.19
13.26 1 Macc 2.70; 9.19-21; 12.52
13.31 1 Macc 11.39, 54; 12.39
13.33 1 Macc 12.33, 35,38
13.34 1 Macc 10.67
13.35 1 Macc 11.30-37
13.37 2 Macc 14.4
13.38 1 Macc 14.7; 15.7
13.39 1 Macc 11.34-35; 15.5,8

[a] Gk *I* [b] Gk *he* [c] Gk *For these*
[d] The word *you* in verses 37-40 is plural
[e] Or *court* [f] 142 B.C.

was removed from Israel, 42 and the
people began to write in their documents and contracts, "In the first
year of Simon the great high priest
and commander and leader of the
Jews."

The Capture of Gazara by Simon

43 In those days Simon[g] encamped against Gazara[h] and surrounded it with troops. He made a
siege engine, brought it up to the
city, and battered and captured
one tower. 44 The men in the siege
engine leaped out into the city,
and a great tumult arose in the
city. 45 The men in the city, with
their wives and children, went up
on the wall with their clothes torn,
and they cried out with a loud
voice, asking Simon to make peace
with them; 46 they said, "Do not
treat us according to our wicked
acts but according to your mercy."
47 So Simon reached an agreement
with them and stopped fighting
against them. But he expelled
them from the city and cleansed
the houses in which the idols were
located, and then entered it with
hymns and praise. 48 He removed
all uncleanness from it, and settled
in it those who observed the law.
He also strengthened its fortifications and built in it a house for
himself.

Simon Regains the Citadel at Jerusalem

49 Those who were in the citadel at Jerusalem were prevented
from going in and out to buy and
sell in the country. So they were
very hungry, and many of them perished from famine. 50 Then they
cried to Simon to make peace with
them, and he did so. But he expelled them from there and
cleansed the citadel from its pollutions. 51 On the twenty-third day of
the second month, in the one hundred seventy-first year,[i] the Jews[j]
entered it with praise and palm
branches, and with harps and cymbals and stringed instruments, and
with hymns and songs, because a
great enemy had been crushed and
removed from Israel. 52 Simon[k] decreed that every year they should
celebrate this day with rejoicing.
He strengthened the fortifications
of the temple hill alongside the citadel, and he and his men lived
there. 53 Simon saw that his son
John had reached manhood, and
so he made him commander of all
the forces; and he lived at Gazara.

Capture of Demetrius

14 In the one hundred
seventy-second year[l] King
Demetrius assembled his forces
and marched into Media to obtain
help, so that he could make war
against Trypho. 2 When King Arsaces of Persia and Media heard that
Demetrius had invaded his territory, he sent one of his generals to
take him alive. 3 The general[k]
went and defeated the army of Demetrius, and seized him and took
him to Arsaces, who put him under
guard.

Eulogy of Simon

4 The land[m] had rest all the
days of Simon.
He sought the good of his
nation;
his rule was pleasing to
them,
as was the honor shown
him, all his days.
5 To crown all his honors he
took Joppa for a harbor,
and opened a way to the
isles of the sea.
6 He extended the borders of
his nation,
and gained full control of
the country.
7 He gathered a host of
captives;
he ruled over Gazara and
Beth-zur and the
citadel,
and he removed its
uncleanness from it;
and there was none to
oppose him.
8 They tilled their land in
peace;

13.42 1 Macc 14.27 **13.43** 1 Macc 4.15; 2 Macc 10.32; 1 Macc 6.20, 51 **13.46** 2 Macc 10.34 **13.48** 1 Macc 14.7 **13.49** 1 Macc 1.33; 10.32; 11.20 **13.51** 1 Macc 13.37; 2 Macc 10.7; Jn 12.13; Rev 7.9; 1 Macc 4.24; 2 Macc 10.38; 1 Macc 1.36 **13.52** 1 Macc 7.49 **13.53** 1 Macc 16.1 **14.1** 1 Macc 11.39; 12.39-48; 15.10-12 **14.2** 1 Macc 15.22 **14.4** Josh 11.23; 1 Kings 5.4; 1 Macc 9.57; 3.3-9 **14.5** 1 Macc 13.11 **14.6** Ex 34.24 **14.7** 1 Macc 13.43-48, 49-50 **14.8** Zech 8.12

g Gk *he* h Cn: Gk *Gaza* i 141 B.C. j Gk *they* k Gk *He* l 140 B.C. m Other ancient authorities add *of Judah*

the ground gave its
increase,
and the trees of the plains
their fruit.
9 Old men sat in the streets;
they all talked together of
good things,
and the youths put on
splendid military attire.
10 He supplied the towns with
food,
and furnished them with
the means of defense,
until his renown spread to
the ends of the earth.
11 He established peace in the
land,
and Israel rejoiced with
great joy.
12 All the people sat under
their own vines and fig
trees,
and there was none to
make them afraid.
13 No one was left in the land
to fight them,
and the kings were crushed
in those days.
14 He gave help to all the
humble among his
people;
he sought out the law,
and did away with all the
renegades and outlaws.
15 He made the sanctuary
glorious,
and added to the vessels of
the sanctuary.

Diplomacy with Rome and Sparta

16 It was heard in Rome, and as
far away as Sparta, that Jonathan
had died, and they were deeply
grieved. 17 When they heard that
his brother Simon had become
high priest in his stead, and that he
was ruling over the country and the
towns in it, 18 they wrote to him on
bronze tablets to renew with him
the friendship and alliance that
they had established with his
brothers Judas and Jonathan.
19 And these were read before the
assembly in Jerusalem.
20 This is a copy of the letter
that the Spartans sent:
"The rulers and the city of the
Spartans to the high priest Simon
and to the elders and the priests
and the rest of the Jewish people,
our brothers, greetings. 21 The envoys who were sent to our people
have told us about your glory and
honor, and we rejoiced at their
coming. 22 We have recorded what
they said in our public decrees, as
follows, 'Numenius son of Antiochus and Antipater son of Jason,
envoys of the Jews, have come to
us to renew their friendship with
us. 23 It has pleased our people to
receive these men with honor and
to put a copy of their words in the
public archives, so that the people
of the Spartans may have a record
of them. And they have sent a copy
of this to the high priest Simon.' "
24 After this Simon sent Numenius to Rome with a large gold
shield weighing one thousand minas, to confirm the alliance with
the Romans.[n]

Official Honors for Simon

25 When the people heard
these things they said, "How shall
we thank Simon and his sons?
26 For he and his brothers and the
house of his father have stood firm;
they have fought and repulsed Israel's enemies and established its
freedom." 27 So they made a record
on bronze tablets and put it on pillars on Mount Zion.
This is a copy of what they
wrote: "On the eighteenth day of
Elul, in the one hundred seventy-
second year,[o] which is the third
year of the great high priest Simon,
28 in Asaramel,[p] in the great assembly of the priests and the people and the rulers of the nation and
the elders of the country, the following was proclaimed to us:
29 "Since wars often occurred
in the country, Simon son of Mattathias, a priest of the sons[q] of
Joarib, and his brothers, exposed
themselves to danger and resisted
the enemies of their nation, in or-

14.9 Zech 8.4 **14.10** 1 Macc 13.33; 12.38,52 **14.11** Lev 26.6 **14.12** 1 Kings 4.25; Mic 4.4; Zech 3.10 **14.13** 1 Macc 10.51-52; 12.31; 13.51 **14.14** Isa 11.3-4; Ezra 7.10; 1 Macc 1.37 **14.16** 1 Macc 8.17-22; 12.4, 2 **14.17** 1 Macc 13.42 **14.18** 1 Macc 8.22 **14.20** 1 Macc 12.5 **14.21** 1 Macc 12.12 **14.22** 1 Macc 12.16; 15.15; 12.10 **14.24** 1 Macc 15.18 **14.26** 1 Macc 2.1-5 **14.27** 1 Macc 8.22; 4.37; 13.42 **14.29** 1 Macc 2.1, 26-27,60, 67-68; 4.41-42; 3.3; 11.51

[n] Gk *them* [o] 140 B.C.
[p] This word resembles the Hebrew words for *the court of the people of God* or *the prince of the people of God* [q] Meaning of Gk uncertain

der that their sanctuary and the
law might be preserved; and they
brought great glory to their nation.
30 Jonathan rallied the[r] nation,
became their high priest, and was
gathered to his people. 31 When
their enemies decided to invade
their country and lay hands on
their sanctuary, 32 then Simon rose
up and fought for his nation. He
spent great sums of his own
money; he armed the soldiers of
his nation and paid them wages.
33 He fortified the towns of Judea,
and Beth-zur on the borders of Judea, where formerly the arms of
the enemy had been stored, and he
placed there a garrison of Jews.
34 He also fortified Joppa, which is
by the sea, and Gazara, which is on
the borders of Azotus, where the
enemy formerly lived. He settled
Jews there, and provided in those
towns[s] whatever was necessary for
their restoration.

35 "The people saw Simon's
faithfulness[t] and the glory that he
had resolved to win for his nation,
and they made him their leader
and high priest, because he had
done all these things and because
of the justice and loyalty that he
had maintained toward his nation.
He sought in every way to exalt his
people. 36 In his days things prospered in his hands, so that the
Gentiles were put out of the[r]
country, as were also those in the
city of David in Jerusalem, who
had built themselves a citadel from
which they used to sally forth and
defile the environs of the sanctuary, doing great damage to its purity. 37 He settled Jews in it and fortified it for the safety of the
country and of the city, and built
the walls of Jerusalem higher.

38 "In view of these things King
Demetrius confirmed him in the
high priesthood, 39 made him one
of his Friends, and paid him high
honors. 40 For he had heard that
the Jews were addressed by the Romans as friends and allies and
brothers, and that the Romans[u]
had received the envoys of Simon
with honor.

41 "The Jews and their priests
have resolved that Simon should
be their leader and high priest forever, until a trustworthy prophet
should arise, 42 and that he should
be governor over them and that he
should take charge of the sanctuary and appoint officials over its
tasks and over the country and the
weapons and the strongholds, and
that he should take charge of the
sanctuary, 43 and that he should be
obeyed by all, and that all contracts in the country should be
written in his name, and that he
should be clothed in purple and
wear gold.

44 "None of the people or
priests shall be permitted to nullify
any of these decisions or to oppose
what he says, or to convene an assembly in the country without his
permission, or to be clothed in purple or put on a gold buckle. 45 Whoever acts contrary to these decisions or rejects any of them shall
be liable to punishment."

46 All the people agreed to
grant Simon the right to act in accordance with these decisions.
47 So Simon accepted and agreed to
be high priest, to be commander
and ethnarch of the Jews and
priests, and to be protector of them
all.[v] 48 And they gave orders to inscribe this decree on bronze tablets, to put them up in a conspicuous place in the precincts of the
sanctuary, 49 and to deposit copies
of them in the treasury, so that Simon and his sons might have
them.

Letter of Antiochus VII

15 Antiochus, son of King Demetrius, sent a letter from
the islands of the sea to Simon, the
priest and ethnarch of the Jews,
and to all the nation; 2 its contents
were as follows: "King Antiochus
to Simon the high priest and ethnarch and to the nation of the
Jews, greetings. 3 Whereas certain
scoundrels have gained control of
the kingdom of our ancestors, and
I intend to lay claim to the king-

14.30 1 Macc 10.20; 11.27; 13.23
14.32 1 Macc 13.43-53
14.33 1 Macc 13.48; 4.29; 14.7
14.34 1 Macc 10.75; 12.33-34; 13.43-48; 14.5-7
14.35 1 Macc 13.42
14.36 1 Macc 14.4-15; 13.49-50; 1.34; 4.41
14.39 1 Macc 2.18
14.40 1 Macc 8.23-32; 15.15-21
14.41 Ps 110.4; Heb 5.6; 1 Macc 4.46; 9.27; Jn 6.14-15; 7.40
14.43 Esth 8.15; 1 Macc 10.20, 62
14.44 1 Macc 10.89; 11.58
14.45 1 Esd 8.22
14.47 1 Macc 15.1
14.48 1 Macc 14.27
15.1 1 Macc 10.67; 14.47
15.3 1 Macc 4.35; 6.29; 2 Macc 10.14, 24

[r] Gk *their* [s] Gk *them*
[t] Other ancient authorities read *conduct*
[u] Gk *they* [v] Or *to preside over them all*

dom so that I may restore it as it
formerly was, and have recruited a
host of mercenary troops and have
equipped warships, 4 and intend to
make a landing in the country so
that I may proceed against those
who have destroyed our country
and those who have devastated
many cities in my kingdom, 5 now
therefore I confirm to you all the
tax remissions that the kings before me have granted you, and a release from all the other payments
from which they have released you.
6 I permit you to mint your own
coinage as money for your country,
7 and I grant freedom to Jerusalem
and the sanctuary. All the weapons
that you have prepared and the
strongholds that you have built
and now hold shall remain yours.
8 Every debt you owe to the royal
treasury and any such future debts
shall be canceled for you from
henceforth and for all time. 9 When
we gain control of our kingdom, we
will bestow great honor on you and
your nation and the temple, so that
your glory will become manifest in
all the earth."

10 In the one hundred seventy-
fourth year[w] Antiochus set out and
invaded the land of his ancestors.
All the troops rallied to him, so
that there were only a few with Trypho. 11 Antiochus pursued him,
and Trypho[x] came in his flight to
Dor, which is by the sea; 12 for he
knew that troubles had converged
on him, and his troops had deserted him. 13 So Antiochus encamped against Dor, and with him
were one hundred twenty thousand warriors and eight thousand
cavalry. 14 He surrounded the town,
and the ships joined battle from
the sea; he pressed the town hard
from land and sea, and permitted
no one to leave or enter it.

Rome Supports the Jews

15 Then Numenius and his
companions arrived from Rome,
with letters to the kings and countries, in which the following was
written: 16 "Lucius, consul of the
Romans, to King Ptolemy, greetings. 17 The envoys of the Jews have
come to us as our friends and allies
to renew our ancient friendship
and alliance. They had been sent
by the high priest Simon and by the
Jewish people 18 and have brought
a gold shield weighing one thousand minas. 19 We therefore have
decided to write to the kings and
countries that they should not
seek their harm or make war
against them and their cities and
their country, or make alliance
with those who war against them.
20 And it has seemed good to us to
accept the shield from them.
21 Therefore if any scoundrels have
fled to you from their country,
hand them over to the high priest
Simon, so that he may punish
them according to their law."

22 The consul[y] wrote the same
thing to King Demetrius and to At-
talus and Ariarathes and Arsaces,
23 and to all the countries, and to
Sampsames,[z] and to the Spartans,
and to Delos, and to Myndos, and
to Sicyon, and to Caria, and to Samos, and to Pamphylia, and to
Lycia, and to Halicarnassus, and to
Rhodes, and to Phaselis, and to
Cos, and to Side, and to Aradus
and Gortyna and Cnidus and Cyprus and Cyrene. 24 They also sent
a copy of these things to the high
priest Simon.

Antiochus VII Threatens Simon

25 King Antiochus besieged
Dor for the second time, continually throwing his forces against it
and making engines of war; and he
shut Trypho up and kept him from
going out or in. 26 And Simon sent
to Antiochus[a] two thousand
picked troops, to fight for him, and
silver and gold and a large amount
of military equipment. 27 But he refused to receive them, and broke
all the agreements he formerly had
made with Simon, and became estranged from him. 28 He sent to
him Athenobius, one of his
Friends, to confer with him, saying, "You hold control of Joppa
and Gazara and the citadel in Jerusalem; they are cities of my king-

15.5 1 Macc 11.34-35; 13.39
15.7 1 Macc 13.38
15.9 1 Macc 11.42; 14.4,21
15.10 1 Macc 11.39; 12.39-48; 13.20-24
15.11 Judg 1.27
15.14 1 Macc 13.49
15.15 1 Macc 12.16; 14.22,40
15.17 1 Macc 6.17-32
15.18 1 Macc 14.24
15.21 Jn 19.7; Acts 9.2
15.22 1 Macc 10.67; 11.9; 13.36; 14.2
15.25 1 Macc 5.20; 2 Macc 12.15, 27
15.27 1 Macc 15.1-9
15.28 1 Macc 14.4-7

[w] 138 B.C. [x] Gk *he* [y] Gk *He*
[z] The name is uncertain [a] Gk *him*

dom. 29You have devastated their
territory, you have done great damage in the land, and you have taken
possession of many places in my
kingdom. 30Now then, hand over
the cities that you have seized and
the tribute money of the places
that you have conquered outside
the borders of Judea; 31or else pay
me five hundred talents of silver
for the destruction that you have
caused and five hundred talents
more for the tribute money of the
cities. Otherwise we will come and
make war on you."
32 So Athenobius, the king's
Friend, came to Jerusalem, and
when he saw the splendor of Simon, and the sideboard with its
gold and silver plate, and his great
magnificence, he was amazed.
When he reported to him the
king's message, 33Simon said to
him in reply: "We have neither
taken foreign land nor seized foreign property, but only the inheritance of our ancestors, which at
one time had been unjustly taken
by our enemies. 34Now that we
have the opportunity, we are firmly
holding the inheritance of our ancestors. 35As for Joppa and Gazara,
which you demand, they were
causing great damage among the
people and to our land; for them
we will give you one hundred talents."
Athenobius[b] did not answer
him a word, 36but returned in
wrath to the king and reported to
him these words, and also the
splendor of Simon and all that he
had seen. And the king was very
angry.

Victory over Cendebeus

37 Meanwhile Trypho em-
barked on a ship and escaped to
Orthosia. 38Then the king made
Cendebeus commander-in-chief of
the coastal country, and gave him
troops of infantry and cavalry. 39He
commanded him to encamp
against Judea, to build up Kedron
and fortify its gates, and to make
war on the people; but the king
pursued Trypho. 40So Cendebeus
came to Jamnia and began to pro-

15.29 1 Macc 12.24-33; 13.43-53 **15.33** Gen 13.14-17; 1 Kings 8.36; Ezek 47.13-14 **15.35** 1 Macc 12.33; 13.43-48 **15.37** 1 Macc 15.10-14 **15.40** 1 Macc 4.15; 5.58; 10.69

16.1 1 Macc 13.53 **16.2** 1 Macc 2.1-5; 14.4-15 **16.3** 1 Macc 3.19; 4.24,55; 12.15 **16.4** 1 Macc 2.1; 13.25,30 **16.8** 1 Macc 3.54; 4.13,40; 15.39 **16.10** 1 Macc 10.84

voke the people and invade Judea
and take the people captive and
kill them. 41He built up Kedron
and stationed horsemen and
troops there, so that they might go
out and make raids along the highways of Judea, as the king had ordered him.

16 John went up from Gazara
and reported to his father
Simon what Cendebeus had done.
2And Simon called in his two eldest sons Judas and John, and said
to them: "My brothers and I and
my father's house have fought the
wars of Israel from our youth until
this day, and things have prospered
in our hands so that we have delivered Israel many times. 3But now I
have grown old, and you by
Heaven's[c] mercy are mature in
years. Take my place and my
brother's, and go out and fight for
our nation, and may the help that
comes from Heaven be with you."
4 So John[d] chose out of the
country twenty thousand warriors
and cavalry, and they marched
against Cendebeus and camped for
the night in Modein. 5Early in the
morning they started out and
marched into the plain, where a
large force of infantry and cavalry
was coming to meet them; and a
stream lay between them. 6Then
he and his army lined up against
them. He saw that the soldiers
were afraid to cross the stream, so
he crossed over first; and when his
troops saw him, they crossed over
after him. 7Then he divided the
army and placed the cavalry in the
center of the infantry, for the cavalry of the enemy were very numerous. 8They sounded the trumpets,
and Cendebeus and his army were
put to flight; many of them fell
wounded and the rest fled into the
stronghold. 9At that time Judas
the brother of John was wounded,
but John pursued them until Cendebeus[e] reached Kedron, which
he had built. 10They also fled into
the towers that were in the fields of
Azotus, and John[e] burned it with
fire, and about two thousand of

[b] Gk *He* [c] Gk *his*
[d] Other ancient authorities read *he* [e] Gk *he*

them fell. He then returned to Judea safely.

Murder of Simon and His Sons

11 Now Ptolemy son of Abubus
had been appointed governor over
the plain of Jericho; he had a large
store of silver and gold, 12 for he
was son-in-law of the high priest.
13 His heart was lifted up; he determined to get control of the country, and made treacherous plans
against Simon and his sons, to do
away with them. 14 Now Simon was
visiting the towns of the country
and attending to their needs, and
he went down to Jericho with his
sons Mattathias and Judas, in the
one hundred seventy-seventh
year,[f] in the eleventh month,
which is the month of Shebat.
15 The son of Abubus received
them treacherously in the little
stronghold called Dok, which he
had built; he gave them a great
banquet, and hid men there.
16 When Simon and his sons were
drunk, Ptolemy and his men rose
up, took their weapons, rushed in
against Simon in the banquet hall
and killed him and his two sons, as
well as some of his servants. 17 So
he committed an act of great
treachery and returned evil for
good.

16.11 Num 22.1; Josh 3.16
16.13 1 Macc 15.25-31
16.16 Dan 5.4,30; Jdt 13.2-10
16.19 1 Macc 15.83
16.21 1 Macc 16.16
16.24 1 Macc 13.42; 14.27

John Succeeds Simon

18 Then Ptolemy wrote a report
about these things and sent it to
the king, asking him to send troops
to aid him and to turn over to him
the towns and the country. 19 He
sent other troops to Gazara to do
away with John; he sent letters to
the captains asking them to come
to him so that he might give them
silver and gold and gifts; 20 and he
sent other troops to take possession of Jerusalem and the temple
hill. 21 But someone ran ahead and
reported to John at Gazara that his
father and brothers had perished,
and that "he has sent men to kill
you also." 22 When he heard this,
he was greatly shocked; he seized
the men who came to destroy him
and killed them, for he had found
out that they were seeking to destroy him.
23 The rest of the acts of John
and his wars and the brave deeds
that he did, and the building of the
walls that he completed, and his
achievements, 24 are written in the
annals of his high priesthood, from
the time that he became high
priest after his father.

f 134 B.C.

2 Maccabees

Title and Background

This book claims to be a condensation of a five-volume work by Jason of Cyrene on the life and times of Judas Maccabeus (2.23). Even more than 1 Maccabees, it stresses the miraculous intervention of God during this critical period of Jewish history.

Author and Date of Writing

We have no evidence of Jason's original five-volume work from which this book claims to be abridged, and no idea who abridged it. But the writing style makes it clear that the author wrote in Greek. The book was likely written during the first half of the first century B.C. by a God-fearing Jew.

Theme and Message

The sanctity of the temple and God's directing of history are unifying themes in this book. God defends his temple from being desecrated by pagans and protects and delivers those who strive for personal holiness. This is one of the first Jewish writings that clearly portray the doctrine of the resurrection of the dead.

Outline

I. Two Letters to the Jews in Egypt (1.1–2.18)
II. God's Protection of the Temple from Desecration (2.19–3.40)
III. God's Judgment Against Those Who Corrupt Judaism (4.1–7.42)
IV. God's Deliverance of the Jews from Wicked Antiochus (8.1–10.9)
V. God's Help of Judas and His Men (10.10–16.39)

A Letter to the Jews in Egypt

1 The Jews in Jerusalem and those in the land of Judea,

To their Jewish kindred in Egypt,

Greetings and true peace.

2 May God do good to you, and may he remember his covenant with Abraham and Isaac and Jacob, his faithful servants. 3 May he give you all a heart to worship him and to do his will with a strong heart and a willing spirit. 4 May he open your heart to his law and his commandments, and may he bring peace. 5 May he hear your prayers and be reconciled to you, and may he not forsake you in time of evil. 6 We are now praying for you here.

7 In the reign of Demetrius, in the one hundred sixty-ninth year,[a] we Jews wrote to you, in the critical distress that came upon us in those years after Jason and his company revolted from the holy land and the kingdom 8 and burned the gate and shed innocent blood. We prayed to the Lord and were heard, and we offered sacrifice and grain offering, and we lit the lamps and set out the loaves. 9 And now see that you keep the festival of booths in the month of Chislev, in the one hundred eighty-eighth year.[b]

A Letter to Aristobulus

10 The people of Jerusalem and of Judea and the senate and Judas,

To Aristobulus, who is of the family of the anointed priests, teacher of King Ptolemy, and to the Jews in Egypt,

Greetings and good health.

11 Having been saved by God out of grave dangers we thank him

1.1 1 Macc 10.25; Acts 15.23; 23.26; Rom 1.7
1.2 Gen 15.18; 26.3; 35.12; Lev 26.42
1.3 Deut 10.20; Jn 4.23-24
1.4 Acts 16.14
1.5 2 Cor 5.18-21
1.7 1 Macc 10.67; 12.48; 13.23; 2 Macc 4.7-22
1.8 1 Macc 4.38; 1.60-61; 2 Macc 6.10; 1 Macc 13.1-42
1.9 Lev 23.33-43; 1 Macc 4.59; 2 Macc 10.1-8
1.10 1 Macc 12.6; 2 Macc 4.44; 1 Macc 1.18; 10.51-59

[a] 143 B.C. [b] 124 B.C.

greatly for taking our side against
the king,[c] 12 for he drove out those
who fought against the holy city.
13 When the leader reached Persia
with a force that seemed irresistible, they were cut to pieces in the
temple of Nanea by a deception
employed by the priests of the goddess[d] Nanea. 14 On the pretext of
intending to marry her, Antiochus
came to the place together with his
Friends, to secure most of its treasures as a dowry. 15 When the
priests of the temple of Nanea had
set out the treasures and Antiochus had come with a few men inside the wall of the sacred pre-
cinct, they closed the temple as
soon as he entered it. 16 Opening a
secret door in the ceiling, they
threw stones and struck down the
leader and his men; they dismembered them and cut off their heads
and threw them to the people outside. 17 Blessed in every way be our
God, who has brought judgment on
those who have behaved impiously.

Fire Consumes Nehemiah's Sacrifice

18 Since on the twenty-fifth day
of Chislev we shall celebrate the
purification of the temple, we
thought it necessary to notify you,
in order that you also may celebrate the festival of booths and the
festival of the fire given when Nehemiah, who built the temple and
the altar, offered sacrifices.
19 For when our ancestors were
being led captive to Persia, the
pious priests of that time took
some of the fire of the altar and secretly hid it in the hollow of a dry
cistern, where they took such precautions that the place was unknown to anyone. 20 But after many
years had passed, when it pleased
God, Nehemiah, having been commissioned by the king of Persia,
sent the descendants of the priests
who had hidden the fire to get it.
And when they reported to us that
they had not found fire but only a
thick liquid, he ordered them to
dip it out and bring it. 21 When the
materials for the sacrifices were
presented, Nehemiah ordered the
priests to sprinkle the liquid on the
wood and on the things laid upon
it. 22 When this had been done and
some time had passed, and when
the sun, which had been clouded
over, shone out, a great fire blazed
up, so that all marveled. 23 And
while the sacrifice was being consumed, the priests offered prayer
—the priests and everyone. Jonathan led, and the rest responded,
as did Nehemiah. 24 The prayer was
to this effect:
"O Lord, Lord God, Creator of
all things, you are awe-inspiring
and strong and just and merciful,
you alone are king and are kind,
25 you alone are bountiful, you
alone are just and almighty and
eternal. You rescue Israel from every evil; you chose the ancestors
and consecrated them. 26 Accept
this sacrifice on behalf of all your
people Israel and preserve your
portion and make it holy. 27 Gather
together our scattered people, set
free those who are slaves among
the Gentiles, look on those who
are rejected and despised, and let
the Gentiles know that you are our
God. 28 Punish those who oppress
and are insolent with pride.
29 Plant your people in your holy
place, as Moses promised."
30 Then the priests sang the
hymns. 31 After the materials of the
sacrifice had been consumed, Nehemiah ordered that the liquid
that was left should be poured on
large stones. 32 When this was
done, a flame blazed up; but when
the light from the altar shone back,
it went out. 33 When this matter became known, and it was reported
to the king of the Persians that, in
the place where the exiled priests
had hidden the fire, the liquid had
appeared with which Nehemiah
and his associates had burned the
materials of the sacrifice, 34 the
king investigated the matter, and
enclosed the place and made it sacred. 35 And with those persons
whom the king favored he exchanged many excellent gifts.

1.13 1 Macc 6.1-4; 2 Macc 9.1-4
1.14 2 Macc 9.2
1.15 1 Macc 6.2
1.17 Ps 72.18-19; Tob 8.15; Jdt 13.17-18; 1 Macc 4.30
1.18 1 Macc 4.52-59; Neh 8.13-18
1.19 2 Kings 24.14-16; 25.20
1.20 Neh 2.7-8
1.22 1 Kings 18.33-38
1.24 Gen 1.1; Isa 42.5; Neh 9.6; Wis 15.1
1.25 Wis 14.4; 16.8; Gen 13.1-3; 22.15-18; Deut 14.2; Mal 1.2
1.26 Deut 32.9; Jer 10.16; 12.10; Sir 17.17; Lev 11.44-45; 19.2
1.27 Ps 147.2; Jer 32.8; Sir 36.11; Bar 5.6
1.28 1 Macc 1.24; 2 Macc 7.36
1.29 Deut 30.4-5

[c] Cn: Gk *as those who array themselves against a king* [d] Gk lacks *the goddess*

36 Nehemiah and his associates called this "nephthar," which means purification, but by most people it is called naphtha.[e]

Jeremiah Hides the Tent, Ark, and Altar

2 One finds in the records that the prophet Jeremiah ordered those who were being deported to take some of the fire, as has been mentioned, 2 and that the prophet, after giving them the law, instructed those who were being deported not to forget the commandments of the Lord, or to be led astray in their thoughts on seeing the gold and silver statues and their adornment. 3 And with other similar words he exhorted them that the law should not depart from their hearts.

4 It was also in the same document that the prophet, having received an oracle, ordered that the tent and the ark should follow with him, and that he went out to the mountain where Moses had gone up and had seen the inheritance of God. 5 Jeremiah came and found a cave-dwelling, and he brought there the tent and the ark and the altar of incense; then he sealed up the entrance. 6 Some of those who followed him came up intending to mark the way, but could not find it. 7 When Jeremiah learned of it, he rebuked them and declared: "The place shall remain unknown until God gathers his people together again and shows his mercy. 8 Then the Lord will disclose these things, and the glory of the Lord and the cloud will appear, as they were shown in the case of Moses, and as Solomon asked that the place should be specially consecrated."

9 It was also made clear that being possessed of wisdom Solomon[f] offered sacrifice for the dedication and completion of the temple. 10 Just as Moses prayed to the Lord, and fire came down from heaven and consumed the sacrifices, so also Solomon prayed, and the fire came down and consumed the whole burnt offerings. 11 And Moses said, "They were consumed because the sin offering had not been eaten." 12 Likewise Solomon also kept the eight days.

13 The same things are reported in the records and in the memoirs of Nehemiah, and also that he founded a library and collected the books about the kings and prophets, and the writings of David, and letters of kings about votive offerings. 14 In the same way Judas also collected all the books that had been lost on account of the war that had come upon us, and they are in our possession. 15 So if you have need of them, send people to get them for you.

16 Since, therefore, we are about to celebrate the purification, we write to you. Will you therefore please keep the days? 17 It is God who has saved all his people, and has returned the inheritance to all, and the kingship and the priesthood and the consecration, 18 as he promised through the law. We have hope in God that he will soon have mercy on us and will gather us from everywhere under heaven into his holy place, for he has rescued us from great evils and has purified the place.

The Compiler's Preface

19 The story of Judas Maccabeus and his brothers, and the purification of the great temple, and the dedication of the altar, 20 and further the wars against Antiochus Epiphanes and his son Eupator, 21 and the appearances that came from heaven to those who fought bravely for Judaism, so that though few in number they seized the whole land and pursued the barbarian hordes, 22 and regained possession of the temple famous throughout the world, and liberated the city, and re-established the laws that were about to be abolished, while the Lord with great kindness became gracious to them— 23 all this, which has been set forth by Jason of Cyrene in five volumes, we shall attempt to condense into a single book. 24 For

2.2 Let Jer 6.6; Jer 10.2; Let Jer 6.4-5, 73
2.3 Jer 31.33
2.4 Ex 25.10-22; 2 Sam 6.1-13; 1 Kings 8.4; Deut 32.49; 34.1-4
2.8 Ex 16.10; Mk 9.2-8; 1 Kings 8.11
2.9 1 Kings 3.3-28; 4.29-34; 8.62-64
2.10 Lev 9.22-24; 2 Chr 7.1
2.11 Lev 10.16-19
2.13 Ezra 3.4-6; 1 Esd 5.46-50
2.14 1 Macc 1.56
2.16 2 Macc 1.18
2.17 1 Macc 4.10-11,24; 12.15; 2 Macc 1.11; Gen 13.14-17; 1 Macc 15.33-34
2.18 Deut 30.2-5; 2 Macc 1.27
2.20 Dan 8.9; 11.21; 1 Macc 1.10; 3.27; 2 Macc 4.7; 1 Macc 6.17
2.21 2 Macc 3.24; Rom 1.14; Col 3.11
2.22 1 Macc 4.52-58
2.23 Lk 1.1-4

[e] Gk *nephthai* [f] Gk *he*

considering the flood of statistics
involved and the difficulty there is
for those who wish to enter upon
the narratives of history because of
the mass of material, 25 we have
aimed to please those who wish to
read, to make it easy for those who
are inclined to memorize, and to
profit all readers. 26 For us who
have undertaken the toil of abbre-
viating, it is no light matter but
calls for sweat and loss of sleep,
27 just as it is not easy for one who
prepares a banquet and seeks the
benefit of others. Nevertheless, to
secure the gratitude of many we
will gladly endure the uncomfort-
able toil, 28 leaving the responsibility for exact details to the com-
piler, while devoting our effort to
arriving at the outlines of the condensation. 29 For as the master
builder of a new house must be
concerned with the whole construction, while the one who undertakes its painting and decoration has to consider only what is
suitable for its adornment, such in
my judgment is the case with us.
30 It is the duty of the original his-
torian to occupy the ground, to discuss matters from every side, and
to take trouble with details, 31 but
the one who recasts the narrative
should be allowed to strive for
brevity of expression and to forego
exhaustive treatment. 32 At this
point therefore let us begin our
narrative, without adding any more
to what has already been said; for it
would be foolish to lengthen the
preface while cutting short the history itself.

Arrival of Heliodorus in Jerusalem

3 While the holy city was inhabited in unbroken peace and
the laws were strictly observed because of the piety of the high priest
Onias and his hatred of wickedness, 2 it came about that the kings
themselves honored the place and
glorified the temple with the finest
presents, 3 even to the extent that
King Seleucus of Asia defrayed
from his own revenues all the expenses connected with the service
of the sacrifices.

4 But a man named Simon, of
the tribe of Benjamin, who had
been made captain of the temple,
had a disagreement with the high
priest about the administration of
the city market. 5 Since he could
not prevail over Onias, he went to
Apollonius of Tarsus,[g] who at that
time was governor of Coelesyria
and Phoenicia, 6 and reported to
him that the treasury in Jerusalem
was full of untold sums of money,
so that the amount of the funds
could not be reckoned, and that
they did not belong to the account
of the sacrifices, but that it was
possible for them to fall under the
control of the king. 7 When Apollonius met the king, he told him of
the money about which he had
been informed. The king[h] chose
Heliodorus, who was in charge of
his affairs, and sent him with commands to effect the removal of the
reported wealth. 8 Heliodorus at
once set out on his journey, osten-
sibly to make a tour of inspection
of the cities of Coelesyria and
Phoenicia, but in fact to carry out
the king's purpose.

9 When he had arrived at Jerusalem and had been kindly welcomed by the high priest of[i] the
city, he told about the disclosure
that had been made and stated
why he had come, and he inquired
whether this really was the situation. 10 The high priest explained
that there were some deposits belonging to widows and orphans,
11 and also some money of Hyrcanus son of Tobias, a man of very
prominent position, and that it totaled in all four hundred talents of
silver and two hundred of gold. To
such an extent the impious Simon
had misrepresented the facts.
12 And he said that it was utterly
impossible that wrong should be
done to those people who had
trusted in the holiness of the place
and in the sanctity and inviolabil-
ity of the temple that is honored
throughout the whole world.

2.25 2 Macc 15.38-39
3.1 1 Macc 12.7-8; 2 Macc 15.12
3.3 Ezra 6.9-10
3.4 2 Macc 4.1
3.5 Acts 9.11; 1 Macc 10.69; 1 Esd 4.48; 6.29
3.9 2 Macc 5.18
3.10 Deut 14.28-29
3.11 Neh 2.10; 13.4-8

[g] Gk *Apollonius son of Tharseas* [h] Gk *He*
[i] Other ancient authorities read *and*

Heliodorus Plans to Rob the Temple

13 But Heliodorus, because of
the orders he had from the king,
said that this money must in any
case be confiscated for the king's
treasury. 14 So he set a day and
went in to direct the inspection of
these funds.

There was no little distress
throughout the whole city. 15 The
priests prostrated themselves before the altar in their priestly vestments and called toward heaven
upon him who had given the law
about deposits, that he should
keep them safe for those who had
deposited them. 16 To see the appearance of the high priest was to
be wounded at heart, for his face
and the change in his color disclosed the anguish of his soul.
17 For terror and bodily trembling
had come over the man, which
plainly showed to those who
looked at him the pain lodged in
his heart. 18 People also hurried out
of their houses in crowds to make
a general supplication because the
holy place was about to be brought
into dishonor. 19 Women, girded
with sackcloth under their breasts,
thronged the streets. Some of the
young women who were kept in-
doors ran together to the gates,
and some to the walls, while others
peered out of the windows. 20 And
holding up their hands to heaven,
they all made supplication.
21 There was something pitiable in
the prostration of the whole popu-
lace and the anxiety of the high
priest in his great anguish.

The Lord Protects His Temple

22 While they were calling upon
the Almighty Lord that he would
keep what had been entrusted safe
and secure for those who had entrusted it, 23 Heliodorus went on
with what had been decided. 24 But
when he arrived at the treasury
with his bodyguard, then and there
the Sovereign of spirits and of all
authority caused so great a manifestation that all who had been so
bold as to accompany him were astounded by the power of God, and
became faint with terror. 25 For
there appeared to them a magnificently caparisoned horse, with a
rider of frightening mien; it rushed
furiously at Heliodorus and struck
at him with its front hoofs. Its rider
was seen to have armor and weapons of gold. 26 Two young men also
appeared to him, remarkably
strong, gloriously beautiful and
splendidly dressed, who stood on
either side of him and flogged him
continuously, inflicting many
blows on him. 27 When he suddenly
fell to the ground and deep darkness came over him, his men took
him up, put him on a stretcher,
28 and carried him away—this man
who had just entered the aforesaid
treasury with a great retinue and
all his bodyguard but was now unable to help himself. They recognized clearly the sovereign power
of God.

Onias Prays for Heliodorus

29 While he lay prostrate,
speechless because of the divine
intervention and deprived of any
hope of recovery, 30 they praised
the Lord who had acted marvelously for his own place. And the
temple, which a little while before
was full of fear and disturbance,
was filled with joy and gladness,
now that the Almighty Lord had
appeared.

31 Some of Heliodorus's friends
quickly begged Onias to call upon
the Most High to grant life to one
who was lying quite at his last
breath. 32 So the high priest, fearing that the king might get the no-
tion that some foul play had been
perpetrated by the Jews with regard to Heliodorus, offered sacrifice for the man's recovery.
33 While the high priest was making
an atonement, the same young
men appeared again to Heliodorus
dressed in the same clothing, and
they stood and said, "Be very grateful to the high priest Onias, since
for his sake the Lord has granted
you your life. 34 And see that you,
who have been flogged by heaven,
report to all people the majestic

3.15 2 Macc 10.4; 13.12; 3 Macc 1.16; 5.50; 1 Macc 3.50; 5.31
3.18 3 Macc 1.17
3.19 Sir 42.9-12; 3 Macc 1.19
3.20 1 Kings 8.54; 1 Tim 2.8
3.24 2 Macc 2.21; 5.2-4; 12.22
3.25 2 Macc 5.2-3; 10.29; 11.8; Rev 19.11
3.26 Lk 24.4; Acts 1.10
3.27 Gen 19.11; Acts 9.8
3.29 Wis 4.19; Lk 4.20; Acts 9.9
3.30 2 Macc 2.21
3.31 Gen 14.18; Dan 3.26; Mk 5.7
3.33 2 Macc 3.26
3.34 Lk 24.31

power of God." Having said this
they vanished.

The Conversion of Heliodorus

35 Then Heliodorus offered sacrifice to the Lord and made very
great vows to the Savior of his life,
and having bidden Onias farewell,
he marched off with his forces to
the king. 36 He bore testimony to
all concerning the deeds of the supreme God, which he had seen
with his own eyes. 37 When the king
asked Heliodorus what sort of person would be suitable to send on
another mission to Jerusalem, he
replied, 38 "If you have any enemy
or plotter against your government,
send him there, for you will get
him back thoroughly flogged, if he
survives at all; for there is certainly
some power of God about the
place. 39 For he who has his dwelling in heaven watches over that
place himself and brings it aid, and
he strikes and destroys those who
come to do it injury." 40 This was
the outcome of the episode of Heliodorus and the protection of the
treasury.

Simon Accuses Onias

4 The previously mentioned Simon, who had informed about
the money against[j] his own country, slandered Onias, saying that it
was he who had incited Heliodorus
and had been the real cause of the
misfortune. 2 He dared to designate as a plotter against the government the man who was the
benefactor of the city, the protector of his compatriots, and a zealot
for the laws. 3 When his hatred pro-
gressed to such a degree that even
murders were committed by one of
Simon's approved agents, 4 Onias
recognized that the rivalry was serious and that Apollonius son of
Menestheus,[k] and governor of
Coelesyria and Phoenicia, was in-
tensifying the malice of Simon.
5 So he appealed to the king, not
accusing his compatriots but having in view the welfare, both public
and private, of all the people. 6 For
he saw that without the king's attention public affairs could not
again reach a peaceful settlement,
and that Simon would not stop his
folly.

Jason's Reforms

7 When Seleucus died and Antiochus, who was called Epiphanes,
succeeded to the kingdom, Jason
the brother of Onias obtained the
high priesthood by corruption,
8 promising the king at an inter-
view[l] three hundred sixty talents
of silver, and from another source
of revenue eighty talents. 9 In addition to this he promised to pay one
hundred fifty more if permission
were given to establish by his authority a gymnasium and a body of
youth for it, and to enroll the people of Jerusalem as citizens of Antioch. 10 When the king assented
and Jason[m] came to office, he at
once shifted his compatriots over
to the Greek way of life.

11 He set aside the existing
royal concessions to the Jews, secured through John the father of
Eupolemus, who went on the mission to establish friendship and alliance with the Romans; and he destroyed the lawful ways of living
and introduced new customs contrary to the law. 12 He took delight
in establishing a gymnasium right
under the citadel, and he induced
the noblest of the young men to
wear the Greek hat. 13 There was
such an extreme of Hellenization
and increase in the adoption of foreign ways because of the surpassing wickedness of Jason, who was
ungodly and no true[n] high priest,
14 that the priests were no longer
intent upon their service at the altar. Despising the sanctuary and
neglecting the sacrifices, they hurried to take part in the unlawful
proceedings in the wrestling arena
after the signal for the discus-
throwing, 15 disdaining the honors
prized by their ancestors and putting the highest value upon Greek
forms of prestige. 16 For this reason
heavy disaster overtook them, and
those whose ways of living they ad-

3.38 Gen 28.16-19
3.39 1 Kings 8.27-30; 2 Chr 6.18; Isa 66.1; Ps 125.1-2; Isa 31.5
4.1 2 Macc 3.4, 24-28
4.4 2 Macc 4.21
4.7 2 Macc 3.3; 1 Macc 1.10; 2 Macc 2.20; 1.7; 3.1; 4.24
4.9 1 Macc 1.14
4.11 2 Macc 3.2-3; 1 Macc 8.17-32; 1.15, 44-50
4.12 1 Macc 1.14
4.13 1 Macc 1.13
4.14 1 Macc 1.41-49

j Gk *and* k Vg Compare verse 21: Meaning of Gk uncertain l Or *by a petition* m Gk *he* n Gk lacks *true*

mired and wished to imitate completely became their enemies and
punished them. 17It is no light
thing to show irreverence to the divine laws—a fact that later events
will make clear.

Jason Introduces Greek Customs

18 When the quadrennial
games were being held at Tyre and
the king was present, 19the vile Jason sent envoys, chosen as being
Antiochian citizens from Jerusalem, to carry three hundred silver
drachmas for the sacrifice to Hercules. Those who carried the
money, however, thought best not
to use it for sacrifice, because that
was inappropriate, but to expend it
for another purpose. 20So this
money was intended by the sender
for the sacrifice to Hercules, but by
the decision of its carriers it was
applied to the construction of tri-
remes.
21 When Apollonius son of
Menestheus was sent to Egypt for
the coronation[o] of Philometor as
king, Antiochus learned that Philometor[p] had become hostile to his
government, and he took measures
for his own security. Therefore
upon arriving at Joppa he proceeded to Jerusalem. 22He was
welcomed magnificently by Jason
and the city, and ushered in with a
blaze of torches and with shouts.
Then he marched his army into
Phoenicia.

Menelaus Becomes High Priest

23 After a period of three years
Jason sent Menelaus, the brother
of the previously mentioned Simon, to carry the money to the
king and to complete the records
of essential business. 24But he,
when presented to the king, extolled him with an air of authority,
and secured the high priesthood
for himself, outbidding Jason by
three hundred talents of silver.
25After receiving the king's orders
he returned, possessing no qualifi-
cation for the high priesthood, but
having the hot temper of a cruel tyrant and the rage of a savage wild
beast. 26So Jason, who after sup-
planting his own brother was sup-
planted by another man, was
driven as a fugitive into the land of
Ammon. 27Although Menelaus
continued to hold the office, he
did not pay regularly any of the
money promised to the king.
28When Sostratus the captain of
the citadel kept requesting
payment—for the collection of the
revenue was his responsibility—
the two of them were summoned
by the king on account of this issue. 29Menelaus left his own
brother Lysimachus as deputy in
the high priesthood, while Sostratus left Crates, the commander
of the Cyprian troops.

The Murder of Onias

30 While such was the state of
affairs, it happened that the people
of Tarsus and of Mallus revolted
because their cities had been given
as a present to Antiochis, the
king's concubine. 31So the king
went hurriedly to settle the trouble, leaving Andronicus, a man of
high rank, to act as his deputy.
32But Menelaus, thinking he had
obtained a suitable opportunity,
stole some of the gold vessels of
the temple and gave them to Andronicus; other vessels, as it happened, he had sold to Tyre and the
neighboring cities. 33When Onias
became fully aware of these acts,
he publicly exposed them, having
first withdrawn to a place of sanctuary at Daphne near Antioch.
34Therefore Menelaus, taking Andronicus aside, urged him to kill
Onias. Andronicus[q] came to
Onias, and resorting to treachery,
offered him sworn pledges and
gave him his right hand; he persuaded him, though still suspicious, to come out from the place
of sanctuary; then, with no regard
for justice, he immediately put him
out of the way.

Andronicus Is Punished

35 For this reason not only
Jews, but many also of other nations, were grieved and displeased

4.18 Josh 19.29; 1 Kings 7.13
4.21 2 Macc 4.4; 9.29; 2 Chr 2.26; 1 Macc 10.75-76; 14.5,34
4.23 2 Macc 5.5
4.24 2 Macc 4.7-8; 11.3
4.26 2 Macc 4.7
4.29 2 Macc 4.39
4.30 Acts 21.39; 22.3
4.31 2 Macc 5.23
4.33 2 Macc 3.1

[o]Meaning of Gk uncertain [p]Gk *he*
[q]Gk *He*

at the unjust murder of the man.
36 When the king returned from the
region of Cilicia, the Jews in the
city[r] appealed to him with regard
to the unreasonable murder of
Onias, and the Greeks shared their
hatred of the crime. 37 Therefore
Antiochus was grieved at heart and
filled with pity, and wept because
of the moderation and good conduct of the deceased. 38 Inflamed
with anger, he immediately
stripped off the purple robe from
Andronicus, tore off his clothes,
and led him around the whole city
to that very place where he had
committed the outrage against
Onias, and there he dispatched the
bloodthirsty fellow. The Lord thus
repaid him with the punishment
he deserved.

Unpopularity of Lysimachus and Menelaus

39 When many acts of sacrilege
had been committed in the city by
Lysimachus with the connivance
of Menelaus, and when report of
them had spread abroad, the popu-
lace gathered against Lysimachus,
because many of the gold vessels
had already been stolen. 40 Since
the crowds were becoming aroused
and filled with anger, Lysimachus
armed about three thousand men
and launched an unjust attack, under the leadership of a certain
Auranus, a man advanced in years
and no less advanced in folly.
41 But when the Jews[s] became
aware that Lysimachus was attacking them, some picked up stones,
some blocks of wood, and others
took handfuls of the ashes that
were lying around, and threw them
in wild confusion at Lysimachus
and his men. 42 As a result, they
wounded many of them, and killed
some, and put all the rest to flight;
the temple robber himself they
killed close by the treasury.

43 Charges were brought
against Menelaus about this inci-
dent. 44 When the king came to
Tyre, three men sent by the senate
presented the case before him.
45 But Menelaus, already as good as
beaten, promised a substantial
bribe to Ptolemy son of Dorymenes
to win over the king. 46 Therefore
Ptolemy, taking the king aside into
a colonnade as if for refreshment,
induced the king to change his
mind. 47 Menelaus, the cause of all
the trouble, he acquitted of the
charges against him, while he sentenced to death those unfortunate
men, who would have been freed
uncondemned if they had pleaded
even before Scythians. 48 And so
those who had spoken for the city
and the villages[t] and the holy vessels quickly suffered the unjust
penalty. 49 Therefore even the Tyrians, showing their hatred of the
crime, provided magnificently for
their funeral. 50 But Menelaus, because of the greed of those in
power, remained in office, growing
in wickedness, having become the
chief plotter against his compatriots.

Jason Tries to Regain Control

5 About this time Antiochus
made his second invasion of
Egypt. 2 And it happened that, for
almost forty days, there appeared
over all the city golden-clad cavalry
charging through the air, in companies fully armed with lances and
drawn swords— 3 troops of cavalry
drawn up, attacks and counterat-
tacks made on this side and on
that, brandishing of shields, mass-
ing of spears, hurling of missiles,
the flash of golden trappings, and
armor of all kinds. 4 Therefore everyone prayed that the apparition
might prove to have been a good
omen.

5 When a false rumor arose that
Antiochus was dead, Jason took no
fewer than a thousand men and
suddenly made an assault on the
city. When the troops on the wall
had been forced back and at last
the city was being taken, Menelaus
took refuge in the citadel. 6 But Jason kept relentlessly slaughtering
his compatriots, not realizing that
success at the cost of one's kindred is the greatest misfortune, but

4.36 1 Macc 11.14; 2 Macc 4.30; Acts 22.3
4.38 Judg 8.26; 1 Macc 10.20, 62; 14.43-44
4.39 2 Macc 4.29
4.44 1 Macc 12.6; 2 Macc 1.10
4.45 1 Macc 3.38; 2 Macc 8.8; 10.12
4.47 3 Macc 7.5; 4 Macc 10.7; Col 3.11
4.50 2 Macc 4.23-24
5.1 Dan 11.29; 1 Macc 1.16-17; 4 Macc 4.22
5.2 2 Macc 3.24-27; 10.29-30; 11.8
5.5 4 Macc 4.22; 2 Macc 4.7-10,23

[r] Or *in each city* [s] Gk *they*
[t] Other ancient authorities read *the people*

imagining that he was setting up trophies of victory over enemies and not over compatriots. 7 He did not, however, gain control of the government; in the end he got only disgrace from his conspiracy, and fled again into the country of the Ammonites. 8 Finally he met a miserable end. Accused[u] before Aretas the ruler of the Arabs, fleeing from city to city, pursued by everyone, hated as a rebel against the laws, and abhorred as the executioner of his country and his compatriots, he was cast ashore in Egypt. 9 There he who had driven many from their own country into exile died in exile, having embarked to go to the Lacedaemonians in hope of finding protection because of their kinship. 10 He who had cast out many to lie unburied had no one to mourn for him; he had no funeral of any sort and no place in the tomb of his ancestors.

11 When news of what had happened reached the king, he took it to mean that Judea was in revolt. So, raging inwardly, he left Egypt and took the city by storm. 12 He commanded his soldiers to cut down relentlessly everyone they met and to kill those who went into their houses. 13 Then there was massacre of young and old, destruction of boys, women, and children, and slaughter of young girls and infants. 14 Within the total of three days eighty thousand were destroyed, forty thousand in hand-to-hand fighting, and as many were sold into slavery as were killed.

Pillage of the Temple

15 Not content with this, Antiochus[v] dared to enter the most holy temple in all the world, guided by Menelaus, who had become a traitor both to the laws and to his country. 16 He took the holy vessels with his polluted hands, and swept away with profane hands the votive offerings that other kings had made to enhance the glory and honor of the place. 17 Antiochus was elated in spirit, and did not perceive that the Lord was angered for a little while because of the sins of those who lived in the city, and that this was the reason he was disregarding the holy place. 18 But if it had not happened that they were involved in many sins, this man would have been flogged and turned back from his rash act as soon as he came forward, just as Heliodorus had been, whom King Seleucus sent to inspect the treasury. 19 But the Lord did not choose the nation for the sake of the holy place, but the place for the sake of the nation. 20 Therefore the place itself shared in the misfortunes that befell the nation and afterward participated in its benefits; and what was forsaken in the wrath of the Almighty was restored again in all its glory when the great Lord became reconciled.

21 So Antiochus carried off eighteen hundred talents from the temple, and hurried away to Antioch, thinking in his arrogance that he could sail on the land and walk on the sea, because his mind was elated. 22 He left governors to oppress the people: at Jerusalem, Philip, by birth a Phrygian and in character more barbarous than the man who appointed him; 23 and at Gerizim, Andronicus; and besides these Menelaus, who lorded it over his compatriots worse than the others did. In his malice toward the Jewish citizens,[w] 24 Antiochus[v] sent Apollonius, the captain of the Mysians, with an army of twenty-two thousand, and commanded him to kill all the grown men and to sell the women and boys as slaves. 25 When this man arrived in Jerusalem, he pretended to be peaceably disposed and waited until the holy sabbath day; then, finding the Jews not at work, he ordered his troops to parade under arms. 26 He put to the sword all those who came out to see them, then rushed into the city with his armed warriors and killed great numbers of people.

27 But Judas Maccabeus, with about nine others, got away to the

5.7 2 Macc 4.26
5.9 1 Macc 12.2, 5-6
5.10 Ps 79.3; Tob 1.18-19; 1 Macc 7.17
5.11 2 Macc 7.3; 9.4; 1 Macc 1.20, 31
5.14 1 Macc 1.32
5.15 1 Macc 1.21
5.16 1 Macc 1.21-23
5.17 2 Macc 6.12-16; 7.33; Neh 9.26-30; Dan 9.11-14
5.18 2 Macc 3.7-8
5.20 2 Macc 10.4; 1.5; 8.29
5.21 1 Macc 1.24; 2 Macc 9.8
5.22 1 Macc 1.29; 2 Macc 8.8
5.23 2 Macc 4.31
5.24 1 Macc 3.10; 1.30
5.25 1 Macc 1.30; 2.34-38
5.27 1 Macc 2.28; 1.48,63; 2 Macc 4.11

u Cn: Gk *Imprisoned* v Gk *he*
w Or *worse than the others did in his malice toward the Jewish citizens*

wilderness, and kept himself and
his companions alive in the mountains as wild animals do; they continued to live on what grew wild, so
that they might not share in the defilement.

The Suppression of Judaism

6 Not long after this, the king
sent an Athenian[x] senator[y]
to compel the Jews to forsake the
laws of their ancestors and no longer to live by the laws of God; [2]also
to pollute the temple in Jerusalem
and to call it the temple of Olym-
pian Zeus, and to call the one in
Gerizim the temple of Zeus-the-
Friend-of-Strangers, as did the
people who lived in that place.
3 Harsh and utterly grievous
was the onslaught of evil. [4]For the
temple was filled with debauchery
and reveling by the Gentiles, who
dallied with prostitutes and had intercourse with women within the
sacred precincts, and besides
brought in things for sacrifice that
were unfit. [5]The altar was covered
with abominable offerings that
were forbidden by the laws. [6]Peo-
ple could neither keep the sabbath, nor observe the festivals of
their ancestors, nor so much as
confess themselves to be Jews.
7 On the monthly celebration of
the king's birthday, the Jews[z]
were taken, under bitter constraint, to partake of the sacrifices;
and when a festival of Dionysus
was celebrated, they were compelled to wear wreathes of ivy and
to walk in the procession in honor
of Dionysus. [8]At the suggestion of
the people of Ptolemais[a] a decree
was issued to the neighboring
Greek cities that they should adopt
the same policy toward the Jews
and make them partake of the sacrifices, [9]and should kill those who
did not choose to change over to
Greek customs. One could see,
therefore, the misery that had
come upon them. [10]For example,
two women were brought in for
having circumcised their children.
They publicly paraded them
around the city, with their babies
hanging at their breasts, and then
hurled them down headlong from
the wall. [11]Others who had assembled in the caves nearby, in order
to observe the seventh day secretly, were betrayed to Philip and
were all burned together, because
their piety kept them from defending themselves, in view of their regard for that most holy day.

Providential Significance of the Persecution

12 Now I urge those who read
this book not to be depressed by
such calamities, but to recognize
that these punishments were designed not to destroy but to discipline our people. [13]In fact, it is a
sign of great kindness not to let the
impious alone for long, but to punish them immediately. [14]For in the
case of the other nations the Lord
waits patiently to punish them until they have reached the full measure of their sins; but he does not
deal in this way with us, [15]in order
that he may not take vengeance on
us afterward when our sins have
reached their height. [16]Therefore
he never withdraws his mercy from
us. Although he disciplines us with
calamities, he does not forsake his
own people. [17]Let what we have
said serve as a reminder; we must
go on briefly with the story.

The Martyrdom of Eleazar

18 Eleazar, one of the scribes in
high position, a man now advanced in age and of noble presence, was being forced to open his
mouth to eat swine's flesh. [19]But
he, welcoming death with honor
rather than life with pollution,
went up to the rack of his own accord, spitting out the flesh, [20]as all
ought to go who have the courage
to refuse things that it is not right
to taste, even for the natural love
of life.
21 Those who were in charge of
that unlawful sacrifice took the
man aside because of their long ac-

6.1 1 Macc 1.41
6.2 Dan 9.27; 11.31; 1 Macc 1.46-47,54; Deut 27.12; Josh 8.33; Jn 4.20
6.4 Rom 1.28; Let Jer 6.11, 43; Lev 11.17; 1 Macc 1.47
6.6 1 Macc 1.43
6.7 2 Macc 14.33; 10.7; 3 Macc 2.29
6.9 1 Macc 1.50
6.10 1 Macc 1.48, 60-61
6.11 1 Macc 1.45; 2.32-38
6.12 Wis 12.1-2, 22; Heb 12.3-11
6.14 Ps 73.4-9, 16-20; Wis 11.9-10; 2 Macc 7.36; 5.17; 7.33
6.16 Ps 94.12-14; Isa 54.7-8; 2 Macc 7.33; 10.4
6.18 3 Macc 6.1; 4 Macc 5.4-6.30; 1 Macc 1.47, 62-63; 2 Macc 7.1
6.19 Heb 11.35; Lev 11.7-8
6.21 4 Macc 6.15

[x]Other ancient authorities read *Antiochian* [y]Or *Geron an Athenian* [z]Gk *they*
[a]Cn: Gk *suggestion of the Ptolemies* (or *of Ptolemy*)

quaintance with him, and privately
urged him to bring meat of his own
providing, proper for him to use,
and to pretend that he was eating
the flesh of the sacrificial meal
that had been commanded by the
king, 22 so that by doing this he
might be saved from death, and be
treated kindly on account of his
old friendship with them. 23 But
making a high resolve, worthy of
his years and the dignity of his old
age and the gray hairs that he had
reached with distinction and his
excellent life even from childhood,
and moreover according to the
holy God-given law, he declared
himself quickly, telling them to
send him to Hades.
24 "Such pretense is not worthy
of our time of life," he said, "for
many of the young might suppose
that Eleazar in his ninetieth year
had gone over to an alien religion,
25 and through my pretense, for the
sake of living a brief moment longer, they would be led astray because of me, while I defile and disgrace my old age. 26 Even if for the
present I would avoid the punishment of mortals, yet whether I live
or die I shall not escape the hands
of the Almighty. 27 Therefore, by
bravely giving up my life now, I will
show myself worthy of my old age
28 and leave to the young a noble
example of how to die a good
death willingly and nobly for the
revered and holy laws."
When he had said this, he went[b]
at once to the rack. 29 Those who a
little before had acted toward him
with goodwill now changed to ill
will, because the words he had uttered were in their opinion sheer
madness.[c] 30 When he was about
to die under the blows, he groaned
aloud and said: "It is clear to the
Lord in his holy knowledge that,
though I might have been saved
from death, I am enduring terrible
sufferings in my body under this
beating, but in my soul I am glad to
suffer these things because I fear
him."
31 So in this way he died, leaving in his death an example of nobility and a memorial of courage,
not only to the young but to the
great body of his nation.

The Martyrdom of Seven Brothers

7 It happened also that seven
brothers and their mother
were arrested and were being compelled by the king, under torture
with whips and thongs, to partake
of unlawful swine's flesh. 2 One of
them, acting as their spokesman,
said, "What do you intend to ask
and learn from us? For we are
ready to die rather than transgress
the laws of our ancestors."
3 The king fell into a rage, and
gave orders to have pans and caldrons heated. 4 These were heated
immediately, and he commanded
that the tongue of their spokesman
be cut out and that they scalp him
and cut off his hands and feet,
while the rest of the brothers and
the mother looked on. 5 When he
was utterly helpless, the king[d] ordered them to take him to the fire,
still breathing, and to fry him in a
pan. The smoke from the pan
spread widely, but the brothers[e]
and their mother encouraged one
another to die nobly, saying, 6 "The
Lord God is watching over us and
in truth has compassion on us, as
Moses declared in his song that
bore witness against the people to
their faces, when he said, 'And he
will have compassion on his servants.' "[f]
7 After the first brother had
died in this way, they brought forward the second for their sport.
They tore off the skin of his head
with the hair, and asked him, "Will
you eat rather than have your body
punished limb by limb?" 8 He replied in the language of his ancestors and said to them, "No." Therefore he in turn underwent tortures
as the first brother had done. 9 And
when he was at his last breath, he
said, "You accursed wretch, you
dismiss us from this present life,
but the King of the universe will
raise us up to an everlasting re-

6.23 Prov 16.31; 20.29; Sir 6.18; 2 Macc 15.13; Mt 11.20; Tob 3.10; Wis 16.13; Sir 28.21
6.25 Rom 14.13-15, 19-21; 1 Cor 8.9-13; 11.28
6.26 Ps 68.20; 2 Macc 7.31; Heb 12.25
6.30 4 Macc 9.29; Mt 5.11-12; Acts 5.41; Col 1.24; Job 28.28; Ps 19.19; 111.10
6.31 Heb 11.35
7.1 4 Macc 8.1-12.19; Jer 15.9; Lev 11.7-8; 2 Macc 6.18
7.2 Dan 3.16-18; Acts 5.29
7.3 2 Macc 5.11; 9.4; Dan 3.19
7.4 4 Macc 10.17
7.6 Ps 1.6; 121.1-4; 145.20; Wis 3.9; Ps 103.13-14; 106.45; Deut 32.36
7.9 Tob 10.13; 13.7; 1 Esd 4.58; Dan 12.2; 1 Cor 6.14; 2 Cor 4.14

[b] Other ancient authorities read *was dragged* [c] Meaning of Gk uncertain [d] Gk *he* [e] Gk *they* [f] Gk *slaves*

newal of life, because we have died
for his laws."
10 After him, the third was the
victim of their sport. When it was
demanded, he quickly put out his
tongue and courageously stretched
forth his hands, 11 and said nobly,
"I got these from Heaven, and because of his laws I disdain them,
and from him I hope to get them
back again." 12 As a result the king
himself and those with him were
astonished at the young man's
spirit, for he regarded his sufferings as nothing.
13 After he too had died, they
maltreated and tortured the fourth
in the same way. 14 When he was
near death, he said, "One cannot
but choose to die at the hands of
mortals and to cherish the hope
God gives of being raised again by
him. But for you there will be no
resurrection to life!"
15 Next they brought forward
the fifth and maltreated him. 16 But
he looked at the king,[g] and said,
"Because you have authority
among mortals, though you also
are mortal, you do what you please.
But do not think that God has forsaken our people. 17 Keep on, and
see how his mighty power will torture you and your descendants!"
18 After him they brought forward the sixth. And when he was
about to die, he said, "Do not deceive yourself in vain. For we are
suffering these things on our own
account, because of our sins
against our own God. Therefore[h]
astounding things have happened.
19 But do not think that you will go
unpunished for having tried to
fight against God!"
20 The mother was especially
admirable and worthy of honorable
memory. Although she saw her
seven sons perish within a single
day, she bore it with good courage
because of her hope in the Lord.
21 She encouraged each of them in
the language of their ancestors.
Filled with a noble spirit, she reinforced her woman's reasoning with
a man's courage, and said to them,
22 "I do not know how you came
into being in my womb. It was not
I who gave you life and breath, nor
I who set in order the elements
within each of you. 23 Therefore the
Creator of the world, who shaped
the beginning of humankind and
devised the origin of all things, will
in his mercy give life and breath
back to you again, since you now
forget yourselves for the sake of his
laws."
24 Antiochus felt that he was
being treated with contempt, and
he was suspicious of her reproach-
ful tone. The youngest brother being still alive, Antiochus[i] not only
appealed to him in words, but
promised with oaths that he would
make him rich and enviable if he
would turn from the ways of his ancestors, and that he would take
him for his Friend and entrust him
with public affairs. 25 Since the
young man would not listen to him
at all, the king called the mother to
him and urged her to advise the
youth to save himself. 26 After
much urging on his part, she undertook to persuade her son.
27 But, leaning close to him, she
spoke in their native language as
follows, deriding the cruel tyrant:
"My son, have pity on me. I carried
you nine months in my womb, and
nursed you for three years, and
have reared you and brought you
up to this point in your life, and
have taken care of you.[j] 28 I beg
you, my child, to look at the
heaven and the earth and see everything that is in them, and recognize that God did not make them
out of things that existed.[k] And in
the same way the human race
came into being. 29 Do not fear this
butcher, but prove worthy of your
brothers. Accept death, so that in
God's mercy I may get you back
again along with your brothers."
30 While she was still speaking,
the young man said, "What are
you[l] waiting for? I will not obey
the king's command, but I obey
the command of the law that was

7.11 Sus 9; 1 Macc 3.19, 50; 2 Macc 12.44; 14.46 **7.14** Dan 12.2; 2 Macc 12.44; 14.46; Jn 5.28-29; Rev 20.12-15 **7.16** Rom 13.1-4 **7.17** 2 Macc 9.5-28 **7.18** Ezra 9.10-11; Bar 1.13; 2 Macc 5.17; 6.12-16 **7.19** Acts 5.39 **7.22** Gen 2.7; Eccl 12.7; Acts 17.25; Ps 139.13-16 **7.23** Gen 1.1; Isa 45.12; Gen 1.26-27; 2.7,21-22; Ps 9.13; Tob 13.2 **7.24** 2 Macc 6.1; 1 Macc 2.18; 10.12; 11.57 **7.27** 4 Macc 13.20 **7.28** Ps 8.3-6; Heb 11.3 **7.29** 2 Macc 7.1-19 **7.30** Lev 11.7-8

[g] Gk *at him* [h] Lat: Other ancient authorities lack *Therefore* [i] Gk *he* [j] Or *have borne the burden of your education* [k] Or *God made them out of things that did not exist*
[l] The Gk here for *you* is plural

given to our ancestors through Moses. 31 But you,[m] who have contrived all sorts of evil against the
Hebrews, will certainly not escape
the hands of God. 32 For we are suffering because of our own sins.
33 And if our living Lord is angry for
a little while, to rebuke and discipline us, he will again be reconciled with his own servants.[n]
34 But you, unholy wretch, you
most defiled of all mortals, do not
be elated in vain and puffed up by
uncertain hopes, when you raise
your hand against the children of
heaven. 35 You have not yet escaped the judgment of the almighty, all-seeing God. 36 For our
brothers after enduring a brief suffering have drunk[o] of ever-flowing
life, under God's covenant; but
you, by the judgment of God, will
receive just punishment for your
arrogance. 37 I, like my brothers,
give up body and life for the laws of
our ancestors, appealing to God to
show mercy soon to our nation and
by trials and plagues to make you
confess that he alone is God, 38 and
through me and my brothers to
bring to an end the wrath of the Almighty that has justly fallen on our
whole nation."

39 The king fell into a rage, and
handled him worse than the others, being exasperated at his scorn.
40 So he died in his integrity, putting his whole trust in the Lord.

41 Last of all, the mother died,
after her sons.

42 Let this be enough, then,
about the eating of sacrifices and
the extreme tortures.

The Revolt of Judas Maccabeus

8 Meanwhile Judas, who was
also called Maccabeus, and
his companions secretly entered
the villages and summoned their
kindred and enlisted those who
had continued in the Jewish faith,
and so they gathered about six
thousand. 2 They implored the
Lord to look upon the people who
were oppressed by all; and to have
pity on the temple that had been
profaned by the godless; 3 to have
mercy on the city that was being
destroyed and about to be leveled
to the ground; to hearken to the
blood that cried out to him; 4 to remember also the lawless destruction of the innocent babies and the
blasphemies committed against
his name; and to show his hatred
of evil.

5 As soon as Maccabeus got his
army organized, the Gentiles could
not withstand him, for the wrath of
the Lord had turned to mercy.
6 Coming without warning, he
would set fire to towns and villages. He captured strategic positions and put to flight not a few of
the enemy. 7 He found the nights
most advantageous for such attacks. And talk of his valor spread
everywhere.

8 When Philip saw that the man
was gaining ground little by little,
and that he was pushing ahead
with more frequent successes, he
wrote to Ptolemy, the governor of
Coelesyria and Phoenicia, to come
to the aid of the king's government. 9 Then Ptolemy[p] promptly
appointed Nicanor son of Patro-
clus, one of the king's chief[q]
Friends, and sent him, in command of no fewer than twenty
thousand Gentiles of all nations,
to wipe out the whole race of Judea. He associated with him Gorgias, a general and a man of experience in military service. 10 Nicanor
determined to make up for the
king the tribute due to the Romans, two thousand talents, by
selling the captured Jews into slavery. 11 So he immediately sent to
the towns on the seacoast, inviting
them to buy Jewish slaves and
promising to hand over ninety
slaves for a talent, not expecting
the judgment from the Almighty
that was about to overtake him.

Preparation for Battle

12 Word came to Judas concerning Nicanor's invasion; and
when he told his companions of
the arrival of the army, 13 those

7.31 Ps 68.20; 2 Macc 6.26; Rom 2.3; Heb 12.25
7.33 2 Macc 5.17; 6.12-16
7.34 1 Macc 1.24; 2 Macc 5.21
7.35 Add Esth 15.2; 2 Macc 9.5
7.36 1 Pet 5.10; 2 Macc 1.28; 7.17-19
7.37 Deut 6.4-5; Mk 12.29; 1 Cor 8.4,6
7.38 1 Macc 3.8
7.39 2 Macc 5.11; 7.3; 9.4
7.40 Heb 11.35; Ps 4.5; 22.4-5; 37.5; 2 Macc 8.18
8.1 1 Macc 2.4; 3.1; 2 Macc 5.27
8.2 1 Macc 1.21-23; 2 Macc 5.15-16
8.3 Gen 4.10; Rev 6.9-10
8.4 Ps 45.6; Heb 1.9
8.5 1 Macc 2.16; 3.1,8
8.6 1 Macc 3.10-25
8.7 1 Macc 3.3
8.8 2 Macc 5.22; 4.45
8.9 1 Macc 3.38; 7.26; 4.1-18
8.10 1 Macc 3.41; 2 Macc 8.25, 34
8.13 1 Macc 3.56

[m] The Gk here for *you* is singular
[n] Gk *slaves* [o] Cn: Gk *fallen* [p] Gk *he*
[q] Gk *one of the first*

who were cowardly and distrustful
of God's justice ran off and got
away. 14 Others sold all their remaining property, and at the same
time implored the Lord to rescue
those who had been sold by the ungodly Nicanor before he ever met
them, 15 if not for their own sake,
then for the sake of the covenants
made with their ancestors, and because he had called them by his
holy and glorious name. 16 But
Maccabeus gathered his forces together, to the number six thousand, and exhorted them not to be
frightened by the enemy and not to
fear the great multitude of Gentiles who were wickedly coming
against them, but to fight nobly,
17 keeping before their eyes the
lawless outrage that the Gentiles[r]
had committed against the holy
place, and the torture of the derided city, and besides, the overthrow of their ancestral way of life.
18 "For they trust to arms and acts
of daring," he said, "but we trust in
the Almighty God, who is able with
a single nod to strike down those
who are coming against us, and
even, if necessary, the whole
world."

19 Moreover, he told them of
the occasions when help came to
their ancestors; how, in the time of
Sennacherib, when one hundred
eighty-five thousand perished,
20 and the time of the battle against
the Galatians that took place in
Babylonia, when eight thousand
Jews[s] fought along with four thousand Macedonians; yet when the
Macedonians were hard pressed,
the eight thousand, by the help
that came to them from heaven,
destroyed one hundred twenty
thousand Galatians[t] and took a
great amount of booty.

Judas Defeats Nicanor

21 With these words he filled
them with courage and made them
ready to die for their laws and their
country; then he divided his army
into four parts. 22 He appointed his
brothers also, Simon and Joseph
and Jonathan, each to command a
division, putting fifteen hundred
men under each. 23 Besides, he appointed Eleazar to read aloud[u]
from the holy book, and gave the
watchword, "The help of God";
then, leading the first division
himself, he joined battle with Nicanor.

24 With the Almighty as their
ally, they killed more than nine
thousand of the enemy, and
wounded and disabled most of Nicanor's army, and forced them all
to flee. 25 They captured the money
of those who had come to buy
them as slaves. After pursuing
them for some distance, they were
obliged to return because the hour
was late. 26 It was the day before
the sabbath, and for that reason
they did not continue their pursuit.
27 When they had collected the
arms of the enemy and stripped
them of their spoils, they kept the
sabbath, giving great praise and
thanks to the Lord, who had preserved them for that day and allotted it to them as the beginning of
mercy. 28 After the sabbath they
gave some of the spoils to those
who had been tortured and to the
widows and orphans, and distributed the rest among themselves
and their children. 29 When they
had done this, they made common
supplication and implored the
merciful Lord to be wholly reconciled with his servants.[v]

Judas Defeats Timothy and Bacchides

30 In encounters with the
forces of Timothy and Bacchides
they killed more than twenty thousand of them and got possession of
some exceedingly high strongholds, and they divided a very large
amount of plunder, giving to those
who had been tortured and to the
orphans and widows, and also to
the aged, shares equal to their
own. 31 They collected the arms of
the enemy,[w] and carefully stored
all of them in strategic places; the
rest of the spoils they carried to Jerusalem. 32 They killed the com-

8.15 Gen 17.7; Ex 24.7-8; Rom 9.4; Deut 28.10; Dan 9.19
8.16 2 Macc 8.1
8.17 1 Macc 1.21-23; 2 Macc 5.15-16; Dan 9.27; 11.31; Mt 24.15; 2 Macc 6.18-7.42
8.18 Ps 20.7; 33.16; 44.6; 37.5-6; 2 Macc 7.40; Ps 2.1-12
8.19 2 Kings 19.35; 1 Macc 7.41; 2 Macc 15.22
8.21 1 Macc 3.58; 2 Macc 15.10
8.22 1 Macc 2.1-5; 3.55
8.23 1 Sam 7.12; 2 Macc 13.15
8.24 2 Macc 11.10; 12.36; 1 Macc 7.43
8.25 2 Macc 8.10-11,34; 1 Macc 4.16
8.27 1 Macc 3.12; 4.23; 7.47; 2.41; 2 Macc 12.38
8.29 2 Macc 1.5; 5.20
8.30 1 Macc 5.6, 11,34; 7.8
8.32 1 Macc 5.12-13

r Gk *they* s Gk lacks *Jews* t Gk lacks *Galatians* u Meaning of Gk uncertain v Gk *slaves* w Gk *their arms*

mander of Timothy's forces, a most
wicked man, and one who had
greatly troubled the Jews. 33 While
they were celebrating the victory in
the city of their ancestors, they
burned those who had set fire to
the sacred gates, Callisthenes and
some others, who had fled into one
little house; so these received the
proper reward for their impiety.[x]
34 The thrice-accursed Nicanor, who had brought the thousand merchants to buy the Jews,
35 having been humbled with the
help of the Lord by opponents
whom he regarded as of the least
account, took off his splendid uni-
form and made his way alone like a
runaway slave across the country
until he reached Antioch, having
succeeded chiefly in the destruction of his own army! 36 So he who
had undertaken to secure tribute
for the Romans by the capture of
the people of Jerusalem proclaimed that the Jews had a Defender, and that therefore the Jews
were invulnerable, because they
followed the laws ordained by him.

The Last Campaign of Antiochus Epiphanes

9 About that time, as it happened, Antiochus had re-
treated in disorder from the region
of Persia. 2 He had entered the city
called Persepolis and attempted to
rob the temples and control the
city. Therefore the people rushed
to the rescue with arms, and Antiochus and his army were defeated,[y]
with the result that Antiochus was
put to flight by the inhabitants and
beat a shameful retreat. 3 While he
was in Ecbatana, news came to
him of what had happened to Nicanor and the forces of Timothy.
4 Transported with rage, he conceived the idea of turning upon the
Jews the injury done by those who
had put him to flight; so he ordered
his charioteer to drive without
stopping until he completed the
journey. But the judgment of
heaven rode with him! For in his
arrogance he said, "When I get
there I will make Jerusalem a cemetery of Jews."
5 But the all-seeing Lord, the
God of Israel, struck him with an
incurable and invisible blow. As
soon as he stopped speaking he
was seized with a pain in his bowels, for which there was no relief,
and with sharp internal tortures—
6 and that very justly, for he had
tortured the bowels of others with
many and strange inflictions. 7 Yet
he did not in any way stop his insolence, but was even more filled
with arrogance, breathing fire in
his rage against the Jews, and giving orders to drive even faster. And
so it came about that he fell out of
his chariot as it was rushing along,
and the fall was so hard as to torture every limb of his body. 8 Thus
he who only a little while before
had thought in his superhuman arrogance that he could command
the waves of the sea, and had imagined that he could weigh the high
mountains in a balance, was
brought down to earth and carried
in a litter, making the power of
God manifest to all. 9 And so the
ungodly man's body swarmed with
worms, and while he was still living
in anguish and pain, his flesh rotted away, and because of the
stench the whole army felt revul-
sion at his decay. 10 Because of his
intolerable stench no one was able
to carry the man who a little while
before had thought that he could
touch the stars of heaven. 11 Then
it was that, broken in spirit, he began to lose much of his arrogance
and to come to his senses under
the scourge of God, for he was tortured with pain every moment.
12 And when he could not endure
his own stench, he uttered these
words, "It is right to be subject to
God; mortals should not think that
they are equal to God."[z]

Antiochus Makes a Promise to God

13 Then the abominable fellow
made a vow to the Lord, who would

8.34 Add Esth 16.15; 2 Macc 15.3; 1 Macc 7.26; 2 Macc 8.9, 23,10-11
8.35 2 Macc 8.24
8.36 Ps 91.1-13; 121.1-8; 125.1-2
9.1 1 Macc 1.10; 2 Macc 4.7
9.2 1 Macc 6.1-3; 2 Macc 1.13; 1 Macc 6.4
9.3 1 Macc 6.5
9.4 2 Macc 5.11; 7.3; 1 Macc 1.24; 2 Macc 5.21; 7.34,36
9.5 Add Esth 15.12; 2 Macc 7.35; Acts 1.18; 1 Macc 6.9
9.8 1 Macc 1.24; 2 Macc 5.21; Ps 65.7; Mk 4.41; Job 38.8-11; Isa 40.12
9.9 Acts 12.23
9.10 Isa 14.12-19
9.12 Jas 4.7; 1 Pet 5.6; Jn 5.18; 10.30,33

x Meaning of Gk uncertain y Gk *they were defeated* z Or *not think thoughts proper only to God*

no longer have mercy on him, stating 14 that the holy city, which he
was hurrying to level to the ground
and to make a cemetery, he was
now declaring to be free; 15 and the
Jews, whom he had not considered
worth burying but had planned to
throw out with their children for
the wild animals and for the birds
to eat, he would make, all of them,
equal to citizens of Athens; 16 and
the holy sanctuary, which he had
formerly plundered, he would
adorn with the finest offerings; and
all the holy vessels he would give
back, many times over; and the expenses incurred for the sacrifices
he would provide from his own revenues; 17 and in addition to all this
he also would become a Jew and
would visit every inhabited place
to proclaim the power of God.
18 But when his sufferings did not
in any way abate, for the judgment
of God had justly come upon him,
he gave up all hope for himself and
wrote to the Jews the following letter, in the form of a supplication.
This was its content:

Antiochus's Letter and Death

19 "To his worthy Jewish citizens, Antiochus their king and
general sends hearty greetings and
good wishes for their health and
prosperity. 20 If you and your children are well and your affairs are as
you wish, I am glad. As my hope is
in heaven, 21 I remember with affection your esteem and goodwill.
On my way back from the region of
Persia I suffered an annoying illness, and I have deemed it necessary to take thought for the general
security of all. 22 I do not despair of
my condition, for I have good hope
of recovering from my illness,
23 but I observed that my father, on
the occasions when he made expe-
ditions into the upper country, appointed his successor, 24 so that, if
anything unexpected happened or
any unwelcome news came, the
people throughout the realm
would not be troubled, for they
would know to whom the government was left. 25 Moreover, I understand how the princes along the
borders and the neighbors of my
kingdom keep watching for oppor-
tunities and waiting to see what
will happen. So I have appointed
my son Antiochus to be king,
whom I have often entrusted and
commended to most of you when I
hurried off to the upper provinces;
and I have written to him what is
written here. 26 I therefore urge and
beg you to remember the public
and private services rendered to
you and to maintain your present
goodwill, each of you, toward me
and my son. 27 For I am sure that he
will follow my policy and will treat
you with moderation and kindness."

28 So the murderer and blasphemer, having endured the more
intense suffering, such as he had
inflicted on others, came to the
end of his life by a most pitiable
fate, among the mountains in a
strange land. 29 And Philip, one of
his courtiers, took his body home;
then, fearing the son of Antiochus,
he withdrew to Ptolemy Philometor in Egypt.

Purification of the Temple

10 Now Maccabeus and his
followers, the Lord leading
them on, recovered the temple and
the city; 2 they tore down the altars
that had been built in the public
square by the foreigners, and also
destroyed the sacred precincts.
3 They purified the sanctuary, and
made another altar of sacrifice;
then, striking fire out of flint, they
offered sacrifices, after a lapse of
two years, and they offered incense
and lighted lamps and set out the
bread of the Presence. 4 When they
had done this, they fell prostrate
and implored the Lord that they
might never again fall into such
misfortunes, but that, if they
should ever sin, they might be disciplined by him with forbearance
and not be handed over to blasphemous and barbarous nations. 5 It
happened that on the same day on
which the sanctuary had been profaned by the foreigners, the purification of the sanctuary took place,
that is, on the twenty-fifth day of

9.16 1 Macc 1.21-23; 2 Macc 5.15-16
9.17 Dan 4.31-35; 2 Macc 7.37
9.18 1 Macc 6.12-13
9.19 3 Jn 2
9.21 Phil 1.3-7; 2 Macc 8.5-11
9.23 1 Macc 3.37; 6.1
9.25 1 Macc 6.15; 2 Macc 10.10
9.28 1 Macc 6.16
9.29 1 Macc 6.14; 2 Macc 14.23; 1 Macc 4.21
10.1 1 Macc 4.34-35
10.2 1 Macc 1.46-47,54; 2 Macc 6.2-5
10.3 1 Macc 4.36; Ex 30.7-8; 25.30
10.4 1 Macc 4.40; 2 Macc 13.12; 5.20; 6.12-20
10.5 1 Macc 4.52; 2 Macc 1.18

the same month, which was Chislev. 6 They celebrated it for eight
days with rejoicing, in the manner
of the festival of booths, remembering how not long before, during
the festival of booths, they had
been wandering in the mountains
and caves like wild animals.
7 Therefore, carrying ivy-wreathed
wands and beautiful branches and
also fronds of palm, they offered
hymns of thanksgiving to him who
had given success to the purifying
of his own holy place. 8 They decreed by public edict, ratified by
vote, that the whole nation of the
Jews should observe these days every year.
9 Such then was the end of Antiochus, who was called Epiphanes.

Accession of Antiochus Eupator

10 Now we will tell what took
place under Antiochus Eupator,
who was the son of that ungodly
man, and will give a brief summary
of the principal calamities of the
wars. 11 This man, when he succeeded to the kingdom, appointed
one Lysias to have charge of the
government and to be chief governor of Coelesyria and Phoenicia.
12 Ptolemy, who was called Ma-
cron, took the lead in showing justice to the Jews because of the
wrong that had been done to them,
and attempted to maintain peaceful relations with them. 13 As a result he was accused before Eupator by the king's Friends. He heard
himself called a traitor at every
turn, because he had abandoned
Cyprus, which Philometor had entrusted to him, and had gone over
to Antiochus Epiphanes. Unable to
command the respect due his office,[a] he took poison and ended
his life.

Campaign in Idumea

14 When Gorgias became governor of the region, he maintained a
force of mercenaries, and at every
turn kept attacking the Jews. 15 Besides this, the Idumeans, who had
control of important strongholds,
were harassing the Jews; they received those who were banished
from Jerusalem, and endeavored
to keep up the war. 16 But Maccabeus and his forces, after making
solemn supplication and imploring
God to fight on their side, rushed
to the strongholds of the Idumeans. 17 Attacking them vigorously, they gained possession of
the places, and beat off all who
fought upon the wall, and slaughtered those whom they encountered, killing no fewer than twenty
thousand.
18 When at least nine thousand
took refuge in two very strong towers well equipped to withstand a
siege, 19 Maccabeus left Simon and
Joseph, and also Zacchaeus and
his troops, a force sufficient to besiege them; and he himself set off
for places where he was more urgently needed. 20 But those with Simon, who were money-hungry,
were bribed by some of those who
were in the towers, and on receiving seventy thousand drachmas let
some of them slip away. 21 When
word of what had happened came
to Maccabeus, he gathered the
leaders of the people, and accused
these men of having sold their kindred for money by setting their enemies free to fight against them.
22 Then he killed these men who
had turned traitor, and immediately captured the two towers.
23 Having success at arms in everything he undertook, he destroyed
more than twenty thousand in the
two strongholds.

Judas Defeats Timothy

24 Now Timothy, who had been
defeated by the Jews before, gathered a tremendous force of mercenaries and collected the cavalry
from Asia in no small number. He
came on, intending to take Judea
by storm. 25 As he drew near, Maccabeus and his men sprinkled dust
on their heads and girded their
loins with sackcloth, in supplication to God. 26 Falling upon the
steps before the altar, they im-

10.6 Lev 23.33-43; 1 Macc 4.59; 2 Macc 1.9
10.7 2 Macc 6.7; 1 Macc 13.51; Jn 12.13; Rev 7.9
10.8 2 Macc 1.18; 2.16
10.10 1 Macc 6.17; 2 Macc 9.25; 13.1
10.11 1 Macc 3.33; 2 Macc 11.1; 13.2; 1 Macc 10.69; 2 Macc 3.5,8
10.12 1 Macc 3.38; 2 Macc 4.45
10.13 2 Macc 4.21
10.14 1 Macc 3.38; 4.1; 2 Macc 8.9; 1 Macc 4.35
10.16 1 Macc 5.1-3
10.19 1 Macc 2.1-5
10.20 2 Chr 19.7; 3 Macc 2.32; 4.19
10.24 1 Macc 5.28-34; 2 Macc 8.30; 1 Macc 4.35; 2 Macc 10.14
10.25 Josh 7.6; 1 Macc 11.71; 2 Macc 14.15
10.26 1 Macc 3.50; 4.10; 2 Macc 8.2, 14; Ex 23.22

[a] Cn: Meaning of Gk uncertain

plored him to be gracious to them
and to be an enemy to their enemies and an adversary to their adversaries, as the law declares.
27 And rising from their prayer they
took up their arms and advanced a
considerable distance from the
city; and when they came near the
enemy they halted. 28 Just as dawn
was breaking, the two armies
joined battle, the one having as
pledge of success and victory not
only their valor but also their reli-
ance on the Lord, while the other
made rage their leader in the fight.
29 When the battle became
fierce, there appeared to the enemy from heaven five resplendent
men on horses with golden bridles,
and they were leading the Jews.
30 Two of them took Maccabeus between them, and shielding him
with their own armor and weapons,
they kept him from being
wounded. They showered arrows
and thunderbolts on the enemy, so
that, confused and blinded, they
were thrown into disorder and cut
to pieces. 31 Twenty thousand five
hundred were slaughtered, besides
six hundred cavalry.
32 Timothy himself fled to a
stronghold called Gazara, especially well garrisoned, where Chaereas was commander. 33 Then Maccabeus and his men were glad, and
they besieged the fort for four days.
34 The men within, relying on the
strength of the place, kept blaspheming terribly and uttering
wicked words. 35 But at dawn of the
fifth day, twenty young men in the
army of Maccabeus, fired with anger because of the blasphemies,
bravely stormed the wall and with
savage fury cut down everyone they
met. 36 Others who came up in the
same way wheeled around against
the defenders and set fire to the
towers; they kindled fires and
burned the blasphemers alive.
Others broke open the gates and
let in the rest of the force, and they
occupied the city. 37 They killed
Timothy, who was hiding in a cistern, and his brother Chaereas, and
Apollophanes. 38 When they had
accomplished these things, with
hymns and thanksgivings they
blessed the Lord who shows great
kindness to Israel and gives them
the victory.

10.28 1 Macc 5.30-34; 2 Macc 7.40; 8.18
10.29 2 Macc 3.25-26; 5.2-3; 11.8
10.32 1 Macc 13.43
10.34 1 Macc 2.6; 7.38,41; 2 Macc 12.14
10.35 Lev 24.16
10.38 1 Macc 4.24; 13.51; Ps 18.31-42; 1 Macc 3.19; 2 Macc 13.15; 15.8,21

Lysias Besieges Beth-zur

11 Very soon after this, Lysias,
the king's guardian and
kinsman, who was in charge of the
government, being vexed at what
had happened, 2 gathered about
eighty thousand infantry and all
his cavalry and came against the
Jews. He intended to make the city
a home for Greeks, 3 and to levy
tribute on the temple as he did on
the sacred places of the other nations, and to put up the high
priesthood for sale every year. 4 He
took no account whatever of the
power of God, but was elated with
his ten thousands of infantry, and
his thousands of cavalry, and his
eighty elephants. 5 Invading Judea,
he approached Beth-zur, which
was a fortified place about five stadia[b] from Jerusalem, and pressed
it hard.
6 When Maccabeus and his
men got word that Lysias[c] was besieging the strongholds, they and
all the people, with lamentations
and tears, prayed the Lord to send
a good angel to save Israel. 7 Maccabeus himself was the first to take
up arms, and he urged the others
to risk their lives with him to aid
their kindred. Then they eagerly
rushed off together. 8 And there,
while they were still near Jerusalem, a horseman appeared at their
head, clothed in white and brandishing weapons of gold. 9 And together they all praised the merciful
God, and were strengthened in
heart, ready to assail not only humans but the wildest animals or
walls of iron. 10 They advanced in
battle order, having their heavenly
ally, for the Lord had mercy on
them. 11 They hurled themselves
like lions against the enemy, and
laid low eleven thousand of them
and sixteen hundred cavalry, and
forced all the rest to flee. 12 Most of
them got away stripped and

11.1 1 Macc 4.26; 2 Macc 10.11
11.3 2 Macc 4.7,24
11.4 1 Macc 1.17; 3.34; 6.30
11.5 1 Macc 4.29, 61; 6.7,26,31
11.6 1 Macc 3.50; 2 Macc 10.26; Ex 23.20; Josh 5.13-15; Judg 6.11; 2 Kings 19.35
11.8 2 Macc 5.2-3; 10.29-30; 3.24-27; Rev. 19.11
11.10 2 Macc 8.24; 12.36
11.11 1 Macc 3.4
11.12 1 Macc 4.34

[b] Meaning of Gk uncertain [c] Gk *he*

wounded, and Lysias himself escaped by disgraceful flight.

Lysias Makes Peace with the Jews

13 As he was not without intelligence, he pondered over the defeat that had befallen him, and realized that the Hebrews were
invincible because the mighty God
fought on their side. So he sent to
them 14 and persuaded them to settle everything on just terms, promising that he would persuade the
king, constraining him to be their
friend.[d] 15 Maccabeus, having regard for the common good, agreed
to all that Lysias urged. For the
king granted every request in behalf of the Jews which Maccabeus
delivered to Lysias in writing.
16 The letter written to the
Jews by Lysias was to this effect:
"Lysias to the people of the
Jews, greetings. 17 John and Absalom, who were sent by you, have
delivered your signed communica-
tion and have asked about the matters indicated in it. 18 I have informed the king of everything that
needed to be brought before him,
and he has agreed to what was possible. 19 If you will maintain your
goodwill toward the government, I
will endeavor in the future to help
promote your welfare. 20 And concerning such matters and their details, I have ordered these men and
my representatives to confer with
you. 21 Farewell. The one hundred
forty-eighth year,[e] Dioscorinthius
twenty-fourth."
22 The king's letter ran thus:
"King Antiochus to his brother
Lysias, greetings. 23 Now that our
father has gone on to the gods, we
desire that the subjects of the
kingdom be undisturbed in caring
for their own affairs. 24 We have
heard that the Jews do not consent
to our father's change to Greek
customs, but prefer their own way
of living and ask that their own
customs be allowed them. 25 Accordingly, since we choose that
this nation also should be free
from disturbance, our decision is
that their temple be restored to
them and that they shall live according to the customs of their ancestors. 26 You will do well, therefore, to send word to them and give
them pledges of friendship, so that
they may know our policy and be of
good cheer and go on happily in
the conduct of their own affairs."
27 To the nation the king's letter was as follows:
"King Antiochus to the senate of
the Jews and to the other Jews,
greetings. 28 If you are well, it is as
we desire. We also are in good
health. 29 Menelaus has informed
us that you wish to return home
and look after your own affairs.
30 Therefore those who go home by
the thirtieth of Xanthicus will have
our pledge of friendship and full
permission 31 for the Jews to enjoy
their own food and laws, just as
formerly, and none of them shall
be molested in any way for what
may have been done in ignorance.
32 And I have also sent Menelaus to
encourage you. 33 Farewell. The
one hundred forty-eighth year,[e]
Xanthicus fifteenth."
34 The Romans also sent them
a letter, which read thus:
"Quintus Memmius and Titus
Manius, envoys of the Romans, to
the people of the Jews, greetings.
35 With regard to what Lysias the
kinsman of the king has granted
you, we also give consent. 36 But as
to the matters that he decided are
to be referred to the king, as soon
as you have considered them, send
some one promptly so that we may
make proposals appropriate for
you. For we are on our way to Antioch. 37 Therefore make haste and
send messengers so that we may
have your judgment. 38 Farewell.
The one hundred forty-eighth
year,[e] Xanthicus fifteenth."

Incidents at Joppa and Jamnia

12 When this agreement had
been reached, Lysias re-
turned to the king, and the Jews
went about their farming.
2 But some of the governors in
various places, Timothy and Apol-

11.13 1 Macc 4.35; 3.19; 2 Macc 10.38; 15.8,21
11.14 1 Macc 6.58-61; 2 Macc 13.23
11.19 1 Macc 10.29-45; 11.33-37
11.22 1 Macc 6.17; 2 Macc 10.10; 13.1
11.23 2 Macc 10.9
11.24 1 Macc 2.44-50; 2 Macc 4.11-16; 6.1
11.25 1 Macc 2.19-20; 2 Macc 7.2,24
11.27 1 Macc 12.6; 2 Macc 1.10
11.28 2 Macc 4.23-50; 13.3-7
11.31 1 Macc 1.47-49
11.34 1 Macc 8.1-16
11.36 1 Macc 8.21-30
12.2 1 Macc 5.34; 2 Macc 8.30; 10.24-37; 1 Macc 7.26; 2 Macc 14.12

[d] Meaning of Gk uncertain [e] 164 B.C.

lonius son of Gennaeus, as well as
Hieronymus and Demophon, and
in addition to these Nicanor the
governor of Cyprus, would not let
them live quietly and in peace.
3 And the people of Joppa did so
ungodly a deed as this: they invited
the Jews who lived among them to
embark, with their wives and children, on boats that they had provided, as though there were no ill
will to the Jews;[f] 4 and this was
done by public vote of the city.
When they accepted, because they
wished to live peaceably and suspected nothing, the people of
Joppa[g] took them out to sea and
drowned them, at least two hundred. 5 When Judas heard of the
cruelty visited on his compatriots,
he gave orders to his men 6 and,
calling upon God, the righteous
judge, attacked the murderers of
his kindred. He set fire to the harbor by night, burned the boats, and
massacred those who had taken
refuge there. 7 Then, because the
city's gates were closed, he withdrew, intending to come again and
root out the whole community of
Joppa. 8 But learning that the people in Jamnia meant in the same
way to wipe out the Jews who were
living among them, 9 he attacked
the Jamnites by night and set fire
to the harbor and the fleet, so that
the glow of the light was seen in
Jerusalem, thirty miles[h] distant.

The Campaign in Gilead

10 When they had gone more
than a mile[i] from there, on their
march against Timothy, at least
five thousand Arabs with five hundred cavalry attacked them. 11 After a hard fight, Judas and his companions, with God's help, were
victorious. The defeated nomads
begged Judas to grant them
pledges of friendship, promising to
give him livestock and to help his
people[j] in all other ways. 12 Judas,
realizing that they might indeed be
useful in many ways, agreed to
make peace with them; and after
receiving his pledges they went
back to their tents.

13 He also attacked a certain
town that was strongly fortified
with earthworks[k] and walls, and
inhabited by all sorts of Gentiles.
Its name was Caspin. 14 Those who
were within, relying on the
strength of the walls and on their
supply of provisions, behaved most
insolently toward Judas and his
men, railing at them and even blaspheming and saying unholy things.
15 But Judas and his men, calling
against the great Sovereign of the
world, who without battering-rams
or engines of war overthrew Jericho in the days of Joshua, rushed
furiously upon the walls. 16 They
took the town by the will of God,
and slaughtered untold numbers,
so that the adjoining lake, a quarter of a mile[l] wide, appeared to be
running over with blood.

Judas Defeats Timothy's Army

17 When they had gone ninety-
five miles[m] from there, they came
to Charax, to the Jews who are
called Toubiani. 18 They did not
find Timothy in that region, for he
had by then left there without ac-
complishing anything, though in
one place he had left a very strong
garrison. 19 Dositheus and Sosipater, who were captains under Maccabeus, marched out and destroyed those whom Timothy had
left in the stronghold, more than
ten thousand men. 20 But Maccabeus arranged his army in divisions, set men[j] in command of
the divisions, and hurried after
Timothy, who had with him one
hundred twenty thousand infantry
and two thousand five hundred
cavalry. 21 When Timothy learned
of the approach of Judas, he sent
off the women and the children
and also the baggage to a place
called Carnaim; for that place was
hard to besiege and difficult of access because of the narrowness of
all the approaches. 22 But when Judas's first division appeared, terror
and fear came over the enemy at
the manifestation to them of him

12.3 Josh 19.46; 1 Macc 10.75; Acts 10.5,8
12.6 1 Macc 10.76; 14.5,34
12.8 1 Macc 5.58; 10.69
12.10 1 Macc 5.39
12.11 Ps 18.31-42; 1 Macc 3.19; 2 Macc 10.38; 13.15; 11.26, 30
12.14 1 Macc 2.6; 7.38,41; 2 Macc 10.34-36
12.15 3 Macc 2.7; 1 Tim 6.15; Rev 17.14; Josh 6.15-21
12.17 1 Macc 5.13
12.20 1 Macc 5.37-44
12.21 Gen 14.5; Am 6.13; 1 Macc 5.26
12.22 2 Macc 3.24; 5.2-4; 15.27

[f] Gk *to them* [g] Gk *they* [h] Gk *two hundred forty stadia* [i] Gk *nine stadia* [j] Gk *them* [k] Meaning of Gk uncertain [l] Gk *two stadia* [m] Gk *seven hundred fifty stadia*

who sees all things. In their flight
they rushed headlong in every direction, so that often they were injured by their own men and
pierced by the points of their own
swords. 23 Judas pressed the pursuit with the utmost vigor, putting
the sinners to the sword, and destroyed as many as thirty thousand.
24 Timothy himself fell into the
hands of Dositheus and Sosipater
and their men. With great guile he
begged them to let him go in
safety, because he held the parents
of most of them, and the brothers
of some, to whom no consideration
would be shown. 25 And when with
many words he had confirmed his
solemn promise to restore them
unharmed, they let him go, for the
sake of saving their kindred.

Judas Wins Other Victories

26 Then Judas[n] marched
against Carnaim and the temple of
Atargatis, and slaughtered twenty-
five thousand people. 27 After the
rout and destruction of these, he
marched also against Ephron, a
fortified town where Lysias lived
with multitudes of people of all na-
tionalities.[o] Stalwart young men
took their stand before the walls
and made a vigorous defense; and
great stores of war engines and
missiles were there. 28 But the
Jews[p] called upon the Sovereign
who with power shatters the might
of his enemies, and they got the
town into their hands, and killed
as many as twenty-five thousand of
those who were in it.
29 Setting out from there, they
hastened to Scythopolis, which is
seventy-five miles[q] from Jerusalem. 30 But when the Jews who
lived there bore witness to the
goodwill that the people of Scythopolis had shown them and their
kind treatment of them in times of
misfortune, 31 they thanked them
and exhorted them to be well disposed to their race in the future
also. Then they went up to Jerusalem, as the festival of weeks was
close at hand.

Judas Defeats Gorgias

32 After the festival called Pentecost, they hurried against Gorgias, the governor of Idumea,
33 who came out with three thousand infantry and four hundred
cavalry. 34 When they joined battle,
it happened that a few of the Jews
fell. 35 But a certain Dositheus, one
of Bacenor's men, who was on
horseback and was a strong man,
caught hold of Gorgias, and grasping his cloak was dragging him off
by main strength, wishing to take
the accursed man alive, when one
of the Thracian cavalry bore down
on him and cut off his arm; so Gorgias escaped and reached Marisa.
36 As Esdris and his men had
been fighting for a long time and
were weary, Judas called upon the
Lord to show himself their ally and
leader in the battle. 37 In the language of their ancestors he raised
the battle cry, with hymns; then he
charged against Gorgias's troops
when they were not expecting it,
and put them to flight.

Prayers for Those Killed in Battle

38 Then Judas assembled his
army and went to the city of Adullam. As the seventh day was coming on, they purified themselves
according to the custom, and kept
the sabbath there.
39 On the next day, as had now
become necessary, Judas and his
men went to take up the bodies of
the fallen and to bring them back
to lie with their kindred in the se-
pulchres of their ancestors. 40 Then
under the tunic of each one of the
dead they found sacred tokens of
the idols of Jamnia, which the law
forbids the Jews to wear. And it became clear to all that this was the
reason these men had fallen. 41 So
they all blessed the ways of the
Lord, the righteous judge, who reveals the things that are hidden;
42 and they turned to supplication,
praying that the sin that had been
committed might be wholly blot-

12.24 2 Macc 12.19
12.26 1 Macc 5.43
12.27 1 Macc 5.46
12.28 2 Macc 12.15
12.29 Jdt 3.10
12.31 Ex 34.22-24; Deut 16.9-12; Tob 2.1
12.32 Acts 2.1; 1 Macc 4.1,5; 2 Macc 8.9; 10.14
12.35 1 Macc 5.66
12.36 2 Macc 8.24; 11.10
12.37 2 Chr 20.21-22; 2 Macc 10.7, 38
12.38 Josh 12.35; 15.35; 1 Macc 2.41; 2 Macc 8.27
12.39 1 Macc 2.70; 9.19; 13.25; 1 Esd 1.31
12.40 2 Macc 10.8; Deut 7.25-26
12.41 Ps 7.11; 50.6; 96.10,13

[n] Gk *he* [o] Meaning of Gk uncertain
[p] Gk *they* [q] Gk *six hundred stadia*

ted out. The noble Judas exhorted
the people to keep themselves free
from sin, for they had seen with
their own eyes what had happened
as the result of the sin of those who
had fallen. 43 He also took up a collection, man by man, to the
amount of two thousand drachmas
of silver, and sent it to Jerusalem
to provide for a sin offering. In doing this he acted very well and honorably, taking account of the resurrection. 44 For if he were not
expecting that those who had
fallen would rise again, it would
have been superfluous and foolish
to pray for the dead. 45 But if he was
looking to the splendid reward that
is laid up for those who fall asleep
in godliness, it was a holy and
pious thought. Therefore he made
atonement for the dead, so that
they might be delivered from their
sin.

Menelaus Is Put to Death

13 In the one hundred forty-
ninth year[r] word came to
Judas and his men that Antiochus
Eupator was coming with a great
army against Judea, 2 and with him
Lysias, his guardian, who had
charge of the government. Each of
them had a Greek force of one
hundred ten thousand infantry,
five thousand three hundred cavalry, twenty-two elephants, and
three hundred chariots armed with
scythes.
3 Menelaus also joined them
and with utter hypocrisy urged Antiochus on, not for the sake of his
country's welfare, but because he
thought that he would be established in office. 4 But the King of
kings aroused the anger of Antiochus against the scoundrel; and
when Lysias informed him that
this man was to blame for all the
trouble, he ordered them to take
him to Beroea and to put him to
death by the method that is customary in that place. 5 For there is
a tower there, fifty cubits high, full
of ashes, and it has a rim running
around it that on all sides inclines
precipitously into the ashes.

12.43 Lev 4.27-35; 6.24-29
12.44 Dan 12.2; 2 Macc 7.14; 14.46; 1 Cor 15.29
12.45 Jn 11.11-12; 1 Cor 15.20; 1 Thess 5.6, 10
13.1 2 Macc 9.25; 10.10; 1 Macc 6.28-31
13.2 2 Macc 10.11; 11.1
13.3 2 Macc 4.23-50; 11.29
13.4 Deut 10.17; Ps 136.31; 1 Tim 6.15; Rev 17.14; 19.16; Acts 17.10
13.6 2 Kings 9.30-35
13.8 2 Macc 4.50
13.9 1 Macc 1.24; 2 Macc 9.4, 7-8,11
13.10 1 Macc 3.50; 4.10; 2 Macc 8.2, 14; 10.26
13.11 1 Macc 2.6; 2 Macc 10.34-36; 12.14
13.12 1 Macc 4.40; 2 Macc 3.15; 10.4
13.13 2 Macc 14.37; 11.10,13
13.14 Rev 2.10; 1 Macc 2.1, 15; 13.25,30
13.15 2 Macc 8.23; 1 Macc 3.19; 2 Macc 10.38; 15.8,21; 1 Macc 6.45-46
13.17 1 Sam 7.12; Ps 46.1; 2 Macc 13.13

6 There they all push to destruction
anyone guilty of sacrilege or notorious for other crimes. 7 By such a
fate it came about that Menelaus
the lawbreaker died, without even
burial in the earth. 8 And this was
eminently just; because he had
committed many sins against the
altar whose fire and ashes were
holy, he met his death in ashes.

A Battle Near the City of Modein

9 The king with barbarous arrogance was coming to show the
Jews things far worse than those
that had been done[s] in his father's
time. 10 But when Judas heard of
this, he ordered the people to call
upon the Lord day and night, now
if ever to help those who were on
the point of being deprived of the
law and their country and the holy
temple, 11 and not to let the people
who had just begun to revive fall
into the hands of the blasphemous
Gentiles. 12 When they had all
joined in the same petition and
had implored the merciful Lord
with weeping and fasting and lying
prostrate for three days without
ceasing, Judas exhorted them and
ordered them to stand ready.
13 After consulting privately
with the elders, he determined to
march out and decide the matter
by the help of God before the
king's army could enter Judea and
get possession of the city. 14 So,
committing the decision to the
Creator of the world and exhorting
his troops to fight bravely to the
death for the laws, temple, city,
country, and commonwealth, he
pitched his camp near Modein.
15 He gave his troops the watchword, "God's victory," and with a
picked force of the bravest young
men, he attacked the king's pavilion at night and killed as many as
two thousand men in the camp. He
stabbed[t] the leading elephant and
its rider. 16 In the end they filled
the camp with terror and confusion and withdrew in triumph.
17 This happened, just as day was

[r] 163 B.C. [s] Or *the worst of the things that had been done* [t] Meaning of Gk uncertain

dawning, because the Lord's help
protected him.

Antiochus Makes a Treaty with the Jews

18 The king, having had a taste
of the daring of the Jews, tried
strategy in attacking their positions. 19 He advanced against Beth-
zur, a strong fortress of the Jews,
was turned back, attacked again,[u]
and was defeated. 20 Judas sent in
to the garrison whatever was necessary. 21 But Rhodocus, a man
from the ranks of the Jews, gave secret information to the enemy; he
was sought for, caught, and put in
prison. 22 The king negotiated a
second time with the people in
Beth-zur, gave pledges, received
theirs, withdrew, attacked Judas
and his men, was defeated; 23 he
got word that Philip, who had been
left in charge of the government,
had revolted in Antioch; he was
dismayed, called in the Jews,
yielded and swore to observe all
their rights, settled with them and
offered sacrifice, honored the
sanctuary and showed generosity
to the holy place. 24 He received
Maccabeus, left Hegemonides as
governor from Ptolemais to Gerar,
25 and went to Ptolemais. The people of Ptolemais were indignant
over the treaty; in fact they were so
angry that they wanted to annul its
terms.[v] 26 Lysias took the public
platform, made the best possible
defense, convinced them, appeased them, gained their goodwill, and set out for Antioch. This
is how the king's attack and with-
drawal turned out.

Alcimus Speaks against Judas

14 Three years later, word
came to Judas and his men
that Demetrius son of Seleucus
had sailed into the harbor of Tripo-
lis with a strong army and a fleet,
2 and had taken possession of the
country, having made away with
Antiochus and his guardian Lysias.
3 Now a certain Alcimus, who
had formerly been high priest but
had willfully defiled himself in the
times of separation,[w] realized that
there was no way for him to be safe
or to have access again to the holy
altar, 4 and went to King Demetrius
in about the one hundred fifty-first
year,[x] presenting to him a crown
of gold and a palm, and besides
these some of the customary olive
branches from the temple. During
that day he kept quiet. 5 But he
found an opportunity that fur-
thered his mad purpose when he
was invited by Demetrius to a
meeting of the council and was
asked about the attitude and intentions of the Jews. He answered:
6 "Those of the Jews who are
called Hasideans, whose leader is
Judas Maccabeus, are keeping up
war and stirring up sedition, and
will not let the kingdom attain
tranquility. 7 Therefore I have laid
aside my ancestral glory—I mean
the high priesthood—and have
now come here, 8 first because I am
genuinely concerned for the interests of the king, and second because I have regard also for my
compatriots. For through the folly
of those whom I have mentioned
our whole nation is now in no
small misfortune. 9 Since you are
acquainted, O king, with the details of this matter, may it please
you to take thought for our country
and our hard-pressed nation with
the gracious kindness that you
show to all. 10 For as long as Judas
lives, it is impossible for the government to find peace." 11 When he
had said this, the rest of the king's
Friends,[y] who were hostile to Judas, quickly inflamed Demetrius
still more. 12 He immediately chose
Nicanor, who had been in command of the elephants, appointed
him governor of Judea, and sent
him off 13 with orders to kill Judas
and scatter his troops, and to in-
stall Alcimus as high priest of the
great[z] temple. 14 And the Gentiles
throughout Judea, who had fled
before[v] Judas, flocked to join Nicanor, thinking that the misfortunes and calamities of the Jews

13.19 1 Macc 4.29; 6.31; 9.52
13.22 1 Macc 6.29
13.23 1 Macc 6.14; 9.29; 6.56, 58-59
13.25 1 Macc 5.15; 10.1; 11.22-24
13.26 1 Macc 6.63
14.1 1 Macc 7.1
14.2 1 Macc 6.17; 7.2; 2 Macc 10.10; 11.1
14.3 1 Macc 7.5; 9.1; 2 Macc 4.11-15
14.4 1 Macc 7.7; 13.37; 2 Macc 10.7
14.6 1 Macc 2.42; 7.13
14.8 1 Macc 7.25
14.12 1 Macc 3.38; 7.26; 2 Macc 8.9; 12.2
14.13 1 Macc 7.9

[u] Or *faltered* [v] Meaning of Gk uncertain
[w] Other ancient authorities read *of mixing*
[x] 161 B.C. [y] Gk *of the Friends* [z] Gk *greatest*

would mean prosperity for themselves.

Nicanor Makes Friends with Judas

15 When the Jews[a] heard of Nicanor's coming and the gathering
of the Gentiles, they sprinkled dust
on their heads and prayed to him
who established his own people
forever and always upholds his
own heritage by manifesting himself. 16 At the command of the
leader, they[b] set out from there
immediately and engaged them in
battle at a village called Dessau.[c]
17 Simon, the brother of Judas, had
encountered Nicanor, but had
been temporarily[d] checked because of the sudden consternation
created by the enemy.

18 Nevertheless Nicanor, hearing of the valor of Judas and his
troops and their courage in battle
for their country, shrank from deciding the issue by bloodshed.
19 Therefore he sent Posidonius,
Theodotus, and Mattathias to give
and receive pledges of friendship.
20 When the terms had been fully
considered, and the leader had informed the people, and it had appeared that they were of one mind,
they agreed to the covenant. 21 The
leaders[e] set a day on which to
meet by themselves. A chariot
came forward from each army;
seats of honor were set in place;
22 Judas posted armed men in readiness at key places to prevent sudden treachery on the part of the enemy; so they duly held the
consultation.

23 Nicanor stayed on in Jerusalem and did nothing out of the
way, but dismissed the flocks of
people that had gathered. 24 And
he kept Judas always in his presence; he was warmly attached to
the man. 25 He urged him to marry
and have children; so Judas[b] married, settled down, and shared the
common life.

Nicanor Turns against Judas

26 But when Alcimus noticed
their goodwill for one another, he
took the covenant that had been
made and went to Demetrius. He
told him that Nicanor was disloyal
to the government, since he had
appointed that conspirator against
the kingdom, Judas, to be his successor. 27 The king became excited
and, provoked by the false accusations of that depraved man, wrote
to Nicanor, stating that he was displeased with the covenant and
commanding him to send Maccabeus to Antioch as a prisoner without delay.

28 When this message came to
Nicanor, he was troubled and
grieved that he had to annul their
agreement when the man had done
no wrong. 29 Since it was not possible to oppose the king, he watched
for an opportunity to accomplish
this by a stratagem. 30 But Maccabeus, noticing that Nicanor was
more austere in his dealings with
him and was meeting him more
rudely than had been his custom,
concluded that this austerity did
not spring from the best motives.
So he gathered not a few of his
men, and went into hiding from
Nicanor. 31 When the latter became
aware that he had been cleverly
outwitted by the man, he went to
the great[f] and holy temple while
the priests were offering the customary sacrifices, and commanded
them to hand the man over.
32 When they declared on oath that
they did not know where the man
was whom he wanted, 33 he
stretched out his right hand toward
the sanctuary, and swore this oath:
"If you do not hand Judas over to
me as a prisoner, I will level this
shrine of God to the ground and
tear down the altar, and build here
a splendid temple to Dionysus."

34 Having said this, he went
away. Then the priests stretched
out their hands toward heaven and
called upon the constant Defender
of our nation, in these words:
35 "O Lord of all, though you have
need of nothing, you were pleased
that there should be a temple for
your habitation among us; 36 so

14.15 Josh 7.6; 1 Macc 11.71; 2 Macc 10.25; 13.10; 3.24; 12.22; 15.27
14.16 1 Macc 2.3; 9.19,62,65
14.19 1 Macc 7.27-28; 2 Macc 11.26, 30; 12.11
14.22 1 Macc 7.15-16; 2 Macc 12.1-4
14.23 2 Macc 14.14
14.26 1 Macc 7.7
14.27 1 Macc 7.35
14.29 1 Macc 7.29
14.30 1 Macc 7.30
14.33 2 Macc 15.32; 1 Macc 7.35; 2 Macc 6.7
14.35 Ps 50.10-12; Acts 17.25; 1 Kings 8.27-39; 9.3
14.36 Isa 6.3; Rev 4.8; 1 Macc 4.36; 2 Macc 10.1-8

[a] Gk *they* [b] Gk *he* [c] Meaning of Gk uncertain [d] Other ancient authorities read *slowly* [e] Gk *They* [f] Gk *greatest*

now, O holy One, Lord of all holiness, keep undefiled forever this
house that has been so recently
purified."

Razis Dies for His Country

37 A certain Razis, one of the elders of Jerusalem, was denounced
to Nicanor as a man who loved his
compatriots and was very well
thought of and for his goodwill was
called father of the Jews. 38 In former times, when there was no min-
gling with the Gentiles, he had
been accused of Judaism, and he
had most zealously risked body
and life for Judaism. 39 Nicanor,
wishing to exhibit the enmity that
he had for the Jews, sent more
than five hundred soldiers to arrest
him; 40 for he thought that by ar-
resting[g] him he would do them an
injury. 41 When the troops were
about to capture the tower and
were forcing the door of the courtyard, they ordered that fire be
brought and the doors burned. Being surrounded, Razis[h] fell upon
his own sword, 42 preferring to die
nobly rather than to fall into the
hands of sinners and suffer out-
rages unworthy of his noble birth.
43 But in the heat of the struggle he
did not hit exactly, and the crowd
was now rushing in through the
doors. He courageously ran up on
the wall, and bravely threw himself
down into the crowd. 44 But as they
quickly drew back, a space opened
and he fell in the middle of the
empty space. 45 Still alive and
aflame with anger, he rose, and
though his blood gushed forth and
his wounds were severe he ran
through the crowd; and standing
upon a steep rock, 46 with his blood
now completely drained from him,
he tore out his entrails, took them
in both hands and hurled them at
the crowd, calling upon the Lord of
life and spirit to give them back to
him again. This was the manner of
his death.

Nicanor's Arrogance

15 When Nicanor heard that
Judas and his troops were
in the region of Samaria, he made
plans to attack them with complete safety on the day of rest.
2 When the Jews who were compelled to follow him said, "Do not
destroy so savagely and barba-
rously, but show respect for the
day that he who sees all things has
honored and hallowed above other
days," 3 the thrice-accursed wretch
asked if there were a sovereign in
heaven who had commanded the
keeping of the sabbath day. 4 When
they declared, "It is the living Lord
himself, the Sovereign in heaven,
who ordered us to observe the seventh day," 5 he replied, "But I am a
sovereign also, on earth, and I
command you to take up arms and
finish the king's business." Nevertheless, he did not succeed in carrying out his abominable design.

Judas Prepares the Jews for Battle

6 This Nicanor in his utter
boastfulness and arrogance had
determined to erect a public monument of victory over Judas and his
forces. 7 But Maccabeus did not
cease to trust with all confidence
that he would get help from the
Lord. 8 He exhorted his troops not
to fear the attack of the Gentiles,
but to keep in mind the former
times when help had come to them
from heaven, and so to look for the
victory that the Almighty would
give them. 9 Encouraging them
from the law and the prophets, and
reminding them also of the struggles they had won, he made them
the more eager. 10 When he had
aroused their courage, he issued
his orders, at the same time pointing out the perfidy of the Gentiles
and their violation of oaths. 11 He
armed each of them not so much
with confidence in shields and
spears as with the inspiration of
brave words, and he cheered them
all by relating a dream, a sort of vision,[g] which was worthy of belief.

12 What he saw was this: Onias,
who had been high priest, a noble
and good man, of modest bearing
and gentle manner, one who spoke

14.37 2 Macc 13.13; 4.2; 14.8
14.38 Judg 9.17; Jdt 13.20
14.41 1 Sam 31.4
14.46 Jn 14.6; Rom 6.4; Rev 1.18; Dan 12.2; 2 Macc 7.11; 12.44; 7.1-19
15.2 Add Esth 15.12; 2 Macc 7.35
15.3 Add Esth 16.15; 2 Macc 8.34
15.4 Ex 20.8-11; Deut 5.12-15
15.6 1 Macc 1.24; 2 Macc 9.4-11
15.7 2 Macc 10.25-28
15.8 1 Macc 7.40-41; 2 Macc 8.19; 1 Macc 3.19; 2 Macc 10.38; 13.15; 15.21
15.9 Mt 22.40; Lk 24.27
15.10 2 Macc 8.19-21; 14.18-27
15.12 1 Macc 12.7-8; 2 Macc 3.1

[g] Meaning of Gk uncertain [h] Gk *he*

fittingly and had been trained from childhood in all that belongs to excellence, was praying with outstretched hands for the whole body of the Jews. 13 Then in the same fashion another appeared, distinguished by his gray hair and dignity, and of marvelous majesty and authority. 14 And Onias spoke, saying, "This is a man who loves the family of Israel and prays much for the people and the holy city—Jeremiah, the prophet of God." 15 Jeremiah stretched out his right hand and gave to Judas a golden sword, and as he gave it he addressed him thus: 16 "Take this holy sword, a gift from God, with which you will strike down your adversaries."

17 Encouraged by the words of Judas, so noble and so effective in arousing valor and awaking courage in the souls of the young, they determined not to carry on a campaign[i] but to attack bravely, and to decide the matter by fighting hand to hand with all courage, because the city and the sanctuary and the temple were in danger. 18 Their concern for wives and children, and also for brothers and sisters[j] and relatives, lay upon them less heavily; their greatest and first fear was for the consecrated sanctuary. 19 And those who had to remain in the city were in no little distress, being anxious over the encounter in the open country.

The Defeat and Death of Nicanor

20 When all were now looking forward to the coming issue, and the enemy was already close at hand with their army drawn up for battle, the elephants[k] strategically stationed and the cavalry deployed on the flanks, 21 Maccabeus, observing the masses that were in front of him and the varied supply of arms and the savagery of the elephants, stretched out his hands toward heaven and called upon the Lord who works wonders; for he knew that it is not by arms, but as the Lord[l] decides, that he gains the victory for those who deserve it. 22 He called upon him in these words: "O Lord, you sent your angel in the time of King Hezekiah of Judea, and he killed fully one hundred eighty-five thousand in the camp of Sennacherib. 23 So now, O Sovereign of the heavens, send a good angel to spread terror and trembling before us. 24 By the might of your arm may these blasphemers who come against your holy people be struck down." With these words he ended his prayer.

25 Nicanor and his troops advanced with trumpets and battle songs, 26 but Judas and his troops met the enemy in battle with invocations to God and prayers. 27 So, fighting with their hands and praying to God in their hearts, they laid low at least thirty-five thousand, and were greatly gladdened by God's manifestation.

28 When the action was over and they were returning with joy, they recognized Nicanor, lying dead, in full armor. 29 Then there was shouting and tumult, and they blessed the Sovereign Lord in the language of their ancestors. 30 Then the man who was ever in body and soul the defender of his people, the man who maintained his youthful goodwill toward his compatriots, ordered them to cut off Nicanor's head and arm and carry them to Jerusalem. 31 When he arrived there and had called his compatriots together and stationed the priests before the altar, he sent for those who were in the citadel. 32 He showed them the vile Nicanor's head and that profane man's arm, which had been boastfully stretched out against the holy house of the Almighty. 33 He cut out the tongue of the ungodly Nicanor and said that he would feed it piecemeal to the birds and would hang up these rewards of his folly opposite the sanctuary. 34 And they all, looking to heaven, blessed the Lord who had manifested himself, saying, "Blessed is he who has kept his own place undefiled!" 35 Judas[m] hung Nicanor's head

15.13 Prov 16.31; 20.29; Sir 6.18; 2 Macc 6.23
15.14 Jer 1.1-3; 2 Macc 2.1-8
15.17 1 Macc 4.36-39
15.18 2 Macc 14.33
15.20 1 Macc 1.17; 60.30,37; 2 Macc 11.4; 13.2
15.21 1 Macc 3.54; 4.10; 5.31; 2 Macc 3.20; Ps 20.7; 33.16-17; 44.6; Prov 16.1; 19.21; 1 Macc 3.19; 2 Macc 15.8
15.22 2 Kings 19.35; 1 Macc 7.40-41; 2 Macc 8.19
15.23 2 Macc 5.2-3; 10.29-30; 11.8
15.24 2 Macc 10.34-35
15.25 1 Macc 3.54; 4.13,40; 6.33
15.27 1 Macc 7.43; 2 Macc 3.24; 12.22
15.28 1 Macc 7.43
15.30 1 Sam 17.54; 1 Macc 7.47
15.31 1 Macc 1.33; 6.18; 11.20-21; 12.36
15.32 1 Macc 7.47; 2 Macc 14.33
15.34 Ps 72.19; 103.1; Tob 3.11; Jdt 13.17-18
15.35 1 Sam 31.9; Jdt 14.1; 1 Macc 7.47

[i] Or *to remain in camp* [j] Gk *for brothers* [k] Gk *animals* [l] Gk *he* [m] Gk *He*

from the citadel, a clear and conspicuous sign to everyone of the
help of the Lord. 36 And they all decreed by public vote never to let
this day go unobserved, but to celebrate the thirteenth day of the
twelfth month—which is called
Adar in the Aramaic language—
the day before Mordecai's day.
37 This, then, is how matters
turned out with Nicanor, and from
that time the city has been in the
possession of the Hebrews. So I
will here end my story.

15.36 1 Macc 7.49; Esth 9.20-21; Add Esth 10.13

15.39 2 Macc 2.23-32

The Compiler's Epilogue

38 If it is well told and to the
point, that is what I myself desired;
if it is poorly done and mediocre,
that was the best I could do. 39 For
just as it is harmful to drink wine
alone, or, again, to drink water
alone, while wine mixed with water is sweet and delicious and en-
hances one's enjoyment, so also
the style of the story delights the
ears of those who read the work.
And here will be the end.

(b) The books from 1 Esdras through 3 Maccabees are recognized as Deuterocanonical Scripture by the Greek and Russian Churches. They are not so recognized by the Roman Catholic Church, but 1 Esdras and the Prayer of Manasseh (together with 2 Esdras) are placed in an appendix to the Latin Vulgate Bible.

1 Esdras

Title and Background

The word "Esdras" is the Greek spelling of "Ezra." This book repeats the content of the canonical Ezra, plus the closing chapters of 2 Chronicles (2 Chr 35.1–36.23) and a few verses from Nehemiah (Neh 7.38–8.12). Only one main section (1 Esd 3.1–4.63) has no counterpart elsewhere in the Bible.

Author and Date of Writing

Most believe the author of this book was translating the canonical Ezra into Greek, perhaps from a Hebrew manuscript that differs from the present Hebrew Ezra. The author may have taken the new section from a Persian folktale. The book was probably written about 100 B.C.

Theme and Message

God punishes his people through their exile in Babylon. But he is faithful to his promise and mercifully guides and equips Zerubbabel and Ezra to lead groups of Jews back to the Promised Land. Eventually the temple is rebuilt and the worship of God restored.

Outline

I. The Final Years of the Nation of Judah (1.1-58)
II. Cyrus Permits the Jews to Return under Zerubbabel (2.1–5.55)
III. The Temple Rebuilt (5.56–7.15)

Josiah Celebrates the Passover

1 Josiah kept the passover to his
Lord in Jerusalem; he killed
the passover lamb on the fourteenth day of the first month, 2 having placed the priests according to
their divisions, arrayed in their
vestments, in the temple of the
Lord. 3 He told the Levites, the
temple servants of Israel, that they
should sanctify themselves to the
Lord and put the holy ark of the
Lord in the house that King Solomon, son of David, had built; 4 and
he said, "You need no longer carry
it on your shoulders. Now worship
the Lord your God and serve his
people Israel; prepare yourselves
by your families and kindred, 5 in
accordance with the directions of
King David of Israel and the magnificence of his son Solomon.
Stand in order in the temple according to the groupings of the ancestral houses of you Levites, who
minister before your kindred the
people of Israel, 6 and kill the passover lamb and prepare the sacrifices for your kindred, and keep
the passover according to the commandment of the Lord that was
given to Moses."
7 To the people who were
present Josiah gave thirty thousand lambs and kids, and three
thousand calves; these were given
from the king's possessions, as he
promised, to the people and the
priests and Levites. 8 Hilkiah,

1.1 2 Chr 35.1-19; Ex 32.6; Num 9.3; 2 Kings 23.21
1.2 1 Chr 23.6; 2 Chr 23.18
1.3 1 Chr 9.2; 15.14; 2 Chr 29.5; 5.7
1.4 1 Chr 23.26; Deut 6.13; Mt 4.10
1.5 1 Chr 9.10-13; 2 Chr 8.14; Ps 134.1
1.6 2 Chr 30.15; Ezra 6.20; Ex 12.14-20

1.7 2 Chr 30.24 **1.8** 2 Chr 34.9

Zechariah, and Jehiel,[a] the chief
officers of the temple, gave to the
priests for the passover two thousand six hundred sheep and three
hundred calves. 9 And Jeconiah
and Shemaiah and his brother Nethanel, and Hashabiah and Ochiel
and Joram, captains over thousands, gave the Levites for the
passover five thousand sheep and
seven hundred calves.

10 This is what took place. The
priests and the Levites, having the
unleavened bread, stood in proper
order according to kindred 11 and
the grouping of the ancestral
houses, before the people, to make
the offering to the Lord as it is written in the book of Moses; this they
did in the morning. 12 They roasted
the passover lamb with fire, as required; and they boiled the sacrifices in bronze pots and caldrons,
with a pleasing odor, 13 and carried
them to all the people. Afterward
they prepared the passover for
themselves and for their kindred
the priests, the sons of Aaron,
14 because the priests were offering
the fat until nightfall; so the Levites prepared it for themselves
and for their kindred the priests,
the sons of Aaron. 15 The temple
singers, the sons of Asaph, were in
their place according to the arrangement made by David, and
also Asaph, Zechariah, and Ed-
dinus, who represented the king.
16 The gatekeepers were at each
gate; no one needed to interrupt
his daily duties, for their kindred
the Levites prepared the passover
for them.

17 So the things that had to do
with the sacrifices to the Lord were
accomplished that day: the passover was kept 18 and the sacrifices
were offered on the altar of the
Lord, according to the command of
King Josiah. 19 And the people of
Israel who were present at that
time kept the passover and the festival of unleavened bread seven
days. 20 No passover like it had
been kept in Israel since the times
of the prophet Samuel; 21 none of
the kings of Israel had kept such a
passover as was kept by Josiah and

1.9 2 Chr 31.12
1.10 Ex 12.15
1.12 Ex 12.8-9; Lev 6.25-28
1.15 1 Chr 25.1-9
1.16 1 Chr 26.1-19
1.18 1 Esd 1.1
1.19 Ex 12.15; 2 Chr 30.21
1.20 2 Kings 23.21-23
1.23 2 Kings 22.2; 2 Chr 35.26
1.25 2 Chr 35.20-27; 2 Kings 23.29; Isa 10.9; Jer 46.2
1.27 Acts 5.39
1.29 Judg 1.27; 2 Kings 23.29; Zech 12.11
1.30 2 Kings 23.30
1.32 Lam 4.20

the priests and Levites and the
people of Judah and all of Israel
who were living in Jerusalem. 22 In
the eighteenth year of the reign of
Josiah this passover was kept.

The End of Josiah's Reign

23 And the deeds of Josiah were
upright in the sight of the Lord, for
his heart was full of godliness. 24 In
ancient times the events of his
reign have been recorded—
concerning those who sinned and
acted wickedly toward the Lord beyond any other people or kingdom,
and how they grieved the Lord[b]
deeply, so that the words of the
Lord fell upon Israel.

25 After all these acts of Josiah,
it happened that Pharaoh, king of
Egypt, went to make war at Carchemish on the Euphrates, and Josiah went out against him. 26 And
the king of Egypt sent word to him
saying, "What have we to do with
each other, O king of Judea? 27 I
was not sent against you by the
Lord God, for my war is at the Euphrates. And now the Lord is with
me! The Lord is with me, urging
me on! Stand aside, and do not oppose the Lord."

28 Josiah, however, did not turn
back to his chariot, but tried to
fight with him, and did not heed
the words of the prophet Jeremiah
from the mouth of the Lord. 29 He
joined battle with him in the plain
of Megiddo, and the commanders
came down against King Josiah.
30 The king said to his servants,
"Take me away from the battle, for
I am very weak." And immediately
his servants took him out of the
line of battle. 31 He got into his second chariot; and after he was
brought back to Jerusalem he died,
and was buried in the tomb of his
ancestors.

32 In all Judea they mourned
for Josiah. The prophet Jeremiah
lamented for Josiah, and the principal men, with the women,[c] have
made lamentation for him to this
day; it was ordained that this
should always be done throughout

[a] Gk *Esyelus* [b] Gk *him* [c] Or *their wives*

the whole nation of Israel. 33 These things are written in the book of the histories of the kings of Judea; and every one of the acts of Josiah, and his splendor, and his understanding of the law of the Lord, and the things that he had done before, and these that are now told, are recorded in the book of the kings of Israel and Judah.

The Last Kings of Judah

34 The men of the nation took Jeconiah[d] son of Josiah, who was twenty-three years old, and made him king in succession to his father Josiah. 35 He reigned three months in Judah and Jerusalem. Then the king of Egypt deposed him from reigning in Jerusalem, 36 and fined the nation one hundred talents of silver and one talent of gold. 37 The king of Egypt made his brother Jehoiakim king of Judea and Jerusalem. 38 Jehoiakim put the nobles in prison, and seized his brother Zarius and brought him back from Egypt.

39 Jehoiakim was twenty-five years old when he began to reign in Judea and Jerusalem; he did what was evil in the sight of the Lord. 40 King Nebuchadnezzar of Babylon came up against him; he bound him with a chain of bronze and took him away to Babylon. 41 Nebuchadnezzar also took some holy vessels of the Lord, and carried them away, and stored them in his temple in Babylon. 42 But the things that are reported about Jehoiakim,[e] and his uncleanness and impiety, are written in the annals of the kings.

43 His son Jehoiachin[f] became king in his place; when he was made king he was eighteen years old, 44 and he reigned three months and ten days in Jerusalem. He did what was evil in the sight of the Lord. 45 A year later Nebuchadnezzar sent and removed him to Babylon, with the holy vessels of the Lord, 46 and made Zedekiah king of Judea and Jerusalem.

1.33 2 Kings 22.8-23.3; 2 Chr 34.14-33
1.34 2 Chr 36.1-10; 2 Kings 23.30; Jer 22.11
1.35 2 Kings 23.31
1.37 2 Kings 23.34
1.39 2 Kings 23.36-37
1.40 2 Kings 24.1; 2 Chr 33.11
1.41 2 Kings 24.13
1.42 2 Kings 24.5
1.43 2 Kings 24.8
1.44 2 Kings 24.9
1.45 2 Kings 24.13
1.46 2 Kings 24.17; 2 Chr 36.11-21; 2 Kings 24.18; Jer 52.1
1.47 2 Kings 24.19; Jer 21.1-7
1.48 2 Kings 25.1; Jer 52.3; Ezek 17.15
1.49 2 Chr 33.3-5; 2 Esd 10.22
1.50 Jer 25.3-4; 35.15; 44.4
1.51 2 Chr 30.10; Jer 5.12-13
1.52 Ezra 5.12; 1 Esd 6.15
1.53 Jer 52.10; 2 Macc 5.13
1.54 1 Kings 25.13-17; Ezra 1.7; Jer 52.17-23
1.55 2 Kings 25.9; Ps 74.7; Jer 52.13
1.56 2 Kings 25.11; Jer 39.9; 52.15

The Fall of Jerusalem

Zedekiah was twenty-one years old, and he reigned eleven years. 47 He also did what was evil in the sight of the Lord, and did not heed the words that were spoken by the prophet Jeremiah from the mouth of the Lord. 48 Although King Nebuchadnezzar had made him swear by the name of the Lord, he broke his oath and rebelled; he stiffened his neck and hardened his heart and transgressed the laws of the Lord, the God of Israel. 49 Even the leaders of the people and of the priests committed many acts of sacrilege and lawlessness beyond all the unclean deeds of all the nations, and polluted the temple of the Lord in Jerusalem—the temple that God had made holy. 50 The God of their ancestors sent his messenger to call them back, because he would have spared them and his dwelling place. 51 But they mocked his messengers, and whenever the Lord spoke, they scoffed at his prophets, 52 until in his anger against his people because of their ungodly acts he gave command to bring against them the kings of the Chaldeans. 53 These killed their young men with the sword around their holy temple, and did not spare young man or young woman,[g] old man or child, for he gave them all into their hands. 54 They took all the holy vessels of the Lord, great and small, the treasure chests of the Lord, and the royal stores, and carried them away to Babylon. 55 They burned the house of the Lord, broke down the walls of Jerusalem, burned their towers with fire, 56 and utterly destroyed all its glorious things. The survivors he led away to Babylon with the sword, 57 and they were servants to him and to his sons until the Persians began to reign, in fulfillment of the word of the Lord by the mouth of Jeremiah, 58 saying, "Until the land

1.57 Jer 27.7; Dan 5.24-31 **1.58** Jer 25.12; 29.10; Lev 25.4; 26.34

d 2 Kings 23.30; 2 Chr 36.1 *Jehoahaz*
e Gk *him* f Gk *Jehoiakim* g Gk *virgin*

has enjoyed its sabbaths, it shall
keep sabbath all the time of its
desolation until the completion of
seventy years."

Cyrus Permits the Exiles to Return

2 In the first year of Cyrus as
king of the Persians, so that
the word of the Lord by the
mouth of Jeremiah might be
accomplished— 2 the Lord stirred
up the spirit of King Cyrus of the
Persians, and he made a proclamation throughout all his kingdom
and also put it in writing:
3 "Thus says Cyrus king of the
Persians: The Lord of Israel, the
Lord Most High, has made me king
of the world, 4 and he has commanded me to build him a house
at Jerusalem, which is in Judea. 5 If
any of you, therefore, are of his
people, may your Lord be with you;
go up to Jerusalem, which is in Judea, and build the house of the
Lord of Israel—he is the Lord who
dwells in Jerusalem, 6 and let each
of you, wherever you may live, be
helped by the people of your place
with gold and silver, 7 with gifts
and with horses and cattle, besides
the other things added as votive
offerings for the temple of the Lord
that is in Jerusalem."
8 Then arose the heads of families of the tribes of Judah and Benjamin, and the priests and the Levites, and all whose spirit the Lord
had stirred to go up to build the
house in Jerusalem for the Lord;
9 their neighbors helped them with
everything, with silver and gold,
with horses and cattle, and with a
very great number of votive offerings from many whose hearts were
stirred.
10 King Cyrus also brought out
the holy vessels of the Lord that
Nebuchadnezzar had carried away
from Jerusalem and stored in his
temple of idols. 11 When King Cyrus of the Persians brought these
out, he gave them to Mithridates,
his treasurer, 12 and by him they
were given to Sheshbazzar,[h] the
governor of Judea. 13 The number
of these was: one thousand gold
cups, one thousand silver cups,
twenty-nine silver censers, thirty
gold bowls, two thousand four
hundred ten silver bowls, and one
thousand other vessels. 14 All the
vessels were handed over, gold and
silver, five thousand four hundred
sixty-nine, 15 and they were carried
back by Sheshbazzar with the returning exiles from Babylon to Jerusalem.

Opposition to Rebuilding Jerusalem

16 In the time of King Artaxerxes of the Persians, Bishlam,
Mithridates, Tabeel, Rehum, Beltethmus, the scribe Shimshai, and
the rest of their associates, living
in Samaria and other places, wrote
him the following letter, against
those who were living in Judea and
Jerusalem:
17 "To King Artaxerxes our
lord, your servants the recorder Rehum and the scribe Shimshai and
the other members of their council, and the judges in Coelesyria
and Phoenicia: 18 Let it now be
known to our lord the king that the
Jews who came up from you to us
have gone to Jerusalem and are
building that rebellious and
wicked city, repairing its market
places and walls and laying the
foundations for a temple. 19 Now if
this city is built and the walls finished, they will not only refuse to
pay tribute but will even resist
kings. 20 Since the building of the
temple is now going on, we think it
best not to neglect such a matter,
21 but to speak to our lord the king,
in order that, if it seems good to
you, search may be made in the
records of your ancestors. 22 You
will find in the annals what has
been written about them, and will
learn that this city was rebellious,
troubling both kings and other cities, 23 and that the Jews were rebels and kept setting up blockades
in it from of old. That is why this
city was laid waste. 24 Therefore we
now make known to you, O lord
and king, that if this city is built

2.1 2 Chr 36.22-23; Ezra 1.1-4; Isa 44.28; 45.1; Dan 6.28; Jer 25.12; 29.10 **2.4** Ezra 5.13 **2.5** Ezra 3.8-10; 6.13-15; 1 Esd 5.56-59; 1 Kings 8.13; Joel 3.17,21; Zech 8.3 **2.7** Num 29.39; 2 Chr 24.8-11 **2.8** Ezra 1.5-11; Phil 2.13 **2.10** 2 Kings 14.13; 2 Chr 36.7; Ezra 5.14; 6.5 **2.12** Ezra 5.14 **2.16** Ezra 4.7-24; Neh 2.1; Add Esth 1.1-2; 1 Esd 8.1; Ezra 4.1-4 **2.17** 1 Macc 10.69; 2 Macc 3.5,8; 4.4 **2.18** Neh 3.1-32; 6.15; Ezra 3.10 **2.21** Ezra 5.17; 6.1 **2.23** 1 Kings 24.1; 25.1

[h] Gk *Sanabassaros*

and its walls finished, you will no
longer have access to Coelesyria
and Phoenicia."
25 Then the king, in reply to the
recorder Rehum, Beltethmus, the
scribe Shimshai, and the others associated with them and living in
Samaria and Syria and Phoenicia,
wrote as follows:
26 "I have read the letter that
you sent me. So I ordered search to
be made, and it has been found
that this city from of old has fought
against kings, 27 that the people in
it were given to rebellion and war,
and that mighty and cruel kings
ruled in Jerusalem and exacted
tribute from Coelesyria and Phoenicia. 28 Therefore I have now issued orders to prevent these people from building the city and to
take care that nothing more be
done 29 and that such wicked proceedings go no further to the an-
noyance of kings."
30 Then, when the letter from
King Artaxerxes was read, Rehum
and the scribe Shimshai and their
associates went quickly to Jerusalem, with cavalry and a large number of armed troops, and began to
hinder the builders. And the building of the temple in Jerusalem
stopped until the second year of
the reign of King Darius of the Persians.

The Debate of the Three Bodyguards

3 Now King Darius gave a great
banquet for all that were under him, all that were born in his
house, and all the nobles of Media
and Persia, 2 and all the satraps
and generals and governors that
were under him in the hundred
twenty-seven satrapies from India
to Ethiopia. 3 They ate and drank,
and when they were satisfied they
went away, and King Darius went
to his bedroom; he went to sleep,
but woke up again.
4 Then the three young men of
the bodyguard, who kept guard
over the person of the king, said to
one another, 5 "Let each of us state
what one thing is strongest; and to
the one whose statement seems
wisest, King Darius will give rich
gifts and great honors of victory.
6 He shall be clothed in purple, and
drink from gold cups, and sleep on
a gold bed,[i] and have a chariot
with gold bridles, and a turban of
fine linen, and a necklace around
his neck; 7 and because of his wisdom he shall sit next to Darius and
shall be called Kinsman of Darius."
8 Then each wrote his own
statement, and they sealed them
and put them under the pillow of
King Darius, 9 and said, "When the
king wakes, they will give him the
writing; and to the one whose
statement the king and the three
nobles of Persia judge to be wisest
the victory shall be given according
to what is written." 10 The first
wrote, "Wine is strongest." 11 The
second wrote, "The king is strongest." 12 The third wrote, "Women
are strongest, but above all things
truth is victor."[j]
13 When the king awoke, they
took the writing and gave it to him,
and he read it. 14 Then he sent and
summoned all the nobles of Persia
and Media and the satraps and
generals and governors and prefects, 15 and he took his seat in the
council chamber, and the writing
was read in their presence. 16 He
said, "Call the young men, and
they shall explain their statements." So they were summoned,
and came in. 17 They said to them,
"Explain to us what you have written."

The Speech about Wine

Then the first, who had spoken
of the strength of wine, began and
said: 18 "Gentlemen, how is wine
the strongest? It leads astray the
minds of all who drink it. 19 It
makes equal the mind of the king
and the orphan, of the slave and
the free, of the poor and the rich.
20 It turns every thought to feasting
and mirth, and forgets all sorrow
and debt. 21 It makes all hearts feel
rich, forgets kings and satraps, and
makes everyone talk in millions.[k]

2.26 1 Esd 2.21
2.27 1 Kings 4.21; Ps 72.8-11
2.30 Ezra 4.24
3.1 Ezra 4.5; 5.6-7; Esth 1.1-4
3.6 Judg 8.26; Esth 6.8-9; 1 Macc 10.20,62,64; Gen 41.43
3.7 1 Esd 4.42
3.12 Prov 23.23; Jn 18.37-38
3.14 1 Esd 3.1
3.18 Prov 20.1; 23.29-35; 31.4-5
3.20 Ps 104.15; Eccl 10.19; Sir 31.28; Prov 31.6-7

[i] Gk *on gold* [j] Or *but truth is victor over all things* [k] Gk *talents*

22 When people drink they forget to
be friendly with friends and kindred, and before long they draw
their swords. 23 And when they recover from the wine, they do not
remember what they have done.
24 Gentlemen, is not wine the
strongest, since it forces people to
do these things?" When he had
said this, he stopped speaking.

The Speech about the King

4 Then the second, who had
spoken of the strength of the
king, began to speak: 2 "Gentlemen, are not men strongest, who
rule over land and sea and all that
is in them? 3 But the king is stronger; he is their lord and master,
and whatever he says to them they
obey. 4 If he tells them to make war
on one another, they do it; and if
he sends them out against the enemy, they go, and conquer mountains, walls, and towers. 5 They kill
and are killed, and do not disobey
the king's command; if they win
the victory, they bring everything
to the king—whatever spoil they
take and everything else. 6 Likewise those who do not serve in the
army or make war but till the soil;
whenever they sow and reap, and
bring some to the king; and they
compel one another to pay taxes to
the king. 7 And yet he is only one
man! If he tells them to kill, they
kill; if he tells them to release, they
release; 8 if he tells them to attack,
they attack; if he tells them to lay
waste, they lay waste; if he tells
them to build, they build; 9 if he
tells them to cut down, they cut
down; if he tells them to plant,
they plant. 10 All his people and his
armies obey him. Furthermore, he
reclines, he eats and drinks and
sleeps, 11 but they keep watch
around him, and no one may go
away to attend to his own affairs,
nor do they disobey him. 12 Gentlemen, why is not the king the strongest, since he is to be obeyed in
this fashion?" And he stopped
speaking.

3.22 Isa 5.11-12; Sir 31.29 **3.23** Prov 31.5; Isa 28.7 **4.3** 2 Sam 3.21; Dan 4.24 **4.5** Eccl 8.2-5 **4.6** Lk 23.2; Rom 13.6 **4.7** 2 Sam 1.13-16; Jer 37.17-21 **4.8** 1 Esd 2.4-9

4.13 Ezra 2.2; 3.2, 8; 1 Esd 5.5,8 **4.14** 1 Esd 4.2-12; 3.18-23 **4.17** Prov 31.13, 19,21, 11-12,23 **4.20** Gen 2.24; Mk 10.7-8; Eph 5.31 **4.24** Am 4.1 **4.25** Gen 24.67; Eph 5.25; Col 3.19 **4.27** 2 Sam 12.1-5; Prov 5.1-14; 7.6-27

The Speech about Women

13 Then the third, who had spoken of women and truth (and this
was Zerubbabel), began to speak:
14 "Gentlemen, is not the king
great, and are not men many, and
is not wine strong? Who is it, then,
that rules them, or has the mastery
over them? Is it not women?
15 Women gave birth to the king
and to every people that rules over
sea and land. 16 From women they
came; and women brought up the
very men who plant the vineyards
from which comes wine. 17 Women
make men's clothes; they bring
men glory; men cannot exist without women. 18 If men gather gold
and silver or any other beautiful
thing, and then see a woman lovely
in appearance and beauty, 19 they
let all those things go, and gape at
her, and with open mouths stare at
her, and all prefer her to gold or silver or any other beautiful thing.
20 A man leaves his own father, who
brought him up, and his own country, and clings to his wife. 21 With
his wife he ends his days, with no
thought of his father or his mother
or his country. 22 Therefore you
must realize that women rule over
you!

"Do you not labor and toil, and
bring everything and give it to
women? 23 A man takes his sword,
and goes out to travel and rob and
steal and to sail the sea and rivers;
24 he faces lions, and he walks in
darkness, and when he steals and
robs and plunders, he brings it
back to the woman he loves. 25 A
man loves his wife more than his
father or his mother. 26 Many men
have lost their minds because of
women, and have become slaves
because of them. 27 Many have perished, or stumbled, or sinned because of women. 28 And now do you
not believe me?

"Is not the king great in his
power? Do not all lands fear to
touch him? 29 Yet I have seen him
with Apame, the king's concubine,
the daughter of the illustrious Bar-
tacus; she would sit at the king's
right hand 30 and take the crown

from the king's head and put it on
her own, and slap the king with her
left hand. 31 At this the king would
gaze at her with mouth agape. If
she smiles at him, he laughs; if she
loses her temper with him, he flatters her, so that she may be reconciled to him. 32 Gentlemen, why are
not women strong, since they do
such things?"

The Speech about Truth

33 Then the king and the nobles looked at one another; and he
began to speak about truth:
34 "Gentlemen, are not women
strong? The earth is vast, and
heaven is high, and the sun is swift
in its course, for it makes the circuit of the heavens and returns to
its place in one day. 35 Is not the
one who does these things great?
But truth is great, and stronger
than all things. 36 The whole earth
calls upon truth, and heaven
blesses her. All God's works[l]
quake and tremble, and with him
there is nothing unrighteous.
37 Wine is unrighteous, the king is
unrighteous, women are unrighteous, all human beings are unrighteous, all their works are unrighteous, and all such things.
There is no truth in them and in
their unrighteousness they will
perish. 38 But truth endures and is
strong forever, and lives and prevails forever and ever. 39 With it
there is no partiality or preference,
but it does what is righteous instead of anything that is unrighteous or wicked. Everyone ap-
proves its deeds, 40 and there is
nothing unrighteous in its judgment. To it belongs the strength
and the kingship and the power
and the majesty of all the ages.
Blessed be the God of truth!"
41 When he stopped speaking, all
the people shouted and said,
"Great is truth, and strongest of
all!"

Zerubbabel's Reward

42 Then the king said to him,
"Ask what you wish, even beyond
what is written, and we will give it
to you, for you have been found to
be the wisest. You shall sit next to
me, and be called my Kinsman."
43 Then he said to the king, "Remember the vow that you made on
the day when you became king, to
build Jerusalem, 44 and to send
back all the vessels that were taken
from Jerusalem, which Cyrus set
apart when he began[m] to destroy
Babylon, and vowed to send them
back there. 45 You also vowed to
build the temple, which the Edomites burned when Judea was laid
waste by the Chaldeans. 46 And
now, O lord the king, this is what I
ask and request of you, and this befits your greatness. I pray therefore
that you fulfill the vow whose fulfillment you vowed to the King of
heaven with your own lips."

47 Then King Darius got up and
kissed him, and wrote letters for
him to all the treasurers and governors and generals and satraps, that
they should give safe conduct to
him and to all who were going up
with him to build Jerusalem.
48 And he wrote letters to all the
governors in Coelesyria and Phoenicia and to those in Lebanon, to
bring cedar timber from Lebanon
to Jerusalem, and to help him
build the city. 49 He wrote in behalf
of all the Jews who were going up
from his kingdom to Judea, in the
interest of their freedom, that no
officer or satrap or governor or
treasurer should forcibly enter
their doors; 50 that all the country
that they would occupy should be
theirs without tribute; that the Idumeans should give up the villages
of the Jews that they held; 51 that
twenty talents a year should be
given for the building of the temple
until it was completed, 52 and an
additional ten talents a year for
burnt offerings to be offered on the
altar every day, in accordance with
the commandment to make seventeen offerings; 53 and that all who
came from Babylonia to build the
city should have their freedom,
they and their children and all the
priests who came. 54 He wrote also
concerning their support and the

4.31 Prov 21.9,19; 25.24
4.34 1 Esd 4.14-32; Ps 103.11; 19.4-6; Eccl 1.5; Sir 43.1-5
4.36 Ps 119.42, 160
4.37 Ps 14.2-3; 53.2-3; Rom 3.10-12
4.38 Ps 119.89; Jn 17.17
4.39 Acts 10.34; Rom 2.11; Eph 6.9
4.40 Jn 8.32; 14.6; 1 Esd 8.25; Isa 45.19
4.42 Esth 5.3; Mk 6.23; 1 Esd 3.7
4.43 2 Chr 36.22-23; Ezra 1.1-4; 6.5; 1 Esd 2.3-7
4.44 Isa 44.28; 45.1-2
4.45 Ps 137.7; Ob 11-14
4.46 Tob 13.7,11, 16
4.47 Ezra 6.3-12; Neh 2.7; 1 Macc 12.4
4.48 Ezra 6.8; Neh 2.8
4.50 1 Macc 11.34-35; 10.15-16; Mk 3.8
4.52 Ezra 6.9-10
4.53 Ezra 1.5,11; 2.1-70

[l] Gk *All the works* [m] Cn: Gk *vowed*

priests' vestments in which[n] they
were to minister. 55 He wrote that
the support for the Levites should
be provided until the day when the
temple would be finished and Jerusalem built. 56 He wrote that land
and wages should be provided for
all who guarded the city. 57 And he
sent back from Babylon all the vessels that Cyrus had set apart; everything that Cyrus had ordered to be
done, he also commanded to be
done and to be sent to Jerusalem.

Zerubbabel's Prayer

58 When the young man went
out, he lifted up his face to heaven
toward Jerusalem, and praised the
King of heaven, saying, 59 "From
you comes the victory; from you
comes wisdom, and yours is the
glory. I am your servant. 60 Blessed
are you, who have given me wisdom; I give you thanks, O Lord of
our ancestors."

61 So he took the letters, and
went to Babylon and told this to all
his kindred. 62 And they praised the
God of their ancestors, because he
had given them release and permission 63 to go up and build Jerusalem and the temple that is called
by his name; and they feasted, with
music and rejoicing, for seven
days.

List of the Returning Exiles

5 After this the heads of ancestral houses were chosen to go
up, according to their tribes, with
their wives and sons and daughters, and their male and female
servants, and their livestock. 2 And
Darius sent with them a thousand
cavalry to take them back to Jerusalem in safety, with the music of
drums and flutes; 3 all their kindred were making merry. And he
made them go up with them.

4 These are the names of the
men who went up, according to
their ancestral houses in the
tribes, over their groups: 5 the
priests, the descendants of Phinehas son of Aaron; Jeshua son of
Jozadak son of Seraiah and Joakim
son of Zerubbabel son of Shealtiel,
of the house of David, of the lineage of Phares, of the tribe of Judah, 6 who spoke wise words before
King Darius of the Persians, in the
second year of his reign, in the
month of Nisan, the first month.

7 These are the Judeans who
came up out of their sojourn in exile, whom King Nebuchadnezzar of
Babylon had carried away to Babylon 8 and who returned to Jerusalem and the rest of Judea, each to
his own town. They came with Zerubbabel and Jeshua, Nehemiah,
Seraiah, Resaiah, Eneneus, Mordecai, Beelsarus, Aspharasus, Ree-
liah, Rehum, and Baanah, their
leaders.

9 The number of those of the
nation and their leaders: the descendants of Parosh, two thousand
one hundred seventy-two. The descendants of Shephatiah, four
hundred seventy-two. 10 The descendants of Arah, seven hundred
fifty-six. 11 The descendants of
Pahath-moab, of the descendants
of Jeshua and Joab, two thousand
eight hundred twelve. 12 The descendants of Elam, one thousand
two hundred fifty-four. The descendants of Zattu, nine hundred
forty-five. The descendants of
Chorbe, seven hundred five. The
descendants of Bani, six hundred
forty-eight. 13 The descendants of
Bebai, six hundred twenty-three.
The descendants of Azgad, one
thousand three hundred twenty-
two. 14 The descendants of Adonikam, six hundred sixty-seven. The
descendants of Bigvai, two thousand sixty-six. The descendants of
Adin, four hundred fifty-four.
15 The descendants of Ater, namely
of Hezekiah, ninety-two. The descendants of Kilan and Azetas,
sixty-seven. The descendants of
Azaru, four hundred thirty-two.
16 The descendants of Annias, one
hundred one. The descendants of
Arom. The descendants of Bezai,
three hundred twenty-three. The
descendants of Arsiphurith, one
hundred twelve. 17 The descendants of Baiterus, three thousand
five. The descendants of Bethlo-

4.57 Ezra 1.7-11; 1 Esd 2.11-14 **4.59** Deut 20.4; 2 Sam 8.6; Ps 20.9; Prov 21.31; Dan 2.21; Wis 7.7; Sir 1.1; Jas 1.5; 1 Chr 29.11; Ps 29.1-3; Mt 6.13 **4.60** Ps 72.18; Dan 2.20; Tob 11.14; 13.17 **4.62** Ex 3.13; Deut 1.11; 2 Chr 34.32-33 **4.63** Ezra 6.22 **5.1** Ex 6.14; Num 1.2; 1 Esd 1.5 **5.2** 1 Kings 9.19; Ezra 8.22; Neh 2.9 **5.4** Ezra 2.1-70; Neh 7.6-73 **5.5** Num 25.7-13; Josh 22.30-32; 1 Chr 9.20; Ezra 3.2,8-9; 5.2; Sir 49.12, 11; 1 Esd 4.13 **5.9** Ezra 8.3; 1 Esd 8.30

[n] Gk *in what priestly vestments*

mon, one hundred twenty-three.
[18]Those from Netophah, fifty-five.
Those from Anathoth, one hundred fifty-eight. Those from Beth-
asmoth, forty-two. [19]Those from
Kiriatharim, twenty-five. Those
from Chephirah and Beeroth,
seven hundred forty-three. [20]The
Chadiasans and Ammidians, four
hundred twenty-two. Those from
Kirama and Geba, six hundred
twenty-one. [21]Those from Maca-
lon, one hundred twenty-two.
Those from Betolio, fifty-two. The
descendants of Niphish, one hundred fifty-six. [22]The descendants
of the other Calamolalus and Ono,
seven hundred twenty-five. The descendants of Jerechus, three hundred forty-five. [23]The descendants
of Senaah, three thousand three
hundred thirty.

24 The priests: the descendants
of Jedaiah son of Jeshua, of the descendants of Anasib, nine hundred
seventy-two. The descendants of
Immer, one thousand and fifty-
two. [25]The descendants of Pashhur, one thousand two hundred
forty-seven. The descendants of
Charme, one thousand seventeen.

26 The Levites: the descendants of Jeshua and Kadmiel and
Bannas and Sudias, seventy-four.
[27]The temple singers: the descendants of Asaph, one hundred
twenty-eight. [28]The gatekeepers:
the descendants of Shallum, the
descendants of Ater, the descendants of Talmon, the descendants
of Akkub, the descendants of Hatita, the descendants of Shobai, in
all one hundred thirty-nine.

29 The temple servants: the descendants of Esau, the descendants of Hasupha, the descendants
of Tabbaoth, the descendants of
Keros, the descendants of Sua, the
descendants of Padon, the descendants of Lebanah, the descendants
of Hagabah, [30]the descendants of
Akkub, the descendants of Uthai,
the descendants of Ketab, the descendants of Hagab, the descendants of Subai, the descendants of
Hana, the descendants of Cathua,
the descendants of Geddur, [31]the
descendants of Jairus, the descendants of Daisan, the descendants
of Noeba, the descendants of Chezib, the descendants of Gazera, the
descendants of Uzza, the descendants of Phinoe, the descendants
of Hasrah, the descendants of Bas-
thai, the descendants of Asnah,
the descendants of Maani, the
descendants of Nephisim, the
descendants of Acuph,[o] the descendants of Hakupha, the
descendants of Asur, the descendants of Pharakim, the descendants of Bazluth, [32]the descendants of Mehida, the descendants
of Cutha, the descendants of Cha-
rea, the descendants of Barkos, the
descendants of Serar, the descendants of Temah, the descendants
of Neziah, the descendants of Hatipha.

33 The descendants of Solomon's servants: the descendants of
Assaphioth, the descendants of Peruda, the descendants of Jaalah,
the descendants of Lozon, the descendants of Isdael, the descendants of Shephatiah, [34]the descendants of Agia, the descendants of
Pochereth-hazzebaim, the descendants of Sarothie, the descendants
of Masiah, the descendants of Gas,
the descendants of Addus, the descendants of Subas, the descendants of Apherra, the descendants
of Barodis, the descendants of
Shaphat, the descendants of Allon.

35 All the temple servants and
the descendants of Solomon's servants were three hundred seventy-
two.

36 The following are those who
came up from Tel-melah and Tel-
harsha, under the leadership of
Cherub, Addan, and Immer,
[37]though they could not prove by
their ancestral houses or lineage
that they belonged to Israel: the
descendants of Delaiah son of Tobiah, and the descendants of Nekoda, six hundred fifty-two.

38 Of the priests the following
had assumed the priesthood but
were not found registered: the descendants of Habaiah, the descendants of Hakkoz, and the descen-

5.24 1 Chr 24.7-18
5.26 1 Chr 23.3-23
5.27 1 Chr 25.1-31; 1 Esd 1.15
5.28 1 Chr 26.1-19; 1 Esd 1.16
5.29 1 Chr 9.2; Ezra 7.7,24; Neh 10.28
5.37 Num 3.10; 16.39-40; Ezra 2.62
5.38 Num 3.10; 16.39-40; 2 Sam 17.27; 2 Kings 2.7

[o] Other ancient authorities read *Acub* or *Acum*

dants of Jaddus who had married
Agia, one of the daughters of Barzillai, and was called by his name.
39 When a search was made in the
register and the genealogy of these
men was not found, they were excluded from serving as priests.
40 And Nehemiah and Attharias[p]
told them not to share in the holy
things until a high priest should
appear wearing Urim and Thummim.[q]

41 All those of Israel, twelve or
more years of age, besides male
and female servants, were forty-
two thousand three hundred sixty;
42 their male and female servants
were seven thousand three hundred thirty-seven; there were two
hundred forty-five musicians and
singers. 43 There were four hundred
thirty-five camels, and seven thousand thirty-six horses, two hundred forty-five mules, and five
thousand five hundred twenty-five
donkeys.

44 Some of the heads of families, when they came to the temple
of God that is in Jerusalem, vowed
that, to the best of their ability,
they would erect the house on its
site, 45 and that they would give to
the sacred treasury for the work a
thousand minas of gold, five thousand minas of silver, and one hundred priests' vestments.

46 The priests, the Levites, and
some of the people[r] settled in Jerusalem and its vicinity; and the
temple singers, the gatekeepers,
and all Israel in their towns.

Worship Begins Again

47 When the seventh month
came, and the Israelites were all in
their own homes, they gathered
with a single purpose in the square
before the first gate toward the
east. 48 Then Jeshua son of Jozadak, with his fellow priests, and
Zerubbabel son of Shealtiel, with
his kinsmen, took their places and
prepared the altar of the God of Israel, 49 to offer burnt offerings
upon it, in accordance with the directions in the book of Moses the
man of God. 50 And some joined
them from the other peoples of the
land. And they erected the altar in
its place, for all the peoples of the
land were hostile to them and were
stronger than they; and they offered sacrifices at the proper times
and burnt offerings to the Lord
morning and evening. 51 They kept
the festival of booths, as it is commanded in the law, and offered the
proper sacrifices every day, 52 and
thereafter the regular offerings and
sacrifices on sabbaths and at new
moons and at all the consecrated
feasts. 53 And all who had made any
vow to God began to offer sacrifices to God, from the new moon of
the seventh month, though the
temple of God was not yet built.
54 They gave money to the masons
and the carpenters, and food and
drink 55 and carts[s] to the Sidonians and the Tyrians, to bring cedar
logs from Lebanon and convey
them in rafts to the harbor of
Joppa, according to the decree
that they had in writing from King
Cyrus of the Persians.

The Foundations of the Temple Laid

56 In the second year after their
coming to the temple of God in Jerusalem, in the second month, Zerubbabel son of Shealtiel and
Jeshua son of Jozadak made a beginning, together with their kindred and the levitical priests and
all who had come back to Jerusalem from exile; 57 and they laid the
foundation of the temple of God
on the new moon of the second
month in the second year after
they came to Judea and Jerusalem.
58 They appointed the Levites who
were twenty or more years of age to
have charge of the work of the
Lord. And Jeshua arose, and his
sons and kindred and his brother
Kadmiel and the sons of Jeshua
Emadabun and the sons of Joda
son of Iliadun, with their sons and
kindred, all the Levites, pressing
forward the work on the house of
God with a single purpose.

5.39 Ezra 2.62
5.40 Ex 28.30; Lev 8.8; Num 27.21
5.44 Prov 3.9; 1 Cor 16.2
5.45 Ex 25.1-2; 1 Chr 29.6-9; Ezra 2.68-69
5.46 Ezra 3.1; Neh 11.1-5
5.47 Ezra 3.1-7; Neh 8.1
5.48 Ezra 2.2; Neh 12.1; Gen 12.7-8; Ex 17.15; 20.24-26; 1 Kings 18.30
5.49 Deut 12.5-6
5.50 Ezra 4.4-5; Num 28.2-4
5.51 Lev 23.33-36; Num 29.12-38; Neh 8.14
5.52 Num 28.3,11, 19,26; 29.39
5.53 Lev 27.1-29
5.54 2 Chr 24.8-11; Ezra 1.6
5.55 2 Chr 2.8-10
5.56 Ezra 3.8-4.3; 1 Esd 5.48; 2.8; 5.1-3
5.57 1 Kings 6.37
5.58 1 Chr 23.24, 27; 1 Esd 5.26

[p] Or *the governor* [q] Gk *Manifestation and Truth* [r] Or *those who were of the people* [s] Meaning of Gk uncertain

So the builders built the temple of the Lord. 59 And the priests stood arrayed in their vestments, with musical instruments and trumpets, and the Levites, the sons of Asaph, with cymbals, 60 praising the Lord and blessing him, according to the directions of King David of Israel; 61 they sang hymns, giving thanks to the Lord, "For his goodness and his glory are forever upon all Israel." 62 And all the people sounded trumpets and shouted with a great shout, praising the Lord for the erection of the house of the Lord. 63 Some of the levitical priests and heads of ancestral houses, old men who had seen the former house, came to the building of this one with outcries and loud weeping, 64 while many came with trumpets and a joyful noise, 65 so that the people could not hear the trumpets because of the weeping of the people.

For the multitude sounded the trumpets loudly, so that the sound was heard far away; 66 and when the enemies of the tribe of Judah and Benjamin heard it, they came to find out what the sound of the trumpets meant. 67 They learned that those who had returned from exile were building the temple for the Lord God of Israel. 68 So they approached Zerubbabel and Jeshua and the heads of the ancestral houses and said to them, "We will build with you. 69 For we obey your Lord just as you do and we have been sacrificing to him ever since the days of King Esarhaddon[t] of the Assyrians, who brought us here." 70 But Zerubbabel and Jeshua and the heads of the ancestral houses in Israel said to them, "You have nothing to do with us in building the house for the Lord our God, 71 for we alone will build it for the Lord of Israel, as Cyrus, the king of the Persians, has commanded us." 72 But the peoples of the land pressed hard[u] upon those in Judea, cut off their supplies, and hindered their building; 73 and by plots and demagoguery and uprisings they prevented the completion of the building as long as King Cyrus lived. They were kept from building for two years, until the reign of Darius.

Work on the Temple Begins Again

6 Now in the second year of the reign of Darius, the prophets Haggai and Zechariah son of Iddo prophesied to the Jews who were in Judea and Jerusalem; they prophesied to them in the name of the Lord God of Israel. 2 Then Zerubbabel son of Shealtiel and Jeshua son of Jozadak began to build the house of the Lord that is in Jerusalem, with the help of the prophets of the Lord who were with them.

3 At the same time Sisinnes the governor of Syria and Phoenicia and Sathrabuzanes and their associates came to them and said, 4 "By whose order are you building this house and this roof and finishing all the other things? And who are the builders that are finishing these things?" 5 Yet the elders of the Jews were dealt with kindly, for the providence of the Lord was over the captives; 6 they were not prevented from building until word could be sent to Darius concerning them and a report made.

7 A copy of the letter that Sisinnes the governor of Syria and Phoenicia, and Sathrabuzanes, and their associates the local rulers in Syria and Phoenicia, wrote and sent to Darius:

8 "To King Darius, greetings. Let it be fully known to our lord the king that, when we went to the country of Judea and entered the city of Jerusalem, we found the elders of the Jews, who had been in exile, 9 building in the city of Jerusalem a great new house for the Lord, of hewn stone, with costly timber laid in the walls. 10 These operations are going on rapidly, and the work is prospering in their hands and being completed with all splendor and care. 11 Then we

5.59 1 Chr 6.31; 16.5-6,42; 25.1
5.61 Tob 13.17; Wis 10.20; Eph 5.19; Col 3.16; 1 Chr 25.3; Ps 100.4; 147.7; 2 Chr 7.3; Ps 145.7
5.64 Ezra 3.12
5.66 Ezra 4.7-10
5.69 2 Kings 17.24,32-33; 19.37
5.70 Neh 2.20
5.71 Ezra 1.1-3; 1 Esd 2.3-7
5.72 Ezra 4.4-6
5.73 Ezra 4.24
6.1 Ezra 4.24-5.17; Hag 1.1-4; 2.1-4; Zech 1.1; 4.9; 6.15
6.2 Ezra 2.2; 3.2; 1 Esd 5.48,56
6.3 1 Esd 6.27
6.4 1 Esd 6.11
6.5 Ezra 7.6,28; Wis 14.3
6.7 Ezra 4.11; 5.6
6.9 1 Esd 5.56-58
6.11 1 Esd 6.4

[t] Gk *Asbasareth* [u] Meaning of Gk uncertain

asked these elders, 'At whose command are you building this house
and laying the foundations of this
structure?' 12 In order that we
might inform you in writing who
the leaders are, we questioned
them and asked them for a list of
the names of those who are at their
head. 13 They answered us, 'We are
the servants of the Lord who created the heaven and the earth.
14 The house was built many years
ago by a king of Israel who was
great and strong, and it was finished. 15 But when our ancestors
sinned against the Lord of Israel
who is in heaven, and provoked
him, he gave them over into the
hands of King Nebuchadnezzar of
Babylon, king of the Chaldeans;
16 and they pulled down the house,
and burned it, and carried the people away captive to Babylon. 17 But
in the first year that Cyrus reigned
over the country of Babylonia, King
Cyrus wrote that this house should
be rebuilt. 18 And the holy vessels
of gold and of silver, which Nebuchadnezzar had taken out of the
house in Jerusalem and stored in
his own temple, these King Cyrus
took out again from the temple in
Babylon, and they were delivered
to Zerubbabel and Sheshbazzar[v]
the governor 19 with the command
that he should take all these vessels back and put them in the temple at Jerusalem, and that this
temple of the Lord should be rebuilt on its site. 20 Then this Sheshbazzar, after coming here, laid the
foundations of the house of the
Lord that is in Jerusalem. Although it has been in process of
construction from that time until
now, it has not yet reached completion.' 21 Now therefore, O king,
if it seems wise to do so, let search
be made in the royal archives of
our lord[w] the king that are in Babylon; 22 if it is found that the building of the house of the Lord in Jerusalem was done with the consent
of King Cyrus, and if it is approved
by our lord the king, let him send
us directions concerning these
things."

Official Permission Granted

23 Then Darius commanded
that search be made in the royal archives that were deposited in Babylon. And in Ecbatana, the fortress
that is in the country of Media, a
scroll[x] was found in which this
was recorded: 24 "In the first year of
the reign of King Cyrus, he ordered
the building of the house of the
Lord in Jerusalem, where they sacrifice with perpetual fire; 25 its
height to be sixty cubits and its
width sixty cubits, with three
courses of hewn stone and one
course of new native timber; the
cost to be paid from the treasury of
King Cyrus; 26 and that the holy
vessels of the house of the Lord,
both of gold and of silver, which
Nebuchadnezzar took out of the
house in Jerusalem and carried
away to Babylon, should be restored to the house in Jerusalem,
to be placed where they had been."
27 So Darius[y] commanded Sisinnes the governor of Syria and
Phoenicia, and Sathrabuzanes,
and their associates, and those
who were appointed as local rulers
in Syria and Phoenicia, to keep
away from the place, and to permit
Zerubbabel, the servant of the Lord
and governor of Judea, and the elders of the Jews to build this house
of the Lord on its site. 28 "And I
command that it be built completely, and that full effort be
made to help those who have returned from the exile of Judea, until the house of the Lord is finished; 29 and that out of the tribute
of Coelesyria and Phoenicia a portion be scrupulously given to these
men, that is, to Zerubbabel the
governor, for sacrifices to the Lord,
for bulls and rams and lambs,
30 and likewise wheat and salt and
wine and oil, regularly every year,
without quibbling, for daily use as
the priests in Jerusalem may indicate, 31 in order that libations may
be made to the Most High God for
the king and his children, and
prayers be offered for their lives."

6.13 Lev 25.55; Ps 113.1; 134.1; Dan 3.26,28; Gen 1.1; Ps 33.6; Isa 42.5; Jdt 13.18
6.14 1 Kings 6.1-38
6.15 Ezra 9.6-7; Neh 9.16-31; Dan 9.4-14
6.16 2 Kings 25.9; 2 Chr 36.19; 1 Esd 1.55; 2 Kings 24.14; 25.11; 2 Chr 36.20; 1 Esd 1.56
6.17 Ezra 1.2-4; 1 Esd 2.3-7
6.18 Ezra 1.7-11; 1 Esd 2.10-15
6.20 Ezra 2.1-2; 1 Esd 4.61-5.6; 5.57
6.21 Ezra 6.1; 1 Esd 6.23
6.23 Ezra 6.1-12; 1 Esd 6.21
6.24 Ezra 1.1; 1 Esd 2.1
6.25 1 Kings 6.36; 1 Esd 8.18
6.26 1 Esd 6.18
6.27 1 Esd 6.3,7
6.29 Ezra 6.8; 1 Esd 2.19; 4.50; 5.49-52
6.31 Bar 1.11; 1 Tim 2.1-2

[v] Gk *Sanabassarus*
[w] Other ancient authorities read *of Cyrus*
[x] Other authorities read *passage*
[y] Gk *he*

32 He commanded that if anyone should transgress or nullify
any of the things herein written,[z]
a beam should be taken out of the
house of the perpetrator, who then
shall be impaled upon it, and all
property forfeited to the king.
33 “Therefore may the Lord,
whose name is there called upon,
destroy every king and nation that
shall stretch out their hands to
hinder or damage that house of the
Lord in Jerusalem.
34 “I, King Darius, have decreed that it be done with all diligence as here prescribed.”

The Temple Is Dedicated

7 Then Sisinnes the governor of
Coelesyria and Phoenicia, and
Sathrabuzanes, and their associates, following the orders of King
Darius, [2]supervised the holy work
with very great care, assisting the
elders of the Jews and the chief officers of the temple. [3]The holy
work prospered, while the prophets Haggai and Zechariah prophesied; [4]and they completed it by
the command of the Lord God of
Israel. So with the consent of Cyrus
and Darius and Artaxerxes, kings
of the Persians, [5]the holy house
was finished by the twenty-third
day of the month of Adar, in the
sixth year of King Darius. [6]And the
people of Israel, the priests, the
Levites, and the rest of those who
returned from exile who joined
them, did according to what was
written in the book of Moses.
[7]They offered at the dedication of
the temple of the Lord one hundred bulls, two hundred rams, four
hundred lambs, [8]and twelve male
goats for the sin of all Israel, according to the number of the
twelve leaders of the tribes of Israel; [9]and the priests and the Levites stood arrayed in their vestments, according to kindred, for
the services of the Lord God of Israel in accordance with the book of
Moses; and the gatekeepers were
at each gate.

6.32 Ezra 7.26; Dan 2.5; 3.29
6.33 Deut 12.5,11; 2 Chr 5.6-10, 20; 1 Esd 4.63
7.1 Ezra 6.13-18; 1 Esd 6.27-31
7.3 Ezra 5.1-2; Hag 1.1-4; Zech 1.4; 1 Esd 6.1
7.7 1 Kings 8.63; 2 Chr 7.5
7.8 Ezra 8.35
7.9 Ex 28.2-4; 1 Macc 3.49; 1 Esd 1.2; 1 Chr 26.1; Ezra 2.42,70
7.10 Ezra 6.19-22; Ex 12.6; 2 Chr 30.1-27; 1 Esd 1.1-21
7.11 2 Chr 29.34; 30.15
7.13 Neh 9.2; 10.28; Ezra 9.11
7.14 Ex 12.15; Lev 23.6-8
8.1 Ezra 7.1-10; 4.7; Neh 2.1; 1 Esd 3.16; Neh 8.1
8.2 Num 25.7-11; 1 Esd 5.5
8.3 2 Chr 23.18; 30.16; Ezra 3.2; 1 Cor 9.9
8.4 1 Esd 8.80
8.5 Ezra 8.1-20; 1 Esd 8.28-40
8.6 Ezra 7.28; 8.18,22,31

The Passover

10 The people of Israel who
came from exile kept the passover
on the fourteenth day of the first
month, after the priests and the
Levites were purified together.
[11]Not all of the returned captives
were purified, but the Levites were
all purified together,[a] [12]and they
sacrificed the passover lamb for all
the returned captives and for their
kindred the priests and for themselves. [13]The people of Israel who
had returned from exile ate it, all
those who had separated themselves from the abominations of
the peoples of the land and sought
the Lord. [14]They also kept the festival of unleavened bread seven
days, rejoicing before the Lord,
[15]because he had changed the will
of the king of the Assyrians concerning them, to strengthen their
hands for the service of the Lord
God of Israel.

Ezra Arrives in Jerusalem

8 After these things, when Artaxerxes, the king of the Persians, was reigning, Ezra came, the
son of Seraiah son of Azariah son
of Hilkiah son of Shallum [2]son of
Zadok son of Ahitub son of Amariah son of Uzzi son of Bukki son of
Abishua son of Phineas son of Eleazar son of Aaron the high[b] priest.
[3]This Ezra came up from Babylon
as a scribe skilled in the law of Moses, which was given by the God of
Israel; [4]and the king showed him
honor, for he found favor before
the king[c] in all his requests.
[5]There came up with him to Jerusalem some of the people of Israel
and some of the priests and Levites
and temple singers and gatekeepers and temple servants, [6]in the
seventh year of the reign of Artaxerxes, in the fifth month (this was
the king's seventh year); for they
left Babylon on the new moon of
the first month and arrived in Jerusalem on the new moon of the fifth
month, by the prosperous journey

[z] Other authorities read *stated above* or *added in writing* [a] Meaning of Gk uncertain
[b] Gk *the first* [c] Gk *him*

that the Lord gave them.[d] 7For
Ezra possessed great knowledge,
so that he omitted nothing from
the law of the Lord or the commandments, but taught all Israel
all the ordinances and judgments.

The King's Mandate

8 The following is a copy of the
written commission from King
Artaxerxes that was delivered to
Ezra the priest and reader of the
law of the Lord:
9 "King Artaxerxes to Ezra the
priest and reader of the law of the
Lord, greeting. 10In accordance
with my gracious decision, I have
given orders that those of the Jewish nation and of the priests and
Levites and others in our realm,
those who freely choose to do so,
may go with you to Jerusalem.
11Let as many as are so disposed,
therefore, leave with you, just as I
and the seven Friends who are my
counselors have decided, 12in order to look into matters in Judea
and Jerusalem, in accordance with
what is in the law of the Lord,
13and to carry to Jerusalem the
gifts for the Lord of Israel that I
and my Friends have vowed, and to
collect for the Lord in Jerusalem
all the gold and silver that may be
found in the country of Babylonia,
14together with what is given by
the nation for the temple of their
Lord that is in Jerusalem, both
gold and silver for bulls and rams
and lambs and what goes with
them, 15so as to offer sacrifices on
the altar of their Lord that is in Jerusalem. 16Whatever you and your
kindred are minded to do with the
gold and silver, perform it in accordance with the will of your God;
17deliver the holy vessels of the
Lord that are given you for the use
of the temple of your God that is in
Jerusalem. 18And whatever else
occurs to you as necessary for the
temple of your God, you may provide out of the royal treasury.
19 "I, King Artaxerxes, have
commanded the treasurers of Syria
and Phoenicia that whatever Ezra
the priest and reader of the law of
the Most High God sends for, they

8.7 Neh 8.1-8
8.8 Ezra 7.11-26
8.11 Esth 1.14
8.13 Ezra 8.25; 1.4; 1 Esd 2.6
8.14 Lev 4.1-21; Deut 12.5-14
8.17 2 Esd 2.10
8.18 Ezra 6.4; 1 Esd 6.25
8.19 1 Esd 8.7; Gen 14.18-22; Ps 7.17; Dan 4.2; 5.18
8.20 Ezra 6.9; 1 Esd 6.30
8.22 1 Macc 10.29-31
8.23 Ex 18.21; Deut 16.18; 1 Esd 6.7; Neh 8.1-8
8.24 1 Esd 6.32
8.25 Ezra 7.27-28; 1 Chr 29.10; Ps 72.19; 1 Esd 4.40; Ezra 6.22
8.26 Add Esth 2.18; 1 Macc 10.65; 11.57
8.27 Ezra 8.18,22, 31; 1 Esd 8.6
8.28 Ezra 8.1-20
8.29 1 Chr 3.22
8.30 Ezra 2.3; 1 Esd 5.9

shall take care to give him, 20up to
a hundred talents of silver, and
likewise up to a hundred cors of
wheat, a hundred baths of wine,
and salt in abundance. 21Let all
things prescribed in the law of God
be scrupulously fulfilled for the
Most High God, so that wrath may
not come upon the kingdom of the
king and his sons. 22You are also
informed that no tribute or any
other tax is to be laid on any of the
priests or Levites or temple singers
or gatekeepers or temple servants
or persons employed in this temple, and that no one has authority
to impose any tax on them.
23 "And you, Ezra, according to
the wisdom of God, appoint judges
and justices to judge all those who
know the law of your God, throughout all Syria and Phoenicia; and
you shall teach it to those who do
not know it. 24All who transgress
the law of your God or the law of
the kingdom shall be strictly punished, whether by death or some
other punishment, either fine or
imprisonment."

Ezra Praises God

25 Then Ezra the scribe said,[e]
"Blessed be the Lord alone, who
put this into the heart of the king,
to glorify his house that is in Jerusalem, 26and who honored me in
the sight of the king and his counselors and all his Friends and nobles. 27I was encouraged by the
help of the Lord my God, and I
gathered men from Israel to go up
with me."

The Leaders Who Returned

28 These are the leaders, according to their ancestral houses
and their groups, who went up with
me from Babylon, in the reign of
King Artaxerxes: 29Of the descendants of Phineas, Gershom. Of the
descendants of Ithamar, Gamael.
Of the descendants of David, Hattush son of Shecaniah. 30Of the descendants of Parosh, Zechariah,
and with him a hundred fifty men

[d] Other authorities add *for him* or *upon him*
[e] Other ancient authorities lack *Then Ezra the scribe said*

enrolled. 31 Of the descendants of
Pahath-moab, Eliehoenai son of
Zerahiah, and with him two hundred men. 32 Of the descendants of
Zattu, Shecaniah son of Jahaziel,
and with him three hundred men.
Of the descendants of Adin, Obed
son of Jonathan, and with him two
hundred fifty men. 33 Of the descendants of Elam, Jeshaiah son of
Gotholiah, and with him seventy
men. 34 Of the descendants of
Shephatiah, Zeraiah son of Michael, and with him seventy men.
35 Of the descendants of Joab,
Obadiah son of Jehiel, and with
him two hundred twelve men. 36 Of
the descendants of Bani, Shelomith son of Josiphiah, and with
him a hundred sixty men. 37 Of the
descendants of Bebai, Zechariah
son of Bebai, and with him twenty-
eight men. 38 Of the descendants of
Azgad, Johanan son of Hakkatan,
and with him a hundred ten men.
39 Of the descendants of Adonikam, the last ones, their names being Eliphelet, Jeuel, and Shemaiah, and with them seventy men.
40 Of the descendants of Bigvai,
Uthai son of Istalcurus, and with
him seventy men.
41 I assembled them at the river
called Theras, and we encamped
there three days, and I inspected
them. 42 When I found there none
of the descendants of the priests or
of the Levites, 43 I sent word to Eli-
ezar, Iduel, Maasmas, 44 Elnathan,
Shemaiah, Jarib, Nathan, Elnathan, Zechariah, and Meshullam,
who were leaders and men of understanding; 45 I told them to go to
Iddo, who was the leading man at
the place of the treasury, 46 and ordered them to tell Iddo and his
kindred and the treasurers at that
place to send us men to serve as
priests in the house of our Lord.
47 And by the mighty hand of our
Lord they brought us competent
men of the descendants of Mahli
son of Levi, son of Israel, namely
Sherebiah[f] with his descendants
and kinsmen, eighteen; 48 also
Hashabiah and Annunus and his
brother Jeshaiah, of the descendants of Hananiah, and their descendants, twenty men; 49 and of
the temple servants, whom David
and the leaders had given for the
service of the Levites, two hundred
twenty temple servants; the list of
all their names was reported.

Ezra Proclaims a Fast

50 There I proclaimed a fast for
the young men before our Lord, to
seek from him a prosperous journey for ourselves and for our children and the livestock that were
with us. 51 For I was ashamed to
ask the king for foot soldiers and
cavalry and an escort to keep us
safe from our adversaries; 52 for we
had said to the king, "The power of
our Lord will be with those who
seek him, and will support them in
every way." 53 And again we prayed
to our Lord about these things, and
we found him very merciful.

The Gifts for the Temple

54 Then I set apart twelve of the
leaders of the priests, Sherebiah
and Hashabiah, and ten of their
kinsmen with them; 55 and I
weighed out to them the silver and
the gold and the holy vessels of the
house of our Lord, which the king
himself and his counselors and the
nobles and all Israel had given. 56 I
weighed and gave to them six hundred fifty talents of silver, and silver vessels worth a hundred talents, and a hundred talents of
gold, 57 and twenty golden bowls,
and twelve bronze vessels of fine
bronze that glittered like gold.
58 And I said to them, "You are holy
to the Lord, and the vessels are
holy, and the silver and the gold
are vowed to the Lord, the Lord of
our ancestors. 59 Be watchful and
on guard until you deliver them to
the leaders of the priests and the
Levites, and to the heads of the ancestral houses of Israel, in Jerusalem, in the chambers of the house
of our Lord." 60 So the priests and
the Levites who took the silver and
the gold and the vessels that had
been in Jerusalem carried them to
the temple of the Lord.

8.41 1 Esd 8.61
8.42 1 Esd 8.5
8.45 Ezra 5.1; Zech 1.1
8.47 Ezra 7.6,9,28; 8.18,22,31; Ex 6.19; 1 Chr 6.19
8.49 1 Chr 9.2; Ezra 2.43; Neh 8.28; 1 Esd 5.29
8.50 Ezra 8.21-23; 2 Chr 20.3; Esth 4.16-17; Isa 58.3,5; 1 Esd 8.6
8.52 1 Chr 22.19; 2 Chr 15.2, 12; 20.3-5
8.53 Ex 34.6; Ps 103.8; Joel 2.13
8.54 Ezra 8.24-30; Neh 8.7; 12.8
8.55 Ezra 1.9-11; 1 Esd 8.13-16
8.58 Lev 21.1-6; 1 Kings 8.4; 1 Macc 4.49
8.59 1 Esd 8.64

[f] Gk *Asbebias*

The Return to Jerusalem

61 We left the river Theras on
the twelfth day of the first month;
and we arrived in Jerusalem by the
mighty hand of our Lord, which
was upon us; he delivered us from
every enemy on the way, and so we
came to Jerusalem. 62 When we
had been there three days, the silver and the gold were weighed and
delivered in the house of our Lord
to the priest Meremoth son of
Uriah; 63 with him was Eleazar son
of Phinehas, and with them were
Jozabad son of Jeshua and Moeth
son of Binnui,[g] the Levites. 64 The
whole was counted and weighed,
and the weight of everything was
recorded at that very time. 65 And
those who had returned from exile
offered sacrifices to the Lord, the
God of Israel, twelve bulls for all
Israel, ninety-six rams, 66 seventy-
two lambs, and as a thank offering
twelve male goats—all as a sacrifice to the Lord. 67 They delivered
the king's orders to the royal stewards and to the governors of Coelesyria and Phoenicia; and these officials[h] honored the people and the
temple of the Lord.

Ezra's Prayer

68 After these things had been
done, the leaders came to me and
said, 69 "The people of Israel and
the rulers and the priests and the
Levites have not put away from
themselves the alien peoples of the
land and their pollutions, the Canaanites, the Hittites, the Perizzites, the Jebusites, the Moabites,
the Egyptians, and the Edomites.
70 For they and their descendants
have married the daughters of
these people,[i] and the holy race
has been mixed with the alien peoples of the land; and from the beginning of this matter the leaders
and the nobles have been sharing
in this iniquity."

71 As soon as I heard these
things I tore my garments and my
holy mantle, and pulled out hair
from my head and beard, and sat
down in anxiety and grief. 72 And
all who were ever moved at[j] the
word of the Lord of Israel gathered
around me, as I mourned over this
iniquity, and I sat grief-stricken
until the evening sacrifice. 73 Then
I rose from my fast, with my garments and my holy mantle torn,
and kneeling down and stretching
out my hands to the Lord 74 I said,

"O Lord, I am ashamed and confused before your face. 75 For our
sins have risen higher than our
heads, and our mistakes have
mounted up to heaven 76 from the
times of our ancestors, and we are
in great sin to this day. 77 Because
of our sins and the sins of our ancestors, we with our kindred and
our kings and our priests were
given over to the kings of the earth,
to the sword and exile and plundering, in shame until this day.
78 And now in some measure mercy
has come to us from you, O Lord,
to leave to us a root and a name in
your holy place, 79 and to uncover a
light for us in the house of the Lord
our God, and to give us food in the
time of our servitude. 80 Even in
our bondage we were not forsaken
by our Lord, but he brought us into
favor with the kings of the Persians, so that they have given us
food 81 and glorified the temple of
our Lord, and raised Zion from desolation, to give us a stronghold in
Judea and Jerusalem.

82 "And now, O Lord, what
shall we say, when we have these
things? For we have transgressed
your commandments, which you
gave by your servants the prophets,
saying, 83 'The land that you are entering to take possession of is a
land polluted with the pollution of
the aliens of the land, and they
have filled it with their uncleanness. 84 Therefore do not give your
daughters in marriage to their descendants, and do not take their
daughters for your descendants;
85 do not seek ever to have peace
with them, so that you may be
strong and eat the good things of
the land and leave it for an inheritance to your children forever.'
86 And all that has happened to us

8.61 Ezra 8.31-36; 1 Esd 8.41, 47
8.62 Neh 2.11
8.64 1 Esd 8.56-57
8.65 Ezra 2.1; 6.16
8.67 1 Macc 10.69; 2 Macc 3.5,8; 1 Esd 2.17; 4.48
8.68 Ezra 9.1-15
8.69 Ezra 6.21; Neh 9.2; 1 Esd 7.13
8.70 Ex 34.15-16; Deut 7.3-4; Neh 13.23-27; Ezra 10.18-24; Neh 13.28
8.71 Job 1.20; Neh 1.4; 1 Macc 2.14; 2 Esd 1.8
8.72 Ezra 10.3; Ex 29.39,41; Num 28.4
8.73 Ex 9.29; Ps 134.2; 1 Tim 2.8
8.74 Ezek 36.32; Dan 9.7-8
8.75 Gen 18.21
8.77 Dan 9.9-15; Bar 1.13,17; Song of Thr 1.6; Deut 28.62-64; 2 Kings 25.21; Tob 3.4-5
8.78 Jer 42.11-12; Bar 4.22-23; 2 Macc 2.7
8.80 1 Esd 8.4
8.81 1 Esd 2.3-7; 6.27-31
8.82 Ex 34.15-16; Lev 18.19-30; Deut 7.3-4
8.85 Josh 9.14-15; Deut 8.7-10

g Gk *Sabannus* h Gk *they*
i Gk *their daughters* j Or *zealous for*

has come about because of our evil
deeds and our great sins. For you,
O Lord, lifted the burden of our
sins 87 and gave us such a root as
this; but we turned back again to
transgress your law by mixing with
the uncleanness of the peoples of
the land. 88 Were you not angry
enough with us to destroy us without leaving a root or seed or name?
89 O Lord of Israel, you are faithful;
for we are left as a root to this day.
90 See, we are now before you in our
iniquities; for we can no longer
stand in your presence because of
these things."

The Plan for Ending Mixed Marriages

91 While Ezra was praying and
making his confession, weeping
and lying on the ground before the
temple, there gathered around him
a very great crowd of men and
women and youths from Jerusalem; for there was great weeping
among the multitude. 92 Then
Shecaniah son of Jehiel, one of the
men of Israel, called out, and said
to Ezra, "We have sinned against
the Lord, and have married foreign
women from the peoples of the
land; but even now there is hope
for Israel. 93 Let us take an oath to
the Lord about this, that we will
put away all our foreign wives, with
their children, 94 as seems good to
you and to all who obey the law of
the Lord. 95 Rise up[k] and take action, for it is your task, and we are
with you to take strong measures."
96 Then Ezra rose up and made the
leaders of the priests and Levites of
all Israel swear that they would do
this. And they swore to it.

The Expulsion of Foreign Wives

9 Then Ezra set out and went
from the court of the temple
to the chamber of Jehohanan son
of Eliashib, 2 and spent the night
there; and he did not eat bread or
drink water, for he was mourning
over the great iniquities of the
multitude. 3 And a proclamation
was made throughout Judea and
Jerusalem to all who had returned
from exile that they should assemble at Jerusalem, 4 and that if any
did not meet there within two or
three days, in accordance with the
decision of the ruling elders, their
livestock would be seized for sacrifice and the men themselves[l] expelled from the multitude of those
who had returned from the captivity.

5 Then the men of the tribe of
Judah and Benjamin assembled at
Jerusalem within three days; this
was the ninth month, on the twentieth day of the month. 6 All the
multitude sat in the open square
before the temple, shivering because of the bad weather that prevailed. 7 Then Ezra stood up and
said to them, "You have broken the
law and married foreign women,
and so have increased the sin of Israel. 8 Now then make confession
and give glory to the Lord the God
of our ancestors, 9 and do his will;
separate yourselves from the peoples of the land and from your foreign wives."

10 Then all the multitude
shouted and said with a loud voice,
"We will do as you have said. 11 But
the multitude is great and it is winter, and we are not able to stand in
the open air. This is not a work we
can do in one day or two, for we
have sinned too much in these
things. 12 So let the leaders of the
multitude stay, and let all those in
our settlements who have foreign
wives come at the time appointed,
13 with the elders and judges of
each place, until we are freed from
the wrath of the Lord over this
matter."

14 Jonathan son of Asahel and
Jahzeiah son of Tikvah[m] undertook the matter on these terms,
and Meshullam and Levi and
Shabbethai served with them as
judges. 15 And those who had returned from exile acted in accordance with all this.

16 Ezra the priest chose for
himself the leading men of their
ancestral houses, all of them by

8.87 Isa 11.10-11; 27.6; 37.31-32; Jer 23.3; 1 Esd 8.68-70; Neh 13.23-27
8.89 Ps 145.13; Isa 49.7; 1 Cor 1.9
8.90 Ps 130.3
8.91 Ezra 10.1-5; Dan 9.20
8.92 1 Esd 8.68-70
8.95 1 Chr 28.10
8.96 Neh 5.12; 10.28-30
9.1 Ezra 10.6-36
9.2 1 Esd 8.71-72
9.6 Neh 8.1,3; 1 Esd 5.47; 9.38
9.8 Josh 7.19; 1 Chr 16.28-29; Ps 96.7-8
9.9 Ex 33.16; Lev 20.24,26; 1 Esd 7.13
9.13 2 Chr 29.10; 30.8
9.14 Ezra 10.15

[k] Other ancient authorities read *as seems good to you." And all who obeyed the law of the Lord rose and said to Ezra, "Rise up*
[l] Gk *he himself*
[m] Gk *Thocanos*

name; and on the new moon of the
tenth month they began their sessions to investigate the matter.
17 And the cases of the men who
had foreign wives were brought to
an end by the new moon of the first
month.

18 Of the priests, those who
were brought in and found to have
foreign wives were: 19 of the descendants of Jeshua son of Jozadak and his kindred, Maaseiah, El-
iezar, Jarib, and Jodan. 20 They
pledged themselves to put away
their wives, and to offer rams in expiation of their error. 21 Of the descendants of Immer: Hanani and
Zebadiah and Maaseiah and Shemaiah and Jehiel and Azariah. 22 Of
the descendants of Pashhur: Elioenai, Maaseiah, Ishmael, and Nathanael, and Gedaliah, and Sal-
thas.

23 And of the Levites: Jozabad
and Shimei and Kelaiah, who was
Kelita, and Pethahiah and Judah
and Jonah. 24 Of the temple singers: Eliashib and Zaccur.[n] 25 Of the
gatekeepers: Shallum and Telem.[o]

26 Of Israel: of the descendants
of Parosh: Ramiah, Izziah, Malchijah, Mijamin, and Eleazar, and Asi-
bias, and Benaiah. 27 Of the descendants of Elam: Mattaniah and
Zechariah, Jezrielus and Abdi, and
Jeremoth and Elijah. 28 Of the descendants of Zamoth: Eliadas, Eliashib, Othoniah, Jeremoth, and
Zabad and Zerdaiah. 29 Of the descendants of Bebai: Jehohanan
and Hananiah and Zabbai and
Emathis. 30 Of the descendants of
Mani: Olamus, Mamuchus, Adaiah, Jashub, and Sheal and Jeremoth. 31 Of the descendants of
Addi: Naathus and Moossias, Lac-
cunus and Naidus, and Bescaspas-
mys and Sesthel, and Belnuus and
Manasseas. 32 Of the descendants
of Annan, Elionas and Asaias and
Melchias and Sabbaias and Simon
Chosamaeus. 33 Of the descendants of Hashum: Mattenai and
Mattattah and Zabad and Eliphelet
and Manasseh and Shimei. 34 Of
the descendants of Bani: Jeremai,
Momdius, Maerus, Joel, Mamdai
and Bedeiah and Vaniah, Caraba-
sion and Eliashib and Mamitane-
mus, Eliasis, Binnui, Elialis,
Shimei, Shelemiah, Nethaniah. Of
the descendants of Ezora: Shashai,
Azarel, Azael, Samatus, Zambris,
Joseph. 35 Of the descendants of
Nooma: Mazitias, Zabad, Iddo,
Joel, Benaiah. 36 All these had married foreign women, and they put
them away together with their children.

Ezra Reads the Law to the People

37 The priests and the Levites
and the Israelites settled in Jerusalem and in the country. On the new
moon of the seventh month, when
the people of Israel were in their
settlements, 38 the whole multitude gathered with one accord in
the open square before the east
gate of the temple; 39 they told Ezra
the chief priest and reader to bring
the law of Moses that had been
given by the Lord God of Israel.
40 So Ezra the chief priest brought
the law, for all the multitude, men
and women, and all the priests to
hear the law, on the new moon of
the seventh month. 41 He read
aloud in the open square before
the gate of the temple from early
morning until midday, in the presence of both men and women; and
all the multitude gave attention to
the law. 42 Ezra the priest and
reader of the law stood on the
wooden platform that had been
prepared; 43 and beside him stood
Mattathiah, Shema, Ananias, Azariah, Uriah, Hezekiah, and Baal-
samus on his right, 44 and on his
left Pedaiah, Mishael, Malchijah,
Lothasubus, Nabariah, and Zechariah. 45 Then Ezra took up the book
of the law in the sight of the multitude, for he had the place of honor
in the presence of all. 46 When he
opened the law, they all stood
erect. And Ezra blessed the Lord
God Most High, the God of hosts,
the Almighty, 47 and the multitude
answered, "Amen." They lifted up
their hands, and fell to the ground
and worshiped the Lord. 48 Jeshua

9.18 1 Esd 8.69; Neh 13.28
9.20 Ezra 10.19
9.37 Neh 7.53-8.12; Ezra 3.1; 1 Esd 5.46
9.38 1 Esd 5.47; 9.6
9.39 Josh 8.31-32; 2 Kings 23.25; Dan 9.13; Jn 1.17
9.40 Deut 31.11-12
9.46 Gen 14.18-20; 24.27; 1 Esd 8.25
9.47 Deut 27.15-26; Neh 5.13; Jdt 13.20; 1 Esd 8.73
9.48 2 Chr 17.7-9

[n] Gk *Bacchurus* [o] Gk *Tolbanes*

and Anniuth and Sherebiah, Jadi-
nus, Akkub, Shabbethai, Hodiah,
Maiannas and Kelita, Azariah and
Jozabad, Hanan, Pelaiah, the Levites, taught the law of the Lord,[p]
at the same time explaining what
was read.

49 Then Attharates[q] said to
Ezra the chief priest and reader,
and to the Levites who were teaching the multitude, and to all,
50 "This day is holy to the Lord"—
now they were all weeping as they
heard the law— 51 "so go your way,
eat the fat and drink the sweet, and
send portions to those who have
none; 52 for the day is holy to the
Lord; and do not be sorrowful, for
the Lord will exalt you." 53 The Levites commanded all the people,
saying, "This day is holy; do not be
sorrowful." 54 Then they all went
their way, to eat and drink and enjoy themselves, and to give portions to those who had none, and
to make great rejoicing; 55 because
they were inspired by the words
which they had been taught. And
they came together.[r]

9.50 Lev 23.36
9.51 Deut 26.13; Neh 5.14-19; Job 29.11-17
9.54 Deut 16.14-15; 26.11

[p] Other ancient authorities add *and read the law of the Lord to the multitude*
[q] Or *the governor*
[r] The Greek text ends abruptly: compare Neh 8.13

Prayer of Manasseh

Title and Background

According to 2 Kings 21.1-18, Manasseh was the worst king that Judah had. However, according to 2 Chr 33.11-13, when he was taken captive to Babylon, he prayed to the Lord. In response, God restored him to his position as king of Judah for a brief time before his death. The Chronicler also said that Manasseh's prayer to God was written down (see 2 Chr 33.18-19). This book claims to be a copy of that prayer.

Author and Date of Writing

This work is probably not the original prayer of Manasseh; rather, it is a later second-century attempt by a pious Jew to compose a prayer Manasseh might have prayed. The only manuscripts available for it are in Greek, though the original writing may have been done in Hebrew.

Theme and Message

God is not only the Creator of the universe and the God of all justice; he is also the Lord of all mercy and forgiveness. On this basis, King Manasseh confesses his many sins and asks for divine pardon and redemption.

Outline

I. Praise to God (1-8)
II. Confession and Request for Pardon (9-15)

Ascription of Praise

1 O Lord Almighty,
God of our ancestors,
of Abraham and Isaac and Jacob
and of their righteous offspring;
2 you who made heaven and earth
with all their order;
3 who shackled the sea by your word of command,
who confined the deep
and sealed it with your terrible and glorious name;
4 at whom all things shudder,
and tremble before your power,
5 for your glorious splendor cannot be borne,
and the wrath of your threat to sinners is unendurable;
6 yet immeasurable and unsearchable
is your promised mercy,
7 for you are the Lord Most High,
of great compassion,
long-suffering, and very merciful,
and you relent at human suffering.
O Lord, according to your great goodness
you have promised repentance and forgiveness
to those who have sinned against you,
and in the multitude of your mercies
you have appointed repentance for sinners,
so that they may be saved.[a]
8 Therefore you, O Lord, God of the righteous,

1 Ex 13.15-16; Dan 2.23; Acts 3.13
2 Gen 1.1; Ps 33.6; Isa 42.5; 45.12
3 Job 38.8-11
4 1 Chr 16.30; Job 26.11; Ps 114.7; Isa 19.16
5 Ex 15.11;Ps 145.5,12; Bar 4.24
6 Ps 103.11-12
7 Ex 34.6-7; Ps 103.8,13; Isa 54.8; Bar 2.27; Ps 103.9-10; Dan 9.9; Sir 18.12; Acts 5.31
8 Mk 2.17; Lk 5.32; 1 Tim 1.15; 2 Chr 33.12-13,19; Lk 15.7; 18.13

[a] Other ancient authorities lack *O Lord, according . . . be saved*

have not appointed
repentance for the
righteous,
for Abraham and Isaac and
Jacob, who did not sin
against you,
but you have appointed
repentance for me, who
am a sinner.

Confession of Sins

9 For the sins I have
committed are more in
number than the sand
of the sea;
my transgressions are
multiplied, O Lord, they
are multiplied!
I am not worthy to look up
and see the height of
heaven
because of the multitude of
my iniquities.
10 I am weighted down with
many an iron fetter,
so that I am rejected[b]
because of my sins,
and I have no relief;
for I have provoked your
wrath
and have done what is evil in
your sight,
setting up abominations and
multiplying offenses.

Supplication for Pardon

11 And now I bend the knee of
my heart,
imploring you for your
kindness.
12 I have sinned, O Lord, I have
sinned,
and I acknowledge my
transgressions.
13 I earnestly implore you,
forgive me, O Lord, forgive
me!
Do not destroy me with my
transgressions!
Do not be angry with me
forever or store up evil
for me;
do not condemn me to the
depths of the earth.
For you, O Lord, are the God
of those who repent,
14 and in me you will manifest
your goodness;
for, unworthy as I am, you
will save me according
to your great mercy,
15 and I will praise you
continually all the days
of my life.
For all the host of heaven
sings your praise,
and yours is the glory
forever. Amen.

9 2 Kings 21.2-9; 2 Chr 33.2-9
10 2 Chr 33.11; 2 Kings 21.10-15
11 Joel 2.13
12 Ps 19.12; 51.3-5; Isa 59.12-13
13 Ps 44.23; 79.5; 85.5; 63.9; 88.5-6
14 1 Tim 1.15-16; Titus 3.5
15 2 Chr 18.18; Ps 103.21; Lk 2.13; 1 Chr 29.10-13; Mt 6.13

[b]Other ancient authorities read *so that I cannot lift up my head*

Psalm 151

Title and Background

Most manuscripts of the Septuagint have 151 psalms, this one being the last one. The translator, however, acknowledged that this one was "outside the number," i.e., not one of the generally accepted 150 psalms.

Author and Date of Writing

Psalm 151 claims to be a psalm of David, written after his defeat of Goliath. A Hebrew copy of it has been found among the Dead Sea Scrolls, indicating that it was originally written in Hebrew. From its contents and style, there is no reason to deny that it may have been an early psalm of David–perhaps his first one.

Theme and Message

David acknowledges both his low position in the family and God's remarkable decisions to have him anointed as king of Israel and to empower him to defeat Goliath.

Outline

I. Young David Chosen to Become King (1-5)
II. Goliath and His Gods Defeated (6-7)

This psalm is ascribed to David as his own composition (though it is outside the number[a]), after he had fought in single combat with Goliath.

1 I was small among my brothers,
and the youngest in my father's house;
I tended my father's sheep.

2 My hands made a harp;
my fingers fashioned a lyre.

3 And who will tell my Lord?
The Lord himself; it is he who hears.[b]

4 It was he who sent his messenger[c]
and took me from my father's sheep,
and anointed me with his anointing oil.

5 My brothers were handsome and tall,
but the Lord was not pleased with them.

6 I went out to meet the Philistine,[d]
and he cursed me by his idols.

7 But I drew his own sword;
I beheaded him, and took away disgrace from the people of Israel.

151.1 1 Sam 16.7, 11
151.2 2 Chr 29.26; 1 Sam 16.18-20,23
151.3 Ps 34.15,17; Prov 15.29; 1 Pet 3.12
151.4 Ps 78.70; 1 Sam 16.3; Ps 89.20
151.5 1 Sam 16.7-10
151.6 1 Sam 17.40, 43
151.7 1 Sam 17.51

[a] Other ancient authorities add *of the one hundred fifty* (psalms)
[b] Other ancient authorities add *everything*; others add *me*; others read *who will hear me*
[c] Or *angel*
[d] Or *foreigner*

3 Maccabees

Title and Background

This book seems to be misnamed, since its events precede the Maccabean period by almost 50 years. The only justification for its title is that the book's theme of God's intervention in the persecution of his people is also prominent in 2 Maccabees.

Author and Date of Writing

The author of this book is unknown, but most scholars consider him to be a conservative Jew living in Alexandria, Egypt, in the first century B.C. The book was likely composed in Greek.

Theme and Message

This book encourages Egyptian Jews to remain steadfast in their faith despite threats of persecution from their Roman rulers. God promises to intervene on behalf of his people, as he has done in the past, if they are threatened with annihilation.

Outline

I. Entry into the Temple Refused to Ptolemy Philopator (1.1–2.24)
II. Ptolemy's Planned Revenge Against Jews in Egypt (2.25–4.21)
III. Execution of the Jews Thwarted by God (5.1–6.29)
IV. Ptolemy's Release of the Jews (6.30–9.23)

The Battle of Raphia

1 When Philopator learned from
those who returned that the
regions that he had controlled had
been seized by Antiochus, he gave
orders to all his forces, both infantry and cavalry, took with him his
sister Arsinoë, and marched out to
the region near Raphia, where the
army of Antiochus was encamped.
2 But a certain Theodotus, determined to carry out the plot he had
devised, took with him the best of
the Ptolemaic arms that had been
previously issued to him,[a] and
crossed over by night to the tent of
Ptolemy, intending single-handed
to kill him and thereby end the
war. 3 But Dositheus, known as the
son of Drimylus, a Jew by birth
who later changed his religion and
apostatized from the ancestral traditions, had led the king away and
arranged that a certain insignifi-
cant man should sleep in the tent;
and so it turned out that this man
incurred the vengeance meant for
the king.[b] 4 When a bitter fight resulted, and matters were turning
out rather in favor of Antiochus,
Arsinoë went to the troops with
wailing and tears, her locks all disheveled, and exhorted them to
defend themselves and their children and wives bravely, promising
to give them each two minas of
gold if they won the battle. 5 And so
it came about that the enemy was
routed in the action, and many
captives also were taken. 6 Now
that he had foiled the plot, Ptolemy[c] decided to visit the neighboring cities and encourage them.
7 By doing this, and by endowing
their sacred enclosures with gifts,
he strengthened the morale of his
subjects.

Philopator Attempts to Enter the Temple

8 Since the Jews had sent some
of their council and elders to greet
him, to bring him gifts of welcome,

1.1 2 Macc 3.12; 7.1; 1 Macc 1.10
1.3 1 Macc 1.11-15,43-49
1.7 1 Macc 10.39-41,44

[a] Or *the best of the Ptolemaic soldiers previously put under his command* [b] Gk *that one* [c] Gk *he*

and to congratulate him on what had happened, he was all the more eager to visit them as soon as possible. 9 After he had arrived in Jerusalem, he offered sacrifice to the supreme God[d] and made thank offerings and did what was fitting for the holy place.[e] Then, upon entering the place and being impressed by its excellence and its beauty, 10 he marveled at the good order of the temple, and conceived a desire to enter the sanctuary. 11 When they said that this was not permitted, because not even members of their own nation were allowed to enter, not even all of the priests, but only the high priest who was pre-eminent over all—and he only once a year—the king was by no means persuaded. 12 Even after the law had been read to him, he did not cease to maintain that he ought to enter, saying, "Even if those men are deprived of this honor, I ought not to be." 13 And he inquired why, when he entered every other temple,[f] no one there had stopped him. 14 And someone answered thoughtlessly that it was wrong to take that as a portent.[g] 15 "But since this has happened," the king[h] said, "why should not I at least enter, whether they wish it or not?"

Jewish Resistance to Ptolemy

16 Then the priests in all their vestments prostrated themselves and entreated the supreme God[d] to aid in the present situation and to avert the violence of this evil design, and they filled the temple with cries and tears; 17 those who remained behind in the city were agitated and hurried out, supposing that something mysterious was occurring. 18 Young women who had been secluded in their chambers rushed out with their mothers, sprinkled their hair with dust,[i] and filled the streets with groans and lamentations. 19 Those women who had recently been arrayed for marriage abandoned the bridal chambers[j] prepared for wedded union, and, neglecting proper modesty, in a disorderly rush flocked together in the city. 20 Mothers and nurses abandoned even newborn children here and there, some in houses and some in the streets, and without a backward look they crowded together at the most high temple. 21 Various were the supplications of those gathered there because of what the king was profanely plotting. 22 In addition, the bolder of the citizens would not tolerate the completion of his plans or the fulfillment of his intended purpose. 23 They shouted to their compatriots to take arms and die courageously for the ancestral law, and created a considerable disturbance in the holy place;[e] and being barely restrained by the old men and the elders,[k] they resorted to the same posture of supplication as the others. 24 Meanwhile the crowd, as before, was engaged in prayer, 25 while the elders near the king tried in various ways to change his arrogant mind from the plan that he had conceived. 26 But he, in his arrogance, took heed of nothing, and began now to approach, determined to bring the aforesaid plan to a conclusion. 27 When those who were around him observed this, they turned, together with our people, to call upon him who has all power to defend them in the present trouble and not to overlook this unlawful and haughty deed. 28 The continuous, vehement, and concerted cry of the crowds[l] resulted in an immense uproar; 29 for it seemed that not only the people but also the walls and the whole earth around echoed, because indeed all at that time[m] preferred death to the profanation of the place.

1.9 2 Macc 3.36; 3 Macc 3.11; 4.16; 5.25; 7.22; 2 Chr 3.1-5.1
1.11 Ex 30.10; Lev 16.2, 11-17; Heb 9.7
1.16 Ex 28.1-43; 39.1-31; 2 Macc 3.15; 5.50
1.17 2 Macc 3.18
1.18 Sir 42.9-12; 2 Macc 3.19
1.19 Joel 2.16; Bar 2.23; 2 Macc 4.6; 2 Esd 16.33-34
1.23 1 Macc 2.40; 3.21; 13.3-4; 2 Macc 8.21
1.24 3 Macc 1.21
1.26 1 Macc 1.24; 2 Macc 5.21; 9.8
1.27 Ps 46.1; 91.1-13

[d] Gk *the greatest God* [e] Gk *the place*
[f] Or *entered the temple precincts*
[g] Or *to boast of this* [h] Gk *he*
[i] Other ancient authorities add *and ashes*
[j] Or *the canopies* [k] Other ancient authorities read *priests* [l] Other ancient authorities read *vehement cry of the assembled crowds*
[m] Other ancient authorities lack *at that time*

The Prayer of the High Priest Simon

2 Then the high priest Simon,
facing the sanctuary, bending
his knees and extending his hands
with calm dignity, prayed as follows:[n] 2“Lord, Lord, king of the
heavens, and sovereign of all creation, holy among the holy ones,
the only ruler, almighty, give attention to us who are suffering grievously from an impious and profane
man, puffed up in his audacity and
power. 3For you, the creator of all
things and the governor of all, are a
just Ruler, and you judge those
who have done anything in insolence and arrogance. 4You destroyed those who in the past committed injustice, among whom
were even giants who trusted in
their strength and boldness, whom
you destroyed by bringing on them
a boundless flood. 5You consumed
with fire and sulfur the people of
Sodom who acted arrogantly, who
were notorious for their vices;[o]
and you made them an example to
those who should come afterward.
6You made known your mighty
power by inflicting many and varied punishments on the audacious
Pharaoh who had enslaved your
holy people Israel. 7And when he
pursued them with chariots and a
mass of troops, you overwhelmed
him in the depths of the sea, but
carried through safely those who
had put their confidence in you,
the Ruler over the whole creation.
8And when they had seen works of
your hands, they praised you, the
Almighty. 9You, O King, when you
had created the boundless and immeasurable earth, chose this city
and sanctified this place for your
name, though you have no need of
anything; and when you had glorified it by your magnificent manifestation,[p] you made it a firm
foundation for the glory of your
great and honored name. 10And
because you love the house of Israel, you promised that if we
should have reverses and tribulation should overtake us, you would
listen to our petition when we
come to this place and pray. 11And
indeed you are faithful and true.
12And because oftentimes when
our fathers were oppressed you
helped them in their humiliation,
and rescued them from great evils,
13see now, O holy King, that because of our many and great sins
we are crushed with suffering, subjected to our enemies, and overtaken by helplessness. 14In our
downfall this audacious and profane man undertakes to violate the
holy place on earth dedicated to
your glorious name. 15For your
dwelling is the heaven of heavens,
unapproachable by human beings.
16But because you graciously bestowed your glory on your people
Israel, you sanctified this place.
17Do not punish us for the defilement committed by these men, or
call us to account for this profanation, otherwise the transgressors
will boast in their wrath and exult
in the arrogance of their tongue,
saying, 18‘We have trampled down
the house of the sanctuary as the
houses of the abominations are
trampled down.’ 19Wipe away our
sins and disperse our errors, and
reveal your mercy at this hour.
20Speedily let your mercies overtake us, and put praises in the
mouth of those who are downcast
and broken in spirit, and give us
peace.”

God’s Punishment of Ptolemy

21 Thereupon God, who over-
sees all things, the first Father of
all, holy among the holy ones, having heard the lawful supplication,
scourged him who had exalted
himself in insolence and audacity.
22He shook him on this side and
that as a reed is shaken by the
wind, so that he lay helpless on the

2.2 Ps 47.6-8; 103.19; Tob 10.13; Acts 17.24; Gen 17.1; 2 Macc 1.25; Rev 1.8; 3 Macc 1.26 **2.3** Gen 1.1; Isa 45.12,18; Eph 3.9; Rev 4.11; Ex 18.11; Ps 31.23; Wis 12.17; 3 Macc 6.9 **2.4** Gen 6.4; Wis 14.6; Sir 16.7; Bar 3.26-28 **2.5** Gen 19.24; Deut 29.23; Wis 10.7; 2 Pet 2.6 **2.6** Ex 9.16; Rom 9.17; Ex 7.14-11.29; 12.29-32; 19.6; 2 Pet 2.9 **2.7** Ex 14.21-28; 2 Macc 12.15; 1 Tim 6.15; Rev 17.14 **2.8** Ex 15.1-21; Ps 105.43; Wis 19.8-9 **2.9** Bar 3.25; 1 Kings 8.29; 9.3; 2 Macc 14.35; Acts 17.25; 2 Chr 7.1-3 **2.10** Deut 4.30; 30.1-6; 1 Kings 18.33-34, 48-50 **2.10** Ps 145.13; 1 Esd 8.89 **2.12** 1 Sam 12.10-11; Ps 22.4-5; 106.43; Neh 9.28 **2.13** Ezra 9.6-9; Ps 106.6-7; Dan 9.11-14; Bar 1.17-20 **2.14** Jdt 9.8 **2.15** 1 Kings 8.27; Isa 66.1; Acts 7.49; Prov 30.4; Bar 3.24 **2.17** 3 Macc 1.26 **2.18** Isa 10.10-11; Dan 8.13; 1 Macc 3.45,51 **2.19** Ps 57.2,9; 1 Jn 1.7,9 **2.20** Neh 9.27-28; Lam 3.22; Sir 18.5; Ps 42.5,11; Num 6.26; Ps 122.6-7 **2.21** Isa 64.8; Eph 3.14-15 **2.22** Mt 11.7; Lk 7.24; 2 Macc 3.25-29; 9.5-9; Acts 12.23

[n] Other ancient authorities lack verse 1
[o] Other ancient authorities read *secret in their vices*
[p] Or *epiphany*

ground and, besides being paralyzed in his limbs, was unable even
to speak, since he was smitten[q] by
a righteous judgment. 23 Then both
friends and bodyguards, seeing the
severe punishment that had overtaken him, and fearing that he
would lose his life, quickly dragged
him out, panic-stricken in their exceedingly great fear. 24 After a
while he recovered, and though he
had been punished, he by no
means repented, but went away uttering bitter threats.

Hostile Measures against the Jews

25 When he arrived in Egypt, he
increased in his deeds of malice,
abetted by the previously mentioned drinking companions and
comrades, who were strangers to
everything just. 26 He was not content with his uncounted licentious
deeds, but even continued with
such audacity that he framed evil
reports in the various localities;
and many of his friends, intently
observing the king's purpose,
themselves also followed his will.
27 He proposed to inflict public disgrace on the Jewish community,[r]
and he set up a stone[s] on the
tower in the courtyard with this inscription: 28 "None of those who do
not sacrifice shall enter their sanctuaries, and all Jews shall be subjected to a registration involving
poll tax and to the status of slaves.
Those who object to this are to be
taken by force and put to death;
29 those who are registered are also
to be branded on their bodies by
fire with the ivy-leaf symbol of Dionysus, and they shall also be reduced to their former limited status." 30 In order that he might not
appear to be an enemy of all, he inscribed below: "But if any of them
prefer to join those who have been
initiated into the mysteries, they
shall have equal citizenship with
the Alexandrians."

31 Now some, however, with an
obvious abhorrence of the price to
be exacted for maintaining the religion of their city,[t] readily gave
themselves up, since they expected to enhance their reputation
by their future association with the
king. 32 But the majority acted
firmly with a courageous spirit and
did not abandon their religion; and
by paying money in exchange for
life they confidently attempted to
save themselves from the registration. 33 They remained resolutely
hopeful of obtaining help, and they
abhorred those who separated
themselves from them, considering them to be enemies of the Jewish nation,[r] and depriving them of
companionship and mutual help.

The Jews and Their Neighbors

3 When the impious king comprehended this situation, he
became so infuriated that not only
was he enraged against those Jews
who lived in Alexandria, but was
still more bitterly hostile toward
those in the countryside; and he
ordered that all should promptly
be gathered into one place, and
put to death by the most cruel
means. 2 While these matters were
being arranged, a hostile rumor
was circulated against the Jewish
nation by some who conspired to
do them ill, a pretext being given
by a report that they hindered others[u] from the observance of their
customs. 3 The Jews, however, continued to maintain goodwill and
unswerving loyalty toward the dynasty; 4 but because they worshiped God and conducted themselves by his law, they kept their
separateness with respect to foods.
For this reason they appeared
hateful to some; 5 but since they
adorned their style of life with the
good deeds of upright people, they
were established in good repute
with everyone. 6 Nevertheless
those of other races paid no heed
to their good service to their nation, which was common talk
among all; 7 instead they gossiped
about the differences in worship
and foods, alleging that these people were loyal neither to the king
nor to his authorities, but were

2.24 2 Macc 9.7
2.25 Prov 20.1; 23.29-35
2.28 Ex 1.8-14; Neh 9.36; 1 Macc 3.41; 2 Macc 8.11
2.29 Gal 6.19; Rev 7.3; 13.16-17; 2 Macc 6.7; 14.33
2.30 Wis 14.23
2.31 1 Macc 1.11-15,52
2.32 1 Macc 1.62-63; 2.19-20; 2 Macc 10.20; 3 Macc 4.19
2.33 2 Jn 10-11
3.1 1 Macc 1.50; 2 Macc 6.9-7.42
3.2 Esth 3.5-11
3.3 3 Macc 6.26; 7.7
3.4 Lev 11.1-47; Deut 14.3-21; 2 Macc 6.18-20
3.5 Deut 4.5-6; Col 4.5; 1 Thess 4.12
3.7 Esth 3.8; Dan 3.12-17; 6.13

[q] Other ancient authorities read *pierced*
[r] Gk *the nation*
[s] Gk *stele*
[t] Meaning of Gk uncertain
[u] Gk *them*

hostile and greatly opposed to his
government. So they attached no
ordinary reproach to them.
8 The Greeks in the city, though
wronged in no way, when they saw
an unexpected tumult around
these people and the crowds that
suddenly were forming, were not
strong enough to help them, for
they lived under tyranny. They did
try to console them, being grieved
at the situation, and expected that
matters would change; 9 for such a
great community ought not be left
to its fate when it had committed
no offense. 10 And already some of
their neighbors and friends and
business associates had taken
some of them aside privately and
were pledging to protect them and
to exert more earnest efforts for
their assistance.

Ptolemy's Decree That All Jews Be Arrested

11 Then the king, boastful of
his present good fortune, and not
considering the might of the supreme God,[v] but assuming that he
would persevere constantly in his
same purpose, wrote this letter
against them:
12 "King Ptolemy Philopator to
his generals and soldiers in Egypt
and all its districts, greetings and
good health:
13 "I myself and our government are faring well. 14 When our
expedition took place in Asia, as
you yourselves know, it was
brought to conclusion, according
to plan, by the gods' deliberate alliance with us in battle, 15 and we
considered that we should not rule
the nations inhabiting Coelesyria
and Phoenicia by the power of the
spear, but should cherish them
with clemency and great benevolence, gladly treating them well.
16 And when we had granted very
great revenues to the temples in
the cities, we came on to Jerusalem also, and went up to honor the
temple of those wicked people,
who never cease from their folly.
17 They accepted our presence by
word, but insincerely by deed, because when we proposed to enter
their inner temple and honor it
with magnificent and most beautiful offerings, 18 they were carried
away by their traditional arrogance, and excluded us from entering; but they were spared the exercise of our power because of the
benevolence that we have toward
all. 19 By maintaining their manifest ill-will toward us, they become
the only people among all nations
who hold their heads high in defiance of kings and their own benefactors, and are unwilling to regard
any action as sincere.
20 "But we, when we arrived in
Egypt victorious, accommodated
ourselves to their folly and did as
was proper, since we treat all nations with benevolence. 21 Among
other things, we made known to all
our amnesty toward their compatriots here, both because of their
alliance with us and the myriad affairs liberally entrusted to them
from the beginning; and we ven-
tured to make a change, by deciding both to deem them worthy of
Alexandrian citizenship and to
make them participants in our regular religious rites.[w] 22 But in their
innate malice they took this in a
contrary spirit, and disdained what
is good. Since they incline constantly to evil, 23 they not only
spurn the priceless citizenship, but
also both by speech and by silence
they abominate those few among
them who are sincerely disposed
toward us; in every situation, in accordance with their infamous way
of life, they secretly suspect that
we may soon alter our policy.
24 Therefore, fully convinced by
these indications that they are ill-
disposed toward us in every way,
we have taken precautions so that,
if a sudden disorder later arises
against us, we shall not have these
impious people behind our backs
as traitors and barbarous enemies.
25 Therefore we have given orders
that, as soon as this letter arrives,
you are to send to us those who live
among you, together with their

3.8 2 Macc 4.25; 4 Macc 1.11
3.11 Ps 59.16; 68.28; Isa 40.10; Jdt 9.14; Esth 3.13
3.12 3 Macc 1.1
3.15 2 Macc 3.5,8; 1 Esd 4.48; 7.1
3.16 3 Macc 1.7, 9
3.18 3 Macc 1.10-12
3.19 Add Esth 13.4-5; 16.2
3.21 3 Macc 2.28-30
3.23 3 Macc 2.32-33,31
3.24 Ex 1.10
3.25 2 Kings 25.7; 2 Chr 33.11; 1 Macc 3.41; Esth 3.13-14; Add Esth 13.6; 3 Macc 3.1

[v] Gk *the greatest God*
[w] Other ancient authorities read *partners of our regular priests*

wives and children, with insulting
and harsh treatment, and bound
securely with iron fetters, to suffer
the sure and shameful death that
befits enemies. 26 For when all of
these have been punished, we are
sure that for the remaining time
the government will be established
for ourselves in good order and in
the best state. 27 But those who
shelter any of the Jews, whether
old people or children or even infants, will be tortured to death
with the most hateful torments, together with their families. 28 Any
who are willing to give information
will receive the property of those
who incur the punishment, and
also two thousand drachmas from
the royal treasury, and will be
awarded their freedom.[x] 29 Every
place detected sheltering a Jew is
to be made unapproachable and
burned with fire, and shall become
useless for all time to any mortal
creature." 30 The letter was written
in the above form.

The Jews Deported to Alexandria

4 In every place, then, where
this decree arrived, a feast at
public expense was arranged for
the Gentiles with shouts and gladness, for the inveterate enmity that
had long ago been in their minds
was now made evident and outspo-
ken. 2 But among the Jews there
was incessant mourning, lamentation, and tearful cries; everywhere
their hearts were burning, and they
groaned because of the unexpected destruction that had suddenly been decreed for them.
3 What district or city, or what habitable place at all, or what streets
were not filled with mourning and
wailing for them? 4 For with such a
harsh and ruthless spirit were they
being sent off, all together, by the
generals in the several cities, that
at the sight of their unusual punishments, even some of their enemies, perceiving the common object of pity before their eyes,
reflected on the uncertainty of life
and shed tears at the most miserable expulsion of these people. 5 For
a multitude of gray-headed old
men, sluggish and bent with age,
was being led away, forced to
march at a swift pace by the violence with which they were driven
in such a shameful manner. 6 And
young women who had just entered the bridal chamber[y] to share
married life exchanged joy for wailing, their myrrh-perfumed hair
sprinkled with ashes, and were carried away unveiled, all together
raising a lament instead of a wedding song, as they were torn by the
harsh treatment of the heathen.[z]
7 In bonds and in public view they
were violently dragged along as far
as the place of embarkation.
8 Their husbands, in the prime of
youth, their necks encircled with
ropes instead of garlands, spent
the remaining days of their marriage festival in lamentations instead of good cheer and youthful
revelry, seeing death immediately
before them.[a] 9 They were brought
on board like wild animals, driven
under the constraint of iron bonds;
some were fastened by the neck to
the benches of the boats, others
had their feet secured by unbreak-
able fetters, 10 and in addition they
were confined under a solid deck,
so that, with their eyes in total
darkness, they would undergo
treatment befitting traitors during
the whole voyage.

The Jews Imprisoned at Schedia

11 When these people had been
brought to the place called
Schedia, and the voyage was concluded as the king had decreed, he
commanded that they should be
enclosed in the hippodrome that
had been built with a monstrous
perimeter wall in front of the city,
and that was well suited to make
them an obvious spectacle to all
coming back into the city and to
those from the city[b] going out into
the country, so that they could nei-

3.26 Add Esth 13.7
3.29 Add Esth 16.24
4.2 Esth 4.1-3
4.4 Am 1.6,13
4.6 Bar 2.23; 1 Macc 1.26-27; 3 Macc 1.19; Lam 5.15; Am 8.10; Tob 2.6
4.8 Isa 61.10; Jdt 15.13
4.9 3 Macc 3.25
4.11 3 Macc 5.46; 6.16; Mt 27.39; Mk 15.29

[x] Gk *crowned with freedom* [y] Or *the canopy*
[z] Other ancient authorities read *as though torn by heathen whelps* [a] Gk *seeing Hades already lying at their feet* [b] Gk *those of them*

ther communicate with the king's
forces nor in any way claim to be
inside the circuit of the city.[c]
12 And when this had happened,
the king, hearing that the Jews'
compatriots from the city frequently went out in secret to lament bitterly the ignoble misfortune of their kindred, 13 ordered in
his rage that these people be dealt
with in precisely the same fashion
as the others, not omitting any detail of their punishment. 14 The entire race was to be registered individually, not for the hard labor that
has been briefly mentioned before,
but to be tortured with the out-
rages that he had ordered, and at
the end to be destroyed in the
space of a single day. 15 The registration of these people was therefore conducted with bitter haste
and zealous intensity from the rising of the sun until its setting,
coming to an end after forty days
but still uncompleted.
16 The king was greatly and
continually filled with joy, organiz-
ing feasts in honor of all his idols,
with a mind alienated from truth
and with a profane mouth, praising
speechless things that are not able
even to communicate or to come
to one's help, and uttering im-
proper words against the supreme
God.[d] 17 But after the previously
mentioned interval of time the
scribes declared to the king that
they were no longer able to take
the census of the Jews because of
their immense number, 18 though
most of them were still in the
country, some still residing in their
homes, and some at the place;[e]
the task was impossible for all the
generals in Egypt. 19 After he had
threatened them severely, charging
that they had been bribed to contrive a means of escape, he was
clearly convinced about the matter
20 when they said and proved that
both the paper[f] and the pens
they used for writing had already
given out. 21 But this was an act of
the invincible providence of him
who was aiding the Jews from
heaven.

Execution of the Jews Is Twice Thwarted

5 Then the king, completely inflexible, was filled with overpowering anger and wrath; so he
summoned Hermon, keeper of the
elephants, 2 and ordered him on
the following day to drug all the
elephants—five hundred in
number—with large handfuls of
frankincense and plenty of unmixed wine, and to drive them in,
maddened by the lavish abundance of drink, so that the Jews
might meet their doom. 3 When he
had given these orders he returned
to his feasting, together with those
of his Friends and of the army who
were especially hostile toward the
Jews. 4 And Hermon, keeper of the
elephants, proceeded faithfully to
carry out the orders. 5 The servants
in charge of the Jews[g] went out in
the evening and bound the hands
of the wretched people and arranged for their continued custody
through the night, convinced that
the whole nation would experience
its final destruction. 6 For to the
Gentiles it appeared that the Jews
were left without any aid, 7 because
in their bonds they were forcibly
confined on every side. But with
tears and a voice hard to silence
they all called upon the Almighty
Lord and Ruler of all power, their
merciful God and Father, praying
8 that he avert with vengeance the
evil plot against them and in a glorious manifestation rescue them
from the fate now prepared for
them. 9 So their entreaty ascended
fervently to heaven.
10 Hermon, however, when he
had drugged the pitiless elephants
until they had been filled with a
great abundance of wine and sati-
ated with frankincense, presented
himself at the courtyard early in
the morning to report to the king
about these preparations. 11 But
the Lord[h] sent upon the king a
portion of sleep, that beneficence
that from the beginning, night and

4.12 3 Macc 3.27; 4.4
4.13 2 Macc 7.3, 39; 9.4,7; 3 Macc 5.1
4.14 3 Macc 2.28
4.16 Esth 1.3-9; Dan 5.1-4; Rom 1.18; Ps 115.3-7; Isa 44.9-20; 46.7; Jer 10.5; Let Jer 6.8-40; 3 Macc 1.9, 16; Acts 12.21-22
4.19 2 Macc 10.20; 3 Macc 2.32
4.21 Wis 14.3; 4 Macc 9.24; 13.19; 17.22
5.1 2 Macc 4.25; 7.3,39; 9.4,7; 3 Macc 4.13
5.3 3 Macc 4.16; Add Esth 2.18; 1 Macc 2.18; 2 Macc 1.14
5.7 3 Macc 2.2; Ps 22.28; 103.19; Add Esth 16.18,21; 2 Macc 2.7; 5.51; Isa 64.8; Tob 13.4; Wis 11.10; Mt 6.9
5.8 2 Macc 2.21; 3.24; 5.2-3; 10.29

[c] Or *claim protection of the walls*; meaning of Gk uncertain [d] Gk *the greatest God*
[e] Other ancient authorities read *on the way*
[f] Or *paper factory* [g] Gk *them* [h] Gk *he*

day, is bestowed by him who grants
it to whomever he wishes. 12 And by
the action of the Lord he was overcome by so pleasant and deep a
sleep[i] that he quite failed in his
lawless purpose and was completely frustrated in his inflexible
plan. 13 Then the Jews, since they
had escaped the appointed hour,
praised their holy God and again
implored him who is easily reconciled to show the might of his all-
powerful hand to the arrogant
Gentiles.
14 But now, since it was nearly
the middle of the tenth hour, the
person who was in charge of the in-
vitations, seeing that the guests
were assembled, approached the
king and nudged him. 15 And when
he had with difficulty roused him,
he pointed out that the hour of the
banquet was already slipping by,
and he gave him an account of the
situation. 16 The king, after considering this, returned to his drinking,
and ordered those present for the
banquet to recline opposite him.
17 When this was done he urged
them to give themselves over to
revelry and to make the present[j]
portion of the banquet joyful by
celebrating all the more. 18 After
the party had been going on for
some time, the king summoned
Hermon and with sharp threats demanded to know why the Jews had
been allowed to remain alive
through the present day. 19 But
when he, with the corroboration of
his Friends, pointed out that while
it was still night he had carried out
completely the order given him,
20 the king,[k] possessed by a savagery worse than that of Phalaris,
said that the Jews[l] were benefited
by today's sleep, "but," he added,
"tomorrow without delay prepare
the elephants in the same way for
the destruction of the lawless
Jews!" 21 When the king had spoken, all those present readily and
joyfully with one accord gave their
approval, and all went to their own
homes. 22 But they did not so much
employ the duration of the night in
sleep as in devising all sorts of insults for those they thought to be
doomed.
23 Then, as soon as the cock
had crowed in the early morning,
Hermon, having equipped[m] the
animals, began to move them
along in the great colonnade.
24 The crowds of the city had been
assembled for this most pitiful
spectacle and they were eagerly
waiting for daybreak. 25 But the
Jews, at their last gasp—since the
time had run out—stretched their
hands toward heaven and with
most tearful supplication and
mournful dirges implored the supreme God[n] to help them again at
once. 26 The rays of the sun were
not yet shed abroad, and while the
king was receiving his Friends,
Hermon arrived and invited him to
come out, indicating that what the
king desired was ready for action.
27 But he, on receiving the report
and being struck by the unusual in-
vitation to come out—since he
had been completely overcome by
incomprehension—inquired what
the matter was for which this had
been so zealously completed for
him. 28 This was the act of God who
rules over all things, for he had implanted in the king's mind a forgetfulness of the things he had previously devised. 29 Then Hermon and
all the king's Friends[o] pointed out
that the animals and the armed
forces were ready, "O king, according to your eager purpose."[p] 30 But
at these words he was filled with
an overpowering wrath, because by
the providence of God his whole
mind had been deranged concerning these matters; and with a
threatening look he said, 31 "If your
parents or children were present, I
would have prepared them to be a
rich feast for the savage animals
instead of the Jews, who give me
no ground for complaint and have

5.12 Gen 2.21; 15.12; 1 Sam 26.12; Job 4.13
5.13 1 Chr 16.25, 36; Ezra 3.11; Ps 96.4; Tob 14.15; 2 Macc 8.2, 14; 10.4,26; Wis 7.23; 11.17
5.16 3 Macc 4.16; 5.3
5.17 Ex 32.18; 2 Macc 6.4; 3 Macc 4.8; Rom 13.13
5.20 3 Macc 5.42, 1-2
5.23 Mt 26.74; Lk 22.60; Jn 18.27
5.25 1 Kings 8.54; 2 Macc 3.20; 1 Tim 2.8; 3 Macc 5.13
5.28 Prov 16.1; 19.21; 21.1; Ps 22.28; 103.19; Add Esth 16.18; 3 Macc 2.7, 51; 3.11-29
5.30 3 Macc 4.13; 5.1; Dan 4.33

[i] Other ancient authorities add *from evening until the ninth hour*
[j] Other ancient authorities read *delayed* (Gk *untimely*) [k] Gk *he* [l] Gk *they*
[m] Or *armed* [n] Gk *the greatest God*
[o] Gk *all the Friends*
[p] Other ancient authorities read *pointed to the beasts and the armed forces, saying, "They are ready, O king, according to your eager purpose."*

exhibited to an extraordinary degree a full and firm loyalty to my ancestors. 32 In fact you would have been deprived of life instead of these, if it were not for an affection arising from our nurture in common and your usefulness." 33 So Hermon suffered an unexpected and dangerous threat, and his eyes wavered and his face fell. 34 The king's Friends one by one sullenly slipped away and dismissed[q] the assembled people to their own occupations. 35 Then the Jews, on hearing what the king had said, praised the manifest Lord God, King of kings, since this also was his aid that they had received.

36 The king, however, reconvened the party in the same manner and urged the guests to return to their celebrating. 37 After summoning Hermon he said in a threatening tone, "How many times, you poor wretch, must I give you orders about these things? 38 Equip[r] the elephants now once more for the destruction of the Jews tomorrow!" 39 But the officials who were at table with him, wondering at his instability of mind, remonstrated as follows: 40 "O king, how long will you put us to the test, as though we are idiots, ordering now for a third time that they be destroyed, and again revoking your decree in the matter?[s] 41 As a result the city is in a tumult because of its expectation; it is crowded with masses of people, and also in constant danger of being plundered."

42 At this the king, a Phalaris in everything and filled with madness, took no account of the changes of mind that had come about within him for the protection of the Jews, and he firmly swore an irrevocable oath that he would send them to death[t] without delay, mangled by the knees and feet of the animals, 43 and would also march against Judea and rapidly level it to the ground with fire and spear, and by burning to the ground the temple inaccessible to him[u] would quickly render it forever empty of those who offered sacrifices there. 44 Then the Friends and officers departed with great joy, and they confidently posted the armed forces at the places in the city most favorable for keeping guard.

45 Now when the animals had been brought virtually to a state of madness, so to speak, by the very fragrant draughts of wine mixed with frankincense and had been equipped with frightful devices, the elephant keeper 46 entered at about dawn into the courtyard—the city now being filled with countless masses of people crowding their way into the hippodrome—and urged the king on to the matter at hand. 47 So he, when he had filled his impious mind with a deep rage, rushed out in full force along with the animals, wishing to witness, with invulnerable heart and with his own eyes, the grievous and pitiful destruction of the aforementioned people.

48 When the Jews saw the dust raised by the elephants going out at the gate and by the following armed forces, as well as by the trampling of the crowd, and heard the loud and tumultuous noise, 49 they thought that this was their last moment of life, the end of their most miserable suspense, and giving way to lamentation and groans they kissed each other, embracing relatives and falling into one another's arms[v]—parents and children, mothers and daughters, and others with babies at their breasts who were drawing their last milk. 50 Not only this, but when they considered the help that they had received before from heaven, they prostrated themselves with one accord on the ground, removing the babies from their breasts, 51 and cried out in a very loud voice, imploring the Ruler over every power to manifest himself and be merciful to them, as they stood now at the gates of death.[t]

5.34 3 Macc 5.3
5.35 1 Tim 6.15; Rev 17.14; 19.16
5.36 3 Macc 5.3,16
5.38 3 Macc 5.2, 10,23
5.41 Job 39.7; 1 Macc 13.44; 3 Macc 3.8
5.42 3 Macc 5.20
5.43 2 Kings 25.9; 2 Chr 36.19; Bar 1.2; Tob 14.4; 1 Esd 1.55
5.46 3 Macc 4.11; 6.16
5.47 3 Macc 4.13; 5.1
5.50 1 Macc 3.19; 12.15; 16.3; 2 Macc 8.20; 3 Macc 4.21; Jdt 4.11; 2 Macc 3.15; 10.4; 3 Macc 1.16
5.51 3 Macc 2.7; 5.7,28; Ps 9.13; 88.3; 107.18

[q] Other ancient authorities read *he dismissed* [r] Or *Arm* [s] Other ancient authorities read *when the matter is in hand* [t] Gk *Hades* [u] Gk *us* [v] Gk *falling upon their necks*

The Prayer of Eleazar

6 Then a certain Eleazar, famous among the priests of the
country, who had attained a ripe
old age and throughout his life had
been adorned with every virtue, directed the elders around him to
stop calling upon the holy God,
and he prayed as follows: 2 "King of
great power, Almighty God Most
High, governing all creation with
mercy, 3 look upon the descendants of Abraham, O Father, upon
the children of the sainted Jacob, a
people of your consecrated portion
who are perishing as foreigners in a
foreign land. 4 Pharaoh with his
abundance of chariots, the former
ruler of this Egypt, exalted with
lawless insolence and boastful
tongue, you destroyed together
with his arrogant army by drowning
them in the sea, manifesting the
light of your mercy on the nation of
Israel. 5 Sennacherib exulting in
his countless forces, oppressive
king of the Assyrians, who had already gained control of the whole
world by the spear and was lifted
up against your holy city, speaking
grievous words with boasting and
insolence, you, O Lord, broke in
pieces, showing your power to
many nations. 6 The three companions in Babylon who had voluntar-
ily surrendered their lives to the
flames so as not to serve vain
things, you rescued unharmed,
even to a hair, moistening the fiery
furnace with dew and turning the
flame against all their enemies.
7 Daniel, who through envious
slanders was thrown down into the
ground to lions as food for wild animals, you brought up to the light
unharmed. 8 And Jonah, wasting
away in the belly of a huge, sea-
born monster, you, Father,
watched over and restored[w] unharmed to all his family. 9 And
now, you who hate insolence, all-
merciful and protector of all, reveal yourself quickly to those of
the nation of Israel[x]—who are being outrageously treated by the
abominable and lawless Gentiles.
10 "Even if our lives have become entangled in impieties in our
exile, rescue us from the hand of
the enemy, and destroy us, Lord,
by whatever fate you choose. 11 Let
not the vain-minded praise their
vanities[y] at the destruction of
your beloved people, saying, 'Not
even their god has rescued them.'
12 But you, O Eternal One, who
have all might and all power,
watch over us now and have mercy
on us who by the senseless insolence of the lawless are being deprived of life in the manner of traitors. 13 And let the Gentiles cower
today in fear of your invincible
might, O honored One, who have
power to save the nation of Jacob.
14 The whole throng of infants and
their parents entreat you with
tears. 15 Let it be shown to all the
Gentiles that you are with us,
O Lord, and have not turned your
face from us; but just as you have
said, 'Not even when they were in
the land of their enemies did I neglect them,' so accomplish it,
O Lord."

Two Angels Rescue the Jews

16 Just as Eleazar was ending
his prayer, the king arrived at the
hippodrome with the animals and
all the arrogance of his forces.
17 And when the Jews observed this
they raised great cries to heaven so
that even the nearby valleys resounded with them and brought an
uncontrollable terror upon the
army. 18 Then the most glorious, almighty, and true God revealed his
holy face and opened the heavenly
gates, from which two glorious angels of fearful aspect descended,
visible to all but the Jews. 19 They
opposed the forces of the enemy
and filled them with confusion and
terror, binding them with immovable shackles. 20 Even the king began to shudder bodily, and he forgot his sullen insolence. 21 The
animals turned back upon the
armed forces following them and

6.1 2 Macc 6.18; 4 Macc 5.4 **6.2** Gen 17.1; Ex 6.3; 1 Esd 9.6; Rev 4.8 **6.3** Gen 12.2-3; Isa 41.8; Lk 1.55,73 **6.4** Ex 14.28; Ps 78.53; 106.11 **6.5** 2 Kings 18.13; 19.35-37; 1 Macc 7.41; 2 Macc 8.19; 15.22 **6.6** Dan 3.16-17; Song of Thr 1.22-27 **6.7** Dan 6.16-22; Bel 31-42 **6.8** Jon 1.17-2.10 **6.9** Ps 91.1-13; 121.1-8 **6.10** Ps 35.17; 71.4; 144.7, 11; 2 Macc 1.25 **6.11** Ps 79.10; 115.2 **6.12** Ps 90.1-2; Sus 42; 2 Macc 1.25; 1 Chr 29.12; Wis 11.17; 3 Macc 5.13; Ps 123.2-3; Hab 3.2; Sir 36.1; Bar 3.2 **6.13** Ps 69.35; Isa 33.22; 59.1,16 **6.15** 2 Chr 13.12; Ps 46.7,11; Lev 26.44; Deut 4.31 **6.16** 3 Macc 4.11; 5.46 **6.18** Ps 76.4; Jdt 16.13; Song of Thr 1.3,22; Wis 18.17; 2 Macc 3.25-29; Mt 28.2-4; Dan 10.7; Acts 22.6-9

[w] Other ancient authorities read *rescued and restored*; others, *mercifully restored*
[x] Other ancient authorities read *to the saints of Israel*
[y] Or *bless their vain gods*

began trampling and destroying
them.
22 Then the king's anger was
turned to pity and tears because of
the things that he had devised beforehand. 23 For when he heard the
shouting and saw them all fallen
headlong to destruction, he wept
and angrily threatened his Friends,
saying, 24 "You are committing
treason and surpassing tyrants in
cruelty; and even me, your benefactor, you are now attempting to
deprive of dominion and life by secretly devising acts of no advantage to the kingdom. 25 Who has
driven from their homes those who
faithfully kept our country's fortresses, and foolishly gathered every one of them here? 26 Who is it
that has so lawlessly encompassed
with outrageous treatment those
who from the beginning differed
from[z] all nations in their goodwill
toward us and often have accepted
willingly the worst of human dangers? 27 Loose and untie their unjust bonds! Send them back to
their homes in peace, begging pardon for your former actions![a]
28 Release the children of the almighty and living God of heaven,
who from the time of our ancestors
until now has granted an unim-
peded and notable stability to our
government." 29 These then were
the things he said; and the Jews,
immediately released, praised
their holy God and Savior, since
they now had escaped death.

The Jews Celebrate Their Deliverance

30 Then the king, when he had
returned to the city, summoned
the official in charge of the revenues and ordered him to provide to
the Jews both wines and everything else needed for a festival of
seven days, deciding that they
should celebrate their rescue with
all joyfulness in that same place in
which they had expected to meet
their destruction. 31 Accordingly
those disgracefully treated and
near to death,[b] or rather, who
stood at its gates, arranged for a
banquet of deliverance instead of a
bitter and lamentable death, and
full of joy they apportioned to cele-
brants the place that had been prepared for their destruction and
burial. 32 They stopped their chant-
ing of dirges and took up the song
of their ancestors, praising God,
their Savior and worker of wonders.[c] Putting an end to all
mourning and wailing, they formed
choruses[d] as a sign of peaceful joy.
33 Likewise also the king, after con-
vening a great banquet to celebrate
these events, gave thanks to
heaven unceasingly and lavishly
for the unexpected rescue that
he[e] had experienced. 34 Those
who had previously believed that
the Jews would be destroyed and
become food for birds, and had joyfully registered them, groaned as
they themselves were overcome by
disgrace, and their fire-breathing
boldness was ignominiously[f]
quenched.
35 The Jews, as we have said
before, arranged the aforementioned choral group[g] and passed
the time in feasting to the accompaniment of joyous thanksgiving
and psalms. 36 And when they had
ordained a public rite for these
things in their whole community
and for their descendants, they instituted the observance of the
aforesaid days as a festival, not for
drinking and gluttony, but because
of the deliverance that had come
to them through God. 37 Then they
petitioned the king, asking for dismissal to their homes. 38 So their
registration was carried out from
the twenty-fifth of Pachon to the
fourth of Epeiph,[h] for forty days;
and their destruction was set for
the fifth to the seventh of
Epeiph,[i] the three days 39 on
which the Lord of all most gloriously revealed his mercy and rescued them all together and un-

6.22 3 Macc 4.13; 5.1,30
6.24 2 Macc 4.2; 3 Macc 3.19
6.26 3 Macc 3.3; 7.7
6.28 Hos 11.1; Wis 18.13; Jn 1.12; 1 Pet 2.9-10; Deut 5.26; Ps 42.2; Jer 10.10; Add Esth 16.16
6.29 Isa 43.3; 60.16; Add Esth 15.2; Sir 51.1
6.30 3 Macc 4.11; 5.46; 6.16
6.31 Job 38.17; Ps 107.18; 3 Macc 5.51; Esth 9.20-22; 1 Macc 4.59
6.32 2 Chr 20.21; Ezra 3.11; Ps 136; Ex 3.20; Neh 9.10; Ps 77.14; Dan 4.2-3
6.34 Gen 40.19; Ezek 39.4; 2 Macc 9.15
6.35 3 Macc 6.32; Ps 100.1-5; Jdt 16.1; Col 3.16
6.36 Esth 9.15; 1 Macc 4.56; 7.49; 2 Macc 10.6
6.39 Ex 15.1,21; Ps 76.4; Isa 12.5

[z] Or *excelled above*
[a] Other ancient authorities read *revoking your former commands* [b] Gk *Hades*
[c] Other ancient authorities read *praising Israel and the wonder-working God*; or *praising Israel's Savior, the wonder-working God*
[d] Or *dances* [e] Other ancient authorities read *they* [f] Other ancient authorities read *completely* [g] Or *dance*
[h] July 7—August 15 [i] August 16—18

harmed. 40 Then they feasted, being provided with everything by the king, until the fourteenth day,[j] on which also they made the petition for their dismissal. 41 The king granted their request at once and wrote the following letter for them to the generals in the cities, magnanimously expressing his concern:

Ptolemy's Letter on Behalf of the Jews

7 "King Ptolemy Philopator to the generals in Egypt and all in authority in his government, greetings and good health:

2 "We ourselves and our children are faring well, the great God guiding our affairs according to our desire. 3 Certain of our friends, frequently urging us with malicious intent, persuaded us to gather together the Jews of the kingdom in a body and to punish them with barbarous penalties as traitors; 4 for they declared that our government would never be firmly established until this was accomplished, because of the ill-will that these people had toward all nations. 5 They also led them out with harsh treatment as slaves, or rather as traitors, and, girding themselves with a cruelty more savage than that of Scythian custom, they tried without any inquiry or examination to put them to death. 6 But we very severely threatened them for these acts, and in accordance with the clemency that we have toward all people we barely spared their lives. Since we have come to realize that the God of heaven surely defends the Jews, always taking their part as a father does for his children, 7 and since we have taken into account the friendly and firm goodwill that they had toward us and our ancestors, we justly have acquitted them of every charge of whatever kind. 8 We also have ordered all people to return to their own homes, with no one in any place[k] doing them harm at all or reproaching them for the irrational things that have happened. 9 For you should know that if we devise any evil against them or cause them any grief at all, we always shall have not a mortal but the Ruler over every power, the Most High God, in everything and inescapably as an antagonist to avenge such acts. Farewell."

The Jews Return Home with Joy

10 On receiving this letter the Jews[l] did not immediately hurry to make their departure, but they requested of the king that at their own hands those of the Jewish nation who had willfully transgressed against the holy God and the law of God should receive the punishment they deserved. 11 They declared that those who for the belly's sake had transgressed the divine commandments would never be favorably disposed toward the king's government. 12 The king[m] then, admitting and approving the truth of what they said, granted them a general license so that freely, and without royal authority or supervision, they might destroy those everywhere in his kingdom who had transgressed the law of God. 13 When they had applauded him in fitting manner, their priests and the whole multitude shouted the Hallelujah and joyfully departed. 14 And so on their way they punished and put to a public and shameful death any whom they met of their compatriots who had become defiled. 15 In that day they put to death more than three hundred men; and they kept the day as a joyful festival, since they had destroyed the profaners. 16 But those who had held fast to God even to death and had received the full enjoyment of deliverance began their departure from the city, crowned with all sorts of very fragrant flowers, joyfully and loudly giving thanks to the one God of their ancestors, the eternal Savior[n] of Israel, in words of praise and all kinds of melodious songs.

6.40 3 Macc 7.18 **7.1** 3 Macc 1.1; 3.12 **7.3** 3 Macc 3.2 **7.4** Esth 3.8; 3 Macc 3.2,7 **7.5** Ex 1.8-14; 2 Macc 8.11; 3 Macc 2.28; 2 Macc 4.47; 4 Macc 10.7 **7.6** Dan 3.24-27; 6.19-23; Zech 8.23; Ps 103.13; Tob 13.4; 3 Macc 5.7; 2 Cor 1.3 **7.7** 3 Macc 3.3; 6.26 **7.8** 3 Macc 6.37, 40-41 **7.9** 2 Macc 1.25; 3 Macc 2.2; Rev 1.5,8; 19.15-16; Gen 14.19; Ps 57.2; Deut 32.35; Rom 12.19; Heb 10.30 **7.10** Esth 8.8-11; Jn 19.31; Deut 13.6-18; 17.2-7 **7.11** Rom 16.18; Phil 3.19 **7.13** Tob 13.17; Rev 19.1,3-4, 6 **7.15** 3 Macc 6.35-36 **7.16** Bar 5.6-9; Deut 6.4-5; 1 Cor 8.4,6; Isa 60.16; Hos 13.4; 3 Macc 6.29, 32

[j] August 25 [k] Other ancient authorities read *way* [l] Gk *they* [m] Gk *He*
[n] Other ancient authorities read *the holy Savior*; others, *the holy one*

17 When they had arrived at
Ptolemais, called "rose-bearing"
because of a characteristic of the
place, the fleet waited for them, in
accordance with the common desire, for seven days. 18 There they
celebrated their deliverance,[o] for
the king had generously provided
all things to them for their journey
until all of them arrived at their
own houses. 19 And when they had
all landed in peace with appropriate thanksgiving, there too in like
manner they decided to observe
these days as a joyous festival during the time of their stay. 20 Then,
after inscribing them as holy on a
pillar and dedicating a place of
prayer at the site of the festival,
they departed unharmed, free, and
overjoyed, since at the king's command they had all of them been
brought safely by land and sea and
river to their own homes. 21 They
also possessed greater prestige
among their enemies, being held
in honor and awe; and they were
not subject at all to confiscation of
their belongings by any one. 22 Besides, they all recovered all of their
property, in accordance with the
registration, so that those who
held any of it restored it to them
with extreme fear.[p] So the supreme God perfectly performed
great deeds for their deliverance.
23 Blessed be the Deliverer of Israel
through all times! Amen.

7.17 1 Macc 5.15, 22; 2 Macc 6.8
7.18 3 Macc 6.40
7.19 3 Macc 6.36
7.20 3 Macc 2.27; 6.39; 7.2-9
7.21 Tob 1.2; Heb 10.34
7.22 2 Macc 3.36; 3 Macc 1.9,16
7.23 2 Sam 22.2; Ps 18.2; 140.7; Rom 11.26

[o] Gk *they made a cup of deliverance*
[p] Other ancient authorities read *with a very large supplement*

(c) The following book is included in the Slavonic Bible as 3 Esdras, but is not found in the Greek. It is included in the Appendix to the Latin Vulgate Bible as 4 Esdras.

2 Esdras

Title and Background

This book claims to be a series of apocalyptic visions (similar in style to Revelation) given to Ezra, the scribe. The visions were intended to help God's people affirm God's power, goodness, and justice in the midst of the wickedness and cruelty of those who ruled over them.

Author and Date of Writing

The book of 2 Esdras was written in three sections at three times. Chapters 3–14 were written in Hebrew by an unknown Palestinian Jew at the end of the first century A.D. About fifty years later, a Christian writer composed chapters 1–2 in Greek as an introduction, and almost a century after that another Greek-speaking Christian wrote the final two chapters.

Theme and Message

One theme of 2 Esdras is the denunciation of the wickedness of the Roman empire. But the central part of this book struggles with, and provides answers to, the problem of evil and suffering in a world created by a loving God. It addresses particularly the suffering of God's people. According to the book, Ezra receives several visions of the signs of the end times and confirmation that the righteous, though few in number, will be saved.

Outline

I. God's Call of Ezra as Prophet (1.1–2.48)
II. Ezra's Prayer (3.1-36)
III. Ezra's Visions from the Angel Uriel (4.1–6.34)
IV. Ezra's Conversation with Uriel (6.35–9.37)
V. Further Visions (9.38–13.58)
VI. Ezra and the Scriptures (14.1-48)
VII. Ezra's Final Prophecies (15.1–16.78)

Comprising what is sometimes called 5 Ezra (chapters 1–2), 4 Ezra (chapters 3–14), and 6 Ezra (chapters 15–16)

The Genealogy of Ezra

1 The book[a] of the prophet
Ezra son of Seraiah son of Azariah son of Hilkiah son of Shallum
son of Zadok son of Ahitub 2 son of
Ahijah son of Phinehas son of Eli
son of Amariah son of Azariah son
of Meraimoth son of Arna son of
Uzzi son of Borith son of Abishua
son of Phinehas son of Eleazar
3 son of Aaron, of the tribe of Levi,
who was a captive in the country of
the Medes in the reign of Artaxerxes, king of the Persians.[b]

1.1 Ezra 7.1-5; 1 Esd 8.1-2 **1.3** Ezra 4.7; 7.1; Neh 2.1; Add Esth 1.1-2 **1.5** Isa 6.9; 50.1; 58.1; 2 Kings 17.41; Ps 78.4-8

Ezra's Prophetic Call

4 The word of the Lord came to
me, saying, 5 "Go, declare to my
people their evil deeds, and to
their children the iniquities that
they have committed against me,

[a] Other ancient authorities read *The second book* [b] Other ancient authorities, which place chapters 1 and 2 after 16.78, lack verses 1-3 and begin the chapter: *The word of the Lord that came to Ezra son of Chusi in the days of King Nebuchadnezzar, saying, "Go,*

so that they may tell[c] their children's children 6 that the sins of
their parents have increased in
them, for they have forgotten me
and have offered sacrifices to
strange gods. 7 Was it not I who
brought them out of the land of
Egypt, out of the house of bondage? But they have angered me and
despised my counsels. 8 Now you,
pull out the hair of your head and
hurl[d] all evils upon them, for they
have not obeyed my law—they are
a rebellious people. 9 How long
shall I endure them, on whom I
have bestowed such great benefits? 10 For their sake I have overthrown many kings; I struck down
Pharaoh with his servants and all
his army. 11 I destroyed all nations
before them, and scattered in the
east the peoples of two provinces,[e] Tyre and Sidon; I killed all
their enemies.

God's Mercies to Israel

12 "But speak to them and say,
Thus says the Lord: 13 Surely it was
I who brought you through the sea,
and made safe highways for you
where there was no road; I gave you
Moses as leader and Aaron as
priest; 14 I provided light for you
from a pillar of fire, and did great
wonders among you. Yet you have
forgotten me, says the Lord.
15 "Thus says the Lord Almighty:[f] The quails were a sign to
you; I gave you camps for your protection, and in them you complained. 16 You have not exulted in
my name at the destruction of your
enemies, but to this day you still
complain.[g] 17 Where are the benefits that I bestowed on you? When
you were hungry and thirsty in the
wilderness, did you not cry out to
me, 18 saying, 'Why have you led us
into this wilderness to kill us? It
would have been better for us to
serve the Egyptians than to die in
this wilderness.' 19 I pitied your
groanings and gave you manna for
food; you ate the bread of angels.
20 When you were thirsty, did I not
split the rock so that waters flowed
in abundance? Because of the heat
I clothed you with the leaves of
trees.[h] 21 I divided fertile lands
among you; I drove out the Canaanites, the Perizzites, and the
Philistines[i] before you. What
more can I do for you? says the
Lord. 22 Thus says the Lord Almighty:[f] When you were in the
wilderness, at the bitter stream,
thirsty and blaspheming my name,
23 I did not send fire on you for your
blasphemies, but threw a tree into
the water and made the stream
sweet.

Israel's Disobedience and Rejection

24 "What shall I do to you,
O Jacob? You, Judah, would not
obey me. I will turn to other nations and will give them my name,
so that they may keep my statutes.
25 Because you have forsaken me, I
also will forsake you. When you
beg mercy of me, I will show you no
mercy. 26 When you call to me, I
will not listen to you; for you have
defiled your hands with blood, and
your feet are swift to commit murder. 27 It is not as though you had
forsaken me; you have forsaken
yourselves, says the Lord.
28 "Thus says the Lord Almighty: Have I not entreated you
as a father entreats his sons or a
mother her daughters or a nurse
her children, 29 so that you should
be my people and I should be your
God, and that you should be my
children and I should be your father? 30 I gathered you as a hen
gathers her chicks under her
wings. But now, what shall I do to
you? I will cast you out from my
presence. 31 When you offer obla-

1.6 Isa 7.10; 51.13; Jer 2.32; 18.15 **1.7** Ex 12.29-35; 20.2; 2 Kings 24.20; Ezra 5.12 **1.8** Ezra 9.3; 1 Esd 8.71; Deut 9.7; Isa 30.9; Jer 6.28; Ezek 2.5-8 **1.10** Ex 14.28 **1.11** Josh 24.8; Am 2.9 **1.13** Ex 14.22,29; 4.14-17; Ps 77.20; 105.26 **1.14** Ex 13.21; 7.3; Deut 6.22; Neh 9.10; Jer 32.20-21 **1.15** Ex 16.13; Ps 105.40 **1.18** Ex 16.3; 17.3; Num 14.2-5 **1.19** Ex 16.14-31; Josh 5.12; Ps 78.25; Wis 16.20 **1.20** Ex 17.6; Num 20.10-11; Wis 11.4 **1.21** Ex 23.28-31; 34.11; Josh 24.18; Ps 78.55; Isa 5.4 **1.23** Ex 15.22-25 **1.24** Mk 12.1-9; Acts 13.45-46; 18.6 **1.25** 2 Chr 15.2; 24.20; Jer 16.10-11 **1.26** Isa 1.15; 59.2,3,7 **1.28** Ps 103.13; Isa 63.16; 64.8

1.29 Deut 7.6; Jer 24.7; Zech 8.8; Heb 8.10 **1.30** Mt 23.37; Lk 13.34; Jer 7.15 **1.31** Isa 1.12-14; Am 5.21-22

[c] Other ancient authorities read *nourish*
[d] Other ancient authorities read *and shake out*
[e] Other ancient authorities read *Did I not destroy the city of Bethsaida because of you, and to the south burn two cities . . . ?*
[f] Other ancient authorities lack *Almighty*
[g] Other ancient authorities read verse 16, *Your pursuer with his army I sank in the sea, but still the people complain also concerning their own destruction.*
[h] Other ancient authorities read *I made for you trees with leaves*
[i] Other ancient authorities read *Perizzites and their children*

tions to me, I will turn my face
from you; for I have rejected your[j]
festal days, and new moons, and
circumcisions of the flesh.[k] 32 I
sent you my servants the prophets,
but you have taken and killed them
and torn their bodies[l] in pieces; I
will require their blood of you, says
the Lord.[m]

33 "Thus says the Lord Almighty: Your house is desolate; I
will drive you out as the wind
drives straw; 34 and your sons will
have no children, because with
you[n] they have neglected my commandment and have done what is
evil in my sight. 35 I will give your
houses to a people that will come,
who without having heard me will
believe. Those to whom I have
shown no signs will do what I have
commanded. 36 They have seen no
prophets, yet will recall their former state.[o] 37 I call to witness the
gratitude of the people that is to
come, whose children rejoice with
gladness;[p] though they do not see
me with bodily eyes, yet with the
spirit they will believe the things I
have said.

38 "And now, father,[q] look
with pride and see the people coming from the east; 39 to them I will
give as leaders Abraham, Isaac,
and Jacob, and Hosea and Amos
and Micah and Joel and Obadiah
and Jonah 40 and Nahum and Habakkuk, Zephaniah, Haggai, Zechariah and Malachi, who is also
called the messenger of the Lord.[r]

God's Judgment on Israel

2 "Thus says the Lord: I brought
this people out of bondage,
and I gave them commandments
through my servants the prophets;
but they would not listen to them,
and made my counsels void. 2 The
mother who bore them[s] says to
them, 'Go, my children, because I
am a widow and forsaken. 3 I
brought you up with gladness; but
with mourning and sorrow I have
lost you, because you have sinned
before the Lord God and have done
what is evil in my sight.[t] 4 But now
what can I do for you? For I am a
widow and forsaken. Go, my children, and ask for mercy from the
Lord.' 5 Now I call upon you, father, as a witness in addition to the
mother of the children, because
they would not keep my covenant,
6 so that you may bring confusion
on them and bring their mother to
ruin, so that they may have no offspring. 7 Let them be scattered
among the nations; let their names
be blotted out from the earth, because they have despised my covenant.

8 "Woe to you, Assyria, who
conceal the unrighteous within
you! O wicked nation, remember
what I did to Sodom and Gomorrah, 9 whose land lies in lumps of
pitch and heaps of ashes.[u] That is
what I will do to those who have
not listened to me, says the Lord
Almighty."

10 Thus says the Lord to Ezra:
"Tell my people that I will give
them the kingdom of Jerusalem,
which I was going to give to Israel.
11 Moreover, I will take back to myself their glory, and will give to
these others the everlasting habitations, which I had prepared for
Israel.[v] 12 The tree of life shall give
them fragrant perfume, and they

1.32 2 Chr 36.16; Mt 23.34-35; Acts 7.52; 2 Sam 4.11; Ezek 3.18,20
1.33 Isa 1.7; 6.11; Jer 12.11; Ezek 15.8
1.35 Isa 11.10; Zech 8.22-23; Rom 10.9-17; 15.12
1.37 Jn 20.29
1.38 2 Esd 2.5
1.39 Hos 1.1
1.40 Mal 1.1; 3.1
2.1 2 Esd 1.7; Am 3.7; Zech 1.6; Rev 10.7
2.2 Isa 54.1; Gal 4.26-27; Bar 4.19; Isa 54.4; Lam 1.1
2.3 Bar 4.11; Lam 1.12; Lk 19.41-44
2.5 2 Esd 1.38; Isa 24.5; Jer 31.32; Ezek 17.18-19
2.6 Mt 24.2; Lk 21.20-24
2.7 Lev 26.33; Deut 4.27; Jer 9.16; Ezek 12.14-15
2.8 Gen 19.24; 3 Macc 2.5; Jude 7
2.10 Hos 1.9; 2.23; 1 Pet 1.10
2.11 2 Esd 1.24; Lk 16.9; Jn 14.2-3; 2 Cor 5.1
2.12 Gen 2.9; 3.22; Rev 2.7; 22.2, 14

[j] Other ancient authorities read *I have not commanded for you*
[k] Other ancient authorities lack *of the flesh*
[l] Other ancient authorities read *the bodies of the apostles*
[m] Other ancient authorities add *Thus says the Lord Almighty: Recently you also laid hands on me, crying out before the judge's seat for him to deliver me to you. You took me as a sinner, not as a father who freed you from slavery, and you delivered me to death by hanging me on the tree; these are the things you have done. Therefore, says the Lord, let my Father and his angels return and judge between you and me; if I have not kept the commandment of the Father, if I have not nourished you, if I have not done the things my Father commanded, I will contend in judgment with you, says the Lord.*
[n] Other ancient authorities lack *with you*
[o] Other ancient authorities read *their iniquities*
[p] Other ancient authorities read *The apostles bear witness to the coming people with joy*
[q] Other ancient authorities read *brother*
[r] Other ancient authorities read *and Jacob, Elijah and Enoch, Zechariah and Hosea, Amos, Joel, Micah, Obadiah, Zephaniah, 40 Nahum, Jonah, Mattia* (or *Mattathias*), *Habakkuk, and twelve angels with flowers*
[s] Other ancient authorities read *They begat for themselves a mother who*
[t] Other ancient authorities read *in his sight*
[u] Other ancient authorities read *Gomorrah, whose land descends to hell*
[v] Lat *for those*

shall neither toil nor become
weary. 13 Go[w] and you will receive;
pray that your days may be few,
that they may be shortened. The
kingdom is already prepared for
you; be on the watch! 14 Call, O call
heaven and earth to witness: I set
aside evil and created good; for I
am the Living One, says the Lord.

Exhortation to Good Works

15 "Mother, embrace your children; bring them up with gladness,
as does a dove; strengthen their
feet, because I have chosen you,
says the Lord. 16 And I will raise up
the dead from their places, and
bring them out from their tombs,
because I recognize my name in
them. 17 Do not fear, mother of
children, for I have chosen you,
says the Lord. 18 I will send you
help, my servants Isaiah and Jeremiah. According to their counsel I
have consecrated and prepared for
you twelve trees loaded with various fruits, 19 and the same number
of springs flowing with milk and
honey, and seven mighty mountains on which roses and lilies
grow; by these I will fill your children with joy.

20 "Guard the rights of the
widow, secure justice for the ward,
give to the needy, defend the orphan, clothe the naked, 21 care for
the injured and the weak, do not
ridicule the lame, protect the
maimed, and let the blind have a
vision of my splendor. 22 Protect
the old and the young within your
walls; 23 When you find any who are
dead, commit them to the grave
and mark it,[x] and I will give you
the first place in my resurrection.
24 Pause and be quiet, my people,
because your rest will come.

25 "Good nurse, nourish your
children; strengthen their feet.
26 Not one of the servants[y] whom I
have given you will perish, for I will
require them from among your
number. 27 Do not be anxious, for
when the day of tribulation and anguish comes, others shall weep
and be sorrowful, but you shall rejoice and have abundance. 28 The
nations shall envy you, but they
shall not be able to do anything
against you, says the Lord. 29 My
power will protect[z] you, so that
your children may not see hell.[a]

30 "Rejoice, O mother, with
your children, because I will deliver you, says the Lord. 31 Remember your children that sleep, because I will bring them out of the
hiding places of the earth, and will
show mercy to them; for I am merciful, says the Lord Almighty.
32 Embrace your children until I
come, and proclaim mercy to
them; because my springs run over,
and my grace will not fail."

Ezra on Mount Horeb

33 I, Ezra, received a command
from the Lord on Mount Horeb to
go to Israel. When I came to them
they rejected me and refused the
Lord's commandment. 34 Therefore I say to you, O nations that
hear and understand, "Wait for
your shepherd; he will give you everlasting rest, because he who will
come at the end of the age is close
at hand. 35 Be ready for the rewards
of the kingdom, because perpetual
light will shine on you forevermore. 36 Flee from the shadow of
this age, receive the joy of your
glory; I publicly call on my savior to
witness.[b] 37 Receive what the Lord
has entrusted to you and be joyful,
giving thanks to him who has
called you to the celestial kingdoms. 38 Rise, stand erect and see
the number of those who have
been sealed at the feast of the
Lord. 39 Those who have departed
from the shadow of this age have
received glorious garments from
the Lord. 40 Take again your full
number, O Zion, and close the list
of your people who are clothed in
white, who have fulfilled the law of

2.13 Mt 7.7-8; Lk 11.9-11; Mt 24.22; Mk 13.20, 23,33-37 **2.14** Deut 30.19; Isa 1.2; Jdt 7.28; Jer 10.10; Dan 6.26; Rev 1.18 **2.15** 2 Esd 2.2; Deut 7.6; 1 Kings 8.44; Isa 42.1 **2.16** Dan 12.2; Jn 5.28; 1 Cor 15.51-55 **2.18** Rev 22.2 **2.19** Ex 3.8; Deut 31.20; Jer 11.5 **2.20** Deut 26.12-13; Isa 1.17; Zech 7.10; Job 31.16-22; Mt 25.34-40 **2.21** Isa 35.5; Lk 4.18; Jn 9.1-25 **2.23** Tob 1.17-19; Sir 38.16 **2.25** Isa 35.3; Heb 12.12-13; Jn 10.28-29; 17.12 **2.27** Jer 51.48; Rev 18.20; 19.1-2 **2.30** Isa 44.23; 61.3; 66.10 **2.31** 2 Macc 7.9; Jn 6.40; 2 Cor 4.14; Ex 34.6; Ps 103.8; Joel 2.13 **2.32** Ps 23.5 **2.33** Ex 3.1; Deut 4.15; 2 Chr 5.10 **2.34** Isa 40.11; Ezek 34.15, 23; Jn 10.11; Heb 13.20

2.35 Isa 60.20; 2 Esd 7.42; Rev 21.23; 22.5 **2.36** Isa 43.10,12; 44.8; Jer 29.23 **2.38** Rev 7.4-8 **2.39** Mt 22.11; Rev 3.5; 7.9 **2.40** Heb 12.22-23; Rev 3.4; 6.11; 7.14

[w] Other ancient authorities read *Seek*
[x] Or *seal it*; or *mark them and commit them to the grave* [y] Or *slaves* [z] Lat *hands will cover* [a] Lat *Gehenna*
[b] Other ancient authorities read *I testify that my savior has been commissioned by the Lord*

the Lord. 41 The number of your
children, whom you desired, is
now complete; implore the Lord's
authority that your people, who
have been called from the beginning, may be made holy."

Ezra Sees the Son of God

42 I, Ezra, saw on Mount Zion a
great multitude that I could not
number, and they all were praising
the Lord with songs. 43 In their
midst was a young man of great
stature, taller than any of the others, and on the head of each of
them he placed a crown, but he
was more exalted than they. And I
was held spellbound. 44 Then I
asked an angel, "Who are these,
my lord?" 45 He answered and said
to me, "These are they who have
put off mortal clothing and have
put on the immortal, and have confessed the name of God. Now they
are being crowned, and receive
palms." 46 Then I said to the angel,
"Who is that young man who is
placing crowns on them and putting palms in their hands?" 47 He
answered and said to me, "He is
the Son of God, whom they confessed in the world." So I began to
praise those who had stood valiantly for the name of the Lord.[c]
48 Then the angel said to me, "Go,
tell my people how great and how
many are the wonders of the Lord
God that you have seen."

Ezra's Prayer of Complaint

3 In the thirtieth year after the
destruction of the city, I was
in Babylon—I, Salathiel, who am
also called Ezra. I was troubled as
I lay on my bed, and my thoughts
welled up in my heart, 2 because I
saw the desolation of Zion and the
wealth of those who lived in Babylon. 3 My spirit was greatly agitated, and I began to speak anxious words to the Most High, and
said, 4 "O sovereign Lord, did you
not speak at the beginning when
you planted[d] the earth—and that
without help—and commanded
the dust[e] 5 and it gave you Adam, a
lifeless body? Yet he was the creation of your hands, and you
breathed into him the breath of
life, and he was made alive in your
presence. 6 And you led him into
the garden that your right hand
had planted before the earth appeared. 7 And you laid upon him
one commandment of yours; but
he transgressed it, and immediately you appointed death for him
and for his descendants. From him
there sprang nations and tribes,
peoples and clans without number. 8 And every nation walked after its own will; they did ungodly
things in your sight and rejected
your commands, and you did not
hinder them. 9 But again, in its
time you brought the flood upon
the inhabitants of the world and
destroyed them. 10 And the same
fate befell all of them: just as death
came upon Adam, so the flood
upon them. 11 But you left one of
them, Noah with his household,
and all the righteous who have descended from him.

12 "When those who lived on
earth began to multiply, they produced children and peoples and
many nations, and again they began to be more ungodly than were
their ancestors. 13 And when they
were committing iniquity in your
sight, you chose for yourself one of
them, whose name was Abraham;
14 you loved him, and to him alone
you revealed the end of the times,
secretly by night. 15 You made an
everlasting covenant with him, and
promised him that you would
never forsake his descendants; and
you gave him Isaac, and to Isaac
you gave Jacob and Esau. 16 You set
apart Jacob for yourself, but Esau
you rejected; and Jacob became a
great multitude. 17 And when you
led his descendants out of Egypt,
you brought them to Mount Sinai.
18 You bent down the heavens and
shook[f] the earth, and moved the

2.41 2 Esd 6.36-37; Rev 6.11; Rom 8.28-30 **2.42** Rev 7.9 **2.43** Rev 1.13-15; 1 Cor 9.25; 2 Tim 4.8; 1 Pet 5.4; Rev 2.10 **2.44** 2 Esd 4.1; Rev 7.13 **2.45** Rev 7.9 **2.47** Mt 10.32; Rom 10.9-10 **2.48** Rev 1.11; 4.1-2 **3.1** 2 Kings 25.1-21; 2 Chr 36.11-20; Ezra 3.2; 5.2 **3.2** Isa 64.10; Jer 4.27; 2 Esd 12.48 **3.4** Gen 1.9-12 **3.5** Gen 2.7 **3.6** Gen 2.8 **3.7** Gen 2.16-17; 3.1-7,22; 2 Esd 7.118; Rom 5.12; 1 Cor 15.21-22; Gen 5.1-32; Acts 17.26 **3.8** Gen 6.5,12; 8.12 **3.9** Gen 6.13-7.24 **3.11** Gen 6.9-13; 8.13-18 **3.12** Gen 10.1-32; 11.1-9 **3.13** Gen 12.1; 17.5 **3.14** Gen 15.5, 12,17 **3.15** Gen 17.7; 21.1-3; 25.21-26 **3.16** Gen 25.23; Mal 1.2-3; Rom 9.12-13

3.17 Ex 12.29-39; 19.1-2 **3.18** Ex 19.16-18; Ps 68.7-8

[c] Other ancient authorities read *to praise and glorify the Lord* [d] Other ancient authorities read *formed* [e] Syr Ethiop: Lat *people* or *world* [f] Syr Ethiop Arab 1 Georg: Lat *set fast*

world, and caused the depths to
tremble, and troubled the times.
19 Your glory passed through the
four gates of fire and earthquake
and wind and ice, to give the law to
the descendants of Jacob, and your
commandment to the posterity of
Israel.
20 "Yet you did not take away
their evil heart from them, so that
your law might produce fruit in
them. 21 For the first Adam, burdened with an evil heart, transgressed and was overcome, as were
also all who were descended from
him. 22 Thus the disease became
permanent; the law was in the
hearts of the people along with the
evil root; but what was good departed, and the evil remained. 23 So
the times passed and the years
were completed, and you raised up
for yourself a servant, named David. 24 You commanded him to
build a city for your name, and
there to offer you oblations from
what is yours. 25 This was done for
many years; but the inhabitants of
the city transgressed, 26 in everything doing just as Adam and all
his descendants had done, for they
also had the evil heart. 27 So you
handed over your city to your enemies.

Babylon Compared with Zion

28 "Then I said in my heart, Are
the deeds of those who inhabit
Babylon any better? Is that why it
has gained dominion over Zion?
29 For when I came here I saw ungodly deeds without number, and
my soul has seen many sinners
during these thirty years.[g] And my
heart failed me, 30 because I have
seen how you endure those who
sin, and have spared those who act
wickedly, and have destroyed your
people, and protected your enemies, 31 and have not shown to anyone how your way may be comprehended.[h] Are the deeds of
Babylon better than those of Zion?
32 Or has another nation known
you besides Israel? Or what tribes
have so believed the covenants as
these tribes of Jacob? 33 Yet their
reward has not appeared and their
labor has borne no fruit. For I have
traveled widely among the nations
and have seen that they abound in
wealth, though they are unmindful
of your commandments. 34 Now
therefore weigh in a balance our
iniquities and those of the inhabitants of the world; and it will be
found which way the turn of the
scale will incline. 35 When have the
inhabitants of the earth not sinned
in your sight? Or what nation has
kept your commandments so well?
36 You may indeed find individuals
who have kept your commandments, but nations you will not
find."

Limitations of the Human Mind

4 Then the angel that had been
sent to me, whose name was
Uriel, answered 2 and said to me,
"Your understanding has utterly
failed regarding this world, and do
you think you can comprehend the
way of the Most High?" 3 Then I
said, "Yes, my lord." And he replied to me, "I have been sent to
show you three ways, and to put
before you three problems. 4 If you
can solve one of them for me, then
I will show you the way you desire
to see, and will teach you why the
heart is evil."
5 I said, "Speak, my lord."
And he said to me, "Go, weigh
for me the weight of fire, or measure for me a blast[i] of wind, or call
back for me the day that is past."
6 I answered and said, "Who of
those that have been born can do
that, that you should ask me about
such things?"
7 And he said to me, "If I had
asked you, 'How many dwellings
are in the heart of the sea, or how
many streams are at the source of
the deep, or how many streams are
above the firmament, or which are
the exits of Hades, or which are the
entrances[j] of paradise?' 8 perhaps
you would have said to me, 'I never
went down into the deep, nor as

3.19 Ex 20.1-21
3.20 Sir 15.14-17; Jer 17.9; 2 Esd 7.48
3.21 Gen 3.1-7; 1 Cor 15.45; Rom 5.12; 1 Cor 15.22
3.23 1 Sam 16.11-13
3.24 2 Sam 5.6-7
3.25 2 Kings 18.12; Isa 24.5; Lam 3.42
3.27 Jer 34.17-22; Bar 4.6; Acts 7.42
3.28 Rev 14.8; 18.1-3,7
3.30 Ps 72.3-14; Jer 20.5-6; Hab 1.13-17
3.32 Wis 18.22; 2 Macc 8.15; Rom 9.4
3.33 Ps 73.3,7-9; Jer 12.1
3.34 Job 31.6; Ps 62.9; Prov 16.2; Dan 5.27
4.1 2 Esd 2.44; 5.20; 10.28
4.2 Isa 40.28; 55.8-9; Rom 11.33
4.4 Jer 17.9; Sir 10.12
4.6 Job 15.14; 25.4; Ps 139.3-6,17
4.8 Rom 10.6-7

[g] Ethiop Arab 1 Arm: Lat Syr *in this thirtieth year* [h] Syr; compare Ethiop: Lat *how this way should be forsaken* [i] Syr Ethiop Arab 1 Arab 2 Georg *a measure*
[j] Syr Compare Ethiop Arab 2 Arm: Lat lacks *of Hades, or which are the entrances*

yet into Hades, neither did I ever ascend into heaven.' 9 But now I have asked you only about fire and wind and the day—things that you have experienced and from which you cannot be separated, and you have given me no answer about them." 10 He said to me, "You cannot understand the things with which you have grown up; 11 how then can your mind comprehend the way of the Most High? And how can one who is already worn out[k] by the corrupt world understand incorruption?"[l] When I heard this, I fell on my face[m] 12 and said to him, "It would have been better for us not to be here than to come here and live in ungodliness, and to suffer and not understand why."

Parable of the Forest and the Sea

13 He answered me and said, "I went into a forest of trees of the plain, and they made a plan 14 and said, 'Come, let us go and make war against the sea, so that it may recede before us and so that we may make for ourselves more forests.' 15 In like manner the waves of the sea also made a plan and said, 'Come, let us go up and subdue the forest of the plain so that there also we may gain more territory for ourselves.' 16 But the plan of the forest was in vain, for the fire came and consumed it; 17 likewise also the plan of the waves of the sea was in vain,[n] for the sand stood firm and blocked it. 18 If now you were a judge between them, which would you undertake to justify, and which to condemn?"

19 I answered and said, "Each made a foolish plan, for the land has been assigned to the forest, and the locale of the sea a place to carry its waves."

20 He answered me and said, "You have judged rightly, but why have you not judged so in your own case? 21 For as the land has been assigned to the forest and the sea to its waves, so also those who inhabit the earth can understand only what is on the earth, and he who is[o] above the heavens can understand what is above the height of the heavens."

The New Age Will Make All Things Clear

22 Then I answered and said, "I implore you, my lord, why[p] have I been endowed with the power of understanding? 23 For I did not wish to inquire about the ways above, but about those things that we daily experience: why Israel has been given over to the Gentiles in disgrace; why the people whom you loved has been given over to godless tribes, and the law of our ancestors has been brought to destruction and the written covenants no longer exist. 24 We pass from the world like locusts, and our life is like a mist,[q] and we are not worthy to obtain mercy. 25 But what will he do for his[r] name that is invoked over us? It is about these things that I have asked."

26 He answered me and said, "If you are alive, you will see, and if you live long,[s] you will often marvel, because the age is hurrying swiftly to its end. 27 It will not be able to bring the things that have been promised to the righteous in their appointed times, because this age is full of sadness and infirmities. 28 For the evil about which[t] you ask me has been sown, but the harvest of it has not yet come. 29 If therefore that which has been sown is not reaped, and if the place where the evil has been sown does not pass away, the field where the good has been sown will not come. 30 For a grain of evil seed was sown in Adam's heart from the beginning, and how much ungodliness it has produced until now—and will produce until the time of threshing comes! 31 Consider now for yourself how much fruit of ungodliness a grain of evil seed has produced. 32 When heads of grain

4.11 Isa 40.28; 55.8-9; Rom 11.33
4.12 2 Esd 7.63
4.19 Gen 1.9-10; Deut 32.8; Prov 8.29; Acts 17.26
4.21 Ps 104.5-9; Jn 3.31; 2 Cor 2.14; Isa 55.8-9
4.23 2 Kings 25.1-21; 2 Chr 36.11-20; 1 Macc 1.6-13; Hab 1.13-17; 2 Esd 3.28-31; 14.21; 3.32
4.24 Hos 13.3; Wis 2.4
4.26 2 Esd 5.55; 1 Cor 7.31; 1 Jn 2.17
4.28 Joel 3.13; Mt 13.24-30, 36-43; Rev 14.14-16
4.30 Sir 15.14-17; 2 Esd 3.20; Rom 5.12; 1 Cor 15.21

[k] Meaning of Lat uncertain [l] Syr Ethiop *the way of the incorruptible?*
[m] Syr Ethiop Arab 1: Meaning of Lat uncertain
[n] Lat lacks *was in vain* [o] Or *those who are*
[p] Syr Ethiop Arm: Meaning of Lat uncertain
[q] Syr Ethiop Arab Georg: Lat *a trembling*
[r] Ethiop adds *holy* [s] Syr: Lat *live*
[t] Syr Ethiop: Meaning of Lat uncertain

without number are sown, how
great a threshing floor they will
fill!"

When Will the New Age Come?

33 Then I answered and said,
"How long?[u] When will these
things be? Why are our years few
and evil?" 34 He answered me and
said, "Do not be in a greater hurry
than the Most High. You, indeed,
are in a hurry for yourself,[v] but the
Highest is in a hurry on behalf of
many. 35 Did not the souls of the
righteous in their chambers ask
about these matters, saying, 'How
long are we to remain here?[w] And
when will the harvest of our reward
come? 36 And the archangel Jere-
miel answered and said, 'When the
number of those like yourselves is
completed;[x] for he has weighed
the age in the balance, 37 and measured the times by measure, and
numbered the times by number;
and he will not move or arouse
them until that measure is fulfilled.' "

38 Then I answered and said,
"But, O sovereign Lord, all of us
also are full of ungodliness. 39 It is
perhaps on account of us that the
time of threshing is delayed for the
righteous—on account of the sins
of those who inhabit the earth."

40 He answered me and said,
"Go and ask a pregnant woman
whether, when her nine months
have been completed, her womb
can keep the fetus within her any
longer."

41 And I said, "No, lord, it cannot."

He said to me, "In Hades the
chambers of the souls are like the
womb. 42 For just as a woman who
is in labor makes haste to escape
the pangs of birth, so also do these
places hasten to give back those
things that were committed to
them from the beginning. 43 Then
the things that you desire to see
will be disclosed to you."

How Much Time Remains?

44 I answered and said, "If I
have found favor in your sight, and
if it is possible, and if I am worthy,
45 show me this also: whether more
time is to come than has passed, or
whether for us the greater part has
gone by. 46 For I know what has
gone by, but I do not know what is
to come."

47 And he said to me, "Stand at
my right side, and I will show you
the interpretation of a parable."

48 So I stood and looked, and
lo, a flaming furnace passed by before me, and when the flame had
gone by I looked, and lo, the smoke
remained. 49 And after this a cloud
full of water passed before me and
poured down a heavy and violent
rain, and when the violent rainstorm had passed, drops still remained in the cloud.[y]

50 He said to me, "Consider it
for yourself; for just as the rain is
more than the drops, and the fire is
greater than the smoke, so the
quantity that passed was far
greater; but drops and smoke remained."

51 Then I prayed and said, "Do
you think that I shall live until
those days? Or who will be alive in
those days?"

52 He answered me and said,
"Concerning the signs about which
you ask me, I can tell you in part;
but I was not sent to tell you concerning your life, for I do not know.

Signs of the End

5 "Now concerning the signs:
lo, the days are coming when
those who inhabit the earth shall
be seized with great terror,[u] and
the way of truth shall be hidden,
and the land shall be barren of
faith. 2 Unrighteousness shall be
increased beyond what you yourself see, and beyond what you
heard of formerly. 3 And the land
that you now see ruling shall be a
trackless waste, and people shall
see it desolate. 4 But if the Most
High grants that you live, you shall

4.33 Zech 1.12; Mk 13.4; Rev 6.10; Gen 47.9; Job 14.1; Eccl 2.23; 2 Esd 7.12
4.35 2 Esd 7.32, 95; Rev 6.9-10
4.36 2 Esd 2.41; Rev 6.11; Dan 5.24-28; 2 Esd 3.34
4.37 Sir 36.10; Rom 11.25
4.39 Gen 18.23-32
4.40 2 Esd 16.37
4.44 Gen 6.8; 18.3,27, 30-31; 2 Esd 5.56; 7.75
4.47 2 Esd 4.3-4; 7.75-76; Rev 4.1; 22.6
4.48 1 Kings 19.11-12
4.52 Mt 16.3; Mk 13.4; Lk 7.21
5.1 Mk 13.14-20; Lk 21.25-26
5.2 Mt 24.12; 2 Thess 2.3, 8-10
5.3 Isa 24.1-3; 60.12; Ezek 29.9-12; Rev 18.17,19
5.4 Mt 24.37-41, 19; Mk 13.24; Rev 8.12

[u] Syr Ethiop: Meaning of Lat uncertain
[v] Syr Ethiop Arab Arm: Meaning of Lat uncertain
[w] Syr Ethiop Arab 2 Georg: Lat *How long do I hope thus?*
[x] Syr Ethiop Arab 2: Lat *number of seeds is completed for you*
[y] Lat *in it*

see it thrown into confusion after
the third period;[z]
and the sun shall suddenly
begin to shine at night,
and the moon during the
day.
5 Blood shall drip from wood,
and the stone shall utter
its voice;
the peoples shall be
troubled,
and the stars shall fall.[a]
6 And one shall reign whom those
who inhabit the earth do not expect, and the birds shall fly away
together; 7 and the Dead Sea[b] shall
cast up fish; and one whom the
many do not know shall make his
voice heard by night, and all shall
hear his voice.[c] 8 There shall be
chaos also in many places, fire
shall often break out, the wild animals shall roam beyond their
haunts, and menstruous women
shall bring forth monsters. 9 Salt
waters shall be found in the sweet,
and all friends shall conquer one
another; then shall reason hide itself, and wisdom shall withdraw
into its chamber, 10 and it shall be
sought by many but shall not be
found, and unrighteousness and
unrestraint shall increase on earth.
11 One country shall ask its neighbor, 'Has righteousness, or anyone
who does right, passed through
you?' And it will answer, 'No.' 12 At
that time people shall hope but
not obtain; they shall labor, but
their ways shall not prosper.
13 These are the signs that I am permitted to tell you, and if you pray
again, and weep as you do now,
and fast for seven days, you shall
hear yet greater things than these."

Conclusion of the Vision

14 Then I woke up, and my body
shuddered violently, and my soul
was so troubled that it fainted.
15 But the angel who had come and
talked with me held me and
strengthened me and set me on my
feet.
16 Now on the second night
Phaltiel, a chief of the people,
came to me and said, "Where have
you been? And why is your face
sad? 17 Or do you not know that Israel has been entrusted to you in
the land of their exile? 18 Rise
therefore and eat some bread, and
do not forsake us, like a shepherd
who leaves the flock in the power
of savage wolves."
19 Then I said to him, "Go away
from me and do not come near me
for seven days; then you may come
to me."
He heard what I said and left me.
20 So I fasted seven days, mourning
and weeping, as the angel Uriel
had commanded me.

Ezra's Second Prayer of Complaint

21 After seven days the
thoughts of my heart were very
grievous to me again. 22 Then my
soul recovered the spirit of understanding, and I began once more to
speak words in the presence of the
Most High. 23 I said, "O sovereign
Lord, from every forest of the earth
and from all its trees you have chosen one vine, 24 and from all the
lands of the world you have chosen
for yourself one region,[d] and from
all the flowers of the world you
have chosen for yourself one lily,
25 and from all the depths of the
sea you have filled for yourself one
river, and from all the cities that
have been built you have consecrated Zion for yourself, 26 and
from all the birds that have been
created you have named for yourself one dove, and from all the
flocks that have been made you
have provided for yourself one
sheep, 27 and from all the multitude of peoples you have gotten for
yourself one people; and to this
people, whom you have loved, you
have given the law that is approved
by all. 28 And now, O Lord, why
have you handed the one over to
the many, and dishonored[e] the

5.5 Hab 2.11; Lk 19.40; Mt 24.19; Mk 13.25 **5.6** 2 Thess 2.8-9; Rev 13.1-18 **5.8** Rev 8.7-9,21; 16.2-21; 18.1 **5.10** Isa 59.14-15; Mt 24.12 **5.13** 2 Esd 6.35; 12.51 **5.14** Dan 7.15; 2 Esd 6.36; Ps 84.2; 107.5; Jon 2.7 **5.15** 2 Esd 2.44; 4.1 **5.16** Rev 5.3-5 **5.17** Ezra 7.6-10; Neh 8.1-8 **5.18** 1 Kings 19.5, 7; Ezek 34.2-6; Zech 11.16; Jn 10.12-13 **5.20** Ezra 9.3-5; 2 Esd 2.3; 4.1; 10.28 **5.23** Ps 80.8-15; Isa 5.1,7; Jer 2.21 **5.24** Gen 12.1; 13.14-17; 28.13-14; Song 2.2; Hos 14.5 **5.25** Ps 46.4-5; Isa 8.6; Ps 48.1-2; 132.13 **5.26** Ps 74.19; Song 2.14; Ps 79.13; Isa 53.7; Jn 10.16 **5.27** Ex 19.5-6; 1 Pet 2.9; Ex 20.1-17; 34.1-27; Sir 45.3-7 **5.28** 1 Esd 8.78, 87; Rom 11.17-18

[z] Literally *after the third*; Ethiop *after three months*; Arm *after the third vision*; Georg *after the third day* [a] Ethiop Compare Syr and Arab: Meaning of Lat uncertain [b] Lat *Sea of Sodom* [c] Cn: Lat *fish; and it shall make its voice heard by night, which the many have not known, but all shall hear its voice.* [d] Ethiop: Lat *pit* [e] Syr Ethiop Arab: Lat *prepared*

one root beyond the others, and
scattered your only one among the
many? 29 And those who opposed
your promises have trampled on
those who believed your covenants. 30 If you really hate your people, they should be punished at
your own hands."

Response to Ezra's Complaints

31 When I had spoken these
words, the angel who had come to
me on a previous night was sent to
me. 32 He said to me, "Listen to
me, and I will instruct you; pay attention to me, and I will tell you
more."
33 Then I said, "Speak, my
lord." And he said to me, "Are you
greatly disturbed in mind over Israel? Or do you love him more than
his Maker does?"
34 I said, "No, my lord, but because of my grief I have spoken; for
every hour I suffer agonies of heart,
while I strive to understand the
way of the Most High and to search
out some part of his judgment."
35 He said to me, "You cannot."
And I said, "Why not, my lord? Why
then was I born? Or why did not my
mother's womb become my grave,
so that I would not see the travail
of Jacob and the exhaustion of the
people of Israel?"
36 He said to me, "Count up for
me those who have not yet come,
and gather for me the scattered
raindrops, and make the withered
flowers bloom again for me; 37 open
for me the closed chambers, and
bring out for me the winds shut up
in them, or show me the picture of
a voice; and then I will explain to
you the travail that you ask to understand."[f]
38 I said, "O sovereign Lord,
who is able to know these things
except he whose dwelling is not
with mortals? 39 As for me, I am
without wisdom, and how can I
speak concerning the things that
you have asked me?"
40 He said to me, "Just as you
cannot do one of the things that
were mentioned, so you cannot
discover my judgment, or the goal
of the love that I have promised to
my people."

Why Successive Generations Have Been Created

41 I said, "Yet, O Lord, you
have charge of those who are alive
at the end, but what will those do
who lived before me, or we, ourselves, or those who come after
us?"
42 He said to me, "I shall liken
my judgment to a circle;[g] just as
for those who are last there is no
slowness, so for those who are first
there is no haste."
43 Then I answered and said,
"Could you not have created at one
time those who have been and
those who are and those who will
be, so that you might show your
judgment the sooner?"
44 He replied to me and said,
"The creation cannot move faster
than the Creator, nor can the world
hold at one time those who have
been created in it."
45 I said, "How have you said to
your servant that you[h] will certainly give life at one time to your
creation? If therefore all creatures
will live at one time[i] and the creation will sustain them, it might
even now be able to support all of
them present at one time."
46 He said to me, "Ask a
woman's womb, and say to it, 'If
you bear ten[j] children, why one
after another?' Request it therefore
to produce ten at one time."
47 I said, "Of course it cannot,
but only each in its own time."
48 He said to me, "Even so I
have given the womb of the earth
to those who from time to time are
sown in it. 49 For as an infant does
not bring forth, and a woman who
has become old does not bring
forth any longer, so I have made
the same rule for the world that I
created."

5.29 Isa 63.18; Jer 12.10; 2 Esd 3.32 **5.31** 2 Esd 4.1 **5.32** 2 Esd 7.49 **5.33** Isa 49.15; 2 Esd 8.48 **5.35** Job 38.1-3; Jdt 8.14; Job 3.11; 10.18-19 **5.37** 2 Esd 4.5 **5.38** 1 Kings 8.27; Isa 66.1; Acts 7.49-50 **5.40** 2 Esd 4.10-11; Ex 15.13; Deut 7.13; 2 Sam 7.15; Rom 8.35-39 **5.44** Jn 1.2-3; Col 1.15-18; Heb 1.2-3 **5.47** Eccl 3.1-8,11; Wis 15.8 **5.48** Isa 66.7-9

[f] Lat *see* [g] Or *crown* [h] Syr Ethiop Arab 1: Meaning of Lat uncertain [i] Lat lacks *If . . . one time* [j] Syr Ethiop Arab 2 Arm: Meaning of Lat uncertain

When and How Will the End Come?

50 Then I inquired and said,
"Since you have now given me the
opportunity, let me speak before
you. Is our mother, of whom you
have told me, still young? Or is she
now approaching old age?"
51 He replied to me, "Ask a
woman who bears children, and
she will tell you. 52 Say to her, 'Why
are those whom you have borne recently not like those whom you
bore before, but smaller in stature?' 53 And she herself will answer
you, 'Those born in the strength of
youth are different from those born
during the time of old age, when
the womb is failing.' 54 Therefore
you also should consider that you
and your contemporaries are
smaller in stature than those who
were before you, 55 and those who
come after you will be smaller than
you, as born of a creation that already is aging and passing the
strength of youth."
56 I said, "I implore you,
O Lord, if I have found favor in
your sight, show your servant
through whom you will visit your
creation."

6 He said to me, "At the beginning of the circle of the earth,
before[k] the portals of the world
were in place, and before the assembled winds blew, 2 and before
the rumblings of thunder sounded,
and before the flashes of lightning
shone, and before the foundations
of paradise were laid, 3 and before
the beautiful flowers were seen,
and before the powers of move-
ments[l] were established, and before the innumerable hosts of angels were gathered together, 4 and
before the heights of the air were
lifted up, and before the measures
of the firmaments were named,
and before the footstool of Zion
was established, 5 and before the
present years were reckoned and
before the imaginations of those
who now sin were estranged, and
before those who stored up treasures of faith were sealed— 6 then
I planned these things, and they
were made through me alone and
not through another; just as the
end shall come through me alone
and not through another."

The Dividing of the Times

7 I answered and said, "What
will be the dividing of the times?
Or when will be the end of the first
age and the beginning of the age
that follows?"
8 He said to me, "From Abraham to Isaac,[m] because from him
were born Jacob and Esau, for Jacob's hand held Esau's heel from
the beginning. 9 Now Esau is the
end of this age, and Jacob is the
beginning of the age that follows.
10 The beginning of a person is the
hand, and the end of a person is
the heel;[n] seek for nothing else,
Ezra, between the heel and the
hand, Ezra!"

More Signs of the End

11 I answered and said,
"O sovereign Lord, if I have found
favor in your sight, 12 show your
servant the last of your signs of
which you showed me a part on a
previous night."
13 He answered and said to me,
"Rise to your feet and you will hear
a full, resounding voice. 14 And if
the place where you are standing is
greatly shaken 15 while the voice is
speaking, do not be terrified; because the word concerns the end,
and the foundations of the earth
will understand 16 that the speech
concerns them. They will tremble
and be shaken, for they know that
their end must be changed."
17 When I heard this, I got to
my feet and listened; a voice was
speaking, and its sound was like
the sound of mighty[o] waters. 18 It
said, "The days are coming when I
draw near to visit the inhabitants
of the earth, 19 and when I require

5.52 Gen 6.4; Num 13.33
5.55 2 Esd 4.26; 1 Cor 7.31
5.56 2 Esd 4.44
6.1 Gen 1.2
6.2 Gen 2.4-9
6.3 Job 38.6-7; Ps 148.2,5; Col 1.16
6.4 Gen 1.6-8; 1 Chr 28.2; Isa 66.1; Mt 5.35
6.5 Gen 2.25
6.6 Ps 139.15-16; Jer 1.5; Eph 1.3,11; Isa 65.17; 2 Pet 3.8-12; Rev 19.6-7, 11-16
6.8 Gen 25.23-26
6.11 Gen 18.27, 30-32; Ex 33.13
6.12 2 Esd 4.51-5.13
6.16 Isa 13.13; Jer 10.10; Hag 2.21; Heb 12.26
6.17 Rev 1.15; 14.2; 19.6
6.19 Rev 18.4-6; 20.11-15

[k] Meaning of Lat uncertain: Compare Syr *The beginning by the hand of humankind, but the end by my own hands. For as before the land of the world existed there, and before*; Ethiop: *At first by the Son of Man, and afterwards I myself. For before the earth and the lands were created, and before* [l] Or *earthquakes*
[m] Other ancient authorities read *to Abraham*
[n] Syr: Meaning of Lat uncertain [o] Lat *many*

from the doers of iniquity the penalty of their iniquity, and when the
humiliation of Zion is complete.
20 When the seal is placed upon the
age that is about to pass away,
then I will show these signs: the
books shall be opened before the
face of the firmament, and all shall
see my judgment[p] together.
21 Children a year old shall speak
with their voices, and pregnant
women shall give birth to premature children at three and four
months, and these shall live and
leap about. 22 Sown places shall
suddenly appear unsown, and full
storehouses shall suddenly be
found to be empty; 23 the trumpet
shall sound aloud, and when all
hear it, they shall suddenly be terrified. 24 At that time friends shall
make war on friends like enemies,
the earth and those who inhabit it
shall be terrified, and the springs
of the fountains shall stand still, so
that for three hours they shall not
flow.
25 "It shall be that whoever remains after all that I have foretold
to you shall be saved and shall see
my salvation and the end of my
world. 26 And they shall see those
who were taken up, who from their
birth have not tasted death; and
the heart of the earth's[q] inhabitants shall be changed and converted to a different spirit. 27 For
evil shall be blotted out, and deceit
shall be quenched; 28 faithfulness
shall flourish, and corruption shall
be overcome, and the truth, which
has been so long without fruit,
shall be revealed."

Conclusion of the Second Vision

29 While he spoke to me, little
by little the place where I was
standing began to rock to and fro.[r]
30 And he said to me, "I have come
to show you these things this
night.[s] 31 If therefore you will pray
again and fast again for seven days,
I will again declare to you greater
things than these,[t] 32 because
your voice has surely been heard by
the Most High; for the Mighty One
has seen your uprightness and has
also observed the purity that you
have maintained from your youth.
33 Therefore he sent me to show
you all these things, and to say to
you: 'Believe and do not be afraid!
34 Do not be quick to think vain
thoughts concerning the former
times; then you will not act hastily
in the last times.' "

The Third Vision

35 Now after this I wept again
and fasted seven days in the same
way as before, in order to complete
the three weeks that had been prescribed for me. 36 Then on the
eighth night my heart was troubled
within me again, and I began to
speak in the presence of the Most
High. 37 My spirit was greatly
aroused, and my soul was in distress.

God's Work in Creation

38 I said, "O Lord, you spoke at
the beginning of creation, and said
on the first day, 'Let heaven and
earth be made,' and your word accomplished the work. 39 Then the
spirit was blowing, and darkness
and silence embraced everything;
the sound of human voices was not
yet there.[u] 40 Then you commanded a ray of light to be brought
out from your store-chambers, so
that your works could be seen.
41 "Again, on the second day,
you created the spirit of the firmament, and commanded it to divide
and separate the waters, so that
one part might move upward and
the other part remain beneath.
42 "On the third day you commanded the waters to be gathered
together in a seventh part of the
earth; six parts you dried up and
kept so that some of them might
be planted and cultivated and be of
service before you. 43 For your word
went forth, and at once the work
was done. 44 Immediately fruit
came forth in endless abundance

6.20 Ex 32.32; Ps 69.28; Dan 7.10; 12.1; Rev 20.12
6.21 Isa 65.19-20
6.23 1 Cor 15.52; 1 Thess 4.16
6.24 Mt 10..34-36; Mk 13.12; Lk 12.49-53
6.25 Mt 10.22; Mk 13.13
6.26 Gen 5.24; 2 Kings 2.11-12; Sir 44.16
6.27 Isa 2.4; 65.25; Ezek 39.25-26
6.28 Isa 11.3-5; 32.15-20; Jer 32.41
6.31 2 Esd 5.19-21
6.32 Ps 50.1; 132.2,5; Isa 1.24; Sir 46.16; Ezra 7.6,10; 1 Esd 8.3,7
6.33 Ex 20.20; Ps 27.1; Isa 41.10; Rev 1.17
6.35 2 Esd 5.13, 21; 12.51; Dan 10.2-3
6.36 Dan 7.15; Sir 40.6; 2 Esd 3.1; 5.14
6.38 Gen 1.1-4; Ps 33.6; Heb 11.3; 2 Pet 3.5
6.39 Gen 1.2
6.40 Gen 1.3; Ps 104.2
6.41 Gen 1.6-8; Ps 104.2-3
6.42 Gen 1.9-10; Ps 104.5-9; Gen 1.12-13; 2.8; 4.2
6.44 Gen 2.9; Ps 104.14-16

[p] Syr: Lat lacks *my judgment*
[q] Syr Compare Ethiop Arab 1 Arm: Lat lacks *earth's*
[r] Syr Ethiop Compare Arab Arm: Meaning of Lat uncertain
[s] Syr Compare Ethiop: Meaning of Lat uncertain
[t] Syr Ethiop Arab 1 Arm: Lat adds *by day*
[u] Syr Ethiop: Lat *was not yet from you*

and of varied appeal to the taste,
and flowers of inimitable color,
and odors of inexpressible fragrance. These were made on the
third day.
45 "On the fourth day you commanded the brightness of the sun,
the light of the moon, and the arrangement of the stars to come
into being; 46 and you commanded
them to serve humankind, about to
be formed.
47 "On the fifth day you commanded the seventh part, where
the water had been gathered together, to bring forth living creatures, birds, and fishes; and so it
was done. 48 The dumb and lifeless
water produced living creatures, as
it was commanded, so that therefore the nations might declare your
wondrous works.
49 "Then you kept in existence
two living creatures;[v] the one you
called Behemoth[w] and the name
of the other Leviathan. 50 And you
separated one from the other, for
the seventh part where the water
had been gathered together could
not hold them both. 51 And you
gave Behemoth[w] one of the parts
that had been dried up on the third
day, to live in it, where there are a
thousand mountains; 52 but to Leviathan you gave the seventh part,
the watery part; and you have kept
them to be eaten by whom you
wish, and when you wish.
53 "On the sixth day you commanded the earth to bring forth before you cattle, wild animals, and
creeping things; 54 and over these
you placed Adam, as ruler over all
the works that you had made; and
from him we have all come, the
people whom you have chosen.

Why Do God's People Suffer?

55 "All this I have spoken before you, O Lord, because you have
said that it was for us that you created this world.[x] 56 As for the other
nations that have descended from
Adam, you have said that they are
nothing, and that they are like spittle, and you have compared their
abundance to a drop from a
bucket. 57 And now, O Lord, these
nations, which are reputed to be as
nothing, domineer over us and devour us. 58 But we your people,
whom you have called your firstborn, only begotten, zealous for
you,[y] and most dear, have been
given into their hands. 59 If the
world has indeed been created for
us, why do we not possess our
world as an inheritance? How long
will this be so?"

Response to Ezra's Questions

7 When I had finished speaking
these words, the angel who
had been sent to me on the former
nights was sent to me again. 2 He
said to me, "Rise, Ezra, and listen
to the words that I have come to
speak to you."
3 I said, "Speak, my lord." And
he said to me, "There is a sea set in
a wide expanse so that it is deep
and vast, 4 but it has an entrance
set in a narrow place, so that it is
like a river. 5 If there are those who
wish to reach the sea, to look at it
or to navigate it, how can they
come to the broad part unless they
pass through the narrow part? 6 Another example: There is a city built
and set on a plain, and it is full of
all good things; 7 but the entrance
to it is narrow and set in a precipitous place, so that there is fire on
the right hand and deep water on
the left. 8 There is only one path lying between them, that is, between
the fire and the water, so that only
one person can walk on the path.
9 If now the city is given to someone as an inheritance, how will the
heir receive the inheritance unless
by passing through the appointed
danger?"
10 I said, "That is right, lord."
He said to me, "So also is Israel's
portion. 11 For I made the world for
their sake, and when Adam transgressed my statutes, what had
been made was judged. 12 And so
the entrances of this world were
made narrow and sorrowful and

6.45 Gen 1.14-19; Ps 104.19
6.46 Ps 8.6-8
6.47 Gen 1.20-23; Ps 104.24-26
6.49 Job 40.15; 3.8; 41.1; Ps 74.14; 104.26; Isa 27.1
6.53 Gen 1.24-25
6.54 Gen 1.26-28; Ps 8.6-8; 104.23; Gen 3.20; 4.1-2; Mal 2.10; Acts 17.26
6.55 2 Esd 7.11
6.56 Gen 5.1-32; 10.1-32; Acts 17.26; Isa 40.15
6.58 Jer 31.9; Sir 36.17; Deut 4.37; 10.15; Hos 11.1
6.59 Deut 19.10; 1 Kings 8.36; Ps 105.11; Lam 5.2
7.1 2 Esd 2.44; 4.1; 5.31
7.3 Ps 104.25
7.7 Mt 7.13-14
7.11 2 Esd 6.55; Gen 3.1-7
7.12 Gen 47.9; Job 14.1; Eccl 2.23; 2 Esd 4.33

v Syr Ethiop: Lat *two souls*
w Other Lat authorities read *Enoch*
x Syr Ethiop Arab 2: Lat *the firstborn world* Compare Arab 1 *first world*
y Meaning of Lat uncertain

toilsome; they are few and evil, full
of dangers and involved in great
hardships. 13 But the entrances of
the greater world are broad and
safe, and yield the fruit of immortality. 14 Therefore unless the living
pass through the difficult and futile experiences, they can never receive those things that have been
reserved for them. 15 Now therefore
why are you disturbed, seeing that
you are to perish? Why are you
moved, seeing that you are mortal?
16 Why have you not considered in
your mind what is to come, rather
than what is now present?"

The Fate of the Ungodly

17 Then I answered and said,
"O sovereign Lord, you have ordained in your law that the righteous shall inherit these things,
but that the ungodly shall perish.
18 The righteous, therefore, can endure difficult circumstances while
hoping for easier ones; but those
who have done wickedly have suffered the difficult circumstances
and will never see the easier ones."
19 He said to me, "You are not a
better judge than the Lord,[z] or
wiser than the Most High! 20 Let
many perish who are now living,
rather than that the law of God
that is set before them be disregarded! 21 For the Lord[a] strictly
commanded those who came into
the world, when they came, what
they should do to live, and what
they should observe to avoid punishment. 22 Nevertheless they were
not obedient, and spoke against
him;

they devised for themselves
vain thoughts,
23 and proposed to
themselves wicked
frauds;
they even declared that the
Most High does not
exist,
and they ignored his ways.
24 They scorned his law,
and denied his covenants;
they have been unfaithful to
his statutes,
and have not performed his
works.

25 "That is the reason, Ezra, that
empty things are for the empty,
and full things are for the full.

The Temporary Messianic Kingdom

26 "For indeed the time will
come, when the signs that I have
foretold to you will come to pass,
that the city that now is not seen
shall appear,[b] and the land that
now is hidden shall be disclosed.
27 Everyone who has been delivered
from the evils that I have foretold
shall see my wonders. 28 For my
son the Messiah[c] shall be revealed
with those who are with him, and
those who remain shall rejoice four
hundred years. 29 After those years
my son the Messiah shall die, and
all who draw human breath.[d]
30 Then the world shall be turned
back to primeval silence for seven
days, as it was at the first beginnings, so that no one shall be left.
31 After seven days the world that is
not yet awake shall be roused, and
that which is corruptible shall perish. 32 The earth shall give up those
who are asleep in it, and the dust
those who rest there in silence;
and the chambers shall give up the
souls that have been committed to
them. 33 The Most High shall be revealed on the seat of judgment,
and compassion shall pass away,
and patience shall be withdrawn.[e]
34 Only judgment shall remain,
truth shall stand, and faithfulness
shall grow strong. 35 Recompense
shall follow, and the reward shall
be manifested; righteous deeds
shall awake, and unrighteous
deeds shall not sleep.[f] *36* The pit[g]

7.13 Heb 12.11; Rev 22.2; 1 Cor 15.53-54; Wis 8.13,17
7.14 Mt 5.11-12; 1 Cor 2.9; Heb 12.3-11
7.16 Rom 8.18; 2 Cor 4.18
7.17 Dan 12.2; Mt 5.5; 25.34; Ps 1.6; 73.17-20; Wis 4.18-19; 1 Cor 2.6; Rev 20.11-14
7.19 Rom 11.25; 12.16; 1 Cor 1.25
7.21 Gen 2.16-17; Deut 30.15-20; Jn 3.16-21
7.22 Neh 9.26; Bar 1.19; Ps 2.1-3; Eccl 7.29
7.23 Ps 14.1; 53.1
7.24 1 Macc 2.49; 2 Esd 7.81; 9.11; Jer 11.10; Ezek 44.7; 2 Chr 12.2; 29.6; Neh 1.8
7.25 Mt 13.12; Lk 19.26
7.26 2 Esd 6.20-24; 13.35; Rev 21.1-2, 9-10; Isa 65.17; 66.22; 2 Pet 3.13
7.28 Lk 1.35; 3.22; 2 Esd 12.34; Rev 20.4-6
7.29 Mt 27.50; Lk 23.46
7.31 2 Pet 3.10,12
7.32 Dan 12.2; Jn 5.28; Rev 20.12-13; 2 Esd 4.35,41
7.33 Mt 25.31-33; Rev 20.11-13
7.35 2 Esd 7.77; 1 Cor 3.13-14; Rev 22.12; Mt 25.35-46; Rev 20.12-13 ***7.36*** Rev 9.1-2; 20.1; Lk 16.23-24; Mt 13.42,50; Rev 9.2; Lk 16.26

[z] Other ancient authorities read *God*; Ethiop Georg *the only One*
[a] Other ancient authorities read *God*
[b] Arm: Lat Syr *that the bride shall appear, even the city appearing*
[c] Syr Arab 1: Ethiop *my Messiah*; Arab 2 *the Messiah*; Arm *the Messiah of God*; Lat *my son Jesus*
[d] Arm *all who have continued in faith and in patience*
[e] Lat *shall gather together*
[f] The passage from verse *36* to verse *105*, formerly missing, has been restored to the text
[g] Syr Ethiop: Lat *place*

of torment shall appear, and opposite it shall be the place of rest;
and the furnace of hell[h] shall be
disclosed, and opposite it the paradise of delight. 37 Then the Most
High will say to the nations that
have been raised from the dead,
'Look now, and understand whom
you have denied, whom you have
not served, whose commandments
you have despised. 38 Look on this
side and on that; here are delight
and rest, and there are fire and torments.' Thus he will[i] speak to
them on the day of judgment — 39 a
day that has no sun or moon or
stars, 40 or cloud or thunder or
lightning, or wind or water or air,
or darkness or evening or morning,
41 or summer or spring or heat or
winter[j] or frost or cold, or hail or
rain or dew, 42 or noon or night, or
dawn or shining or brightness or
light, but only the splendor of the
glory of the Most High, by which all
shall see what has been destined.
43 It will last as though for a week of
years. 44 This is my judgment and
its prescribed order; and to you
alone I have shown these things."

Only a Few Will Be Saved

45 I answered and said,
"O sovereign Lord, I said then
and[k] I say now: Blessed are those
who are alive and keep your commandments! 46 But what of those
for whom I prayed? For who among
the living is there that has not
sinned, or who is there among
mortals that has not transgressed
your covenant? 47 And now I see
that the world to come will bring
delight to few, but torments to
many. 48 For an evil heart has
grown up in us, which has alienated us from God,[l] and has
brought us into corruption and the
ways of death, and has shown us
the paths of perdition and removed
us far from life — and that not
merely for a few but for almost all
who have been created."
49 He answered me and said,
"Listen to me, Ezra,[m] and I will instruct you, and will admonish you
once more. 50 For this reason the
Most High has made not one world
but two. 51 Inasmuch as you have
said that the righteous are not
many but few, while the ungodly
abound, hear the explanation for
this.
52 "If you have just a few precious stones, will you add to them
lead and clay?"[n] 53 I said, "Lord,
how could that be?" 54 And he said
to me, "Not only that, but ask the
earth and she will tell you; defer to
her, and she will declare it to you.
55 Say to her, 'You produce gold
and silver and bronze, and also
iron and lead and clay; 56 but silver
is more abundant than gold, and
bronze than silver, and iron than
bronze, and lead than iron, and
clay than lead.' 57 Judge therefore
which things are precious and desirable, those that are abundant or
those that are rare?"
58 I said, "O sovereign Lord,
what is plentiful is of less worth,
for what is more rare is more precious."
59 He answered me and said,
"Consider within yourself[o] what
you have thought, for the person
who has what is hard to get rejoices more than the person who
has what is plentiful. 60 So also will
be the judgment[p] that I have
promised; for I will rejoice over the
few who shall be saved, because it
is they who have made my glory to
prevail now, and through them my
name has now been honored. 61 I
will not grieve over the great number of those who perish; for it is
they who are now like a mist, and
are similar to a flame and smoke —
they are set on fire and burn hotly,
and are extinguished."

Lamentation of Ezra, with Response

62 I replied and said, "O earth,
what have you brought forth, if the
mind is made out of the dust like
the other created things? 63 For it

7.37 Mt 25.31-46 **7.41** Gen 8.22 **7.42** Isa 60.19-20; 2 Esd 2.35; Rev 21.23 **7.45** Ps 1.1-2; 119.1-3 **7.46** Ps 14.2-3; Rom 3.10-18, 23; Gal 3.22 **7.47** 2 Esd 8.3; Mt 7.14; 22.14; 7.13 **7.48** Jer 17.9; 2 Esd 3.20; Gen 3.19; Rom 5.12; 6.23 **7.49** 2 Esd 5.32 **7.54** Job 12.7-12 **7.57** 2 Chr 9.1, 9-10; Isa 54.12; 1 Cor 3.12 **7.59** Mt 13.44-46 **7.60** Lk 15.7,10 **7.61** 2 Esd 4.24; Jas 4.14; Mt 3.12; 5.22; 2 Thess 1.8; Jude 7; Rev 20.14 **7.62** Gen 1.11-12; 2.7 **7.63** 2 Esd 4.12

[h] Lat Syr Ethiop *Gehenna*
[i] Syr Ethiop Arab 1: Lat *you shall* [j] Or *storm*
[k] Syr: Lat *And I answered, "I said then, O Lord, and* [l] Cn: Lat Syr Ethiop *from these*
[m] Syr Arab 1 Georg: Lat Ethiop lack *Ezra*
[n] Arab 1: Meaning of Lat Syr Ethiop uncertain
[o] Syr Ethiop Arab 1: Meaning of Lat uncertain
[p] Syr Arab 1: Lat *creation*

would have been better if the dust
itself had not been born, so that
the mind might not have been
made from it. 64 But now the mind
grows with us, and therefore we are
tormented, because we perish and
we know it. 65 Let the human race
lament, but let the wild animals of
the field be glad; let all who have
been born lament, but let the cattle and the flocks rejoice. 66 It is
much better with them than with
us; for they do not look for a judgment, and they do not know of any
torment or salvation promised to
them after death. 67 What does it
profit us that we shall be preserved
alive but cruelly tormented? 68 For
all who have been born are entangled in[q] iniquities, and are full of
sins and burdened with transgressions. 69 And if after death we were
not to come into judgment, perhaps it would have been better for
us."

70 He answered me and said,
"When the Most High made the
world and Adam and all who have
come from him, he first prepared
the judgment and the things that
pertain to the judgment. 71 But
now, understand from your own
words—for you have said that the
mind grows with us. 72 For this reason, therefore, those who live on
earth shall be tormented, because
though they had understanding,
they committed iniquity; and
though they received the commandments, they did not keep
them; and though they obtained
the law, they dealt unfaithfully
with what they received. 73 What,
then, will they have to say in the
judgment, or how will they answer
in the last times? 74 How long the
Most High has been patient with
those who inhabit the world!—and
not for their sake, but because of
the times that he has foreor-
dained."

State of the Dead before Judgment

75 I answered and said, "If I
have found favor in your sight,
O Lord, show this also to your servant: whether after death, as soon
as everyone of us yields up the
soul, we shall be kept in rest until
those times come when you will renew the creation, or whether we
shall be tormented at once?"

76 He answered me and said,
"I will show you that also, but do
not include yourself with those
who have shown scorn, or number
yourself among those who are tormented. 77 For you have a treasure
of works stored up with the Most
High, but it will not be shown to
you until the last times. 78 Now
concerning death, the teaching is:
When the decisive decree has gone
out from the Most High that a person shall die, as the spirit leaves
the body to return again to him
who gave it, first of all it adores the
glory of the Most High. 79 If it is one
of those who have shown scorn and
have not kept the way of the Most
High, who have despised his law
and hated those who fear God—
80 such spirits shall not enter into
habitations, but shall immediately
wander about in torments, always
grieving and sad, in seven ways.
81 The first way, because they have
scorned the law of the Most High.
82 The second way, because they
cannot now make a good repentance so that they may live. 83 The
third way, they shall see the reward
laid up for those who have trusted
the covenants of the Most High.
84 The fourth way, they shall consider the torment laid up for themselves in the last days. 85 The fifth
way, they shall see how the habitations of the others are guarded by
angels in profound quiet. 86 The
sixth way, they shall see how some
of them will cross over[r] into torments. 87 The seventh way, which
is worse[s] than all the ways that
have been mentioned, because
they shall utterly waste away in
confusion and be consumed with
shame,[t] and shall wither with fear
at seeing the glory of the Most
High in whose presence they
sinned while they were alive, and

7.65 Job 14.1; Ps 90.9-10; Jas 4.9
7.68 Ps 14.2-3; 2 Esd 7.46; Rom 3.10-18
7.69 2 Cor 5.10; Heb 9.27
7.70 Mal 2.10; Acts 17.26
7.72 Rom 2.17-24; 9.31
7.74 Isa 30.18; Rom 2.4; 2 Pet 3.9
7.75 Eccl 12.7; Lk 23.46; 16.22-24
7.76 2 Esd 7.24
7.77 2 Esd 8.33, 36; 1 Cor 3.12-13; 2 Esd 7.35
7.78 Gen 3.19; Job 34.14-15; Eccl 12.7
7.80 2 Esd 2.11; Lk 16.9; Jn 14.2-3; 2 Cor 5.1
7.81 2 Esd 7.24, 76; 9.11
7.82 Lk 16.26-31
7.83 Lk 16.23
7.84 Rev 20.11-14
7.85 Lk 16.23
7.87 Rev 11.11-13; Mt 25.31; Acts 10.42; 2 Tim 4.1

q Syr *defiled with* r Cn: Meaning of Lat uncertain s Lat Syr Ethiop *greater* t Syr Ethiop: Meaning of Lat uncertain in whose presence they are to be judged in the last times.

88 "Now this is the order of those who have kept the ways of the Most High, when they shall be separated from their mortal body.[u] *89*During the time that they lived in it,[v] they laboriously served the Most High, and withstood danger every hour so that they might keep the law of the Lawgiver perfectly. *90*Therefore this is the teaching concerning them: *91*First of all, they shall see with great joy the glory of him who receives them, for they shall have rest in seven orders. *92*The first order, because they have striven with great effort to overcome the evil thought that was formed with them, so that it might not lead them astray from life into death. *93*The second order, because they see the perplexity in which the souls of the ungodly wander and the punishment that awaits them. *94*The third order, they see the witness that he who formed them bears concerning them, that throughout their life they kept the law with which they were entrusted. *95*The fourth order, they understand the rest that they now enjoy, being gathered into their chambers and guarded by angels in profound quiet, and the glory waiting for them in the last days. *96*The fifth order, they rejoice that they have now escaped what is corruptible and shall inherit what is to come; and besides they see the straits and toil[w] from which they have been delivered, and the spacious liberty that they are to receive and enjoy in immortality. *97*The sixth order, when it is shown them how their face is to shine like the sun, and how they are to be made like the light of the stars, being incorruptible from then on. *98*The seventh order, which is greater than all that have been mentioned, because they shall rejoice with boldness, and shall be confident without confusion, and shall be glad without fear, for they press forward to see the face of him whom they served in life and from whom they are to receive their reward when glorified. *99*This is the order of the souls of the righteous, as henceforth is announced;[x] and the previously mentioned are the ways of torment that those who would not give heed shall suffer hereafter."

100 Then I answered and said, "Will time therefore be given to the souls, after they have been separated from the bodies, to see what you have described to me?"

101 He said to me, "They shall have freedom for seven days, so that during these seven days they may see the things of which you have been told, and afterwards they shall be gathered in their habitations."

No Intercession for the Ungodly

102 I answered and said, "If I have found favor in your sight, show further to me, your servant, whether on the day of judgment the righteous will be able to intercede for the ungodly or to entreat the Most High for them— *103*fathers for sons or sons for parents, brothers for brothers, relatives for their kindred, or friends for those who are most dear."

104 He answered me and said, "Since you have found favor in my sight, I will show you this also. The day of judgment is decisive[y] and displays to all the seal of truth. Just as now a father does not send his son, or a son his father, or a master his servant, or a friend his dearest friend, to be ill[z] or sleep or eat or be healed in his place, *105*so no one shall ever pray for another on that day, neither shall anyone lay a burden on another;[a] for then all shall bear their own righteousness and unrighteousness."

36 *106* I answered and said, "How then do we find that first Abraham prayed for the people of Sodom, and Moses for our ancestors who sinned in the desert, 37 *107*and Joshua after him for Israel

7.88 Job 34.14-15; Eccl 12.7; 2 Esd 7.78
7.89 Ps 119.69-72; Dan 1.8-15; 3.8-26; 6.10-23; Heb 11.32-38
7.91 Heb 4.9-11
7.92 Sir 15.14-17
7.93 Lk 16.22-26
7.94 Mt 10.32; Rev 3.5
7.95 2 Esd 4.35; Jn 14.2-3; 2 Cor 5.1; Rev 21.1-22.5
7.96 Mt 25.34; 2 Esd 7.17, 13
7.97 Dan 12.3; 2 Esd 7.125; Mt 13.43; 1 Cor 15.51-54
7.98 Rev 19.6-8; Mt 5.8; Heb 12.14; 1 Jn 3.2; Rev 22.4; Lk 6.23,35; 2 Cor 3.14; 4.5; Rev 22.12
7.101 2 Esd 7.80,95
7.102 2 Esd 4.44; Gen 18.23-33; Num 14.13-19; Rom 8.34; Heb 7.25
7.104 Mt 25.31-46; Jn 5.28-29; Heb 9.27-28; Rev 20.11-15
7.105 Deut 24.16; Jer 31.30; Ezek 18.1-32
7.36 106 Gen 18.23-32; Ex 32.11-13; Num 14.13-19
7.37 107 Josh 7.6-7

[u] Lat *the corruptible vessel*
[v] Syr: Ethiop: Meaning of Lat uncertain
[w] Syr Ethiop: Lat *fullness* [x] Syr: Meaning of Lat uncertain [y] Lat *bold*
[z] Syr Ethiop Arm: Lat *to understand*
[a] Syr Ethiop: Lat lacks *on that . . . another*

in the days of Achan, [38] *108*and
Samuel in the days of Saul,[b] and
David for the plague, and Solomon
for those at the dedication,
[39] *109*and Elijah for those who received the rain, and for the one
who was dead, that he might live,
[40] *110*and Hezekiah for the people
in the days of Sennacherib, and
many others prayed for many?
[41] *111*So if now, when corruption
has increased and unrighteousness
has multiplied, the righteous have
prayed for the ungodly, why will it
not be so then as well?"

42 *112* He answered me and
said, "This present world is not the
end; the full glory does not[c] remain in it;[d] therefore those who
were strong prayed for the weak.
[43] *113*But the day of judgment will
be the end of this age and the beginning[e] of the immortal age to
come, in which corruption has
passed away, [44] *114*sinful indulgence has come to an end, unbelief
has been cut off, and righteousness has increased and truth has
appeared. [45] *115*Therefore no one
will then be able to have mercy on
someone who has been con-
demned in the judgment, or to
harm[f] someone who is victorious."

Lamentation over the Fate of Most People

46 *116* I answered and said,
"This is my first and last comment:
it would have been better if the
earth had not produced Adam, or
else, when it had produced him,
had restrained him from sinning.
[47] *117*For what good is it to all
that they live in sorrow now and
expect punishment after death?
[48] *118*O Adam, what have you done?
For though it was you who sinned,
the fall was not yours alone, but
ours also who are your descendants. [49] *119*For what good is it to
us, if an immortal time has been
promised to us, but we have done
deeds that bring death? [50] *120*And
what good is it that an everlasting
hope has been promised to us, but
we have miserably failed? [51] *121*Or
that safe and healthful habitations

7.38 *108* 1 Sam 7.9; 12.23; 2 Sam 24.17; 1 Kings 8.22-53
7.39 *109* 1 Kings 17.20-21; 18.42,45
7.40 *110* 2 Kings 19.15-19
7.43 *113* Mt 13.39-42, 49; 2 Esd 2.34; 6.7; 1 Cor 15.42, 52-53
7.44 *114* Mt 25.41-46; 2 Pet 3.13
7.45 *115* Jn 10.28-29; 1 Jn 5.18
7.46 *116* 2 Esd 3.4-36; Gen 1.27; 2.7
7.47 *117* Gen 3.16-19
7.48 *118* 2 Esd 3.7; 4.30-31; Rom 5.12,18
7.49 *119* Rom 6.16,21, 23; Rev 2.19-23
7.51 *121* 2 Esd 2.11; 7.80
7.53 *123* Ezek 47.12; Rev 22.2
7.55 *125* Dan 12.2; 2 Esd 7.97; Mt 3.43; 8.12; 22.13; Jude 13
7.58 *128* Rev 2.7,11, 17,26-27; 3.5, 12,21
7.59 *129* Deut 30.19
7.60 *130* 2 Chr 36.16; Mt 23.29-37; Acts 7.51-52
7.61 *131* Lk 15.7,10
7.62 *132* Ex 34.6-7; Ps 103.8-12; Isa 55.6-7
7.63 *133* Ps 78.34-35; Am 5.14-15; Lk 18.9-14; Rev 2.5
7.64 *134* 2 Pet 3.9; 2 Esd 7.74

have been reserved for us, but we
have lived wickedly? [52] *122*Or that
the glory of the Most High will defend those who have led a pure life,
but we have walked in the most
wicked ways? [53] *123*Or that a paradise shall be revealed, whose fruit
remains unspoiled and in which
are abundance and healing, but we
shall not enter it [54] *124*because we
have lived in perverse ways?[g]
[55] *125*Or that the faces of those who
practiced self-control shall shine
more than the stars, but our faces
shall be blacker than darkness?
[56] *126*For while we lived and committed iniquity we did not consider
what we should suffer after death."

57 *127* He answered and said,
"This is the significance of the
contest that all who are born on
earth shall wage: [58] *128*if they are
defeated they shall suffer what you
have said, but if they are victorious
they shall receive what I have
said.[h] [59] *129*For this is the way of
which Moses, while he was alive,
spoke to the people, saying,
'Choose life for yourself, so that
you may live!' [60] *130*But they did not
believe him or the prophets after
him, or even myself who have spoken to them. [61] *131*Therefore there
shall not be[i] grief at their destruction, so much as joy over those to
whom salvation is assured."

Ezra Appeals to God's Mercy

62 *132* I answered and said, "I
know, O Lord, that the Most High
is now called merciful, because he
has mercy on those who have not
yet come into the world; [63] *133*and
gracious, because he is gracious to
those who turn in repentance to
his law; [64] *134*and patient, because
he shows patience toward those
who have sinned, since they are his
own creatures; [65] *135*and bountiful,
because he would rather give than

7.65 *135* Acts 20.35

[b] Syr Ethiop Arab 1: Lat Arab 2 Arm lack *in the days of Saul* [c] Lat lacks *not* [d] Or *the glory does not continuously abide in it*
[e] Syr Ethiop: Lat lacks *the beginning*
[f] Syr Ethiop: Lat *overwhelm* [g] Cn: Lat Syr *places* [h] Syr Ethiop Arab 1: Lat *what I say*
[i] Syr: Lat *there was not*

take away;[j] 66 *136* and abundant in
compassion, because he makes his
compassions abound more and
more to those now living and to
those who are gone and to those
yet to come — 67 *137* for if he did not
make them abound, the world with
those who inhabit it would not
have life — 68 *138* and he is called
the giver, because if he did not give
out of his goodness so that those
who have committed iniquities
might be relieved of them, not
one ten-thousandth of humankind
could have life; 69 *139* and the judge,
because if he did not pardon those
who were created by his word and
blot out the multitude of their
sins,[k] 70 *140* there would probably
be left only very few of the innumerable multitude."

8 He answered me and said,
"The Most High made this
world for the sake of many, but the
world to come for the sake of only
a few. 2 But I tell you a parable,
Ezra. Just as, when you ask the
earth, it will tell you that it provides a large amount of clay from
which earthenware is made, but
only a little dust from which gold
comes, so is the course of the
present world. 3 Many have been
created, but only a few shall be
saved."

Ezra Again Appeals to God's Mercy

4 I answered and said, "Then
drink your fill of understanding,[l]
O my soul, and drink wisdom,
O my heart. 5 For not of your own
will did you come into the world,[m]
and against your will you depart,
for you have been given only a
short time to live. 6 O Lord above
us, grant to your servant that we
may pray before you, and give us a
seed for our heart and cultivation
of our understanding so that fruit
may be produced, by which every
mortal who bears the likeness[n] of
a human being may be able to live.
7 For you alone exist, and we are a
work of your hands, as you have declared. 8 And because you give life
to the body that is now fashioned
in the womb, and furnish it with
members, what you have created is
preserved amid fire and water, and
for nine months the womb[o] endures your creature that has been
created in it. 9 But that which
keeps and that which is kept shall
both be kept by your keeping.[m]
And when the womb gives up again
what has been created in it, 10 you
have commanded that from the
members themselves (that is, from
the breasts) milk, the fruit of the
breasts, should be supplied, 11 so
that what has been fashioned may
be nourished for a time; and afterwards you will still guide it in your
mercy. 12 You have nurtured it in
your righteousness, and instructed
it in your law, and reproved it in
your wisdom. 13 You put it to death
as your creation, and make it live
as your work. 14 If then you will
suddenly and quickly[p] destroy
what with so great labor was fashioned by your command, to what
purpose was it made? 15 And now I
will speak out: About all humankind you know best; but I will
speak about your people, for whom
I am grieved, 16 and about your inheritance, for whom I lament, and
about Israel, for whom I am sad,
and about the seed of Jacob, for
whom I am troubled. 17 Therefore I
will pray before you for myself and
for them, for I see the failings of us
who inhabit the earth; 18 and now
also[q] I have heard of the swiftness
of the judgment that is to come.
19 Therefore hear my voice and understand my words, and I will
speak before you."

Ezra's Prayer

The beginning of the words of
Ezra's prayer,[r] before he was
taken up. He said: 20 "O Lord, you
who inhabit eternity,[s] whose eyes
are exalted[t] and whose upper
chambers are in the air, 21 whose

7.66 *136* Ps 103.13; Sir 18.13-14; Bar 2.27
7.68 *138* Jn 3.27; Jas 1.17
7.69 *139* Ps 96.13; 98.9; Acts 17.30-31; Ps 51.1,9; 1 Jn 1.7-9
8.3 2 Esd 7.47; Mt 7.14; 22.14
8.4 Prov 1.2-7; Sir 1.14-20
8.5 Gen 47.9; Ps 90.10
8.6 Ps 1.3; Mt 3.8; Jn 15.2-5; Gal 5.22-23; Gen 5.3
8.7 Deut 4.5; Isa 44.6; 1 Cor 8.4-6; Isa 29.23; 45.11; 60.21
8.8 Ps 139.15
8.10 Ex 2.9; Song 8.1; 3 Macc 5.49
8.13 Deut 32.39; 1 Sam 2.6; Isa 26.19
8.14 Gen 2.7; Ps 139.14-15
8.16 Ex 34.9; Ps 28.9; 78.71; Jer 10.16
8.18 2 Esd 7.102-115
8.19 Gen 5.24; 2 Kings 2.11
8.20 Ps 90.1-2; 104.3; Am 9.6
8.21 Ps 11.4; 47.8; Isa 6.1; Rev 4.3-5; Isa 6.3

[j] Or *he is ready to give according to requests* [k] Lat *contempts* [l] Syr: Lat *Then release understanding* [m] Syr: Meaning of Lat uncertain [n] Syr: Lat *place* [o] Lat *what you have formed* [p] Syr: Lat *will with a light command* [q] Syr: Lat *but* [r] Syr Ethiop; Lat *beginning of Ezra's words* [s] Or *you who abide forever* [t] Another Lat text reads *whose are the highest heavens*

throne is beyond measure and
whose glory is beyond comprehension, before whom the hosts of angels stand trembling 22and at
whose command they are changed
to wind and fire,[u] whose word is
sure and whose utterances are certain, whose command is strong
and whose ordinance is terrible,
23whose look dries up the depths
and whose indignation makes the
mountains melt away, and whose
truth is established[v] forever—
24hear, O Lord, the prayer of your
servant, and give ear to the petition
of your creature; attend to my
words. 25For as long as I live I will
speak, and as long as I have understanding I will answer. 26O do not
look on the sins of your people, but
on those who serve you in truth.
27Do not take note of the endeavors of those who act wickedly, but
of the endeavors of those who have
kept your covenants amid afflictions. 28Do not think of those who
have lived wickedly in your sight,
but remember those who have willingly acknowledged that you are to
be feared. 29Do not will the destruction of those who have the
ways of cattle, but regard those
who have gloriously taught your
law.[w] 30Do not be angry with those
who are deemed worse than wild
animals, but love those who have
always put their trust in your glory.
31For we and our ancestors have
passed our lives in ways that bring
death;[x] but it is because of us sinners that you are called merciful.
32For if you have desired to have
pity on us, who have no works of
righteousness, then you will be
called merciful. 33For the righteous, who have many works laid
up with you, shall receive their reward in consequence of their own
deeds. 34But what are mortals, that
you are angry with them; or what is
a corruptible race, that you are so
bitter against it? 35For in truth
there is no one among those who
have been born who has not acted
wickedly; among those who have
existed[y] there is no one who has
not done wrong. 36For in this,
O Lord, your righteousness and
goodness will be declared, when
you are merciful to those who have
no store of good works."

Response to Ezra's Prayer

37 He answered me and said,
"Some things you have spoken
rightly, and it will turn out according to your words. 38For indeed I
will not concern myself about the
fashioning of those who have
sinned, or about their death, their
judgment, or their destruction;
39but I will rejoice over the creation of the righteous, over their
pilgrimage also, and their salvation, and their receiving their reward. 40As I have spoken, therefore, so it shall be.
41 "For just as the farmer sows
many seeds in the ground and
plants a multitude of seedlings,
and yet not all that have been sown
will come up[z] in due season, and
not all that were planted will take
root; so also those who have been
sown in the world will not all be
saved."
42 I answered and said, "If I
have found favor in your sight, let
me speak. 43If the farmer's seed
does not come up, because it has
not received your rain in due season, or if it has been ruined by too
much rain, it perishes.[a] 44But people, who have been formed by your
hands and are called your own image because they are made like
you, and for whose sake you have
formed all things—have you also
made them like the farmer's seed?
45Surely not, O Lord[b] above! But
spare your people and have mercy
on your inheritance, for you have
mercy on your own creation."

8.22 Ps 104.4; Heb 1.7; Ps 119.89; Isa 40.8; 1 Pet 1.25
8.23 Ex 14.21,29; Isa 50.2; 51.10; Mic 1.4; Sir 16.18-19; Isa 45.19; Dan 4.37; Jn 17.17
8.24 Ps 17.1; 55.2
8.26 Ps 25.7; 51.9; Deut 10.12; Ps 2.11; Lk 4.8; 1 Thess 1.9
8.27 1 Macc 2.20; 2 Esd 3.32; 7.83
8.29 Ezra 7.10; Neh 8.1-9; Mt 7.29
8.31 Ex 34.6; Ps 103.8-10; 2 Esd 2.31; Rom 11.32
8.32 Rom 3.10-18
8.33 2 Esd 7.77; Mt 5.12; 1 Cor 3.14; 2 Cor 5.10; Col 3.24
8.34 Ps 8.4
8.35 Ps 14.3-4; 53.3-4
8.39 Gen 47.9; 2 Cor 5.6-8; Heb 11.13-16; Isa 52.7-8; Lk 15.7,10; 19.9; 2 Esd 8.33
8.41 Mt 13.3-8; Mk 4.3-9; Lk 13.23-30
8.42 2 Esd 4.44
8.43 1 Kings 17.1; 18.1-6; Ps 65.9-13; Isa 30.23
8.44 Gen 1.26-27; 5.2
8.45 Joel 2.17; Ex 34.9; Add Esth 13.15,17; 2 Esd 8.16

[u] Syr: Lat *they whose service takes the form of wind and fire* [v] Arab 2: Other authorities read *truth bears witness* [w] Syr *have received the brightness of your law*
[x] Syr Ethiop: Meaning of Lat uncertain
[y] Syr: Meaning of Lat uncertain
[z] Syr Ethiop *will live*; Lat *will be saved*
[a] Cn: Compare Syr Arab 1 Arm Georg 2: Meaning of Lat uncertain
[b] Ethiop Arab Compare Syr: Lat lacks *O Lord*

Ezra's Final Appeal for Mercy

46 He answered me and said,
"Things that are present are for
those who live now, and things
that are future are for those who
will live hereafter. 47 For you come
far short of being able to love my
creation more than I love it. But
you have often compared yourself[c] to the unrighteous. Never do
so! 48 But even in this respect you
will be praiseworthy before the
Most High, 49 because you have
humbled yourself, as is becoming
for you, and have not considered
yourself to be among the righteous. You will receive the greatest
glory, 50 for many miseries will af-
fect those who inhabit the world in
the last times, because they have
walked in great pride. 51 But think
of your own case, and inquire concerning the glory of those who are
like yourself, 52 because it is for you
that paradise is opened, the tree of
life is planted, the age to come is
prepared, plenty is provided, a city
is built, rest is appointed,[d] goodness is established and wisdom
perfected beforehand. 53 The root
of evil[e] is sealed up from you, illness is banished from you, and
death[f] is hidden; Hades has fled
and corruption has been forgotten;[g] 54 sorrows have passed away,
and in the end the treasure of
immortality is made manifest.
55 Therefore do not ask any more
questions about the great number
of those who perish. 56 For when
they had opportunity to choose,
they despised the Most High, and
were contemptuous of his law, and
abandoned his ways. 57 Moreover,
they have even trampled on his
righteous ones, 58 and said in their
hearts that there is no God—
though they knew well that they
must die. 59 For just as the things
that I have predicted await[h] you,
so the thirst and torment that are
prepared await them. For the Most
High did not intend that anyone
should be destroyed; 60 but those
who were created have themselves
defiled the name of him who made
them, and have been ungrateful to
him who prepared life for them
now. 61 Therefore my judgment is
now drawing near; 62 I have not
shown this to all people, but only
to you and a few like you."
Then I answered and said,
63 "O Lord, you have already shown
me a great number of the signs that
you will do in the last times, but
you have not shown me when you
will do them."

8.47 2 Esd 5.33 **8.49** 2 Kings 22.19; Lk 18.13-14; Mt 23.12; Lk 14.11; Jas 4.6 **8.50** 2 Tim 3.1-9 **8.52** 2 Esd 7.123; Rev 2.7; 22.1-2; Heb 11.16; Rev 21.2, 9-21; Heb 4.9-11 **8.53** 1 Tim 6.10; Rev 6.8; 20.14 **8.54** Rev 21.4; 2 Esd 7.13 **8.56** Josh 24.15; Sir 15.15-16; 2 Esd 7.129 **8.57** Ps 56.1-2; Am 2.7; 5.11 **8.58** Ps 14.1; 53.1 **8.59** Lk 16.23-24; 4 Macc 9.9; 13.15; Rev 14.11; 18.7; Mt 18.14; 1 Tim 2.4 **8.60** Rom 1.21 **8.63** 2 Esd 4.51-5.13; 6.11-24; 4.33 **9.2** Mt 24.33; Mk 15.29 **9.3** Mt 24.7; Mk 13.8; Lk 21.11; Mt 24.6; Lk 21.9 **9.5** Gen 1.1 **9.6** Mt 24.29; 2 Thess 2.9 **9.7** Jas 2.14-26; Gal 2.15-21; Phil 3.8-11; 2 Tim 1.8-10 **9.8** Mt 24.13; Rev 2.7 **9.9** Rev 17.8; 18.9-10; 2 Esd 7.36-38; 4 Macc 9.9; 10.11

More about the Signs of the End

9 He answered me and said,
"Measure carefully in your
mind, and when you see that some
of the predicted signs have occurred, 2 then you will know that it
is the very time when the Most
High is about to visit the world that
he has made. 3 So when there shall
appear in the world earthquakes,
tumult of peoples, intrigues of nations, wavering of leaders, confusion of princes, 4 then you will
know that it was of these that the
Most High spoke from the days
that were of old, from the beginning. 5 For just as with everything
that has occurred in the world, the
beginning is evident,[i] and the end
manifest; 6 so also are the times of
the Most High: the beginnings are
manifest in wonders and mighty
works, and the end in penalties[j]
and in signs.
7 It shall be that all who will be
saved and will be able to escape on
account of their works, or on account of the faith by which they
have believed, 8 will survive the
dangers that have been predicted,
and will see my salvation in my
land and within my borders, which
I have sanctified for myself from
the beginning. 9 Then those who
have now abused my ways shall be
amazed, and those who have rejected them with contempt shall
live in torments. 10 For as many as

[c] Syr Ethiop: Lat *brought yourself near*
[d] Syr Ethiop: Lat *allowed* [e] Lat lacks *of evil*
[f] Syr Ethiop Arm: Lat lacks *death*
[g] Syr: Lat *Hades and corruption have fled into oblivion*; or *corruption has fled into Hades to be forgotten* [h] Syr: Lat *will receive*
[i] Syr: Ethiop *is in the word*; Meaning of Lat uncertain [j] Syr: Lat Ethiop *in effects*

did not acknowledge me in their
lifetime, though they received my
benefits, 11 and as many as scorned
my law while they still had freedom, and did not understand but
despised it[k] while an opportunity
of repentance was still open to
them, 12 these must in torment
acknowledge it[k] after death.
13 Therefore, do not continue to be
curious about how the ungodly will
be punished; but inquire how the
righteous will be saved, those to
whom the age belongs and for
whose sake the age was made."[l]

The Argument Recapitulated

14 I answered and said, 15 "I
said before, and I say now, and will
say it again: there are more who
perish than those who will be
saved, 16 as a wave is greater than a
drop of water."

17 He answered me and said,
"As is the field, so is the seed; and
as are the flowers, so are the colors; and as is the work, so is the
product; and as is the farmer, so is
the threshing floor. 18 For there
was a time in this age when I was
preparing for those who now exist,
before the world was made for
them to live in, and no one opposed me then, for no one existed;
19 but now those who have been
created in this world, which is supplied both with an unfailing table
and an inexhaustible pasture,[m]
have become corrupt in their ways.
20 So I considered my world, and
saw that it was lost. I saw that my
earth was in peril because of the
devices of those who[n] had come
into it. 21 And I saw and spared
some[o] with great difficulty, and
saved for myself one grape out of a
cluster, and one plant out of a
great forest.[p] 22 So let the multitude perish that has been born in
vain, but let my grape and my plant
be saved, because with much labor
I have perfected them.

23 "Now, if you will let seven
days more pass—do not, however,
fast during them, 24 but go into a
field of flowers where no house has
been built, and eat only of the
flowers of the field, and taste no
meat and drink no wine, but eat
only flowers, 25 and pray to the
Most High continually. Then I will
come and talk with you."

The Abiding Glory of the Mosaic Law

26 So I went, as he directed me,
into the field that is called Ardat;[q]
there I sat among the flowers and
ate of the plants of the field, and
the nourishment they afforded satisfied me. 27 After seven days, while
I lay on the grass, my heart was
troubled again as it was before.
28 Then my mouth was opened, and
I began to speak before the Most
High, and said, 29 "O Lord, you
showed yourself among us, to our
ancestors in the wilderness when
they came out from Egypt and
when they came into the untrodden and unfruitful wilderness;
30 and you said, 'Hear me, O Israel,
and give heed to my words,
O descendants of Jacob. 31 For I
sow my law in you, and it shall
bring forth fruit in you, and you
shall be glorified through it forever.' 32 But though our ancestors
received the law, they did not keep
it and did not observe the[r] statutes; yet the fruit of the law did not
perish—for it could not, because it
was yours. 33 Yet those who received it perished, because they
did not keep what had been sown
in them. 34 Now this is the general
rule that, when the ground has received seed, or the sea a ship, or
any dish food or drink, and when it
comes about that what was sown
or what was launched or what was
put in is destroyed, 35 they are destroyed, but the things that held
them remain; yet with us it has not
been so. 36 For we who have received the law and sinned will perish, as well as our hearts that received it; 37 the law, however, does
not perish but survives in its glory."

9.11 2 Esd 7.24, 81; Isa 55.6-7; Wis 12.10,20; Acts 17.30-31; 2 Pet 3.9
9.12 Mt 25.41-46
9.13 Ezek 3.19,21; 2 Esd 7.45-60; Mt 19.23-26; Rom 10.9-10
9.15 2 Esd 7.47; 8.3
9.18 Ps 90.2; Prov 8.25-26; Eph 1.4
9.19 Gen 6.11-12; Ps 14.1; Rom 3.10
9.21 Isa 59.1,16; 63.5
9.22 Ps 80.8-11; Isa 5.7
9.23 2 Esd 5.13, 19-21; 6.31, 35
9.24 2 Macc 5.27; Deut 32.37-38; Dan 1.8-16
9.29 Ex 19.9; 24.10; Deut 4.12
9.30 Deut 6.3-4; 31.12-13; 4.1, 30; 7.12
9.31 Ps 1.3; Mt 13.3-9; Jn 15.1-6
9.32 Ps 119.89; Mt 24.34-35; 2 Esd 8.22
9.36 Jer 7.24-29; 18.9-10; Ezek 33.13, 18
9.37 Rom 7.12

[k] Or *me* [l] Syr: Lat *saved, and whose is the age and for whose sake the age was made and when* [m] Cn: Lat *law* [n] Cn: Lat *devices that* [o] Lat *them* [p] Syr Ethiop Arab 1: Lat *tribe* [q] Syr Ethiop *Arpad*; Arm *Ardab* [r] Lat *my*

The Vision of a Weeping Woman

38 When I said these things in
my heart, I looked around,[s] and
on my right I saw a woman; she was
mourning and weeping with a loud
voice, and was deeply grieved at
heart; her clothes were torn, and
there were ashes on her head.
39 Then I dismissed the thoughts
with which I had been engaged,
and turned to her 40 and said to her,
"Why are you weeping, and why are
you grieved at heart?"
41 She said to me, "Let me
alone, my lord, so that I may weep
for myself and continue to mourn,
for I am greatly embittered in spirit
and deeply distressed."
42 I said to her, "What has happened to you? Tell me."
43 And she said to me, "Your
servant was barren and had no
child, though I lived with my husband for thirty years. 44 Every hour
and every day during those thirty
years I prayed to the Most High,
night and day. 45 And after thirty
years God heard your servant, and
looked upon my low estate, and
considered my distress, and gave
me a son. I rejoiced greatly over
him, I and my husband and all my
neighbors;[t] and we gave great
glory to the Mighty One. 46 And I
brought him up with much care.
47 So when he grew up and I came
to take a wife for him, I set a day
for the marriage feast.

10 "But it happened that
when my son entered his
wedding chamber, he fell down
and died. 2 So all of us put out our
lamps, and all my neighbors[t] attempted to console me; I remained
quiet until the evening of the second day. 3 But when all of them had
stopped consoling me, encouraging me to be quiet, I got up in the
night and fled, and I came to this
field, as you see. 4 And now I intend
not to return to the town, but to
stay here; I will neither eat nor
drink, but will mourn and fast continually until I die."
5 Then I broke off the reflections with which I was still engaged, and answered her in anger
and said, 6 "You most foolish of
women, do you not see our mourning, and what has happened to us?
7 For Zion, the mother of us all, is
in deep grief and great distress. 8 It
is most appropriate to mourn now,
because we are all mourning, and
to be sorrowful, because we are all
sorrowing; you are sorrowing for
one son, but we, the whole world,
for our mother.[u] 9 Now ask the
earth, and she will tell you that it is
she who ought to mourn over so
many who have come into being
upon her. 10 From the beginning all
have been born of her, and others
will come; and, lo, almost all go[v]
to perdition, and a multitude of
them will come to doom. 11 Who
then ought to mourn the more, she
who lost so great a multitude, or
you who are grieving for one alone?
12 But if you say to me, 'My lamentation is not like the earth's, for I
have lost the fruit of my womb,
which I brought forth in pain and
bore in sorrow; 13 but it is with the
earth according to the way of the
earth—the multitude that is now
in it goes as it came'; 14 then I say
to you, 'Just as you brought forth
in sorrow, so the earth also has
from the beginning given her fruit,
that is, humankind, to him who
made her.' 15 Now, therefore, keep
your sorrow to yourself, and bear
bravely the troubles that have
come upon you. 16 For if you acknowledge the decree of God to be
just, you will receive your son back
in due time, and will be praised
among women. 17 Therefore go into
the town to your husband."
18 She said to me, "I will not do
so; I will not go into the city, but I
will die here."
19 So I spoke again to her, and
said, 20 "Do not do that, but let
yourself be persuaded—for how
many are the adversities of Zion?—
and be consoled because of the
sorrow of Jerusalem. 21 For you see
how our sanctuary has been laid
waste, our altar thrown down, our

9.38 Ruth 1.19-21; Job 2.8; Jer 6.26; Jdt 9.1
9.43 Gen 11.30; 25.21; 29.31; 2 Esd 10.45-46
9.45 Gen 30.23; 1 Sam 2.1,7; Lk 1.25; 2 Esd 6.32
9.47 Gen 24.1-4; Sir 7.25
10.1 Tob 3.8
10.7 Gal 4.26
10.9 Rom 8.22
10.10 2 Esd 7.47-48; 8.3
10.12 Gen 3.16; Isa 13.8; Jn 16.21
10.14 Gen 2.7; Sir 17.1; Gen 1.1; Isa 42.5; 45.12
10.16 Ps 111.7; 145.17; Prov 8.15
10.21 2 Kings 25.9; 2 Chr 36.19; Jdt 5.18; 1 Esd 1.55

[s] Syr Arab Arm: Lat *I looked about me with my eyes* [t] Literally *all my citizens*
[u] Compare Syr: Meaning of Lat uncertain
[v] Literally *walk*

temple destroyed; 22 our harp has
been laid low, our song has been
silenced, and our rejoicing has
been ended; the light of our lampstand has been put out, the ark of
our covenant has been plundered,
our holy things have been polluted,
and the name by which we are
called has been almost profaned;
our children[w] have suffered abuse,
our priests have been burned to
death, our Levites have gone into
exile, our virgins have been defiled, and our wives have been ravished; our righteous men[x] have
been carried off, our little ones
have been cast out, our young men
have been enslaved and our strong
men made powerless. 23 And, worst
of all, the seal of Zion has been deprived of its glory, and given over
into the hands of those that hate
us. 24 Therefore shake off your
great sadness and lay aside your
many sorrows, so that the Mighty
One may be merciful to you again,
and the Most High may give you
rest, a respite from your troubles."
25 While I was talking to her,
her face suddenly began to shine
exceedingly; her countenance
flashed like lightning, so that I was
too frightened to approach her,
and my heart was terrified. While[y]
I was wondering what this meant,
26 she suddenly uttered a loud and
fearful cry, so that the earth shook
at the sound. 27 When I looked up,
the woman was no longer visible to
me, but a city was being built,[z]
and a place of huge foundations
showed itself. I was afraid, and
cried with a loud voice and said,
28 "Where is the angel Uriel, who
came to me at first? For it was he
who brought me into this overpowering bewilderment; my end has
become corruption, and my prayer
a reproach."

Uriel's Interpretation of the Vision

29 While I was speaking these
words, the angel who had come to
me at first came to me, and when
he saw me 30 lying there like a
corpse, deprived of my understanding, he grasped my right hand
and strengthened me and set me
on my feet, and said to me,
31 "What is the matter with you?
And why are you troubled? And
why are your understanding and
the thoughts of your mind troubled?"
32 I said, "It was because you
abandoned me. I did as you directed, and went out into the field,
and lo, what I have seen I saw, and
can still see, I am unable to explain."
33 He said to me, "Stand up
like a man, and I will instruct you."
34 I said, "Speak, my lord; only
do not forsake me, so that I may
not die before my time.[a] 35 For I
have seen what I did not know, and
I hear[b] what I do not understand
36 —or is my mind deceived, and
my soul dreaming? 37 Now therefore I beg you to give your servant
an explanation of this bewildering
vision."
38 He answered me and said,
"Listen to me, and I will teach you,
and tell you about the things that
you fear; for the Most High has revealed many secrets to you. 39 He
has seen your righteous conduct,
and that you have sorrowed continually for your people and mourned
greatly over Zion. 40 This therefore
is the meaning of the vision. 41 The
woman who appeared to you a little while ago, whom you saw
mourning and whom you began to
console 42 (you do not now see the
form of a woman, but there appeared to you a city being built)[c]
43 and who told you about the misfortune of her son—this is the interpretation: 44 The woman whom
you saw is Zion, which you now behold as a city being built.[d] 45 And
as for her telling you that she was
barren for thirty years, the reason
is that there were three thousand[e]

10.22 Ps 137.2-3; Isa 14.11; Rev 18.22; Ezek 26.13; Rev 1.5; 2 Kings 25.13-17; 1 Macc 1.21-23; 1 Esd 1.49; 2 Chr 36.20; Neh 7.6; Jer 13.16; Ezek 25.3; Gen 34.5; Lam 2.10; Isa 13.16; Lam 2.11-12; 4.4; Ezra 9.9; Add Esth 7.4; 2 Macc 5.24
10.23 1 Sam 4.21-22; Jer 2.11; Hos 4.7
10.24 2 Esd 6.32; 2.31; 8.31
10.25 Mt 17.2; Rev 1.14; Lk 2.9
10.27 Zech 2.1-5; Heb 11.10; Rev 21.9-21
10.28 2 Esd 4.1; 5.20
10.29 2 Esd 4.1
10.30 Dan 10.9; Rev 1.17
10.32 2 Esd 9.23-26; 2 Cor 12.3-4
10.33 2 Esd 5.15; 6.13,17
10.37 2 Esd 13.21, 51
10.38 Ex 4.15; Ps 25.12; 94.12; Gen 18.17; Am 3.7; Mt 13.11
10.39 2 Esd 8.49; 12.7; Ezra 9.3-5; 2 Esd 5.20; 10.8
10.41 2 Esd 9.40, 42; 10.20
10.42 2 Esd 10.27

10.45 2 Esd 9.45

w Ethiop *free men* x Syr *our seers*
y Syr Ethiop Arab 1: Lat lacks *I was too . . . terrified. While* z Lat: Syr Ethiop Arab 1 Arab 2 Arm *but there was an established city*
a Syr Ethiop Arab: Lat *die to no purpose*
b Other ancient authorities read *have heard*
c Lat: Syr Ethiop Arab 1 Arab 2 Arm *an established city* d Cn: Lat *an established city*
e Most Lat Mss read *three*

years in the world before any offering was offered in it.[f] 46 And after
three thousand[g] years Solomon
built the city, and offered offerings; then it was that the barren
woman bore a son. 47 And as for her
telling you that she brought him up
with much care, that was the period of residence in Jerusalem.
48 And as for her saying to you, 'My
son died as he entered his wedding
chamber,' and that misfortune had
overtaken her,[h] this was the destruction that befell Jerusalem.
49 So you saw her likeness, how she
mourned for her son, and you began to console her for what had
happened.[i] 50 For now the Most
High, seeing that you are sincerely
grieved and profoundly distressed
for her, has shown you the brilliance of her glory, and the loveli-
ness of her beauty. 51 Therefore I
told you to remain in the field
where no house had been built,
52 for I knew that the Most High
would reveal these things to you.
53 Therefore I told you to go into
the field where there was no foundation of any building, 54 because
no work of human construction
could endure in a place where the
city of the Most High was to be revealed.

55 "Therefore do not be afraid,
and do not let your heart be terrified; but go in and see the splendor
or[j] the vastness of the building, as
far as it is possible for your eyes to
see it, 56 and afterward you will
hear as much as your ears can hear.
57 For you are more blessed than
many, and you have been called to
be with[k] the Most High as few
have been. 58 But tomorrow night
you shall remain here, 59 and the
Most High will show you in those
dream visions what the Most High
will do to those who inhabit the
earth in the last days."

So I slept that night and the following one, as he had told me.

The Vision of the Eagle

11 On the second night I had
a dream: I saw rising from
the sea an eagle that had twelve
feathered wings and three heads.
2 I saw it spread its wings over[l] the
whole earth, and all the winds of
heaven blew upon it, and the
clouds were gathered around it.[m]
3 I saw that out of its wings there
grew opposing wings; but they became little, puny wings. 4 But its
heads were at rest; the middle
head was larger than the other
heads, but it too was at rest with
them. 5 Then I saw that the eagle
flew with its wings, and it reigned
over the earth and over those who
inhabit it. 6 And I saw how all
things under heaven were subjected to it, and no one spoke
against it—not a single creature
that was on the earth. 7 Then I saw
the eagle rise upon its talons, and
it uttered a cry to its wings, saying,
8 "Do not all watch at the same
time; let each sleep in its own
place, and watch in its turn; 9 but
let the heads be reserved for the
last."

10 I looked again and saw that
the voice did not come from its
heads, but from the middle of its
body. 11 I counted its rival wings,
and there were eight of them. 12 As
I watched, one wing on the right
side rose up, and it reigned over all
the earth. 13 And after a time its
reign came to an end, and it disappeared, so that even its place was
no longer visible. Then the next
wing rose up and reigned, and it
continued to reign a long time.
14 While it was reigning its end
came also, so that it disappeared
like the first. 15 And a voice
sounded, saying to it, 16 "Listen to
me, you who have ruled the earth
all this time; I announce this to
you before you disappear. 17 After
you no one shall rule as long as you
have ruled, not even half as long."

18 Then the third wing raised itself up, and held the rule as the
earlier ones had done, and it also
disappeared. 19 And so it went with

10.46 2 Chr 1.14-15; 2.1; 3.1-2 **10.48** 2 Kings 25.8-17; 2 Chr 36.17-19; Jer 52.12-23; 2 Esd 10.21-23 **10.49** Ex 25.9,40; Heb 8.5 **10.50** Isa 60.19-20; Rev 21.9-22.5 **10.54** Heb 11.10, 16; 13.14 **10.56** 1 Cor 2.9; 2 Cor 12.4 **10.59** Rev 1.9-11; 4.1 **11.1** Dan 7.3-8; Rev 13.1; Ezek 17.3,7; Rev 4.7; 8.13 **11.2** Dan 7.2; 2 Esd 13.2; Rev 7.1 **11.3** 2 Esd 12.17 **11.6** Rev 13.5, 12-17 **11.10** 2 Esd 12.17 **11.12** Rev 13.1; 17.9-13 **11.18** Dan 2.36-40; 7.17-24

[f] Cn: Lat Syr Arab Arm *her* [g] Syr Ethiop Arab Arm: Lat *three* [h] Or *him* [i] Most Lat Mss and Arab 1 add *these were the things to be opened to you* [j] Other ancient authorities read *and* [k] Or *been named by* [l] Arab 2 Arm: Lat Syr Ethiop *in* [m] Syr: Compare Ethiop Arab: Lat lacks *the clouds* and *around it*

all the wings; they wielded power one after another and then were never seen again. 20 I kept looking, and in due time the wings that followed[n] also rose up on the right[o] side, in order to rule. There were some of them that ruled, yet disappeared suddenly; 21 and others of them rose up, but did not hold the rule.

22 And after this I looked and saw that the twelve wings and the two little wings had disappeared, 23 and nothing remained on the eagle's body except the three heads that were at rest and six little wings.

24 As I kept looking I saw that two little wings separated from the six and remained under the head that was on the right side; but four remained in their place. 25 Then I saw that these little wings[p] planned to set themselves up and hold the rule. 26 As I kept looking, one was set up, but suddenly disappeared; 27 a second also, and this disappeared more quickly than the first. 28 While I continued to look the two that remained were planning between themselves to reign together; 29 and while they were planning, one of the heads that were at rest (the one that was in the middle) suddenly awoke; it was greater than the other two heads. 30 And I saw how it allied the two heads with itself, 31 and how the head turned with those that were with it and devoured the two little wings[p] that were planning to reign. 32 Moreover this head gained control of the whole earth, and with much oppression dominated its inhabitants; it had greater power over the world than all the wings that had gone before.

33 After this I looked again and saw the head in the middle suddenly disappear, just as the wings had done. 34 But the two heads remained, which also in like manner ruled over the earth and its inhabitants. 35 And while I looked, I saw the head on the right side devour the one on the left.

11.28 Rev 13.1, 11-15
11.32 2 Esd 12.24
11.37 Dan 7.4; 2 Esd 12.31-39; 11.1
11.39 Dan 7.2-6; Rev 13.1,11
11.40 Rev 13.12-15; 17.9-13; 13.16-18; 17.6; 18.24, 23; 19.20
11.42 Heb 10.32-34
11.43 Dan 4.28-31; 5.20,22-23; 3 Macc 2.3; 4 Macc 9.30-32; 2 Esd 6.32
11.45 Rev 17.15-17; 18.1-8,21-24
11.46 Rev 11.16-18; 19.1-7; Gen 1.1

A Lion Roused from the Forest

36 Then I heard a voice saying to me, "Look in front of you and consider what you see." 37 When I looked, I saw what seemed to be a lion roused from the forest, roaring; and I heard how it uttered a human voice to the eagle, and spoke, saying, 38 "Listen and I will speak to you. The Most High says to you, 39 'Are you not the one that remains of the four beasts that I had made to reign in my world, so that the end of my times might come through them? 40 You, the fourth that has come, have conquered all the beasts that have gone before; and you have held sway over the world with great terror, and over all the earth with grievous oppression; and for so long you have lived on the earth with deceit.[q] 41 You have judged the earth, but not with truth, 42 for you have oppressed the meek and injured the peaceable; you have hated those who tell the truth, and have loved liars; you have destroyed the homes of those who brought forth fruit, and have laid low the walls of those who did you no harm. 43 Your insolence has come up before the Most High, and your pride to the Mighty One. 44 The Most High has looked at his times; now they have ended, and his ages have reached completion. 45 Therefore you, eagle, will surely disappear, you and your terrifying wings, your most evil little wings, your malicious heads, your most evil talons, and your whole worthless body, 46 so that the whole earth, freed from your violence, may be refreshed and relieved, and may hope for the judgment and mercy of him who made it.' "

12 While the lion was saying these words to the eagle, I looked 2 and saw that the remaining head had disappeared. The two wings that had gone over to it rose

[n] Syr Arab 2 *the little wings*
[o] Some Ethiop Mss read *left*
[p] Syr: Lat *underwings*
[q] Syr Arab Arm: Lat Ethiop *The fourth came, however, and conquered . . . and held sway . . . and for so long lived*

up and[r] set themselves up to
reign, and their reign was brief and
full of tumult. 3When I looked
again, they were already vanishing.
The whole body of the eagle was
burned, and the earth was exceedingly terrified.
Then I woke up in great perplexity of mind and great fear, and I
said to my spirit, 4"You have
brought this upon me, because you
search out the ways of the Most
High. 5I am still weary in mind and
very weak in my spirit, and not
even a little strength is left in me,
because of the great fear with
which I have been terrified tonight.
6Therefore I will now entreat the
Most High that he may strengthen
me to the end."

The Interpretation of the Vision

7 Then I said, "O sovereign
Lord, if I have found favor in your
sight, and if I have been accounted
righteous before you beyond many
others, and if my prayer has indeed
come up before your face,
8strengthen me and show me, your
servant, the interpretation and
meaning of this terrifying vision so
that you may fully comfort my soul.
9For you have judged me worthy to
be shown the end of the times and
the last events of the times."
10 He said to me, "This is the
interpretation of this vision that
you have seen: 11The eagle that
you saw coming up from the sea is
the fourth kingdom that appeared
in a vision to your brother Daniel.
12But it was not explained to him
as I now explain to you or have explained it. 13The days are coming
when a kingdom shall rise on
earth, and it shall be more terrifying than all the kingdoms that
have been before it. 14And twelve
kings shall reign in it, one after another. 15But the second that is to
reign shall hold sway for a longer
time than any other one of the
twelve. 16This is the interpretation
of the twelve wings that you saw.
17 "As for your hearing a voice
that spoke, coming not from the
eagle's[s] heads but from the midst
of its body, this is the interpretation: 18In the midst of[t] the time of
that kingdom great struggles shall
arise, and it shall be in danger of
falling; nevertheless it shall not fall
then, but shall regain its former
power.[u] 19As for your seeing eight
little wings[v] clinging to its wings,
this is the interpretation: 20Eight
kings shall arise in it, whose times
shall be short and their years swift;
21two of them shall perish when
the middle of its time draws near;
and four shall be kept for the time
when its end approaches, but two
shall be kept until the end.
22 "As for your seeing three
heads at rest, this is the interpretation: 23In its last days the Most
High will raise up three kings,[w]
and they[x] shall renew many things
in it, and shall rule the earth 24and
its inhabitants more oppressively
than all who were before them.
Therefore they are called the heads
of the eagle, 25because it is they
who shall sum up his wickedness
and perform his last actions. 26As
for your seeing that the large head
disappeared, one of the kings[y]
shall die in his bed, but in agonies.
27But as for the two who remained,
the sword shall devour them. 28For
the sword of one shall devour him
who was with him; but he also
shall fall by the sword in the last
days.
29 As for your seeing two little
wings[z] passing over to[a] the head
which was on the right side, 30this
is the interpretation: It is these
whom the Most High has kept for
the eagle's[s] end; this was the
reign which was brief and full of tumult, as you have seen.
31 "And as for the lion whom
you saw rousing up out of the forest and roaring and speaking to the
eagle and reproving him for his unrighteousness, and as for all his
words that you have heard, 32this is
the Messiah[b] whom the Most
High has kept until the end of

12.3 2 Esd 11.45 **12.4** 1 Cor 2.10-16 **12.5** Dan 7.15,28; 8.27 **12.7** 2 Esd 4.44; 8.49; 10.39; 2 Chr 33.18-19; Ps 6.9; Acts 10.2-4, 31; Rev 8.4 **12.8** 2 Esd 4.45; 5.56; 6.12 **12.11** Dan 7.7 **12.14** Rev 17.9-14 **12.17** 2 Esd 11.10

12.18 Rev 13.3-4 **12.19** 2 Esd 11.3,11 **12.23** 2 Tim 3.1; Rev 17.15-18 **12.24** 2 Esd 11.30-32, 40-44 **12.27** Rev 19.15-16 **12.30** 2 Esd 12.2-3 **12.31** 2 Esd 11.37-46 **12.32** Gen 49.9; Mic 5.8; Rev 5.5; 2 Esd 13.26; 2 Sam 7.12, 14,16; Isa 9.6-7; Jer 23.5; Lk 1.32-33; Rev 22.16; 2 Esd 13.37

r Ethiop: Lat lacks *rose up and* s Lat *his*
t Syr Arm: Lat *After* u Ethiop Arab 1 Arm: Lat Syr *its beginning* v Syr: Lat *underwings*
w Syr Ethiop Arab Arm: Lat *kingdoms*
x Syr Ethiop Arm: Lat *he* y Lat *them*
z Arab 1: Lat *underwings* a Syr Ethiop: Lat lacks *to* b Literally *anointed one*

days, who will arise from the offspring of David, and will come and
speak[c] with them. He will denounce them for their ungodliness
and for their wickedness, and will
display before them their contemptuous dealings. 33 For first he
will bring them alive before his
judgment seat, and when he has
reproved them, then he will destroy them. 34 But in mercy he will
set free the remnant of my people,
those who have been saved
throughout my borders, and he will
make them joyful until the end
comes, the day of judgment, of
which I spoke to you at the beginning. 35 This is the dream that you
saw, and this is its interpretation.
36 And you alone were worthy to
learn this secret of the Most High.
37 Therefore write all these things
that you have seen in a book, put
it[d] in a hidden place; 38 and you
shall teach them to the wise
among your people, whose hearts
you know are able to comprehend
and keep these secrets. 39 But as
for you, wait here seven days more,
so that you may be shown whatever
it pleases the Most High to show
you." Then he left me.

The People Come to Ezra

40 When all the people heard
that the seven days were past and I
had not returned to the city, they
all gathered together, from the
least to the greatest, and came to
me and spoke to me, saying,
41 "How have we offended you, and
what harm have we done you, that
you have forsaken us and sit in this
place? 42 For of all the prophets you
alone are left to us, like a cluster of
grapes from the vintage, and like a
lamp in a dark place, and like a
haven for a ship saved from a
storm. 43 Are not the disasters that
have befallen us enough? 44 Therefore if you forsake us, how much
better it would have been for us if
we also had been consumed in the
burning of Zion. 45 For we are no
better than those who died there."
And they wept with a loud voice.
Then I answered them and said,
46 "Take courage, O Israel; and do
not be sorrowful, O house of Jacob; 47 for the Most High has you in
remembrance, and the Mighty One
has not forgotten you in your struggle. 48 As for me, I have neither forsaken you nor withdrawn from you;
but I have come to this place to
pray on account of the desolation
of Zion, and to seek mercy on account of the humiliation of our[e]
sanctuary. 49 Now go to your
homes, every one of you, and after
these days I will come to you." 50 So
the people went into the city, as I
told them to do. 51 But I sat in the
field seven days, as the angel[f] had
commanded me; and I ate only of
the flowers of the field, and my
food was of plants during those
days.

The Man from the Sea

13 After seven days I dreamed
a dream in the night. 2 And
lo, a wind arose from the sea and
stirred up[g] all its waves. 3 As I kept
looking the wind made something
like the figure of a man come up
out of the heart of the sea. And I
saw[h] that this man flew[i] with the
clouds of heaven; and wherever he
turned his face to look, everything
under his gaze trembled, 4 and
whenever his voice issued from his
mouth, all who heard his voice
melted as wax melts[j] when it feels
the fire.
5 After this I looked and saw
that an innumerable multitude of
people were gathered together
from the four winds of heaven to
make war against the man who
came up out of the sea. 6 And I
looked and saw that he carved out
for himself a great mountain, and
flew up on to it. 7 And I tried to see
the region or place from which the
mountain was carved, but I could
not.
8 After this I looked and saw
that all who had gathered together

12.33 Dan 12.2; Jn 5.28-29; Dan 7.13-14; Mt 25.41-46; Rev 20.11-14
12.34 2 Esd 7.28; Rev 19.1-7
12.35 2 Esd 11.1
12.37 Jer 30.2; Rev 1.11
12.38 2 Esd 14.46; 10.38; 1 Cor 2.9-13
12.39 2 Esd 5.13; 6.31; 9.23,27
12.40 2 Esd 9.23,27
12.42 2 Esd 1.1; Ps 119.105; 2 Pet 1.19
12.44 2 Kings 25.9; 2 Chr 36.19
2.45 1 Kings 19.4
12.46 Hag 2.4; Bar 4.5,21,27, 30
12.48 Isa 64.10; 2 Esd 3.2
12.49 2 Esd 12.39
12.51 2 Esd 5.13, 21; 6.35; 9.23,24
13.1 2 Esd 11.2
13.3 Dan 7.13; Rev 1.13; Ps 18.10; 104.3; Isa 19.1; Rev 1.7
13.4 Ps 68.2; Mic 1.4; Jdt 16.15
13.5 2 Esd 13.34; Rev 16.16; 19.19; 12.7, 17
13.6 Dan 2.45

c Syr: Lat lacks *of days . . . and speak*
d Ethiop Arab 1 Arab 2 Arm: Lat Syr *them*
e Syr Ethiop: Lat *your* f Literally *he*
g Other ancient authorities read *I saw a wind arise from the sea and stir up*
h Syr: Lat lacks *the wind . . . I saw*
i Syr Ethiop Arab Arm: Lat *grew strong*
j Syr: Lat *burned as the earth rests*

against him, to wage war with him,
were filled with fear, and yet they
dared to fight. 9When he saw the
onrush of the approaching multitude, he neither lifted his hand nor
held a spear or any weapon of war;
10but I saw only how he sent forth
from his mouth something like a
stream of fire, and from his lips a
flaming breath, and from his
tongue he shot forth a storm of
sparks.[k] 11All these were mingled
together, the stream of fire and the
flaming breath and the great
storm, and fell on the onrushing
multitude that was prepared to
fight, and burned up all of them, so
that suddenly nothing was seen of
the innumerable multitude but
only the dust of ashes and the
smell of smoke. When I saw it, I
was amazed.

12 After this I saw the same
man come down from the mountain and call to himself another
multitude that was peaceable.
13Then many people[l] came to
him, some of whom were joyful
and some sorrowful; some of them
were bound, and some were bringing others as offerings.

The Interpretation of the Vision

Then I woke up in great terror,
and prayed to the Most High, and
said, 14"From the beginning you
have shown your servant these
wonders, and have deemed me
worthy to have my prayer heard by
you; 15now show me the interpretation of this dream also. 16For as
I consider it in my mind, alas for
those who will be left in those
days! And still more, alas for those
who are not left! 17For those who
are not left will be sad 18because
they understand the things that are
reserved for the last days, but cannot attain them. 19But alas for
those also who are left, and for that
very reason! For they shall see
great dangers and much distress,
as these dreams show. 20Yet it is
better[m] to come into these
things,[n] though incurring peril,
than to pass from the world like a
cloud, and not to see what will
happen in the last days."

13.10 2 Thess 2.8; Rev 19.13-15; Isa 11.4
13.11 Rev 19.20-21; 20.14-15
13.12 Rev 7.9
13.13 Rev 7.10; 19.1-9; 6.10; Isa 66.20
13.14 2 Esd 9.25-37
13.15 2 Esd 12.8
13.16 Mt 24.37-42
13.19 Mt 24.15-28; Mk 13.14-23; Lk 21.20-24
13.20 Ps 90.5-6; Wis 2.4; 2 Esd 7.61
13.21 2 Esd 12.10, 16-17; 14.8
13.23 Jas 2.14-26
13.26 2 Esd 12.32; Gal 4.4; Lk 2.10; Rom 8.19-25
13.27 2 Esd 13.9-11
13.31 Isa 19.2; Mt 24.7
13.32 2 Esd 5.1-13; 6.11-28; Mk 13.4-8; 2 Esd 7.28; Mt 24.30; Mk 13.26-27
13.33 Jn 5.25
13.34 Rev 16.16; 19.19
13.36 2 Esd 7.26; Rev 21.1-2, 9-10; Dan 2.34,45; 2 Esd 13.6

He answered me and said, 21"I
will tell you the interpretation of
the vision, and I will also explain
to you the things that you have
mentioned. 22As for what you said
about those who survive, and concerning those who do not survive,[o]
this is the interpretation: 23The
one who brings the peril at that
time will protect those who fall
into peril, who have works and
faith toward the Almighty. 24Un-
derstand therefore that those who
are left are more blessed than
those who have died.

25 "This is the interpretation of
the vision: As for your seeing a man
come up from the heart of the sea,
26this is he whom the Most High
has been keeping for many ages,
who will himself deliver his creation; and he will direct those who
are left. 27And as for your seeing
wind and fire and a storm coming
out of his mouth, 28and as for his
not holding a spear or weapon of
war, yet destroying the onrushing
multitude that came to conquer
him, this is the interpretation:
29The days are coming when the
Most High will deliver those who
are on the earth. 30And bewilderment of mind shall come over
those who inhabit the earth.
31They shall plan to make war
against one another, city against
city, place against place, people
against people, and kingdom
against kingdom. 32When these
things take place and the signs occur that I showed you before, then
my Son will be revealed, whom you
saw as a man coming up from the
sea.[p]

33 "Then, when all the nations
hear his voice, all the nations shall
leave their own lands and the warfare that they have against one another; 34and an innumerable multitude shall be gathered together,
as you saw, wishing to come and
conquer him. 35But he shall stand
on the top of Mount Zion. 36And

[k] Meaning of Lat uncertain [l] Lat Syr Arab 2 literally *the faces of many people* [m] Ethiop Compare Arab 2: Lat *easier* [n] Syr: Lat *this* [o] Syr Arab 1: Lat lacks *and . . . not survive* [p] Syr and most Lat Mss lack *from the sea*

Zion shall come and be made manifest to all people, prepared and built, as you saw the mountain carved out without hands. 37 Then he, my Son, will reprove the assembled nations for their ungodliness (this was symbolized by the storm), 38 and will reproach them to their face with their evil thoughts and the torments with which they are to be tortured (which were symbolized by the flames), and will destroy them without effort by means of the law[q] (which was symbolized by the fire).

39 "And as for your seeing him gather to himself another multitude that was peaceable, 40 these are the nine[r] tribes that were taken away from their own land into exile in the days of King Hoshea, whom Shalmaneser, king of the Assyrians, made captives; he took them across the river, and they were taken into another land. 41 But they formed this plan for themselves, that they would leave the multitude of the nations and go to a more distant region, where no human beings had ever lived, 42 so that there at least they might keep their statutes that they had not kept in their own land. 43 And they went in by the narrow passages of the Euphrates river. 44 For at that time the Most High performed signs for them, and stopped the channels of the river until they had crossed over. 45 Through that region there was a long way to go, a journey of a year and a half; and that country is called Arzareth.[s]

46 "Then they lived there until the last times; and now, when they are about to come again, 47 the Most High will stop[t] the channels of the river again, so that they may be able to cross over. Therefore you saw the multitude gathered together in peace. 48 But those who are left of your people, who are found within my holy borders, shall be saved.[u] 49 Therefore when he destroys the multitude of the nations that are gathered together, he will defend the people who remain. 50 And then he will show them very many wonders."

51 I said, "O sovereign Lord, explain this to me: Why did I see the man coming up from the heart of the sea?"

52 He said to me, "Just as no one can explore or know what is in the depths of the sea, so no one on earth can see my Son or those who are with him, except in the time of his day.[v] 53 This is the interpretation of the dream that you saw. And you alone have been enlightened about this, 54 because you have forsaken your own ways and have applied yourself to mine, and have searched out my law; 55 for you have devoted your life to wisdom, and called understanding your mother. 56 Therefore I have shown you these things; for there is a reward laid up with the Most High. For it will be that after three more days I will tell you other things, and explain weighty and wondrous matters to you."

57 Then I got up and walked in the field, giving great glory and praise to the Most High for the wonders that he does[w] from time to time, 58 and because he governs the times and whatever things come to pass in their seasons. And I stayed there three days.

The Lord Commissions Ezra

14 On the third day, while I was sitting under an oak, suddenly a voice came out of a bush opposite me and said, "Ezra, Ezra!" 2 And I answered, "Here I am, Lord," and I rose to my feet. 3 Then he said to me, "I revealed myself in a bush and spoke to Moses when my people were in bondage in Egypt; 4 and I sent him and led[x] my people out of Egypt; and I led him up on Mount Sinai, where I kept him with me many days. 5 I told him many wondrous things, and showed him the secrets of the

13.37 2 Esd 12.32-33
13.38 2 Esd 7.38, 47,80; 4 Macc 9.9; Rev 14.10; 20.10; 2 Esd 13.10-11
13.39 2 Esd 13.12
13.40 2 Kings 17.1-6
13.42 2 Kings 17.7-18
13.44 Josh 3.14-16; 2 Kings 2.8, 14
13.46 Rev 7.4-8
13.47 Isa 11.15-16
13.49 Rev 19.11-21
13.52 2 Esd 7.28; 14.9; Mt 24.36; Mk 13.26,32; Mt 24.31; 25.31
13.54 Ezra 7.7,10; Neh 8.1-3
13.55 Sir 15.2
13.56 Jer 31.16; Mt 5.12; 1 Cor 3.14; 2 Esd 7.35,83
13.57 2 Esd 9.24; 12.51; Ps 77.14; 136.4; Dan 4.2-3; Wis 8.8
13.58 Ps 31.15; Dan 2.21; Acts 1.7; 1 Thess 5.1
14.1 Ex 3.4
14.3 Ex 3.6-4.17
14.4 Ex 12.29-36; 20.2; 19.1-2; 24.15-18; 34.28

q Syr: Lat *effort and the law* r Other Lat Mss *ten;* Syr Ethiop Arab 1 Arm *nine and a half* s That is *Another Land* t Syr: Lat *stops* u Syr: Lat lacks *shall be saved* v Syr: Ethiop *except when his time and his day have come.* Lat lacks *his* w Lat *did* x Syr Arab 1 Arab 2 *he led*

times and declared to him[y] the
end of the times. Then I commanded him, saying, 6 'These
words you shall publish openly,
and these you shall keep secret.'
7 And now I say to you: 8 Lay up in
your heart the signs that I have
shown you, the dreams that you
have seen, and the interpretations
that you have heard; 9 for you shall
be taken up from among humankind, and henceforth you shall live
with my Son and with those who
are like you, until the times are
ended. 10 The age has lost its
youth, and the times begin to grow
old. 11 For the age is divided into
twelve parts, and nine[z] of its parts
have already passed, 12 as well as
half of the tenth part; so two of its
parts remain, besides half of the
tenth part.[a] 13 Now therefore, set
your house in order, and reprove
your people; comfort the lowly
among them, and instruct those
that are wise.[b] And now renounce
the life that is corruptible, 14 and
put away from you mortal
thoughts; cast away from you the
burdens of humankind, and divest
yourself now of your weak nature;
15 lay to one side the thoughts that
are most grievous to you, and hurry
to escape from these times. 16 For
evils worse than those that you
have now seen happen shall take
place hereafter. 17 For the weaker
the world becomes through old
age, the more shall evils be increased upon its inhabitants.
18 Truth shall go farther away, and
falsehood shall come near. For the
eagle[c] that you saw in the vision is
already hurrying to come."

Ezra's Concern to Restore the Scriptures

19 Then I answered and said,
"Let me speak[d] in your presence,
Lord. 20 For I will go, as you have
commanded me, and I will reprove
the people who are now living; but
who will warn those who will be
born hereafter? For the world lies
in darkness, and its inhabitants are
without light. 21 For your law has
been burned, and so no one knows
the things which have been done
or will be done by you. 22 If then I
have found favor with you, send
the holy spirit into me, and I will
write everything that has happened
in the world from the beginning,
the things that were written in your
law, so that people may be able to
find the path, and that those who
want to live in the last days may do
so."

23 He answered me and said,
"Go and gather the people, and tell
them not to seek you for forty days.
24 But prepare for yourself many
writing tablets, and take with you
Sarea, Dabria, Selemia, Ethanus,
and Asiel—these five, who are
trained to write rapidly; 25 and you
shall come here, and I will light in
your heart the lamp of understanding, which shall not be put out until what you are about to write is
finished. 26 And when you have finished, some things you shall make
public, and some you shall deliver
in secret to the wise; tomorrow at
this hour you shall begin to write."

Ezra's Last Words to the People

27 Then I went as he com-
manded me, and I gathered all the
people together, and said, 28 "Hear
these words, O Israel. 29 At first our
ancestors lived as aliens in Egypt,
and they were liberated from there
30 and received the law of life,
which they did not keep, which
you also have transgressed after
them. 31 Then land was given to
you for a possession in the land of
Zion; but you and your ancestors
committed iniquity and did not
keep the ways that the Most High
commanded you. 32 And since he is
a righteous judge, in due time he
took from you what he had given.
33 And now you are here, and your

14.9 Gen 5.24; 2 Kings 2.11-12; 2 Esd 6.26; 7.28; 13.32, 52 **14.10** 2 Esd 5.53 **14.12** Dan 12.7; Rev 10.5-6 **14.13** 2 Sam 17.23; 2 Kings 20.1; Isa 38.1; 1 Tim 5.20; 2 Tim 4.2; Titus 1.13; Isa 40.1; 61.2; 1 Cor 15.42, 53 **14.14** 2 Cor 5.4 **14.16** Mt 24.8 **14.17** Rev 6.1-17; 8.1-9.20 **14.18** Mt 24.5; 2 Thess 2.9-11; 1 Tim 4.1; 2 Esd 11.1-12.3 **14.20** Jn 3.19; Eph 5.8; 1 Jn 2.11 **14.21** 2 Esd 4.23 **14.22** 2 Esd 4.44; Ps 43.3; 51.11; Isa 61.1; 2 Pet 1.20-21; 2 Esd 12.37; Ps 119.105; Prov 6.23 **14.23** Ex 24.18; 34.28; Deut 9.9,18 **14.24** 2 Esd 14.44 **14.25** Ps 18.28; Prov 6.23; 2 Esd 12.42; 2 Pet 1.19; Prov 20.27; 24.20 **14.29** Gen 15.13; 47.4; Deut 26.5; Ex 12.29-36 **14.30** Ex 20.1-17; Deut 4.5-6; Ex 32.1-6

14.31 2 Kings 17.7-20; 24.2-4 **14.32** Ps 7.11; 67.4; Jer 11.20; 2 Kings 25.21; Jer 52.27-31; 2 Esd 13.40; 13.45

[y] Syr Ethiop Arab Arm: Lat lacks *declared to him* [z] Cn: Lat Ethiop *ten*
[a] Syr lacks verses 11, 12: Ethiop *For the world is divided into ten parts, and has come to the tenth, and half of the tenth remains. Now . . .*
[b] Lat lacks *and . . . wise* [c] Syr Ethiop Arab Arm: Meaning of Lat uncertain
[d] Most Lat Mss lack *Let me speak*

people[e] are farther in the interior.[f] 34 If you, then, will rule over
your minds and discipline your
hearts, you shall be kept alive, and
after death you shall obtain mercy.
35 For after death the judgment will
come, when we shall live again;
and then the names of the righteous shall become manifest, and
the deeds of the ungodly shall be
disclosed. 36 But let no one come to
me now, and let no one seek me for
forty days."

The Restoration of the Scriptures

37 So I took the five men, as he
commanded me, and we pro-
ceeded to the field, and remained
there. 38 And on the next day a
voice called me, saying, "Ezra,
open your mouth and drink what I
give you to drink." 39 So I opened
my mouth, and a full cup was offered to me; it was full of something like water, but its color was
like fire. 40 I took it and drank; and
when I had drunk it, my heart
poured forth understanding, and
wisdom increased in my breast, for
my spirit retained its memory,
41 and my mouth was opened and
was no longer closed. 42 Moreover,
the Most High gave understanding
to the five men, and by turns they
wrote what was dictated, using
characters that they did not
know.[g] They sat forty days; they
wrote during the daytime, and ate
their bread at night. 43 But as for
me, I spoke in the daytime and was
not silent at night. 44 So during the
forty days, ninety-four[h] books
were written. 45 And when the forty
days were ended, the Most High
spoke to me, saying, "Make public
the twenty-four[i] books that you
wrote first, and let the worthy and
the unworthy read them; 46 but
keep the seventy that were written
last, in order to give them to the
wise among your people. 47 For in
them is the spring of understanding, the fountain of wisdom, and
the river of knowledge." 48 And I
did so.[j]

14.34 Sir 32.14; 1 Pet 1.13; 5.8
14.35 2 Cor 5.10; Heb 9.27; Dan 12.2; 2 Macc 7.9; Jn 5.28-29; 1 Cor 15.52-55; Mt 25.41-46; Rev 20.12
14.36 2 Esd 14.23
14.37 2 Esd 14.24; 9.24; 13.57
14.38 Ezek 3.1-3
14.40 Jn 4.10,14; 7.37-38
14.44 2 Esd 14.24
14.46 2 Esd 12.38
14.47 Isa 58.11; Jn 4.14; Prov 13.14; 16.22
15.1 Deut 18.18; Isa 51.16; Jer 1.9
15.2 Ps 111.7; Rev 21.5; 22.6
15.4 Ezek 3.18-20; Jn 8.21,24
15.5 Isa 51.17-20; Ezek 6.11-12; Sir 39.18-21; Rev 6.8
15.6 Dan 8.23; 2 Macc 6.14
15.8 Gen 4.10; 2 Macc 8.3; Heb 12.24; Rev 6.10
15.9 Deut 32.35-36; Lk 18.7-8; Heb 10.30; Rev 19.2
15.10 Ps 44.22; Isa 53.7; Rom 8.36
15.11 Deut 4.34,37; 5.15; Ps 89.10,13; Ex 7.14-12.32; Jdt 5.12

Vengeance on the Wicked

15 [k]Speak in the ears of my
people the words of the
prophecy that I will put in your
mouth, says the Lord, 2 and cause
them to be written on paper; for
they are trustworthy and true. 3 Do
not fear the plots against you, and
do not be troubled by the unbelief
of those who oppose you. 4 For all
unbelievers shall die in their unbelief.[l]
5 Beware, says the Lord, I am
bringing evils upon the world, the
sword and famine, death and destruction, 6 because iniquity has
spread throughout every land, and
their harmful doings have reached
their limit. 7 Therefore, says the
Lord, 8 I will be silent no longer
concerning their ungodly acts that
they impiously commit, neither
will I tolerate their wicked practices. Innocent and righteous
blood cries out to me, and the
souls of the righteous cry out continually. 9 I will surely avenge
them, says the Lord, and will receive to myself all the innocent
blood from among them. 10 See, my
people are being led like a flock to
the slaughter; I will not allow them
to live any longer in the land of
Egypt, 11 but I will bring them out
with a mighty hand and with an
uplifted arm, and will strike Egypt
with plagues, as before, and will
destroy all its land.
12 Let Egypt mourn, and its
foundations, because of the plague
of chastisement and castigation
that the Lord will bring upon it.

[e] Lat *brothers* [f] Syr Ethiop Arm: Lat *are among you* [g] Syr Compare Ethiop Arab 2 Arm: Meaning of Lat uncertain [h] Syr Ethiop Arab 1 Arm: Meaning of Lat uncertain [i] Syr Arab 1: Lat lacks *twenty-four* [j] Syr adds *in the seventh year of the sixth week, five thousand years and three months and twelve days after creation. At that time Ezra was caught up, and taken to the place of those who are like him, after he had written all these things. And he was called the scribe of the knowledge of the Most High for ever and ever.* Ethiop Arab 1 Arm have a similar ending [k] Chapters 15 and 16 (except 15.57-59, which has been found in Greek) are extant only in Lat [l] Other ancient authorities add *and all who believe shall be saved by their faith*

13 Let the farmers that till the
ground mourn, because their seed
shall fail to grow[m] and their trees
shall be ruined by blight and hail
and by a terrible tempest. 14 Alas
for the world and for those who live
in it! 15 For the sword and misery
draw near them, and nation shall
rise up to fight against nation, with
swords in their hands. 16 For there
shall be unrest among people;
growing strong against one another, they shall in their might
have no respect for their king or
the chief of their leaders. 17 For a
person will desire to go into a city,
and shall not be able to do so.
18 Because of their pride the cities
shall be in confusion, the houses
shall be destroyed, and people
shall be afraid. 19 People shall have
no pity for their neighbors, but
shall make an assault upon[n] their
houses with the sword, and plunder their goods, because of hunger
for bread and because of great tribulation.

20 See how I am calling together all the kings of the earth to
turn to me, says God, from the rising sun and from the south, from
the east and from Lebanon; to turn
and repay what they have given
them. 21 Just as they have done to
my elect until this day, so I will do,
and will repay into their bosom.
Thus says the Lord God: 22 My right
hand will not spare the sinners,
and my sword will not cease from
those who shed innocent blood on
earth. 23 And a fire went forth from
his wrath, and consumed the foundations of the earth and the sinners, like burnt straw. 24 Alas for
those who sin and do not observe
my commandments, says the
Lord;[o] 25 I will not spare them. Depart, you faithless children! Do not
pollute my sanctuary. 26 For God[p]
knows all who sin against him;
therefore he will hand them over to
death and slaughter. 27 Already calamities have come upon the
whole earth, and you shall remain
in them; God[p] will not deliver you,
because you have sinned against
him.

A Terrifying Vision of Warfare

28 What a terrifying sight, appearing from the east! 29 The nations of the dragons of Arabia shall
come out with many chariots, and
from the day that they set out,
their hissing shall spread over the
earth, so that all who hear them
will fear and tremble. 30 Also the
Carmonians, raging in wrath, shall
go forth like wild boars[q] from the
forest, and with great power they
shall come and engage them in
battle, and with their tusks they
shall devastate a portion of the
land of the Assyrians with their
teeth. 31 And then the dragons,[r]
remembering their origin, shall become still stronger; and if they
combine in great power and turn to
pursue them, 32 then these shall be
disorganized and silenced by their
power, and shall turn and flee.[s]
33 And from the land of the Assyrians an enemy in ambush shall attack them and destroy one of
them, and fear and trembling shall
come upon their army, and indeci-
sion upon their kings.

Judgment on Babylon

34 See the clouds from the east,
and from the north to the south!
Their appearance is exceedingly
threatening, full of wrath and
storm. 35 They shall clash against
one another and shall pour out a
heavy tempest on the earth, and
their own tempest;[t] and there
shall be blood from the sword as
high as a horse's belly 36 and a
man's thigh and a camel's hock.
37 And there shall be fear and great
trembling on the earth; those who
see that wrath shall be horror-
stricken, and they shall be seized
with trembling. 38 After that, heavy
storm clouds shall be stirred up
from the south, and from the
north, and another part from the
west. 39 But the winds from the
east shall prevail over the cloud

15.14 2 Esd 13.16, 19
15.15 Jdt 7.32; Mt 24.7; Mk 13.8; Lk 21.10
15.16 Mt 10.34-36; Lk 12.52-53; 2 Tim 3.1-8
15.18 2 Esd 16.10; Lk 21.26; Rev 18.10,15
15.19 Mt 24.21; Rev 7.14
15.20 Jer 25.5; 26.1-3; Tob 13.6
15.21 Deut 32.41-43; Ps 28.4; Jer 25.14; 51.24,56
15.22 Isa 47.3; Jer 21.7; Ezek 7.4,9
15.23 2 Pet 3.10,12; Jude 7
15.26 Ps 139.1-6; Add Esth 15.2; 2 Macc 7.35; 9.5
15.27 Sir 10.13; 2 Esd 16.5, 14-18; Rev 6.1-9.21
15.28 Isa 41.2; 46.11; Rev 16.12-16
15.29 Jer 25.9,18; Wis 17.9
15.30 Ps 80.13
15.34 2 Esd 15.28; Isa 14.31; 41.25; Jer 1.13-15; Ezek 23.24
15.35 Rev 14.20
15.37 Isa 33.14; Ezek 26.16; Joel 2.1; 2 Esd 16.18
15.38 Dan 11.5-6,9, 11

m Lat lacks *to grow* n Cn: Lat *shall empty*
o Other ancient authorities read *God*
p Other ancient authorities read *the Lord*
q Other ancient authorities lack *like wild boars*
r Cn: Lat *dragon* s Other ancient authorities read *turn their face to the north*
t Meaning of Lat uncertain

that was[u] raised in wrath, and shall dispel it; and the tempest[v] that was to cause destruction by the east wind shall be driven violently toward the south and west. 40 Great and mighty clouds, full of wrath and tempest, shall rise and destroy all the earth and its inhabitants, and shall pour out upon every high and lofty place[w] a terrible tempest, 41 fire and hail and flying swords and floods of water, so that all the fields and all the streams shall be filled with the abundance of those waters. 42 They shall destroy cities and walls, mountains and hills, trees of the forests, and grass of the meadows, and their grain. 43 They shall go on steadily to Babylon and blot it out. 44 They shall come to it and surround it; they shall pour out on it the tempest[v] and all its fury;[x] then the dust and smoke shall reach the sky, and all who are around it shall mourn for it. 45 And those who survive shall serve those who have destroyed it.

Judgment on Asia

46 And you, Asia, who share in the splendor of Babylon and the glory of her person— 47 woe to you, miserable wretch! For you have made yourself like her; you have decked out your daughters for prostitution to please and glory in your lovers, who have always lusted after you. 48 You have imitated that hateful one in all her deeds and devices.[y] Therefore God[z] says, 49 I will send evils upon you: widowhood, poverty, famine, sword, and pestilence, bringing ruin to your houses, bringing destruction and death. 50 And the glory of your strength shall wither like a flower when the heat shall rise that is sent upon you. 51 You shall be weakened like a wretched woman who is beaten and wounded, so that you cannot receive your mighty lovers. 52 Would I have dealt with you so violently, says the Lord, 53 if you had not killed my chosen people continually, exulting and clapping your hands and talking about their death when you were drunk?

54 Beautify your face! 55 The reward of a prostitute is in your lap; therefore you shall receive your recompense. 56 As you will do to my chosen people, says the Lord, so God will do to you, and will hand you over to adversities. 57 Your children shall die of hunger, and you shall fall by the sword; your cities shall be wiped out, and all your people who are in the open country shall fall by the sword. 58 Those who are in the mountains and highlands[a] shall perish of hunger, and they shall eat their own flesh in hunger for bread and drink their own blood in thirst for water. 59 Unhappy above all others, you shall come and suffer fresh miseries. 60 As they pass by they shall crush the hateful[b] city, and shall destroy a part of your land and abolish a portion of your glory, when they return from devastated Babylon. 61 You shall be broken down by them like stubble,[c] and they shall be like fire to you. 62 They shall devour you and your cities, your land and your mountains; they shall burn with fire all your forests and your fruitful trees. 63 They shall carry your children away captive, plunder your wealth, and mar the glory of your countenance.

Further Denunciations

16 Woe to you, Babylon and Asia! Woe to you, Egypt and Syria! 2 Bind on sackcloth and cloth of goats' hair,[d] and wail for your children, and lament for them; for your destruction is at

2 Esd 15.46; Isa 19.1-17; Jer 46.2-26; Ezek 29.3-30.26; Isa 17.1-14; Jer 49.23-27; Am 1.3-5

15.40 Jer 4.13; Ezek 30.3; Joel 2.2; Zeph 1.15
15.42 Gen 7.17-23; Isa 8.7-8; Dan 11.10,40
15.43 1 Pet 5.13; Rev 18.1-3
15.44 Isa 34.10; Rev 14.11; 19.3; Jer 50.46; Rev 18.9-19
15.47 Rev 14.8; 18.2; Ezek 16.15-34; 23.5-21; Rev 17.4-6
15.49 Ezek 16.35-43; 23.22-49; Rev 18.7-8
15.53 Jer 50.11; 3 Macc 6.5; Lam 2.15; Ezek 25.6; Nam 3.19
15.55 Ezek 25.7; Am 1.3-2.3
15.56 Jer 50.8-16; 51.1-58; Hab 2.3-19
15.57 Jer 5.17; Lam 1.15; 2.11-12,21; 4.4-5; Isa 1.20; 3.25; Jer 11.22; Ezek 30.6
15.59 2 Esd 8.50; Jas 5.1
15.61 Ex 15.7; Isa 47.14; Joel 2.5
15.63 Jer 20.4; 48.46; 1 Macc 1.32; 8.10; 2 Esd 16.46; 2 Chr 14.14; Jer 30.16; Ezek 29.19; 1 Macc 7.47
16.1 Isa 13.1-14. 23; 21.1-10; 47.1-15; Jer 50.1-51.58; Rev 18.1-24;

[u] Literally *that he* [v] Meaning of Lat uncertain [w] Or *eminent person*
[x] Other ancient authorities add *until they destroy it to its foundations*
[y] Other ancient authorities add *you have followed after that one about to gratify her magnates and leaders so that you may be made proud and be pleased by her fornications*
[z] Other ancient authorities read *the Lord*
[a] Gk: Lat omits *and highlands*
[b] Another reading is *idle* or *unprofitable*
[c] Other ancient authorities read *like dry straw*
[d] Other ancient authorities lack *cloth of goats' hair*

hand. 3 The sword has been sent
upon you, and who is there to turn
it back? 4 A fire has been sent upon
you, and who is there to quench it?
5 Calamities have been sent upon
you, and who is there to drive them
away? 6 Can one drive off a hungry
lion in the forest, or quench a fire
in the stubble once it has started
to burn?[e] 7 Can one turn back an
arrow shot by a strong archer?
8 The Lord God sends calamities,
and who will drive them away?
9 Fire will go forth from his wrath,
and who is there to quench it?
10 He will flash lightning, and who
will not be afraid? He will thunder,
and who will not be terrified?
11 The Lord will threaten, and who
will not be utterly shattered at his
presence? 12 The earth and its
foundations quake, the sea is
churned up from the depths, and
its waves and the fish with them
shall be troubled at the presence of
the Lord and the glory of his power.
13 For his right hand that bends the
bow is strong, and his arrows that
he shoots are sharp and when they
are shot to the ends of the world
will not miss once. 14 Calamities
are sent forth and shall not return
until they come over the earth.
15 The fire is kindled, and shall not
be put out until it consumes the
foundations of the earth. 16 Just as
an arrow shot by a mighty archer
does not return, so the calamities
that are sent upon the earth shall
not return. 17 Alas for me! Alas for
me! Who will deliver me in those
days?

The Horror of the Last Days

18 The beginning of sorrows,
when there shall be much lamentation; the beginning of famine,
when many shall perish; the beginning of wars, when the powers
shall be terrified; the beginning of
calamities, when all shall tremble.
What shall they do, when the calamities come? 19 Famine and
plague, tribulation and anguish are
sent as scourges for the correction
of humankind. 20 Yet for all this
they will not turn from their iniquities, or ever be mindful of the
scourges. 21 Indeed, provisions will
be so cheap upon earth that people
will imagine that peace is assured
for them, and then calamities shall
spring up on the earth – the sword,
famine, and great confusion. 22 For
many of those who live on the
earth shall perish by famine; and
those who survive the famine shall
die by the sword. 23 And the dead
shall be thrown out like dung, and
there shall be no one to console
them; for the earth shall be left
desolate, and its cities shall be demolished. 24 No one shall be left to
cultivate the earth or to sow it.
25 The trees shall bear fruit, but
who will gather it? 26 The grapes
shall ripen, but who will tread
them? For in all places there shall
be great solitude; 27 a person will
long to see another human being,
or even to hear a human voice.
28 For ten shall be left out of a city;
and two, out of the field, those who
have hidden themselves in thick
groves and clefts in the rocks.
29 Just as in an olive orchard three
or four olives may be left on every
tree, 30 or just as when a vineyard is
gathered, some clusters may be
left[f] by those who search carefully
through the vineyard, 31 so in those
days three or four shall be left by
those who search their houses with
the sword. 32 The earth shall be left
desolate, and its fields shall be
plowed up,[g] and its roads and all
its paths shall bring forth thorns,
because no sheep will go along
them. 33 Virgins shall mourn because they have no bridegrooms;
women shall mourn because they
have no husbands; their daughters
shall mourn, because they have no
help. 34 Their bridegrooms shall be
killed in war, and their husbands
shall perish of famine.

God's People Must Prepare for the End

35 Listen now to these things,
and understand them, you who are

16.3 2 Esd 15.15, 57
16.4 2 Esd 15.23, 41,61-62
16.5 2 Esd 15.27
16.6 2 Esd 15.61
16.8 Isa 14.26-27; 45.7; Am 3.6
16.10 Ps 144.6; Ezek 21.10, 28; 2 Esd 15.18; Ps 18.13; 29.3-4; Isa 29.6
16.12 Ps 18.15
16.13 Ps 7.13; 18.14; 144.6; Ezek 5.15-16
16.15 2 Pet 3.10,12
16.16 Wis 5.12
16.18 Mt 24.7-8; Mk 13.8; 2 Esd 15.33, 37
16.19 Prov 3.11-12; Isa 9.8-21; Am 4.6-12; Heb 12.5-7
16.20 Judg 2.16-18; 2 Kings 17.14-18; Ps 106.13-43
16.21 Jer 6.14; 8.11; 2 Esd 15.27; 16.5; Rev 8.7-9.21
16.22 Am 5.18-20
16.23 2 Kings 9.37; Ps 83.10; Jer 8.2; 9.22; Isa 24.1; Jer 51.62; Mic 7.13
16.28 Mt 24.40-41; Mk 13.14-16; Lk 23.30
16.33 Jer 7.34; 16.9; 25.10-11; 3 Macc 1.19; Rev 18.10
16.35 Ps 113.1; Isa 56.6; 65.13-15

e Other ancient authorities read *fire when dry straw has been set on fire*
f Other ancient authorities read *a cluster may remain exposed*
g Other ancient authorities read *be for briers*

servants of the Lord. 36 This is word
of the Lord; receive it and do not
disbelieve what the Lord says.[h]
37 The calamities draw near, and
are not delayed. 38 Just as a pregnant woman, in the ninth month
when the time of her delivery
draws near, has great pains
around her womb for two or three
hours beforehand, but when the
child comes forth from the womb,
there will not be a moment's
delay, 39 so the calamities will
not delay in coming upon the
earth, and the world will groan,
and pains will seize it on every
side.
40 Hear my words, O my people; prepare for battle, and in the
midst of the calamities be like
strangers on the earth. 41 Let the
one who sells be like one who will
flee; let the one who buys be like
one who will lose; 42 let the one
who does business be like one who
will not make a profit; and let the
one who builds a house be like one
who will not live in it; 43 let the one
who sows be like one who will not
reap; so also the one who prunes
the vines, like one who will not
gather the grapes; 44 those who
marry, like those who will have no
children; and those who do not
marry, like those who are widowed.
45 Because of this those who labor,
labor in vain; 46 for strangers shall
gather their fruits, and plunder
their goods, overthrow their
houses, and take their children
captive; for in captivity and famine
they will produce their children.[i]
47 Those who conduct business, do
so only to have it plundered; the
more they adorn their cities, their
houses and possessions, and their
persons, 48 the more angry I will be
with them for their sins, says the
Lord. 49 Just as a respectable and
virtuous woman abhors a prostitute, 50 so righteousness shall abhor iniquity, when she decks herself out, and shall accuse her to her
face when he comes who will defend the one who searches out every sin on earth.

The Power and Wisdom of God

51 Therefore do not be like her
or her works. 52 For in a very short
time iniquity will be removed from
the earth, and righteousness will
reign over us. 53 Sinners must not
say that they have not sinned;[j] for
God[k] will burn coals of fire on the
head of everyone who says, "I
have not sinned before God and
his glory." 54 The Lord[l] certainly
knows everything that people do;
he knows their imaginations and
their thoughts and their hearts.
55 He said, "Let the earth be
made," and it was made, and "Let
the heaven be made," and it was
made. 56 At his word the stars were
fixed in their places, and he knows
the number of the stars. 57 He
searches the abyss and its treasures; he has measured the sea and
its contents; 58 he has confined the
sea in the midst of the waters;[m]
and by his word he has suspended
the earth over the water. 59 He has
spread out the heaven like a dome
and made it secure upon the waters; 60 he has put springs of water
in the desert, and pools on the tops
of the mountains, so as to send rivers from the heights to water the
earth. 61 He formed human beings
and put a heart in the midst of
each body, and gave each person
breath and life and understanding
62 and the spirit[n] of Almighty
God,[o] who surely made all things
and searches out hidden things in
hidden places. 63 He knows your
imaginations and what you think
in your hearts! Woe to those who
sin and want to hide their sins!
64 The Lord will strictly examine all
their works, and will make a public
spectacle of all of you. 65 You shall

16.38 Jer 4.31; 6.24; 13.21; 2 Esd 4.40 **16.39** Rev 18.9-19 **16.40** Gen 23.4; Ps 39.12; Heb 11.9, 13-16; 1 Pet 2.11 **16.41** 1 Cor 7.29-31 **16.45** Jer 4.30; 6.29 **16.46** 2 Esd 15.19, 63 **16.48** Deut 9.7; 2 Kings 22.13; Rom 1.18 **16.50** Mt 24.30-31; Acts 17.31; Titus 2.13; Rev 22.20; 1 Sam 16.7; Jer 11.20; 17.10 **16.52** 2 Pet 3.13 **16.53** 1 Jn 1.8,10; Prov 25.21-22; Rom 12.19-20 **16.54** Ps 139.1-6; 2 Esd 15.26 **16.55** Gen 1.1-3; Ps 148.5; 33.6 **16.56** Gen 1.14-18; Am 5.8 **16.57** Sir 1.3; 42.18; Lk 8.31 **16.58** Gen 1.9-10 **16.59** Gen 1.6-8; Ps 104.2-3 **16.60** Ps 104.10,33, 35; Isa 41.18 **16.61** Gen 1.26-27; 2.7; Ps 139.13-15; Prov 4.23 **16.62** Gen 2.7; Eccl 12.7 **16.63** Gen 6.5 **16.65** Isa 44.11; 65.13; Jer 17.13; Let Jer 6.26,39; Jer 2.9; Rom 2.15

[h] Cn: Lat *do not believe the gods of whom the Lord speaks* [i] Other ancient authorities read *therefore those who are married may know that they will produce children for captivity and famine* [j] Other ancient authorities add *or the unjust done injustice* [k] Lat *for he* [l] Other ancient authorities read *Lord God* [m] Other ancient authorities read *confined the world between the waters and the waters* [n] Or *breath* [o] Other ancient authorities read *of the Lord Almighty*

be put to shame when your sins
come out before others, and your
own iniquities shall stand as your
accusers on that day. 66 What will
you do? Or how will you hide your
sins before the Lord and his glory?
67 Indeed, God[p] is the judge; fear
him! Cease from your sins, and forget your iniquities, never to commit them again; so God[p] will lead
you forth and deliver you from all
tribulation.

Impending Persecution of God's People

68 The burning wrath of a great
multitude is kindled over you; they
shall drag some of you away and
force you to eat what was sacrificed to idols. 69 And those who
consent to eat shall be held in derision and contempt, and shall be
trampled under foot. 70 For in
many places[q] and in neighboring
cities there shall be a great upris-
ing against those who fear the
Lord. 71 They shall[r] be like mani-
acs, sparing no one, but plundering
and destroying those who continue
to fear the Lord.[s] 72 For they shall
destroy and plunder their goods,
and drive them out of house and
home. 73 Then the tested quality of
my elect shall be manifest, like
gold that is tested by fire.

Promise of Divine Deliverance

74 Listen, my elect ones, says
the Lord; the days of tribulation
are at hand, but I will deliver you
from them. 75 Do not fear or doubt,
for God[p] is your guide. 76 You who
keep my commandments and precepts, says the Lord God, must not
let your sins weigh you down, or
your iniquities prevail over you.
77 Woe to those who are choked by
their sins and overwhelmed by
their iniquities! They are like a
field choked with underbrush and
its path[t] overwhelmed with
thorns, so that no one can pass
through. 78 It is shut off and given
up to be consumed by fire.

16.67 Gen 18.26; Ps 94.2; Isa 33.22; 1.16-17; Jer 25.5; Isa 49.10; 57.18 **16.68** Mt 10.17-18; 24.9; Mk 13.9; 2 Macc 6.18; 4 Macc 5.2; 1 Cor 8.1 **16.70** Rev 2.10; 3.10; 6.9-10; 12.17 **16.72** 2 Esd 15.63; Heb 10.34 **16.73** Zech 13.9; Sir 2.5; 1 Pet 1.7 **16.74** 2 Esd 2.27; 15.19 **16.75** Ps 48.14; 73.24; Isa 58.11 **16.76** Heb 12.1 **16.77** Mt 13.7,22; Mk 4.7,18-19

16.78 Mt 7.19; 13.40-42; Heb 6.7-8

[p] Other ancient authorities read *the Lord*
[q] Meaning of Lat uncertain
[r] Other ancient authorities read *For people, because of their misfortunes, shall*
[s] Other ancient authorities read *fear God*
[t] Other ancient authorities read *seed*

(d) The following book appears in an appendix to the Greek Bible.

4 Maccabees

Title and Background

This book takes its name from the Maccabean period, in which its events took place. It is essentially a sermon that extols and commemorates the martyrdom of Eleazar and of a mother with her seven sons (recorded in 2 Macc 6.12–7.42). The sermon may first have been preached on the Feast of Dedication (cf. 1.10), the festival that celebrated the Maccabees gaining control of and purifying the temple.

Author and Date of Writing

The unknown author of 4 Maccabees was obviously well-versed in the Greek language and in Greek philosophy, but thoroughly Jewish in his thinking. The book was likely written in Greek between 63 B.C. and A.D. 70.

Theme and Message

The main intent of the book is to demonstrate that Jewish wisdom, which can be obtained only from God through his Law, is fully compatible with the Greek philosophy that reason is the supreme guide of human behavior. To the author, only Judaism embodies true philosophy.

Outline

I. The Supremacy of Reason (1.1–3.5)
II. The Examples of King David and the High Priest Onias (3.6–4.14)
III. The Example of Eleazar (4.15–7.23)
IV. The Example of a Mother and her Seven Sons (8.1–17.6)
V. Concluding Perspectives (17.7–18.24)

The Author's Definition of His Task

1 The subject that I am about to
discuss is most philosophical,
that is, whether devout reason is
sovereign over the emotions. So it
is right for me to advise you to pay
earnest attention to philosophy.
2 For the subject is essential to everyone who is seeking knowledge,
and in addition it includes the
praise of the highest virtue—I
mean, of course, rational judgment. 3 If, then, it is evident that
reason rules over those emotions
that hinder self-control, namely,
gluttony and lust, 4 it is also clear
that it masters the emotions that
hinder one from justice, such as
malice, and those that stand in the
way of courage, namely anger, fear,
and pain. 5 Some might perhaps
ask, "If reason rules the emotions,
why is it not sovereign over forgetfulness and ignorance?" Their attempt at argument is ridiculous![a]
6 For reason does not rule its own
emotions, but those that are opposed to justice, courage, and self-
control;[b] and it is not for the purpose of destroying them, but so
that one may not give way to them.
7 I could prove to you from
many and various examples that
reason[c] is dominant over the emotions, 8 but I can demonstrate it
best from the noble bravery of
those who died for the sake of virtue, Eleazar and the seven brothers
and their mother. 9 All of these, by

1.1 4 Macc 1.13; 2.24; 6.31-35; 13.1
1.2 4 Macc 1.18
1.3 4 Macc 1.18; Gal 5.22-23
1.4 4 Macc 1.18; Mic 6.8; Josh 1.6-7; 4 Macc 1.18
1.5 4 Macc 2.24-3.1
1.8 2 Macc 6.18; 3 Macc 6.1; 2 Macc 7.1-41

[a] Or *They are attempting to make my argument ridiculous!* [b] Other ancient authorities add *and rational judgment*
[c] Other ancient authorities read *devout reason*

despising sufferings that bring
death, demonstrated that reason
controls the emotions. 10 On this
anniversary[d] it is fitting for me to
praise for their virtues those who,
with their mother, died for the
sake of nobility and goodness, but
I would also call them blessed for
the honor in which they are held.
11 All people, even their torturers,
marveled at their courage and endurance, and they became the
cause of the downfall of tyranny
over their nation. By their endurance they conquered the tyrant,
and thus their native land was purified through them. 12 I shall
shortly have an opportunity to
speak of this; but, as my custom is,
I shall begin by stating my main
principle, and then I shall turn to
their story, giving glory to the all-
wise God.

The Supremacy of Reason

13 Our inquiry, accordingly, is
whether reason is sovereign over
the emotions. 14 We shall decide
just what reason is and what emotion is, how many kinds of emotions there are, and whether reason rules over all these. 15 Now
reason is the mind that with sound
logic prefers the life of wisdom.
16 Wisdom, next, is the knowledge
of divine and human matters and
the causes of these. 17 This, in turn,
is education in the law, by which
we learn divine matters reverently
and human affairs to our advantage. 18 Now the kinds of wisdom
are rational judgment, justice,
courage, and self-control. 19 Rational judgment is supreme over all of
these, since by means of it reason
rules over the emotions. 20 The two
most comprehensive types[e] of the
emotions are pleasure and pain;
and each of these is by nature concerned with both body and soul.
21 The emotions of both pleasure
and pain have many conse-
quences. 22 Thus desire precedes
pleasure and delight follows it.
23 Fear precedes pain and sorrow
comes after. 24 Anger, as a person
will see by reflecting on this experience, is an emotion embracing
pleasure and pain. 25 In pleasure
there exists even a malevolent ten-
dency, which is the most complex
of all the emotions. 26 In the soul
it is boastfulness, covetousness,
thirst for honor, rivalry, and malice; 27 in the body, indiscriminate
eating, gluttony, and solitary gor-
mandizing.

28 Just as pleasure and pain are
two plants growing from the body
and the soul, so there are many off-
shoots of these plants,[f] 29 each of
which the master cultivator, reason, weeds and prunes and ties up
and waters and thoroughly irri-
gates, and so tames the jungle of
habits and emotions. 30 For reason
is the guide of the virtues, but over
the emotions it is sovereign.

Observe now, first of all, that rational judgment is sovereign over
the emotions by virtue of the restraining power of self-control.
31 Self-control, then, is dominance
over the desires. 32 Some desires
are mental, others are physical,
and reason obviously rules over
both. 33 Otherwise, how is it that
when we are attracted to forbidden
foods we abstain from the pleasure
to be had from them? Is it not because reason is able to rule over
appetites? I for one think so.
34 Therefore when we crave seafood
and fowl and animals and all sorts
of foods that are forbidden to us by
the law, we abstain because of
domination by reason. 35 For the
emotions of the appetites are restrained, checked by the temperate mind, and all the impulses of
the body are bridled by reason.

Compatibility of the Law with Reason

2 And why is it amazing that the
desires of the mind for the enjoyment of beauty are rendered
powerless? 2 It is for this reason,
certainly, that the temperate Joseph is praised, because by mental
effort[g] he overcame sexual desire.
3 For when he was young and in his
prime for intercourse, by his rea-

1.11 Jas 1.2-3; 3 Macc 6.16-28; 4 Macc 4.15; 5.1; Mal 3.2-3; 4 Macc 6.28-29; 17.21
1.13 4 Macc 1.1; 13.1
1.16 Prov 1.1-7; 4 Macc 1.21
1.17 Ezra 7.6,10; Sir 21.21; 34.9
1.18 Wis 8.7
1.24 Mt 5.21-22; Eph 4.26-27, 31; Jas 1.19-20
1.26 Rom 7.8; Col 3.5; Rom 1.29-31; Gal 5.19-21
1.27 3 Macc 7.11; Phil 3.19
1.34 Lev 11.1-31; Deut 14.3-21; Acts 10.10-14; Gal 5.22-23
2.1 Song 1.15-16; 4.1,7; 4 Macc 8.5
2.2 Gen 39.7-12

[d] Gk *At this time* [e] Or *sources*
[f] Other ancient authorities read *these emotions*
[g] Other ancient authorities add *in reasoning*

son he nullified the frenzy[h] of the
passions. 4 Not only is reason
proved to rule over the frenzied
urge of sexual desire, but also over
every desire.[i] 5 Thus the law says,
"You shall not covet your neighbor's wife or anything that is your
neighbor's." 6 In fact, since the law
has told us not to covet, I could
prove to you all the more that reason is able to control desires.

Just so it is with the emotions
that hinder one from justice. 7 Otherwise how could it be that someone who is habitually a solitary
gormandizer, a glutton, or even a
drunkard can learn a better way,
unless reason is clearly lord of the
emotions? 8 Thus, as soon as one
adopts a way of life in accordance
with the law, even though a lover
of money, one is forced to act contrary to natural ways and to lend
without interest to the needy and
to cancel the debt when the seventh year arrives. 9 If one is greedy,
one is ruled by the law through reason so that one neither gleans the
harvest nor gathers the last grapes
from the vineyard.

In all other matters we can recognize that reason rules the emotions. 10 For the law prevails even
over affection for parents, so that
virtue is not abandoned for their
sakes. 11 It is superior to love for
one's wife, so that one rebukes her
when she breaks the law. 12 It takes
precedence over love for children,
so that one punishes them for mis-
deeds. 13 It is sovereign over the relationship of friends, so that one
rebukes friends when they act
wickedly. 14 Do not consider it par-
adoxical when reason, through the
law, can prevail even over enmity.
The fruit trees of the enemy are not
cut down, but one preserves the
property of enemies from marauders and helps raise up what has
fallen.[j]

15 It is evident that reason rules
even[k] the more violent emotions:
lust for power, vainglory, boasting,
arrogance, and malice. 16 For the
temperate mind repels all these
malicious emotions, just as it repels anger—for it is sovereign over
even this. 17 When Moses was angry
with Dathan and Abiram, he did
nothing against them in anger, but
controlled his anger by reason.
18 For, as I have said, the temperate
mind is able to get the better of the
emotions, to correct some, and to
render others powerless. 19 Why
else did Jacob, our most wise father, censure the households of
Simeon and Levi for their irrational
slaughter of the entire tribe of the
Shechemites, saying, "Cursed be
their anger"? 20 For if reason could
not control anger, he would not
have spoken thus. 21 Now when
God fashioned human beings, he
planted in them emotions and inclinations, 22 but at the same time
he enthroned the mind among the
senses as a sacred governor over
them all. 23 To the mind he gave
the law; and one who lives subject
to this will rule a kingdom that is
temperate, just, good, and courageous.

24 How is it then, one might
say, that if reason is master of the
emotions, it does not control for-
3 getfulness and ignorance?
1 But this argument is entirely
ridiculous; for it is evident that
reason rules not over its own emotions, but over those of the body.
2 No one of us[l] can eradicate that
kind of desire, but reason can provide a way for us not to be enslaved
by desire. 3 No one of us can eradicate anger from the mind, but reason can help to deal with anger.
4 No one of us can eradicate malice, but reason can fight at our side
so that we are not overcome by
malice. 5 For reason does not uproot the emotions but is their antagonist.

King David's Thirst

6 Now this can be explained
more clearly by the story of King
David's thirst. 7 David had been attacking the Philistines all day long,
and together with the soldiers of
his nation had killed many of

2.5 Ex 20.17; Deut 5.28; Rom 7.7-8
2.8 1 Tim 6.10; Ex 22.25; Lev 25.35-37; Deut 23.19-20; 15.1-3
2.9 Lev 19.9-10; Deut 20.19-20
2.11 Lk 14.26
2.12 Mt 10.37; Lk 14.26; Prov 13.24; 23.13-14; Sir 22.6
2.13 Prov 12.26; 27.6; 28.23
2.14 Deut 20.18-20; Ex 23.4-5
2.15 Rom 1.29-31
2.16 Gal 5.16-21; Eph 4.31-32
2.17 Num 16.1-35; Sir 45.18
2.19 Gen 34.25-30; 49.7
2.22 2 Sam 7.3; Eccl 1.17; 2.3
2.24 4 Macc 1.1, 13; 6.31-35; 13.1
3.3 Gen 4.6-7; Eph 4.26
3.6 2 Sam 23.13-17; 1 Chr 11.15-19

[h] Or *gadfly* [i] Or *all covetousness*
[j] Or *the beasts that have fallen*
[k] Other ancient authorities read *through*
[l] Gk *you*

them. 8Then when evening fell,
he[m] came, sweating and quite exhausted, to the royal tent, around
which the whole army of our ancestors had encamped. 9Now all
the rest were at supper, 10but the
king was extremely thirsty, and
though springs were plentiful
there, he could not satisfy his
thirst from them. 11But a certain
irrational desire for the water in
the enemy's territory tormented
and inflamed him, undid and consumed him. 12When his guards
complained bitterly because of the
king's craving, two staunch young
soldiers, respecting[n] the king's desire, armed themselves fully, and
taking a pitcher climbed over the
enemy's ramparts. 13Eluding the
sentinels at the gates, they went
searching throughout the enemy
camp 14and found the spring, and
from it boldly brought the king a
drink. 15But David,[o] though he
was burning with thirst, considered it an altogether fearful danger
to his soul to drink what was regarded as equivalent to blood.
16Therefore, opposing reason to
desire, he poured out the drink as
an offering to God. 17For the temperate mind can conquer the
drives of the emotions and quench
the flames of frenzied desires; 18it
can overthrow bodily agonies even
when they are extreme, and by nobility of reason spurn all domination by the emotions.

An Attempt on the Temple Treasury

19 The present occasion now
invites us to a narrative demonstration of temperate reason.

20 At a time when our ancestors
were enjoying profound peace because of their observance of the
law and were prospering, so that
even Seleucus Nicanor, king of
Asia, had both appropriated money
to them for the temple service and
recognized their commonwealth—
21just at that time certain persons
attempted a revolution against the
public harmony and caused many
and various disasters.

3.14 2 Sam 23.16; 1 Chr 11.18
3.15 Lev 17.10; 2 Sam 23.17
3.18 4 Macc 6.34-35; 8.28
3.20 2 Macc 3.1; 3.3
3.21 2 Macc 3.4-6

4.1 3 Macc 3.4; 2 Macc 3.1
4.2 2 Macc 3.5
4.4 2 Macc 3.7
4.5 2 Macc 3.8
4.6 2 Macc 3.9-11
4.7 2 Macc 3.14-15
4.9 2 Macc 3.15, 18,20
4.10 1 Macc 3.25-26; 10.29; 3 Macc 6.18
4.11 2 Macc 3.27-28,31

4 Now there was a certain Simon, a political opponent of
the noble and good man, Onias,
who then held the high priesthood
for life. When despite all manner of
slander he was unable to injure
Onias in the eyes of the nation, he
fled the country with the purpose
of betraying it. 2So he came to Apollonius, governor of Syria, Phoenicia, and Cilicia, and said, 3"I
have come here because I am loyal
to the king's government, to report
that in the Jerusalem treasuries
there are deposited tens of thousands in private funds, which are
not the property of the temple but
belong to King Seleucus." 4When
Apollonius learned the details of
these things, he praised Simon for
his service to the king and went up
to Seleucus to inform him of the
rich treasure. 5On receiving authority to deal with this matter, he
proceeded quickly to our country
accompanied by the accursed Simon and a very strong military
force. 6He said that he had come
with the king's authority to seize
the private funds in the treasury.
7The people indignantly protested
his words, considering it outrageous that those who had committed deposits to the sacred treasury
should be deprived of them, and
did all that they could to prevent it.
8But, uttering threats, Apollonius
went on to the temple. 9While the
priests together with women and
children were imploring God in the
temple to shield the holy place
that was being treated so contemptuously, 10and while Apollonius
was going up with his armed forces
to seize the money, angels on
horseback with lightning flashing
from their weapons appeared from
heaven, instilling in them great
fear and trembling. 11Then Apollonius fell down half dead in the
temple area that was open to all,
stretched out his hands toward
heaven, and with tears begged the
Hebrews to pray for him and propi-
tiate the wrath of the heavenly
army. 12For he said that he had

[m] Other ancient authorities read *he hurried and* [n] Or *embarrassed because of* [o] Gk *he*

committed a sin deserving of
death, and that if he were spared
he would praise the blessedness of
the holy place before all people.
13 Moved by these words, the high
priest Onias, although otherwise
he had scruples about doing so,
prayed for him so that King Seleucus would not suppose that Apollonius had been overcome by human treachery and not by divine
justice. 14 So Apollonius,[p] having
been saved beyond all expecta-
tions, went away to report to the
king what had happened to him.

Antiochus's Persecution of the Jews

15 When King Seleucus died,
his son Antiochus Epiphanes succeeded to the throne, an arrogant
and terrible man, 16 who removed
Onias from the priesthood and appointed Onias's[q] brother Jason as
high priest. 17 Jason[r] agreed that if
the office were conferred on him
he would pay the king three thousand six hundred sixty talents an-
nually. 18 So the king appointed
him high priest and ruler of the nation. 19 Jason[r] changed the nation's way of life and altered its
form of government in complete violation of the law, 20 so that not
only was a gymnasium constructed
at the very citadel[s] of our native
land, but also the temple service
was abolished. 21 The divine justice
was angered by these acts and
caused Antiochus himself to make
war on them. 22 For when he was
warring against Ptolemy in Egypt,
he heard that a rumor of his death
had spread and that the people of
Jerusalem had rejoiced greatly. He
speedily marched against them,
23 and after he had plundered them
he issued a decree that if any of
them were found observing the
ancestral law they should die.
24 When, by means of his decrees,
he had not been able in any way to
put an end to the people's observance of the law, but saw that all
his threats and punishments were
being disregarded 25 —even to the
extent that women, because they
had circumcised their sons, were
thrown headlong from heights
along with their infants, though
they had known beforehand that
they would suffer this— 26 when, I
say, his decrees were despised by
the people, he himself tried
through torture to compel everyone in the nation to eat defiling
foods and to renounce Judaism.

Antiochus's Encounter with Eleazar

5 The tyrant Antiochus, sitting
in state with his counselors on
a certain high place, and with his
armed soldiers standing around
him, 2 ordered the guards to seize
each and every Hebrew and to
compel them to eat pork and food
sacrificed to idols. 3 If any were not
willing to eat defiling food, they
were to be broken on the wheel
and killed. 4 When many persons
had been rounded up, one man, Eleazar by name, leader of the flock,
was brought[t] before the king. He
was a man of priestly family,
learned in the law, advanced in
age, and known to many in the tyrant's court because of his philosophy.[u]
5 When Antiochus saw him he
said, 6 "Before I begin to torture
you, old man, I would advise you to
save yourself by eating pork, 7 for I
respect your age and your gray
hairs. Although you have had them
for so long a time, it does not seem
to me that you are a philosopher
when you observe the religion of
the Jews. 8 When nature has
granted it to us, why should you
abhor eating the very excellent
meat of this animal? 9 It is senseless not to enjoy delicious things
that are not shameful, and wrong
to spurn the gifts of nature. 10 It
seems to me that you will do something even more senseless if, by
holding a vain opinion concerning
the truth, you continue to despise
me to your own hurt. 11 Will you
not awaken from your foolish philosophy, dispel your futile reason-

4.13 2 Macc 3.32-34 **4.14** 2 Macc 3.35-39 **4.15** 1 Macc 1.10, 24; 2 Macc 5.21; 7.36; 9.4,7-8; 4 Macc 1.11 **4.16** 2 Macc 4.7 **4.17** 2 Macc 4.8 **4.20** 2 Macc 4.9-12; 1 Macc 1.41-49; 2 Macc 4.13-14 **4.21** 2 Macc 4.16-17 **4.22** 1 Macc 1.17; 2 Macc 5.1, 5 **4.23** 1 Macc 1.50 **4.24** 1 Macc 2.19-41 **4.25** 1 Macc 1.60-61; 2 Macc 6.10 **4.26** 2 Macc 6.18; 7.1; 4 Macc 5.2,6 **5.1** 4 Macc 1.11 **5.2** 2 Macc 6.18; 7.1; Acts 15.29; 1 Cor 8.1 **5.4** 2 Macc 6.18-31; 3 Macc 6.1; 4 Macc 6.5 **5.7** Prov 16.31; 20.29; Wis 4.8-9; Sir 6.18; Acts 25.19; 26.5; 4 Macc 9.6-7 **5.9** 1 Tim 4.3-5

[p] Gk *he* [q] Gk *his* [r] Gk *He* [s] Or *high place* [t] Or *was the first of the flock to be brought* [u] Other ancient authorities read *his advanced age*

ings, adopt a mind appropriate to
your years, philosophize according
to the truth of what is beneficial,
12 and have compassion on your old
age by honoring my humane advice? 13 For consider this: if there is
some power watching over this religion of yours, it will excuse you
from any transgression that arises
out of compulsion."

14 When the tyrant urged him
in this fashion to eat meat unlaw-
fully, Eleazar asked to have a word.
15 When he had received permission to speak, he began to address
the people as follows: 16 "We,
O Antiochus, who have been persuaded to govern our lives by the
divine law, think that there is no
compulsion more powerful than
our obedience to the law. 17 Therefore we consider that we should
not transgress it in any respect.
18 Even if, as you suppose, our law
were not truly divine and we had
wrongly held it to be divine, not
even so would it be right for us to
invalidate our reputation for piety.
19 Therefore do not suppose that it
would be a petty sin if we were to
eat defiling food; 20 to transgress
the law in matters either small or
great is of equal seriousness, 21 for
in either case the law is equally despised. 22 You scoff at our philosophy as though living by it were
irrational, 23 but it teaches us
self-control, so that we master all
pleasures and desires, and it also
trains us in courage, so that we endure any suffering willingly; 24 it instructs us in justice, so that in all
our dealings we act impartially,[v]
and it teaches us piety, so that with
proper reverence we worship the
only living God.

25 "Therefore we do not eat defiling food; for since we believe
that the law was established by
God, we know that in the nature of
things the Creator of the world in
giving us the law has shown sympathy toward us. 26 He has permitted us to eat what will be most
suitable for our lives,[w] but he has
forbidden us to eat meats that
would be contrary to this. 27 It
would be tyrannical for you to
compel us not only to transgress
the law, but also to eat in such a
way that you may deride us for eating defiling foods, which are most
hateful to us. 28 But you shall have
no such occasion to laugh at me,
29 nor will I transgress the sacred
oaths of my ancestors concerning
the keeping of the law, 30 not even
if you gouge out my eyes and burn
my entrails. 31 I am not so old and
cowardly as not to be young in reason on behalf of piety. 32 Therefore
get your torture wheels ready and
fan the fire more vehemently! 33 I
do not so pity my old age as to
break the ancestral law by my own
act. 34 I will not play false to you,
O law that trained me, nor will I renounce you, beloved self-control.
35 I will not put you to shame,
philosophical reason, nor will I reject you, honored priesthood and
knowledge of the law. 36 You,
O king,[x] shall not defile the honorable mouth of my old age, nor my
long life lived lawfully. 37 My ancestors will receive me as pure, as one
who does not fear your violence
even to death. 38 You may tyrannize
the ungodly, but you shall not
dominate my religious principles,
either by words or through deeds."

Martyrdom of Eleazar

6 When Eleazar in this manner
had made eloquent response
to the exhortations of the tyrant,
the guards who were standing by
dragged him violently to the instruments of torture. 2 First they
stripped the old man, though he
remained adorned with the grace-
fulness of his piety. 3 After they had
tied his arms on each side they
flogged him, 4 while a herald who
faced him cried out, "Obey the
king's commands!" 5 But the courageous and noble man, like a true
Eleazar, was unmoved, as though
being tortured in a dream; 6 yet
while the old man's eyes were
raised to heaven, his flesh was being torn by scourges, his blood
flowing, and his sides were being
cut to pieces. 7 Although he fell to

5.12 2 Macc 6.27-28 **5.13** 2 Macc 7.35; 9.5; 3 Macc 2.21; 2 Macc 6.26; 4 Macc 8.14 **5.16** Ex 24.7; Josh 24.16-18; Ps 1.1-2; 119.1-8 **5.19** 4 Macc 5.8-13 **5.20** Rom 3.9-10; Jas 2.10-12 **5.23** 4 Macc 1.2-4, 18; Acts 24.25; Gal 5.22-23; 2 Pet 1.6; Acts 5.41; Col 1.24; 1 Pet 4.12-13, 16 **5.24** Ex 23.3; Deut 1.17; Wis 5.18; 1 Tim 5.21; Deut 6.4; Ps 84.2; Dan 6.26; Bel 25 **5.25** Ex 20.1 **5.26** Lev 11.1-47; Deut 14.3-21 **5.28** Ex 24.7; Josh 24.16-18; Neh 10.28-29 **5.32** 4 Macc 5.3; 8.13; 9.12; Dan 3.19-22 **5.37** 4 Macc 13.17 **6.3** Jn 19.1; Acts 5.40; 16.22-23 **6.5** 2 Macc 6.18; 8.23; 3 Macc 6.1 **6.6** 4 Macc 6.23; Acts 7.55; 4 Macc 9.12

[v] Or *so that we hold in balance all our habitual inclinations* [w] Or *souls* [x] Gk lacks *O king*

the ground because his body could
not endure the agonies, he kept his
reason upright and unswerving.
8 One of the cruel guards rushed at
him and began to kick him in the
side to make him get up again after
he fell. 9 But he bore the pains and
scorned the punishment and endured the tortures. 10 Like a noble
athlete the old man, while being
beaten, was victorious over his torturers; 11 in fact, with his face
bathed in sweat, and gasping heavily for breath, he amazed even his
torturers by his courageous spirit.
12 At that point, partly out of
pity for his old age, 13 partly out of
sympathy from their acquaintance
with him, partly out of admiration
for his endurance, some of the
king's retinue came to him and
said, 14 "Eleazar, why are you so
irrationally destroying yourself
through these evil things? 15 We
will set before you some cooked
meat; save yourself by pretending
to eat pork."
16 But Eleazar, as though more
bitterly tormented by this counsel,
cried out: 17 "Never may we, the
children of Abraham,[y] think so
basely that out of cowardice we
feign a role unbecoming to us!
18 For it would be irrational if having lived in accordance with truth
up to old age and having maintained in accordance with law the
reputation of such a life, we should
now change our course 19 and ourselves become a pattern of impiety
to the young by setting them an example in the eating of defiling
food. 20 It would be shameful if we
should survive for a little while and
during that time be a laughingstock to all for our cowardice,
21 and be despised by the tyrant as
unmanly by not contending even to
death for our divine law. 22 Therefore, O children of Abraham, die
nobly for your religion! 23 And you,
guards of the tyrant, why do you
delay?"
24 When they saw that he was
so courageous in the face of the afflictions, and that he had not been
changed by their compassion, the
guards brought him to the fire.
25 There they burned him with maliciously contrived instruments,
threw him down, and poured stink-
ing liquids into his nostrils.
26 When he was now burned to his
very bones and about to expire, he
lifted up his eyes to God and said,
27 "You know, O God, that though I
might have saved myself, I am dying in burning torments for the
sake of the law. 28 Be merciful to
your people, and let our punishment suffice for them. 29 Make my
blood their purification, and take
my life in exchange for theirs."
30 After he said this, the holy man
died nobly in his tortures; even in
the tortures of death he resisted,
by virtue of reason, for the sake of
the law.
31 Admittedly, then, devout
reason is sovereign over the emotions. 32 For if the emotions had
prevailed over reason, we would
have testified to their domination.
33 But now that reason has conquered the emotions, we properly
attribute to it the power to govern.
34 It is right for us to acknowledge
the dominance of reason when it
masters even external agonies. It
would be ridiculous to deny it.[z] 35 I
have proved not only that reason
has mastered agonies, but also
that it masters pleasures and in no
respect yields to them.

An Encomium on Eleazar

7 For like a most skillful pilot,
the reason of our father Eleazar steered the ship of religion over
the sea of the emotions, 2 and
though buffeted by the stormings
of the tyrant and overwhelmed by
the mighty waves of tortures, 3 in
no way did he turn the rudder of
religion until he sailed into the
haven of immortal victory. 4 No city
besieged with many ingenious war
machines has ever held out as did
that most holy man. Although his
sacred life was consumed by tortures and racks, he conquered the
besiegers with the shield of his devout reason. 5 For in setting his
mind firm like a jutting cliff, our

6.10 1 Cor 9.24-27; 2 Tim 2.5; Heb 12.1 **6.15** 2 Macc 6.21-22 **6.17** Ps 105.6; Isa 41.8; 3 Macc 6.3; Jn 8.39 **6.19** 2 Macc 6.27-28 **6.20** 2 Macc 6.24-25 **6.22** 2 Macc 6.26-28 **6.23** 2 Macc 7.30; 4 Macc 9.1 **6.26** Ps 123.1; Isa 51.6; 1 Esd 4.58 **6.29** 4 Macc 1.11; 17.21; Isa 53.5-12; Mk 10.45; Jn 11.49-52 **6.31** 4 Macc 1.1, 13; 2.24; 13.1 **6.33** 4 Macc 7.10, 16 **6.34** 4 Macc 8.28 **7.1** 4 Macc 5.4-6.30 **7.2** 4 Macc 1.11 **7.3** 4 Macc 13.6-7; 15.31-32

y Or *O children of Abraham* z Syr: Meaning of Gk uncertain

father Eleazar broke the maddening waves of the emotions. 6 O priest, worthy of the priesthood, you neither defiled your sacred teeth nor profaned your stomach, which had room only for reverence and purity, by eating defiling foods. 7 O man in harmony with the law and philosopher of divine life! 8 Such should be those who are administrators of the law, shielding it with their own blood and noble sweat in sufferings even to death. 9 You, father, strengthened our loyalty to the law through your glorious endurance, and you did not abandon the holiness that you praised, but by your deeds you made your words of divine[a] philosophy credible. 10 O aged man, more powerful than tortures; O elder, fiercer than fire; O supreme king over the passions, Eleazar! 11 For just as our father Aaron, armed with the censer, ran through the multitude of the people and conquered the fiery[b] angel, 12 so the descendant of Aaron, Eleazar, though being consumed by the fire, remained unmoved in his reason. 13 Most amazing, indeed, though he was an old man, his body no longer tense and firm,[c] his muscles flabby, his sinews feeble, he became young again 14 in spirit through reason; and by reason like that of Isaac he rendered the many-headed rack ineffective. 15 O man of blessed age and of venerable gray hair and of law-abiding life, whom the faithful seal of death has perfected!

16 If, therefore, because of piety an aged man despised tortures even to death, most certainly devout reason is governor of the emotions. 17 Some perhaps might say, "Not all have full command of their emotions, because not all have prudent reason." 18 But as many as attend to religion with a whole heart, these alone are able to control the passions of the flesh, 19 since they believe that they, like our patriarchs Abraham and Isaac and Jacob, do not die to God, but live to God. 20 No contradiction therefore arises when some persons appear to be dominated by their emotions because of the weakness of their reason. 21 What person who lives as a philosopher by the whole rule of philosophy, and trusts in God, 22 and knows that it is blessed to endure any suffering for the sake of virtue, would not be able to overcome the emotions through godliness? 23 For only the wise and courageous are masters of their emotions.

7.6 2 Macc 6.19-20 **7.8** Ezra 7.10; Neh 8.1-8; Mal 2.7 **7.9** Ps 101.1-4; Prov 16.6; 3 Macc 3.3-4; 2 Macc 6.28 **7.10** 4 Macc 6.32-34 **7.11** Num 16.46-50 **7.12** 4 Macc 6.24-26 **7.14** Gen 22.1-14 **7.15** 4 Macc 5.7 **7.16** 4 Macc 6.31-33 **7.19** Mt 22.32; Mk 12.26; Lk 20.38; Rom 6.10; 14.8; Gal 2.19

Seven Brothers Defy the Tyrant

8 For this is why even the very young, by following a philosophy in accordance with devout reason, have prevailed over the most painful instruments of torture. 2 For when the tyrant was conspicuously defeated in his first attempt, being unable to compel an aged man to eat defiling foods, then in violent rage he commanded that others of the Hebrew captives be brought, and that any who ate defiling food would be freed after eating, but if any were to refuse, they would be tortured even more cruelly.

3 When the tyrant had given these orders, seven brothers—handsome, modest, noble, and accomplished in every way—were brought before him along with their aged mother. 4 When the tyrant saw them, grouped about their mother as though a chorus, he was pleased with them. And struck by their appearance and nobility, he smiled at them, and summoned them nearer and said, 5 "Young men, with favorable feelings I admire each and every one of you, and greatly respect the beauty and the number of such brothers. Not only do I advise you not to display the same madness as that of the old man who has just been tortured, but I also exhort you to yield to me and enjoy my friendship. 6 Just as I am able to punish those who disobey my orders, so I can be a benefactor to those who obey me. 7 Trust me, then, and you will

8.2 4 Macc 5.4-7; 2 Macc 5.11; 7.3; 4 Macc 18.20 **8.3** 2 Macc 7.1-42; 4 Macc 17.9 **8.4** 4 Macc 13.8; 14.7-8; 18.23 **8.5** 4 Macc 2.1; 1 Macc 2.18; 10.65; 11.57; 2 Macc 7.24; 3 Macc 2.23 **8.6** 3 Macc 6.24; Lk 22.25

[a] Other ancient authorities lack *divine*
[b] Other ancient authorities lack *fiery*
[c] Gk *the tautness of the body already loosed*

have positions of authority in my government if you will renounce the ancestral tradition of your national life. 8 Enjoy your youth by adopting the Greek way of life and by changing your manner of living. 9 But if by disobedience you rouse my anger, you will compel me to destroy each and every one of you with dreadful punishments through tortures. 10 Therefore take pity on yourselves. Even I, your enemy, have compassion for your youth and handsome appearance. 11 Will you not consider this, that if you disobey, nothing remains for you but to die on the rack?"

12 When he had said these things, he ordered the instruments of torture to be brought forward so as to persuade them out of fear to eat the defiling food. 13 When the guards had placed before them wheels and joint-dislocators, rack and hooks[d] and catapults[e] and caldrons, braziers and thumbscrews and iron claws and wedges and bellows, the tyrant resumed speaking: 14 "Be afraid, young fellows; whatever justice you revere will be merciful to you when you transgress under compulsion."

15 But when they had heard the inducements and saw the dreadful devices, not only were they not afraid, but they also opposed the tyrant with their own philosophy, and by their right reasoning nullified his tyranny. 16 Let us consider, on the other hand, what arguments might have been used if some of them had been cowardly and unmanly. Would they not have been the following? 17 "O wretches that we are and so senseless! Since the king has summoned and exhorted us to accept kind treatment if we obey him, 18 why do we take pleasure in vain resolves and venture upon a disobedience that brings death? 19 O men and brothers, should we not fear the instruments of torture and consider the threats of torments, and give up this vain opinion and this arrogance that threatens to destroy us? 20 Let us take pity on our youth and have compassion on our mother's age; 21 and let us seriously consider that if we disobey we are dead! 22 Also, divine justice will excuse us for fearing the king when we are under compulsion. 23 Why do we banish ourselves from this most pleasant life and deprive ourselves of this delightful world? 24 Let us not struggle against compulsion[f] or take hollow pride in being put to the rack. 25 Not even the law itself would arbitrarily put us to death for fearing the instruments of torture. 26 Why does such contentiousness excite us and such a fatal stubbornness please us, when we can live in peace if we obey the king?"

27 But the youths, though about to be tortured, neither said any of these things nor even seriously considered them. 28 For they were contemptuous of the emotions and sovereign over agonies, 29 so that as soon as the tyrant had ceased counseling them to eat defiling food, all with one voice together, as from one mind, said:

9 "Why do you delay, O tyrant? For we are ready to die rather than transgress our ancestral commandments; 2 we are obviously putting our forebears to shame unless we should practice ready obedience to the law and to Moses[g] our counselor. 3 Tyrant and counselor of lawlessness, in your hatred for us do not pity us more than we pity ourselves.[h] 4 For we consider this pity of yours, which insures our safety through transgression of the law, to be more grievous than death itself. 5 You are trying to terrify us by threatening us with death by torture, as though a short time ago you learned nothing from Eleazar. 6 And if the aged men of the Hebrews because of their religion lived piously[i] while enduring torture, it would be even more fitting that we young men should die despising your coercive tortures, which our aged instructor also

8.8 2 Macc 4.10-15; 6.8-9
8.10 4 Macc 12.2
8.11 2 Macc 6.19, 28; 4 Macc 7.14
8.13 4 Macc 5.32; 11.10; 1 Macc 6.51; 4 Macc 9.26; 11.9
8.14 4 Macc 5.13
8.15 4 Macc 1.11; 11.24-25
8.19 4 Macc 8.13; 1 Macc 1.24; 2 Macc 9.4, 7-8; 13.9
8.20 4 Macc 8.8
8.22 4 Macc 5.13; 8.14
8.23 Eccl 2.9-10; 11.9; 4 Macc 8.8
8.28 4 Macc 3.18; 6.34-35
8.29 4 Macc 8.4; 13.13
9.1 4 Macc 6.23; 4.23-24; 5.16-17,33
9.3 4 Macc 1.11; 5.1; 8.15
9.4 4 Macc 8.10
9.5 4 Macc 5.1-6.30
9.6 Heb 11.35-37; Dan 3.8-23

[d] Meaning of Gk uncertain
[e] Here and elsewhere in 4 Macc an instrument of torture
[f] Or *fate*
[g] Other ancient authorities read *knowledge*
[h] Meaning of Gk uncertain
[i] Other ancient authorities read *died*

overcame. 7 Therefore, tyrant, put
us to the test; and if you take our
lives because of our religion, do
not suppose that you can injure us
by torturing us. 8 For we, through
this severe suffering and endurance, shall have the prize of virtue
and shall be with God, on whose
account we suffer; 9 but you, because of your bloodthirstiness toward us, will deservedly undergo
from the divine justice eternal torment by fire."

The Torture of the First and Second Brothers

10 When they had said these
things, the tyrant was not only indignant, as at those who are disobedient, but also infuriated, as at
those who are ungrateful. 11 Then
at his command the guards
brought forward the eldest, and
having torn off his tunic, they
bound his hands and arms with
thongs on each side. 12 When they
had worn themselves out beating
him with scourges, without accom-
plishing anything, they placed him
upon the wheel. 13 When the noble
youth was stretched out around
this, his limbs were dislocated,
14 and with every member disjointed he denounced the tyrant,
saying, 15 "Most abominable tyrant, enemy of heavenly justice,
savage of mind, you are mangling
me in this manner, not because I
am a murderer, or as one who acts
impiously, but because I protect
the divine law." 16 And when the
guards said, "Agree to eat so that
you may be released from the tortures," 17 he replied, "You abominable lackeys, your wheel is not so
powerful as to strangle my reason.
Cut my limbs, burn my flesh, and
twist my joints; 18 through all these
tortures I will convince you that
children of the Hebrews alone are
invincible where virtue is concerned." 19 While he was saying
these things, they spread fire under
him, and while fanning the
flames[j] they tightened the wheel
further. 20 The wheel was completely smeared with blood, and
the heap of coals was being
quenched by the drippings of gore,
and pieces of flesh were falling off
the axles of the machine. 21 Although the ligaments joining his
bones were already severed, the
courageous youth, worthy of Abraham, did not groan, 22 but as
though transformed by fire into immortality, he nobly endured the
rackings. 23 "Imitate me, brothers,"
he said. "Do not leave your post in
my struggle[k] or renounce our courageous family ties. 24 Fight the sacred and noble battle for religion.
Thereby the just Providence of our
ancestors may become merciful to
our nation and take vengeance on
the accursed tyrant." 25 When he
had said this, the saintly youth
broke the thread of life.

26 While all were marveling at
his courageous spirit, the guards
brought in the next eldest, and after fitting themselves with iron
gauntlets having sharp hooks, they
bound him to the torture machine
and catapult. 27 Before torturing
him, they inquired if he were willing to eat, and they heard his noble
decision.[l] 28 These leopard-like
beasts tore out his sinews with the
iron hands, flayed all his flesh up
to his chin, and tore away his
scalp. But he steadfastly endured
this agony and said, 29 "How sweet
is any kind of death for the religion
of our ancestors!" 30 To the tyrant
he said, "Do you not think, you
most savage tyrant, that you are
being tortured more than I, as you
see the arrogant design of your tyranny being defeated by our endurance for the sake of religion? 31 I
lighten my pain by the joys that
come from virtue, 32 but you suffer
torture by the threats that come
from impiety. You will not escape,
you most abominable tyrant, the
judgments of the divine wrath."

The Torture of the Third and Fourth Brothers

10 When he too had endured
a glorious death, the third

9.7 Wis 2.17,19 **9.8** Wis 10.12; 4 Macc 17.12; 1 Cor 9.24; 2 Tim 4.6-8; Mt 5.12; Jas 5.10 **9.9** Mt 5.22; 2 Thess 1.9; Jude 7; Rev 20.14 **9.10** 2 Macc 5.11; 7.3; 4 Macc 8.2 **9.11** 2 Macc 7.4 **9.12** 4 Macc 6.3,6; 5.3,32; 8.13 **9.15** 4 Macc 4.23-24; 5.16-17; 9.1 **9.18** 4 Macc 9.8 **9.19** 2 Macc 7.5 **9.22** 1 Cor 15.51-52; 2 Cor 3.18; Phil 3.21 **9.23** 4 Macc 13.9; 1 Cor 4.16; 11.1; 1 Thess 1.6 **9.24** 1 Tim 6.12; 2 Tim 4.7; 4 Macc 13.19; 17.22; 12.18 **9.26** 2 Macc 7.7-9; 4 Macc 8.13 **9.28** 1 Cor 15.32 **9.29** 2 Macc 6.30 **9.32** 4 Macc 10.11; 2 Tim 2.16; Titus 2.12; Ps 21.9; Jer 21.12; Rom 2.5,8; 1 Thess 2.16 **10.1** 2 Macc 7.10-12

[j] Meaning of Gk uncertain
[k] Other ancient authorities read *post forever*
[l] Other ancient authorities read *having heard his noble decision, they tore him to shreds*

was led in, and many repeatedly
urged him to save himself by tasting the meat. 2 But he shouted, "Do
you not know that the same father
begot me as well as those who
died, and the same mother bore
me, and that I was brought up on
the same teachings? 3 I do not renounce the noble kinship that
binds me to my brothers."[m] 5 Enraged by the man's boldness, they
disjointed his hands and feet with
their instruments, dismembering
him by prying his limbs from their
sockets, 6 and breaking his fingers
and arms and legs and elbows.
7 Since they were not able in any
way to break his spirit,[n] they abandoned the instruments[o] and
scalped him with their fingernails
in a Scythian fashion. 8 They immediately brought him to the wheel,
and while his vertebrae were being
dislocated by this, he saw his own
flesh torn all around and drops of
blood flowing from his entrails.
9 When he was about to die, he
said, 10 "We, most abominable tyrant, are suffering because of our
godly training and virtue, 11 but
you, because of your impiety and
bloodthirstiness, will undergo unceasing torments."
12 When he too had died in a
manner worthy of his brothers,
they dragged in the fourth, saying,
13 "As for you, do not give way to
the same insanity as your brothers,
but obey the king and save yourself." 14 But he said to them, "You
do not have a fire hot enough to
make me play the coward. 15 No—
by the blessed death of my brothers, by the eternal destruction of
the tyrant, and by the everlasting
life of the pious, I will not renounce our noble family ties.
16 Contrive tortures, tyrant, so that
you may learn from them that I am
a brother to those who have just
now been tortured." 17 When he
heard this, the bloodthirsty, mur-
derous, and utterly abominable
Antiochus gave orders to cut out
his tongue. 18 But he said, "Even if
you remove my organ of speech,
God hears also those who are
mute. 19 See, here is my tongue; cut
it off, for in spite of this you will
not make our reason speechless.
20 Gladly, for the sake of God, we
let our bodily members be mutilated. 21 God will visit you swiftly,
for you are cutting out a tongue
that has been melodious with divine hymns."

10.2 4 Macc 8.3; 14.12 **10.5** Acts 4.13; 2 Cor 3.12 **10.7** 2 Macc 4.47; 3 Macc 7.5 **10.8** 4 Macc 9.12 **10.10** 4 Macc 9.8, 18; 17.12 **10.11** 4 Macc 9.32 **10.12** 2 Macc 6.13-14 **10.15** 4 Macc 9.9; 2 Thess 1.9; Dan 12.2; 2 Esd 2.11; Mt 25.46; Jn 3.15-16,36 **10.17** 2 Macc 7.4 **10.19** 2 Macc 7.10 **10.21** Isa 29.6; 2 Esd 6.18-19; 9.2; Lk 19.44 **11.1** 2 Macc 7.15-17 **11.2** 4 Macc 9.8; 10.10 **11.5** Isa 40.26; Sir 24.8; 2 Macc 1.24; 3 Macc 3.2 **11.9** 4 Macc 8.13 **11.10** 4 Macc 5.32; 8.13 **11.12** Rom 5.3-4; 2 Cor 6.4; Heb 10.36; Jas 5.10-11 **11.13** 2 Macc 7.18-19

The Torture of the Fifth and Sixth Brothers

11 When he too died, after being cruelly tortured, the
fifth leaped up, saying, 2 "I will not
refuse, tyrant, to be tortured for
the sake of virtue. 3 I have come of
my own accord, so that by murder-
ing me you will incur punishment
from the heavenly justice for even
more crimes. 4 Hater of virtue,
hater of humankind, for what act
of ours are you destroying us in this
way? 5 Is it because[p] we revere the
Creator of all things and live according to his virtuous law? 6 But
these deeds deserve honors, not
tortures."[q] 9 While he was saying
these things, the guards bound
him and dragged him to the catapult; 10 they tied him to it on his
knees, and fitting iron clamps on
them, they twisted his back[r]
around the wedge on the wheel,[s]
so that he was completely curled
back like a scorpion, and all his
members were disjointed. 11 In this
condition, gasping for breath and
in anguish of body, 12 he said, "Tyrant, they are splendid favors that
you grant us against your will, because through these noble sufferings you give us an opportunity to
show our endurance for the law."
13 When he too had died, the
sixth, a mere boy, was led in. When
the tyrant inquired whether he was
willing to eat and be released, he

[m] Other ancient authorities add verse 4 *So if you have any instrument of torture, apply it to my body; for you cannot touch my soul, even if you wish."* [n] Gk *to strangle him* [o] Other ancient authorities read *they tore off his skin* [p] Other ancient authorities read *Or does it seem evil to you that* [q] Other authorities add verses 7 and 8, *7 If you but understood human feelings and had hope of salvation from God— 8 but, as it is, you are a stranger to God and persecute those who serve him."* [r] Gk *loins* [s] Meaning of Gk uncertain

said, 14“I am younger in age than
my brothers, but I am their equal
in mind. 15Since to this end we
were born and bred, we ought likewise to die for the same principles.
16So if you intend to torture me for
not eating defiling foods, go on torturing!” 17When he had said this,
they led him to the wheel. 18He
was carefully stretched tight upon
it, his back was broken, and he was
roasted[t] from underneath. 19To
his back they applied sharp spits
that had been heated in the fire,
and pierced his ribs so that his
entrails were burned through.
20While being tortured he said,
“O contest befitting holiness, in
which so many of us brothers have
been summoned to an arena of sufferings for religion, and in which
we have not been defeated! 21For
religious knowledge, O tyrant, is
invincible. 22I also, equipped with
nobility, will die with my brothers,
23and I myself will bring a great
avenger upon you, you inventor
of tortures and enemy of those
who are truly devout. 24We six
boys have paralyzed your tyranny.
25Since you have not been able to
persuade us to change our mind or
to force us to eat defiling foods, is
not this your downfall? 26Your fire
is cold to us, and the catapults
painless, and your violence powerless. 27For it is not the guards of
the tyrant but those of the divine
law that are set over us; therefore,
unconquered, we hold fast to reason.”

The Torture of the Seventh Brother

12 When he too, thrown into
the caldron, had died a
blessed death, the seventh and
youngest of all came forward.
2Even though the tyrant had been
vehemently reproached by the
brothers, he felt strong compassion for this child when he saw
that he was already in fetters. He
summoned him to come nearer
and tried to persuade him, saying,
3“You see the result of your brothers' stupidity, for they died in torments because of their disobedience. 4You too, if you do not obey,
will be miserably tortured and die
before your time, 5but if you yield
to persuasion you will be my friend
and a leader in the government of
the kingdom.” 6When he had thus
appealed to him, he sent for the
boy's mother to show compassion
on her who had been bereaved of
so many sons and to influence her
to persuade the surviving son to
obey and save himself. 7But when
his mother had exhorted him in
the Hebrew language, as we shall
tell a little later, 8he said, “Let me
loose, let me speak to the king and
to all his friends that are with
him.” 9Extremely pleased by the
boy's declaration, they freed him
at once. 10Running to the nearest
of the braziers, 11he said, “You profane tyrant, most impious of all the
wicked, since you have received
good things and also your kingdom
from God, were you not ashamed
to murder his servants and torture
on the wheel those who practice
religion? 12Because of this, justice
has laid up for you intense and
eternal fire and tortures, and these
throughout all time[u] will never let
you go. 13As a man, were you not
ashamed, you most savage beast,
to cut out the tongues of men who
have feelings like yours and are
made of the same elements as you,
and to maltreat and torture them
in this way? 14Surely they by dying
nobly fulfilled their service to God,
but you will wail bitterly for having
killed without cause the contes-
tants for virtue.” 15Then because
he too was about to die, he said,
16“I do not desert the excellent example[v] of my brothers, 17and I call
on the God of our ancestors to be
merciful to our nation;[w] 18but on
you he will take vengeance both in
this present life and when you are
dead.” 19After he had uttered these
imprecations, he flung himself
into the braziers and so ended his
life.[x]

11.14 4 Macc 3.17; 8.29
11.17 4 Macc 5.32
11.20 4 Macc 6.10; 16.16; 17.11
11.21 4 Macc 1.16-17
11.22 4 Macc 1.8-10; 9.13, 24,27
11.24 4 Macc 1.11; 8.15; 9.30
11.27 4 Macc 1.1; 6.31-35
12.1 2 Macc 7.24-40
12.2 4 Macc 8.10; 2 Macc 7.24
12.5 2 Macc 7.24; 4 Macc 8.5
12.6 2 Macc 7.25-26
12.7 2 Macc 7.21, 27-29; 4 Macc 16.15; Acts 21.40; 4 Macc 16.16-23
12.11 Mt 5.45; Rom 13.1; Jas 1.17
12.12 Ps 96.13; 98.9; 4 Macc 9.9; Mt 25.46; Mk 9.48
12.13 2 Macc 7.4; 4 Macc 10.17; Wis 7.1-6; Acts 14.15
12.14 4 Macc 11.20
12.16 4 Macc 9.23
12.17 Ex 3.13, 15-16; Tob 8.5; Acts 24.14
12.18 Nah 1.2; 4 Macc 9.24; Rom 12.19; 2 Thess 1.8
12.19 4 Macc 17.1

t Other ancient authorities add *by fire*
u Gk *throughout the whole age*
v Other ancient authorities read *the witness*
w Other ancient authorities read *my race*
x Gk *and so gave up*; other ancient authorities read *gave up his spirit* or *his soul*

Reason's Sovereignty in the Seven

13 Since, then, the seven
brothers despised suffer-
ings even unto death, everyone
must concede that devout reason
is sovereign over the emotions.
2 For if they had been slaves to
their emotions and had eaten defiling food, we would say that they
had been conquered by these emotions. 3 But in fact it was not so. Instead, by reason, which is praised
before God, they prevailed over
their emotions. 4 The supremacy of
the mind over these cannot be
overlooked, for the brothers[y] mastered both emotions and pains.
5 How then can one fail to confess
the sovereignty of right reason over
emotion in those who were not
turned back by fiery agonies? 6 For
just as towers jutting out over harbors hold back the threatening
waves and make it calm for those
who sail into the inner basin, 7 so
the seven-towered right reason of
the youths, by fortifying the harbor
of religion, conquered the tempest
of the emotions. 8 For they consti-
tuted a holy chorus of religion and
encouraged one another, saying,
9 "Brothers, let us die like brothers
for the sake of the law; let us imitate the three youths in Assyria
who despised the same ordeal of
the furnace. 10 Let us not be cowardly in the demonstration of our
piety." 11 While one said, "Courage,
brother," another said, "Bear up
nobly," 12 and another reminded
them, "Remember whence you
came, and the father by whose
hand Isaac would have submitted
to being slain for the sake of religion." 13 Each of them and all of
them together looking at one another, cheerful and undaunted,
said, "Let us with all our hearts
consecrate ourselves to God, who
gave us our lives,[z] and let us use
our bodies as a bulwark for the law.
14 Let us not fear him who thinks
he is killing us, 15 for great is the
struggle of the soul and the danger
of eternal torment lying before
those who transgress the commandment of God. 16 Therefore let
us put on the full armor of self-
control, which is divine reason.
17 For if we so die,[a] Abraham and
Isaac and Jacob will welcome us,
and all the fathers will praise us."
18 Those who were left behind said
to each of the brothers who were
being dragged away, "Do not put
us to shame, brother, or betray the
brothers who have died before us."
19 You are not ignorant of the
affection of family ties, which the
divine and all-wise Providence has
bequeathed through the fathers to
their descendants and which was
implanted in the mother's womb.
20 There each of the brothers spent
the same length of time and was
shaped during the same period of
time; and growing from the same
blood and through the same life,
they were brought to the light of
day. 21 When they were born after
an equal time of gestation, they
drank milk from the same fountains. From such embraces
brotherly-loving souls are nourished; 22 and they grow stronger
from this common nurture and
daily companionship, and from
both general education and our
discipline in the law of God.
23 Therefore, when sympathy
and brotherly affection had been
so established, the brothers were
the more sympathetic to one another. 24 Since they had been educated by the same law and trained
in the same virtues and brought up
in right living, they loved one another all the more. 25 A common
zeal for nobility strengthened their
goodwill toward one another, and
their concord, 26 because they
could make their brotherly love
more fervent with the aid of their
religion. 27 But although nature
and companionship and virtuous
habits had augmented the affection of family ties, those who were
left endured for the sake of religion, while watching their brothers
being maltreated and tortured to
death.

[y] Gk *they* [z] Or *souls*
[a] Other ancient authorities read *suffer*

13.1 4 Macc 1.1, 13; 2.24; 6.31-35
13.4 Eccl 1.17,22; 4 Macc 2.16, 18,22
13.6 4 Macc 7.1-3; 15.31-32
13.8 4 Macc 8.4; 14.7; 18.23
13.9 Dan 3.8-30; Song of Thr 1-22
13.12 Isa 51.1-2; Gen 22.1-19; Wis 10.5; 4 Macc 14.20; Heb 11.17-19
13.13 4 Macc 8.4,27
13.14 Mt 10.28; Lk 12.4
13.15 Lk 16.23; Rev 14.10-11
13.16 Eph 6.11,13
13.17 Mt 8.11; Lk 16.22; 4 Macc 5.37
13.18 Heb 11.35-40
13.19 4 Macc 9.24; 17.22
13.20 Ps 139.13-16
13.21 2 Esd 8.10; 4 Macc 7.27
13.22 Deut 6.7-9; Ps 78.1-7; Sir 1.27; Eph 6.4
13.24 Ezra 7.6,10; 4 Macc 1.17; Acts 22.3; 4 Macc 9.8, 18; 10.10; 17.12
13.25 4 Macc 1.10; 8.3-4; 9.13, 24,27; 8.4,29; 13.13

14 Furthermore, they encouraged them to face the torture, so that they not only despised
their agonies, but also mastered
the emotions of brotherly love.
2 O reason,[b] more royal than
kings and freer than the free!
3 O sacred and harmonious concord of the seven brothers on behalf of religion! 4 None of the seven
youths proved coward or shrank
from death, 5 but all of them, as
though running the course toward
immortality, hastened to death by
torture. 6 Just as the hands and feet
are moved in harmony with the
guidance of the mind, so those
holy youths, as though moved by
an immortal spirit of devotion,
agreed to go to death for its sake.
7 O most holy seven, brothers in
harmony! For just as the seven
days of creation move in choral
dance around religion, 8 so these
youths, forming a chorus, encircled the sevenfold fear of tortures
and dissolved it. 9 Even now, we
ourselves shudder as we hear of
the suffering of these young men;
they not only saw what was happening, not only heard the direct
word of threat, but also bore the
sufferings patiently, and in agonies
of fire at that. 10 What could be
more excruciatingly painful than
this? For the power of fire is intense and swift, and it consumed
their bodies quickly.

An Encomium on the Mother of the Seven

11 Do not consider it amazing
that reason had full command over
these men in their tortures, since
the mind of woman despised even
more diverse agonies, 12 for the
mother of the seven young men
bore up under the rackings of each
one of her children.
13 Observe how complex is a
mother's love for her children,
which draws everything toward an
emotion felt in her inmost parts.
14 Even unreasoning animals, as
well as human beings, have a sympathy and parental love for their
offspring. 15 For example, among
birds, the ones that are tame protect their young by building on the
housetops, 16 and the others, by
building in precipitous chasms and
in holes and tops of trees, hatch
the nestlings and ward off the intruder. 17 If they are not able to
keep the intruder[c] away, they do
what they can to help their young
by flying in circles around them in
the anguish of love, warning them
with their own calls. 18 And why is
it necessary to demonstrate sympathy for children by the example
of unreasoning animals, 19 since
even bees at the time for making
honeycombs defend themselves
against intruders and, as though
with an iron dart, sting those who
approach their hive and defend it
even to the death? 20 But sympathy
for her children did not sway the
mother of the young men; she was
of the same mind as Abraham.

15 O reason of the children,
tyrant over the emotions!
O religion, more desirable to the
mother than her children! 2 Two
courses were open to this mother,
that of religion, and that of preserving her seven sons for a time,
as the tyrant had promised. 3 She
loved religion more, the religion
that preserves them for eternal life
according to God's promise.[d] 4 In
what manner might I express the
emotions of parents who love their
children? We impress upon the
character of a small child a wondrous likeness both of mind and of
form. Especially is this true of
mothers, who because of their
birth pangs have a deeper sympathy toward their offspring than do
the fathers. 5 Considering that
mothers are the weaker sex and
give birth to many, they are more
devoted to their children.[e] 6 The
mother of the seven boys, more
than any other mother, loved her
children. In seven pregnancies she
had implanted in herself tender
love toward them, 7 and because of
the many pains she suffered with
each of them she had sympathy for

14.2 4 Macc 1.1, 13; 13.1 **14.4** Rev 12.11 **14.5** 1 Cor 9.24-6; Heb 12.1 **14.7** Gen 1.3-2.3 **14.8** 4 Macc 8.4; 13.8; 18.23 **14.9** 4 Macc 11.12 **14.12** 2 Macc 7.41; 4 Macc 8.3; 12.6-7 **14.13** Isa 49.15; 66.13; Sir 4.10; 4 Macc 15.4 **14.15** Mt 6.26 **14.19** Sir 11.3 **14.20** Gen 22.1-19; Wis 10.5; 4 Macc 13.12; Heb 11.17-19 **15.2** Deut 30.15; Jer 21.8 **15.3** Heb 11.26; 13.13; 4 Macc 10.15; Mt 25.46; Gal 6.8 **15.4** 4 Macc 14.13 **15.5** 1 Pet 3.7 **15.6** 2 Macc 7.27; 4 Macc 13.20

[b] Or *O minds* [c] Gk *it* [d] Gk *according to God* [e] Or *For to the degree that mothers are weaker and the more children they bear, the more they are devoted to their children.*

them; 8 yet because of the fear of
God she disdained the temporary
safety of her children. 9 Not only
so, but also because of the nobility
of her sons and their ready obedience to the law, she felt a greater
tenderness toward them. 10 For
they were righteous and self-
controlled and brave and magnani-
mous, and loved their brothers and
their mother, so that they obeyed
her even to death in keeping the
ordinances.

11 Nevertheless, though so
many factors influenced the
mother to suffer with them out of
love for her children, in the case of
none of them were the various tortures strong enough to pervert her
reason. 12 But each child separately
and all of them together the
mother urged on to death for religion's sake. 13 O sacred nature and
affection of parental love, yearning
of parents toward offspring, nurture and indomitable suffering by
mothers! 14 This mother, who saw
them tortured and burned one by
one, because of religion did not
change her attitude. 15 She
watched the flesh of her children
being consumed by fire, their toes
and fingers scattered[f] on the
ground, and the flesh of the head
to the chin exposed like masks.

16 O mother, tried now by more
bitter pains than even the birth
pangs you suffered for them!
17 O woman, who alone gave birth
to such complete devotion!
18 When the firstborn breathed his
last, it did not turn you aside, nor
when the second in torments
looked at you piteously nor when
the third expired; 19 nor did you
weep when you looked at the eyes
of each one in his tortures gazing
boldly at the same agonies, and
saw in their nostrils the signs of
the approach of death. 20 When you
saw the flesh of children burned
upon the flesh of other children,
severed hands upon hands,
scalped heads upon heads, and
corpses fallen on other corpses,
and when you saw the place filled
with many spectators of the tortur-
ings, you did not shed tears. 21 Neither the melodies of sirens nor the
songs of swans attract the attention of their hearers as did the
voices of the children in torture
calling to their mother. 22 How
great and how many torments the
mother then suffered as her sons
were tortured on the wheel and
with the hot irons! 23 But devout
reason, giving her heart a man's
courage in the very midst of her
emotions, strengthened her to disregard, for the time, her parental
love.

24 Although she witnessed the
destruction of seven children and
the ingenious and various rackings, this noble mother disregarded all these[g] because of faith
in God. 25 For as in the council
chamber of her own soul she saw
mighty advocates—nature, family,
parental love, and the rackings of
her children— 26 this mother held
two ballots, one bearing death and
the other deliverance for her children. 27 She did not approve the deliverance that would preserve the
seven sons for a short time, 28 but
as the daughter of God-fearing
Abraham she remembered his for-
titude.

29 O mother of the nation, vindicator of the law and champion of
religion, who carried away the
prize of the contest in your heart!
30 O more noble than males in
steadfastness, and more courageous than men in endurance!
31 Just as Noah's ark, carrying the
world in the universal flood,
stoutly endured the waves, 32 so
you, O guardian of the law, overwhelmed from every side by the
flood of your emotions and the violent winds, the torture of your
sons, endured nobly and withstood
the wintry storms that assail religion.

16 If, then, a woman, ad-
vanced in years and mother
of seven sons, endured seeing her
children tortured to death, it must
be admitted that devout reason is
sovereign over the emotions.

[f] Or *quivering* [g] Other ancient authorities read *having bidden them farewell, surrendered them*

15.8 Heb 11.25
15.9 4 Macc 13.25
15.10 4 Macc 1.30-31; 5.23, 34; 13.16; Phil 2.9
15.12 2 Macc 7.27-29; 4 Macc 12.7; 16.16-22
15.15 4 Macc 9.20, 28; 10.8; 11.18-19
15.17 4 Macc 16.13; 17.6
15.18 4 Macc 9.25, 27-28; 10.12
15.22 4 Macc 5.3, 32; 8.13; 9.12; 10.8; 11.17
15.23 4 Macc 17.2; 14.13-20
15.24 4 Macc 7.14; 8.11,13,24; 9.22; 14.12
15.26 Deut 30.15; Sir 37.16-18; 2 Esd 7.127-131; 4 Macc 15.2
15.28 4 Macc 13.12; 17.6
15.29 4 Macc 9.8; 17.12
15.31 Gen 6.14-7.24; Wis 14.6; 1 Pet 3.20; 4 Macc 7.1-3; 13.6-7
16.1 4 Macc 1.1; 2.24; 13.1

2 Thus I have demonstrated not
only that men have ruled over the
emotions, but also that a woman
has despised the fiercest tortures.
3 The lions surrounding Daniel
were not so savage, nor was the
raging fiery furnace of Mishael so
intensely hot, as was her innate parental love, inflamed as she saw
her seven sons tortured in such
varied ways. 4 But the mother
quenched so many and such great
emotions by devout reason.
5 Consider this also: If this
woman, though a mother, had
been fainthearted, she would have
mourned over them and perhaps
spoken as follows: 6 "O how
wretched am I and many times unhappy! After bearing seven children, I am now the mother of none!
7 O seven childbirths all in vain,
seven profitless pregnancies, fruitless nurturings and wretched nurs-
ings! 8 In vain, my sons, I endured
many birth pangs for you, and the
more grievous anxieties of your upbringing. 9 Alas for my children,
some unmarried, others married
and without offspring.[h] I shall not
see your children or have the happiness of being called grandmother. 10 Alas, I who had so many
and beautiful children am a widow
and alone, with many sorrows.[i]
11 And when I die, I shall have none
of my sons to bury me."
12 Yet that holy and God-
fearing mother did not wail with
such a lament for any of them, nor
did she dissuade any of them from
dying, nor did she grieve as they
were dying. 13 On the contrary, as
though having a mind like adamant and giving rebirth for immortality to the whole number of her
sons, she implored them and urged
them on to death for the sake of
religion. 14 O mother, soldier of
God in the cause of religion, elder
and woman! By steadfastness you
have conquered even a tyrant, and
in word and deed you have proved
more powerful than a man. 15 For
when you and your sons were arrested together, you stood and
watched Eleazar being tortured,
and said to your sons in the Hebrew language, 16 "My sons, noble
is the contest to which you are
called to bear witness for the nation. Fight zealously for our ancestral law. 17 For it would be shameful if, while an aged man endures
such agonies for the sake of religion, you young men were to be
terrified by tortures. 18 Remember
that it is through God that you
have had a share in the world and
have enjoyed life, 19 and therefore
you ought to endure any suffering
for the sake of God. 20 For his sake
also our father Abraham was zealous to sacrifice his son Isaac, the
ancestor of our nation; and when
Isaac saw his father's hand wielding a knife[j] and descending upon
him, he did not cower. 21 Daniel
the righteous was thrown to the lions, and Hananiah, Azariah, and
Mishael were hurled into the fiery
furnace and endured it for the sake
of God. 22 You too must have the
same faith in God and not be
grieved. 23 It is unreasonable for
people who have religious knowledge not to withstand pain."
24 By these words the mother of
the seven encouraged and persuaded each of her sons to die
rather than violate God's commandment. 25 They knew also that
those who die for the sake of God
live to God, as do Abraham and
Isaac and Jacob and all the patriarchs.

17 Some of the guards said
that when she also was
about to be seized and put to death
she threw herself into the flames
so that no one might touch her
body.
2 O mother, who with your
seven sons nullified the violence of
the tyrant, frustrated his evil designs, and showed the courage of
your faith! 3 Nobly set like a roof on
the pillars of your sons, you held
firm and unswerving against the
earthquake of the tortures. 4 Take
courage, therefore, O holy-minded
mother, maintaining firm an enduring hope in God. 5 The moon in
heaven, with the stars, does not

16.3 Dan 6.16-23; 3.19-26; 4 Macc 13.9; 16.21; 14.13-20; 15.4,11
16.7 4 Macc 15.6
16.9 Prov 17.6
16.11 1 Sam 31.8-13; Tob 1.18; 1 Macc 7.17; Wis 18.12
16.12 1 Thess 4.13
16.13 4 Macc 15.17; Jn 3.5; Gal 4.19
16.14 4 Macc 1.11; 9.8,30; 15.30
16.15 2 Macc 6.18-31; 4 Macc 5.4-6.30; 2 Macc 7.21, 27; 4 Macc 12.7
16.16 4 Macc 6.10; 11.20; 17.11; Heb 12.1
16.19 2 Macc 7.29
16.20 Gen 22.1-9; 4 Macc 13.12; 14.20
16.21 Dan 6.1-23; 4 Macc 16.3; 18.13; Dan 3.8-30; 4 Macc 13.9; 16.3; 18.12
16.22 Rev 12.11
16.25 4 Macc 7.19; Mt 22.32; Mk 12.26-27; Lk 20.37
17.1 2 Macc 7.41; 4 Macc 12.19
17.2 4 Macc 1.11; 16.14; 15.23
17.4 Josh 1.7,9; 1 Thess 1.3; Heb 6.11; 1 Pet 1.3

[h] Gk *without benefit* [i] Or *much to be pitied*
[j] Gk *sword*

stand so august as you, who, after
lighting the way of your star-like
seven sons to piety, stand in honor
before God and are firmly set in
heaven with them. 6 For your children were true descendants of father Abraham.[k]

The Effect of the Martyrdoms

7 If it were possible for us to
paint the history of your religion as
an artist might, would not those
who first beheld it have shuddered
as they saw the mother of the
seven children enduring their varied tortures to death for the sake of
religion? 8 Indeed it would be
proper to inscribe on their tomb
these words as a reminder to the
people of our nation:[l]
9 "Here lie buried an aged
priest and an aged woman and
seven sons, because of the violence of the tyrant who wished to
destroy the way of life of the Hebrews. 10 They vindicated their nation, looking to God and enduring
torture even to death."
11 Truly the contest in which
they were engaged was divine,
12 for on that day virtue gave the
awards and tested them for their
endurance. The prize was immortality in endless life. 13 Eleazar was
the first contestant, the mother of
the seven sons entered the compe-
tition, and the brothers contended.
14 The tyrant was the antagonist,
and the world and the human race
were the spectators. 15 Reverence
for God was victor and gave the
crown to its own athletes. 16 Who
did not admire the athletes of the
divine[m] legislation? Who were not
amazed?
17 The tyrant himself and all
his council marveled at their[n] endurance, 18 because of which they
now stand before the divine throne
and live the life of eternal blessedness. 19 For Moses says, "All who
are consecrated are under your
hands." 20 These, then, who have
been consecrated for the sake of
God,[o] are honored, not only with
this honor, but also by the fact that
because of them our enemies did
not rule over our nation, 21 the tyrant was punished, and the homeland purified—they having become, as it were, a ransom for the
sin of our nation. 22 And through
the blood of those devout ones and
their death as an atoning sacrifice,
divine Providence preserved Israel
that previously had been mistreated.
23 For the tyrant Antiochus,
when he saw the courage of their
virtue and their endurance under
the tortures, proclaimed them to
his soldiers as an example for their
own endurance, 24 and this made
them brave and courageous for infantry battle and siege, and he ravaged and conquered all his enemies.

18 O Israelite children, offspring of the seed of Abraham, obey this law and exercise piety in every way, 2 knowing that
devout reason is master of all emotions, not only of sufferings from
within, but also of those from without.
3 Therefore those who gave over
their bodies in suffering for the
sake of religion were not only admired by mortals, but also were
deemed worthy to share in a divine
inheritance. 4 Because of them the
nation gained peace, and by reviving observance of the law in the
homeland they ravaged the enemy.
5 The tyrant Antiochus was both
punished on earth and is being
chastised after his death. Since in
no way whatever was he able to
compel the Israelites to become
pagans and to abandon their ancestral customs, he left Jerusalem
and marched against the Persians.

The Mother's Address to Her Children

6 The mother of seven sons expressed also these principles to her

17.6 4 Macc 13.12; 15.28; Rom 4.9-12; Gal 3.29
17.9 4 Macc 5.4; 8.3,8
17.10 4 Macc 9.1-8; Heb 11.35-37
17.11 4 Macc 6.10; 11.20; 16.16
17.12 4 Macc 9.18; 10.10; 9.8,30; 11.12; 15.29; 1 Cor 9.24-27; Rev 2.7
17.14 4 Macc 5.1; 18.5
17.15 Josh 24.14; Tob 4.5; 4 Macc 11.5; Heb 12.28; 2 Tim 4.8; Jas 1.12; 1 Pet 5.4
17.17 4 Macc 1.11; 17.12
17.19 Num 3.13; 8.17
17.20 Jn 12.26
17.21 1 Macc 6.8-16; 2 Macc 9.28; 4 Macc 1.11; 6.28-29; Mk 10.45; Jn 11.49-52; 1 Tim 2.6
17.22 Rom 3.25; Heb 9.11-15; 1 Pet 1.19; 1 Jn 2.2; 4 Macc 9.24; 13.19
17.23 4 Macc 1.11; 5.1; 8.2-4
18.1 4 Macc 6.17; 17.6
18.2 4 Macc 1.1,13
18.3 2 Esd 7.17.96; Acts 20.32; Col 1.12
18.5 4 Macc 5.1; 18.22-23; 1 Macc 3.37; 6.1; 2 Macc 9.1

18.6 2 Macc 7.22-29

[k] Gk *For your childbearing was from Abraham the father*; other ancient authorities read *For . . . Abraham the servant* [l] Or *as a memorial to the heroes of our people*
[m] Other ancient authorities read *true*
[n] Other ancient authorities add *virtue and*
[o] Other ancient authorities lack *for the sake of God*

children: [7] "I was a pure virgin and
did not go outside my father's
house; but I guarded the rib from
which woman was made.[p] [8] No se-
ducer corrupted me on a desert
plain, nor did the destroyer, the deceitful serpent, defile the purity of
my virginity. [9] In the time of my
maturity I remained with my husband, and when these sons had
grown up their father died. A happy
man was he, who lived out his life
with good children, and did not
have the grief of bereavement.
[10] While he was still with you, he
taught you the law and the prophets. [11] He read to you about Abel
slain by Cain, and Isaac who was
offered as a burnt offering, and
about Joseph in prison. [12] He told
you of the zeal of Phinehas, and he
taught you about Hananiah, Azariah, and Mishael in the fire. [13] He
praised Daniel in the den of the lions and blessed him. [14] He reminded you of the scripture of Isaiah, which says, 'Even though you
go through the fire, the flame shall
not consume you.' [15] He sang to
you songs of the psalmist David,
who said, 'Many are the afflictions
of the righteous.' [16] He recounted
to you Solomon's proverb, 'There
is a tree of life for those who do his
will.' [17] He confirmed the query of
Ezekiel, 'Shall these dry bones
live?' [18] For he did not forget to
teach you the song that Moses
taught, which says, [19] 'I kill and I
make alive: this is your life and the
length of your days.' "

20 O bitter was that day—and
yet not bitter—when that bitter tyrant of the Greeks quenched fire
with fire in his cruel caldrons, and
in his burning rage brought those
seven sons of the daughter of Abraham to the catapult and back again
to more[q] tortures, [21] pierced the
pupils of their eyes and cut out
their tongues, and put them to
death with various tortures. [22] For
these crimes divine justice pursued and will pursue the accursed
tyrant. [23] But the sons of Abraham
with their victorious mother are
gathered together into the chorus
of the fathers, and have received
pure and immortal[r] souls from
God, [24] to whom be glory forever
and ever. Amen.

18.7 Sir 42.9-12; 2 Macc 3.19; 3 Macc 1.19; Gen 2.22
18.8 Deut 22.25-27
18.10 Deut 6.7-9; Ps 78.5-7
18.11 Gen 4.2-15; 22.1-19; 4 Macc 13.12; 14.20; Heb 11.17-19; Gen 39.1-23
18.12 Num 25.1-9; Dan 3.8-27; 4 Macc 13.9; 16.3,21
18.13 Dan 6.1-23; 4 Macc 16.3, 21
18.14 Isa 43.2
18.15 Ps 34.19
18.16 Prov 3.18
18.17 Ezek 37.2-3
18.18 Deut 32.39; 30.20
18.20 2 Macc 7.3; 4 Macc 8.2; 8.13
18.21 2 Macc 7.4,10; 4 Macc 10.17,19
18.23 4 Macc 13.12; 17.6; 8.4; 13.8; 14.7-8
18.24 Rom 16.27; Gal 1.5; 1 Tim 4.18; 1 Pet 5.11

[p] Gk *the rib that was built*
[q] Other ancient authorities read *to all his*
[r] Other ancient authorities read *victorious*

THE NEW COVENANT
commonly called

The New Testament

OF OUR LORD AND SAVIOR JESUS CHRIST

NEW
REVISED
STANDARD
VERSION

THE GOSPEL ACCORDING TO

Matthew

Title and Background

The Gospel of Matthew was so named to distinguish it from the other Gospel accounts. There is only one gospel message, but four accounts of it. So we have here Matthew's version of the "good news" from God. Matthew's name means "gift of the LORD."

Author and Date of Writing

All four of the canonical Gospels are anonymous, but the early church fathers were unanimous in holding that Matthew was the author of this Gospel. Also known as Levi, he was a tax collector. The Gospel was most likely written shortly after the destruction of Jerusalem in A.D. 70.

Theme and Message

Matthew's main purpose is to demonstrate to his Jewish readers that Jesus is their Messiah. He quotes the Old Testament often and uses the phrase "kingdom of heaven" frequently. The whole Gospel is woven around five great discourses: (1) chapters 5-7; (2) chapter 10; (3) chapter 13; (4) chapter 18; (5) chapters 24-25.

Outline

I. The Birth and Early Years of Jesus (1.1–2.23)
II. The Beginnings of Jesus' Ministry (3.1–4.11)
III. Jesus' Ministry in Galilee (4.12–14.12)
IV. Jesus' Withdrawals From Galilee (14.13–17.20)
V. Jesus' Last Ministry in Galilee (17.22–18.35)
VI. Jesus' Ministry in Judea and Perea (19.1–20.34)
VII. Passion Week (21:1–27.66)
VIII. The Resurrection (28.1-20)

The Genealogy of Jesus the Messiah

1 An account of the genealogy[a]
of Jesus the Messiah,[b] the son
of David, the son of Abraham.
2 Abraham was the father of
Isaac, and Isaac the father of Jacob, and Jacob the father of Judah
and his brothers, 3 and Judah the
father of Perez and Zerah by Tamar,
and Perez the father of Hezron,
and Hezron the father of Aram, 4 and
Aram the father of Aminadab, and
Aminadab the father of Nahshon,
and Nahshon the father of Salmon,
5 and Salmon the father of Boaz by
Rahab, and Boaz the father of Obed
by Ruth, and Obed the father of
Jesse, 6 and Jesse the father of King
David.
And David was the father of Solomon by the wife of Uriah, 7 and
Solomon the father of Rehoboam,
and Rehoboam the father of Abijah, and Abijah the father of
Asaph,[c] 8 and Asaph[c] the father of
Jehoshaphat, and Jehoshaphat the
father of Joram, and Joram the father of Uzziah, 9 and Uzziah the father of Jotham, and Jotham the father of Ahaz, and Ahaz the father of
Hezekiah, 10 and Hezekiah the father of Manasseh, and Manasseh
the father of Amos,[d] and Amos[d]
the father of Josiah, 11 and Josiah

1.1 Ps 132.11; Isa 11.1; Lk 1.32; Jn 7.42; Acts 2.30; 13.23; Rom 1.3; Gen 12.3; 22.18; Gal 3.16 **1.2** Gen 21.2,3; 25.26; 29.35 **1.3** Gen 38.27ff; Ruth 4.18ff; 1 Chr 2.5, 9ff **1.6** 1 Sam 16.1; 17.1; 2 Sam 12.24 **1.7** 1 Chr 3.10 **1.10** 2 Kings 20.21; 1 Chr 3.13 **1.11** 2 Kings 24.14-16; Jer 27.20; 39.9; Dan 1.2

[a] Or *birth* [b] Or *Jesus Christ* [c] Other ancient authorities read *Asa* [d] Other ancient authorities read *Amon*

the father of Jechoniah and his brothers, at the time of the deportation to Babylon.

12 And after the deportation to Babylon: Jechoniah was the father of Salathiel, and Salathiel the father of Zerubbabel, 13 and Zerubbabel the father of Abiud, and Abiud the father of Eliakim, and Eliakim the father of Azor, 14 and Azor the father of Zadok, and Zadok the father of Achim, and Achim the father of Eliud, 15 and Eliud the father of Eleazar, and Eleazar the father of Matthan, and Matthan the father of Jacob, 16 and Jacob the father of Joseph the husband of Mary, of whom Jesus was born, who is called the Messiah.[e]

17 So all the generations from Abraham to David are fourteen generations; and from David to the deportation to Babylon, fourteen generations; and from the deportation to Babylon to the Messiah,[e] fourteen generations.

The Birth of Jesus the Messiah

18 Now the birth of Jesus the Messiah[f] took place in this way. When his mother Mary had been engaged to Joseph, but before they lived together, she was found to be with child from the Holy Spirit. 19 Her husband Joseph, being a righteous man and unwilling to expose her to public disgrace, planned to dismiss her quietly. 20 But just when he had resolved to do this, an angel of the Lord appeared to him in a dream and said, "Joseph, son of David, do not be afraid to take Mary as your wife, for the child conceived in her is from the Holy Spirit. 21 She will bear a son, and you are to name him Jesus, for he will save his people from their sins." 22 All this took place to fulfill what had been spoken by the Lord through the prophet:

23 "Look, the virgin shall
conceive and bear a
son,
and they shall name him
Emmanuel,"

which means, "God is with us." 24 When Joseph awoke from sleep, he did as the angel of the Lord commanded him; he took her as his wife, 25 but had no marital relations with her until she had borne a son;[g] and he named him Jesus.

1.12 1 Chr 3.17, 19
1.16 Lk 1.27
1.17 vv. 11,12
1.18-25pp Lk 1.26-35; 2.1-7
1.19 Deut 24.1
1.21 Lk 2.21; 2.11; Jn 1.29; Acts 4.12; 13.23,38
1.23 Isa 7.14
1.25 Ex 13.2; Lk 2.21
2.1 Lk 2.4-7; 1.5
2.2 Jer 23.5; Zech 9.9; Mk 15.2; Jn 1.49
2.5 Jn 7.42
2.6 Mic 5.2; Jn 21.16
2.11 Mt 1.18; 12.46; Ps 72.10; Isa 60.2

The Visit of the Wise Men

2 In the time of King Herod, after Jesus was born in Bethlehem of Judea, wise men[h] from the East came to Jerusalem, 2 asking, "Where is the child who has been born king of the Jews? For we observed his star at its rising,[i] and have come to pay him homage." 3 When King Herod heard this, he was frightened, and all Jerusalem with him; 4 and calling together all the chief priests and scribes of the people, he inquired of them where the Messiah[e] was to be born. 5 They told him, "In Bethlehem of Judea; for so it has been written by the prophet:

6 'And you, Bethlehem, in the
land of Judah,
are by no means least
among the rulers of
Judah;
for from you shall come a
ruler
who is to shepherd[j] my
people Israel.' "

7 Then Herod secretly called for the wise men[h] and learned from them the exact time when the star had appeared. 8 Then he sent them to Bethlehem, saying, "Go and search diligently for the child; and when you have found him, bring me word so that I may also go and pay him homage." 9 When they had heard the king, they set out; and there, ahead of them, went the star that they had seen at its rising,[i] until it stopped over the place where the child was. 10 When they saw that the star had stopped,[k] they were overwhelmed with joy. 11 On entering the house, they saw the child with Mary his mother;

[e] Or *the Christ* [f] Or *Jesus Christ* [g] Other ancient authorities read *her firstborn son* [h] Or *astrologers*; Gk *magi* [i] Or *in the East* [j] Or *rule* [k] Gk *saw the star*

and they knelt down and paid him homage. Then, opening their treasure chests, they offered him gifts of gold, frankincense, and myrrh. 12 And having been warned in a dream not to return to Herod, they left for their own country by another road.

The Escape to Egypt

13 Now after they had left, an angel of the Lord appeared to Joseph in a dream and said, "Get up, take the child and his mother, and flee to Egypt, and remain there until I tell you; for Herod is about to search for the child, to destroy him." 14 Then Joseph[l] got up, took the child and his mother by night, and went to Egypt, 15 and remained there until the death of Herod. This was to fulfill what had been spoken by the Lord through the prophet, "Out of Egypt I have called my son."

The Massacre of the Infants

16 When Herod saw that he had been tricked by the wise men,[m] he was infuriated, and he sent and killed all the children in and around Bethlehem who were two years old or under, according to the time that he had learned from the wise men.[m] 17 Then was fulfilled what had been spoken through the prophet Jeremiah:

18 "A voice was heard in
Ramah,
wailing and loud
lamentation,
Rachel weeping for her
children;
she refused to be consoled,
because they are no
more."

The Return from Egypt

19 When Herod died, an angel of the Lord suddenly appeared in a dream to Joseph in Egypt and said, 20 "Get up, take the child and his mother, and go to the land of Israel, for those who were seeking the child's life are dead." 21 Then Joseph[l] got up, took the child and his mother, and went to the land of Israel. 22 But when he heard that Archelaus was ruling over Judea in place of his father Herod, he was afraid to go there. And after being warned in a dream, he went away to the district of Galilee. 23 There he made his home in a town called Nazareth, so that what had been spoken through the prophets might be fulfilled, "He will be called a Nazorean."

The Proclamation of John the Baptist

3 In those days John the Baptist appeared in the wilderness of Judea, proclaiming, 2 "Repent, for the kingdom of heaven has come near."[n] 3 This is the one of whom the prophet Isaiah spoke when he said,

"The voice of one crying out
in the wilderness:
'Prepare the way of the Lord,
make his paths straight.' "

4 Now John wore clothing of camel's hair with a leather belt around his waist, and his food was locusts and wild honey. 5 Then the people of Jerusalem and all Judea were going out to him, and all the region along the Jordan, 6 and they were baptized by him in the river Jordan, confessing their sins.

7 But when he saw many Pharisees and Sadducees coming for baptism, he said to them, "You brood of vipers! Who warned you to flee from the wrath to come? 8 Bear fruit worthy of repentance. 9 Do not presume to say to yourselves, 'We have Abraham as our ancestor'; for I tell you, God is able from these stones to raise up children to Abraham. 10 Even now the ax is lying at the root of the trees; every tree therefore that does not bear good fruit is cut down and thrown into the fire.

11 "I baptize you with[o] water for repentance, but one who is more powerful than I is coming after me; I am not worthy to carry his sandals. He will baptize you with[o] the Holy Spirit and fire. 12 His win-

2.12 Mt 2.22; Acts 10.22; Heb 11.7
2.13 v. 19
2.14 Hos 11.1; Ex 4.22
2.18 Jer 31.15
2.19-23pp Lk 1.26
2.19 Mt 1.20; v. 13
2.22 v. 12; Mt 3.13; Lk 2.39
2.23 Lk 1.26; Isa 11.1; Mk 1.24
3.1-12pp Mk 1.1-8; Lk 3.2-17; Jn 1.6-8; 19-28
3.2 Dan 2.44; Mt 4.7; 10.7
3.3 Isa 40.3; Mk 1.3; Lk 3.4; Jn 1.23; Lk 1.76
3.4 2 Kings 1.8; Zech 13.4; Lev 11.22
3.6 Acts 19.4,18
3.7 Mt 12.34; 23.33; Rom 5.9; 1 Thes 1.10
3.8 Acts 26.20
3.9 Jn 8.33,39; Acts 13.26; Rom 4.1,11, 16
3.10 Mt 7.19
3.11 Acts 1.5; 11.16; 19.4; Isa 4.4; Acts 2.3,4
3.12 Mal 3.3; Mt 13.30

l Gk *he* m Or *astrologers;* Gk *magi*
n Or *is at hand* o Or *in*

nowing fork is in his hand, and he
will clear his threshing floor and
will gather his wheat into the granary; but the chaff he will burn
with unquenchable fire."

The Baptism of Jesus

13 Then Jesus came from Galilee to John at the Jordan, to be
baptized by him. 14 John would
have prevented him, saying, "I
need to be baptized by you, and do
you come to me?" 15 But Jesus answered him, "Let it be so now; for
it is proper for us in this way to fulfill all righteousness." Then he
consented. 16 And when Jesus had
been baptized, just as he came up
from the water, suddenly the heavens were opened to him and he saw
the Spirit of God descending like a
dove and alighting on him. 17 And a
voice from heaven said, "This is my
Son, the Beloved,[p] with whom I
am well pleased."

The Temptation of Jesus

4 Then Jesus was led up by the
Spirit into the wilderness to be
tempted by the devil. 2 He fasted
forty days and forty nights, and afterwards he was famished. 3 The
tempter came and said to him, "If
you are the Son of God, command
these stones to become loaves of
bread." 4 But he answered, "It is
written,

'One does not live by bread
alone,
but by every word that
comes from the mouth
of God.' "

5 Then the devil took him to the
holy city and placed him on the
pinnacle of the temple, 6 saying to
him, "If you are the Son of God,
throw yourself down; for it is written,

'He will command his angels
concerning you,'
and 'On their hands they
will bear you up,
so that you will not dash
your foot against a
stone.' "

7 Jesus said to him, "Again it is
written, 'Do not put the Lord your
God to the test.' "

8 Again, the devil took him to a
very high mountain and showed
him all the kingdoms of the world
and their splendor; 9 and he said to
him, "All these I will give you, if
you will fall down and worship
me." 10 Jesus said to him, "Away
with you, Satan! for it is written,

'Worship the Lord your God,
and serve only him.' "

11 Then the devil left him, and suddenly angels came and waited on
him.

Jesus Begins His Ministry in Galilee

12 Now when Jesus[q] heard that
John had been arrested, he withdrew to Galilee. 13 He left Nazareth
and made his home in Capernaum
by the sea, in the territory of Zebulun and Naphtali, 14 so that what
had been spoken through the
prophet Isaiah might be fulfilled:

15 "Land of Zebulun, land of
Naphtali,
on the road by the sea,
across the Jordan,
Galilee of the
Gentiles—
16 the people who sat in
darkness
have seen a great light,
and for those who sat in the
region and shadow of
death
light has dawned."

17 From that time Jesus began to
proclaim, "Repent, for the kingdom of heaven has come near."[r]

Jesus Calls the First Disciples

18 As he walked by the Sea of
Galilee, he saw two brothers, Simon, who is called Peter, and Andrew his brother, casting a net into
the sea—for they were fishermen.
19 And he said to them, "Follow me,
and I will make you fish for people." 20 Immediately they left their
nets and followed him. 21 As he
went from there, he saw two other

3.13-17pp Mk 1.9-11; Lk 3.21,22
3.13 Jn 1.31-34
3.16 Isa 11.2; 42.1; Jn 1.32
3.17 Ps 2.7; Mt 12.18; 17.5; Mk 9.7; Lk 9.35
4.1-11pp Mk 1.12,13; Lk 4.1-13
4.2 Ex 34.28; 1 Kings 19.8
4.3 1 Thes 3.5
4.4 Deut 8.3
4.5 Neh 11.1; Dan 9.24; Mt 27.53; Rev 21.10
4.6 Ps 91.11,12
4.7 Deut 6.16
4.10 1 Chr 21.1; Deut 6.13
4.11 Mt 26.53; Lk 22.43; Heb 1.14
4.12-17pp Mk 1.14,15; Lk 4.14,15; Jn 4.43-45
4.15 Isa 9.1,2
4.16 Isa 42.7; Lk 2.32
4.17 Mt 3.2; 10.7
4.18-25pp Lk 5.1-11
4.18 Jn 1.35-42
4.20 Mt 10.28; Lk 18.28

p Or *my beloved Son* q Gk *he* r Or *is at hand*

brothers, James son of Zebedee
and his brother John, in the boat
with their father Zebedee, mending
their nets, and he called them.
22 Immediately they left the boat
and their father, and followed him.

Jesus Ministers to Crowds of People

23 Jesus[s] went throughout Galilee, teaching in their synagogues
and proclaiming the good news[t] of
the kingdom and curing every disease and every sickness among the
people. 24 So his fame spread
throughout all Syria, and they
brought to him all the sick, those
who were afflicted with various diseases and pains, demoniacs, epileptics, and paralytics, and he
cured them. 25 And great crowds
followed him from Galilee, the Decapolis, Jerusalem, Judea, and
from beyond the Jordan.

The Beatitudes

5 When Jesus[u] saw the crowds,
he went up the mountain; and
after he sat down, his disciples
came to him. 2 Then he began to
speak, and taught them, saying:
3 "Blessed are the poor in spirit,
for theirs is the kingdom of heaven.
4 "Blessed are those who
mourn, for they will be comforted.
5 "Blessed are the meek, for
they will inherit the earth.
6 "Blessed are those who hunger and thirst for righteousness, for
they will be filled.
7 "Blessed are the merciful, for
they will receive mercy.
8 "Blessed are the pure in heart,
for they will see God.
9 "Blessed are the peacemakers, for they will be called children
of God.
10 "Blessed are those who are
persecuted for righteousness' sake,
for theirs is the kingdom of heaven.
11 "Blessed are you when people revile you and persecute you
and utter all kinds of evil against
you falsely[v] on my account. 12 Rejoice and be glad, for your reward is
great in heaven, for in the same

4.23 Mk 1.39; Lk 4.15,44; Mt 9.35; 13.54; Mk 1.21; 1.34 **4.24** Lk 2.2; Mt 8.16,28, 33; Mk 1.32; Lk 8.36; Mt 17.15; 8.6; 9.2,6 **4.25** Mk 3.7,8; Lk 6.17 **5.1-7.29pp** Lk 6.20-49 **5.1-12pp** Lk 6.20-23 **5.1** Mk 3.13; Jn 6.3 **5.3** Mk 10.14; Lk 22.29 **5.4** Isa 61.2,3 **5.6** Isa 55.1,2 **5.8** Heb 12.14; 1 Jn 3.2 **5.9** Rom 8.14 **5.10** 1 Pet 3.14 **5.11** 1 Pet 4.14 **5.12** Acts 7.52; 1 Thes 2.15; Jas 5.10 **5.13** Mk 9.50; Lk 14.34,35 **5.14** Phil 2.15 **5.15** Mk 4.21; Lk 8.16 **5.16** 1 Pet 2.12 **5.17** Rom 3.31; Gal 3.24 **5.18** Lk 16.17 **5.19** Jas 2.10 **5.21f** Ex 20.13; Deut 5.17 **5.22** 1 Jn 3.15; Jas 2.20

way they persecuted the prophets
who were before you.

Salt and Light

13 "You are the salt of the earth;
but if salt has lost its taste, how can
its saltiness be restored? It is no
longer good for anything, but is
thrown out and trampled under
foot.
14 "You are the light of the
world. A city built on a hill cannot
be hid. 15 No one after lighting a
lamp puts it under the bushel basket, but on the lampstand, and it
gives light to all in the house. 16 In
the same way, let your light shine
before others, so that they may see
your good works and give glory to
your Father in heaven.

The Law and the Prophets

17 "Do not think that I have
come to abolish the law or the
prophets; I have come not to abolish but to fulfill. 18 For truly I tell
you, until heaven and earth pass
away, not one letter,[w] not one
stroke of a letter, will pass from the
law until all is accomplished.
19 Therefore, whoever breaks[x] one
of the least of these commandments, and teaches others to do
the same, will be called least in the
kingdom of heaven; but whoever
does them and teaches them will
be called great in the kingdom of
heaven. 20 For I tell you, unless
your righteousness exceeds that of
the scribes and Pharisees, you will
never enter the kingdom of heaven.

Concerning Anger

21 "You have heard that it was
said to those of ancient times, 'You
shall not murder'; and 'whoever
murders shall be liable to judgment.' 22 But I say to you that if you
are angry with a brother or sister,[y]
you will be liable to judgment; and
if you insult[z] a brother or sister,[a]
you will be liable to the council;
and if you say, 'You fool,' you will

[s] Gk *He* [t] Gk *gospel* [u] Gk *he* [v] Other ancient authorities lack *falsely* [w] Gk *one iota* [x] Or *annuls* [y] Gk *a brother*; other ancient authorities add *without cause* [z] Gk *say Raca to* (an obscure term of abuse) [a] Gk *a brother*

be liable to the hell[b] of fire. 23So
when you are offering your gift at
the altar, if you remember that
your brother or sister[c] has something against you, 24leave your gift
there before the altar and go; first
be reconciled to your brother or sister,[c] and then come and offer your
gift. 25Come to terms quickly with
your accuser while you are on the
way to court[d] with him, or your accuser may hand you over to the
judge, and the judge to the guard,
and you will be thrown into prison.
26Truly I tell you, you will never get
out until you have paid the last
penny.

Concerning Adultery

27 "You have heard that it was
said, 'You shall not commit adultery.' 28But I say to you that everyone who looks at a woman with lust
has already committed adultery
with her in his heart. 29If your right
eye causes you to sin, tear it out
and throw it away; it is better for
you to lose one of your members
than for your whole body to be
thrown into hell.[b] 30And if your
right hand causes you to sin, cut it
off and throw it away; it is better for
you to lose one of your members
than for your whole body to go into
hell.[b]

Concerning Divorce

31 "It was also said, 'Whoever
divorces his wife, let him give her a
certificate of divorce.' 32But I say to
you that anyone who divorces his
wife, except on the ground of unchastity, causes her to commit
adultery; and whoever marries a divorced woman commits adultery.

Concerning Oaths

33 "Again, you have heard that
it was said to those of ancient
times, 'You shall not swear falsely,
but carry out the vows you have
made to the Lord.' 34But I say to
you, Do not swear at all, either by
heaven, for it is the throne of God,
35or by the earth, for it is his footstool, or by Jerusalem, for it is the
city of the great King. 36And do not
swear by your head, for you cannot
make one hair white or black. 37Let
your word be 'Yes, Yes' or 'No, No';
anything more than this comes
from the evil one.[e]

Concerning Retaliation

38 "You have heard that it was
said, 'An eye for an eye and a tooth
for a tooth.' 39But I say to you, Do
not resist an evildoer. But if anyone
strikes you on the right cheek, turn
the other also; 40and if anyone
wants to sue you and take your
coat, give your cloak as well; 41and
if anyone forces you to go one mile,
go also the second mile. 42Give to
everyone who begs from you, and
do not refuse anyone who wants to
borrow from you.

Love for Enemies

43 "You have heard that it was
said, 'You shall love your neighbor
and hate your enemy.' 44But I say
to you, Love your enemies and pray
for those who persecute you, 45so
that you may be children of your
Father in heaven; for he makes his
sun rise on the evil and on the
good, and sends rain on the righteous and on the unrighteous.
46For if you love those who love
you, what reward do you have? Do
not even the tax collectors do the
same? 47And if you greet only your
brothers and sisters,[f] what more
are you doing than others? Do not
even the Gentiles do the same?
48Be perfect, therefore, as your
heavenly Father is perfect.

Concerning Almsgiving

6 "Beware of practicing your piety before others in order to be
seen by them; for then you have no
reward from your Father in heaven.
2 "So whenever you give alms,
do not sound a trumpet before you,
as the hypocrites do in the synagogues and in the streets, so that
they may be praised by others. Truly I tell you, they have received
their reward. 3But when you give
alms, do not let your left hand
know what your right hand is do-

5.23 Mt 8.4; 23.19 **5.25** Prov 25.8; Lk 12.57-59 **5.27-32pp** Mk 10.11; Lk 16.18 **5.27** Ex 20.14; Deut 5.18 **5.28** Job 31.1; Prov 6.25 **5.29** Mt 18.9; Mk 9.43-47 **5.31** Deut 24.1-4; Mk 10.11, 12; Lk 16.18 **5.33** Lev 19.12; Num 30.2; Deut 23.21; Mt 23.16 **5.34** Jas 5.12; Isa 66.1 **5.38** Ex 21.24; Lev 24.20; Deut 19.21 **5.39** Prov 24.29; Lk 6.29; Rom 12.17, 19; 1 Cor 6.7; 1 Pet 3.9 **5.42** Deut 15.8; Lk 6.30 **5.43** Lev 19.18; Deut 23.6; Ps 41.10 **5.44** Rom 12.14; Acts 7.60; 1 Cor 4.12; 1 Pet 2.23 **5.45** Job 25.3 **5.48** Lev 19.2; Col 1.28; Jas 1.4 **6.1** Mt 23.5 **6.2** Rom 12.8

b Gk *Gehenna* c Gk *your brother*
d Gk lacks *to court* e Or *evil*
f Gk *your brothers*

ing, 4 so that your alms may be
done in secret; and your Father
who sees in secret will reward
you.[g]

Concerning Prayer

5 "And whenever you pray, do
not be like the hypocrites; for they
love to stand and pray in the synagogues and at the street corners, so
that they may be seen by others.
Truly I tell you, they have received
their reward. 6 But whenever you
pray, go into your room and shut
the door and pray to your Father
who is in secret; and your Father
who sees in secret will reward
you.[g]
7 "When you are praying, do not
heap up empty phrases as the Gentiles do; for they think that they
will be heard because of their many
words. 8 Do not be like them, for
your Father knows what you need
before you ask him.
9 "Pray then in this way:
Our Father in heaven,
hallowed be your name.
10 Your kingdom come.
Your will be done,
on earth as it is in
heaven.
11 Give us this day our daily
bread.[h]
12 And forgive us our debts,
as we also have forgiven
our debtors.
13 And do not bring us to the
time of trial,[i]
but rescue us from the
evil one.[j]
14 For if you forgive others their
trespasses, your heavenly Father
will also forgive you; 15 but if you do
not forgive others, neither will your
Father forgive your trespasses.

Concerning Fasting

16 "And whenever you fast, do
not look dismal, like the hypocrites, for they disfigure their faces
so as to show others that they are
fasting. Truly I tell you, they have
received their reward. 17 But when
you fast, put oil on your head and
wash your face, 18 so that your fasting may be seen not by others but
by your Father who is in secret; and
your Father who sees in secret will
reward you.[g]

Concerning Treasures

19 "Do not store up for yourselves treasures on earth, where
moth and rust[k] consume and
where thieves break in and steal;
20 but store up for yourselves treasures in heaven, where neither
moth nor rust[k] consumes and
where thieves do not break in and
steal. 21 For where your treasure is,
there your heart will be also.

The Sound Eye

22 "The eye is the lamp of the
body. So, if your eye is healthy,
your whole body will be full of
light; 23 but if your eye is unhealthy,
your whole body will be full of
darkness. If then the light in you is
darkness, how great is the darkness!

Serving Two Masters

24 "No one can serve two masters; for a slave will either hate the
one and love the other, or be devoted to the one and despise the other. You cannot serve God and
wealth.[l]

Do Not Worry

25 "Therefore I tell you, do not
worry about your life, what you will
eat or what you will drink,[m] or
about your body, what you will
wear. Is not life more than food,
and the body more than clothing?
26 Look at the birds of the air; they
neither sow nor reap nor gather
into barns, and yet your heavenly
Father feeds them. Are you not of
more value than they? 27 And can
any of you by worrying add a single
hour to your span of life?[n] 28 And
why do you worry about clothing?
Consider the lilies of the field, how
they grow; they neither toil nor

6.4 Col 3.23,24
6.5 Mk 11.25; Lk 18.10-14
6.6 2 Kings 4.33
6.7 Eccl 5.2; 1 Kings 18.26, 29
6.10 Mt 26.39,42
6.11 Prov 30.8
6.12 Mt 18.21
6.13 Jn 17.15; 2 Thes 3.3; Jas 1.13
6.14 Mk 11.25, 26; Eph 4.32; Col 3.13
6.15 Mt 18.35
6.16 Isa 58.5
6.18 vv. 4,6
6.19 Prov 23.4; 1 Tim 6.17 Heb 13.5; Jas 5.1
6.20 Lk 12.33,34; 18.22; 1 Tim 6.19; 1 Pet 1.4
6.22 Mt 20.15; Mk 7.22; Lk 11.34-36
6.24 Lk 16.13
6.25 Ps 55.22; Phil 4.6; 1 Pet 5.7
6.26 Job 38.41; Ps 147.9; Lk 12.24
6.27 Ps 39.5

[g] Other ancient authorities add *openly*
[h] Or *our bread for tomorrow* [i] Or *us into temptation* [j] Or *from evil.* Other ancient authorities add, in some form, *For the kingdom and the power and the glory are yours forever. Amen.* [k] Gk *eating* [l] Gk *mammon*
[m] Other ancient authorities lack *or what you will drink* [n] Or *add one cubit to your height*

spin, 29 yet I tell you, even Solomon in all his glory was not clothed like one of these. 30 But if God so clothes the grass of the field, which is alive today and tomorrow is thrown into the oven, will he not much more clothe you—you of little faith? 31 Therefore do not worry, saying, 'What will we eat?' or 'What will we drink?' or 'What will we wear?' 32 For it is the Gentiles who strive for all these things; and indeed your heavenly Father knows that you need all these things. 33 But strive first for the kingdom of God[o] and his[p] righteousness, and all these things will be given to you as well.

34 "So do not worry about tomorrow, for tomorrow will bring worries of its own. Today's trouble is enough for today.

Judging Others

7 "Do not judge, so that you may not be judged. 2 For with the judgment you make you will be judged, and the measure you give will be the measure you get. 3 Why do you see the speck in your neighbor's[q] eye, but do not notice the log in your own eye? 4 Or how can you say to your neighbor,[r] 'Let me take the speck out of your eye,' while the log is in your own eye? 5 You hypocrite, first take the log out of your own eye, and then you will see clearly to take the speck out of your neighbor's[q] eye.

Profaning the Holy

6 "Do not give what is holy to dogs; and do not throw your pearls before swine, or they will trample them under foot and turn and maul you.

Ask, Search, Knock

7 "Ask, and it will be given you; search, and you will find; knock, and the door will be opened for you. 8 For everyone who asks receives, and everyone who searches finds, and for everyone who knocks, the door will be opened. 9 Is there anyone among you who, if your child asks for bread, will give a stone? 10 Or if the child asks for a fish, will give a snake? 11 If you then, who are evil, know how to give good gifts to your children, how much more will your Father in heaven give good things to those who ask him!

The Golden Rule

12 "In everything do to others as you would have them do to you; for this is the law and the prophets.

The Narrow Gate

13 "Enter through the narrow gate; for the gate is wide and the road is easy[s] that leads to destruction, and there are many who take it. 14 For the gate is narrow and the road is hard that leads to life, and there are few who find it.

A Tree and Its Fruit

15 "Beware of false prophets, who come to you in sheep's clothing but inwardly are ravenous wolves. 16 You will know them by their fruits. Are grapes gathered from thorns, or figs from thistles? 17 In the same way, every good tree bears good fruit, but the bad tree bears bad fruit. 18 A good tree cannot bear bad fruit, nor can a bad tree bear good fruit. 19 Every tree that does not bear good fruit is cut down and thrown into the fire. 20 Thus you will know them by their fruits.

Concerning Self-Deception

21 "Not everyone who says to me, 'Lord, Lord,' will enter the kingdom of heaven, but only the one who does the will of my Father in heaven. 22 On that day many will say to me, 'Lord, Lord, did we not prophesy in your name, and cast out demons in your name, and do many deeds of power in your name?' 23 Then I will declare to them, 'I never knew you; go away from me, you evildoers.'

Hearers and Doers

24 "Everyone then who hears these words of mine and acts on

6.29 1 Kings 10.4-7 **6.30** Mt 8.26; 14.31; 16.8 **6.32** v. 8 **6.33** Mt 19.28; Mk 10.29, 30; Lk 18.29,30 **7.1-6pp** Lk 6.37-42 **7.1** Mk 4.24; Rom 2.1; 14.10; 1 Cor 4.3 **7.6** Prov 9.7,8; Acts 13.45 **7.7** Mk 11.24; Jn 15.7; 16.23,24; Jas 4.3; 1 Jn 3.22; 5.14,15 **7.8** Jer 29.12,13

7.12 Lk 6.31; Rom 13.8-10; Gal 5.14 **7.13** Lk 13.24 **7.15** Jer 23.16; Mt 24.11, 24; Mk 13.22; 2 Pet 2.1; 1 Jn 4.1; Rev 16.13; 19.20; 20.10; Acts 20.29 **7.16** Mt 12.33; Mk 3.10; Jas 3.12 **7.19** Mt 3.10; Lk 3.9; Jn 15.2,6 **7.21** Hos 8.2 Mt 25.11, 12; Acts 19.13; Rom 2.13; Jas 1.22 **7.22** Mt 25.12; Lk 13.25-27 **7.23** Ps 6.8; Mt 25.12; Lk 13.25,27 **7.24** Lk 6.47-49; Jas 1.22-25

[o] Other ancient authorities lack *of God*
[p] Or *its* [q] Gk *brother's* [r] Gk *brother*
[s] Other ancient authorities read *for the road is wide and easy*

them will be like a wise man who
built his house on rock. 25 The rain
fell, the floods came, and the winds
blew and beat on that house, but it
did not fall, because it had been
founded on rock. 26 And everyone
who hears these words of mine and
does not act on them will be like a
foolish man who built his house on
sand. 27 The rain fell, and the floods
came, and the winds blew and beat
against that house, and it fell — and
great was its fall!"
28 Now when Jesus had finished saying these things, the
crowds were astounded at his
teaching, 29 for he taught them as
one having authority, and not as
their scribes.

Jesus Cleanses a Leper

8 When Jesus[t] had come down
from the mountain, great
crowds followed him; 2 and there
was a leper[u] who came to him and
knelt before him, saying, "Lord, if
you choose, you can make me
clean." 3 He stretched out his hand
and touched him, saying, "I do
choose. Be made clean!" Immediately his leprosy[u] was cleansed.
4 Then Jesus said to him, "See that
you say nothing to anyone; but go,
show yourself to the priest, and offer the gift that Moses commanded, as a testimony to them."

Jesus Heals a Centurion's Servant

5 When he entered Capernaum,
a centurion came to him, appealing
to him 6 and saying, "Lord, my servant is lying at home paralyzed, in
terrible distress." 7 And he said to
him, "I will come and cure him."
8 The centurion answered, "Lord, I
am not worthy to have you come
under my roof; but only speak the
word, and my servant will be
healed. 9 For I also am a man under
authority, with soldiers under me;
and I say to one, 'Go,' and he goes,
and to another, 'Come,' and he
comes, and to my slave, 'Do this,'
and the slave does it." 10 When
Jesus heard him, he was amazed
and said to those who followed
him, "Truly I tell you, in no one[v] in
Israel have I found such faith. 11 I
tell you, many will come from east
and west and will eat with Abraham and Isaac and Jacob in the
kingdom of heaven, 12 while the
heirs of the kingdom will be thrown
into the outer darkness, where
there will be weeping and gnashing
of teeth." 13 And to the centurion
Jesus said, "Go; let it be done for
you according to your faith." And
the servant was healed in that
hour.

Jesus Heals Many at Peter's House

14 When Jesus entered Peter's
house, he saw his mother-in-law lying in bed with a fever; 15 he
touched her hand, and the fever
left her, and she got up and began
to serve him. 16 That evening they
brought to him many who were
possessed with demons; and he
cast out the spirits with a word, and
cured all who were sick. 17 This was
to fulfill what had been spoken
through the prophet Isaiah, "He
took our infirmities and bore our
diseases."

Would-Be Followers of Jesus

18 Now when Jesus saw great
crowds around him, he gave orders
to go over to the other side. 19 A
scribe then approached and said,
"Teacher, I will follow you wherever you go." 20 And Jesus said to
him, "Foxes have holes, and birds
of the air have nests; but the Son of
Man has nowhere to lay his head."
21 Another of his disciples said to
him, "Lord, first let me go and bury
my father." 22 But Jesus said to
him, "Follow me, and let the dead
bury their own dead."

Jesus Stills the Storm

23 And when he got into the
boat, his disciples followed him.
24 A windstorm arose on the sea, so
great that the boat was being
swamped by the waves; but he was
asleep. 25 And they went and woke

7.28 Mt 11.1; 13.53; 19.1; 26.1; 13.54; Mk 1.22; 6.2; Lk 4.32; Jn 7.46
8.1-4pp Mk 1.40-45; Lk 5.12-16
8.2 Mt 9.18; 15.25; 18.26; 20.20; Jn 9.38
8.4 Lev 14.3,4, 10; Mk 3.12; 5.43; 7.36; 8.30; 9.9
8.5-13pp Lk 7.1-10
8.8 Ps 107.20
8.11 Isa 49.12; 59.19; Mal 1.11; Lk 13.29; Acts 10.45
8.12 Mt 13.42, 50; 22.13; 25.30; Lk 13.28
8.14-17pp Mk 1.29-34; Lk 4.28-41
8.14 1 Cor 9.5
8.17 Isa 53.4
8.18-22pp Lk 9.57-62
8.18 Mk 4.35; Lk 8.22
8.22 Mt 9.9; Jn 1.43; 21.19
8.23-27pp Mk 4.36-41; Lk 8.22-25

[t] Gk *he* [u] The terms *leper* and *leprosy* can refer to several diseases [v] Other ancient authorities read *Truly I tell you, not even*

him up, saying, "Lord, save us! We
are perishing!" 26 And he said to
them, "Why are you afraid, you of
little faith?" Then he got up and rebuked the winds and the sea; and
there was a dead calm. 27 They were
amazed, saying, "What sort of man
is this, that even the winds and the
sea obey him?"

Jesus Heals the Gadarene Demoniacs

28 When he came to the other
side, to the country of the Gadarenes,[w] two demoniacs coming out
of the tombs met him. They were
so fierce that no one could pass
that way. 29 Suddenly they shouted,
"What have you to do with us, Son
of God? Have you come here to torment us before the time?" 30 Now a
large herd of swine was feeding at
some distance from them. 31 The
demons begged him, "If you cast us
out, send us into the herd of
swine." 32 And he said to them,
"Go!" So they came out and entered the swine; and suddenly, the
whole herd rushed down the steep
bank into the sea and perished in
the water. 33 The swineherds ran
off, and on going into the town,
they told the whole story about
what had happened to the demoniacs. 34 Then the whole town came
out to meet Jesus; and when they
saw him, they begged him to leave
9 their neighborhood. 1 And after getting into a boat he
crossed the sea and came to his
own town.

Jesus Heals a Paralytic

2 And just then some people
were carrying a paralyzed man lying on a bed. When Jesus saw their
faith, he said to the paralytic,
"Take heart, son; your sins are forgiven." 3 Then some of the scribes
said to themselves, "This man is
blaspheming." 4 But Jesus, perceiving their thoughts, said, "Why do
you think evil in your hearts? 5 For
which is easier, to say, 'Your sins
are forgiven,' or to say, 'Stand up
and walk'? 6 But so that you may
know that the Son of Man has authority on earth to forgive sins"—
he then said to the paralytic—
"Stand up, take your bed and go to
your home." 7 And he stood up and
went to his home. 8 When the
crowds saw it, they were filled with
awe, and they glorified God, who
had given such authority to human
beings.

The Call of Matthew

9 As Jesus was walking along,
he saw a man called Matthew sitting at the tax booth; and he said to
him, "Follow me." And he got up
and followed him.
10 And as he sat at dinner[x] in
the house, many tax collectors and
sinners came and were sitting[y]
with him and his disciples. 11 When
the Pharisees saw this, they said to
his disciples, "Why does your
teacher eat with tax collectors and
sinners?" 12 But when he heard
this, he said, "Those who are well
have no need of a physician, but
those who are sick. 13 Go and learn
what this means, 'I desire mercy,
not sacrifice.' For I have come to
call not the righteous but sinners."

The Question about Fasting

14 Then the disciples of John
came to him, saying, "Why do we
and the Pharisees fast often,[z] but
your disciples do not fast?" 15 And
Jesus said to them, "The wedding
guests cannot mourn as long as the
bridegroom is with them, can they?
The days will come when the bridegroom is taken away from them,
and then they will fast. 16 No one
sews a piece of unshrunk cloth on
an old cloak, for the patch pulls
away from the cloak, and a worse
tear is made. 17 Neither is new wine
put into old wineskins; otherwise,
the skins burst, and the wine is
spilled, and the skins are destroyed; but new wine is put into
fresh wineskins, and so both are
preserved."

8.26 Mt. 6.30; 14.31; 16.8; Ps 65.7; 89.9; 107.29
8.28-9.1pp Mk 5.1-20; Lk 8.26-39
8.29 Judg 11.12; 2 Sam 16.10; Mk 1.24; Jn 2.4
8.34 see 1 Kings 17.18; Lk 5.8; Acts 16.39
9.1 Mt 4.13
9.2-8pp Mk 2.1-12; Lk 5.17-26
9.2 Mt 9.22; Mk 6.50; 10.49; Acts 23.11
9.4 Mt 12.25; Lk 6.8; 9.47; 11.17
9.8 Mt 5.16; 15.31; Lk 7.16; 13.13; 17.15; 23.47; Jn 15.8; Acts 4.21; 11.18; 21.20
9.9-13pp Mk 2.13-17; Lk 5.27-32
9.11 Mt 11.19; Gal 2.15
9.13 Hos 6.6; Mic 6.6-8; Mt 12.7; 1 Tim 1.15
9.14-17pp Mk 2.18-22; Lk 5.33-39
9.14 Lk 18.12
9.15 Jn 3.29; Acts 13.2,3; 14.23
9.16 Lk 5.36

[w] Other ancient authorities read *Gergesenes*; others, *Gerasenes* [x] Gk *reclined* [y] Gk *were reclining* [z] Other ancient authorities lack *often*

A Girl Restored to Life and a Woman Healed

18 While he was saying these
things to them, suddenly a leader
of the synagogue[a] came in and
knelt before him, saying, "My
daughter has just died; but come
and lay your hand on her, and she
will live." 19 And Jesus got up and
followed him, with his disciples.
20 Then suddenly a woman who had
been suffering from hemorrhages
for twelve years came up behind
him and touched the fringe of his
cloak, 21 for she said to herself, "If
I only touch his cloak, I will be
made well." 22 Jesus turned, and
seeing her he said, "Take heart,
daughter; your faith has made you
well." And instantly the woman
was made well. 23 When Jesus came
to the leader's house and saw the
flute players and the crowd making
a commotion, 24 he said, "Go away;
for the girl is not dead but sleeping." And they laughed at him.
25 But when the crowd had been
put outside, he went in and took
her by the hand, and the girl got up.
26 And the report of this spread
throughout that district.

Jesus Heals Two Blind Men

27 As Jesus went on from there,
two blind men followed him, crying
loudly, "Have mercy on us, Son of
David!" 28 When he entered the
house, the blind men came to him;
and Jesus said to them, "Do you
believe that I am able to do this?"
They said to him, "Yes, Lord."
29 Then he touched their eyes and
said, "According to your faith let it
be done to you." 30 And their eyes
were opened. Then Jesus sternly
ordered them, "See that no one
knows of this." 31 But they went
away and spread the news about
him throughout that district.

Jesus Heals One Who Was Mute

32 After they had gone away, a
demoniac who was mute was
brought to him. 33 And when the
demon had been cast out, the one
who had been mute spoke; and the
crowds were amazed and said,
"Never has anything like this been
seen in Israel." 34 But the Pharisees
said, "By the ruler of the demons
he casts out the demons."[b]

The Harvest Is Great, the Laborers Few

35 Then Jesus went about all
the cities and villages, teaching in
their synagogues, and proclaiming
the good news of the kingdom, and
curing every disease and every sickness. 36 When he saw the crowds,
he had compassion for them, because they were harassed and helpless, like sheep without a shepherd. 37 Then he said to his
disciples, "The harvest is plentiful,
but the laborers are few; 38 therefore ask the Lord of the harvest to
send out laborers into his harvest."

The Twelve Apostles

10 Then Jesus[c] summoned
his twelve disciples and
gave them authority over unclean
spirits, to cast them out, and to
cure every disease and every sickness. 2 These are the names of the
twelve apostles: first, Simon, also
known as Peter, and his brother
Andrew; James son of Zebedee,
and his brother John; 3 Philip and
Bartholomew; Thomas and Matthew the tax collector; James son
of Alphaeus, and Thaddaeus;[d] 4 Simon the Cananaean, and Judas Iscariot, the one who betrayed him.

The Mission of the Twelve

5 These twelve Jesus sent out
with the following instructions:
"Go nowhere among the Gentiles,
and enter no town of the Samaritans, 6 but go rather to the lost
sheep of the house of Israel. 7 As
you go, proclaim the good news,
'The kingdom of heaven has come
near.'[e] 8 Cure the sick, raise the
dead, cleanse the lepers,[f] cast out
demons. You received without payment; give without payment. 9 Take

9.18-26pp Mk 5.21-43; Lk 8.40-56
9.18 Mt 8.2; Jn 9.38
9.20 Mt 14.36; Mk 3.10
9.21 see Lk 6.19
9.22 Mk 10.52; Lk 7.50; 17.19; 18.42; Mt 9.29; 15.28
9.23 see 2 Chr 35.25; Jer 9.17; 16.6; Ezek 24.17
9.24 Jn 11.13; Acts 20.10
9.27 Mt 15.22; Mk 10.47, 48; Lk 18.38,39
9.29 see v. 22; Mt 8.13
9.30 Mt 8.4; 17.9
9.31 Mk 7.36
9.32 Mt 12.22-24; Lk 11.14
9.34 Mt 12.24; Mk 3.22; Lk 11.15
9.35 Mk 6.6; Lk 13.22
9.36 Mk 6.34; Ezek 34.5; Zech 10.2
9.37 Lk 10.2; Jn 4.35
10.1-15pp Mk 6.7-13; Lk 9.1-16
10.1 Mk 3.13-15; Lk 6.14-16; Acts 1.13
10.4 Lk 6.15; Acts 1.13; Jn 13.26
10.5 Lk 9.52; Acts 8.5,25
10.6 Mt 15.24; Ezek 34.5
10.7 Mt 3.2; Lk 10.9

[a] Gk lacks *of the synagogue* [b] Other ancient authorities lack this verse [c] Gk *he* [d] Other ancient authorities read *Lebbaeus*, or *Lebbaeus called Thaddaeus* [e] Or *is at hand* [f] The terms *leper* and *leprosy* can refer to several diseases

no gold, or silver, or copper in your
belts, 10 no bag for your journey, or
two tunics, or sandals, or a staff; for
laborers deserve their food.
11 Whatever town or village you enter, find out who in it is worthy, and
stay there until you leave. 12 As you
enter the house, greet it. 13 If the
house is worthy, let your peace
come upon it; but if it is not worthy, let your peace return to you.
14 If anyone will not welcome you or
listen to your words, shake off the
dust from your feet as you leave
that house or town. 15 Truly I tell
you, it will be more tolerable for
the land of Sodom and Gomorrah
on the day of judgment than for
that town.

Coming Persecutions

16 "See, I am sending you out
like sheep into the midst of wolves;
so be wise as serpents and innocent as doves. 17 Beware of them,
for they will hand you over to councils and flog you in their synagogues; 18 and you will be dragged
before governors and kings because of me, as a testimony to
them and the Gentiles. 19 When
they hand you over, do not worry
about how you are to speak or what
you are to say; for what you are to
say will be given to you at that
time; 20 for it is not you who speak,
but the Spirit of your Father speaking through you. 21 Brother will betray brother to death, and a father
his child, and children will rise
against parents and have them put
to death; 22 and you will be hated by
all because of my name. But the
one who endures to the end will be
saved. 23 When they persecute you
in one town, flee to the next; for
truly I tell you, you will not have
gone through all the towns of Israel
before the Son of Man comes.
24 "A disciple is not above the
teacher, nor a slave above the master; 25 it is enough for the disciple
to be like the teacher, and the slave
like the master. If they have called
the master of the house Beelzebul,
how much more will they malign
those of his household!

10.10 1 Cor 9.7; 1 Tim 5.18
10.14 Lk 10.10,11; Acts 13.51; 18.6
10.15 Mt 11.22
10.16-23pp Lk 21.12-19
10.16 Lk 10.3; Rom 16.19
10.18 Acts 25.24-26
10.20 2 Sam 23.2; Jn 16.7-11; Acts 4.8
10.22 Lk 21.17; Dan 12.12; Mt 24.13; Mk 13.13
10.24 Lk 6.40; Jn 13.16; 15.20
10.25 Mt 12.24; Mk 3.22; Lk 11.15
10.26 Mk 4.22; Lk 8.17; 12.2,3
10.28 Isa 8.12,13; Heb 10.31
10.30 Lk 21.18; Acts 27.34
10.32 Rom 10.9; 2 Tim 2.12; Rev 3.5
10.34 Lk 12.51-53; Mk 13.12
10.35 Mic 7.6
10.36 Mic 7.6
10.37 Lk 14.26
10.38 Mt 16.24
10.39 Mt 16.25; Lk 17.33; Jn 12.25
10.40 Lk 9.48; Jn 12.44; Gal 4.14

Whom to Fear

26 "So have no fear of them; for
nothing is covered up that will not
be uncovered, and nothing secret
that will not become known.
27 What I say to you in the dark, tell
in the light; and what you hear
whispered, proclaim from the
housetops. 28 Do not fear those who
kill the body but cannot kill the
soul; rather fear him who can destroy both soul and body in hell.[g]
29 Are not two sparrows sold for a
penny? Yet not one of them will fall
to the ground apart from your Father. 30 And even the hairs of your
head are all counted. 31 So do not
be afraid; you are of more value
than many sparrows.
32 "Everyone therefore who acknowledges me before others, I
also will acknowledge before my
Father in heaven; 33 but whoever
denies me before others, I also will
deny before my Father in heaven.

Not Peace, but a Sword

34 "Do not think that I have
come to bring peace to the earth; I
have not come to bring peace, but
a sword.
35 For I have come to set a
 man against his father,
and a daughter against her
 mother,
and a daughter-in-law
 against her
 mother-in-law;
36 and one's foes will be
 members of one's own
 household.
37 Whoever loves father or mother
more than me is not worthy of me;
and whoever loves son or daughter
more than me is not worthy of me;
38 and whoever does not take up the
cross and follow me is not worthy
of me. 39 Those who find their life
will lose it, and those who lose
their life for my sake will find it.

Rewards

40 "Whoever welcomes you welcomes me, and whoever welcomes
me welcomes the one who sent me.
41 Whoever welcomes a prophet in

g Gk *Gehenna*

the name of a prophet will receive
a prophet's reward; and whoever
welcomes a righteous person in the
name of a righteous person will receive the reward of the righteous;
42 and whoever gives even a cup of
cold water to one of these little
ones in the name of a disciple—
truly I tell you, none of these will
lose their reward."

11 Now when Jesus had finished instructing his twelve
disciples, he went on from there to
teach and proclaim his message in
their cities.

Messengers from John the Baptist

2 When John heard in prison
what the Messiah[h] was doing, he
sent word by his[i] disciples 3 and
said to him, "Are you the one who
is to come, or are we to wait for another?" 4 Jesus answered them,
"Go and tell John what you hear
and see: 5 the blind receive their
sight, the lame walk, the lepers[j]
are cleansed, the deaf hear, the
dead are raised, and the poor have
good news brought to them. 6 And
blessed is anyone who takes no offense at me."

Jesus Praises John the Baptist

7 As they went away, Jesus began to speak to the crowds about
John: "What did you go out into the
wilderness to look at? A reed shak-
en by the wind? 8 What then did you
go out to see? Someone[k] dressed
in soft robes? Look, those who
wear soft robes are in royal palaces.
9 What then did you go out to see?
A prophet?[l] Yes, I tell you, and
more than a prophet. 10 This is the
one about whom it is written,

'See, I am sending my
messenger ahead of
you,
who will prepare your way
before you.'

11 Truly I tell you, among those
born of women no one has arisen
greater than John the Baptist; yet
the least in the kingdom of heaven
is greater than he. 12 From the days
of John the Baptist until now the
kingdom of heaven has suffered violence,[m] and the violent take it by
force. 13 For all the prophets and
the law prophesied until John
came; 14 and if you are willing to accept it, he is Elijah who is to come.
15 Let anyone with ears[n] listen!

16 "But to what will I compare
this generation? It is like children
sitting in the marketplaces and
calling to one another,
17 'We played the flute for you,
and you did not dance;
we wailed, and you did not
mourn.'
18 For John came neither eating nor
drinking, and they say, 'He has a
demon'; 19 the Son of Man came
eating and drinking, and they say,
'Look, a glutton and a drunkard, a
friend of tax collectors and sinners!' Yet wisdom is vindicated by
her deeds."[o]

Woes to Unrepentant Cities

20 Then he began to reproach
the cities in which most of his
deeds of power had been done, because they did not repent. 21 "Woe
to you, Chorazin! Woe to you, Bethsaida! For if the deeds of power
done in you had been done in Tyre
and Sidon, they would have repented long ago in sackcloth and ashes.
22 But I tell you, on the day of judgment it will be more tolerable for
Tyre and Sidon than for you. 23 And
you, Capernaum,
will you be exalted to
heaven?
No, you will be brought
down to Hades.
For if the deeds of power done in
you had been done in Sodom, it
would have remained until this
day. 24 But I tell you that on the day
of judgment it will be more tolerable for the land of Sodom than for
you."

10.42 Mt 25.40; Heb 6.10
11.2-19pp Lk 7.18-35
11.2 Mt 14.3; Mk 6.17; Lk 9.7ff
11.3 Jn 11.27
11.5 Isa 35.4-6; 61.1; Lk 4.18,19
11.6 Isa 8.14,15; Rom 9.32; 1 Pet 2.8
11.7 Mt 3.1
11.9 Lk 1.76
11.10 Mal 3.1; Mk 1.2
11.14 Mal 4.5; Mt 17.12; Lk 1.17
11.15 Mt 13.9,43; Mk 4.23; Rev 13.9
11.19 Mt 9.11; Lk 15.2
11.21 Jon 3.7,8
11.22 v. 24; Mt 10.15
11.23 Isa 14.13; Lam 2.1
11.24 Mt 10.15

[h] Or *the Christ* [i] Other ancient authorities read *two of his* [j] The terms *leper* and *leprosy* can refer to several diseases [k] Or *Why then did you go out? To see someone* [l] Other ancient authorities read *Why then did you go out? To see a prophet?* [m] Or *has been coming violently* [n] Other ancient authorities add *to hear* [o] Other ancient authorities read *children*

Jesus Thanks His Father

25 At that time Jesus said, "I
thank[p] you, Father, Lord of heaven
and earth, because you have hidden these things from the wise and
the intelligent and have revealed
them to infants; 26 yes, Father, for
such was your gracious will.[q] 27 All
things have been handed over to
me by my Father; and no one
knows the Son except the Father,
and no one knows the Father except the Son and anyone to whom
the Son chooses to reveal him.

28 Come to me, all you that are
weary and are carrying heavy burdens, and I will give you rest.
29 Take my yoke upon you, and
learn from me; for I am gentle and
humble in heart, and you will find
rest for your souls. 30 For my yoke is
easy, and my burden is light."

Plucking Grain on the Sabbath

12 At that time Jesus went
through the grainfields on
the sabbath; his disciples were
hungry, and they began to pluck
heads of grain and to eat. 2 When
the Pharisees saw it, they said to
him, "Look, your disciples are doing what is not lawful to do on the
sabbath." 3 He said to them, "Have
you not read what David did when
he and his companions were hungry? 4 He entered the house of God
and ate the bread of the Presence,
which it was not lawful for him or
his companions to eat, but only for
the priests. 5 Or have you not read
in the law that on the sabbath the
priests in the temple break the sabbath and yet are guiltless? 6 I tell
you, something greater than the
temple is here. 7 But if you had
known what this means, 'I desire
mercy and not sacrifice,' you would
not have condemned the guiltless.
8 For the Son of Man is lord of the
sabbath."

The Man with a Withered Hand

9 He left that place and entered
their synagogue; 10 a man was there
with a withered hand, and they
asked him, "Is it lawful to cure on
the sabbath?" so that they might
accuse him. 11 He said to them,
"Suppose one of you has only one
sheep and it falls into a pit on the
sabbath; will you not lay hold of it
and lift it out? 12 How much more
valuable is a human being than a
sheep! So it is lawful to do good on
the sabbath." 13 Then he said to the
man, "Stretch out your hand." He
stretched it out, and it was restored, as sound as the other. 14 But
the Pharisees went out and conspired against him, how to destroy
him.

God's Chosen Servant

15 When Jesus became aware of
this, he departed. Many crowds[r]
followed him, and he cured all of
them, 16 and he ordered them not
to make him known. 17 This was to
fulfill what had been spoken
through the prophet Isaiah:
18 "Here is my servant, whom I
have chosen,
my beloved, with whom my
soul is well pleased.
I will put my Spirit upon
him,
and he will proclaim
justice to the Gentiles.
19 He will not wrangle or cry
aloud,
nor will anyone hear his
voice in the streets.
20 He will not break a bruised
reed
or quench a smoldering
wick
until he brings justice to
victory.
21 And in his name the
Gentiles will hope."

Jesus and Beelzebul

22 Then they brought to him a
demoniac who was blind and mute;
and he cured him, so that the one
who had been mute could speak
and see. 23 All the crowds were
amazed and said, "Can this be the
Son of David?" 24 But when the
Pharisees heard it, they said, "It is
only by Beelzebul, the ruler of the

11.25 1 Cor 1.26-29 **11.27** Mt 28.18; Jn 3.35; 13.3; 17.2 **11.28** Jer 31.25; Jn 7.37 **11.29** Jn 13.15; Phil 2.5; 1 Pet 2.21; 1 Jn 2.6; Jer 6.16 **12.1-8pp** Mk 2.23-28; Lk 6.1-5 **12.1** Deut 23.25 **12.2** v. 10; Lk 13.14; 14.3; Jn 5.10; 7.23; 9.16 **12.3** 1 Sam 21.6 **12.4** Ex 25.30; Lev 24.5,9 **12.5** Num 28.9, 10 **12.6** vv. 41,42 **12.7** Hos 6.6; Mt 9.13 **12.9-14pp** Mk 3.1-6; Lk 6.6-11 **12.10** Lk 13.14; 14.3; Jn 9.16 **12.11** Lk 14.5 **12.12** Mt 10.31 **12.14** Mt 27.1; Jn 5.18; 11.53 **12.15-21pp** Mk 3.7-12 **12.15** Mt 10.23; 19.2 **12.16** Mt 9.30 **12.18** Isa 42.1-4 **12.22-37pp** Mk 3.20-30; Lk 11.14-23 **12.22** Mt 9.32,33 **12.23** Mt 9.27 **12.24** Mt 9.34; 10.25; Jn 7.20; 8.52; 10.20

[p] Or *praise* [q] Or *for so it was well-pleasing in your sight* [r] Other ancient authorities lack *crowds*

demons, that this fellow casts out
the demons." 25 He knew what they
were thinking and said to them,
"Every kingdom divided against itself is laid waste, and no city or
house divided against itself will
stand. 26 If Satan casts out Satan,
he is divided against himself; how
then will his kingdom stand? 27 If I
cast out demons by Beelzebul, by
whom do your own exorcists[s] cast
them out? Therefore they will be
your judges. 28 But if it is by the
Spirit of God that I cast out demons, then the kingdom of God
has come to you. 29 Or how can one
enter a strong man's house and
plunder his property, without first
tying up the strong man? Then indeed the house can be plundered.
30 Whoever is not with me is against
me, and whoever does not gather
with me scatters. 31 Therefore I tell
you, people will be forgiven for every sin and blasphemy, but blasphemy against the Spirit will not be
forgiven. 32 Whoever speaks a word
against the Son of Man will be forgiven, but whoever speaks against
the Holy Spirit will not be forgiven,
either in this age or in the age to
come.

A Tree and Its Fruit

33 "Either make the tree good,
and its fruit good; or make the tree
bad, and its fruit bad; for the tree is
known by its fruit. 34 You brood of
vipers! How can you speak good
things, when you are evil? For out
of the abundance of the heart the
mouth speaks. 35 The good person
brings good things out of a good
treasure, and the evil person brings
evil things out of an evil treasure.
36 I tell you, on the day of judgment
you will have to give an account for
every careless word you utter; 37 for
by your words you will be justified,
and by your words you will be condemned."

The Sign of Jonah

38 Then some of the scribes and
Pharisees said to him, "Teacher,
we wish to see a sign from you."
39 But he answered them, "An evil
and adulterous generation asks for
a sign, but no sign will be given to
it except the sign of the prophet Jonah. 40 For just as Jonah was three
days and three nights in the belly of
the sea monster, so for three days
and three nights the Son of Man
will be in the heart of the earth.
41 The people of Nineveh will rise
up at the judgment with this generation and condemn it, because
they repented at the proclamation
of Jonah, and see, something greater than Jonah is here! 42 The queen
of the South will rise up at the judgment with this generation and condemn it, because she came from
the ends of the earth to listen to
the wisdom of Solomon, and see,
something greater than Solomon is
here!

The Return of the Unclean Spirit

43 "When the unclean spirit has
gone out of a person, it wanders
through waterless regions looking
for a resting place, but it finds
none. 44 Then it says, 'I will return
to my house from which I came.'
When it comes, it finds it empty,
swept, and put in order. 45 Then it
goes and brings along seven other
spirits more evil than itself, and
they enter and live there; and the
last state of that person is worse
than the first. So will it be also with
this evil generation."

The True Kindred of Jesus

46 While he was still speaking
to the crowds, his mother and his
brothers were standing outside,
wanting to speak to him. 47 Someone told him, "Look, your mother
and your brothers are standing outside, wanting to speak to you."[t]
48 But to the one who had told him
this, Jesus[u] replied, "Who is my
mother, and who are my brothers?"
49 And pointing to his disciples, he
said, "Here are my mother and my
brothers! 50 For whoever does the
will of my Father in heaven is my
brother and sister and mother."

12.25 Mt 9.4
12.27 Mt 9.34; 10.25; Acts 19.13
12.28 Dan 2.44; 7.14; Lk 1.33; 17.20,21
12.30 Mk 9.40; Lk 9.50
12.31 Lk 12.10
12.32 Mt 11.19; 13.55; Jn 7.12,52
12.33 Mt 7.17; Lk 6.43,44
12.34 Mt 3.7; 23.33; Lk 6.45
12.38-45pp Lk 11.29-32
12.38 Mt 16.1; Mk 8.11,12; Jn 2.18; 6.30; 1 Cor 1.22
12.39 Mt 16.4
12.40 Jon 1.17
12.41 Jon 1.2; 3.5
12.42 1 Kings 10.2; 2 Chr 9.1
12.45 2 Pet 2.20
12.46-50pp Mk 3.31-35; Lk 8.19-21
12.46 Mt 13.55; Mk 6.3; Jn 2.12; 7.3, 5; Acts 1.4; 1 Cor 9.5; Gal 1.9
12.50 Jn 15.14

[s] Gk *sons* [t] Other ancient authorities lack verse 47 [u] Gk *he*

The Parable of the Sower

13 That same day Jesus went
out of the house and sat beside the sea. 2 Such great crowds
gathered around him that he got
into a boat and sat there, while the
whole crowd stood on the beach.
3 And he told them many things in
parables, saying: "Listen! A sower
went out to sow. 4 And as he sowed,
some seeds fell on the path, and
the birds came and ate them up.
5 Other seeds fell on rocky ground,
where they did not have much soil,
and they sprang up quickly, since
they had no depth of soil. 6 But
when the sun rose, they were
scorched; and since they had no
root, they withered away. 7 Other
seeds fell among thorns, and the
thorns grew up and choked them.
8 Other seeds fell on good soil and
brought forth grain, some a hundredfold, some sixty, some thirty.
9 Let anyone with ears[v] listen!"

The Purpose of the Parables

10 Then the disciples came and
asked him, "Why do you speak to
them in parables?" 11 He answered,
"To you it has been given to know
the secrets[w] of the kingdom of
heaven, but to them it has not been
given. 12 For to those who have,
more will be given, and they will
have an abundance; but from those
who have nothing, even what they
have will be taken away. 13 The reason I speak to them in parables is
that 'seeing they do not perceive,
and hearing they do not listen, nor
do they understand.' 14 With them
indeed is fulfilled the prophecy of
Isaiah that says:

'You will indeed listen, but
never understand,
and you will indeed look,
but never perceive.
15 For this people's heart has
grown dull,
and their ears are hard of
hearing,
and they have shut their
eyes;
so that they might not
look with their eyes,
and listen with their ears,
and understand with their
heart and turn—
and I would heal them.'

16 But blessed are your eyes, for
they see, and your ears, for they
hear. 17 Truly I tell you, many
prophets and righteous people
longed to see what you see, but did
not see it, and to hear what you
hear, but did not hear it.

The Parable of the Sower Explained

18 "Hear then the parable of the
sower. 19 When anyone hears the
word of the kingdom and does not
understand it, the evil one comes
and snatches away what is sown in
the heart; this is what was sown on
the path. 20 As for what was sown
on rocky ground, this is the one
who hears the word and immediately receives it with joy; 21 yet such
a person has no root, but endures
only for a while, and when trouble
or persecution arises on account of
the word, that person immediately
falls away.[x] 22 As for what was
sown among thorns, this is the one
who hears the word, but the cares
of the world and the lure of wealth
choke the word, and it yields nothing. 23 But as for what was sown on
good soil, this is the one who hears
the word and understands it, who
indeed bears fruit and yields, in
one case a hundredfold, in another
sixty, and in another thirty."

The Parable of Weeds among the Wheat

24 He put before them another
parable: "The kingdom of heaven
may be compared to someone who
sowed good seed in his field; 25 but
while everybody was asleep, an enemy came and sowed weeds among
the wheat, and then went away.
26 So when the plants came up and
bore grain, then the weeds appeared as well. 27 And the slaves of
the householder came and said to
him, 'Master, did you not sow good
seed in your field? Where, then, did
these weeds come from?' 28 He an-

13.1-9pp Mk 4.1-9; Lk 8.4-8
13.2 Lk 5.3
13.8 Gen 26.12
13.9 Mt 11.15
13.10-17pp Mk 4.10-12; Lk 8.9-10
13.11 Mt 11.25; 19.11; Jn 6.65; 1 Cor 2.10; 1 Jn 2.27
13.12 Mt 25.29; Lk 19.26
13.13 Jer 5.21; Ezek 12.2
13.14 Isa 6.9,10; Ezek 12.2; Jn 12.40; Acts 28.26, 27; Rom 11.8
13.15 Heb 5.11
13.16 Mt 16.17; Lk 10.23,24; Jn 20.29
13.17 Heb 11.13; 1 Pet 1.10, 11
13.18-23pp Mk 4.13-20; Lk 8.11-15
13.19 Mt 4.23
13.21 Mt 11.6
13.22 Rom 12.2; 1 Cor 1.20; 2 Cor 4.4; Gal 1.4; Eph 2.2; Mt 19.23; 1 Tim 6.9, 10,17
13.23 v. 8
13.24 Lk 13.18,20

[v] Other ancient authorities add *to hear*
[w] Or *mysteries*
[x] Gk *stumbles*

swered, 'An enemy has done this.'
The slaves said to him, 'Then do
you want us to go and gather
them?' 29 But he replied, 'No; for in
gathering the weeds you would uproot the wheat along with them.
30 Let both of them grow together
until the harvest; and at harvest
time I will tell the reapers, Collect
the weeds first and bind them in
bundles to be burned, but gather
the wheat into my barn.' "

The Parable of the Mustard Seed

31 He put before them another
parable: "The kingdom of heaven is
like a mustard seed that someone
took and sowed in his field; 32 it is
the smallest of all the seeds, but
when it has grown it is the greatest
of shrubs and becomes a tree, so
that the birds of the air come and
make nests in its branches."

The Parable of the Yeast

33 He told them another parable: "The kingdom of heaven is like
yeast that a woman took and mixed
in with[y] three measures of flour
until all of it was leavened."

The Use of Parables

34 Jesus told the crowds all
these things in parables; without a
parable he told them nothing.
35 This was to fulfill what had been
spoken through the prophet:[z]

"I will open my mouth to
speak in parables;
I will proclaim what has
been hidden from the
foundation of the
world."[a]

Jesus Explains the Parable of the Weeds

36 Then he left the crowds and
went into the house. And his disciples approached him, saying, "Explain to us the parable of the weeds
of the field." 37 He answered, "The
one who sows the good seed is the
Son of Man; 38 the field is the
world, and the good seed are the
children of the kingdom; the weeds
are the children of the evil one,
39 and the enemy who sowed them
is the devil; the harvest is the end
of the age, and the reapers are angels. 40 Just as the weeds are collected and burned up with fire, so
will it be at the end of the age.
41 The Son of Man will send his angels, and they will collect out of his
kingdom all causes of sin and all
evildoers, 42 and they will throw
them into the furnace of fire, where
there will be weeping and gnashing
of teeth. 43 Then the righteous will
shine like the sun in the kingdom
of their Father. Let anyone with
ears[b] listen!

Three Parables

44 "The kingdom of heaven is
like treasure hidden in a field,
which someone found and hid;
then in his joy he goes and sells all
that he has and buys that field.

45 "Again, the kingdom of heav-
en is like a merchant in search of
fine pearls; 46 on finding one pearl
of great value, he went and sold all
that he had and bought it.

47 "Again, the kingdom of heav-
en is like a net that was thrown into
the sea and caught fish of every
kind; 48 when it was full, they drew
it ashore, sat down, and put the
good into baskets but threw out the
bad. 49 So it will be at the end of the
age. The angels will come out and
separate the evil from the righteous
50 and throw them into the furnace
of fire, where there will be weeping
and gnashing of teeth.

Treasures New and Old

51 "Have you understood all
this?" They answered, "Yes."
52 And he said to them, "Therefore
every scribe who has been trained
for the kingdom of heaven is like
the master of a household who
brings out of his treasure what is
new and what is old." 53 When
Jesus had finished these parables,
he left that place.

The Rejection of Jesus at Nazareth

54 He came to his hometown

13.30 Mt 3.12
13.31,32pp Mk 4.30-32; Lk 13.18,19
13.31 Isa 2.2, 3; Mic 4.1
13.32 Ps 104.12; Ezek 17.23; 31.6; Dan 4.12
13.33-35pp Lk 13.20,21
13.33 Gen 18.6; Gal 5.9
13.34 Mk 4.33,34
13.35 Ps 78.2; Rom 16.25, 26; 1 Cor 2.7; Eph 3.9; Col 1.26
13.38 Mt 24.14; 28.19; Lk 24.47; Jn 8.44; 1 Jn 3.10
13.39 Joel 3.13; Mt 24.3; 28.20; Rev 14.15
13.40 1 Cor 10.11; Heb 9.26
13.41 Mt 24.31
13.42 Mt 8.12; v. 50; Mt 24.51; 25.30; Lk 13.28
13.43 Dan 12.3; Mt 11.15
13.44 see Phil 3.7, 8; Isa 55.1
13.47 Mt 22.10
13.49 Mt 25.32
13.50 v. 42
13.53 Mt 7.28; 11.1; 19.1; 26.1
13.54-58pp Mk 6.1-6; Lk 4.16-30
13.54 Mt 4.23; 7.28

[y] Gk *hid in* [z] Other ancient authorities read *the prophet Isaiah* [a] Other ancient authorities lack *of the world* [b] Other ancient authorities add *to hear*

and began to teach the people[c] in
their synagogue, so that they were
astounded and said, "Where did
this man get this wisdom and these
deeds of power? 55 Is not this the
carpenter's son? Is not his mother
called Mary? And are not his brothers James and Joseph and Simon
and Judas? 56 And are not all his
sisters with us? Where then did this
man get all this?" 57 And they took
offense at him. But Jesus said to
them, "Prophets are not without
honor except in their own country
and in their own house." 58 And he
did not do many deeds of power
there, because of their unbelief.

The Death of John the Baptist

14 At that time Herod the ruler[d] heard reports about
Jesus; 2 and he said to his servants,
"This is John the Baptist; he has
been raised from the dead, and for
this reason these powers are at
work in him." 3 For Herod had arrested John, bound him, and put
him in prison on account of Herodias, his brother Philip's wife,[e]
4 because John had been telling
him, "It is not lawful for you to
have her." 5 Though Herod[f] wanted to put him to death, he feared
the crowd, because they regarded
him as a prophet. 6 But when Herod's birthday came, the daughter of
Herodias danced before the company, and she pleased Herod 7 so
much that he promised on oath to
grant her whatever she might ask.
8 Prompted by her mother, she said,
"Give me the head of John the Baptist here on a platter." 9 The king
was grieved, yet out of regard for
his oaths and for the guests, he
commanded it to be given; 10 he
sent and had John beheaded in the
prison. 11 The head was brought on
a platter and given to the girl, who
brought it to her mother. 12 His disciples came and took the body and
buried it; then they went and told
Jesus.

Feeding the Five Thousand

13 Now when Jesus heard this,
he withdrew from there in a boat to
a deserted place by himself. But
when the crowds heard it, they followed him on foot from the towns.
14 When he went ashore, he saw a
great crowd; and he had compassion for them and cured their sick.
15 When it was evening, the disciples came to him and said, "This is
a deserted place, and the hour is
now late; send the crowds away so
that they may go into the villages
and buy food for themselves."
16 Jesus said to them, "They need
not go away; you give them something to eat." 17 They replied, "We
have nothing here but five loaves
and two fish." 18 And he said,
"Bring them here to me." 19 Then
he ordered the crowds to sit down
on the grass. Taking the five loaves
and the two fish, he looked up to
heaven, and blessed and broke the
loaves, and gave them to the disciples, and the disciples gave them to
the crowds. 20 And all ate and were
filled; and they took up what was
left over of the broken pieces,
twelve baskets full. 21 And those
who ate were about five thousand
men, besides women and children.

Jesus Walks on the Water

22 Immediately he made the
disciples get into the boat and go
on ahead to the other side, while
he dismissed the crowds. 23 And after he had dismissed the crowds,
he went up the mountain by himself to pray. When evening came,
he was there alone, 24 but by this
time the boat, battered by the
waves, was far from the land,[g] for
the wind was against them. 25 And
early in the morning he came walking toward them on the sea. 26 But
when the disciples saw him walking on the sea, they were terrified,
saying, "It is a ghost!" And they
cried out in fear. 27 But immediately Jesus spoke to them and said,
"Take heart, it is I; do not be
afraid."
28 Peter answered him, "Lord, if

13.55 Lk 3.23; Jn 6.42
13.57 Jn 4.44
14.1-12pp Mk 6.14-29; Lk 9.7-9
14.1 Mk 8.15; Lk 3.1,19; 8.3; 13.31; 23.7,8; Acts 4.27; 12.1
14.3 Lk 3.19,20
14.4 Lev 18.16; 20.21
14.5 Mt 21.26; Lk 20.6
14.13-21pp Mk 6.30-44; Lk 9.10-17; Jn 6.1-13
14.14 Mt 9.36
14.17 Mt 16.9
14.19 1 Sam 9.13; Mt 15.36; Mk 14.22; Lk 24.30
14.22-36pp Mk 6.45-52; Jn 6.15-21
14.23 Lk 6.12; 9.28
14.26 see Lk 24.37
14.27 Mt 9.2; 17.7; 28.10; Rev 1.17

c Gk *them* d Gk *tetrarch* e Other ancient authorities read *his brother's wife*
f Gk *he* g Other ancient authorities read *was out on the sea*

it is you, command me to come to
you on the water." 29 He said,
"Come." So Peter got out of the
boat, started walking on the water,
and came toward Jesus. 30 But
when he noticed the strong wind,[h]
he became frightened, and beginning to sink, he cried out, "Lord,
save me!" 31 Jesus immediately
reached out his hand and caught
him, saying to him, "You of little
faith, why did you doubt?" 32 When
they got into the boat, the wind
ceased. 33 And those in the boat
worshiped him, saying, "Truly you
are the Son of God."

Jesus Heals the Sick in Gennesaret

34 When they had crossed over,
they came to land at Gennesaret.
35 After the people of that place recognized him, they sent word
throughout the region and brought
all who were sick to him, 36 and
begged him that they might touch
even the fringe of his cloak; and all
who touched it were healed.

The Tradition of the Elders

15 Then Pharisees and scribes
came to Jesus from Jerusalem and said, 2 "Why do your disciples break the tradition of the elders? For they do not wash their
hands before they eat." 3 He answered them, "And why do you
break the commandment of God
for the sake of your tradition? 4 For
God said,[i] 'Honor your father and
your mother,' and, 'Whoever
speaks evil of father or mother
must surely die.' 5 But you say that
whoever tells father or mother,
'Whatever support you might have
had from me is given to God,'[j]
then that person need not honor
the father.[k] 6 So, for the sake of
your tradition, you make void the
word[l] of God. 7 You hypocrites!
Isaiah prophesied rightly about you
when he said:

8 'This people honors me with
their lips,
but their hearts are far
from me;
9 in vain do they worship me,
teaching human precepts
as doctrines.'"

Things That Defile

10 Then he called the crowd to
him and said to them, "Listen and
understand: 11 it is not what goes
into the mouth that defiles a person, but it is what comes out of the
mouth that defiles." 12 Then the
disciples approached and said to
him, "Do you know that the Pharisees took offense when they heard
what you said?" 13 He answered,
"Every plant that my heavenly Father has not planted will be uprooted. 14 Let them alone; they are
blind guides of the blind.[m] And if
one blind person guides another,
both will fall into a pit." 15 But Peter said to him, "Explain this parable to us." 16 Then he said, "Are you
also still without understanding?
17 Do you not see that whatever
goes into the mouth enters the
stomach, and goes out into the
sewer? 18 But what comes out of the
mouth proceeds from the heart,
and this is what defiles. 19 For out
of the heart come evil intentions,
murder, adultery, fornication,
theft, false witness, slander.
20 These are what defile a person,
but to eat with unwashed hands
does not defile."

The Canaanite Woman's Faith

21 Jesus left that place and
went away to the district of Tyre
and Sidon. 22 Just then a Canaanite
woman from that region came out
and started shouting, "Have mercy
on me, Lord, Son of David; my
daughter is tormented by a demon." 23 But he did not answer her
at all. And his disciples came and
urged him, saying, "Send her away,
for she keeps shouting after us."
24 He answered, "I was sent only to
the lost sheep of the house of Israel." 25 But she came and knelt be-

14.31 Mt 6.30; 8.26; 16.8 **14.33** Ps 2.7; Mt 16.16; 26.63; Lk 4.41; Jn 11.27; Acts 8.37; Rom 1.4 **14.36** Mt 9.20; Mk 3.10 **15.1-20pp** Mk 7.1-23 **15.2** Lk 11.38 **15.4** Ex 20.12; Deut 5.16; Eph 6.2 **15.5** Ex 21.17; Lev 20.9; Deut 27.16 **15.9** Col 2.18-22 **15.11** Acts 10.14, 15; 1 Tim 4.3 **15.13** Isa 60.21; Jn 15.2; 1 Cor 3.9ff **15.14** Mt 23.16; Lk 6.39; Rom 2.19 **15.15** Mt 13.36 **15.16** Mt 16.9 **15.18** Mt 12.34; Jas 3.6 **15.19** Gal 5.19-21; 1 Cor 6.9, 10; Rom 14.14 **15.21-28pp** Mk 7.24-30 **15.22** Mt 9.27; 4.24 **15.24** Mt 10.6,23 **15.25** Mt 8.2; 18.26; 20.20; Jn 9.38

[h] Other ancient authorities read *the wind*
[i] Other ancient authorities read *commanded, saying*
[j] Or *is an offering*
[k] Other ancient authorities add *or the mother*
[l] Other ancient authorities read *law*; others, *commandment*
[m] Other ancient authorities lack *of the blind*

fore him, saying, "Lord, help me."
26 He answered, "It is not fair to
take the children's food and throw
it to the dogs." 27 She said, "Yes,
Lord, yet even the dogs eat the
crumbs that fall from their masters' table." 28 Then Jesus answered her, "Woman, great is your
faith! Let it be done for you as you
wish." And her daughter was
healed instantly.

Jesus Cures Many People

29 After Jesus had left that
place, he passed along the Sea of
Galilee, and he went up the mountain, where he sat down. 30 Great
crowds came to him, bringing with
them the lame, the maimed, the
blind, the mute, and many others.
They put them at his feet, and he
cured them, 31 so that the crowd
was amazed when they saw the
mute speaking, the maimed whole,
the lame walking, and the blind
seeing. And they praised the God of
Israel.

Feeding the Four Thousand

32 Then Jesus called his disciples to him and said, "I have compassion for the crowd, because
they have been with me now for
three days and have nothing to eat;
and I do not want to send them
away hungry, for they might faint
on the way." 33 The disciples said to
him, "Where are we to get enough
bread in the desert to feed so great
a crowd?" 34 Jesus asked them,
"How many loaves have you?" They
said, "Seven, and a few small fish."
35 Then ordering the crowd to sit
down on the ground, 36 he took the
seven loaves and the fish; and after
giving thanks he broke them and
gave them to the disciples, and the
disciples gave them to the crowds.
37 And all of them ate and were
filled; and they took up the broken
pieces left over, seven baskets full.
38 Those who had eaten were four
thousand men, besides women and
children. 39 After sending away the
crowds, he got into the boat and
went to the region of Magadan.[n]

15.28 Mt 9.22,28; Mk 10.52; Lk 7.50; 17.19
15.29-31pp Mk 7.31-37
15.30 Lk 7.22
15.31 Mt 9.8
15.32-39pp Mk 8.1-9
15.32 Mt 9.36
15.36 Mt 14.19; 1 Sam 9.13

16.1-12pp Mk 8.11-12
16.1 Mt 12.38; Lk 11.16,29; 12.54-56
16.4 Jon 3.4,5; Mt 12.39
16.6 Lk 12.1
16.8 Mt 6.30; 8.26; 14.31
16.9 Mt 14.17-21
16.10 Mt 15.34-38
16.13-20pp Mk 8.27-30; Lk 9.18-21
16.14 Mt 14.2; Jn 1.21

The Demand for a Sign

16 The Pharisees and Sadducees came, and to test
Jesus[o] they asked him to show
them a sign from heaven. 2 He answered them, "When it is evening,
you say, 'It will be fair weather, for
the sky is red.' 3 And in the morning, 'It will be stormy today, for the
sky is red and threatening.' You
know how to interpret the appearance of the sky, but you cannot interpret the signs of the times.[p] 4 An
evil and adulterous generation asks
for a sign, but no sign will be given
to it except the sign of Jonah."
Then he left them and went away.

The Yeast of the Pharisees and Sadducees

5 When the disciples reached
the other side, they had forgotten
to bring any bread. 6 Jesus said to
them, "Watch out, and beware of
the yeast of the Pharisees and Sadducees." 7 They said to one another, "It is because we have brought
no bread." 8 And becoming aware
of it, Jesus said, "You of little faith,
why are you talking about having
no bread? 9 Do you still not perceive? Do you not remember the
five loaves for the five thousand,
and how many baskets you gathered? 10 Or the seven loaves for the
four thousand, and how many baskets you gathered? 11 How could
you fail to perceive that I was not
speaking about bread? Beware of
the yeast of the Pharisees and Sadducees!" 12 Then they understood
that he had not told them to beware of the yeast of bread, but of
the teaching of the Pharisees and
Sadducees.

Peter's Declaration about Jesus

13 Now when Jesus came into
the district of Caesarea Philippi, he
asked his disciples, "Who do people say that the Son of Man is?"
14 And they said, "Some say John
the Baptist, but others Elijah, and

[n] Other ancient authorities read *Magdala* or *Magdalan* [o] Gk *him* [p] Other ancient authorities lack [2]*When it is . . . of the times*

still others Jeremiah or one of the
prophets." 15He said to them, "But
who do you say that I am?" 16Si-
mon Peter answered, "You are the
Messiah,[q] the Son of the living
God." 17And Jesus answered him,
"Blessed are you, Simon son of Jonah! For flesh and blood has not
revealed this to you, but my Father
in heaven. 18And I tell you, you are
Peter,[r] and on this rock[s] I will
build my church, and the gates of
Hades will not prevail against it. 19I
will give you the keys of the kingdom of heaven, and whatever you
bind on earth will be bound in
heaven, and whatever you loose on
earth will be loosed in heaven."
20Then he sternly ordered the disciples not to tell anyone that he
was[t] the Messiah.[q]

Jesus Foretells His Death and Resurrection

21 From that time on, Jesus began to show his disciples that he
must go to Jerusalem and undergo
great suffering at the hands of the
elders and chief priests and
scribes, and be killed, and on the
third day be raised. 22And Peter
took him aside and began to rebuke him, saying, "God forbid it,
Lord! This must never happen to
you." 23But he turned and said to
Peter, "Get behind me, Satan! You
are a stumbling block to me; for
you are setting your mind not on
divine things but on human
things."

The Cross and Self-Denial

24 Then Jesus told his disciples,
"If any want to become my followers, let them deny themselves and
take up their cross and follow me.
25For those who want to save their
life will lose it, and those who lose
their life for my sake will find it.
26For what will it profit them if
they gain the whole world but forfeit their life? Or what will they give
in return for their life?
27 "For the Son of Man is to
come with his angels in the glory of
his Father, and then he will repay
everyone for what has been done.
28Truly I tell you, there are some
standing here who will not taste
death before they see the Son of
Man coming in his kingdom."

The Transfiguration

17 Six days later, Jesus took
with him Peter and James
and his brother John and led them
up a high mountain, by themselves. 2And he was transfigured
before them, and his face shone
like the sun, and his clothes became dazzling white. 3Suddenly
there appeared to them Moses and
Elijah, talking with him. 4Then Peter said to Jesus, "Lord, it is good
for us to be here; if you wish, I[u] will
make three dwellings[v] here, one
for you, one for Moses, and one for
Elijah." 5While he was still speaking, suddenly a bright cloud overshadowed them, and from the
cloud a voice said, "This is my Son,
the Beloved;[w] with him I am well
pleased; listen to him!" 6When the
disciples heard this, they fell to the
ground and were overcome by fear.
7But Jesus came and touched
them, saying, "Get up and do not
be afraid." 8And when they looked
up, they saw no one except Jesus
himself alone.
9 As they were coming down the
mountain, Jesus ordered them,
"Tell no one about the vision until
after the Son of Man has been
raised from the dead." 10And the
disciples asked him, "Why, then,
do the scribes say that Elijah must
come first?" 11He replied, "Elijah
is indeed coming and will restore
all things; 12but I tell you that Elijah has already come, and they did
not recognize him, but they did to
him whatever they pleased. So also
the Son of Man is about to suffer at
their hands." 13Then the disciples
understood that he was speaking to
them about John the Baptist.

Jesus Cures a Boy with a Demon

14 When they came to the
crowd, a man came to him, knelt

16.16 Mt 14.33; Jn 6.69; 11.27
16.17 1 Cor 15.50; Gal 1.6; Eph 6.12
16.18 Jn 1.42
16.19 Mt 18.18; Jn 20.23
16.20 Mk 3.12; 5.43; 7.36; 9.9
16.21-28pp Mk 8.31-9.1; Lk 9.22-27
16.21 Mt 17.22, 23; 20.17-19; Lk 17.25
16.24 Mt 10.38, 39; Lk 14.27; 17.33; Jn 12.25
16.27 Mt 10.33; Lk 12.9; 1 Jn 2.18; Rom 2.6; Rev 22.12
16.28 Mt 10.23; 1 Cor 16.22; 1 Thes 4.15-18; Rev 1.7; Jas 5.7
17.1-13pp Mk 9.2-13; Lk 9.28-36
17.1 Mt 26.37; Mk 5.37; 13.2
17.5 2 Pet 1.17; Mt 3.17; Isa 42.1; Acts 3.22,23
17.7 Mt 14.27
17.9 Mt 8.4; 16.20; Mk 3.12; 5.43; 7.36
17.10 Mal 4.5; Mt 11.14
17.11 Mal 4.6; Lk 1.16,17
17.12 Mt 11.14; 14.3,10; 16.21
17.14-21pp Mk 9.14-29; Lk 9.37-43

[q] Or *the Christ* [r] Gk *Petros* [s] Gk *petra*
[t] Other ancient authorities add *Jesus*
[u] Other ancient authorities read *we*
[v] Or *tents* [w] Or *my beloved Son*

before him, 15 and said, "Lord, have
mercy on my son, for he is an epileptic and he suffers terribly; he often falls into the fire and often into
the water. 16 And I brought him to
your disciples, but they could not
cure him." 17 Jesus answered, "You
faithless and perverse generation,
how much longer must I be with
you? How much longer must I put
up with you? Bring him here to
me." 18 And Jesus rebuked the demon,[x] and it[y] came out of him,
and the boy was cured instantly.
19 Then the disciples came to Jesus
privately and said, "Why could we
not cast it out?" 20 He said to them,
"Because of your little faith. For
truly I tell you, if you have faith the
size of a[z] mustard seed, you will
say to this mountain, 'Move from
here to there,' and it will move; and
nothing will be impossible for
you."[a]

Jesus Again Foretells His Death and Resurrection

22 As they were gathering[b] in
Galilee, Jesus said to them, "The
Son of Man is going to be betrayed
into human hands, 23 and they will
kill him, and on the third day he
will be raised." And they were
greatly distressed.

Jesus and the Temple Tax

24 When they reached Capernaum, the collectors of the temple
tax[c] came to Peter and said, "Does
your teacher not pay the temple
tax?"[c] 25 He said, "Yes, he does."
And when he came home, Jesus
spoke of it first, asking, "What do
you think, Simon? From whom do
kings of the earth take toll or tribute? From their children or from
others?" 26 When Peter[d] said,
"From others," Jesus said to him,
"Then the children are free.
27 However, so that we do not give
offense to them, go to the sea and
cast a hook; take the first fish that
comes up; and when you open its
mouth, you will find a coin;[e] take
that and give it to them for you and
me."

17.15 Mt 4.24
17.20 Mt 21.21; Mk 11.23; Lk 17.6; 1 Cor 12.9
17.22,23pp Mk 9.30-32; Lk 9.43-45
17.22 Mt 16.21; 20.17; Lk 18.31; 24.6,7
17.24 Ex 30.13; 38.26
17.25 Rom 13.7; Mt 22.17,19
17.27 Mt 5.29,30; 18.6,8; Lk 17.2; Jn 6.61; 1 Cor 8.13

18.1-9pp Mk 9.33-37; Lk 9.46-48
18.3 Mt 19.14; Mk 10.15; Lk 18.17; 1 Pet 2.2
18.4 Mt 20.27; 23.11
18.5 Mt 10.40; Lk 18.17
18.6 Lk 17.1,2
18.7 Lk 17.1; 1 Cor 11.19
18.8 Mt 5.29,30; Mk 9.43,45
18.9 Mt 5.29; Mk 9.47; Mt 17.27
18.10-14pp Lk 15.4-7
18.10 Ps 34.7; Acts 12.11; Heb 1.14

True Greatness

18 At that time the disciples
came to Jesus and asked,
"Who is the greatest in the kingdom of heaven?" 2 He called a
child, whom he put among them,
3 and said, "Truly I tell you, unless
you change and become like children, you will never enter the kingdom of heaven. 4 Whoever becomes
humble like this child is the greatest in the kingdom of heaven.
5 Whoever welcomes one such
child in my name welcomes me.

Temptations to Sin

6 "If any of you put a stumbling
block before one of these little
ones who believe in me, it would be
better for you if a great millstone
were fastened around your neck
and you were drowned in the depth
of the sea. 7 Woe to the world because of stumbling blocks! Occasions for stumbling are bound to
come, but woe to the one by whom
the stumbling block comes!

8 "If your hand or your foot
causes you to stumble, cut it off
and throw it away; it is better for
you to enter life maimed or lame
than to have two hands or two feet
and to be thrown into the eternal
fire. 9 And if your eye causes you to
stumble, tear it out and throw it
away; it is better for you to enter
life with one eye than to have two
eyes and to be thrown into the
hell[f] of fire.

The Parable of the Lost Sheep

10 "Take care that you do not
despise one of these little ones; for,
I tell you, in heaven their angels
continually see the face of my Father in heaven.[g] 12 What do you
think? If a shepherd has a hundred
sheep, and one of them has gone
astray, does he not leave the

[x] Gk *it* or *him* [y] Gk *the demon*
[z] Gk *faith as a grain of* [a] Other ancient authorities add verse 21, *But this kind does not come out except by prayer and fasting*
[b] Other ancient authorities read *living*
[c] Gk *didrachma* [d] Gk *he* [e] Gk *stater*; the stater was worth two didrachmas
[f] Gk *Gehenna* [g] Other ancient authorities add verse 11, *For the Son of Man came to save the lost*

ninety-nine on the mountains and
go in search of the one that went
astray? 13 And if he finds it, truly I
tell you, he rejoices over it more
than over the ninety-nine that never went astray. 14 So it is not the will
of your[h] Father in heaven that one
of these little ones should be lost.

Reproving Another Who Sins

15 "If another member of the
church[i] sins against you,[j] go and
point out the fault when the two of
you are alone. If the member[k] listens to you, you have regained that
one. 16 But if you are not listened
to, take one or two others along
with you, so that every word may be
confirmed by the evidence of two
or three witnesses. 17 If the member[k] refuses to listen to them, tell
it to the church; and if the offender[k] refuses to listen even to the
church, let such a one be to you as
a Gentile and a tax collector.
18 Truly I tell you, whatever you
bind on earth will be bound in
heaven, and whatever you loose on
earth will be loosed in heaven.
19 Again, truly I tell you, if two of
you agree on earth about anything
you ask, it will be done for you by
my Father in heaven. 20 For where
two or three are gathered in my
name, I am there among them."

Forgiveness

21 Then Peter came and said to
him, "Lord, if another member of
the church[l] sins against me, how
often should I forgive? As many as
seven times?" 22 Jesus said to him,
"Not seven times, but, I tell you,
seventy-seven[m] times.

The Parable of the Unforgiving Servant

23 "For this reason the kingdom
of heaven may be compared to a
king who wished to settle accounts
with his slaves. 24 When he began
the reckoning, one who owed him
ten thousand talents[n] was brought
to him; 25 and, as he could not pay,
his lord ordered him to be sold, together with his wife and children
and all his possessions, and payment to be made. 26 So the slave fell
on his knees before him, saying,
'Have patience with me, and I will
pay you everything.' 27 And out of
pity for him, the lord of that slave
released him and forgave him the
debt. 28 But that same slave, as he
went out, came upon one of his fellow slaves who owed him a hundred denarii;[o] and seizing him by
the throat, he said, 'Pay what you
owe.' 29 Then his fellow slave fell
down and pleaded with him, 'Have
patience with me, and I will pay
you.' 30 But he refused; then he
went and threw him into prison until he would pay the debt. 31 When
his fellow slaves saw what had happened, they were greatly distressed, and they went and reported to their lord all that had taken
place. 32 Then his lord summoned
him and said to him, 'You wicked
slave! I forgave you all that debt because you pleaded with me.
33 Should you not have had mercy
on your fellow slave, as I had mercy
on you?' 34 And in anger his lord
handed him over to be tortured until he would pay his entire debt.
35 So my heavenly Father will also
do to every one of you, if you do not
forgive your brother or sister[p] from
your heart."

Teaching about Divorce

19 When Jesus had finished
saying these things, he left
Galilee and went to the region of
Judea beyond the Jordan. 2 Large
crowds followed him, and he cured
them there.

3 Some Pharisees came to him,
and to test him they asked, "Is it
lawful for a man to divorce his wife
for any cause?" 4 He answered,
"Have you not read that the one
who made them at the beginning
'made them male and female,'
5 and said, 'For this reason a man

18.15 Lev 19.17; Lk 17.3; Gal 6.1; Jas 5.19,20
18.16 Deut 19.15; Jn 8.17; 2 Cor 13.1; Heb 10.28
18.17 1 Cor 6.1-6; 2 Thes 3.6, 14
18.18 Mt 16.19; Jn 20.23
18.19 Mt 5.24; 1 Jn 5.14
18.21 Gen 4.24; Lk 17.4
18.22 Mt 6.14; Mk 11.25; Col 3.13
18.23 Mt 25.19
18.25 Lk 7.42; 2 Kings 4.1; Neh 5.5,8
18.26 Mt 8.2
18.35 Mt 6.14; Mk 11.26; Jas 2.13
19.1 Mk 10.1; Jn 10.40
19.2 Mt 4.23
19.3-12pp Mk 10.2-12
19.3 Mt 5.31
19.4 Gen 1.27; 5.2
19.5 Gen 2.24; 1 Cor 6.16; Eph 5.31

[h] Other ancient authorities read *my* [i] Gk *If your brother* [j] Other ancient authorities lack *against you* [k] Gk *the brother* [l] Gk *if my brother* [m] Or *seventy times seven* [n] A talent was worth more than fifteen years' wages of a laborer [o] The denarius was the usual day's wage for a laborer [p] Gk *brother*

shall leave his father and mother and be joined to his wife, and the two shall become one flesh'? [6]So they are no longer two, but one flesh. Therefore what God has joined together, let no one separate." [7]They said to him, "Why then did Moses command us to give a certificate of dismissal and to divorce her?" [8]He said to them, "It was because you were so hard-hearted that Moses allowed you to divorce your wives, but from the beginning it was not so. [9]And I say to you, whoever divorces his wife, except for unchastity, and marries another commits adultery."[q]

10 His disciples said to him, "If such is the case of a man with his wife, it is better not to marry." [11]But he said to them, "Not everyone can accept this teaching, but only those to whom it is given. [12]For there are eunuchs who have been so from birth, and there are eunuchs who have been made eunuchs by others, and there are eunuchs who have made themselves eunuchs for the sake of the kingdom of heaven. Let anyone accept this who can."

Jesus Blesses Little Children

13 Then little children were being brought to him in order that he might lay his hands on them and pray. The disciples spoke sternly to those who brought them; [14]but Jesus said, "Let the little children come to me, and do not stop them; for it is to such as these that the kingdom of heaven belongs." [15]And he laid his hands on them and went on his way.

The Rich Young Man

16 Then someone came to him and said, "Teacher, what good deed must I do to have eternal life?" [17]And he said to him, "Why do you ask me about what is good? There is only one who is good. If you wish to enter into life, keep the commandments." [18]He said to him, "Which ones?" And Jesus said, "You shall not murder; You shall not commit adultery; You shall not steal; You shall not bear false witness; [19]Honor your father and mother; also, You shall love your neighbor as yourself." [20]The young man said to him, "I have kept all these;[r] what do I still lack?" [21]Jesus said to him, "If you wish to be perfect, go, sell your possessions, and give the money[s] to the poor, and you will have treasure in heaven; then come, follow me." [22]When the young man heard this word, he went away grieving, for he had many possessions.

23 Then Jesus said to his disciples, "Truly I tell you, it will be hard for a rich person to enter the kingdom of heaven. [24]Again I tell you, it is easier for a camel to go through the eye of a needle than for someone who is rich to enter the kingdom of God." [25]When the disciples heard this, they were greatly astounded and said, "Then who can be saved?" [26]But Jesus looked at them and said, "For mortals it is impossible, but for God all things are possible."

27 Then Peter said in reply, "Look, we have left everything and followed you. What then will we have?" [28]Jesus said to them, "Truly I tell you, at the renewal of all things, when the Son of Man is seated on the throne of his glory, you who have followed me will also sit on twelve thrones, judging the twelve tribes of Israel. [29]And everyone who has left houses or brothers or sisters or father or mother or children or fields, for my name's sake, will receive a hundredfold,[t] and will inherit eternal life. [30]But many who are first will be last, and the last will be first.

The Laborers in the Vineyard

20 "For the kingdom of heaven is like a landowner who went out early in the morning to hire laborers for his vineyard. [2]Af-

19.7 Deut 24.1-4; Mt 5.31
19.9 Mk 5.32; Lk 16.18; 1 Cor 7.10-13
19.11 1 Cor 7.7-9
19.13-15pp Mk 10.13-16; Lk 18.15-17
19.14 Mt 18.3; 1 Cor 14.20; 1 Pet 2.2
19.16-30pp Mk 10.17-31; Lk 18.18-30
19.16 Lev 18.5; Lk 10.25
19.18 Ex 20.13; Deut 5.17; Rom 13.9; Jas 2.11
19.19 Lev 19.18; Mt 22.39; Rom 13.9; Gal 5.14
19.21 Mt 6.20; Lk 12.33; 16.9; Acts 2.45; 4.34,35
19.23 Mt 13.22; 1 Cor 1.26; 1 Tim 6.9, 10
19.26 Gen 18.14; Job 42.2; Jer 32.17; Zech 8.6
19.27 Mt 4.20; Lk 5.11
19.28 Mt 20.21; Lk 22.28-30; Rev 3.21
19.30 Mt 20.16; Lk 13.30
20.1 Mt 13.24; 21.28,33

[q] Other ancient authorities read *except on the ground of unchastity, causes her to commit adultery*; others add at the end of the verse *and he who marries a divorced woman commits adultery* [r] Other ancient authorities add *from my youth* [s] Gk lacks *the money*
[t] Other ancient authorities read *manifold*

ter agreeing with the laborers for
the usual daily wage,[u] he sent
them into his vineyard. 3 When he
went out about nine o'clock, he
saw others standing idle in the
marketplace; 4 and he said to them,
'You also go into the vineyard, and
I will pay you whatever is right.' So
they went. 5 When he went out
again about noon and about three
o'clock, he did the same. 6 And
about five o'clock he went out and
found others standing around; and
he said to them, 'Why are you
standing here idle all day?' 7 They
said to him, 'Because no one has
hired us.' He said to them, 'You
also go into the vineyard.' 8 When
evening came, the owner of the
vineyard said to his manager, 'Call
the laborers and give them their
pay, beginning with the last and
then going to the first.' 9 When
those hired about five o'clock
came, each of them received the
usual daily wage.[u] 10 Now when
the first came, they thought they
would receive more; but each of
them also received the usual daily
wage.[u] 11 And when they received
it, they grumbled against the landowner, 12 saying, 'These last
worked only one hour, and you
have made them equal to us who
have borne the burden of the day
and the scorching heat.' 13 But he
replied to one of them, 'Friend, I
am doing you no wrong; did you not
agree with me for the usual daily
wage?[u] 14 Take what belongs to
you and go; I choose to give to this
last the same as I give to you. 15 Am
I not allowed to do what I choose
with what belongs to me? Or are
you envious because I am generous?'[v] 16 So the last will be first,
and the first will be last."[w]

A Third Time Jesus Foretells His Death and Resurrection

17 While Jesus was going up to
Jerusalem, he took the twelve disciples aside by themselves, and
said to them on the way, 18 "See, we
are going up to Jerusalem, and the
Son of Man will be handed over to
the chief priests and scribes, and
they will condemn him to death;
19 then they will hand him over to
the Gentiles to be mocked and
flogged and crucified; and on the
third day he will be raised."

The Request of the Mother of James and John

20 Then the mother of the sons
of Zebedee came to him with her
sons, and kneeling before him, she
asked a favor of him. 21 And he said
to her, "What do you want?" She
said to him, "Declare that these
two sons of mine will sit, one at
your right hand and one at your
left, in your kingdom." 22 But Jesus
answered, "You do not know what
you are asking. Are you able to
drink the cup that I am about to
drink?"[x] They said to him, "We are
able." 23 He said to them, "You will
indeed drink my cup, but to sit at
my right hand and at my left, this is
not mine to grant, but it is for those
for whom it has been prepared by
my Father."

24 When the ten heard it, they
were angry with the two brothers.
25 But Jesus called them to him and
said, "You know that the rulers of
the Gentiles lord it over them, and
their great ones are tyrants over
them. 26 It will not be so among
you; but whoever wishes to be great
among you must be your servant,
27 and whoever wishes to be first
among you must be your slave;
28 just as the Son of Man came not
to be served but to serve, and to
give his life a ransom for many."

Jesus Heals Two Blind Men

29 As they were leaving Jericho,
a large crowd followed him.
30 There were two blind men sitting
by the roadside. When they heard
that Jesus was passing by, they
shouted, "Lord,[y] have mercy on
us, Son of David!" 31 The crowd
sternly ordered them to be quiet;

20.8 Lev 19.13; Deut 24.15
20.12 Jon 4.8; Lk 12.55; Jas 1.11
20.13 Mt 22.12; 26.50
20.15 Deut 15.9; Mt 6.23; Mk 7.22
20.16 Mt 19.30
20.17-19pp Mk 10.32-34; Lk 18.31-34
20.18 Mt 16.21
20.19 Mt 16.21; 27.2; Acts 2.23; 3.13
20.20-28pp Mk 10.35-45
20.20 Mt 4.21; 8.2; 9.18; Jn 9.38
20.21 Mt 19.28
20.22 Mt 26.39, 42; Lk 22.42; Jn 18.11
20.23 Acts 12.2; Rev 1.9; Mt 25.34
20.24 Lk 22.24,25
20.25 Lk 22.25-27
20.26 Mt 23.11; Mk 9.35; Lk 9.48
20.28 Jn 13.4; Phil 2.7; Jn 13.14; Isa 53.10; 1 Tim 2.6; Titus 2.14; 1 Pet 1.19; Mt 26.28; Heb 9.28
20.29-34pp Mk 10.46-52; Lk 18.35-43
20.30 Mt 9.27

[u] Gk *a denarius* [v] Gk *is your eye evil because I am good?* [w] Other ancient authorities add *for many are called but few are chosen* [x] Other ancient authorities add *or to be baptized with the baptism that I am baptized with?* [y] Other ancient authorities lack *Lord*

but they shouted even more loudly,
"Have mercy on us, Lord, Son of
David!" 32 Jesus stood still and
called them, saying, "What do you
want me to do for you?" 33 They
said to him, "Lord, let our eyes be
opened." 34 Moved with compassion, Jesus touched their eyes. Immediately they regained their sight
and followed him.

Jesus' Triumphal Entry into Jerusalem

21 When they had come near
Jerusalem and had reached
Bethphage, at the Mount of Olives,
Jesus sent two disciples, 2 saying to
them, "Go into the village ahead of
you, and immediately you will find
a donkey tied, and a colt with her;
untie them and bring them to me.
3 If anyone says anything to you,
just say this, 'The Lord needs
them.' And he will send them immediately.[z]" 4 This took place to
fulfill what had been spoken
through the prophet, saying,

5 "Tell the daughter of Zion,
Look, your king is coming to
you,
humble, and mounted on a
donkey,
and on a colt, the foal of
a donkey."

6 The disciples went and did as
Jesus had directed them; 7 they
brought the donkey and the colt,
and put their cloaks on them, and
he sat on them. 8 A very large
crowd[a] spread their cloaks on the
road, and others cut branches from
the trees and spread them on the
road. 9 The crowds that went ahead
of him and that followed were
shouting,

"Hosanna to the Son of
David!
Blessed is the one who
comes in the name of
the Lord!
Hosanna in the highest
heaven!"

10 When he entered Jerusalem, the
whole city was in turmoil, asking,
"Who is this?" 11 The crowds were
saying, "This is the prophet Jesus
from Nazareth in Galilee."

Jesus Cleanses the Temple

12 Then Jesus entered the temple[b] and drove out all who were
selling and buying in the temple,
and he overturned the tables of the
money changers and the seats of
those who sold doves. 13 He said to
them, "It is written,

'My house shall be called a
house of prayer';
but you are making it a
den of robbers."

14 The blind and the lame came
to him in the temple, and he cured
them. 15 But when the chief priests
and the scribes saw the amazing
things that he did, and heard[c] the
children crying out in the temple,
"Hosanna to the Son of David,"
they became angry 16 and said to
him, "Do you hear what these are
saying?" Jesus said to them, "Yes;
have you never read,

'Out of the mouths of infants
and nursing babies
you have prepared praise
for yourself'?"

17 He left them, went out of the city
to Bethany, and spent the night
there.

Jesus Curses the Fig Tree

18 In the morning, when he returned to the city, he was hungry.
19 And seeing a fig tree by the side
of the road, he went to it and found
nothing at all on it but leaves. Then
he said to it, "May no fruit ever
come from you again!" And the fig
tree withered at once. 20 When the
disciples saw it, they were amazed,
saying, "How did the fig tree wither
at once?" 21 Jesus answered them,
"Truly I tell you, if you have faith
and do not doubt, not only will you
do what has been done to the fig
tree, but even if you say to this
mountain, 'Be lifted up and thrown
into the sea,' it will be done.
22 Whatever you ask for in prayer
with faith, you will receive."

21.1-11pp Mk 11.1-11; Lk 19.29-44; Jn 12.12-19 **21.5** Isa 62.11; Zech 9.9 **21.8** 2 Kings 9.13 **21.9** Ps 118.26; v. 15; Mt 23.39 **21.11** Jn 6.14; 7.40; Acts 3.22; Mk 6.15; Lk 13.33 **21.12-17pp** Mk 11.15-19; Lk 19.45-48 **21.12** Ex 30.13; Deut 14.25 **21.13** Isa 56.7; Jer 7.11 **21.15** v. 9; Lk 19.39 **21.16** Ps 8.2 **21.18-22pp** Mk 11.12-14, 20-25 **21.21** Mt 17.20; Lk 17.6; Jas 1.6 **21.22** Mt 7.7; Jn 14.13,14; 16.23; Jas 5.16

[z] Or *'The Lord needs them and will send them back immediately.'* [a] Or *Most of the crowd*
[b] Other ancient authorities add *of God*
[c] Gk lacks *heard*

The Authority of Jesus Questioned

23 When he entered the temple,
the chief priests and the elders of
the people came to him as he was
teaching, and said, "By what authority are you doing these things,
and who gave you this authority?"
24 Jesus said to them, "I will also
ask you one question; if you tell me
the answer, then I will also tell you
by what authority I do these things.
25 Did the baptism of John come
from heaven, or was it of human origin?" And they argued with one
another, "If we say, 'From heaven,'
he will say to us, 'Why then did you
not believe him?' 26 But if we say,
'Of human origin,' we are afraid of
the crowd; for all regard John as a
prophet." 27 So they answered
Jesus, "We do not know." And he
said to them, "Neither will I tell
you by what authority I am doing
these things.

The Parable of the Two Sons

28 "What do you think? A man
had two sons; he went to the first
and said, 'Son, go and work in the
vineyard today.' 29 He answered, 'I
will not'; but later he changed his
mind and went. 30 The father[d]
went to the second and said the
same; and he answered, 'I go, sir';
but he did not go. 31 Which of the
two did the will of his father?" They
said, "The first." Jesus said to
them, "Truly I tell you, the tax collectors and the prostitutes are going into the kingdom of God ahead
of you. 32 For John came to you in
the way of righteousness and you
did not believe him, but the tax
collectors and the prostitutes believed him; and even after you saw
it, you did not change your minds
and believe him.

The Parable of the Wicked Tenants

33 "Listen to another parable.
There was a landowner who planted a vineyard, put a fence around
it, dug a wine press in it, and built
a watchtower. Then he leased it to
tenants and went to another coun-

21.23-27pp Mk 11.27-33; Lk 20.1-8
21.23 Acts 4.7; 7.27
21.26 Mt 14.5; Mk 6.20
21.28 v. 33; Mt 20.21
21.31 Lk 7.29,50
21.32 Mt 3.1ff; Lk 7.29,30; 3.12,13
21.33-46pp Mk 12.1-12; Lk 20.9-19
21.33 Ps 80.8; Isa 5.1-7; Mt 25.14,15
21.34 Mt 22.3
21.35 2 Chr 24.21; Mt 23.34, 37; Heb 11.36, 37
21.38 Ps 2.8; Heb 1.2; Mt 26.3; 27.1
21.41 Mt 8.11; Acts 13.46; 18.6; 28.28
21.42 Ps 118.22, 23; Acts 4.11; 1 Pet 2.7
21.43 Mt 8.12
21.46 vv. 26,11
22.1-14pp Mk 12.13-17; Lk 20.19-26
22.2 Mt 13.24

try. 34 When the harvest time had
come, he sent his slaves to the tenants to collect his produce. 35 But
the tenants seized his slaves and
beat one, killed another, and
stoned another. 36 Again he sent
other slaves, more than the first;
and they treated them in the same
way. 37 Finally he sent his son to
them, saying, 'They will respect my
son.' 38 But when the tenants saw
the son, they said to themselves,
'This is the heir; come, let us kill
him and get his inheritance.' 39 So
they seized him, threw him out of
the vineyard, and killed him.
40 Now when the owner of the vineyard comes, what will he do to
those tenants?" 41 They said to
him, "He will put those wretches to
a miserable death, and lease the
vineyard to other tenants who will
give him the produce at the harvest
time."

42 Jesus said to them, "Have
you never read in the scriptures:

'The stone that the builders
    rejected
  has become the
    cornerstone;[e]
this was the Lord's doing,
  and it is amazing in our
    eyes'?

43 Therefore I tell you, the kingdom
of God will be taken away from you
and given to a people that produces
the fruits of the kingdom.[f] 44 The
one who falls on this stone will be
broken to pieces; and it will crush
anyone on whom it falls."[g]

45 When the chief priests and
the Pharisees heard his parables,
they realized that he was speaking
about them. 46 They wanted to arrest him, but they feared the
crowds, because they regarded him
as a prophet.

The Parable of the Wedding Banquet

22 Once more Jesus spoke to
them in parables, saying:
2 "The kingdom of heaven may be
compared to a king who gave a

[d] Gk *He* [e] Or *keystone* [f] Gk *the fruits of it* [g] Other ancient authorities lack verse 44

wedding banquet for his son. 3He
sent his slaves to call those who
had been invited to the wedding
banquet, but they would not come.
4Again he sent other slaves, saying,
'Tell those who have been invited:
Look, I have prepared my dinner,
my oxen and my fat calves have
been slaughtered, and everything is
ready; come to the wedding banquet.' 5But they made light of it
and went away, one to his farm, another to his business, 6while the
rest seized his slaves, mistreated
them, and killed them. 7The king
was enraged. He sent his troops,
destroyed those murderers, and
burned their city. 8Then he said to
his slaves, 'The wedding is ready,
but those invited were not worthy.
9Go therefore into the main
streets, and invite everyone you
find to the wedding banquet.'
10Those slaves went out into the
streets and gathered all whom they
found, both good and bad; so the
wedding hall was filled with guests.
11 "But when the king came in
to see the guests, he noticed a man
there who was not wearing a wedding robe, 12and he said to him,
'Friend, how did you get in here
without a wedding robe?' And he
was speechless. 13Then the king
said to the attendants, 'Bind him
hand and foot, and throw him into
the outer darkness, where there
will be weeping and gnashing of
teeth.' 14For many are called, but
few are chosen."

The Question about Paying Taxes

15 Then the Pharisees went and
plotted to entrap him in what he
said. 16So they sent their disciples
to him, along with the Herodians,
saying, "Teacher, we know that you
are sincere, and teach the way of
God in accordance with truth, and
show deference to no one; for you
do not regard people with partiality. 17Tell us, then, what you think.
Is it lawful to pay taxes to the emperor, or not?" 18But Jesus, aware
of their malice, said, "Why are you
putting me to the test, you hypocrites? 19Show me the coin used for
the tax." And they brought him a
denarius. 20Then he said to them,
"Whose head is this, and whose title?" 21They answered, "The emperor's." Then he said to them,
"Give therefore to the emperor the
things that are the emperor's, and
to God the things that are God's."
22When they heard this, they were
amazed; and they left him and
went away.

The Question about the Resurrection

23 The same day some Sadducees came to him, saying there is
no resurrection;[h] and they asked
him a question, saying, 24"Teacher, Moses said, 'If a man dies childless, his brother shall marry the
widow, and raise up children for his
brother.' 25Now there were seven
brothers among us; the first married, and died childless, leaving the
widow to his brother. 26The second
did the same, so also the third,
down to the seventh. 27Last of all,
the woman herself died. 28In the
resurrection, then, whose wife of
the seven will she be? For all of
them had married her."
29 Jesus answered them, "You
are wrong, because you know neither the scriptures nor the power of
God. 30For in the resurrection they
neither marry nor are given in marriage, but are like angels[i] in heav-
en. 31And as for the resurrection of
the dead, have you not read what
was said to you by God, 32'I am the
God of Abraham, the God of Isaac,
and the God of Jacob'? He is God
not of the dead, but of the living."
33And when the crowd heard it,
they were astounded at his teaching.

The Greatest Commandment

34 When the Pharisees heard
that he had silenced the Sadducees, they gathered together, 35and
one of them, a lawyer, asked him a
question to test him. 36"Teacher,

22.3 Mt 21.34 **22.4** Mt 21.36 **22.7** Lk 19.27 **22.8** Mt 10.11,13 **22.10** Mt 13.47 **22.11** 2 Cor 5.3; Eph 4.24; Col 3.10,12; Rev 3.4; 16.15; 19.8 **22.12** Mt 20.13; 26.50 **22.13** Mt 8.12; Lk 13.28 **22.16** Mk 3.6; 8.15 **22.17** Mt 17.25

22.21 Rom 13.7 **22.23-33pp** Mk 12.18-27; Lk 20.27-38 **22.23** Acts 23.8 **22.24** Deut 25.5 **22.29** Jn 20.9 **22.32** Ex 3.6,16; Acts 7.32; Heb 11.16 **22.33** Mt 7.28 **22.34-40pp** Mk 12.28-34 **22.35** Lk 7.30; 10.25; 11.45; 14.3

[h] Other ancient authorities read *who say that there is no resurrection* [i] Other ancient authorities add *of God*

JEWISH SECTS

PHARISEES

Their roots can be traced to the second century B.C. — to the Hasidim.

1. Along with the Torah, they accepted as equally inspired and authoritative, all material contained within the oral tradition.
2. On free will and determination, they held to a mediating view that made it impossible for either free will or the sovereignty of God to cancel out the other.
3. They accepted a rather developed hierarchy of angels and demons.
4. They taught that there was a future for the dead.
5. They believed in the immortality of the soul and in reward and retribution after death.
6. They were champions of human equality.
7. The emphasis of their teaching was ethical rather than theological.

SADDUCEES

They probably had their beginning during the Hasmonean period (166-63 B.C.). Their demise occurred c. A.D. 70 with the fall of Jerusalem.

1. They denied that the oral law was authoritative and binding.
2. They interpreted Mosaic law more literally than did the Pharisees.
3. They were very exacting in Levitical purity.
4. They attributed all to free will.
5. They argued there is neither resurrection of the dead nor a future life.
6. They rejected a belief in angels and demons.
7. They rejected the idea of a spiritual world.
8. Only the books of Moses were canonical Scripture.

ESSENES

They probably originated among the Hasidim, along with the Pharisees, from whom they later separated (I Maccabees 2:42; 7:13). They were a group of very strict and zealous Jews who took part with the Maccabeans in a revolt against the Syrians, c. 165-155 B.C.

1. They followed a strict observance of the purity laws of the Torah.
2. They were notable for their communal ownership of property.
3. They had a strong sense of mutual responsibility.
4. Daily worship was an important feature along with a daily study of their sacred scriptures.
5. Solemn oaths of piety and obedience had to be taken.
6. Sacrifices were offered on holy days and during sacred seasons.
7. Marriage was not condemned in principle but was avoided.
8. They attributed all that happened to fate.

ZEALOTS

They originated during the reign of Herod the Great c. 6 B.C. and ceased to exist in A.D. 73 at Masada.

1. They opposed payment of tribute for taxes to a pagan emperor, saying that allegiance was due only to God.
2. They held a fierce loyalty to the Jewish traditions.
3. They were opposed to the use of the Greek language in Palestine.
4. They prophesied the coming of the time of salvation.

which commandment in the law is
the greatest?" 37 He said to him,
" 'You shall love the Lord your God
with all your heart, and with all
your soul, and with all your mind.'
38 This is the greatest and first commandment. 39 And a second is like
it: 'You shall love your neighbor as
yourself.' 40 On these two commandments hang all the law and
the prophets."

The Question about David's Son

41 Now while the Pharisees
were gathered together, Jesus
asked them this question: 42 "What
do you think of the Messiah?[j]
Whose son is he?" They said to
him, "The son of David." 43 He said
to them, "How is it then that David
by the Spirit[k] calls him Lord, saying,

44 'The Lord said to my Lord,
"Sit at my right hand,
until I put your enemies
under your feet" '?

45 If David thus calls him Lord, how
can he be his son?" 46 No one was
able to give him an answer, nor
from that day did anyone dare to
ask him any more questions.

Jesus Denounces Scribes and Pharisees

23 Then Jesus said to the
crowds and to his disciples,
2 "The scribes and the Pharisees sit
on Moses' seat; 3 therefore, do
whatever they teach you and follow
it; but do not do as they do, for they
do not practice what they teach.
4 They tie up heavy burdens, hard
to bear,[l] and lay them on the
shoulders of others; but they themselves are unwilling to lift a finger
to move them. 5 They do all their
deeds to be seen by others; for they
make their phylacteries broad and
their fringes long. 6 They love to
have the place of honor at banquets and the best seats in the synagogues, 7 and to be greeted with
respect in the marketplaces, and to
have people call them rabbi. 8 But
you are not to be called rabbi, for
you have one teacher, and you are
all students.[m] 9 And call no one
your father on earth, for you have
one Father—the one in heaven.
10 Nor are you to be called instructors, for you have one instructor,
the Messiah.[n] 11 The greatest
among you will be your servant.
12 All who exalt themselves will be
humbled, and all who humble
themselves will be exalted.

13 "But woe to you, scribes and
Pharisees, hypocrites! For you lock
people out of the kingdom of heav-
en. For you do not go in yourselves,
and when others are going in, you
stop them.[o] 15 Woe to you, scribes
and Pharisees, hypocrites! For you
cross sea and land to make a single
convert, and you make the new
convert twice as much a child of
hell[p] as yourselves.

16 "Woe to you, blind guides,
who say, 'Whoever swears by the
sanctuary is bound by nothing, but
whoever swears by the gold of the
sanctuary is bound by the oath.'
17 You blind fools! For which is
greater, the gold or the sanctuary
that has made the gold sacred?
18 And you say, 'Whoever swears by
the altar is bound by nothing, but
whoever swears by the gift that is
on the altar is bound by the oath.'
19 How blind you are! For which is
greater, the gift or the altar that
makes the gift sacred? 20 So whoever swears by the altar, swears by it
and by everything on it; 21 and whoever swears by the sanctuary,
swears by it and by the one who
dwells in it; 22 and whoever swears
by heaven, swears by the throne of
God and by the one who is seated
upon it.

23 "Woe to you, scribes and
Pharisees, hypocrites! For you tithe
mint, dill, and cummin, and have
neglected the weightier matters of
the law: justice and mercy and
faith. It is these you ought to have

22.37 Deut 6.5 **22.39** Lev 19.18; Mt 19.19; Rom 13.9; Gal 5.14; Jas 2.8 **22.40** Mt 7.12 **22.41-46pp** Mk 12.35-37; Lk 20.41-44 **22.42** Mt 9.27 **22.44** Ps 110.1; Acts 2.34; Heb 1.13; 10.13 **22.46** Mk 12.34; Lk 20.40 **23.1-12pp** Mk 12.38-40; Lk 20.45-47 **23.2** Ezra 7.6,25; Neh 8.4 **23.4** Lk 11.46; Acts 15.10; Gal 6.13 **23.5** Mt 6.1,2,5, 16; Deut 6.8 **23.6** Lk 11.43; 14.7; 20.46 **23.8** Jas 3.1 **23.9** Mal 1.6 **23.11** Mt 20.26 **23.12** Lk 14.11; 18.14; Jas 4.6; 1 Pet 5.5 **23.13** Lk 11.52 **23.16** v. 24; Mt 15.14; 5.33-35 **23.17** Ex 30.29 **23.19** Ex 29.37 **23.22** Ps 11.4; Mt 5.34 **23.23** Mt 11.42; Lev 27.30; Mic 6.8

[j] Or *Christ* [k] Gk *in spirit* [l] Other ancient authorities lack *hard to bear* [m] Gk *brothers* [n] Or *the Christ* [o] Other authorities add here (or after verse 12) verse 14, *Woe to you, scribes and Pharisees, hypocrites! For you devour widows' houses and for the sake of appearance you make long prayers; therefore you will receive the greater condemnation* [p] Gk *Gehenna*

practiced without neglecting the
others. 24 You blind guides! You
strain out a gnat but swallow a
camel!
25 "Woe to you, scribes and
Pharisees, hypocrites! For you
clean the outside of the cup and of
the plate, but inside they are full of
greed and self-indulgence. 26 You
blind Pharisee! First clean the inside of the cup,[q] so that the outside also may become clean.
27 "Woe to you, scribes and
Pharisees, hypocrites! For you are
like whitewashed tombs, which on
the outside look beautiful, but inside they are full of the bones of the
dead and of all kinds of filth. 28 So
you also on the outside look righteous to others, but inside you are
full of hypocrisy and lawlessness.
29 "Woe to you, scribes and
Pharisees, hypocrites! For you
build the tombs of the prophets
and decorate the graves of the righteous, 30 and you say, 'If we had
lived in the days of our ancestors,
we would not have taken part with
them in shedding the blood of the
prophets.' 31 Thus you testify
against yourselves that you are descendants of those who murdered
the prophets. 32 Fill up, then, the
measure of your ancestors. 33 You
snakes, you brood of vipers! How
can you escape being sentenced to
hell?[r] 34 Therefore I send you
prophets, sages, and scribes, some
of whom you will kill and crucify,
and some you will flog in your synagogues and pursue from town to
town, 35 so that upon you may come
all the righteous blood shed on
earth, from the blood of righteous
Abel to the blood of Zechariah son
of Barachiah, whom you murdered
between the sanctuary and the altar. 36 Truly I tell you, all this will
come upon this generation.

The Lament over Jerusalem

37 "Jerusalem, Jerusalem, the
city that kills the prophets and
stones those who are sent to it!
How often have I desired to gather
your children together as a hen
gathers her brood under her wings,
and you were not willing! 38 See,
your house is left to you, desolate.[s] 39 For I tell you, you will not
see me again until you say,
'Blessed is the one who comes in
the name of the Lord.'"

The Destruction of the Temple Foretold

24 As Jesus came out of the
temple and was going
away, his disciples came to point
out to him the buildings of the
temple. 2 Then he asked them,
"You see all these, do you not? Truly I tell you, not one stone will be
left here upon another; all will be
thrown down."

Signs of the End of the Age

3 When he was sitting on the
Mount of Olives, the disciples
came to him privately, saying, "Tell
us, when will this be, and what will
be the sign of your coming and of
the end of the age?" 4 Jesus answered them, "Beware that no one
leads you astray. 5 For many will
come in my name, saying, 'I am the
Messiah!'[t] and they will lead many
astray. 6 And you will hear of wars
and rumors of wars; see that you
are not alarmed; for this must take
place, but the end is not yet. 7 For
nation will rise against nation, and
kingdom against kingdom, and
there will be famines[u] and earthquakes in various places: 8 all this
is but the beginning of the birthpangs.

Persecutions Foretold

9 "Then they will hand you over
to be tortured and will put you to
death, and you will be hated by all
nations because of my name.
10 Then many will fall away,[v] and
they will betray one another and
hate one another. 11 And many
false prophets will arise and lead
many astray. 12 And because of the
increase of lawlessness, the love of
many will grow cold. 13 But the one

23.24 v. 16
23.25 Mk 7.4; Lk 11.39
23.27 Lk 11.44; Acts 23.3
23.29 Lk 11.47,48
23.31 Acts 7.51,52
23.32 1 Thes 2.16
23.33 Mt 3.7; 5.22
23.34 Lk 11.49; 2 Chr 36.15, 16
23.35 Gen 4.8; Heb 11.4; Zech 1.1; 2 Chr 24.21
23.36 Mt 10.23; 24.34
23.37-39pp Lk 13.34-35
23.37 2 Chr 24.21
23.39 Ps 118.26; Mt 21.9
24.1-14pp Mk 13.3-13; Lk 21.5-19
24.1 Mk 13.1
24.2 Mt 26.61; 27.39,40; Lk 19.44; Jn 2.19
24.4 Jer 29.8; 2 Thes 2.3
24.5 vv. 11,23, 24; 1 Jn 2.18
24.7 Isa 19.2; Hag 2.22; Zech 14.13
24.9 Mt 10.17, 22; Jn 15.18; 16.2
24.10 Mt 11.6
24.11 Mt 7.15; Acts 20.29; 1 Tim 4.1
24.13 Mt 10.22; Rev 2.7

[q] Other ancient authorities add *and of the plate* [r] Gk *Gehenna* [s] Other ancient authorities lack *desolate* [t] Or *the Christ* [u] Other ancient authorities add *and pestilences* [v] Or *stumble*

who endures to the end will be
saved. 14 And this good news[w] of
the kingdom will be proclaimed
throughout the world, as a testimony to all the nations; and then the
end will come.

The Desolating Sacrilege

15 "So when you see the desolating sacrilege standing in the
holy place, as was spoken of by the
prophet Daniel (let the reader understand), 16 then those in Judea
must flee to the mountains; 17 the
one on the housetop must not go
down to take what is in the house;
18 the one in the field must not turn
back to get a coat. 19 Woe to those
who are pregnant and to those who
are nursing infants in those days!
20 Pray that your flight may not be
in winter or on a sabbath. 21 For at
that time there will be great suffering, such as has not been from the
beginning of the world until now,
no, and never will be. 22 And if
those days had not been cut short,
no one would be saved; but for the
sake of the elect those days will be
cut short. 23 Then if anyone says to
you, 'Look! Here is the Messiah!'[x]
or 'There he is!'—do not believe it.
24 For false messiahs[y] and false
prophets will appear and produce
great signs and omens, to lead
astray, if possible, even the elect.
25 Take note, I have told you beforehand. 26 So, if they say to you,
'Look! He is in the wilderness,' do
not go out. If they say, 'Look! He is
in the inner rooms,' do not believe
it. 27 For as the lightning comes
from the east and flashes as far as
the west, so will be the coming of
the Son of Man. 28 Wherever the
corpse is, there the vultures will
gather.

The Coming of the Son of Man

29 "Immediately after the suffering of those days
the sun will be darkened,
and the moon will not give
its light;
the stars will fall from
heaven,
and the powers of heaven
will be shaken.
30 Then the sign of the Son of Man
will appear in heaven, and then all
the tribes of the earth will mourn,
and they will see 'the Son of Man
coming on the clouds of heaven'
with power and great glory. 31 And
he will send out his angels with a
loud trumpet call, and they will
gather his elect from the four
winds, from one end of heaven to
the other.

The Lesson of the Fig Tree

32 "From the fig tree learn its
lesson: as soon as its branch becomes tender and puts forth its
leaves, you know that summer is
near. 33 So also, when you see all
these things, you know that he[z] is
near, at the very gates. 34 Truly I tell
you, this generation will not pass
away until all these things have
taken place. 35 Heaven and earth
will pass away, but my words will
not pass away.

The Necessity for Watchfulness

36 "But about that day and hour
no one knows, neither the angels of
heaven, nor the Son,[a] but only the
Father. 37 For as the days of Noah
were, so will be the coming of the
Son of Man. 38 For as in those days
before the flood they were eating
and drinking, marrying and giving
in marriage, until the day Noah entered the ark, 39 and they knew
nothing until the flood came and
swept them all away, so too will be
the coming of the Son of Man.
40 Then two will be in the field; one
will be taken and one will be left.
41 Two women will be grinding
meal together; one will be taken
and one will be left. 42 Keep awake
therefore, for you do not know on
what day[b] your Lord is coming.
43 But understand this: if the owner
of the house had known in what
part of the night the thief was coming, he would have stayed awake
and would not have let his house

24.14 Rom 10.18; Col 1.6,23
24.15-28pp Mk 13.14-23; Lk 21.20-24
24.15 Dan 9.27; 11.31; 12.11; Acts 21.28
24.21 Dan 12.1; Joel 2.2
24.22 Isa 65.8,9
24.23 Lk 17.23; 21.8
24.24 2 Thes 2.9-11; Rev 13.13
24.27 Lk 17.24
24.29-31pp Mk 13.24-27; Lk 21.25-28
24.29 Isa 13.10; Ezek 32.7; Joel 2.10; Rev 8.12
24.30 Dan 7.13; Mt 16.27; Rev 1.7
24.31 Isa 27.13; Zech 9.14; 1 Cor 15.52; 1 Thes 4.16
24.32-35pp Mk 13.28-31; Lk 21.29-33
24.33 Jas 5.9
24.34 Mt 16.28; 23.36
24.35 Mt 5.18
24.37 Gen 6.5; 7.6-23; Lk 17.26,27
24.40 Lk 17.34,35
24.42 Mt 25.13; Lk 12.40
24.43 1 Thes 5.2; 2 Pet 3.10; Rev 3.3; 16.15

[w] Or *gospel* [x] Or *the Christ* [y] Or *christs* [z] Or *it* [a] Other ancient authorities lack *nor the Son* [b] Other ancient authorities read *at what hour*

be broken into. 44 Therefore you also must be ready, for the Son of Man is coming at an unexpected hour.

The Faithful or the Unfaithful Slave

45 "Who then is the faithful and wise slave, whom his master has put in charge of his household, to give the other slaves[c] their allowance of food at the proper time? 46 Blessed is that slave whom his master will find at work when he arrives. 47 Truly I tell you, he will put that one in charge of all his possessions. 48 But if that wicked slave says to himself, 'My master is delayed,' 49 and he begins to beat his fellow slaves, and eats and drinks with drunkards, 50 the master of that slave will come on a day when he does not expect him and at an hour that he does not know. 51 He will cut him in pieces[d] and put him with the hypocrites, where there will be weeping and gnashing of teeth.

The Parable of the Ten Bridesmaids

25 "Then the kingdom of heaven will be like this. Ten bridesmaids[e] took their lamps and went to meet the bridegroom.[f] 2 Five of them were foolish, and five were wise. 3 When the foolish took their lamps, they took no oil with them; 4 but the wise took flasks of oil with their lamps. 5 As the bridegroom was delayed, all of them became drowsy and slept. 6 But at midnight there was a shout, 'Look! Here is the bridegroom! Come out to meet him.' 7 Then all those bridesmaids[e] got up and trimmed their lamps. 8 The foolish said to the wise, 'Give us some of your oil, for our lamps are going out.' 9 But the wise replied, 'No! there will not be enough for you and for us; you had better go to the dealers and buy some for yourselves.' 10 And while they went to buy it, the bridegroom came, and those who were ready went with him into the wedding banquet; and the door was shut. 11 Later the other bridesmaids[e] came also, saying, 'Lord, lord, open to us.' 12 But he replied, 'Truly I tell you, I do not know you.' 13 Keep awake therefore, for you know neither the day nor the hour.[g]

The Parable of the Talents

14 "For it is as if a man, going on a journey, summoned his slaves and entrusted his property to them; 15 to one he gave five talents,[h] to another two, to another one, to each according to his ability. Then he went away. 16 The one who had received the five talents went off at once and traded with them, and made five more talents. 17 In the same way, the one who had the two talents made two more talents. 18 But the one who had received the one talent went off and dug a hole in the ground and hid his master's money. 19 After a long time the master of those slaves came and settled accounts with them. 20 Then the one who had received the five talents came forward, bringing five more talents, saying, 'Master, you handed over to me five talents; see, I have made five more talents.' 21 His master said to him, 'Well done, good and trustworthy slave; you have been trustworthy in a few things, I will put you in charge of many things; enter into the joy of your master.' 22 And the one with the two talents also came forward, saying, 'Master, you handed over to me two talents; see, I have made two more talents.' 23 His master said to him, 'Well done, good and trustworthy slave; you have been trustworthy in a few things, I will put you in charge of many things; enter into the joy of your master.' 24 Then the one who had received the one talent also came forward, saying, 'Master, I knew that you were a harsh man, reaping where you did not sow, and

24.44 1 Thes 5.6
24.45-51pp Lk 12.42-46
24.45 Mt 25.21,23
24.46 Rev 16.15
24.49 Lk 21.34
24.51 Mt 8.12; 13.42,50; 25.30
25.1 Mt 13.24; Lk 12.35-38; Rev 19.7; 21.2,9
25.2 Mt 7.24; 10.16; 24.45
25.5 1 Thes 5.6
25.7 Lk 12.35
25.10 Lk 13.25; Rev 19.9
25.11 Mt 7.21-23
25.13 Mt 24.42, 44; Mk 13.35; Lk 12.40; 1 Thes 5.6
25.14 Lk 19.12; Mt 21.33
25.15 Mt 18.23, 24; Lk 19.13
25.19 Mt 18.23
25.21 Mt 24.45, 47; Lk 16.10
25.23 v. 21
25.24 2 Thes 2.9-11; 2 Tim 2.19

c Gk *to give them* d Or *cut him off*
e Gk *virgins* f Other ancient authorities add *and the bride* g Other ancient authorities add *in which the Son of Man is coming* h A talent was worth more than fifteen years' wages of a laborer

gathering where you did not scatter
seed; 25 so I was afraid, and I went
and hid your talent in the ground.
Here you have what is yours.' 26 But
his master replied, 'You wicked
and lazy slave! You knew, did you,
that I reap where I did not sow, and
gather where I did not scatter?
27 Then you ought to have invested
my money with the bankers, and
on my return I would have received
what was my own with interest.
28 So take the talent from him, and
give it to the one with the ten talents. 29 For to all those who have,
more will be given, and they will
have an abundance; but from those
who have nothing, even what they
have will be taken away. 30 As for
this worthless slave, throw him
into the outer darkness, where
there will be weeping and gnashing
of teeth.'

The Judgment of the Nations

31 "When the Son of Man
comes in his glory, and all the angels with him, then he will sit on
the throne of his glory. 32 All the nations will be gathered before him,
and he will separate people one
from another as a shepherd separates the sheep from the goats,
33 and he will put the sheep at his
right hand and the goats at the left.
34 Then the king will say to those at
his right hand, 'Come, you that are
blessed by my Father, inherit the
kingdom prepared for you from the
foundation of the world; 35 for I was
hungry and you gave me food, I was
thirsty and you gave me something
to drink, I was a stranger and you
welcomed me, 36 I was naked and
you gave me clothing, I was sick
and you took care of me, I was in
prison and you visited me.' 37 Then
the righteous will answer him,
'Lord, when was it that we saw you
hungry and gave you food, or
thirsty and gave you something to
drink? 38 And when was it that we
saw you a stranger and welcomed
you, or naked and gave you clothing? 39 And when was it that we saw
you sick or in prison and visited
you?' 40 And the king will answer
them, 'Truly I tell you, just as you
did it to one of the least of these
who are members of my family,[i]
you did it to me.' 41 Then he will say
to those at his left hand, 'You that
are accursed, depart from me into
the eternal fire prepared for the
devil and his angels; 42 for I was
hungry and you gave me no food, I
was thirsty and you gave me nothing to drink, 43 I was a stranger and
you did not welcome me, naked
and you did not give me clothing,
sick and in prison and you did not
visit me.' 44 Then they also will answer, 'Lord, when was it that we
saw you hungry or thirsty or a
stranger or naked or sick or in prison, and did not take care of you?'
45 Then he will answer them, 'Truly
I tell you, just as you did not do it
to one of the least of these, you did
not do it to me.' 46 And these will go
away into eternal punishment, but
the righteous into eternal life."

The Plot to Kill Jesus

26 When Jesus had finished
saying all these things, he
said to his disciples, 2 "You know
that after two days the Passover is
coming, and the Son of Man will be
handed over to be crucified."
3 Then the chief priests and the
elders of the people gathered in the
palace of the high priest, who was
called Caiaphas, 4 and they conspired to arrest Jesus by stealth
and kill him. 5 But they said, "Not
during the festival, or there may be
a riot among the people."

The Anointing at Bethany

6 Now while Jesus was at Bethany in the house of Simon the leper,[j] 7 a woman came to him with
an alabaster jar of very costly ointment, and she poured it on his
head as he sat at the table. 8 But
when the disciples saw it, they
were angry and said, "Why this
waste? 9 For this ointment could
have been sold for a large sum, and
the money given to the poor."

25.27 Lk 17.24 **25.29** Mt 13.12; Mk 4.25; Lk 8.18 **25.30** Mt 8.12; 3.42,50; 22.13; Lk 13.28 **25.31** Mt 16.27; 19.28 **25.32** Ezek 34.17, 20 **25.34** Lk 12.32; 1 Cor 6.9; 15.50; Gal 5.21; Rev 13.8; 17.8 **25.35** Isa 58.7; Ezek 18.7; Jas 1.27; Heb 13.2 **25.36** Jas 2.15,16; 2 Tim 1.16 **25.40** Prov 14.31; 19.17; Mt 10.42; Heb 6.10 **25.41** Mt 7.23; Mk 9.48; Lk 16.24; Jude 7; 2 Pet 2.4 **25.45** Prov 14.31; 17.5 **25.46** Dan 12.2; Jn 5.29; Rom 2.7; Gal 6.8 **26.1-5, 14-16pp** Mk 14.1-2, 10-11; Lk 22.1-6 **26.1** Mt 7.28; 11.1; 13.53; 19.1 **26.2** Jn 13.1 **26.3** Ps 2.2; Jn 11.47-53 **26.4** Mt 12.14 **26.5** Mt 27.24 **26.6-13pp** Mk 14.3-9; Jn 12.1-8 **26.6** Mt 21.17

[i] Gk *these my brothers* [j] The terms *leper* and *leprosy* can refer to several diseases

10 But Jesus, aware of this, said to
them, "Why do you trouble the
woman? She has performed a good
service for me. 11 For you always
have the poor with you, but you will
not always have me. 12 By pouring
this ointment on my body she has
prepared me for burial. 13 Truly I
tell you, wherever this good news[k]
is proclaimed in the whole world,
what she has done will be told in
remembrance of her."

Judas Agrees to Betray Jesus

14 Then one of the twelve, who
was called Judas Iscariot, went to
the chief priests 15 and said, "What
will you give me if I betray him to
you?" They paid him thirty pieces
of silver. 16 And from that moment
he began to look for an opportunity
to betray him.

The Passover with the Disciples

17 On the first day of Unleavened Bread the disciples came to
Jesus, saying, "Where do you want
us to make the preparations for you
to eat the Passover?" 18 He said,
"Go into the city to a certain man,
and say to him, 'The Teacher says,
My time is near; I will keep the
Passover at your house with my disciples.' " 19 So the disciples did as
Jesus had directed them, and they
prepared the Passover meal.
20 When it was evening, he took
his place with the twelve;[l] 21 and
while they were eating, he said,
"Truly I tell you, one of you will betray me." 22 And they became greatly distressed and began to say to
him one after another, "Surely not
I, Lord?" 23 He answered, "The one
who has dipped his hand into the
bowl with me will betray me. 24 The
Son of Man goes as it is written of
him, but woe to that one by whom
the Son of Man is betrayed! It
would have been better for that one
not to have been born." 25 Judas,
who betrayed him, said, "Surely
not I, Rabbi?" He replied, "You
have said so."

The Institution of the Lord's Supper

26 While they were eating,
Jesus took a loaf of bread, and after
blessing it he broke it, gave it to the
disciples, and said, "Take, eat; this
is my body." 27 Then he took a cup,
and after giving thanks he gave it to
them, saying, "Drink from it, all of
you; 28 for this is my blood of the[m]
covenant, which is poured out for
many for the forgiveness of sins. 29 I
tell you, I will never again drink of
this fruit of the vine until that day
when I drink it new with you in my
Father's kingdom."
30 When they had sung the
hymn, they went out to the Mount
of Olives.

Peter's Denial Foretold

31 Then Jesus said to them,
"You will all become deserters because of me this night; for it is written,

'I will strike the shepherd,
and the sheep of the flock
will be scattered.'

32 But after I am raised up, I will go
ahead of you to Galilee." 33 Peter
said to him, "Though all become
deserters because of you, I will never desert you." 34 Jesus said to him,
"Truly I tell you, this very night, before the cock crows, you will deny
me three times." 35 Peter said to
him, "Even though I must die with
you, I will not deny you." And so
said all the disciples.

Jesus Prays in Gethsemane

36 Then Jesus went with them
to a place called Gethsemane; and
he said to his disciples, "Sit here
while I go over there and pray."
37 He took with him Peter and the
two sons of Zebedee, and began to
be grieved and agitated. 38 Then he
said to them, "I am deeply grieved,
even to death; remain here, and
stay awake with me." 39 And going
a little farther, he threw himself on
the ground and prayed, "My Father, if it is possible, let this cup
pass from me; yet not what I want
but what you want." 40 Then he
came to the disciples and found

26.11 Deut 15.11
26.12 Jn 19.40
26.15 Ex 21.32 Zech 11.12
26.17-19pp Mk 14.12-16; Lk 22.7-13
26.18 Jn 7.6,8; 12.23; 13.1; 17.1
26.19 Deut 16.5-8
26.20-25pp Mk 14.17-21; Lk 22.14-18
26.23 Ps 41.9; Lk 22.21; Jn 13.18; Isa 53; Dan 9.26; Lk 24.25; Acts 17.2,3; 1 Cor 15.3
26.26-29pp Mk. 14.22-25; Lk 22.19-24
26.26 1 Cor 10.16; 11.23-25
26.28 Ex 24.6-8; Mt 20.28; Mk 1.4; Heb 9.20
26.30-35pp Mk 14.27-31; Lk 22.31-34
26.30 Mk 14.26
26.31 Jn 16.32; Mt 11.6; Zech 13.7
26.32 Mt 28.7,10, 16
26.34 Jn 13.38
26.35 Jn 13.37
26.36-46pp Mk 14.32-42; Lk 22.39-46
26.37 Mt 4.21
26.38 Jn 12.27
26.39 Jn 12.27; Mt 20.22; Jn 6.38; Phil 2.8
26.40 v. 38

k Or *gospel*
l Other ancient authorities add *disciples*
m Other ancient authorities add *new*

them sleeping; and he said to Peter, "So, could you not stay awake
with me one hour? 41 Stay awake
and pray that you may not come
into the time of trial;[n] the spirit indeed is willing, but the flesh is
weak." 42 Again he went away for
the second time and prayed, "My
Father, if this cannot pass unless I
drink it, your will be done."
43 Again he came and found them
sleeping, for their eyes were heavy.
44 So leaving them again, he went
away and prayed for the third time,
saying the same words. 45 Then he
came to the disciples and said to
them, "Are you still sleeping and
taking your rest? See, the hour is at
hand, and the Son of Man is betrayed into the hands of sinners.
46 Get up, let us be going. See, my
betrayer is at hand."

The Betrayal and Arrest of Jesus

47 While he was still speaking,
Judas, one of the twelve, arrived;
with him was a large crowd with
swords and clubs, from the chief
priests and the elders of the people. 48 Now the betrayer had given
them a sign, saying, "The one I will
kiss is the man; arrest him." 49 At
once he came up to Jesus and said,
"Greetings, Rabbi!" and kissed
him. 50 Jesus said to him, "Friend,
do what you are here to do." Then
they came and laid hands on Jesus
and arrested him. 51 Suddenly, one
of those with Jesus put his hand on
his sword, drew it, and struck the
slave of the high priest, cutting off
his ear. 52 Then Jesus said to him,
"Put your sword back into its place;
for all who take the sword will perish by the sword. 53 Do you think
that I cannot appeal to my Father,
and he will at once send me more
than twelve legions of angels?
54 But how then would the scriptures be fulfilled, which say it must
happen in this way?" 55 At that hour
Jesus said to the crowds, "Have
you come out with swords and
clubs to arrest me as though I were
a bandit? Day after day I sat in the
temple teaching, and you did not
arrest me. 56 But all this has taken
place, so that the scriptures of the
prophets may be fulfilled." Then
all the disciples deserted him and
fled.

Jesus before the High Priest

57 Those who had arrested
Jesus took him to Caiaphas the
high priest, in whose house the
scribes and the elders had gathered. 58 But Peter was following
him at a distance, as far as the
courtyard of the high priest; and
going inside, he sat with the guards
in order to see how this would end.
59 Now the chief priests and the
whole council were looking for
false testimony against Jesus so
that they might put him to death,
60 but they found none, though
many false witnesses came forward. At last two came forward
61 and said, "This fellow said, 'I am
able to destroy the temple of God
and to build it in three days.' "
62 The high priest stood up and
said, "Have you no answer? What is
it that they testify against you?"
63 But Jesus was silent. Then the
high priest said to him, "I put you
under oath before the living God,
tell us if you are the Messiah,[o] the
Son of God." 64 Jesus said to him,
"You have said so. But I tell you,

From now on you will see
the Son of Man
seated at the right hand of
Power
and coming on the clouds
of heaven."

65 Then the high priest tore his
clothes and said, "He has blasphemed! Why do we still need witnesses? You have now heard his
blasphemy. 66 What is your verdict?" They answered, "He deserves death." 67 Then they spat in
his face and struck him; and some
slapped him, 68 saying, "Prophesy
to us, you Messiah![o] Who is it that
struck you?"

Peter's Denial of Jesus

69 Now Peter was sitting outside in the courtyard. A servant-girl
came to him and said, "You also

26.41 Mt 6.13; Lk 11.4
26.42 Jn 4.34; 5.30; 6.38
26.45 v. 18; Jn 12.23,27; 13.1; 17.1
26.47-56pp Mk 14.43-50; Lk 22.47-53; Jn 18.1-11
26.49 v. 25
26.50 Mt 20.13; 22.12
26.52 Gen 9.6; Rev 13.10
26.53 2 Kings 6.17; Dan 7.10
26.54 v. 24; Lk 24.25,44, 46
26.56 v. 54
26.57-68pp Mk 14.53-65; Jn 18.12-14, 19-25
26.58 Jn 18.15
26.60 Ps 27.12; 35.11; Acts 6.13; Deut 19.15
26.61 Mt 27.40
26.63 Isa 53.7; Mt 27.12, 14; Lev 5.1; Jn 18.33
26.64 Ps 110.1; Dan 7.13; Mt 16.27,28
26.65 Num 14.6; Acts 14.14; Lev 24.16
26.66 Jn 19.7
26.67 Isa 53.3; Mt 27.30; Jn 19.3
26.69-75pp Mk 14.66-72; Lk 22.55-63; Jn 18.15-18, 25-27

[n] Or *into temptation* [o] Or *Christ*

were with Jesus the Galilean."
70 But he denied it before all of
them, saying, "I do not know what
you are talking about." 71 When he
went out to the porch, another
servant-girl saw him, and she said
to the bystanders, "This man was
with Jesus of Nazareth."[p] 72 Again
he denied it with an oath, "I do not
know the man." 73 After a little
while the bystanders came up and
said to Peter, "Certainly you are
also one of them, for your accent
betrays you." 74 Then he began to
curse, and he swore an oath, "I do
not know the man!" At that moment the cock crowed. 75 Then Peter remembered what Jesus had
said: "Before the cock crows, you
will deny me three times." And he
went out and wept bitterly.

Jesus Brought before Pilate

27 When morning came, all
the chief priests and the elders of the people conferred together against Jesus in order to
bring about his death. 2 They
bound him, led him away, and
handed him over to Pilate the governor.

The Suicide of Judas

3 When Judas, his betrayer, saw
that Jesus[q] was condemned, he repented and brought back the thirty
pieces of silver to the chief priests
and the elders. 4 He said, "I have
sinned by betraying innocent[r]
blood." But they said, "What is that
to us? See to it yourself." 5 Throwing down the pieces of silver in the
temple, he departed; and he went
and hanged himself. 6 But the chief
priests, taking the pieces of silver,
said, "It is not lawful to put them
into the treasury, since they are
blood money." 7 After conferring
together, they used them to buy
the potter's field as a place to bury
foreigners. 8 For this reason that
field has been called the Field of
Blood to this day. 9 Then was fulfilled what had been spoken
through the prophet Jeremiah,[s]
"And they took[t] the thirty pieces
of silver, the price of the one on
whom a price had been set,[u] on
whom some of the people of Israel
had set a price, 10 and they gave[v]
them for the potter's field, as the
Lord commanded me."

Pilate Questions Jesus

11 Now Jesus stood before the
governor; and the governor asked
him, "Are you the King of the
Jews?" Jesus said, "You say so."
12 But when he was accused by the
chief priests and elders, he did not
answer. 13 Then Pilate said to him,
"Do you not hear how many accusations they make against you?"
14 But he gave him no answer, not
even to a single charge, so that the
governor was greatly amazed.

Barabbas or Jesus?

15 Now at the festival the governor was accustomed to release a
prisoner for the crowd, anyone
whom they wanted. 16 At that time
they had a notorious prisoner,
called Jesus[w] Barabbas. 17 So after
they had gathered, Pilate said to
them, "Whom do you want me to
release for you, Jesus[w] Barabbas or
Jesus who is called the Messiah?"[x]
18 For he realized that it was out of
jealousy that they had handed him
over. 19 While he was sitting on the
judgment seat, his wife sent word
to him, "Have nothing to do with
that innocent man, for today I have
suffered a great deal because of a
dream about him." 20 Now the chief
priests and the elders persuaded
the crowds to ask for Barabbas and
to have Jesus killed. 21 The governor again said to them, "Which of
the two do you want me to release
for you?" And they said, "Barabbas." 22 Pilate said to them, "Then
what should I do with Jesus who is
called the Messiah?"[x] All of them
said, "Let him be crucified!"
23 Then he asked, "Why, what evil
has he done?" But they shouted all

26.75 v. 34; Jn 13.38 **27.1-2pp** Mk 15.1; Lk 23.1; Jn 18.28 **27.2** Mt 20.19; Acts 3.13 **27.3** Mt 26.14,15 **27.4** v. 24 **27.5** Acts 1.18 **27.8** Acts 1.19 **27.9f** Zech 11.12, 13 **27.11-26pp** Mk 15.2-15; Lk 23.3-25; Jn 18.29-40 **27.12** Mt 26.63; Jn 19.9 **27.13** Mt 26.62; Jn 19.10 **27.14** 1 Tim 6.13 **27.19** Acts 12.21; v. 24 **27.20** Acts 3.14

[p] Gk *the Nazorean* [q] Gk *he* [r] Other ancient authorities read *righteous* [s] Other ancient authorities read *Zechariah* or *Isaiah* [t] Or *I took* [u] Or *the price of the precious One* [v] Other ancient authorities read *I gave* [w] Other ancient authorities lack *Jesus* [x] Or *the Christ*

the more, "Let him be crucified!"

Pilate Hands Jesus over to Be Crucified

24 So when Pilate saw that he
could do nothing, but rather that a
riot was beginning, he took some
water and washed his hands before
the crowd, saying, "I am innocent
of this man's blood;[y] see to it yourselves." 25 Then the people as a
whole answered, "His blood be on
us and on our children!" 26 So he
released Barabbas for them; and after flogging Jesus, he handed him
over to be crucified.

The Soldiers Mock Jesus

27 Then the soldiers of the governor took Jesus into the governor's headquarters,[z] and they
gathered the whole cohort around
him. 28 They stripped him and put a
scarlet robe on him, 29 and after
twisting some thorns into a crown,
they put it on his head. They put a
reed in his right hand and knelt before him and mocked him, saying,
"Hail, King of the Jews!" 30 They
spat on him, and took the reed and
struck him on the head. 31 After
mocking him, they stripped him of
the robe and put his own clothes
on him. Then they led him away to
crucify him.

The Crucifixion of Jesus

32 As they went out, they came
upon a man from Cyrene named Simon; they compelled this man to
carry his cross. 33 And when they
came to a place called Golgotha
(which means Place of a Skull),
34 they offered him wine to drink,
mixed with gall; but when he tasted it, he would not drink it. 35 And
when they had crucified him, they
divided his clothes among themselves by casting lots;[a] 36 then they
sat down there and kept watch over
him. 37 Over his head they put the
charge against him, which read,
"This is Jesus, the King of the
Jews."
38 Then two bandits were crucified with him, one on his right and
one on his left. 39 Those who passed
by derided[b] him, shaking their
heads 40 and saying, "You who
would destroy the temple and
build it in three days, save yourself!
If you are the Son of God, come
down from the cross." 41 In the
same way the chief priests also,
along with the scribes and elders,
were mocking him, saying, 42 "He
saved others; he cannot save himself.[c] He is the King of Israel; let
him come down from the cross
now, and we will believe in him.
43 He trusts in God; let God deliver
him now, if he wants to; for he said,
'I am God's Son.'" 44 The bandits
who were crucified with him also
taunted him in the same way.

The Death of Jesus

45 From noon on, darkness
came over the whole land[d] until
three in the afternoon. 46 And
about three o'clock Jesus cried
with a loud voice, "Eli, Eli, lema sa-
bachthani?" that is, "My God, my
God, why have you forsaken me?"
47 When some of the bystanders
heard it, they said, "This man is
calling for Elijah." 48 At once one of
them ran and got a sponge, filled it
with sour wine, put it on a stick,
and gave it to him to drink. 49 But
the others said, "Wait, let us see
whether Elijah will come to save
him."[e] 50 Then Jesus cried again
with a loud voice and breathed his
last.[f] 51 At that moment the curtain of the temple was torn in two,
from top to bottom. The earth
shook, and the rocks were split.
52 The tombs also were opened, and
many bodies of the saints who had
fallen asleep were raised. 53 After
his resurrection they came out of
the tombs and entered the holy city
and appeared to many. 54 Now
when the centurion and those with

27.24 Mt 26.5; Deut 21.6-8; Ps 26.6; v. 19
27.25 Josh 2.19; Acts 5.28
27.26 Isa 53.5
27.27-31pp Mk 15.16-20
27.27 Jn 18.28,33; Acts 10.1
27.29 Ps 69.19; Isa 53.3
27.30 Mt 26.67; Mk 10.34; 14.65
27.31 Isa 53.7
27.32-44pp Mk 15.21-32; Lk 23.32-43; Jn 19.17-24
27.32 Heb 13.12
27.34 Ps 69.21
27.35 Ps 22.18
27.36 v. 54
27.38 Isa 53.12
27.39 Ps 22.7; 109.25
27.40 Mt 26.61; Acts 6.14; Jn 2.19
27.42 Jn 1.49; 12.13
27.43 Ps 22.8
27.45-56pp Mk 15.33-41; Lk 23.41-49; Jn 19.28-37
27.45 Am 8.9
27.46 Ps 22.1
27.48 Ps 69.21
27.51 Ex 26.31; Heb 9.3; v. 54
27.54 Mt 3.17; 17.5

[y] Other ancient authorities read *this righteous blood*, or *this righteous man's blood*
[z] Gk *the praetorium*
[a] Other ancient authorities add *in order that what had been spoken through the prophet might be fulfilled, "They divided my clothes among themselves, and for my clothing they cast lots."*
[b] Or *blasphemed*
[c] Or *is he unable to save himself?*
[d] Or *earth*
[e] Other ancient authorities add *And another took a spear and pierced his side, and out came water and blood*
[f] Or *gave up his spirit*

him, who were keeping watch over
Jesus, saw the earthquake and
what took place, they were terrified
and said, "Truly this man was
God's Son!"[g]

55 Many women were also
there, looking on from a distance;
they had followed Jesus from Galilee and had provided for him.
56 Among them were Mary Magdalene, and Mary the mother of
James and Joseph, and the mother
of the sons of Zebedee.

The Burial of Jesus

57 When it was evening, there
came a rich man from Arimathea,
named Joseph, who was also a disciple of Jesus. 58 He went to Pilate
and asked for the body of Jesus;
then Pilate ordered it to be given to
him. 59 So Joseph took the body
and wrapped it in a clean linen
cloth 60 and laid it in his own new
tomb, which he had hewn in the
rock. He then rolled a great stone
to the door of the tomb and went
away. 61 Mary Magdalene and the
other Mary were there, sitting opposite the tomb.

The Guard at the Tomb

62 The next day, that is, after
the day of Preparation, the chief
priests and the Pharisees gathered
before Pilate 63 and said, "Sir, we
remember what that impostor said
while he was still alive, 'After three
days I will rise again.' 64 Therefore
command the tomb to be made secure until the third day; otherwise
his disciples may go and steal him
away, and tell the people, 'He has
been raised from the dead,' and the
last deception would be worse than
the first." 65 Pilate said to them,
"You have a guard[h] of soldiers; go,
make it as secure as you can."[i]
66 So they went with the guard and
made the tomb secure by sealing
the stone.

The Resurrection of Jesus

28 After the sabbath, as the
first day of the week was
dawning, Mary Magdalene and the
other Mary went to see the tomb.
2 And suddenly there was a great
earthquake; for an angel of the
Lord, descending from heaven,
came and rolled back the stone and
sat on it. 3 His appearance was like
lightning, and his clothing white as
snow. 4 For fear of him the guards
shook and became like dead men.
5 But the angel said to the women,
"Do not be afraid; I know that you
are looking for Jesus who was crucified. 6 He is not here; for he has
been raised, as he said. Come, see
the place where he[j] lay. 7 Then go
quickly and tell his disciples, 'He
has been raised from the dead,[k]
and indeed he is going ahead of you
to Galilee; there you will see him.'
This is my message for you." 8 So
they left the tomb quickly with fear
and great joy, and ran to tell his disciples. 9 Suddenly Jesus met them
and said, "Greetings!" And they
came to him, took hold of his feet,
and worshiped him. 10 Then Jesus
said to them, "Do not be afraid; go
and tell my brothers to go to Galilee; there they will see me."

The Report of the Guard

11 While they were going, some
of the guard went into the city and
told the chief priests everything
that had happened. 12 After the
priests[l] had assembled with the
elders, they devised a plan to give a
large sum of money to the soldiers,
13 telling them, "You must say, 'His
disciples came by night and stole
him away while we were asleep.'
14 If this comes to the governor's
ears, we will satisfy him and keep
you out of trouble." 15 So they took
the money and did as they were directed. And this story is still told
among the Jews to this day.

The Commissioning of the Disciples

16 Now the eleven disciples
went to Galilee, to the mountain to
which Jesus had directed them.
17 When they saw him, they worshiped him; but some doubted.
18 And Jesus came and said to

27.55 Lk 8.2,3
27.56 Mk 15.40, 47; Lk 24.10
27.57-61pp Mk 15.42-47; Lk 23.50-56; Jn 19.38-42
27.57 Acts 13.29
27.60 Mt 28.2; Mk 16.4
27.63 Mt 16.21; 17.23; 20.19; Mk 8.31; 10.34; Lk 9.22; 18.33; 24.6,7; Jn 2.19
27.66 v. 60; Mt 28.11-15
28.1-10pp Mk 16.1-8; Lk 24.1-11; Jn 20.1-18
28.1 Lk 8.2; Mt 27.56
28.2 Mt 27.51,60
28.3 Dan 7.9; 10.6; Mk 9.3; Jn 20.12; Acts 1.10
28.5 v. 10; Mt 14.27
28.6 Mt 12.40; 16.21; 17.23; 20.19
28.7 Mt 26.32; v. 16
28.9 Jn 20.14-18
28.10 Rom 8.29; Heb 2.11
28.11 Mt 27.65,66
28.14 Mt 27.2
28.16-20pp Mk 16.15-18
28.16 v. 7; Mt 26.32
28.18 Dan 7.13, 14; Lk 10.22; Phil 2.9,10; 1 Pet 3.22

[g] Or *a son of God* [h] Or *Take a guard* [i] Gk *you know how* [j] Other ancient authorities read *the Lord* [k] Other ancient authorities lack *from the dead* [l] Gk *they*

them, "All authority in heaven and
on earth has been given to me.
19 Go therefore and make disciples
of all nations, baptizing them in
the name of the Father and of the
Son and of the Holy Spirit, 20 and
teaching them to obey everything
that I have commanded you. And
remember, I am with you always, to
the end of the age."[m]

28.19 Lk 24.47; Acts 1.8
28.20 Acts 2.42; Mt 18.20; Acts 18.10

[m] Other ancient authorities add *Amen*

THE GOSPEL ACCORDING TO

Mark

Title and Background

The early church fathers agreed that Mark's Gospel reproduces the preaching of Peter. Peter's personality can be found on almost every page, and the main characteristic of this Gospel is action.

Author and Date of Writing

John Mark was the son of Mary (Acts 12.12) and the cousin of Barnabas (Col 4.10). He accompanied Paul and Barnabas on their first missionary journey (Acts 13.5). Paul spoke of him as his companion in Rome and paid high tribute to his service (2 Tim 4.11). It is believed that Mark is the first of the Gospels to be written, possibly when Christians were beginning to suffer persecution under Emperor Nero. It would therefore be dated about A.D. 65.

Theme and Message

The book of Mark stresses the facts and actions of Jesus rather than his words or sayings. Although it is the shortest of the four Gospels, it is often the most detailed. Jewish customs are carefully explained for Roman readers. One of Mark's purposes was to demonstrate the deity of Christ. He tells the stories of Christ's ministry, especially his miracles. Mark spends one-third of the book telling the events of Christ's last week on earth, ending with his death and resurrection.

Outline

I. The Beginnings of Jesus' Ministry (1.1-13)
II. Jesus' Ministry in Galilee (1.14–6.29)
III. Withdrawals From Galilee (6.30–9.32)
IV. Final Ministry in Galilee (9.33-50)
V. Jesus' Ministry in Judea and Perea (10.1-52)
VI. The Passion of Jesus (11.1–15.47)
VII. The Resurrection of Jesus (16.1-20)

The Proclamation of John the Baptist

1 The beginning of the good
news[a] of Jesus Christ, the Son
of God.[b]
2 As it is written in the prophet
Isaiah,[c]
"See, I am sending my
messenger ahead of
you,[d]
who will prepare your way;
3 the voice of one crying out in
the wilderness:
'Prepare the way of the
Lord,
make his paths straight,' "
4 John the baptizer appeared[e] in
the wilderness, proclaiming a baptism of repentance for the forgiveness of sins.
5 And people from the
whole Judean countryside and all
the people of Jerusalem were going
out to him, and were baptized by
him in the river Jordan, confessing
their sins.
6 Now John was clothed
with camel's hair, with a leather
belt around his waist, and he ate
locusts and wild honey.
7 He proclaimed, "The one who is more
powerful than I is coming after me;
I am not worthy to stoop down and
untie the thong of his sandals.
8 I

1.1-8pp Mt 3.1-12; Lk 3.2-17; Jn 1.6-8,19-28
1.1 Mt 4.3
1.2 Mal 3.1; Mt 11.10; Lk 7.27
1.3 Isa 40.3
1.4 Acts 13.24; Lk 1.77
1.6 Lev 11.22
1.7 Acts 13.25
1.8 Acts 1.5; Isa 44.3; Joel 2.28

[a] Or *gospel* [b] Other ancient authorities lack *the Son of God* [c] Other ancient authorities read *in the prophets* [d] Gk *before your face* [e] Other ancient authorities read *John was baptizing*

have baptized you with[f] water; but
he will baptize you with[f] the Holy
Spirit."

The Baptism of Jesus

9 In those days Jesus came from
Nazareth of Galilee and was baptized by John in the Jordan. 10 And
just as he was coming up out of the
water, he saw the heavens torn
apart and the Spirit descending
like a dove on him. 11 And a voice
came from heaven, "You are my
Son, the Beloved;[g] with you I am
well pleased."

The Temptation of Jesus

12 And the Spirit immediately
drove him out into the wilderness.
13 He was in the wilderness forty
days, tempted by Satan; and he was
with the wild beasts; and the angels waited on him.

The Beginning of the Galilean Ministry

14 Now after John was arrested,
Jesus came to Galilee, proclaiming
the good news[h] of God,[i] 15 and
saying, "The time is fulfilled, and
the kingdom of God has come
near;[j] repent, and believe in the
good news."[h]

Jesus Calls the First Disciples

16 As Jesus passed along the
Sea of Galilee, he saw Simon and
his brother Andrew casting a net
into the sea—for they were fishermen. 17 And Jesus said to them,
"Follow me and I will make you
fish for people." 18 And immediately they left their nets and followed
him. 19 As he went a little farther,
he saw James son of Zebedee and
his brother John, who were in their
boat mending the nets. 20 Immediately he called them; and they left
their father Zebedee in the boat
with the hired men, and followed
him.

The Man with an Unclean Spirit

21 They went to Capernaum;
and when the sabbath came, he entered the synagogue and taught.
22 They were astounded at his
teaching, for he taught them as one
having authority, and not as the
scribes. 23 Just then there was in
their synagogue a man with an unclean spirit, 24 and he cried out,
"What have you to do with us,
Jesus of Nazareth? Have you come
to destroy us? I know who you are,
the Holy One of God." 25 But Jesus
rebuked him, saying, "Be silent,
and come out of him!" 26 And the
unclean spirit, convulsing him and
crying with a loud voice, came out
of him. 27 They were all amazed,
and they kept on asking one another, "What is this? A new teaching—
with authority! He[k] commands
even the unclean spirits, and they
obey him." 28 At once his fame began to spread throughout the surrounding region of Galilee.

Jesus Heals Many at Simon's House

29 As soon as they[l] left the synagogue, they entered the house of
Simon and Andrew, with James
and John. 30 Now Simon's mother-
in-law was in bed with a fever, and
they told him about her at once.
31 He came and took her by the
hand and lifted her up. Then the
fever left her, and she began to
serve them.
32 That evening, at sundown,
they brought to him all who were
sick or possessed with demons.
33 And the whole city was gathered
around the door. 34 And he cured
many who were sick with various
diseases, and cast out many demons; and he would not permit the
demons to speak, because they
knew him.

A Preaching Tour in Galilee

35 In the morning, while it was
still very dark, he got up and went
out to a deserted place, and there
he prayed. 36 And Simon and his
companions hunted for him.
37 When they found him, they said
to him, "Everyone is searching for
you." 38 He answered, "Let us go on

1.9-11pp Mt 3.13-17; Lk 3.21,22
1.9 Mt 2.23
1.10 Jn 1.32
1.11 Ps 2.7; Isa 42.1
1.12,13pp Mt 4.1-11; Lk 4.1-13
1.14,15pp Mt 4.12-17; Lk 4.14,15; Jn 4.43-45
1.14 Mt 4.23
1.15 Gal 4.4; Eph 1.10; Acts 20.21
1.16-20pp Mt 4.18-22; Lk 5.1-11
1.18 Mt 19.27
1.21-28pp Lk 4.31-37
1.21 Mt 4.23
1.22 Mt 7.28
1.24 Mt 8.29; Mk 10.47; 14.67; Jn 6.69; Acts 3.14
1.25 v. 34
1.27 Mk 10.24, 32
1.29-31pp Mt 8.14-17; Lk 4.38-41
1.29 vv. 21,23
1.32-34pp Mt 8.16-17; Lk 4.40-41
1.32 Mk 4.24
1.34 Mt 4.23; Mk 3.12; Acts 16.17, 18
1.35 Mt 14.23; Lk 5.16
1.38 Isa 61.1

[f] Or *in* [g] Or *my beloved Son*
[h] Or *gospel* [i] Other ancient authorities read *of the kingdom* [j] Or *is at hand*
[k] Or *A new teaching! With authority he*
[l] Other ancient authorities read *he*

to the neighboring towns, so that I may proclaim the message there also; for that is what I came out to do." 39 And he went throughout Galilee, proclaiming the message in their synagogues and casting out demons.

Jesus Cleanses a Leper

40 A leper[m] came to him begging him, and kneeling[n] he said to him, "If you choose, you can make me clean." 41 Moved with pity,[o] Jesus[p] stretched out his hand and touched him, and said to him, "I do choose. Be made clean!" 42 Immediately the leprosy[m] left him, and he was made clean. 43 After sternly warning him he sent him away at once, 44 saying to him, "See that you say nothing to anyone; but go, show yourself to the priest, and offer for your cleansing what Moses commanded, as a testimony to them." 45 But he went out and began to proclaim it freely, and to spread the word, so that Jesus[p] could no longer go into a town openly, but stayed out in the country; and people came to him from every quarter.

Jesus Heals a Paralytic

2 When he returned to Capernaum after some days, it was reported that he was at home. 2 So many gathered around that there was no longer room for them, not even in front of the door; and he was speaking the word to them. 3 Then some people[q] came, bringing to him a paralyzed man, carried by four of them. 4 And when they could not bring him to Jesus because of the crowd, they removed the roof above him; and after having dug through it, they let down the mat on which the paralytic lay. 5 When Jesus saw their faith, he said to the paralytic, "Son, your sins are forgiven." 6 Now some of the scribes were sitting there, questioning in their hearts, 7 "Why does this fellow speak in this way? It is blasphemy! Who can forgive sins but God alone?" 8 At once Jesus perceived in his spirit that they were discussing these questions among themselves; and he said to them, "Why do you raise such questions in your hearts? 9 Which is easier, to say to the paralytic, 'Your sins are forgiven,' or to say, 'Stand up and take your mat and walk'? 10 But so that you may know that the Son of Man has authority on earth to forgive sins"—he said to the paralytic— 11 "I say to you, stand up, take your mat and go to your home." 12 And he stood up, and immediately took the mat and went out before all of them; so that they were all amazed and glorified God, saying, "We have never seen anything like this!"

Jesus Calls Levi

13 Jesus[r] went out again beside the sea; the whole crowd gathered around him, and he taught them. 14 As he was walking along, he saw Levi son of Alphaeus sitting at the tax booth, and he said to him, "Follow me." And he got up and followed him.

15 And as he sat at dinner[s] in Levi's[t] house, many tax collectors and sinners were also sitting[u] with Jesus and his disciples—for there were many who followed him. 16 When the scribes of[v] the Pharisees saw that he was eating with sinners and tax collectors, they said to his disciples, "Why does he eat[w] with tax collectors and sinners?" 17 When Jesus heard this, he said to them, "Those who are well have no need of a physician, but those who are sick; I have come to call not the righteous but sinners."

The Question about Fasting

18 Now John's disciples and the Pharisees were fasting; and people[q] came and said to him, "Why do John's disciples and the disciples of the Pharisees fast, but your

1.39 Mt 4.23-25
1.40-45pp Mt 8.1-4; Lk 5.12-16
1.40 Mk 10.17
1.44 Lev 13.49; 14.2-32
1.45 Lk 5.15; Mt 28.15; Mk 2.13; Lk 5.17; Jn 6.2
2.1-12pp Mt 9.1-8; Lk 5.17-26
2.2 v. 13
2.3 Mt 4.24
2.7 Isa 43.25
2.12 Mt 9.33
2.13-17pp Mt 9.9-13; Lk 5.27-32
2.13 Mk 1.45
2.14 Mt 8.22
2.16 Acts 23.9
2.17 Lk 19.10; 1 Tim 1.15
2.18-22pp Mt 9.14-17; Lk 5.33-39

[m] The terms *leper* and *leprosy* can refer to several diseases [n] Other ancient authorities lack *kneeling* [o] Other ancient authorities read *anger* [p] Gk *he* [q] Gk *they* [r] Gk *He* [s] Gk *reclined* [t] Gk *his* [u] Gk *reclining* [v] Other ancient authorities read *and* [w] Other ancient authorities add *and drink*

disciples do not fast?" 19 Jesus said
to them, "The wedding guests cannot fast while the bridegroom is
with them, can they? As long as
they have the bridegroom with
them, they cannot fast. 20 The days
will come when the bridegroom is
taken away from them, and then
they will fast on that day.

21 "No one sews a piece of unshrunk cloth on an old cloak; otherwise, the patch pulls away from
it, the new from the old, and a
worse tear is made. 22 And no one
puts new wine into old wineskins;
otherwise, the wine will burst the
skins, and the wine is lost, and so
are the skins; but one puts new
wine into fresh wineskins."[x]

Pronouncement about the Sabbath

23 One sabbath he was going
through the grainfields; and as they
made their way his disciples began
to pluck heads of grain. 24 The
Pharisees said to him, "Look, why
are they doing what is not lawful on
the sabbath?" 25 And he said to
them, "Have you never read what
David did when he and his companions were hungry and in need of
food? 26 He entered the house of
God, when Abiathar was high
priest, and ate the bread of the
Presence, which it is not lawful for
any but the priests to eat, and he
gave some to his companions."
27 Then he said to them, "The sabbath was made for humankind, and
not humankind for the sabbath;
28 so the Son of Man is lord even of
the sabbath."

The Man with a Withered Hand

3 Again he entered the synagogue, and a man was there
who had a withered hand. 2 They
watched him to see whether he
would cure him on the sabbath, so
that they might accuse him. 3 And
he said to the man who had the
withered hand, "Come forward."
4 Then he said to them, "Is it lawful
to do good or to do harm on the
sabbath, to save life or to kill?" But
they were silent. 5 He looked
around at them with anger; he was
grieved at their hardness of heart
and said to the man, "Stretch out
your hand." He stretched it out,
and his hand was restored. 6 The
Pharisees went out and immediately conspired with the Herodians
against him, how to destroy him.

A Multitude at the Seaside

7 Jesus departed with his disciples to the sea, and a great multitude from Galilee followed him;
8 hearing all that he was doing, they
came to him in great numbers from
Judea, Jerusalem, Idumea, beyond
the Jordan, and the region around
Tyre and Sidon. 9 He told his disciples to have a boat ready for him
because of the crowd, so that they
would not crush him; 10 for he had
cured many, so that all who had
diseases pressed upon him to
touch him. 11 Whenever the unclean spirits saw him, they fell
down before him and shouted,
"You are the Son of God!" 12 But he
sternly ordered them not to make
him known.

Jesus Appoints the Twelve

13 He went up the mountain
and called to him those whom he
wanted, and they came to him.
14 And he appointed twelve, whom
he also named apostles,[y] to be
with him, and to be sent out to proclaim the message, 15 and to have
authority to cast out demons. 16 So
he appointed the twelve:[z] Simon
(to whom he gave the name Peter);
17 James son of Zebedee and John
the brother of James (to whom he
gave the name Boanerges, that is,
Sons of Thunder); 18 and Andrew,
and Philip, and Bartholomew, and
Matthew, and Thomas, and James
son of Alphaeus, and Thaddaeus,
and Simon the Cananaean, 19 and
Judas Iscariot, who betrayed him.

Jesus and Beelzebul

Then he went home; 20 and the

2.20 Lk 17.22
2.23-28pp Mt 12.1-8 Lk 6.1-5
2.23 Deut 23.25
2.26 1 Sam 21.1-6; 2 Sam 8.17; Ex 29.32, 33; Lev 24.9
2.27 Ex 23.12; Deut 5.14
3.1-6pp Mt 12.9-14; Lk 6.6-11
3.1 Mk 1.21,39
3.2 Lk 14.1; 20.20; Mt 12.10
3.6 Mt 12.14; 22.16; Mk 12.13
3.7-12pp Mt 12.15-21
3.7 Mt 4.25
3.8 Mt 11.21
3.10 Mt 4.23; Mk 5.29,34; 6.56; 8.22
3.11 Mk 1.23,24; Lk 4.41; Mt 14.33
3.12 Mk 1.25,34
3.13-19pp Mt 10.1-4; Lk 6.12-16
3.13 Mt 5.1; Lk 9.1
3.16 Jn 1.42
3.20-27pp Mt 12.22-45; Lk 11.14-23
3.20 Mk 6.31

[x] Other ancient authorities lack *but one puts new wine into fresh wineskins* [y] Other ancient authorities lack *whom he also named apostles* [z] Other ancient authorities lack *So he appointed the twelve*

crowd came together again, so that
they could not even eat. 21When
his family heard it, they went out to
restrain him, for people were saying, "He has gone out of his mind."
22And the scribes who came down
from Jerusalem said, "He has Beelzebul, and by the ruler of the demons he casts out demons." 23And
he called them to him, and spoke
to them in parables, "How can Satan cast out Satan? 24If a kingdom
is divided against itself, that kingdom cannot stand. 25And if a house
is divided against itself, that house
will not be able to stand. 26And if
Satan has risen up against himself
and is divided, he cannot stand,
but his end has come. 27But no one
can enter a strong man's house and
plunder his property without first
tying up the strong man; then indeed the house can be plundered.
28 "Truly I tell you, people will
be forgiven for their sins and whatever blasphemies they utter; 29but
whoever blasphemes against the
Holy Spirit can never have forgiveness, but is guilty of an eternal
sin"— 30for they had said, "He has
an unclean spirit."

The True Kindred of Jesus

31 Then his mother and his
brothers came; and standing outside, they sent to him and called
him. 32A crowd was sitting around
him; and they said to him, "Your
mother and your brothers and sisters[a] are outside, asking for you."
33And he replied, "Who are my
mother and my brothers?" 34And
looking at those who sat around
him, he said, "Here are my mother
and my brothers! 35Whoever does
the will of God is my brother and
sister and mother."

The Parable of the Sower

4 Again he began to teach beside the sea. Such a very large
crowd gathered around him that he
got into a boat on the sea and sat
there, while the whole crowd was
beside the sea on the land. 2He began to teach them many things in
parables, and in his teaching he
said to them: 3"Listen! A sower
went out to sow. 4And as he sowed,
some seed fell on the path, and the
birds came and ate it up. 5Other
seed fell on rocky ground, where it
did not have much soil, and it
sprang up quickly, since it had no
depth of soil. 6And when the sun
rose, it was scorched; and since it
had no root, it withered away.
7Other seed fell among thorns, and
the thorns grew up and choked it,
and it yielded no grain. 8Other seed
fell into good soil and brought forth
grain, growing up and increasing
and yielding thirty and sixty and a
hundredfold." 9And he said, "Let
anyone with ears to hear listen!"

The Purpose of the Parables

10 When he was alone, those
who were around him along with
the twelve asked him about the
parables. 11And he said to them,
"To you has been given the secret[b]
of the kingdom of God, but for
those outside, everything comes in
parables; 12in order that
'they may indeed look, but
not perceive,
and may indeed listen, but
not understand;
so that they may not turn
again and be forgiven.' "
13 And he said to them, "Do
you not understand this parable?
Then how will you understand all
the parables? 14The sower sows the
word. 15These are the ones on the
path where the word is sown: when
they hear, Satan immediately
comes and takes away the word
that is sown in them. 16And these
are the ones sown on rocky ground:
when they hear the word, they immediately receive it with joy. 17But
they have no root, and endure only
for a while; then, when trouble or
persecution arises on account of
the word, immediately they fall
away.[c] 18And others are those
sown among the thorns: these are
the ones who hear the word, 19but
the cares of the world, and the lure
of wealth, and the desire for other

3.21 Jn 10.20; Acts 26.24
3.22 Mt 9.34; 10.25; Jn 7.20; 8.48,52
3.23 Mk 4.2ff
3.27 Isa 49.24,25
3.28 Lk 12.10
3.31-35pp Mt 12.46-50; Lk 8.19-21
3.31 Mt 12.46; Lk 8.19
4.1-9pp Mt 13.1-9; Lk 8.4-8
4.1 Mk 2.13; 3.7
4.2 Mk 3.23
4.8 Jn 15.5; Col 1.6
4.9 Mt 11.15
4.10-12pp Mt 13.10-17; Lk 8.9-10
4.11 1 Cor 5.12; Col 4.5; 1 Thes 4.12; 1 Tim 3.7
4.12 Isa 6.9; Jn 12.40; Acts 28.26; Rom 11.8
4.15 Mk 2.23,26

[a] Other ancient authorities lack *and sisters*
[b] Or *mystery* [c] Or *stumble*

things come in and choke the
word, and it yields nothing. 20 And
these are the ones sown on the
good soil: they hear the word and
accept it and bear fruit, thirty and
sixty and a hundredfold."

A Lamp under a Bushel Basket

21 He said to them, "Is a lamp
brought in to be put under the
bushel basket, or under the bed,
and not on the lampstand? 22 For
there is nothing hidden, except to
be disclosed; nor is anything secret, except to come to light. 23 Let
anyone with ears to hear listen!"
24 And he said to them, "Pay attention to what you hear; the measure
you give will be the measure you
get, and still more will be given
you. 25 For to those who have, more
will be given; and from those who
have nothing, even what they have
will be taken away."

The Parable of the Growing Seed

26 He also said, "The kingdom
of God is as if someone would scatter seed on the ground, 27 and
would sleep and rise night and day,
and the seed would sprout and
grow, he does not know how. 28 The
earth produces of itself, first the
stalk, then the head, then the full
grain in the head. 29 But when the
grain is ripe, at once he goes in with
his sickle, because the harvest has
come."

The Parable of the Mustard Seed

30 He also said, "With what can
we compare the kingdom of God,
or what parable will we use for it?
31 It is like a mustard seed, which,
when sown upon the ground, is the
smallest of all the seeds on earth;
32 yet when it is sown it grows up
and becomes the greatest of all
shrubs, and puts forth large
branches, so that the birds of the
air can make nests in its shade."

The Use of Parables

33 With many such parables he
spoke the word to them, as they
were able to hear it; 34 he did not
speak to them except in parables,
but he explained everything in private to his disciples.

Jesus Stills a Storm

35 On that day, when evening
had come, he said to them, "Let us
go across to the other side." 36 And
leaving the crowd behind, they
took him with them in the boat,
just as he was. Other boats were
with him. 37 A great windstorm
arose, and the waves beat into the
boat, so that the boat was already
being swamped. 38 But he was in
the stern, asleep on the cushion;
and they woke him up and said to
him, "Teacher, do you not care that
we are perishing?" 39 He woke up
and rebuked the wind, and said to
the sea, "Peace! Be still!" Then the
wind ceased, and there was a dead
calm. 40 He said to them, "Why are
you afraid? Have you still no faith?"
41 And they were filled with great
awe and said to one another, "Who
then is this, that even the wind and
the sea obey him?"

Jesus Heals the Gerasene Demoniac

5 They came to the other side of
the sea, to the country of the
Gerasenes.[d] 2 And when he had
stepped out of the boat, immediately a man out of the tombs with
an unclean spirit met him. 3 He
lived among the tombs; and no one
could restrain him any more, even
with a chain; 4 for he had often
been restrained with shackles and
chains, but the chains he wrenched
apart, and the shackles he broke in
pieces; and no one had the
strength to subdue him. 5 Night
and day among the tombs and on
the mountains he was always howling and bruising himself with
stones. 6 When he saw Jesus from a
distance, he ran and bowed down
before him; 7 and he shouted at the
top of his voice, "What have you to
do with me, Jesus, Son of the Most
High God? I adjure you by God, do
not torment me." 8 For he had said

4.21-25pp Mt 5.15; Lk 8.16; 11.33
4.22 Mt 10.26; Lk 8.17; 12.2
4.23 Mt 11.15
4.24 Mt 7.2; Lk 6.38
4.25 Mt 13.12; 25.29; Lk 8.18; 19.26
4.26 Mt 13.24
4.29 Rev 14.15
4.30-34pp Mt 13.31,32; Lk 13.18,19
4.30 Mt 13.24
4.33 Jn 16.12
4.34 Mt 13.34; Jn 16.25
4.35-41pp Mt 8.23-27; Lk 8.22-25
4.36 Mk 5.2,21
4.40 Mt 14.31, 32; Mk 16.14
5.1-20pp Mt 8.28-34; Lk 8.26-39
5.2 Mt 4.1; 1.23
5.6 Mt 4.9; 18.26
5.7 Mt 8.29; 4.3; Lk 8.28; Acts 16.17; Heb 7.1

[d] Other ancient authorities read *Gergesenes*; others, *Gadarenes*

to him, "Come out of the man, you
unclean spirit!" 9 Then Jesus[e]
asked him, "What is your name?"
He replied, "My name is Legion; for
we are many." 10 He begged him
earnestly not to send them out of
the country. 11 Now there on the
hillside a great herd of swine was
feeding; 12 and the unclean spirits[f]
begged him, "Send us into the
swine; let us enter them." 13 So he
gave them permission. And the unclean spirits came out and entered
the swine; and the herd, numbering about two thousand, rushed
down the steep bank into the sea,
and were drowned in the sea.

14 The swineherds ran off and
told it in the city and in the country. Then people came to see what
it was that had happened. 15 They
came to Jesus and saw the demoniac sitting there, clothed and in his
right mind, the very man who had
had the legion; and they were
afraid. 16 Those who had seen what
had happened to the demoniac and
to the swine reported it. 17 Then
they began to beg Jesus[g] to leave
their neighborhood. 18 As he was
getting into the boat, the man who
had been possessed by demons
begged him that he might be with
him. 19 But Jesus[e] refused, and
said to him, "Go home to your
friends, and tell them how much
the Lord has done for you, and
what mercy he has shown you."
20 And he went away and began to
proclaim in the Decapolis how
much Jesus had done for him; and
everyone was amazed.

A Girl Restored to Life and a Woman Healed

21 When Jesus had crossed
again in the boat[h] to the other
side, a great crowd gathered
around him; and he was by the sea.
22 Then one of the leaders of the
synagogue named Jairus came and,
when he saw him, fell at his feet
23 and begged him repeatedly, "My
little daughter is at the point of
death. Come and lay your hands on
her, so that she may be made well,
and live." 24 So he went with him.

5.15 vv. 16,18; Mt 4.24; v. 9
5.18 Acts 16.39
5.20 Mk 7.31; Mt 4.25
5.21-43pp Mt 9.18-26; Lk 8.40-56
5.21 Mt 9.1
5.22 Lk 8.49; 13.14; Acts 13.15; 18.8,17
5.23 Mk 6.5; 7.32; 8.23; Acts 9.17; 28.8
5.25 Lev 15.25
5.29 v. 34
5.30 Lk 5.17
5.34 Lk 7.50; 8.48; Acts 16.36; Jas 2.16
5.35 v. 22
5.36 Lk 8.50
5.37 Mt 17.1; 26.37
5.38 v. 22
5.39 Jn 11.11

And a large crowd followed him
and pressed in on him. 25 Now
there was a woman who had been
suffering from hemorrhages for
twelve years. 26 She had endured
much under many physicians, and
had spent all that she had; and she
was no better, but rather grew
worse. 27 She had heard about
Jesus, and came up behind him in
the crowd and touched his cloak,
28 for she said, "If I but touch his
clothes, I will be made well." 29 Immediately her hemorrhage
stopped; and she felt in her body
that she was healed of her disease.
30 Immediately aware that power
had gone forth from him, Jesus
turned about in the crowd and said,
"Who touched my clothes?" 31 And
his disciples said to him, "You see
the crowd pressing in on you; how
can you say, 'Who touched me?' "
32 He looked all around to see who
had done it. 33 But the woman,
knowing what had happened to
her, came in fear and trembling,
fell down before him, and told him
the whole truth. 34 He said to her,
"Daughter, your faith has made
you well; go in peace, and be
healed of your disease."

35 While he was still speaking,
some people came from the leader's house to say, "Your daughter is
dead. Why trouble the teacher any
further?" 36 But overhearing[i] what
they said, Jesus said to the leader
of the synagogue, "Do not fear,
only believe." 37 He allowed no one
to follow him except Peter, James,
and John, the brother of James.
38 When they came to the house of
the leader of the synagogue, he saw
a commotion, people weeping and
wailing loudly. 39 When he had entered, he said to them, "Why do
you make a commotion and weep?
The child is not dead but sleeping."
40 And they laughed at him. Then
he put them all outside, and took
the child's father and mother and
those who were with him, and went

[e] Gk *he* [f] Gk *they* [g] Gk *him*
[h] Other ancient authorities lack *in the boat*
[i] Or *ignoring*; other ancient authorities read *hearing*

in where the child was. 41 He took
her by the hand and said to her,
"Talitha cum," which means, "Little girl, get up!" 42 And immediately
the girl got up and began to walk
about (she was twelve years of age).
At this they were overcome with
amazement. 43 He strictly ordered
them that no one should know this,
and told them to give her something to eat.

The Rejection of Jesus at Nazareth

6 He left that place and came to
his hometown, and his disciples followed him. 2 On the sabbath
he began to teach in the synagogue, and many who heard him
were astounded. They said, "Where
did this man get all this? What is
this wisdom that has been given to
him? What deeds of power are being done by his hands! 3 Is not this
the carpenter, the son of Mary[j]
and brother of James and Joses
and Judas and Simon, and are not
his sisters here with us?" And they
took offense[k] at him. 4 Then Jesus
said to them, "Prophets are not
without honor, except in their
hometown, and among their own
kin, and in their own house." 5 And
he could do no deed of power
there, except that he laid his hands
on a few sick people and cured
them. 6 And he was amazed at their
unbelief.

The Mission of the Twelve

Then he went about among the
villages teaching. 7 He called the
twelve and began to send them out
two by two, and gave them authority over the unclean spirits. 8 He ordered them to take nothing for
their journey except a staff; no
bread, no bag, no money in their
belts; 9 but to wear sandals and not
to put on two tunics. 10 He said to
them, "Wherever you enter a
house, stay there until you leave
the place. 11 If any place will not
welcome you and they refuse to
hear you, as you leave, shake off
the dust that is on your feet as a
testimony against them." 12 So they

5.41 Lk 7.14; Acts 9.40
5.43 Mt 8.4
6.1-6pp Mt 13.53-58; Lk 4.16-30
6.2 Mt 4.23; 7.28; Mk 1.21
6.3 Mt 12.46; 11.6
6.4 Jn 4.44
6.6 Mt 9.35; Lk 13.22
6.7-13pp Mt 10.1-15; Lk 9.1-6
6.7 Mk 3.13; Lk 10.1
6.12 Mt 11.1; Lk 9.6
6.13 Jas 5.14
6.14-29pp Mt 14.1-12; Lk 9.7-9
6.15 Mt 16.14; Mk 8.28; Mt 21.11
6.16 Lk 3.19
6.18 Lev 18.16; 20.21
6.20 Mt 21.26
6.21 Esther 1.3; 2.18
6.23 Esther 5.3, 6; 7.2

went out and proclaimed that all
should repent. 13 They cast out
many demons, and anointed with
oil many who were sick and cured
them.

The Death of John the Baptist

14 King Herod heard of it, for
Jesus'[l] name had become known.
Some were[m] saying, "John the baptizer has been raised from the
dead; and for this reason these
powers are at work in him." 15 But
others said, "It is Elijah." And others said, "It is a prophet, like one of
the prophets of old." 16 But when
Herod heard of it, he said, "John,
whom I beheaded, has been
raised."

17 For Herod himself had sent
men who arrested John, bound
him, and put him in prison on account of Herodias, his brother Philip's wife, because Herod[n] had
married her. 18 For John had been
telling Herod, "It is not lawful for
you to have your brother's wife."
19 And Herodias had a grudge
against him, and wanted to kill
him. But she could not, 20 for Herod
feared John, knowing that he was a
righteous and holy man, and he
protected him. When he heard
him, he was greatly perplexed;[o]
and yet he liked to listen to him.
21 But an opportunity came when
Herod on his birthday gave a banquet for his courtiers and officers
and for the leaders of Galilee.
22 When his daughter Herodias[p]
came in and danced, she pleased
Herod and his guests; and the king
said to the girl, "Ask me for whatever you wish, and I will give it."
23 And he solemnly swore to her,
"Whatever you ask me, I will give
you, even half of my kingdom."
24 She went out and said to her
mother, "What should I ask for?"
She replied, "The head of John the
baptizer." 25 Immediately she

[j] Other ancient authorities read *son of the carpenter and of Mary* [k] Or *stumbled* [l] Gk *his* [m] Other ancient authorities read *He was* [n] Gk *he* [o] Other ancient authorities read *he did many things* [p] Other ancient authorities read *the daughter of Herodias herself*

rushed back to the king and requested, "I want you to give me at once the head of John the Baptist on a platter." [26]The king was deeply grieved; yet out of regard for his oaths and for the guests, he did not want to refuse her. [27]Immediately the king sent a soldier of the guard with orders to bring John's[q] head. He went and beheaded him in the prison, [28]brought his head on a platter, and gave it to the girl. Then the girl gave it to her mother. [29]When his disciples heard about it, they came and took his body, and laid it in a tomb.

Feeding the Five Thousand

30 The apostles gathered around Jesus, and told him all that they had done and taught. [31]He said to them, "Come away to a deserted place all by yourselves and rest a while." For many were coming and going, and they had no leisure even to eat. [32]And they went away in the boat to a deserted place by themselves. [33]Now many saw them going and recognized them, and they hurried there on foot from all the towns and arrived ahead of them. [34]As he went ashore, he saw a great crowd; and he had compassion for them, because they were like sheep without a shepherd; and he began to teach them many things. [35]When it grew late, his disciples came to him and said, "This is a deserted place, and the hour is now very late; [36]send them away so that they may go into the surrounding country and villages and buy something for themselves to eat." [37]But he answered them, "You give them something to eat." They said to him, "Are we to go and buy two hundred denarii[r] worth of bread, and give it to them to eat?" [38]And he said to them, "How many loaves have you? Go and see." When they had found out, they said, "Five, and two fish." [39]Then he ordered them to get all the people to sit down in groups on the green grass. [40]So they sat down in groups of hundreds and of fifties. [41]Taking the five loaves and the two fish, he looked up to heaven, and blessed and broke the loaves, and gave them to his disciples to set before the people; and he divided the two fish among them all. [42]And all ate and were filled; [43]and they took up twelve baskets full of broken pieces and of the fish. [44]Those who had eaten the loaves numbered five thousand men.

Jesus Walks on the Water

45 Immediately he made his disciples get into the boat and go on ahead to the other side, to Bethsaida, while he dismissed the crowd. [46]After saying farewell to them, he went up on the mountain to pray.

47 When evening came, the boat was out on the sea, and he was alone on the land. [48]When he saw that they were straining at the oars against an adverse wind, he came towards them early in the morning, walking on the sea. He intended to pass them by. [49]But when they saw him walking on the sea, they thought it was a ghost and cried out; [50]for they all saw him and were terrified. But immediately he spoke to them and said, "Take heart, it is I; do not be afraid." [51]Then he got into the boat with them and the wind ceased. And they were utterly astounded, [52]for they did not understand about the loaves, but their hearts were hardened.

Healing the Sick in Gennesaret

53 When they had crossed over, they came to land at Gennesaret and moored the boat. [54]When they got out of the boat, people at once recognized him, [55]and rushed about that whole region and began to bring the sick on mats to wherever they heard he was. [56]And wherever he went, into villages or cities or farms, they laid the sick in the marketplaces, and begged him that they might touch even the fringe of

6.30-44pp Mt 14.13-21; Lk 9.10-17; Jn 6.1-13
6.31 Mk 3.20
6.32 v. 45
6.34 Mt 9.36
6.37 2 Kings 4.42-44
6.38 Mt 15.34; Mk 8.5
6.41 Mt 26.26; Mk 14.22; Lk 24.30,31
6.45-52pp Mt. 14.22-32; Jn 6.15-21
6.45 v. 32; Mt 11.21; Mk 8.22
6.48 Mt 13.35; 24.43
6.50 Mt 9.2
6.51 v. 32
6.52 Mk 8.17,18; 3.5
6.53-56pp Mt 14.34-36
6.53 Jn 6.24,25
6.56 Mk 3.10; Mt 9.20

[q] Gk *his* [r] The denarius was the usual day's wage for a laborer

his cloak; and all who touched it
were healed.

The Tradition of the Elders

7 Now when the Pharisees and
some of the scribes who had
come from Jerusalem gathered
around him, 2 they noticed that
some of his disciples were eating
with defiled hands, that is, without
washing them. 3 (For the Pharisees,
and all the Jews, do not eat unless
they thoroughly wash their
hands,[s] thus observing the tradition of the elders; 4 and they do not
eat anything from the market unless they wash it;[t] and there are
also many other traditions that
they observe, the washing of cups,
pots, and bronze kettles.[u]) 5 So the
Pharisees and the scribes asked
him, "Why do your disciples not
live[v] according to the tradition of
the elders, but eat with defiled
hands?" 6 He said to them, "Isaiah
prophesied rightly about you hypocrites, as it is written,

'This people honors me with
their lips,
but their hearts are far
from me;
7 in vain do they worship me,
teaching human precepts
as doctrines.'

8 You abandon the commandment
of God and hold to human tradition."
9 Then he said to them, "You
have a fine way of rejecting the
commandment of God in order to
keep your tradition! 10 For Moses
said, 'Honor your father and your
mother'; and, 'Whoever speaks evil
of father or mother must surely
die.' 11 But you say that if anyone
tells father or mother, 'Whatever
support you might have had from
me is Corban' (that is, an offering
to God[w]) — 12 then you no longer
permit doing anything for a father
or mother, 13 thus making void the
word of God through your tradition
that you have handed on. And you
do many things like this."
14 Then he called the crowd
again and said to them, "Listen to
me, all of you, and understand:

7.1-23pp Mt 15.1-20
7.3 v. 5; Acts 10.14, 28; 11.8
7.4 Mt 23.25; Lk 11.39
7.5 vv. 3,8,9,13; Gal 1.14
7.6 Isa 29.13
7.8 vv. 5,9,13
7.9 vv. 5,8,13
7.10 Ex 20.12; Deut 5.6; Ex 21.17; Lev 20.9
7.11 Mt 23.18
7.13 vv. 5,8,9
7.17 Mk 9.28
7.19 Rom 14.1-12; Col 2.16; Lk 11.41; Acts 10.15; 11.9
7.22 Mt 6.23; 20.15
7.24-30pp Mt 15.21-28
7.24 Mt 11.21

15 there is nothing outside a person
that by going in can defile, but the
things that come out are what defile."[x]
17 When he had left the crowd
and entered the house, his disciples asked him about the parable.
18 He said to them, "Then do you
also fail to understand? Do you not
see that whatever goes into a person from outside cannot defile,
19 since it enters, not the heart but
the stomach, and goes out into the
sewer?" (Thus he declared all foods
clean.) 20 And he said, "It is what
comes out of a person that defiles.
21 For it is from within, from the human heart, that evil intentions
come: fornication, theft, murder,
22 adultery, avarice, wickedness,
deceit, licentiousness, envy, slander, pride, folly. 23 All these evil
things come from within, and they
defile a person."

The Syrophoenician Woman's Faith

24 From there he set out and
went away to the region of Tyre.[y]
He entered a house and did not
want anyone to know he was there.
Yet he could not escape notice,
25 but a woman whose little daughter had an unclean spirit immediately heard about him, and she
came and bowed down at his feet.
26 Now the woman was a Gentile, of
Syrophoenician origin. She begged
him to cast the demon out of her
daughter. 27 He said to her, "Let the
children be fed first, for it is not fair
to take the children's food and
throw it to the dogs." 28 But she answered him, "Sir,[z] even the dogs
under the table eat the children's
crumbs." 29 Then he said to her,
"For saying that, you may go — the
demon has left your daughter."
30 So she went home, found the

[s] Meaning of Gk uncertain [t] Other ancient authorities read *and when they come from the marketplace, they do not eat unless they purify themselves* [u] Other ancient authorities add *and beds* [v] Gk *walk* [w] Gk lacks *to God*
[x] Other ancient authorities add verse 16, *"Let anyone with ears to hear listen"* [y] Other ancient authorities add *and Sidon*
[z] Or *Lord*; other ancient authorities prefix *Yes*

child lying on the bed, and the demon gone.

Jesus Cures a Deaf Man

31 Then he returned from the
region of Tyre, and went by way of
Sidon towards the Sea of Galilee, in
the region of the Decapolis. 32 They
brought to him a deaf man who had
an impediment in his speech; and
they begged him to lay his hand on
him. 33 He took him aside in private, away from the crowd, and put
his fingers into his ears, and he
spat and touched his tongue.
34 Then looking up to heaven, he
sighed and said to him, "Ephpha-
tha," that is, "Be opened." 35 And
immediately his ears were opened,
his tongue was released, and he
spoke plainly. 36 Then Jesus[a] ordered them to tell no one; but the
more he ordered them, the more
zealously they proclaimed it.
37 They were astounded beyond
measure, saying, "He has done everything well; he even makes the
deaf to hear and the mute to
speak."

Feeding the Four Thousand

8 In those days when there was
again a great crowd without
anything to eat, he called his disciples and said to them, 2 "I have
compassion for the crowd, because
they have been with me now for
three days and have nothing to eat.
3 If I send them away hungry to
their homes, they will faint on the
way—and some of them have
come from a great distance." 4 His
disciples replied, "How can one
feed these people with bread here
in the desert?" 5 He asked them,
"How many loaves do you have?"
They said, "Seven." 6 Then he ordered the crowd to sit down on the
ground; and he took the seven
loaves, and after giving thanks he
broke them and gave them to his
disciples to distribute; and they
distributed them to the crowd.
7 They had also a few small fish;
and after blessing them, he ordered
that these too should be distributed. 8 They ate and were filled; and
they took up the broken pieces left
over, seven baskets full. 9 Now
there were about four thousand
people. And he sent them away.
10 And immediately he got into the
boat with his disciples and went to
the district of Dalmanutha.[b]

The Demand for a Sign

11 The Pharisees came and began to argue with him, asking him
for a sign from heaven, to test him.
12 And he sighed deeply in his spirit
and said, "Why does this generation ask for a sign? Truly I tell you,
no sign will be given to this generation." 13 And he left them, and getting into the boat again, he went
across to the other side.

The Yeast of the Pharisees and of Herod

14 Now the disciples[c] had forgotten to bring any bread; and they
had only one loaf with them in the
boat. 15 And he cautioned them,
saying, "Watch out—beware of the
yeast of the Pharisees and the yeast
of Herod."[d] 16 They said to one another, "It is because we have no
bread." 17 And becoming aware of
it, Jesus said to them, "Why are you
talking about having no bread? Do
you still not perceive or understand? Are your hearts hardened?
18 Do you have eyes, and fail to see?
Do you have ears, and fail to hear?
And do you not remember? 19 When
I broke the five loaves for the five
thousand, how many baskets full of
broken pieces did you collect?"
They said to him, "Twelve." 20 "And
the seven for the four thousand,
how many baskets full of broken
pieces did you collect?" And they
said to him, "Seven." 21 Then he
said to them, "Do you not yet understand?"

Jesus Cures a Blind Man at Bethsaida

22 They came to Bethsaida.
Some people[e] brought a blind man

7.31-37pp Mt 15.29-31 **7.32** Mk 5.23; Mt 9.32; Lk 11.14 **7.33** Mk 8.23 **7.34** Mk 6.41; 8.12 **7.35** Isa 35.5,6 **7.36** Mk 1.44; 5.43 **8.1-10pp** Mt 15.32-39 **8.2** Mt 9.36 **8.5** Mk 6.38 **8.7** Mt 14.19; Mk 6.41 **8.11-21pp** Mt 16.1-10 **8.11** Mt 12.38, 39; Lk 11.29; Jn 6.30 **8.12** Mk 7.34 **8.15** Lk 12.1; Mk 12.13 **8.17** Mk 6.52; Isa 6.9,10 **8.19** Mt 14.20; Mk 6.43; Lk 9.17; Jn 6.13 **8.20** vv. 6-9; Mt 15.37 **8.21** Mk 6.52 **8.22** Mt 11.21; Mk 6.45; Lk 9.10

[a] Gk *he* [b] Other ancient authorities read *Mageda* or *Magdala* [c] Gk *they* [d] Other ancient authorities read *the Herodians* [e] Gk *They*

to him and begged him to touch
him. 23 He took the blind man by
the hand and led him out of the village; and when he had put saliva on
his eyes and laid his hands on him,
he asked him, "Can you see anything?" 24 And the man[f] looked up
and said, "I can see people, but
they look like trees, walking."
25 Then Jesus[f] laid his hands on
his eyes again; and he looked intently and his sight was restored,
and he saw everything clearly.
26 Then he sent him away to his
home, saying, "Do not even go into
the village."[g]

Peter's Declaration about Jesus

27 Jesus went on with his disciples to the villages of Caesarea Philippi; and on the way he asked his
disciples, "Who do people say that
I am?" 28 And they answered him,
"John the Baptist; and others, Elijah; and still others, one of the
prophets." 29 He asked them, "But
who do you say that I am?" Peter
answered him, "You are the Messiah."[h] 30 And he sternly ordered
them not to tell anyone about him.

Jesus Foretells His Death and Resurrection

31 Then he began to teach them
that the Son of Man must undergo
great suffering, and be rejected by
the elders, the chief priests, and
the scribes, and be killed, and after
three days rise again. 32 He said all
this quite openly. And Peter took
him aside and began to rebuke
him. 33 But turning and looking at
his disciples, he rebuked Peter and
said, "Get behind me, Satan! For
you are setting your mind not on
divine things but on human
things."

34 He called the crowd with his
disciples, and said to them, "If any
want to become my followers, let
them deny themselves and take up
their cross and follow me. 35 For
those who want to save their life
will lose it, and those who lose
their life for my sake, and for the
sake of the gospel,[i] will save it.
36 For what will it profit them to

8.23 Mk 7.33; 5.23 **8.26** Mt 8.4 **8.27-30pp** Mt 16.13-20; Lk 9.18-21 **8.27** Jn 6.66-69 **8.28** Mk 6.14 **8.29** Jn 6.69; 11.27 **8.30** Mk 9.9 **8.31-9.1pp** Mt 16.21-28; Lk 9.22-27 **8.32** Jn 18.20 **8.33** Mt 4.10 **8.34** Mt 10.38; Lk 14.27 **8.35** Mt 10.39; Lk 17.33; Jn 12.25

8.38 Mt 10.33; Lk 12.9; Mt 8.20; Mk 13.26 **9.1** Mt 24.30; 25.31; Mk 13.30; Lk 22.18 **9.2-13pp** Mt 17.1-8; Lk 9.28-36 **9.2** Mk 5.37; 13.3 **9.3** Mt 28.3 **9.5** Mt 23.7 **9.7** 2 Pet 1.17, 18; Mk 1.11 **9.9** Mk 5.43; 7.36; 8.30 **9.11** Mt 11.14 **9.12** Ps 22.6; Lk 23.11; Phil 2.7

gain the whole world and forfeit
their life? 37 Indeed, what can they
give in return for their life? 38 Those
who are ashamed of me and of my
words[j] in this adulterous and sinful generation, of them the Son of
Man will also be ashamed when he
comes in the glory of his Father
9 with the holy angels." 1 And he
said to them, "Truly I tell you,
there are some standing here who
will not taste death until they see
that the kingdom of God has come
with[k] power."

The Transfiguration

2 Six days later, Jesus took with
him Peter and James and John,
and led them up a high mountain
apart, by themselves. And he was
transfigured before them, 3 and his
clothes became dazzling white,
such as no one[l] on earth could
bleach them. 4 And there appeared
to them Elijah with Moses, who
were talking with Jesus. 5 Then Peter said to Jesus, "Rabbi, it is good
for us to be here; let us make three
dwellings,[m] one for you, one for
Moses, and one for Elijah." 6 He did
not know what to say, for they were
terrified. 7 Then a cloud overshadowed them, and from the cloud
there came a voice, "This is my
Son, the Beloved;[n] listen to him!"
8 Suddenly when they looked
around, they saw no one with them
any more, but only Jesus.

The Coming of Elijah

9 As they were coming down the
mountain, he ordered them to tell
no one about what they had seen,
until after the Son of Man had risen
from the dead. 10 So they kept the
matter to themselves, questioning
what this rising from the dead
could mean. 11 Then they asked
him, "Why do the scribes say that
Elijah must come first?" 12 He said
to them, "Elijah is indeed coming

[f] Gk *he* [g] Other ancient authorities add *or tell anyone in the village* [h] Or *the Christ* [i] Other ancient authorities read *lose their life for the sake of the gospel* [j] Other ancient authorities read *and of mine* [k] Or *in* [l] Gk *no fuller* [m] Or *tents* [n] Or *my beloved Son*

first to restore all things. How then is it written about the Son of Man, that he is to go through many sufferings and be treated with contempt? 13 But I tell you that Elijah has come, and they did to him whatever they pleased, as it is written about him."

The Healing of a Boy with a Spirit

14 When they came to the disciples, they saw a great crowd around them, and some scribes arguing with them. 15 When the whole crowd saw him, they were immediately overcome with awe, and they ran forward to greet him. 16 He asked them, "What are you arguing about with them?" 17 Someone from the crowd answered him, "Teacher, I brought you my son; he has a spirit that makes him unable to speak; 18 and whenever it seizes him, it dashes him down; and he foams and grinds his teeth and becomes rigid; and I asked your disciples to cast it out, but they could not do so." 19 He answered them, "You faithless generation, how much longer must I be among you? How much longer must I put up with you? Bring him to me." 20 And they brought the boy[o] to him. When the spirit saw him, immediately it convulsed the boy,[o] and he fell on the ground and rolled about, foaming at the mouth. 21 Jesus[p] asked the father, "How long has this been happening to him?" And he said, "From childhood. 22 It has often cast him into the fire and into the water, to destroy him; but if you are able to do anything, have pity on us and help us." 23 Jesus said to him, "If you are able! — All things can be done for the one who believes." 24 Immediately the father of the child cried out,[q] "I believe; help my unbelief!" 25 When Jesus saw that a crowd came running together, he rebuked the unclean spirit, saying to it, "You spirit that keeps this boy from speaking and hearing, I command you, come out of him, and never enter him again!" 26 After crying out and convulsing him terribly, it came out, and the boy was like a corpse, so that most of them said, "He is dead." 27 But Jesus took him by the hand and lifted him up, and he was able to stand. 28 When he had entered the house, his disciples asked him privately, "Why could we not cast it out?" 29 He said to them, "This kind can come out only through prayer."[r]

Jesus Again Foretells His Death and Resurrection

30 They went on from there and passed through Galilee. He did not want anyone to know it; 31 for he was teaching his disciples, saying to them, "The Son of Man is to be betrayed into human hands, and they will kill him, and three days after being killed, he will rise again." 32 But they did not understand what he was saying and were afraid to ask him.

Who Is the Greatest?

33 Then they came to Capernaum; and when he was in the house he asked them, "What were you arguing about on the way?" 34 But they were silent, for on the way they had argued with one another who was the greatest. 35 He sat down, called the twelve, and said to them, "Whoever wants to be first must be last of all and servant of all." 36 Then he took a little child and put it among them; and taking it in his arms, he said to them, 37 "Whoever welcomes one such child in my name welcomes me, and whoever welcomes me welcomes not me but the one who sent me."

Another Exorcist

38 John said to him, "Teacher, we saw someone[s] casting out demons in your name, and we tried to stop him, because he was not following us." 39 But Jesus said, "Do not stop him; for no one who does

9.13 Mt 11.14; Lk 1.17
9.14-29pp Mt 17.14-21; Lk 9.37-43
9.15 Mk 14.33; 16.5,6
9.20 Mk 1.26
9.23 Mk 11.23; Lk 17.6; Jn 11.40
9.25 v. 15
9.28 Mk 7.17
9.30-32pp Mt 17.22-23 Lk 9.43-45
9.31 Mt 16.21; Mk 8.31
9.32 Jn 12.16
9.33-50pp Mt 18.1-5; Lk 9.46-48
9.34 Lk 22.24
9.35 Mt 20.26, 27; Mk 10.43; Lk 22.26
9.36 Mk 10.16
9.37 Mt 10.40; Jn 12.44; 13.20
9.38 Num 11.27-29

[o] Gk *him* [p] Gk *He* [q] Other ancient authorities add *with tears* [r] Other ancient authorities add *and fasting* [s] Other ancient authorities add *who does not follow us*

a deed of power in my name will be
able soon afterward to speak evil of
me. 40 Whoever is not against us is
for us. 41 For truly I tell you, whoever gives you a cup of water to drink
because you bear the name of
Christ will by no means lose the reward.

Temptations to Sin

42 "If any of you put a stumbling block before one of these little ones who believe in me,[t] it
would be better for you if a great
millstone were hung around your
neck and you were thrown into the
sea. 43 If your hand causes you to
stumble, cut it off; it is better for
you to enter life maimed than to
have two hands and to go to hell,[u]
to the unquenchable fire.[v] 45 And
if your foot causes you to stumble,
cut it off; it is better for you to enter
life lame than to have two feet and
to be thrown into hell.[u,v] 47 And if
your eye causes you to stumble,
tear it out; it is better for you to
enter the kingdom of God with one
eye than to have two eyes and to be
thrown into hell,[u] 48 where their
worm never dies, and the fire is
never quenched.
49 "For everyone will be salted
with fire.[w] 50 Salt is good; but if salt
has lost its saltiness, how can you
season it?[x] Have salt in yourselves,
and be at peace with one another."

Teaching about Divorce

10 He left that place and went
to the region of Judea and[y]
beyond the Jordan. And crowds
again gathered around him; and, as
was his custom, he again taught
them.
2 Some Pharisees came, and to
test him they asked, "Is it lawful for
a man to divorce his wife?" 3 He answered them, "What did Moses
command you?" 4 They said, "Moses allowed a man to write a certificate of dismissal and to divorce
her." 5 But Jesus said to them, "Because of your hardness of heart he
wrote this commandment for you.
6 But from the beginning of creation, 'God made them male and
female.' 7 'For this reason a man
shall leave his father and mother
and be joined to his wife,[z] 8 and
the two shall become one flesh.' So
they are no longer two, but one
flesh. 9 Therefore what God has
joined together, let no one separate."
10 Then in the house the disciples asked him again about this
matter. 11 He said to them, "Whoever divorces his wife and marries
another commits adultery against
her; 12 and if she divorces her husband and marries another, she
commits adultery."

Jesus Blesses Little Children

13 People were bringing little
children to him in order that he
might touch them; and the disciples spoke sternly to them. 14 But
when Jesus saw this, he was indignant and said to them, "Let the little children come to me; do not
stop them; for it is to such as these
that the kingdom of God belongs.
15 Truly I tell you, whoever does not
receive the kingdom of God as a little child will never enter it." 16 And
he took them up in his arms, laid
his hands on them, and blessed
them.

The Rich Man

17 As he was setting out on a
journey, a man ran up and knelt before him, and asked him, "Good
Teacher, what must I do to inherit
eternal life?" 18 Jesus said to him,
"Why do you call me good? No one
is good but God alone. 19 You know
the commandments: 'You shall not
murder; You shall not commit
adultery; You shall not steal; You
shall not bear false witness; You
shall not defraud; Honor your father and mother.' " 20 He said to
him, "Teacher, I have kept all these
since my youth." 21 Jesus, looking

9.40 Mt 12.30
9.41 Mt 10.42
9.42 Lk 17.1,2; 1 Cor 8.12
9.43 Mt 5.29,30; 5.22; 25.41
9.45 Mt 5.22
9.47 Mt 5.29
9.48 Isa 66.24
9.49 Lev 2.13
9.50 Mt 5.13; Lk 14.34,35; Col 4.6; Rom 12.18; 2 Cor 13.11; 1 Thes 5.13
10.1 Mt 19.1; Jn 10.40; 11.7
10.2-12pp Mt 19.3-12
10.4 Deut 24.1-4; Mt 5.31; 19.7
10.6 Gen 1.27; 5.2
10.7 Gen 2.24; 1 Cor 6.16
10.11 Mt 5.32; Lk 16.18; Rom 7.3; 1 Cor 7.10, 11
10.13-16pp Mt 19.13-15; Lk 18.15-17
10.15 Mt 18.3; 1 Cor 14.20; 1 Pet 2.2
10.16 Mk 9.36
10.17-31pp Mt 19.16-30; Lk 18.18-30
10.17 Mk 1.40; Lk 10.25; Eph 1.18
10.19 Ex 20.12-16; Deut 5.16-20
10.21 Mt 6.20; Lk 12.33; Acts 2.35; 4.34,35

[t] Other ancient authorities lack *in me* [u] Gk *Gehenna* [v] Verses 44 and 46 (which are identical with verse 48) are lacking in the best ancient authorities [w] Other ancient authorities either add or substitute *and every sacrifice will be salted with salt* [x] Or *how can you restore its saltiness?* [y] Other ancient authorities lack *and* [z] Other ancient authorities lack *and be joined to his wife*

at him, loved him and said, "You
lack one thing; go, sell what you
own, and give the money[a] to the
poor, and you will have treasure in
heaven; then come, follow me."
22 When he heard this, he was
shocked and went away grieving,
for he had many possessions.
23 Then Jesus looked around
and said to his disciples, "How
hard it will be for those who have
wealth to enter the kingdom of
God!" 24 And the disciples were
perplexed at these words. But
Jesus said to them again, "Children, how hard it is[b] to enter the
kingdom of God! 25 It is easier for a
camel to go through the eye of a
needle than for someone who is
rich to enter the kingdom of God."
26 They were greatly astounded and
said to one another,[c] "Then who
can be saved?" 27 Jesus looked at
them and said, "For mortals it is
impossible, but not for God; for
God all things are possible."
28 Peter began to say to him,
"Look, we have left everything and
followed you." 29 Jesus said, "Truly
I tell you, there is no one who has
left house or brothers or sisters or
mother or father or children or
fields, for my sake and for the sake
of the good news,[d] 30 who will not
receive a hundredfold now in this
age—houses, brothers and sisters,
mothers and children, and fields
with persecutions—and in the age
to come eternal life. 31 But many
who are first will be last, and the
last will be first."

A Third Time Jesus Foretells His Death and Resurrection

32 They were on the road, going
up to Jerusalem, and Jesus was
walking ahead of them; they were
amazed, and those who followed
were afraid. He took the twelve
aside again and began to tell them
what was to happen to him, 33 saying, "See, we are going up to Jerusalem, and the Son of Man will be
handed over to the chief priests
and the scribes, and they will condemn him to death; then they will
hand him over to the Gentiles;
34 they will mock him, and spit
upon him, and flog him, and kill
him; and after three days he will
rise again."

The Request of James and John

35 James and John, the sons of
Zebedee, came forward to him and
said to him, "Teacher, we want you
to do for us whatever we ask of
you." 36 And he said to them, "What
is it you want me to do for you?"
37 And they said to him, "Grant us
to sit, one at your right hand and
one at your left, in your glory."
38 But Jesus said to them, "You do
not know what you are asking. Are
you able to drink the cup that I
drink, or be baptized with the baptism that I am baptized with?"
39 They replied, "We are able."
Then Jesus said to them, "The cup
that I drink you will drink; and with
the baptism with which I am baptized, you will be baptized; 40 but to
sit at my right hand or at my left is
not mine to grant, but it is for those
for whom it has been prepared."
41 When the ten heard this,
they began to be angry with James
and John. 42 So Jesus called them
and said to them, "You know that
among the Gentiles those whom
they recognize as their rulers lord it
over them, and their great ones are
tyrants over them. 43 But it is not so
among you; but whoever wishes to
become great among you must be
your servant, 44 and whoever wishes
to be first among you must be slave
of all. 45 For the Son of Man came
not to be served but to serve, and to
give his life a ransom for many."

The Healing of Blind Bartimaeus

46 They came to Jericho. As he
and his disciples and a large crowd
were leaving Jericho, Bartimaeus
son of Timaeus, a blind beggar, was
sitting by the roadside. 47 When he
heard that it was Jesus of Nazareth,
he began to shout out and say,

10.23 Mt 19.23; Lk 18.24
10.24 Ps 52.7; 62.10; 1 Tim 6.17
10.27 Jer 32.17
10.28 Mt 4.20-22
10.29 Mt 6.33
10.31 Mt 20.16; Lk 13.30
10.32-34pp Mt 20.17-19; Lk 18.31-34
10.32 Mk 8.31; 9.31; Lk 9.22
10.34 Mt 26.67; 27.30; Mk 14.65
10.35-45pp Mt 20.20-28
10.37 Mt 19.28; Lk 22.30
10.38 Lk 12.50; Jn 18.11
10.39 Acts 12.2; Rev 1.9;
10.41; Lk 22.25-27
10.43 Mt 9.35
10.45 Jn 13.14; 1 Tim 2.5, 6
10.46-52pp Mt 20.29-34; Lk 18.35-43
10.47 Mt 9.27

[a] Gk lacks *the money* [b] Other ancient authorities add *for those who trust in riches*
[c] Other ancient authorities read *to him*
[d] Or *gospel*

"Jesus, Son of David, have mercy
on me!" 48 Many sternly ordered
him to be quiet, but he cried out
even more loudly, "Son of David,
have mercy on me!" 49 Jesus stood
still and said, "Call him here." And
they called the blind man, saying
to him, "Take heart; get up, he is
calling you." 50 So throwing off his
cloak, he sprang up and came to
Jesus. 51 Then Jesus said to him,
"What do you want me to do for
you?" The blind man said to him,
"My teacher,[e] let me see again."
52 Jesus said to him, "Go; your faith
has made you well." Immediately
he regained his sight and followed
him on the way.

Jesus' Triumphal Entry into Jerusalem

11 When they were approaching Jerusalem, at Bethphage and Bethany, near the Mount of
Olives, he sent two of his disciples
2 and said to them, "Go into the village ahead of you, and immediately
as you enter it, you will find tied
there a colt that has never been ridden; untie it and bring it. 3 If anyone says to you, 'Why are you doing
this?' just say this, 'The Lord needs
it and will send it back here immediately.' " 4 They went away and
found a colt tied near a door, outside in the street. As they were untying it, 5 some of the bystanders
said to them, "What are you doing,
untying the colt?" 6 They told them
what Jesus had said; and they allowed them to take it. 7 Then they
brought the colt to Jesus and threw
their cloaks on it; and he sat on it.
8 Many people spread their cloaks
on the road, and others spread
leafy branches that they had cut in
the fields. 9 Then those who went
ahead and those who followed
were shouting,

"Hosanna!
 Blessed is the one who
  comes in the name of
  the Lord!
10 Blessed is the coming
  kingdom of our
  ancestor David!
 Hosanna in the highest
  heaven!"

11 Then he entered Jerusalem
and went into the temple; and
when he had looked around at everything, as it was already late, he
went out to Bethany with the
twelve.

Jesus Curses the Fig Tree

12 On the following day, when
they came from Bethany, he was
hungry. 13 Seeing in the distance a
fig tree in leaf, he went to see
whether perhaps he would find
anything on it. When he came to it,
he found nothing but leaves, for it
was not the season for figs. 14 He
said to it, "May no one ever eat fruit
from you again." And his disciples
heard it.

Jesus Cleanses the Temple

15 Then they came to Jerusalem. And he entered the temple
and began to drive out those who
were selling and those who were
buying in the temple, and he overturned the tables of the money
changers and the seats of those
who sold doves; 16 and he would
not allow anyone to carry anything
through the temple. 17 He was
teaching and saying, "Is it not written,

'My house shall be called a
  house of prayer for all
  the nations'?
 But you have made it a den
  of robbers."

18 And when the chief priests and
the scribes heard it, they kept looking for a way to kill him; for they
were afraid of him, because the
whole crowd was spellbound by his
teaching. 19 And when evening
came, Jesus and his disciples[f]
went out of the city.

The Lesson from the Withered Fig Tree

20 In the morning as they
passed by, they saw the fig tree
withered away to its roots. 21 Then
Peter remembered and said to him,
"Rabbi, look! The fig tree that you

10.51 Jn 20.16; Mt 23.7
10.52 Mt 9.22; Mk 5.34; Lk 7.50; 8.48; 17.19
11.1-11pp Mt 21.1-11; Lk 19.29-44; Jn 12.12-19
11.1 Mt 21.17
11.4 Mk 14.16
11.9 Ps 118.26; Mt 23.39
11.11 Mt 21.10, 11,17
11.12-14, 20-25pp Mt 21.18-22
11.12 Lk 13.6-9
11.15-19pp Mt 21.12-17; Lk 19.45-48
11.17 Isa 56.7; Jer 7.11
11.18 Mt 21.46; 7.28; Mk 1.22; Lk 4.32
11.20 Mt 21.19
11.21 Mt 23.7

[e] Aramaic *Rabbouni* [f] Gk *they*: other ancient authorities read *he*

cursed has withered." 22 Jesus answered them, "Have[g] faith in God.
23 Truly I tell you, if you say to this
mountain, 'Be taken up and
thrown into the sea,' and if you do
not doubt in your heart, but believe
that what you say will come to
pass, it will be done for you. 24 So I
tell you, whatever you ask for in
prayer, believe that you have received[h] it, and it will be yours.
25 Whenever you stand praying,
forgive, if you have anything
against anyone; so that your Father
in heaven may also forgive you your
trespasses."[i]

Jesus' Authority Is Questioned

27 Again they came to Jerusalem. As he was walking in the temple, the chief priests, the scribes,
and the elders came to him 28 and
said, "By what authority are you
doing these things? Who gave you
this authority to do them?" 29 Jesus
said to them, "I will ask you one
question; answer me, and I will tell
you by what authority I do these
things. 30 Did the baptism of John
come from heaven, or was it of human origin? Answer me." 31 They
argued with one another, "If we
say, 'From heaven,' he will say,
'Why then did you not believe
him?' 32 But shall we say, 'Of human origin'?"—they were afraid of
the crowd, for all regarded John as
truly a prophet. 33 So they answered
Jesus, "We do not know." And
Jesus said to them, "Neither will I
tell you by what authority I am doing these things."

The Parable of the Wicked Tenants

12 Then he began to speak to
them in parables. "A man
planted a vineyard, put a fence
around it, dug a pit for the wine
press, and built a watchtower; then
he leased it to tenants and went to
another country. 2 When the season
came, he sent a slave to the tenants
to collect from them his share of
the produce of the vineyard. 3 But
they seized him, and beat him, and
sent him away empty-handed.

11.22 Mt 17.20
11.23 Mt 21.21; Lk 17.6
11.24 Mt 7.7; Jn 14.13,14; 15.7; 16.23, 24; Jas 1.5, 6
11.25 Mt 6.14,15; Col 3.13
11.27-33pp Mt 21.23-27; Lk 20.1-8
11.32 Mt 14.5
12.1-12pp Mt 21.33-46; Lk 20.9-19
12.1 Isa 5.1-7
12.6 cf. Heb 1.1-3
12.10 Ps 118.22, 23; Acts 4.11; 1 Pet 2.7
12.12 Mt 21.45, 46; Mk 11.18; Mt 22.22
12.13-17pp Mt 22.15-22; Lk 20.20-26
12.13 Mk 3.6; Lk 11.54

4 And again he sent another slave to
them; this one they beat over the
head and insulted. 5 Then he sent
another, and that one they killed.
And so it was with many others;
some they beat, and others they
killed. 6 He had still one other, a
beloved son. Finally he sent him to
them, saying, 'They will respect my
son.' 7 But those tenants said to
one another, 'This is the heir;
come, let us kill him, and the inheritance will be ours.' 8 So they
seized him, killed him, and threw
him out of the vineyard. 9 What
then will the owner of the vineyard
do? He will come and destroy the
tenants and give the vineyard to
others. 10 Have you not read this
scripture:

'The stone that the builders
rejected
has become the
cornerstone;[j]
11 this was the Lord's doing,
and it is amazing in our
eyes'?"

12 When they realized that he
had told this parable against them,
they wanted to arrest him, but they
feared the crowd. So they left him
and went away.

The Question about Paying Taxes

13 Then they sent to him some
Pharisees and some Herodians to
trap him in what he said. 14 And
they came and said to him, "Teacher, we know that you are sincere,
and show deference to no one; for
you do not regard people with partiality, but teach the way of God in
accordance with truth. Is it lawful
to pay taxes to the emperor, or not?
15 Should we pay them, or should
we not?" But knowing their hypocrisy, he said to them, "Why are you
putting me to the test? Bring me a
denarius and let me see it." 16 And
they brought one. Then he said to
them, "Whose head is this, and

[g] Other ancient authorities read *"If you have*
[h] Other ancient authorities read *are receiving*
[i] Other ancient authorities add verse 26, *"But if you do not forgive, neither will your Father in heaven forgive your trespasses."*
[j] Or *keystone*

whose title?" They answered, "The
emperor's." 17 Jesus said to them,
"Give to the emperor the things
that are the emperor's, and to God
the things that are God's." And
they were utterly amazed at him.

The Question about the Resurrection

18 Some Sadducees, who say
there is no resurrection, came to
him and asked him a question, saying, 19 "Teacher, Moses wrote for us
that 'if a man's brother dies, leaving a wife but no child, the man[k]
shall marry the widow and raise up
children for his brother.' 20 There
were seven brothers; the first married and, when he died, left no children; 21 and the second married her
and died, leaving no children; and
the third likewise; 22 none of the
seven left children. Last of all the
woman herself died. 23 In the resurrection[l] whose wife will she be?
For the seven had married her."
24 Jesus said to them, "Is not
this the reason you are wrong, that
you know neither the scriptures
nor the power of God? 25 For when
they rise from the dead, they neither marry nor are given in marriage, but are like angels in heaven.
26 And as for the dead being raised,
have you not read in the book of
Moses, in the story about the bush,
how God said to him, 'I am the God
of Abraham, the God of Isaac, and
the God of Jacob'? 27 He is God not
of the dead, but of the living; you
are quite wrong."

The First Commandment

28 One of the scribes came near
and heard them disputing with one
another, and seeing that he answered them well, he asked him,
"Which commandment is the first
of all?" 29 Jesus answered, "The
first is, 'Hear, O Israel: the Lord
our God, the Lord is one; 30 you
shall love the Lord your God with
all your heart, and with all your
soul, and with all your mind, and
with all your strength.' 31 The second is this, 'You shall love your
neighbor as yourself.' There is no
other commandment greater than
these." 32 Then the scribe said to
him, "You are right, Teacher; you
have truly said that 'he is one, and
besides him there is no other';
33 and 'to love him with all the
heart, and with all the understanding, and with all the strength,' and
'to love one's neighbor as
oneself,'—this is much more important than all whole burnt offerings and sacrifices." 34 When Jesus
saw that he answered wisely, he
said to him, "You are not far from
the kingdom of God." After that no
one dared to ask him any question.

The Question about David's Son

35 While Jesus was teaching in
the temple, he said, "How can the
scribes say that the Messiah[m] is
the son of David? 36 David himself,
by the Holy Spirit, declared,

'The Lord said to my Lord,
"Sit at my right hand,
until I put your enemies
under your feet." '

37 David himself calls him Lord; so
how can he be his son?" And the
large crowd was listening to him
with delight.

Jesus Denounces the Scribes

38 As he taught, he said, "Beware of the scribes, who like to
walk around in long robes, and to
be greeted with respect in the marketplaces, 39 and to have the best
seats in the synagogues and places
of honor at banquets! 40 They devour widows' houses and for the
sake of appearance say long
prayers. They will receive the greater condemnation."

The Widow's Offering

41 He sat down opposite the
treasury, and watched the crowd
putting money into the treasury.
Many rich people put in large
sums. 42 A poor widow came and
put in two small copper coins,
which are worth a penny. 43 Then
he called his disciples and said to
them, "Truly I tell you, this poor
widow has put in more than all

12.17 Rom 13.7
12.18-27pp Mt 22.23-33; Lk 20.27-38
12.19 Deut 25.5
12.25 1 Cor 15.42, 49,52
12.26 Ex 3.6
12.28-34pp Mt 22.34-40
12.28 Lk 10.25-28; 20.39
12.29 Deut 6.4
12.31 Lev 19.18; Rom 13.9; Gal 5.14; Jas 2.8
12.32 Deut 4.39; Isa 45.6,14; 46.9
12.33 1 Sam 15.22; Hos 6.6; Mic 6.6-8
12.34 Mt 22.46
12.35-37pp Mt 22.41-46; Lk 20.41-44
12.35 Mt 26.55; 9.27
12.36 Ps 110.1; Acts 2.34, 35; Heb 1.13
12.37 Jn 12.9
12.38-40pp Mt 23.1-12; Lk 20.45-47
12.38 Lk 11.43
12.41 Jn 8.20; 2 Kings 12.9
12.43 2 Cor 8.12

[k] Gk *his brother* [l] Other ancient authorities add *when they rise* [m] Or *the Christ*

those who are contributing to the
treasury. 44 For all of them have
contributed out of their abundance; but she out of her poverty
has put in everything she had, all
she had to live on."

The Destruction of the Temple Foretold

13 As he came out of the temple, one of his disciples
said to him, "Look, Teacher, what
large stones and what large buildings!" 2 Then Jesus asked him, "Do
you see these great buildings? Not
one stone will be left here upon another; all will be thrown down."
3 When he was sitting on the
Mount of Olives opposite the temple, Peter, James, John, and Andrew asked him privately, 4 "Tell
us, when will this be, and what will
be the sign that all these things are
about to be accomplished?" 5 Then
Jesus began to say to them, "Beware that no one leads you astray.
6 Many will come in my name and
say, 'I am he!'[n] and they will lead
many astray. 7 When you hear of
wars and rumors of wars, do not be
alarmed; this must take place, but
the end is still to come. 8 For nation
will rise against nation, and kingdom against kingdom; there will be
earthquakes in various places;
there will be famines. This is but
the beginning of the birthpangs.

Persecution Foretold

9 "As for yourselves, beware; for
they will hand you over to councils;
and you will be beaten in synagogues; and you will stand before
governors and kings because of me,
as a testimony to them. 10 And the
good news[o] must first be proclaimed to all nations. 11 When
they bring you to trial and hand you
over, do not worry beforehand
about what you are to say; but say
whatever is given you at that time,
for it is not you who speak, but the
Holy Spirit. 12 Brother will betray
brother to death, and a father his
child, and children will rise against
parents and have them put to
death; 13 and you will be hated by

13.1-13pp Mt 24.1-14; Lk 21.5-19
13.2 Lk 19.44; Mk 14.58; 15.29; Acts 6.14
13.3 Mk 5.37; 9.2
13.5 Eph 5.6; 1 Thes 2.3
13.6 Jn 8.24
13.9 Mt 10.17
13.11 Mt 10.19; Lk 12.11
13.12 Mic 7.6; Mt 10.21
13.13 Jn 15.21; Mt 10.22; Rev 2.10
13.14-23pp Mt 24.15-28; Lk 21.20-24
13.14 Dan 9.27; 11.31; 12.11
13.17 Lk 23.29
13.19 Dan 9.26; 12.1; Joel 2.2
13.21 Lk 17.23; 21.8
13.22 Mt 7.15; Jn 4.48
13.23 2 Pet 3.17
13.24-27pp Mt 24.29-31; Lk 21.25-28
13.24 Zeph 1.15
13.26 Dan 7.13; Mt 16.27; Mk 14.62; 1 Thes 4.16; 2 Thes 1.7, 10

all because of my name. But the
one who endures to the end will be
saved.

The Desolating Sacrilege

14 "But when you see the desolating sacrilege set up where it
ought not to be (let the reader understand), then those in Judea
must flee to the mountains; 15 the
one on the housetop must not go
down or enter the house to take
anything away; 16 the one in the
field must not turn back to get a
coat. 17 Woe to those who are pregnant and to those who are nursing
infants in those days! 18 Pray that it
may not be in winter. 19 For in
those days there will be suffering,
such as has not been from the beginning of the creation that God
created until now, no, and never
will be. 20 And if the Lord had not
cut short those days, no one would
be saved; but for the sake of the
elect, whom he chose, he has cut
short those days. 21 And if anyone
says to you at that time, 'Look!
Here is the Messiah!'[p] or 'Look!
There he is!'—do not believe it.
22 False messiahs[q] and false
prophets will appear and produce
signs and omens, to lead astray, if
possible, the elect. 23 But be alert; I
have already told you everything.

The Coming of the Son of Man

24 "But in those days, after that
suffering,

the sun will be darkened,
and the moon will not give
its light,
25 and the stars will be falling
from heaven,
and the powers in the
heavens will be shaken.

26 Then they will see 'the Son of
Man coming in clouds' with great
power and glory. 27 Then he will
send out the angels, and gather his
elect from the four winds, from the
ends of the earth to the ends of
heaven.

The Lesson of the Fig Tree

28 "From the fig tree learn its

[n] Gk *I am* [o] Gk *gospel* [p] Or *the Christ* [q] Or *christs*

lesson: as soon as its branch becomes tender and puts forth its
leaves, you know that summer is
near. 29 So also, when you see these
things taking place, you know that
he[r] is near, at the very gates.
30 Truly I tell you, this generation
will not pass away until all these
things have taken place. 31 Heaven
and earth will pass away, but my
words will not pass away.

The Necessity for Watchfulness

32 "But about that day or hour
no one knows, neither the angels in
heaven, nor the Son, but only the
Father. 33 Beware, keep alert;[s] for
you do not know when the time will
come. 34 It is like a man going on a
journey, when he leaves home and
puts his slaves in charge, each with
his work, and commands the doorkeeper to be on the watch. 35 Therefore, keep awake—for you do not
know when the master of the house
will come, in the evening, or at
midnight, or at cockcrow, or at
dawn, 36 or else he may find you
asleep when he comes suddenly.
37 And what I say to you I say to all:
Keep awake."

The Plot to Kill Jesus

14 It was two days before the
Passover and the festival of
Unleavened Bread. The chief
priests and the scribes were looking for a way to arrest Jesus[t] by
stealth and kill him; 2 for they said,
"Not during the festival, or there
may be a riot among the people."

The Anointing at Bethany

3 While he was at Bethany in
the house of Simon the leper,[u] as
he sat at the table, a woman came
with an alabaster jar of very costly
ointment of nard, and she broke
open the jar and poured the ointment on his head. 4 But some were
there who said to one another in
anger, "Why was the ointment
wasted in this way? 5 For this ointment could have been sold for
more than three hundred denarii,[v]
and the money given to the poor."
And they scolded her. 6 But Jesus
said, "Let her alone; why do you
trouble her? She has performed a
good service for me. 7 For you always have the poor with you, and
you can show kindness to them
whenever you wish; but you will
not always have me. 8 She has done
what she could; she has anointed
my body beforehand for its burial.
9 Truly I tell you, wherever the good
news[w] is proclaimed in the whole
world, what she has done will be
told in remembrance of her."

Judas Agrees to Betray Jesus

10 Then Judas Iscariot, who was
one of the twelve, went to the chief
priests in order to betray him to
them. 11 When they heard it, they
were greatly pleased, and promised
to give him money. So he began to
look for an opportunity to betray
him.

The Passover with the Disciples

12 On the first day of Unleavened Bread, when the Passover
lamb is sacrificed, his disciples
said to him, "Where do you want us
to go and make the preparations
for you to eat the Passover?" 13 So
he sent two of his disciples, saying
to them, "Go into the city, and a
man carrying a jar of water will
meet you; follow him, 14 and wherever he enters, say to the owner of
the house, 'The Teacher asks,
Where is my guest room where I
may eat the Passover with my disciples?' 15 He will show you a large
room upstairs, furnished and
ready. Make preparations for us
there." 16 So the disciples set out
and went to the city, and found everything as he had told them; and
they prepared the Passover meal.
17 When it was evening, he
came with the twelve. 18 And when
they had taken their places and
were eating, Jesus said, "Truly I tell
you, one of you will betray me, one
who is eating with me." 19 They began to be distressed and to say to

13.28-31pp Mt 24.32-35; Lk 21.29-33
13.30 Mk 9.1
13.31 Mt 5.18; Lk 16.17
13.32-37pp Mt 24.32-35; Lk 21.29-33
13.32 Acts 1.7
13.33 Eph 6.18; Col 4.2; 1 Thes 5.6
13.34 Mt 25.14
13.35 Lk 12.35-40
14.1,2,10,11pp Mt 26.1-5, 14-16; Lk 22.1-6
14.1 Jn 11.55; 13.1; Mt 12.14
14.3-9pp Mt 26.6-13; Jn 12.1-8
14.3 Lk 7.37-39; Mt 21.17
14.7 Deut 15.11
14.8 Jn 19.20
14.10 Lk 22.3,4; Jn 6.71
14.12-16pp Mt 26.17-19 Lk 22.7-13
14.12 Ex 12.11
14.17-21pp Mt 26.20-25; Lk 22.14-18
14.18 vv. 44,45

[r] Or *it* [s] Other ancient authorities add *and pray* [t] Gk *him* [u] The terms *leper* and *leprosy* can refer to several diseases
[v] The denarius was the usual day's wage for a laborer [w] Or *gospel*

him one after another, "Surely, not
I?" 20 He said to them, "It is one of
the twelve, one who is dipping
bread[x] into the bowl[y] with me.
21 For the Son of Man goes as it is
written of him, but woe to that one
by whom the Son of Man is betrayed! It would have been better
for that one not to have been born."

The Institution of the Lord's Supper

22 While they were eating, he
took a loaf of bread, and after
blessing it he broke it, gave it to
them, and said, "Take; this is my
body." 23 Then he took a cup, and
after giving thanks he gave it to
them, and all of them drank from
it. 24 He said to them, "This is my
blood of the[z] covenant, which is
poured out for many. 25 Truly I tell
you, I will never again drink of the
fruit of the vine until that day when
I drink it new in the kingdom of
God."

Peter's Denial Foretold

26 When they had sung the
hymn, they went out to the Mount
of Olives. 27 And Jesus said to
them, "You will all become deserters; for it is written,

'I will strike the shepherd,
and the sheep will be
scattered.'

28 But after I am raised up, I will go
before you to Galilee." 29 Peter said
to him, "Even though all become
deserters, I will not." 30 Jesus said
to him, "Truly I tell you, this day,
this very night, before the cock
crows twice, you will deny me three
times." 31 But he said vehemently,
"Even though I must die with you,
I will not deny you." And all of
them said the same.

Jesus Prays in Gethsemane

32 They went to a place called
Gethsemane; and he said to his
disciples, "Sit here while I pray."
33 He took with him Peter and
James and John, and began to be
distressed and agitated. 34 And said
to them, "I am deeply grieved, even
to death; remain here, and keep
awake." 35 And going a little farther, he threw himself on the
ground and prayed that, if it were
possible, the hour might pass from
him. 36 He said, "Abba,[a] Father, for
you all things are possible; remove
this cup from me; yet, not what I
want, but what you want." 37 He
came and found them sleeping;
and he said to Peter, "Simon, are
you asleep? Could you not keep
awake one hour? 38 Keep awake
and pray that you may not come
into the time of trial;[b] the spirit indeed is willing, but the flesh is
weak." 39 And again he went away
and prayed, saying the same words.
40 And once more he came and
found them sleeping, for their eyes
were very heavy; and they did not
know what to say to him. 41 He
came a third time and said to them,
"Are you still sleeping and taking
your rest? Enough! The hour has
come; the Son of Man is betrayed
into the hands of sinners. 42 Get up,
let us be going. See, my betrayer is
at hand."

The Betrayal and Arrest of Jesus

43 Immediately, while he was
still speaking, Judas, one of the
twelve, arrived; and with him there
was a crowd with swords and clubs,
from the chief priests, the scribes,
and the elders. 44 Now the betrayer
had given them a sign, saying, "The
one I will kiss is the man; arrest
him and lead him away under
guard." 45 So when he came, he
went up to him at once and said,
"Rabbi!" and kissed him. 46 Then
they laid hands on him and arrested him. 47 But one of those who
stood near drew his sword and
struck the slave of the high priest,
cutting off his ear. 48 Then Jesus
said to them, "Have you come out
with swords and clubs to arrest me
as though I were a bandit? 49 Day
after day I was with you in the temple teaching, and you did not arrest
me. But let the scriptures be ful-

14.22-25pp Mt 26.26-29; Lk 22.19-24
14.22 Mk 6.41; 8.6; Lk 24.30; 1 Cor 11.23-25
14.23 1 Cor 10.16
14.24 Ex 24.8; Heb 9.20
14.26-31pp Mt 26.30-35; Lk 22.31-34
14.26 Mt 21.1
14.27 Zech 13.7
14.28 Mk 16.7
14.29 Jn 13.37,38
14.30 vv. 66-72; Jn 13.38
14.32-42pp Mt 26.36-46; Lk 22.39-46
14.34 Jn 12.27
14.35 v. 41
14.36 Rom 8.15; Gal 4.6; Jn 5.30; 6.38
14.38 Mt 6.13; Lk 11.4; Rom 7.23; Gal 5.17
14.41 v. 35; Jn 13.1
14.43-52pp Mt 26.47-56; Lk 22.47-53; Jn 18.1-11
14.45 Mt 23.7
14.49 Mk 12.35; Isa 53.7ff; Lk 19.47; Jn 18.19-21

[x] Gk lacks *bread* [y] Other ancient authorities read *same bowl* [z] Other ancient authorities add *new* [a] Aramaic for *Father* [b] Or *into temptation*

filled." 50 All of them deserted him
and fled.
51 A certain young man was following him, wearing nothing but a
linen cloth. They caught hold of
him, 52 but he left the linen cloth
and ran off naked.

Jesus before the Council

53 They took Jesus to the high
priest; and all the chief priests, the
elders, and the scribes were assembled. 54 Peter had followed him at a
distance, right into the courtyard of
the high priest; and he was sitting
with the guards, warming himself
at the fire. 55 Now the chief priests
and the whole council were looking
for testimony against Jesus to put
him to death; but they found none.
56 For many gave false testimony
against him, and their testimony
did not agree. 57 Some stood up and
gave false testimony against him,
saying, 58 "We heard him say, 'I will
destroy this temple that is made
with hands, and in three days I will
build another, not made with
hands.' " 59 But even on this point
their testimony did not agree.
60 Then the high priest stood up before them and asked Jesus, "Have
you no answer? What is it that they
testify against you?" 61 But he was
silent and did not answer. Again
the high priest asked him, "Are you
the Messiah,[c] the Son of the
Blessed One?" 62 Jesus said, "I am;
and

'you will see the Son of Man
seated at the right hand of
the Power,'
and 'coming with the clouds
of heaven.' "

63 Then the high priest tore his
clothes and said, "Why do we still
need witnesses? 64 You have heard
his blasphemy! What is your decision?" All of them condemned him
as deserving death. 65 Some began
to spit on him, to blindfold him,
and to strike him, saying to him,
"Prophesy!" The guards also took
him over and beat him.

Peter Denies Jesus

66 While Peter was below in the
courtyard, one of the servant-girls
of the high priest came by. 67 When
she saw Peter warming himself, she
stared at him and said, "You also
were with Jesus, the man from
Nazareth." 68 But he denied it, saying, "I do not know or understand
what you are talking about." And
he went out into the forecourt.[d]
Then the cock crowed.[e] 69 And the
servant-girl, on seeing him, began
again to say to the bystanders,
"This man is one of them." 70 But
again he denied it. Then after a little while the bystanders again said
to Peter, "Certainly you are one of
them; for you are a Galilean." 71 But
he began to curse, and he swore an
oath, "I do not know this man you
are talking about." 72 At that moment the cock crowed for the second time. Then Peter remembered
that Jesus had said to him, "Before
the cock crows twice, you will deny
me three times." And he broke
down and wept.

Jesus before Pilate

15 As soon as it was morning,
the chief priests held a
consultation with the elders and
scribes and the whole council.
They bound Jesus, led him away,
and handed him over to Pilate. 2 Pilate asked him, "Are you the King
of the Jews?" He answered him,
"You say so." 3 Then the chief
priests accused him of many
things. 4 Pilate asked him again,
"Have you no answer? See how
many charges they bring against
you." 5 But Jesus made no further
reply, so that Pilate was amazed.

Pilate Hands Jesus over to Be Crucified

6 Now at the festival he used to
release a prisoner for them, anyone
for whom they asked. 7 Now a man
called Barabbas was in prison with
the rebels who had committed
murder during the insurrection.
8 So the crowd came and began to
ask Pilate to do for them according
to his custom. 9 Then he answered

14.50 Ps 88.8; v. 27
14.53-65pp Mt 26.57-68; Jn 18.12-14, 19-25
14.54 v. 68; Mt 26.3; Jn 18.18
14.58 Mk 15.29; Jn 2.19; Acts 6.14
14.61 Isa 53.7
14.62 Dan 7.13; Mt 24.30; Mk 13.26
14.63 Num 14.6; Acts 14.14
14.64 Lev 24.16
14.65 Mk 10.34; Esther 7.8; Lk 22.64
14.66-72pp Mt 26.69-75; Lk 22.55-62; Jn 18.15-18, 25-27
14.66 vv. 30,54
14.67 v. 54; Mk 1.24
14.68 v. 54
14.70 v. 68; Acts 2.7
14.72 v. 30
15.1-15pp Mt 27.11-26; Lk 23.3-25; Jn 18.29-40
15.1 Mt 5.22; Lk 22.66; 23.1; Jn 18.28
15.5 Isa 53.7
15.6 Mt 27.15; Lk 23.17; Jn 18.39

[c] Or *the Christ* [d] Or *gateway* [e] Other ancient authorities lack *Then the cock crowed*

them, "Do you want me to release
for you the King of the Jews?"
10 For he realized that it was out of
jealousy that the chief priests had
handed him over. 11 But the chief
priests stirred up the crowd to have
him release Barabbas for them instead. 12 Pilate spoke to them
again, "Then what do you wish me
to do[f] with the man you call[g] the
King of the Jews?" 13 They shouted
back, "Crucify him!" 14 Pilate asked
them, "Why, what evil has he
done?" But they shouted all the
more, "Crucify him!" 15 So Pilate,
wishing to satisfy the crowd, released Barabbas for them; and after
flogging Jesus, he handed him over
to be crucified.

The Soldiers Mock Jesus

16 Then the soldiers led him
into the courtyard of the palace
(that is, the governor's headquarters[h]); and they called together the
whole cohort. 17 And they clothed
him in a purple cloak; and after
twisting some thorns into a crown,
they put it on him. 18 And they began saluting him, "Hail, King of the
Jews!" 19 They struck his head with
a reed, spat upon him, and knelt
down in homage to him. 20 After
mocking him, they stripped him of
the purple cloak and put his own
clothes on him. Then they led him
out to crucify him.

The Crucifixion of Jesus

21 They compelled a passer-by,
who was coming in from the country, to carry his cross; it was Simon
of Cyrene, the father of Alexander
and Rufus. 22 Then they brought
Jesus[i] to the place called Golgotha (which means the place of a
skull). 23 And they offered him wine
mixed with myrrh; but he did not
take it. 24 And they crucified him,
and divided his clothes among
them, casting lots to decide what
each should take.

25 It was nine o'clock in the
morning when they crucified him.
26 The inscription of the charge
against him read, "The King of the
Jews." 27 And with him they crucified two bandits, one on his right
and one on his left.[j] 29 Those who
passed by derided[k] him, shaking
their heads and saying, "Aha! You
who would destroy the temple and
build it in three days, 30 save yourself, and come down from the
cross!" 31 In the same way the chief
priests, along with the scribes,
were also mocking him among
themselves and saying, "He saved
others; he cannot save himself.
32 Let the Messiah,[l] the King of Israel, come down from the cross
now, so that we may see and believe." Those who were crucified
with him also taunted him.

The Death of Jesus

33 When it was noon, darkness
came over the whole land[m] until
three in the afternoon. 34 At three
o'clock Jesus cried out with a loud
voice, "Eloi, Eloi, lema sabachtha-
ni?" which means, "My God, my
God, why have you forsaken me?"[n]
35 When some of the bystanders
heard it, they said, "Listen, he is
calling for Elijah." 36 And someone
ran, filled a sponge with sour wine,
put it on a stick, and gave it to him
to drink, saying, "Wait, let us see
whether Elijah will come to take
him down." 37 Then Jesus gave a
loud cry and breathed his last.
38 And the curtain of the temple
was torn in two, from top to bottom. 39 Now when the centurion,
who stood facing him, saw that in
this way he[o] breathed his last, he
said, "Truly this man was God's
Son!"[p]

40 There were also women looking on from a distance; among
them were Mary Magdalene, and
Mary the mother of James the
younger and of Joses, and Salome.
41 These used to follow him and

15.11 Acts 3.14
15.15 Jn 19.1,16
15.16-20pp Mt 27.27-31
15.16 Acts 10.1
15.21-32pp Mt 27.32-44; Lk 23.32-43; Jn 19.17-24
15.21 Lk 23.26; Rom 16.13
15.24 Ps 22.18
15.29 Ps 22.7; Mk 13.2; 14.58; Jn 2.19
15.31 Ps 22.8
15.32 vv. 26,27
15.33-41pp Mt 27.45-50; Lk 23.44-49; Jn 19.28-37
15.34 Ps 22.1
15.36 Ps 69.21
15.38 Heb 10.19, 20
15.39 Mk 1.11; 9.7
15.40 Ps 38.11; Jn 19.25; Mk 16.1
15.41 Lk 8.1-3

[f] Other ancient authorities read *what should I do* [g] Other ancient authorities lack *the man you call* [h] Gk *the praetorium* [i] Gk *him* [j] Other ancient authorities add verse 28, *And the scripture was fulfilled that says, "And he was counted among the lawless."* [k] Or *blasphemed* [l] Or *the Christ* [m] Or *earth* [n] Other ancient authorities read *made me a reproach* [o] Other ancient authorities add *cried out and* [p] Or *a son of God*

provided for him when he was in
Galilee; and there were many other
women who had come up with him
to Jerusalem.

The Burial of Jesus

42 When evening had come, and
since it was the day of Preparation,
that is, the day before the sabbath,
43 Joseph of Arimathea, a respected
member of the council, who was
also himself waiting expectantly
for the kingdom of God, went boldly to Pilate and asked for the body
of Jesus. 44 Then Pilate wondered if
he were already dead; and summoning the centurion, he asked
him whether he had been dead for
some time. 45 When he learned
from the centurion that he was
dead, he granted the body to Joseph. 46 Then Joseph[q] bought a
linen cloth, and taking down the
body,[r] wrapped it in the linen
cloth, and laid it in a tomb that had
been hewn out of the rock. He then
rolled a stone against the door of
the tomb. 47 Mary Magdalene and
Mary the mother of Joses saw
where the body[r] was laid.

The Resurrection of Jesus

16 When the sabbath was
over, Mary Magdalene, and
Mary the mother of James, and Salome bought spices, so that they
might go and anoint him. 2 And
very early on the first day of the
week, when the sun had risen, they
went to the tomb. 3 They had been
saying to one another, "Who will
roll away the stone for us from the
entrance to the tomb?" 4 When
they looked up, they saw that the
stone, which was very large, had already been rolled back. 5 As they
entered the tomb, they saw a young
man, dressed in a white robe, sitting on the right side; and they
were alarmed. 6 But he said to
them, "Do not be alarmed; you are
looking for Jesus of Nazareth, who
was crucified. He has been raised;
he is not here. Look, there is the
place they laid him. 7 But go, tell
his disciples and Peter that he is
going ahead of you to Galilee; there
you will see him, just as he told
you." 8 So they went out and fled
from the tomb, for terror and
amazement had seized them; and
they said nothing to anyone, for
they were afraid.[s]

15.42-47pp Mt 27.57-61; Lk 23.50-56; Jn 19.38-42
15.42 Deut 21.22, 23; Mt 27.62
15.43 Acts 13.50; 17.12; Lk 2.25,38
15.45 v. 39
16.1-8pp Mt 28.1-10; Lk 24.1-11; Jn 20.1-18
16.1 Lk 23.56; Jn 19.39
16.3 Mk 15.46
16.5 Mk 9.15
16.6 v. 5; Mk 1.24
16.7 Mk 14.28; Jn 21.1-23
16.9 Jn 20.11-18
16.12 Lk 24.13-35
16.14 Lk 24.36-38; Jn 20.26

The Shorter Ending of Mark

⟦And all that had been commanded them they told briefly to
those around Peter. And afterward
Jesus himself sent out through
them, from east to west, the sacred
and imperishable proclamation of
eternal salvation.[t]⟧

The Longer Ending of Mark

Jesus Appears to Mary Magdalene

9 ⟦Now after he rose early on the
first day of the week, he appeared
first to Mary Magdalene, from
whom he had cast out seven demons. 10 She went out and told
those who had been with him,
while they were mourning and
weeping. 11 But when they heard
that he was alive and had been
seen by her, they would not believe
it.

Jesus Appears to Two Disciples

12 After this he appeared in another form to two of them, as they
were walking into the country.
13 And they went back and told the
rest, but they did not believe them.

Jesus Commissions the Disciples

14 Later he appeared to the
eleven themselves as they were sitting at the table; and he upbraided
them for their lack of faith and
stubbornness, because they had
not believed those who saw him af-

[q] Gk *he* [r] Gk *it* [s] Some of the most ancient authorities bring the book to a close at the end of verse 8. One authority concludes the book with the shorter ending; others include the shorter ending and then continue with verses 9-20. In most authorities verses 9-20 follow immediately after verse 8, though in some of these authorities the passage is marked as being doubtful. [t] Other ancient authorities add *Amen*

ter he had risen.[u] 15 And he said to
them, "Go into all the world and
proclaim the good news[v] to the
whole creation. 16 The one who believes and is baptized will be saved;
but the one who does not believe
will be condemned. 17 And these
signs will accompany those who
believe: by using my name they will
cast out demons; they will speak in
new tongues; 18 they will pick up
snakes in their hands,[w] and if they
drink any deadly thing, it will not
hurt them; they will lay their hands
on the sick, and they will recover."

The Ascension of Jesus

19 So then the Lord Jesus, after
he had spoken to them, was taken
up into heaven and sat down at the
right hand of God. 20 And they went
out and proclaimed the good news
everywhere, while the Lord worked
with them and confirmed the message by the signs that accompanied
it.[x]]

16.15 Mt 28.18-20; Lk 24.47,48
16.19 Lk 24.50,51; Acts 1.9-11

[u] Other ancient authorities add, in whole or in part, *And they excused themselves, saying, "This age of lawlessness and unbelief is under Satan, who does not allow the truth and power of God to prevail over the unclean things of the spirits. Therefore reveal your righteousness now"—thus they spoke to Christ. And Christ replied to them, "The term of years of Satan's power has been fulfilled, but other terrible things draw near. And for those who have sinned I was handed over to death, that they may return to the truth and sin no more, that they may inherit the spiritual and imperishable glory of righteousness that is in heaven."*
[v] Or *gospel* [w] Other ancient authorities lack *in their hands* [x] Other ancient authorities add *Amen*

THE GOSPEL ACCORDING TO

Luke

Title and Background

The Gospel of Luke has been called the most beautiful book ever written. Luke's writing shows him to be a highly educated man, one who wrote from a Greek background and viewpoint. He wrote especially with Gentiles in mind, for he explained Jewish customs and traced the genealogy of Jesus back to Adam.

Author and Date of Writing

Though the author's name does not appear in the book, early church tradition ascribes this Gospel to Luke, "the beloved physician" (Col 4.14). It is a companion volume to the book of Acts, and the language and structure of these books indicate that both were written by the same person.

Luke was probably a Gentile by birth, well educated in Greek culture, a physician by profession and a companion of Paul at various times. Since Luke probably used Mark as one of his sources (cf. Lk 1.1-4), he likely wrote this book shortly after A.D. 70.

Theme and Message

Luke tells us in the first four verses that he wrote this Gospel to give Theophilus (likely a government official) the true and complete story of Jesus' life. One of his interests in writing this book was to show that Jesus loved all kinds of people. In the parables especially, he wrote about the poor and oppressed. The theme of joy is felt throughout the book, as Christ's coming brought joy and the hope of salvation to a sinful world.

Outline

I. The Preface (1.1-4)
II. The Coming of Jesus (1.5–2.52)
III. Jesus' Preparation for His Ministry (3.1–4.13)
IV. Jesus' Ministry in Galilee (4.14–9.9)
V. Jesus' Withdrawals From Galilee (9.10-50)
VI. Jesus' Ministry in Judea (9.51–13.21)
VII. Jesus' Ministry in and near Perea (13.22–19.27)
VIII. Jesus' Sacrifice and Triumph (19.28–24.53)

Dedication to Theophilus

1 Since many have undertaken
to set down an orderly account
of the events that have been fulfilled among us, 2 just as they were
handed on to us by those who from
the beginning were eyewitnesses
and servants of the word, 3 I too decided, after investigating everything carefully from the very first,[a]
to write an orderly account for you,
most excellent Theophilus, 4 so
that you may know the truth concerning the things about which you
have been instructed.

1.2 Heb 2.3; 1 Pet 5.1; 2 Pet 1.16; 1 Jn 1.1; Mk 1.1; Jn 15.27
1.3 Acts 11.4; 18.23; 1.1
1.4 Jn 20.31
1.5 Mt 2.1; 1 Chr 24.10
1.6 Gen 7.1; 1 Kings 9.4; 2 Kings 20.3

The Birth of John the Baptist Foretold

5 In the days of King Herod of
Judea, there was a priest named
Zechariah, who belonged to the
priestly order of Abijah. His wife
was a descendant of Aaron, and her
name was Elizabeth. 6 Both of them
were righteous before God, living
blamelessly according to all the
commandments and regulations of
the Lord. 7 But they had no children, because Elizabeth was bar-

[a] Or *for a long time*

ren, and both were getting on in
years.
8 Once when he was serving as
priest before God and his section
was on duty, 9 he was chosen by lot,
according to the custom of the
priesthood, to enter the sanctuary
of the Lord and offer incense.
10 Now at the time of the incense
offering, the whole assembly of the
people was praying outside.
11 Then there appeared to him an
angel of the Lord, standing at the
right side of the altar of incense.
12 When Zechariah saw him, he was
terrified; and fear overwhelmed
him. 13 But the angel said to him,
"Do not be afraid, Zechariah, for
your prayer has been heard. Your
wife Elizabeth will bear you a son,
and you will name him John. 14 You
will have joy and gladness, and
many will rejoice at his birth, 15 for
he will be great in the sight of
the Lord. He must never drink
wine or strong drink; even before
his birth he will be filled with
the Holy Spirit. 16 He will turn
many of the people of Israel to
the Lord their God. 17 With the
spirit and power of Elijah he
will go before him, to turn the
hearts of parents to their children, and the disobedient to the
wisdom of the righteous, to make
ready a people prepared for the
Lord." 18 Zechariah said to the angel, "How will I know that this is
so? For I am an old man, and my
wife is getting on in years." 19 The
angel replied, "I am Gabriel. I
stand in the presence of God, and
I have been sent to speak to you
and to bring you this good news.
20 But now, because you did not
believe my words, which will
be fulfilled in their time, you
will become mute, unable to
speak, until the day these things
occur."
21 Meanwhile the people were
waiting for Zechariah, and wondered at his delay in the sanctuary.
22 When he did come out, he could
not speak to them, and they realized that he had seen a vision in the
sanctuary. He kept motioning to

1.8 1 Chr 24.19; 2 Chr 8.14
1.9 Ex 30.7,8; 1 Chr 23.13; 2 Chr 29.11
1.10 Lev 16.17
1.13 vv. 30,60,63
1.14 v. 58
1.15 Num 6.3; Judg 13.4; Lk 7.33; Jer 1.5; Gal 1.15
1.16 Mal 4.5,6
1.17 Mt 11.14; 17.13
1.18 Gen 17.17; v. 34
1.19 Dan 8.16; 9.21-23; Mt 18.10
1.20 Ezek 3.26; 24.27
1.22 v. 62
1.25 Gen 30.23; Isa 4.1
1.26-38pp Mt 1.18-25
1.26 Mt 2.23
1.27 Mt 1.16; v. 19
1.28 Dan 9.23; 10.19
1.31 Isa 7.14; Lk 2.21
1.32 Mk 5.7; Isa 9.6,7; Jer 23.5; Rev 3.7
1.33 Dan 2.44; 7.14,27; Mt 28.18; Heb 1.8
1.35 v. 32; Mk 1.24; Mt 4.3
1.37 Gen 18.14; Jer 32.17; Mt 19.26; Mk 10.27; Lk 18.27; Rom 4.21

them and remained unable to
speak. 23 When his time of service
was ended, he went to his home.
24 After those days his wife Elizabeth conceived, and for five
months she remained in seclusion.
She said, 25 "This is what the Lord
has done for me when he looked
favorably on me and took away the
disgrace I have endured among my
people."

The Birth of Jesus Foretold

26 In the sixth month the angel
Gabriel was sent by God to a town
in Galilee called Nazareth, 27 to a
virgin engaged to a man whose
name was Joseph, of the house of
David. The virgin's name was Mary.
28 And he came to her and said,
"Greetings, favored one! The Lord
is with you."[b] 29 But she was much
perplexed by his words and pondered what sort of greeting this
might be. 30 The angel said to her,
"Do not be afraid, Mary, for you
have found favor with God. 31 And
now, you will conceive in your
womb and bear a son, and you will
name him Jesus. 32 He will be great,
and will be called the Son of the
Most High, and the Lord God will
give to him the throne of his ancestor David. 33 He will reign over the
house of Jacob forever, and of his
kingdom there will be no end."
34 Mary said to the angel, "How can
this be, since I am a virgin?"[c]
35 The angel said to her, "The Holy
Spirit will come upon you, and the
power of the Most High will over-
shadow you; therefore the child to
be born[d] will be holy; he will be
called Son of God. 36 And now, your
relative Elizabeth in her old age
has also conceived a son; and this
is the sixth month for her who was
said to be barren. 37 For nothing
will be impossible with God."
38 Then Mary said, "Here am I, the
servant of the Lord; let it be with
me according to your word." Then
the angel departed from her.

[b] Other ancient authorities add *Blessed are you among women* [c] Gk *I do not know a man*
[d] Other ancient authorities add *of you*

Mary Visits Elizabeth

39 In those days Mary set out
and went with haste to a Judean
town in the hill country, 40 where
she entered the house of Zechariah
and greeted Elizabeth. 41 When
Elizabeth heard Mary's greeting,
the child leaped in her womb. And
Elizabeth was filled with the Holy
Spirit 42 and exclaimed with a loud
cry, "Blessed are you among wom-
en, and blessed is the fruit of your
womb. 43 And why has this happened to me, that the mother of my
Lord comes to me? 44 For as soon as
I heard the sound of your greeting,
the child in my womb leaped for
joy. 45 And blessed is she who believed that there would be[e] a fulfillment of what was spoken to her
by the Lord."

Mary's Song of Praise

46 And Mary[f] said,
"My soul magnifies the Lord,
47 and my spirit rejoices in
God my Savior,
48 for he has looked with favor
on the lowliness of his
servant.
Surely, from now on all
generations will call me
blessed;
49 for the Mighty One has done
great things for me,
and holy is his name.
50 His mercy is for those who
fear him
from generation to
generation.
51 He has shown strength with
his arm;
he has scattered the proud
in the thoughts of their
hearts.
52 He has brought down the
powerful from their
thrones,
and lifted up the lowly;
53 he has filled the hungry with
good things,
and sent the rich away
empty.
54 He has helped his servant
Israel,
in remembrance of his
mercy,
55 according to the promise he
made to our ancestors,
to Abraham and to his
descendants forever."
56 And Mary remained with her
about three months and then returned to her home.

The Birth of John the Baptist

57 Now the time came for Elizabeth to give birth, and she bore a
son. 58 Her neighbors and relatives
heard that the Lord had shown his
great mercy to her, and they rejoiced with her.
59 On the eighth day they came
to circumcise the child, and they
were going to name him Zechariah
after his father. 60 But his mother
said, "No; he is to be called John."
61 They said to her, "None of your
relatives has this name." 62 Then
they began motioning to his father
to find out what name he wanted to
give him. 63 He asked for a writing
tablet and wrote, "His name is
John." And all of them were
amazed. 64 Immediately his mouth
was opened and his tongue freed,
and he began to speak, praising
God. 65 Fear came over all their
neighbors, and all these things
were talked about throughout the
entire hill country of Judea. 66 All
who heard them pondered them
and said, "What then will this child
become?" For, indeed, the hand of
the Lord was with him.

Zechariah's Prophecy

67 Then his father Zechariah
was filled with the Holy Spirit and
spoke this prophecy:
68 "Blessed be the Lord God of
Israel,
for he has looked favorably
on his people and
redeemed them.
69 He has raised up a mighty
savior[g] for us
in the house of his servant
David,

1.39 v. 65
1.41 v. 67
1.42 Judg 5.24; Lk 11.27,28
1.43 Lk 2.11
1.46 1 Sam 2.1-10; Ps 34.2,3
1.47 Ps 35.9; 1 Tim 1.1; 2.3; Titus 2.10; Jude 25
1.48 Ps 138.6; Lk 11.27
1.49 Ps 71.19; 111.9
1.50 Ps 103.17
1.51 Ps 98.1; Isa 40.10; Ps 33.10; 1 Pet 5.5
1.52 Job 5.11
1.53 Ps 34.10
1.54 Ps 98.3
1.55 Gen 17.19; Ps 132.11; Gal 3.16
1.58 Gen 19.19
1.59 Gen 17.12; Lev 12.3
1.62 v. 22
1.63 v. 13
1.64 v. 20
1.66 Lk 2.19,51; Gen 39.2; Acts 11.21
1.67 v. 41; Joel 2.28
1.68 Ps 72.18; 111.9; Lk 7.16
1.69 Ps 18.2; 89.17; 132.17; Ezek 29.21

[e] Or *believed, for there will be* [f] Other ancient authorities read *Elizabeth* [g] Gk *a horn of salvation*

70 as he spoke through the
mouth of his holy
prophets from of old,
71 that we would be saved
from our enemies and
from the hand of all
who hate us.
72 Thus he has shown the
mercy promised to our
ancestors,
and has remembered his
holy covenant,
73 the oath that he swore to our
ancestor Abraham,
to grant us 74 that we, being
rescued from the hands
of our enemies,
might serve him without
fear, 75 in holiness and
righteousness
before him all our days.
76 And you, child, will be called
the prophet of the Most
High;
for you will go before the
Lord to prepare his ways,
77 to give knowledge of
salvation to his people
by the forgiveness of their
sins.
78 By the tender mercy of our
God,
the dawn from on high will
break upon[h] us,
79 to give light to those who sit
in darkness and in the
shadow of death,
to guide our feet into the
way of peace."

80 The child grew and became
strong in spirit, and he was in the
wilderness until the day he appeared publicly to Israel.

The Birth of Jesus

2 In those days a decree went
out from Emperor Augustus
that all the world should be registered. 2 This was the first registration and was taken while Quirinius
was governor of Syria. 3 All went to
their own towns to be registered.
4 Joseph also went from the town of
Nazareth in Galilee to Judea, to the
city of David called Bethlehem, because he was descended from the
house and family of David. 5 He
went to be registered with Mary, to
whom he was engaged and who was
expecting a child. 6 While they were
there, the time came for her to deliver her child. 7 And she gave birth
to her firstborn son and wrapped
him in bands of cloth, and laid him
in a manger, because there was no
place for them in the inn.

The Shepherds and the Angels

8 In that region there were shepherds living in the fields, keeping
watch over their flock by night.
9 Then an angel of the Lord stood
before them, and the glory of the
Lord shone around them, and they
were terrified. 10 But the angel said
to them, "Do not be afraid; for
see—I am bringing you good news
of great joy for all the people: 11 to
you is born this day in the city of
David a Savior, who is the Messiah,[i] the Lord. 12 This will be a sign
for you: you will find a child
wrapped in bands of cloth and lying
in a manger." 13 And suddenly there
was with the angel a multitude of
the heavenly host,[j] praising God
and saying,
14 "Glory to God in the highest
heaven,
and on earth peace among
those whom he
favors!"[k]

15 When the angels had left
them and gone into heaven, the
shepherds said to one another,
"Let us go now to Bethlehem and
see this thing that has taken place,
which the Lord has made known to
us." 16 So they went with haste and
found Mary and Joseph, and the
child lying in the manger. 17 When
they saw this, they made known
what had been told them about
this child; 18 and all who heard it
were amazed at what the shepherds told them. 19 But Mary treasured all these words and pondered
them in her heart. 20 The shepherds
returned, glorifying and praising

1.70 Jer 23.5; Dan 9.24; Acts 3.21; Rom 1.2; Mic 7.20; Ps 105.8,9; 106.45; Ezek 16.60
1.74 Rom 6.18; Heb 9.14
1.75 Eph 4.24; Titus 2.12
1.76 Mal 3.1; 4.5; Mt 11.9,10
1.77 Mk 1.4
1.79 Mt 9.2; Mk 4.16; Acts 26.18
1.80 Lk 2.40,52
2.1-7pp Mt 1.18-25
2.1 Lk 3.1
2.4 Lk 1.27
2.9 Lk 1.11; Acts 5.19
2.10 Mt 14.27
2.11 Jn 4.42; Mt 1.16; 16.16; Lk 1.43; Acts 2.36
2.12 1 Sam 2.34; 2 Kings 19.29; Isa 7.14
2.13 Dan 7.10; Rev 5.11
2.14 Isa 57.19; Lk 1.79; Rom 5.1; Eph 1.9; Phil 2.13
2.19 v. 51
2.20 Mt 9.8

[h] Other ancient authorities read *has broken upon* [i] Or *the Christ* [j] Gk *army*
[k] Other ancient authorities read *peace, good will among people*

God for all they had heard and seen, as it had been told them.

Jesus Is Named

21 After eight days had passed, it was time to circumcise the child; and he was called Jesus, the name given by the angel before he was conceived in the womb.

Jesus Is Presented in the Temple

22 When the time came for their purification according to the law of Moses, they brought him up to Jerusalem to present him to the Lord 23 (as it is written in the law of the Lord, "Every firstborn male shall be designated as holy to the Lord"), 24 and they offered a sacrifice according to what is stated in the law of the Lord, "a pair of turtledoves or two young pigeons."

25 Now there was a man in Jerusalem whose name was Simeon;[l] this man was righteous and devout, looking forward to the consolation of Israel, and the Holy Spirit rested on him. 26 It had been revealed to him by the Holy Spirit that he would not see death before he had seen the Lord's Messiah.[m] 27 Guided by the Spirit, Simeon[n] came into the temple; and when the parents brought in the child Jesus, to do for him what was customary under the law, 28 Simeon[o] took him in his arms and praised God, saying,

29 "Master, now you are
dismissing your
servant[p] in peace,
according to your word;
30 for my eyes have seen your
salvation,
31 which you have prepared in
the presence of all
peoples,
32 a light for revelation to the
Gentiles
and for glory to your
people Israel."

33 And the child's father and mother were amazed at what was being said about him. 34 Then Simeon[l] blessed them and said to his mother Mary, "This child is destined for the falling and the rising of many in Israel, and to be a sign that will be opposed 35 so that the inner thoughts of many will be revealed—and a sword will pierce your own soul too."

2.21 Lk 1.59; 1.31 **2.22** Lev 12.2-6 **2.23** Ex 13.2,12; Num 3.13 **2.25** v. 38; Lk 23.51 **2.26** Ps 89.48; Heb 11.5 **2.27** v. 22 **2.29** v. 26 **2.30** Isa 52.10; Lk 3.6 **2.32** Isa 42.6; 49.6; Acts 13.47; 26.23 **2.34** Mt 21.44; 1 Cor 1.23, 24; 2 Cor 2.16; 1 Pet 2.7,8

2.36 Acts 21.9; Josh 19.24; 1 Tim 5.9 **2.37** Acts 13.3; 1 Tim 5.5 **2.38** v. 25; Lk 24.21 **2.39** v. 51 **2.40** v. 52; Lk 1.80 **2.41** Ex 23.15; Deut 16.1-6 **2.47** Mt 7.28; Mk 1.22; Lk 4.22,32; Jn 7.15,46 **2.48** Mk 3.31-35

36 There was also a prophet, Anna[q] the daughter of Phanuel, of the tribe of Asher. She was of a great age, having lived with her husband seven years after her marriage, 37 then as a widow to the age of eighty-four. She never left the temple but worshiped there with fasting and prayer night and day. 38 At that moment she came, and began to praise God and to speak about the child[r] to all who were looking for the redemption of Jerusalem.

The Return to Nazareth

39 When they had finished everything required by the law of the Lord, they returned to Galilee, to their own town of Nazareth. 40 The child grew and became strong, filled with wisdom; and the favor of God was upon him.

The Boy Jesus in the Temple

41 Now every year his parents went to Jerusalem for the festival of the Passover. 42 And when he was twelve years old, they went up as usual for the festival. 43 When the festival was ended and they started to return, the boy Jesus stayed behind in Jerusalem, but his parents did not know it. 44 Assuming that he was in the group of travelers, they went a day's journey. Then they started to look for him among their relatives and friends. 45 When they did not find him, they returned to Jerusalem to search for him. 46 After three days they found him in the temple, sitting among the teachers, listening to them and asking them questions. 47 And all who heard him were amazed at his understanding and his answers. 48 When his parents[s] saw him they were astonished; and his mother

[l] Gk *Symeon* [m] Or *the Lord's Christ* [n] Gk *In the Spirit, he* [o] Gk *he* [p] Gk *slave* [q] Gk *Hanna* [r] Gk *him* [s] Gk *they*

said to him, "Child, why have you
treated us like this? Look, your father and I have been searching for
you in great anxiety." 49 He said to
them, "Why were you searching for
me? Did you not know that I must
be in my Father's house?"[t] 50 But
they did not understand what he
said to them. 51 Then he went down
with them and came to Nazareth,
and was obedient to them. His
mother treasured all these things
in her heart.

52 And Jesus increased in wisdom and in years,[u] and in divine
and human favor.

The Proclamation of John the Baptist

3 In the fifteenth year of the
reign of Emperor Tiberius,
when Pontius Pilate was governor
of Judea, and Herod was ruler[v] of
Galilee, and his brother Philip ruler[v] of the region of Ituraea and
Trachonitis, and Lysanias ruler[v] of
Abilene, 2 during the high priesthood of Annas and Caiaphas, the
word of God came to John son of
Zechariah in the wilderness. 3 He
went into all the region around the
Jordan, proclaiming a baptism of
repentance for the forgiveness of
sins, 4 as it is written in the book
of the words of the prophet Isaiah,

"The voice of one crying out
in the wilderness:
'Prepare the way of the Lord,
make his paths straight.
5 Every valley shall be filled,
and every mountain and
hill shall be made low,
and the crooked shall be
made straight,
and the rough ways made
smooth;
6 and all flesh shall see the
salvation of God.' "

7 John said to the crowds that
came out to be baptized by him,
"You brood of vipers! Who warned
you to flee from the wrath to come?
8 Bear fruits worthy of repentance.
Do not begin to say to yourselves,
'We have Abraham as our ancestor'; for I tell you, God is able from
these stones to raise up children to
Abraham. 9 Even now the ax is lying
at the root of the trees; every tree
therefore that does not bear good
fruit is cut down and thrown into
the fire."

10 And the crowds asked him,
"What then should we do?" 11 In reply he said to them, "Whoever has
two coats must share with anyone
who has none; and whoever has
food must do likewise." 12 Even tax
collectors came to be baptized, and
they asked him, "Teacher, what
should we do?" 13 He said to them,
"Collect no more than the amount
prescribed for you." 14 Soldiers also
asked him, "And we, what should
we do?" He said to them, "Do not
extort money from anyone by
threats or false accusation, and be
satisfied with your wages."

15 As the people were filled
with expectation, and all were
questioning in their hearts concerning John, whether he might be
the Messiah,[w] 16 John answered all
of them by saying, "I baptize you
with water; but one who is more
powerful than I is coming; I am not
worthy to untie the thong of his
sandals. He will baptize you with[x]
the Holy Spirit and fire. 17 His winnowing fork is in his hand, to clear
his threshing floor and to gather
the wheat into his granary; but the
chaff he will burn with unquenchable fire."

18 So, with many other exhortations, he proclaimed the good news
to the people. 19 But Herod the ruler,[v] who had been rebuked by him
because of Herodias, his brother's
wife, and because of all the evil
things that Herod had done, 20 added to them all by shutting up John
in prison.

The Baptism of Jesus

21 Now when all the people
were baptized, and when Jesus also
had been baptized and was praying, the heaven was opened, 22 and
the Holy Spirit descended upon

2.49 Jn 2.16
2.50 Mk 9.32; Lk 9.45
2.51 vv. 19,39
2.52 v. 40; 1 Sam 2.26
3.1-20pp Mt 3.1-12; Mk 1.1-8; Jn 1.6-8,19-28
3.1 Mt 27.2; 14.1
3.2 Jn 11.49; 18.13; Acts 4.6; Mt 26.3
3.4 Isa 40.3-5
3.6 Ps 98.2; Isa 52.10; Lk 2.30
3.7 Mt 12.34; 23.33
3.8 Jn 8.33,39
3.9 Mt 7.19; Heb 6.7,8
3.10 Acts 2.37
3.11 Jas 2.15,16
3.12 Lk 7.29
3.13 Lk 19.8
3.14 Ex 23.1; Lev 19.11
3.15 Acts 13.25
3.16 Acts 1.5; 11.16; 19.4
3.17 Isa 30.24; Mic 4.12; Mt 13.30
3.19 Mt 14.3,4; Mk 6.17,18
3.21,22pp Mt 3.13-17; Mk 1.9-11
3.21 Lk 5.16; 6.12; 9.18,28; 11.1
3.22 Ps 2.7; Isa 42.1; Lk 9.35; Acts 10.38; 2 Pet 1.17

[t] Or *be about my Father's interests?*
[u] Or *in stature* [v] Gk *tetrarch* [w] Or *the Christ* [x] Or *in*

him in bodily form like a dove. And
a voice came from heaven, "You are
my Son, the Beloved;[y] with you I
am well pleased."[z]

The Ancestors of Jesus

23 Jesus was about thirty years
old when he began his work. He
was the son (as was thought) of Joseph son of Heli, 24 son of Matthat,
son of Levi, son of Melchi, son
of Jannai, son of Joseph, 25 son of
Mattathias, son of Amos, son of
Nahum, son of Esli, son of Naggai,
26 son of Maath, son of Mattathias,
son of Semein, son of Josech,
son of Joda, 27 son of Joanan, son
of Rhesa, son of Zerubbabel, son of
Shealtiel,[a] son of Neri, 28 son of
Melchi, son of Addi, son of Cosam,
son of Elmadam, son of Er, 29 son of
Joshua, son of Eliezer, son of Jo-
rim, son of Matthat, son of Levi,
30 son of Simeon, son of Judah, son
of Joseph, son of Jonam, son of Eliakim, 31 son of Melea, son of Men-
na, son of Mattatha, son of Nathan,
son of David, 32 son of Jesse, son of
Obed, son of Boaz, son of Sala,[b]
son of Nahshon, 33 son of Amminadab, son of Admin, son of Arni,[c]
son of Hezron, son of Perez, son of
Judah, 34 son of Jacob, son of Isaac,
son of Abraham, son of Terah, son
of Nahor, 35 son of Serug, son of
Reu, son of Peleg, son of Eber, son
of Shelah, 36 son of Cainan, son of
Arphaxad, son of Shem, son of
Noah, son of Lamech, 37 son of Methuselah, son of Enoch, son of Jared, son of Mahalaleel, son of Cainan, 38 son of Enos, son of Seth, son
of Adam, son of God.

The Temptation of Jesus

4 Jesus, full of the Holy Spirit,
returned from the Jordan and
was led by the Spirit in the wilderness, 2 where for forty days he was
tempted by the devil. He ate nothing at all during those days, and
when they were over, he was famished. 3 The devil said to him, "If
you are the Son of God, command
this stone to become a loaf of
bread." 4 Jesus answered him, "It is
written, 'One does not live by bread
alone.' "
5 Then the devil[d] led him up
and showed him in an instant all
the kingdoms of the world. 6 And
the devil[d] said to him, "To you I
will give their glory and all this authority; for it has been given over to
me, and I give it to anyone I please.
7 If you, then, will worship me, it
will all be yours." 8 Jesus answered
him, "It is written,

'Worship the Lord your God,
and serve only him.' "

9 Then the devil[d] took him to
Jerusalem, and placed him on the
pinnacle of the temple, saying to
him, "If you are the Son of God,
throw yourself down from here,
10 for it is written,

'He will command his angels
concerning you,
to protect you,'

11 and

'On their hands they will
bear you up,
so that you will not dash
your foot against a
stone.' "

12 Jesus answered him, "It is said,
'Do not put the Lord your God to
the test.' " 13 When the devil had
finished every test, he departed
from him until an opportune time.

The Beginning of the Galilean Ministry

14 Then Jesus, filled with the
power of the Spirit, returned to
Galilee, and a report about him
spread through all the surrounding
country. 15 He began to teach in
their synagogues and was praised
by everyone.

The Rejection of Jesus at Nazareth

16 When he came to Nazareth,
where he had been brought up, he
went to the synagogue on the sabbath day, as was his custom. He
stood up to read, 17 and the scroll of

3.23 Mt 4.17; Acts 1.1; Jn 8.57; Lk 1.27
3.27 Mt 1.12
3.31 2 Sam 5.14; 1 Chr 3.5
3.32 Ruth 4.18ff; 1 Chr 2.10ff
3.34 Gen 11.24, 26
3.36 Gen 11.12; 5.6ff
3.38 Gen 5.1,2
4.1-13pp Mt 4.1-11; Mk 1.12,13
4.1 v. 14; Lk 2.27
4.2 Ex 34.28; 1 Kings 19.8
4.4 Deut 8.3
4.6 Jn 12.31; 14.30; 1 Jn 5.19
4.8 Deut 6.13
4.10 Ps 91.11,12
4.12 Deut 6.16
4.13 Jn 14.30; Heb 4.15
4.14,15pp Mt 4.12-17; Mk 1.14,15; Jn 4.43-45
4.14 Mt 9.26
4.15 Mt 9.35; 11.1
4.16 Mt 13.54; Mk 6.1; Acts 13.14-16

[y] Or *my beloved Son* [z] Other ancient authorities read *You are my Son, today I have begotten you* [a] Gk *Salathiel* [b] Other ancient authorities read *Salmon* [c] Other ancient authorities read *Amminadab, son of Aram*; others vary widely [d] Gk *he*

the prophet Isaiah was given to
him. He unrolled the scroll and
found the place where it was written:
18 "The Spirit of the Lord is
upon me,
because he has anointed
me
to bring good news to the
poor.
He has sent me to proclaim
release to the captives
and recovery of sight to the
blind,
to let the oppressed go
free,
19 to proclaim the year of the
Lord's favor."
20 And he rolled up the scroll, gave
it back to the attendant, and sat
down. The eyes of all in the synagogue were fixed on him. 21 Then
he began to say to them, "Today
this scripture has been fulfilled in
your hearing." 22 All spoke well of
him and were amazed at the gracious words that came from his
mouth. They said, "Is not this Joseph's son?" 23 He said to them,
"Doubtless you will quote to me
this proverb, 'Doctor, cure yourself!' And you will say, 'Do here
also in your hometown the things
that we have heard you did at Capernaum.' " 24 And he said, "Truly I
tell you, no prophet is accepted in
the prophet's hometown. 25 But the
truth is, there were many widows in
Israel in the time of Elijah, when
the heaven was shut up three years
and six months, and there was a severe famine over all the land; 26 yet
Elijah was sent to none of them except to a widow at Zarephath in Sidon. 27 There were also many lepers[e] in Israel in the time of the
prophet Elisha, and none of them
was cleansed except Naaman the
Syrian." 28 When they heard this,
all in the synagogue were filled
with rage. 29 They got up, drove him
out of the town, and led him to the
brow of the hill on which their
town was built, so that they might
hurl him off the cliff. 30 But he
passed through the midst of them
and went on his way.

The Man with an Unclean Spirit

31 He went down to Capernaum, a city in Galilee, and was
teaching them on the sabbath.
32 They were astounded at his
teaching, because he spoke with
authority. 33 In the synagogue there
was a man who had the spirit of an
unclean demon, and he cried out
with a loud voice, 34 "Let us alone!
What have you to do with us, Jesus
of Nazareth? Have you come to destroy us? I know who you are, the
Holy One of God." 35 But Jesus rebuked him, saying, "Be silent, and
come out of him!" When the demon had thrown him down before
them, he came out of him without
having done him any harm. 36 They
were all amazed and kept saying to
one another, "What kind of utterance is this? For with authority and
power he commands the unclean
spirits, and out they come!" 37 And
a report about him began to reach
every place in the region.

Healings at Simon's House

38 After leaving the synagogue
he entered Simon's house. Now Simon's mother-in-law was suffering
from a high fever, and they asked
him about her. 39 Then he stood
over her and rebuked the fever, and
it left her. Immediately she got up
and began to serve them.
40 As the sun was setting, all
those who had any who were sick
with various kinds of diseases
brought them to him; and he laid
his hands on each of them and
cured them. 41 Demons also came
out of many, shouting, "You are the
Son of God!" But he rebuked them
and would not allow them to
speak, because they knew that he
was the Messiah.[f]

Jesus Preaches in the Synagogues

42 At daybreak he departed and
went into a deserted place. And the
crowds were looking for him; and
when they reached him, they wanted to prevent him from leaving

4.18 Isa 61.1,2; Mt 12.18
4.19 Lev 25.10
4.20 v. 17
4.22 Ps 45.2; Mt 13.54, 55; Mk 6.2, 3; Jn 6.42; 7.15
4.23 Mk 1.21ff; 2.1ff; v. 16
4.24 Mt 13.57; Mk 6.4; Jn 4.44
4.25 1 Kings 17.1, 8-16; 18.1; Jas 5.17,18
4.27 2 Kings 5.1-14
4.29 Num 15.35; Acts 7.58; Heb 13.12
4.30 Jn 8.59; 10.39
4.31-37pp Mk 1.21-28
4.31 Mt 4.13
4.32 Mt 7.28; Mk 11.18; Jn 7.46
4.34 v. 41; Ps 16.10; Dan 9.24
4.35 vv. 39,41; Mt 8.26; Mk 4.39; Lk 8.24
4.36 v. 32
4.37 v. 14
4.38,39pp Mt 8.14-17; Mk 1.29-34
4.39 vv. 35,41
4.40-44pp Mt 8.16-17; Mk 1.32-34
4.40 Mk 5.23; Mt 4.23
4.41 Mt 4.3; 8.4
4.42 Mk 1.35-38

[e] The terms *leper* and *leprosy* can refer to several diseases [f] Or *the Christ*

them. 43 But he said to them, "I must proclaim the good news of the kingdom of God to the other cities also; for I was sent for this purpose." 44 So he continued proclaiming the message in the synagogues of Judea.[g]

Jesus Calls the First Disciples

5 Once while Jesus[h] was standing beside the lake of Gennesaret, and the crowd was pressing in on him to hear the word of God, 2 he saw two boats there at the shore of the lake; the fishermen had gone out of them and were washing their nets. 3 He got into one of the boats, the one belonging to Simon, and asked him to put out a little way from the shore. Then he sat down and taught the crowds from the boat. 4 When he had finished speaking, he said to Simon, "Put out into the deep water and let down your nets for a catch." 5 Simon answered, "Master, we have worked all night long but have caught nothing. Yet if you say so, I will let down the nets." 6 When they had done this, they caught so many fish that their nets were beginning to break. 7 So they signaled their partners in the other boat to come and help them. And they came and filled both boats, so that they began to sink. 8 But when Simon Peter saw it, he fell down at Jesus' knees, saying, "Go away from me, Lord, for I am a sinful man!" 9 For he and all who were with him were amazed at the catch of fish that they had taken; 10 and so also were James and John, sons of Zebedee, who were partners with Simon. Then Jesus said to Simon, "Do not be afraid; from now on you will be catching people." 11 When they had brought their boats to shore, they left everything and followed him.

Jesus Cleanses a Leper

12 Once, when he was in one of the cities, there was a man covered with leprosy.[i] When he saw Jesus, he bowed with his face to the ground and begged him, "Lord, if you choose, you can make me clean." 13 Then Jesus[h] stretched out his hand, touched him, and said, "I do choose. Be made clean." Immediately the leprosy[i] left him. 14 And he ordered him to tell no one. "Go," he said, "and show yourself to the priest, and, as Moses commanded, make an offering for your cleansing, for a testimony to them." 15 But now more than ever the word about Jesus[j] spread abroad; many crowds would gather to hear him and to be cured of their diseases. 16 But he would withdraw to deserted places and pray.

Jesus Heals a Paralytic

17 One day, while he was teaching, Pharisees and teachers of the law were sitting near by (they had come from every village of Galilee and Judea and from Jerusalem); and the power of the Lord was with him to heal.[k] 18 Just then some men came, carrying a paralyzed man on a bed. They were trying to bring him in and lay him before Jesus;[j] 19 but finding no way to bring him in because of the crowd, they went up on the roof and let him down with his bed through the tiles into the middle of the crowd[l] in front of Jesus. 20 When he saw their faith, he said, "Friend,[m] your sins are forgiven you." 21 Then the scribes and the Pharisees began to question, "Who is this who is speaking blasphemies? Who can forgive sins but God alone?" 22 When Jesus perceived their questionings, he answered them, "Why do you raise such questions in your hearts? 23 Which is easier, to say, 'Your sins are forgiven you,' or to say, 'Stand up and walk'? 24 But so that you may know that the Son of Man has authority on earth to forgive sins"—he said to the one who was paralyzed—"I say to you, stand up and take your bed and go to your home." 25 Immediately he stood up before them, took what he had

4.44 Mt 4.18-22; Mk 1.16-20; Jn 1.40-42
5.1-11pp Mt 4.18-22; Mk 1.16-20
5.3 Mt 13.1,2; Mk 4.1
5.4 Jn 21.6
5.5 Lk 8.24,45; 9.33,49; 17.13
5.10 Mt 14.27
5.11 v. 28; Mt 19.29
5.12-16pp Mt 8.1-4; Mk 1.40-45
5.12 Lk 17.11-19
5.15 Mt 9.26; Lk 4.14,37
5.16 Mt 14.23; Mk 6.46; Lk 3.21; 6.12; 9.18,28; 11.1
5.17-26pp Mt 9.1-8; Mk 2.1-12
5.17 Mt 15.1; Mk 5.30; Lk 6.19
5.19 Mt 24.17
5.20 Lk 7.48,49
5.21 Isa 43.25

g Other ancient authorities read *Galilee*
h Gk *he*
i The terms *leper* and *leprosy* can refer to several diseases
j Gk *him*
k Other ancient authorities read *was present to heal them*
l Gk *into the midst*
m Gk *Man*

been lying on, and went to his
home, glorifying God. 26 Amazement seized all of them, and they
glorified God and were filled with
awe, saying, "We have seen strange
things today."

Jesus Calls Levi

27 After this he went out and
saw a tax collector named Levi, sitting at the tax booth; and he said to
him, "Follow me." 28 And he got up,
left everything, and followed him.
29 Then Levi gave a great banquet for him in his house; and
there was a large crowd of tax collectors and others sitting at the table[n] with them. 30 The Pharisees
and their scribes were complaining
to his disciples, saying, "Why do
you eat and drink with tax collectors and sinners?" 31 Jesus answered, "Those who are well have
no need of a physician, but those
who are sick; 32 I have come to call
not the righteous but sinners to repentance."

The Question about Fasting

33 Then they said to him,
"John's disciples, like the disciples
of the Pharisees, frequently fast
and pray, but your disciples eat and
drink. 34 Jesus said to them, "You
cannot make wedding guests fast
while the bridegroom is with them,
can you? 35 The days will come
when the bridegroom will be taken
away from them, and then they will
fast in those days." 36 He also told
them a parable: "No one tears a
piece from a new garment and sews
it on an old garment; otherwise the
new will be torn, and the piece
from the new will not match the
old. 37 And no one puts new wine
into old wineskins; otherwise the
new wine will burst the skins and
will be spilled, and the skins will be
destroyed. 38 But new wine must be
put into fresh wineskins. 39 And no
one after drinking old wine desires
new wine, but says, 'The old is
good.'"[o]

The Question about the Sabbath

6 One sabbath[p] while Jesus[q]
was going through the grainfields, his disciples plucked some
heads of grain, rubbed them in
their hands, and ate them. 2 But
some of the Pharisees said, "Why
are you doing what is not lawful[r]
on the sabbath?" 3 Jesus answered,
"Have you not read what David did
when he and his companions were
hungry? 4 He entered the house of
God and took and ate the bread of
the Presence, which it is not lawful
for any but the priests to eat, and
gave some to his companions?"
5 Then he said to them, "The Son of
Man is lord of the sabbath."

The Man with a Withered Hand

6 On another sabbath he entered the synagogue and taught,
and there was a man there whose
right hand was withered. 7 The
scribes and the Pharisees watched
him to see whether he would cure
on the sabbath, so that they might
find an accusation against him.
8 Even though he knew what they
were thinking, he said to the man
who had the withered hand, "Come
and stand here." He got up and
stood there. 9 Then Jesus said to
them, "I ask you, is it lawful to do
good or to do harm on the sabbath,
to save life or to destroy it?" 10 After
looking around at all of them, he
said to him, "Stretch out your
hand." He did so, and his hand was
restored. 11 But they were filled
with fury and discussed with one
another what they might do to
Jesus.

Jesus Chooses the Twelve Apostles

12 Now during those days he
went out to the mountain to pray;
and he spent the night in prayer to
God. 13 And when day came, he
called his disciples and chose
twelve of them, whom he also
named apostles: 14 Simon, whom
he named Peter, and his brother
Andrew, and James, and John, and
Philip, and Bartholomew, 15 and

5.26 Lk 7.16
5.27-32pp Mt 9.9-13; Mk 2.13-17
5.28 v. 11
5.29 Lk 15.1
5.30 Acts 23.9
5.32 1 Tim 1.15
5.33-39pp Mt 9.14-17; Mk 2.18-22
5.33 Lk 7.18; Jn 3.25,26
5.35 Lk 9.22; 17.22
6.1-5pp Mt 12.1-8; Mk 2.23-28
6.1 Deut 23.25
6.2 Ex 20.10; 23.12; Deut 5.14
6.3 1 Sam 21.6
6.4 Lev 24.9
6.6-11pp Mt 12.9-14; Mk 3.1-6
6.6 Lk 13.14; 14.3; Jn 9.16
6.8 Mt 9.4
6.12-16pp Mt 10.1-4; Mk 3.13-19
6.12 Mt 14.23; Lk 9.28
6.13 Mk 6.30

[n] Gk *reclining* [o] Other ancient authorities read *better*; others lack verse 39 [p] Other ancient authorities read *On the second first sabbath* [q] Gk *he* [r] Other ancient authorities add *to do*

Matthew, and Thomas, and James
son of Alphaeus, and Simon, who
was called the Zealot, 16 and Judas
son of James, and Judas Iscariot,
who became a traitor.

Jesus Teaches and Heals

17 He came down with them
and stood on a level place, with a
great crowd of his disciples and a
great multitude of people from all
Judea, Jerusalem, and the coast of
Tyre and Sidon. 18 They had come
to hear him and to be healed of
their diseases; and those who were
troubled with unclean spirits were
cured. 19 And all in the crowd were
trying to touch him, for power
came out from him and healed all
of them.

Blessings and Woes

20 Then he looked up at his disciples and said:
"Blessed are you who are
poor,
for yours is the kingdom of
God.
21 "Blessed are you who are
hungry now,
for you will be filled.
"Blessed are you who weep
now,
for you will laugh.
22 "Blessed are you when people hate you, and when they ex-
clude you, revile you, and defame
you[s] on account of the Son of
Man. 23 Rejoice in that day and leap
for joy, for surely your reward is
great in heaven; for that is what
their ancestors did to the prophets.
24 "But woe to you who are rich,
for you have received your
consolation.
25 "Woe to you who are full
now,
for you will be hungry.
"Woe to you who are
laughing now,
for you will mourn and
weep.
26 "Woe to you when all speak
well of you, for that is what their
ancestors did to the false prophets.

Love for Enemies

27 "But I say to you that listen,
Love your enemies, do good to
those who hate you, 28 bless those
who curse you, pray for those who
abuse you. 29 If anyone strikes you
on the cheek, offer the other also;
and from anyone who takes away
your coat do not withhold even
your shirt. 30 Give to everyone who
begs from you; and if anyone takes
away your goods, do not ask for
them again. 31 Do to others as you
would have them do to you.
32 "If you love those who love
you, what credit is that to you? For
even sinners love those who love
them. 33 If you do good to those
who do good to you, what credit is
that to you? For even sinners do
the same. 34 If you lend to those
from whom you hope to receive,
what credit is that to you? Even
sinners lend to sinners, to receive
as much again. 35 But love your enemies, do good, and lend, expecting nothing in return.[t] Your reward will be great, and you will be
children of the Most High; for he is
kind to the ungrateful and the
wicked. 36 Be merciful, just as your
Father is merciful.

Judging Others

37 "Do not judge, and you will
not be judged; do not condemn,
and you will not be condemned.
Forgive, and you will be forgiven;
38 give, and it will be given to you. A
good measure, pressed down,
shaken together, running over, will
be put into your lap; for the measure you give will be the measure
you get back."
39 He also told them a parable:
"Can a blind person guide a blind
person? Will not both fall into a
pit? 40 A disciple is not above the
teacher, but everyone who is fully
qualified will be like the teacher.
41 Why do you see the speck in your
neighbor's[u] eye, but do not notice
the log in your own eye? 42 Or how
can you say to your neighbor,[v]
'Friend,[v] let me take out the speck
in your eye,' when you yourself do

6.16 Jude 1
6.17 Mt 4.25; Mk 3.7,8
6.19 Mt 9.21; 14.36; Mk 3.10; Lk 5.17
6.21 Isa 61.3
6.22 1 Pet 4.14; Jn 9.22; 16.2
6.23 Acts 5.41; Col 1.24; Mal 4.2; Acts 7.51
6.24 Jas 5.1; Lk 16.25
6.25 Isa 65.13; Prov 14.13
6.26 Jn 15.19
6.27-36pp Mt 5.43-48
6.27 v. 35; Rom 12.20
6.28 Lk 23.34; Acts 7.60
6.30 Deut 15.7,8, 10; Prov 21.26
6.31 Mt 7.12
6.35 vv. 27,30
6.37-45pp Mt 7.1-5
6.37 Rom 2.1
6.38 Mk 4.24; Jas 2.13
6.39 Mt 15.4
6.40 Mt 10.24; Jn 13.16; 15.20

[s] Gk *cast out your name as evil* [t] Other ancient authorities read *despairing of no one* [u] Gk *brother's* [v] Gk *brother*

not see the log in your own eye?
You hypocrite, first take the log out
of your own eye, and then you will
see clearly to take the speck out of
your neighbor's[w] eye.

A Tree and Its Fruit

43 "No good tree bears bad
fruit, nor again does a bad tree bear
good fruit; 44 for each tree is known
by its own fruit. Figs are not gathered from thorns, nor are grapes
picked from a bramble bush. 45 The
good person out of the good treasure of the heart produces good,
and the evil person out of evil treasure produces evil; for it is out of
the abundance of the heart that the
mouth speaks.

The Two Foundations

46 "Why do you call me 'Lord,
Lord,' and do not do what I tell
you? 47 I will show you what someone is like who comes to me, hears
my words, and acts on them.
48 That one is like a man building a
house, who dug deeply and laid the
foundation on rock; when a flood
arose, the river burst against that
house but could not shake it, because it had been well built.[x]
49 But the one who hears and does
not act is like a man who built a
house on the ground without a
foundation. When the river burst
against it, immediately it fell, and
great was the ruin of that house."

Jesus Heals a Centurion's Servant

7 After Jesus[y] had finished all
his sayings in the hearing of
the people, he entered Capernaum.
2 A centurion there had a slave
whom he valued highly, and who
was ill and close to death. 3 When
he heard about Jesus, he sent some
Jewish elders to him, asking him to
come and heal his slave. 4 When
they came to Jesus, they appealed
to him earnestly, saying, "He is
worthy of having you do this for
him, 5 for he loves our people, and
it is he who built our synagogue for
us." 6 And Jesus went with them,
but when he was not far from the
house, the centurion sent friends
to say to him, "Lord, do not trouble
yourself, for I am not worthy to
have you come under my roof;
7 therefore I did not presume to
come to you. But only speak the
word, and let my servant be healed.
8 For I also am a man set under authority, with soldiers under me;
and I say to one, 'Go,' and he goes,
and to another, 'Come,' and he
comes, and to my slave, 'Do this,'
and the slave does it." 9 When Jesus
heard this he was amazed at him,
and turning to the crowd that followed him, he said, "I tell you, not
even in Israel have I found such
faith." 10 When those who had been
sent returned to the house, they
found the slave in good health.

Jesus Raises the Widow's Son at Nain

11 Soon afterwards[z] he went to
a town called Nain, and his disciples and a large crowd went with
him. 12 As he approached the gate
of the town, a man who had died
was being carried out. He was his
mother's only son, and she was a
widow; and with her was a large
crowd from the town. 13 When the
Lord saw her, he had compassion
for her and said to her, "Do not
weep." 14 Then he came forward
and touched the bier, and the bearers stood still. And he said, "Young
man, I say to you, rise!" 15 The dead
man sat up and began to speak,
and Jesus[y] gave him to his mother.
16 Fear seized all of them; and they
glorified God, saying, "A great
prophet has risen among us!" and
"God has looked favorably on his
people!" 17 This word about him
spread throughout Judea and all
the surrounding country.

Messengers from John the Baptist

18 The disciples of John reported all these things to him. So John
summoned two of his disciples
19 and sent them to the Lord to ask,

6.43 Mt 7.16,18, 20
6.44 Mt 12.33
6.45 Mt 12.34, 35; Mk 7.20
6.46-49pp Mt 7.24-27
6.46 Mt 7.21
6.47 Jas 1.22-25
7.1-10pp Mt 8.5-13
7.1 Mt 7.28
7.9 v. 50
7.11 1 Kings 17.17-24; 2 Kings 4.32-37; Mk 5.21-24, 35-43; Jn 11.1-44
7.13 v. 19; Lk 10.1; 11.1,39; 12.42; 13.15; 17.5,6; 18.6; 19.8; 22.61; 24.34
7.14 Lk 8.54; Jn 11.43; Acts 9.40
7.16 Lk 1.65; Jn 6.14; Lk 1.68
7.18-35pp Mt 11.2-19

[w] Gk *brother's* [x] Other ancient authorities read *founded upon the rock* [y] Gk *he* [z] Other ancient authorities read *Next day*

"Are you the one who is to come, or
are we to wait for another?"
20When the men had come to him,
they said, "John the Baptist has
sent us to you to ask, 'Are you the
one who is to come, or are we to
wait for another?'" 21Jesus[a] had
just then cured many people of diseases, plagues, and evil spirits, and
had given sight to many who were
blind. 22And he answered them,
"Go and tell John what you have
seen and heard: the blind receive
their sight, the lame walk, the lepers[b] are cleansed, the deaf hear,
the dead are raised, the poor have
good news brought to them. 23And
blessed is anyone who takes no offense at me."

24 When John's messengers
had gone, Jesus[c] began to speak to
the crowds about John:[d] "What
did you go out into the wilderness
to look at? A reed shaken by the
wind? 25What then did you go out
to see? Someone[e] dressed in soft
robes? Look, those who put on fine
clothing and live in luxury are in
royal palaces. 26What then did you
go out to see? A prophet? Yes, I tell
you, and more than a prophet.
27This is the one about whom it is
written,

'See, I am sending my
messenger ahead of
you,
who will prepare your way
before you.'

28I tell you, among those born of
women no one is greater than
John; yet the least in the kingdom
of God is greater than he." 29(And
all the people who heard this, including the tax collectors, acknowledged the justice of God,[f]
because they had been baptized
with John's baptism. 30But by refusing to be baptized by him, the
Pharisees and the lawyers rejected
God's purpose for themselves.)

31 "To what then will I compare
the people of this generation, and
what are they like? 32They are like
children sitting in the marketplace
and calling to one another,

'We played the flute for you,
and you did not dance;
we wailed, and you did not
weep.'

33For John the Baptist has come
eating no bread and drinking no
wine, and you say, 'He has a demon'; 34the Son of Man has come
eating and drinking, and you say,
'Look, a glutton and a drunkard, a
friend of tax collectors and sinners!' 35Nevertheless, wisdom is
vindicated by all her children."

A Sinful Woman Forgiven

36 One of the Pharisees asked
Jesus[d] to eat with him, and he
went into the Pharisee's house and
took his place at the table. 37And a
woman in the city, who was a sinner, having learned that he was eating in the Pharisee's house,
brought an alabaster jar of ointment. 38She stood behind him at
his feet, weeping, and began to
bathe his feet with her tears and to
dry them with her hair. Then she
continued kissing his feet and
anointing them with the ointment.
39Now when the Pharisee who had
invited him saw it, he said to himself, "If this man were a prophet, he
would have known who and what
kind of woman this is who is touching him—that she is a sinner."
40Jesus spoke up and said to him,
"Simon, I have something to say to
you." "Teacher," he replied,
"Speak." 41"A certain creditor had
two debtors; one owed five hundred denarii,[g] and the other fifty.
42When they could not pay, he canceled the debts for both of them.
Now which of them will love him
more?" 43Simon answered, "I suppose the one for whom he canceled
the greater debt." And Jesus[c] said
to him, "You have judged rightly."
44Then turning toward the woman,
he said to Simon, "Do you see this
woman? I entered your house; you
gave me no water for my feet, but
she has bathed my feet with her
tears and dried them with her hair.

7.21 Mt 4.23; Mk 3.10
7.22 Isa 29.18, 19; 35.5,6; Lk 4.18
7.27 Mal 3.1; Mk 1.2
7.29 Mt 21.32; Lk 3.12
7.30 Acts 20.27
7.33 Lk 1.15
7.34 Lk 5.29; 15.1,2
7.36ff Mt 26.6-13; Mk 14.3-9; Jn 12.1-8
7.39 v. 16; Lk 24.19; Jn 6.14
7.41 Mt 18.28
7.44 Gen 18.4; 19.2; 43.24; Judg 19.21; 1 Tim 5.10

[a] Gk *He* [b] The terms *leper* and *leprosy* can refer to several diseases [c] Gk *he* [d] Gk *him* [e] Or *Why then did you go out? To see someone* [f] Or *praised God* [g] The denarius was the usual day's wage for a laborer

45 You gave me no kiss, but from the
time I came in she has not stopped
kissing my feet. 46 You did not
anoint my head with oil, but she
has anointed my feet with ointment. 47 Therefore, I tell you, her
sins, which were many, have been
forgiven; hence she has shown
great love. But the one to whom little is forgiven, loves little." 48 Then
he said to her, "Your sins are forgiv-
en." 49 But those who were at the
table with him began to say among
themselves, "Who is this who even
forgives sins?" 50 And he said to the
woman, "Your faith has saved you;
go in peace."

Some Women Accompany Jesus

8 Soon afterwards he went on
through cities and villages,
proclaiming and bringing the good
news of the kingdom of God. The
twelve were with him, 2 as well as
some women who had been cured
of evil spirits and infirmities: Mary,
called Magdalene, from whom sev-
en demons had gone out, 3 and Joanna, the wife of Herod's steward
Chuza, and Susanna, and many
others, who provided for them[h]
out of their resources.

The Parable of the Sower

4 When a great crowd gathered
and people from town after town
came to him, he said in a parable:
5 "A sower went out to sow his seed;
and as he sowed, some fell on the
path and was trampled on, and the
birds of the air ate it up. 6 Some fell
on the rock; and as it grew up, it
withered for lack of moisture.
7 Some fell among thorns, and the
thorns grew with it and choked it.
8 Some fell into good soil, and when
it grew, it produced a hundredfold." As he said this, he called out,
"Let anyone with ears to hear listen!"

The Purpose of the Parables

9 Then his disciples asked him
what this parable meant. 10 He
said, "To you it has been given to
know the secrets[i] of the kingdom
of God; but to others I speak[j] in
parables, so that
'looking they may not
perceive,
and listening they may not
understand.'

The Parable of the Sower Explained

11 "Now the parable is this: The
seed is the word of God. 12 The ones
on the path are those who have
heard; then the devil comes and
takes away the word from their
hearts, so that they may not believe
and be saved. 13 The ones on the
rock are those who, when they hear
the word, receive it with joy. But
these have no root; they believe
only for a while and in a time of
testing fall away. 14 As for what fell
among the thorns, these are the
ones who hear; but as they go on
their way, they are choked by the
cares and riches and pleasures of
life, and their fruit does not mature. 15 But as for that in the good
soil, these are the ones who, when
they hear the word, hold it fast in
an honest and good heart, and bear
fruit with patient endurance.

A Lamp under a Jar

16 "No one after lighting a lamp
hides it under a jar, or puts it under
a bed, but puts it on a lampstand,
so that those who enter may see
the light. 17 For nothing is hidden
that will not be disclosed, nor is
anything secret that will not become known and come to light.
18 Then pay attention to how you
listen; for to those who have, more
will be given; and from those who
do not have, even what they seem
to have will be taken away."

The True Kindred of Jesus

19 Then his mother and his
brothers came to him, but they
could not reach him because of the
crowd. 20 And he was told, "Your
mother and your brothers are
standing outside, wanting to see
you." 21 But he said to them, "My
mother and my brothers are those
who hear the word of God and do
it."

7.46 Ps 23.5 **7.48** Mt 9.2; Mk 2.5; Lk 5.20 **7.50** Mt 9.22; Mk 5.34; Lk 8.48 **8.1** Mt 4.23 **8.2** Mt 27.55,56 **8.4-8pp** Mt 13.1-8; Mk 4.1-9 **8.8** Mt 11.15 **8.9,10pp** Mt 13.1-17; Mk 4.10-12 **8.10** Isa 6.9,10; Jer 5.21; Ezek 12.2 **8.11-18pp** Mt 13.18-23; Mk 4.13-20 **8.11** 1 Thes 2.13; 1 Pet 1.23 **8.16** Mt 5.15; Mk 4.21; Lk 11.33 **8.17** Mt 10.26; Mk 4.22; Lk 12.2 **8.18** Mt 13.12; 25.29; Lk 19.26 **8.19-21pp** Mt 12.46-50; Mk 3.31-35 **8.21** Lk 11.28; Jn 15.14

h Other ancient authorities read *him*
i Or *mysteries* j Gk lacks *I speak*

Jesus Calms a Storm

22 One day he got into a boat
with his disciples, and he said to
them, "Let us go across to the other
side of the lake." So they put out,
23 and while they were sailing he
fell asleep. A windstorm swept
down on the lake, and the boat was
filling with water, and they were in
danger. 24 They went to him and
woke him up, shouting, "Master,
Master, we are perishing!" And he
woke up and rebuked the wind and
the raging waves; they ceased, and
there was a calm. 25 He said to
them, "Where is your faith?" They
were afraid and amazed, and said
to one another, "Who then is this,
that he commands even the winds
and the water, and they obey him?"

Jesus Heals the Gergesene Demoniac

26 Then they arrived at the
country of the Gerasenes,[k] which
is opposite Galilee. 27 As he
stepped out on land, a man of the
city who had demons met him. For
a long time he had worn[l] no
clothes, and he did not live in a
house but in the tombs. 28 When he
saw Jesus, he fell down before him
and shouted at the top of his voice,
"What have you to do with me,
Jesus, Son of the Most High God?
I beg you, do not torment me"—
29 for Jesus[m] had commanded the
unclean spirit to come out of the
man. (For many times it had seized
him; he was kept under guard and
bound with chains and shackles,
but he would break the bonds and
be driven by the demon into the
wilds.) 30 Jesus then asked him,
"What is your name?" He said, "Legion"; for many demons had entered him. 31 They begged him not
to order them to go back into the
abyss.

32 Now there on the hillside a
large herd of swine was feeding;
and the demons[n] begged Jesus[o] to
let them enter these. So he gave
them permission. 33 Then the demons came out of the man and entered the swine, and the herd
rushed down the steep bank into
the lake and was drowned.

34 When the swineherds saw
what had happened, they ran off
and told it in the city and in the
country. 35 Then people came out
to see what had happened, and
when they came to Jesus, they
found the man from whom the demons had gone sitting at the feet of
Jesus, clothed and in his right
mind. And they were afraid.
36 Those who had seen it told them
how the one who had been possessed by demons had been
healed. 37 Then all the people of
the surrounding country of the
Gerasenes[k] asked Jesus[o] to leave
them; for they were seized with
great fear. So he got into the boat
and returned. 38 The man from
whom the demons had gone
begged that he might be with him;
but Jesus[m] sent him away, saying,
39 "Return to your home, and declare how much God has done for
you." So he went away, proclaiming throughout the city how much
Jesus had done for him.

A Girl Restored to Life and a Woman Healed

40 Now when Jesus returned,
the crowd welcomed him, for they
were all waiting for him. 41 Just
then there came a man named Jairus, a leader of the synagogue. He
fell at Jesus' feet and begged him
to come to his house, 42 for he had
an only daughter, about twelve
years old, who was dying.

As he went, the crowds pressed
in on him. 43 Now there was a woman who had been suffering from
hemorrhages for twelve years; and
though she had spent all she had
on physicians,[p] no one could cure
her. 44 She came up behind him
and touched the fringe of his
clothes, and immediately her hemorrhage stopped. 45 Then Jesus

8.22-25pp Mt 8.23-27; Mk 4.36-41
8.22 Mk 6.47-52; Jn 6.16-21
8.24 Lk 5.5; 4.39
8.26-39pp Mt 8.28-34; Mk 6.1-20
8.28 Mk 1.24
8.31 Rom 10.7; Rev 20.1,3
8.33 vv. 22,23
8.35 Lk 10.39
8.36 Mt 4.24
8.37 Acts 16.39
8.40-56pp Mt 9.18-26; Mk 5.21-43
8.45 Lk 5.5

[k] Other ancient authorities read *Gadarenes*; others, *Gergesenes* [l] Other ancient authorities read *a man of the city who had had demons for a long time met him. He wore* [m] Gk *he* [n] Gk *they* [o] Gk *him*
[p] Other ancient authorities lack *and had spent all she had on physicians*

asked, "Who touched me?" When
all denied it, Peter[q] said, "Master,
the crowds surround you and press
in on you." 46 But Jesus said,
"Someone touched me; for I noticed that power had gone out from
me." 47 When the woman saw that
she could not remain hidden, she
came trembling; and falling down
before him, she declared in the
presence of all the people why she
had touched him, and how she had
been immediately healed. 48 He
said to her, "Daughter, your faith
has made you well; go in peace."
49 While he was still speaking,
someone came from the leader's
house to say, "Your daughter is
dead; do not trouble the teacher
any longer." 50 When Jesus heard
this, he replied, "Do not fear. Only
believe, and she will be saved."
51 When he came to the house, he
did not allow anyone to enter with
him, except Peter, John, and
James, and the child's father and
mother. 52 They were all weeping
and wailing for her; but he said,
"Do not weep; for she is not dead
but sleeping." 53 And they laughed
at him, knowing that she was dead.
54 But he took her by the hand and
called out, "Child, get up!" 55 Her
spirit returned, and she got up at
once. Then he directed them to
give her something to eat. 56 Her
parents were astounded; but he ordered them to tell no one what had
happened.

The Mission of the Twelve

9 Then Jesus[r] called the twelve
together and gave them power
and authority over all demons and
to cure diseases, 2 and he sent them
out to proclaim the kingdom of
God and to heal. 3 He said to them,
"Take nothing for your journey, no
staff, nor bag, nor bread, nor
money—not even an extra tunic.
4 Whatever house you enter, stay
there, and leave from there. 5 Wherever they do not welcome you, as
you are leaving that town shake the
dust off your feet as a testimony
against them." 6 They departed and
went through the villages, bringing
the good news and curing diseases
everywhere.

Herod's Perplexity

7 Now Herod the ruler[s] heard
about all that had taken place, and
he was perplexed, because it was
said by some that John had been
raised from the dead, 8 by some
that Elijah had appeared, and by
others that one of the ancient
prophets had arisen. 9 Herod said,
"John I beheaded; but who is this
about whom I hear such things?"
And he tried to see him.

Feeding the Five Thousand

10 On their return the apostles
told Jesus[t] all they had done. He
took them with him and withdrew
privately to a city called Bethsaida.
11 When the crowds found out
about it, they followed him; and he
welcomed them, and spoke to
them about the kingdom of God,
and healed those who needed to be
cured.
12 The day was drawing to a
close, and the twelve came to him
and said, "Send the crowd away, so
that they may go into the surrounding villages and countryside, to
lodge and get provisions; for we are
here in a deserted place." 13 But he
said to them, "You give them something to eat." They said, "We have
no more than five loaves and two
fish—unless we are to go and buy
food for all these people." 14 For
there were about five thousand
men. And he said to his disciples,
"Make them sit down in groups of
about fifty each." 15 They did so
and made them all sit down. 16 And
taking the five loaves and the two
fish, he looked up to heaven, and
blessed and broke them, and gave
them to the disciples to set before
the crowd. 17 And all ate and were
filled. What was left over was gathered up, twelve baskets of broken
pieces.

8.46 Lk 5.17; 6.19 **8.48** Lk 7.50; 17.19; 18.42 **8.49** v. 41 **8.52** Lk 23.27; Jn 11.11,13 **8.54** Lk 7.14; Jn 11.43 **8.56** Mt 8.4; Mk 3.12; 7.36; Lk 9.21 **9.1-6pp** Mt 10.1-15; Mk 6.7-13 **9.1** Mk 3.13,14 **9.2** Lk 10.1,9 **9.3** Lk 10.4; 22.35 **9.5** Acts 13.51 **9.7-9pp** Mt 14.1-12; Mk 6.14-39 **9.7** v. 19 **9.8** Mt 16.14 **9.9** Lk 23.8 **9.10-17pp** Mt 14.13-21; Mk 6.30-44; Jn 6.1-13 **9.10** v. 17 **9.13** 2 Kings 4.42-44 **9.16** Lk 22.19; 24.30,31; Acts 2.42; 20.11; 27.35

[q] Other ancient authorities add *and those who were with him* [r] Gk *he* [s] Gk *tetrarch* [t] Gk *him*

Peter's Declaration about Jesus

18 Once when Jesus[u] was praying alone, with only the disciples
near him, he asked them, "Who do
the crowds say that I am?" 19 They
answered, "John the Baptist; but
others, Elijah; and still others, that
one of the ancient prophets has
arisen." 20 He said to them, "But
who do you say that I am?" Peter
answered, "The Messiah[v] of God."

Jesus Foretells His Death and Resurrection

21 He sternly ordered and commanded them not to tell anyone,
22 saying, "The Son of Man must
undergo great suffering, and be rejected by the elders, chief priests,
and scribes, and be killed, and on
the third day be raised."
23 Then he said to them all, "If
any want to become my followers,
let them deny themselves and take
up their cross daily and follow me.
24 For those who want to save their
life will lose it, and those who lose
their life for my sake will save it.
25 What does it profit them if they
gain the whole world, but lose or
forfeit themselves? 26 Those who
are ashamed of me and of my
words, of them the Son of Man will
be ashamed when he comes in his
glory and the glory of the Father
and of the holy angels. 27 But truly
I tell you, there are some standing
here who will not taste death before they see the kingdom of God."

The Transfiguration

28 Now about eight days after
these sayings Jesus[u] took with him
Peter and John and James, and
went up on the mountain to pray.
29 And while he was praying, the appearance of his face changed, and
his clothes became dazzling white.
30 Suddenly they saw two men, Moses and Elijah, talking to him.
31 They appeared in glory and were
speaking of his departure, which
he was about to accomplish at Jerusalem. 32 Now Peter and his companions were weighed down with
sleep; but since they had stayed
awake,[w] they saw his glory and the
two men who stood with him.
33 Just as they were leaving him,
Peter said to Jesus, "Master, it is
good for us to be here; let us make
three dwellings,[x] one for you, one
for Moses, and one for Elijah"—
not knowing what he said. 34 While
he was saying this, a cloud came
and overshadowed them; and they
were terrified as they entered the
cloud. 35 Then from the cloud came
a voice that said, "This is my Son,
my Chosen;[y] listen to him!"
36 When the voice had spoken,
Jesus was found alone. And they
kept silent and in those days told
no one any of the things they had
seen.

Jesus Heals a Boy with a Demon

37 On the next day, when they
had come down from the mountain, a great crowd met him. 38 Just
then a man from the crowd shouted, "Teacher, I beg you to look at
my son; he is my only child. 39 Suddenly a spirit seizes him, and all at
once he[z] shrieks. It convulses him
until he foams at the mouth; it
mauls him and will scarcely leave
him. 40 I begged your disciples to
cast it out, but they could not."
41 Jesus answered, "You faithless
and perverse generation, how
much longer must I be with you
and bear with you? Bring your son
here." 42 While he was coming, the
demon dashed him to the ground
in convulsions. But Jesus rebuked
the unclean spirit, healed the boy,
and gave him back to his father.
43 And all were astounded at the
greatness of God.

Jesus Again Foretells His Death

While everyone was amazed at
all that he was doing, he said to his
disciples, 44 "Let these words sink
into your ears: The Son of Man is
going to be betrayed into human
hands." 45 But they did not understand this saying; its meaning was
concealed from them, so that they
could not perceive it. And they

[u] Gk *he* [v] Or *The Christ* [w] Or *but when they were fully awake* [x] Or *tents*
[y] Other ancient authorities read *my Beloved*
[z] Or *it*

9.18-27pp Mt 16.13-28; Mk 8.27-9.1
9.18 Jn 1.49; 6.66-69; 11.27
9.19 vv. 7,8; Mk 9.11-13
9.20 Jn 6.69
9.21 Mt 16.20
9.22 vv. 43-45; Lk 18.31-34
9.23 Mt 10.38; Lk 14.27
9.24 Mt 10.39
9.25 Jn 12.25
9.26 Mt 10.33; Lk 12.9; 2 Tim 2.12; 1 Jn 2.28
9.27 Lk 22.18; Jn 21.22
9.28-36pp Mt 17.1-8; Mk 9.2-13
9.28 Lk 3.21; 5.16; 6.12
9.31 2 Pet 1.15
9.32 Mt 26.43; Mk 14.40
9.33 Lk 5.8; 8.24,45; 17.13
9.35 2 Pet 1.17, 18; Mt 3.17
9.36 Mt 17.9
9.37-42pp Mt 17.14-21; Mk 9.14-29
9.43-45pp Mt 17.22,23; Mk 9.30-32
9.43 2 Pet 1.16
9.44 v. 22
9.45 Lk 2.50; 18.34

were afraid to ask him about this
saying.

True Greatness

46 An argument arose among
them as to which one of them was
the greatest. 47 But Jesus, aware of
their inner thoughts, took a little
child and put it by his side, 48 and
said to them, "Whoever welcomes
this child in my name welcomes
me, and whoever welcomes me
welcomes the one who sent me; for
the least among all of you is the
greatest."

Another Exorcist

49 John answered, "Master, we
saw someone casting out demons
in your name, and we tried to stop
him, because he does not follow
with us." 50 But Jesus said to him,
"Do not stop him; for whoever is
not against you is for you."

A Samaritan Village Refuses to Receive Jesus

51 When the days drew near for
him to be taken up, he set his face
to go to Jerusalem. 52 And he sent
messengers ahead of him. On their
way they entered a village of the
Samaritans to make ready for him;
53 but they did not receive him, because his face was set toward Jerusalem. 54 When his disciples James
and John saw it, they said, "Lord,
do you want us to command fire to
come down from heaven and consume them?"[a] 55 But he turned
and rebuked them. 56 Then[b] they
went on to another village.

Would-Be Followers of Jesus

57 As they were going along the
road, someone said to him, "I will
follow you wherever you go." 58 And
Jesus said to him, "Foxes have
holes, and birds of the air have
nests; but the Son of Man has nowhere to lay his head." 59 To another he said, "Follow me." But he
said, "Lord, first let me go and bury
my father." 60 But Jesus[c] said to
him, "Let the dead bury their own
dead; but as for you, go and proclaim the kingdom of God." 61 An-

9.46-50pp Mt 18.1-5; Mk 9.33-37
9.48 Mt 10.40; Jn 12.44; 13.20; Mt 23.11,12
9.49 Mk 9.38
9.50 Mt 12.30
9.51 Lk 13.22; 17.11; 18.31; 19.11,28
9.52 Mt 10.5; Jn 4.4
9.54 Mk 3.17; 1 Kings 1.10, 12
9.57-62pp Mt 8.18-22
9.59 Mt 8.21,22
10.1 Mt 10.1; Mk 6.7; Lk 9.1,2,51, 52
10.2 Mt 9.37,38; Jn 4.35
10.3 Mt 10.16
10.4 Mt 10.9,10; Mk 6.8; Lk 9.3
10.5 Mk 10.12
10.7 Mt 10.10; 1 Cor 9.14; 1 Tim 5.18
10.9 Mt 3.2; 10.7
10.11 Mt 10.14; Mk 6.11; Lk 9.5
10.12 Mt 10.15; 11.24
10.13 Mt 11.21; Lk 6.24-26

other said, "I will follow you, Lord;
but let me first say farewell to those
at my home." 62 Jesus said to him,
"No one who puts a hand to the
plow and looks back is fit for the
kingdom of God."

The Mission of the Seventy

10 After this the Lord appointed seventy[d] others and
sent them on ahead of him in pairs
to every town and place where he
himself intended to go. 2 He said to
them, "The harvest is plentiful, but
the laborers are few; therefore ask
the Lord of the harvest to send out
laborers into his harvest. 3 Go on
your way. See, I am sending you out
like lambs into the midst of wolves.
4 Carry no purse, no bag, no sandals; and greet no one on the road.
5 Whatever house you enter, first
say, 'Peace to this house!' 6 And if
anyone is there who shares in
peace, your peace will rest on that
person; but if not, it will return to
you. 7 Remain in the same house,
eating and drinking whatever they
provide, for the laborer deserves to
be paid. Do not move about from
house to house. 8 Whenever you enter a town and its people welcome
you, eat what is set before you;
9 cure the sick who are there, and
say to them, 'The kingdom of God
has come near to you.'[e] 10 But
whenever you enter a town and
they do not welcome you, go out
into its streets and say, 11 'Even the
dust of your town that clings to our
feet, we wipe off in protest against
you. Yet know this: the kingdom of
God has come near.'[f] 12 I tell you,
on that day it will be more tolerable
for Sodom than for that town.

Woes to Unrepentant Cities

13 "Woe to you, Chorazin! Woe
to you, Bethsaida! For if the deeds
of power done in you had been
done in Tyre and Sidon, they would

[a] Other ancient authorities add *as Elijah did* [b] Other ancient authorities read *rebuked them, and said, "You do not know what spirit you are of, 56for the Son of Man has not come to destroy the lives of human beings but to save them." Then* [c] Gk *he* [d] Other ancient authorities read *seventy-two* [e] Or *is at hand for you* [f] Or *is at hand*

have repented long ago, sitting in
sackcloth and ashes. 14 But at the
judgment it will be more tolerable
for Tyre and Sidon than for you.
15 And you, Capernaum,
will you be exalted to
heaven?
No, you will be brought
down to Hades.

16 "Whoever listens to you listens to me, and whoever rejects
you rejects me, and whoever rejects
me rejects the one who sent me."

The Return of the Seventy

17 The seventy[g] returned with
joy, saying, "Lord, in your name
even the demons submit to us!"
18 He said to them, "I watched Satan fall from heaven like a flash of
lightning. 19 See, I have given you
authority to tread on snakes and
scorpions, and over all the power of
the enemy; and nothing will hurt
you. 20 Nevertheless, do not rejoice
at this, that the spirits submit to
you, but rejoice that your names
are written in heaven."

Jesus Rejoices

21 At that same hour Jesus[h] rejoiced in the Holy Spirit[i] and said,
"I thank[j] you, Father, Lord of
heaven and earth, because you
have hidden these things from the
wise and the intelligent and have
revealed them to infants; yes, Father, for such was your gracious
will.[k] 22 All things have been handed over to me by my Father; and no
one knows who the Son is except
the Father, or who the Father is except the Son and anyone to whom
the Son chooses to reveal him."

23 Then turning to the disciples, Jesus[h] said to them privately,
"Blessed are the eyes that see what
you see! 24 For I tell you that many
prophets and kings desired to see
what you see, but did not see it,
and to hear what you hear, but did
not hear it."

The Parable of the Good Samaritan

25 Just then a lawyer stood up
to test Jesus.[l] "Teacher," he said,
"what must I do to inherit eternal
life?" 26 He said to him, "What is
written in the law? What do you
read there?" 27 He answered, "You
shall love the Lord your God with
all your heart, and with all your
soul, and with all your strength,
and with all your mind; and your
neighbor as yourself." 28 And he
said to him, "You have given the
right answer; do this, and you will
live."

29 But wanting to justify himself, he asked Jesus, "And who is
my neighbor?" 30 Jesus replied, "A
man was going down from Jerusalem to Jericho, and fell into the
hands of robbers, who stripped
him, beat him, and went away,
leaving him half dead. 31 Now by
chance a priest was going down
that road; and when he saw him, he
passed by on the other side. 32 So
likewise a Levite, when he came to
the place and saw him, passed by
on the other side. 33 But a Samaritan while traveling came near him;
and when he saw him, he was
moved with pity. 34 He went to him
and bandaged his wounds, having
poured oil and wine on them. Then
he put him on his own animal,
brought him to an inn, and took
care of him. 35 The next day he took
out two denarii,[m] gave them to the
innkeeper, and said, 'Take care of
him; and when I come back, I will
repay you whatever more you
spend.' 36 Which of these three, do
you think, was a neighbor to the
man who fell into the hands of the
robbers?" 37 He said, "The one who
showed him mercy." Jesus said to
him, "Go and do likewise."

Jesus Visits Martha and Mary

38 Now as they went on their
way, he entered a certain village,
where a woman named Martha
welcomed him into her home.
39 She had a sister named Mary,
who sat at the Lord's feet and listened to what he was saying. 40 But

10.15 Mt 11.23
10.16 Mt 10.40; Mk 9.37; Lk 9.48; Jn 13.20
10.17 v. 1
10.18 Jn 12.31; Rev 9.1; 12.8,9
10.19 Acts 28.5
10.20 Ex 32.32; Ps 69.28; Dan 12.1; Phil 4.3; Heb 12.23; Rev 13.8; 21.27
10.21 Mt 11.25; 1 Cor 1.26-29
10.22 Mt 28.18; Jn 3.35; 17.2
10.23 Mt 13.16
10.24 1 Pet 1.10
10.25 Mt 19.16; Mk 10.17; Lk 18.18
10.27 Deut 6.5; Lev 19.18; Rom 13.9; Gal 5.14; Jas 2.8
10.28 Lev 18.5; Mt 19.17
10.29 Lk 16.15
10.33 Lk 9.52; Jn 4.9
10.38 Jn 11.1; 12.2,3
10.39 Lk 8.35; Acts 22.3

[g] Other ancient authorities read *seventy-two* [h] Gk *he* [i] Other authorities read *in the spirit* [j] Or *praise* [k] Or *for so it was well-pleasing in your sight* [l] Gk *him* [m] The denarius was the usual day's wage for a laborer

Martha was distracted by her many
tasks; so she came to him and
asked, "Lord, do you not care that
my sister has left me to do all the
work by myself? Tell her then to
help me." 41 But the Lord answered
her, "Martha, Martha, you are worried and distracted by many things;
42 there is need of only one thing.[n]
Mary has chosen the better part,
which will not be taken away from
her."

The Lord's Prayer

11 He was praying in a certain
place, and after he had finished, one of his disciples said to
him, "Lord, teach us to pray, as
John taught his disciples." 2 He
said to them, "When you pray, say:

Father,[o] hallowed be your
name.
Your kingdom come.[p]
3 Give us each day our daily
bread.[q]
4 And forgive us our sins,
for we ourselves forgive
everyone indebted to
us.
And do not bring us to the
time of trial."[r]

Perseverance in Prayer

5 And he said to them, "Suppose one of you has a friend, and
you go to him at midnight and say
to him, 'Friend, lend me three
loaves of bread; 6 for a friend of
mine has arrived, and I have nothing to set before him.' 7 And he answers from within, 'Do not bother
me; the door has already been
locked, and my children are with
me in bed; I cannot get up and give
you anything.' 8 I tell you, even
though he will not get up and give
him anything because he is his
friend, at least because of his per-
sistence he will get up and give him
whatever he needs.

9 "So I say to you, Ask, and it
will be given you; search, and you
will find; knock, and the door will
be opened for you. 10 For everyone
who asks receives, and everyone
who searches finds, and for everyone who knocks, the door will be
opened. 11 Is there anyone among
you who, if your child asks for[s] a
fish, will give a snake instead of a
fish? 12 Or if the child asks for an
egg, will give a scorpion? 13 If you
then, who are evil, know how to
give good gifts to your children,
how much more will the heavenly
Father give the Holy Spirit[t] to
those who ask him!"

Jesus and Beelzebul

14 Now he was casting out a demon that was mute; when the demon had gone out, the one who
had been mute spoke, and the
crowds were amazed. 15 But some
of them said, "He casts out demons
by Beelzebul, the ruler of the demons." 16 Others, to test him, kept
demanding from him a sign from
heaven. 17 But he knew what they
were thinking and said to them,
"Every kingdom divided against itself becomes a desert, and house
falls on house. 18 If Satan also is divided against himself, how will his
kingdom stand? —for you say that
I cast out the demons by Beelzebul.
19 Now if I cast out the demons by
Beelzebul, by whom do your exorcists[u] cast them out? Therefore
they will be your judges. 20 But if it
is by the finger of God that I cast
out the demons, then the kingdom
of God has come to you. 21 When a
strong man, fully armed, guards his
castle, his property is safe. 22 But
when one stronger than he attacks
him and overpowers him, he takes
away his armor in which he trusted
and divides his plunder. 23 Whoever
is not with me is against me, and
whoever does not gather with me
scatters.

10.42 Ps 27.4 **11.1** Mk 1.35; Lk 3.21 **11.4** Mt 18.35; Mk 11.25 **11.8** Lk 18.1-6 **11.9** Mt 7.7-11; 18.19; 21.22; Mk 11.24; Jas 1.5-8; 1 Jn 5.14, 15 **11.14-28pp** Mt 12.22-45; Mk 3.20-30 **11.14** Mt 9.32-34 **11.16** Mt 16.1; Mk 8.11 **11.17** Jn 2.25 **11.20** Ex 8.19 **11.23** Lk 9.50

[n] Other ancient authorities read *few things are necessary, or only one* [o] Other ancient authorities read *Our Father in heaven* [p] A few ancient authorities read *Your Holy Spirit come upon us and cleanse us.* Other ancient authorities add *Your will be done, on earth as in heaven* [q] Or *our bread for tomorrow* [r] Or *us into temptation.* Other ancient authorities add *but rescue us from the evil one* (or *from evil*) [s] Other ancient authorities add *bread, will give a stone; or if your child asks for* [t] Other ancient authorities read *the Father give the Holy Spirit from heaven* [u] Gk *sons*

The Return of the Unclean Spirit

24 “When the unclean spirit has gone out of a person, it wanders through waterless regions looking for a resting place, but not finding any, it says, ‘I will return to my house from which I came.’ 25 When it comes, it finds it swept and put in order. 26 Then it goes and brings seven other spirits more evil than itself, and they enter and live there; and the last state of that person is worse than the first.”

True Blessedness

27 While he was saying this, a woman in the crowd raised her voice and said to him, “Blessed is the womb that bore you and the breasts that nursed you!” 28 But he said, “Blessed rather are those who hear the word of God and obey it!”

The Sign of Jonah

29 When the crowds were increasing, he began to say, “This generation is an evil generation; it asks for a sign, but no sign will be given to it except the sign of Jonah. 30 For just as Jonah became a sign to the people of Nineveh, so the Son of Man will be to this generation. 31 The queen of the South will rise at the judgment with the people of this generation and condemn them, because she came from the ends of the earth to listen to the wisdom of Solomon, and see, something greater than Solomon is here! 32 The people of Nineveh will rise up at the judgment with this generation and condemn it, because they repented at the proclamation of Jonah, and see, something greater than Jonah is here!

The Light of the Body

33 “No one after lighting a lamp puts it in a cellar,[v] but on the lampstand so that those who enter may see the light. 34 Your eye is the lamp of your body. If your eye is healthy, your whole body is full of light; but if it is not healthy, your body is full of darkness. 35 Therefore consider whether the light in you is not darkness. 36 If then your whole body is full of light, with no part of it in darkness, it will be as full of light as when a lamp gives you light with its rays.”

Jesus Denounces Pharisees and Lawyers

37 While he was speaking, a Pharisee invited him to dine with him; so he went in and took his place at the table. 38 The Pharisee was amazed to see that he did not first wash before dinner. 39 Then the Lord said to him, “Now you Pharisees clean the outside of the cup and of the dish, but inside you are full of greed and wickedness. 40 You fools! Did not the one who made the outside make the inside also? 41 So give for alms those things that are within; and see, everything will be clean for you.

42 “But woe to you Pharisees! For you tithe mint and rue and herbs of all kinds, and neglect justice and the love of God; it is these you ought to have practiced, without neglecting the others. 43 Woe to you Pharisees! For you love to have the seat of honor in the synagogues and to be greeted with respect in the marketplaces. 44 Woe to you! For you are like unmarked graves, and people walk over them without realizing it.”

45 One of the lawyers answered him, “Teacher, when you say these things, you insult us too.” 46 And he said, “Woe also to you lawyers! For you load people with burdens hard to bear, and you yourselves do not lift a finger to ease them. 47 Woe to you! For you build the tombs of the prophets whom your ancestors killed. 48 So you are witnesses and approve of the deeds of your ancestors; for they killed them, and you build their tombs. 49 Therefore also the Wisdom of God said, ‘I will send them prophets and apostles, some of whom they will kill and persecute,’ 50 so that this generation may be charged with the blood of all the prophets shed since the foundation of the world, 51 from the

11.26 Heb 10.26; 2 Pet 2.20
11.27 Lk 23.29
11.28 Lk 8.21; Jn 15.14
11.29-32pp Mt 12.38-42
11.29 Mt 16.4; Mk 8.12; v. 16
11.31 1 Kings 10.1; 2 Chr 9.1
11.32 Jon 3.5
11.33 Mt 5.15; Mk 4.21; Lk 8.16
11.34 Mt 6.22,23
11.37 Lk 7.36; 14.1
11.38 Mk 7.3,4
11.39 Mt 23.25,26
11.41 Lk 12.33; Mk 7.19; Titus 1.15
11.42 Mt 23.23; Lk 18.12
11.43 Mt 23.6,7; Mk 12.38, 39; Lk 20.46
11.44 Mt 23.27
11.46 Mt 23.4
11.47 Mt 23.29-32; Acts 7.51-53
11.49 Mt 23.34-36; 1 Cor 1.24; Col 2.3
11.51 Gen 4.8; 2 Chr 24.20, 21

[v] Other ancient authorities add *or under the bushel basket*

blood of Abel to the blood of Zechariah, who perished between the
altar and the sanctuary. Yes, I tell
you, it will be charged against this
generation. 52 Woe to you lawyers!
For you have taken away the key of
knowledge; you did not enter yourselves, and you hindered those who
were entering."
53 When he went outside, the
scribes and the Pharisees began to
be very hostile toward him and to
cross-examine him about many
things, 54 lying in wait for him, to
catch him in something he might
say.

A Warning against Hypocrisy

12 Meanwhile, when the
crowd gathered by the
thousands, so that they trampled
on one another, he began to speak
first to his disciples, "Beware of the
yeast of the Pharisees, that is, their
hypocrisy. 2 Nothing is covered up
that will not be uncovered, and
nothing secret that will not become known. 3 Therefore whatever
you have said in the dark will be
heard in the light, and what you
have whispered behind closed
doors will be proclaimed from the
housetops.

Exhortation to Fearless Confession

4 "I tell you, my friends, do not
fear those who kill the body, and
after that can do nothing more.
5 But I will warn you whom to fear:
fear him who, after he has killed,
has authority[w] to cast into hell.[x]
Yes, I tell you, fear him! 6 Are not
five sparrows sold for two pennies?
Yet not one of them is forgotten in
God's sight. 7 But even the hairs of
your head are all counted. Do not
be afraid; you are of more value
than many sparrows.
8 "And I tell you, everyone who
acknowledges me before others,
the Son of Man also will acknowledge before the angels of God; 9 but
whoever denies me before others
will be denied before the angels of
God. 10 And everyone who speaks a
word against the Son of Man will be

11.52 Mt 23.13 **11.54** Mk 12.13 **12.1** Mt 16.6; Mk 8.15; Mt 16.12 **12.2** Mt 10.26, 27; Mk 4.22; Lk 8.17; Eph 5.13 **12.4** Mt 10.28-33; Jn 15.14,15 **12.5** Heb 10.31 **12.7** Mt 12.12; Lk 21.18; Acts 27.34 **12.8** Mk 8.38; 2 Tim 2.12; 1 Jn 2.23 **12.10** Mt 12.31, 32; Mk 3.28,29

12.11 Mt 10.19; Mk 13.11; Lk 21.14 **12.14** Mic 6.8; Rom 2.1,3 **12.19** Eccl 11.9; Jas 5.5 **12.20** Jer 17.11; Job 27.8; Ps 39.6 **12.21** v. 33 **12.24** Job 38.41 **12.25** Ps 39.5

forgiven; but whoever blasphemes
against the Holy Spirit will not be
forgiven. 11 When they bring you
before the synagogues, the rulers,
and the authorities, do not worry
about how[y] you are to defend
yourselves or what you are to say;
12 for the Holy Spirit will teach you
at that very hour what you ought to
say."

The Parable of the Rich Fool

13 Someone in the crowd said
to him, "Teacher, tell my brother to
divide the family inheritance with
me." 14 But he said to him, "Friend,
who set me to be a judge or arbitra-
tor over you?" 15 And he said to
them, "Take care! Be on your guard
against all kinds of greed; for one's
life does not consist in the abundance of possessions." 16 Then he
told them a parable: "The land of a
rich man produced abundantly.
17 And he thought to himself, 'What
should I do, for I have no place to
store my crops?' 18 Then he said, 'I
will do this: I will pull down my
barns and build larger ones, and
there I will store all my grain and
my goods. 19 And I will say to my
soul, 'Soul, you have ample goods
laid up for many years; relax, eat,
drink, be merry.' 20 But God said to
him, 'You fool! This very night your
life is being demanded of you. And
the things you have prepared,
whose will they be?' 21 So it is with
those who store up treasures for
themselves but are not rich toward
God."

Do Not Worry

22 He said to his disciples,
"Therefore I tell you, do not worry
about your life, what you will eat,
or about your body, what you will
wear. 23 For life is more than food,
and the body more than clothing.
24 Consider the ravens: they neither
sow nor reap, they have neither
storehouse nor barn, and yet God
feeds them. Of how much more value are you than the birds! 25 And
can any of you by worrying add a

[w] Or *power* [x] Gk *Gehenna* [y] Other ancient authorities add *or what*

single hour to your span of life?[z] 26 If then you are not able to do so small a thing as that, why do you worry about the rest? 27 Consider the lilies, how they grow: they neither toil nor spin;[a] yet I tell you, even Solomon in all his glory was not clothed like one of these. 28 But if God so clothes the grass of the field, which is alive today and tomorrow is thrown into the oven, how much more will he clothe you—you of little faith! 29 And do not keep striving for what you are to eat and what you are to drink, and do not keep worrying. 30 For it is the nations of the world that strive after all these things, and your Father knows that you need them. 31 Instead, strive for his[b] kingdom, and these things will be given to you as well.

32 "Do not be afraid, little flock, for it is your Father's good pleasure to give you the kingdom. 33 Sell your possessions, and give alms. Make purses for yourselves that do not wear out, an unfailing treasure in heaven, where no thief comes near and no moth destroys. 34 For where your treasure is, there your heart will be also.

Watchful Slaves

35 "Be dressed for action and have your lamps lit; 36 be like those who are waiting for their master to return from the wedding banquet, so that they may open the door for him as soon as he comes and knocks. 37 Blessed are those slaves whom the master finds alert when he comes; truly I tell you, he will fasten his belt and have them sit down to eat, and he will come and serve them. 38 If he comes during the middle of the night, or near dawn, and finds them so, blessed are those slaves.

39 "But know this: if the owner of the house had known at what hour the thief was coming, he[c] would not have let his house be broken into. 40 You also must be ready, for the Son of Man is coming at an unexpected hour."

12.27 1 Kings 10.4-7
12.30 Mt 6.8
12.32 Jn 21.15-17
12.33 Mt 19.21; Mk 6.20
12.34 Mt 6.21
12.35 Mt 25.1-13; Mk 13.33-37; Eph 6.14
12.37 Mt 24.42, 46; Lk 17.8; Jn 13.4
12.39 Mt 24.43; 1 Thes 5.2; 2 Pet 3.10; Rev 3.3; 16.15
12.40 Mt 24.44; Mk 13.33; Lk 21.36
12.41-48pp Mt 24.45-51
12.42 Lk 7.13
12.47 Num 15.30; Deut 25.2
12.48 Lev 5.17
12.50 Mk 10.38; Jn 12.27
12.51 Mt 10.34-36; v. 49
12.53 Mic 7.6; Mt 10.21

The Faithful or the Unfaithful Slave

41 Peter said, "Lord, are you telling this parable for us or for everyone?" 42 And the Lord said, "Who then is the faithful and prudent manager whom his master will put in charge of his slaves, to give them their allowance of food at the proper time? 43 Blessed is that slave whom his master will find at work when he arrives. 44 Truly I tell you, he will put that one in charge of all his possessions. 45 But if that slave says to himself, 'My master is delayed in coming,' and if he begins to beat the other slaves, men and women, and to eat and drink and get drunk, 46 the master of that slave will come on a day when he does not expect him and at an hour that he does not know, and will cut him in pieces,[d] and put him with the unfaithful. 47 That slave who knew what his master wanted, but did not prepare himself or do what was wanted, will receive a severe beating. 48 But the one who did not know and did what deserved a beating will receive a light beating. From everyone to whom much has been given, much will be required; and from the one to whom much has been entrusted, even more will be demanded.

Jesus the Cause of Division

49 "I came to bring fire to the earth, and how I wish it were already kindled! 50 I have a baptism with which to be baptized, and what stress I am under until it is completed! 51 Do you think that I have come to bring peace to the earth? No, I tell you, but rather division! 52 From now on five in one household will be divided, three against two and two against three; 53 they will be divided:

father against son
  and son against father,
mother against daughter

[z] Or *add a cubit to your stature* [a] Other ancient authorities read *Consider the lilies; they neither spin nor weave* [b] Other ancient authorities read *God's* [c] Other ancient authorities add *would have watched and* [d] Or *cut him off*

and daughter against
mother,
mother-in-law against her
daughter-in-law
and daughter-in-law against
mother-in-law."

Interpreting the Time

54 He also said to the crowds,
"When you see a cloud rising in the
west, you immediately say, 'It is going to rain'; and so it happens.
55 And when you see the south wind
blowing, you say, 'There will be
scorching heat'; and it happens.
56 You hypocrites! You know how to
interpret the appearance of earth
and sky, but why do you not know
how to interpret the present time?

Settling with Your Opponent

57 "And why do you not judge
for yourselves what is right?
58 Thus, when you go with your accuser before a magistrate, on the
way make an effort to settle the
case,[e] or you may be dragged before the judge, and the judge hand
you over to the officer, and the officer throw you in prison. 59 I tell you,
you will never get out until you
have paid the very last penny."

Repent or Perish

13 At that very time there
were some present who
told him about the Galileans
whose blood Pilate had mingled
with their sacrifices. 2 He asked
them, "Do you think that because
these Galileans suffered in this way
they were worse sinners than all
other Galileans? 3 No, I tell you; but
unless you repent, you will all perish as they did. 4 Or those eighteen
who were killed when the tower of
Siloam fell on them — do you think
that they were worse offenders
than all the others living in Jerusalem? 5 No, I tell you; but unless you
repent, you will all perish just as
they did."

The Parable of the Barren Fig Tree

6 Then he told this parable: "A
man had a fig tree planted in his
vineyard; and he came looking for

12.54 Mt 16.2
12.55 Mt 20.12
12.56 Mt 16.3
12.58 Mt 5.25,26
12.59 Mk 12.42
13.1 Mt 27.2
13.2 Jn 9.2,3
13.6 Mt 21.19
13.7 Mt 3.10; 7.19; Lk 3.9
13.11 v. 16
13.13 Mk 5.23
13.14 Ex 20.9; Lk 6.7; 14.3
13.15 Lk 7.13; 14.5
13.16 Lk 19.9
13.18,19pp Mt 13.31,32; Mk 4.30-32

fruit on it and found none. 7 So he
said to the gardener, 'See here! For
three years I have come looking for
fruit on this fig tree, and still I find
none. Cut it down! Why should it
be wasting the soil?' 8 He replied,
'Sir, let it alone for one more year,
until I dig around it and put manure on it. 9 If it bears fruit next
year, well and good; but if not, you
can cut it down.' "

Jesus Heals a Crippled Woman

10 Now he was teaching in one
of the synagogues on the sabbath.
11 And just then there appeared a
woman with a spirit that had crippled her for eighteen years. She
was bent over and was quite unable
to stand up straight. 12 When Jesus
saw her, he called her over and
said, "Woman, you are set free
from your ailment." 13 When he laid
his hands on her, immediately she
stood up straight and began praising God. 14 But the leader of the
synagogue, indignant because
Jesus had cured on the sabbath,
kept saying to the crowd, "There
are six days on which work ought to
be done; come on those days and
be cured, and not on the sabbath
day." 15 But the Lord answered him
and said, "You hypocrites! Does
not each of you on the sabbath untie his ox or his donkey from the
manger, and lead it away to give it
water? 16 And ought not this woman, a daughter of Abraham whom
Satan bound for eighteen long
years, be set free from this bondage
on the sabbath day?" 17 When he
said this, all his opponents were
put to shame; and the entire crowd
was rejoicing at all the wonderful
things that he was doing.

The Parable of the Mustard Seed

18 He said therefore, "What is
the kingdom of God like? And to
what should I compare it? 19 It is
like a mustard seed that someone
took and sowed in the garden; it
grew and became a tree, and the
birds of the air made nests in its
branches."

[e] Gk *settle with him*

The Parable of the Yeast

20 And again he said, "To what
should I compare the kingdom of
God? 21 It is like yeast that a woman
took and mixed in with[f] three
measures of flour until all of it was
leavened."

The Narrow Door

22 Jesus[g] went through one
town and village after another,
teaching as he made his way to Jerusalem. 23 Someone asked him,
"Lord, will only a few be saved?"
He said to them, 24 "Strive to enter
through the narrow door; for many,
I tell you, will try to enter and will
not be able. 25 When once the owner of the house has got up and shut
the door, and you begin to stand
outside and to knock at the door,
saying, 'Lord, open to us,' then in
reply he will say to you, 'I do not
know where you come from.'
26 Then you will begin to say, 'We
ate and drank with you, and you
taught in our streets.' 27 But he will
say, 'I do not know where you come
from; go away from me, all you evildoers!' 28 There will be weeping and
gnashing of teeth when you see
Abraham and Isaac and Jacob and
all the prophets in the kingdom of
God, and you yourselves thrown
out. 29 Then people will come from
east and west, from north and
south, and will eat in the kingdom
of God. 30 Indeed, some are last
who will be first, and some are first
who will be last."

The Lament over Jerusalem

31 At that very hour some Pharisees came and said to him, "Get
away from here, for Herod wants to
kill you." 32 He said to them, "Go
and tell that fox for me,[h] 'Listen, I
am casting out demons and performing cures today and tomorrow,
and on the third day I finish my
work. 33 Yet today, tomorrow, and
the next day I must be on my way,
because it is impossible for a
prophet to be killed outside of Jerusalem.' 34 Jerusalem, Jerusalem,
the city that kills the prophets and
stones those who are sent to it!
How often have I desired to gather
your children together as a hen
gathers her brood under her wings,
and you were not willing! 35 See,
your house is left to you. And I tell
you, you will not see me until the
time comes when[i] you say,
'Blessed is the one who comes in
the name of the Lord.' "

Jesus Heals the Man with Dropsy

14 On one occasion when
Jesus[j] was going to the
house of a leader of the Pharisees
to eat a meal on the sabbath, they
were watching him closely. 2 Just
then, in front of him, there was a
man who had dropsy. 3 And Jesus
asked the lawyers and Pharisees,
"Is it lawful to cure people on the
sabbath, or not?" 4 But they were
silent. So Jesus[j] took him and
healed him, and sent him away.
5 Then he said to them, "If one of
you has a child[k] or an ox that has
fallen into a well, will you not immediately pull it out on a sabbath
day?" 6 And they could not reply to
this.

Humility and Hospitality

7 When he noticed how the
guests chose the places of honor,
he told them a parable. 8 "When
you are invited by someone to a
wedding banquet, do not sit down
at the place of honor, in case someone more distinguished than you
has been invited by your host; 9 and
the host who invited both of you
may come and say to you, 'Give this
person your place,' and then in disgrace you would start to take the
lowest place. 10 But when you are
invited, go and sit down at the lowest place, so that when your host
comes, he may say to you, 'Friend,
move up higher'; then you will be
honored in the presence of all who
sit at the table with you. 11 For all
who exalt themselves will be humbled, and those who humble themselves will be exalted."

13.20,21pp Mt 13.31,32
13.22 Lk 9.51
13.24 Mt 7.13
13.25 Mt 25.10-12; 7.23
13.27 Mt 7.23; 25.41
13.28 Mt 8.11,12
13.30 Mt 19.30; Mk 10.31
13.32 Heb 2.10; 7.28
13.34 Mt 23.37-39; Lk 19.41
13.35 Ps 118.26; Mt 21.9; Lk 19.38
14.1 Mk 3.2
14.3 Mt 12.10; Mk 3.4; Lk 6.9
14.5 Ex 23.5; Lk 13.15
14.7 Mt 23.6
14.8 Prov 25.6,7
14.10 Prov 25.6,7
14.11 Mt 23.12; LK 18.14; Jas 4.6; 1 Pet 5.5,6

[f] Gk *hid in* [g] Gk *He* [h] Gk lacks *for me* [i] Other ancient authorities lack *the time comes when* [j] Gk *he* [k] Other ancient authorities read *a donkey*

12 He said also to the one who
had invited him, "When you give a
luncheon or a dinner, do not invite
your friends or your brothers or
your relatives or rich neighbors, in
case they may invite you in return,
and you would be repaid. 13 But
when you give a banquet, invite the
poor, the crippled, the lame, and
the blind. 14 And you will be
blessed, because they cannot repay
you, for you will be repaid at the
resurrection of the righteous."

The Parable of the Great Dinner

15 One of the dinner guests, on
hearing this, said to him, "Blessed
is anyone who will eat bread in the
kingdom of God!" 16 Then Jesus[l]
said to him, "Someone gave a great
dinner and invited many. 17 At the
time for the dinner he sent his
slave to say to those who had been
invited, 'Come; for everything is
ready now.' 18 But they all alike began to make excuses. The first said
to him, 'I have bought a piece of
land, and I must go out and see it;
please accept my regrets.' 19 Another said, 'I have bought five yoke of
oxen, and I am going to try them
out; please accept my regrets.'
20 Another said, 'I have just been
married, and therefore I cannot
come.' 21 So the slave returned and
reported this to his master. Then
the owner of the house became angry and said to his slave, 'Go out at
once into the streets and lanes of
the town and bring in the poor, the
crippled, the blind, and the lame.'
22 And the slave said, 'Sir, what you
ordered has been done, and there
is still room.' 23 Then the master
said to the slave, 'Go out into the
roads and lanes, and compel people to come in, so that my house
may be filled. 24 For I tell you,[m]
none of those who were invited will
taste my dinner.' "

The Cost of Discipleship

25 Now large crowds were traveling with him; and he turned and
said to them, 26 "Whoever comes to
me and does not hate father and
mother, wife and children, brothers and sisters, yes, and even life
itself, cannot be my disciple.
27 Whoever does not carry the cross
and follow me cannot be my disciple. 28 For which of you, intending
to build a tower, does not first sit
down and estimate the cost, to see
whether he has enough to complete it? 29 Otherwise, when he has
laid a foundation and is not able to
finish, all who see it will begin to
ridicule him, 30 saying, 'This fellow
began to build and was not able to
finish.' 31 Or what king, going out to
wage war against another king, will
not sit down first and consider
whether he is able with ten thousand to oppose the one who comes
against him with twenty thousand?
32 If he cannot, then, while the other is still far away, he sends a dele-
gation and asks for the terms of
peace. 33 So therefore, none of you
can become my disciple if you do
not give up all your possessions.

About Salt

34 "Salt is good; but if salt has
lost its taste, how can its saltiness
be restored?[n] 35 It is fit neither for
the soil nor for the manure pile;
they throw it away. Let anyone with
ears to hear listen!"

The Parable of the Lost Sheep

15 Now all the tax collectors
and sinners were coming
near to listen to him. 2 And the
Pharisees and the scribes were
grumbling and saying, "This fellow
welcomes sinners and eats with
them."

3 So he told them this parable:
4 "Which one of you, having a hundred sheep and losing one of them,
does not leave the ninety-nine in
the wilderness and go after the one
that is lost until he finds it? 5 When
he has found it, he lays it on his
shoulders and rejoices. 6 And when
he comes home, he calls together
his friends and neighbors, saying to
them, 'Rejoice with me, for I have
found my sheep that was lost.'

14.13 v. 21
14.15-24pp Mt 22.1-14
14.15 Rev 19.9
14.17 Prov 9.2,5
14.20 Deut 24.5; 1 Cor 7.33
14.21 v. 13
14.24 Mt 21.43; Acts 13.46
14.25 Mt 10.37,38
14.27 Mt 16.24; Mk 8.34; Lk 9.23
14.33 Lk 18.29,30; Phil 3.7; Heb 11.26
14.34 Mt 5.13; Mk 9.50
14.35 Mt 11.15
15.1 Lk 5.29
15.2 Mt 9.11
15.3-7pp Mt 18.10-14

[l] Gk *he*
[m] The Greek word for *you* here is plural
[n] Or *how can it be used for seasoning?*

7 Just so, I tell you, there will be
more joy in heaven over one sinner
who repents than over ninety-nine
righteous persons who need no repentance.

The Parable of the Lost Coin

8 "Or what woman having ten
silver coins,[o] if she loses one of
them, does not light a lamp, sweep
the house, and search carefully until she finds it? 9 When she has
found it, she calls together her
friends and neighbors, saying, 'Rejoice with me, for I have found the
coin that I had lost.' 10 Just so, I tell
you, there is joy in the presence of
the angels of God over one sinner
who repents."

The Parable of the Prodigal and His Brother

11 Then Jesus[p] said, "There
was a man who had two sons.
12 The younger of them said to his
father, 'Father, give me the share of
the property that will belong to
me.' So he divided his property between them. 13 A few days later the
younger son gathered all he had
and traveled to a distant country,
and there he squandered his property in dissolute living. 14 When he
had spent everything, a severe famine took place throughout that
country, and he began to be in
need. 15 So he went and hired himself out to one of the citizens of
that country, who sent him to his
fields to feed the pigs. 16 He would
gladly have filled himself with[q] the
pods that the pigs were eating; and
no one gave him anything. 17 But
when he came to himself he said,
'How many of my father's hired
hands have bread enough and to
spare, but here I am dying of hunger! 18 I will get up and go to my father, and I will say to him, "Father,
I have sinned against heaven and
before you; 19 I am no longer worthy
to be called your son; treat me like
one of your hired hands." ' 20 So he
set off and went to his father. But
while he was still far off, his father
saw him and was filled with compassion; he ran and put his arms
around him and kissed him.
21 Then the son said to him, 'Father, I have sinned against heaven
and before you; I am no longer worthy to be called your son.'[r] 22 But
the father said to his slaves,
'Quickly, bring out a robe—the
best one—and put it on him; put a
ring on his finger and sandals on
his feet. 23 And get the fatted calf
and kill it, and let us eat and celebrate; 24 for this son of mine was
dead and is alive again; he was lost
and is found!' And they began to
celebrate.

25 "Now his elder son was in the
field; and when he came and approached the house, he heard music and dancing. 26 He called one of
the slaves and asked what was going on. 27 He replied, 'Your brother
has come, and your father has
killed the fatted calf, because he
has got him back safe and sound.'
28 Then he became angry and refused to go in. His father came out
and began to plead with him. 29 But
he answered his father, 'Listen! For
all these years I have been working
like a slave for you, and I have never disobeyed your command; yet
you have never given me even a
young goat so that I might celebrate with my friends. 30 But when
this son of yours came back, who
has devoured your property with
prostitutes, you killed the fatted
calf for him!' 31 Then the father[p]
said to him, 'Son, you are always
with me, and all that is mine is
yours. 32 But we had to celebrate
and rejoice, because this brother of
yours was dead and has come to
life; he was lost and has been
found.' "

The Parable of the Dishonest Manager

16 Then Jesus[p] said to the
disciples, "There was a rich
man who had a manager, and
charges were brought to him that
this man was squandering his prop-

15.7 v. 10; Lk 19.10; Jas 5.20 **15.10** v. 7 **15.11** Mt 21.28 **15.12** Deut 21.17 **15.20** Gen 45.14; 46.29; Acts 20.37 **15.21** Ps 51.4 **15.22** Zech 3.4; Gen 41.42 **15.24** v. 32; 1 Tim 5.6; Eph 2.1; 5.14 **15.30** v. 12 **15.32** v. 24 **16.1** Lk 15.13

[o] Gk *drachmas*, each worth about a day's wage for a laborer [p] Gk *he* [q] Other ancient authorities read *filled his stomach with* [r] Other ancient authorities add *treat me as one of your hired servants*

erty. 2 So he summoned him and
said to him, 'What is this that I hear
about you? Give me an accounting
of your management, because you
cannot be my manager any longer.'
3 Then the manager said to himself,
'What will I do, now that my master
is taking the position away from
me? I am not strong enough to dig,
and I am ashamed to beg. 4 I have
decided what to do so that, when I
am dismissed as manager, people
may welcome me into their
homes.' 5 So, summoning his master's debtors one by one, he asked
the first, 'How much do you owe
my master?' 6 He answered, 'A hundred jugs of olive oil.' He said to
him, 'Take your bill, sit down
quickly, and make it fifty.' 7 Then
he asked another, 'And how much
do you owe?' He replied, 'A hundred containers of wheat.' He said
to him, 'Take your bill and make it
eighty.' 8 And his master commended the dishonest manager because he had acted shrewdly; for
the children of this age are more
shrewd in dealing with their own
generation than are the children of
light. 9 And I tell you, make friends
for yourselves by means of dishonest wealth[s] so that when it is gone,
they may welcome you into the
eternal homes.[t]
10 "Whoever is faithful in a very
little is faithful also in much; and
whoever is dishonest in a very little
is dishonest also in much. 11 If then
you have not been faithful with the
dishonest wealth,[s] who will entrust to you the true riches? 12 And
if you have not been faithful with
what belongs to another, who will
give you what is your own? 13 No
slave can serve two masters; for a
slave will either hate the one and
love the other, or be devoted to the
one and despise the other. You
cannot serve God and wealth."[s]

The Law and the Kingdom of God

14 The Pharisees, who were lovers of money, heard all this, and
they ridiculed him. 15 So he said to
them, "You are those who justify
yourselves in the sight of others;
but God knows your hearts; for
what is prized by human beings is
an abomination in the sight of God.
16 "The law and the prophets
were in effect until John came;
since then the good news of the
kingdom of God is proclaimed, and
everyone tries to enter it by force.[u]
17 But it is easier for heaven and
earth to pass away, than for one
stroke of a letter in the law to be
dropped.
18 "Anyone who divorces his
wife and marries another commits
adultery, and whoever marries a
woman divorced from her husband
commits adultery.

The Rich Man and Lazarus

19 "There was a rich man who
was dressed in purple and fine lin-
en and who feasted sumptuously
every day. 20 And at his gate lay a
poor man named Lazarus, covered
with sores, 21 who longed to satisfy
his hunger with what fell from the
rich man's table; even the dogs
would come and lick his sores.
22 The poor man died and was carried away by the angels to be with
Abraham.[v] The rich man also died
and was buried. 23 In Hades, where
he was being tormented, he looked
up and saw Abraham far away with
Lazarus by his side.[w] 24 He called
out, 'Father Abraham, have mercy
on me, and send Lazarus to dip the
tip of his finger in water and cool
my tongue; for I am in agony in
these flames.' 25 But Abraham said,
'Child, remember that during your
lifetime you received your good
things, and Lazarus in like manner
evil things; but now he is comforted here, and you are in agony. 26 Besides all this, between you and us a
great chasm has been fixed, so that
those who might want to pass from
here to you cannot do so, and no
one can cross from there to us.'
27 He said, 'Then, father, I beg you

16.8 Jn 12.36; Eph 5.8; 1 Thes 5.5
16.9 Mt 6.19,24; 19.21; Lk 11.41; 12.33
16.10 Mt 25.21; Lk 19.17
16.11 v. 9
16.13 Mt 6.24
16.14 2 Tim 3.2; Lk 23.35
16.15 Lk 10.29; 1 Sam 16.7; Prov 21.2; Acts 1.24
16.16 Mt 11.12, 13; 4.23
16.17 Isa 40.8; Mt 5.17,18; Lk 21.33
16.18 Mt 5.31,32; 19.19; Mk 10.11; 1 Cor 7.10, 11
16.20 Acts 3.2
16.22 Jn 13.23
16.23 Mt 11.23
16.24 v. 30; Mt 25.41
16.25 Lk 6.24

[s] Gk *mammon* [t] Gk *tents*
[u] Or *everyone is strongly urged to enter it*
[v] Gk *to Abraham's bosom* [w] Gk *in his bosom*

to send him to my father's house—
28 for I have five brothers—that he
may warn them, so that they will
not also come into this place of torment.' 29 Abraham replied, 'They
have Moses and the prophets; they
should listen to them.' 30 He said,
'No, father Abraham; but if someone goes to them from the dead,
they will repent.' 31 He said to him,
'If they do not listen to Moses and
the prophets, neither will they be
convinced even if someone rises
from the dead.' "

Some Sayings of Jesus

17 Jesus[x] said to his disciples, "Occasions for stumbling are bound to come, but woe
to anyone by whom they come! 2 It
would be better for you if a millstone were hung around your neck
and you were thrown into the sea
than for you to cause one of these
little ones to stumble. 3 Be on your
guard! If another disciple[y] sins,
you must rebuke the offender, and
if there is repentance, you must
forgive. 4 And if the same person
sins against you seven times a day,
and turns back to you seven times
and says, 'I repent,' you must forgive."

5 The apostles said to the Lord,
"Increase our faith!" 6 The Lord replied, "If you had faith the size of
a[z] mustard seed, you could say to
this mulberry tree, 'Be uprooted
and planted in the sea,' and it
would obey you.

7 "Who among you would say to
your slave who has just come in
from plowing or tending sheep in
the field, 'Come here at once and
take your place at the table'?
8 Would you not rather say to him,
'Prepare supper for me, put on your
apron and serve me while I eat and
drink; later you may eat and drink'?
9 Do you thank the slave for doing
what was commanded? 10 So you
also, when you have done all that
you were ordered to do, say, 'We
are worthless slaves; we have done
only what we ought to have
done!' "

16.29 Lk 4.17; Jn 5.45-47; Acts 15.21
16.30 Lk 3.8; 19.9
17.1 Mt 18.6,7; Mk 9.42; 1 Cor 11.19
17.2 1 Cor 8.12
17.3 Mt 18.15
17.4 Mt 18.21,22
17.5 Mk 6.30
17.6 Mt 17.20; 21.21; Mk 9.23; Lk 7.13
17.8 Lk 12.37
17.11 Lk 9.51,52; Jn 4.3,4
17.12 Lev 13.46
17.14 Lev 13.2; 14.2; Mt 8.4
17.15 Mt 9.8
17.16 Mt 10.5
17.19 Mt 9.22; Mk 5.34; Lk 7.50; 8.48; 18.42
17.20 Lk 19.11; Acts 1.6
17.21 v. 23
17.22 Mt 9.15; Mk 2.20; Lk 5.35
17.23 Mt 24.23; Mk 13.21; Lk 21.8
17.24 Mt 24.27
17.25 Mt 16.21; Lk 9.22
17.26 Mt 24.37-39; Gen ch. 7

Jesus Cleanses Ten Lepers

11 On the way to Jerusalem
Jesus[a] was going through the region between Samaria and Galilee.
12 As he entered a village, ten lepers[b] approached him. Keeping
their distance, 13 they called out,
saying, "Jesus, Master, have mercy
on us!" 14 When he saw them, he
said to them, "Go and show yourselves to the priests." And as they
went, they were made clean.
15 Then one of them, when he saw
that he was healed, turned back,
praising God with a loud voice.
16 He prostrated himself at Jesus'[c]
feet and thanked him. And he was
a Samaritan. 17 Then Jesus asked,
"Were not ten made clean? But the
other nine, where are they? 18 Was
none of them found to return and
give praise to God except this foreigner?" 19 Then he said to him,
"Get up and go on your way; your
faith has made you well."

The Coming of the Kingdom

20 Once Jesus[a] was asked by
the Pharisees when the kingdom of
God was coming, and he answered,
"The kingdom of God is not coming with things that can be observed; 21 nor will they say, 'Look,
here it is!' or 'There it is!' For, in
fact, the kingdom of God is
among[d] you."

22 Then he said to the disciples,
"The days are coming when you
will long to see one of the days of
the Son of Man, and you will not
see it. 23 They will say to you, 'Look
there!' or 'Look here!' Do not go, do
not set off in pursuit. 24 For as the
lightning flashes and lights up the
sky from one side to the other, so
will the Son of Man be in his day.[e]
25 But first he must endure much
suffering and be rejected by this
generation. 26 Just as it was in the
days of Noah, so too it will be in the
days of the Son of Man. 27 They
were eating and drinking, and mar-

[x] Gk *He* [y] Gk *your brother* [z] Gk *faith as a grain of* [a] Gk *he* [b] The terms *leper* and *leprosy* can refer to several diseases [c] Gk *his* [d] Or *within* [e] Other ancient authorities lack *in his day*

rying and being given in marriage,
until the day Noah entered the ark,
and the flood came and destroyed
all of them. 28 Likewise, just as it
was in the days of Lot: they were
eating and drinking, buying and
selling, planting and building,
29 but on the day that Lot left Sodom, it rained fire and sulfur from
heaven and destroyed all of them
30 – it will be like that on the day
that the Son of Man is revealed.
31 On that day, anyone on the
housetop who has belongings in
the house must not come down to
take them away; and likewise anyone in the field must not turn back.
32 Remember Lot's wife. 33 Those
who try to make their life secure
will lose it, but those who lose their
life will keep it. 34 I tell you, on that
night there will be two in one bed;
one will be taken and the other left.
35 There will be two women grinding meal together; one will be tak-
en and the other left."[f] 37 Then
they asked him, "Where, Lord?" He
said to them, "Where the corpse is,
there the vultures will gather."

The Parable of the Widow and the Unjust Judge

18 Then Jesus[g] told them a
parable about their need to
pray always and not to lose heart.
2 He said, "In a certain city there
was a judge who neither feared God
nor had respect for people. 3 In that
city there was a widow who kept
coming to him and saying, 'Grant
me justice against my opponent.'
4 For a while he refused; but later
he said to himself, 'Though I have
no fear of God and no respect for
anyone, 5 yet because this widow
keeps bothering me, I will grant her
justice, so that she may not wear
me out by continually coming.' "[h]
6 And the Lord said, "Listen to what
the unjust judge says. 7 And will not
God grant justice to his chosen
ones who cry to him day and night?
Will he delay long in helping them?
8 I tell you, he will quickly grant justice to them. And yet, when the
Son of Man comes, will he find
faith on earth?"

The Parable of the Pharisee and the Tax Collector

9 He also told this parable to
some who trusted in themselves
that they were righteous and regarded others with contempt:
10 "Two men went up to the temple
to pray, one a Pharisee and the other a tax collector. 11 The Pharisee,
standing by himself, was praying
thus, 'God, I thank you that I am
not like other people: thieves,
rogues, adulterers, or even like this
tax collector. 12 I fast twice a week;
I give a tenth of all my income.'
13 But the tax collector, standing
far off, would not even look up to
heaven, but was beating his breast
and saying, 'God, be merciful to
me, a sinner!' 14 I tell you, this man
went down to his home justified
rather than the other; for all who
exalt themselves will be humbled,
but all who humble themselves will
be exalted."

Jesus Blesses Little Children

15 People were bringing even
infants to him that he might touch
them; and when the disciples saw
it, they sternly ordered them not to
do it. 16 But Jesus called for them
and said, "Let the little children
come to me, and do not stop them;
for it is to such as these that the
kingdom of God belongs. 17 Truly I
tell you, whoever does not receive
the kingdom of God as a little child
will never enter it."

The Rich Ruler

18 A certain ruler asked him,
"Good Teacher, what must I do to
inherit eternal life?" 19 Jesus said
to him, "Why do you call me good?
No one is good but God alone.
20 You know the commandments:
'You shall not commit adultery;
You shall not murder; You shall not
steal; You shall not bear false witness; Honor your father and mother.' " 21 He replied, "I have kept all
these since my youth." 22 When

17.28 Gen 18.20-33; 19.24,25
17.30 2 Thes 1.7
17.31 Mt 24.17, 18; Mk 13.15, 16
17.32 Gen 19.26
17.33 Mt 10.39; 16.25; Mk 8.35; Lk 9.24
17.34 Mt 24.40,41
17.37 Mt 24.28
18.1 Lk 11.5-8; Rom 12.12; Eph 6.18; Col 4.2; 1 Thes 5.17
18.5 Lk 11.8
18.6 Lk 7.13
18.7 Rev 6.10; Rom 8.33; Col 3.12; 2 Tim 2.10
18.9 Lk 16.15
18.11 Mt 6.5; Mk 11.25
18.12 Mt 9.14; Lk 11.42
18.13 Lk 23.48
18.14 Mt 23.12; Lk 14.11; 1 Pet 5.6
18.15-17pp Mt 19.13-15; Mk 10.13-16
18.17 Mt 18.3
18.18-30pp Mt 19.16-30; Mk 10.17-31
18.18 Lk 10.25
18.20 Ex 20.12-16; Deut 5.16-20; Rom 13.9
18.22 Lk 12.33; Mt 19.21

[f] Other ancient authorities add verse 36, *"Two will be in the field; one will be taken and the other left."* [g] Gk *he* [h] Or *so that she may not finally come and slap me in the face*

Jesus heard this, he said to him, "There is still one thing lacking. Sell all that you own and distribute the money[i] to the poor, and you will have treasure in heaven; then come, follow me." 23 But when he heard this, he became sad; for he was very rich. 24 Jesus looked at him and said, "How hard it is for those who have wealth to enter the kingdom of God! 25 Indeed, it is easier for a camel to go through the eye of a needle than for someone who is rich to enter the kingdom of God."

26 Those who heard it said, "Then who can be saved?" 27 He replied, "What is impossible for mortals is possible for God."

28 Then Peter said, "Look, we have left our homes and followed you." 29 And he said to them, "Truly I tell you, there is no one who has left house or wife or brothers or parents or children, for the sake of the kingdom of God, 30 who will not get back very much more in this age, and in the age to come eternal life."

A Third Time Jesus Foretells His Death and Resurrection

31 Then he took the twelve aside and said to them, "See, we are going up to Jerusalem, and everything that is written about the Son of Man by the prophets will be accomplished. 32 For he will be handed over to the Gentiles; and he will be mocked and insulted and spat upon. 33 After they have flogged him, they will kill him, and on the third day he will rise again." 34 But they understood nothing about all these things; in fact, what he said was hidden from them, and they did not grasp what was said.

Jesus Heals a Blind Beggar Near Jericho

35 As he approached Jericho, a blind man was sitting by the roadside begging. 36 When he heard a crowd going by, he asked what was happening. 37 They told him, "Jesus of Nazareth[j] is passing by." 38 Then he shouted, "Jesus, Son of David, have mercy on me!" 39 Those who were in front sternly ordered him to be quiet; but he shouted even more loudly, "Son of David, have mercy on me!" 40 Jesus stood still and ordered the man to be brought to him; and when he came near, he asked him, 41 "What do you want me to do for you?" He said, "Lord, let me see again." 42 Jesus said to him, "Receive your sight; your faith has saved you." 43 Immediately he regained his sight and followed him, glorifying God; and all the people, when they saw it, praised God.

Jesus and Zacchaeus

19 He entered Jericho and was passing through it. 2 A man was there named Zacchaeus; he was a chief tax collector and was rich. 3 He was trying to see who Jesus was, but on account of the crowd he could not, because he was short in stature. 4 So he ran ahead and climbed a sycamore tree to see him, because he was going to pass that way. 5 When Jesus came to the place, he looked up and said to him, "Zacchaeus, hurry and come down; for I must stay at your house today." 6 So he hurried down and was happy to welcome him. 7 All who saw it began to grumble and said, "He has gone to be the guest of one who is a sinner." 8 Zacchaeus stood there and said to the Lord, "Look, half of my possessions, Lord, I will give to the poor; and if I have defrauded anyone of anything, I will pay back four times as much." 9 Then Jesus said to him, "Today salvation has come to this house, because he too is a son of Abraham. 10 For the Son of Man came to seek out and to save the lost."

The Parable of the Ten Pounds

11 As they were listening to this, he went on to tell a parable, because he was near Jerusalem, and because they supposed that the kingdom of God was to appear immediately. 12 So he said, "A no-

18.24 Prov 11.28 **18.27** Gen 18.14; Job 42.2; Jer 32.17; Lk 1.37 **18.28** Lk 5.11 **18.30** Mt 12.32 **18.31-34pp** Mt 20.17-19; Mk 10.32-34 **18.31** Lk 9.51; Ps 22 **18.32** Mt 16.21; 27.2; Lk 23.1 **18.34** Mk 9.32; Lk 9.45 **18.35-43pp** Mt 20.29-34; Mk 10.46-52 **18.38** Mt 9.27 **18.39** v. 38 **18.42** Mt 9.22; Mk 5.34; Lk 17.19 **18.43** Mt 9.8; Lk 13.17 **19.1** Lk 18.35 **19.4** 1 Kings 10.27; 1 Chr 27.28; Isa 9.10 **19.7** Mt 9.11; Lk 5.30 **19.8** Lk 7.13; 3.14; Ex 22.1; Lev 6.5; Num 5.7; 2 Sam 12.6 **19.9** Lk 3.8; 13.16; Rom 4.16; Gal 3.7 **19.10** Mt 18.11 **19.11** Acts 1.6 **19.12** Mt 25.14-30; Mk 13.34

[i] Gk lacks *the money* [j] Gk *the Nazorean*

bleman went to a distant country
to get royal power for himself and
then return. 13 He summoned ten
of his slaves, and gave them ten
pounds,[k] and said to them, 'Do
business with these until I come
back.' 14 But the citizens of his
country hated him and sent a dele-
gation after him, saying, 'We do not
want this man to rule over us.'
15 When he returned, having received royal power, he ordered
these slaves, to whom he had given
the money, to be summoned so
that he might find out what they
had gained by trading. 16 The first
came forward and said, 'Lord, your
pound has made ten more pounds.'
17 He said to him, 'Well done, good
slave! Because you have been trustworthy in a very small thing, take
charge of ten cities.' 18 Then the
second came, saying, 'Lord, your
pound has made five pounds.' 19 He
said to him, 'And you, rule over five
cities.' 20 Then the other came, saying, 'Lord, here is your pound. I
wrapped it up in a piece of cloth,
21 for I was afraid of you, because
you are a harsh man; you take what
you did not deposit, and reap what
you did not sow.' 22 He said to him,
'I will judge you by your own words,
you wicked slave! You knew, did
you, that I was a harsh man, taking
what I did not deposit and reaping
what I did not sow? 23 Why then did
you not put my money into the
bank? Then when I returned, I
could have collected it with interest.' 24 He said to the bystanders,
'Take the pound from him and give
it to the one who has ten pounds.'
25 (And they said to him, 'Lord, he
has ten pounds!') 26 'I tell you, to all
those who have, more will be given;
but from those who have nothing,
even what they have will be taken
away. 27 But as for these enemies of
mine who did not want me to be
king over them—bring them here
and slaughter them in my presence.' "

Jesus' Triumphal Entry into Jerusalem

28 After he had said this, he
went on ahead, going up to Jerusalem.
29 When he had come near
Bethphage and Bethany, at the
place called the Mount of Olives,
he sent two of the disciples, 30 saying, "Go into the village ahead of
you, and as you enter it you will
find tied there a colt that has never
been ridden. Untie it and bring it
here. 31 If anyone asks you, 'Why
are you untying it?' just say this,
'The Lord needs it.' " 32 So those
who were sent departed and found
it as he had told them. 33 As they
were untying the colt, its owners
asked them, "Why are you untying
the colt?" 34 They said, "The Lord
needs it." 35 Then they brought it to
Jesus; and after throwing their
cloaks on the colt, they set Jesus
on it. 36 As he rode along, people
kept spreading their cloaks on the
road. 37 As he was now approaching
the path down from the Mount of
Olives, the whole multitude of the
disciples began to praise God joyfully with a loud voice for all the
deeds of power that they had seen,
38 saying,
"Blessed is the king
who comes in the name of
the Lord!
Peace in heaven,
and glory in the highest
heaven!"
39 Some of the Pharisees in the
crowd said to him, "Teacher, order
your disciples to stop." 40 He answered, "I tell you, if these were silent, the stones would shout out."

Jesus Weeps over Jerusalem

41 As he came near and saw the
city, he wept over it, 42 saying, "If
you, even you, had only recognized
on this day the things that make for
peace! But now they are hidden
from your eyes. 43 Indeed, the days
will come upon you, when your enemies will set up ramparts around
you and surround you, and hem
you in on every side. 44 They will
crush you to the ground, you and
your children within you, and they

19.17 Lk 16.10 **19.21** Mt 25.24 **19.22** 2 Sam 1.16; Job 15.6; Mt 25.26 **19.26** Mt 13.12; Lk 8.18 **19.28-40pp** Mt 21.1-11; Mk 11.1-11; Jn 12.12-19 **19.28** Mk 10.32; Mt 21.17; Lk 21.37

19.32 Lk 22.13 **19.36** 2 Kings 9.13 **19.38** Ps 118.26; Lk 13.35; 2.14 **19.39** Mt 21.15,16 **19.40** Hab 2.11 **19.41** Lk 13.34,35 **19.43** Isa 29.3; Jer 6.6; Ezek 4.2; Lk 21.20 **19.44** Mt 24.2; Mk 13.2; Lk 21.6; 1 Pet 2.12

[k] The mina, rendered here by *pound,* was about three months' wages for a laborer

will not leave within you one stone
upon another; because you did not
recognize the time of your visitation from God."[l]

Jesus Cleanses the Temple

45 Then he entered the temple
and began to drive out those who
were selling things there; 46 and he
said, "It is written,

'My house shall be a house
of prayer';
but you have made it a den
of robbers."

47 Every day he was teaching in
the temple. The chief priests, the
scribes, and the leaders of the people kept looking for a way to kill
him; 48 but they did not find anything they could do, for all the people were spellbound by what they
heard.

The Authority of Jesus Questioned

20 One day, as he was teaching the people in the temple and telling the good news, the
chief priests and the scribes came
with the elders 2 and said to him,
"Tell us, by what authority are you
doing these things? Who is it who
gave you this authority?" 3 He answered them, "I will also ask you a
question, and you tell me: 4 Did the
baptism of John come from heav-
en, or was it of human origin?"
5 They discussed it with one another, saying, "If we say, 'From heav-
en,' he will say, 'Why did you not
believe him?' 6 But if we say, 'Of
human origin,' all the people will
stone us; for they are convinced
that John was a prophet." 7 So they
answered that they did not know
where it came from. 8 Then Jesus
said to them, "Neither will I tell
you by what authority I am doing
these things."

The Parable of the Wicked Tenants

9 He began to tell the people
this parable: "A man planted a
vineyard, and leased it to tenants,
and went to another country for a
long time. 10 When the season
came, he sent a slave to the tenants
in order that they might give him
his share of the produce of the
vineyard; but the tenants beat him
and sent him away empty-handed.
11 Next he sent another slave; that
one also they beat and insulted and
sent away empty-handed. 12 And he
sent still a third; this one also they
wounded and threw out. 13 Then
the owner of the vineyard said,
'What shall I do? I will send my beloved son; perhaps they will respect him.' 14 But when the tenants
saw him, they discussed it among
themselves and said, 'This is the
heir; let us kill him so that the inheritance may be ours.' 15 So they
threw him out of the vineyard and
killed him. What then will the owner of the vineyard do to them? 16 He
will come and destroy those tenants and give the vineyard to others." When they heard this, they
said, "Heaven forbid!" 17 But he
looked at them and said, "What
then does this text mean:

'The stone that the builders
rejected
has become the
cornerstone'?[m]

18 Everyone who falls on that stone
will be broken to pieces; and it will
crush anyone on whom it falls."
19 When the scribes and chief
priests realized that he had told
this parable against them, they
wanted to lay hands on him at that
very hour, but they feared the people.

The Question about Paying Taxes

20 So they watched him and
sent spies who pretended to be
honest, in order to trap him by
what he said, so as to hand him
over to the jurisdiction and authority of the governor. 21 So they asked
him, "Teacher, we know that you
are right in what you say and teach,
and you show deference to no one,
but teach the way of God in accordance with truth. 22 Is it lawful for
us to pay taxes to the emperor, or
not?" 23 But he perceived their
craftiness and said to them,

19.45-48pp Mt 21.12-17; Mk 11.15-19
19.46 Isa 56.7
19.47 Mt 26.55; Mk 11.18; Jn 7.19
20.1-8pp Mt 21.23-27; Mk 11.27-33
20.1 Mt 26.55; Lk 8.1
20.2 Jn 2.18; Acts 4.7; 7.27
20.6 Mt 14.5; Lk 7.29
20.9-18pp Mt 21.33-46; Mk 12.1-12
20.9 Isa 5.1-7; Mt 25.14
20.16 Lk 19.27; Rom 3.4,6, 31
20.17 Ps 118.22, 23; 1 Pet 2.6
20.18 Isa 8.14,15
20.19-26pp Mt 22.15-22; Mk 12.13-17
20.19 Lk 19.47
20.21 Jn 3.2

[l] Gk lacks *from God* [m] Or *keystone*

24 "Show me a denarius. Whose head and whose title does it bear?" They said, "The emperor's." 25 He said to them, "Then give to the emperor the things that are the emperor's, and to God the things that are God's." 26 And they were not able in the presence of the people to trap him by what he said; and being amazed by his answer, they became silent.

The Question about the Resurrection

27 Some Sadducees, those who say there is no resurrection, came to him 28 and asked him a question, "Teacher, Moses wrote for us that if a man's brother dies, leaving a wife but no children, the man[n] shall marry the widow and raise up children for his brother. 29 Now there were seven brothers; the first married, and died childless; 30 then the second 31 and the third married her, and so in the same way all seven died childless. 32 Finally the woman also died. 33 In the resurrection, therefore, whose wife will the woman be? For the seven had married her."

34 Jesus said to them, "Those who belong to this age marry and are given in marriage; 35 but those who are considered worthy of a place in that age and in the resurrection from the dead neither marry nor are given in marriage. 36 Indeed they cannot die anymore, because they are like angels and are children of God, being children of the resurrection. 37 And the fact that the dead are raised Moses himself showed, in the story about the bush, where he speaks of the Lord as the God of Abraham, the God of Isaac, and the God of Jacob. 38 Now he is God not of the dead, but of the living; for to him all of them are alive." 39 Then some of the scribes answered, "Teacher, you have spoken well." 40 For they no longer dared to ask him another question.

The Question about David's Son

41 Then he said to them, "How can they say that the Messiah[o] is David's son? 42 For David himself says in the book of Psalms,

'The Lord said to my Lord,
"Sit at my right hand,
43 until I make your enemies
your footstool."'

44 David thus calls him Lord; so how can he be his son?"

Jesus Denounces the Scribes

45 In the hearing of all the people he said to the[p] disciples, 46 "Beware of the scribes, who like to walk around in long robes, and love to be greeted with respect in the marketplaces, and to have the best seats in the synagogues and places of honor at banquets. 47 They devour widows' houses and for the sake of appearance say long prayers. They will receive the greater condemnation."

The Widow's Offering

21 He looked up and saw rich people putting their gifts into the treasury; 2 he also saw a poor widow put in two small copper coins. 3 He said, "Truly I tell you, this poor widow has put in more than all of them; 4 for all of them have contributed out of their abundance, but she out of her poverty has put in all she had to live on."

The Destruction of the Temple Foretold

5 When some were speaking about the temple, how it was adorned with beautiful stones and gifts dedicated to God, he said, 6 "As for these things that you see, the days will come when not one stone will be left upon another; all will be thrown down."

Signs and Persecutions

7 They asked him, "Teacher, when will this be, and what will be the sign that this is about to take place?" 8 And he said, "Beware that you are not led astray; for many will come in my name and say, 'I am

20.25 Rom 13.7; Lk 23.2
20.27-40pp Mt 22.23-33; Mk 12.18-27
20.27 Acts 23.6,8
20.28 Deut 25.5
20.36 Rom 8.16, 17; 1 Jn 3.1,2
20.37 Ex 3.6
20.38 Rom 6.10, 11
20.40 Mt 22.46; Mk 12.34
20.41-44pp Mt 22.41-46; Mk 12.35-37
20.42 Ps 110.1; Acts 2.34
20.45-47pp Mt 23.1-12; Mk 12.38-40
20.46 Lk 11.43
21.1 Mk 12.41-44
21.2 Mk 12.42
21.5-19pp Mt 24.1-14; Mk 13.3-13
21.5 Mk 13.1
21.6 Lk 19.44
21.8 Mk 13.21; Lk 17.23

[n] Gk *his brother* [o] Or *the Christ*
[p] Other ancient authorities read *his*

he!'[q] and, 'The time is near!'[r] Do
not go after them.
9 "When you hear of wars and
insurrections, do not be terrified;
for these things must take place
first, but the end will not follow immediately." 10 Then he said to
them, "Nation will rise against nation, and kingdom against kingdom; 11 there will be great earthquakes, and in various places
famines and plagues; and there will
be dreadful portents and great
signs from heaven.
12 "But before all this occurs,
they will arrest you and persecute
you; they will hand you over to synagogues and prisons, and you will
be brought before kings and governors because of my name. 13 This
will give you an opportunity to testify. 14 So make up your minds not
to prepare your defense in advance;
15 for I will give you words[s] and a
wisdom that none of your opponents will be able to withstand or
contradict. 16 You will be betrayed
even by parents and brothers, by
relatives and friends; and they will
put some of you to death. 17 You
will be hated by all because of my
name. 18 But not a hair of your head
will perish. 19 By your endurance
you will gain your souls.

The Destruction of Jerusalem Foretold

20 "When you see Jerusalem
surrounded by armies, then know
that its desolation has come near.[t]
21 Then those in Judea must flee to
the mountains, and those inside
the city must leave it, and those
out in the country must not enter
it; 22 for these are days of vengeance, as a fulfillment of all that is
written. 23 Woe to those who are
pregnant and to those who are
nursing infants in those days! For
there will be great distress on the
earth and wrath against this people; 24 they will fall by the edge of
the sword and be taken away as
captives among all nations; and Jerusalem will be trampled on by the
Gentiles, until the times of the
Gentiles are fulfilled.

21.10 2 Chr 15.6; Isa 19.2
21.12 Jn 16.2
21.13 Phil 1.12
21.14 Lk 12.11,12
21.15 Lk 12.12
21.16 Lk 12.52,53
21.17 Mt 10.22
21.18 Mt 10.30; Lk 12.7
21.19 Rev 2.7
21.20-24pp Mt 24.15-28; Mk 13.14-23
21.20 Lk 19.43
21.21 Lk 17.31
21.22 Isa 63.4; Dan 9.24-27; Zech 11.1
21.24 Isa 63.18; Dan 8.13; 9.27; 12.7; Rom 11.25; Rev 11.2
21.25-28pp Mt 24.29-31; Mk 13.24-27
21.25 2 Pet 3.10, 12
21.27 Rev 1.7; 14.14
21.28 Lk 18.7
21.29-33pp Mt 24.32-35; Mk 13.28-31
21.31 Mt 3.2
21.33 Lk 16.17
21.34-38pp Mt 24.36-51; Mk 13.32-37
21.34 Mk 4.19; Lk 12.45; 1 Thes 5.6, 7
21.36 Lk 18.1
21.37 Lk 19.47; Mk 11.19

The Coming of the Son of Man

25 "There will be signs in the
sun, the moon, and the stars, and
on the earth distress among nations confused by the roaring of the
sea and the waves. 26 People will
faint from fear and foreboding of
what is coming upon the world, for
the powers of the heavens will be
shaken. 27 Then they will see 'the
Son of Man coming in a cloud' with
power and great glory. 28 Now when
these things begin to take place,
stand up and raise your heads, because your redemption is drawing
near."

The Lesson of the Fig Tree

29 Then he told them a parable:
"Look at the fig tree and all the
trees; 30 as soon as they sprout
leaves you can see for yourselves
and know that summer is already
near. 31 So also, when you see these
things taking place, you know that
the kingdom of God is near. 32 Truly
I tell you, this generation will not
pass away until all things have tak-
en place. 33 Heaven and earth will
pass away, but my words will not
pass away.

Exhortation to Watch

34 "Be on guard so that your
hearts are not weighed down with
dissipation and drunkenness and
the worries of this life, and that day
catch you unexpectedly, 35 like a
trap. For it will come upon all who
live on the face of the whole earth.
36 Be alert at all times, praying that
you may have the strength to escape all these things that will take
place, and to stand before the Son
of Man."
37 Every day he was teaching in
the temple, and at night he would
go out and spend the night on the
Mount of Olives, as it was called.
38 And all the people would get up
early in the morning to listen to
him in the temple.

[q] Gk *I am* [r] Or *at hand* [s] Gk *a mouth* [t] Or *is at hand*

The Plot to Kill Jesus

22 Now the festival of Unleavened Bread, which is called the Passover, was near. 2 The chief priests and the scribes were looking for a way to put Jesus[u] to death, for they were afraid of the people.

3 Then Satan entered into Judas called Iscariot, who was one of the twelve; 4 he went away and conferred with the chief priests and officers of the temple police about how he might betray him to them. 5 They were greatly pleased and agreed to give him money. 6 So he consented and began to look for an opportunity to betray him to them when no crowd was present.

The Preparation of the Passover

7 Then came the day of Unleavened Bread, on which the Passover lamb had to be sacrificed. 8 So Jesus[v] sent Peter and John, saying, "Go and prepare the Passover meal for us that we may eat it." 9 They asked him, "Where do you want us to make preparations for it?" 10 "Listen," he said to them, "when you have entered the city, a man carrying a jar of water will meet you; follow him into the house he enters 11 and say to the owner of the house, 'The teacher asks you, "Where is the guest room, where I may eat the Passover with my disciples?"' 12 He will show you a large room upstairs, already furnished. Make preparations for us there." 13 So they went and found everything as he had told them; and they prepared the Passover meal.

The Institution of the Lord's Supper

14 When the hour came, he took his place at the table, and the apostles with him. 15 He said to them, "I have eagerly desired to eat this Passover with you before I suffer; 16 for I tell you, I will not eat it[w] until it is fulfilled in the kingdom of God." 17 Then he took a cup, and after giving thanks he said, "Take this and divide it among yourselves; 18 for I tell you that from now on I will not drink of the fruit of the vine until the kingdom of God comes." 19 Then he took a loaf of bread, and when he had given thanks, he broke it and gave it to them, saying, "This is my body, which is given for you. Do this in remembrance of me." 20 And he did the same with the cup after supper, saying, "This cup that is poured out for you is the new covenant in my blood.[x] 21 But see, the one who betrays me is with me, and his hand is on the table. 22 For the Son of Man is going as it has been determined, but woe to that one by whom he is betrayed!" 23 Then they began to ask one another, which one of them it could be who would do this.

The Dispute about Greatness

24 A dispute also arose among them as to which one of them was to be regarded as the greatest. 25 But he said to them, "The kings of the Gentiles lord it over them; and those in authority over them are called benefactors. 26 But not so with you; rather the greatest among you must become like the youngest, and the leader like one who serves. 27 For who is greater, the one who is at the table or the one who serves? Is it not the one at the table? But I am among you as one who serves.

28 "You are those who have stood by me in my trials; 29 and I confer on you, just as my Father has conferred on me, a kingdom, 30 so that you may eat and drink at my table in my kingdom, and you will sit on thrones judging the twelve tribes of Israel.

Jesus Predicts Peter's Denial

31 "Simon, Simon, listen! Satan has demanded[y] to sift all of you like wheat, 32 but I have prayed for you that your own faith may not fail; and you, when once you have

22.1-6pp Mt 26.1-5, 14-16; Mk 14.1-2, 10-11
22.1 Jn 11.47-53
22.2 Mt 12.14
22.3 Jn 13.2
22.5 Zech 11.12
22.7-13pp Mt 26.17-19; Mk 14.12-16
22.7 Ex 12.18-20; Deut 16.5-8
22.8 Lk 19.29; Acts 3.1
22.14-30pp Mt 26.20-29; Mk 14.17-25
22.16 Lk 14.15; Rev 19.9
22.21 Mt 26.21-24; Mk 14.18-21; Jn 13.21-30
22.22 Acts 2.23; 4.28
22.24 Mk 9.34; Lk 9.46
22.25 Mt 20.25-28; Mk 10.42-45
22.26 Lk 9.48; 1 Pet 5.5
22.27 Lk 12.37
22.28 Heb 2.18; 4.15
22.29 Lk 12.32; 2 Tim 2.12
22.30 Lk 14.15; Rev 19.9; Mt 19.28; Rev 3.21
22.31-38pp Mt 26.30-35; Mk 14.27-31
22.31 Job 1.6-12; Am 9.9
22.32 Jn 17.9,15; 21.15-17

[u] Gk *him* [v] Gk *he* [w] Other ancient authorities read *never eat it again* [x] Other ancient authorities lack, in whole or in part, verses 19b-20 (*which is given . . . in my blood*) [y] Or *has obtained permission*

turned back, strengthen your
brothers." 33 And he said to him,
"Lord, I am ready to go with you to
prison and to death!" 34 Jesus[z]
said, "I tell you, Peter, the cock will
not crow this day, until you have
denied three times that you know
me."

Purse, Bag, and Sword

35 He said to them, "When I
sent you out without a purse, bag,
or sandals, did you lack anything?"
They said, "No, not a thing." 36 He
said to them, "But now, the one
who has a purse must take it, and
likewise a bag. And the one who
has no sword must sell his cloak
and buy one. 37 For I tell you, this
scripture must be fulfilled in me,
'And he was counted among the
lawless'; and indeed what is written about me is being fulfilled."
38 They said, "Lord, look, here are
two swords." He replied, "It is
enough."

Jesus Prays on the Mount of Olives

39 He came out and went, as
was his custom, to the Mount of
Olives; and the disciples followed
him. 40 When he reached the place,
he said to them, "Pray that you may
not come into the time of trial."[a]
41 Then he withdrew from them
about a stone's throw, knelt down,
and prayed, 42 "Father, if you are
willing, remove this cup from me;
yet, not my will but yours be done."
⟦43 Then an angel from heaven appeared to him and gave him
strength. 44 In his anguish he
prayed more earnestly, and his
sweat became like great drops of
blood falling down on the
ground.⟧[b] 45 When he got up from
prayer, he came to the disciples
and found them sleeping because
of grief, 46 and he said to them,
"Why are you sleeping? Get up and
pray that you may not come into
the time of trial."[a]

The Betrayal and Arrest of Jesus

47 While he was still speaking,
suddenly a crowd came, and the
one called Judas, one of the twelve,
was leading them. He approached
Jesus to kiss him; 48 but Jesus said
to him, "Judas, is it with a kiss that
you are betraying the Son of Man?"
49 When those who were around
him saw what was coming, they
asked, "Lord, should we strike with
the sword?" 50 Then one of them
struck the slave of the high priest
and cut off his right ear. 51 But
Jesus said, "No more of this!" And
he touched his ear and healed him.
52 Then Jesus said to the chief
priests, the officers of the temple
police, and the elders who had
come for him, "Have you come out
with swords and clubs as if I were a
bandit? 53 When I was with you day
after day in the temple, you did not
lay hands on me. But this is your
hour, and the power of darkness!"

Peter Denies Jesus

54 Then they seized him and led
him away, bringing him into the
high priest's house. But Peter was
following at a distance. 55 When
they had kindled a fire in the middle of the courtyard and sat down
together, Peter sat among them.
56 Then a servant-girl, seeing him in
the firelight, stared at him and
said, "This man also was with
him." 57 But he denied it, saying,
"Woman, I do not know him." 58 A
little later someone else, on seeing
him, said, "You also are one of
them." But Peter said, "Man, I am
not!" 59 Then about an hour later
still another kept insisting, "Surely
this man also was with him; for he
is a Galilean." 60 But Peter said,
"Man, I do not know what you are
talking about!" At that moment,
while he was still speaking, the
cock crowed. 61 The Lord turned
and looked at Peter. Then Peter remembered the word of the Lord,
how he had said to him, "Before
the cock crows today, you will deny
me three times." 62 And he went
out and wept bitterly.

22.35 Mt 10.9; Lk 9.3; 10.4
22.37 Isa 53.12; Mk 15.28
22.39-46pp Mt 26.36-46; Mk 14.32-43
22.39 Lk 21.37
22.40 Mt 6.13
22.42 Mk 10.38; Jn 5.30; 18.11
22.46 v. 40
22.47-53pp Mt 26.47-56; Mk 14.43-50; Jn 18.1-11
22.49 v. 38
22.52 vv. 4,37
22.53 Jn 12.27
22.54-71pp Mt 26.69-75; Mk 14.66-72; Jn 18.15-18, 25-27
22.54 Mt 26.58; Mk 14.54
22.61 v. 34

[z] Gk *He* [a] Or *into temptation* [b] Other ancient authorities lack verses 43 and 44

The Mocking and Beating of Jesus

63 Now the men who were holding Jesus began to mock him and
beat him; 64 they also blindfolded
him and kept asking him, "Prophesy! Who is it that struck you?"
65 They kept heaping many other
insults on him.

Jesus before the Council

66 When day came, the assembly of the elders of the people, both
chief priests and scribes, gathered
together, and they brought him to
their council. 67 They said, "If you
are the Messiah,[c] tell us." He replied, "If I tell you, you will not believe; 68 and if I question you, you
will not answer. 69 But from now on
the Son of Man will be seated at the
right hand of the power of God."
70 All of them asked, "Are you,
then, the Son of God?" He said to
them, "You say that I am." 71 Then
they said, "What further testimony
do we need? We have heard it ourselves from his own lips!"

Jesus before Pilate

23 Then the assembly rose as
a body and brought Jesus[d]
before Pilate. 2 They began to accuse him, saying, "We found this
man perverting our nation, forbid-
ding us to pay taxes to the emperor,
and saying that he himself is the
Messiah, a king."[e] 3 Then Pilate
asked him, "Are you the king of the
Jews?" He answered, "You say so."
4 Then Pilate said to the chief
priests and the crowds, "I find no
basis for an accusation against this
man." 5 But they were insistent and
said, "He stirs up the people by
teaching throughout all Judea,
from Galilee where he began even
to this place."

Jesus before Herod

6 When Pilate heard this, he
asked whether the man was a Galilean. 7 And when he learned that he
was under Herod's jurisdiction, he
sent him off to Herod, who was
himself in Jerusalem at that time.
8 When Herod saw Jesus, he was
very glad, for he had been wanting
to see him for a long time, because
he had heard about him and was
hoping to see him perform some
sign. 9 He questioned him at some
length, but Jesus[f] gave him no answer. 10 The chief priests and the
scribes stood by, vehemently accusing him. 11 Even Herod with his
soldiers treated him with contempt
and mocked him; then he put an
elegant robe on him, and sent him
back to Pilate. 12 That same day
Herod and Pilate became friends
with each other; before this they
had been enemies.

Jesus Sentenced to Death

13 Pilate then called together
the chief priests, the leaders, and
the people, 14 and said to them,
"You brought me this man as one
who was perverting the people; and
here I have examined him in your
presence and have not found this
man guilty of any of your charges
against him. 15 Neither has Herod,
for he sent him back to us. Indeed,
he has done nothing to deserve
death. 16 I will therefore have him
flogged and release him."[g]
18 Then they all shouted out together, "Away with this fellow! Release Barabbas for us!" 19 (This was
a man who had been put in prison
for an insurrection that had taken
place in the city, and for murder.)
20 Pilate, wanting to release Jesus,
addressed them again; 21 but they
kept shouting, "Crucify, crucify
him!" 22 A third time he said to
them, "Why, what evil has he
done? I have found in him no
ground for the sentence of death; I
will therefore have him flogged and
then release him." 23 But they kept
urgently demanding with loud
shouts that he should be crucified;
and their voices prevailed. 24 So Pilate gave his verdict that their demand should be granted. 25 He released the man they asked for, the
one who had been put in prison for

22.63 Mt 26.67, 68; Mk 14.65; Jn 18.22,23
22.66 Mt 27.1; Mk 15.1
22.67 Mt 26.63-66; Mk 14.61-63; Jn 18.19-21
22.70 Mt 27.11; Lk 23.3
23.1-25pp Mt 27.11-26; Mk 15.2-15; Jn 18.29-40
23.1 Mt 27.2; Mk 15.1; Jn 18.28
23.2 Lk 20.22; Jn 19.12
23.3 Lk 22.70; 1 Tim 6.13
23.4 1 Pet 2.22
23.7 Lk 3.1
23.8 Lk 9.9; Mt 14.1; Mk 6.14
23.11 Mk 15.17-19; Jn 19.2,3
23.12 Acts 4.27
23.14 vv. 2,4
23.16 Mt 27.26; Mk 15.15; Jn 19.1
23.18 Mt 27.20-23; Mk 15.11-14; Jn 18.38-40; 19.14,15; Acts 3.13,14
23.22 v. 16

c Or *the Christ* d Gk *him* e Or *is an anointed king* f Gk *he* g Here, or after verse 19, other ancient authorities add verse 17, *Now he was obliged to release someone for them at the festival*

insurrection and murder, and he
handed Jesus over as they wished.

The Crucifixion of Jesus

26 As they led him away, they
seized a man, Simon of Cyrene,
who was coming from the country,
and they laid the cross on him, and
made him carry it behind Jesus.
27 A great number of the people followed him, and among them were
women who were beating their
breasts and wailing for him. 28 But
Jesus turned to them and said,
"Daughters of Jerusalem, do not
weep for me, but weep for yourselves and for your children. 29 For
the days are surely coming when
they will say, 'Blessed are the barren, and the wombs that never
bore, and the breasts that never
nursed.' 30 Then they will begin to
say to the mountains, 'Fall on us';
and to the hills, 'Cover us.' 31 For if
they do this when the wood is
green, what will happen when it is
dry?"

32 Two others also, who were
criminals, were led away to be put
to death with him. 33 When they
came to the place that is called The
Skull, they crucified Jesus[h] there
with the criminals, one on his right
and one on his left. ⟦34 Then Jesus
said, "Father, forgive them; for
they do not know what they are doing."⟧[i] And they cast lots to divide
his clothing. 35 And the people
stood by, watching; but the leaders
scoffed at him, saying, "He saved
others; let him save himself if he is
the Messiah[j] of God, his chosen
one!" 36 The soldiers also mocked
him, coming up and offering him
sour wine, 37 and saying, "If you are
the King of the Jews, save yourself!" 38 There was also an inscription over him,[k] "This is the King of
the Jews."

39 One of the criminals who
were hanged there kept deriding[l]
him and saying, "Are you not the
Messiah?[j] Save yourself and us!"
40 But the other rebuked him, saying, "Do you not fear God, since
you are under the same sentence of
condemnation? 41 And we indeed
have been condemned justly, for
we are getting what we deserve for
our deeds, but this man has done
nothing wrong." 42 Then he said,
"Jesus, remember me when you
come into[m] your kingdom." 43 He
replied, "Truly I tell you, today you
will be with me in Paradise."

The Death of Jesus

44 It was now about noon, and
darkness came over the whole
land[n] until three in the afternoon,
45 while the sun's light failed;[o] and
the curtain of the temple was torn
in two. 46 Then Jesus, crying with a
loud voice, said, "Father, into your
hands I commend my spirit." Having said this, he breathed his last.
47 When the centurion saw what
had taken place, he praised God
and said, "Certainly this man was
innocent."[p] 48 And when all the
crowds who had gathered there for
this spectacle saw what had taken
place, they returned home, beating
their breasts. 49 But all his acquaintances, including the women
who had followed him from Galilee, stood at a distance, watching
these things.

The Burial of Jesus

50 Now there was a good and
righteous man named Joseph,
who, though a member of the
council, 51 had not agreed to their
plan and action. He came from the
Jewish town of Arimathea, and he
was waiting expectantly for the
kingdom of God. 52 This man went
to Pilate and asked for the body of
Jesus. 53 Then he took it down,
wrapped it in a linen cloth, and laid
it in a rock-hewn tomb where no
one had ever been laid. 54 It was the
day of Preparation, and the sabbath was beginning.[q] 55 The wom-
en who had come with him from

23.26-31pp Mk 15.21 **23.26** Jn 19.17 **23.27** Lk 8.52 **23.28** Lk 19.41-44; 21.23,24 **23.30** Isa 2.19; Hos 10.8; Rev 6.16 **23.31** Ezek 20.47 **23.32-38pp** Mt 27.32-44; Mk 15.21-32; Jn 19.17-24 **23.32** Isa 53.12 **23.34** Ps 22.18; Acts 7.60 **23.35** Ps 22.17 **23.36** Ps 69.21; Mt 27.48 **23.39** vv. 35,37 **23.41** vv. 4,14,22 **23.43** 2 Cor 12.3, 4; Rev 2.7 **23.44-49pp** Mt 27.45-50; Mk 15.33-41; Jn 19.28-37 **23.45** Ex 26.31-35; Heb 9.8; 10.19 **23.46** Ps 31.5; 1 Pet 2.23 **23.47** Mt 27.54 **23.49** Ps 38.11; Lk 8.2 **23.50-56pp** Mt 27.57-61; Mk 15.42-47; Jn 19.38-42 **23.51** Lk 2.25 **23.54** Mt 27.62 **23.55** v. 49

[h] Gk *him* [i] Other ancient authorities lack the sentence *Then Jesus . . . what they are doing* [j] Or *the Christ* [k] Other ancient authorities add *written in Greek and Latin and Hebrew* (that is, *Aramaic*)
[l] Or *blaspheming* [m] Other ancient authorities read *in* [n] Or *earth* [o] Or *the sun was eclipsed.* Other ancient authorities read *the sun was darkened* [p] Or *righteous*
[q] Gk *was dawning*

Galilee followed, and they saw the tomb and how his body was laid. 56 Then they returned, and prepared spices and ointments.

On the sabbath they rested according to the commandment.

The Resurrection of Jesus

24 But on the first day of the week, at early dawn, they came to the tomb, taking the spices that they had prepared. 2 They found the stone rolled away from the tomb, 3 but when they went in, they did not find the body.[r] 4 While they were perplexed about this, suddenly two men in dazzling clothes stood beside them. 5 The women[s] were terrified and bowed their faces to the ground, but the men[t] said to them, "Why do you look for the living among the dead? He is not here, but has risen.[u] 6 Remember how he told you, while he was still in Galilee, 7 that the Son of Man must be handed over to sinners, and be crucified, and on the third day rise again." 8 Then they remembered his words, 9 and returning from the tomb, they told all this to the eleven and to all the rest. 10 Now it was Mary Magdalene, Joanna, Mary the mother of James, and the other women with them who told this to the apostles. 11 But these words seemed to them an idle tale, and they did not believe them. 12 But Peter got up and ran to the tomb; stooping and looking in, he saw the linen cloths by themselves; then he went home, amazed at what had happened.[v]

The Walk to Emmaus

13 Now on that same day two of them were going to a village called Emmaus, about seven miles[w] from Jerusalem, 14 and talking with each other about all these things that had happened. 15 While they were talking and discussing, Jesus himself came near and went with them, 16 but their eyes were kept from recognizing him. 17 And he said to them, "What are you discussing with each other while you walk along?" They stood still, looking sad.[x] 18 Then one of them, whose name was Cleopas, answered him, "Are you the only stranger in Jerusalem who does not know the things that have taken place there in these days?" 19 He asked them, "What things?" They replied, "The things about Jesus of Nazareth,[y] who was a prophet mighty in deed and word before God and all the people, 20 and how our chief priests and leaders handed him over to be condemned to death and crucified him. 21 But we had hoped that he was the one to redeem Israel.[z] Yes, and besides all this, it is now the third day since these things took place. 22 Moreover, some women of our group astounded us. They were at the tomb early this morning, 23 and when they did not find his body there, they came back and told us that they had indeed seen a vision of angels who said that he was alive. 24 Some of those who were with us went to the tomb and found it just as the women had said; but they did not see him." 25 Then he said to them, "Oh, how foolish you are, and how slow of heart to believe all that the prophets have declared! 26 Was it not necessary that the Messiah[a] should suffer these things and then enter into his glory?" 27 Then beginning with Moses and all the prophets, he interpreted to them the things about himself in all the scriptures.

28 As they came near the village to which they were going, he walked ahead as if he were going on. 29 But they urged him strongly, saying, "Stay with us, because it is almost evening and the day is now nearly over." So he went in to stay with them. 30 When he was at the table with them, he took bread, blessed and broke it, and gave it to

23.56 Mk 16.1; Ex 12.16; 20.10
24.1-11pp Mt 28.1-10; Mk 16.1-8; Jn 20.1-18
24.1 Lk 23.56
24.4 Acts 1.10; 12.7
24.6 Mt 17.22, 23; Mk 9.30,31; Lk 9.22
24.8 Jn 2.22
24.9 v. 46
24.10 Lk 8.1-3
24.11 v. 35
24.15 v. 36
24.16 Jn 21.4
24.18 Jn 19.25
24.19 Mt 21.11; Lk 7.16; 13.33; Acts 3.22
24.20 Lk 23.13
24.21 Lk 1.68
24.22 vv. 9,10
24.24 v. 12
24.26 Heb 2.10; 1 Pet 1.11
24.27 Gen 3.15; Num 21.9; Deut 18.15; Isa 7.14; 9.6; 40.10,11; ch. 53; Ezek 34.23; Dan 9.24; Mic 7.20; Mal 3.1
24.28 Mk 6.48
24.30 Mt 14.19

[r] Other ancient authorities add *of the Lord Jesus* [s] Gk *They* [t] Gk *but they* [u] Other ancient authorities lack *He is not here, but has risen* [v] Other ancient authorities lack verse 12 [w] Gk *sixty stadia;* other ancient authorities read *a hundred sixty stadia* [x] Other ancient authorities read *walk along, looking sad?"* [y] Other ancient authorities read *Jesus the Nazorean* [z] Or *to set Israel free* [a] Or *the Christ*

RESURRECTION APPEARANCES

Event	Date	Matthew	Mark	Luke	John	Acts	I Corinthians
At the empty tomb outside Jerusalem	Early Sunday morning	28:1-10	16:1-8	24:1-12	20:1-9		
To Mary Magdalene at the tomb	Early Sunday morning		16:9-11		20:11-18		
To two travelers on the road to Emmaus	Sunday at midday			24:13-32			
To Peter in Jerusalem	During the day on Sunday			24:34			15:5
To the ten disciples in the upper room	Sunday evening		16:14	24:36-43	20:19-25		
To the eleven disciples in the upper room	One week later				20:26-31		15:5
To seven disciples fishing on the Sea of Galilee	One day at daybreak				21:1-23		
To the eleven disciples on the mountain in Galilee	Some time later	28:16-20	16:15-18				
To more than 500	Some time later						15:6
To James	Some time later						15:7
At the Ascension on the Mt. of Olives	Forty days after the resurrection			24:44-51		1:3-8	

them. 31 Then their eyes were
opened, and they recognized him;
and he vanished from their sight.
32 They said to each other, "Were
not our hearts burning within us[b]
while he was talking to us on the
road, while he was opening the
scriptures to us?" 33 That same
hour they got up and returned to
Jerusalem; and they found the
eleven and their companions gathered together. 34 They were saying,
"The Lord has risen indeed, and he
has appeared to Simon!" 35 Then
they told what had happened on
the road, and how he had been
made known to them in the breaking of the bread.

Jesus Appears to His Disciples

36 While they were talking
about this, Jesus himself stood
among them and said to them,
"Peace be with you."[c] 37 They were
startled and terrified, and thought
that they were seeing a ghost. 38 He
said to them, "Why are you frightened, and why do doubts arise in
your hearts? 39 Look at my hands
and my feet; see that it is I myself.
Touch me and see; for a ghost does
not have flesh and bones as you see
that I have." 40 And when he had
said this, he showed them his
hands and his feet.[d] 41 While in
their joy they were disbelieving and
still wondering, he said to them,
"Have you anything here to eat?"
42 They gave him a piece of broiled
fish, 43 and he took it and ate in
their presence.

24.33 Acts 1.14 **24.34** 1 Cor 15.5 **24.36-43pp** Jn 20.19-25 **24.37** Mk 6.49 **24.39** Jn 20.27 **24.41** Jn 21.5 **24.43** Acts 10.41
24.44-49pp Jn 20.21; Acts 1.8 **24.44** Mt 16.21; Mk 8.31; Lk 9.22; 18.31 **24.46** Isa 50.6; Hos 6.2; 1 Cor 15.3, 4 **24.47** Acts 5.31; 13.38; Mt 28.19 **24.48** Acts 1.8 **24.49** Jn 14.16; Acts 1.4 **24.50-53pp** Mk 16.19,20 **24.50** Acts 1.12 **24.51** 2 Kings 2.11 **24.53** Acts 2.46

44 Then he said to them,
"These are my words that I spoke
to you while I was still with you—
that everything written about me in
the law of Moses, the prophets, and
the psalms must be fulfilled."
45 Then he opened their minds to
understand the scriptures, 46 and
he said to them, "Thus it is written,
that the Messiah[e] is to suffer and
to rise from the dead on the third
day, 47 and that repentance and forgiveness of sins is to be proclaimed
in his name to all nations,[f] beginning from Jerusalem. 48 You are
witnesses of these things. 49 And
see, I am sending upon you what
my Father promised; so stay here
in the city until you have been
clothed with power from on high."

The Ascension of Jesus

50 Then he led them out as far
as Bethany, and, lifting up his
hands, he blessed them. 51 While
he was blessing them, he withdrew
from them and was carried up into
heaven.[g] 52 And they worshiped
him, and[h] returned to Jerusalem
with great joy; 53 and they were continually in the temple blessing
God.[i]

[b] Other ancient authorities lack *within us*
[c] Other ancient authorities lack *and said to them, "Peace be with you."*
[d] Other ancient authorities lack verse 40
[e] Or *the Christ*
[f] Or *nations. Beginning from Jerusalem you are witnesses*
[g] Other ancient authorities lack *and was carried up into heaven*
[h] Other ancient authorities lack *worshiped him, and*
[i] Other ancient authorities add *Amen*

THE GOSPEL ACCORDING TO

John

Title and Background

The Gospel of John gets its name from the person who undoubtedly wrote it—the apostle John. His name means "The LORD is gracious." He was greatly influenced by the Old Testament. The prologue, for example, with its account of the origin of light and life, reminds us of the Genesis account of creation.

Author and Date of Writing

The apostle John is "the disciple whom Jesus loved" (13.23; 19.26; 20.2; 21.7,20,24). He knew Jewish life well and referred often to Jewish customs. John's account has many touches that were based on the recollections of an eyewitness. The date of writing was probably about A.D. 85 or a little later.

Theme and Message

The writer states his main goal clearly in 20.31: "so that you may come to believe that Jesus is the Messiah." He may have had Greek readers in mind. Along with this evangelistic purpose, John wanted to make clear to his readers both that Jesus was God and that Jesus had come in the flesh.

Outline

I. Prologue (1.1-18)
II. Beginnings of Jesus' Ministry (1.19-51)
III. Jesus' Ministry: Signs and Discourses (2.1–11.57)
IV. Passion Week (12.1–19.42)
V. The Resurrection (20.1-29)
VI. Statement of Purpose (20.30-31)
VII. Epilogue (21.1-25)

The Word Became Flesh

1 In the beginning was the
Word, and the Word was with
God, and the Word was God. 2 He
was in the beginning with God. 3 All
things came into being through
him, and without him not one
thing came into being. What has
come into being 4 in him was life,[a]
and the life was the light of all people. 5 The light shines in the darkness, and the darkness did not
overcome it.
6 There was a man sent from
God, whose name was John. 7 He
came as a witness to testify to the
light, so that all might believe
through him. 8 He himself was not
the light, but he came to testify to
the light. 9 The true light, which enlightens everyone, was coming into
the world.[b]
10 He was in the world, and the
world came into being through
him; yet the world did not know
him. 11 He came to what was his
own,[c] and his own people did not
accept him. 12 But to all who received him, who believed in his
name, he gave power to become
children of God, 13 who were born,
not of blood or of the will of the
flesh or of the will of man, but of
God.

1.1 Col 1.17; 1 Jn 1.1; Phil 2.6 **1.3** Col 1.16; Heb 1.2 **1.4** Jn 5.26; 11.25; 14.6 **1.5** Jn 3.19; 9.5; 12.46 **1.6-8pp** Mt 3.1-12; Mk 1.1-8; Lk 3.2-17 **1.7** Acts 19.4 **1.8** v. 20 **1.9** Isa 49.6; 1 Jn 2.8 **1.10** Col 1.16; Heb 1.2

1.12 Gal 3.26; Jn 3.18; 1 Jn 5.13
1.13 Jn 3.5,6; Jas 1.18; 1 Pet 1.23

[a] Or [3]*through him. And without him not one thing came into being that has come into being.* [4]*In him was life*
[b] Or *He was the true light that enlightens everyone coming into the world*
[c] Or *to his own home*

14 And the Word became flesh
and lived among us, and we have
seen his glory, the glory as of a father's only son,[d] full of grace and
truth. 15 (John testified to him and
cried out, "This was he of whom I
said, 'He who comes after me ranks
ahead of me because he was before
me.' ") 16 From his fullness we have
all received, grace upon grace.
17 The law indeed was given
through Moses; grace and truth
came through Jesus Christ. 18 No
one has ever seen God. It is God the
only Son,[e] who is close to the Father's heart,[f] who has made him
known.

The Testimony of John the Baptist

19 This is the testimony given
by John when the Jews sent priests
and Levites from Jerusalem to ask
him, "Who are you?" 20 He confessed and did not deny it, but confessed, "I am not the Messiah."[g]
21 And they asked him, "What
then? Are you Elijah?" He said, "I
am not." "Are you the prophet?"
He answered, "No." 22 Then they
said to him, "Who are you? Let us
have an answer for those who sent
us. What do you say about yourself?" 23 He said,

"I am the voice of one crying
out in the wilderness,
'Make straight the way of the
Lord,' "

as the prophet Isaiah said.
24 Now they had been sent from
the Pharisees. 25 They asked him,
"Why then are you baptizing if you
are neither the Messiah,[g] nor Elijah, nor the prophet?" 26 John answered them, "I baptize with water.
Among you stands one whom you
do not know, 27 the one who is coming after me; I am not worthy to untie the thong of his sandal." 28 This
took place in Bethany across the
Jordan where John was baptizing.

The Lamb of God

29 The next day he saw Jesus
coming toward him and declared,
"Here is the Lamb of God who
takes away the sin of the world!

1.14 Rom 1.3; Gal 4.4; 1 Tim 3.16; Heb 2.14
1.15 v. 30
1.16 Eph 1.23; Col 1.19
1.17 Rom 3.24
1.18 Ex 33.20; Jn 6.46; 1 Jn 4.9
1.20 Jn 3.28; Lk 3.15,16
1.21 Mt 11.14; 16.14; Deut 18.15
1.23 Mt 3.1; Mk 1.3; Lk 3.4; Isa 40.3
1.26 Acts 1.5
1.27 vv. 15,30
1.28 Jn 3.26; 10.40
1.29 Isa 53.7; 1 Pet 1.19
1.30 vv. 15,27
1.32 Mt 3.16; Mk 1.10; Lk 3.22
1.33 Mt 3.11; Acts 1.5
1.34 v. 49
1.35 v. 29
1.36 v. 29
1.38 v. 49
1.40 Mt 4.18-22; Mk 1.16-20; Lk 5.2-11
1.41 Dan 9.25; Jn 4.25
1.42 Jn 21.15-17; 1 Cor 15.5; Mt 16.18
1.43 Mt 10.3; Jn 6.5,7; 12.21,22; 14.8,9

30 This is he of whom I said, 'After
me comes a man who ranks ahead
of me because he was before me.'
31 I myself did not know him; but I
came baptizing with water for this
reason, that he might be revealed
to Israel." 32 And John testified, "I
saw the Spirit descending from
heaven like a dove, and it remained
on him. 33 I myself did not know
him, but the one who sent me to
baptize with water said to me, 'He
on whom you see the Spirit descend and remain is the one who
baptizes with the Holy Spirit.'
34 And I myself have seen and have
testified that this is the Son of
God."[h]

The First Disciples of Jesus

35 The next day John again was
standing with two of his disciples,
36 and as he watched Jesus walk by,
he exclaimed, "Look, here is the
Lamb of God!" 37 The two disciples
heard him say this, and they followed Jesus. 38 When Jesus turned
and saw them following, he said to
them, "What are you looking for?"
They said to him, "Rabbi" (which
translated means Teacher), "where
are you staying?" 39 He said to
them, "Come and see." They came
and saw where he was staying, and
they remained with him that day. It
was about four o'clock in the afternoon. 40 One of the two who heard
John speak and followed him was
Andrew, Simon Peter's brother.
41 He first found his brother Simon
and said to him, "We have found
the Messiah" (which is translated
Anointed[i]). 42 He brought Simon[j]
to Jesus, who looked at him and
said, "You are Simon son of John.
You are to be called Cephas"
(which is translated Peter[k]).

Jesus Calls Philip and Nathanael

43 The next day Jesus decided

[d] Or *the Father's only Son* [e] Other ancient authorities read *It is an only Son, God,* or *It is the only Son* [f] Gk *bosom* [g] Or *the Christ* [h] Other ancient authorities read *is God's chosen one* [i] Or *Christ* [j] Gk *him* [k] From the word for *rock* in Aramaic (*kepha*) and Greek (*petra*), respectively

to go to Galilee. He found Philip
and said to him, "Follow me."
44 Now Philip was from Bethsaida,
the city of Andrew and Peter.
45 Philip found Nathanael and said
to him, "We have found him about
whom Moses in the law and also
the prophets wrote, Jesus son of
Joseph from Nazareth." 46 Nathanael said to him, "Can anything
good come out of Nazareth?" Philip said to him, "Come and see."
47 When Jesus saw Nathanael coming toward him, he said of him,
"Here is truly an Israelite in whom
there is no deceit!" 48 Nathanael
asked him, "Where did you get to
know me?" Jesus answered, "I saw
you under the fig tree before Philip
called you." 49 Nathanael replied,
"Rabbi, you are the Son of God!
You are the King of Israel!" 50 Jesus
answered, "Do you believe because
I told you that I saw you under the
fig tree? You will see greater things
than these." 51 And he said to him,
"Very truly, I tell you,[1] you will see
heaven opened and the angels of
God ascending and descending
upon the Son of Man."

The Wedding at Cana

2 On the third day there was a
wedding in Cana of Galilee,
and the mother of Jesus was there.
2 Jesus and his disciples had also
been invited to the wedding.
3 When the wine gave out, the
mother of Jesus said to him, "They
have no wine." 4 And Jesus said to
her, "Woman, what concern is that
to you and to me? My hour has not
yet come." 5 His mother said to the
servants, "Do whatever he tells
you." 6 Now standing there were six
stone water jars for the Jewish rites
of purification, each holding twenty or thirty gallons. 7 Jesus said to
them, "Fill the jars with water."
And they filled them up to the
brim. 8 He said to them, "Now draw
some out, and take it to the chief
steward." So they took it. 9 When
the steward tasted the water that
had become wine, and did not
know where it came from (though
the servants who had drawn the
water knew), the steward called the
bridegroom 10 and said to him, "Everyone serves the good wine first,
and then the inferior wine after the
guests have become drunk. But you
have kept the good wine until
now." 11 Jesus did this, the first of
his signs, in Cana of Galilee, and
revealed his glory; and his disciples
believed in him.

12 After this he went down to
Capernaum with his mother, his
brothers, and his disciples; and
they remained there a few days.

Jesus Cleanses the Temple

13 The Passover of the Jews was
near, and Jesus went up to Jerusalem. 14 In the temple he found people selling cattle, sheep, and doves,
and the money changers seated at
their tables. 15 Making a whip of
cords, he drove all of them out of
the temple, both the sheep and the
cattle. He also poured out the
coins of the money changers and
overturned their tables. 16 He told
those who were selling the doves,
"Take these things out of here!
Stop making my Father's house a
marketplace!" 17 His disciples remembered that it was written,
"Zeal for your house will consume
me." 18 The Jews then said to him,
"What sign can you show us for doing this?" 19 Jesus answered them,
"Destroy this temple, and in three
days I will raise it up." 20 The Jews
then said, "This temple has been
under construction for forty-six
years, and will you raise it up in
three days?" 21 But he was speaking
of the temple of his body. 22 After
he was raised from the dead, his
disciples remembered that he had
said this; and they believed the
scripture and the word that Jesus
had spoken.

23 When he was in Jerusalem
during the Passover festival, many
believed in his name because they
saw the signs that he was doing.
24 But Jesus on his part would not
entrust himself to them, because
he knew all people 25 and needed

1.44 Jn 12.21 **1.45** Jn 21.2; Lk 24.27; Mt 2.23; Lk 2.4 **1.46** Jn 7.41,42 **1.47** Ps 32.2; 73.1; Rom 9.4,6 **1.49** vv. 38,34; Mt 2.2; Mk 15.32; Jn 12.13 **1.51** Gen 28.12; Mt 3.16; Lk 3.21; Mt 8.20 **2.1** Jn 4.46; 21.2 **2.4** Jn 19.26; 7.6,30; 8.20 **2.6** Mk 7.3,4; Jn 3.25 **2.9** Jn 4.46

2.11 Jn 1.14 **2.12** Mt 4.13; 12.46 **2.13-25pp** Mk 11.15-19; Lk 19.45-48 **2.13** Jn 6.4; 11.55; Deut 16.1-6; Lk 2.41 **2.16** Lk 2.49 **2.17** Ps 69.9 **2.18** Mt 12.38 **2.19** Mt 26.61; 27.40; Mk 14.58 **2.21** 1 Cor 6.19 **2.22** Lk 24.8; Jn 12.16; 14.26 **2.23** v. 13 **2.25** Jn 6.61,64; 13.21

[1] Both instances of the Greek word for *you* in this verse are plural

no one to testify about anyone; for
he himself knew what was in everyone.

Nicodemus Visits Jesus

3 Now there was a Pharisee
named Nicodemus, a leader of
the Jews. 2 He came to Jesus[m] by
night and said to him, "Rabbi, we
know that you are a teacher who
has come from God; for no one can
do these signs that you do apart
from the presence of God." 3 Jesus
answered him, "Very truly, I tell
you, no one can see the kingdom of
God without being born from
above."[n] 4 Nicodemus said to him,
"How can anyone be born after
having grown old? Can one enter a
second time into the mother's
womb and be born?" 5 Jesus answered, "Very truly, I tell you, no
one can enter the kingdom of God
without being born of water and
Spirit. 6 What is born of the flesh is
flesh, and what is born of the Spirit
is spirit.[o] 7 Do not be astonished
that I said to you, 'You[p] must be
born from above.'[q] 8 The wind[o]
blows where it chooses, and you
hear the sound of it, but you do not
know where it comes from or where
it goes. So it is with everyone who
is born of the Spirit." 9 Nicodemus
said to him, "How can these things
be?" 10 Jesus answered him, "Are
you a teacher of Israel, and yet you
do not understand these things?

11 "Very truly, I tell you, we
speak of what we know and testify
to what we have seen; yet you[r] do
not receive our testimony. 12 If I
have told you about earthly things
and you do not believe, how can
you believe if I tell you about heavenly things? 13 No one has ascended into heaven except the one who
descended from heaven, the Son of
Man.[s] 14 And just as Moses lifted
up the serpent in the wilderness, so
must the Son of Man be lifted up,
15 that whoever believes in him may
have eternal life.[t]

16 "For God so loved the world
that he gave his only Son, so that
everyone who believes in him may
not perish but may have eternal
life.

17 "Indeed, God did not send
the Son into the world to condemn
the world, but in order that the
world might be saved through him.
18 Those who believe in him are not
condemned; but those who do not
believe are condemned already, because they have not believed in the
name of the only Son of God. 19 And
this is the judgment, that the light
has come into the world, and people loved darkness rather than light
because their deeds were evil.
20 For all who do evil hate the light
and do not come to the light, so
that their deeds may not be exposed. 21 But those who do what is
true come to the light, so that it
may be clearly seen that their
deeds have been done in God."[t]

Jesus and John the Baptist

22 After this Jesus and his disciples went into the Judean countryside, and he spent some time there
with them and baptized. 23 John
also was baptizing at Aenon near
Salim because water was abundant
there; and people kept coming and
were being baptized 24 —John, of
course, had not yet been thrown
into prison.

25 Now a discussion about purification arose between John's disciples and a Jew.[u] 26 They came to
John and said to him, "Rabbi, the
one who was with you across the
Jordan, to whom you testified, here
he is baptizing, and all are going to
him." 27 John answered, "No one
can receive anything except what
has been given from heaven. 28 You
yourselves are my witnesses that I
said, 'I am not the Messiah,[v] but I
have been sent ahead of him.' 29 He
who has the bride is the bridegroom. The friend of the bride-

3.1 Jn 7.50; 19.39; Lk 23.13; Jn 7.26
3.2 Jn 9.16,33; Acts 2.22; 10.38
3.3 Titus 3.5; Jas 1.18; 1 Pet 1.23; 1 Jn 3.9
3.5 Eph 5.26; Titus 3.5
3.6 Jn 1.13; 1 Cor 15.50
3.8 1 Cor 2.11
3.9 Jn 6.52,60
3.10 Lk 2.46
3.11 Jn 7.16,17
3.13 Prov 30.4; Acts 2.34; Rom 10.6; Eph 4.9
3.14 Num 21.9; Jn 8.28; 12.34
3.15 v. 36; Jn 20.21; 1 Jn 5.11-13
3.16 Rom 5.8; 1 Jn 4.9
3.17 Jn 5.36,38; 8.15; 12.47; 1 Jn 4.14
3.18 Jn 5.24; 1 Jn 4.9
3.19 Jn 1.4; 8.12
3.20 Eph 5.11,13
3.21 1 Jn 1.6
3.22 Jn 4.2
3.24 Mt 4.12; 14.3
3.25 Jn 2.6
3.26 Jn 1.7,28
3.27 1 Cor 4.7; Heb 5.4
3.28 Jn 1.20,23
3.29 Mk 2.19,20; Mt 25.1; Jn 15.11; 16.24

m Gk *him* n Or *born anew*
o The same Greek word means both *wind* and *spirit* p The Greek word for *you* here is plural q Or *anew* r The Greek word for *you* here and in verse 12 is plural s Other ancient authorities add *who is in heaven*
t Some interpreters hold that the quotation concludes with verse 15 u Other ancient authorities read *the Jews* v Or *the Christ*

groom, who stands and hears him,
rejoices greatly at the bridegroom's
voice. For this reason my joy has
been fulfilled. 30 He must increase,
but I must decrease."[w]

The One Who Comes from Heaven

31 The one who comes from
above is above all; the one who is of
the earth belongs to the earth and
speaks about earthly things. The
one who comes from heaven is
above all. 32 He testifies to what he
has seen and heard, yet no one accepts his testimony. 33 Whoever has
accepted his testimony has certified[x] this, that God is true. 34 He
whom God has sent speaks the
words of God, for he gives the Spirit
without measure. 35 The Father
loves the Son and has placed all
things in his hands. 36 Whoever believes in the Son has eternal life;
whoever disobeys the Son will not
see life, but must endure God's
wrath.

Jesus and the Woman of Samaria

4 Now when Jesus[y] learned
that the Pharisees had heard,
"Jesus is making and baptizing
more disciples than John" 2 —
although it was not Jesus himself
but his disciples who baptized—
3 he left Judea and started back to
Galilee. 4 But he had to go through
Samaria. 5 So he came to a Samaritan city called Sychar, near the plot
of ground that Jacob had given to
his son Joseph. 6 Jacob's well was
there, and Jesus, tired out by his
journey, was sitting by the well. It
was about noon.

7 A Samaritan woman came to
draw water, and Jesus said to her,
"Give me a drink." 8 (His disciples
had gone to the city to buy food.)
9 The Samaritan woman said to
him, "How is it that you, a Jew, ask
a drink of me, a woman of Samaria?" (Jews do not share things
in common with Samaritans.)[z]
10 Jesus answered her, "If you knew
the gift of God, and who it is that is
saying to you, 'Give me a drink,'

3.31 Jn 8.23; 1 Jn 4.5
3.32 v. 11; Jn 8.26; 15.15
3.33 Rom 4.11; 15.28; Eph 1.13; 4.30
3.34 Mt 12.18; Lk 4.18
3.35 Mt 28.18; Jn 5.20,22; 17.2
3.36 Jn 5.24; 6.47
4.1 Jn 3.22,26
4.3 Jn 3.22
4.4 Lk 9.52
4.5 Gen 33.19; 48.22; Josh 24.32
4.8 vv. 5,39
4.9 Mt 10.5; Lk 9.52,53; Jn 8.48
4.10 Isa 44.3; Jn 7.37; Rev 21.6; 22.17
4.12 v. 6
4.14 Jn 6.35; 7.38
4.15 Jn 6.34
4.19 Lk 7.39
4.20 Deut 11.29; Josh 8.33; Lk 9.53
4.21 Mal 1.11; 1 Tim 2.8
4.22 2 Kings 17.28-41; Isa 2.3; Rom 3.1,2; 9.4,5
4.23 Jn 5.25; Phil 3.3
4.24 Phil 3.3
4.25 Jn 1.41; Mt 1.16

you would have asked him, and he
would have given you living water."
11 The woman said to him, "Sir, you
have no bucket, and the well is
deep. Where do you get that living
water? 12 Are you greater than our
ancestor Jacob, who gave us the
well, and with his sons and his
flocks drank from it?" 13 Jesus said
to her, "Everyone who drinks of
this water will be thirsty again,
14 but those who drink of the water
that I will give them will never be
thirsty. The water that I will give
will become in them a spring of water gushing up to eternal life."
15 The woman said to him, "Sir, give
me this water, so that I may never
be thirsty or have to keep coming
here to draw water."

16 Jesus said to her, "Go, call
your husband, and come back."
17 The woman answered him, "I
have no husband." Jesus said to
her, "You are right in saying, 'I have
no husband'; 18 for you have had
five husbands, and the one you
have now is not your husband.
What you have said is true!" 19 The
woman said to him, "Sir, I see that
you are a prophet. 20 Our ancestors
worshiped on this mountain, but
you[a] say that the place where people must worship is in Jerusalem."
21 Jesus said to her, "Woman, believe me, the hour is coming when
you will worship the Father neither
on this mountain nor in Jerusalem.
22 You worship what you do not
know; we worship what we know,
for salvation is from the Jews.
23 But the hour is coming, and is
now here, when the true worshipers will worship the Father in spirit
and truth, for the Father seeks
such as these to worship him.
24 God is spirit, and those who worship him must worship in spirit and
truth." 25 The woman said to him,
"I know that Messiah is coming"
(who is called Christ). "When he

[w] Some interpreters hold that the quotation continues through verse 36 [x] Gk *set a seal to* [y] Other ancient authorities read *the Lord*
[z] Other ancient authorities lack this sentence
[a] The Greek word for *you* here and in verses 21 and 22 is plural

comes, he will proclaim all things
to us." 26 Jesus said to her, "I am
he,[b] the one who is speaking to
you."

27 Just then his disciples came.
They were astonished that he was
speaking with a woman, but no one
said, "What do you want?" or,
"Why are you speaking with her?"
28 Then the woman left her water
jar and went back to the city. She
said to the people, 29 "Come and
see a man who told me everything
I have ever done! He cannot be the
Messiah,[c] can he?" 30 They left the
city and were on their way to him.

31 Meanwhile the disciples
were urging him, "Rabbi, eat something." 32 But he said to them, "I
have food to eat that you do not
know about." 33 So the disciples
said to one another, "Surely no one
has brought him something to
eat?" 34 Jesus said to them, "My
food is to do the will of him who
sent me and to complete his work.
35 Do you not say, 'Four months
more, then comes the harvest'? But
I tell you, look around you, and see
how the fields are ripe for harvesting. 36 The reaper is already receiving[d] wages and is gathering fruit
for eternal life, so that sower and
reaper may rejoice together. 37 For
here the saying holds true, 'One
sows and another reaps.' 38 I sent
you to reap that for which you did
not labor. Others have labored, and
you have entered into their labor."

39 Many Samaritans from that
city believed in him because of the
woman's testimony, "He told me
everything I have ever done." 40 So
when the Samaritans came to him,
they asked him to stay with them;
and he stayed there two days.
41 And many more believed because of his word. 42 They said to
the woman, "It is no longer because of what you said that we believe, for we have heard for ourselves, and we know that this is
truly the Savior of the world."

Jesus Returns to Galilee

43 When the two days were
over, he went from that place to

4.26 Mt 26.63, 64; Mk 14.61, 62; Jn 8.24
4.27 v. 8
4.29 vv. 17,18; Jn 7.26,31
4.32 Mt 4.4
4.34 Jn 5.30; 6.38; 17.4; 19.30
4.35 Mt 9.37; Lk 10.2
4.36 Rom 1.13; v. 14
4.37 Job 31.8; Mic 6.15 2
4.39 v. 29
4.42 1 Jn 4.14; 1 Tim 4.10; 2 Tim 1.10
4.43-45pp Mt 4.12-17; Mk 1.14,15; Lk 4.14,15
4.43 v. 40
4.44 Mt 13.57; Mk 6.4; Lk 4.24
4.45 Jn 2.23
4.46 Jn 2.1-11
4.47 vv. 3,54
4.48 Dan 4.2; Mk 13.22; Acts 2.19, 22,43; 4.30; Rom 15.19; Heb 2.4
4.53 Acts 11.14
4.54 Jn 2.11
5.2 Neh 3.1; 12.39

Galilee 44 (for Jesus himself had
testified that a prophet has no hon-
or in the prophet's own country).
45 When he came to Galilee, the
Galileans welcomed him, since
they had seen all that he had done
in Jerusalem at the festival; for
they too had gone to the festival.

Jesus Heals an Official's Son

46 Then he came again to Cana
in Galilee where he had changed
the water into wine. Now there was
a royal official whose son lay ill in
Capernaum. 47 When he heard that
Jesus had come from Judea to Galilee, he went and begged him to
come down and heal his son, for he
was at the point of death. 48 Then
Jesus said to him, "Unless you[e]
see signs and wonders you will not
believe." 49 The official said to him,
"Sir, come down before my little
boy dies." 50 Jesus said to him, "Go;
your son will live." The man believed the word that Jesus spoke to
him and started on his way. 51 As he
was going down, his slaves met him
and told him that his child was
alive. 52 So he asked them the hour
when he began to recover, and they
said to him, "Yesterday at one in
the afternoon the fever left him."
53 The father realized that this was
the hour when Jesus had said to
him, "Your son will live." So he
himself believed, along with his
whole household. 54 Now this was
the second sign that Jesus did after
coming from Judea to Galilee.

Jesus Heals on the Sabbath

5 After this there was a festival
of the Jews, and Jesus went up
to Jerusalem.

2 Now in Jerusalem by the
Sheep Gate there is a pool, called
in Hebrew[f] Beth-zatha,[g] which
has five porticoes. 3 In these lay
many invalids—blind, lame, and

[b] Gk *I am* [c] Or *the Christ*
[d] Or 35. . . *the fields are already ripe for harvesting.* 36 *The reaper is receiving* [e] Both instances of the Greek word for *you* in this verse are plural [f] That is, *Aramaic*
[g] Other ancient authorities read *Bethesda*, others *Bethsaida*

paralyzed.[h] 5 One man was there
who had been ill for thirty-eight
years. 6 When Jesus saw him lying
there and knew that he had been
there a long time, he said to him,
"Do you want to be made well?"
7 The sick man answered him, "Sir,
I have no one to put me into the
pool when the water is stirred up;
and while I am making my way,
someone else steps down ahead of
me." 8 Jesus said to him, "Stand up,
take your mat and walk." 9 At once
the man was made well, and he
took up his mat and began to walk.
Now that day was a sabbath.
10 So the Jews said to the man who
had been cured, "It is the sabbath;
it is not lawful for you to carry your
mat." 11 But he answered them,
"The man who made me well said
to me, 'Take up your mat and
walk.'" 12 They asked him, "Who is
the man who said to you, 'Take it
up and walk'?" 13 Now the man who
had been healed did not know who
it was, for Jesus had disappeared
in[i] the crowd that was there.
14 Later Jesus found him in the
temple and said to him, "See, you
have been made well! Do not sin
any more, so that nothing worse
happens to you." 15 The man went
away and told the Jews that it was
Jesus who had made him well.
16 Therefore the Jews started persecuting Jesus, because he was doing
such things on the sabbath. 17 But
Jesus answered them, "My Father
is still working, and I also am working." 18 For this reason the Jews
were seeking all the more to kill
him, because he was not only
breaking the sabbath, but was also
calling God his own Father, thereby making himself equal to God.

The Authority of the Son

19 Jesus said to them, "Very truly, I tell you, the Son can do nothing on his own, but only what he
sees the Father doing; for whatever
the Father[j] does, the Son does
likewise. 20 The Father loves the
Son and shows him all that he himself is doing; and he will show him
greater works than these, so that
you will be astonished. 21 Indeed,
just as the Father raises the dead
and gives them life, so also the Son
gives life to whomever he wishes.
22 The Father judges no one but has
given all judgment to the Son, 23 so
that all may honor the Son just as
they honor the Father. Anyone who
does not honor the Son does not
honor the Father who sent him.
24 Very truly, I tell you, anyone who
hears my word and believes him
who sent me has eternal life, and
does not come under judgment,
but has passed from death to life.
25 "Very truly, I tell you, the
hour is coming, and is now here,
when the dead will hear the voice
of the Son of God, and those who
hear will live. 26 For just as the Father has life in himself, so he has
granted the Son also to have life in
himself; 27 and he has given him authority to execute judgment, because he is the Son of Man. 28 Do
not be astonished at this; for the
hour is coming when all who are in
their graves will hear his voice
29 and will come out—those who
have done good, to the resurrection
of life, and those who have done
evil, to the resurrection of condemnation.

Witnesses to Jesus

30 "I can do nothing on my own.
As I hear, I judge; and my judgment
is just, because I seek to do not my
own will but the will of him who
sent me.
31 "If I testify about myself, my
testimony is not true. 32 There is
another who testifies on my behalf,
and I know that his testimony to
me is true. 33 You sent messengers
to John, and he testified to the
truth. 34 Not that I accept such human testimony, but I say these
things so that you may be saved.
35 He was a burning and shining

5.8 Mt 9.6; Mk 2.11; Lk 5.24
5.9 Jn 9.14
5.10 vv. 15,16; Neh 13.19; Jer 17.21; Mt 12.2; Mk 2.24; Jn 7.23; 9.16
5.14 Mk 2.5; Jn 8.11
5.17 Jn 9.4; 14.10
5.18 Jn 7.1,19; 10.30,33
5.19 Jn 8.28; 12.49; 14.10
5.20 Jn 3.35; 14.12
5.21 Rom 4.17; 8.11; Jn 11.25
5.22 Jn 9.39; Acts 17.31
5.23 Lk 10.16; 1 Jn 2.23
5.24 Jn 3.18; 12.44; 20.31; 1 Jn 5.13; 3.14
5.25 Jn 4.21; 6.60; 8.43,47
5.26 Jn 6.57
5.27 Acts 10.42; 17.31
5.29 Dan 12.2; Acts 24.15; Mt 25.46
5.30 Jn 8.16; 4.34; 6.38
5.31 Jn 8.14
5.32 Jn 8.18
5.33 Jn 1.7,15, 19,27,32
5.34 1 Jn 5.9
5.35 2 Pet 1.19; Mt 21.26

[h] Other ancient authorities add, wholly or in part, *waiting for the stirring of the water;* [4] *for an angel of the Lord went down at certain seasons into the pool, and stirred up the water; whoever stepped in first after the stirring of the water was made well from whatever disease that person had.* [i] Or *had left because of* [j] Gk *that one*

lamp, and you were willing to rejoice for a while in his light. 36 But
I have a testimony greater than
John's. The works that the Father
has given me to complete, the very
works that I am doing, testify on
my behalf that the Father has sent
me. 37 And the Father who sent me
has himself testified on my behalf.
You have never heard his voice or
seen his form, 38 and you do not
have his word abiding in you, because you do not believe him
whom he has sent.

39 "You search the scriptures
because you think that in them you
have eternal life; and it is they that
testify on my behalf. 40 Yet you refuse to come to me to have life. 41 I
do not accept glory from human
beings. 42 But I know that you do
not have the love of God in[k] you.
43 I have come in my Father's
name, and you do not accept me; if
another comes in his own name,
you will accept him. 44 How can you
believe when you accept glory from
one another and do not seek the
glory that comes from the one who
alone is God? 45 Do not think that I
will accuse you before the Father;
your accuser is Moses, on whom
you have set your hope. 46 If you believed Moses, you would believe
me, for he wrote about me. 47 But if
you do not believe what he wrote,
how will you believe what I say?"

Feeding the Five Thousand

6 After this Jesus went to the
other side of the Sea of Galilee, also called the Sea of Tiberias.[l] 2 A large crowd kept following
him, because they saw the signs
that he was doing for the sick.
3 Jesus went up the mountain and
sat down there with his disciples.
4 Now the Passover, the festival of
the Jews, was near. 5 When he
looked up and saw a large crowd
coming toward him, Jesus said to
Philip, "Where are we to buy bread
for these people to eat?" 6 He said
this to test him, for he himself
knew what he was going to do.
7 Philip answered him, "Six

5.36 1 Jn 5.9; Jn 10.25; 14.11; 15.24
5.37 Jn 8.18; Deut 4.12; 1 Tim 1.17
5.38 Jn 3.17
5.39 Lk 24.25,27; Acts 13.27
5.41 v. 44
5.43 Mt 24.5
5.44 Rom 2.29
5.45 Jn 9.28; Rom 2.17
5.46 Gen 3.15; Lk 24.27; Acts 26.22
5.47 Lk 16.29,31
6.1-14pp Mt 14.13-21; Mk 6.30-44; Lk 9.10-17
6.2 Jn 2.11
6.3 v. 15
6.4 Jn 2.13
6.5 Jn 1.43
6.6 2 Cor 13.5
6.8 Jn 1.40
6.9 2 Kings 4.43
6.11 v. 23; Mt 15.36
6.14 Gen 49.10; Deut 18.15, 18; Mt 11.3; 21.11
6.15-21pp Mt 14.22-32; Mk 6.45-52
6.15 Jn 18.36

months' wages[m] would not buy
enough bread for each of them to
get a little." 8 One of his disciples,
Andrew, Simon Peter's brother,
said to him, 9 "There is a boy here
who has five barley loaves and two
fish. But what are they among so
many people?" 10 Jesus said,
"Make the people sit down." Now
there was a great deal of grass in
the place; so they[n] sat down, about
five thousand in all. 11 Then Jesus
took the loaves, and when he had
given thanks, he distributed them
to those who were seated; so also
the fish, as much as they wanted.
12 When they were satisfied, he told
his disciples, "Gather up the fragments left over, so that nothing
may be lost." 13 So they gathered
them up, and from the fragments of
the five barley loaves, left by those
who had eaten, they filled twelve
baskets. 14 When the people saw
the sign that he had done, they began to say, "This is indeed the
prophet who is to come into the
world."

15 When Jesus realized that
they were about to come and take
him by force to make him king, he
withdrew again to the mountain by
himself.

Jesus Walks on the Water

16 When evening came, his disciples went down to the sea, 17 got
into a boat, and started across the
sea to Capernaum. It was now dark,
and Jesus had not yet come to
them. 18 The sea became rough because a strong wind was blowing.
19 When they had rowed about
three or four miles,[o] they saw
Jesus walking on the sea and coming near the boat, and they were
terrified. 20 But he said to them, "It
is I;[p] do not be afraid." 21 Then
they wanted to take him into the
boat, and immediately the boat
reached the land toward which
they were going.

[k] Or *among* [l] Gk *of Galilee of Tiberius*
[m] Gk *Two hundred denarii*; the denarius was the usual day's wage for a laborer
[n] Gk *the men* [o] Gk *about twenty-five or thirty stadia* [p] Gk *I am*

The Bread from Heaven

22 The next day the crowd that
had stayed on the other side of the
sea saw that there had been only
one boat there. They also saw that
Jesus had not got into the boat
with his disciples, but that his disciples had gone away alone.
23 Then some boats from Tiberias
came near the place where they
had eaten the bread after the Lord
had given thanks.[q] 24 So when the
crowd saw that neither Jesus nor
his disciples were there, they
themselves got into the boats and
went to Capernaum looking for
Jesus.

25 When they found him on the
other side of the sea, they said to
him, "Rabbi, when did you come
here?" 26 Jesus answered them,
"Very truly, I tell you, you are looking for me, not because you saw
signs, but because you ate your fill
of the loaves. 27 Do not work for the
food that perishes, but for the food
that endures for eternal life, which
the Son of Man will give you. For it
is on him that God the Father has
set his seal." 28 Then they said to
him, "What must we do to perform
the works of God?" 29 Jesus answered them, "This is the work of
God, that you believe in him whom
he has sent." 30 So they said to him,
"What sign are you going to give us
then, so that we may see it and believe you? What work are you performing? 31 Our ancestors ate the
manna in the wilderness; as it is
written, 'He gave them bread from
heaven to eat.' " 32 Then Jesus said
to them, "Very truly, I tell you, it
was not Moses who gave you the
bread from heaven, but it is my Father who gives you the true bread
from heaven. 33 For the bread of
God is that which[r] comes down
from heaven and gives life to the
world." 34 They said to him, "Sir,
give us this bread always."

35 Jesus said to them, "I am the
bread of life. Whoever comes to me
will never be hungry, and whoever
believes in me will never be thirsty.
36 But I said to you that you have
seen me and yet do not believe.
37 Everything that the Father gives
me will come to me, and anyone
who comes to me I will never drive
away; 38 for I have come down from
heaven, not to do my own will, but
the will of him who sent me. 39 And
this is the will of him who sent me,
that I should lose nothing of all
that he has given me, but raise it up
on the last day. 40 This is indeed the
will of my Father, that all who see
the Son and believe in him may
have eternal life; and I will raise
them up on the last day."

41 Then the Jews began to complain about him because he said, "I
am the bread that came down from
heaven." 42 They were saying, "Is
not this Jesus, the son of Joseph,
whose father and mother we know?
How can he now say, 'I have come
down from heaven'?" 43 Jesus answered them, "Do not complain
among yourselves. 44 No one can
come to me unless drawn by the
Father who sent me; and I will raise
that person up on the last day. 45 It
is written in the prophets, 'And
they shall all be taught by God.' Everyone who has heard and learned
from the Father comes to me.
46 Not that anyone has seen the Father except the one who is from
God; he has seen the Father. 47 Very
truly, I tell you, whoever believes
has eternal life. 48 I am the bread of
life. 49 Your ancestors ate the manna in the wilderness, and they died.
50 This is the bread that comes
down from heaven, so that one may
eat of it and not die. 51 I am the living bread that came down from
heaven. Whoever eats of this bread
will live forever; and the bread that
I will give for the life of the world is
my flesh."

52 The Jews then disputed
among themselves, saying, "How
can this man give us his flesh to
eat?" 53 So Jesus said to them,
"Very truly, I tell you, unless you
eat the flesh of the Son of Man and

6.22 vv. 2,16ff **6.23** vv. 1,11 **6.24** Mt 14.34; Mk 6.53 **6.26** vv. 24,30 **6.27** Isa 55.2; v. 54; Jn 4.14; 3.35 **6.29** 1 Jn 3.23; Jn 3.17 **6.30** Mt 12.38; Mk 8.11 **6.31** Ex 16.15; Num 11.8; Neh 9.15; Ps 78.24 **6.33** v. 50 **6.34** Jn 4.15 **6.35** vv. 48,51; Jn 4.14 **6.36** v. 26 **6.37** v. 39; Jn 17.2 **6.38** Jn 4.34; 5.30 **6.39** Jn 10.28; 17.12; 18.9 **6.40** vv. 27,47, 54; Jn 3.15, 16 **6.42** Lk 4.22; Jn 7.27,28; vv. 38,62 **6.44** Jer 31.3; Hos 11.4; Jn 12.32 **6.45** Isa 54.13; Jer 31.34; Heb 8.10; 10.16 **6.46** Jn 1.18; 5.37; 7.29; 8.19 **6.47** Jn 3.16,18, 36; 5.24; 11.26 **6.48** vv. 35,51 **6.49** v. 31 **6.50** v. 33 **6.51** Heb 10.10

6.52 Jn 9.16; 10.19 **6.53** Mt 26.26,28

q Other ancient authorities lack *after the Lord had given thanks* r Or *he who*

drink his blood, you have no life in
you. 54 Those who eat my flesh and
drink my blood have eternal life,
and I will raise them up on the last
day; 55 for my flesh is true food and
my blood is true drink. 56 Those
who eat my flesh and drink my
blood abide in me, and I in them.
57 Just as the living Father sent me,
and I live because of the Father, so
whoever eats me will live because
of me. 58 This is the bread that
came down from heaven, not like
that which your ancestors ate, and
they died. But the one who eats
this bread will live forever." 59 He
said these things while he was
teaching in the synagogue at Capernaum.

The Words of Eternal Life

60 When many of his disciples
heard it, they said, "This teaching
is difficult; who can accept it?"
61 But Jesus, being aware that his
disciples were complaining about
it, said to them, "Does this offend
you? 62 Then what if you were to see
the Son of Man ascending to where
he was before? 63 It is the spirit that
gives life; the flesh is useless. The
words that I have spoken to you are
spirit and life. 64 But among you
there are some who do not believe." For Jesus knew from the
first who were the ones that did not
believe, and who was the one that
would betray him. 65 And he said,
"For this reason I have told you
that no one can come to me unless
it is granted by the Father."
66 Because of this many of his
disciples turned back and no longer went about with him. 67 So
Jesus asked the twelve, "Do you
also wish to go away?" 68 Simon Peter answered him, "Lord, to whom
can we go? You have the words of
eternal life. 69 We have come to believe and know that you are the
Holy One of God."[s] 70 Jesus answered them, "Did I not choose
you, the twelve? Yet one of you is a
devil." 71 He was speaking of Judas
son of Simon Iscariot,[t] for he,
though one of the twelve, was going to betray him.

6.54 Jn 4.14
6.56 Jn 15.4; 1 Jn 3.24; 4.15,16
6.57 Jn 3.17
6.58 vv. 49-51
6.60 v. 66
6.61 Mt 11.6
6.62 Jn 3.13; 17.5
6.63 2 Cor 3.6
6.64 Jn 2.25
6.65 vv. 37,44; Jn 3.27
6.66 v. 60
6.67 Mt 10.2
6.68 Mt 16.16; Acts 5.20
6.69 Mk 8.29; Lk 9.20
6.70 Jn 15.16,19; 13.27
6.71 Jn 13.26; Mk 14.10
7.1 Jn 5.18
7.2 Lev 23.34; Deut 16.16
7.3 Mt 12.46; Mk 3.31
7.5 Mk 3.21
7.6 Mt 26.18; vv. 8,30
7.7 Jn 15.18,19; 3.19,20
7.8 v. 6
7.11 Jn 11.56
7.12 vv. 40-43
7.13 Jn 9.22; 12.42; 19.38
7.14 v. 28
7.15 Mt 13.54; Mk 6.2; Lk 4.22
7.16 Jn 3.11; 8.28; 12.49
7.17 Jn 8.43

The Unbelief of Jesus' Brothers

7 After this Jesus went about in
Galilee. He did not wish[u] to
go about in Judea because the
Jews were looking for an opportunity to kill him. 2 Now the Jewish
festival of Booths[v] was near. 3 So
his brothers said to him, "Leave
here and go to Judea so that your
disciples also may see the works
you are doing; 4 for no one who
wants[w] to be widely known acts in
secret. If you do these things, show
yourself to the world." 5 (For not
even his brothers believed in him.)
6 Jesus said to them, "My time has
not yet come, but your time is always here. 7 The world cannot hate
you, but it hates me because I testify against it that its works are evil.
8 Go to the festival yourselves. I am
not[x] going to this festival, for my
time has not yet fully come." 9 After
saying this, he remained in Galilee.

Jesus at the Festival of Booths

10 But after his brothers had
gone to the festival, then he also
went, not publicly but as it were[y]
in secret. 11 The Jews were looking
for him at the festival and saying,
"Where is he?" 12 And there was
considerable complaining about
him among the crowds. While
some were saying, "He is a good
man," others were saying, "No, he
is deceiving the crowd." 13 Yet no
one would speak openly about him
for fear of the Jews.
14 About the middle of the festival Jesus went up into the temple
and began to teach. 15 The Jews
were astonished at it, saying, "How
does this man have such learning,[z]
when he has never been taught?"
16 Then Jesus answered them, "My
teaching is not mine but his who
sent me. 17 Anyone who resolves to
do the will of God will know wheth-

[s] Other ancient authorities read *the Christ, the Son of the living God* [t] Other ancient authorities read *Judas Iscariot son of Simon;* others, *Judas son of Simon from Karyot* (Kerioth) [u] Other ancient authorities read *was not at liberty* [v] Or *Tabernacles* [w] Other ancient authorities read *wants it* [x] Other ancient authorities add *yet* [y] Other ancient authorities lack *as it were* [z] Or *this man know his letters*

er the teaching is from God or
whether I am speaking on my own.
18 Those who speak on their own
seek their own glory; but the one
who seeks the glory of him who
sent him is true, and there is nothing false in him.
19 "Did not Moses give you the
law? Yet none of you keeps the law.
Why are you looking for an opportunity to kill me?" 20 The crowd answered, "You have a demon! Who is
trying to kill you?" 21 Jesus answered them, "I performed one
work, and all of you are astonished.
22 Moses gave you circumcision (it
is, of course, not from Moses, but
from the patriarchs), and you circumcise a man on the sabbath. 23 If
a man receives circumcision on the
sabbath in order that the law of
Moses may not be broken, are you
angry with me because I healed a
man's whole body on the sabbath?
24 Do not judge by appearances, but
judge with right judgment."

Is This the Christ?

25 Now some of the people of
Jerusalem were saying, "Is not this
the man whom they are trying to
kill? 26 And here he is, speaking
openly, but they say nothing to
him! Can it be that the authorities
really know that this is the Messiah?[a] 27 Yet we know where this
man is from; but when the Messiah[a] comes, no one will know
where he is from." 28 Then Jesus
cried out as he was teaching in the
temple, "You know me, and you
know where I am from. I have not
come on my own. But the one who
sent me is true, and you do not
know him. 29 I know him, because I
am from him, and he sent me."
30 Then they tried to arrest him, but
no one laid hands on him, because
his hour had not yet come. 31 Yet
many in the crowd believed in him
and were saying, "When the Messiah[a] comes, will he do more signs
than this man has done?"[b]

Officers Are Sent to Arrest Jesus

32 The Pharisees heard the
crowd muttering such things about
him, and the chief priests and
Pharisees sent temple police to arrest him. 33 Jesus then said, "I will
be with you a little while longer,
and then I am going to him who
sent me. 34 You will search for me,
but you will not find me; and where
I am, you cannot come." 35 The
Jews said to one another, "Where
does this man intend to go that we
will not find him? Does he intend
to go to the Dispersion among the
Greeks and teach the Greeks?
36 What does he mean by saying,
'You will search for me and you will
not find me' and 'Where I am, you
cannot come'?"

Rivers of Living Water

37 On the last day of the festival, the great day, while Jesus was
standing there, he cried out, "Let
anyone who is thirsty come to me,
38 and let the one who believes in
me drink. As[c] the scripture has
said, 'Out of the believer's heart[d]
shall flow rivers of living water.' "
39 Now he said this about the Spirit,
which believers in him were to receive; for as yet there was no Spirit,[e] because Jesus was not yet glorified.

Division among the People

40 When they heard these
words, some in the crowd said,
"This is really the prophet." 41 Others said, "This is the Messiah."[a]
But some asked, "Surely the Messiah[a] does not come from Galilee,
does he? 42 Has not the scripture
said that the Messiah[a] is descended from David and comes from
Bethlehem, the village where David lived?" 43 So there was a division in the crowd because of him.
44 Some of them wanted to arrest
him, but no one laid hands on him.

The Unbelief of Those in Authority

45 Then the temple police went
back to the chief priests and Phari-

7.18 Jn 5.41; 8.50 **7.19** Ex 24.3; Jn 1.17; 11.53 **7.20** Jn 8.48; 10.20 **7.22** Lev 12.3; Gen 17.10 **7.23** Mk 3.5 **7.24** Lev 19.15; Jn 8.15 **7.26** v. 48 **7.27** Mt 13.55; Mk 6.3; Lk 4.22 **7.28** Jn 8.14; 8.26; 1.18 **7.29** Mt 11.27; Jn 10.15 **7.30** Mt 21.46; Jn 8.20 **7.31** Jn 8.30; Mt 12.23 **7.33** Jn 13.33; 16.16-19 **7.34** Jn 8.21; 13.33 **7.35** Jas 1.1; 1 Pet 1.1 **7.37** Lev 23.36; Isa 55.1; Rev 22.17 **7.38** Isa 12.3; Jn 4.10,14 **7.39** Joel 2.28; Acts 2.17, 33; Jn 20.22; 12.23 **7.40** Mt 21.11; Jn 1.21 **7.41** Jn 1.46 **7.42** Jer 23.5; Mic 5.2; Mt 2.5; Lk 2.4 **7.43** Jn 9.16; 10.19 **7.44** v. 30

[a] Or *the Christ* [b] Other ancient authorities read *is doing* [c] Or *come to me and drink. 38The one who believes in me, as* [d] Gk *out of his belly* [e] Other ancient authorities read *for as yet the Spirit* (others, *Holy Spirit*) *had not been given*

sees, who asked them, "Why did
you not arrest him?" 46 The police
answered, "Never has anyone spoken like this!" 47 Then the Pharisees replied, "Surely you have not
been deceived too, have you?
48 Has any one of the authorities or
of the Pharisees believed in him?
49 But this crowd, which does not
know the law—they are accursed."
50 Nicodemus, who had gone to
Jesus[f] before, and who was one of
them, asked, 51 "Our law does not
judge people without first giving
them a hearing to find out what
they are doing, does it?" 52 They replied, "Surely you are not also from
Galilee, are you? Search and you
will see that no prophet is to arise
from Galilee."

The Woman Caught in Adultery

⟦53 Then each of them went home,
8 1 while Jesus went to the
Mount of Olives. 2 Early in the
morning he came again to the temple. All the people came to him and
he sat down and began to teach
them. 3 The scribes and the Pharisees brought a woman who had
been caught in adultery; and making her stand before all of them,
4 they said to him, "Teacher, this
woman was caught in the very act
of committing adultery. 5 Now in
the law Moses commanded us to
stone such women. Now what do
you say?" 6 They said this to test
him, so that they might have some
charge to bring against him. Jesus
bent down and wrote with his finger on the ground. 7 When they
kept on questioning him, he
straightened up and said to them,
"Let anyone among you who is
without sin be the first to throw a
stone at her." 8 And once again he
bent down and wrote on the
ground.[g] 9 When they heard it, they
went away, one by one, beginning
with the elders; and Jesus was left
alone with the woman standing before him. 10 Jesus straightened up
and said to her, "Woman, where
are they? Has no one condemned
you?" 11 She said, "No one, sir."[h]

7.46 Mt 7.28,29
7.47 v. 12
7.48 Jn 12.42
7.51 Deut 17.6; 19.15
8.5 Lev 20.10; Deut 22.22
8.7 Deut 17.7; Rom 2.1
8.9 Rom 2.22
8.11 Jn 3.18; 5.14
8.12 Jn 1.4; 9.5; 12.35
8.13 Jn 5.31
8.14 Jn 18.37; 13.3; 16.28; 7.28; 9.29
8.15 Jn 7.24; 3.17
8.16 Jn 5.30
8.17 Deut 17.6; Mt 18.16
8.18 Jn 5.37
8.19 Jn 14.7; 16.3
8.20 Mk 12.41; Jn 7.30
8.21 Jn 7.34
8.23 Jn 3.31; 17.14
8.24 Mk 13.6; Jn 4.26; 13.19

And Jesus said, "Neither do I condemn you. Go your way, and from
now on do not sin again."⟧[i]

Jesus the Light of the World

12 Again Jesus spoke to them,
saying, "I am the light of the world.
Whoever follows me will never
walk in darkness but will have the
light of life." 13 Then the Pharisees
said to him, "You are testifying on
your own behalf; your testimony is
not valid." 14 Jesus answered,
"Even if I testify on my own behalf,
my testimony is valid because I
know where I have come from and
where I am going, but you do not
know where I come from or where
I am going. 15 You judge by human
standards;[j] I judge no one. 16 Yet
even if I do judge, my judgment is
valid; for it is not I alone who judge,
but I and the Father[k] who sent me.
17 In your law it is written that the
testimony of two witnesses is valid.
18 I testify on my own behalf, and
the Father who sent me testifies on
my behalf." 19 Then they said to
him, "Where is your Father?" Jesus
answered, "You know neither me
nor my Father. If you knew me, you
would know my Father also." 20 He
spoke these words while he was
teaching in the treasury of the temple, but no one arrested him, because his hour had not yet come.

Jesus Foretells His Death

21 Again he said to them, "I am
going away, and you will search for
me, but you will die in your sin.
Where I am going, you cannot
come." 22 Then the Jews said, "Is
he going to kill himself? Is that
what he means by saying, 'Where I
am going, you cannot come'?"
23 He said to them, "You are from
below, I am from above; you are of
this world, I am not of this world.
24 I told you that you would die in

[f] Gk *him* [g] Other ancient authorities add *the sins of each of them* [h] Or *Lord*
[i] The most ancient authorities lack 7.53—8.11; other authorities add the passage here or after 7.36 or after 21.25 or after Luke 21.38, with variations of text; some mark the passage as doubtful. [j] Gk *according to the flesh*
[k] Other ancient authorities read *he*

your sins, for you will die in your
sins unless you believe that I am
he."[l] 25 They said to him, "Who are
you?" Jesus said to them, "Why do
I speak to you at all?[m] 26 I have
much to say about you and much to
condemn; but the one who sent me
is true, and I declare to the world
what I have heard from him."
27 They did not understand that he
was speaking to them about the
Father. 28 So Jesus said, "When you
have lifted up the Son of Man, then
you will realize that I am he,[l] and
that I do nothing on my own, but I
speak these things as the Father instructed me. 29 And the one who
sent me is with me; he has not left
me alone, for I always do what is
pleasing to him." 30 As he was saying these things, many believed in
him.

True Disciples

31 Then Jesus said to the Jews
who had believed in him, "If you
continue in my word, you are truly
my disciples; 32 and you will know
the truth, and the truth will make
you free." 33 They answered him,
"We are descendants of Abraham
and have never been slaves to anyone. What do you mean by saying,
'You will be made free'?"
34 Jesus answered them, "Very
truly, I tell you, everyone who commits sin is a slave to sin. 35 The
slave does not have a permanent
place in the household; the son has
a place there forever. 36 So if the
Son makes you free, you will be
free indeed. 37 I know that you are
descendants of Abraham; yet you
look for an opportunity to kill me,
because there is no place in you for
my word. 38 I declare what I have
seen in the Father's presence; as
for you, you should do what you
have heard from the Father."[n]

Jesus and Abraham

39 They answered him, "Abraham is our father." Jesus said to
them, "If you were Abraham's children, you would be doing[o] what
Abraham did, 40 but now you are
trying to kill me, a man who has

8.26
Jn 7.28;
3.32; 15.15
8.28
Jn 3.14;
12.32; 5.19;
3.11
8.29
Jn 4.34;
5.30; 6.38
8.30
Jn 7.31;
10.42; 11.45
8.31
Jn 15.7;
2 Jn 9
8.32
Rom 8.2;
Jas 2.12
8.33
Mt 3.9
8.34
Rom 6.16;
2 Pet 2.19
8.35
Gal 4.30
8.37
vv. 39,40
8.38
Jn 5.19,30;
14.10,24
8.39
Rom 9.7;
Gal 3.7
8.40
v. 26
8.41
Isa 63.16;
64.8
8.42
1 Jn 5.1;
Jn 16.27,28;
17.8; 7.28
8.44
1 Jn 3.8;
vv. 38,41;
1 Jn 2.4;
Mt 12.34
8.47
1 Jn 4.6
8.48
v. 52;
Jn 7.20;
10.20
8.50
Jn 5.41
8.51
Jn 14.23;
15.20; 17.6;
Mt 16.28;
Heb 11.5
8.52
Jn 7.20;
14.23; 15.20;
17.6
8.53
Jn 4.12
8.54
v. 50;
Jn 16.14
8.55
Jn 7.28,29;
15.10

told you the truth that I heard from
God. This is not what Abraham did.
41 You are indeed doing what your
father does." They said to him, "We
are not illegitimate children; we
have one father, God himself."
42 Jesus said to them, "If God were
your Father, you would love me, for
I came from God and now I am
here. I did not come on my own,
but he sent me. 43 Why do you not
understand what I say? It is because you cannot accept my word.
44 You are from your father the
devil, and you choose to do your father's desires. He was a murderer
from the beginning and does not
stand in the truth, because there is
no truth in him. When he lies, he
speaks according to his own nature, for he is a liar and the father
of lies. 45 But because I tell the
truth, you do not believe me.
46 Which of you convicts me of sin?
If I tell the truth, why do you not
believe me? 47 Whoever is from God
hears the words of God. The reason
you do not hear them is that you
are not from God."
48 The Jews answered him,
"Are we not right in saying that you
are a Samaritan and have a demon?" 49 Jesus answered, "I do not
have a demon; but I honor my Father, and you dishonor me. 50 Yet I
do not seek my own glory; there is
one who seeks it and he is the
judge. 51 Very truly, I tell you, whoever keeps my word will never see
death." 52 The Jews said to him,
"Now we know that you have a demon. Abraham died, and so did the
prophets; yet you say, 'Whoever
keeps my word will never taste
death.' 53 Are you greater than our
father Abraham, who died? The
prophets also died. Who do you
claim to be?" 54 Jesus answered, "If
I glorify myself, my glory is nothing.
It is my Father who glorifies me, he
of whom you say, 'He is our God,'
55 though you do not know him. But

[l] Gk *I am* [m] Or *What I have told you from the beginning* [n] Other ancient authorities read *you do what you have heard from your father* [o] Other ancient authorities read *If you are Abraham's children, then do*

I know him; if I would say that I do not know him, I would be a liar like you. But I do know him and I keep his word. 56 Your ancestor Abraham rejoiced that he would see my day; he saw it and was glad." 57 Then the Jews said to him, "You are not yet fifty years old, and have you seen Abraham?"[p] 58 Jesus said to them, "Very truly, I tell you, before Abraham was, I am." 59 So they picked up stones to throw at him, but Jesus hid himself and went out of the temple.

A Man Born Blind Receives Sight

9 As he walked along, he saw a man blind from birth. 2 His disciples asked him, "Rabbi, who sinned, this man or his parents, that he was born blind?" 3 Jesus answered, "Neither this man nor his parents sinned; he was born blind so that God's works might be revealed in him. 4 We[q] must work the works of him who sent me[r] while it is day; night is coming when no one can work. 5 As long as I am in the world, I am the light of the world." 6 When he had said this, he spat on the ground and made mud with the saliva and spread the mud on the man's eyes, 7 saying to him, "Go, wash in the pool of Siloam" (which means Sent). Then he went and washed and came back able to see. 8 The neighbors and those who had seen him before as a beggar began to ask, "Is this not the man who used to sit and beg?" 9 Some were saying, "It is he." Others were saying, "No, but it is someone like him." He kept saying, "I am the man." 10 But they kept asking him, "Then how were your eyes opened?" 11 He answered, "The man called Jesus made mud, spread it on my eyes, and said to me, 'Go to Siloam and wash.' Then I went and washed and received my sight." 12 They said to him, "Where is he?" He said, "I do not know."

The Pharisees Investigate the Healing

13 They brought to the Pharisees the man who had formerly been blind. 14 Now it was a sabbath day when Jesus made the mud and opened his eyes. 15 Then the Pharisees also began to ask him how he had received his sight. He said to them, "He put mud on my eyes. Then I washed, and now I see." 16 Some of the Pharisees said, "This man is not from God, for he does not observe the sabbath." But others said, "How can a man who is a sinner perform such signs?" And they were divided. 17 So they said again to the blind man, "What do you say about him? It was your eyes he opened." He said, "He is a prophet."

18 The Jews did not believe that he had been blind and had received his sight until they called the parents of the man who had received his sight 19 and asked them, "Is this your son, who you say was born blind? How then does he now see?" 20 His parents answered, "We know that this is our son, and that he was born blind; 21 but we do not know how it is that now he sees, nor do we know who opened his eyes. Ask him; he is of age. He will speak for himself." 22 His parents said this because they were afraid of the Jews; for the Jews had already agreed that anyone who confessed Jesus[s] to be the Messiah[t] would be put out of the synagogue. 23 Therefore his parents said, "He is of age; ask him."

24 So for the second time they called the man who had been blind, and they said to him, "Give glory to God! We know that this man is a sinner." 25 He answered, "I do not know whether he is a sinner. One thing I do know, that though I was blind, now I see." 26 They said to him, "What did he do to you? How did he open your eyes?" 27 He answered them, "I have told you already, and you would not listen. Why do you want to hear it again? Do you also want to become his

8.56 Mt 13.17; Heb 11.13
8.58 Jn 1.1; 17.5, 24; Rev 1.8
8.59 Jn 10.31; 11.8; 12.36
9.2 v. 34; Lk 13.2; Ex 20.5; Ezek 18.20
9.3 Jn 11.4
9.4 Jn 11.9; 12.35
9.5 Jn 1.4; 8.12; 12.46
9.6 Mk 7.33; 8.23
9.7 v. 11; Lk 13.4; Jn 11.37
9.11 v. 7
9.14 Jn 5.9
9.15 v. 10
9.16 Mt 12.2; Jn 7.43; 10.19
9.17 v. 15; Mt 21.11
9.18 v. 22
9.22 Jn 7.13; 12.42; v. 34; Lk 6.22
9.23 v. 21
9.24 Josh 7.19; 1 Sam 6.5; v. 16
9.27 v. 15; Jn 5.25

[p] Other ancient authorities read *has Abraham seen you?* [q] Other ancient authorities read *I* [r] Other ancient authorities read *us* [s] Gk *him* [t] Or *the Christ*

disciples?" 28 Then they reviled
him, saying, "You are his disciple,
but we are disciples of Moses. 29 We
know that God has spoken to Moses, but as for this man, we do not
know where he comes from." 30 The
man answered, "Here is an aston-
ishing thing! You do not know
where he comes from, and yet he
opened my eyes. 31 We know that
God does not listen to sinners, but
he does listen to one who worships
him and obeys his will. 32 Never
since the world began has it been
heard that anyone opened the eyes
of a person born blind. 33 If this
man were not from God, he could
do nothing." 34 They answered him,
"You were born entirely in sins,
and are you trying to teach us?"
And they drove him out.

Spiritual Blindness

35 Jesus heard that they had
driven him out, and when he found
him, he said, "Do you believe in the
Son of Man?"[u] 36 He answered,
"And who is he, sir?[v] Tell me, so
that I may believe in him." 37 Jesus
said to him, "You have seen him,
and the one speaking with you is
he." 38 He said, "Lord,[v] I believe."
And he worshiped him. 39 Jesus
said, "I came into this world for
judgment so that those who do not
see may see, and those who do see
may become blind." 40 Some of the
Pharisees near him heard this and
said to him, "Surely we are not
blind, are we?" 41 Jesus said to
them, "If you were blind, you
would not have sin. But now that
you say, 'We see,' your sin remains.

Jesus the Good Shepherd

10 "Very truly, I tell you, anyone who does not enter the
sheepfold by the gate but climbs in
by another way is a thief and a bandit. 2 The one who enters by the
gate is the shepherd of the sheep.
3 The gatekeeper opens the gate for
him, and the sheep hear his voice.
He calls his own sheep by name
and leads them out. 4 When he has
brought out all his own, he goes
ahead of them, and the sheep follow him because they know his
voice. 5 They will not follow a
stranger, but they will run from
him because they do not know the
voice of strangers." 6 Jesus used
this figure of speech with them, but
they did not understand what he
was saying to them.

7 So again Jesus said to them,
"Very truly, I tell you, I am the gate
for the sheep. 8 All who came before me are thieves and bandits;
but the sheep did not listen to
them. 9 I am the gate. Whoever enters by me will be saved, and will
come in and go out and find pasture. 10 The thief comes only to
steal and kill and destroy. I came
that they may have life, and have it
abundantly.

11 "I am the good shepherd.
The good shepherd lays down his
life for the sheep. 12 The hired
hand, who is not the shepherd and
does not own the sheep, sees the
wolf coming and leaves the sheep
and runs away—and the wolf
snatches them and scatters them.
13 The hired hand runs away because a hired hand does not care
for the sheep. 14 I am the good
shepherd. I know my own and my
own know me, 15 just as the Father
knows me and I know the Father.
And I lay down my life for the
sheep. 16 I have other sheep that do
not belong to this fold. I must bring
them also, and they will listen to
my voice. So there will be one
flock, one shepherd. 17 For this reason the Father loves me, because I
lay down my life in order to take it
up again. 18 No one takes[w] it from
me, but I lay it down of my own accord. I have power to lay it down,
and I have power to take it up
again. I have received this command from my Father."

19 Again the Jews were divided
because of these words. 20 Many of
them were saying, "He has a de-

9.28 Jn 5.45 **9.29** Jn 8.14 **9.31** Job 27.8,9; Ps 34.15; 66.18; Prov 15.29; 28.9; Isa 1.15; Jer 11.11; Zech 7.13 **9.33** v. 16 **9.34** v. 2 **9.35** Mt 14.33; 16.16; Mk 1.1; Jn 10.36 **9.36** Rom 10.14 **9.37** Jn 4.26 **9.38** Mt 28.9 **9.39** Jn 5.22,27; 3.19; Mt 13.13; 15.14 **9.40** Rom 2.19 **9.41** Jn 15.22,24 **10.2** Mk 6.34; vv. 11,12 **10.3** vv. 16,27,9 **10.4** v. 3 **10.6** Jn 16.25 **10.7** Jer 23.1,2; Ezek 34.2 **10.10** Jn 5.40 **10.11** Isa 40.11; Ezek 34.11-16; 23; Heb 13.20; 1 Pet 5.4; Rev 7.17; 1 Jn 3.16; Jn 15.13 **10.12** Zech 11.16, 17 **10.14** vv. 11,27 **10.15** Mt 11.27 **10.16** Isa 56.8; Jn 11.52; Eph 2.14; 1 Pet 2.25 **10.17** Isa 53.7,8, 12 **10.18** Jn 2.19; 15.10; Heb 5.8 **10.19** Jn 7.43; 9.16 **10.20** Jn 7.20; 8.48; Mk 3.21

[u] Other ancient authorities read *the Son of God*
[v] *Sir* and *Lord* translate the same Greek word
[w] Other ancient authorities read *has taken*

mon and is out of his mind. Why
listen to him?" 21 Others were saying, "These are not the words of
one who has a demon. Can a demon open the eyes of the blind?"

Jesus Is Rejected by the Jews

22 At that time the festival of
the Dedication took place in Jerusalem. It was winter, 23 and Jesus
was walking in the temple, in the
portico of Solomon. 24 So the Jews
gathered around him and said to
him, "How long will you keep us in
suspense? If you are the Messiah,[x]
tell us plainly." 25 Jesus answered,
"I have told you, and you do not
believe. The works that I do in my
Father's name testify to me; 26 but
you do not believe, because you do
not belong to my sheep. 27 My
sheep hear my voice. I know them,
and they follow me. 28 I give them
eternal life, and they will never perish. No one will snatch them out of
my hand. 29 What my Father has
given me is greater than all else,
and no one can snatch it out of the
Father's hand.[y] 30 The Father and I
are one."

31 The Jews took up stones
again to stone him. 32 Jesus replied,
"I have shown you many good
works from the Father. For which
of these are you going to stone
me?" 33 The Jews answered, "It is
not for a good work that we are going to stone you, but for blasphemy, because you, though only a human being, are making yourself
God." 34 Jesus answered, "Is it not
written in your law,[z] 'I said, you
are gods'? 35 If those to whom the
word of God came were called
'gods'—and the scripture cannot
be annulled— 36 can you say that
the one whom the Father has sanctified and sent into the world is
blaspheming because I said, 'I am
God's Son'? 37 If I am not doing the
works of my Father, then do not believe me. 38 But if I do them, even
though you do not believe me, believe the works, so that you may
know and understand[a] that the
Father is in me and I am in the Father." 39 Then they tried to arrest
him again, but he escaped from
their hands.

40 He went away again across
the Jordan to the place where John
had been baptizing earlier, and he
remained there. 41 Many came to
him, and they were saying, "John
performed no sign, but everything
that John said about this man was
true." 42 And many believed in him
there.

The Death of Lazarus

11 Now a certain man was ill,
Lazarus of Bethany, the village of Mary and her sister Martha.
2 Mary was the one who anointed
the Lord with perfume and wiped
his feet with her hair; her brother
Lazarus was ill. 3 So the sisters sent
a message to Jesus,[b] "Lord, he
whom you love is ill." 4 But when
Jesus heard it, he said, "This illness does not lead to death; rather
it is for God's glory, so that the Son
of God may be glorified through it."
5 Accordingly, though Jesus loved
Martha and her sister and Lazarus,
6 after having heard that Lazarus[c]
was ill, he stayed two days longer in
the place where he was.

7 Then after this he said to the
disciples, "Let us go to Judea
again." 8 The disciples said to him,
"Rabbi, the Jews were just now trying to stone you, and are you going
there again?" 9 Jesus answered,
"Are there not twelve hours of daylight? Those who walk during the
day do not stumble, because they
see the light of this world. 10 But
those who walk at night stumble,
because the light is not in them."
11 After saying this, he told them,
"Our friend Lazarus has fallen
asleep, but I am going there to
awaken him." 12 The disciples said
to him, "Lord, if he has fallen
asleep, he will be all right."
13 Jesus, however, had been speaking about his death, but they

10.21 Jn 9.32,33; Ex 4.11
10.23 Acts 3.11; 5.12
10.25 Jn 5.36
10.26 Jn 8.47
10.27 vv. 4,14
10.28 Jn 17.2,3; 1 Jn 2.25; Jn 6.37,39
10.29 Jn 14.28; 17.2,6ff
10.30 Jn 17.21ff
10.31 Jn 8.59
10.33 Jn 5.18
10.34 Ps 82.6
10.36 Jn 6.69; 3.17; Jn 5.17,18
10.37 Jn 15.24
10.38 Jn 14.10,11; 17.21
10.39 Jn 7.30; 8.59
10.40 Jn 1.28
10.41 Jn 2.11; 3.30
10.42 Jn 7.31; 11.45
11.1 Mk 11.1; Lk 10.38
11.2 Mk 14.3; Lk 7.38; Jn 12.3
11.3 Lk 7.13
11.4 v. 40; Jn 9.3
11.7 Jn 10.40
11.8 Jn 10.31
11.9 Lk 13.33; Jn 9.4; 12.35
11.11 v. 3; Mt 27.52; Mk 5.39; Acts 7.60
11.13 Mt 9.24; Lk 8.52

x Or *the Christ* y Other ancient authorities read *My Father who has given them to me is greater than all, and no one can snatch them out of the Father's hand* z Other ancient authorities read *in the law* a Other ancient authorities lack *and understand*; others read *and believe* b Gk *him* c Gk *he*

thought that he was referring merely to sleep. 14 Then Jesus told them
plainly, "Lazarus is dead. 15 For
your sake I am glad I was not there,
so that you may believe. But let us
go to him." 16 Thomas, who was
called the Twin,[d] said to his fellow
disciples, "Let us also go, that we
may die with him."

Jesus the Resurrection and the Life

17 When Jesus arrived, he
found that Lazarus[e] had already
been in the tomb four days. 18 Now
Bethany was near Jerusalem, some
two miles[f] away, 19 and many of
the Jews had come to Martha and
Mary to console them about their
brother. 20 When Martha heard that
Jesus was coming, she went and
met him, while Mary stayed at
home. 21 Martha said to Jesus,
"Lord, if you had been here, my
brother would not have died. 22 But
even now I know that God will give
you whatever you ask of him."
23 Jesus said to her, "Your brother
will rise again." 24 Martha said to
him, "I know that he will rise again
in the resurrection on the last day."
25 Jesus said to her, "I am the resurrection and the life.[g] Those who
believe in me, even though they
die, will live, 26 and everyone who
lives and believes in me will never
die. Do you believe this?" 27 She
said to him, "Yes, Lord, I believe
that you are the Messiah,[h] the Son
of God, the one coming into the
world."

Jesus Weeps

28 When she had said this, she
went back and called her sister
Mary, and told her privately, "The
Teacher is here and is calling for
you." 29 And when she heard it, she
got up quickly and went to him.
30 Now Jesus had not yet come to
the village, but was still at the
place where Martha had met him.
31 The Jews who were with her in
the house, consoling her, saw Mary
get up quickly and go out. They followed her because they thought
that she was going to the tomb to
weep there. 32 When Mary came
where Jesus was and saw him, she
knelt at his feet and said to him,
"Lord, if you had been here, my
brother would not have died."
33 When Jesus saw her weeping,
and the Jews who came with her
also weeping, he was greatly disturbed in spirit and deeply moved.
34 He said, "Where have you laid
him?" They said to him, "Lord,
come and see." 35 Jesus began to
weep. 36 So the Jews said, "See how
he loved him!" 37 But some of them
said, "Could not he who opened
the eyes of the blind man have kept
this man from dying?"

Jesus Raises Lazarus to Life

38 Then Jesus, again greatly
disturbed, came to the tomb. It was
a cave, and a stone was lying
against it. 39 Jesus said, "Take away
the stone." Martha, the sister of
the dead man, said to him, "Lord,
already there is a stench because
he has been dead four days."
40 Jesus said to her, "Did I not tell
you that if you believed, you would
see the glory of God?" 41 So they
took away the stone. And Jesus
looked upward and said, "Father, I
thank you for having heard me. 42 I
knew that you always hear me, but
I have said this for the sake of the
crowd standing here, so that they
may believe that you sent me."
43 When he had said this, he cried
with a loud voice, "Lazarus, come
out!" 44 The dead man came out,
his hands and feet bound with
strips of cloth, and his face
wrapped in a cloth. Jesus said to
them, "Unbind him, and let him
go."

The Plot to Kill Jesus

45 Many of the Jews therefore,
who had come with Mary and had
seen what Jesus did, believed in
him. 46 But some of them went to
the Pharisees and told them what
he had done. 47 So the chief priests
and the Pharisees called a meeting

11.16 Mt 10.3; Jn 20.24-28 **11.17** v. 39 **11.18** v. 1 **11.19** Job 2.11 **11.21** vv. 2,32 **11.22** Jn 9.31 **11.24** Dan 12.2; Jn 5.28,29; Acts 24.15 **11.25** Jn 1.4; 5.26; 14.6; 3.36 **11.26** Jn 6.47; 8.51 **11.27** Mt 16.16; Jn 6.14 **11.28** Mt 26.18; Lk 22.11 **11.30** v. 20 **11.31** v. 19

11.32 v. 21 **11.33** v. 38; Jn 12.27; 13.21 **11.35** Lk 19.41 **11.37** Jn 9.6,7 **11.38** v. 33; Mt 27.60; Mk 15.46; Lk 24.2; Jn 20.1 **11.39** v. 17 **11.40** vv. 4,23 **11.41** Jn 17.1; Mt 11.25 **11.42** Jn 12.30; 3.17 **11.44** Jn 19.40; 20.7 **11.45** v. 19; Jn 2.23 **11.47** v. 57; Mt 26.3

[d] Gk *Didymus* [e] Gk *he* [f] Gk *fifteen stadia* [g] Other ancient authorities lack *and the life* [h] Or *the Christ*

of the council, and said, "What are we to do? This man is performing many signs. 48 If we let him go on like this, everyone will believe in him, and the Romans will come and destroy both our holy place[i] and our nation." 49 But one of them, Caiaphas, who was high priest that year, said to them, "You know nothing at all! 50 You do not understand that it is better for you to have one man die for the people than to have the whole nation destroyed." 51 He did not say this on his own, but being high priest that year he prophesied that Jesus was about to die for the nation, 52 and not for the nation only, but to gather into one the dispersed children of God. 53 So from that day on they planned to put him to death.

54 Jesus therefore no longer walked about openly among the Jews, but went from there to a town called Ephraim in the region near the wilderness; and he remained there with the disciples.

55 Now the Passover of the Jews was near, and many went up from the country to Jerusalem before the Passover to purify themselves. 56 They were looking for Jesus and were asking one another as they stood in the temple, "What do you think? Surely he will not come to the festival, will he?" 57 Now the chief priests and the Pharisees had given orders that anyone who knew where Jesus[j] was should let them know, so that they might arrest him.

Mary Anoints Jesus

12 Six days before the Passover Jesus came to Bethany, the home of Lazarus, whom he had raised from the dead. 2 There they gave a dinner for him. Martha served, and Lazarus was one of those at the table with him. 3 Mary took a pound of costly perfume made of pure nard, anointed Jesus' feet, and wiped them[k] with her hair. The house was filled with the fragrance of the perfume. 4 But Judas Iscariot, one of his disciples (the one who was about to betray him), said, 5 "Why was this perfume not sold for three hundred denarii[l] and the money given to the poor?" 6 (He said this not because he cared about the poor, but because he was a thief; he kept the common purse and used to steal what was put into it.) 7 Jesus said, "Leave her alone. She bought it[m] so that she might keep it for the day of my burial. 8 You always have the poor with you, but you do not always have me."

The Plot to Kill Lazarus

9 When the great crowd of the Jews learned that he was there, they came not only because of Jesus but also to see Lazarus, whom he had raised from the dead. 10 So the chief priests planned to put Lazarus to death as well, 11 since it was on account of him that many of the Jews were deserting and were believing in Jesus.

Jesus' Triumphal Entry into Jerusalem

12 The next day the great crowd that had come to the festival heard that Jesus was coming to Jerusalem. 13 So they took branches of palm trees and went out to meet him, shouting,

"Hosanna!
Blessed is the one who
comes in the name of
the Lord—
the King of Israel!"

14 Jesus found a young donkey and sat on it; as it is written:

15 "Do not be afraid, daughter
of Zion.
Look, your king is coming,
sitting on a donkey's colt!"

16 His disciples did not understand these things at first; but when Jesus was glorified, then they remembered that these things had been written of him and had been done to him. 17 So the crowd that had been with him when he called Lazarus out of the tomb and raised him from the dead continued to

11.49 Mt 26.3; Jn 18.13,14
11.50 Jn 18.14
11.52 Isa 49.6; Jn 10.16
11.53 Mt 26.4
11.54 Jn 7.1; 2 Chr 13.19
11.55 Mt 26.1,2; Mk 14.1; Lk 22.1; Jn 12.1; Num 9.10; 2 Chr 30.17, 18
11.56 Jn 7.11
12.1-11pp Mt 26.6-13; Mk 14.3-9
12.1 Lk 7.37-39; Jn 11.55
12.2 Lk 10.38
12.3 Jn 11.2; Mk 14.3
12.4 Jn 6.71
12.6 Jn 13.29; Lk 8.3
12.7 Jn 19.40
12.8 Mt 26.11; Mk 14.7
12.9 Mk 12.37; Mt 11.43,44
12.11 v. 18; Jn 11.45
12.12-19pp Mt 21.1-11; Mk 11.1-11; Lk 19.29-44
12.13 Ps 118.25, 26; Jn 1.49
12.15 Zech 9.9
12.16 Mk 9.32; Jn 2.22; 14.26; 7.39

[i] Or *our temple*; Greek *our place* [j] Gk *he*
[k] Gk *his feet* [l] Three hundred denarii would be nearly a year's wages for a laborer
[m] Gk lacks *She bought it*

testify.[n] 18 It was also because they
heard that he had performed this
sign that the crowd went to meet
him. 19 The Pharisees then said to
one another, "You see, you can do
nothing. Look, the world has gone
after him!"

Some Greeks Wish to See Jesus

20 Now among those who went
up to worship at the festival were
some Greeks. 21 They came to Philip, who was from Bethsaida in Galilee, and said to him, "Sir, we wish
to see Jesus." 22 Philip went and
told Andrew; then Andrew and
Philip went and told Jesus. 23 Jesus
answered them, "The hour has
come for the Son of Man to be glorified. 24 Very truly, I tell you, unless a grain of wheat falls into the
earth and dies, it remains just a
single grain; but if it dies, it bears
much fruit. 25 Those who love their
life lose it, and those who hate
their life in this world will keep it
for eternal life. 26 Whoever serves
me must follow me, and where I
am, there will my servant be also.
Whoever serves me, the Father will
honor.

Jesus Speaks about His Death

27 "Now my soul is troubled.
And what should I say—'Father,
save me from this hour'? No, it is
for this reason that I have come to
this hour. 28 Father, glorify your
name." Then a voice came from
heaven, "I have glorified it, and I
will glorify it again." 29 The crowd
standing there heard it and said
that it was thunder. Others said,
"An angel has spoken to him."
30 Jesus answered, "This voice has
come for your sake, not for mine.
31 Now is the judgment of this
world; now the ruler of this world
will be driven out. 32 And I, when I
am lifted up from the earth, will
draw all people[o] to myself." 33 He
said this to indicate the kind of
death he was to die. 34 The crowd
answered him, "We have heard
from the law that the Messiah[p] remains forever. How can you say
that the Son of Man must be lifted
up? Who is this Son of Man?"
35 Jesus said to them, "The light is
with you for a little longer. Walk
while you have the light, so that the
darkness may not overtake you. If
you walk in the darkness, you do
not know where you are going.
36 While you have the light, believe
in the light, so that you may become children of light."

The Unbelief of the People

After Jesus had said this, he departed and hid from them. 37 Although he had performed so many
signs in their presence, they did
not believe in him. 38 This was to
fulfill the word spoken by the
prophet Isaiah:

"Lord, who has believed our
message,
and to whom has the arm
of the Lord been
revealed?"

39 And so they could not believe,
because Isaiah also said,

40 "He has blinded their eyes
and hardened their heart,
so that they might not look
with their eyes,
and understand with their
heart and turn—
and I would heal them."

41 Isaiah said this because[q] he saw
his glory and spoke about him.
42 Nevertheless many, even of the
authorities, believed in him. But
because of the Pharisees they did
not confess it, for fear that they
would be put out of the synagogue;
43 for they loved human glory more
than the glory that comes from
God.

Summary of Jesus' Teaching

44 Then Jesus cried aloud:
"Whoever believes in me believes
not in me but in him who sent me.
45 And whoever sees me sees him
who sent me. 46 I have come as light

12.18 v. 11 **12.19** Jn 11.47,48 **12.20** Jn 7.35; Acts 11.20 **12.21** Jn 1.44 **12.23** Jn 13.1,32; 17.1; Mk 14.35, 41 **12.24** 1 Cor 15.36 **12.25** Mt 10.39; Mk 8.35; Lk 9.24; 14.26 **12.26** Jn 14.3; 17.24; 1 Thes 4.17 **12.27** Mt 26.38, 39; Mk 14.34; Jn 11.33 **12.28** Mt 3.17; 17.5; Mk 1.11; 9.7; Lk 3.22; 9.35 **12.30** Jn 11.42 **12.31** Jn 16.11; 14.30; 2 Cor 4.4; Eph 2.2 **12.32** Jn 3.14; 8.28; 6.44 **12.33** Jn 18.32 **12.34** Ps 110.4; Isa 9.7; Ezek 37.25; Dan 7.14 **12.35** Eph 5.8 **12.36** Lk 16.8; Jn 8.59 **12.37** Jn 2.11 **12.38** Isa 53.1; Rom 10.16 **12.40** Isa 6.9,10; Mt 13.14 **12.41** Isa 6.1 **12.42** Jn 7.48,13; 9.22 **12.43** Jn 5.44 **12.44** Mt 10.40; Jn 5.24 **12.45** Jn 14.9 **12.46** Jn 1.4; 3.19; 8.12; 9.5

[n] Other ancient authorities read *with him began to testify that he had called. . .from the dead* [o] Other ancient authorities read *all things* [p] Or *the Christ* [q] Other ancient witnesses read *when*

into the world, so that everyone
who believes in me should not remain in the darkness. 47 I do not
judge anyone who hears my words
and does not keep them, for I came
not to judge the world, but to save
the world. 48 The one who rejects
me and does not receive my word
has a judge; on the last day the
word that I have spoken will serve
as judge, 49 for I have not spoken on
my own, but the Father who sent
me has himself given me a commandment about what to say and
what to speak. 50 And I know that
his commandment is eternal life.
What I speak, therefore, I speak
just as the Father has told me."

Jesus Washes the Disciples' Feet

13 Now before the festival of
the Passover, Jesus knew
that his hour had come to depart
from this world and go to the Father. Having loved his own who
were in the world, he loved them to
the end. 2 The devil had already put
it into the heart of Judas son of Simon Iscariot to betray him. And
during supper 3 Jesus, knowing
that the Father had given all things
into his hands, and that he had
come from God and was going to
God, 4 got up from the table,[r] took
off his outer robe, and tied a towel
around himself. 5 Then he poured
water into a basin and began to
wash the disciples' feet and to wipe
them with the towel that was tied
around him. 6 He came to Simon
Peter, who said to him, "Lord, are
you going to wash my feet?" 7 Jesus
answered, "You do not know now
what I am doing, but later you will
understand." 8 Peter said to him,
"You will never wash my feet."
Jesus answered, "Unless I wash
you, you have no share with me."
9 Simon Peter said to him, "Lord,
not my feet only but also my hands
and my head!" 10 Jesus said to him,
"One who has bathed does not
need to wash, except for the feet,[s]
but is entirely clean. And you[t] are
clean, though not all of you." 11 For
he knew who was to betray him; for
this reason he said, "Not all of you
are clean."

12 After he had washed their
feet, had put on his robe, and had
returned to the table, he said to
them, "Do you know what I have
done to you? 13 You call me Teacher and Lord—and you are right, for
that is what I am. 14 So if I, your
Lord and Teacher, have washed
your feet, you also ought to wash
one another's feet. 15 For I have set
you an example, that you also
should do as I have done to you.
16 Very truly, I tell you, servants[u]
are not greater than their master,
nor are messengers greater than
the one who sent them. 17 If you
know these things, you are blessed
if you do them. 18 I am not speaking
of all of you; I know whom I have
chosen. But it is to fulfill the scripture, 'The one who ate my bread[v]
has lifted his heel against me.' 19 I
tell you this now, before it occurs,
so that when it does occur, you may
believe that I am he.[w] 20 Very truly,
I tell you, whoever receives one
whom I send receives me; and whoever receives me receives him who
sent me."

Jesus Foretells His Betrayal

21 After saying this Jesus was
troubled in spirit, and declared,
"Very truly, I tell you, one of you
will betray me." 22 The disciples
looked at one another, uncertain of
whom he was speaking. 23 One of
his disciples—the one whom Jesus
loved—was reclining next to him;
24 Simon Peter therefore motioned
to him to ask Jesus of whom he was
speaking. 25 So while reclining next
to Jesus, he asked him, "Lord, who
is it?" 26 Jesus answered, "It is the
one to whom I give this piece of
bread when I have dipped it in the
dish."[x] So when he had dipped the
piece of bread, he gave it to Judas

12.47 Jn 3.17 **12.48** Lk 10.16; Mt 10.15 **12.49** Jn 14.31 **12.50** Jn 8.28 **13.1** Jn 11.55; 12.23; 16.28 **13.2** Jn 6.70,71; Mk 14.10 **13.3** Mt 28.18; Heb 2.8; Jn 8.42; 16.28 **13.4** Lk 22.27 **13.5** Lk 7.44 **13.8** Jn 3.5; 9.7 **13.10** Jn 15.3 **13.11** Jn 6.64
13.13 Lk 6.46; Phil 2.11 **13.14** 1 Pet 5.5 **13.15** 1 Pet 2.21 **13.16** Mt 10.24; Lk 6.40; Jn 15.20 **13.17** Lk 11.28; Jas 1.25 **13.18** Ps 41.9; Mt 26.23 **13.19** Jn 14.29; 16.4; 8.24 **13.20** Mt 10.40; Lk 10.16 **13.21-30pp** Mt 26.21-26; Mk 14.18-21; Lk 22.21-23 **13.21** Jn 12.27 **13.23** Jn 19.26; 20.2; 21.7,20 **13.25** Jn 21.20 **13.26** Jn 6.71

[r] Gk *from supper* [s] Other ancient authorities lack *except for the feet*
[t] The Greek word for *you* here is plural
[u] Gk *slaves* [v] Other ancient authorities read *ate bread with me* [w] Gk *I am*
[x] Gk *dipped it*

son of Simon Iscariot.[y] 27 After he
received the piece of bread,[z] Satan
entered into him. Jesus said to
him, "Do quickly what you are going to do." 28 Now no one at the table knew why he said this to him.
29 Some thought that, because Judas had the common purse, Jesus
was telling him, "Buy what we need
for the festival"; or, that he should
give something to the poor. 30 So,
after receiving the piece of bread,
he immediately went out. And it
was night.

The New Commandment

31 When he had gone out, Jesus
said, "Now the Son of Man has
been glorified, and God has been
glorified in him. 32 If God has been
glorified in him,[a] God will also glorify him in himself and will glorify
him at once. 33 Little children, I am
with you only a little longer. You
will look for me; and as I said to the
Jews so now I say to you, 'Where I
am going, you cannot come.' 34 I
give you a new commandment,
that you love one another. Just as I
have loved you, you also should
love one another. 35 By this everyone will know that you are my disciples, if you have love for one another."

Jesus Foretells Peter's Denial

36 Simon Peter said to him,
"Lord, where are you going?" Jesus
answered, "Where I am going, you
cannot follow me now; but you will
follow afterward." 37 Peter said to
him, "Lord, why can I not follow
you now? I will lay down my life for
you." 38 Jesus answered, "Will you
lay down your life for me? Very truly, I tell you, before the cock crows,
you will have denied me three
times.

Jesus the Way to the Father

14 "Do not let your hearts be
troubled. Believe[b] in God,
believe also in me. 2 In my Father's
house there are many dwelling
places. If it were not so, would I
have told you that I go to prepare a
place for you?[c] 3 And if I go and
prepare a place for you, I will come
again and will take you to myself,
so that where I am, there you may
be also. 4 And you know the way to
the place where I am going."[d]
5 Thomas said to him, "Lord, we do
not know where you are going. How
can we know the way?" 6 Jesus said
to him, "I am the way, and the
truth, and the life. No one comes to
the Father except through me. 7 If
you know me, you will know[e] my
Father also. From now on you do
know him and have seen him."

8 Philip said to him, "Lord,
show us the Father, and we will be
satisfied." 9 Jesus said to him,
"Have I been with you all this time,
Philip, and you still do not know
me? Whoever has seen me has seen
the Father. How can you say, 'Show
us the Father'? 10 Do you not believe that I am in the Father and
the Father is in me? The words that
I say to you I do not speak on my
own; but the Father who dwells in
me does his works. 11 Believe me
that I am in the Father and the Father is in me; but if you do not,
then believe me because of the
works themselves. 12 Very truly, I
tell you, the one who believes in
me will also do the works that I do
and, in fact, will do greater works
than these, because I am going to
the Father. 13 I will do whatever you
ask in my name, so that the Father
may be glorified in the Son. 14 If in
my name you ask me[f] for anything, I will do it.

The Promise of the Holy Spirit

15 "If you love me, you will
keep[g] my commandments. 16 And I
will ask the Father, and he will give
you another Advocate,[h] to be with

13.27 Lk 22.3 **13.29** Jn 12.5,6 **13.31** Jn 7.39; 14.13; 1 Pet 4.11 **13.32** Jn 17.1 **13.33** Jn 7.33,34 **13.34** Lev 19.18; Jn 15.12; 1 Pet 1.22; 1 Jn 2.7; 3.11; 4.10 **13.35** 1 Jn 3.14; 4.20 **13.36** Jn 21.18; 2 Pet 1.14 **13.37** Mt 26.33-35; Mk 14.29-31; Lk 22.33,34 **13.38** Jn 18.27 **14.1** Jn 16.23,24 **14.2** Jn 13.33 **14.3** Jn 12.26 **14.5** Jn 11.16 **14.6** Jn 10.9; 8.32; 1.4; 11.25 **14.7** Jn 8.19 **14.9** Jn 12.45 **14.10** Jn 10.38; 5.19; 12.49 **14.11** Jn 5.36; 10.38 **14.12** Mt 21.21; Lk 10.17 **14.13** Jn 15.7,16; 16.23; Jas 1.5 **14.15** Jn 15.10; 1 Jn 5.3 **14.16** Jn 15.26; 16.7; 1 Jn 2.1

[y] Other ancient authorities read *Judas Iscariot son of Simon*; others, *Judas son of Simon from Karyot* (Kerioth) [z] Gk *After the piece of bread* [a] Other ancient authorities lack *If God has been glorified in him* [b] Or *You believe* [c] Or *If it were not so, I would have told you; for I go to prepare a place for you* [d] Other ancient authorities read *Where I am going you know, and the way you know* [e] Other ancient authorities read *If you had known me, you would have known* [f] Other ancient authorities lack *me* [g] Other ancient authorities read *me, keep* [h] Or *Helper*

you forever. 17 This is the Spirit of truth, whom the world cannot receive, because it neither sees him nor knows him. You know him, because he abides with you, and he will be in[i] you.

18 "I will not leave you orphaned; I am coming to you. 19 In a little while the world will no longer see me, but you will see me; because I live, you also will live. 20 On that day you will know that I am in my Father, and you in me, and I in you. 21 They who have my commandments and keep them are those who love me; and those who love me will be loved by my Father, and I will love them and reveal myself to them." 22 Judas (not Iscariot) said to him, "Lord, how is it that you will reveal yourself to us, and not to the world?" 23 Jesus answered him, "Those who love me will keep my word, and my Father will love them, and we will come to them and make our home with them. 24 Whoever does not love me does not keep my words; and the word that you hear is not mine, but is from the Father who sent me.

25 "I have said these things to you while I am still with you. 26 But the Advocate,[j] the Holy Spirit, whom the Father will send in my name, will teach you everything, and remind you of all that I have said to you. 27 Peace I leave with you; my peace I give to you. I do not give to you as the world gives. Do not let your hearts be troubled, and do not let them be afraid. 28 You heard me say to you, 'I am going away, and I am coming to you.' If you loved me, you would rejoice that I am going to the Father, because the Father is greater than I. 29 And now I have told you this before it occurs, so that when it does occur, you may believe. 30 I will no longer talk much with you, for the ruler of this world is coming. He has no power over me; 31 but I do as the Father has commanded me, so that the world may know that I love the Father. Rise, let us be on our way.

14.17 Jn 16.13; 1 Jn 4.6; 1 Cor 2.14
14.18 vv. 3,28
14.19 Jn 7.33; 16.16; 6.57
14.20 Jn 10.38
14.21 1 Jn 2.5; 5.3
14.22 Acts 1.13; 10.14,41
14.23 1 Jn 2.24; Rev 3.20
14.24 Jn 7.16; 8.28; 12.49
14.26 Jn 15.26; 16.7,13; 1 Jn 2.20, 27
14.27 Jn 16.33; Phil 4.7; Col 3.15
14.28 vv. 3,18; Jn 5.18; 10.29,30; Phil 2.6
14.29 Jn 13.19
14.30 Jn 12.31
14.31 Jn 10.18; 12.49; 18.1

15.1 Isa 5.1-7; Ezek 19.10
15.3 Jn 13.10; 17.17; Eph 5.26
15.4 1 Jn 2.6
15.5 v. 16
15.6 v. 2
15.7 Jn 14.13; 16.23
15.8 Mt 5.16; Jn 8.31
15.10 Jn 14.15,23
15.11 Jn 17.13
15.12 Jn 13.34
15.13 Rom 5.7,8; Jn 10.11
15.14 Mt 12.50
15.15 Jn 8.26

Jesus the True Vine

15 "I am the true vine, and my Father is the vinegrower. 2 He removes every branch in me that bears no fruit. Every branch that bears fruit he prunes[k] to make it bear more fruit. 3 You have already been cleansed[k] by the word that I have spoken to you. 4 Abide in me as I abide in you. Just as the branch cannot bear fruit by itself unless it abides in the vine, neither can you unless you abide in me. 5 I am the vine, you are the branches. Those who abide in me and I in them bear much fruit, because apart from me you can do nothing. 6 Whoever does not abide in me is thrown away like a branch and withers; such branches are gathered, thrown into the fire, and burned. 7 If you abide in me, and my words abide in you, ask for whatever you wish, and it will be done for you. 8 My Father is glorified by this, that you bear much fruit and become[l] my disciples. 9 As the Father has loved me, so I have loved you; abide in my love. 10 If you keep my commandments, you will abide in my love, just as I have kept my Father's commandments and abide in his love. 11 I have said these things to you so that my joy may be in you, and that your joy may be complete.

12 "This is my commandment, that you love one another as I have loved you. 13 No one has greater love than this, to lay down one's life for one's friends. 14 You are my friends if you do what I command you. 15 I do not call you servants[m] any longer, because the servant[n] does not know what the master is doing; but I have called you friends, because I have made known to you everything that I have heard from my Father. 16 You did not choose me but I chose you. And I appointed you to go and bear fruit, fruit that will last, so that the Father will give you whatever you

15.16 Jn 6.70; 14.13

[i] Or *among* [j] Or *Helper* [k] The same Greek root refers to pruning and cleansing [l] Or *be* [m] Gk *slaves* [n] Gk *slave*

ask him in my name. 17 I am giving
you these commands so that you
may love one another.

The World's Hatred

18 "If the world hates you, be
aware that it hated me before it
hated you. 19 If you belonged to the
world,[o] the world would love you
as its own. Because you do not belong to the world, but I have chosen
you out of the world—therefore
the world hates you. 20 Remember
the word that I said to you, 'Servants[p] are not greater than their
master.' If they persecuted me,
they will persecute you; if they kept
my word, they will keep yours also.
21 But they will do all these things
to you on account of my name, because they do not know him who
sent me. 22 If I had not come and
spoken to them, they would not
have sin; but now they have no excuse for their sin. 23 Whoever hates
me hates my Father also. 24 If I had
not done among them the works
that no one else did, they would
not have sin. But now they have
seen and hated both me and my
Father. 25 It was to fulfill the word
that is written in their law, 'They
hated me without a cause.'
26 "When the Advocate[q]
comes, whom I will send to you
from the Father, the Spirit of truth
who comes from the Father, he will
testify on my behalf. 27 You also are
to testify because you have been
with me from the beginning.

16 "I have said these things to
you to keep you from stumbling. 2 They will put you out of the
synagogues. Indeed, an hour is
coming when those who kill you
will think that by doing so they are
offering worship to God. 3 And they
will do this because they have not
known the Father or me. 4 But I
have said these things to you so
that when their hour comes you
may remember that I told you
about them.

The Work of the Spirit

"I did not say these things to you
from the beginning, because I was
with you. 5 But now I am going to
him who sent me; yet none of you
asks me, 'Where are you going?'
6 But because I have said these
things to you, sorrow has filled your
hearts. 7 Nevertheless I tell you the
truth: it is to your advantage that I
go away, for if I do not go away, the
Advocate[q] will not come to you;
but if I go, I will send him to you.
8 And when he comes, he will prove
the world wrong about[r] sin and
righteousness and judgment:
9 about sin, because they do not believe in me; 10 about righteousness,
because I am going to the Father
and you will see me no longer;
11 about judgment, because the ruler of this world has been condemned.
12 "I still have many things to
say to you, but you cannot bear
them now. 13 When the Spirit of
truth comes, he will guide you into
all the truth; for he will not speak
on his own, but will speak whatever
he hears, and he will declare to you
the things that are to come. 14 He
will glorify me, because he will
take what is mine and declare it to
you. 15 All that the Father has is
mine. For this reason I said that he
will take what is mine and declare
it to you.

Sorrow Will Turn into Joy

16 "A little while, and you will
no longer see me, and again a little
while, and you will see me."
17 Then some of his disciples said
to one another, "What does he
mean by saying to us, 'A little
while, and you will no longer see
me, and again a little while, and
you will see me'; and 'Because I am
going to the Father'?" 18 They said,
"What does he mean by this 'a little
while'? We do not know what he is
talking about." 19 Jesus knew that
they wanted to ask him, so he said
to them, "Are you discussing
among yourselves what I meant
when I said, 'A little while, and you

15.17 v. 12 **15.18** 1 Jn 3.13 **15.19** Jn 17.14 **15.20** Mt 10.24; Lk 6.40; Jn 13.16 **15.21** Mt 12.24; Lk 6.40; Jn 13.16 **15.22** Jn 9.41; Rom 1.20 **15.23** 1 Jn 2.23 **15.24** Jn 5.36 **15.25** Ps 35.19; 69.4 **15.26** Jn 14.16,17, 26; 1 Jn 2.1; 5.7 **15.27** Lk 24.48; Acts 2.32; 3.15; 5.32; 10.39; 13.31; 1 Jn 4.14 **16.1** Jn 15.18-27; Mt 11.6 **16.2** Jn 9.22; Acts 26.9, 10; Isa 66.5; Rev 6.9 **16.3** Jn 15.21; 17.25; 1 Jn 3.1 **16.4** Jn 13.19; 15.27 **16.5** Jn 7.33; 13.36; 14.5 **16.7** Jn 7.39; 14.16,26; 15.26 **16.9** Jn 15.22 **16.10** Acts 3.14; 7.52; 17.31; 1 Pet 3.18 **16.11** Jn 12.31 **16.12** Mk 4.33 **16.13** Jn 14.17,26 **16.14** Jn 7.39 **16.15** Jn 17.10 **16.16** Jn 7.33; 14.18-24; 13.3 **16.17** vv. 16,5 **16.19** Mk 9.32

[o] Gk *were of the world* [p] Gk *Slaves*
[q] Or *Helper* [r] Or *convict the world of*

will no longer see me, and again a
little while, and you will see me'?
20 Very truly, I tell you, you will
weep and mourn, but the world will
rejoice; you will have pain, but your
pain will turn into joy. 21 When a
woman is in labor, she has pain,
because her hour has come. But
when her child is born, she no longer remembers the anguish because of the joy of having brought
a human being into the world. 22 So
you have pain now; but I will see
you again, and your hearts will rejoice, and no one will take your joy
from you. 23 On that day you will
ask nothing of me.[s] Very truly, I
tell you, if you ask anything of the
Father in my name, he will give it
to you.[t] 24 Until now you have not
asked for anything in my name. Ask
and you will receive, so that your
joy may be complete.

Peace for the Disciples

25 "I have said these things to
you in figures of speech. The hour
is coming when I will no longer
speak to you in figures, but will tell
you plainly of the Father. 26 On that
day you will ask in my name. I do
not say to you that I will ask the
Father on your behalf; 27 for the Father himself loves you, because you
have loved me and have believed
that I came from God.[u] 28 I came
from the Father and have come
into the world; again, I am leaving
the world and am going to the Father."

29 His disciples said, "Yes, now
you are speaking plainly, not in any
figure of speech! 30 Now we know
that you know all things, and do
not need to have anyone question
you; by this we believe that you
came from God." 31 Jesus answered
them, "Do you now believe? 32 The
hour is coming, indeed it has come,
when you will be scattered, each
one to his home, and you will leave
me alone. Yet I am not alone because the Father is with me. 33 I
have said this to you, so that in me
you may have peace. In the world
you face persecution. But take
courage; I have conquered the
world!"

Jesus Prays for His Disciples

17 After Jesus had spoken
these words, he looked up
to heaven and said, "Father, the
hour has come; glorify your Son so
that the Son may glorify you, 2 since
you have given him authority over
all people,[v] to give eternal life to
all whom you have given him. 3 And
this is eternal life, that they may
know you, the only true God, and
Jesus Christ whom you have sent.
4 I glorified you on earth by finishing the work that you gave me to
do. 5 So now, Father, glorify me in
your own presence with the glory
that I had in your presence before
the world existed.

6 "I have made your name
known to those whom you gave me
from the world. They were yours,
and you gave them to me, and they
have kept your word. 7 Now they
know that everything you have giv-
en me is from you; 8 for the words
that you gave to me I have given to
them, and they have received them
and know in truth that I came from
you; and they have believed that
you sent me. 9 I am asking on their
behalf; I am not asking on behalf of
the world, but on behalf of those
whom you gave me, because they
are yours. 10 All mine are yours, and
yours are mine; and I have been
glorified in them. 11 And now I am
no longer in the world, but they are
in the world, and I am coming to
you. Holy Father, protect them in
your name that you have given
me, so that they may be one, as we
are one. 12 While I was with them, I
protected them in your name that[w]
you have given me. I guarded them,
and not one of them was lost except the one destined to be lost,[x]
so that the scripture might be fulfilled. 13 But now I am coming to

16.20 Lk 23.27; Jn 20.20 **16.21** 1 Thes 5.3 **16.22** vv. 6,16 **16.23** Mt 7.7; Jn 14.13; 15.16 **16.24** Jn 15.11 **16.25** Jn 10.6; Mt 13.34 **16.27** Jn 14.21,23 **16.28** Jn 13.3 **16.29** v. 25 **16.30** Jn 8.42 **16.32** Mt 26.31; Mk 14.27 **16.33** Jn 14.27; Col 1.20; Rom 8.37; Rev 3.21

17.1 Jn 12.23; 13.32 **17.2** Dan 7.14; Heb 2.8; Jn 6.37 **17.3** Jn 5.44; 3.34; 6.29,57 **17.4** Jn 13.31; 4.34; 14.31 **17.5** Jn 1.1; Phil 2.6 **17.6** Jn 6.37,39 **17.8** Jn 8.28; 16.27 **17.9** Lk 22.32; Jn 14.16 **17.10** Jn 16.15 **17.11** Jn 13.1; 7.33; Rev 19.12; Jn 10.30 **17.12** Heb 2.13; Jn 6.39; 18.9; 6.70

[s] Or *will ask me no question* [t] Other ancient authorities read *Father, he will give it to you in my name* [u] Other ancient authorities read *the Father* [v] Gk *flesh* [w] Other ancient authorities read *protected in your name those whom* [x] Gk *except the son of destruction*

you, and I speak these things in the
world so that they may have my joy
made complete in themselves.[y] 14 I
have given them your word, and the
world has hated them because they
do not belong to the world, just as
I do not belong to the world. 15 I am
not asking you to take them out of
the world, but I ask you to protect
them from the evil one.[z] 16 They do
not belong to the world, just as I do
not belong to the world. 17 Sanctify
them in the truth; your word is
truth. 18 As you have sent me into
the world, so I have sent them into
the world. 19 And for their sakes I
sanctify myself, so that they also
may be sanctified in truth.

20 "I ask not only on behalf of
these, but also on behalf of those
who will believe in me through
their word, 21 that they may all be
one. As you, Father, are in me and
I am in you, may they also be in
us,[a] so that the world may believe
that you have sent me. 22 The glory
that you have given me I have given
them, so that they may be one, as
we are one, 23 I in them and you in
me, that they may become completely one, so that the world may
know that you have sent me and
have loved them even as you have
loved me. 24 Father, I desire that
those also, whom you have given
me, may be with me where I am, to
see my glory, which you have given
me because you loved me before
the foundation of the world.

25 "Righteous Father, the world
does not know you, but I know you;
and these know that you have sent
me. 26 I made your name known to
them, and I will make it known, so
that the love with which you have
loved me may be in them, and I in
them."

The Betrayal and Arrest of Jesus

18 After Jesus had spoken
these words, he went out
with his disciples across the Kidron
valley to a place where there was a
garden, which he and his disciples
entered. 2 Now Judas, who betrayed him, also knew the place,
because Jesus often met there with
his disciples. 3 So Judas brought a
detachment of soldiers together
with police from the chief priests
and the Pharisees, and they came
there with lanterns and torches
and weapons. 4 Then Jesus, knowing all that was to happen to him,
came forward and asked them,
"Whom are you looking for?" 5 They
answered, "Jesus of Nazareth."[b]
Jesus replied, "I am he."[c] Judas,
who betrayed him, was standing
with them. 6 When Jesus[d] said to
them, "I am he,"[c] they stepped
back and fell to the ground. 7 Again
he asked them, "Whom are you
looking for?" And they said, "Jesus
of Nazareth."[b] 8 Jesus answered, "I
told you that I am he.[c] So if you are
looking for me, let these men go."
9 This was to fulfill the word that he
had spoken, "I did not lose a single
one of those whom you gave me."
10 Then Simon Peter, who had a
sword, drew it, struck the high
priest's slave, and cut off his right
ear. The slave's name was Mal-
chus. 11 Jesus said to Peter, "Put
your sword back into its sheath.
Am I not to drink the cup that the
Father has given me?"

Jesus before the High Priest

12 So the soldiers, their officer,
and the Jewish police arrested
Jesus and bound him. 13 First they
took him to Annas, who was the
father-in-law of Caiaphas, the high
priest that year. 14 Caiaphas was
the one who had advised the Jews
that it was better to have one person die for the people.

Peter Denies Jesus

15 Simon Peter and another disciple followed Jesus. Since that
disciple was known to the high
priest, he went with Jesus into the
courtyard of the high priest, 16 but
Peter was standing outside at the
gate. So the other disciple, who
was known to the high priest, went
out, spoke to the woman who

17.14 Jn 15.19; 8.23 **17.15** Mt 6.13 **17.16** v. 14 **17.17** Jn 15.3 **17.18** Jn 20.21 **17.19** Jn 15.13 **17.21** Jn 10.38 **17.22** Jn 14.20 **17.24** Jn 12.26; Mt 25.34; v. 5 **17.25** Jn 15.21; 16.3; 7.29; Jn 16.27 **17.26** v. 6; Jn 15.9 **18.1-11pp** Mt 26.47-56; Mk 14.43-50; Lk 22.27-53 **18.1** 2 Sam 15.23 **18.2** Lk 21.37; 22.39 **18.3** Acts 1.16 **18.4** Jn 6.64; 13.1,11; v. 7 **18.7** v. 4 **18.9** Jn 17.12 **18.11** Mt 20.22 **18.13** Mt 26.57; Mk 14.53; Lk 22.54 **18.14** Jn 11.49-51 **18.15-18pp** Mt 26.69-75; Mk 14.66-72; Lk 22.55-62 **18.15** Mt 26.58; Mk 14.54; Lk 22.54

[y] Or *among themselves* [z] Or *from evil*
[a] Other ancient authorities read *be one in us*
[b] Gk *the Nazorean* [c] Gk *I am* [d] Gk *he*

guarded the gate, and brought Peter in. 17 The woman said to Peter, "You are not also one of this man's disciples, are you?" He said, "I am not." 18 Now the slaves and the police had made a charcoal fire because it was cold, and they were standing around it and warming themselves. Peter also was standing with them and warming himself.

The High Priest Questions Jesus

19 Then the high priest questioned Jesus about his disciples and about his teaching. 20 Jesus answered, "I have spoken openly to the world; I have always taught in synagogues and in the temple, where all the Jews come together. I have said nothing in secret. 21 Why do you ask me? Ask those who heard what I said to them; they know what I said." 22 When he had said this, one of the police standing nearby struck Jesus on the face, saying, "Is that how you answer the high priest?" 23 Jesus answered, "If I have spoken wrongly, testify to the wrong. But if I have spoken rightly, why do you strike me?" 24 Then Annas sent him bound to Caiaphas the high priest.

Peter Denies Jesus Again

25 Now Simon Peter was standing and warming himself. They asked him, "You are not also one of his disciples, are you?" He denied it and said, "I am not." 26 One of the slaves of the high priest, a relative of the man whose ear Peter had cut off, asked, "Did I not see you in the garden with him?" 27 Again Peter denied it, and at that moment the cock crowed.

Jesus before Pilate

28 Then they took Jesus from Caiaphas to Pilate's headquarters.[e] It was early in the morning. They themselves did not enter the headquarters,[e] so as to avoid ritual defilement and to be able to eat the Passover. 29 So Pilate went out to them and said, "What accusation do you bring against this man?" 30 They answered, "If this man were not a criminal, we would not have handed him over to you." 31 Pilate said to them, "Take him yourselves and judge him according to your law." The Jews replied, "We are not permitted to put anyone to death." 32 (This was to fulfill what Jesus had said when he indicated the kind of death he was to die.)

33 Then Pilate entered the headquarters[e] again, summoned Jesus, and asked him, "Are you the King of the Jews?" 34 Jesus answered, "Do you ask this on your own, or did others tell you about me?" 35 Pilate replied, "I am not a Jew, am I? Your own nation and the chief priests have handed you over to me. What have you done?" 36 Jesus answered, "My kingdom is not from this world. If my kingdom were from this world, my followers would be fighting to keep me from being handed over to the Jews. But as it is, my kingdom is not from here." 37 Pilate asked him, "So you are a king?" Jesus answered, "You say that I am a king. For this I was born, and for this I came into the world, to testify to the truth. Everyone who belongs to the truth listens to my voice." 38 Pilate asked him, "What is truth?"

Jesus Sentenced to Death

After he had said this, he went out to the Jews again and told them, "I find no case against him. 39 But you have a custom that I release someone for you at the Passover. Do you want me to release for you the King of the Jews?" 40 They shouted in reply, "Not this man, but Barabbas!" Now Barabbas was a bandit.

19 Then Pilate took Jesus and had him flogged. 2 And the soldiers wove a crown of thorns and put it on his head, and they dressed him in a purple robe. 3 They kept coming up to him, saying, "Hail, King of the Jews!" and striking him on the face. 4 Pilate went out again and said to them, "Look, I am bringing him out to you to let you know that I find no case against

[e] Gk *the praetorium*

18.17 v. 25
18.18 Mk 14.54, 67; Jn 21.9
18.19 Mt 26.59-68; Mk 14.55-65; Lk 22.63-71
18.20 Mt 26.55; Jn 7.26
18.22 v. 3; Jn 19.3
18.23 Mt 5.39; Acts 23.2-5
18.24 v. 13
18.25 v. 18
18.26 v. 10
18.27 Jn 13.38
18.28-19.16pp Mt 27.11-16; Mk 15.2-15; Lk 23.3-25
18.28 Mt 27.1,2; Mk 15.1; Lk 23.1; Jn 11.55; Acts 11.3
18.32 Mt 20.19; Jn 12.32,33
18.33 vv. 28,29; Jn 19.9; Lk 23.3
18.36 Mt 26.53; Lk 17.21; Jn 6.15
18.37 Jn 8.47; 1 Jn 3.19; 4.6
18.38 Jn 19.4,6
18.39 Mt 27.15-18, 20-23; Mk 15.6-15; Lk 23.18-25
18.40 Acts 3.14
19.1 Mt 27.26
19.2 Mt 27.27-30; Mk 15.16-19
19.3 Jn 18.22
19.4 v. 6; Jn 18.38

him." 5 So Jesus came out, wearing
the crown of thorns and the purple
robe. Pilate said to them, "Here is
the man!" 6 When the chief priests
and the police saw him, they shouted, "Crucify him! Crucify him!" Pilate said to them, "Take him yourselves and crucify him; I find no
case against him." 7 The Jews answered him, "We have a law, and
according to that law he ought to
die because he has claimed to be
the Son of God."
8 Now when Pilate heard this,
he was more afraid than ever. 9 He
entered his headquarters[f] again
and asked Jesus, "Where are you
from?" But Jesus gave him no answer. 10 Pilate therefore said to
him, "Do you refuse to speak to
me? Do you not know that I have
power to release you, and power to
crucify you?" 11 Jesus answered
him, "You would have no power
over me unless it had been given
you from above; therefore the one
who handed me over to you is
guilty of a greater sin." 12 From
then on Pilate tried to release him,
but the Jews cried out, "If you release this man, you are no friend of
the emperor. Everyone who claims
to be a king sets himself against the
emperor."
13 When Pilate heard these
words, he brought Jesus outside
and sat[g] on the judge's bench at a
place called The Stone Pavement,
or in Hebrew[h] Gabbatha. 14 Now it
was the day of Preparation for the
Passover; and it was about noon.
He said to the Jews, "Here is your
King!" 15 They cried out, "Away
with him! Away with him! Crucify
him!" Pilate asked them, "Shall I
crucify your King?" The chief
priests answered, "We have no king
but the emperor." 16 Then he handed him over to them to be crucified.

The Crucifixion of Jesus

So they took Jesus; 17 and carrying the cross by himself, he went
out to what is called The Place of
the Skull, which in Hebrew[h] is
called Golgotha. 18 There they crucified him, and with him two others, one on either side, with Jesus
between them. 19 Pilate also had an
inscription written and put on the
cross. It read, "Jesus of Nazareth,[i]
the King of the Jews." 20 Many of
the Jews read this inscription, because the place where Jesus was
crucified was near the city; and it
was written in Hebrew,[h] in Latin,
and in Greek. 21 Then the chief
priests of the Jews said to Pilate,
"Do not write, 'The King of the
Jews,' but, 'This man said, I am
King of the Jews.'" 22 Pilate answered, "What I have written I have
written." 23 When the soldiers had
crucified Jesus, they took his
clothes and divided them into four
parts, one for each soldier. They
also took his tunic; now the tunic
was seamless, woven in one piece
from the top. 24 So they said to one
another, "Let us not tear it, but
cast lots for it to see who will get
it." This was to fulfill what the
scripture says,

"They divided my clothes
among themselves,
and for my clothing they
cast lots."

25 And that is what the soldiers did.
Meanwhile, standing near the
cross of Jesus were his mother, and
his mother's sister, Mary the wife
of Clopas, and Mary Magdalene.
26 When Jesus saw his mother and
the disciple whom he loved standing beside her, he said to his mother, "Woman, here is your son."
27 Then he said to the disciple,
"Here is your mother." And from
that hour the disciple took her into
his own home.
28 After this, when Jesus knew
that all was now finished, he said
(in order to fulfill the scripture), "I
am thirsty." 29 A jar full of sour wine
was standing there. So they put a
sponge full of the wine on a branch
of hyssop and held it to his mouth.
30 When Jesus had received the
wine, he said, "It is finished." Then
he bowed his head and gave up his
spirit.

19.5 v. 2
19.6 Acts 3.13
19.7 Lev 24.16; Mt 26.63-66; Jn 5.18; 10.33
19.9 Isa 53.7; Mt 27.12,14
19.11 Rom 13.1; Jn 18.28ff
19.12 Lk 23.2
19.13 Mt 27.19
19.14 Mt 27.62; Mk 15.25; vv. 19,21
19.16 Mt 27.26; Mk 15.15; Lk 23.25
19.17-27pp Mt 27.32-44; Mk 15.21-32; Lk 23.32-43
19.17 Lk 23.26
19.21 v. 14
19.24 Ex 28.32; Ps 22.18
19.25 Mt 27.55, 56; Mk 15.40, 41; Lk 23.49; 24.18; Jn 20.1,18
19.26 Jn 13.23; 20.2; 21.20; 2.4
19.28-37pp Mt 27.45-50; Mk 15.33-41; Lk 23.44-49
19.28 Jn 13.1; 17.4; Ps 69.21
19.30 Jn 17.4

f Gk *the praetorium*
g Or *seated him*
h That is, *Aramaic*
i Gk *the Nazorean*

Jesus' Side Is Pierced

31 Since it was the day of Preparation, the Jews did not want the
bodies left on the cross during the
sabbath, especially because that
sabbath was a day of great solem-
nity. So they asked Pilate to have
the legs of the crucified men broken and the bodies removed.
32 Then the soldiers came and
broke the legs of the first and of the
other who had been crucified with
him. 33 But when they came to
Jesus and saw that he was already
dead, they did not break his legs.
34 Instead, one of the soldiers
pierced his side with a spear, and at
once blood and water came out.
35 (He who saw this has testified so
that you also may believe. His testimony is true, and he knows[j] that
he tells the truth.) 36 These things
occurred so that the scripture
might be fulfilled, "None of his
bones shall be broken." 37 And
again another passage of scripture
says, "They will look on the one
whom they have pierced."

The Burial of Jesus

38 After these things, Joseph of
Arimathea, who was a disciple of
Jesus, though a secret one because
of his fear of the Jews, asked Pilate
to let him take away the body of
Jesus. Pilate gave him permission;
so he came and removed his body.
39 Nicodemus, who had at first
come to Jesus by night, also came,
bringing a mixture of myrrh and aloes, weighing about a hundred
pounds. 40 They took the body of
Jesus and wrapped it with the
spices in linen cloths, according to
the burial custom of the Jews.
41 Now there was a garden in the
place where he was crucified, and
in the garden there was a new tomb
in which no one had ever been laid.
42 And so, because it was the Jewish day of Preparation, and the
tomb was nearby, they laid Jesus
there.

The Resurrection of Jesus

20 Early on the first day of the
week, while it was still
dark, Mary Magdalene came to the
tomb and saw that the stone had
been removed from the tomb. 2 So
she ran and went to Simon Peter
and the other disciple, the one
whom Jesus loved, and said to
them, "They have taken the Lord
out of the tomb, and we do not
know where they have laid him."
3 Then Peter and the other disciple
set out and went toward the tomb.
4 The two were running together,
but the other disciple outran Peter
and reached the tomb first. 5 He
bent down to look in and saw the
linen wrappings lying there, but he
did not go in. 6 Then Simon Peter
came, following him, and went into
the tomb. He saw the linen wrappings lying there, 7 and the cloth
that had been on Jesus' head, not
lying with the linen wrappings but
rolled up in a place by itself. 8 Then
the other disciple, who reached the
tomb first, also went in, and he saw
and believed; 9 for as yet they did
not understand the scripture, that
he must rise from the dead. 10 Then
the disciples returned to their
homes.

Jesus Appears to Mary Magdalene

11 But Mary stood weeping outside the tomb. As she wept, she
bent over to look[k] into the tomb;
12 and she saw two angels in white,
sitting where the body of Jesus had
been lying, one at the head and the
other at the feet. 13 They said to
her, "Woman, why are you weeping?" She said to them, "They have
taken away my Lord, and I do not
know where they have laid him."
14 When she had said this, she
turned around and saw Jesus
standing there, but she did not
know that it was Jesus. 15 Jesus
said to her, "Woman, why are you
weeping? Whom are you looking
for?" Supposing him to be the gardener, she said to him, "Sir, if you
have carried him away, tell me
where you have laid him, and I will
take him away." 16 Jesus said to

19.31 Deut 21.23; Ex 12.16
19.32 v. 18
19.34 1 Jn 5.6,8
19.35 Jn 15.27; 21.24
19.36 Ex 12.46; Num 9.12; Ps 34.20
19.37 Zech 12.10
19.38-42pp Mt 27.57-61; Mk 15.42-47; Lk 23.50-56
19.39 Jn 3.1; 7.50
19.40 Jn 11.44; Mt 26.12; Jn 20.5,7; Lk 24.12
19.42 vv. 14,31, 20,41
20.1-10pp Mt 28.1-10; Mk 16.1-8; Lk 24.1-11
20.1 Mt 27.60,66
20.2 Jn 13.23; 19.26; 21.7, 20,24
20.3 Lk 24.12
20.5 Jn 19.40
20.8 v. 4
20.9 Mt 22.29; Lk 24.26,46
20.11 Mk 16.5; v. 5
20.12 Mt 28.2,3; Mk 16.5; Lk 24.4
20.13 v. 2
20.14 Mt 28.9; Jn 21.4
20.15 v. 13

[j] Or *there is one who knows* [k] Gk lacks *to look*

her, "Mary!" She turned and said to
him in Hebrew,[l] "Rabbouni!"
(which means Teacher). 17 Jesus
said to her, "Do not hold on to me,
because I have not yet ascended to
the Father. But go to my brothers
and say to them, 'I am ascending to
my Father and your Father, to my
God and your God.' " 18 Mary Magdalene went and announced to the
disciples, "I have seen the Lord";
and she told them that he had said
these things to her.

Jesus Appears to the Disciples

19 When it was evening on that
day, the first day of the week, and
the doors of the house where the
disciples had met were locked for
fear of the Jews, Jesus came and
stood among them and said,
"Peace be with you." 20 After he
said this, he showed them his
hands and his side. Then the disciples rejoiced when they saw the
Lord. 21 Jesus said to them again,
"Peace be with you. As the Father
has sent me, so I send you."
22 When he had said this, he
breathed on them and said to
them, "Receive the Holy Spirit. 23 If
you forgive the sins of any, they are
forgiven them; if you retain the sins
of any, they are retained."

Jesus and Thomas

24 But Thomas (who was called
the Twin[m]), one of the twelve, was
not with them when Jesus came.
25 So the other disciples told him,
"We have seen the Lord." But he
said to them, "Unless I see the
mark of the nails in his hands, and
put my finger in the mark of the
nails and my hand in his side, I will
not believe."

26 A week later his disciples
were again in the house, and
Thomas was with them. Although
the doors were shut, Jesus came
and stood among them and said,
"Peace be with you." 27 Then he
said to Thomas, "Put your finger
here and see my hands. Reach out
your hand and put it in my side. Do
not doubt but believe." 28 Thomas
answered him, "My Lord and my
God!" 29 Jesus said to him, "Have
you believed because you have
seen me? Blessed are those who
have not seen and yet have come to
believe."

The Purpose of This Book

30 Now Jesus did many other
signs in the presence of his disciples, which are not written in this
book. 31 But these are written so
that you may come to believe[n] that
Jesus is the Messiah,[o] the Son of
God, and that through believing
you may have life in his name.

Jesus Appears to Seven Disciples

21 After these things Jesus
showed himself again to
the disciples by the Sea of Tiberias;
and he showed himself in this way.
2 Gathered there together were Simon Peter, Thomas called the
Twin,[m] Nathanael of Cana in Galilee, the sons of Zebedee, and two
others of his disciples. 3 Simon Peter said to them, "I am going fishing." They said to him, "We will go
with you." They went out and got
into the boat, but that night they
caught nothing.

4 Just after daybreak, Jesus
stood on the beach; but the disciples did not know that it was Jesus.
5 Jesus said to them, "Children, you
have no fish, have you?" They answered him, "No." 6 He said to
them, "Cast the net to the right
side of the boat, and you will find
some." So they cast it, and now
they were not able to haul it in because there were so many fish.
7 That disciple whom Jesus loved
said to Peter, "It is the Lord!" When
Simon Peter heard that it was the
Lord, he put on some clothes, for
he was naked, and jumped into the
sea. 8 But the other disciples came
in the boat, dragging the net full of
fish, for they were not far from the
land, only about a hundred yards[p]
off.

20.17 Mt 28.10; v. 27; Jn 7.33
20.18 Lk 24.10,13
20.19-25pp Lk 24.36-43
20.19 Lk 24.36-39; vv. 21,26
20.20 Lk 24.39,40; Jn 16.20,22
20.21 Mt 28.19; Jn 17.18,19
20.23 Mt 16.19; 18.18
20.24 Jn 11.16
20.25 v. 20
20.26 v. 21
20.27 v. 25; Lk 24.40
20.29 1 Pet 1.8
20.30 Jn 21.25
20.31 Jn 19.35; 3.15
21.1 Jn 20.19,26; 6.1
21.2 Jn 11.16; 1.45; Mt 4.21; Mk 1.19; Lk 5.10
21.3 Lk 5.5
21.4 Jn 20.14
21.5 Lk 24.41
21.6 Lk 5.4,6,7
21.7 Jn 13.23; 20.2; v. 20

[l] That is, *Aramaic* [m] Gk *Didymus*
[n] Other ancient authorities read *may continue to believe* [o] Or *the Christ* [p] Gk *two hundred cubits*

9 When they had gone ashore,
they saw a charcoal fire there, with
fish on it, and bread. 10 Jesus said
to them, "Bring some of the fish
that you have just caught." 11 So Simon Peter went aboard and hauled
the net ashore, full of large fish, a
hundred fifty-three of them; and
though there were so many, the net
was not torn. 12 Jesus said to them,
"Come and have breakfast." Now
none of the disciples dared to ask
him, "Who are you?" because they
knew it was the Lord. 13 Jesus came
and took the bread and gave it to
them, and did the same with the
fish. 14 This was now the third time
that Jesus appeared to the disciples after he was raised from the
dead.

Jesus and Peter

15 When they had finished
breakfast, Jesus said to Simon Peter, "Simon son of John, do you
love me more than these?" He said
to him, "Yes, Lord; you know that I
love you." Jesus said to him, "Feed
my lambs." 16 A second time he
said to him, "Simon son of John, do
you love me?" He said to him, "Yes,
Lord; you know that I love you."
Jesus said to him, "Tend my
sheep." 17 He said to him the third
time, "Simon son of John, do you
love me?" Peter felt hurt because
he said to him the third time, "Do
you love me?" And he said to him,
"Lord, you know everything; you
know that I love you." Jesus said to
him, "Feed my sheep. 18 Very truly,
I tell you, when you were younger,
you used to fasten your own belt
and to go wherever you wished. But
when you grow old, you will stretch
out your hands, and someone else
will fasten a belt around you and
take you where you do not wish to
go." 19 (He said this to indicate the
kind of death by which he would
glorify God.) After this he said to
him, "Follow me."

Jesus and the Beloved Disciple

20 Peter turned and saw the disciple whom Jesus loved following
them; he was the one who had reclined next to Jesus at the supper
and had said, "Lord, who is it that
is going to betray you?" 21 When Peter saw him, he said to Jesus,
"Lord, what about him?" 22 Jesus
said to him, "If it is my will that he
remain until I come, what is that to
you? Follow me!" 23 So the rumor
spread in the community[q] that
this disciple would not die. Yet
Jesus did not say to him that he
would not die, but, "If it is my will
that he remain until I come, what is
that to you?"[r]

24 This is the disciple who is
testifying to these things and has
written them, and we know that his
testimony is true. 25 But there are
also many other things that Jesus
did; if every one of them were written down, I suppose that the world
itself could not contain the books
that would be written.

21.9 vv. 10,13
21.13 v. 9
21.14 Jn 20.19,26
21.15 Jn 13.37; Mt 26.33; Mk 14.29
21.16 Mt 2.6; Acts 20.28; 1 Pet 5.2; Rev 7.17
21.17 Jn 16.30; v. 16
21.19 2 Pet 1.14
21.20 v. 7; Jn 13.25
21.22 Mt 16.27, 28; 25.31; 1 Cor 4.5; 11.26; Rev 2.25; 3.11; 22.7,20
21.23 Acts 1.15
21.24 Jn 15.27; 19.35
21.25 Jn 20.30

[q] Gk *among the brothers* [r] Other ancient authorities lack *what is that to you*

THE *Acts* OF THE APOSTLES

Title and Background

The book of Acts provides the basic history of the spread of Christianity during the thirty years immediately following the death and resurrection of Jesus Christ. It serves as a link between the Gospels and the letters. It can be called "The Acts of the Holy Spirit," because it teaches about the coming and the work of the Spirit.

Author and Date of Writing

Although the author does not name himself, evidence outside the Scriptures and inferences from the book itself lead to the conclusion that the author was Luke. It is a companion volume to the Gospel of Luke (cf. Lk 1.1-4 and Acts 1.1-2), and it was written after that book (that is, shortly after A.D. 70).

Theme and Message

The theme of the work is best summarized in 1.8. Luke weaves together different interests and emphases as he relates the beginnings and expansion of the church. The design of the book revolves around (1) key persons: Peter and Paul; (2) important topics and events: the role of the Holy Spirit, pioneer missionary outreach to new fields, conversions, the growth of the church, and life in the Christian community; (3) significant problems: conflict between Jewish and Gentile Christians, persecution of the church by some Jewish elements, trials before Jews and Romans, confrontations with Gentiles, and other hardships in the ministry; (4) geographical advances: from Jerusalem to Rome.

Outline

- I. Peter and the Beginnings of the Church in Palestine (1.1–12.25)
  - A. "Throughout Judea, Galilee, and Samaria" (1.1–9.31; see 9.31)
  - B. "As far as Phoenicia, Cyprus, and Antioch" (9.32–12.25; see 11.19)
- II. Paul and the Expansion of the Church From Antioch to Rome (13.1–28.31)
  - A. "Through the Region of Phrygia and Galatia" (13.1–15.35; see 16.6)
  - B. "Over to Macedonia" (15.36–21.16; see 16.9)
  - C. "To Rome" (21.17–28.31; see 28.14)

The Promise of the Holy Spirit

1 In the first book, Theophilus, I
wrote about all that Jesus did
and taught from the beginning
2 until the day when he was taken
up to heaven, after giving instructions through the Holy Spirit to the
apostles whom he had chosen. 3 After his suffering he presented himself alive to them by many convincing proofs, appearing to them
during forty days and speaking
about the kingdom of God. 4 While
staying[a] with them, he ordered
them not to leave Jerusalem, but to
wait there for the promise of the
Father. "This," he said, "is what
you have heard from me; 5 for John
baptized with water, but you will
be baptized with[b] the Holy Spirit
not many days from now."

The Ascension of Jesus

6 So when they had come together, they asked him, "Lord, is
this the time when you will restore
the kingdom to Israel?" 7 He replied, "It is not for you to know the
times or periods that the Father

1.1 Lk 1.1-4
1.2 Mt 28.19
1.3 Mt 28.17; Lk 24.34,36; 1 Cor 15.5-7
1.4 Lk 24.49; Jn 14.16
1.5 Acts 11.16
1.6 Mt 24.3
1.7 Mt 24.36; Mk 13.32

[a] Or *eating* [b] Or *by*

has set by his own authority. 8 But
you will receive power when the
Holy Spirit has come upon you;
and you will be my witnesses in Jerusalem, in all Judea and Samaria,
and to the ends of the earth."
9 When he had said this, as they
were watching, he was lifted up,
and a cloud took him out of their
sight. 10 While he was going and
they were gazing up toward heaven,
suddenly two men in white robes
stood by them. 11 They said, "Men
of Galilee, why do you stand looking up toward heaven? This Jesus,
who has been taken up from you
into heaven, will come in the same
way as you saw him go into heav-
en."

Matthias Chosen to Replace Judas

12 Then they returned to Jerusalem from the mount called Olivet, which is near Jerusalem, a sabbath day's journey away. 13 When
they had entered the city, they
went to the room upstairs where
they were staying, Peter, and John,
and James, and Andrew, Philip and
Thomas, Bartholomew and Matthew, James son of Alphaeus, and
Simon the Zealot, and Judas son
of[c] James. 14 All these were constantly devoting themselves to
prayer, together with certain wom-
en, including Mary the mother of
Jesus, as well as his brothers.
15 In those days Peter stood up
among the believers[d] (together the
crowd numbered about one hundred twenty persons) and said,
16 "Friends,[e] the scripture had to
be fulfilled, which the Holy Spirit
through David foretold concerning
Judas, who became a guide for
those who arrested Jesus— 17 for
he was numbered among us and
was allotted his share in this ministry." 18 (Now this man acquired a
field with the reward of his wickedness; and falling headlong,[f] he
burst open in the middle and all his
bowels gushed out. 19 This became
known to all the residents of Jerusalem, so that the field was called
in their language Hakeldama, that

1.8 Acts 2.1-4; Lk 24.48; Jn 15.27 **1.9** Lk 24.51; v. 2 **1.10** Lk 24.4; Jn 20.12 **1.11** Mt 24.30; Mk 13.26; Jn 14.3 **1.13** Acts 9.37, 39; 20.8; Mt 10.2-4; Mk 3.16-19; Lk 6.14-16 **1.14** Acts 2.1,46; Lk 23.49,55; Mt 12.46 **1.15** Jn 21.23; Acts 6.3; 9.30 **1.16** Jn 13.18 **1.17** Jn 6.70,71; v. 25; Acts 20.24; 21.19 **1.18** Mt 27.3-10; 26.14,15 **1.20** Ps 69.25; 109.8 **1.21** Lk 24.3 **1.22** Mk 1.1; v. 8; Acts 2.32 **1.24** 1 Sam 16.7; Jer 17.10; Acts 15.8; Rom 8.27 **1.26** Lev 16.8 **2.1** Lev 23.15; Deut 16.9; Acts 1.14 **2.2** Acts 4.31 **2.4** Acts 4.8,31; 9.17; 13.9,52; 1 Cor 12.10, 11; 14.21 **2.5** Acts 8.2 **2.7** v. 12; Acts 1.11

is, Field of Blood.) 20 "For it is written in the book of Psalms,

'Let his homestead become
desolate,
and let there be no one to
live in it';
and
'Let another take his
position of overseer.'

21 So one of the men who have accompanied us during all the time
that the Lord Jesus went in and out
among us, 22 beginning from the
baptism of John until the day when
he was taken up from us—one of
these must become a witness with
us to his resurrection." 23 So they
proposed two, Joseph called Barsabbas, who was also known as
Justus, and Matthias. 24 Then they
prayed and said, "Lord, you know
everyone's heart. Show us which
one of these two you have chosen
25 to take the place[g] in this ministry and apostleship from which Judas turned aside to go to his own
place." 26 And they cast lots for
them, and the lot fell on Matthias;
and he was added to the eleven
apostles.

The Coming of the Holy Spirit

2 When the day of Pentecost
had come, they were all together in one place. 2 And suddenly
from heaven there came a sound
like the rush of a violent wind, and
it filled the entire house where they
were sitting. 3 Divided tongues, as
of fire, appeared among them, and
a tongue rested on each of them.
4 All of them were filled with the
Holy Spirit and began to speak in
other languages, as the Spirit gave
them ability.
5 Now there were devout Jews
from every nation under heaven living in Jerusalem. 6 And at this
sound the crowd gathered and was
bewildered, because each one
heard them speaking in the native
language of each. 7 Amazed and astonished, they asked, "Are not all
these who are speaking Galileans?

[c] Or *the brother of* [d] Gk *brothers*
[e] Gk *Men, brothers* [f] Or *swelling up*
[g] Other ancient authorities read *the share*

8 And how is it that we hear, each of
us, in our own native language?
9 Parthians, Medes, Elamites, and
residents of Mesopotamia, Judea
and Cappadocia, Pontus and Asia,
10 Phrygia and Pamphylia, Egypt
and the parts of Libya belonging to
Cyrene, and visitors from Rome,
both Jews and proselytes, 11 Cretans and Arabs—in our own languages we hear them speaking
about God's deeds of power." 12 All
were amazed and perplexed, saying
to one another, "What does this
mean?" 13 But others sneered and
said, "They are filled with new
wine."

Peter Addresses the Crowd

14 But Peter, standing with the
eleven, raised his voice and addressed them, "Men of Judea and
all who live in Jerusalem, let this
be known to you, and listen to what
I say. 15 Indeed, these are not
drunk, as you suppose, for it is only
nine o'clock in the morning. 16 No,
this is what was spoken through
the prophet Joel:

17 'In the last days it will be,
God declares,
that I will pour out my Spirit
upon all flesh,
and your sons and your
daughters shall
prophesy,
and your young men shall
see visions,
and your old men shall
dream dreams.
18 Even upon my slaves, both
men and women,
in those days I will pour
out my Spirit;
and they shall prophesy.
19 And I will show portents in
the heaven above
and signs on the earth
below,
blood, and fire, and
smoky mist.
20 The sun shall be turned to
darkness
and the moon to blood,
before the coming of the
Lord's great and
glorious day.
21 Then everyone who calls on
the name of the Lord
shall be saved.'

22 "You that are Israelites,[h] listen to what I have to say: Jesus of
Nazareth,[i] a man attested to you
by God with deeds of power, wonders, and signs that God did
through him among you, as you
yourselves know— 23 this man,
handed over to you according to
the definite plan and foreknowledge of God, you crucified and
killed by the hands of those outside
the law. 24 But God raised him up,
having freed him from death,[j] because it was impossible for him to
be held in its power. 25 For David
says concerning him,

'I saw the Lord always before
me,
for he is at my right hand
so that I will not be
shaken;
26 therefore my heart was glad,
and my tongue rejoiced;
moreover my flesh will live
in hope.
27 For you will not abandon my
soul to Hades,
or let your Holy One
experience corruption.
28 You have made known to me
the ways of life;
you will make me full of
gladness with your
presence.'

29 "Fellow Israelites,[k] I may
say to you confidently of our ancestor David that he both died and was
buried, and his tomb is with us to
this day. 30 Since he was a prophet,
he knew that God had sworn with
an oath to him that he would put
one of his descendants on his
throne. 31 Foreseeing this, David[l]
spoke of the resurrection of the
Messiah,[m] saying,

'He was not abandoned to
Hades,
nor did his flesh
experience corruption.'

32 This Jesus God raised up, and of
that all of us are witnesses. 33 Being

2.9 1 Pet 1.1; Acts 6.9; 16.6; Rom 16.5; 1 Cor 16.19; 2 Cor 1.8
2.12 v. 7
2.13 1 Cor 14.23
2.15 1 Thes 5.7
2.17 Joel 2.28-32; Zech 12.10; Jn 7.38; Acts 10.45; 21.9
2.18 Acts 21.4,9, 10
2.20 Mt 24.29; Mk 13.24; Lk 21.25
2.21 Rom 10.13
2.22 Jn 3.2; Acts 10.38; Jn 4.48
2.23 Mt 26.24; Lk 22.22; Acts 3.18; 4.28; 3.13
2.24 Acts 3.15; Rom 4.24; 2 Cor 4.14; Eph 1.20; Col 2.12; Heb 13.20; 1 Pet 1.21
2.25 Ps 16.8-11
2.27 Mt 11.23; Acts 13.35
2.29 Acts 7.8,9; 13.36; 1 Kings 2.10; Neh 3.16
2.30 2 Sam 7.12, 13; Ps 132.11; Rom 1.3
2.31 Ps 16.10
2.32 v. 24; Acts 1.8
2.33 Acts 5.31; 1.4; Jn 7.39; 14.26; 15.26; Acts 10.45

[h] Gk *Men, Israelites* [i] Gk *the Nazorean* [j] Gk *the pains of death* [k] Gk *Men, brothers* [l] Gk *he* [m] Or *the Christ*

COUNTRIES OF PEOPLE MENTIONED AT PENTECOST

therefore exalted at[n] the right
hand of God, and having received
from the Father the promise of the
Holy Spirit, he has poured out this
that you both see and hear. 34 For
David did not ascend into the heavens, but he himself says,
'The Lord said to my Lord,
"Sit at my right hand,
35 until I make your enemies
your footstool." '
36 Therefore let the entire house of
Israel know with certainty that God
has made him both Lord and Messiah,[o] this Jesus whom you crucified."

The First Converts

37 Now when they heard this,
they were cut to the heart and said
to Peter and to the other apostles,
"Brothers,[p] what should we do?"
38 Peter said to them, "Repent, and
be baptized every one of you in the
name of Jesus Christ so that your
sins may be forgiven; and you will
receive the gift of the Holy Spirit.
39 For the promise is for you, for
your children, and for all who are
far away, everyone whom the Lord
our God calls to him." 40 And he
testified with many other arguments and exhorted them, saying,
"Save yourselves from this corrupt
generation." 41 So those who welcomed his message were baptized,
and that day about three thousand
persons were added. 42 They devoted themselves to the apostles'
teaching and fellowship, to the
breaking of bread and the prayers.

Life among the Believers

43 Awe came upon everyone,
because many wonders and signs
were being done by the apostles.
44 All who believed were together
and had all things in common;
45 they would sell their possessions
and goods and distribute the proceeds[q] to all, as any had need.
46 Day by day, as they spent much
time together in the temple, they
broke bread at home[r] and ate their
food with glad and generous[s]
hearts, 47 praising God and having
the goodwill of all the people. And
day by day the Lord added to their
number those who were being
saved.

Peter Heals a Crippled Beggar

3 One day Peter and John were
going up to the temple at the
hour of prayer, at three o'clock in
the afternoon. 2 And a man lame
from birth was being carried in.
People would lay him daily at the
gate of the temple called the Beautiful Gate so that he could ask for
alms from those entering the temple. 3 When he saw Peter and John
about to go into the temple, he
asked them for alms. 4 Peter looked
intently at him, as did John, and
said, "Look at us." 5 And he fixed
his attention on them, expecting to
receive something from them. 6 But
Peter said, "I have no silver or gold,
but what I have I give you; in the
name of Jesus Christ of Nazareth,[t]
stand up and walk." 7 And he took
him by the right hand and raised
him up; and immediately his feet
and ankles were made strong.
8 Jumping up, he stood and began
to walk, and he entered the temple
with them, walking and leaping
and praising God. 9 All the people
saw him walking and praising God,
10 and they recognized him as the
one who used to sit and ask for
alms at the Beautiful Gate of the
temple; and they were filled with
wonder and amazement at what
had happened to him.

Peter Speaks in Solomon's Portico

11 While he clung to Peter and
John, all the people ran together to
them in the portico called Solomon's Portico, utterly astonished.
12 When Peter saw it, he addressed
the people, "You Israelites,[u] why
do you wonder at this, or why do
you stare at us, as though by our
own power or piety we had made
him walk? 13 The God of Abraham,
the God of Isaac, and the God of
Jacob, the God of our ancestors has

2.34 Ps 110.1; Mt 22.44
2.37 Lk 3.10; Acts 9.6; 16.30
2.38 Lk 24.47; Acts 3.19; 5.31; 8.12,16; 22.16
2.39 Isa 57.19; Joel 2.32; Acts 10.45; Eph 2.13
2.43 Acts 5.12
2.44 Acts 4.32,34
2.46 Acts 5.42; 20.7; 1 Cor 10.16
2.47 Acts 4.33; Rom 14.18; Acts 5.14; 11.24
3.1 Acts 2.46; Ps 55.17
3.2 Acts 14.8; Lk 16.20; v. 10
3.4 Acts 10.4
3.6 Acts 4.10
3.9 Acts 4.16,21
3.10 Jn 9.8
3.11 Lk 22.8; Jn 10.23; Acts 5.12
3.13 Isa 52.13; Acts 5.30; Mt 27.2; Acts 2.23; Lk 23.4

[n] Or *by* [o] Or *Christ* [p] Gk *Men, brothers* [q] Gk *them* [r] Or *from house to house* [s] Or *sincere* [t] Gk *the Nazorean* [u] Gk *Men, Israelites*

glorified his servant[v] Jesus, whom
you handed over and rejected in
the presence of Pilate, though he
had decided to release him. 14 But
you rejected the Holy and Righteous One and asked to have a
murderer given to you, 15 and you
killed the Author of life, whom God
raised from the dead. To this we are
witnesses. 16 And by faith in his
name, his name itself has made
this man strong, whom you see and
know; and the faith that is through
Jesus[w] has given him this perfect
health in the presence of all of you.
17 "And now, friends,[x] I know
that you acted in ignorance, as did
also your rulers. 18 In this way God
fulfilled what he had foretold
through all the prophets, that his
Messiah[y] would suffer. 19 Repent
therefore, and turn to God so that
your sins may be wiped out, 20 so
that times of refreshing may come
from the presence of the Lord, and
that he may send the Messiah[z] appointed for you, that is, Jesus,
21 who must remain in heaven until
the time of universal restoration
that God announced long ago
through his holy prophets. 22 Moses
said, 'The Lord your God will raise
up for you from your own people[x]
a prophet like me. You must listen
to whatever he tells you. 23 And it
will be that everyone who does not
listen to that prophet will be utterly rooted out of the people.' 24 And
all the prophets, as many as have
spoken, from Samuel and those after him, also predicted these days.
25 You are the descendants of the
prophets and of the covenant that
God gave to your ancestors, saying
to Abraham, 'And in your descendants all the families of the earth
shall be blessed.' 26 When God
raised up his servant,[v] he sent him
first to you, to bless you by turning
each of you from your wicked
ways."

Peter and John before the Council

4 While Peter and John[a] were
speaking to the people, the
priests, the captain of the temple,
and the Sadducees came to them,
2 much annoyed because they were
teaching the people and proclaiming that in Jesus there is the resurrection of the dead. 3 So they arrested them and put them in custody
until the next day, for it was already evening. 4 But many of those
who heard the word believed; and
they numbered about five thousand.
5 The next day their rulers, elders, and scribes assembled in Jerusalem, 6 with Annas the high
priest, Caiaphas, John,[b] and Alexander, and all who were of the
high-priestly family. 7 When they
had made the prisoners[c] stand in
their midst, they inquired, "By
what power or by what name did
you do this?" 8 Then Peter, filled
with the Holy Spirit, said to them,
"Rulers of the people and elders,
9 if we are questioned today because of a good deed done to someone who was sick and are asked
how this man has been healed,
10 let it be known to all of you, and
to all the people of Israel, that this
man is standing before you in good
health by the name of Jesus Christ
of Nazareth,[d] whom you crucified,
whom God raised from the dead.
11 This Jesus[e] is

'the stone that was rejected
by you, the builders;
it has become the
cornerstone.'[f]

12 There is salvation in no one else,
for there is no other name under
heaven given among mortals by
which we must be saved."
13 Now when they saw the boldness of Peter and John and realized
that they were uneducated and ordinary men, they were amazed and
recognized them as companions of
Jesus. 14 When they saw the man
who had been cured standing beside them, they had nothing to say
in opposition. 15 So they ordered

3.14 Mk 1.24; Acts 4.27; 7.52; Mk 15.11; Lk 23.18-25
3.15 Acts 5.31; 2.24,32
3.17 Lk 23.34; Acts 13.27
3.18 Acts 2.23; Lk 24.27; Acts 17.3; 26.23
3.21 Acts 1.11; Mt 17.11; Lk 1.70
3.22 Deut 18.15; Acts 7.37
3.23 Deut 18.19
3.25 Acts 2.39; Rom 9.4,8; Gen 12.3; 28.14
3.26 Acts 13.46; 2.24; v. 22
4.1 Lk 22.4; Mt 3.7; Acts 6.12
4.2 Acts 17.18; 23.8
4.3 Acts 5.18
4.4 Acts 2.41
4.5 Lk 23.13
4.6 Lk 3.2; Mt 26.3
4.8 Acts 13.9; Lk 23.13; v. 5
4.10 Acts 3.6; 2.24
4.11 Ps 118.22; Isa 28.16; Mt 21.42
4.12 Mt 1.21; Acts 10.43; 1 Tim 2.5, 6
4.13 v. 31; Mt 11.25; 1 Cor 1.27
4.15 Mt 5.22

v Or *child* w Gk *him* x Gk *brothers*
y Or *his Christ* z Or *the Christ*
a Gk *While they* b Other ancient authorities read *Jonathan* c Gk *them*
d Gk *the Nazorean* e Gk *This*
f Or *keystone*

them to leave the council while
they discussed the matter with one
another. 16 They said, "What will
we do with them? For it is obvious
to all who live in Jerusalem that a
notable sign has been done
through them; we cannot deny it.
17 But to keep it from spreading further among the people, let us warn
them to speak no more to anyone
in this name." 18 So they called
them and ordered them not to
speak or teach at all in the name of
Jesus. 19 But Peter and John answered them, "Whether it is right
in God's sight to listen to you rather than to God, you must judge;
20 for we cannot keep from speaking about what we have seen and
heard." 21 After threatening them
again, they let them go, finding no
way to punish them because of the
people, for all of them praised God
for what had happened. 22 For the
man on whom this sign of healing
had been performed was more than
forty years old.

The Believers Pray for Boldness

23 After they were released,
they went to their friends[g] and reported what the chief priests and
the elders had said to them.
24 When they heard it, they raised
their voices together to God and
said, "Sovereign Lord, who made
the heaven and the earth, the sea,
and everything in them, 25 it is you
who said by the Holy Spirit through
our ancestor David, your servant:[h]
'Why did the Gentiles rage,
and the peoples imagine
vain things?
26 The kings of the earth took
their stand,
and the rulers have
gathered together
against the Lord and
against his Messiah.'[i]
27 For in this city, in fact, both Herod and Pontius Pilate, with the
Gentiles and the peoples of Israel,
gathered together against your holy
servant[h] Jesus, whom you anointed, 28 to do whatever your hand and
your plan had predestined to take
place. 29 And now, Lord, look at
their threats, and grant to your servants[j] to speak your word with all
boldness, 30 while you stretch out
your hand to heal, and signs and
wonders are performed through the
name of your holy servant[h] Jesus."
31 When they had prayed, the place
in which they were gathered together was shaken; and they were
all filled with the Holy Spirit and
spoke the word of God with boldness.

The Believers Share Their Possessions

32 Now the whole group of
those who believed were of one
heart and soul, and no one claimed
private ownership of any possessions, but everything they owned
was held in common. 33 With great
power the apostles gave their testimony to the resurrection of the
Lord Jesus, and great grace was
upon them all. 34 There was not a
needy person among them, for as
many as owned lands or houses
sold them and brought the proceeds of what was sold. 35 They laid
it at the apostles' feet, and it was
distributed to each as any had
need. 36 There was a Levite, a native of Cyprus, Joseph, to whom
the apostles gave the name Barnabas (which means "son of encouragement"). 37 He sold a field that
belonged to him, then brought the
money, and laid it at the apostles'
feet.

Ananias and Sapphira

5 But a man named Ananias,
with the consent of his wife
Sapphira, sold a piece of property;
2 with his wife's knowledge, he kept
back some of the proceeds, and
brought only a part and laid it at
the apostles' feet. 3 "Ananias," Peter asked, "why has Satan filled
your heart to lie to the Holy Spirit
and to keep back part of the proceeds of the land? 4 While it remained unsold, did it not remain
your own? And after it was sold,
were not the proceeds at your dis-

4.16 Jn 11.47; Acts 3.7-10
4.18 Acts 5.40
4.19 Acts 5.28,29
4.20 Acts 1.8; 2.32
4.24 2 Kings 19.15
4.25 Ps 2.1; Acts 1.16
4.26 Heb 1.9
4.27 v. 30; Lk 4.18; Jn 10.36; Mt 14.1; Lk 23.12
4.28 Acts 2.23
4.29 vv. 13,31; Acts 9.27; 13.46; 28.31
4.30 Acts 2.43; 5.12; 3.6,16; v. 27
4.31 Acts 2.2,4; v. 29
4.32 Acts 5.12; 2.44
4.33 Acts 1.8; 1.22
4.34 Acts 2.45
4.35 v. 37; Acts 5.2; 2.45; 6.1
4.37 v. 35; Acts 5.2
5.2 Acts 4.37
5.3 Deut 23.21; Lk 22.3; Jn 13.2,7; v. 9

[g] Gk *their own* [h] Or *child* [i] Or *his Christ* [j] Gk *slaves*

might give repentance to Israel and
forgiveness of sins. 32 And we are
witnesses to these things, and so is
the Holy Spirit whom God has giv-
en to those who obey him."
33 When they heard this, they
were enraged and wanted to kill
them. 34 But a Pharisee in the council named Gamaliel, a teacher of
the law, respected by all the people, stood up and ordered the men
to be put outside for a short time.
35 Then he said to them, "Fellow Israelites,[o] consider carefully what
you propose to do to these men.
36 For some time ago Theudas rose
up, claiming to be somebody, and a
number of men, about four hundred, joined him; but he was killed,
and all who followed him were dispersed and disappeared. 37 After
him Judas the Galilean rose up at
the time of the census and got people to follow him; he also perished,
and all who followed him were
scattered. 38 So in the present case,
I tell you, keep away from these
men and let them alone; because if
this plan or this undertaking is of
human origin, it will fail; 39 but if it
is of God, you will not be able to
overthrow them – in that case you
may even be found fighting against
God!"
They were convinced by him,
40 and when they had called in the
apostles, they had them flogged.
Then they ordered them not to
speak in the name of Jesus, and let
them go. 41 As they left the council,
they rejoiced that they were considered worthy to suffer dishonor
for the sake of the name. 42 And every day in the temple and at home[p]
they did not cease to teach and
proclaim Jesus as the Messiah.[q]

Seven Chosen to Serve

6 Now during those days, when
the disciples were increasing
in number, the Hellenists complained against the Hebrews because their widows were being neglected in the daily distribution of
food. 2 And the twelve called together the whole community of the
disciples and said, "It is not right
that we should neglect the word of
God in order to wait on tables.[r]
3 Therefore, friends,[s] select from
among yourselves seven men of
good standing, full of the Spirit and
of wisdom, whom we may appoint
to this task, 4 while we, for our part,
will devote ourselves to prayer and
to serving the word." 5 What they
said pleased the whole community,
and they chose Stephen, a man full
of faith and the Holy Spirit, together with Philip, Prochorus, Nicanor,
Timon, Parmenas, and Nicolaus, a
proselyte of Antioch. 6 They had
these men stand before the apostles, who prayed and laid their
hands on them.
7 The word of God continued to
spread; the number of the disciples
increased greatly in Jerusalem, and
a great many of the priests became
obedient to the faith.

The Arrest of Stephen

8 Stephen, full of grace and
power, did great wonders and signs
among the people. 9 Then some of
those who belonged to the synagogue of the Freedmen (as it was
called), Cyrenians, Alexandrians,
and others of those from Cilicia
and Asia, stood up and argued with
Stephen. 10 But they could not
withstand the wisdom and the
Spirit[t] with which he spoke.
11 Then they secretly instigated
some men to say, "We have heard
him speak blasphemous words
against Moses and God." 12 They
stirred up the people as well as the
elders and the scribes; then they
suddenly confronted him, seized
him, and brought him before the
council. 13 They set up false witnesses who said, "This man never
stops saying things against this
holy place and the law; 14 for we
have heard him say that this Jesus
of Nazareth[u] will destroy this
place and will change the customs
that Moses handed on to us."

5.32 Lk 24.48; Jn 15.26; Rom 8.16
5.33 Acts 2.37; 7.54
5.38 Mt 15.13
5.39 Acts 7.51; 9.5; 11.17
5.40 Mt 10.17; Mk 13.9
5.41 1 Pet 4.13, 16; Jn 15.21
5.42 Acts 2.46; 8.35; 11.20; 17.18; Gal 1.16
6.1 Acts 2.41, 47; 9.29; 11.20; 4.35
6.3 Jn 21.23; Acts 1.15
6.5 Acts 11.19, 24; 8.5,26; 21.8
6.6 Acts 1.24; 8.17; 9.17; 13.3; 1 Tim 4.14; 5.22; 2 Tim 1.6
6.7 Acts 12.24; 19.20; Acts 13.8; 14.22; Gal 1.23; 6.10
6.10 Lk 21.15; Acts 5.39
6.11 Mt 26.59,60
6.13 Acts 7.58; 21.28
6.14 Mt 26.61; 15.1; 21.21; 26.3; 28.17

[o] Gk *Men, Israelites* [p] Or *from house to house* [q] Or *the Christ* [r] Or *keep accounts* [s] Gk *brothers* [t] Or *spirit* [u] Gk *the Nazorean*

posal? How is it that you have contrived this deed in your heart? You
did not lie to us[k] but to God!"
5 Now when Ananias heard these
words, he fell down and died. And
great fear seized all who heard of it.
6 The young men came and
wrapped up his body,[l] then carried him out and buried him.
7 After an interval of about
three hours his wife came in, not
knowing what had happened. 8 Peter said to her, "Tell me whether
you and your husband sold the
land for such and such a price."
And she said, "Yes, that was the
price." 9 Then Peter said to her,
"How is it that you have agreed together to put the Spirit of the Lord
to the test? Look, the feet of those
who have buried your husband are
at the door, and they will carry you
out." 10 Immediately she fell down
at his feet and died. When the
young men came in they found her
dead, so they carried her out and
buried her beside her husband.
11 And great fear seized the whole
church and all who heard of these
things.

The Apostles Heal Many

12 Now many signs and wonders were done among the people
through the apostles. And they
were all together in Solomon's Portico. 13 None of the rest dared to
join them, but the people held
them in high esteem. 14 Yet more
than ever believers were added to
the Lord, great numbers of both
men and women, 15 so that they
even carried out the sick into the
streets, and laid them on cots and
mats, in order that Peter's shadow
might fall on some of them as he
came by. 16 A great number of people would also gather from the
towns around Jerusalem, bringing
the sick and those tormented by
unclean spirits, and they were all
cured.

The Apostles Are Persecuted

17 Then the high priest took action; he and all who were with him
(that is, the sect of the Sadducees),
being filled with jealousy, 18 arrested the apostles and put them in the
public prison. 19 But during the
night an angel of the Lord opened
the prison doors, brought them
out, and said, 20 "Go, stand in the
temple and tell the people the
whole message about this life."
21 When they heard this, they entered the temple at daybreak and
went on with their teaching.
When the high priest and those
with him arrived, they called together the council and the whole
body of the elders of Israel, and
sent to the prison to have them
brought. 22 But when the temple
police went there, they did not find
them in the prison; so they returned and reported, 23 "We found
the prison securely locked and the
guards standing at the doors, but
when we opened them, we found
no one inside." 24 Now when the
captain of the temple and the chief
priests heard these words, they
were perplexed about them, wondering what might be going on.
25 Then someone arrived and announced, "Look, the men whom
you put in prison are standing in
the temple and teaching the people!" 26 Then the captain went with
the temple police and brought
them, but without violence, for
they were afraid of being stoned by
the people.
27 When they had brought
them, they had them stand before
the council. The high priest questioned them, 28 saying, "We gave
you strict orders not to teach in this
name,[m] yet here you have filled Jerusalem with your teaching and
you are determined to bring this
man's blood on us." 29 But Peter
and the apostles answered, "We
must obey God rather than any human authority.[n] 30 The God of our
ancestors raised up Jesus, whom
you had killed by hanging him on a
tree. 31 God exalted him at his right
hand as Leader and Savior that he

5.5 vv. 10,11 **5.6** Jn 19.40 **5.8** v. 2 **5.9** v. 3 **5.10** v. 5 **5.11** v. 5; Acts 19.17 **5.12** Acts 2.43; 3.11; 4.32 **5.13** Acts 2.47; 4.21 **5.14** Acts 2.47; 11.24 **5.15** Mt 9.21; 14.36; Acts 19.12 2 **5.17** Acts 15.5; 4.1 **5.18** Acts 4.3 **5.19** Acts 12.7; 16.26 **5.20** Jn 6.63,68 **5.21** Acts 4.5,6; vv. 27,34,41 **5.24** Acts 4.1 **5.26** Acts 4.21 **5.28** Acts 4.18; 2.33,36; 3.15; 7.52; Mt 23.35; 27.25 **5.29** Acts 4.19 **5.30** Acts 3.13, 15; 22.14; 10.39; 13.29; Gal 3.13; 1 Pet 2.24 **5.31** Acts 2.33; Heb 2.10; Acts 3.15

k Gk *to men* l Meaning of Gk uncertain
m Other ancient authorities read *Did we not give you strict orders not to teach in this name?*
n Gk *than men*

15 And all who sat in the council
looked intently at him, and they
saw that his face was like the face
of an angel.

Stephen's Speech to the Council

7 Then the high priest asked
him, "Are these things so?"
2 And Stephen replied:
"Brothers[v] and fathers, listen to
me. The God of glory appeared to
our ancestor Abraham when he was
in Mesopotamia, before he lived in
Haran, 3 and said to him, 'Leave
your country and your relatives and
go to the land that I will show you.'
4 Then he left the country of the
Chaldeans and settled in Haran.
After his father died, God had him
move from there to this country in
which you are now living. 5 He did
not give him any of it as a heritage,
not even a foot's length, but promised to give it to him as his possession and to his descendants after
him, even though he had no child.
6 And God spoke in these terms,
that his descendants would be resident aliens in a country belonging
to others, who would enslave them
and mistreat them during four hundred years. 7 'But I will judge the
nation that they serve,' said God,
'and after that they shall come out
and worship me in this place.'
8 Then he gave him the covenant of
circumcision. And so Abraham[w]
became the father of Isaac and circumcised him on the eighth day;
and Isaac became the father of Jacob, and Jacob of the twelve patriarchs.
9 "The patriarchs, jealous of Joseph, sold him into Egypt; but God
was with him, 10 and rescued him
from all his afflictions, and enabled
him to win favor and to show wisdom when he stood before Pharaoh, king of Egypt, who appointed
him ruler over Egypt and over all
his household. 11 Now there came a
famine throughout Egypt and Canaan, and great suffering, and our
ancestors could find no food. 12 But
when Jacob heard that there was
grain in Egypt, he sent our ancestors there on their first visit. 13 On
the second visit Joseph made himself known to his brothers, and Joseph's family became known to
Pharaoh. 14 Then Joseph sent and
invited his father Jacob and all his
relatives to come to him, seventy-
five in all; 15 so Jacob went down to
Egypt. He himself died there as
well as our ancestors, 16 and their
bodies[x] were brought back to Shechem and laid in the tomb that
Abraham had bought for a sum of
silver from the sons of Hamor in
Shechem.
17 "But as the time drew near
for the fulfillment of the promise
that God had made to Abraham,
our people in Egypt increased and
multiplied 18 until another king
who had not known Joseph ruled
over Egypt. 19 He dealt craftily with
our race and forced our ancestors
to abandon their infants so that
they would die. 20 At this time Moses was born, and he was beautiful
before God. For three months he
was brought up in his father's
house; 21 and when he was abandoned, Pharaoh's daughter adopted him and brought him up as her
own son. 22 So Moses was instructed in all the wisdom of the Egyptians and was powerful in his words
and deeds.
23 "When he was forty years old,
it came into his heart to visit his
relatives, the Israelites.[y] 24 When
he saw one of them being wronged,
he defended the oppressed man
and avenged him by striking down
the Egyptian. 25 He supposed that
his kinsfolk would understand that
God through him was rescuing
them, but they did not understand.
26 The next day he came to some of
them as they were quarreling and
tried to reconcile them, saying,
'Men, you are brothers; why do you
wrong each other?' 27 But the man
who was wronging his neighbor
pushed Moses[z] aside, saying,
'Who made you a ruler and a judge
over us? 28 Do you want to kill me
as you killed the Egyptian yester-

7.2 Acts 22.1; Ps 29.3; Gen 11.31; 15.7
7.3 Gen 12.1
7.4 Gen 12.5
7.5 Gen 12.7; 17.8; 26.3
7.6 Gen 15.13, 14; Ex 12.40
7.7 Ex 3.12
7.8 Gen 17.9-11; 21.2-4; 25.26; 29.31ff
7.9 Gen 37.4, 11,28; 39.2, 21,23
7.10 Gen 41.37; 42.6
7.11 Gen 41.54
7.12 Gen 42.1,2
7.13 Gen 45.1-4
7.14 Gen 45.9, 10; 46.26,27; Deut 10.22
7.15 Gen 46.5; 49.33; Ex 1.6
7.16 Gen 23.16; 33.19; Josh 24.32
7.17 Ex 1.7-9; Ps 105.24, 25
7.19 Ex 1.10,11, 15-22
7.22 1 Kings 4.30; Isa 19.11
7.23 Ex 2.11,12

[v] Gk *Men, brothers* [w] Gk *he*
[x] Gk *they* [y] Gk *his brothers, the sons of Israel* [z] Gk *him*

day?' 29 When he heard this, Moses
fled and became a resident alien in
the land of Midian. There he became the father of two sons.
30 "Now when forty years had
passed, an angel appeared to him
in the wilderness of Mount Sinai,
in the flame of a burning bush.
31 When Moses saw it, he was
amazed at the sight; and as he approached to look, there came the
voice of the Lord: 32 'I am the God
of your ancestors, the God of Abraham, Isaac, and Jacob.' Moses began to tremble and did not dare to
look. 33 Then the Lord said to him,
'Take off the sandals from your
feet, for the place where you are
standing is holy ground. 34 I have
surely seen the mistreatment of my
people who are in Egypt and have
heard their groaning, and I have
come down to rescue them. Come
now, I will send you to Egypt.'
35 "It was this Moses whom
they rejected when they said, 'Who
made you a ruler and a judge?' and
whom God now sent as both ruler
and liberator through the angel
who appeared to him in the bush.
36 He led them out, having performed wonders and signs in
Egypt, at the Red Sea, and in the
wilderness for forty years. 37 This is
the Moses who said to the Israelites, 'God will raise up a prophet
for you from your own people[a] as
he raised me up.' 38 He is the one
who was in the congregation in the
wilderness with the angel who
spoke to him at Mount Sinai, and
with our ancestors; and he received
living oracles to give to us. 39 Our
ancestors were unwilling to obey
him; instead, they pushed him
aside, and in their hearts they
turned back to Egypt, 40 saying to
Aaron, 'Make gods for us who will
lead the way for us; as for this Moses who led us out from the land of
Egypt, we do not know what has
happened to him.' 41 At that time
they made a calf, offered a sacrifice
to the idol, and reveled in the
works of their hands. 42 But God
turned away from them and handed them over to worship the host of
heaven, as it is written in the book
of the prophets:

'Did you offer to me slain
victims and sacrifices
forty years in the
wilderness, O house of
Israel?
43 No; you took along the tent
of Moloch,
and the star of your god
Rephan,
the images that you made
to worship;
so I will remove you beyond
Babylon.'

44 "Our ancestors had the tent
of testimony in the wilderness, as
God[b] directed when he spoke to
Moses, ordering him to make it according to the pattern he had seen.
45 Our ancestors in turn brought it
in with Joshua when they dispossessed the nations that God drove
out before our ancestors. And it
was there until the time of David,
46 who found favor with God and
asked that he might find a dwelling
place for the house of Jacob.[c]
47 But it was Solomon who built a
house for him. 48 Yet the Most High
does not dwell in houses made
with human hands;[d] as the prophet says,

49 'Heaven is my throne,
and the earth is my
footstool.
What kind of house will you
build for me, says the
Lord,
or what is the place of my
rest?
50 Did not my hand make all
these things?'

51 "You stiff-necked people,
uncircumcised in heart and ears,
you are forever opposing the Holy
Spirit, just as your ancestors used
to do. 52 Which of the prophets did
your ancestors not persecute? They
killed those who foretold the coming of the Righteous One, and now
you have become his betrayers and
murderers. 53 You are the ones that

7.30 Ex 3.1,2 **7.32** Ex 3.6 **7.33** Ex 3.5; Josh 5.15 **7.34** Ex 3.7 **7.35** Ex 14.19 **7.36** Ex 12.41; 14.21 **7.37** Deut 18.15, 18; Acts 3.22 **7.38** Ex 19.17; Isa 63.9; Rom 3.2; Heb 5.12; 1 Pet 4.11 **7.40** Ex 32.1,23 **7.41** Ex 32.4,6; Ps 106.19 **7.42** Ezek 20.25, 39; Am 5.25,26 **7.44** Ex 25.9,40 **7.45** Josh 3.14-17; Ps 44.2 **7.46** 2 Sam 7.8-16; Ps 132.1-5 **7.48** 1 Kings 8.27; 2 Chr 2.6 **7.49** Isa 66.1,2; Mt 5.34,35 **7.51** Lev 26.41; Jer 6.10; 9.26 **7.52** 2 Chr 36.16; Mt 23.31, 37; Acts 3.14 **7.53** Ex 20.1; Heb 2.2

[a] Gk *your brothers* [b] Gk *he* [c] Other ancient authorities read *for the God of Jacob* [d] Gk *with hands*

received the law as ordained by angels, and yet you have not kept it."

The Stoning of Stephen

54 When they heard these
things, they became enraged and
ground their teeth at Stephen.[e]
55 But filled with the Holy Spirit, he
gazed into heaven and saw the glory of God and Jesus standing at the
right hand of God. 56 "Look," he
said, "I see the heavens opened
and the Son of Man standing at the
right hand of God!" 57 But they covered their ears, and with a loud
shout all rushed together against
him. 58 Then they dragged him out
of the city and began to stone him;
and the witnesses laid their coats
at the feet of a young man named
Saul. 59 While they were stoning
Stephen, he prayed, "Lord Jesus,
receive my spirit." 60 Then he knelt
down and cried out in a loud voice,
"Lord, do not hold this sin against
them." When he had said this, he
8 died.[f] 1 And Saul approved of
their killing him.

Saul Persecutes the Church

That day a severe persecution
began against the church in Jerusalem, and all except the apostles
were scattered throughout the
countryside of Judea and Samaria.
2 Devout men buried Stephen and
made loud lamentation over him.
3 But Saul was ravaging the church
by entering house after house;
dragging off both men and women,
he committed them to prison.

Philip Preaches in Samaria

4 Now those who were scattered
went from place to place, proclaiming the word. 5 Philip went down to
the city[g] of Samaria and proclaimed the Messiah[h] to them.
6 The crowds with one accord listened eagerly to what was said by
Philip, hearing and seeing the signs
that he did, 7 for unclean spirits,
crying with loud shrieks, came out
of many who were possessed; and
many others who were paralyzed or
lame were cured. 8 So there was
great joy in that city.
9 Now a certain man named Simon had previously practiced magic in the city and amazed the people of Samaria, saying that he was
someone great. 10 All of them, from
the least to the greatest, listened to
him eagerly, saying, "This man is
the power of God that is called
Great." 11 And they listened eagerly
to him because for a long time he
had amazed them with his magic.
12 But when they believed Philip,
who was proclaiming the good
news about the kingdom of God
and the name of Jesus Christ, they
were baptized, both men and wom-
en. 13 Even Simon himself believed.
After being baptized, he stayed
constantly with Philip and was
amazed when he saw the signs and
great miracles that took place.
14 Now when the apostles at Jerusalem heard that Samaria had
accepted the word of God, they
sent Peter and John to them. 15 The
two went down and prayed for
them that they might receive the
Holy Spirit 16 (for as yet the Spirit
had not come[i] upon any of them;
they had only been baptized in the
name of the Lord Jesus). 17 Then
Peter and John[j] laid their hands
on them, and they received the
Holy Spirit. 18 Now when Simon
saw that the Spirit was given
through the laying on of the apostles' hands, he offered them money, 19 saying, "Give me also this
power so that anyone on whom I
lay my hands may receive the Holy
Spirit." 20 But Peter said to him,
"May your silver perish with you,
because you thought you could obtain God's gift with money! 21 You
have no part or share in this, for
your heart is not right before God.
22 Repent therefore of this wickedness of yours, and pray to the Lord
that, if possible, the intent of your
heart may be forgiven you. 23 For I
see that you are in the gall of bitterness and the chains of wickedness." 24 Simon answered, "Pray for
me to the Lord, that nothing of

7.55 Acts 6.5
7.56 Mt 3.16; Dan 7.13
7.58 Lk 4.29; Lev 24.16; Deut 13.9, 10
7.59 Acts 9.14
7.60 Acts 9.40
8.1 Acts 7.58; 11.19
8.2 Gen 23.2; 50.10; 2 Sam 3.31
8.3 Acts 7.58; 22.4; 25.10, 11; 1 Cor 15.9; Gal 1.13; Phil 3.6; 1 Tim 1.13
8.4 v. 1; Acts 15.35
8.5 Acts 6.5
8.7 Mt 4.24
8.9 Acts 13.6; 5.36
8.10 Acts 14.11; 28.6
8.12 Acts 1.3; 2.38
8.13 v. 6; Acts 19.11
8.14 v. 1
8.15 Acts 2.38
8.16 Acts 19.2; Mt 28.19; Acts 10.48; 19.5
8.17 Acts 6.6; 2.4
8.20 Acts 2.38; Mt 10.8; 2 Kings 5.16
8.21 Ps 78.37
8.23 Isa 58.6; Heb 12.15

[e] Gk *him* [f] Gk *fell asleep* [g] Other ancient authorities read *a city* [h] Or *the Christ* [i] Gk *fallen* [j] Gk *they*

what you[k] have said may happen
to me."
25 Now after Peter and John[l]
had testified and spoken the word
of the Lord, they returned to Jerusalem, proclaiming the good news
to many villages of the Samaritans.

Philip and the Ethiopian Eunuch

26 Then an angel of the Lord
said to Philip, "Get up and go toward the south[m] to the road that
goes down from Jerusalem to
Gaza." (This is a wilderness road.)
27 So he got up and went. Now there
was an Ethiopian eunuch, a court
official of the Candace, queen of
the Ethiopians, in charge of her entire treasury. He had come to Jerusalem to worship 28 and was returning home; seated in his chariot, he
was reading the prophet Isaiah.
29 Then the Spirit said to Philip,
"Go over to this chariot and join
it." 30 So Philip ran up to it and
heard him reading the prophet Isaiah. He asked, "Do you understand
what you are reading?" 31 He replied, "How can I, unless someone
guides me?" And he invited Philip
to get in and sit beside him. 32 Now
the passage of the scripture that he
was reading was this:

"Like a sheep he was led to
the slaughter,
and like a lamb silent
before its shearer,
so he does not open his
mouth.
33 In his humiliation justice
was denied him.
Who can describe his
generation?
For his life is taken away
from the earth."

34 The eunuch asked Philip, "About
whom, may I ask you, does the
prophet say this, about himself or
about someone else?" 35 Then Philip began to speak, and starting with
this scripture, he proclaimed to
him the good news about Jesus.
36 As they were going along the
road, they came to some water; and
the eunuch said, "Look, here is water! What is to prevent me from being baptized?"[n] 38 He commanded
the chariot to stop, and both of
them, Philip and the eunuch, went
down into the water, and Philip[o]
baptized him. 39 When they came
up out of the water, the Spirit of the
Lord snatched Philip away; the eunuch saw him no more, and went
on his way rejoicing. 40 But Philip
found himself at Azotus, and as he
was passing through the region, he
proclaimed the good news to all
the towns until he came to Caesarea.

The Conversion of Saul

9 Meanwhile Saul, still breathing threats and murder against
the disciples of the Lord, went to
the high priest 2 and asked him for
letters to the synagogues at Damascus, so that if he found any
who belonged to the Way, men or
women, he might bring them
bound to Jerusalem. 3 Now as he
was going along and approaching
Damascus, suddenly a light from
heaven flashed around him. 4 He
fell to the ground and heard a voice
saying to him, "Saul, Saul, why do
you persecute me?" 5 He asked,
"Who are you, Lord?" The reply
came, "I am Jesus, whom you are
persecuting. 6 But get up and enter
the city, and you will be told what
you are to do." 7 The men who were
traveling with him stood speechless because they heard the voice
but saw no one. 8 Saul got up from
the ground, and though his eyes
were open, he could see nothing;
so they led him by the hand and
brought him into Damascus. 9 For
three days he was without sight,
and neither ate nor drank.
10 Now there was a disciple in
Damascus named Ananias. The
Lord said to him in a vision, "Ananias." He answered, "Here I am,
Lord." 11 The Lord said to him,

8.25 Lk 16.28; v. 40
8.26 Acts 5.19; v. 5
8.27 Ps 68.31; Zeph 3.10; Jn 12.20
8.29 Acts 10.19; 11.12; 13.2; 20.23; 21.11
8.32 Isa 53.7,8
8.35 Mt 5.2; Lk 24.27; Acts 17.2; 18.28; 5.42
8.36 Acts 10.47
8.39 1 Kings 18.12; 2 Kings 2.16; Ezek 3.12, 14
9.1 Acts 8.3; 22.4-16; 26.9-18
9.3 Acts 22.6; 26.12; 1 Cor 15.8
9.4 Acts 22.7; 26.14
9.7 Acts 22.9; 26.13,14
9.8 Acts 22.11; Gal 1.17
9.10 Acts 22.12
9.11 Acts 21.39; 22.3

[k] The Greek word for *you* and the verb *pray* are plural [l] Gk *after they* [m] Or *go at noon* [n] Other ancient authorities add all or most of verse 37, *And Philip said, "If you believe with all your heart, you may." And he replied, "I believe that Jesus Christ is the Son of God."* [o] Gk *he*

"Get up and go to the street called
Straight, and at the house of Judas
look for a man of Tarsus named
Saul. At this moment he is praying,
12 and he has seen in a vision[p] a
man named Ananias come in and
lay his hands on him so that he
might regain his sight." 13 But Ananias answered, "Lord, I have heard
from many about this man, how
much evil he has done to your
saints in Jerusalem; 14 and here he
has authority from the chief priests
to bind all who invoke your name."
15 But the Lord said to him, "Go, for
he is an instrument whom I have
chosen to bring my name before
Gentiles and kings and before the
people of Israel; 16 I myself will
show him how much he must suffer
for the sake of my name." 17 So Ananias went and entered the house.
He laid his hands on Saul[q] and
said, "Brother Saul, the Lord Jesus,
who appeared to you on your way
here, has sent me so that you may
regain your sight and be filled with
the Holy Spirit." 18 And immediately something like scales fell from
his eyes, and his sight was restored.
Then he got up and was baptized,
19 and after taking some food, he regained his strength.

Saul Preaches in Damascus

For several days he was with the
disciples in Damascus, 20 and immediately he began to proclaim
Jesus in the synagogues, saying,
"He is the Son of God." 21 All who
heard him were amazed and said,
"Is not this the man who made hav-
oc in Jerusalem among those who
invoked this name? And has he not
come here for the purpose of bringing them bound before the chief
priests?" 22 Saul became increas-
ingly more powerful and confounded the Jews who lived in Damascus
by proving that Jesus[r] was the
Messiah.[s]

Saul Escapes from the Jews

23 After some time had passed,
the Jews plotted to kill him, 24 but
their plot became known to Saul.
They were watching the gates day
and night so that they might kill
him; 25 but his disciples took him
by night and let him down through
an opening in the wall,[t] lowering
him in a basket.

Saul in Jerusalem

26 When he had come to Jerusalem, he attempted to join the
disciples; and they were all afraid
of him, for they did not believe that
he was a disciple. 27 But Barnabas
took him, brought him to the apostles, and described for them how
on the road he had seen the Lord,
who had spoken to him, and how in
Damascus he had spoken boldly in
the name of Jesus. 28 So he went in
and out among them in Jerusalem,
speaking boldly in the name of the
Lord. 29 He spoke and argued with
the Hellenists; but they were attempting to kill him. 30 When the
believers[u] learned of it, they
brought him down to Caesarea and
sent him off to Tarsus.

31 Meanwhile the church
throughout Judea, Galilee, and Samaria had peace and was built up.
Living in the fear of the Lord and in
the comfort of the Holy Spirit, it increased in numbers.

The Healing of Aeneas

32 Now as Peter went here and
there among all the believers,[v] he
came down also to the saints living
in Lydda. 33 There he found a man
named Aeneas, who had been bedridden for eight years, for he was
paralyzed. 34 Peter said to him, "Aeneas, Jesus Christ heals you; get up
and make your bed!" And immediately he got up. 35 And all the residents of Lydda and Sharon saw him
and turned to the Lord.

Peter in Lydda and Joppa

36 Now in Joppa there was a
disciple whose name was Tabitha,
which in Greek is Dorcas.[w] She
was devoted to good works and acts

9.14 v. 21; Acts 7.59; 1 Cor 1.2; 2 Tim 2.22
9.15 Acts 13.2; Eph 3.7,8; Gal 2.7,8; Acts 25.22, 23; 26.1
9.16 Acts 20.23; 21.11; 2 Cor 11.23
9.17 Acts 22.12, 13; 8.17; 2.4; 4.31
9.19 Acts 26.20
9.21 Acts 8.3; Gal 1.13,23
9.22 Acts 18.28
9.23 Acts 23.12; 25.3
9.24 2 Cor 11.32, 33
9.26 Acts 22.17; Gal 1.17,18
9.27 Acts 4.36; vv. 20,22
9.29 Acts 6.1; 11.20; 2 Cor 11.26
9.31 Acts 8.1
9.32 v. 13
9.34 Acts 3.6,16; 4.10
9.35 1 Chr 5.16; Acts 11.21
9.36 Jn 1.3; 1 Tim 2.10; Titus 3.8

[p] Other ancient authorities lack *in a vision*
[q] Gk *him* [r] Gk *that this* [s] Or *the Christ* [t] Gk *through the wall*
[u] Gk *brothers* [v] Gk *all of them*
[w] The name Tabitha in Aramaic and the name Dorcas in Greek mean *a gazelle*

of charity. [37]At that time she became ill and died. When they had
washed her, they laid her in a room
upstairs. [38]Since Lydda was near
Joppa, the disciples, who heard
that Peter was there, sent two men
to him with the request, "Please
come to us without delay." [39]So
Peter got up and went with them;
and when he arrived, they took him
to the room upstairs. All the widows stood beside him, weeping and
showing tunics and other clothing
that Dorcas had made while she
was with them. [40]Peter put all of
them outside, and then he knelt
down and prayed. He turned to the
body and said, "Tabitha, get up."
Then she opened her eyes, and seeing Peter, she sat up. [41]He gave her
his hand and helped her up. Then
calling the saints and widows, he
showed her to be alive. [42]This became known throughout Joppa,
and many believed in the Lord.
[43]Meanwhile he stayed in Joppa
for some time with a certain Simon, a tanner.

Peter and Cornelius

10 In Caesarea there was a
man named Cornelius, a
centurion of the Italian Cohort, as
it was called. [2]He was a devout
man who feared God with all his
household; he gave alms generously to the people and prayed constantly to God. [3]One afternoon at
about three o'clock he had a vision
in which he clearly saw an angel of
God coming in and saying to him,
"Cornelius." [4]He stared at him in
terror and said, "What is it, Lord?"
He answered, "Your prayers and
your alms have ascended as a memorial before God. [5]Now send men
to Joppa for a certain Simon who is
called Peter; [6]he is lodging with Simon, a tanner, whose house is by
the seaside." [7]When the angel who
spoke to him had left, he called two
of his slaves and a devout soldier
from the ranks of those who served
him, [8]and after telling them everything, he sent them to Joppa.

9 About noon the next day, as
they were on their journey and approaching the city, Peter went up
on the roof to pray. [10]He became
hungry and wanted something to
eat; and while it was being prepared, he fell into a trance. [11]He
saw the heaven opened and something like a large sheet coming
down, being lowered to the ground
by its four corners. [12]In it were all
kinds of four-footed creatures and
reptiles and birds of the air. [13]Then
he heard a voice saying, "Get up,
Peter; kill and eat." [14]But Peter
said, "By no means, Lord; for I have
never eaten anything that is profane or unclean." [15]The voice said
to him again, a second time, "What
God has made clean, you must not
call profane." [16]This happened
three times, and the thing was suddenly taken up to heaven.

17 Now while Peter was greatly
puzzled about what to make of the
vision that he had seen, suddenly
the men sent by Cornelius appeared. They were asking for Simon's house and were standing by
the gate. [18]They called out to ask
whether Simon, who was called Peter, was staying there. [19]While Peter was still thinking about the vision, the Spirit said to him, "Look,
three[x] men are searching for you.
[20]Now get up, go down, and go with
them without hesitation; for I have
sent them." [21]So Peter went down
to the men and said, "I am the one
you are looking for; what is the reason for your coming?" [22]They answered, "Cornelius, a centurion, an
upright and God-fearing man, who
is well spoken of by the whole Jewish nation, was directed by a holy
angel to send for you to come to his
house and to hear what you have to
say." [23]So Peter[y] invited them in
and gave them lodging.

The next day he got up and went
with them, and some of the believers[z] from Joppa accompanied
him. [24]The following day they
came to Caesarea. Cornelius was
expecting them and had called together his relatives and close

9.37 Acts 1.13 **9.38** Acts 11.26 **9.39** Acts 6.1 **9.40** Mt 9.25; Acts 7.60; Mk 5.41,42 **9.41** v. 13 **9.43** Acts 10.6 **10.2** vv. 22,35 **10.3** Acts 9.10; 3.1; 5.19 **10.4** Acts 3.4; Rev 8.4; Mt 26.13 **10.6** Acts 9.43 **10.9** Acts 11.5-14; Mt 24.17 **10.10** Acts 22.17 **10.11** Acts 7.56; Rev 19.11 **10.14** Acts 9.5; Lev 11.4; 20.25; Deut 14.3,7; Ezek 4.14 **10.15** v. 28; Mt 15.11; Rom 14.14, 17,20; 1 Cor 10.25; 1 Tim 4.4; Titus 1.15 **10.17** v. 3 **10.19** Acts 11.12 **10.20** Acts 15.7 **10.22** v. 2; Acts 11.14 **10.23** v. 45; Acts 11.12

[x] One ancient authority reads *two*; others lack the word [y] Gk *he* [z] Gk *brothers*

friends. 25 On Peter's arrival Cornelius met him, and falling at his feet, worshiped him. 26 But Peter made him get up, saying, "Stand up; I am only a mortal." 27 And as he talked with him, he went in and found that many had assembled; 28 and he said to them, "You yourselves know that it is unlawful for a Jew to associate with or to visit a Gentile; but God has shown me that I should not call anyone profane or unclean. 29 So when I was sent for, I came without objection. Now may I ask why you sent for me?"

30 Cornelius replied, "Four days ago at this very hour, at three o'clock, I was praying in my house when suddenly a man in dazzling clothes stood before me. 31 He said, 'Cornelius, your prayer has been heard and your alms have been remembered before God. 32 Send therefore to Joppa and ask for Simon, who is called Peter; he is staying in the home of Simon, a tanner, by the sea.' 33 Therefore I sent for you immediately, and you have been kind enough to come. So now all of us are here in the presence of God to listen to all that the Lord has commanded you to say."

Gentiles Hear the Good News

34 Then Peter began to speak to them: "I truly understand that God shows no partiality, 35 but in every nation anyone who fears him and does what is right is acceptable to him. 36 You know the message he sent to the people of Israel, preaching peace by Jesus Christ—he is Lord of all. 37 That message spread throughout Judea, beginning in Galilee after the baptism that John announced: 38 how God anointed Jesus of Nazareth with the Holy Spirit and with power; how he went about doing good and healing all who were oppressed by the devil, for God was with him. 39 We are witnesses to all that he did both in Judea and in Jerusalem. They put him to death by hanging him on a tree; 40 but God raised him on the third day and allowed him to appear, 41 not to all the people but to us who were chosen by God as witnesses, and who ate and drank with him after he rose from the dead. 42 He commanded us to preach to the people and to testify that he is the one ordained by God as judge of the living and the dead. 43 All the prophets testify about him that everyone who believes in him receives forgiveness of sins through his name."

Gentiles Receive the Holy Spirit

44 While Peter was still speaking, the Holy Spirit fell upon all who heard the word. 45 The circumcised believers who had come with Peter were astounded that the gift of the Holy Spirit had been poured out even on the Gentiles, 46 for they heard them speaking in tongues and extolling God. Then Peter said, 47 "Can anyone withhold the water for baptizing these people who have received the Holy Spirit just as we have?" 48 So he ordered them to be baptized in the name of Jesus Christ. Then they invited him to stay for several days.

Peter's Report to the Church at Jerusalem

11 Now the apostles and the believers[a] who were in Judea heard that the Gentiles had also accepted the word of God. 2 So when Peter went up to Jerusalem, the circumcised believers[b] criticized him, 3 saying, "Why did you go to uncircumcised men and eat with them?" 4 Then Peter began to explain it to them, step by step, saying, 5 "I was in the city of Joppa praying, and in a trance I saw a vision. There was something like a large sheet coming down from heaven, being lowered by its four corners; and it came close to me. 6 As I looked at it closely I saw four-footed animals, beasts of prey, reptiles, and birds of the air. 7 I also heard a voice saying to me, 'Get up, Peter; kill and eat.' 8 But I replied, 'By no means, Lord; for nothing profane or unclean has ever en-

10.26 Acts 24.14, 15; Rev 19.10
10.28 Jn 4.9; 18.28; Acts 11.3; 15.8,9
10.30 Acts 1.10; Mt 28.3; Mk 16.5; Lk 24.4
10.34 Deut 10.17; Rom 2.11; Eph 6.9; Col 3.25; 1 Pet 1.17
10.35 Acts 15.9
10.36 Isa 57.19; Mt 28.18; Rom 10.12; Eph 1.20,22
10.38 Acts 2.22; Jn 3.2
10.39 Lk 24.48; Acts 5.30
10.40 Acts 2.24
10.41 Jn 14.17,22; 21.13
10.42 Mt 28.19, 20; Rom 14.9; 2 Cor 5.10; 1 Pet 4.5
10.43 Isa 53.11; Acts 26.22; 15.9; Rom 10.11; Gal 3.22
10.44 Acts 4.31; 8.15,16; 11.15; 15.8
10.45 v. 23; Acts 11.18
10.47 Acts 8.36; 11.17
10.48 1 Cor 1.17; Acts 2.38; 8.16; 19.5
11.2 Acts 10.45
11.3 Acts 10.28; Gal 2.12
11.4 Lk 1.3
11.5 Acts 10.9-32

[a] Gk *brothers* [b] Gk lacks *believers*

tered my mouth.' 9 But a second
time the voice answered from heav-
en, 'What God has made clean, you
must not call profane.' 10 This happened three times; then everything
was pulled up again to heaven. 11 At
that very moment three men, sent
to me from Caesarea, arrived at the
house where we were. 12 The Spirit
told me to go with them and not to
make a distinction between them
and us.[c] These six brothers also
accompanied me, and we entered
the man's house. 13 He told us how
he had seen the angel standing in
his house and saying, 'Send to Joppa and bring Simon, who is called
Peter; 14 he will give you a message
by which you and your entire
household will be saved.' 15 And as
I began to speak, the Holy Spirit
fell upon them just as it had upon
us at the beginning. 16 And I remembered the word of the Lord,
how he had said, 'John baptized
with water, but you will be baptized with the Holy Spirit.' 17 If then
God gave them the same gift that
he gave us when we believed in the
Lord Jesus Christ, who was I that I
could hinder God?" 18 When they
heard this, they were silenced. And
they praised God, saying, "Then
God has given even to the Gentiles
the repentance that leads to life."

The Church in Antioch

19 Now those who were scattered because of the persecution
that took place over Stephen traveled as far as Phoenicia, Cyprus,
and Antioch, and they spoke the
word to no one except Jews. 20 But
among them were some men of Cyprus and Cyrene who, on coming to
Antioch, spoke to the Hellenists[d]
also, proclaiming the Lord Jesus.
21 The hand of the Lord was with
them, and a great number became
believers and turned to the Lord.
22 News of this came to the ears of
the church in Jerusalem, and they
sent Barnabas to Antioch. 23 When
he came and saw the grace of God,
he rejoiced, and he exhorted them
all to remain faithful to the Lord
with steadfast devotion; 24 for he
was a good man, full of the Holy
Spirit and of faith. And a great
many people were brought to the
Lord. 25 Then Barnabas went to
Tarsus to look for Saul, 26 and when
he had found him, he brought him
to Antioch. So it was that for an entire year they met with[e] the church
and taught a great many people,
and it was in Antioch that the disciples were first called "Christians."

27 At that time prophets came
down from Jerusalem to Antioch.
28 One of them named Agabus
stood up and predicted by the Spirit that there would be a severe famine over all the world; and this took
place during the reign of Claudius.
29 The disciples determined that
according to their ability, each
would send relief to the believers[f]
living in Judea; 30 this they did,
sending it to the elders by Barnabas and Saul.

James Killed and Peter Imprisoned

12 About that time King Herod laid violent hands upon
some who belonged to the church.
2 He had James, the brother of
John, killed with the sword. 3 After
he saw that it pleased the Jews, he
proceeded to arrest Peter also.
(This was during the festival of Unleavened Bread.) 4 When he had
seized him, he put him in prison
and handed him over to four
squads of soldiers to guard him, intending to bring him out to the
people after the Passover. 5 While
Peter was kept in prison, the
church prayed fervently to God for
him.

Peter Delivered from Prison

6 The very night before Herod
was going to bring him out, Peter,
bound with two chains, was sleeping between two soldiers, while
guards in front of the door were
keeping watch over the prison.
7 Suddenly an angel of the Lord ap-

11.9 Acts 10.15
11.12 Acts 8.29; 15.9; 10.23
11.13 Acts 10.30
11.15 Acts 10.44; 2.4
11.16 Mt 3.11; Jn 1.26,33; Acts 1.5; Joel 2.28; 3.18
11.17 Acts 10.45, 47
11.18 Rom 10.12, 13; 2 Cor 7.10
11.19 Acts 8.1,4
11.20 Acts 4.36; 6.5; 13.1; 5.42
11.21 Lk 1.66; Acts 2.47; 9.35
11.23 Acts 13.43; 14.22
11.24 Acts 6.5; v. 21; Acts 5.14
11.25 Acts 9.11,30
11.26 Acts 26.28
11.27 Acts 18.22; 1 Cor 12.28
11.28 Acts 21.10
11.29 Rom 15.26; 1 Cor 16.1; 2 Cor 9.1
11.30 Acts 12.25; 14.23
12.2 Mt 4.21; 20.23
12.3 Acts 24.27; Ex 12.15; 23.15
12.5 Eph 6.18; 1 Thes 5.17
12.6 Acts 21.33
12.7 Acts 5.19; 16.26

[c] Or *not to hesitate* [d] Other ancient authorities read *Greeks* [e] Or *were guests of* [f] Gk *brothers*

peared and a light shone in the cell.
He tapped Peter on the side and
woke him, saying, "Get up quickly." And the chains fell off his
wrists. 8 The angel said to him,
"Fasten your belt and put on your
sandals." He did so. Then he said
to him, "Wrap your cloak around
you and follow me." 9 Peter[g] went
out and followed him; he did not
realize that what was happening
with the angel's help was real; he
thought he was seeing a vision.
10 After they had passed the first
and the second guard, they came
before the iron gate leading into
the city. It opened for them of its
own accord, and they went outside
and walked along a lane, when suddenly the angel left him. 11 Then
Peter came to himself and said,
"Now I am sure that the Lord has
sent his angel and rescued me from
the hands of Herod and from all
that the Jewish people were expecting."

12 As soon as he realized this,
he went to the house of Mary, the
mother of John whose other name
was Mark, where many had gathered and were praying. 13 When he
knocked at the outer gate, a maid
named Rhoda came to answer.
14 On recognizing Peter's voice, she
was so overjoyed that, instead of
opening the gate, she ran in and
announced that Peter was standing
at the gate. 15 They said to her,
"You are out of your mind!" But she
insisted that it was so. They said,
"It is his angel." 16 Meanwhile Peter continued knocking; and when
they opened the gate, they saw him
and were amazed. 17 He motioned
to them with his hand to be silent,
and described for them how the
Lord had brought him out of the
prison. And he added, "Tell this to
James and to the believers."[h]
Then he left and went to another
place.

18 When morning came, there
was no small commotion among
the soldiers over what had become
of Peter. 19 When Herod had
searched for him and could not
find him, he examined the guards
and ordered them to be put to
death. Then Peter[i] went down
from Judea to Caesarea and stayed
there.

The Death of Herod

20 Now Herod was angry with
the people of Tyre and Sidon. So
they came to him in a body; and
after winning over Blastus, the
king's chamberlain, they asked for
a reconciliation, because their
country depended on the king's
country for food. 21 On an appointed day Herod put on his royal
robes, took his seat on the platform, and delivered a public address to them. 22 The people kept
shouting, "The voice of a god, and
not of a mortal!" 23 And immediately, because he had not given the
glory to God, an angel of the Lord
struck him down, and he was eaten
by worms and died.

24 But the word of God continued to advance and gain adherents.
25 Then after completing their mission Barnabas and Saul returned
to[j] Jerusalem and brought with
them John, whose other name was
Mark.

Barnabas and Saul Commissioned

13 Now in the church at Antioch there were prophets
and teachers: Barnabas, Simeon
who was called Niger, Lucius of Cyrene, Manaen a member of the
court of Herod the ruler,[k] and
Saul. 2 While they were worshiping
the Lord and fasting, the Holy Spirit said, "Set apart for me Barnabas
and Saul for the work to which I
have called them." 3 Then after
fasting and praying they laid their
hands on them and sent them off.

The Apostles Preach in Cyprus

4 So, being sent out by the Holy
Spirit, they went down to Seleucia;
and from there they sailed to Cyprus. 5 When they arrived at Sala-
mis, they proclaimed the word of

12.9 Acts 9.10
12.10 Acts 16.26
12.11 Lk 15.17; Dan 3.28; 6.22; 2 Cor 1.10; 2 Pet 2.9
12.12 Acts 15.37; v. 5
12.13 Jn 18.16,17
12.14 Lk 24.41
12.15 Gen 48.16; Mt 18.10
12.17 Acts 13.16; 19.33; 21.40
12.19 Acts 16.27; 27.42
12.20 Mt 11.21; 1 Kings 5.9, 11; Ezek 27.17
12.23 1 Sam 25.38; 2 Sam 24.17
12.24 Acts 6.7; 19.20
12.25 Acts 13.5, 13; 15.37
13.1 Acts 11.22-26
13.2 Acts 9.15; 22.21; 14.26
13.3 Acts 6.65; 14.26
13.4 vv. 2,3; Acts 4.36
13.5 Acts 9.20

[g] Gk *He* [h] Gk *brothers* [i] Gk *he*
[j] Other ancient authorities read *from*
[k] Gk *tetrarch*

God in the synagogues of the Jews.
And they had John also to assist
them. 6 When they had gone
through the whole island as far as
Paphos, they met a certain magician, a Jewish false prophet,
named Bar-Jesus. 7 He was with the
proconsul, Sergius Paulus, an intelligent man, who summoned Barnabas and Saul and wanted to hear
the word of God. 8 But the magician
Elymas (for that is the translation
of his name) opposed them and
tried to turn the proconsul away
from the faith. 9 But Saul, also
known as Paul, filled with the Holy
Spirit, looked intently at him 10 and
said, "You son of the devil, you enemy of all righteousness, full of all
deceit and villainy, will you not
stop making crooked the straight
paths of the Lord? 11 And now
listen—the hand of the Lord is
against you, and you will be blind
for a while, unable to see the sun."
Immediately mist and darkness
came over him, and he went about
groping for someone to lead him by
the hand. 12 When the proconsul
saw what had happened, he believed, for he was astonished at the
teaching about the Lord.

Paul and Barnabas in Antioch of Pisidia

13 Then Paul and his companions set sail from Paphos and came
to Perga in Pamphylia. John, however, left them and returned to Jerusalem; 14 but they went on from
Perga and came to Antioch in Pi-
sidia. And on the sabbath day they
went into the synagogue and sat
down. 15 After the reading of the
law and the prophets, the officials
of the synagogue sent them a message, saying, "Brothers, if you have
any word of exhortation for the
people, give it." 16 So Paul stood up
and with a gesture began to speak:

"You Israelites,[l] and others who
fear God, listen. 17 The God of this
people Israel chose our ancestors
and made the people great during
their stay in the land of Egypt, and
with uplifted arm he led them out
of it. 18 For about forty years he put
up with[m] them in the wilderness.
19 After he had destroyed seven nations in the land of Canaan, he gave
them their land as an inheritance
20 for about four hundred fifty
years. After that he gave them
judges until the time of the prophet
Samuel. 21 Then they asked for a
king; and God gave them Saul son
of Kish, a man of the tribe of Benjamin, who reigned for forty years.
22 When he had removed him, he
made David their king. In his testimony about him he said, 'I have
found David, son of Jesse, to be a
man after my heart, who will carry
out all my wishes.' 23 Of this man's
posterity God has brought to Israel
a Savior, Jesus, as he promised;
24 before his coming John had already proclaimed a baptism of repentance to all the people of Israel.
25 And as John was finishing his
work, he said, 'What do you suppose that I am? I am not he. No, but
one is coming after me; I am not
worthy to untie the thong of the
sandals[n] on his feet.'

26 "My brothers, you descendants of Abraham's family, and
others who fear God, to us[o] the
message of this salvation has been
sent. 27 Because the residents of Jerusalem and their leaders did not
recognize him or understand the
words of the prophets that are read
every sabbath, they fulfilled those
words by condemning him. 28 Even
though they found no cause for a
sentence of death, they asked Pilate to have him killed. 29 When
they had carried out everything
that was written about him, they
took him down from the tree and
laid him in a tomb. 30 But God
raised him from the dead; 31 and for
many days he appeared to those
who came up with him from Galilee to Jerusalem, and they are now
his witnesses to the people. 32 And
we bring you the good news that
what God promised to our ancestors 33 he has fulfilled for us, their

13.6 Acts 8.9
13.7 vv. 8,12
13.8 Acts 8.9; vv. 7,12; Acts 6.7
13.9 Acts 4.8
13.10 Mt 13.38; Jn 8.44; Hos 14.9
13.11 Ex 9.3
13.12 vv. 7,8; Acts 8.25
13.13 Acts 15.38
13.14 Acts 14.19, 21; 16.13
13.17 Deut 7.6-8
13.18 Ex 16.35; Deut 1.31
13.19 Deut 7.1; Josh 19.51
13.20 Judg 2.16; 1 Sam 3.20
13.21 1 Sam 8.5; 10.1
13.22 1 Sam 13.14; 15.23,26
13.23 Isa 11.1; Mt 1.21; Rom 11.26
13.24 Mt 3.1; Lk 3.3
13.25 Mt 3.11; Lk 3.16
13.27 Lk 23.13; Acts 3.17; Lk 24.27
13.28 Mt 27.22
13.29 Lk 18.31; Mt 27.59
13.30 Mt 28.6
13.31 Mt 28.16; Lk 24.48
13.32 Gen 3.15; Rom 4.13
13.33 Ps 2.7

[l] Gk *Men, Israelites* [m] Other ancient authorities read *cared for* [n] Gk *untie the sandals* [o] Other ancient authorities read *you*

children, by raising Jesus; as also it
is written in the second psalm,
'You are my Son;
today I have begotten you.'
34 As to his raising him from the
dead, no more to return to corruption, he has spoken in this way,
'I will give you the holy
promises made to
David.'
35 Therefore he has also said in another psalm,
'You will not let your Holy
One experience
corruption.'
36 For David, after he had served
the purpose of God in his own generation, died,[p] was laid beside his
ancestors, and experienced corruption; 37 but he whom God raised up
experienced no corruption. 38 Let it
be known to you therefore, my
brothers, that through this man
forgiveness of sins is proclaimed to
you; 39 by this Jesus[q] everyone who
believes is set free from all those
sins[r] from which you could not be
freed by the law of Moses. 40 Beware, therefore, that what the
prophets said does not happen to
you:
41 'Look, you scoffers!
Be amazed and perish,
for in your days I am doing a
work,
a work that you will never
believe, even if
someone tells you.' "
42 As Paul and Barnabas[s] were
going out, the people urged them
to speak about these things again
the next sabbath. 43 When the
meeting of the synagogue broke
up, many Jews and devout converts
to Judaism followed Paul and Barnabas, who spoke to them and
urged them to continue in the
grace of God.
44 The next sabbath almost the
whole city gathered to hear the
word of the Lord.[t] 45 But when the
Jews saw the crowds, they were
filled with jealousy; and blaspheming, they contradicted what was
spoken by Paul. 46 Then both Paul
and Barnabas spoke out boldly,
saying, "It was necessary that the

13.34 Isa 55.3
13.35 Ps 16.10; Acts 2.27
13.36 Acts 2.29; 1 Kings 2.10
13.38 Lk 24.47
13.39 Rom 3.28; Acts 10.43
13.40 Jn 6.45
13.41 Hab 1.5
13.42 v. 14
13.43 Acts 11.23; 14.22
13.45 Acts 18.6; 1 Pet 4.4; Jude 10
13.46 v. 26; Acts 3.26; 18.6; 28.28
13.47 Isa 49.6; Lk 2.32
13.48 Acts 2.47; Rom 3.28ff
13.51 Mt 10.14; Mk 6.11; Lk 9.5; Acts 18.6
13.52 Acts 2.4
14.1 Acts 13.51; 13.5; 2.47; 18.4
14.3 Heb 2.4; Jn 4.48
14.4 Acts 17.4,5; v. 14
14.5 2 Tim 3.11
14.6 Mt 10.23

word of God should be spoken first
to you. Since you reject it and judge
yourselves to be unworthy of eternal life, we are now turning to the
Gentiles. 47 For so the Lord has
commanded us, saying,
'I have set you to be a light
for the Gentiles,
so that you may bring
salvation to the ends of
the earth.' "
48 When the Gentiles heard
this, they were glad and praised the
word of the Lord; and as many as
had been destined for eternal life
became believers. 49 Thus the word
of the Lord spread throughout the
region. 50 But the Jews incited the
devout women of high standing
and the leading men of the city,
and stirred up persecution against
Paul and Barnabas, and drove them
out of their region. 51 So they shook
the dust off their feet in protest
against them, and went to Iconium. 52 And the disciples were filled
with joy and with the Holy Spirit.

Paul and Barnabas in Iconium

14 The same thing occurred in
Iconium, where Paul and
Barnabas[s] went into the Jewish
synagogue and spoke in such a way
that a great number of both Jews
and Greeks became believers. 2 But
the unbelieving Jews stirred up the
Gentiles and poisoned their minds
against the brothers. 3 So they remained for a long time, speaking
boldly for the Lord, who testified to
the word of his grace by granting
signs and wonders to be done
through them. 4 But the residents
of the city were divided; some sided with the Jews, and some with
the apostles. 5 And when an attempt was made by both Gentiles
and Jews, with their rulers, to mistreat them and to stone them, 6 the
apostles[s] learned of it and fled to
Lystra and Derbe, cities of Lycao-
nia, and to the surrounding country; 7 and there they continued proclaiming the good news.

[p] Gk *fell asleep* [q] Gk *this* [r] Gk *all*
[s] Gk *they* [t] Other ancient authorities read *God*

Paul and Barnabas in Lystra and Derbe

8 In Lystra there was a man sitting who could not use his feet and
had never walked, for he had been
crippled from birth. 9 He listened to
Paul as he was speaking. And Paul,
looking at him intently and seeing
that he had faith to be healed,
10 said in a loud voice, "Stand upright on your feet." And the man[u]
sprang up and began to walk.
11 When the crowds saw what Paul
had done, they shouted in the Lyc-
aonian language, "The gods have
come down to us in human form!"
12 Barnabas they called Zeus, and
Paul they called Hermes, because
he was the chief speaker. 13 The
priest of Zeus, whose temple was
just outside the city,[v] brought
oxen and garlands to the gates; he
and the crowds wanted to offer sacrifice. 14 When the apostles Barnabas and Paul heard of it, they tore
their clothes and rushed out into
the crowd, shouting, 15 "Friends,[w]
why are you doing this? We are
mortals just like you, and we bring
you good news, that you should
turn from these worthless things to
the living God, who made the heav-
en and the earth and the sea and all
that is in them. 16 In past generations he allowed all the nations to
follow their own ways; 17 yet he has
not left himself without a witness
in doing good—giving you rains
from heaven and fruitful seasons,
and filling you with food and your
hearts with joy." 18 Even with these
words, they scarcely restrained the
crowds from offering sacrifice to
them.
19 But Jews came there from
Antioch and Iconium and won over
the crowds. Then they stoned Paul
and dragged him out of the city,
supposing that he was dead. 20 But
when the disciples surrounded
him, he got up and went into the
city. The next day he went on with
Barnabas to Derbe.

The Return to Antioch in Syria

21 After they had proclaimed
the good news to that city and had
made many disciples, they returned to Lystra, then on to Iconium and Antioch. 22 There they
strengthened the souls of the disciples and encouraged them to continue in the faith, saying, "It is
through many persecutions that we
must enter the kingdom of God."
23 And after they had appointed elders for them in each church, with
prayer and fasting they entrusted
them to the Lord in whom they had
come to believe.
24 Then they passed through Pi-
sidia and came to Pamphylia.
25 When they had spoken the word
in Perga, they went down to Atta-
lia. 26 From there they sailed back
to Antioch, where they had been
commended to the grace of God for
the work[x] that they had completed. 27 When they arrived, they
called the church together and related all that God had done with
them, and how he had opened a
door of faith for the Gentiles.
28 And they stayed there with the
disciples for some time.

The Council at Jerusalem

15 Then certain individuals
came down from Judea and
were teaching the brothers, "Unless you are circumcised according
to the custom of Moses, you cannot
be saved." 2 And after Paul and Barnabas had no small dissension and
debate with them, Paul and Barnabas and some of the others were
appointed to go up to Jerusalem to
discuss this question with the
apostles and the elders. 3 So they
were sent on their way by the
church, and as they passed through
both Phoenicia and Samaria, they
reported the conversion of the
Gentiles, and brought great joy to
all the believers.[y] 4 When they
came to Jerusalem, they were welcomed by the church and the apostles and the elders, and they reported all that God had done with
them. 5 But some believers who be-

14.8 Acts 3.2
14.9 Acts 3.4; 10.4; Mt 9.28,29
14.11 Acts 8.10; 28.6
14.15 Acts 10.26; Jas 5.17; 1 Sam 12.21; Jer 14.22; 1 Cor 8.4; Gen 1.1; Ps 146.6; Rev 14.7
14.16 Ps 81.12; Acts 17.30; 1 Pet 4.3
14.17 Acts 17.27; Rom 1.20; Deut 11.14; Job 5.10; Ps 65.10
14.19 Acts 13.45; 2 Cor 11.25; 2 Tim 3.11
14.20 vv. 22,28
14.22 Acts 11.23; 13.43; Jn 16.33; 1 Thes 3.3; 2 Tim 3.12
14.23 Titus 1.5; Acts 11.30; 13.3; 20.32
14.26 Acts 11.19; 13.1,3; 15.40
14.27 Acts 15.4, 12; 21.19; 1 Cor 16.9; 2 Cor 2.12; Col 4.3
15.1 v. 24; Gal 2.12; v. 5; Gal 5.2; Acts 6.14
15.2 v. 7; Gal 2.2; Acts 11.30
15.3 Acts 20.38; Rom 15.24; 1 Cor 16.6, 11; Acts 14.27
15.4 v. 12; Acts 14.27

[u] Gk *he* [v] Or *The priest of Zeus-Outside-the-City* [w] Gk *Men*
[x] Or *committed in the grace of God to the work* [y] Gk *brothers*

longed to the sect of the Pharisees
stood up and said, "It is necessary
for them to be circumcised and ordered to keep the law of Moses."
6 The apostles and the elders
met together to consider this matter. 7 After there had been much debate, Peter stood up and said to
them, "My brothers,[z] you know
that in the early days God made a
choice among you, that I should be
the one through whom the Gentiles would hear the message of the
good news and become believers.
8 And God, who knows the human
heart, testified to them by giving
them the Holy Spirit, just as he did
to us; 9 and in cleansing their
hearts by faith he has made no distinction between them and us.
10 Now therefore why are you putting God to the test by placing on
the neck of the disciples a yoke
that neither our ancestors nor we
have been able to bear? 11 On the
contrary, we believe that we will be
saved through the grace of the Lord
Jesus, just as they will."
12 The whole assembly kept silence, and listened to Barnabas
and Paul as they told of all the
signs and wonders that God had
done through them among the
Gentiles. 13 After they finished
speaking, James replied, "My
brothers,[z] listen to me. 14 Simeon
has related how God first looked favorably on the Gentiles, to take
from among them a people for his
name. 15 This agrees with the words
of the prophets, as it is written,
16 'After this I will return,
and I will rebuild the
dwelling of David,
which has fallen;
from its ruins I will rebuild
it,
and I will set it up,
17 so that all other peoples may
seek the Lord—
even all the Gentiles over
whom my name has
been called.
Thus says the Lord, who
has been making these
things 18 known from
long ago.'[a]
19 Therefore I have reached the decision that we should not trouble
those Gentiles who are turning to
God, 20 but we should write to them
to abstain only from things polluted by idols and from fornication
and from whatever has been strangled[b] and from blood. 21 For in every city, for generations past, Moses has had those who proclaim
him, for he has been read aloud every sabbath in the synagogues."

The Council's Letter to Gentile Believers

22 Then the apostles and the elders, with the consent of the whole
church, decided to choose men
from among their members[c] and
to send them to Antioch with Paul
and Barnabas. They sent Judas
called Barsabbas, and Silas, leaders among the brothers, 23 with the
following letter: "The brothers,
both the apostles and the elders, to
the believers[d] of Gentile origin in
Antioch and Syria and Cilicia,
greetings. 24 Since we have heard
that certain persons who have gone
out from us, though with no instructions from us, have said things
to disturb you and have unsettled
your minds,[e] 25 we have decided
unanimously to choose representatives[f] and send them to you, along
with our beloved Barnabas and
Paul, 26 who have risked their lives
for the sake of our Lord Jesus
Christ. 27 We have therefore sent
Judas and Silas, who themselves
will tell you the same things by
word of mouth. 28 For it has seemed
good to the Holy Spirit and to us to
impose on you no further burden
than these essentials: 29 that you
abstain from what has been sacrificed to idols and from blood and
from what is strangled[g] and from
fornication. If you keep yourselves

15.7 Acts 10.19, 20; 20.24
15.8 Acts 1.24; 10.44,47
15.9 Acts 10.28, 34,43; 11.12
15.10 Mt 23.4; Gal 5.1
15.11 Rom 3.24; Eph 2.5-8; Titus 2.11; 3.4,5
15.12 Jn 4.48; Acts 14.27
15.13 Acts 12.17
15.15 Acts 13.40
15.16 Am 9.11,12; Jer 12.15
15.20 v. 29; 1 Cor 8.7-13; 10.7,8,14-28; Rev 2.14,20; Gen 9.4; Lev 3.17; Deut 12.16, 23
15.21 Acts 13.15; 2 Cor 3.14, 15
15.22 Acts 11.20; vv. 27,32,40
15.23 vv. 1,41; Acts 23.26; Jas 1.1
15.24 v. 1; Gal 1.7; 5.10
15.26 Acts 14.19; 1 Cor 15.30
15.29 v. 20; Acts 21.25; Lev 17.14

[z] Gk *Men, brothers* [a] Other ancient authorities read *things. 18Known to God from of old are all his works.'* [b] Other ancient authorities lack *and from whatever has been strangled* [c] Gk *from among them* [d] Gk *brothers* [e] Other ancient authorities add *saying, 'You must be circumcised and keep the law,'* [f] Gk *men* [g] Other ancient authorities lack *and from what is strangled*

from these, you will do well. Farewell."
30 So they were sent off and
went down to Antioch. When they
gathered the congregation together, they delivered the letter.
31 When its members[h] read it, they
rejoiced at the exhortation. 32 Judas and Silas, who were themselves
prophets, said much to encourage
and strengthen the believers.[i]
33 After they had been there for
some time, they were sent off in
peace by the believers[i] to those
who had sent them.[j] 35 But Paul
and Barnabas remained in Antioch, and there, with many others,
they taught and proclaimed the
word of the Lord.

Paul and Barnabas Separate

36 After some days Paul said to
Barnabas, "Come, let us return and
visit the believers[i] in every city
where we proclaimed the word of
the Lord and see how they are doing." 37 Barnabas wanted to take
with them John called Mark. 38 But
Paul decided not to take with them
one who had deserted them in
Pamphylia and had not accompanied them in the work. 39 The disagreement became so sharp that
they parted company; Barnabas
took Mark with him and sailed
away to Cyprus. 40 But Paul chose
Silas and set out, the believers[i]
commending him to the grace of
the Lord. 41 He went through Syria
and Cilicia, strengthening the
churches.

Timothy Joins Paul and Silas

16 Paul[k] went on also to Derbe and to Lystra, where
there was a disciple named Timothy, the son of a Jewish woman
who was a believer; but his father
was a Greek. 2 He was well spoken
of by the believers[i] in Lystra and
Iconium. 3 Paul wanted Timothy to
accompany him; and he took him
and had him circumcised because
of the Jews who were in those
places, for they all knew that his
father was a Greek. 4 As they went
from town to town, they delivered
to them for observance the decisions that had been reached by the
apostles and elders who were in Jerusalem. 5 So the churches were
strengthened in the faith and increased in numbers daily.

Paul's Vision of the Man of Macedonia

6 They went through the region
of Phrygia and Galatia, having been
forbidden by the Holy Spirit to
speak the word in Asia. 7 When they
had come opposite Mysia, they attempted to go into Bithynia, but
the Spirit of Jesus did not allow
them; 8 so, passing by Mysia, they
went down to Troas. 9 During the
night Paul had a vision: there stood
a man of Macedonia pleading with
him and saying, "Come over to
Macedonia and help us." 10 When
he had seen the vision, we immediately tried to cross over to Macedonia, being convinced that God had
called us to proclaim the good
news to them.

The Conversion of Lydia

11 We set sail from Troas and
took a straight course to Samo-
thrace, the following day to Neapo-
lis, 12 and from there to Philippi,
which is a leading city of the district[l] of Macedonia and a Roman
colony. We remained in this city for
some days. 13 On the sabbath day
we went outside the gate by the river, where we supposed there was a
place of prayer; and we sat down
and spoke to the women who had
gathered there. 14 A certain woman
named Lydia, a worshiper of God,
was listening to us; she was from
the city of Thyatira and a dealer in
purple cloth. The Lord opened her
heart to listen eagerly to what was
said by Paul. 15 When she and her
household were baptized, she
urged us, saying, "If you have
judged me to be faithful to the
Lord, come and stay at my home."
And she prevailed upon us.

15.33 Acts 16.36; 1 Cor 16.11; Heb 11.31
15.36ff Acts 13.4, 13,14,51; 14.1,6,24,25
15.37 Acts 12.12
15.38 Acts 13.13
15.41 Acts 16.5
16.1 Acts 14.6; 19.22; Rom 16.21; 1 Cor 4.17; 2 Tim 1.2; 1.5
16.3 Gal 2.3
16.4 Acts 15.28, 29; 15.2; 11.30
16.5 Acts 15.41
16.6 Acts 18.23; 2.9
16.7 v. 8; Lk 24.49; Rom 8.9; Gal 4.6
16.8 v. 11; 2 Cor 2.12; 2 Tim 4.13
16.9 Acts 9.10; 18.5; 20.1,3; 27.2
16.10 2 Cor 2.13
16.11 v. 8; 2 Tim 4.13
16.12 Phil 1.1; Acts 18.5; 19.21,22,29; 20.1,3; 27.2
16.13 Acts 13.14
16.14 Lk 24.45
16.15 Acts 11.14; Lk 24.29

[h] Gk *When they* [i] Gk *brothers* [j] Other ancient authorities add verse 34, *But it seemed good to Silas to remain there* [k] Gk *He*
[l] Other authorities read *a city of the first district*

Paul and Silas in Prison

16 One day, as we were going to
the place of prayer, we met a slave
girl who had a spirit of divination
and brought her owners a great
deal of money by fortune-telling.
17 While she followed Paul and us,
she would cry out, "These men are
slaves of the Most High God, who
proclaim to you[m] a way of salvation." 18 She kept doing this for
many days. But Paul, very much
annoyed, turned and said to the
spirit, "I order you in the name of
Jesus Christ to come out of her."
And it came out that very hour.

19 But when her owners saw
that their hope of making money
was gone, they seized Paul and Silas and dragged them into the marketplace before the authorities.
20 When they had brought them before the magistrates, they said,
"These men are disturbing our city;
they are Jews 21 and are advocating
customs that are not lawful for us
as Romans to adopt or observe."
22 The crowd joined in attacking
them, and the magistrates had
them stripped of their clothing and
ordered them to be beaten with
rods. 23 After they had given them a
severe flogging, they threw them
into prison and ordered the jailer to
keep them securely. 24 Following
these instructions, he put them in
the innermost cell and fastened
their feet in the stocks.

25 About midnight Paul and Silas were praying and singing hymns
to God, and the prisoners were listening to them. 26 Suddenly there
was an earthquake, so violent that
the foundations of the prison were
shaken; and immediately all the
doors were opened and everyone's
chains were unfastened. 27 When
the jailer woke up and saw the prison doors wide open, he drew his
sword and was about to kill himself, since he supposed that the
prisoners had escaped. 28 But Paul
shouted in a loud voice, "Do not
harm yourself, for we are all here."
29 The jailer[n] called for lights, and
rushing in, he fell down trembling
before Paul and Silas. 30 Then he
brought them outside and said,
"Sirs, what must I do to be saved?"
31 They answered, "Believe on the
Lord Jesus, and you will be saved,
you and your household." 32 They
spoke the word of the Lord[o] to him
and to all who were in his house.
33 At the same hour of the night he
took them and washed their
wounds; then he and his entire
family were baptized without delay. 34 He brought them up into the
house and set food before them;
and he and his entire household rejoiced that he had become a believer in God.

35 When morning came, the
magistrates sent the police, saying,
"Let those men go." 36 And the jailer reported the message to Paul,
saying, "The magistrates sent word
to let you go; therefore come out
now and go in peace." 37 But Paul
replied, "They have beaten us in
public, uncondemned, men who
are Roman citizens, and have
thrown us into prison; and now are
they going to discharge us in secret? Certainly not! Let them come
and take us out themselves." 38 The
police reported these words to the
magistrates, and they were afraid
when they heard that they were Roman citizens; 39 so they came and
apologized to them. And they took
them out and asked them to leave
the city. 40 After leaving the prison
they went to Lydia's home; and
when they had seen and encouraged the brothers and sisters[p]
there, they departed.

The Uproar in Thessalonica

17 After Paul and Silas[q] had
passed through Amphipo-
lis and Apollonia, they came to
Thessalonica, where there was a
synagogue of the Jews. 2 And Paul
went in, as was his custom, and on
three sabbath days argued with
them from the scriptures, 3 explaining and proving that it was neces-

16.16 Deut 18.11; 1 Sam 28.3, 7
16.17 Mk 5.7
16.19 Acts 19.25, 26; 15.40; 17.6,7; Jas 2.6
16.20 Acts 17.6
16.22 2 Cor 11.23, 25; 1 Thes 2.2
16.23 vv. 27,36
16.24 Jer 20.2,3
16.25 Eph 5.19
16.26 Acts 4.31; 5.19; 12.7,10
16.27 Acts 12.19
16.30 Acts 2.37; 9.6; 22.10
16.31 Jn 3.16,36; 6.47; 1 Jn 5.10
16.33 v. 25
16.34 Acts 11.14
16.36 vv. 23,27
16.37 Acts 22.25-27
16.38 Acts 22.29
16.39 Mt 8.34
16.40 v. 14
17.1 Acts 27.2; 1 Thes 1.1; 2 Thes 1.1
17.2 Acts 9.20; 13.14; 16.13; 19.8
17.3 Lk 24.26,46; Acts 18.28; Gal 3.1

[m] Other ancient authorities read *to us*
[n] Gk *He* [o] Other ancient authorities read *word of God* [p] Gk *brothers* [q] Gk *they*

sary for the Messiah[r] to suffer and
to rise from the dead, and saying,
"This is the Messiah,[r] Jesus whom
I am proclaiming to you." 4 Some of
them were persuaded and joined
Paul and Silas, as did a great many
of the devout Greeks and not a few
of the leading women. 5 But the
Jews became jealous, and with the
help of some ruffians in the marketplaces they formed a mob and
set the city in an uproar. While they
were searching for Paul and Silas to
bring them out to the assembly,
they attacked Jason's house.
6 When they could not find them,
they dragged Jason and some believers[s] before the city authorities,[t] shouting, "These people
who have been turning the world
upside down have come here also,
7 and Jason has entertained them
as guests. They are all acting contrary to the decrees of the emperor,
saying that there is another king
named Jesus." 8 The people and
the city officials were disturbed
when they heard this, 9 and after
they had taken bail from Jason and
the others, they let them go.

Paul and Silas in Beroea

10 That very night the believers[s] sent Paul and Silas off to Beroea; and when they arrived, they
went to the Jewish synagogue.
11 These Jews were more receptive
than those in Thessalonica, for
they welcomed the message very
eagerly and examined the scriptures every day to see whether
these things were so. 12 Many of
them therefore believed, including
not a few Greek women and men of
high standing. 13 But when the
Jews of Thessalonica learned that
the word of God had been proclaimed by Paul in Beroea as well,
they came there too, to stir up and
incite the crowds. 14 Then the believers[s] immediately sent Paul
away to the coast, but Silas and
Timothy remained behind.
15 Those who conducted Paul
brought him as far as Athens; and
after receiving instructions to have
Silas and Timothy join him as soon
as possible, they left him.

Paul in Athens

16 While Paul was waiting for
them in Athens, he was deeply distressed to see that the city was full
of idols. 17 So he argued in the synagogue with the Jews and the devout
persons, and also in the marketplace[u] every day with those who
happened to be there. 18 Also some
Epicurean and Stoic philosophers
debated with him. Some said,
"What does this babbler want to
say?" Others said, "He seems to be
a proclaimer of foreign divinities."
(This was because he was telling
the good news about Jesus and the
resurrection.) 19 So they took him
and brought him to the Areopagus
and asked him, "May we know
what this new teaching is that you
are presenting? 20 It sounds rather
strange to us, so we would like to
know what it means." 21 Now all
the Athenians and the foreigners
living there would spend their time
in nothing but telling or hearing
something new.

22 Then Paul stood in front of
the Areopagus and said, "Athenians, I see how extremely religious
you are in every way. 23 For as I
went through the city and looked
carefully at the objects of your worship, I found among them an altar
with the inscription, 'To an unknown god.' What therefore you
worship as unknown, this I proclaim to you. 24 The God who made
the world and everything in it, he
who is Lord of heaven and earth,
does not live in shrines made by
human hands, 25 nor is he served by
human hands, as though he needed anything, since he himself gives
to all mortals life and breath and
all things. 26 From one ancestor[v]
he made all nations to inhabit the
whole earth, and he allotted the
times of their existence and the
boundaries of the places where

17.4 Acts 15.22, 27,32,40
17.5 v. 13; Rom 16.21
17.6 Acts 16.19, 20
17.7 Lk 23.2; Jn 19.12
17.9 v. 5
17.10 v. 14; Acts 20.4; v. 2
17.11 Isa 34.16; Lk 16.29; Jn 5.39
17.14 vv. 6,10; Acts 16.1
17.15 Acts 15.3; vv. 16,21, 22; Acts 18.5
17.16 2 Pet 2.8
17.18 1 Cor 4.10; Acts 4.2
17.19 Acts 23.19; v. 22
17.24 Isa 42.5; Acts 14.15; Mt 11.25; Acts 7.48
17.25 Ps 50.10-12; Isa 42.5; 57.16; Zech 12.1
17.26 Mal 2.10; Deut 32.8

[r] Or *the Christ* [s] Gk *brothers* [t] Gk *politarchs* [u] Or *civic center*; Gk *agora* [v] Gk *From one*; other ancient authorities read *From one blood*

they would live, 27 so that they
would search for God[w] and perhaps grope for him and find him —
though indeed he is not far from
each one of us. 28 For 'In him we
live and move and have our being';
as even some of your own poets
have said,
'For we too are his offspring.'
29 Since we are God's offspring, we
ought not to think that the deity is
like gold, or silver, or stone, an image formed by the art and imagination of mortals. 30 While God has
overlooked the times of human ignorance, now he commands all
people everywhere to repent, 31 because he has fixed a day on which
he will have the world judged in
righteousness by a man whom he
has appointed, and of this he has
given assurance to all by raising
him from the dead."
32 When they heard of the resurrection of the dead, some
scoffed; but others said, "We will
hear you again about this." 33 At
that point Paul left them. 34 But
some of them joined him and became believers, including Dionysius the Areopagite and a woman
named Damaris, and others with
them.

Paul in Corinth

18 After this Paul[x] left Athens
and went to Corinth.
2 There he found a Jew named Aquila, a native of Pontus, who had
recently come from Italy with his
wife Priscilla, because Claudius
had ordered all Jews to leave
Rome. Paul[y] went to see them,
3 and, because he was of the same
trade, he stayed with them, and
they worked together — by trade
they were tentmakers. 4 Every sabbath he would argue in the synagogue and would try to convince
Jews and Greeks.
5 When Silas and Timothy arrived from Macedonia, Paul was
occupied with proclaiming the
word,[z] testifying to the Jews that
the Messiah[a] was Jesus. 6 When
they opposed and reviled him, in
protest he shook the dust from his
clothes[b] and said to them, "Your
blood be on your own heads! I am
innocent. From now on I will go to
the Gentiles." 7 Then he left the
synagogue[c] and went to the house
of a man named Titius[d] Justus, a
worshiper of God; his house was
next door to the synagogue. 8 Crispus, the official of the synagogue,
became a believer in the Lord, together with all his household; and
many of the Corinthians who heard
Paul became believers and were
baptized. 9 One night the Lord said
to Paul in a vision, "Do not be
afraid, but speak and do not be silent; 10 for I am with you, and no
one will lay a hand on you to harm
you, for there are many in this city
who are my people." 11 He stayed
there a year and six months, teaching the word of God among them.
12 But when Gallio was proconsul of Achaia, the Jews made a
united attack on Paul and brought
him before the tribunal. 13 They
said, "This man is persuading people to worship God in ways that are
contrary to the law." 14 Just as Paul
was about to speak, Gallio said to
the Jews, "If it were a matter of
crime or serious villainy, I would be
justified in accepting the complaint of you Jews; 15 but since it is
a matter of questions about words
and names and your own law, see
to it yourselves; I do not wish to be
a judge of these matters." 16 And he
dismissed them from the tribunal.
17 Then all of them[e] seized Sosthenes, the official of the synagogue,
and beat him in front of the tribunal. But Gallio paid no attention to
any of these things.

Paul's Return to Antioch

18 After staying there for a considerable time, Paul said farewell
to the believers[f] and sailed for Syria, accompanied by Priscilla and
Aquila. At Cenchreae he had his

[w] Other ancient authorities read *the Lord*
[x] Gk *he* [y] Gk *He* [z] Gk *with the word*
[a] Or *the Christ* [b] Gk *reviled him, he shook out his clothes* [c] Gk *left there* [d] Other ancient authorities read *Titus* [e] Other ancient authorities read *all the Greeks*
[f] Gk *brothers*

17.27 Rom 1.20; Acts 14.17
17.28 Col 1.17; Heb 1.3,5
17.29 Isa 40.18ff
17.30 v. 23; Acts 14.16; Rom 3.25; Lk 24.47; Titus 2.11, 12; 1 Pet 1.14
17.31 Mt 10.15; Acts 10.42; Lk 22.22; Acts 22.4
17.34 vv. 19,22
18.1 Acts 17.15; 1 Cor 1.2
18.2 Rom 16.3; 1 Cor 16.19; 2 Tim 4.19; Acts 11.28
18.3 Acts 20.34; 1 Cor 4.12; 1 Thes 2.9; 2 Thes 3.8
18.4 Acts 17.2
18.5 Acts 17.14, 15; 16.9; 20.21; v. 28; Acts 17.3
18.6 Acts 13.45, 51; 2 Sam 1.16; Ezek 18.13; Acts 20.26; 13.46
18.7 Acts 16.14
18.8 1 Cor 1.14
18.9 Acts 23.11
18.10 Mt 28.20
18.14 Acts 23.29; 25.11,19
18.17 1 Cor 1.1
18.18 Num 6.18; Acts 21.24; Rom 16.1

hair cut, for he was under a vow.
19 When they reached Ephesus, he
left them there, but first he himself
went into the synagogue and had a
discussion with the Jews. 20 When
they asked him to stay longer, he
declined; 21 but on taking leave of
them, he said, "I[g] will return to
you, if God wills." Then he set sail
from Ephesus.
22 When he had landed at Caesarea, he went up to Jerusalem[h]
and greeted the church, and then
went down to Antioch. 23 After
spending some time there he departed and went from place to
place through the region of Galatia[i] and Phrygia, strengthening all
the disciples.

Ministry of Apollos

24 Now there came to Ephesus
a Jew named Apollos, a native of
Alexandria. He was an eloquent
man, well-versed in the scriptures.
25 He had been instructed in the
Way of the Lord; and he spoke with
burning enthusiasm and taught accurately the things concerning
Jesus, though he knew only the
baptism of John. 26 He began to
speak boldly in the synagogue; but
when Priscilla and Aquila heard
him, they took him aside and explained the Way of God to him
more accurately. 27 And when he
wished to cross over to Achaia, the
believers[j] encouraged him and
wrote to the disciples to welcome
him. On his arrival he greatly
helped those who through grace
had become believers, 28 for he
powerfully refuted the Jews in public, showing by the scriptures that
the Messiah[k] is Jesus.

Paul in Ephesus

19 While Apollos was in Corinth, Paul passed through
the interior regions and came to
Ephesus, where he found some disciples. 2 He said to them, "Did you
receive the Holy Spirit when you
became believers?" They replied,
"No, we have not even heard that
there is a Holy Spirit." 3 Then he
said, "Into what then were you baptized?" They answered, "Into
John's baptism." 4 Paul said, "John
baptized with the baptism of repentance, telling the people to believe in the one who was to come
after him, that is, in Jesus." 5 On
hearing this, they were baptized in
the name of the Lord Jesus. 6 When
Paul had laid his hands on them,
the Holy Spirit came upon them,
and they spoke in tongues and
prophesied— 7 altogether there
were about twelve of them.
8 He entered the synagogue and
for three months spoke out boldly,
and argued persuasively about the
kingdom of God. 9 When some
stubbornly refused to believe and
spoke evil of the Way before the
congregation, he left them, taking
the disciples with him, and argued
daily in the lecture hall of Tyrannus.[l] 10 This continued for two
years, so that all the residents of
Asia, both Jews and Greeks, heard
the word of the Lord.

The Sons of Sceva

11 God did extraordinary miracles through Paul, 12 so that when
the handkerchiefs or aprons that
had touched his skin were brought
to the sick, their diseases left
them, and the evil spirits came out
of them. 13 Then some itinerant
Jewish exorcists tried to use the
name of the Lord Jesus over those
who had evil spirits, saying, "I adjure you by the Jesus whom Paul
proclaims." 14 Seven sons of a Jewish high priest named Sceva were
doing this. 15 But the evil spirit said
to them in reply, "Jesus I know,
and Paul I know; but who are you?"
16 Then the man with the evil spirit
leaped on them, mastered them
all, and so overpowered them that
they fled out of the house naked
and wounded. 17 When this became
known to all residents of Ephesus,
both Jews and Greeks, everyone

18.21 1 Cor 4.19
18.22 Acts 11.19
18.23 Acts 16.6; 14.22; 15.32, 41
18.24 Acts 19.1; 1 Cor 1.12; 3.5,6; 4.6; Titus 3.13
18.25 Rom 12.11; Acts 19.3
18.27 vv. 12,18
18.28 Acts 9.22; 17.3; v. 5
19.1 1 Cor 1.12; 3.5,6; Acts 18.1, 19-24
19.3 Acts 18.25
19.4 Mt 3.11; Acts 13.24, 25
19.6 Acts 6.6; 8.17; 2.4; 10.46
19.8 Acts 17.2; 18.4; 1.3; 28.23
19.9 Acts 14.4; 2 Tim 1.15; Acts 9.2; v. 30
19.10 Acts 20.31; vv. 22,26, 27; Acts 13.12
19.11 Acts 8.13
19.12 Acts 5.15
19.13 Mt 12.27; Mk 9.38; Lk 9.49
19.17 Acts 2.43; 5.5,11

[g] Other ancient authorities read *I must at all costs keep the approaching festival in Jerusalem, but I* [h] Gk *went up* [i] Gk *the Galatian region* [j] Gk *brothers* [k] Or *the Christ* [l] Other ancient authorities read *of a certain Tyrannus, from eleven o'clock in the morning to four in the afternoon*

was awestruck; and the name of
the Lord Jesus was praised. 18 Also
many of those who became believers confessed and disclosed their
practices. 19 A number of those who
practiced magic collected their
books and burned them publicly;
when the value of these books[m]
was calculated, it was found to
come to fifty thousand silver coins.
20 So the word of the Lord grew
mightily and prevailed.

The Riot in Ephesus

21 Now after these things had
been accomplished, Paul resolved
in the Spirit to go through Macedonia and Achaia, and then to go on
to Jerusalem. He said, "After I have
gone there, I must also see Rome."
22 So he sent two of his helpers,
Timothy and Erastus, to Macedonia, while he himself stayed for
some time longer in Asia.

23 About that time no little disturbance broke out concerning the
Way. 24 A man named Demetrius, a
silversmith who made silver
shrines of Artemis, brought no little business to the artisans.
25 These he gathered together, with
the workers of the same trade, and
said, "Men, you know that we get
our wealth from this business.
26 You also see and hear that not
only in Ephesus but in almost the
whole of Asia this Paul has persuaded and drawn away a considerable number of people by saying
that gods made with hands are not
gods. 27 And there is danger not
only that this trade of ours may
come into disrepute but also that
the temple of the great goddess Artemis will be scorned, and she will
be deprived of her majesty that
brought all Asia and the world to
worship her."

28 When they heard this, they
were enraged and shouted, "Great
is Artemis of the Ephesians!" 29 The
city was filled with the confusion;
and people[n] rushed together to the
theater, dragging with them Gaius
and Aristarchus, Macedonians who
were Paul's travel companions.
30 Paul wished to go into the crowd,
but the disciples would not let him;
31 even some officials of the province of Asia,[o] who were friendly to
him, sent him a message urging
him not to venture into the theater.
32 Meanwhile, some were shouting
one thing, some another; for the assembly was in confusion, and most
of them did not know why they had
come together. 33 Some of the
crowd gave instructions to Alexander, whom the Jews had pushed
forward. And Alexander motioned
for silence and tried to make a defense before the people. 34 But
when they recognized that he was a
Jew, for about two hours all of
them shouted in unison, "Great is
Artemis of the Ephesians!" 35 But
when the town clerk had quieted
the crowd, he said, "Citizens of
Ephesus, who is there that does
not know that the city of the Ephesians is the temple keeper of the
great Artemis and of the statue that
fell from heaven?[p] 36 Since these
things cannot be denied, you ought
to be quiet and do nothing rash.
37 You have brought these men here
who are neither temple robbers nor
blasphemers of our[q] goddess. 38 If
therefore Demetrius and the artisans with him have a complaint
against anyone, the courts are
open, and there are proconsuls; let
them bring charges there against
one another. 39 If there is anything
further[r] you want to know, it must
be settled in the regular assembly.
40 For we are in danger of being
charged with rioting today, since
there is no cause that we can give
to justify this commotion." 41 When
he had said this, he dismissed the
assembly.

Paul Goes to Macedonia and Greece

20 After the uproar had
ceased, Paul sent for the
disciples; and after encouraging
them and saying farewell, he left

19.20 Acts 6.7; 12.24
19.21 Rom 15.24-28
19.22 Acts 13.5; Rom 16.23; 2 Tim 4.20; v. 10
19.23 v. 9
19.24 Acts 16.16, 19
19.26 Ps 115.4; Isa 44.10-20; Jer 10.3; Acts 17.29
19.28 Acts 18.19
19.29 Rom 16.23; 1 Cor 1.4; Acts 20.4; 27.2; Col 4.10; Philem 24
19.32 Acts 21.34
19.33 1 Tim 1.20; 2 Tim 4.14; Acts 12.17
19.35 Acts 18.19
19.37 Rom 2.22
19.38 Acts 13.7
20.1 Acts 11.26; 1 Cor 16.5; 1 Tim 1.3

[m] Gk *them* [n] Gk *they* [o] Gk *some of the Asiarchs* [p] Meaning of Gk uncertain
[q] Other ancient authorities read *your*
[r] Other ancient authorities read *about other matters*

for Macedonia. 2When he had gone
through those regions and had giv-
en the believers[s] much encouragement, he came to Greece, 3where
he stayed for three months. He was
about to set sail for Syria when a
plot was made against him by the
Jews, and so he decided to return
through Macedonia. 4He was accompanied by Sopater son of Pyr-
rhus from Beroea, by Aristarchus
and Secundus from Thessalonica,
by Gaius from Derbe, and by Timothy, as well as by Tychicus and
Trophimus from Asia. 5They went
ahead and were waiting for us in
Troas; 6but we sailed from Philippi
after the days of Unleavened Bread,
and in five days we joined them in
Troas, where we stayed for seven
days.

Paul's Farewell Visit to Troas

7 On the first day of the week,
when we met to break bread, Paul
was holding a discussion with
them; since he intended to leave
the next day, he continued speaking until midnight. 8There were
many lamps in the room upstairs
where we were meeting. 9A young
man named Eutychus, who was sitting in the window, began to sink
off into a deep sleep while Paul
talked still longer. Overcome by
sleep, he fell to the ground three
floors below and was picked up
dead. 10But Paul went down, and
bending over him took him in his
arms, and said, "Do not be
alarmed, for his life is in him."
11Then Paul went upstairs, and after he had broken bread and eaten,
he continued to converse with
them until dawn; then he left.
12Meanwhile they had taken the
boy away alive and were not a little
comforted.

The Voyage from Troas to Miletus

13 We went ahead to the ship
and set sail for Assos, intending to
take Paul on board there; for he
had made this arrangement, intending to go by land himself.
14When he met us in Assos, we
took him on board and went to Mit-
ylene. 15We sailed from there, and
on the following day we arrived opposite Chios. The next day we
touched at Samos, and[t] the day after that we came to Miletus. 16For
Paul had decided to sail past Ephesus, so that he might not have to
spend time in Asia; he was eager to
be in Jerusalem, if possible, on the
day of Pentecost.

Paul Speaks to the Ephesian Elders

17 From Miletus he sent a message to Ephesus, asking the elders
of the church to meet him. 18When
they came to him, he said to them:
"You yourselves know how I
lived among you the entire time
from the first day that I set foot in
Asia, 19serving the Lord with all humility and with tears, enduring the
trials that came to me through the
plots of the Jews. 20I did not shrink
from doing anything helpful, proclaiming the message to you and
teaching you publicly and from
house to house, 21as I testified to
both Jews and Greeks about repentance toward God and faith toward
our Lord Jesus. 22And now, as a
captive to the Spirit,[u] I am on my
way to Jerusalem, not knowing
what will happen to me there, 23ex-
cept that the Holy Spirit testifies to
me in every city that imprisonment
and persecutions are waiting for
me. 24But I do not count my life of
any value to myself, if only I may
finish my course and the ministry
that I received from the Lord Jesus,
to testify to the good news of God's
grace.
25 "And now I know that none
of you, among whom I have gone
about proclaiming the kingdom,
will ever see my face again.
26Therefore I declare to you this
day that I am not responsible for
the blood of any of you, 27for I did
not shrink from declaring to you
the whole purpose of God. 28Keep
watch over yourselves and over all

20.3 v. 19; Acts 23.12; 25.3; 2 Cor 11.26
20.4 Acts 19.29; 27.2; 16.1; Eph 6.21; Col 4.7; 2 Tim 4.12; Titus 3.12; Acts 21.29; 2 Tim 4.20
20.6 Acts 16.8; 2 Cor 2.12; 2 Tim 4.13
20.7 1 Cor 16.2; Rev 1.10
20.8 Acts 1.13
20.10 1 Kings 17.21; Mt 9.23,24
20.15 v. 17; 2 Tim 4.20
20.16 Acts 18.19; 21.4,12; 19.21; 2.1; 1 Cor 16.8
20.17 Acts 11.30
20.18 Acts 18.19; 19.1,10
20.20 v. 27
20.21 Acts 18.5; 2.38; 24.24; 26.18
20.22 v. 16
20.23 Acts 21.4,11
20.24 Acts 21.13; 2 Cor 4.16; Acts 1.17; 2 Cor 4.1; Gal 1.1; Titus 1.3
20.25 v. 38
20.26 Acts 18.6; 2 Cor 7.2
20.27 v. 20; Acts 13.36
20.28 1 Tim 4.16; 1 Pet 5.2; 1 Cor 12.28; 1 Pet 1.19; 20.29; Mt 7.15

[s] Gk *given them* [t] Other ancient authorities add *after remaining at Trogyllium* [u] Or *And now, bound in the spirit*

the flock, of which the Holy Spirit
has made you overseers, to shepherd the church of God[v] that he
obtained with the blood of his own
Son.[w] 29 I know that after I have
gone, savage wolves will come in
among you, not sparing the flock.
30 Some even from your own group
will come distorting the truth in order to entice the disciples to follow
them. 31 Therefore be alert, remembering that for three years I did not
cease night or day to warn everyone
with tears. 32 And now I commend
you to God and to the message of
his grace, a message that is able to
build you up and to give you the
inheritance among all who are
sanctified. 33 I coveted no one's silver or gold or clothing. 34 You know
for yourselves that I worked with
my own hands to support myself
and my companions. 35 In all this I
have given you an example that by
such work we must support the
weak, remembering the words of
the Lord Jesus, for he himself said,
'It is more blessed to give than to
receive.' "
36 When he had finished speaking, he knelt down with them all
and prayed. 37 There was much
weeping among them all; they embraced Paul and kissed him,
38 grieving especially because of
what he had said, that they would
not see him again. Then they
brought him to the ship.

Paul's Journey to Jerusalem

21 When we had parted from
them and set sail, we came
by a straight course to Cos, and the
next day to Rhodes, and from there
to Patara.[x] 2 When we found a ship
bound for Phoenicia, we went on
board and set sail. 3 We came in
sight of Cyprus; and leaving it on
our left, we sailed to Syria and
landed at Tyre, because the ship
was to unload its cargo there. 4 We
looked up the disciples and stayed
there for seven days. Through the
Spirit they told Paul not to go on to
Jerusalem. 5 When our days there
were ended, we left and proceeded
on our journey; and all of them,
with wives and children, escorted
us outside the city. There we knelt
down on the beach and prayed
6 and said farewell to one another.
Then we went on board the ship,
and they returned home.
7 When we had finished[y] the
voyage from Tyre, we arrived at
Ptolemais; and we greeted the believers[z] and stayed with them for
one day. 8 The next day we left and
came to Caesarea; and we went
into the house of Philip the evangelist, one of the seven, and stayed
with him. 9 He had four unmarried
daughters[a] who had the gift of
prophecy. 10 While we were staying
there for several days, a prophet
named Agabus came down from
Judea. 11 He came to us and took
Paul's belt, bound his own feet and
hands with it, and said, "Thus says
the Holy Spirit, 'This is the way the
Jews in Jerusalem will bind the
man who owns this belt and will
hand him over to the Gentiles.' "
12 When we heard this, we and the
people there urged him not to go
up to Jerusalem. 13 Then Paul answered, "What are you doing,
weeping and breaking my heart?
For I am ready not only to be bound
but even to die in Jerusalem for the
name of the Lord Jesus." 14 Since
he would not be persuaded, we remained silent except to say, "The
Lord's will be done."
15 After these days we got ready
and started to go up to Jerusalem.
16 Some of the disciples from Caesarea also came along and brought
us to the house of Mnason of Cyprus, an early disciple, with whom
we were to stay.

Paul Visits James at Jerusalem

17 When we arrived in Jerusalem, the brothers welcomed us
warmly. 18 The next day Paul went
with us to visit James; and all the
elders were present. 19 After greeting them, he related one by one the
things that God had done among

20.31 Acts 19.10
20.32 Acts 14.23; 9.31; 26.18; Eph 1.18; Col 1.12; 3.24; 1 Pet 1.4
20.33 1 Cor 9.12; 2 Cor 7.2; 11.9; 12.17
20.34 Acts 18.3
20.35 Rom 15.1
20.36 Acts 9.40; 21.5
20.37 Gen 45.14
20.38 v. 25; Acts 15.3
21.2 Acts 11.19
21.4 v. 11; Acts 20.23
21.5 Acts 20.36
21.7 Acts 12.20; 1.15
21.8 Eph 4.11; 2 Tim 4.5; Acts 6.5; 8.26,40
21.9 Acts 2.17; Lk 2.36
21.10 Acts 11.28
21.11 v. 33; Acts 20.23
21.13 Acts 20.24
21.14 Mt 26.42; Lk 22.42
21.16 vv. 3,4
21.17 Acts 15.4
21.18 Acts 12.17; 15.13
21.19 Acts 14.27; 1.17; 20.24

[v] Other ancient authorities read *of the Lord*
[w] Or *with his own blood;* Gk *with the blood of his Own*
[x] Other ancient authorities add *and Myra*
[y] Or *continued*
[z] Gk *brothers*
[a] Gk *four daughters, virgins,*

the Gentiles through his ministry.
20 When they heard it, they praised
God. Then they said to him, "You
see, brother, how many thousands
of believers there are among the
Jews, and they are all zealous for
the law. 21 They have been told
about you that you teach all the
Jews living among the Gentiles to
forsake Moses, and that you tell
them not to circumcise their children or observe the customs.
22 What then is to be done? They
will certainly hear that you have
come. 23 So do what we tell you. We
have four men who are under a
vow. 24 Join these men, go through
the rite of purification with them,
and pay for the shaving of their
heads. Thus all will know that
there is nothing in what they have
been told about you, but that you
yourself observe and guard the law.
25 But as for the Gentiles who have
become believers, we have sent a
letter with our judgment that they
should abstain from what has been
sacrificed to idols and from blood
and from what is strangled[b] and
from fornication." 26 Then Paul
took the men, and the next day,
having purified himself, he entered
the temple with them, making public the completion of the days of
purification when the sacrifice
would be made for each of them.

Paul Arrested in the Temple

27 When the seven days were almost completed, the Jews from
Asia, who had seen him in the temple, stirred up the whole crowd.
They seized him, 28 shouting, "Fellow Israelites, help! This is the man
who is teaching everyone everywhere against our people, our law,
and this place; more than that, he
has actually brought Greeks into
the temple and has defiled this
holy place." 29 For they had previously seen Trophimus the Ephesian with him in the city, and they
supposed that Paul had brought
him into the temple. 30 Then all the
city was aroused, and the people
rushed together. They seized Paul
and dragged him out of the temple,
and immediately the doors were
shut. 31 While they were trying to
kill him, word came to the tribune
of the cohort that all Jerusalem
was in an uproar. 32 Immediately he
took soldiers and centurions and
ran down to them. When they saw
the tribune and the soldiers, they
stopped beating Paul. 33 Then the
tribune came, arrested him, and ordered him to be bound with two
chains; he inquired who he was
and what he had done. 34 Some in
the crowd shouted one thing, some
another; and as he could not learn
the facts because of the uproar, he
ordered him to be brought into the
barracks. 35 When Paul[c] came to
the steps, the violence of the mob
was so great that he had to be carried by the soldiers. 36 The crowd
that followed kept shouting, "Away
with him!"

Paul Defends Himself

37 Just as Paul was about to be
brought into the barracks, he said
to the tribune, "May I say something to you?" The tribune[d] replied, "Do you know Greek?
38 Then you are not the Egyptian
who recently stirred up a revolt and
led the four thousand assassins out
into the wilderness?" 39 Paul replied, "I am a Jew, from Tarsus in
Cilicia, a citizen of an important
city; I beg you, let me speak to the
people." 40 When he had given him
permission, Paul stood on the
steps and motioned to the people
for silence; and when there was a
great hush, he addressed them in
the Hebrew[e] language, saying:

22 "Brothers and fathers, listen to the defense that I
now make before you."
2 When they heard him addressing them in Hebrew,[e] they became
even more quiet. Then he said:
3 "I am a Jew, born in Tarsus in
Cilicia, but brought up in this city
at the feet of Gamaliel, educated
strictly according to our ancestral
law, being zealous for God, just as

21.20 Acts 22.3; Rom 10.2; Gal 1.14 **21.21** v. 28; 1 Cor 7.18, 19 **21.23** Acts 18.18 **21.24** v. 26; Acts 24.18 **21.25** Acts 15.20, 29 **21.26** Num 6.13; Acts 24.18 **21.27** Acts 24.18; 26.21 **21.28** Acts 24.5,6 **21.29** Acts 20.4; 18.19 **21.30** Acts 26.21; 16.19

21.32 Acts 23.27 **21.33** Acts 20.23; v. 11 **21.34** Acts 19.32; v. 37 **21.36** Lk 23.18; Jn 19.15; Acts 22.22 **21.37** v. 34 **21.38** Acts 5.36; Mt 24.26 **21.39** Acts 9.11; 22.3 **21.40** Acts 12.17; 22.2; 26.14 **22.1** Acts 7.2 **22.2** Acts 21.40 **22.3** Acts 21.39; 20.4; Lk 10.39; Acts 26.5; 21.20

[b] Other ancient authorities lack *and from what is strangled* [c] Gk *he* [d] Gk *He* [e] That is, *Aramaic*

all of you are today. 4 I persecuted this Way up to the point of death by binding both men and women and putting them in prison, 5 as the high priest and the whole council of elders can testify about me. From them I also received letters to the brothers in Damascus, and I went there in order to bind those who were there and to bring them back to Jerusalem for punishment.

Paul Tells of His Conversion

6 "While I was on my way and approaching Damascus, about noon a great light from heaven suddenly shone about me. 7 I fell to the ground and heard a voice saying to me, 'Saul, Saul, why are you persecuting me?' 8 I answered, 'Who are you, Lord?' Then he said to me, 'I am Jesus of Nazareth[f] whom you are persecuting.' 9 Now those who were with me saw the light but did not hear the voice of the one who was speaking to me. 10 I asked, 'What am I to do, Lord?' The Lord said to me, 'Get up and go to Damascus; there you will be told everything that has been assigned to you to do.' 11 Since I could not see because of the brightness of that light, those who were with me took my hand and led me to Damascus.

12 "A certain Ananias, who was a devout man according to the law and well spoken of by all the Jews living there, 13 came to me; and standing beside me, he said, 'Brother Saul, regain your sight!' In that very hour I regained my sight and saw him. 14 Then he said, 'The God of our ancestors has chosen you to know his will, to see the Righteous One and to hear his own voice; 15 for you will be his witness to all the world of what you have seen and heard. 16 And now why do you delay? Get up, be baptized, and have your sins washed away, calling on his name.'

Paul Sent to the Gentiles

17 "After I had returned to Jerusalem and while I was praying in the temple, I fell into a trance 18 and saw Jesus[g] saying to me, 'Hurry and get out of Jerusalem quickly, because they will not accept your testimony about me.' 19 And I said, 'Lord, they themselves know that in every synagogue I imprisoned and beat those who believed in you. 20 And while the blood of your witness Stephen was shed, I myself was standing by, approving and keeping the coats of those who killed him.' 21 Then he said to me, 'Go, for I will send you far away to the Gentiles.'"

Paul and the Roman Tribune

22 Up to this point they listened to him, but then they shouted, "Away with such a fellow from the earth! For he should not be allowed to live." 23 And while they were shouting, throwing off their cloaks, and tossing dust into the air, 24 the tribune directed that he was to be brought into the barracks, and ordered him to be examined by flogging, to find out the reason for this outcry against him. 25 But when they had tied him up with thongs,[h] Paul said to the centurion who was standing by, "Is it legal for you to flog a Roman citizen who is uncondemned?" 26 When the centurion heard that, he went to the tribune and said to him, "What are you about to do? This man is a Roman citizen." 27 The tribune came and asked Paul,[g] "Tell me, are you a Roman citizen?" And he said, "Yes." 28 The tribune answered, "It cost me a large sum of money to get my citizenship." Paul said, "But I was born a citizen." 29 Immediately those who were about to examine him drew back from him; and the tribune also was afraid, for he realized that Paul was a Roman citizen and that he had bound him.

Paul before the Council

30 Since he wanted to find out what Paul[i] was being accused of by the Jews, the next day he released him and ordered the chief priests and the entire council to

22.4 Acts 8.3; 26.9-11; Phil 3.6; 1 Tim 1.13
22.5 Lk 22.66; Acts 4.5; 9.2; 26.10,12
22.6 Acts 9.3; 26.12,13
22.9 Acts 9.7; 26.13
22.10 Acts 16.30
22.11 Acts 9.8
22.12 Acts 9.17; 10.22
22.14 Acts 3.13; 5.30; 9.15; 26.16; 1 Cor 9.1; 15.8; Acts 7.52
22.15 Acts 23.11; 26.16
22.16 Acts 2.38; Heb 10.22; Acts 9.14; Rom 10.13
22.17 Acts 9.26; 10.10
22.19 v. 4; Acts 8.3; 26.11; Mt 10.17
22.20 Lk 11.48; Acts 8.1; Rom 1.32
22.21 Acts 9.15
22.22 Acts 21.36; 25.24
22.23 Acts 7.58; 2 Sam 16.13
22.24 Acts 21.34
22.25 Acts 16.37
22.29 vv. 24,25
22.30 Acts 23.28; 21.33

[f] Gk *the Nazorean* [g] Gk *him* [h] Or *up for the lashes* [i] Gk *he*

meet. He brought Paul down and
had him stand before them.

23 While Paul was looking intently at the council he
said, "Brothers,[j] up to this day I
have lived my life with a clear conscience before God." 2 Then the
high priest Ananias ordered those
standing near him to strike him on
the mouth. 3 At this Paul said to
him, "God will strike you, you
whitewashed wall! Are you sitting
there to judge me according to the
law, and yet in violation of the law
you order me to be struck?" 4 Those
standing nearby said, "Do you dare
to insult God's high priest?" 5 And
Paul said, "I did not realize, brothers, that he was high priest; for it is
written, 'You shall not speak evil of
a leader of your people.' "

6 When Paul noticed that some
were Sadducees and others were
Pharisees, he called out in the
council, "Brothers, I am a Pharisee,
a son of Pharisees. I am on trial
concerning the hope of the resurrection[k] of the dead." 7 When he
said this, a dissension began between the Pharisees and the Sadducees, and the assembly was divided. 8 (The Sadducees say that
there is no resurrection, or angel,
or spirit; but the Pharisees acknowledge all three.) 9 Then a great
clamor arose, and certain scribes of
the Pharisees' group stood up and
contended, "We find nothing
wrong with this man. What if a spirit or an angel has spoken to him?"
10 When the dissension became violent, the tribune, fearing that they
would tear Paul to pieces, ordered
the soldiers to go down, take him
by force, and bring him into the
barracks.

11 That night the Lord stood
near him and said, "Keep up your
courage! For just as you have testified for me in Jerusalem, so you
must bear witness also in Rome."

The Plot to Kill Paul

12 In the morning the Jews
joined in a conspiracy and bound
themselves by an oath neither to
eat nor drink until they had killed
Paul. 13 There were more than forty
who joined in this conspiracy.
14 They went to the chief priests
and elders and said, "We have
strictly bound ourselves by an oath
to taste no food until we have
killed Paul. 15 Now then, you and
the council must notify the tribune
to bring him down to you, on the
pretext that you want to make a
more thorough examination of his
case. And we are ready to do away
with him before he arrives."

16 Now the son of Paul's sister
heard about the ambush; so he
went and gained entrance to the
barracks and told Paul. 17 Paul
called one of the centurions and
said, "Take this young man to the
tribune, for he has something to report to him." 18 So he took him,
brought him to the tribune, and
said, "The prisoner Paul called me
and asked me to bring this young
man to you; he has something to
tell you." 19 The tribune took him
by the hand, drew him aside privately, and asked, "What is it that
you have to report to me?" 20 He answered, "The Jews have agreed to
ask you to bring Paul down to the
council tomorrow, as though they
were going to inquire more thoroughly into his case. 21 But do not
be persuaded by them, for more
than forty of their men are lying in
ambush for him. They have bound
themselves by an oath neither to
eat nor drink until they kill him.
They are ready now and are waiting
for your consent." 22 So the tribune
dismissed the young man, ordering
him, "Tell no one that you have informed me of this."

Paul Sent to Felix the Governor

23 Then he summoned two of
the centurions and said, "Get ready
to leave by nine o'clock tonight for
Caesarea with two hundred soldiers, seventy horsemen, and two
hundred spearmen. 24 Also provide
mounts for Paul to ride, and take
him safely to Felix the governor."
25 He wrote a letter to this effect:

23.1 Acts 22.30; 24.16; 2 Cor 1.12; 2 Tim 1.3
23.2 Jn 18.22
23.3 Mt 23.27; Lev 19.35; Deut 25.1,2; Jn 7.51
23.5 Ex 22.28
23.6 Acts 26.5; Phil 3.5; Acts 24.15, 16; 26.8
23.8 Mt 22.23; Mk 12.18; Lk 20.27
23.9 Acts 25.25; 26.31; 22.7, 17,18
23.10 Acts 21.34
23.11 Acts 18.9; 19.21; 28.23
23.12 vv. 21,30; Acts 25.3
23.14 v. 21
23.15 Acts 22.30
23.16 Acts 21.34; v. 10
23.18 Eph 3.1
23.20 vv. 14,15
23.21 vv.12,14
23.23 v. 33
23.24 Acts 24.1,3, 10; 25.14

[j] Gk *Men, brothers* [k] Gk *concerning hope and resurrection*

26 “Claudius Lysias to his Excellency the governor Felix, greetings. 27This man was seized by the
Jews and was about to be killed by
them, but when I had learned that
he was a Roman citizen, I came
with the guard and rescued him.
28Since I wanted to know the
charge for which they accused him,
I had him brought to their council.
29I found that he was accused concerning questions of their law, but
was charged with nothing deserving death or imprisonment.
30When I was informed that there
would be a plot against the man, I
sent him to you at once, ordering
his accusers also to state before
you what they have against him.[l]”
31 So the soldiers, according to
their instructions, took Paul and
brought him during the night to
Antipatris. 32The next day they let
the horsemen go on with him,
while they returned to the barracks. 33When they came to Caesarea and delivered the letter to the
governor, they presented Paul also
before him. 34On reading the letter, he asked what province he belonged to, and when he learned
that he was from Cilicia, 35he said,
“I will give you a hearing when your
accusers arrive.” Then he ordered
that he be kept under guard in Herod’s headquarters.[m]

Paul before Felix at Caesarea

24 Five days later the high
priest Ananias came down
with some elders and an attorney, a
certain Tertullus, and they reported their case against Paul to the
governor. 2When Paul[n] had been
summoned, Tertullus began to accuse him, saying:
“Your Excellency,[o] because of
you we have long enjoyed peace,
and reforms have been made for
this people because of your fore-
sight. 3We welcome this in every
way and everywhere with utmost
gratitude. 4But, to detain you no
further, I beg you to hear us briefly
with your customary graciousness.
5We have, in fact, found this man a
pestilent fellow, an agitator among
all the Jews throughout the world,
and a ringleader of the sect of the
Nazarenes.[p] 6He even tried to profane the temple, and so we seized
him.[q] 8By examining him yourself
you will be able to learn from him
concerning everything of which we
accuse him.”
9 The Jews also joined in the
charge by asserting that all this was
true.

Paul’s Defense before Felix

10 When the governor motioned
to him to speak, Paul replied:
“I cheerfully make my defense,
knowing that for many years you
have been a judge over this nation.
11As you can find out, it is not more
than twelve days since I went up to
worship in Jerusalem. 12They did
not find me disputing with anyone
in the temple or stirring up a crowd
either in the synagogues or
throughout the city. 13Neither can
they prove to you the charge that
they now bring against me. 14But
this I admit to you, that according
to the Way, which they call a sect,
I worship the God of our ancestors,
believing everything laid down according to the law or written in the
prophets. 15I have a hope in God —
a hope that they themselves also
accept — that there will be a resurrection of both[r] the righteous and
the unrighteous. 16Therefore I do
my best always to have a clear conscience toward God and all people.
17Now after some years I came to
bring alms to my nation and to offer sacrifices. 18While I was doing
this, they found me in the temple,
completing the rite of purification,
without any crowd or disturbance.
19But there were some Jews from
Asia — they ought to be here before
you to make an accusation, if they
have anything against me. 20Or let
these men here tell what crime

23.26 Acts 24.3; 15.23
23.27 Acts 21.32, 33; 22.25-29
23.28 Acts 22.30
23.29 Acts 18.15; 25.19; 26.31
23.30 vv. 20,21; Acts 24.19; 25.16
23.32 v. 23
23.33 vv. 23,24,26
23.34 Acts 21.39
23.35 Acts 24.19; 25.16; 24.27
24.1 Acts 23.2, 30,35
24.3 Acts 23.26; 26.25
24.5 Acts 16.20; 17.6; 21.28
24.6 Acts 21.28
24.9 1 Thes 2.16
24.10 Acts 23.24
24.11 Acts 21.26
24.12 Acts 25.8; 28.17
24.13 Acts 25.7
24.14 Acts 9.2; v. 5; Acts 3.13; 26.22; 28.23
24.15 Acts 23.6; 28.20; Dan 12.2; Jn 5.28,29
24.16 Acts 23.1
24.17 Acts 11.29, 30; Rom 15.25-28; 2 Cor 8.1-4; Gal 2.10
24.18 Acts 21.26, 27
24.19 Acts 23.30

[l] Other ancient authorities add *Farewell* [m] Gk *praetorium* [n] Gk *he* [o] Gk lacks *Your Excellency* [p] Gk *Nazoreans* [q] Other ancient authorities add *and we would have judged him according to our law. 7But the chief captain Lysias came and with great violence took him out of our hands, 8commanding his accusers to come before you.* [r] Other ancient authorities read *of the dead, both of*

they had found when I stood before
the council, 21 unless it was this
one sentence that I called out
while standing before them, 'It is
about the resurrection of the dead
that I am on trial before you today.' "
22 But Felix, who was rather
well informed about the Way, ad-
journed the hearing with the comment, "When Lysias the tribune
comes down, I will decide your
case." 23 Then he ordered the centurion to keep him in custody, but
to let him have some liberty and
not to prevent any of his friends
from taking care of his needs.

Paul Held in Custody

24 Some days later when Felix
came with his wife Drusilla, who
was Jewish, he sent for Paul and
heard him speak concerning faith
in Christ Jesus. 25 And as he discussed justice, self-control, and
the coming judgment, Felix became frightened and said, "Go
away for the present; when I have
an opportunity, I will send for you."
26 At the same time he hoped that
money would be given him by Paul,
and for that reason he used to send
for him very often and converse
with him.
27 After two years had passed,
Felix was succeeded by Porcius
Festus; and since he wanted to
grant the Jews a favor, Felix left
Paul in prison.

Paul Appeals to Caesar

25 Three days after Festus had
arrived in the province, he
went up from Caesarea to Jerusalem 2 where the chief priests and
the leaders of the Jews gave him a
report against Paul. They appealed
to him 3 and requested, as a favor to
them against Paul,[s] to have him
transferred to Jerusalem. They
were, in fact, planning an ambush
to kill him along the way. 4 Festus
replied that Paul was being kept at
Caesarea, and that he himself intended to go there shortly. 5 "So,"
he said, "let those of you who have
the authority come down with me,
and if there is anything wrong
about the man, let them accuse
him."
6 After he had stayed among
them not more than eight or ten
days, he went down to Caesarea;
the next day he took his seat on the
tribunal and ordered Paul to be
brought. 7 When he arrived, the
Jews who had gone down from Jerusalem surrounded him, bringing
many serious charges against him,
which they could not prove. 8 Paul
said in his defense, "I have in no
way committed an offense against
the law of the Jews, or against the
temple, or against the emperor."
9 But Festus, wishing to do the
Jews a favor, asked Paul, "Do you
wish to go up to Jerusalem and be
tried there before me on these
charges?" 10 Paul said, "I am appealing to the emperor's tribunal;
this is where I should be tried. I
have done no wrong to the Jews, as
you very well know. 11 Now if I am
in the wrong and have committed
something for which I deserve to
die, I am not trying to escape
death; but if there is nothing to
their charges against me, no one
can turn me over to them. I appeal
to the emperor." 12 Then Festus, after he had conferred with his council, replied, "You have appealed to
the emperor; to the emperor you
will go."

Festus Consults King Agrippa

13 After several days had
passed, King Agrippa and Bernice
arrived at Caesarea to welcome
Festus. 14 Since they were staying
there several days, Festus laid
Paul's case before the king, saying,
"There is a man here who was left
in prison by Felix. 15 When I was in
Jerusalem, the chief priests and
the elders of the Jews informed me
about him and asked for a sentence
against him. 16 I told them that it
was not the custom of the Romans
to hand over anyone before the ac-

24.21 Acts 23.6
24.23 Acts 23.35; 28.16; 23.16; 27.3
24.25 Gal 5.23; Acts 10.42
24.27 Acts 25.1,4, 9,14; 12.3; 23.35
25.2 Acts 24.1; v. 15
25.3 Acts 23.12, 15
25.4 Acts 24.23
25.7 Mk 15.3; Lk 23.2,10; Acts 24.5,13
25.8 Acts 6.13; 24.12; 28.17
25.9 Acts 24.27; v. 20
25.11 v. 25; Acts 26.32; 28.19
25.14 Acts 24.27
25.15 Acts 24.1; v. 2
25.16 vv. 4,5

[s] Gk *him*

cused had met the accusers face to
face and had been given an opportunity to make a defense against
the charge. 17 So when they met
here, I lost no time, but on the next
day took my seat on the tribunal
and ordered the man to be brought.
18 When the accusers stood up,
they did not charge him with any of
the crimes[t] that I was expecting.
19 Instead they had certain points
of disagreement with him about
their own religion and about a certain Jesus, who had died, but
whom Paul asserted to be alive.
20 Since I was at a loss how to investigate these questions, I asked
whether he wished to go to Jerusalem and be tried there on these
charges.[u] 21 But when Paul had appealed to be kept in custody for the
decision of his Imperial Majesty, I
ordered him to be held until I could
send him to the emperor." 22 Agrippa said to Festus, "I would like to
hear the man myself." "Tomorrow," he said, "you will hear him."

Paul Brought before Agrippa

23 So on the next day Agrippa
and Bernice came with great pomp,
and they entered the audience hall
with the military tribunes and the
prominent men of the city. Then
Festus gave the order and Paul was
brought in. 24 And Festus said,
"King Agrippa and all here present
with us, you see this man about
whom the whole Jewish community petitioned me, both in Jerusalem and here, shouting that he
ought not to live any longer. 25 But
I found that he had done nothing
deserving death; and when he appealed to his Imperial Majesty, I
decided to send him. 26 But I have
nothing definite to write to our sovereign about him. Therefore I have
brought him before all of you, and
especially before you, King Agrippa, so that, after we have examined
him, I may have something to
write — 27 for it seems to me unreasonable to send a prisoner without
indicating the charges against
him."

25.17 vv. 6,10
25.19 Acts 18.15; 23.29
25.20 v. 9
25.21 vv. 11,12
25.22 Acts 9.15
25.23 v. 13; Acts 26.30
25.24 vv. 2,3,7; Acts 22.22
25.25 Acts 23.9, 29; 26.31,32

26.1 Acts 9.15; 25.22
26.3 Acts 6.14; 25.19; v. 7
26.4 Gal 1.13,14; Phil 3.5
26.5 Acts 22.3; 23.6; Phil 3.5
26.6 Acts 23.6; 13.32; Rom 15.8; Titus 2.13
26.7 Jas 1.1; 1 Thes 3.10; 1 Tim 5.5
26.9 Jn 16.2; 1 Tim 1.13; Jn 15.21
26.10 Acts 8.3; Gal 1.13; Acts 9.14,21
26.12 Acts 9.3; 22.6

Paul Defends Himself before Agrippa

26 Agrippa said to Paul, "You
have permission to speak
for yourself." Then Paul stretched
out his hand and began to defend
himself:
2 "I consider myself fortunate
that it is before you, King Agrippa,
I am to make my defense today
against all the accusations of the
Jews, 3 because you are especially
familiar with all the customs and
controversies of the Jews; therefore
I beg of you to listen to me patiently.
4 "All the Jews know my way of
life from my youth, a life spent
from the beginning among my own
people and in Jerusalem. 5 They
have known for a long time, if they
are willing to testify, that I have belonged to the strictest sect of our
religion and lived as a Pharisee.
6 And now I stand here on trial on
account of my hope in the promise
made by God to our ancestors, 7 a
promise that our twelve tribes hope
to attain, as they earnestly worship
day and night. It is for this hope,
your Excellency,[v] that I am accused by Jews! 8 Why is it thought
incredible by any of you that God
raises the dead?
9 "Indeed, I myself was convinced that I ought to do many
things against the name of Jesus of
Nazareth.[w] 10 And that is what I did
in Jerusalem; with authority received from the chief priests, I not
only locked up many of the saints
in prison, but I also cast my vote
against them when they were being
condemned to death. 11 By punishing them often in all the synagogues I tried to force them to blaspheme; and since I was so furiously
enraged at them, I pursued them
even to foreign cities.

Paul Tells of His Conversion

12 "With this in mind, I was
traveling to Damascus with the authority and commission of the

[t] Other ancient authorities read *with anything*
[u] Gk *on them* [v] Gk *O king* [w] Gk *the Nazorean*

chief priests, 13 when at midday
along the road, your Excellency,[x] I
saw a light from heaven, brighter
than the sun, shining around me
and my companions. 14 When we
had all fallen to the ground, I heard
a voice saying to me in the Hebrew[y] language, 'Saul, Saul, why
are you persecuting me? It hurts
you to kick against the goads.' 15 I
asked, 'Who are you, Lord?' The
Lord answered, 'I am Jesus whom
you are persecuting. 16 But get up
and stand on your feet; for I have
appeared to you for this purpose, to
appoint you to serve and testify to
the things in which you have seen
me[z] and to those in which I will
appear to you. 17 I will rescue you
from your people and from the
Gentiles—to whom I am sending
you 18 to open their eyes so that
they may turn from darkness to
light and from the power of Satan
to God, so that they may receive
forgiveness of sins and a place
among those who are sanctified by
faith in me.'

Paul Tells of His Preaching

19 "After that, King Agrippa, I
was not disobedient to the heavenly vision, 20 but declared first to
those in Damascus, then in Jerusalem and throughout the countryside of Judea, and also to the Gentiles, that they should repent and
turn to God and do deeds consistent with repentance. 21 For this reason the Jews seized me in the temple and tried to kill me. 22 To this
day I have had help from God, and
so I stand here, testifying to both
small and great, saying nothing but
what the prophets and Moses said
would take place: 23 that the Messiah[a] must suffer, and that, by being
the first to rise from the dead, he
would proclaim light both to our
people and to the Gentiles."

Paul Appeals to Agrippa to Believe

24 While he was making this defense, Festus exclaimed, "You are
out of your mind, Paul! Too much
learning is driving you insane!"
25 But Paul said, "I am not out of
my mind, most excellent Festus,
but I am speaking the sober truth.
26 Indeed the king knows about
these things, and to him I speak
freely; for I am certain that none of
these things has escaped his notice, for this was not done in a corner. 27 King Agrippa, do you believe
the prophets? I know that you believe." 28 Agrippa said to Paul, "Are
you so quickly persuading me to
become a Christian?"[b] 29 Paul replied, "Whether quickly or not, I
pray to God that not only you but
also all who are listening to me today might become such as I am—
except for these chains."

30 Then the king got up, and
with him the governor and Bernice
and those who had been seated
with them; 31 and as they were leaving, they said to one another, "This
man is doing nothing to deserve
death or imprisonment." 32 Agrippa
said to Festus, "This man could
have been set free if he had not appealed to the emperor."

Paul Sails for Rome

27 When it was decided that
we were to sail for Italy,
they transferred Paul and some
other prisoners to a centurion of
the Augustan Cohort, named Julius. 2 Embarking on a ship of Adra-
myttium that was about to set sail
to the ports along the coast of Asia,
we put to sea, accompanied by Aristarchus, a Macedonian from
Thessalonica. 3 The next day we
put in at Sidon; and Julius treated
Paul kindly, and allowed him to go
to his friends to be cared for. 4 Putting out to sea from there, we
sailed under the lee of Cyprus, because the winds were against us.
5 After we had sailed across the sea
that is off Cilicia and Pamphylia,
we came to Myra in Lycia. 6 There
the centurion found an Alexandrian ship bound for Italy and put
us on board. 7 We sailed slowly for

26.14 Acts 9.7; 21.40 **26.16** Ezek 2.1; Dan 10.11; Acts 22.14, 15 **26.17** Jer 1.8,19; Acts 22.21 **26.18** Isa 35.5; 42.7; Eph 5.8; Col 1.13; 1 Pet 2.9; Lk 24.47; Acts 2.38; 20.32 **26.20** Acts 9.19-29; 22.17-20; 13.46; 9.15; 3.19; Mt 3.8; Lk 3.8 **26.21** Acts 21.30, 31 **26.22** Lk 24.27,44; Acts 24.14 **26.23** Mt 26.24; 1 Cor 15.20; Col 1.18; Rev 1.5; Lk 2.32 **26.24** 2 Kings 9.11; Jn 10.20; 1 Corr 1.23 **26.25** Acts 23.26; 24.3 **26.30** Acts 25.33 **26.31** Acts 23.29 **26.32** Acts 28.18; 25.11 **27.1** Acts 25.12, 25; 10.1 **27.2** Acts 19.29; 16.9; 17.1 **27.3** Acts 24.23; 28.16 **27.4** v. 7 **27.5** Acts 6.9; 13.13 **27.6** Acts 28.11; v. 1 **27.7** vv. 4,12,13

[x] Gk *O king* [y] That is, *Aramaic* [z] Other ancient authorities read *the things that you have seen* [a] Or *the Christ* [b] Or *Quickly you will persuade me to play the Christian*

a number of days and arrived with
difficulty off Cnidus, and as the
wind was against us, we sailed under the lee of Crete off Salmone.
8 Sailing past it with difficulty, we
came to a place called Fair Havens,
near the city of Lasea.
9 Since much time had been
lost and sailing was now dangerous, because even the Fast had already gone by, Paul advised them,
10 saying, "Sirs, I can see that the
voyage will be with danger and
much heavy loss, not only of the
cargo and the ship, but also of our
lives." 11 But the centurion paid
more attention to the pilot and to
the owner of the ship than to what
Paul said. 12 Since the harbor was
not suitable for spending the winter, the majority was in favor of putting to sea from there, on the
chance that somehow they could
reach Phoenix, where they could
spend the winter. It was a harbor of
Crete, facing southwest and north-
west.

The Storm at Sea

13 When a moderate south wind
began to blow, they thought they
could achieve their purpose; so
they weighed anchor and began to
sail past Crete, close to the shore.
14 But soon a violent wind, called
the northeaster, rushed down from
Crete.[c] 15 Since the ship was
caught and could not be turned
head-on into the wind, we gave way
to it and were driven. 16 By running
under the lee of a small island
called Cauda[d] we were scarcely
able to get the ship's boat under
control. 17 After hoisting it up they
took measures[e] to undergird the
ship; then, fearing that they would
run on the Syrtis, they lowered the
sea anchor and so were driven.
18 We were being pounded by the
storm so violently that on the next
day they began to throw the cargo
overboard, 19 and on the third day
with their own hands they threw
the ship's tackle overboard.
20 When neither sun nor stars appeared for many days, and no small
tempest raged, all hope of our being saved was at last abandoned.
21 Since they had been without
food for a long time, Paul then
stood up among them and said,
"Men, you should have listened to
me and not have set sail from Crete
and thereby avoided this damage
and loss. 22 I urge you now to keep
up your courage, for there will be
no loss of life among you, but only
of the ship. 23 For last night there
stood by me an angel of the God to
whom I belong and whom I worship, 24 and he said, 'Do not be
afraid, Paul; you must stand before
the emperor; and indeed, God has
granted safety to all those who are
sailing with you.' 25 So keep up your
courage, men, for I have faith in
God that it will be exactly as I have
been told. 26 But we will have to run
aground on some island."
27 When the fourteenth night
had come, as we were drifting
across the sea of Adria, about midnight the sailors suspected that
they were nearing land. 28 So they
took soundings and found twenty
fathoms; a little farther on they
took soundings again and found fifteen fathoms. 29 Fearing that we
might run on the rocks, they let
down four anchors from the stern
and prayed for day to come. 30 But
when the sailors tried to escape
from the ship and had lowered the
boat into the sea, on the pretext of
putting out anchors from the bow,
31 Paul said to the centurion and
the soldiers, "Unless these men
stay in the ship, you cannot be
saved." 32 Then the soldiers cut
away the ropes of the boat and set
it adrift.
33 Just before daybreak, Paul
urged all of them to take some
food, saying, "Today is the fourteenth day that you have been in
suspense and remaining without
food, having eaten nothing.
34 Therefore I urge you to take some
food, for it will help you survive; for
none of you will lose a hair from

27.9 Lev 23.27-29 **27.10** v. 21 **27.13** vv. 7,12 **27.14** Mk 4.37 **27.17** vv. 26,29 **27.18** Jon 1.5; v. 38 **27.21** vv. 10,7,12, 13 **27.22** vv. 25,36 **27.23** Acts 23.11; 5.19; Rom 1.9 **27.24** Acts 23.11; v. 44 **27.25** vv. 22,36; Rom 4.20, 21 **27.26** Acts 28.1 **27.30** v. 16 **27.34** 1 Kings 1.52; Mt 10.30; Lk 12.7; 21.18

[c] Gk *it* [d] Other ancient authorities read *Clauda* [e] Gk *helps*

your heads." 35 After he had said
this, he took bread; and giving
thanks to God in the presence of
all, he broke it and began to eat.
36 Then all of them were encouraged and took food for themselves.
37 (We were in all two hundred
seventy-six[f] persons in the ship.)
38 After they had satisfied their
hunger, they lightened the ship by
throwing the wheat into the sea.

The Shipwreck

39 In the morning they did not
recognize the land, but they noticed a bay with a beach, on which
they planned to run the ship
ashore, if they could. 40 So they cast
off the anchors and left them in the
sea. At the same time they loosened the ropes that tied the
steering-oars; then hoisting the
foresail to the wind, they made for
the beach. 41 But striking a reef,[g]
they ran the ship aground; the bow
stuck and remained immovable,
but the stern was being broken up
by the force of the waves. 42 The
soldiers' plan was to kill the prisoners, so that none might swim away
and escape; 43 but the centurion,
wishing to save Paul, kept them
from carrying out their plan. He ordered those who could swim to
jump overboard first and make for
the land, 44 and the rest to follow,
some on planks and others on
pieces of the ship. And so it was
that all were brought safely to land.

Paul on the Island of Malta

28 After we had reached safety, we then learned that the
island was called Malta. 2 The natives showed us unusual kindness.
Since it had begun to rain and was
cold, they kindled a fire and welcomed all of us around it. 3 Paul
had gathered a bundle of brushwood and was putting it on the fire,
when a viper, driven out by the
heat, fastened itself on his hand.
4 When the natives saw the creature
hanging from his hand, they said to
one another, "This man must be a
murderer; though he has escaped

27.35 1 Sam 9.13; Mt 15.36; Mk 8.6; Jn 6.11; 1 Tim 4.3, 4
27.36 vv. 22,25
27.38 v. 18
27.39 Acts 28.1
27.40 v. 29
27.41 2 Cor 11.25
27.42 Acts 12.19
27.43 v. 3
27.44 vv. 22,31
28.1 Acts 27.26, 39
28.2 Rom 1.14; 1 Cor 14.11; Col 3.11
28.4 Lk 13.2,4
28.5 Lk 10.19
28.6 Acts 14.11
28.8 Jas 5.14,15; Mk 5.23
28.11 Acts 27.6
28.14 Acts 1.15
28.16 Acts 24.23; 27.3

from the sea, justice has not allowed him to live." 5 He, however,
shook off the creature into the fire
and suffered no harm. 6 They were
expecting him to swell up or drop
dead, but after they had waited a
long time and saw that nothing unusual had happened to him, they
changed their minds and began to
say that he was a god.

7 Now in the neighborhood of
that place were lands belonging to
the leading man of the island,
named Publius, who received us
and entertained us hospitably for
three days. 8 It so happened that
the father of Publius lay sick in bed
with fever and dysentery. Paul visited him and cured him by praying
and putting his hands on him. 9 After this happened, the rest of the
people on the island who had diseases also came and were cured.
10 They bestowed many honors on
us, and when we were about to sail,
they put on board all the provisions
we needed.

Paul Arrives at Rome

11 Three months later we set
sail on a ship that had wintered at
the island, an Alexandrian ship
with the Twin Brothers as its fig-
urehead. 12 We put in at Syracuse
and stayed there for three days;
13 then we weighed anchor and
came to Rhegium. After one day
there a south wind sprang up, and
on the second day we came to Puteoli. 14 There we found believers[h]
and were invited to stay with them
for seven days. And so we came to
Rome. 15 The believers[h] from
there, when they heard of us, came
as far as the Forum of Appius and
Three Taverns to meet us. On seeing them, Paul thanked God and
took courage.

16 When we came into Rome,
Paul was allowed to live by himself,
with the soldier who was guarding
him.

[f] Other ancient authorities read *seventy-six*; others, *about seventy-six* [g] Gk *place of two seas* [h] Gk *brothers*

Paul and Jewish Leaders in Rome

17 Three days later he called together the local leaders of the
Jews. When they had assembled,
he said to them, "Brothers, though
I had done nothing against our people or the customs of our ancestors, yet I was arrested in Jerusalem and handed over to the
Romans. 18 When they had examined me, the Romans[i] wanted to
release me, because there was no
reason for the death penalty in my
case. 19 But when the Jews object-
ed, I was compelled to appeal to
the emperor—even though I had
no charge to bring against my nation. 20 For this reason therefore I
have asked to see you and speak
with you,[j] since it is for the sake of
the hope of Israel that I am bound
with this chain." 21 They replied,
"We have received no letters from
Judea about you, and none of the
brothers coming here has reported
or spoken anything evil about you.
22 But we would like to hear from
you what you think, for with regard
to this sect we know that everywhere it is spoken against."

Paul Preaches in Rome

23 After they had set a day to
meet with him, they came to him at
his lodgings in great numbers.
From morning until evening he explained the matter to them, testifying to the kingdom of God and trying to convince them about Jesus
both from the law of Moses and
from the prophets. 24 Some were
convinced by what he had said,
while others refused to believe.
25 So they disagreed with each other; and as they were leaving, Paul
made one further statement: "The
Holy Spirit was right in saying to
your ancestors through the prophet
Isaiah,

26 'Go to this people and say,
You will indeed listen, but
never understand,
and you will indeed look,
but never perceive.
27 For this people's heart has
grown dull,
and their ears are hard of
hearing,
and they have shut their
eyes;
so that they might not
look with their eyes,
and listen with their ears,
and understand with their
heart and turn—
and I would heal them.'

28 Let it be known to you then that
this salvation of God has been sent
to the Gentiles; they will listen."[k]

30 He lived there two whole
years at his own expense[l] and welcomed all who came to him, 31 proclaiming the kingdom of God and
teaching about the Lord Jesus
Christ with all boldness and without hindrance.

28.17 Acts 13.50; 25.8; 6.14
28.18 Acts 22.24; 26.31,32; 23.29
28.19 Acts 25.11
28.20 Acts 26.6,7, 29; Eph 3.1; 4.1; 6.20; 2 Tim 1.16
28.21 Acts 22.5
28.22 Acts 24.14; 1 Pet 2.12; 4.14
28.23 Acts 17.3; 19.8
28.24 Acts 14.4
28.26 Isa 6.9,10; Mt 13.14, 15; Rom 11.8
28.28 Mt 21.41, 43; Acts 13.46, 47; Rom 11.11
28.31 v. 23; Eph 6.19; 2 Tim 2.9

[i] Gk *they* [j] Or *I have asked you to see me and speak with me* [k] Other ancient authorities add verse 29, *And when he had said these words, the Jews departed, arguing vigorously among themselves* [l] Or *in his own hired dwelling*

THE LETTER OF PAUL TO THE

Romans

Title and Background

When Paul wrote this letter, he was probably in Corinth on his third missionary journey. His work in the eastern Mediterranean was almost finished, and he greatly desired to visit the church in Rome. At this time, however, he could not go to Rome, so he sent a letter there, intending to visit Rome while en route on a mission to Spain. This letter served as a theological introduction to that hoped-for personal ministry.

Author and Date of Writing

The writer of this letter was the apostle Paul; it was probably written in the early spring of A.D. 57.

Theme and Message

Paul's primary theme in Romans is the basic gospel–God's plan of salvation and righteousness for the whole human race, Jew and Gentile alike (see 1.16-17). "The gospel of God" (1.1) includes justification by faith, but it also embraces such related ideas as guilt, sanctification, and security. Romans is the most comprehensive and systematic statement of the Christian faith in the Bible.

Outline

I. Introduction (1.1-15)
II. Theme: Righteousness from God (1.16-17)
III. The Unrighteousness of All Humanity (1.18–3.20)
IV. Righteousness Imputed: Justification (3.21–5.21)
V. Righteousness Imparted: Sanctification (6.1–8.39)
VI. God's Righteousness Vindicated : The Problem of Israel's Rejection (9.1–11.36)
VII. Righteousness Practiced (12.1–15.13)
VIII. Conclusion (15.14-33)
IX. Commendation and Greetings (16.1-27)

Salutation

1 Paul, a servant[a] of Jesus
Christ, called to be an apostle,
set apart for the gospel of God,
2 which he promised beforehand
through his prophets in the holy
scriptures, 3 the gospel concerning
his Son, who was descended from
David according to the flesh 4 and
was declared to be Son of God with
power according to the spirit[b] of
holiness by resurrection from the
dead, Jesus Christ our Lord,
5 through whom we have received
grace and apostleship to bring
about the obedience of faith
among all the Gentiles for the sake
of his name, 6 including yourselves
who are called to belong to Jesus
Christ,
7 To all God's beloved in Rome,
who are called to be saints:
Grace to you and peace from
God our Father and the Lord Jesus
Christ.

1.1 1 Cor 1.1; Acts 9.15; 2 Cor 11.7
1.2 Acts 26.6; Gal 3.8
1.3 Jn 1.14
1.4 Acts 13.33; Heb 9.14
1.5 Gal 1.16; Acts 6.7; 9.15
1.7 1 Cor 1.2, 3; Gal 1.3; Eph 1.2
1.8 Phil 1.3; Acts 16.19

Prayer of Thanksgiving

8 First, I thank my God through
Jesus Christ for all of you, because
your faith is proclaimed throughout the world. 9 For God, whom I

1.9 Phil 1.8; Acts 24.14; Eph 1.16

[a] Gk *slave* [b] Or *Spirit*

serve with my spirit by announcing
the gospel[c] of his Son, is my witness that without ceasing I remember you always in my prayers,
10 asking that by God's will I may
somehow at last succeed in coming
to you. 11 For I am longing to see
you so that I may share with you
some spiritual gift to strengthen
you— 12 or rather so that we may
be mutually encouraged by each
other's faith, both yours and mine.
13 I want you to know, brothers and
sisters,[d] that I have often intended
to come to you (but thus far have
been prevented), in order that I
may reap some harvest among you
as I have among the rest of the
Gentiles. 14 I am a debtor both
to Greeks and to barbarians, both
to the wise and to the foolish
15 —hence my eagerness to proclaim the gospel to you also who
are in Rome.

The Power of the Gospel

16 For I am not ashamed of the
gospel; it is the power of God for
salvation to everyone who has
faith, to the Jew first and also to
the Greek. 17 For in it the righteousness of God is revealed through
faith for faith; as it is written, "The
one who is righteous will live by
faith."[e]

The Guilt of Humankind

18 For the wrath of God is revealed from heaven against all ungodliness and wickedness of those
who by their wickedness suppress
the truth. 19 For what can be known
about God is plain to them, because God has shown it to them.
20 Ever since the creation of the
world his eternal power and divine
nature, invisible though they are,
have been understood and seen
through the things he has made. So
they are without excuse; 21 for
though they knew God, they did
not honor him as God or give
thanks to him, but they became futile in their thinking, and their
senseless minds were darkened.
22 Claiming to be wise, they became
fools; 23 and they exchanged the
glory of the immortal God for images resembling a mortal human
being or birds or four-footed animals or reptiles.
24 Therefore God gave them up
in the lusts of their hearts to impurity, to the degrading of their bodies among themselves, 25 because
they exchanged the truth about
God for a lie and worshiped and
served the creature rather than the
Creator, who is blessed forever!
Amen.
26 For this reason God gave
them up to degrading passions.
Their women exchanged natural
intercourse for unnatural, 27 and in
the same way also the men, giving
up natural intercourse with wom-
en, were consumed with passion
for one another. Men committed
shameless acts with men and received in their own persons the due
penalty for their error.
28 And since they did not see fit
to acknowledge God, God gave
them up to a debased mind and to
things that should not be done.
29 They were filled with every kind
of wickedness, evil, covetousness,
malice. Full of envy, murder, strife,
deceit, craftiness, they are gossips,
30 slanderers, God-haters,[f] insolent, haughty, boastful, inventors
of evil, rebellious toward parents,
31 foolish, faithless, heartless, ruthless. 32 They know God's decree,
that those who practice such
things deserve to die—yet they not
only do them but even applaud
others who practice them.

The Righteous Judgment of God

2 Therefore you have no excuse,
whoever you are, when you
judge others; for in passing judgment on another you condemn
yourself, because you, the judge,
are doing the very same things.
2 You say,[g] "We know that God's
judgment on those who do such
things is in accordance with truth."
3 Do you imagine, whoever you are,

1.10 Rom 15.32 **1.11** Rom 15.23 **1.13** Rom 15.22 **1.14** 1 Cor 9.16; Acts 28.2 **1.15** Rom 12.18; 15.20 **1.16** 2 Tim 1.8; 1 Cor 1.18; Acts 3.26; Rom 2.9 **1.17** Rom 3.21; Gal 3.11; Heb 10.38 **1.18ff** Eph 5.6; Col 3.6 **1.19** Acts 14.17 **1.20** Ps 19.1-6 **1.21** Jer 2.5; Eph 4.17,18 **1.22** Jer 10.14 **1.23** Ps 106.20; Jer 2.11; Acts 17.29

1.24 Eph 4.18, 19; 1 Pet 4.3 **1.25** Isa 44.20; Jer 10.14; Rom 9.5 **1.26** Lev 18.22; Eph 4.19; 1 Thes 4.5 **1.27** Lev 18.22; 20.13 **1.28** Eph 4.19 **1.30** Ps 5.5; 2 Tim 3.2 **1.31** 2 Tim 3.3 **1.32** Rom 6.21; Acts 8.1; 22.20 **2.1** Rom 1.20; 2 Sam 12.5-7; Mt 7.1,2

[c] Gk *my spirit in the gospel* [d] Gk *brothers* [e] Or *The one who is righteous through faith will live* [f] Or *God-hated* [g] Gk lacks *You say*

that when you judge those who do such things and yet do them yourself, you will escape the judgment of God? 4 Or do you despise the riches of his kindness and forbearance and patience? Do you not realize that God's kindness is meant to lead you to repentance? 5 But by your hard and impenitent heart you are storing up wrath for yourself on the day of wrath, when God's righteous judgment will be revealed. 6 For he will repay according to each one's deeds: 7 to those who by patiently doing good seek for glory and honor and immortality, he will give eternal life; 8 while for those who are self-seeking and who obey not the truth but wickedness, there will be wrath and fury. 9 There will be anguish and distress for everyone who does evil, the Jew first and also the Greek, 10 but glory and honor and peace for everyone who does good, the Jew first and also the Greek. 11 For God shows no partiality.

12 All who have sinned apart from the law will also perish apart from the law, and all who have sinned under the law will be judged by the law. 13 For it is not the hearers of the law who are righteous in God's sight, but the doers of the law who will be justified. 14 When Gentiles, who do not possess the law, do instinctively what the law requires, these, though not having the law, are a law to themselves. 15 They show that what the law requires is written on their hearts, to which their own conscience also bears witness; and their conflicting thoughts will accuse or perhaps excuse them 16 on the day when, according to my gospel, God, through Jesus Christ, will judge the secret thoughts of all.

The Jews and the Law

17 But if you call yourself a Jew and rely on the law and boast of your relation to God 18 and know his will and determine what is best because you are instructed in the law, 19 and if you are sure that you are a guide to the blind, a light to those who are in darkness, 20 a corrector of the foolish, a teacher of children, having in the law the embodiment of knowledge and truth, 21 you, then, that teach others, will you not teach yourself? While you preach against stealing, do you steal? 22 You that forbid adultery, do you commit adultery? You that abhor idols, do you rob temples? 23 You that boast in the law, do you dishonor God by breaking the law? 24 For, as it is written, "The name of God is blasphemed among the Gentiles because of you."

25 Circumcision indeed is of value if you obey the law; but if you break the law, your circumcision has become uncircumcision. 26 So, if those who are uncircumcised keep the requirements of the law, will not their uncircumcision be regarded as circumcision? 27 Then those who are physically uncircumcised but keep the law will condemn you that have the written code and circumcision but break the law. 28 For a person is not a Jew who is one outwardly, nor is true circumcision something external and physical. 29 Rather, a person is a Jew who is one inwardly, and real circumcision is a matter of the heart — it is spiritual and not literal. Such a person receives praise not from others but from God.

3 Then what advantage has the Jew? Or what is the value of circumcision? 2 Much, in every way. For in the first place the Jews[h] were entrusted with the oracles of God. 3 What if some were unfaithful? Will their faithlessness nullify the faithfulness of God? 4 By no means! Although everyone is a liar, let God be proved true, as it is written,

"So that you may be justified
in your words,
and prevail in your
judging."[i]

5 But if our injustice serves to con-

2.4 Eph 1.7; 2.7; Rom 11.22; 3.25; Ex 34.6; 2 Pet 3.9 **2.5** Deut 32.34; Jude 6 **2.6** Mt 16.27; 1 Cor 3.8; 2 Cor 5.10 **2.8** Gal 5.20; 2 Thes 2.12 **2.9** 1 Pet 4.17 **2.10** 1 Pet 1.7; v. 9 **2.11** Deut 10.17; Gal 2.6; Eph 6.9 **2.12** Rom 3.19; 1 Cor 9.21 **2.13** Jas 1.22,23, 25 **2.14ff** v. 15 **2.15** vv. 14,27 **2.16** Eccl 12.14; 1 Cor 4.5; Acts 10.42; 1 Tim 1.11 **2.17** v. 23; Mic 3.11; Rom 9.4 **2.18** Phil 1.10 **2.20** Rom 6.17; 2 Tim 1.13 **2.21** Mt 23.3,4 **2.22** Acts 19.37 **2.23** v. 17 **2.24** Isa 52.5 **2.25** Gal 5.3 **2.26** 1 Cor 7.19; Eph 2.11; Rom 8.4 **2.27** Mt 12.41 **2.28** Mt 3.9; Jn 8.39; Rom 9.6; Gal 6.15 **2.29** Col 2.11; 2 Cor 10.18; 1 Pet 3.4

3.2 Deut 4.8; Ps 147.19 **3.3** Heb 4.2; 2 Tim 2.13 **3.4** Jn 3.33; Ps 116.11; 51.4 **3.5** Rom 6.19; Gal 3.15

[h] Gk *they* [i] Gk *when you are being judged*

firm the justice of God, what
should we say? That God is unjust
to inflict wrath on us? (I speak in a
human way.) 6 By no means! For
then how could God judge the
world? 7 But if through my falsehood God's truthfulness abounds
to his glory, why am I still being
condemned as a sinner? 8 And why
not say (as some people slander us
by saying that we say), "Let us do
evil so that good may come"? Their
condemnation is deserved!

None Is Righteous

9 What then? Are we any better
off?[j] No, not at all; for we have already charged that all, both Jews
and Greeks, are under the power of
sin, 10 as it is written:

"There is no one who is
righteous, not even one;
11 there is no one who has
understanding,
there is no one who seeks
God.
12 All have turned aside,
together they have
become worthless;
there is no one who shows
kindness,
there is not even one."
13 "Their throats are opened
graves;
they use their tongues to
deceive."
"The venom of vipers is
under their lips."
14 "Their mouths are full of
cursing and bitterness."
15 "Their feet are swift to shed
blood;
16 ruin and misery are in their
paths,
17 and the way of peace they
have not known."
18 "There is no fear of God
before their eyes."

19 Now we know that whatever
the law says, it speaks to those who
are under the law, so that every
mouth may be silenced, and the
whole world may be held accountable to God. 20 For "no human being will be justified in his sight" by
deeds prescribed by the law, for

3.6 Gen 18.25 **3.7** v. 4 **3.8** Rom 6.1 **3.9** Gal 3.22 **3.10** Ps 14.1-3 **3.13** Ps 5.9 **3.14** Ps 10.7; 140.3 **3.15** Isa 59.7,8 **3.18** Ps 36.1 **3.19** Jn 10.34; Rom 2.12 **3.20** Ps 143.2; Acts 13.39; Gal 2.16; Rom 7.7

3.21 Rom 1.17; 9.30; 1.2; Acts 10.43 **3.22** Rom 10.12; Gal 3.28; Col 3.11 **3.23** Gal 3.22 **3.24** Rom 4.16; Eph 1.7; 2.8; Col 1.14; Heb 9.12,15 **3.25** 1 Jn 2.2; Heb 9.14, 28; 1 Pet 1.19 **3.27** Rom 2.17, 23; 4.2; 1 Cor 1.29-31; Eph 2.9 **3.28** Acts 13.39; Eph 2.9 **3.29** Rom 9.24; Acts 10.34, 35 **3.30** Gal 3.8 **4.2** 1 Cor 1.31 **4.3** Gen 15.6; Gal 3.6; Jas 2.23 **4.4** Rom 11.6

through the law comes the knowledge of sin.

Righteousness through Faith

21 But now, apart from law, the
righteousness of God has been disclosed, and is attested by the law
and the prophets, 22 the righteousness of God through faith in Jesus
Christ[k] for all who believe. For
there is no distinction, 23 since all
have sinned and fall short of the
glory of God; 24 they are now justified by his grace as a gift, through
the redemption that is in Christ
Jesus, 25 whom God put forward as
a sacrifice of atonement[l] by his
blood, effective through faith. He
did this to show his righteousness,
because in his divine forbearance
he had passed over the sins previously committed; 26 it was to prove
at the present time that he himself
is righteous and that he justifies
the one who has faith in Jesus.[m]

27 Then what becomes of boasting? It is excluded. By what law? By
that of works? No, but by the law of
faith. 28 For we hold that a person is
justified by faith apart from works
prescribed by the law. 29 Or is God
the God of Jews only? Is he not the
God of Gentiles also? Yes, of Gentiles also, 30 since God is one; and
he will justify the circumcised on
the ground of faith and the uncircumcised through that same faith.
31 Do we then overthrow the law by
this faith? By no means! On the
contrary, we uphold the law.

The Example of Abraham

4 What then are we to say was
gained by[n] Abraham, our ancestor according to the flesh? 2 For
if Abraham was justified by works,
he has something to boast about,
but not before God. 3 For what does
the scripture say? "Abraham believed God, and it was reckoned to
him as righteousness." 4 Now to
one who works, wages are not reckoned as a gift but as something

[j] Or *at any disadvantage?* [k] Or *through the faith of Jesus Christ* [l] Or *a place of atonement* [m] Or *who has the faith of Jesus* [n] Other ancient authorities read *say about*

due. 5 But to one who without
works trusts him who justifies the
ungodly, such faith is reckoned as
righteousness. 6 So also David
speaks of the blessedness of those
to whom God reckons righteousness apart from works:
7 "Blessed are those whose
iniquities are forgiven,
and whose sins are
covered;
8 blessed is the one against
whom the Lord will not
reckon sin."
9 Is this blessedness, then, pronounced only on the circumcised,
or also on the uncircumcised? We
say, "Faith was reckoned to Abraham as righteousness." 10 How
then was it reckoned to him? Was
it before or after he had been circumcised? It was not after, but before he was circumcised. 11 He received the sign of circumcision as a
seal of the righteousness that he
had by faith while he was still uncircumcised. The purpose was to
make him the ancestor of all who
believe without being circumcised
and who thus have righteousness
reckoned to them, 12 and likewise
the ancestor of the circumcised
who are not only circumcised but
who also follow the example of the
faith that our ancestor Abraham
had before he was circumcised.

God's Promise Realized through Faith

13 For the promise that he
would inherit the world did not
come to Abraham or to his descendants through the law but through
the righteousness of faith. 14 If it is
the adherents of the law who are to
be the heirs, faith is null and the
promise is void. 15 For the law
brings wrath; but where there is no
law, neither is there violation.
16 For this reason it depends on
faith, in order that the promise may
rest on grace and be guaranteed to
all his descendants, not only to the
adherents of the law but also to
those who share the faith of Abraham (for he is the father of all of us,
17 as it is written, "I have made you

4.7 Ps 32.1,2
4.8 2 Cor 5.19
4.9 Rom 3.30; v. 3
4.11 Gen 17.10; Lk 19.9
4.13 Gen 17.4-6; Gal 3.29
4.14 Gal 3.18
4.15 Rom 3.20; 7.8,10,11; Gal 3.10
4.16 Rom 3.24; 9.8; 15.8
4.17 Gen 17.5; 1 Cor 1.28
4.18 Gen 15.5
4.19 Gen 17.17; Heb 11.11
4.21 Gen 18.14; Heb 11.19
4.23 Rom 15.4; 1 Cor 9.10; 10.11
4.24 Rom 10.9; Acts 2.24
4.25 Isa 53.5,6; 2 Cor 5.21; 1 Cor 15.17
5.1 Rom 3.28
5.2 Eph 2.18; 1 Cor 15.1; Heb 3.6
5.3 2 Cor 12.10; Jas 1.2,3
5.5 Phil 1.20; Eph 1.13
5.6 Gal 4.4; Rom 4.25

the father of many nations")—in
the presence of the God in whom
he believed, who gives life to the
dead and calls into existence the
things that do not exist. 18 Hoping
against hope, he believed that he
would become "the father of many
nations," according to what was
said, "So numerous shall your descendants be." 19 He did not weak-
en in faith when he considered his
own body, which was already[o] as
good as dead (for he was about a
hundred years old), or when he
considered the barrenness of Sarah's womb. 20 No distrust made
him waver concerning the promise
of God, but he grew strong in his
faith as he gave glory to God, 21 being fully convinced that God was
able to do what he had promised.
22 Therefore his faith[p] "was reckoned to him as righteousness."
23 Now the words, "it was reckoned
to him," were written not for his
sake alone, 24 but for ours also. It
will be reckoned to us who believe
in him who raised Jesus our Lord
from the dead, 25 who was handed
over to death for our trespasses and
was raised for our justification.

Results of Justification

5 Therefore, since we are justified by faith, we[q] have peace
with God through our Lord Jesus
Christ, 2 through whom we have obtained access[r] to this grace in
which we stand; and we[s] boast in
our hope of sharing the glory of
God. 3 And not only that, but we[s]
also boast in our sufferings, knowing that suffering produces endurance, 4 and endurance produces
character, and character produces
hope, 5 and hope does not disap-
point us, because God's love has
been poured into our hearts
through the Holy Spirit that has
been given to us.
6 For while we were still weak,
at the right time Christ died for the
ungodly. 7 Indeed, rarely will any-

[o] Other ancient authorities lack *already*
[p] Gk *Therefore it* [q] Other ancient authorities read *let us* [r] Other ancient authorities add *by faith* [s] Or *let us*

one die for a righteous person—
though perhaps for a good person
someone might actually dare to
die. 8 But God proves his love for us
in that while we still were sinners
Christ died for us. 9 Much more
surely then, now that we have been
justified by his blood, will we be
saved through him from the wrath
of God.[t] 10 For if while we were enemies, we were reconciled to God
through the death of his Son, much
more surely, having been reconciled, will we be saved by his life.
11 But more than that, we even
boast in God through our Lord
Jesus Christ, through whom we
have now received reconciliation.

Adam and Christ

12 Therefore, just as sin came
into the world through one man,
and death came through sin, and
so death spread to all because all
have sinned— 13 sin was indeed in
the world before the law, but sin is
not reckoned when there is no law.
14 Yet death exercised dominion
from Adam to Moses, even over
those whose sins were not like the
transgression of Adam, who is a
type of the one who was to come.
15 But the free gift is not like
the trespass. For if the many died
through the one man's trespass,
much more surely have the grace of
God and the free gift in the grace of
the one man, Jesus Christ, abounded for the many. 16 And the free gift
is not like the effect of the one
man's sin. For the judgment following one trespass brought condemnation, but the free gift following many trespasses brings
justification. 17 If, because of the
one man's trespass, death exercised dominion through that one,
much more surely will those who
receive the abundance of grace and
the free gift of righteousness exercise dominion in life through the
one man, Jesus Christ.
18 Therefore just as one man's
trespass led to condemnation for
all, so one man's act of righteousness leads to justification and life
for all. 19 For just as by the one
man's disobedience the many were
made sinners, so by the one man's
obedience the many will be made
righteous. 20 But law came in, with
the result that the trespass multiplied; but where sin increased,
grace abounded all the more, 21 so
that, just as sin exercised dominion in death, so grace might also
exercise dominion through justification[u] leading to eternal life
through Jesus Christ our Lord.

Dying and Rising with Christ

6 What then are we to say?
Should we continue in sin in
order that grace may abound? 2 By
no means! How can we who died to
sin go on living in it? 3 Do you not
know that all of us who have been
baptized into Christ Jesus were
baptized into his death? 4 Therefore we have been buried with him
by baptism into death, so that, just
as Christ was raised from the dead
by the glory of the Father, so we too
might walk in newness of life.
5 For if we have been united
with him in a death like his, we will
certainly be united with him in a
resurrection like his. 6 We know
that our old self was crucified with
him so that the body of sin might
be destroyed, and we might no longer be enslaved to sin. 7 For whoever has died is freed from sin. 8 But
if we have died with Christ, we believe that we will also live with him.
9 We know that Christ, being raised
from the dead, will never die again;
death no longer has dominion over
him. 10 The death he died, he died
to sin, once for all; but the life he
lives, he lives to God. 11 So you also
must consider yourselves dead to
sin and alive to God in Christ Jesus.
12 Therefore, do not let sin exercise dominion in your mortal
bodies, to make you obey their passions. 13 No longer present your
members to sin as instruments[v] of
wickedness, but present yourselves
to God as those who have been

5.8 Jn 15.13; 1 Pet 3.18; 1 Jn 3.16
5.9 Rom 3.5,25; Heb 9.14; 1 Thes 1.10
5.10 Rom 11.28; Col 1.21,22; 2 Cor 5.18; Rom 8.34
5.12 Gen 2.17; 3.6,19; 1 Cor 15.21; Rom 6.23
5.13 Rom 4.15
5.14 1 Cor 15.22, 45
5.15 vv. 12,18, 19; Isa 53.11; Acts 15.11
5.17 2 Tim 2.12; Rev 22.5
5.18 v. 12; Rom 4.25
5.19 v. 12; Rom 11.32; Phil 2.8
5.20 Rom 7.7,8; Gal 3.19; 1 Tim 1.14
5.21 vv. 12,14; Jn 1.17; Rom 6.23
6.1 Rom 3.5,8; v. 15
6.2 Rom 7.4,6; Gal 2.19; Col 3.3; 1 Pet 2.24
6.3 Acts 2.38; 8.16; 19.5
6.4 Col 2.12; Gal 6.15; Eph 4.22-24; Col 3.10
6.6 Eph 4.22; Col 3.9; Gal 2.20; Rom 7.24
6.9 Rev 1.18
6.10 Heb 7.27
6.11 v. 2; Gal 2.19
6.12 v. 14
6.13 Rom 7.5; Col 3.5; Rom 12.1

[t] Gk *the wrath* [u] Or *righteousness*
[v] Or *weapons*

brought from death to life, and
present your members to God as
instruments[w] of righteousness.
14 For sin will have no dominion
over you, since you are not under
law but under grace.

Slaves of Righteousness

15 What then? Should we sin
because we are not under law but
under grace? By no means! 16 Do
you not know that if you present
yourselves to anyone as obedient
slaves, you are slaves of the one
whom you obey, either of sin,
which leads to death, or of obedience, which leads to righteousness? 17 But thanks be to God that
you, having once been slaves of sin,
have become obedient from the
heart to the form of teaching to
which you were entrusted, 18 and
that you, having been set free from
sin, have become slaves of righteousness. 19 I am speaking in human terms because of your natural
limitations.[x] For just as you once
presented your members as slaves
to impurity and to greater and
greater iniquity, so now present
your members as slaves to righteousness for sanctification.

20 When you were slaves of sin,
you were free in regard to righteousness. 21 So what advantage
did you then get from the things of
which you now are ashamed? The
end of those things is death. 22 But
now that you have been freed from
sin and enslaved to God, the advantage you get is sanctification. The
end is eternal life. 23 For the wages
of sin is death, but the free gift of
God is eternal life in Christ Jesus
our Lord.

An Analogy from Marriage

7 Do you not know, brothers
and sisters[y]—for I am speaking to those who know the law—
that the law is binding on a person
only during that person's lifetime?
2 Thus a married woman is bound
by the law to her husband as long
as he lives; but if her husband dies,
she is discharged from the law concerning the husband. 3 Accordingly, she will be called an adulteress
if she lives with another man while
her husband is alive. But if her husband dies, she is free from that law,
and if she marries another man,
she is not an adulteress.

4 In the same way, my friends,[y]
you have died to the law through
the body of Christ, so that you may
belong to another, to him who has
been raised from the dead in order
that we may bear fruit for God.
5 While we were living in the flesh,
our sinful passions, aroused by the
law, were at work in our members
to bear fruit for death. 6 But now we
are discharged from the law, dead
to that which held us captive, so
that we are slaves not under the old
written code but in the new life of
the Spirit.

The Law and Sin

7 What then should we say?
That the law is sin? By no means!
Yet, if it had not been for the law,
I would not have known sin. I
would not have known what it is to
covet if the law had not said, "You
shall not covet." 8 But sin, seizing
an opportunity in the commandment, produced in me all kinds of
covetousness. Apart from the law
sin lies dead. 9 I was once alive
apart from the law, but when the
commandment came, sin revived
10 and I died, and the very commandment that promised life
proved to be death to me. 11 For sin,
seizing an opportunity in the commandment, deceived me and
through it killed me. 12 So the law is
holy, and the commandment is
holy and just and good.

13 Did what is good, then, bring
death to me? By no means! It was
sin, working death in me through
what is good, in order that sin
might be shown to be sin, and
through the commandment might
become sinful beyond measure.

The Inner Conflict

14 For we know that the law is
spiritual; but I am of the flesh, sold

6.14 Rom 8.2; Gal 5.18
6.16 Rom 11.2; Mt 6.24; Jn 8.34; 2 Pet 2.19
6.17 Rom 1.8; 2 Tim 1.13
6.18 Jn 8.32; Rom 8.2
6.19 Rom 3.5; 6.13; 12.1
6.20 Mt 6.24; Jn 8.34
6.21 Rom 7.5; 8.6,13,21
6.22 Jn 8.32; 1 Cor 7.22; 1 Pet 2.16
6.23 Rom 5.12; 5.21; Gal 6.7,8
7.2 1 Cor 7.39
7.3 Mt 5.32
7.4 Rom 6.2,11; Gal 2.19; Col 1.22
7.5 Rom 6.13, 21; Gal 5.19; Jas 1.15
7.6 Rom 2.29; 2 Cor 3.6
7.7 Ex 20.17; Deut 5.21; Rom 3.20; 5.20
7.8 v. 11; 1 Cor 15.56
7.10 Lev 18.5; Rom 10.5; Gal 3.12
7.12 1 Tim 1.8

[w] Or *weapons* [x] Gk *the weakness of your flesh* [y] Gk *brothers*

into slavery under sin.[z] 15 I do not
understand my own actions. For I
do not do what I want, but I do the
very thing I hate. 16 Now if I do what
I do not want, I agree that the law
is good. 17 But in fact it is no longer
I that do it, but sin that dwells
within me. 18 For I know that nothing good dwells within me, that is,
in my flesh. I can will what is right,
but I cannot do it. 19 For I do not do
the good I want, but the evil I do
not want is what I do. 20 Now if I do
what I do not want, it is no longer
I that do it, but sin that dwells
within me.
21 So I find it to be a law that
when I want to do what is good, evil
lies close at hand. 22 For I delight in
the law of God in my inmost self,
23 but I see in my members another
law at war with the law of my mind,
making me captive to the law of sin
that dwells in my members.
24 Wretched man that I am! Who
will rescue me from this body of
death? 25 Thanks be to God through
Jesus Christ our Lord!
So then, with my mind I am a
slave to the law of God, but with my
flesh I am a slave to the law of sin.

Life in the Spirit

8 There is therefore now no condemnation for those who are
in Christ Jesus. 2 For the law of the
Spirit[a] of life in Christ Jesus has
set you[b] free from the law of sin
and of death. 3 For God has done
what the law, weakened by the
flesh, could not do: by sending his
own Son in the likeness of sinful
flesh, and to deal with sin,[c] he
condemned sin in the flesh, 4 so
that the just requirement of the law
might be fulfilled in us, who walk
not according to the flesh but according to the Spirit.[a] 5 For those
who live according to the flesh set
their minds on the things of the
flesh, but those who live according
to the Spirit[a] set their minds on
the things of the Spirit.[a] 6 To set
the mind on the flesh is death, but
to set the mind on the Spirit[a] is life
and peace. 7 For this reason the
mind that is set on the flesh is hostile to God; it does not submit to
God's law—indeed it cannot, 8 and
those who are in the flesh cannot
please God.
9 But you are not in the flesh;
you are in the Spirit,[a] since the
Spirit of God dwells in you. Anyone
who does not have the Spirit of
Christ does not belong to him.
10 But if Christ is in you, though the
body is dead because of sin, the
Spirit[a] is life because of righteousness. 11 If the Spirit of him who
raised Jesus from the dead dwells
in you, he who raised Christ[d] from
the dead will give life to your mortal bodies also through[e] his Spirit
that dwells in you.
12 So then, brothers and sisters,[f] we are debtors, not to the
flesh, to live according to the
flesh— 13 for if you live according
to the flesh, you will die; but if by
the Spirit you put to death the
deeds of the body, you will live.
14 For all who are led by the Spirit of
God are children of God. 15 For you
did not receive a spirit of slavery to
fall back into fear, but you have received a spirit of adoption. When
we cry, "Abba![g] Father!" 16 it is
that very Spirit bearing witness[h]
with our spirit that we are children
of God, 17 and if children, then
heirs, heirs of God and joint heirs
with Christ— if, in fact, we suffer
with him so that we may also be
glorified with him.

Future Glory

18 I consider that the sufferings
of this present time are not worth
comparing with the glory about to
be revealed to us. 19 For the creation waits with eager longing for
the revealing of the children of

7.15 Gal 5.17
7.16 v. 12
7.17 v. 20
7.18 v. 25
7.19 v. 15
7.20 v. 17
7.21 vv. 23,25
7.22 Ps 1.2; 2 Cor 4.16; Eph 3.16
7.23 Gal 5.17
7.24 Rom 6.6; 8.2
7.25 1 Cor 15.57
8.1 Rom 5.16
8.2 1 Cor 15.45; Rom 6.14, 18; Jn 8.32, 36
8.3 Acts 13.39; Heb 7.18; Ph 2.7; Heb 2.14
8.4 Gal 5.16,25
8.5 Gal 5.19-25
8.6 Rom 6.21; Gal 6.8
8.7 Jas 4.4
8.8 Rom 7.5
8.9 1 Cor 3.16; Gal 4.6; Phil 1.19; 1 Jn 4.13
8.10 Gal 2.20; Eph 3.17
8.11 Acts 2.24; Jn 5.21; 1 Cor 6.14
8.13 Gal 6.8; Col 3.5
8.14 Gal 5.18
8.15 2 Tim 1.7; Heb 2.15; Gal 4.5,6
8.16 2 Cor 1.22; Eph 1.13
8.17 Gal 4.7; 2 Tim 2.12; 1 Pet 4.13
8.18 2 Cor 4.17; Col 3.4; 1 Pet 5.1
8.19 Col 3.4; 1 Pet 1.7,13; 1 Jn 3.2

[z] Gk *sold under sin* [a] Or *spirit* [b] Here the Greek word *you* is singular number; other ancient authorities read *me* or *us* [c] Or *and as a sin offering* [d] Other ancient authorities read *the Christ* or *Christ Jesus* or *Jesus Christ* [e] Other ancient authorities read *on account of* [f] Gk *brothers* [g] Aramaic for *Father* [h] Or [15] *a spirit of adoption, by which we cry, "Abba! Father!"* [16] *The Spirit itself bears witness*

God; 20 for the creation was subjected to futility, not of its own will but by the will of the one who subjected it, in hope 21 that the creation itself will be set free from its bondage to decay and will obtain the freedom of the glory of the children of God. 22 We know that the whole creation has been groaning in labor pains until now; 23 and not only the creation, but we ourselves, who have the first fruits of the Spirit, groan inwardly while we wait for adoption, the redemption of our bodies. 24 For in[i] hope we were saved. Now hope that is seen is not hope. For who hopes[j] for what is seen? 25 But if we hope for what we do not see, we wait for it with patience.

26 Likewise the Spirit helps us in our weakness; for we do not know how to pray as we ought, but that very Spirit intercedes[k] with sighs too deep for words. 27 And God,[l] who searches the heart, knows what is the mind of the Spirit, because the Spirit[m] intercedes for the saints according to the will of God.[n]

28 We know that all things work together for good[o] for those who love God, who are called according to his purpose. 29 For those whom he foreknew he also predestined to be conformed to the image of his Son, in order that he might be the firstborn within a large family.[p] 30 And those whom he predestined he also called; and those whom he called he also justified; and those whom he justified he also glorified.

God's Love in Christ Jesus

31 What then are we to say about these things? If God is for us, who is against us? 32 He who did not withhold his own Son, but gave him up for all of us, will he not with him also give us everything else? 33 Who will bring any charge against God's elect? It is God who justifies. 34 Who is to condemn? It is Christ Jesus, who died, yes, who was raised, who is at the right hand of God, who indeed intercedes for us.[q] 35 Who will separate us from the love of Christ? Will hardship, or distress, or persecution, or famine, or nakedness, or peril, or sword? 36 As it is written,

"For your sake we are being
killed all day long;
we are accounted as sheep
to be slaughtered."

37 No, in all these things we are more than conquerors through him who loved us. 38 For I am convinced that neither death, nor life, nor angels, nor rulers, nor things present, nor things to come, nor powers, 39 nor height, nor depth, nor anything else in all creation, will be able to separate us from the love of God in Christ Jesus our Lord.

God's Election of Israel

9 I am speaking the truth in Christ—I am not lying; my conscience confirms it by the Holy Spirit— 2 I have great sorrow and unceasing anguish in my heart. 3 For I could wish that I myself were accursed and cut off from Christ for the sake of my own people,[r] my kindred according to the flesh. 4 They are Israelites, and to them belong the adoption, the glory, the covenants, the giving of the law, the worship, and the promises; 5 to them belong the patriarchs, and from them, according to the flesh, comes the Messiah,[s] who is over all, God blessed forever.[t] Amen.

6 It is not as though the word of God had failed. For not all Israelites truly belong to Israel, 7 and not all of Abraham's children are his true descendants; but "It is through Isaac that descendants shall be named for you." 8 This means that it is not the children of

8.20 Gen 3.17-19; Eccl 1.2 **8.21** Acts 3.21; Rom 6.21; 2 Pet 3.13; Rev 21.1 **8.23** 2 Cor 1.22; 5.2,4; Gal 5.5 **8.26** Mt 20.22; Eph 6.18 **8.27** Ps 139.1,2; Lk 16.15; Rev 2.23 **8.28** v. 32 **8.29** Rom 11.2; 1 Pet 1.2, 20; Eph 1.5, 11; Phil 3.21; Heb 1.6 **8.30** Eph 1.5,11; Rom 9.24; 1 Cor 6.11 **8.31** Rom 4.1; Ps 118.6 **8.32** Jn 3.16; Rom 5.8; 4.25 **8.33** Lk 18.7; Isa 50.8,9 **8.34** Col 3.1; Heb 1.3; 7.25; 9.24; 1 Jn 2.1 **8.36** Ps 44.22; 2 Cor 4.11 **8.37** 1 Cor 15.57; Rev 1.5 **8.38** Eph 1.21; 1 Pet 3.22 **9.1** 2 Cor 1.23; 11.10; 1 Tim 2.7 **9.3** Ex 32.32 **9.4** Acts 3.25; Ps 147.19; Heb 9.1 **9.5** Col 1.16-19; Jn 1.1; Rom 1.25 **9.6** Num 23.19; Rom 2.28, 29; Gal 6.16 **9.7** Gal 4.23; Heb 11.18 **9.8** Rom 8.14; Gal 3.29; 4.28

[i] Or *by* [j] Other ancient authorities read *awaits* [k] Other ancient authorities add *for us* [l] Gk *the one* [m] Gk *he* or *it* [n] Gk *according to God* [o] Other ancient authorities read *God makes all things work together for good*, or *in all things God works for good* [p] Gk *among many brothers* [q] Or *Is it Christ Jesus . . . for us?* [r] Gk *my brothers* [s] Or *the Christ* [t] Or *Messiah, who is God over all, blessed forever*; or *Messiah. May he who is God over all be blessed forever*

the flesh who are the children of
God, but the children of the promise are counted as descendants.
9For this is what the promise said,
"About this time I will return and
Sarah shall have a son." 10Nor is
that all; something similar happened to Rebecca when she had
conceived children by one husband, our ancestor Isaac. 11Even
before they had been born or had
done anything good or bad (so that
God's purpose of election might
continue, 12not by works but by his
call) she was told, "The elder shall
serve the younger." 13As it is written,

"I have loved Jacob,
but I have hated Esau."

14 What then are we to say? Is
there injustice on God's part? By
no means! 15For he says to Moses,

"I will have mercy on whom
I have mercy,
and I will have compassion
on whom I have
compassion."

16So it depends not on human will
or exertion, but on God who shows
mercy. 17For the scripture says to
Pharaoh, "I have raised you up for
the very purpose of showing my
power in you, so that my name may
be proclaimed in all the earth."
18So then he has mercy on whomever he chooses, and he hardens
the heart of whomever he chooses.

God's Wrath and Mercy

19 You will say to me then,
"Why then does he still find fault?
For who can resist his will?" 20But
who indeed are you, a human being, to argue with God? Will what is
molded say to the one who molds
it, "Why have you made me like
this?" 21Has the potter no right
over the clay, to make out of the
same lump one object for special
use and another for ordinary use?
22What if God, desiring to show his
wrath and to make known his power, has endured with much patience the objects of wrath that are
made for destruction; 23and what if
he has done so in order to make
known the riches of his glory for
the objects of mercy, which he has
prepared beforehand for glory—
24including us whom he has called,
not from the Jews only but also
from the Gentiles? 25As indeed he
says in Hosea,

"Those who were not my
people I will call 'my
people,'
and her who was not
beloved I will call
'beloved.' "

26 "And in the very place where
it was said to them,
'You are not my
people,'
there they shall be called
children of the living
God."

27 And Isaiah cries out concerning Israel, "Though the number of
the children of Israel were like the
sand of the sea, only a remnant of
them will be saved; 28for the Lord
will execute his sentence on the
earth quickly and decisively."[u]
29And as Isaiah predicted,

"If the Lord of hosts had not
left survivors[v] to us,
we would have fared like
Sodom
and been made like
Gomorrah."

Israel's Unbelief

30 What then are we to say?
Gentiles, who did not strive for
righteousness, have attained it,
that is, righteousness through
faith; 31but Israel, who did strive
for the righteousness that is based
on the law, did not succeed in fulfilling that law. 32Why not? Because they did not strive for it on
the basis of faith, but as if it were
based on works. They have stumbled over the stumbling stone, 33as
it is written,

"See, I am laying in Zion a
stone that will make
people stumble, a rock
that will make them
fall,

9.9 Gen 18.10 **9.10** Gen 25.21 **9.11** Rom 4.17; 8.28 **9.12** Gen 25.23 **9.13** Mal 1.2,3 **9.14** 2 Chr 19.7 **9.15** Ex 33.19 **9.16** Eph 2.8 **9.17** Ex 9.16 **9.19** 2 Chr 20.6; Job 23.13; Dan 4.35 **9.20** Isa 29.16; 64.8 **9.21** 2 Tim 2.20 **9.22** Rom 2.4 **9.23** Eph 3.16; Rom 8.29, 30 **9.24** Rom 3.29 **9.25** Hos 2.23; 1 Pet 2.10 **9.26** Hos 1.10 **9.27** Isa 10.22, 23; Gen 22.17; Hos 1.10 **9.29** Isa 1.4; 13.19; Jer 50.40 **9.30** Rom 10.6; Gal 2.16; Heb 11.7 **9.31** Rom 10.2,3; Gal 5.4 **9.32** 1 Pet 2.6,8 **9.33** Isa 28.16; Mt 21.42; Rom 10.11

u Other ancient authorities read *for he will finish his work and cut it short in righteousness, because the Lord will make the sentence shortened on the earth* v Or *descendants;* Gk *seed*

and whoever believes in
him[w] will not be put to
shame."

10 Brothers and sisters,[x] my
heart's desire and prayer to
God for them is that they may be
saved. 2 I can testify that they have
a zeal for God, but it is not enlightened. 3 For, being ignorant of the
righteousness that comes from
God, and seeking to establish their
own, they have not submitted to
God's righteousness. 4 For Christ is
the end of the law so that there may
be righteousness for everyone who
believes.

Salvation Is for All

5 Moses writes concerning the
righteousness that comes from the
law, that "the person who does
these things will live by them."
6 But the righteousness that comes
from faith says, "Do not say in your
heart, 'Who will ascend into heav-
en?' " (that is, to bring Christ
down) 7 "or 'Who will descend into
the abyss?' " (that is, to bring
Christ up from the dead). 8 But
what does it say?

"The word is near you,
on your lips and in your
heart"

(that is, the word of faith that we
proclaim); 9 because[y] if you confess with your lips that Jesus is
Lord and believe in your heart that
God raised him from the dead, you
will be saved. 10 For one believes
with the heart and so is justified,
and one confesses with the mouth
and so is saved. 11 The scripture
says, "No one who believes in him
will be put to shame." 12 For there
is no distinction between Jew and
Greek; the same Lord is Lord of all
and is generous to all who call on
him. 13 For, "Everyone who calls on
the name of the Lord shall be
saved."

14 But how are they to call on
one in whom they have not believed? And how are they to believe
in one of whom they have never
heard? And how are they to hear
without someone to proclaim him?
15 And how are they to proclaim
him unless they are sent? As it is
written, "How beautiful are the
feet of those who bring good news!"
16 But not all have obeyed the good
news;[z] for Isaiah says, "Lord, who
has believed our message?" 17 So
faith comes from what is heard,
and what is heard comes through
the word of Christ.[a]

18 But I ask, have they not
heard? Indeed they have; for

"Their voice has gone out to
all the earth,
and their words to the ends
of the world."

19 Again I ask, did Israel not understand? First Moses says,

"I will make you jealous of
those who are not a
nation;
with a foolish nation I will
make you angry."

20 Then Isaiah is so bold as to say,

"I have been found by those
who did not seek me;
I have shown myself to
those who did not ask
for me."

21 But of Israel he says, "All day
long I have held out my hands to a
disobedient and contrary people."

Israel's Rejection Is Not Final

11 I ask, then, has God rejected his people? By no
means! I myself am an Israelite, a
descendant of Abraham, a member
of the tribe of Benjamin. 2 God has
not rejected his people whom he
foreknew. Do you not know what
the scripture says of Elijah, how he
pleads with God against Israel?
3 "Lord, they have killed your
prophets, they have demolished
your altars; I alone am left, and
they are seeking my life." 4 But
what is the divine reply to him? "I
have kept for myself seven thousand who have not bowed the knee
to Baal." 5 So too at the present
time there is a remnant, chosen by
grace. 6 But if it is by grace, it is no
longer on the basis of works, other-

10.2 Acts 21.20 **10.3** Rom 1.17; Phil 3.9 **10.4** Gal 3.24; Rom 7.1-4 **10.5** Neh 9.29; Ezek 20.11, 13,21; Rom 7.10 **10.7** Heb 13.20 **10.8** Deut 30.14 **10.9** Mt 10.32; Lk 12.8; Acts 16.31 **10.11** Isa 28.16; Rom 9.33 **10.12** Rom 3.22, 29; Gal 3.28; Acts 10.36 **10.13** Joel 2.32; Acts 2.21 **10.15** Isa 52.7

10.16 Heb 4.2; Isa 53.1; Jn 12.38 **10.17** Gal 3.2,5; Col 3.16 **10.18** Ps 19.4; Col 1.6,23; 1 Thes 1.8 **10.19** Deut 32.21; Rom 11.11 **10.20** Isa 65.1; Rom 9.30 **10.21** Isa 65.2 **11.1** 1 Sam 12.22; Jer 31.37; 2 Cor 11.22; Phil 3.5 **11.2** Ps 94.19; 1 Kings 19.10; Rom 8.29 **11.4** 1 Kings 19.18 **11.5** 2 Kings 19.4; Rom 9.27 **11.6** Rom 4.4

[w] Or *trusts in it* [x] Gk *Brothers*
[y] Or *namely, that* [z] Or *gospel*
[a] Or *about Christ*; other ancient authorities read *of God*

wise grace would no longer be
grace.[b]
7 What then? Israel failed to obtain what it was seeking. The elect
obtained it, but the rest were hardened, 8 as it is written,
"God gave them a sluggish
spirit,
eyes that would not see
and ears that would not
hear,
down to this very day."
9 And David says,
"Let their table become a
snare and a trap,
a stumbling block and a
retribution for them;
10 let their eyes be darkened so
that they cannot see,
and keep their backs
forever bent."

The Salvation of the Gentiles

11 So I ask, have they stumbled
so as to fall? By no means! But
through their stumbling[c] salvation
has come to the Gentiles, so as to
make Israel[d] jealous. 12 Now if
their stumbling[c] means riches for
the world, and if their defeat means
riches for Gentiles, how much
more will their full inclusion mean!
13 Now I am speaking to you
Gentiles. Inasmuch then as I am an
apostle to the Gentiles, I glorify my
ministry 14 in order to make my own
people[e] jealous, and thus save
some of them. 15 For if their rejection is the reconciliation of the
world, what will their acceptance
be but life from the dead! 16 If the
part of the dough offered as first
fruits is holy, then the whole batch
is holy; and if the root is holy, then
the branches also are holy.
17 But if some of the branches
were broken off, and you, a wild olive shoot, were grafted in their
place to share the rich root[f] of the
olive tree, 18 do not boast over the
branches. If you do boast, remember that it is not you that support
the root, but the root that supports
you. 19 You will say, "Branches were
broken off so that I might be grafted in." 20 That is true. They were
broken off because of their unbelief, but you stand only through
faith. So do not become proud, but
stand in awe. 21 For if God did not
spare the natural branches, perhaps he will not spare you.[g]
22 Note then the kindness and the
severity of God: severity toward
those who have fallen, but God's
kindness toward you, provided you
continue in his kindness; otherwise you also will be cut off. 23 And
even those of Israel,[h] if they do not
persist in unbelief, will be grafted
in, for God has the power to graft
them in again. 24 For if you have
been cut from what is by nature a
wild olive tree and grafted, contrary
to nature, into a cultivated olive
tree, how much more will these
natural branches be grafted back
into their own olive tree.

All Israel Will Be Saved

25 So that you may not claim to
be wiser than you are, brothers and
sisters,[i] I want you to understand
this mystery: a hardening has come
upon part of Israel, until the full
number of the Gentiles has come
in. 26 And so all Israel will be saved;
as it is written,
"Out of Zion will come the
Deliverer;
he will banish ungodliness
from Jacob."
27 "And this is my covenant
with them,
when I take away their
sins."
28 As regards the gospel they are enemies of God[j] for your sake; but as
regards election they are beloved,
for the sake of their ancestors; 29 for
the gifts and the calling of God are
irrevocable. 30 Just as you were
once disobedient to God but have
now received mercy because of
their disobedience, 31 so they have
now been disobedient in order
that, by the mercy shown to you,

11.7 Rom 9.18, 31 **11.8** Isa 29.10; Deut 29.4; Mt 13.13,14 **11.9** Ps 69.22,23 **11.11** Acts 13.46; Rom 10.19 **11.12** v. 25 **11.13** Acts 9.15; Rom 15.16 **11.14** Rom 10.19; 1 Cor 7.16; 9.22 **11.15** Lk 15.24,32 **11.16** Lev 23.10; Num 15.18 **11.17** Jer 11.17; Acts 2.39; Eph 2.11,12 **11.20** Rom 12.16; 2 Cor 1.24 **11.22** 1 Cor 15.2; Heb 3.6; Jn 15.2 **11.23** 2 Cor 3.16 **11.25** 1 Cor 2.7-10; Eph 3.3-5,9; Rom 9.18 **11.26** Isa 59.20,21 **11.27** Isa 27.9 **11.28** Deut 7.8; 10.15; Rom 5.10; 9.5 **11.29** Num 23.19 **11.30** Eph 2.2

[b] Other ancient authorities add *But if it is by works, it is no longer on the basis of grace, otherwise work would no longer be work*
[c] Gk *transgression* [d] Gk *them*
[e] Gk *my flesh* [f] Other ancient authorities read *the richness* [g] Other ancient authorities read *neither will he spare you*
[h] Gk lacks *of Israel* [i] Gk *brothers*
[j] Gk lacks *of God*

they too may now[k] receive mercy.
32 For God has imprisoned all in
disobedience so that he may be
merciful to all.
33 O the depth of the riches and
wisdom and knowledge of God!
How unsearchable are his judgments and how inscrutable his
ways!

34 "For who has known the
mind of the Lord?
Or who has been his
counselor?"
35 "Or who has given a gift to
him,
to receive a gift in return?"

36 For from him and through him
and to him are all things. To him be
the glory forever. Amen.

The New Life in Christ

12 I appeal to you therefore,
brothers and sisters,[l] by
the mercies of God, to present your
bodies as a living sacrifice, holy
and acceptable to God, which is
your spiritual[m] worship. 2 Do not
be conformed to this world,[n] but
be transformed by the renewing of
your minds, so that you may discern what is the will of God—what
is good and acceptable and perfect.[o]
3 For by the grace given to me I
say to everyone among you not to
think of yourself more highly than
you ought to think, but to think
with sober judgment, each according to the measure of faith that God
has assigned. 4 For as in one body
we have many members, and not
all the members have the same
function, 5 so we, who are many,
are one body in Christ, and individually we are members one of another. 6 We have gifts that differ according to the grace given to us:
prophecy, in proportion to faith;
7 ministry, in ministering; the
teacher, in teaching; 8 the exhorter,
in exhortation; the giver, in generosity; the leader, in diligence; the
compassionate, in cheerfulness.

Marks of the True Christian

9 Let love be genuine; hate what
is evil, hold fast to what is good;
10 love one another with mutual affection; outdo one another in
showing honor. 11 Do not lag in
zeal, be ardent in spirit, serve the
Lord.[p] 12 Rejoice in hope, be patient in suffering, persevere in
prayer. 13 Contribute to the needs
of the saints; extend hospitality to
strangers.
14 Bless those who persecute
you; bless and do not curse them.
15 Rejoice with those who rejoice,
weep with those who weep. 16 Live
in harmony with one another; do
not be haughty, but associate with
the lowly;[q] do not claim to be wiser than you are. 17 Do not repay
anyone evil for evil, but take
thought for what is noble in the
sight of all. 18 If it is possible, so far
as it depends on you, live peaceably with all. 19 Beloved, never
avenge yourselves, but leave room
for the wrath of God;[r] for it is written, "Vengeance is mine, I will repay, says the Lord." 20 No, "if your
enemies are hungry, feed them; if
they are thirsty, give them something to drink; for by doing this you
will heap burning coals on their
heads." 21 Do not be overcome by
evil, but overcome evil with good.

Being Subject to Authorities

13 Let every person be subject
to the governing authori-
ties; for there is no authority except from God, and those authorities that exist have been instituted
by God. 2 Therefore whoever resists
authority resists what God has appointed, and those who resist will
incur judgment. 3 For rulers are not
a terror to good conduct, but to
bad. Do you wish to have no fear of
the authority? Then do what is
good, and you will receive its approval; 4 for it is God's servant for
your good. But if you do what is

11.32 Rom 3.9; Gal 3.22,23 **11.33** Eph 3.8; Ps 92.5 **11.34** Isa 40.13, 14; 1 Cor 2.16; Job 36.22 **11.36** 1 Cor 8.6; Heb 2.10; Rom 16.27; Heb 13.21 **12.1** 2 Cor 10.1,2 Rom 6.13, 16,19; 1 Pet 2.5 **12.2** 1 Pet 1.14; 1 Jn 2.15; Eph 4.23; 5.10 **12.3** Rom 15.15; 2 Cor 10.13; Eph 4.7 **12.4** 1 Cor 12.12-14; Eph 4.4,16 **12.6** 1 Cor 7.7; 12.4,10; 1 Pet 4.10, 11 **12.7** 1 Cor 12.28; 14.26 **12.8** Acts 15.32; Mt 6.1-3; 1 Tim 5.17; 2 Cor 9.7 **12.12** Heb 10.32, 36; Acts 1.14 **12.13** Rom 15.25; Heb 13.2 **12.14** Mt 5.44; Lk 6.28 **12.16** Rom 15.5; 11.25 **12.17** Prov 20.22; 2 Cor 8.21 **12.18** Mk 9.50; Rom 14.19 **12.19** Lev 19.18; Heb 10.30 **12.20** Prov 25.21, 22; Mt 5.44; Lk 6.27 **13.1** Titus 3.1; 1 Pet 2.13; Jn 19.11; Dan 2.21 **13.2** Titus 3.1 **13.3** 1 Pet 2.14 **13.4** 1 Thes 4.6

[k] Other ancient authorities lack *now*
[l] Gk *brothers* [m] Or *reasonable*
[n] Gk *age* [o] Or *what is the good and acceptable and perfect will of God* [p] Other ancient authorities read *serve the opportune time* [q] Or *give yourselves to humble tasks*
[r] Gk *the wrath*

wrong, you should be afraid, for the
authority[s] does not bear the sword
in vain! It is the servant of God to
execute wrath on the wrongdoer.
5 Therefore one must be subject,
not only because of wrath but also
because of conscience. 6 For the
same reason you also pay taxes, for
the authorities are God's servants,
busy with this very thing. 7 Pay
to all what is due them—taxes
to whom taxes are due, revenue to
whom revenue is due, respect
to whom respect is due, honor to
whom honor is due.

Love for One Another

8 Owe no one anything, except
to love one another; for the one
who loves another has fulfilled the
law. 9 The commandments, "You
shall not commit adultery; You
shall not murder; You shall not
steal; You shall not covet"; and any
other commandment, are summed
up in this word, "Love your neighbor as yourself." 10 Love does no
wrong to a neighbor; therefore, love
is the fulfilling of the law.

An Urgent Appeal

11 Besides this, you know what
time it is, how it is now the moment for you to wake from sleep.
For salvation is nearer to us now
than when we became believers;
12 the night is far gone, the day is
near. Let us then lay aside the
works of darkness and put on the
armor of light; 13 let us live honorably as in the day, not in reveling
and drunkenness, not in debauchery and licentiousness, not in quarreling and jealousy. 14 Instead, put
on the Lord Jesus Christ, and make
no provision for the flesh, to gratify
its desires.

Do Not Judge Another

14 Welcome those who are
weak in faith,[t] but not for
the purpose of quarreling over
opinions. 2 Some believe in eating
anything, while the weak eat only
vegetables. 3 Those who eat must
not despise those who abstain, and
those who abstain must not pass
judgment on those who eat; for
God has welcomed them. 4 Who are
you to pass judgment on servants
of another? It is before their own
lord that they stand or fall. And
they will be upheld, for the Lord[u]
is able to make them stand.

5 Some judge one day to be better than another, while others
judge all days to be alike. Let all be
fully convinced in their own minds.
6 Those who observe the day, observe it in honor of the Lord. Also
those who eat, eat in honor of the
Lord, since they give thanks to
God; while those who abstain, abstain in honor of the Lord and give
thanks to God.

7 We do not live to ourselves,
and we do not die to ourselves. 8 If
we live, we live to the Lord, and if
we die, we die to the Lord; so then,
whether we live or whether we die,
we are the Lord's. 9 For to this end
Christ died and lived again, so that
he might be Lord of both the dead
and the living.

10 Why do you pass judgment
on your brother or sister?[v] Or you,
why do you despise your brother or
sister?[v] For we will all stand before
the judgment seat of God.[w] 11 For it
is written,

"As I live, says the Lord,
every knee shall bow to
me,
and every tongue shall give
praise to[x] God."

12 So then, each of us will be accountable to God.[y]

Do Not Make Another Stumble

13 Let us therefore no longer
pass judgment on one another, but
resolve instead never to put a stumbling block or hindrance in the way
of another.[z] 14 I know and am persuaded in the Lord Jesus that nothing is unclean in itself; but it is unclean for anyone who thinks it
unclean. 15 If your brother or sister[v] is being injured by what you
eat, you are no longer walking in

[s] Gk *it* [t] Or *conviction* [u] Other ancient authorities read *for God* [v] Gk *brother* [w] Other ancient authorities read *of Christ* [x] Or *confess* [y] Other ancient authorities lack *to God* [z] Gk *of a brother*

13.5 Eccl 8.2; 1 Pet 2.19
13.7 Mt 22.21; Mk 12.17; Lk 20.25
13.8 Gal 5.14; Col 3.14; Jas 2.8
13.9 Ex 20.13, 14; Mt 19.19
13.10 Mt 22.39,40
13.11ff 1 Cor 7.29, 30; 15.34; Eph 5.14; 1 Thes 5.5, 6
13.12 1 Jn 2.8; Eph 5.11; 1 Thes 5.8
13.13 1 Thes 4.12; Gal 5.21; Eph 5.18
13.14 Gal 3.27; Eph 4.24; Gal 5.16
14.1 1 Cor 8.9; 9.22
14.2 1 Tim 4.4; Titus 1.15
14.3 Col 2.16
14.4 Jas 4.12
14.5 Gal 4.10
14.6 1 Cor 10.31; 1 Tim 4.3
14.7 2 Cor 5.15; Gal 2.20; Phil 1.20,21
14.8 Phil 1.20
14.9 2 Cor 5.15; Acts 10.36
14.10 2 Cor 5.10
14.11 Isa 45.23; Phil 2.10,11
14.12 Mt 12.36; 1 Pet 4.5
14.13 Mt 7.1; 1 Cor 8.13
14.14 Acts 10.15; 1 Cor 8.7
14.15 Eph 5.2; 1 Cor 8.11

love. Do not let what you eat cause the ruin of one for whom Christ died. 16 So do not let your good be spoken of as evil. 17 For the kingdom of God is not food and drink but righteousness and peace and joy in the Holy Spirit. 18 The one who thus serves Christ is acceptable to God and has human approval. 19 Let us then pursue what makes for peace and for mutual upbuilding. 20 Do not, for the sake of food, destroy the work of God. Everything is indeed clean, but it is wrong for you to make others fall by what you eat; 21 it is good not to eat meat or drink wine or do anything that makes your brother or sister[a] stumble.[b] 22 The faith that you have, have as your own conviction before God. Blessed are those who have no reason to condemn themselves because of what they approve. 23 But those who have doubts are condemned if they eat, because they do not act from faith;[c] for whatever does not proceed from faith[c] is sin.[d]

Please Others, Not Yourselves

15 We who are strong ought to put up with the failings of the weak, and not to please ourselves. 2 Each of us must please our neighbor for the good purpose of building up the neighbor. 3 For Christ did not please himself; but, as it is written, "The insults of those who insult you have fallen on me." 4 For whatever was written in former days was written for our instruction, so that by steadfastness and by the encouragement of the scriptures we might have hope. 5 May the God of steadfastness and encouragement grant you to live in harmony with one another, in accordance with Christ Jesus, 6 so that together you may with one voice glorify the God and Father of our Lord Jesus Christ.

The Gospel for Jews and Gentiles Alike

7 Welcome one another, therefore, just as Christ has welcomed you, for the glory of God. 8 For I tell you that Christ has become a servant of the circumcised on behalf of the truth of God in order that he might confirm the promises given to the patriarchs, 9 and in order that the Gentiles might glorify God for his mercy. As it is written,

"Therefore I will confess[e]
you among the
Gentiles,
and sing praises to your
name";

10 and again he says,

"Rejoice, O Gentiles, with
his people";

11 and again,

"Praise the Lord, all you
Gentiles,
and let all the peoples
praise him";

12 and again Isaiah says,

"The root of Jesse shall
come,
the one who rises to rule
the Gentiles;
in him the Gentiles shall
hope."

13 May the God of hope fill you with all joy and peace in believing, so that you may abound in hope by the power of the Holy Spirit.

Paul's Reason for Writing So Boldly

14 I myself feel confident about you, my brothers and sisters,[f] that you yourselves are full of goodness, filled with all knowledge, and able to instruct one another. 15 Nevertheless on some points I have written to you rather boldly by way of reminder, because of the grace given me by God 16 to be a minister of Christ Jesus to the Gentiles in the priestly service of the gospel of God, so that the offering of the Gentiles may be acceptable, sanctified by the Holy Spirit. 17 In Christ Jesus, then, I have reason to boast of my work for God. 18 For I will not

14.16 1 Cor 10.30
14.17 1 Cor 8.8; Rom 15.13
14.18 2 Cor 8.21
14.19 Ps 34.14; Heb 12.14; Rom 15.2
14.20 v. 15; 1 Cor 8.9-12
14.21 1 Cor 8.13
14.22 1 Jn 3.21
15.1 Rom 14.1; Gal 6.1,2
15.2 1 Cor 10.33; Rom 14.19
15.3 Ps 69.9; 2 Cor 8.9
15.4 Rom 4.23, 24; 2 Tim 3.16, 17
15.5 Rom 12.16; 1 Cor 1.10
15.6 Rev 1.6
15.7 Rom 14.1
15.8 Mt 15.24; Acts 3.25, 26; Rom 3.3; 2 Cor 1.20
15.9 Ps 18.49; 2 Sam 22.50
15.10 Deut 32.43
15.11 Ps 117.1
15.12 Isa 11.10; Mt 12.21; Rev 5.5; 22.16
15.13 Rom 14.17; 1 Thes 1.5
15.14 2 Pet 1.12; 1 Cor 8.1, 7,10
15.15 Rom 12.3; Eph 3.7,8
15.16 Acts 9.15; Rom 11.13; Phil 2.17
15.17 Phil 3.3; Heb 2.17; 5.1
15.18 Acts 15.12; 21.19; Rom 1.5; 16.26

[a] Gk *brother* [b] Other ancient authorities add *or be upset or be weakened* [c] Or *conviction* [d] Other authorities, some ancient, add here 16.25-27 [e] Or *thank* [f] Gk *brothers*

venture to speak of anything except what Christ has accomplished[g] through me to win obedience from the Gentiles, by word
and deed, [19]by the power of signs
and wonders, by the power of the
Spirit of God,[h] so that from Jerusalem and as far around as Illyricum
I have fully proclaimed the good
news[i] of Christ. [20]Thus I make it
my ambition to proclaim the good
news,[i] not where Christ has already been named, so that I do not
build on someone else's foundation, [21]but as it is written,

"Those who have never been
told of him shall see,
and those who have never
heard of him shall
understand."

Paul's Plan to Visit Rome

22 This is the reason that I have
so often been hindered from coming to you. [23]But now, with no further place for me in these regions,
I desire, as I have for many years, to
come to you [24]when I go to Spain.
For I do hope to see you on my journey and to be sent on by you, once
I have enjoyed your company for a
little while. [25]At present, however,
I am going to Jerusalem in a ministry to the saints; [26]for Macedonia
and Achaia have been pleased to
share their resources with the poor
among the saints at Jerusalem.
[27]They were pleased to do this, and
indeed they owe it to them; for if
the Gentiles have come to share in
their spiritual blessings, they ought
also to be of service to them in material things. [28]So, when I have
completed this, and have delivered
to them what has been collected,[j]
I will set out by way of you to Spain;
[29]and I know that when I come to
you, I will come in the fullness of
the blessing[k] of Christ.

30 I appeal to you, brothers and
sisters,[l] by our Lord Jesus Christ
and by the love of the Spirit, to join
me in earnest prayer to God on my
behalf, [31]that I may be rescued
from the unbelievers in Judea, and
that my ministry[m] to Jerusalem
may be acceptable to the saints,
[32]so that by God's will I may come
to you with joy and be refreshed in
your company. [33]The God of peace
be with all of you.[n] Amen.

Personal Greetings

16 I commend to you our sister Phoebe, a deacon[o] of
the church at Cenchreae, [2]so that
you may welcome her in the Lord
as is fitting for the saints, and help
her in whatever she may require
from you, for she has been a benefactor of many and of myself as
well.

3 Greet Prisca and Aquila, who
work with me in Christ Jesus, [4]and
who risked their necks for my life,
to whom not only I give thanks, but
also all the churches of the Gentiles. [5]Greet also the church in
their house. Greet my beloved
Epaenetus, who was the first convert[p] in Asia for Christ. [6]Greet
Mary, who has worked very hard
among you. [7]Greet Andronicus and
Junia,[q] my relatives[r] who were in
prison with me; they are prominent
among the apostles, and they were
in Christ before I was. [8]Greet Ampliatus, my beloved in the Lord.
[9]Greet Urbanus, our co-worker in
Christ, and my beloved Stachys.
[10]Greet Apelles, who is approved in
Christ. Greet those who belong to
the family of Aristobulus. [11]Greet
my relative[s] Herodion. Greet
those in the Lord who belong to the
family of Narcissus. [12]Greet those
workers in the Lord, Tryphaena
and Tryphosa. Greet the beloved
Persis, who has worked hard in the
Lord. [13]Greet Rufus, chosen in the
Lord; and greet his mother—a
mother to me also. [14]Greet Asyn-
critus, Phlegon, Hermes, Patrobas,
Hermas, and the brothers and sis-

15.19 Acts 19.11; 2 Cor 12.12 **15.20** 2 Cor 10.15, 16 **15.21** Isa 52.15 **15.22** Rom 1.13 **15.23** Acts 19.21; Rom 1.11 **15.24** v. 28; Acts 15.3 **15.25** Acts 19.21; 24.27 **15.26** 2 Cor 8.1; 9.2; 1 Thes 1.7, 8 **15.27** 1 Cor 9.11 **15.30** Gal 5.22; 2 Cor 1.11; Col 4.12 **15.32** Rom 1.10; Acts 18.21; 1 Cor 16.18 **15.33** Rom 16.20; 2 Cor 13.11; Phil 4.9; Heb 13.20 **16.1** Acts 18.18 **16.2** Phil 2.29; Rom 15.15, 31 **16.3** Acts 18.2; 2 Tim 4.19 **16.5** 1 Cor 16.15, 19; Col 4.15 **16.9** 2 Cor 5.17 **16.10** 2 Cor 5.17 **16.11** vv. 7,21; 1 Cor 1.11

[g] Gk *speak of those things that Christ has not accomplished* [h] Other ancient authorities read *of the Spirit* or *of the Holy Spirit* [i] Or *gospel* [j] Gk *have sealed to them this fruit* [k] Other ancient authorities add *of the gospel* [l] Gk *brothers* [m] Other ancient authorities read *my bringing of a gift* [n] One ancient authority adds 16.25-27 here [o] Or *minister* [p] Gk *first fruits* [q] Or *Junias;* other ancient authorities read *Julia* [r] Or *compatriots* [s] Or *compatriot*

ters[t] who are with them. 15 Greet
Philologus, Julia, Nereus and his
sister, and Olympas, and all the
saints who are with them. 16 Greet
one another with a holy kiss. All
the churches of Christ greet you.

Final Instructions

17 I urge you, brothers and sisters,[t] to keep an eye on those who
cause dissensions and offenses, in
opposition to the teaching that you
have learned; avoid them. 18 For
such people do not serve our Lord
Christ, but their own appetites,[u]
and by smooth talk and flattery
they deceive the hearts of the
simple-minded. 19 For while your
obedience is known to all, so that I
rejoice over you, I want you to be
wise in what is good and guileless
in what is evil. 20 The God of peace
will shortly crush Satan under your
feet. The grace of our Lord Jesus
Christ be with you.[v]
21 Timothy, my co-worker,
greets you; so do Lucius and Jason
and Sosipater, my relatives.[w]
22 I Tertius, the writer of this
letter, greet you in the Lord.[x]
23 Gaius, who is host to me and
to the whole church, greets you.
Erastus, the city treasurer, and our
brother Quartus, greet you.[y]

Final Doxology

25 Now to God[z] who is able to
strengthen you according to my
gospel and the proclamation of
Jesus Christ, according to the revelation of the mystery that was kept
secret for long ages 26 but is now
disclosed, and through the prophetic writings is made known to
all the Gentiles, according to the
command of the eternal God, to
bring about the obedience of
faith— 27 to the only wise God,
through Jesus Christ, to whom[a] be
the glory forever! Amen.[b]

16.15 vv. 2,14 **16.16** 1 Cor 16.20; 2 Cor 13.12; 1 Thes 5.26 **16.17** 1 Tim 1.3; 6.3; Gal 1.8, 9; 2 Thes 3.6, 14; 2 Jn 10 **16.18** Phil 3.19; Col 2.4 **16.19** Rom 1.8; Mt 10.16; 1 Cor 14.20 **16.20** Rom 15.33; Gen 3.15; 1 Cor 16.23; 1 Thes 5.28 **16.21** Acts 16.1; 13.1; 17.5; 20.4; vv. 7, 11

[t] Gk *brothers* [u] Gk *their own belly* [v] Other ancient authorities lack this sentence [w] Or *compatriots* [x] Or *I Tertius, writing this letter in the Lord, greet you* [y] Other ancient authorities add verse 24, *The grace of our Lord Jesus Christ be with all of you. Amen.* [z] Gk *the one* [a] Other ancient authorities lack *to whom*. The verse then reads, *to the only wise God be the glory through Jesus Christ forever. Amen.* [b] Other ancient authorities lack 16.25-27 or include it after 14.23 or 15.33; others put verse 24 after verse 27

THE FIRST LETTER OF PAUL TO THE

Corinthians

Title and Background

Located between the Corinthian Gulf and the Saronic Gulf, the city of Corinth was a wealthy trading center. It was also a wicked city, known for its vice throughout the Roman world. Because the church in Corinth was new, it was hard for the Christians there not to act like their neighbors. Consequently, they were facing some serious problems.

Author and Date of Writing

Few question Paul's authorship of this letter (see 1.1). It was written about A.D. 55, toward the close of Paul's three-year residency in Ephesus.

Theme and Message

The letter revolves around a series of problems in Christian conduct permeating the church at Corinth. Thus it deals with progressive sanctification, the continuing development of holiness of character. Obviously Paul was personally concerned with the Corinthians' problems, revealing a true pastor's (shepherd's) heart. In spite of the concentration on problems, the book contains some of the most familiar and beloved chapters in the entire Bible–e.g., ch. 13 (on love) and ch. 15 (on the resurrection).

Outline

I. Introduction: Greetings and Thanksgiving (1.1-9)
II. Divisions in the Church (1.10–4.21)
III. Moral and Ethical Disorders (5.1–6.20)
IV. Instruction on Marriage (7.1-40)
V. Instruction on Christian Freedom (8.1–11.1)
VI. Instruction on Public Worship (11.2–14.40)
  A. Propriety in Worship (11.2-16)
  B. The Lord's Supper (11.17-34)
  C. Spiritual Gifts (12.1–14.40)
VII. Instruction on the Resurrection (15.1-58)
VIII. Conclusion: Practical and Personal Matters (16.1-24)

Salutation

1 Paul, called to be an apostle of
Christ Jesus by the will of
God, and our brother Sosthenes,

2 To the church of God that is in
Corinth, to those who are sanctified in Christ Jesus, called to be
saints, together with all those who
in every place call on the name of
our Lord Jesus Christ, both their
Lord[a] and ours:

3 Grace to you and peace from
God our Father and the Lord Jesus
Christ.

4 I give thanks to my[b] God always for you because of the grace of
God that has been given you in
Christ Jesus, 5 for in every way you
have been enriched in him, in
speech and knowledge of every
kind— 6 just as the testimony of[c]
Christ has been strengthened
among you— 7 so that you are not
lacking in any spiritual gift as you
wait for the revealing of our Lord
Jesus Christ. 8 He will also

1.1 Rom 1.1; 2 Cor 1.1; Eph 1.1; Col 1.1; Acts 18.17 **1.2** Acts 18.1; Rom 1.7; Acts 7.59 **1.3** Rom 1.7 **1.4** Rom 1.8 **1.5** 2 Cor 9.11; 8.7 **1.6** 2 Tim 1.8; Rev 1.2 **1.7** Phil 3.20; Titus 2.13; 2 Pet 3.12

[a] Gk *theirs* [b] Other ancient authorities lack *my* [c] Or *to*

strengthen you to the end, so that you may be blameless on the day of our Lord Jesus Christ. [9]God is faithful; by him you were called into the fellowship of his Son, Jesus Christ our Lord.

Divisions in the Church

10 Now I appeal to you, brothers and sisters,[d] by the name of our Lord Jesus Christ, that all of you be in agreement and that there be no divisions among you, but that you be united in the same mind and the same purpose. [11]For it has been reported to me by Chloe's people that there are quarrels among you, my brothers and sisters.[e] [12]What I mean is that each of you says, "I belong to Paul," or "I belong to Apollos," or "I belong to Cephas," or "I belong to Christ." [13]Has Christ been divided? Was Paul crucified for you? Or were you baptized in the name of Paul? [14]I thank God[f] that I baptized none of you except Crispus and Gaius, [15]so that no one can say that you were baptized in my name. [16](I did baptize also the household of Stephanas; beyond that, I do not know whether I baptized anyone else.) [17]For Christ did not send me to baptize but to proclaim the gospel, and not with eloquent wisdom, so that the cross of Christ might not be emptied of its power.

Christ the Power and Wisdom of God

18 For the message about the cross is foolishness to those who are perishing, but to us who are being saved it is the power of God. [19]For it is written,

"I will destroy the wisdom of the wise,
and the discernment of the discerning I will thwart."

[20]Where is the one who is wise? Where is the scribe? Where is the debater of this age? Has not God made foolish the wisdom of the world? [21]For since, in the wisdom of God, the world did not know God through wisdom, God decided, through the foolishness of our proclamation, to save those who believe. [22]For Jews demand signs and Greeks desire wisdom, [23]but we proclaim Christ crucified, a stumbling block to Jews and foolishness to Gentiles, [24]but to those who are the called, both Jews and Greeks, Christ the power of God and the wisdom of God. [25]For God's foolishness is wiser than human wisdom, and God's weakness is stronger than human strength.

26 Consider your own call, brothers and sisters:[d] not many of you were wise by human standards,[g] not many were powerful, not many were of noble birth. [27]But God chose what is foolish in the world to shame the wise; God chose what is weak in the world to shame the strong; [28]God chose what is low and despised in the world, things that are not, to reduce to nothing things that are, [29]so that no one[h] might boast in the presence of God. [30]He is the source of your life in Christ Jesus, who became for us wisdom from God, and righteousness and sanctification and redemption, [31]in order that, as it is written, "Let the one who boasts, boast in[i] the Lord."

Proclaiming Christ Crucified

2 When I came to you, brothers and sisters,[d] I did not come proclaiming the mystery[j] of God to you in lofty words or wisdom. [2]For I decided to know nothing among you except Jesus Christ, and him crucified. [3]And I came to you in weakness and in fear and in much trembling. [4]My speech and my proclamation were not with plausible words of wisdom,[k] but with a demonstration of the Spirit and of power, [5]so that your faith might rest not on human wisdom but on the power of God.

1.9 Isa 49.7; 1 Jn 1.3
1.10 2 Cor 13.11; Rom 12.16
1.13 2 Cor 11.4; Mt 28.19; Acts 2.38
1.14 Acts 18.8; Rom 16.23
1.16 1 Cor 16.15
1.17 Jn 4.2; Acts 10.48; 1 Cor 2.1, 4,13
1.18 Acts 17.18; 1 Cor 15.2; Rom 1.16
1.19 Isa 29.14
1.20 Isa 33.18; Rom 1.22
1.21 Gal 1.15; 1 Tim 4.16; Heb 7.25
1.22 Mt 12.38
1.23 Gal 5.11; 1 Cor 2.14
1.24 Rom 1.4; Col 2.3
1.26 Rom 11.29
1.27 Jas 2.5
1.29 Eph 2.9
1.30 1 Cor 6.11; 1 Thes 5.23; Eph 1.7,14; Rom 3.24
1.31 Jer 9.23,24; 2 Cor 10.17
2.1 1 Cor 1.17
2.2 Gal 6.14; 1 Cor 1.23
2.4 Rom 15.19; 1 Cor 4.20
2.5 2 Cor 4.7; 6.7

d Gk *brothers* e Gk *my brothers* f Other ancient authorities read *I am thankful* g Gk *according to the flesh* h Gk *no flesh* i Or *of* j Other ancient authorities read *testimony* k Other ancient authorities read *the persuasiveness of wisdom*

The True Wisdom of God

6 Yet among the mature we do
speak wisdom, though it is not a
wisdom of this age or of the rulers
of this age, who are doomed to perish. 7 But we speak God's wisdom,
secret and hidden, which God decreed before the ages for our glory.
8 None of the rulers of this age understood this; for if they had, they
would not have crucified the Lord
of glory. 9 But, as it is written,

"What no eye has seen, nor
 ear heard,
nor the human heart
 conceived,
what God has prepared for
 those who love him"—

10 these things God has revealed to
us through the Spirit; for the Spirit
searches everything, even the
depths of God. 11 For what human
being knows what is truly human
except the human spirit that is
within? So also no one compre-
hends what is truly God's except
the Spirit of God. 12 Now we have
received not the spirit of the world,
but the Spirit that is from God, so
that we may understand the gifts
bestowed on us by God. 13 And we
speak of these things in words not
taught by human wisdom but
taught by the Spirit, interpreting
spiritual things to those who are
spiritual.[l]

14 Those who are unspiritual[m]
do not receive the gifts of God's
Spirit, for they are foolishness to
them, and they are unable to understand them because they are
spiritually discerned. 15 Those who
are spiritual discern all things, and
they are themselves subject to no
one else's scrutiny.

16 "For who has known the
 mind of the Lord
so as to instruct him?"

But we have the mind of Christ.

On Divisions in the Corinthian Church

3 And so, brothers and sisters,[n]
I could not speak to you as
spiritual people, but rather as people of the flesh, as infants in Christ.
2 I fed you with milk, not solid food,
for you were not ready for solid
food. Even now you are still not
ready, 3 for you are still of the flesh.
For as long as there is jealousy and
quarreling among you, are you not
of the flesh, and behaving according to human inclinations? 4 For
when one says, "I belong to Paul,"
and another, "I belong to Apollos,"
are you not merely human?

5 What then is Apollos? What is
Paul? Servants through whom you
came to believe, as the Lord assigned to each. 6 I planted, Apollos
watered, but God gave the growth.
7 So neither the one who plants nor
the one who waters is anything, but
only God who gives the growth.
8 The one who plants and the one
who waters have a common purpose, and each will receive wages
according to the labor of each. 9 For
we are God's servants, working together; you are God's field, God's
building.

10 According to the grace of
God given to me, like a skilled master builder I laid a foundation, and
someone else is building on it.
Each builder must choose with
care how to build on it. 11 For no
one can lay any foundation other
than the one that has been laid;
that foundation is Jesus Christ.
12 Now if anyone builds on the
foundation with gold, silver, precious stones, wood, hay, straw—
13 the work of each builder will become visible, for the Day will disclose it, because it will be revealed
with fire, and the fire will test what
sort of work each has done. 14 If
what has been built on the foundation survives, the builder will receive a reward. 15 If the work is
burned up, the builder will suffer
loss; the builder will be saved, but
only as through fire.

16 Do you not know that you are
God's temple and that God's Spirit
dwells in you?[o] 17 If anyone destroys God's temple, God will de-

2.6 Eph 4.13; Phil 3.15; 1 Cor 1.20; 1.28
2.8 Acts 7.2; Jas 2.1
2.9 Isa 64.4; 65.17
2.10 Mt 16.17; Eph 3.3,5; Jn 14.26
2.11 Prov 20.27; Jer 17.9
2.12 Rom 8.15; 1 Cor 1.27
2.13 1 Cor 1.17
2.14 1 Cor 1.18; Jas 3.15
2.16 Isa 40.13; Jn 15.15
3.1 1 Cor 2.15; Rom 7.14; 1 Cor 2.14; Heb 5.13
3.2 Heb 5.12, 13; 1 Pet 2.2
3.3 1 Cor 1.11; Gal 5.20; Jas 3.16
3.4 1 Cor 1.12
3.8 Ps 62.12; Gal 6.4,5
3.9 2 Cor 6.1; Isa 61.3; Eph 2.20-22; 1 Pet 2.5
3.10 Rom 12.3; 15.20; 1 Cor 15.10
3.11 Isa 28.6; Eph 2.20
3.13 1 Cor 4.5; 2 Thes 1.7-10
3.14 1 Cor 4.5; 9.17
3.15 Job 23.10; Jude 23
3.16 1 Cor 6.19; 2 Cor 6.16

[l] Or *interpreting spiritual things in spiritual language,* or *comparing spiritual things with spiritual* [m] Or *natural* [n] Gk *brothers*
[o] In verses 16 and 17 the Greek word for *you* is plural

stroy that person. For God's temple
is holy, and you are that temple.
18 Do not deceive yourselves. If
you think that you are wise in this
age, you should become fools so
that you may become wise. 19 For
the wisdom of this world is foolishness with God. For it is written,

"He catches the wise in their
craftiness,"

20 and again,

"The Lord knows the
thoughts of the wise,
that they are futile."

21 So let no one boast about human
leaders. For all things are yours,
22 whether Paul or Apollos or Cephas or the world or life or death or
the present or the future—all belong to you, 23 and you belong to
Christ, and Christ belongs to God.

The Ministry of the Apostles

4 Think of us in this way, as servants of Christ and stewards of
God's mysteries. 2 Moreover, it is
required of stewards that they be
found trustworthy. 3 But with me it
is a very small thing that I should
be judged by you or by any human
court. I do not even judge myself. 4 I
am not aware of anything against
myself, but I am not thereby acquitted. It is the Lord who judges
me. 5 Therefore do not pronounce
judgment before the time, before
the Lord comes, who will bring to
light the things now hidden in
darkness and will disclose the purposes of the heart. Then each one
will receive commendation from
God.
6 I have applied all this to Apollos and myself for your benefit,
brothers and sisters,[p] so that you
may learn through us the meaning
of the saying, "Nothing beyond
what is written," so that none of
you will be puffed up in favor of one
against another. 7 For who sees
anything different in you?[q] What
do you have that you did not receive? And if you received it, why
do you boast as if it were not a gift?
8 Already you have all you want!
Already you have become rich!
Quite apart from us you have become kings! Indeed, I wish that you
had become kings, so that we
might be kings with you! 9 For I
think that God has exhibited us
apostles as last of all, as though
sentenced to death, because we
have become a spectacle to the
world, to angels and to mortals.
10 We are fools for the sake of
Christ, but you are wise in Christ.
We are weak, but you are strong.
You are held in honor, but we in
disrepute. 11 To the present hour
we are hungry and thirsty, we are
poorly clothed and beaten and
homeless, 12 and we grow weary
from the work of our own hands.
When reviled, we bless; when persecuted, we endure; 13 when slandered, we speak kindly. We have
become like the rubbish of the
world, the dregs of all things, to
this very day.

Fatherly Admonition

14 I am not writing this to make
you ashamed, but to admonish you
as my beloved children. 15 For
though you might have ten thousand guardians in Christ, you do
not have many fathers. Indeed, in
Christ Jesus I became your father
through the gospel. 16 I appeal to
you, then, be imitators of me. 17 For
this reason I sent[r] you Timothy,
who is my beloved and faithful
child in the Lord, to remind you of
my ways in Christ Jesus, as I teach
them everywhere in every church.
18 But some of you, thinking that I
am not coming to you, have become arrogant. 19 But I will come to
you soon, if the Lord wills, and I
will find out not the talk of these
arrogant people but their power.
20 For the kingdom of God depends
not on talk but on power. 21 What
would you prefer? Am I to come to
you with a stick, or with love in a
spirit of gentleness?

3.18 Isa 5.21; 1 Cor 8.2 **3.19** Job 5.13; 1 Cor 1.20 **3.20** Ps 94.11 **3.21** 1 Cor 4.6; Rom 8.32 **3.23** 1 Cor 15.23; 2 Cor 10.7; Gal 3.29 **4.1** 2 Cor 6.4; 1 Cor 9.17; Rom 11.25; 16.25 **4.4** 2 Cor 1.12; Rom 2.13 **4.5** Rom 2.1; 2 Cor 10.18; Rom 2.29 **4.6** 1 Cor 1.19, 31; 3.19,20; 1.12; 3.4 **4.7** Rom 12.3,6 **4.8** Rev 3.17,18 **4.9** 1 Cor 15.31; 2 Cor 11.23; Rom 8.36; Heb 10.33 **4.10** 1 Cor 1.18; Acts 17.18; 1 Cor 3.18 **4.11** Rom 8.35; 2 Cor 11.23-27 **4.12** Acts 18.3; 1 Pet 3.9; Jn 15.20; Rom 8.35 **4.14** 1 Thes 2.11 **4.15** 1 Cor 1.30; Philem 10 **4.16** Phil 3.17; 1 Thes 1.6; 2 Thes 3.9 **4.19** Acts 19.21; 2 Cor 1.15; Rom 15.32 **4.20** 1 Thes 1.5 **4.21** 2 Cor 1.23; 13.10

[p] Gk *brothers* [q] Or *Who makes you different from another?* [r] Or *am sending*

Sexual Immorality Defiles the Church

5 It is actually reported that
there is sexual immorality
among you, and of a kind that is
not found even among pagans; for
a man is living with his father's
wife. 2 And you are arrogant!
Should you not rather have
mourned, so that he who has done
this would have been removed
from among you?
3 For though absent in body, I
am present in spirit; and as if
present I have already pronounced
judgment 4 in the name of the Lord
Jesus on the man who has done
such a thing.[s] When you are assembled, and my spirit is present
with the power of our Lord Jesus,
5 you are to hand this man over to
Satan for the destruction of the
flesh, so that his spirit may be
saved in the day of the Lord.[t]
6 Your boasting is not a good
thing. Do you not know that a little
yeast leavens the whole batch of
dough? 7 Clean out the old yeast so
that you may be a new batch, as
you really are unleavened. For our
paschal lamb, Christ, has been sacrificed. 8 Therefore, let us celebrate
the festival, not with the old yeast,
the yeast of malice and evil, but
with the unleavened bread of sincerity and truth.

Sexual Immorality Must Be Judged

9 I wrote to you in my letter not
to associate with sexually immoral
persons— 10 not at all meaning the
immoral of this world, or the
greedy and robbers, or idolaters,
since you would then need to go
out of the world. 11 But now I am
writing to you not to associate with
anyone who bears the name of
brother or sister[u] who is sexually
immoral or greedy, or is an idolater, reviler, drunkard, or robber. Do
not even eat with such a one. 12 For
what have I to do with judging
those outside? Is it not those who
are inside that you are to judge?
13 God will judge those outside.

5.1 Lev 18.8; Deut 22.30; 2 Cor 7.12 **5.2** 1 Cor 4.18; 2 Cor 7.7 **5.3** Col 2.5 **5.4** 2 Thes 3.6; 2 Cor 2.10 **5.5** 1 Tim 1.20 **5.6** Jas 4.16; Gal 5.9 **5.7** 1 Pet 1.19 **5.8** Deut 16.3; Mk 8.15 **5.9** 2 Cor 6.14; Eph 5.11; 2 Thes 3.14 **5.10** 1 Cor 10.27 **5.11** 2 Thes 3.6; 1 Cor 10.7, 14,20,21 **5.12** Mk 4.11; 1 Cor 6.1-4 **5.13** Deut 13.5; 21.21

6.1 Mt 18.17 **6.2** Dan 7.22; Mt 19.28; Lk 22.30 **6.4** 1 Cor 5.12 **6.5** 1 Cor 15.34; Acts 1.15 **6.6** 2 Cor 6.14, 15 **6.7** Mt 5.39,40; Rom 12.17 **6.8** 1 Thes 4.6 **6.9** Gal 5.21; 1 Tim 1.10; Rev 22.15 **6.11** Eph 2.2; Col 3.7; Titus 3.3 **6.12** 1 Cor 10.23 **6.13** Mt 15.17; Eph 5.23

"Drive out the wicked person from
among you."

Lawsuits among Believers

6 When any of you has a griev-
ance against another, do you
dare to take it to court before the
unrighteous, instead of taking it
before the saints? 2 Do you not
know that the saints will judge the
world? And if the world is to be
judged by you, are you incompe-
tent to try trivial cases? 3 Do you
not know that we are to judge
angels—to say nothing of ordinary
matters? 4 If you have ordinary
cases, then, do you appoint as
judges those who have no standing
in the church? 5 I say this to your
shame. Can it be that there is no
one among you wise enough to decide between one believer[u] and
another, 6 but a believer[u] goes to
court against a believer[u]—and before unbelievers at that?
7 In fact, to have lawsuits at all
with one another is already a defeat
for you. Why not rather be
wronged? Why not rather be defrauded? 8 But you yourselves
wrong and defraud—and believers[v] at that.
9 Do you not know that wrongdoers will not inherit the kingdom
of God? Do not be deceived! Fornicators, idolaters, adulterers, male
prostitutes, sodomites, 10 thieves,
the greedy, drunkards, revilers,
robbers—none of these will inherit
the kingdom of God. 11 And this is
what some of you used to be. But
you were washed, you were sanctified, you were justified in the name
of the Lord Jesus Christ and in the
Spirit of our God.

Glorify God in Body and Spirit

12 "All things are lawful for
me," but not all things are beneficial. "All things are lawful for me,"
but I will not be dominated by anything. 13 "Food is meant for the
stomach and the stomach for

[s] Or *on the man who has done such a thing in the name of the Lord Jesus* [t] Other ancient authorities add *Jesus* [u] Gk *brother* [v] Gk *brothers*

food,"[w] and God will destroy both
one and the other. The body is
meant not for fornication but for
the Lord, and the Lord for the body.
14 And God raised the Lord and will
also raise us by his power. 15 Do you
not know that your bodies are
members of Christ? Should I therefore take the members of Christ
and make them members of a prostitute? Never! 16 Do you not know
that whoever is united to a prostitute becomes one body with her?
For it is said, "The two shall be one
flesh." 17 But anyone united to the
Lord becomes one spirit with him.
18 Shun fornication! Every sin that a
person commits is outside the
body; but the fornicator sins
against the body itself. 19 Or do you
not know that your body is a temple[x] of the Holy Spirit within you,
which you have from God, and that
you are not your own? 20 For you
were bought with a price; therefore
glorify God in your body.

Directions concerning Marriage

7 Now concerning the matters
about which you wrote: "It is
well for a man not to touch a woman." 2 But because of cases of sexual immorality, each man should
have his own wife and each woman
her own husband. 3 The husband
should give to his wife her conjugal
rights, and likewise the wife to her
husband. 4 For the wife does not
have authority over her own body,
but the husband does; likewise the
husband does not have authority
over his own body, but the wife
does. 5 Do not deprive one another
except perhaps by agreement for a
set time, to devote yourselves to
prayer, and then come together
again, so that Satan may not tempt
you because of your lack of self-
control. 6 This I say by way of con-
cession, not of command. 7 I wish
that all were as I myself am. But
each has a particular gift from God,
one having one kind and another a
different kind.

8 To the unmarried and the widows I say that it is well for them to

6.14 Rom 6.5,8; 8.11; 2 Cor 4.14; Eph 1.19
6.15 Rom 12.5; 1 Cor 12.27
6.16 Gen 2.4; Mt 19.5; Eph 5.31
6.17 Jn 17.21-23; Gal 2.20
6.18 Rom 6.12; Heb 13.4; 1 Thes 4.4
6.19 Jn 2.21; Rom 14.7,8
6.20 1 Cor 7.23; 1 Pet 1.18, 19; Rev 5.9
7.1 vv. 8,26
7.3 1 Pet 3.7
7.5 Ex 19.15; 1 Sam 21.4, 5; 1 Thes 3.5
7.6 2 Cor 8.8
7.7 v. 8; 1 Cor 9.5; 12.11; Mt 19.12
7.8 vv. 1,26
7.9 1 Tim 5.14
7.10 Mal 2.14; Mt 5.32; 19.3-9; Mk 10.11; Lk 16.18
7.12 v. 6; 2 Cor 11.17
7.14 Mal 2.15
7.15 Rom 14.19; 1 Cor 14.33
7.16 1 Pet 3.1
7.17 Rom 12.3; 1 Cor 4.17; 14.33; 2 Cor 8.18; 11.28
7.18 Acts 15.1,2
7.19 Gal 5.6; 6.15; Rom 2.25
7.20 v. 24

remain unmarried as I am. 9 But if
they are not practicing self-control,
they should marry. For it is better
to marry than to be aflame with
passion.

10 To the married I give this
command—not I but the Lord—
that the wife should not separate
from her husband 11 (but if she
does separate, let her remain unmarried or else be reconciled to her
husband), and that the husband
should not divorce his wife.

12 To the rest I say—I and not
the Lord—that if any believer[y] has
a wife who is an unbeliever, and
she consents to live with him, he
should not divorce her. 13 And if
any woman has a husband who is
an unbeliever, and he consents to
live with her, she should not divorce him. 14 For the unbelieving
husband is made holy through his
wife, and the unbelieving wife is
made holy through her husband.
Otherwise, your children would be
unclean, but as it is, they are holy.
15 But if the unbelieving partner
separates, let it be so; in such a
case the brother or sister is not
bound. It is to peace that God has
called you.[z] 16 Wife, for all you
know, you might save your husband. Husband, for all you know,
you might save your wife.

The Life That the Lord Has Assigned

17 However that may be, let
each of you lead the life that the
Lord has assigned, to which God
called you. This is my rule in all the
churches. 18 Was anyone at the
time of his call already circumcised? Let him not seek to remove
the marks of circumcision. Was
anyone at the time of his call uncircumcised? Let him not seek circumcision. 19 Circumcision is nothing, and uncircumcision is
nothing; but obeying the commandments of God is everything.
20 Let each of you remain in the

[w] The quotation may extend to the word *other* [x] Or *sanctuary* [y] Gk *brother*
[z] Other ancient authorities read *us*

condition in which you were
called.
21 Were you a slave when
called? Do not be concerned about
it. Even if you can gain your freedom, make use of your present
condition now more than ever.[a]
22 For whoever was called in the
Lord as a slave is a freed person belonging to the Lord, just as whoever
was free when called is a slave of
Christ. 23 You were bought with a
price; do not become slaves of human masters. 24 In whatever condition you were called, brothers and
sisters,[b] there remain with God.

The Unmarried and the Widows

25 Now concerning virgins, I
have no command of the Lord, but
I give my opinion as one who by the
Lord's mercy is trustworthy. 26 I
think that, in view of the impending[c] crisis, it is well for you to remain as you are. 27 Are you bound
to a wife? Do not seek to be free.
Are you free from a wife? Do not
seek a wife. 28 But if you marry, you
do not sin, and if a virgin marries,
she does not sin. Yet those who
marry will experience distress in
this life,[d] and I would spare you
that. 29 I mean, brothers and sisters,[b] the appointed time has
grown short; from now on, let even
those who have wives be as though
they had none, 30 and those who
mourn as though they were not
mourning, and those who rejoice as
though they were not rejoicing, and
those who buy as though they had
no possessions, 31 and those who
deal with the world as though they
had no dealings with it. For the
present form of this world is passing away.
32 I want you to be free from
anxieties. The unmarried man is
anxious about the affairs of the
Lord, how to please the Lord; 33 but
the married man is anxious about
the affairs of the world, how to
please his wife, 34 and his interests
are divided. And the unmarried
woman and the virgin are anxious
about the affairs of the Lord, so
that they may be holy in body and
spirit; but the married woman is
anxious about the affairs of the
world, how to please her husband.
35 I say this for your own benefit,
not to put any restraint upon you,
but to promote good order and unhindered devotion to the Lord.
36 If anyone thinks that he is
not behaving properly toward his
fiancé,[e] if his passions are strong,
and so it has to be, let him marry as
he wishes; it is no sin. Let them
marry. 37 But if someone stands
firm in his resolve, being under no
necessity but having his own desire
under control, and has determined
in his own mind to keep her as his
fiancé,[e] he will do well. 38 So
then, he who marries his fiancé[e]
does well; and he who refrains from
marriage will do better.
39 A wife is bound as long as her
husband lives. But if the husband
dies,[f] she is free to marry anyone
she wishes, only in the Lord. 40 But
in my judgment she is more
blessed if she remains as she is.
And I think that I too have the Spirit of God.

Food Offered to Idols

8 Now concerning food sacrificed to idols: we know that
"all of us possess knowledge."
Knowledge puffs up, but love
builds up. 2 Anyone who claims to
know something does not yet have
the necessary knowledge; 3 but
anyone who loves God is known by
him.
4 Hence, as to the eating of food
offered to idols, we know that "no
idol in the world really exists," and
that "there is no God but one." 5 Indeed, even though there may be so-
called gods in heaven or on earth—
as in fact there are many gods and
many lords— 6 yet for us there is
one God, the Father, from whom
are all things and for whom we exist, and one Lord, Jesus Christ,
through whom are all things and
through whom we exist.

7.22 Jn 8.32,36; Philem 16; Eph 6.6
7.23 1 Cor 6.20
7.25 2 Cor 8.8, 10; 1 Tim 1.13, 16
7.26 vv. 1,8
7.29 Rom 13.11, 12; v. 31
7.31 1 Cor 9.18; 1 Jn 2.17
7.32 1 Tim 5.5
7.34 Lk 10.40
7.38 Heb 13.4
7.39 Rom 7.2; 2 Cor 6.14
7.40 v. 25
8.1 Acts 15.20; Rom 15.14; 14.3,10
8.2 1 Cor 3.18; 13.8,9,12; 1 Tim 6.4
8.3 Gal 4.9; Rom 8.29
8.4 1 Cor 10.19; Deut 6.4; Eph 4.6
8.6 Mal 2.10; Rom 11.36; Phil 2.11

[a] Or *avail yourself of the opportunity*
[b] Gk *brothers* [c] Or *present* [d] Gk *in the flesh* [e] Gk *virgin* [f] Gk *falls asleep*

7 It is not everyone, however,
who has this knowledge. Since
some have become so accustomed
to idols until now, they still think
of the food they eat as food offered
to an idol; and their conscience,
being weak, is defiled. 8 “Food will
not bring us close to God.”[g] We are
no worse off if we do not eat, and
no better off if we do. 9 But take
care that this liberty of yours does
not somehow become a stumbling
block to the weak. 10 For if others
see you, who possess knowledge,
eating in the temple of an idol,
might they not, since their conscience is weak, be encouraged to
the point of eating food sacrificed
to idols? 11 So by your knowledge
those weak believers for whom
Christ died are destroyed.[h] 12 But
when you thus sin against members of your family,[i] and wound
their conscience when it is weak,
you sin against Christ. 13 Therefore,
if food is a cause of their falling,[j]
I will never eat meat, so that I may
not cause one of them[k] to fall.

The Rights of an Apostle

9 Am I not free? Am I not an
apostle? Have I not seen Jesus
our Lord? Are you not my work in
the Lord? 2 If I am not an apostle to
others, at least I am to you; for you
are the seal of my apostleship in
the Lord.

3 This is my defense to those
who would examine me. 4 Do we
not have the right to our food and
drink? 5 Do we not have the right to
be accompanied by a believing
wife,[l] as do the other apostles and
the brothers of the Lord and Cephas? 6 Or is it only Barnabas and I
who have no right to refrain from
working for a living? 7 Who at any
time pays the expenses for doing
military service? Who plants a vineyard and does not eat any of its
fruit? Or who tends a flock and
does not get any of its milk?

8 Do I say this on human authority? Does not the law also say
the same? 9 For it is written in the
law of Moses, “You shall not muzzle an ox while it is treading out the
grain.” Is it for oxen that God is
concerned? 10 Or does he not speak
entirely for our sake? It was indeed
written for our sake, for whoever
plows should plow in hope and
whoever threshes should thresh in
hope of a share in the crop. 11 If we
have sown spiritual good among
you, is it too much if we reap your
material benefits? 12 If others share
this rightful claim on you, do not
we still more?

Nevertheless, we have not made
use of this right, but we endure
anything rather than put an obstacle in the way of the gospel of
Christ. 13 Do you not know that
those who are employed in the
temple service get their food from
the temple, and those who serve at
the altar share in what is sacrificed
on the altar? 14 In the same way, the
Lord commanded that those who
proclaim the gospel should get
their living by the gospel.

15 But I have made no use of
any of these rights, nor am I writing
this so that they may be applied in
my case. Indeed, I would rather die
than that—no one will deprive me
of my ground for boasting! 16 If I
proclaim the gospel, this gives me
no ground for boasting, for an obligation is laid on me, and woe to me
if I do not proclaim the gospel!
17 For if I do this of my own will, I
have a reward; but if not of my own
will, I am entrusted with a commission. 18 What then is my reward?
Just this: that in my proclamation
I may make the gospel free of
charge, so as not to make full use of
my rights in the gospel.

19 For though I am free with respect to all, I have made myself a
slave to all, so that I might win
more of them. 20 To the Jews I became as a Jew, in order to win
Jews. To those under the law I be-

8.7 1 Cor 10.28; Rom 14.14
8.8 Rom 14.17
8.9 Gal 5.13; Rom 14.1, 13,20
8.10 1 Cor 10.28, 32
8.11 Rom 14.15, 20
8.13 Rom 14.21; 2 Cor 11.29
9.1 2 Cor 12.12; Acts 9.3,17; 18.9; 22.14, 18; 23.11; 1 Cor 3.6; 4.15
9.2 2 Cor 3.2, 3
9.4 1 Thes 2.6; 2 Thes 3.8, 9
9.5 1 Cor 7.7, 8; Mt 12.46; 8.14
9.6 Acts 4.36
9.7 2 Cor 10.4; 1 Tim 1.18; Deut 20.6; Prov 27.18
9.9 Deut 25.4; 1 Tim 5.18
9.11 Rom 15.27
9.12 2 Cor 6.3; 11.12
9.13 Lev 6.16; Deut 18.1
9.14 Mt 10.10; Lk 10.7
9.15 Acts 18.3; 2 Cor 11.10
9.16 Rom 1.14; Acts 9.15
9.17 1 Cor 3.8, 14; Gal 2.7; Phil 1.16, 17; Col 1.25
9.18 2 Cor 11.7; 12.13; 1 Cor 7.31
9.19 Gal 5.13; Mt 18.15; 1 Pet 3.1
9.20 Acts 16.3; 21.23; Rom 11.14; Gal 2.19

[g] The quotation may extend to the end of the verse [h] Gk *the weak brother . . . is destroyed* [i] Gk *against the brothers* [j] Gk *my brother's falling* [k] Gk *cause my brother* [l] Gk *a sister as wife*

came as one under the law (though I myself am not under the law) so that I might win those under the law. 21 To those outside the law I became as one outside the law (though I am not free from God's law but am under Christ's law) so that I might win those outside the law. 22 To the weak I became weak, so that I might win the weak. I have become all things to all people, that I might by all means save some. 23 I do it all for the sake of the gospel, so that I may share in its blessings.

24 Do you not know that in a race the runners all compete, but only one receives the prize? Run in such a way that you may win it. 25 Athletes exercise self-control in all things; they do it to receive a perishable wreath, but we an imperishable one. 26 So I do not run aimlessly, nor do I box as though beating the air; 27 but I punish my body and enslave it, so that after proclaiming to others I myself should not be disqualified.

Warnings from Israel's History

10 I do not want you to be unaware, brothers and sisters,[m] that our ancestors were all under the cloud, and all passed through the sea, 2 and all were baptized into Moses in the cloud and in the sea, 3 and all ate the same spiritual food, 4 and all drank the same spiritual drink. For they drank from the spiritual rock that followed them, and the rock was Christ. 5 Nevertheless, God was not pleased with most of them, and they were struck down in the wilderness.

6 Now these things occurred as examples for us, so that we might not desire evil as they did. 7 Do not become idolaters as some of them did; as it is written, "The people sat down to eat and drink, and they rose up to play." 8 We must not indulge in sexual immorality as some of them did, and twenty-three thousand fell in a single day. 9 We must not put Christ[n] to the test, as some of them did, and were destroyed by serpents. 10 And do not complain as some of them did, and were destroyed by the destroyer. 11 These things happened to them to serve as an example, and they were written down to instruct us, on whom the ends of the ages have come. 12 So if you think you are standing, watch out that you do not fall. 13 No testing has overtaken you that is not common to everyone. God is faithful, and he will not let you be tested beyond your strength, but with the testing he will also provide the way out so that you may be able to endure it.

14 Therefore, my dear friends,[o] flee from the worship of idols. 15 I speak as to sensible people; judge for yourselves what I say. 16 The cup of blessing that we bless, is it not a sharing in the blood of Christ? The bread that we break, is it not a sharing in the body of Christ? 17 Because there is one bread, we who are many are one body, for we all partake of the one bread. 18 Consider the people of Israel;[p] are not those who eat the sacrifices partners in the altar? 19 What do I imply then? That food sacrificed to idols is anything, or that an idol is anything? 20 No, I imply that what pagans sacrifice, they sacrifice to demons and not to God. I do not want you to be partners with demons. 21 You cannot drink the cup of the Lord and the cup of demons. You cannot partake of the table of the Lord and the table of demons. 22 Or are we provoking the Lord to jealousy? Are we stronger than he?

Do All to the Glory of God

23 "All things are lawful," but not all things are beneficial. "All things are lawful," but not all things build up. 24 Do not seek your own advantage, but that of the other. 25 Eat whatever is sold in the meat market without raising any question on the ground of con-

9.21 Rom 2.12, 14; Gal 3.2; 1 Cor 7.22
9.24 2 Tim 4.7; Heb 12.1
9.25 Eph 6.12; 1 Tim 6.12
9.27 Rom 8.13; Col 3.5; Rom 6.18
10.1 Ex 13.21; 14.22,29; Rom 1.13
10.3 Ex 16.4,35
10.4 Ex 17.6; Num 20.11
10.5 Num 14.29, 30; Heb 3.17
10.6 Num 11.4, 34; Ps 106.14
10.7 Ex 32.4,6
10.8 Num 25.1ff
10.9 Num 21.5,6
10.10 Num 16.41, 49; Ex 12.23
10.11 Rom 13.11; Phil 4.5
10.12 Rom 11.20
10.13 2 Pet 2.9
10.14 2 Cor 6.17
10.16 Mt 26.26; Acts 2.42
10.17 Rom 12.5; 1 Cor 12.27
10.18 Lev 7.6
10.20 Deut 32.17; Ps 106.37; Rev 9.20
10.21 2 Cor 6.15, 16
10.22 Deut 32.21; Eccl 6.10; Isa 45.9
10.23 1 Cor 6.12; Rom 14.19
10.24 v. 33; Rom 15.1,2; Phil 2.4,21
10.25 1 Cor 8.7

[m] Gk *brothers* [n] Other ancient authorities read *the Lord* [o] Gk *my beloved* [p] Gk *Israel according to the flesh*

science, 26 for "the earth and its fullness are the Lord's." 27 If an unbeliever invites you to a meal and you are disposed to go, eat whatever is set before you without raising any question on the ground of conscience. 28 But if someone says to you, "This has been offered in sacrifice," then do not eat it, out of consideration for the one who informed you, and for the sake of conscience— 29 I mean the other's conscience, not your own. For why should my liberty be subject to the judgment of someone else's conscience? 30 If I partake with thankfulness, why should I be denounced because of that for which I give thanks?

31 So, whether you eat or drink, or whatever you do, do everything for the glory of God. 32 Give no offense to Jews or to Greeks or to the church of God, 33 just as I try to please everyone in everything I do, not seeking my own advantage, but that of many, so that they may be saved. **11** 1 Be imitators of me, as I am of Christ.

Head Coverings

2 I commend you because you remember me in everything and maintain the traditions just as I handed them on to you. 3 But I want you to understand that Christ is the head of every man, and the husband[q] is the head of his wife,[r] and God is the head of Christ. 4 Any man who prays or prophesies with something on his head disgraces his head, 5 but any woman who prays or prophesies with her head unveiled disgraces her head—it is one and the same thing as having her head shaved. 6 For if a woman will not veil herself, then she should cut off her hair; but if it is disgraceful for a woman to have her hair cut off or to be shaved, she should wear a veil. 7 For a man ought not to have his head veiled, since he is the image and reflection[s] of God; but woman is the reflection[s] of man. 8 Indeed, man was not made from woman, but woman from man. 9 Neither was man created for the sake of woman, but woman for the sake of man. 10 For this reason a woman ought to have a symbol of[t] authority on her head,[u] because of the angels. 11 Nevertheless, in the Lord woman is not independent of man or man independent of woman. 12 For just as woman came from man, so man comes through woman; but all things come from God. 13 Judge for yourselves: is it proper for a woman to pray to God with her head unveiled? 14 Does not nature itself teach you that if a man wears long hair, it is degrading to him, 15 but if a woman has long hair, it is her glory? For her hair is given to her for a covering. 16 But if anyone is disposed to be contentious—we have no such custom, nor do the churches of God.

Abuses at the Lord's Supper

17 Now in the following instructions I do not commend you, because when you come together it is not for the better but for the worse. 18 For, to begin with, when you come together as a church, I hear that there are divisions among you; and to some extent I believe it. 19 Indeed, there have to be factions among you, for only so will it become clear who among you are genuine. 20 When you come together, it is not really to eat the Lord's supper. 21 For when the time comes to eat, each of you goes ahead with your own supper, and one goes hungry and another becomes drunk. 22 What! Do you not have homes to eat and drink in? Or do you show contempt for the church of God and humiliate those who have nothing? What should I say to you? Should I commend you? In this matter I do not commend you!

The Institution of the Lord's Supper

23 For I received from the Lord

10.26 Ps 24.1
10.29 Rom 14.16
10.30 Rom 14.6; 1 Tim 4.3, 4
10.31 Col 3.17; 1 Pet 4.11
10.32 1 Cor 8.13
10.33 Rom 15.2; 1 Cor 9.22; 13.5
11.1 1 Cor 4.16
11.2 1 Cor 4.17; 2 Thes 2.15
11.3 Eph 1.22; 4.15; 5.23; 1 Cor 3.23
11.4 Acts 13.1; 1 Thes 5.20
11.5 Acts 21.9; Deut 21.12
11.7 Gen 1.26
11.8 Gen 2.21-23
11.9 Gen 2.18
11.10 Gen 24.65
11.12 2 Cor 5.18; Rom 11.36
11.13 Lk 12.57
11.16 1 Cor 7.17
11.17 vv. 2,22
11.18 1 Cor 1.10-12
11.19 Mt 18.7; Lk 17.1; 1 Tim 4.1; Deut 13.3; 1 Jn 2.19
11.21 2 Pet 2.13; Jude 12
11.22 1 Cor 10.32; Jas 2.6
11.23 1 Cor 15.3; Mt 26.26-28; Mk 14.22-24; Lk 22.17-20

[q] The same Greek word means *man* or *husband* [r] Or *head of the woman*
[s] Or *glory* [t] Gk lacks *a symbol of*
[u] Or *have freedom of choice regarding her head*

what I also handed on to you, that
the Lord Jesus on the night when
he was betrayed took a loaf of
bread, 24 and when he had given
thanks, he broke it and said, "This
is my body that is for[v] you. Do this
in remembrance of me." 25 In the
same way he took the cup also, after supper, saying, "This cup is the
new covenant in my blood. Do this,
as often as you drink it, in remembrance of me." 26 For as often as
you eat this bread and drink the
cup, you proclaim the Lord's death
until he comes.

Partaking of the Supper Unworthily

27 Whoever, therefore, eats the
bread or drinks the cup of the Lord
in an unworthy manner will be an-
swerable for the body and blood of
the Lord. 28 Examine yourselves,
and only then eat of the bread and
drink of the cup. 29 For all who eat
and drink[w] without discerning the
body,[x] eat and drink judgment
against themselves. 30 For this reason many of you are weak and ill,
and some have died.[y] 31 But if we
judged ourselves, we would not be
judged. 32 But when we are judged
by the Lord, we are disciplined[z] so
that we may not be condemned
along with the world.
33 So then, my brothers and sisters,[a] when you come together to
eat, wait for one another. 34 If you
are hungry, eat at home, so that
when you come together, it will not
be for your condemnation. About
the other things I will give instructions when I come.

Spiritual Gifts

12 Now concerning spiritual
gifts,[b] brothers and sis-
ters,[a] I do not want you to be uninformed. 2 You know that when you
were pagans, you were enticed and
led astray to idols that could not
speak. 3 Therefore I want you to understand that no one speaking by
the Spirit of God ever says "Let
Jesus be cursed!" and no one can
say "Jesus is Lord" except by the
Holy Spirit.

11.25 2 Cor 3.6; Lk 22.20 **11.26** 1 Cor 4.5; Jn 14.3; Acts 1.11; Rev 1.7 **11.27** Heb 10.29 **11.28** 2 Cor 13.5 **11.31** Ps 32.5; 1 Jn 1.9 **11.32** Ps 94.12; Heb 12.7-10; 1 Cor 1.20 **11.34** vv. 21,22; 1 Cor 4.19 **12.1** 1 Cor 14.1, 37; Rom 1.13 **12.2** Eph 2.11, 12; 1 Pet 4.3; 1 Thes 1.9; Ps 115.5 **12.3** 1 Jn 4.2,3; Rom 9.3; 10.9 **12.4** Rom 12.4-7; Heb 2.4 **12.5** Eph 4.11 **12.7** Eph 4.7 **12.8** 1 Cor 2.6, 7; Rom 15.4; 2 Cor 8.7 **12.9** Mt 17.19, 20; 2 Cor 4.13; vv. 28,30 **12.10** Gal 3.5; Rom 12.6; 1 Jn 4.1; Acts 2.4; 1 Cor 13.1 **12.11** 2 Cor 10.13; Heb 2.4 **12.12** Rom 12.4; Gal 3.16 **12.13** Eph 2.18; Gal 3.28; Col 3.11; Jn 7.37-39 **12.18** vv. 28,11

4 Now there are varieties of
gifts, but the same Spirit; 5 and
there are varieties of services, but
the same Lord; 6 and there are varieties of activities, but it is the same
God who activates all of them in everyone. 7 To each is given the manifestation of the Spirit for the common good. 8 To one is given
through the Spirit the utterance of
wisdom, and to another the utterance of knowledge according to the
same Spirit, 9 to another faith by
the same Spirit, to another gifts of
healing by the one Spirit, 10 to another the working of miracles, to
another prophecy, to another the
discernment of spirits, to another
various kinds of tongues, to another the interpretation of tongues.
11 All these are activated by one and
the same Spirit, who allots to each
one individually just as the Spirit
chooses.

One Body with Many Members

12 For just as the body is one
and has many members, and all the
members of the body, though
many, are one body, so it is with
Christ. 13 For in the one Spirit we
were all baptized into one body—
Jews or Greeks, slaves or free—and
we were all made to drink of one
Spirit.
14 Indeed, the body does not
consist of one member but of
many. 15 If the foot would say, "Because I am not a hand, I do not belong to the body," that would not
make it any less a part of the body.
16 And if the ear would say, "Because I am not an eye, I do not belong to the body," that would not
make it any less a part of the body.
17 If the whole body were an eye,
where would the hearing be? If the
whole body were hearing, where
would the sense of smell be? 18 But
as it is, God arranged the members
in the body, each one of them, as

[v] Other ancient authorities read *is broken for* [w] Other ancient authorities add *in an unworthy manner,* [x] Other ancient authorities read *the Lord's body* [y] Gk *fallen asleep* [z] Or *When we are judged, we are being disciplined by the Lord* [a] Gk *brothers* [b] Or *spiritual persons*

he chose. 19 If all were a single
member, where would the body be?
20 As it is, there are many members,
yet one body. 21 The eye cannot say
to the hand, "I have no need of
you," nor again the head to the
feet, "I have no need of you." 22 On
the contrary, the members of the
body that seem to be weaker are indispensable, 23 and those members
of the body that we think less honorable we clothe with greater hon-
or, and our less respectable members are treated with greater
respect; 24 whereas our more respectable members do not need
this. But God has so arranged the
body, giving the greater honor to
the inferior member, 25 that there
may be no dissension within the
body, but the members may have
the same care for one another. 26 If
one member suffers, all suffer together with it; if one member is
honored, all rejoice together with
it.
27 Now you are the body of
Christ and individually members of
it. 28 And God has appointed in the
church first apostles, second
prophets, third teachers; then
deeds of power, then gifts of healing, forms of assistance, forms of
leadership, various kinds of
tongues. 29 Are all apostles? Are all
prophets? Are all teachers? Do all
work miracles? 30 Do all possess
gifts of healing? Do all speak in
tongues? Do all interpret? 31 But
strive for the greater gifts. And I
will show you a still more excellent
way.

The Gift of Love

13 If I speak in the tongues of
mortals and of angels, but
do not have love, I am a noisy gong
or a clanging cymbal. 2 And if I have
prophetic powers, and understand
all mysteries and all knowledge,
and if I have all faith, so as to remove mountains, but do not have
love, I am nothing. 3 If I give away
all my possessions, and if I hand
over my body so that I may boast,[c]
but do not have love, I gain nothing.
4 Love is patient; love is kind;
love is not envious or boastful or
arrogant 5 or rude. It does not insist
on its own way; it is not irritable or
resentful; 6 it does not rejoice in
wrongdoing, but rejoices in the
truth. 7 It bears all things, believes
all things, hopes all things, endures
all things.
8 Love never ends. But as for
prophecies, they will come to an
end; as for tongues, they will cease;
as for knowledge, it will come to an
end. 9 For we know only in part, and
we prophesy only in part; 10 but
when the complete comes, the partial will come to an end. 11 When I
was a child, I spoke like a child, I
thought like a child, I reasoned like
a child; when I became an adult, I
put an end to childish ways. 12 For
now we see in a mirror, dimly,[d] but
then we will see face to face. Now
I know only in part; then I will
know fully, even as I have been fully known. 13 And now faith, hope,
and love abide, these three; and
the greatest of these is love.

Gifts of Prophecy and Tongues

14 Pursue love and strive for
the spiritual gifts, and especially that you may prophesy.
2 For those who speak in a tongue
do not speak to other people but to
God; for nobody understands
them, since they are speaking mysteries in the Spirit. 3 On the other
hand, those who prophesy speak to
other people for their upbuilding
and encouragement and consolation. 4 Those who speak in a tongue
build up themselves, but those
who prophesy build up the church.
5 Now I would like all of you to
speak in tongues, but even more to
prophesy. One who prophesies is
greater than one who speaks in
tongues, unless someone inter-
prets, so that the church may be
built up.
6 Now, brothers and sisters,[e] if
I come to you speaking in tongues,
how will I benefit you unless I
speak to you in some revelation or

12.20 v. 14 **12.27** Eph 1.23; 4.12; Col 1.18,24; Eph 5.30; Rom 12.5 **12.28** Eph 4.11; 2.30; 3.5; Rom 12.6,8; vv. 9,10 **12.30** v. 10 **12.31** 1 Cor 14.1, 39 **13.2** Acts 13.1; 1 Cor 14.1; Mt 7.22; 1 Cor 12.9; Mt 17.20; 21.21 **13.3** Mt 6.2 **13.4** Prov 10.12; 1 Pet 4.8 **13.5** 1 Cor 10.24; 2 Cor 5.19 **13.6** 2 Jn 4 **13.7** Rom 15.1; 1 Cor 9.12 **13.8** vv. 1,2 **13.9** 1 Cor 8.2 **13.12** 2 Cor 5.7; Phil 3.12; 1 Jn 3.2; 1 Cor 8.3 **13.13** 1 Cor 16.14 **14.1** 1 Cor 16.14; 12.31; 12.1; 13.2 **14.2** Acts 10.46; 1 Cor 12.10, 28,30; 13.1 **14.3** vv. 5,12,17, 26; Acts 4.36 **14.5** Num 11.29 **14.6** v. 26; 1 Cor 12.8; Rom 6.17

c Other ancient authorities read *body to be burned* d Gk *in a riddle* e Gk *brothers*

knowledge or prophecy or teaching? 7 It is the same way with lifeless instruments that produce
sound, such as the flute or the
harp. If they do not give distinct
notes, how will anyone know what
is being played? 8 And if the bugle
gives an indistinct sound, who will
get ready for battle? 9 So with yourselves; if in a tongue you utter
speech that is not intelligible, how
will anyone know what is being
said? For you will be speaking into
the air. 10 There are doubtless many
different kinds of sounds in the
world, and nothing is without
sound. 11 If then I do not know the
meaning of a sound, I will be a foreigner to the speaker and the
speaker a foreigner to me. 12 So
with yourselves; since you are eager for spiritual gifts, strive to excel
in them for building up the church.

13 Therefore, one who speaks in
a tongue should pray for the power
to interpret. 14 For if I pray in a
tongue, my spirit prays but my
mind is unproductive. 15 What
should I do then? I will pray with
the spirit, but I will pray with the
mind also; I will sing praise with
the spirit, but I will sing praise with
the mind also. 16 Otherwise, if you
say a blessing with the spirit, how
can anyone in the position of an
outsider say the "Amen" to your
thanksgiving, since the outsider
does not know what you are saying? 17 For you may give thanks well
enough, but the other person is not
built up. 18 I thank God that I speak
in tongues more than all of you;
19 nevertheless, in church I would
rather speak five words with my
mind, in order to instruct others
also, than ten thousand words in a
tongue.

20 Brothers and sisters,[f] do not
be children in your thinking; rather, be infants in evil, but in thinking be adults. 21 In the law it is written,

"By people of strange
tongues
and by the lips of
foreigners
I will speak to this people;
yet even then they will not
listen to me,"

says the Lord. 22 Tongues, then, are
a sign not for believers but for unbelievers, while prophecy is not for
unbelievers but for believers. 23 If,
therefore, the whole church comes
together and all speak in tongues,
and outsiders or unbelievers enter,
will they not say that you are out of
your mind? 24 But if all prophesy,
an unbeliever or outsider who enters is reproved by all and called to
account by all. 25 After the secrets
of the unbeliever's heart are disclosed, that person will bow down
before God and worship him, declaring, "God is really among you."

Orderly Worship

26 What should be done then,
my friends?[f] When you come together, each one has a hymn, a lesson, a revelation, a tongue, or an
interpretation. Let all things be
done for building up. 27 If anyone
speaks in a tongue, let there be
only two or at most three, and each
in turn; and let one interpret. 28 But
if there is no one to interpret, let
them be silent in church and speak
to themselves and to God. 29 Let
two or three prophets speak, and
let the others weigh what is said.
30 If a revelation is made to someone else sitting nearby, let the first
person be silent. 31 For you can all
prophesy one by one, so that all
may learn and all be encouraged.
32 And the spirits of prophets are
subject to the prophets, 33 for God
is a God not of disorder but of
peace.

(As in all the churches of the
saints, 34 women should be silent in
the churches. For they are not permitted to speak, but should be subordinate, as the law also says. 35 If
there is anything they desire to
know, let them ask their husbands
at home. For it is shameful for a
woman to speak in church.[g] 36 Or
did the word of God originate with
you? Or are you the only ones it has
reached?)

14.8 Num 10.9 **14.9** 1 Cor 9.26 **14.11** Acts 28.2 **14.12** vv. 4,5,17, 26 **14.15** Eph 5.19; Col 3.16 **14.16** 1 Chr 16.36; Ps 106.48; Mt 15.36; 1 Cor 11.24 **14.17** Rom 14.19 **14.20** Eph 4.14; Heb 5.12, 13; Ps 131.2; Rom 16.19; 1 Pet 2.2 **14.21** Jn 10.34; Isa 28.11,12 **14.22** v. 1 **14.23** Acts 2.13 **14.25** Jn 4.19; Lk 17.16; Isa 45.14; Zech 8.23 **14.26** 1 Cor 12.7-10; 2 Cor 12.19; Eph 4.12 **14.29** 1 Cor 12.10 **14.32** 1 Jn 4.1 **14.33** v. 40; 1 Cor 4.17; 11.16 **14.34** 1 Tim 2.11, 12; 1 Pet 3.1; Gen 3.16

[f] Gk *brothers* [g] Other ancient authorities put verses 34-35 after verse 40

37 Anyone who claims to be a
prophet, or to have spiritual powers, must acknowledge that what I
am writing to you is a command of
the Lord. 38 Anyone who does not
recognize this is not to be recognized. 39 So, my friends,[h] be eager
to prophesy, and do not forbid
speaking in tongues; 40 but all
things should be done decently
and in order.

The Resurrection of Christ

15 Now I would remind you,
brothers and sisters,[i] of
the good news[j] that I proclaimed
to you, which you in turn received,
in which also you stand, 2 through
which also you are being saved, if
you hold firmly to the message that
I proclaimed to you—unless you
have come to believe in vain.
3 For I handed on to you as of
first importance what I in turn had
received: that Christ died for our
sins in accordance with the scriptures, 4 and that he was buried, and
that he was raised on the third day
in accordance with the scriptures,
5 and that he appeared to Cephas,
then to the twelve. 6 Then he appeared to more than five hundred
brothers and sisters[i] at one time,
most of whom are still alive,
though some have died.[k] 7 Then he
appeared to James, then to all the
apostles. 8 Last of all, as to one untimely born, he appeared also to
me. 9 For I am the least of the apostles, unfit to be called an apostle,
because I persecuted the church of
God. 10 But by the grace of God I am
what I am, and his grace toward me
has not been in vain. On the contrary, I worked harder than any of
them—though it was not I, but the
grace of God that is with me.
11 Whether then it was I or they, so
we proclaim and so you have come
to believe.

The Resurrection of the Dead

12 Now if Christ is proclaimed
as raised from the dead, how can
some of you say there is no resurrection of the dead? 13 If there is no
resurrection of the dead, then
Christ has not been raised; 14 and if
Christ has not been raised, then
our proclamation has been in vain
and your faith has been in vain.
15 We are even found to be mis-
representing God, because we testified of God that he raised
Christ—whom he did not raise if it
is true that the dead are not raised.
16 For if the dead are not raised,
then Christ has not been raised.
17 If Christ has not been raised,
your faith is futile and you are still
in your sins. 18 Then those also who
have died[k] in Christ have perished.
19 If for this life only we have hoped
in Christ, we are of all people most
to be pitied.
20 But in fact Christ has been
raised from the dead, the first fruits
of those who have died.[k] 21 For
since death came through a human
being, the resurrection of the dead
has also come through a human being; 22 for as all die in Adam, so all
will be made alive in Christ. 23 But
each in his own order: Christ the
first fruits, then at his coming
those who belong to Christ. 24 Then
comes the end,[l] when he hands
over the kingdom to God the Father, after he has destroyed every
ruler and every authority and power. 25 For he must reign until he has
put all his enemies under his feet.
26 The last enemy to be destroyed is
death. 27 For "God[m] has put all
things in subjection under his
feet." But when it says, "All things
are put in subjection," it is plain
that this does not include the one
who put all things in subjection under him. 28 When all things are subjected to him, then the Son himself
will also be subjected to the one
who put all things in subjection under him, so that God may be all in
all.
29 Otherwise, what will those
people do who receive baptism on
behalf of the dead? If the dead are

14.37 2 Cor 10.7; 1 Jn 4.6 **14.39** 1 Cor 12.31 **14.40** v. 33 **15.1** Gal 1.11; Rom 2.16; 5.2 **15.2** Rom 1.16; 11.22; Gal 3.4 **15.3** 1 Cor 11.23; 1 Pet 2.24; Isa 53.5-12; Lk 24.25-27; Acts 26.22, 23 **15.4** Mt 16.21; Ps 16.8-10; Acts 2.24,25 **15.5** Lk 24.34; 1 Cor 1.12; Mt 28.17 **15.7** Lk 24.33,36, 37; Acts 1.3, 4 **15.8** Acts 9.3-8; 1 Cor 9.1; Gal 1.16 **15.9** Eph 3.8; 1 Tim 1.15; Acts 8.3 **15.10** Eph 3.7,8; 2 Cor 11.23; 3.5; Gal 2.8; Phil 2.13 **15.12** Acts 17.32; 23.8; 2 Tim 2.18 **15.14** 1 Thes 4.14 **15.15** Acts 2.24 **15.17** Rom 4.25 **15.18** 1 Thes 4.16 **15.19** 2 Tim 3.12 **15.20** 1 Pet 1.3; v. 23; Acts 26.23; Rev 1.5 **15.21** Rom 5.12 **15.24** Dan 7.14,27 **15.25** Ps 110.1 **15.26** 2 Tim 1.10; Rev 20.14

15.27 Ps 8.6; Mt 28.18; Heb 2.8 **15.28** Phil 3.21; 1 Cor 3.23

[h] Gk *my brothers* [i] Gk *brothers*
[j] Or *gospel* [k] Gk *fallen asleep*
[l] Or *Then come the rest* [m] Gk *he*

not raised at all, why are people
baptized on their behalf?
30 And why are we putting ourselves in danger every hour? 31 I die
every day! That is as certain, brothers and sisters,[n] as my boasting of
you—a boast that I make in Christ
Jesus our Lord. 32 If with merely human hopes I fought with wild animals at Ephesus, what would I
have gained by it? If the dead are
not raised,
"Let us eat and drink,
for tomorrow we die."
33 Do not be deceived:
"Bad company ruins good
morals."
34 Come to a sober and right mind,
and sin no more; for some people
have no knowledge of God. I say
this to your shame.

The Resurrection Body

35 But someone will ask, "How
are the dead raised? With what
kind of body do they come?"
36 Fool! What you sow does not
come to life unless it dies. 37 And as
for what you sow, you do not sow
the body that is to be, but a bare
seed, perhaps of wheat or of some
other grain. 38 But God gives it a
body as he has chosen, and to each
kind of seed its own body. 39 Not all
flesh is alike, but there is one flesh
for human beings, another for animals, another for birds, and another for fish. 40 There are both heavenly bodies and earthly bodies, but
the glory of the heavenly is one
thing, and that of the earthly is another. 41 There is one glory of the
sun, and another glory of the
moon, and another glory of the
stars; indeed, star differs from star
in glory.
42 So it is with the resurrection
of the dead. What is sown is perishable, what is raised is imperishable. 43 It is sown in dishonor, it is
raised in glory. It is sown in weakness, it is raised in power. 44 It is
sown a physical body, it is raised a
spiritual body. If there is a physical
body, there is also a spiritual body.
45 Thus it is written, "The first man,
Adam, became a living being"; the
last Adam became a life-giving
spirit. 46 But it is not the spiritual
that is first, but the physical, and
then the spiritual. 47 The first man
was from the earth, a man of dust;
the second man is[o] from heaven.
48 As was the man of dust, so are
those who are of the dust; and as is
the man of heaven, so are those
who are of heaven. 49 Just as we
have borne the image of the man of
dust, we will[p] also bear the image
of the man of heaven.
50 What I am saying, brothers
and sisters,[n] is this: flesh and
blood cannot inherit the kingdom
of God, nor does the perishable inherit the imperishable. 51 Listen, I
will tell you a mystery! We will not
all die,[q] but we will all be changed,
52 in a moment, in the twinkling of
an eye, at the last trumpet. For the
trumpet will sound, and the dead
will be raised imperishable, and we
will be changed. 53 For this perishable body must put on imperisha-
bility, and this mortal body must
put on immortality. 54 When this
perishable body puts on imperisha-
bility, and this mortal body puts on
immortality, then the saying that is
written will be fulfilled:
"Death has been swallowed
up in victory."
55 "Where, O death, is your
victory?
Where, O death, is your
sting?"
56 The sting of death is sin, and the
power of sin is the law. 57 But
thanks be to God, who gives us the
victory through our Lord Jesus
Christ.
58 Therefore, my beloved,[r] be
steadfast, immovable, always excelling in the work of the Lord, because you know that in the Lord
your labor is not in vain.

The Collection for the Saints

16 Now concerning the collection for the saints: you
should follow the directions I gave

15.30 2 Cor 11.26
15.31 Rom 8.36; 2 Cor 4.10; 11.23
15.32 2 Cor 1.8; Lk 12.19
15.34 1 Thes 4.5; 1 Cor 6.5
15.35 Rom 9.19; Ezek 37.3
15.36 Jn 12.24
15.38 Gen 1.11
15.42 Dan 12.3; Mt 13.43
15.43 Phil 3.21
15.45 Gen 2.7; Rom 5.14; 8.2
15.47 Jn 3.31; Gen 2.7; 3.19
15.49 Gen 5.3; Rom 8.29; 1 Jn 3.2
15.50 Mt 16.17; Jn 3.3,5
15.51 1 Thes 4.15-17; Phil 3.21
15.52 Mt 24.31; Jn 5.25; 1 Thes 4.16
15.53 2 Cor 5.4
15.54 Isa 25.7; Heb 2.14; Rev 20.14
15.55 Hos 13.14
15.56 Rom 5.12; 4.15; 5.13
15.58 2 Pet 3.14; 1 Cor 16.10
16.1 Acts 24.17; 9.13; 16.6

[n] Gk *brothers* [o] Other ancient authorities add *the Lord* [p] Other ancient authorities read *let us* [q] Gk *fall asleep* [r] Gk *beloved brothers*

to the churches of Galatia. 2 On the first day of every week, each of you is to put aside and save whatever extra you earn, so that collections need not be taken when I come. 3 And when I arrive, I will send any whom you approve with letters to take your gift to Jerusalem. 4 If it seems advisable that I should go also, they will accompany me.

Plans for Travel

5 I will visit you after passing through Macedonia—for I intend to pass through Macedonia— 6 and perhaps I will stay with you or even spend the winter, so that you may send me on my way, wherever I go. 7 I do not want to see you now just in passing, for I hope to spend some time with you, if the Lord permits. 8 But I will stay in Ephesus until Pentecost, 9 for a wide door for effective work has opened to me, and there are many adversaries.

10 If Timothy comes, see that he has nothing to fear among you, for he is doing the work of the Lord just as I am; 11 therefore let no one despise him. Send him on his way in peace, so that he may come to me; for I am expecting him with the brothers.

12 Now concerning our brother Apollos, I strongly urged him to visit you with the other brothers, but he was not at all willing[s] to come now. He will come when he has the opportunity.

Final Messages and Greetings

13 Keep alert, stand firm in your faith, be courageous, be strong. 14 Let all that you do be done in love.

15 Now, brothers and sisters,[t] you know that members of the household of Stephanas were the first converts in Achaia, and they have devoted themselves to the service of the saints; 16 I urge you to put yourselves at the service of such people, and of everyone who works and toils with them. 17 I rejoice at the coming of Stephanas and Fortunatus and Achaicus, because they have made up for your absence; 18 for they refreshed my spirit as well as yours. So give recognition to such persons.

19 The churches of Asia send greetings. Aquila and Prisca, together with the church in their house, greet you warmly in the Lord. 20 All the brothers and sisters[t] send greetings. Greet one another with a holy kiss.

21 I, Paul, write this greeting with my own hand. 22 Let anyone be accursed who has no love for the Lord. Our Lord, come![u] 23 The grace of the Lord Jesus be with you. 24 My love be with all of you in Christ Jesus.[v]

16.2 Acts 20.7; 2 Cor 9.4, 5
16.3 2 Cor 8.18, 19
16.5 Acts 19.21
16.6 Acts 15.3
16.7 Acts 18.21
16.10 Acts 16.1; 19.22; 1 Cor 15.58
16.11 1 Tim 4.12; Acts 15.33
16.12 Acts 18.24; 1 Cor 1.12; 3.5,6
16.13 Phil 1.27; 2 Thes 2.15; Eph 6.10
16.14 1 Cor 14.1
16.15 Rom 16.5; 2 Cor 8.4; Heb 6.10
16.16 Heb 13.1
16.17 2 Cor 7.6, 7; 11.9
16.18 2 Cor 7.13; Phil 2.29
16.19 Acts 16.6; Rom 16.5
16.22 Eph 6.24; Rom 9.3
16.23 Rom 16.20

[s] Or *it was not at all God's will for him*
[t] Gk *brothers*
[u] Gk *Marana tha*. These Aramaic words can also be read *Maran atha*, meaning *Our Lord has come*
[v] Other ancient authorities add *Amen*

THE SECOND LETTER OF PAUL TO THE

Corinthians

Title and Background

This letter was probably written from Macedonia a few months after the first letter. The divisions and problems spoken of in 1 Corinthians were still present in the church at Corinth. False teachers were challenging both Paul's personal integrity and his authority as an apostle. They insisted that he was not a genuine apostle and that he was putting into his own pocket the money they had collected for the poverty-stricken believers in Jerusalem.

Author and Date of Writing

The apostle Paul wrote this letter. It is stamped with his style and contains more autobiographical material than any of his other writings. The available evidence indicates that 2 Corinthians was written in the fall of A.D. 55.

Theme and Message

Paul shows his feelings in this letter more than in any other, going from despair to ecstatic joy. It falls naturally into three sections: (1) Paul explains the reasons for the change of his itinerary (chs. 1-7); (2) he encourages the Corinthians to complete the collection in preparation for his arrival (chs. 8-9); (3) he stresses the certainty of his coming, his authenticity as an apostle, and his readiness as an apostle to excercise discipline if necessary (chs. 10-13).

Outline

I. Introduction: Greetings and Thanksgiving (1.1-11)
II. Paul's Explanation of His Conduct and Apostolic Ministry (1.12–7.16)
III. The Collection for the Christians at Jerusalem (8.1–9.15)
IV. Paul's Vindication of His Apostolic Authority (10.1–13.10)
V. Conclusion (13.11-14)

Salutation

1 Paul, an apostle of Christ
Jesus by the will of God, and
Timothy our brother,
To the church of God that is in
Corinth, including all the saints
throughout Achaia:
2 Grace to you and peace from
God our Father and the Lord Jesus
Christ.

Paul's Thanksgiving after Affliction

3 Blessed be the God and Father
of our Lord Jesus Christ, the Father
of mercies and the God of all consolation, 4 who consoles us in all
our affliction, so that we may be
able to console those who are in
any affliction with the consolation
with which we ourselves are consoled by God. 5 For just as the sufferings of Christ are abundant for
us, so also our consolation is abundant through Christ. 6 If we are being afflicted, it is for your consolation and salvation; if we are being
consoled, it is for your consolation,
which you experience when you
patiently endure the same sufferings that we are also suffering.
7 Our hope for you is unshaken; for
we know that as you share in our
sufferings, so also you share in our
consolation.
8 We do not want you to be unaware, brothers and sisters,[a] of the
affliction we experienced in Asia;
for we were so utterly, unbearably

1.1 Col 1.1; 1 Tim 1.1; 1 Cor 1.1
1.2 Rom 1.7; 1 Cor 1.3; Gal 1.3
1.3 Eph 1.3; 1 Pet 1.3; Rom 15.5
1.4 2 Cor 7.6, 7,13
1.5 2 Cor 4.10; Col 1.24
1.6 2 Cor 4.15
1.7 Rom 8.17; 2 Tim 2.12
1.8 Acts 19.23; 1 Cor 15.32

[a] Gk *brothers*

crushed that we despaired of life itself. 9 Indeed, we felt that we had received the sentence of death so that we would rely not on ourselves but on God who raises the dead. 10 He who rescued us from so deadly a peril will continue to rescue us; on him we have set our hope that he will rescue us again, 11 as you also join in helping us by your prayers, so that many will give thanks on our[b] behalf for the blessing granted us through the prayers of many.

The Postponement of Paul's Visit

12 Indeed, this is our boast, the testimony of our conscience: we have behaved in the world with frankness[c] and godly sincerity, not by earthly wisdom but by the grace of God—and all the more toward you. 13 For we write you nothing other than what you can read and also understand; I hope you will understand until the end— 14 as you have already understood us in part—that on the day of the Lord Jesus we are your boast even as you are our boast.

15 Since I was sure of this, I wanted to come to you first, so that you might have a double favor;[d] 16 I wanted to visit you on my way to Macedonia, and to come back to you from Macedonia and have you send me on to Judea. 17 Was I vacillating when I wanted to do this? Do I make my plans according to ordinary human standards,[e] ready to say "Yes, yes" and "No, no" at the same time? 18 As surely as God is faithful, our word to you has not been "Yes and No." 19 For the Son of God, Jesus Christ, whom we proclaimed among you, Silvanus and Timothy and I, was not "Yes and No"; but in him it is always "Yes." 20 For in him every one of God's promises is a "Yes." For this reason it is through him that we say the "Amen," to the glory of God. 21 But it is God who establishes us with you in Christ and has anointed us, 22 by putting his seal on us and giving us his Spirit in our hearts as a first installment.

23 But I call on God as witness against me: it was to spare you that I did not come again to Corinth. 24 I do not mean to imply that we lord it over your faith; rather, we are workers with you for your joy, because you stand firm in the faith.

2

1 So I made up my mind not to make you another painful visit. 2 For if I cause you pain, who is there to make me glad but the one whom I have pained? 3 And I wrote as I did, so that when I came, I might not suffer pain from those who should have made me rejoice; for I am confident about all of you, that my joy would be the joy of all of you. 4 For I wrote you out of much distress and anguish of heart and with many tears, not to cause you pain, but to let you know the abundant love that I have for you.

Forgiveness for the Offender

5 But if anyone has caused pain, he has caused it not to me, but to some extent—not to exaggerate it—to all of you. 6 This punishment by the majority is enough for such a person; 7 so now instead you should forgive and console him, so that he may not be overwhelmed by excessive sorrow. 8 So I urge you to reaffirm your love for him. 9 I wrote for this reason: to test you and to know whether you are obedient in everything. 10 Anyone whom you forgive, I also forgive. What I have forgiven, if I have forgiven anything, has been for your sake in the presence of Christ. 11 And we do this so that we may not be outwitted by Satan; for we are not ignorant of his designs.

Paul's Anxiety in Troas

12 When I came to Troas to proclaim the good news of Christ, a door was opened for me in the

1.9 Jer 17.5,7
1.10 2 Pet 2.9
1.11 Rom 15.30; Phil 1.19; 2 Cor 4.15
1.12 2 Cor 2.17; 1 Cor 2.4, 13
1.14 1 Cor 1.8
1.15 1 Cor 4.19; Rom 1.11; 15.29
1.16 1 Cor 16.5-7
1.17 2 Cor 10.2, 3
1.18 1 Cor 1.9; 2 Cor 2.17
1.19 Mt 16.16; 1 Thes 1.1; Heb 13.8
1.20 Rom 15.8,9; 1 Cor 14.16
1.21 1 Cor 1.8; 1 Jn 2.20, 27
1.22 Eph 1.13
1.23 Gal 1.20; 1 Cor 4.21; 2 Cor 2.3
1.24 1 Pet 5.3; Rom 11.20; 1 Cor 15.1
2.1 2 Cor 1.23
2.2 2 Cor 7.8
2.3 2 Cor 12.21; 7.16; 8.22
2.4 2 Cor 7.8, 9,12
2.5 1 Cor 5.1, 2
2.6 1 Cor 5.4, 5
2.7 Gal 6.1; Eph 4.32
2.9 Phil 2.22; 2 Cor 7.15; 10.6
2.11 Mt 4.10; Lk 22.31; 2 Cor 4.4; 1 Pet 5.8
2.12 Acts 16.8; 1 Cor 16.9

[b] Other ancient authorities read *your*
[c] Other ancient authorities read *holiness*
[d] Other ancient authorities read *pleasure*
[e] Gk *according to the flesh*

Lord; 13 but my mind could not rest
because I did not find my brother
Titus there. So I said farewell to
them and went on to Macedonia.
14 But thanks be to God, who in
Christ always leads us in triumphal
procession, and through us spreads
in every place the fragrance that
comes from knowing him. 15 For we
are the aroma of Christ to God
among those who are being saved
and among those who are perishing; 16 to the one a fragrance from
death to death, to the other a fragrance from life to life. Who is sufficient for these things? 17 For we
are not peddlers of God's word like
so many;[f] but in Christ we speak
as persons of sincerity, as persons
sent from God and standing in his
presence.

Ministers of the New Covenant

3 Are we beginning to commend
ourselves again? Surely we do
not need, as some do, letters of recommendation to you or from you,
do we? 2 You yourselves are our letter, written on our[g] hearts, to be
known and read by all; 3 and you
show that you are a letter of Christ,
prepared by us, written not with
ink but with the Spirit of the living
God, not on tablets of stone but on
tablets of human hearts.
4 Such is the confidence that we
have through Christ toward God.
5 Not that we are competent of ourselves to claim anything as coming
from us; our competence is from
God, 6 who has made us competent
to be ministers of a new covenant,
not of letter but of spirit; for the
letter kills, but the Spirit gives life.
7 Now if the ministry of death,
chiseled in letters on stone tablets,[h] came in glory so that the
people of Israel could not gaze at
Moses' face because of the glory of
his face, a glory now set aside,
8 how much more will the ministry
of the Spirit come in glory? 9 For if
there was glory in the ministry of
condemnation, much more does
the ministry of justification
abound in glory! 10 Indeed, what
once had glory has lost its glory because of the greater glory; 11 for if
what was set aside came through
glory, much more has the permanent come in glory!
12 Since, then, we have such a
hope, we act with great boldness,
13 not like Moses, who put a veil
over his face to keep the people of
Israel from gazing at the end of the
glory that[i] was being set aside.
14 But their minds were hardened.
Indeed, to this very day, when they
hear the reading of the old covenant, that same veil is still there,
since only in Christ is it set aside.
15 Indeed, to this very day whenever
Moses is read, a veil lies over their
minds; 16 but when one turns to the
Lord, the veil is removed. 17 Now
the Lord is the Spirit, and where
the Spirit of the Lord is, there is
freedom. 18 And all of us, with unveiled faces, seeing the glory of the
Lord as though reflected in a mirror, are being transformed into the
same image from one degree of glory to another; for this comes from
the Lord, the Spirit.

Treasure in Clay Jars

4 Therefore, since it is by God's
mercy that we are engaged in
this ministry, we do not lose heart.
2 We have renounced the shameful
things that one hides; we refuse to
practice cunning or to falsify God's
word; but by the open statement of
the truth we commend ourselves to
the conscience of everyone in the
sight of God. 3 And even if our gospel is veiled, it is veiled to those
who are perishing. 4 In their case
the god of this world has blinded
the minds of the unbelievers, to
keep them from seeing the light of
the gospel of the glory of Christ,
who is the image of God. 5 For we
do not proclaim ourselves; we proclaim Jesus Christ as Lord and ourselves as your slaves for Jesus'
sake. 6 For it is the God who said,
"Let light shine out of darkness,"

2.13 2 Cor 7.5, 6; Mk 6.46; Rom 15.26 **2.14** Rom 6.17; Eph 5.2; Phil 4.18; 1 Cor 12.8 **2.15** Eph 5.2; Phil 4.18; 2 Cor 4.3 **2.16** Jn 9.39; 1 Pet 2.7 **2.17** 2 Cor 4.2; 1.12; 12.19 **3.1** 2 Cor 5.12; 12.11; Acts 18.27 **3.2** 1 Cor 9.2 **3.3** Jer 31.33; Ezek 11.19 **3.4** Eph 3.12 **3.5** 2 Cor 2.16; 1 Cor 15.10 **3.6** Heb 8.6,8; Gal 3.10; Jn 6.63 **3.7** Ex 34.29-35 **3.9** v. 7; Rom 1.17; 3.21 **3.12** 2 Cor 7.4; Eph 6.19 **3.13** v. 7; Ex 34.33 **3.14** Rom 11.7; Acts 13.15; v. 6 **3.16** Rom 11.23 **3.17** 1 Cor 15.45; Isa 61.1,2; Jn 8.32 **3.18** 1 Cor 13.12; 2 Cor 4.4, 6; Rom 8.29 **4.1** 2 Cor 3.6; 1 Cor 7.25 **4.2** 2 Cor 2.17 **4.3** 2 Cor 2.12; 3.14; 1 Cor 1.18 **4.4** Jn 12.31; Col 1.15; Jn 1.18

4.5 1 Cor 1.13,23; 9.19 **4.6** Gen 1.3; 2 Pet 1.19

[f] Other ancient authorities read *like the others*
[g] Other ancient authorities read *your*
[h] Gk *on stones* [i] Gk *of what*

who has shone in our hearts to give
the light of the knowledge of the
glory of God in the face of Jesus
Christ.

7 But we have this treasure in
clay jars, so that it may be made
clear that this extraordinary power
belongs to God and does not come
from us. 8 We are afflicted in every
way, but not crushed; perplexed,
but not driven to despair; 9 persecuted, but not forsaken; struck
down, but not destroyed; 10 always
carrying in the body the death of
Jesus, so that the life of Jesus may
also be made visible in our bodies.
11 For while we live, we are always
being given up to death for Jesus'
sake, so that the life of Jesus may
be made visible in our mortal flesh.
12 So death is at work in us, but life
in you.

13 But just as we have the same
spirit of faith that is in accordance
with scripture—"I believed, and so
I spoke"—we also believe, and so
we speak, 14 because we know that
the one who raised the Lord Jesus
will raise us also with Jesus, and
will bring us with you into his presence. 15 Yes, everything is for your
sake, so that grace, as it extends to
more and more people, may increase thanksgiving, to the glory of
God.

Living by Faith

16 So we do not lose heart. Even
though our outer nature is wasting
away, our inner nature is being renewed day by day. 17 For this slight
momentary affliction is preparing
us for an eternal weight of glory beyond all measure, 18 because we
look not at what can be seen but at
what cannot be seen; for what can
be seen is temporary, but what cannot be seen is eternal.

5 For we know that if the earthly
tent we live in is destroyed, we
have a building from God, a house
not made with hands, eternal in
the heavens. 2 For in this tent we
groan, longing to be clothed with
our heavenly dwelling— 3 if indeed, when we have taken it off[j]
we will not be found naked. 4 For
while we are still in this tent, we
groan under our burden, because
we wish not to be unclothed but to
be further clothed, so that what is
mortal may be swallowed up by
life. 5 He who has prepared us for
this very thing is God, who has giv-
en us the Spirit as a guarantee.

6 So we are always confident;
even though we know that while we
are at home in the body we are
away from the Lord— 7 for we walk
by faith, not by sight. 8 Yes, we do
have confidence, and we would
rather be away from the body and
at home with the Lord. 9 So whether we are at home or away, we make
it our aim to please him. 10 For all
of us must appear before the judgment seat of Christ, so that each
may receive recompense for what
has been done in the body, whether
good or evil.

The Ministry of Reconciliation

11 Therefore, knowing the fear
of the Lord, we try to persuade others; but we ourselves are well
known to God, and I hope that we
are also well known to your consciences. 12 We are not commending ourselves to you again, but giving you an opportunity to boast
about us, so that you may be able
to answer those who boast in outward appearance and not in the
heart. 13 For if we are beside ourselves, it is for God; if we are in our
right mind, it is for you. 14 For the
love of Christ urges us on, because
we are convinced that one has died
for all; therefore all have died.
15 And he died for all, so that those
who live might live no longer for
themselves, but for him who died
and was raised for them.

16 From now on, therefore, we
regard no one from a human point
of view;[k] even though we once
knew Christ from a human point of
view,[k] we know him no longer in
that way. 17 So if anyone is in
Christ, there is a new creation: everything old has passed away; see,

4.7 2 Cor 5.1; 1 Cor 2.5
4.8 2 Cor 7.5; 6.12
4.9 Jn 15.20; Heb 13.5; Ps 37.24
4.10 Gal 6.17; Rom 8.17
4.11 Rom 8.36
4.12 2 Cor 13.9
4.13 Ps 116.10
4.14 1 Thes 4.14
4.16 Rom 7.22; Col 3.10
4.17 Rom 8.18; 1 Pet 1.6
4.18 Rom 8.24; Heb 11.1
5.1 2 Pet 1.13, 14
5.2 Rom 8.23; v. 4
5.4 1 Cor 15.53, 54
5.5 Rom 8.23; 2 Cor 1.22
5.6 Heb 11.13, 14
5.7 1 Cor 13.12
5.8 Phil 1.23
5.10 Rom 14.10; Eph 6.8
5.11 Heb 10.31; Jude 23; 2 Cor 4.2
5.12 2 Cor 3.1; 1.14
5.13 2 Cor 11.1, 16,17
5.14 Acts 18.5; Rom 5.15; Gal 2.20
5.15 Rom 14.7-9
5.16 2 Cor 11.18; Phil 3.4; Jn 8.15
5.17 Rom 16.7; Gal 5.6; Rev 21.4,5

[j] Other ancient authorities read *put it on*
[k] Gk *according to the flesh*

everything has become new! 18 All
this is from God, who reconciled us
to himself through Christ, and has
given us the ministry of reconciliation; 19 that is, in Christ God was
reconciling the world to himself,[l]
not counting their trespasses
against them, and entrusting the
message of reconciliation to us.
20 So we are ambassadors for
Christ, since God is making his appeal through us; we entreat you on
behalf of Christ, be reconciled to
God. 21 For our sake he made him
to be sin who knew no sin, so that
in him we might become the righteousness of God.

6 As we work together with
him,[m] we urge you also not to
accept the grace of God in vain.
2 For he says,

"At an acceptable time I
have listened to you,
and on a day of salvation I
have helped you."

See, now is the acceptable time;
see, now is the day of salvation!
3 We are putting no obstacle in anyone's way, so that no fault may be
found with our ministry, 4 but as
servants of God we have commended ourselves in every way: through
great endurance, in afflictions,
hardships, calamities, 5 beatings,
imprisonments, riots, labors,
sleepless nights, hunger; 6 by purity, knowledge, patience, kindness,
holiness of spirit, genuine love,
7 truthful speech, and the power of
God; with the weapons of righteousness for the right hand and for
the left; 8 in honor and dishonor, in
ill repute and good repute. We are
treated as impostors, and yet are
true; 9 as unknown, and yet are well
known; as dying, and see—we are
alive; as punished, and yet not
killed; 10 as sorrowful, yet always
rejoicing; as poor, yet making many
rich; as having nothing, and yet
possessing everything.

11 We have spoken frankly to
you Corinthians; our heart is wide
open to you. 12 There is no restric-
tion in our affections, but only in
yours. 13 In return—I speak as to

5.18 Col 1.20; Rom 5.10
5.20 2 Cor 3.6; Eph 6.20; 2 Cor 6.1
5.21 1 Pet 2.22; 1 Jn 3.5; Gal 3.13
6.1 1 Cor 3.9; 2 Cor 5.20; Heb 12.15
6.2 Isa 49.8
6.3 Rom 14.13; 1 Cor 9.12; 10.32
6.5 2 Cor 11.23
6.7 2 Cor 4.2; 10.4; Eph 6.11,13
6.9 Rom 8.36; 2 Cor 1.8-10; 4.10,11
6.10 Rom 8.32; 1 Cor 3.21
6.11 Ezek 33.22; 2 Cor 7.3; Isa 60.5
6.13 1 Cor 4.14
6.14 Deut 7.2,3; 1 Cor 5.9, 10; Eph 5.7, 11; 1 Jn 1.6
6.16 1 Cor 3.16; Jer 31.1; Ezek 37.27
6.17 Isa 52.11; Rev 18.4
6.18 Hos 1.10; Isa 43.6
7.1 2 Cor 6.17, 18
7.2 2 Cor 6.12, 13
7.3 2 Cor 6.11, 12
7.4 2 Cor 1.4, 14; 3.12
7.5 2 Cor 2.13; 4.8; Deut 32.25

children—open wide your hearts
also.

The Temple of the Living God

14 Do not be mismatched with
unbelievers. For what partnership
is there between righteousness and
lawlessness? Or what fellowship is
there between light and darkness?
15 What agreement does Christ
have with Beliar? Or what does a
believer share with an unbeliever?
16 What agreement has the temple
of God with idols? For we[n] are the
temple of the living God; as God
said,

"I will live in them and walk
among them,
and I will be their God,
and they shall be my
people.
17 Therefore come out from
them,
and be separate from them,
says the Lord,
and touch nothing unclean;
then I will welcome you,
18 and I will be your father,
and you shall be my sons
and daughters,
says the Lord Almighty."

7 Since we have these promises,
beloved, let us cleanse ourselves from every defilement of
body and of spirit, making holiness
perfect in the fear of God.

Paul's Joy at the Church's Repentance

2 Make room in your hearts[o] for
us; we have wronged no one, we
have corrupted no one, we have
taken advantage of no one. 3 I do
not say this to condemn you, for I
said before that you are in our
hearts, to die together and to live
together. 4 I often boast about you;
I have great pride in you; I am filled
with consolation; I am overjoyed in
all our affliction.

5 For even when we came into
Macedonia, our bodies had no rest,

[l] Or *God was in Christ reconciling the world to himself* [m] Gk *As we work together*
[n] Other ancient authorities read *you*
[o] Gk lacks *in your hearts*

but we were afflicted in every
way—disputes without and fears
within. 6 But God, who consoles
the downcast, consoled us by the
arrival of Titus, 7 and not only by
his coming, but also by the consolation with which he was consoled
about you, as he told us of your
longing, your mourning, your zeal
for me, so that I rejoiced still more.
8 For even if I made you sorry with
my letter, I do not regret it (though
I did regret it, for I see that I grieved
you with that letter, though only
briefly). 9 Now I rejoice, not because you were grieved, but because your grief led to repentance;
for you felt a godly grief, so that you
were not harmed in any way by us.
10 For godly grief produces a repentance that leads to salvation and
brings no regret, but worldly grief
produces death. 11 For see what
earnestness this godly grief has
produced in you, what eagerness to
clear yourselves, what indignation,
what alarm, what longing, what
zeal, what punishment! At every
point you have proved yourselves
guiltless in the matter. 12 So although I wrote to you, it was not on
account of the one who did the
wrong, nor on account of the one
who was wronged, but in order that
your zeal for us might be made
known to you before God. 13 In this
we find comfort.

In addition to our own consolation, we rejoiced still more at the
joy of Titus, because his mind has
been set at rest by all of you. 14 For
if I have been somewhat boastful
about you to him, I was not disgraced; but just as everything we
said to you was true, so our boasting to Titus has proved true as well.
15 And his heart goes out all the
more to you, as he remembers the
obedience of all of you, and how
you welcomed him with fear and
trembling. 16 I rejoice, because I
have complete confidence in you.

Encouragement to Be Generous

8 We want you to know, brothers and sisters,[p] about the
grace of God that has been granted
to the churches of Macedonia; 2 for
during a severe ordeal of affliction,
their abundant joy and their extreme poverty have overflowed in a
wealth of generosity on their part.
3 For, as I can testify, they voluntar-
ily gave according to their means,
and even beyond their means,
4 begging us earnestly for the privilege[q] of sharing in this ministry to
the saints— 5 and this, not merely
as we expected; they gave themselves first to the Lord and, by the
will of God, to us, 6 so that we
might urge Titus that, as he had already made a beginning, so he
should also complete this generous
undertaking[r] among you. 7 Now as
you excel in everything—in faith,
in speech, in knowledge, in utmost
eagerness, and in our love for
you[s]—so we want you to excel
also in this generous undertaking.[r]

8 I do not say this as a command, but I am testing the genuineness of your love against the
earnestness of others. 9 For you
know the generous act[t] of our
Lord Jesus Christ, that though he
was rich, yet for your sakes he became poor, so that by his poverty
you might become rich. 10 And in
this matter I am giving my advice:
it is appropriate for you who began
last year not only to do something
but even to desire to do
something— 11 now finish doing it,
so that your eagerness may be
matched by completing it according to your means. 12 For if the eagerness is there, the gift is acceptable according to what one
has—not according to what one
does not have. 13 I do not mean that
there should be relief for others
and pressure on you, but it is a
question of a fair balance between
14 your present abundance and
their need, so that their abundance
may be for your need, in order that
there may be a fair balance. 15 As it
is written,

[p] Gk *brothers* [q] Gk *grace* [r] Gk *this grace* [s] Other ancient authorities read *your love for us* [t] Gk *the grace*

7.6 2 Cor 1.3, 4; v. 13; 2 Cor 2.13
7.8 2 Cor 2.2, 4
7.10 Acts 11.18
7.11 2 Cor 2.6; Rom 3.5
7.12 v. 8; 2 Cor 2.3, 9; 1 Cor 5.1, 2
7.13 v. 6; 1 Cor 16.18
7.14 vv. 4,6
7.15 2 Cor 2.9; Phil 2.12
7.16 2 Thes 3.4
8.1 Acts 16.9
8.2 2 Cor 9.11
8.3 1 Cor 16.2
8.4 Acts 24.17; Rom 15.25, 26,31; 2 Cor 9.1
8.6 v. 17; 2 Cor 12.18; vv. 16,23,10
8.7 2 Cor 9.8; 1 Cor 1.5; 12.13
8.8 1 Cor 7.6
8.9 2 Cor 13.14; Phil 2.6,7
8.10 1 Cor 7.25; 2 Cor 9.2; 1 Cor 16.2, 3
8.11 2 Cor 9.2
8.12 Mk 12.43, 44; Lk 21.3
8.14 2 Cor 9.12
8.15 Ex 16.18

"The one who had much did
not have too much,
and the one who had little
did not have too little."

Commendation of Titus

16 But thanks be to God who put in the heart of Titus the same eagerness for you that I myself have. 17 For he not only accepted our appeal, but since he is more eager than ever, he is going to you of his own accord. 18 With him we are sending the brother who is famous among all the churches for his proclaiming the good news;[u] 19 and not only that, but he has also been appointed by the churches to travel with us while we are administering this generous undertaking[v] for the glory of the Lord himself[w] and to show our goodwill. 20 We intend that no one should blame us about this generous gift that we are administering, 21 for we intend to do what is right not only in the Lord's sight but also in the sight of others. 22 And with them we are sending our brother whom we have often tested and found eager in many matters, but who is now more eager than ever because of his great confidence in you. 23 As for Titus, he is my partner and co-worker in your service; as for our brothers, they are messengers[x] of the churches, the glory of Christ. 24 Therefore openly before the churches, show them the proof of your love and of our reason for boasting about you.

The Collection for Christians at Jerusalem

9 Now it is not necessary for me to write you about the ministry to the saints, 2 for I know your eagerness, which is the subject of my boasting about you to the people of Macedonia, saying that Achaia has been ready since last year; and your zeal has stirred up most of them. 3 But I am sending the brothers in order that our boasting about you may not prove to have been empty in this case, so that you may be ready, as I said you would be; 4 otherwise, if some Macedonians come with me and find that you are not ready, we would be humiliated—to say nothing of you—in this undertaking.[y] 5 So I thought it necessary to urge the brothers to go on ahead to you, and arrange in advance for this bountiful gift that you have promised, so that it may be ready as a voluntary gift and not as an extortion.

6 The point is this: the one who sows sparingly will also reap sparingly, and the one who sows bountifully will also reap bountifully. 7 Each of you must give as you have made up your mind, not reluctantly or under compulsion, for God loves a cheerful giver. 8 And God is able to provide you with every blessing in abundance, so that by always having enough of everything, you may share abundantly in every good work. 9 As it is written,

"He scatters abroad, he gives
to the poor;
his righteousness[z] endures
forever."

10 He who supplies seed to the sower and bread for food will supply and multiply your seed for sowing and increase the harvest of your righteousness.[z] 11 You will be enriched in every way for your great generosity, which will produce thanksgiving to God through us; 12 for the rendering of this ministry not only supplies the needs of the saints but also overflows with many thanksgivings to God. 13 Through the testing of this ministry you glorify God by your obedience to the confession of the gospel of Christ and by the generosity of your sharing with them and with all others, 14 while they long for you and pray for you because of the surpassing grace of God that he has given you. 15 Thanks be to God for his indescribable gift!

Paul Defends His Ministry

10 I myself, Paul, appeal to you by the meekness and

8.17 v. 6
8.18 2 Cor 12.18
8.19 1 Cor 16.3, 4; vv. 4,6,11
8.21 Rom 12.17; 14.18
8.23 Phil 2.25
8.24 2 Cor 7.14; 9.2
9.1 2 Cor 8.4
9.2 2 Cor 7.4; Rom 15.26; Acts 18.12; 2 Cor 8.10
9.3 1 Cor 16.2
9.4 Rom 15.26
9.5 Gen 33.11; 1 Sam 25.27; Phil 4.17; 2 Cor 12.17, 18
9.6 Gal 6.7,9
9.7 Deut 15.7, 10; Ex 25.2; Rom 12.8; 2 Cor 8.12
9.8 Eph 3.20; Phil 4.19
9.9 Ps 112.9
9.10 Isa 55.10; Hos 10.12
9.11 1 Cor 1.5, 11
9.12 2 Cor 8.14
9.13 2 Cor 8.4; Rom 15.31; Mt 9.8; 2 Cor 2.12
9.15 2 Cor 2.14; Rom 5.15, 16
10.1 Gal 5.2; Rom 12.1

u Or *the gospel* v Gk *this grace* w Other ancient authorities lack *himself* x Gk *apostles* y Other ancient authorities add *of boasting* z Or *benevolence*

gentleness of Christ—I who am
humble when face to face with you,
but bold toward you when I am
away!— 2 I ask that when I am
present I need not show boldness
by daring to oppose those who
think we are acting according to
human standards.[a] 3 Indeed, we
live as human beings,[b] but we do
not wage war according to human
standards;[a] 4 for the weapons of
our warfare are not merely human,[c] but they have divine power
to destroy strongholds. We destroy
arguments 5 and every proud obstacle raised up against the knowledge of God, and we take every
thought captive to obey Christ.
6 We are ready to punish every disobedience when your obedience is
complete.
7 Look at what is before your
eyes. If you are confident that you
belong to Christ, remind yourself of
this, that just as you belong to
Christ, so also do we. 8 Now, even if
I boast a little too much of our authority, which the Lord gave for
building you up and not for tearing
you down, I will not be ashamed of
it. 9 I do not want to seem as though
I am trying to frighten you with my
letters. 10 For they say, "His letters
are weighty and strong, but his
bodily presence is weak, and his
speech contemptible." 11 Let such
people understand that what we
say by letter when absent, we will
also do when present.
12 We do not dare to classify or
compare ourselves with some of
those who commend themselves.
But when they measure themselves
by one another, and compare
themselves with one another, they
do not show good sense. 13 We,
however, will not boast beyond
limits, but will keep within the
field that God has assigned to us,
to reach out even as far as you.
14 For we were not overstepping our
limits when we reached you; we
were the first to come all the way to
you with the good news[d] of Christ.
15 We do not boast beyond limits,
that is, in the labors of others; but
our hope is that, as your faith in-

10.2 1 Cor 4.21; 2 Cor 13.2, 10
10.3 v. 2
10.4 1 Tim 1.18; 2 Tim 2.3; Acts 7.22; 1 Cor 2.5; Jer 1.10
10.5 1 Cor 1.19; Isa 2.11,12; 2 Cor 9.13
10.6 2 Cor 2.9
10.7 Jn 7.24; 1 Cor 1.12; 14.37
10.8 2 Cor 7.4; 13.10
10.10 1 Cor 2.3; Gal 4.13,14; 1 Cor 1.17
10.12 2 Cor 3.1; 5.12
10.13 v. 15
10.14 2 Cor 2.12
10.15 Rom 15.20; 2 Thes 1.3
10.17 Jer 9.24; 1 Cor 1.31
10.18 Rom 2.29; 1 Cor 4.5
11.1 vv. 16,17, 21; 2 Cor 5.13
11.2 Hos 2.19; Eph 5.26, 27; 2 Cor 4.14
11.3 Gen 3.4; Jn 8.44
11.4 1 Cor 3.11; Rom 8.15; Gal 1.6-8
11.5 2 Cor 12.11; Gal 2.6
11.6 1 Cor 1.17; Eph 3.4; 2 Cor 4.2
11.7 2 Cor 12.13; 1 Cor 9.18
11.8 Phil 4.15,18
11.9 2 Cor 12.13, 14

creases, our sphere of action
among you may be greatly enlarged, 16 so that we may proclaim
the good news[d] in lands beyond
you, without boasting of work already done in someone else's
sphere of action. 17 "Let the one
who boasts, boast in the Lord."
18 For it is not those who commend
themselves that are approved, but
those whom the Lord commends.

Paul and the False Apostles

11 I wish you would bear with
me in a little foolishness.
Do bear with me! 2 I feel a divine
jealousy for you, for I promised you
in marriage to one husband, to
present you as a chaste virgin to
Christ. 3 But I am afraid that as the
serpent deceived Eve by its cunning, your thoughts will be led
astray from a sincere and pure[e] devotion to Christ. 4 For if someone
comes and proclaims another
Jesus than the one we proclaimed,
or if you receive a different spirit
from the one you received, or a different gospel from the one you accepted, you submit to it readily
enough. 5 I think that I am not in
the least inferior to these super-
apostles. 6 I may be untrained in
speech, but not in knowledge; certainly in every way and in all things
we have made this evident to you.
7 Did I commit a sin by humbling myself so that you might be
exalted, because I proclaimed
God's good news[f] to you free of
charge? 8 I robbed other churches
by accepting support from them in
order to serve you. 9 And when I was
with you and was in need, I did not
burden anyone, for my needs were
supplied by the friends[g] who came
from Macedonia. So I refrained and
will continue to refrain from burdening you in any way. 10 As the
truth of Christ is in me, this boast
of mine will not be silenced in the

11.10 Rom 9.1; 1 Cor 9.15; Acts 18.12

[a] Gk *according to the flesh* [b] Gk *in the flesh* [c] Gk *fleshly* [d] Or *the gospel*
[e] Other ancient authorities lack *and pure*
[f] Gk *the gospel of God* [g] Gk *brothers*

regions of Achaia. 11 And why? Because I do not love you? God knows
I do!

12 And what I do I will also continue to do, in order to deny an opportunity to those who want an opportunity to be recognized as our
equals in what they boast about.
13 For such boasters are false apostles, deceitful workers, disguising
themselves as apostles of Christ.
14 And no wonder! Even Satan disguises himself as an angel of light.
15 So it is not strange if his ministers also disguise themselves as
ministers of righteousness. Their
end will match their deeds.

Paul's Sufferings as an Apostle

16 I repeat, let no one think that
I am a fool; but if you do, then accept me as a fool, so that I too may
boast a little. 17 What I am saying in
regard to this boastful confidence,
I am saying not with the Lord's authority, but as a fool; 18 since many
boast according to human standards,[h] I will also boast. 19 For you
gladly put up with fools, being wise
yourselves! 20 For you put up with it
when someone makes slaves of
you, or preys upon you, or takes advantage of you, or puts on airs, or
gives you a slap in the face. 21 To
my shame, I must say, we were too
weak for that!

But whatever anyone dares to
boast of—I am speaking as a
fool—I also dare to boast of that.
22 Are they Hebrews? So am I. Are
they Israelites? So am I. Are they
descendants of Abraham? So am I.
23 Are they ministers of Christ? I am
talking like a madman—I am a better one: with far greater labors, far
more imprisonments, with countless floggings, and often near
death. 24 Five times I have received
from the Jews the forty lashes minus one. 25 Three times I was beat-
en with rods. Once I received a
stoning. Three times I was shipwrecked; for a night and a day I was
adrift at sea; 26 on frequent journeys, in danger from rivers, danger
from bandits, danger from my own
people, danger from Gentiles, danger in the city, danger in the wilderness, danger at sea, danger from
false brothers and sisters;[i] 27 in
toil and hardship, through many a
sleepless night, hungry and thirsty,
often without food, cold and naked. 28 And, besides other things, I
am under daily pressure because of
my anxiety for all the churches.
29 Who is weak, and I am not weak?
Who is made to stumble, and I am
not indignant?

30 If I must boast, I will boast of
the things that show my weakness.
31 The God and Father of the Lord
Jesus (blessed be he forever!)
knows that I do not lie. 32 In Damascus, the governor[j] under King
Aretas guarded the city of Damascus in order to[k] seize me, 33 but I
was let down in a basket through a
window in the wall,[l] and escaped
from his hands.

Paul's Visions and Revelations

12 It is necessary to boast;
nothing is to be gained by
it, but I will go on to visions and
revelations of the Lord. 2 I know a
person in Christ who fourteen years
ago was caught up to the third
heaven—whether in the body or
out of the body I do not know; God
knows. 3 And I know that such a
person—whether in the body or
out of the body I do not know; God
knows— 4 was caught up into Paradise and heard things that are not
to be told, that no mortal is permitted to repeat. 5 On behalf of such a
one I will boast, but on my own behalf I will not boast, except of my
weaknesses. 6 But if I wish to boast,
I will not be a fool, for I will be
speaking the truth. But I refrain
from it, so that no one may think
better of me than what is seen in
me or heard from me, 7 even considering the exceptional character
of the revelations. Therefore, to
keep[m] me from being too elated, a
thorn was given me in the flesh, a
messenger of Satan to torment me,

11.11 2 Cor 12.15
11.12 1 Cor 9.12
11.13 Gal 1.7; 2 Pet 2.1; Phil 3.2
11.15 Phil 3.19
11.16 v. 1
11.17 1 Cor 7.6, 12,25; Acts 9.24,25
11.18 Phil 3.3,4
11.21 2 Cor 10.10; Phil 3.4
11.22 Acts 6.1; Phil 3.5; Rom 9.4
11.23 1 Cor 15.10; Acts 16.23; 2 Cor 6.5
11.24 Deut 25.3
11.25 Acts 16.22; 14.19
11.26 Acts 9.23; 14.5; 21.31; Gal 2.4
11.27 1 Thes 2.9; 1 Cor 4.11; 2 Cor 6.5
11.29 1 Cor 9.22
11.30 1 Cor 2.3
11.31 Gal 1.20; Rom 9.5
11.32 Acts 9.24,25
12.1 Co 11.30; v. 7; Gal 1.12; 2.2
12.2 Rom 16.7; Eph 4.10; 2 Cor 11.11
12.4 Lk 23.43
12.6 2 Cor 10.8; 11.16

[h] Gk *according to the flesh* [i] Gk *brothers*
[j] Gk *ethnarch* [k] Other ancient authorities read *and wanted to* [l] Gk *through the wall*
[m] Other ancient authorities read *To keep*

to keep me from being too elated.[n]
8 Three times I appealed to the
Lord about this, that it would leave
me, 9 but he said to me, "My grace
is sufficient for you, for power[o] is
made perfect in weakness." So, I
will boast all the more gladly of my
weaknesses, so that the power of
Christ may dwell in me. 10 Therefore I am content with weaknesses,
insults, hardships, persecutions,
and calamities for the sake of
Christ; for whenever I am weak,
then I am strong.

Paul's Concern for the Corinthian Church

11 I have been a fool! You forced
me to it. Indeed you should have
been the ones commending me, for
I am not at all inferior to these
super-apostles, even though I am
nothing. 12 The signs of a true apostle were performed among you with
utmost patience, signs and wonders and mighty works. 13 How have
you been worse off than the other
churches, except that I myself did
not burden you? Forgive me this
wrong!

14 Here I am, ready to come to
you this third time. And I will not
be a burden, because I do not want
what is yours but you; for children
ought not to lay up for their parents, but parents for their children.
15 I will most gladly spend and be
spent for you. If I love you more, am
I to be loved less? 16 Let it be assumed that I did not burden you.
Nevertheless (you say) since I was
crafty, I took you in by deceit.
17 Did I take advantage of you
through any of those whom I sent
to you? 18 I urged Titus to go, and
sent the brother with him. Titus
did not take advantage of you, did
he? Did we not conduct ourselves
with the same spirit? Did we not
take the same steps?

19 Have you been thinking all
along that we have been defending
ourselves before you? We are
speaking in Christ before God. Everything we do, beloved, is for the
sake of building you up. 20 For I fear
that when I come, I may find you

12.8 Mt 26.44 **12.9** Phil 4.13; 2 Cor 11.30; 1 Pet 4.14 **12.10** Rom 5.3; 2 Cor 6.4; 2 Thes 1.4 **12.11** 2 Cor 11.1, 5 **12.12** Rom 15.18, 19 **12.13** 1 Cor 9.12, 18; 2 Cor 11.7 **12.14** 2 Cor 13.1; 1 Cor 10.24, 33; 4.14,15; Prov 19.14 **12.15** Phil 2.17; 1 Thes 2.8 **12.18** 2 Cor 8.6, 16,18 **12.19** Rom 9.1; 2 Cor 10.8 **12.20** 2 Cor 2.1-4; 1 Cor 1.11; 3.3 **12.21** 2 Cor 2.1, 4; 13.2; Gal 5.19 **13.1** 2 Cor 12.14; Deut 19.15; Mt 18.16 **13.3** Mt 10.20; 1 Cor 5.4; 2 Cor 9.8; 10.4 **13.4** Phil 2.7,8; 1 Pet 3.18; Rom 6.4,8; v. 9 **13.5** Jn 6.6; 1 Cor 11.28; 9.27 **13.9** 2 Cor 11.30; 12.10 **13.10** 2 Cor 2.3; Titus 1.13; 2 Cor 10.8

not as I wish, and that you may find
me not as you wish; I fear that there
may perhaps be quarreling, jealousy, anger, selfishness, slander, gossip, conceit, and disorder. 21 I fear
that when I come again, my God
may humble me before you, and
that I may have to mourn over
many who previously sinned and
have not repented of the impurity,
sexual immorality, and licentiousness that they have practiced.

Further Warning

13 This is the third time I am
coming to you. "Any charge
must be sustained by the evidence
of two or three witnesses." 2 I
warned those who sinned previously and all the others, and I warn
them now while absent, as I did
when present on my second visit,
that if I come again, I will not be
lenient— 3 since you desire proof
that Christ is speaking in me. He is
not weak in dealing with you, but is
powerful in you. 4 For he was crucified in weakness, but lives by the
power of God. For we are weak in
him,[p] but in dealing with you we
will live with him by the power of
God.

5 Examine yourselves to see
whether you are living in the faith.
Test yourselves. Do you not realize
that Jesus Christ is in you?—
unless, indeed, you fail to meet the
test! 6 I hope you will find out that
we have not failed. 7 But we pray to
God that you may not do anything
wrong—not that we may appear to
have met the test, but that you may
do what is right, though we may
seem to have failed. 8 For we cannot do anything against the truth,
but only for the truth. 9 For we rejoice when we are weak and you are
strong. This is what we pray for,
that you may become perfect. 10 So
I write these things while I am away
from you, so that when I come, I
may not have to be severe in using
the authority that the Lord has giv-

[n] Other ancient authorities lack *to keep me from being too elated* [o] Other ancient authorities read *my power* [p] Other ancient authorities read *with him*

en me for building up and not for
tearing down.

Final Greetings and Benediction

11 Finally, brothers and sisters,[q] farewell.[r] Put things in order, listen to my appeal,[s] agree
with one another, live in peace;
and the God of love and peace will
be with you. 12 Greet one another
with a holy kiss. All the saints greet
you.
13 The grace of the Lord Jesus
Christ, the love of God, and the
communion of[t] the Holy Spirit be
with all of you.

13.11 Rom 15.33; Eph 6.23
13.13 Phil 4.22

[q] Gk *brothers* [r] Or *rejoice*
[s] Or *encourage one another* [t] Or *and the sharing in*

THE LETTER OF PAUL TO THE

Galatians

Title and Background

Judaizers were Jewish Christians who believed, among other things, that a number of the ceremonial practices of the Old Testament were still binding on the New Testament church. Following Paul's successful campaign in Galatia, they insisted that Gentile converts to Christianity abide by certain Old Testament practices, especially circumcision. The Judaizers argued that Paul was not an authentic apostle and that out of a desire to make the message more appealing to Gentiles, he had removed from the gospel certain legal requirements. Paul responds by writing this letter.

Author and Date of Writing

The opening verse identifies the author as the apostle Paul. Various dates have been given for the writing of this letter, but it was probably one of his earliest letters, written near A.D. 50.

Theme and Message

Galatians stands as an eloquent and vigorous defense for the essential New Testament truth that we are justified by faith in Jesus Christ–by nothing less and nothing more. Furthermore, we are sanctified by depending on the grace of Christ and by experiencing the power of the Holy Spirit working within us. Some have called this letter the *Magna Charta* of Christian liberty.

Outline

I. Introduction: Greetings and Denunciation (1.1-9)
II. Authentication of the Apostle of Liberty and Faith (1.10–2.21)
III. Justification of the Doctrine of Liberty and Faith (3.1–4.31)
IV. Practice of the Life of Liberty and Faith (5.1–6.10)
V. Conclusion (6.11-18)

Salutation

1 Paul an apostle—sent neither
by human commission nor
from human authorities, but
through Jesus Christ and God the
Father, who raised him from the
dead— 2 and all the members of
God's family[a] who are with me,
To the churches of Galatia:
3 Grace to you and peace from
God our Father and the Lord Jesus
Christ, 4 who gave himself for our
sins to set us free from the present
evil age, according to the will of our
God and Father, 5 to whom be the
glory forever and ever. Amen.

There Is No Other Gospel

6 I am astonished that you are
so quickly deserting the one who
called you in the grace of Christ
and are turning to a different
gospel— 7 not that there is another
gospel, but there are some who are
confusing you and want to pervert
the gospel of Christ. 8 But even if
we or an angel[b] from heaven
should proclaim to you a gospel
contrary to what we proclaimed to
you, let that one be accursed! 9 As
we have said before, so now I repeat, if anyone proclaims to you a
gospel contrary to what you received, let that one be accursed!
10 Am I now seeking human approval, or God's approval? Or am I

1.1 2 Cor 1.1; vv. 11,12; Acts 9.6; 2.24
1.2 Phil 4.21; 1 Cor 16.1
1.3 Rom 1.7
1.4 Rom 4.25; Gal 2.20; 2 Cor 4.4
1.5 Rom 16.27
1.6 Gal 5.8; 2 Cor 11.4
1.7 Acts 15.24; Gal 5.10
1.8 2 Cor 11.4, 14; Rom 9.3
1.9 Rom 16.17 **1.10** 1 Thes 2.4

[a] Gk *all the brothers* [b] Or *a messenger*

trying to please people? If I were
still pleasing people, I would not be
a servant[c] of Christ.

Paul's Vindication of His Apostleship

11 For I want you to know,
brothers and sisters,[d] that the gospel that was proclaimed by me is
not of human origin; 12 for I did not
receive it from a human source, nor
was I taught it, but I received it
through a revelation of Jesus
Christ.

13 You have heard, no doubt, of
my earlier life in Judaism. I was violently persecuting the church of
God and was trying to destroy it. 14 I
advanced in Judaism beyond many
among my people of the same age,
for I was far more zealous for the
traditions of my ancestors. 15 But
when God, who had set me apart
before I was born and called me
through his grace, was pleased 16 to
reveal his Son to me,[e] so that I
might proclaim him among the
Gentiles, I did not confer with any
human being, 17 nor did I go up to
Jerusalem to those who were already apostles before me, but I
went away at once into Arabia, and
afterwards I returned to Damascus.

18 Then after three years I did
go up to Jerusalem to visit Cephas
and stayed with him fifteen days;
19 but I did not see any other apostle except James the Lord's brother. 20 In what I am writing to you,
before God, I do not lie! 21 Then I
went into the regions of Syria and
Cilicia, 22 and I was still unknown
by sight to the churches of Judea
that are in Christ; 23 they only heard
it said, "The one who formerly was
persecuting us is now proclaiming
the faith he once tried to destroy."
24 And they glorified God because
of me.

Paul and the Other Apostles

2 Then after fourteen years I
went up again to Jerusalem
with Barnabas, taking Titus along
with me. 2 I went up in response to
a revelation. Then I laid before
them (though only in a private
meeting with the acknowledged
leaders) the gospel that I proclaim
among the Gentiles, in order to
make sure that I was not running,
or had not run, in vain. 3 But even
Titus, who was with me, was not
compelled to be circumcised,
though he was a Greek. 4 But because of false believers[f] secretly
brought in, who slipped in to spy
on the freedom we have in Christ
Jesus, so that they might enslave
us — 5 we did not submit to them
even for a moment, so that the
truth of the gospel might always remain with you. 6 And from those
who were supposed to be acknowledged leaders (what they actually
were makes no difference to me;
God shows no partiality) — those
leaders contributed nothing to me.
7 On the contrary, when they saw
that I had been entrusted with the
gospel for the uncircumcised, just
as Peter had been entrusted with
the gospel for the circumcised 8 (for
he who worked through Peter making him an apostle to the circumcised also worked through me in
sending me to the Gentiles), 9 and
when James and Cephas and John,
who were acknowledged pillars,
recognized the grace that had been
given to me, they gave to Barnabas
and me the right hand of fellowship, agreeing that we should go to
the Gentiles and they to the circumcised. 10 They asked only one
thing, that we remember the poor,
which was actually what I was[g] eager to do.

Paul Rebukes Peter at Antioch

11 But when Cephas came to
Antioch, I opposed him to his face,
because he stood self-condemned;
12 for until certain people came
from James, he used to eat with the
Gentiles. But after they came, he
drew back and kept himself separate for fear of the circumcision
faction. 13 And the other Jews
joined him in this hypocrisy, so
that even Barnabas was led astray
by their hypocrisy. 14 But when I

1.11 1 Cor 15.1
1.12 vv. 1,16; Eph 3.3
1.13 Acts 8.3; 9.21
1.14 Acts 22.3; Col 2.8
1.15 Isa 49.1,5; Jer 1.5; Acts 9.15; Rom 1.1
1.16 Acts 9.20; Eph 6.12
1.18 Acts 9.22, 23,26,27
1.19 Mt 13.55
1.21 Acts 9.30
1.22 1 Thes 2.14; Rom 16.7
2.1 Acts 15.2
2.2 Acts 15.12; Gal 1.6; Phil 2.16
2.3 2 Cor 2.13; Acts 16.3; 1 Cor 9.21
2.4 Acts 15.1; 2 Cor 11.26
2.5 v. 14; Col 1.5
2.6 Gal 6.3; Rom 2.11; 2 Cor 12.11
2.7 1 Thes 2.4; Acts 13.46
2.9 Rom 12.3; Gal 1.16
2.10 Acts 11.29, 30; 24.17
2.11 Acts 11.10
2.12 Acts 11.2,3
2.13 v. 1
2.14 vv. 5,9,11

c Gk *slave* d Gk *brothers* e Gk *in me*
f Gk *false brothers* g Or *had been*

saw that they were not acting consistently with the truth of the gospel, I said to Cephas before them all, "If you, though a Jew, live like a Gentile and not like a Jew, how can you compel the Gentiles to live like Jews?"[h]

Jews and Gentiles Are Saved by Faith

15 We ourselves are Jews by birth and not Gentile sinners; 16 yet we know that a person is justified[i] not by the works of the law but through faith in Jesus Christ.[j] And we have come to believe in Christ Jesus, so that we might be justified by faith in Christ,[k] and not by doing the works of the law, because no one will be justified by the works of the law. 17 But if, in our effort to be justified in Christ, we ourselves have been found to be sinners, is Christ then a servant of sin? Certainly not! 18 But if I build up again the very things that I once tore down, then I demonstrate that I am a transgressor. 19 For through the law I died to the law, so that I might live to God. I have been crucified with Christ; 20 and it is no longer I who live, but it is Christ who lives in me. And the life I now live in the flesh I live by faith in the Son of God,[l] who loved me and gave himself for me. 21 I do not nullify the grace of God; for if justification[m] comes through the law, then Christ died for nothing.

Law or Faith

3 You foolish Galatians! Who has bewitched you? It was before your eyes that Jesus Christ was publicly exhibited as crucified! 2 The only thing I want to learn from you is this: Did you receive the Spirit by doing the works of the law or by believing what you heard? 3 Are you so foolish? Having started with the Spirit, are you now ending with the flesh? 4 Did you experience so much for nothing?—if it really was for nothing. 5 Well then, does God[n] supply you with the Spirit and work miracles among you by your doing the works of the law, or by your believing what you heard?

6 Just as Abraham "believed God, and it was reckoned to him as righteousness," 7 so, you see, those who believe are the descendants of Abraham. 8 And the scripture, foreseeing that God would justify the Gentiles by faith, declared the gospel beforehand to Abraham, saying, "All the Gentiles shall be blessed in you." 9 For this reason, those who believe are blessed with Abraham who believed.

10 For all who rely on the works of the law are under a curse; for it is written, "Cursed is everyone who does not observe and obey all the things written in the book of the law." 11 Now it is evident that no one is justified before God by the law; for "The one who is righteous will live by faith."[o] 12 But the law does not rest on faith; on the contrary, "Whoever does the works of the law[p] will live by them." 13 Christ redeemed us from the curse of the law by becoming a curse for us—for it is written, "Cursed is everyone who hangs on a tree"— 14 in order that in Christ Jesus the blessing of Abraham might come to the Gentiles, so that we might receive the promise of the Spirit through faith.

The Promise to Abraham

15 Brothers and sisters,[q] I give an example from daily life: once a person's will[r] has been ratified, no one adds to it or annuls it. 16 Now the promises were made to Abraham and to his offspring;[s] it does not say, "And to offsprings,"[t] as of many; but it says, "And to your offspring,"[s] that is, to one person, who is Christ. 17 My point is this: the law, which came four hundred thirty years later, does not annul a

2.15 Phil 3.4,5; Mt 9.11 **2.16** Acts 13.39; Rom 1.17; 3.20 **2.17** v. 15; Gal 3.21 **2.19** Rom 8.2; 6.14; 2 Cor 5.15; 1 Thes 5.10 **2.20** 1 Pet 4.2; Eph 5.2; Titus 2.14 **2.21** Gal 3.21 **3.1** Gal 1.2; 5.7; 1 Cor 1.23 **3.2** Acts 2.38; Rom 10.16, 17 **3.3** Gal 4.9; Heb 7.16 **3.4** 1 Cor 15.2 **3.5** Phil 1.19; 1 Cor 12.10; Rom 10.17 **3.6** Gen 15.6; Rom 4.3; Jas 2.23 **3.7** v. 9 **3.8** Gen 12.3; Acts 3.25 **3.9** Rom 4.16; v. 7 **3.10** Deut 27.26 **3.11** Gal 2.16; Hab 2.4; Heb 10.38 **3.12** Lev 18.5; Rom 10.5 **3.13** Gal 4.5; Acts 5.30; Deut 21.23 **3.14** Rom 4.9; Joel 2.28; Acts 2.33 **3.15** Heb 9.17 **3.16** Gen 12.3; 13.15; Acts 3.25 **3.17** Ex 12.40; Rom 4.13

[h] Some interpreters hold that the quotation extends into the following paragraph
[i] Or *reckoned as righteous;* and so elsewhere
[j] Or *the faith of Jesus Christ*
[k] Or *the faith of Christ*
[l] Or *by the faith of the Son of God*
[m] Or *righteousness*
[n] Gk *he*
[o] Or *The one who is righteous through faith will live*
[p] Gk *does them*
[q] Gk *Brothers*
[r] Or *covenant* (as in verse 17)
[s] Gk *seed*
[t] Gk *seeds*

covenant previously ratified by
God, so as to nullify the promise.
18 For if the inheritance comes
from the law, it no longer comes
from the promise; but God granted
it to Abraham through the promise.

The Purpose of the Law

19 Why then the law? It was
added because of transgressions,
until the offspring[u] would come to
whom the promise had been made;
and it was ordained through angels
by a mediator. 20 Now a mediator
involves more than one party; but
God is one.
21 Is the law then opposed to
the promises of God? Certainly not!
For if a law had been given that
could make alive, then righteousness would indeed come through
the law. 22 But the scripture has imprisoned all things under the power
of sin, so that what was promised
through faith in Jesus Christ[v]
might be given to those who believe.
23 Now before faith came, we
were imprisoned and guarded under the law until faith would be revealed. 24 Therefore the law was our
disciplinarian until Christ came, so
that we might be justified by faith.
25 But now that faith has come, we
are no longer subject to a disciplinarian, 26 for in Christ Jesus you are
all children of God through faith.
27 As many of you as were baptized
into Christ have clothed yourselves with Christ. 28 There is no
longer Jew or Greek, there is
no longer slave or free, there is no
longer male and female; for all of
you are one in Christ Jesus. 29 And
if you belong to Christ, then
you are Abraham's offspring,[u] heirs
according to the promise.

4 My point is this: heirs, as long
as they are minors, are no better than slaves, though they are the
owners of all the property; 2 but
they remain under guardians and
trustees until the date set by the
father. 3 So with us; while we were
minors, we were enslaved to the elemental spirits[w] of the world. 4 But
when the fullness of time had
come, God sent his Son, born of a
woman, born under the law, 5 in order to redeem those who were under the law, so that we might receive adoption as children. 6 And
because you are children, God has
sent the Spirit of his Son into our[x]
hearts, crying, "Abba![y] Father!"
7 So you are no longer a slave but a
child, and if a child then also an
heir, through God.[z]

Paul Reproves the Galatians

8 Formerly, when you did not
know God, you were enslaved to
beings that by nature are not gods.
9 Now, however, that you have
come to know God, or rather to be
known by God, how can you turn
back again to the weak and beggarly elemental spirits?[a] How can you
want to be enslaved to them again?
10 You are observing special days,
and months, and seasons, and
years. 11 I am afraid that my work
for you may have been wasted.
12 Friends,[b] I beg you, become
as I am, for I also have become as
you are. You have done me no
wrong. 13 You know that it was because of a physical infirmity that I
first announced the gospel to you;
14 though my condition put you to
the test, you did not scorn or despise me, but welcomed me as an
angel of God, as Christ Jesus.
15 What has become of the good
will you felt? For I testify that, had
it been possible, you would have
torn out your eyes and given them
to me. 16 Have I now become your
enemy by telling you the truth?
17 They make much of you, but for
no good purpose; they want to ex-
clude you, so that you may make
much of them. 18 It is good to be
made much of for a good purpose
at all times, and not only when I am
present with you. 19 My little children, for whom I am again in the

3.18 Rom 4.14; 8.17
3.19 Acts 7.53; Deut 5.5
3.20 Heb 8.6; 9.15; 12.24
3.21 Gal 2.17,21
3.22 Rom 3.9-19; 11.32
3.23 Rom 11.32
3.24 Rom 10.4; 1 Cor 4.15; Gal 2.16
3.26 Jn 1.12; Rom 8.14
3.27 Rom 6.3; 13.14
3.28 Col 3.11; Jn 10.16; Eph 2.14,15
3.29 1 Cor 3.23; Gal 4.28
4.3 Col 2.8,20; Heb 5.12
4.4 Eph 1.10; Mt 5.17
4.5 Eph 1.7; Jn 1.12; Eph 1.5
4.6 Rom 5.5; 8.15
4.8 Eph 2.12; 1 Thes 4.5; Rom 1.25; 1 Cor 12.2
4.9 1 Cor 8.3; Col 2.20
4.10 Rom 14.5
4.11 1 Thes 3.5
4.12 Gal 6.18
4.13 1 Cor 2.3
4.14 Mt 10.40; Lk 10.16
4.16 Am 5.10
4.18 vv. 13,14
4.19 1 Jn 2.1; 1 Cor 4.15; Eph 4.13

[u] Gk *seed* [v] Or *through the faith of Jesus Christ* [w] Or *the rudiments* [x] Other ancient authorities read *your* [y] Aramaic for *Father* [z] Other ancient authorities read *an heir of God through Christ* [a] Or *beggarly rudiments* [b] Gk *Brothers*

pain of childbirth until Christ is
formed in you, 20 I wish I were
present with you now and could
change my tone, for I am perplexed
about you.

The Allegory of Hagar and Sarah

21 Tell me, you who desire to be
subject to the law, will you not listen to the law? 22 For it is written
that Abraham had two sons, one by
a slave woman and the other by a
free woman. 23 One, the child of
the slave, was born according to
the flesh; the other, the child of the
free woman, was born through the
promise. 24 Now this is an allegory:
these women are two covenants.
One woman, in fact, is Hagar, from
Mount Sinai, bearing children for
slavery. 25 Now Hagar is Mount Sinai in Arabia[c] and corresponds to
the present Jerusalem, for she is in
slavery with her children. 26 But the
other woman corresponds to the
Jerusalem above; she is free, and
she is our mother. 27 For it is written,

"Rejoice, you childless one,
 you who bear no
 children,
burst into song and shout,
 you who endure no
 birthpangs;
for the children of the
 desolate woman are
 more numerous
than the children of the
 one who is married."

28 Now you,[d] my friends,[e] are children of the promise, like Isaac.
29 But just as at that time the child
who was born according to the
flesh persecuted the child who was
born according to the Spirit, so it is
now also. 30 But what does the
scripture say? "Drive out the slave
and her child; for the child of the
slave will not share the inheritance
with the child of the free woman."
31 So then, friends,[e] we are children, not of the slave but of the free
5 woman. 1 For freedom Christ
has set us free. Stand firm,
therefore, and do not submit again
to a yoke of slavery.

4.21 Lk 16.29 **4.22** Gen 16.15; 21.2,9 **4.23** Rom 9.7; Gen 18.10; Heb 11.11 **4.24** Deut 33.2 **4.26** Isa 2.2; Heb 12.22; Rev 3.12 **4.27** Isa 54.1 **4.28** Acts 3.25; Rom 9.8 **4.29** Gen 21.9 **4.30** Gen 21.10-12 **5.1** Jn 8.32; Acts 15.10
5.2 Acts 15.1 **5.3** Gal 3.10 **5.4** Heb 12.15; 2 Pet 3.17 **5.5** Rom 8.23, 24; 2 Tim 4.8 **5.6** 1 Cor 7.19; Jas 2.18 **5.7** 1 Cor 9.24; Gal 3.1 **5.8** Gal 1.6 **5.9** 1 Cor 5.6 **5.10** 2 Cor 2.3; Gal 1.7 **5.11** Gal 4.29; 6.12; 1 Cor 1.23 **5.13** 1 Cor 8.9; 1 Pet 2.16; 1 Cor 9.19 **5.14** Lev 19.18; Mt 7.12; 22.39; Rom 13.8 **5.16** Rom 8.4; vv. 24,25; Eph 2.3 **5.17** Rom 7.15-23

The Nature of Christian Freedom

2 Listen! I, Paul, am telling you
that if you let yourselves be circumcised, Christ will be of no benefit to you. 3 Once again I testify to
every man who lets himself be circumcised that he is obliged to obey
the entire law. 4 You who want to be
justified by the law have cut yourselves off from Christ; you have
fallen away from grace. 5 For
through the Spirit, by faith, we eagerly wait for the hope of righteousness. 6 For in Christ Jesus neither
circumcision nor uncircumcision
counts for anything; the only thing
that counts is faith working[f]
through love.

7 You were running well; who
prevented you from obeying the
truth? 8 Such persuasion does not
come from the one who calls you.
9 A little yeast leavens the whole
batch of dough. 10 I am confident
about you in the Lord that you will
not think otherwise. But whoever it
is that is confusing you will pay the
penalty. 11 But my friends,[e] why
am I still being persecuted if I am
still preaching circumcision? In
that case the offense of the cross
has been removed. 12 I wish those
who unsettle you would castrate
themselves!

13 For you were called to freedom, brothers and sisters;[e] only do
not use your freedom as an opportunity for self-indulgence,[g] but
through love become slaves to one
another. 14 For the whole law is
summed up in a single commandment, "You shall love your neighbor as yourself." 15 If, however, you
bite and devour one another, take
care that you are not consumed by
one another.

The Works of the Flesh

16 Live by the Spirit, I say, and
do not gratify the desires of the
flesh. 17 For what the flesh desires
is opposed to the Spirit, and what

c Other ancient authorities read *For Sinai is a mountain in Arabia* d Other ancient authorities read *we* e Gk *brothers* f Or *made effective* g Gk *the flesh*

the Spirit desires is opposed to the
flesh; for these are opposed to each
other, to prevent you from doing
what you want. 18 But if you are led
by the Spirit, you are not subject to
the law. 19 Now the works of the
flesh are obvious: fornication, impurity, licentiousness, 20 idolatry,
sorcery, enmities, strife, jealousy,
anger, quarrels, dissensions, factions, 21 envy,[h] drunkenness, carousing, and things like these. I am
warning you, as I warned you before: those who do such things will
not inherit the kingdom of God.

The Fruit of the Spirit

22 By contrast, the fruit of the
Spirit is love, joy, peace, patience,
kindness, generosity, faithfulness,
23 gentleness, and self-control.
There is no law against such things.
24 And those who belong to Christ
Jesus have crucified the flesh with
its passions and desires. 25 If we live
by the Spirit, let us also be guided
by the Spirit. 26 Let us not become
conceited, competing against one
another, envying one another.

Bear One Another's Burdens

6 My friends,[i] if anyone is detected in a transgression, you
who have received the Spirit
should restore such a one in a spirit
of gentleness. Take care that you
yourselves are not tempted. 2 Bear
one another's burdens, and in this
way you will fulfill[j] the law of
Christ. 3 For if those who are nothing think they are something, they
deceive themselves. 4 All must test
their own work; then that work,
rather than their neighbor's work,
will become a cause for pride. 5 For
all must carry their own loads.
6 Those who are taught the
word must share in all good things
with their teacher.
7 Do not be deceived; God is not
mocked, for you reap whatever you
sow. 8 If you sow to your own flesh,
you will reap corruption from the
flesh; but if you sow to the Spirit,
you will reap eternal life from the
Spirit. 9 So let us not grow weary in
doing what is right, for we will reap
at harvest-time, if we do not give
up. 10 So then, whenever we have
an opportunity, let us work for the
good of all, and especially for those
of the family of faith.

Final Admonitions and Benediction

11 See what large letters I make
when I am writing in my own hand!
12 It is those who want to make a
good showing in the flesh that try
to compel you to be circumcised—
only that they may not be persecuted for the cross of Christ. 13 Even
the circumcised do not themselves
obey the law, but they want you to
be circumcised so that they may
boast about your flesh. 14 May I
never boast of anything except the
cross of our Lord Jesus Christ, by
which[k] the world has been crucified to me, and I to the world.
15 For[l] neither circumcision nor
uncircumcision is anything; but a
new creation is everything! 16 As for
those who will follow this rule—
peace be upon them, and mercy,
and upon the Israel of God.
17 From now on, let no one
make trouble for me; for I carry the
marks of Jesus branded on my
body.
18 May the grace of our Lord
Jesus Christ be with your spirit,
brothers and sisters.[m] Amen.

5.18 Rom 6.14 **5.19** Eph 5.3; Col 3.5 **5.21** 1 Cor 6.9 **5.22** Eph 5.9; Col 3.12-15; 1 Cor 13.7 **5.24** Rom 6.6 **5.25** Rom 8.4 **5.26** Phil 2.3 **6.2** Rom 15.1; Jas 2.8 **6.3** Rom 12.3; 1 Cor 8.2; 2 Cor 3.5 **6.4** 1 Cor 11.28; Phil 1.26 **6.6** 1 Cor 9.11 **6.7** 1 Cor 6.9; Job 13.9 **6.8** Hos 8.7; Jas 3.18 **6.9** 1 Cor 15.58; Heb 3.6; Rev 2.10 **6.10** Jn 9.4; Titus 3.8; Eph 2.19 **6.12** Mt 23.27, 28; Acts 15.1; Gal 5.11 **6.13** Rom 2.25; Phil 3.3 **6.14** Gal 2.20; Rom 6.2,6 **6.15** 2 Cor 5.17 **6.17** 2 Cor 1.5

[h] Other ancient authorities add *murder*
[i] Gk *Brothers* [j] Other ancient authorities read *in this way fulfill* [k] Or *through whom*
[l] Other ancient authorities add *in Christ Jesus*
[m] Gk *brothers*

THE LETTER OF PAUL TO THE

Ephesians

Title and Background

Ephesus was the most important city in western Asia Minor (now Turkey). Because it was at an intersection of major trade routes, it became a commercial center. It also boasted a pagan temple dedicated to the Roman goddess Diana (Greek name: Artemis). Paul made Ephesus a center for evangelism for about three years. This letter was probably not sent merely to the church at Ephesus but also to the various churches in the province of Asia, where Paul conducted his third missionary journey.

Author and Date of Writing

Most scholars believe that Paul wrote this letter about A.D. 60, during his two-year imprisonment in Rome.

Theme and Message

Unlike several of Paul's other letters, Ephesians does not address any particular error or heresy. Paul wrote so that his readers might better understand the dimensions of God's eternal purpose and grace and come to appreciate the high goals God has for the church.

One of Paul's themes is that of unity, that all Christians are one family in Jesus and they should act with love toward each other. He also writes about the church–not a church building, but the church that is made up of all Christians throughout the ages.

Outline

I. Greetings (1.1-2)
II. The Glory and Headship of Christ (1.3-14)
III. Prayer That Christians May Realize God's Purpose and Power (1.15-23)
IV. Steps Toward the Fulfillment of God's Purpose (2.1–3.21)
V. Ways to Fulfill God's Purpose in the Church (4.1–6.20)
VI. Conclusion (6.21-24)

Salutation

1 Paul, an apostle of Christ
Jesus by the will of God,
To the saints who are in Ephesus
and are faithful[a] in Christ Jesus:
2 Grace to you and peace from
God our Father and the Lord Jesus
Christ.

Spiritual Blessings in Christ

3 Blessed be the God and Father
of our Lord Jesus Christ, who has
blessed us in Christ with every spiritual blessing in the heavenly
places, 4 just as he chose us in
Christ[b] before the foundation of
the world to be holy and blameless

1.1 2 Cor 1.1; 1 Cor 1.1; Phil 1.1; Col 1.1,2
1.2 Rom 1.7
1.3 2 Cor 1.3; Eph 2.6; 3.10; 6.12
1.4 Eph 5.27; Col 1.22; Eph 4.2,15, 16
1.5 Rom 8.29f
1.7 Col 1.14
1.9 Rom 16.25

before him in love. 5 He destined us
for adoption as his children
through Jesus Christ, according to
the good pleasure of his will, 6 to
the praise of his glorious grace that
he freely bestowed on us in the Beloved. 7 In him we have redemption
through his blood, the forgiveness
of our trespasses, according to the
riches of his grace 8 that he lavished
on us. With all wisdom and insight
9 he has made known to us the mystery of his will, according to his
good pleasure that he set forth in

[a] Other ancient authorities lack *in Ephesus*, reading *saints who are also faithful* [b] Gk *in him*

Christ, 10 as a plan for the fullness
of time, to gather up all things in
him, things in heaven and things
on earth. 11 In Christ we have also
obtained an inheritance,[c] having
been destined according to the
purpose of him who accomplishes
all things according to his counsel
and will, 12 so that we, who were
the first to set our hope on Christ,
might live for the praise of his glory. 13 In him you also, when you had
heard the word of truth, the gospel
of your salvation, and had believed
in him, were marked with the seal
of the promised Holy Spirit;
14 this[d] is the pledge of our inheritance toward redemption as God's
own people, to the praise of his glory.

Paul's Prayer

15 I have heard of your faith in
the Lord Jesus and your love[e] toward all the saints, and for this reason 16 I do not cease to give thanks
for you as I remember you in my
prayers. 17 I pray that the God of our
Lord Jesus Christ, the Father of
glory, may give you a spirit of wisdom and revelation as you come to
know him, 18 so that, with the eyes
of your heart enlightened, you may
know what is the hope to which he
has called you, what are the riches
of his glorious inheritance among
the saints, 19 and what is the immeasurable greatness of his power
for us who believe, according to the
working of his great power. 20 God[f]
put this power to work in Christ
when he raised him from the dead
and seated him at his right hand in
the heavenly places, 21 far above all
rule and authority and power and
dominion, and above every name
that is named, not only in this age
but also in the age to come. 22 And
he has put all things under his feet
and has made him the head over all
things for the church, 23 which is
his body, the fullness of him who
fills all in all.

From Death to Life

2 You were dead through the
trespasses and sins 2 in which
you once lived, following the
course of this world, following
the ruler of the power of the air, the
spirit that is now at work among
those who are disobedient. 3 All of
us once lived among them in the
passions of our flesh, following the
desires of flesh and senses, and we
were by nature children of wrath,
like everyone else. 4 But God, who
is rich in mercy, out of the great
love with which he loved us 5 even
when we were dead through our
trespasses, made us alive together
with Christ[g]—by grace you have
been saved— 6 and raised us up
with him and seated us with him in
the heavenly places in Christ Jesus,
7 so that in the ages to come he
might show the immeasurable
riches of his grace in kindness toward us in Christ Jesus. 8 For by
grace you have been saved through
faith, and this is not your own doing; it is the gift of God— 9 not the
result of works, so that no one may
boast. 10 For we are what he has
made us, created in Christ Jesus for
good works, which God prepared
beforehand to be our way of life.

One in Christ

11 So then, remember that at
one time you Gentiles by birth,[h]
called "the uncircumcision" by
those who are called "the
circumcision"—a physical circumcision made in the flesh by human
hands— 12 remember that you
were at that time without Christ,
being aliens from the commonwealth of Israel, and strangers to
the covenants of promise, having
no hope and without God in the
world. 13 But now in Christ Jesus
you who once were far off have
been brought near by the blood of
Christ. 14 For he is our peace; in his
flesh he has made both groups into
one and has broken down the di-

1.10 Gal 4.4; Col 1.16,20
1.11 Eph 3.11; Rom 9.11; Heb 6.17
1.12 vv. 6,14
1.13 Col 1.5; Eph 4.30
1.14 2 Cor 1.22; Acts 20.32
1.15 Col 1.4; Eph 3.18
1.16 Rom 1.8,9; Col 1.3,9
1.17 Jn 20.17; Col 1.9
1.18 Acts 26.18; Eph 4.4
1.19 Col 1.29; Eph 6.10
1.20 Acts 2.24; Heb 1.3
1.21 Phil 2.9,10
1.22 Mt 28.18; Eph 4.15; 5.23
1.23 Rom 12.5; Col 2.17
2.1 v. 5; Jn 5.24
2.2 Eph 6.12; 5.6
2.3 Gal 5.16,17; Rom 2.14; 5.10
2.4 Rom 10.12
2.5 vv. 1,8
2.6 Eph 1.20
2.7 Titus 3.4
2.8 Gal 2.16; v. 5
2.9 Rom 3.20, 28; 2 Tim 1.9
2.10 Eph 4.24; Titus 2.14
2.11 Rom 2.28; Col 2.11
2.12 1 Thes 4.5; Gal 4.8
2.13 Acts 2.39; Col 1.20 **2.14** Col 3.15; 1 Cor 12.13

c Or *been made a heritage* d Other ancient authorities read *who* e Other ancient authorities lack *and your love* f Gk *He* g Other ancient authorities read *in Christ* h Gk *in the flesh*

viding wall, that is, the hostility between us. 15 He has abolished the law with its commandments and ordinances, that he might create in himself one new humanity in place of the two, thus making peace, 16 and might reconcile both groups to God in one body[i] through the cross, thus putting to death that hostility through it.[j] 17 So he came and proclaimed peace to you who were far off and peace to those who were near; 18 for through him both of us have access in one Spirit to the Father. 19 So then you are no longer strangers and aliens, but you are citizens with the saints and also members of the household of God, 20 built upon the foundation of the apostles and prophets, with Christ Jesus himself as the cornerstone.[k] 21 In him the whole structure is joined together and grows into a holy temple in the Lord; 22 in whom you also are built together spiritually[l] into a dwelling place for God.

Paul's Ministry to the Gentiles

3 This is the reason that I Paul am a prisoner for[m] Christ Jesus for the sake of you Gentiles— 2 for surely you have already heard of the commission of God's grace that was given me for you, 3 and how the mystery was made known to me by revelation, as I wrote above in a few words, 4 a reading of which will enable you to perceive my understanding of the mystery of Christ. 5 In former generations this mystery[n] was not made known to humankind, as it has now been revealed to his holy apostles and prophets by the Spirit: 6 that is, the Gentiles have become fellow heirs, members of the same body, and sharers in the promise in Christ Jesus through the gospel.

7 Of this gospel I have become a servant according to the gift of God's grace that was given me by the working of his power. 8 Although I am the very least of all the saints, this grace was given to me to bring to the Gentiles the news of the boundless riches of Christ, 9 and to make everyone see[o] what is the plan of the mystery hidden for ages in[p] God who created all things; 10 so that through the church the wisdom of God in its rich variety might now be made known to the rulers and authorities in the heavenly places. 11 This was in accordance with the eternal purpose that he has carried out in Christ Jesus our Lord, 12 in whom we have access to God in boldness and confidence through faith in him.[q] 13 I pray therefore that you[r] may not lose heart over my sufferings for you; they are your glory.

Prayer for the Readers

14 For this reason I bow my knees before the Father,[s] 15 from whom every family[t] in heaven and on earth takes its name. 16 I pray that, according to the riches of his glory, he may grant that you may be strengthened in your inner being with power through his Spirit, 17 and that Christ may dwell in your hearts through faith, as you are being rooted and grounded in love. 18 I pray that you may have the power to comprehend, with all the saints, what is the breadth and length and height and depth, 19 and to know the love of Christ that surpasses knowledge, so that you may be filled with all the fullness of God.

20 Now to him who by the power at work within us is able to accomplish abundantly far more than all we can ask or imagine, 21 to him be glory in the church and in Christ Jesus to all generations, forever and ever. Amen.

Unity in the Body of Christ

4 I therefore, the prisoner in the Lord, beg you to lead a life worthy of the calling to which you

2.15 Col 1.21,22; Gal 6.15
2.16 Col 1.20,22
2.17 Isa 57.19; Ps 148.14
2.18 Eph 3.12; 1 Cor 12.13; Col 1.12
2.19 Phil 3.20; Gal 6.10
2.20 Mt 16.18; Rev 21.14
2.21 1 Cor 3.16, 17
3.1 Acts 23.18; Eph 4.1
3.2 Col 1.25; 1 Tim 1.4
3.3 Acts 22.17; Gal 1.12; Rom 16.25
3.4 1 Cor 4.1
3.5 Rom 16.26
3.6 Gal 3.29; Eph 2.15,16
3.8 1 Cor 15.9; Gal 1.16; Col 1.27
3.9 Col 1.26,27
3.10 1 Pet 1.12; 1 Cor 2.7; Eph 1.21
3.12 Heb 4.16; Eph 2.18
3.13 2 Cor 4.1
3.14 Phil 2.10
3.16 Eph 1.18; Col 1.11; Rom 7.22
3.17 Jn 14.23; Col 1.23
3.18 Eph 1.18; Job 11.8,9
3.19 Col 2.10; Eph 1.23
3.20 Rom 16.25
3.21 Rom 11.36
4.1 Eph 3.1; Col 1.10

[i] Or *reconcile both of us in one body for God*
[j] Or *in him*, or *in himself* [k] Or *keystone*
[l] Gk *in the Spirit* [m] Or *of* [n] Gk *it*
[o] Other ancient authorities read *to bring to light* [p] Or *by* [q] Or *the faith of him*
[r] Or *I* [s] Other ancient authorities add *of our Lord Jesus Christ* [t] Gk *fatherhood*

have been called, 2 with all humility and gentleness, with patience,
bearing with one another in love,
3 making every effort to maintain
the unity of the Spirit in the bond
of peace. 4 There is one body and
one Spirit, just as you were called
to the one hope of your calling,
5 one Lord, one faith, one baptism,
6 one God and Father of all, who is
above all and through all and in all.
7 But each of us was given grace
according to the measure of
Christ's gift. 8 Therefore it is said,
"When he ascended on high
he made captivity itself
a captive;
he gave gifts to his
people."
9 (When it says, "He ascended,"
what does it mean but that he had
also descended[u] into the lower
parts of the earth? 10 He who descended is the same one who ascended far above all the heavens,
so that he might fill all things.)
11 The gifts he gave were that some
would be apostles, some prophets,
some evangelists, some pastors
and teachers, 12 to equip the saints
for the work of ministry, for building up the body of Christ, 13 until all
of us come to the unity of the faith
and of the knowledge of the Son of
God, to maturity, to the measure of
the full stature of Christ. 14 We
must no longer be children, tossed
to and fro and blown about by every
wind of doctrine, by people's trickery, by their craftiness in deceitful
scheming. 15 But speaking the truth
in love, we must grow up in every
way into him who is the head, into
Christ, 16 from whom the whole
body, joined and knit together by
every ligament with which it is
equipped, as each part is working
properly, promotes the body's
growth in building itself up in love.

The Old Life and the New

17 Now this I affirm and insist
on in the Lord: you must no longer
live as the Gentiles live, in the futility of their minds. 18 They are darkened in their understanding, alienated from the life of God because of
their ignorance and hardness of
heart. 19 They have lost all sensitivi-
ty and have abandoned themselves
to licentiousness, greedy to practice every kind of impurity. 20 That
is not the way you learned Christ!
21 For surely you have heard about
him and were taught in him, as
truth is in Jesus. 22 You were taught
to put away your former way of life,
your old self, corrupt and deluded
by its lusts, 23 and to be renewed in
the spirit of your minds, 24 and to
clothe yourselves with the new self,
created according to the likeness of
God in true righteousness and holiness.

Rules for the New Life

25 So then, putting away falsehood, let all of us speak the truth to
our neighbors, for we are members
of one another. 26 Be angry but do
not sin; do not let the sun go down
on your anger, 27 and do not make
room for the devil. 28 Thieves must
give up stealing; rather let them labor and work honestly with their
own hands, so as to have something to share with the needy. 29 Let
no evil talk come out of your
mouths, but only what is useful for
building up,[v] as there is need, so
that your words may give grace to
those who hear. 30 And do not
grieve the Holy Spirit of God, with
which you were marked with a seal
for the day of redemption. 31 Put
away from you all bitterness and
wrath and anger and wrangling and
slander, together with all malice,
32 and be kind to one another, tenderhearted, forgiving one another,
as God in Christ has forgiven you.[w]

5 1 Therefore be imitators of
God, as beloved children,
2 and live in love, as Christ loved
us[x] and gave himself up for us, a
fragrant offering and sacrifice to
God.

4.2 Col 3.12; Eph 1.4 **4.3** Col 3.14 **4.4** 1 Cor 12.12; Eph 2.16; 1.18 **4.6** Rom 11.36 **4.7** Rom 12.3 **4.8** Ps 68.18; Judg 5.12; Col 2.15 **4.9** Jn 3.13 **4.11** 1 Cor 12.28 **4.12** 2 Cor 13.9; Eph 1.23; 1 Cor 12.27 **4.13** Col 2.2; 1 Cor 14.20; Col 1.28 **4.14** 1 Cor 14.20; Jas 1.6; Eph 6.11 **4.15** 2 Cor 4.2; Eph 1.22; Col 1.18 **4.17** Col 3.7; 1 Pet 4.3; Rom 1.21 **4.18** Eph 2.1,12; 2 Cor 3.14 **4.19** 1 Tim 4.2; Rom 1.24; Col 3.5 **4.22** 1 Pet 2.1; Rom 6.6 **4.23** Col 3.10 **4.24** Rom 6.4; 2 Cor 5.17 **4.25** Zech 8.16; Rom 12.5 **4.26** Ps 37.8 **4.27** 2 Cor 2.10, 11 **4.28** Acts 20.35; Lk 3.11 **4.30** 1 Thes 5.19; Rom 8.23 **4.31** Col 3.8; Titus 3.3 **4.32** 2 Cor 2.10; Mt 6.14,15

5.1 Lk 6.36 **5.2** 1 Thes 4.9; Gal 1.4; 2 Cor 2.15

[u] Other ancient authorities add *first* [v] Other ancient authorities read *building up faith* [w] Other ancient authorities read *us* [x] Other ancient authorities read *you*

Renounce Pagan Ways

3 But fornication and impurity
of any kind, or greed, must not
even be mentioned among you, as
is proper among saints. 4Entirely
out of place is obscene, silly, and
vulgar talk; but instead, let there
be thanksgiving. 5Be sure of this,
that no fornicator or impure person, or one who is greedy (that is,
an idolater), has any inheritance in
the kingdom of Christ and of God.
6 Let no one deceive you with
empty words, for because of these
things the wrath of God comes on
those who are disobedient. 7There-
fore do not be associated with
them. 8For once you were darkness, but now in the Lord you are
light. Live as children of light—
9for the fruit of the light is found in
all that is good and right and true.
10Try to find out what is pleasing to
the Lord. 11Take no part in the unfruitful works of darkness, but instead expose them. 12For it is
shameful even to mention what
such people do secretly; 13but everything exposed by the light becomes visible, 14for everything that
becomes visible is light. Therefore
it says,

"Sleeper, awake!
Rise from the dead,
and Christ will shine on
you."

15 Be careful then how you live,
not as unwise people but as wise,
16making the most of the time, because the days are evil. 17So do not
be foolish, but understand what
the will of the Lord is. 18Do not get
drunk with wine, for that is debauchery; but be filled with the
Spirit, 19as you sing psalms and
hymns and spiritual songs among
yourselves, singing and making
melody to the Lord in your hearts,
20giving thanks to God the Father
at all times and for everything in
the name of our Lord Jesus Christ.

The Christian Household

21 Be subject to one another
out of reverence for Christ.
22 Wives, be subject to your
husbands as you are to the Lord.
23For the husband is the head of
the wife just as Christ is the head of
the church, the body of which he is
the Savior. 24Just as the church is
subject to Christ, so also wives
ought to be, in everything, to their
husbands.
25 Husbands, love your wives,
just as Christ loved the church and
gave himself up for her, 26in order
to make her holy by cleansing her
with the washing of water by the
word, 27so as to present the church
to himself in splendor, without a
spot or wrinkle or anything of the
kind—yes, so that she may be holy
and without blemish. 28In the
same way, husbands should love
their wives as they do their own
bodies. He who loves his wife loves
himself. 29For no one ever hates
his own body, but he nourishes and
tenderly cares for it, just as Christ
does for the church, 30because we
are members of his body.[y] 31"For
this reason a man will leave his father and mother and be joined to
his wife, and the two will become
one flesh." 32This is a great mystery, and I am applying it to Christ
and the church. 33Each of you,
however, should love his wife as
himself, and a wife should respect
her husband.

Children and Parents

6 Children, obey your parents in
the Lord,[z] for this is right.
2"Honor your father and
mother"—this is the first commandment with a promise: 3"so
that it may be well with you and
you may live long on the earth."
4 And, fathers, do not provoke
your children to anger, but bring
them up in the discipline and instruction of the Lord.

Slaves and Masters

5 Slaves, obey your earthly masters with fear and trembling, in singleness of heart, as you obey
Christ; 6not only while being

5.3 Rom 6.13; Col 3.5; 1 Cor 5.1
5.5 1 Cor 6.9; Col 3.5
5.6 Jer 29.8; Rom 1.18
5.8 Jn 8.12; Lk 16.8
5.9 Gal 5.22
5.11 1 Cor 5.9; Rom 6.21
5.12 Rom 1.24
5.14 Isa 60.1; Jn 5.25
5.16 Col 4.5; Eph 6.13
5.17 Rom 12.2; 1 Thes 4.3
5.18 Prov 20.1; Lk 1.15
5.19 Col 3.16; Acts 16.25
5.20 Ps 34.1; Heb 13.15
5.22 Gen 3.16; Eph 6.5
5.23 1 Cor 11.3; Col 1.18; Eph 1.23
5.24 Col 3.18
5.25 Col 3.19
5.26 Titus 3.5
5.27 Col 1.22; Eph 1.4
5.28 v. 25
5.30 1 Cor 6.15; Eph 1.23
5.31 Gen 2.24; Mt 19.5; 1 Cor 6.16
5.32 Col 3.19; 1 Pet 3.6
6.1 Col 3.20
6.2 Deut 5.16
6.4 Col 3.21; Gen 18.19
6.5 Col 3.22; 1 Tim 6.1; Phil 2.12; 1 Chr 29.17

[y] Other ancient authorities add *of his flesh and of his bones* [z] Other ancient authorities lack *in the Lord*

watched, and in order to please them, but as slaves of Christ, doing the will of God from the heart. [7]Render service with enthusiasm, as to the Lord and not to men and women, [8]knowing that whatever good we do, we will receive the same again from the Lord, whether we are slaves or free.

9 And, masters, do the same to them. Stop threatening them, for you know that both of you have the same Master in heaven, and with him there is no partiality.

The Whole Armor of God

10 Finally, be strong in the Lord and in the strength of his power. [11]Put on the whole armor of God, so that you may be able to stand against the wiles of the devil. [12]For our[a] struggle is not against enemies of blood and flesh, but against the rulers, against the authorities, against the cosmic powers of this present darkness, against the spiritual forces of evil in the heavenly places. [13]Therefore take up the whole armor of God, so that you may be able to withstand on that evil day, and having done everything, to stand firm. [14]Stand therefore, and fasten the belt of truth around your waist, and put on the breastplate of righteousness. [15]As shoes for your feet put on whatever will make you ready to proclaim the gospel of peace. [16]With all of these,[b] take the shield of faith, with which you will be able to quench all the flaming arrows of the evil one. [17]Take the helmet of salvation, and the sword of the Spirit, which is the word of God.

18 Pray in the Spirit at all times in every prayer and supplication. To that end keep alert and always persevere in supplication for all the saints. [19]Pray also for me, so that when I speak, a message may be given to me to make known with boldness the mystery of the gospel,[c] [20]for which I am an ambassador in chains. Pray that I may declare it boldly, as I must speak.

Personal Matters and Benediction

21 So that you also may know how I am and what I am doing, Tychicus will tell you everything. He is a dear brother and a faithful minister in the Lord. [22]I am sending him to you for this very purpose, to let you know how we are, and to encourage your hearts.

23 Peace be to the whole community,[d] and love with faith, from God the Father and the Lord Jesus Christ. [24]Grace be with all who have an undying love for our Lord Jesus Christ.[e]

6.7 Col 3.23
6.9 Lev 25.43; Jn 13.13; Col 3.25
6.10 1 Cor 16.13; Eph 1.19
6.11 1 Cor 16.21
6.12 1 Cor 9.25; Rom 8.38
6.13 2 Cor 10.4; Eph 5.16
6.14 Isa 11.5; 59.17
6.15 Isa 52.7
6.16 1 Jn 5.4
6.17 Isa 59.17; Heb 4.12
6.18 Lk 18.1; Mt 26.41; Phil 1.4
6.19 Acts 4.29; 2 Cor 3.12
6.20 2 Cor 5.20; Phil 1.20
6.21 Acts 20.4
6.23 1 Pet 5.14; Gal 5.6

[a] Other ancient authorities read *your* [b] Or *In all circumstances* [c] Other ancient authorities lack *of the gospel* [d] Gk *to the brothers* [e] Other ancient authorities add *Amen*

THE LETTER OF PAUL TO THE

Philippians

Title and Background

Philippians was written by Paul while he was in prison. The church at Philippi had sent Paul a gift by way of Epaphroditus, their messenger. Epaphroditus became sick, and the Philippian Christians were concerned about him. This made Epaphroditus all the more eager to return home. Paul therefore wrote this letter to his Christian friends in Philippi, expressing his gratitude for their love and help.

Author and Date of Writing

The first verse of Philippians tells us that Paul was the author, and the writing itself reveals the stamp of genuineness. The many personal references of the author fit what we know of Paul from other New Testament books. The most widely accepted date for the writing of the letter is about A.D. 61, during Paul's Roman imprisonment.

Theme and Message

The theme of the book is "joy" or "rejoicing in the Lord." The word "joy" in its various forms occurs sixteen times. There were also perils to watch out for because the church had many enemies, both inside and outside. Paul warns the Philippians of the present dangers of a self-seeking attitude and of pride, both of which could lead to harmful divisions. In Philippians can also be found the most profound statement of the meaning of the incarnation (2.5-11).

Outline

I. Greetings, Thanksgiving, and Prayer (1.1-11)
II. Paul's Personal Circumstances (1.12-26)
III. Exhortations (1.27–2.18)
  A. Live a Life Worthy of the Gospel (1.27-30)
  B. Follow the Servant Attitude of Christ (2.1-18)
IV. Paul's Associates in the Gospel (2.19-30)
V. Warnings Against Judaizers and Libertines (3.1–4.1)
VI. Final Exhortations, Thanks, and Conclusion (4.2-23)

Salutation

1 Paul and Timothy, servants[a]
of Christ Jesus,
To all the saints in Christ Jesus
who are in Philippi, with the bishops[b] and deacons:[c]
2 Grace to you and peace from
God our Father and the Lord Jesus
Christ.

Paul's Prayer for the Philippians

3 I thank my God every time I
remember you, 4 constantly praying
with joy in every one of my prayers
for all of you, 5 because of your
sharing in the gospel from the first
day until now. 6 I am confident of
this, that the one who began a good
work among you will bring it to
completion by the day of Jesus
Christ. 7 It is right for me to think
this way about all of you, because
you hold me in your heart,[d] for all
of you share in God's grace[e] with
me, both in my imprisonment and
in the defense and confirmation of
the gospel. 8 For God is my witness,
how I long for all of you with the

1.1 2 Cor 1.1; Acts 16.1; 1 Cor 1.2
1.2 1 Pet 1.2
1.3 1 Cor 1.4
1.4 Rom 1.9
1.5 Acts 2.42; 16.17
1.6 v. 10
1.7 2 Pet 1.13; 2 Cor 7.3; vv. 13,14,17
1.8 Rom 1.9; Gal 1.20

[a] Gk *slaves* [b] Or *overseers* [c] Or *overseers and helpers* [d] Or *because I hold you in my heart* [e] Gk *in grace*

compassion of Christ Jesus. 9 And this is my prayer, that your love may overflow more and more with knowledge and full insight 10 to help you to determine what is best, so that in the day of Christ you may be pure and blameless, 11 having produced the harvest of righteousness that comes through Jesus Christ for the glory and praise of God.

Paul's Present Circumstances

12 I want you to know, beloved[f] that what has happened to me has actually helped to spread the gospel, 13 so that it has become known throughout the whole imperial guard[g] and to everyone else that my imprisonment is for Christ; 14 and most of the brothers and sisters,[f] having been made confident in the Lord by my imprisonment, dare to speak the word[h] with greater boldness and without fear.

15 Some proclaim Christ from envy and rivalry, but others from goodwill. 16 These proclaim Christ out of love, knowing that I have been put here for the defense of the gospel; 17 the others proclaim Christ out of selfish ambition, not sincerely but intending to increase my suffering in my imprisonment. 18 What does it matter? Just this, that Christ is proclaimed in every way, whether out of false motives or true; and in that I rejoice.

Yes, and I will continue to rejoice, 19 for I know that through your prayers and the help of the Spirit of Jesus Christ this will turn out for my deliverance. 20 It is my eager expectation and hope that I will not be put to shame in any way, but that by my speaking with all boldness, Christ will be exalted now as always in my body, whether by life or by death. 21 For to me, living is Christ and dying is gain. 22 If I am to live in the flesh, that means fruitful labor for me; and I do not know which I prefer. 23 I am hard pressed between the two: my desire is to depart and be with Christ, for that is far better; 24 but to remain in the flesh is more necessary for you. 25 Since I am convinced of this, I know that I will remain and continue with all of you for your progress and joy in faith, 26 so that I may share abundantly in your boasting in Christ Jesus when I come to you again.

27 Only, live your life in a manner worthy of the gospel of Christ, so that, whether I come and see you or am absent and hear about you, I will know that you are standing firm in one spirit, striving side by side with one mind for the faith of the gospel, 28 and are in no way intimidated by your opponents. For them this is evidence of their destruction, but of your salvation. And this is God's doing. 29 For he has graciously granted you the privilege not only of believing in Christ, but of suffering for him as well— 30 since you are having the same struggle that you saw I had and now hear that I still have.

Imitating Christ's Humility

2 If then there is any encouragement in Christ, any consolation from love, any sharing in the Spirit, any compassion and sympathy, 2 make my joy complete: be of the same mind, having the same love, being in full accord and of one mind. 3 Do nothing from selfish ambition or conceit, but in humility regard others as better than yourselves. 4 Let each of you look not to your own interests, but to the interests of others. 5 Let the same mind be in you that was[i] in Christ Jesus,

6 who, though he was in the
form of God,
did not regard equality
with God
as something to be
exploited,
7 but emptied himself,
taking the form of a slave,
being born in human
likeness.
And being found in human
form,

1.9 1 Thes 3.12; Col 1.9
1.13 Phil 4.22
1.14 v. 7
1.15 Phil 2.3
1.16 1 Cor 9.17; v. 12
1.17 Phil 2.3
1.19 2 Cor 1.11
1.20 Rom 8.19; 5.5; Eph 6.19
1.23 2 Cor 5.8; 2 Tim 4.6
1.26 2 Cor 1.14; 5.12
1.28 2 Thes 1.5; Rom 8.17
1.29 Mt 5.12; Acts 14.22
1.30 1 Thes 2.2; Col 2.1; Acts 16.19
2.1 2 Cor 13.13; Col 3.12
2.2 Jn 3.29; Rom 12.16; 1 Pet 3.8
2.3 Gal 5.26; Rom 12.10; 1 Pet 5.5
2.4 Rom 15.1,2
2.5 Mt 11.29; 1 Pet 2.21
2.6 Jn 1.1; 2 Cor 4.4; Jn 5.18
2.7 Jn 1.14; Gal 4.4; Heb 2.17

[f] Gk *brothers* [g] Gk *whole praetorium*
[h] Other ancient authorities read *word of God*
[i] Or *that you have*

8 he humbled himself
and became obedient to
the point of death—
even death on a cross.

9 Therefore God also highly
exalted him
and gave him the name
that is above every name,
10 so that at the name of Jesus
every knee should bend,
in heaven and on earth and
under the earth,
11 and every tongue should
confess
that Jesus Christ is Lord,
to the glory of God the
Father.

Shining as Lights in the World

12 Therefore, my beloved, just
as you have always obeyed me, not
only in my presence, but much
more now in my absence, work out
your own salvation with fear and
trembling; 13 for it is God who is at
work in you, enabling you both to
will and to work for his good pleasure.
14 Do all things without murmuring and arguing, 15 so that you
may be blameless and innocent,
children of God without blemish in
the midst of a crooked and perverse
generation, in which you shine like
stars in the world. 16 It is by your
holding fast to the word of life that
I can boast on the day of Christ that
I did not run in vain or labor in vain.
17 But even if I am being poured out
as a libation over the sacrifice and
the offering of your faith, I am glad
and rejoice with all of you— 18 and
in the same way you also must be
glad and rejoice with me.

Timothy and Epaphroditus

19 I hope in the Lord Jesus to
send Timothy to you soon, so that
I may be cheered by news of you.
20 I have no one like him who will
be genuinely concerned for your
welfare. 21 All of them are seeking
their own interests, not those of
Jesus Christ. 22 But Timothy's[j]
worth you know, how like a son
with a father he has served with me

2.8 Mt 26.39; Jn 10.18; Heb 5.8
2.9 Acts 2.33; Heb 2.9; Eph 1.20,21
2.10 Mt 28.18; Rom 14.11
2.11 Jn 13.13; Acts 2.36
2.12f Phil 1.5; Eph 6.5
2.13 2 Cor 3.5
2.14 1 Cor 10.10; Rom 14.1
2.15 Mt 5.45; Eph 5.1; 5.8
2.16 2 Cor 1.14; 1 Thes 2.19
2.17 2 Tim 4.6; Rom 15.16; Col 1.24
2.19 Rom 16.21
2.20 1 Cor 16.10
2.21 1 Cor 10.24; 13.5
2.22 1 Cor 4.17; 1 Tim 1.2
2.24 Phil 1.25
2.25 Phil 4.18; Philem 2
2.26 Phil 1.8
2.29 1 Cor 16.18; 1 Tim 5.17
2.30 1 Cor 16.17
3.1 Phil 4.4
3.2 Gal 5.15; 2 Cor 11.13
3.3 Rom 2.28, 29; Gal 6.14,15
3.5 Rom 11.1; 2 Cor 11.22
3.6 Acts 22.3; Rom 10.5; Lk 1.6

in the work of the gospel. 23 I hope
therefore to send him as soon as I
see how things go with me; 24 and I
trust in the Lord that I will also
come soon.
25 Still, I think it necessary to
send to you Epaphroditus—my
brother and co-worker and fellow
soldier, your messenger[k] and minister to my need; 26 for he has been
longing for[l] all of you, and has
been distressed because you heard
that he was ill. 27 He was indeed so
ill that he nearly died. But God had
mercy on him, and not only on him
but on me also, so that I would not
have one sorrow after another. 28 I
am the more eager to send him,
therefore, in order that you may rejoice at seeing him again, and that
I may be less anxious. 29 Welcome
him then in the Lord with all joy,
and honor such people, 30 because
he came close to death for the work
of Christ,[m] risking his life to make
up for those services that you could
not give me.

3 Finally, my brothers and sisters,[n] rejoice[o] in the Lord.

Breaking with the Past

To write the same things to you
is not troublesome to me, and for
you it is a safeguard.
2 Beware of the dogs, beware of
the evil workers, beware of those
who mutilate the flesh![p] 3 For it is
we who are the circumcision, who
worship in the Spirit of God[q] and
boast in Christ Jesus and have no
confidence in the flesh— 4 even
though I, too, have reason for confidence in the flesh.
If anyone else has reason to be
confident in the flesh, I have more:
5 circumcised on the eighth day, a
member of the people of Israel, of
the tribe of Benjamin, a Hebrew
born of Hebrews; as to the law, a
Pharisee; 6 as to zeal, a persecutor

[j] Gk *his* [k] Gk *apostle* [l] Other ancient authorities read *longing to see* [m] Other ancient authorities read *of the Lord* [n] Gk *my brothers* [o] Or *farewell* [p] Gk *the mutilation* [q] Other ancient authorities read *worship God in spirit*

of the church; as to righteousness
under the law, blameless.
7 Yet whatever gains I had,
these I have come to regard as loss
because of Christ. 8 More than that,
I regard everything as loss because
of the surpassing value of knowing
Christ Jesus my Lord. For his sake
I have suffered the loss of all
things, and I regard them as rubbish, in order that I may gain Christ
9 and be found in him, not having a
righteousness of my own that
comes from the law, but one that
comes through faith in Christ,[r] the
righteousness from God based on
faith. 10 I want to know Christ[s] and
the power of his resurrection and
the sharing of his sufferings by becoming like him in his death, 11 if
somehow I may attain the resurrection from the dead.

Pressing toward the Goal

12 Not that I have already obtained this or have already reached
the goal;[t] but I press on to make it
my own, because Christ Jesus has
made me his own. 13 Beloved,[u] I do
not consider that I have made it my
own;[v] but this one thing I do: forgetting what lies behind and straining forward to what lies ahead, 14 I
press on toward the goal for the
prize of the heavenly[w] call of God
in Christ Jesus. 15 Let those of us
then who are mature be of the
same mind; and if you think differently about anything, this too God
will reveal to you. 16 Only let us
hold fast to what we have attained.
17 Brothers and sisters,[u] join in
imitating me, and observe those
who live according to the example
you have in us. 18 For many live as
enemies of the cross of Christ; I
have often told you of them, and
now I tell you even with tears.
19 Their end is destruction; their
god is the belly; and their glory is in
their shame; their minds are set on
earthly things. 20 But our citizenship[x] is in heaven, and it is from
there that we are expecting a Savior, the Lord Jesus Christ. 21 He will
transform the body of our humiliation[y] that it may be conformed to
the body of his glory,[z] by the power that also enables him to make all
things subject to himself.
4 1 Therefore, my brothers and
sisters,[a] whom I love and long for,
my joy and crown, stand firm in the
Lord in this way, my beloved.

Exhortations

2 I urge Euodia and I urge Syntyche to be of the same mind in the
Lord. 3 Yes, and I ask you also, my
loyal companion,[b] help these
women, for they have struggled beside me in the work of the gospel,
together with Clement and the rest
of my co-workers, whose names are
in the book of life.
4 Rejoice[c] in the Lord always;
again I will say, Rejoice.[c] 5 Let your
gentleness be known to everyone.
The Lord is near. 6 Do not worry
about anything, but in everything
by prayer and supplication with
thanksgiving let your requests be
made known to God. 7 And the
peace of God, which surpasses all
understanding, will guard your
hearts and your minds in Christ
Jesus.

8 Finally, beloved,[d] whatever is
true, whatever is honorable, whatever is just, whatever is pure, whatever is pleasing, whatever is com-
mendable, if there is any
excellence and if there is anything
worthy of praise, think about[e]
these things. 9 Keep on doing the
things that you have learned and
received and heard and seen in me,
and the God of peace will be with
you.

Acknowledgment of the Philippians' Gift

10 I rejoice[f] in the Lord greatly
that now at last you have revived
your concern for me; indeed, you

3.7 Mt 13.44; Lk 14.33
3.8 Eph 4.13; 2 Pet 1.3
3.9 Rom 10.5; 9.30
3.10 Rom 6.3-5; 8.17
3.11 Acts 26.7
3.12 1 Tim 6.12; 1 Cor 13.10; Acts 9.5,6
3.13 Lk 9.62; 1 Cor 9.24
3.14 Heb 6.1; 2 Tim 1.9
3.15 1 Cor 2.6; Gal 5.10
3.16 Rom 12.16; Gal 6.16
3.17 1 Cor 4.16; 1 Pet 5.3
3.18 Acts 20.31; Gal 6.14
3.19 2 Cor 11.15; Rom 16.18; 6.21; 8.5,6
3.20 Eph 2.19; Col 3.1; 1 Cor 1.7
3.21 1 Cor 15.43; Col 3.4; Eph 1.19
4.1 Phil 1.8; 1 Cor 16.13; Phil 1.27
4.2 Phil 2.2
4.3 Rom 16.3; Lk 10.20; Rev 3.5
4.4 Rom 12.12; Phil 3.1
4.5 Heb 10.37; Jas 5.8,9
4.6 Mt 6.25; Eph 6.18
4.7 Jn 14.27; Col 3.15; 1 Pet 1.5
4.8 1 Pet 2.12; 1 Thes 5.22
4.9 Phil 3.17; Rom 15.33

[r] Or *through the faith of Christ* [s] Gk *him*
[t] Or *have already been made perfect*
[u] Gk *Brothers* [v] Other ancient authorities read *my own yet* [w] Gk *upward*
[x] Or *commonwealth* [y] Or *our humble bodies* [z] Or *his glorious body* [a] Gk *my brothers* [b] Or *loyal Syzygus*
[c] Or *Farewell* [d] Gk *brothers*
[e] Gk *take account of* [f] Gk *I rejoiced*

were concerned for me, but had no
opportunity to show it.[g] 11 Not that
I am referring to being in need; for
I have learned to be content with
whatever I have. 12 I know what it is
to have little, and I know what it is
to have plenty. In any and all circumstances I have learned the secret of being well-fed and of going
hungry, of having plenty and of being in need. 13 I can do all things
through him who strengthens me.
14 In any case, it was kind of you to
share my distress.
15 You Philippians indeed know
that in the early days of the gospel,
when I left Macedonia, no church
shared with me in the matter of giving and receiving, except you
alone. 16 For even when I was in
Thessalonica, you sent me help for
my needs more than once. 17 Not
that I seek the gift, but I seek the
profit that accumulates to your account. 18 I have been paid in full
and have more than enough; I am
fully satisfied, now that I have received from Epaphroditus the gifts
you sent, a fragrant offering, a sacrifice acceptable and pleasing to
God. 19 And my God will fully satisfy every need of yours according to
his riches in glory in Christ Jesus.
20 To our God and Father be glory
forever and ever. Amen.

4.11 1 Tim 6.6
4.12 1 Cor 4.11; 2 Cor 11.9
4.13 Jn 15.5; 2 Cor 12.9
4.14 Phil 1.7
4.15 2 Cor 11.8, 9
4.16 Acts 17.1; 1 Thes 2.9
4.17 Titus 3.14
4.18 Phil 2.25; 2 Cor 2.14
4.19 Ps 23.1; 2 Cor 9.8; Eph 1.7
4.20 Gal 1.4; Rom 11.36

Final Greetings and Benediction

21 Greet every saint in Christ
Jesus. The friends[h] who are with
me greet you. 22 All the saints greet
you, especially those of the emper-
or's household.
23 The grace of the Lord Jesus
Christ be with your spirit.[i]

[g] Gk lacks *to show it* [h] Gk *brothers*
[i] Other ancient authorities add *Amen*

THE LETTER OF PAUL TO THE

Colossians

Title and Background

During Paul's three-year ministry in Ephesus, Epaphras had been converted and had carried the gospel to Colosse. The young church that resulted then became the target of a heretical attack (the Colossian heresy), which led to Epaphras's visit to Paul in Rome and ultimately to the writing of this letter.

Author and Date of Writing

Because of the many parallels between Ephesians and Colossians, it seems likely that Paul wrote Colossians at the same time as Ephesians and from the same place, that is, from Rome. It should be dated about A.D. 60, during Paul's first Roman imprisonment.

Theme and Message

Paul's purpose is to refute the Colossian heresy. To accomplish this goal he exalts Christ and states that he is the supreme Lord of all. His theme, in other words, is the complete adequacy of Christ as contrasted with the emptiness of mere human philosophy. For "in him the whole fullness of diety dwells bodily," and we "have come to fullness in him" (2.9-10).

Outline

I. Greetings, Thanksgiving, and Prayer (1.1-14)
II. The Supremacy of Christ (1.15-23)
III. Paul's Labor for the Church (1.24–2.7)
IV. Freedom from Human Regulations through Life with Christ (2.8-23)
V. Rules for Holy Living (3.1–4.6)
VI. Final Greetings and Conclusion (4.7-18)

Salutation

1 Paul, an apostle of Christ
Jesus by the will of God, and
Timothy our brother,
2 To the saints and faithful
brothers and sisters[a] in Christ in
Colossae:
Grace to you and peace from
God our Father.

Paul Thanks God for the Colossians

3 In our prayers for you we always thank God, the Father of our
Lord Jesus Christ, 4 for we have
heard of your faith in Christ Jesus
and of the love that you have for all
the saints, 5 because of the hope
laid up for you in heaven. You have
heard of this hope before in the
word of the truth, the gospel 6 that
has come to you. Just as it is bearing fruit and growing in the whole
world, so it has been bearing fruit
among yourselves from the day you
heard it and truly comprehended
the grace of God. 7 This you learned
from Epaphras, our beloved fellow
servant.[b] He is a faithful minister
of Christ on your[c] behalf, 8 and he
has made known to us your love in
the Spirit.
9 For this reason, since the day
we heard it, we have not ceased
praying for you and asking that you
may be filled with the knowledge of
God's[d] will in all spiritual wisdom
and understanding, 10 so that you
may lead lives worthy of the Lord,
fully pleasing to him, as you bear

1.1 Eph 1.1 **1.2** Rom 1.7 **1.3** Eph 1.16 **1.4** Eph 1.15; Gal 5.6 **1.5** 1 Thes 5.8; 1 Pet 1.4 **1.6** Mt 24.14; Jn 15.16 **1.7** Philem 23; Col 4.7 **1.8** Rom 15.30 **1.9** Eph 1.15-17; Rom 12.2 **1.10** Eph 4.1; 1 Thes 4.1; Rom 1.13

[a] Gk *brothers* [b] Gk *slave* [c] Other ancient authorities read *our* [d] Gk *his*

fruit in every good work and as you
grow in the knowledge of God.
11 May you be made strong with all
the strength that comes from his
glorious power, and may you be
prepared to endure everything with
patience, while joyfully 12 giving
thanks to the Father, who has enabled[e] you[f] to share in the inheritance of the saints in the light.
13 He has rescued us from the power of darkness and transferred us
into the kingdom of his beloved
Son, 14 in whom we have redemption, the forgiveness of sins.[g]

The Supremacy of Christ

15 He is the image of the invisible God, the firstborn of all creation; 16 for in[h] him all things in
heaven and on earth were created,
things visible and invisible, whether thrones or dominions or rulers or
powers—all things have been created through him and for him. 17 He
himself is before all things, and in[h]
him all things hold together. 18 He
is the head of the body, the church;
he is the beginning, the firstborn
from the dead, so that he might
come to have first place in everything. 19 For in him all the fullness
of God was pleased to dwell, 20 and
through him God was pleased to
reconcile to himself all things,
whether on earth or in heaven, by
making peace through the blood of
his cross.

21 And you who were once estranged and hostile in mind, doing
evil deeds, 22 he has now reconciled[i] in his fleshly body[j] through
death, so as to present you holy
and blameless and irreproachable
before him— 23 provided that you
continue securely established and
steadfast in the faith, without shift-
ing from the hope promised by the
gospel that you heard, which has
been proclaimed to every creature
under heaven. I, Paul, became a
servant of this gospel.

Paul's Interest in the Colossians

24 I am now rejoicing in my sufferings for your sake, and in my
flesh I am completing what is lacking in Christ's afflictions for the
sake of his body, that is, the
church. 25 I became its servant according to God's commission that
was given to me for you, to make
the word of God fully known, 26 the
mystery that has been hidden
throughout the ages and generations but has now been revealed to
his saints. 27 To them God chose to
make known how great among the
Gentiles are the riches of the glory
of this mystery, which is Christ in
you, the hope of glory. 28 It is he
whom we proclaim, warning everyone and teaching everyone in all
wisdom, so that we may present everyone mature in Christ. 29 For this
I toil and struggle with all the ener-
gy that he powerfully inspires within me.

2 For I want you to know how
much I am struggling for you,
and for those in Laodicea, and for
all who have not seen me face to
face. 2 I want their hearts to be encouraged and united in love, so
that they may have all the riches of
assured understanding and have
the knowledge of God's mystery,
that is, Christ himself,[k] 3 in whom
are hidden all the treasures of wisdom and knowledge. 4 I am saying
this so that no one may deceive you
with plausible arguments. 5 For
though I am absent in body, yet I
am with you in spirit, and I rejoice
to see your morale and the firm-
ness of your faith in Christ.

Fullness of Life in Christ

6 As you therefore have received
Christ Jesus the Lord, continue to
live your lives[l] in him, 7 rooted and
built up in him and established in
the faith, just as you were taught,
abounding in thanksgiving.

8 See to it that no one takes you
captive through philosophy and

1.11 Eph 3.16; 4.2; Acts 5.41
1.12 Eph 5.20; 1.11
1.13 Eph 6.12; 2 Pet 1.11
1.15 2 Cor 4.4; Rev 3.14
1.16 Heb 1.2; Eph 1.20, 21; Heb 2.10
1.17 Jn 1.1; 8.58
1.18 Eph 1.22, 23; Rev 1.5
1.19 Jn 1.16
1.20 2 Cor 5.18; Eph 2.13,14
1.21 Rom 5.10; Eph 2.3
1.22 Rom 7.4; Eph 2.15; 5.27
1.23 Eph 3.17; Rom 10.18
1.25 Eph 3.2
1.26 Eph 3.3,4
1.27 2 Cor 2.14; Rom 9.23; 1 Tim 1.1
1.28 Col 3.16; 1 Cor 2.6, 7
1.29 1 Cor 15.10; Col 2.1; Eph 1.19
2.1 Col 1.29; 4.12
2.2 Phil 3.8
2.3 Isa 45.3; Rom 11.33
2.5 1 Thes 2.17; 1 Cor 14.40; 1 Pet 5.9
2.6 1 Thes 4.1
2.7 Eph 2.21
2.8 1 Cor 8.9; 1 Tim 6.20; Gal 4.3

[e] Other ancient authorities read *called* [f] Other ancient authorities read *us* [g] Other ancient authorities add *through his blood* [h] Or *by* [i] Other ancient authorities read *you have now been reconciled* [j] Gk *in the body of his flesh* [k] Other ancient authorities read *of the mystery of God, both of the Father and of Christ* [l] Gk *to walk*

empty deceit, according to human tradition, according to the elemental spirits of the universe,[m] and not according to Christ. 9 For in him the whole fullness of deity dwells bodily, 10 and you have come to fullness in him, who is the head of every ruler and authority. 11 In him also you were circumcised with a spiritual circumcision,[n] by putting off the body of the flesh in the circumcision of Christ; 12 when you were buried with him in baptism, you were also raised with him through faith in the power of God, who raised him from the dead. 13 And when you were dead in trespasses and the uncircumcision of your flesh, God[o] made you[p] alive together with him, when he forgave us all our trespasses, 14 erasing the record that stood against us with its legal demands. He set this aside, nailing it to the cross. 15 He disarmed[q] the rulers and authorities and made a public example of them, triumphing over them in it.

16 Therefore do not let anyone condemn you in matters of food and drink or of observing festivals, new moons, or sabbaths. 17 These are only a shadow of what is to come, but the substance belongs to Christ. 18 Do not let anyone disqualify you, insisting on self-abasement and worship of angels, dwelling[r] on visions,[s] puffed up without cause by a human way of thinking,[t] 19 and not holding fast to the head, from whom the whole body, nourished and held together by its ligaments and sinews, grows with a growth that is from God.

Warnings against False Teachers

20 If with Christ you died to the elemental spirits of the universe,[m] why do you live as if you still belonged to the world? Why do you submit to regulations, 21 "Do not handle, Do not taste, Do not touch"? 22 All these regulations refer to things that perish with use; they are simply human commands and teachings. 23 These have indeed an appearance of wisdom in promoting self-imposed piety, humility, and severe treatment of the body, but they are of no value in checking self-indulgence.[u]

The New Life in Christ

3 So if you have been raised with Christ, seek the things that are above, where Christ is, seated at the right hand of God. 2 Set your minds on things that are above, not on things that are on earth, 3 for you have died, and your life is hidden with Christ in God. 4 When Christ who is your[v] life is revealed, then you also will be revealed with him in glory.

5 Put to death, therefore, whatever in you is earthly: fornication, impurity, passion, evil desire, and greed (which is idolatry). 6 On account of these the wrath of God is coming on those who are disobedient.[w] 7 These are the ways you also once followed, when you were living that life.[x] 8 But now you must get rid of all such things—anger, wrath, malice, slander, and abusive[y] language from your mouth. 9 Do not lie to one another, seeing that you have stripped off the old self with its practices 10 and have clothed yourselves with the new self, which is being renewed in knowledge according to the image of its creator. 11 In that renewal[z] there is no longer Greek and Jew, circumcised and uncircumcised, barbarian, Scythian, slave and free; but Christ is all and in all!

12 As God's chosen ones, holy and beloved, clothe yourselves with compassion, kindness, humility, meekness, and patience. 13 Bear with one another and, if

2.9 Jn 1.14; Col 1.19 **2.10** Eph 1.21,22 **2.11f** Rom 2.29; Phil 3.3; Rom 6.6; Gal 5.24 **2.12** Rom 6.4,5; Acts 2.24 **2.13** Eph 2.1 **2.14** Eph 2.15 **2.15** Gen 3.15; Isa 53.12; Eph 6.12 **2.16** Rom 14.3; 14.17; 14.5; Gal 4.10,11 **2.17** Heb 8.5 **2.18** Phil 3.14; v. 23 **2.19** Eph 1.22; 4.16 **2.20** Rom 6.3,5; Gal 4.3,9 **2.22** 1 Cor 6.13; Isa 29.13; Titus 1.14 **2.23** Rom 13.14; 1 Tim 4.8

3.1 Ps 110.1; Rom 8.34 **3.2** Phil 3.19,20 **3.3** Rom 6.2; 2 Cor 5.14 **3.4** 1 Jn 3.2; Jn 14.6 **3.5** Rom 6.13; Eph 5.3,5 **3.6** Rom 1.18; Eph 5.6 **3.7** Eph 2.2 **3.8** Eph 4.22,29 **3.9** Eph 4.25; 4.22 **3.10** Rom 12.2; Eph 4.23; 2.10 **3.11** Gal 3.28; Eph 1.23 **3.12** Gal 5.22,23; Phil 2.3; 2 Cor 6.6 **3.13** Eph 4.2,32

[m] Or *the rudiments of the world* [n] Gk *a circumcision made without hands* [o] Gk *he* [p] Other ancient authorities read *made us;* others, *made* [q] Or *divested himself of* [r] Other ancient authorities read *not dwelling* [s] Meaning of Gk uncertain [t] Gk *by the mind of his flesh* [u] Or *are of no value, serving only to indulge the flesh* [v] Other authorities read *our* [w] Other ancient authorities lack *on those who are disobedient* (Gk *the children of disobedience*) [x] Or *living among such people* [y] Or *filthy* [z] Gk *its creator,* [11]*where*

anyone has a complaint against another, forgive each other; just as the Lord[a] has forgiven you, so you also must forgive. 14 Above all, clothe yourselves with love, which binds everything together in perfect harmony. 15 And let the peace of Christ rule in your hearts, to which indeed you were called in the one body. And be thankful. 16 Let the word of Christ[b] dwell in you richly; teach and admonish one another in all wisdom; and with gratitude in your hearts sing psalms, hymns, and spiritual songs to God.[c] 17 And whatever you do, in word or deed, do everything in the name of the Lord Jesus, giving thanks to God the Father through him.

Rules for Christian Households

18 Wives, be subject to your husbands, as is fitting in the Lord. 19 Husbands, love your wives and never treat them harshly.

20 Children, obey your parents in everything, for this is your acceptable duty in the Lord. 21 Fathers, do not provoke your children, or they may lose heart. 22 Slaves, obey your earthly masters[d] in everything, not only while being watched and in order to please them, but wholeheartedly, fearing the Lord.[d] 23 Whatever your task, put yourselves into it, as done for the Lord and not for your masters,[e] 24 since you know that from the Lord you will receive the inheritance as your reward; you serve[f] the Lord Christ. 25 For the wrongdoer will be paid back for whatever wrong has been done, and there is

4 no partiality. 1 Masters, treat your slaves justly and fairly, for you know that you also have a Master in heaven.

Further Instructions

2 Devote yourselves to prayer, keeping alert in it with thanksgiving. 3 At the same time pray for us as well that God will open to us a door for the word, that we may declare the mystery of Christ, for which I am in prison, 4 so that I may reveal it clearly, as I should.

5 Conduct yourselves wisely toward outsiders, making the most of the time.[g] 6 Let your speech always be gracious, seasoned with salt, so that you may know how you ought to answer everyone.

Final Greetings and Benediction

7 Tychicus will tell you all the news about me; he is a beloved brother, a faithful minister, and a fellow servant[h] in the Lord. 8 I have sent him to you for this very purpose, so that you may know how we are[i] and that he may encourage your hearts; 9 he is coming with Onesimus, the faithful and beloved brother, who is one of you. They will tell you about everything here.

10 Aristarchus my fellow prisoner greets you, as does Mark the cousin of Barnabas, concerning whom you have received instructions—if he comes to you, welcome him. 11 And Jesus who is called Justus greets you. These are the only ones of the circumcision among my co-workers for the kingdom of God, and they have been a comfort to me. 12 Epaphras, who is one of you, a servant[h] of Christ Jesus, greets you. He is always wrestling in his prayers on your behalf, so that you may stand mature and fully assured in everything that God wills. 13 For I testify for him that he has worked hard for you and for those in Laodicea and in Hierapolis. 14 Luke, the beloved physician, and Demas greet you. 15 Give my greetings to the brothers and sisters[j] in Laodicea, and to Nympha and the church in her house. 16 And when this letter has been read among you, have it read also in the church of the Laodice-

3.14 Eph 4.3
3.15 Phil 4.7; 1 Cor 7.15; Eph 4.4
3.16 Eph 5.19
3.17 1 Cor 10.31; Eph 5.20
3.18 Eph 5.22-6.9
3.19 Eph 5.25
3.20 Eph 6.1
3.21 Eph 6.4
3.22 Eph 6.5,6; Philem 16
3.24 Eph 6.8; 1 Cor 7.22
3.25 Eph 6.8,9; Acts 10.34
4.1 Lev 25.43, 53; Eph 6.9
4.2 Rom 12.12; Eph 6.18; Phil 4.6
4.3 Eph 6.19; 1 Cor 16.9; Eph 6.20
4.5 Eph 5.15,16
4.6 Eph 4.29; Mk 9.50; 1 Pet 3.15
4.7 Eph 6.21,22
4.9 Philem 10
4.10 Acts 19.29; 15.37; 4.36
4.11 Acts 11.2; Rom 16.3
4.12 Col 1.7; Rom 15.30; Phil 3.15
4.13 Col 2.1
4.14 2 Tim 4.10, 11; Philem 24
4.15 Rom 16.5

[a] Other ancient authorities read *just as Christ*
[b] Other ancient authorities read *of God*, or *of the Lord*
[c] Other ancient authorities read *to the Lord*
[d] In Greek the same word is used for *master* and *Lord*
[e] Gk *not for men*
[f] Or *you are slaves of*, or *be slaves of*
[g] Or *opportunity*
[h] Gk *slave*
[i] Other authorities read *that I may know how you are*
[j] Gk *brothers*

ans; and see that you read also the
letter from Laodicea. 17 And say to
Archippus, "See that you complete
the task that you have received in
the Lord."

4.17 Philem 2; 2 Tim 4.5
4.18 1 Cor 16.21; Heb 13.3; 13.25

18 I, Paul, write this greeting
with my own hand. Remember my
chains. Grace be with you.[k]

[k] Other ancient authorities add *Amen*

THE FIRST LETTER OF PAUL TO THE

Thessalonians

Title and Background

Paul founded the church at Thessalonica during his second missionary journey. He had taught there just three weeks when he had to leave suddenly because of the opposition of the Jews. Recent converts from paganism were thus left with little pastoral support in the midst of persecution. Paul wrote to give encouragement to them.

Author and Date of Writing

Both external and internal evidence support the view that Paul wrote 1 Thessalonians. It is generally dated about A.D. 51. Except for the possibility of an early date for Galatians (A.D. 48-49), 1 Thessalonians is Paul's earliest canonical letter.

Theme and Message

Although the thrust of each letter is varied, the subject of what happens at the return of Christ is predominant in both Thessalonian letters. Every chapter of 1 Thessalonians ends with a reference to the second coming of Christ, with chapter 4 giving it major consideration. Christians are encouraged to eagerly await that day of days.

Outline

I. Greetings and Thanksgiving (1.1-10)
II. Paul's Defense of His Actions and Absence (2.1–3.13)
III. Exhortations (4.1–5.22)
  A. About One's Personal Life (4.1-12)
  B. About Christ's Coming (4.13–5.11)
  C. About Church Life (5.12-22)
IV. Concluding Prayer, Greetings, and Benediction (5.23-28)

Salutation

1 Paul, Silvanus, and Timothy,
To the church of the Thessalo-
nians in God the Father and the
Lord Jesus Christ:
Grace to you and peace.

The Thessalonians' Faith and Example

2 We always give thanks to God
for all of you and mention you in
our prayers, constantly 3 remembering before our God and Father
your work of faith and labor of love
and steadfastness of hope in our
Lord Jesus Christ. 4 For we know,
brothers and sisters[a] beloved by
God, that he has chosen you, 5 because our message of the gospel
came to you not in word only, but
also in power and in the Holy Spirit
and with full conviction; just as you
know what kind of persons we
proved to be among you for your
sake. 6 And you became imitators
of us and of the Lord, for in spite of
persecution you received the word
with joy inspired by the Holy Spirit,
7 so that you became an example to
all the believers in Macedonia and
in Achaia. 8 For the word of the
Lord has sounded forth from you
not only in Macedonia and Achaia,
but in every place your faith in God
has become known, so that we
have no need to speak about it.

1.1 2 Thes 1.1; 2 Cor 1.19; Acts 16.1; 17.1; Rom 1.7
1.2 2 Thes 1.3; Rom 1.8,9
1.3 2 Thes 1.11; 1.3
1.5 2 Thes 2.14; Col 2.2; 2 Thes 3.7
1.6 1 Cor 4.16; 11.1; Acts 17.5-10; 13.52
1.8 Rom 10.18; 1.8; 2 Thes 1.4

[a] Gk *brothers*

9 For the people of those regions[b]
report about us what kind of welcome we had among you, and how
you turned to God from idols, to
serve a living and true God, 10 and
to wait for his Son from heaven,
whom he raised from the dead—
Jesus, who rescues us from the
wrath that is coming.

Paul's Ministry in Thessalonica

2 You yourselves know, brothers
and sisters,[c] that our coming
to you was not in vain, 2 but though
we had already suffered and been
shamefully mistreated at Philippi,
as you know, we had courage in our
God to declare to you the gospel of
God in spite of great opposition.
3 For our appeal does not spring
from deceit or impure motives or
trickery, 4 but just as we have been
approved by God to be entrusted
with the message of the gospel,
even so we speak, not to please
mortals, but to please God who
tests our hearts. 5 As you know and
as God is our witness, we never
came with words of flattery or with
a pretext for greed; 6 nor did we
seek praise from mortals, whether
from you or from others, 7 though
we might have made demands as
apostles of Christ. But we were
gentle[d] among you, like a nurse
tenderly caring for her own children. 8 So deeply do we care for you
that we are determined to share
with you not only the gospel of God
but also our own selves, because
you have become very dear to us.
9 You remember our labor and
toil, brothers and sisters;[c] we
worked night and day, so that we
might not burden any of you while
we proclaimed to you the gospel of
God. 10 You are witnesses, and God
also, how pure, upright, and
blameless our conduct was toward
you believers. 11 As you know, we
dealt with each one of you like a
father with his children, 12 urging
and encouraging you and pleading
that you lead a life worthy of God,
who calls you into his own kingdom and glory.
13 We also constantly give
thanks to God for this, that when
you received the word of God that
you heard from us, you accepted it
not as a human word but as what it
really is, God's word, which is also
at work in you believers. 14 For you,
brothers and sisters,[c] became imitators of the churches of God in
Christ Jesus that are in Judea, for
you suffered the same things from
your own compatriots as they did
from the Jews, 15 who killed both
the Lord Jesus and the prophets,[e]
and drove us out; they displease
God and oppose everyone 16 by hindering us from speaking to the
Gentiles so that they may be saved.
Thus they have constantly been
filling up the measure of their sins;
but God's wrath has overtaken
them at last.[f]

Paul's Desire to Visit the Thessalonians Again

17 As for us, brothers and sisters,[c] when, for a short time, we
were made orphans by being separated from you—in person, not in
heart—we longed with great eagerness to see you face to face. 18 For
we wanted to come to you—
certainly I, Paul, wanted to again
and again—but Satan blocked our
way. 19 For what is our hope or joy
or crown of boasting before our
Lord Jesus at his coming? Is it not
you? 20 Yes, you are our glory and
joy!

3 Therefore when we could bear
it no longer, we decided to be
left alone in Athens; 2 and we sent
Timothy, our brother and co-
worker for God in proclaiming[g] the
gospel of Christ, to strengthen and
encourage you for the sake of your
faith, 3 so that no one would be
shaken by these persecutions. Indeed, you yourselves know that
this is what we are destined for. 4 In
fact, when we were with you, we

1.9 1 Cor 12.2; Gal 4.8 **1.10** 2 Pet 3.12; Acts 2.24; Rom 5.9 **2.1** 1 Thes 1.5, 9 **2.2** Acts 16.22; 1 Thes 1.5; Phil 1.30 **2.3** 2 Cor 7.2 **2.4** 2 Cor 2.17; Gal 2.7; 1.10 **2.5** Acts 20.33; Rom 1.9 **2.6** 2 Cor 4.5; 1 Cor 9.1, 2 **2.7** v. 11; Gal 4.19 **2.8** 2 Cor 12.15; 1 Jn 3.16 **2.9** Acts 20.34; 2 Thes 3.8; 2 Cor 12.13 **2.10** 1 Thes 1.5. 2 Cor 1.12 **2.11** 1 Cor 4.14; v. 7 **2.12** Eph 4.1; 1 Pet 5.10 **2.13** 1 Thes 1.2; Gal 4.14 **2.14** Acts 17.5; 2 Thes 1.4 **2.15** Acts 2.23; 7.52 **2.16** Acts 9.23; 13.45,50ff; Mt 23.32 **2.17** 1 Cor 5.3; 1 Thes 3.10 **2.18** Rom 15.22; 1.13 **2.19** 2 Cor 1.14; Phil 4.1; 1 Thes 3.13 **2.20** 2 Cor 1.14 **3.1** v. 5; Acts 17.15 **3.2** 2 Cor 1.1; Col 1.1 **3.3** Acts 9.16; 14.22 **3.4** Acts 20.24; 1 Thes 2.14

[b] Gk *For they* [c] Gk *brothers* [d] Other ancient authorities read *infants* [e] Other ancient authorities read *their own prophets* [f] Or *completely* or *forever* [g] Gk lacks *proclaiming*

told you beforehand that we were
to suffer persecution; so it turned
out, as you know. 5 For this reason,
when I could bear it no longer, I
sent to find out about your faith; I
was afraid that somehow the
tempter had tempted you and that
our labor had been in vain.

Timothy's Encouraging Report

6 But Timothy has just now
come to us from you, and has
brought us the good news of your
faith and love. He has told us also
that you always remember us kindly and long to see us—just as we
long to see you. 7 For this reason,
brothers and sisters,[h] during all
our distress and persecution we
have been encouraged about you
through your faith. 8 For we now
live, if you continue to stand firm
in the Lord. 9 How can we thank
God enough for you in return for all
the joy that we feel before our God
because of you? 10 Night and day
we pray most earnestly that we may
see you face to face and restore
whatever is lacking in your faith.
11 Now may our God and Father
himself and our Lord Jesus direct
our way to you. 12 And may the Lord
make you increase and abound in
love for one another and for all, just
as we abound in love for you. 13 And
may he so strengthen your hearts in
holiness that you may be blameless
before our God and Father at the
coming of our Lord Jesus with all
his saints.

A Life Pleasing to God

4 Finally, brothers and sisters,[h]
we ask and urge you in the
Lord Jesus that, as you learned
from us how you ought to live and
to please God (as, in fact, you are
doing), you should do so more and
more. 2 For you know what instructions we gave you through the Lord
Jesus. 3 For this is the will of God,
your sanctification: that you abstain from fornication; 4 that each
one of you know how to control
your own body[i] in holiness and
honor, 5 not with lustful passion,
like the Gentiles who do not know
God; 6 that no one wrong or exploit
a brother or sister[j] in this matter,
because the Lord is an avenger in
all these things, just as we have already told you beforehand and solemnly warned you. 7 For God did
not call us to impurity but in holiness. 8 Therefore whoever rejects
this rejects not human authority
but God, who also gives his Holy
Spirit to you.
9 Now concerning love of the
brothers and sisters,[h] you do not
need to have anyone write to you,
for you yourselves have been
taught by God to love one another;
10 and indeed you do love all the
brothers and sisters[h] throughout
Macedonia. But we urge you, beloved,[h] to do so more and more,
11 to aspire to live quietly, to mind
your own affairs, and to work with
your hands, as we directed you,
12 so that you may behave properly
toward outsiders and be dependent
on no one.

The Coming of the Lord

13 But we do not want you to be
uninformed, brothers and sisters,[h]
about those who have died,[k] so
that you may not grieve as others
do who have no hope. 14 For since
we believe that Jesus died and rose
again, even so, through Jesus, God
will bring with him those who have
died.[k] 15 For this we declare to you
by the word of the Lord, that we
who are alive, who are left until the
coming of the Lord, will by no
means precede those who have
died.[k] 16 For the Lord himself, with
a cry of command, with the archangel's call and with the sound of
God's trumpet, will descend from
heaven, and the dead in Christ will
rise first. 17 Then we who are alive,
who are left, will be caught up in
the clouds together with them to
meet the Lord in the air; and so we
will be with the Lord forever.
18 Therefore encourage one another
with these words.

3.5 1 Cor 11.3; Gal 2.2
3.6 Acts 18.5; 1 Thes 1.3
3.7 2 Cor 1.4
3.8 Phil 4.1
3.9 1 Thes 1.2
3.10 2 Tim 1.3; 2 Cor 13.9
3.11 2 Thes 3.5
3.12 1 Thes 4.1, 10
3.13 1 Cor 1.8; 1 Thes 2.19; 4.17
4.1 Phil 1.27; 1 Thes 2.12; Col 1.10
4.3 1 Cor 6.18; Col 3.5
4.4 1 Cor 7.2; 1 Pet 3.7
4.5 Col 3.5; Eph 4.17; 1 Cor 15.34
4.6 1 Cor 6.8; Heb 13.4
4.7 Lev 11.44; 1 Pet 1.15; 1 Thes 2.3
4.8 Rom 5.5
4.9 Rom 12.10; 1 Thes 5.1
4.10 1 Thes 1.7; 3.12
4.11 Eph 4.28; 2 Thes 3.10-12
4.12 Rom 13.13
4.13 Eph 2.12
4.14 1 Cor 15.13, 23
4.15 1 Kings 13.17; 20.35; 1 Cor 15.51, 52
4.16 Mt 24.31; 1 Cor 15.23; 2 Thes 2.1
4.17 1 Cor 15.52; Acts 1.9; Rev 11.12; Jn 12.26

[h] Gk *brothers* [i] Or *how to take a wife for himself* [j] Gk *brother* [k] Gk *fallen asleep*

5 Now concerning the times and
the seasons, brothers and sisters,[l] you do not need to have anything written to you. 2 For you yourselves know very well that the day
of the Lord will come like a thief in
the night. 3 When they say, "There
is peace and security," then sudden destruction will come upon
them, as labor pains come upon a
pregnant woman, and there will be
no escape! 4 But you, beloved,[l] are
not in darkness, for that day to surprise you like a thief; 5 for you are
all children of light and children of
the day; we are not of the night or
of darkness. 6 So then let us not fall
asleep as others do, but let us keep
awake and be sober; 7 for those who
sleep sleep at night, and those who
are drunk get drunk at night. 8 But
since we belong to the day, let us
be sober, and put on the breastplate of faith and love, and for a
helmet the hope of salvation. 9 For
God has destined us not for wrath
but for obtaining salvation through
our Lord Jesus Christ, 10 who died
for us, so that whether we are
awake or asleep we may live with
him. 11 Therefore encourage one
another and build up each other, as
indeed you are doing.

Final Exhortations, Greetings, and Benediction

12 But we appeal to you, brothers and sisters,[l] to respect those
who labor among you, and have
charge of you in the Lord and admonish you; 13 esteem them very
highly in love because of their
work. Be at peace among yourselves. 14 And we urge you, beloved,[l] to admonish the idlers, encourage the faint hearted, help the
weak, be patient with all of them.
15 See that none of you repays evil
for evil, but always seek to do good
to one another and to all. 16 Rejoice
always, 17 pray without ceasing,
18 give thanks in all circumstances;
for this is the will of God in Christ
Jesus for you. 19 Do not quench the
Spirit. 20 Do not despise the words
of prophets,[m] 21 but test everything; hold fast to what is good;
22 abstain from every form of evil.
23 May the God of peace himself sanctify you entirely; and may
your spirit and soul and body be
kept sound[n] and blameless at the
coming of our Lord Jesus Christ.
24 The one who calls you is faithful,
and he will do this.
25 Beloved,[o] pray for us.
26 Greet all the brothers and
sisters[l] with a holy kiss. 27 I solemnly command you by the Lord
that this letter be read to all of
them.[p]
28 The grace of our Lord Jesus
Christ be with you.[q]

5.1 Acts 1.7; 1 Thes 4.9 **5.2** 1 Cor 1.8; 2 Pet 3.10 **5.3** Hos 13.13 **5.4** Acts 26.18; 1 Jn 2.8 **5.6** Rom 13.11; 1 Pet 1.13 **5.7** Acts 2.15; 2 Pet 2.13 **5.8** Eph 6.14, 23,17 **5.9** 2 Thes 2.13, 14; Rom 14.9 **5.10** 2 Cor 5.15 **5.12** 1 Tim 5.17; Heb 13.17 **5.14** 2 Thes 3.11; Rom 14.1 **5.15** Rom 12.17; 1 Pet 3.9; Gal 6.10; 2.13,14; Rom 14.9 **5.16** Phil 4.4 **5.19** Eph 4.30 **5.21** 1 Cor 14.29; 1 Jn 4.1 **5.23** Rom 15.33 **5.24** 1 Cor 1.9 **5.25** Eph 6.19 **5.27** Col 4.16

l Gk *brothers* m Gk *despise prophecies* n Or *complete* o Gk *Brothers* p Gk *to all the brothers* q Other ancient authorities add *Amen*

THE SECOND LETTER OF PAUL TO

Thessalonians

Title and Background

See Introduction to 1 Thessalonians.

Author and Date of Writing

Because of its similarity to 1 Thessalonians, this letter must have been written not long after the first one, about A.D. 51 or 52.

Theme and Message

Like 1 Thessalonians, this letter deals extensively with the doctrine of the last things. In fact, 18 of the 47 verses in 2 Thessalonians deal with this subject. Some people had misunderstood Paul and were sure Jesus was coming very soon. They had even stopped working and were just waiting for his return. Paul writes to correct this misunderstanding.

Outline

I. Greetings, Thanksgiving, and Prayer (1.1-12)
II. Instruction on Christ's Coming and Christian Conduct (2.1-17)
III. Request for Prayer and Warning against Idleness (3.1-15)
IV. Final Greetings and Benediction (3.16-18)

Salutation

1 Paul, Silvanus, and Timothy,
To the church of the Thessalo-
nians in God our Father and the
Lord Jesus Christ:
2 Grace to you and peace from
God our[a] Father and the Lord
Jesus Christ.

Thanksgiving

3 We must always give thanks to
God for you, brothers and sisters,[b]
as is right, because your faith is
growing abundantly, and the love
of everyone of you for one another
is increasing. 4 Therefore we ourselves boast of you among the
churches of God for your steadfastness and faith during all your persecutions and the afflictions that
you are enduring.

The Judgment at Christ's Coming

5 This is evidence of the righteous judgment of God, and is intended to make you worthy of the
kingdom of God, for which you are
also suffering. 6 For it is indeed just
of God to repay with affliction
those who afflict you, 7 and to give
relief to the afflicted as well as to
us, when the Lord Jesus is revealed
from heaven with his mighty angels
8 in flaming fire, inflicting vengeance on those who do not know
God and on those who do not obey
the gospel of our Lord Jesus.
9 These will suffer the punishment
of eternal destruction, separated
from the presence of the Lord and
from the glory of his might, 10 when
he comes to be glorified by his
saints and to be marveled at on
that day among all who have believed, because our testimony to
you was believed. 11 To this end we
always pray for you, asking that our
God will make you worthy of his
call and will fulfill by his power every good resolve and work of faith,
12 so that the name of our Lord
Jesus may be glorified in you, and
you in him, according to the grace

1.1 1 Thes 1.1; 2 Cor 1.19; Acts 16.1 **1.2** Rom 1.7; 1 Cor 1.3 **1.3** 1 Thes 1.2; 3.12 **1.4** 2 Cor 7.14; 1 Thes 1.3; 2.14 **1.5** Phil 1.28; 1 Thes 2.14 **1.6** Col 3.25; Rev 6.10 **1.7** 1 Thes 4.16; Jude 14 **1.8** Gal 4.8; Rom 2.8 **1.9** Phil 3.19; 2 Pet 3.7; 2 Thes 2.8 **1.10** Jn 17.10; 1 Cor 3.13; 1.6 **1.11** v. 5; 1 Thes 1.3 **1.12** Phil 2.9ff

[a] Other ancient authorities read *the*
[b] Gk *brothers*

of our God and the Lord Jesus
Christ.

The Man of Lawlessness

2 As to the coming of our Lord
Jesus Christ and our being
gathered together to him, we beg
you, brothers and sisters,[c] 2 not to
be quickly shaken in mind or
alarmed, either by spirit or by word
or by letter, as though from us, to
the effect that the day of the Lord
is already here. 3 Let no one deceive
you in any way; for that day will not
come unless the rebellion comes
first and the lawless one[d] is revealed, the one destined for destruction.[e] 4 He opposes and exalts
himself above every so-called god
or object of worship, so that he
takes his seat in the temple of God,
declaring himself to be God. 5 Do
you not remember that I told you
these things when I was still with
you? 6 And you know what is now
restraining him, so that he may be
revealed when his time comes.
7 For the mystery of lawlessness is
already at work, but only until the
one who now restrains it is removed. 8 And then the lawless one
will be revealed, whom the Lord
Jesus[f] will destroy[g] with the
breath of his mouth, annihilating
him by the manifestation of his
coming. 9 The coming of the lawless one is apparent in the working
of Satan, who uses all power, signs,
lying wonders, 10 and every kind of
wicked deception for those who are
perishing, because they refused to
love the truth and so be saved.
11 For this reason God sends them a
powerful delusion, leading them to
believe what is false, 12 so that all
who have not believed the truth
but took pleasure in unrighteousness will be condemned.

Chosen for Salvation

13 But we must always give
thanks to God for you, brothers and
sisters[c] beloved by the Lord, because God chose you as the first
fruits[h] for salvation through sanctification by the Spirit and through
belief in the truth. 14 For this purpose he called you through our
proclamation of the good news,[i]
so that you may obtain the glory of
our Lord Jesus Christ. 15 So then,
brothers and sisters,[c] stand firm
and hold fast to the traditions that
you were taught by us, either by
word of mouth or by our letter.
16 Now may our Lord Jesus
Christ himself and God our Father,
who loved us and through grace
gave us eternal comfort and good
hope, 17 comfort your hearts and
strengthen them in every good
work and word.

Request for Prayer

3 Finally, brothers and sisters,[c]
pray for us, so that the word of
the Lord may spread rapidly and be
glorified everywhere, just as it is
among you, 2 and that we may be
rescued from wicked and evil people; for not all have faith. 3 But the
Lord is faithful; he will strengthen
you and guard you from the evil
one.[j] 4 And we have confidence in
the Lord concerning you, that you
are doing and will go on doing the
things that we command. 5 May the
Lord direct your hearts to the love
of God and to the steadfastness of
Christ.

Warning against Idleness

6 Now we command you, be-
loved,[c] in the name of our Lord
Jesus Christ, to keep away from believers who are[k] living in idleness
and not according to the tradition
that they[l] received from us. 7 For
you yourselves know how you
ought to imitate us; we were not
idle when we were with you, 8 and
we did not eat anyone's bread without paying for it; but with toil and
labor we worked night and day, so
that we might not burden any of
you. 9 This was not because we do

2.1 1 Thes 4.15-17; Mk 13.27
2.2 Eph 5.6; 2 Thes 3.17; 1 Cor 1.8
2.3 Eph 5.6-8; Dan 7.25; 8.25; 11.36; Rev 13.5ff; Jn 17.12
2.4 1 Cor 8.5; Isa 14.13, 14; Ezek 28.2
2.7 Rev 17.5,7
2.8 Dan 7.10; Rev 19.15
2.9 Mt 24.24; Jn 4.48
2.10 1 Cor 1.18
2.11 Rom 1.28; Mt 24.5; 1 Tim 4.1
2.12 Rom 1.32
2.13 Eph 1.4; 1 Pet 1.2
2.14 1 Pet 5.10
2.15 1 Cor 16.13; 11.2
2.16 1 Thes 3.11; Jn 3.16
2.17 1 Thes 3.2; 2 Thes 3.3
3.1 1 Thes 4.1; 5.25; 1.8
3.2 Rom 15.31
3.3 1 Cor 1.9; 1 Thes 5.24; 2 Pet 2.9
3.4 2 Cor 2.3; Gal 5.10
3.5 1 Chr 29.18
3.6 1 Cor 5.4, 11; 2 Thes 2.15
3.7 1 Thes 1.6
3.8 1 Thes 2.9; Acts 18.3; Eph 4.28
3.9 1 Cor 9.4ff

[c] Gk *brothers* [d] Gk *the man of lawlessness*; other ancient authorities read *the man of sin* [e] Gk *the son of destruction* [f] Other ancient authorities lack *Jesus* [g] Other ancient authorities read *consume* [h] Other ancient authorities read *from the beginning* [i] Or *through our gospel* [j] Or *from evil* [k] Gk *from every brother who is* [l] Other ancient authorities read *you*

not have that right, but in order to
give you an example to imitate.
10 For even when we were with you,
we gave you this command: Anyone unwilling to work should not
eat. 11 For we hear that some of you
are living in idleness, mere busybodies, not doing any work. 12 Now
such persons we command and exhort in the Lord Jesus Christ to do
their work quietly and to earn their
own living. 13 Brothers and sisters,[m] do not be weary in doing
what is right.
14 Take note of those who do
not obey what we say in this letter;
have nothing to do with them, so

3.10 1 Thes 4.11
3.11 1 Tim 5.13
3.12 1 Thes 4.1, 11; Eph 4.28
3.13 Gal 6.9
3.14 Mt 18.17
3.15 Gal 6.1; 1 Thes 5.14
3.16 Rom 15.33; Ruth 2.4
3.17 1 Cor 16.21
3.18 Rom 16.20; 1 Thes 5.28

that they may be ashamed. 15 Do
not regard them as enemies, but
warn them as believers.[n]

Final Greetings and Benediction

16 Now may the Lord of peace
himself give you peace at all times
in all ways. The Lord be with all of
you.
17 I, Paul, write this greeting
with my own hand. This is the mark
in every letter of mine; it is the way
I write. 18 The grace of our Lord
Jesus Christ be with all of you.[o]

[m] Gk *Brothers* [n] Gk *a brother* [o] Other ancient authorities add *Amen*

THE FIRST LETTER OF PAUL TO

Timothy

Title and Background

During his (assumed) fourth missionary journey, Paul had instructed Timothy to care for the church at Ephesus while he went on to Macedonia (1 Tim 1.3). When Paul realized he might not return to Ephesus in the near future, he wrote this first letter to Timothy, to encourage the young pastor in the tasks that awaited him.

Author and Date of Writing

Both early church tradition and the salutations of the Pastoral Letters testify that Paul wrote this letter, though not all scholars are convinced of his authorship today. It was probably written about A.D. 64, at least eight years after Paul's three-year stay in Ephesus.

Theme and Message

The letter was written to Timothy to give him instructions regarding the church. The two main responsibilities Paul had given his young assistant were to refute false teachings and to supervise the affairs of the growing Ephesian church. A major problem in this church was a heresy that combined Gnosticism, decadent Judaism, and false asceticism.

Outline

I. Warning Against False Teachers (1.1-11)
II. The Lord's Grace to Paul (1.12-17)
III. The Purpose of Paul's Instructions (1.18-20)
IV. Instructions for the Church (2.1–3.16)
V. Dealing With False Teachers (4.1-16)
VI. Dealing With Different Groups (5.1–6.2)
VII. Miscellaneous Matters (6.3-21)

Salutation

1 Paul, an apostle of Christ
Jesus by the command of God
our Savior and of Christ Jesus our
hope,
2 To Timothy, my loyal child in
the faith:
Grace, mercy, and peace from
God the Father and Christ Jesus
our Lord.

Warning against False Teachers

3 I urge you, as I did when I was
on my way to Macedonia, to remain in Ephesus so that you may
instruct certain people not to teach
any different doctrine, 4 and not to
occupy themselves with myths and
endless genealogies that promote
speculations rather than the divine
training[a] that is known by faith.
5 But the aim of such instruction is
love that comes from a pure heart,
a good conscience, and sincere
faith. 6 Some people have deviated
from these and turned to meaningless talk, 7 desiring to be teachers
of the law, without understanding
either what they are saying or the
things about which they make as-
sertions.
8 Now we know that the law is
good, if one uses it legitimately.
9 This means understanding that
the law is laid down not for the innocent but for the lawless and disobedient, for the godless and sinful, for the unholy and profane, for
those who kill their father or moth-

1.1 Acts 9.15; Col 1.27
1.2 Acts 16.1; 2 Tim 1.2
1.3 Acts 20.1; Gal 1.6,7
1.4 Titus 1.14; 1 Tim 6.4
1.5 2 Tim 2.22
1.6 Titus 1.10
1.7 Jas 3.1; 1 Tim 6.4
1.8 Rom 7.12
1.9 Gal 3.19; 1 Pet 4.18

[a] Or *plan*

er, for murderers, 10 fornicators,
sodomites, slave traders, liars, per-
jurers, and whatever else is contrary to the sound teaching 11 that
conforms to the glorious gospel of
the blessed God, which he entrusted to me.

Gratitude for Mercy

12 I am grateful to Christ Jesus
our Lord, who has strengthened
me, because he judged me faithful
and appointed me to his service,
13 even though I was formerly a
blasphemer, a persecutor, and a
man of violence. But I received
mercy because I had acted igno-
rantly in unbelief, 14 and the grace
of our Lord overflowed for me with
the faith and love that are in Christ
Jesus. 15 The saying is sure and
worthy of full acceptance, that
Christ Jesus came into the world to
save sinners—of whom I am the
foremost. 16 But for that very reason
I received mercy, so that in me, as
the foremost, Jesus Christ might
display the utmost patience, making me an example to those who
would come to believe in him for
eternal life. 17 To the King of the
ages, immortal, invisible, the only
God, be honor and glory forever
and ever.[b] Amen.

18 I am giving you these instructions, Timothy, my child, in accordance with the prophecies made
earlier about you, so that by following them you may fight the good
fight, 19 having faith and a good
conscience. By rejecting conscience, certain persons have suffered shipwreck in the faith;
20 among them are Hymenaeus and
Alexander, whom I have turned
over to Satan, so that they may
learn not to blaspheme.

Instructions concerning Prayer

2 First of all, then, I urge that
supplications, prayers, inter-
cessions, and thanksgivings be
made for everyone, 2 for kings and
all who are in high positions, so
that we may lead a quiet and
peaceable life in all godliness and
dignity. 3 This is right and is acceptable in the sight of God our Savior,
4 who desires everyone to be saved
and to come to the knowledge of
the truth. 5 For

there is one God;
there is also one mediator
between God and
humankind,
Christ Jesus, himself human,
6 who gave himself a ransom
for all

—this was attested at the right
time. 7 For this I was appointed a
herald and an apostle (I am telling
the truth,[c] I am not lying), a teacher of the Gentiles in faith and truth.

8 I desire, then, that in every
place the men should pray, lifting
up holy hands without anger or argument; 9 also that the women
should dress themselves modestly
and decently in suitable clothing,
not with their hair braided, or with
gold, pearls, or expensive clothes,
10 but with good works, as is proper
for women who profess reverence
for God. 11 Let a woman[d] learn in
silence with full submission. 12 I
permit no woman[d] to teach or to
have authority over a man;[e] she is
to keep silent. 13 For Adam was
formed first, then Eve; 14 and Adam
was not deceived, but the woman
was deceived and became a transgressor. 15 Yet she will be saved
through childbearing, provided
they continue in faith and love and
holiness, with modesty.

Qualifications of Bishops

3 The saying is sure:[f] whoever
aspires to the office of bishop[g] desires a noble task. 2 Now a
bishop[h] must be above reproach,
married only once,[i] temperate,
sensible, respectable, hospitable,
an apt teacher, 3 not a drunkard,
not violent but gentle, not quarrelsome, and not a lover of money.
4 He must manage his own house-

1.10 2 Tim 4.3; Titus 1.9
1.11 Gal 2.7
1.12 2 Cor 12.9; Col 1.25
1.13 Acts 8.3
1.14 Rom 5.20; 2 Tim 1.13
1.15 2 Tim 2.11; Titus 3.8
1.16 v. 13; Eph 2.7
1.17 Col 1.15; Rom 11.36
1.18 1 Tim 4.14; 2 Tim 2.2, 3
1.19 1 Tim 6.12, 21
1.20 2 Tim 2.17; 4.14
2.2 Ezra 6.10; Rom 13.1
2.3 Rom 12.2; 1 Tim 4.10
2.4 Jn 3.16; 2 Tim 2.25
2.5 Gal 3.20; Heb 9.15
2.6 Mk 10.45; 1 Cor 1.6; Gal 4.4
2.7 Eph 3.7,8; Gal 1.16
2.8 Ps 134.2
2.9 1 Pet 3.3
2.11 1 Cor 14.34
2.13 Gen 1.27; 1 Cor 11.8
2.14 Gen 3.6; 2 Cor 11.3
2.15 1 Tim 1.14
3.1 1 Tim 1.15; Acts 20.28
3.2 Titus 1.6-8; 2 Tim 2.24
3.3 2 Tim 2.24; 1 Pet 5.2
3.4 Titus 1.6

[b] Gk *to the ages of the ages* [c] Other ancient authorities add *in Christ* [d] Or *wife* [e] Or *her husband* [f] Some interpreters place these words at the end of the previous paragraph. Other ancient authorities read *The saying is commonly accepted* [g] Or *overseer* [h] Or *an overseer* [i] Gk *the husband of one wife*

hold well, keeping his children
submissive and respectful in every
way— 5 for if someone does not
know how to manage his own
household, how can he take care of
God's church? 6 He must not be a
recent convert, or he may be puffed
up with conceit and fall into the
condemnation of the devil. 7 Moreover, he must be well thought of by
outsiders, so that he may not fall
into disgrace and the snare of the
devil.

Qualifications of Deacons

8 Deacons likewise must be serious, not double-tongued, not indulging in much wine, not greedy
for money; 9 they must hold fast to
the mystery of the faith with a clear
conscience. 10 And let them first be
tested; then, if they prove themselves blameless, let them serve as
deacons. 11 Women[j] likewise must
be serious, not slanderers, but temperate, faithful in all things. 12 Let
deacons be married only once,[k]
and let them manage their children
and their households well; 13 for
those who serve well as deacons
gain a good standing for themselves and great boldness in the
faith that is in Christ Jesus.

The Mystery of Our Religion

14 I hope to come to you soon,
but I am writing these instructions
to you so that, 15 if I am delayed,
you may know how one ought to
behave in the household of God,
which is the church of the living
God, the pillar and bulwark of the
truth. 16 Without any doubt, the
mystery of our religion is great:

He[l] was revealed in flesh,
  vindicated[m] in spirit,[n]
    seen by angels,
proclaimed among Gentiles,
  believed in throughout the
    world,
  taken up in glory.

False Asceticism

4 Now the Spirit expressly says
that in later[o] times some will
renounce the faith by paying attention to deceitful spirits and teachings of demons, 2 through the hypocrisy of liars whose consciences
are seared with a hot iron. 3 They
forbid marriage and demand abstinence from foods, which God created to be received with thanksgiving by those who believe and know
the truth. 4 For everything created
by God is good, and nothing is to be
rejected, provided it is received
with thanksgiving; 5 for it is sanctified by God's word and by prayer.

A Good Minister of Jesus Christ

6 If you put these instructions
before the brothers and sisters,[p]
you will be a good servant[q] of
Christ Jesus, nourished on the
words of the faith and of the sound
teaching that you have followed.
7 Have nothing to do with profane
myths and old wives' tales. Train
yourself in godliness, 8 for, while
physical training is of some value,
godliness is valuable in every way,
holding promise for both the
present life and the life to come.
9 The saying is sure and worthy of
full acceptance. 10 For to this end
we toil and struggle,[r] because we
have our hope set on the living
God, who is the Savior of all people, especially of those who believe.

11 These are the things you
must insist on and teach. 12 Let no
one despise your youth, but set the
believers an example in speech and
conduct, in love, in faith, in purity.
13 Until I arrive, give attention to
the public reading of scripture,[s] to
exhorting, to teaching. 14 Do not
neglect the gift that is in you,
which was given to you through
prophecy with the laying on of
hands by the council of elders.[t]
15 Put these things into practice,
devote yourself to them, so that all
may see your progress. 16 Pay close
attention to yourself and to your

3.5 v. 15
3.6 1 Tim 6.4
3.7 1 Cor 5.12; 2 Tim 2.26
3.8 Acts 6.3; Titus 2.3
3.9 1 Tim 1.19
3.11 2 Tim 3.3; Titus 2.3
3.13 Mt 25.21
3.15 Eph 2.21; v. 5; 1 Tim 4.10; Gal 2.9
3.16 Jn 1.14; 1 Pet 3.18; Acts 1.9
4.1 Jn 16.13; 2 Thes 2.3; 2 Tim 3.1; 3.13; Rev 9.20
4.2 Eph 4.19
4.3 1 Cor 7.28; Heb 13.4; Gen 1.29; Rom 14.6
4.4 Rom 14.14
4.6 2 Cor 11.23; 1 Tim 1.10; 2 Tim 3.10
4.7 2 Tim 2.16; Heb 5.14
4.8 1 Tim 6.6; Ps 37.4; Rom 8.28
4.10 1 Cor 4.11; 1 Tim 2.4
4.11 1 Tim 5.7; 6.2
4.12 Titus 2.7; 1 Pet 5.3; 1 Tim 1.14
4.14 2 Tim 1.6; 1 Tim 1.18; 5.22; Acts 6.6
4.16 Acts 20.28; Ezek 33.9

[j] Or *Their wives,* or *Women deacons*
[k] Gk *be husbands of one wife*
[l] Gk *Who;* other ancient authorities read *God;* others, *Which*
[m] Or *justified*
[n] Or *by the Spirit*
[o] Or *the last*
[p] Gk *brothers*
[q] Or *deacon*
[r] Other ancient authorities read *suffer reproach*
[s] Gk *to the reading*
[t] Gk *by the presbytery*

teaching; continue in these things,
for in doing this you will save both
yourself and your hearers.

Duties toward Believers

5 Do not speak harshly to an
older man,[u] but speak to him
as to a father, to younger men as
brothers, 2 to older women as
mothers, to younger women as
sisters—with absolute purity.
3 Honor widows who are really
widows. 4 If a widow has children or
grandchildren, they should first
learn their religious duty to their
own family and make some repayment to their parents; for this is
pleasing in God's sight. 5 The real
widow, left alone, has set her hope
on God and continues in supplications and prayers night and day;
6 but the widow[v] who lives for pleasure is dead even while she lives.
7 Give these commands as well, so
that they may be above reproach.
8 And whoever does not provide for
relatives, and especially for family
members, has denied the faith and
is worse than an unbeliever.
9 Let a widow be put on the list
if she is not less than sixty years old
and has been married only once;[w]
10 she must be well attested for her
good works, as one who has
brought up children, shown hospitality, washed the saints' feet,
helped the afflicted, and devoted
herself to doing good in every way.
11 But refuse to put younger widows
on the list; for when their sensual
desires alienate them from Christ,
they want to marry, 12 and so they
incur condemnation for having violated their first pledge. 13 Besides
that, they learn to be idle, gadding
about from house to house; and
they are not merely idle, but also
gossips and busybodies, saying
what they should not say. 14 So I
would have younger widows marry,
bear children, and manage their
households, so as to give the adversary no occasion to revile us. 15 For
some have already turned away to
follow Satan. 16 If any believing
woman[x] has relatives who are really widows, let her assist them; let
the church not be burdened, so
that it can assist those who are real
widows.
17 Let the elders who rule well
be considered worthy of double
honor,[y] especially those who labor
in preaching and teaching; 18 for
the scripture says, "You shall not
muzzle an ox while it is treading
out the grain," and, "The laborer
deserves to be paid." 19 Never accept any accusation against an elder except on the evidence of two
or three witnesses. 20 As for those
who persist in sin, rebuke them in
the presence of all, so that the rest
also may stand in fear. 21 In the
presence of God and of Christ
Jesus and of the elect angels, I
warn you to keep these instructions without prejudice, doing
nothing on the basis of partiality.
22 Do not ordain[z] anyone hastily,
and do not participate in the sins of
others; keep yourself pure.
23 No longer drink only water,
but take a little wine for the sake of
your stomach and your frequent
ailments.
24 The sins of some people are
conspicuous and precede them to
judgment, while the sins of others
follow them there. 25 So also good
works are conspicuous; and even
when they are not, they cannot remain hidden.

6 Let all who are under the yoke
of slavery regard their masters
as worthy of all honor, so that the
name of God and the teaching may
not be blasphemed. 2 Those who
have believing masters must not be
disrespectful to them on the
ground that they are members of
the church;[a] rather they must
serve them all the more, since
those who benefit by their service
are believers and beloved.[b]

5.1 Lev 19.32 **5.3** vv. 5,16 **5.4** Eph 6.1,2 **5.5** vv. 3,16; 1 Cor 7.32; Lk 2.37 **5.6** Jas 5.5 **5.7** 1 Tim 4.11 **5.8** Gal 6.10; Titus 1.16 **5.10** Acts 16.15; Heb 13.2; Lk 7.44; v. 16 **5.13** 2 Thes 3.11; Titus 1.11 **5.14** 1 Cor 7.9; Titus 2.5 **5.16** vv. 3,5 **5.17** Phil 2.29; Rom 12.8; Acts 28.10 **5.18** 1 Cor 9.9; Lev 19.13; Deut 24.14, 15; Mt 10.10 **5.19** Deut 19.15 **5.20** Titus 1.13; Deut 13.11 **5.21** 1 Tim 6.13; 2 Tim 2.14 **5.22** Acts 6.6; 2 Tim 1.6; Eph 5.11 **5.23** 1 Tim 3.8 **6.1** Titus 2.9; 1 Pet 2.18; Titus 2.5,8 **6.2** Gal 3.28; Philem 16; 1 Tim 4.11

[u] Or *an elder*, or *a presbyter* [v] Gk *she* [w] Gk *the wife of one husband* [x] Other ancient authorities read *believing man or woman*; others, *believing man* [y] Or *compensation* [z] Gk *Do not lay hands on* [a] Gk *are brothers* [b] Or *since they are believers and beloved, who devote themselves to good deeds*

False Teaching and True Riches

Teach and urge these duties.
3 Whoever teaches otherwise and
does not agree with the sound
words of our Lord Jesus Christ and
the teaching that is in accordance
with godliness, 4 is conceited, understanding nothing, and has a
morbid craving for controversy and
for disputes about words. From
these come envy, dissension, slander, base suspicions, 5 and wrangling among those who are depraved in mind and bereft of the
truth, imagining that godliness is a
means of gain.[c] 6 Of course, there
is great gain in godliness combined
with contentment; 7 for we brought
nothing into the world, so that[d] we
can take nothing out of it; 8 but if
we have food and clothing, we will
be content with these. 9 But those
who want to be rich fall into temptation and are trapped by many
senseless and harmful desires that
plunge people into ruin and destruction. 10 For the love of money
is a root of all kinds of evil, and in
their eagerness to be rich some
have wandered away from the faith
and pierced themselves with many
pains.

The Good Fight of Faith

11 But as for you, man of God,
shun all this; pursue righteousness, godliness, faith, love, endurance, gentleness. 12 Fight the good
fight of the faith; take hold of the
eternal life, to which you were
called and for which you made[e]
the good confession in the presence of many witnesses. 13 In the
presence of God, who gives life to
all things, and of Christ Jesus, who
in his testimony before Pontius Pilate made the good confession, I
charge you 14 to keep the commandment without spot or blame
until the manifestation of our Lord
Jesus Christ, 15 which he will bring
about at the right time—he who is
the blessed and only Sovereign, the
King of kings and Lord of lords. 16 It
is he alone who has immortality
and dwells in unapproachable
light, whom no one has ever seen or
can see; to him be honor and eternal dominion. Amen.

17 As for those who in the
present age are rich, command
them not to be haughty, or to set
their hopes on the uncertainty of
riches, but rather on God who richly provides us with everything for
our enjoyment. 18 They are to do
good, to be rich in good works, generous, and ready to share, 19 thus
storing up for themselves the treasure of a good foundation for the
future, so that they may take hold
of the life that really is life.

Personal Instructions and Benediction

20 Timothy, guard what has
been entrusted to you. Avoid the
profane chatter and contradictions
of what is falsely called knowledge;
21 by professing it some have
missed the mark as regards the
faith.

Grace be with you.[f]

6.3 2 Tim 1.13; Titus 1.1
6.4 1 Cor 8.2; 2 Tim 2.14
6.5 1 Cor 11.16; Titus 1.11; 2 Pet 2.3
6.6 Phil 4.11; Heb 13.5
6.7 Job 1.21
6.8 Heb 13.5
6.9 1 Tim 3.7; 1.19
6.10 1 Tim 3.3; Jas 5.19
6.12 1 Cor 9.25, 26; 1 Tim 1.18; Heb 13.23
6.13 1 Tim 5.21; Jn 18.37
6.14 Phil 1.6; 2 Thes 2.8
6.15 1 Tim 1.11, 17; Rev 17.14; 19.16
6.16 1 Tim 1.17; Jn 1.18; Eph 3.21
6.17 Lk 12.20,21; 1 Tim 4.10; Acts 14.17
6.18 1 Tim 5.10; Rom 12.8, 13
6.20 2 Tim 1.14; 2.16

[c] Other ancient authorities add *Withdraw yourself from such people* [d] Other ancient authorities read *world—it is certain that* [e] Gk *confessed* [f] The Greek word for *you* here is plural; in other ancient authorities it is singular. Other ancient authorities add *Amen*

THE SECOND LETTER OF PAUL TO

Timothy

Title and Background

After Paul's release from prison in Rome in A.D. 62-63 and after his (assumed) fourth missionary journey, during which he wrote 1 Timothy and Titus, he was again imprisoned in Rome under Emperor Nero about 66-67. He was languishing in a cold dungeon, chained like a common criminal. Paul knew that his work was done and that his life was nearly at an end.

Author and Date of Writing

The first verse states that the author is Paul, and numerous references in the letter confirm this, though like 1 Timothy, Paul's authorship is disputed. It was probably written about A.D. 66.

Theme and Message

Paul had three reasons for writing to Timothy at this time: (1) Paul was lonely because many of his friends had deserted him. He wanted very much for Timothy to join him. (2) He was concerned about the welfare of the churches during this time of persecution under Nero, and he admonished Timothy to guard the gospel and, if necessary, to suffer for it. (3) He wanted to write to the Ephesian church through Timothy.

Outline

I. Paul's Concern for Timothy (1.1-14)
II. Paul's Situation (1.15-18)
III. Instructions to Timothy (2.1-26)
IV. Warning About the Last Days (3.1-17)
V. Paul's Charge, Requests, and Greetings (4.1-22)

Salutation

1 Paul, an apostle of Christ
Jesus by the will of God, for
the sake of the promise of life that
is in Christ Jesus,
2 To Timothy, my beloved child:
Grace, mercy, and peace from
God the Father and Christ Jesus
our Lord.

Thanksgiving and Encouragement

3 I am grateful to God—whom I
worship with a clear conscience, as
my ancestors did—when I remember you constantly in my prayers
night and day. 4 Recalling your
tears, I long to see you so that I may
be filled with joy. 5 I am reminded
of your sincere faith, a faith that
lived first in your grandmother Lois
and your mother Eunice and now,
I am sure, lives in you. 6 For this
reason I remind you to rekindle the
gift of God that is within you
through the laying on of my hands;
7 for God did not give us a spirit of
cowardice, but rather a spirit of
power and of love and of self-
discipline.
8 Do not be ashamed, then, of
the testimony about our Lord or of
me his prisoner, but join with me in
suffering for the gospel, relying on
the power of God, 9 who saved us
and called us with a holy calling,
not according to our works but according to his own purpose and
grace. This grace was given to us in
Christ Jesus before the ages began,
10 but it has now been revealed

1.1 2 Cor 1.1; Eph 3.6; Titus 1.2 **1.2** 1 Tim 1.2 **1.3** Rom 1.8,9; 1 Thes 1.2, 21; Acts 20.37 **1.4** 2 Tim 4.9 **1.5** 1 Tim 1.5; Acts 16.1 **1.6** 1 Tim 4.14 **1.7** Rom 8.15; Jn 14.27 **1.8** Rom 1.16; Eph 3.1; 2 Tim 2.3, 9; 4.5 **1.9** Heb 3.1; Rom 16.25 **1.10** Eph 1.9; 1 Cor 15.54

through the appearing of our Savior
Christ Jesus, who abolished death
and brought life and immortality to
light through the gospel. 11 For this
gospel I was appointed a herald
and an apostle and a teacher,[a]
12 and for this reason I suffer as I do.
But I am not ashamed, for I know
the one in whom I have put my
trust, and I am sure that he is able
to guard until that day what I have
entrusted to him.[b] 13 Hold to the
standard of sound teaching that
you have heard from me, in the
faith and love that are in Christ
Jesus. 14 Guard the good treasure
entrusted to you, with the help of
the Holy Spirit living in us.
15 You are aware that all who
are in Asia have turned away from
me, including Phygelus and Her-
mogenes. 16 May the Lord grant
mercy to the household of Onesiphorus, because he often refreshed me and was not ashamed
of my chain; 17 when he arrived in
Rome, he eagerly[c] searched for me
and found me 18 —may the Lord
grant that he will find mercy from
the Lord on that day! And you know
very well how much service he rendered in Ephesus.

A Good Soldier of Christ Jesus

2 You then, my child, be strong
in the grace that is in Christ
Jesus; 2 and what you have heard
from me through many witnesses
entrust to faithful people who will
be able to teach others as well.
3 Share in suffering like a good soldier of Christ Jesus. 4 No one serving in the army gets entangled in
everyday affairs; the soldier's aim is
to please the enlisting officer. 5 And
in the case of an athlete, no one is
crowned without competing according to the rules. 6 It is the farmer who does the work who ought to
have the first share of the crops.
7 Think over what I say, for the Lord
will give you understanding in all
things.
8 Remember Jesus Christ,
raised from the dead, a descendant
of David—that is my gospel, 9 for
which I suffer hardship, even to the
point of being chained like a criminal. But the word of God is not
chained. 10 Therefore I endure everything for the sake of the elect, so
that they may also obtain the salvation that is in Christ Jesus, with
eternal glory. 11 The saying is sure:

If we have died with him, we
will also live with him;
12 if we endure, we will also
reign with him;
if we deny him, he will also
deny us;
13 if we are faithless, he
remains faithful—
for he cannot deny himself.

A Worker Approved by God

14 Remind them of this, and
warn them before God[d] that they
are to avoid wrangling over words,
which does no good but only ruins
those who are listening. 15 Do your
best to present yourself to God as
one approved by him, a worker who
has no need to be ashamed, rightly
explaining the word of truth.
16 Avoid profane chatter, for it will
lead people into more and more
impiety, 17 and their talk will
spread like gangrene. Among them
are Hymenaeus and Philetus,
18 who have swerved from the truth
by claiming that the resurrection
has already taken place. They are
upsetting the faith of some. 19 But
God's firm foundation stands,
bearing this inscription: "The Lord
knows those who are his," and,
"Let everyone who calls on the
name of the Lord turn away from
wickedness."
20 In a large house there are
utensils not only of gold and silver
but also of wood and clay, some for
special use, some for ordinary.
21 All who cleanse themselves of
the things I have mentioned[e] will
become special utensils, dedicated
and useful to the owner of the
house, ready for every good work.
22 Shun youthful passions and pur-

1.11 1 Tim 2.7
1.12 Titus 3.8; 1 Tim 6.20
1.13 Titus 1.9; Rom 2.20; 1 Tim 1.14
1.14 Rom 8.9,11
1.15 Acts 19.10; 2 Tim 4.10, 11,16
1.16 2 Tim 4.19
1.18 2 Thes 1.10; Heb 6.10
2.1 2 Tim 1.2; Eph 6.10
2.2 2 Tim 1.13; 1 Tim 6.12; 1.18; 1.12
2.3 1 Tim 1.18
2.4 2 Pet 2.20
2.5 1 Cor 9.25
2.8 Acts 2.24; Mt 1.1; Rom 2.16
2.9 Acts 9.16; Phil 1.7; Acts 28.31
2.10 Eph 3.13; 2 Cor 1.6
2.12 1 Pet 4.13; Mt 10.33
2.13 Rom 3.3; Num 23.19
2.14 1 Tim 5.21; 6.4
2.15 Jas 1.12
2.16 1 Tim 4.7
2.17 1 Tim 1.20
2.18 1 Cor 15.12
2.19 Isa 28.16, 17; 1 Tim 3.15; Jn 10.14; 1 Cor 1.2
2.20 Rom 9.21
2.21 Isa 52.11; 2 Tim 3.17
2.22 1 Tim 6.11; 1.14; 1.5

[a] Other ancient authorities add *of the Gentiles*
[b] Or *what has been entrusted to me*
[c] Or *promptly*
[d] Other ancient authorities read *the Lord*
[e] Gk *of these things*

sue righteousness, faith, love, and
peace, along with those who call on
the Lord from a pure heart. 23 Have
nothing to do with stupid and
senseless controversies; you know
that they breed quarrels. 24 And the
Lord's servant[f] must not be quarrelsome but kindly to everyone, an
apt teacher, patient, 25 correcting
opponents with gentleness. God
may perhaps grant that they will repent and come to know the truth,
26 and that they may escape from
the snare of the devil, having been
held captive by him to do his will.[g]

Godlessness in the Last Days

3 You must understand this,
that in the last days distressing times will come. 2 For people
will be lovers of themselves, lovers
of money, boasters, arrogant, abusive, disobedient to their parents,
ungrateful, unholy, 3 inhuman, im-
placable, slanderers, profligates,
brutes, haters of good, 4 treacherous, reckless, swollen with conceit,
lovers of pleasure rather than lovers of God, 5 holding to the outward
form of godliness but denying its
power. Avoid them! 6 For among
them are those who make their way
into households and captivate silly
women, overwhelmed by their sins
and swayed by all kinds of desires,
7 who are always being instructed
and can never arrive at a knowledge
of the truth. 8 As Jannes and Jambres opposed Moses, so these people, of corrupt mind and counterfeit faith, also oppose the truth.
9 But they will not make much
progress, because, as in the case of
those two men,[h] their folly will become plain to everyone.

Paul's Charge to Timothy

10 Now you have observed my
teaching, my conduct, my aim in
life, my faith, my patience, my love,
my steadfastness, 11 my persecutions and suffering the things that
happened to me in Antioch, Iconium, and Lystra. What persecutions
I endured! Yet the Lord rescued me
from all of them. 12 Indeed, all who
want to live a godly life in Christ
Jesus will be persecuted. 13 But
wicked people and impostors will
go from bad to worse, deceiving
others and being deceived. 14 But
as for you, continue in what you
have learned and firmly believed,
knowing from whom you learned it,
15 and how from childhood you
have known the sacred writings
that are able to instruct you for salvation through faith in Christ
Jesus. 16 All scripture is inspired by
God and is[i] useful for teaching, for
reproof, for correction, and for
training in righteousness, 17 so that
everyone who belongs to God may
be proficient, equipped for every
good work.

4 In the presence of God and of
Christ Jesus, who is to judge
the living and the dead, and in view
of his appearing and his kingdom,
I solemnly urge you: 2 proclaim the
message; be persistent whether the
time is favorable or unfavorable;
convince, rebuke, and encourage,
with the utmost patience in teaching. 3 For the time is coming when
people will not put up with sound
doctrine, but having itching ears,
they will accumulate for themselves teachers to suit their own
desires, 4 and will turn away from
listening to the truth and wander
away to myths. 5 As for you, always
be sober, endure suffering, do the
work of an evangelist, carry out
your ministry fully.

6 As for me, I am already being
poured out as a libation, and the
time of my departure has come. 7 I
have fought the good fight, I have
finished the race, I have kept the
faith. 8 From now on there is reserved for me the crown of righteousness, which the Lord, the
righteous judge, will give me on
that day, and not only to me but
also to all who have longed for his
appearing.

2.23 1 Tim 6.4; Titus 3.9
2.24 1 Tim 3.3; Titus 1.7; 1 Tim 3.2
2.25 Gal 6.1; 1 Pet 3.15
2.26 1 Tim 3.7
3.1 1 Tim 4.1
3.2 2 Pet 2.3; Rom 1.30
3.3 Rom 1.31; Titus 1.8
3.4 2 Pet 2.10; Phil 3.19
3.5 2 Thes 3.6
3.6 Titus 1.11
3.7 2 Tim 2.25
3.8 Ex 7.11; Acts 13.8; 1 Tim 6.5
3.9 Ex 7.12
3.10 1 Tim 4.6; Phil 2.22
3.11 Acts 13.45; 14.2,19
3.12 Ps 34.19; Mt 16.24; 1 Thes 3.3
3.13 2 Tim 2.16; Titus 3.3
3.14 2 Tim 1.13
3.15 2 Tim 1.5; Jn 5.39
3.16 Rom 15.4; 2 Pet 1.20, 21
3.17 1 Tim 6.11; 2 Tim 2.21
4.1 1 Tim 5.21; Acts 10.42
4.2 1 Tim 5.20; Titus 1.13; 1 Tim 4.13
4.3 2 Tim 3.1, 6; 1 Tim 1.10
4.5 Acts 21.8
4.6 Phil 2.17; 1.23
4.7 Phil 3.14; 1 Tim 6.12 **4.8** Jas 1.12; 1 Pet 5.4; 2 Tim 1.12

[f] Gk *slave* [g] Or *by him, to do his* (that is, God's) *will* [h] Gk lacks *two men*
[i] Or *Every scripture inspired by God is also*

Personal Instructions

9 Do your best to come to me
soon, 10 for Demas, in love with this
present world, has deserted me and
gone to Thessalonica; Crescens has
gone to Galatia,[j] Titus to Dalmatia. 11 Only Luke is with me. Get
Mark and bring him with you, for
he is useful in my ministry. 12 I have
sent Tychicus to Ephesus. 13 When
you come, bring the cloak that I left
with Carpus at Troas, also the
books, and above all the parch-
ments. 14 Alexander the copper-
smith did me great harm; the Lord
will pay him back for his deeds.
15 You also must beware of him, for
he strongly opposed our message.
16 At my first defense no one
came to my support, but all deserted me. May it not be counted
against them! 17 But the Lord stood
by me and gave me strength, so
that through me the message
might be fully proclaimed and all
the Gentiles might hear it. So I was
rescued from the lion's mouth.
18 The Lord will rescue me from every evil attack and save me for his
heavenly kingdom. To him be the
glory forever and ever. Amen.

Final Greetings and Benediction

19 Greet Prisca and Aquila, and
the household of Onesiphorus.
20 Erastus remained in Corinth;
Trophimus I left ill in Miletus.
21 Do your best to come before winter. Eubulus sends greetings to
you, as do Pudens and Linus and
Claudia and all the brothers and
sisters.[k]
22 The Lord be with your spirit.
Grace be with you.[l]

4.10 Col 4.14; 1 Jn 2.15
4.11 2 Tim 1.15; Col 4.14; Acts 12.12
4.14 Acts 19.33; Rom 12.19; Ps 119.98, 99
4.16 Acts 7.60
4.17 Acts 23.11; 2 Pet 2.9
4.18 Ps 121.7; Rom 11.36
4.19 Acts 18.2
4.20 Acts 19.22
4.21 v. 9
4.22 Gal 6.18; Philem 25

[j] Other ancient authorities read *Gaul*
[k] Gk *all the brothers* [l] The Greek word for *you* here is plural. Other ancient authorities add *Amen*

THE LETTER OF PAUL TO

Titus

Title and Background

When Paul left Antioch to discuss "his" gospel with the Jerusalem leaders, he took Titus with him (Gal 2.1-3). Presumably Titus, who is not referred to in Acts, worked with Paul at Ephesus during the third missionary journey. From there the apostle sent him to Corinth, to help that church with its work (2 Cor 7.6-7; 8.17). Following Paul's release from his first Roman imprisonment, he and Titus worked briefly in Crete (Titus 1.5), after which he commissioned Titus to remain there as his representative and to complete some needed work.

Author and Date of Writing

Paul probably wrote this letter to Titus from Corinth about A.D. 64. See also the Introduction to 1 Timothy.

Theme and Message

Paul wrote Titus to give him personal authorization and guidance in meeting opposition, instructions about faith and conduct, and warnings about false teachers. He also informed Titus of his future plans for him.

Outline

I. Concerning Elders (1.1-9)
II. Concerning False Teachers (1.10-16)
III. Concerning Various Groups (2.1-15)
IV. Concerning Believers in General (3.1-8)
V. Concerning Response to Spiritual Error (3.9-15)

Salutation

1 Paul, a servant[a] of God and an
apostle of Jesus Christ, for the
sake of the faith of God's elect and
the knowledge of the truth that is
in accordance with godliness, 2 in
the hope of eternal life that God,
who never lies, promised before
the ages began — 3 in due time he
revealed his word through the proclamation with which I have been
entrusted by the command of God
our Savior,
4 To Titus, my loyal child in the
faith we share:
Grace[b] and peace from God the
Father and Christ Jesus our Savior.

Titus in Crete

5 I left you behind in Crete for
this reason, so that you should put
in order what remained to be done,
and should appoint elders in every
town, as I directed you: 6 someone
who is blameless, married only
once,[c] whose children are believers, not accused of debauchery and
not rebellious. 7 For a bishop,[d] as
God's steward, must be blameless;
he must not be arrogant or quick-
tempered or addicted to wine or violent or greedy for gain; 8 but he
must be hospitable, a lover of
goodness, prudent, upright, devout, and self-controlled. 9 He must
have a firm grasp of the word that
is trustworthy in accordance with
the teaching, so that he may be
able both to preach with sound
doctrine and to refute those who
contradict it.
10 There are also many rebel-

1.1 Rom 1.1; 2 Cor 1.1; 1 Tim 2.4; 6.3
1.2 2 Tim 1.1; Rom 16.25
1.3 2 Tim 1.10; 1 Thes 2.4
1.4 2 Cor 2.13; Eph 1.2; 1 Tim 1.2
1.5 Acts 27.7; 14.23; 11.30
1.6 1 Tim 3.2-4
1.7 1 Cor 4.1; Eph 5.18
1.8 1 Tim 3.2; 2 Tim 3.3
1.9 1 Tim 1.19; 1.10
1.10 1 Tim 1.6; Acts 11.2

[a] Gk *slave* [b] Other ancient authorities read *Grace, mercy,* [c] Gk *husband of one wife* [d] Or *an overseer*

lious people, idle talkers and deceivers, especially those of the circumcision; 11 they must be
silenced, since they are upsetting
whole families by teaching for sordid gain what it is not right to
teach. 12 It was one of them, their
very own prophet, who said,

"Cretans are always liars,
vicious brutes, lazy
gluttons."

13 That testimony is true. For this
reason rebuke them sharply, so
that they may become sound in the
faith, 14 not paying attention to
Jewish myths or to commandments of those who reject the
truth. 15 To the pure all things are
pure, but to the corrupt and unbelieving nothing is pure. Their very
minds and consciences are corrupted. 16 They profess to know
God, but they deny him by their actions. They are detestable, disobedient, unfit for any good work.

Teach Sound Doctrine

2 But as for you, teach what is
consistent with sound doctrine. 2 Tell the older men to be
temperate, serious, prudent, and
sound in faith, in love, and in endurance.

3 Likewise, tell the older wom-
en to be reverent in behavior, not to
be slanderers or slaves to drink;
they are to teach what is good, 4 so
that they may encourage the young
women to love their husbands, to
love their children, 5 to be self-
controlled, chaste, good managers
of the household, kind, being submissive to their husbands, so that
the word of God may not be dis-
credited.

6 Likewise, urge the younger
men to be self-controlled. 7 Show
yourself in all respects a model of
good works, and in your teaching
show integrity, gravity, 8 and sound
speech that cannot be censured;
then any opponent will be put to
shame, having nothing evil to say
of us.

9 Tell slaves to be submissive to
their masters and to give satisfaction in every respect; they are not
to talk back, 10 not to pilfer, but to
show complete and perfect fidelity,
so that in everything they may be
an ornament to the doctrine of God
our Savior.

11 For the grace of God has appeared, bringing salvation to all,[e]
12 training us to renounce impiety
and worldly passions, and in the
present age to live lives that are
self-controlled, upright, and godly,
13 while we wait for the blessed
hope and the manifestation of the
glory of our great God and Savior,[f]
Jesus Christ. 14 He it is who gave
himself for us that he might redeem us from all iniquity and purify for himself a people of his own
who are zealous for good deeds.

15 Declare these things; exhort
and reprove with all authority.[g]
Let no one look down on you.

Maintain Good Deeds

3 Remind them to be subject to
rulers and authorities, to be
obedient, to be ready for every good
work, 2 to speak evil of no one, to
avoid quarreling, to be gentle, and
to show every courtesy to everyone.
3 For we ourselves were once foolish, disobedient, led astray, slaves
to various passions and pleasures,
passing our days in malice and
envy, despicable, hating one another. 4 But when the goodness and
loving kindness of God our Savior
appeared, 5 he saved us, not because of any works of righteousness that we had done, but according to his mercy, through the
water[h] of rebirth and renewal by
the Holy Spirit. 6 This Spirit he
poured out on us richly through
Jesus Christ our Savior, 7 so that,
having been justified by his grace,
we might become heirs according
to the hope of eternal life. 8 The
saying is sure.

I desire that you insist on these
things, so that those who have
come to believe in God may be
careful to devote themselves to

1.11 2 Tim 3.6; 1 Tim 6.5
1.12 Acts 17.28
1.13 2 Cor 13.10; Titus 2.2
1.14 1 Tim 1.4; Isa 29.13
1.15 Lk 11.39,41; Rom 14.23
1.16 1 Jn 2.4; 2 Tim 3.5, 8
2.1 Titus 1.9
2.2 Titus 1.13
2.3 1 Tim 3.8
2.5 1 Cor 14.34; Eph 5.22; 1 Tim 6.1
2.7 1 Tim 4.12
2.8 1 Tim 6.3
2.9 Eph 6.5
2.10 Mt 5.16
2.11 Rom 5.15; 1 Tim 2.4
2.12 Titus 3.3; 2 Tim 3.12
2.13 2 Thes 2.8; 2 Pet 1.1
2.14 1 Tim 2.6; Heb 9.14; Ex 19.5; Eph 2.10
3.1 Rom 13.1; 2 Tim 2.21
3.2 Eph 4.31; 2 Tim 2.24, 25
3.3 1 Cor 6.11; 1 Pet 4.3
3.4 Titus 2.11; 1 Tim 2.3
3.5 Rom 3.20; Eph 5.26; Rom 12.2
3.6 Rom 5.5
3.7 Rom 3.24; 8.17,24
3.8 1 Tim 1.15; Titus 2.14

[e] Or *has appeared to all, bringing salvation*
[f] Or *of the great God and our Savior*
[g] Gk *commandment*
[h] Gk *washing*

good works; these things are excellent and profitable to everyone.
9 But avoid stupid controversies,
genealogies, dissensions, and
quarrels about the law, for they are
unprofitable and worthless. 10 After
a first and second admonition,
have nothing more to do with anyone who causes divisions, 11 since
you know that such a person is perverted and sinful, being self-
condemned.

Final Messages and Benediction

12 When I send Artemas to you,
or Tychicus, do your best to come
to me at Nicopolis, for I have decided to spend the winter there.
13 Make every effort to send Zenas
the lawyer and Apollos on their
way, and see that they lack nothing. 14 And let people learn to devote themselves to good works in
order to meet urgent needs, so that
they may not be unproductive.

15 All who are with me send
greetings to you. Greet those who
love us in the faith.

Grace be with all of you.[i]

3.9 1 Tim 1.4; 2 Tim 2.14
3.10 Rom 16.17
3.12 Acts 20.4; 2 Tim 4.9, 10
3.13 Acts 18.24
3.14 v. 8
3.15 Col 4.18

[i] Other ancient authorities add *Amen*

THE LETTER OF PAUL TO

Philemon

Title and Background

Philemon was a believer in Colosse who, along with other Christians, was a slave owner. One of his slaves, Onesimus, had apparently stolen from him and then run away, which under Roman law was punishable by death. But Onesimus met Paul and through his ministry became a Christian. Now he was willing to return to his master.

Author and Date of Writing

Paul wrote this short letter about A.D. 60 from prison in Rome and sent it to Colosse with Onesimus and Tychicus.

Theme and Message

Paul wrote this personal appeal to ask Philemon to welcome Onesimus as a Christian brother, not as a slave. Now that Onesimus (whose name means "useful") was a believer, he was really useful.

Outline

I. Greetings (1-3)
II. Thanksgiving and Prayer (4-7)
III. Paul's Plea for Onesimus (8-21)
IV. Conclusion (22-25)

Salutation

1 Paul, a prisoner of Christ
Jesus, and Timothy our brother,[a]
To Philemon our dear friend and
co-worker, 2 to Apphia our sister,[b]
to Archippus our fellow soldier,
and to the church in your house:
3 Grace to you and peace from
God our Father and the Lord Jesus
Christ.

Philemon's Love and Faith

4 When I remember you[c] in my
prayers, I always thank my God
5 because I hear of your love for all
the saints and your faith toward the
Lord Jesus. 6 I pray that the sharing
of your faith may become effective
when you perceive all the good that
we[d] may do for Christ. 7 I have indeed received much joy and encouragement from your love, because the hearts of the saints have
been refreshed through you, my
brother.

1 Eph 3.1; 2 Cor 1.1; Phil 2.25
2 Col 4.17; Phil 2.25; Rom 16.5
4 Rom 1.8,9
5 Eph 1.15; Col 1.4
7 v. 20; 2 Cor 7.13
10 Col 4.9; 1 Cor 4.14, 15
13 Phil 1.7
14 1 Pet 5.2; 2 Cor 9.7

Paul's Plea for Onesimus

8 For this reason, though I am
bold enough in Christ to command
you to do your duty, 9 yet I would
rather appeal to you on the basis of
love—and I, Paul, do this as an old
man, and now also as a prisoner of
Christ Jesus.[e] 10 I am appealing to
you for my child, Onesimus, whose
father I have become during my imprisonment. 11 Formerly he was
useless to you, but now he is indeed useful[f] both to you and to
me. 12 I am sending him, that is, my
own heart, back to you. 13 I wanted
to keep him with me, so that he
might be of service to me in your
place during my imprisonment for
the gospel; 14 but I preferred to do
nothing without your consent, in

[a] Gk *the brother* [b] Gk *the sister* [c] From verse 4 through verse 21, *you* is singular
[d] Other ancient authorities read *you* (plural)
[e] Or *as an ambassador of Christ Jesus, and now also his prisoner* [f] The name Onesimus means *useful* or (compare verse 20) *beneficial*

order that your good deed might be
voluntary and not something
forced. 15 Perhaps this is the reason
he was separated from you for a
while, so that you might have him
back forever, 16 no longer as a slave
but more than a slave, a beloved
brother—especially to me but how
much more to you, both in the
flesh and in the Lord.
17 So if you consider me your
partner, welcome him as you would
welcome me. 18 If he has wronged
you in any way, or owes you anything, charge that to my account.
19 I, Paul, am writing this with my
own hand: I will repay it. I say nothing about your owing me even your
own self. 20 Yes, brother, let me
have this benefit from you in the
Lord! Refresh my heart in Christ.
21 Confident of your obedience, I
am writing to you, knowing that
you will do even more than I say.
22 One thing more—prepare a
guest room for me, for I am hoping
through your prayers to be restored
to you.

Final Greetings and Benediction

23 Epaphras, my fellow prisoner
in Christ Jesus, sends greetings to
you,[g] 24 and so do Mark, Aristarchus, Demas, and Luke, my fellow
workers.
25 The grace of the Lord Jesus
Christ be with your spirit.[h]

16 Mt 23.8; 1 Tim 6.2; Col 3.22
17 2 Cor 8.23
21 2 Cor 2.3
22 Acts 28.23; Phil 1.25; 2.24; 2 Cor 1.11
23 Col 1.7
24 Acts 12.12; Col 4.10
25 2 Tim 4.22

[g] Here *you* is singular [h] Other ancient authorities add *Amen*

THE LETTER TO THE

Hebrews

Title and Background

The first-century church underwent much persecution, and this letter was written in that setting. The persecution had not yet resulted in martyrdom, but it was severe. The intended readers seem to have been Jewish Christians who were thinking of abandoning their faith and of lapsing back into Judaism. So the author exhorts them to hold fast to their confession of Christ as Savior and Lord.

Author and Date of Writing

The author of this letter does not identify himself, but he was obviously well known to the original recipients. For many years Paul was considered to be the author, but since the Reformation it has been widely recognized that Paul could not have been the author. Apollos and Barnabas are those most often suggested. The book was written prior to the fall of Jerusalem in A.D. 70.

Theme and Message

The theme of Hebrews is the absolute supremacy and sufficiency of Jesus Christ as revealer and as mediator of God's grace. The prologue presents Christ as God's full and final revelation. Hebrews could be called "the book of better things," since the two Greek words for "better" and "superior" occur fifteen times in the letter. Practical applications of this theme are given throughout the book.

Outline

I. Christ's Superior Revelation (1.1-4)
II. Christ's Superiority Over Angels (1.5–2.18)
III. Christ's Superiority Over Moses (3.1–4.13)
IV. Christ's Superiority Over Aaronic Priests (4.14–7.28)
V. Christ's Superior Sacrifice (8.1–10.39)
VI. Plea for Persevering Faith (11.1–12.29)
VII. Conclusion (13.1-25)

God Has Spoken by His Son

1 Long ago God spoke to our ancestors in many and various
ways by the prophets, 2 but in these
last days he has spoken to us by a
Son,[a] whom he appointed heir of
all things, through whom he also
created the worlds. 3 He is the reflection of God's glory and the exact imprint of God's very being,
and he sustains[b] all things by his
powerful word. When he had made
purification for sins, he sat down at
the right hand of the Majesty on
high, 4 having become as much superior to angels as the name he has
inherited is more excellent than
theirs.

1.2 Gal 4.4; Heb 2.3; Ps 2.8; Jn 1.3; 1 Cor 8.6 **1.3** Jn 1.14; Col 1.17; Heb 7.27; 8.1 **1.4** Eph 1.21; Phil 2.9,10 **1.5** Ps 2.7 **1.6** Heb 10.5; Deut 32.43 **1.7** Ps 104.4

The Son Is Superior to Angels

5 For to which of the angels did
God ever say,
"You are my Son;
today I have begotten
you"?
Or again,
"I will be his Father,
and he will be my Son"?
6 And again, when he brings the
firstborn into the world, he says,
"Let all God's angels worship
him."
7 Of the angels he says,
"He makes his angels winds,
and his servants flames of
fire."

[a] Or *the Son* [b] Or *bears along*

[8]But of the Son he says,
"Your throne, O God,[c] is
forever and ever,
and the righteous scepter is
the scepter of your[d]
kingdom.
[9] You have loved righteousness
and hated wickedness;
therefore God, your God, has
anointed you
with the oil of gladness
beyond your
companions."
[10]And,
"In the beginning, Lord, you
founded the earth,
and the heavens are the
work of your hands;
[11] they will perish, but you
remain;
they will all wear out like
clothing;
[12] like a cloak you will roll
them up,
and like clothing[e] they will
be changed.
But you are the same,
and your years will never
end."
[13]But to which of the angels has he
ever said,
"Sit at my right hand
until I make your enemies
a footstool for your
feet"?
[14]Are not all angels[f] spirits in the
divine service, sent to serve for the
sake of those who are to inherit salvation?

Warning to Pay Attention

2 Therefore we must pay greater
attention to what we have
heard, so that we do not drift away
from it. [2]For if the message declared through angels was valid,
and every transgression or disobedience received a just penalty,
[3]how can we escape if we neglect
so great a salvation? It was declared at first through the Lord,
and it was attested to us by those
who heard him, [4]while God added
his testimony by signs and wonders
and various miracles, and by gifts
of the Holy Spirit, distributed according to his will.

1.8 Ps 45.6,7
1.9 Phil 2.9; Isa 61.1,3
1.10 Ps 102.25
1.11 Isa 34.4
1.12 Heb 13.8
1.13 Ps 110.1; Heb 10.13
1.14 Ps 103.20; Heb 5.9
2.2 Heb 1.1; Acts 7.53; Heb 10.28, 35
2.3 Heb 10.29; 1.1; Lk 1.2
2.4 Jn 4.48; 1 Cor 12.4; Eph 1.5
2.5 Heb 6.5
2.6 Ps 8.4-6
2.8 Mt 28.18; 1 Cor 15.27; 15.25
2.9 Phil 2.7-9; Acts 2.33; Jn 3.16; 1 Jn 2.2
2.10 Lk 24.46; Rom 11.36; Acts 3.15; 5.31; Lk 13.32
2.11 Heb 10.10; Acts 17.26; Jn 20.17
2.12 Ps 22.22
2.13 Isa 8.17,18; Jn 10.29

Exaltation through Abasement

5 Now God[g] did not subject the
coming world, about which we are
speaking, to angels. [6]But someone
has testified somewhere,
"What are human beings that
you are mindful of
them,[h]
or mortals, that you care
for them?[i]
[7] You have made them for a
little while lower[j] than
the angels;
you have crowned them
with glory and honor,[k]
[8] subjecting all things under
their feet."
Now in subjecting all things to
them, God[g] left nothing outside
their control. As it is, we do not yet
see everything in subjection to
them, [9]but we do see Jesus, who
for a little while was made lower[l]
than the angels, now crowned with
glory and honor because of the suffering of death, so that by the grace
of God[m] he might taste death for
everyone.
10 It was fitting that God,[g] for
whom and through whom all things
exist, in bringing many children to
glory, should make the pioneer of
their salvation perfect through sufferings. [11]For the one who sanctifies and those who are sanctified
all have one Father.[n] For this reason Jesus[g] is not ashamed to call
them brothers and sisters,[o] [12]say-
ing,
"I will proclaim your name
to my brothers and
sisters,[o]
in the midst of the
congregation I will
praise you."
[13]And again,

[c] Or *God is your throne* [d] Other ancient authorities read *his* [e] Other ancient authorities lack *like clothing* [f] Gk *all of them* [g] Gk *he* [h] Gk *What is man that you are mindful of him?* [i] Gk *or the son of man that you care for him?* In the Hebrew of Psalm 8.4-6 both *man* and *son of man* refer to all humankind [j] Or *them only a little lower* [k] Other ancient authorities add *and set them over the works of your hands* [l] Or *who was made a little lower* [m] Other ancient authorities read *apart from God* [n] Gk *are all of one* [o] Gk *brothers*

"I will put my trust in him."
And again,
"Here am I and the children
whom God has given
me."
14 Since, therefore, the children share flesh and blood, he himself likewise shared the same
things, so that through death he
might destroy the one who has the
power of death, that is, the devil,
15 and free those who all their lives
were held in slavery by the fear of
death. 16 For it is clear that he did
not come to help angels, but the
descendants of Abraham. 17 Therefore he had to become like his
brothers and sisters[p] in every respect, so that he might be a merciful and faithful high priest in the
service of God, to make a sacrifice
of atonement for the sins of the
people. 18 Because he himself was
tested by what he suffered, he is
able to help those who are being
tested.

Moses a Servant, Christ a Son

3 Therefore, brothers and sisters,[p] holy partners in a heavenly calling, consider that Jesus,
the apostle and high priest of our
confession, 2 was faithful to the one
who appointed him, just as Moses
also "was faithful in all[q] God's[r]
house." 3 Yet Jesus[s] is worthy of
more glory than Moses, just as the
builder of a house has more honor
than the house itself. 4 (For every
house is built by someone, but the
builder of all things is God.) 5 Now
Moses was faithful in all God's[r]
house as a servant, to testify to the
things that would be spoken later.
6 Christ, however, was faithful over
God's[r] house as a son, and we are
his house if we hold firm[t] the confidence and the pride that belong
to hope.

Warning against Unbelief

7 Therefore, as the Holy Spirit
says,
"Today, if you hear his voice,
8 do not harden your hearts as
in the rebellion,
as on the day of testing in
the wilderness,
9 where your ancestors put me
to the test,
though they had seen my
works 10 for forty years.
Therefore I was angry with
that generation,
and I said, 'They always go
astray in their hearts,
and they have not known
my ways.'
11 As in my anger I swore,
'They will not enter my
rest.' "
12 Take care, brothers and sisters,[p]
that none of you may have an evil,
unbelieving heart that turns away
from the living God. 13 But exhort
one another every day, as long as it
is called "today," so that none of
you may be hardened by the deceitfulness of sin. 14 For we have become partners of Christ, if only we
hold our first confidence firm to
the end. 15 As it is said,
"Today, if you hear his voice,
do not harden your hearts as
in the rebellion."
16 Now who were they who heard
and yet were rebellious? Was it not
all those who left Egypt under the
leadership of Moses? 17 But with
whom was he angry forty years?
Was it not those who sinned,
whose bodies fell in the wilderness? 18 And to whom did he swear
that they would not enter his rest,
if not to those who were disobedient? 19 So we see that they were unable to enter because of unbelief.

The Rest That God Promised

4 Therefore, while the promise
of entering his rest is still
open, let us take care that none of
you should seem to have failed to
reach it. 2 For indeed the good news
came to us just as to them; but the
message they heard did not benefit
them, because they were not united by faith with those who listened.[u] 3 For we who have believed

2.14 Mt 16.17; Jn 1.14; 1 Cor 15.54-57; 1 Jn 3.8
2.15 Rom 8.15; 2 Tim 1.7
2.17 Phil 2.7; Heb 4.15; 5.1,2; 1 Jn 2.2; 4.10
2.18 Heb 4.15
3.1 Heb 2.11; Phil 3.14; Rom 15.8; Heb 10.21
3.3 2 Cor 3.7-11
3.4 Eph 2.10; Heb 1.2
3.5 Num 12.7; Ex 14.31; Deut 18.18, 19
3.6 Heb 1.2; 1 Cor 3.16; Rom 5.2; Col 1.23
3.7 Heb 9.8; Ps 95.7
3.9 Acts 7.36
3.11 Heb 4.3,5
3.12 Heb 12.25; 9.14
3.13 Heb 10.24, 25; Eph 4.22
3.14 v. 6
3.15 v. 7
3.16 Num 14.2
3.17 Num 14.29; Ps 106.26
3.18 Num 14.23; Heb 4.6
3.19 Jn 3.36
4.1 Heb 12.15
4.2 1 Thes 2.13
4.3 Ps 95.11; Heb 3.11

[p] Gk *brothers* [q] Other ancient authorities lack *all* [r] Gk *his* [s] Gk *this one*
[t] Other ancient authorities add *to the end*
[u] Other ancient authorities read *it did not meet with faith in those who listened*

enter that rest, just as God[v] has
said,

"As in my anger I swore,
'They shall not enter my
rest,' "

though his works were finished at
the foundation of the world. 4 For
in one place it speaks about the
seventh day as follows, "And God
rested on the seventh day from all
his works." 5 And again in this
place it says, "They shall not enter
my rest." 6 Since therefore it remains open for some to enter it,
and those who formerly received
the good news failed to enter because of disobedience, 7 again he
sets a certain day—"today"—
saying through David much later,
in the words already quoted,

"Today, if you hear his voice,
do not harden your hearts."

8 For if Joshua had given them rest,
God[v] would not speak later about
another day. 9 So then, a sabbath
rest still remains for the people of
God; 10 for those who enter God's
rest also cease from their labors as
God did from his. 11 Let us therefore make every effort to enter that
rest, so that no one may fall
through such disobedience as
theirs.

12 Indeed, the word of God is
living and active, sharper than any
two-edged sword, piercing until it
divides soul from spirit, joints from
marrow; it is able to judge the
thoughts and intentions of the
heart. 13 And before him no creature is hidden, but all are naked
and laid bare to the eyes of the one
to whom we must render an account.

Jesus the Great High Priest

14 Since, then, we have a great
high priest who has passed through
the heavens, Jesus, the Son of God,
let us hold fast to our confession.
15 For we do not have a high priest
who is unable to sympathize with
our weaknesses, but we have one
who in every respect has been tested[w] as we are, yet without sin.
16 Let us therefore approach the
throne of grace with boldness, so
that we may receive mercy and find
grace to help in time of need.

5 Every high priest chosen from
among mortals is put in
charge of things pertaining to God
on their behalf, to offer gifts and
sacrifices for sins. 2 He is able to
deal gently with the ignorant and
wayward, since he himself is subject to weakness; 3 and because of
this he must offer sacrifice for his
own sins as well as for those of the
people. 4 And one does not presume to take this honor, but takes
it only when called by God, just as
Aaron was.

5 So also Christ did not glorify
himself in becoming a high priest,
but was appointed by the one who
said to him,

"You are my Son,
today I have begotten you";

6 as he says also in another place,

"You are a priest forever,
according to the order of
Melchizedek."

7 In the days of his flesh, Jesus[v]
offered up prayers and supplications, with loud cries and tears, to
the one who was able to save him
from death, and he was heard because of his reverent submission.
8 Although he was a Son, he learned
obedience through what he suffered; 9 and having been made perfect, he became the source of eternal salvation for all who obey him,
10 having been designated by God a
high priest according to the order
of Melchizedek.

Warning against Falling Away

11 About this[x] we have much to
say that is hard to explain, since
you have become dull in understanding. 12 For though by this time
you ought to be teachers, you need
someone to teach you again the basic elements of the oracles of God.
You need milk, not solid food; 13 for
everyone who lives on milk, being
still an infant, is unskilled in the
word of righteousness. 14 But solid
food is for the mature, for those
whose faculties have been trained

4.4 Gen 2.2; Ex 20.11
4.5 Ps 95.11; Heb 3.11
4.6 Heb 3.18,19
4.7 Ps 95.7,8; Heb 3.7,8
4.8 Josh 22.4; Heb 1.1
4.10 v. 4
4.11 Heb 3.18
4.12 Jer 23.29; Eph 6.17; 1 Cor 14.24, 25
4.13 Ps 33.13-15; Job 26.6
4.14 Heb 3.1; 7.26; 10.23
4.15 Heb 2.18; 2 Cor 5.21; 1 Pet 2.22
4.16 Eph 2.18
5.1 Heb 8.3,4; 7.27
5.2 Heb 2.18; Jas 5.19; Heb 7.28
5.3 Heb 7.27; 9.7
5.4 2 Chr 26.18; Ex 28.1
5.5 Jn 8.54; Ps 2.7; Heb 1.1,5
5.6 Ps 110.4; Heb 7.17
5.7 Mt 26.39, 53; 27.46; Mk 14.36; 15.34
5.8 Heb 3.6; Phil 2.8
5.9 Heb 2.10
5.10 vv. 5,6
5.12 Gal 4.3; Heb 6.1; Acts 7.38; 1 Cor 3.2
5.13 1 Cor 3.1
5.14 Isa 7.15

[v] Gk *he* [w] Or *tempted* [x] Or *him*

by practice to distinguish good
from evil.

The Peril of Falling Away

6 Therefore let us go on toward
perfection,[y] leaving behind
the basic teaching about Christ,
and not laying again the foundation: repentance from dead works
and faith toward God, 2 instruction
about baptisms, laying on of
hands, resurrection of the dead,
and eternal judgment. 3 And we will
do[z] this, if God permits. 4 For it is
impossible to restore again to repentance those who have once
been enlightened, and have tasted
the heavenly gift, and have shared
in the Holy Spirit, 5 and have tasted
the goodness of the word of God
and the powers of the age to come,
6 and then have fallen away, since
on their own they are crucifying
again the Son of God and are holding him up to contempt. 7 Ground
that drinks up the rain falling on it
repeatedly, and that produces a
crop useful to those for whom it is
cultivated, receives a blessing from
God. 8 But if it produces thorns and
thistles, it is worthless and on the
verge of being cursed; its end is to
be burned over.
9 Even though we speak in this
way, beloved, we are confident of
better things in your case, things
that belong to salvation. 10 For God
is not unjust; he will not overlook
your work and the love that you
showed for his sake[a] in serving the
saints, as you still do. 11 And we
want each one of you to show the
same diligence so as to realize the
full assurance of hope to the very
end, 12 so that you may not become
sluggish, but imitators of those
who through faith and patience inherit the promises.

The Certainty of God's Promise

13 When God made a promise
to Abraham, because he had no
one greater by whom to swear,
he swore by himself, 14 saying, "I
will surely bless you and multiply
you." 15 And thus Abraham,[b] having patiently endured, obtained
the promise. 16 Human beings, of
course, swear by someone greater
than themselves, and an oath given
as confirmation puts an end to all
dispute. 17 In the same way, when
God desired to show even more
clearly to the heirs of the promise
the unchangeable character of his
purpose, he guaranteed it by an
oath, 18 so that through two unchangeable things, in which it is
impossible that God would prove
false, we who have taken refuge
might be strongly encouraged to
seize the hope set before us. 19 We
have this hope, a sure and steadfast
anchor of the soul, a hope that enters the inner shrine behind the
curtain, 20 where Jesus, a forerun-
ner on our behalf, has entered, having become a high priest forever
according to the order of
Melchizedek.

The Priestly Order of Melchizedek

7 This "King Melchizedek of Salem, priest of the Most High
God, met Abraham as he was returning from defeating the kings
and blessed him"; 2 and to him
Abraham apportioned "one-tenth
of everything." His name, in the
first place, means "king of righteousness"; next he is also king of
Salem, that is, "king of peace."
3 Without father, without mother,
without genealogy, having neither
beginning of days nor end of life,
but resembling the Son of God, he
remains a priest forever.
4 See how great he is! Even[c]
Abraham the patriarch gave him a
tenth of the spoils. 5 And those descendants of Levi who receive the
priestly office have a commandment in the law to collect tithes[d]
from the people, that is, from their
kindred,[e] though these also are
descended from Abraham. 6 But
this man, who does not belong to
their ancestry, collected tithes[d]
from Abraham and blessed him

6.1 Phil 3.12-14; Heb 5.12; 9.14
6.2 Acts 19.3,4; 6.6; 17.31,32
6.3 Acts 18.21
6.4ff Heb 10.26, 32; Eph 2.8; Gal 3.2,5
6.5 Heb 2.5
6.6 Heb 10.26-29
6.7 Ps 65.10
6.8 Gen 3.17,18
6.10 Mt 10.42; 25.40; 2 Thes 1.6, 7; 1 Thes 1.3; Rom 15.25
6.11 Heb 3.6,14; Col 2.2
6.12 Heb 10.36
6.13 Gen 22.16, 17; Lk 1.73
6.16 Gal 3.15; Ex 22.11
6.17 Heb 11.9; Ps 110.4
6.18 Titus 1.2; Heb 7.19
6.19 Lev 16.2; Heb 9.7
6.20 Heb 4.14; 5.6
7.1 Gen 14.18-20
7.3 vv. 6,28
7.4 Gen 14.20
7.5 Num 18.21, 26
7.6 Gen 14.19; Rom 4.13

[y] Or *toward maturity* [z] Other ancient authorities read *let us do* [a] Gk *for his name* [b] Gk *he* [c] Other ancient authorities lack *Even* [d] Or *a tenth* [e] Gk *brothers*

who had received the promises. 7 It is beyond dispute that the inferior is blessed by the superior. 8 In the one case, tithes are received by those who are mortal; in the other, by one of whom it is testified that he lives. 9 One might even say that Levi himself, who receives tithes, paid tithes through Abraham, 10 for he was still in the loins of his ancestor when Melchizedek met him.

Another Priest, Like Melchizedek

11 Now if perfection had been attainable through the levitical priesthood—for the people received the law under this priesthood—what further need would there have been to speak of another priest arising according to the order of Melchizedek, rather than one according to the order of Aaron? 12 For when there is a change in the priesthood, there is necessarily a change in the law as well. 13 Now the one of whom these things are spoken belonged to another tribe, from which no one has ever served at the altar. 14 For it is evident that our Lord was descended from Judah, and in connection with that tribe Moses said nothing about priests.

15 It is even more obvious when another priest arises, resembling Melchizedek, 16 one who has become a priest, not through a legal requirement concerning physical descent, but through the power of an indestructible life. 17 For it is attested of him,

"You are a priest forever,
  according to the order of
    Melchizedek."

18 There is, on the one hand, the abrogation of an earlier commandment because it was weak and ineffectual 19 (for the law made nothing perfect); there is, on the other hand, the introduction of a better hope, through which we approach God.

20 This was confirmed with an oath; for others who became priests took their office without an oath, 21 but this one became a priest with an oath, because of the one who said to him,

"The Lord has sworn
  and will not change his
    mind,
'You are a priest forever' "—

22 accordingly Jesus has also become the guarantee of a better covenant.

23 Furthermore, the former priests were many in number, because they were prevented by death from continuing in office; 24 but he holds his priesthood permanently, because he continues forever. 25 Consequently he is able for all time to save[f] those who approach God through him, since he always lives to make intercession for them.

26 For it was fitting that we should have such a high priest, holy, blameless, undefiled, separated from sinners, and exalted above the heavens. 27 Unlike the other[g] high priests, he has no need to offer sacrifices day after day, first for his own sins, and then for those of the people; this he did once for all when he offered himself. 28 For the law appoints as high priests those who are subject to weakness, but the word of the oath, which came later than the law, appoints a Son who has been made perfect forever.

Mediator of a Better Covenant

8 Now the main point in what we are saying is this: we have such a high priest, one who is seated at the right hand of the throne of the Majesty in the heavens, 2 a minister in the sanctuary and the true tent[h] that the Lord, and not any mortal, has set up. 3 For every high priest is appointed to offer gifts and sacrifices; hence it is necessary for this priest also to have something to offer. 4 Now if he were on earth, he would not be a priest at all, since there are priests who offer gifts according to the law. 5 They offer worship in a sanctuary that is a

7.8 Heb 5.6; 6.20
7.11 vv. 18,19; Heb 8.7; 10.1; v. 17
7.13 vv. 14,11
7.14 Isa 11.1; Mt 1.3; Lk 3.33; Rom 1.3; Rev 5.5
7.16 Heb 9.10,14
7.17 Ps 110.4; Heb 5.6; 6.20; v.21
7.18 Rom 8.3; Gal 4.9
7.19 Acts 13.39; Rom 3.20; Gal 2.16; Heb 9.9; 6.18; 8.6; 4.16
7.21 Ps 110.4
7.22 Heb 8.6; 9.15; 12.24
7.24 v. 28
7.25 v. 19; Rom 8.34; Heb 9.24
7.26 Heb 4.15; 8.1
7.27 Heb 5.1,3; 9.12; Eph 5.2; Heb 9.14,28
7.28 Heb 5.2; 1.2; 2.10
8.1 Heb 2.17; 1.3
8.2 Heb 9.11,24
8.3 Heb 5.1; 9.14
8.4 Heb 5.1
8.5 Col 2.17; Heb 9.23; 10.1; Ex 25.40; Heb 11.7; 12.25

f Or *able to save completely* g Gk lacks *other* h Or *tabernacle*

sketch and shadow of the heavenly
one; for Moses, when he was about
to erect the tent,[i] was warned,
"See that you make everything according to the pattern that was
shown you on the mountain." 6 But
Jesus[j] has now obtained a more
excellent ministry, and to that degree he is the mediator of a better
covenant, which has been enacted
through better promises. 7 For if
that first covenant had been fault-
less, there would have been no
need to look for a second one.
8 God[k] finds fault with them
when he says:

"The days are surely coming,
says the Lord,
when I will establish a new
covenant with the
house of Israel
and with the house of
Judah;
9 not like the covenant that I
made with their
ancestors,
on the day when I took
them by the hand to
lead them out of the
land of Egypt;
for they did not continue in
my covenant,
and so I had no concern for
them, says the Lord.
10 This is the covenant that I
will make with the
house of Israel
after those days, says the
Lord:
I will put my laws in their
minds,
and write them on their
hearts,
and I will be their God,
and they shall be my
people.
11 And they shall not teach one
another
or say to each other, 'Know
the Lord,'
for they shall all know me,
from the least of them to
the greatest.
12 For I will be merciful toward
their iniquities,
and I will remember their
sins no more."

8.6 1 Tim 2.5; Heb 7.22
8.7 Heb 7.11,18
8.8 Jer 31.31-34
8.9 Ex 19.5,6
8.10 Heb 10.16; 2 Cor 3.3; Zech 8.8
8.11 Isa 54.13; Jn 6.45; 1 Jn 2.27
8.12 Heb 10.17
8.13 2 Cor 5.17
9.1 Ex 25.8
9.2 Ex 25.8,9, 23-39
9.3 Ex 26.31-33
9.4 Ex 30.1-5; 25.10ff; 16.32,33; Num 17.10
9.5 Ex 25.17ff
9.6 Num 28.3
9.7 Lev 16.11ff; Ex 30.10; Heb 5.2,3
9.8 Heb 10.19, 20; Jn 14.6
9.9 Heb 11.19; 5.1; Gal 3.21
9.10 Lev 11.2ff; Col 2.16; Heb 7.16
9.11ff Heb 2.17; 10.1; 8.2

13 In speaking of "a new covenant,"
he has made the first one obsolete.
And what is obsolete and growing
old will soon disappear.

The Earthly and the Heavenly Sanctuaries

9 Now even the first covenant
had regulations for worship
and an earthly sanctuary. 2 For a
tent[i] was constructed, the first
one, in which were the lampstand,
the table, and the bread of the
Presence;[l] this is called the Holy
Place. 3 Behind the second curtain
was a tent[i] called the Holy of Ho-
lies. 4 In it stood the golden altar of
incense and the ark of the covenant
overlaid on all sides with gold, in
which there were a golden urn
holding the manna, and Aaron's
rod that budded, and the tablets of
the covenant; 5 above it were the
cherubim of glory overshadowing
the mercy seat.[m] Of these things
we cannot speak now in detail.
6 Such preparations having
been made, the priests go continually into the first tent[i] to carry out
their ritual duties; 7 but only the
high priest goes into the second,
and he but once a year, and not
without taking the blood that he
offers for himself and for the sins
committed unintentionally by the
people. 8 By this the Holy Spirit indicates that the way into the sanctuary has not yet been disclosed as
long as the first tent[i] is still standing. 9 This is a symbol[n] of the
present time, during which gifts
and sacrifices are offered that cannot perfect the conscience of the
worshiper, 10 but deal only with
food and drink and various baptisms, regulations for the body imposed until the time comes to set
things right.
11 But when Christ came as a
high priest of the good things that
have come,[o] then through the
greater and perfect[p] tent[i] (not
made with hands, that is, not of

[i] Or *tabernacle* [j] Gk *he* [k] Gk *He*
[l] Gk *the presentation of the loaves*
[m] Or *the place of atonement* [n] Gk *parable*
[o] Other ancient authorities read *good things to come* [p] Gk *more perfect*

this creation), 12 he entered once
for all into the Holy Place, not with
the blood of goats and calves, but
with his own blood, thus obtaining
eternal redemption. 13 For if the
blood of goats and bulls, with the
sprinkling of the ashes of a heifer,
sanctifies those who have been defiled so that their flesh is purified,
14 how much more will the blood of
Christ, who through the eternal
Spirit[q] offered himself without
blemish to God, purify our[r] conscience from dead works to worship the living God!

15 For this reason he is the mediator of a new covenant, so that
those who are called may receive
the promised eternal inheritance,
because a death has occurred that
redeems them from the transgressions under the first covenant.[s]
16 Where a will[s] is involved, the
death of the one who made it must
be established. 17 For a will[s] takes
effect only at death, since it is not
in force as long as the one who
made it is alive. 18 Hence not even
the first covenant was inaugurated
without blood. 19 For when every
commandment had been told to all
the people by Moses in accordance
with the law, he took the blood of
calves and goats,[t] with water and
scarlet wool and hyssop, and sprinkled both the scroll itself and all
the people, 20 saying, "This is the
blood of the covenant that God
has ordained for you." 21 And in
the same way he sprinkled with the
blood both the tent[u] and all the
vessels used in worship. 22 Indeed,
under the law almost everything is
purified with blood, and without
the shedding of blood there is no
forgiveness of sins.

Christ's Sacrifice Takes Away Sin

23 Thus it was necessary for the
sketches of the heavenly things to
be purified with these rites, but the
heavenly things themselves need
better sacrifices than these. 24 For
Christ did not enter a sanctuary
made by human hands, a mere
copy of the true one, but he entered into heaven itself, now to appear in the presence of God on our
behalf. 25 Nor was it to offer himself
again and again, as the high priest
enters the Holy Place year after
year with blood that is not his own;
26 for then he would have had to
suffer again and again since the
foundation of the world. But as it
is, he has appeared once for all at
the end of the age to remove sin by
the sacrifice of himself. 27 And just
as it is appointed for mortals to die
once, and after that the judgment,
28 so Christ, having been offered
once to bear the sins of many, will
appear a second time, not to deal
with sin, but to save those who are
eagerly waiting for him.

Christ's Sacrifice Once for All

10 Since the law has only a
shadow of the good things
to come and not the true form of
these realities, it[v] can never, by
the same sacrifices that are continually offered year after year, make
perfect those who approach. 2 Otherwise, would they not have ceased
being offered, since the worshipers, cleansed once for all, would no
longer have any consciousness of
sin? 3 But in these sacrifices there
is a reminder of sin year after year.
4 For it is impossible for the blood
of bulls and goats to take away
sins. 5 Consequently, when Christ[w]
came into the world, he said,

"Sacrifices and offerings you
have not desired,
but a body you have
prepared for me;
6 in burnt offerings and sin
offerings
you have taken no
pleasure.
7 Then I said, 'See, God, I
have come to do your
will, O God'
(in the scroll of the book[x]
it is written of me)."

9.12 Heb 7.27; 10.4 **9.13** Num 19.9, 17,18 **9.14** 1 Jn 1.7; 1 Pet 3.18; Titus 2.14 **9.15** 1 Tim 2.5; Heb 3.1; 7.22 **9.17** Gal 3.15 **9.18** Ex 24.6 **9.19** Ex 24.65ff; Lev 14.4,7 **9.20** Ex 24.8; Mt 26.28 **9.21** Lev 8.15 **9.22** Lev 17.11 **9.23** Heb 8.5 **9.24** Heb 6.20; 8.2; 7.25; 1 Jn 2.1 **9.25** v. 7; Heb 10.19 **9.26** Heb 4.3; 7.27; 1.2 **9.27** Gen 3.19; 2 Cor 5.10 **9.28** Rom 6.10; 1 Pet 2.24; Titus 2.13 **10.1** Heb 9.9,11, 23 **10.3** Heb 9.7 **10.4** Mic 6.6,7 **10.5** Ps 40.6-8; Heb 1.6; 1 Pet 2.24 **10.7** Jer 36.2

[q] Other ancient authorities read *Holy Spirit*
[r] Other ancient authorities read *your*
[s] The Greek word used here means both *covenant* and *will*
[t] Other ancient authorities lack *and goats*
[u] Or *tabernacle*
[v] Other ancient authorities read *they*
[w] Gk *he*
[x] Meaning of Gk uncertain

8 When he said above, "You have
neither desired nor taken pleasure
in sacrifices and offerings and
burnt offerings and sin offerings"
(these are offered according to the
law), 9 then he added, "See, I have
come to do your will." He abolishes
the first in order to establish the
second. 10 And it is by God's will[y]
that we have been sanctified
through the offering of the body of
Jesus Christ once for all.

11 And every priest stands day
after day at his service, offering
again and again the same sacrifices
that can never take away sins.
12 But when Christ[z] had offered for
all time a single sacrifice for sins,
"he sat down at the right hand of
God," 13 and since then has been
waiting "until his enemies would
be made a footstool for his feet."
14 For by a single offering he has
perfected for all time those who are
sanctified. 15 And the Holy Spirit
also testifies to us, for after saying,
16 "This is the covenant that I
will make with them
after those days, says the
Lord:
I will put my laws in their
hearts,
and I will write them on
their minds,"
17 he also adds,
"I will remember[a] their sins
and their lawless deeds
no more."
18 Where there is forgiveness of
these, there is no longer any offering for sin.

A Call to Persevere

19 Therefore, my friends,[b]
since we have confidence to enter
the sanctuary by the blood of
Jesus, 20 by the new and living way
that he opened for us through the
curtain (that is, through his flesh),
21 and since we have a great priest
over the house of God, 22 let us approach with a true heart in full assurance of faith, with our hearts
sprinkled clean from an evil conscience and our bodies washed
with pure water. 23 Let us hold fast
to the confession of our hope without wavering, for he who has promised is faithful. 24 And let us consider how to provoke one another to
love and good deeds, 25 not neglecting to meet together, as is the habit
of some, but encouraging one another, and all the more as you see
the Day approaching.

26 For if we willfully persist in
sin after having received the knowledge of the truth, there no longer
remains a sacrifice for sins, 27 but a
fearful prospect of judgment, and a
fury of fire that will consume the
adversaries. 28 Anyone who has violated the law of Moses dies without
mercy "on the testimony of two or
three witnesses." 29 How much
worse punishment do you think
will be deserved by those who have
spurned the Son of God, profaned
the blood of the covenant by which
they were sanctified, and outraged
the Spirit of grace? 30 For we know
the one who said, "Vengeance is
mine, I will repay." And again,
"The Lord will judge his people."
31 It is a fearful thing to fall into the
hands of the living God.

32 But recall those earlier days
when, after you had been enlightened, you endured a hard struggle
with sufferings, 33 sometimes being
publicly exposed to abuse and persecution, and sometimes being
partners with those so treated.
34 For you had compassion for
those who were in prison, and you
cheerfully accepted the plundering
of your possessions, knowing that
you yourselves possessed something better and more lasting. 35 Do
not, therefore, abandon that confidence of yours; it brings a great reward. 36 For you need endurance,
so that when you have done the
will of God, you may receive what
was promised.
37 For yet "in a very little
while,

10.8 vv. 5,6; Mk 12.33 **10.9** v. 7 **10.10** Jn 17.19; Heb 7.27; 1 Pet 2.24 **10.11** Heb 5.1; v. 4 **10.12** Heb 1.3 **10.13** Ps 110.1. Heb 1.13 **10.14** v. 1 **10.15** Heb 3.7 **10.16** Jer 31.33,34 **10.17** Heb 8.12 **10.19** Eph 2.18; Heb 9.8,12 **10.20** Heb 9.8,3 **10.21** Heb 2.17; 1 Tim 3.15 **10.22** Heb 4.16; Eph 3.12; Heb 9.14; Ezek 36.25 **10.23** Heb 4.14; 1 Cor 1.9 **10.24** Heb 13.1; Titus 3.8 **10.25** Acts 2.42; Heb 3.13; Phil 4.5 **10.26** Num 15.30; 2 Pet 2.20 **10.27** Heb 9.27; Isa 26.11 **10.28** Deut 17.2-6; Heb 2.2 **10.29** Heb 2.3; 6.6; 13.20; Eph 4.30; Heb 6.4 **10.30** Deut 32.35, 36; Rom 12.19 **10.32** Heb 6.4; Phil 1.29,30 **10.33** 1 Cor 4.9; 1 Thes 2.14 **10.34** Heb 9.15 **10.35** Heb 2.1

10.36 Lk 21.19; Col 3.24 **10.37** Hab 2.3, 4; Lk 18.8

[y] Gk *by that will* [z] Gk *this one*
[a] Gk *on their minds and I will remember*
[b] Gk *Therefore, brothers*

the one who is coming will
come and will not
delay;
38 but my righteous one will
live by faith.
My soul takes no pleasure
in anyone who shrinks
back."
39 But we are not among those who
shrink back and so are lost, but
among those who have faith and so
are saved.

The Meaning of Faith

11 Now faith is the assurance
of things hoped for, the
conviction of things not seen. 2 Indeed, by faith[c] our ancestors received approval. 3 By faith we understand that the worlds were
prepared by the word of God, so
that what is seen was made from
things that are not visible.[d]

The Examples of Abel, Enoch, and Noah

4 By faith Abel offered to God a
more acceptable[e] sacrifice than
Cain's. Through this he received
approval as righteous, God himself
giving approval to his gifts; he died,
but through his faith[f] he still
speaks. 5 By faith Enoch was taken
so that he did not experience
death; and "he was not found, because God had taken him." For it
was attested before he was taken
away that "he had pleased God."
6 And without faith it is impossible
to please God, for whoever would
approach him must believe that he
exists and that he rewards those
who seek him. 7 By faith Noah,
warned by God about events as yet
unseen, respected the warning and
built an ark to save his household;
by this he condemned the world
and became an heir to the righteousness that is in accordance
with faith.

The Faith of Abraham

8 By faith Abraham obeyed
when he was called to set out for a
place that he was to receive as an
inheritance; and he set out, not
knowing where he was going. 9 By
faith he stayed for a time in the
land he had been promised, as in a
foreign land, living in tents, as did
Isaac and Jacob, who were heirs
with him of the same promise.
10 For he looked forward to the city
that has foundations, whose archi-
tect and builder is God. 11 By faith
he received power of procreation,
even though he was too old—and
Sarah herself was barren—because
he considered him faithful who
had promised.[g] 12 Therefore from
one person, and this one as good as
dead, descendants were born, "as
many as the stars of heaven and as
the innumerable grains of sand by
the seashore."
13 All of these died in faith
without having received the promises, but from a distance they saw
and greeted them. They confessed
that they were strangers and foreigners on the earth, 14 for people
who speak in this way make it clear
that they are seeking a homeland.
15 If they had been thinking of the
land that they had left behind, they
would have had opportunity to return. 16 But as it is, they desire a
better country, that is, a heavenly
one. Therefore God is not ashamed
to be called their God; indeed, he
has prepared a city for them.
17 By faith Abraham, when put
to the test, offered up Isaac. He
who had received the promises was
ready to offer up his only son, 18 of
whom he had been told, "It is
through Isaac that descendants
shall be named for you." 19 He considered the fact that God is able
even to raise someone from the
dead—and figuratively speaking,
he did receive him back. 20 By faith
Isaac invoked blessings for the future on Jacob and Esau. 21 By faith
Jacob, when dying, blessed each of
the sons of Joseph, "bowing in worship over the top of his staff." 22 By
faith Joseph, at the end of his life,

10.38 Rom 1.17; Gal 3.11
10.39 2 Pet 2.20; Acts 16.30
11.1 Rom 8.24; 2 Cor 4.18; 5.7
11.2 vv. 4,39
11.3 Gen 1.1; Jn 1.3; Heb 6.5
11.4 Gen 4.4,10; 1 Jn 3.12; Heb 12.24
11.5 Gen 5.21-24
11.6 Heb 7.19
11.7 Gen 6.13-22
11.8 Gen 12.1-4; Acts 7.2-4
11.9 Gen 12.8; 18.1,9; Heb 6.17
11.10 Heb 12.22; 13.14; Rev 21.2
11.11 Gen 17.19; 18.11-14; 21.2
11.12 Rom 4.19; Gen 22.17; 32.12
11.13 Gen 23.4; Ps 39.12
11.16 Ex 3.6,15; Phil 3.20; Heb 13.14
11.17 Gen 22.1-10; Jas 2.21
11.18 Gen 21.12; Rom 9.7
11.19 Rom 4.21
11.21 Gen 48.5, 16,20
11.22 Gen 50.24, 25; Ex 13.19

[c] Gk *by this* [d] Or *was not made out of visible things* [e] Gk *greater* [f] Gk *through it* [g] Other ancient authorities read *By faith Sarah herself, though barren, received power to conceive, even when she was too old, because she considered him faithful who had promised.*

6 for the Lord disciplines those
whom he loves,
and chastises every child
whom he accepts."
7 Endure trials for the sake of discipline. God is treating you as children; for what child is there whom
a parent does not discipline? 8 If
you do not have that discipline in
which all children share, then you
are illegitimate and not his children. 9 Moreover, we had human
parents to discipline us, and we respected them. Should we not be
even more willing to be subject to
the Father of spirits and live? 10 For
they disciplined us for a short time
as seemed best to them, but he disciplines us for our good, in order
that we may share his holiness.
11 Now, discipline always seems
painful rather than pleasant at the
time, but later it yields the peaceful fruit of righteousness to those
who have been trained by it.
12 Therefore lift your drooping
hands and strengthen your weak
knees, 13 and make straight paths
for your feet, so that what is lame
may not be put out of joint, but
rather be healed.

Warnings against Rejecting God's Grace

14 Pursue peace with everyone,
and the holiness without which no
one will see the Lord. 15 See to it
that no one fails to obtain the grace
of God; that no root of bitterness
springs up and causes trouble, and
through it many become defiled.
16 See to it that no one becomes
like Esau, an immoral and godless
person, who sold his birthright for
a single meal. 17 You know that later, when he wanted to inherit the
blessing, he was rejected, for he
found no chance to repent,[r] even
though he sought the blessing[s]
with tears.
18 You have not come to something[t] that can be touched, a blazing fire, and darkness, and gloom,
and a tempest, 19 and the sound of
a trumpet, and a voice whose words
made the hearers beg that not another word be spoken to them.

12.6 Ps 94.12; Jas 1.12
12.7 Deut 8.5
12.8 1 Pet 5.9
12.9 Lk 18.2; Num 16.22; Isa 38.16
12.10 2 Pet 1.4
12.11 1 Pet 1.6; Jas 3.17,18
12.12 Isa 35.3
12.13 Prov 4.26; Gal 6.1
12.14 Rom 14.19; 6.22; Mt 5.8
12.15 Gal 5.4; Deut 29.18; Heb 3.12
12.16 Gen 25.33
12.17 Gen 27.30-40
12.18 Ex 19.12-22; Deut 4.11
12.19 Ex 20.19; Deut 5.5
12.20 Ex 19.12,13
12.21 Ex 19.16
12.22 Phil 3.20; Gal 4.26
12.23 Lk 10.20; Phil 3.12
12.24 1 Tim 2.5; Gen 4.10; Heb 11.4
12.25 Heb 2.2,3; 8.5; 11.7
12.26 Ex 19.18; Hag 2.6
12.27 1 Cor 7.31; 2 Pet 3.10
12.28 Dan 2.44; Heb 13.15
12.29 Deut 4.24
13.1 Rom 12.10; 1 Thes 4.9; 1 Pet 1.22
13.2 1 Pet 4.9; Gen 18.3
13.3 Mt 25.36; Col 4.18

20 (For they could not endure the
order that was given, "If even an
animal touches the mountain, it
shall be stoned to death." 21 Indeed, so terrifying was the sight
that Moses said, "I tremble with
fear.") 22 But you have come to
Mount Zion and to the city of the
living God, the heavenly Jerusalem, and to innumerable angels in
festal gathering, 23 and to the assembly[u] of the firstborn who are
enrolled in heaven, and to God the
judge of all, and to the spirits of the
righteous made perfect, 24 and to
Jesus, the mediator of a new covenant, and to the sprinkled blood
that speaks a better word than the
blood of Abel.
25 See that you do not refuse
the one who is speaking; for if they
did not escape when they refused
the one who warned them on earth,
how much less will we escape if we
reject the one who warns from
heaven! 26 At that time his voice
shook the earth; but now he has
promised, "Yet once more I will
shake not only the earth but also
the heaven." 27 This phrase, "Yet
once more," indicates the removal
of what is shaken—that is, created
things—so that what cannot be
shaken may remain. 28 Therefore,
since we are receiving a kingdom
that cannot be shaken, let us give
thanks, by which we offer to God
an acceptable worship with reverence and awe; 29 for indeed our God
is a consuming fire.

Service Well-Pleasing to God

13 Let mutual love continue.
2 Do not neglect to show
hospitality to strangers, for by doing that some have entertained angels without knowing it. 3 Remember those who are in prison, as
though you were in prison with
them; those who are being tortured, as though you yourselves

[r] Or *no chance to change his father's mind* [s] Gk *it* [t] Other ancient authorities read *a mountain* [u] Or *angels, and to the festal gathering* [23] *and assembly*

made mention of the exodus of the Israelites and gave instructions about his burial.[h]

The Faith of Moses

23 By faith Moses was hidden by his parents for three months after his birth, because they saw that the child was beautiful; and they were not afraid of the king's edict.[i] 24 By faith Moses, when he was grown up, refused to be called a son of Pharaoh's daughter, 25 choosing rather to share ill-treatment with the people of God than to enjoy the fleeting pleasures of sin. 26 He considered abuse suffered for the Christ[j] to be greater wealth than the treasures of Egypt, for he was looking ahead to the reward. 27 By faith he left Egypt, unafraid of the king's anger; for he persevered as though[k] he saw him who is invisible. 28 By faith he kept the Passover and the sprinkling of blood, so that the destroyer of the firstborn would not touch the firstborn of Israel.[l]

The Faith of Other Israelite Heroes

29 By faith the people passed through the Red Sea as if it were dry land, but when the Egyptians attempted to do so they were drowned. 30 By faith the walls of Jericho fell after they had been encircled for seven days. 31 By faith Rahab the prostitute did not perish with those who were disobedient,[m] because she had received the spies in peace.

32 And what more should I say? For time would fail me to tell of Gideon, Barak, Samson, Jephthah, of David and Samuel and the prophets— 33 who through faith conquered kingdoms, administered justice, obtained promises, shut the mouths of lions, 34 quenched raging fire, escaped the edge of the sword, won strength out of weakness, became mighty in war, put foreign armies to flight. 35 Women received their dead by resurrection. Others were tortured, refusing to accept release, in order to obtain a better resurrection. 36 Others suffered mocking and flogging, and even chains and imprisonment. 37 They were stoned to death, they were sawn in two,[n] they were killed by the sword; they went about in skins of sheep and goats, destitute, persecuted, tormented— 38 of whom the world was not worthy. They wandered in deserts and mountains, and in caves and holes in the ground.

39 Yet all these, though they were commended for their faith, did not receive what was promised, 40 since God had provided something better so that they would not, apart from us, be made perfect.

The Example of Jesus

12 Therefore, since we are surrounded by so great a cloud of witnesses, let us also lay aside every weight and the sin that clings so closely,[o] and let us run with perseverance the race that is set before us, 2 looking to Jesus the pioneer and perfecter of our faith, who for the sake of[p] the joy that was set before him endured the cross, disregarding its shame, and has taken his seat at the right hand of the throne of God.

3 Consider him who endured such hostility against himself from sinners,[q] so that you may not grow weary or lose heart. 4 In your struggle against sin you have not yet resisted to the point of shedding your blood. 5 And you have forgotten the exhortation that addresses you as children—

"My child, do not regard
lightly the discipline of
the Lord,
or lose heart when you are
punished by him;

11.23 Ex 2.2; 1.16 **11.24** Ex 2.10 **11.25** v. 37 **11.26** Heb 13.13; 2.2 **11.27** Ex 12.50, 51; v. 13 **11.28** Ex 12.21 **11.29** Ex 14.21-31 **11.30** Josh 6.12-21 **11.31** Josh 2.9ff; 6.23; Jas 2.25 **11.33** 2 Sam 7.11; Judg 14.5; 1 Sam 17.34; Dan 6.22 **11.34** 2 Kings 20.7; Judg 15.8 **11.35** 1 Kings 17.22; Acts 22.25 **11.36** Jer 20.2 **11.37** 1 Kings 21.13; Acts 7.58; 2 Kings 1.8 **11.38** 1 Kings 18.4 **11.40** Heb 5.9 **12.1** 1 Cor 9.24; Heb 10.36 **12.2** Phil 2.8,9; Heb 1.3,13; 1 Pet 3.22 **12.3** Mt 10.24; Gal 6.9 **12.4** Heb 10.32-34; 1 Cor 10.13 **12.5** Prov 3.11,12

[h] Gk *his bones* [i] Other ancient authorities add *By faith Moses, when he was grown up, killed the Egyptian, because he observed the humiliation of his people* (Gk *brothers*) [j] Or *the Messiah* [k] Or *because* [l] Gk *would not touch them* [m] Or *unbelieving* [n] Other ancient authorities add *they were tempted* [o] Other ancient authorities read *sin that easily distracts* [p] Or *who instead of* [q] Other ancient authorities read *such hostility from sinners against themselves*

were being tortured.[v] 4 Let marriage be held in honor by all, and let the marriage bed be kept undefiled; for God will judge fornicators and adulterers. 5 Keep your lives free from the love of money, and be content with what you have; for he has said, "I will never leave you or forsake you." 6 So we can say with confidence,

"The Lord is my helper;
  I will not be afraid.
What can anyone do to me?"

7 Remember your leaders, those who spoke the word of God to you; consider the outcome of their way of life, and imitate their faith. 8 Jesus Christ is the same yesterday and today and forever. 9 Do not be carried away by all kinds of strange teachings; for it is well for the heart to be strengthened by grace, not by regulations about food,[w] which have not benefited those who observe them. 10 We have an altar from which those who officiate in the tent[x] have no right to eat. 11 For the bodies of those animals whose blood is brought into the sanctuary by the high priest as a sacrifice for sin are burned outside the camp. 12 Therefore Jesus also suffered outside the city gate in order to sanctify the people by his own blood. 13 Let us then go to him outside the camp and bear the abuse he endured. 14 For here we have no lasting city, but we are looking for the city that is to come. 15 Through him, then, let us continually offer a sacrifice of praise to God, that is, the fruit of lips that confess his name. 16 Do not neglect to do good and to share what you have, for such sacrifices are pleasing to God.

17 Obey your leaders and submit to them, for they are keeping watch over your souls and will give an account. Let them do this with joy and not with sighing—for that would be harmful to you.

18 Pray for us; we are sure that we have a clear conscience, desiring to act honorably in all things. 19 I urge you all the more to do this, so that I may be restored to you very soon.

Benediction

20 Now may the God of peace, who brought back from the dead our Lord Jesus, the great shepherd of the sheep, by the blood of the eternal covenant, 21 make you complete in everything good so that you may do his will, working among us[y] that which is pleasing in his sight, through Jesus Christ, to whom be the glory forever and ever. Amen.

Final Exhortation and Greetings

22 I appeal to you, brothers and sisters,[z] bear with my word of exhortation, for I have written to you briefly. 23 I want you to know that our brother Timothy has been set free; and if he comes in time, he will be with me when I see you. 24 Greet all your leaders and all the saints. Those from Italy send you greetings. 25 Grace be with all of you.[a]

13.4 1 Cor 6.9; Rev 22.15
13.5 Phil 4.11; Deut 31.6,8; Josh 1.5
13.7 v. 17; Heb 6.12
13.8 Heb 1.12
13.9 Eph 4.14; Col 2.7,16
13.10 1 Cor 9.13; 10.18
13.11 Ex 29.14; Lev 16.27
13.12 Jn 19.17
13.13 Heb 11.26
13.14 Phil 3.20; Heb 10.34; 12.22
13.15 1 Pet 2.5; Hos 14.2
13.17 Isa 62.6; Acts 20.28
13.18 1 Thes 5.25; Acts 24.16
13.19 Philem 22
13.20 Rom 15.33; Zech 9.11
13.21 1 Pet 5.10; Phil 2.13
13.23 1 Thes 3.2; 1 Tim 6.12
13.24 v. 7
13.25 Col 4.18; Titus 3.15

[v] Gk *were in the body* [w] Gk *not by foods* [x] Or *tabernacle* [y] Other ancient authorities read *you* [z] Gk *brothers* [a] Other ancient authorities add *Amen*

THE LETTER OF

James

Title and Background

The book of James has a distinctively Jewish nature that suggests it was composed when the church was still predominantly Jewish. It reflects a simple church order, and no reference is made to the controversy over Gentile circumcision. The seven New Testament letters from James through the book of Jude are called the General Letters because they are addressed to Christians in general and not to a particular church.

Author and Date of Writing

The author identifies himself as James, and he was probably the brother of Jesus and the leader of the Jerusalem council. At first James did not believe in Jesus and even challenged him and misunderstood his mission. Later he became very prominent in the church. The book of James was written about A.D. 48, and certainly before 50.

Theme and Message

As the pastor and leader of the Jerusalem church, James wrote to instruct and encourage his dispersed people in the face of their difficulties. The letter is concerned mainly with the practical aspects of the Christian faith, consisting of maxims and counsel for everyday conduct. Many of his statements bear similarity to Jesus' Sermon on the Mount (Mt 5-7). The letter discusses true religion, true faith, and true wisdom.

Outline

I. Trials and Temptations (1.1-18)
II. Listening and Doing (1.19-27)
III. Favoritism Forbidden (2.1-13)
IV. Faith and Works (2.14-26)
V. Taming the Tongue (3.1-12)
VI. Two Kinds of Wisdom (3.13-18)
VII. Warning Against Worldliness (4.1-17)
VIII. Warning to Rich Oppressors (5.1-6)
IX. Miscellaneous Exhortations (5.7-20)

Salutation

1 James, a servant[a] of God and
of the Lord Jesus Christ,
To the twelve tribes in the Dispersion:
Greetings.

Faith and Wisdom

2 My brothers and sisters,[b]
whenever you face trials of any
kind, consider it nothing but joy,
3 because you know that the testing
of your faith produces endurance;
4 and let endurance have its full effect, so that you may be mature
and complete, lacking in nothing.
5 If any of you is lacking in wisdom, ask God, who gives to all generously and ungrudgingly, and it
will be given you. 6 But ask in faith,
never doubting, for the one who
doubts is like a wave of the sea,
driven and tossed by the wind;
7, 8 for the doubter, being double-
minded and unstable in every way,

1.1 Acts 12.17; Titus 1.1; Acts 26.7; Deut 32.26; Jn 7.35; 1 Pet 1.1 **1.2** Mt 5.12; Heb 10.34; 1 Pet 1.6 **1.3** Rom 5.3 **1.4** Col 4.12; 1 Thes 5.23 **1.5** 1 Kings 3.9; Prov 2.3; 1 Jn 5.14 **1.6** Mk 11.24 **1.7** Jas 4.8

[a] Gk *slave* [b] Gk *brothers*

must not expect to receive anything from the Lord.

Poverty and Riches

9 Let the believer[c] who is lowly
boast in being raised up, 10 and the
rich in being brought low, because
the rich will disappear like a flower
in the field. 11 For the sun rises with
its scorching heat and withers the
field; its flower falls, and its beauty
perishes. It is the same way with
the rich; in the midst of a busy life,
they will wither away.

Trial and Temptation

12 Blessed is anyone who endures temptation. Such a one has
stood the test and will receive the
crown of life that the Lord[d] has
promised to those who love him.
13 No one, when tempted, should
say, "I am being tempted by God";
for God cannot be tempted by evil
and he himself tempts no one.
14 But one is tempted by one's own
desire, being lured and enticed by
it; 15 then, when that desire has
conceived, it gives birth to sin, and
that sin, when it is fully grown,
gives birth to death. 16 Do not be
deceived, my beloved.[e]

17 Every generous act of giving,
with every perfect gift, is from
above, coming down from the Father of lights, with whom there is
no variation or shadow due to
change.[f] 18 In fulfillment of his
own purpose he gave us birth by
the word of truth, so that we would
become a kind of first fruits of his
creatures.

Hearing and Doing the Word

19 You must understand this,
my beloved:[e] let everyone be quick
to listen, slow to speak, slow to anger; 20 for your anger does not
produce God's righteousness.
21 Therefore rid yourselves of all
sordidness and rank growth of
wickedness, and welcome with
meekness the implanted word that
has the power to save your souls.

22 But be doers of the word, and
not merely hearers who deceive
themselves. 23 For if any are hearers
of the word and not doers, they are
like those who look at themselves[g]
in a mirror; 24 for they look at themselves and, on going away, immediately forget what they were like.
25 But those who look into the perfect law, the law of liberty, and persevere, being not hearers who forget but doers who act — they will be
blessed in their doing.

26 If any think they are religious, and do not bridle their
tongues but deceive their hearts,
their religion is worthless. 27 Religion that is pure and undefiled before God, the Father, is this: to care
for orphans and widows in their
distress, and to keep oneself unstained by the world.

Warning against Partiality

2 My brothers and sisters,[h] do
you with your acts of favoritism really believe in our glorious
Lord Jesus Christ?[i] 2 For if a person with gold rings and in fine
clothes comes into your assembly,
and if a poor person in dirty clothes
also comes in, 3 and if you take notice of the one wearing the fine
clothes and say, "Have a seat here,
please," while to the one who is
poor you say, "Stand there," or,
"Sit at my feet,"[j] 4 have you not
made distinctions among yourselves, and become judges with evil
thoughts? 5 Listen, my beloved
brothers and sisters.[k] Has not God
chosen the poor in the world to be
rich in faith and to be heirs of the
kingdom that he has promised to
those who love him? 6 But you have
dishonored the poor. Is it not the
rich who oppress you? Is it not they
who drag you into court? 7 Is it not
they who blaspheme the excellent
name that was invoked over you?

8 You do well if you really fulfill
the royal law according to the
scripture, "You shall love your
neighbor as yourself." 9 But if you

1.10 1 Cor 7.31; 1 Pet 1.24
1.11 Isa 40.6-8; Ps 102.4,11
1.12 Heb 12.5; Jas 2.5
1.15 Job 15.35; Ps 7.14; Rom 6.21, 23
1.16 1 Cor 6.9; v. 19
1.17 Jn 3.27; Mal 3.6
1.18 Jn 1.13; Eph 1.12; Rev 14.4
1.19 Prov 5.1,2; 10.19
1.21 Eph 4.22; 1 Pet 2.1; Eph 1.13; Titus 2.11
1.22 Mt 7.21; Rom 2.13; 1 Jn 3.7
1.23 Lk 6.47; 1 Cor 13.12
1.25 2 Cor 3.18; Jas 2.12; Jn 13.17
1.26 Ps 34.13; 1 Pet 3.10
1.27 Mt 25.36; Rom 12.2; 1 Jn 5.18
2.1 Prov 24.23; Mt 22.16; 1 Cor 2.8
2.2 v. 3
2.3 v. 2
2.4 Jn 7.24
2.5 1 Cor 1.26-28; Lk 12.21; Jas 1.12
2.6 1 Cor 11.22; Acts 8.3
2.8 Lev 19.18; Mt 22.39

[c] Gk *brother* [d] Gk *he*; other ancient authorities read *God* [e] Gk *my beloved brothers* [f] Other ancient authorities read *variation due to a shadow of turning* [g] Gk *at the face of his birth* [h] Gk *My brothers* [i] Or *hold the faith of our glorious Lord Jesus Christ without acts of favoritism* [j] Gk *Sit under my footstool* [k] Gk *brothers*

show partiality, you commit sin
and are convicted by the law as
transgressors. 10 For whoever keeps
the whole law but fails in one point
has become accountable for all of
it. 11 For the one who said, "You
shall not commit adultery," also
said, "You shall not murder." Now
if you do not commit adultery but
if you murder, you have become a
transgressor of the law. 12 So speak
and so act as those who are to be
judged by the law of liberty. 13 For
judgment will be without mercy to
anyone who has shown no mercy;
mercy triumphs over judgment.

Faith without Works Is Dead

14 What good is it, my brothers
and sisters,[l] if you say you have
faith but do not have works? Can
faith save you? 15 If a brother or sister is naked and lacks daily food,
16 and one of you says to them, "Go
in peace; keep warm and eat your
fill," and yet you do not supply
their bodily needs, what is the good
of that? 17 So faith by itself, if it has
no works, is dead.

18 But someone will say, "You
have faith and I have works." Show
me your faith apart from your
works, and I by my works will show
you my faith. 19 You believe that
God is one; you do well. Even the
demons believe—and shudder.
20 Do you want to be shown, you
senseless person, that faith apart
from works is barren? 21 Was not
our ancestor Abraham justified by
works when he offered his son
Isaac on the altar? 22 You see that
faith was active along with his
works, and faith was brought to
completion by the works. 23 Thus
the scripture was fulfilled that
says, "Abraham believed God, and
it was reckoned to him as righteousness," and he was called the
friend of God. 24 You see that a person is justified by works and not by
faith alone. 25 Likewise, was not
Rahab the prostitute also justified
by works when she welcomed the
messengers and sent them out by
another road? 26 For just as the
body without the spirit is dead, so
faith without works is also dead.

Taming the Tongue

3 Not many of you should become teachers, my brothers
and sisters,[l] for you know that we
who teach will be judged with
greater strictness. 2 For all of us
make many mistakes. Anyone who
makes no mistakes in speaking is
perfect, able to keep the whole
body in check with a bridle. 3 If we
put bits into the mouths of horses
to make them obey us, we guide
their whole bodies. 4 Or look at
ships: though they are so large that
it takes strong winds to drive them,
yet they are guided by a very small
rudder wherever the will of the pilot directs. 5 So also the tongue is a
small member, yet it boasts of
great exploits.

How great a forest is set ablaze
by a small fire! 6 And the tongue is
a fire. The tongue is placed among
our members as a world of iniquity;
it stains the whole body, sets on
fire the cycle of nature,[m] and is itself set on fire by hell.[n] 7 For every
species of beast and bird, of reptile
and sea creature, can be tamed and
has been tamed by the human species, 8 but no one can tame the
tongue—a restless evil, full of
deadly poison. 9 With it we bless
the Lord and Father, and with it we
curse those who are made in the
likeness of God. 10 From the same
mouth come blessing and cursing.
My brothers and sisters,[o] this
ought not to be so. 11 Does a spring
pour forth from the same opening
both fresh and brackish water?
12 Can a fig tree, my brothers and
sisters,[p] yield olives, or a grapevine
figs? No more can salt water yield
fresh.

Two Kinds of Wisdom

13 Who is wise and understanding among you? Show by your good
life that your works are done with
gentleness born of wisdom. 14 But if

2.10 Mt 5.19; Gal 3.10
2.11 Ex 20.13, 14; Deut 5.17, 18
2.12 Jas 1.25
2.13 Mt 5.7; 18.32-35
2.14 Mt 7.26; Jas 1.22ff
2.15 Lk 3.11
2.16 1 Jn 3.17, 18
2.18 Jas 3.13
2.19 Deut 6.4; Mt 8.29; Lk 4.34
2.20 v. 17
2.21 Gen 22.9
2.22 Heb 11.17
2.23 Gen 15.6; Rom 4.3; 2 Chr 20.7; Isa 41.8
2.25 Josh 2.1ff; Heb 11.31
2.26 v. 20
3.1 Mt 23.8; Lk 6.37
3.2 1 Kings 8.46; 1 Pet 3.10; Mt 12.37; Jas 1.26
3.3 Ps 32.9
3.5 Prov 12.18; Ps 12.3
3.6 Prov 16.27; Mt 15.11, 18,19
3.8 Ps 140.3; Rom 3.13
3.9 Gen 1.26
3.12 Mt 7.16
3.13 Gal 6.4; Jas 2.18
3.14 Rom 2.8; v. 16; 1 Tim 2.4; Jas 5.19

[l] Gk *brothers*
[m] Or *wheel of birth*
[n] Gk *Gehenna*
[o] Gk *My brothers*
[p] Gk *my brothers*

you have bitter envy and selfish
ambition in your hearts, do not be
boastful and false to the truth.
15 Such wisdom does not come
down from above, but is earthly,
unspiritual, devilish. 16 For where
there is envy and selfish ambition,
there will also be disorder and
wickedness of every kind. 17 But the
wisdom from above is first pure,
then peaceable, gentle, willing to
yield, full of mercy and good fruits,
without a trace of partiality or hypocrisy. 18 And a harvest of righteousness is sown in peace for[q]
those who make peace.

Friendship with the World

4 Those conflicts and disputes
among you, where do they
come from? Do they not come from
your cravings that are at war within
you? 2 You want something and do
not have it; so you commit murder.
And you covet[r] something and
cannot obtain it; so you engage in
disputes and conflicts. You do not
have, because you do not ask. 3 You
ask and do not receive, because
you ask wrongly, in order to spend
what you get on your pleasures.
4 Adulterers! Do you not know that
friendship with the world is enmity
with God? Therefore whoever
wishes to be a friend of the world
becomes an enemy of God. 5 Or do
you suppose that it is for nothing
that the scripture says, "God[s]
yearns jealously for the spirit that
he has made to dwell in us"? 6 But
he gives all the more grace; therefore it says,

"God opposes the proud,
but gives grace to the
humble."

7 Submit yourselves therefore to
God. Resist the devil, and he will
flee from you. 8 Draw near to God,
and he will draw near to you.
Cleanse your hands, you sinners,
and purify your hearts, you double-
minded. 9 Lament and mourn and
weep. Let your laughter be turned
into mourning and your joy into de-
jection. 10 Humble yourselves before the Lord, and he will exalt you.

Warning against Judging Another

11 Do not speak evil against one
another, brothers and sisters.[t]
Whoever speaks evil against another or judges another, speaks evil
against the law and judges the law;
but if you judge the law, you are not
a doer of the law but a judge.
12 There is one lawgiver and judge
who is able to save and to destroy.
So who, then, are you to judge your
neighbor?

Boasting about Tomorrow

13 Come now, you who say,
"Today or tomorrow we will go to
such and such a town and spend a
year there, doing business and
making money." 14 Yet you do not
even know what tomorrow will
bring. What is your life? For you are
a mist that appears for a little while
and then vanishes. 15 Instead you
ought to say, "If the Lord wishes,
we will live and do this or that."
16 As it is, you boast in your arrogance; all such boasting is evil.
17 Anyone, then, who knows the
right thing to do and fails to do it,
commits sin.

Warning to Rich Oppressors

5 Come now, you rich people,
weep and wail for the miseries
that are coming to you. 2 Your
riches have rotted, and your
clothes are moth-eaten. 3 Your gold
and silver have rusted, and their
rust will be evidence against you,
and it will eat your flesh like fire.
You have laid up treasure[u] for the
last days. 4 Listen! The wages of the
laborers who mowed your fields,
which you kept back by fraud, cry
out, and the cries of the harvesters
have reached the ears of the Lord of
hosts. 5 You have lived on the earth
in luxury and in pleasure; you have
fattened your hearts in a day of
slaughter. 6 You have condemned
and murdered the righteous one,
who does not resist you.

3.15 Jas 1.17; 1 Tim 4.1
3.16 Gal 5.20
3.17 1 Cor 2.6; Rom 12.9; 1 Pet 1.22
3.18 Prov 11.18; Isa 32.17
4.1 Titus 3.9; Rom 7.23
4.3 Ps 18.41; 1 Jn 3.22; 5.14
4.4 Jas 1.27; 1 Jn 2.15; Jn 15.19
4.5 Gen 6.5; Num 11.29
4.6 Ps 138.6; Prov 3.34
4.7 1 Pet 5.6-9
4.8 2 Chr 15.2; Isa 1.16; Jas 1.8
4.9 Lk 6.25
4.10 Mt 23.12
4.11 1 Pet 2.1
4.12 Mt 10.28; Rom 14.4
4.13 Prov 27.1
4.14 Job 7.7; Ps 102.3
4.15 Acts 18.21
4.16 1 Cor 5.6
4.17 Lk 12.47; Jn 9.41
5.1 Lk 6.24
5.2 Job 13.28; Mt 6.20
5.3 vv. 7,8
5.4 Lev 19.13; Deut 24.15; Rom 9.29
5.5 Am 6.1; Jer 12.3; 25.34

q Or *by* r Or *you murder and you covet* s Gk *He* t Gk *brothers* u Or *will eat your flesh, since you have stored up fire*

Patience in Suffering

7 Be patient, therefore, beloved,[v] until the coming of the
Lord. The farmer waits for the precious crop from the earth, being
patient with it until it receives the
early and the late rains. 8 You also
must be patient. Strengthen your
hearts, for the coming of the Lord
is near.[w] 9 Beloved,[x] do not grumble against one another, so that
you may not be judged. See, the
Judge is standing at the doors! 10 As
an example of suffering and patience, beloved,[v] take the prophets who spoke in the name of the
Lord. 11 Indeed we call blessed
those who showed endurance. You
have heard of the endurance of
Job, and you have seen the purpose
of the Lord, how the Lord is compassionate and merciful.

12 Above all, my beloved,[v] do
not swear, either by heaven or by
earth or by any other oath, but let
your "Yes" be yes and your "No" be
no, so that you may not fall under
condemnation.

The Prayer of Faith

13 Are any among you suffering? They should pray. Are any
cheerful? They should sing songs of
praise. 14 Are any among you sick?
They should call for the elders of
the church and have them pray
over them, anointing them with oil
in the name of the Lord. 15 The
prayer of faith will save the sick,
and the Lord will raise them up;
and anyone who has committed
sins will be forgiven. 16 Therefore
confess your sins to one another,
and pray for one another, so that
you may be healed. The prayer of
the righteous is powerful and effective. 17 Elijah was a human being
like us, and he prayed fervently
that it might not rain, and for three
years and six months it did not rain
on the earth. 18 Then he prayed
again, and the heaven gave rain
and the earth yielded its harvest.

19 My brothers and sisters,[y] if
anyone among you wanders from
the truth and is brought back by
another, 20 you should know that
whoever brings back a sinner from
wandering will save the sinner's[z]
soul from death and will cover a
multitude of sins.

5.7 Deut 11.14; Jer 5.24
5.8 1 Pet 4.7
5.9 Jas 4.11,12; Mt 24.33
5.10 Mt 5.12
5.11 Mt 5.10; Job 1.21,22; 42.10; Num 14.18
5.12 Mt 5.34-37
5.13 v. 10; Ps 50.15; Col 3.16
5.14 Mk 6.13
5.16 Mt 3.6; 1 Pet 2.24; Jn 9.31
5.17 Acts 14.15; 1 Kings 17.1; Lk 4.25
5.18 1 Kings 18.42, 45
5.19 Mt 18.15
5.20 Rom 11.14; 1 Pet 4.8

v Gk *brothers* w Or *is at hand*
x Gk *Brothers* y Gk *My brothers*
z Gk *his*

THE FIRST LETTER OF

Peter

Title and Background

The recipients of this letter had been suffering various trials and afflictions, and the possibility of greater and more severe difficulties was very real. This letter was addressed to Christians who were scattered throughout the Roman world.

Author and Date of Writing

The author identifies himself as the apostle Peter, and the contents and character of the letter tend to support his authorship. Moreover, the letter reflects the history and terminology of the Gospels and Acts, notably Peter's speeches. It was written about A.D. 64.

Theme and Message

1 Peter touches on various doctrines and has much to say about Christian life and duties. It has been characterized as a letter of separation, of suffering and persecution, of suffering and glory, of hope, of pilgrimage, of courage, and as a letter dealing with the true grace of God. It contains numerous exhortations.

Outline

I. Greetings (1.1-2)
II. Praise for God's Grace and Salvation (1.3-12)
III. Holy Living (1.13–5.11)
IV. The Purpose of the Letter (5.12)
V. Closing Greetings (5.13-14)

Salutation

1 Peter, an apostle of Jesus
Christ,
To the exiles of the Dispersion in
Pontus, Galatia, Cappadocia, Asia,
and Bithynia, 2 who have been chosen and destined by God the Father
and sanctified by the Spirit to be
obedient to Jesus Christ and to be
sprinkled with his blood:
May grace and peace be yours in
abundance.

A Living Hope

3 Blessed be the God and Father
of our Lord Jesus Christ! By his
great mercy he has given us a new
birth into a living hope through the
resurrection of Jesus Christ from
the dead, 4 and into an inheritance
that is imperishable, undefiled,
and unfading, kept in heaven for
you, 5 who are being protected by
the power of God through faith for
a salvation ready to be revealed in
the last time. 6 In this you rejoice,[a]
even if now for a little while you
have had to suffer various trials,
7 so that the genuineness of your
faith—being more precious than
gold that, though perishable, is
tested by fire—may be found to result in praise and glory and honor
when Jesus Christ is revealed. 8 Although you have not seen[b] him,
you love him; and even though you
do not see him now, you believe in
him and rejoice with an indescribable and glorious joy, 9 for you are
receiving the outcome of your
faith, the salvation of your souls.
10 Concerning this salvation,
the prophets who prophesied of the
grace that was to be yours made
careful search and inquiry, 11 inquiring about the person or time

1.1 2 Pet 2.1; Acts 2.5,9
1.2 2 Thes 2.13; Heb 10.22; 2 Pet 1.2
1.3 2 Cor 1.3; Jas 1.18; 1 Cor 15.20
1.4 Col 3.24
1.5 Jn 10.28
1.6 Rom 5.2; 1 Pet 5.10; Jas 1.2
1.7 Jas 1.3; Ps 66.10; Rom 2.7
1.8 1 Jn 4.20; Jn 20.29
1.9 Rom 6.22
1.10 Mt 13.17; 26.24
1.11 2 Pet 1.21; Isa ch. 53

[a] Or *Rejoice in this* [b] Other ancient authorities read *known*

that the Spirit of Christ within
them indicated when it testified in
advance to the sufferings destined
for Christ and the subsequent glory. 12 It was revealed to them that
they were serving not themselves
but you, in regard to the things that
have now been announced to you
through those who brought you
good news by the Holy Spirit sent
from heaven—things into which
angels long to look!

A Call to Holy Living

13 Therefore prepare your
minds for action;[c] discipline yourselves; set all your hope on the
grace that Jesus Christ will bring
you when he is revealed. 14 Like
obedient children, do not be conformed to the desires that you formerly had in ignorance. 15 Instead,
as he who called you is holy, be
holy yourselves in all your conduct;
16 for it is written, "You shall be
holy, for I am holy."

17 If you invoke as Father the
one who judges all people impartially according to their deeds, live
in reverent fear during the time of
your exile. 18 You know that you
were ransomed from the futile
ways inherited from your ancestors, not with perishable things like
silver or gold, 19 but with the precious blood of Christ, like that of a
lamb without defect or blemish.
20 He was destined before the foundation of the world, but was revealed at the end of the ages for
your sake. 21 Through him you have
come to trust in God, who raised
him from the dead and gave him
glory, so that your faith and hope
are set on God.

22 Now that you have purified
your souls by your obedience to the
truth[d] so that you have genuine
mutual love, love one another
deeply[e] from the heart.[f] 23 You
have been born anew, not of perishable but of imperishable seed,
through the living and enduring
word of God.[g] 24 For

"All flesh is like grass
and all its glory like the
flower of grass.
The grass withers,
and the flower falls,
25 but the word of the Lord
endures forever."

That word is the good news that
was announced to you.

The Living Stone and a Chosen People

2 Rid yourselves, therefore, of
all malice, and all guile, insin-
cerity, envy, and all slander. 2 Like
newborn infants, long for the pure,
spiritual milk, so that by it you may
grow into salvation— 3 if indeed
you have tasted that the Lord is
good.

4 Come to him, a living stone,
though rejected by mortals yet chosen and precious in God's sight,
and 5 like living stones, let yourselves be built[h] into a spiritual
house, to be a holy priesthood, to
offer spiritual sacrifices acceptable
to God through Jesus Christ. 6 For
it stands in scripture:

"See, I am laying in Zion a
stone,
a cornerstone chosen and
precious;
and whoever believes in
him[i] will not be put to
shame."

7 To you then who believe, he is
precious; but for those who do not
believe,

"The stone that the builders
rejected
has become the very head
of the corner,"

8 and

"A stone that makes them
stumble,
and a rock that makes
them fall."

They stumble because they disobey the word, as they were destined to do.

9 But you are a chosen race, a
royal priesthood, a holy nation,
God's own people,[j] in order that

1.12 Dan 9.24; Eph 3.10 **1.13** Eph 6.14; 1 Thes 5.6 **1.14** Rom 12.2; Eph 4.18 **1.15** 2 Cor 7.1 **1.16** Lev 11.44 **1.17** Deut 10.17; Heb 12.28 **1.18** 1 Cor 6.20; Ezek 20.18 **1.19** Ex 12.5 **1.20** Eph 1.4; Heb 9.26 **1.22** Jas 4.8; Heb 13.1 **1.23** Jn 3.3; 1.13; Heb 4.12 **1.24** Isa 40.6-9; Jas 1.10,11 **1.25** Jn 1.1 **2.1** Eph 4.22; Jas 1.21; 4.11 **2.2** Mk 10.15; 1 Cor 3.2 **2.3** Heb 6.5; Titus 3.4 **2.4** v. 7 **2.5** Heb 13.15; Phil 4.18 **2.6** Isa 28.16; Eph 2.20 **2.7** Ps 118.22; Mt 21.42 **2.8** Isa 8.14; 1 Cor 1.23; Rom 9.22 **2.9** Deut 10.15; Acts 26.18

[c] Gk *gird up the loins of your mind* [d] Other ancient authorities add *through the Spirit* [e] Or *constantly* [f] Other ancient authorities read *a pure heart* [g] Or *through the word of the living and enduring God* [h] Or *you yourselves are being built* [i] Or *it* [j] Gk *a people for his possession*

you may proclaim the mighty acts
of him who called you out of darkness into his marvelous light.
10 Once you were not a people,
but now you are God's
people;
once you had not received
mercy,
but now you have received
mercy.

Live as Servants of God

11 Beloved, I urge you as aliens
and exiles to abstain from the desires of the flesh that wage war
against the soul. 12 Conduct yourselves honorably among the Gentiles, so that, though they malign
you as evildoers, they may see your
honorable deeds and glorify God
when he comes to judge.[k]
13 For the Lord's sake accept
the authority of every human institution,[l] whether of the emperor as
supreme, 14 or of governors, as sent
by him to punish those who do
wrong and to praise those who do
right. 15 For it is God's will that by
doing right you should silence the
ignorance of the foolish. 16 As servants[m] of God, live as free people,
yet do not use your freedom as a
pretext for evil. 17 Honor everyone.
Love the family of believers.[n] Fear
God. Honor the emperor.

The Example of Christ's Suffering

18 Slaves, accept the authority
of your masters with all deference,
not only those who are kind and
gentle but also those who are
harsh. 19 For it is a credit to you if,
being aware of God, you endure
pain while suffering unjustly. 20 If
you endure when you are beaten
for doing wrong, what credit is
that? But if you endure when you
do right and suffer for it, you have
God's approval. 21 For to this you
have been called, because Christ
also suffered for you, leaving you
an example, so that you should follow in his steps.
22 "He committed no sin,
and no deceit was found in
his mouth."

2.10 Hos 1.9,10 **2.11** Rom 12.1; Ps 39.12; Gal 5.16; Jas 4.1 **2.12** Phil 2.15; 1 Pet 3.16; Mt 5.16 **2.13** Rom 13.1 **2.14** Rom 13.4,3 **2.15** 1 Pet 3.17; Titus 2.8 **2.16** Gal 5.1; 1 Cor 7.22 **2.17** Rom 12.10; Heb 13.1 **2.18** Eph 6.5 **2.19** Rom 13.5 **2.20** 1 Pet 3.17 **2.21** Mt 16.24; Acts 14.22 **2.22** Isa 53.9

2.23 Isa 53.7; Heb 12.3; Lk 23.46 **2.24** Heb 9.28; Rom 6.2; Isa 53.5 **2.25** Isa 53.6; 1 Pet 5.4 **3.1** Eph 5.22; 1 Cor 7.16 **3.3** 1 Tim 2.9; Isa 3.18-23 **3.4** Rom 7.22 **3.5** 1 Tim 5.5 **3.6** Gen 18.12 **3.7** Eph 5.25; 1 Thes 4.4; Mt 5.23ff **3.8** Phil 2.3; 1 Pet 5.5 **3.9** Rom 12.17; Heb 6.14

23 When he was abused, he did not
return abuse; when he suffered, he
did not threaten; but he entrusted
himself to the one who judges justly. 24 He himself bore our sins in his
body on the cross,[o] so that, free
from sins, we might live for righteousness; by his wounds[p] you
have been healed. 25 For you were
going astray like sheep, but now
you have returned to the shepherd
and guardian of your souls.

Wives and Husbands

3 Wives, in the same way, accept the authority of your husbands, so that, even if some of
them do not obey the word, they
may be won over without a word by
their wives' conduct, 2 when they
see the purity and reverence of
your lives. 3 Do not adorn yourselves outwardly by braiding your
hair, and by wearing gold ornaments or fine clothing; 4 rather, let
your adornment be the inner self
with the lasting beauty of a gentle
and quiet spirit, which is very precious in God's sight. 5 It was in this
way long ago that the holy women
who hoped in God used to adorn
themselves by accepting the authority of their husbands. 6 Thus
Sarah obeyed Abraham and called
him lord. You have become her
daughters as long as you do what is
good and never let fears alarm you.
7 Husbands, in the same way,
show consideration for your wives
in your life together, paying honor
to the woman as the weaker sex,[q]
since they too are also heirs of the
gracious gift of life—so that nothing may hinder your prayers.

Suffering for Doing Right

8 Finally, all of you, have unity
of spirit, sympathy, love for one another, a tender heart, and a humble
mind. 9 Do not repay evil for evil or
abuse for abuse; but, on the contrary, repay with a blessing. It is for

[k] Gk *God on the day of visitation*
[l] Or *every institution ordained for human beings* [m] Gk *slaves* [n] Gk *Love the brotherhood* [o] Or *carried up our sins in his body to the tree* [p] Gk *bruise*
[q] Gk *vessel*

this that you were called—that you
might inherit a blessing. 10 For

"Those who desire life
and desire to see good
days,
let them keep their tongues
from evil
and their lips from
speaking deceit;
11 let them turn away from evil
and do good;
let them seek peace and
pursue it.
12 For the eyes of the Lord are
on the righteous,
and his ears are open to
their prayer.
But the face of the Lord is
against those who do
evil."

13 Now who will harm you if
you are eager to do what is good?
14 But even if you do suffer for doing
what is right, you are blessed. Do
not fear what they fear,[r] and do
not be intimidated, 15 but in your
hearts sanctify Christ as Lord. Always be ready to make your defense to anyone who demands from
you an accounting for the hope
that is in you; 16 yet do it with gentleness and reverence.[s] Keep your
conscience clear, so that, when you
are maligned, those who abuse you
for your good conduct in Christ
may be put to shame. 17 For it is
better to suffer for doing good, if
suffering should be God's will,
than to suffer for doing evil. 18 For
Christ also suffered[t] for sins once
for all, the righteous for the unrighteous, in order to bring you[u] to
God. He was put to death in the
flesh, but made alive in the spirit,
19 in which also he went and made
a proclamation to the spirits in
prison, 20 who in former times did
not obey, when God waited patiently in the days of Noah, during
the building of the ark, in which a
few, that is, eight persons, were
saved through water. 21 And baptism, which this prefigured, now
saves you—not as a removal of dirt
from the body, but as an appeal to
God for[v] a good conscience,
through the resurrection of Jesus

3.10 Ps 34.12-16; Jas 1.26; 1 Pet 2.1, 22
3.13 Prov 16.7
3.14 1 Pet 2.19ff; Isa 8.12,13
3.15 Col 4.6; 1 Pet 1.3; 1.17
3.16 Heb 13.18; 1 Pet 2.12, 15
3.17 1 Pet 2.20, 15
3.18 1 Pet 2.21; 2 Cor 13.4; Eph 3.12; 1 Pet 4.1,6
3.19 1 Pet 4.6
3.20 Gen 6.3,5; Heb 11.7; Gen 8.18
3.21 Titus 3.5; Heb 9.14; 1 Pet 1.3
3.22 Rom 8.34, 38
4.1 1 Pet 3.18; Gal 5.24
4.2 Gal 2.20; Rom 6.11
4.3 Eph 4.17
4.4 1 Pet 3.16
4.5 Acts 10.42; 2 Tim 4.1
4.6 1 Pet 3.19
4.7 Rom 13.11; 1 Pet 1.13
4.8 Heb 13.1; 1 Cor 13.7
4.9 Heb 13.2; 2 Cor 9.7
4.10 Rom 12.6,7; 1 Cor 4.1
4.11 Eph 6.10; 5.20; 1 Tim 6.16

Christ, 22 who has gone into heaven
and is at the right hand of God,
with angels, authorities, and powers made subject to him.

Good Stewards of God's Grace

4 Since therefore Christ suffered in the flesh,[w] arm yourselves also with the same intention
(for whoever has suffered in the
flesh has finished with sin), 2 so as
to live for the rest of your earthly
life[x] no longer by human desires
but by the will of God. 3 You have
already spent enough time in doing
what the Gentiles like to do, living
in licentiousness, passions, drunkenness, revels, carousing, and lawless idolatry. 4 They are surprised
that you no longer join them in the
same excesses of dissipation, and
so they blaspheme.[y] 5 But they will
have to give an accounting to him
who stands ready to judge the living and the dead. 6 For this is the
reason the gospel was proclaimed
even to the dead, so that, though
they had been judged in the flesh
as everyone is judged, they might
live in the spirit as God does.

7 The end of all things is near;[z]
therefore be serious and discipline
yourselves for the sake of your
prayers. 8 Above all, maintain constant love for one another, for love
covers a multitude of sins. 9 Be hospitable to one another without
complaining. 10 Like good stewards
of the manifold grace of God, serve
one another with whatever gift
each of you has received. 11 Whoever speaks must do so as one speaking the very words of God; whoever
serves must do so with the strength
that God supplies, so that God may
be glorified in all things through
Jesus Christ. To him belong the
glory and the power forever and
ever. Amen.

[r] Gk *their fear* [s] Or *respect* [t] Other ancient authorities read *died* [u] Other ancient authorities read *us* [v] Or *a pledge to God from* [w] Other ancient authorities add *for us*; others, *for you* [x] Gk *rest of the time in the flesh* [y] Or *they malign you* [z] Or *is at hand*

Suffering as a Christian

12 Beloved, do not be surprised at the fiery ordeal that is taking place among you to test you, as though something strange were happening to you. 13 But rejoice insofar as you are sharing Christ's sufferings, so that you may also be glad and shout for joy when his glory is revealed. 14 If you are reviled for the name of Christ, you are blessed, because the spirit of glory,[a] which is the Spirit of God, is resting on you.[b] 15 But let none of you suffer as a murderer, a thief, a criminal, or even as a mischief maker. 16 Yet if any of you suffers as a Christian, do not consider it a disgrace, but glorify God because you bear this name. 17 For the time has come for judgment to begin with the household of God; if it begins with us, what will be the end for those who do not obey the gospel of God? 18 And

"If it is hard for the
righteous to be saved,
what will become of the
ungodly and the
sinners?"

19 Therefore, let those suffering in accordance with God's will entrust themselves to a faithful Creator, while continuing to do good.

Tending the Flock of God

5 Now as an elder myself and a witness of the sufferings of Christ, as well as one who shares in the glory to be revealed, I exhort the elders among you 2 to tend the flock of God that is in your charge, exercising the oversight,[c] not under compulsion but willingly, as God would have you do it[d]—not for sordid gain but eagerly. 3 Do not lord it over those in your charge, but be examples to the flock. 4 And when the chief shepherd appears, you will win the crown of glory that never fades away. 5 In the same way, you who are younger must accept the authority of the elders.[e] And all of you must clothe yourselves with humility in your dealings with one another, for

"God opposes the proud,
but gives grace to the
humble."

6 Humble yourselves therefore under the mighty hand of God, so that he may exalt you in due time. 7 Cast all your anxiety on him, because he cares for you. 8 Discipline yourselves, keep alert.[f] Like a roaring lion your adversary the devil prowls around, looking for someone to devour. 9 Resist him, steadfast in your faith, for you know that your brothers and sisters[g] in all the world are undergoing the same kinds of suffering. 10 And after you have suffered for a little while, the God of all grace, who has called you to his eternal glory in Christ, will himself restore, support, strengthen, and establish you. 11 To him be the power forever and ever. Amen.

Final Greetings and Benediction

12 Through Silvanus, whom I consider a faithful brother, I have written this short letter to encourage you and to testify that this is the true grace of God. Stand fast in it. 13 Your sister church[h] in Babylon, chosen together with you, sends you greetings; and so does my son Mark. 14 Greet one another with a kiss of love.

Peace to all of you who are in Christ.[i]

4.12 1 Pet 1.6,7
4.13 Phil 3.10; Rom 8.17
4.14 Mt 5.11
4.15 1 Thes 4.11
4.16 Acts 5.41
4.17 Jer 25.29; Mal 3.5
4.18 Prov 11.31; Lk 23.31
4.19 2 Tim 1.12
5.1 Lk 24.48; 1 Pet 1.5, 7; Rev 1.9
5.2 Jn 21.16; 1 Cor 9.17; 1 Tim 3.3, 8; Titus 1.7
5.3 Ezek 34.4; Phil 3.17
5.4 Heb 13.20; 2 Tim 4.8
5.5 Jas 4.6; Isa 57.15
5.6 Jas 4.10
5.7 Ps 37.5; Mt 6.25; Heb 13.5
5.8 Lk 21.34; Job 1.7
5.9 Jas 4.7; Col 2.5; Acts 14.22
5.10 Heb 13.21; 2 Thes 2.17
5.12 2 Cor 1.19; Heb 13.22
5.13 Acts 12.12
5.14 Rom 16.16; Eph 6.23

[a] Other ancient authorities add *and of power* [b] Other ancient authorities add *On their part he is blasphemed, but on your part he is glorified* [c] Other ancient authorities lack *exercising the oversight* [d] Other ancient authorities lack *as God would have you do it* [e] Or *of those who are older* [f] Or *be vigilant* [g] Gk *your brotherhood* [h] Gk *She who is* [i] Other ancient authorities add *Amen*

THE SECOND LETTER OF

Peter

Title and Background

The recipients of this letter were probably the same group of Christians addressed in Peter's first letter. They were in danger of being confused by false teachers.

Author and Date of Writing

The author identifies himself as Simon Peter. He asserts that this is his second letter to the readers (3.1) and refers to Paul as "our beloved brother" (3.15). The character of the letter is compatible with the claim that it was written by Peter. If this is so, it was written about A.D. 66. Some, however, maintain that it is a much later work.

Theme and Message

Peter as a "shepherd" of Christ's sheep is particularly concerned about the false teachers and evildoers who have come into the church. He teaches the church how to deal with these false teachers, but he also recommends to his readers a wholesome combination of Christian faith and practice. The Lord is certain to return, so the believers are to be watchful!

Outline

I. Introduction (1.1-2)
II. Growth in Christian Virtues (1.3-11)
III. Peter's Message (1.12-21)
IV. Warning Against False Teachers (2.1-22)
V. Christ's Return (3.1-16)
VI. Conclusion (3.17-18)

Salutation

1 Simeon[a] Peter, a servant[b]
and apostle of Jesus Christ,
To those who have received a
faith as precious as ours through
the righteousness of our God and
Savior Jesus Christ:[c]
2 May grace and peace be yours
in abundance in the knowledge of
God and of Jesus our Lord.

The Christian's Call and Election

3 His divine power has given us
everything needed for life and godliness, through the knowledge of
him who called us by[d] his own glory and goodness. 4 Thus he has giv-
en us, through these things, his
precious and very great promises,
so that through them you may escape from the corruption that is in
the world because of lust, and may
become participants of the divine
nature. 5 For this very reason, you
must make every effort to support
your faith with goodness, and
goodness with knowledge, 6 and
knowledge with self-control, and
self-control with endurance, and
endurance with godliness, 7 and
godliness with mutual[e] affection,
and mutual[e] affection with love.
8 For if these things are yours and
are increasing among you, they
keep you from being ineffective
and unfruitful in the knowledge of
our Lord Jesus Christ. 9 For anyone
who lacks these things is nearsighted and blind, and is forgetful of the

1.1 Rom 1.1; 1 Pet 1.1; Rom 1.12; 3.21-26; Titus 2.13
1.2 1 Pet 1.2; vv. 3,8
1.3 1 Pet 1.5; 1 Thes 2.12
1.4 2 Cor 7.1; Eph 4.24; 1 Jn 3.2; 2 Pet 2.18-20
1.5 2 Pet 3.18; Col 2.3
1.6 Acts 24.25; Lk 21.19; v. 3
1.7 1 Thes 3.12
1.8 Jn 15.2; Titus 3.14
1.9 1 Jn 2.11; Eph 5.26; 1 Jn 1.7

[a] Other ancient authorities read *Simon*
[b] Gk *slave*
[c] Or *of our God and the Savior Jesus Christ*
[d] Other ancient authorities read *through*
[e] Gk *brotherly*

cleansing of past sins. 10 Therefore,
brothers and sisters,[f] be all the
more eager to confirm your call and
election, for if you do this, you will
never stumble. 11 For in this way,
entry into the eternal kingdom of
our Lord and Savior Jesus Christ
will be richly provided for you.
12 Therefore I intend to keep on
reminding you of these things,
though you know them already and
are established in the truth that
has come to you. 13 I think it right,
as long as I am in this body,[g] to
refresh your memory, 14 since I
know that my death[h] will come
soon, as indeed our Lord Jesus
Christ has made clear to me. 15 And
I will make every effort so that after
my departure you may be able at
any time to recall these things.

Eyewitnesses of Christ's Glory

16 For we did not follow cleverly
devised myths when we made
known to you the power and coming of our Lord Jesus Christ, but we
had been eyewitnesses of his majesty. 17 For he received honor and
glory from God the Father when
that voice was conveyed to him by
the Majestic Glory, saying, "This is
my Son, my Beloved,[i] with whom
I am well pleased." 18 We ourselves
heard this voice come from heaven,
while we were with him on the holy
mountain.
19 So we have the prophetic
message more fully confirmed. You
will do well to be attentive to this
as to a lamp shining in a dark place,
until the day dawns and the morning star rises in your hearts. 20 First
of all you must understand this,
that no prophecy of scripture is a
matter of one's own interpretation,
21 because no prophecy ever came
by human will, but men and wom-
en moved by the Holy Spirit spoke
from God.[j]

False Prophets and Their Punishment

2 But false prophets also arose
among the people, just as
there will be false teachers among
you, who will secretly bring in destructive opinions. They will even
deny the Master who bought
them—bringing swift destruction
on themselves. 2 Even so, many will
follow their licentious ways, and
because of these teachers[k] the way
of truth will be maligned. 3 And in
their greed they will exploit you
with deceptive words. Their condemnation, pronounced against
them long ago, has not been idle,
and their destruction is not asleep.
4 For if God did not spare the
angels when they sinned, but cast
them into hell[l] and committed
them to chains[m] of deepest darkness to be kept until the judgment;
5 and if he did not spare the ancient
world, even though he saved Noah,
a herald of righteousness, with sev-
en others, when he brought a flood
on a world of the ungodly; 6 and if
by turning the cities of Sodom and
Gomorrah to ashes he condemned
them to extinction[n] and made
them an example of what is coming
to the ungodly;[o] 7 and if he rescued
Lot, a righteous man greatly distressed by the licentiousness of the
lawless 8 (for that righteous man,
living among them day after day,
was tormented in his righteous
soul by their lawless deeds that he
saw and heard), 9 then the Lord
knows how to rescue the godly
from trial, and to keep the unrighteous under punishment until the
day of judgment 10—especially
those who indulge their flesh in depraved lust, and who despise authority.
Bold and willful, they are not
afraid to slander the glorious
ones,[p] 11 whereas angels, though
greater in might and power, do not
bring against them a slanderous
judgment from the Lord.[q] 12 These

1.12 1 Jn 2.21 **1.13** 2 Cor 5.1 **1.14** 2 Tim 4.6; Jn 21.18,19 **1.16** 1 Tim 1.4; Mt 17.1; Mk 9.2 **1.17** Mt 3.17; Lk 9.35 **1.18** Mt 17.6 **1.19** 1 Pet 1.10, 11; Ps 119.105; Rev 22.16 **1.20f** Rom 12.6 **1.21** 2 Tim 3.16; 1 Pet 1.11; Acts 1.16 **2.1** 1 Tim 4.1; Jude 18; 1 Cor 6.20 **2.3** 1 Tim 6.5; 2 Cor 2.17; Deut 32.35 **2.4** Jude 6; Jn 8.44; Rev 20.1,2 **2.5** Gen 7.1; Heb 11.7; 1 Pet 3.20 **2.6** Gen 19.24; Jude 7; Num 26.10 **2.7** Gen 19.16; 2 Pet 3.17 **2.9** 1 Cor 10.13; Jude 6 **2.10** 2 Pet 3.3; Jude 8; Titus 1.7 **2.11** Jude 9 **2.12** Jude 10

[f] Gk *brothers* [g] Gk *tent* [h] Gk *the putting off of my tent* [i] Other ancient authorities read *my beloved Son* [j] Other ancient authorities read *but moved by the Holy Spirit saints of God spoke* [k] Gk *because of them* [l] Gk *Tartaros* [m] Other ancient authorities read *pits* [n] Other ancient authorities lack *to extinction* [o] Other ancient authorities read *an example to those who were to be ungodly* [p] Or *angels*; Gk *glories* [q] Other ancient authorities read *before the Lord*; others lack the phrase

people, however, are like irrational
animals, mere creatures of instinct, born to be caught and
killed. They slander what they do
not understand, and when those
creatures are destroyed,[r] they also
will be destroyed, 13 suffering[s] the
penalty for doing wrong. They
count it a pleasure to revel in the
daytime. They are blots and blemishes, reveling in their dissipation[t]
while they feast with you. 14 They
have eyes full of adultery, insatiable for sin. They entice unsteady
souls. They have hearts trained in
greed. Accursed children! 15 They
have left the straight road and have
gone astray, following the road of
Balaam son of Bosor,[u] who loved
the wages of doing wrong, 16 but
was rebuked for his own transgression; a speechless donkey spoke with a human voice
and restrained the prophet's madness.

17 These are waterless springs
and mists driven by a storm; for
them the deepest darkness has
been reserved. 18 For they speak
bombastic nonsense, and with licentious desires of the flesh they
entice people who have just[v] escaped from those who live in error.
19 They promise them freedom, but
they themselves are slaves of corruption; for people are slaves to
whatever masters them. 20 For if,
after they have escaped the defilements of the world through the
knowledge of our Lord and Savior
Jesus Christ, they are again entangled in them and overpowered, the
last state has become worse for
them than the first. 21 For it would
have been better for them never to
have known the way of righteousness than, after knowing it, to turn
back from the holy commandment
that was passed on to them. 22 It
has happened to them according to
the true proverb,

"The dog turns back to its
own vomit,"

and,

"The sow is washed only to
wallow in the mud."

2.13 Rom 13.13; Jude 12; 1 Cor 11.20, 21
2.14 v. 18; Jude 11; v. 3; Eph 2.3
2.15 Num 22.5,7; Jude 11
2.16 Num 22.21, 23,28,30,31
2.17 Jude 12,13
2.18 Jude 16
2.19f Jn 8.34; Rom 6.16
2.20 Mt 12.45; Lk 11.26; 2 Pet 1.2
2.21 Heb 6.4ff; 2 Pet 3.2; Jude 3
2.22 Prov 26.11
3.3 1 Tim 4.1; Jude 18; 2 Pet 2.10
3.4 Isa 5.9; Jer 17.15; Ezek 12.22; Mt 24.48; Acts 7.60; Mt 10.6
3.5 Gen 1.6,9; Heb 11.3; Ps 24.2; Col 1.17
3.6 Gen 7.21,22
3.7 v. 10; 2 Thes 1.7; 1 Cor 3.13
3.8 Ps 90.4
3.9 Heb 10.37; Isa 30.18; 1 Pet 3.20; Rom 2.4
3.10 Mt 24.43; 1 Thes 5.2; Mt 24.35; Rev 21.1

The Promise of the Lord's Coming

3 This is now, beloved, the second letter I am writing to you;
in them I am trying to arouse your
sincere intention by reminding you
2 that you should remember the
words spoken in the past by the
holy prophets, and the commandment of the Lord and Savior spoken
through your apostles. 3 First of all
you must understand this, that in
the last days scoffers will come,
scoffing and indulging their own
lusts 4 and saying, "Where is the
promise of his coming? For ever
since our ancestors died,[w] all
things continue as they were from
the beginning of creation!" 5 They
deliberately ignore this fact, that
by the word of God heavens existed
long ago and an earth was formed
out of water and by means of water,
6 through which the world of that
time was deluged with water and
perished. 7 But by the same word
the present heavens and earth have
been reserved for fire, being kept
until the day of judgment and destruction of the godless.

8 But do not ignore this one
fact, beloved, that with the Lord
one day is like a thousand years,
and a thousand years are like one
day. 9 The Lord is not slow about
his promise, as some think of slowness, but is patient with you,[x] not
wanting any to perish, but all to
come to repentance. 10 But the day
of the Lord will come like a thief,
and then the heavens will pass
away with a loud noise, and the elements will be dissolved with fire,
and the earth and everything that is
done on it will be disclosed.[y]

11 Since all these things are to
be dissolved in this way, what sort
of persons ought you to be in leading lives of holiness and godliness,

[r] Gk *in their destruction* [s] Other ancient authorities read *receiving* [t] Other ancient authorities read *love feasts* [u] Other ancient authorities read *Beor* [v] Other ancient authorities read *actually* [w] Gk *our fathers fell asleep* [x] Other ancient authorities read *on your account* [y] Other ancient authorities read *will be burned up*

[12]waiting for and hastening[z] the
coming of the day of God, because
of which the heavens will be set
ablaze and dissolved, and the elements will melt with fire? [13]But, in
accordance with his promise, we
wait for new heavens and a new
earth, where righteousness is at
home.

Final Exhortation and Doxology

14 Therefore, beloved, while
you are waiting for these things,
strive to be found by him at peace,
without spot or blemish; [15]and regard the patience of our Lord as
salvation. So also our beloved
brother Paul wrote to you according to the wisdom given him,
[16]speaking of this as he does in all
his letters. There are some things
in them hard to understand, which
the ignorant and unstable twist to
their own destruction, as they do
the other scriptures. [17]You therefore, beloved, since you are forewarned, beware that you are not
carried away with the error of the
lawless and lose your own stability.
[18]But grow in the grace and knowledge of our Lord and Savior Jesus
Christ. To him be the glory both
now and to the day of eternity.
Amen.[a]

3.12 1 Cor 1.7; Titus 2.13; Ps 50.3; Isa 34.4; v. 10
3.13 Isa 65.17; 66.22; Rev 21.1
3.14 2 Pet 1.10; 1 Cor 15.58; Phil 2.15
3.15 v. 9; 1 Cor 3.10; Eph 3.3
3.16 v. 14; Heb 5.11; 2 Pet 2.14; v. 2
3.17 1 Cor 10.12; 2 Pet 2.18; Rev 2.5

[z] Or *earnestly desiring* [a] Other ancient authorities lack *Amen*

THE FIRST LETTER OF

John

Title and Background

False teachers were trying to mislead first-century Christians by denying, among other things, the true humanity of Christ. This view came to be called Gnosticism and is the background of much of 1 John.

Author and Date of Writing

The author is John son of Zebedee–the apostle and the author of the Gospel of John. He was a first cousin of Jesus. The letter is difficult to date with precision, but many factors indicate that it was written near the end of the first century, probably around A.D. 90.

Theme and Message

John had two basic purposes in mind in this letter: (1) to expose false teachers, and (2) to give believers assurance of salvation. In keeping with his intention to combat Gnostic teachers, John specifically struck at their total lack of morality; and by giving eyewitness testimony to the human nature of the Son of God, he sought to confirm his readers' belief in the incarnate Christ. He tells his readers that if he is successful in doing this, it would give him great joy.

Outline

I. The Reality of the Incarnation (1.1-4)
II. Fellowship With the Father and the Son (1.5–2.28)
III. Divine Sonship (2.29–4.6)
IV. Ethics and Christ (4.7–5.12)
V. Great Christian Certainties (5.13-21)

The Word of Life

1 We declare to you what was
from the beginning, what we
have heard, what we have seen
with our eyes, what we have looked
at and touched with our hands,
concerning the word of life— 2 this
life was revealed, and we have seen
it and testify to it, and declare to
you the eternal life that was with
the Father and was revealed to
us— 3 we declare to you what we
have seen and heard so that you
also may have fellowship with us;
and truly our fellowship is with the
Father and with his Son Jesus
Christ. 4 We are writing these
things so that our[a] joy may be
complete.

God Is Light

5 This is the message we have
heard from him and proclaim to
you, that God is light and in him
there is no darkness at all. 6 If we
say that we have fellowship with
him while we are walking in darkness, we lie and do not do what is
true; 7 but if we walk in the light as
he himself is in the light, we have
fellowship with one another, and
the blood of Jesus his Son cleanses
us from all sin. 8 If we say that we
have no sin, we deceive ourselves,
and the truth is not in us. 9 If we
confess our sins, he who is faithful
and just will forgive us our sins and
cleanse us from all unrighteousness. 10 If we say that we have not
sinned, we make him a liar, and his
word is not in us.

1.1 Jn 1.1,14; 2 Pet 1.16; Jn 20.27 **1.2** Jn 1.1-4; Rom 16.26; Jn 21.24 **1.3** Acts 4.20; 1 Cor 1.9 **1.4** 1 Jn 2.1; Jn 3.29 **1.5** 1 Jn 3.11 **1.6** 2 Cor 6.14; Jn 8.55; 3.21 **1.7** Heb 9.14; 1 Pet 1.19; Rev 1.5 **1.8** Job 15.14; Prov 20.9; Jas 3.2; 1 Jn 2.4 **1.9** Ps 51.2 **1.10** 1 Jn 5.10; 2.14

[a] Other ancient authorities read *your*

Christ Our Advocate

2 My little children, I am writing
these things to you so that you
may not sin. But if anyone does sin,
we have an advocate with the Father, Jesus Christ the righteous;
2 and he is the atoning sacrifice for
our sins, and not for ours only but
also for the sins of the whole world.
3 Now by this we may be sure
that we know him, if we obey his
commandments. 4 Whoever says, "I
have come to know him," but does
not obey his commandments, is a
liar, and in such a person the truth
does not exist; 5 but whoever obeys
his word, truly in this person the
love of God has reached perfection.
By this we may be sure that we are
in him: 6 whoever says, "I abide in
him," ought to walk just as he
walked.

A New Commandment

7 Beloved, I am writing you no
new commandment, but an old
commandment that you have had
from the beginning; the old commandment is the word that you
have heard. 8 Yet I am writing you a
new commandment that is true in
him and in you, because[b] the darkness is passing away and the true
light is already shining. 9 Whoever
says, "I am in the light," while hating a brother or sister,[c] is still in
the darkness. 10 Whoever loves a
brother or sister[d] lives in the light,
and in such a person[e] there is no
cause for stumbling. 11 But whoever
hates another believer[f] is in the
darkness, walks in the darkness,
and does not know the way to go,
because the darkness has brought
on blindness.

12 I am writing to you, little
children,
because your sins are
forgiven on account of
his name.
13 I am writing to you, fathers,
because you know him who
is from the beginning.
I am writing to you, young
people,
because you have
conquered the evil one.
14 I write to you, children,
because you know the
Father.
I write to you, fathers,
because you know him who
is from the beginning.
I write to you, young people,
because you are strong
and the word of God abides
in you,
and you have overcome
the evil one.

15 Do not love the world or the
things in the world. The love of the
Father is not in those who love
the world; 16 for all that is in the
world—the desire of the flesh, the
desire of the eyes, the pride in
riches—comes not from the Father
but from the world. 17 And the
world and its desire[g] are passing
away, but those who do the will of
God live forever.

Warning against Antichrists

18 Children, it is the last hour!
As you have heard that antichrist is
coming, so now many antichrists
have come. From this we know that
it is the last hour. 19 They went out
from us, but they did not belong to
us; for if they had belonged to us,
they would have remained with us.
But by going out they made it plain
that none of them belongs to us.
20 But you have been anointed by
the Holy One, and all of you have
knowledge.[h] 21 I write to you, not
because you do not know the truth,
but because you know it, and you
know that no lie comes from the
truth. 22 Who is the liar but the one
who denies that Jesus is the
Christ?[i] This is the antichrist, the
one who denies the Father and the
Son. 23 No one who denies the Son
has the Father; everyone who confesses the Son has the Father also.
24 Let what you heard from the beginning abide in you. If what you
heard from the beginning abides in
you, then you will abide in the Son
and in the Father. 25 And this is

2.1 Rom 8.34; Heb 7.25
2.2 Rom 3.25; Jn 1.29
2.5 Jn 14.23; 1 Jn 4.12, 13
2.6 Jn 15.4; 1 Pet 2.21
2.7 1 Jn 3.2; 2 Jn 5; 1 Jn 3.11
2.8 Eph 5.8; 1 Thes 5.5; Jn 1.9
2.9 2 Pet 1.9
2.10 1 Jn 3.14; v. 11
2.11 Jn 12.35
2.12 Lk 24.47
2.13 1 Jn 1.1; v. 14
2.14 1 Jn 1.1; Eph 6.10; Jn 5.38
2.15 Rom 12.2; Mt 6.24; Jas 4.4
2.16 Rom 13.14; Prov 27.20; Jas 4.16
2.17 1 Cor 7.31
2.18 1 Pet 4.7; 1 Jn 4.1,3
2.19 Acts 20.30; Mt 24.24; 1 Cor 11.19
2.20 2 Cor 1.21; Acts 3.14; Jn 14.26
2.21 2 Pet 1.12; 1 Jn 3.19
2.23 Jn 14.7
2.24 2 Jn 6; Jn 14.23
2.25 Jn 17.3

[b] Or *that* [c] Gk *hating a brother* [d] Gk *loves a brother* [e] Or *in it* [f] Gk *hates a brother* [g] Or *the desire for it* [h] Other ancient authorities read *you know all things* [i] Or *the Messiah*

what he has promised us,[j] eternal
life.
26 I write these things to you
concerning those who would deceive you. 27 As for you, the anointing that you received from him
abides in you, and so you do not
need anyone to teach you. But as
his anointing teaches you about all
things, and is true and is not a lie,
and just as it has taught you, abide
in him.[k]
28 And now, little children,
abide in him, so that when he is
revealed we may have confidence
and not be put to shame before him
at his coming.

Children of God

29 If you know that he is righteous, you may be sure that everyone who does right has been born
3 of him. 1 See what love the Father has given us, that we
should be called children of God;
and that is what we are. The reason
the world does not know us is that
it did not know him. 2 Beloved, we
are God's children now; what we
will be has not yet been revealed.
What we do know is this: when he[k]
is revealed, we will be like him, for
we will see him as he is. 3 And all
who have this hope in him purify
themselves, just as he is pure.
4 Everyone who commits sin is
guilty of lawlessness; sin is lawlessness. 5 You know that he was revealed to take away sins, and in
him there is no sin. 6 No one who
abides in him sins; no one who sins
has either seen him or known him.
7 Little children, let no one deceive
you. Everyone who does what is
right is righteous, just as he is righteous. 8 Everyone who commits sin
is a child of the devil; for the devil
has been sinning from the beginning. The Son of God was revealed
for this purpose, to destroy the
works of the devil. 9 Those who
have been born of God do not sin,
because God's seed abides in
them;[l] they cannot sin, because
they have been born of God. 10 The
children of God and the children of
the devil are revealed in this way:
all who do not do what is right are
not from God, nor are those who do
not love their brothers and sisters.[m]

Love One Another

11 For this is the message you
have heard from the beginning,
that we should love one another.
12 We must not be like Cain who
was from the evil one and murdered his brother. And why did he
murder him? Because his own
deeds were evil and his brother's
righteous. 13 Do not be astonished,
brothers and sisters,[n] that the
world hates you. 14 We know that
we have passed from death to life
because we love one another. Whoever does not love abides in death.
15 All who hate a brother or sister[m]
are murderers, and you know that
murderers do not have eternal life
abiding in them. 16 We know love
by this, that he laid down his life
for us—and we ought to lay down
our lives for one another. 17 How
does God's love abide in anyone
who has the world's goods and sees
a brother or sister[o] in need and yet
refuses help?
18 Little children, let us love,
not in word or speech, but in truth
and action. 19 And by this we will
know that we are from the truth
and will reassure our hearts before
him 20 whenever our hearts condemn us; for God is greater than
our hearts, and he knows everything. 21 Beloved, if our hearts do
not condemn us, we have boldness
before God; 22 and we receive from
him whatever we ask, because we
obey his commandments and do
what pleases him.
23 And this is his commandment, that we should believe in the
name of his Son Jesus Christ and
love one another, just as he has
commanded us. 24 All who obey his
commandments abide in him, and
he abides in them. And by this we

2.26 2 Jn 7 **2.27** Jn 14.26,17 **2.28** 1 Jn 3.2, 21; 4.17; Mk 8.38; 1 Thes 2.19 **2.29** 1 Jn 3.7,9; 4.7 **3.1** Jn 1.12; 16.3 **3.2** Rom 8.15; 2 Cor 4.17; Rom 8.29; 2 Pet 1.4; 2 Cor 3.18 **3.4** Rom 4.15; 1 Jn 5.17 **3.5** Isa 53.5,6; 2 Cor 5.21 **3.7** 1 Jn 2.1, 26,29 **3.8** Jn 8.44; 16.11; Heb 2.14 **3.9** 1 Jn 5.18; 1 Pet 1.23 **3.10** 1 Jn 2.29

3.11 1 Jn 1.5; Jn 13.34,35; 2 Jn 5 **3.13** Jn 15.18 **3.14** Jn 5.24; 1 Jn 2.9, 11 **3.15** Mt 5.21,22; Jn 8.44; Gal 5.20,21 **3.16** Jn 3.16; 13.1; 15.13 **3.17** Deut 15.7; 1 Jn 4.20 **3.18** Rom 12.9; Jas 1.22 **3.19** 1 Jn 2.21 **3.20** 1 Cor 4.4 **3.21** 1 Jn 5.14 **3.22** Mt 7.7; 21.22; 1 Jn 2.3 **3.23** 1 Jn 2.8

3.24 Rom 8.9; 1 Jn 4.13

j Other ancient authorities read *you* k Or *it*
l Or *because the children of God abide in him*
m Gk *his brother* n Gk *brothers*
o Gk *brother*

know that he abides in us, by the
Spirit that he has given us.

Testing the Spirits

4 Beloved, do not believe every
spirit, but test the spirits to
see whether they are from God; for
many false prophets have gone out
into the world. 2 By this you know
the Spirit of God: every spirit that
confesses that Jesus Christ has
come in the flesh is from God, 3 and
every spirit that does not confess
Jesus[p] is not from God. And this is
the spirit of the antichrist, of which
you have heard that it is coming;
and now it is already in the world.
4 Little children, you are from God,
and have conquered them; for the
one who is in you is greater than
the one who is in the world. 5 They
are from the world; therefore what
they say is from the world, and the
world listens to them. 6 We are from
God. Whoever knows God listens to
us, and whoever is not from God
does not listen to us. From this we
know the spirit of truth and the
spirit of error.

God Is Love

7 Beloved, let us love one another, because love is from God; everyone who loves is born of God and
knows God. 8 Whoever does not
love does not know God, for God is
love. 9 God's love was revealed
among us in this way: God sent his
only Son into the world so that we
might live through him. 10 In this is
love, not that we loved God but
that he loved us and sent his Son to
be the atoning sacrifice for our
sins. 11 Beloved, since God loved us
so much, we also ought to love one
another. 12 No one has ever seen
God; if we love one another, God
lives in us, and his love is perfected
in us.

13 By this we know that we
abide in him and he in us, because
he has given us of his Spirit. 14 And
we have seen and do testify that the
Father has sent his Son as the Savior of the world. 15 God abides in
those who confess that Jesus is the

4.1 Mt 24.4; 2 Pet 2.1; 1 Jn 2.18
4.2 1 Cor 12.3; 1 Jn 2.23
4.3 2 Jn 7; 1 Jn 2.22; 2 Thes 2.7
4.4 1 Jn 5.4
4.5 Jn 3.31; 15.19
4.6 Jn 8.47; 1 Cor 14.37; Jn 14.17; 1 Tim 4.1
4.7 1 Jn 3.10, 11
4.8 v. 16
4.9 Jn 3.16; 1 Jn 5.11
4.10 Rom 5.8,10; 1 Jn 2.2
4.11 Jn 3.16; 15.12
4.12 Jn 1.18; 1 Tim 6.16; 1 Jn 2.5
4.13 1 Jn 3.24
4.15 Rom 10.9
4.16 v. 8; 1 Jn 3.24
4.17 1 Jn 2.28
4.18 Rom 8.15; v. 12
4.19 v. 10
4.20 1 Jn 2.4; 1.6; 3.17
5.1 Jn 1.12; 1 Jn 2.22, 23; Jn 1.13; 8.42
5.2 1 Jn 2.5
5.3 Jn 14.15; 1 Jn 2.5; 2 Jn 6
5.4 Jn 16.33
5.5 1 Jn 4.15
5.6 Jn 19.34
5.7 Jn 15.26

Son of God, and they abide in God.
16 So we have known and believe
the love that God has for us.
God is love, and those who abide
in love abide in God, and God
abides in them. 17 Love has been
perfected among us in this: that we
may have boldness on the day of
judgment, because as he is, so are
we in this world. 18 There is no fear
in love, but perfect love casts out
fear; for fear has to do with punishment, and whoever fears has not
reached perfection in love. 19 We
love[q] because he first loved us.
20 Those who say, "I love God," and
hate their brothers or sisters,[r] are
liars; for those who do not love a
brother or sister[s] whom they have
seen, cannot love God whom they
have not seen. 21 The commandment we have from him is this:
those who love God must love their
brothers and sisters[r] also.

Faith Conquers the World

5 Everyone who believes that
Jesus is the Christ[t] has been
born of God, and everyone who
loves the parent loves the child.
2 By this we know that we love the
children of God, when we love God
and obey his commandments. 3 For
the love of God is this, that we obey
his commandments. And his commandments are not burdensome,
4 for whatever is born of God conquers the world. And this is the victory that conquers the world, our
faith. 5 Who is it that conquers the
world but the one who believes
that Jesus is the Son of God?

Testimony concerning the Son of God

6 This is the one who came by
water and blood, Jesus Christ, not
with the water only but with the
water and the blood. And the Spirit
is the one that testifies, for the
Spirit is the truth. 7 There are three

[p] Other ancient authorities read *does away with Jesus* (Gk *dissolves Jesus*) [q] Other ancient authorities add *him*; others add *God* [r] Gk *brothers* [s] Gk *brother* [t] Or *the Messiah*

that testify:[u] 8 the Spirit and the
water and the blood, and these
three agree. 9 If we receive human
testimony, the testimony of God is
greater; for this is the testimony of
God that he has testified to his
Son. 10 Those who believe in the
Son of God have the testimony in
their hearts. Those who do not believe in God[v] have made him a liar
by not believing in the testimony
that God has given concerning his
Son. 11 And this is the testimony:
God gave us eternal life, and this
life is in his Son. 12 Whoever has the
Son has life; whoever does not have
the Son of God does not have life.

Epilogue

13 I write these things to you
who believe in the name of the Son
of God, so that you may know that
you have eternal life.
14 And this is the boldness we
have in him, that if we ask anything
according to his will, he hears us.
15 And if we know that he hears us
in whatever we ask, we know that
we have obtained the requests
made of him. 16 If you see your
brother or sister[w] committing what
is not a mortal sin, you will ask,
and God[x] will give life to such a
one—to those whose sin is not
mortal. There is sin that is mortal;
I do not say that you should pray
about that. 17 All wrongdoing is sin,
but there is sin that is not mortal.
18 We know that those who are
born of God do not sin, but the one
who was born of God protects
them, and the evil one does not
touch them. 19 We know that we are
God's children, and that the whole
world lies under the power of the
evil one. 20 And we know that the
Son of God has come and has given
us understanding so that we may
know him who is true;[y] and we are
in him who is true, in his Son Jesus
Christ. He is the true God and eternal life.
21 Little children, keep yourselves from idols.[z]

5.8 Mt 18.16 **5.9** Jn 8.17,18; Mt 3.16,17 **5.10** Rom 8.16; Gal 4.6; Jn 3.33 **5.11** 1 Jn 2.25; Jn 1.4 **5.12** Jn 3.36 **5.13** Jn 20.31; 1 Jn 1.1,2 **5.14** 1 Jn 3.21, 22; Mt 7.7 **5.16** Jas 5.15; Heb 6.4,6 **5.17** 1 Jn 3.4 **5.18** 1 Jn 3.9; Jn 14.30 **5.19** 1 Jn 4.6; Gal 1.4 **5.20** Lk 24.45; Jn 17.3; Rev 3.7 **5.21** 1 Cor 10.14

[u] A few other authorities read (with variations) [7] *There are three that testify in heaven, the Father, the Word, and the Holy Spirit, and these three are one.* [8] *And there are three that testify on earth:* [v] Other ancient authorities read *in the Son* [w] Gk *your brother* [x] Gk *he* [y] Other ancient authorities read *know the true God* [z] Other ancient authorities add *Amen*

THE SECOND LETTER OF

John

Title and Background

During the first two centuries A.D. the gospel was taken from place to place by traveling evangelists and teachers. Believers customarily took these missionaries into their homes and gave them provisions for their journey when they left. Since Gnostic teachers also relied on this practice, 2 John was written to urge discernment in supporting traveling teachers.

Author and Date of Writing

John wrote this letter shortly after his first letter, about A.D. 90.

Theme and Message

John writes of how important it is for Christians to love one another. To love means to obey God's commandments, and God's commandments in turn tell us to live lives of love. John again emphasizes the importance of the doctrine that Jesus is God's Son—both God and man. Christians should separate themselves from those who teach otherwise.

Outline

I. Greeting (1-3)
II. Commendation (4)
III. Exhortation and Warning (5-11)
IV. Conclusion (12-13)

Salutation

1 The elder to the elect lady and
her children, whom I love in the
truth, and not only I but also all
who know the truth, 2 because of
the truth that abides in us and will
be with us forever:
3 Grace, mercy, and peace will
be with us from God the Father and
from[a] Jesus Christ, the Father's
Son, in truth and love.

Truth and Love

4 I was overjoyed to find some of
your children walking in the truth,
just as we have been commanded
by the Father. 5 But now, dear lady,
I ask you, not as though I were writing you a new commandment, but
one we have had from the beginning, let us love one another. 6 And
this is love, that we walk according
to his commandments; this is the
commandment just as you have
heard it from the beginning—you
must walk in it.
7 Many deceivers have gone out
into the world, those who do not
confess that Jesus Christ has come
in the flesh; any such person is the
deceiver and the antichrist! 8 Be on
your guard, so that you do not lose
what we[b] have worked for, but may
receive a full reward. 9 Everyone
who does not abide in the teaching
of Christ, but goes beyond it, does
not have God; whoever abides in
the teaching has both the Father
and the Son. 10 Do not receive into
the house or welcome anyone who
comes to you and does not bring
this teaching; 11 for to welcome is
to participate in the evil deeds of
such a person.

1 3 Jn 1; 1 Jn 3.18; Jn 8.32
2 2 Pet 1.12; 1 Jn 1.8
3 1 Tim 1.2
4 3 Jn 3,4
5 1 Jn 2.7; 3.11
6 1 Jn 2.5; 2.24
7 1 Jn 4.1-3; 2.22
8 Mk 13.9; 1 Cor 3.8; Heb 10.32
9 1 Jn 2.23
10 Rom 16.17
11 1 Tim 5.22

[a] Other ancient authorities add *the Lord*
[b] Other ancient authorities read *you*

Final Greetings

12 Although I have much to
write to you, I would rather not use
paper and ink; instead I hope to
come to you and talk with you face
to face, so that our joy may be complete.
13 The children of your elect
sister send you their greetings.[c]

12 3 Jn 13, 14; 1 Jn 1.4
13 v. 1

[c] Other ancient authorities add *Amen*

THE THIRD LETTER OF

John

Title and Background

Itinerant teachers sent out by John were rejected by Diotrephes, a dictatorial leader in one of the churches in the province of Asia. This man had gone so far as to excommunicate members who showed hospitality to John's messengers.

Author and Date of Writing

The letter was probably written about the same time as 1 and 2 John, around A.D. 90. The apostle John is the author.

Theme and Message

John writes to Gaius, his personal friend and a leader in the church. He wants to praise and thank him for his help and to encourage him. He also reproves Diotrephes for not cooperating and for rebelling against John's leadership. In a later visit John will deal with him personally.

Outline

I. Greeting (1-2)
II. Commendation of Gaius (3-8)
III. Condemnation of Diotrephes (9-10)
IV. Exhortation to Gaius (11)
V. Example of Demetrius (12)
VI. Conclusion (13-14)

Salutation

1 The elder to the beloved Gaius, whom I love in truth.

Gaius Commended for His Hospitality

2 Beloved, I pray that all may go
well with you and that you may be
in good health, just as it is well
with your soul. 3 I was overjoyed
when some of the friends[a] arrived
and testified to your faithfulness to
the truth, namely how you walk in
the truth. 4 I have no greater joy
than this, to hear that my children
are walking in the truth.

5 Beloved, you do faithfully
whatever you do for the friends,[a]
even though they are strangers to
you; 6 they have testified to your
love before the church. You will do
well to send them on in a manner
worthy of God; 7 for they began
their journey for the sake of
Christ,[b] accepting no support from
non-believers.[c] 8 Therefore we
ought to support such people, so
that we may become co-workers
with the truth.

1 2 Jn 1
3 2 Jn 4; vv. 5,10
4 1 Cor 4.15; Philem 10
5 Rom 12.13; Heb 13.2
6 Acts 15.3; Titus 3.13
7 Acts 5.41; 20.33,35
9 2 Jn 9
10 2 Jn 12; v. 5; Jn 9.34
11 Ps 37.27; 1 Jn 2.29; 3.6,9
12 1 Tim 3.7; Jn 21.24

Diotrephes and Demetrius

9 I have written something to
the church; but Diotrephes, who
likes to put himself first, does not
acknowledge our authority. 10 So if
I come, I will call attention to what
he is doing in spreading false
charges against us. And not content with those charges, he refuses
to welcome the friends,[a] and even
prevents those who want to do so
and expels them from the church.

11 Beloved, do not imitate what
is evil but imitate what is good.
Whoever does good is from God;
whoever does evil has not seen
God. 12 Everyone has testified favorably about Demetrius, and so
has the truth itself. We also testify

[a] Gk *brothers* [b] Gk *for the sake of the name* [c] Gk *the Gentiles*

for him,[d] and you know that our
testimony is true.

Final Greetings

13 I have much to write to you,
but I would rather not write with
pen and ink; 14 instead I hope to see
you soon, and we will talk together
face to face.
15 Peace to you. The friends
send you their greetings. Greet the
friends there, each by name.

13 2 Jn 12
14 1 Pet 5.14

[d] Gk lacks *for him*

THE LETTER OF

Jude

Title and Background

Jude originated as a personal letter from a leader in the apostolic church to one or more of the congregations dispersed throughout the Roman Empire. The dangers facing the church at this time were not those of outright persecution and extinction but of heresy and distortion of the faith.

Author and Date of Writing

The author identifies himself as Jude, another form of the Hebrew name Judah. He was most likely Judas, the brother of our Lord Jesus. The letter was probably written about A.D. 65.

Theme and Message

Although Jude was eager to write to his readers about salvation, he thought he must instead warn them about certain immoral, false teachers circulating among them, who were perverting the grace of God. They were apparently trying to convince believers that being saved by grace gave them license to sin, since their sins would no longer be held against them. It has been thought that these false teachers were Gnostics, probably forerunners of second-century, fully developed Gnosticism.

Outline

I. Introduction (1-2)
II. Occasion for the Letter (3-4)
III. Warning Against False Teachers (5-16)
IV. Exhortation to Believers (17-23)
V. Concluding Doxology (24-25)

Salutation

1 Jude,[a] a servant[b] of Jesus
Christ and brother of James,
To those who are called, who are
beloved[c] in[d] God the Father and
kept safe for[d] Jesus Christ:
2 May mercy, peace, and love be
yours in abundance.

Occasion of the Letter

3 Beloved, while eagerly preparing to write to you about the salvation we share, I find it necessary to
write and appeal to you to contend
for the faith that was once for all
entrusted to the saints. 4 For certain intruders have stolen in among
you, people who long ago were designated for this condemnation as
ungodly, who pervert the grace of
our God into licentiousness and
deny our only Master and Lord,
Jesus Christ.[e]

1 Acts 1.13; 1 Pet 1.5
2 1 Pet 1.2; 2 Pet 1.2
3 Titus 1.4; 1 Tim 6.12
4 Gal 2.4; 2 Pet 2.1; Rom 9.22; 2 Pet 2.1
5 Num 14.29; Ps 106.26
6 Jn 8.44; 2 Pet 2.4; Rev 20.10
7 2 Pet 2.6; Gen 19.24

Judgment on False Teachers

5 Now I desire to remind you,
though you are fully informed, that
the Lord, who once for all saved[f] a
people out of the land of Egypt, afterward destroyed those who did
not believe. 6 And the angels who
did not keep their own position,
but left their proper dwelling, he
has kept in eternal chains in deepest darkness for the judgment of
the great Day. 7 Likewise, Sodom
and Gomorrah and the surrounding
cities, which, in the same manner
as they, indulged in sexual immorality and pursued unnatural lust,[g]

[a] Gk *Judas* [b] Gk *slave* [c] Other ancient authorities read *sanctified* [d] Or *by*
[e] Or *the only Master and our Lord Jesus Christ*
[f] Other ancient authorities read *though you were once for all fully informed, that Jesus* (or *Joshua*) *who saved* [g] Gk *went after other flesh*

serve as an example by undergoing
a punishment of eternal fire.
8 Yet in the same way these
dreamers also defile the flesh, reject authority, and slander the glorious ones.[h] 9 But when the archangel Michael contended with the
devil and disputed about the body
of Moses, he did not dare to bring
a condemnation of slander[i]
against him, but said, "The Lord rebuke you!" 10 But these people
slander whatever they do not understand, and they are destroyed by
those things that, like irrational
animals, they know by instinct.
11 Woe to them! For they go the way
of Cain, and abandon themselves
to Balaam's error for the sake of
gain, and perish in Korah's rebellion. 12 These are blemishes[j] on
your love-feasts, while they feast
with you without fear, feeding
themselves.[k] They are waterless
clouds carried along by the winds;
autumn trees without fruit, twice
dead, uprooted; 13 wild waves of the
sea, casting up the foam of their
own shame; wandering stars, for
whom the deepest darkness has
been reserved forever.
14 It was also about these that
Enoch, in the seventh generation
from Adam, prophesied, saying,
"See, the Lord is coming[l] with ten
thousands of his holy ones, 15 to execute judgment on all, and to convict everyone of all the deeds of ungodliness that they have
committed in such an ungodly way,
and of all the harsh things that ungodly sinners have spoken against
him." 16 These are grumblers and
malcontents; they indulge their
own lusts; they are bombastic in
speech, flattering people to their
own advantage.

8 2 Pet 2.10
9 Dan 10.13; Zech 3.2
10 2 Pet 2.12; Phil 3.19
11 Gen 4.3-8; 1 Jn 3.12; Num 22.7; 2 Pet 2.15; Num 16.1-3, 31-35
12 2 Pet 2.13; 1 Cor 11.20ff; Eph 4.14; Mt 15.13
13 Isa 57.20; Phil 3.19; 2 Pet 2.17
14 Gen 5.18; Deut 33.2; Dan 7.10
15 2 Pet 2.6ff; 1 Tim 1.9
16 2 Pet 2.18
17 2 Pet 3.2
18 1 Tim 4.1; 2 Pet 2.1
19 1 Cor 2.14, 15; Jas 3.15
20 Col 2.7; Eph 6.18
21 Titus 2.13; 2 Pet 3.12
23 Am 4.11; Zech 3.2-5
24 Rom 16.25; Eph 3.20; Col 1.22
25 1 Tim 1.17; Rom 11.36

Warnings and Exhortations

17 But you, beloved, must remember the predictions of the
apostles of our Lord Jesus Christ;
18 for they said to you, "In the last
time there will be scoffers, indulging their own ungodly lusts." 19 It is
these worldly people, devoid of the
Spirit, who are causing divisions.
20 But you, beloved, build yourselves up on your most holy faith;
pray in the Holy Spirit; 21 keep
yourselves in the love of God; look
forward to the mercy of our Lord
Jesus Christ that leads to[m] eternal
life. 22 And have mercy on some
who are wavering; 23 save others by
snatching them out of the fire; and
have mercy on still others with
fear, hating even the tunic defiled
by their bodies.[n]

Benediction

24 Now to him who is able to
keep you from falling, and to make
you stand without blemish in the
presence of his glory with rejoicing,
25 to the only God our Savior,
through Jesus Christ our Lord, be
glory, majesty, power, and authority, before all time and now and forever. Amen.

[h] Or *angels*; Gk *glories* [i] Or *condemnation for blasphemy* [j] Or *reefs* [k] Or *without fear. They are shepherds who care only for themselves* [l] Gk *came* [m] Gk *Christ to* [n] Gk *by the flesh*. The Greek text of verses 22-23 is uncertain at several points

THE

Revelation

TO JOHN

Title and Background

Since Roman authorities at this time were beginning to enforce the cult of emperor worship, Christians–who held that Christ, not the emperor, was Lord–were facing increasing hostility. Some in the church were advocating a policy of compromise; this had to be corrected lest its subtle influence undermine believers' determination to stand fast in the perilous days that lay ahead.

Author and Date of Writing

Four times the author identifies himself as John, and John was held to be the author from as early as the second century. Whether or not this was the same John as the one who wrote the Gospel cannot be determined for certain. Most scholars hold that the book was written about A.D. 95.

Theme and Message

John writes to encourage the faithful to resist staunchly the demands that they worship the emperor. He informs his readers that the final showdown between God and Satan is imminent. Satan will increase his persecution of believers, but they must stand fast, even to death. They are sealed against any spiritual harm and will soon be vindicated when Christ returns, when the wicked are forever destroyed, and when God's people enter an eternity of glory and blessedness.

Outline

I. Jesus Among the Seven Churches (1.1-20)
II. Letters to the Seven Churches (2.1–3.22)
III. The Throne, the Scroll, and the Lamb (4.1–5.14)
IV. The Seven Seals (6.1–8.1)
V. The Seven Trumpets (8.2–11.19)
VI. Various Personages and Events (12.1–14.20)
VII. The Seven Bowls (15.1–16.21)
VIII. Babylon: The Great Whore (17.1–19.5)
IX. The Wedding of the Lamb (19.6-10)
X. The Return of Christ (19.11-21)
XI. The Thousand Years (20.1-6)
XII. Satan's Doom (20.7-10)
XIII. Great White Throne Judgment (20.11-15)
XIV. New Heaven, New Earth, New Jerusalem (21.1–22.5)
XV. Conclusion (22.6-21)

Introduction and Salutation

1 The revelation of Jesus Christ,
which God gave him to show
his servants[a] what must soon take
place; he made[b] it known by sending
his angel to his servant[c] John,
2 who testified to the word of God
and to the testimony of Jesus
Christ, even to all that he saw.
3 Blessed is the one who reads
aloud the words of the prophecy,
and blessed are those who hear and
who keep what is written in it; for
the time is near.

1.1 Jn 12.49; Rev 22.16
1.2 1 Cor 1.6; Rev 12.17
1.3 Lk 11.28; Rev 22.10

[a] Gk *slaves* [b] Gk *and he made*
[c] Gk *slave*

4 John to the seven churches
that are in Asia:
Grace to you and peace from him
who is and who was and who is to
come, and from the seven spirits
who are before his throne, 5 and
from Jesus Christ, the faithful witness, the firstborn of the dead, and
the ruler of the kings of the earth.
To him who loves us and freed[d]
us from our sins by his blood, 6 and
made[e] us to be a kingdom, priests
serving[f] his God and Father, to
him be glory and dominion forever
and ever. Amen.
7 Look! He is coming with the
clouds;
every eye will see him,
even those who pierced him;
and on his account all the
tribes of the earth will
wail.
So it is to be. Amen.
8 "I am the Alpha and the Omega," says the Lord God, who is and
who was and who is to come, the
Almighty.

A Vision of Christ

9 I, John, your brother who
share with you in Jesus the persecution and the kingdom and the
patient endurance, was on the island called Patmos because of the
word of God and the testimony of
Jesus.[g] 10 I was in the spirit[h] on
the Lord's day, and I heard behind
me a loud voice like a trumpet
11 saying, "Write in a book what you
see and send it to the seven
churches, to Ephesus, to Smyrna,
to Pergamum, to Thyatira, to Sardis, to Philadelphia, and to Laodicea."
12 Then I turned to see whose
voice it was that spoke to me, and
on turning I saw seven golden
lampstands, 13 and in the midst of
the lampstands I saw one like the
Son of Man, clothed with a long
robe and with a golden sash across
his chest. 14 His head and his hair
were white as white wool, white as
snow; his eyes were like a flame of
fire, 15 his feet were like burnished
bronze, refined as in a furnace, and
his voice was like the sound of
many waters. 16 In his right hand he
held seven stars, and from his
mouth came a sharp, two-edged
sword, and his face was like the sun
shining with full force.
17 When I saw him, I fell at his
feet as though dead. But he placed
his right hand on me, saying, "Do
not be afraid; I am the first and the
last, 18 and the living one. I was
dead, and see, I am alive forever
and ever; and I have the keys of
Death and of Hades. 19 Now write
what you have seen, what is, and
what is to take place after this. 20 As
for the mystery of the seven stars
that you saw in my right hand,
and the seven golden lampstands:
the seven stars are the angels
of the seven churches, and the
seven lampstands are the seven
churches.

The Message to Ephesus

2 "To the angel of the church in
Ephesus write: These are the
words of him who holds the seven
stars in his right hand, who walks
among the seven golden lampstands:
2 "I know your works, your toil
and your patient endurance. I
know that you cannot tolerate evildoers; you have tested those who
claim to be apostles but are not,
and have found them to be false. 3 I
also know that you are enduring
patiently and bearing up for the
sake of my name, and that you have
not grown weary. 4 But I have this
against you, that you have abandoned the love you had at first.
5 Remember then from what you
have fallen; repent, and do the
works you did at first. If not, I will
come to you and remove your
lampstand from its place, unless
you repent. 6 Yet this is to your
credit: you hate the works of the
Nicolaitans, which I also hate. 7 Let
anyone who has an ear listen to
what the Spirit is saying to the

1.4 Jn 1.1; Rev 3.1; 4.5
1.5 Rev 3.14; Col 1.18; Ps 89.27; Rev 17.14; Jn 13.34; Heb 9.14
1.6 1 Pet 2.5; Rev 5.10; Rom 11.36
1.7 Zech 12.10
1.8 Rev 21.6; 4.8; 16.7
1.9 Phil 4.14; 2 Tim 2.12
1.10 Rev 4.1,2
1.11 vv. 8,17
1.12 Ex 25.27; Zech 4.2
1.13 Ezek 1.26; Dan 7.13; 10.5
1.14 Dan 7.9; 10.6; Rev 19.12
1.15 Dan 10.6; Ezek 43.2
1.16 Rev 2.1; 3.1; Heb 4.12; Rev 2.12,16
1.17 Ezek 1.28; Dan 8.18; 10.10; Isa 41.4
1.18 Rom 6.9; Rev 4.9; 20.1
1.20 Zech 4.2
2.1 Rev 1.16; 1.13
2.2 Rev 3.1,8; 1 Jn 4.1; 2 Cor 11.13
2.3 Jn 15.21
2.4 Mt 24.12
2.5 vv. 16,22,2; Rev 1.20
2.6 v. 15
2.7 Mt 11.15; Rev 3.6,13; 22.2,14; Gen 2.9

[d] Other ancient authorities read *washed*
[e] Gk *and he made* [f] Gk *priests to*
[g] Or *testimony to Jesus* [h] Or *in the Spirit*

churches. To everyone who conquers, I will give permission to eat
from the tree of life that is in the
paradise of God.

The Message to Smyrna

8 "And to the angel of the
church in Smyrna write: These are
the words of the first and the last,
who was dead and came to life:
9 "I know your affliction and
your poverty, even though you are
rich. I know the slander on the part
of those who say that they are Jews
and are not, but are a synagogue of
Satan. 10 Do not fear what you are
about to suffer. Beware, the devil is
about to throw some of you into
prison so that you may be tested,
and for ten days you will have affliction. Be faithful until death,
and I will give you the crown of life.
11 Let anyone who has an ear listen
to what the Spirit is saying to the
churches. Whoever conquers will
not be harmed by the second
death.

The Message to Pergamum

12 "And to the angel of the
church in Pergamum write: These
are the words of him who has the
sharp two-edged sword:
13 "I know where you are living,
where Satan's throne is. Yet you
are holding fast to my name, and
you did not deny your faith in me[i]
even in the days of Antipas my witness, my faithful one, who was
killed among you, where Satan
lives. 14 But I have a few things
against you: you have some there
who hold to the teaching of Balaam, who taught Balak to put a
stumbling block before the people
of Israel, so that they would eat
food sacrificed to idols and practice fornication. 15 So you also have
some who hold to the teaching of
the Nicolaitans. 16 Repent then. If
not, I will come to you soon and
make war against them with the
sword of my mouth. 17 Let anyone
who has an ear listen to what the
Spirit is saying to the churches. To
everyone who conquers I will give
some of the hidden manna, and I
will give a white stone, and on the
white stone is written a new name
that no one knows except the one
who receives it.

The Message to Thyatira

18 "And to the angel of the
church in Thyatira write: These are
the words of the Son of God, who
has eyes like a flame of fire, and
whose feet are like burnished
bronze:
19 "I know your works—your
love, faith, service, and patient endurance. I know that your last
works are greater than the first.
20 But I have this against you: you
tolerate that woman Jezebel, who
calls herself a prophet and is teaching and beguiling my servants[j] to
practice fornication and to eat food
sacrificed to idols. 21 I gave her time
to repent, but she refuses to repent
of her fornication. 22 Beware, I am
throwing her on a bed, and those
who commit adultery with her I am
throwing into great distress, unless
they repent of her doings; 23 and I
will strike her children dead. And
all the churches will know that I
am the one who searches minds
and hearts, and I will give to each
of you as your works deserve. 24 But
to the rest of you in Thyatira, who
do not hold this teaching, who have
not learned what some call 'the
deep things of Satan,' to you I say,
I do not lay on you any other burden; 25 only hold fast to what you
have until I come. 26 To everyone
who conquers and continues to do
my works to the end,
    I will give authority over the
        nations;
27 to rule[k] them with an iron
        rod,
    as when clay pots are
        shattered—
28 even as I also received authority
from my Father. To the one who
conquers I will also give the morning star. 29 Let anyone who has an

2.8 Rev 1.11,17,18
2.9 Rev 1.9; Jas 2.5; Rev 3.9
2.10 Rev 3.10; Dan 1.12
2.11 Rev 20.14; 21.8
2.12 Rev 1.11,16
2.13 Rev 14.12; v. 9
2.14 Num 24.14; 2 Pet 2.15; Jude 11; 1 Cor 8.9; 10.19,20; 6.13
2.15 v. 6
2.16 2 Thes 2.8; Rev 1.16
2.17 Jn 6.49,50; Isa 62.2; Rev 19.12
2.18 Rev 1.11,14,15
2.19 v. 2
2.20 1 Kings 16.31; 21.25; 2 Kings 9.7; Acts 15.20
2.21 Rom 2.4; Rev 9.20
2.22 Rev 17.2; 18.9
2.23 Jer 11.20; Acts 1.24; Rom 8.27; Ps 62.12
2.24 Acts 15.28
2.26 Heb 3.6; Ps 2.8; Rev 3.21
2.27 Rev 12.5; Isa 30.14; Jer 19.11
2.28 Rev 22.16

[i] Or *deny my faith* [j] Gk *slaves* [k] Or *to shepherd*

ear listen to what the Spirit is saying to the churches.

The Message to Sardis

3 "And to the angel of the
church in Sardis write: These
are the words of him who has the
seven spirits of God and the seven
stars:

"I know your works; you have a
name of being alive, but you are
dead. 2 Wake up, and strengthen
what remains and is on the point of
death, for I have not found your
works perfect in the sight of my
God. 3 Remember then what you received and heard; obey it, and repent. If you do not wake up, I will
come like a thief, and you will not
know at what hour I will come to
you. 4 Yet you have still a few persons in Sardis who have not soiled
their clothes; they will walk with
me, dressed in white, for they are
worthy. 5 If you conquer, you will be
clothed like them in white robes,
and I will not blot your name out of
the book of life; I will confess your
name before my Father and before
his angels. 6 Let anyone who has an
ear listen to what the Spirit is saying to the churches.

The Message to Philadelphia

7 "And to the angel of the
church in Philadelphia write:

These are the words of the
holy one, the true one,
who has the key of David,
who opens and no one will
shut,
who shuts and no one
opens:

8 "I know your works. Look, I
have set before you an open door,
which no one is able to shut. I
know that you have but little power, and yet you have kept my word
and have not denied my name. 9 I
will make those of the synagogue of
Satan who say that they are Jews
and are not, but are lying—I will
make them come and bow down
before your feet, and they will learn
that I have loved you. 10 Because
you have kept my word of patient
endurance, I will keep you from the
hour of trial that is coming on the
whole world to test the inhabitants
of the earth. 11 I am coming soon;
hold fast to what you have, so that
no one may seize your crown. 12 If
you conquer, I will make you a pillar in the temple of my God; you
will never go out of it. I will write on
you the name of my God, and the
name of the city of my God, the
new Jerusalem that comes down
from my God out of heaven, and my
own new name. 13 Let anyone who
has an ear listen to what the Spirit
is saying to the churches.

The Message to Laodicea

14 "And to the angel of the
church in Laodicea write: The
words of the Amen, the faithful and
true witness, the origin[1] of God's
creation:

15 "I know your works; you are
neither cold nor hot. I wish that
you were either cold or hot. 16 So,
because you are lukewarm, and
neither cold nor hot, I am about to
spit you out of my mouth. 17 For
you say, 'I am rich, I have prospered, and I need nothing.' You do
not realize that you are wretched,
pitiable, poor, blind, and naked.
18 Therefore I counsel you to buy
from me gold refined by fire so that
you may be rich; and white robes to
clothe you and to keep the shame
of your nakedness from being seen;
and salve to anoint your eyes so
that you may see. 19 I reprove and
discipline those whom I love. Be
earnest, therefore, and repent.
20 Listen! I am standing at the door,
knocking; if you hear my voice and
open the door, I will come in to you
and eat with you, and you with me.
21 To the one who conquers I will
give a place with me on my throne,
just as I myself conquered and sat
down with my Father on his
throne. 22 Let anyone who has an
ear listen to what the Spirit is saying to the churches."

3.1 Rev 1.4,16; 2.2; 1 Tim 5.6
3.3 1 Thes 5.2, 6; 2 Pet 3.10
3.4 Acts 1.15; Jude 23; Rev 6.11; 7.9,13
3.5 Mt 10.32
3.6 Rev 2.7
3.7 Acts 3.14; 1 Jn 5.20; Isa 22.22
3.8 Acts 14.27; Rev 2.13
3.9 Rev 2.9; Isa 49.23; 43.4
3.10 2 Pet 2.9; Rev 16.14; 6.10; 17.8
3.11 Rev 22.7,12, 20; 2.25,10
3.12 Gal 2.9; Rev 22.4; 21.2
3.13 v. 6
3.14 Isa 65.16
3.15 v. 1
3.17 Hos 12.8; Zech 11.5; 1 Cor 4.8
3.18 Isa 55.1; Mt 13.44; Rev 7.13
3.19 Prov 3.11; Heb 12.5,6; Rev 2.5
3.20 Mt 24.33; Lk 12.36; Jn 14.23
3.21 Rev 2.7; Mt 19.28; Rev 5.5
3.22 Rev 2.7

[1] Or *beginning*

The Heavenly Worship

4 After this I looked, and there in heaven a door stood open! And the first voice, which I had heard speaking to me like a trumpet, said, "Come up here, and I will show you what must take place after this." 2 At once I was in the spirit,[m] and there in heaven stood a throne, with one seated on the throne! 3 And the one seated there looks like jasper and carnelian, and around the throne is a rainbow that looks like an emerald. 4 Around the throne are twenty-four thrones, and seated on the thrones are twenty-four elders, dressed in white robes, with golden crowns on their heads. 5 Coming from the throne are flashes of lightning, and rumblings and peals of thunder, and in front of the throne burn seven flaming torches, which are the seven spirits of God; 6 and in front of the throne there is something like a sea of glass, like crystal.

Around the throne, and on each side of the throne, are four living creatures, full of eyes in front and behind: 7 the first living creature like a lion, the second living creature like an ox, the third living creature with a face like a human face, and the fourth living creature like a flying eagle. 8 And the four living creatures, each of them with six wings, are full of eyes all around and inside. Day and night without ceasing they sing,

"Holy, holy, holy,
the Lord God the Almighty,
who was and is and is to
come."

9 And whenever the living creatures give glory and honor and thanks to the one who is seated on the throne, who lives forever and ever, 10 the twenty-four elders fall before the one who is seated on the throne and worship the one who lives forever and ever; they cast their crowns before the throne, singing,

11 "You are worthy, our Lord
and God,
to receive glory and honor
and power,
for you created all things,
and by your will they
existed and were
created."

The Scroll and the Lamb

5 Then I saw in the right hand of the one seated on the throne a scroll written on the inside and on the back, sealed[n] with seven seals; 2 and I saw a mighty angel proclaiming with a loud voice, "Who is worthy to open the scroll and break its seals?" 3 And no one in heaven or on earth or under the earth was able to open the scroll or to look into it. 4 And I began to weep bitterly because no one was found worthy to open the scroll or to look into it. 5 Then one of the elders said to me, "Do not weep. See, the Lion of the tribe of Judah, the Root of David, has conquered, so that he can open the scroll and its seven seals."

6 Then I saw between the throne and the four living creatures and among the elders a Lamb standing as if it had been slaughtered, having seven horns and seven eyes, which are the seven spirits of God sent out into all the earth. 7 He went and took the scroll from the right hand of the one who was seated on the throne. 8 When he had taken the scroll, the four living creatures and the twenty-four elders fell before the Lamb, each holding a harp and golden bowls full of incense, which are the prayers of the saints. 9 They sing a new song:

"You are worthy to take the
scroll
and to open its seals,
for you were slaughtered and
by your blood you
ransomed for God
saints from[o] every tribe
and language and
people and nation;

4.1 Rev 1.10; 11.12; 1.19 **4.2** Rev 1.10; Isa 6.1; Ezek 1.26-28; Dan 7.9 **4.4** Rev 11.16; 3.4,5 **4.5** Rev 8.5; 16.18; 1.4; Zech 4.2 **4.6** Rev 15.2; Ezek 1.5 **4.7** Ezek 1.10; 10.14 **4.8** Isa 6.2,3; Rev 1.8,4 **4.9** Ps 47.8; Rev 10.6; 15.7 **4.10** Rev 5.8,14; vv. 2,9,4 **4.11** Rev 5.12; Gen 1.1; Eph 3.9; Rev 10.6

5.1 vv. 7.13; Ezek 2.9,10; Isa 29.11; Dan 12.4 **5.2** Rev 10.1 **5.5** Gen 49.9; Heb 7.14; Isa 11.1,10; Rom 15.12; Rev 22.16 **5.6** Rev 4.6; Isa 53.7; Rev 13.8; Zech 3.9; 4.10; Rev 4.5 **5.7** v. 1 **5.8** Rev 14.2; Ps 141.2 **5.9** Ps 40.3; Rev 4.11; 1 Cor 6.20; Heb 9.12

m Or *in the Spirit* n Or *written on the inside, and sealed on the back* o Gk *ransomed for God from*

10 you have made them to be a
kingdom and priests
serving[p] our God,
and they will reign on
earth."
11 Then I looked, and I heard
the voice of many angels surrounding the throne and the living creatures and the elders; they numbered myriads of myriads and
thousands of thousands, 12 singing
with full voice,
"Worthy is the Lamb that
was slaughtered
to receive power and wealth
and wisdom and might
and honor and glory and
blessing!"
13 Then I heard every creature in
heaven and on earth and under the
earth and in the sea, and all that is
in them, singing,
"To the one seated on the
throne and to the Lamb
be blessing and honor and
glory and might
forever and ever!"
14 And the four living creatures
said, "Amen!" And the elders fell
down and worshiped.

The Seven Seals

6 Then I saw the Lamb open one
of the seven seals, and I heard
one of the four living creatures call
out, as with a voice of thunder,
"Come!"[q] 2 I looked, and there was
a white horse! Its rider had a bow;
a crown was given to him, and he
came out conquering and to conquer.
3 When he opened the second
seal, I heard the second living creature call out, "Come!"[q] 4 And out
came[r] another horse, bright red;
its rider was permitted to take
peace from the earth, so that people would slaughter one another;
and he was given a great sword.
5 When he opened the third
seal, I heard the third living creature call out, "Come!"[q] I looked,
and there was a black horse! Its rider held a pair of scales in his hand,
6 and I heard what seemed to be a
voice in the midst of the four living
creatures saying, "A quart of wheat
for a day's pay,[s] and three quarts
of barley for a day's pay,[s] but do
not damage the olive oil and the
wine!"
7 When he opened the fourth
seal, I heard the voice of the fourth
living creature call out, "Come!"[q]
8 I looked and there was a pale
green horse! Its rider's name was
Death, and Hades followed with
him; they were given authority over
a fourth of the earth, to kill with
sword, famine, and pestilence, and
by the wild animals of the earth.
9 When he opened the fifth seal,
I saw under the altar the souls of
those who had been slaughtered
for the word of God and for the testimony they had given; 10 they cried
out with a loud voice, "Sovereign
Lord, holy and true, how long will
it be before you judge and avenge
our blood on the inhabitants of the
earth?" 11 They were each given a
white robe and told to rest a little
longer, until the number would be
complete both of their fellow servants[t] and of their brothers and
sisters,[u] who were soon to be
killed as they themselves had been
killed.
12 When he opened the sixth
seal, I looked, and there came a
great earthquake; the sun became
black as sackcloth, the full moon
became like blood, 13 and the stars
of the sky fell to the earth as the fig
tree drops its winter fruit when
shaken by a gale. 14 The sky vanished like a scroll rolling itself up,
and every mountain and island was
removed from its place. 15 Then the
kings of the earth and the magnates and the generals and the rich
and the powerful, and everyone,
slave and free, hid in the caves and
among the rocks of the mountains,
16 calling to the mountains and
rocks, "Fall on us and hide us from
the face of the one seated on the
throne and from the wrath of the
Lamb; 17 for the great day of their
wrath has come, and who is able to
stand?"

5.10 Ex 19.6; Isa 61.6
5.11 Dan 7.10; Heb 12.22
5.12 Rev 4.11
5.13 Phil 2.10; v. 3; 1 Tim 6.16; Rev 1.6; 6.16; 7.10
5.14 Rev 19.4; 4.9,10
6.1 Rev 5.5-7,1; 14.2; 19.6
6.2 Zech 6.3; Rev 19.11; Zech 6.11; Rev 14.14
6.3 Rev 4.7
6.4 Zech 6.2
6.5 Rev 4.7; Zech 6.2
6.6 Rev 4.6,7; 9.4
6.7 Rev 4.7
6.8 Zech 6.3; Hos 13.14; Ezek 5.12
6.9 Rev 14.18; 16.7; 20.4; 1.9; 12.17
6.10 Zech 1.12; Ps 79.5; Rev 3.7; 19.2
6.11 Rev 3.5; 7.9; 14.13; Heb 11.40
6.12 Rev 16.18; Mt 24.29; Joel 2.31; Acts 2.20
6.13 Rev 8.10; 9.1; Isa 34.4
6.14 Isa 34.4; Jer 3.23; 4.24; Rev 16.10
6.15 Isa 2.10,19
6.16 Hos 10.8; Lk 23.30; Rev 9.6
6.17 Zeph 1.14; Rev 16.14; Ps 76.7

p Gk *priests to* q Or *"Go!"* r Or *went*
s Gk *a denarius* t Gk *slaves*
u Gk *brothers*

The 144,000 of Israel Sealed

7 After this I saw four angels
standing at the four corners of
the earth, holding back the four
winds of the earth so that no wind
could blow on earth or sea or
against any tree. 2 I saw another angel ascending from the rising of the
sun, having the seal of the living
God, and he called with a loud
voice to the four angels who had
been given power to damage earth
and sea, 3 saying, "Do not damage
the earth or the sea or the trees,
until we have marked the servants[v] of our God with a seal on
their foreheads."
4 And I heard the number of
those who were sealed, one hundred forty-four thousand, sealed
out of every tribe of the people of
Israel:

5 From the tribe of Judah twelve
thousand sealed,
from the tribe of Reuben twelve
thousand,
from the tribe of Gad twelve
thousand,
6 from the tribe of Asher twelve
thousand,
from the tribe of Naphtali
twelve thousand,
from the tribe of Manasseh
twelve thousand,
7 from the tribe of Simeon
twelve thousand,
from the tribe of Levi twelve
thousand,
from the tribe of Issachar
twelve thousand,
8 from the tribe of Zebulun
twelve thousand,
from the tribe of Joseph twelve
thousand,
from the tribe of Benjamin
twelve thousand sealed.

The Multitude from Every Nation

9 After this I looked, and there
was a great multitude that no one
could count, from every nation,
from all tribes and peoples and languages, standing before the throne
and before the Lamb, robed in
white, with palm branches in their
hands. 10 They cried out in a loud
voice, saying,

"Salvation belongs to our
God who is seated on
the throne, and to the
Lamb!"

11 And all the angels stood around
the throne and around the elders
and the four living creatures, and
they fell on their faces before the
throne and worshiped God, 12 singing,

"Amen! Blessing and glory
and wisdom
and thanksgiving and honor
and power and might
be to our God forever and
ever! Amen."

13 Then one of the elders addressed me, saying, "Who are
these, robed in white, and where
have they come from?" 14 I said to
him, "Sir, you are the one that
knows." Then he said to me,
"These are they who have come out
of the great ordeal; they have
washed their robes and made them
white in the blood of the Lamb.

15 For this reason they are
before the throne of
God,
and worship him day and
night within his temple,
and the one who is seated
on the throne will
shelter them.
16 They will hunger no more,
and thirst no more;
the sun will not strike
them,
nor any scorching heat;
17 for the Lamb at the center of
the throne will be their
shepherd,
and he will guide them to
springs of the water of
life,
and God will wipe away
every tear from their
eyes."

The Seventh Seal and the Golden Censer

8 When the Lamb opened the
seventh seal, there was silence
in heaven for about half an hour.

7.1 Rev 9.4 **7.3** Rev 6.6; Ezek 9.4; Rev 22.4 **7.4ff** Rev 9.16; 14.1 **7.9** Rom 11.25; Rev 5.9; 3.5, 18; 4.4; 6.11 **7.10** Ps 3.8; Rev 12.10; 19.1; 5.13 **7.11** Rev 4.6 **7.12** Rev 5.12-14 **7.13** v. 9 **7.14** Mt 24.21; Zech 3.3-5; Heb 9.14; 1 Jn 1.7 **7.15** Isa 4.5,6; Rev 21.3 **7.16** Isa 49.10; Ps 121.5,6; Rev 21.4 **7.17** Ps 23.1; Jn 10.11,14; Isa 25.8 **8.1** Rev 6.1

[v] Gk *slaves*

2 And I saw the seven angels who
stand before God, and seven trumpets were given to them.
3 Another angel with a golden
censer came and stood at the altar;
he was given a great quantity of incense to offer with the prayers of all
the saints on the golden altar that
is before the throne. 4 And the
smoke of the incense, with the
prayers of the saints, rose before
God from the hand of the angel.
5 Then the angel took the censer
and filled it with fire from the altar
and threw it on the earth; and there
were peals of thunder, rumblings,
flashes of lightning, and an earthquake.

The Seven Trumpets

6 Now the seven angels who had
the seven trumpets made ready to
blow them.
7 The first angel blew his trumpet, and there came hail and fire,
mixed with blood, and they were
hurled to the earth; and a third of
the earth was burned up, and a
third of the trees were burned up,
and all green grass was burned up.
8 The second angel blew his
trumpet, and something like a
great mountain, burning with fire,
was thrown into the sea. 9 A third of
the sea became blood, a third of
the living creatures in the sea died,
and a third of the ships were destroyed.
10 The third angel blew his
trumpet, and a great star fell from
heaven, blazing like a torch, and it
fell on a third of the rivers and on
the springs of water. 11 The name of
the star is Wormwood. A third of
the waters became wormwood, and
many died from the water, because
it was made bitter.
12 The fourth angel blew his
trumpet, and a third of the sun was
struck, and a third of the moon,
and a third of the stars, so that a
third of their light was darkened; a
third of the day was kept from shining, and likewise the night.
13 Then I looked, and I heard an
eagle crying with a loud voice as it
flew in midheaven, "Woe, woe, woe

8.2 1 Cor 15.52; 1 Thes 4.16
8.3 Rev 7.2; 5.8; Ex 30.1; Rev 6.9
8.4 Ps 141.2
8.5 Lev 16.12; Rev 4.5; 6.12
8.6 v. 2
8.7 Ezek 38.22; Rev 9.4
8.8 Jer 51.25; Rev 16.3
8.10 Isa 14.12; Rev 9.1; 16.4
8.11 Jer 9.15; 23.15
8.12 Rev 6.12,13
8.13 Rev 14.6; 19.17; 9.12; 11.14
9.1 Rev 8.10; Lk 8.31; Rev 17.8; 20.1
9.2 Gen 19.28; Ex 19.18; Joel 2.2,10
9.3 Ex 10.12-15; v. 10
9.4 Rev 6.6; 8.7; 7.2,3
9.5 vv. 10,3
9.6 Job 3.21; Jer 8.3; Rev 6.16
9.7 Joel 2.4; Nah 3.17; Dan 7.8
9.8 Joel 1.6
9.9 Joel 2.5
9.10 vv. 5,19
9.11 Eph 2.2; v. 1
9.12 Rev 8.13
9.13 Ex 30.1-3; Rev 8.3
9.14 Rev 16.12

to the inhabitants of the earth, at
the blasts of the other trumpets
that the three angels are about to
blow!"
9 And the fifth angel blew his
trumpet, and I saw a star that
had fallen from heaven to earth,
and he was given the key to the
shaft of the bottomless pit; 2 he
opened the shaft of the bottomless
pit, and from the shaft rose smoke
like the smoke of a great furnace,
and the sun and the air were darkened with the smoke from the
shaft. 3 Then from the smoke came
locusts on the earth, and they were
given authority like the authority of
scorpions of the earth. 4 They were
told not to damage the grass of the
earth or any green growth or any
tree, but only those people who do
not have the seal of God on their
foreheads. 5 They were allowed to
torture them for five months, but
not to kill them, and their torture
was like the torture of a scorpion
when it stings someone. 6 And in
those days people will seek death
but will not find it; they will long to
die, but death will flee from them.
7 In appearance the locusts
were like horses equipped for battle. On their heads were what
looked like crowns of gold; their
faces were like human faces, 8 their
hair like women's hair, and their
teeth like lions' teeth; 9 they had
scales like iron breastplates, and
the noise of their wings was like the
noise of many chariots with horses
rushing into battle. 10 They have
tails like scorpions, with stingers,
and in their tails is their power to
harm people for five months.
11 They have as king over them the
angel of the bottomless pit; his
name in Hebrew is Abaddon,[w] and
in Greek he is called Apollyon.[x]
12 The first woe has passed.
There are still two woes to come.
13 Then the sixth angel blew his
trumpet, and I heard a voice from
the four[y] horns of the golden altar
before God, 14 saying to the sixth

[w] That is, *Destruction* [x] That is, *Destroyer*
[y] Other ancient authorities lack *four*

angel who had the trumpet, "Release the four angels who are
bound at the great river Euphrates." 15 So the four angels were released, who had been held ready
for the hour, the day, the month,
and the year, to kill a third of humankind. 16 The number of the
troops of cavalry was two hundred
million; I heard their number.
17 And this was how I saw the
horses in my vision: the riders wore
breastplates the color of fire and of
sapphire[z] and of sulfur; the heads
of the horses were like lions' heads,
and fire and smoke and sulfur
came out of their mouths. 18 By
these three plagues a third of humankind was killed, by the fire and
smoke and sulfur coming out of
their mouths. 19 For the power of
the horses is in their mouths and in
their tails; their tails are like serpents, having heads; and with them
they inflict harm.

20 The rest of humankind, who
were not killed by these plagues,
did not repent of the works of their
hands or give up worshiping demons and idols of gold and silver
and bronze and stone and wood,
which cannot see or hear or walk.
21 And they did not repent of their
murders or their sorceries or their
fornication or their thefts.

The Angel with the Little Scroll

10 And I saw another mighty
angel coming down from
heaven, wrapped in a cloud, with a
rainbow over his head; his face was
like the sun, and his legs like pillars of fire. 2 He held a little scroll
open in his hand. Setting his right
foot on the sea and his left foot on
the land, 3 he gave a great shout,
like a lion roaring. And when he
shouted, the seven thunders
sounded. 4 And when the seven
thunders had sounded, I was about
to write, but I heard a voice from
heaven saying, "Seal up what the
seven thunders have said, and do
not write it down." 5 Then the angel
whom I saw standing on the sea
and the land

9.15 v. 18
9.16 Rev 5.11; 7.4
9.17 v. 18; Rev 11.5
9.18 vv. 15,17
9.20 Deut 31.29; 1 Cor 10.20; Ps 115.4; 135.15; Dan 5.23
9.21 Rev 2.21; 18.23; 17.2,5
10.1 Rev 5.2; Mt 17.2; Rev 1.16,15
10.3 Isa 31.4; Rev 4.5
10.4 Dan 8.26; 12.4,9; Rev 22.10
10.5 Ex 6.8; Dan 12.7
10.6 Rev 4.11; 14.7; 16.17
10.7 Rev 11.15; Rom 16.25
10.8 v. 4
10.9 Jer 15.16; Ezek 2.8
10.10 Ezek 3.3
10.11 Rev 11.1; Ezek 37.4,9
11.1 Ezek 40.3; Rev 21.15
11.2 Ezek 40.17; Lk 21.24; Rev 13.5
11.3 Rev 19.10; 12.6
11.4 Ps 52.8; Jer 11.16; Zech 4.3; Mt 11.14
11.5 2 Kings 1.10; Jer 5.14; Num 16.29

raised his right hand to
heaven
6 and swore by him who lives
forever and ever,
who created heaven and what is in
it, the earth and what is in it, and
the sea and what is in it: "There
will be no more delay, 7 but in the
days when the seventh angel is to
blow his trumpet, the mystery of
God will be fulfilled, as he announced to his servants[a] the
prophets."

8 Then the voice that I had
heard from heaven spoke to me
again, saying, "Go, take the scroll
that is open in the hand of the angel who is standing on the sea and
on the land." 9 So I went to the angel and told him to give me the little scroll; and he said to me, "Take
it, and eat; it will be bitter to your
stomach, but sweet as honey in
your mouth." 10 So I took the little
scroll from the hand of the angel
and ate it; it was sweet as honey in
my mouth, but when I had eaten it,
my stomach was made bitter.

11 Then they said to me, "You
must prophesy again about many
peoples and nations and languages
and kings."

The Two Witnesses

11 Then I was given a measuring rod like a staff, and I
was told, "Come and measure the
temple of God and the altar and
those who worship there, 2 but do
not measure the court outside the
temple; leave that out, for it is giv-
en over to the nations, and they
will trample over the holy city for
forty-two months. 3 And I will grant
my two witnesses authority to
prophesy for one thousand two
hundred sixty days, wearing sackcloth."

4 These are the two olive trees
and the two lampstands that stand
before the Lord of the earth. 5 And
if anyone wants to harm them, fire
pours from their mouth and consumes their foes; anyone who
wants to harm them must be killed

[z] Gk *hyacinth* [a] Gk *slaves*

in this manner. 6 They have authority to shut the sky, so that no rain
may fall during the days of their
prophesying, and they have authority over the waters to turn them
into blood, and to strike the earth
with every kind of plague, as often
as they desire.
7 When they have finished their
testimony, the beast that comes up
from the bottomless pit will make
war on them and conquer them
and kill them, 8 and their dead bodies will lie in the street of the great
city that is prophetically[b] called
Sodom and Egypt, where also their
Lord was crucified. 9 For three and
a half days members of the peoples
and tribes and languages and nations will gaze at their dead bodies
and refuse to let them be placed in
a tomb; 10 and the inhabitants of
the earth will gloat over them and
celebrate and exchange presents,
because these two prophets had
been a torment to the inhabitants
of the earth.
11 But after the three and a half
days, the breath[c] of life from God
entered them, and they stood on
their feet, and those who saw them
were terrified. 12 Then they[d] heard
a loud voice from heaven saying to
them, "Come up here!" And they
went up to heaven in a cloud while
their enemies watched them. 13 At
that moment there was a great
earthquake, and a tenth of the city
fell; seven thousand people were
killed in the earthquake, and the
rest were terrified and gave glory to
the God of heaven.
14 The second woe has passed.
The third woe is coming very soon.

The Seventh Trumpet

15 Then the seventh angel blew
his trumpet, and there were loud
voices in heaven, saying,
"The kingdom of the world
has become the
kingdom of our Lord
and of his Messiah,[e]
and he will reign forever and
ever."
16 Then the twenty-four elders
who sit on their thrones before God
fell on their faces and worshiped
God, 17 singing,
"We give you thanks, Lord
God Almighty,
who are and who were,
for you have taken your great
power
and begun to reign.
18 The nations raged,
but your wrath has come,
and the time for judging
the dead,
for rewarding your servants,[f]
the prophets
and saints and all who fear
your name,
both small and great,
and for destroying those who
destroy the earth."
19 Then God's temple in heaven
was opened, and the ark of his covenant was seen within his temple;
and there were flashes of lightning,
rumblings, peals of thunder, an
earthquake, and heavy hail.

The Woman and the Dragon

12 A great portent appeared in
heaven: a woman clothed
with the sun, with the moon under
her feet, and on her head a crown of
twelve stars. 2 She was pregnant
and was crying out in birthpangs,
in the agony of giving birth. 3 Then
another portent appeared in heav-
en: a great red dragon, with seven
heads and ten horns, and seven diadems on his heads. 4 His tail swept
down a third of the stars of heaven
and threw them to the earth. Then
the dragon stood before the woman
who was about to bear a child, so
that he might devour her child as
soon as it was born. 5 And she gave
birth to a son, a male child, who is
to rule[g] all the nations with a rod
of iron. But her child was snatched
away and taken to God and to his
throne; 6 and the woman fled into
the wilderness, where she has a
place prepared by God, so that
there she can be nourished for one
thousand two hundred sixty days.

11.6 1 Kings 17.1; Ex 7.17,19
11.7 Rev 13.1; 9.1,2; Dan 7.21
11.8 Rev 14.8; Isa 1.9; Heb 13.12
11.10 Rev 3.10; Esther 9.19, 22
11.11 Ezek 37.5,9, 10,14
11.12 Rev 4.1; 2 Kings 2.11; Acts 1.9
11.13 Rev 6.12; 14.7; 16.11
11.14 Rev 9.12
11.15 Rev 10.7; 16.17; 19.1; 12.10; Dan 2.44; 7.14,27
11.16 Rev 4.4; 5.8
11.17 Rev 1.8; 19.6
11.18 Ps 2.1; Dan 7.9,10; Rev 10.7; 19.5
11.19 Rev 15.5,8; 8.5; 16.21
12.2 Isa 66.7; Gal 4.19
12.3 Rev 13.1; Dan 7.7; Rev 19.12
12.4 Rev 8.7,12; Dan 8.10
12.5 Ps 2.9; Rev 2.27; 2 Cor 12.2
12.6 Rev 11.3

[b] Or *allegorically*; Gk *spiritually* [c] Or *the spirit* [d] Other ancient authorities read *I* [e] Gk *Christ* [f] Gk *slaves* [g] Or *to shepherd*

Michael Defeats the Dragon

7 And war broke out in heaven;
Michael and his angels fought
against the dragon. The dragon and
his angels fought back, 8 but they
were defeated, and there was no
longer any place for them in heav-
en. 9 The great dragon was thrown
down, that ancient serpent, who is
called the Devil and Satan, the deceiver of the whole world—he was
thrown down to the earth, and his
angels were thrown down with him.
10 Then I heard a loud voice in
heaven, proclaiming,

"Now have come the
salvation and the power
and the kingdom of our
God
and the authority of his
Messiah,[h]
for the accuser of our
comrades[i] has been
thrown down,
who accuses them day and
night before our God.
11 But they have conquered
him by the blood of the
Lamb
and by the word of their
testimony,
for they did not cling to life
even in the face of
death.
12 Rejoice then, you heavens
and those who dwell in
them!
But woe to the earth and the
sea,
for the devil has come
down to you
with great wrath,
because he knows that his
time is short!"

The Dragon Fights Again on Earth

13 So when the dragon saw that
he had been thrown down to the
earth, he pursued[j] the woman
who had given birth to the male
child. 14 But the woman was given
the two wings of the great eagle, so
that she could fly from the serpent
into the wilderness, to her place
where she is nourished for a time,
and times, and half a time. 15 Then
from his mouth the serpent poured
water like a river after the woman,
to sweep her away with the flood.
16 But the earth came to the help of
the woman; it opened its mouth
and swallowed the river that the
dragon had poured from his mouth.
17 Then the dragon was angry with
the woman, and went off to make
war on the rest of her children,
those who keep the commandments of God and hold the testimony of Jesus.

The First Beast

18 Then the dragon[k] took his
stand on the sand of the seashore.

13 1 And I saw a beast rising out
of the sea, having ten horns
and seven heads; and on its horns
were ten diadems, and on its
heads were blasphemous names.
2 And the beast that I saw was like
a leopard, its feet were like a
bear's, and its mouth was like a
lion's mouth. And the dragon gave
it his power and his throne and
great authority. 3 One of its heads
seemed to have received a death-
blow, but its mortal wound[l] had
been healed. In amazement the
whole earth followed the beast.
4 They worshiped the dragon, for
he had given his authority to
the beast, and they worshiped the
beast, saying, "Who is like the
beast, and who can fight against it?"
5 The beast was given a mouth
uttering haughty and blasphemous
words, and it was allowed to exercise authority for forty-two
months. 6 It opened its mouth to
utter blasphemies against God,
blaspheming his name and his
dwelling, that is, those who dwell
in heaven. 7 Also it was allowed to
make war on the saints and to conquer them.[m] It was given authority
over every tribe and people and
language and nation, 8 and all the
inhabitants of the earth will worship it, everyone whose name has
not been written from the founda-

12.7 Dan 10.13; Rev 20.2
12.9 Gen 3.1,4; Rev 20.2,3, 8,10; Jn 12.31
12.10 Rev 11.15; Job 1.9-11; Zech 3.1
12.11 Rom 16.20; Lk 14.26
12.12 Ps 96.11; Isa 49.13; Rev 18.20; 8.13; 10.6
12.13 vv. 3,5
12.14 Ex 19.4; Dan 7.25; 12.7
12.15 Isa 59.19
12.17 Gen 3.15; Rev 11.7; 14.12; 1.2,9
13.1 Dan 7.1-6; Rev 17.3
13.2 Rev 16.10
13.3 Rev 17.8
13.4 Rev 18.18
13.5 Dan 7.8,11, 25; Rev 11.2
13.6 Rev 12.12
13.7 Dan 7.21; Rev 11.7; 5.9
13.8 Phil 4.3; Rev 3.5; 17.8; 5.6

h Gk *Christ* i Gk *brothers*
j Or *persecuted* k Gk *Then he*; other ancient authorities read *Then I stood*
l Gk *the plague of its death* m Other ancient authorities lack this sentence

tion of the world in the book of life of the Lamb that was slaughtered.[n]

9 Let anyone who has an ear listen:

10 If you are to be taken
captive,
into captivity you go;
if you kill with the sword,
with the sword you must
be killed.

Here is a call for the endurance and faith of the saints.

The Second Beast

11 Then I saw another beast that rose out of the earth; it had two horns like a lamb and it spoke like a dragon. 12 It exercises all the authority of the first beast on its behalf, and it makes the earth and its inhabitants worship the first beast, whose mortal wound[o] had been healed. 13 It performs great signs, even making fire come down from heaven to earth in the sight of all; 14 and by the signs that it is allowed to perform on behalf of the beast, it deceives the inhabitants of earth, telling them to make an image for the beast that had been wounded by the sword[p] and yet lived; 15 and it was allowed to give breath[q] to the image of the beast so that the image of the beast could even speak and cause those who would not worship the image of the beast to be killed. 16 Also it causes all, both small and great, both rich and poor, both free and slave, to be marked on the right hand or the forehead, 17 so that no one can buy or sell who does not have the mark, that is, the name of the beast or the number of its name. 18 This calls for wisdom: let anyone with understanding calculate the number of the beast, for it is the number of a person. Its number is six hundred sixty-six.[r]

The Lamb and the 144,000

14 Then I looked, and there was the Lamb, standing on Mount Zion! And with him were one hundred forty-four thousand who had his name and his Father's name written on their foreheads. 2 And I heard a voice from heaven like the sound of many waters and like the sound of loud thunder; the voice I heard was like the sound of harpists playing on their harps, 3 and they sing a new song before the throne and before the four living creatures and before the elders. No one could learn that song except the one hundred forty-four thousand who have been redeemed from the earth. 4 It is these who have not defiled themselves with women, for they are virgins; these follow the Lamb wherever he goes. They have been redeemed from humankind as first fruits for God and the Lamb, 5 and in their mouth no lie was found; they are blameless.

The Messages of the Three Angels

6 Then I saw another angel flying in midheaven, with an eternal gospel to proclaim to those who live[s] on the earth — to every nation and tribe and language and people. 7 He said in a loud voice, "Fear God and give him glory, for the hour of his judgment has come; and worship him who made heaven and earth, the sea and the springs of water."

8 Then another angel, a second, followed, saying, "Fallen, fallen is Babylon the great! She has made all nations drink of the wine of the wrath of her fornication."

9 Then another angel, a third, followed them, crying with a loud voice, "Those who worship the beast and its image, and receive a mark on their foreheads or on their hands, 10 they will also drink the wine of God's wrath, poured unmixed into the cup of his anger, and they will be tormented with fire and sulfur in the presence of the holy angels and in the presence of the Lamb. 11 And the smoke of their torment goes up forever and

13.9 Mk 4.23; Rev 2.7
13.10 Isa 33.1; Mt 26.52; Rev 14.12
13.11 Rev 11.7
13.12 vv. 4,14; Rev 14.9,11; v. 3
13.13 Mt 24.24; Rev 16.14; 1 Kings 18.38; Rev 20.9
13.14 Rev 12.9; 2 Thes 2.9, 10
13.15 Dan 3.5; Rev 16.2
13.16 Rev 11.18; 19.5,18; 14.9
13.17 Rev 14.9,11; 15.2
13.18 Rev 17.9; 15.2; 21.17
14.1 Rev 5.6; Ps 2.6; Rev 3.12; 7.3
14.2 Rev 1.15; 5.8
14.3 Rev 5.9; v. 1
14.4 2 Cor 11.2; Rev 3.4; 5.9; Jas 1.18
14.5 Ps 32.2; Zeph 3.13; Eph 5.27
14.6 Rev 8.13; 3.10; 5.9
14.7 Rev 15.4; 11.13; 4.11; 8.10
14.8 Isa 21.9; Jer 51.8; Rev 18.2; 17.5; 18.10
14.9 Rev 13.14-16
14.10 Isa 51.17; Jer 25.15; Rev 18.6; 20.10; 19.20
14.11 Isa 34.10; Rev 19.3; 4.8; 13.17

n Or *written in the book of life of the Lamb that was slaughtered from the foundation of the world* o Gk *whose plague of its death* p Or *that had received the plague of the sword* q Or *spirit* r Other ancient authorities read *six hundred sixteen* s Gk *sit*

ever. There is no rest day or night
for those who worship the beast
and its image and for anyone who
receives the mark of its name."
12 Here is a call for the endurance of the saints, those who keep
the commandments of God and
hold fast to the faith of[t] Jesus.
13 And I heard a voice from
heaven saying, "Write this: Blessed
are the dead who from now on die
in the Lord." "Yes," says the Spirit,
"they will rest from their labors, for
their deeds follow them."

Reaping the Earth's Harvest

14 Then I looked, and there was
a white cloud, and seated on the
cloud was one like the Son of Man,
with a golden crown on his head,
and a sharp sickle in his hand!
15 Another angel came out of the
temple, calling with a loud voice to
the one who sat on the cloud, "Use
your sickle and reap, for the hour to
reap has come, because the harvest
of the earth is fully ripe." 16 So the
one who sat on the cloud swung his
sickle over the earth, and the earth
was reaped.
17 Then another angel came out
of the temple in heaven, and he too
had a sharp sickle. 18 Then another
angel came out from the altar, the
angel who has authority over fire,
and he called with a loud voice to
him who had the sharp sickle, "Use
your sharp sickle and gather the
clusters of the vine of the earth, for
its grapes are ripe." 19 So the angel
swung his sickle over the earth and
gathered the vintage of the earth,
and he threw it into the great wine
press of the wrath of God. 20 And
the wine press was trodden outside
the city, and blood flowed from the
wine press, as high as a horse's bridle, for a distance of about two
hundred miles.[u]

The Angels with the Seven Last Plagues

15 Then I saw another portent
in heaven, great and amazing: seven angels with seven
plagues, which are the last, for with
them the wrath of God is ended.
2 And I saw what appeared to be
a sea of glass mixed with fire, and
those who had conquered the beast
and its image and the number of its
name, standing beside the sea of
glass with harps of God in their
hands. 3 And they sing the song of
Moses, the servant[v] of God, and
the song of the Lamb:

"Great and amazing are your
deeds,
Lord God the Almighty!
Just and true are your ways,
King of the nations![w]
4 Lord, who will not fear
and glorify your name?
For you alone are holy.
All nations will come
and worship before you,
for your judgments have
been revealed."

5 After this I looked, and the
temple of the tent[x] of witness in
heaven was opened, 6 and out of
the temple came the seven angels
with the seven plagues, robed in
pure bright linen,[y] with golden
sashes across their chests. 7 Then
one of the four living creatures gave
the seven angels seven golden
bowls full of the wrath of God, who
lives forever and ever; 8 and the
temple was filled with smoke from
the glory of God and from his power, and no one could enter the temple until the seven plagues of the
seven angels were ended.

The Bowls of God's Wrath

16 Then I heard a loud voice
from the temple telling the
seven angels, "Go and pour out on
the earth the seven bowls of the
wrath of God."
2 So the first angel went and
poured his bowl on the earth, and
a foul and painful sore came on
those who had the mark of the
beast and who worshiped its image.
3 The second angel poured his

14.12 Rev 13.10; 12.17
14.13 Rev 20.6; 1 Cor 15.18; 1 Thes 4.16
14.14 Dan 7.13; Rev 1.13; 6.2
14.15 Joel 3.13; Jer 51.33; Rev 13.12
14.18 Rev 16.8; Joel 3.13
14.19 Rev 19.15
14.20 Isa 63.3; Heb 13.12; Rev 11.8
15.1 Rev 12.1,3; 16.1; Lev 26.21; Rev 14.10
15.2 Rev 4.6; 13.14,15; 5.8
15.3 Deut 32.3,4; Ps 111.2; 145.17; Hos 14.9
15.4 Jer 10.7; Isa 66.23
15.5 Rev 11.19; Num 1.50
15.6 Rev 14.15; v. 1; Rev 1.13
15.7 Rev 4.6,9; 10.6
15.8 Ex 40.34; 1 Kings 8.10; Isa 6.4
16.1 Rev 15.1
16.2 Rev 8.7; Ex 9.9-11; Rev 13.15-17
16.3 Rev 8.8,9; Ex 17.17-21

[t] Or *to their faith in* [u] Gk *one thousand six hundred stadia* [v] Gk *slave* [w] Other ancient authorities read *the ages* [x] Or *tabernacle* [y] Other ancient authorities read *stone*

bowl into the sea, and it became
like the blood of a corpse, and every living thing in the sea died.
4 The third angel poured his
bowl into the rivers and the springs
of water, and they became blood.
5 And I heard the angel of the waters say,

"You are just, O Holy One,
who are and were,
for you have judged these
things;
6 because they shed the blood
of saints and prophets,
you have given them blood
to drink.
It is what they deserve!"

7 And I heard the altar respond,

"Yes, O Lord God, the
Almighty,
your judgments are true
and just!"

8 The fourth angel poured his
bowl on the sun, and it was allowed
to scorch them with fire; 9 they
were scorched by the fierce heat,
but they cursed the name of God,
who had authority over these
plagues, and they did not repent
and give him glory.
10 The fifth angel poured his
bowl on the throne of the beast,
and its kingdom was plunged into
darkness; people gnawed their
tongues in agony, 11 and cursed the
God of heaven because of their
pains and sores, and they did not
repent of their deeds.
12 The sixth angel poured his
bowl on the great river Euphrates,
and its water was dried up in order
to prepare the way for the kings
from the east. 13 And I saw three
foul spirits like frogs coming from
the mouth of the dragon, from the
mouth of the beast, and from the
mouth of the false prophet.
14 These are demonic spirits, performing signs, who go abroad to the
kings of the whole world, to assemble them for battle on the great day
of God the Almighty. 15 ("See, I am
coming like a thief! Blessed is the
one who stays awake and is
clothed,[z] not going about naked
and exposed to shame.") 16 And
they assembled them at the place
that in Hebrew is called Harmagedon.
17 The seventh angel poured his
bowl into the air, and a loud voice
came out of the temple, from the
throne, saying, "It is done!" 18 And
there came flashes of lightning,
rumblings, peals of thunder, and a
violent earthquake, such as had
not occurred since people were
upon the earth, so violent was that
earthquake. 19 The great city was
split into three parts, and the cities
of the nations fell. God remembered great Babylon and gave her
the wine-cup of the fury of his
wrath. 20 And every island fled
away, and no mountains were to
be found; 21 and huge hailstones,
each weighing about a hundred
pounds,[a] dropped from heaven on
people, until they cursed God for
the plague of the hail, so fearful
was that plague.

The Great Whore and the Beast

17 Then one of the seven angels who had the seven
bowls came and said to me,
"Come, I will show you the judgment of the great whore who is
seated on many waters, 2 with
whom the kings of the earth have
committed fornication, and with
the wine of whose fornication the
inhabitants of the earth have become drunk." 3 So he carried me
away in the spirit[b] into a wilderness, and I saw a woman sitting on
a scarlet beast that was full of blasphemous names, and it had seven
heads and ten horns. 4 The woman
was clothed in purple and scarlet,
and adorned with gold and jewels
and pearls, holding in her hand a
golden cup full of abominations
and the impurities of her fornication; 5 and on her forehead was
written a name, a mystery: "Babylon the great, mother of whores
and of earth's abominations."

16.4 Rev 8.10; Ex 7.17-21 **16.5** Rev 15.3; 11.17; 15.4 **16.6** Rev 17.6; 18.24; Isa 49.26 **16.7** Rev 6.9; 14.18; 15.3; 19.2 **16.8** Rev 8.12; 14.18 **16.9** Rev 2.21; 11.13 **16.10** Rev 13.2; 9.2; 11.10 **16.11** vv. 9,21; Rev 11.13; 2.21 **16.12** Rev 9.14; Isa 41.2 **16.13** Rev 12.3; 13.1; 19.20 **16.14** 1 Tim 4.1; Rev 13.13; 3.10; 17.14 **16.15** 1 Thes 5.2; 2 Cor 5.3 **16.16** Rev 19.19; 9.11; 2 Kings 23.29, 30 **16.17** Eph 2.2; Rev 11.15; 14.15; 21.6 **16.18** Rev 4.5; 6.12; Dan 12.1 **16.19** Rev 17.18; 14.8; 18.5; 14.10 **16.20** Rev 6.14 **16.21** Rev 11.19; Ex 9.23 **17.1** Rev 21.9; 16.19; 19.2; Jer 51.13 **17.2** Rev 18.3; 14.8 **17.3** Rev 12.3,6, 14 **17.4** Jer 51.7; Rev 18.16; 18.6

17.5 2 Thes 2.7; Rev 14.8; 16.19; 18.9 **17.6** Rev 18.24; 13.15; 12.11

[z] Gk *and keeps his robes* [a] Gk *weighing about a talent* [b] Or *in the Spirit*

6 And I saw that the woman was
drunk with the blood of the saints
and the blood of the witnesses to
Jesus.

When I saw her, I was greatly
amazed. 7 But the angel said to me,
"Why are you so amazed? I will tell
you the mystery of the woman, and
of the beast with seven heads and
ten horns that carries her. 8 The
beast that you saw was, and is not,
and is about to ascend from the
bottomless pit and go to destruction. And the inhabitants of the
earth, whose names have not been
written in the book of life from the
foundation of the world, will be
amazed when they see the beast,
because it was and is not and is to
come.

9 "This calls for a mind that has
wisdom: the seven heads are seven
mountains on which the woman is
seated; also, they are seven kings,
10 of whom five have fallen, one is
living, and the other has not yet
come; and when he comes, he
must remain only a little while.
11 As for the beast that was and is
not, it is an eighth but it belongs to
the seven, and it goes to destruction. 12 And the ten horns that you
saw are ten kings who have not yet
received a kingdom, but they are to
receive authority as kings for one
hour, together with the beast.
13 These are united in yielding their
power and authority to the beast;
14 they will make war on the Lamb,
and the Lamb will conquer them,
for he is Lord of lords and King of
kings, and those with him are
called and chosen and faithful."

15 And he said to me, "The waters that you saw, where the whore
is seated, are peoples and multitudes and nations and languages.
16 And the ten horns that you saw,
they and the beast will hate the
whore; they will make her desolate
and naked; they will devour her
flesh and burn her up with fire.
17 For God has put it into their
hearts to carry out his purpose by
agreeing to give their kingdom to
the beast, until the words of God
will be fulfilled. 18 The woman you
saw is the great city that rules over
the kings of the earth."

17.7 vv. 5,3,9 **17.8** Rev 11.7; 13.10; 3.10; 13.3,8 **17.9** Rev 13.18 **17.11** v. 8 **17.12** Dan 7.20; Rev 13.1; 18.10,17,19 **17.13** v. 17 **17.14** Rev 16.14; 1 Tim 6.15; Rev 19.16; Mt 22.14 **17.15** Isa 8.7; Rev 5.9; 13.7 **17.16** Rev 18.17, 19; Ezek 16.37, 39; Rev 19.18; 18.8 **17.17** 2 Thes 2.11; Rev 10.7 **17.18** Rev 16.19

The Fall of Babylon

18 After this I saw another angel coming down from
heaven, having great authority; and
the earth was made bright with his
splendor. 2 He called out with a
mighty voice,

"Fallen, fallen is Babylon the
great!
It has become a dwelling
place of demons,
a haunt of every foul spirit,
a haunt of every foul bird,
a haunt of every foul and
hateful beast.[c]
3 For all the nations have
drunk[d]
of the wine of the wrath of
her fornication,
and the kings of the earth
have committed
fornication with her,
and the merchants of the
earth have grown rich
from the power[e] of her
luxury."

4 Then I heard another voice
from heaven saying,

"Come out of her, my people,
so that you do not take
part in her sins,
and so that you do not share
in her plagues;
5 for her sins are heaped high
as heaven,
and God has remembered
her iniquities.
6 Render to her as she herself
has rendered,
and repay her double for
her deeds;
mix a double draught for
her in the cup she mixed.
7 As she glorified herself and
lived luxuriously,
so give her a like measure
of torment and grief.
Since in her heart she says,

18.1 Rev 17.1; 10.1; Ezek 43.2 **18.2** Rev 14.8; Isa 13.21, 22; Jer 50.39 **18.3** Rev 14.8; Jer 25.15,27 **18.4** Isa 48.20; Jer 50.8; 2 Cor 6.17 **18.5** Jer 51.9; Rev 16.19 **18.6** Ps 137.8; Jer 50.15; Rev 14.10; 16.19 **18.7** Ezek 28.2-8; Isa 47.7,8; Zeph 2.15

[c] Other ancient authorities lack the words *a haunt of every foul beast* and attach the words *and hateful* to the previous line so as to read *a haunt of every foul and hateful bird* [d] Other ancient authorities read *she has made all nations drink* [e] Or *resources*

'I rule as a queen;
I am no widow,
and I will never see grief,'
8 therefore her plagues will
come in a single day—
pestilence and mourning
and famine—
and she will be burned with
fire;
for mighty is the Lord God
who judges her."

9 And the kings of the earth,
who committed fornication and
lived in luxury with her, will weep
and wail over her when they see the
smoke of her burning; 10 they will
stand far off, in fear of her torment,
and say,

"Alas, alas, the great city,
Babylon, the mighty city!
For in one hour your
judgment has come."

11 And the merchants of the
earth weep and mourn for her,
since no one buys their cargo anymore, 12 cargo of gold, silver, jewels
and pearls, fine linen, purple, silk
and scarlet, all kinds of scented
wood, all articles of ivory, all articles of costly wood, bronze, iron,
and marble, 13 cinnamon, spice, incense, myrrh, frankincense, wine,
olive oil, choice flour and wheat,
cattle and sheep, horses and chariots, slaves—and human lives.[f]

14 "The fruit for which your
soul longed
has gone from you,
and all your dainties and
your splendor
are lost to you,
never to be found again!"

15 The merchants of these wares,
who gained wealth from her, will
stand far off, in fear of her torment,
weeping and mourning aloud,

16 "Alas, alas, the great city,
clothed in fine linen,
in purple and scarlet,
adorned with gold,
with jewels, and with
pearls!
17 For in one hour all this
wealth has been laid
waste!"

And all shipmasters and seafar-
ers, sailors and all whose trade is

18.8 Isa 47.9; Rev 17.16; Jer 50.34; Rev 11.17
18.9 Rev 17.2; Jer 50.46; v. 18; Rev 19.3
18.10 vv. 15,17, 16,19
18.11 v. 3; Ezek 27.27
18.12 Rev 17.4
18.13 Ezek 27.13
18.15 Ezek 27.36, 31
18.16 Rev 17.4
18.17 Rev 17.16; Isa 23.14; Ezek 27.29
18.18 Ezek 27.30; Rev 13.4
18.19 Josh 7.6; Job 2.12; Ezek 27.30
18.20 Isa 44.23; Jer 51.48; Rev 19.2
18.21 Jer 51.63; Rev 12.8
18.22 Isa 24.8; Ezek 26.13; Jer 25.10
18.23 Jer 25.10; 7.34; 16.9; Isa 23.8; Nah 3.4
18.24 Rev 17.6; Jer 51.49

on the sea, stood far off 18 and cried
out as they saw the smoke of her
burning,

"What city was like the great
city?"

19 And they threw dust on their
heads, as they wept and mourned,
crying out,

"Alas, alas, the great city,
where all who had ships at
sea
grew rich by her wealth!
For in one hour she has been
laid waste.
20 Rejoice over her, O heaven,
you saints and apostles and
prophets!
For God has given judgment
for you against her."

21 Then a mighty angel took up
a stone like a great millstone and
threw it into the sea, saying,

"With such violence Babylon
the great city
will be thrown down,
and will be found no more;
22 and the sound of harpists
and minstrels and of
flutists and trumpeters
will be heard in you no
more;
and an artisan of any trade
will be found in you no
more;
and the sound of the
millstone
will be heard in you no
more;
23 and the light of a lamp
will shine in you no more;
and the voice of bridegroom
and bride
will be heard in you no
more;
for your merchants were the
magnates of the earth,
and all nations were
deceived by your
sorcery.
24 And in you[g] was found the
blood of prophets and
of saints,
and of all who have been
slaughtered on earth."

[f] Or *chariots, and human bodies and souls*
[g] Gk *her*

The Rejoicing in Heaven

19 After this I heard what
seemed to be the loud
voice of a great multitude in heav-
en, saying,
"Hallelujah!
Salvation and glory and
power to our God,
2 for his judgments are true
and just;
he has judged the great
whore
who corrupted the earth
with her fornication,
and he has avenged on her
the blood of his
servants."[h]
3 Once more they said,
"Hallelujah!
The smoke goes up from her
forever and ever."
4 And the twenty-four elders and
the four living creatures fell down
and worshiped God who is seated
on the throne, saying,
"Amen. Hallelujah!"
5 And from the throne came a
voice saying,
"Praise our God,
all you his servants,[h]
and all who fear him,
small and great."
6 Then I heard what seemed to be
the voice of a great multitude, like
the sound of many waters and like
the sound of mighty thunderpeals,
crying out,
"Hallelujah!
For the Lord our God
the Almighty reigns.
7 Let us rejoice and exult
and give him the glory,
for the marriage of the Lamb
has come,
and his bride has made
herself ready;
8 to her it has been granted to
be clothed
with fine linen, bright and
pure"—
for the fine linen is the righteous
deeds of the saints.
9 And the angel said[i] to me,
"Write this: Blessed are those who
are invited to the marriage supper
of the Lamb." And he said to me,
"These are true words of God."
10 Then I fell down at his feet to
worship him, but he said to me,
"You must not do that! I am a fellow servant[j] with you and your
comrades[k] who hold the testimony of Jesus.[l] Worship God! For the
testimony of Jesus[l] is the spirit of
prophecy."

The Rider on the White Horse

11 Then I saw heaven opened,
and there was a white horse! Its rider is called Faithful and True, and
in righteousness he judges and
makes war. 12 His eyes are like a
flame of fire, and on his head are
many diadems; and he has a name
inscribed that no one knows but
himself. 13 He is clothed in a robe
dipped in[m] blood, and his name is
called The Word of God. 14 And the
armies of heaven, wearing fine lin-
en, white and pure, were following
him on white horses. 15 From his
mouth comes a sharp sword with
which to strike down the nations,
and he will rule[n] them with a rod
of iron; he will tread the wine press
of the fury of the wrath of God the
Almighty. 16 On his robe and on his
thigh he has a name inscribed,
"King of kings and Lord of lords."

The Beast and Its Armies Defeated

17 Then I saw an angel standing
in the sun, and with a loud voice he
called to all the birds that fly in
midheaven, "Come, gather for the
great supper of God, 18 to eat the
flesh of kings, the flesh of captains,
the flesh of the mighty, the flesh of
horses and their riders—flesh of
all, both free and slave, both small
and great." 19 Then I saw the beast
and the kings of the earth with
their armies gathered to make war
against the rider on the horse and
against his army. 20 And the beast
was captured, and with it the false
prophet who had performed in its
presence the signs by which he de-

[h] Gk *slaves* [i] Gk *he said* [j] Gk *slave* [k] Gk *brothers* [l] Or *to Jesus* [m] Other ancient authorities read *sprinkled with* [n] Or *will shepherd*

19.1 Rev 11.15; 4.11; 7.10,12; 12.10
19.2 Deut 32.43; Rev 6.10
19.3 Isa 34.10; Rev 14.11
19.4 Rev 4.4,6; 5.14
19.5 Ps 134.1; Rev 11.18; 20.12
19.6 Rev 11.15, 17; 14.2
19.7 Mt 22.2; 25.10; 2 Cor 11.2; Eph 5.32; Rev 21.2,9
19.8 Rev 15.4
19.9 v. 10; Rev 1.19; Lk 14.15; Rev 21.5
19.10 Rev 22.8; Acts 10.26; Rev 22.9; 12.17
19.11 Rev 15.5; 6.2; 3.14; Isa 11.4
19.12 Rev 1.14; 6.2; 2.17
19.13 Isa 63.2,3; Jn 1.1
19.14 v. 8
19.15 Isa 11.4; 2 Thes 2.8; Ps 2.9; Rev 2.27; 14.19,20
19.16 Dan 2.47; Rev 17.14
19.17 Rev 8.13; Ezek 39.17
19.18 Ezek 39.18-20; Rev 11.18
19.19 Rev 11.7; 16.14,16
19.20 Rev 16.13; 13.12ff; Dan 7.11; Rev 20.10; 14.10; 21.8

ceived those who had received the
mark of the beast and those who
worshiped its image. These two
were thrown alive into the lake of
fire that burns with sulfur. 21And
the rest were killed by the sword of
the rider on the horse, the sword
that came from his mouth; and all
the birds were gorged with their
flesh.

The Thousand Years

20 Then I saw an angel coming down from heaven,
holding in his hand the key to the
bottomless pit and a great chain.
2He seized the dragon, that ancient
serpent, who is the Devil and Satan, and bound him for a thousand
years, 3and threw him into the pit,
and locked and sealed it over him,
so that he would deceive the nations no more, until the thousand
years were ended. After that he
must be let out for a little while.
4 Then I saw thrones, and those
seated on them were given authority to judge. I also saw the souls of
those who had been beheaded for
their testimony to Jesus[o] and for
the word of God. They had not worshiped the beast or its image and
had not received its mark on their
foreheads or their hands. They
came to life and reigned with
Christ a thousand years. 5(The rest
of the dead did not come to life until the thousand years were ended.)
This is the first resurrection.
6Blessed and holy are those who
share in the first resurrection. Over
these the second death has no
power, but they will be priests of
God and of Christ, and they will
reign with him a thousand years.

Satan's Doom

7 When the thousand years are
ended, Satan will be released from
his prison 8and will come out to deceive the nations at the four corners of the earth, Gog and Magog,
in order to gather them for battle;
they are as numerous as the sands
of the sea. 9They marched up over
the breadth of the earth and surrounded the camp of the saints and
the beloved city. And fire came
down from heaven[p] and consumed
them. 10And the devil who had deceived them was thrown into the
lake of fire and sulfur, where the
beast and the false prophet were,
and they will be tormented day and
night forever and ever.

The Dead Are Judged

11 Then I saw a great white
throne and the one who sat on it;
the earth and the heaven fled from
his presence, and no place was
found for them. 12And I saw the
dead, great and small, standing before the throne, and books were
opened. Also another book was
opened, the book of life. And the
dead were judged according to
their works, as recorded in the
books. 13And the sea gave up the
dead that were in it, Death and Hades gave up the dead that were in
them, and all were judged according to what they had done. 14Then
Death and Hades were thrown into
the lake of fire. This is the second
death, the lake of fire; 15and anyone whose name was not found
written in the book of life was
thrown into the lake of fire.

The New Heaven and the New Earth

21 Then I saw a new heaven
and a new earth; for the
first heaven and the first earth had
passed away, and the sea was no
more. 2And I saw the holy city, the
new Jerusalem, coming down out
of heaven from God, prepared as a
bride adorned for her husband.
3And I heard a loud voice from the
throne saying,

"See, the home[q] of God is
among mortals.
He will dwell[q] with them as
their God;[r]
they will be his peoples,[s]

19.21 vv. 11,19, 15,17 **20.1** Rev 10.1; 1.18; 9.1 **20.2** 2 Pet 2.4; Jude 6; Rev 12.9 **20.3** Dan 6.17; Rev 12.9 **20.4** Dan 7.9,22, 27; Rev 6.9; 13.12,15,16 **20.5** Lk 14.14; Phil 3.11; 1 Thes 4.16 **20.6** Rev 14.13; 2.11; 21.8; 1.6 **20.7** v. 2 **20.8** Ezek 38.2; 39.1; Rev 16.14; Heb 11.12 **20.9** Ezek 38.9, 22; 39.6 **20.10** vv. 3,8 **20.11f** Rev 4.2; 21.1; Dan 2.35; Rev 12.8 **20.12** Mt 16.27; Rev 2.3; 22.12 **20.13** Rev 6.8; Isa 26.19; Rev 2.23 **20.14** 1 Cor 15.26; Rev 6.8 **21.1** Isa 65.17; 2 Pet 3.13; Rev 20.11 **21.2** Heb 11.10; 12.22; Rev 3.12 **21.3** Ezek 37.27; 2 Cor 6.16; Rev 7.15

[o] Or *for the testimony of Jesus* [p] Other ancient authorities read *from God, out of heaven,* or *out of heaven from God* [q] Gk *tabernacle* [r] Other ancient authorities lack *as their God* [s] Other ancient authorities read *people*

and God himself will be with
them;[t]
4 he will wipe every tear from
their eyes.
Death will be no more;
mourning and crying and
pain will be no more,
for the first things have
passed away."

5 And the one who was seated
on the throne said, "See, I am making all things new." Also he said,
"Write this, for these words are
trustworthy and true." 6 Then he
said to me, "It is done! I am the Alpha and the Omega, the beginning
and the end. To the thirsty I will
give water as a gift from the spring
of the water of life. 7 Those who
conquer will inherit these things,
and I will be their God and they will
be my children. 8 But as for the
cowardly, the faithless,[u] the polluted, the murderers, the fornicators, the sorcerers, the idolaters,
and all liars, their place will be in
the lake that burns with fire and
sulfur, which is the second death."

Vision of the New Jerusalem

9 Then one of the seven angels
who had the seven bowls full of the
seven last plagues came and said to
me, "Come, I will show you the
bride, the wife of the Lamb." 10 And
in the spirit[v] he carried me away to
a great, high mountain and showed
me the holy city Jerusalem coming
down out of heaven from God. 11 It
has the glory of God and a radiance
like a very rare jewel, like jasper,
clear as crystal. 12 It has a great,
high wall with twelve gates, and at
the gates twelve angels, and on the
gates are inscribed the names of
the twelve tribes of the Israelites;
13 on the east three gates, on the
north three gates, on the south
three gates, and on the west three
gates. 14 And the wall of the city has
twelve foundations, and on them
are the twelve names of the twelve
apostles of the Lamb.

15 The angel[w] who talked to me
had a measuring rod of gold to
measure the city and its gates and
walls. 16 The city lies foursquare, its

21.4 Rev 7.17; 1 Cor 15.26; Rev 20.14; Isa 35.10; 65.19
21.5 Rev 4.9; 20.11; Isa 43.19; Rev 19.9
21.6 Rev 16.17; 1.8; 22.13; Jn 4.10
21.7 Rev 2.7; v. 3
21.8 Heb 12.14; Rev 22.15; 19.20; 2.11
21.9 Rev 15.1,6, 7; 20.14ff
21.10 Rev 1.10; Ezek 40.2; Rev 17.3
21.11 Rev 15.8; 22.5; 4.6
21.12 Ezek 48.31-34
21.14 Mt 16.18; Eph 2.20
21.15 Rev 11.1
21.18 vv. 11,19, 21; Rev 4.6
21.19 Isa 54.11, 12; vv. 11, 18; Rev 4.3
21.20 Rev 4.3
21.21 vv. 15,25,18
21.22 Jn 4.21,23; Rev 1.8; 5.6
21.23 Isa 24.23; 60.19,20; Rev 22.5
21.24 Isa 60.3,5
21.25 Isa 60.11; Zech 14.7; Rev 22.5
21.27 Isa 52.1; Joel 3.17; Rev 22.14; 3.5
22.1 Ezek 47.1; Zech 14.8; Rev 4.6
22.2 Gen 2.9; Rev 2.7; Ezek 47.12

length the same as its width; and
he measured the city with his rod,
fifteen hundred miles;[x] its length
and width and height are equal.
17 He also measured its wall, one
hundred forty-four cubits[y] by human measurement, which the angel was using. 18 The wall is built of
jasper, while the city is pure gold,
clear as glass. 19 The foundations of
the wall of the city are adorned
with every jewel; the first was jasper, the second sapphire, the third
agate, the fourth emerald, 20 the
fifth onyx, the sixth carnelian, the
seventh chrysolite, the eighth beryl, the ninth topaz, the tenth chrys-
oprase, the eleventh jacinth, the
twelfth amethyst. 21 And the twelve
gates are twelve pearls, each of the
gates is a single pearl, and the
street of the city is pure gold, trans-
parent as glass.

22 I saw no temple in the city,
for its temple is the Lord God the
Almighty and the Lamb. 23 And the
city has no need of sun or moon to
shine on it, for the glory of God is
its light, and its lamp is the Lamb.
24 The nations will walk by its light,
and the kings of the earth will bring
their glory into it. 25 Its gates will
never be shut by day—and there
will be no night there. 26 People will
bring into it the glory and the honor
of the nations. 27 But nothing unclean will enter it, nor anyone who
practices abomination or falsehood, but only those who are written in the Lamb's book of life.

The River of Life

22 Then the angel[z] showed
me the river of the water of
life, bright as crystal, flowing from
the throne of God and of the Lamb
2 through the middle of the street of
the city. On either side of the river
is the tree of life[a] with its twelve
kinds of fruit, producing its fruit
each month; and the leaves of the

[t] Other ancient authorities add *and be their God* [u] Or *the unbelieving* [v] Or *in the Spirit* [w] Gk *He* [x] Gk *twelve thousand stadia* [y] That is, almost seventy-five yards [z] Gk *he* [a] Or *the Lamb. [2]In the middle of the street of the city, and on either side of the river, is the tree of life*

tree are for the healing of the nations. 3 Nothing accursed will be
found there any more. But the
throne of God and of the Lamb will
be in it, and his servants[b] will worship him; 4 they will see his face,
and his name will be on their foreheads. 5 And there will be no more
night; they need no light of lamp or
sun, for the Lord God will be their
light, and they will reign forever
and ever.
6 And he said to me, "These
words are trustworthy and true, for
the Lord, the God of the spirits of
the prophets, has sent his angel to
show his servants[b] what must soon
take place."
7 "See, I am coming soon!
Blessed is the one who keeps the
words of the prophecy of this
book."

Epilogue and Benediction

8 I, John, am the one who heard
and saw these things. And when I
heard and saw them, I fell down to
worship at the feet of the angel who
showed them to me; 9 but he said to
me, "You must not do that! I am a
fellow servant[c] with you and your
comrades[d] the prophets, and with
those who keep the words of this
book. Worship God!"
10 And he said to me, "Do not
seal up the words of the prophecy
of this book, for the time is near.
11 Let the evildoer still do evil, and
the filthy still be filthy, and the
righteous still do right, and the
holy still be holy."

12 "See, I am coming soon; my
reward is with me, to repay according to everyone's work. 13 I am the
Alpha and the Omega, the first and
the last, the beginning and the
end."
14 Blessed are those who wash
their robes,[e] so that they will have
the right to the tree of life and may
enter the city by the gates. 15 Outside are the dogs and sorcerers and
fornicators and murderers and
idolaters, and everyone who loves
and practices falsehood.
16 "It is I, Jesus, who sent my
angel to you with this testimony for
the churches. I am the root and the
descendant of David, the bright
morning star."
17 The Spirit and the bride say,
"Come."
And let everyone who hears
say, "Come."
And let everyone who is
thirsty come.
Let anyone who wishes take
the water of life as a
gift.
18 I warn everyone who hears
the words of the prophecy of this
book: if anyone adds to them, God
will add to that person the plagues
described in this book; 19 if anyone
takes away from the words of the
book of this prophecy, God will
take away that person's share in
the tree of life and in the holy city,
which are described in this book.
20 The one who testifies to
these things says, "Surely I am
coming soon."
Amen. Come, Lord Jesus!
21 The grace of the Lord Jesus
be with all the saints. Amen.[f]

22.3 Zech 14.11; Rev 7.15
22.4 Mt 5.8; Rev 14.1
22.5 Rev 21.25, 23; Dan 7.27
22.6 Rev 1.1; 19.19; 21.5
22.7 Rev 3.11; 1.3
22.8 Rev 1.1; 19.10
22.9 Rev 19.10; 1.1; vv. 10, 18,19; Rev 21.2
22.10 Dan 8.26; Rev 1.3
22.11 Dan 12.10; Ezek 3.27
22.12 Isa 40.10; Jer 17.10; Rev 2.23
22.13 Rev 1.8,17; 21.6
22.15 Gal 5.19ff; Col 3.6; Phil 3.2
22.16 Rev 1.1; 5.5; Zech 6.12; 2 Pet 1.19; Rev 2.28
22.17 Rev 2.7; 21.2; Isa 55.1; Rev 21.6
22.18 Deut 4.2; Prov 30.6; Rev 15.6; 16.21
22.20 Rev 1.2; 2 Tim 4.8; Rom 16.20; 2 Thes 3.18

[b] Gk *slaves* [c] Gk *slave* [d] Gk *brothers*
[e] Other ancient authorities read *do his commandments* [f] Other ancient authorities lack *all*; others lack *the saints*; others lack *Amen*

Study Helps

PARABLES OF THE BIBLE

PARABLES OF THE OLD TESTAMENT

Parable	Reference
The trees	Judg 9.7–15
The ewe lamb	2 Sam 12.1–4
Two sons	2 Sam 14.1–24
Thorn bush and cedar	2 Kings 14.8–14
The vineyard	Isa 5.1–7
Almond branch and boiling pot	Jer 1.11–19
Linen loincloth	Jer 13.1–11
Wine-jars	Jer 13.12–14
Potter and clay	Jer 18.1–10
Two baskets of figs	Jer 24.1–10
Cup of God's wrath	Jer 25.15–38
Useless vine	Ezek 15.1–8
Boiling pot	Ezek 24.1–4
Valley of dry bones	Ezek 37.1–14
Measuring line	Zech 2.1–13
Golden lampstand and two olive trees	Zech 4.1–14
Flying scroll	Zech 5.1–4

THE PARABLES OF JESUS

Parable	Matthew	Mark	Luke
Lamp under a bushel basket	5.14–15	4.21–22	8.16; 11.33
Wise and foolish builders	7.24–27		6.47–49
Unshrunk cloth on an old cloak	9.16	2.21	5.36
New wine in old wineskins	9.17	2.22	5.37–38
Sower and the soils	13.3–8,18–23	4.3–8,14–20	8.5–8,11–15
Weeds	13.24–30,36–43		
Mustard seed	13.31–32	4.30–32	13.18–19
Yeast	13.33		13.20–21
Hidden treasure	13.44		
Valuable pearl	13.45–46		
Net	13.47–50		
Master of a household	13.52		
Lost sheep	18.12–14		15.4–7
Unforgiving servant	18.23–34		
Laborers in the vineyard	20.1–16		
Two sons	21.28–32		
Tenants	21.33–44	12.1–11	20.9–18
Wedding banquet	22.2–14		
Fig tree	24.32–35	13.28–29	21.29–31
Faithful and wise slave	24.45–51		12.42–48

THE PARABLES OF JESUS *(cont.)*

Parable	Matthew	Mark	Luke
Ten bridesmaids	25.1–13		
Talents (pounds)	25.14–30		19.12–27
Sheep and goats	25.31–46		
Growing seed		4.26–29	
Watchful slaves		13.35–37	12.35–40
Creditor			7.41–43
Good Samaritan			10.30–37
Friend in need			11.5–8
Rich fool			12.16–21
Barren fig tree			13.6–9
Lowest seat at the banquet			14.7–14
Great dinner			14.16–24
Cost of discipleship			14.28–33
Lost coin			15.8–10
Prodigal son			15.11–32
Dishonest manager			16.1–8
Rich man and Lazarus			16.19–31
Master and his slave			17.7–10
Persistent widow			18.2–8
Pharisee and tax collector			18.10–14

MIRACLES OF THE BIBLE

MIRACLES OF THE OLD TESTAMENT

Miracle	Reference
Burning bush	Ex 3.1–14
Staff becoming a snake	Ex 4.1–5; 7.8–13
Leprous hand	Ex 4.6–12
Ten plagues	Ex 8.14—12.30
Dividing of the Red Sea	Ex 14.21–31
Water from the rock	Ex 17.1–9
Destruction of Korah	Num 16.31–35
Aaron's staff budding	Num 17.1–19
Water from the rock in Kadesh	Num 20.9–11
Bronze serpent	Num 21.4–9
Balaam's donkey	Num 22.20–35
Jordan divided	Josh 3.7–17
Fall of Jericho	Josh 6.1–20
Sun standing still	Josh 10.1–14
Slain lion	Judg 14.5–10
Dagon's temple pulled down	Judg 16.23–30
Thunder and rain	1 Sam 12.16–18
Jeroboam's hand withered and restored	1 Kings 13.6
Elijah fed by ravens	1 Kings 17.1–6
Widow's meal and oil	1 Kings 17.8–16
Widow's son raised from the dead	1 Kings 17.17–24
Sacrifice consumed by fire	1 Kings 18.30–39
Rain in answer to prayer	1 Kings 18.41–45
Jordan divided	2 Kings 2.1–8
Water made wholesome	2 Kings 2.19–22
Widow's oil multiplied	2 Kings 4.1–7
Shunammite's son restored to life	2 Kings 4.8–37
Poison stew rendered harmless	2 Kings 4.38–41
Feeding of one hundred men	2 Kings 4.42–44
Naaman healed of leprosy	2 Kings 5.1–19
Floating ax head	2 Kings 6.1–7
Blinded eyes	2 Kings 6.8–23
Dead man restored to life	2 Kings 13.21
Hezekiah healed	2 Kings 20.1–7
Three men delivered from blazing furnace	Dan 3.23–27
Daniel delivered from the den of lions	Dan 6.10–23
Sea stilled when Jonah cast in	Jon 1.15
Jonah delivered from fish's mouth	Jon 2.10
Withering of the bush	Jon 4.6–7

THE MIRACLES OF JESUS

	Matthew	Mark	Luke	John
Healing Miracles				
Man with leprosy	8.2–4	1.40–42	5.12–13	
Roman centurion's servant	8.5–13		7.1–10	
Peter's mother-in-law	8.14–15	1.30–31	4.38–39	
Two Gadarena demoniacs	8.28–34	5.1–15	8.27–35	
Paralyzed man	9.2–7	2.3–12	5.18–25	
Woman with hemorrhages	9.20–22	5.25–29	8.43–48	
Two blind men	9.27–31			
Mute, demon-possessed man	9.32–33			
Man with a withered hand	12.10–13	3.1–5	6.6–10	
Blind, mute, demon-possessed man	12.22		11.14	
Canaanite woman's daughter	15.21–28	7.24–30		
Boy with a demon	17.14–18	9.17–29	9.38–43	
Two blind men (including Bartimaeus)	20.29–34	10.46–52	18.35–43	
Deaf man with speech impediment		7.31–37		
Possessed man in synagogue		1.23–26	4.33–35	
Blind man at Bethsaida		8.22–26		
Crippled woman			13.11–13	
Man with dropsy			14.1–4	
Ten men with leprosy			17.11–19	
The high priest's slave			22.50–51	
Official's son at Capernaum				4.46–54
Sick man at pool of Beth-zatha				5.1–9
Man born blind				9.1–7
Miracles showing power over nature				
Calming the storm	8.23–27	4.37–41	8.22–25	
Walking on water	14.25	6.48–51		6.19–21
Feeding of the 5000	14.15–21	6.35–44	9.12–17	6.5–13
Feeding of the 4000	15.32–38	8.1–9		
Coin in fish	17.24–27			
Fig tree withered	21.18–22	11.12–14, 20–25		
Large catch of fish			5.4–11	
Water turned into wine				2.1–11
Another large catch of fish				21.1–11
Miracles of raising the dead				
Jairus's daughter	9.18–19, 23–25	5.22–24, 38–42	8.41–42, 49–56	
Widow's son at Nain			7.11–15	
Lazarus				11.1–44

MIRACLES OF THE APOSTLES

Miracle	Acts
Crippled beggar healed (by Peter)	3.6–9
Death of Ananias and Sapphira	5.1–10
Saul's sight restored	9.17–18
Healing of Aeneas	9.33–35
Raising of Dorcas	9.36–41
Elymas blinded	13.8–11
Crippled man healed (by Paul)	14.8–10
Demon cast out of a girl	16.16–18
Raising of Eutychus	20.9–10
Unharmed by viper	28.3–5
Healing of Publius's father	28.7–9

MINISTRY OF JESUS

THE YEAR OF INAUGURATION Event	Place	Matthew	Mark	Luke	John
Jesus baptized	Jordan River	3.13–17	1.9–11	3.21–23	1.29–39
Jesus tempted by Satan	Wilderness	4.1–11	1.12–13	4.1–13	
Jesus' first miracle	Cana				2.1–11
Jesus and Nicodemus	Judea				3.1–21
Jesus talks to a Samaritan woman	Samaria				4.5–42
Jesus heals an official's son	Cana				4.46–54
The people of Nazareth try to kill Jesus	Nazareth			4.16–31	

THE YEAR OF POPULARITY Event	Place	Matthew	Mark	Luke	John
Jesus calls four fishermen	Sea of Galilee	4.18–22	1.16–20	5.1–11	
Jesus heals Peter's mother-in-law	Capernaum	8.14–17	1.29–34	4.38–41	
Jesus begins preaching in Galilee	Galilee	4.23–25	1.35–39	4.42–44	
Matthew decides to follow Jesus	Capernaum	9.9–13	2.13–17	5.27–32	
Jesus chooses twelve disciples	Galilee	10.2–4	3.13–19	6.12–15	
Jesus preaches the Sermon on the Mount	Galilee	5.1—7.29		6.20–49	
A sinful woman anoints Jesus	Capernaum			7.36–50	
Jesus travels again through Galilee	Galilee			8.1–3	
Jesus tells parables about the kingdom	Galilee	13.1–52	4.1–34	8.4–18	
Jesus quiets the storm	Sea of Galilee	8.23–27	4.35–41	8.22–25	
Jairus's daughter raised to life by Jesus	Capernaum	9.18–26	5.21–43	8.40–56	
Jesus sends out the twelve	Galilee	9.35—11.1	6.6–13	9.1–6	

THE YEAR OF OPPOSITION Event	Place	Matthew	Mark	Luke	John
John the Baptist killed by Herod	Machaerus in Judea	14.1–12	6.14–29	9.7–9	
Jesus feeds the 5000	Near Bethsaida	14.13–21	6.30–44	9.10–17	6.1–14
Jesus walks on water	Sea of Galilee	14.22–23	6.45–52		6.16–21
Jesus feeds the 4000	Sea of Galilee	15.32–39	8.1–9		
Peter confesses Jesus as the Son of God	Caesarea Philippi	16.13–20	8.27–30	9.18–21	
Jesus predicts his death	Caesarea Philippi	16.21–26	8.31–37	9.22–25	
Jesus is transfigured	Mount Hermon	17.1–13	9.2–13	9.28–36	

THE MINISTRY OF JESUS *(cont.)*

THE YEAR OF OPPOSITION *(cont.)* Event	Place	Matthew	Mark	Luke	John
Jesus pays his temple taxes	Capernaum	17.24–27			
Jesus attends the Feast of Tabernacles	Jerusalem				7.11–52
Jesus heals a man born blind	Jerusalem				9.1–41
Jesus visits Mary and Martha	Bethany			10.38–42	
Jesus raises Lazarus from the dead	Bethany				11.1–44
Jesus begins his last trip to Jerusalem	Border road			17.11	
Jesus blesses the little children	Transjordan	19.13–15	10.13–16	18.15–17	
Jesus talks to the rich young man	Transjordan	19.16–30	10.17–31	18.18–30	
Jesus again predicts his death	Near the Jordan	20.17–19	10.32–34	18.31–34	
Jesus heals blind Bartimaeus	Jericho	20.29–34	10.46–52	18.35–43	
Jesus talks to Zacchaeus	Jericho			19.1–10	
Jesus visits Mary and Martha again	Bethany				11.55—12.1

THE LAST WEEK Event	Place	Day of week	Matthew	Mark	Luke	John
The triumphal entry	Jerusalem	Sunday	21.1–11	11.1–10	19.29–44	12.12–19
Jesus curses the fig tree	Jerusalem	Monday	21.18–19	11.12–14		
Jesus cleanses the temple	Jerusalem	Monday	21.12–13	11.15–18	19.45–48	
The authority of Jesus questioned	Jerusalem	Tuesday	21.23–27	11.27–33	20.1–8	
Jesus teaches in the temple	Jerusalem	Tuesday	21.28—23.29	12.1–44	20.9—21.4	
Jesus' feet anointed	Bethany	Tuesday	26.6–13	14.3–9		12.2–11
The plot against Jesus	Jerusalem	Wednesday	26.14–16	14.10–11	22.3–6	
The Last Supper	Jerusalem	Thursday	26.17–29	14.12–25	22.7–20	13.1–38
Jesus comforts his disciples	Jerusalem	Thursday				14.1—16.33
Jesus' high priestly prayer	Jerusalem	Thursday				17.1–26
Gethsemane	Jerusalem	Thursday	26.36–46	14.32–42	22.40–46	
Jesus' arrest and trial	Jerusalem	Friday	26.47—27.26	14.43—15.15	22.47—23.25	18.2—19.16
Jesus' crucifixion and death	Golgotha	Friday	27.27–56	15.16–41	23.26–49	19.17–30
The burial of Jesus	Garden tomb	Friday	27.57–66	15.42–47	23.50–56	19.31–42

PROMISES AND PERSPECTIVES FROM THE BIBLE

Promises from the Bible

GOD'S PROMISE OF:

Love—Matthew 10.30-31; John 3.16; John 15.9,13; 1 John 4.9
Forgiveness—Luke 15.3-7; Acts 10.43; Ephesians 1.7; 1 John 1.9
Salvation—Matthew 1.21; Acts 16.31; Ephesians 2.8; Hebrews 7.25
the Holy Spirit—Luke 11.13; John 14.16-17; Acts 2.38; Romans 8.11
Everlasting Life—John 6.40; John 10.28; 1 Corinthians 15.51-52; 1 Thessalonians 4.17
Peace—John 14.27; Romans 5.1-2; Ephesians 2.14; 2 Thessalonians 3.16
Joy—John 15.10-11; John 16.22; Romans 16.13; 1 Peter 1.8
Freedom—John 8.34-36; Romans 6.6,14,20-22; 2 Corinthians 3.17; Revelation 1.5
Growth—Philippians 1.6; 2 Corinthians 3.18; Ephesians 4.14-15; 2 Peter 1.3-4
Encouragement—1 Thessalonians 5.23; 2 Thessalonians 2.16-17; Hebrews 6.10; 1 Peter 2.9
Excellence—Matthew 20.26-28; John 14.12; John 15.15-16; 2 Corinthians 3.5-6
Strength—1 Corinthians 1.8; Ephesians 3.20; 2 Thessalonians 3.3; 1 Peter 5.10
Blessing—John 1.16; John 10.10; Romans 8.28; Ephesians 1.3
His Presence—Matthew 18.20; Matthew 28.20; John 6.37; Romans 8.38-39
Answered Prayer—Matthew 7.7-11; Matthew 21.22; 1 Peter 3.12; 1 John 5.14-15
Christ's Return—John 14.2-3; Acts 1.11; 1 Thessalonians 4.16-17; Revelation 1.7

GOD'S PROMISE WHEN YOU:

Feel Guilty—Romans 8.1-2; 1 Corinthians 6.11; Ephesians 3.12; Hebrews 10.22-23
Feel Dejected—Matthew 11.28-30; Romans 8.26-27; Hebrews 4.16; James 4.8,10
Are Disappointed—Matthew 19.25-26; Mark 9.21-24; John 15.7; Ephesians 3.20
Are Persecuted—Matthew 5.10-12; 2 Corinthians 4.8-12; 2 Timothy 1.11-12; 1 Peter 3.13-14
Are Anxious—Matthew 6.25; Matthew 11.28-29; Philippians 4.6-7; 1 Peter 5.7
Are Sick—Matthew 8.16-17; John 16.33; Romans 8.37-39; James 5.14-15
Are Impatient—Romans 2.7; 1 Timothy 1.16; Hebrews 6.12; 1 Peter 3.9
Are Confused—John 8.12; John 14.27; 1 Corinthians 2.15-16; James 1.5
Are Tempted—1 Corinthians 10.13; Hebrews 2.18; Hebrews 4.15-16; 1 Peter 5.8-10
Are Weak—Romans 8.26; 1 Corinthians 1.7-9; 2 Corinthians 4.7-9; 2 Corinthians 12.9-10
Are Afraid—Romans 8.37-39; 2 Corinthians 1.10; 2 Timothy 1.7; Hebrews 13.6
Obey—Matthew 16.27; John 8.31-32; John 14.21, 23; James 1.25
Are In Need—John 6.35; 2 Corinthians 9.10-11; Ephesians 3.20-21; Philippians 4.19
Grieve—Matthew 5.4; John 16.20-22; 1 Thessalonians 4.13-14; Revelation 21.3-4
Suffer—John 16.33; Romans 8.16-17; 1 Peter 2.20-21; 1 Peter 4.12-13
Fail—Romans 3.23-24; Romans 5.8; Hebrews 10.36; 1 John 1.8-9
Doubt—John 3.18; John 11.25-26; Romans 4.5; 1 John 4.15-16

PERSPECTIVES FROM THE BIBLE

WHAT THE BIBLE SAYS ABOUT:

Adultery—Matthew 5.27-32; Galatians 5.13-26; Ephesians 4.17–5.3
Ambition—Matthew 16.21-27; Mark 9.33-37; Mark 10.35-45; Philippians 2.1-4
Anger—Matthew 5.21-26; Ephesians 4.25–5.2; James 1.19-27
Anxiety—Luke 12.22-34; Philippians 4.4-9; Hebrews 13.5-6
Atonement—Romans 3.21-26; 2 Corinthians 5.14-21; Hebrews 9; 1 Peter 2.22-25
Baptism—Matthew 3.1-12; Matthew 28.16-20; Romans 6.1-5
Bible Reading—2 Timothy 3.14-17; Hebrews 4.12; James 1.19-27
Blood of Christ—Matthew 26.27-29; Hebrews 9.11-28
Body of Christ—Mark 14.22-24; 1 Corinthians 12.12-31; Hebrews 2.14-18
Celibacy—Matthew 19.4-12; 1 Corinthians 7.32-40; 1 Timothy 4.1-5
Children—Matthew 18.1-9; Mark 10.13-16; Ephesians 6.1-4
Compassion—John 11.17-44; 2 Corinthians 1.3-7; 1 John 3.11-24
Conversion—John 3.1-21; 2 Corinthians 5.17-19; Ephesians 2.1-10
Creation—Romans 1.18-23; Romans 8.18-27; Colossians 1.15-17
Cross—Mark 8.31–9.1; Luke 23.26-49
Death—John 12.23-26; Romans 6.1-23; 1 Corinthians 15
Discipleship—Luke 14.25-34; John 15.1-17; John 21.15-19
Discipline—1 Corinthians 11.27-32; Hebrews 12.1-13; Revelation 3.19
Divorce—Matthew 19.1-12; Mark 10.2-12; 1 Corinthians 7.10-16
Eternal Life—Matthew 19.16-30; John 3.1-21; Romans 6.15-23
Faith—Matthew 6.25-34; Romans 3.21–5.11; Hebrews 11
Freedom—John 8.31-41; Romans 8.1-17; Galatians 4.21–5.26
Friendship—John 14.23–15.17; Colossians 3.12-17; 1 John 1.1-7
Giving—Matthew 6.1-4; 2 Corinthians 8–9
Grace—Luke 15.11-31; Romans 5; Ephesians 2
Greed—Luke 12.13-21; 1 Timothy 6.3-10; James 5.1-6
Happiness—Matthew 5.1-12; John 13.1-17; Philippians 4.4-9
Heaven—Matthew 6.19-24; Matthew 25.31-46; Philippians 3.12–4.1
Holy Spirit—John 14.15-31; John 16.5-16; Acts 2; Romans 8.1-17
Hope—Romans 5.1-11; Colossians 1.3-27; 1 Peter 1.3-9
Hospitality—Luke 14.12-14; Romans 12.13; 1 Peter 4.9
Hypocrisy—Matthew 6.1-24; Matthew 23; James 1.22-27
Joy—Luke 15; James 1.2-18; 1 Peter 4.12-19
Justification—Romans 3.21-31; Romans 4.1–5.11; Galatians 2.15-21
Loneliness—Matthew 26.36-46; 2 Timothy 4.16-18
Lord's Supper—Luke 22.7-23; John 13; 1 Corinthians 11.17-34
Love—Mark 12.28-34; 1 Corinthians 13; 1 John 4.7-21
Marriage—Matthew 19.1-12; 1 Corinthians 7; Ephesians 5.22-33
Peace—John 14.25-27; Romans 5.1-11; Ephesians 2.14-18; Philippians 4.4-9
Poor—Matthew 25.31-46; Luke 1.39-56; James 2.1-13
Profanity—Ephesians 4.29-32; James 3.1-12
Reconciliation—Matthew 5.23-26; 2 Corinthians 5.11–6.2; Ephesians 2.11-22
Repentance—Matthew 4.12-17; Luke 18.9-14; Acts 2.38-41
Resurrection—Matthew 27.57–28.20; 1 Corinthians 15
Revenge—Matthew 5.38-47; Romans 12.17-21
Reward—Matthew 5.3-12; Mark 10.29-31; 1 Corinthians 3.10-15
Salvation—Luke 19.1-10; Acts 16.16-34; Ephesians 2.1-10
Sanctification—2 Corinthians 7.1; 1 Thessalonians 5.23; 2 Peter 1.3-11

Second Coming—Matthew 24; John 14.1-4; 1 Corinthians 15.12-28; 1 Thessalonians 4.13–5.11
Stewardship—Matthew 25.14-30; Luke 12.35-48
Suffering—Romans 8.12-17; 1 Peter 3.8-22; 1 Peter 4.12-19
Unity—John 17; Ephesians 4.1-16

WHAT TO READ WHEN:

The Future Seems Hopeless—1 Corinthians 15.20-28; 1 Peter 1.1-9; 1 Peter 5.10-11; Revelation 11.15-19
Seeking God's Direction—Romans 12.1-3; Ephesians 5.15-17; Colossians 1.9-14; James 1.5-8
You Need Comfort—2 Corinthians 1.3-7; 2 Corinthians 7.6-13
Others Disagree With You—Matthew 7.1-5; Romans 12.9-21; Romans 14.1–15.7; 2 Corinthians 5.11-21
The World Seems Enticing—2 Corinthians 6.14–7.1; James 1.26-27; James 4.4-10; 1 John 2.15-17
You Need Assurance of Salvation—John 3.14-21; John 11.25-26; Acts 16.31-34; 1 John 5.9-13
Others Have Sinned Against You—Matthew 6.14-15; Matthew 18.21-35; Colossians 3.12-14; James 2.12-13
You Are Tempted to be Bitter—1 Corinthians 13; Ephesians 4.29–5.2; Hebrews 12.14-15
You Are Tempted to Neglect Public Worship—Acts 2.42-47; Hebrews 10.19-25
Your Faith Needs Strengthening—Romans 5.1-11; 1 Corinthians 9.24-27; Hebrews 10.19-25,35-39; Hebrews 11.1–12.13
You Need to Control Your Tongue—Matthew 15.1-20; James 3.1-12
You Are Prone to Judge Others—Matthew 7.1-5; 1 Corinthians 4.1-5; James 2.1-13; James 4.11-12
You Have Been Cheated—Matthew 18.15-17; 1 Corinthians 6.1-8; James 5.1-8
Things Are Going Well—Luke 12.13-21; 1 Timothy 6.3-19; Hebrews 13.5; James 2.1-17
You Wonder About Your Spiritual Gifts—Romans 12.3-8; 1 Corinthians 1.4-9; 1 Corinthians 12.1–14.25; 1 Peter 4.7-11
You Are Starting a New Job—Matthew 5.13-16; Romans 12.1-2; Galatians 5.13-26; Ephesians 1.3-14
You Are in a Position of Responsibility—Mark 10.35-45; Luke 7.1-10; 1 Corinthians 16.13-14; Galatians 6.9-10
You Are Establishing a New Home—Ephesians 5.22–6.4; Colossians 3.18-21; 1 Peter 3.1-7
You Have Been Quarreling—1 Corinthians 3; Ephesians 4.1-6, 4.15–5.2; 2 Timothy 2.14-26; James 4.1-12
You Are Challenged by Dark Forces—Romans 8.38-39; 2 Corinthians 4.7-18; Ephesians 6.10-18; 2 Timothy 4.6-7
You Are Jealous—Galatians 5.13-15,19-21; James 3.13-18
You Struggle With Laziness—Ephesians 5.15-16; Philippians 2.12-13; 1 Thessalonians 4.1-12; 2 Thessalonians 3.6-15
You Struggle With Lust—Matthew 5.27-30; Romans 7.7-25; Romans 13.8-14; James 1.13-18
You Are Angry—Matthew 5.21-22; Matthew 18.21-35; Ephesians 4.25–5.2; James 1.19-21
You Desire Revenge—Matthew 5.38-42; Romans 12.17-21; 1 Thessalonians 5.12-15; 1 Peter 3.8-14
You Are Proud—Matthew 25.34-40; Mark 10.35-45; Romans 12.3; Philippians 2.1-11
You Struggle With Addiction—Romans 6.1-23; Romans 12.1-2; 1 Corinthians 6.12-20; Philippians 3.17–4.1
You Are Greedy—Luke 12.13-21; 2 Corinthians 9.6-15; Ephesians 5.3-7; 1 John 3.16-18
You Desire to Learn How to Pray—Matthew 6.5-15; Mark 11.22-25; Luke 18.9-14; Philippians 4.4-7
You Struggle With Apathy—Matthew 25.1-13; Luke 12.35-48; 1 Thessalonians 5.1-11; Revelation 3.1-6,14-22

CONCORDANCE

TO THE OLD AND NEW TESTAMENTS

Concordance to the NRSV

This concordance to the New Revised Standard Version of the Bible began with the one found in the RSV Harper Study Bible. Each verse used in that earlier concordance was examined for changes that scholars made in the NRSV text, and these changes have been incorporated in this concordance.

The RSV Harper Study Bible concordance was the product of extensive research. Incorporated into it were (a) Bible verses relating to approximately three hundred carefully selected doctrinal and practical topics (such as *grace, justify, redemption, faith, hope, love,* etc.), and (b) the favorite Bible verses and golden texts from several Sunday School curriculum courses. In other words, almost any verse that the average user might want to look up should be found within this concordance.

Note the following features of this concordance:

1. For each verse quoted, an italicized single letter is used to designate the word entry.

2. The texts chosen for each word entry have been placed in Bible book order.

3. Occasionally the verses under a word entry contain different forms of that entry (for example, under the word ABIDE, they contain "abide," "abides," or "abode"); the alternative forms have been placed in parentheses after the key word entry. The context given in each verse will clue the reader which form of the word entry fits the italicized letter.

4. Many Bible names have been placed in a paragraph style, giving the most important references to events in that person's life.

5. Sometimes a verse is taken from a footnote reading rather than the main text of the NRSV. When this is the case, the verse reference has an "n" after it.

A concordance of this type is naturally limited and cannot be expected to meet the needs of every user. Nevertheless, in the extent of coverage, relevance of inclusion, and objectivity of selection, it should prove to be a valuable tool for Bible reading, study, and comprehension.

AARON

Brother of Moses, Ex 4.14; 7.1; commended for his eloquence, Ex 4.14; chosen to assist Moses, Ex 4.16,27-28; co-leader with Moses, Ex 5.1; 8.25; supported Moses' arms, Ex 17.12; set apart as priest, Ex 28; Heb 5.4; made a golden calf, Ex 32; Acts 7.40-41; found fault with Moses, Num 12; his rod budded, Num 17; Heb 9.4; with Moses disobedient at Meribah, Num 20.10-53; died on Mount Hor, Num 20.26-29.

ABANDON (ABANDONED)

Deut 4.31 a merciful God, he will neither *a* you
29.25 they *a* the covenant of the LORD, the
32.15 He *a* God who made him, and scoffed
2 Kings 22.17 Because they have *a* me and have made
2 Chr 12. 1 he *a* the law of the LORD, he and all
13.10 the LORD is our God, and we have not *a*
Ps 37.33 The LORD will not *a* them to their
Isa 54. 7 For a brief moment I *a* you, but with
Jer 22. 9 "Because they *a* the covenant of the
Acts 2.27 you will not *a* my soul to Hades, or let
Rev 2. 4 you, that you have *a* the love you had

ABASE

Job 40.11 look on all who are proud, and *a* them.
Ezek 21.26 that which is low, *a* that which is high.

ABEL

Gen 4. 2 Now *A* was a keeper of sheep, and Cain
4. 8 Cain said to his brother *A*, "Let us go
4.25 for me another child instead of *A*,
Mt 23.35 from the blood of righteous *A* to the
Heb 11. 4 By faith *A* offered to God a more
12.24 a better word than the blood of *A*.

ABHOR

Job 19.19 All my intimate friends *a* me, and those
30.10 They *a* me, they keep aloof from me;

ABHORRENT

Deut 12.31 every *a* thing that the LORD hates
17. 1 for that is *a* to the LORD your God.
1 Sam 27.12 "He has made himself utterly *a* to his

ABIATHAR

1 Sam 22.20 Ahitub, *A*, escaped and fled after David.
23. 6 When *A* . . . fled to David at Keilah, he

1 Sam 30. 7 David said to the priest *A* son of
2 Sam 15.29 So Zadok and *A* carried the ark of God
20.25 was secretary; Zadok and *A* were priests;
Mk 2.26 when *A* was high priest, and ate the

ABIDE (ABIDES ABODE)

Gen 6. 3 My spirit shall not *a* in mortals forever,
Ps 15. 1 O LORD, who may *a* in your tent? Who
68.16 at the mount that God desired for his *a*,
91. 1 who *a* in the shadow of the Almighty,
Prov 3.33 but he blesses the *a* of the righteous.
Hag 2. 5 My spirit *a* among you; do not fear. For
Jn 15. 4 *A* in me, as I *a* in you. Just as the
1 Cor 13.13 So faith, hope, and love *a*, these three;
1 Jn 2.24 *a* in you, then you will *a* in the Son
3. 6 No one who *a* in him sins; no one who
2 Jn 2 because of the truth that *a* in us and

ABILITY

Ex 31. 3 I have filled him . . . with *a*,
Mt 25.15 another one, to each according to his *a*.

ABIMELECH

Gen 20. 2 King *A* of Gerar sent and took Sarah.

ABISHAI

Sought to kill Saul, 1 Sam 26.5-9; pursued Abner, 2 Sam 2.18,24; desired to kill Shimei, 2 Sam 16.9-11; 19.21; one of David's key warriors, 2 Sam 23.18-19; slew the Edomites, 1 Chr 18.12.

ABLE

Num 13.30 it, for we are well *a* to overcome it."
14.16 is because the LORD was not *a* to bring
Josh 23. 9 no one has been *a* to withstand you to
1 Sam 6.20 "Who is *a* to stand before the LORD, this
2 Chr 25. 9 "The LORD is *a* to give you much more
Dan 3.17 is *a* to deliver us from the furnace of
6.20 been *a* to deliver you from the lions?
Mt 3. 9 God is *a* from these stones to raise up
9.28 "Do you believe that I am *a* to do this?"
20.22 Are you *a* to drink the cup that I am
Lk 12.26 you are not *a* to do so small a thing
2 Cor 9. 8 And God is *a* to provide you with every
Eph 3.20 within us is *a* to accomplish abundantly
Heb 2.18 suffered, he is *a* to help those who are

ABNER

Captain of Saul's host, 1 Sam 14.50; made Ish-bosheth king, 2 Sam 2.8-11; fought David's forces, 2 Sam 2.12-32; made a league with David, 2 Sam 3.6-21; slain by Joab, 2 Sam 3.22-30; mourned by David, 2 Sam 3.31-39.

ABOLISH (ABOLISHED)

Hos 2.18 I will *a* the bow, the sword, and war
2 Tim 1.10 Jesus, who *a* death and brought life and

ABOMINABLE

Ps 14. 1 They are corrupt, they do *a* deeds; there

ABOMINATION (ABOMINATIONS)

Lev 18.30 my charge not to commit any of these *a*
Prov 6.16 seven that are an *a* to him: haughty
11. 1 A false balance is an *a* to the LORD, but
17.15 are both alike an *a* to the LORD.
20.23 Differing weights are an *a* to the LORD,
28. 9 to the law, even one's prayer are an *a*.
Isa 1.13 offerings is futile; incense is an *a* to me.
Ezek 8. 9 "Go in, and see the vile *a* that they are
11.18 it all its detestable things and all its *a*.
16. 2 make known to Jerusalem her *a*,
Dan 9.27 in their place shall be an *a* that
11.31 and set up the *a* that makes desolate.
Mal 2.11 *a* has been committed in Israel and in
Rev 17. 4 a golden cup full of *a* and and the

ABOUND (ABOUNDED ABOUNDS)

Ps 72. 7 may righteousness flourish and peace *a*,
Prov 28.20 The faithful will *a* with blessings, but
Rom 3. 7 God's truthfulness *a* to his glory,
5.20 where sin increased, grace *a* all the

ABRAHAM

Born, Gen 11.26; married Sarai, Gen 11.29; migrated from Ur to Haran, Gen 11.31; called by God, Gen 12.1-5; Heb 11.8; went to Egypt, Gen 12.10-20; separated from Lot, Gen 13.7-11; rescued Lot, Gen 14.13-16; God's covenant with him, Gen 15.18; 17.1-21; Ishmael is born to him, Gen 16.15-16; entertained angels, Gen 18.1-21; interceded for Sodom, Gen 18.22-33; banished Hagar and Ishmael, Gen 21.9-21; offered up Isaac, Gen 22.1-14; buried Sarah, Gen 23; married Keturah, Gen 25.1; death and burial, Gen 25.8-10.

Gen 17. 5 your name shall be *A*; for I have made
20. 1 *A* journeyed toward . . . the Negeb,
22. 1 God tested *A*. He said to him, "*A*!" And
Mt 3. 9 'We have *A* as our ancestor'; for I tell
Lk 16.22 carried away by the angels to be with *A*.
Jn 8.58 truly, I tell you, before *A* was, I am."
Heb 11. 8 By faith *A* obeyed when he was called

ABSALOM

Third son of David, 2 Sam 3.3; avenged Tamar and fled, 2 Sam 13.20-39; returned to Jerusalem, 2 Sam 14.23-33; conspired against David, 2 Sam 15.1-12; slain by Joab, 2 Sam 18.9-17; mourned by David, 2 Sam 18.33.

ABSENT

1 Cor 5. 3 though *a* in body, I am present in spirit;
Col 2. 5 though I am *a* in body, yet I am with

ABSTAIN

Acts 15.20 write to them to *a* only from things
1 Thess 5.22 what is good; *a* from every form of evil.

ABUNDANCE

Ps 37.16 one has than the *a* of many wicked.
105. 40 and gave them food from heaven in *a*.
Mt 12.34 For out of the *a* of the heart the mouth
Mk 12.15 life does not consist in the *a* of
Lk 21. 4 have contributed out of their *a*, but she
2 Cor 9. 8 to provide you with every blessing in *a*,

ABUNDANT (ABUNDANTLY)

Gen 30.30 before I came, and it has increased *a*;
Jn 10.10 that they may have life, and have it *a*.
2 Cor 8. 2 their *a* joy and their extreme poverty

ABUSE

Ex 22.22 You shall not *a* any widow or orphan.

ACCEPT (ACCEPTED)

Gen 4. 7 If you do well, will you not be *a*? But if
Deut 33.11 substance, and *a* the work of his hands;
2 Kings 5.26 Is this a time to *a* money and to *a*
Job 42. 8 I will *a* his prayer not to deal with you
Prov 2. 1 child, if you *a* my words and treasure
Jer 14.12 and grain offering, I do not *a* them;
Ezek 43.27 offerings of well-being; and I will *a* you,
Hos 14. 2 away all guilt; *a* that which is good,
Am 5.22 and grain offerings, I will not *a* them;
Mt 19.12 of heaven. Let anyone *a* this who can.
Lk 4.24 no prophet is *a* in the prophet's
Jn 5.43 my Father's name and you do not *a* me;
Acts 22.18 they will not *a* your testimony about
1 Pet 2.13 For the Lord's sake *a* the authority of
3. 1 *a* the authority of your husbands, so

ACCEPTABLE

Lev 22.20 a blemish, for it will not be *a* for you.
2 Cor 6. 2 "At an *a* time I have listened to you,

ACCESS

Rom 5. 2 through whom we have obtained *a* to
Eph 2.18 him both of us have *a* in one Spirit
3.12 in whom we have *a* to God in boldness

ACCORD
Zeph 3. 9 of the LORD and serve him with one *a*.
Acts 8. 6 with one *a* listened eagerly to what was

ACCOUNT (ACCOUNTS ACCOUNTING)
Mt 1. 1 An *a* of the genealogy of Jesus the
12.36 you will have to give an *a* for every
18.23 who wished to settle *a* with his slaves.
Lk 16. 2 Give me an *a* of your management,
Philem 18 owes you anything, charge that to my *a*.

ACCOUNTABLE
Rom 14.12 So then, each of us will be *a* to God.

ACCURSED
Isa 65.20 short of a hundred will be considered *a*.
Jer 48.10 *A* is the one who is slack in doing the
Rom 9. 3 For I could wish that I myself were *a*
1 Cor 16.22 Let anyone be *a* who has no love for
Gal 1. 8 to what you received, let that one be *a*!

ACCUSATION (ACCUSATIONS)
Mt 27.13 how many *a* they make against you?"
Lk 23. 4 crowds, "I find no basis for an *a* against
Jn 18.29 them and said, "What *a* do you bring

ACCUSE (ACCUSED)
Jer 2. 9 *a* you, and I *a* your children's children.
Hos 4. 4 Yet let no one contend, and let none *a*,
Zech 3. 1 standing at his right hand to *a* him.
Mt 12.10 the sabbath?" so that they might *a* him.
27.12 when he was *a* by the chief priests and
Mk 15. 3 the chief priests *a* him of many things.
Acts 23.28 charge for which they had *a* him, I had

ACCUSER
Mt 5.25 Come to terms quickly with your *a*
Lk 12.58 when you go with your *a* before the

ACHAIA
Acts 18.12 Gallio was proconsul of *A*, the Jews
19.21 Spirit to go through Macedonia and *A*,
Rom 15.26 Macedonia and *A* have been pleased to
2 Cor 9. 2 saying that *A* has been ready since last
1 Thess 1. 7 all the believers in Macedonia and in *A*.

ACKNOWLEDGE (ACKNOWLEDGED ACKNOWLEDGES)
Deut 4.35 that you would *a* that the LORD is God;
4.39 So *a* today and take to heart that the
Job 40.14 Then I will also *a* to you that your own
Ps 32. 5 Then I *a* my sin to you , and I did not
Prov 3. 6 In all your ways *a* him, and he will
Jer 3.13 Only *a* your guilt, that you have
14.20 We *a* our wickedness, O LORD, the
Dan 11.39 who *a* him he shall make more wealthy,
Hos 5.15 until they *a* their guilt and seek my
Mt 10.32 who *a* me before others, I will also *a*
Lk 12. 8 who *a* me before others, the Son of

ACQUIRED
Ex 15.16 until the people whom you *a* passed by.
Ruth 4. 9 I have *a* from the hand of Naomi all
4.10 I have *a* Ruth the Moabite . . . to be my
Eccl 1.16 "I have *a* great wisdom, surpassing all

ACQUIT (ACQUITTED)
Deut 5.11 not *a* anyone who misuses his name.
Isa 5.23 who *a* the guilty for a bribe, and deprive
1 Cor 4. 4 against myself, but I am not thereby *a*.

ACQUITTAL
Ps 69.27 guilt; may they have no *a* from you.

ACT (ACTED ACTING ACTS)
Ps 119.126 It is time for the LORD to *a*, for your law
Jer 22. 3 Thus says the LORD: *A* with justice and
Ezek 20.14 But I *a* for the sake of my name, so
Mic 3. 4 time, because they have *a* wickedly.
Lk 6.47 to me, hears my words and *a* on them.
2 Cor 10. 2 to oppose those who think we are *a*
Jas 2.12 so *a* as those who are to be judged by

ACTION (ACTIONS)
1 Sam 2. 3 knowledge, and by him *a* are weighed.
Dan 11.32 their God shall stand firm and take *a*.
1 Jn 3.18 in word or speech, but in truth and *a*.

ACTIVATES
1 Cor 12. 6 is the the same God who *a* all of them

ACTS (n)
Ps 103. 7 to Moses, his *a* to the people of Israel.
Prov 20.11 make themselves known by their *a*,

ADAM
Gen 3.21 God made garments of skins for *A* and
5. 1 This is a list of the descendants of *A*.
5. 3 When *A* had lived one hundred thirty
Lk 3.38 Enos, son of Seth, son of *A*, son of God.
Rom 5.14 death exercised dominion from *A* to
1 Cor 15.22 as all die in *A*, so all will be made alive
15.45 "The first man, *A*, became a living
1 Tim 2.13 For *A* was formed first, then Eve; and *A*

ADD (ADDED ADDS)
Gen 30.24 "May the LORD *a* to me another son!"
Deut 4. 2 You must neither *a* anything to what I
12.32 I command you; do not *a* to it
Prov 30. 6 Do not *a* to his words, or else he will
Heb 2. 4 God *a* his testimony by signs and
Rev 22.18 this book: if any one *a* to them, God

ADMIRED
Esth 2.15 Now Esther was *a* by all who saw her.

ADMITTED
Deut 23. 1 is cut off shall be *a* to the assembly

ADMONISH
1 Cor 4.14 ashamed, but to *a* you as my beloved
1 Thess 5.14 we urge you, beloved to *a* the idlers,

ADMONITION
Prov 15.31 The ear that heeds wholesome *a* will

ADOPTION
Rom 8.23 groan inwardly while we wait for *a* , the
8.15 fear, but you have received a spirit of *a*.
9. 4 Israelites, and to them belong the *a*, the
Gal 4. 5 so that we might receive *a* as children.

ADORNED
Prov 14.18 The simple are *a* with folly, but the
Rev 21. 2 prepared as a bride *a* for her husband.

ADULTERERS
Hos 7. 4 They are all *a*; they are like a heated
Mal 3. 5 against the sorcerers, against the *a*,
Jas 4. 4 *A*! Do you not know that friendship

ADULTERESS
Hos 3. 1 a woman who has a lover and is an *a*,
Rom 7. 3 an *a* if she lives with another man

ADULTERY (ADULTERIES)
Ex 20.14 You shall not commit *a*.
Lev 20.10 If a man commits *a* with a wife of his
Deut 5.18 Neither shall you commit *a*.
Prov 6.32 But he who commits *a* has no sense; he
Jer 3. 8 for all the *a* of that faithless one, Israel,
5. 7 I fed them to the full, they committed *a*
13.27 your abominations, your *a* and your
Mt 5.27 it was said, 'You shall not commit *a*.'
5.28 committed *a* with her in his heart.
19. 9 and marries another, commits *a*.
Mk 7.21 come fornication, theft, murder, *a*,
10.11 marries another, commits *a* against her;
Lk 16.18 his wife and marries another commits *a*,

Jn 8. 3 a woman who had been caught in *a*;
2 Pet 2.14 They have eyes full of *a*, insatiable for

ADVANCE (ADVANCED)

Esth 2. 9 and *a* her and her maids to the best
Acts 12.24 But the word of God continued to *a* and

ADVANTAGE

Job 35. 3 If you ask, "What *a* have I? How am I
Eccl 3.19 humans have no *a* over the animals; for
5. 9 this is an *a* for a land: a king for a
7.11 an *a* to those who see the sun.
Rom 3. 1 Then what *a* has the Jew? Or what is
1 Cor 10.33 everything I do, not seeking my own *a*,

ADVERSARY (ADVERSARIES)

Ezra 4. 1 When the *a* of Judah and Benjamin
Ps 27.12 Do not give me up to the will of my *a*;
Am 3. 1 An *a* shall surround the land, and strip

ADVERSITY

Ps 10. 6 all generations we shall not meet *a*."
Prov 24.10 If you faint in the day of *a*, your
Isa 48.10 I have tested you in the furnace of *a*.

ADVICE

Num 31.16 These women here, on Balaam's *a*,
1 Kings 12. 8 But he disregarded the *a* that the older
2 Chr 10. 8 he rejected the *a* that the older men
Ps 1. 1 who do not follow the *a* of the wicked,
Prov 8.14 I have good *a* and sound wisdom; I have
12. 5 just; the *a* of the wicked is treacherous.
19.20 Listen to *a* and accept instruction, that
Eccl 4.13 foolish king, who will no longer take *a*.
2 Cor 8.10 in this matter I am giving my *a*: it is

ADVOCATE

Jn 14.16 and he will give you another *A*, to be
15.26 "When the *A* comes, whom I will send
16. 7 go away, the *A* will not come to you;
1 Jn 2. 1 we have an *a* with the Father, Jesus

AFFLICT (AFFLICTED)

Deut 28.27 LORD will *a* you with the boils of Egypt,
Job 34.28 to him, and he heard the cry of the *a*—
36. 6 wicked alive, but gives the *a* their right.
Ps 9.12 he does not forget the cry of the *a*.
34. 2 in the LORD; let the *a* hear and be glad.
94. 5 people, O LORD, and *a* your heritage.
Isa 53. 7 *a*, yet he did not open his mouth; like a
58.10 hungry and satisfy the needs of the *a*,
Mic 4. 6 driven away, and those whom I have *a*.
Nah 1.12 I have *a* you, I will *a* you no more.
2 Cor 1. 6 If we are being *a*, it is for your
4. 8 We are *a* in every way, but not crushed;

AFFLICTION (AFFLICTIONS)

Gen 16.11 for the LORD has given heed to your *a*.
29.32 the LORD has looked upon my *a*;
31.42 God saw my *a* and the labor of my
Deut 16. 3 the bread of *a* —because you came out
28.59 your offspring with severe and lasting *a*
Job 30.16 within me; days of *a* have taken hold
Ps 22.24 For he did not despise or abhor the *a* of
34.19 Many are the *a* of the righteous; but the
Isa 30.20 bread of adversity and the water of *a*,
Lam 3. 1 I am one who has seen *a* under the rod
2 Cor 1. 4 who consoles us in all our *a*, so that we
6. 4 way: through great endurance, in *a*,
7. 4 consolation; I am overjoyed in all our *a*.
Col 1.24 completing what is lacking in Christ's *a*
Rev 2. 9 "I know your *a* and your poverty, even

AFFORD

Lev 27. 8 to what each one making a vow can *a*.

AFRAID

Gen 3.10 I was *a*, because I was naked; and I hid
32. 7 Then Jacob was greatly *a* and
43.18 Now the men were *a* because they were
Ex 2.14 Then Moses was *a* and thought, "Surely
3. 6 his face, for he was *a* to look at God.
14.13 "Do not be *a*, stand firm, and see the
Num 12. 8 Why then were you not *a* to speak
Deut 13.11 Then all Israel shall hear and be *a*, and
17.13 All the people shall hear and be *a*, and
1 Sam 18.12 Saul was *a* of David, because the LORD
2 Sam 1.14 "Were you not *a* to lift your hand to
2 Kings 25.24 Do not be *a* because of the Chaldean
1 Chr 13.12 David was *a* of God that day; he said,
2 Chr 20. 3 Jehoshaphat was *a*; he set himself to
Ezra 4. 4 of Judah, and made them *a* to build,
Ps 3. 6 I am not *a* of ten thousands of people
27. 1 of my life; of whom shall I be *a*?
56. 3 when I am *a*, I put my trust in you.
119.120 of you, and I am *a* of your judgments.
Isa 10.24 do not be *a* of the Assyrians when they
12. 2 salvation; I will trust, and will not be *a*,
41.10 do not be *a*, for I am your God; I will
Jer 36.24 was *a*, nor did they tear their garments.
Zeph 3.13 down, and no one shall make them *a*.
Zech 8.13 Do not be *a*, but let your hands be
Mt 1.20 do not be *a* to take Mary as your wife,
10.31 So do not be *a*; you are of more value
28. 5 angel said to the women, "Do not be *a*;
Mk 6.50 said, "Take heart, it is I; do not be *a*."
11.18 to kill him; for they were *a* of him,
Lk 19.21 for I was *a* of you, because you are a
Jn 9.22 this because they were *a* of the Jews;
12.15 "Do not be *a*, daughter of Zion. Look,
14.27 be troubled, and do not let them be *a*.
19. 8 when Pilate heard this, he was more *a*
Acts 9.26 disciples; and they were all *a* of him,
27.24 'Do not be *a*, Paul; you must stand
Heb 11.23 and they were not *a* of the king's edict.

AFFRONT

Prov 17. 9 who forgives an *a* fosters friendship,

AGE (AGES)

Prov 8.23 *A* ago I was set up, at the first, before
Mt 13.40 fire, so it will be at the end of the *a*.

AGED

Job 12.12 Is wisdom with the *a*, and
15.10 gray-haired and the *a* are on our side,
29. 8 withdrew, and the *a* rose up and stood;

AGITATED

Mk 14.33 John, and began to be distressed and *a*.

AGONY

Isa 13. 8 Pangs and *a* will seize them; they will

AGREE (AGREED)

Gen 23.16 Abraham *a* with Ephron; and Abraham
Dan 1.14 So he *a* to this proposal and tested
Mt 18.19 if two of you *a* on earth about anything
20.13 did you not *a* with me for the usual
Mk 14.56 him, and their testimony did not *a*.
Acts 5. 9 you have *a* together to put the Spirit of
Rom 7.16 I do not want, I *a* that the law is good.

AGREEABLE

Lev 10.19 would it have been *a* to the LORD?

AGREEMENT

Isa 28.15 death, and with Sheol we have an *a*;
2 Cor 6.15 What *a* does Christ have with Belial? Or
6.16 What *a* has the temple of God with

AGRIPPA

Acts 25.13 King *A* and Bernice arrived at Caesarea
26. 1 *A* said to Paul, "You have permission to
26.27 King *A*, do you believe the prophets? I

AH

Isa 5. 8 *A*, you who join house to house, who

APPEARING
2 Tim 4. 8 also to all who have longed for his *a*.

APPLAUD
Rom 1.32 but even *a* others who practice them.

APPLE (APPLES)
Deut 32.10 him, guarded him as the *a* of his eye.
Ps 17. 8 Guard me as the *a* of the eye; hide me
Prov 7. 2 keep my teachings as the *a* of your eye;
25.11 A word fitly spoken is like *a* of gold in a
Song 2. 3 As an *a* tree among the trees of the
Zech 2. 8 touches you touches the *a* of my eye.

APPLY
Prov 23.12 *A* your mind to instruction and your ear

APPOINT (APPOINTED)
2 Sam 7.10 I will *a* a place for my people Israel and
2 Chr 11.15 and had *a* his own priests for the high
Neh 5.14 I was *a* to be their governor in the land
Job 30.23 death, and to the house *a* for all living.
Ps 7. 6 O my God; you have *a* a judgment.
Jon 4. 6 The LORD God *a* a bush, and made it
4. 7 God *a* a worm that attacked the bush,
Mk 3.14 he *a* twelve, whom he also named
Lk 10. 1 this the Lord *a* seventy others and sent
Jn 15.16 I chose you. And I *a* you to go and bear
Acts 3.20 may send the Messiah *a* for you, that is,
2 Tim 1.11 For this gospel I was *a* a herald and an
Heb 1. 2 us by a Son, whom he *a* the heir of all

APPROACH
Jer 30.21 for who would otherwise dare to *a* me?
Ezek 42.13 where the priests who *a* the LORD shall
Heb 10.22 let us *a* with a true heart in full

APPROVAL
Rom 13. 3 what is good, and you will receive its *a*;
Heb 11. 2 by faith our ancestors received *a*.

APPROVED (APPROVING)
1 Sam 18. 5 the people, even the servants of Saul, *a*.
Eccl 9. 7 for God has long ago *a* what you do.
Acts 8. 1 Saul *a* of their killing him. That day a
22.20 I myself was standing by, *a* and keeping
2 Tim 2.15 yourself to God as one *a* by him,

AQUILA
Acts 18. 2 There he found a Jew named *A*, a
18.18 Syria, accompanied by Priscilla and *A*.
18.26 when Priscilla and *A* heard him, they
Rom 16. 3 Greet Prisca and *A*, who work with me
1 Cor 16.19 *A* and Prisca, together with the church
2 Tim 4.19 Greet Prisca and *A*, and the household

ARABIA
1 Kings 10.15 and from all the kings of *A* and the
Gal 1.17 but I went away at once into *A*; and
4.25 Hagar is Mount Sinai in *A* and

ARAM (ARAMEANS)
2 Kings 5. 1 of the army of the king of *A*,
6.23 the *A* no longer came raiding into the
Isa 7. 8 the head of *A* is Damascus, and the
Am 9. 7 from Caphtor and the *A* from Kir?

ARARAT
Gen 8. 4 ark came to rest on the mountains of *A*.

ARBITRATE
Mic 4. 3 and shall *a* between strong nations

ARCHANGEL (ARCHANGEL'S)
1 Thess 4.16 with the *a* call, and with the sound of
Jude 9 when the *a* Michael contended with the

ARGUE (ARGUED ARGUES ARGUING)
Isa 3.13 The LORD rises to *a* his case; he stands
Job 13. 3 and I desire to *a* my case with God.
40. 2 Anyone who *a* with God must respond."
Prov 25. 9 *A* your case with your neighbor directly,
Mk 9.33 "What were you *a* about on the way?"
11.31 They *a* with one another, "If we say,
Acts 9.29 He spoke and *a* with the Hellenists; but
17. 2 on three sabbath days *a* with them from
17.17 he *a* in the synagogue with the Jews
18. 4 sabbath he would *a* in the synagogue

ARGUMENT (ARGUMENTS)
2 Cor 10. 4 We destroy *a* and every proud obstacle
Col 2. 4 one may deceive you with plausable *a*.
1 Tim 2. 8 up holy hands without anger or *a*;

ARIMATHEA
Mt 27.57 came a rich man from *A*, named
Jn 19.38 things, Joseph of *A*, who was a disciple

ARISE
Num 10.35 Moses would say, "*A*, O LORD, let your
Isa 60. 1 *A*, shine; for your light has come, and

ARK
Gen 6.14 Make yourself an *a* of cypress wood;
8. 4 the *a* came to rest on the mountains of
Ex 25.10 They shall make an *a* of acacia wood;
37. 1 Bezalel made the *a* of acacia wood; it
Num 10.33 with the *a* of the covenant of the LORD
Josh 3. 3 "When you see the *a* of the covenant of
6.11 the *a* of the LORD went around the city,
Judg 20.27 (for the *a* of the covenant of God was
1 Sam 4. 3 Let us bring the *a* of the covenant of
4.11 The *a* of God was captured; and the two
5. 2 Philistines took the *a* of God and
6.13 they looked up and saw the *a*, they
6.19 when they greeted the *a* of the LORD;
14.18 to Ahijah, "Bring the *a* of God here."
2 Sam 6. 2 to bring up from there the *a* of God,
15.24 Levites, carrying the *a* of the covenant
1 Chr 13. 3 let us bring again the *a* of our God to
16. 1 They brought in the *a* of God, and set it
2 Chr 5. 4 came, and the Levites carried the *a*.
Jer 3.16 no more say, "The *a* of the covenant of
Heb 9. 4 of incense and the *a* of the covenant
Rev 11.19 *a* of his covenant was seen within his

ARM (ARMS)
2 Chr 32. 8 With him is an *a* of flesh; but with us is
Job 40. 9 Have you an *a* like God, and can you
Ps 44. 3 nor did their own *a* give them victory;
98. 1 and his holy *a* have gotten him victory.
Isa 40.10 with might, and his *a* rules for him;
Mk 9.36 them; and taking it in his *a*, he said
10.16 he took them up in his *a*, laid his
Jn 12.38 and to whom has the *a* of the Lord

ARMOR
1 Sam 17.38 Saul clothed David with his *a*; he put a
Eph 6.11 Put on the whole *a* of God, so that you

ARMY (ARMIES)
Josh 5.14 as commander of the *a* of the LORD I
2 Kings 25. 5 the *a* of the Chaldeans pursued the
1 Chr 12.22 there was a great *a*, like an *a* of God.
Ps 27. 3 Though an *a* encamp against me, my
44. 9 us, and have not gone out with our *a*.
Joel 2.25 my great *a*, which I sent against you.

AROMA
2 Cor 2.15 we are the *a* of Christ to God among

AROUSED
Jer 32.31 This city has *a* my anger and wrath,

ARRESTED
Mt 4.12 Jesus heard that John had been *a*,
Mk 1.14 after John was *a*, Jesus came to Galilee,

ARROGANCE

Jas 4.16 you boast in your *a*; all such boasting is

ARROGANT

Ps 36.11 Do not let the foot of the *a* tread on me,
119. 51 The *a* utterly deride me, but I do not
119. 78 Let the *a* be put to shame, because
Prov 16. 5 All those who are *a* are an abomination
Mal 3.15 Now we count the *a* happy; evildoers
1 Cor 4.18 am not coming to you, have become *a*,
5. 2 And you are *a*! Should you not rather

ARROGANTLY

Dan 8.11 against the prince of the host it acted *a*;

ARROW (ARROWS)

1 Sam 20.20 I will shoot three *a* to the side of it, as
2 Kings 13.17 "The LORD's *a* of victory, the *a* of victory
Job 6. 4 For the *a* of the Almighty are in me; my
Ps 7.13 weapons, making his *a* fiery shafts.
18.14 he sent out his *a*, and scattered them;
38. 2 your *a* have sunk into me, and your
45. 5 Your *a* are sharp in the heart of the
Prov 7.23 the trap until an *a* pierces its entrails.
Isa 5.28 their *a* are sharp, all their bows bent,
Ezek 5.16 deadly *a* of famine, *a* for destruction,

ARTISAN (ARTISANS)

Isa 41. 7 The *a* encourages the goldsmith, and
44.11 and the *a* too are merely human.

ASCEND (ASCENDED ASCENDING)

Judg 13.20 angel of the LORD *a* in the flame of the
Ps 24. 3 Who shall *a* the hill of the LORD? And
68.18 You *a* the high mount, leading captives
139. 8 If I *a* to heaven, you are there; if I make
Prov 30. 4 Who has *a* to heaven and come down?
Isa 14.13 "I will *a* to heaven; I will raise my
Jn 3.13 No one has *a* into heaven except the
6.62 were to see the Son of man *a* to where
20.17 because I have not yet *a* to the Father.
Rom 10. 6 in your heart, 'Who will *a* into heaven?' "
Eph 4. 9 "He *a*," what does it mean but that he

ASHAMED

Gen 2.25 wife were both naked, and were not *a*.
Ezra 9. 6 "O my God, I am too *a* and embarrassed
Ps 25. 3 be *a* who are wantonly treacherous.
34. 5 radiant; so your faces shall never be *a*.
Jer 6.15 yet they were not *a*, they did not know
8.12 they were not at all *a*, they did not
12.13 shall be *a* of their harvests because of
Mk 8.38 Those who are *a* of me and of my words
Lk 9.26 Those who are *a* of me and of my
Rom 1.16 I am not *a* of the gospel; it is the power
1 Cor 4.14 I am not writing this to make you *a*,
2 Tim 1. 8 Do not be *a*, then, of the testimony
1.12 But I am not *a*, for I know the one in

ASHER

Gen 30.13 call me happy"; so she named him *A*.
Num 1.13 from *A*, Pagiel son of Ochran;
Deut 33.24 And of *A* he said, Most blessed of sons
Judg 5.17 *A* sat still at the coast of the sea,

ASHES

Gen 18.27 to the Lord, I who am but dust and *a*.
Job 13.12 Your maxims are proverbs of *a*, your
30.19 and I have become like dust and *a*.

ASIA

Acts 2. 9 Judea and Cappadocia, Pontus and *A*,
6. 9 those from Cilicia and *A*, stood up and
16. 6 the Holy Spirit to speak the word in *A*.
19.10 all the residents of *A*, both Jews and
19.27 her majesty that brought all *A* and the
Rom 16. 5 was the first convert in *A* for Christ.
1 Cor 16.19 The churches of *A* send greetings.
1 Pet 1. 1 Galatia, Cappadocia, *A*, and Bithynia,
Rev 1. 4 to the seven churches that are in *A*:

ASK (ASKED ASKING)

Ex 11. 2 that every man is to *a* his neighbor
12.35 They had *a* the Egyptians for jewelry of
1 Sam 1.20 for she said, "I have *a* him of the LORD."
1 Kings 3. 5 God said, "*A* what I should give you."
2 Chr 1. 7 said to him, "*A* what I should give you."
Ps 2. 8 *A* of me, and I will make the nations
27. 4 One thing I *a* of the LORD, that will I
106. 15 he gave them what they *a*, but sent a
Prov 30. 7 Two things I *a* of you; do not deny
Isa 1.12 who *a* this from your hand? Trample my
7.11 to Ahaz, saying, *A* a sign of the LORD
65. 1 be sought out by those who did not *a*,
Jer 50. 5 They shall *a* the way to Zion, with faces
Zech 10. 1 *A* rain from the LORD in the season of
Mt 6. 8 knows what you need before you *a* him.
7. 7 "*A*, and it will be given you; search, and
9.38 *a* the Lord of the harvest to send out
21.22 Whatever you *a* for in prayer with faith,
27.58 to Pilate and *a* for the body of Jesus;
Mk 6.22 the girl, "*A* me for whatever you wish,
10.35 you to do for us whatever we *a* of you."
Lk 10. 2 laborers are few; therefore *a* the Lord of
11. 9 I say to you, *A*, and it will be given you;
11.13 give the Holy Spirit to those who *a*
23.52 to Pilate and *a* for the body of Jesus.
Jn 14.13 I will do whatever you *a* in my name, so
14.16 And I will *a* the Father, and he will give
15. 7 and my words abide in you, *a* for
16.24 *A* and you will receive, so that your joy
17. 9 I am *a* on their behalf; I am not *a* on
17.15 world, but I *a* that you protect them
17.20 "I *a* not only on behalf of these, but
Eph 3.20 far more than all that we *a* or
Jas 1. 5 any of you is lacking wisdom, *a* God,
4. 2 You do not have, because you do not *a*.
1 Jn 3.22 we receive from him whatever we *a*,
5.14 if we *a* anything according to his will,
5.16 not a mortal sin, you will *a*, and God

ASLEEP

1 Kings 18.27 or perhaps he is *a* and must be
Mt 8.24 swamped by the waves; but he was *a*.
Mk 4.38 he was in the stern, *a* on the cushion;
13.36 else he may find you *a* when he comes
Lk 8.23 and while they were sailing he fell *a*. A
Jn 11.11 "Our friend Lazarus has fallen *a*, but I
1 Thess 5. 6 then let us not fall *a* as others do, but

ASSEMBLE (ASSEMBLED)

Gen 49. 2 *A* and hear, O sons of Jacob, listen to
Lev 8. 3 *a* the whole congregation at the
Num 1.18 they *a* the whole congregation together.
1 Kings 8. 1 Solomon *a* the elders of Israel and all
2 Chr 5. 2 Solomon *a* the elders of Israel and all
Neh 9. 1 people of Israel were *a* with fasting and
Isa 45.20 *A* yourselves and come together, draw
Ezek 11.17 and *a* you out of the countries where
39. 1 to all the wild animals: *A* and come,
1 Cor 5. 4 When you are *a*, and my spirit is

ASSEMBLY

Lev 23.36 it is a solemn *a*; you shall not work at
1 Chr 29.20 David said to the whole *a*, "Bless the
2 Chr 23. 3 the whole *a* made a covenant with the
Ps 7. 7 Let the *a* of the peoples be gathered
149. 1 song, his praise in the *a* of the faithful.
Joel 2.15 fast; call a solemn *a*; gather the people.
Acts 19.39 it must be settled in the regular *a*.
Heb 12.23 to the *a* of the firstborn who are
Jas 2. 2 and in fine clothes comes into your *a*,

ASSURANCE

Acts 17.31 he has given *a* to all by raising him
Heb 6.11 to realize the full *a* of hope to the very

Heb 11. 1 faith is the *a* of things hoped for, the

ASSYRIA

Gen 2.14 river is Tigris, which flows east of *A*.
2 Kings 15.29 King Tiglath-pileser of *A* came and
19.20 to me about King Sennacherib of *A*.
Isa 7.18 and for the bee that is in the land of *A*.
Hos 7.11 they call upon Egypt, they go to *A*.
14. 3 *A* shall not save us; we will not ride

ASTONISHED

2 Chr 7.21 exalted, everyone passing by will be *a*,
Dan 3.24 King Nebuchadnezzar was *a* and rose
Mt 7.28 the crowds were *a* at his teaching.

ASTOUNDED

Lk 4.32 They were *a* at his teaching, because he

ASTRAY

Ps 58. 3 The wicked go *a* from the womb; they
95.10 "They are a people whose hearts go *a*,
119. 67 Before I was humbled when I went *a*;
Isa 9.16 those who lead this people led them *a*,
Hos 4.12 a spirit of whoredom has led them *a*,
Mt 24. 5 Messiah,' and they will lead many *a*.
Mk 13. 5 "Beware that no one leads you *a*. Many
Lk 21. 8 "Beware that you are not led *a*; for

ASUNDER

Ps 2. 3 "Let us burst their bonds *a*, and cast

ATHENS (ATHENIANS)

Acts 17.15 conducted Paul brought him as far as *A*;
17.22 "*A*, I see how extremely religious you
18. 1 After this Paul left *A* and went to
1 Thess 3. 1 longer, we decided to be left alone in *A*;

ATONE (ATONED)

Prov 16. 6 loyalty and faithfulness iniquity is *a* for,
Dan 9.24 to put an end to sin, and to *a* for

ATONEMENT

Ex 29.36 shall offer a bull as a sin offering for *a*.
32.30 perhaps I can make *a* for your sin."
Lev 1. 4 shall be acceptable in your behalf as *a*
8.15 he consecrated it, to make *a* for it.
9. 7 make *a* for yourself and for the people;
14.18 priest shall make *a* on his behalf before
16.34 everlasting statute for you, to make *a*
17.11 for, as life, it is the blood that makes *a*.
23.27 of this seventh month is the day of *a*.
Num 16.46 the congregation and make *a* for them.
31.50 to make *a* for ourselves before the LORD.
2 Chr 29.24 at the altar, to make *a* for all Israel.
Ezek 45.20 so you shall make *a* for the temple.

ATTACK

Isa 7. 1 of Israel went up to *a* Jerusalem,

ATTEND

Jer 9.25 when I will *a* to all those who are

ATTENTION

Acts 18.17 But Gallio paid no *a* to these things.
27.11 centurion paid more *a* to the pilot and
Heb 2. 1 pay greater *a* to what we have heard,

ATTENTIVE

Neh 1.11 Lord, let your ear be *a* to the prayer of
Prov 4.20 My child, be *a* to my words; incline
5. 1 My child, be *a* to my wisdom, incline

ATTESTED

Acts 2.22 of Nazareth, a man *a* to you by God
Rom 3.21 been disclosed, and is *a* by the law and
Heb 11. 5 it was *a* before he was taken away that

ATTORNEY

Acts 24. 1 elders and an *a*, a certain Tertullus,

AUTHORITIES

Rom 13. 1 every person be subject to governing *a*;
Titus 3. 1 them to be be subject to rulers and *a*,

AUTHORITY

Isa 9. 6 given to us; *a* rests upon his shoulders;
22.21 I will commit your *a* to his hand, and
Mt 7.29 taught them as one having *a*, and not
8. 9 I also am a man under *a*, with soldiers
9. 6 Son of man has *a* on earth to forgive
21.23 "By what *a* are you doing these things,
28.18 "All *a* in heaven and on earth has been
Mk 1.22 he taught them as one having *a*, and
2.10 Son of Man has *a* on earth to forgive
3.15 and to have *a* to cast out demons.
11.28 "By what *a* are you doing these things?
Lk 4. 6 you I will give their glory and all this *a*;
4.36 with *a* and power he commands the
5.24 that the Son of Man has *a* on earth
10.19 I have given you *a* to tread on snakes
20. 2 by what *a* are you doing these things?
Jn 5.27 has given him *a* to execute judgment,
Acts 9.14 he has *a* from the chief priests to bind
Rom 13. 1 there is no *a* except from God, and
2 Cor 10. 8 if I boast a little too much of our *a*,
Rev 2.26 the end, I will give *a* over the nations,
12.10 of our God and the *a* of his Messiah,
13. 2 it his power and his throne and great *a*.

AVARICE

Mk 7.22 adultery, *a*, wickedness, deceit,

AVENGE (AVENGED)

2 Kings 9. 7 that I may *a* on Jezebel the blood
Isa 1.24 my enemies, and *a* myself on my foes!
Joel 3.21 I will *a* their blood, and I will not clear
Rom 12.19 never *a* yourselves, but leave room for
Rev 19. 2 and he has *a* on her the blood of his

AVENGER

Num 35.12 shall be for you a refuge from the *a*,
1 Thess 4. 6 because the Lord is an *a* in all these

AVOID

Prov 4.15 not walk in the way of evildoers. *A* it;
14.27 so that one may *a* the snares of death.
2 Tim 2.16 *A* such profane chatter, for it will lead
Titus 3. 2 of no one, to *a* quarreling, to be gentle,

AWAKE (AWAKES)

Ps 57. 8 *A*, my soul! *A*, O harp and lyre! I will *a*
73.20 They are like a dream when one *a*, an
Isa 52. 1 *A*, *a*, put on your strength, O Zion! Put
Mt 24.42 Keep *a* therefore, for you do not know
25.13 Keep *a* therefore, for you know neither
26.38 remain here, and stay *a* with me."
26.42 Stay *a* and pray that you may not come
Mk 14.34 even to death; remain here, and keep *a*."
Rev 16.15 Blessed is the one who stays *a* and is

AWAKEN

Song 8. 4 do not stir up or *a* love until it is ready!
Jn 11.11 asleep, but I am going there to *a* him."

AWARE

1 Pet 2.19 if, being *a* of God, you endure pain

AWE

Ps 33. 8 of the world stand in *a* of him.
119.161 but my heart stands in *a* of your words.
Mt 9. 8 crowds saw it, they were filled with *a*,

AX (AXES)

2 Kings 6. 5 a log, his *a* head fell into the water;
1 Chr 20. 3 to work with saws and iron picks and *a*.
Ps 74. 5 they hacked the wooden trellis with *a*.
Isa 10.15 Shall the *a* vaunt itself over the one
Mt 3.10 now the *a* is lying at the root of the
Lk 3. 9 Even now the *a* is lying at the root of

AZAZEL

Lev 16. 8 lot for the LORD and the other lot for *A*.

B

BAAL (BAALS)

Judg 2.13 abandoned the LORD, and worshiped *B*
6.31 "Will you contend for *B*? Or will you
10.13 our God and have worshiped the *B*."
1 Kings 16.31 and went and served *B*, and worshiped
2 Kings 17.16 all the host of heaven, and served *B*.
Jer 2. 8 the prophets prophesied by *B*, and went
Hos 2. 8 her silver and gold that they used for *B*.

BABEL

Gen 11. 9 Therefore it was called *B*, because there

BABES (BABIES)

Ps 8. 2 Out of the mouths of *b* and infants you
Isa 3. 4 princes, and *b* shall rule over them.
Mt 21.16 of the mouth of infants and nursing *b*

BABYLON (BABYLONIA)

2 Kings 17.24 king of Assyria brought people from *B*,
1 Chr 9. 1 Judah was taken into exile in *B* because
Ezra 1.11 were brought up from *B* to Jerusalem.
Ps 137. 1 By the rivers of *B*— there we sat down
Isa 48.20 Go out from *B*, flee from Chaldea,
Mt 1.11 at the time of the deportation to *B*.
1 Pet 5.13 Your sister church in *B*, chosen together
Rev 14. 8 fallen is *B* the great! She has made all

BACK (BACKS)

Ps 18.40 You have made my enemies turn their *b*
Isa 38.17 you have cast all my sins behind your *b*.

BACKSLIDING

Jer 8. 5 away turned away in perpetual *b*?

BALAAM

Num 22. 5 He sent messengers to *B* son of Beor at
23. 1 Then *B* said to Balak, "Build me seven
24. 1 Now *B* saw that it pleased the LORD to
31. 8 they also slew *B* the son of Beor with
Mic 6. 5 what *B* the son of Beor answered him,
2 Pet 2.15 gone astray, following the road of *B*, son
Rev 2.14 who hold to the teaching of *B*, who

BALANCE (BALANCES)

Job 6. 2 and all my calamity laid in the *b*!
Prov 11. 1 A false *b* is an abomination to the LORD,
Isa 40.12 in scales and the hills in a *b*?
Ezek 5. 1 and your beard; then take *b* for
Hos 12. 7 A trader, in whose hands are false *b*, he

BALDHEAD

2 Kings 2.23 at him, saying, "Go away, *b*! Go away, *b*!"

BAND

Jer 9. 2 they are all adulterers, a *b* of traitors.

BANDIT (BANDITS)

Mk 14.48 clubs to arrest me as though I were a *b*?
15.27 with him they crucified two *b*, one of
Jn 18.40 but Barabbas!" Now Barabbas was a *b*.
2 Cor 11.26 from rivers, danger from *b*, danger from

BANDS

Lk 2. 7 wrapped him in *b* of cloth, and laid him

BANISH

Eccl 11.10 *B* anxiety from your mind, and put away

BANQUET (BANQUETING)

Song 2. 4 He brought me to the *b* house, and his
Dan 5.10 lords, came into the *b* hall. The queen
Lk 5.29 Levi gave a great *b* for him in his house;

BAPTISM (BAPTISMS)

Mt 21.25 Did the *b* of John come from heaven, or
Mk 10.38 with the *b* that I am baptized with?"
11.30 Did the *b* of John come from heaven, or
Lk 3. 3 proclaiming a *b* of repentance for the
12.50 I have a *b* with which to be baptized,
20. 4 Did the *b* of John come from heaven, or
1 Cor 15.29 do who receive *b* on behalf of the dead?
Eph 4. 5 one Lord, one faith, one *b*, one God and
Col 2.12 when you were buried with him in *b*,
Heb 6. 2 toward God, with instruction about *b*,
9.10 only with food and drink and various *b*,
1 Pet 3.21 *b*, which this prefigured, now saves

BAPTIZE (BAPTIZED BAPTIZING)

Mt 3. 6 they were *b* by him in the river Jordan,
3.11 "I *b* you with water for repentance, but
28.19 *b* them in the name of the Father
Mk 16.16 The one who believes and is *b* will be
Lk 3.16 "I *b* you with water; but one who is
7.29 justice of God, because they had been *b*
Jn 1.26 John answered them, "I *b* with water.
3.23 John also was *b* at Aenon near Salim
4. 1 "Jesus is making and *b* more disciples
Acts 1. 5 you will be *b* with the Holy Spirit not
8.12 they were *b*, both men and women.
8.38 down into the water, and Philip *b* him.
9.18 restored. Then he got up and was *b*,
16.15 When she and her household were *b*,
22.16 Get up and be *b*, and have your sins
Rom 6. 3 have been *b* into Christ Jesus were *b*
1 Cor 1.13 Or were you *b* in the name of Paul?
1.17 Christ did not send me to *b* but to
10. 2 all were *b* into Moses in the cloud and
12.13 Spirit we were all *b* into one body—
Gal 3.27 *b* into Christ have clothed yourselves

BAPTIZER

Mk 1. 4 John the *b* appeared in the wilderness,
6.14 saying, "John the *b* has been raised

BARABBAS

Mt 27.21 to release for you?" And they said, "*B*."
Mk 15. 7 a man called *B* was in prison with the
15.11 to have him release *B* for them instead.
15.15 satisfy the crowd, released *B* for them;
Jn 18.40 in reply, "Not this man, but *B*!" Now *B*

BAREFOOT

2 Sam 15.30 with his head covered and walking *b*;
Isa 20. 3 Isaiah has walked naked and *b* for three

BARNABAS

Benevolent, Acts 4.36-37; introduced Paul to the apostles, Acts 9.26-27; preached at Antioch, Acts 11.22-24; ministered with Paul at Antioch, Acts 11.25-26; took relief offerings to Judea, Acts 11.29-30; accompanied Paul on his first missionary journey, Acts 13.1—14.28; attended the Council of Jerusalem, Acts 15.1-31; separated from Paul, Acts 15.36-41.

BARNS

Prov 3.10 then your *b* will be filled with plenty,
Mt 6.26 neither sow nor reap nor gather into *b*,
Lk 12.18 I will pull down my *b*, and build larger

BARREN

Gen 11.30 Now Sarai was *b*; she had no child.
29.31 he opened her womb; but Rachel was *b*.
Judg 13. 2 Manoah; and his wife was *b*, having
Ps 113. 9 He gives the *b* woman a home, making
Isa 54. 1 Sing, O *b* one who did not bear; burst
Lk 1. 7 Elizabeth was *b*, and both were getting

BARRIERS

Isa 59. 2 your iniquities have been *b* between you

BARTHOLOMEW

Mt 10. 3 Philip and *B*; Thomas and Matthew the
Lk 6.14 and John, and Philip, and *B*, and
Acts 1.13 Philip and Thomas, *B* and Matthew,

BARUCH

Jer 32.12 I gave the deed of purchase to *B* son of
36. 4 and *B* wrote on a scroll at Jeremiah's
36.18 *B* answered them, "He dictated all these
43. 3 but *B* son of Neraiah is inciting you
45. 1 the prophet Jeremiah spoke to *B* son of

BASIN

Ex 30.18 You shall make a bronze *b* with a
38. 8 He made the bronze *b* with its stand of

BASKET (BASKETS)

Ex 2. 3 she got a papyrus *b* for him, and
Jer 24. 1 two *b* of figs placed before the temple
Am 8. 1 GOD showed me — a *b* of summer fruit.
Mt 13.48 put the good into *b* but threw out the
14.20 over of the broken pieces, twelve *b* full.
15.37 the broken pieces left over, seven *b* full.
Mk 8.19 how many *b* full of broken pieces did
Acts 9.25 in the wall, lowering him in a *b*.
2 Cor 11.33 I was let down in a *b* through a window

BATHED (BATHING)

2 Sam 11. 2 that he saw from the roof a woman *b*;
Ezek 16. 9 Then I *b* you with water and washed off

BATHSHEBA

Taken by David, 2 Sam 11.1-5; gave birth to Solomon, 2 Sam 12.24; interceded for Solomon's succession on the throne, 1 Kings 1.15-31; petitioned for Adonijah, 1 Kings 2.12-25.

BATTLE

Num 31. 7 They did *b* against Midian, as the LORD
1 Sam 4.16 "I have just come from the *b*; I fled
1 Kings 8.44 "If you people go out to *b* against their
2 Chr 20.15 for the *b* is not yours but God's.
1 Cor 14. 8 sound, who will get ready for *b*?
Rev 16.14 to assemble them for *b* on the great day

BEAR (BEARS) (n)

1 Sam 17.34 whenever a lion or a *b* came, and took a
2 Kings 2.24 Then two she-*b* came out of the woods
Dan 7. 5 a second one, that looked like a *b*.

BEAR (BEARS BORE) (v)

Gen 4.13 "My punishment is greater than I can *b*!
43. 9 you, then let me *b* the blame forever.
44.32 then I shall *b* the blame in the sight of
Ex 28.12 Aaron shall *b* their names before the
28.30 Aaron shall *b* the judgment of the
Num 18. 1 shall *b* responsibility for the offenses
Esth 8. 6 how can I *b* to see the calamity that is
Ps 55.12 enemies who taunt me—I could *b* that;
68.19 Blessed be the Lord, who daily *b* us up;
Isa 53.11 and he shall *b* their iniquities.
Jer 44.22 longer *b* the sight of your evil doings,
Gal 6. 2 *B* one another's burdens, and in this
1 Pet 2.24 He himself *b* our sins in his body on

BEAST

Rev 13.11 Then I saw another *b* that rose out of
17. 8 *b* that you saw was, and is not, and is

BEATINGS

Isa 1. 5 Why do you seek further *b*? Why do you

BEAUTIFUL

Gen 12.11 that you are a woman *b* in appearance;
2 Sam 11. 2 woman bathing; the woman was very *b*.
Esth 2. 7 the girl was fair and *b*, and when her
Ps 48. 2 His holy mountain, *b* in elevation, is
Song 1. 5 I am black and *b*, O daughters of
6. 4 You are *b* as Tirzah, my love, comely as
Isa 4. 2 day the branch of the LORD shall be *b*
Jer 13.20 flock that was given you, your *b* flock?
Ezek 16.13 You grew exceedingly *b*, fit to be a

BEAUTIFY

Jer 4.30 In vain you *b* yourself. Your lovers

BEAUTY

Ps 27. 4 to behold the *b* of the LORD, and to
45.11 house, and the king will desire your *b*.
Prov 6.25 Do not desire her *b* in your heart, and
31.30 Charm is deceitful, and *b* is vain, but a
Ezek 27. 3 Tyre, you have said, "I am perfect in *b*."
28.17 Your heart was proud because of your *b*;
1 Pet 3. 4 lasting *b* of a gentle and quiet spirit,

BED (BEDS)

Job 7.13 When I say, "My *b* will comfort me, my
Isa 28.20 the *b* is too short to stretch oneself on
Am 6. 4 Alas for those who lie upon *b* of ivory,
Mt 9. 6 "Stand up, take your *b* and go to your
Lk 5.19 him down with his *b* through the tiles

BEE (BEES)

Deut 1.44 out against you and chased you as *b* do.
Judg 14. 8 a swarm of *b* in the body of the lion,
Isa 7.18 for the *b* that is in the land of Assyria.

BEELZEBUL

Mt 12.24 "It is only by *B*, the ruler of demons,
Mk 3.22 "He has *B*, and by the ruler of the

BEER-SHEBA

Gen 21.14 wandered about in the wilderness of *B*.
21.32 When they had made a covenant at *B*,
22.19 together to *B*; and Abraham lived at *B*.
46. 1 and came to *B*, he offered sacrifices to
1 Sam 3.20 all Israel from Dan to *B* knew that
1 Chr 21. 2 number Israel, from *B* to Dan, and bring
Am 5. 5 not enter into Gilgal or cross over to *B*;

BEFITS

Ps 33. 1 O you righteous. Praise *b* the upright.

BEG

Gal 4.12 Friends, I *b* you, become as I am, for I

BEGGAR

Mk 10.46 a blind *b*, was sitting by the roadside.
Jn 9. 8 those who had seen him before as a *b*,

BEGINNING

Gen 1. 1 In the *b* when God created the heavens
Ex 12. 2 shall mark for you the *b* of months;
Ps 111. 10 The fear of the LORD is the *b* of wisdom;
Prov 1. 7 The fear of the LORD is the *b* of
4. 7 The *b* of wisdom is this: Get wisdom,
Mt 24. 8 all this is but the *b* of the birthpangs.
Mk 1. 1 The *b* of the good news of Jesus Christ,
Jn 1. 1 In the *b* was the Word, and the Word

BEGUILING

Rev 2.20 and is teaching and *b* my servants

BEHAVE (BEHAVED BEHAVING)

1 Cor 3. 3 and *b* according to human inclinations?
7.36 he is not *b* properly toward his fiancee,
2 Cor 1.12 we have *b* in the world with frankness
1 Tim 3.15 ought to *b* in the household of God,

BEHAVIOR

1 Sam 21.13 he changed his *b* before them; he

BEHEADED

Mt 14.10 he sent and had John *b* in the prison.
Mk 6.16 it, he said, "John, whom I *b*, has been

BEHEMOTH

Job 40.15 "Look at *B*, which I made just as I

BEHOLD

Ps 17.15 As for me, I shall *b* your face in
46. 8 Come, *b* the works of the LORD; see
97. 6 and all the peoples *b* his glory.

BEINGS

Job 1. 6 One day the heavenly *b* came to present
38. 7 and all the heavenly *b* shouted for joy?

BELIEVE

Gen 45.26 He was stunned; he could not *b* them.
Ex 4. 5 "so that they may *b* that the LORD, the
2 Chr 20.20 you will be established; *b* his prophets,"
Job 9.16 I do not *b* that he would listen to my
Ps 27.13 I *b* that I shall see the goodness of the
119. 66 for I *b* in your commandments.
Prov 14.15 The simple *b* everything, but the clever
26.25 an enemy speaks graciously, do not *b*
Isa 43.10 that you may know and *b* me and
Jer 12. 6 do not *b* them, though they speak
Hab 1. 5 that you would not *b* if you were told.
Mt 9.28 "Do you *b* that I am able to do this?"
21.25 to us, 'Why then did you not *b* him?'
27.42 the cross now, and we will *b* in him.
Mk 1.15 near; repent, and *b* in the good news."
5.36 of the synagogue, "Do not fear, only *b*."
11.24 ask for in prayer, *b* that you receive it,
13.21 or 'Look! There he is!'—do not *b* it.
16.11 had been seen by her, they would not *b*
Lk 1.20 because you did not *b* my words, which
8.13 no root, they *b* for a while and in a
8.50 not fear. Only *b*, and she shall be saved."
20. 5 he will say, 'Why did you not *b* him?'
22.67 He replied, "If I tell you, you will not *b*;
24.25 how slow of heart to *b* all that the
Jn 1. 7 light, so that all might *b* through him.
3.18 who *b* in him are not condemned;
4.42 we *b*, for we have heard for ourselves,
5.46 If you believed Moses, you would *b* me,
6.69 We have come to *b* and know that you
9.35 he said, "Do you *b* in the Son of man?"
10.26 but you do not *b*, because you do not
10.38 though you do not *b* me, *b* the works,
11.15 glad I was not there, so that you may *b*.
12.37 in their presence, they did not *b* in him.
14. 1 be troubled. *B* in God, *b* also in me.
17.20 on behalf of those who will *b* in me
19.35 has testified so that you also may *b*.
20.25 and my hand in his side, I will not *b*."
20.29 have not seen and yet have come to *b*."
Acts 8.37n Philip said, "If you *b* with all your heart,
15.11 we *b* that we will be saved through the
16.31 "*B* in the Lord Jesus, and you will be
26.27 King Agrippa, do you *b* the prophets? I
Rom 3.22 faith in Jesus Christ for all who *b*.
10. 9 and *b* in your heart that God raised him
1 Cor 1.21 our proclamation, to save those who *b*.
Heb 11. 6 approach him must *b* that he exists
1 Jn 5.10 Those who *b* in the Son of God have

BELIEVED (BELIEVES BELIEVING)

Gen 15. 6 And he *b* the LORD; and the LORD
Ex 4.31 The people *b*; and when they heard that
14.31 *b* in the LORD and in his servant Moses.
Ps 106. 12 Then they *b* his words; they sang his
Isa 53. 1 Who has *b* what we have heard? And to
Mk 9.23 things can be done for the one who *b*."
16.16n The one who *b* and is baptized will be
Lk 1.45 blessed is she who *b* that there would
Jn 2.22 they *b* the scripture and the word that
3.15 up, that whoever *b* in him may have
4.39 Many Samaritans from that city *b* in
4.50 The man *b* the word that Jesus spoke to
4.53 will live." So he himself *b*, along with his
5.24 anyone who hears my word and *b* him
7. 5 (For not even his brothers *b* in him.)
7.31 Yet many in the crowd *b* in him and
11.45 and had seen what Jesus did, *b* in him.
20. 8 first, also went in, and he saw and *b*;
Acts 4. 4 many of those who heard the word *b*;
9.42 throughout Joppa, and many *b* in the
10.43 everyone who *b* in him receives
13.12 saw what had happened, he *b*,
17.12 Many of them therefore *b*, including not
Rom 9.33 whoever *b* in him will not be put to
10.11 one who *b* in him will be put to shame."
1 Cor 13. 7 It bears all things, *b* all things, hopes
Gal 3. 6 Just as Abraham "*b* God, and it was
Phil 1.29 not only of *b* in Christ, but of suffering
Titus 3. 8 so that those who have *b* in God may
1 Jn 5. 1 who *b* that Jesus is the Christ has been

BELIEVER (BELIEVERS)

Acts 5.14 more than ever *b* were added to the
9.30 when the *b* learned of it, they brought
11.21 a great number became *b* and turned to
11.29 send relief to the *b* living in Judea;
14. 1 of both Jews and Greeks became *b*.
15. 3 and brought great joy to all the *b*.
16. 1 son of a Jewish woman who was a *b*;
17.34 him and became *b*, including Dionysius
18. 8 official of the synagogue, became a *b*
1 Cor 6. 6 but a *b* goes to court against a *b*
8.11 So by your knowledge those weak *b* for
1 Thess 2.13 word, which is also at work in you *b*.
2 Thess 3.15 them as enemies, but warn them as *b*.
1 Jn 2.11 Whoever hates another *b* is in the

BELLY

Gen 3.14 upon your *b* you shall go, and dust shall
Jon 2. 2 me; out of the *b* of Sheol I cried,

BELONG (BELONGED BELONGS)

Ps 82. 8 the earth; for all the nations *b* to you!
Mic 7.14 with your staff, the flock that *b* to you,
Rom 7. 4 you may *b* to another, to him who has
Col 2.20 you live as if you still *b* to the world?

BELOVED

Deut 33.12 The *b* of the LORD rests in safety—the
Neh 13.26 he was *b* by his God, and God made
Ps 127. 2 anxious toil; for he gives sleep to his *b*.
Song 1.14 My *b* is to me a cluster of henna
2.16 My *b* is mine and I am his; he pastures
5. 9 What is your *b* more than another *b*, O
6. 3 I am my beloved's and my *b* is mine; he
8. 5 the wilderness, leaning upon her *b*?
Dan 10.11 He said to me, "Daniel, greatly *b*, pay
Mt 3.17 "This is my Son, the *B*, with whom I am
17. 5 "This is my Son, the *B*; with him I am
Mk 1.11 "You are my Son, the *B*; with you I am
9. 7 "This is my Son, the *B*; listen to him."
12. 6 still one other, a *b* son. Finally he sent
Lk 3.22 "You are my Son, the *B*; with you I am
Rom 9.25 and her who was not *b* I will call '*b*.' "
11.28 as regards election they are *b*, for the
16. 8 Greet Ampliatus, my *b* in the Lord.
Eph 1. 6 that he freely bestowed on us in the *B*.
1 Tim 6. 2 by their service are believers and *b*.
2 Pet 1.17 "This is my Son, my *B*, with whom I am
Jude 20 you, *b*, build yourselves up on your

BELTS

Job 12.21 princes, and looses the *b* of the strong.
Isa 11. 5 Righteousness shall be the *b* around his
Mt 3. 4 hair with a leather *b* around his waist,
Mk 6. 8 no bread, no bag, no money in their *b*;
Acts 21.11 us and took Paul's *b*, and bound his

BEND

Phil 2.10 the name of Jesus every knee should *b*,

BENEFICIAL

1 Cor 6.12 lawful for me," but not all things are *b*.
10.23 are lawful," but not all things are *b*.

BENEFIT (BENEFITS)

Ps 103. 2 my soul, and do not forget all his *b*—
1 Cor 7.35 I say this for your own *b*, not to put any
Gal 5. 2 Christ will be of no *b* to you.

BEN-HADAD I

King of Syria, 1 Kings 15.18; made alliance with Asa, 1 Kings 15.19; ravaged cities in northern Israel, 1 Kings 15.20-21. (See also 2 Chr 16.4.)

BEN-HADAD II

King of Syria, 1 Kings 20.1; besieged Samaria, 1 Kings 20.1; defeated twice by Ahab, 1 Kings 20.2-30; granted conditions of peace, 1 Kings 20.31-34.

BEN-HADAD III

King of Syria, 2 Kings 13.3,24; oppressed cities of Israel, 2 Kings 13.3-13; defeated by Jehoahaz, king of Israel, 2 Kings 13.22-25.

BENJAMIN

Born, Gen 35.16-18; brought to Egypt, Gen 43; accused of theft but interceded for by Judah, Gen 44; blessed by Jacob, Gen 49.27.

Tribe of Benjamin: blessed by Moses, Deut 33.12; allotted its territory, Josh 18.11-28; decimated almost to extinction, Judg 20; rebuilt through new wives and families, Judg 21; Saul, the first king of Israel, and Paul, the apostle, from this tribe, 1 Sam 9.1; Phil 3.5.

BEREAVE (BEREAVED)

Gen 42.36 "I am the one you have *b* of children:
Jer 15. 7 have *b* them, I have destroyed my
Hos 9.12 I will *b* them until no one is left.

BESET

Ps 109. 3 They *b* me with words of hate, and

BESIDE

Ps 23. 2 pastures; he leads me *b* still waters;

BESIEGE (BESIEGED)

Deut 20.12 war against you, then you shall *b* it;
28.52 It shall *b* you in all your towns until
2 Chr 6.28 if their enemies *b* them in any of the
Eccl 9.14 it. A great king came against it and *b* it,
Isa 1. 8 in a cucumber field, like a *b* city.
Jer 52. 5 city was *b* untill the eleventh year of

BEST

Phil 1.10 insight to help you determine what is *b*,

BESTIR

Ps 35.23 Wake up! *B* yourself for my defense, for

BESTOWED

Acts 28.10 They *b* many honors on us, and when
1 Cor 2.12 we may understand the gifts *b* on us
Eph 1. 6 glorious grace which he freely *b* on us

BETHANY

Mt 21.17 out of the city to *B* and lodged there.
26. 6 while Jesus was at *B* in the house of
Lk 19.29 come near Bethphage and *B*, at the
24.50 led them out as far as *B*, and lifting up
Jn 11. 1 a certain man was ill, Lazarus of *B*, the
12. 1 Jesus came to *B*, the home of Lazarus,

BETHEL

Gen 12. 8 east of *B*, and pitched his tent, with *B*
28.19 He called that place *B*; but the name of
31.13 I am the God of *B*, where you anointed
Josh 8. 9 ambush, and lay between *B* and Ai, to
1 Sam 7.16 He went on a circuit year by year to *B*,
1 Kings 12.29 He set one in *B*, and the other he put
13.11 there lived an old prophet in *B*. One of
Ezra 2.28 Of *B* and Ai, two hundred twenty-three.
Am 4. 4 Come to *B*—and transgress; to
7.10 Then Amaziah, the priest of *B*, sent to
7.13 never again prophesy at *B*, for it is the

BETHLEHEM

Gen 35.19 on the way to Ephrath (that is, *B*),
Ruth 1.19 until they came to *B*. When they came
1 Sam 16. 4 the LORD commanded, and came to *B*.
17.15 from Saul to his father's sheep at *B*.
2 Sam 23.16 drew water from the well of *B* that was
Mic 5. 2 But you, O *B* of Ephrathah, who are
Mt 2. 1 after Jesus was born in *B* of Judea, wise
2. 6 'And you, *B*, in the land of Judah, are
Lk 2. 4 to the city of David called *B*, because
Jn 7.42 comes from *B*, the village where David

BETHSAIDA

Mt 11.21 Woe to you, *B*! For if the deeds of
Mk 6.45 and go on ahead to the other side, to *B*,
8.22 They came to *B*. Some people brought a
Lk 9.10 withdrew privately to a city called *B*.

BETRAY (BETRAYED BETRAYING)

Mt 17.22 "The Son of Man is going to be *b* into
26.16 to look for an opportunity to *b* him.
26.24 that one by whom the Son of man is *b*!
26.45 the Son of Man is *b* into the hands of
27. 4 "I have sinned in *b* innocent blood." But
Mk 3.19 and Judas Iscariot, who *b* him.
13.12 Brother will *b* brother to death, and a
14.11 to look for an opportunity to *b* him.
14.18 "Truly I tell you, one of you will *b* me,
14.41 the Son of Man is *b* into the hands of
Lk 21.16 You will be *b* even by parents and
22. 4 about how he might *b* him to them.
Jn 13.11 For he knew who was to *b* him; for this
18. 2 Judas, who *b* him, also knew the place,
1 Cor 11.23 on the night when he was *b* took a

BETTER

Job 35. 3 How am I *b* off than if I had sinned?
Eccl 3.12 nothing *b* for them than to be happy
Phil 2. 3 but in humility regard others *b* than
Heb 8. 6 he is the mediator of a *b* covenant,
9.23 themselves need *b* sacrifices than these.

BEWARE

Eccl 12.12 Of anything beyond these, my child, *b*.
Mt 7.15 "*B* of false prophets, who come to you
16. 6 out, and *b* of the yeast of the Pharisees
Mk 8.15 out—*b* of the yeast of the Pharisees
12.38 "*B* of the scribes, who like to walk

BIND (BINDS BOUND)

Gen 44.30 then, as his life is *b* up in the boy's life,
Job 26. 8 He *b* up the waters in his thick clouds,
Ps 147. 3 bokenhearted, and *b* up their wounds.
Prov 6.21 *B* them upon your heart always; tie
Ezek 34.16 the strayed, and I will *b* up the injured,
Mt 16.19 whatever you *b* on earth will be bound
18.18 whatever you *b* on earth will be bound
1 Cor 7.27 Are you *b* to a wife? Do not seek to be

BIRD (BIRDS BIRD'S)

Gen 1.20 let *b* fly above the earth across the
Deut 22. 6 If you come on a *b* nest, in any tree or
Ps 11. 1 to me, "Flee like a *b* to the mountains;
102. 7 I lie awake; I am like a lonely *b* on the
124. 7 have escaped like a *b* from the snare
Prov 1.17 the net baited while the *b* is looking on;
Isa 31. 5 Like *b* hovering overhead, so the LORD
Jer 12. 9 Are the *b* of prey all around her? Go,
Am 3. 5 Does a *b* fall into a snare on the earth,
Mt 8.20 have holes, and *b* of the air have nests;
13.32 *b* of the air come and make nests in its
Mk 4.32 so that the *b* of the air can make nests
Lk 9.58 and *b* of the air have nests; but the Son
13.19 the *b* of the air made nests in its

BIRTH

Deut 32.18 you forgot the God who gave you *b*.
Ezek 16. 3 Your origin and your *b* were in the land
Mt 1.18 Now the *b* of Jesus the Messiah took

Eph 1. 3 who has *b* us in Christ with every
Jas 5.11 we call *b* those who showed endurance.
1 Pet 3.14 suffer for doing what is right, you are *b*.
Rev 14.13 "Write this: *B* are the dead who from
22. 7 *B* is the one who keeps the words of
22.14 *B* are those who wash their robes, so

BLESSING (BLESSINGS)

Gen 22.18 of the earth gain *b* for themselves,
Lev 25.21 I will order my *b* upon you in the sixth
Deut 11.26 I am setting before you today a *b* and a
23. 5 God turned the curse into a *b* for you,
27.12 shall stand on Mount Gerizim for the *b*
28. 2 all these *b* shall come upon you and
Josh 8.34 all the words of the law, *b* and curses,
Ps 21. 3 For you meet him with rich *b*; you set a
Prov 10.22 The *b* of the LORD makes rich, and he
11.11 By the *b* of the upright a city is exalted,
Isa 19.24 Assyria, a *b* in the midst of the earth,
65.16 whoever invokes a *b* in the land shall
Ezek 34.26 their season; they shall be showers of *b*.
44.30 order that a *b* may rest on your house.
Mal 3.10 pour down for you an overflowing *b*.
Rom 15.29 come in the fullness of the *b* of Christ.
1 Cor 10.16 The cup of *b* which we bless, is it not a
Jas 3.10 the same mouth come *b* and cursing.

BLIND (n and adj)

Deut 28.29 at noon as *b* people grope in darkness,
2 Sam 5. 8 to attack the lame and the *b*, those
Job 29.15 I was eyes to the *b*, and feet to the
Ps 146. 8 LORD opens the eyes of the *b*. The LORD
Isa 29.18 darkness the eyes of the *b* shall see.
35. 5 Then the eyes of the *b* shall be opened,
42. 7 the nations, to open the eyes that are *b*,
42.16 I will lead the *b* by a road they do not
42.19 Who is *b* but my servant, or deaf like
43. 8 the people who are *b*, yet have eyes,
56.10 Israel's sentinels are *b*, they are all
59.10 We grope like the *b* along a wall,
Mal 1. 8 When you offer *b* animals in sacrifice, is
Mt 9.27 two *b* men followed him, crying loudly,
11. 5 the *b* receive their sight, the lame walk,
12.22 brought to him a demoniac who was *b*
15.14 them alone; they are *b* guides of the *b*.
15.30 the lame, the maimed, the *b*, the mute,
20.30 two *b* men sitting by the roadside.
23.16 "Woe to you, *b* guides, who say,
Mk 8.22 Some people brought a *b* man to him
10.51 And the *b* man said to him, "My
Lk 4.18 and recovering of sight to the *b*,
6.39 "Can a *b* person guide a *b* person? Will
7.21 had given sight to many who were *b*.
14.13 poor, the crippled, the lame, and the *b*,
18.35 Jericho, a *b* man was sitting by the
Jn 9. 1 along, he saw a man *b* from birth.
9.20 this is our son, and that he was born *b*;
9.25 know, that though I was *b*, now I see."
9.39 and those who do see may become *b*."
10.21 Can a demon open the eyes of the *b*?"
Rom 2.19 you are a guide to the *b*, a light to
2 Pet 1. 9 lacks these things is nearsighted and *b*,
Rev 3.17 wretched, pitiable, poor, *b*, and naked.

BLIND (BLINDED BLINDS) (v)

Deut 16.19 for a bribe *b* the eyes of the wise and
1 Sam 12. 3 I taken a bribe to *b* my eyes with it?
2 Cor 4. 4 god of this world has *b* the minds of the

BLINDLY

Lam 4.14 *b* they wandered through the streets, so

BLINDNESS

Gen 19.11 they struck with *b* the men who were at
2 Kings 6.18 said, "Strike this people, please, with *b*."
Zech 12. 4 horse with panic, and its rider with *b*.
1 Jn 2.11 because the darkness has brought on *b*.

BLOOD

Gen 4.10 your brother's *b* is crying out to me
9. 4 not eat flesh with its life, that is, its *b*.
9. 6 Whoever sheds the *b* of a human, by a
42.22 now there comes a reckoning for his *b*."
Ex 7.17 in the Nile, and it shall be turned to *b*.
24. 8 "See the *b* of the covenant that the
29.12 shall take some of the *b* of the bull and
Lev 16.14 He shall take some of the *b* of the bull,
17.11 life, it is the *b* that makes atonement.
Deut 12.16 The *b*, however, you must not eat; you
1 Sam 14.32 and the troops ate them with the *b*.
Ps 105. 29 He turned their waters into *b*, and
Ezek 3.18 but their *b* I will require at your hand.
Mt 23.30 in shedding the *b* of the prophets.'
23.35 from the *b* of righteous Abel to the *b* of
26.28 this is my *b* of the covenant, which is
27.24 saying, "I am innocent of this man's *b*;
Mk 14.24 "This is my *b* of the covenant, which is
Lk 11.51 from the *b* of Abel to the *b* of
22.20 out for you is the new covenant in my *b*
Jn 6.53 of Man and drink his *b*, you have no life
Acts 1.19 Hakeldama, that is, Field of *B*.)
18. 6 "Your *b* be upon your heads! I am
Rom 5. 9 we have been justified by his *b*, will we
1 Cor 15.50 flesh and *b* cannot inherit the kingdom
Eph 1. 7 we have redemption through his *b*, the
2.13 been brought near by the *b* of Christ.
Heb 9. 7 and not without taking the *b* that he
9.12 but his own *b*, thus obtaining eternal
10.19 to enter the sanctuary by the *b* of Jesus,
10.29 profaned the *b* of the covenant by
1 Pet 1.19 with the precious *b* of Christ, like that
1 Jn 1. 7 the *b* of Jesus his Son cleanses us from
5. 6 only but with the water and the *b*.
Rev 7.14 made them white in the *b* of the Lamb.
11. 6 over the waters to turn them into *b*,
12.11 conquered him by the *b* of the Lamb
19. 2 and he has avenged on her the *b* of his

BLOODSHED

Isa 5. 7 he expected justice, but saw *b*;
Jer 48.10 one who keeps back the sword from *b*.

BLOT (BLOTS BLOTTED)

Ex 32.32 if not, *b* me out of the book that you
Deut 9.14 and *b* out their name from under
25.19 shall *b* out the remembrance of Amalek
29.20 LORD will *b* out their names from under
2 Kings 14.27 had not said he would *b* out the name
Ps 51. 1 mercy *b* out my transgressions.
109. 14 not let the sin of his mother be *b* out.
Isa 6. 7 guilt has departed and your sin is *b* out."
43.25 I am He who *b* out your transgressions
Jer 18.23 do not *b* out their sin from your sight.

BLOW

Num 10. 5 When you *b* an alarm, the camp on the
Song 4.16 O south wind! *B* upon my garden,

BOAST (BOASTING) (n)

Ps 34. 2 My soul makes its *b* in the LORD; let the
Rom 3.27 Then what becomes of *b*? It is
2 Cor 7.14 true, so our *b* to Titus has proved true
8.24 of your love and of our reason for *b*
11.10 this *b* of mine shall not be silenced in

BOAST (BOASTED BOASTS) (v)

Ps 10. 3 the wicked *b* of the desires of their
38.16 rejoice over me, those who *b* against
44. 8 In God we have *b* continually, and we
Prov 20.14 says the buyer, then goes away and *b*.
25.14 rain is one who *b* of a gift never given.
27. 1 Do not *b* about tomorrow, for you do
Jer 9.24 let those who *b* *b* in this, that they
Rom 2.17 the law and *b* of your relation to God
2.23 You that *b* in the law, do you dishonor

Rom 5. 2 and we *b* in our hope of sharing the
5.11 we even *b* in God through our Lord
11.18 do not *b* over the branches. If you do *b*,
1 Cor 1.31 written, "Let one who *b*, *b* in the Lord."
3.21 So let no one *b* about human leaders.
2 Cor 7. 4 I often *b* about you; I have great pride
10.17 "Let the one who *b*, *b* in the Lord." For
11.21 as a fool—I also dare to *b* of that.
Gal 6.14 I never *b* of anything except the cross
Eph 2. 9 result of works, so that no one may *b*.
Jas 1. 9 Let the believer who is lowly *b* in being

BOAT

Mt 4.22 they left the *b* and their father, and
Mk 3. 9 He told his disciples to have a *b* ready
Lk 8.22 day he got into a *b* with his disciples,
Jn 6.21 and immediately the *b* reached the land

BODILY

Lk 3.22 Spirit descended on him in *b* form like
Col 2. 9 the whole fullness of deity dwells *b*,

BODY (BODIES)

Gen 47.18 of my lord but our *b* and our lands.
1 Sam 31.12 took the *b* of Saul and the *b* of his sons
Isa 37.36 morning dawned, they were all dead *b*.
Mt 10.28 Do not fear those who can kill the *b*
26.26 and said, "Take, eat; this is my *b*."
27.58 to Pilate and asked for the *b* of Jesus;
Mk 6.29 about it, they came and took his *b*,
14.22 to them, and said, "Take; this is my *b*."
15.43 to Pilate and asked for the *b* of Jesus.
Lk 22.19 saying, "This is my *b*, which is given for
Jn 2.21 he was speaking of the temple of his *b*.
Rom 12. 4 as in one *b* we have many members,
1 Cor 6.13 *b* is meant not for fornication but for
6.15 that your *b* are members of Christ?
6.19 your *b* is a temple of the Holy Spirit
12.12 For just as the *b* is one and has many
12.24 God has so arranged the *b*, giving the
12.27 Now you are the *b* of Christ and
15.35 With what kind of *b* do they come?"
Gal 6.17 the marks of Jesus branded on my *b*.
Eph 1.23 the church, which is his *b*, the fullness
4. 4 There is one *b* and one Spirit, just as
4.16 the whole *b*, joined and knit together by
5.30 because we are members of his *b*.
Phil 3.21 transform the *b* of our humiliation that
Col 1.18 He is the head of the *b*, the church; he
2.19 head, from whom the whole *b*,
Heb 10. 5 but a *b* you have prepared for me;
Jude 9 disputed about the *b* of Moses, he did
Rev 11. 8 dead *b* will lie in the street of the great

BOG

Ps 40. 2 from the desolate pit, out of the miry *b*,

BOIL (v)

Deut 14.21 shall not *b* a kid in its mother's milk.

BOILS (n)

Ex 9. 9 shall cause festering *b* on humans and
Deut 28.27 LORD will afflict you with the *b* of Egypt,

BOLD

Prov 21.29 The wicked put on a *b* face, but the

BOLDNESS

Acts 4.13 when they saw the *b* of Peter and John
4.29 servants to speak thy word with all *b*,
28.31 about the Lord Jesus Christ with all *b*
2 Cor 3.12 have such a hope, we act with great *b*,
Eph 3.12 have access to God in *b* and confidence
Phil 1.14 dare to speak the word with greater *b*
1 Jn 4.17 we may have *b* on the day of judgment,
5.14 this is the *b* we have in him, that if we

BOND (BONDS)

Ps 69.33 does not despise his own that are in *b*.
Isa 58. 6 to loose the *b* of injustice, to undo the
Eph 4. 3 the unity of the Spirit in the *b* of peace.

BONE (BONES)

Gen 50.25 comes to you, you shall carry up my *b*
Ex 13.19 Moses took with him the *b* of Joseph
Num 9.12 of it until morning, nor break a *b* of it;
Josh 24.32 The *b* of Joseph, which the Israelites
2 Kings 13.21 man touched the *b* of Elisha, he came
1 Chr 11. 1 and said, "See, we are your *b* and flesh.
Ps 22.17 I can count all my *b*. They stare and
34.20 He keeps all their *b*; not one of them
Jer 8. 1 the *b* of the kings of Judah, the *b* of its
Ezek 37. 7 a rattling, and the *b* came together,
Jn 19.36 fulfilled, "None of his *b* shall be broken."

BOOK (BOOKS)

Ex 24. 7 took the *b* of the covenant, and read it
Num 21.14 is said in the *B* of the Wars of the Lord,
Deut 31.26 "Take this *b* of the law and put it
Josh 1. 8 This *b* of the law shall not depart out of
8.31 is written in the *b* of the law of Moses,
2 Kings 22. 8 I have found the *b* of the law in the
23. 2 all the words of the *b* of the covenant
2 Chr 34.16 Shaphan brought the *b* to the king, and
Neh 7. 5 I found the *b* of the genealogy of those
8. 1 Ezra to bring the *b* of the law of Moses
Job 19.23 down! O that they were inscribed in a *b*!
Ps 139. 16 In your *b* were written, all the days that
Eccl 12.12 Of making many *b* there is no end, and
Isa 30. 8 them on a tablet, inscribe it in a *b*,
34.16 Seek and read from the *b* of the LORD:
Jer 25.13 everything written in this *b*, which
Dan 7.10 in judgment, and the *b* were opened.
9. 2 perceived in the *b* the number of years
10.21 you what is inscribed in the *b* of truth.
12. 1 everyone who is found written in the *b*.
Mal 3.16 a *b* of remembrance was written before
Jn 20.30 are not written in this *b*. But these
21.25 itself could not contain the *b* that
Acts 19.19 magic collected their *b* and burned
Phil 4. 3 whose names are in the *b* of life.
2 Tim 4.13 also the *b*, and above all the
Rev 1.11 "Write in a *b* what you see and send it
3. 5 I will not blot your name out of the *b* of
13. 8 of the world in the *b* of life of the Lamb
20.12 Also another *b* was opened, the *b* of
21.27 who are written in the Lamb's *b* of life.

BOOTH (BOOTHS)

Gen 33.17 a house, and made *b* for his cattle;
Lev 23.34 there shall be the festival of *b* to the
23.42 You shall live in *b* for seven days; all
Deut 16.13 You shall keep the festival of *b* for
Neh 8.14 Israel should live in *b* during the festival
Am 9.11 I will raise up the *b* of David that has
Jon 4. 5 city, and made a *b* for himself there.
Jn 7. 2 Now the Jewish festival of *B* was near

BOOTY

Num 31.32 The *b* remaining from the spoil that the

BORN

1 Kings 13. 2 'A son shall be *b* to the house of David,
Job 14. 1 "A mortal *b* of woman, few of days, and
25. 4 How can one *b* of woman be pure?
Eccl 3. 2 time to be *b*, and a time to die, a time
Isa 9. 6 For a child has been *b* for us, a son is
Jer 1. 5 before you were *b* I consecrated you;
Mt 1.16 husband of Mary, of whom Jesus was *b*,
2. 1 after Jesus was *b* in Bethlehem of
11.11 among those *b* of women no one has
Lk 1.35 child to be *b* will be holy; he will be
Jn 1.13 of God, who were *b*, not of blood or
3. 3 of God without being *b* from above.
9.34 "You were *b* entirely in sins, and you
16.21 her child is *b*, she no longer remembers
1 Pet 1.23 You have been *b* anew, not of

1 Jn 3. 9 Those who have been *b* of God do not
5.18 know that those *b* of God do not sin,

BORROW

2 Kings 4. 3 "Go outside, *b* vessels from all your
Ps 37.21 The wicked *b*, and do not pay back, but
Mt 5.42 do not refuse anyone who wants to *b*

BORROWER

Prov 22. 7 and the *b* is the slave of the lender.
Isa 24. 2 as with the lender, so with the *b*; as

BOSOM

Prov 6.27 Can fire be carried in the *b* without
Isa 40.11 in his arms, and carry them in his *b*,
66.11 deeply with delight from her glorious *b*.

BOTHER (BOTHERING)

Lk 11. 7 "Do not *b* me; the door has already
18. 5 because this widow keeps *b* me, I will

BOTTLE

Ps 33. 7 gathered the waters of the sea as in a *b*;
56. 8 of my tossings; put my tears in your *b*.

BOUGH (BOUGHS)

Gen 49.22 Joseph is a fruitful *b*, a fruitful *b* by a
Ezek 31.12 have fallen, and its *b* lie broken in all

BOUNDARY (BOUNDARIES)

Deut 19.14 not remove your neighbor's *b* marker,
32. 8 he fixed the *b* of the peoples according

BOUNDLESS

Eph 3. 8 to the Gentiles the news of the *b* riches

BOUNDS

Ps 74.17 You have fixed all the *b* of the earth;

BOUNTY

Ps 65.11 You crown the year with your *b*; your
116. 12 I return to the LORD for all his *b* to me?

BOW (n)

Gen 9.13 I set my *b* in the cloud, and it shall be
21.20 and became an expert with the *b*.
Ps 44. 6 For not in my *b* do I trust, nor can my
46. 9 he breaks the *b*, and shatters the spear;
Hos 1. 5 On that day I will break the *b* of Israel

BOW (BOWED BOWING)

Gen 33. 6 they and their children, and *b* down;
42. 6 Joseph's brothers came and *b*
43.28 And they *b* their heads and did
49. 8 your father's sons shall *b* down before
Ex 23.24 you shall not *b* down to their gods, or
Deut 5. 9 You shall not *b* down to them or
26.10 and *b* down before the LORD your God.
1 Kings 19.18 all the knees that have not *b* to Baal,
2 Kings 4.37 and fell at his feet, *b* to the ground;
Ps 5. 7 I will *b* down toward your holy temple
81. 9 you shall not *b* down to a foreign god.
86. 9 you have made shall come and *b* down
Zeph 1. 5 who *b* down on the roofs to the host of
Jn 19.30 Then he *b* his head and gave up his
Rev 3. 9 and *b* down before your feet, and they

BOWL (BOWLS)

2 Kings 2.20 "Bring me a new *b*, and put salt in it."
Mt 26.23 has dipped his hand in the *b* with me,
Rev 16. 1 earth the seven *b* of the wrath of God."

BOY (BOYS)

Gen 44.34 to my father if the *b* is not with me?
48.16 bless the *b*; and in them let my name
1 Sam 20.21 Then I will send the *b*, saying, 'Go, find
17.33 to fight against him; for you are just a *b*
2 Kings 5.14 was restored like the flesh of a young *b*,
2 Chr 34. 3 while he was still a *b*, he began to seek
Prov 22.15 Folly is bound up in the heart of a *b*,

Isa 3. 4 I will make *b* their princes, and babes
Jer 1. 6 know how to speak, for I am only a *b*."
Zech 8. 5 city shall be of *b* and girls playing in its
Jn 6. 9 is a *b* here who has five barley loaves

BRANCH (BRANCHES)

Isa 4. 2 day the *b* of the LORD shall be beautiful
11. 1 and a *b* shall grow out of his roots.
Jer 23. 5 I will raise up for David a righteous *B*,
33.15 I will cause a righteous *B* to spring up
Zech 3. 8 I am going to bring my servant the *B*.
Mk 11. 8 and others spread leafy *b* that they had
Jn 12.13 So they took *b* of palm trees and went
15. 2 He removes every *b* in me that bears no
Rom 11.18 do not boast over the *b*. If you do boast,

BREACH

Ps 106. 23 Moses, his chosen one, stood in the *b*
Ezek 22.30 stand in the *b* before me on behalf of

BREAD

Ex 16. 4 I am going to rain *b* from heaven for
Deut 8. 3 one does not live by *b* alone, but by
1 Sam 21. 6 no *b* there except the *b* of the Presence,
Prov 4.17 For they eat the *b* of wickedness and
22. 9 are blessed, for they share their *b* with
Eccl 11. 1 Send out your *b* upon the waters, for
Isa 3. 1 all support of *b*, and all support of
Jer 37.21 loaf of *b* was given him daily from the
Ezek 4.17 Lacking *b* and water, they will look at
Mt 4. 3 these stones to become loaves of *b*."
12. 4 of God and ate the *b* of the Presence,
15.33 "Where are we to get enough *b* in the
26.26 Jesus took a loaf of *b*, and after
Mk 8. 4 can one feed these people with *b* here
14.22 he took a loaf of *b*, and after blessing it
Lk 4. 3 this stone to become a loaf of *b*."
22.19 he took a loaf of *b*, and when he had
24.30 he took *b*, blessed and broke it, and
Jn 6.32 not Moses who gave you the *b* from
6.35 "I am the *b* of life; Whoever comes to
13.26 the one to whom I give this piece of *b*
21.13 Jesus came and took the *b* and gave it
Acts 20. 7 of the week, when we met to break *b*,
1 Cor 10.16 The *b* that we break, is it not a sharing
11.23 when he was betrayed took a loaf of *b*,

BREAK (BREAKING BROKE BROKEN)

Gen 17.14 from his people; he has *b* my covenant."
Num 9.12 of it until morning, nor *b* a bone of it;
Deut 7. 5 *b* down their altars, smash their pillars,
Ezra 9.14 shall we *b* your commandments again
Job 16.12 at ease, and he *b* me in two; he seized
17.11 My days are past, my plans are *b* off,
Ps 34.20 their bones; not one of them will be *b*.
102. 23 He has *b* my strength in midcourse; he
119.126 LORD to act, for your law has been *b*.
Prov 18.14 sickness; a *b* spirit—who can bear?
Jer 19.11 So will I *b* this people and this city, as
33.20 If any of you could *b* my covenant with
Hos 8. 1 have *b* my covenant, and transgressed
Jn 19.33 already dead, they did not *b* his legs.
Acts 21.13 are you doing, weeping and *b* my heart?
Rom 2.27 code and circumcision but *b* the law.

BREASTPLATE

Isa 59.17 He put on righteousness like a *b*, and a
Eph 6.14 and put on the *b* of righteousness.
1 Thess 5. 8 and put on the *b* of faith and love,

BREASTS

Song 4. 5 Your two *b* are like two fawns, twins of
Isa 32.12 Beat upon your *b* for the present fields,

BREATH

Job 32. 8 the *b* of the Almighty, that makes for
Ps 18.15 rebuke, O LORD, at the blast of the *b* of
33. 6 and all their host by the *b* of his mouth.

Ps 62. 9 Those of low estate are but a *b*, those
94.11 thoughts, that they are but an empty *b*.
144. 4 They are like a *b*; their days are like a
146. 4 their *b* departs they return to the earth;
Eccl 3.19 They all have the same *b*, and humans
11. 5 as you do not know how the *b* comes
12. 7 and the *b* returns to God who gave it.
Isa 11. 4 and with the *b* of his lips he shall kill
40. 7 fades, when the *b* of the LORD blows
Ezek 37. 5 to these bones: I will cause *b* to enter
37. 9 "Prophesy to the *b*, prophesy, mortal,
Rev 13.15 to give *b* to the image of the beast

BREATHE (BREATHED BREATHES BREATHING)

Gen 2. 7 *b* into his nostrils the breath of life; and
Ps 27.12 against me, and they are *b* out violence.
150. 6 Let everything that *b* praise the LORD!
Acts 9. 1 Saul, still *b* threats and murder against

BREEZE

Gen 3. 8 the garden at the time of the evening *b*,

BRIBE (BRIBES)

Ex 23. 8 take no *b*, for a *b* blinds the officials,
Deut 16.19 not accept *b*, for a *b* blinds the eyes
1 Sam 8. 3 gain; they took *b* and perverted justice.
12. 3 from whose hand have I taken a *b* to
Ps 26.10 and whose right hands are full of *b*.
Prov 15.27 but those who hate *b* will live.
17. 8 A *b* is like a magic stone in the eyes of
Am 5.12 who take a *b*, and push aside the needy
Mic 3.11 Its rulers give judgment for a *b*, its
7. 3 the official and the judge ask for a *b*,

BRIBERY

Job 15.34 and fire consumes the tents of *b*.

BRICK (BRICKS)

Gen 11. 3 "Come, let us make *b*, and burn them
Ex 5. 7 longer give the people straw to make *b*,
Isa 9.10 "The *b* have fallen, but we will build
Ezek 4. 1 take a *b* and set it before you. On it

BRIDE

Song 4. 9 sister, my *b*, you have ravished my heart
Isa 61.10 garland, and as a *b* adorns herself with
Jer 2.32 forget her ornaments, or a *b* her attire?
7.34 mirth and gladness, the voice of the *b*
Rev 21. 2 from God, prepared as a *b* adorned for
21. 9 I will show you the *b*, the wife of the

BRIDEGROOM

Ex 4.26 "Truly you are a *b* of blood to me!"
Ps 19. 5 which comes out like a *b* from his
Mt 9.15 mourn as long as the *b* is with them,
Mk 2.19 cannot fast while the *b* is with them
Lk 5.34 wedding guests fast while the *b* is with
Jn 3.29 The friend of the *b*, who stands and

BRIDESMAIDS

Mt 25. 1 Ten *b* took their lamps and went to

BRIDLE

Ps 32. 9 temper must be curbed with bit and *b*,
Jas 1.26 are religious, and do not *b* their tongues
3. 2 keep the whole body in check with a *b*.

BRIGHT (BRIGHTER)

Job 11.17 your life will be *b* than the noonday; its
Acts 26.13 a light from heaven, *b* than the sun,
Rev 22.16 of David, the *b* morning star."

BRING (BRINGING BRINGS BROUGHT)

Gen 28.15 will *b* you back to this land; for I will
45.19 wives, and *b* your father, and come.
Ex 13.11 "When the LORD has *b* you into the land
Num 24. 8 God *b* him out of Egypt, is like the
27. 5 Moses *b* their case before the LORD.
Job 33.30 to *b* back their soul from the Pit, so
Ps 64. 9 they will tell what God has *b* about,
Isa 49.22 they shall *b* your sons in their bosom,
52. 7 announces peace, who *b* good news,
60. 5 abundance of the sea shall be *b* to you,
61. 1 he has sent me to *b* good news to the
Jer 21. 4 I will *b* them together into the center of
Am 5.25 Did you *b* to me sacrifices and offerings
Nah 1.15 the feet of one who *b* good tidings,
Mal 3.10 *B* the full tithe into the storehouse, so
Mt 6.13 And do not *b* us to the time of trial, but
10.34 the earth; I have not come to *b* peace,
Lk 2.10 —I am *b* you good news of great joy for
4.18 me to *b* good news to the poor.
Jn 1.42 He *b* Simon to Jesus, who looked at
Jas 5.19 from the truth and is *b* back by another,

BROKENHEARTED

Ps 34.18 The LORD is near to the *b*, and saves the
Isa 61. 1 to the oppressed, to bind up the *b*, to

BRONZE

Gen 4.22 who made all kinds of *b* and iron tools.
Num 21. 9 Moses made a serpent of *b*, and put it
Jer 15.20 you to this people a fortified wall of *b*;
Dan 2.32 of silver, its middle and thighs of *b*,

BROOD

Mt 23.37 as a hen gathers her *b* under her wings,
Lk 3. 7 "You *b* of vipers! Who warned you to

BROOKS

Jer 31. 9 I will let them walk by *b* of water, in a

BROTHER (BROTHERS BROTHER'S)

Gen 4. 8 Cain rose up against his *b* Abel, and
20.16 I have given your *b* a thousand pieces of
27.45 until your *b* anger against you turns
37.11 So his *b* were jealous of him, but his
37.27 lay our hands on him, for he is our *b*,
45. 4 "I am your *b*, Joseph, whom you sold
49. 8 Judah, your *b* shall praise you; your
Num 20.14 "Thus says your *b* Israel: You know all
Deut 25. 5 Her husband's *b* shall go in to her,
Judg 9. 5 house at Ophrah, and killed his *b*
1 Sam 17.22 the ranks, and went and greeted his *b*.
1 Kings 2.15 has turned about and become my *b*,
13.30 mourned over him, saying, "Alas, my *b*!"
20.32 he said, "Is he still live? He is my *b*."
1 Chr 5. 2 Judah became prominent among his *b*
Ps 22.22 will tell of your name to my *b* and
Mal 1. 2 you loved us?" Is not Esau Jacob's *b*?
Mt 5.22 if you are angry with a *b* or sister, you
10.21 *B* will betray *b* to death, and a father
12.46 his mother and his *b* were standing
12.50 the will of my Father in heaven is my *b*,
13.55 are not his *b* James and Joseph and
20.24 it, they were angry with the two *b*.
28.10 go and tell my *b* to go to Galilee; there
Mk 3.35 does the will of God is my *b* and sister
12.19 widow and raise up children for his *b*.
13.12 *B* will betray *b* to death, and a father
Lk 8.20 mother and your *b* are standing outside,
Jn 7. 5 (For not even his *b* believed in him.)
Acts 7.13 Joseph made himself known to his *b*,
7.26 you are *b*; why do you wrong each
9.17 hands on Saul and said, "*B* Saul, the
Rom 14.10 Why do you pass judgment on your *b* or
14.21 that makes your *b* or sister stumble.
1 Cor 5.11 with anyone who bears the name of *b* or
2 Cor 8.18 we are sending the *b* who is famous
Gal 1.19 apostle except James the Lord's *b*.
1 Thess 4. 6 that no one wrong or exploit a *b* or
Philem 16 but more than a slave, a beloved *b*
1 Jn 3.17 sees a *b* or sister in need, yet refuses to
4.20 "I love God," and hates their *b* or sisters,

BRUISED

Isa 42. 3 a *b* reed he will not break, and a dimly

BUCKET

Isa 40.15 the nations are like a drop from a *b*,

BUILD (BUILDING BUILDS BUILT)

1 Kings 6. 1 he began to *b* the house of the LORD.
1 Chr 17.12 He shall *b* a house for me, and I will
22.19 Go and *b* the sanctuary of the LORD God
2 Chr 2. 6 who is able to *b* him a house, since
Neh 2.18 to me. Then they said, "Let us start *b*!"
Ps 127. 1 Unless the LORD *b* the house, those who
Prov 9. 1 Wisdom has *b* her house, she has hewn
14. 1 The wise woman *b* her house, but the
24. 3 By wisdom a house is *b*, and by
Eccl 2. 4 works; I *b* houses and planted vineyards
Isa 61. 4 They shall *b* up the ancient ruins, they
Jer 29. 5 *B* houses and live in them; plant
Dan 4.30 magnificent Babylon, which I have *b* as
Hab 2.12 for you who *b* a town by bloodshed,
Hag 1. 8 hills and bring wood and *b* the house,
Mal 1. 4 They may *b*, but I will tear down, until
Mt 16.18 on this rock I will *b* my church, and the
Lk 6.48 like a man *b* a house, who dug deeply
14.30 fellow began to *b*, and was not able
Acts 20.32 a message that is able to *b* you up and
1 Cor 10.23 are lawful," but not all things *b* up.
14.12 to excel in them for *b* up the church.
14.26 Let all things be done for *b* up. If
2 Cor 10. 8 which the Lord gave for *b* you up
12.19 do, beloved, is for the sake of *b* you up.
Eph 2.20 household of God, *b* upon the
1 Thess 5.11 one another and *b* up each other,
Jude 20 beloved, *b* yourselves up on most holy

BUILDERS

Ps 118. 22 The stone that the *b* rejected has
Lk 20.17 stone that the *b* rejected has become

BUILDING (BUILDINGS)

Mk 13. 1 what large stones and what large *b*!"
1 Cor 3. 9 together; you are God's field, God's *b*.

BULWARK (BULWARKS)

Ps 8. 2 you have founded a *b* because of your
Isa 26. 1 city; he sets up victory like walls and *b*.
Jer 50.15 surrendered; her *b* have fallen, her walls

BURDEN (BURDENS) (n)

Num 11.11 that you lay the *b* of all this people on
Ps 38. 4 my head; they weigh like a *b* too heavy
55.22 Cast your *b* on the LORD, and he will
66.11 us into the net; you laid *b* on our backs;
Isa 9. 4 the yoke of their *b*, and the bar across
10.27 On that day his *b* will be removed from
Jer 17.21 that you do not bear a *b* on the sabbath
23.33 asks you, "What is the *b* of the LORD?
23.36 the *b* is everyone's own word, and so
Mt 11.30 For my yoke is easy, and my *b* is light."
20.12 equal to us who have borne the *b* of the
23. 4 They tie up heavy *b*, hard to bear, and
Lk 11.46 you load people with *b* hard to bear,
Acts 15.28 impose on you no further *b* than these
Gal 6. 2 Bear one another's *b*, and in this way
Rev 2.24 I say, I do not lay upon you any other *b*;

BURDEN (BURDENED BURDENING)

Isa 43.24 But you have *b* me with your sins; you
2 Cor 11. 9 and will continue to refrain from *b* you
12.13 except that I myself did not *b* you?
2 Thess 3. 8 day, so that we might not *b* any of you.

BURIAL

Mk 14. 8 anointed my body beforehand for its *b*.

BURN (BURNED BURNING)

Josh 11.11 who breathed, and he *b* Hazor with fire.
Ps 38. 7 my loins are filled with *b*, and there is
39. 3 While I mused, the fire *b*; then I spoke
Jer 20. 9 like a *b* fire shut up in my bones,
36.25 urged the king not to *b* the scroll, he
39. 8 Chaldeans *b* the king's house and the
52.13 He *b* the house of the LORD, the king's
Lam 2. 3 he has *b* like a flaming fire in Jacob,
Mt 13.30 first and bind them in bundles to be *b*,
Lk 24.32 "Were not our hearts *b* within us while
Acts 19.19 their books and *b* them publicly;
1 Cor 3.15 If the work is *b* up, the builder will

BURNT OFFERING (BURNT OFFERINGS)

Gen 8.20 clean bird, and offered *b* on the altar.
22. 7 are here, but where is the lamb for a *b*?"
Ex 29.18 it is a *b* to the LORD; it is a pleasing
Lev 1. 3 If the offering is a *b* from the herd, you
1.17 the wood that is on the fire; it is a *b*,
6. 9 This is the ritual of the *b*. The *b* itself
Judg 13.16 if you want to prepare a *b*, then offer it
1 Sam 7. 9 lamb and offered it as a whole *b*
13.12 so I forced myself, and offered the *b*."
15.22 Has the LORD as great delight in *b* and
2 Sam 24.24 I will not offer *b* to the LORD my God
2 Kings 3.27 succeed him, and offered him as a *b*
1 Chr 16.40 to offer *b* to the LORD on the altar of *b*
21.26 and presented *b* and offerings of
Ezra 3. 4 and offered the daily *b* by number
Ps 40. 6 ear. *B* and sin offering you have not
50. 8 you; your *b* are continually before me.
51.16 if I were to give a *b*, you would not be
Isa 1.11 I have had enough of *b* of rams and the
Jer 7.21 Add your *b* to your sacrifices, and eat
Ezek 46.12 provides a freewill offering, either a *b*
Dan 8.11 it took the regular *b* away from him and
Mic 6. 6 Shall I come before him with *b*, with

BURY (BURIED)

Gen 23.19 Abraham *b* Sarah his wife in the cave of
35.29 and his sons Esau and Jacob *b* him.
47.29 truly with me. Do not *b* me in Egypt.
Deut 34. 6 He was *b* in a valley in the land of
Mt 8.21 "Lord, first let me go and *b* my father."
Lk 9.59 "Lord, first let me go and *b* my father."
Rom 6. 4 we have been *b* with him by baptism
1 Cor 15. 4 he was *b*, and that he was raised on the
Col 2.12 when you were *b* with him in baptism,

BUSH

Ex 3. 2 to him in a flame of fire out of a *b*;
Jon 4. 6 God appointed a *b*, and made it come
Lk 20.37 showed, in the story about the *b*,
Acts 7.30 Sinai, in the flame of a burning *b*.

BUSHEL

Mt 5.15 lighting a lamp puts it under a *b* basket,
Mk 4.21 brought in to be put under a *b* basket,

BUSY

1 Kings 20.40 While your servant was *b* here and
Ps 141. 4 to *b* myself with wicked deeds in

BUSYBODIES

2 Thess 3.11 in idleness, mere *b*, not doing any work.
1 Tim 5.13 not merely idle, but also gossips and *b*,

BUY (BOUGHT)

Ex 21. 2 When you *b* a male Hebrew slave, he
2 Sam 24.24 "No, but I will *b* them from you for a
1 Chr 21.24 "No; I will *b* them for the full price. I
Neh 5. 8 have *b* back our Jewish kindred who
Hos 3. 2 I *b* her for fifteen shekels of silver and a
1 Cor 6.20 you were *b* with a price; therefore
7.23 You were *b* with a price; do not become
2 Pet 2. 1 even deny the Master who *b* them—

BUYER

Deut 28.68 female slaves, but there will be no *b*.

BYWORD

Deut 28.37 and a *b* among all the peoples where
2 Chr 7.20 make it a proverb and a *b* among all

Job 17. 6 "He has made me a *b* of the peoples,
Ps 44.14 have made us a *b* among the nations,

C

CAESAREA

Mt 16.13 came into the district of *C* Philippi,
Mk 8.27 disciples to the villages of *C* Philippi;
Acts 8.40 to all the towns until he came to *C*.
10. 1 In *C* there was a man named Cornelius,
11.11 three men, sent to me from *C*, arrived
18.22 When he had landed at *C*, he went up
23.33 When they came to *C* and delivered the
25. 4 replied that Paul was being kept at *C*,

CAIAPHAS

High priest, Mt 26.3, 57; Lk 3.2; Jn 18.13; prophesied that Jesus should die, 11.49-53; 18.14; took part in the trial of Jesus, Mt 26.62-66 (Mk 14.60-64; Jn 18.19-24,28); present at examination of Peter and John, Acts 4.6-21.

CAIN (CAIN'S)

Gen 4. 1 Eve, and she conceived and bore *C*,
4. 3 *C* brought to the LORD an offering of the
4. 8 *C* rose up against his brother Abel, and
4.16 *C* went away from the presence of the
4.25 instead of Abel, for *C* had killed him."
Heb 11. 4 God a more acceptable sacrifice than *C*.
1 Jn 3.12 not be like *C* who was from the evil one
Jude 11 they go the way of *C*, and abandon

CAKE (CAKES)

Gen 18. 6 of choice flour, knead it, and make *c*."
Hos 7. 8 the peoples; Ephraim is a *c* not turned.

CALAMITY

Job 6.30 my tongue? Cannot my taste discern *c*?
Ps 18.18 They confronted me in the day of my *c*;
Prov 1.26 I also will laugh at your *c*; I will mock
Jer 48.16 The *c* of Moab is near at hand and his
Dan 9.14 So the LORD kept watch over this *c* until
Ob 13 gate of my people on the day of their *c*;

CALEB

Sent with the spies, Num 13.16; exhorted the people, Num 13.30; 14.6-10; was promised entrance into Canaan, Num 14.22-38 (32.10-12; Deut 1.34-36); Num 26.65; received Hebron as an inheritance, Josh 14.6-15; 15.13-19; Judg 1.20.

CALF (CALVES)

Gen 18. 7 herd, and took a *c*, tender and good,
Ex 32. 4 it in a mold, and cast an image of a *c*;
32.24 it into the fire, and out came this *c*!"
1 Kings 12.28 took counsel, and made two *c* of gold.
Ps 106. 19 They made a *c* at Horeb and worshiped
Hos 13. 2 to these," they say. People are kissing *c*!
Lk 15.23 get the fatted *c* and kill it, and let us
Acts 7.41 they made a *c*, offered a sacrifice to the

CALL (CALLING CALLS)

Job 13.22 Then *c*, and I will answer; or let me
14.15 You would *c*, and I would answer you;
Ps 50. 4 He *c* to the heavens above and to the
53. 4 they eat bread, and do not *c* upon God?
55.16 But I *c* upon God; and the LORD will
80.18 us life, and we will *c* on your name.
91.15 When they *c* to me, I will answer them;
102. 2 answer me speedily in the day when I *c*.
105. 1 give thanks to the LORD, *c* on his name,
116. 2 I will *c* on him as long as I live.
145. 18 the LORD is near to all who *c* on him, to
Prov 8. 1 Does not wisdom *c*, does not
Isa 45. 4 I *c* you by your name, I surname you,
55. 6 be found, *c* upon him while he is near;
64. 7 There is no one who *c* upon your name,
65.24 Before they *c* I will answer, while they
Jer 3.19 I thought you would *c* me, My Father,
33. 3 *C* to me and I will answer you, and will
Joel 2.15 sanctify a fast; *c* a solemn assembly;
2.32 who *c* on the name of the LORD
Mk 10.49 to him, "Take heart; get up, he is *c* you.
15.35 it, they said "Listen, he is *c* for Elijah."
Lk 15. 6 he *c* together his friends and neighbors,
Jn 10. 3 his voice. He *c* his own sheep by name
Acts 2.21 who *c* on the name of the Lord
Rom 10.12 all and is generous to all who *c* on him.
10.14 how are they to *c* on one in whom they
11.29 gifts and the *c* of God are irrevocable.
1 Cor 1.26 Consider your own *c*, brothers and
2 Tim 2.22 who *c* upon the Lord from a pure heart.
2 Pet 1.10 eager to confirm your *c* and election,

CALLED

Gen 13. 4 there Abram *c* on the name of the LORD.
22.14 So Abraham *c* that place "The LORD will
Ex 3. 4 God *c* to him out of the bush, "Moses,
Judg 16.28 Then Samson *c* to the LORD and said,
1 Sam 3. 4 the Lord *c*,"Samuel! Samuel!" and he
Prov 1.24 Because I have *c* and you refused, have
Song 5. 6 him; I *c* him, but he gave no answer.
Isa 41. 9 earth, and *c* from its farthest corners,
42. 6 the LORD, I have *c* you in righteousness,
49. 1 The LORD *c* me before I was born, while
Jer 35.17 I have *c* to them and they have not
Mt 2.15 prophet, "Out of Egypt have I *c* my son."
Mk 3.13 the hills, and *c* to him those whom he
6. 7 He *c* the twelve and began to send
Lk 1.32 and will be *c* the Son of the Most High,
9. 1 Jesus *c* the twelve together and gave
Acts 11.26 the disciples were first *c* "Christians."
28.17 he *c* together the local leaders of the
Rom 1. 6 yourselves who are *c* to belong to Jesus
8.30 whom he predestined he also *c*; and
1 Cor 1.24 to those who are *c*, both Jews and
7.15 It is to peace that God has *c* you.
Gal 1. 6 quickly deserting the one who *c* you in
5.13 you were *c* to freedom, brothers and
Heb 5. 4 it only when *c* by God, just as Aaron
11. 8 faith Abraham obeyed when he was *c*
Jas 2.23 and he was *c* the friend of God.
Jude 1 To those who are *c*, who are beloved in

CALM

Mt 8.26 and the sea; and there was a dead *c*.
Mk 4.39 wind ceased, and there was a dead *c*.
Lk 8.24 waves; they ceased, and there was a *c*.

CAMEL (CAMELS CAMEL'S)

Gen 24.10 the servant took ten of his master's *c*
Mt 3. 4 John wore clothing of *c* hair with a
19.24 easier for a *c* to go through the eye of a
23.24 You strain out a gnat but swallow a *c*!
Mk 10.25 It is easier for a *c* to go through the eye
Lk 18.25 easier for a *c* to go through the eye of a

CAMP

Num 2. 2 The Israelites shall *c* each in their
4. 5 When the *c* is to set out, Aaron and his
5. 2 put out of the *c* everyone who is

CANA

Jn 2. 1 there was a wedding in *C* in Galilee,
4.46 he came again to *C* in Galilee where he
21. 2 the Twin, Nathanael of *C* in Galilee,

CANAAN (CANAANITE)

Gen 9.22 Ham, the father of *C*, saw the
9.25 "Cursed be *C*; lowest of slaves shall he
11.31 the Chaldeans to go into the land of *C*;
12. 5 they set forth to go to the land of *C*.
42. 5 the famine had reached the land of *C*.
Ex 6. 4 with them, to give them the land of *C*,
Deut 32.49 view the land of *C*, which I am giving to
Ps 106. 38 whom they sacrificed to the idols of *C*;

Mt 15.22 a *C* woman from that region came out

CANCELED

Lk 7.42 they could not pay, he *c* the debts

CAPABLE

Prov 31.10 A *c* wife who can find? She is far more

CAPERNAUM

Mt 4.13 left Nazareth and made his home in *C*
8. 5 When he entered *C*, a centurion came
11.23 and you *C*, will you be exalted to
17.24 When they reaced *C*, the collectors of
Mk 2. 1 When he returned to *C* after some days,
Lk 7. 1 the hearing of the people, he entered *C*.
10.15 you *C*, will you be exalted to heaven?
Jn 4.46 a royal official whose son lay ill in *C*.
6.59 he was teaching in the synagogue at *C*.

CAPTIVE (CAPTIVES)

Gen 14.14 that his nephew had been taken *c*,
Deut 21.11 you see among the *c* a beautiful woman
Ezra 2. 1 province who came from those *c* exiles
Ps 68.18 the high mount, leading *c* in thy train,
Isa 20. 4 of Assyria lead away the Egyptians as *c*
52. 2 from your neck, O *c* daughter Zion!
Jer 13.17 the LORD's flock has been taken *c*.
20. 4 he shall carry them *c* to Babylon, and
Lk 21.24 be taken away as *c* among all nations;
Rom 7.23 making me *c* to the law of sin that
2 Cor 10. 5 and we take every thought *c* to obey
Eph 4. 8 on high he made captivity itself a *c*;
Rev 13.10 If you are to be taken *c*, into captivity

CAPTIVITY

Isa 46. 2 the burden, but themselves go into *c*.
Jer 15. 2 famine, and those destined for *c*, to *c*.
22.22 and your lovers shall go into *c*;
Ezek 39.23 Israel went into *c* for their iniquity,

CAPTORS

Ps 137. 3 our *c* asked us for songs, and our
Isa 14. 2 will take captive those who were their *c*,

CARE (CARED CARES)

Deut 32.10 *c* for him, guarded him as the apple of
Ps 8. 4 of them, mortals that you *c* for them?
142. 4 refuge remains to me; no one *c* for me.
Jer 30.17 an outcast: "It is Zion, no one *c* for her!"
Mk 4.38 do you not *c* that we are perishing?"
4.19 but the *c* of the world, and the lure of
Lk 8.14 they are choked by the *c* and riches and
10.34 him to an inn, and took *c* of him.
1 Cor 3.10 must choose with *c* how to build it.
12.25 but the members may have the same *c*
Heb 2. 6 them, or mortals, that you *c* for them?

CAREFUL

Deut 5.32 You must therefore be *c* to do as the
2 Kings 10.31 Jehu was not *c* to follow the law of the

CARELESS

Prov 14.16 the fool throws off restraint and is *c*.
Mt 12.36 have to give an account for every *c* word

CARMEL

Josh 12.22 one; the king of Jokneam in *C*, one;
1 Sam 15.12 "Saul went to *C*, where he set up a
25. 5 "Go up to *C*, and go to Nabal, and greet
1 Kings 18.19 all Israel assemble for me at Mount *C*,
Song 7. 5 Your head crowns you like *C*, and your
Isa 35. 2 to it, the majesty of *C* and Sharon.

CARPENTER (CARPENTER'S)

Isa 44.13 The *c* stretches a line, marks it out with
Mt 13.55 Is not this the *c* son? Is not his mother
Mk 6. 3 Is not this the *c*, the son of Mary and

CARRY (CARRIED CARRIES CARRYING)

Gen 50.25 comes to you, you shall *c* up my bones
Deut 1.31 your God *c* you, just as one *c* a child,
2 Kings 24.14 He *c* away all Jerusalem, all the
2 Chr 36. 7 Nebuchadnezzar also *c* some of the
Ps 49.17 when they die they will *c* nothing away;
Eccl 5.15 for their toil, which they may *c* away
Isa 46. 4 even when you turn gray I will *c* you.
63. 9 he lifted them up and *c* them all the
Jer 20. 5 and seize them, and *c* them to Babylon.
Mk 15.21 to *c* his cross; it was Simon of Cyrene,
Lk 14.27 Whoever does not *c* the cross and follow
24.51 from them and was *c* up into heaven.
Jn 19.17 *c* the cross by himself, he went out to
Acts 13.29 they had *c* out all that was written
2 Cor 4.10 always *c* in the body the death of Jesus,
Rev 17.17 to *c* out his purpose by agreeing to give

CASE

Num 27. 5 Moses brought their *c* before the LORD.
Job 13.18 I have indeed prepared my *c*; I know
23. 4 I would lay my *c* before him, and fill my
Prov 18.17 one who first states a *c* seems right,
25. 9 Argue your *c* with your neighbor
Isa 41.21 Set forth your *c*, says the LORD; bring
Jn 18.38 and told them, "I find no *c* against him.
19. 4 you know that I find no *c* against him."
19. 6 crucify him; I find no *c* against him."
Acts 25.14 Festus laid Paul's *c* before the king,

CAST (CASTING CASTS)

Gen 21.10 "*C* out this slave woman with her son;
2 Kings 21.14 I will *c* off the remnant of my heritage,
Ps 42. 5 Why are you *c* down, O my soul, and
43. 5 Why are you *c* down, O my soul, and
55.22 *C* your burden on the LORD, and he will
Prov 21.12 wicked; he *c* the wicked down to ruin.
Jer 7.15 I will *c* you out of my sight, just as I *c*
Mk 3.15 and to have authority to *c* out demons.
3.22 and by the ruler of the demons he *c* out
9.28 privately, "Why could we not *c* it out?"
Lk 9.49 we saw a man *c* out demons in your
11.15 "He *c* out demons by Beelzebul, the
Jn 21. 6 "*C* the net to the right side of the boat,

CASTLE

Lk 11.21 a strong man, fully armed, guards his *c*,

CATCH (CATCHES CATCHING CAUGHT)

Jer 5.26 they set a trap; they *c* human beings.
Lk 5.10 from now on you will be *c* people."
1 Cor 3.19 "He *c* the wise in their craftiness,
2 Cor 12. 2 ago was *c* up to the third heaven—
1 Thess 4.17 will be *c* up in the clouds together with

CATTLE

Gen 1.25 God made . . . the *c* of every kind, and
Job 18. 3 Why are we counted as *c*? Why are we

CAUSE

Job 5. 8 seek God, to God I would commit my *c*.
Ps 35. 7 without *c* they hid their net for me;
69. 4 my head those who hate me without *c*;
119.154 Plead my *c* and redeem me; give me life
140. 12 LORD maintains the *c* of the needy, and
Prov 23.11 strong; he will plead their *c* against you.
Isa 51.22 God who pleads the *c* of his people:
Jer 5.28 they do not judge with justice the *c* of
Jn 15.25 their law, 'They hated me without a *c*.'

CAVE (CAVES)

Gen 19.30 Zoar; so he lived in a *c* with his two
23.19 buried Sarah his wife in the *c* of the
25. 9 buried him in the *c* of Machpelah, in
49.29 Bury me with my ancestors—in the *c*
50.13 buried him in the *c* of the field at
1 Sam 13. 6 people hid themselves in *c* and in holes
22. 1 there and escaped to the *c* of Adullam;

1 Kings 18. 4 hundred prophets, hid them fifty to a *c*,
19. 9 At that place he came to a *c*, and spent
Isa 2.19 Enter the *c* of the rocks and the holes

CEASE (CEASED CEASES CEASING)

1 Sam 7. 8 "Do not *c* to cry out to the LORD our
12.23 against the LORD by *c* to pray for you;
Ezra 4.23 and by force and power made them *c*.
Job 3.17 There the wicked *c* from troubling, and
Ps 46. 9 He makes wars *c* to the end of the
Prov 22.10 goes out; quarreling and abuse will *c*.
Isa 1.16 *c* to do evil, learn to do good; seek
Lam 3.22 The steadfast love of the LORD never *c*,
Dan 9.27 he shall make sacrifice and offering *c*;
Jon 1.15 the sea; and the sea *c* from its raging.
Mk 6.51 into the boat with them and the wind *c*.
Rev 4. 8 Day and night without *c* they sing,

CEDAR (CEDARS)

Judg 9.15 bramble and devour the *c* of Lebanon.'
Ps 29. 5 voice of the LORD breaks the *c*; the LORD
Song 1.17 the beams of our house are *c*, our
Isa 2.13 against all the *c* of Lebanon, lofty and
9.10 down, but we will put *c* in their place."
Ezek 31. 3 Consider Assyria, a *c* of Lebanon, with

CELLAR

Lk 11.33 lighting a lamp puts it in a *c*, but on

CENSUS

Num 1. 2 Take a *c* of the whole congregation of
26. 2 Take a *c* of the whole congregation of
Acts 5.37 rose up at the time of the *c* and got

CENTURION

Mt 8. 5 a *c* came to him, appealing to him and
27.54 *c* and those with him, who were
Mk 15.39 Now when the *c*, who stood facing him,
Lk 7. 2 A *c* there had a slave whom he valued
23.47 When the *c* saw what had taken place,

CEPHAS

1 Cor 15. 5 that he appeared to *C*, then to the

CERTIFIED

Jn 3.33 testimony has *c* this, that God is true.

CHAFF

Job 21.18 wind, and like *c* that the storm carries
Ps 1. 4 are not so but are like *c* which the wind
35. 5 them be like *c* before the wind, with
Isa 17.13 they will flee far away, chased like *c* on
29. 5 the multitude of tyrants like flying *c*.
33.11 You conceive *c*, you bring forth stubble;
41.15 and you shall make the hills like *c*.
Dan 2.35 broken in pieces and became like the *c*
Hos 13. 3 like *c* that swirls from the threshing
Mt 3.12 but the *c* he will burn with . . . fire.
Lk 3.17 but the *c* he will burn with . . . fire.

CHAIN (CHAINS)

Mk 5. 3 restrain him anymore, even with a *c*;
Acts 26.29 become as I am—except for these *c*."
28.20 of Israel that I am bound with this *c*."
2 Tim 1.16 me and was not ashamed of my *c*;

CHANGE (CHANGED)

Gen 31.41 and you have *c* my wages ten times.
35. 2 purify yourselves, and *c* your clothes;
Ex 13.17 they may *c* their minds and return to
32.12 *c* your mind and do not bring disaster
Num 23.19 or a mortal, that he should *c* his mind.
Esth 9. 1 which had been *c* to a day when the
Ps 102. 26 a garment. You *c* them like clothing,
Jer 2.11 Has a nation *c* its gods, even though
13.23 Can Ethiopians *c* their skin or leopards
18. 8 turns from its evil, I will *c* my mind
26.13 the LORD will *c* his mind about the
26.19 did not the LORD *c* his mind about the
Dan 4.16 his mind be *c* from that of a human,
Hos 4. 7 me; they *c* their glory into shame.
Mal 3. 6 For I the LORD do not *c*; therefore you,
Mt 18. 3 unless you *c* and become like children,
21.29 not'; but later he *c* his mind and went.
1 Cor 15.51 We will not all die, but we will all be *c*,
Heb 7.21 Lord has sworn and will not *c* his mind,

CHANNELS

Job 28.10 They cut out *c* in the rocks, and their
Ps 18.15 the *c* of the sea were seen, and the

CHARACTER

Rom 5. 4 endurance produces *c*, and *c* produces
Heb 6.17 the unchangeable *c* of his purpose,

CHARGE (CHARGED CHARGES)

Gen 28. 1 Jacob and blessed him, and *c* him,
Deut 3.28 But *c* Joshua, and encourage and
33. 4 Moses *c* us with the law, as a
1 Kings 2. 1 to die drew near, he *c* Solomon his son,
Neh 5. 7 I brought *c* against the nobles and the
Ezra 1. 2 he has *c* me to build him a house at
Mt 27.37 over his head they put the *c* against
Mk 13.34 he leaves home and puts his slaves in *c*,
Lk 11.50 may be *c* with the blood of all
Acts 25. 7 bringing many serious *c* against him,
25.18 they did not *c* him with any of the
25.27 without indicating the *c* against
Rom 3. 9 for we have already *c* that all, both Jews
8.33 will bring any *c* against God's elect?

CHARIOT (CHARIOTS)

Josh 17.16 who live in the plain have *c* of iron,
2 Kings 2.11 a *c* of fire and horses of fire separated
6.17 of horses and *c* of fire round all Elisha.
Ps 20. 7 Some take pride in *c*, and some in
Isa 31. 1 who rely on horses, who trust in *c*
Joel 2. 5 As with the rumbling of *c*, they leap on
Nah 2. 4 The *c* race madly through the streets,
Hab 3. 8 you drove your horses, your *c* to victory?
Zech 6. 1 up and saw four *c* came out from

CHARM

Isa 47.11 upon you, which you cannot *c* away;

CHARMER (CHARMERS)

Ps 58. 5 it does not hear the voice of *c* or of the
Eccl 10.11 charmed, there is no advantage in a *c*.

CHASE (CHASED)

Lev 26. 7 You shall give *c* to your enemies, and
Deut 1.44 out against you and *c* you as bees do.
Neh 13.28 the Horonite; I *c* him away from me.

CHASTENING

Isa 26.16 poured out a prayer when your *c* was on

CHASTISE

Ps 39.11 You *c* mortals in punishment for sin,
Jer 30.11 I will *c* you in just measure, and I will
46.28 I will *c* you in just measure, and I will

CHEAT

Lev 25.17 You shall not *c* one another, but you

CHEDORLAOMER

Gen 14. 1 King Arioch of Ellasar, King *C* of Elam,

CHEEK (CHEEKS)

1 Kings 22.24 up to Micaiah, slapped him on the *c*,
2 Chr 18.23 up to Micaiah, slapped him on the *c*,
Song 1.10 Your *c* are comely with ornaments, your
Isa 50. 6 my *c* to those who pulled out the beard;
Lam 3.30 to give one's *c* to the smiter, and be
Mt 5.39 if anyone strikes you on the right *c*,

CHEER

Job 9.27 my sad countenance and be of good *c*,'

CHEERFUL
Prov 15.13 A glad heart makes a *c* countenance,
17.22 A *c* heart is a good medicine, but a
2 Cor 9. 7 compulsion, for God loves a *c* giver.

CHEERFULNESS
Rom 12. 8 in diligence; the compassionate, in *c*.

CHERISHED
Ps 66.18 If I had *c* iniquity in my heart, the Lord
Ezek 35. 5 Because you *c* an ancient enmity, and

CHERUB (CHERUBIM)
Gen 3.24 of the garden of Eden he placed the *c*,
Ex 25.18 You shall make two *c* of gold; you shall
26. 1 make them with *c* skillfully worked
2 Sam 22.11 He rode on a *c*, and flew; he was seen
1 Kings 6.23 he made two *c* of olivewood, each ten
Isa 37.16 Israel, who are enthroned above the *c*,
Ezek 9. 3 God of Israel had gone up from the *c*
10. 3 Now the *c* were standing on the south
28.14 With an anointed *c* as guardian I placed
Heb 9. 5 above it were the *c* of glory

CHEST
Zech 13. 6 "What are these wounds on your *c*?" the

CHEW (CHEWS)
Lev 11.26 or does not *c* the cud is unclean
Deut 14. 6 and *c* the cud, among the animals, you

CHILD
Ruth 4.16 Naomi took the *c* and laid him in her
1 Kings 3. 7 although I am only a little *c*; I do not
Ps 131. 2 like a weaned *c* with its mother; my
Prov 2. 1 My *c*, if you accept my words and
10. 1 A wise *c* makes a glad father but a
23.19 Hear, my *c*, and be wise, and direct
23.26 My *c*, give me your heart, and let your
27.11 Be wise, my *c*, and make my heart glad,
29.15 a mother is disgraced by a neglected *c*.
Isa 9. 6 For a *c* has been born for us, a son is
11. 6 together, and a little *c* shall lead them.
Ezek 18.20 A *c* shall not suffer for the iniquity of a
Hos 11. 1 Israel was a *c*, I loved him, and out of
Mt 1.18 found to be with *c* from the Holy Spirit.
2. 8 "Go and search diligently for the *c*; and
7. 9 who if your *c* asks for bread, will give a
18. 2 He called a *c*, whom he put among
Mk 9.36 he took a little *c* and put it among
13.12 brother to death, and a father his *c*,
Lk 1.41 greeting, the *c* leaped in her womb.
1.66 said, "What then will this *c* become?"
1.76 you, *c*, will be called the prophet of the
1.80 the *c* grew and became strong in spirit,
2.40 the *c* grew and became strong, filled
2.48 his mother said to him, "*C*, why have
11.11 if your *c* asks for a fish, will give a
8.54 by the hand and called out, "*C*, get up!"
9.47 thoughts, took a little *c* and put it by
1 Cor 13.11 I was a *c*, I spoke like a *c*, I thought
Gal 4. 7 but a *c*, and if a *c* then also an heir,
1 Tim 1. 2 To Timothy, my loyal *c* in the faith:
2 Tim 1. 2 To Timothy, my beloved *c*: Grace,
Heb 12. 5 "My *c*, do not regard lightly the
1 Jn 5. 1 who loves the parent loves the *c*.
Rev 12. 4 that he might devour her *c* as soon as it

CHILDBEARING
1 Tim 2.15 she will be saved through *c*, provided

CHILDHOOD
2 Tim 3.15 how from *c* you have known the sacred

CHILDLESS
Gen 15. 2 what will you give me, for I continue *c*,
Gal 4.27 "Rejoice, you *c* one, you who bear no

CHILDREN (CHILDREN'S)
Gen 18.19 chosen him, that he may charge his *c*
33. 5 "The *c* whom God has graciously given
Ex 12.26 when your *c* ask you, "What do you
Num 14.18 the iniquity of the parents upon the *c*
Deut 1.39 your *c*, who today do not yet know right
4.10 on the earth, and may teach their *c* so";
6. 7 Recite them to your *c* and talk about
11. 2 Remember today that it was not your *c*
12.25 go well with you and your *c* after you,
32.46 give them as a command to your *c*,
1 Kings 9. 6 you or your *c*, and do not keep my
2 Kings 14. 6 nor *c* be put to death for the parents;
2 Chr 6.16 if only your *c* keep to their way, to walk
25. 4 he did not put their *c* to death,
Job 8. 4 If your *c* sinned against him, he
Ps 89.30 If his *c* forsake my law and and do not
103. 17 fear him, and his righteousness to *c c*,
128. 3 your *c* will be like olive shoots around
128. 6 May you see your *c c*! Peace be upon
Prov 4. 1 Listen, *c*, to a father's instruction, and
13.22 good leave an inheritance to their *c c*,
13.24 Those who spare the rod hate their *c*,
17.25 Foolish *c* are a grief to their father and
19.26 their mother are *c* who cause shame
20.11 Even *c* make themselves known by their
22. 6 Train *c* in the right way, and when old,
29.17 Discipline your *c*, and they will give you
31.28 Her *c* rise up and call her happy; her
Isa 1. 2 I reared *c* and brought them up, but
8.18 I and the *c* whom the LORD has given
30. 9 rebellious people, faithless *c*, *c* who will
49.20 The *c* born in the time of your
54.13 All your *c* shall be taught by the LORD,
66. 8 as Zion was in labor she delivered her *c*.
Jer 31.29 grapes, and the *c* teeth are set on edge."
Ezek 5.10 midst, and *c* shall eat their parents;
18. 2 grapes, and the *c* teeth are set on edge"?
23.39 they had slaughtered their *c* for their
Hos 1.10 be said to them, "*C* of the living God."
Joel 1. 3 Tell your *c* of it, and let your *c* tell their
Mal 4. 6 will turn the hearts of parents to their *c*
Mt 2.16 and he sent and killed all the *c*
3. 9 these stones to raise up *c* to Abraham.
5. 9 for they will be called *c* of God.
7.11 know how to give good gifts to your *c*,
17.26 Jesus said to him, "Then the *c* are free.
19.13 Then little *c* were being brought to him
19.14 "Let the little *c* come to me, and do not
21.15 heard the *c* crying out in the temple,
Mk 7.27 said to her, "Let the *c* be fed first, for it
10.14 "Let the little *c* come to me; do not
Lk 1.17 to turn the hearts of parents to their *c*,
3. 8 is able from these stones to raise up *c*
6.35 and you will be *c* of the Most High;
7.32 like *c* sitting in the marketplace and
16. 8 the *c* of this age are more shrewd in
18.16 "Let the little *c* come to me, and do not
Jn 1.12 he gave power to become *c* of God,
8.39 "If you were Abraham's *c*, you would be
12.36 so that you may become *c* of light."
13.33 Little *c*, I am with you only a little
Acts 2.39 promise is for you, for your *c*, and for
Rom 8.14 led by the Spirit of God are *c* of God.
8.16 we are *c* of God, and if *c*, then heirs,
9. 8 but the *c* of the promise are counted
1 Cor 7.14 Otherwise, your *c* would be unclean,
14.20 do not be *c* in your thinking; rather, be
2 Cor 12.14 *c* ought not to lay up for their parents,
Gal 3.26 Jesus you are all *c* of God through faith.
4.28 my friends, are *c* of promise, like Isaac.
Eph 1. 5 adoption as his *c* through Jesus Christ,
2. 3 and we were by nature *c* of wrath,
4.14 We must no longer be *c*, tossed to and
6. 1 *C*, obey your parents in the Lord, for
Phil 2.15 *c* of God without blemish in the midst

Col 3.20 *C*, obey your parents in everything, for
1 Thess 5. 5 you are all *c* of light and *c* of the day;
1 Pet 1.14 Like obedient *c*, do not be conformed
1 Jn 2.18 *C*, it is the last hour! As you have heard
3. 1 us, that we should be called *c* of God;
2 Jn 4 some of your *c* walking in the truth,

CHOKE (CHOKED)

Mt 13.22 lure of wealth *c* the word, and it yields
Mk 4. 7 thorns, the thorns grew up and *c* it,
4.19 other things come in and *c* the word,
Lk 8. 7 and the thorns grew with it and *c* it.
8.14 their way, they are *c* by the cares and

CHOOSE (CHOOSES CHOOSING)

Num 16. 7 man whom the LORD *c* shall be the holy
17. 5 staff of the man whom I *c* shall sprout;
Deut 12. 5 God will *c* out of all your tribes as his
14.24 LORD your God will *c* to set his name
17.15 a king whom the LORD your God will *c*.
30.19 *C* life so that you and your descendants
Josh 24.15 *c* this day whom you will serve, whether
1 Sam 17. 8 *C* a man for yourselves, and let him
2 Sam 24.12 Three things I offer you; *c* one of them,
1 Chr 21.10 Three things I offer you; *c* one of them,
Ps 16. 4 who *c* another god multiply their
25.12 will teach them the way they should *c*.
65. 4 Happy are those whom you *c* and bring
Prov 1.29 and did not *c* the fear of the LORD,
Isa 7.15 how to refuse the evil and *c* the good.
58. 5 Is such the fast that I *c*, a day to
Zech 1.17 comfort Zion and again *c* Jerusalem.
Mt 20.15 to do what I *c* with what belongs
Mk 1.40 he said to him, "If you *c*, you can make
Jn 15.16 You did not *c* me, but I chose you. And
Acts 15.25 to *c* representatives and send them to
Heb 11.25 daughter, *c* rather to share ill-treatment

CHORAZIN

Mt 11.21 "Woe to you, *C*! Woe to you, Bethsaida!
Lk 10.13 "Woe to you, *C*! Woe to you, Bethsaida!

CHOSE (CHOSEN) (v)

Gen 13.11 So Lot *c* for himself all the plain of the
18.19 No, for I have *c* him, that he may
Ex 18.25 Moses *c* able men from all Israel and
Num 1.16 were the ones *c* from the congregation,
Deut 4.37 your ancestors, he *c* their descendants
7. 7 the LORD set his heart on you and *c* you,
18. 5 LORD your God has *c* Levi out of all your
1 Sam 2.28 I *c* him out of all the tribes of Israel to
10.24 see the one one whom the LORD has *c*?
1 Kings 3. 8 midst of the people whom you have *c*,
11.13 the sake of Jerusalem, which I have *c*."
2 Kings 23.27 I will reject this city that I have *c*,
1 Chr 28.10 LORD has *c* you to build a house as the
2 Chr 29.11 for the LORD has *c* you to stand in his
Ps 47. 4 He *c* our heritage for us, the pride of
78.68 But he *c* the tribe of Judah, Mount
119. 30 I have *c* the way of faithfulness; I set
119.173 to help me, for I have *c* your precepts.
Prov 22. 1 A good name is to be *c* rather than
Isa 41. 8 my servant, Jacob, whom I have *c*,
43.10 my servant whom I have *c*, so that you
49. 7 the Holy One of Israel, who has *c* you."
66. 3 These have *c* their own ways, and in
Jer 33.24 "The two families that the LORD *c* have
Hag 2.23 you like a signet ring; for I have *c* you,
Mt 12.18 Here is my servant, whom I have *c*, my
22.14 For many are called, but few are *c*."
Lk 6.13 and *c* twelve of them, whom he also
14. 7 how the guests *c* the places of honor,
Jn 13.18 I know whom I have *c*. But it is to
Acts 6. 5 they *c* Stephen, a man full of faith and
9.15 instrument whom I have *c* to bring my
22.14 ancestors has *c* you to know his will,
1 Cor 1.27 God *c* what is foolish in the world to
1 Cor 12.18 members in the body, each one as he *c*.
Eph 1. 4 just as he *c* us in Christ before the
1 Thess 1. 4 beloved by God, that he has *c* you,
2 Thess 2.13 God *c* you as the first fruits for
1 Pet 1. 2 who have been *c* and destined by God

CHOSEN (n and adj)

1 Chr 16.13 Israel, children of Jacob, his *c* ones.
Ps 89. 3 "I have made a covenant with my *c* one,
105. 43 out with joy, his *c* ones with singing.
106. 23 had not Moses, his *c* one, stood in the
Isa 42. 1 my *c*, in whom my soul delights;
45. 4 Jacob, and Israel my *c*, I call you
65. 9 my *c* shall inherit it, and my servants
65.22 my *c* shall long enjoy the work of their
Lk 9.35 said, "This is my Son, my *C*; listen to
Col 3.12 As God's *c* ones, holy and beloved,
1 Pet 2. 9 you are a *c* race, a royal priesthood, a

CHRISTIAN (CHRISTIANS)

Acts 11.26 that the disciples were first called "*C*."
26.28 quickly persuading me to become a *C*?"
1 Pet 4.16 Yet if any of you suffers as a *C*, do not

CHURCH (CHURCHES)

Mt 16.18 on this rock I will build my *c*, and the
18.17 to listen to them, tell it to the *c*;
Acts 9.31 the *c* throughout Judea, Galilee, and
11.22 News of this came to the ears of the *c*
12. 1 upon some who belonged to the *c*.
12. 5 Peter was kept in prison, the *c* prayed
16. 5 So the *c* were strengthened in the faith
Rom 16. 5 Greet also the *c* in their house.
1 Cor 10.32 to Jews or to Greeks or to the *c* of God,
12.28 God has appointed in the *c* first
14. 4 but those who prophesy build up the *c*.
15. 9 an apostle, because I persecuted the *c*
2 Cor 8. 1 has been granted to the *c* of Macedonia;
Eph 1.22 head over all things for the *c*, which is
3.21 to him be glory in the *c* and in Christ
5.24 Just as the *c* is subject to Christ, so
1 Tim 3. 5 how can he take care of God's *c*?
5.16 let the *c* not be burdened, so that it can
Philem 2 soldier, and to the *c* in your house:
3 Jn 10 to do so and expels them from the *c*.
Rev 1. 4 John to the seven *c* that are in Asia:
2.23 all the *c* will know that I am the one

CIRCLE

Prov 8.27 there, when he drew a *c* on the face of
Isa 40.22 is he who sits above the *c* of the earth,

CIRCUMCISE (CIRCUMCISED)

Gen 17.10 you: Every male among you shall be *c*.
34.24 and every male was *c*, all who went out
Deut 10.16 *C*, then, the foreskin of your heart, and
30. 6 God will *c* your heart and the heart of
Josh 5. 3 made flint knives and *c* the Israelites
Jer 4. 4 *C* yourselves to the LORD, remove the
Jn 7.22 and you *c* a man on the sabbath.
Acts 11. 2 the *c* believers criticized him,
15. 1 "Unless you are *c* according to the
Gal 2. 3 with me, was not compelled to be *c*,
Col 2.11 were *c* with a spiritual circumcision,

CIRCUMCISION

Ex 4.26 she said, "A bridegroom of blood by *c*."
Rom 2.26 their uncircumcision be regarded as *c*?
4.11 He received the sign of *c* as a seal of
1 Cor 7.19 *C* is nothing, and uncircumcision is
Gal 5. 6 in Christ Jesus neither *c* nor
Eph 2.11 by those who are called "the *c*"—

CISTERN (CISTERNS)

Prov 5.15 Drink water from your own *c*, flowing
Jer 2.13 water, and dug out *c* for themselves,
38. 6 and threw him into the *c* of Malchiah,

CITIZENSHIP
Phil 3.20 But our *c* is in heaven, and it is from

CITY (CITIES)
Num 35. 6 the Levites shall include six *c* of refuge,
Deut 19. 2 you shall set apart three *c* in the land
Josh 6. 3 You shall march around the *c*, all the
20. 2 'Appoint the *c* of refuge, of which I
2 Kings 25. 4 a breach was made in the *c* wall; the
Ps 46. 4 whose streams make glad the *c* of God,
48. 1 to be praised in the *c* of our God.
Prov 11.10 blessing of the upright a *c* is exalted,
Eccl 9.14 a little *c* with few people in it. A great
Isa 1.26 shall be called the *c* of righteousness,
Jer 39. 2 the month, a breach was made in the *c*.
Lam 1. 1 How lonely sits the *c* that once was full
Ezek 33.21 came to me and said, "The *c* has fallen."
Dan 9.19 because your *c* and your people bear
Zech 8. 3 Jerusalem shall be called the faithful *c*,
Mt 5.14 world. A *c* built on a hill cannot be hid.
Mk 1.33 the whole *c* was gathered around the
Lk 19.19 said to him, 'And you, rule over five *c*.'
Acts 17.16 to see that the *c* was full of idols.
Heb 11.10 he looked forward to the *c* that has
Rev 3.12 God, and the name of the *c* of my God,
21. 2 the holy *c*, new Jerusalem, coming
21.15 of gold to measure the *c* and its gates

CLAIMS
1 Cor 14.37 Anyone who *c* to be a prophet, or to

CLAN
Num 27. 4 of our father be taken away from his *c*

CLAY
Job 10. 9 that you have fashioned me like *c*;
13.12 ashes, your defenses are defenses of *c*.
33. 6 are; I too was formed from a piece of *c*.
Isa 29.16 Shall the potter be regarded as the *c*?
45. 9 Does the *c* say to the one who fashions
64. 8 we are the *c*, and you are our potter; we
Jer 18. 6 Just like the *c* in the potter's hand, so

CLEAN
Gen 7. 2 with you seven pairs of all *c* animals,
Deut 14.11 You may eat any *c* birds.
2 Kings 5.14 the flesh of a young boy, and he was *c*.
Job 14. 4 Who can bring a *c* thing out of an
15.14 What are mortals that they can be *c*? Or
25. 4 How can one born of woman be *c*?
33. 9 You say, "I am *c*, without transgression;
Ps 24. 4 Those who have *c* hands and pure
73.13 in vain I have kept my heart *c* and
Prov 20. 9 Who can say, "I have made my heart *c*;
Isa 1.16 Wash yourselves; make yourselves *c*;
Jer 13.27 long will it be before you are made *c*?
Mt 8. 2 if you choose, you can make me *c*."
23.25 you *c* the outside of the cup and of the
Mk 1.40 "If you choose, you can make me *c*."
Lk 5.12 if you choose, you can make me *c*."
11.41 and see, everything will be *c* for you.
17.14 And as they went they were made *c*
Acts 10.15 "What God has made *c*, you must not
11. 9 'What God has made *c*, you must not
Rom 14.20 Everything is indeed *c*, but it is wrong

CLEANNESS
Ps 18.20 according to the *c* of my hands he

CLEANSE (CLEANSED CLEANSES CLEANSING)
Lev 14.11 The priest who *c* shall set the person to
Num 8. 6 from among the Israelites and *c* them.
Deut 32.43 hate him, and *c* the land for his people.
2 Chr 29.16 part of the house of the LORD to *c* it,
Job 9.30 with soap and *c* my hands with lye,
Ps 51. 2 my iniquity, and *c* me from my sin.
Prov 20.30 Blows that wound *c* away evil; beatings
Isa 4. 4 and *c* the bloodstains of Jerusalem from
Jer 33. 8 I will *c* them from all the guilt of their
Ezek 22.24 You are a land that is not *c*, not rained
36.25 from all your idols I will *c* you. A new
37.23 and will *c* them. Then they shall be my
Dan 11.35 they may be refined, purified, and *c*,
Mt 10. 8 the sick, raise the dead, *c* the lepers,
Lk 4.27 none of them was *c*, except Naaman
Jn 15. 3 You have already been *c* by the word
2 Cor 7. 1 let us *c* ourselves from every defilement
Eph 5.26 to make her holy by *c* her with the
Jas 4. 8 *C* your hands, you sinners, and purify

CLEAR (CLEARED)
Gen 44.16 can we speak? How can we *c* ourselves?
Ps 19.12 their errors? *C* me from hidden faults.
80. 9 You *c* the ground for it; it took deep
Lk 3.17 to *c* his threshing floor, and to gather

CLEFT-FOOTED
Lev 11. 3 and is *c* and chews the cud—such you

CLING (CLINGS)
Gen 2.24 his father and mother and *c* to his wife,
Job 19.20 My bones *c* to my skin and flesh, and I
Ps 119. 25 My soul *c* to the dust; revive me
119. 31 I *c* to your decrees, O LORD; let me not
Rev 12.11 for they did not *c* to life even in the

CLOAK (CLOAKS)
Ruth 3. 9 spread your *c* over your servant, for you
1 Sam 24. 4 stealthily cut off a corner of Saul's *c*.
Ezek 16. 8 and I spread the edge of my *c* over you,
Mt 5.40 and take your coat, give your *c* as well;
21. 8 A very large crowd spread their *c* on the
Mk 2.21 a pice of unshrunk cloth on an old *c*;
5.27 him in the crowd and touched his *c*.
6.56 might touch even the fringe of his *c*;
11. 8 Many people spread their *c* on the road,
Lk 19.36 kept spreading their *c* on the road.
2 Tim 4.13 When you come, bring the *c* that I left

CLOTH
Isa 64. 6 our righteous deeds are like a flthy *c*.
Mt 9.16 a piece of unshrunk *c* on an old cloak,
Lk 2. 7 son and wrapped him in bands of *c*,

CLOTHE (CLOTHED CLOTHES)
Gen 3.21 for the man and his wife, and *c* them.
2 Chr 28.15 with the booty they *c* all that were
Job 29.14 I put on righteousness, and it *c* me; my
Ps 30.11 off my sackcloth and *c* me with joy,
Isa 22.21 will *c* him with your robe and bind your
Zech 3. 5 a clean turban on his head and *c* him
Mt 6.30 if God so *c* the grass of the field, which
6.29 all his glory was not *c* like one of these.
Mk 5.15 saw the demoniac sitting there, *c* and in
15.17 they *c* him in a purple cloak; and after
Lk 8.35 feet of Jesus, *c* and in his right mind;
12.27 all his glory was not *c* like one of these.
12.28 if God so *c* the grass of the field, which
2 Cor 5. 2 to be *c* with our heavenly dwelling—
Eph 4.24 and to *c* yourselves with a new self,
Col 3.12 *c* yourselves with compassion, kindness,
Rev 16.15 is the one who stays awake and is *c*,

CLOTHES (CLOTHING)
Deut 8. 4 The *c* on your back did not wear out
Job 31.19 I have seen anyone perish for lack of *c*,
Ps 22.18 they divide my *c* among themselves, and
Prov 25.20 Like a moth in *c* or a worm in wood,
27.26 lambs will provide your *c*, and the goats
Mt 6.25 than food, and the body more than *c*?
7.15 prophets, who come to you in sheep's *c*
17. 2 sun, and his *c* became dazzling white.
27.35 they divided his *c* among themselves by
Mk 15.24 divided his *c* among them, casting lots
Lk 8.44 touched the fringe of his *c*, and
23.34 doing. And they cast lots to divide his *c*.

Jn 19.24 themselves, and for my *c* they cast lots."
Acts 9.39 and other *c* that Dorcas had made
1 Pet 3. 3 by wearing gold ornaments or fine *c*;

CLOUD (CLOUDS)

Gen 9.13 I set my bow in the *c*, and it shall be a
Ex 13.21 a pillar of *c* by day, to lead them along
40.34 Then the *c* covered the tent of meeting,
Num 9.15 the *c* covered the tabernacle, the tent of
12. 5 LORD came down in a pillar of *c*, and
Deut 31.15 the pillar of *c* stood at the entrance to
Isa 4. 5 over its places of assembly a *c* by day
Mt 17. 5 suddenly a bright *c* overshadowed them,
Mk 9. 7 Then a *c* overshadowed them, and from
Acts 1. 9 up, and a *c* took him out of their sight.
1 Cor 10. 2 all were baptized into Moses in the *c*

COAL (COALS)

Ps 18. 8 glowing *c* flamed forth from him.
140. 10 Let burning *c* fall on them! Let them be
Prov 25.22 you will heap *c* of fire on their heads,
Isa 6. 6 seraphs flew to me, holding a live *c* that
Rom 12.20 you will heap burning *c* on their heads."

COAT (COATS)

Mt 5.40 sue you and take your *c*, give your cloak
Lk 3.11 "Whoever has two *c* must share with
6.29 takes away your *c* do not withhold even
Acts 22.20 and keeping the *c* of those who killed

COAX

Judg 14.15 said to Samson's wife, "*C* your husband
16. 5 "*C* him, and find out what makes his

COCK

Mt 26.74 the man!" At that moment the *c* crowed.
Mk 14.30 before the *c* crows twice, you will deny
14.68 into the forecourt. Then the *c* crowed.
Lk 22.34 Peter, the *c* will not crow this day, until
22.60 he was still speaking, the *c* crowed.
Jn 13.38 before the *c* crows, you will have denied

COIN (COINS)

Mt 17.27 you open its mouth you will find a *c*;
Mk 12.42 came and put in two small copper *c*,
Lk 21. 2 a poor widow put in two small copper *c*.

COLD

Mt 24.12 the love of many will grow *c*.
Rev 3.16 are lukewarm, and neither *c* nor hot,

COLLECT (COLLECTED)

Gen 47.14 Joseph *c* all the money to be found in
Mt 13.41 they will *c* out of his kingdom all

COLLECTION

1 Cor 16. 1 concerning the *c* for the saints: you

COLT

Zech 9. 9 and riding on a donkey, on a *c*, the foal
Mk 11. 2 you will find tied there a *c* that has
Lk 19.30 will find tied there a *c* that has never

COME

Gen 24.31 "*C* in, O blessed of the LORD. Why do
Num 10.29 *c* with us, and we will treat you well;
Ps 66.16 *C* and hear, all you who fear God, and I
100. 2 *C* into his presence with singing.
Prov 2.19 those who go to her never *c* back, nor
25. 7 for it is better to be told, "*C* up here,"
Song 7.11 *C*, my beloved, let us go forth into the
Isa 1.18 *C* now, let us argue it out, says the
2. 3 *C*, let us go up to the mountain of the
2. 5 of Jacob, *c*, let us walk in the light
26.20 *C*, my people, enter your chambers, and
35. 4 recompense. He will *c* and save you."
55. 1 you that have no money, *c*, buy and eat!
Jer 2.27 their trouble they say, "*C* and save us!"
Hos 6. 1 "*C*, let us return to the LORD; for it is he
Mic 4. 2 "*C*, let us go up to the mountain of the
Mal 3. 1 you seek will suddenly *c* to his temple;
Mt 6.10 Your kingdom *c*, Your will be done, on
8. 9 to another, '*C*,' and he *c*, and to my
11. 3 "Are you the one who is to *c*, or are we
11.28 *C* to me, all you that are weary and are
24. 5 For many will *c* in my name, saying, 'I
Mk 6.31 "*C* away to a deserted place all by
13. 6 Many will *c* in my name and say, 'I am
Jn 1.39 He said to them, "*C* and see." They came
4.29 "*C* and see a man who told me
7.28 I am from. I have not *c* on my own.
7.37 "Let anyone who is thirsty *c* to me, and
11.43 cried with a loud voice, "Lazarus, *c* out!"
Acts 1.11 will *c* in the same way as you saw him
16. 9 "*C* over to Macedonia and help us."
Rom 15.23 years, to *c* to you when I go to Spain.
1 Cor 16.22 has no love for the Lord. Our Lord, *c*!
2 Tim 4. 9 Do your best to *c* to me soon, for
Heb 12.22 But you have *c* to Mount Zion and to
Rev 18. 4 "*C* out of her, my people, so that you
22.17 Spirit and the Bride say, "*C*." And let

COMES (CAME COMING)

1 Sam 28.13 a divine being *c* up out of the ground."
2 Sam 19.15 king *c* back to the Jordan; and Judah *c*
Ps 50. 3 God *c*, and does not keep silence,
96.13 for he is *c*, he is *c* to judge the earth.
118. 26 Blessed is the one who *c* in the name of
Isa 63. 1 "Who is this that *c* from Edom, from
Dan 6. 6 and satraps conspired and *c* to the king
Mal 4. 1 the day is *c*, burning like an oven, when
4. 5 the great and terrible day of the LORD *c*.
Mt 21. 9 Blessed is the one who *c* in the name of
23.39 'Blessed is the one who *c* in the name
24.42 not know on what day your Lord is *c*.
25.31 "When the Son of Man *c* in his glory,
26.64 of Power and *c* on the clouds of heaven."
Mk 3.13 whom he wanted, and they *c* to him.
8.38 also be ashamed when he *c* in the glory
10.45 Son of Man *c* not to be served but to
13.26 they will see the Son of man *c* in clouds
14.62 and '*c* with the clouds of heaven.' "
Lk 12.40 Son of Man is *c* at an unexpected hour."
13.35 the one who *c* in the name of the Lord!' "
21.27 'Son of Man *c* in a cloud' with power
Jn 6.35 "Whoever *c* to me will never be hungry,
6.37 who *c* to me I will never drive away;
12.13 Blessed is the one who *c* in the name of
14.18 not leave you orphaned; I am *c* to you.
1 Cor 11.26 proclaim the Lord's death until he *c*.
2 Cor 13. 1 This is the third time I am *c* to you.
Heb 10.37 the one who is *c* one will come and
Jude 14 "See, the Lord is *c* with ten thousands
Rev 1. 7 Look! he is *c* with the clouds; every eye
3.11 I am *c* soon; hold fast to what you have,
22.12 I am *c* soon, my reward is with me, to
22.20 these things says, "Surely I am *c* soon."

COMELY

Song 6. 4 my love, *c* as Jerusalem, terrible as an

COMFORT (n)

Ps 119. 50 This is my *c* in my distress, that your
2 Cor 7.13 to you before God. In this we find *c*.
2 Thess 2.16 grace gave us eternal *c* and good hope,

COMFORT (COMFORTED COMFORTS)

Gen 24.67 So Isaac was *c* after his mother's death.
37.35 sought to *c* him; but he refused to be *c*,
Job 2.11 together to go and console and *c* him.
21.34 will you *c* me with empty nothings?
Ps 23. 4 your rod and your staff—they *c* me.
77. 2 wearying; my soul refuses to be *c*.
86.17 you, LORD, have helped me and *c* me.
Isa 12. 1 your anger turned away, and you *c* me.
40. 1 *C*, O *c* my people, says your God. Speak

Isa 49.13 For the LORD has *c* his people, and will
51. 3 For the LORD will *c* Zion; he will *c* all
51.12 I am he who *c* you; why then are you
52. 9 for the LORD has *c* his people, he has
61. 2 of our God; to *c* all who mourn;
66.13 As a mother *c* her child, so I will *c* you;
Lam 1. 2 all her lovers she has no one to *c* her;
Lk 16.25 but now he is *c* here, and you are in

COMFORTERS

Job 16. 2 such things; miserable *c* are you all.
Ps 69.20 was none; and for *c*, but I found none.
Nah 3. 7 her? Where shall I seek *c* for you?

COMING (n)

Mt 24. 3 what will be the sign of your *c* and of
24.27 so will be the *c* of the Son of Man.
24.37 so will be the *c* of the Son of Man.
Lk 12.45 'My master is delayed in *c*.' and if he
1 Cor 15.23 fruits, then at his *c* those who belong to
1 Thess 2.19 boasting before our Lord Jesus at his *c*?
3.13 at the *c* of our Lord Jesus with all his
4.15 who are alive, who are left until the *c* of
5.23 and blameless at the *c* of our Lord
2 Thess 2. 1 As to the *c* of our Lord Jesus Christ and
Jas 5. 7 beloved, until the *c* of the Lord.
2 Pet 1.16 to you the power and *c* of our Lord
3. 4 "Where is the promise of his *c*? For ever
1 Jn 2.28 be put to shame before him at his *c*.

COMMAND (n)

Num 9.18 At the *c* of the LORD the Israelites would
20.24 you rebelled against my *c* at the waters
22.18 I could not go beyond the *c* of the LORD
Ps 68.11 The Lord gives the *c*; great is the
Eccl 8. 2 Keep the king's *c* because of your
1 Cor 7.10 To the married I give *c* —not I but the
14.37 what I am writing to you is a *c* of the

COMMAND (COMMANDED COMMANDS)

Gen 2.16 God *c* the man, "You may freely eat of
6.22 did this; he did all that God *c* him.
Ex 7. 2 You shall speak all that I *c* you, and
39.32 just as the LORD had *c* Moses.
Lev 8.36 did all the things that the LORD *c*
Deut 4.13 his covenant, which he *c* you to
28. 8 LORD will *c* the blessing upon you in
Josh 1. 9 I hereby *c* you: Be strong and
11.15 As the LORD *c* . . . Moses, so Moses *c*
Ps 33. 9 it came to be; he *c*, and it stood firm.
148. 5 LORD, for he *c* and they were created.
Jer 1. 7 and you shall speak whatever I *c* you.
11. 4 to my voice, and do all that I *c* you.
26. 2 to them all the words that I *c* you;
Mt 4. 6 'He will *c* his angels concerning you,'
28.20 them to obey everything I have *c* you.
Lk 8.25 this, that he *c* even the winds and the
9.54 do you want us to *c* fire to come down
Jn 15.14 You are my friends if you do what I *c*
1 Cor 9.14 Lord *c* that those who proclaim the
1 Tim 6.17 age are rich, *c* them not to be haughty,

COMMANDER (COMMANDERS COMMANDER'S)

Gen 21.22 with Phicol the *c* of his army, said to
Deut 20. 9 then the *c* shall take charge of them.
33.21 for there a *c* allotment was reserved; he
Josh 5.14 as *c* of the army of the LORD have I now

COMMANDMENT (COMMANDMENTS)

Ex 34.28 the words of the covenant, the ten *c*.
Lev 27.34 These are the *c* that the LORD gave to
Deut 4.13 you to observe, that is, the ten *c*;
1 Kings 2. 3 keeping his statutes, his *c*, his
Ezra 9.14 shall we break your *c* again and
Ps 119.151 near, O LORD, and all your *c* are true.
Prov 4. 4 fast to my words; keep my *c*, and live;
13.13 who respect the *c* will be rewarded.
Eccl 12.13 Fear God, and keep his *c*; for that is the
Mt 19.17 you wish to enter into life, keep the *c*."
Jn 13.34 I give you a new *c*, that you love one
Rom 7.12 law is holy, and the *c* is holy and just
1 Jn 2. 7 no new *c*, but an old *c* that you have
5. 3 his *c*. And his *c* are not burdensome,
2 Jn 5 though I were writing you a new *c*, but

COMMEND (COMMENDED COMMENDS)

Prov 12. 8 One is *c* for good sense, but a perverse
Eccl 8.15 I *c* enjoyment, for there is nothing
Lk 16. 8 his master *c* the dishonest manager
23.46 "Father, into your hands I *c* my spirit!"
Acts 20.32 now I *c* you to God and to the message
Rom 16. 1 I *c* to you our sister Phoebe, a deacon
2 Cor 3. 1 Are we beginning to *c* ourselves again?
10.12 with some of those who *c* themselves.
10.18 approved, but those whom the Lord *c*.

COMMISSION

1 Cor 9.17 of my own will, I am entrusted with a *c*.
Eph 3. 2 of the *c* of God's grace that was given
Col 1.25 became its servant according to God's *c*

COMMIT (COMMITTED)

Josh 22.31 you have not *c* this treachery against
1 Kings 15. 3 he *c* all the sins that his father did
Neh 2.18 they *c* themselves to the common good.
Job 5. 8 God, and to God I would *c* my cause.
Ps 31. 5 Into your hand I *c* my spirit; you have
37. 5 *C* your way to the LORD; trust in him
Prov 16. 3 *C* your work to the LORD, and your plans
Jer 20.12 them, for to you have I *c* my cause.
Ezek 17.20 for the treason he has *c* against me.
Dan 9. 7 of the treachery that they have *c*

COMMON

Acts 2.44 were together and had all things in *c*;
4.32 everything they owned was held in *c*.
1 Cor 10.13 overtaken you that is not *c* to everyone.

COMMONWEALTH

Eph 2.12 Christ, being aliens from the *c* of Israel,

COMMUNE

Ps 77. 6 I *c* with my heart in the night; I

COMMUNION

2 Cor 13.13 and the *c* of the Holy Spirit be with all

COMMUNITY

Jn 21.23 rumor spread in the *c* that this disciple

COMPANION (COMPANIONS)

Josh 14. 8 my *c* who went up with me made the
Judg 14.20 Samson's wife was given to his *c*, who
Job 6.15 My *c* are treacherous like a torrent-bed,
Ps 119. 63 I am a *c* of all who fear you, of those
Prov 13.20 wise, but the *c* of fools suffers harm.
28. 7 but *c* of gluttons shame their parents.
Song 8.13 my *c* are listening for your voice;
Mal 2.14 though she is your *c* and your wife by
Phil 4. 3 Yes, and I ask you, my loyal *c*, help

COMPANY

Ps 50.18 see one, and you keep *c* with adulterers.
111. 1 in the *c* of the upright, in the
Jer 15.17 I did not sit in the *c* of merrymakers,
1 Cor 15.33 be deceived: "Bad *c* ruins good morals."

COMPARE (COMPARED)

Ps 40. 5 none can *c* with you. Were I to proclaim
89. 6 who in the skies can be *c* to the LORD?
Isa 46. 5 and *c* me, as though we were alike?
Mt 11.16 to what will I *c* this generation? It is
2 Cor 10.12 We do not dare to classify or *c* ourselves

COMPASSION

Deut 13.17 show you *c*, and in his *c* multiply you,
Judg 21. 6 Israelites had *c* for Benjamin their kin,

Judg 21.15 people had *c* on Benjamin because the
2 Kings 13.23 gracious to them and had *c* on them;
2 Chr 30. 9 kindred and your children will find *c*
36.15 he had *c* on his people and on his
Ps 103. 13 As a father has *c* on his children, so the
135. 14 his people, and have *c* on his servants.
Isa 14. 1 the LORD will have *c* on Jacob and will
54. 7 you, but with great *c* I will gather you.
Jer 12.15 them up, I will again have *c* on them,
Dan 1. 9 allowed Daniel to receive favor and *c*
Mic 7.19 He will again have *c* upon us; he will
Zech 12.10 I will pour out a spirit of *c* and
Mt 9.36 he saw the crowds, he had *c* for them,
14.14 and he had *c* for them and cured their
15.32 "I have *c* for the crowd, because they
20.34 Moved with *c*, Jesus touched their eyes.
Mk 6.34 he saw a great crowd; and he had *c* on
8. 2 "I have *c* for the crowd, because they
Lk 7.13 he had *c* for her and said to her, and
15.20 father saw him and was filled with *c*;
Heb 10.34 For you had *c* for those who were in

COMPASSIONATE

Ex 22.27 cries out to me, I will listen, for I am *c*.
Ps 78.38 he, being *c*, forgave their iniquity, and
Jas 5.11 Lord, how the Lord is *c* and merciful.

COMPEL (COMPELLED)

Mt 27.32 they *c* this man to carry his cross.
Lk 14.23 and lanes, and *c* the people to come in,
Gal 2. 3 with me, was not *c* to be circumcised,
2.14 Jew, how can you *c* the Gentiles to live

COMPETE

Jer 12. 5 you, how will you *c* with horses?
1 Cor 9.24 in a race the runners all *c*, but only one

COMPETENT

2 Cor 3. 5 Not that we are *c* of ourselves to claim

COMPLAIN (COMPLAINED)

Gen 21.25 Abraham *c* to Abimelech about a well
Ex 16. 2 the Israelites *c* against Moses and Aaron
Num 11. 1 people *c* in the hearing of the LORD
14. 2 Israelites *c* against Moses and Aaron;
14.27 long shall this wicked congregation *c*
Job 7.11 of my spirit; I will *c* in the bitterness of
Jn 6.41 the Jews began to *c* about him because
Acts 6. 1 Hellenists *c* against the Hebrews
1 Cor 10.10 do not *c* as some of them did, and were

COMPLAINT

Job 23. 2 "Today also my *c* is bitter; his hand is
Ps 55.17 and at noon I utter my *c* and moan, and
142. 2 I pour out my *c* before him; I tell my
Dan 6. 4 to find grounds for *c* against Daniel
Hab 2. 1 what he will answer concerning my *c*.

COMPLETE (COMPLETED COMPLETING)

Gen 15.16 the iniquity of the Amorites is not yet *c*."
Jn 5.36 that the Father has given me to *c*,
Rom 15.28 when I have *c* this, and have delievered
2 Cor 8.11 by *c* it according to your means.
Jas 1. 4 so that you may be mature and *c*,

COMPLETELY

Jn 17.23 that they may become *c* one, so that

COMPLETION

Jas 2.22 faith was brought to *c* by the works,

COMPREHEND

Job 37. 5 he does great things that we cannot *c*.
Eph 3.18 I pray that you may have power to *c*,

COMPUTE

Lev 25.50 They shall *c* with the purchaser the

CONCEAL (CONCEALED CONCEALS)

Job 31.33 if I have *c* my transgressions as others
Prov 12.23 One who is clever *c* knowledge, but the
25. 2 It is the glory of God to *c* things, but
28.13 No one who *c* transgressions will

CONCEIT

Job 37.24 regard any who are wise in their own *c*."

CONCEITED

1 Tim 6. 4 is *c*, understanding nothing, and has a

CONCEIVE (CONCEIVED)

Gen 4. 1 his wife Eve, and she *c* and bore Cain,
Ps 35.20 they *c* deceitful words against those

CONCERNED

Jon 4.10 LORD said, "You are *c* about the bush,
Phil 2.20 will be genuinely *c* for your welfare.

CONCOCT

Prov 16.27 Scoundrels *c* evil, and their speech is

CONCUBINE (CONCUBINES)

Judg 19. 2 his *c* became angry with him, and she
2 Sam 16.22 Absalom went in to his father's *c* in the

CONDEMN (CONDEMNED CONDEMNS)

Job 34.29 When he is quiet, who can *c*? When he
40. 8 you *c* me that you may be justified?
Ps 34.22 those who take refuge in him will be *c*.
37.33 or let them be *c* when they are brought
94.21 righteous, and *c* the innocent to death.
109. 31 to save them from those who would *c*
Prov 12. 2 LORD, but those who devise evil he *c*.
Mt 20.18 scribes, and they will *c* him to death;
Mk 10.33 scribes, and they will *c* him to death,
Lk 11.32 judgment with this generation and *c* it;
Jn 3.17 not to *c* the world, but in order that
8.10 where are they? Has no one *c* you?"
Rom 8.34 Who is to *c*? Is it Christ Jesus, who
Col 2.16 do not let anyone *c* you in the matters
1 Jn 3.21 if our hearts do not *c* us, we have

CONDEMNATION

Rom 5.18 as one man's trespass led to *c* for all,
8. 1 is now no *c* for those who are in Christ

CONDITION

1 Cor 7.20 you remain in the *c* in which you were

CONDUCT

Job 11. 4 you say, "My *c* is pure, and I am clean
Ps 112. 5 lend, who *c* their affairs with justice.
Prov 10.23 wise *c* is a pleasure to a person of
Col 4. 5 *C* yourselves wisely toward outsiders,
1 Pet 2.12 *C* yourselves honorably among the
3.16 those who abuse you for your good *c* in

CONDUIT

2 Kings 18.17 and stood by the *c* of the upper pool,
20.20 how he made the pool and the *c* and
Isa 36. 2 He stood by the *c* of the upper pool on

CONFERRED

Mt 27. 1 and elders of the people *c* together
Lk 22.29 on you just as my Father has *c* on me,

CONFESS (CONFESSED CONFESSES CONFESSING)

Lev 5. 5 you shall *c* the sin that you have
26.40 But if they *c* their iniquity and the
Num 5. 7 *c* the sin that has been committed. The
1 Kings 8.33 turn again to you, *c* your name, pray
Ps 32. 5 "I will *c* my transgressions to the LORD,"
Prov 28.13 but one who *c* and forsakes them will
Mt 3. 6 by him in the river Jordan, *c* their sins.
Mk 1. 5 by him in the river Jordan, *c* their sins.
Jn 1.20 He *c* and did not deny it, but *c*, "I am

Jn 9.22 anyone who *c* Jesus to be the Messiah
Acts 19.18 many of those who became believers *c*
Rom 10. 9 if you *c* with your lips that Jesus is
10.10 one *c* with the mouth and is so saved.
15. 9 I will *c* you among the Gentiles,
Phil 2.11 every tongue should *c* that Jesus Christ
Heb 11.13 They *c* that they were strangers and
Jas 5.16 *c* your sins to one another, and pray for
1 Jn 1. 9 we *c* our sins, he who is faithful and
4.15 abides in those who *c* that Jesus is the
Rev 3. 5 I will *c* your name before my Father and

CONFESSION

Ezra 10. 1 Ezra prayed and made *c*, weeping and
10.11 Now make *c* to the LORD the God of
Dan 9. 4 made *c*, saying, "Ah, Lord, great and
1 Tim 6.13 made the good *c*, I charge you to keep
Heb 4.14 Son of God, let us hold fast to our *c*.

CONFIDENCE

2 Kings 18.19 of Assyria: On what do you base this *c*
Prov 3.26 the LORD will be your *c* and will keep
11.13 who is trustworthy in spirit keeps a *c*.
Isa 36. 4 On what do you base this *c* of yours?
Mic 7. 5 in a friend, have no *c* in a loved one;
Phil 3. 4 I, too, have reason for *c* in the flesh,
2 Thess 3. 4 we have *c* in the Lord concerning you,

CONFIDENT

Ps 27. 3 war rise up against me, yet I will be *c*.
2 Cor 5. 6 So we are always *c*; even though we
10. 7 If you are *c* that you belong to Christ,
Gal 5.10 I am *c* about you in the Lord that you
Phil 1. 6 I am *c* of this, that the one who began
Heb 6. 9 beloved, we are *c* of better things in

CONFIRMS (CONFIRMED)

Ps 119.106 I have sworn an oath and *c* it, to
Isa 44.26 who *c* the word of his servant, and
Mt 18.16 every word may be *c* by the evidence of
Mk 16.20n *c* the message by the signs that

CONFLICTS

Jas 4. 1 Those *c* and disputes among you, where

CONFORMED

Rom 12. 2 Do not be *c* to this world but be
Phil 3.21 it may be *c* to the body of his glory,
1 Pet 1.14 do not be *c* to the desires that you

CONFRONT

Deut 31.21 this song shall *c* them as a witness,
Ps 17.13 Rise up, O LORD, *c* them, overthrow

CONFUSING

Gal 1. 7 but there are some who are *c* you and

CONFUSION

Ex 23.27 will throw into *c* all the people against
Esth 3.15 but the city of Susa was thrown into *c*.

CONFUTED

Job 32.12 there was in fact no one that *c* Job, no

CONGREGATION

Lev 4.13 If the whole *c* of Israel errs
Num 1. 2 Take a census of the whole *c* of
35.24 the *c* shall judge between the slayer and
Ps 22.22 and sisters; in the midst of the *c* I will
26.12 level ground; in the great *c* I will bless
40.10 and your faithfulness from the great *c*.
107. 32 Let them extol him in the *c* of the
Acts 7.38 in the *c* in the wilderness with the
Heb 2.12 in the midst of the *c* I will praise

CONQUER (CONQUERED CONQUERING CONQUERS)

Jn 16.33 But take courage; I have *c* the world!"
Heb 11.33 who through faith *c* kingdoms,
1 Jn 4. 4 you are from God, and have *c* them; for
5. 4 And this is the victory that *c* the world,
Rev 2.17 To everyone who *c* I will give some of
3. 5 If you *c* you will be clothed like them in
3.21 one who *c*, I will give a place with me
5. 5 Judah, the Root of David, has *c*, so that
6. 2 to him, and he came out *c* and to *c*.
12.11 have *c* him by the blood of the Lamb
15. 2 those who had *c* the beast and its
17.14 the Lamb will *c* them, for he is Lord of
21. 7 who *c* will inherit these things, and I

CONQUERORS

Rom 8.37 we are more than *c* through him who

CONSCIENCE

Acts 23. 1 I have lived my life with a clear *c* before
24.16 I do my best always to have a clear *c*
Rom 2.15 to which their own *c* also bears witness;
9. 1 —I am not lying; my *c* confirms it by
13. 5 because of wrath but also because of *c*.
1 Cor 8.10 since their *c* is weak, be encouraged to
10.29 I mean the other's *c*, not your own. For
1 Tim 1.19 good fight, having faith and a good *c*.
2 Tim 1. 3 God—whom I worship with a clear *c*,
Heb 9. 9 cannot perfect the *c* of the worshiper,
1 Pet 3.16 Keep your *c* clear, so that, when you
3.21 but as an appeal to God for a good *c*,

CONSCIENTIOUS

2 Chr 29.34 —for the Levites were more *c* than the

CONSECRATE (CONSECRATED CONSECRATES CONSECRATING)

Ex 13. 2 "*C* to me all the firstborn; whatever is
19.10 "Go to the people and *c* them today and
28.41 ordain them and *c* them, so that they
29. 1 is what you shall do to them to *c* them,
Lev 8.10 and all that was in it, and *c* them.
20. 7 *C* yourselves therefore, and be holy; for
27.14 If a person *c* a house to the LORD, the
Num 8.17 in the land of Egypt I *c* them for myself,
Deut 15.19 herd and flock you shall *c* to the LORD
1 Chr 29. 5 will offer willingly, *c* themselves today
Jer 1. 5 you, and before you were born I *c* you;

CONSECRATION

Num 6. 7 their *c* to God is upon the head.

CONSENT (CONSENTED CONSENTS)

Prov 1.10 child, if sinners entice you, do not *c*.
Lk 22. 6 he *c* and began to look for a way to
Acts 15.22 elders, with the *c* of the whole church,
1 Cor 7.12 and she *c* to live with him, he should

CONSIDER (CONSIDERED CONSIDERS)

Judg 19.30 until this day? *C* it, take counsel, and
Ruth 1. 6 the LORD had *c* his people and given
1 Sam 12.24 for *c* what great things he has done for
Job 1. 8 to Satan, "Have you *c* my servant Job?
37.14 stop and *c* the wondrous works of God.
Ps 41. 1 Happy are those who *c* the poor; The
90.11 Who *c* the power of your anger? Your
119. 95 to destroy me, but I *c* your decrees.
Prov 6. 6 you lazybones; *c* its ways, and be wise.
24.32 Then I saw and *c* it; I looked and
Isa 44.19 No one *c*, nor is there knowledge or
Hag 1. 5 *C* how you have fared. You have sown
2.15 But now, *c* what will come to pass from
Mt 6.28 *C* the lilies of the field, how they grow;
Lk 12.24 *C* the ravens: they neither sow nor reap,
Acts 20.24 I do not *c* my life of any value to
Rom 6.11 you also must *c* yourselves dead to sin
Heb 3. 1 *c* that Jesus, the apostle and high priest
10.24 let us *c* how to provoke one another to
11.11 barren—because he *c* him faithful who
11.19 He *c* the fact that God is able even to
12. 3 *C* him who endured such hostility

Jas 1. 2 trials of any kind, *c* it nothing but joy,

CONSIGNED

Isa 38.10 I am *c* to the gates of Sheol for the

CONSISTENT (CONSISTENTLY)

Gal 2.14 they were not acting *c* with the truth
Titus 2. 1 teach what is *c* with sound doctrine.

CONSOLATION (CONSOLATIONS)

Job 15.11 Are the *c* of God too small for you, or
21. 2 to my words, and let this be your *c*.
Jer 16. 7 anyone give them the cup of *c* to drink
Ezek 16.54 you have done, becoming a *c* to them.
Zech 10. 2 tell false dreams, and give empty *c*.
Lk 2.25 looking forward to the *c* of Israel,
2 Cor 1. 3 Father of of mercies and God of all *c*,

CONSOLE (CONSOLED)

Ezek 14.22 you will be *c* for the evil that I have
Jn 11.19 to Martha and Mary to *c* them about
2 Cor 7. 6 downcast, *c* us by the arrival of Titus,

CONSPIRACY

2 Sam 15.12 The *c* grew in strength, and the people
Isa 8.12 Do not call *c* all that this people call *c*,
Acts 23.13 more than forty who joined in this *c*.

CONSPIRE (CONSPIRED)

Gen 37.18 came near to them, they *c* to kill him.
1 Kings 16. 9 his his servant Zimri . . . *c* against him.
Ps 2. 1 Why do the nations *c*, and the peoples
Am 7.10 "Amos has *c* against you in the very

CONSTRAINS

Job 32.18 full of words; the spirit within me *c* me.

CONSULT (CONSULTED CONSULTS)

1 Chr 13. 1 David *c* with the commanders of the
Isa 8.19 if the people say to you, "*C* the ghosts
31. 1 to the Holy One of Israel or *c* the LORD!
Ezek 14. 3 them; shall I let myself be *c* by them?
20. 3 Why are you coming? To *c* me? As I
21.21 shakes the arrows, he *c* the teraphim,
Hos 4.12 My people *c* a piece of wood, and their

CONSUME (CONSUMED CONSUMES CONSUMING)

Num 16.21 so that I may *c* them in a moment.
Job 1.16 the sheep and the servants, and *c* them;
20.26 them; what is left in their tent will be *c*.
Ps 59.13 *c* them in wrath, *c* them until they are
90. 7 For we are *c* by your anger; by your
Mt 6.20 where neither moth nor rust *c* and
Heb 12.29 and awe; for indeed our God is a *c* fire.

CONTAIN

1 Kings 8.27 and the highest heaven cannot *c* you,
Jn 21.25 world itself could not *c* the books that

CONTEMPLATE

Isa 52.15 which they had not heard they shall *c*.

CONTEMPT

Gen 16. 4 she looked with *c* on her mistress.
Esth 1.17 to look with *c* upon their husbands,
Job 12. 5 Those at ease have *c* for misfortune, but
Isa 9. 1 he brought into *c* the land of Zebulun
Lk 18. 9 righteous and regarded others with *c*:
1 Cor 11.22 Or do you show *c* for the church of God

CONTEND

Judg 6.31 "Will you *c* for Baal? Or will you defend
Job 10. 2 me; let me know why you *c* against me.
13.19 Who is there that will *c* with me? For
Ps 35. 1 *C*, O LORD, with those who *c* with me;
Isa 49.25 I will *c* with those who *c* with you, and
Hos 4. 4 Yet let no one *c*, and let none accuse,
Jude 3 appeal to you to *c* for the faith that was

CONTENT

Josh 7. 7 Would that we had been *c* to settle
2 Cor 12.10 Therefore I am *c* with weaknesses,
Phil 4.11 need; for I have learned to be *c* with
1 Tim 6. 8 and clothing, we will be *c* with these.

CONTENTIOUS

Prov 21.19 land than with a *c* and fretful wife.
27.15 on a rainy day and a *c* wife are alike;

CONTINUALLY

Ps 34. 1 his praise shall *c* be in my mouth.

CONTINUE (CONTINUED)

Ps 36.10 O *c* your steadfast love to those who
Jer 31. 3 I have *c* my faithfulness to you.
Jn 8.31 "If you *c* in my word, you are truly my
Acts 13.43 them and urged them to *c* in the grace
Rom 6. 1 we *c* in sin that grace may abound?
Phil 1.25 I will remain and *c* with all of you for
2 Tim 3.14 for you, *c* in what you have learned and

CONTRIBUTIONS

2 Chr 31.12 Faithfully brought in the *c*, the tithes

CONTRITE

Ps 51.17 a broken and *c* heart, O God, you will
Isa 66. 2 to the humble and *c* in spirit, who

CONTRITION

Jer 44.10 They have shown no *c* or fear to this

CONTROL (CONTROLLED)

Gen 45. 1 Joseph could no longer *c* himself before
Prov 16.32 one whose temper is *c* than one who
1 Cor 7.37 necessity but having his desire under *c*,
1 Thess 4. 4 you know how to *c* your body in
Heb 2. 8 them, God left nothing outside their *c*.

CONTROVERSY

Mic 6. 2 Hear, you mountains, the *c* of the LORD,

CONVERT (CONVERTS)

Mt 23.15 cross sea and land to make a single *c*,
Rom 16. 5 Epaenetus, who was the first *c* in Asia
1 Cor 16.15 were the first *c* in Achaia, and
1 Tim 3. 6 He must not be a recent *c*, or he may

CONVICT (CONVICTS)

Jer 2.19 you, and your apostasies will *c* you.
Jn 8.46 Which of you *c* me of sin? If I tell the
Jude 15 to *c* everyone of all the deeds of

CONVINCE (CONVINCED)

Acts 18. 4 and would try to *c* Jews and Greeks.
Rom 4.21 fully *c* that God was able to do what he
8.38 I am *c* that neither death, nor life, nor
14. 5 Let all be fully *c* in their own minds.

CONVOCATION

Lev 23. 3 is a sabbath of complete rest, a holy *c*;
Num 28.26 of weeks, you shall have a holy *c*;

COOKED

2 Kings 6.29 we *c* my son and ate him. The next day

COOL

Prov 17.27 who is *c* in spirit has understanding.

COPY

Josh 8.32 wrote on the stones a *c* of the law
Esth 4. 8 Mordecai also gave him a *c* of the

CORBAN

Mk 7.11 might have had from me is *C*' (that is,

CORD (CORDS)

Ps 18. 4 The *c* of death encompassed me, the
129. 4 he has cut the *c* of the wicked.
Eccl 4.12 A threefold *c* is not quickly broken.

Eccl 12. 6 before the silver *c* is snapped, and the
Hos 11. 4 I led them with *c* of human kindness,

CORINTH

Acts 18. 1 this Paul left Athens and went to *C*.
19. 1 While Apollos was at *C*, Paul passed
1 Cor 1. 2 church of God that is in *C*, to those

CORNELIUS

Acts 10. 1 there was a man named *C*, a centurion
10. 3 of God coming in and saying to him, "*C*."
10.24 *C* was expecting them and had called
10.31 '*C*, your prayer has been heard and

CORNER

Acts 26.26 his notice, for this was not done in a *c*.
1 Pet 2. 7 has become the very head of the *c*,"

CORNERSTONE

Eph 2.20 with Christ Jesus himself as the *c*,
1 Pet 2. 6 Zion a stone, a *c* chosen and precious;

CORPSE

Mt 24.28 Wherever the *c* is, there the vultures

CORRECT

Jer 10.24 *C* me, O LORD, but in just measure; not

CORRECTION

Jer 2.30 down your children; they accepted no *c*.
5. 3 them, but they refused to take *c*.
Zeph 3. 2 to no voice; it has accepted no *c*.
3. 7 the city will fear me, it will accept *c*;

CORRUPT (CORRUPTED)

Gen 6.11 Now the earth was *c* in God's sight, and
Hos 9. 9 They have deeply *c* themselves as in the
Mal 2. 8 you have *c* the covenant of Levi,

CORRUPTION

Dan 6. 4 find no grounds for complaint or any *c*,
Acts 2.27 or let your Holy One experience *c*.
13.35 not let your Holy One experience *c*.'

CORRUPTLY

Deut 4.16 do not act *c* by making an idol for

COST

2 Sam 24.24 to the LORD my God that *c* me nothing."
1 Chr 21.24 offer burnt offerings that *c* me nothing."
Ezra 6. 4 timber; let the *c* be paid from the royal
Lk 14.28 not first sit down and estimate the *c*,

COUNCIL (COUNCILS)

Job 15. 8 Have you listened in the *c* of God? And
Ps 82. 1 God has taken his place in the divine *c*;
89. 7 a God feared in the *c* of the holy ones,
Jer 23.18 For who has stood in the *c* of the LORD
Mt 10.17 they will hand you over to *c* and flog
Lk 23.50 though a member of the *c*, had not

COUNSEL (COUNSELED COUNSELS)

Ex 18.19 Now listen to me. I will give you *c*, and
2 Sam 17. 7 time the *c* which Ahithophel has given
Job 26. 2 you have *c* one who has no wisdom,
38. 2 "Who is this that darkens *c* by words
Ps 2. 2 the rulers take *c* together, against the
33.10 brings the *c* of the nations to nothing;
33.11 *c* of the LORD stands forever, the
73.24 You guide me with your *c*, and
106. 13 his works; they did not wait for his *c*.
Prov 15.22 Without *c*, plans go wrong, but with
Isa 11. 2 the spirit of *c* and might, the spirit of
28.29 LORD of hosts; he is wonderful in *c*, and
Jer 7.24 evil will they walked in their own *c*,
18.18 from the priest, nor *c* from the wise,
32.19 of hosts, great in *c* and mighty in deed;
Dan 4.27 O king, let my *c* be acceptable to you:
Eph 1.11 all things according to his *c* and will,

COUNSELOR (COUNSELORS)

2 Chr 22. 3 his mother was his *c* in doing wickedly.
25.16 "Have we made you a royal *c*? Stop!
Ps 119. 24 decrees are my delight, they are my *c*.
Isa 1.26 at the first, your *c* as at the beginning.
3. 3 dignitary, *c* and the skillful magician
9. 6 and he is named Wonderful *C*, Mighty
40.13 LORD, or as his *c* has instructed him?
41.28 among these there is no *c* who, when I
Mic 4. 9 Has your *c* perished, that pangs have

COUNT (COUNTED COUNTING)

Gen 15. 5 *c* the stars, if you are able to *c* them."
Num 23.10 Who can *c* the dust of Jacob, or number
2 Sam 24. 1 "Go, *c* the people of Israel and Judah."
Ps 90.12 So teach us to *c* our days that we may
139. 18 I try to *c* them—they are more than
Mk 15.28n says, "And he was *c* among the lawless."
Lk 22.37 'And he was *c* among the lawless'; and
2 Cor 5.19 world to himself, not *c* their trespasses

COUNTENANCE

Gen 4. 5 So Cain was very angry, and his *c* fell.
Job 29.24 light of my *c* they did not extinguish.
Prov 15.13 A glad heart makes a cheerful *c*, but by

COUNTRY

Heb 11.16 they desire a better *c*, that is, a

COURAGE

1 Sam 4. 9 Take *c*, and be men, O Philistines, in
1 Chr 28.20 "Be strong and of good *c*, and act. Do
2 Chr 15. 8 he took *c*, and put away the abominable
Ps 27.14 be strong, and let your heart take *c*;
31.24 Be strong, and let your heart take *c*, all
Ezek 22.14 Can your *c* endure, or can your hands
Jn 16.33 But take *c*; I have conquered
Acts 23.11 "Keep up your *c*! For just as you have
27.22 I urge you now to keep up your *c*, for
27.25 So keep up your *c*, men, for I have faith
28.15 them, Paul thanked God and took *c*.

COURAGEOUS (COURAGEOUSLY)

Josh 1. 6 Be strong and *c*; for you shall put this
1. 9 Be strong and *c*; do not be frightened or
10.25 be strong and *c*; for thus the LORD will
2 Sam 10.12 Be strong, and let us be *c* for the sake
2 Chr 19.11 Deal *c*, and may the LORD be with the
1 Cor 16.13 stand firm in your faith, be *c*, be strong.

COURSE

Ps 19. 5 like a strong man runs its *c* with joy.
Acts 20.24 if only I may finish my *c* and the

COURT

Ex 27. 9 You shall make the *c* of the tabernacle.
1 Cor 4. 3 be judged by you or by any human *c*.
6. 1 do you dare to take it to *c* before the

COVENANT

Gen 6.18 I will establish my *c* with you; and you
9. 9 I am establishing my *c* with you and
17. 2 I will make my *c* between me and you,
21.27 Abimelech, and the two men made a *c*.
26.28 and us, and let us make a *c* with you,
31.44 Come now, let us make a *c*, you and I;
Ex 2.24 God remembered his *c* with Abraham,
6. 4 I also established my *c* with them, to
23.32 You shall make no *c* with them and
24. 8 "See the blood of the *c* that the LORD
25.16 You shall put into the ark the *c* that I
34.28 wrote . . . the words of the *c*, the ten
Lev 26. 9 you; and I will maintain my *c* with you.
26.25 you, executing vengeance for the *c*;
26.42 I will remember also my *c* with Isaac,
Num 25.12 say, 'I hereby grant him my *c* of peace.
Deut 4.31 he will not forget the *c* with your
5. 3 our ancestors did the LORD make this *c*,

Deut 7. 2 Make no *c* with them and show them
7. 9 the faithful God who maintains *c* loyalty
7.12 God will maintain with you the *c* loyalty
17. 2 the LORD your God, and transgress his *c*
29. 1 These are the words of the *c* that the
29.12 to enter into the *c* of the LORD your
29.25 it is because they abandoned the *c* of
33. 9 observed your word, and kept your *c*.
Josh 24.25 So Joshua made a *c* with the people
Judg 2. 1 I said, 'I will never break my *c* with
2. 2 do not make a *c* with the inhabitants of
1 Sam 18. 3 Jonathan made a *c* with David, because
20. 8 brought your servant into a sacred *c*
2 Sam 3.21 they may make a *c* with you, and that
5. 3 David made a *c* with them at Hebron
23. 5 he has made with me an everlasting *c*,
1 Kings 8.23 keeping *c* and showing steadfast love for
19.10 Israelites have forsaken your *c*, thrown
2 Kings 11. 4 He made a *c* with them and put them
11.17 Jehoiada made a *c* between the LORD
23. 2 book of the *c* that had been found in
23. 3 book. All the people joined in the *c*.
1 Chr 16.15 Remember his *c* forever, the word that
2 Chr 6.14 keeping *c* in steadfast love with your
15.12 They entered into a *c* to seek the LORD,
21. 7 of the *c* that he had made with David,
34.31 his place and made a *c* before the LORD,
Ezra 10. 3 let us make a *c* with our God to send
Ps 25.10 for those who keep his *c* and
25.14 and he makes his *c* known to them.
44.17 not forgotten you, or been false to your *c*.
50. 5 faithful ones, who made a *c* with me by
55.20 on a friend and violated a *c* with me.
74.20 Have regard for your *c*, for the dark
78.37 toward him; they were not true to his *c*.
83. 5 accord; against thee they make a *c*—
89. 3 "I have made a *c* with my chosen one,
103. 18 to those who keep his *c* and remember
105. 10 a statute, to Israel as an everlasting *c*,
106. 45 their sake he remembered his *c*, and
132. 12 If your sons keep my *c* and my decrees
Prov 2.17 of her youth and forgets her sacred *c*;
Isa 28.18 your *c* with death will be annulled,
42. 6 I have given you as a *c* to the people, a
59.21 as for me, this is my *c* with them, says
61. 8 I will make an everlasting *c* with them.
Jer 11.10 the house of Judah have broken the *c*
14.21 and do not break your *c* with us.
22. 9 "Because they abandoned the *c* of the
31.31 when I will make a new *c* with the
32.40 I will make an everlasting *c* with them,
33.21 then could my *c* with my servant David
50. 5 *c* that will never be forgotten.
Ezek 16.60 yet I will remember my *c* with you in
17.14 that by keeping his *c* it might stand.
37.26 I will make a *c* of peace with them; it
Dan 9.27 He shall make a strong *c* with many for
11.28 his heart shall be set against the holy *c*.
Hos 6. 7 But at Adam they transgressed the *c*;
Mal 2. 4 to you, that my *c* with Levi may hold,
2.14 is your companion and your wife by *c*.
Mt 26.28 this is my blood of the *c*, which is
Mk 14.24 "This is my blood of the *c*, which is
Lk 1.72 and has remembered his holy *c*,
Acts 3.25 of the prophets and of the *c*
7. 8 Then he gave him the *c* of circumcision.
Rom 11.27 "And this is my *c* with them, when I
1 Cor 11.25 "This cup is the new *c* in my blood. Do
2 Cor 3. 6 competent to be ministers of a new *c*,
3.14 when they hear the reading of the old *c*,
Gal 3.17 does not annul a *c* previously ratified by
Heb 7.22 also become the guarantee of a better *c*.
8. 8 when I will establish a new *c* with the
9.15 reason he is the mediator of a new *c*,
10.16 is the *c* that I will make with them
Rev 11.19 the ark of his *c* was seen within his

COVENANTS

Hos 10. 4 words; with empty oaths they make *c*;
Eph 2.12 strangers to the *c* of promise, having no

COVER (COVERED COVERING COVERS)

Gen 7.20 mountains, *c* them fifteen cubits deep.
24.65 So she took her veil and *c* herself.
Ex 33.22 I will *c* you with my hand until I have
Num 9.15 the cloud *c* the tabernacle, the tent of
16.42 the cloud had *c* it, and the glory of the
Ps 5.12 LORD; you *c* them with favor as a shield.
91. 4 he will *c* you with his pinions, and
Prov 10.12 stirs up strife, but love *c* all offenses.
Isa 6. 2 with two they *c* their faces, and with
11. 9 of the LORD as the waters *c* the sea.
Hos 10. 8 They shall say to the mountains, *C* us,
Mt 10.26 nothing is *c* up that will not be
Lk 12. 2 Nothing is *c* up that will not be
23.30 'Fall on us'; and to the hills, '*C* us.'

COVERING (n)

Ps 18.11 He made darkness his *c* around him, his
Isa 28.20 on it, and the *c* too narrow to wrap

COVET (COVETED)

Ex 20.17 You shall not *c* your neighbor's house;
Deut 5.21 Neither shall you *c* your neighbor's
Josh 7.21 fifty shekels, then I *c* them and took
Mic 2. 2 They *c* fields, and seize them; houses,
Acts 20.33 I *c* no one's silver or gold or clothing.
Rom 7. 7 the law had not said, "You shall not *c*."
13. 9 You shall not steal, You shall not *c*,"

COVETOUSNESS

Isa 57.17 Because of their wicked *c* I was angry; I
Rom 1.29 kind of wickedness, evil, *c*, malice.
7. 8 produced in me all kinds of *c*.

CO-WORKERS

Col 4.11 among my *c* for the kingdom of God,
3 Jn 8 that we may become *c* with the truth.

CRAFT

Isa 2.16 Tarshish, and against all the beautiful *c*.

CRAFTINESS

Job 5.13 He takes the wise in their own *c*; and
1 Cor 3.19 written, "He catches the wise in their *c*,"
Eph 4.14 by their *c* in deceitful scheming.

CRAFTY

Job 5.12 He frustrates the devices of the *c*, so
15. 5 and you choose the tongue of the *c*.

CRAVING (CRAVINGS)

Prov 21.25 The *c* of the lazy person is fatal, for lazy
Jas 4. 1 they come from your *c* that are at war

CREATE (CREATED CREATES)

Gen 1. 1 when God *c* the heavens and the earth,
1.21 God *c* the great sea monsters and every
1.27 God *c* humankind in his own image, in
Deut 32. 6 Is not he your father, who *c* you, who
Ps 51.10 *C* in me a clean heart, O God, and put
104. 30 you send forth your Spirit, they are *c*;
148. 5 for he commanded and they were *c*.
Prov 8.22 The LORD *c* me at the beginning of his
Isa 4. 5 Then the LORD will *c* over the whole site
40.26 your eyes on high and see: who *c* these?
41.20 this, the Holy One of Israel has *c* it.
42. 5 says God, the LORD, who *c* the heavens
43. 7 whom I *c* for my glory, whom I formed
45. 7 I form light and *c* darkness, I make
45.18 thus says the LORD, who *c* the heavens
65.17 For I am about to *c* new heavens and a
Jer 31.22 For the LORD has *c* a new thing on the
Am 4.13 *c* the wind, and reveals his thoughts to
Eph 2.10 us, *c* in Christ Jesus for good works,
Col 1.16 —all things have been *c* through him

1 Tim 4. 4 For everything *c* by God is good, and
Rev 4.11 for you *c* all things, and by your will
10. 6 who *c* heaven and what is in it, the

CREATION
Mk 13.19 not been from the beginning of the *c*
Rom 8.21 the *c* itself will be set free from its
8.22 the whole *c* has been groaning in labor
2 Cor 5.17 if anyone is in Christ, there is a new *c*:
Gal 6.15 is anything; but a new *c* is everything!
2 Pet 3. 4 as they were from the beginning of *c*!"

CREATOR
Eccl 12. 1 Remember your *C* in the days of your
Isa 40.28 God, *C* of the ends of the earth.
43.15 Holy One, the *C* of Israel, your King.
Rom 1.25 served the creature rather than the *C*,

CREATURES
Gen 1.20 waters bring forth swarms of living *c*,
Ezek 10.17 for the spirit of the living *c* was in
Rev 4. 6 four living *c*, full of eyes in front and

CREDIT
Deut 24.13 it will be to your *c* before the LORD your

CREDITOR (CREDITORS)
Deut 15. 2 every *c* shall remit the claim that is
Isa 50. 1 Or which of my *c* is it to whom I have
Lk 7.41 "A certain *c* had two debtors; one owed

CREEPING
Gen 1.24 cattle and *c* things and wild animals of

CRETE
Acts 27.12 It was a harbor of *C*, facing southwest
Titus 1. 5 I left you behind in *C* for this reason, so

CRIME (CRIMES)
Gen 50.17 I beg you, forgive the *c* of your brothers
Deut 24.16 only for their own *c* may persons be put
Judg 9.56 God repaid Abimelech for the *c* he
Ezek 7.23 the land is full of bloody *c*; the city is

CRIMINAL
Judg 20. 3 us, how did this *c* act come about?"

CRIMSON
Josh 2.18 tie this *c* cord in the window through

CRINGE (CRINGING)
Ps 18.44 obeyed me; foreigners came *c* to me.
66. 3 great power, your enemies *c* before you.

CRIPPLED
Acts 14. 8 walked, for he had been *c* from birth.
2 Sam 4. 4 Jonathan had a son who was *c* in his
9. 3 a son of Jonathan; he is *c* in his feet."

CRISIS
1 Cor 7.26 in view of the impending *c*, it is well for

CROOKED
Prov 2.15 those whose paths are *c*, and who are
Eccl 1.15 What is *c* cannot be made straight, and
7.13 can make straight what he has made *c*?
Isa 59. 8 Their roads they have made *c*; no one

CROPS
Lk 12.17 I do, for I have no place to store my *c*?'
2 Tim 2. 6 ought to have the first share of the *c*.

CROSS
Mt 10.38 whoever does not take the *c* and follow
16.24 and take up their *c* and follow me.
27.32 they compelled this man to carry his *c*.
Mk 8.34 deny themselves and take up their *c*
15.21 to carry his *c*; it was Simon of Cyrene,
15.30 yourself, and come down from the *c*!"
Lk 9.23 themselves and take up their *c* daily
Lk 14.27 does not carry the *c* and follow me
23.26 laid the *c* on him, and made him carry
Jn 19.17 and carrying the *c* by himself, he went
1 Cor 1.17 so that the *c* of Christ be emptied of its
Gal 5.11 the offense of the *c* has been removed.
6.12 they may not be persecuted for the *c*
6.14 I never boast of anything except the *c*
Phil 2. 8 the point of death—even death on a *c*.
3.18 many live as enemies of the *c* of Christ;
Col 2.14 He set this aside, nailing it to the *c*.
Heb 12. 2 endured the *c*, disregarding its shame,
1 Pet 2.24 bore our sins in his body on the *c*,

CROSS-EXAMINE
Lk 11.53 to *c* him about many things, lying in

CROSSING
Josh 3.17 entire nation finished *c* over the Jordan.

CROWD (CROWDS)
Mt 4.25 And great *c* followed him from Galilee,
Mk 8. 2 "I have compassion on the *c*, because
12.37 the large *c* was listening to him with

CROWN (CROWNED)
2 Chr 23.11 out the king's son, put the *c* on him,
Ps 8. 5 God, and *c* them with glory and honor.
21. 3 rich blessings; you set a *c* of fine gold
65.11 You *c* the year with your bounty; your
Prov 4. 9 she will bestow on you a beautiful *c*."
12. 4 A good wife is the *c* of her husband, but
16.31 Gray hair is a *c* of glory; it is gained in
Isa 62. 3 You shall be a *c* of beauty in the hand
Lam 5.16 *c* has fallen from our head; woe to us,
Ezek 16.12 ears, and a beautiful *c* upon your head.
Zech 6.11 make a *c*, and set it on the head of the
2 Tim 4. 8 reserved for me the *c* of righteousness,
Rev 3.11 have so that no one may seize your *c*.
14.14 Son of Man, with a golden *c* on his

CROWS
Mk 14.30 very night, before the cock *c* twice, you

CRUCIBLE
Prov 17. 3 The *c* is for silver, and the furnace is for

CRUCIFY (CRUCIFIED)
Mt 20.19 to be mocked and flogged and *c*;
23.34 some of whom you will kill and *c*, and
27.22 All of them said, "Let him be *c*."
27.35 when they had *c* him, they divided his
28. 5 you are looking for Jesus who was *c*.
Mk 15.13 They shouted back, "*C* him!"
15.20 him. Then they led him out to *c* him.
16. 6 for Jesus of Nazareth, who was *c*.
Lk 23.21 but they kept shouting, "*C*, *c*, him!"
23.33 The Skull, they *c* Jesus there with the
Jn 19. 6 saw him, they shouted, "*C* him, *c* him!"
19.10 to release you, and power to *c* you?"
19.18 There they *c* him, and with him two
Acts 2.23 you *c* and killed by the hands of those
Rom 6. 6 our old self was *c* with him so that the
1 Cor 1.13 been divided? Was Paul *c* for you?
2. 2 you except Jesus Christ and him *c*.
2. 8 had, they would not have *c* the Lord
2 Cor 13. 4 For he was *c* in weakness, but lives by
Gal 2.19 I have been *c* with Christ; and it is no
3. 1 Jesus Christ was publicly exhibited as *c*!
6.14 by which the world has been *c* to me,
Rev 11. 8 and Egypt, where also their Lord was *c*.

CRUEL (CRUELLY)
Job 30.21 You have turned *c* to me; with the
39.16 It deals *c* with its young, as if they were
Prov 11.17 but the *c* do themselves harm.

CRUMBS
Mt 15.27 yet even the dogs eat the *c* that fall
Mk 7.28 under the table eat the children's *c*."

CRUSH (CRUSHED)

Job 20.19 they have *c* and abandoned the poor,
Ps 18.29 By you I can *c* a troop; and by my God I
Lam 1.15 a time against me to *c* my young men;
Mk 3. 9 crowd, so that they would not *c* him;
Lk 20.18 and it will *c* anyone on whom it falls."
Rom 16.20 The God of peace will shortly *c* Satan

CRY (CRIED CRYING)

Gen 4.10 Listen, your brother's blood is *c* out to
27.34 Esau heard his father's words, he *c* out
Ex 2. 6 the child. He was *c*, and she took pity
22.23 *c* out to me, I will surely heed their *c*;
Lev 13.45 upper lip and *c* out, "Unclean, unclean."
1 Sam 7. 9 Samuel *c* out to the LORD for Israel, and
5.11 Samuel was angry; and he *c* out to the
Job 19. 7 Even when I *c* out, 'Violence!' I am not
Ps 5. 2 Listen to the sound of my *c*, my King
18. 6 to my God I *c* for help. From his temple
88. 1 when, at night, I *c* out in your presence,
99. 6 his name. They *c* to the LORD, and he
102. 1 prayer, O LORD; let my *c* come to you.
107. 28 they *c* to the LORD in their trouble,
119.145 With my whole heart I *c*; answer me, O
120. 1 In my distress I *c* to the LORD, that he
130. 1 Out of the depths I *c* to you, O LORD.
Isa 42. 2 He will not *c* or lift up his voice, or
Jon 1. 2 that great city, and *c* against it;
Mt 12.19 He will not wrangle or *c* aloud, nor will

CUNNING

2 Cor 4. 2 we refuse to practice *c* or to falsify

CUP

Gen 44. 2 Put my *c*, the silver *c*, in the top of the
Ps 11. 6 wind shall be the portion of their *c*.
16. 5 LORD is my chosen portion and my *c*;
23. 5 anoint head with oil; my *c* overflows.
75. 8 For in the hand of the LORD there is a *c*
116. 13 I will lift up the *c* of salvation and call
Isa 51.17 the *c* of his wrath, who have drunk to
Jer 25.28 And if they refuse to accept the *c* from
Hab 2.16 The *c* in the LORD's right hand will
Mt 10.42 whoever gives even a *c* of cold water to
20.22 Are you able to drink the *c* that I am
23.25 you clean the outside of the *c* and of
26.27 Then he took a *c*, and after giving
26.39 if it is possible, let this *c* pass from me;
Mk 9.41 whoever gives you a *c* of water to drink
10.38 Are you able to drink the *c* that I drink,
14.23 Then he took a *c*, and after giving
14.36 are possible; remove this *c* from me;
Lk 11.39 you Pharisees clean the outside of the *c*
22.17 he took a *c*, and after giving thanks he
22.42 you are willing, remove this *c* from me;
Jn 18.11 the *c* that the Father has given me?"
1 Cor 10.16 The *c* of blessing which we bless, is it
11.25 "This *c* is the new covenant in my
Rev 16.19 her the wine-*c* of the fury of his wrath.

CUPBEARER

Gen 40. 9 So the chief *c* told his dream to Joseph,

CURDS

Gen 18. 8 he took *c* and milk and the calf that he
Isa 7.15 He shall eat *c* and honey by the time he

CURE (CURED CURING)

Mt 4.23 *c* every disease and every sickness
8.16 with a word, and *c* all who were sick.
10. 8 *C* the sick, raise the dead, cleanse the
12.15 followed him, and he *c* all of them.
14.14 compassion for them and *c* their sick.
17.16 disciples, but they could not *c* him."
Lk 4.23 to me this proverb, 'Doctor, *c* yourself!'
4.40 his hands on each of them and *c* them.
7.21 Jesus had just then *c* many people of
8. 2 as some women who had been *c* of evil
Lk 13.14 come on those days and be *c*, and not
14. 3 "Is it lawful to *c* people on the sabbath,
Acts 28. 8 him and *c* him by praying and putting
28. 9 who had diseases also came and were *c*.

CURSE (CURSES CURSING CURSINGS) (n)

Deut 11.26 before you today a blessing and a *c*:
21.23 anyone hung on a tree is under God's *c*.
27.13 shall stand on Mount Ebal for the *c*:
Josh 8.34 the words of the law, blessings and *c*,
Prov 3.33 The LORD's *c* is on the house of the
Jer 25.18 a waste, an object of hissing and a *c*,
Zech 5. 3 "This is the *c* that goes out over the
8.13 you have been a *c* among the nations,
Mal 2. 2 then I will send the *c* on you and I will
Rom 3.14 "Their mouths are full of *c* and
Gal 3.10 on the works of the law are under a *c*;
Jas 3.10 the same mouth come blessing and *c*.

CURSE (CURSED CURSES CURSING) (v)

Gen 3.14 *c* are you among all animals and among
4.11 you are *c* from the ground, which has
12. 3 and the one who *c* you I will *c*; and in
49. 7 *C* be their anger, for it is fierce, and
Ex 21.17 Whoever *c* father or mother shall be put
Num 22. 6 Come now, *c* this people for me, since
23. 8 How can I *c* whom God has not *c*? How
Josh 6.26 "*C* before the LORD be anyone who tries
1 Sam 14.24 "*C* be anyone who eats food before it is
2 Sam 16. 5 was Shimei son of Gera; he came out *c*.
1 Kings 21.13 saying, "Naboth *c* God and the king."
2 Kings 2.24 and saw them, he *c* them in the name
Job 1.11 he has, and he will *c* you to your face."
2. 9 in your integrity? *C* God, and die."
3. 1 his mouth and *c* the day of his birth.
Ps 109. 17 He loved to *c*; let curses come on him.
Prov 20.20 If you *c* father or mother, your lamp will
Eccl 10.20 Do not *c* the king, even in your thought,
Jer 17. 5 *C* are those who trust in mere mortals
20.14 *C* be the day on which I was born! The
Mk 11.21 "Rabbi, look! The fig tree that you *c* has
Lk 6.28 bless those who *c* you, pray for those
1 Cor 12. 3 Spirit of God ever says "Let Jesus be *c*!"
Gal 3.13 "*C* is everyone who hangs on a tree"
Rev 16. 9 they *c* the name of God, who had

CURTAIN (CURTAINS)

Ex 26. 1 make the tabernacle with ten *c* of fine
Lev 16. 2 into the sanctuary inside the *c* before
Mt 27.51 the *c* of the temple was torn in two,
Mk 15.38 the *c* of the temple was torn in two,
Lk 23.45 failed; and the *c* of the temple was torn
Heb 9. 3 Behind the second *c* was a tent called
10.20 the *c* (that is, through his flesh),

CUSH

Gen 2.13 that flows around the whole land of *C*.

CUSTOM (CUSTOMS)

Ezra 7.24 shall not be lawful to impose tribute, *c*,
Jer 10. 3 For the *c* of the peoples are false: a tree
Lk 4.16 on the sabbath day, as was his *c*.

CUT

1 Kings 18.28 aloud, and *c* themselves with swords
Isa 14.22 will *c* off from Babylon name and
Dan 9.26 an anointed one shall be *c* off and shall
Mk 9.43 If your hand causes you to sin, *c* it off;
Acts 2.37 they heard this, they were *c* to the heart

CYMBALS (CYMBALS)

Ps 150. 5 Praise him with clanging *c*; praise him
1 Cor 13. 1 love, I am a noisy gong or a clanging *c*.

CYPRUS

Acts 4.36 a Levite, a native of *C*, Joseph, to whom
11.19 Stephen traveled as far as Phoenicia, *C*
13. 4 and from there they sailed to *C*.

Acts 15.39 Mark with him and sailed away to *C*.
27. 4 sailed under the lee of *C*, because the

CYRUS

Ezra 1. 1 In the first year of King *C* of Persia, in
4. 3 as King *C* of Persia has commanded
5.13 King *C* of Babylon, in the first year of
Isa 44.28 who says of *C*, "He is my shepherd, and
45. 1 says the LORD to his anointed, to *C*,
Dan 1.21 there until the first year of King *C*.

D

DAILY

Lk 9.23 and take up their cross *d* and follow
11. 3 Give us each day our *d* bread.

DAMASCUS

Gen 14.15 pursued them to Hobah, north of *D*.
2 Sam 8. 6 put garrisons among the Arameans of *D*;
Isa 7. 8 For the head of Aram is *D*, and the
Zech 9. 1 land of Hadrach and will rest upon *D*.
Acts 9. 2 him for letters to the synagogues at *D*,
22.10 'Get up and go to *D*; there you will be
2 Cor 11.32 under King Aretas guarded the city of *D*
Gal 1.17 Arabia, and afterwards I returned to *D*.

DAN (Son of Jacob)

Born, Gen 30.6; blessed by Jacob, Gen 49.16-17.

Tribe of Dan: blessed by Moses, Deut 33.22; allotted territory, Josh 19.40-48; migrated north, Judg 18; became center of idolatry, 1 Kings 12.28-30.

DAN (the city)

Gen 14.14 them, and went in pursuit as far as *D*.
Judg 18.29 They named the city *D*, after their
20. 1 came out, from *D* to Beersheba,
1 Sam 3.20 all Israel from *D* to Beersheba knew

DANCE (DANCED DANCING)

Ex 32.19 and the *d*, Moses' anger burned hot,
Judg 21.21 young women of Shiloh come out to *d*
2 Sam 6.14 David *d* before the LORD with all his
Ps 30.11 You have turned my mourning into *d*;
Lam 5.15 our *d* has been turned to mourning.
Mt 11.17 the flute for you and you did not *d*;
14. 6 the daughter of Herodias *d* before the
Mk 6.22 his daughter Herodias came in and *d*,
Lk 7.32 the flute for you, and you did not *d*;

DANGER

1 Cor 15.30 we putting ourselves in *d* every hour?

DANIEL (BELTESHAZZAR)

Trained in the king's palace, Dan 1.1-7; abstained from the king's food, Dan 1.8-16; interpreted Nebuchadnezzar's dreams, Dan 2; 4; interpreted the handwriting on the wall, Dan 5.10-29; delivered from the lion's den, Dan 6; visions and dreams, Dan 7—8; 10—12; prayed for his people, Dan 9.

DARE

Rom 5. 7 person someone might actually *d* to die.
1 Cor 6. 1 do you *d* take it to court before the

DARIUS

Ezra 4. 5 of Persia and until the reign of King *D*
6. 1 Then King *D* made a decree, and they
Dan 5.31 *D* the Mede received the kingdom,
6.28 Daniel prospered during the reign of *D*
Hag 1. 1 In the second year of King *D*, in the
Zech 1. 1 eighth month, in the second year of *D*,

DARK

Job 24.16 In the *d* they dig through houses; by
Mt 10.27 What I say to you in the *d*, tell in the
2 Pet 1.19 to this as a lamp shining in a *d* place,

DARKEN (DARKENED DARKENS)

Job 38. 2 "Who is this that *d* counsel by words
Eccl 12. 2 the stars are *d* and the clouds return
Am 8. 9 noon, and *d* the earth in broad daylight.
Mk 13.24 the sun will be *d*, and the moon will

DARKEST

Ps 23. 4 though I walk through the *d* valley,

DARKNESS

Gen 1. 5 light Day, and the *d* he called Night.
15.12 and terrifying *d* descended upon him.
Ex 10.21 may be *d* over the land of Egypt, a *d*
Job 10.21 return, to the land of gloom and deep *d*,
24.17 are friends with the terrors of deep *d*.
Ps 44.19 of jackals, and covered us with deep *d*.
139. 12 even the *d* is not dark to you; the night
Isa 8.22 earth, but will see only distress and *d*,
Jer 13.16 the LORD your God before he brings *d*,
Joel 2. 2 it is near—a day of *d* and gloom, a day
Mt 6.23 If then the light in you is *d*, how great
22.13 throw him into the outer *d*, where there
25.30 throw him into the outer *d*, where there
27.45 noon on, *d* came over the whole land
Mk 15.33 was noon, *d* came over the whole land
Lk 23.44 noon, and *d* came over the whole land
1 Pet 2. 9 called you out of *d* into his marvelous

DAUGHTER (DAUGHTERS)

Gen 20.12 the *d* of my father but not the *d* of my
Ruth 1.12 Turn back, my *d*, go your way, for I am
Esth 2. 7 Mordecai adopted her as his own *d*.
Ps 144. 12 our *d* like corner pillars, cut for the
Isa 3.17 with scabs the heads of the *d* of Zion,
Zech 9. 9 greatly, O *d* Zion! Shout aloud, O *d*
Mt 9.18 "My *d* has just died; but come and lay
21. 5 "Tell the *d* of Zion, Look, your king is
Mk 5.23 "My little *d* is at the point of death.
7.29 may go—the demon has left your *d*."
Lk 8.42 he had an only *d*, about twelve years
Acts 7.21 abandoned, Pharaoh's *d* adopted him
Heb 11.24 to be called the son of Pharaoh's *d*,

DAVID

Anointed by Samuel, 1 Sam 16.1-13; played the harp for Saul, 1 Sam 16.14-23; killed Goliath, 1 Sam 17; won Jonathan's friendship, 1 Sam 18.1-4; incurred Saul's jealousy, 1 Sam 18.5-9; married Michal, 1 Sam 18.20-29; fled from Saul, 1 Sam 19—22; fought the Philistines, 1 Sam 23; spared Saul at En-gedi, 1 Sam 24; David and Abigail, 1 Sam 25; spared Saul at Ziph, 1 Sam 26; lived among the Philistines, 1 Sam 27.1—28.2; 29; defeated the Amalekites, 1 Sam 30; made king over Judah, 2 Sam 2.1-7; made king over Israel, 2 Sam 5.1-16; brought the ark to Jerusalem, 2 Sam 6; God's covenant with David, 2 Sam 7; extended his kingdom, 2 Sam 8; David and Bath-sheba, 2 Sam 11.1—12.25; fled Absalom's revolt, 2 Sam 15—16; returned to Jerusalem, 2 Sam 19; David's song, 2 Sam 22.1—23.7; numbered Israel and Judah, 2 Sam 24; charged Solomon, 1 Kings 2.1-9; died, 1 Kings 2.10-12. (See also 1 Chr 11—29.)

Ps 78.70 He chose his servant *D*, and took him
Jer 23. 5 when I will raise up for *D* a righteous
Ezek 34.23 over them one shepherd, my servant *D*,
Mt 12. 3 Have you not read what *D* did when he
Mk 2.25 "Have you never read what *D* did when
Lk 1.32 will give him the throne of his father *D*,
Acts 2.25 For *D* says concerning him, 'I saw the
Rom 1. 3 who was descended from *D* according to
Rev 5. 5 of Judah, the Root of *D*, has conquered,

DAWN

Ps 119.147 I rise before *d* and cry for help; I put
Isa 58. 8 light shall break forth like the *d*, and
Lk 1.78 our God, the *d* from on high will break

DAWNING

Mt 28. 1 as the first day of the week was *d*, Mary

DAY (DAYS)

Gen 1. 5 God called the light *D*, and the
2. 3 God blessed the seventh *d* and hallowed
Deut 33.25 and as your *d*, so is your strength.
Josh 10.14 There has been no *d* like it before or
2 Kings 7. 9 This is a *d* of good news; if we are
Job 15.23 They know that a *d* of darkness is ready
Ps 19. 2 *D* to *d* pours forth speech, and night to
42. 8 By *d* the LORD commands his steadfast
74.16 Yours is the *d*, yours also the night; you
90.12 So teach us to count our *d* that we may
102. 11 My *d* are like an evening shadow; I
118. 24 This is the *d* that the LORD has made;
145. 2 Every *d* I will bless you, and praise your
Isa 2.12 LORD of hosts has a *d* against all that is
11.10 On that *d* the root of Jesse shall stand
12. 1 You will say in that *d*: "I will give
13. 6 Wail, for the *d* of the LORD is near; it
34. 8 the LORD has a *d* of vengeance, a year of
37. 3 "This *d* is a *d* of distress, of rebuke, and
Jer 46.10 That *d* is the *d* of the Lord GOD of
Ezek 30. 3 a *d* is near, the *d* of the LORD is near;
Joel 1.15 for the *d*! For the *d* of the LORD is near,
2.11 the *d* of the LORD is great; terrible
Am 5.18 Why do you want the *d* of the LORD? It
Zeph 1.14 great *d* of the LORD is near, near and
Zech 14. 1 a *d* is coming for the LORD, when the
Mal 3. 2 who can endure the *d* of his coming,
4. 1 the *d* is coming, burning like an oven,
Mk 13.32 "But about that *d* or hour no one
Jn 8.56 rejoiced that he would see my *d*;
Acts 5.42 every *d* in the temple and at home they
Rom 13.13 let us live honorably as in the *d*, not in
1 Cor 15.31 in danger every hour? I die every *d*!
16. 2 On the first *d* of every week, each of
2 Cor 1.14 on the *d* of the Lord Jesus we are your
6. 2 you, on a *d* of salvation I have helped
Phil 1. 6 bring it to completion by the *d* of Jesus
1 Thess 5. 2 the *d* of the Lord will come like a thief
Heb 10.25 the more as you see the *D* approaching.
2 Pet 3.10 the *d* of the Lord will come like a thief,

DEACONS

Phil 1. 1 are in Philippi, with the bishops' and *d*:
1 Tim 3. 8 *D* likewise must be serious, not

DEAD

Num 14.29 your *d* bodies shall fall in this very
16.48 He stood between the *d* and the living;
2 Kings 19.35 dawned, they were all *d* bodies.
Eccl 9. 3 live, and after that they go to the *d*.
Mt 8.22 me, and let the *d* bury their own *d*."
9.24 away; for the girl is not *d* but sleeping."
11. 5 the deaf hear, the *d* are raised, and the
22.32 He is not God of the *d*, but of the
Mk 5.39 weep? The child is not *d* but sleeping."
15.44 Pilate wondered if he were already *d*;
Lk 8.49 "Your daughter is *d*; do not trouble the
9.60 "Let the *d* bury their own *d*; but as for
15.24 son of mine was *d*, and is alive again;
Acts 14.19 out of the city, supposing that he was *d*.
20. 9 below and was picked up *d*. But Paul
Rom 8.10 though the body is *d* because of sin, the
1 Cor 15.29 who receive baptism on behalf of the *d*?
Eph 2. 1 You were *d* through the trespasses and
Jude 12 autumn trees without fruit, twice *d*,
Rev 3. 1 a name of being alive, but you are *d*.
14.13 Blessed are the *d* who from now on die
20.12 I saw the *d*, great and small, standing

DEAF

Lev 19.14 You shall not revile the *d* or put a
Isa 29.18 In that day the *d* shall hear the words
Mk 7.32 They brought to him a *d* man who had
7.37 makes the *d* hear and the dumb speak."

DEAL (DEALT)

Gen 12.16 for her sake he *d* well with Abram; and
21. 1 The LORD *d* with Sarah as he had said,
Ps 103. 10 not *d* with us according to our sins,
147. 20 has not *d* thus with any other nation;

DEAR

Ps 39.11 sin, consuming like a moth what is *d*
102. 14 For your servants hold its stones *d*, and

DEATH

Num 11.15 going to treat me, put me to *d* at once
23.10 Let me die the *d* of the upright, and let
Deut 30.15 life and prosperity, *d* and adversity.
2 Sam 15.21 whether for *d* or for life, there also your
22. 6 me, the snares of *d* confronted me.
Job 38.17 Have the gates of *d* been revealed to
Ps 116. 3 The snares of *d* encompassed me; the
116. 15 of the LORD is the *d* of his faithful ones.
Prov 14.12 to a person, but its end is the way to *d*.
Jer 21. 8 you the way of life and the way of *d*.
Ezek 18.32 I have no pleasure in the *d* of anyone,
Hos 13.14 from *D*? O *D*, where are your plagues?
Mk 5.23 daughter is at the point of *d*. Come and
14.55 testimony against Jesus to put him to *d*;
Lk 1.79 sit darkness and in the shadow of *d*,
9.27 some standing here who will not taste *d*
22. 2 looking for a way to put Jesus to *d*,
Jn 12.33 to indicate the kind of *d* he was to die.
21.19 to indicate the kind of *d* by which he
Rom 5.14 *d* excercised dominion from Adam to
8.13 you put to *d* the deeds of the body,
8.38 I am sure that neither *d*, nor life, nor
1 Cor 15.54 be fulfilled: "*D* has been swallowed up
15.55 "Where, O *d*, is your victory? Where, O
2 Cor 2.16 to the one a fragrance from *d* to *d*, to
Col 3. 5 Put to *d*, therefore, whatever in you is
2 Tim 1.10 Christ Jesus, who abolished *d* and
2 Pet 1.14 since I know that my *d* will come soon,
Rev 2.11 will not be harmed by the second *d*.

DEBORAH

Judg 4. 4 *D*, a prophetess, the wife of Lappidoth,
4.14 *D* said to Barak, "Up! For this is the day
5. 1 Then *D* and Barak . . . sang on that day,

DEBT (DEBTS)

1 Sam 22. 2 in distress, and everyone who was in *d*,
2 Kings 4. 7 "Go sell the oil and pay your *d*, and you
Neh 10.31 year and the exaction of every *d*.
Mt 18.27 released him and forgave him the *d*.

DEBTORS

Lk 7.41 "A certain creditor had two *d*; one owed
16. 5 summoning his master's *d* one by one,
Rom 8.12 we are *d*, not to the flesh, to live

DECEIT

Job 15.35 forth evil and their heart prepares *d*."
27. 4 and my tongue will not utter *d*.
Ps 10. 7 mouths are filled with cursing and *d*
17. 1 give ear to my prayer from lips free of *d*.
32. 2 and in whose spirit there is no *d*.
34.13 evil, and your lips from speaking *d*.
50.19 rein for evil, and your tongue frames *d*.
Prov 12.20 *D* is in the mind of those who plan evil,
Isa 53. 9 and there was no *d* in his mouth.
Jer 14.14 and the *d* of their own minds.
Am 8. 5 and practice *d* with false balances,
Mk 7.22 wickedness, *d*, licentiousness, envy,
Jn 1.47 truly an Israelite in whom there is no *d*!"
Rom 1.29 Full of envy, murder, strife, *d*, craftiness
2 Cor 12.16 since I was crafty, I took you in by *d*.
1 Thess 2. 3 our appeal does not spring from *d* or

DECEITFUL

Ps 5. 6 the LORD abhors the bloodthirsty and *d*.
52. 4 love all words that devour, O *d* tongue.
Prov 31.30 Charm is *d*, and beauty is vain, but a
Nah 3. 1 City of bloodshed, utterly *d*, full of
2 Cor 11.13 boasters are false apostles, *d* workers,
Eph 4.14 by their craftiness in *d* scheming.

DECEITFULNESS

Heb 3.13 of you may be hardened by the *d* of sin.

DECEIVE (DECEIVED DECEIVES DECEIVING)

Gen 29.25 for Rachel? Why then have you *d* me?"
Lev 6. 2 trespass against the LORD by *d* a
Josh 9.22 "Why did you *d* us, saying, 'We are very
1 Sam 19.17 "Why have you *d* me like this, and let
1 Kings 13.18 and drink water." But he was *d* him.
2 Kings 18.29 'Do not let Hezekiah *d* you, for he will
Job 12.16 wisdom; the *d* and the deceiver are his.
13. 9 you *d* him, as one person *d* another?
Prov 26.19 one who *d* his neighbor and says, "I am
Jer 4.10 GOD, how utterly you have *d* this people
9. 5 They all *d* their neighbors, and no one
37. 9 Do not *d* yourselves, saying, "The
Lam 1.19 I called to my lovers but they *d* me; my
Jn 7.12 were saying, "No, he is *d* the crowd."
7.47 "Surely, you have not been *d* too, have
Rom 16.18 by smooth talk and flattery they will *d*
1 Cor 6. 9 Do not be *d*! Fornicators, idolaters,
15.33 Do not be *d*: "Bad company ruins good
2 Cor 11. 3 afraid that as the serpent *d* Eve by its
Gal 6. 7 Do not be *d*; God is not mocked, for
Eph 5. 6 Let no one *d* you with empty words, for
Col 2. 4 may *d* you with plausible arguments.
2 Thess 2. 3 Let no one *d* you in any way; for that
1 Tim 2.14 Adam was not *d*, but the woman was *d*
Rev 18.23 and all nations were *d* by your sorcery.

DECEIVER (DECEIVERS)

Titus 1.10 rebellious people, idle talkers and *d*,
2 Jn 7 such person is the *d* and the antichrist.
Rev 12. 9 and Satan, the *d* of the whole world

DECENTLY

1 Cor 14.40 but all things should be done *d* and in

DECIDE (DECIDED)

1 Chr 21.12 Now *d* what answer I shall return to the
2 Chr 2. 1 Solomon *d* to build a temple for the
Isa 11. 4 and *d* with equity for the meek of the
1 Cor 2. 2 I *d* to know nothing among you except

DECISION (DECISIONS)

Deut 17. 8 If any judicial *d* is too difficult for you
17. 9 they shall announce to you the *d* in the
Prov 16.10 Inspired *d* are on the lips of a king; his
Joel 3.14 multitudes, in the valley of *d*! For the
Acts 16. 4 the *d* that had been reached by the

DECLARE (DECLARED)

1 Chr 16.24 *D* his glory among the nations, his
Ps 96. 3 *D* his glory among the nations his
145. 6 proclaimed, and I will *d* your greatness.
Isa 48. 3 "The former things I *d* long ago, they
66.19 shall *d* my glory among the nations.
Mt 7.23 Then I will *d* to them, 'I never knew
Jn 16.13 and he will *d* to you the things that are
Rom 1. 4 and was *d* to be Son of God with power

DECREE (DECREED DECREES)

Ezra 6. 8 I make a *d* regarding what you shall do
Job 20.29 God, the heritage *d* for him by God."
Ps 2. 7 I will tell of the *d* of the LORD: He said
19. 7 the *d* of the LORD are sure, making wise
78. 5 He established a *d* in Jacob, and
93. 5 Your *d* are very sure; holiness befits
99. 7 they kept his *d*, and the statutes that he
Isa 10. 1 Ah, you who make iniquitous *d*, who
Dan 4.24 O king, and it is a *d* of the Most High
6.26 I make a *d*, that in all my royal
9.24 "Seventy weeks are *d* for your people
Lk 2. 1 *d* went out from Emperor Augustus that
Acts 17. 7 acting contrary to the *d* of the emperor,
1 Cor 2. 7 hidden, which God *d* before the ages

DEDICATE (DEDICATED)

2 Sam 8.11 these also King David *d* to the LORD,
1 Kings 7.51 the things that David his father had *d*,
8.63 of Israel *d* the house of the LORD.
1 Chr 26.27 From booty won in battles they *d* gifts
2 Chr 2. 4 my God and *d* it to him for offering

DEDICATION

Num 7.10 presented offerings for the *d* of the altar
Ezra 6.17 They offered at the *d* of this house of
Neh 12.27 at the *d* of the wall of Jerusalem they
Dan 3. 2 and come to the *d* of the statue
Jn 10.22 time the festival of the *D* took place

DEED (DEEDS)

Deut 11. 7 seen every great *d* that the LORD did.
Judg 6.13 where are all his wonderful *d* that our
Job 34.11 and according to their *d* he will repay
Ps 150. 2 Praise him for his mighty *d*; praise him
Eccl 12.14 God will bring every *d* into judgment,
Jer 25.14 I will repay them according to their *d*
Lk 23.41 are getting what we deserve for our *d*,
Jn 3.19 than light because their *d* were evil.
Rom 3.20 in his sight" by *d* prescribed by the law,
8.13 you put to death the *d* of the body
Rev 14.13 their labors, for their *d* follow them."

DEEP

Job 11. 7 "Can you find out the *d* things of God?
Ps 42. 7 *D* calls to *d* at the thunder of your
92. 5 O LORD! Your thoughts are very *d*!
104. 6 You cover it with the *d* as a garment;
Prov 8.28 he established the fountains of the *d*,
Dan 2.22 He reveals *d* and hidden things; he
Lk 5. 4 into the *d* water and let down your nets
Rev 2.24 what some call 'the *d* things of Satan,'

DEFEAT

1 Cor 6. 7 at all with one another is already a *d*

DEFECT

Dan 1. 4 young men without physical *d* and

DEFEND

2 Kings 19.34 For I will *d* this city to save it, for my
20. 6 I will *d* this city for my own sake and
Ps 45. 4 for the cause of truth and to *d* the right;
Prov 31. 9 righteously, *d* the rights of the poor
Isa 37.35 I will *d* this city to save it, for my own
Lk 12.11 worry about how you are to *d* yourselves

DEFENSE

Acts 22. 1 fathers, listen to the *d* that I now make
Phil 1. 7 in the *d* and confirmation of the gospel.

DEFENSELESS

Ps 141. 8 in you I seek refuge; leave me not *d*.

DEFER (DEFERRED)

Lev 19.32 rise before the aged, and *d* to the old;
Prov 13.12 Hope *d* makes the heart sick, but a
Isa 48. 9 For my name's sake I *d* my anger, for

DEFILE (DEFILED DEFILES DEFILING)

Lev 15.31 in their uncleanness by *d* my tabernacle
18.24 Do not *d* yourselves in any of these
Num 19.13 not purify themselves, *d* the tabernacle
19.20 they have *d* the sanctuary of the LORD.
35.34 You shall not *d* the land in which you
Neh 13.29 they have *d* the priesthood, the
Ps 79. 1 they have *d* your holy temple; they have
Jer 2. 7 But when you entered you *d* my land,

Ezek 5.11 you have *d* my sanctuary with all your
20.31 you *d* yourselves with all your idols to
23.38 they have *d* my sanctuary on the same
37.23 They shall never again *d* themselves
43. 8 they were *d* my holy name by their
Dan 1. 8 not *d* himself with the royal rations of
Hos 5. 3 you have played the whore; Israel is *d*.
Mt 15.18 from the heart, and this is what *d*.
Mk 7.15 *d*, the things that come out are what *d*."
7.20 is what comes out of a person that *d*.
1 Cor 8. 7 and their conscience, being weak, is *d*.

DEFRAUD (DEFRAUDED)

Lev 6. 2 robbery, or if you have *d* his neighbor,
19.13 You shall not *d* your neighbor; you shall
Lk 19. 8 if I have *d* anyone of anything I will pay
1 Cor 6. 7 be wronged? Why not rather be *d*?

DEFY

1 Sam 17.10 "Today I *d* the ranks of Israel! Give me

DEGRADING

Rom 1.24 to impurity, to the *d* of their bodies

DELAY

Hab 2. 3 for it; it will surely come, it will not *d*.

DELIGHT (DELIGHTS) (n)

Gen 3. 6 for food, and that it was a *d* to the eyes,
Deut 28.63 as the LORD took *d* in making you
30. 9 will again take *d* in prospering you,
1 Sam 19. 1 son Jonathan took great *d* in David.
15.22 "Has the LORD as great *d* in burnt
Job 27.10 Will they take *d* in the Almighty? Will
34. 9 profits one nothing to take *d* in God.'
Ps 1. 2 but their *d* is in the law of the LORD,
36. 8 give them drink from the river of your *d*.
37. 4 Take *d* in the LORD, and he will give you
51.16 For you have no *d* in sacrifice; if I were
119. 77 that I may live; for your law is my *d*.
Prov 8.30 I was daily his *d*, rejoicing before him
11.20 but those of blameless ways are his *d*.
15. 8 but the prayer of the upright is his *d*.
16.13 Righteous lips are the *d* of a king, and
Song 2. 3 With great *d* I sat in his shadow, and
Ezek 24.16 take away from you the *d* of your eyes;

DELIGHT (DELIGHTED DELIGHTS) (v)

2 Sam 22.20 he delivered me, because he *d* in me.
1 Kings 10. 9 be the LORD your God, who has *d* in you
Job 22.26 you will *d* yourself in the Almighty,
Ps 5. 4 you are not a God who *d* in wickedness;
37.23 firm by the LORD, when he *d* in our way;
40. 8 I *d* to do your will, O my God; your law
44. 3 of your countenance, for you *d* in them.
51.19 then you will *d* in right sacrifices, in
112. 1 who greatly *d* in his commandmants.
Prov 1.22 How long will scoffers *d* in their
3.12 loves, as a father the son in whom he *d*.
Isa 1.11 I do not *d* in the blood of bulls, or of
55. 2 is good, and *d* yourselves in rich food.
58. 2 they seek me and *d* to know my ways,
62. 4 for the LORD *d* in you, and your land
Mic 7.18 because he *d* in showing clemency.
Mal 3. 1 the covenant in whom you *d*—indeed,
Rom 7.22 I *d* in the law of God, in my inmost

DELIVER

Gen 32.11 *D* me, please, from the hand of my
Ex 3. 8 I have come down to *d* them from the
5.23 done nothing at all to *d* your people."
25.22 I will *d* to you all my commands for the
Josh 2.13 to them, and *d* our lives from death."
Judg 7. 7 hundred men that lapped I will *d* you,
Ps 3. 7 Rise up, O LORD! *D* me, O my God! For
6. 4 Turn, O LORD, save my life; *d* me for the
33.19 to *d* their soul from death, and to keep
59. 1 *D* me from my enemies, O my God;
Eccl 8. 8 wickedness *d* those who practice it.
Isa 43.13 is no one who can *d* from my hand;
50. 2 redeem? Or have I no power to *d*?
Jer 1. 8 of them, for I am with you to *d* you,
Dan 3.17 serve is able to *d* us from the furnace
6.16 God, whom you faithfully serve, *d* you!"

DELIVERS (DELIVERED DELIVERING)

Gen 14.20 Most High, who has *d* your enemies
Ex 18. 9 to Israel, in *d* them from the Egyptians.
Judg 2.18 he *d* them from the hand of their
6. 9 I *d* you from the hand of the Egyptians,
7. 2 me, saying, 'My own hand has *d* me.'
2 Sam 19. 9 "The king *d* us from the hands of our
22.18 He *d* me from my strong enemy, from
22.20 place; he *d* me, because he delighted
Job 29.12 because I *d* the poor who cried, and the
Ps 18.17 He *d* me from my strong enemy, and
33.16 a warrior is not *d* by his great strength.
34. 4 me, and *d* me from all my fears.
54. 7 For he has *d* me from every trouble,
106. 10 of the foe, and *d* them from the hand of
107. 6 and he *d* them from their distress;
116. 8 For you have *d* my soul from death, my
138. 7 your hand, and your right hand *d* me.
Prov 11. 4 wrath, but righteousness *d* from death.
11. 8 The righteous are *d* from trouble, and
Eccl 9.15 man, and he by his wisdom *d* the city.
Dan 12. 1 But at that time your people shall be *d*,
Rom 15.28 *d* to them what has been collected,

DELIVERANCE

Ex 14.13 stand firm, and see the *d* that the LORD
1 Sam 11. 9 time the sun is hot, you shall have *d*.' "
11.13 today the LORD has brought *d* to Israel."
Ps 3. 8 *D* belongs to the LORD; may your
9.14 of daughter Zion, rejoice in your *d*.
22.31 proclaim his *d* to a people yet unborn,
32. 7 you surround me with glad cries of *d*.
53. 6 O that *d* for Israel would come from
Isa 46.13 I bring near my *d*, it is not far off, and
51. 5 I will bring near my *d* swiftly, my
Jon 2. 9 vowed I will pay. *D* belongs to the LORD!"
Phil 1.19 Jesus Christ this will turn out for my *d*.

DELIVERER

Judg 3. 9 LORD raised up a *d* for the Israelites,
2 Sam 22. 2 LORD is my rock, my fortress, and my *d*,
Ps 18. 2 LORD is my rock, my fortress, and my *d*,
140. 7 O LORD, my LORD, my strong *d*, you have

DELUDED

Isa 44.20 a *d* mind has led him astray, and he

DELUSION

Isa 41.29 No, they are all a *d*; their works are
2 Thess 2.11 reason God sends them a powerful *d*,

DEMANDED

Lk 12.20 very night your life is being *d* of you.
12.48 been entrusted, even more will be *d*.

DEMON (DEMONS)

Mt 15.22 David, my daughter is tormented by a *d*."
Mk 1.34 various diseases, and cast out many *d*;
3.22 and by the ruler of the *d* he casts out *d*."
9.38 someone casting out *d* in your name,
Lk 7.33 no wine, and you say, 'He has a *d*';
11.14 casting out a *d* that was mute; when
Jn 7.20 crowd answered, "You have a *d*! Who is
1 Cor 10.20 pagans sacrifice, they sacrifice to *d* and
1 Tim 4. 1 to deceitful spirits and teachings of *d*,
Jas 2.19 well. Even the *d* believe—and shudder.
Rev 9.20 or give up worshiping *d* and idols of
18. 2 It has become a dwelling place of *d*,

DEMONSTRATION

1 Cor 2. 4 but with a *d* of the Spirit and of power,

DEN

Jer 7.11 become a *d* of robbers in your sight?
Mt 21.13 but you are making it a *d* of robbers."

DENARIUS

Mk 12.15 to the test? Bring me a *d*, and let me
Lk 20.24 "Show me a *d*. Whose head and whose

DENOUNCED

Dan 3. 8 came forward and *d* the Jews.

DENY (DENIED DENIES)

Ezra 8.21 that we might *d* ourselves before our
Mt 10.33 others, I also will *d* before my Father
16.24 let them *d* themselves and take up their
26.34 cock crows, you will *d* me three times."
26.70 he *d* it before all of them, saying, "I do
Mk 8.34 let them *d* themselves and take up their
14.30 crows twice, you will *d* me three times."
14.68 he *d* it, saying, "I do not know or
Lk 12. 9 whoever *d* me before others will be
22.34 have *d* three times that you know me."
22.57 But he *d* it, saying, "Woman, I do not
Jn 18.25 are you?" He *d* it and said, "I am not."
1 Tim 5. 8 has *d* the faith and is worse than an
2 Tim 2.12 with him; if we *d* him, he also will *d*
Titus 1.16 God, but they *d* him by their actions.
2 Pet 2. 1 They will even *d* the Master who bought
1 Jn 2.22 antichrist, the one who *d* the Father
Rev 2.13 my name, and you did not *d* your faith

DEPART (DEPARTED)

Ps 18.21 and have not wickedly *d* from my God.
34.14 *D* from evil, and do good; seek peace,
Isa 52.11 *D*, *d*, go out from there! Touch no
Mt 25.41 *d* from me into the eternal fire prepared

DEPARTURE

Lk 9.31 in glory and were speaking of his *d*,
2 Pet 1.15 after my *d* you may be able at any time

DEPRAVED

1 Tim 6. 5 among those who are *d* in mind

DEPRIVE

Isa 5.23 and *d* the innocent of their rights!
1 Cor 7. 5 Do not *d* one another except perhaps by
9.15 —no one will *d* me of my ground for

DEPTHS

Ps 130. 1 Out of the *d* I cry to you , O LORD. Lord,
1 Cor 2.10 searches everything, even the *d* of God.

DERBE

Acts 14. 6 of it and fled to Lystra and *D*, cities
16. 1 Paul went on also to *D* and to Lystra,
20. 4 by Gaius of *D*, and by Timothy, as well

DERIDED

Mt 27.39 Those who passed by *d* him, shaking
Mk 15.29 Those who passed by *d* him, shaking

DESCEND (DESCENDED)

Ex 34. 5 The LORD *d* in the cloud and stood with
Lk 3.22 the Holy Spirit *d* upon him in bodily
1 Thess 4.16 will *d* from heaven, and the dead in
Heb 7.14 evident that our Lord was *d* from Judah,

DESCENDANTS

Gen 5. 1 This is a list of the *d* of Adam. When
10. 1 These are the *d* of Noah's sons, Shem,
Deut 4.40 well-being and that of your *d* after you,
Ps 89. 4 'I will establish your *d* forever, and
Rom 4.18 was said, "So numerous shall your *d* be."
9. 7 is through Isaac that *d* shall be named
Gal 3. 7 who believe are the *d* of Abraham.

DESERT

Ps 107. 4 Some wandered in *d* wastes, finding no
Isa 21.13 the scrub of the *d* plain you will lodge,
35. 6 in the wilderness, and streams in the *d*;
41.19 I will set in the *d* the cyprus, the plane
42.11 *d* and the towns lift up their voice, the
51. 3 her *d* like the garden of the LORD; joy

DESERTED (DESERTING)

Mt 14.13 from there in a boat to a *d* place
26.56 Then all the disciples *d* him and fled.
Mk 6.31 "Come away to a *d* place all by
14.50 All of them *d* him and fled.
Gal 1. 6 are so quickly *d* him the one called you
2 Tim 4.10 has *d* me and gone to Thessalonica;

DESERTERS

Mt 26.31 "You will all become *d* because of me

DESERVE (DESERVED DESERVES DESERVING)

Deut 19. 6 although a death sentence was not *d*,
Mt 10.10 or a staff; for laborers *d* their food.
26.66 verdict?" They answered, "He *d* death."
Mk 14.64 All of them condemned him as *d* death.
1 Tim 5.18 "The laborer *d* to be paid." Never accept
Rev 16. 6 them blood to drink. It is what they *d*!"

DESIGNATED

Heb 5.10 having been *d* by God a high priest

DESIGNS

2 Cor 2.11 Satan; for we are not ignorant of his *d*.

DESIRE (DESIRES) (n)

Gen 3.16 your *d* shall be for your husband, and
Deut 12. 8 today, all of us according to our own *d*,
1 Sam 9.20 And on whom is all Israel's *d* fixed, if
2 Sam 23. 5 cause to prosper all my help and my *d*?
2 Chr 9.12 granted the queen of Sheba every *d* that
Job 17.11 plans are broken off, the *d* of my heart.
Ps 10.17 LORD, you will hear the *d* of the meek;
37. 4 and he will give you the *d* of your heart.
140. 8 Grant not, O LORD, the *d* of the wicked;
145. 16 your hand, satisfying the *d* of every
145. 19 He fulfills the *d* of all who fear him; he
Prov 10.24 the *d* of the righteous will be granted.
11.23 The *d* of the righteous ends only in
13.12 sick, but a *d* fulfilled is a tree of life.
13.19 A *d* realized is sweet to the soul, but to
Eccl 6. 9 sight of eyes than the wandering of *d*;
12. 5 and *d* fails; because all must go to their
Song 7.10 I am my beloved's, and his *d* is for me.
Isa 26. 8 name and your renown are the soul's *d*.
Rom 10. 1 and sisters, my heart's *d* and prayer
Eph 2. 3 following the *d* of flesh and senses, and
1 Jn 2.16 the *d* of the flesh, the *d* of the eyes, the

DESIRE (DESIRED DESIRES) (v)

Esth 1. 8 of his palace to do as each one *d*.
Job 21.14 'Leave us alone! We do not *d* to know
Ps 19.10 More to be *d* are they than gold, even
40. 6 Sacrifice and offering you do not *d*; but
45.11 house, and the king will *d* your beauty.
51. 6 You *d* truth in the inward being;
73.25 And there is nothing on earth that I *d*
Prov 6.25 Do not *d* her beauty in your heart, and
21.10 The souls of the wicked *d* evil; their
Isa 53. 2 in his appearance that we should *d* him.
Lk 10.24 and kings *d* to see what you see!
22.15 eagerly *d* to eat this passover with you
Gal 4.21 me, you who *d* to be subject to the law,
5.17 the flesh *d* is opposed to the Spirit,

DESOLATE

Ps 68. 6 God gives the *d* a home to live in; he
Isa 1. 7 aliens devour your land; it is *d*, as
24. 1 to lay waste the earth and make it *d*,
Mt 23.38 See, your house is left to you, *d*.

DESOLATION

Jer 4.27 The whole land shall be a *d*; yet I will

Lk 21.20 armies, know that its *d* has come near.

DESPERATE

Ps 88.15 youth up. I suffer your terrors; I am *d*.

DESPISE (DESPISED DESPISING)

Gen 25.34 his way. Thus Esau *d* his birthright.
Num 6.16 the LORD; and she *d* him in her heart.
14.11 How long will this people *d* me? And
15.31 Because of having *d* the word of the
16.30 know that these men have *d* the LORD."
2 Kings 17.15 They *d* his statutes, and his covenant
2 Chr 36.16 the messengers of God, *d* his words,
Neh 4. 4 Hear, O our God, for we are *d*; turn
Job 5.17 therefore do not *d* the discipline of the
19.18 Even young children *d* me; when I rise,
42. 6 therefore I *d* myself, and repent in dust
Ps 22. 6 not human; scorned by others, and *d*
106. 24 Then they *d* the pleasant land, having
119.141 I am small and *d*, yet I do not forget
Prov 1. 7 fools *d* wisdom and instruction.
3.11 My child, do not *d* the LORD's discipline
13.13 Those who *d* the word bring destruction
Isa 1. 4 who have *d* the Holy One of Israel, who
5.24 and have *d* the word of the Holy One
49. 7 to one deeply *d*, abhorred by the
52. 5 continually, all day long my name is *d*.
53. 3 He was *d* and rejected by others; a man
Jer 4.30 you beautify yourself. Your lovers *d* you;
49.15 among the nations, *d* by humankind.
Am 5.21 I hate, I *d* your festivals, and I take no
Zech 4.10 whoever has *d* the day of small things
Mt 6.24 be devoted to the one and *d* the other.
18.10 you do not *d* one of these little ones;
Lk 16.13 be devoted to the one and *d* the other.
1 Cor 1.28 God chose what is low and *d* in the
16.11 let no one *d* him. Send him on his way
Gal 4.14 you did not scorn or *d* me, but
2 Pet 2.10 in depraved lust, and who *d* authority.

DESPOILED

Ps 12. 5 "Because the poor are *d*, because the

DESTINE (DESTINED)

Isa 65.12 I will *d* you to the sword, and all of you
Acts 13.48 many as had been *d* for eternal life
Eph 1. 5 He *d* us for adoption as his children
1 Thess 5. 9 For God has *d* us not for wrath but for
1 Pet 1.20 He was *d* before the foundation of the

DESTITUTE

Ps 102. 17 He will regard the prayer of the *d*, and
Heb 11.37 and goats, *d*, persecuted, tormented—

DESTROY (DESTROYED DESTROYING DESTROYS)

Gen 20. 4 "Lord, will you *d* an innocent people?
Num 33.52 *d* all their figured stones, *d* all their
Deut 7. 2 them, then you must utterly *d* them.
Josh 11.20 that they might be utterly *d*, and might
1 Sam 15. 3 and utterly *d* all that they have;
2 Kings 8.19 LORD would not *d* Judah, for the sake of
Ps 57. 1 take refuge, until the *d* storms pass by.
101. 8 by morning I will *d* all the wicked
Prov 1.32 and the complacency of fools *d* them;
14.11 The house of the wicked is *d*, but the
Jer 5.17 they shall *d* with the sword your
Lam 2. 2 The Lord has *d* without mercy all the
Ezek 9. 8 will you *d* all who remain of Israel as
Hos 4. 6 My people are *d* for lack of knowledge;
Mt 26.61 'I am able to *d* the temple of God and
Mk 12. 9 He will come and *d* the tenants, and
14.58 "We heard him say, 'I will *d* this temple
Lk 12.33 no thief comes near and no moth *d*.
Jn 2.19 "*D* this temple, and in three days I will
1 Cor 3.17 If anyone *d* God's temple, God will *d*
2 Thess 2. 8 whom the Lord Jesus will *d* with the
Heb 2.14 through death he might *d* the one who
2 Pet 2.12 creatures are *d*, they also will be *d*,
Rev 11.18 great, and for *d* those who *d* the earth."

DESTROYERS

Jer 22. 7 I will prepare *d* against you, all with

DESTRUCTION

Prov 16.18 Pride goes before *d*, and a haughty
Isa 28.22 have heard a decree of *d* from the Lord
Lam 2.11 ground because of the *d* of my people,
1 Cor 5. 5 man over to Satan for the *d* of the flesh,

DETERMINE (DETERMINED)

1 Sam 20. 7 angry, then know that evil is *d* by him.
2 Chr 25.16 "I know that God has *d* to destroy you,
Esth 7. 7 saw that the king had *d* to destroy him.
Job 14. 5 Since their days are *d*, and the number
Dan 11.36 completed, for what is *d* shall be done.
Lk 22.22 Son of Man is going as it has been *d*,
Rom 2.18 know his will and *d* what is best
1 Cor 7.37 and has *d* in his own mind to keep her
Phil 1.10 full insight to help you *d* what is best,

DETEST

Num 21. 5 no water, and we *d* this miserable food."

DETESTABLE

Lev 11.10 that are in the waters, they are *d* to you
Ezek 20. 7 Cast away the *d* things your eyes feast
Hos 9.10 and become *d* like the thing they loved.

DEVIL

Mt 4. 1 the wilderness to be tempted by the *d*.
13.39 enemy who sowed them is the *d*; the
Lk 8.12 the *d* comes and takes away the word
Jn 8.44 You are from your father the *d*, and you
13. 2 The *d* had already put it into the heart
Eph 4.27 and do not make room for the *d*.
Jas 4. 7 to God. Resist the *d*, and he will flee
1 Pet 5. 8 roaring lion your adversary the *d* prowls
1 Jn 3. 8 *d* has been sinning from the beginning.
3. 8 purpose, to destroy the works of the *d*.
Rev 2.10 Beware, the *d* is about to throw some of
12.12 the *d* has come down to you with great
20.10 the *d* who had deceived them was

DEVIOUS

Jer 17. 9 The heart is *d* above all else; it is

DEVISE

Prov 24. 2 for their minds *d* violence, and their
Ezek 11. 2 these are the men who *d* iniquity and
Mic 2. 1 Alas for those who *d* wickedness and

DEVOTE (DEVOTED)

Lev 27.28 every *d* thing is most holy to the LORD.
Num 18.14 Every *d* thing in Israel shall be yours.
Josh 6.18 to covet and take any of the *d* things
7. 1 broke faith in regard to the *d* things;
Ezek 44.29 and every *d* thing in Israel shall be
Mic 4.13 and shall *d* their gain to the LORD,
Titus 3. 8 may be careful to *d* themselves to good

DEVOTION

1 Chr 29. 3 because of my *d* to the house of my
Acts 11.23 faithful to the Lord with steadfast *d*;
2 Cor 11. 3 from a sincere and pure *d* to Christ.

DEVOUR (DEVOURED DEVOURING DEVOURS)

2 Sam 2.26 "Is the sword to keep *d* forever? Do you
Prov 21.20 the house of the wise, but the fool *d* it.
Isa 1.20 and rebel, you shall be *d* by the sword;
9.20 satisfied; they *d* the flesh of their own
Jer 30.16 Therefore all who *d* you shall be *d*, and
Hos 7. 7 are as an oven, and they *d* their rulers.
Mt 23.14n For you *d* widows' houses and for the

DEVOUT

Lk 2.25 Simeon, this man was righteous and *d*,

Acts 2. 5 there were *d* Jews from every nation
10. 2 He was a *d* man who feared God with
22.12 certain Ananias, who was a *d* man

DEW

Judg 6.37 if there is *d* on the fleece alone, and it
Ps 133. 3 It is like the *d* of Hermon, which falls
Prov 3.20 open, and the clouds drop down the *d*.
19.12 but his favor is like *d* on the grass.
Hos 6. 4 cloud, like the *d* that goes away early.
13. 3 mist or like the *d* that goes away early,
14. 5 I will be as the *d* to Israel; he shall

DIE (DIES DYING)

Gen 2.17 in the day that you eat of it you shall *d*."
Num 16.29 If these people *d* a natural death, or if a
26.65 them, "They shall *d* in the wilderness."
Deut 4.22 I am going to *d* in this land without
32.50 you shall *d* there on the mountain
Judg 16.30 said, "Let me *d* with the Philistines."
Job 3.11 "Why did I not *d* at birth, come forth
12. 2 the people, and wisdom will *d* with you.
14.10 But mortals *d*, and are laid low; humans
21.23 One *d* in full prosperity, being wholly at
Ps 41. 5 wonder in malice when I will *d*,
118. 17 I shall not *d*, but I shall live, and
Prov 10.21 feed many, but fools *d* for lack of sense.
19.16 who are heedless of their ways will *d*.
Eccl 2.16 How can the wise *d* just like fools?
Ezek 33.11 evil ways; why will you *d*, O house of
Mk 14.31 "Even though I must *d* with you, I will
Jn 8.24 for you will *d* in your sins unless you
11.16 us also go, that we may *d* with him."
12.24 grain; but if it *d*, it bears much fruit.
21.23 that this disciple would not *d*.
Rom 6. 9 raised from the dead, will never *d* again;
14. 8 if we *d*, we *d* to the Lord; so then,
1 Cor 15.31 in danger every hour? I *d* every day!
2 Cor 6. 9 as *d*, and see—we are alive; as
Phil 1.21 to me, living is Christ, and *d* is gain.

DIED

Gen 7.21 all flesh *d* that moved on the earth,
25. 8 Abraham . . . *d* in a good old age, an old
35.29 Isaac . . . *d* and was gathered to his
Ex 2.23 After a long time the king of Egypt *d*.
Deut 34. 5 Then Moses . . . *d* there in the land of
Josh 24.29 Joshua son of Nun . . . *d*, being one
1 Sam 31. 6 Saul and his three sons . . . *d* together
2 Sam 18.33 Would that I had *d* instead of you, O
1 Kings 22.37 So the king *d*, and was brought to
2 Kings 4.20 child sat on her lap till noon, and he *d*.
1 Chr 10.13 Saul *d* for his unfaithfulness; he was
Ezek 24.18 the morning, and at evening my wife *d*.
Lk 7.12 a man who had *d* was being carried out.
Acts 7.60 them." When he had said this, he *d*.
Rom 5. 6 the right time Christ *d* for the ungodly.
6. 2 can we who *d* to sin go on living in it?
7. 4 you have *d* to the law through the body
7.10 and I *d*, and the very commandment
1 Cor 8.11 for whom Christ *d* are destroyed.
11.30 you are weak and ill, and some have *d*.
15. 3 that Christ *d* for our sins in accordance
15. 6 are still alive, though some have *d*.
2 Cor 5.14 that one has *d* for all; therefore all have
Gal 2.19 through the law I *d* to the law, so that I
1 Thess 4.13 about those who have *d*, so that you
Rev 16. 3 and every living thing in the sea *d*.

DIFFERENCE

Ezek 44.23 people the *d* between the holy and the

DIFFERENT

1 Cor 4. 7 who sees anything *d* in you? What do
Gal 1. 6 Christ and are turning to a *d* gospel—

DIG (DIGS DUG)

Gen 26.22 moved from there and *d* another well,
Prov 26.27 Whoever *d* a pit will fall into it, and a
Eccl 10. 8 Whoever *d* a pit will fall into it; and
Mt 25.18 went off and *d* a hole in the ground
Lk 16. 3 I am not strong enough to *d*, and I am

DILIGENT (DILEGENTLY)

Deut 11.22 If you will *d* observe this entire
28.58 If you do not *d* observe all the words of
Prov 12.24 The hand of the *d* will rule, while the
13. 4 while the appetite of the *d* is richly
21. 5 The plans of the *d* lead surely to

DIM

Ps 69. 3 is parched. My eyes grow *d* with waiting

DINE

Gen 43.16 ready, for the men are to *d* with me
Lk 11.37 a Pharisee asked him to *d* with him; so

DINNER

Prov 15.17 Better is a *d* of vegetables where love is
Mt 22. 4 I have prepared my *d*, my oxen and my
Lk 14.12 or *d*, do not invite your friends or your
14.16 gave a great *d*, and invited many.

DIPPED

Mt 26.23 "The one who has *d* his hand into the
Jn 13.26 of bread when I have *d* it in the dish."

DIRECT (DIRECTED DIRECTS)

1 Sam 7. 3 *D* your heart to the LORD, and serve him
1 Chr 29.18 people, and *d* their hearts toward you.
Ps 119.128 I *d* my steps by all your precepts; I hate
Prov 16. 9 plans the way, but the LORD *d* the steps.
Isa 40.13 Who has *d* the Spirit of the LORD, or as
Mt 28.16 mountain to which Jesus had *d* them.
Acts 10.22 was *d* by a holy angel to send for you to

DIRECTION

Josh 9.14 and did not ask *d* from the LORD.

DISAPPOINTED

Job 41. 9 Any hope of capturing it will be *d*; were

DISASTER

Prov 24.22 for *d* comes from them suddenly, and
Jer 17.18 bring on them the day of *d*; destroy
44.11 I am determined to bring *d* on you, to
Am 3. 6 Does *d* befall a city, unless the LORD has
Zeph 3.15 in your midst; you shall fear *d* no more.

DISCERN (DISCERNED DISCERNING)

1 Kings 3. 9 able to *d* between good and evil;
Ps 139. 2 I rise up; you *d* my thoughts from far
Rom 12. 2 you may *d* what is the will of God—
1 Cor 1.19 the discernment of the *d* I will thwart."
2.14 them because they are spiritually *d*.
11.29 who eat and drink without *d* the body,

DISCERNMENT

1 Cor 1.19 wise, and the *d* of the discerning I will

DISCHARGED

Rom 7. 2 her husband dies she is *d* from the law
7. 6 But now we are *d* from the law, dead to

DISCIPLE (DISCIPLES)

Isa 8.16 seal the teaching among my *d*.
Mt 10. 1 Jesus summoned his twelve *d* and gave
10.24 "A *d* is not above the teacher, nor a
14.19 *d*, and the *d* gave them to the crowds.
15. 2 "Why do your *d* break the tradition of
17.16 I brought him to your *d*, but they could
21. 1 the Mount of Olives, Jesus sent two *d*,
28. 7 tell his *d*, 'He has been raised from the
28.19 Go therefore and make *d* of all nations,
Mk 3. 7 Jesus departed with his *d* to the sea,
6.45 he made his *d* get into the boat and go
8. 6 gave them to his *d* to distribute and

Mk 9.31 he was teaching his *d*, saying to them,
10.13 them, and the *d* spoke sternly to them.
Lk 6.40 A *d* is not above the teacher, but
7.18 John summoned two of his *d* and sent
9.16 broke them, and gave them to the *d* to
14.33 cannot become my *d* if you do not give
17. 3 your guard! If another *d* sins, rebuke the
19.29 he sent two of the *d*, saying, "Go into
22.39 of Olives; and the *d* followed him.
Jn 2.11 his glory; and his *d* believed in him.
3.25 arose between John's *d* and a Jew.
6.66 many of his *d* turned back and no
8.31 in my word, you are truly my *d*;
9.28 are his *d*, but we are *d* of Moses.
13.35 that you are my *d*, if you have love for
15. 8 you bear much fruit and become my *d*.
19.26 Jesus saw his mother and the *d* whom
19.38 Joseph of Arimathea, who was a *d* of
20. 2 went to Simon Peter and the other *d*,
20.19 where the *d* had met were locked for
21. 4 the *d* did not know that it was Jesus.
Acts 9.10 was a *d* at Damascus named Ananias.

DISCIPLINARIAN

Gal 3.24 the law was our *d* until Christ came, so
3.25 come, we are no longer subject to a *d*,

DISCIPLINE (n)

Job 5.17 do not despise the *d* of the Almighty.
Ps 50.17 For you hate *d*, and you cast my words
Prov 3.11 do not despise the LORD's *d* or be weary
15.10 There is severe *d* for one who forsakes
23.13 Do not withhold *d* from your children; if
Heb 12. 5 do not regard lightly the *d* of the Lord,
12.11 *d* always seems painful rather than

DISCIPLINE (DISCIPLINED DISCIPLINES)

Deut 4.36 he made you hear his voice to *d* you.
8. 5 as a parent *d* a child so the LORD your
1 Kings 12.11 My father *d* you with whips, but I will *d*
Ps 6. 1 in your anger, nor *d* me in your wrath.
38. 1 in your anger, nor *d* me in your wrath!
94.10 He who *d* the nations, he teaches
94.12 Happy are those whom you *d*, O LORD,
Prov 19.18 *D* your children while there is hope; do
29.17 *D* your children, and they will give you
Jer 31.18 "You *d* me, and I took the *d*; I was like
Hos 7.12 I will *d* them according to the report
1 Cor 11.32 we are *d* so that we may not be
Heb 12. 9 we had human parents to *d* us, and we
1 Pet 1.13 your minds for action; *d* yourselves;
Rev 3.19 I reprove and *d* those whom I love. Be

DISCLOSED

Mk 4.22 there is nothing hidden, except to be *d*;

DISCORD

Prov 6.19 falsely, and one who sows *d* in a family.

DISCOURAGE

Num 32. 7 Why will you *d* the hearts of the

DISCOVER

Ps 44.21 to a strange god, would not God *d* this?

DISCRETION

1 Chr 22.12 may the LORD grant you *d* and

DISEASE (DISEASED DISEASES)

Ex 15.26 I will not bring upon you any of the *d*
Deut 7.15 all the dread *d* of Egypt that you
1 Kings 15.23 But in his old age he was *d* in his feet.
2 Chr 16.12 yet even in his *d* he did not seek the
21.18 him in his bowels with an incurable *d*.
Ps 106. 15 but sent a wasting *d* among them.
Mt 4.23 curing every *d* and every sickness
8.17 "He took our infirmities and bore our *d*."
Mk 3.10 so that all who had *d* pressed upon him
5.29 her body that she was healed of her *d*.
Lk 6.18 to hear him and to be healed of their *d*;

DISGRACE

Josh 5. 9 rolled away from you the *d* of Egypt."
2 Kings 19. 3 is a day of distress, of rebuke, and of *d*;
Job 10.15 for I am filled with *d* and look upon my
Ps 44.15 All day long my *d* is before me, and
Prov 3.35 will inherit honor, but stubborn fools, *d*.
18. 3 comes also; and with dishonor comes *d*.
Jer 31.19 because I bore the *d* of my youth."
Ezek 22. 4 I have made you a *d* to the nations,
Mt 1.19 and unwilling to expose her to public *d*,
Lk 1.25 me and took away the *d* I have endured

DISGRACEFUL

Deut 22.21 she committed a *d* act in Israel by
1 Cor 11. 6 if it is *d* for a woman to have her hair

DISGUISE (DISGUISED DISGUISING)

1 Kings 14. 2 said to his wife, "Go, *d* yourself,
20.38 the road, *d* himself with a bandage over
2 Chr 18.29 "I will *d* myself and go into battle, but
35.22 him, but *d* himself in order to fight
2 Cor 11.13 workers, *d* themselves as apostles

DISH

Lk 11.39 the *d*, but inside you are full of greed

DISHONEST

Ex 18.21 God, are trustworthy, and hate *d* gain;
Jer 22.17 eyes and heart are only on your *d* gain,
Ezek 22.13 together at the *d* gain you have made,
Lk 16. 8 master commended the *d* manager
16.11 not been faithful with the *d* wealth,

DISHONOR

Ps 109. 29 May my accusers be clothed with *d*;
Jer 2.25 in our shame, and let our *d* cover us;
14.21 sake; do not *d* your glorious throne;

DISINHERIT

Num 14.12 strike them with pestilence and *d* them,

DISLOYALTY

Hos 14. 4 I will heal their *d*; I will love them

DISMAYED

Job 21. 6 When I think of it I am *d*, and
Dan 8.27 But I was *d* by the vision and did not

DISOBEDIENCE

Rom 5.19 just as by one man's *d* many were made

DISOBEDIENT

Lk 1.17 the *d* to the wisdom of the righteous, to
Acts 26.19 that, King Agrippa, I was not *d* to the
Rom 10.21 long I have held out my hands to a *d*
Eph 2. 2 is now at work among those who are *d*.
Titus 3. 3 For we ourselves were once foolish, *d*,
Heb 3.18 his rest, if not to those who were *d*?

DISOBEY (DISOBEYED)

Deut 17.12 anyone who presumes to *d* the priest
1 Kings 13.21 "Because you have *d* the word of the
13.26 "It is the man of God who *d* the word of
Prov 24.21 the king, and do not *d* either of them;
Lk 15.29 and I never *d* your command; yet you

DISORDER

1 Cor 14.33 God is a God not of *d* but of peace.

DISPLAYED

Ps 77.14 have *d* your might among the peoples.

DISPERSE (DISPERSED)

Isa 11.12 of Israel, and gather the *d* of Judah
Ezek 22.15 and *d* you through the countries,
36.19 and they were *d* through the countries;

DISPERSION
Jn 7.35 intend to go to the *D* among the Greeks
1 Pet 1. 1 To the exiles of the *D* in Pontus,

DISPLEASE (DISPLEASED DISPLEASING)
Gen 38.10 he did was *d* in the sight of the LORD,
48.17 hand on the head of Ephraim, it *d* him;
Num 22.34 if it is *d* to you, I will return home."
1 Sam 8. 6 But the thing *d* Samuel when they said,
2 Sam 11.27 things that David had done *d* the LORD.
1 Kings 1. 6 had never at any time *d* him by asking,
1 Chr 21. 7 God was *d* with this thing, and he
Prov 24.18 or else the LORD will see it and be *d*,
Isa 59.15 The LORD saw it, and it *d* him that there
Jon 4. 1 very *d* to Jonah, and he became angry.
1 Thess 2.15 they *d* God and oppose everyone by

DISPLEASURE
Num 14.34 forty years, and you shall know my *d*."

DISPOSSESS (DISPOSSESSED)
Deut 9. 1 go in and *d* nations larger and mightier
Acts 7.45 with Joshua when they *d* the nations

DISPUTE (DISPUTES)
Deut 19.17 then both parties to the *d* shall appear
Eccl 6.10 they are not able to *d* with those who
Lk 22.24 A *d* also arose among them as to which
2 Cor 7. 5 every way — *d* without and fear within.

DISQUALIFY (DISQUALIFIED)
1 Cor 9.27 to others I myself should not be *d*.
Col 2.18 Do not let anyone *d* you, insisting on

DISREPUTE
Acts 19.27 that this trade of ours may come into *d*
1 Cor 4.10 You are held in honor, but we in *d*. To

DISSENSION (DISSENSIONS)
Rom 16.17 keep an eye on those who cause *d* and
1 Cor 12.25 there may be no *d* within the body, but
Titus 3. 9 genealogies, *d*, and quarrels

DISSOLVED
2 Pet 3.10 elements will be *d* with fire, and the
3.11 all these things are to be *d* in this way,

DISTANCE
Lk 22.54 house. But Peter was following at a *d*.

DISTINCT
Ex 33.16 way, we shall be *d*, I and your people,

DISTINCTION (DISTINCTIONS)
Ex 8.23 I will make a *d* between my people and
11. 7 know that the LORD makes a *d* between
Lev 11.47 to make a *d* between the unclean and
20.25 make a *d* between the clean animal and
Ezek 22.26 have made no *d* between the holy and
Acts 15. 9 has made no *d* between them and us.
Rom 3.22 for all who believe. For there is no *d*,
10.12 there is no *d* between Jew and Greek;
Jas 2. 4 have you not made *d* among yourselves,

DISTINGUISH (DISTINGUISHED)
Lev 10.10 You are to *d* between the holy and the
Song 5.10 and ruddy, *d* among ten thousand.
Ezek 44.23 how to *d* between the unclean and
Dan 6. 3 Daniel *d* himself above all the other
Heb 5.14 trained by practice to *d* good from evil.

DISTRACTED
Lk 10.41 Martha, you are worried and *d* by many

DISTRESS
Deut 4.30 In your *d*, when all these things have
Judg 10.14 them deliver you in the time of your *d*."
1 Sam 22. 2 Everyone who was in *d*, and everyone
2 Sam 16.12 be that the LORD will look upon my *d*,
2 Kings 14.26 LORD saw that the *d* of Israel was very
2 Chr 15. 4 but when in their *d* they turned to the
28.22 of his *d* he became yet more faithless
33.12 he was in *d* he entreated the favor
Neh 9. 9 saw the *d* of our ancesters in Egypt and
Ps 4. 1 You gave me room when I was in *d*. Be
107. 6 and he delivered them from their *d*;
116. 3 hold on me; I suffered *d* and anguish.
120. 1 In my *d* I cry to the LORD, that he may
Prov 1.27 when *d* and anguish come upon you.
Isa 8.22 earth, but will see only *d* and darkness.
26.16 LORD, in *d* they sought you, they poured
63. 9 he became their savior in all their *d*.
Jer 30. 7 none like it; it is a time of *d* for Jacob;
Jon 2. 2 I called to the LORD out of my *d*, and he
Lk 21.23 For there will be great *d* on the earth
1 Cor 7.28 who marry will experience *d* in this life,
2 Cor 2. 4 I wrote you out of much *d* and anguish
Rev 2.22 I am throwing into great *d*, unless they

DISTRESSED (DISTRESSING)
Gen 21.11 The matter was very *d* to Abraham on
45. 5 And now do not be *d*, or angry with
1 Sam 1.10 She was deeply *d* and prayed to the
Dan 4.19 was called Beltashazzar, was severely *d*
6.14 heard the charge, he was very much *d*.
Mt 17.23 will be raised." And they were greatly *d*.
2 Pet 2. 7 Lot, a righteous man greatly *d* by the

DISTRIBUTED
Josh 13.32 the inheritances that Moses *d* in the
Heb 2. 4 by gifts of the Holy Spirit, *d* according

DISTURBED
1 Sam 28.15 said to Saul, "Why have you *d* me by
Jn 11.38 Then Jesus, again greatly *d*, came to the
Acts 17. 8 and the city officials were *d* when they

DIVIDE (DIVIDED DIVIDES DIVIDING)
Ex 14.21 into dry land; and the waters were *d*.
Num 31.27 *D* the booty into two parts, between the
Josh 19.51 of meeting. So they finished *d* the land.
2 Sam 1.23 In life and in death they were not *d*;
1 Kings 3.25 "*D* the living boy in two; then give half
Neh 9.11 you *d* the sea before them, so that they
Isa 53.12 and he shall *d* the spoil with the strong;
Ezek 37.22 and never again shall they be *d* into two
Mt 12.25 every kingdom *d* against itself is laid
Mk 3.24 If a kingdom is *d* against itself, that
15.24 him, and *d* his clothes among them.
Lk 11.17 every kingdom *d* against itself becomes
12.13 "Teacher, tell my brother to *d* the
12.53 one household will be *d*, father against
22.17 "Take this, and *d* it among yourselves;
Jn 10.19 Again the Jews were *d* because of these
19.24 "They *d* my clothes among themselves,
1 Cor 1.13 Has Christ been *d*? Was Paul crucified
Heb 4.12 piercing until it *d* soul from spirit,

DIVINATION
Gen 30.27 I have learned by *d* that the LORD has
Num 22. 7 departed with fees for *d* in their hand;
Ezek 12.24 longer be any false vision or flattering *d*
Acts 16.16 slave girl who had a spirit of *d* and

DIVINE
2 Pet 1. 4 become participants of the *d* nature.

DIVISION (DIVISIONS)
1 Chr 24. 1 The *d* of the sons of Aaron were these.
Lk 12.51 the earth? No, I tell you, but rather *d*;
1 Cor 1.10 and that there be no *d* among you,
11.18 I hear that there are *d* among you;

DIVORCE (DIVORCES)
Deut 24. 1 he writes her a certificate of *d*, puts it
Jer 3. 8 I had sent her away with a decree of *d*;
Mt 19. 7 whoever *d* his wife, except for

Mk 10. 4 a certificate of dismissal and to *d* her."
1 Cor 7.13 to live with her, she should not *d* him.

DO (DONE)

Gen 2. 3 rested from all the work that he had *d*
2 Chr 29.36 of what God had *d* for the people;
Eccl 9. 7 God has long ago approved what you *d*.
Isa 63. 7 because of all that the LORD has *d* for
Zeph 2. 3 of the land, who *d* his commands;
Mt 7.12 as you would have them *d* to you;
16.27 will repay everyone for what has been *d*.
Acts 21.19 that God had *d* among the Gentiles

DOCTOR

Lk 4.23 to me this proverb, '*D*, cure yourself!'

DOCTRINE (DOCTRINES)

Mk 7. 7 me, teaching human precepts as *d*.'
Eph 4.14 fro and blown about by every wind of *d*,
1 Tim 1. 3 people not to teach any different *d*,
Titus 1. 9 to preach with sound *d* and to refute
2.10 may be an ornament to the *d* of God

DOCUMENT

Isa 29.11 for you like the words of a sealed *d*.

DOERS

Rom 2.13 the *d* of the law who will be justified.
Jas 1.22 But be *d* of the word, and not merely

DOG (DOGS)

Judg 7. 5 who lap with their tongues, as a *d* laps,
2 Sam 9. 8 should look upon a dead *d* such as I?"
1 Kings 21.19 Naboth, *d* will also lick up your blood."
2 Kings 8.13 "What is your servant, who is a mere *d*,
Ps 59. 6 evening they come back, howling like *d*
Prov 26.17 who takes a passing *d* by the ears.
Eccl 9. 4 for a living *d* is better than a dead
Isa 56.10 they are all silent *d* that cannot bark;
Mt 7. 6 "Do not give what is holy to *d*; and do
15.26 children's food and throw it to the *d*."
Mk 7.28 even the *d* under the table eat the
Lk 16.21 the *d* would come and lick his sores.
Phil 3. 2 Beware of the *d*, beware of the evil
2 Pet 2.22 "The *d* turns back to its own vomit,"

DOME

Gen 1. 6 "Let there be a *d* in the midst of the

DOMINATED

1 Cor 6.12 for me," but I will not be *d* by anything.

DOMINION

Ps 22.28 For *d* belongs to the LORD, and he rules
72. 8 May he have *d* from sea to sea, and
103. 22 all his works, in all places of his *d*.
Ezek 30.18 dark, when I break there the *d* of Egypt,
Dan 6.26 be destroyed, and his *d* has no end.
Zech 9.10 nations; his *d* shall be from sea to sea,
Rom 5.21 grace also might exercise *d* through
6. 9 again; death no longer has *d* over him.
6.12 Do not let sin exercise *d* in your mortal

DONKEY (DONKEY'S)

Num 22.23 The *d* saw the angel of the LORD
22.28 mouth of the *d*, and it said to Balaam,
Mt 21. 5 humble, and mounted on an *d*, and on
Jn 12.15 your king is coming, sitting on a *d* colt!"
2 Pet 2.16 a speechless *d* spoke with human voice

DOOR (DOORS)

Ps 24. 7 O gates! and be lifted up, O ancient *d*!
Prov 18.16 A gift opens *d*; it gives access to the
Isa 45. 2 I will break in pieces the *d* of bronze
Hos 2.15 make the Valley of Achor a *d* of hope.
Lk 12. 3 have whispered behind closed *d* will be
13.24 "Strive to enter through the narrow *d*;
13.25 knock at the *d*, saying, 'Lord, open to
Acts 14.27 opened a *d* of faith for the Gentiles.
1 Cor 16. 9 a wide *d* for effective work has opened
Col 4. 3 God will open to us a *d* for the word,
Rev 3. 8 Look, I have set before you an open *d*,
3.20 I am standing at the *d*, knocking; if you
4. 1 and there in heaven a *d* stood open!

DOORKEEPER

Ps 84.10 I would rather be a *d* in the house of

DOORPOSTS

Ex 12. 7 blood and put it on the two *d* and the

DORCAS

Acts 9.36 name was Tabitha, which in Greek is *D*.
9.39 other clothing that *D* had made while

DOUBLE

Gen 43.15 they took *d* the money with them, as
2 Kings 2. 9 let me inherit a *d* share of your spirit."
Ps 12. 2 with flattering lips and a *d* heart they
Isa 40. 2 from the LORD's hand *d* for all her sins.
Zech 9.12 I declare that I will restore to you *d*.

DOUBT (DOUBTS)

Deut 28.66 Your life shall hang in *d* before you;
Mt 21.21 if you have faith and do not *d*, not only
Mk 11.23 sea and if you do not *d* in your heart,
Jn 20.27 put it in my side. Do not *d* but believe."
Rom 14.23 those who have *d* are condemned if

DOVE (DOVES)

Gen 8. 8 he sent out a *d* from him, to see if the
Ps 55. 6 "O that I had wings like a *d*! I would fly
Song 5.12 His eyes are like *d* beside springs of
Hos 7.11 Ephraim has become like a *d*, silly and
Mt 3.16 the Spirit of God descending like a *d*
Lk 3.22 upon him in bodily form like a *d*,
Jn 1.32 Spirit descending from heaven like a *d*,

DOWNFALL

Prov 29.16 but the righteous will look upon their *d*.
Ezek 32.10 each one of them, on the day of your *d*.

DOWNTRODDEN

Ps 74.21 Do not let the *d* be put to shame; let
147. 6 The LORD lifts up the *d*, he casts the

DRAGON

Ezek 32. 2 but you are like a *d* in the seas;
Rev 12. 3 a great red *d*, with seven heads and ten

DRAW (DRAWN DREW)

Gen 24.11 time when women go out to *d* water.
24.19 "I will *d* for your camels also, until they
Ps 18.16 took me; he *d* me out of mighty waters.
30. 1 you, O LORD, for you have *d* me up,
69.18 *D* near to me, redeem me, set me free
Song 1. 4 *D* me after you, let us make haste. The
Isa 34. 1 *D* near, O nations, to hear, O peoples,
Acts 7.17 as the time *d* near for the fulfillment of
Jas 4. 8 *D* near to God and he will *d* near to

DRAWERS

Josh 9.21 hewers of wood and *d* of water for all

DREAD

Isa 7.16 before whose two kings you are in *d*
8.12 and do not fear what it fears or be in *d*.

DREAM (DREAMED DREAMS)

Gen 28.12 he *d* that there was a ladder set up on
31.24 God came to Laban . . . in a *d* by night,
37. 5 Joseph had a *d*, and when he told it to
40. 5 One night they both *d* — the cupbearer
41. 8 Pharaoh told them his *d*, but there was
42. 9 Joseph also remembered the *d* that he
Num 12. 6 them in visions; I speak to them in *d*.
Deut 13. 1 or those who divine by *d* appear among
Judg 7.13 "I had a *d*; and in it a cake of barley

1 Kings 3. 5 the LORD appeared to Solomon in a *d*
Eccl 5. 7 With many *d* come vanities and a
Isa 29. 8 a hungry person *d* of eating and wakes
Jer 23.28 Let the prophet who has a *d* tell the *d*,
Dan 2. 1 Nebuchadnezzar *d* such *d* that his spirit
Joel 2.28 your old men shall *d d*, and your young
Mt 1.20 of the Lord appeared to him in a *d*
27.19 a great deal because of a *d* about him."
Acts 2.17 see visions, and your old men shall *d d*.

DREAMER

Gen 37.19 said to one another, "Here comes this *d*.

DRENCH

Ezek 32. 6 I will *d* the land with your flowing

DRINK (n)

Ps 36. 8 and you give them *d* from the river of
Prov 31. 6 Give strong *d* to one who is perishing,
Lk 1.15 He must never drink wine or strong *d*,
Jn 4. 7 and Jesus said to her, "Give me a *d*."
Titus 2. 3 not to be slanderers or slaves to *d*;

DRINK (DRANK DRINKING)

Gen 19.32 Come, let us make our father *d* wine,
24.14 say, '*D*, and I will water your camels'
Lev 10. 8 *D* no wine nor strong drink, neither you
2 Sam 23.15 that someone would give me water to *d*
Ps 60. 3 given us wine to *d* that made us reel.
110. 7 He will *d* from the stream by the path;
Prov 5.15 *D* water from your own cistern, flowing
25.21 if they are thirsty, give them water to *d*;
Song 5. 1 Eat, friends, *d*, and be drunk with love.
Jer 25.17 nations to whom the LORD sent me *d* it:
35. 6 But they answered, "We will *d* no wine,
Hab 2.15 for you who make your neighbors *d*,
Mt 11.18 John came neither eating nor *d*, and
24.38 before the flood they were eating and *d*,
27.34 they offered him wine to *d*, mixed with
Mk 14.23 it to them, and all of them *d* from it.
Lk 7.33 *d* no wine; and you say, 'He has a
12.29 eat and what you are to *d*, and do not
Jn 4.14 those who *d* of the water that I will give
1 Cor 10. 4 they *d* from the spiritual rock that
10.31 So, whether you eat or *d*, or whatever
11.26 this bread and *d* the cup, you proclaim
12.13 we were all made to *d* of one Spirit.
1 Tim 5.23 No longer *d* only water, but take a little

DRIVE (DRIVES DRIVING DROVE)

Gen 31.18 and he *d* away all his livestock, all the
Ex 14.21 The LORD *d* the sea back by a strong
Judg 1.27 Manasseh did not *d* out the inhabitants
2 Kings 9.20 son of Nimshi; for he *d* like a maniac."
Ps 35. 5 with the angel of the LORD *d* them on.
44. 2 with your own hand *d* out the nations,
Isa 59.19 stream that the wind of the LORD *d* on.
Mt 21.12 and *d* out all who were selling and
Jn 9.34 trying to teach us?" And they *d* him out.

DROSS

Ps 119.119 the wicked of the earth you count as *d*;
Prov 25. 4 Take away the *d* from the silver, and
Isa 1.22 Your silver has become *d*, your wine is
1.25 I will smelt away your *d* as with lye and

DROUGHT

Hag 1.11 I have called for a *d* on the land and

DROWNED

Mt 18. 6 your neck and you were *d* in the depth
Mk 5.13 into the sea, and were *d* in the sea.
Lk 8.33 the steep bank into the lake and was *d*.

DRUNK

Gen 9.21 wine and became *d*, and he lay
2 Sam 11.13 in his presence and he made him *d*;
Isa 29. 9 Be *d*, but not with wine; stagger, but
51.17 wrath, who have *d* to the dregs the bowl
Acts 2.15 Indeed, these men are not *d*, as you

DRUNKARD (DRUNKARDS)

Ps 69.12 gate, and the *d* make songs about me.
Isa 19.14 Egypt stagger in all its doings as a *d*
28. 1 the proud garland of the *d* of Ephraim,
Mt 11.19 a glutton and a *d*, a friend of tax
24.49 slaves, and eats and drinks with *d*,
Lk 7.34 'Look, a glutton and a *d*, a friend of tax
1 Cor 5.11 or is an idolater, reviler, *d*, or robber.

DRUNKENNESS

Eccl 10.17 time— for strength, and not for *d*!
Ezek 23.33 You shall be filled with *d* and sorrow. A

DRY (DRIED DRYING)

Gen 8.13 saw that the face of the ground was *d*.
Josh 2.10 heard how the LORD *d* up the water of
3.17 the priests . . . stood on *d* ground in the
Isa 44.27 deep, "Be *d*— I will *d* up your rivers";
Joel 1.12 the trees of the field are *d* up;

DUE

Rom 4. 4 reckoned as a gift but as something *d*.

DULL

Acts 28.27 For this people's heart has grown *d*,
Heb 5.11 you have become *d* in understanding.

DUST

Gen 2. 7 LORD God formed man from the *d* of the
3.14 and *d* you shall eat all the days of your
3.19 you are *d*, and to *d* you shall return."
13.16 your offspring like the *d* of the earth;
18.27 to the Lord, I who am but *d* and ashes.
Job 34.15 together, and all mortals return to *d*.
38.38 when the *d* runs into a mass and the
Ps 90. 3 You turn us back to *d*, and say, "Turn
103. 14 made; he remembers that we are *d*.
104. 29 breath, they die and return to their *d*.
Eccl 3.20 all are from the *d*, and all turn to *d*
12. 7 the *d* returns to the earth as it was, and
Mt 10.14 shake off the *d* from your feet as you
Lk 10.11 *d* of your town that clings to our feet,

DUTY

Deut 25. 5 performing the *d* of a husband's brother
1 Tim 5. 4 first learn their religious *d* to their own

DWELL (DWELLS)

Ex 29.45 I will *d* among the Israelites, and I will
1 Kings 6.13 I will *d* among the children of Israel,
8.27 will God indeed *d* on the earth? Even
Ps 23. 6 I shall *d* in the house of the LORD my
Isa 33. 5 The LORD is exalted, he *d* on high; he
Jn 14.10 own; but the Father who *d* in me does
Rom 7.17 I that do it, but sin that *d* within me.
1 Cor 3.16 temple and that God's Spirit *d* in you?
Eph 3.17 Christ may *d* in your hearts through
Jas 4. 5 for the spirit that he has made to *d*
Rev 21. 3 He will *d* with them as their God; they

DWELLING (DWELLINGS)

Job 23. 3 him, that I might come even to his *d*!
Ps 43. 3 me to your holy hill and to your *d*!
78.60 He abandoned his *d* at Shiloh, the tent
Isa 11.10 of him, and his *d* shall be glorious.
Mt 17. 4 I will make three *d* here, one for you,
Mk 9. 5 let us make three *d*, one for you, one
Lk 9.33 let us make three *d*, one for you, one
Acts 28.30n in his own hired *d* and welcome all who

DWELLING PLACE

Deut 33.27n The eternal God is a *d*, he shatters
Ps 84. 1 How lovely is your *d*, O LORD of hosts!
90. 1 Lord, you have been our *d* in all
132. 5 for the LORD, a *d* for the Mighty One
132. 7 "Let us go to his *d*; let us worship at his
Ezek 37.27 My *d* shall be with them; and I will be

DWINDLED
Isa 24. 6 inhabitants of the earth *d*, and few

E

EAGER (EAGERNESS)
Rom 1.15 —hence my *e* to proclaim the gospel to
1 Cor 14.39 friends, be *e* to prophesy, and do not
2 Cor 8.16 heart of Titus the same *e* for you that I

EAGLE (EAGLES)
Lev 11.13 they are an abomination: the *e*, the
Job 39.27 it at your command that the *e* mounts
Prov 30.19 I do not understand: the way of an *e* in
Isa 40.31 they shall mount up with wings like *e*,
Ezek 10.14 of a lion, and the fourth that of an *e*.
17. 2 A great *e*, with great wings and long

EAR (EARS)
Ex 21. 6 his master shall pierce his *e* with an
Job 42. 5 heard of you by the hearing of the *e*,
Ps 34.15 and his *e* are open to their cry.
40. 6 but you have given me an open *e*.
94. 9 who planted the *e*, does he not hear?
135. 17 they have *e*, but they do not hear, and
Prov 2. 2 making your *e* attentive to wisdom and
Jer 5.21 not see, who have *e*, but do not hear.
Ezek 12. 2 who have *e* to hear but do not hear;
Mt 13. 9 Let anyone with *e*, listen!"
26.51 of the high priest, cutting off his *e*.
Mk 4. 9 said, Let anyone with *e* to hear listen!
4.23 Let anyone with *e* to hear listen!"
14.47 of the high priest, cutting off his *e*.
Lk 14.35 away. Let anyone with *e* to hear listen!
22.50 of the high priest and cut off his right *e*.
Jn 18.10 priest's slave, and cut off his right *e*.
1 Cor 2. 9 "What no eye has seen, nor *e* heard, nor
12.16 And if the *e* would say, "Because I am
Rev 2.29 Let anyone who had an *e* listen to what

EARN
1 Cor 16. 2 aside and save whatever extra you *e*,

EARTH
Gen 1. 1 God created the heavens and the *e*,
1.10 God called the dry land *E*, and the
Josh 3.11 Lord of all the *e* is going to pass before
Job 26. 7 the void, and hangs the *e* upon nothing.
Ps 24. 1 The *e* is the LORD's and all that is in it,
33. 5 the *e* is full of the steadfast love of the
65. 9 You visit the *e* and water it, you greatly
Isa 6. 3 of hosts; the whole *e* is full of his glory."
Jer 4.27 Because of this the *e* shall mourn, and
Ezek 34.27 fruit, and the *e* shall yield its increase.
Hab 2.20 holy temple; let all the *e* keep silence
3.12 In fury you trod the *e*, in anger you
Zeph 3. 8 my passion all the *e* shall be consumed.
Mt 27.51 The *e* shook, and the rocks were split.
Mk 4.28 The *e* produces of itself, first the stalk,
1 Cor 10.26 for "the *e* and its fullness are the
15.47 first man was from the *e*, a man of dust;
2 Pet 3.13 wait for a new heavens and a new *e*,
Rev 6. 4 was permitted to take peace from the *e*,

EARTHLY
2 Cor 1.12 not by *e* wisdom but by the grace of
5. 1 if the *e* tent we live in is destroyed, we

EARTHQUAKE (EARTHQUAKES)
1 Kings 19.11 after the wind an *e*, but the LORD was
Isa 29. 6 with thunder and *e* and great noise,
Am 1. 1 Joash of Israel, two years before the *e*.
Mt 28. 2 suddenly there was a great *e*; for an
Mk 13. 8 there will be *e* in various places; there
Lk 21.11 there will be great *e*, and in various
Acts 16.26 there was an *e*, so violent that the
Rev 16.18 of thunder, and a violent *e*, such as

EASE
Job 3.26 I am not at *e*, nor am I quiet; I have no
Ps 73.12 are the wicked; always at *e*, they
Am 6. 1 Alas for those who are at *e* in Zion, and

EAST
Mt 2. 1 wise men from the *E* came to
8.11 many will come from *e* and west and
Lk 13.29 people will come from *e* and west,

EASY (EASIER)
Mt 7.13 the road is *e* that leads to destruction,
9. 5 which is *e*, to say, 'Your sins are
11.30 For my yoke is *e*, and my burden is

EAT (ATE EATEN EATING)
Gen 2.17 tree of knowledge . . . you shall not *e*,
43.32 the Egyptians could not *e* with the
Ex 12.15 days you shall *e* unleavened bread;
32. 6 the people sat down to *e* and drink, and
Lev 7.26 You must not *e* any blood whatever,
19.26 You shall not *e* anything with its blood
Deut 12. 7 you shall *e* in the presence of the LORD
1 Sam 9.24 guests." So Saul *a* with Samuel that day.
14.32 and the troops *a* them with the blood.
Ps 14. 4 all the evildoers who *e* up my people as
Prov 23. 1 you sit down to *e* with a ruler, observe
Isa 1.19 you shall *e* the good of the land;
22.13 wine. "Let us *e* and drink, for tomorrow
Jer 15.16 Your words were found, and I *a* them,
Ezek 2. 8 open your mouth and *e* what I give you.
3. 1 *e* this scroll, and go, speak to the house
Dan 4.33 from human society, *a* grass like oxen,
Mt 9.11 "Why does your teacher *e* with tax
15.38 Those who had *e* were four thousand
24.38 before the flood they were *e* and
26.26 and said, "Take, *e*; this is my body."
Mk 14.14 guest room where I may *e* the Passover
Lk 5.30 "Why do you *e* and drink with tax
12.19 many years; relax, *e*, drink, be merry.'
17.27 They were *e* and drinking, and marrying
24.43 and he took it and *a* in their presence.
Jn 4.31 were urging him, "Rabbi, *e* something."
Acts 10.13 voice saying, "Get up, Peter; kill and *e*."
11. 7 to me, 'Get up, Peter; kill and *e*.'
Rom 14. 3 Those who *e* must not despise those
1 Cor 10.27 *e* whatever is set before you without
10.31 So, whether you *e* or drink, or whatever
15.32 "Let us *e* and drink, for tomorrow we
2 Thess 3.10 anyone unwilling to work should not *e*.
Rev 3.20 I will come in to you and *e* with you,

EBENEZER
1 Sam 7.12 and named it *E*; for he said, "Thus far

EDEN
Gen 2. 8 God planted a garden in *E*, in the east;
Isa 51. 3 and will make her wilderness like *E*,
Ezek 28.13 You were in *E*, the garden of God; every
Joel 2. 3 them the land is like the garden of *E*,

EDOM (EDOMITES)
Gen 25.30 famished!" (Therefore he was called *E*.)
36. 9 descendants of Esau, ancestor of the *E*,
Num 20.21 *E* refused to give Israel passage through
2 Sam 8.14 He put garrisons in *E*; throughout all *E*
Ps 108. 9 is my washbasin; on *E* I hurl my shoe;
Isa 63. 1 "Who is this that comes from *E*, from
Am 9.12 that they may possess the remnant of *E*

EGYPT
Gen 12.10 Abram went down to *E* to reside there
37.28 of silver. And they took Joseph to *E*.
41.33 wise, and set him over the land of *E*.
45.13 father how greatly I am honored in *E*,
Ex 7. 4 I will lay my hand upon *E* and bring my
13.14 of hand the LORD brought us out of *E*,
1 Kings 3. 1 alliance with Pharaoh king of *E*;

Hos 11. 1 him, and out of *E* I called my son.
Mt 2.13 and flee to *E*, and remain there until I
2.15 "Out of *E* have I called my son."
Heb 11.26 greater wealth than the treasures of *E*,

ELDER (ELDERS)

Gen 25.23 the other, the *e* shall serve the younger."
Lev 4.15 The *e* of the congregation shall lay their
Num 11.16 "Gather for me seventy of the *e* of
Ruth 4. 2 Boaz took ten men of the *e* of the city,
Prov 31.23 city gates, taking his seat among the *e*
Mt 16.21 great suffering at the hands of the *e*
Lk 7. 3 sent some Jewish *e* to him, asking him
Acts 20.17 asking the *e* of the church to meet him.
Rom 9.12 was told, "The *e* will serve the younger."
1 Tim 4.14 laying on of hands by the council of *e*.
5.17 Let the *e* who rule well be considered
Titus 1. 5 and should appoint *e* in every town, as I
Jas 5.14 sick? They should call for the *e* of the
1 Pet 5. 1 I exhort the *e* among you to tend the
2 Jn 1 The *e* to the elect lady and her
3 Jn 1 The *e* to the beloved Garius, whom I
Rev 4. 4 on the thrones were twenty-four *e*,
19. 4 the twenty-four *e* and the four living

ELECT

Mt 24.22 for the sake of the *e* those days will be
24.31 they will gather his *e* from the four
Mk 13.20 but for the sake of the *e*, whom he
13.27 gather his *e* from the four winds, from
Rom 8.33 will bring any charge against God's *e*?
11. 7 The *e* obtained it, but the rest were
2 Tim 2.10 endure everything for the sake of the *e*,

ELECTION

Rom 9.11 that God's purpose of *e* might continue,
11.28 as regards *e* they are beloved, for the
2 Pet 1.10 more eager to confirm your call and *e*,

ELEMENTS

2 Pet 3.10 the *e* will be dissolved with fire, and the
3.12 dissolved, and the *e* will melt with fire!

ELEVEN

Mk 16.14 Later he appeared to the *e* themselves
Lk 24.33 found the *e* and their companions

ELI

1 Sam 1. 3 where two sons of *E* . . . were priests of
1. 9 Now *E* the priest was sitting on the seat
1.25 bull, and they brought the child to *E*.
2.11 Lord, in the presence of the priest *E*.
3. 1 was ministering to the Lord under *E*.
4.11 and the two sons of *E* . . . died.
4.15 *E* was ninety-eight years old and his

ELIJAH

Predicted the drought, 1 Kings 17.1; fed by ravens, 1 Kings 17.2-7; fed by the widow of Zarephath, 1 Ki 17.8-16; revived the son of the widow, 1 Kings 17.17-24; met Ahab, 1 Kings 18.1-19; triumphed over the prophets of Baal, 1 Kings 18.20-40; prayed for rain, 1 Kings 18.41-46; fled to Mount Horeb, 1 Kings 19.1-8; heard the still small voice, 1 Kings 19.9-18; chose Elisha, 1 Kings 19.19-21; reproved Ahab, 1 Kings 21.17-29; called fire from heaven, 2 Kings 1.3-16; taken up into heaven, 2 Kings 2.1-11.

Mal 4. 5 I will send you the prophet *E* before the
Mt 11.14 to accept it, he is *E* who is to come.
17. 3 appeared to them Moses and *E*, talking
Mk 9.13 I tell you that *E* has come, and they did
15.35 it, they said, "Listen, he is calling for *E*."
Lk 1.17 With the spirit and power of *E* he will
9.54n heaven and consume them as *E* did?"
Jn 1.21 "What then? Are you *E*?" He said, "I am
Jas 5.17 *E* was a human being like us, and he

ELISHA

Called, 1 Kings 19.19-21; succeeded Elijah, 2 Kings 2.1-15; purified the water, 2 Kings 2.19-22; cursed the children, 2 Kings 2.23-25; prophesied victory over the Moabites, 2 Kings 3; increased the widow's oil, 2 Kings 4.1-7; restored the life of the Shunammite's son, 2 Kings 4.8-37; purified the pot of stew, 2 Kings 4.38-41; fed a multitude, 2 Kings 4.42-44; healed Naaman's leprosy, 2 Kings 5; caused Syrians' blindness, 2 Kings 6.8-23; promised food in time of famine, 2 Kings 6.24–7.2; prophesied Hazael's cruelty, 2 Kings 8.7-15; anointed Jehu, 2 Kings 9.1-10; prophesied victory over Syria, 2 Kings 13.14-19; death and burial, 2 Kings 13.20; bones of Elisha, 2 Kings 13.21.

ELIZABETH

Lk 1. 5 of Aaron, and her name was *E*.
1.13 your wife *E* will bear you a son, and you
1.40 the house of Zechariah and greeted *E*.

ELOQUENT

Ex 4.10 O my Lord, I have never been *e*, neither
1 Cor 1.17 the gospel, and not with *e* wisdom,

EMBLEMS

Ps 74. 7 holy place; they set up their *e* there.

EMBRACED

Gen 48.10 him; and he kissed them and *e* them.
Song 2. 6 my head, and that his right hand *e* me!

EMMANUEL (see IMMANUEL)

EMMAUS

Lk 24.13 of them were going to a village called *E*,

EMPEROR (EMPEROR'S)

Mt 22.21 "Give therefore to the *e* the things that
Jn 19.12 to be a king sets himself against the *e*."
Acts 25.10 "I am appealing to the *e* tribunal; this is
Phil 4.22 you especially those of the *e* household.

EMPTY

Job 35.13 God does not hear an *e* cry, nor does
Mt 6. 7 do not heap up *e* phrases as the

ENABLE

Eccl 6. 2 yet God does not *e* them to enjoy these

ENCAMP (ENCAMPS)

Job 19.12 against me, and *e* round about my tent.
Ps 27. 3 Though an army *e* against me, my heart
34. 7 The angel of the Lord *e* around those
Isa 29. 3 like David I will *e* against you; I will

ENCOMPASSES

Jer 31.22 thing on the earth: a woman *e* a man.

ENCOURAGE (ENCOURAGED)

Deut 1.38 *e* him, for he is the one who will secure
3.28 charge Joshua, and *e* and strengthen
2 Chr 32. 8 were *e* by the words of King Hezekiah
Job 16. 5 I could *e* you with my mouth, and the
Ezek 13.22 you have *e* the wicked not to turn from
Eph 6.22 know how we are, and to *e* your hearts.
Col 2. 2 I want their hearts to be *e* and united
1 Thess 4.18 *e* one another with these words.
Titus 2. 4 *e* the young women to love their

ENCOURAGEMENT

Acts 4.36 Barnabas (which means "son of *e*").
Phil 2. 1 If then there is any *e* in Christ, any

END (ENDS) (n)

Gen 6.13 determined to make an *e* of all flesh,
Ps 2. 8 and the *e* of the earth your possession.
19. 4 and their words to the *e* of the world.
39. 4 "Lord, let me know my *e*, and what is
90. 9 our years come to an *e* like a sigh.
Eccl 4. 8 yet there is no *e* to all their toil, and
12.13 The *e* of the matter; all has been heard.
Lam 4.18 our *e* drew near; our days were

Ezek 7. 2 An *e*! The *e* has come upon the four
Dan 11.45 shall come to his *e*, with no one to help
Am 8. 2 The *e* has come upon my people Israel;
Mt 24. 3 of your coming and of the *e* of the age?"
24.14 the nations; and then the *e* will come.
28.20 am with you always, to the *e* of the age."
Jn 13. 1 in the world, he loved them to the *e*.
Acts 1. 8 and Samaria, and to the *e* of the earth."
Rom 10. 4 For Christ is the *e* of the law so that
1 Cor 13. 8 as for knowledge, it will come to an *e*.
Heb 6.16 as confirmation puts an *e* to all dispute.
1 Pet 4. 7 The *e* of all things is near; therefore be
4.17 what will be the *e* for those who do not

END (ENDS) (v)

Mt 26.58 guards in order to see how this would *e*.
1 Cor 13. 8 Love never *e*; But as for prophesies,
Heb 1.12 the same, and your years will never *e*."

ENDURANCE

Lk 21.19 By your *e* you will gain your souls.
Rom 5. 4 produces *e*, and *e* produces character,
2 Cor 6. 4 every way: through great *e*, in
Heb 10.36 For you need *e*, so that when you have
Jas 1. 3 the testing of your faith produces *e*.
2 Pet 1. 6 and self-control with *e*, and *e* with
Rev 14.12 Here is a call for the *e* of the saints,

ENDURE (ENDURED ENDURES)

Job 8.15 if one lays hold of it, it will not *e*.
Ps 72.17 May his name *e* forever, his fame
100. 5 his steadfast love *e* forever, and his
102. 26 They will perish, but you *e*; they will all
111. 3 work, and his righteousness *e* forever.
118. 2 Israel say, "His steadfast love *e* forever."
136. 2 of gods, for his steadfast love *e* forever.
Ezek 22.14 Can your courage *e*, or can your hands
Nah 1. 6 Who can *e* the heat of his anger? His
Mal 3. 2 who can *e* the day of his coming, and
Mt 10.22 But the one who *e* to the end will be
24.13 But the one who *e* to the end will be
Mk 4.17 have no root and *e* only for a while;
13.13 the one who *e* to the end will be saved.
Jn 6.27 for the food that *e* for eternal life,
1 Cor 13. 7 all things, hopes all things, *e* all things.
10.13 way out so that you may be able to *e* it.
2 Tim 2.12 if we *e*, we will also reign with him; if
Heb 12. 2 *e* the cross, disregarding its shame, and
Jas 1.12 Blessed is anyone who *e* temptation.
1 Pet 2.20 If you *e* when you are beaten for doing

ENEMY (ENEMIES)

Lev 26.32 devastate the land, so that your *e* who
Deut 28.25 cause you to be defeated before your *e*;
Judg 5.31 "So perish all your *e*, O LORD! But may
1 Kings 21.20 to Elijah, "Have you found me, O my *e*?"
Esth 9.22 the Jews gained relief from their *e*,
Job 13.24 hide your face, and count me as your *e*?
Ps 72. 9 before him, and his *e* lick the dust.
92. 9 your *e*, O LORD, for your *e* shall perish;
Prov 16. 7 he causes even their *e* to be at peace
24.17 Do not rejoice when your *e* fall, and do
25.21 If your *e* are hungry, give them bread to
Mt 5.43 love your neighbor and hate your *e*.'
22.44 until I put your *e* under your feet" '?
Lk 6.27 Love your *e*, do good to those who hate
Rom 12.20 "if your *e* are hungry, feed them; if they
1 Cor 15.26 The last *e* to be destroyed is death. For
Gal 4.16 become your *e* by telling you the truth?
Phil 3.18 many live as *e* of the cross; I have often

ENGAGE (ENGAGED)

Ex 22.16 a man seduces a virgin who is not *e*
Deut 2. 5 not to *e* in battle with them, for I will
20. 7 Has anyone become *e* to a woman but
Mt 1.18 Mary had been *e* to Joseph, but before
Lk 1.27 to a virgin *e* to a man whose name was
2. 5 registered with Mary, to whom he was *e*

ENGRAVE

Ex 28.11 you shall *e* the two stones with the
Zech 3. 9 seven facets, I will *e* its inscription,

ENJOY

Isa 65.22 and my chosen shall long *e* the work of
Heb 11.25 of God than to *e* the fleeting pleasures

ENJOYMENT

Eccl 2.24 to eat and drink and find *e* in their toil.
5.18 fitting is to eat and drink and find *e* in

ENLARGE (ENLARGED)

Ps 119. 32 for you *e* my understanding.
Isa 54. 2 *E* the sight of your tent, and let the
2 Cor 10.15 of action among you may be greatly *e*,

ENLIGHTENED

Rom 10. 2 they have a zeal for God, but it is not *e*.
Heb 10.32 after you had been *e*, you endured a

ENLIGHTENING

Ps 19. 8 of the LORD is clear, *e* the eyes;

ENOCH

Gen 4.18 To *E* was born Irad; and Irad was the
5.18 years he became the father of *E*.
5.22 *E* walked with God after the birth of
5.24 *E* walked with God; then he was no
Lk 3.37 of Methuselah, son of *E*, son of Jared,
Heb 11. 5 By faith *E* was taken so that he did not
Jude 14 It was also about these that *E*, in the

ENRAGED

Isa 8.21 when they are hungry, they will be *e*
34. 2 LORD is *e* against all the nations, and

ENRICH (ENRICHED)

1 Sam 17.25 the king will greatly *e* the man who kills
1 Cor 1. 5 in every way you have been *e* in him, in
2 Cor 9.11 You will be *e* in every way for your great

ENROLLED

Num 1.19 So he *e* them in the wilderness of Sinai.
2.33 the Levites were not *e* among the other
Heb 12.23 of the firstborn who are *e* in heaven,

ENSIGNS

Num 2. 2 under *e* by their ancestral houses; they

ENSLAVED

Rom 6. 6 and we might no longer be *e* to sin.
Gal 4. 3 while we were minors, we were *e* to the

ENTANGLED

2 Sam 22. 6 the cords of Sheol *e* me, the snares of
Ps 18. 5 the cords of Sheol *e* me; the snares of

ENTER (ENTERED)

Gen 7.13 day Noah with his sons . . . *e* the ark,
Ex 40.35 Moses was not able to *e* the tent of
Num 20.24 For he shall not *e* the land that I have
Deut 29.12 to *e* into the covenant of the LORD your
Ps 95.11 anger I swore, "They shall not *e* my rest."
100. 4 *E* his gates with thanksgiving, and his
Isa 26.20 Come, my people, *e* your chambers, and
Mt 5.20 you will never *e* the kingdom of
7.13 "*E* through the narrow gate; for the gate
7.21 to me, 'Lord, Lord,' will *e* the kingdom
19.24 hard for a rich person to *e* the kingdom
Mk 3.27 no one can *e* a strong man's house and
10.23 who have wealth to *e* the kingdom
Lk 11.52 you did not *e* yourselves, and you
Jn 3. 5 no one can *e* the kingdom of God

ENTHRONED

Ps 9. 7 But the LORD sits *e* forever, he has
80. 1 You who are *e* upon the cherubrim,
123. 1 eyes, O you who are *e* in the heavens!

ENTICE (ENTICED)

1 Kings 22.20 LORD said, 'Who will *e* Ahab, so that he
2 Chr 18.21 LORD said, "You are to *e* him, and you
Job 31. 9 "If my heart has been *e* by a woman,
Prov 1.10 child, if sinners *e* you, do not consent.
16.29 The violent *e* their neighbors, and lead
Jer 20. 7 O LORD, you have *e* me, and I was *e*;

ENTREAT (ENTREATED)

Judg 13. 8 Manoah *e* the LORD, and said, "O LORD, I
Zech 7. 2 to *e* the favor of the LORD, and to ask
2 Cor 5.20 we *e* you on behalf of Christ, be

ENTREATY

2 Chr 33.19 His prayer, and how God received his *e*,
Ezra 8.23 God for this, and he listened to our *e*.

ENTRUST (ENTRUSTED ENTRUSTING)

Num 12. 7 Moses; he is *e* with all my house.
Lk 16.11 who will *e* to you the true riches?
Jn 2.24 his part would not *e* himself to them,
Rom 3. 2 place the Jews were *e* with the oracles
1 Cor 9.17 my own will, I am *e* with a commission.
2 Cor 5.19 and *e* to us the message of
1 Tim 6.20 Timothy, guard what has been *e* to you.
2 Tim 1.12 to guard until that day what I *e* to him.
2. 2 many witnesses *e* to faithful people
1 Pet 4.19 will *e* themselves to a faithful Creator,

ENVIOUS

Ps 37. 1 do not be *e* of wrongdoers, for they will
73. 3 For I was *e* of the arrogant; I saw the
1 Cor 13. 4 love is kind; love is not *e* or boastful or

ENVOY (ENVOYS)

2 Chr 32.31 of the *e* of the officials of Babylon,
Prov 13.17 brings trouble, but a faithful *e*, healing.
Isa 33. 7 the streets; the *e* of peace weep bitterly.

ENVY (ENVIED)

Gen 26.14 so that the Philistines *e* him.
30. 1 bore Jacob no children, she *e* her sister;
Prov 3.31 Do not *e* the violent and do not choose
23.17 Do not let your heart *e* sinners, but
24. 1 Do not *e* the wicked, nor desire to be

EPHESUS

Acts 18.19 When they reached *E*, he left them
19. 1 to *E*, where he found some disciples.
20.16 For Paul had decided to sail past *E*, so
1 Cor 15.32 hopes I fought with wild animals at *E*,
1 Tim 1. 3 remain in *E* so that you may instruct
Rev 2. 1 "To the angel of the church in *E* write:

EPHRAIM (EPHRAIMITES)

Gen 41.52 The second he named *E*, "For God has
48. 1 him his two sons, Manasseh and *E*.
Num 7.48 son of Ammihud, the leader of the *E*:
Judg 1.29 *E* did not drive out the Canaanites who
Ps 78.67 he did not choose the tribe of *E*;
Hos 4.17 *E* is joined to idols—let him alone.
7. 8 *E* mixes himself with the peoples; *E* is
11. 8 How can I give you up, *E*? How can I

EPILEPTIC (EPILEPTICS)

Mt 4.24 demoniacs, *e*, and paralytics, and he
17.15 have mercy on my son, for he is an *e*

EQUAL

Jn 5.18 thereby making himself *e* with God.

EQUITY

Ps 98. 9 righteousness, and the peoples with *e*.
99. 4 lover of justice, you have established *e*;

ERECT (ERECTED)

Gen 33.20 There he *e* an altar and called it
Lev 26. 1 idols and *e* no carved images or pillars,

ERR

Prov 14.22 Do they not *e* that plan evil? Those who

ERROR (ERRORS)

Lev 5.18 atonement on your behalf for the *e* that
Num 15.25 sin offering before the LORD, for their *e*.
Job 19. 4 I have erred, my *e* remains with me.
Ps 19.12 But who can detect their *e*? Clear me
Eccl 10. 5 sun, as great an *e* as if it proceeded
Rom 1.27 own persons the due penalty for their *e*.

ESAU

Born, Gen 25.24-26; sold his birthright, Gen 25.29-34; married Hittite women, Gen 26.34; lost Isaac's blessing, Gen 27.30-40; hated Jacob, Gen 27.41; married Mahalath, Gen 28.9; reconciled with Jacob, Gen 33.1-15.

ESCAPE (ESCAPED ESCAPES)

1 Sam 22.20 named Abiathar, *e* and fled after David.
Esth 4.13 palace you will *e* any more than all the
Ps 124. 7 We have *e* like a bird from the snare of
Eccl 7.26 one who pleases God *e* her, but the
Jer 44.14 to settle in the land of Egypt shall *e*
Ezek 24.26 on that day, one who has *e* will come to
33.21 someone who had *e* from Jerusalem
Ob 17 be those that *e*, and it shall be holy;
1 Thess 5. 3 woman, and there will be no *e*!
Heb 2. 3 how can we *e* if we neglect so great a
2 Pet 2.20 they have *e* the defilements of the world

ESTABLISH (ESTABLISHED ESTABLISHES)

Gen 17. 7 I will *e* my covenant between me and
17.21 my covenant I will *e* with Isaac, whom
Deut 28. 9 LORD will *e* you as his holy people, as he
29.13 that he may *e* you today as his people,
32. 6 created you, who made you and *e* you?
2 Sam 5.12 perceived that the LORD had *e* him king
7.12 your body, and I will *e* his kingdom.
1 Kings 2.12 David, and his kingdom was firmly *e*.
9. 5 I will *e* your royal throne over Israel
1 Chr 17.14 and his throne shall be *e* forever.
Ps 8. 3 the moon and the stars that you have *e*;
74.16 night; you *e* the luminaries and the sun.
99. 4 King, lover of justice, you have *e* equity;
Prov 3.19 by understanding he *e* the heavens;
Isa 2. 2 LORD's house shall be *e* as the highest
9. 7 his kingdom. He will *e* and uphold it
16. 5 throne shall be *e* in steadfast love in
Jer 10.12 power, who *e* the world by his wisdom,
51.15 power, who *e* the world by his wisdom,
2 Cor 1.21 it is God who *e* us with you in Christ
1 Pet 5.10 restore, support, strengthen, and *e* you.

ESTATE

Prov 20.21 An *e* quickly acquired in the beginning

ESTEEM

1 Thess 5.13 *e* them very highly in love because of

ESTHER

Esth 2. 7 is *E*, his cousin, for she had neither
9.32 The command of Queen *E* fixed these

ETERNAL

Mt 18. 8 feet and to be thrown into the *e* fire.
19.16 good deed must I do to have *e* life?"
19.29 a hundredfold, and will inherit *e* life.
25.41 depart from me into the *e* fire prepared
Mk 3.29 have forgivness, but is guilty of an *e* sin"
10.17 what must I do to inherit *e* life?"
Lk 10.25 said, "what must I do to inherit *e* life?"
16. 9 may welcome you into the *e* homes.
Jn 3.16 him may not perish but may have *e* life.
12.25 life in this world will keep it for *e* life.
12.50 I know that his commandment is *e* life.
17. 2 people, to give *e* life to all whom you
Acts 13.46 to be unworthy of *e* life, we are now
13.48 as had been destined for *e* life became

Rom 2. 7 and immortality, he will give *e* life;
5.21 justification leading to *e* life through
2 Cor 4.18 but what cannot be seen is *e*.
Titus 1. 2 in hope of *e* life that God, who never
1 Jn 2.25 this is what he has promised us, *e* life.
5.13 that you may know that you have *e* life.
5.20 Christ. He is the true God and *e* life.

ETERNITY

Isa 57.15 the high and lofty one who inhabits *e*,

ETHIOPIA (ETHIOPIAN)

Ps 68.31 Egypt; let *E* hasten to stretch out its
Isa 43. 3 *E* and Seba in exchange for you.
Acts 8.27 an *E* eunuch, a court official of the

EUNUCH (EUNUCHS)

Mt 19.12 *e* who have made themselves *e* for the
Acts 8.27 an Ethiopian *e*, a court official of the

EUPHRATES

Gen 2.14 of Assyria. And the fourth river is the *E*.
15.18 the river of Egypt to . . . the river *E*,
Josh 1. 4 the river *E*, all the land of the Hittites,
24. 2 lived beyond the *E* and served other
Jer 13. 4 go now to the *E*, and hide it there in a
Rev 16.12 poured his bowl on the great river *E*,

EVANGELIST (EVANGELISTS)

Acts 21. 8 we went into the house of Philip the *e*,
Eph 4.11 some prophets, some *e*, some pastors
2 Tim 4. 5 do the work of an *e*, carry out your

EVE

Gen 3.20 The man named his wife *E*, because she
4. 1 Now the man knew his wife *E*, and she
2 Cor 11. 3 afraid that as the serpent deceived *E*
1 Tim 2.13 For Adam was formed first, then *E*; and

EVENING

Mt 8.16 That *e* they brought to him many who
Mk 1.32 That *e*, at sundown, they brought to
14.17 When it was *e*, he came with the

EVERLASTING

Gen 9.16 remember the *e* covenant between God
17. 7 for an *e* covenant, to be God to you and
21.33 on the name of the LORD, the *E* God.
Ps 139. 24 way in me, and lead me in the way *e*.
145. 13 Your kingdom is an *e* kingdom, and
Isa 9. 6 Mighty God, *E* Father, Prince
26. 4 for in the LORD GOD you have an *e* rock.
60.19 LORD will be your *e* light, and your God
Ezek 16.60 I will establish with you an *e* covenant.
Dan 12. 2 of the earth shall awake, some to *e* life,
Hab 1.12 Are you not from of *e*, O LORD my God,

EVIL

Deut 13. 5 you shall purge the *e* from your midst.
Judg 4. 1 Israelites again did what was *e* in the
10. 6 Israelites again did what was *e* in the
1 Sam 20. 7 that *e* has been determined by him.
1 Kings 11. 6 Solomon did what was *e* in the sight of
16.25 Omri did what was *e* in the sight of the
2 Chr 33. 6 He did much *e* in the sight of the LORD,
33. 9 that they did more *e* than the nations
Neh 9.28 had rest, they again did *e* before you,
Ps 7.14 See how they conceive *e*, and are
28. 4 and according to the *e* of their deeds;
35. 4 confounded who devise *e* against me.
91.10 no *e* shall befall you, no scourge come
140. 11 in the land; let *e* speedily hunt down
Prov 6.18 plans, feet that hurry to run to *e*,
Eccl 8.11 the human heart is fully set to do *e*.
Isa 5.20 Ah, you who call *e* good and good *e*,
Jer 9. 3 for they proceed from *e* to *e*, and they
16.10 pronounced all this great *e* against us?
Ezek 33.11 turn back, turn back from your *e* ways;
Dan 12. 4 back and forth, and *e* shall increase."
Nah 1.11 gone out who plots *e* against the LORD,
Mt 7.11 If you then, who are *e*, know how to
12.45 brings along seven other spirits more *e*
13.49 and separate the *e* from the righteous
15.19 out of the heart come *e* intentions,
27.23 he asked, "Why, what *e* has he done?"
Mk 15.14 asked them, "Why, what *e* has he done?"
Lk 11.13 who are *e*, know how to give good gifts
11.26 seven other spirits more *e* than itself,
Jn 7. 7 I testify against it that its works are *e*.
17.15 ask you to protect them from the *e* one.
Acts 23. 5 'You shall not speak *e* of a leader of
Rom 2. 9 and distress for everyone who does *e*,
3. 8 "Let us do *e* so that good may come?"
7.19 but the *e* I do not want is what I do.
1 Cor 5. 8 the old yeast, the yeast of malice and *e*,
Eph 4.29 Let no *e* talk come out of your mouths,
1 Thess 5.15 See that none of you repays *e* for *e*, but
1 Tim 6.10 of money is the root of all kinds of *e*,
Titus 3. 2 every good work, to speak *e* of no one,
1 Jn 2.13 because you have conquered the *e* one.

EVILDOER (EVILDOERS)

Prov 4.14 and do not walk in the way of *e*.
Mt 7.23 knew you; go away from me, you *e*.'
Lk 13.27 come from; go away from me, all you *e*!'
Rev 22.11 Let the *e* still do evil, and the filthy still

EXALT (EXALTED EXALTING EXALTS)

Ex 9.17 You are still *e* yourself against my
Josh 3. 7 "This day I will begin to *e* you in the
4.14 On that day the LORD *e* Joshua in the
1 Kings 1. 5 Now Adonijah son of Haggith *e* himself,
1 Chr 29.25 The LORD highly *e* Solomon in the sight
Job 36.22 See, God is *e* in his power; who is a
Ps 18.46 rock, and *e* be the God of my salvation,
35.26 let those who *e* themselves against me
46.10 among the nations, I am *e* in the earth."
57. 5 Be *e*, O God, above the heavens. Let
108. 5 Be *e*, O God, above the heavens, and let
138. 2 for you have *e* your name and your word
148. 13 for his name alone is *e*; his glory is
Prov 4. 8 Prize her highly, and she will *e* you; she
14.34 Righteousness *e* a nation, but sin is a
Isa 2.11 humbled; and the LORD alone will be *e*
Ezek 21.26 *E* that which is low, abase that which is
Lk 14.11 all who *e* themselves will be humbled,
Acts 5.31 God *e* him at his right hand as Leader
Phil 1.20 Christ will be *e* now as always in my
2. 9 Therefore God also highly *e* him and

EXAMINE (EXAMINED EXAMINES)

Ezra 10.16 month they sat down to *e* the matter.
Prov 5.21 of the LORD, and he *e* all their paths.
Lam 3.40 Let us test and *e* our ways, and return
Lk 23.14 I have *e* him in your presence and have
Acts 12.19 find him, he *e* the guards and ordered
17.11 eagerly and *e* the scriptures every day
22.24 and ordered him to be *e* by flogging,
1 Cor 9. 3 is my defense to those who would *e* me.
11.28 *E* yourselves, and then only eat of the
2 Cor 13. 5 *E* yourselves to see whether you are

EXAMPLE (EXAMPLES)

Jn 13.15 I have set you an *e*, that you also
1 Cor 10. 6 these things occurred as *e* for us, so
10.11 happened to them to serve as an *e*,
1 Thess 1. 7 so that you became an *e* to all the
2 Thess 3. 9 but in order to give you an *e* to imitate.
1 Tim 1.16 the utmost patience, making me an *e* to
4.12 but set the believers an *e* in speech and
1 Pet 2.21 also suffered for you, leaving you an *e*,
5. 3 in your charge, but be *e* to the flock.

EXCEEDS

Mt 5.20 unless your righteousness *e* that of the

EZRA

Ezra 7. 6 *E* went up from Babylonia. He was a
7.10 For *E* had set his heart to study the law
10. 1 While *E* prayed and made confession,
Neh 8. 1 They told *E* the scribe to bring the book

F

FACE (FACES)

Ex 33.11 the LORD used to speak to Moses *f* to *f*,
33.23 my back; but my *f* shall not be seen."
34.29 the skin of his *f* shone because he has
Num 6.25 the LORD make his *f* to shine upon you,
Deut 5. 4 LORD spoke with you *f* to *f* at the
34.10 like Moses, whom the LORD knew *f* to *f*.
2 Kings 14. 8 "Come, let us look one another in the *f*."
Ezra 9.15 though no one can *f* you because of
Ps 4. 6 Let the light of your *f* shine on us,
24. 6 who seek the *f* of the God of Jacob.
27. 8 Your *f*, LORD, do I seek. Do not hide
31.16 Let your *f* shine on your servant; save
34.16 The *f* of the LORD is against evildoers, to
67. 1 us and make his *f* to shine upon us,
119.135 Make your *f* shine upon your servant,
Song 2.14 let me see your *f*, let me hear your
Mt 6.16 hypocrites, for they disfigure their *f* so
2 Cor 3. 7 Israel could not gaze at Moses' *f*

FACTIONS

1 Cor 11.19 there have to be *f* among you, so it will

FAIL (FAILED)

Josh 23.14 not one thing has *f* of all the good
1 Sam 17.32 "Let no one's heart *f* because of him;
1 Kings 2. 4 not *f* you a successor on the throne
Job 19.14 and my close friends have *f* me;

FAINT

Song 5. 8 beloved, tell him this: I am *f* with love.
Isa 7. 4 and do not let your heart be *f* because
40.29 He gives power to the *f*, and strengthens
42. 4 He will not *f* or be crushed until he has
Lam 1.13 me back; he has left me stunned, *f*
Mt 15.32 hungry, for they might *f* on the way.
Mk 8. 3 to their homes, they will *f* on the way;

FAIR (FAIREST)

Prov 1. 9 for they are a *f* garland for your head,
Song 1. 8 If you do not know, O *f* among women,

FAITH

Deut 32.51 because both of you broke *f* with me
Josh 7. 1 Israelites broke *f* in regard to the
Ps 78.22 Israel, because they had no *f* in God,
Isa 7. 9 If you do not stand firm in *f*, you shall
Hab 2. 4 them, but the righteous live by their *f*.
Mt 8.10 in no one in Israel have I found such *f*.
8.13 it be done for you according to your *f*."
8.26 "Why are you afraid, you of little *f*?"
15.28 "Woman, great is your *f*! Let it be done
17.20 said to them, "Because of your little *f*.
21.21 if you have *f* and do not doubt, not only
Mk 2. 5 when Jesus saw their *f*, he said to the
4.40 are you afraid? Have you still no *f*?"
5.34 "Daughter, your *f* has made you well; go
11.22 Jesus answered them, "Have *f* in God.
Lk 5.20 When he saw their *f* he said, "Friend,
7. 9 not even in Israel have I found such *f*."
8.48 "Daughter, your *f* has made you well; go
12.28 will he clothe you—you of little *f*?
17. 5 said to the Lord, "Increase our *f*!"
17.19 on your way; your *f* has made you well."
18. 8 of Man comes, will he find *f* on earth?"
18.42 your sight; your *f* has saved you."
22.32 prayed for you that your own *f* may not
Acts 14. 9 and seeing that he had *f* to be healed,
14.27 had opened a door of *f* for the Gentiles.
20.21 God and *f* toward our Lord Jesus.
Acts 26.18 those who are sanctified by *f* in me.'
27.25 for I have *f* in God that it will be
Rom 1. 8 because your *f* is proclaimed throughout
1.16 God for salvation to everyone who has *f*
3.31 Do we then overthrow the law by this *f*?
4.16 For this reason it depends on *f*, in order
4.19 He did not weaken in *f* when he
5. 1 since we are justified by *f*, we have
12. 3 according to the measure of *f* that God
14. 1 Welcome those who are weak in *f*, but
14.23 whatever does not proceed from *f* is sin.
1 Cor 12. 9 to another *f* by the same Spirit, to
2 Cor 4.13 we have the same spirit of *f* that is in
Gal 1.23 the *f* he once tried to destroy."
2.16 that we may be justified by *f* in Christ,
5. 6 the only thing that counts is *f* working
6.10 especially for those of the family of *f*.
Eph 1.15 I have heard of your *f* in the Lord Jesus
2. 8 by grace you have been saved through *f*,
6.16 take the shield of *f*, with which you will
Col 1. 4 we have heard of your *f* in Christ Jesus
1 Thess 1. 3 your work of *f* and labor of love and
3. 7 encouraged about you through your *f*.
1 Tim 3.13 themselves and great boldness in the *f*
5. 8 has denied the *f* and is worse than an
6.12 Fight the good fight of the *f*; take hold
2 Tim 1. 5 I am reminded of your sincere *f*, a *f* that
Philem 6 sharing of your *f* may become effective
Heb 4. 2 not united in *f* with those who listened.
10.38 but my righteous one will live by *f*.
11. 1 Now *f* is the assurance of things hoped
11.33 who through *f* conquered kingdoms,
13. 7 of their way of life, and imitate their *f*.
Jas 2.18 and I by my works will show you my *f*.
2.22 You see that *f* was active along with his
1 Pet 1. 7 the genuineness of your *f*— being more
Jude 3 you to contend for the *f* that was once
Rev 14.12 of God and hold fast to the *f* of Jesus.

FAITHFUL

1 Sam 2.35 I will raise up for myself a *f* priest, who
22.14 among your servants is so *f* as David?
2 Chr 31.20 he did what was good and right and *f*
Neh 7. 2 —for he was a *f* man and feared God
9. 8 you found his heart *f* before you, and
Ps 4. 3 the LORD has set apart the *f* for himself;
16.10 up to Sheol, or let the *f* one see the Pit.
30. 4 O you his *f* ones, and give thanks to his
31.23 The LORD preserves the *f*, but
32. 6 let all who are *f* offer prayer to you;
37.28 justice; he will not forsake his *f* ones.
50. 5 "Gather to me my *f* ones, who made a
78. 8 steadfast, whose spirit was not *f* to God.
79. 2 the flesh of your *f* to the wild animals
101. 6 I will look with favor on the *f* in the
116. 15 of the LORD is the death of his *f* ones.
Prov 2. 8 and preserving the way of his *f* ones.
Isa 1.21 How the *f* city has become a whore! She
25. 1 things, plans formed of old, *f* and sure.
Dan 6. 4 he was *f*, and no negligence or
Hos 11.12 Judah still walks with God, and is *f* to
Mt 24.45 "Who then is the *f* and wise slave,
Lk 12.42 is the *f* and prudent manager whom his
16.10 whoever is *f* in a very little is *f* also in
Acts 11.23 them all to remain *f* to the Lord
1 Cor 1. 9 God is *f*; by him you were called into
10.13 God is *f*, and he will not let you be
Col 1. 7 He is a *f* minister of Christ on your
1 Thess 5.24 The one who calls you is *f*, and he will
2 Thess 3. 3 But the Lord is *f*; he will strengthen you
2 Tim 2. 2 entrust to *f* people who will be able to
Heb 11.11 barren— because he considered him *f*
Rev 2.10 Be *f* until death, and I will give you the
19.11 horse! Its rider is called *F* and True,

FAITHFULNESS

Ps 36. 5 to the heavens, your *f* to the clouds.

Ps 40.10 I have spoken of your *f* and your
57.10 heavens; your *f* extends to the clouds.
85.11 *F* will spring up from the ground, and
88.11 in the grave, or your *f* in Abaddon?
89. 2 forever; your *f* is as firm as the heavens.
89.33 my steadfast love, or be false to my *f*.
92. 2 in the morning, and your *f* by night,
117. 2 us, and the *f* of the LORD endures
119. 90 Your *f* endures to all generations; you
119.138 decrees in righteousnsss and in all *f*.
143. 1 give ear to my supplications in your *f*;
Jer 31. 3 therefore I have continued my *f* to you.
Lam 3.23 are new every morning; great is your *f*.
Hos 4. 1 There is no *f* or loyalty, and no

FAITHLESS (FAITHLESSLY)

Ezek 15. 8 desolate, because they have acted *f*,
Prov 13.15 favor, but the way of the *f* is their ruin.
Jer 3. 6 seen what she did, that *f* one, Israel,
Mt 17.17 "You *f* and perverse generation, how
Lk 9.41 "You *f* and perverse generation, how
Rev 21. 8 as for the cowardly, the *f*, the polluted,

FAITHLESSNESS

Ezra 9. 2 in this *f* the officials and leaders have
Rom 3. 3 Will their *f* nullify the faithfulness of

FALL (FALLEN FELL)

Num 14. 5 Moses and Aaron *f* on their faces before
16. 4 When Moses heard it, he *f* on his face.
16.22 They *f* on their faces, and said, "O God,
16.45 in a moment." And they *f* on their faces.
1 Sam 3.19 let none of his words *f* to the ground.
25.23 *f* before David on her face, bowing to
2 Sam 1.25 How the mighty have *f* in the midst of
Ps 37.24 we stumble, we shall not *f* headlong,
53. 3 They have all *f* away, they are all alike
106. 26 would make them *f* in the wilderness,
141. 10 Let the wicked *f* into their own nets,
Prov 24.17 Do not rejoice when your enemies *f*,
Isa 14.12 How you are *f* from heaven, O Day Star,
21. 9 "*F*, *f* is Babylon; and all the images of
Jer 51. 8 Suddenly Babylon has *f* and is
Hos 10. 8 Cover us, and to the hills, *F* on us.
Mic 7. 8 when I *f*, I shall rise; when I sit in
Mt 24.10 Then many will *f* away, and they will
Mk 4.17 of the word, immediately they *f* away.
Rom 11.11 So I ask, have they stumbled so as to *f*?
Gal 5. 4 from Christ; you have *f* away from grace.
Heb 4.11 one may *f* through such disobedience
6. 6 the age to come, and then have *f* away,
1 Pet 2. 8 stumble, and a rock that makes them *f*."
Rev 1.17 saw him, I *f* at his feet as though dead.
14. 8 "*F*, *f* is Babylon the great! She has made

FALLING (n)

Lk 2.34 this child is set for the *f* and the rising
1 Cor 8.13 if food is a cause of their *f*, I will never

FALSE (FALSELY)

Gen 21.23 swear . . . that you will not deal *f* with
Deut 32. 5 his degenerate children have dealt *f*
2 Chr 26.16 he was *f* to the LORD his God, and
Job 31.28 judges, for I should have been *f* to God
Ps 119. 29 Put *f* ways far from me; and graciously
119.104 therefore I hate every *f* way.
Prov 6.19 lying witness who testifies *f*, and one
Jer 51.17 for their images are *f*; and there is no
Hos 10. 2 Their heart is *f*; now they must bear
Mt 7.15 "Beware of *f* prophets, who come to you
24.24 For *f* messiahs and *f* prophets will
Phil 1.18 way, whether out of *f* motives or true;
2 Thess 2.11 leading them to believe what is *f*,

FALSEHOOD

Job 21.34 is nothing left of your answers but *f*."
Ps 62. 4 They take pleasure in *f*; they bless with
119.163 I hate and abhor *f*, but I love your law.
Prov 30. 8 Remove far from me *f* and lying; give
Isa 5.18 who drag iniquity along with cords of *f*,
Ezek 13. 6 They have envisioned *f* and lying
Eph 4.25 putting away *f*, let all of us speak the

FALSIFY

2 Cor 4. 2 to practice cunning or to *f* God's word;

FAME

Mk 1.28 At once his *f* began to spread

FAMILY (FAMILIES)

Gen 12. 3 in you all the *f* of the earth shall be
Job 19.13 "He has put my *f* far from me, and my
22. 6 pledges from your *f* for no reason,
Ps 107. 41 distress, and makes their *f* like flocks.
Jer 31. 1 I will be the God of all the *f* of Israel,
Am 3. 2 have I known of all the *f* of the earth;
Mt 25.40 of these who are members of my *f*, you
Gal 6.10 all, especially for those of the *f* of faith.

FAMINE

Gen 12.10 there was a *f* in the land. So Abram
41.30 them there will arise seven years of *f*,
47.20 fields, because *f* was severe upon them;
Ruth 1. 1 judges ruled there was a *f* in the land,
2 Sam 21. 1 a *f* in the days of David for three years,
1 Kings 18. 2 to Ahab. The *f* was severe in Samaria.
2 Kings 6.25 continued, *f* in Samaria became so great
25. 3 the *f* became so severe in the city that
1 Chr 21.12 either three years of *f*; or three months
Job 5.20 In *f* he will redeem you from death, and
Ps 105. 16 When he summoned *f* against the land,
Jer 14.15 "Sword and *f* shall not come on this
24.10 I will send sword, *f*, and pestilence
Lam 5.10 as an oven from the scorching heat of *f*.
Am 8.11 not a *f* of bread, or a thirst for water,
Acts 11.28 would be a severe *f* over all the world;

FAR

Lk 15.20 while he was still *f* off, his father saw

FAST (FASTING) (n)

2 Chr 20. 3 proclaimed a *f* throughout all Judah.
Ezra 8.21 I proclaimed a *f* there, at the river
Neh 9. 1 people of Israel were assembled with *f*
Esth 4. 3 mourning among the Jews, with *f* and
4.16 hold a *f* on my behalf, and neither eat
Ps 109. 24 My knees are weak through *f*; my body
Joel 2.12 return to me with all your heart, with *f*,
Jon 3. 5 believed God; they proclaimed a *f*,
Zech 8.19 The *f* of the fourth month, and the *f* of
Mt 17.21n not come out except by prayer and *f*."
Mk 9.29n can come out only through prayer and *f*."

FAST (FASTED FASTING) (v)

1 Sam 7. 6 They *f* that day, and said, "We have
Neh 1. 4 for days, *f* and praying before the God
Isa 58. 3 "Why do we *f*, but you do not see? Why
Zech 7. 5 seventy years, was it for me that you *f*?
Mt 4. 2 He *f* forty days and forty nights, and
6.16 so as to show others that they are *f*.
9.14 *f* often, but your disciples do not *f*?"
Mk 2.18 Pharisees *f*, but your disciples do not *f*?"
Lk 5.33 frequently *f* and pray, but your disciples

FATAL

Jer 17.16 service, nor have I desired the *f* day.

FATE

Eccl 3.19 the *f* of humans and the *f* of animals is
9. 2 since the same *f* comes to all, to the

FATHER (FATHERS FATHER'S)

Gen 2.24 Therefore a man leaves his *f* and his
5. 3 Adam . . . became the *f* of a son in his
50. 5 let me go up, so that I may bury my *f*;
Deut 32. 6 Is not he your *f*, who created you, who
1 Sam 2.25 would not listen to the voice of their *f*;

1 Sam 22. 3 “Pray let my f and my mother come to
2 Sam 7.14 I will be his f, and he shall be a son to
1 Kings 1. 6 His f had never at any time displeased
1 Chr 17.13 I will be a f to him, and he shall be a
Job 29.16 I was a f to the needy, and I
38.28 “Has the rain a f, or who has begotten
Ps 27.10 If my f and my mother forsake me, the
68. 5 F of the orphans and protector of
103. 13 As a f has compassion for his children,
Prov 1. 8 Hear, my child, your f instruction, and
10. 1 A wise child makes a glad f, but a
23.22 Listen to your f who begot you, and do
28.24 Anyone who robs f or mother and says,
Isa 64. 8 Yet, O LORD, you are our F; we are the
Mal 2.10 Have we not all one f? Has not one God
Mt 5.45 that you may be children of your F in
5.48 therefore, as your heavenly F is perfect.
6. 9 in this way: Our F in heaven, hallowed
7.21 only the one who does the will of my F
10.32 I also will acknowledge before my F in
10.37 Whoever loves f or mother more than
19. 5 a man shall leave his f and mother and
23. 9 call no man your f on earth, for you
Mk 7.11 you say that if anyone tells f or mother,
10. 7 leave his f and mother and be joined
Lk 2.49 know that I must be in my F house?”
9.59 “Lord, first let me go and bury my f.”
11.13 heavenly F give the Holy Spirit to those
12.53 will be divided, f against son and son
14.26 to me and does not hate f and mother,
Jn 12.49 but the F who sent me has himself
1 Cor 4.15 I became your f through the gospel.
2 Cor 6.18 I will be your f, and you will be my sons
Eph 6. 4 F, do not provoke your children to
Col 3.21 F, do not provoke your children, or they
Heb 7. 3 Without f, without mother, without
Jas 1.17 coming down from the F of lights, with
1 Jn 2.13 I am writing to you, f, because you

FAULT

1 Sam 29. 3 to me I have found no f in him to this
Rom 9.19 “Why then does he still find f? For who
2 Cor 6. 3 so that no f may be found with our
Heb 8. 8 God finds f with them when he says:

FAVOR

Gen 6. 8 But Noah found f in the sight of the
18. 3 if I find f with you, do not pass by your
32. 5 in order that I may find f in your sight.’ ”
33. 8 answered, “To find f with my lord.”
Ex 3.21 I will bring this people into such f with
11. 3 The LORD gave the people f in the sight
12.36 The LORD had given the people f in the
33.12 and you have also found f in my sight.’
Lev 26. 9 I will look with f upon you and make
Num 11.15 if I have found f in your sight—and do
Judg 6.17 If now I have found f with you, then
Ruth 2.10 “Why have I found f in your sight, that
2 Sam 14.22 knows that I have found f in your sight,
15.25 If I find f in the eyes of the LORD, he
Ezra 9. 8 for a brief moment f has been shown by
Esth 5. 8 If I have won the king’s f, and if it
Job 20.10 children will seek the f of the poor,
Ps 84.11 sun and shield; he bestows f and honor.
90.17 Let the f of the Lord our God be upon
115. 12 the people of Tyre will seek your f with
Prov 3. 4 So you will find f and good repute in
3.34 scornful, but to the humble he shows f.
11.27 Whoever diligently seeks good seeks f,
16.15 his f is like the clouds that bring the
18.22 good thing, and obtains f from the LORD.
Eccl 10.12 words spoken by the wise bring them f,
Isa 60.10 you down, but in my f I have had mercy
Jer 16.13 day and night, for I will show you no f.
Lk 1.30 Mary, for you have found f with God.
2.40 and the f of God was upon him.
2.52 in years, and in divine and human f.

Acts 7.46 David, who found f with God and asked
24.27 to grant the Jews a f, Felix left Paul in
2 Cor 1.15 first, so that you might have a double f;

FAVORABLE

1 Kings 22. 8 he never prophesies anything f about
22.13 with one accord are f to the king;
Ps 85. 1 LORD, you were f to your land; you

FAVORED

Lk 1.28 “Greetings, f one! The Lord is with you.”

FEAR (FEARS) (n)

Ex 14.10 In great f the Israelites cried out to the
Deut 2.25 to put the dread and f of you upon the
2 Chr 20.29 The f of God came on all the kingdoms
26. 5 who instructed him in the f of God;
Esth 8.17 because the f of the Jews had fallen
Job 28.28 the f of the Lord, that is wisdom;
Ps 2.11 Serve the LORD with f, with trembling
19. 9 the f of the LORD is pure, enduring
36. 1 there is no f of God before their eyes.
Prov 1. 7 The f of the LORD is the beginning of
9.10 The f of the LORD is the beginning of
14.27 The f of the LORD is a fountain of life,
19.23 The f of the LORD is life indeed; filled
29.25 The f of others lays a snare, but one
Isa 8.13 let him be your f, and let him be your
Mt 14.26 “It is a ghost!” And they cried out for f.
Jn 20.19 had met were locked for f of the Jews,
Rom 3.18 “There is no f of God before their eyes.”
13. 3 you wish to have no f of the authority?
1 Cor 2. 3 and in f and in much trembling.
2 Cor 5.11 knowing the f of the Lord, we try to
7. 5 way—disputes without and f within.
7.15 welcomed him with f and trembling.
1 Jn 4.18 There is no f in love, but perfect love

FEAR (FEARED FEARS) (v)

Gen 42.18 “Do this and you will live, for I f God:
Ex 1.17 because the midwives f God, he gave
9.20 of Pharaoh who f the word of the LORD
18.21 among all the people, men who f God,
Num 14. 9 and the LORD is with us; do not f them.
Deut 1.21 promised you; do not f or be dismayed.”
5.29 to f me and to keep all my
6. 2 may f the LORD your God all the days of
31. 8 or forsake you. Do not f or be dismayed.”
Josh 8. 1 the LORD said to Joshua, “Do not f or be
1 Sam 15.24 because I f the people and obeyed their
2 Chr 20.15 says the LORD to you: ‘Do not f or be
Ps 25.14 of the LORD is for those who f him,
46. 2 we will not f, though the earth
102. 15 The nations will f the name of the LORD,
111. 5 He provides food for those who f him;
119. 38 your promise, which is for those who f
Prov 3. 7 own eyes; f the LORD, and turn away
24.21 My child, f the LORD and the king, and
31.30 but a woman who f the LORD is to be
Eccl 5. 7 and a multitude of words; but f God.
8.12 it will be well with those who f God,
12.13 F God, and keep his commandments;
Isa 41.10 do not f, for I am with you, do not be
50.10 Who among you f the LORD and obeys
Jer 5.24 say in their hearts, “Let us f the LORD
33. 9 they shall f and tremble because of all
46.27 have no f, my servant Jacob, and do not
Dan 6.26 tremble and f before the God of Daniel:
Mt 14. 5 he f the crowd, because they regarded
Mk 6.20 Herod f John, knowing he was a
Lk 1.50 His mercy is for those who f him from
12. 5 I will warn you whom to f: f him who,
Acts 10. 2 He was a devout man who f God with
Rev 15. 4 Lord, who will not f and glorify your

FEAST (FEASTED FEASTING FEASTS)

Esth 9.17 they rested and made that a day of f
Ps 36. 8 They f on the abundance of your house,

Ps 63. 5 My soul is satisfied with a rich *f*, and
Isa 25. 6 for all peoples a *f* of rich food, a *f* of
Lam 4. 5 Those who *f* on delicacies perish in the
Am 8.10 I will turn your *f* into mourning, and all

FEEBLE

Neh 4. 2 "What are these *f* Jews doing? Will they
Isa 13. 7 Therefore all hands will be *f*, and every

FEED (FED)

Ex 16.32 may see the food with which I *f* you
Deut 8.16 and *f* you in the wilderness with manna
1 Kings 17. 9 commanded a widow there to *f* you."
Prov 10.21 The lips of the righteous *f* many, but
Isa 40.11 He will *f* his flock like a shepherd; he
58.14 I will *f* you with the heritage of your
61. 5 Strangers shall stand and *f* your flocks,
Jer 50.19 and it shall *f* on Carmel and in Bashan,
Ezek 34. 2 Should not shepherds *f* the sheep? You
Hos 13. 5 I who *f* you in the wilderness, in the
Mic 5. 4 he shall stand and *f* his flock in the
Mk 8. 4 "How can one *f* these people with bread
Jn 21.17 you." Jesus said to him, "*F* my sheep.

FELLOW

Gen 19. 9 "This *f* came here as an alien, and he
Ex 2.13 "Why do you strike your *f* Hebrew?"
Acts 22.22 then they shouted, "Away with such a *f*
Eph 3. 6 the Gentiles are *f* heirs, members of the
Phil 2.25 co-worker and *f* soldier, your messenger

FELLOWSHIP

Acts 2.42 the apostles' teaching and *f*, to the
1 Cor 1. 9 by him you were called into the *f* of his
Gal 2. 9 to Barnabas and me the right hand of *f*,
1 Jn 1. 3 that you also may have *f* with us; and

FESTIVAL (FESTIVALS)

Ex 23.14 in a year you shall hold a *f* for me.
Lev 23. 2 These are the appointed *f* of the LORD
23.41 You shall keep it as a *f* to the LORD
Num 29.39 offer to the LORD at your appointed *f*,
1 Kings 8.65 Solomon held the *f* at that time, and all
Dan 5. 1 King Belshazzar made a great *f* for a
Mt 26. 5 "Not during the *f*, or there may be a riot
27.15 Now at the *f* the governor was
Mk 15. 6 Now at the *f* he used to release a
Lk 2.41 to Jerusalem for the *f* of the Passover.
22. 1 the *f* of Unleavened Bread which is

FEVER

Mk 1.30 mother-in-law was in bed with a *f*,
Lk 4.38 was suffering from a high *f*,
Jn 4.52 at one in the afternoon the *f* left him."
Acts 28. 8 father of Publius lay sick in bed with *f*

FEW

Eccl 5. 2 earth; therefore let your words be *f*.
Mt 7.14 leads to life, and there are *f* who find it.
Lk 13.23 him, "Lord, will only a *f* be saved?"

FIELD

Isa 5. 8 who add *f* to *f*, until there is room for
Jer 32. 7 "Buy my *f* that is at Anathoth, for the
Mt 13.44 of heaven is like treasure hidden in a *f*,
Acts 1.19 the *f* was called in their language
1 Cor 3. 9 you are God's *f*, God's building.

FIERCE

Song 8. 6 strong as death, passion *f* as the grave.

FIG TREE (FIG TREES)

Song 2.13 The *f* puts forth its figs, and the vines
Isa 34. 4 on a vine, or fruit withering on a *f*.
Joel 1. 7 waste my vines, and splintered my *f*;
Hab 3.17 Though the *f* does not blossom, and no
Mic 4. 4 their own vines and under their own *f*,
Mt 21.19 you again!" And the *f* withered at once.
Mk 11.13 Seeing in the distance a *f* in leaf, he
Mk 13.28 "From the *f* learn its lesson: as soon as
Lk 13. 6 A man had a *f* planted in his vineyard;
21.29 "Look at the *f* and all the trees; as soon
Jn 1.48 "I saw you under the *f* before Philip
Jas 3.12 Can a *f*, my brothers and sister, yield

FIGHT (FIGHTING)

Ex 14.14 The LORD will *f* for you, and you have
Deut 1.30 God . . . is the one who will *f* for you,
20. 4 God who goes before you, to *f* for you
2 Chr 11. 4 LORD: You shall not go up or *f* against
Isa 31. 4 the LORD of hosts will come down to *f*
58. 4 Look, you fast only to quarrel and to *f*
Jer 1.19 They will *f* against you; but they shall
21. 5 I myself will *f* against you with
Zech 14.14 other; even Judah will *f* at Jerusalem.
Jn 18.36 my followers would be *f*, to keep me
Acts 5.39 you may even be found *f* against God!"
1 Tim 1.19 following them, you may *f* the good *f*.
6.12 *F* the good *f* of the faith; take hold of

FIGS

Jer 8.13 grapes on the vine, nor *f* on the fig tree;
24. 1 The LORD showed me two baskets of *f*

FILL (FILLED)

Gen 1.22 multiply and *f* the waters in the seas,
1.28 multiply, and *f* the earth and subdue it;
Ex 40.35 the glory of the LORD *f* the tabernacle.
Num 14.21 all the earth shall be *f* with the glory of
Deut 14.29 in your towns, may come and eat their *f*
1 Kings 8.11 for the glory of the LORD *f* the house of
2 Kings 24. 4 he *f* Jerusalem with innocent blood, and
2 Chr 5.14 glory of the LORD *f* the house of God.
Prov 7.18 Come, let us take our *f* of love until
Isa 27. 6 shoots, and *f* the whole world with fruit.
Ezek 43. 5 and the glory of the LORD *f* the temple.
44. 4 lo! the glory of the LORD *f* the temple
Hab 2.14 the earth will be *f* with the knowledge
Lk 1.53 he has *f* the hungry with good things,
3. 5 Every valley shall be *f*, and every
Jn 2. 7 said to them, "*F* the jars with water."
6.26 because you ate your *f* of the loaves.
Acts 2. 4 All of them were *f* with the Holy Spirit
5.28 you have *f* Jerusalem with your teaching
Eph 5.18 is debauchery; but be *f* with the Spirit,

FINAL

Ezek 21.25 come, the time of your *f* punishment,

FIND (FINDS FOUND)

Num 32.23 and be sure your sin will *f* you out.
Deut 4.29 you will *f* him if you search after him
32.10n He *f* him in a desert land, in a howling
1 Sam 25.28 evil shall not be *f* in you so long as you
2 Chr 34.15 Shaphan, "I have *f* the book of the law
Neh 8.14 they *f* it written in the law, which the
Job 23. 3 Oh, that I knew where I might *f* him,
33.24 down into the Pit; I have *f* a ransom;
Prov 8.35 For whoever *f* me *f* life and obtains
18.22 He who *f* a wife *f* a good thing, and
Song 3. 4 when I *f* him whom my soul loves.
Jer 15.16 Your words were *f*, and I ate them, and
29.14 I will let you *f* me, says the LORD, and I
Lk 15. 9 Rejoice with me, for I have *f* the coin
15.24 and is alive again; he was lost, and is *f*.
Jn 1.41 said to him. "We have *f* the Messiah"
1.45 "We have *f* him about whom Moses in
9.35 had driven him out, and when he *f* him,
Rev 20.15 not *f* written in the book of life was

FINE

Ex 2. 2 that he was a *f* child, she hid him three

FINGER (FINGERS)

Ex 8.19 said to Pharaoh, "This is the *f* of God!"
31.18 of stone, written with the *f* of God.
Deut 9.10 stone tablets written with the *f* of God;

Ps 8. 3 at your heavens, the work of your *f*,
Dan 5. 5 the *f* of a human hand appeared and
Mt 23. 4 are unwilling to lift a *f* to move them.
Lk 11.20 if it is by the *f* of God that I cast out
11.46 do not lift one *f* to ease them.

FINISH (FINISHED FINISHING)

Gen 2. 1 Thus the heavens and the earth were *f*,
1 Kings 6.14 So Solomon built the house, and *f* it.
1 Chr 28.20 the service of the house of the LORD is *f*.
Ezra 6.15 and this house was *f* on the third day of
Neh 6.15 So the wall was *f* on the twenty-fifth
Dan 9.24 to *f* the transgression, to put an end to
Lk 13.32 and on the third day I *f* my work.
Jn 17. 4 on earth by *f* the work that you gave
19.30 he said, "It is *f*." Then he bowed his
Acts 20.24 if only I may *f* my course and the
2 Tim 4. 7 good fight, I have *f* the race, I have kept
1 Pet 4. 1 has suffered in the flesh has *f* with sin),

FIRE

Gen 19.24 and Gomorrah sulfur and *f* from the
Lev 9.24 *F* came out from the LORD and
10. 1 they offered unholy *f* before the LORD,
Deut 4.12 the LORD spoke to you out of the *f*.
4.24 the LORD your God is a devouring *f*, a
5. 4 to face at the mountain, out of the *f*.
Josh 8.19 took it, and at once set the city on *f*.
Judg 1. 8 put it to the sword and set the city on *f*.
1 Kings 18.38 Then the *f* of the LORD fell and
19.12 a *f*, but the LORD was not in the *f*;
2 Kings 2.11 a chariot of *f* and horses of *f* separated
2 Chr 7. 1 Solomon had ended his prayer, *f* came
Ps 66.12 we went through *f* and through water;
83.14 As *f* consumes the forest, as the flame
Prov 26.20 For lack of wood the *f* goes out, and
Isa 43. 2 when you walk through *f* you shall not
66.24 not die, their *f* shall not be quenched,
Jer 20. 9 like a burning *f* shut up in my bones;
23.29 Is not my word like *f*, says the LORD,
36.23 the entire scroll was consumed in the *f*
Lam 1.13 "From on high he sent *f*; it went deep
Dan 3.25 walking in the middle of the *f*,
Mt 3.10 fruit is cut down and thrown into the *f*.
3.11 baptize you with the Holy Spirit and *f*.
25.41 depart from me into the eternal *f*
Lk 3.16 baptize you with the Holy Spirit and *f*.
9.54 do you want us to command *f* to come
12.49 "I came to bring *f* to the earth, and how
Jn 21. 9 ashore, they saw a charcoal *f* there,
Acts 28. 5 shook off the creature into the *f* and
1 Cor 3.13 be revealed with *f*, and the *f* will test
3.15 will be saved, but only as through *f*.
2 Thess 1. 8 with his mighty angels in flaming *f*,
Heb 12.29 for indeed our God is a consuming *f*.
Jas 3. 6 And the tongue is a *f*. The tongue is
Jude 7 undergoing a punishment of eternal *f*.
23 others by snatching them out of the *f*;
Rev 21. 8 will be in the lake that burns with *f*

FIRMAMENT

Ps 19. 1 God; and the *f* proclaims his handiwork.

FIRST

Isa 41. 4 I, the LORD, am *f*, and will be with the
Mt 6.33 strive *f* for the kingdom of God and his
19.30 many who are *f* will be last, and the last
Mk 9.35 "Whoever wants to be *f* must be last of
Lk 9.59 "Lord, *f* let me go and bury my father."
Rom 16. 5 who was the *f* convert in Asia
1 Cor 15.47 The *f* man was from the earth, a man of
16.15 were the *f* converts in Achaia,
2 Cor 8. 5 they gave themselves *f* to the Lord and,
3 Jn 9 Diotrephes, who likes to put himself *f*,
Rev 1.17 not be afraid; I am the *f* and the last,
20. 5 were ended.) This is the *f* resurrection.

FIRST FRUITS

Ex 34.26 the *f* of your ground you shall bring to
Lev 2.14 a grain offering of *f* to the LORD, you
23.10 shall bring the sheaf of the *f* of your
Num 28.26 On the day of the *f*, when you offer a
Prov 3. 9 and with the *f* of all your produce.
Rom 11.16 dough offered as *f* is holy, then the
1 Cor 15.20 the dead, the *f* of those who have died.
2 Thess 3.13 God chose you as the *f* for salvation
Jas 1.18 we would become a kind of *f* of his

FIRSTBORN

Ex 11. 5 Every *f* in the land of Egypt shall die,
Num 3.45 the Levites as substitutes for all the *f*
8.17 For all the *f* among the Israelites are
Ps 78.51 He struck all the *f* in Egypt, the first
89.27 I will make him the *f*, the highest of the
Col 1.15 the invisible God, the *f* of all creation;

FIRSTLING

Lev 27.26 A *f* of animals . . . which as a *f* belongs

FISH

Gen 1.26 let them have dominion over the *f* of
Ex 7.21 the *f* in the river died. The river stank
Isa 19. 8 Those who *f* will mourn; all who cast
Jon 1.17 provided a large *f* to swallow up Jonah;
2.10 spoke to the *f*, and it spewed Jonah out
Mt 7.10 Or if the child asks for a *f*, will give a
14.17 nothing here but five loaves and two *f*."
15.34 They said, "Seven, and a few small *f*."
17.27 take the first *f* that comes up; and when
Mk 1.17 me, and I will make you *f* for people."
6.38 found out, they said, "Five, and two *f*."
8. 7 They had also a few small *f*; and after
Lk 11.11 if your child asks for a *f*, will give a
Jn 6. 9 who has five barley loaves and two *f*.
21. 6 haul it in because there were so many *f*.

FISHERMEN

Jer 16.16 I am now sending for many *f*, says the
Mk 1.16 a net in the sea — for they were *f*.

FIVE

Mt 16. 9 you not remember the *f* loaves for the *f*
Mk 6.38 found out, they said, "*F*, and two fish."
6.44 loaves were numbered *f* thousand men.
Lk 9.13 "We have no more than *f* loaves and two
Jn 4.18 for you have had *f* husbands, and the

FIXED

Lk 4.20 of all in the synagogue were *f* on him.
Acts 17.31 because he has *f* a day on which he will

FLAME

Isa 10.17 become a fire, and his Holy One a *f*;
43. 2 and the *f* shall not consume you.

FLASHES

Song 8. 6 as the grave. Its *f* are *f* of fire, a raging
Rev 4. 5 from the throne are *f* of lightning,

FLATTER (FLATTERING FLATTERS)

Job 32.22 For I do not know how to *f*— or my
Ps 12. 2 other; with *f* lips and a double heart
36. 2 For they *f* themselves in their own eyes
Prov 26.28 its victims, and a *f* mouth works ruin.
28.23 favor than one who *f* with the tongue.
29. 5 Whoever *f* a neighbor is spreading a net

FLAVOR

Job 6. 6 is there any *f* in the juice of mallows?

FLEE (FLED)

Ex 2.15 But Moses *f* from Pharaoh. He settled
Deut 19. 5 the killer may *f* to one of these cities
1 Kings 2.29 "Joab has *f* to the tent of the LORD and
Ps 11. 1 how can you say to me, "*F* like a bird to
143. 9 my enemies; I have *f* to you for refuge.

Prov 28. 1 The wicked *f* when no one pursues, but
Jer 6. 1 *F* for safety, O children of Benjamin,
Jon 1. 3 Jonah set out to *f* to Tarshish from the
Zech 14. 5 you shall *f* as you *f* from the earthquake
Mt 2.13 child and his mother, and *f* to Egypt,
10.23 you in one town, *f* to the next;
Lk 3. 7 Who warned you to *f* from the wrath
21.21 those in Judea must *f* to the mountains,
1 Cor 10.14 dear friends, *f* from the worship of idols.

FLEECE

Judg 6.37 I am going to lay a *f* of wool on the

FLEET

1 Kings 9.26 Solomon built a *f* of ships at
10.11 Moreover, the *f* of Hiram, which carried

FLEETING

Ps 39. 4 my days; let me know how *f* my life is.
Heb 11.25 God than to enjoy the *f* pleasures of sin.

FLESH

1 Chr 11. 1 and said, "See, we are your bone and *f*.
2 Chr 32. 8 With him is an arm of *f*; but with us is
Job 19.26 destroyed, then in my *f* I shall see God,
Ps 145. 21 and all *f* will bless his holy name
Mt 26.41 indeed is willing, but the *f* is weak."
Mk 14.38 indeed is willing, but the *f* is weak."
Lk 3. 6 and all *f* shall see the salvation of God.' "
Jn 1.14 the Word became *f* and lived among us,
6.51 give for the life of the world is my *f*."
6.63 the spirit that gives life; the *f* is useless.
Rom 7.14 but I am of the *f*, sold into slavery
7.18 good dwells within me, that is, in my *f*.
8. 3 his own Son in the likeness of sinful *f*,
8. 6 To set the mind on the *f* is death, but
8. 9 But you are not in the *f*, you are in the
9. 5 according to the *f*, comes the Messiah,
1 Cor 3. 1 but rather as people of the *f*, as infants
5. 5 to Satan for the destruction of the *f*,
15.39 Not all *f* is alike, but there is one *f* for
15.50 *f* and blood cannot inherit the kingdom
2 Cor 12. 7 a thorn was given me in the *f*, a
Gal 5.17 the *f* desires is opposed to the Spirit,
Phil 3. 4 too, have reason for confidence in the *f*.

FLESHPOTS

Ex 16. 3 when we sat by the *f* and ate our fill of

FLOAT (FLOATED)

Gen 7.18 and the ark *f* on the face of the waters.
2 Kings 6. 6 threw it in there, and made the iron *f*.

FLOCK

Gen 30.41 the stronger of the *f* were breeding,
Ps 68.10 your *f* found a dwelling in it; in your
77.20 You lead your people like a *f* by the
79.13 Then we your people, the *f* of your
Isa 40.11 He will feed his *f* like a shepherd; he
Ezek 36.38 Like the *f* for sacrifices, like the *f* at
Lk 12.32 "Do not be afraid, little *f*, for it is the
1 Pet 5. 2 among you to tend to the *f* of God

FLOGGED (FLOGGING)

Mt 20.19 to be mocked and *f* and crucified;
27.26 and after *f* Jesus, he handed him over
Lk 18.33 After they have *f* him, they will kill him,
23.16 therefore have him *f* and release him."
Jn 19. 1 Then Pilate took Jesus and had him *f*
Acts 22.24 ordered him to be examined by *f*, to

FLOOD (FLOODS)

Gen 6.17 I am going to bring a *f* of waters on the
9.11 never again shall there be a *f* to destroy
Ps 6. 6 every night I *f* my bed with my tears.
29.10 The LORD sits enthroned over the *f*; the
Mt 7.27 The rain fell, and the *f* came, and the
Lk 17.27 ark, and the *f* came and destroyed all

FLOWING

Rev 22. 1 as crystal, *f* from the throne of God

FLOWER (FLOWERS)

Job 14. 2 comes up like a *f* and withers, flees like
Song 2.12 The *f* appear on the earth, the time of
Isa 40. 7 The grass withers, the *f* fades, when the

FLY (FLIES)

Ex 8.21 I will send swarms of *f* on you, your
Eccl 10. 1 Dead *f* make the perfumer's ointment
Isa 7.18 that day the LORD will whistle for the *f*

FOES

2 Sam 24.13 will you flee three months before your *f*
Ps 3. 1 O LORD, how many are my *f*! Many are
108. 13 it is he who will tread down our *f*.
Mt 10.36 and one's *f* will be members of one's

FOLD

Jer 50. 6 have gone, they have forgotten their *f*.
Jn 10.16 sheep, that do not belong to this *f*.

FOLLOW

Lev 20.23 You shall not *f* the practices of the
26. 3 If you *f* my statues and keep my
Deut 5.33 You must *f* exactly the path that the
13. 4 your God you shall *f*, him alone you
1 Sam 8. 3 his sons did not *f* in his ways, but
1 Kings 18.21 If the LORD is God, *f* him; but if Baal,
2 Kings 10.31 Jehu was not careful to *f* the law of the
Ps 38.20 my adversaries because I *f* after good.
Eccl 11. 9 *F* the inclination of your heart and the
Ezek 11.20 they may *f* my statutes and keep my
20.19 your God; *f* my statutes, and be careful
37.24 They shall *f* my ordinances and be
Mt 4.19 "*F* me, and I will make you fish for
8.19 "Teacher, I will *f* you wherever you go."
8.22 "*F* me, and let the dead bury their own
9. 9 tax booth; and he said to him, "*F* me."
Mk 2.14 tax booth; and he said to him, "*F* me."
5.37 allowed no one to *f* him except Peter,
15.41 These used to *f* him and provided for
Lk 5.27 tax booth; and he said to him, "*F* me."
9.23 and take up their cross daily and *f*
9.49 him, because he does not *f* with us."
9.57 to him, "I will *f* you wherever you go."
18.22 treasure in heaven; then come, *f* me."
Jn 1.43 He found Philip and said to him, "*F* me."
10. 4 the sheep *f* him, because they know his
10.27 my voice. I know them, and they *f* me.
12.26 Whoever serves me, must *f* me, and
13.37 "Lord, why can I not *f* you now? I will
21.19 God.) After this he said to him, "*F* me."
Rom 4.12 who also *f* the example of the faith that

FOLLOWED (FOLLOWING)

Num 32.12 for they have unreservedly *f* the LORD.'
Josh 14. 8 yet I wholeheartedly *f* the LORD my God.
2 Kings 17.15 they *f* the nations that were around
Jer 9.14 but have stubbornly *f* their own hearts
Ezek 11.12 whose statutes you have not *f*, and
Mic 6.16 of Ahab, and you have *f* their counsels.
Mt 26.58 Peter was *f* him at a distance, as far as
Mk 1.18 they left their nets and *f* him.
10.28 we have left everything and *f* you."
14.54 Peter had *f* him at a distance, right into
Lk 18.28 we have left our homes and *f* you."
22.54 house. But Peter was *f* at a distance.
Jn 1.40 John speak, and *f* him was Andrew,
18.15 Peter and another disciple *f* Jesus.

FOLLOWERS

Mt 16.24 "If any want to become my *f*, let them
Mk 8.34 "If any want to become my *f*, let them

FOLLY (FOLLIES)

1 Sam 25.25 Nabal is his name, and *f* is with him;

Ps 73. 7 fatness; their hearts overflow with *f.*
Prov 24. 9 The devising of *f* is sin, and the scoffer
26.11 his vomit is a fool who reverts to his *f.*

FOOD (FOODS)
Gen 1.29 in its fruit; you shall have them for *f.*
3. 6 woman saw that the tree was good for *f,*
Num 21. 5 no *f* and no water, and we detest this
Lam 4. 4 children beg for *f,* but no one gives
Mt 15.26 It is not fair to take the children's *f* and
Mk 7.27 not fair to take the children's *f* and
Lk 12.23 For life is more than *f,* and the body
Jn 4.32 "I have *f* to eat that you do not know
1 Cor 6.13 "*F* is meant for the stomach and the
9. 4 not have the right to our *f* and drink?
1 Tim 4. 3 marriage and demand abstinence from *f,*
6. 8 have *f* and clothing, we will be content

FOOL (FOOLS)
1 Sam 26.21 I have been a *f,* and have made a great
2 Sam 3.33 saying, "Should Abner die as a *f* dies?
Job 5. 2 Surely vexation kills the *f,* and jealousy
Ps 14. 1 *F* say in their hearts, "There is no God."
49.10 *f* and dolt perish together and leave
53. 1 *F* say in their hearts, "There is no God."
Prov 10. 8 but a babbling *f* will come to ruin.
13.16 intelligently, but the *f* displays folly.
14. 7 Leave the presence of a *f,* for there you
14. 9 *F* mock at the guilt offering, but the
16.22 has it, but folly is the punishment of *f.*
17.12 of its cubs than to confront a *f* in folly.
24. 7 Wisdom is too high for *f;* in the gate
26. 1 in harvest, so honor is not fitting for a *f.*
26. 5 Answer *f* according to their folly, or they
Eccl 2.15 happens to the *f* will happen to me
4. 5 *F* fold their hands, and consume their
7.17 not be too wicked, and do not be a *f;*
Isa 35. 8 no traveler, not even *f,* shall go astray.
Mt 5.22 if you say, 'You *f!*' you will be liable to
Lk 11.40 You *f!* Did not the one who made the
12.20 'you *f!* This very night your life is being
Rom 1.22 Claiming to be wise, they became *f,* and
1 Cor 4.10 We are *f* for the sake of Christ, but you

FOOLISH
Isa 44.25 the wise, and makes their knowledge *f;*
Jer 4.22 "For my people are *f,* they do not know
Mt 7.26 will be like a *f* man who built his house
Lk 24.25 "Oh, how *f* you are, and how slow of

FOOLISHNESS
1 Cor 1.21 through the *f* of our proclamation,
2.14 of God's Spirit, for they are *f* to them,

FOOT (FEET)
Ps 2.12 with trembling kiss his *f,* or he will be
8. 6 you have put all things under their *f,*
119. 59 of your ways, turn my *f* to your decrees;
119.105 Your word is a lamp to my *f* and a light
121. 3 He will not let your *f* be moved, he who
Song 7. 1 How graceful are your *f* in sandals, O
Nah 1.15 mountains the *f* of one who brings good
Mt 22.44 until I put your enemies under your *f*" '?
28. 9 him, took hold of his *f,* and worshiped
Mk 9.45 if your *f* causes you to stumble, cut it
12.36 until I put your enemies under your *f.*" '
Lk 7.38 to bathe his *f* with her tears and to dry
10.39 Mary, who sat at the Lord's *f* and
24.39 Look at my hands and my *f;* see that it
Jn 12. 3 anointed Jesus' *f* and wiped them with
13. 5 began to wash the disciples' *f* and to
Rom 3.15 Their *f* are swift to shed blood, ruin and
1 Cor 12.15 If the *f* would say, "Because I am not a
15.25 he has put all his enemies under his *f.*

FOOT-RUNNERS
Jer 12. 5 If you have raced *f* and they have

FOOTSTOOL
Ps 110. 1 hand until I make your enemies your *f.*"
Isa 66. 1 is my throne and the earth is my *f;*
Lk 20.43 hand, until I make your enemies a *f.*" '
Acts 2.35 hand, until I make your enemies your *f.*" '
Heb 10.13 "until his enemies would be made a *f*

FORBEARANCE
Rom 3.25 in his divine *f* he passed over the sins

FORBID (FORBIDDEN)
1 Cor 14.39 and do not *f* speaking in tongues;
Acts 16. 6 been *f* by the Holy Spirit to speak the

FORCE (FORCED FORCES)
Deut 33.27 the ancient gods, shatters the *f* of old;
1 Sam 13.12 so I *f* myself, and offered the burnt
Prov 12.24 while the lazy will be put to *f* labor.
Mt 11.12 violence, and the violent take it by *f.*
Jn 6.15 and take him by *f* to make him king,
2 Cor 12.11 I have been a fool! You *f* me to it.

FOREHEAD (FOREHEADS)
Ezek 3. 7 have a hard *f* and a stubborn heart.
9. 4 and put a mark on the *f* of the those
Rev 13.16 to be marked on the right hand or the *f,*

FOREIGN
Ezra 10.11 have trespassed and married *f* women,
Ps 137. 4 we sing the LORD's song in a *f* land?

FOREIGNER (FOREIGNERS)
Deut 23.20 On loans to a *f* you may charge interest,
1 Kings 8.41 "Likewise when a *f,* who is not of your
Ezek 44. 7 to all your abominations in admitting *f,*
Lk 17.18 and give praise to God except this *f?*"
1 Cor 14.11 of a sound, I will be a *f* to the speaker

FOREKNEW
Rom 8.29 those whom he *f* he also predestined to
11. 2 has not rejected his people whom he *f.*

FOREKNOWLEDGE
Acts 2.23 definite plan and *f* of God, you crucified

FORFEIT (FORFEITED)
Deut 22. 9 the whole yield will have to be *f,* both
Mk 8.36 to gain the whole world and *f* their life?

FORGET (FORGETS FORGETTING FORGOT FORGOTTEN)
Gen 40.23 did not remember Joseph, but *f* him.
Deut 4.31 he will not *f* the covenant with your
6.12 take care that you do not *f* the LORD,
8.11 Take care that you do not *f* the LORD, by
Judg 3. 7 *f* the LORD their God, and worshiping
1 Sam 12. 9 they *f* the LORD their God; and he sold
Ps 10.11 They think in their heart, "God has *f,* he
42. 9 to God, my rock, "Why have you *f* me?
44.24 Why do you *f* our affliction and
44.17 come upon us, yet we have not *f* you
45.10 *f* your people and your father's house,
74.19 animals; do not *f* the life of your poor
77. 9 Has God *f* to be gracious? Has he in
103. 2 my soul, and do not *f* all his benefits—
106. 13 But they soon *f* his works; they did not
119. 16 in your statutes; I will not *f* your word.
137. 5 If I *f* you, O Jerusalem, let my right
Prov 2.17 of her youth and *f* her sacred covenant;
3. 1 My child, do not *f* my teaching, but let
31. 7 let them drink and *f* their poverty, and
Isa 17.10 you have *f* the God of your salvation,
44.21 my servant; O Israel, you will not be *f*
49.14 has forsaken me, my Lord has *f* me."
51.13 You have *f* the LORD, your Maker, who
65.11 the LORD, who *f* my holy mountain,
Jer 2.32 Yet my people have *f* me, days without
13.25 because you have *f* me and trusted
18.15 But my people have *f* me, they burn

Jer 23.27 plan to make my people *f* my name
30.14 All your lovers have *f* you; they care
50. 6 they have gone, they have *f* their fold.
Lam 5.20 Why have you *f* us completely? Why
Hos 4. 6 you have *f* the law of your God, I also
Mk 8.14 the disciples had *f* to bring bread; and
Lk 12. 6 Yet not one of them is *f* in God's sight.
Phil 3.13 I do; *f* what lies behind and straining

FORGIVE

Gen 50.17 I beg you, *f* the crime of your brothers
Ex 32.32 if you will only *f* their sin —but if not,
Num 14.19 *F* the iniquity of this people according
14.20 said, "I do *f*, just as you have asked;
30. 8 bound herself; and the LORD will *f* her.
Josh 24.19 God; he will not *f* your transgressions
1 Sam 25.28 Please *f* the trespass of your servant; for
1 Kings 8.30 heaven your dwelling place; heed and *f*.
8.39 *f*, and act, and render to all whose
2 Chr 6.21 heaven your dwelling place; hear and *f*.
7.14 and will *f* their sin and heal their land.
Ps 25.18 and my trouble, and *f* all my sins.
79. 9 deliver us, and *f* our sins, for your
85. 2 You *f* the iniquity of your people; you
Isa 2. 9 is brought low—-do not *f* them!
Jer 31.34 for I will *f* their iniquity, and remember
33. 8 I will *f* all the guilt of their sin and
36. 3 so that I may *f* their iniquity and their
Mt 6.12 And *f* us our debts, as we also have
6.15 not *f* others, neither will your Father *f*
18.35 one of you, if you do not *f* your brother
Mk 2. 7 Who can *f* sins but God alone?"
11.25 Whenever you stand praying, *f*, if you
Lk 6.37 condemned. *F*, and you will be forgiven;
11. 4 And *f* us our sins, for we ourselves *f*
17. 3 and if there is repentance you must *f*.
23.34 Jesus said, "Father, *f* them; for they do
Jn 20.23 If you *f* the sins of any, they are
2 Cor 2. 7 instead you should *f* and console him,
1 Jn 1. 9 and just will *f* us our sins and cleanse

FORGIVES (FORGAVE FORGIVEN FORGIVING)

Ex 34. 7 *f* iniquity and transgression and sin, yet
Lev 4.20 for them, and they shall be *f*.
19.22 the sin he committed shall be *f* him.
Num 14.18 love, *f* iniquity and transgression,
15.25 of the Israelites, and they shall be *f*;
Ps 32. 1 are those whose transgression is *f*,
78.38 being compassionate, *f* their iniquity,
99. 8 you were a *f* God to them, but an
103. 3 who *f* all your iniquity, who heals all
Prov 17. 9 One who *f* an affront fosters friendship,
Isa 33.24 the people who live there will be *f* their
Lam 3.42 and rebelled, and you have not *f*.
Mt 9. 2 "Take heart, son; your sins are *f*."
12.31 will be *f* for every sin and blasphemy,
18.27 slave released him and *f* him the debt.
18.32 You wicked slave! I *f* you all that debt
Mk 2. 5 to the paralytic, "Son, your sins are *f*."
3.28 people will be *f* for their sins and
Lk 5.20 he said, "Friend, your sins are *f* you."
12.10 a word against the Son of Man will be *f*;
Acts 2.38 Jesus Christ so that your sins may be *f*;
8.22 the intent of your heart may be *f*
Rom 4. 7 are those whose iniquities are *f*,
Eph 4.32 one another, as God in Christ has *f* you.
Col 2.13 when he *f* us all our trespasses, erasing
1 Jn 2.12 your sins are *f* on account of his name.

FORGIVENESS

Ps 130. 4 But there is *f* with you, so that you may
Dan 9. 9 the Lord our God belong mercy and *f*,
Acts 10.43 everyone who believes in him receives *f*
13.38 that through this man *f* of sins is
26.18 so that they may receive *f* of sins and a
Col 1.14 we have redemption, the *f* of sins.
Heb 9.22 the shedding of blood there is no *f*

FORK

Jer 15. 7 winnowed them with a winnowing *f*
Lk 3.17 winnowing *f* is in his hand, to clear his

FORM (FORMED FORMS)

Gen 2. 7 God *f* man from the dust of the ground,
2.19 God *f* every animal of the field and
Job 33. 6 are; I too was *f* from a piece of clay.
Isa 43. 1 you, O Jacob, he who *f* you, O Israel:
44. 2 who made you, who *f* you in the womb
Jer 1. 5 "Before I *f* you in the womb I knew you,
Am 4.13 lo, the one who *f* the mountains,
Gal 4.19 of childbirth until Christ be *f* in you,
Acts 14.11 gods have come down to us in human *f*!"
1 Cor 7.31 the present *f* of this world is passing
Phil 2. 6 though he was in the *f* of God, did not
2 Tim 3. 5 holding to the outward *f* of godliness

FORMER

Isa 41.22 Tell us the *f* things, what they are, so
48. 3 The *f* things I declared long ago, they

FORNICATION

Acts 15.20 to abstain only from . . . *f* and from

FORNICATORS

1 Cor 6. 9 Do not be deceived! *F*, idolaters,

FORSAKE (FORSAKEN FORSAKING)

Deut 31. 8 with you; he will not fail you or *f* you.
Josh 1. 5 be with you; I will not fail you or *f* you.
1 Sam 8. 8 *f* me and serving other gods, so also
1 Kings 9. 9 'Because they have *f* the LORD their
11.33 because he has *f* me, worshiped Astarte
18.18 because you have *f* the commandments
1 Chr 28. 9 but if you *f* him, he will abandon you
2 Chr 7.19 if you turn aside and *f* my statutes and
Ps 9.10 O LORD, have not *f* those who seek you.
22. 1 My God, my God, why have you *f* me?
27. 9 Do not cast me off, do not *f* me, O God
37.25 yet I have not seen the righteous *f* or
37.28 justice; he will not *f* his faithful ones.
71.11 and seize that person whom God has *f*,
94.14 For the LORD will not *f* his people; he
119. 8 your statutes; do not utterly *f* me.
Prov 3. 3 not let loyalty and faithfulness *f* you;
6.20 and do not *f* your mother's teaching.
Isa 1. 4 deal corruptly, who have *f* the LORD,
1.28 who *f* the LORD shall be consumed.
2. 6 you have *f* the ways of your people, O
55. 7 let the wicked *f* their way, and the
Jer 1.16 them, for all their wickedness in *f* me;
2.17 brought this upon yourself by *f* the LORD
5.19 you have *f* me and served foreign gods
16.11 It is because your ancestors have *f* me,
Ezek 8.12 not see us, the LORD has *f* the land.' "
Am 5. 2 maiden Israel; *f* on her land, with no
Mt 27.46 "My God, my God, why have you *f* me?"
Mk 15.34 "My God, my God, why have you *f* me?"
2 Cor 4. 9 persecuted, but not *f*; struck down, but

FORTRESS

Ps 31. 2 of refuge for me, a strong *f* to save me.
31. 3 You are indeed my rock and my *f*; for
59. 9 watch for you; for you, O God, are my *f*.
144. 2 my rock and my *f*, my stronghold and
Prov 10.15 The wealth of the rich is their *f*; the
Dan 11.38 strongest *f* by the help of a foreign god.

FORTUNES

Deut 30. 3 God will restore your *f* and have
Job 42.10 LORD restored the *f* of Job, when he had
Ps 14. 7 When the LORD restores the *f* of his
53. 6 When God restores the *f* of his people,
85. 1 your land; you restored the *f* of Jacob.
126. 1 When the LORD restored the *f* of Zion,
Jer 31.23 and in its towns when I restore their *f*:
33. 7 I will restore the *f* of Judah and the *f* of

Am 9.14 I will restore the *f* of my people Israel,
Zeph 2. 7 be mindful of them and restore their *f*.
3.20 when I restore your *f* before your eyes,

FORTY

Gen 7. 4 rain upon the earth *f* days and *f* nights;
Ex 24.18 on the mountain *f* days and *f* nights.
Num 14.33 shepherds in the wilderness for *f* years,
Deut 2. 7 These *f* years the LORD your God has
9.11 At the end of *f* days and *f* nights the
25. 3 *F* lashes may be given but not more; if
29. 5 I have led you *f* years in the wilderness.

FOUNDATION (FOUNDATIONS)

Ezra 3. 6 But the *f* of the temple of the LORD was
3.11 because the *f* of the house of the LORD
Job 38. 4 were you when I laid the *f* of the earth?
Ps 11. 3 If the *f* are destroyed, what can the
18. 7 the earth reeled and rocked; the *f* also
102. 25 Long ago you laid the *f* of the earth,
Isa 24.18 opened, and the *f* of the earth tremble.
28.16 See, I am laying in Zion a *f* stone, a
40.21 not understood from the *f* of the earth?
54.11 antimony, and lay your *f* with sapphires.
Hag 2.18 the day that the *f* of the LORD's temple
Mt 13.35 been hidden from the *f* of the world."
Rom 15.20 that I do not build on someone else's *f*,
1 Cor 3.11 no one can lay any *f* other than the one
2 Tim 2.19 But God's firm *f* stands, bearing this

FOUNDED

Ps 24. 2 he has *f* it upon the seas, and
Prov 3.19 The LORD by wisdom *f* the earth; by

FOUNTAIN (FOUNTAINS)

Gen 7.11 all the *f* of the great deep burst forth,
Ps 36. 9 with you is the *f* of life; in your light we
Prov 14.27 The fear of the LORD is a *f* of life, so
16.22 Wisdom is a *f* of life to one who has it,
18. 4 waters; the *f* of wisdom is a gushing
25.26 Like a muddied spring or a polluted *f*
Eccl 12. 6 pitcher is broken at the *f*, and the
Song 4.12 my bride, a garden locked, a *f* sealed.
Jer 2.13 they have forsaken me, the *f* of living
9. 1 of water, and my eyes a *f* of tears,
17.13 forsaken the *f* of living water, the LORD.
Joel 3.18 a *f* shall come forth from the house of
Zech 13. 1 that day a *f* shall be opened for the

FOX (FOXES)

Judg 15. 4 and caught three hundred *f*, and took
Neh 4. 3 *f* going up on it would break
Song 2.15 Catch us the *f*, the little *f*, that spoil the
Mt 8.20 "*F* have holes, and birds of the air have
Lk 9.58 "*F* have holes, and birds of the air have
13.32 "Go and tell that *f* for me, 'Listen, I am

FRAGRANCE

Song 7.13 The mandrakes give forth *f*, and over
2 Cor 2.14 the *f* that comes from knowing him.

FRANKINCENSE

Isa 60. 6 They shall bring gold and *f*, and shall
Mt 2.11 they offered him gifts of gold, *f*, and

FREE (FREED)

Gen 44.10 my slave, but the rest of you shall go *f*.
Ex 21. 5 children; I will not go out a *f* person,"
Num 32.22 and be *f* of obligation to the LORD and
Deut 15.13 a male slave out from you a *f* person
Ps 146. 7 The LORD sets the prisoners *f*; the LORD
Ezek 13.20 and let the lives go *f*, the lives that you
Lk 1.64 his tongue *f*, and he began to speak,
Jn 8.32 the truth and the truth will make you *f*.'
8.36 So if the Son makes you *f*, you will be *f*
Acts 13.39 you could not be *f* by the law of Moses.
Rom 5.15 But the *f* gift is not like the trespass.
6. 7 For whoever has died is *f* from sin. But
Rom 6.18 you, having been set *f* from sin, have
1 Cor 7.39 the husband dies, she is *f* to marry
9. 1 Am I not *f*? Am I not an apostle? Have I
2 Cor 11. 7 God's good news to you *f* of charge?
Gal 1. 4 our sins to set us *f* from the present evil
3.28 or Greek, there is no longer slave or *f*,
Heb 2.15 *f* those who all their lives were held in
Rev 1. 5 us and *f* us from our sins by his blood,

FREEDOM

Rom 8.21 and will obtain the *f* of glory of the
1 Cor 7.21 Even if you can gain your *f*, make use
2 Cor 3.17 the Spirit of the Lord is, there is *f*.
Gal 2. 4 in to spy on the *f* we have in Christ
5. 1 For *f* Christ has set us free. Stand firm,
5.13 you were called to *f*, brothers and
1 Pet 2.16 yet do not use your *f* as pretext for evil.
2 Pet 2.19 They promise them *f*, but they

FREELY

Gen 2.16 "You may *f* eat of every tree of the
Prov 11.24 Some give *f*, yet grow all the richer;

FREEWILL OFFERING (FREEWILL OFFERINGS)

Lev 7.16 or a *f*, it shall be eaten on the day that
Deut 16.10 contributing a *f* in proportion to the
Ezra 1. 4 animals, besides *f* for the house of God
2.68 of families made *f* for the house of God,

FRIEND (FRIENDS)

Ex 33.11 face to face, as one speaks to a *f*.
Judg 5.31 may your *f* be like the sun as it rises in
2 Chr 20. 7 to the descendants of your *f* Abraham?
Job 6.14 "Those who withhold kindness from a *f*
6.27 the orphan, and bargain over your *f*.
16.20 My *f* scorn me; my eye pours out tears
19.14 relatives and my close *f* have failed me;
42.10 of Job when he had prayed for his *f*;
Ps 35.14 my bosom, as though I grieved for my *f*
41. 9 Even my bosom *f* in whom I trusted,
55.13 my equal, my companion, my familiar *f*.
88.18 have caused *f* and neighbor to shun me;
Prov 16.28 strife, and a whisperer separates close *f*.
17.17 A *f* loves at all times, and kinsfolk are
18.24 Some *f* play at friendship but a true *f*
19. 4 Wealth brings many *f*, but the poor are
19. 6 generous, and everyone is a *f* to a giver
22.24 Make no *f* with those given to anger,
27. 6 Well meant are the wounds a *f* inflicts,
Jer 3. 4 "My father, you are the *f* of my
Mic 7. 5 Put no trust in a *f*, have no confidence
Mt 11.19 a *f* of tax collectors and sinners!'
20.13 '*F*, I am doing you no wrong; did you
26.50 to him, "*F*, do what you are here to do."
Mk 5.19 "Go home to your *f*, and tell them how
Lk 7.34 and a drunkard, a *f* of tax collectors and
11. 5 '*F*, lend me three loaves of bread; for a
12. 4 my *f*, do not fear those who kill the
14.10 say to you, '*F*, move up higher'; then
16. 9 make *f* by means of dishonest wealth so
Jn 11.11 "Our *f* Lazarus has fallen asleep, but I
15.13 this, to lay down one's life for one's *f*.
19.12 this man, you are no *f* of the emporer.
2 Cor 11. 9 needs were supplied by the *f* who came
Jas 2.23 and he was called the *f* of God.

FRIENDSHIP

Job 29. 4 when the *f* of God was upon my tent;
Ps 25.14 The *f* of the LORD is for those who fear
Jas 4. 4 know that *f* with the world is enmity

FRIGHTENED

Dan 4. 5 I saw a dream that *f* me. My fantasies
Mt 2. 3 When king Herod heard this, he was *f*,
Lk 24.38 "Why are you *f*, and why do doubts arise

FRINGE

Mt 9.20 him and touched the *f* of his cloak,

Mt 14.36 might touch even the *f* of his cloak;

FROGS

Ex 8. 2 I will plague your whole country with *f*.
Ps 105. 30 Their land swarmed with *f*, even in the

FRUIT (FRUITS)

Num 13.26 and showed them the *f* of the land.
Deut 30. 9 in the *f* of your body, in the *f* of your
Ps 1. 3 water, which yield their *f* in its season,
Prov 1.31 they shall eat the *f* of their way
8.19 My *f* is better than gold, even fine gold,
11.30 The *f* of the righteous is a tree of life,
Song 4.13 of pomegranates with all choicest *f*,
Jer 21.14 you according to the *f* of your doings,
Mic 6. 7 the *f* of my body for the sin of my soul?"
Hab 3.17 not blossom, and no *f* is on the vines;
Mt 7.16 You will know them by their *f*. Are
21.43 that produces the *f* of the kingdom."
Mk 4.20 hear the word and accept it and bear *f*,
11.14 "May no one ever eat *f* from you again."
Lk 1.42 and blessed is the *f* of your womb!
3. 9 not bear good *f* is cut down and thrown
6.43 "No good tree bears bad *f*, nor again
8.15 and bear *f* with patient endurance.
Jn 12.24 grain; but if it dies, it bears much *f*.
15. 5 abide in me and I in them bear much *f*,
Gal 5.22 the *f* of the Spirit is love, joy, peace,
Col 1.10 as you bear *f* in every good work and as
Heb 12.11 it yields the peaceful *f* of righteousness
Rev 18.14 *f* for which your soul longed has gone
22. 2 twelve kinds of *f*, producing its *f* each

FRUSTRATE (FRUSTRATES)

Ezra 4. 5 they bribed officials to *f* their plan
Job 5.12 He *f* the devices of the crafty, so that

FUGITIVE

Gen 4.12 you will be a *f* and a wanderer on the

FULFILL (FULFILLED FULFILLING FULFILLS)

Gen 26. 3 I will *f* the oath that I swore to your
Deut 9. 5 to *f* the promise which the LORD made
1 Kings 2.27 thus *f* the word of the LORD that he had
2 Chr 6.10 the LORD has *f* his promise that he
36.21 to *f* the word of the LORD by the mouth
Ps 20. 5 May the LORD *f* all your petitions.
138. 8 The LORD will *f* his purpose for me; your
145. 19 He *f* the desire of all who fear him; he
Jer 28. 6 may the LORD *f* the words that you have
33.14 I will *f* the promise I made to the house
Mt 3.15 for us in this way to *f* all righteousness."
5.17 I have come not to abolish but to *f*.
8.17 *f* what had been spoken through the
21. 4 took place to *f* what had been spoken
26.56 scriptures of the prophets might be *f*."
Mk 1.15 "The time is *f*, and the kingdom of God
14.49 arrest me. But let the scriptures be *f*."
15.28n the scripture was *f* that says, "And he
Lk 1. 1 the events that have been *f* among us,
4.21 "Today this scripture has been *f* in your
22.16 I will not eat it until it is *f* in the
24.44 the prophets, and the psalms must be *f*."
Jn 3.29 For this reason my joy has been *f*.
17.12 be lost, so that the scripture might be *f*.
19.24 get it." This was to *f* what the scripture
Rom 9.31 the law, did not succeed in *f* that law.
13. 8 who loves one another has *f* the law.

FULL

Isa 6. 3 hosts; the whole earth is *f* of his glory."
Rom 11.25 until the *f* number of the Gentiles
Jas 1. 4 let endurance have its *f* effect, so that

FULLY

Lk 6.40 everyone who is *f* qualified will be like

FULLERS'

Mal 3. 2 he is like refiner's fire and like *f* soap;

FULLNESS

Jn 1.16 From his *f* have we all received, grace
Rom 15.29 you, I will come in the *f* of the blessing
Gal 4. 4 But when the *f* of time had come, God
Eph 3.19 you may be filled with all the *f* of God.
Col 2. 9 in him the whole *f* of deity dwells
2.10 you have come to *f* in him, who is the

FURNACE

Ps 12. 6 that are pure, silver refined in a *f*
21. 9 You will make them like a fiery *f* when
Prov 27.21 is for silver, and the *f* is for gold,
Isa 31. 9 is in Zion, and whose *f* is in Jerusalem.
48.10 I have tested you in the *f* of adversity.
Dan 3.19 He ordered the *f* heated up seven times
Mt 13.42 they will throw them into the *f* of fire,

FURY

Isa 42.13 a soldier, like a warrior he stirs up his *f*;
Ezek 21.17 strike hand to hand, I will satisfy my *f*;
Lk 6.11 they were filled with *f* and discussed

FUTILE

Isa 1.13 courts no more; bringing offerings is *f*;
Rom 1.21 they became *f* in their thinking, and
1 Cor 15.17 your faith is *f* and you are still in your

FUTILITY

Rom 8.20 creation was subjected to *f*, not of its
Eph 4.17 Gentiles live, in the *f* of their minds.

G

GABRIEL

Dan 8.16 "*G*, help this man understand the
9.21 in prayer, the man *G*, whom I had seen
Lk 1.19 "I am *G*. I stand in the presence of God,
1.26 In the sixth month the angel *G* was

GAD

Gen 30.11 "Good fortune!" so she named him *G*.
46.16 The children of *G*: Ziphion, Haggi,
Deut 33.20 he said: Blessed be the enlargement of *G*!

GADITES

Num 32.33 Moses gave to them—to the *G* and to

GAIN (GAINED GAINING)

Ps 119. 36 my heart to your decrees, and not to *g*.
Prov 1. 3 for *g* instruction in wise dealing,
9. 9 righteous and they will *g* in learning.
Eccl 1. 3 What do people *g* from all the toil at
2.11 was nothing to be *g* under the sun.
5.16 go and what *g* do they have for toiling
Mic 4.13 devote their *g* to the LORD, their wealth
Hab 2. 9 Alas for you who get evil *g* for your
Mt 16.26 it profit them if they *g* the whole world
Lk 9.25 them if they *g* the whole world, but lose
19.15 find out what that had *g* by trading.
2 Cor 12. 1 to boast; nothing is to be *g* by it, but I
Phil 1.21 to me, living is Christ and dying is *g*.
3. 8 as rubbish, in order that I may *g* Christ

GALATIA

Acts 16. 6 through the region of Phrygia and *G*,
18.23 through the region of *G* and Phrygia,
1 Cor 16. 1 directions I gave to the churches of *G*.
Gal 1. 2 To the churches of *G*: Grace to you and
1 Pet 1. 1 exiles of the Dispersion in Pontus, *G*,

GALILEAN

Mt 26.69 said, "You also were with Jesus the *G*."
Mk 14.70 you are one of them; for you are a *G*."
Lk 23. 6 he asked whether the man was a *G*.

GALILEE
Josh 20. 7 they set apart Kedesh in *G* in the hill
Isa 9. 1 the land beyond the Jordan, *G* of the
Mt 2.22 he went away to the district of *G*.
4.12 has been arrested, he withdrew to *G*.
4.15 across the Jordan, *G* of the Gentiles—
Mk 3. 7 a great multitude from *G* followed him;
16. 7 he is going ahead of you to *G*; there you
Lk 2. 4 went up from the town of Nazareth in *G*
Jn 2. 1 there was a wedding in Cana in *G*, and
4. 3 he left Judea and started back to *G*.
7.52 you not also from *G*, are you? Search
Acts 1.11 "Men of *G*, why do you stand looking

GALLIO
Acts 18.12 But when *G* was proconsul of Achaia,
18.17 But *G* paid no attention to any of these

GALLOWS
Esth 5.14 "Let a *g* fifty cubits high be made, and

GAMALIEL
Acts 5.34 Pharisee in the council named *G*, a
22. 3 brought up in this city at the feet of *G*,

GAME
Gen 27. 3 go out to the field, and hunt *g* for me.

GAP
Neh 6. 1 the wall and there was no *g* left in it

GARDEN
Gen 2. 8 God planted a *g* in Eden, in the east;
13.10 everywhere like the *g* of the LORD,
Song 4.12 A *g* locked is my sister, my bride, a *g*
Isa 1.30 leaf withers, and like a *g* without water.
Ezek 28.13 You were in Eden, the *g* of God; every
31. 8 The cedars in the *g* of God could not
36.35 desolate has become like the *g* of Eden;
Joel 2. 3 them the land is like the *g* of Eden,
Jn 19.41 where he was crucified, and in the *g*

GARDENER
Jn 20.15 Supposing him to be the *g*, she said to

GARLAND
Isa 28. 1 the proud *g* of the drunkards of
28. 5 the LORD of hosts will be a *g* of glory,

GARLIC
Num 11. 5 the leeks, the onions, and the *g*;

GARMENT (GARMENTS)
Gen 3.21 God made *g* of skins for the man and
39.13 saw that he had left his *g* in her hand,
Deut 22. 5 nor shall a man put on a woman's *g*;
Job 13.28 rotten thing, like a *g* that is moth-eaten.
Prov 20.16 Take the *g* of the one who has given
Eccl 9. 8 Let your *g* be always white; do not let
Song 5. 3 I had put off my *g*, how could I put it
Lk 5.36 "No one tears a piece from a new *g* and

GATE (GATES)
Neh 2.13 down and its *g* that had been destroyed
Job 38.17 Have the *g* of death been revealed to
Ps 24. 7 Lift up your heads, O *g*! and be lifted
122. 2 standing within your *g*, O Jerusalem.
Isa 26. 2 Open the *g*, so that the righteous nation
Mk 13.29 you know that he is near, at the very *g*.
Jn 10. 7 I tell you, I am the *g* for the sheep.
10. 9 I am the *g*; whoever enters by me will
Heb 13.12 Jesus also suffered outside the city *g* in

GATEWAY
Gen 19. 1 Lot was sitting in the *g* of Sodom.

GATHER (GATHERED GATHERING GATHERS)
Gen 1. 9 "Let the waters . . . be *g* together into
41.35 Let them *g* all the food of these good
Ex 16.16 "*G* as much of it as each of you needs,
Num 15.32 found a man *g* sticks on the sabbath
Deut 30. 4 there the LORD your God will *g* you,
Ps 106. 47 God, and *g* us from among the nations,
107. 3 and *g* in from the lands, from the east
Prov 10. 5 A child who *g* in summer is prudent,
Eccl 2. 8 I also *g* for myself silver and gold and
Isa 49. 5 him, and that Israel might be *g* to him,
56. 8 who *g* the outcasts of Israel, I will
Jer 4. 5 and say, "*G* together, and let us go
9.22 the reaper, and no one shall *g* them."
23. 3 I myself will *g* the remnant of my flock
29.14 *g* you from all the nations and all the
31.10 who scattered Israel will *g* him, and will
32.37 I am going to *g* them from all the lands
Ezek 22.19 dross, I will *g* you into the midst of
Joel 3.11 nations all around, *g* yourselves there.
Mic 7. 1 who, after the summer fruit has been *g*,
Zeph 3.19 I will save the lame and *g* the outcast,
Mt 12.30 whoever does not *g* with me scatters.
18.20 two or three are *g* in my name, I am
Mk 13.27 and *g* his elect from the four winds,
Lk 11.23 whoever does not *g* with me scatters.
13.34 I have *g* your children together as a hen
Jn 6.12 "*G* up the fragments left over, so that
11.52 to *g* into one the dispersed children of
Eph 1.10 of time, to *g* up all things in him,

GAZA
Gen 10.19 extended from Sidon . . . as far as *G*,
Judg 1.18 Judah took *G* with its territory,
16. 1 Samson went to *G*, where he saw a
Zech 9. 5 shall see it and be afraid; *G* too,
Acts 8.26 that goes down from Jerusalem to *G*."

GENEALOGY (GENEALOGIES)
Mt 1. 1 An account of the *g* of Jesus the
1 Tim 1. 4 with myths and endless *g* that promote
Heb 7. 3 father, without mother, without *g*,

GENERATION (GENERATIONS)
Gen 2. 4 are the *g* of the heavens and the earth
Ps 100. 5 forever, and his faithfulness to all *g*.
Eccl 1. 4 A *g* goes, and a *g* comes, but the earth
Mt 12.39 evil and adulterous *g* asks for a sign,
Mk 8.38 words in this adulterous and sinful *g*,

GENEROUS (GENEROUSLY)
Ps 112. 5 It is well with those who deal *g* and
Acts 2.46 ate their food with glad and *g* hearts,
2 Cor 8. 9 For you know the *g* act of our Lord
1 Tim 6.18 good, to be rich in good works, *g*, and

GENTILE (GENTILES)
Mt 10. 5 "Go nowhere among the *G*, and enter
Mk 7.26 the woman was a *G*, of Syrophoenician
Acts 4.25 'Why did the *G* rage, and the peoples
11.18 even to the *G* the repentance that leads
Gal 3. 8 that God would justify the *G* by faith,

GENTLE
Mt 11.29 I am *g* and humble in heart, and you
1 Thess 2. 7 we were *g* among you, like a nurse
Titus 3. 2 avoid quarrelling, to be *g*, and to show
1 Pet 3. 4 lasting beauty of a *g* and quiet spirit,

GENTLENESS
1 Cor 4.21 a stick, or with love in a spirit of *g*?
2 Cor 10. 1 you by the meekness and *g* of Christ—
Gal 6. 1 restore such a one in a spirit of *g*.
Eph 4. 2 called, with all humility and *g*, with

GENUINENESS
1 Pet 1. 7 so that the *g* of your faith, —being more

GET (GETTING GOT)
Lk 15.27 he has *g* him back safe and sound.'
18.30 who will not *g* back very much more in
23.41 we are *g* what we deserve for our deeds,

GETHSEMANE

Mt 26.36 went with them to a place called *G*;
Mk 14.32 They went a place which was called *G*;

GHOST

Mt 14.26 they were terrified, saying, "It is a *g*!"
Mk 6.49 on the sea, they thought it was a *g*,
Lk 24.37 and thought that they were seeing a *g*.

GIBEAH

Judg 19.12 of Israel; but we will continue on to *G*."
1 Sam 10.26 Saul also went to his home at *G*, and
14.16 Saul's lookouts in *G* of Benjamin were
Isa 10.29 Ramah trembles, *G* of Saul has fled.

GIDEON

Judg 6.11 as his son *G* was beating out wheat in
7. 1 (that is, *G*) and all the troops that were
7.19 *G* and the hundred who were with him
8. 4 Then *G* came to the Jordan and crossed
8.23 *G* said to them, "I will not rule over
8.32 *G* the son of Joash died at a good old
Heb 11.32 time would fail me to tell of *G*, Barak,

GIFT (GIFTS)

Gen 33.11 Please accept my *g* that I brought you,
Num 8.19 I have given the Levites as a *g* to Aaron
1 Sam 2.20 by this woman for the *g* that she made
Ps 45.12 of Tyre will seek your favor with *g*,
68.18 receiving *g* among the people, even
68.29 at Jerusalem kings bear *g* to you.
72.10 the kings of Sheba and Seba bring *g*.
Prov 18.16 A *g* opens doors; it gives access to the
21.14 A *g* in secret averts anger; and a
Eccl 3.13 God's *g* that all should eat and drink
Isa 1.23 Everyone loves a bribe and runs after *g*.
Mt 7.11 If you . . . know how to give good *g* to
Lk 11.13 who are evil, know how to give good *g*
21. 1 people putting their *g* into the treasury;
Acts 2.38 you will receive the *g* of the Holy Spirit.
8.20 you could obtain *g* of God with money!
11.17 then God gave them the same *g* that he
Rom 4. 4 wages are not reckoned as a *g* but as
6.23 but the free *g* of God is eternal life in
12. 6 We have *g* that differ according to the
1 Cor 7. 7 each has a particular *g* from God, one
12. 4 there are varieties of *g*, but the same
14. 1 love and strive for the spiritual *g*,
16. 3 with letters to take your *g* to Jerusalem.
2 Cor 9.15 be to God for his indescribable *g*!
Eph 3. 7 according to the *g* of God's grace
4. 7 according to the measure of Christ's *g*.
Phil 4.17 Not that I seek the *g*; but I seek the
1 Tim 4.14 Do not neglect the *g* that is in you,
Heb 2. 4 and by *g* of the Holy Spirit, distributed
1 Pet 4.10 serve one another with whatever *g* each

GILEAD

Gen 31.21 his face toward the hill country of *G*.
Deut 3.15 To Machir I gave *G*.
34. 1 him the whole land: *G* as far as Dan,
Josh 12. 2 of the Ammonites, that is, half of *G*,
Ps 60. 7 *G* is mine, and Manasseh is mine;
Jer 8.22 Is there no balm in *G*? Is there no

GILGAL

Josh 4.19 they camped in *G* on the east border of
10. 9 having marched up all night from *G*.
1 Sam 7.16 on a circuit year by year to Bethel, *G*,
13. 4 were called out to join Saul at *G*.
Am 4. 4 to *G*—and multiply transgression;

GIRD (GIRDED)

Ex 29. 5 and *g* him with the decorated band of
2 Sam 22.40 For you *g* me with strength for the
Ps 45. 3 *G* your sword on your thigh, O mighty

GIRL (GIRLS GIRL'S)

Judg 19. 4 the *g* father, made him stay, and he
2 Kings 5. 2 had taken a young *g* captive from the
Ps 68.25 between them *g* playing tambourines:
Prov 30.19 seas, and the way of a man with a *g*.
Zech 8. 5 city shall be of boys and *g* playing in its
Mt 9.24 away; for the *g* is not dead but sleeping."

GIVE

Gen 13.15 all the land that you see I will *g* to you
Ex 22.29 firstborn of your sons you shall *g* to me.
30.15 *g* more, and the poor shall not *g* less,
Deut 1.35 the good land which I swore to *g* to
6.10 to Jacob, to *g* you—a land with fine,
28.65 LORD will *g* you a trembling heart,
Judg 8. 5 "Please *g* some loaves of bread to my
1 Sam 28.19 the LORD will *g* Israel along with you
2 Kings 12.11 They would *g* the money that was
Ps 16.10 you do not *g* me up to Sheol, or let
105. 11 "To you I will *g* the land of Canaan as
119. 34 *G* me understanding, that I may keep
Prov 21.26 covet, but the righteous *g* and do not
23.26 My child, *g* me your heart, and let your
Hos 11. 8 How can I *g* you up, Ephraim? How can
Mt 6.11 *G* us this day our daily bread.
14.16 go away; you *g* them something to eat."
16.19 I *g* you the keys of the kingdom of
22.21 "*G* therefore to the emperor the things
Mk 6.37 them, "You *g* them something to eat."
12.17 them, "*G* to the emperor the things that
Lk 6.38 *g*, and it will be given to you. A good
14.33 my disciple if you do not *g* up all of
20.25 "Then *g* to the emperor the things that
Jn 4. 7 and Jesus said to her, "*G* me a drink."
6.34 said to him, "Sir, *g* us this bread always."
10.28 I *g* them eternal life, and they will never
14.16 he will *g* you another Advocate, to be
Acts 20.35 said, 'It is more blessed to *g* than to
Rom 8.32 will he not with him also *g* us
1 Cor 7. 3 husband should *g* to his wife her
Eph 1.17 of glory, may *g* you a spirit of wisdom

GIVES (GAVE GIVEN GIVING)

Num 21.34 of him, for I have *g* him into your hand,
Deut 2.33 our God *g* him over to us; and we
2 Chr 13.16 and God *g* them into their hands.
Judg 16.23 "Our god has *g* Samson our enemy into
Job 1.21 the LORD *g*, and the LORD has taken
35.10 is God my Maker, who *g* strength
Ps 37.21 the righteous are generous and keep *g*;
68.11 The Lord *g* the command; great is the
136. 25 who *g* food to all flesh, for his steadfast
Prov 2. 6 For the LORD *g* wisdom; from his mouth
12.26 The righteous *g* good advice to friends,
28.27 Whoever *g* to the poor lack nothing, but
Eccl 2.26 the one who pleases him God *g* wisdom
12. 7 and the breath returns to God who *g* it.
Mt 13.12 For to those who have, more will be *g*,
15. 5 might have had from me is *g* to God,'
Mk 4.25 For those who have, more will be *g*; and
Lk 8.18 to those who have, more will be *g*; and
12.48 whom much has been *g*, much will be
Jn 5.22 one but has *g* all judgment to the Son,
2 Cor 9. 9 "He scatters abroad, he *g* to the poor;
Gal 1. 4 Christ, who *g* himself for our sins to set
2.20 who loved me and *g* himself for me.
Phil 4.15 shared with me in the matter of *g*
1 Jn 3.24 in us, by the Spirit that he has *g* us.

GLAD

Ps 9. 2 I will be *g* and exult in you; I will sing
40.16 may all who seek you rejoice and be *g*
46. 4 a river whose streams make *g* the city of
105. 38 Egypt was *g* when they departed, for
122. 1 I was *g* when they said to me, "Let us
Prov 15.13 A *g* heart makes a cheerful
Isa 25. 9 let us be *g* and rejoice in his salvation.

Isa 65.18 But be *g* and rejoice forever in what I
Phil 2.17 of your faith, I am *g* and rejoice with all

GLADNESS

Esth 9.19 of Adar as a day of *g* and feasting,
Ps 4. 7 You have put more *g* in my heart more
100. 2 Worship the LORD with *g*; come into his
Isa 16.10 Joy and *g* are taken away from the
61. 3 ashes, the oil of *g* instead of mourning,
Jer 7.34 to an end the sound of mirth and *g*,

GLORIFY (GLORIFIED)

Ezra 7.27 of the king to *g* the house of the LORD
Ps 50.15 I will deliver you, and you shall *g* me."
Isa 44.23 redeemed Jacob, and will be *g* in Israel.
49. 3 my servant, Israel, in whom I will be *g*."
55. 5 the Holy One of Israel, for he has *g* you.
60. 7 my altar, and I will *g* my glorious house.
Lk 5.26 they *g* God and were filled with awe,
7.16 they *g* God, saying, "A great prophet has
Jn 7.39 no Spirit, because Jesus was not yet *g*.
12.28 Father, *g* your name." Then a voice came
13.31 said, "Now the Son of Man has been *g*
14.13 so that the Father may be *g* in the Son.
15. 8 Father is *g* by this, that you bear much
17. 1 the hour has come; *g* your Son so that
Rom 11.13 apostle to the Gentiles. I *g* my ministry
1 Cor 6.20 a price; therefore *g* God in your body.
Rev 15. 4 who will not fear and *g* your name?

GLORIOUS (GLORIOUSLY)

Ps 87. 3 *G* things are spoken of you, O city of
Isa 12. 5 praises to the LORD, for he has done *g*;

GLORY

Ex 16. 7 you shall see the *g* of the LORD, because
24.16 The *g* of the LORD settled on Mount
40.34 the *g* of the LORD filled the tabernacle.
Num 14.21 shall be filled with the *g* of the LORD
16.19 the *g* of the LORD appeared to the whole
Deut 5.24 God has shown us his *g* and greatness,
Josh 7.19 give *g* to the LORD God of Israel and
1 Sam 4.21 "The *g* has departed from Israel,"
15.29 the *G* of Israel will not recant or change
1 Kings 8.11 for the *g* of the LORD filled the house of
1 Chr 16.24 Declare his *g* among the nations, his
29.11 are the greatness, the power, the *g*,
2 Chr 5.14 for the *g* of the LORD filled the house of
Ps 8. 1 You have set your *g* above the heavens.
19. 1 heavens are telling the *g* of God; and
21. 5 His *g* is great through your help;
29. 1 beings, ascribe to the LORD *g* and
97. 6 and all the peoples behold his *g*.
106. 47 to your holy name and *g* in your praise.
115. 1 but to your name give *g*, for the sake of
Isa 24.15 Therefore in the east give *g* to the LORD;
35. 2 The *g* of Lebanon shall be given to it,
35. 2 They shall see the *g* of the LORD, the
40. 5 the *g* of the LORD shall be revealed,
42. 8 my *g* I give to no other, nor my praise
Jer 33. 9 a *g* before all the nations of the earth
Ezek 1.28 of the likeness of the *g* of the LORD.
3.12 me up, and as the *g* of the LORD rose
3.23 and the *g* of the LORD stood there, like
9. 3 the *g* of the God of Israel had gone up
10.18 the *g* of the LORD went out from the
28.22 O Sidon, and I will gain *g* in your midst
39.21 I will display my *g* among the nations;
43. 2 And there, the *g* of the God of Israel
Dan 7.14 was given dominion and *g* and kingship,
Hab 2.14 the knowledge of the *g* of the LORD,
Mt 24.30 of heaven' with power and great *g*.
Lk 2.14 "*G* to God in the highest heaven , and
Jn 5.41 I do accept *g* from human beings.
7.18 speak on their own seek their own *g*;
8.50 Yet I do not seek my own *g*; there is
11. 4 lead to death; rather it is for God's *g*,
Jn 12.43 for they loved human *g* more than the *g*
17. 5 with the *g* that I had in your presence
17.24 to see my *g* which you have given me
Rom 1.23 exchanged the *g* of the immortal God
3.23 sinned and fall short of the *g* of God;
8.18 not worth comparing with the *g* about
11.36 things. To him be the *g* forever. Amen.
1 Cor 15.43 It is sown in dishonor, it is raised in *g*.
2 Cor 3.11 more has the permanent come in *g*.
Phil 3.21 may be conformed to the body of his *g*,
Col 1.27 which is Christ in you, the hope of *g*.
2 Thess 1. 9 of the Lord and from the *g* of his might,
2.14 that you may obtain the *g* of our Lord
2 Pet 1. 3 of him who called by his own *g*
Rev 7.12 "Amen! Blessing and *g* and wisdom and
14. 7 "Fear God and give him *g*, for the hour

GNASH (GNASHED GNASHING)

Job 16. 9 and hated me; he has *g* his teeth at me;
Ps 35.16 and more, *g* at me with their teeth.
Lam 2.16 they hiss, they *g* their teeth, they cry:
Mt 24.51 there will be weeping and *g* of teeth.

GNAT (GNATS)

Ex 8.16 become *g* throughout the whole land
Mt 23.24 guides, You strain out a *g* but swallow

GO (GOING)

Gen 7. 1 "*G* into the ark, you and all your
24.58 "Will you *g* with this man?" She said, "I
Ex 5. 1 'Let my people *g*, so that they may
9.13 'Let my people *g*, so that they may
Num 14. 4 choose a captain, and *g* back to Egypt."
2 Kings 5.10 "*G*, wash in the Jordan seven times, and
Ps 143. 8 Teach me the way I should *g*, for to you
Eccl 5.15 they shall *g* again, naked as they came,
Isa 2. 3 "Come, let us *g* up to the mountain of
6. 9 "*G*, and say to this people: 'Keep
48.20 *G* out from Babylon, flee from Chaldea,
Jer 42. 3 show us where we should *g* and what
Hos 11.10 They shall *g* after the LORD, who roars
Am 7.15 LORD said to me, '*G*, prophesy to my
Mic 4. 2 "Come, let us *g* up to the mountain of
Mal 3.14 or by *g* about as mourners before the
Mt 6. 6 whenever you pray, *g* into your room
28. 7 Then *g* quickly and tell his disciples,
28.19 *G* therefore and make disciples of all
Mk 5.19 "*G* home to your friends, and tell them
16. 7 But *g*, tell his disciples and Peter that
16.15n "*G* into all the world and proclaim the
Lk 9.60 as for you, *g* and proclaim the kingdom
Jn 6.68 "Lord, to whom can we *g*? You have the

GOADS

Eccl 12.11 sayings of the wise are like *g*, and like
Acts 26.14 me? It hurts you to kick against the *g*.'

GOAL

Phil 3.12 this or have already reached the *g*;

GOAT-DEMONS

Lev 17. 7 no longer offer their sacrifices for *g*,
2 Chr 11.15 for the high places, and for the *g*,
Isa 34.14 with hyenas, *g* shall call to each other;

GOD

Gen 1. 1 when *G* created the heavens and
3. 5 and you will be like *G*, knowing good
8. 1 *G* remembered Noah and all the wild
50.25 "When *G* comes to you, you shall carry
Ex 2.24 *G* heard their groaning, and *G*
13.17 *G* did not lead them by way of the land
Josh 10.42 the LORD *G* of Israel fought for Israel.
2 Sam 7.23 on earth whose *G* went to redeem it as
1 Kings 8.28 O LORD my *G*, heeding the cry and the
11.23 *G* raised up another adversary against
2 Chr 36.15 The LORD, the *G* of their ancestors, sent
36.16 they kept mocking the messengers of *G*,

Ps 8. 5 have made them a little lower than G,
22. 1 G, my G, why have you forsaken me?
Isa 12. 2 the LORD G is my strength and my
26. 4 LORD G you have an everlasting rock.
40. 1 O comfort my people, says your G.
Dan 3.25 the fourth has the appearance of a g."
Hag 1.14 the house of the LORD of hosts, their G,
Mal 3. 8 Will anyone rob G? Yet you are robbing
Mk 15.34 "My G, my G, why have you forsaken
Jn 20.28 answered him. "My Lord and my G!"
Acts 2.32 This Jesus G raised up, and of that all
28. 6 minds and began to say that he was a g.
1 Cor 14.33 for G is not a G of disorder but of
2 Cor 4. 4 case the g of this world has blinded
Eph 2. 4 But G, who is rich in mercy, out of the
2. 8 your own doing; it is the gift of G—
4.24 created according to the likeness of G
5. 1 be imitators of G, as beloved children,
Titus 2.11 the grace of G has appeared, bringing
2.13 the glory of our great G and Savior
Rev 21.22 its temple is the Lord G the Almighty
22. 1 as crystal, flowing from the throne of G

GODLESS

Job 8.13 forget God; hope of the g shall perish.
13.16 that the g shall not come before him.
20. 5 the joy of the g is but for a moment?
27. 8 For what is the hope of the g when God
36.13 "The g in heart cherish anger; they do
Prov 11. 9 the g would destroy their neighbors,
Isa 9.17 for everyone was g and an evildoer, and
10. 6 Against a g nation I send him, and
33.14 are afraid; trembling has seized the g:

GODLINESS

1 Tim 6. 3 teaching that is in accordance with g,
6. 5 imagining that g is a means of gain.
2 Tim 3. 5 holding the outward form of g but
2 Pet 1. 7 g with mutual affection, and mutual

GODLY

Ps 12. 1 there is no longer anyone who is g; the
52. 1 one, of mischief done against the g?
2 Tim 3.12 all who want to live a g life in Christ

GODS

Gen 31.19 Rachel stole her father's household g.
31.30 father's house, why did you steal my g?"
31.34 Rachel had taken the household g and
1 Kings 20.23 "Their g are g of the hills, and so they
Ps 82. 6 "You are g, children of the Most High,
Isa 37.19 have hurled their g into the fire; though
Jer 5.19 served foreign g in your land, so you
16.20 Can mortals make for themselves g?
Dan 4. 8 is endowed with a spirit of the holy g—
Acts 7.40 saying to Aaron, "Make g for us who
1 Cor 8. 5 though there may be so-called g in

GOLD

Gen 2.11 whole land of Havilah, where there is g;
Num 31.52 all the g of the offering that they
Job 22.25 if the Almighty is your g and your
31.24 "If I have made g my trust, or called
Ps 19.10 More to be desired are they than g,
Prov 8.10 and knowledge rather than choice g;
25.11 spoken is like apples of g in a setting of
Isa 60. 6 They shall bring g and frankincense,
Lam 4. 1 How the g has grown dim, how the pure
Dan 2.32 head of that statue was of fine g, its
Acts 3. 6 "I have no silver and g, but what I have
Rev 21.18 while the city is pure g, clear as glass.

GOLGOTHA

Mt 27.33 they came to a place called G (which
Mk 15.22 brought Jesus to the place called G
Jn 19.17 the Skull, which in Hebrew is called G.

GOLIATH

1 Sam 17. 4 of the Philistines, a champion named G,
17.23 the Philistine of Gath, G by name, came
21. 9 "The sword of G the Philistine, whom

GOMORRAH

Gen 13.10 before the LORD had destroyed . . . G.
14.10 as kings of Sodom and G fled, some fell
19.24 the LORD rained on . . . G sulfur and fire
Deut 29.23 like the destruction of Sodom and G,
Isa 1. 9 been like Sodom, and become like G.
Mt 10.15 of Sodom and G than for that town.
Jude 6 Likewise, Sodom and G and the

GOOD

Gen 1. 4 God saw that the light was g; and God
1.31 he had made, and indeed, it was very g.
Deut 1.23 The plan seemed g to me, and I
1 Chr 19.13 may the LORD do what seems g to him."
Ps 14. 3 perverse; there is no one that does g,
16. 2 my Lord; I have no g apart from you."
25. 8 G and upright is the LORD; therefore he
37.27 Depart from evil, and do g; so you shall
92. 1 It is g to give thanks to the LORD, to
133. 1 g and pleasant it is when kindred live
Prov 31.12 She does him g, and not harm, all the
Eccl 7. 1 g name is better than precious
Isa 5.20 you who call evil g and g evil, who put
48.17 God, who teaches you for your own g,
Hos 14. 2 accept that which is g, and we will offer
Am 5.15 Hate evil, and love g, and establish
Mic 3. 2 you who hate the g and love the evil,
Mt 13. 8 Other seeds fell on g soil and brought
13.48 put the g into baskets but threw out the
25.21 "Well done, g and trustworthy slave; you
Mk 4. 8 Other seed fell into g soil and brought
10.18 call me g? No one is g but God alone.
Lk 6. 9 is it lawful to do g or to do harm on the
8. 8 Some fell into g soil, and when it grew,
9.33 "Master, it is g for us to be here; let us
Jn 1.46 "Can anything g come out of Nazareth?"
Rom 3. 8 "Let us do evil so that g may come?"
7.18 I know that nothing g dwells within me,
8.28 all things work together for g for those
14.16 do not let your g be spoken of as evil.
16.19 I want you to be wise in what is g and
1 Pet 2. 3 you have tasted that the Lord is g.

GOOD NEWS

Mt 26.13 wherever this g is proclaimed in the
Mk 1. 1 The beginning of the g of Jesus Christ,
1.14 into Galilee, proclaiming the g of God,
13.10 the g must first be preached to all
Acts 14. 7 there they continued proclaiming the g.
20.24 Jesus, to testify to the g of God's grace.
1 Cor 15. 1 of the g that I proclaimed to you, which
2 Cor 10.14 all the way to you with the g of Christ.

GOODNESS

Ps 23. 6 Surely g and mercy shall follow me all
31.19 O how abundant is your g, that you
Zech 9.17 what g and beauty are his! Grain shall
2 Pet 1. 5 support your faith with g, and g with

GOSPEL

Mt 24.14n this g of the kingdom will be
26.13n wherever this g is proclaimed in the
Mk 1. 1n The beginning of the g of Jesus Christ,
1.14n into Galilee, proclaiming the g of God,
13.10n the g must first be preached to all
14. 9n wherever the g is proclaimed in the
16.15n world and proclaim the g to the whole
Rom 1. 1 an apostle, set apart for the g of God,
1.16 I am not ashamed of the g; it is the
2.16 day when, according to my g, God,
16.25 to strengthen you according to my g
2 Cor 9.13 to the confession of the g of Christ

Gal 1. 6 and are turning to a different *g*—
1.11 the *g* that was proclaimed by me is not
2. 7 with the *g* for the uncircumcised,
Eph 1.13 word of truth, the *g* of your salvation,
6.15 you ready to proclaim the *g* of peace;
Phil 1.27 your life in a manner worthy of the *g*
Col 1.23 from the hope promised by the *g*
1 Thess 1. 5 of the *g* came to you not in word only,
1 Tim 1.11 teaching that conforms to the glorious *g*
2 Tim 1. 8 but join with me in suffering for the *g*,
1 Pet 4. 6 *g* was proclaimed even to the dead, so
Rev 14. 6 angel . . . with an eternal *g* to proclaim

GOSSIP (GOSSIPS)

Prov 11.13 A *g* goes about telling secrets, but on
20.19 A *g* reveals secrets; therefore do not
Rom 1.29 strife, deceit, craftiness, they are *g*,
1 Tim 5.13 they are not merely idle, but also *g* and

GOVERNOR (GOVERNORS)

Gen 42. 6 Joseph was *g* over the land; it was he
Neh 5.14 I was appointed to be their *g* in the
Jer 40. 7 Gedaliah son of Ahikam *g* in the
Mal 1. 8 wrong? Try presenting that to your *g*;
Mk 13. 9 you will stand before *g* and kings

GRACE

Ps 45. 2 of men; *g* is poured upon your lips;
Jer 31. 2 found *g* in the wilderness; when Israel
Zech 4. 7 top stone amid shouts of '*G*, *g* to it!' "
Jn 1.14 a father's only son, full of *g* and truth.
Acts 4.33 Jesus, and great *g* was upon them all.
13.43 urged them to continue in the *g* of God.
14. 3 testified to the word of his *g*, by
14.26 commended to the *g* of God for the
15.40 commending him to the *g* of the Lord.
Rom 1. 5 through whom we have received *g* and
3.24 they are now justified by his *g* as a gift,
4.16 in order that the promise may rest on *g*
5. 2 access to this *g* in which we stand,
5.15 much more surely have the *g* of God
5.20 but where sin increased, *g* abounded all
6. 1 we continue in sin in order that *g*
15.15 because of the *g* given me by God
1 Cor 3.10 According to the *g* of God given to me,
15.10 by the *g* of God I am what I am, and
2 Cor 4.15 so that *g*, as it extends to more and
12. 9 "My *g* is sufficient for you, for power is
13.13 The *g* of the Lord Jesus Christ, the love
Gal 1. 6 the one who called you in the *g*
5. 4 Christ; you have fallen away from *g*.
Eph 1. 7 according to the riches of his *g*
2. 7 show the immeasurable riches of his *g*
2 Thess 2.16 and through *g* gave us eternal comfort
1 Tim 1.14 the *g* of our Lord overflowed for me
Titus 2.11 For the *g* of God has appeared, bringing
3. 7 so that, having been justified by his *g*,
Heb 4.16 approach the throne of *g* with boldness,
13. 9 for the heart to be strengthened by *g*,
Jas 4. 6 But he gives all the more *g*; therefore it
1 Pet 4.10 Like good stewards of the manifold *g* of
5. 5 the proud, but gives *g* to the humble."
5.10 God of all *g*, who has called you to his
2 Pet 3.18 grow in the *g* and knowledge of our
Jude 4 who pervert the *g* of our God into

GRACEFUL

Song 7. 1 How *g* are your feet in sandals, O

GRACIOUS

Num 6.25 face shine upon you, and be *g* to you;
2 Kings 13.23 the LORD was *g* to them and had
Ps 67. 1 May God be *g* to us and bless us and
103. 8 The LORD is merciful and *g*, slow to
145. 8 The LORD is *g* and merciful, slow to
147. 1 praises to our God; for he is *g*, and a
Prov 22.11 love a pure heart and are *g* in speech
Isa 33. 2 O LORD, be *g* to us; we wait for you. Be

Joel 2.13 your God, for he is *g* and merciful,
Lk 4.22 were amazed at the *g* words that came
Col 4. 6 Let your speech always be *g*, seasoned

GRAIN

Prov 14. 4 Where there are no oxen, there is no *g*;
Mk 4.28 the head, then the full *g* in the head.
Lk 6. 1 his disciples plucked some heads of *g*,
Acts 7.12 Jacob heard that there was *g* in Egypt,
1 Cor 15.37 perhaps of wheat or of some other *g*.

GRAIN OFFERING

Lev 2. 1 When anyone brings a *g* to the LORD,
6.14 This is the ritual of the *g*: The sons of

GRAINFIELDS

Mt 12. 1 Jesus through the *g* on the sabbath; his

GRANT (GRANTED)

1 Sam 1.17 God of Israel *g* your petition you have
2 Chr 9.12 Solomon *g* to the queen of Sheba every
Prov 10.24 but the desire of the righteous will be *g*.
Acts 27.24 God has *g* safety to all those who are

GRAPES

Num 13.23 a branch with a single cluster of *g*,
Isa 5. 2 he expected it to yield *g*, but it yielded
Jer 31.29 say: "The parents have eaten sour *g*,
Ezek 18. 2 parents have eaten sour *g*, and the
Hos 9.10 Like *g* in the wilderness, I found Israel.
Am 9.13 reaps, and the treader of *g* the one who

GRASS

Ps 37. 2 they will soon fade like the *g*, and
103. 15 As for mortals, their days are like *g*;
Isa 5.24 as dry *g* sinks down in the flame, so
40. 6 All people are *g*, and their constancy is
Dan 4.33 from human society, ate *g* like oxen,
Lk 12.28 if God so clothes the *g* of the field,
1 Pet 1.24 "All flesh is like *g* and all its glory like
Rev 8. 7 up, and all green *g* was burnt up.

GRASSHOPPERS

Num 13.33 to ourselves we seemed like *g*, and so
Isa 40.22 the earth, and its inhabitants are like *g*;
Nah 3.17 Your guards are like *g*, your scribes like

GRAVE (GRAVES)

Ps 49.14 straight to the *g* they descend, and their
Ezek 32.23 Its company is all around its *g*, all of
37.12 your *g*, and bring you up from your *g*,
Lk 11.44 you are like unmarked *g*, and people
Jn 5.28 all who are in their *g* will hear his voice

GREAT (GREATER GREATEST)

2 Sam 5.10 David became *g* and *g*, for the LORD, the
7.22 you are *g*, O LORD God; for there is no
1 Chr 11. 9 David became *g* and *g*, for the Lord of
17.19 you have done all these *g* deeds,
Job 37.23 find him; he is *g* in power and justice,
Ps 40.16 say continually, "*G* is the LORD!"
70. 4 your salvation say evermore, "God is *g*!"
Eccl 2. 9 So I became *g* and surpassed all who
Jer 45. 5 you, do you seek *g* things for yourself?
Joel 2.21 rejoice, for the LORD has done *g* things!
Mal 1. 5 this, and you shall say, "*G* is the LORD
Mt 5.19 them will be called *g* in the kingdom
12. 6 something *g* than the temple is here.
12.42 see, something *g* than Solomon is here.
15.28 "Woman, *g* is your faith! Let it be done
18. 1 asked, "Who is the *g* in the kingdom
Mk 9.34 argued with one another who was the *g*.
Lk 1.15 he will be *g* in the sight of the Lord. He
22.24 of them was to be regarded as the *g*.
1 Cor 13.13 these three; and the *g* of these is love.
Rev 2.19 that your last works are *g* than the first.
18.16 "Alas, alas, the *g* city, clothed in fine

GREATNESS

Deut 3.24 only begun to show your servant your *g*
Ps 145. 3 to be praised; his *g* is unsearchable.
150. 2 him according to his surpassing *g*!
Ezek 31. 2 hordes: Whom are you like in your *g*?
38.23 I will display my *g* and my holiness and

GREECE

Dan 8.21 The male goat is the king of *G*, and the
11. 2 stir up all against the kingdom of *G*.
Zech 9.13 sons, O Zion, against your sons, O *G*,
Acts 20. 2 he came to *G*, where he stayed for three

GREED

Lk 12.15 Be on your guard against all kinds of *g*;
1 Thess 2. 5 words of flattery or with a pretext for *g*;
2 Pet 2. 3 in their *g* they will exploit you with
2.14 souls. They have hearts trained in *g*.

GREEDY

1 Sam 2.29 "Why then look with *g* eye at my
Prov 1.19 is the end of all who are *g* for gain;
Jer 6.13 of them, everyone is *g* for unjust gain;
8.10 greatest everyone is *g* for unjust gain;
1 Cor 5.11 or sister who is sexually immoral or *g*,
6.10 thieves, the *g*, drunkards, revilers,
Eph 5. 5 one who is *g* (that is, an idolater), has

GREEK (GREEKS)

Jn 12.20 to worship at the festival were some *G*.
Acts 14. 1 of both Jews and *G* became believers.
16. 1 was a believer; but his father was a *G*.
19.10 of Asia, both Jews and *G* heard the
20.21 as I testified to both Jews and to *G*
Rom 1.14 I am a debtor both to *G* and to
1 Cor 1.22 demand signs and *G* desire wisdom,

GREET (GREETED GREETING)

1 Sam 6.19 when they *g* the ark of the LORD; and he
Mt 23. 7 to be *g* with respect in the
Mk 12.38 and to be *g* with respect in the
Lk 1.29 pondered what sort of *g* this might be.
1.41 When Elizabeth heard Mary's *g*, the
11.43 be *g* with respect in the marketplaces.
Rom 16.16 *G* one another with a holy kiss. All the
1 Cor 16.21 I, Paul, write this *g* with my own hand.
Heb 11.13 from a distance they saw and *g* them.

GRIEF

Prov 14.13 the heart is sad, and the end of joy is *g*.
17.25 Foolish children are a *g* to their father
2 Cor 7.10 godly *g* produces a repentance that

GRIEVE (GRIEVED GRIEVING)

Gen 6. 6 on the earth, and it *g* him to his heart.
1 Sam 16. 1 "How long will you *g* over Saul? I have
Ps 78.40 the wilderness and *g* him in the desert!
Isa 63.10 But they rebelled and *g* his holy spirit;
Am 6. 6 but are not *g* over the ruin of Joseph!
Mt 14. 9 The king was *g*; yet out of regard for his
Mk 3. 5 he was *g* at their hardness of heart and
10.22 went away *g*; for he had many
14.34 "I am deeply *g*, even to death; remain
Eph 4.30 do not *g* the Holy Spirit of God, with
1 Thess 4.13 so that you may not *g* as others do who

GROAN (GROANING GROANS)

Ps 79.11 the *g* of the prisoners come before you;
Prov 29. 2 but when the wicked rule, the people *g*.
Ezek 30.24 of Pharaoh, and he will *g* before him
Joel 1.18 How the animals *g*! The herds of cattle
Acts 7.34 are in Egypt and have heard their *g*,

GROPE

Job 5.14 and *g* at noonday as in the night.
12.25 They *g* in the dark without light; he
Isa 59.10 We *g* like the blind along a wall,

GROUND

Judg 16.21 shackles; and he *g* at the mill in prison.
Lk 23.22 in him no *g* for the sentence of death;
Acts 7.54 enraged and *g* their teeth at Stephen.

GROUPS

Mk 6.39 all the people to sit down in *g* on the

GROW (GREW)

1 Sam 2.21 the boy Samuel *g* up in the presence of
3.19 As Samuel *g* up, the LORD was with him
Isa 9. 7 His authority shall *g* continually, and
53. 2 he *g* up before him like a young plant,
Lk 1.80 The child *g* and became strong in spirit,
2.40 The child *g* and became strong, filled
Acts 19.20 So the word of the Lord *g* mightily and

GRUMBLED

Deut 1.27 you *g* in your tents and said, "It is
Ps 106. 25 They *g* in their tents, and did not obey

GUARANTEE

2 Cor 5. 5 God, who has given us the Spirit as a *g*.

GUARD (GUARDS)

1 Sam 2. 9 He will *g* the feet of his faithful ones,
Neh 4. 9 to our God, and set a *g* as a protection
Job 7.12 the Dragon, that you set a *g* over me?
Ps 91.11 his angels concerning you to *g* you
97.10 he *g* the lives of his faithful; he rescues
140. 4 *G* me, O LORD, from the hands of the
141. 3 Set a *g* over my mouth, O LORD; keep
Prov 2.11 over you; and understanding will *g* you.
4. 6 keep you; love her, and she will *g* you.
13. 3 Those who *g* their mouths preserve their
Eccl 5. 1 *G* your steps when you go to the house
Mt 5.25 to the judge, and the judge to the *g*,
Phil 4. 7 will *g* your hearts and your minds in
1 Tim 6.20 *g* what has been entrusted to you.

GUARDIAN (GUARDIANS)

Gal 4. 2 they remain under *g* and trustees until
1 Cor 4.15 might have ten thousand *g* in Christ,
1 Pet 2.25 to the shepherd and *g* of your souls.

GUEST (GUESTS)

Ps 39.12 For I am your passing *g*, an alien, like
Zeph 1. 7 a sacrifice, he has consecrated his *g*.
Mt 22.10 bad; so wedding hall was filled with *g*.
Lk 22.11 "Where is the *g* room, where I may eat

GUIDANCE

Job 37.12 They turn round and round by his *g*, to
Prov 11.14 Where there is no *g*, a nation falls, but
24. 6 for by wise *g* you can wage your war,

GUIDE (GUIDED GUIDES)

Deut 32.12 the LORD alone *g* him; no foreign god
Ps 31. 3 for your name's sake lead me and *g*
48.14 and ever. He will be our *g* forever.
67. 4 people with equity and *g* the nations
73.24 You *g* me with your counsel, and
78.52 sheep, and *g* them in the wilderness
Isa 42.16 they have not known I will *g* them.
58.11 The LORD will *g* you continually, and
Mt 15.14 if one blind person *g* another, both will
Lk 6.39 "Can a blind person *g* a blind person?
Jn 16.13 truth comes he will *g* you into all truth;
Acts 1.16 Judas, who became a *g* for those who
Rom 2.19 are sure that you are a *g* to the blind,
Gal 5.25 the Spirit, let us also be *g* by the Spirit.

GUILE

Prov 26.26 though hatred is covered with *g*, the

GUILT

Lev 4.22 "When a ruler sins, . . . and incurs *g*,
1 Chr 21. 3 this? Why should he bring *g* on Israel?"
Ps 25.11 O LORD, pardon my *g*, for it is great.

Ezek 16.49 This was the *g* of your sister Sodom:
Hos 13. 1 in Israel; but he incurred *g* through Baal
Zech 3. 9 I will remove the *g* of this land in a

GUILT OFFERING

Lev 7. 1 This is the ritual of the *g*. It is most

GUILTLESS

2 Sam 3.28 kingdom are forever *g* before the LORD
2 Cor 7.11 point you have proved yourselves *g* in

GUILTY

Lev 5. 4 know it , you shall in any of these be *g*.
Ps 68.21 of those who walk in their *g* ways.
Isa 5.23 who acquit the *g* for a bribe, and
50. 9 who helps me; who will declare me *g*?
Jer 2. 3 All who ate of it were held *g*; disaster
12. 1 Why does the way of the *g* prosper?
Ezek 22. 4 have become *g* by the blood that you
Hos 4.15 O Israel, do not let Judah become *g*.
Lk 23.14 have not found this man *g* of any of

H

HABAKKUK

Hab 1. 1 The oracle that the prophet *H* saw. O
3. 1 A prayer of the prophet *H* according to

HADES

Mt 16.18 and the gates of *H* will not prevail
Lk 16.23 In *H*, where he was being tormented, he
Acts 2.27 For you will not abandon my soul to *H*,
Rev 6. 8 was Death, and *H* followed with him;
20.14 Death and *H* were thrown into the lake

HAGAR

Gen 16. 1 Egyptian slave-girl whose name was *H*,
16.15 *H* bore Abram a son; and Abram named
21. 9 Sarah saw the son of *H* the Egyptian,
21.14 and a skin of water, and gave it to *H*,
Gal 4.24 is *H*, from Mount Sinai, bearing

HAGGAI

Ezra 5. 1 Now the prophets, *H* and Zechariah son
6.14 the prophesying of the prophet *H*
Hag 1. 1 came by the prophet *H* to Zerubbabel
2. 1 of the LORD came by the prophet *H*,

HAIL (HAILSTONES)

Ex 9.18 I will cause the heaviest *h* to fall that
Josh 10.11 more who died because of the *h* than

HAIR (HAIRS)

Ps 40.12 they are more than the *h* of my head,
Prov 23. 7 like a *h* in the throat, so are they. "Eat
Isa 3.24 and instead of well-set *h*, baldness;
Mt 10.30 even the *h* of your head are all counted.
Lk 7.38 her tears and to dry them with her *h*.
12. 7 even the *h* of your head are all counted.
1 Cor 11.15 if a woman has long *h*, it is her glory?

HALLOW (HALLOWED)

Gen 2. 3 God blessed the seventh day and *h* it,
Ezek 20.20 and *h* my sabbaths that they may be a
Mt 6. 9 Our Father in heaven, *h* be your name.
Lk 11. 2 "Father, *h* be your name. Your kingdom

HAMATH

Isa 36.19 Where are the gods of *H* and Arpad?
Am 6. 2 and see; from there go to *H* the great;

HAMMER

Judg 4.21 and took a *h* in her hand, and went
1 Kings 6. 7 so that neither *h* nor axe nor any tool
Jer 23.29 like fire, says the LORD, and like a *h*
50.23 the *h* of the whole earth is cut down

HAND (n)

Gen 9. 2 the sea; into your *h* they are delivered.
48.17 saw that his father laid his right *h* on
Ex 3.19 you go unless compelled by a mighty *h*.
4. 2 "What is that in your *h*?" He said, "A
15.12 You stretched out your right *h*, the
17.11 whenever he lowered his *h*, Amalek
Lev 4.24 lay his *h* upon the head of of the goat;
Num 21.34 of him, for I have given him into your *h*,
Deut 2.15 the LORD's own *h* was against them, to
4.34 by war, by a mighty *h* and an
5.15 from there with a mighty *h* and an
26. 8 brought us out of Egypt with a mighty *h*
1 Sam 5. 6 The *h* of the LORD was heavy on the
12.15 then the *h* of the LORD will be against
18.17 "I will not raise a *h* against him; let the
23.16 there he strengthened his *h* through the
2 Sam 3.18 Israel from the *h* of the Philistines
24.14 let us fall into the *h* of the LORD, for his
1 Chr 4.10 and that your *h* might be with me, and
Ezra 7.28 I took courage, for the *h* of the LORD my
Job 8.20 person, nor take the *h* of evildoers.
12. 9 does not know that the *h* of the LORD
19.21 for the *h* of God has touched me!
40.14 your own right *h* can give you victory.
Ps 31.15 My times are in your *h*; deliver me from
32. 4 day and night your *h* was heavy on me;
74.11 why do you keep your *h* in your bosom?
104. 28 when you open your *h*, they are filled
106. 10 them from the *h* of the enemy.
118. 16 right *h* of the LORD is exalted; the right
Eccl 9. 1 their deeds are in the *h* of God; whether
9.10 Whatever your *h* finds to do, do with
Isa 5.25 away, and his *h* is stretched out still.
8.11 to me while his *h* was strong upon me,
9.12 turned away; his *h* is stretched out still.
9.17 turned away, his *h* is stretched out still.
14.27 His *h* is stretched out, and who will
40.12 the waters in the hollow of his *h*
59. 1 See, the LORD's *h* is not too short to
Ezek 3.14 my spirit, the *h* of the LORD was being
3.22 *h* of the LORD was upon me there; and
13. 9 My *h* will be against the prophets who
20.33 a mighty *h* and an outstretched arm,
25.16 stretch out my *h* against the Philistines,
33.22 *h* of the LORD had been upon me the
37. 1 The *h* of the LORD came upon me, and
Dan 5. 5 fingers of a human *h* appeared and
Mt 3.12 His winnowing fork is in his *h*, and he
5.30 if your right *h* causes you to sin, cut if
6. 3 left *h* know what your right *h* is doing,
18. 8 "If your *h* or your foot causes you to
Mk 3. 5 said to the man, "Stretch out your *h*." He
9.43 If your *h* causes you to stumble, cut it
Lk 6. 6 man there whose right *h* was withered.
6.10 He did so, and the *h* was restored.
Jn 20.25 of the nails and my *h* in his side, I will
Acts 11.21 The *h* of the Lord was with them, and a
13.11 the *h* of the Lord is against you, and
1 Cor 5. 5 you are to *h* this man over to Satan for
2 Thess 3.17 Paul, write this greeting with my own *h*.

HANDS (n)

Num 27.23 he laid his *h* on him and commissioned
Job 10. 8 Your *h* fashioned and made me; and
34.19 poor, for they are all the work of his *h*?
Ps 24. 4 who have clean *h* and pure hearts, who
115. 7 They have *h*, but do not feel; feet, but
Prov 31.20 and reaches out her *h* to the needy.
Jer 32.28 this city into the *h* of the Chaldeans
Mt 15.20 to eat with unwashed *h* does not defile."
Mk 7. 2 his disciples were eating with defiled *h*,
Lk 15.19 son; treat me like one of your hired *h*."
24.39 Look at my *h* and my feet; see that it is
Jn 13. 9 feet only but also my *h* and my head!"
20.20 he showed them his *h* and his side.
20.25 I see the mark of the nails in his *h*,
Rom 10.21 I have held out my *h* to a disobedient
2 Cor 5. 1 a house not made with *h*, eternal in the
1 Jn 1. 1 have looked at and touched with our *h*,

HANDED
Deut 3. 2 for I have *h* him over to you, along with
Mt 11.27 "All things have been *h* over to me by
20.18 the Son of Man will be *h* over to the
26. 2 of Man will be *h* over to be crucified.
27. 2 led him away, and *h* him over to Pilate
Mk 15. 1 led him away and *h* him over to Pilate.
Lk 18.32 he will be *h* over to the Gentiles; and

HANDSOME
Ps 45. 2 You are the most *h* of men; grace is

HANG (HANGED HANGING HANGS HUNG)
Deut 21.23 for anyone *h* on a tree is under God's
2 Sam 17.23 set his house in order, and *h* himself;
18.10 told Joab, "I saw Absalom *h* in an oak."
Esth 6. 4 to the king about having Mordecai *h*
7. 9 And the king said, "*H* him on that."
Job 26. 7 the void, and *h* the earth upon nothing.
Ps 137. 2 On the willows there we *h* up our harps.
Mt 27. 5 departed; and he went and *h* himself.
Acts 10.39 put him to death by *h* him on a tree;

HANNAH
1 Sam 1. 2 two wives; the name of the one was *H*,
1.13 *H* was praying silently; only her lips
2. 1 *H* prayed and said, "My heart exults in
2.21 the LORD took note of *H*; she conceived

HAPPY
Deut 24. 5 at home one year, to be *h* with the wife
33.29 *H* are you, O Israel! Who is like you, a
1 Kings 10. 8 *H* are your wives! *H* are these your
2 Chr 9. 7 *H* are your people! *H* are these your
Job 5.17 "How *h* is the one whom God reproves;
Ps 1. 1 *H* are those who do not follow the
32. 1 *H* are those whose transgression is
34. 8 is good; *h* are those who take refuge
41. 1 *H* are those who consider the poor; the
127. 5 *H* is the man who has his quiver full of
144. 15 *H* are the people whose God is the
146. 5 *H* are those whose help is the God of
Prov 3.13 *H* are those who find wisdom, and
8.32 to me: *h* are those who keep my ways.
28.14 *H* is the one who is never without fear,
31.28 Her children rise up and call her *h*; her
Mal 3.15 we count the arrogant *h*; evildoers not

HARD (HARDER)
Jer 32.17 arm! Nothing is too *h* for you.
Mt 7.14 road is *h* that leads to life, and there
1 Cor 15.10 I worked *h* than any of them—
2 Pet 3.16 some things in them *h* to understand,

HARDEN (HARDENED HARDENS)
Ex 4.21 but I will *h* his heart, so that he will
7. 3 I will *h* Pharaoh's heart, and I will
8.32 But Pharaoh *h* his heart this time also,
Deut 2.30 LORD your God had *h* his spirit and
Josh 11.20 it was the LORD's doing to *h* their hearts
1 Sam 6. 6 Why should you *h* your hearts as the
Ps 95. 8 Do not *h* your hearts, as at Meribah, as
Isa 63.17 stray from your ways and *h* our heart,
Dan 5.20 spirit was *h* so that he acted proudly, he
Mk 6.52 the loaves, but their hearts were *h*.
Jn 12.40 has blinded their eyes and *h* their heart,
Rom 9.18 and he *h* the heart of whomever he
11. 7 elect obtained it, but the rest were *h*,
2 Cor 3.14 But their minds were *h*. Indeed, to this
Heb 3. 8 do not *h* your hearts as in the rebellion,

HARDENING
Rom 11.25 a *h* has come upon part of Israel, until

HARD-HEARTED
Deut 15. 7 do not be *h* or tight-fisted toward your
Mt 19. 8 because you were so *h* that Moses

HARDNESS
Mk 3. 5 he was grieved at their *h* of heart and
10. 5 "Because of your *h* of heart he wrote
Eph 4.18 of their ignorance and *h* of heart.

HARDSHIP
Rom 8.35 Will *h*, or distress, or persecution, or

HARM
Gen 44.29 one also from me, and *h* comes to him,
Jer 25. 6 of your hands. Then I will do you no *h*."
39.12 look after him well and do him no *h*,
Lk 6. 9 to do good or to do *h* on the sabbath,
Acts 16.28 "Do not *h* yourself, for we are all here."

HARMAGEDON
Rev 16.16 at the place that in Hebrew is called *H*.

HARMONY
Rom 15. 5 grant you to live in *h* with one another,
Col 3.14 binds everything together in perfect *h*.

HARP (HARPS)
Ps 108. 2 Awake, O *h* and lyre! I will awake the
137. 2 On the willows there we hung up our *h*.
1 Cor 14. 7 notes, such as the flute or the *h*.
Rev 5. 8 each holding a *h* and golden bowls full
14. 2 the sound of harpists playing on their *h*,

HARSH (HARSHLY)
Ruth 1.21 when the LORD dealt *h* with me and the
Mt 25.24 I knew that you were a *h* man, reaping

HARVEST (HARVESTS)
Gen 8.22 as the earth endures, seedtime and *h*,
Lev 23.10 and you reap its *h*, you shall bring the
Prov 25.13 snow in the time of *h* are faithful
Isa 9. 3 rejoice before you as with joy at the *h*,
16. 9 for the shout over your fruit *h* and your
Jer 5.17 They shall eat up your *h* and your food;
8.20 "The *h* is past, the summer is ended,
12.13 They shall be ashamed of their *h*
Joel 3.13 Put in the sickle, for the *h* is ripe. Go
Mt 9.37 "The *h* is plentiful, but the laborers are
13.30 both of them grow together until the *h*;
Mk 4.29 the sickle, because the *h* has come."
Lk 10. 2 of the *h* to send out laborers into his *h*.
Jn 4.35 'Four months more, then comes the *h*'?
Rom 1.13 that I may reap some *h* among you
2 Cor 9.10 increase the *h* of your righteousness.
Phil 1.11 having produced the *h* of righteousness
Rev 14.15 because the *h* of the earth is fully ripe."

HASTE
Ps 38.22 Make *h* to help me, O Lord, my
70. 1 deliver me. O LORD, make *h* to help me!
Lk 2.16 went with *h*, and found Mary and

HATE (HATED HATES)
Gen 27.41 Now Esau *h* Jacob because of the
Ps 26. 5 I *h* the company of evildoers, and will
68. 1 let those who *h* him flee before
69. 4 are those who *h* me without cause;
101. 3 I *h* the work of those who fall away; it
106. 41 so that those who *h* them ruled them.
119.113 I *h* the doubled-minded, but I love your
Prov 6.16 six things that the LORD *h*, seven that
19. 7 If the poor are *h* even by their kin, how
Eccl 2.18 I *h* all my toil in which I had toiled
Jer 44. 4 to do this abominable thing that I *h*!"
Am 5.15 *H* evil and love good, and establish
Mal 1. 3 I have loved Jacob but I have *h* Esau; I
Mt 10.22 you will be *h* by all because of my
24. 9 you will be *h* by all nations because of
Mk 13.13 you will be *h* by all because of my
Lk 6.22 "Blessed are you when people *h* you,
14.26 comes to me and does not *h* father and
21.17 You will be *h* by all because of my

Jn 15.18 “If the world *h* you, be aware that it *h*
15.25 their law, ‘They *h* me without a cause.’
17.14 and the world has *h* them because they
Rom 7.15 what I want, but I do the very thing I *h*.
9.13 “I have loved Jacob, but I have *h* Esau.”
12. 9 *h* what is evil, hold fast to what is good;
Eph 5.29 no one ever *h* his own body, but he
Heb 1. 9 loved righteousness and *h* wickedness;
1 Jn 4.20 say, “I love God,” and *h* their brothers or

HATRED

Num 35.20 if someone pushes another from *h*, or
Ps 25.19 foes, and with what violent *h* they hate
Prov 8.13 fear of the LORD is *h* of evil. Pride and

HAUGHTY

Prov 6.17 *h* eyes, a lying tongue, and hands that
Isa 3.16 Because the daughters of Zion are *h*
5.15 low, and the eyes of the *h* are humbled.
Jer 13.15 Hear and give ear; do not be *h*, for the
Rom 12.16 do not be *h*, but associate with the

HAWK

Lev 11.16 the sea gull, the *h* of any kind;
Job 39.26 “Is it by your wisdom that the *h* soars,

HEAD

Gen 28.11 of the place, he put it under his *h*
1 Sam 17.51 killed him; then he cut off his *h* with it.
2 Kings 4.19 He complained to his father, “Oh, my *h*,
Song 7. 5 Your *h* crowns you like Carmel, and
Mt 14. 8 “Give me the *h* of John the Baptist here
Mk 6.28 brought his *h* on a platter, and gave it
Jn 13. 9 feet only but also my hands and my *h*!”
1 Cor 11. 3 Christ is the *h* of every man, and the
Eph 1.22 and has made him the *h* over all things
5.23 the husband is the *h* of the wife just as
Col 1.18 He is the *h* of the body, the church; he

HEAL (HEALED HEALS)

Gen 20.17 prayed to God; and God *h* Abimelech,
Ex 15.26 Egyptians; for I am the LORD who *h* you.”
Num 12.13 cried to the LORD, “O God, please *h* her.”
Deut 32.39 I kill and I make alive; I wound and I *h*;
2 Chr 7.14 will forgive their sin and *h* their land.
Ps 30. 2 to you for help, and you have *h* me.
41. 4 me; *h* me, for I have sinned against you.”
103. 3 your iniquity, who *h* all your diseases,
107. 20 he sent out his word and *h* them, and
147. 3 He *h* the brokenhearted, and binds up
Isa 30.26 and *h* the wounds inflicted by his blow.
53. 5 us whole, and by his bruises we are *h*.
57.19 near, says the LORD; and I will *h* them.
Jer 3.22 children, I will *h* your faithlessness.
17.14 *H* me, O LORD, and I shall be *h*; save
30.17 health to you, and your wounds I will *h*,
33. 6 I will *h* them and reveal to them
51. 9 We tried to *h* Babylon, but she could
Hos 5.13 is not able to cure you or *h* your wound.
7. 1 when I would *h* Israel, the corruption of
11. 3 but they did not know that I *h* them.
14. 4 I will *h* their disloyalty; I will love them
Mt 13.15 heart and turn— and I would *h* them.’
Mk 6.56 cloak; and all who touched it were *h*.
Lk 6.18 hear him and to be *h* of their diseases;
8.47 and how she had been immediately *h*.
9. 2 proclaim the kingdom of God and to *h*.
22.51 this!” And he touched his ear and *h* him.
Jn 4.47 him to come down and *h* his son,
5.13 man who had been *h* did not know who
Acts 14. 9 and seeing that he had faith to be *h*,
1 Pet 2.24 by his wounds you have been *h*.

HEALING

Prov 3. 8 It will be *h* for your flesh and a
29. 1 will suddenly be broken beyond *h*.
Jer 8.15 find no good, for a time of *h*, but found
14.19 us down so that there is no *h* for us?
46.11 many medicines; there is no *h* for you.
Ezek 47.12 will be for food, and their leaves for *h*.”
Mal 4. 2 shall rise, with *h* in its wings.
1 Cor 12. 9 to another gifts of *h* by the one Spirit,
12.28 then deeds of power, then gifts of *h*,
Rev 22. 2 of the trees are for the *h* of the nations.

HEALTH (HEALTHY)

Ps 38. 3 is no *h* in my bones because of my sin.
Prov 16.24 to the soul and *h* to the body.
Jer 30.17 For I will restore *h* to you, and your
Lk 11.34 when your eye is *h*, your whole body is
Acts 3.16 Jesus has given him this perfect *h* in
3 Jn 2 well with you and that you may be in *h*,

HEAP

Josh 3.13 cut off; they shall stand in a single *h*.”
Job 27.16 Though they *h* up silver like dust, and
Ps 39. 6 they *h* up, and do not know who
Prov 25.22 you will *h* coals of fire on their heads,
Jer 9.11 I will make Jerusalem a *h* of ruins, a

HEAR (HEARD HEARS)

Gen 21.17 God *h* the voice of the boy; and the
Ex 2.24 God *h* their groaning, and God
Deut 4.10 I will let them *h* my words, so that they
5. 1 *H*, O Israel, the statutes and ordinances
6. 4 *H*, O Israel: The LORD is our God, the
31.12 that they may *h* and learn to fear the
2 Sam 5.24 When you *h* the sound of marching in
22. 7 From his temple he *h* my voice, and my
1 Kings 8.39 then *h* in heaven your dwelling place,
2 Kings 19.16 Incline your ear, O LORD, and *h*; open
2 Chr 6.27 may you *h* in heaven, forgive the sin of
7.12 “I have *h* your prayer, and have chosen
33.13 received his entreaty, and *h* his plea,
Neh 8. 9 people wept when they *h* the words of
Job 42. 4 ‘*H*, and I will speak; I will question
Ps 6. 9 The LORD has *h* my supplication; the
34.17 the righteous cry for help, the LORD *h*,
49. 1 *H* this, all peoples; give ear, all
Prov 1. 8 *H*, my child, your father’s instruction,
Isa 1. 2 *H*, O heavens, and listen, O earth; for
33.13 *H*, you who are far away, what I have
40.28 Have you not known? Have you not *h*?
64. 4 From ages past no one has *h*, no ear
66. 8 Who has *h* of such a thing? Who has
Jer 18. 2 and there I will let you *h* my words.”
31.18 I *h* Ephraim pleading: “You disciplined
Ezek 3.27 Let those who will *h*, *h*; and let those
12. 2 see, who have ears to *h*, but do not *h*;
33.31 and they *h* your words, but they will not
Mic 1. 2 *H*, you peoples, all of you; listen, O
Mt 11. 4 “Go and tell John what you *h* and see:
Mk 4.24 to them, “Pay attention to what you *h*;
Lk 6.18 They had come to *h* him and to be
7.22 tell John what you have seen and *h*:
Jn 5.24 anyone who *h* my word and believes
10. 3 the sheep *h* his voice. He calls his own
12.47 I do not judge anyone who *h* my words
Acts 4.20 about what we have seen and *h*.”
10.44 the Holy Spirit fell on all who *h*
19.10 of Asia, both Jews and Greeks, *h* the
Rom 10.14 And how are they to *h* without someone
15.21 and those who have never *h* of him
1 Jn 1. 1 what we have *h*, what we have seen
Rev 1. 3 blessed are those who *h* and who keep

HEARING (n)

Gen 23.10 Abraham in the *h* of the Hittites,
Neh 13. 1 the book of Moses in the *h* of the
1 Cor 12.17 were an eye, where would the *h* be?

HEART

Gen 8.21 the inclination of the human *h* is evil
Ex 28.30 judgment . . . on his *h* before the LORD
35. 5 let whoever is of a generous *h* bring the
Deut 6. 5 love the LORD your God with all your *h*,

Deut 7. 7 people that the LORD set his *h* on you
10.12 serve the LORD your God with all your *h*
10.15 yet the LORD set his *h* in love on your
17.17 for himself, or else his *h* will turn away;
28.65 LORD will give you a trembling *h*, failing
30. 6 God will circumcise your *h* and the *h*
30.14 mouth and in your *h* for you to observe.
1 Sam 7. 3 Direct your *h* to the LORD, and serve
10. 9 God gave him another *h*; and all these
13.14 has sought out a man after his own *h*;
16. 7 but the LORD looks on the *h*."
25.37 his *h* died within him; he became like a
2 Sam 17.10 whose *h* is like the *h* of a lion, will
24.10 David was stricken to the *h* because he
1 Kings 3. 6 in uprightness of *h* toward you; and you
8.48 if they repent with all their *h* and soul
11. 9 with Solomon, because his *h* had turned
15.14 the *h* of Asa was true to the LORD all his
2 Kings 14.10 your *h* has lifted you up. Be content
22.19 because your *h* was penitent and you
23.25 turned to the LORD with all his *h*, with
1 Chr 28. 9 him with single mind and willing *h*;
29.17 I know, my God, that you search the *h*,
2 Chr 16. 9 to strengthen those whose *h* is true
17. 6 His *h* was courageous in the ways of the
25.19 your *h* has lifted you up in boastfulness.
32.25 his *h* was proud. Therefore wrath came
Ezra 6.22 turned the *h* of the king of Assyria to
7.10 Ezra had set his *h* to study the law of
Neh 2. 2 sick? This can only be sadness of the *h*."
2.12 had put into my *h* to do for Jerusalem.
Job 11.13 "If you direct your *h* rightly, you will
23.16 God has made my *h* faint; the Almighty
31. 9 "If my *h* has been enticed by a woman,
36.13 "The godless in *h* cherish anger; they do
Ps 19. 8 of the LORD are right, rejoicing the *h*;
44.21 this? For he knows the secrets of the *h*.
45. 1 My *h* overflows with a goodly theme; I
51.10 Create in me a clean *h*, O God, and put
55.21 than butter, but with a *h* set on war;
57. 7 My *h* is steadfast, O God, my *h* is
69.20 Insults have broken my *h*, so that I am
77. 6 I commune with my *h* in the night; I
78.18 They tested God in their *h* by
101. 2 I will walk with integrity of *h* within my
102. 4 My *h* is stricken and withered like grass;
104. 15 wine to gladden the human *h*, oil to
108. 1 My *h* is steadfast, O God, my *h* is
109. 22 needy, and my *h* is pierced within me.
119. 11 I treasure your word in my *h*, so that I
143. 4 within me; my *h* within me is appalled.
Prov 2.10 wisdom will come into your *h*, and
3. 3 write them on the tablet of your *h*.
4.23 Keep your *h* with all vigilance, for from
6.18 a *h* that devises wicked plans, feet that
18.12 Before destruction one's *h* is haughty,
20. 9 Who can say, I have made my *h* clean; I
21. 1 king's *h* is a stream of water in the
23.26 My child, give me your *h*, and let your
26.23 vessel are smooth lips with an evil *h*.
27.19 face, so one human *h* reflects another.
Eccl 5. 2 nor let your *h* be quick to utter a word
10. 2 The *h* of the wise inclines to the right,
Song 8. 6 Set me as a seal upon your *h*, as a seal
Isa 1. 5 head is sick, and the whole *h* faint.
38. 3 you in faithfulness with a whole *h*,
42.25 burned him, but he did not take it to *h*.
63.17 stray from your ways and harden our *h*,
Jer 3.10 did not return to me with her whole *h*,
3.15 give you shepherds after my own *h*, who
4.14 Jerusalem, wash your *h* clean of
4.19 My *h* is beating wildly; I cannot keep
17. 9 The *h* is devious above all else; it is
32.39 I will give them one *h* and one way,
Ezek 11.19 I will give them one *h*, and put a new
16.30 How sick is your *h*, says the Lord GOD,
28. 2 Because your *h* is proud and you have
Ezek 33.31 lips, but their *h* is set on their gain.
36.26 remove from your body the *h* of stone
44. 7 uncircumcised in *h* and flesh,
Dan 5.22 his son, have not humbled your *h*,
Hos 10. 2 Their *h* is false; now they must bear
Joel 2.12 return to me with all your *h*, with
Am 2.16 who are stout of *h* among the mighty
Mt 5. 8 "Blessed are the pure in *h*, for they will
5.28 committed adultery with her in his *h*.
6.21 treasure is, there your *h* will be also.
9. 2 "Take *h*, son; your sins are forgiven."
13.15 this people's *h* has grown dull, and their
14.27 said, "Take *h*, it is I; do not be afraid."
15.19 out of the *h* come evil intentions,
Mk 6.50 said, "Take *h*, it is I; do not be afraid."
7.21 it is . . . from the human *h*, that evil
10. 5 "Because of your hardness of *h* he wrote
12.30 love the Lord your God with all your *h*,
Lk 2.19 words and pondered them in her *h*.
2.51 treasured all these things in her *h*.
6.45 out of the good treasure of the *h*
Jn 1.18 only Son, who is close to the Father's *h*,
7.38 "Out of the believer's *h* shall flow rivers
Acts 1.24 "Lord, you know everyone's *h*. Show us
2.26 therefore my *h* was glad, and my tongue
4.32 who believed were of one *h* and soul,
7.23 came into his *h* to visit his relatives, the
7.51 people, uncircumcised in *h* and ears,
8.21 this, for your *h* is not right before God.
13.22 son of Jesse, to be a man after my *h*,
15. 8 God who knows the human *h* testified
16.14 Lord opened her *h* to listen eagerly to
21.13 you doing, weeping and breaking my *h*?
28.27 For this people's *h* has grown dull, and
Rom 8.27 God, who searches the *h*, knows what is
9. 2 sorrow and unceasing anguish in my *h*.
10. 9 believe in your *h* that God raised him
1 Cor 2. 9 ear heard, nor the human *h* conceived,
2 Cor 4. 1 in this ministry, we do not lose *h*.
6.11 to you Corinthians; our *h* is wide open
7.15 his *h* goes out all the more to you, as
1 Tim 1. 5 is love that comes from a pure *h*,
Heb 4.12 the thoughts and intentions of the *h*.
1 Pet 1.22 love one another deeply from the *h*.

HEARTS

Ex 25. 2 from all those whose *h* prompt them to
Josh 5. 1 they had crossed over, their *h* melted,
24.23 you, and incline your *h* to the LORD,
2 Sam 15. 6 so Absalom stole the *h* of the people of
1 Kings 18.37 and that you have turned their *h* back."
Ps 14. 1 Fools say in their *h*, "There is no God."
24. 4 who have clean hands and pure *h*,
53. 1 Fools say in their *h*, there is no God."
95. 8 Do not harden your *h*, as at Meribah, as
112. 8 Their *h* are steady, they will not be
Isa 29.13 their lips, while their *h* are far from me,
51. 7 who have kept my teaching in your *h*;
Jer 17. 5 whose *h* turn away from the LORD.
31.33 them and I will write it on their *h*;
Zech 7.12 They made their *h* adamant in order not
Mal 4. 6 He will turn the *h* of parents to their
Mt 15. 8 their lips, but their *h* are far from me;
Mk 2. 8 do you raise such question in your *h*?
6.52 the loaves, but their *h* were hardened.
7. 6 their lips, but their *h* are far from me;
8.17 or understand? Are your *h* hardened?
Lk 1.17 turn the *h* of parents to their children,
24.32 "Were not our *h* burning within us while
Jn 12.40 blinded their eyes and hardened their *h*,
14. 1 "Do not let your *h* be troubled. Believe
14.27 Do not let your *h* be troubled, and do
Rom 2.15 the law requires is written on their *h*,
2 Thess 3. 5 May the Lord direct your *h* to the love
Heb 3. 8 do not harden your *h* as in the
3.10 'They always go astray in their *h*, and
4. 7 hear his voice, do not harden your *h*."

Heb 8.10 their minds, and write them on their *h*,
1 Jn 3.20 whenever our *h* condemn us; for God is
Rev 2.23 am the one who searches minds and *h*,

HEAVEN (HEAVENS)

Ex 16. 4 I am going to rain bread from *h* for you;
20.22 yourselves that I spoke with you from *h*.
Deut 30.12 It is not in *h*, that you should say, "Who
1 Kings 8.27 Even *h* and the highest *h* cannot
2 Chr 6.18 *h* and the highest *h* cannot contain you,
Ps 19. 1 The *h* are telling the glory of God; and
103. 11 as the *h* are high above the earth, so
119. 89 forever; your word is firmly fixed in *h*.
139. 8 I ascend to *h*, you are there; if I make
Isa 14.12 How you are fallen from *h*, O Day Star,
24. 4 and withers; the *h* languish together
66. 1 *H* is my throne and the earth is my
Hag 1.10 *h* above you have withheld the dew, and
Mt 5.18 until *h* and earth pass away, not one
6. 9 "Pray then in this way: Our father in *h*,
Mk 1.10 he saw the *h* torn apart and the Spirit
13.31 *H* and earth will pass away, but my
16.19n Jesus . . . was taken up into *h* and sat
Lk 21.26 for the powers of the *h* will be shaken.
21.33 *H* and earth will pass away, but my
Acts 9. 3 suddenly a light from *h* flashed
1 Cor 15.49 also bear the image of the man of *h*.
2 Cor 12. 2 ago was caught up to the third *h*—
1 Pet 3.22 Christ, who has gone into *h* and is at
2 Pet 3. 5 by the word of God *h* existed long ago
3.13 we wait for new *h* and a new earth,
Rev 4. 1 and there in *h* a door stood open!
19. 1 voice of a great multitude in *h*, saying,
21. 1 I saw a new *h* and a new earth; for the

HEAVENLY

Jn 3.12 you believe if I tell you about *h* things?
2 Cor 5. 2 to be clothed with our *h* dwelling—
Eph 1. 3 every spiritual blessing in the *h* places,

HEAVY

1 Kings 14. 6 For I am charged with *h* tidings for you.
Ps 32. 4 day and night your hand was *h* on me;
Eccl 6. 1 the sun, and it lies *h* upon humankind:
Mt 11.28 are weary and are carrying *h* burdens,

HEBRON

Gen 13.18 by the oaks of Mamre, which are at *H*;
Judg 1.10 against the Canaanites who lived in *H*
2 Sam 2.11 that David was king in *H* over the house

HEED (HEEDED)

Ex 5. 2 Who is the LORD, that I should *h* him
Deut 4.30 return to the LORD your God and *h* him.
7.12 If you *h* these ordinances, by diligently
13. 8 you must not yield to or *h* any such
Judg 6.10 But you have not given *h* to my voice."
1 Sam 12.15 if you will not *h* the voice of the LORD,
2 Chr 11. 4 they *h* the word of the LORD and turned
Ps 31. 7 you have taken *h* of my adversities,
Prov 1.23 Give *h* to my reproof; I will pour out my
Eccl 9.17 words of the wise are more to be *h*
Jer 8. 6 I have given *h* and listened, but they do
11. 3 Cursed be anyone who does not *h* the
26. 5 to *h* the words of my servants the

HEEL

Gen 3.15 your head, and you will strike his *h*."
25.26 out, with his hand gripping Esau's *h*;
Ps 41. 9 my bread, has lifted the *h* against me.

HEIFER

Gen 15. 9 "Bring me a *h* three years old, a female
Num 19. 2 to bring you a red *h* without defect, in
Judg 14.18 "If you had not plowed with my *h*, you

HEIGHT

Rom 8.39 nor *h*, nor depth, nor anything else in

HEIR (HEIRS)

Gen 15. 3 and so a slave . . . is to be my *h*."
Jer 49. 1 Has Israel no sons? Has he no *h*? Why
Mt 21.38 'This is the *h*; come, let us kill him and
Mk 12. 7 'This is the *h*; come, let us kill him, and
Lk 20.14 'This is the *h*; let us kill him so that
Rom 8.17 if children, then *h*, *h* of God and joint *h*
Gal 4. 1 *h*, as long as they are minors, are no
Eph 3. 6 the Gentiles have become fellow *h*,
Heb 11. 7 world and became an *h* to righteousness

HELL

Mt 5.22 fool!' you will be liable to the *h* of fire.
5.29 your whole body to be thrown into *h*.
18. 9 eyes and to be thrown into the *h* of fire.
Lk 12. 5 has killed, has authority to cast into *h*.

HELLENISTS

Acts 6. 1 *H* complained against the Hebrews
9.29 spoke and argued with the *H*; but they

HELMET

Isa 59.17 and a *h* of salvation on his head;
Eph 6.17 Take the *h* of salvation, and the sword
1 Thess 5. 8 love, and for a *h* the hope of salvation.

HELP (n)

2 Sam 22.36 salvation, and your *h* made me great.
Ps 18.35 supported me; your *h* made me great.
42. 5 God; for I shall again praise him, my *h*
42.11 God; for I shall again praise him, my *h*
70. 5 You are my *h* and my deliverer; O LORD,
121. 2 My *h* comes from the LORD, who made
Isa 30. 7 Egypt's *h* is worthless and empty,
Acts 26.22 To this day I have had *h* from God, and
Phil 4.16 I was in in Thessalonica, you sent me *h*

HELP (HELPED HELPS) (v)

Ex 2.19 "An Egyptian *h* us against the
Deut 28.31 your enemies, without anyone to *h* you.
2 Kings 14.26 bond or free, and no one to *h* Israel.
2 Chr 14.11 *H* us, O LORD our God, for we rely on
26. 7 God *h* him against the Philistines,
Ps 106. 4 people; *h* me when you deliver them;
107. 12 labor; they fell down, with none to *h*.
109. 26 *H* me, O LORD my God! Save me
Isa 49. 8 you, on a day of salvation I have *h* you;
50. 7 The Lord GOD *h* me; therefore I have
Hos 13. 9 destroy you, O Israel; who can *h* you?
Mt 15.25 knelt before him, saying, "Lord, *h* me."

HELPER

Gen 2.18 I will make him a *h* as his partner."
Ps 10.14 and you have been the *h* of the orphan.
30.10 be gracious to me! O LORD, be my *h*!"
Heb 13. 6 "The Lord is my *h*, I will not be afraid.

HELPLESS

Jer 6.24 our hands fall *h*; anguish has taken hold

HEM

Ps 139. 5 You *h* me in, behind and before, and lay

HEMORRHAGES

Mk 5.25 been suffering from *h* for twelve years,
Lk 8.43 been suffering from *h* for twelve years;

HERALD

2 Chr 36.22 Persia so that he sent a *h* throughout
Ezra 1. 1 Persia so that he sent a *h* throughout
1 Tim 2. 7 right time. For this I was appointed a *h*

HERE

Isa 40. 9 to the cities of Judah, "*H* is your God!"

HERITAGE

1 Kings 8.53 to be your *h*, just as you promised
Job 31. 2 and my *h* from the Almighty on high?
Ps 2. 8 I will make the nations your *h*, and the

Ps 16. 6 in pleasant places; I have a goodly *h*.
33.12 people whom he has chosen as his *h*.
94.14 his people; he will not abandon his *h*;
Jer 12. 7 my house, I have abandoned my *h*;
17. 4 By your own act you shall lose the *h*
50.11 though you exult, O plunderers of my *h*,

HERMON

Deut 3. 8 Jordan, from Wadi Arnon to Mount *H*
4.48 as far as Mount Sirion (that is, H),
Josh 11.17 the valley of Lebanon below Mount *H*.
12. 1 from the Wadi Arnon to Mount *H*, with
Ps 89.12 them; Tabor and *H* joyously praise
133. 3 It is like the dew of *H*, which falls on
Song 4. 8 Amana, from the peak of Senir and *H*,

HEROD

Mt 2. 1 In the time of King *H*, after Jesus was
2.13 for *H* is about to search for the child, to
2.16 When *H* saw that he had been tricked
2.19 When *H* died, an angel of the Lord
14. 1 At that time *H* the ruler heard reports
Mk 6.14 King *H* heard of it, for Jesus' name had
8.15 of the Pharisees and the yeast of *H*."
Lk 3. 1 and *H* was ruler of Galilee, and his
13.31 away from here, for *H* wants to kill you."
23. 7 he sent him off to *H*, who was himself
Acts 4.27 in this city, both *H* and Pontius Pilate,
12. 1 King *H* laid violent hands upon some
12.20 Now *H* was angry with the people of
12.21 day *H* put on his royal robes, took his

HEZEKIAH

2 Kings 16.20 city of David; his son *H* succeeded him.
19.14 *H* received the letter from the hand of
20. 1 In those days *H* became sick and was at
2 Chr 30. 1 *H* sent word to all Israel and Judah,
30.18 But *H* had prayed for them, saying,
32.30 *H* closed the upper outlet of the waters
Isa 39. 1 envoys with letters and a present to *H*,

HIDE (HID HIDDEN HIDES HIDING)

Gen 3. 8 the man and his wife *h* themselves from
18.17 "Shall I *h* from Abraham what I am
Ex 2. 2 a fine baby, she *h* him three months.
2.12 he killed the Egyptian and *h* him in the
3. 6 Moses *h* his face, for he was afraid to
Josh 2. 4 woman took the two men and *h* them.
1 Sam 3.17 Do not *h* it from me. May God do so to
10.22 "See, he has *h* himself among the
2 Chr 22.11 —*h* him from Athaliah, so that she did
Ps 10. 1 do you *h* yourself in times of trouble?
13. 1 forever? How long will you *h* your face
17. 8 eye; *h* me in the shadow of your wings,
19.12 their error? Clear me from *h* faults.
27. 5 he will *h* me in his shelter in the day of
27. 9 Do not *h* your face from me. Do not
30. 7 you *h* your face; I was dismayed.
40.10 I have not *h* your saving help within my
55. 1 do not *h* yourself from my supplication.
89.46 O Lord? Will you *h* yourself forever?
104. 29 When you *h* your face, they are
119.114 You are my *h* place and my shield; I
Prov 27. 5 Better is open rebuke than *h* love.
Isa 1.15 your hands, I will *h* my eyes from you;
2.10 *h* in the dust from the terror of the
32. 2 will be like a *h* place from the wind,
40.27 "My way is *h* from the Lord, and my
45.15 you are a God who *h* himself, O God of
49. 2 in the shadow of his hand he *h* me;
64. 5 because you *h* yourself we transgressed.
65.16 former troubles are forgotten and are *h*
Jer 13. 5 So I went, and *h* it by the Euphrates, as
36.26 prophet Jeremiah. But the Lord *h* them.
Ezek 39.29 I will never again *h* my face from them,
Am 9. 3 they *h* themselves on the top of Carmel,
Mt 5.14 A city built on a hill cannot be *h*.
25.18 the ground and *h* his master's money.
Mk 4.22 For there is nothing *h*, except to be
Lk 8.17 nothing is *h* that will not be disclosed,
10.21 have *h* these things from the wise and
Heb 4.13 before him no creature is *h*, but all are

HIGH (HIGHER)

Ezra 9. 6 our iniquities have risen *h* than our
Eccl 10. 6 folly is set in many *h* places, and the
Ezek 17.24 low the *h* tree, I make *h* the low tree;

HIGH PRIEST

Mk 2.26 when Abiathar was *h*, and ate the bread
14.53 They took Jesus to the *h*; and all the
Jn 18.19 the *h* questioned Jesus about his
Acts 5.17 Then the *h* took action; he and all who
23. 4 "Do you dare to insult God's *h*?" And
Heb 2.17 be a merciful and faithful *h* in the
3. 1 Jesus, the apostle and *h* of our
4.14 have a great *h* who has passed through
5. 5 did not glorify himself in becoming a *h*,

HIGHWAY (HIGHWAYS)

Ps 84. 5 you, in whose heart are the *h* to Zion.
Isa 11.16 so there shall be a *h* from Assyria for
19.23 there will be a *h* from Egypt to Assyria,
35. 8 A *h* shall be there, and it shall be called
49.11 a road, and my *h* shall be raised up.

HILL (HILLS)

Deut 2. 3 skirting this *h* country long enough.
1 Kings 20.23 "Their gods are gods of the *h*, and so
Ps 24. 3 Who shall ascend the *h* of the Lord?

HINDER

1 Sam 14. 6 nothing can *h* the Lord from saving by

HIP

Gen 32.25 him on the *h* socket; and Jacob's *h*

HIRAM

2 Sam 5.11 King *H* of Tyre sent messengers to
1 Kings 5. 1 Now *H* king of Tyre sent his servants to
7.13 King Solomon invited and received *H*
7.40 *H* also made the pots, the shovels, and
9.12 when *H* came from Tyre to see the
1 Chr 14. 1 King *H* of Tyre sent messengers to

HIRED

Deut 23. 4 because they *h* against you Balaam son
2 Chr 24.12 they *h* masons and carpenters to restore
Lk 15.19 son; treat me like one of your *h* hands."

HITTITE (HITTITES)

Gen 15.20 the *H*, the Perizzites, the Rephaim,
23.10 Ephron the *H* answered Abraham in the
Ex 3. 8 country of the Canaanites, the *H*, the
23.23 brings you to the Amorites, the *H*, the
Deut 7. 1 away many nations before you—the *H*,
1 Kings 9.20 who were left of the Amorites, the *H*,
2 Kings 7. 6 has hired against us the kings of the *H*
Ezra 9. 1 from the Canaanites, the *H*, the

HOLD (HELD HOLDING)

Gen 17. 8 the land of Canaan, for a perpetual *h*;
48. 4 offspring after you for a perpetual *h*.'
Deut 30.20 God, obeying him, and *h* fast to him;
Josh 22. 5 to *h* fast to him, and to serve him with
23. 8 but *h* fast to the Lord your God, as you
Job 27. 6 I *h* fast my righteousness, and will not
Ps 119.101 I *h* back my feet from every evil way, in
Isa 65. 2 I *h* out my hands all day long to a
Jer 26. 2 I command you; do not *h* back a word.
Ezek 44.28 give them no *h* in Israel; I am their *h*.
Jn 20.17 "Do not *h* on to me, because I have not
Rom 3.28 we *h* that a person is justified by faith
12. 9 hate what is evil, *h* fast to what is good;

HOLE (HOLES)

Ezek 8. 7 I looked, and there was a *h* in the wall.
Hag 1. 6 wages to put them into a bag with *h*.

HOLINESS

Ex 15.11 Who is like you, majestic in *h*, awesome
Ps 93. 5 very sure; *h* befits your house, O LORD,
Ezek 20.41 I will manifest my *h* among you in the
36.23 you I display my *h* before their eyes.
38.16 through you, O Gog, I display my *h*
Lk 1.75 serve him without fear, in *h* and
2 Cor 7. 1 making *h* perfect in the fear of God.
Eph 4.24 of God in true righteousness and *h*.
1 Thess 4. 7 did not call us to impurity but in *h*.
Heb 12.14 and the *h* without which no one will

HOLLOW

Isa 40.12 the waters in the *h* of his hand

HOLY

Ex 3. 5 on which you are standing is *h* ground."
19. 6 me a priestly kingdom and a *h* nation.
26.33 for you the *h* place from the most *h*.
28.36 engraving of a signet, "*H* to the LORD."
39.30 engraving of a signet, "*H* to the LORD."
Lev 10. 3 who are near me I will show myself *h*,
10.10 distinguish between the *h* and the
11.44 therefore, and be *h*, for I am *h*.
19. 2 You shall be *h*, for I the LORD your God
20.26 You shall be *h* to me; for I the LORD am
21. 6 They shall be *h* to their God, and not
22. 2 that they may not profane my *h* name;
Num 4.20 not go in to look on the *h* things even
6. 5 they shall be *h*; they shall let the locks
16. 3 All the congregation are *h*, everyone of
Deut 5.12 Observe the sabbath day and keep it *h*,
7. 6 For you are a people *h* to the LORD your
14. 2 For you are a people *h* to the LORD your
23.14 your camp must be *h*, so that he may
1 Sam 2. 2 "There is no *H* One like the LORD, no
Ezra 8.28 "You are *h* to the LORD, and the vessels
Neh 13.22 the gates, to keep the sabbath day *h*.
Job 5. 1 To which of the *h* ones will you turn?
Ps 16. 3 As for the *h* ones in the land, they are
22. 3 Yet you are *h*, enthroned on the praises
30. 4 ones, and give thanks to his *h* name.
34. 9 O fear the LORD, you his *h* ones, for
48. 1 in the city of our God. His *h* mountain,
96. 9 Worship the LORD in *h* splendor; tremble
99. 3 your great and awesome name. *H* is he!
134. 2 Lift up your hands to the *h* place, and
Isa 5.16 God shows himself *h* by righteousness.
6. 3 "*H*, *h*, *h* is the LORD of hosts; the earth
8.13 of hosts, him you shall regard as *h*;
35. 8 there, and it shall be called the *H* Way;
62. 9 gather it shall drink it in my *h* courts.
62.12 They shall be called, "The *H* People,
Jer 2. 3 Israel was *h* to the LORD, the first fruits
17.22 but keep the sabbath day *h*, as I
51.51 aliens have come into the *h* places of
Ezek 42.20 between the *h* and the common.
Dan 7.18 the *h* ones of the Most High shall
7.27 given to the people of the *h* ones of the
8.13 Then I heard a *h* one speaking, and
8.24 powerful and the people of the *h* ones.
12. 7 the shattering of the power of the *h*
Zech 14. 5 will come, and all the *h* ones with him.
Mt 7. 6 "Do not give what is *h* to dogs; and do
24.15 sacrilege standing in the *h* place,
Mk 6.20 that he was a righteous and *h* man,
Lk 2.23 first born male shall be designated as *h*
Acts 7.33 the place where you are standing is *h*
Rom 7.12 So the law is *h*, and the commandment
12. 1 bodies as a living sacrifice, *h* and
1 Cor 7.14 the unbelieving husband is made *h*
7.34 so that they may be *h* in body and in
Eph 1. 4 of the world to be *h* and blameless
Eph 5.26 in order to make her *h*, by cleansing her
5.27 that she may be *h* and without blemish.
Heb 7.26 such a high priest, *h*, blameless,
1 Pet 1.15 called you is *h*, be *h* yourselves in all
Jude 14 coming with ten thousand of his *h* ones,
Rev 3. 7 These are the words of the *h* one, the
4. 8 "*H*, *h*, *h*, is the Lord God the Almighty,
21. 2 I saw the *h* city, the new Jerusalem,

HOLY ONE

Prov 9.10 and knowledge of the *H* is insight.
Isa 41.14 LORD; your Redeemer is the *H* of Israel.
43.14 LORD, your Redeemer, the *H* of Israel:
Hab 1.12 not from of old, O LORD my God, my *H*?
Jn 6.69 and know that you are the *H* of God."
Acts 13.35 not let your *H* experience corruption.'

HOLY SPIRIT

Ps 51.11 and do not take your *h* from me.
Mt 1.18 was found to be with child from the *H*.
Mk 1. 8 but he will baptize you with the *H*."
Eph 1.13 with the seal of the promised *H*,
2 Pet 1.21 men and women moved by the *H* spoke

HOME

Ps 68. 6 God gives the desolate a *h* to live in; he
Mk 5.19 "Go *h* to your friends, and tell them
8.26 he sent him away to his *h*, saying, "Do
Lk 8.39 "Return to your *h*, and declare how
Jn 14.23 to them and make our *h* with them.
19.27 hour the disciple took her to his own *h*.
1 Cor 11.34 If you are hungry, eat at *h*, so that when
14.35 know, let them ask their husbands at *h*.
2 Cor 5. 6 while we are at *h* in the body we are
Rev 21. 3 "See, the *h* of God is among mortals.

HOMELAND

Heb 11.14 make it clear that they are seeking a *h*.

HOMETOWN

Mk 6. 1 He left that place and came to his *h*,

HONEST

Lev 19.36 You shall have *h* balances, *h* weights, an
Deut 25.15 You shall have only a full and *h* weight;
Prov 16.11 *H* balances and scales are the LORD's;
Ezek 45.10 You shall have *h* balances, an *h* ephah,
Lk 8.15 hold it fast in an *h* and good heart

HONESTY

Gen 30.33 So my *h* will answer for me later, when

HONEY

Ex 3. 8 land, a land flowing with milk and *h*,
16.31 taste of it was like wafers made with *h*.
Deut 32.13 he nursed him with *h* from the crags,
1 Sam 14.29 because I tasted a little of this *h*.
Ps 19.10 sweeter also than *h*, and drippings of
81.16 wheat and with *h* from the rock I would
119.103 your words to my taste, sweeter than *h*
Prov 24.13 My child, eat *h*, for it is good, and the
Song 4.11 *h* and milk are under your tongue;
Isa 7.15 He shall eat curds and *h* by the time he
Ezek 3. 3 and in my mouth it was as sweet as *h*.
Rev 10.10 sweet as *h* in my mouth, but when I

HONOR (n)

Num 22.17 I will surely do you great *h*, and
2 Sam 6.22 spoken, by them I shall be held in *h*."
2 Chr 1.11 not asked for possessions, wealth, *h*,
Esth 6. 3 "What *h* or distinction has been
Ps 96. 6 *H* and majesty are before him; strength
104. 1 are very great. You are clothed with *h*
Prov 15.33 in wisdom, and humility goes before *h*.
29.23 one who is lowly in spirit will obtain *h*.
Dan 2. 6 from me gifts and rewards and great *h*.
Mt 13.57 "Prophets are not without *h* except in
Mk 6. 4 "Prophets are not without *h*, except in
Lk 14. 7 how the guests chose the places of *h*,

Rom 2. 7 doing good seek for glory and *h* and
12.10 outdo one another in showing *h*.
13. 7 respect is due, *h* to whom *h* is due.
1 Cor 4.10 You are held in *h*, but we in disrepute.
2 Cor 6. 8 in *h* and dishonor, in ill repute and
1 Tim 6.16 see; to him be *h* and eternal dominion.

HONOR (HONORED HONORS) (v)

Gen 34.19 he was the most *h* of all his family.
Ex 20.12 *H* your father and your mother, so that
Deut 5.16 *H* your father and your mother, as the
1 Sam 2.30 those who *h* me I will *h*, and those who
15.30 "I have sinned; yet *h* me now before the
1 Chr 4. 9 Jabez was *h* more than his brothers;
Ps 50.23 thanksgiving as their sacrifice *h* me;
Prov 3. 9 *H* the LORD with your substance and
Isa 29.13 and *h* me with their lips, while their
43.23 offerings, or *h* me with your sacrifices.
58.13 if you *h* it, not going your own ways,
Jer 30.19 I will make them *h*, and they shall not
Dan 11.38 He shall *h* the god of fortresses instead
Mal 1. 6 A son *h* his father, and servants their
Mt 15. 4 God said, '*H* your father and your
15. 8 'This people *h* me with their lips, but
19.19 *H* your father and mother; also, You
Mk 7.10 said, "*H* your father and your mother';
Lk 14.10 will be *h* in the presence of all who sit
Jn 5.23 all may *h* the Son, just as they *h* the
8.49 I *h* my father, and you dishonor me.
Eph 6. 2 is right. "*H* your father and mother"—
Phil 2.29 Lord with all joy, and *h* such people,
1 Tim 5. 3 *H* widows who are really widows. If a

HONORABLE

Phil 4. 8 is true, whatever is *h*, whatever is just,

HOPE (n)

Ezra 10. 2 but even now there is *h* for Israel in
Job 5.16 So the poor have *h*, and injustice shuts
13.15 See, he will kill me; I have no *h*; but I
14.19 the earth; you destroy the *h* of mortals.
17.15 where then is my *h*? Who will see my *h*?
19.10 gone, he has uprooted my *h* like a tree.
27. 8 what is the *h* of the godless when God
Ps 65. 5 you are the *h* of all the ends of the
78. 7 so that they should set their *h* in God,
146. 5 God of Jacob, whose *h* is in the LORD
Prov 10.28 The *h* of the righteous ends in gladness,
13.12 *H* deferred makes the heart sick, but a
19.18 your children while there is *h*;
29.20 There is more *h* for a fool than for
Isa 20. 5 because of Ethiopia their *h* and Egypt
Jer 14.22 We set our *h* on you, for it is you who
31.17 There is *h* for your future, says the
Ezek 37.11 bones are dried up, and our *h* is lost;
Hos 2.15 make the Valley of Achor a door of *h*.
Acts 28.20 since it is for the sake of the *h* of Israel
Rom 4.18 Hoping against *h*, he believed that he
12.12 Rejoice in *h*, be patient in suffering,
1 Cor 15.19 for in this life only we have *h* in Christ,
Eph 1.12 who were the first to set our *h* on Christ
1.18 is the *h* to which he has called you,
Col 1. 5 of the *h* laid up for you in heaven.
1.23 from the *h* promised by the gospel
1.27 which is Christ in you, the *h* of glory.
1 Thess 1. 3 love and steadfastness of *h* in our Lord
2.19 what is our *h* or joy or crown of
Titus 2.13 godly, while we wait for the blessed *h*,
Heb 6.18 encouraged to seize the *h* set before us.
10.23 us hold fast the confession of our *h*
1 Pet 1. 3 has given us a new birth into a living *h*
1 Jn 3. 3 who have this *h* in him purify

HOPE (HOPED HOPES) (v)

Ps 33.18 him, on those who *h* in his steadfast
33.22 LORD, be upon us even as we *h* in you.
42. 5 within me? *H* in God; for I shall again
43. 5 *H* in God; for I shall again praise him,
56. 6 steps. As they have *h* to have my life,
71.14 But I will *h* continually, and will praise
119.74 rejoice, because I have *h* in your word.
119.166 I *h* for your salvation, O LORD, and I
Lam 3.18 and all that I had *h* for from the LORD."
Mt 12.21 And in his name will the Gentiles *h*."
Lk 6.34 to those from whom you *h* to receive,
24.21 we had *h* that he was the one to
Rom 8.24 is not hope. For who *h* for what is seen?
15.12 Gentiles; in him the Gentiles shall *h*."
1 Cor 15.19 for in this life only we have *h* in Christ,

HORN (HORNS)

1 Kings 1.50 up and went to grasp the *h* of the altar.
2.28 the LORD and grasped the *h* of the altar.
Jer 48.25 The *h* of Moab is cut off, and his arm is
Ezek 29.21 I will cause a *h* to sprout up for the
Dan 3. 5 when you hear the sound of the *h*, pipe,
7. 7 that preceded it, and it had ten *h*.
8. 3 two *h*. Both *h* were long, but one was
Zech 1.18 I looked up and saw four *h*. I asked the
Rev 17.12 the ten *h* that you saw are ten kings

HORSE (HORSES)

Deut 17.16 he must not acquire many *h* for himself,
Josh 11. 6 you shall hamstring their *h*, and burn
1 Kings 10.28 Solomon's import of *h* was from Egypt
2 Chr 1.16 Solomon's *h* were imported from Egypt
9.25 Solomon had four thousand stalls for *h*
Job 39.18 aloft, it laughs at the *h* and its rider.
Ps 32. 9 Do not be like a *h* or a mule, without
33.17 The war *h* is a vain hope for victory,
Prov 21.31 *h* is made ready for the day of battle,
26. 3 A whip for the *h*, a bridle for the
Am 6.12 Do *h* run on rocks? Does one plow the
Zech 1. 8 the night I saw a man riding on a red *h*!
6. 2 The first chariot had red *h*, the second
Jas 3. 3 put bits into the mouths of *h* to make

HOSANNAH

Mt 21.15 "*H* to the Son of David!" they became
Mk 11. 9 shouting, "*H*! Blessed is the one who

HOSEA

Hos 1. 1 word of the LORD that came to *H* son of
Rom 9.25 As indeed he says in *H*, "Those who

HOSPITABLE

1 Tim 3. 2 temperate, sensible, respectable, *h*, an
Titus 1. 8 he must be *h*, a lover of goodness,
1 Pet 4. 9 Be *h* to one another without

HOSPITALITY

Rom 12.13 of the saints; extend *h* to strangers.

HOSTILE

Rom 8. 7 that is set on the flesh is *h* to God;
Col 1.21 were once estranged and *h* in mind,

HOSTILITY

Deut 15. 9 view your needy neighbor with *h* and

HOSTS

2 Sam 7.26 'The LORD of *h* is God over Israel'; and
Ps 24.10 is this King of glory? The LORD of *h*,
Isa 1. 9 If the LORD of *h* had not left us a few

HOUR

Mt 20.12 'These last worked only one *h*, and you
25.13 for you know neither the day nor the *h*.
Mk 13.32 about that day or *h* no one knows,
14.35 possible, the *h* might pass from him.
14.41 The *h* has come; the Son of man is
Lk 22.53 But this is your *h*, and the power of
Jn 4.21 me, the *h* is coming when you will
7.30 him, because his *h* had not yet come.
12.23 "The *h* has come for the Son of Man to
12.27 I say—'Father, save me from this *h*'?

Jn 16.32 The *h* is coming, indeed it has come,

HOUSE (HOUSES)

Lev 27.14 If a person consecrates a *h* to the LORD,
Deut 8.12 eaten your fill and built fine *h* and live
2 Sam 7.11 to you that the LORD will make you a *h*.
2 Kings 25. 9 burned the *h* of the LORD, the king's *h*,
1 Chr 17. 5 I have not lived in a *h* since the day I
17.10 to you that the LORD will build you a *h*.
22. 5 and the *h* that is to be built for the
28. 2 planned to build a *h* of rest for the ark
2 Chr 5.14 for the glory of the LORD filled the *h* of
22.12 hidden in the *h* of God, while Athaliah
24. 4 Joash decided to restore the *h* of
29.18 "We have cleansed all the *h* of the LORD,
Ezra 3.11 the foundation of the *h* of the LORD
6.15 this *h* was finished on the third day of
Neh 13.11 said, "Why is the *h* of God forsaken?"
Job 8.14 is gossamer, a spider's *h* their trust.
Ps 42. 4 led them in procession to the *h* of God,
52. 8 like a green olive tree in the *h* of God.
69. 9 zeal for your *h* that has consumed me;
84.10 be a doorkeeper in the *h* of my God
92.13 They are planted in the *h* of the LORD;
122. 1 to me, "Let us go to the *h* of the LORD!"
Prov 25.24 in a *h* shared with a contentious wife.
Eccl 7. 2 better to go to the *h* of mourning than
Isa 2. 3 the LORD, to the *h* of the God of Jacob;
6. 4 who called, and the *h* filled with smoke.
22.24 him the whole weight of his ancestral *h*,
38. 1 Set your *h* in order; for you shall die;
Jer 16. 5 Do not enter the *h* of mourning, or go
26. 9 'This *h* shall be like Shiloh, and this
52.13 He burned the *h* of the LORD, the king's
Ezek 10. 4 the *h*; the *h* was filled with the cloud,
Joel 3.18 fountain shall come forth from the *h* of
Hag 1. 4 paneled *h*, while this *h* lies in ruins?
1. 9 Because my *h* lies in ruins, while all of
Mt 21.13 "My *h* shall be called a *h* of prayer'; but
Mk 5.38 When they came to the *h* of the leader
6.10 "Whenever you enter a *h*, stay there
11.17 'My *h* shall be called a *h* of prayer for
Lk 2.49 know that I must be in my Father's *h*?"
6.48 like a man building a *h*, who dug deeply
9. 4 Whatever *h* you enter, stay there and
10. 7 to be paid. Do not go from *h* to *h*.
11.17 becomes a desert, and *h* falls on *h*.
13.35 See, your *h* is left to you. And I tell you,
19.46 'My *h* shall be a *h* of prayer'; but you
Jn 2.16 making my father's *h* a market place!"
Acts 7.48 Most High does not dwell in *h* made
20.20 teaching you publicly and from *h* to *h*,
1 Cor 16.19 with the church in their *h*, greet you

HOUSEHOLD

Josh 24.15 me and my *h*, we will serve the LORD."
Prov 31.21 for all her *h* are clothed in crimson.
31.27 She looks well to the ways of her *h*, and
Mt 10.36 foes will be members of one's own *h*.
13.52 is like the master of a *h* who brings out
Jn 4.53 believed, along with his whole *h*.
Acts 16.31 and you will be saved, you and your *h*."
Phil 4.22 you, especially those of the emperor's *h*.
1 Tim 3. 4 He must manage his own *h* well,
3.15 one ought to behave in the *h* of God,

HOUSETOP (HOUSETOPS)

Prov 21. 9 live in a corner of the *h* than in a house
Mt 10.27 hear whispered, proclaim from the *h*.
24.17 the one on the *h* must not go down to
Mk 13.15 the one on the *h* must not go down or
Lk 12. 3 doors will be proclaimed from the *h*.

HUMAN

Job 4.17 Can *h* beings be pure before their
5. 7 but *h* beings are born to trouble just as
7.17 What are *h* beings, that you make so
Ps 9.20 the nations know that they are only *h*.
144. 3 what are *h* beings that you regard them,
Prov 27.19 face, so one *h* heart reflects another.
Jer 10.23 that the way of *h* beings is not in their
Dan 2.34 stone was cut out, not by *h* hands, and
7.13 I saw one like a *h* being coming with
Rom 3.20 "no *h* being will be justified in his sight"
1 Cor 2.13 in words not taught by *h* wisdom but
3. 3 behaving according to *h* inclinations?
3.21 So let no one boast about *h* leaders. For
2 Cor 10. 3 Indeed, we live as *h* beings, but we do
10. 4 of our warfare are not merely *h*,
Gal 1. 1 Paul an apostle—sent by neither *h*
Heb 2. 6 "What are *h* beings that you are mindful

HUMAN RACE

Prov 8.31 inhabited world and delighting in the *h*.

HUMANITY

Eph 2.15 might create in himself one new *h* in

HUMANKIND

Gen 1.26 God said, "Let us make *h* in our image,

HUMBLE (HUMBLED HUMBLES)

Ex 10. 3 How long will you refuse to *h* yourself
Lev 26.41 if then their uncircumcised heart is *h*
Deut 8. 2 in order to *h* you, testing you to know
1 Kings 21.29 how Ahab has *h* himself before me?
2 Kings 22.19 and you *h* yourself before the LORD,
2 Chr 7.14 are called by my name *h* themselves,
12. 6 of Israel and the king *h* themselves
30.11 and Zebulun *h* themselves and came to
32.26 Hezekiah *h* himself for the pride of his
34.27 patient and you *h* yourself before God
Ps 55.19 from of old, will hear and *h* them—
119. 67 Before I was *h* I went astray; but now I
119. 75 and that in faithfulness you have *h* me.
Isa 5.15 low, and the eyes of the haughty are *h*.
Dan 5.22 And you, Belshazzar his son, have not *h*
10.12 and to *h* yourself before your God,
Mt 18. 4 Whoever becomes *h* like this child is
23.12 all those who *h* themselves will be
Lk 18.14 all who *h* themselves will be exalted."
2 Cor 12.21 again, my God may *h* me before you,
Phil 2. 8 he *h* himself and became obedient
Jas 4.10 *H* yourselves before the Lord, and he
1 Pet 5. 6 *H* yourselves therefore under the mighty

HUMBLE (adj)

Num 12. 3 Now the man Moses was very *h*, more
2 Sam 22.28 You deliver a *h* people, but your eyes
Job 22.29 you say it is pride; for he saves the *h*.
Ps 18.27 you deliver a *h* people, but the haughty
25. 9 He leads the *h* in what is right, and
149. 4 his people; he adorns the *h* with victory.
Isa 57.15 those who are contrite and *h* in spirit,
Zeph 2. 3 Seek the LORD, all you *h* of the land,
3.12 the midst of you a people *h* and lowly.
Zech 9. 9 victorious is he, *h* and riding on a
Mt 21. 5 your king is coming to you, *h*, and
1 Pet 3. 8 another, a tender heart, and a *h* mind.

HUMILITY

Prov 15.33 if wisdom, and *h* goes before honor.
22. 4 reward for *h* and fear of the LORD is
Phil 2. 3 but in *h* regard others as better than

HUNGER

Ps 34.10 young lions suffer want and *h*, but those
Isa 49.10 they shall not *h* or thirst, neither
Jer 38. 9 him in the cistern to die there of *h*,
Lam 2.19 lives of your children, who faint for *h*
Ezek 34.29 they shall no more be consumed with *h*
Mt 5. 6 who *h* and thirst for righteousness,
Acts 27.38 had satisfied their *h*, they lightened
2 Cor 6. 5 labors, sleepless nights, *h*; by purity,
Rev 7.16 They will *h* no more, and thirst no

HUNGRY

1 Sam 2. 5 but those who were *h* are fat with spoil.
Ps 50.12 "If I were *h*, I would not tell you, for the
107. 9 the thirsty, and the *h* he fills with good
Prov 6.30 satisfy their appetite when they are *h*.
Isa 8.21 the land, greatly distressed and *h*;
Mt 21.18 when he returned to the city, he was *h*.
Mk 2.25 when he and his companions were *h*
11.12 they came from Bethany, he was *h*.
Lk 1.53 filled the *h* with good things, and sent
6.21 "Blessed are you who are *h* now, for you
Jn 6.35 whoever comes to me will never be *h*,
Acts 10.10 roof to pray. He became *h* and wanted
1 Cor 4.11 To the present hour we are *h* and
11.34 If you are *h*, eat at home, so that when
2 Cor 11.27 *h* and thirsty, often without food, cold
Phil 4.12 secret of being well-fed and of going *h*,

HUNT (HUNTED)

Ezek 13.18 lives! Will you *h* down lives among my
Job 10.16 Bold as a lion you *h* me; you repeat
Ps 140. 11 let evil speedily *h* down the violent!
Jer 50.17 Israel is a *h* sheep driven away by lions.

HUNTER

Gen 10. 9 He was a mighty *h* before the LORD;
25.27 Esau was a skillful *h*, a man of the

HURAM

2 Chr 2.11 Then King *H* of Tyre answered in a

HURRIEDLY

Prov 19. 2 one who moves too *h* misses the way.

HURRY

Gen 19.22 *H*, escape there, for I can do nothing

HURT

1 Chr 4.10 and that you would keep me from *h* and
Eccl 8. 9 authority over another to the other's *h*.
Isa 11. 9 They will not *h* or destroy on all my
Jer 8.21 For the *h* of my poor people I am *h*, I

HUSBAND (HUSBANDS HUSBAND'S)

Gen 3. 6 she also gave some to her *h*, who was
18.12 I have grown old, and my *h* is old,
Deut 25. 5 Her *h* brother shall go in to her, taking
Esth 1.17 to look with contempt upon their *h*,
Prov 31.23 Her *h* is known in the city gates, taking
Isa 54. 5 For your Maker is your *h*, the LORD of
Jer 31.32 that they broke, though I was their *h*,
Mt 1.16 father of Joseph the *h* of Mary, of whom
Jn 4.16 said to her, "Go, call your *h*, and come
Rom 7. 2 woman is bound by law to her *h*
1 Cor 7. 2 own wife and each woman her own *h*.
7.14 the unbelieving *h* is made holy through
7.34 of the world, how to please her *h*.
Eph 5.25 *H*, love your wives, just as Christ loved
5.33 and a wife should respect her *h*.
Col 3.19 *H*, love your wives, and never treat
1 Tim 3.2n be above reproach, the *h* of one wife,
1 Pet 3. 7 *H*, in the same way, show consideration

HYMN (HYMNS)

Mt 26.30 When they had sung the *h*, they went
Mk 14.26 When they had sung the *h*, they went
1 Cor 14.26 together, each one has a *h*, a lesson,
Eph 5.19 as you sing psalms and *h* and spiritual
Col 3.16 sing psalms, *h*, and spiritual songs

HYPOCRISY

Lk 12. 1 yeast of the Pharisees, that is, their *h*.

HYPOCRITE (HYPOCRITES)

Mt 6. 2 sound a trumpet before you, as the *h* do
6. 5 you pray, do not be like the *h*;
6.16 you fast, do not look dismal, like the *h*,
7. 5 You *h*, first take the log out of your own
15. 7 You *h*! Isaiah prophesied rightly about
23.13 woe to you, scribes and Pharisees, *h*!
23.23 "Woe to you, scribes and Pharisees, *h*!
Mk 7. 6 Isaiah prophesied rightly about you *h*,
Lk 13.15 "You *h*! does not each of you on the

HYSSOP

Ex 12.22 Take a bunch of *h*, dip it in the blood
Ps 51. 7 Purge me with *h*, and I shall be clean;
Jn 19.29 sponge full of the wine on a branch of *h*

I

IDLE

Mt 20. 3 he saw others standing *i* in the

IDLENESS

2 Thess 3. 6 away from believers who are living in *i*
3.11 some of you are living in *i*, mere

IDOL (IDOLS)

Ex 20. 4 You shall not make for yourself an *i*,
Lev 26. 1 You shall make for yourselves no *i* and
Deut 5. 8 You shall not make for yourself an *i*,
Judg 17. 3 for my son, to make an *i* of cast metal.
18.30 Danites set up the *i* for themselves.
1 Sam 19.13 Michal took an *i* and laid it on the bed;
1 Chr 16.26 For all the gods of the peoples are *i*,
2 Chr 15. 8 put away the abominable *i* from all the
Ps 31. 6 those who pay regard to worthless *i*,
78.58 they moved him to jealousy with their *i*.
106. 38 they sacrificed to the *i* of Canaan;
Isa 2. 8 Their land is filled with *i*; they bow
2.18 The *i* shall utterly pass away. Enter the
19. 3 they will consult the *i* and the spirits of
40.19 An *i*?—A workman casts it, and a
44. 9 All who make *i* are nothing, and the
48. 5 that you would not say, "My *i* did them,
Jer 50.38 land of images, and they go mad over *i*.
Ezek 14. 4 who take their *i* into their hearts and
20.18 nor defile yourselves with their *i*.
Hos 4.17 Ephraim is joined to *i*— let him alone.
8. 4 they made *i* for their own destruction.
Mic 1. 7 with fire, and all her *i* I will lay waste;
Acts 15.20 to abstain only from things polluted by *i*
17.16 to see that the city was full of *i*.
21.25 from what has been sacrificed to *i*
1 Cor 8. 1 concerning food offered to *i*: we know
10.19 to *i* is anything, or that an *i* is anything?
1 Thess 1. 9 you turned to God from *i*, to serve a
1 Jn 5.21 Little children, keep yourselves from *i*.

IDOLATER (IDOLATERS)

1 Cor 6. 9 Do not be deceived! Fornicators, *i*,
Eph 5. 5 or one who is greedy (that is, an *i*), has

IGNORANCE (IGNORANT)

Ps 73.22 I was stupid and *i*, I was like a brute
Acts 17.30 has overlooked the times of human *i*,
Eph 4.18 because of their *i* and hardness of heart.

IGNORED

Deut 33. 9 he *i* his kin, and did not acknowledge

ILL

Lk 7. 2 whom he valued highly, and who was *i*
Jn 11. 3 to Jesus, "Lord, he whom you love is *i*."
1 Cor 11.30 this reason many of you are weak and *i*,
Phil 2.26 because you heard that he was *i*.

ILLNESS

Deut 7.15 LORD will turn away from you every *i*;
2 Kings 8. 8 him, whether I shall recover from this *i*."
Ps 41. 3 sickbed; in their *i* you heal all their
Jn 11. 4 "This *i* does not lead to death; rather it

ILL-TREATMENT

Heb 11.25 choosing rather to share *i* with the

IMAGE (IMAGES)

Gen 1.26 "Let us make humankind in our *i*,
Num 33.52 destroy all their molten *i*, and demolish
1 Sam 6. 5 you must make *i* of your tumors and *i*
1 Cor 11. 7 since he is the *i* and reflection of God;
Col 1.15 He is the *i* of the invisible God, the
3.10 according to the *i* of its creator.

IMAGINE

Eph 3.20 far more than all that we ask or *i*,

IMITATE (IMITATING)

Phil 3.17 join in *i* me, and observe those who live
3 Jn 11 Beloved, do not *i* what is evil but *i* what

IMITATORS

1 Cor 4.16 I appeal to you, then, be *i* of me. For
11. 1 be saved. Be *i* of me, as I am of Christ.
Eph 5. 1 be *i* of God, as beloved children, and
1 Thess 1. 6 you became *i* of us and of the Lord, for
Heb 6.12 but *i* of those who through faith

IMMANUEL (EMMANUEL)

Isa 7.14 shall bear a son, and shall name him *I*.
8. 8 will fill the breadth of your land, O *I*.
Mt 1.23 and they shall name him *E*," which

IMMORALITY

1 Cor 5. 1 that there is sexual *i* among you,

IMMORTAL (IMMORTALITY)

Rom 1.23 exchanged the glory of the *i* God for
1 Cor 15.53 and this mortal body must put on *i*.

IMPERISHABLE

1 Cor 15.42 is sown is perishable, what is raised is *i*.
1 Pet 1. 4 into an inheritance that is *i*, undefiled,

IMPLORE

2 Kings 20. 3 "Remember now, O LORD, I *i* you, how I

IMPOSSIBLE

Gen 11. 6 they propose to do will now be *i*
Lk 1.37 "For nothing will be *i* with God."
Heb 10. 4 it is *i* for the blood of bulls and goats to

IMPRISONED

Jer 37.15 Jeremiah, and they beat him and *i* him
Acts 22.19 I *i* and beat those who believed
Rom 11.32 God has *i* all in disobedience, so that

IMPRISONMENT (IMPRISONMENTS)

Acts 20.23 city that *i* and persecutions are waiting
2 Cor 6. 5 hardships, calamities, beatings, *i*, riots,
11.23 greater labors, far more *i*, with countless
Phil 1.13 to everyone else that my *i* is for Christ;
Heb 11.36 and flogging, and even chains and *i*.

IMPURE (IMPURITY)

Zech 13. 1 to cleanse them from sin and *i*.
Rom 1.24 them up in the lusts of their hearts to *i*,
2 Cor 12.21 have not repented of the *i*, sexual
Eph 4.19 greedy to practice every kind of *i*.
1 Thess 2. 3 does not spring from deceit or *i* motives

IMPUTE (IMPUTES)

1 Sam 22.15 Do not let the king *i* anything to his
Ps 32. 2 those to whom the LORD *i* no iniquity,

INCENSE

Ex 30. 1 shall make an altar on which to offer *i*;
30.35 make an *i* blended as by the perfumer,
37.25 He made an altar of *i* of acacia wood,
Num 16.17 of you take his censer, and put *i* on it,
2 Chr 26.16 to make an offering on the altar of *i*.
Ps 141. 2 Let my prayer be counted as *i* before
Ezek 8.11 the fragrant cloud of *i* was ascending.
Mal 1.11 in every place *i* is offered to my name,
Lk 1. 9 the sanctuary of the Lord and offer *i*.

INCITED

1 Chr 21. 1 and *i* David to count the people of
Acts 13.50 But the Jews *i* the devout women of

INCLINATION

Gen 6. 5 every *i* of the thoughts of their hearts
8.21 for the *i* of the human heart is evil from

INCLINE (INCLINING)

1 Kings 8.58 but *i* our hearts to him, to walk in all
Prov 2. 2 and *i* your heart to understanding;
Dan 9.18 *I* your ear, O my God, and hear. Open

INCOME

Prov 3.14 for her *i* is better than silver, and her

INCREASE (INCREASED INCREASES)

Ps 71.21 You will *i* my honor, and comfort me
115. 14 May the LORD give you *i*, both you and
Prov 16.21 and pleasant speech *i* persuasiveness.
Eccl 5.11 When goods *i*, they who eat them *i*; and
Isa 26.15 But you have *i* the nation, O LORD, you
Ezek 34.27 the earth shall yield its *i*. They shall be
Lk 2.52 Jesus *i* in wisdom and in years, and in
Jn 3.30 He must *i*, but I must decrease."
Acts 16. 5 in the faith and *i* in numbers daily.
1 Thess 3.12 the Lord make you *i* and abound in love

INCREDIBLE

Acts 26. 8 Why is it thought *i* by any of you that

INDICATE (INDICATES INDICATING)

Jn 21.19 said this to *i* the kind of death by which
Acts 25.27 a prisoner without *i* the charges against
Heb 9. 8 By this the Holy Spirit *i* that the way

INDICTMENT

Job 31.35 that I had the *i* written by my adversary!
Hos 4. 1 LORD has an *i* against the inhabitants
12. 2 LORD has an *i* against Judah, and will

INDIGNANT

Mk 10.14 when Jesus saw this, he was *i* and said

INDISPENSABLE

1 Cor 12.22 the body that seem to be weaker are *i*,

INDULGE

2 Pet 2.10 who *i* their flesh in depraved lust, and

INFANT (INFANTS)

Hos 11. 4 like those who lift *i* to their cheeks.
Isa 13.16 Their *i* will be dashed to pieces before
Mt 11.25 intelligent and have revealed them to *i*;
Lk 10.21 and revealed them to *i*; yes, for such
18.15 bringing even *i* to him that he might
1 Cor 3. 1 as people of the flesh, as *i* in Christ.
Heb 5.13 who lives on milk, being still an *i*,

INFERIOR

Job 12. 3 I am not *i* to you. Who does not know
2 Cor 12.11 I am not at all *i* to these super-apostles,

INFIRMITIES

Ps 41. 3 in their illness you heal all their *i*.

INFORMED

Jude 5 to remind you, though you are fully *i*,

INFURIATED

Esth 3. 5 or do obeisance to him, Haman was *i*.

INHABITS (INHABITED)

Isa 57.15 the high and lofty one who *i* eternity,
Jer 17.25 and this city shall be *i* forever.

INHERIT

Lev 20.24 You shall *i* their land, and I will give it
Num 33.54 to your ancestral tribes you shall *i*.
34.13 This is the land that you shall *i* by lot,

Ps 37. 9 but those who wait for the LORD shall *i*
Zech 2.12 The LORD will *i* Judah as his portion in
Mt 25.34 *i* the kingdom prepared for you from the
Mk 10.17 what must I do to *i* eternal life?"
Lk 10.25 said, "what must I do to *i* eternal life?"
18.18 what must I do to *i* eternal life?"
Rom 4.13 the promise that he would *i* the world

INHERITANCE

Num 27. 8 you shall pass his *i* on to his daughter.
Deut 18. 1 Levi, shall have no . . . *i* within Israel;
20.16 God is giving you as an *i*, you must not
Josh 13.14 by fire to the LORD . . . are their *i*,
1 Kings 21. 3 that I should give you my ancestral *i*."
1 Chr 16.18 land of Canaan as your portion for an *i*."
Ps 105. 11 land of Canaan as your portion for an *i*."
Prov 13.22 The good leave an *i* to their children's
Lam 5. 2 Our *i* has been turned over to strangers,
Ezek 47.14 and this land shall fall to you as your *i*.
Acts 20.32 up and to give you the *i* among all who
Gal 3.18 For if the *i* comes from the law, it no
Eph 1.18 of his glorious *i* among the saints,
Col 3.24 you will receive the *i* as your reward;
1 Pet 1. 4 into an *i* which is imperishable,

INIQUITY (INIQUITIES)

Ex 34. 7 forgiving *i* and transgression and sin, yet
34. 7 visiting the *i* of the parents upon the
2 Sam 7.14 When he commits *i*, I will punish him
Ezra 9. 6 our *i* have risen higher than our heads,
Job 34.32 if I have done *i*, I will do it no more'?
Ps 51. 9 face from my sins, and blot out all my *i*.
66.18 If I had cherished *i* in my heart, the
106. 43 and were brought low through their *i*.
Prov 5.22 The *i* of the wicked ensnare them, and
Isa 53. 6 the LORD has laid on him the *i* of us all.
Ezek 36.33 day that I cleanse you from all your *i*,
39.23 of Israel went into captivity for their *i*,
Titus 2.14 redeem us from all *i* and purify for

INJURED

Ezek 34.16 and I will bind up the *i*, and I will

INJUSTICE

Prov 22. 8 Whoever sows *i* will reap calamity, and
Isa 58. 6 that I choose: to loose the bonds of *i*,
Rom 9.14 Is there *i* on God's part? By no means!

INK

Jer 36.18 and I wrote them with *i* on the scroll."
2 Cor 3. 3 written not with *i* but with the Spirit of
2 Jn 12 rather not use paper and *i*; instead I

INN

Lk 2. 7 there was no place for them in the *i*.
10.34 brought him to an *i*, and took care of

INNOCENT

Gen 20. 4 said, Lord, will you destroy an *i* people?
Deut 19.13 you shall purge the guilt of *i* blood from
2 Kings 24. 4 filled Jerusalem with *i* blood, and the
Job 4. 7 now, who that was *i* ever perished?
9.28 for I know you will not hold me *i*.
17. 8 and the *i* stir themselves up against
27.17 wear it, and the *i* will divide the silver.
34. 5 Job has said, 'I am *i*, and God has
Ps 19.13 I shall be blameless, and *i* of great
Isa 3.10 Tell the *i* how fortunate they are, for
Jer 2.35 "I am *i*; surely his anger has turned
19. 4 filled this place with the blood of the *i*,
Jon 1.14 life. Do not make us guilty of *i* blood;
Mt 10.16 so be wise as serpents and *i* as doves.
27.24 "I am *i* of this man's blood; see to it
Lk 23.47 God and said, "Certainly this man was *i*!"
1 Tim 1. 9 law is not laid down for the *i* but for

INQUIRE (INQUIRED)

Gen 25.22 do I live?" So she went to *i* of the LORD.
Ex 18.15 the people come to me to *i* of God.
Deut 12.30 do not *i* concerning their gods, saying,
Judg 20.18 to Bethel, where they *i* of God, "Which
1 Sam 14.37 So Saul *i* of God, "Shall I go down after
23. 2 David *i* of the LORD, "Shall I go and
2 Sam 2. 1 David *i* of the LORD, "Shall I go up into
5.19 David *i* of the LORD, "Shall I go up
2 Kings 22.13 "Go, *i* of the LORD for me, for the
1 Chr 14.10 David *i* of God, "Shall I go up against
2 Chr 34.21 "Go, *i* of the LORD for me and for those
Jer 8. 2 which they have *i* of and worshiped;
21. 2 "Please *i* of the LORD on our behalf, for

INSANE

Acts 26.25 Too much learning is driving you *i*!"

INSCRIBED

Job 19.23 down! O that they were *i* in a book!
Dan 5.25 hand was sent and this writing was *i*.
10.21 tell you what is *i* in the book of truth.

INSCRIPTION

Mk 15.26 The *i* of the charge against him read,
Lk 23.38 There was also an *i* over him, "This is
Jn 19.19 Pilate also had an *i* written and put on

INSIGHT

Dan 1. 4 endowed with knowledge and *i*, and

INSIST

Eph 4.17 I affirm and *i* on in the Lord; you must

INSOLENT

Ps 19.13 Keep back your servant also from the *i*;

INSPIRED

2 Tim 3.16 All scripture is *i* by God and is useful

INSTALLMENT

2 Cor 1.22 us his Spirit in our hearts as a first *i*.

INSTINCTIVELY

Rom 2.14 do *i* what the law requires, these,

INSTRUCT (INSTRUCTED)

2 Chr 26. 5 days of Zechariah, who *i* him in the fear
Ps 32. 8 I will *i* you and teach you the way you
Lk 1. 4 the things of which you have been *i*.
Acts 7.22 Moses was *i* in all the wisdom of the
1 Tim 1. 3 *i* certain people not to teach any
2 Tim 3. 7 who are always being *i* and can never
3.15 writings that are able to *i* you for

INSTRUCTION

Job 36.10 He opens their ears to *i*, and commands
Prov 8.10 Take my *i* instead of silver, and
Isa 29.24 and those who grumble will accept *i*.
Mic 4. 2 out of Zion shall go forth *i*, and the
Mal 2. 6 True *i* was in his mouth, and no wrong

INSTRUCTORS

Mt 23.10 Nor are you to be called *i*, for you have

INSTRUMENT (INSTRUMENTS)

1 Chr 15.16 as the singers to play on musical *i*,
Am 6. 5 and like David improvise on *i* of music;
Acts 9.15 he is an *i* whom I have chosen to bring

INSULT (INSULTS)

Gen 39.14 has brought among us a Hebrew to *i* us!
Ps 69. 9 the *i* of those who *i* you have fallen on
69.20 *I* have broken my heart, so that I am in
Prov 17. 5 Those who mock the poor *i* their Maker;
Isa 50. 6 out the beard; I hid not my face from *i*
Hos 12.14 on him and pay him back for his *i*.
Lk 11.45 when you say these things, you *i* us too."
Acts 23. 4 "Do you dare to *i* God's high priest?"
Rom 15. 3 "The *i* of those who *i* you have fallen on
2 Cor 12.10 I am content with weaknesses, *i*,

INTEGRITY

Job 2. 9 "Do you still persist in your *i*? Curse
Titus 2. 7 and in your teaching show *i*, gravity,

INTEND

1 Kings 5. 5 I *i* to build a house for the name of the
2 Cor 8.21 we *i* to do what is right not only in the

INTENTIONS

Mt 15.19 For out of the heart come evil *i*,

INTERCEDE (INTERCEDED INTERCEDES)

Deut 9.20 but I *i* also on behalf of Aaron at the
Jer 27.18 them, then let them *i* with the LORD
Rom 8.26 that very Spirit *i* with sighs too deep for

INTERCESSION

1 Sam 2.25 sins against the LORD, who can make *i*?"
Isa 53.12 many, and made *i* for the transgressors.
Heb 7.25 he always lives to make *i* for them.

INTEREST

Lev 25.36 Do not take *i* in advance or otherwise
Neh 5.10 and grain. Let us stop this taking of *i*.
Ps 15. 5 who do not lend money at *i*, and do not

INTERMARRY

Josh 23.12 left here among you, and *i* with them,

INTERPRET (INTERPRETED)

Lk 12.56 how to *i* the appearance of earth and
24.27 he *i* to them the things about himself in
1 Cor 14.27 three, and each in turn; and let one *i*.

INTERPRETATION

Dan 2. 4 the dream, and we will reveal the *i*."
2.36 dream; now we will tell the king its *i*.
4.18 you, Belteshazzar, declare the *i*, since
5.12 Daniel be called, and he will give the *i*."
2 Pet 1.20 of scripture is a matter of one's own *i*,

INTERPRETER

Gen 42.23 since he spoke with them through an *i*.

INTERVALS

2 Kings 20. 9 advanced ten *i*; shall it retreat ten *i*?"

INTERVENED

Jer 15.11 I have *i* in your life for good, surely I

INVISIBLE

Rom 1.20 divine nature, *i* though they are, have
Col 1.15 He is the image of the *i* God, the
1 Tim 1.17 of the ages, immortal, *i*, the only God,

INVITED

Jn 2. 2 had also been *i* to the wedding.
Rev 19. 9 Blessed are those who are *i* to the

INVOKE

Gen 4.26 people began to *i* the name of the LORD.
12. 8 to the LORD and *i* the name of the LORD.

IRON

Josh 17.16 who live in the plain have chariots of *i*,
2 Kings 6. 6 threw it in there, and made the *i* float.
1 Chr 20. 3 set them to work with saws and *i* picks
Ps 105. 18 fetters, his neck was put in a collar of *i*;
Prov 27.17 *I* sharpens *i*, and one person sharpens
Jer 28.13 broken wooden bars only to forge *i* bars
Dan 2.35 Then the *i*, the clay, the bronze, the

IRON-SMELTER

Deut 4.20 brought you out of the *i*, out of Egypt,

IRONSMITH

Isa 44.12 The *i* fashions it and works over the

ISAAC

His birth foretold, Gen 18.1-15; born, Gen 21.1-7; offered to God, Gen 22.1-19; married Rebekah, Gen 24; father of twins, Gen 25.19-26; dwelt in Gerar, Gen 26.1-6; Isaac and Abimelech, Gen 26.7-33; blessed Jacob, Gen 27.1-40; death and burial, Gen 35.29.

Gen 21. 3 Abraham gave the name *I* to his son
Gal 4.28 are children of the promise, like *I*.
Heb 11.20 By faith *I* invoked blessings for the

ISAIAH

Called, Isa 6; father of two sons, Isa 7.3; 8.3; prophesied during the reign of Uzziah, Jotham, Ahaz, and Hezekiah, Isa 1.1; counselled Ahaz, Isa 7; counselled Hezekiah, 2 Kings 19—20 (Isa 37—39).

Mt 3. 3 is the one of whom the prophet *I* spoke
15. 7 *I* prophesied rightly about you when he
Lk 4.17 the scroll of the prophet *I* was given to
Acts 8.28 it and heard him reading the prophet *I*.

ISHMAEL

Gen 16.11 shall bear a son; you shall call him *I*,
17.18 God, "O that *I* might live in your sight!"
25.12 These are the descendants of *I*,

ISRAEL

Gen 32.28 shall no longer be called Jacob, but *I*,
Ex 1. 1 of the sons of *I* who came to Egypt
4.22 says the LORD, *I* is my first-born son.
1 Sam 7. 6 And Samuel judged the people of *I* at
1 Kings 4. 1 King Solomon was king over all *I*,
12.19 *I* has been in rebellion against the
17. 1 the LORD the God of *I* lives, before
1 Chr 14. 8 David had been anointed king over all *I*,
2 Chr 30. 1 the passover to the Lord the God of *I*.
Ezra 7. 7 Some of the people of *I*, and some of
Ps 25.22 Redeem *I*, O God, out of all its
103. 7 to Moses, his acts to the people of *I*.
Isa 1. 3 but *I* does not know, my people do not
Mt 2. 6 a ruler who is to shepherd my people *I*.' "
27.42 He is the King of *I*; let him come down
Lk 2.25 looking forward to the consolation of *I*,
Acts 1. 6 when you will restore the kingdom to *I*?"
Rom 11.26 so all *I* will be saved; as it is written,
Eph 2.12 aliens from the commonwealth of *I*,
Heb 8. 8 a new covenant with the house of *I*

ISRAELITES

Ex 14. 8 he pursued the *I*, who were going out
19. 1 after the *I* had gone out of the land of
Josh 4. 8 The *I* did as Joshua commanded. They
Rev 21.12 the names of the twelve tribes of the *I*;

ISSACHAR

Gen 30.18 to my husband"; so she named him *I*.
49.14 *I* is a strong donkey, lying down
Num 26.23 The descendants of *I* by their clans: of
Rev 7. 7 from the tribe of *I* twelve thousand,

IVORY

1 Kings 10.18 king also made a great *i* throne, and
22.39 the *i* house that he built, and all the
Ps 45. 8 From *i* palaces stringed instruments
Am 3.15 the houses of *i* shall perish, and the
6. 4 Alas for those who lie on beds of *i*, and

J

JABBOK

Gen 32.22 children, and crossed the ford of the *J*.
Deut 3.16 up to the *J*, the wadi being boundary of
Josh 12. 2 as far as the river *J*, the boundary of the

JACKALS

Ezek 13. 4 Your prophets have been like *j* among

JACOB (JACOB'S)

Born, Gen 25.19-26; obtained Esau's birthright, Gen 25.27-34; received Isaac's blessing, Gen 27.1-29; fled from Esau, Gen 27.41—28.5; dream at Bethel and his vow, Gen 28.10-22; served Laban for Rachel and Leah, Gen 29.1-30; dealings with Laban, Gen 30.25-43; departure from Paddan-aram, Gen 31; wrestled at Peniel, Gen 32.24-32; reconciled with Esau, Gen 33.1-16; blessed by God at Bethel, Gen 35.1-15; went down to Egypt, Gen 46—47; blessed Ephraim and Manasseh, Gen 48; blessed his own sons, Gen 49.1-27; death and burial, Gen 49.28—50.14.

Num 24.17 a star shall come out of *J*, and a scepter
Hos 12.12 *J* fled to the land of Aram, there Israel
Mt 8.11 Isaac and *J* in the kingdom of heaven,
Rom 9.13 is written, "I have loved *J*, but I have
Heb 11.21 By faith *J*, when dying, blessed each of
Jn 4. 6 *J* well was there, and Jesus, tired out by

JAIRUS

Mk 5.22 leaders of the synagogue named *J* came
Lk 8.41 there came a man named *J*, a leader of

JAMES

Mt 4.21 from there, he saw two other brothers, *J*
10. 3 tax collector; *J* son of Alphaeus, and
Acts 1.13 Matthew, *J* son of Alphaeus, and Simon
1 Cor 15. 7 Then he appeared to *J*, then to all the

JAPHETH

Gen 9.27 May God make space for *J*, and let him

JAR (JARS)

Judg 7.16 and empty *j*, with torches inside the *j*,
1 Kings 17.14 "The *j* of meal will not be emptied, and
Mk 14.13 a man carrying a *j* of water will meet
Lk 22.10 a man carrying a *j* of water will meet
Jn 4.28 So the woman left her water *j* and went
2 Cor 4. 7 we have this treasure in clay *j*, so that it

JAWBONE

Judg 15.15 Then he found a fresh *j* of a donkey,

JEALOUS

Gen 37.11 his brothers were *j* of him, but his
Num 11.29 said to him, "Are you *j* for my sake?
Deut 4.24 your God is a devouring fire, a *j* God.
5. 9 for I the LORD your God am a *j* God,
6.15 who is present with you, is a *j* God;
32.21 They made me *j* with what is no god,
Josh 24.19 He is a *j* God; he will not forgive your
Ps 79. 5 forever? Will your *j* wrath burn like fire?
106. 16 They were *j* of Moses in the camp, and
Ezek 39.25 Israel; and I will be *j* for my holy name.
Joel 2.18 Then the LORD became *j* for his land,
Nah 1. 2 A *j* and avenging God is the LORD, the
Zech 8. 2 I am *j* for Zion with great jealousy, and
Acts 7. 9 "The patriarchs, *j* of Joseph, sold him
Rom 11.11 to the Gentiles, so as to make Israel *j*.

JEALOUSY

Num 5.14 if the spirit of *j* comes on him, and he
1 Kings 14.22 they provoked him to *j* with their sins
Prov 6.34 *j* arouses a husband's fury, and he
Isa 11.13 The *j* of Ephraim shall depart, the
Ezek 5.13 I, the LORD, have spoken in my *j*, when I
8. 3 to the seat of the image of *j*, which
Mt 27.18 it was out of *j* that they handed him
Mk 15.10 it was out of *j* that the chief priests had
1 Cor 3. 3 as long as there is *j* and quarreling
2 Cor 11. 2 I feel a divine *j* for you, for I promised

JEHOSHAPHAT

1 Kings 15.24 father David; his son *J* succeeded him.
22. 7 But *J* said, "Is there no other prophet of
2 Chr 20. 1 some of the Meunites, came against *J*
20.30 the realm of *J* was quiet, for his God
21. 1 *J* slept with his ancestors and was
Joel 3. 2 and bring them down to the valley of *J*,

JEPHTHAH

Judg 11. 1 *J* . . . was a mighty warrior. Gilead was
11.30 *J* made a vow to the LORD, and said, "If
12. 1 said to *J*, "Why did you cross over to
1 Sam 12.11 LORD sent . . . *J*, and Samson, and
Heb 11.32 me to tell of Gideon, Barak, Samson, *J*,

JEREMIAH

Called, Jer 1.1-10; vision of almond rod and boiling pot, Jer 1.11-19; sign of the waist cloth, Jer 13.1-11; sign of the potter's vessel, Jer 18; sign of the earthen flask, Jer 19; put in stocks, Jer 20.1-6; sign of the basket of figs, Jer 24; his life threatened, Jer 26; sign of purchase of field, Jer 32.6-44; prophesied to Rechabites, Jer 35; wrote prophecies, Jer 36; imprisoned, Jer 32.1-5; 37.11—38.28; released, Jer 39.11-14; 40.1-6; taken into Egypt, Jer 43.1-7.

Mt 16.14 but others Elijah, and still others *J* or

JERICHO

Josh 2. 1 "Go, view the land, especially *J*." So they
6. 2 I have handed *J* over to you, along with
1 Kings 16.34 In his days Hiel of Bethel built *J*; he
Mk 10.46 and a large crowd were leaving *J*,
Heb 11.30 By faith the walls of *J* fell after they

JEROBOAM

1 Kings 11.26 *J* son of Nebat . . . rebelled against the
12. 2 When *J* the son of Nebat heard of it
12.25 *J* built Shechem in the hill country of
13. 1 While *J* was standing by the altar to
14. 1 At that time Abijah son of *J* fell sick.
14.20 that *J* reigned was twenty-two years;
14.30 was war between Rehoboam and *J*
15.25 Nadab the son of *J* began to reign over
15.34 walking in the way of *J* and in the sin
2 Kings 14.23 *J* the son of Joash of Israel began to
14.28 Now the rest of the acts of *J*, and all
14.29 *J* slept with his ancestors, the kings of
Hos 1. 1 in the days of King *J* son of Joash of
Am 7.10 the priest of Bethel, sent to King *J*

JERUSALEM

Judg 19.10 and arrived opposite Jebus (that is, *J*).
2 Sam 5. 5 at *J* he reigned over all Israel and Judah
2 Kings 21. 4 LORD had said, "In *J* I will put my name."
2 Chr 20.28 They came to *J*, with harps and lyres
36.19 broke down the wall of *J*, burned all its
36.23 charged me to build him a house at *J*,
Ezra 3. 8 their arrival at the house of God at *J*,
Ps 51.18 good pleasure; rebuild the walls of *J*,
122. 6 Pray for the peace of *J*! "May they
137. 5 If I forget you, O *J*, let my right hand
Isa 31. 5 so the LORD of hosts will protect *J*;
40. 9 strength, O *J*, herald of good tidings,
Mt 23.37 "*J*, *J*, the city that kills the prophets
Acts 1. 8 my witnesses in *J*, in all Judea and
15. 2 to go up to *J* to discuss this question
Rom 15.26 with the poor among the saints at *J*.
Gal 4.26 corresponds to the *J* above; she is free,
Heb 12.22 to the city of the God, the heavenly *J*,
Rev 21. 2 saw the holy city, the new *J*, coming

JESUS

His birth foretold, Lk 1.26-38; born, Mt 1.18-25; Lk 2.1-7; circumcised, Lk 2.21; presented in the temple, Lk 2.22-38; visited by the wise men, Mt 2.1-12; fled to Egypt, Mt 2.13-18; brought to Nazareth, Mt 2.19-23 (Lk 2.39); boyhood visit to Jerusalem, Lk 2.41-50; his brothers and sisters, Mt 13.55-56 (Mk 6.3); baptized, Mt 3.13-17 (Mk 1.9-11; Lk 3.21-22; Jn 1.31-34); tempted by the devil, Mt 4.1-11 (Mk 1.12-13; Lk 4.1-13); called his disciples, Mt 4.18-22 (Mk 1.16-20; Lk 5.1-11); Mt 9.9 (Mk 2.13-14; Lk 5.27-28); Jn 1.35-51; commissioned the twelve, Mt 10.1-4 (Mk 3.13-19; Lk 6.12-16); Sermon on the Mount, Mt 5—7 (Lk 6.17-49); sent out disciples, Mt 9.35—11.1 (Mk 6.7-13; Lk 9.1-6; 10.1-24); foretold his death and resurrection, Mt 16.21-28 (Mk 8.31-38; Lk 9.22-27); Mt 17.22-23 (Mk 9.30-32; Lk 9.43-45); Mt

20.17-28 (Mk 10.32-45; Lk 18.31-34); transfigured, Mt 17.1-8 (Mk 9.2-8; Lk 9.28-36); triumphal entry into Jerusalem, Mt 21.1-11 (Mk 11.1-11; Lk 19.29-44; Jn 12.12-19); instituted the Lord's supper, Mt 26.26-29 (Mk 14.22-25; Lk 22.17-20; 1 Cor 11.23-26); betrayed, arrested, and forsaken, Mt 26.47-57 (Mk 14.43-53; Lk 22.47-54; Jn 18.2-13); crucified, Mt 27.31-56 (Mk 15.20-41; Lk 23.26-49; Jn 19.16-30); appeared after his resurrection, Mt 28.9-20 (Mk 16.9-18n; Lk 24.13-49; Jn 20.11-31); Acts 1.3-8; 1 Cor 15.5-7; ascended to heaven, Lk 24.50-53 (Mk 16.19n); Acts 1.9-11.

JETHRO

Ex 3. 1 keeping the flock of his father-in-law *J*,
4.18 Moses went back to . . . *J* and said to
18. 1 *J*, the priest of Midian . . . heard of all
18.12 *J* . . . brought a burnt offering and

JEW (JEWS)

Ezra 4.12 king that the *J* who came up from you
Neh 1. 2 I asked them about the *J* that survived,
Esth 2. 5 was a *J* in the citadel of Susa whose
Dan 3. 8 came forward and denounced the *J*.
Mt 2. 2 child who has been born king of the *J*?
27.11 "Are you the King of the *J*?" Jesus said,
27.37 read, "This is Jesus, the King of the *J*."
Jn 11. 8 the *J* were just now trying to stone you,
Acts 18. 5 testifying to the *J* that the Messiah was
19.10 Asia, both *J* and Greeks, heard the word
Rom 3. 9 all both *J* and Greeks, are under the
9.24 called, not from the *J* only but also
1 Cor 1.22 For *J* demand signs and Greeks desire
9.20 To the *J* I became a *J*, in order to win
10.32 Give no offense to *J* or to Greeks or to

JEWELS (JEWELRY)

Gen 24.53 the servant brought forth *j* of silver and
Ex 3.22 neighbor . . . for *j* of silver and of gold,
Prov 8.11 for wisdom is better than *j*, and all that

JEWISH

Jn 18.12 officer, and the *J* police arrested Jesus

JEZREEL

Josh 19.18 Its territory included *J*, Chesulloth,
1 Kings 21. 1 had a vineyard in *J*, beside the palace
Hos 1. 4 the house of Jehu for the blood of *J*,
2.22 and the oil, and they shall answer *J*;

JOAB

Murdered Abner, 2 Sam 3.22-30; set Uriah in the forefront, 2 Sam 11.6-22; reconciled David and Absalom, 2 Sam 14.28-33; killed Absalom, 2 Sam 18.9-17; pursued Sheba and slew Amasa, 2 Sam 20.4-22; put to death by Solomon, 1 Kings 2.28-34.

JOB

Job 1. 1 in the land of Uz whose name was *J*.
2. 3 "Have you considered my servant *J*?
42. 8 go to my servant *J*, and offer up for
42.10 the LORD restored the fortunes of *J*
42.17 And *J* died, old and full of days.
Ezek 14.14 even if Noah, Daniel, and *J*, these
Jas 5.11 You have heard of the endurance of *J*,

JOEL

Joel 1. 1 The word of the LORD that came to *J*
Acts 2.16 what was spoken through the prophet *J*:

JOHN (the Baptist)

Birth foretold, Lk 1.5-25; born, Lk 1.57-66; preached and baptized, Mt 3.1-12 (Mk 1.4-11; Lk 3.1-17; Jn 1.6-8, 19-28); imprisoned, Mt 14.3-4 (Mk 6.17-18; Lk 3.19-20); sent messengers to Jesus, Mt 11.1-6 (Lk 7.18-23); commended by Jesus, Mt 11.7-15 (Lk 7.24-35); beheaded and buried, Mt 14.6-12 (Mk 6.17-29).

JOHN (the Apostle)

Called, Mt 4.21 (Mk 1.19; Lk 5.10); sent out with the twelve, Mt 10.2 (Mk 3.17); desire for revenge rebuked, Lk 9.51-56; selfish request rejected, Mt 20.20-24 (Mk 10.35-41); healed and preached in the temple, Acts 3.1—4.22.

JOIN (JOINED)

2 Kings 23. 3 book. All the people *j* in the covenant.
Dan 11.34 help, and many shall *j* them insincerely.
Zech 2.11 Many nations shall *j* themselves to the
Mt 19. 5 and be *j* to his wife, and the two shall
19. 6 what God has *j* together, let no one
Mk 10. 7 father and mother and be *j* to his wife,
10. 9 Therefore what God has *j* together, let

JONAH

2 Kings 14.25 which he spoke by his servant *J* son of
Jon 1. 1 Now the word of the LORD came to *J*
2. 1 Then *J* prayed to the LORD his God from
3. 1 of the LORD came to *J* a second time,
4. 1 But this was very displeasing to *J*, and
Mt 12.40 as *J* was three days and three nights in
16. 4 will be given to it except the sign of *J*."
Lk 11.30 just as *J* became a sign to the people of
11.32 see, something greater than *J* is here!

JONATHAN

Smote the Philistine garrison, 1 Sam 13.2-4; 14.1-15; unknowingly transgressed Saul's oath, 1 Sam 14.24-30; rescued by the people, 1 Sam 14.36-46; made a covenant with David, 1 Sam 18.1-5; friendship with David, 1 Sam 20; killed by the Philistines, 1 Sam 31.2; mourned by David, 2 Sam 1.17-27; covenant with him remembered by David, 2 Sam 9.

JOPPA

2 Chr 2.16 and bring it to you in rafts by sea to *J*;
Jon 1. 3 He went down to *J* and found a ship
Acts 9.36 Now in *J* there was a disciple whose
10. 5 send men to *J* for a certain Simon who

JORDAN

Gen 13.10 that the plain of the *J* was well watered
Deut 1. 1 Moses spoke to all Israel beyond the *J*
4.21 he vowed that I should not cross the *J*
Josh 4. 1 nation had finished crossing over the *J*,
2 Sam 19.15 king came back to the *J*; and Judah
2 Kings 5.10 wash in the *J* seven times, and your
Job 40.23 it is confident though *J* rushes against
Ps 42. 6 from the land of the *J* and of Hermon,
Mt 3. 6 were baptized by him in the river *J*,
3.13 came from Galilee to John at the *J*,
19. 1 to the region of Judea beyond the *J*.
Jn 3.26 the one who was with you across the *J*,
10.40 away again across the *J* to the place

JOSEPH (Son of Jacob)

Born, Gen 30.22-24; incurred jealousy by his dreams, Gen 37.5-11; sold into Egypt, Gen 37.12-28; refused Potiphar's wife, Gen 39.1-18; imprisoned, Gen 39.19-23; interpreted the prisoners' dreams, Gen 40; interpreted Pharaoh's dreams, Gen 41.1-36; made ruler over Egypt, Gen 41.37-49,53-57; married, had two sons, Gen 41.50-52; met his brothers, Gen 42—43; made himself known to them, Gen 45; saw his father again, Gen 46.28-34; died, Gen 50.22-26; buried in Shechem, Josh 24.32.

Deut 33.13 And of *J* he said, Blessed by the LORD
Ps 105. 17 He had sent a man ahead of them, *J*,
Heb 11.22 By faith *J*, at the end of his life, made

JOSEPH (Husband of Mary, Jesus' mother)

Betrothed to Mary, Mk 1.18 (Lk 1.27); instructed by an angel, Mt 1.19-21; went to Bethlehem, Lk 2.4; fled into Egypt, Mt 2.13-15; returned to Nazareth, Mt 2.19-23.

JOSEPH (of Arimathea)

Mt 27.57 rich man from Arimathea, named *J*,
Jn 19.38 After these things, *J* of Arimathea, who

Ex 2.14 Do you mean to *k* me as you *k* the
Num 31.17 *k* every male among the little ones,
1 Kings 21.19 Have you *k*, and also taken possession?"
2 Kings 6.21 "Father, shall I *k* them? Shall I *k* them?"
Job 13.15 See, he will *k* me; I have no hope; but I
Ps 44.22 Because of you we are being *k* all day
Mt 10.28 can *k* the body but cannot *k* the soul;
21.38 'This is the the heir; come, let us *k* him
23.37 "Jerusalem, Jerusalem, the city that *k*
Mk 8.31 scribes, and be *k*, and after three days
10.34 flog him, and *k* him; and after three
Lk 12. 4 do not fear those who *k* the body
19.47 people kept looking for a way to *k* him;
20.15 him out of the vineyard and *k* him.
Jn 5.18 were seeking all the more to *k* him,
Acts 2.23 you crucified and *k* by the hands of
11. 7 saying to me, 'Get up, Peter; *k* and eat.'
Rev 2.13 Antipas . . . was *k* among you, where

KIN

Lev 25.25 If anyone of your *k* falls into difficulty
Deut 23. 7 of the Edomites, for they are your *k*.
Ruth 2.20 a relative of ours, one of our nearest *k*."
3. 9 over your servant, for you are next-of-*k*."
4.14 not left you this day without next-of-*k*;
2 Sam 19.12 You are my *k*; you are my bone and my
Prov 18.24 friend sticks closer than one's nearest *k*.
Jer 9. 4 and put no trust in any of your *k*; for all
Neh 5. 8 but now you are selling your own *k* who

KIND (KINDLY)

Josh 2.12 since I have dealt *k* with you, swear to
Prov 11.17 Those who are *k* reward themselves, but
14.21 happy are those who are *k* to the poor.
19.17 whoever is *k* to the poor lends to the
Eph 4.32 and be *k* to one another, tenderhearted,
2 Tim 2.24 must not be quarrelsome but *k* to

KINDNESS

Gen 19.19 shown me great *k* in saving my life;
2 Sam 9. 1 I may show *k* for Jonathan's sake?"
Job 6.14 "Those who withhold *k* from a friend
Zech 7. 9 show *k* and mercy to one another;
Rom 2. 4 that God's *k* is meant to lead you
3.12 there is no one who shows *k*, there is
11.22 the *k* and severity of God: severity
Titus 3. 4 the goodness and loving *k* of God our

KINDRED

Gen 13. 8 between you and me, . . . for we are *k*.
1 Kings 12.24 shall not go up or fight against your *k*
1 Chr 13. 2 let us send abroad to our *k* who remain
2 Chr 11. 4 shall not go up or fight against your *k*.
Ps 69. 8 I have become a stranger to my *k*, an
Prov 27.10 is a neighbor who is nearby than *k* who

KING

Ex 2.23 After a long time, the *k* of Egypt died.
Deut 17.14 and you say, "I will set a *k* over me, like
Judg 18. 1 In those days there was no *k* in Israel.
21.25 In those days there was no *k* in Israel;
1 Sam 2.10 he will give strength to his *k*, and exalt
8. 5 appoint for us, then, a *k* to govern us,
10.24 all the people shouted, "Long live the *k*!"
11.15 there they made Saul *k* before the LORD,
12.12 though the LORD your God was your *k*.
23.17 you shall be *k* over Israel, and I shall be
2 Sam 19.10 say nothing about bringing the *k* back?"
2 Kings 11.12 they proclaimed him *k*, and anointed
1 Chr 16.31 say among the nations, "The LORD is *k*!"
Job 41.34 is lofty; it is *k* over all that are proud."
Ps 2. 6 "I have set my *k* on Zion, my holy hill."
5. 2 Listen to the sound of my cry, my *K*
10.16 The LORD is *k* forever and ever; the
24. 7 doors! that the *K* of glory may come in.
44. 4 You are my *K* and my God; you
47. 8 God is *k* over the nations; God sits on
72. 1 Give the *k* your justice, O God, and
93. 1 The LORD is *k*, he is robed in majesty;
97. 1 The LORD is *k*! Let the earth rejoice; let
149. 2 the children of Zion rejoice in their *K*.
Eccl 8. 4 the word of the *k* is powerful, and who
10.16 you, O land, when your *k* is a servant,
Isa 32. 1 See, a *k* will reign in righteousness, and
43.15 Holy One, the Creator of Israel, your *K*.
Jer 10. 7 Who would not fear you, O *K* of the
29.16 the *k* who sits on the throne of David,
30. 9 the LORD their God and David their *k*,
51.57 sleep and never wake, says the *K*,
Dan 2. 4 The Chaldeans said to the *k* (in
2.37 You, O *k*, the *k* of kings— to whom the
Hos 3. 5 the LORD their God, and David their *k*;
Mic 2.13 Their *k* will pass on before them, the
Zech 9. 9 Lo, your *k* comes to you; triumphant
Mt 22. 2 to a *k* who gave a wedding banquet
25.34 the *k* will say to those at his right hand,
Lk 19.38 "Blessed is the *k* who comes in the
23. 3 asked him, "Are you the *k* of the Jews?"
Jn 1.49 the Son of God! You are the *K* of Israel!"
6.15 by force to make him *k*, he withdrew
12.13 the name of the Lord—the *K* of Israel!"
18.37 "So you are a *k*?" Jesus answered, "You
19.14 He said to the Jews, "Here is your *K*!"
Acts 7.18 another *k* who had not known Joseph
17. 7 that there is another *k* named Jesus."
1 Tim 1.17 To the *K* of ages, immortal, invisible,
Rev 9.11 have as *k* over them the angel of the
19.16 inscribed, "*K* of kings and Lord of lords."

KINGDOM

Ex 19. 6 but you shall be for me a priestly *k* and
1 Sam 13.14 your *k* shall not continue; the LORD has
2 Sam 7.12 your body, and I will establish his *k*.
1 Chr 17.11 own sons, and I will establish his *k*.
29.11 yours is the *k*, O LORD, and you are
Ps 145. 12 and the glorious splendor of your *k*.
Isa 9. 7 peace for the throne of David and his *k*.
Dan 4. 3 His *k* is an everlasting *k*, and his
4.17 High is sovereign over the *k* of mortals;
4.31 The *k* has departed from you! You shall
11. 4 his *k* shall be broken and divided
Ob 21 Easu; and the *k* shall be the LORD's.
Mt 3. 2 "Repent, for the *k* of heaven has come
4.17 "Repent, for the *k* of heaven has come
4.23 proclaiming the good news of the *k* and
6.33 strive first for the *k* of God and his
8.11 and Isaac and Jacob in the *k* of heaven,
10. 7 news, 'The *k* of heaven has come near.'
18. 3 you will never enter the *k* of heaven.
19.14 as these that the *k* of heaven belongs."
21.43 *k* of God will be taken away from you
24. 7 will rise against nation, and *k* against *k*,
25.34 inherit the *k* prepared for you from the
26.29 drink it new with you in my Father's *k*."
Mk 1.15 the *k* of God has come near; repent,
4.26 "The *k* of God is as if someone would
9. 1 not taste death until they see that the *k*
11.10 Blessed is the coming *k* of our ancestor
12.34 "You are not far from the *k* of God."
13. 8 will rise against nation, and *k* against *k*;
14.25 that day when I drink it new in the *k*
Lk 4.43 I must proclaim the good news of the *k*
8.10 been given to know the secrets of the *k*
9.11 them, and spoke to them about the *k*
9.62 the plow and looks back is fit for the *k*
10. 9 to them, 'The *k* of God has come near
11.17 "Every *k* divided against itself becomes
12.31 strive for his *k*, and these things will be
16.16 good news of the *k* of God is
17.21 For in fact, the *k* of God is among you.
18.16 for it to such as these that the *k* of God
18.29 or children, for the sake of the *k*
21.10 will rise against nation, and *k* against *k*;
21.31 place, you know the *k* of God is near.
22.29 just as my father conferred on me, a *k*,

Jn 3. 5 enter the *k* of God without being born
Acts 1. 6 when you will restore the *k* to Israel?"
14.22 that we must enter the *k* of God."
19. 8 argued persuasively about the *k* of God.
28.23 testifying to the *k* of God and trying to
Rom 14.17 the *k* of God is not food and drink but
1 Cor 4.20 the *k* of God depends not on talk but
6.10 of these will inherit the *k* of God.
15.24 end, when he hands over the *k* to God
15.50 flesh and blood cannot inherit the *k* of
Eph 5. 5 has any inheritance in the *k* of Christ
2 Thess 1. 5 to make you worthy of the *k* of God,
Heb 12.28 are receiving a *k* that cannot be shaken,
2 Pet 1.11 entry into the eternal *k* of our Lord and
Rev 1. 6 made us to be a *k*, priests serving his
11.15 *k* of the world has become the *k* of our

KINGDOMS

Dan 8.22 four *k* shall arise from his nation, but
Hag 2.22 earth, and to overthrow the throne of *k*;
Mt 4. 8 showed him all the *k* of the world and
Lk 4. 5 him in an instant all the *k* of the world.

KINGS (KING'S)

2 Chr 23.11 he brought out the *k* son, put the crown
Ps 102. 15 LORD, all the *k* of the earth your glory.
Prov 8.15 By me *k* reign, and rulers decree what is
21. 1 The *k* heart is a stream of water in the
31. 4 It is not for *k*, O Lemuel, it is not for *k*
Dan 7.17 "As for these four great beasts, four *k*
1 Cor 4. 8 Quite apart from us you have become *k*!
1 Tim 2. 2 for *k* and all who are in high positions,
Rev 16.12 prepare the way for the *k* from the east.

KINGSHIP

1 Sam 10.16 But about the matter of the *k*, of which
Dan 7.27 The *k* and the dominion and the

KINSFOLK

Judg 20.23 again draw near to battle against our *k*
Prov 17.17 times, and *k* are born to share adversity.

KISHON

Judg 5.21 The torrent *K* swept them away, the

KISS (KISSED KISSES KISSING)

Gen 29.11 Then Jacob *k* Rachel, and wept aloud.
33. 4 him, and fell on his neck and *k* him,
45.15 he *k* all his brothers and wept upon
48.10 brought them near him; and he *k* them
Ruth 1.14 Orpah *k* her mother-in-law, but Ruth
1 Sam 20.41 and they *k* each other, and wept with
2 Sam 14.33 the king; and the king *k* Absalom.
Ps 2.12 *k* his feet, or he will be angry, and you
85.10 meet; righteousness and peace will *k*
Prov 7.13 She seizes him and *k* him, and with
24.26 who gives an honest answer gives a *k* on
Song 1. 2 Let him *k* me with the *k* of his mouth!
Hos 13. 2 to these," they say. People are *k* calves!
Mt 26.48 "The one I will *k* is the man; arrest him."
Mk 14.44 "The one I will *k* is the man; arrest him
Lk 7.45 You gave me no *k*, but from the time I
15.20 put his arms around him and *k* him.
22.47 them. He approached Jesus to *k* him;
Acts 20.37 they embraced Paul and *k* him, grieving
Rom 16.16 Greet one another with a holy *k*. All the
1 Cor 16.20 Greet one another with a holy *k*.
1 Pet 5.14 Greet one another with a *k* of love.

KNEE (KNEES)

1 Kings 19.18 all the *k* that have not bowed to Baal,
Ezra 9. 5 fell on my *k*, spread out my hands to
Isa 45.23 "To me every *k* shall bow, every tongue
Dan 6.10 on his *k* three times a day to pray to his
Lk 5. 8 Peter saw it he fell down at Jesus' *k*,
Rom 14.11 every *k* shall bow to me, and every

KNEEL (KNELT)

Gen 24.11 He made the camels *k* down outside
1 Kings 8.54 the altar of the LORD, where he had *k*
Ps 95. 6 bow down, let us *k* before the LORD, our

KNIFE

Gen 22. 6 he himself carried the fire and the *k*.
22.10 his hand and took the *k* to kill his son.
Prov 23. 2 put a *k* to your throat if you have a big

KNOCK (KNOCKING)

Mt 7. 7 will find; *k*, and the door will be opened
Lk 11. 9 will find; *k*, and the door will be opened
13.25 and to *k* at the door, saying, 'Lord,
Acts 12.16 Peter continued *k*; and when they
Rev 3.20 I am standing at the door, *k*; if you hear

KNOW

Ex 1. 8 arose over Egypt, who did not *k* Joseph.
7. 5 Egyptians shall *k* that I am the LORD,
18.11 Now I *k* that the LORD is greater than all
29.46 they shall *k* that I am the LORD their
31.13 that you may *k* that I, the LORD, sanctify
Lev 23.43 may *k* that I made the people
Judg 2.10 who did not *k* the LORD or the work that
1 Sam 17.47 all this assembly may *k* that the LORD
2 Sam 7.20 to you? For you *k* your servant, O Lord
1 Kings 8.43 may *k* your name and fear you, as do
8.60 of the earth may *k* that the LORD is God;
20.13 and you shall *k* that I am the LORD."
1 Chr 28. 9 son Solomon, *k* the God of your father,
Job 8. 9 are but of yesterday, and we *k* nothing,
19.25 I *k* that my Redeemer lives, and that at
24.16 themselves up; they do not *k* the light.
30.23 I *k* that you will bring me to death, and
Ps 25. 4 Make me to *k* your ways, O LORD; teach
46.10 "Be still, and *k* that I am God! I am
56. 9 I call. This I *k*, that God is for me.
73.11 they say, "How can God *k*? Is there
89.15 are the people who *k* the festal shout,
100. 3 *K* that the LORD is God. It is he that
109. 27 *k* that this is your hand; you, O LORD,
142. 3 When my spirit is faint, you *k* my way.
Prov 28.22 rich and does not *k* that loss is sure to
Eccl 3.14 I *k* that whatever God does endures
8. 5 and the wise mind will *k* the time and
Isa 1. 3 Israel does not *k*, my people do not
37.20 may *k* that you alone are the LORD."
41.20 so that all may see and *k*, all may
49.26 all flesh shall *k* that I am the LORD
52. 6 Therefore my people shall *k* my name;
52. 6 that day they shall *k* that it is I who
55. 5 You shall call nations that you do not *k*,
Jer 8. 7 but my people do not *k* the ordinance
12. 3 But you, O LORD, *k* me; you see me and
24. 7 a heart to *k* that I am the LORD; and
31.34 or say to each other, "*K* the LORD," for
Ezek 6.14 Then they shall *k* that I am the LORD.
17.21 wind; and you shall *k* that I, the LORD,
29.21 Then they shall *k* that I am the LORD.
32.15 in it, they shall *k* that I am the LORD.
34.27 and they shall *k* that I am the LORD,
37.28 nations shall *k* that I the LORD sanctify
39. 7 nations shall *k* that I am the LORD, the
Hos 6. 3 Let us *k*, let us press on to *k* the LORD;
11. 3 but they did not *k* that I healed them.
14. 9 those who are discerning *k* them.
Joel 2.27 You shall *k* that I am in the midst of
Mic 4.12 they do not *k* the thoughts of the LORD;
Mt 6. 3 your left hand *k* what your right hand
9. 6 that you may *k* that the Son of Man has
24.50 him and at an hour he does not *k*.
Mk 2.10 *k* that the Son of Man has authority on
12.24 you *k* neither the scriptures nor the
13.35 you do not *k* when the master of the
Lk 4.34 us? I *k* who you are, the Holy One
5.24 that you may *k* that the Son of Man has

Lk 13.27 say, 'I do not *k* where you come from;
20.21 "Teacher, we *k* that you are right in
Jn 10.14 I *k* my own and my own *k* me,
13.35 By this everyone will *k* that you are my
17. 3 life, that they *k* you, the only true God,
17.23 the world may *k* that you have sent me
Acts 19.15 "Jesus I *k*, and Paul I *k*; but who are
1 Cor 3.16 Do you not *k* that you are God's temple
Gal 4. 9 however, that you have come to *k* God,
Eph 1.18 you may *k* what is the hope to which he
Phil 3.10 I want to *k* Christ and the power of his
2 Tim 1.12 I *k* the one in whom I have put my
Heb 8.11 or say to each other, '*K* the Lord,'
1 Jn 4. 6 From this we *k* the spirit of truth and
5.13 you may *k* that you have eternal life.
1 Jn 5.19 We *k* that we are God's children, and
Rev 2. 2 "I *k* your works, your toil and patient

KNOWS (KNEW KNOWN)

Job 23.10 he *k* the way that I take; when he has
Ps 76. 1 In Judah God is *k*, his name is great in
103. 14 he *k* how we are made; he remembers
Isa 19.21 will make himself *k* to the Egyptians;
Am 3. 2 You only have I *k* of all the families of
Zech 11.11 watching me, *k* that it was the word
Mt 6. 8 for your Father *k* what you need before
6.32 heavenly Father *k* that you need all
12.33 fruit bad; for the tree is *k* by its fruit.
Mk 3.12 ordered them not to make him *k*.
13.32 about that day or hour no one *k*,
Jn 1.18 Father's heart, who has made him *k*.
2.25 for he himself *k* what was in everyone.
Acts 7.13 Joseph made himself *k* to his brothers,
7.18 another king who had not *k* Joseph
15. 8 God, who *k* the human heart, testified
Rom 1.21 for though they *k* God, they did not
Col 1.25 make the word of God fully *k*, the
2 Pet 2.21 better for them never to have *k* the way
Rev 1. 1 he made it *k* by sending his angel to his

KNOWLEDGE

Gen 2. 9 and the tree of the *k* of good and evil.
Num 24.16 knows the *k* of the Most High, who sees
Ps 139. 6 Such *k* is too wonderful for me; it is so
Prov 1. 4 simple, *k* and prudence to the young—
9.10 and the *k* of the Holy One is insight.
14. 6 but *k* is easy for one who understands.
15. 2 tongue of the wise dispenses *k*, but the
30. 3 wisdom, nor have I *k* of the holy ones.
Isa 5.13 My people go into exile without *k*; their
11. 9 earth will be full of the *k* of the LORD
Dan 1.17 To these four young men God gave *k*
Hos 4. 6 My people are destroyed for lack of *k*;
Lk 1.77 give *k* of salvation to his people by the
11.52 For you have taken away the key of *k*;
1 Cor 1. 5 in him, in speech and *k* of every kind—
8. 1 *K* puffs up, but love builds up. Anyone
8.11 by your *k* those weak believers for
2 Cor 6. 6 by purity, *k*, patience, kindness,
1 Tim 2. 4 saved and to come to the *k* of the truth.

KORAH (KORAH'S)

Num 16. 1 Now *K* the son of Izhar son of Kohath
16.49 those who died in the affair of *K*.
Jude 11 sake of gain, and perish in *K* rebellion.

L

LABAN

Gen 24.29 brother whose name was *L*; and *L* ran
27.43 flee at once to my brother *L* in Haran,
28. 5 to Paddan-aram, to *L* son of Bethuel
29. 5 "Do you know *L* son of Nahor?" They
30.25 Jacob said to *L*, "Send me away, that I
31. 2 Jacob saw that *L* did not regard him as
31.20 Jacob deceived *L* the Aramean in that
31.48 *L* said, "This heap is a witness between
31.55 *L* arose, and kissed his grandchildren

LABOR (LABORS) (n)

Ex 2.11 out to the people and saw their forced *l*.
Ps 48. 6 of them there, pains as of a woman in *l*.
Prov 12.14 things, and manual *l* has its reward.
Isa 21. 3 me, like the pangs of a woman in *l*;
66. 7 "Before she was in *l* she gave birth;
Jer 6.24 hold of us, pain as of a woman in *l*.
Jn 16.21 When a woman is in *l*, she has pain,
Rom 8.22 whole creation has been groaning in *l*
1 Cor 15.58 that in the Lord your *l* is not in vain.
1 Thess 2. 9 You remember our *l* and toil, brothers
5. 3 as *l* pains come upon a pregnant
Heb 4.10 rest also cease from their *l* as God did

LABOR (v)

Deut 5.13 Six days you shall *l*, and do all your
Ps 127. 1 the house, those who build it *l* in vain.
Prov 21.25 is fatal, for lazy hands refuse to *l*.
Hab 2.13 that peoples *l* only to feed the flames,

LABORERS

Eccl 5.12 Sweet is the sleep of *l*, whether they eat
Mt 20. 1 in the morning to hire *l* for his vineyard.
Lk 10. 2 harvest is plentiful, but the *l* are few;
Jas 5. 4 wages of the *l* who mowed your fields,

LACERATE

Deut 14. 1 you must not *l* yourselves or shave your

LACK (LACKED LACKING)

Deut 2. 7 has been with you; you have *l* nothing."
Eccl 6. 2 honor, so that they *l* nothing of all that
Mk 10.21 "You *l* one thing; go, sell what you own,
Lk 18.22 "There is still one thing *l*. Sell all that
22.35 bag, or sandals, did you *l* anything?"

LAKE

Lk 8.33 steep bank into the *l* and were drowned.
Rev 19.20 two were thrown alive into the *l* of fire
20.10 devil . . . was thrown into the *l* of fire

LAMB (LAMBS)

Gen 22. 7 but where is the *l* for a burnt offering?"
Ex 12. 5 Your *l* shall be without blemish, a
29.39 One *l* you shall offer in the morning,
2 Sam 12. 3 man had nothing but one little ewe *l*,
Isa 53. 7 like a *l* that is led to the slaughter, and
65.25 The wolf and the *l* shall feed together,
Jer 11.19 But I was like a gentle *l* led to the
Lk 10. 3 I am sending you out like *l* into the
Jn 1.29 "Here is the *L* of God, who takes away
21.15 love you." Jesus said to him, "Feed my *l*."
1 Pet 1.19 of Christ, like that of a *l* without defect
Rev 5. 6 a *L* standing as if it had been
5.12 "Worthy is the *L* that was slaughtered to
6.16 the throne and from the wrath of the *L*;
7.10 saying, "Salvation belongs . . . to the *L*!"
14. 1 there was the *L*, standing on Mount
17.14 they will make war on the *L*, and the *L*
19. 7 marriage of the *L* has come, and his
21. 9 show you the bride, the wife of the *L*."
21.14 names of the twelve apostles of the *L*.
21.23 God is its light, and its lamp is the *L*.

LAME

2 Sam 5. 8 attack the *l* and the blind, those whom
Isa 35. 6 then the *l* shall leap like a deer, and
Mt 15.31 maimed whole, the *l* walking, and the
Acts 3. 2 a man *l* from birth was being carried in.

LAMENT (LAMENTED)

1 Sam 7. 2 all the house of Israel *l* after the LORD.
Joel 1. 8 *L* like a virgin dressed in sackcloth for

LAMENTATION

2 Sam 1.17 David intoned this *l* over Saul and his
Jer 6.26 as for an only child, most bitter *l*:
Ezek 27. 2 Now you, mortal, raise a *l* over Tyre,

Am 5. 1 this word that I take up over you in *l*,

LAMP (LAMPS)

Ex 27.20 so that a *l* may be set up to burn
1 Sam 3. 3 *l* of God had not yet gone out, and
2 Sam 22.29 you are my *l*, O LORD, the LORD lightens
1 Kings 11.36 David may always have a *l* before me
15. 4 God gave him a *l* in Jerusalem, setting
2 Kings 4.10 table, a chair, and a *l*, so that he can
8.19 since he promised to give a *l* to him
Job 18. 6 their tent, the *l* above them is put out.
29. 3 when his *l* shone over my head, and by
Ps 18.28 It is you who light my *l*; the LORD, my
119.105 Your word is a *l* to my feet and a light
Prov 6.23 For the commandment is a *l* and the
20.20 your *l* will go out in utter darkness.
20.27 The human spirit is the *l* of the LORD,
24.20 no future; the *l* of the wicked go out.
31.18 Her *l* does not go out at night. She puts
Mt 5.15 No one after lighting a *l* puts it under
6.22 "The eye is the *l* of the body. So, if your
Mk 4.21 "Is a *l* brought in to be put under a
Lk 8.16 "No one after lighting a *l* hides it under
11.33 "No one after lighting a *l* puts it in a
11.34 Your eye is the *l* of your body. If your
12.35 dressed for action and have your *l* lit;
Jn 5.35 He was a burning and shining *l*, and
Rev 21.23 of God is its light, and its *l* is the Lamb.

LAMPSTAND (LAMPSTANDS)

Ex 25.31 You shall make a *l* of pure gold. The
37.17 He also made the *l* of pure gold. The
Lev 24. 4 He shall set up the lamps on the *l* of
Num 8. 2 lamps shall give light in front of the *l*."
Zech 4. 2 "I see a *l* all of gold, with a bowl on the
Rev 1.12 and on turning I saw seven golden *l*,

LAND (LANDS)

Gen 13.15 all the *l* which you see I will give to you
35.12 The *l* that I gave to Abraham and Isaac
47.18 of my lord but our bodies and our *l*.
50.24 out of this *l* to the *l* that he swore to
Ex 6. 8 I will bring you into the *l* that I swore
Lev 18.25 Thus the *l* became defiled; and I
25.23 The *l* shall not be sold in perpetuity, for
Num 13.26 and showed them the fruit of the *l*.
32. 5 let this *l* be given to your servants for a
32.22 and this *l* shall be your possession
33.54 You shall apportion the *l* by lot
35.34 You shall not defile the *l* in which you
Deut 8. 7 God is bringing you into a good *l*, a *l*
11.10 *l* that you are about to enter to occupy
11.11 *l* that you are crossing over to occupy is
29.24 "Why has the LORD done thus to this *l*?
Josh 13. 1 much of the *l* still remains to be
24.13 I gave you a *l* on which you had not
Neh 9.24 decendants went in and possessed the *l*,
Isa 38.11 not see the LORD in the *l* of the living;
Jer 2. 7 you entered you defiled my *l*, and made
22.29 O *l*, *l*, *l*, hear the word of the LORD!
Ezek 33.24 of these waste places in the *l*
36. 6 prophesy concerning the *l* of Israel, and
45. 1 When you allot the *l* as an inheritance,
Hos 9. 3 shall not remain in the *l* of the LORD;
Acts 7. 3 relatives and go to the *l* that I will show
20.13 intending to go by *l* himself.
2 Cor 10.16 proclaim the good news in *l* beyond

LANDMARK (LANDMARKS)

Job 24. 2 The wicked remove *l*; they seize flocks
Prov 22.28 Do not remove the ancient *l* that your
23.10 Do not remove an ancient *l* or encroach

LANGUAGE

Gen 11. 1 Now the whole earth had one *l* and the
Neh 13.24 they could not speak the *l* of Judah,
Jer 5.15 a nation whose *l* you do not know,
Ezek 3. 5 of obscure speech and a difficult *l*,
Acts 2. 6 them speaking in the native *l* of each.

LANGUISH (LANGUISHES LANGUISHING)

Ps 6. 2 O LORD, for I am *l*; O LORD, heal me,
119. 81 My soul *l* for your salvation; I hope in
Isa 19. 8 who spread nets on the water will *l*.

LASHES

2 Cor 11.24 from the Jews the forty *l* minus one.

LAST

Mt 12.45 the *l* state of that person is worse than
19.30 are first will be *l*, and the *l* will be first."
Mk 10.31 are first will be *l*, and the *l* will be first."
15.37 gave a loud cry and breathed his *l*.
Lk 13.30 some are *l* who will be first, and some
2 Tim 3. 1 this, that in the *l* days distressing times
Heb 1. 2 but in these *l* days he has spoken to us
Rev 1.17 not be afraid; I am the first and the *l*,

LAUGH (LAUGHED LAUGHS)

Gen 17.17 Abraham fell on his face and *l*, and said
18.12 So Sarah *l* to herself, saying, "After I
2 Chr 30.10 Zebulun; but they *l* them to scorn, and
Job 5.22 At destruction and famine you shall *l*,
41.29 as chaff; it *l* at the rattle of javelins.
Ps 2. 4 He who sits in the heavens *l*; the LORD
37.13 but the LORD *l* at the wicked, for he sees
52. 6 see, and fear, and will *l* at the evildoer,
59. 8 But you *l* at them, O LORD; you hold all
Prov 1.26 I also will *l* at your calamity; I will
31.25 clothing, and she *l* at the time to come.
Mt 9.24 girl is not dead but sleeping." And they *l*
Mk 5.40 And they *l* at him. But he put them all
Lk 6.21 are you who weep now, for you will *l*.
8.53 they *l* at him, knowing that she was

LAUGHTER

Gen 21. 6 "God has brought *l* for me; everyone
Prov 14.13 Even in *l* the heart is sad, and the end
Eccl 2. 2 I said of *l*, "It is mad," and of pleasure,
7. 3 Sorrow is better than *l*, for by sadness

LAW (LAWS)

Num 5.29 This is the *l* in cases of jealousy, when
6.13 This is the *l* for the nazirites when the
Deut 1. 5 Moses undertook to expound this *l* as
17.18 have a copy of this *l* written for him
31. 9 Then Moses wrote down this *l*, and gave
31.11 you shall read this *l* before all Israel in
31.26 "Take this book of the *l* and put it
Josh 1. 8 This book of the *l* shall not depart out
8.34 he read all the words of the *l*, blessings
2 Chr 12. 1 strong, he abandoned the *l* of the LORD,
Neh 9.13 gave them right ordinances and true *l*,
Ps 1. 2 but their delight is in the *l* of the LORD,
19. 7 The *l* of the LORD is perfect, reviving the
119. 44 I will keep your *l* continually, forever
Prov 29. 9 If the wise go to *l* with fools, there is
Jer 31.33 I will put my *l* within them, and I will
Dan 6. 5 it in connection with the *l* of his God."
Mt 5.17 think that I have come to abolish the *l*
11.13 all the prophets and the *l* prophesied
Lk 5.17 Pharisees and teachers of the *l* sitting
16.17 in the letter of the *l* to become void.
24.44 everything written about me in the *l*
Acts 13.15 After the reading of the *l* and the
Rom 2.12 all who have sinned under the *l* will be
4.15 For the *l* brings wrath, but where there
7.22 I delight in the *l* of God in my
8. 2 set you free from the *l* of sin and death.
10. 4 For Christ is the end of the *l* so that
1 Cor 9.21 To those outside the *l* I became as one
Gal 3.10 on the works of the *l* are under a curse;
3.19 Why then the *l*? It was added because
3.23 and guarded under the *l* until faith
4.21 to the *l*, will you not listen to the *l*?
5.14 the whole *l* is summed up in a single

Gal 6. 2 this way you will fulfill the *l* of Christ.
1 Tim 1. 8 Now we know that the *l* is good, if one
Heb 7.19 (for the *l* made nothing perfect);
Jas 1.25 who looks into the perfect *l*, the *l* of
2. 9 are convicted by the *l* as transgressors.
4.11 judges the *l*; but if you judge the *l*, you

LAWFUL
Mt 12. 2 what is not *l* to do on the sabbath."
12.12 So it is *l* to do good on the sabbath."
14. 4 him, "It is not *l* for you to have her."
Mk 6.18 telling Herod, "It is not *l* for you to have
1 Cor 6.12 "All things are *l* for me," but not all

LAWLESS
Mk 15.28n says, "And he was counted among the *l*."
Lk 22.37 me, 'And he was counted among the *l*';
2 Thess 2. 3 comes first and the *l* one is revealed,
2. 8 then the *l* one will be revealed, whom

LAWLESSNESS
2 Thess 2. 7 the mystery of *l* is already at work, but
1 Jn 3. 4 Everyone who commits sin is guilty of *l*;

LAWYER (LAWYERS)
Lk 10.25 a *l* stood up to test Jesus. "Teacher," he
11.46 he said, "Woe also to you *l*! For you

LAY
Deut 9.18 I *l* prostrate before the LORD as before,
Prov 9. 6 *L* aside immaturity, and live, and walk
10.14 The wise *l* up knowledge, but the
Mt 8.20 Son of Man has nowhere to *l* his head."
1 Cor 3.11 no one can *l* any foundation other than

LAZARUS
Lk 16.20 at his gate lay a poor man named *L*,
Jn 11. 1 a certain man was ill, *L* of Bethany,
11.43 cried with a loud voice, "*L*, come out."
12. 1 the home of *L*, whom he had raised
12.10 chief priests planned to put *L* to death
12.17 been with him when he called *L* out

LAZY
Ex 5.17 He said, "You are *l*, *l*; that is why you
Prov 13. 4 appetite of the *l* craves, and gets
21.25 craving of the *l* person is fatal, for *l*
22.13 The *l* person says, "There is a lion
26.15 *l* person buries a hand in the dish, and
26.16 *l* person is wiser in self-esteem than

LAZYBONES
Prov 6. 6 Go to the ant, you *l*; consider its ways,

LEAD (LEADS LED)
Gen 24.27 the LORD has *l* me on the way to the
33.14 of his servant, and I will *l* on slowly,
Ex 13.18 So God *l* the people by the roundabout
Josh 24. 3 *l* him through all the land of Canaan
1 Sam 12. 2 with you. I have *l* you from my youth
Ps 5. 8 *L* me, O LORD, in your righteousness
23. 2 he *l* me beside still waters; he restores
25. 5 *L* me in your truth, and teach me, for
61. 2 *L* me to the rock that is higher than I;
78.14 In the daytime he *l* them with a cloud,
107. 7 he *l* them by a straight way, until they
136. 16 *l* his people through the wilderness,
Isa 11. 6 together, and a little child shall *l* them.
40.11 bosom, and gently *l* the mother sheep.
48.17 for your own good, who *l* you in the way
63.14 Thus you *l* your people, to make for
Jer 2. 6 of Egypt, who *l* us in the wilderness,
Hos 11. 4 I *l* them with cords of human kindness,
Mt 4. 1 Jesus was *l* up by the Spirit into the
Lk 4.29 town and *l* him to the brow of the hill
Acts 8.32 "Like a sheep he was *l* to the slaughter,
Rom 8.14 all who are *l* by the Spirit of God are
1 Cor 7.17 each of you *l* the life that the Lord has
Gal 5.18 if you are *l* by the Spirit, you are not

Eph 4. 1 beg you to *l* a life worthy of the calling
Col 1.10 that you may *l* lives worthy of the Lord,
1 Thess 2.12 pleading that you *l* a life worthy of God,

LEADER
Mt 9.18 *l* of the synagogue came in and knelt
Lk 8.41 named Jairus, the *l* of the synagogue.
13.14 the *l* of the synagogue, indignant

LEAF (LEAVES)
Gen 3. 7 they sewed fig *l* together and made
Job 13.25 Will you frighten a windblown *l* and
Ezek 47.12 Their *l* will not wither nor their fruit
Mk 11.13 he found nothing but *l*, for it was not
13.28 and puts forth its *l*, you know that

LEAGUE
Job 5.23 you shall be in *l* with the stones of the

LEAH
Gen 29.16 the name of the elder was *L*, and the
29.30 and he loved Rachel more than *L*. He
30. 9 When *L* saw that she had ceased
31. 4 called Rachel and *L* into the field where
35.23 The sons of *L*: Reuben (Jacob's
Ruth 4.11 Rachel and *L*, who together built up the

LEAN
Isa 48. 2 the holy city, and *l* on the God of Israel;

LEAP (LEAPED)
2 Sam 22.30 and by my God I can *l* over a wall.
Lk 1.41 greeting, the child *l* in her womb.

LEARN (LEARNED)
Gen 30.27 I have *l* by divination that the LORD has
Deut 31.12 hear and *l* to fear the LORD your God
Ps 119. 7 when I *l* your righteous ordinances.
119. 71 that I was humbled, so that I might *l*
Prov 8. 5 O simple ones, *l* prudence; acquire
Isa 1.17 *l* to do good; seek justice, rescue the
26. 9 inhabitants of the world *l* righteousness.
Jer 10. 2 Do not *l* the way of the nations, or be
Dan 5.21 until he *l* that the Most High God has
Mt 9.13 Go and *l* what this means, 'I desire
11.29 Take my yoke upon you, and *l* from me;
Phil 4. 9 on doing the things that you have *l*
4.11 need; for I have *l* to be content with
1 Thess 4. 1 as you *l* from us how you ought to live
Heb 5. 8 was a Son, he *l* obedience through what
Rev 14. 3 No one could *l* that song except the

LEARNING
Prov 1. 5 Let the wise also hear and gain in *l*,
Jn 7.15 "How does this man have such *l*, when
Acts 26.24 Paul! Too much *l* is driving you insane!"

LEAST
Judg 6.15 Manasseh, and I am the *l* in my family."
1 Sam 9.21 a Benjaminite, from the *l* of the tribes
Mt 2. 6 by no means *l* among the rulers of
5.19 same, will be called *l* in the kingdom
11.11 the *l* in the kingdom of heaven is
Lk 7.28 John; yet the *l* in the kingdom of God is
9.48 for the *l* among all of you is the
1 Cor 15. 9 I am the *l* of the apostles, unfit to be
Eph 3. 8 I am the very *l* of all the saints,

LEAVE (LEFT)
Judg 16.20 did not know that the LORD had *l* him.
1 Kings 19.10 I alone am *l*, and they are seeking my
2 Kings 2. 2 and as you yourself live, I will not *l* you."
4.30 yourself live, I will not *l* without you."
Job 22.17 They said to God; '*L* us alone,' and
Ezek 9. 8 *l* alone, I fell prostrate on my face, and
Mt 4.22 they *l* the boat and their father, and
19.27 "Look, we have *l* everything and
Mk 1.18 they *l* their nets and followed him.
1.20 they *l* their father Zebedee in the boat

Mk 10. 7 man shall *l* his father and mother and
Lk 5.11 to shore, they *l* everything and followed
8.37 the Gerasenes asked Jesus to *l* them;

LEAVEN

Ex 12.15 you shall remove *l* from your houses,
Lev 2.11 bring to the LORD shall be made with *l*,

LEBANON

Deut 1. 7 land of the Canaanites and the *L*, as far
Judg 9.15 bramble and devour the cedars of *L*.'
1 Kings 5. 6 command that cedars from *L* be cut for
10.17 them in the House of the Forest of *L*.
Ezra 3. 7 to bring cedar trees from *L* to the sea,
Ps 29. 5 cedars; the LORD breaks the cedars of *L*.
Song 5.15 His appearance is like *L*, choice as the
Isa 10.34 with an ax, and *L* with its majestic trees
60.13 glory of *L* shall come to you, the
Jer 18.14 Does the snow of *L* leave the crags of

LEFT (n and adj)

Gen 13. 9 the right hand, then I will go to the *l*."
Mt 6. 3 do not let your *l* hand know what your
20.21 at your right hand and one at your *l*,

LEGION (LEGIONS)

Mt 26.53 send me more than twelve *l* of angels?
Mk 5. 9 "My name is *L*; for we are many."

LEGS

Dan 2.33 its *l* of iron, its feet partly of iron and
Jn 19.33 already dead, they did not break his *l*.

LEHI

Judg 15.19 that is at *L*, and water came from it.
2 Sam 23.11 Philistines gathered together at *L*,

LEND (LENDING LENT LENDS)

Ex 22.25 If you *l* money to my people, to the
Deut 28.12 You will *l* to many nations, but you will
1 Sam 1.28 I have *l* him to the LORD; as long as he
Ps 37.26 They are ever giving liberally and *l*, and
Prov 19.17 is kind to the poor *l* to the LORD,
Jer 15.10 I have not *l*, nor have I borrowed, yet all
Lk 6.34 if you *l* to those from whom you hope

LENGTH

Gen 6.15 *l* of the ark three hundred cubits, its
Ezek 40. 5 The *l* of the measuring reed in the
Eph 3.18 saints, what is the breadth and *l* and

LEOPARD (LEOPARDS)

Isa 11. 6 lamb, the *l* shall lie down with the kid,
Jer 13.23 change their skin or the *l* their spots?
Dan 7. 6 as I watched, another appeared, like a *l*.

LEPER (LEPERS)

Mt 8. 2 a *l* who came to him and knelt before
11. 5 the lame walk, the *l* are cleansed, the
26. 6 at Bethany in the house of Simon the *l*,
Mk 1.40 A *l* came to him begging him, and
14. 3 in the house of Simon the *l*, as he sat
Lk 4.27 many *l* in Israel in the time of the
7.22 lame walk, *l* are cleansed, the deaf hear,
17.12 ten *l* approached him. Keeping their

LEPROSY

2 Kings 5. 1 a mighty warrior, suffered from *l*.
5.27 the *l* of Naaman shall cling to you, and
Lk 5.12 there was a man covered with *l*. When

LEPROUS

Ex 4. 6 when he took it out, his hand was *l*, as
Lev 13. 2 and it turns into a *l* disease on the skin
14. 2 This shall be the ritual for the *l* person
14.34 and I put a *l* disease in a house in the
Num 5. 2 put out of the camp everyone who is *l*,
12.10 Miriam was *l*, as white as snow. And
2 Kings 7. 3 there were four *l* men outside the city
15. 5 LORD struck the king, so that he was *l*
2 Chr 26.19 angry with the priests a *l* disease broke

LETTER (LETTERS)

2 Sam 11.14 David wrote a *l* to Joab, and sent it by
1 Kings 21. 8 she wrote *l* in Ahab's name and sealed
2 Kings 5. 6 He brought the *l* to the king of Israel,
2 Chr 21.12 A *l* came to him from the prophet
30. 1 wrote *l* also to Ephraim and Manasseh,
Ezra 5. 5 and then answer was returned by *l*
Neh 6. 5 sent his servant to me with an open *l*
Isa 37.14 Hezekiah received the *l* from the hand
Jer 29. 1 of the *l* that the prophet Jeremiah
Acts 9. 2 for *l* to the synagogues at Damascus,
15.23 with the following *l*: "The brothers, both
15.30 together, they delivered the *l*.
22. 5 received *l* to the brothers in Damascus,
23.25 the governor." He wrote a *l* to this effect:
23.33 and delivered the *l* to the governor,
2 Cor 3. 1 need, as some do, *l* of recommendation
3. 2 You yourselves are our *l*, written on our
3. 6 of spirit; for the *l* kills, but the Spirit
10. 9 I am trying to frighten you with my *l*.
Gal 6.11 See what large *l* I make when I am
Col 4.16 when this *l* has been read among you,
2 Thess 2. 2 either by spirit or by word or by *l*,
3.14 who do not obey what we say in this *l*;
3.17 This is the mark in every *l* of mine; it
2 Pet 3.16 speaking of this as he does in all his *l*.

LEVI

Gen 29.34 three sons"; therefore he was named *L*.
Ex 2. 1 Now a man from the house of *L* went
Num 1.49 Only the tribe of *L* you shall not enroll,
Deut 10. 8 the LORD set apart the tribe of *L* to carry

LEVIATHAN

Job 41. 1 "Can you draw out *L* with a fishhook, or
Isa 27. 1 strong sword will punish *L* the fleeing

LEVITES

Josh 14. 4 no portion was given to the *L* in the
2 Chr 31. 2 to his service, the priests and the *L*,
34. 9 which the *L*, the keepers of the
35. 3 He said to the *L* who taught all Israel

LIAR (LIARS)

Ps 116. 11 in my consternation, "Everyone is a *l*."
Jn 8.55 not know him, I would be a *l* like you.
Rom 3. 4 Although everyone is a *l*, let God be
1 Jn 5.10 made him a *l* by not believing in the
Rev 21. 8 and all *l*, their place will be in the lake

LIBERTY

Lev 25.10 shall proclaim *l* throughout the land
Ps 119. 45 I shall walk at *l*, for I have sought your
Jer 34. 8 to make a proclamation of *l* to them,
Ezek 46.17 his to the year of *l*; then it shall revert
1 Cor 8. 9 take care that this *l* of yours does not
10.29 why should my *l* be subject to the

LIE (LIES)

Num 23.19 is not a human being, that he should *l*,
Ps 4. 8 I will both *l* down and sleep in peace;
119. 69 The arrogant smear me with *l*, but with
Prov 14. 5 A faithful witness does not *l*, but a false
Isa 28.15 we have made *l* our refuge, and in
59. 3 your lips have spoken *l*, your tongue
Jer 27.10 For they are prophesying a *l* to you,
Jn 8.44 When he *l*, he speaks according to his
Acts 5. 3 has Satan filled your heart to *l* to the
Rom 1.25 exchanged the truth about God for a *l*
Col 3. 9 Do not *l* to one another, seeing that you
Rev 14. 5 in their mouth no *l* was found; they are

LIFE

Gen 1.30 everything that has the breath of *l*, I
2. 9 tree of *l* also in the midst of the garden,

Lev 17.11 For the *l* of the flesh is in the blood;
Deut 30.15 I have set before you today *l* and
30.20 for that means *l* to you and length of
1 Sam 2. 6 The LORD kills and brings to *l*; he brings
25.29 to seek your *l*, the *l* of my lord shall be
2 Sam 15.21 whether for death or for *l*, there also
1 Kings 20.42 your *l* shall be for his *l*, and your people
2 Kings 13.21 the bones of Elisha, he came to *l*,
Job 7. 7 "Remember that my *l* is a breath; my
33. 4 the breath of the Almighty gives me *l*.
33.30 Pit, so that they may see the light of *l*.
Ps 16.11 You show me the path of *l*. In your
34.12 Which of you desires *l*, and covets many
36. 9 For with you is the fountain of *l*; in
63. 3 your steadfast love is better than *l*,
94.21 together against the *l* of the righteous,
Prov 3.22 and they will be *l* for your soul
4.22 they are *l* to those who find them, and
8.35 For whoever finds me finds *l* and
12.28 In the path of righteousness there is *l*,
14.27 The fear of the LORD is a fountain of *l*,
Eccl 2.17 I hated *l*, because what is done under
9. 9 Enjoy *l* with the wife whom you love,
Isa 4. 3 has been recorded for *l* in Jerusalem,
38.17 held back my *l* from the pit of
Jer 8. 3 Death shall be preferred to *l* by all the
21. 8 I am setting before you the way of *l* and
Ezek 3.21 warning; and you will have saved your *l*.
Jon 4. 3 now, O LORD, please take my *l* from me,
Mt 7.14 and the road is hard that leads to *l*,
10.39 those who lose their *l* for my sake will
16.26 gain the whole world and forfeit their *l*?
25.46 but the righteous into eternal *l*."
Mk 8.35 those who want to save their *l* will lose
8.36 gain the whole world and forfeit their *l*?
10.30 and in the age to come eternal *l*.
Lk 9.24 who want to save their *l* will lose it, and
12.22 do not worry about your *l*, what you will
18.18 what must I do to inherit eternal *l*?"
Jn 1. 4 In him was *l*, and the *l* was the light of
3.36 believes in the Son has eternal *l*;
4.14 spring of water gushing up to eternal *l*."
5.24 believes him who sent me has eternal *l*,
6.68 we go? You have the words of eternal *l*.
10.10 I came that they may have *l*, and have
10.15 Father. I lay down my *l* for the sheep.
10.28 I give them eternal *l*, and they will
11.25 "I am the resurrection and the *l*. Those
14. 6 "I am the way and the truth, and the *l*;
17. 3 this is eternal *l*, that they know you, the
20.31 that through believing you may have *l*
Acts 5.20 people the whole message about this *l*."
17.25 he himself gives to all mortals *l* and
Rom 6.13 who have been brought from death to *l*,
6.23 but the free gift of God is eternal *l*
8.10 the Spirit is *l* because of righteousness.
8.38 neither death, nor *l*, nor angels, nor
2 Cor 2.16 to the other a fragrance from *l* to *l*.
3. 6 for the letter kills, but the Spirit gives *l*.
4.10 that the *l* of Jesus may be made visible
4.12 So death is at work in us, but *l* in you.
Gal 1.13 no doubt, of my earlier *l* in Judaism.
2.20 the *l* I now live in the flesh I live by
Eph 2.10 prepared beforehand to be our way of *l*.
Col 3. 3 and your *l* is hidden with Christ in God.
1 Tim 2. 2 lead a quiet and peaceable *l* in all
Heb 7.16 the power of an indestructible *l*.
Jas 4.14 What is your *l*? for you are a mist that
1 Pet 3.10 "Those who desire *l* and desire to see
1 Jn 3.14 we have passed from death to *l* because
3.16 by this, that he laid down his *l* for us
Rev 2. 7 give permission to eat from the tree of *l*
3. 5 not blot your name out of the book of *l*;
11.11 breath of *l* from God entered them, and
12.11 they did not cling to *l* even in the face
13. 8 in the book of *l* of the Lamb that was
20. 4 They came to *l*, and reigned with Christ
Rev 21. 6 a gift from the spring of the water of *l*.
21.27 are written in the Lamb's book of *l*.
22.17 who wishes take the water of *l* as a gift.

LIFT (LIFTED LIFTING)

Ps 24. 7 *L* up your heads, O gates! and be *l* up,
25. 1 To you, O LORD, I *l* up my soul. O my
75. 6 not from the wilderness comes *l* up; but
86. 4 for to you, O LORD, I *l* up my soul.
121. 1 I *l* up my eyes to the hills—from where
131. 1 O LORD, my heart is not *l* up, my eyes
134. 2 *L* up your hands to the holy place, and
Lk 1.52 from their thrones, and *l* up the lowly;
Jn 3.14 so must the Son of man be *l* up, that
8.28 "When you have *l* up the Son of Man,
12.32 And I, when I am *l* up from the earth,

LIGHT (LIGHTS)

Gen 1. 3 said, "Let there be *l*"; and there was *l*.
1.15 let there be *l* in the dome of the sky to
Ex 10.23 but all the Israelites had *l* where they
Lev 24. 2 the lamp, that a *l* may be kept burning
2 Sam 23. 4 is like the *l* of morning, like the sun
Job 24.16 themselves up; they do not know the *l*.
Ps 27. 1 The LORD is my *l* and my salvation;
37. 6 make your vindication shine like the *l*,
43. 3 O send out your *l* and your truth; let
49.19 who will never more see the *l*.
97.11 *L* dawns for the righteous, and joy for
119.105 is a lamp to my feet and a *l* to my path.
119.130 The unfolding of your words gives *l*; it
139. 12 as the day, for darkness is as *l* to you.
Prov 4.18 of the righteous is like the *l* of dawn,
13. 9 The *l* of the righteous rejoices, but the
Eccl 11. 7 *L* is sweet, and it is pleasant for the
Isa 2. 5 come, let us walk in the *l* of the LORD!
5.20 put darkness for *l* and *l* for darkness,
42. 6 to the people, a *l* to the nations,
45. 7 I form *l* and create darkness, I make
49. 6 I will give you as a *l* to the nations, that
58. 8 Then your *l* shall break forth like the
60. 1 Arise, shine; for your *l* has come, and
60. 3 Nations shall come to your *l*, and kings
Mic 7. 8 in darkness, the LORD will be a *l* to me.
Mt 4.16 who sat in darkness have seen a great *l*,
5.16 let your *l* shine before others, so that
Lk 1.79 *l* to those who sit in darkness and in
2.32 a *l* for revelation to the Gentiles and for
12. 3 said in the dark will be heard in the *l*,
Jn 1. 5 The *l* shines in the darkness, and the
3.19 that the *l* has come into the world,
8.12 "I am the *l* of the world. Whoever
9. 5 in the world, I am the *l* of the world."
12.35 believe in the *l*, so that you may
Acts 9. 3 suddenly a *l* from heaven flashed
13.47 have set you to be a *l* for the Gentiles,
22. 6 a great *l* from heaven suddenly shone
26.13 your Excellency, I saw a *l* from heaven,
26.18 that they may turn from darkness to *l*
Rom 13.12 of darkness and put on the armor of *l*;
1 Cor 4. 5 comes, who will bring to *l* the things
2 Cor 4. 4 to keep them from seeing the *l* of the
4. 6 "Let *l* shine out of darkness," who has
6.14 is there between *l* and darkness?
Eph 5. 8 darkness, but now in the Lord you are *l*.
5.14 for everything that becomes visible is *l*.
Jas 1.17 coming down from the father of *l*, with
1 Pet 2. 9 out of darkness into his marvelous *l*.
1 Jn 1. 5 that God is *l* and in him there is no
1. 7 but if we walk in the *l*, as he himself is
2. 8 away and the true *l* is already shining.
Rev 22. 5 they need no *l* of lamp or sun, for the

LIGHTNING (LIGHTNINGS)

Ps 18.14 and scattered them; he flashed forth *l*,
Mt 24.27 as the *l* comes from the east and flashes
Lk 17.24 as the *l* flashes and lights up the sky

Rev 8. 5 of thunder, rumblings, flashes of *l*, and

LIKENESS

Gen 5. 1 he made them in the *l* of God.
Isa 40.18 liken God, or what *l* compare with him?
Rom 8. 3 his own Son in the *l* of sinful flesh,
Phil 2. 7 form of a slave, being born in human *l*.

LILY (LILIES)

Song 2. 2 As a *l* among brambles, so is my love
Mt 6.28 Consider the *l* of the field, how they
Lk 12.27 Consider the *l*, how they grow; they

LINEN

Mk 15.46 the body, wrapped it in the *l* cloth,
Rev 19. 8 with fine *l*, bright and pure" —for the

LION (LIONS LION'S)

1 Sam 17.34 whenever a *l* or a bear came, and took a
2 Sam 23.20 went down and killed a *l* in a pit on a
1 Kings 13.24 he went away, a *l* met him on the road
1 Chr 11.22 killed a *l* in a pit on a day when snow
Ps 7. 2 or like a *l* they will tear me apart; they
22.21 dog! Save me from the mouth of the *l*!
104. 21 The young *l* roar for their prey, seeking
Prov 26.13 The lazy person says, "There is a *l* in
Jer 12. 8 has become to me like a *l* in the forest;
Dan 6.16 brought and thrown into the den of *l*.
7. 4 first was like a *l* and had eagle's wings.
Hos 5.14 I will be like a *l* to Ephraim, and like a
Am 5.19 not light; as if someone fled from a *l*,
2 Tim 4.17 it. So I was rescued from the *l* mouth.
Heb 11.33 shut the mouths of *l*, quenched the
1 Pet 5. 8 Like a roaring *l* your adversary the devil
Rev 5. 5 the *L* of the tribe of Judah, the Root of

LIPS

Ps 12. 4 will prevail; our *l* are our own—who is
34.13 evil, and your *l* from speaking deceit.
Prov 12.19 Truthful *l* endure forever, but a lying
16.13 Righteous *l* are the delight of a king,
20.15 but the *l* informed by knowledge are a
Song 4. 3 Your *l* are like a crimson thread, and
Isa 29.13 honor me with their *l*, while their hearts
Mt 15. 8 This people honors me with their *l*, but
Mk 7. 6 'This people honors me with their *l*, but
Rom 3.13 "The venom of vipers is under their *l*."
10. 8 "The word is near you, on your *l* and in

LISTED

Judg 8.14 questioned him; and he *l* for him the

LISTEN (LISTENED LISTENING LISTENS)

Ex 23.21 Be attentive to him and *l* to his voice;
Josh 5. 6 not having *l* to the voice of the LORD. To
Judg 13. 9 God *l* to Manoah, and the angel of God
1 Sam 8.19 the people refused to *l* to the voice of
2 Kings 21. 9 But they did not *l*, Manasseh misled
Job 36.11 If they *l*, and serve him, they complete
Prov 12.15 way is right, but the wise *l* to advice.
23.22 *L* to your father who begot you, and do
Eccl 5. 1 to draw near to *l* is better than the
Isa 6. 9 'Keep *l*, but do not comprehend; keep
51. 1 *L* to me, you that pursue righteousness,
Jer 12.17 But if any nation will not *l*, then I will
17.24 But if you *l* to me, says the LORD, and
18.10 not *l* to my voice, then I will change my
26. 3 It may be that they will *l*, all of them,
Dan 9.19 forgive; O Lord, *l* and act and do not
Mal 3.16 The LORD took note and *l*, and a book of
Mk 9. 7 "This is my Son, the Beloved; *l* to him!"
Lk 9.35 "This is my Son, my Chosen; *l* to him!"
10.16 "Whoever *l* to you *l* to me, and whoever
Jn 10.16 them also, and they will *l* to my voice.
Acts 28.26 You will indeed *l*, but never understand,
Jas 1.19 let everyone be quick to *l*, slow to

LITTLE

Ps 37.16 Better is a *l* that the righteous one has
Prov 13.11 but those who gather *l* by *l* will increase
Isa 28.10 line, line upon line, here a *l*, there a *l*."
Mic 5. 2 who are one of the *l* clans of Judah,
Mt 6.30 much more clothe you—you of *l* faith?
8.26 "Why are you afraid, you of *l* faith?"
10.42 cold water to one of these *l* ones in the
14.31 him, "You of *l* faith, why did you doubt?"
16. 8 "You of *l* faith, why are you talking
18. 6 stumbling block before one of these *l*
Lk 7.47 the one to whom *l* is forgiven, loves *l*."
17. 2 to cause one of these *l* ones to stumble.
2 Cor 8.15 the one who had *l* did not have too *l*."

LIVE (v)

Gen 13. 6 so great that they could not *l* together,
Ex 1.17 them, but they let the boys *l*.
9.16 this is why I have let you *l*: to show you
33.20 face; for no one shall not see me and *l*."
Lev 18. 5 by doing so one shall *l*: I am the LORD.
Num 21. 9 look at the serpent of bronze and *l*.
Deut 4. 1 that you may *l* to enter and occupy the
5.24 to someone and the person may still *l*.
5.33 that you may *l*, and that it may go well
8. 1 that you may *l* and increase, and go in
8. 3 one does not *l* by bread alone, but by
16.20 that you may *l* and occupy the land that
30.20 that you may *l* in the land that the LORD
Josh 15.63 the Jebusites *l* with the people of Judah
1 Sam 10.24 all the people shouted, "Long *l* the king!"
1 Kings 1.34 and say, 'Long *l* King Solomon!'
Job 14.14 If mortals die, will they *l* again? All the
Ps 27. 4 to *l* in the house of the LORD all the
84. 4 Happy are those who *l* in your house,
91. 1 You who *l* in the shelter of the Most
107. 36 there he lets the hungry *l*, and they
119. 17 so that I may *l* and observe your word.
119.144 give me understanding that I may *l*.
133. 1 it is when kindred *l* together in unity!
146. 2 I will praise the LORD as long as I *l*; I
Prov 4. 4 words; keep my commandments, and *l*;
9. 6 Lay aside immaturity, and *l*, and walk
21. 9 It is better to *l* in a corner of the
Isa 26.19 Your dead shall *l*, their corpses shall
33.14 among us can *l* with the devouring fire?
55. 3 come to me; listen, so that you may *l*;
Jer 27.12 and serve him and his people, and *l*.
Ezek 16. 6 you lay in your blood, I said to you, "*L*,
18. 9 a one is righteous, he shall surely *l*,
18.22 that they have done they shall *l*.
20.11 by whose observance everyone shall *l*.
33.19 is lawful and right, they shall *l* by it.
37. 3 said to me, "Mortal, can these bones *l*?"
Hos 6. 2 raise us up, that we may *l* before him.
12. 9 I will make you *l* in tents again, as in
14. 7 They shall again *l* beneath my shadow,
Am 5.14 Seek good and not evil, that you may *l*;
Mt 4. 4 "One does not *l* by bread alone, but by
9.18 lay your hand on her, and she will *l*."
Mk 7. 5 disciples not *l* according to the tradition
12.44 everything she had, all she had to *l* on."
Lk 4. 4 'One does not *l* by bread alone.'
10.28 the right answer; do this, and you will *l*."
Jn 6.58 But the one who eats this bread will *l*
14.19 will see me; because I *l*, you also will *l*.
Acts 17.28 For 'In him we *l* and move and have
Rom 8.13 if you *l* according to the flesh, you will
10. 5 who does these things will *l* by them."
13.13 let us *l* honorably as in the day, not in
14. 7 We do not *l* to ourselves, and we do not
Gal 3.11 one who is righteous will *l* by faith."
5.16 *L* by the Spirit, I say, and do not gratify
5.25 If we *l* by the Spirit, let us also be
Eph 4.17 no longer *l* as the Gentiles *l*, in the
5. 2 *l* in love, as Christ loved us and gave
5. 8 you are light. *L* as children of light—

Col 2. 6 continue to *l* your lives in him, rooted
2 Tim 2.11 died with him, we will also *l* with him;
Titus 2.12 to *l* lives that are self-controlled,

LIVES (LIVED LIVING) (v)
Gen 14.12 took Lot . . . who *l* in Sodom, and his
19.30 in Zoar; so he *l* in a cave with his two
2 Sam 7. 2 I am *l* in a house of cedar, but the ark
Job 19.25 I know that my Redeemer *l*, and at the
Lk 1. 6 righteous before God, *l* blamelessly
Jn 1.14 Word became flesh and *l* among us, and
Acts 9.31 *L* in the fear of the Lord and in the
Eph 2. 2 trespasses and sins in which you once *l*,
Phil 1.21 For to me, *l* is Christ and dying is
1 Pet 4. 3 Gentiles like to do, *l* in licentiousness,
1 Jn 4.12 if we love one another, God *l* in us, and

LIVES (n)
Prov 11.30 a tree of life, but violence takes *l* away.
Jer 51. 6 of Babylon, save your *l*, each of you!
Ezek 13.18 you hunt down *l* among my people, and
Acts 15.26 who have risked their *l* for the sake of
Heb 13. 5 Keep your *l* free from love of money,
2 Pet 3.11 in leading *l* of holiness and godliness,

LIVING (n and adj)
Gen 2. 7 of life; and the man became a *l* being.
Num 16.48 He stood between the dead and the *l*;
Josh 3.10 among you is the *l* God who without
1 Sam 17.36 he has defied the armies of the *l* God."
2 Kings 19. 4 of Assyria has sent to mock the *l* God,
Ps 42. 2 My soul thirsts for God, for the *l* God.
66. 9 who has kept us among the *l*, and has
69.28 be blotted out of the book of the *l*;
Eccl 4. 2 already died, more fortunate than the *l*
9. 5 the *l* know that they will die, but the
Isa 8.19 their gods, the dead on behalf of the *l*,
38.19 The *l*, the *l*, they thank you, as I do this
Jer 10.10 is the *l* God and the everlasting King.
Zech 14. 8 that day *l* waters shall flow out of
Mt 22.32 He is God not of the dead, but of the *l*."
Mk 12.27 He is God not of the dead, but of the *l*;
Lk 15.13 squandered his property in dissolute *l*.
24. 5 do you look for the *l* among the dead?
Jn 4.10 and he would have given you *l* water."
6.51 I am the *l* bread that came down from
6.57 the *l* Father sent me, and I live because
1 Cor 15.45 "The first man, Adam, became a *l* being";
1 Thess 1. 9 from idols, to serve a *l* and true God,
1 Tim 4.10 we have our hope set on the *l* God, who
Heb 3.12 heart that turns away from the *l* God.
Rev 1.18 and the *l* one. I was dead, and see, I am

LIZARD
Lev 11.29 . . . the great *l* according to its kind,
Prov 30.28 the *l* can be grasped in the hand, yet it

LOAN (LOANS)
Deut 23.19 shall not charge interest on *l* to another
24.10 When you make your neighbor a *l* of

LOATHE (LOATHED)
Job 10. 1 "I *l* my life; I will give free utterance to
Ps 95.10 For forty years I *l* that generation and
139. 21 I not *l* those who rise up against you?
Ezek 36.31 you shall *l* yourselves for your iniquities

LOAVES
Mt 14.17 nothing here but five *l* and two fish."
15.34 "How many *l* have you?" They said,
Mk 6.38 "How many *l* have you? Go and see."
8. 5 asked them, "How many *l* do you have?"
Lk 9.13 "We have no more than five *l* and two
11. 5 'Friend, lend me three *l* of bread; for a
Jn 6. 9 here who has five barley *l* and two fish.
6.26 but because you ate your fill of the *l*.

LOCK
Mt 23.13 For you *l* people out of the kingdom of

LOCUST (LOCUSTS)
Ex 10. 4 tomorrow I will bring *l* into your
Lev 11.22 of them you may eat: the *l* according to
Judg 6. 5 even bring their tents, as thick as *l*;
Ps 105. 34 He spoke, and the *l* came, and young *l*
Prov 30.27 the *l* have no king, yet all of them
Joel 1. 4 What the cutting *l* left, the swarming *l*
Am 7. 1 he was forming *l* at the time the latter
Mt 3. 4 and his food was *l* and wild honey.
Mk 1. 6 his waist, and he ate *l* and wild honey.
Rev 9. 3 from the smoke came *l* on the earth,

LODGE (LODGED)
Ruth 1.16 you go, I will go; Where you *l*, I will *l*;
1 Sam 7. 2 day that the ark was *l* at Kiriath-jearim,

LOFTY
Job 22.12 See the highest stars, how *l* they are!
Isa 57.15 high and *l* one who inhabits eternity,
1 Cor 2. 1 the mystery of God to you in *l* words or

LONELY
Ps 25.16 gracious to me, for I am *l* and afflicted.

LONG (LONGED LONGING LONGS)
Job 3.21 to the bitter in soul, who *l* for death,
Ps 42. 1 As a deer *l* for flowing streams, so my
84. 2 My soul *l*, indeed it faints for the courts
119. 20 is consumed with *l* for your ordinances
119. 40 I have *l* for your precepts; in your
Mt 13.17 righteous people *l* to see what you see,
Lk 17.22 days are coming when you will *l* to see
Rom 8.19 creation waits with eager *l* for the
Rev 18.14 "The fruit for which your soul *l* has

LOOK (LOOKED LOOKING LOOKS)
Gen 13.14 eyes now, and *l* from the place where
15. 5 "*L* toward heaven, and count the stars,
19.17 "Flee for your life; do not *l* back or stop
19.26 But Lot's wife . . . *l* back, and she
22.13 Abraham *l* up and saw a ram, caught in
Num 21. 9 person would *l* at the serpent of bronze
Deut 26.15 *L* down from your holy habitation, from
1 Sam 16. 7 "Do not *l* on his appearance or on the
2 Sam 22.42 They *l*, but there was no one to save
Job 36.25 All people have *l* on it; everyone
Ps 8. 3 When I *l* at your heavens, the work of
33.13 The LORD *l* down from heaven, he sees
84. 9 O God; *l* on the face of your anointed.
102. 19 from heaven the LORD *l* at the earth,
104. 27 These all *l* to you, to give them their
119.153 *L* on my misery and rescue me, for I do
Isa 22.11 But you did not *l* to him who did it, or
33.20 *L* on Zion, the city of our appointed
42.18 and you that are blind, *l* up and see!
51. 1 *L* to the rock from which you were
51. 6 the heavens, and *l* at the earth beneath;
63. 5 I *l*, but there was no helper; I stared,
Mic 7. 7 But as for me, I will *l* to the LORD, I will
Hab 1.13 evil, and you cannot *l* on wrongdoing;
Hag 1. 9 You have *l* for much, and, lo, it came to
Mt 5.28 who *l* at a woman with lust had already
6.16 whenever you fast, do not *l* dismal, like
13.14 you will indeed *l*, but never perceive.
23.28 on the outside *l* righteous to others,
Mk 4.12 'they may indeed *l*, but not perceive,
Lk 1.48 for he has *l* with favor on the lowliness
2.25 *l* forward to consolation of Israel,
9.38 "Teacher, I beg you to *l* at my son; he is
13. 7 I have come *l* for fruit on this fig tree,
24. 5 "Why do you *l* for the living among the
Jn 6.26 you are *l* for me, not because you saw
18. 4 and asked them, "Whom are you *l* for?"
20.15 are you weeping? Whom are you *l* for?"
Acts 1.11 why do you stand *l* up toward heaven?

Acts 28.26 you will indeed *l* but never perceive.
2 Cor 10. 7 *L* at what is before your eyes. If you are
Heb 11.10 he *l* forward to the city that has
12. 2 *l* to Jesus the pioneer and perfector of
Jas 1.25 those who *l* into the perfect law, the

LOOSE (LOOSED LOOSES)

Job 12.21 on princes, and *l* the belt of the strong.
Ps 78.49 He let *l* on them his fierce anger, wrath,
116. 16 You have *l* my bonds. I will offer to you
Prov 5. 3 For the lips of a *l* woman drip honey,
Isa 58. 6 I choose: to *l* the bonds of injustice,
Mt 16.19 whatever you *l* on earth will be *l* in
18.18 whatever you *l* on earth will be *l* in

LORD

Gen 2. 4 day that the *L* God made the earth and
6. 8 Noah found favor in the sight of the *L*.
12. 1 Now the *L* said to Abram, "Go from
Ex 6. 3 by my name 'The *L*' I did not make
12.51 very day the *L* brought the Israelites
15. 1 the Israelites sang this song to the *L*:
Deut 34.10 Moses, whom the *L* knew face to face.
1 Kings 1.31 said, "May my *l* King David live forever!"
Ps 1. 2 but their delight is in the law of the *L*,
83.18 that you alone, whose name is the *L*,
84. 1 is your dwelling place, O *L* of hosts!
Isa 53. 6 and the *L* has laid on him the iniquity
Mt 12. 8 For the Son of Man is *l* of the sabbath."
Mk 1. 3 Prepare the way of the *L*, make his
Jn 14. 5 "*L*, we do not know where you are
20.28 answered him, "My *L* and my God!"
Acts 2.36 God has made him both *L* and Messiah,
1 Cor 12. 3 no one can say "Jesus is *L*" except by
Phil 2.11 should confess that Jesus Christ is *L*,
Heb 1.10 beginning, *L*, you founded the earth,
Rev 19. 6 "Hallelujah! for the *L* our God the

LORD JESUS

Acts 15.11 be saved through the grace of the *L*,
16.31 "Believe on the *L*, and you will be

LORD JESUS CHRIST

Acts 11.17 he gave us when we believed in the *L*,
Rom 5. 1 we have peace with God through our *L*.
1 Cor 15.57 who gives us the victory through our *L*.
2 Cor 8. 9 you know the generous act of our *L*,
2 Pet 1.16 to you the power and coming of our *L*,

LORD OF HOSTS

Ps 46. 7 The *L* is with us; the God of Jacob is
Isa 8.13 the *L*, him you shall regard as holy; let

LORDS

1 Cor 8. 5 fact there are many gods and many *l*—

LOSE (LOSES LOST)

Ps 119.176 I have gone astray like a *l* sheep; seek
Eccl 5.14 riches were *l* in a bad venture; though
Isa 6. 5 "Woe is me! I am *l*, for I am a man of
Ezek 37.11 bones are dried up, and our hope is *l*;
Mt 10. 6 go rather to the *l* sheep of the house of
10.39 Those who find their life will *l* it, and
15.24 was sent only to the *l* sheep of the
16.25 who want to save their life will *l* it,
18.14 that one of these little ones should be *l*.
Mk 8.35 it, and those who *l* their life for my sake
Lk 9.24 those who *l* their life for my sake will
15. 8 if she *l* one of them, does not light a
15.24 is alive again; he was *l*, and is found!'
17.33 it, but those who *l* their life will keep it.
Jn 6.39 should *l* nothing of all that he has given
18. 9 "I did not *l* a single one of those whom

LOST (n)

Ezek 34.16 I will seek the *l*, and I will bring back
Mt 18.11n For the Son of Man came to save the *l*.
Lk 19.10 Man came to seek out and to save the *l*."

LOT

Accompanied Abram to Canaan, Gen 11.31—12.5; separated from Abram to live at Sodom, Gen 13; rescued by Abram, Gen 14.1-16; sheltered angels, Gen 19.1-11; fled to Zoar, Gen 19.15-23; Lot and his daughters, Gen 19.30-38.

Gen 12. 4 and *L* went with him. Abram was
14.16 brought back his nephew *L* with his
19. 1 *L* was sitting in the gateway of Sodom.
Lk 17.28 just as it was in the days of *L*: they
2 Pet 2. 7 if he rescued *L*, a righteous man greatly

LOT (LOTS)

Lev 16. 8 Aaron shall cast *l* on the two goats, one
1 Sam 14.42 Then Saul said, "Cast the *l* between me
Ps 22.18 and for my clothing they cast *l*.
Prov 1.14 Throw in your *l* among us; we will all
16.33 The *l* is cast into the lap, but the
Eccl 3.22 enjoy their work, for that is their *l*;
Ob 11 his gates and cast *l* for Jerusalem,
Jon 1. 7 they cast lots, and the *l* fell on Jonah.
Mt 27.35 clothes among themselves by casting *l*;
Lk 1. 9 he was chosen by *l*, according to the
Jn 19.24 "Let us not tear it, but cast *l* for it to
Acts 1.26 and the *l* fell on Matthias; and he was

LOVE (n)

1 Sam 20.14 show me the faithful *l* of the LORD;
2 Sam 7.15 I will not take my steadfast *l* from him,
Prov 7.18 let us take our fill of *l* until morning;
10.12 stirs up strife, but *l* covers all offenses.
15.17 is a dinner of vegetables where *l* is
27. 5 Better is open rebuke than hidden *l*.
Song 1. 2 For your *l* is better than wine, your
1.15 you are beautiful, my *l*; ah, you are
4. 1 How beautiful you are, my *l*, how very
4.10 How much better is your *l* than wine,
5. 1 Eat, friends, drink, and be drunk with *l*.
8. 6 for *l* is strong as death, passion fierce as
8. 7 Many waters cannot quench *l*, neither
Isa 63. 9 in his *l* and in his pity he redeemed
Ezek 33.32 To them you are like a singer of *l* songs,
Hos 6. 4 Your *l* is like a morning cloud, like the
11. 4 of human kindness, with bands of *l*.
Mt 24.12 the *l* of many will grow cold.
Lk 11.42 and neglect justice and the *l* of God;
Jn 15.13 No one has greater *l* than this, to lay
17.26 so that the *l* with which you have loved
Rom 5. 5 God's *l* has been poured into our hearts
5. 8 But God proves his *l* for us in that while
8.39 be able to separate us from the *l* of God
12. 9 Let *l* be genuine; hate what is evil, hold
1 Cor 8. 1 Knowledge puffs up, but *l* builds up.
13. 1 but do not have *l*, I am a noisy gong or
13.13 three; and the greatest of these is *l*.
2 Cor 5.14 the *l* of Christ urges us on, because we
6. 6 kindness, holiness of spirit, genuine *l*,
8. 8 I am testing the genuineness of your *l*
8.24 show them the proof of your *l* and of
13.13 Christ, the *l* of God, and the
Gal 5. 6 that counts is faith working through *l*.
5.13 through *l* become slaves to one another.
Eph 1.15 your *l* toward all the saints, and for this
3.19 *l* of Christ that surpasses knowledge,
4.15 speaking the truth in *l*, we must grow
5. 2 live in *l*, as Christ loved us and gave
Phil 1. 9 is my prayer, that your *l* may overflow
1.16 These proclaim Christ out of *l*, knowing
Col 1. 4 Jesus and of the *l* that you have for all
3.14 Above all, clothe yourselves with *l*,
1 Thess 1. 3 your work of faith and labor of *l* and
4. 9 concerning *l* of the brothers and sisters,
2 Tim 4.10 Demas, in *l* with this present world, has
Heb 13. 1 Let mutual *l* continue. Do not neglect
1 Pet 4. 8 another, for *l* covers a multitude of sins.
1 Jn 3. 1 See what *l* the Father has given us, that
3.16 We know *l* by this, that he laid down

Jude 12 These are blemishes on your *l*-feasts,
Rev 2. 4 that you have abandoned the *l* you had

LOVE (v)

Ex 20. 6 generation of those who *l* me and keep
21. 5 "I *l* my master, my wife, and my
Lev 19.18 you shall *l* your neighbor as yourself: I
Deut 5.10 generation of those who *l* me
6. 5 You shall *l* the LORD your God with all
7.13 he will *l* you, bless you, and multiply
10.12 to *l* him, to serve the LORD your God
10.19 You shall also *l* the stranger, for you
13. 3 to know whether you indeed *l* the LORD
30. 6 so that you will *l* the LORD your God
Josh 23.11 very careful . . . to *l* the LORD your God.
2 Chr 19. 2 wicked and *l* those who hate the LORD?
Neh 1. 5 *l* with those who *l* him and keep his
Ps 18. 1 I *l* you, O LORD, my strength. The LORD
31.23 *L* the LORD, all you his saints. The LORD
45. 7 you *l* righteousness and hate
60. 5 that those whom you *l* may be rescued.
70. 4 Let those who *l* your salvation say
91.14 Those who *l* me, I will deliver; I will
116. 1 I *l* the LORD, because he has heard my
119. 97 Oh, how I *l* your law! It is my
Prov 4. 6 keep you; *l* her, and she will guard you.
8.17 I *l* those who *l* me, and those who seek
20.13 Do not *l* sleep, or else you will come to
22.11 who *l* a pure heart and are gracious
Eccl 3. 8 time to *l*, and a time to hate; a time for
9. 9 life with the wife whom you *l*, all the
Isa 61. 8 For I the LORD *l* justice, I hate robbery
Hos 3. 1 *l* a woman who has a lover and is an
9.15 I will *l* them no more; all their officials
14. 4 I will *l* them freely, for my anger has
Am 5.15 Hate evil and *l* good, and establish
Mic 3. 2 you who hate the good and *l* the evil,
6. 8 do justice, to *l* kindness, and to walk
Mt 5.43 'You shall *l* your neighbor and hate
19.19 You shall *l* your neighbor as yourself."
22.37 "You shall *l* the Lord your God with all
23. 6 They *l* to have the place of honor at
Mk 12.30 you shall *l* the Lord your God with all
Lk 6.27 *L* your enemies, do good to those who
6.32 "If you *l* those who *l* you, what credit is
10.27 "You shall *l* the Lord your God with all
16.13 will either hate the one and *l* the other,
Jn 8.42 God were your Father, you would *l* me,
11. 3 to Jesus, "Lord, he whom you *l* is ill."
12.25 Those who *l* their life will lose it, and
13.34 commandment, that you *l* one another.
14.15 "If you *l* me, you will keep my
14.21 and keep them are those who *l* me;
15.12 that you *l* one another as I have *l* you.
21.15 "Yes, Lord; you know that I *l* you." Jesus
Rom 8.28 together for good for those who *l* God,
13. 8 one anything, except to *l* one another;
1 Cor 2. 9 God has prepared for those who *l* him"
2 Cor 12.15 If I *l* you more, am I to be *l* less? Let it
Eph 5.25 Husbands, *l* your wives, just as Christ
Col 3.19 Husbands, *l* your wives, and never treat
Titus 2. 4 the young women to *l* their husbands,
Jas 2. 5 he has promised to those who *l* him?
1 Pet 1. 8 you have not seen him, you *l* him;
2.17 everyone. *L* the family of believers.
1 Jn 2.15 Do not *l* the world or the things in the
3.11 that we should *l* one another.
4. 7 let us *l* one another, because *l* is from
4.19 We *l*, because he first loved us.
5. 2 we *l* God and obey his commandments.
Rev 3.19 I reprove and discipline those whom I *l*.

LOVES (LOVED)

Gen 24.67 she became his wife; and he *l* her. So
25.28 Isaac *l* Esau . . . , but Rebekah *l* Jacob.
37. 3 Now Israel *l* Joseph more than any
44.20 mother's children, and his father *l* him.'
Deut 4.37 because he *l* your ancestors, he chose
15.16 because he *l* you and your household,
23. 5 you, because the LORD your God *l* you.)
1 Sam 1. 5 gave a double portion, because he *l* her,
16.21 Saul *l* him greatly, and he became his
18. 1 and Jonathan *l* him as his own soul.
18.16 all Israel and Judah *l* David; for it was
18.28 and that Saul's daughter Michal *l* him,
20.17 him, for he *l* him as he *l* his own life.
1 Kings 3. 3 Solomon *l* the LORD, walking in the
10. 9 Because the LORD *l* Israel forever, he has
11. 1 Solomon *l* many foreign women along
2 Chr 2.11 "Because the LORD *l* his people he has
Ps 78.68 tribe of Judah, Mount Zion, which he *l*.
97.10 The LORD *l* those who hate evil; he
Prov 3.12 for the LORD reproves the one he *l*, as a
12. 1 Whoever *l* discipline *l* knowledge, but
15. 9 he *l* the one who pursues righteousness.
17.17 A friend *l* at all times, and kinsfolk are
17.19 One who *l* transgression *l* strife; one
21.17 Whoever *l* pleasure will suffer want;
Song 3. 1 at night I sought him whom my soul *l*;
Isa 48.14 LORD *l* him; he shall perform his
Jer 31. 3 I have *l* you with an everlasting love;
Hos 11. 1 When Israel was a child, I *l* him, and
Mal 1. 2 I have *l* you, says the LORD. But you say,
Mt 10.37 Whoever *l* father or mother more than
Mk 10.21 Jesus, looking at him, *l* him and said,
Lk 7. 5 he *l* our people, and it is he who built
7.47 forgiven, hence she has shown great *l*.
Jn 3.16 "For God so *l* the world that he gave his
5.20 The Father *l* the Son and shows him all
10.17 For this reason the Father *l* me,
11.36 So the Jews said, "See how he *l* him!"
12.43 for they *l* human glory more than the
13. 1 were in the world, he *l* them to the end.
15. 9 As the Father has *l* me, so I have *l* you;
16.27 for the Father himself *l* you, because
17.23 that you have sent me and have *l* them
19.26 and the disciple whom he *l* standing
Rom 9.13 "I have *l* Jacob, but I have hated Esau."
1 Cor 8. 3 but anyone who *l* God is known by him.
2 Cor 9. 7 compulsion, for God *l* a cheerful giver.
Gal 2.20 in the Son of God, who *l* me and gave
Eph 2. 4 out of the great love with which he *l* us
Heb 1. 9 You have *l* righteousness and hated
1 Jn 2.10 whoever *l* a brother or sister lives in the
Rev 1. 5 To him who *l* us and freed us from our

LOVELY

Ps 84. 1 How *l* is your dwelling place, O LORD of

LOVER (LOVERS)

Eccl 5.10 the *l* of money will not be satisfied with
Jer 4.30 Your *l* despise you; they seek your life.
22.22 and your *l* shall go into captivity;
30.14 All your *l* have forgotten you; they care
Ezek 16.33 but you gave your gifts to all your *l*,
23.22 I will rouse against you your *l* from
Hos 8. 9 alone; Ephraim has bargained for *l*.
2 Tim 3. 2 people will be *l* of themselves, *l* of

LOVE-SONG

Isa 5. 1 beloved my *l* concerning his vineyard:

LOW (LOWEST)

Isa 2.11 eyes of people will be brought *l*,
10.33 down, and the lofty will be brought *l*.
26. 5 city he lays *l*. He lays it *l* to the ground,
Lk 14. 9 you would start to take the *l* place.

LOWLY

Prov 16.19 It is better to be of a *l* spirit among the
29.23 one who is *l* in spirit will obtain honor.
Zeph 3.12 the midst of you a people humble and *l*.

LOYAL (LOYALLY)

Deut 18.13 You must remain completely *l* to the

2 Sam 22.26 "With the *l* you show yourself *l*; with the
1 Chr 19. 2 "I will deal *l* with Hanun son of Nahash,
Ps 18.25 With the *l* you show yourself *l*; with the

LOYALTY

Ruth 3.10 this last instance of your *l* is better than
2 Sam 2. 5 because you showed this *l* to Saul your
Prov 19.22 What is desirable in a person is *l*, and it

LUKE

Col 4.14 *L*, the beloved physician, and Demas
2 Tim 4.11 Only *L* is with me. Get Mark and bring
Philem 24 Demas, and *L*, my fellow workers.

LUKEWARM

Rev 3.16 because you are *l*, and neither cold nor

LUMP

Isa 38.21 had said, "Let them take a *l* of figs,

LURE

Mk 4.19 cares of the world, and the *l* of wealth,

LUST

Mt 5.28 everyone who looks at a woman with *l*

LYING

Ps 31.18 Let the *l* lips be stilled that speak
109. 2 me, speaking against me with *l* tongues.
Prov 6.17 haughty eyes, a *l* tongue, and hands

LYRE

Gen 4.21 ancestor of all those who play the *l* and
Ps 33. 2 Praise the LORD with the *l*, make the

LYSTRA

Acts 14. 6 of it and fled to *L* and Derbe, cities
14.21 they returned to *L*, then on to Iconium
16. 1 Paul went on also to Derbe and to *L*,
2 Tim 3.11 and *L*. What persecutions I endured!

M

MACEDONIA

Acts 16. 9 stood a man of *M* pleading with him
18. 5 Silas and Timothy arrived from *M*, Paul
19.22 his helpers, Timothy and Erastus, to *M*,
Rom 15.26 *M* and Achaia have been pleased to
2 Cor 9. 2 boasting about you to the people of *M*,
Phil 4.15 when I left *M*, no church shared with
1 Thess 1. 8 sounded forth from you not only in *M*

MAD

Deut 28.34 driven *m* by the sight that your eyes
1 Sam 21.13 he pretended to be *m* in their presence.

MADE

Eph 2.10 For we are what he has *m* us, created in

MADNESS

Eccl 2.12 to consider wisdom and *m* and folly;

MAGGOT (MAGGOTS)

Job 25. 6 much less mortal, who is a *m*, and a
Hos 5.12 Therefore I am like *m* to Ephraim, and

MAGNIFICENT

1 Chr 22. 5 for the LORD must be exceedingly *m*,

MAGNIFY (MAGNIFIED MAGNIFIES)

2 Sam 7.26 your name will be *m* forever in the
1 Chr 17.24 name will be established and *m* forever
Ps 34. 3 O *m* the LORD with me, and let us exalt
Isa 10.15 or the saw *m* itself against the one who
42.21 *m* his teaching and make it glorious.
Lk 1.47 "My soul *m* the Lord, and my spirit

MAGOG

Ezek 38. 2 your face toward Gog, of the land of *M*,
Rev 20. 8 Gog and *M*, in order to gather them for

MAID

Prov 30.23 and a *m* when she succeeds her

MAIDEN (MAIDENS)

Song 1. 3 poured out; therefore the *m* love you.
Am 5. 2 Fallen, no more to rise, is *m* Israel;

MAINTAIN

Job 16.21 he would *m* the right of a mortal with

MAINTENANCE

1 Chr 26.27 dedicated gifts for the *m* of the house of

MAJESTIC

Ps 8. 1 Sovereign, how *m* is your name in all
8. 9 Sovereign, how *m* is your name in all

MAJESTY

Job 13.11 Will not his *m* terrify you, and the dread
40.10 "Deck yourself with *m* and dignity;
Isa 33.21 there the LORD in *m* will be for us a
Lam 1. 6 daughter Zion has departed all her *m*.
Dan 4.30 mighty power and for my glorious *m*?"
4.36 and my *m* and splendor were restored to
Mic 5. 4 LORD, in the *m* of the name of the LORD
Acts 19.27 she will be deprived of her *m* that

MAKER

Gen 14.19 God Most High, *m* of heaven and earth;
Job 35.10 no one says, 'Where is God my *M*, who
Ps 95. 6 let us kneel before the LORD, our *M*!
Isa 17. 7 On that day people will regard their *M*,
45. 9 "Woe to you who strive with your *M*,
54. 5 For your *M* is your husband, the LORD of

MALACHI

Mal 1. 1 The word of the LORD to Israel by *M*.

MALE

Gen 1.27 them; *m* and female he created them.
17.10 Every *m* among you shall be
Gal 3.28 there is no longer *m* nor female; for all

MALTA

Acts 28. 1 learned that the island was called *M*.

MAN (MEN)

Gen 2. 7 God formed *m* from the dust of the
2.19 the *m* called every living creature,
3. 8 the *m* and his wife hid themselves from
1 Sam 4. 9 Take courage, and be *m*, O Philistines,
2 Sam 12. 7 Nathan said to David, "You are the *m*!
Rom 5.12 sin came into the world through one *m*,
1 Cor 11. 8 *m* was not made from woman, but

MAN OF GOD

Judg 13. 6 told her husband, "A *m* came to me,
1 Sam 2.27 A *m* came to Eli and said to him, "Thus
9. 6 "There is a *m* in this town; he is a man
1 Kings 13. 1 a *m* came out of Judah by the word of
13.26 "It is the *m* who disobeyed the word of
17.24 now I know that you are a *m*, and that
20.28 A *m* approached and said to the king of
2 Kings 1.10 "If I am a *m*, let fire come down from
7.17 in the gate, just as the *m* had said
2 Chr 25. 7 a *m* came to him and said, "O king, do

MANAGEMENT

Lk 16. 2 Give me an accounting of your *m*,

MANAGER

Mt 20. 8 the owner of the vineyard said to his *m*,
Lk 12.42 is the faithful and prudent *m* whom his
16. 1 a rich man who had a *m*, and charges

MANASSEH

Gen 41.51 Joseph named the firstborn *M*, "For," he
48. 1 with him his two sons, *M* and Ephraim.
Num 1.34 The descendants of *M*, their lineage, in

Deut 3.13 I give to the half-tribe of *M* the rest of
Judg 6.15 my clan is the weakest in *M*, and I am
2 Kings 21. 1 *M* was twelve years old when he began
21.16 *M* shed very much innocent blood, until
21.18 *M* slept with his ancestors, and was
23.12 the altars that *M* had made in the two
2 Chr 33. 1 *M* was twelve years old when he began
33.13 Then *M* knew that the LORD indeed
33.23 humble himself before the LORD, as *M*

MANDRAKES

Gen 30.14 Reuben went and found *m* in the field,
Song 7.13 The *m* give forth fragrance, and over our

MANGER

Lk 2. 7 and laid him in a *m*, because there was

MANIFESTED

Ps 90.16 Let your work be *m* to your servants,

MANIFESTATION

1 Cor 12. 7 To each is given the *m* of the Spirit for
1 Tim 6.14 spot or blame until the *m* of our Lord

MANNA

Ex 16.31 Israel called it *m*; it was like coriander
16.35 Israelites ate *m* forty years, until they
Num 11. 6 there is nothing at all but this *m* to
Josh 5.12 The *m* ceased on the day they ate the
Ps 78.24 he rained down on them *m* to eat, and
Jn 6.31 Our ancestors ate *m* in the wilderness;
Rev 2.17 I will give some of the hidden *m*,

MANTLE

2 Kings 2.13 He picked up the *m* of Elijah that had

MARK

Cousin of Barnabas, Col 4.10; lived in Jerusalem, Acts 12.12; accompanied Barnabas and Paul to Antioch, Acts 12.25; began missionary work, Acts 13.5; deserted the group at Perga, Acts 13.13; subject of contention, Acts 15.37-38; went with Barnabas to Cyprus, Acts 15.39; ministered to Paul in Rome, Col 4.10; Philem 24; companion of Peter, 1 Pet 5.13.

MARK (MARKED MARKS)

Gen 4.15 LORD put a *m* on Cain, so that no one
Ps 37.37 *M* the blameless, and behold the
50.22 "*M* this, then, you who forget God, or I
130. 3 If you, O LORD, should *m* iniquities,
Ezek 9. 4 put a *m* upon the foreheads of those
Hab 1.12 O LORD, you have *m* them for judgment;
Gal 6.17 the *m* of Jesus branded on my body.
Rev 13.16 and slave, to be *m* on the right hand or
14. 9 and receive a *m* on their foreheads or
19.20 received the *m* of the beast and those

MARKET (MARKETS)

Ezek 27.15 coastlands were your own special *m*,
1 Cor 10.25 Eat whatever is sold in the meat *m*

MARKETPLACE (MARKETPLACES)

Lk 7.32 like children sitting in the *m* and calling
20.46 love to be greeted in the *m*, and to have
Acts 17.17 and also in the *m* every day with those

MARRIAGE (MARRIAGES)

Gen 34. 9 Make *m* with us; give your daughters to
Deut 24. 1 Suppose a man enters into *m* with a
2 Cor 11. 2 I promised you in *m* to one husband, to
1 Tim 4. 3 They forbid *m* and demand abstinence
Heb 13. 4 Let *m* be held in honor by all, and let

MARRY (MARRIED MARRIES)

Num 12. 1 of the Cushite woman whom he had *m*,
Mal 2.11 *m* the daughter of a foreign god. May
Mt 5.32 and whoever *m* a divorced woman
19. 9 and *m* another commits adultery."
Mk 10.11 divorces his wife and *m* another
12.25 they rise from the dead, they neither *m*
Lk 16.18 who divorces his wife and *m* another
20.35 from the dead neither *m* nor are given
1 Cor 7.10 To the *m* I give this command, — not I
7.33 the *m* man is anxious about the affairs

MARTHA

Lk 10.38 *M* welcomed him into her house.
Jn 11. 1 the village of Mary and her sister *M*.
11.24 *M* said to him, "I know that he will rise
12. 2 they gave a dinner for him. *M* served,

MARVELOUS

Job 5. 9 unsearchable, *m* things without number.
9.10 and *m* things without number.
Ps 118. 23 This is the LORD's doing; it is *m* in our

MARY (Mother of Jesus)

Betrothed to Joseph, Mt 1.18 (Lk 1.27); Jesus' birth foretold to her, Lk 1.26-38; visited Elizabeth, Lk 1.39-45; The Song of Mary, Lk 1.46-55; went to Bethlehem, Lk 2.4-5; birth of Jesus, Mt 1.25 (Lk 2.7); found Jesus in the temple, Lk 2.41-51; attended the marriage at Cana, Jn 2.1-5; concerned over Jesus' ministry, Mk 3.31-35; at the cross, Jn 19.25-27; in the upper room, Acts 1.14.

MARY (Magdalene)

Healed of demons, Lk 8.2; stood by the cross, Mt 27.56 (Mk 15.40; Jn 19.25); watched Jesus' burial, Mt 27.61 (Mk 15.47); came early to the tomb, Mt 28.1 (Mk 16.1; Lk 24.1-10; Jn 20.1); saw the risen Lord, Mt 28.9 (Mk 16.9n; Jn 20.11-18).

MARY (of Bethany)

Listened to the Lord's teaching, Lk 10.38-42; present at the raising of Lazarus, Jn 11.1-45; anointed Jesus, Jn 12.1-8.

MASTER (MASTERS)

Gen 39. 3 His *m* saw that the LORD was with him,
Ex 21. 5 "I love my *m*, my wife, and my children;
Prov 27.18 who takes care of a *m* will be honored.
Jer 3.14 I am your *m*; I will take you, one from a
Dan 1. 3 commanded his palace *m* Ashpenaz
Mt 6.24 "No one can serve two *m*; for a slave
Eph 6. 9 both of you have the same *M* in heaven,
1 Tim 6. 2 Those who have believing *m* must not
1 Pet 2.18 Slaves, accept the authority of your *m*

MATTHEW

Mt 9. 9 he saw a man called *M* sitting at the
10. 3 Thomas and *M* the tax collector; James
Mk 3.18 and *M*, and Thomas, and James son of
Lk 6.15 and *M*, and Thomas, and James son of
Acts 1.13 and Thomas, Bartholomew and *M*,

MATURE (MATURITY)

1 Cor 2. 6 Yet among the *m* we do speak wisdom,
Eph 4.13 to *m*, to the measure of the full stature

MEASURE (MEASURED MEASURING)

Ps 39. 4 my end, and what is the *m* of my days;
Isa 40.12 Who has *m* the waters in the hollow of
Jer 31.37 If the heavens above can be *m*, and the
Zech 2. 1 looked up and saw a man with a *m* line
Mk 4.24 the *m* you give will be the *m* you get,
Lk 6.38 for the *m* you give will be the *m* you get
Rev 11. 1 "Come and *m* the temple of God and
21.15 had a *m* rod of gold to *m* the city and

MEDE (MEDES)

2 Kings 17. 6 of Gozan, and in the cities of the *M*.
Esth 1.19 the laws of the Persians and the *M*
Jer 51.11 up the spirit of the kings of the *M*,
Dan 5.28 and given to the *M* and Persians."
6. 8 according to the law of the *M* and the
9. 1 by birth a *M*, who became king over the

MEDIA

Ezra 6. 2 province of *M*, that a scroll was found
Esth 1. 3 The army of Persia and *M* and the
10. 2 written in the annals of the kings of *M*
Dan 8.20 the two horns, these are the kings of *M*

MEDIATOR

Job 33.23 be for one of them an angel, a *m*,
Gal 3.20 Now a *m* involves more than one party;
1 Tim 2. 5 one *m* between God and humankind,
Heb 9.15 reason he is the *m* of a new covenant,
12.24 to Jesus, the *m* of a new covenant, and

MEDITATE

Josh 1. 8 you shall *m* on it day and night, so that
Ps 1. 2 and on his law they *m* day and night.
63. 6 I think of you on my bed, and *m* on you
77.12 I will *m* on all your work, and muse on
119. 15 I will *m* on your precepts, and fix my
119. 78 as for me, I will *m* on your precepts.
143. 5 deeds, I *m* on the works of your hands.

MEDITATION

Job 15. 4 of God, and hindering *m* before God.
Ps 19.14 and the *m* of my heart be acceptable
49. 3 speak wisdom; the *m* of my heart shall
104. 34 May my *m* be pleasing to him, for I
119. 97 I love your law! It is my *m* all day long.

MEEK

Ps 10.17 you will hear the desire of the *m*; you
37.11 But the *m* shall inherit the land, and
Isa 29.19 The *m* shall obtain fresh joy in the
Mt 5. 5 "Blessed are the *m*, for they will inherit

MEEKNESS

2 Cor 10. 1 by the *m* and gentleness of Christ—
Jas 1.21 welcome with *m* the implanted word

MEET

Ex 25.22 There I will *m* with you, and from above
Am 4.12 to you, prepare to *m* your God, O Israel!
Mt 8.34 the whole town came out to *m* Jesus;
1 Thess 4.17 with them to *m* the Lord in the air;
Heb 10.25 not neglecting to *m* together, as is the

MEETING

Ps 74. 8 they burned all the *m* places of God in

MEGIDDO

Josh 12.21 of Taanach, one; the king of *M*, one;
17.11 the inhabitants of *M* and its villages
1 Kings 4.12 in Taanach, *M*, and all Bethshean,
2 Kings 9.27 Then he fled to *M*, and died there.
23.29 when Pharaoh Neco met him at *M*, he
Zech 12.11 for Hadad-rimmon in the plain of *M*.

MELCHIZEDEK

Gen 14.18 King *M* of Salem brought out bread and
Ps 110. 4 forever according to the order of *M*."
Heb 5. 6 forever, according to the order of *M*."
6.20 forever according to the order of *M*.
7. 1 This "King *M* of Salem, priest of the
7.10 loins of his ancestor when *M* met him.
7.15 another priest arises, resembling *M*,

MELT (MELTED MELTS)

Ex 15.15 all the inhabitants of Canaan *m* away.
Josh 2.11 As soon as we heard it, our hearts *m*,
5. 1 they had crossed over, their hearts *m*,
7. 5 The hearts of the people *m* and turned
Ps 22.14 my heart is like wax; it is *m* within my
97. 5 The mountains *m* like wax before the
147. 18 He sends out his word, and *m* them; he
Ezek 22.22 *m* in a smelter, so you shall be *m* in it;

MEMBER (MEMBERS)

Mt 18.15 "If another *m* of the church sins against
18.21 if another *m* of the church sins against
Rom 6.13 No longer present your *m* to sin as
12. 4 as in one body we have many *m*, and
1 Cor 6.15 know that your bodies are *m* of Christ?
Eph 5.30 church, because we are *m* of his body.

MEMORIAL

Josh 4. 7 shall be to the Israelites a *m* forever."
Acts 10. 4 prayers and alms have ascended as a *m*

MEMORY

Deut 32.26 out the *m* of them from humankind;
Job 18.17 Their *m* perishes from the earth, and
Ps 109. 15 may his *m* be cut off from the earth.
Prov 10. 7 The *m* of the righteous is a blessing,
Eccl 9. 5 reward, and even the *m* of them is lost.

MENE

Dan 5.25 that was inscribed: *M*, *M*, TEKEL, and

MEPHIBOSHETH

Crippled by a fall, 2 Sam 4.4; dined continually at the royal table, 2 Sam 9; reported to David as a deserter, 2 Sam 16.1-4; cleared himself before David, 2 Sam 19.24-30.

MERCHANT (MERCHANTS)

Nah 3.16 You increased your *m* more than the
Mt 13.45 is like a *m* in search of fine pearls;
Rev 18. 3 the *m* of the earth have grown rich from

MERCIFUL

Gen 19.16 LORD being *m* to him, and they brought
1 Kings 20.31 kings of the house of Israel are *m* kings;
Ps 86.15 you, O Lord, are a God *m* and gracious,
Jon 4. 2 that you are a gracious God and *m*,
Mt 5. 7 "Blessed are the *m*, for they will receive
Lk 6.36 Be *m*, just as your Father is *m*.
Heb 8.12 I will be *m* toward their iniquities, and I

MERCY (MERCIES)

Gen 43.14 may God Almighty grant you *m* before
Ex 33.19 will show *m* on whom I will show *m*.
Deut 7. 2 with them and show them no *m*.
1 Chr 21.13 of the LORD, for his *m* is very great;
Neh 1.11 today, and grant him *m* in the sight of
Ps 51. 1 Have *m* on me, O God, according to
103. 4 crowns you with steadfast love and *m*,
Jer 31.20 for him; I will surely have *m* on him,
42.12 I will grant you *m*, and he will have *m*
Lam 3.22 ceases, his *m* never come to an end;
Dan 2.18 told them to seek *m* from the God of
Hab 3. 2 known; in wrath may you remember *m*.
Mt 9.13 means, 'I desire *m* and not sacrifice.'
12. 7 means, 'I desire *m* and not sacrifice,'
15.22 "Have *m* on me, Lord, Son of David; my
20.30 they shouted, "Lord, have *m* on us, Son
23.23 of the law, justice and *m* and faith.
Mk 5.19 for you, and what *m* he has shown you."
Lk 1.50 His *m* is on those who fear him from
1.72 he has shown *m* promised to our
10.37 He said, "The one who showed him *m*."
16.24 'Father Abraham, have *m* on me, and
18.38 "Jesus, Son of David, have *m* on me!
Rom 9.15 "I will have *m* on whom I have *m*, and I
9.18 he has *m* upon whomever he chooses,
9.23 riches of his glory for the objects of *m*,
11.30 but have now received *m* because of
2 Cor 4. 1 by God's *m* that we are engaged in this
Phil 2.27 But God had *m* on him, and not only on

MERCY SEAT

Ex 25.22 meet with you, and from above the *m*,
Lev 16. 2 inside the curtain before the *m* that is

MEROM

Josh 11. 5 at the waters of *M*, to fight with Israel.
11. 7 by the waters of *M*, and fell upon them.

MESSAGE

Judg 3.20 and said, "I have a *m* from God for you."
Hag 1.13 spoke to the people with the LORD's *m*,
Mk 16.20n confirmed the *m* by the signs that
Acts 5.20 and tell the people the whole *m* about
15. 7 Gentiles would hear the *m* of the good
17.11 they welcomed the *m* very eagerly and
20.32 you to God and to the *m* of his grace,
2 Tim 4. 2 I solemnly urge you: proclaim the *m*; be
2 Pet 1.19 we have the prophetic *m* more fully
1 Jn 1. 5 This is the *m* we have heard from him

MESSENGER (MESSENGERS)

Gen 32. 3 Jacob sent *m* before him to his brother
2 Chr 36.15 sent persistently to them by his *m*,
Prov 25.13 harvest are faithful *m* to those who send
Jer 49.14 a *m* has been sent among the nations:
Ezek 30. 9 On that day, *m* shall go out from me in
Mal 2. 7 his mouth, for he is the *m* of the LORD
3. 1 I am sending my *m* to prepare the way
Mt 11.10 I am sending my *m* ahead of you, who
Mk 1. 2 I am sending my *m* ahead of you, who
Lk 7.27 "See, I am sending my *m* ahead of you,
9.52 And he sent *m* ahead of him. On their
2 Cor 12. 7 was given me in the flesh, a *m* of Satan

MESSIAH

Mt 1.16 Jesus was born, who is called the *M*.
16.16 Peter answered, "You are the *M*, the
Jn 1.41 and said to him, "We have found the *M*"
4.25 said to him, "I know that *M* is coming"

METHUSELAH

Gen 5.27 Thus all the days of *M* were nine

MICAH

Jer 26.18 "*M* of Moresheth, who prophesied
Mic 1. 1 word of the LORD that came to *M* of

MICHAL

Married to David, 1 Sam 18.20-30; helped David escape, 1 Sam 19.12-17; restored to David, 2 Sam 3.13-16; rebuked for despising David, 2 Sam 6.12-23.

1 Sam 14.49 and the name of the younger, *M*.
2 Sam 3.13 unless you bring Saul's daughter *M*
1 Chr 15.29 *M* daughter of Saul looked out of the

MICHMASH

1 Sam 13. 2 two thousand were with Saul in *M* and
14. 5 crag rose on the north in front of *M*,
Isa 10.28 Migron, at *M* he stores his baggage;

MIDIAN

Gen 25. 2 She bore him . . . *M*, Ishbak, and Shuah.
Ex 2.15 Moses . . . settled in the land of *M*, and
4.19 The LORD said to Moses in *M*, "Go back
18. 1 Jethro, the priest of *M* . . . heard of all
Num 22. 4 Moab said to the elders of *M*, "This
Judg 6. 1 them into the hand of *M* seven years.
7. 8 The camp of *M* was below him in the
1 Kings 11.18 They set out from *M* and came to
Ps 83. 9 Do to them as you did to *M*, as to
Isa 9. 4 you have broken as on the day of *M*.
10.26 against them, as when he struck *M* at

MIDIANITE

Gen 37.28 When some *M* traders passed by, they

MIDNIGHT

Judg 16. 3 But Samson lay only until *m*. Then at *m*
Ps 119. 62 At *m* I rise to praise you, because of
Acts 16.25 About *m* Paul and Silas were praying
20. 7 day, he continued speaking until *m*.

MIDWIVES

Ex 1.15 king of Egypt said to the Hebrew *m*,

MIGHT

Judg 6.14 "Go in this *m* of yours and deliver Israel
1 Sam 2. 9 darkness; for not by *m* does one prevail.
Job 39.19 "Do you give the horse its *m*? Do you
Ps 59.16 But I will sing of your *m*; I will sing
118. 14 The LORD is my strength and my *m*; he
Isa 12. 2 the LORD GOD is my strength and my *m*;
Eccl 9.10 your hand finds to do, do with your *m*;
Hab 1.11 become guilty; their own *m* is their god!
Zech 4. 6 Not by *m*, nor by power, but by my

MIGHTY (MIGHTIER)

2 Sam 1.25 How the *m* have fallen in the midst of
Job 21. 7 reach old age, and grow *m* in power?
36. 5 "Surely God is *m* and does not despise
Ps 71.16 I will come praising the *m* deeds of the
Prov 24. 5 Wise warriors are *m* than strong ones,
Isa 1.24 LORD of hosts, the *M* One of Israel: Ah,
9. 6 Wonderful Counselor, *M* God,
63. 1 is I, announcing vindication, *m* to save."

MILE

Mt 5.41 you to go one *m*, go also the second *m*.

MILITARY

1 Cor 9. 7 pays the expenses for doing *m* service?

MILK

Gen 18. 8 Then he took curds and *m* and the calf
Ex 3. 8 land, a land flowing with *m* and honey,
Judg 4.19 she opened a skin of *m* and gave him a
Job 10.10 Did you not pour me out like *m* and
1 Cor 3. 2 I fed you with *m*, not solid food, for you
9. 7 a flock and does not get any of its *m*?
Heb 5.12 You need *m*, not solid food; for

MILLSTONE

Judg 9.53 But a certain woman threw an upper *m*
Mt 18. 6 great *m* were fastened around your neck
Mk 9.42 better for you if a great *m* were hung
Lk 17. 2 better for you if a *m* were hung around

MIND (MINDS)

Gen 37.11 but his father kept the matter in *m*.
Deut 29. 4 has not given you a *m* to understand,
2 Sam 7. 3 do all that you have in *m*; for the LORD
1 Kings 3. 9 there an understanding *m* to govern
2 Kings 6.11 *m* of the king of Aram was greatly
1 Chr 17. 2 "Do all that you have in *m*, for God is
2 Chr 6. 7 David had it in *m* to build a house for
Neh 4. 6 height; for the people had a *m* to work.
Ps 77.11 I will call to *m* the deeds of the LORD; I
Prov 14.30 A tranquil *m* gives life to the flesh, but
16. 9 The human *m* plans his way, but the
17.20 The crooked of *m* do not prosper, and
Isa 6.10 Make the *m* of this people dull, and
26. 3 Those of steadfast *m* you keep in peace
44.20 deluded *m* has led him astray, and he
Jer 23.16 They speak visions of their own *m*, not
Dan 4.16 his *m* be changed from that of a human,
Mk 5.15 sitting there, clothed and in his right *m*,
Rom 8. 7 the *m* that is set on the flesh is hostile
11.34 "For who has known the *m* of the Lord?
1 Cor 2.16 him?" But we have the *m* of Christ.
14.15 spirit, but I will pray with the *m* also.
14.19 rather speak five words with my *m*,
2 Cor 3.15 Moses is read, a veil lies over their *m*;
9. 7 must give as you have made up your *m*,
Phil 2. 5 Let the same *m* be in you that was in
4. 2 I urge Syntyche to be of the same *m*
Col 3. 2 Set your *m* on things that are above, not

MINDFUL

Ps 25. 6 Be *m* of your mercy, O LORD, and of
115. 12 The LORD has been *m* of us; he will
Zeph 2. 7 their God will be *m* of them and restore

MINISTER (MINISTERED MINISTERING MINISTERS)

Deut 18. 7 he may *m* in the name of the LORD his
1 Sam 2.11 while the boy remained to *m* to the
3. 1 Samuel was *m* to the LORD under Eli.
1 Chr 6.32 They *m* with song before the tabernacle
Ps 104. 4 your messengers, fire and flame your *m*.
Isa 56. 6 themselves to the LORD, to *m* to him,
60.10 walls, and their kings shall *m* to you;
Ezek 44.11 They shall be *m* in my sanctuary, having
Rom 15.16 me by God to be a *m* of Christ Jesus
2 Cor 11.23 Are they *m* of Christ? I am talking like a
Col 4. 7 he is a beloved brother, a faithful *m*,

MINISTRY

Rom 11.13 apostle to the Gentiles, I glorify my *m*.
12. 7 in proportion to faith; *m*, in ministering;
15.25 going to Jerusalem in a *m* to the saints;
Eph 4.12 equip the saints for the work of *m*, for

MIRACLES

1 Chr 16.12 wonderful works he has done, his *m*,
1 Cor 12.10 to another the working of *m*, to another
Gal 3. 5 with the Spirit and work *m* among you

MIRIAM

Song of Miriam, Ex 15.20-21; became leprous for criticizing Moses, Num 12.1-10; her leprosy healed, Num 12.11-16; died in Kadesh, Num 20.1.

MIRROR (MIRRORS)

Ex 38. 8 from the *m* of the women who served at
Job 37.18 out the skies, hard as a molten *m*?
1 Cor 13.12 now we see in a *m*, dimly, but then we
Jas 1.23 those who look at themselves in a *m*.

MISCHIEF

Judg 15. 3 when I do *m* to the Philistines, I will be
Ps 7.14 evil, and are pregnant with *m*, and bring
36. 4 They plot *m* while on their beds; they
1 Pet 4.15 thief, a criminal, or even as a *m* maker.

MISERABLE

Job 16. 2 such things; *m* comforters are you all.

MISERY

Ex 3. 7 "I have observed the *m* of my people
Num 11.15 sight—and do not let me see my *m*."

MISFORTUNE

Prov 13.21 *M* pursues sinners, but prosperity

MISLEAD

2 Kings 4.28 for a son? Did I not say, Do not *m* me?"

MISS (MISSED)

Judg 20.16 could sling a stone at a hair and not *m*.
1 Sam 20.18 you will be *m*, because your place will
Job 5.24 shall inspect your fold and *m* nothing.
Prov 8.36 but those who *m* me injure themselves;

MIST

Jas 4.14 you are a *m* that appears for a little

MISTAKE

Jer 42.20 you today that you have made a fatal *m*.

MIZPAH

Gen 31.49 and the pillar *M*, for he said, "The LORD
Judg 11.11 all his words before the LORD at *M*.
1 Sam 7. 5 "Gather all Israel at *M*, and I will pray
10.17 summoned the people to the LORD at *M*
Jer 41.10 the rest of the people who were in *M*,

MOCK (MOCKED MOCKING MOCKS)

Gen 27.12 I shall seem to be *m* him, and bring a
Judg 16.10 you have *m* me, and told me lies; please
1 Kings 18.27 At noon Elijah *m* them, saying, "Cry
2 Kings 19. 4 of Assyria has sent to *m* the living God,
2 Kings 19.22 "Whom have you *m* and reviled? Against
2 Chr 36.16 kept *m* the messengers of God, despising
Job 21. 3 speak; then after I have spoken, *m* on.
Ps 22. 7 All who see me *m* at me, they make
Prov 17. 5 who *m* the poor insult their Maker;
Isa 37. 4 of Assyria has sent to *m* the living God,
Jer 20. 7 all day long; everyone *m* me.
Ezek 22. 5 those who are far from you will *m* you,
Mt 27.29 before him and *m* him, saying, "Hail,
Mk 10.34 they will *m* him, and spit upon him,
15.31 along with the scribes, were also *m* him
Lk 18.32 Gentiles; and he will be *m* and insulted
23.36 The soldiers also *m* him, coming up and

MOCKERY

Ezek 5.15 You shall be a *m* and a taunt, a warning
Joel 2.19 more make you a *m* among the nations.

MOLECH

Lev 18.21 of your offspring to sacrifice them to *M*,
2 Kings 23.10 pass through fire as an offering to *M*.

MONEY

Num 3.49 Moses took the redemption *m* from
Deut 14.25 you may turn it into *m*. With the *m*
2 Kings 12.11 would give the *m* that was weighed
Eccl 5.10 The lover of *m* will not be satisfied with
7.12 of wisdom is like the protection of *m*;
10.19 gladdens life, and *m* meets every need.
Mt 27. 6 the treasury, since they are blood *m*."
28.12 a plan to give a large sum of *m* to the
Lk 16.14 Pharisees, who were also lovers of *m*,
Acts 4.37 then brought the *m*, and laid it at the
8.18 he offered them *m*, saying, "Give me
1 Tim 6.10 love of *m* is a root of all kinds of evils,
Heb 13. 5 Keep your lives free from love of *m*, and

MONEY CHANGERS

Mt 21.12 overturned the tables of the *m* and the
Mk 11.15 overturned the tables of the *m* and the
Jn 2.14 doves, and the *m* seated at their tables.

MOON

Song 6.10 fair as the *m*, bright as the sun, terrible
Isa 13.10 rising, and the *m* will not shed its light.
30.26 light of the *m* will be like the light of
Jer 31.35 and the fixed order of the *m* and the
Ezek 32. 7 cloud, and the *m* shall not give its light.
Mt 24.29 and the *m* will not give its light,
Acts 2.20 turned to darkness and the *m* to blood,
1 Cor 15.41 another glory of the *m*, and another

MORALS

1 Cor 15.33 deceived: "Bad company ruins good *m*."

MORDECAI

Counseled Esther, Esth 2.5-20; informed Esther of a conspiracy, Esth 2.21-23; refused to reverence Haman, Esth 3.2-6; arrayed in royal apparel, Esth 6.1-11; promoted next to the king, Esth 8.1-2; 10.3; reversed Haman's decree, Esth 8.3—9.4; decreed feast of Purim, Esth 9.20-31.

MORIAH

Gen 22. 2 go to land of *M*, and offer him there as
2 Chr 3. 1 of the LORD in Jerusalem on Mount *M*,

MORNING

Ps 5. 3 O LORD, in the *m* you hear my voice; in
30. 5 for the night, but joy comes with the *m*.
Isa 21.12 The sentinel says: "*M* comes, and also
Mk 1.35 In the *m*, while it was still very dark, he
Rev 2.28 who conquers I will also give the *m* star.
22.16 descendant of David, the bright *m* star."

MORSEL

Prov 17. 1 Better is a dry *m* with quiet than a

MORTAL (MORTALS)

Job 4.17 'Can *m* be righteous before God? Can
14.10 But *m* die, and are laid low; humans
15.14 What are *m*, that they can be clean? Or
Ps 8. 4 of them, *m* that you care for him?
Ezek 2. 1 O *m*, stand up on your feet, and I will
3.17 *M*, I have made you a sentinel for the
20. 3 *M* speak to the elders of Israel, and say
30.21 *M* I have broken the arm of Pharaoh
Job 9.32 he is not a *m*, as I am, that I might
14. 1 "A *m*, born of a woman, few of days and
Am 4.13 reveals his thoughts to *m*, makes the
Acts 14.15 We are *m* just like you, and we bring
Rom 6.12 sin exercise dominion in your *m* bodies,
1 Cor 15.53 this *m* body must put on immortality.
1 Jn 5.16 There is sin that is *m*; I do not say that

MOSES (MOSES')

Born, Ex 2.1-2; adopted by Pharaoh's daughter, Ex 2.5-10; trained at the Egyptian court, Acts 7.22; killed an Egyptian, Ex 2.11-12; Fled to Midian, Ex 2.15-20; married Zipporah, Ex 2.21-22; called by God, Ex 3.1—4.17; returned to Egypt, Ex 4.18-31; interceded with Pharaoh, Ex 5—11; led the Israelites across the Red Sea, Ex 14; sang for triumph, Ex 15.1-18; appointed rulers, Ex 18.13-26; met God on Mount Sinai, Ex 19.3-13; 24—31; enraged by Israel's idolatry, Ex 32; talked with the LORD, Ex 33—34; built the tabernacle, Ex 35—40; numbered the people, Num 1; vindicated before Aaron and Miriam, Num 12; sent twelve spies to Canaan, Num 13.1-20; consecrated Joshua as his successor, Num 27.18-23; Deut 31.23; recounted Israel's history, Deut 1—3; exhorted Israel to obedience, Deut 4.1-40; song of Moses, Deut 32.1-43; viewed Canaan, Deut 3.23-27; 32.48-52; 34.1-4; blessed the tribes, Deut 33; death and burial in Moab, Deut 34.5-7. (See also Acts 7.20-44.)

Josh 1. 5 As I was with *M*, so I will be with you; I
Ps 77.20 a flock by the hand of *M* and Aaron.
103. 7 He made his ways known to *M*, his acts
106. 23 he would destroy them—had not *M*,
Isa 63.12 arm to march at the right hand of *M*,
Jer 15. 1 Though *M* and Samuel stood before me,
Mt 17. 3 there appeared to them *M* and Elijah,
19. 8 *M* allowed you to divorce your wives,
Mk 7.10 For *M* said, 'Honor your father and
Lk 16.29 Abraham replied, 'They have *M* and the
24.27 beginning with *M* and all the prophets,
Jn 1.17 The law indeed was given through *M*;
3.14 just as *M* lifted up the serpent in the
5.46 If you believed *M*, you would believe
Acts 3.22 *M* said, 'The Lord your God will raise
Rom 5.14 exercised dominion from Adam to *M*,
1 Cor 10. 2 all were baptized into *M* in the cloud
2 Cor 3. 7 Israel could not gaze at *M* face because
3.15 whenever *M* is read, a veil lies over
2 Tim 3. 8 As Jannes and Jambres opposed *M*, so
Heb 3. 2 just as *M* also "was faithful in all God's
11.23 By faith *M* was hidden by his parents
Jude 9 devil and disputed about the body of *M*,
Rev 15. 3 they sing the song of *M*, the servant of

MOTH

Ps 39.11 for sin, consuming like a *m* what is dear
Mt 6.19 on earth, where *m* and rust consume

MOTHER (MOTHERS MOTHER'S)

Gen 3.20 because she was the *m* of all living.
Ex 2. 8 the girl went and called the child's *m*.
Judg 5. 7 arose, Deborah, arose as a *m* in Israel.
1 Sam 2.19 His *m* used to make for him a little
1 Kings 3.27 living boy; do not kill him. She is his *m*."
2 Chr 15.16 Asa even removed his *m* Maacah from
Ps 113. 9 a home, making her the joyous *m*
Prov 4. 3 my father, tender, and my *m* favorite,
Isa 66.13 As a *m* comforts her child, so I will
Mt 12.48 Jesus replied, "Who is my *m*, and who
12.50 heaven is my brother and sister and *m*."
Mt 19. 5 man shall leave his father and *m* and be
Mk 3.33 replied, "Who are my *m* and brothers?"
7.10 said, 'Honor your father and your *m*';
Jn 19.27 he said to the disciple, "Here is your *m*."
Gal 4.26 above; she is free, and she is our *m*.
1 Tim 5. 2 to older women as *m*, to younger
2 Tim 1. 5 Lois and your *m* Eunice and now, I am

MOTHER-IN-LAW

Ruth 3. 1 Naomi her *m* said to her, "My daughter,
Mk 1.30 Simon's *m* was in bed with a fever, and

MOUNT OF OLIVES

Zech 14. 4 that day his feet shall stand on the *M*,
Mt 21. 1 Bethphage, at the *M*, Jesus sent
24. 3 When he was sitting on the *M*, the
26.30 sung the hymn, they went out to the *M*.
Lk 21.37 and spend the night on the *M*, as it was
Jn 8. 1 went home, while Jesus went to the *M*.

MOUNTAIN (MOUNTAINS)

Deut 1. 6 "You have stayed long enough at this *m*.
Ps 36. 6 Your righteousness is like the mighty *m*
46. 2 should change, though the *m* shake
68.15 O mighty *m*, *m* of Bashan; O
Isa 2. 2 days to come the *m* of the LORD's house
11. 9 not hurt or destroy in all my holy *m*;
25. 6 On this *m* the LORD of hosts will make
30.29 of the flute to go to the *m* of the LORD,
45. 2 I will go before you and level the *m*, I
Ezek 6. 3 You *m* of Israel, hear the word of the
20.40 on my holy *m*, the *m* height of Israel,
Dan 2.35 that struck the statue became a great *m*
Ob 16 For as you have drunk on my holy *m*,
Mic 1. 4 Then the *m* will melt under him and
4. 1 be established as the highest of the *m*,
6. 2 Hear, you *m*, the controversy of the
Nah 1.15 On the *m* the feet of one who brings
Zech 8. 3 LORD of hosts shall be called the holy *m*.
Mt 4. 8 devil took him to a very high *m* and
5. 1 he went up on the *m*; and after he sat
17. 1 brother John and led them up a high *m*,
Mk 6.46 to them, he went up on the *m* to pray.
11.23 if you say to this *m*, 'Be taken up and
13.14 then those in Judea must flee to the *m*;
Lk 9.28 James and went up on the *m* to pray.
Jn 6.15 him king, he withdrew again to the *m*
1 Cor 13. 2 if I have all faith, so as to remove *m*,

MOURN (MOURNED MOURNING)

Gen 37.34 his loins, and *m* for his son many days.
2 Sam 1.12 They *m* and wept, and fasted until
13.37 David *m* for his son day after day.
Dan 10. 2 time I, Daniel, had been *m* for three
Am 5.16 They shall call the farmers to *m*, and
8.10 I will turn your feasts into *m*, and all
Mt 5. 4 "Blessed are those who *m*, for they will
1 Cor 7.30 those who *m* as though they were not
Rev 21. 4 Death will be no more; *m* and crying

MOURNFULLY

Ps 43. 2 Why must I walk about *m* because of

MOUTH (MOUTHS)

Deut 8. 3 that comes from the *m* of the LORD.
2 Kings 4.34 the child, putting his *m* upon his *m*,
Job 40. 4 I answer you? I lay my hand on my *m*.
Ps 34. 1 his praise shall continually be in my *m*.
71. 8 My *m* is filled with your praise, and
109. 2 and deceitful *m* are opened against me,
135. 16 They have *m*, but they do not speak;
141. 3 Set a guard over my *m*, O LORD, keep
Prov 30.32 devising evil, put your hand on your *m*.
Isa 6. 7 The seraph touched my *m* with it and
Mal 2. 6 True instruction was in his *m*, and no
Rom 3.14 "Their *m* are full of cursing and
3.19 that every *m* may be silenced, and the

MOVE (MOVED MOVING)

Deut 19.14 You must not *m* your neighbor's
2 Sam 7. 6 I have been *m* about in a tent and a
1 Chr 17. 6 I have *m* about among all Israel,
Ps 16. 8 he is at my right hand, I shall not be *m*.
21. 7 of the Most High he shall not be *m*.
46. 5 the midst of the city; it shall not be *m*;
121. 3 He will not let your foot be *m*, he who
Acts 17.28 For 'In him we live and *m* and have our
2 Pet 1.21 men and women *m* by the Holy Spirit

MUD

Jn 9. 6 made *m* with the saliva and spread the

MULTIPLY (MULTIPLIED)

Gen 1.22 the seas, and let birds *m* on the earth."
9. 1 "Be fruitful and *m*, and fill the earth.
35.11 be fruitful and *m*; a nation and a
Deut 7.13 he will love you, bless you, and *m* you;
Isa 9. 3 You have *m* the nation, you have

MULTITUDE (MULTITUDES)

Gen 2. 1 the earth were finished, and all their *m*.
Ps 42. 4 of thanksgiving, a *m* keeping festival.
Joel 3.14 *M*, *m*, in the valley of decision! For the
1 Pet 4. 8 one another, for love covers a *m* of sins.
Rev 7. 9 was a great *m* that no one could count,

MURDER (MURDERS)

Ex 20.13 You shall not *m*.
Deut 5.17 You shall not *m*.
Mt 5.21 and 'whoever *m* shall be liable to
15.19 of the heart come evil intentions, *m*,
19.18 Jesus said, "You shall not *m*; You shall
Mk 15. 7 with the rebels who had committed *m*
Lk 23.19 who had been put in prison . . . for *m*.)

MURDERER

Jn 8.44 He was a *m* from the beginning and
Acts 3.14 and asked to have a *m* given to you,

MURMURED (MURMURING)

Josh 9.18 the congregation *m* against the leaders.
Phil 2.14 Do all things without *m* or arguing, so

MUSTARD

Mt 13.31 is like a *m* seed that someone took and
17.20 if you have faith the size of a *m* seed,
Mk 4.31 It is like a *m* seed, which, when sown
Lk 13.19 It is like a *m* seed that someone took
17. 6 "If you had faith the size of a *m* seed,

MUTE

Ps 38.13 not hear; like the *m*, who cannot speak.
Mt 9.32 a demoniac who was *m* was brought to
12.22 who had been *m* could speak and see.
15.30 lame, the maimed, the blind, the *m*,
Mk 7.37 the deaf to hear and the *m* to speak."
Lk 1.20 you will be *m*, unable to speak, until
11.14 the one who had been *m* spoke, and the

MUZZLE

Ps 39. 1 I will keep a *m* on my mouth, as long as

MYRRH

Ps 45. 8 your robes are all fragrant with *m* and
Mt 2.11 him gifts of gold, frankincense, and *m*.
Mk 15.23 they offered him wine mixed with *m*;

MYRTLE

Isa 55.13 of the brier shall come up the *m*;
Zech 1. 8 He was standing among the *m* trees in

MYSTERY (MYSTERIES)

Dan 2.18 the God of heaven concerning this *m*,
Rom 11.25 I want you to understand this *m*: a
16.25 according to the revelation of the *m*
1 Cor 4. 1 of Christ and stewards of God's *m*.
13. 2 prophetic powers, and understand all *m*
15.51 Listen, I will tell you a *m*! We will not
Eph 1. 9 has made known to us the *m* of his will,
3. 4 my understanding the *m* of Christ.
5.32 This is a great *m*, and I am applying it
6.19 with boldness the *m* of the gospel,
Col 1.26 the *m* that has been hidden throughout
2. 2 and have the knowledge of God's *m*,
2 Thess 2. 7 the *m* of lawlessness is already at work,
1 Tim 3. 9 must hold fast to the *m* of the faith
3.16 doubt, the *m* of our religion is great:
Rev 10. 7 the *m* of God will be fulfilled, as he
17. 5 was written a name, a *m*: "Babylon the

MYTHS

1 Tim 1. 4 not to occupy themselves with *m* and
Titus 1.14 not paying attention to Jewish *m* or to
2 Pet 1.16 we did not follow cleverly devised *m*

N

NAAMAN

2 Kings 5. 1 *N*, commander of the army of the king
Lk 4.27 them was cleansed except *N* the Syrian."

NAHUM

Nah 1. 1 Nineveh. The book of the vision of *N* of

NAILING

Col 2.14 He set this aside, *n* it to the cross. He

NAILS

Eccl 12.11 like *n* firmly fixed are the collected
Jn 20.25 "Unless I see the mark of the *n* in his

NAKED

Job 1.21 "*N* I came from my mother's womb, and
24.10 They go about *n*, without clothing;
Eccl 5.15 so they shall go again, *n* as they came;
Isa 20. 3 Isaiah has walked *n* and barefoot
58. 7 when you see the *n*, to cover them, and
Ezek 16.39 objects and leave you *n* and bare.
Mk 14.52 but he left the linen cloth and ran off *n*.

NAKEDNESS

Lev 18. 7 shall not uncover the *n* of your father,
Isa 47. 3 Your *n* shall be uncovered, and your

NAME

Gen 12. 8 the LORD and invoked the *n* of the LORD.
32.29 "Please tell me your *n*." But he said,
Ex 3.13 ask me, 'What is his *n*?' what shall I
6. 3 by my *n* 'the LORD' I did not make
9.16 and to make my *n* resound through all
15. 3 The LORD is a warrior; the LORD is his *n*.
20. 7 make wrongful use of the *n* of the LORD
34. 5 there, and proclaimed the *n*, "The LORD."
Lev 24.11 son blasphemed the *N* in a curse.
Deut 5.11 shall not make wrongful use of the *n* of
28.10 that you are called by the *n* of the LORD,
28.58 fearing this glorious and awesome *n*,
32. 3 I will proclaim the *n* of the LORD;
Josh 7. 9 Then what will you do for your great *n*?"
Judg 13.17 "What is your *n*, so that we may honor
2 Sam 12.28 take the city, and it be called by my *n*."
1 Kings 9. 3 have built, and put my *n* there forever;
1 Chr 16. 2 he blessed the people in the *n* of the
17. 8 I will make for you a *n*, like the *n* of the
29.13 to you and praise your glorious *n*.
Ps 8. 9 our Sovereign, how majestic is your *n* in
9.10 those who know your *n* put their trust
72.17 May his *n* endure forever, his fame
102. 12 your *n* endures to all generations.
118. 26 one who comes in the *n* of the LORD.
138. 2 you have exalted your *n* and your word
Prov 18.10 The *n* of the LORD is a strong tower; the
22. 1 A good *n* is to be chosen rather than
Eccl 7. 1 A good *n* is better than precious
Isa 30.27 *n* of the LORD comes from far away,

Isa 40.26 numbers them, calling them all by *n*;
44. 5 "The LORD's," and adopt the *n* of Israel.
52. 5 all day long my *n* is despised.
56. 5 I will give them an everlasting *n* better
62. 2 you shall be called by a new *n* that the
Jer 7.11 this house, which is called by my *n*,
10. 6 are great, and your *n* is great in might.
14.14 prophets are prophesying lies in my *n*;
Ezek 36.21 But I had concern for my holy *n*, which
39.25 and I will be jealous for my holy *n*.
Hos 12. 5 the God of hosts, the LORD is his *n*!
Joel 2.32 Then everyone who calls upon the *n* of
Am 6.10 We must not mention the *n* of the LORD."
9.12 all the nations who are called by my *n*,
Mt 7.22 Lord, did we not prophesy in your *n*,
28.19 baptizing them in the *n* of the Father
Mk 9.38 someone casting out demons in your *n*,
13. 6 Many will come in my *n* and say, 'I am
Lk 1.31 bear a son, and you will *n* him Jesus.
9.49 saw some casting out demons in your *n*,
11. 2 pray, say: "Father, hallowed be your *n*.
Jn 5.43 I have come in my father's *n*, and you
12.28 Father, glorify your *n*." Then a voice
16.23 you ask anything of the Father in my *n*,
Acts 3.16 by faith in his *n*, his *n* itself has made
4.10 in good health by the *n* of Jesus Christ
4.12 there is no other *n* under heaven given
4.30 performed through the *n* of your holy
8.12 and the *n* of Jesus Christ, they were
9.15 chosen to bring my *n* before Gentiles
19.17 and the *n* of the Lord Jesus was
21.13 die in Jerusalem for the *n* of the Lord
Rom 2.24 "The *n* of God is blasphemed among the
9.17 you, so that my *n* may be proclaimed in
Phil 2. 9 gave him the *n* that is above every *n*,
Col 3.17 do everything in the *n* of the Lord
2 Tim 2.19 everyone who calls on the *n* of the Lord
Heb 1. 4 the *n* he has inherited is more excellent
Jas 2. 7 blaspheme the excellent *n* that was
1 Pet 4.14 If you are reviled for the *n* of Christ,
Rev 2.17 on the white stone is written a new *n*
15. 4 who will not fear and glorify your *n*?

NAMED (NAMES)

Gen 2.20 The man gave *n* to all cattle, and to the
Ex 28. 9 engrave on them the *n* of the sons of
Mt 1.25 had borne a son; and he *n* him Jesus.
10. 2 the *n* of the twelve apostles: first,
Lk 10.20 you, but rejoice that your *n* are written
Phil 4. 3 whose *n* are in the book of life.

NAPHTALI

Gen 30. 8 have prevailed"; so she named him *N*.
49.21 *N* is a doe let loose that bears lovely
Deut 33.23 of *N* he said: O *N*, sated with favor, full
Judg 1.33 *N* did not drive out the inhabitants of
Ps 68.27 princes of Zebulun, the princes of *N*.
Isa 9. 1 the land of Zebulun and the land of *N*,
Mt 4.13 land of *N*, on the road by the sea,

NAPHTALITES

Num 26.50 These are the *N* by their clans: the

NARROW

Mt 7.13 "Enter through the *n* gate; for the gate
Lk 13.24 "Strive to enter through the *n* door; for

NATHAN

Counseled David about the people, 2 Sam 7.2-17 (1 Chr 17.1-15); rebuked David, 2 Sam 12.1-23; anointed Solomon as king, 1 Kings 1.8-45.

NATHANAEL

Jn 1.45 Philip found *N*, and said to him, "We

NATION

Gen 12. 2 I will make of you a great *n*, and I will
18.18 shall become a great and mighty *n*,
46. 3 Egypt, for I will make of you a great *n*
Deut 4. 7 what other great *n* has a god so near to
4.34 to take a *n* for himself from the midst
26. 5 and there he became a *n*, mighty and
28.49 LORD will bring a *n* from far away, from
2 Sam 7.23 Is there another *n* on earth whose God
Ps 106. 5 I may rejoice in the gladness of your *n*,
Prov 14.34 Righteousness exalts a *n*, but sin is a
Isa 2. 4 *n* shall not lift up sword against *n*,
9. 3 You have multiplied the *n*, you have
Jer 7.28 This is the *n* that did not obey the voice
31.36 Israel would cease to be a *n* before me
Ezek 37.22 I will make them one *n* in the land, on
Mt 21.43 given to a *n* that produces the fruits of
Acts 10.35 in every *n* anyone who fears him and

NATIONS

Gen 10. 5 language, by their families, in their *n*.
17. 5 you the ancestor of a multitude of *n*.
22.18 all the *n* of the earth gain blessing for
26. 4 all the *n* of the earth shall gain blessing
Lev 25.44 from the *n* around you that you may
1 Sam 8. 5 then, a king to govern us, like other *n*."
1 Chr 16.24 Declare his glory among the *n*, his
16.35 gather and rescue us from among the *n*,
Ps 18.43 You made me the head of the *n*;
33.10 brings the counsel of the *n* to nothing;
67. 4 Let the *n* be glad and sing for joy, for
79. 6 Pour out your anger on the *n* that do
96. 3 Declare his glory among the *n*, his
110. 6 He will execute judgment among the *n*,
126. 2 then it was said among the *n*, "The LORD
Isa 2. 2 the hills; all the *n* shall stream to it.
40.15 the *n* are like a drop from a bucket, and
49. 6 I will give you as a light to the *n*, that
60. 3 *N* shall come to your light, and kings to
66.18 I am coming to gather all *n* and
66.19 shall declare my glory among the *n*.
Jer 4. 2 then *n* shall be blessed by him, and by
27. 7 All the *n* shall serve him and his son
Ezek 7.24 the worst of the *n* to take possession
11.16 removed them far away among the *n*,
36.23 the *n* shall know that I am the LORD,
39.21 I will display my glory among the *n*; and
Joel 2.17 a mockery, a byword among the *n*.
3. 2 I will gather all the *n* and bring them
3.12 Let the *n* rouse themselves, and come
Mic 5.15 vengeance on the *n* that did not obey.
Hab 1. 5 Look at the *n*, and see! Be astonished!
Zech 14. 2 I will gather all the *n* against Jerusalem
Mal 1.11 setting my name is great among the *n*,
3.12 all *n* will count you happy, for you will
Mt 24. 9 be hated by all *n* because of my name.
Mk 11.17 called a house of prayer for all the *n*"?
Lk 24.47 is to be proclaimed in his name to all *n*,
Rev 11.18 The *n* raged, but your wrath has come,
18.23 and all *n* were deceived by your sorcery.
21.24 The *n* will walk by its light, and the

NATURE

Rom 11.24 from what is by *n* a wild olive tree and

NAZARETH

Mt 2.23 made his home in a town called *N*,
4.13 He left *N* and made his home in
21.11 is the prophet Jesus from *N* in Galilee."
26.71 "This man was with Jesus of *N*."
Mk 16. 6 you are looking for Jesus of *N*, who was
Jn 1.45 wrote, Jesus son of Joseph from *N*."
Acts 2.22 Jesus of *N*, a man attested to you by
10.38 how God anointed Jesus of *N* with the
22. 8 said to me, 'I am Jesus of *N* whom you

NAZIRITE

Num 6. 2 the vow of a *n*, to separate themselves
Judg 13. 5 the boy shall be a *n* to God from birth.

NINEVEH

Gen 10.11 land he went into Assyria, and built *N*,
Jon 1. 2 "Go at once to *N*, that great city, and
4.11 And should I not be concerned about *N*,
Nah 2. 8 *N* is like a pool whose waters run away.
Mt 12.41 the people of *N* will rise up at the
Lk 11.30 became a sign to the people of *N*,
11.32 The people of *N* will rise up at the

NOAH

Born, Gen 5.29; walked with God, Gen 6.9; built the ark, Gen 6.11-22; preserved through the flood, Gen 7.1–8.19; built an altar, Gen 8.20-22; covenant with God, Gen 9.8-17; his drunkenness, Gen 9.20-21; prophesied concerning his sons, Gen 9.22-27; died, Gen 9.28-29.

NOBLE

Prov 8. 6 Hear, for I will speak *n* things, and from
1 Cor 1.26 powerful, not many were of *n* birth.

NOISE

Ps 66. 1 Make a joyful *n* to God, all the earth;
100. 1 Make a joyful *n* to the LORD, all the
Jer 10.22 Hear, a *n*! Listen, it is coming—a great

NOON

Acts 10. 9 About *n* the next day, as they were on

NORTH

Isa 41.25 I stirred up one from the *n*, and he has
43. 6 I will say to the *n*, "Give them up," and

NOTHING

Job 1. 9 the LORD, "Does Job fear God for *n*?
Ezek 12.22 prolonged and every vision comes to *n*"?
Hag 2. 3 to you now? Is it not in your sight as *n*?
1 Cor 13. 3 boast, but do have not love, I gain *n*.

NOTICE

Ex 13.19 "God will surely take *n* of you, and then

NUMBER (NUMBERED)

1 Chr 21. 2 "Go, *n* Israel, from Beer-sheba to Dan,
Job 14.16 then you would not *n* my steps, you
Isa 53.12 death, and was *n* with the transgressors;
Acts 2.47 day by day the Lord added to their *n*
Rev 13.18 of the beast, for it is the *n* of a person.

O

OAK (OAKS)

Isa 1.30 shall be like an *o*, whose leaf withers,
6.13 or an *o* whose stump remains standing
61. 3 They will be called *o* of righteousness,

OATH

Gen 24. 8 then you will be free from this *o* of
24.41 her to you, you will be free from my *o*.'
Num 5.19 the priest shall make her take an *o*,
Ps 15. 4 who stand by their *o* even to their hurt;
Neh 10.29 a curse and an *o* to walk in God's law,
Zech 8.17 love no false *o*; for all these are things
Lk 1.73 *o* which he swore to our ancestor
Acts 23.21 by an *o* neither to eat nor drink until
Heb 7.20 this one became a priest with an *o*,

OBADIAH

Ob 1 The vision of *O*. Thus says the Lord GOD

OBEDIENCE

Gen 49.10 to him; and the *o* of the peoples is his.
Rom 1. 5 apostleship to bring about *o* of faith
16.19 while your *o* is known to all, so that I

OBEDIENT

Isa 1.19 If you are willing and *o*, you shall eat
Lk 2.51 and was *o* to them. His mother
Acts 6. 7 of the priests became *o* to the faith.
Phil 2. 8 and became *o* to the point of death—
1 Pet 1. 2 sanctified by the Spirit to be *o* to Jesus

OBEY (OBEYED OBEYING)

Gen 22.18 because you have *o* my voice."
26. 5 because Abraham *o* my voice and kept
27.13 my son; only *o* my word, and go, get
27.43 my son, *o* my voice; flee at once to my
Ex 19. 5 if you will *o* my voice and keep my
Deut 12.28 Be careful to *o* all these words that I
13. 4 his voice you shall *o*, him shall you
21.20 "This son of ours . . . will not *o* us. He
28.13 if you *o* the commandments of the LORD
28.45 because you did not *o* the LORD your
30. 2 you and your children *o* him with all
30. 8 Then you shall again *o* the LORD,
34. 9 the Israelites *o* him, doing as the LORD
Josh 1.17 Moses in all things, so we will *o* you.
1 Sam 15.19 Why then did you not *o* the voice of the
15.22 Surely, to *o* is better than sacrifice, and
2 Kings 18.12 because they did not *o* the voice of the
Neh 9.17 they refused to *o*, and were not mindful
Jer 3.13 green tree, and have not *o* my voice,
7.23 I gave them, "*O* my voice, and I
7.28 is the nation that did not *o* the voice
26.13 your doings, and *o* the voice of the LORD
32.23 But they did not *o* your voice or follow
35. 8 We have *o* the charge of our ancestor
38.20 Just *o* the voice of the LORD in what I
42. 6 or good, we will *o* the voice of the LORD
43. 4 and all the people did not *o* the voice
Dan 7.27 and all dominions shall serve and *o*
Hag 1.12 all the remnant of the people, *o* the
Zech 6.15 This will happen if you diligently *o* the
Mt 8.27 that even the winds and the sea *o* him?"
28.20 teaching them to *o* everything that I
Mk 1.27 the unclean spirits, and they *o* him."
4.41 this, that even wind and the sea *o* him?"
Lk 8.25 winds and the waters, and they *o* him?"
Acts 5.29 "We must *o* God rather than human
Rom 2. 8 and who *o* not the truth but
2 Cor 10. 5 take every thought captive to *o* Christ.
Gal 5. 7 who prevented you from *o* the truth?
2 Thess 3.14 note of those who do not *o* what we say
Heb 5. 9 of eternal salvation for all who *o* him,
11. 8 By faith Abraham *o* when he was called
13.17 *O* your leaders and submit to them, for
1 Pet 3. 6 Thus Sarah *o* Abraham and called him
4.17 end for those who do not *o* the gospel

OBJECT

Rom 9.21 of the same lump one *o* for special use

OBLIGED

Gal 5. 3 that he is *o* to obey the entire law.

OBSERVE (OBSERVES OBSERVING)

Ex 12.17 You shall *o* the festival of unleavened
31.16 shall keep the sabbath, *o* the sabbath
Deut 4. 6 You must *o* them diligently, for this will
17.19 diligently *o* all the words of this law,
Ps 33.15 hearts of them all, and *o* all their deeds.
105. 45 might keep his statutes and *o* his laws.
106. 3 Happy are those who *o* justice, who do
119. 34 your law and *o* it with my whole heart.
Eccl 11. 4 Whoever *o* the wind will not sow; and
Gal 4.10 You are *o* special days, and months, and

OCCUPATION

Gen 46.33 calls you, and says, 'What is your *o*?'
Jon 1. 8 What is your *o*? Where do you come

OCCUPY

Deut 3.18 God has given you this land to *o*, all
6.18 that you may go in and *o* the good land

OFFEND (OFFENDED)

Gen 40. 1 and his baker *o* their lord the king of
Prov 18.19 An ally *o* is stronger than a city; such

Jn 6.61 it, said to them, "Does this *o* you?

OFFENSE

Mt 11. 6 is anyone who takes no *o* at me."
15.12 the Pharisees took *o* when they heard
Mk 6. 3 here with us?" And they took *o* at him.
Lk 7.23 is anyone who takes no *o* at me."
Acts 25. 8 in no way committed an *o* against the
1 Cor 10.32 Give no *o* to Jews or to Greeks or to the
Gal 5.11 the *o* of the cross has been removed.

OFFER (OFFERED)

Gen 22. 2 and *o* him there as a burnt offering
46. 1 he *o* sacrifices to the God of his father
Ex 34.25 You shall not *o* the blood of my
Lev 10. 1 and they *o* unholy fire before the LORD,
22.20 shall not *o* anything that has a blemish,
Judg 5. 9 Israel who *o* themselves willingly among
2 Sam 24.22 *o* up what seems good to him; here are
1 Chr 29. 9 mind they had *o* freely to the LORD;
2 Chr 8.12 Solomon *o* up burnt offerings to the
Ezra 7.15 counselors have freely *o* to the God of
Neh 11. 2 who willingly *o* to live in Jerusalem.
Ps 4. 5 *O* right sacrifices, and put your trust in
27. 6 I will *o* in his tent sacrifices with shouts
50.14 *O* to God a sacrifice of thanksgiving,
Jon 1.16 they *o* a sacrifice to the LORD and made
Mt 5.24 or sister, and then come and *o* your gift.
Acts 7.42 'Did you *o* to me slain victims and
1 Cor 8. 4 as to the eating of food *o* to idols, we
Heb 11. 4 By faith Abel *o* to God a more
11.17 when put to the test, *o* up Isaac.
12.28 we *o* to God an acceptable worship

OFFERING (OFFERINGS)

Ex 35. 5 Take from among you an *o* to the LORD;
1 Chr 16.29 due his name; bring an *o*, and come
Ps 20. 3 May he remember all your *o*, and regard
Isa 66.20 kindred from all the nations as an *o*
Jer 11.12 out to the gods to whom they make *o*,
Ezek 44.30 every *o* of all kinds shall belong to the
Mal 3. 4 the *o* of Judah and Jerusalem will be
Rom 15.16 so that the *o* of the Gentiles may be

OFFICER

Jer 20. 1 was chief *o* in the house of the LORD,

OFFICIAL (OFFICIALS)

Jer 26.10 When the *o* of Judah heard these
Mic 7. 3 the *o* and the judge ask for a bribe, and
Acts 18.17 Sosthenes, the *o* of the synagogue,

OFFSPRING

Gen 3.15 the woman, between your *o* and hers;
12. 7 said, "To your *o* I will give this land."
17. 8 I will give you, and your *o* after you, the
21.12 is through Isaac that *o* shall be named
26. 4 and will give to your *o* all these lands;
Job 5.25 be many, your *o* like the grass of the
Mal 2.15 what does the one God desire? Godly *o*.
Acts 17.28 poets have said, 'For we too are his *o*.'

OIL

Ex 30.25 make of these a sacred anointing *o*
2 Kings 4. 2 nothing in the house, except a jar of *o*."
Ps 23. 5 you anoint my head with *o*; my cup
45. 7 has anointed you with the *o* of gladness
Isa 1. 6 drained or bound up or softened with *o*.
Mt 25. 4 but the wise took flasks of *o* with their
Mk 6.13 anointed with *o* many who were sick

OINTMENT (OINTMENTS)

Eccl 10. 1 Dead flies make the perfumer's *o* give
Mt 26. 7 alabaster jar of very costly *o*, and she
Mk 14. 3 with an an alabaster jar of very costly *o*
Lk 23.56 returned, and prepared spices and *o*.

OLD (OLDER)

Josh 23. 2 said to them, "I am now *o* and well
2 Chr 10. 8 rejected the advice that the *o* men gave
Mt 9.16 piece of unshrunk cloth on an *o* cloak,
Mk 2.21 piece of unshrunk cloth on an *o* cloak;
Lk 3.23 Jesus was about thirty years *o* when he
2 Cor 3.14 they hear the reading of the *o* covenant,

OLIVE

Gen 8.11 in its beak was a freshly plucked *o* leaf;
Deut 24.20 When you beat your *o* trees, do not
Ps 128. 3 your children will be like *o* shoots
Hos 14. 6 his beauty shall be like the *o* tree, and
Zech 4. 3 And by it there are two *o* trees, one on
Rom 11.17 you, a wild *o* shoot, were grafted in
Rev 11. 4 These are the two *o* trees and the two

OLIVET

Acts 1.12 to Jerusalem from the mount called *O*,

ONE

Gen 2.24 to his wife, and they become *o* flesh.
Mk 10. 8 the two shall become *o* flesh.' So they
Acts 17.26 From *o* ancestor he made all nations to
1 Cor 8. 6 and *o* Lord, Jesus Christ, through whom
Eph 5.31 wife, and the two will become *o* flesh."

ONESIMUS

Col 4. 9 he is coming with *O*, the faithful and
Philem 10 I am appealing to you for my child, *O*,

OPEN (OPENED OPENS)

Gen 3. 5 your eyes will be *o*, and you will be like
3. 7 the eyes of both were *o*, and they knew
Num 22.28 the LORD *o* the mouth of the donkey,
Judg 11.35 I have *o* my mouth to the LORD, and I
2 Kings 6.17 LORD *o* the eyes of the servant, and he
Job 33.16 then he *o* their ears, and terrifies them
Ps 51.15 Lord, *o* my lips, and my mouth will
104. 28 when you *o* your hand, they are filled
119. 18 *O* my eyes, so that I may behold
Prov 20.13 *o* your eyes, and you will have plenty of
31.26 She *o* her mouth with wisdom, and the
Song 5. 2 "*O* to me, my sister, my love, my dove,
5. 6 I *o* to my beloved but my beloved had
Isa 22.22 he shall *o*, and no one shall shut; he
26. 2 *O* the gates, so that the righteous
50. 5 The Lord GOD has *o* my ear, and I was
60.11 Your gates shall always be *o*; day and
Ezek 3. 2 So I *o* my mouth, and he gave me the
Dan 9.18 *O* your eyes and look at our desolation
Mt 3.16 the heavens were *o* to him and he saw
9.30 And their eyes were *o*. Then Jesus
13.35 "I will *o* my mouth to speak in parables;
27.52 The tombs also were *o*, and many
Lk 24.31 their eyes were *o* and they recognized
24.45 he *o* their minds to understand the
Jn 9.14 Jesus made the mud and *o* his eyes.
Acts 14.27 and how he had *o* a door of faith for
16.14 The Lord *o* her heart to listen eagerly to
26.18 I am sending you to *o* their eyes so that
1 Cor 16. 9 door for effective work has *o* to me,
2 Cor 2.12 Christ, a door was *o* for me in the Lord;
Rev 3. 8 I have set before you an *o* door, which
6. 1 I saw the Lamb *o* one of the seven seals,

OPENLY

Mk 1.45 Jesus could no longer go into a town *o*,
Jn 7.13 Yet no one would speak *o* about him for

OPPORTUNITY

Acts 24.25 when I have an *o*, I will send for you.
Phil 4.10 were concerned for me, but had no *o* to

OPPOSE (OPPOSED OPPOSES)

Gal 2.11 Cephas came to Antioch, I *o* him to
2 Thess 2. 4 He *o* and exalts himself above every
2 Tim 3. 8 and counterfeit faith, also *o* the truth.
1 Pet 5. 5 "God *o* the proud, but gives grace to the

OPPRESS (OPPRESSED OPPRESSES OPPRESSING)

Gen 15.13 they shall be *o* for four hundred years;
Ex 23. 9 You shall not *o* a resident alien; you
Ps 42. 9 mournfully because the enemy *o* me?
Prov 14.31 who *o* the poor insult their Maker,
22.16 *O* the poor in order to enrich oneself,
28. 3 A ruler who *o* the poor is a beating rain
Jer 7. 6 if you do not *o* the alien, the orphan,
Ezek 18.12 *o* the poor and needy, commits robbery,
Hos 12. 7 hands are false balances, he loves to *o*.
Am 4. 1 who *o* the poor, who crush the needy,
Mic 2. 2 they *o* the householder and house,
Zech 7.10 do not *o* the widow, the orphan, the
Mal 3. 5 against those who *o* the hired workers

OPPRESSED (n)

Ps 69.32 Let the *o* see it and be glad; you who
76. 9 to save all the *o* of the earth.
Isa 1.17 seek justice, rescue the *o*, defend the
51.14 The *o* shall speedily be released; they
61. 1 sent me to bring good news to the *o*,
Dan 4.27 and your iniquities with mercy to the *o*,

OPPRESSION (OPPRESSIONS)

Ps 55.11 *o* and fraud do not depart from its
Eccl 4. 1 I saw all the *o* that are practiced under
7. 7 *o* makes the wise foolish, and a bribe
Isa 30.12 reject this word, and put your trust in *o*
Jer 22.17 blood, and for practicing *o* and violence.

OPPRESSOR

Ps 72. 4 to the needy, and crush the *o*.
Isa 14. 4 How the *o* has ceased! How his
51.13 But where is the fury of the *o*?
Zech 9. 8 no *o* shall again overrun them, for now I

ORACLE (ORACLES)

Isa 13. 1 The *o* concerning Babylon that Isaiah
17. 1 An *o* concerning Damascus. See,
19. 1 An *o* concerning Egypt. See, the LORD is
21. 1 *o* concerning the wilderness of the sea.
21.13 The *o* concerning the desert plain. In
23. 1 The *o* concerning Tyre. Wail, O ships of
Nah 1. 1 An *o* concerning Nineveh. The book of
Hab 1. 1 The *o* that the prophet Habakkuk saw.
Zech 9. 1 An *O*. The word of the LORD is against
12. 1 An *O*. The word of the LORD concerning
Mal 1. 1 An *o*. The word of the LORD to Israel by
Rom 3. 2 the Jews were entrusted with the *o*
Heb 5.12 the basic elements of the *o* of God.

ORDAIN (ORDAINED)

Ex 28.41 shall anoint them and *o* them and
32.29 Today you have *o* yourselves for the
2 Sam 17.14 the LORD had *o* to defeat the good
Isa 26.12 O LORD, you will *o* peace for us, for
Lam 3.37 and have it done, if the Lord has *o* it?
Acts 10.42 that he is the one *o* by God as judge
Gal 3.19 it was *o* through angels by a mediator.

ORDEAL

2 Cor 8. 2 during a severe *o* of affliction, their
Rev 7.14 they who have come out of the great *o*;

ORDER (ORDERED ORDERS)

Lev 25.21 I will *o* my blessing for you in the sixth
Ps 110. 4 according to the *o* of Melchizedek."
Mt 12.44 it finds it empty, swept, and put in *o*.
17. 9 Jesus *o* them, "Tell no one about the
Mk 5.43 strictly *o* them that no one should know
9. 9 he *o* them to tell no one about what
Lk 8.56 but he *o* them to tell no one what had
Acts 5.28 "We gave you strict *o* not to teach in his
1 Cor 14.40 should be done decently and in *o*.

ORDINANCES

Deut 4. 8 nation has . . . *o* as just as this entire
Job 38.33 Do you know the *o* of the heavens? Can

ORGANIZED

1 Chr 24. 3 David *o* them according to the
2 Chr 23.18 the levitical priests whom David had *o*

ORNAMENT

Titus 2.10 they may be an *o* to the doctrine of God

ORPHAN (ORPHANS)

Deut 10.18 who executes justice for the *o* and
14.29 the resident aliens, the *o*, and the
Job 6.27 You would even cast lots over the *o*,
22. 9 and the arms of the *o* you have crushed.
24. 9 There are those who snatch the *o* child
29.12 cried, and the *o* who had no helper.
Ps 10.14 you; you have been the helper of the *o*.
Jer 49.11 Leave your *o*, I will keep them alive;

OUT

1 Cor 10.13 he will also provide the way *o* so that

OUTWITTED

2 Cor 2.11 this so that we may not be *o* by Satan;

OVEN

Lk 12.28 and tomorrow is thrown into the *o*,

OVERCOME

Rom 12.21 not be *o* by evil, but *o* evil with good.

OVERFLOW (OVERFLOWED OVERFLOWING OVERFLOWS)

Ps 73. 7 with fatness; their hearts *o* with follies.
Mal 3.10 and pour down for you an *o* blessing.
2 Cor 9.12 saints but also *o* in many thanksgivings
1 Tim 1.14 grace of our Lord *o* for me with the

OVERLOOK (OVERLOOKED)

Acts 17.30 has *o* the times of human ignorance,
Heb 6.10 is not unjust; he will not *o* your work

OVERPOWERS

Lk 11.22 he attacks him and *o* him, he takes

OVERSEERS

Acts 20.28 which the Holy Spirit has made you *o*,

OVERTHROW

Jer 1.10 to destroy and to *o*, to build and to
Hag 2.22 earth, and to *o* the throne of kingdoms;
Rom 3.31 Do we then *o* law by this faith? By no

OVERWHELM (OVERWHELMED OVERWHELMS)

Ps 55. 5 come upon me, and horror *o* me.
88. 7 me, and you *o* me with all your waves.
2 Cor 2. 7 he may not be *o* by excessive sorrow.

OWE (OWED)

Mt 18.24 one who *o* him ten thousand talents
Rom 13. 8 *O* no one anything, except to love one

OWN

Ex 15.17 on the mountain of your *o* possession,
Phil 3.12 Christ Jesus has made me his *o*.

OWNER

Isa 1. 3 The ox knows its *o*, and the donkey its
2 Tim 2.21 and useful to the *o* of the house,

OX

Ex 21.28 "When an *o* gores a man or a woman to
Num 22. 4 around us, as the *o* licks up the grass of
Deut 25. 4 You shall not muzzle an *o* while it is
Prov 7.22 her, and goes like an *o* to the slaughter,
Isa 1. 3 The *o* knows its owner, and the donkey
Lk 14. 5 *o* that has fallen into a well, will you
1 Cor 9. 9 "You shall not muzzle an *o* while it is
1 Tim 5.18 you shall not muzzle an *o* when it is

P

PAIN
Job 14.22 They feel only the *p* of their own
Eccl 2.23 all their days are full of *p*, and their
11.10 put away *p* from your body; for youth
Jer 30.15 Your *p* is incurable. Because your guilt
Jn 16.20 have *p*, but your *p* will turn into joy.
2 Cor 2. 2 if I cause you *p*, who is there to make
Gal 4.19 for whom I am again in the *p* of

PAINTED
2 Kings 9.30 Jezebel . . . *p* her eyes, and adorned her
Ezek 23.40 them you bathed yourself, *p* your eyes,

PALACE (PALACES)
Ps 45. 8 From ivory *p* stringed instruments make
45.15 along as they enter the *p* of the king.

PALM
Ps 92.12 The righteous flourish like the *p* tree,
Song 7. 8 I say I will climb the *p* tree and lay
Jn 12.13 they took branches of *p* trees and went

PANGS
Gen 3.16 greatly increase your *p* in childbearing;
Jer 13.21 Will not *p* take hold of you, like those
Hos 13.13 *p* of childbirth come for him, but he is

PANIC
Isa 28.16 foundation: "One who trusts will not *p*."

PARABLE (PARABLES)
Ps 78. 2 I will open my mouth in a *p*; I will utter
Mt 13. 3 he told them many things in *p*, saying,
Mk 4.30 of God, or what *p* will we use for it?
4.34 he did not speak to them except in *p*,
Lk 8.11 *p* is this: The seed is the word of God.

PARADISE
Lk 23.43 tell you, today you will be with me in *P*."
2 Cor 12. 3 was caught up into *P* and heard things

PARALYTIC (PARALYTICS)
Mt 4.24 epileptics, and *p*, and he cured them.
9. 2 Jesus saw their faith, he said to the *p*,

PARALYZED
Mt 8. 6 "Lord, my servant is lying at home *p*, in
Mk 2. 3 people came, bringing to him a *p* man,
Lk 5.18 carrying a *p* man on a bed. They were
Acts 9.33 bedridden for eight years, for he was *p*.

PARDON (PARDONING)
Ex 34. 9 *p* our iniquity and our sin, and take us
Deut 29.20 LORD will be unwilling to *p* them, for
1 Sam 15.25 *p* my sin, and return with me, so that I
2 Kings 5.18 may the LORD *p* your servant on one
24. 4 and the LORD was not willing to *p*.
2 Chr 30.18 for them saying, "The good LORD *p* all
Job 7.21 Why do you not *p* my transgression and
Ps 25.11 sake, O LORD, *p* my guilt, for it is great.
Isa 55. 7 to our God, for he will abundantly *p*.
Jer 5. 1 truth—so that I may *p* Jerusalem.
5. 7 How can I *p* you? Your children have
50.20 be found; for I will *p* the remnant that I
Mic 7.18 Who is a God like you, *p* iniquity and

PARENT (PARENTS)
Deut 24.16 shall children be put to death for the *p*;
2 Kings 14. 6 *p* shall not be put to death for the
Prov 17.21 gets trouble; the *p* of a fool has no joy.
Ezek 18.20 nor a *p* suffer for the iniquity of a child;
Mal 4. 6 turn the hearts of *p* to their children
Mt 10.21 children will rise against *p* and have
Lk 1.17 go before him, to turn the hearts of *p* to
2.41 every year his *p* went to Jerusalem for
Jn 9. 2 who sinned, this man or his *p*, that he
9.18 they called the *p* of the man who had
2 Cor 12.14 up for their *p*, but *p* for their children.
Eph 6. 1 Children, obey your *p* in the Lord, for
2 Tim 3. 2 disobedient to their *p*, ungrateful,

PARTAKE
Ezra 2.63 were not to *p* of the most holy food,
Neh 7.65 not to *p* of the most holy food, until a
1 Cor 10.17 one body, for we all *p* of the one bread.

PARTED
2 Kings 2. 8 the water was *p* to the one side and to

PARTIAL
Lev 19.15 you shall not be *p* to the poor or defer
Deut 1.17 You must not be *p* in judging; hear out
10.17 the great God . . . is not *p* and takes no
Prov 18. 5 It is not right be *p* to the guilty, or to

PARTIALITY
Deut 16.19 distort justice; you must not show *p*;
2 Chr 19. 7 with the LORD our God, or *p*, or taking
Prov 24.23 *P* in judging is not good. Whoever says
28.21 To show *p* is not good—yet for a piece
Acts 10.34 I truly understand that God shows no *p*,
Rom 2.11 also the Greek. For God shows no *p*.
Gal 2. 6 God shows no *p*)—those leaders
Eph 6. 9 in heaven, and with him there is no *p*.
1 Tim 5.21 doing nothing on the basis of *p*.
Jas 2. 9 if you show *p*, you commit sin and are

PARTNER (PARTNERS)
Prov 29.24 To be a *p* of a thief is to hate one's
Lk 5. 7 signaled their *p* in the other boat to
1 Cor 10.20 I do not want you to be *p* with demons.
Philem 17 if you consider me your *p*, welcome him

PARTNERSHIP
2 Cor 6.14 what *p* is there between righteousness

PARTRIDGE
1 Sam 26.20 like one who hunts a *p* in the
Jer 17.11 Like the *p* hatching what it did not lay,

PASCHAL
1 Cor 5. 7 For our *p* lamb, Christ, has been

PASS (PASSED)
Ex 12.23 LORD will *p* over that door and will not
Josh 3. 4 go, for you have not *p* this way before.
Ps 31.12 I have *p* out of mind like one who is
Prov 9.15 calling to those who *p* by, who are
Eccl 6.12 vain life, which they *p* like a shadow?
Isa 14.24 as I have planned, so shall it come to *p*:
43. 2 When you *p* through the waters, I will
Lam 1.12 all you who *p* by? Look and see if there
Mt 24.35 will *p* away, but my words will not *p*
Mk 1.16 As Jesus *p* along the Sea of Galilee, he
13.31 Heaven and earth will *p* away, but my
Lk 10.31 he saw him, he *p* by on the other side.
1 Jn 3.14 know that we have *p* from death to life

PASSION (PASSIONS)
Prov 14.30 to the flesh, but *p* makes the bones rot.
Song 8. 6 is strong as death, *p* fierce as the grave.
Rom 1.27 were consumed with *p* for one another.
1 Cor 7.36 if his *p* are strong, and so it has to be,
Eph 2. 3 lived among them in the *p* of our flesh,

PASSOVER
Ex 12.11 eat it hurriedly. It is the *p* of the LORD.
Lev 23. 5 twilight, there shall be a *p* offering to
Num 9. 5 They kept the *p* in the first month, on
28.16 there shall be a *p* offering to the LORD.
Deut 16. 1 by keeping the *p* for the LORD your God,
Josh 5.11 On the day after the *p*, on that very day,
2 Kings 23.21 "Keep the *p* to the LORD your God as
2 Chr 30. 1 Jerusalem to keep the *p* to the LORD the
35.17 of Israel who were present kept the *p* at
Ezra 6.19 month the returned exiles kept the *p*.

Mt 26. 2 after two days the *P* is coming, and the
Mk 14. 1 It was two days before the *P* and the
14.14 I may eat the *P* with my disciples?'
Lk 22. 7 Bread, on which the *P* lamb had
Jn 13. 1 before the festival of the *P*, Jesus knew
18.39 that I release someone for you at the *P*.
Heb 11.28 By faith he kept the *P* and the

PASTORS
Eph 4.11 some evangelists, some *p* and teachers.

PASTURE (PASTURES)
Ps 23. 2 He makes me lie down in green *p*; he
Jer 50.19 I will restore Israel to its *p*, and it shall

PATH (PATHS)
Job 8.13 the *p* of all who forget God; the hope of
Ps 8. 8 whatever passes along the *p* of the seas.
17. 5 My steps have held fast to your *p*, my
119. 35 me in the *p* of your commandmants,
119.105 a lamp to my feet and a light to my *p*.
Prov 4.18 But the *p* of the righteous is like the
15.24 For the wise the *p* of life leads upward,
Isa 40.14 and who taught him the *p* of justice?
42.16 by *p* they have not known I will guide
45.13 and I will make all his *p* straight;
Jer 31. 9 walk by brooks of water, in a straight *p*
Mt 13. 4 some seeds fell on the *p*, and the birds
Mk 4. 4 some seed fell on the *p*, and the birds

PATHWAYS
Hab 3. 6 his ancient *p* the everlasting hills sank

PATIENCE
Mic 2. 7 Is the LORD's *p* exhausted? Are these his
Mt 18.29 with him, "Have *p* with me, and I will
Rom 8.25 we do not see, we wait for it with *p*.
9.22 has endured with much *p* the objects of
Col 3.12 kindness, humility, meekness, and *p*.
Jas 5.10 As an example of suffering and *p*,
2 Pet 3.15 regard the *p* of our Lord as salvation. So

PATIENT
Lk 8.15 heart, and bear fruit with *p* endurance.
Rom 12.12 Rejoice in hope, be *p* in suffering,
1 Cor 13. 4 Love is *p*; love is kind; love is not
Jas 5. 8 be *p*. Strengthen your hearts, for the
Rev 2. 2 works, your toil and your *p* endurance.
2.19 love, faith, service, and *p* endurance.

PATMOS
Rev 1. 9 was on the island called *P* because of

PAUL

Born in Tarsus, Acts 22.3; educated under Gamaliel, Acts 22.3; consented to Stephen's death, Acts 7.58; 8.1 (22.20); persecuted the church, Acts 8.3; 9.1-2 (22.4-5; 26.10-11; 1 Cor 15.9; Gal 1.13; Phil. 3.6); went into Arabia, Gal 1.17; preached in Damascus, Gal 1.17; went up to Jerusalem, Acts 9.26-28; Gal 1.18-19; name changed to Paul, Acts 13.9; missionary work, Acts 13—14; 15.36—18.22; 18.23—21.17; attended the Council of Jerusalem, Acts 15.1-29; Gal. 2.1-10; arrested in Jerusalem, Acts 21.27-40; imprisoned in Caesarea, Acts 23.23-35; defended himself before Felix, Acts 24; appealed to Caesar, Acts 25.10-12; defended himself before Agrippa, Acts 26; journeyed to Rome, Acts 27.1—28.16; preached during imprisonment, Acts 28.17-31.

1 Cor 1.13 been divided? Was *P* crucified for you?
3. 4 For when one says, "I belong to *P*," and
2 Pet 3.15 our beloved brother *P* wrote to you

PAWN
Ex 22.26 If you take your neighbor's cloak in *p*,

PAY (PAID PAYING PAYS)
Gen 50.15 bears a grudge against us and *p* us back
Num 20.19 and our livestock, then we will *p* for it.
Ps 66.13 I will *p* you my vows, those that my lips
116. 18 I will *p* my vows to the LORD in the
137. 8 Happy shall they be who *p* you back
Isa 40. 2 served her term, that her penalty is *p*,
Joel 3. 4 Are you *p* me back for something? If
Rom 13. 7 *P* all what is due them—taxes to whom
2 Tim 4.14 great harm; the Lord will *p* him back

PAYMENT
Lev 25.52 they shall make *p* for their redemption.
Ezek 16.34 *p*, while no *p* was given to you; you
Mt 10. 8 You received without *p*, give without *p*.

PEACE
Lev 26. 6 I will grant *p* in the land, and you shall
Num 6.26 countenance upon you, and give you *p*.
Deut 20.10 to fight against it, offer it terms of *p*.
Judg 6.23 "*P* be to you; do not fear, you shall not
1 Sam 10.27 him no present. But he held his *p*.
1 Kings 2.33 there shall be *p* from the LORD
2 Kings 20.19 "Why not, if there will be *p* and security
1 Chr 12.18 son of Jesse! *P*, *p* to you, and *p* to the
19.19 by Israel, they made *p* with David,
22. 9 he shall be a man of *p*. I will give him *p*
2 Chr 14. 6 in those years, for the LORD gave him *p*.
Job 52.3 the wild animals shall be at *p* with you.
Ps 35.20 For they do not speak *p*, but they
85.10 will meet; righteousness and *p* will kiss
119.165 Great *p* have those who love your law;
120. 7 I am for *p*; but when I speak, they are
122. 6 Pray for the *p* of Jerusalem: "May they
Prov 3.17 lay hold of her; and all her paths are *p*.
Song 8.10 I was in his eyes as one who brings *p*.
Isa 9. 7 there shall be endless *p* for the throne
26. 3 you keep in *p* —in *p* because they trust
26.12 O LORD, you will ordain *p* for us, for
27. 5 let it make *p* with me, let it make *p*
32. 1 The effect of righteousness will be *p*,
36.16 king of Assyria: 'Make your *p* with me
39. 8 will be *p* and security in my days."
48.22 "There is no *p*," says the LORD, "for the
52. 7 feet of the messenger who announces *p*,
54.10 my covenant of *p* shall not be removed,
55.12 go out in joy, and be led back in *p*;
57.19 *P*, *p*, to the far and the near, says the
60.17 I will anoint *P* as your overseer and
Jer 6.14 saying, "*P*, *p*," when there is no *p*.
8.11 saying, "*P*, *p*," when there is no *p*.
14.19 We look for *p*, but find no good; for a
Ezek 7.25 will seek *p*, but there shall be none.
13.10 people, saying, "*P*," when there is no *p*;
13.16 saw visions of *p* for it, when there was
34.25 I will make with them a covenant of *p*
37.26 I will make a covenant of *p* with them;
Mic 3. 5 who lead my people astray, who cry "*P*"
5. 5 the earth; and he shall be the one of *p*.
Nah 1.15 brings good tidings, who proclaims *p*!
Zech 9.10 and he shall command *p* to the nations;
Mt 10.34 I have not come to bring *p*, but a sword.
Mk 4.39 said to the sea, "*P*! Be still!" Then the
9.50 and be at *p* with one another."
Lk 1.79 to guide our feet into the way of *p*."
2.14 and on earth *p* among those whom he
7.50 "Your faith has saved you; go in *p*."
8.48 your faith has made you well; go in *p*."
10. 5 you enter, first say, '*P* to this house!'
12.51 I have come to give *p* on earth? No,
24.36 them and said to them, "*P* be with you!"
Jn 14.27 *P* I leave with you; my *p* I give to you. I
16.33 to you so that in me you may have *p*.
20.19 among them and said, "*P* be with you."
20.21 said to them again, "*P* be with you.
Acts 10.36 Israel, preaching *p* through Jesus Christ
Rom 5. 1 faith, we have *p* with God through our
14.19 us then pursue what makes for *p* and
16.20 The God of *p* will shortly crush Satan
2 Cor 1. 2 Grace to you and *p* from God our

Eph 2.14 for he is our *p*; in his flesh he has made
2.15 in place of the two, thus making *p*
2.17 proclaimed *p* to you who were far off
Phil 4. 7 the *p* of God, which surpasses all
4. 9 me, and the God of *p* will be with you.
Col 1.20 *p* through the blood of his cross.
3.15 let the *p* of Christ rule in your hearts,
Heb 13.20 may the God of *p*, who brought back
1 Pet 3.11 do good; let them seek *p* and pursue it.
Rev 6. 4 rider was permitted to take *p* from the

PEACEABLY

Gen 37. 4 him, and could not speak *p* to him.
1 Kings 2.13 asked, "Do you come *p*?" He said, "*P*."
Rom 12.18 far as it depends on you, live *p* with all.

PEACEMAKERS

Mt 5. 9 "Blessed are the *p*, for they will be

PEARLS

Mt 7. 6 and do not throw your *p* before swine,
13.45 is like a merchant in search of fine *p*,

PEN

Job 19.24 O that with an iron *p* and with lead
Ps 45. 1 to the king; my tongue is like the *p* of a
Jer 8. 8 the false *p* of the scribes has made it
17. 1 sin of Judah is written with an iron *p*;
3 Jn 13 but I would rather not write with *p* and

PENNY

Mt 10.29 Are now two sparrows sold for a *p*? Yet
Mk 12.42 copper coins, which are worth a *p*.

PENTECOST

Acts 2. 1 When the day of *P* had come, they were
1 Cor 16. 8 But I will stay in Ephesus until *P*,

PEOPLE

Ex 2.11 he went out to his *p* and saw their
6. 7 I will take you as my *p*, and I will be
7.16 "Let my *p* go, so that they may worship
15.16 until your *p*, O LORD, passed by, . . . the
32.11 your wrath burn hot against your *p*,
33.13 Consider too that this nation is your *p*."
Lev 26.12 be your God, and you shall be my *p*.
Num 14.14 you, O LORD, are in the midst of this *p*;
Deut 9.27 attention to the stubbornness of this *p*,
14. 2 you are a *p* holy to the LORD your God;
26.18 to be a treasured *p*, as he promised you,
29.13 he may establish you today as his *p*,
32. 9 LORD's own portion was his *p*, Jacob his
Judg 2. 7 The *p* worshiped the LORD all the days
Ruth 1. 6 LORD had considered his *p* and given
1.16 your *p* shall be my *p*, and your God, my
1 Sam 27.12 himself utterly abhorrent to his *p* Israel;
2 Sam 3.18 my servant David I will save my *p* Israel
7.24 established your *p* Israel to be your *p*
1 Kings 8.16 Since the day that I brought my *p* Israel
22. 4 my *p* are your *p*, my horses are your
2 Kings 3. 7 I am with you, my *p* are your *p*, my
11.17 and *p*, that they should be the LORD's *p*;
1 Chr 17. 9 I will appoint a place for my *p* Israel,
17.21 your *p* whom you redeemed from Egypt?
17.22 made your *p* Israel to be your *p* forever;
2 Chr 7.14 if my *p* who are called by my name
36.15 because he had compassion on his *p*
Ps 78.52 Then he led out his *p* like sheep, he
100. 3 we are his; we are his *p*, and the sheep
106. 40 of the LORD was kindled against his *p*,
110. 3 Your *p* will offer themselves willingly on
125. 2 Jerusalem, so the LORD surrounds his *p*,
144. 15 blessings fall; happy the *p* whose God is
148. 14 He has raised up a horn for his *p*,
149. 4 For the LORD takes pleasure in his *p*; he
Isa 2. 6 you have forsaken the ways of your *p*,
3.12 My *p*—children are their oppressors,
5.13 my *p* go into exile without knowledge;
Isa 9. 2 The *p* who walked in darkness have
40. 5 revealed, and all *p* shall see it together,
40. 6 "What shall I cry?" All *p* are grass, and
47. 6 I was angry with my *p*, I profaned my
58. 1 Announce to my *p* their rebellion, to
63. 8 "Surely they are my *p*, children who will
65.19 in Jerusalem, and delight in my *p*;
Jer 2.13 my *p* have committed two evils: they
7.23 be your God, and you shall be my *p*;
13.11 might be for me a *p*, a name, a praise,
18.15 But my *p* have forgotten me, they burn
24. 7 they shall be my *p* and I will be their
30.22 And you shall be my *p*, and I will be
32.38 They shall be my *p*, and I will be their
Ezek 11.20 Then they shall be my *p*, and I will be
14.11 Then they shall be my *p*, and I will be
36.28 and you shall be my *p*, and I will be
Hos 1.10 it was said to them, "You are not my *p*,"
2.23 I will say to Lo-ammi, "You are my *p*";
Joel 2.18 for his land, and had pity on his *p*.
Am 9. 7 like the Ethiopians to me, O *p* of Israel?
Mic 6. 2 LORD has a controversy with his *p*, and
Acts 18.10 are many in this city who are my *p*."
Rom 9.25 who were not my *p* I will call 'my *p*,'
1 Pet 2.10 were not a *p*, but now you are God's *p*;

PEOPLES

1 Kings 8.60 all the *p* of the earth may know that the
Ps 67. 5 Let the *p* praise you, O God; let all the
Mic 4. 1 *P* shall stream to it, and many nations

PERCEIVE (PERCEIVED PERCEIVES)

Judg 6.22 Gideon *p* that it was the angel of the
Ps 73.17 sanctuary of God; then I *p* their end.
138. 6 but the haughty he *p* from far away.
Isa 64. 4 no ear has *p*, no eye has seen any God
Mt 13.14 and you will indeed look, but never *p*.
Mk 4.12 'they may indeed look, but not *p*, and
8.17 no bread? Do you still not *p* or

PERFECT

2 Sam 22.31 This God—his way is *p*; the promise of
Job 36. 4 not false; one who is *p* in knowledge is
Ps 18.30 This God—his way is *p*; the promise of
Song 6. 9 My dove, my *p* one, is only one, the
Mt 5.48 Be *p*, therefore, as your heavenly Father
19.21 "If you wish to be *p*, go, sell your
Heb 2.10 the pioneer of their salvation *p* through
5. 9 having been made *p*, he became the
7.28 a Son who has been made *p* forever.
9. 9 are offered that cannot *p* the conscience
Jas 1.17 every *p* gift is from above, coming down

PERFECTION

Ps 50. 2 Out of Zion, the *p* of beauty, God
119. 96 I have seen a limit to all *p*, but your
Heb 6. 1 let us go on toward *p*, leaving behind
7.11 Now if *p* had been attainable through
1 Jn 2. 5 person the love of God has reached *p*.

PERFORM (PERFORMED)

2 Kings 23. 3 to *p* the words of this covenant that
Ps 76.11 vows to the LORD your God, and *p* them;
Isa 41. 4 Who has *p* and done this, calling the

PERIL

Lam 5. 9 We get our bread at the *p* of our lives,

PERISH (PERISHED PERISHES PERISHING)

Lev 26.38 You shall *p* among the nations, and the
Num 24.20 was Amalek, but its end is to *p* forever."
Deut 4.26 you will soon utterly *p* from the land
8.19 warn you today that you shall surely *p*.
Josh 23.16 and you shall *p* quickly from the good
Judg 5.31 "So *p* all your enemies, O LORD! But
Esth 4.16 it is against the law; and if I *p*, I *p*."
Job 20. 7 they will *p* forever like their own dung;
Ps 9. 3 back, they stumbled and *p* before you.

Ps 37.20 But the wicked *p*, the enemies of the
73.27 those who are far from you will *p*; you
102. 26 They will *p*, but you endure; they will
Prov 11. 7 When the wicked die, their hope *p*, and
28.28 but when they *p*, the righteous increase.
Jer 8.14 our God has doomed us to *p*, and he
Jon 3. 9 his fierce anger, so that we do not *p*."
Mt 26.52 who take the sword will *p* by the sword.
Lk 13. 3 but unless you repent, you will all *p* as
2 Cor 4. 3 is veiled, it is veiled to those who are *p*.
Heb 1.11 they will *p*, but you remain; they will all

PERISHABLE

1 Cor 9.25 they do it to receive a *p* wreath, but we
15.42 What is sown is *p*, what is raised is
1 Pet 1.18 not with *p* things like silver or gold, but

PERMITS (PERMITTED)

Jn 18.31 "We are not *p* to put anyone to death."
1 Cor 16. 7 some time with you, if the Lord *p*.
Heb 6. 3 we will do this, if God *p*. For it is

PERPLEXED

Lk 9. 7 Herod . . . was *p* , because it was said by
24. 4 While they were *p* about this, suddenly
2 Cor 4. 8 crushed; *p*, but not driven to despair;

PERSECUTE (PERSECUTED PERSECUTING)

Mt 5.10 are those who are *p* for righteousness'
5.11 when people revile you and *p* you and
10.23 When they *p* you in one town, flee to
Lk 11.49 some of whom they will kill and *p*,'
21.12 they will arrest and *p* you; they will
Jn 5.16 Therefore the Jews started *p* Jesus,
15.20 If they *p* me, they will *p* you; if they
Acts 7.52 the prophets did your ancestors not *p*?
9. 4 to him, "Saul, Saul, why do you *p* me?"
22. 4 I *p* this Way up to the point of death,
22. 7 to me, 'Saul, Saul, why are you *p* me?'
Rom 12.14 Bless those who *p* you; bless and do not
1 Cor 4.12 reviled, we bless; when *p*, we endure;
15. 9 apostle, because I *p* the church of God.
2 Cor 4. 9 driven to despair; *p*, but not forsaken;
Gal 1.13 I was violently *p* the church of God and
4.29 *p* the child born according to the Spirit,
6.12 may not be *p* for the cross of Christ.
2 Tim 3.12 a godly life in Christ Jesus will be *p*.

PERSECUTION (PERSECUTIONS)

Mt 13.21 when trouble or *p* arises on account of
Mk 10.30 and fields with *p* —and in the age to
Jn 16.33 In the world you face *p*. But take
Acts 8. 1 day a severe *p* arose against the church
11.19 who were scattered because of the *p*
14.22 "It is through many *p* that we must
1 Thess 3. 4 beforehand that we were to suffer *p*;
2 Thess 1. 4 faith during all your *p* and the
2 Tim 3. 1 and Lystra. What *p* I endured! Yet the
Rev 1. 9 share with you in Jesus the *p* and the

PERSECUTORS

Jer 17.18 Let my *p* be shamed, but do not let me

PERSEVERE (PERSEVERED)

Dan 12.12 Happy are those who *p* and attain the
Heb 11.27 he *p* as though he saw him who is

PERSIA

Ezra 1. 1 In the first year of King Cyrus of *P*, in
4. 7 wrote to King Artaxerxes of *P*;
4.24 year of the reign of King Darius of *P*.
Esth 1. 3 The army of *P* and Media and the
Dan 10.13 with the prince of the kingdom of *P*,

PERSON

Deut 1.16 judge rightly between one *p* and
4.42 who unintentionally kills another *p*,
19. 4 has killed another *p* unintentionally
Prov 27.17 and one *p* sharpens the wits of another.

Ezek 18. 4 it is only the *p* who sins that shall die.

PERSUADE (PERSUADED PERSUADING)

Acts 17. 4 Some of them were *p*, and joined Paul
18.13 man is *p* people to worship God in ways
19.26 Paul has *p* and drawn away a
2 Cor 5.11 the fear of the Lord, we try to *p* others;

PERVERSE (PERVERSELY)

Ex 32. 7 at once! Your people, . . . have acted *p*;
Ps 14. 3 all gone astray, they are all alike *p*;

PERVERSITY

Ezek 9. 9 and the city full of *p*; for they say, 'The

PERVERT (PERVERTED PERVERTING)

Job 8. 3 Or does the Almighty *p* the right?
34.12 and the Almighty will not *p* justice.
Jer 3.21 children, because they have *p* their way,
23.36 so you *p* the words of the living God,
Mic 3. 9 who abhor justice and *p* all equity,
Lk 23. 2 "We found this man *p* our nation,

PESTERED

Judg 16.16 day, and *p* him, he was tired to death.

PESTILENCE

Ex 9. 3 will strike with a deadly *p* your livestock
Deut 28.21 The LORD will make the *p* cling to you
2 Sam 24.13 there be three days' *p* in your land?
Ps 91. 6 files by, or the *p* that stalks in darkness,
Jer 29.17 let loose on them sword, famine, and *p*,

PETER (CEPHAS SIMON SIMEON)

Called to be a fisher of men, Mt 4.18-20 (Mk 1.16-18; Lk 5.1-11); also named Cephas, which means "rock," Jn 1.42n; sent out with the twelve, Mt 10.2 (Mk 3.16); walked on the sea, Mt 14.28-33; confessed Jesus as the Christ, Mt 16.13-20 (Mk 8.27-30; Lk 9.18-22); interceded for by the Lord, Lk 22.31-32; cut off the servant's ear, Jn 18.10-11; denied Jesus three times, Mt 26.69-75 (Mk 14.66-72; Lk 22.54-62; Jn 18.15-18,25-27); "Feed my sheep," Jn 21.15-19; addressed the disciples, Acts 1.15-26; preached on Pentecost, Acts 2.14-42; healed the lame man, Acts 3.1-10; witnessed in Solomon's portico, Acts 3.11-26; preached to the Council, Acts 4.1-12; imprisoned and released, Acts 5.17-42; denounced Simon Magus, Acts 8.14-24; visited Cornelius after the vision, Acts 10; reported to the Jerusalem Church, Acts 11.1-18; imprisoned and delivered, Acts 12.1-19; at the Council of Jerusalem, Acts 15.6-12; visited by Paul, Gal 1.18; blamed by Paul, Gal 2.11-14; Peter's wife's mother, Mt 8.14 (Mk 1.30; Lk 4.38); his wife, 1 Cor 9.5.

PETITIONS

Ps 20. 5 banners. May the LORD fulfill all your *p*.

PHARISEE (PHARISEES)

Mt 3. 7 when he saw many *P* and Sadducees
5.20 exceeds that of the scribes and *P*,
9.11 When the *P* saw this, they said to his
12. 2 When the *P* saw it, they said to him,
12.14 the *P* went out and conspired against
16. 6 and beware of the yeast of the *P* and
19. 3 Some *P* came to him, and to test him
22.15 the *P* went and plotted to entrap him in
23. 2 scribes and the *P* sit on Moses' seat;
27.62 priests and the *P* gathered before Pilate
Jn 3. 1 Now there was a *P* named Nicodemus,
8. 3 The scribes and the *P* brought a woman
Acts 15. 5 the *P* stood up and said, "It is necessary
23. 6 were Sadducees and the others were *P*,

PHILEMON

Philem 1 To *P* our dear friend and co-worker, to

PHILIP

Mt 10. 3 *P* and Bartholomew; Thomas and
Jn 1.43 He found *P* and said to him, "Follow

Jn 6. 5 Jesus said to *P*, "Where are we to buy
12.21 some Greeks. They came to *P*, who was
14. 8 *P* said to him, "Lord, show us the
Acts 1.13 and Andrew, *P* and Thomas,
8. 5 *P* went down to a city of Samaria, and
8.40 But *P* found himself at Azotus, and as
21. 8 we went into the house of *P* the

PHILIPPI

Acts 16.12 and from there to *P*, which is a leading
20. 6 we sailed from *P* after the days of
Phil 1. 1 the saints in Christ Jesus who are in *P*,
1 Thess 2. 2 and been shamefully mistreated at *P*,

PHILISTIA

Ex 15.14 pangs seized the inhabitants of *P*.
Joel 3. 4 and Sidon, and all the regions of *P*?
Zech 9. 6 I will make an end of the pride of *P*.

PHILISTINES

Gen 26. 1 to Gerar, to King Abimelech of the *P*.
Judg 16.21 the *P* seized him and gouged out his
1 Sam 4. 1 In those days the *P* mustered for war
5. 1 When the *P* captured the ark of God,
7. 3 deliver you out of the hand of the *P*."
31. 1 Now the *P* fought against Israel; and
2 Sam 8. 1 David attacked the *P* and subdued
Isa 2. 6 the east and of soothsayers like the *P*,
14.29 Do not rejoice, all you *P*, that the rod
Am 9. 7 the *P* from Caphtor and the Arameans

PHILOSOPHERS

Acts 17.18 Epicurean and Stoic *p* debated with

PHILOSOPHY

Col 2. 8 you captive through *p* and empty deceit,

PHYSICAL

1 Cor 15.44 If there is a *p* body, there is also a
Gal 4.13 was because of a *p* infirmity that I first

PHYSICIAN (PHYSICIANS)

Gen 50. 2 his father. So the *p* embalmed Israel.
Job 13. 4 with lies; all of you are worthless *p*.
Jer 8.22 no balm in Gilead? Is there no *p* there?
Mt 9.12 who are well have no need of a *p*,
Mk 2.17 who are well have no need of a *p*,
5.26 She had endured much under many *p*,
Lk 5.31 who are well have no need of a *p*,
8.43 she had spent all she had on *p*, no one
Col 4.14 Luke, the beloved *p*, and Demas greet

PIECES

Mk 6.43 took up twelve baskets full of broken *p*
8.19 how many baskets full of broken *p* did
Lk 9.17 gathered up, twelve baskets of broken *p*.

PIERCE (PIERCED)

Zech 12.10 they look on the one whom they have *p*,
Lk 2.35 —and a sword will *p* your own soul
Jn 19.34 Instead, one of the soldiers *p* his side
Rev 1. 7 shall see him, even those who *p* him;

PIETY

Mt 6. 1 "Beware of practicing your *p* before
Acts 3.12 as though by our own power or *p* we

PIG (PIGS PIG'S)

Lev 11. 7 The *p*, for even though it has divided
Prov 11.22 a gold ring in a *p* snout is a beautiful
Lk 15.15 who sent him to his fields to feed the *p*.

PIGEON (PIGEONS)

Gen 15. 9 me . . . a turtledove, and a young *p*."
Lev 1.14 shall choose your offering from . . . *p*.

PILATE

Governor of Judea, Lk 3.1; killed some Galileans, Lk 13.1; sentenced Jesus to be crucified, Mt 27.1-25 (Mk 15.1-15; Lk 23.1-26; Jn 18.28—19.22); Jesus suffered under Pontius Pilate, Acts 3.13; 13.28; 1 Tim 6.13.

PILLAR (PILLARS)

Gen 19.26 back, and she became a *p* of salt.
28.18 set it up for a *p* and poured oil on the
Ex 13.21 in front of them in a *p* of cloud by day,
Judg 16.26 "Let me feel the *p* on which the house
2 Sam 18.18 set up for himself the *p* that is in the
2 Kings 10.26 They brought out the *p* that was in the
Neh 9.12 and by night with a *p* of fire, to give
Gal 2. 9 who were acknowledged *p*, recognized

PIONEER

Heb 2.10 should make the *p* of their salvation
12. 2 looking to Jesus the *p* and perfecter of

PIT

Ps 16.10 Sheol, or let your faithful one see the *P*.
Ezek 28. 8 They shall thrust you down to the *P*,
Jon 2. 6 yet you brought up my life from the *P*,

PITY (PITIED)

Ex 2. 6 He was crying, and she took *p* on him;
Deut 7.16 showing them no *p*; you shall not serve
Job 19.21 have *p* on me, O you my friends, for the
27.22 It hurls at them without *p*; they flee
Ps 72.13 He has *p* on the weak and needy, and
Isa 49.10 he who has *p* on them will lead them,
Ezek 7. 4 will not spare you, I will have no *p*. I
8.18 eye will not spare, nor will I have *p*; and
16. 5 No eye *p* you, to do any of these things
Hos 1. 7 I will have *p* on the house of Judah,
Joel 2.18 for his land, and had *p* on his people.
Zech 11. 6 For I will no longer have *p* on the
Mt 18.27 out of *p* for him, the lord of that slave
Mk 1.41 Moved with *p*, Jesus stretched out his
9.22 do anything, have *p* on us and help us."
Lk 10.33 he saw him, he was moved with *p*.
1 Cor 15.19 we are of all people most to be *p*.

PLACE (PLACES)

Gen 8. 9 the dove found no *p* to set its foot, and
Mt 24.34 until all these things have taken *p*.
Lk 2. 7 there was no *p* for them in the inn.
Jn 14. 2 my Father's house are many dwelling *p*.

PLAGUE (PLAGUES)

Gen 12.17 his house with great *p* because of Sarai,
Ex 11. 1 "I will bring one more *p* upon Pharaoh
Num 11.33 struck the people with a very great *p*.
14.37 the land died by a *p* before the LORD.
16.47 where the *p* had already begun among
25. 9 those that died by the *p* were
1 Chr 21.22 —so that the *p* may be averted from
Ps 106. 30 and interceded, and the *p* was stopped.
Zech 14.12 This shall be the *p* with which the LORD

PLAN (PLANNED PLANS)

1 Chr 28. 2 I had *p* to build a house of rest for the
Ezra 4. 5 they bribed officials to frustrate their *p*,
Job 17.11 past, my *p* are broken off, the desires of
21.16 *p* of the wicked are repugnant to me.
Ps 83. 3 They lay crafty *p* against your people;
Prov 15.26 Evil *p* are an abomination to the LORD,
19.21 human mind may devise many *p*, but it
20.18 *P* are established by taking advice; wage
Isa 5.19 let the *p* of the Holy One of Israel
14.26 This is the *p* that is *p* concerning the
19.17 fear because of the *p* that the LORD of
30. 1 LORD, who carry out a *p*, but not mine;
Jer 18.11 you and devising a *p* against you.
29.11 For surely I know the *p* I have for you,
Acts 2.23 according to the definite *p* and
5.38 if this *p* or this undertaking is of human
Eph 1.10 a *p* for the fullness of time, to gather up
3. 9 what is the *p* of the mystery hidden for

PLANT (PLANTED PLANTS)
Gen 1.11 "Let the earth put forth vegetation, *p*
2. 5 when no *p* of the field was yet in the
Ex 15.17 You brought them in and *p* them on the
1 Chr 17. 9 for my people Israel, and will *p* them,
Job 12. 8 ask the *p* of the earth, and they will
Ps 44. 2 drove out the nations, but them you *p*;
80.15 this vine, stock that your right hand *p*.
Jer 2.21 Yet I *p* you as a choice vine, from the
32.41 I will *p* them in this land in
Am 9.15 I will *p* them upon their land, and they
Mt 15.13 Father has not *p* will be uprooted.
1 Cor 3. 6 I *p*, Apollos watered, but God gave the
9. 7 Who *p* a vineyard and does not eat any

PLATFORM
Neh 8. 4 The scribe Ezra stood on a wooden *p*
Acts 12.21 took his seat on the *p*, and delivered a

PLATTER
Mk 6.25 the head of John the Baptist on a *p*."

PLAY (PLAYING)
Gen 21. 9 borne to Abraham, *p* with her son Isaac.
Isa 11. 8 child shall *p* over the hole of the asp,

PLEA
Jer 42. 2 "Be good enough to listen to our *p*, and

PLEAD (PLEADS)
Ps 5. 3 my voice; in the morning I *p* my case to
119.154 *P* my cause and redeem me; give me
Prov 22.23 the LORD *p* their cause and despoils of
Isa 51.22 God who *p* the cause of his people:
Hos 2. 2 *P* with your mother, *p*— for she is not
Lk 15.28 came out and began to *p* with him,

PLEADINGS
Ps 28. 6 for he has heard the sound of my *p*.

PLEASANT
Gen 2. 9 God made to grow every tree that is *p*
Ps 16. 6 lines have fallen for me in *p* places;
106. 24 Then they despised the *p* land, having
133. 1 good and *p* it is when kindred live
Prov 2.10 and knowledge will be *p* to your soul;
9.17 is sweet, and bread eaten in secret is *p*."

PLEASANTNESS
Prov 3.17 Her ways are ways of *p*, and all her

PLEASE (PLEASED PLEASES)
Num 14. 8 If the LORD is *p* with us, he will bring us
Judg 14. 3 "Get her for me, because she *p* me."
1 Sam 12.22 it has *p* the LORD to make you a people
18.26 David was well *p* to be the king's
2 Sam 3.36 just as everything the king did *p* all the
7.29 may it *p* you to bless the house of your
17. 4 The advice *p* Absalom and all the elders
1 Kings 3.10 It *p* the Lord that Solomon had asked
1 Chr 17.27 may it *p* you to bless the house of your
Neh 2. 6 So it *p* the king to send me, and I set
Esth 2. 4 let the girl who *p* the king be queen
Job 6. 9 that it would *p* God to crush me, that
Ps 135. 6 Whatever the LORD *p* he does, in heaven
Prov 16. 7 When the ways of people *p* the LORD, he
Eccl 7.26 one who *p* God escapes her, but the
8. 3 unpleasant, for he does whatever he *p*.
Isa 42.21 The LORD was *p*, for the sake of his
Jon 1.14 "*P*, O LORD, we pray, do not let us
Mic 6. 7 the LORD be *p* with thousands of rams,
Mal 1. 8 he be *p* with you or show you favor?
Mt 3.17 my Beloved, with whom I am well *p*."
17. 5 my Beloved, with whom I am well *p*;"
Mk 1.11 Son, the Beloved; with you I am well *p*."
Lk 3.22 Son, the Beloved; with you I am well *p*."
Rom 8. 8 who are in the flesh cannot *p* God.
15. 1 of the weak, and not to *p* ourselves.
1 Cor 7.32 affairs of the Lord, how to *p* the Lord;
10. 5 God was not *p* with most of them, and
10.33 just as I try to *p* everyone in everything
2 Cor 5. 9 or away, we make it our aim to *p* him.
Gal 1.10 Or am I trying to *p* people? If I were
1.15 his grace, was *p* to reveal his Son
Col 1.19 all the fullness of God was *p* to dwell,
1 Thess 2. 4 speak, not to *p* mortals, but to *p* God
2 Tim 2. 4 aim is to *p* the enlisting officer.
Heb 11. 5 he was taken away that "he had *p* God."
1 Jn 3.22 his commandments and do what *p* him.

PLEASING
Eccl 12.10 The Teacher sought to find *p* words,
Jn 8.29 alone, for I always do what is *p* to him."
Eph 5.10 Try to find out what is *p* to the Lord.
Phil 4. 8 is just, whatever is pure, whatever is *p*,
4.18 offering, a sacrifice acceptable and *p*
Col 1.10 lead lives worthy of the Lord, fully *p*
Heb 13.16 have, for such sacrifices are *p* to God.

PLEASURE (PLEASURES)
Job 22. 3 Is it any *p* to the Almighty if you are
Ps 16.11 fullness of joy; in your right hand are *p*
147. 11 but the LORD takes *p* in those who fear
149. 4 the LORD takes *p* in his people; he
Prov 21.17 Whoever loves *p* will suffer want;
Eccl 2. 1 "Come now, I will make a test of *p*;
2.10 I kept my heart from no *p*, for my heart
5. 4 for he has no *p* in fools. Fulfill what
Ezek 18.23 Have I any *p* in the death of the
33.11 I have no *p* in the death of the wicked,
Hag 1. 8 the house, that I may take *p* in it and
Mal 1.10 on my altar in vain! I have no *p* in you,
Lk 8.14 choked by the cares and riches and *p* of
12.32 it is your Father's good *p* to give you
Phil 2.13 both to will and to work for his good *p*.
2 Thess 2.12 but took *p* in unrighteousness will be
Heb 10. 6 and sin offerings you have no *p*.
11.25 of God than to enjoy the fleeting *p*
Jas 5. 5 lived on the earth in luxury and in *p*;

PLEDGE
Lev 6. 2 neighbor in a matter of a deposit or a *p*,
Deut 24. 6 take a mill or an upper millstone in *p*,
24.12 sleep in the garment given you as the *p*;
2 Chr 34.32 and in Benjamin *p* themselves
Prov 20.16 seize the *p* given as surety for
27.13 seize the *p* given as surety for
Ezek 33.15 If the wicked restores the *p*, give back
Am 2. 8 every altar on garments taken in *p*;
Eph 1.14 Spirit; this is the *p* of our inheritance

PLENTY
Gen 41.29 There will come seven years of great *p*
Prov 12.11 Those who till their land will have *p* of
Phil 4.12 of having *p* and of being in need.

PLOT (PLOTTED)
Neh 4.15 enemies heard that their *p* was known
Isa 7. 5 son of Remaliah, has *p* evil against you
Nah 1. 9 Why do you *p* against the LORD? He will
Mt 22.15 Pharisees went and *p* to entrap him in

PLOW (PLOWED)
Deut 22.10 shall not *p* with an ox and a donkey
Job 4. 8 those who *p* iniquity and sow trouble
Ps 129. 3 The plowers *p* upon my back; they
Prov 20. 4 The lazy person does not *p* in season;
Isa 28.24 those who *p* for sowing *p* continually?
Jer 26.18 Zion shall be *p* as a field; Jerusalem
Hos 10.13 You have *p* wickedness, you have
Mic 3.12 of you Zion shall be *p* as a field;
Lk 9.62 puts a hand to the *p* and looks back
1 Cor 9.10 whoever plows should *p* in hope and

PLOWSHARES
Joel 3.10 Beat your *p* into swords, and your

Mic 4. 3 they shall beat their swords into *p*, and

PLUCK

Jer 12.14 and I will *p* up the house of Judah from

PLUMB LINE

Am 7. 7 beside a wall built with a *p*, with a *p* in

PLUNDER (PLUNDERED PLUNDERING)

Gen 34.27 *p* the city, because their sister had been
Ex 3.22 and so you shall *p* the Egyptians."
12.36 asked. And so they *p* the Egyptians.
Num 31.53 (The troops had all taken *p* for
2 Kings 7.16 out, and *p* the camp of the Arameans.
Isa 17.14 us, and the lot of those who *p* us.
Hab 2. 8 Because you have *p* many nations, all
Mt 12.29 strong man's house and *p* his property,
Heb 10.34 accepted the *p* of your possessions,

POLICE

Jn 7.46 The *p* answered, "Never has anyone

POMP

Ps 49.12 Mortals cannot abide in their *p*; they
Isa 14.11 Your *p* is brought down to Sheol, and

PONDER (PONDERED)

Ps 4. 4 not sin; *p* it on your beds, and be silent.
48. 9 We *p* your steadfast love, O God, in the
Lk 2.19 treasured all these words and *p* them

POOL (POOLS)

Isa 42.15 the rivers into islands, and dry up the *p*.
Jn 5. 2 by the Sheep Gate there is a *p*,
9. 7 him, "Go, wash in the *p* of Siloam"

POOR

Ex 23.11 so that the *p* of your people may eat;
30.15 the *p* shall not give less, than the half
Lev 19.10 you shall leave them for the *p* and the
23.22 you shall leave them for the *p* and for
1 Sam 2. 8 He raises up the *p* from the dust; he
2 Sam 12. 3 the *p* man had nothing but one little
Job 5.16 So the *p* have hope, and injustice shuts
20.19 have crushed and abandoned the *p*,
24. 4 off the road; the *p* of the earth all hide
29.12 because I delivered the *p* who cried,
31.16 If I have withheld anything that the *p*
Ps 9.18 forgotten, nor the hope of the *p* perish
10. 2 arrogance the wicked persecute the *p*—
22.26 The *p* shall eat and be satisfied; those
34. 6 This *p* soul cried, and was heard by the
40.17 As for me, I am *p* and needy, but the
41. 1 Happy are those who consider the *p*;
72. 4 May he defend the cause of the *p* of the
86. 1 and answer me, for I am *p* and needy.
109. 22 For I am *p* and needy, and my heart is
113. 7 He raises the *p* from the dust, and lifts
Prov 10.15 the poverty of the *p* is their ruin.
19. 1 Better the *p* walking in integrity than
19. 7 If the *p* are hated even by their kin,
22. 2 The rich and the *p* have this in
29.14 If a king judges the *p* with equity, his
Isa 3.14 the spoil of the *p* is in your houses.
11. 4 with righteousness he shall judge the *p*,
25. 4 you have been a refuge to the *p*, a
Am 4. 1 who oppress the *p*, who crush the
5.11 because you trample upon the *p* and
8. 6 buying the *p* for silver and the needy for
Mt 5. 3 "Blessed are the *p* in spirit, for theirs is
11. 5 the *p* have good news brought to them.
19.21 and give the money to the *p*,
26.11 you always have the *p* with you, but you
Mk 10.21 sell what you own, and give to the *p*,
14. 5 denarii, and the money given to the *p*."
Lk 4.18 me to bring good news to the *p*.
6.20 "Blessed are you who are *p*, for yours is
14.13 when you give a banquet, invite the *p*,
Lk 16.20 at his gate lay a *p* man named Lazarus,
18.22 distribute the money to the *p*, and you
19. 8 possessions, Lord, I will give to the *p*;
Jn 12. 5 denarii and the money given to the *p*?"
12. 8 You always have the *p* with you, but
2 Cor 6.10 rejoicing; as *p*, yet making many rich;
8. 9 was rich, yet for your sake he became *p*,
9. 9 "He scatters abroad, he gives to the *p*;
Gal 2.10 one thing, that we remember the *p*,
Jas 2. 5 God chosen the *p* in the world to be
Rev 3.17 you are wretched, pitiable, *p*, blind, and

POOREST

2 Kings 25.12 guard left some of the *p* people of the

PORTENT (PORTENTS)

Ps 71. 7 I have been as a *p* to many, but you are
Joel 2.30 I will show *p* in the heavens and on the
Acts 2.19 I will show *p* in the heaven above and
Rev 12. 1 A great *p* appeared in heaven: a woman
15. 1 I saw another *p* in heaven, great and

PORTION (PORTIONS)

Deut 32. 9 LORD's own *p* is his people, Jacob his
1 Sam 1. 5 to Hannah he gave a double *p*, because
2 Sam 20. 1 "We have no *p* in David, no share in the
Neh 8.10 send *p* of them to those for whom
Job 20.29 This is the *p* of the wicked from God,
Ps 16. 5 The LORD is my chosen *p* and my cup;
119. 57 The LORD is my *p*; I promise to keep
142. 5 "You are my refuge, my *p* in the land of
Jer 10.16 like these is the LORD, the *p* of Jacob,
Lam 3.24 LORD is my *p*," says my soul, "therefore I

POSSESS (POSSESSING)

Num 14.24 he went, and his descendants shall *p* it.
36. 8 continue to *p* their ancestral inheritance
Deut 33.23 of the LORD, *p* the west and the south.
Judg 11.24 Should you not *p* what your god
18. 9 slow to go, but enter in and *p* the land.
Neh 9.15 you told them to go in to *p* the land
Ps 25.13 and their children shall *p* the land.
Isa 14. 2 Israel will *p* the nations as male and
34.17 they shall *p* it forever, from generation
54. 3 your descendants will *p* the nations and
60.21 righteous; they shall *p* the land forever.
Ezek 33.26 wife; shall you then *p* the land?
36.12 people Israel— and they shall *p* you,
Dan 7.18 kingdom and *p* the kingdom forever—
Zech 8.12 remnant of this people to *p* all these
2 Cor 6.10 as having nothing, yet *p* everything.

POSSESSION (POSSESSIONS)

Ex 19. 5 you shall be my treasured *p* out of all
Lev 25.34 be sold; for that is their *p* for all time.
Num 32.22 this land shall be your *p* before the
Deut 1. 8 go in and take *p* of the land that I
1.39 I will give it, and they shall take *p* of it.
4.20 to become a people of his very own *p*,
14. 2 earth to be his people, his treasured *p*.
15. 4 your God is giving you as a *p* to occupy
21.16 the day when he wills his *p* to his sons,
Josh 1.11 to go in to take *p* of the land that the
18. 3 slack about going in and taking *p* of the
2 Chr 20.11 us by coming to drive us out of your *p*
Ps 78.55 he apportioned them for a *p* and settled
135. 4 Jacob for himself, Israel as his own *p*.
Eccl 2. 7 I had also great *p* of herds and flocks,
Jer 32.23 and they entered and took *p* of it.
Ob 17 house of Jacob shall take *p* of those
Mal 3.17 my special *p* on the day when I act, and
Mt 19.22 went away grieving; for he had many *p*.
24.47 will put that one in charge of all his *p*.
Lk 12.15 does not consist in the abundance of *p*."

POSSIBLE

Mt 19.26 impossible, but for God all things are *p*."
Mk 10.27 not for God; for God all things are *p*."

Mk 14.35 prayed that, if it were *p*, the hour might
Lk 18.27 is impossible for mortals is *p* for God."

POSTERITY

Ps 22.30 *P* shall serve him; future generations
109. 13 May his *p* be cut off; may his name be

POT (POTS)

2 Kings 4.40 "O man of God, there is death in the *p*!"
Jer 1.13 "I see a boiling *p*, tilted away from the
Rev 2.27 iron rod, as when clay *p* are shattered

POTTER (POTTER'S)

Ps 2. 9 and dash them in pieces like a *p* vessel."
Isa 30.14 is like that of a *p* vessel that is smashed
41.25 rulers as mortar, as the *p* treads clay.
45. 9 your Maker, earthen vessels with the *p*!
Jer 18. 2 "Come, go down to the *p* house, and
18. 6 like the clay in the *p* hand, so are you
19. 1 the LORD: Go and buy a *p* earthenware
Lam 4. 2 as earthen pots, the work of a *p* hands!
Mt 27. 7 they used them to buy the *p* field as a
Rom 9.21 Has the *p* no right over the clay, to

POUR (POURED POURING)

1 Sam 1.15 I have been *p* out my soul before the
7. 6 drew water and *p* it out before the LORD,
2 Sam 23.16 not drink of it; he *p* it out to the LORD,
1 Chr 11.18 not drink of it; he *p* it out to the LORD,
Ps 42. 4 things I remember, as I *p* out my soul:
Isa 32.15 until a spirit from on high is *p* out on
44. 3 *p* water on the thirsty land, and streams
Jer 6.11 *P* it out on the children in the street,
7.20 My anger and my wrath will be *p* out on
10.25 *P* out your wrath on the nations that do
Ezek 7. 8 now I will *p* out my wrath upon you;
Hos 5.10 them I will *p* out my wrath like water.
Joel 2.28 I will *p* out my spirit on all flesh;
Zech 12.10 I will *p* out a spirit of compassion and
Mt 26. 7 ointment, and she *p* it on his head
Mk 14. 3 the jar and *p* the ointment on his head.
Acts 2.17 I will *p* out my Spirit upon all flesh,
Rom 5. 5 God's love has been *p* into our hearts

POVERTY

Prov 6.11 and *p* will come upon you like a robber,
13.18 *P* and disgrace are for the one who
24.34 and *p* will come upon you like a robber,
28.19 worthless pursuits will have plenty of *p*.
Mk 12.44 but she out of her *p* has put in
2 Cor 8. 2 joy and their extreme *p* have overflowed
Rev 2. 9 I know your affliction and your *p*, even

POWER

Lev 26.37 you shall have no *p* to stand against
Num 11.23 "Is the LORD's *p* limited? Now you shall
1 Chr 29.11 Yours, O LORD, are the greatness, the *p*,
2 Chr 25. 8 for God has *p* to help or to overthrow."
Job 23. 6 with me in the greatness of his *p*?
26.14 But the thunder of his *p* who can
Ps 21.13 strength! We will sing and praise your *p*.
49.15 ransom my soul from the *p* of Sheol,
66. 3 of your great *p*, your enemies cringe
67. 2 earth, your saving *p* among all nations.
68.34 Ascribe *p* to God, whose majesty is over
145. 11 of your kingdom, and tell of your *p*,
Prov 3.27 it is due, when it is in your *p* to do
Eccl 8. 8 No one has *p* over the wind to restrain
Isa 40.26 great in strength, mighty in *p*, not one
40.29 He gives *p* to the faint, and strengthens
Jer 16.21 time I am going to teach them my *p*
32.17 heavens and the earth by your great *p*
Dan 8.24 He shall grow strong in *p*, shall cause
Mic 3. 8 as for me, I am filled with *p*, with the
Zech 4. 6 by might, nor by *p*, but by my spirit,
Mt 6.13n and the *p* and the glory are yours
22.29 neither the scriptures nor the *p* of God.
Mk 5.30 aware that *p* had gone forth from him,
9. 1 the kingdom of God has come with *p*."
9.39 for no one who does a deed of *p* in my
12.24 neither the scriptures nor the *p* of God?
14.62 of Man seated at the right hand of *P*,'
Lk 1.35 and the *p* of the Most High will
5.17 and the *p* of the Lord was with him to
6.19 touch him, for *p* came out of him and
8.46 I noticed that *p* had gone out from me."
19.12 country to get royal *p* for himself
21.27 coming in a cloud' with *p* and great
22.53 this is your hour, and the *p* of darkness!"
22.69 at the right hand of the *p* of God."
24.49 have been clothed with *p* from on high
Jn 10.18 I have *p* to lay it down, and I have *p* to
19.10 that I have *p* to release you, and *p* to
Acts 1. 8 you will receive *p* when the Holy Spirit
2.11 them speaking about God's deeds of *p*."
3.12 as though by our own *p* or piety we
4.33 with great *p* the apostles gave their
6. 8 Stephen, full of grace and *p*, did great
8.10 "This man is the *p* of God that is called
26.18 from the *p* of Satan to God, so they
Rom 1.16 the gospel; it is the *p* of God for
15.13 you may abound in hope by the *p* of the
15.19 wonders, by the *p* of the Spirit of God,
1 Cor 1.18 who are being saved it is the *p* of God.
2. 4 with a demonstration of Spirit and of *p*,
2. 5 on human wisdom but on the *p* of God.
5. 4 is present with the *p* of our Lord Jesus,
15.24 every ruler and every authority and *p*.
15.43 It is sown in weakness, it is raised in *p*.
2 Cor 6. 7 truthful speech, and the *p* of God; with
12. 9 so that the *p* of Christ may dwell in me.
12. 9 you, for *p* is made perfect in weakness."
13. 4 in weakness, but lives by the *p* of God.
Eph 1.19 greatness of his *p* in us who believe,
3.20 to him who by the *p* at work within us
Phil 3.10 Christ and the *p* of his resurrection
1 Thess 1. 5 not in word only, but also in *p* and in
Heb 2.14 destroy the one who has the *p* of death,
1 Pet 1. 5 are being protected by the *p* of God
2 Pet 1. 3 His divine *p* has given us everything
Rev 11.17 for you have taken your great *p* and
17.13 These are united in yielding their *p* and

POWERFUL

Lk 3.16 one who is more *p* than I is coming; I

PRAISE (PRAISES) (n)

Deut 10.21 He is your *p*; he is your God, who has
1 Chr 16. 7 David first appointed the singing of *p* to
Ps 47. 6 Sing *p* to God, sing *p*; sing *p* to our
48.10 God, like your *p*, reaches to the ends of
61. 8 So I will always sing *p* to your name, as
65. 1 *P* is due to you, O God, in Zion; and to
71. 8 My mouth is filled with your *p*, and
119.108 Accept my offerings of *p*, O LORD, and
Rom 14.11 to me, and every tongue shall give *p*
Jas 5.13 cheerful? They should sing songs of *p*.

PRAISE (PRAISED PRAISING) (v)

1 Chr 16.25 great is the LORD, and greatly to be *p*;
29.13 we give thanks to you and *p* your
Ps 33. 2 *P* the LORD with the lyre; make melody
71.22 I will also *p* you with the harp for your
76.10 Human wrath serves only to *p* you,
113. 1 *P* the LORD! *P*, O servants of the LORD; *p*
119. 62 At midnight I rise to *p* you, because of
147. 12 *P* the LORD, O Jerusalem! *P* your God, O
148. 2 *P* him, all his angels; *p* him, all his
150. 6 Let everything that breathes *p* the LORD!
Prov 27. 2 Let another *p* you, and not your own
Isa 38.18 cannot thank you, death cannot *p* you;
Dan 4.34 I blessed the Most High, and *p* and
Lk 1.64 freed, and he began to speak, *p* God.
2.28 took him in his arms and *p* God,
Acts 11.18 they were silenced. And they *p* God,

Acts 19.17 and the name of the Lord Jesus was *p*.
Rom 15.11 "*P* the Lord, all you Gentiles, and let all

PRAY

Ex 8. 8 "*P* to the LORD to take away the frogs
1 Sam 12.19 "*P* to the LORD your God for your
12.23 the LORD by ceasing to *p* for you;
2 Sam 7.27 servant has found courage to *p* this
15.31 David said, "O LORD, I *p* you, turn the
24.17 Let your hand, I *p*, be against me and
1 Kings 8.33 confess your name, *p* and plead with
1 Chr 17.25 has found it possible to *p* before you.
Job 42. 8 Job shall *p* for you, for I will accept his
Ps 122. 6 *P* for the peace of Jerusalem: "May they
Isa 16.12 his sanctuary to *p*, he will not prevail.
Jer 7.16 As for you, do not *p* for this people, do
11.14 As for you, do not *p* for this people, or
29.12 come and *p* to me, and I will hear you.
37. 3 Jeremiah saying, "*P* for us to the LORD
Dan 6.10 three times a day to *p* to his God and
Mt 5.44 and *p* for those who persecute you,
6. 5 they love to stand and *p* in the
6. 9 "*P* then in this way: Our Father in
14.23 up into the mountains by himself to *p*.
19.13 he might lay his hands on them and *p*.
24.20 *P* that your flight may not be in winter
26.36 "Sit here while I go over there and *p*."
26.41 Stay awake and *p* that you may not
Mk 6.46 he went up on the mountain to *p*.
13.18 *P* that it may not be in winter.
13.33n Beware, keep alert and *p*; for you do
14.32 said to his disciples, "Sit here while I *p*."
14.38 Keep aware and *p* that you may not
Lk 5.16 withdraw to deserted places and *p*.
5.33 the Pharisees, frequently fast and *p*, but
6.12 he went out to the mountain to *p*; and
6.28 curse you, *p* for those who abuse you.
9.28 and went up on the mountain to *p*.
11. 1 "Lord, teach us to *p*, as John taught his
18. 1 them a parable about their need to *p*
Acts 8.24 Simon answered, "*P* for me to the Lord,
Rom 8.26 we do not know how to *p* as we ought,
1 Cor 11.13 to *p* to God with her head unveiled?
14.15 spirit, but I will *p* with the mind also;
2 Cor 13. 7 *p* to God that you may not do anything
Eph 6.18 *P* in the Spirit at all times in every
1 Thess 3.10 Night and day we *p* most earnestly that
5.17 Rejoice always, *p* without ceasing, give
2 Thess 1.11 To this end we always *p* for you, asking
1 Tim 2. 8 that in every place the men should *p*,
Heb 13.18 *P* for us; we are sure that we have a
Jas 5.13 among you suffering? They should *p*.
Jude 20 most holy faith; *p* in the Holy Spirit;

PRAYS (PRAYED PRAYING)

Gen 20.17 Then Abraham *p* to God; and God
Num 11. 2 Moses *p* to the LORD, and the fire
Deut 9.26 I *p* to the LORD and said, "Lord GOD, do
1 Sam 1.10 was deeply distressed and *p* to the LORD,
1.27 For this child I *p*; and the LORD granted
8. 6 to govern us." And Samuel *p* to the LORD,
2 Kings 4.33 on the two of them, and *p* to the LORD.
6.17 Elisha *p*: "O LORD, please open his eyes
19.15 Hezekiah *p* before the LORD, and said,
20. 2 turned his face to the wall and *p* to the
2 Chr 32.20 the prophet Isaiah son of Amoz *p*
33.13 He *p* to him, and God received his
Neh 1. 4 for days, fasting and *p* before the God
4. 9 we *p* to our God, and set a guard as a
Job 42.10 the fortunes of Job, when he had *p* for
33.26 Then he *p* to God, and is accepted by
Ps 35.13 I *p* with head bowed on my bosom,
Isa 37.15 And Hezekiah *p* to the LORD, saying: "O
38. 2 turned his face to the wall, and *p*
45.20 and keep *p* to a god that cannot save.
Dan 6. 7 whoever *p* to anyone, divine or human,
Jon 2. 1 Then Jonah *p* to the LORD his God from
Mt 26.44 he went away and *p* for the third time,
Mk 1.35 out to a deserted place, and there he *p*.
Lk 1.10 assembly of people was *p* outside.
3.21 been baptized and was *p*, the heaven
9.18 when Jesus was *p* alone, with only the
18.11 standing by himself, was *p* thus,
22.41 knelt down, and *p*, "Father, if you are
Acts 1.24 they *p* and said, "Lord, you know
4.31 When they had *p*, the place in which
8.15 The two went down and *p* for them that
9.11 named Saul. At this moment he is *p*,
9.40 outside, and then he knelt down and *p*.
10.30 I was *p* in my house when suddenly a
12. 5 kept in prison; the church *p* fervently
12.12 where many had gathered and were *p*.
13. 3 after fasting and *p* they laid their hands
16.25 Paul and Silas were *p* and singing
21. 5 we knelt down on the beach and *p*
28. 8 Paul visited him and cured him by *p*
Col 1. 9 we have not ceased *p* for you and

PRAYER

Gen 25.21 LORD granted his *p*, and his wife
2 Chr 6.19 Regard your servant's *p* and his plea, O
30.27 heard; their *p* came to his holy dwelling
Ps 6. 9 my supplication; the LORD accepts my *p*.
17. 1 my cry; give ear to my *p* from lips free
32. 6 let all who are faithful offer *p* to you; at
42. 8 night his song is with me, a *p* to the
65. 2 O you who answer *p*! To you all flesh
72.15 May *p* be made for him continually and
102. 17 He will regard the *p* of the destitute,
109. 4 they accuse me, even as I make *p* for
141. 2 Let my *p* be counted as incense before
Prov 15. 8 but the *p* of the upright is his delight.
15.29 but he hears the *p* of the righteous.
Isa 26.16 they sought you, they poured out a *p*
37. 4 therefore lift up your *p* for the remnant
56. 7 be called a house of *p* for all peoples.
Lam 3. 8 call and cry for help, he shuts out my *p*;
3.44 a cloud so that no *p* can pass through.
Dan 9. 3 to the Lord God, to seek an answer by *p*
Mt 17.21n kind does not come out except by *p*
21.13 My house shall be called a house of *p*';
21.22 Whatever you ask for in *p* with faith,
Mk 9.29 kind can come out only through *p*."
11.17 'My house shall be called a house of *p*
11.24 whatever you ask for in *p*, believe that
Lk 1.13 Zechariah, for your *p* has been heard.
19.46 'My house shall be a house of *p*'; but
Acts 1.14 constantly devoting themselves to *p*,
3. 1 temple at the hour of *p*, three o'clock in
6. 4 for our part, will devote ourselves to *p*
14.23 with *p* and fasting, they entrusted them
16.13 we supposed there was a place of *p*;
Rom 12.12 be patient in suffering, persevere in *p*.
15.30 Spirit, to join me in earnest *p* to God
1 Cor 7. 5 for a set time, to devote yourselves to *p*,
Phil 4. 6 in everything by *p* and supplication with
Col 4. 2 Devote yourselves to *p*, keeping alert in
Jas 5.16 The *p* of the righteous is powerful and

PRAYERS

Mt 23.14n sake of appearance you make long *p*;
Mk 12.40 for the sake of appearance say long *p*.
Lk 20.47 for the sake of appearance say long *p*.
Acts 2.42 to the breaking of bread and the *p*.
10. 4 "Your *p* and your alms have ascended as
Rom 1. 9 ceasing I remember you always in my *p*,
2 Cor 1.11 You also join in helping us by your *p*,
Phil 1. 4 joy in every one of my *p* for all of you,
Col 4.12 always wrestling in his *p* on your behalf,
1 Tim 2. 1 I urge that supplications, *p*,
5. 5 in supplications and *p* night and day;
2 Tim 1. 3 I remember you constantly in my *p*
Heb 5. 7 Jesus offered up *p* and supplications,
1 Pet 3. 7 life—so that nothing may hinder your *p*.

1 Pet 4. 7 yourselves for the sake of your *p*.
Rev 5. 8 incense, which are the *p* of the saints.

PREACH (PREACHING)

Mic 2. 6 "Do not *p*"—thus they *p*—"one should
Rom 2.21 While you *p* against stealing, do you
1 Tim 5.17 those who labor in *p* and teaching;

PREACHER

Mic 2.11 a one would be the *p* for this people!

PRECEPT (PRECEPTS)

Ps 19. 8 the *p* of the LORD are right, rejoicing the
111. 7 and just; all his *p* are trustworthy.
119. 63 who fear you, of those who keep your *p*.
119. 93 I will never forget your *p*, for by them
Prov 4. 2 for I give you good *p*; do not forsake my
Isa 28.10 For it is *p* upon *p*, *p* upon *p*, line upon

PRECIOUS

Job 28.10 rocks and their eyes see every *p* thing.
Ps 36. 7 How *p* is your steadfast love, O God! All
72.14 life; and *p* is their blood in his sight.
116. 15 *P* in the sight of the LORD is the death
133. 2 like the *p* oil on the head, running
Prov 3.15 She is more *p* than jewels, and nothing
20.15 informed by knowledge are a *p* jewel.
31.10 can find? She is far more *p* than jewels.
Isa 43. 4 you are *p* in my sight, and honored, and
1 Pet 1. 7 of your faith—being more *p* than gold
2. 6 a stone, a cornerstone chosen and *p*;
2 Pet 1. 1 who have received a faith as *p* as ours

PREDESTINED

Acts 4.28 hand and your plan had *p* to take place
Rom 8.30 those whom he *p* he also called; and

PREDICTED

2 Kings 23.17 and *p* these things that you have done
Rom 9.29 And as Isaiah *p*, "If the Lord of hosts

PREDICTION

Isa 44.26 and fulfills the *p* of his messengers;

PREGNANT

Ex 21.22 injure a *p* woman so that there is a
Mt 24.19 Woe to those who are *p* and to those
Rev 12. 2 she was *p* and was crying out in

PREPARATION (PREPARATIONS)

2 Chr 35. 4 Make *p* by your ancestral houses by
Mt 26.17 "Where do you want us to make *p* for
Mk 14.12 and make *p* for you to eat the Passover?"
15.42 since it was the day of *P*, that is, the
Lk 23.54 It was the day of *P*, and the sabbath

PREPARE (PREPARED PREPARES)

Neh 8.10 to those for whom nothing is *p*, for this
Ps 132. 17 David; I have *p* a lamp for my anointed
147. 8 with clouds, *p* rain for the earth,
Isa 30.33 For his burning place has long been *p*;
40. 3 "In the wilderness *p* the way of the
62.10 the gates, *p* the way for the people;
Am 4.12 to you, *p* to meet your God, O Israel!"
Zeph 1. 7 the LORD has *p* a sacrifice, he has
Mt 20.23 for whom it has been *p* by my Father."
Mk 1. 3 '*P* the way of the Lord, make his paths
10.40 it is for those for whom it has been *p*."
Lk 1.17 to make ready a people *p* for the Lord."
1.76 will go before the Lord to *p* his ways,
2.31 which you have *p* in the presence of all
3. 4 '*P* the way of the Lord, make his paths
7.27 of you, who will *p* your way before you."
12.47 but did not *p* himself or do what was
Jn 14. 3 And if I go and *p* a place for you, I will
Rom 9.23 which he has *p* beforehand for glory—
1 Cor 2. 9 what God has *p* for those who love
Philem 22 —*p* a guest room for me, for I am
Heb 10. 5 desired, but a body you have *p* for me;

PRESENCE

Gen 4.16 Cain went away from the *p* of the LORD,
Ex 33.15 "If your *p* will not go, do not carry us
Ps 16.11 in your *p* there is fullness of joy; in your
114. 7 Tremble, O earth at the *p* of the LORD,
Jon 1.10 he was fleeing from the *p* of the LORD,
Lk 1.19 I am Gabriel. I stand in the *p* of God,
Acts 10.33 all of us are here in the *p* of God to
Heb 9.24 now to appear in the *p* of God on our
Jude 24 you stand without blemish before the *p*

PRESENT (PRESENTED)

Gen 32.13 him he took a *p* for his brother Esau,
47. 2 took five men and *p* them to Pharaoh.
Num 7.12 The one who *p* his offering the first day
Josh 15.19 "Give me a *p*; since you have set me in
2 Kings 16. 8 and sent a *p* to the king of Assyria.
Jer 40. 5 gave him an allowance of food and a *p*,
Lk 2.22 up to Jerusalem to *p* him to the Lord
Rom 6.19 now *p* your members as slaves to
12. 1 of God, to *p* your bodies as a living
2 Cor 11. 2 husband, to *p* you as a chaste virgin to
Eph 5.27 so as to *p* the church to himself in
Col 1.22 to *p* you holy and blameless and
1.28 we may *p* everyone mature in Christ.

PRESERVE (PRESERVED PRESERVES PRESERVING)

Gen 45. 5 for God sent me before you to *p* life.
1 Sam 30.23 he has *p* us and handed over to us the
Ps 25.21 May integrity and uprightness *p* me, for
32. 7 you *p* me from trouble; you surround
64. 1 *p* my life from the dread enemy,
119.149 voice; O LORD, in your justice *p* my life.
138. 7 you *p* me against the wrath of my
Prov 2. 8 and *p* the way of his faithful ones.
16.17 those who guard their way *p* their lives.
20.28 Loyalty and faithfulness *p* the king, and

PRESS (PRESSED)

Ruth 1.16 "Do not *p* me to leave you or to turn
Hos 6. 3 us know, let us *p* on to know the LORD;
Phil 1.23 I am hard *p* between the two: my desire
3.14 I *p* on toward the goal for the prize of

PRESSURE

2 Cor 8.13 be relief for others and *p* on you,

PREVAILED

Gen 32.28 with God and with humans, and have *p*."
Ex 17.11 Moses held up his hand, Israel *p*;
Hos 12. 4 strove with the angel and *p*, he wept

PREVENT (PREVENTED)

Mt 3.14 John would have *p* him, saying, "I need
Acts 8.37 What is to *p* me from being baptized?"

PRICE

Gen 23.13 I will give the *p* of the field; accept it
Isa 55. 1 and milk without money and without *p*.
1 Cor 6.20 For you were bought with a *p*; therefore
7.23 You were bought with a *p*; do not

PRIDE

Job 33.17 their deeds, and keep them from *p*,
Ps 20. 7 our *p* is in the name of the LORD our
Prov 8.13 *P* and arrogance and the way of evil and
11. 2 When *p* comes, then comes disgrace;
16.18 *P* goes before destruction, and a
Isa 9. 9 but in *p* and arrogance of heart they
Jer 48.29 We have heard of the *p* of Moab—he is
Ezek 7.10 The rod has blossomed, *p* has budded.
Hos 5. 5 Israel's *p* testifies against him; Ephraim
Zeph 2.10 shall be their lot in return for their *p*,
Mk 7.22 licentiousness, envy, slander, *p*, folly.

PRIEST (PRIESTS)

Gen 14.18 King Melchizedek . . . was *p* of God

Isa 30. 5 through a people that cannot *p* them,
Mt 16.26 what will it *p* them if they gain the
Mk 8.36 what will it *p* them to gain the whole

PROLIFIC

Ex 1. 7 But the Israelites were fruitful and *p*;

PROMINENT

1 Chr 5. 2 though Judah became *p* among his

PROMISE (PROMISES) (n)

2 Chr 1. 9 God, let your *p* to my father David now
Ps 77. 8 Are his *p* at an end for all time?
106. 24 pleasant land, having no faith in his *p*.
119. 82 My eyes fail with watching for your *p*; I
Acts 1. 4 wait there for the *p* of the Father. "This,"
2.39 *p* is for you, for your children, and for
7.17 drew near for the fulfillment of the *p*
13.34 will give you the holy *p* given to David.'
26. 6 on trial on account of my hope in the *p*
Rom 4.13 the *p* that he would inherit the world
4.16 that the *p* may rest on grace and be
9. 8 but the children of the *p* are counted as
15. 8 confirm the *p* given to the patriarchs,
2 Cor 1.20 him every one of the *p* of God is a "Yes."
7. 1 Since we have these *p*, beloved, let us
Gal 3.16 the *p* were made to Abraham and to his
3.21 the law then opposed to the *p* of God?
4.23 free woman, was born through the *p*.
4.28 friends, are children of the *p*, like Isaac.
Eph 3. 6 and sharers in the *p* in Christ Jesus
Heb 4. 1 while the *p* of entering his rest is still
6.12 faith and patience inherit the *p*.
8. 6 has been enacted through better *p*.
2 Pet 1. 4 his precious and very great *p*, so that
3. 4 "Where is the *p* of his coming? For ever
3. 9 Lord is not slow about his *p*, as some

PROMISE (PROMISED) (v)

Deut 1.11 more and bless you, as he has *p* you!
12.20 enlarges your territory, as he has *p* you,
19. 8 will give you all the land that he *p* your
Josh 23. 5 their land, as the LORD your God *p* you.
2 Sam 7.28 you have *p* this good thing to your
1 Kings 5.12 gave Solomon wisdom, as he *p* him.
8.56 people Israel according to all that he *p*;
2 Chr 6.10 on the throne of Israel, as the LORD *p*,
Jer 32.42 them all the good fortune that I now *p*
Lk 24.49 I am sending you what my Father *p*; so
Acts 7. 5 but *p* to give it to him as his possession
13.32 news that what God *p* to our ancestors
Rom 1. 2 which he *p* beforehand through his
4.21 that God was able to do what he *p*.
Titus 1. 2 life that God, who never lies, *p* before
Heb 9.15 may receive the *p* eternal inheritance,
10.36 of God, you may receive what was *p*.
11.39 did not receive what was *p*, since God
Jas 1.12 the Lord has *p* to those who love him.
2 Pet 2.19 They *p* them freedom, but they

PRONOUNCED

Jer 44.26 my name shall no more be *p* on the lips

PROOF (PROOFS)

Ps 95. 9 tested me, and put me to the *p*,
Acts 1. 3 alive to them by many convincing *p*,
2 Cor 8.24 show them the *p* of your love and of our
13. 3 desire *p* that Christ is speaking in me.

PROPHECY

Prov 29.18 Where there is no *p*, the people cast off
Lk 1.67 with the Holy Spirit and spoke this *p*:
Rom 12. 6 given to us: *p*, in proportion to faith;
1 Cor 12.10 the working of miracles, to another *p*,
Rev 22. 7 keeps the words of the *p* of this book.

PROPHESY (PROPHESIED PROPHESIES PROPHESYING)

Num 11.25 the spirit rested upon them, they *p*.
1 Chr 25. 1 who should *p* with lyres, harps, and
2 Chr 18. 7 him, for he never *p* anything favorable
Isa 30.10 speak to us smooth things, *p* illusions,
Jer 5.31 the prophets *p* falsely, and the priests
11.21 "You shall not *p* in the name of the
14.14 The prophets are *p* lies in my name; I
19.14 where the LORD had sent him to *p*,
23.13 they *p* by Baal and led my people Israel
23.21 ran; I did not speak to them, yet they *p*.
23.32 I am against those who *p* lying dreams,
25.30 "You, therefore, shall *p* against them all
26.18 "Micah of Moresheth, who *p* during the
29. 9 for it is a lie that they are *p* to you in
32. 3 "Why do you *p* and say, Thus says the
Ezek 4. 7 your arm bared you shall *p* against it.
11. 4 Therefore *p* against them, *p*, O mortal."
13. 2 *p* against the prophets of Israel, who are
21. 2 sanctuaries; *p* against the land of Israel
36. 1 *p* to the mountains of Israel, and say: O
37. 4 "*P* to these bones, and say to them: O
38.14 mortal, *p*, and say to Gog, Thus says the
Am 2.12 the prophets, saying, "You shall not *p*."
7.12 of Judah, earn your bread there, and *p*
Mt 7.22 'Lord, Lord, did we not *p* in your name,
26.68 saying, "*P* to us, you Messiah! Who is it
Mk 14.65 and to strike him, saying to him, "*P*!"
Lk 22.64 him, "*P*! Who is it that struck you?"
Acts 2.17 sons and your daughters shall *p*, and
19. 6 them, and they spoke in tongues and *p*.
1 Cor 13. 9 only in part, and we *p* only in part;
14. 5 speak in tongues, but even more to *p*.
Jude 14 *p*, saying, "See, the Lord is coming with
Rev 10.11 "You must *p* again about many peoples

PROPHET

Gen 20. 7 return the man's wife; for he is a *p*, and
Ex 7. 1 and your brother shall be your *p*.
Deut 18.15 God will raise up for you a *p* like me
34.10 has there arisen a *p* in Israel like Moses
Judg 6. 8 the LORD sent a *p* to the Israelites; and
1 Sam 3.20 knew that Samuel was a trustworthy *p*
1 Kings 13.11 Now there lived an old *p* in Bethel. One
22. 7 "Is there no other *p* of the LORD here of
2 Kings 5. 8 he may learn that there is a *p* in Israel."
2 Chr 18. 6 Is there no other *p* of the LORD here of
28. 9 a *p* of the LORD was there, whose name
36.12 humble himself before the *p* Jeremiah
Ps 74. 9 there is no longer any *p*, and there is no
Jer 8.10 unjust gain; from *p* to priest everyone
Ezek 2. 5 they shall know that there has been a *p*
14. 9 I, the LORD, have deceived that *p*, and I
33.33 know that a *p* has been among them.
Hos 9. 7 "The *p* is a fool, the man of the spirit is
12.13 By a *p* the LORD brought Israel up from
Am 7.14 Amos answered Amaziah, "I am no *p*,
Mt 10.41 welcomes a *p* in the name of a *p* will
21. 4 what had been spoken through the *p*,
21.11 "This is the *p* Jesus from Nazareth in
Mk 11.32 for all regarded John as truly a *p*.
Lk 4.24 no *p* is accepted in the prophet's
7.16 saying, "A great *p* has arisen among us:"
20. 6 they are convinced that John was a *p*."
Jn 1.21 "Are you the *p*?" He answered, "No."
4.19 said to him, Sir, I see that you are a *p*.
7.40 in the crowd said, "This is really the *p*."
Acts 7.37 God will raise up a *p* for you from your
Titus 1.12 of them, their very own *p*, who said,
Rev 19.20 with it the false *p* who had performed

PROPHETESS

Judg 4. 4 Deborah, a *p*, the wife of Lappidoth,
Isa 8. 3 And I went to the *p*, and she conceived

PROPHETIC
1 Cor 13. 2 And if I have *p* powers, and understand
2 Pet 1.19 the *p* message more fully confirmed.

PROPHETS
Num 11.29 Would that all the LORD's people were *p*,
12. 6 When there were *p* among you, I the
Deut 13. 1 If *p* or those who divine by dreams
1 Sam 10. 5 you will meet a band of *p* coming down
10.11 son of Kish? Is Saul also among the *p*?"
19.24 it is said, "Is Saul also among the *p*?"
2 Kings 24. 2 that he spoke by his servants the *p*.
2 Chr 20.20 you will be established; believe his *p*."
Neh 9.30 them by your Spirit through your *p*;
Isa 9.15 head, and *p* who teach lies are the tail;
Jer 4. 9 shall be appalled and the *p* astounded.
5.13 The *p* are nothing but wind, for the
7.25 persistently sent all my servants the *p*
27. 9 therefore, must not listen to your *p*,
44. 4 sent to you all my servants the *p*,
Lam 2.14 *p* have seen for you false and deceptive
4.13 It was for the sins of her *p* and the
Zeph 3. 4 Its *p* are reckless, faithless persons; its
Mt 13.57 "*P* are not without honor except in their
23.37 the city that kills the *p* and stones
24.24 false messiahs and false *p* will appear
Mk 6. 4 "*P* are not without honor, except in
8.28 Elijah; and still others, one of the *p*."
Lk 6.26 what their ancestors did to the false *p*.
9.19 that one of the ancient *p* has arisen."
10.24 many *p* and kings desired to see what
13.34 Jerusalem, the city that kills the *p* and
24.44 Moses, the *p*, and the psalms must be
Acts 13.15 After the reading of the law and the *p*,
Rom 11. 3 "Lord, they have killed your *p*, they
1 Cor 12.28 the church first apostles, second *p*,
14.32 And the spirits of *p* are subject to the *p*,
Eph 4.11 that some would be apostles, some *p*,
1 Pet 1.10 the *p* who prophesied of the grace
2 Pet 2. 1 false *p* also arose among the people,
Rev 10. 7 as he announced to his servants the *p*."

PROSPER (PROSPERED PROSPERS)
Gen 39.23 whatever he did, the LORD made it *p*.
1 Kings 2. 3 that you may *p* in all that you do and
2 Kings 18. 7 was with him; wherever he went, he *p*.
2 Chr 26. 5 he sought the LORD, God made him *p*.
31.21 God, he did with all his heart, and he *p*.
Ezra 5. 8 done diligently and *p* in their hands.
Ps 1. 3 not wither. In all that they do, they *p*.
37. 7 do not fret over those who *p* in their
90.17 our hands—O *p* the work of our hands!
122. 6 of Jerusalem: "May they *p* who love you!
Prov 17. 8 who give it; wherever they turn they *p*.
28.13 one who conceals transgressions will *p*,
Isa 48.15 brought him, and he will *p* in his way.
53.10 him the will of the LORD shall *p*.
54.17 that is fashioned against you shall *p*,
Jer 2.37 trust, and you will not *p* through them.
12. 1 Why does the way of the guilty *p*? Why
Dan 6.28 Daniel *p* during the reign of Darius and

PROSPERITY
Job 21.23 One dies in full *p*, being wholly at ease
Ps 25.13 They will abide in *p*, and their children
30. 6 As for me, I said in my *p*, "I shall never
37.11 and delight themselves in abundant *p*.
Eccl 7.14 In the day of *p* be joyful, and in the day
Isa 48.18 your *p* would have been like a river,
66.12 LORD: I will extend *p* to her like a river,
Hag 2. 9 of hosts; and in this place I will give *p*,

PROSPEROUS
Josh 1. 8 Only then shall you make your way *p*,

PROSTITUTE
Gen 38.15 he thought her to be a *p*, for she had
Josh 6.17 Only Rahab the *p* and all who are with
Judg 16. 1 went to Gaza, where he saw a *p* and
Prov 7.10 comes toward him, decked out like a *p*,
23.27 "For a *p* is a deep pit; an adulteress is a
Heb 11.31 By faith Rahab the *p* did not perish
Jas 2.25 Rahab the *p* also justified by works

PROSTRATED
1 Chr 29.20 bowed their heads and *p* themselves

PROTECT (PROTECTED PROTECTS)
Josh 24.17 He *p* us along all the way that we went,
Ps 16. 1 *P* me, O God, for in you I take refuge.
20. 1 The name of the God of Jacob *p* you!
41. 2 The LORD *p* them and keeps them alive;
59. 1 my God, *p* me from those who rise up
116. 6 The LORD *p* the simple; when I was
Isa 31. 5 he will *p* and deliver it, he will spare
Zech 9.15 LORD of hosts will *p* them, and they
Jn 17.11 Father, *p* them in your name that you
1 Pet 1. 5 who are being *p* by the power of God

PROUD
2 Chr 26.16 when he had become strong he grew *p*,
Job 40.11 look on all who are *p*, and abase them.
41.34 is lofty; it is king over all that are *p*."
Ps 123. 4 who are at ease, the contempt of the *p*.
Prov 21. 4 Haughty eyes and a *p* heart—the lamp
Ob 3 Your *p* heart has deceived you, you that
Lk 1.51 he has scattered the *p* in the thoughts
Jas 4. 6 "God opposes the *p*, but gives grace to

PROVE (PROVING)
Ps 26. 2 *P* me, O LORD, and try me; test my heart
Jn 16. 8 he will *p* the world wrong about sin and
Acts 9.22 by *p* that Jesus was the Messiah.
17. 3 and *p* that it was necessary for the
24.13 Neither can they *p* to you the charge
25. 7 against him, which they could not *p*.

PROVERB (PROVERBS)
Deut 28.37 shall become an object of horror, a *p*,
1 Sam 10.12 Therefore it became a *p*, "Is Saul also
1 Kings 4.32 He composed three thousand *p*, and his
9. 7 Israel will become a *p* and a taunt
Ps 49. 4 I will incline my ear to a *p*; I will solve
Prov 1. 6 skill, to understand a *p* and a figure,
26. 9 drunkard is a *p* in the mouth of a fool.
Ezek 12.22 Mortal, what is this *p* of yours about
16.44 use this *p* about you, "Like mother, like
Lk 4.23 quote me this *p*, 'Doctor, cure yourself!'

PROVIDE (PROVIDED PROVIDES)
Gen 22. 8 "God himself will *p* the lamb for a burnt
45.11 I will *p* for you there—since there are
47.12 And Joseph *p* his father, his brothers,
1 Chr 22.14 I have *p* for the house of the LORD one
29. 2 I have *p* for the house of my God, so far
Job 38.41 Who *p* for the raven its prey, when its
Prov 31.15 still night and *p* food for her household
Jon 1.17 But the LORD *p* a large fish to swallow
Mt 27.55 Jesus from Galilee and had *p* for him.

PROVISION (PROVISIONS)
Gen 45.23 with grain, bread, and *p* for his father
Josh 9. 4 they went and prepared *p*, and took
1 Kings 4.22 Solomon's *p* for one day was thirty cors
Rom 13.14 and make no *p* for the flesh, to gratify

PROVOKE (PROVOKED PROVOKING)
Deut 9.22 you have *p* the LORD to wrath.
32.21 what is no god, *p* me with their idols.
Judg 2.12 to them, and they *p* the LORD to anger.
1 Sam 1. 6 Her rival used to *p* her severely, to
1 Kings 14.22 they *p* him to jealousy with their sins
22.53 he *p* the LORD, the God of Israel, to
2 Kings 14.10 why should you *p* trouble so that you
17.17 in the sight of the Lord, *p* him to anger.

2 Chr 25.19 at home; why should you *p* trouble so
28.25 offerings to other gods, *p* to anger the
Ps 78.41 and again, and *p* the Holy One of Israel.
78.58 they *p* him to anger with their high
Isa 65. 3 people who *p* me to my face
Jer 7.19 Is it I whom they *p*? says the LORD.
44. 8 Why do you *p* me to anger with the
1 Cor 10.22 Or are we *p* the Lord to jealousy? Are
Eph 6. 4 fathers, do not *p* your children to anger,
Heb 10.24 consider how to *p* one another to love

PRUDENCE

Prov 5. 2 so that you may hold on to *p*, and your

PRUDENT

Prov 19.14 parents, but a *p* wife is from the LORD.
Am 5.13 Therefore the *p* will keep silent in such

PSALMS

Lk 24.44 prophets, and the *p* must be fulfilled."
Eph 5.19 as you sing *p* and hymns and spiritual
Col 3.16 in your hearts sing *p*, hymns, and

PUFFED (PUFFS)

1 Cor 4. 6 so that none of you will be *p* up in
8. 1 Knowledge *p* up, but love builds up.

PULLED

Jer 38.13 the ropes and *p* him out of the cistern.

PUNISH (PUNISHED)

Ex 32.34 punishment, I will *p* them for their sin."
Lev 26.18 I will continue to *p* you sevenfold for
26.28 I in turn will *p* you myself sevenfold for
Ps 89.32 then I will *p* their transgression with the
Isa 10.12 he will *p* the arrogant boasting of the
13.11 *p* the world for its evil, and the wicked
24.21 day the LORD will *p* the host of heaven
Jer 5. 9 Shall I not *p* them for these things?
9. 9 Shall I not *p* them for these things?
21.14 I will *p* you according to the fruit of
51.47 when I will *p* the images of Babylon;
Hos 2.13 I will *p* her for the festival days of the
8.13 their iniquity, and *p* their sins;
9. 9 their iniquity, he will *p* their sins.
10.10 against the wayward people to *p* them;
12. 2 and will *p* Jacob according to his ways,
Am 3.14 On the day I *p* Israel for its
2 Cor 6. 9 are alive; as *p*, and yet not killed;

PUNISHMENT

Gen 4.13 LORD, "My *p* is greater than I can bear.
Isa 10. 3 What will you do on the day of *p*, in the
53. 5 upon him was the *p* that made us
Lam 4. 6 hs been greater than the *p* of Sodom,
Ezek 4. 5 and so you shall bear the *p* of the
14.10 they shall bear their *p*— the *p* of the
Hos 9. 7 The days of *p* have come, the days of
Hab 1.12 O Rock, have established them for *p*.
2 Cor 2. 6 *p* by the majority is enough for such a
2 Thess 1. 9 will suffer the *p* of eternal destruction,

PURCHASE (PURCHASED)

Gen 25.10 the field that Abraham *p* from the
Jer 32.12 and I gave the deed of *p* to Baruch son

PURE (PURER)

2 Sam 22.27 With the *p* you show yourself *p*, and
Job 4.17 human beings be *p* before their Maker?
8. 6 if you are *p* and upright, surely then he
11. 4 you say, "My conduct is *p*, and I am
Ps 12. 6 of the LORD are promises that are *p*,
18.26 with the *p* you show yourself *p*; and
19. 9 the fear of the LORD is *p*, enduring
24. 4 who have clean hands and *p* hearts,
73. 1 the upright, to those who are *p* in heart.
119. 9 can young people keep their way *p*?
Prov 15.26 to the LORD, but gracious words are *p*.
16. 2 one's ways may be *p* in one's own eyes,
30.12 are those who are *p* in their own eyes
Hab 1.13 Your eyes are too *p* to behold evil, and
Mt 5. 8 "Blessed are the *p* in heart, for they will
2 Cor 11. 3 led astray from a sincere and *p* devotion
1 Tim 5.22 in the sins of others; keep yourself *p*.
Titus 1.15 To the *p* all things are *p*, but to the

PURGE (PURGED)

2 Chr 34. 5 their altars, and *p* Judah and Jerusalem.
Ps 51. 7 *P* me with hyssop, and I shall be clean;
Ezek 20.38 I will *p* out the rebels among you, and

PURIFICATION

Lk 2.22 when the time came for their *p*
Jn 3.25 a discussion about *p* arose between
Heb 1. 3 When he had made *p* for sins, he sat

PURIFY (PURIFIED)

Num 19.13 who has died, and do not *p* themselves,
31.20 You shall *p* every garment, every article
Neh 12.30 and the Levites *p* themselves; and they
Isa 52.11 out from the midst of it, *p* yourselves,
Dan 12.10 Many shall be *p*, cleansed, and refined,
Mal 3. 3 he will *p* the descendants of Levi and
Acts 21.26 having *p* himself, he entered the temple
Heb 9.14 *p* our conscience from dead works to
9.22 law almost everything is *p* with blood,
1 Pet 1.22 you have *p* your souls by your
1 Jn 3. 3 have this hope in him *p* themselves,

PURITY

1 Pet 3. 2 see the *p* and reverence of your lives.

PURPOSE (PURPOSES)

Prov 20. 5 The *p* in the human mind are like deep
Isa 46.10 "My *p* shall stand, and I will fulfill my
Jer 51.29 for the LORD's *p* against Babylon stand,
Lk 7.30 and the lawyers rejected God's *p* for
Acts 20.27 declaring to you the whole *p* of God.
Eph 1.11 *p* of him who accomplishes all things
3.11 was in accordance with the eternal *p*
2 Tim 1. 9 to our works but according to his own *p*
Heb 6.17 the unchangeable character of his *p*,
Rev 17.17 put into their hearts to carry out his *p*

PURSUE (PURSUED PURSUES)

Ex 14. 8 Pharoah . . . *p* the Israelites, who were
Job 19.22 Why do you, like God, *p* me, never
Ps 83.15 so *p* them with your tempest and terrify
109. 16 kindness, but *p* the poor and needy
Prov 21.21 Whoever *p* righteousness and kindness
Jer 29.18 I will *p* them with the sword, with
Lam 3.66 *P* them in anger and destroy them from
Am 1.11 he *p* his brother with the sword,
Acts 26.11 at them, I *p* them even to foreign cities.
Rom 14.19 Let us then *p* what makes for peace and
1 Tim 6.11 *p* righteousness, godliness, faith, love,
Heb 12.14 *P* peace with everyone, and the holiness

PUT

Rom 13.14 Instead, *p* on the Lord Jesus Christ, and
2 Cor 11.20 you *p* up with it when someone makes
Eph 4.22 to *p* away your former way of life,

Q

QUARREL (QUARRELED QUARRELING QUARRELS)

Ex 17. 3 The people *q* with Moses, and said,
Prov 17.14 out water; so stop before the *q* breaks
19.13 and a wife's *q* is a continual dripping of
1 Cor 1.11 people that there are *q* among you,
3. 3 as there is jealousy and *q* among you,
2 Cor 12.20 I fear that there may perhaps be *q*,

QUEEN

Esth 2.17 head and made her *q* instead of Vashti.
Ps 45. 9 honor; at your right hand stands the *q*
Mt 12.42 The *q* of the South will rise up at the

Lk 11.31 The *q* of the South will rise at the

QUENCH (QUENCHED)

Song 8. 7 Many waters cannot *q* love, neither can
Isa 1.31 burn together, with no one to *q* them.
42. 3 and a dimly burning wick he will not *q*;
Mt 12.20 a bruised reed or *q* a smoldering wick
Mk 9.48 worm never dies, and the fire is never *q*.
1 Thess 5.19 Do not *q* the Spirit. Do not despise the

QUESTION (QUESTIONING QUESTIONS)

1 Kings 10. 1 she came to test him with hard *q*.
2 Chr 9. 1 to Jerusalem to test him with hard *q*,
Isa 45.11 Will you *q* me about my children,
Mk 2. 8 do you raise such *q* in your hearts?
Lk 3.15 were *q* in their hearts concerning John

QUICK-TEMPERED

Prov 14.17 One who is *q* acts foolishly, and the

QUIET (QUIETLY)

Job 34.29 When he is *q*, who can condemn? When
Eccl 4. 6 Better is a handful with *q* than two
Mt 1.19 disgrace, planned to dismiss her *q*.
1 Thess 4.11 to aspire to live *q*, to mind your own

QUIETNESS

Isa 32.17 the result of righteousness, *q* and trust

QUIVER

Ps 127. 5 Happy is the man who has his *q* full of

R

RACE

Eccl 9.11 under the sun the *r* is not to the swift,
1 Cor 9.24 in a *r* the runners all compete, but only
Heb 12. 1 let us run with perserverance the *r* that

RACHEL

Gen 29. 6 and here is his daughter *R*, coming with
29.16 and the name of the younger was *R*.
29.18 Jacob loved *R*; so he said, "I will serve
29.30 to *R* also, and he loved *R* more than
30.22 Then God remembered *R*, and God
31.34 *R* had taken the household gods and
35.19 So *R* died, and she was buried on the
Ruth 4.11 like *R* and Leah, who together built up
Mt 2.18 *R* weeping for her children; she refused

RADIANT

Ps 34. 5 Look to him, and be *r*; so your faces
Isa 60. 5 Then you shall see and be *r*; your heart
Jer 31.12 and they shall be *r* over the goodness of

RAFTS

1 Kings 5. 9 I will make it into *r* to go by sea to the
2 Chr 2.16 bring it to you as *r* by sea to Joppa; you

RAGES (RAGED RAGING)

Prov 19. 3 to ruin, yet the heart *r* against the LORD.
Isa 37.28 and coming in, and your *r* against me.
Rev 11.18 The nations *r*, but your wrath has come,

RAIL

Num 16.11 What is Aaron that you *r* against him?"

RAIN (RAINS)

Gen 2. 5 God had not caused it to *r* upon the
7. 4 For in seven days I will send *r* on the
Lev 26. 4 I will give you your *r* in their season,
Deut 11.14 then he will give the *r* for your land in
28.12 to give the *r* of your land in its season
1 Kings 8.35 there is no *r* because they have sinned
17. 1 shall be neither dew nor *r* these years,
18.41 for there is a sound of the rushing *r*."
Job 5.10 He gives *r* on the earth and sends
38.28 "Has the *r* a father, or who has begotten
Ps 68. 9 *R* in abundance, O God, you showered
Isa 44.14 plants a cedar and the *r* nourishes it.
45. 8 and let the skies *r* down righteousness;
55.10 as the *r* and the snow come down from
Jer 5.24 our God, who gives the *r* in its season,
Joel 2.23 abundant *r*, the early and the latter *r*, as
Am 4. 7 I also withheld the *r* from you when
Zech 10. 1 Ask *r* from the LORD in the season of
14.17 of hosts, there will be no *r* upon them.
Mt 5.45 sends *r* on the righteous and on the
7.25 The *r* fell, the floods came, and the
Acts 14.17 giving you *r* from heaven and fruitful
Rev 11. 6 that no *r* may fall during the days of

RAINBOW

Rev 4. 3 around the throne is a *r* that looks like

RAISE (RAISED RAISES)

Ps 41.10 to me, and *r* me up, that I may repay
148. 14 He has *r* up a horn for his people,
Mt 14. 2 Baptist; he has been *r* from the dead,
16.21 and be killed, and on the third day be *r*.
17. 9 Son of Man has been *r* from the dead.
20.19 and on the third day he will be *r*."
26.32 after I am *r* up, I will go ahead of you
27.64 people, 'He has been *r* from the dead,
28. 6 He is not here; for he has been *r*, as he
Mk 6.14 "John the baptizer has been *r* from the
14.28 after I am *r* up, I will go before you to
16. 6 He has been *r*; he is not here. Look,
Lk 9. 7 that John had been *r* from the dead
21.28 take place, stand up and *r* your heads,
Jn 5.21 just as the father *r* the dead and gives
6.39 given me, but *r* it up at the last day.
Acts 3.15 Author of life, whom God *r* from the
10.40 God *r* him on the third day and allowed
13.30 But God *r* him from the dead;
26. 8 by any of you that God *r* the dead?
Rom 9.17 to Pharaoh, "I have *r* you up for the very
1 Cor 6.14 And God *r* the Lord and will also *r* us
15. 4 that he was *r* on the third day in
15.13 of the dead, then Christ has not been *r*;
2 Cor 4.14 the one who *r* the Lord Jesus will *r* us
Eph 1.20 when he *r* him from the dead and
2. 6 *r* us up with him and seated us with
Col 3. 1 if you have been *r* with Christ, seek the
2 Tim 2. 8 Remember Jesus Christ, *r* from the
Jas 5.15 the sick, and the Lord will *r* them up;
1 Pet 1.21 to trust in God, who *r* him from the

RAM

Gen 15. 9 Bring me . . . a *r* three years old, a
22.13 and saw a *r*, caught in a thicket by its

RAMAH

1 Sam 1.19 they went back to their house at *R*.
2.11 Then Elkanah went home to *R*, while
8. 4 together and came to Samuel at *R*,
19.18 and escaped; he came to Samuel at *R*,
28. 3 mourned for him and buried him in *R*,
2 Chr 16. 1 against Judah, and built *R*, to prevent
Isa 10.29 *R* trembles, Gibeah of Saul has fled. Cry
Jer 31.15 A voice is heard in *R*, lamentation and
Mt 2.18 "A voice was heard in *R*, wailing and

RAMOTH-GILEAD

1 Kings 22. 6 "Shall I go to battle against *R*, or shall I
2 Kings 9. 1 flask of oil in your hand, and go to *R*.

RAMPART

Hab 2. 1 watchpost, and station myself on the *r*,

RANK

Gen 49. 3 of my vigor, excelling in *r* and excelling

RANSOM (RANSOMED)

Ex 30.12 all of them shall give a *r* for their lives
1 Sam 14.45 So the people *r* Jonathan, and he did
Job 6.23 hand'? Or, '*R* me from the hand
33.24 down into the Pit; I have found a *r*;

Job 36.18 not let the greatness of the *r* turn you
Ps 49. 7 Truly, no *r* avails for one's life, there is
49. 8 For the *r* of life is costly, and can never
Prov 21.18 The wicked is a *r* for the righteous, and
Isa 43. 3 I give Egypt as your *r*, Ethiopia and
Hos 13.14 Shall I *r* them from the power of Sheol?
Mt 20.28 serve, and to give his life a *r* for many."
Mk 10.45 serve, and to give his life a *r* for many."
1 Tim 2. 6 human, who gave himself as a *r* for all
1 Pet 1.18 You know that you were *r* from the
Rev 5. 9 by your blood you *r* for God saints from

RARE

1 Sam 3. 1 word of the LORD was *r* in those days;
Isa 13.12 I will make mortals more *r* than fine

RASH

Job 6. 3 sea; therefore my words have been *r*.
Eccl 5. 2 Never be *r* with your mouth, nor let

RAVAGED (RAVAGING)

Nah 2. 2 though ravagers have *r* them and ruined
Acts 8. 3 But Saul was *r* the church by entering

RAVEN (RAVENS)

Gen 8. 7 and sent out the *r*; and it went to and
1 Kings 17. 4 commanded the *r* to feed you there."
Job 38.41 Who provides for the *r* its prey, when its
Lk 12.24 Consider the *r*: they neither sow nor

RAVENOUS

Prov 27. 7 but to a *r* appetite even the bitter

RAVISH (RAVISHED)

Judg 19.24 *R* them and do whatever you want to
Song 4. 9 you have *r* my heart with a glance of

RAZOR

Num 6. 5 vow no *r* shall come upon the head;
Ps 52. 2 Your tongue is like a sharp *r*, you
Isa 7.20 the Lord will shave with a *r* hired
Ezek 5. 1 sword; use it as a barber's *r* and run it

READ (READING READS)

Deut 17.19 he shall *r* in it all the days of his life,
31.11 you shall *r* this law before all Israel in
2 Kings 23. 2 he *r* in their hearing all the words of
Neh 8. 3 he *r* from it facing the square before the
13. 1 they *r* from the book of Moses in the
Isa 29.11 "*R* this," they say, "I cannot, for it is
34.16 *r* from the book of the LORD: Not one of
Jer 36. 6 house you shall *r* the words of the LORD
36.21 and Jehudi *r* it to the king and all the
Dan 5. 7 "Whoever can *r* this writing and tell me
5.17 I will *r* the writing to the king and let
Hab 2. 2 on tablets, so that a runner may *r* it.
Mt 21.42 "Have you never *r* in the scriptures:
Mk 12.10 Have you not *r* this scripture: 'The
12.26 have you not *r* in the book of Moses, in
Lk 6. 3 "Have you not *r* what David did when
Acts 8.28 his chariot, he was *r* the prophet Isaiah.
2 Cor 3. 2 on our hearts, to be known and *r* by all;
Rev 1. 3 Blessed is the one who *r* aloud the

READY

Song 2. 7 not stir up or awaken love until it is *r*.
3. 5 not stir up or awaken love until it is *r*.
8. 4 not stir up or awaken love until it is *r*.
Mt 22. 4 and everything is *r*; come to my
22. 8 'The wedding is *r*, but those invited
24.44 you also must be *r*, for the Son of Man
25.10 those who were *r* went with him into
1 Cor 14. 8 sound, who will get *r* for battle?
2 Cor 9. 2 saying that Achaia has been *r* since last

REALIZED

Mk 15.10 he *r* that it was out of jealousy that the
Lk 20.19 and chief priests *r* that he had told this

REALM

Dan 11. 5 shall rule a *r* greater than his own *r*.

REAP (REAPS)

Lev 19. 9 *r* . . . , you shall not *r* to the very edges
23.22 *r* . . . , you shall not *r* to the very edges
Job 4. 8 iniquity and sow trouble *r* the same.
Ps 126. 5 who sow in tears *r* with shouts of joy.
Prov 22. 8 Whoever sows injustice will *r* calamity,
Eccl 11. 4 whoever regards the clouds will not *r*.
Mic 6.15 You shall sow, but not *r*; you shall tread
Mt 6.26 they neither sow nor *r* nor gather into
Jn 4.37 holds true, 'One sows and another *r*.'
1 Cor 9.11 too much if we *r* your material benefits?
Gal 6. 7 mocked, for you *r* whatever you sow.
Rev 14.15 *r*, for the hour to *r* has come, because

REBEKAH (REBECCA)

Gen 22.23 Bethuel became the father of *R*. These
24.15 he had finished speaking, there was *R*,
24.59 So they sent away their sister *R* and her
24.67 He took *R*, and she became his wife,
25.28 was fond of game; but *R* loved Jacob.
27. 5 *R* was listening when Isaac spoke to his
49.31 there Isaac and his wife *R* were buried;
Rom 9.10 to *R* when she had conceived children

REBEL (REBELS) (n)

Num 20.10 "Listen, you *r*, shall we bring water for
Isa 1.23 Your princes are *r* and companions of
1.28 *r* and sinners shall be destroyed
48. 8 and that from birth you were called a *r*.

REBEL (REBELLED REBELLING REBELS)

Num 14. 9 do not *r* against the LORD; and do not
16.41 of the Israelites *r* against Moses
20.24 because you *r* against my command at
27.14 because you *r* against my word in the
Deut 1.26 You *r* against the command of the LORD
1.43 You *r* against the command of the LORD
2 Kings 3. 5 of Moab *r* against the king of Israel.
Neh 2.19 are doing? Are you *r* against the king?"
Job 24.13 There are those who *r* against the light,
Ps 5.10 them out, for they have *r* against you.
78.17 against him, *r* against the Most High
78.40 How often they *r* against him in the
107. 11 for they had *r* against the words of God,
Prov 28. 2 When a land *r* it has many rulers; but
Isa 1. 2 them up, but they have *r* against me.
1.20 but if you refuse and *r*, you shall be
36. 5 now rely, that you have *r* against me?
63.10 they *r* and grieved his holy spirit;
Jer 4.17 of a field, because she has *r* against me,
Ezek 2. 3 nation of rebels, who have *r* against me;
20.13 Israel *r* against me in the wilderness;
Hos 13.16 because she has *r* against her God;

REBELLION

Josh 22.16 yourselves an altar today in *r* against
1 Sam 15.23 *r* is no less a sin than divination, and
1 Kings 12.19 Israel has been in *r* against the house of
2 Chr 10.19 So Israel has been in *r* against the
Job 34.37 For he adds *r* to his sin; he claps his
Jer 29.32 for he has spoken *r* against the LORD.

REBELLIOUS

Deut 21.18 and *r* son who will not obey his father
Ezra 4.15 this is a *r* city, hurtful to kings and
Isa 30. 1 Oh, *r* children, says the LORD, who carry
Ezek 17.12 Say now to the *r* house: Do you not

REBUILD (REBUILT)

Ezra 1. 3 in Judah, and *r* the house of the LORD,
Neh 4. 6 So we *r* the wall, and all the wall was
Job 12.14 If he tears down, no one can *r*; if he
Ps 51.18 *r* the walls of Jerusalem, then you will

REBUKE (n)

Job 26.11 tremble, and are astounded at his *r*.
Ps 76. 6 At your *r*, O God of Jacob, both rider
104. 7 At your *r* they flee; at the sound of your
Prov 17.10 A *r* strikes deeper into a discerning
27. 5 Better is open *r* than hidden love. Well

REBUKE (REBUKED) (v)

Gen 31.42 and the labor of my hands, and *r* you
37.10 to his brothers, his father *r* him, and
1 Chr 16.21 them; he *r* kings on their account,
Job 13.10 He will surely *r* you if in secret you
Ps 6. 1 O LORD, do not *r* me in your anger, or
38. 1 O LORD, do not *r* me in your anger, or
50. 8 Not for your sacrifices do I *r* you; your
105. 14 them; he *r* kings on their account,
106. 9 He *r* the Red Sea, and it became dry; he
119. 21 You *r* the insolent, accursed ones, who
Prov 24.25 who *r* the wicked will have delight,
Jer 29.27 why have you not *r* Jeremiah of
Zech 3. 2 "The LORD *r* you, O Satan! The LORD
Mt 16.22 took him aside and began to *r* him,
17.18 Jesus *r* the demon, and it came out of
Mk 8.32 took him aside and began to *r* him.
9.25 he *r* the unclean spirit, saying to it,
Lk 4.35 Jesus *r* him, saying "Be silent, and
9.42 Jesus *r* the unclean spirit, healed the
9.55 But he turned and *r* them. Then they
Jude 9 against him, but said, "The Lord *r* you!"

RECEIVE (RECEIVED RECEIVES)

Job 2.10 at the hand of God, and not *r* the bad?"
22.22 *R* instruction from his mouth, and lay
27.13 and the heritage that oppressors *r* from
35. 7 to him; and what does he *r* from your
Ps 24. 5 They will *r* blessing from the LORD, and
49.15 the power of Sheol, for he will *r* me.
73.24 and afterward you will *r* me with honor.
Mt 7. 8 For everyone who asks *r*, and everyone
20.10 came, they thought they would *r* more;
21.22 ask for in prayer with faith, you will *r*."
Mk 4.16 the word, they immediately *r* it with joy;
10.15 does not *r* the kingdom as a little child
10.30 who will not *r* a hundredfold now in
Lk 6.34 sinners lend to sinners, to *r* as much
9.53 but they did not *r* him, because his face
11.10 For everyone who asks *r*, and everyone
18.42 to him, "*R* your sight; your faith has
Jn 1.12 But to all who *r* him, who believed in
3.27 "No one can *r* anything except what has
13.20 and whoever *r* me *r* him who sent me."
20.22 "*R* the Holy Spirit. If you forgive the
Acts 19. 2 "Did you *r* the Holy Spirit when you
1 Cor 2.14 who are unspiritual do not *r* the gifts of
11.23 I *r* from the Lord what I also handed on
15. 3 what I in turn had *r*: that Christ died
Gal 3. 2 Did you *r* the Spirit by doing the works
3.14 that we might *r* the promise of the
4. 5 so that we might *r* adoption as children.
6. 1 who have *r* the Spirit should restore
Col 2. 6 therefore have *r* Christ Jesus the Lord,
1 Thess 1. 6 of persecution you *r* the word with joy
2 Jn 8 worked for, but may *r* a full reward.

RECEPTIVE

Acts 17.11 These Jews were more *r* than those in

RECITE

Deut 6. 7 *R* them to your children and talk about

RECKONS (RECKONED RECKONING)

Gen 15. 6 the LORD; and the LORD *r* it to him as
42.22 So now there comes a *r* for his blood."
Ps 106. 31 that has been *r* to him as righteousness
Prov 18.24 When he began the *r*, one who owed
Rom 4. 3 "Abraham believed God, and it was *r* to
4. 6 to whom God *r* righteousness apart

Rom 4. 9 "Faith was *r* to Abraham as
4.22 his faith was "*r* to him as righteousness."
5.13 but sin is not *r* when there is no law.

RECOGNIZED

Gen 42. 8 Although Joseph had *r* his brothers,

RECOMPENSED

2 Sam 22.25 the LORD has *r* me according to my
Ps 18.24 Therefore the LORD has *r* me according

RECONCILE (RECONCILED)

Mt 5.24 first be *r* to your brother or sister, and
Rom 5.10 enemies, we were *r* to God through the
1 Cor 7.11 unmarried or else be *r* to her husband),
2 Cor 5.18 is from God, who *r* us to himself
Eph 2.16 might *r* both groups to God in one body
Col 1.20 was pleased to *r* to himself all things,

RECONCILIATION

Rom 5.11 through whom we have now received *r*.
11.15 if their rejection is the *r* of the world,

RECOUNT

Ps 118. 17 not die, but I shall live, and *r* the deeds
Isa 63. 7 I will *r* the gracious deeds of the LORD,

RECOVER

2 Kings 8. 8 him, whether I shall *r* from this illness."
Isa 11.11 yet a second time to *r* the remnant

RED SEA

Ex 10.19 the locusts and drove them into the *R*;
15. 4 his picked officers were sunk in the *R*.
15.22 ordered Israel to set out from the *R*,
Josh 4.23 God did to the *R*, which he dried up for
Ps 106. 9 He rebuked the *R*, and it became dry;
Acts 7.36 wonders and signs in Egypt, at the *R*,
Heb 11.29 faith the people passed through the *R*

REDEEM (REDEEMED REDEEMS)

Gen 48.16 the angel who has *r* me from all harm,
Ex 6. 6 I will *r* you with an outstretched arm
15.13 love you led the people whom you *r*;
21. 8 then he shall let her be *r*; he shall have
34.20 if a donkey you shall *r* with a lamb,
Num 18.15 first-born of human beings you shall *r*,
Deut 7. 8 and *r* you from the house of slavery,
9.26 whom you *r* in your greatness, whom
Ruth 4. 4 If you will *r* it, *r* it; but if you will not,
2 Sam 4. 9 As the LORD lives, who has *r* my life out
7.23 whose God went to *r* it as a people,
1 Chr 17.21 whom God went to *r* to be his people,
Neh 1.10 your people, whom you *r* by your great
Job 5.20 In famine he will *r* you from death, and
33.28 He has *r* my soul from going down to
Ps 25.22 *R* Israel, O God, out of all its troubles.
26.11 integrity; *r* me, and be gracious to me.
31. 5 my spirit; you have *r* me, O LORD,
34.22 The LORD *r* the life of his servants; none
44.26 Rise up, come to our help. *R* us for the
69.18 Draw near to me, *r* me, set me free
77.15 With your strong arm you *r* your people,
103. 4 diseases, who *r* your life from the Pit,
130. 7 love, and with him is great power to *r*.
Isa 1.27 Zion shall be *r* by justice, and those in
43. 1 O Israel: Do not fear, for I have *r* you;
48.20 say, "The LORD has *r* his servant Jacob!"
52. 3 and you shall be *r* without money.
Jer 15.21 the wicked, and *r* you from the grasp of
Hos 7.13 I would *r* them, but they speak lies
Mic 6. 4 and *r* you from the house of slavery;
Zech 10. 8 and gather them in, for I have *r* them,
Lk 1.68 favorably on his people and *r* them.
24.21 hoped that he was the one to *r* Israel.
Gal 3.13 Christ *r* us from the curse of the law by
4. 5 to *r* those who were under the law,
Titus 2.14 us that he might *r* us from all iniquity

REDEEMED (n)

Ps 107. 2 Let the *r* of the LORD say so, those he *r*
Isa 35. 9 found there, but the *r* shall walk there.
51.10 of the sea a way for the *r* to cross over?
62.12 "The Holy People, The *R* of the LORD";

REDEEMER

Job 19.25 For I know that my *R* lives, and that at
Ps 19.14 to you, O LORD, my rock and my *r*.
78.35 their rock, the Most High God their *r*.
Prov 23.11 for their *R* is strong; he will plead their
Isa 41.14 says the LORD; your *R* is the Holy One
44. 6 King of Israel, and his *R*, the LORD of
47. 4 Our *R*—the LORD of hosts is his
54. 8 on you, says the LORD, your *R*.
59.20 he will come to Zion as *R*, to those in
Jer 50.34 Their *R* is strong; the LORD of hosts is

REDEMPTION

Ex 21.30 is imposed for the *r* of the victim's life.
Lev 25.24 you shall provide for the *r* of the land.
25.29 sale; the right of *r* shall be for one year.
25.52 they shall make payment for their *r*.
Num 3.49 So Moses took the *r* money from those
Ruth 4. 6 Take my right of *r* yourself, for I cannot
Ps 111. 9 He sent *r* to his people; he has
Jer 32. 7 Anathoth, for the right of *r* by purchase
Lk 2.38 were looking for the *r* of Jerusalem.
21.28 heads, because your *r* is drawing near."
Rom 3.24 through the *r* which is in Christ Jesus,
1 Cor 1.30 and sanctification and *r*, in order that,
Eph 1. 7 we have *r* through his blood, the
4.30 marked with a seal for the day of *r*.
Heb 9.12 his own blood, thus obtaining eternal *r*.

REED

2 Kings 18.21 Egypt, that broken *r* of a staff, which
Isa 42. 3 bruised *r* he will not break, and a dimly
Ezek 40. 3 a measuring *r* in his hand; and he was
Mt 11. 7 to look at? A *r* shaken by the wind?
12.20 He will not break a bruised *r* or quench
Lk 7.24 to look at? A *r* shaken by the wind?

REFINE (REFINED REFINES)

Isa 48.10 See, I have *r* you, but not like silver; I
Jer 9. 7 I will now *r* and test them, for what else
Zech 13. 9 into the fire, *r* them as one *r* silver,
Rev 3.18 buy from me gold *r* by fire so that you

REFLECTS (REFLECTION)

Prov 27.19 the face, so one human heart *r* another.
Heb 1. 3 He is the *r* of God's glory and the exact

REFRESH (REFRESHED)

Gen 18. 5 a little bread, that you may *r* yourselves,
Ex 23.12 slave and the resident alien may be *r*.
Prov 25.13 them; they *r* the spirit of their masters.
Song 2. 5 *r* me with apples; for I am faint with
Rom 15.32 you with joy and be *r* in your company.
1 Cor 16.18 for they *r* my spirit as well as yours. So
2 Tim 1.16 of Onesiphorus, because he often *r* me
Philem 7 of the saints have been *r* through you.
2 Pet 1.13 as I am in this body, to *r* your memory,

REFUGE

Num 35. 6 shall include six cities of *r*, where you
35.11 select cities to be cities of *r* for you,
Deut 32.37 gods, the rock in which they took *r*,
Josh 20. 2 'Appoint the cities of *r*, of which I
Ruth 2.12 under whose wings you have come for *r*!"
Ps 2.12 kindled. Happy are all who take *r*
7. 1 O LORD my God, in you I take *r*; save
14. 6 of the poor, but the LORD is their *r*.
16. 1 Protect me. O God, for in you I take *r*. I
31. 1 In you, O LORD, I seek *r*; do not let me
46. 1 God is our *r* and strength, a very
57. 1 the shadow of your wings I will take *r*,
61. 3 for you are my *r*, a strong tower against

Ps 61. 4 tent forever, find *r* under the shelter of
71. 1 In you, O LORD, I take *r*; never let me be
71. 7 to many, but you are my strong *r*.
73.28 made the Lord GOD my *r*, to tell of all
91. 2 say to the LORD, "My *r* and my fortress;
118. 8 better to take *r* in the LORD than to put
142. 4 notice of me; no *r* remains to me; no
Prov 14.32 the righteous find a *r* in their integrity.
30. 5 true; he is a shield to those who take *r*
Isa 4. 6 and a *r* and a shelter from the storm
25. 4 you have been a *r* to the poor, a *r* to
28.15 we have made lies our *r*, and in
33.16 their *r* will be the fortresses of rocks;
57.13 whoever takes *r* in me shall possess the
Jer 16.19 stronghold, my *r* in the day of trouble,
17.17 me; you are my *r* in the day of disaster;
Joel 3.16 the LORD is a *r* for his people, a
Nah 1. 7 he protects those who take *r* in him,
Zeph 3.12 They shall seek *r* in the name of the

REFUSE (REFUSED)

Gen 39. 8 But he *r* and said to his master's wife,
Num 20.21 Thus Edom *r* to give Israel passage
1 Sam 8.19 the people *r* to listen to the voice of
Neh 9.17 they *r* to obey, and were not mindful of
Esth 1.12 But Queen Vashti *r* to come at the
Ps 78.10 but *r* to walk according to his law.
Prov 1.24 Because I have called and you *r*, have
Isa 7.15 the time he knows how to *r* the evil and
Jer 5. 3 them, but they *r* to take correction.
9. 6 upon deceit! They *r* to know me, says
13.10 evil people, who *r* to hear my words,
Hos 11. 5 because they have *r* to return to me.
Zech 7.11 But they *r* to listen, and turned a
2 Thess 2.10 because they *r* to love the truth and so
Heb 11.24 grown up, *r* to be called the son of
12.25 you do not *r* the one who is speaking;

REFUTE (REFUTED)

Acts 18.28 he powerfully *r* the Jews in public,
Titus 1. 9 and to *r* those who contradict it.

REGARD (REGARDED REGARDS)

Gen 4. 4 the LORD had *r* for Abel and his offering,
1 Kings 8.28 *R* your servant's prayer and his plea, O
Job 34.19 nor *r* the rich more than the poor, for
37.24 he does not *r* any who are wise in their
Ps 80.14 heaven, and see; have *r* for this vine,
106. 44 he *r* their distress, when he heard their
Isa 17. 7 people will *r* their Maker, and their eyes
Jer 24. 5 I will *r* as good the exiles from Judah,
Mk 12.14 you do not *r* people with partiality, but
Phil 3. 8 I *r* everything as loss because of the

REGISTER (REGISTERED)

Num 3.10 you shall make a *r* of Aaron and his
Lk 2. 1 Augustus that all the world should be *r*.

REGRET

1 Sam 15.11 "I *r* that I have made Saul king, for he

REGULAR

Dan 8.11 took the *r* burnt offering away from him

REGULATIONS

Num 9. 3 according to its statutes and all its *r*

REHOBOAM

1 Kings 11.43 David; and his son *R* succeeded him.
12. 1 *R* went to Shechem, for all Israel had
14.21 *R* was forty-one years old when he
15. 6 war between *R* and Jeroboam continued
Mt 1. 7 Solomon the father of *R*, and *R* the

REIGN (REIGNED REIGNS)

Gen 37. 8 "Are you indeed to *r* over us? Are you
Ex 15.18 The LORD will *r* forever and ever."
1 Sam 11.12 is it that said, 'Shall Saul *r* over us?'
1 Kings 2.11 time that David *r* over Israel was forty

Job 34.30 so that the godless should not *r*, or
Ps 146. 10 The LORD will *r* forever, your God, O
Prov 8.15 By me kings *r*, and rulers decree what is
Eccl 4.14 One can indeed come out of prison to *r*,
Isa 24.23 for the LORD of hosts will *r* on Mount
32. 1 king will *r* in righteousness, and princes
Jer 23. 5 and he shall *r* as king and deal wisely,
Lam 5.19 But you, O LORD, *r* forever; your throne
Mic 4. 7 the LORD will *r* over them in Mount Zion
Lk 1.33 He will *r* over the house of Jacob
1 Cor 15.25 he must *r* until he has put all his
Rev 11.15 Messiah, and he will *r* forever and ever."
19. 6 For the Lord our God the Almighty *r*.
20. 4 life and *r* with Christ a thousand years.

REJECT (REJECTED REJECTING REJECTS)

Num 11.20 you have *r* the LORD who is among you,
1 Sam 8. 7 not *r* you, but they have *r* me from
10.19 today you have *r* your God, who saves
Ps 36. 4 way that is not good; they do not *r* evil.
118. 22 The stone that the builders *r* has
Prov 10.17 life, but one who *r* a rebuke goes astray.
Isa 30.12 Because you *r* this word, and put your
Jer 2.37 the LORD has *r* those in whom you trust,
6.19 and as for my teaching, they have *r* it.
6.30 They are called "*r* silver," for the LORD
7.29 the LORD has *r* and forsaken the
Lam 5.22 unless you have utterly *r* us, and are
Ezek 5. 6 her, *r* my ordinances and not following
Hos 4. 6 knowledge, I *r* you from being a priest
Am 2. 4 because they have *r* the law
Mt 21.42 stone that the builders *r* has become
Mk 7. 9 have a fine way of *r* the commandment
12.10 stone that the builders *r* has become
Lk 9.22 be *r* by the elders, chief priests, and
10.16 *r* you *r* me, whoever *r* me *r* the one who
17.25 suffering and be *r* by this generation.
20.17 stone that the builders *r* has become
Jn 12.48 The one who *r* me and does not receive
Rom 11. 1 I ask then, has God *r* his people? By no

REJOICE

Lev 23.40 you shall *r* before the LORD your God for
Deut 16.11 *R* before the LORD your God—you and
1 Chr 16.10 the hearts of those who seek the LORD *r*.
Ps 5.11 But let all who take refuge in you *r*; let
33. 1 *R* in the LORD, O you righteous. Praise
35. 9 Then my soul shall *r* in the LORD,
58.10 The righteous will *r* when they see
85. 6 again, so that your people may *r* in you?
118. 24 has made; let us *r* and be glad in it.
149. 2 let the children of Zion *r* in their King!
Prov 5.18 blessed, and *r* in the wife of your youth,
29. 2 righteous are in authority, the people *r*;
Isa 1.10 I will greatly *r* in the LORD, my whole
35. 1 be glad, the desert shall *r* and blossom;
41.16 Then you shall *r* in the LORD; in the
62. 5 the bride, so shall your God *r* over you.
66.10 *R* with Jerusalem, and be glad for her,
Jer 31.13 shall the young women *r* in the dance,
Lam 2.17 he has made the enemy *r* over you, and
Ezek 7.12 let not the buyer *r*, nor the seller
Joel 2.23 of Zion, be glad and *r* in the LORD
Hab 3.18 yet I will *r* in the LORD; I will exult in
Zech 9. 9 *R* greatly, O daughter Zion! Shout
Mt 5.12 *R* and be glad, for your reward is great
Lk 6.23 *R* in that day and leap for joy, for surely
10.20 do not *r* at this, that the spirits submit
Jn 14.28 If you loved me, you would *r* that I am
Rom 12.15 *R* with those who *r*, weep with those
15.10 he says, "*R*, O Gentiles, with his people";
1 Cor 7.30 those who *r* as though they were not
13. 6 it does not *r* in wrongdoing, but rejoices
Phil 1.18 of false motives or true; and in that I *r*.
3. 1 my brothers and sisters, *r* in the Lord.
4. 4 *R* in the Lord always; again I will say,
1 Thess 5.16 *R* always, pray without ceasing, give
1 Pet 1. 8 see him now, you believe in him and *r*
4.13 But *r* insofar as you are sharing Christ's

REJOICES (REJOICED REJOICING)

Num 10.10 Also on your days of *r*, at your
1 Sam 6.13 the ark, they went with *r* to meet it.
1 Chr 29. 9 Then the people *r* because these had
Esth 8.15 while the city of Susa shouted and *r*.
Ps 19. 8 of the LORD are right, *r* the heart;
Prov 11.10 goes well with the righteous, the city *r*;
15.30 The light of the eyes *r* the heart, and
Mt 18.13 he *r* over it more than over the
Lk 1.47 Lord, and my spirit *r* in God my Savior,
13.17 crowd was *r* at all the wonderful things
15. 5 it, he lays it on his shoulders and *r*.
Jn 8.56 Abraham *r* that he would see my day;
Acts 16.34 he and his entire household *r* that he

REKINDLE

2 Tim 1. 6 remind you to *r* the gift of God that is

RELAX

Lk 12.19 goods laid up for many years; *r*, eat,

RELEASE (RELEASED)

Job 14.14 I would wait, until my *r* should come.
Mk 15. 6 he used to *r* a prisoner for them,
15.15 Pilate . . . *r* Barabbas for them; and after
Lk 23.16 therefore have him flogged and *r* him."
Jn 18.39 have a custom that I *r* someone for you
Rev 20. 7 Satan will be *r* from his prison and will

RELENT (RELENTED)

2 Sam 24.16 LORD *r* concerning the evil, and said to
1 Chr 21.15 the LORD took note and *r* concerning the
Am 7. 3 The LORD *r* concerning this; "It shall not
Jon 3. 9 God may *r* and change his mind;

RELIEF

Gen 5.29 this one shall bring us *r* from our work
Job 32.20 I must speak, so that I may find *r*; I
Acts 11.29 each would send *r* to the believers

RELIGION

Acts 26. 5 belonged to the strictest sect of our *r*
1 Tim 3.16 any doubt, the mystery of our *r* is great:
Jas 1.27 *R* that is pure and undefiled before

RELIGIOUS

Acts 17.22 I see how how extremely *r* you are
Jas 1.26 If any think they are *r*, and do not

RELY (RELYING)

2 Kings 18.21 you are *r* now on Egypt, that broken
18.30 let Hezekiah make you to *r* on the LORD
2 Chr 14.11 God, for we *r* on you, and in your name
16. 7 and did not *r* on the LORD your God,
Isa 59. 4 they *r* on empty pleas, they speak lies,
2 Cor 1. 9 so that we would *r* not on ourselves but

REMAIN (REMAINED REMAINS)

Gen 49.24 Yet his bow *r* taut, and his arms were
Josh 13. 1 much of the land still *r* to be possessed.
1 Sam 1.22 of the LORD, and *r* there forever;
5. 7 of the God of Israel must not *r* with us;
Ps 101. 7 No one who practices deceit shall *r* in
Eccl 1. 4 comes, but the earth *r* forever.
Jer 42.10 If you will only *r* in this land, then I
Hos 3. 4 Israelites shall *r* many days without king
Mk 14.34 deeply grieved, even to death; *r* here,
Lk 10. 7 *R* in the same house, eating and
Jn 21.22 If it is my will that he *r* until I come,
1 Cor 7.24 brothers and sisters, there *r* with God.
1 Jn 2.19 to us, they would have *r* with us.

REMEMBER

Gen 9.15 I will *r* my covenant that is between me
41. 9 said to Pharaoh, "I *r* my faults today.
Ex 13. 3 "*R* this day on which you came out of

Ex 32.13 *R* Abraham, Isaac, and Israel, your
Lev 26.42 *r* my covenant with Jacob; I will *r* also
Num 11. 5 We *r* the fish we used to eat in Egypt
15.39 when you see it, you will *r* all the
Deut 7.18 Just *r* what the LORD your God did to
9. 7 *R* . . . how you provoked the LORD your
15.15 *R* that you were a slave in the land of
16.12 *R* that you were a slave in Egypt, and
24.18 *R* that you were a slave in Egypt and
32. 7 *R* the days of old, consider the years
Judg 8.34 Israelites did not *r* the LORD their God,
16.28 "Lord GOD, *r* me and strengthen me only
1 Sam 1.11 on the misery of your servant, and *r* me,
2 Kings 20. 3 "*R* now, O LORD, I implore you, how I
1 Chr 16.12 *R* the wonderful works he has done, his
2 Chr 6.42 *R* your steadfast love for your servant
24.22 Joash did not *r* the kindness that
Neh 1. 8 *R* the word that you commanded your
4.14 *R* the LORD, who is great and awesome,
5.19 *R* for my good, O my God, all that I
6.14 *R* Tobiah and Sanballat, O my God,
13.14 *R* me, O my God, concerning this, and
Ps 42. 6 cast down within me; therefore I *r* you
74. 2 *R* your congregation, which you
79. 8 Do not *r* against us the iniquities of our
89.47 *R* how short my time is— for whatever
105. 5 *R* the wonderful works he has done, his
137. 7 *R*, O LORD, against the Edomites the day
Prov 31. 7 poverty, and *r* their misery no more.
Eccl 11. 8 *r* that the days of darkness will be
12. 1 *R* your creator in the days of your
Isa 38. 3 "*R* now, O LORD, I implore you, how I
43.18 Do not *r* the former things, or consider
43.25 my own sake, and I will not *r* your sins.
46. 8 *R* this and consider, recall it to mind,
Jer 2. 2 I *r* the devotion of your youth, your love
18.20 *R* how I stood before you to speak good
Ezek 16.22 you did not *r* the days of your youth,
20.43 There you shall *r* your ways and all the
36.31 Then you will *r* your evil ways, and your
Hos 7. 2 consider that I *r* all their wickedness.
Am 1. 9 and did not *r* the covenant of kinship.
Mic 6. 5 O my people, *r* now what King Balak of
Hab 3. 2 it known; in wrath may you *r* mercy.
Zech 10. 9 yet in far countries they shall *r* me,
Mal 4. 4 *R* the teaching of my servant Moses, the
Mt 5.23 if you *r* that your brother or sister has
Lk 16.25 Abraham said, "Child, *r* that during your
17.32 field must not turn back. *R* Lot's wife.
23.42 "Jesus, *r* me when you come into your
Jn 15.20 *R* the word that I said to you, 'Servants
Gal 2.10 only one thing, that we *r* the poor,
Eph 2.11 So then, *r* that at one time you Gentiles
2 Tim 2. 8 *R* Jesus Christ, raised from the dead, a
Heb 8.12 and I will *r* their sins no more."
13. 3 *R* those who are in prison, as though
Jude 17 beloved, must *r* the predictions of the
Rev 3. 3 *R* then what you received and heard;

REMEMBERS (REMEMBERED REMEMBERING)

Gen 8. 1 God *r* Noah and all the wild animals
19.29 God *r* Abraham, and sent Lot out of the
30.22 Then God *r* Rachel, and God heeded
42. 9 Joseph also *r* the dreams that he had
Ex 2.24 God *r* his covenant with Abraham,
6. 5 as slaves, and I have *r* my covenant.
20.24 place where I cause my name to be *r*
Num 10. 9 so that you may be *r* before the LORD
Esth 9.28 These days should be *r* and kept
Ps 78.35 They *r* that God was their rock, the
98. 3 He has *r* his steadfast love and
112. 6 never be moved; they will be *r* forever.
136. 23 It is he who *r* us in our low estate, for
Eccl 1.11 The people of long ago are not *r*, nor
Isa 65.17 former things shall not be *r* or come to
Lam 1. 7 Jerusalem *r*, in the day of her affliction
Ezek 23.19 increased her whorings, *r* the days of
Jon 2. 7 I *r* the LORD; and my prayer came to
Mt 26.75 Peter *r* what Jesus had said: "Before the
Lk 24. 8 Then they *r* his words, and returning
Rev 18. 5 as heaven, and God has *r* her iniquities.

REMEMBRANCE

Ex 28.12 Aaron shall bear their names . . . for *r*.
39. 7 the ephod, to be stones of *r* for the sons
1 Kings 17.18 have come to me to bring my sin to *r*,
Ps 6. 5 For in death there is no *r* of you; in
Mal 3.16 a book of *r* was written before him of
Mt 26.13 she has done will be told in *r* of her."
Lk 22.19 is given for you. Do this in *r* of me."
1 Cor 11.24 body that is for you. Do this in *r* of me."

REMIND

Isa 62. 6 You who *r* the LORD, take no rest, and

REMINDER

Ex 13. 9 your hand and as a *r* on your forehead,
17.14 "Write this as a *r* in a book and recite it
30.16 it will be a *r* to the Israelites of the
Num 10.10 they shall serve as a *r* on your behalf

REMISSION

Deut 15. 1 year you shall grant a *r* of debts.
31.10 seventh year, in the scheduled year of *r*,

REMNANT

2 Kings 19.30 The surviving *r* of the house of Judah
21.14 I will cast off the *r* of my heritage, and
2 Chr 30. 6 he may turn again to the *r* of you who
Ezra 9. 8 our God, who has left us a *r*, and given
Isa 10.20 On that day the *r* of Israel and the
37. 4 lift up your prayer for the *r* that is left."
37.31 surviving *r* of the house of Judah shall
46. 3 of Jacob, all the *r* of the house of Israel,
Jer 23. 3 I myself will gather the *r* of my flock
31. 7 O LORD, your people, the *r* of Israel."
40.11 king of Babylon had left a *r* in Judah
Am 5.15 will be gracious to the *r* of Joseph.
9.12 that they may possess the *r* of Edom
Mic 4. 7 The lame I will make the *r*, and those
5. 8 among the nations the *r* of Jacob,
7.18 of the *r* of your possession?
Zeph 3.13 the *r* of Israel; they shall do no wrong
Zech 8. 6 though it seems impossible to the *r*
8.12 cause the *r* of this people to possess
Rom 9.27 the sea, only a *r* of them will be saved;
11. 5 time there is a *r*, chosen by grace.

REMOVE (REMOVED REMOVES)

2 Kings 23.27 LORD said, "I will *r* Judah also out of my
Ps 103. 12 the west, so far he *r* our transgressions
Prov 22.28 Do not *r* the ancient landmark that your
Isa 54.10 may depart and the hills be *r*, but
Zech 3. 9 I will *r* the guilt of this land in a single

RENDER (RENDERED)

Ps 28. 4 of their hands; *r* them their due reward.
Isa 59.18 to the coastlands he will *r* requital.
Rev 18. 6 *R* to her as she herself has *r*, and repay

RENEW (RENEWED)

1 Sam 11.14 go to Gilgal, and there *r* the kingship."
Ps 103. 5 so that your youth is *r* like the eagle's.
Isa 40.31 wait for the LORD shall *r* their strength,
Lam 5.21 may be restored; *r* our days as of old—
Zeph 3.17 with gladness, he will *r* you in his love;
Col 3.10 which is being *r* in knowledge according

RENEWAL

Mt 19.28 at the *r* of all things, when the Son of

RENOUNCE

Ps 10. 3 greedy for gain curse and *r* the LORD.

RENOWN (RENOWNED)

Gen 6. 4 heroes that were of old, warriors of *r*.

Ps 135. 13 forever, your *r*, O LORD, throughout all
Isa 62. 7 and makes it *r* throughout the earth.

REPAIR (REPAIRED REPAIRING REPAIRS)

1 Kings 18.30 First he *r* the altar of the LORD that had
2 Kings 12. 5 let them *r* the house wherever any need
12.14 given to the workers who were *r* the
22. 5 at the house of the LORD, *r* the house,
Neh 3. 4 made *r*. Next to them Meshullam
Prov 6.15 in a moment, damage beyond *r*.

REPAY

Ezek 23.49 They shall *r* you for your lewdness, and
Job 34.11 according to their deeds he will *r* them,
Ps 35.12 They *r* me evil for good; my soul is
62.12 LORD. For you *r* to all according to their
103. 10 to our sins, nor *r* us according to our
Jer 16.18 And I will doubly *r* their iniquity and
25.14 I will *r* them according to their deeds
50.29 *R* her according to her deeds; just as
Hos 4. 9 their ways, and *r* them for their deeds.
Joel 2.25 I will *r* you for the years that the
Rom 2. 6 he will *r* according to each one's deeds:

REPENT (REPENTED REPENTS)

1 Kings 8.47 have been taken captive, and *r*, and
2 Chr 6.38 if they *r* with all their heart and soul in
Job 42. 6 therefore I despise myself, and *r* in dust
Isa 1.27 those in her who *r*, by righteousness.
Jer 8. 6 no one *r* of wickedness, saying, "What
Ezek 14. 6 Thus says the Lord GOD: *R* and turn
18.30 *R* and turn away from all your
Mt 3. 2 "*R*, for the kingdom of heaven has come
4.17 proclaim, "*R*, for the kingdom of heaven
11.20 had been done, because they did not *r*.
12.41 they *r* at the preaching of Jonah, and
27. 3 he *r* and brought back the thirty pieces
Mk 6.12 out and proclaimed that all should *r*.
Lk 10.13 and Sidon, they would have *r* long ago,
11.32 they *r* at the preaching of Jonah,
13. 3 but unless you *r* you will all perish as
16.30 to them from the dead, they will *r*.'
Acts 2.38 Peter said to them, "*R*, and be baptized
3.19 *R* therefore, and turn to God so that
17.30 commands all people everywhere to *r*,
2 Tim 2.25 grant that they will *r* and come to know
Heb 12.17 for he found no chance to *r*, even
Rev 2. 5 *r*, and do the works you did at first. If
2.16 *R* then. If not, I will come to you soon
2.21 I gave her time to *r*, but she refuses to *r*
9.20 The rest of humankind . . . did not *r* of
16. 9 and they did not *r* and give him glory.

REPENTANCE

Mt 3. 8 Bear fruit worthy of *r*.
Mk 1. 4 proclaiming a baptism of *r* for the
Lk 3. 3 proclaiming a baptism of *r* for the
3. 8 Bear fruits worthy of *r*. Do not begin to
5.32 call not the righteous but sinners to *r*."
15. 7 righteous persons who need no *r*.
24.47 that *r* and forgiveness of sins is to be
Acts 5.31 he might give *r* to Israel and forgiveness
11.18 given even to the Gentiles the *r* that
20.21 to both Jews and Greeks about *r*
26.20 to God and do deeds consistent with *r*.
Rom 2. 4 kindness is meant to lead you to *r*?

REPORT (REPORTS)

Dan 11.44 *r* from the east and the north shall
Mt 14. 1 At that time Herod the ruler heard *r*
Acts 25. 2 of the Jews gave him a *r* against Paul.

REPROACH (REPROACHES)

Gen 30.23 and said, "God has taken away my *r*";
Ruth 2.15 the standing sheaves, and do not *r* her.
Prov 27.11 so that I may answer whoever *r* me.
Jer 20. 8 become for me a *r* and derision all day
1 Tim 3. 2 a bishop must be above *r*, married only

REPROOF

Prov 1.23 Give heed to my *r*; I will pour out my
5.12 discipline, and my heart despised *r*!
13.18 but one who heeds *r* is honored.
29.15 The rod and *r* give wisdom, but a

REPROVE (REPROVED)

Prov 19.25 *r* the intelligent, and they will gain
29. 1 who is often *r*, yet remains stubborn,
1 Cor 14.24 outsider who enters is *r* by all and

REPUTE

1 Sam 18.23 that I am a poor man and of no *r*?"

REQUEST

Esth 5. 3 is it Queen Esther? What is your *r*?
7. 3 the lives of my people—that is my *r*.
Job 6. 8 "O that I might have my *r*, and that God
Ps 21. 2 and have not withheld the *r* of his lips.
Dan 2.49 Daniel made *r* of the king, and he

REQUIRE (REQUIRED)

Deut 10.12 God *r* of you? Only to fear the LORD
Ezra 7.20 whatever else is *r* for the house of your
Ezek 3.18 but their blood I will *r* at your hand.
33. 6 but their blood I will *r* at the sentinel's
Mic 6. 8 what does the LORD *r* of you but to do

RESCUE (RESCUED RESCUES RESCUING)

Num 35.25 the congregation shall *r* the slayer from
1 Sam 30.18 had taken; and David *r* his two wives.
1 Chr 16.35 gather and *r* us from among the
Ps 35.17 you look on? *R* me from their ravages,
37.40 The LORD helps them and *r* them; he *r*
69.14 help *r* me from sinking in the mire;
71. 2 your righteousness deliver me and *r* me;
71.23 to you; my soul also, which you have *r*.
136. 24 and *r* us from our foes, for his steadfast
Prov 24.11 if you hold back from *r* those taken
Isa 1.17 seek justice, *r* the oppressed, defend the
Jer 30. 7 for Jacob; yet he shall be *r* from it.
Ezek 34.10 I will *r* my sheep from their mouths, so
Dan 8. 4 it, and no one could *r* from its power;
Acts 7.25 that God through him was *r* them,
12.11 the Lord has sent his angel and *r* me
Rom 7.24 Who will *r* me from this body of death?
2 Cor 1.10 He who *r* us from so deadly a peril will
Col 1.13 He has *r* us from the power of darkness
2 Tim 4.18 The Lord will *r* me from every evil
2 Pet 2. 7 and if he *r* Lot, a righteous man greatly

RESERVED

2 Pet 3. 7 heavens and earth have been *r* for fire,

RESIDE (RESIDES RESIDING)

Lev 19.33 When an alien *r* with you in your land,
Num 9.14 Any alien *r* among you who wishes to
2 Chr 6.18 "But will God indeed *r* with mortals on
Job 11.14 and do not let wickedness *r* in your

RESIST (RESISTED)

Job 9. 4 —who has *r* him, and succeeded?—
Jas 4. 7 *R* the devil, and he will flee from you.
1 Pet 5. 9 *R* him, steadfast in your faith, for you

RESOLVED

Dan 1. 8 Daniel *r* that he would not defile

RESOURCES

Ezra 2.69 According to their *r* they gave to the

RESPECT

Dan 11.37 He shall pay no *r* to the gods of his
Mt 21.37 to them, saying, 'They will *r* my son.'
Mk 12. 6 to them, saying, 'They will *r* my son.'
Lk 20.13 beloved son; perhaps they will *r* him.'
Eph 5.33 and a wife should *r* her husband.

RESPONSIBLE

Acts 20.26 this day that I am not *r* for the blood of

REST (n)

Lev 16.31 a sabbath of complete *r* to you, and you
25. 4 there shall be a sabbath of complete *r*
Deut 3.20 When the LORD gives *r* to your kindred,
12.10 when he gives you *r* from your enemies
25.19 God has given you *r* from all your
Josh 1.15 until the LORD gives *r* to your kindred as
11.23 And the land had *r* from war.
23. 1 LORD had given *r* to Israel from all their
Judg 3.11 the land had *r* forty years. Then Othniel
5.31 in its might." And land had *r* forty years.
2 Sam 7. 1 LORD had given him *r* from all his
2 Kings 25.11 Babylon— all the *r* of the population.
1 Chr 28. 2 I had planned to build a house of *r* for
Neh 9.28 after they had *r*, they again did evil
Job 3.17 troubling, and there the weary are at *r*.
11.18 be protected and take your *r* in safety.
Ps 95.11 I swore, "They shall not enter my *r*."
116. 7 Return, O my soul, to your *r*, for the
Isa 30.15 In returning and *r* you shall be saved;
Mic 5. 3 then the *r* of his kindred shall return to
Mt 11.28 heavy burdens, and I will give you *r*.
Mk 14.41 you still sleeping and taking your *r*?
2 Cor 7. 5 Macedonia, our bodies had no *r*, but we
Heb 3.11 I swore, 'They will not enter my *r*.' "
4. 9 a sabbath *r* still remains for the people
Rev 11.13 the *r* were terrified and gave glory to

REST (RESTED RESTS)

Gen 2. 2 he *r* on the seventh day from all the
18. 4 feet, and *r* yourselves under the tree,
Ex 23.12 work, but on seventh day you shall *r*;
Lev 26.34 the land shall *r*, and enjoy its sabbath
Deut 33.12 the beloved *r* between his shoulders.
Ruth 3.18 the man will not *r*, but will settle the
2 Kings 2.15 "The spirit of Elijah *r* on Elisha."
Eccl 2.23 even at night their minds do not *r*.
Isa 11. 2 spirit of the LORD shall *r* on him, the
Dan 12.13 you, go your way, and *r*; you shall rise
Heb 4. 4 "And God *r* on the seventh day from all
Rev 14.13 "they will *r* from their labors, for their

RESTING PLACE

Isa 66. 1 build for me, and what is my *r*?
Lk 11.24 waterless regions looking for a *r*,

RESTORE (RESTORED RESTORES)

2 Kings 8. 1 the woman whose son he had *r* to life,
2 Chr 24. 4 afterward Joash decided to *r* the house
33.16 He also *r* the altar of the LORD and
Ps 23. 3 he *r* my soul. He leads me in right
80.19 *R* us, O LORD God of hosts; let your face
85. 4 *R* us again, O God of our salvation, and
Isa 1.26 I will *r* your judges as at the first, and
Jer 8.22 health of my poor people not been *r*?
33.26 For I will *r* their fortunes, and will have
Lam 5.21 *R* us to yourself, O LORD, that we may
Dan 8.14 then the sanctuary shall be *r* to its
9.25 went out to *r* and rebuild Jerusalem
Mt 12.13 He stretched it out, and it was *r*, as
17.11 is indeed coming and will *r* all things;
Lk 6.10 hand." He did so, and his hand was *r*.
Acts 1. 6 the time when you will *r* the kingdom
Gal 6. 1 the Spirit should *r* such a one in a spirit
Heb 6. 4 it is impossible to *r* again to repentance

RESTRAIN (RESTRAINED RESTRAINING)

Ex 36. 6 So people were *r* from bringing;
1 Sam 3.13 God, and he did not *r* them.
Job 7.11 I will not *r* my mouth; I will speak in
Isa 64.12 all this, will you *r* yourself, O LORD?
2 Thess 2. 6 you know what is now *r* him, so that he

RESTRAINT

Prov 29.18 is no prophecy, the people cast off *r*,
14.16 from evil, but the fool throws off *r* and
1 Cor 7.35 own benefit, not to put any *r* upon you,

RESURRECTION

Mt 22.23 came to him, saying there is no *r*;
Mk 12.18 Sadducees, who say that there is no *r*,
Lk 14.14 will be repaid at the *r* of the righteous."
20.27 those who say that there is no *r*,
Jn 5.29 who have done good, to the *r* of life,
11.25 said to her, "I am the *r* and the life.
Acts 1.22 must become a witness with us to his *r*."
2.31 David spoke of the *r* of the Messiah,
17.18 the good news about Jesus and the *r*.)
23. 6 the hope of the *r* of the dead."
24.15 that there will be a *r* of both the
Rom 6. 5 be united with him in a *r* like his.
1 Cor 15.12 of you say there is no *r* of the dead?
2 Tim 2.18 truth by claiming that the *r* has already
Heb 11.35 Women received their dead by *r*. Others
1 Pet 1. 3 a living hope through the *r* of Jesus
Rev 20. 5 years were ended.) This is the first *r*.

RETAIN

Num 36. 7 Israelites shall *r* the inheritance of their

RETRIBUTION

Jer 15.15 visit me, and bring down *r* for me on

RETURN (RETURNED RETURNING RETURNS)

Gen 16. 9 said to her, "*R* to your mistress, and
20. 7 Now then, *r* the man's wife; for he is a
31. 3 Jacob, "*R* to the land of your ancestors
32. 9 '*R* to your country and to your kindred,
44. 4 "Why have you *r* evil for good? Why
50.14 Joseph *r* to Egypt with his brothers and
Num 10.36 "*R*, O LORD of the ten thousand
Deut 4.30 you will *r* to the LORD your God and
22. 2 the owner claims it; then you shall *r* it.
30. 2 and *r* to the LORD your God, and you
Josh 22. 9 half-tribe of Manasseh *r* home, parting
1 Sam 7. 3 "If you are *r* to the LORD with all your
Job 10.21 before I go, never to *r*, to the land of
22.23 If you *r* to the Almighty, you will be
Ps 51.13 your ways, and sinners will *r* to you.
116. 7 *R*, O my soul, to your rest; for the LORD
116. 12 What shall I *r* to the LORD for all his
Eccl 12. 7 and the breath *r* to God who gave it.
Song 6.13 *R*, *r*, O Shulammite! *R*, *r*, that we may
Isa 35.10 ransomed of the LORD shall *r*, and come
44.22 like mist; *r* to me, for I have redeemed
51.11 ransomed of the LORD shall *r*, and come
55.11 it shall not *r* to me empty, but it shall
Jer 3. 1 many lovers; and would you *r* to me?
3.12 *R*, faithless Israel, says the LORD. I will
4. 1 If you *r*, O Israel, says the LORD, if you *r*
24. 7 shall *r* to me with their whole heart.
30.10 Jacob shall *r* and have quiet and ease,
Hos 2. 7 "I will go and *r* to my first husband, for
6. 1 "Come, let us *r* to the LORD; for it is he
14. 1 *R*, O Israel, to the LORD your God, for
Am 4. 8 not satisfied; yet you did not *r* to me,
Zech 1. 3 *R* to me, says the LORD of hosts, and I
Mal 3. 7 *R* to me, and I will *r* to you, says the
Lk 8.39 "*R* to your home, and declare how much
11.24 it says, 'I will *r* to my house from which
17.18 Was none of them found to *r* and give
Acts 15.16 'After this I will *r*, and I will rebuild the

REUBEN

Born, Gen 29.32; found mandrakes for Leah, Gen 30.14; rescued Joseph, Gen 37.21-22; blessed by Jacob, Gen 49.3-4.

Tribe of Reuben: blessed by Moses, Deut 33.6.

REVEAL (REVEALED REVEALING REVEALS)

Deut 29.29 but the *r* things belong to us and to our
1 Sam 3. 7 of the LORD had not yet been *r* to him.
3.21 LORD *r* himself to Samuel at Shiloh by

1 Sam 9.15 Saul came, the LORD had *r* to Samuel:
Ps 98. 2 he has *r* his vindication in the sight of
Prov 20.19 A gossip *r* secrets; therefore do not
Isa 22.14 LORD of hosts has *r* himself in my ears:
53. 1 whom has the arm of the LORD been *r*?
56. 1 will come, and my deliverance be *r*.
Dan 2.19 the mystery was *r* to Daniel in a vision
2.28 God in heaven who *r* mysteries, and he
Am 3. 7 God does nothing, without *r* his secret
Mt 11.25 intelligent and have *r* them to infants;
11.27 to whom the Son chooses to *r* him.
16.17 flesh and blood has not *r* this to you,
Lk 2.26 It had been *r* to him by the Holy Spirit
2.35 the inner thoughts of many will be *r*."
10.21 intelligent and have *r* them to infants;
10.22 to whom the Son chooses to *r* him."
17.30 on the day that the Son of man is *r*.
Jn 1.31 this reason, that he might be *r* to Israel."
12.38 whom has the arm of the Lord been *r*?"
Rom 1.17 righteousness of God is *r* through faith
8.19 longing for the *r* of the children of God;
1 Cor 1. 7 gift as you wait for the *r* of our Lord
2.10 God has *r* to us through the Spirit;
3.13 because it will be *r* with fire, and the
Gal 1.16 grace, was pleased to *r* his Son to me,
Col 3. 4 is *r*, then you also will be *r* with him
2 Thess 1. 7 when the Lord Jesus is *r* from heaven
1 Pet 1.12 It was *r* to them that they were serving
1.13 Jesus Christ will bring you when he is *r*.
4.13 and shout for joy when his glory is *r*.
1 Jn 1. 2 this life was *r*, and we have seen it and
3. 2 what we shall be has not yet been *r*.
4. 9 God's love was *r* among us in this way:

REVEL

Ex 32. 6 down to eat and drink, and rose up to *r*.

REVELATION

Rom 16.25 you according to the *r* of the mystery
Gal 1.12 I received it through a *r* of Jesus Christ.
2. 2 I went up in response to a *r*. Then I laid
Eph 3. 3 was made known to me by *r*, as I wrote

REVENGE

Judg 15. 7 not stop until I have taken *r* on you."
16.28 with this one act of *r* I may pay back
Esth 8.13 were to be ready on that day to take *r*
Prov 6.34 he shows no restraint when he takes *r*.
Jer 20.10 against him, and take our *r* on him."

REVENUE

Ezra 4.13 or toll, and the royal *r* will be reduced.
Isa 23. 3 waters; your *r* was the grain of Shihor,
Rom 13. 7 taxes are due, *r* to whom *r* is due,

REVERE (REVERED)

Josh 24.14 "Now therefore *r* the LORD, and serve
1 Chr 16.25 to be praised; he is *r* above all gods.
Mal 3.16 those who *r* the LORD spoke with one

REVERENCE

Lev 19.30 keep my sabbaths and *r* my sanctuary: I
26. 2 keep my sabbaths and *r* my sanctuary: I
1 Pet 3. 2 they see the purity and *r* of your lives.
3.15 in you; yet do it with gentleness and *r*.

REVERENT

Titus 2. 3 the older women to be *r* in behavior,

REVILE (REVILED)

Ex 22.28 "You shall not *r* God, or curse a leader
2 Kings 19.22 Whom have you mocked and *r*? Against
Ps 74.10 to scoff? Is the enemy to *r* your name
Isa 65. 7 the mountains and *r* me upon the hills,
Mt 5.11 "Blessed are you when people *r* you and
1 Cor 4.12 When *r*, we bless; when persecuted, we
1 Pet 4.14 If you are *r* for the name of Christ, you

REVIVE (REVIVED REVIVING)

Gen 45.27 him, the spirit of their father Jacob *r*.
Judg 15.19 he drank, his spirit returned, and he *r*.
1 Kings 17.22 child came into him again, and he *r*.
Neh 4. 2 Will they *r* the stones out of the heaps
Ps 19. 7 law of the LORD is perfect, *r* the soul;
85. 6 Will you not *r* us again, so that your
119. 25 the dust; *r* me according to your word.
Isa 57.15 in spirit, to *r* the spirit of the humble,
Lam 1.11 treasures for food to *r* their strength.
Hos 6. 2 After two days he will *r* us; on the third
Hab 3. 2 In our own time *r* it; in our own time
Phil 4.10 at last you have *r* your concern for me;

REWARD

Gen 15. 1 your shield; your *r* shall be very great."
1 Sam 24.19 So may the LORD *r* you with good for
Ps 19.11 in keeping them there is great *r*.
58.11 "Surely there is a *r* for the righteous;
109. 5 So they *r* me evil for good, and hatred
Isa 40.10 his *r* is with him, and his recompense
Mt 5.12 be glad, for your *r* is great in heaven,
5.46 who love you, what *r* do you have?
6. 6 Father who sees in secret will *r* you.
10.41 of a prophet will receive a prophet's *r*;
Mk 9.41 of Christ will by no means lose the *r*.
Lk 6.35 nothing in return." Your *r* will be great,
1 Cor 9.18 What then is my *r*? Just this: that in my

RIBS

Gen 2.21 then he took one of his *r* and closed up

RICH (RICHER)

Gen 13. 2 Now Abram was very *r* in livestock, in
14.23 might not say, 'I have made Abram *r*.'
Ex 30.15 The *r* shall not give more, and the poor
2 Sam 12. 2 The *r* man had very many flocks and
Job 15.29 they will not be *r*, and their wealth will
Prov 10.22 The blessing of the LORD makes *r*, and
11.24 Some give freely, yet grow all the *r*;
14.20 neighbors, but the *r* have many friends.
22. 2 The *r* and the poor have this in
23. 4 Do not wear yourself out to get *r*; be
Mt 19.23 be hard for a *r* person to enter the
27.57 there came a *r* man from Arimathea,
Mk 10.25 who is *r* to enter the kingdom of God.
Lk 1.53 good things, and sent the *r* away empty.
6.24 "But woe to you who are *r*, for you have
12.16 land of a *r* man produced abundantly.
16. 1 "There was a *r* man who had a manager,
16.19 "There was a *r* man, who was dressed in
18.23 this, he became sad, for he was very *r*.
1 Cor 4. 8 you want! Already you have become *r*!
1 Tim 6. 9 who want to be *r* fall into temptation
6.17 who are in the present age *r*, command
Jas 1.10 the *r* will disappear like a flower in the
5. 1 you *r* people, weep and wail for the
Rev 2. 9 your poverty, even though you are *r*.
3.17 For you say, 'I am *r*, I have prospered,
18. 3 merchants of the earth have grown *r*

RICHES

1 Kings 10.23 excelled all the kings of the earth in *r*
Job 20.15 They swallow down *r* and vomit them
Ps 119. 14 way of your decrees as much as in all *r*.
Prov 11. 4 *R* do not profit in the day of wrath, but
11.16 destitute, but the aggressive gain *r*.
11.28 Those who trust in their *r* will wither,
27.24 for *r* do not last forever; nor a crown for
Jer 48.36 for the *r* they gained have perished.
Rom 2. 4 the *r* of his kindness and forbearance
11.12 if their stumbling means *r* for the world,
11.33 O the depth of the *r* and wisdom and
Eph 3. 8 the news of the boundless *r* of Christ,
3.16 according to the *r* of his glory, he may
Phil 4.19 need of yours according to his *r* in glory

RIDDLE

Judg 14.12 "Let me now put a *r* to you. If you can
14.19 to those who had explained the *r*.

RIDICULE (RIDICULED)

Lk 14.29 to finish, all who see it begin to *r* him,
16.14 money, heard all this, and they *r* him.

RIGHT

Gen 13. 9 then I will go to the *r*; or if you take the
38.26 "She is more in the *r* than I, since I did
Deut 6.25 has commanded us, we will be in the *r*."
Judg 17. 6 people did what was *r* in their own eyes.
21.25 people did what was *r* in their own eyes.
2 Chr 24. 2 Joash did what was *r* in the sight of the
Job 33.12 in this you are not *r*. I will answer you:
35. 2 be just? You say, 'I am *r* before God.'
36. 6 alive, but gives the afflicted their *r*.
42. 7 not spoken of me what is *r*, as my
Ps 17. 2 come; let your eyes see the *r*.
58. 1 you indeed decree what is *r*, you gods?
Isa 43.26 your case, so that you may be proved *r*.
Lam 1.18 The LORD is in the *r*, for I have rebelled
Hab 2. 4 Look at the proud! Their spirit is not *r*
Mt 20.21 one at your *r* hand and one at your left,
Mk 16.19n and sat down at the *r* hand of God.
Acts 2.33 exalted at the *r* hand of God, and
7.55 of God and Jesus standing at the *r* hand
10.35 him and does what is *r* is acceptable
2 Cor 5.13 for God; if we are in our *r* mind, it is for
8.21 we intend to do what is *r* not only in
Eph 1.20 the dead and seated him at his *r* hand
Jas 4.17 who knows the *r* thing to do and fails to
1 Jn 2.29 everyone who does *r* is born of him.

RIGHTS

Prov 29. 7 The righteous know the *r* of the poor;
31. 9 righteously, defend the *r* of the poor
Jer 5.28 they do not defend the *r* of the needy.
1 Cor 9.18 to make full use of my *r* in the gospel.

RIGHTEOUS

Gen 6. 9 Noah was a *r* man, blameless in his
18.24 Suppose there are fifty *r* within the city;
1 Sam 24.17 "You are more *r* than I; for you have
1 Kings 8.32 vindicating the *r* by rewarding them
Job 4.17 'Can mortals be *r* before God? Can
17. 9 Yet the *r* hold to their way, and they
25. 4 then can a mortal be *r* before God?
32. 1 Job, because he was *r* in his own eyes.
Ps 1. 6 the LORD watches over the way of the *r*,
7.11 God is a *r* judge, and a God who has
11. 3 are destroyed, what can the *r* do?"
14. 5 for God is with the comapny of the *r*.
37.29 The *r* shall inherit the land, and live in
64.10 Let the *r* rejoice in the LORD, and take
68. 3 But let the *r* be joyful; let them exult
71.15 My mouth will tell of your *r* acts, of
92.12 The *r* flourish like the palm tree, and
97.11 Light dawns for the *r*, and joy for the
119.137 You are *r*, O LORD, and your judgments
141. 5 Let the *r* strike me; let the faithful
143. 2 for no one living is *r* before you.
Prov 4.18 But the path of the *r* is like the light of
10. 7 The memory of the *r* is a blessing, but
10.16 The wage of the *r* leads to life, the gain
10.28 The hope of the *r* ends in gladness, but
12.13 their lips, but the *r* escape from trouble.
12.26 The *r* gives good advice to friends, but
15. 6 In the house of the *r* there is much
18.10 tower; the *r* run into it and are safe.
20. 7 The *r* walk in integrity— happy are the
21.15 justice is done, it is a joy to the *r*,
25.26 the *r* who give way before the wicked.
28. 1 pursues, but the *r* are as bold as a lion.
28.28 but when they perish, the *r* increase.
Eccl 3.17 God will judge the *r* and the wicked, for
Eccl 7.20 there is no one on the earth so *r* as to
8.14 that there are *r* people who are treated
9. 2 the same fate comes to all, to the *r* and
Isa 26. 2 Open the gates, so that the *r* nation
53.11 *r* one, my servant, shall make many *r*,
57. 1 The *r* perish, and no one takes it to
64. 6 all our *r* deeds are like a filthy cloth.
Jer 33.15 time I will cause a *r* Branch to spring
Ezek 3.21 you warn the *r* not to sin, they shall
18. 5 If a man is *r* and does what is lawful
18.24 But when the *r* turn away from their
18.26 When the *r* turn away from their
Hab 2. 4 in them, but the *r* live by their faith.
Mt 1.19 Her husband Joseph, being a *r* man and
5.45 and sends rain on the *r* and on the
Mk 6.20 knowing that he was a *r* and holy man,
Lk 1. 6 Both of them were *r* before God, living
2.25 Simeon; this man was *r* and devout,
18. 9 *r* and regarded others with contempt:
Rom 1.17 "The one who is *r* will live by faith."
3.10 "There is no one who is *r*, not even one;
3.26 that he himself is *r* and that he justifies
5. 7 rarely will anyone die for a *r* person
5.19 obedience the many will be made *r*.
Gal 3.11 for "The one who is *r* will live by faith."
Heb 10.38 delay; but my *r* one will live by faith.
Jas 5. 6 condemned and murdered the *r* one,
1 Pet 3.18 once for all, the *r* for the unrighteous,
4.18 If it is hard for the *r* to be saved, what
2 Pet 2. 7 if he rescued Lot, a *r* man greatly
2. 8 (for that *r* man, living among them day
Rev 19. 8 fine linen is the *r* deeds of the saints.

RIGHTEOUSNESS

Gen 15. 6 and the LORD reckoned it to him as *r*.
18.19 way of the LORD by doing *r* and justice;
Deut 9. 4 "It is because of my *r* that the LORD has
1 Sam 26.23 The LORD rewards everyone for his *r* and
Job 27. 6 I hold fast my *r*, and will not let it go;
29.14 I put on *r*, and it clothed me; my justice
36. 3 far away and ascribe *r* to my Maker.
37.23 and abundant *r* he will not violate.
Ps 33. 5 He loves *r* and justice; the earth is full
36. 6 Your *r* is like the mighty mountains,
45. 7 equity; you love *r* and hate wickedness.
50. 6 The heavens declare his *r*, for God
71.19 Your power and your *r*, O God, reach
89.14 *R* and justice are the foundation of your
89.16 name all day long, and extol your *r*.
96.13 He will judge the world with *r*, and the
106. 31 And that has been reckoned to him as *r*
112. 3 houses, and their *r* endures forever.
119.142 Your *r* is an everlasting *r*, and your law
Prov 2. 9 Then you will understand *r* and justice
10. 2 do not profit, but *r* delivers from death.
11.19 Whoever is steadfast in *r* will live, but
12.28 In the path of *r* is life, in walking its
14.34 *R* exalts a nation, but sin is a reproach
16.12 evil, for the throne is established by *r*.
21.21 Whoever pursues *r* and kindness will
Eccl 7.15 righteous people who perish in their *r*,
Isa 5. 7 but saw bloodshed; *r*, but heard a cry!
11. 4 hear; but with *r* he shall judge the poor,
32.16 and *r* abide in the fruitful field.
33. 5 high; he filled Zion with justice and *r*;
45.24 shall be said of me, are *r* and strength;
54.14 In *r* you shall be established; you shall
57.12 I will concede your *r* and your works,
58. 2 as if they were a nation that practiced *r*
59.17 put on *r* like a breastplate, and a
61. 3 spirit. They will be called oaks of *r*,
61.10 he has covered me with the robe of *r*,
Jer 22. 3 Act with justice and *r*, and deliver from
23. 6 he will be called: "The LORD is our *r*."
Ezek 14.14 save only their own lives by their *r*,
18.22 for the *r* that they have done they shall
33.12 *r* of the righteous shall not save them

Dan 4.27 atone for your sins with *r*, and your
9. 7 "*R* is on your side, O Lord, but open to
9.18 before you on the ground of our *r*, but
Hos 10.12 Sow for yourselves *r*; reap steadfast love;
Am 5.24 and *r* like an everflowing stream.
Mt 3.15 proper for us in this way to fulfill all *r*."
5.20 unless your *r* exceeds that of the scribes
21.32 John came to you in the way of *r* and
Lk 1.75 fear, in holiness and *r* before him
Jn 16. 8 wrong about sin and *r* and judgment:
Acts 17.31 he will have the world judged in *r* by a
Rom 1.17 in it the *r* of God is revealed through
3.21 law, the *r* of God has been disclosed,
4. 3 God, and it was reckoned to him as *r*."
4. 6 whom God reckons *r* apart from works:
5.18 one man's act of *r* leads to justification
6.19 present your members as slaves to *r* for
9.30 Gentiles who did not strive for *r*, have
10. 3 being ignorant of the *r* that comes from
1 Cor 1.30 for us wisdom from God, and *r* and
2 Cor 5.21 so that we might become the *r* of God.
Gal 3. 6 God, and it was reckoned to him as *r*."
3.21 *r* would indeed come through the law.
Eph 4.24 likeness of God in true *r* and holiness.
Phil 3. 9 Christ, the *r* from God based on faith.
1 Tim 6.11 all this; pursue *r*, godliness, faith, love,
2 Tim 3.16 for correction, and for training in *r*,
Heb 11. 7 an heir to the *r* that is in accordance
Jas 1.20 your anger does not produce God's *r*.
3.18 harvest of *r* is sown in peace for those

RING (RINGS)

Gen 35. 4 had, and the *r* that were in their ears;
Ex 32. 2 "Take off the gold *r* that are on the ears
Esth 3.10 the king took his signet *r* from his hand
Lk 15.22 put a *r* on his finger and sandals on his

RIOT

Mt 26. 5 the festival, or there may be a *r* among
Mk 14. 2 the festival, or there may be a *r* among

RISE (RISEN RISING)

Gen 13.17 *R* up, walk through the length and the
Ps 9.19 *R* up, O LORD! Let not mortals prevail;
17.13 *R* up, O LORD, confront them, overthrow
44.26 *R* up, come to our help. Redeem us for
68. 1 Let God *r* up, let his enemies be
113. 3 From the *r* of the sun to its setting the
Prov 24.16 though they fall seven times, they will *r*
Isa 30.18 therefore he will *r* up to show mercy
52. 2 the dust, *r* up, O captive Jerusalem;
58.10 your light *r* in the darkness and your
Mk 8.31 be killed, and after three days *r* again.
9. 9 the Son of Man had *r* from the dead.
9.31 days after being killed, he will *r* again."
Lk 2.34 for the falling and *r* of many in Israel,
7.14 he said, "Young man, I say to you, *r*."
24. 5 the dead? He is not here, but has *r*
24. 7 crucified, and on the third day *r* again."
24.34 "The Lord has *r* indeed, and he has
Jn 11.23 said to her, "Your brother will *r* again."
Acts 26.23 by being the first to *r* from the dead, he
Eph 5.14 "Sleeper, awake! *R* from the dead, and
1 Thess 4.16 and the dead in Christ will *r* first.

RITUAL

Lev 6. 9 This is the *r* of the burnt offering.
6.14 This is the *r* of the grain offering: The
6.25 This is the *r* of the sin offering. The sin
7. 1 This is the *r* of the guilt offering. It is
7.11 This is *r* of the sacrifice of the offering

RIVER (RIVERS)

Gen 2.10 A *r* flows out of Eden to water the
Ps 46. 4 There is a *r* whose streams make glad
107. 33 He turns *r* into a desert, springs of
137. 1 By the *r* of Babylon—there we sat
Isa 7.20 with a razor hired beyond the *R*—
33.21 for us a place of broad *r* and streams,
41.18 open *r* on the bare heights, and
48.18 prosperity would have been like a *r*,
66.12 I will extend prosperity to her like a *r*,
Lam 3.48 My eyes flow with *r* of tears because of
Rev 22. 1 showed me the *r* of the water of life,

ROAD (ROADS ROADSIDE)

Mt 2.12 left for their own country by another *r*.
Mk 10.46 a blind beggar, was sitting by the *r*.
Lk 14.23 'Go out into the *r* and lanes, and

ROAR (ROARS)

1 Chr 16.32 Let the sea *r*, and all that fills it; let the
Ps 96.11 and let the earth rejoice; let the sea *r*,
Hos 11.10 go after the LORD, who *r* like a lion;
Am 1. 2 The LORD *r* from Zion, and utters his
3. 4 Does a lion *r* in the forest, when it has

ROB (ROBBED ROBBING ROBS)

Prov 22.22 Do not *r* the poor because they are
28.24 Anyone who *r* father or mother and
Mal 3. 8 Will anyone *r* God? Yet you are *r* me!
2 Cor 11. 8 I *r* other churches by accepting support

ROBBERS

Jer 7.11 called by my name, become a den of *r*
Mk 11.17 But you have made it a den of *r*."
Lk 10.30 fell into the hands of *r*, who stripped
Acts 19.37 men here who are neither temple *r* nor

ROBE (ROBES)

Gen 37. 3 he had made him a long *r* with sleeves.
37.23 they stripped him of his *r*, the long *r*
37.31 a goat, and dipped the *r* in the blood.
Ex 39.22 He also made the *r* of the ephod all of
1 Sam 15.27 Saul caught hold of the hem of his *r*,
Ps 45. 8 your *r* are all fragrant with myrrh and
45.13 in her chamber with gold-woven *r*;
Isa 22.21 will clothe him with your *r* and bind
61.10 covered me with the *r* of righteousness,
Mt 22.11 there who was not wearing a wedding *r*,
Lk 15.22 'Quickly, bring out a *r*—the best
Jn 13. 4 took off his outer *r*, and tied a towel
19. 5 the crown of thorns and the purple *r*.
Rev 6.11 They were each given a white *r* and told

ROCK

Ex 17. 6 Strike the *r*, and water will come out of
Num 20. 8 command the *r* before their eyes to
20.11 up his hand and struck the *r* twice
Deut 32. 4 The *R*, his work is perfect, and all his
32.31 their *r* is not as our *R*; our enemies are
1 Sam 2. 2 besides you; there is no *R* like our God.
2 Sam 22. 2 "The LORD is my *r*, my fortress, and my
Ps 18. 2 The LORD is my *r*, and my fortress, and
18.31 And who is a *r* besides our God?—
27. 5 of his tent; he will set me high on a *r*.
28. 1 LORD, I call; my *r*, do not refuse to hear
40. 2 and set my feet upon a *r*, making my
61. 2 Lead me to the *r* that is higher than I;
62. 6 He alone is my *r* and my salvation, my
71. 3 Be to me a *r* of refuge, a strong fortress,
78.16 He made streams come out of the *r*,
89.26 my God, and the *R* of my salvation!'
92.15 that the LORD is upright; he is my *r*,
105. 41 He opened the *r*, and water gushed out;
114. 8 who turns the *r* into a pool of water,
Isa 17.10 not remembered the *R* of your refuge;
32. 2 the shade of a great *r* in a weary land.
51. 1 to the *r* from which you were hewn,
Jer 23.29 and like a hammer that breaks a *r* in
Mt 7.24 a wise man who built his house on *r*.
16.18 and on this *r* I will build my church,
Lk 6.48 deeply and laid the foundation on *r*;
1 Cor 10. 4 they drank from the spiritual *r* that

ROD

Ps 2. 9 You shall break them with a *r* of iron,
Prov 13.24 who spare the *r* hate their children,
22.15 boy, but the *r* of discipline drives it far
23.14 If you beat them with the *r*, you will
26. 3 donkey, and a *r* for the back of fools.
Isa 10. 5 Assyria, the *r* of my anger— the club in
1 Cor 4.21 Am I to come to you with a *r*, or with

ROLL

Mk 16. 3 "Who will *r* away the stone for us from
Heb 1.12 like a cloak you will *r* them up, and like

ROMAN (ROMANS)

Jn 11.48 and the *R* will come and destroy both
Acts 16.21 that are not lawful for us as *R* to adopt
22.25 for you to flog a *R* citizen who is
25.16 not the custom of the *R* to hand over

ROME

Acts 2.10 Cyrene, and visitors from *R*, both Jews
18. 2 had ordered all Jews to leave *R*.
23.11 so you must bear witness also at *R*."
28.16 When we came into *R*, Paul was
Rom 1. 7 To all God's beloved in *R*, who are
1.15 the gospel to you also who are in *R*.
2 Tim 1.17 he arrived in *R*, he eagerly searched

ROOF

Gen 6.16 Make a *r* for the ark, and finish it to a
Mk 2. 4 they removed the *r* above him; and after
Acts 10. 9 Peter went up on the *r* to pray. He

ROOM

Ps 4. 1 You gave me *r* when I was in distress.
Mt 6. 6 whenever you pray, go into your *r* and
Lk 14.22 has been done, and still there is *r*.'
22.12 He will show you a large *r* upstairs,
Acts 1.13 they went up to the *r* upstairs where
Philem 22 —prepare a guest *r* for me, for I am

ROOT (ROOTED)

1 Kings 14.15 he will *r* up Israel out of this good land
Prov 2.22 land, and the treacherous will be *r* out
12. 3 but the *r* of the righteous will never be
Isa 11.10 On that day the *r* of Jesse shall stand
37.31 Judah shall again take *r* downward, and
40.24 scarcely has their stem taken *r* in the
Mt 3.10 ax is lying at the *r* of the trees; every
Rom 15.12 Isaiah says, "The *r* of Jesse shall come,
Eph 3.17 as you are being *r* and grounded in love.
Col 2. 7 *r* and built up in him and established in
1 Tim 6.10 For the love of money is the *r* of all
Rev 22.16 I am the *r* and the descendant of David,

ROPE (ROPES)

Josh 2.15 she let them down by a *r* through a
Jer 38.13 they drew Jeremiah up by the *r* and

ROSE

Song 2. 1 I am a *r* of Sharon, a lily of the valleys.

ROUSE

Joel 3.12 Let the nations *r* themselves, and come

ROYAL

Esth 4.14 perhaps you have come to *r* dignity for

RUDE

1 Cor 13. 5 not envious or boastful or arrogant or *r*.

RUIN (RUINS)

Deut 13.16 It shall remain a perpetual *r*, never to
Ps 35. 8 Let *r* come upon them unawares. And
89.40 walls; you have laid his strongholds in *r*.
Prov 19. 3 One's own folly leads to *r*, yet the heart
Isa 25. 2 the city a heap, the fortified city a *r*;
Jer 25.11 This whole land shall become a *r* and a
46.19 Memphis shall become a waste, a *r*,
Ezek 21.27 A *r*, a *r*, a *r*—I will make it! (Such has
Am 6. 6 but are not grieved over the *r* of Joseph!

RULE (n)

1 Cor 7.17 you. This is my *r* in all the churches.
Gal 6.16 As for those who will follow this *r*—
Eph 1.21 far above all *r* and authority and power

RULE (RULED RULES) (v)

Gen 1.16 day and the lesser light to *r* the night
3.16 your husband, and he shall *r* over you."
Deut 15. 6 you will *r* over many nations, but they
Judg 8.23 not *r* over you; the LORD will *r* over you."
2 Chr 1.10 people, for who can *r* this great people
9.26 He *r* over all the kings from the
Ps 22.28 to the LORD, and he *r* over the nations.
89. 9 You *r* the raging of the sea; when its
106. 41 that those who hated them *r* over them.
110. 2 scepter. *R* in the midst of your foes.
Prov 19.10 in luxury, much less for a slave to *r*
Isa 3. 4 princes, and babes shall *r* over them.
26.13 lords besides you have *r* over us, but we
40.10 with might, and his arm *r* for him;
Ezek 34. 4 force and harshness you have *r* them.
Dan 11. 3 arise, who shall *r* with great dominion
Mic 5. 2 forth for me one who is to *r* in Israel,
Lk 19.14 saying, 'We do not want this man to *r*
Rev 2.27 to *r* them with an iron rod, as when
12. 5 male child, who is to *r* all the nations
19.15 he will *r* them with a rod of iron; he

RULER (RULERS)

Gen 45. 8 house and *r* over all the land of Egypt.
45.26 Joseph is still alive! He is even *r* over
Lev 4.22 When a *r* sins, doing unintentionally
Ps 2.10 be wise; be warned, O *r* of the earth.
Prov 6. 7 Without having any chief or officer or *r*,
23. 1 When you sit down to eat with a *r*,
29.12 If a *r* listens to falsehood, all his
Isa 33.22 the LORD is our judge, the LORD is our *r*,
40.23 makes the *r* of the earth as nothing.
Jer 2. 8 know me; the *r* transgressed against me;
Jn 12.31 the *r* of this world will be driven out.
16.11 *r* of this world has been condemned.
Acts 4. 8 Spirit said to them, "*R* of the people
7.10 appointed him *r* over Egypt and over all
Rom 13. 3 For *r* are not a terror to good conduct,
1 Cor 2. 8 None of the *r* of this age understood
15.24 after he has destroyed every *r* and every
Rev 1. 5 dead, and the *r* of kings of the earth.

RUMOR (RUMORS)

2 Kings 19. 7 he shall hear a *r* and return to his own
Isa 37. 7 so that he shall hear a *r*, and return to
Mt 24. 6 you will hear of wars and *r* of wars; see

RUN (RAN RUNNING RUNS)

Gen 16. 6 with her, and she *r* away from her.
Neh 6.11 "Should a man like me *r* away? Would a
Ps 119. 32 I *r* the way of your commandments, for
147. 15 to the earth; his word *r* swiftly.
Jer 5. 1 *R* to and fro through the streets of
Dan 12. 4 Many shall be *r* back and forth, and evil
Mt 28. 8 and great joy, and *r* to tell his disciples.
Jn 20. 2 So she *r* and went to Simon Peter and
Gal 2. 2 that I was not *r*, or had not *r*, in vain.
5. 7 You were *r* well; who prevented you
Heb 12. 1 let us *r* with perseverance the race that

RUNNER (RUNNERS)

Job 9.25 "My days are swifter than a *r*; they flee
Hab 2. 2 in plain tablets, so that a *r* may read it.
1 Cor 9.24 in a race the *r* all compete, but only

RUTH

Ruth 1. 4 Orpah, and the name of the other *R*.
2. 2 *R* the Moabite said to Naomi, "Let me
3. 9 "I am *R*, your servant; spread your cloak

Ruth 4.13 Boaz took *R* and she became his wife.
Mt 1. 5 Boaz the father of Obed by *R*, and Obed

S

SABBATH (SABBATHS)

Ex 16.26 day, which is a *s*, there will be none."
20. 8 Remember the *s* day, and keep it holy.
31.16 shall keep the *s*, observing the *s*
Lev 16.31 a *s* of complete rest to you, and you
19.30 You shall keep my *s* and reverence my
25. 4 there shall be a *s* of complete rest for
26. 2 You shall keep my *s* and reverence my
Num 15.32 a man gathering sticks on the *s* day.
Deut 5.12 Observe the *s* day and keep it holy, as
Neh 13.17 that you are doing, profaning the *s* day?
Isa 56. 2 who keeps the *s*, not profaning it, and
58.13 If you refrain from trampling the *s*, from
66.23 from *s* to *s*, all flesh shall come to
Jer 17.21 do not bear a burden on the *s* day or
Ezek 20.12 I gave them my *s*, as a sign between me
44.24 festivals, and they shall keep my *s* holy.
Mt 12. 1 went through the grainfields on the *s*;
24.20 flight may not be in winter or on a *s*.
28. 1 After the *s*, as the first day of the week
Mk 2.23 One *s* he was going through the
3. 2 to see if he would cure him on the *s*,
16. 1 When the *s* was over, Mary Magdalene,
Lk 4.16 he went to the synagogue on the *s* day,
6. 1 One *s* while Jesus was going through
13.14 because Jesus had cured on the *s*,
14. 1 to eat a meal on the *s*, they were
Jn 5.10 "It is the *s*; it is not lawful for you to
7.23 If a man receives circumcision on the *s*
9.14 was a *s* day when Jesus made the mud
Acts 16.13 On the *s* day we went outside the gate

SACKCLOTH

1 Kings 20.32 So they tied *s* around their waists, put
21.27 he fasted, lay in the *s*, and went about
2 Kings 19. 1 tore his clothes, covered himself with *s*,
Esth 4. 1 tore his clothes and put on *s* and ashes,
Ps 35.13 for me, when they were sick, I wore *s*;
69.11 When I made *s* my clothing, I became a
Isa 20. 2 loose the *s* from your loins and take the
37. 1 tore his clothes, covered himself with *s*,
Jon 3. 5 and everyone, great and small, put on *s*.
Lk 10.13 long ago, sitting in *s* and ashes.

SACRED

Ezek 44. 8 have not kept charge of my *s* offerings;
2 Tim 3.15 you have known the *s* writings

SACRIFICE (SACRIFICES) (n)

1 Sam 15.22 to obey is better than *s*, and to heed
1 Chr 29.21 the next day they offered *s* and burnt
Ps 40. 6 *S* and offering you do not desire, but
51.16 For you have no delight in *s*; if I were
Prov 15. 8 *s* of the wicked is an abomination to
21. 3 is more acceptable to the LORD than *s*.
21.27 The *s* of the wicked is an abomination;
Eccl 5. 1 is better than the *s* offered by fools;
Isa 1.11 What to me is the multitude of your *s*?
Jer 6.20 not acceptable, nor are your *s* pleasing
Dan 9.27 he shall make *s* and offering cease;
Hos 6. 6 For I desire steadfast love and not *s*,
8.13 Though they offer choice *s*, though they
Am 4. 4 bring your *s* every morning, your tithes
Mal 1. 8 When you offer blind animals in *s*, is
Mt 9.13 what this means, 'I desire mercy, not *s*.'
12. 7 this means, 'I desire mercy, and not *s*,'
Mk 12.33 than all whole burnt offerings and *s*."
Lk 2.24 they offered a *s* according to what is
Rom 12. 1 present your bodies as a living *s*, holy
3.25 Christ, whom God put forward as a *s*
Eph 5. 2 for us, a fragrant offering and *s* to God.
Phil 4.18 offering, a *s* acceptable and pleasing
Heb 2.17 to make a *s* of atonement for the sins of
Heb 9.26 age to remove sin by the *s* of himself.
10.12 offered for all time a single *s* for sins,
1 Jn 2. 2 he is the atoning *s* for our sins, and not
4.10 his Son to be the atoning *s* for our sins.

SACRIFICE (SACRIFICED) (v)

Ex 3.18 wilderness, so that we may *s* to the
Deut 15.21 you shall not *s* it to the LORD your God;
1 Kings 13. 2 he shall *s* on you the priests of the high
Ps 54. 6 With a freewill offering I will *s* to you; I
Eccl 9. 2 to those who *s* and those who do not *s*.
Jon 2. 9 the voice of thanksgiving will *s* to you;
1 Cor 5. 7 our paschal lamb, Christ, has been *s*.
10.20 that what pagans *s* they *s* to demons

SACRILEGE

Mt 24.15 "So when you see the desolating *s*
Mk 13.14 when you see the desolating *s* set up

SADDUCEES

Mt 3. 7 Pharisees and *S* coming for baptism,
16. 1 The Pharisees and *S* came, and to test
16. 6 of the yeast of the Pharisees and *S*."
22.23 The same day some *S* came to him,
Acts 4. 1 and the *S* came to them, much annoyed
5.17 sect of the *S*), being filled with jealousy,
23. 6 Paul noticed that some were *S* and

SAFE (SAFELY)

Ps 18.32 me with strength, and made my way *s*.
119.117 Hold me up, that I may be *s* and have
Acts 23.24 Paul to ride, and take him *s* to Felix

SAFETY

Ps 4. 8 alone, O LORD, make me lie down in *s*.
12. 5 "I will place them in the *s* for which
Isa 14.30 will graze, and the needy lie down in *s*;

SAGES

Isa 19.12 Where now are your *s*? Let them tell

SAIL (SAILED)

Acts 13. 4 and from there they *s* to Cyprus.
18.18 and *s* for Syria, accompanied by Priscilla
27. 1 was decided that we were to *s* for Italy,

SAINTS (SAINTS')

Mt 27.52 bodies of the *s* who had fallen asleep
Acts 9.13 how much evil he has done to your *s* in
26.10 I not only locked up many of the *s* in
Rom 12.13 Contribute to the needs of the *s*; extend
15.25 to Jerusalem in a ministry to the *s*;
1 Cor 1. 2 called to be *s*, together with all those
6. 2 know that the *s* will judge the world?
2 Cor 9. 1 to you about the ministry for the *s*,
Eph 5. 3 among you, as is proper among *s*.
Col 1.26 but has now been revealed to his *s*.
1 Tim 5.10 shown hospitality, washed the *s* feet,
Philem 7 the hearts of the *s* have been refreshed
Rev 8. 3 with the prayers of all the *s* on the
13. 7 it was allowed to make war on the *s*
14.12 is a call for the endurance of the *s*,
16. 6 they shed the blood of *s* and prophets,
20. 9 surrounded the camp of the *s* and the

SALT (SALTED)

Gen 19.26 back, and she became a pillar of *s*.
Mt 5.13 "You are the *s* of the earth; but if the
Mk 9.49 For everyone will be *s* with fire.
Lk 14.34 "*S* is good; but if *s* has lost its taste,

SALVATION

Gen 49.18 I wait for your *s*, O LORD.
Ex 15. 2 and he has become my *s*; this is my
2 Sam 22. 3 my shield and the horn of my *s*, my
1 Chr 16.23 Tell of his *s* from day to day. Declare
Ps 13. 5 love; my heart shall rejoice in your *s*.
27. 1 The LORD is my light and my *s*; whom
35. 3 pursuers; say to my soul, "I am your *s*!"

Ps 37.39 The *s* of the righteous is from the LORD;
50.23 the right way I will show the *s* of God."
51.12 Restore to me the joy of your *s*, and
62. 1 waits in silence; from him comes my *s*.
70. 4 Let those who love your *s* say evermore,
91.16 will satisfy them, and show them my *s*.
116. 13 I will lift up the cup of *s* and call on
118. 14 and my might; he has become my *s*.
119.123 My eyes fail from watching for your *s*,
Isa 12. 2 God is my *s*; I will trust, and will not be
33. 2 morning, our *s* in the time of trouble.
45. 8 the earth open, that *s* may spring up,
45.17 is saved by the LORD with everlasting *s*;
51. 6 but my *s* will be forever, and my
52. 7 who announces *s*, who says to Zion,
56. 1 for soon my *s* will come, and my
60.18 you shall call your walls *S*, and your
Jer 3.23 in the LORD our God is the *s* of Israel.
Lam 3.26 that one should wait quietly for the *s* of
Mic 7. 7 LORD, I will wait for the God of my *s*;
Hab 3.18 LORD; I will exult in the God of my *s*.
Lk 1.77 give knowledge of *s* to his people by the
2.30 for my eyes have seen your *s*,
3. 6 and all flesh shall see the *s* of God."
19. 9 "Today *s* has come to this house,
Jn 4.22 what we know, for *s* is from the Jews.
Acts 4.12 There is *s* in no one else, for there is no
13.47 may bring *s* to the ends of the earth.' "
28.28 this *s* of God has been sent to the
Rom 1.16 the gospel; it is the power of God for *s*
13.11 For *s* is nearer to us now than when we
2 Cor 6. 2 time; see, now is the day of *s*.
Eph 1.13 the word of truth, the gospel of your *s*,
Phil 1.28 of their destruction, but of your *s*.
2.12 work out your own *s* with fear and
1 Thess 5. 9 for obtaining *s* through our Lord Jesus
Heb 1.14 the sake of those who are to inherit *s*?
1 Pet 1. 9 of your faith, the *s* of your souls.
2 Pet 3.15 regard the patience of our Lord as *s*. So
Jude 3 write to you about the *s* we share, I find
Rev 7.10 "*S* belongs to our God who is seated on
12.10 "Now have come the *s* and the power
19. 1 "Hallelujah! *S* and glory and power to

SAMARIA

1 Kings 16.24 He bought the hill of *S* from Shemer for
16.29 Ahab . . . reigned over Israel in *S*
2 Kings 17. 6 king of Assyria captured *S*; he carried
Isa 7. 9 The head of Ephraim is *S*, and the head
Ezek 16.46 Your elder sister is *S*, who lived with
Hos 8. 5 Your calf is rejected, O *S*. My anger
Mic 1. 6 Therefore I will make *S* a heap in the
Lk 17.11 the region between *S* and Galilee.
Jn 4. 4 But he had to go through *S*. So he came
Acts 1. 8 in Jerusalem, in all Judea and *S*,
8. 5 Philip went down to the city of *S*, and

SAMARITAN (SAMARITANS)

Mt 10. 5 and enter no town of the *S*, but go
Jn 4. 7 A *S* woman came to draw water, and
Acts 8.25 good news to many villages of the *S*.

SAME

Eccl 9. 2 is vanity, since the *s* fate comes to all,

SAMSON

Judg 13.24 woman bore a son, and named him *S*.
14. 1 Once *S* went down to Timnah, and at
15. 1 *S* went to visit his wife, bringing along a
16. 1 Once *S* went to Gaza, where he saw a
16.30 Then *S* said, "Let me die with the
Heb 11.32 fail me to tell of Gideon, Barak, *S*

SAMUEL

Born, 1 Sam 1.19-20; dedicated to God, 1 Sam 1.21-28; ministered before God, 1 Sam 2.11,18-21; called, 1 Sam 3.1-18; judged Israel, 1 Sam 7.3-17; warned Israel for requesting a king, 1 Sam 8.10-18; anointed Saul king, 1 Sam 10.1-8; reasoned with Israel, 1 Sam 12; reproved Saul, 1 Sam 13.8-15; 15.10-23; hewed Agag in pieces, 1 Sam 15.33; anointed David, 1 Sam 16.1-13; died, 1 Sam 25.1; 28.3.

Jer 15. 1 Though Moses and *S* stood before me,
Acts 3.24 from *S* and those after him, also
13.20 judges until the time of the prophet *S*.

SANCTIFICATION

1 Cor 1.30 righteousness and *s* and redemption, in
1 Thess 4. 3 this is the will of God, your *s*: that you

SANCTIFY (SANCTIFIED SANCTIFIES)

Ex 29.43 there, and it will be *s* by my glory;
Lev 22.32 my holy name, that I may be *s* among
Josh 3. 5 "*S* yourselves; for tomorrow the LORD
7.13 Proceed to *s* the people, and say, '*S*
1 Chr 15.14 the priests and the Levites *s* themselves
2 Chr 29. 5 to me, Levites! *S* yourselves, and *s*
Isa 29.23 in his midst, they will *s* my name;
Ezek 20.12 they might know that I the LORD *s* them.
Joel 1.14 *S* a fast, call a solemn assembly. Gather
Jn 17.17 to the world. *S* them in the truth; your
Acts 26.18 and a place among those who are *s* by
1 Cor 1. 2 to those who are *s* in Christ Jesus,
6.11 you were washed, you were *s*, you were
1 Thess 5.23 May the God of peace himself *s* you
Heb 2.11 the one who *s* and those who are *s*
9.13 of the ashes of a heifer, *s* those
10.10 have been *s* through the offering of the
10.14 perfected for all time those who are *s*.
13.12 order to *s* the people by his own blood.

SANCTUARY

Ex 25. 8 have them make me a *s*, so that I may
36. 1 in the construction of the *s* shall work
Lev 12. 4 any holy thing, or come into the *s*,
21.12 outside the *s* and thus profane the *s* of
1 Chr 22.19 Go and build the *s* of the LORD God so
28.10 chosen you to build a house as the *s*;
2 Chr 26.18 Go out of the *s*; for you have done
Ps 20. 2 May he send you help from the *s*, and
63. 2 So I have looked upon you in the *s*,
73.17 task, until I went into the *s* of God;
74. 7 They set your *s* on fire; they desecrated
114. 2 Judah became God's *s*, Israel his
Isa 8.14 He will become a *s*, a stone one strikes
16.12 when he comes to his *s* to pray, he will
Jer 17.12 from the beginning, the shrine of our *s*!
Lam 1.10 has even seen the nations invade her *s*,
2. 7 has scorned his altar, disowned his *s*;
Ezek 5.11 because you have defiled my *s* with all
11.16 yet I have been a *s* to them for a little
23.38 they have defiled my *s* on the same day
24.21 I will profane my *s*, the pride of your
48. 8 the west, with the *s* in the middle of it.
Dan 8.14 then the *s* shall be restored to its
9.17 your face shine upon your desolated *s*.
Am 7.13 prophesy at Bethel, for it is the king's *s*,
Mal 2.11 Judah has profaned the *s* of the LORD,
Heb 9. 1 regulations for worship and an earthly *s*.
9. 8 way into the *s* has not yet been
10.19 confidence to enter the *s* by the blood

SAND

Gen 22.17 as . . . *s* that is on the seashore."
32.12 make your offspring as the *s* of the sea,"
Prov 27. 3 is heavy, and *s* is weighty, but a fool's
Isa 10.22 people Israel were like the *s* of the sea,
Hos 1.10 the people of Israel shall be like the *s*
Mt 7.26 man who built his house upon the *s*;
Rom 9.27 children of Israel were like the *s* of the
Heb 11.12 and as the innumerable grains of *s* by

SANDAL (SANDALS)

Ex 3. 5 Remove the *s* from your feet, for the
Deut 25. 9 pull his *s* off his foot, spit in his face,

Josh 5.15 "Remove the *s* from your feet, for the
Ruth 4. 7 took off his *s* and gave it to the other;
Mk 1. 7 down and untie the thong of his *s*.
6. 9 but to wear *s* and not to put on two
Lk 3.16 not worthy to untie the thong of his *s*.
15.22 a ring on his finger and *s* on his feet.
Acts 7.33 'Take off the *s* from your feet, for the
13.25 not worthy to untie the thong of the *s*

SARAH (SARAH'S SARAI)

Wife of Abraham, Gen 11.29; barren, Gen 11.30; Sarai and Hagar, Gen 16.1-6; represented as Abraham's sister, Gen 12.10-20; 20.1-18; name changed to Sarah, Gen 17.15; laughed at the LORD's promise, Gen 18.9-15; bore Isaac, Gen 21.1-8; jealous of Ishmael, Gen 21.9-11; died at Hebron, Gen 23.2; buried in Machpelah, Gen 23.19.

Gen 11.30 Now *S* was barren; she had no child.
16. 1 *S*, Abram's wife, bore him no children.
18. 9 "Where is your wife *S*?" And he said,
21. 1 LORD dealt with *S* as he had said, and
Rom 4.19 considered the barrenness of *S* womb.
Heb 11.11 too old —and *S* herself was barren—
1 Pet 3. 6 Thus *S* obeyed Abraham, and called

SATAN

1 Chr 21. 1 *S* stood up against Israel, and incited
Job 1. 6 the LORD, and *S* also came among them.
2. 1 and *S* also came among them to present
Zech 3. 1 *S* standing at his right hand to accuse
Mt 4.10 Jesus said to him, "Away with you, *S*!
12.26 If *S* casts out *S*, he is divided against
16.23 and said to Peter, "Get behind me, *S*!
Lk 10.18 to them, "I watched *S* fall from heaven
Acts 5. 3 asked, "Why has *S* filled your heart
2 Cor 2.11 so we may not be outwitted by *S*; for we
11.14 Even *S* disguises himself as an angel of
Rev 2. 9 and are not, but are a synagogue of *S*.
12. 9 serpent, who is called the Devil and *S*,
20. 2 ancient serpent, who is the Devil and *S*,

SATISFACTION

Isa 53.11 he shall find *s* through his knowledge.

SATISFY (SATISFIED SATISFIES)

Josh 22.30 and the Manassites spoke, they were *s*.
Ps 22.26 The poor shall eat and be *s*; those who
65. 4 be *s* with the goodness of your house,
90.14 *S* us in the morning with your steadfast
104. 13 the earth is *s* with the fruit of your
107. 9 For he *s* the thirsty, and the hungry he
132. 15 provisions; I will *s* its poor with bread.
Prov 27.20 never *s*, and human eyes are never *s*.
30.15 give," they cry. Three things are never *s*;
Eccl 1. 8 the eye is not *s* with seeing, or the ear
5.10 of money will not be *s* with money;
Isa 55. 2 your labor for that which does not *s*?
58.11 and *s* your needs in parched places,
Jer 31.14 my people shall be *s* with my bounty,
31.25 I will *s* the weary, and all who are faint
Ezek 7.19 They shall not *s* their hunger or fill
Mic 6.14 You shall eat, but not be *s*, and there
Mt 28.14 we will *s* him and keep you out of
Lk 3.14 accusations, and be *s* with your wages."
Jn 14. 8 show us the Father, and we will be *s*."
Acts 27.38 they had *s* their hunger, they lightened
Phil 4.19 my God will fully *s* every need of yours

SAUL (King of Israel)

Son of Kish, 1 Sam 9.1-2; met Samuel, 1 Sam 9.5-24; anointed by Samuel, 1 Sam 10.1-8; prophesied with the prophets, 1 Sam 10.9-13; chosen king at Mizpah, 1 Sam 10.20-24; defeated the Ammonites, 1 Sam 11.5-11; made king in Gilgal, 1 Sam 11.12-15; reproved for his burnt offering, 1 Sam 13.8-15; built an altar, 1 Sam 14.35; rejected as king, 1 Sam 15.11-30; refreshed by David's harp playing, 1 Sam 16.14-23; became jealous of David, 1 Sam 18.6-30; sought to kill David, 1 Sam 19.1-17; killed the priests of Nob, 1 Sam 22.11-19; spared by David, 1 Sam 24.1-7; 26.1-12; consulted the woman of Endor, 1 Sam 28.3-25; died and buried, 1 Sam 31.

Acts 13.21 asked for a king; and God gave them *S*

SAUL (Paul)

Acts 13. 9 But *S*, also known as Paul, filled with

SAVE

Deut 23.14 to *s* you and to hand over your enemies
1 Sam 4. 3 may come among us and *s* us from the
17.47 the LORD does not *s* by sword and spear;
2 Kings 19.19 So now, O LORD our God, *s* us, I pray
19.34 I will defend this city to *s* it, for my
1 Chr 16.35 Say also: "*S* us, O God of our salvation,
2 Chr 20. 9 in our distress, and you will hear and *s*.'
Ps 28. 9 O *s* your people, and bless your
69.35 God will *s* Zion and rebuild the cities of
76. 9 judgment, to *s* all the oppressed
86. 2 to you; *s* your servant who trusts
116. 4 of the LORD: "O LORD, I pray, *s* my life!"
Prov 2.12 It will *s* you from the way of evil, from
6. 5 *s* yourself like a gazelle from the hunter,
23.14 them with a rod, you will *s* their lives
Isa 25. 9 waited for him, so that he might *s* us.
36.18 you by saying, The LORD will *s* us.
37.20 God, *s* us from his hand, so that all the
44.17 it and says, "*S* me, for you are my god!"
47.15 own paths; there is no one to *s* you.
63. 1 I, announcing vindication, mighty to *s*."
Jer 15.20 for I am with you to *s* you and deliver
17.14 be healed; *s* me, and I shall be saved;
30.10 I am going to *s* you from far away, and
39.17 I will *s* you on that day, says the LORD,
46.27 I am going to *s* you from far away, and
51. 6 of Babylon, *s* your lives, each of you!
Ezek 3.18 their wicked way in order to *s* their life,
7.19 Their silver and gold cannot *s* them on
34.22 I will *s* my flock, and they will no
Hos 13.10 now is your king, that he may *s* you?
14. 3 Assyria shall not *s* us; we will not ride
Am 2.14 strength, nor shall the mighty *s* their
Hab 3.13 You came forth to *s* your people, to *s*
Zeph 3.19 And I will *s* the lame and gather the
Mt 1.21 name him Jesus, for he will *s* his people
8.25 saying, "Lord, *s* us! We are perishing!"
14.30 to sink, he cried out, "Lord, *s* me!"
16.25 who want to *s* their life will lose it,
18.11n For the Son of man came to *s* the lost
27.40 and build it in three days, *s* yourself!
Mk 8.35 those who want to *s* their life will lose
15.30 *s* yourself, and come down from the
Lk 9.24 those who want to *s* their life will lose
9.56n lives of human beings but to *s* them."
1 Cor 7.16 you might *s* your husband. Husband, for
9.22 that I might by all means *s* some.
1 Tim 1.15 came into the world to *s* sinners—
4.16 will *s* both yourself and your hearers.
Heb 7.25 all time to *s* those who approach God
9.28 but to *s* those who are eagerly waiting
Jas 5.20 will *s* the sinner's soul from death
Jude 23 *s* others by snatching them out of the

SAVES (SAVED SAVING)

Ex 14.30 Thus the LORD *s* Israel that day from the
Num 10. 9 your God and be *s* from your enemies.
Deut 33.29 Who is like you, a people *s* by the LORD,
1 Sam 14. 6 nothing can hinder the LORD from *s* by
2 Sam 22. 4 praised, and I am *s* from my enemies.
1 Kings 1.29 "As the LORD lives, who has *s* my life
2 Chr 32.22 So the LORD *s* Hezekiah and the
Job 5.15 But he *s* the needy from the sword of
Ps 18. 3 so I shall be *s* from my enemies.
34. 6 and was heard by the LORD, and was *s*
80. 3 let your face shine, that we may be *s*.
106. 8 Yet he *s* them for his name's sake, so
107. 19 and he *s* them from their distress;

Isa 30.15 In returning and rest you shall be *s*;
Jer 8.20 the summer is ended, and we are not *s*."
23. 6 In his days Judah will be *s* and Israel
33.16 In those days Judah will be *s* and
Ezek 3.19 iniquity; but you will have *s* your life.
Ob 21 have been *s* shall go up to Mount Zion
Mic 6. 5 you may know the *s* acts of the LORD."
Mt 19.25 and said, "Then who can be *s*?"
24.13 one who endures to the end will be *s*.
Mk 10.26 to one another, "Then who can be *s*?"
Lk 7.50 to the woman, "Your faith has *s* you; go
13.23 asked him, "Lord, will only a few be *s*?"
18.26 who heard it said, "Then who can be *s*?"
23.35 "He *s* others; let him save himself if he
Jn 5.34 I say these things so that you may be *s*.
Acts 2.21 on the name of the Lord shall be *s*.'
11.14 and your entire household will be *s*.'
15. 1 the custom of Moses, you cannot be *s*."
15.11 that we will be *s* through the grace of
16.30 and said, "Sirs, what must I do to be *s*?"
27.31 men stay in the ship, you cannot be *s*."
Rom 5. 9 we be *s* through him from the wrath
8.24 For in hope we were *s*. Now hope that
10. 1 to God for them is that they may be *s*.
10. 9 raised him from the dead, you will be *s*.
11.26 And so all Israel will be *s*; as it is
1 Cor 1.18 but to us who are being *s* it is the
3.15 the builder will be *s*, but only as
5. 5 so that his spirit may be *s* in the day of
10.33 but that of many, so that they may be *s*.
15. 2 through which you also are being *s*, if
1 Thess 2.16 to the Gentiles so that they may be *s*.
2 Tim 1. 9 of God, who *s* us and called us with a
Titus 3. 5 he *s* us, not because of any works of
1 Pet 3.20 is, eight persons, were *s* through water.
4.18 If it is hard for the righteous to be *s*,
Jude 5 once for all *s* a people out of the land

SAVIOR

2 Kings 13. 5 the LORD gave Israel a *s*, so that they
Ps 106. 21 They forgot God, their *S*, who had done
Isa 19.20 he will send them a *s*, and will defend
43. 3 God, the Holy One of Israel, your *S*.
43.11 the LORD, and besides me there is no *s*.
45.21 a righteous God and *S*; there is no one
60.16 shall know that I, the LORD, am your *S*
Jer 14. 8 O hope of Israel, its *s* in time of
Hos 13. 4 but me, and besides me there is no *s*.
Lk 1.47 and my spirit rejoices in God my *S*,
1.69 He has raised up a mighty *s* for us in
2.11 is born this day in the city of David a *S*,
Acts 13.23 God has brought to Israel a *S*, Jesus, as
1 Tim 2. 3 acceptable in the sight of God our *S*,
4.10 living God, who is the *S* of all people,
1 Jn 4.14 has sent his Son as the *S* of the world.
Jude 25 only God, our *S*, through Jesus Christ

SAY (SAYING)

Lk 5. 5 nothing. Yet if you *s* so, I will let down
1 Tim 1.15 The *s* is sure and worthy of full
4. 9 The *s* is sure and worthy of full

SCALES

Prov 16.11 Honest balances and *s* are the LORD's;
20.23 to the LORD, and false *s* are not good.
Dan 5.27 you have been weighed on the *s*
Mic 6.11 Can I tolerate wicked *s* and a bag of
Rev 6. 5 Its rider held a pair of *s* in his hand,

SCARLET

Isa 1.18 though your sins are like *s*, they shall
Mt 27.28 stripped him and put a *s* robe on him,

SCATTER (SCATTERED SCATTERS)

Gen 49. 7 them in Jacob, and *s* them in Israel.
Lev 26.33 I will *s* you among the nations, and I
Deut 4.27 The LORD will *s* you among the peoples;
28.64 The LORD will *s* you among all peoples,
Jer 9.16 I will *s* them among the nations that
10.21 not prospered, and all their flock is *s*.
13.24 I will *s* you like chaff driven by the
18.17 east, I will *s* them before the enemy.
Ezek 11.16 though I *s* them among the countries,
20.23 in the wilderness that I would *s* them
Zech 1.21 "These are the horns that *s* Judah, so
7.14 I *s* them with a whirlwind all the
10. 9 Though I *s* them among the nations, yet
Jn 10.12 wolf snatches them and *s* them.
16.32 indeed it has come, when you will be *s*,
Acts 8. 4 those who were *s* went from place to

SCEPTER

Gen 49.10 The *s* shall not depart from Judah, nor
Num 21.18 people dug, with the *s*, with the staff."
24.17 a *s* shall rise out of Israel; it shall crush
Ps 45. 6 and ever. Your royal *s* is a *s* of equity;
60. 7 Ephraim is my helmet; Judah is my *s*.

SCHEMES

Job 10. 3 hands and favor the *s* of the wicked?

SCOFFED

Deut 32.15 him, and *s* at the Rock of his salvation.
Acts 17.32 resurrection of the dead, some *s*; but

SCOFFER (SCOFFERS)

Ps 1. 1 sinners tread, or sit in the seat of *s*;
Prov 1.22 How long will *s* delight in in their
13. 1 but a *s* does not listen to rebuke.
14. 6 A *s* seeks wisdom in vain, but
15.12 *S* do not like to be rebuked; they will
19.25 Strike a *s*, and the simple will learn
Isa 29.20 be no more, and the *s* shall cease to be;
Acts 13.41 'Look, you *s*! Be amazed and perish, for

SCOLDED

Mk 14. 5 given to the poor." And they *s* her.

SCORCH (SCORCHED)

Mt 13. 6 But when the sun rose, they were *s*; and
Rev 16. 8 and it was allowed to *s* them with fire;

SCORN (SCORNED)

2 Sam 12.14 this deed you have utterly *s* the LORD,
2 Chr 30.10 they laughed them to *s*, and mocked
Ps 31.11 I am the *s* of all my adversaries, a
89.41 he has become the *s* of his neighbors.
Ezek 23.32 wide; you shall be *s* and derided, it
Jer 6.10 of the LORD is to them an object of *s*;
Mic 6.16 so you shall bear the *s* of my people.
Gal 4.14 you did not *s* or despise me, but

SCOURGE

Job 5.21 be hidden from the *s* of the tongue,

SCRIBE (SCRIBES)

Ezra 7.12 Ezra, the *s* of the law of the God of
Mt 8.19 A *s* then approached and said, "Teacher,
13.52 every *s* who has been trained for the
23. 2 "The *s* and the Pharisees sit on Moses'
Mk 3.22 *s* who came down from Jerusalem said,
9.14 them, and some *s* arguing with them.
12.38 "Beware of the *s*, who like to walk
1 Cor 1.20 is the one who is wise? Where is the *s*?

SCRIPTURE (SCRIPTURES)

Mt 21.42 "Have you never read in the *s*: 'The
22.29 you know neither the *s* nor the power of
26.54 But how then would the *s* be fulfilled,
Mk 12.10 Have you not read this *s*: 'The stone
12.24 you know neither the *s* nor the power of
14.49 not arrest me. But let the *s* be fulfilled."
15.28n the *s* was fulfilled which says, "And he
Lk 4.21 "Today this *s* has been fulfilled in your
24.32 road, while he was opening the *s* to us?"
24.45 opened their minds to understand the *s*,
Jn 2.22 they believed the *s* and the word that

Jn 5.39 You search the *s* because you think that
10.35 —and the *s* cannot be annulled—
13.18 to fulfill the *s*, 'The one who ate my
17.12 be lost, so that the *s* might be fulfilled.
19.24 This was to fulfill what the *s* says,
19.28 (in order to fulfill the *s*), "I am thirsty."
19.37 of *s* says, "They will look on the one
Acts 8.35 starting with this *s*, he proclaimed to
17. 2 argued with them from the *s*, explaining
17.11 examined the *s* every day to see
18.24 an eloquent man, well-versed in the *s*.
Rom 9.17 For the *s* says to Pharaoh, "I have raised
15. 4 of the *s* we might have hope.
1 Cor 15. 3 for our sins in accordance with the *s*,
Gal 3. 8 the *s*, foreseeing that God would justify
3.22 the *s* has imprisoned all things under
4.30 does the *s* say? "Drive out the slave
Jas 2. 8 fulfill the royal law according to the *s*,
2.23 Thus the *s* was fulfilled that says,
4. 5 that it is for nothing that the *s* says,
2 Pet 1.20 no prophecy of *s* is a matter of one's
3.16 own destruction, as they do the other *s*.

SCROLL

Ps 40. 7 I am; in the *s* of the book it is written
Isa 34. 4 rot away, and the skies roll up like a *s*.
Jer 36. 2 Take a *s* and write on it all the words
36.18 me, and I wrote them with ink on the *s*."
36.23 the entire *s* was consumed in the fire
36.32 Then Jeremiah took another *s* and gave
51.60 Jeremiah wrote in a *s* all the disasters
Ezek 2. 9 out to me, and a written *s* was in it;
Zech 5. 1 Again I looked up and saw a flying *s*.
Lk 4.17 read and the *s* of the prophet Isaiah was
Heb 9.19 sprinkled both the *s* itself and all the
10. 7 (in the *s* of the book it is written of
Rev 5. 1 *s* written on the inside and on the back,
6.14 The sky vanished like a *s* rolling itself
10. 2 He had a little *s* open in his hand.
10. 9 told him to give me the little *s*; and he

SEA (SEAS)

Gen 1.10 that were gathered together he called *S*.
Ex 14.21 The LORD drove the *s* back by a strong
2 Chr 2.16 bring it to you as rafts by *s* to Joppa;
Neh 9.11 you divided the *s* before them, so that
Eccl 1. 7 run to the *s*, but the *s* is not full;
Mt 8.24 A windstorm arose on the *s*, so great
Mk 6.48 early in the morning, walking on the *s*.
Jn 6.19 they saw Jesus walking on the *s* and
1 Cor 10. 2 into Moses in the cloud and in the *s*,
Rev 15. 2 standing beside the *s* of glass with
21. 1 passed away, and the *s* was no more.

SEA OF GALILEE

Mt 4.18 As he walked by the *S*, he saw two
15.29 he passed along the *S*, and he went up
Jn 6. 1 Jesus went to the other side of the *S*,

SEAL (SEALS) (n)

Jn 6.27 him that God the Father has set his *s*."
Rom 4.11 the sign of circumcision as a *s* of the
1 Cor 9. 2 you; for you are the *s* of my apostleship
2 Cor 1.22 by putting his *s* on us and giving us his
Eph 1.13 with the *s* of the promised Holy Spirit;
4.30 you were marked with a *s* for the day of
Rev 6. 1 Lamb opened one of the seven *s*, and I
7. 3 marked the servants of our God with a *s*
8. 1 the Lamb opened the seventh *s*, there
9. 4 who have not the *s* of God on their

SEAL (SEALED SEALING)

Esth 8. 8 the king, and *s* it with the king's ring;
Job 14.17 my transgression would be *s* up in a
Isa 29.11 for you like the words of a *s* document.
Dan 9.24 to *s* both vision and prophet, and to
12. 4 the words and the secret and the book *s*
12. 9 the words are to remain secret and *s*
Mt 27.66 made the tomb secure by *s* the stone.
Rev 5. 1 and on the back, *s* with seven seals;
10. 4 "*S* up what the seven thunders have
22.10 "Do not *s* up the words of the prophecy

SEARCH (SEARCHED SEARCHES SEARCHING)

Job 5.27 See, we have *s* this out; it is true. Hear,
Ps 139. 1 O LORD, you have *s* me and known me.
139. 23 *S* me, O God, and know my heart; test
Jer 17.10 the LORD test the mind and *s* the heart,
29.13 When you *s* for me, you will find me; if
Am 9. 3 from there I will *s* out and take them;
Zeph 1.12 that time I will *s* Jerusalem with lamps,
Mt 2. 8 "Go and *s* diligently for the child, and
7. 7 *s*, and you will find; knock, and the
18.12 and go in *s* of the one that went astray?
Mk 1.37 they said to him, "Everyone is *s* for you."
Jn 5.39 "You *s* the scriptures because you think
7.34 You will *s* for me, but you will not find
7.52 *S* and you will see that no prophet is to
8.21 and you will *s* for me, but you will not
Acts 17.27 so that they would *s* for God, and
Rom 8.27 God, who *s* the heart, knows what is in
1 Cor 2.10 for the Spirit *s* everything, even the
Rev 2.23 I am the one who *s* minds and hearts,

SEASON (SEASONS)

Gen 1.14 and let them be for signs and for *s* and
Eccl 3. 1 For everything there is a *s*, and a time
Mk 9.50 has lost its saltness, how can you *s* it?"

SEAT (SEATED)

2 Kings 25.28 gave him a *s* above the seats of the
Job 29. 7 of the city, I took my *s* in the square,
Mk 14.62 see the Son of Man *s* at the right hand
Lk 11.43 for you love the *s* of honor in the

SECRET (SECRETS)

Deut 29.29 The *s* things belong to the LORD our
2 Sam 15.10 Absalom sent *s* messengers throughout
Ps 44.21 this? For he knows the *s* of the heart.
90. 8 our *s* sins in the light of your
Prov 11.13 A gossip goes about telling *s*, but one
Eccl 12.14 deed into judgment, including every *s*
Isa 45.19 I did not speak in *s*, in a land of
48.16 I have not spoken in *s*, from the time it
Jer 23.24 Who can hide in *s* places so that I
Am 3. 7 without revealing his *s* to his servants
Mt 6. 4 so that your alms may be done in *s*; and
13.11 given to know the *s* of the kingdom
Mk 4.11 has been given the *s* of the kingdom
4.22 is anything *s*, except to come to light.
Rom 2.16 Christ, will judge the *s* thoughts of all.
1 Cor 2. 7 we speak God's wisdom, *s* and hidden,
14.25 After the *s* of the unbeliever's heart are

SECRETLY

Gen 31.27 Why did you flee *s* and deceive me and
2 Kings 17. 9 Israel did *s* things that were not right
Jer 37.17 The king questioned him *s* in his house,
Mt 2. 7 Then Herod *s* called for the wise men

SECT

Acts 24. 5 a ringleader of the *s* of the Nazarenes.
28.22 with regard to this *s* we know that

SECURE (SECURELY)

Judg 18. 7 people who were there living *s*, after the
Ps 112. 7 their hearts are firm, *s* in the LORD.
Lk 17.33 who try to make their life *s* will lose it,

SECURITY

Job 24.23 He gives them *s*, and they are
Isa 38.14 O LORD, I am oppressed; be my *s*!

SEE (SEEING SEEN SEES)

Gen 16.13 God and remained alive after *s* him?"
45.28 alive. I must go and *s* him before I die."
Deut 34. 4 I have let you *s* it with your eyes, but

1 Sam 9.16 I have *s* the suffering of my people,
16. 7 for the LORD does not *s* as mortals *s*;
Job 19.26 then in my flesh I shall *s* God,
Prov 27.12 The clever *s* danger and hide; but the
28.11 poor person *s* through the pose.
Eccl 11. 7 it is pleasant for the eyes to *s* the sun.
Isa 5.12 of the LORD, or *s* the work of his hands!
29.15 who say, "Who *s* us? Who knows us?"
44.18 eyes are shut, so that they cannot *s*,
52.10 ends of the earth shall *s* the salvation
53.10 he shall *s* his offspring, and shall
Mal 3.18 you shall *s* the difference between the
Mt 4.16 who sat in darkness have *s* a great light,
5. 8 the pure in heart, for they will *s* God.
6. 1 before others in order to be *s* by them;
11. 4 "Go and tell John what you hear and *s*:
28. 6 Come, *s* the place where he lay.
Lk 3. 6 all flesh shall *s* the salvation of God.' "
7.22 "Go and tell John what you have *s* and
Jn 3.21 may be clearly *s* that their deeds have
4.35 around you, *s* how the fields are ripe
8.51 keeps my word, will never *s* death."
9.25 know, that though I was blind, now I *s*."
9.39 so that those who do not *s* may *s*,
12.21 said to him, "Sir, we wish to *s* Jesus."
16.16 again a little while, and you will *s* me."
17.24 be with me where I am, to *s* my glory,
20.25 "Unless I *s* the mark of the nails in his
Acts 4.20 from speaking about what we have *s*
9.27 on the road he had *s* the Lord, who had
1 Cor 13.12 now we *s* in a mirror, dimly, but then
2 Cor 3.18 all of us, with unveiled face, *s* the glory
4. 4 keep them from *s* the light of the gospel
Heb 2. 9 but we do *s* Jesus, who for a little while
1 Jn 1. 1 have heard, what we have *s* with our
3. 2 be like him, for we will *s* him as he is
Rev 1. 7 every eye will *s* him, even those who

SEED

Gen 1.29 I have given you every plant yielding *s*
Ps 126. 6 out weeping, bearing the *s* for sowing,
Eccl 11. 6 In the morning sow your *s*, and at
Mt 13.24 someone who sowed good *s* in his field;
13.38 the good *s* are the children of the
Mk 4.26 of God is as if someone would scatter *s*
1 Jn 3. 9 sin, because God's *s* abides in them;

SEEK (SEEKS SOUGHT)

Num 10.33 day's journey, to *s* out a resting place
Deut 4.29 From there you will *s* the LORD your
1 Sam 22.23 the one who *s* my life *s* your life; you
1 Chr 16.11 *S* the LORD and his strength, *s* his
28. 9 If you *s* him, he will be found by you;
2 Chr 7.14 pray, *s* my face, and turn from their
14. 4 and commanded Judah to *s* the LORD,
16.12 yet even in his disease he did not *s* the
19. 3 land, and have set your heart to *s* God."
31.21 to *s* his God, he did with all his heart;
Ps 9.10 have not forsaken those who *s* you.
14. 2 are any who are wise; who *s* after God.
24. 6 who *s* the face of the God of Jacob.
27. 8 my heart says, "*s* his face!" Your face,
40.16 But may all who *s* you rejoice and be
53. 2 are any who are wise, who *s* after God.
54. 3 risen against me, the ruthless *s* my life
63. 1 you are my God, I *s* you, my soul thirsts
69.32 glad; who *s* God, let your hearts revive.
105. 3 hearts of those who *s* the LORD rejoice.
119. 2 who *s* him with their whole heart, who
122. 9 of the LORD our God, I will *s* your good.
Prov 1.28 they will *s* me diligently, but will not
Eccl 1.13 mind to *s* and to search out by wisdom
3.15 is; and God *s* out what has gone by.
12.10 The Teacher *s* to find pleasing words,
Song 3. 1 at night I *s* him whom my soul loves;
Isa 9.13 who struck them, or *s* the LORD of hosts.
26. 9 night, my spirit within me earnestly *s*
34.16 *S* and read from the book of the LORD:
45.19 the offspring of Jacob, "*S* me in chaos."
55. 6 *S* the LORD while he may be found, call
Jer 45. 5 you, do you *s* great things for yourself?
Lam 3.25 wait for him, to the soul that *s* him.
Ezek 7.25 will *s* peace, but there shall be none.
22.30 I *s* for anyone among them who would
34.12 so will I *s* out my sheep. I will rescue
Dan 9. 3 the Lord God, to *s* an answer by prayer
Hos 3. 5 Israelites shall return and *s* the LORD
5.15 acknowledge their guilt and *s* my face.
Am 5. 4 Israel: *S* me and live; but do not *s*
5.14 *S* good, and not evil, that you may live;
Zeph 2. 3 *S* the LORD, all you humble of the land,
Zech 8.22 nations shall come to *s* the LORD of
Lk 11. 9 *s*, and you will find; knock, and the
19.10 Son of Man came to *s* and to save the
Jn 4.23 truth, for the Father *s* such as these
5.30 I *s* to do not my own will, but the will
8.50 Yet I do not *s* my own glory; there is
Acts 15.17 that all other peoples may *s* the Lord—
Rom 3.11 there is no one who *s* God. All have
11. 3 I alone am left, and they *s* my life."
Col 3. 1 *s* the things that are above, where

SEER (SEERS)

1 Sam 9. 9 a prophet was formerly called a *s*.)
Isa 30.10 say to the *s*, "Do not see"; and to the
Mic 3. 7 the *s* shall be disgraced, and the

SELF-CONDEMNED

Gal 2.11 him to his face, because he stood *s*.

SELF-CONTROL

Prov 25.28 without walls, is one who lacks *s*.
Acts 24.25 he discussed justice, *s*, and the coming
1 Cor 7. 9 if they are not practicing *s*, they should
9.25 Athletes exercise *s* in all things; they do

SELFISH (SELFISHNESS)

2 Cor 12.20 anger, *s*, slander, gossip, conceit, and
Phil 2. 3 Do nothing from *s* ambition or conceit,

SELL (SELLS SOLD)

Gen 25.31 Jacob said, "First *s* me your birthright."
31.15 For he has *s* us, and he has been using
37.28 and *s* him to the Ishmaelites for twenty
41.56 the storehouses, and *s* to the Egyptians,
45. 4 brother, Joseph, whom you *s* into Egypt.
Lev 25.23 The land shall not be *s* in perpetuity,
27.28 may be *s* or redeemed; every devoted
Judg 2.14 he *s* them into the power of their
1 Kings 21.25 Ahab, who *s* himself to do what was evil
2 Kings 17.17 they *s* themselves to do evil in the sight
Esth 7. 4 we have been *s*, I and my people, to be
Ps 44.12 You have *s* your people for a trifle,
105. 17 of them, Joseph, who was *s* as a slave.
Am 2. 6 because they *s* the righteous for silver,
Mt 13.44 in his joy he goes and *s* all that he has
Lk 12.33 *S* your possessions, and give alms. Make
Acts 4.34 many as owned lands or houses *s* them
7. 9 patriarchs, jealous of Joseph, *s* him
Rom 7.14 but I am of the flesh, *s* into slavery

SEND (SENDING SENDS SENT)

Gen 45. 5 for God *s* me before you to preserve life.
Ex 3.10 Come now, I will *s* you to Pharaoh to
Ps 43. 3 O *s* out your light and your truth; let
57. 3 He will *s* from heaven and save me, he
147. 15 He *s* out his command to the earth; his
Eccl 11. 1 *S* out your bread upon the waters, for
Isa 6. 8 go for us?" And I said, "Here am I; *s* me!"
Jer 26.12 "It is the LORD who *s* me to prophesy
Mal 3. 1 I am *s* my messenger to prepare the way
Mt 9.38 to *s* out laborers into his harvest."
10. 5 These twelve Jesus *s* out, with the
10.40 me welcomes the one who *s* me.
11. 2 he *s* word by his disciples and said to

Mt 13.41 The Son of Man will *s* his angels, and
Mk 1. 2 "See, I am *s* my messenger ahead of
5.12 spirits begged him, "*S* us to the swine;
11. 1 of Olives, he *s* two of his disciples,
Lk 19.29 of Olives, he *s* two of the disciples,
Jn 6.57 the living Father *s* me, and I live
17. 8 and they have believed that you *s* me.
17.18 As you have *s* me into the world, so I
20.21 the Father has *s* me, even so I *s* you."
1 Cor 1.17 Christ did not *s* me to baptize but to
2 Cor 2.17 as persons *s* from God and standing in
Gal 4. 4 of time had come, God *s* his Son,
4. 6 God has *s* the Spirit of his Son into our
1 Jn 4. 9 God *s* his only Son into the world so

SENNACHERIB

2 Kings 18.13 *S* king of Assyria came up against all
19.16 hear the words of *S*, which he has sent
19.36 *S* of Assyria left, went home, and lived
2 Chr 32. 1 King *S* of Assyria came and invaded
Isa 37.17 hear all the words of *S*, which he has
37.37 Then *S* king of Assyria left, went home,

SENSE

1 Sam 25.33 Blessed be your good *s*, and blessed be

SENTINEL (SENTINELS)

2 Sam 18.25 The *s* shouted and told the king. The
Isa 21.11 "*S*, what of the night? *S*, what of the
62. 6 your walls, O Jerusalem, I have set *s*;
Jer 6.17 I raised up *s* for you: "Give heed to the
31. 6 For there shall be a day when *s* will call
Ezek 3.17 I have made you a *s* for the house of
33. 6 But if the *s* sees the sword coming and
Hos 9. 8 prophet is a *s* for my God over Ephraim,

SEPARATE (SEPARATED SEPARATES)

Gen 1. 4 and God *s* the light from the darkness.
1.14 of the sky to *s* the day from the night;
13.11 eastward; thus they *s* from each other.
Ex 26.33 the veil shall *s* for you the holy place
Lev 15.31 of Israel *s* from their uncleanness,
20.24 God. I have *s* you from the peoples.
1 Kings 8.53 for you have *s* them from among all the
Ezra 9. 1 Levites have not *s* themselves from the
10.11 do his will; *s* yourselves from the
Neh 13. 3 they *s* from Israel all those of foreign
Mt 19. 6 God has joined together, let no one *s*."
25.32 he will *s* the people one from another
Rom 8.35 Who will *s* us from the love of Christ?
8.39 will be able to *s* us from the love of God
1 Cor 7.15 if the unbelieving partner *s*, let it be so;
2 Cor 6.17 them, be *s* from them, says the Lord,
Gal 2.12 *s* for fear of the circumcision faction.

SEPARATION

Ezek 42.20 to make a *s* between the holy and the

SERAPHS

Isa 6. 2 *S* were in attendance above him; each

SERPENT (SERPENTS)

Gen 3. 1 Now the *s* was more crafty than any
Num 21. 6 LORD sent poisonous *s* among the
21. 8 "Make a poisonous *s*, and set it on a
2 Kings 18. 4 broke in pieces the bronze *s* that Moses
Prov 23.32 the last it bites like a *s*, and stings like
Isa 27. 1 will punish Leviathan the fleeing *s*,
Jn 3.14 Just as Moses lifted up the *s* in the
2 Cor 11. 3 *s* deceived Eve by its cunning, your
Rev 20. 2 the dragon, that ancient *s*, who is the

SERVANT (SERVANTS)

Lev 25.42 For they are my *s*, whom I brought out
25.55 Israel are *s*; they are my *s* whom I
Num 12. 7 Not so with my *s* Moses; he is entrusted
1 Sam 25.24 please let your *s* speak in your ears, and
2 Sam 14. 6 Your *s* had two sons, and they fought
1 Kings 12. 7 "If you will be a *s* to this people today
2 Kings 24. 2 that he spoke by his *s* the prophets.
Job 2. 3 "Have you considered my *s* Job? There
42. 8 my *s* Job shall pray for you, for I will
Ps 19.13 Keep back your *s* also from the
78.70 He chose his *s* David, and took him
86.16 to me; give your strength to your *s*,
109. 28 be put to shame; may your *s* be glad.
143. 12 all my adversaries, for I am your *s*.
Prov 30.10 Do not slander a *s* to a master, or the
Isa 41. 8 But you, Israel, my *s*, Jacob, whom I
42. 1 Here is my *s*, whom I uphold, my
42.19 Who is blind but my *s*, or deaf like my
43.10 LORD, and my *s* whom I have chosen,
44. 1 But now hear, O Jacob my *s*, Israel
52.13 my *s* shall prosper; he shall be exalted
66.14 that the hand of the LORD is with his *s*,
Jer 7.25 persistently sent all my *s* the prophets
25. 4 sent you all his *s* the prophets,
25. 9 Babylon, my *s*, and I will bring them
30.10 have no fear, my *s* Jacob, says the LORD,
Ezek 34.23 one shepherd, my *s* David, and he shall
Dan 6.20 Daniel, *s* of the living God, has your
Zech 3. 8 I am going to bring my *s* the Branch.
Mt 23.11 The greatest among you will be your *s*.
Mk 9.35 be first must be last of all and *s* of all."
10.43 great among you must be your *s*,
Lk 1.38 said, "Here am I, the *s* of the Lord;
1.54 He has helped his *s* Israel, in
2.29 now you are dismissing your *s* in peace,
Jn 13.16 *s* are not greater than their master, nor
15.15 I do not call you *s* any longer, because
Acts 3.26 When God raised up his *s*, he sent him
4.25 through our ancestor David, your *s*:
4.27 gathered against your holy *s* Jesus,
Rom 1. 1 Paul, a *s* of Jesus Christ, called to be an
13. 4 approval, for it is God's *s* for your good.
Col 1.23 I, Paul, became a *s* of this gospel.
2 Tim 2.24 the Lord's *s* must not be quarrelsome
Heb 3. 5 house as a *s*, to testify to the things
Rev 7. 3 marked the *s* of our God with a seal on
22. 3 will be in it, and his *s* will worship him;

SERVANT-GIRL

Mt 26.71 another *s* saw him, and she said to the

SERVE (SERVED SERVES SERVING)

Gen 25.23 the other, the elder shall *s* the younger."
Ex 14.12 us alone and let us *s* the Egyptians'?
28. 1 to *s* me as priests —Aaron and Aaron's
Deut 6.13 him you shall *s*, and by his name alone
20.11 people in it shall *s* you at forced labor.
28.36 where you shall *s* other gods, of wood
Josh 22. 5 to *s* him with all your heart and with all
24. 2 beyond the Euphrates and *s* other gods.
24.15 and my household, we will *s* the LORD."
1 Sam 7. 4 the Astartes, and they *s* the LORD only.
2 Sam 22.44 people whom I had not known *s* me.
1 Kings 12. 4 that he placed on us, and we will *s* you."
2 Kings 17.12 they *s* idols, of which the LORD had said
25.24 live in the land, *s* the king of Babylon,
1 Chr 28. 9 and *s* him with single mind and willing
Job 21.15 is the Almighty, that we should *s* him?
Ps 2.11 *S* the LORD with fear, with trembling
106. 36 They *s* their idols, which became a
Isa 60.12 that will not *s* you shall perish;
Jer 25.11 nations shall *s* the king of Babylon
27. 7 All the nations shall *s* him and his son
30. 9 But they shall *s* the LORD their God and
Dan 3.18 we will not *s* your gods and we will not
7.10 A thousand thousands *s* him, and ten
Mal 3.14 You have said, "It is vain to *s* God.
Mt 8.15 her and she got up and began to *s* him.
20.28 of man came not to be served but to *s*,
Mk 1.31 fever left her; and she began to *s* them.
Lk 4.39 Immediately she got up and began to *s*
16.13 No slave can *s* two masters; for a slave

Lk 22.26 youngest, and the leader like one who *s*.
Jn 12.26 Whoever *s* me must follow me, and
Acts 6. 4 ourselves to prayer and to *s* the word."
26.16 purpose, to appoint you to *s* and testify
Rom 16.18 such people do not *s* our Lord Christ,
Phil 2.22 a father he has *s* with me in the work of
Heb 1.14 in the divine service, sent to *s* for the
6.10 you showed for his sake in *s* the saints,

SERVICE

Ex 1.14 made their lives bitter with hard *s* in
Num 3. 7 of meeting, doing *s* at the tabernacle;
Job 7. 1 "Do not human beings have a hard *s* on
1 Cor 9.13 who are employed in the temple *s* get
16.15 themselves to the *s* of the saints;

SETH

Gen 4.25 she bore a son and named him *S*, for
5. 3 to his image, and named him *S*.
Lk 3.38 son of Enos, son of *S*, the son of Adam,

SETTLED

Gen 13.12 Abram *s* in the land of Canaan, while

SEVEN

Josh 6. 4 march around the city *s* times, the
Ps 119.164 *S* times a day I praise you for your
Mt 16.10 Or the *s* loaves for the four thousand,
18.21 should I forgive? As many as *s* times?"
22.25 Now there were *s* brothers among us;
Lk 20.29 Now there were *s* brothers; the first
Rev 3. 1 has the *s* spirits of God and the *s* stars:

SEVENFOLD

Gen 4.24 If Cain is avenged *s*, truly Lamech
Lev 26.18 continue to punish you *s* for your sins,
Prov 6.31 if they are caught, they will pay *s*; they

SEVENTH

Gen 2. 2 on the *s* day God finished his work that
Ex 20.10 the *s* day is a sabbath to the LORD your
Heb 4. 4 "And God rested on the *s* day from all

SEVENTY

Jer 25.11 shall serve the king of Babylon *s* years.
29.10 when Babylon's *s* years are completed
Dan 9. 2 of Jerusalem, namely, *s* years.
9.24 "*S* weeks are decreed for your people
Lk 10. 1 the Lord appointed *s* others and sent

SEVERE

Gen 12.10 an alien, for famine was *s* in the land.
2 Cor 13.10 I may not have to be *s* in using the

SEX

1 Pet 3. 7 honor to the woman as the weaker *s*,

SHADOW

2 Kings 20.10 rather let the *s* retreat ten intervals."
1 Chr 29.15 our days on earth are like a *s*, and there
Job 14. 2 a flower and withers, flees like a *s* and
Ps 102. 11 My days are like an evening *s*; I wither
Eccl 6.12 their vain life, which they pass like a *s*?
Song 2. 3 With great delight I sat in his *s*, and his
Acts 5.15 that Peter's *s* might fall on some of
Col 2.17 These are only a *s* of what is to come,
Heb 10. 1 Since the law has only a *s* of the good

SHADRACH

Dan 1. 7 Hananiah he called *S*, Mishael he called
2.49 and he appointed *S*, Meshach, and
3.12 the affairs of the province of Babylon: *S*,
3.23 *S*, Meshach, and Abednego, fell down,
3.30 Then the king promoted *S*, Meshach,

SHAKE (SHAKEN SHAKES SHOOK)

Judg 16.20 out as at other times and *s* myself free."
Ps 29. 8 The voice of the LORD *s* the
Am 9. 9 and *s* the house of Israel among all the
Hab 3. 6 He stopped and *s* the earth; he looked
Hag 2. 6 I will *s* the heavens and the earth and
Mt 10.14 *s* off the dust from your feet as you
Acts 2.25 at my right hand so that I will not be *s*;
4.31 they were gathered together was *s*;
Heb 12.26 I will *s* not only the earth but also the

SHAME

2 Sam 19. 5 covered with *s* the faces of all your
2 Chr 32.21 So he returned in *s* to his own land.
Ps 4. 2 you people, shall my honor suffer *s*?
22. 5 you they trusted, and were not put to *s*.
31. 1 refuge; do not let me ever be put to *s*;
31.17 Do not let me ever be put to *s*, O LORD,
53. 5 will be put to *s*, for God has rejected
109. 29 may they be wrapped in their own *s* as
119. 6 Then I shall not be put to *s*, having my
Prov 25. 8 end, when your neighbor puts you to *s*?
Isa 23. 9 glory, to *s* all the honored of the earth,
30. 3 of Pharaoh shall become your *s*,
45.17 you shall not be put to *s* or confounded
49.23 who wait for me shall not be put to *s*.
54. 4 for you will forget the *s* of your youth,
61. 7 Because their *s* was double, and
Jer 50. 2 Babylon is taken, Bel is put to *s*,
Ezek 7.18 *S* shall be on all faces, baldness on all
Hos 4. 7 me; they changed their glory into *s*.
10. 6 Ephraim shall be put to *s*, and Israel
Joel 2.26 my people shall never again be put to *s*.
Lk 13.17 all his opponents were put to *s*; and the
1 Cor 6. 5 I say this to your *s*. Can it be that there
15.34 knowledge of God. I say this to your *s*.
1 Jn 2.28 not be put to *s* before him at the time

SHAMEFUL

2 Cor 4. 2 We have renounced the *s* things that

SHARE (SHARED SHARING)

1 Kings 12.16 "What *s* have we in David? We have no
Jn 4. 9 (Jews do not *s* things in common with
Rom 15.26 to *s* their resources with the poor
15.27 Gentiles have come to *s* in their
1 Cor 9.13 who serve at the altar *s* in what is
10.16 is it not a *s* in the body of Christ?
2 Cor 1. 7 as you *s* in our sufferings, so also you
9.13 by the generosity of your *s* with them
Gal 6. 6 who are taught the word must *s* in all
Phil 1. 5 because of your *s* in the gospel from the
2. 1 from love, any *s* in the Spirit,
3.10 and the *s* of his sufferings by becoming
4.15 Macedonia, no church *s* with me in the
Col 1.12 you to *s* in the inheritance of the saints
Heb 2.14 the children *s* flesh and blood, he
13.16 to do good and to *s* what you have,
1 Pet 4.13 insofar as you are *s* Christ's sufferings,

SHARP

Ps 45. 5 Your arrows are *s* in the heart of the
140. 3 They make their tongue *s* as a snake's,

SHATTER (SHATTERED SHATTERING)

Ps 68.21 God will *s* the heads of his enemies, the
Dan 12. 7 when the *s* of the power of the holy
Ob 9 Your warriors shall be *s*, O Teman, so
Mal 1. 4 says, "We are *s* but we will rebuild

SHAVE (SHAVED SHAVING)

2 Sam 10. 4 David's envoys, *s* off half the beard
Isa 7.20 Lord will *s* with a razor hired beyond
Ezek 44.20 They shall not *s* their heads or let their
Acts 21.24 them, and pay for the *s* of their heads.

SHEAVES

Ps 126. 6 with shouts of joy, carrying their *s*.

SHEBA

1 Kings 10. 1 When the queen of *S* heard of the fame
Ps 72.10 may the kings of *S* and Seba bring gifts.

Jer 6.20 me is frankincense that comes from *S*,

SHECHEM

Gen 37.12 to pasture their father's flock near *S*.
Judg 9.41 kinsfolk, so they could not live on at *S*.
Acts 7.16 their bodies were brought back to *S* and

SHED

Deut 21. 7 "Our hands did not *s* this blood, nor
2 Kings 21.16 Manasseh *s* very much innocent blood,

SHEEP

Num 27.17 may not be like *s* without a shepherd."
1 Sam 16.19 me your son David who is with the *s*."
2 Sam 7. 8 from following the *s* to be prince over
24.17 but these *s*, what have they done? Let
1 Kings 22.17 like *s* that have no shepherd;
1 Chr 21.17 But these *s*, what have they done? Let
2 Chr 18.16 mountains, like *s* without a shepherd;
Ps 44.11 You have made us like *s* for slaughter,
44.22 and accounted as *s* for the slaughter.
49.14 Like *s* they are appointed for Sheol;
74. 1 does your anger smoke against the *s*
78.52 Then he led out his people like *s*, and
95. 7 of his pasture, and the *s* of his hand.
100. 3 are his people, and the *s* of his pasture.
119.176 I have gone astray like a lost *s*; seek out
Isa 53. 6 we like *s* have gone astray; we have all
Jer 12. 3 Pull them out like *s* for the slaughter,
23. 1 destroy and scatter the *s* of my pasture!
50. 6 My people have been lost *s*; their
Ezek 34.31 You are my *s*, the *s* of my pasture and I
Mt 9.36 and helpless, like *s* without a shepherd.
10. 6 to the lost *s* of the house of Israel.
12.11 has only one *s* and it falls into a pit on
25.32 as a shepherd separates the *s* from the
26.31 and the *s* of the flock will be scattered.'
Mk 14.27 shepherd, and the *s* will be scattered.'
Lk 15. 4 having a hundred *s*, and losing one of
Jn 10.15 Father. And I lay down my life for the *s*.
10.27 My *s* hear my voice. I know them and
21.16 love you." Jesus said to him, "Tend my *s*."
Acts 8.32 "Like a *s* he was led to the slaughter,
Rom 8.36 are accounted as *s* to be slaughtered."
1 Pet 2.25 you were going astray like *s*, but now

SHEEPFOLD (SHEEPFOLDS)

Ps 78.70 servant David, and took him from the *s*;
Jn 10. 1 who does not enter the *s* by the gate

SHEET

Acts 10.11 something like a large *s* coming down,

SHEKEL

Ex 30.13 half a *s* according to the *s* of the

SHELTER

Ps 27. 5 For he will hide me in his *s* in the day
31.20 In the *s* of your presence you hide them
91. 1 You who live in the *s* of the Most High,
Isa 25. 4 a *s* from the rainstorm and a shade

SHEM

Gen 9.26 "Blessed by the LORD my God be *S*; and

SHEOL

Job 26. 6 *S* is naked before God, and Abaddon
Ps 9.17 The wicked shall depart to *S*, all the
16.10 For you do not give me up to *S*, or let
139. 8 if I make my bed in *S*, you are there. If
Prov 5. 5 to death; her steps follow the path to *S*.
7.27 Her house is the way to *S*, going down
15.11 *S* and Abaddon lie open before the
Isa 5.14 *S* has enlarged its appetite and opened
14. 9 *S* beneath is stirred up to meet you
28.15 and with *S* we have an agreement;
57. 9 far away, and sent down even to *S*.
Ezek 32.21 out of the midst of *S*: "They have come
Hos 13.14 O *S*, where is your destruction?

SHEPHERD (SHEPHERDS)

Gen 46.32 The men are *s*, for they have been
Num 14.33 your children shall be *s* in the
27.17 LORD may not be like sheep without a *s*."
2 Sam 5. 2 you who shall be *s* of my people Israel,
Ps 23. 1 The LORD is my *s*, I shall not want. He
80. 1 Give ear, O *S* of Israel, you who lead
Isa 40.11 feed his flock like a *s*; he will gather
44.28 says of Cyrus, "He is my *s*, and he shall
56.11 *s* also have no understanding; they have
63.11 them up out of the sea with the *s*
Jer 10.21 For the *s* are stupid, and do not inquire
23. 1 Woe to the *s* who destroy and scatter
23. 4 I will raise up *s* over them who will *s*
25.34 Wail, you *s*, and cry out; roll in ashes,
51.23 with you I smash *s* and their flocks;
Ezek 34. 2 prophesy against the *s* of Israel:
34. 7 you *s*, hear the word of the LORD:
34.23 I will set up over them one *s*, my
Am 1. 1 Amos, who was among the *s* of Tekoa,
Mic 7.14 *S* your people with your staff, the flock
Nah 3.18 Your *s* are asleep, O king of Assyria;
Zech 10. 2 like sheep; they suffer for lack of a *s*.
11. 7 I became the *s* of the flock doomed to
11.16 a *s* who does not care for the perishing,
13. 7 "Awake, O sword, against my *s*, against
Mt 2. 6 a ruler who is to *s* my people Israel.' "
9.36 and helpless, like sheep without a *s*.
26.31 "I will strike the *s*, and the sheep of the
Mk 6.34 they were like sheep without a *s*;
14.27 'I will strike the *s*, and the sheep will
Lk 2. 8 there were *s* living in the fields, keeping
2.20 The *s* returned, glorifying and praising
Jn 10. 2 The one who enters by the gate is the *s*
10.11 "I am the good *s*. The good *s* lays down
Acts 20.28 you overseers, to *s* the church of God
Heb 13.20 Jesus, the great *s* of the sheep, by the
1 Pet 5. 4 when the chief *s* appears, you will win
Rev 7.17 will be their *s*, and he will guide them

SHIBBOLETH

Judg 12. 6 "Then say *S*," and he said, "Sibboleth,"

SHIELD

2 Sam 22. 3 my *s* and the horn of my salvation, my
Ps 3. 3 But you, O LORD, are a *s* around me, my
5.12 you cover them with favor as with a *s*.
7.10 God is my *s*, who saves the upright in
18. 2 my rock in whom I take refuge, my *s*,
18.30 true; he is a *s* for all who take refuge
18.35 have given me the *s* of your salvation,
28. 7 The LORD is my strength and my *s*; in
35. 2 Take hold of *s* and buckler, and rise up
84.11 the LORD God is a sun and *s*; he bestows
89.18 For our *s* belongs to the LORD, our king
91. 4 his faithfulness is a *s* and buckler. You
115. 9 in the LORD! He is their help and their *s*.
Prov 2. 7 the upright; he is a *s* to those who walk
Zech 12. 8 LORD will *s* the inhabitants of Jerusalem
Eph 6.16 take the *s* of faith, with which you will

SHILOH

Josh 18. 8 lots for you here before the LORD in *S*."
1 Sam 1. 3 to sacrifice to the LORD of hosts at *S*,
14. 3 the priest of the LORD in *S*, carrying an
Ps 78.60 He abandoned his dwelling at *S*, the
Jer 26. 6 I will make this house like *S*, and I will

SHINE (SHINED)

Num 6.25 the LORD make his face to *s* upon you,
Job 22.28 for you, and light will *s* on your ways.
Eccl 8. 1 Wisdom makes one's face *s*, and the
Isa 9. 2 of deep darkness— on them light has *s*.
Dan 12. 3 Those who are wise shall *s* like the
Zech 9.16 of a crown they shall *s* on his land.
Mt 5.16 same way, let your light *s* before others,
13.43 Then the righteous will *s* like the sun in

Eph 5.14 from the dead, and Christ will *s* on you."
Phil 2.15 in which you *s* like stars in the world.

SHIP (SHIPS)

1 Kings 22.48 Jehoshaphat made *s* of the Tarshish
Ps 104. 26 There go the *s*, and Leviathan that you
107. 23 Some went down to the sea in *s*, doing
Prov 30.19 way of a *s* on the high seas, and the
Ezek 30. 9 messengers shall go out from me in *s* to

SHIPWRECK (SHIPWRECKED)

2 Cor 11.25 Three times I was *s*; for a night and a
1 Tim 1.19 persons have suffered *s* in the faith;

SHIRT

Lk 6.29 your coat do not withhold even your *s*

SHORT (SHORTENED)

Isa 50. 2 Is my hand *s*, that it cannot redeem?
Mt 24.22 And if those days had not been cut *s*,
Mk 13.20 if the Lord had not cut *s* those days, no

SHOUT (SHOUTED SHOUTS)

Josh 6.16 "*S*; for the LORD has given you the city.
Isa 12. 6 *S* aloud and sing for joy, O royal Zion,
42.13 he cries out, he *s* aloud, he shows
Mt 20.30 passing by, they *s*, "Lord, have mercy
Lk 19.40 were silent, the stones would *s* out."

SHOW (SHOWED SHOWN SHOWS)

Ex 33.18 Moses said, "*S* me your glory, I pray."
Deut 34. 1 the LORD *s* him the whole land: Gilead
Mic 6. 8 He has *s* you, O mortal, what is good;
7.15 land of Egypt, *s* us marvelous things.
Mt 8. 4 but go, *s* yourself to the priest, and
Lk 1.72 he has *s* the mercy promised to our
24.40 said this, he *s* them his hands and his
Jn 14. 8 "Lord, *s* us the Father, and we will be
Acts 10.28 but God has *s* me that I should not call
Rom 3.25 He did this to *s* his righteousness,
5. 8 But God *s* his love for us in that while
Gal 2. 6 God *s* no partiality)—those leaders

SHOWERS

Jer 3. 3 Therefore the *s* have been withheld, and
Ezek 34.26 their season; they shall be *s* of blessing.
Hos 6. 3 he will come to us like the *s*, like the
Mic 5. 7 dew from the LORD, like *s* on the grass,

SHRIVELED

Ps 22.16 My hands and feet have *s*; I can count

SHUN

1 Cor 6.18 *S* fornication! Every sin that a person
1 Tim 6.11 for you, man of God, *s* all this; pursue

SHUT

Gen 7.16 him; and the LORD *s* him in.
Isa 22.22 open, and no one shall *s*; he shall *s*,

SICK

2 Kings 20. 1 Hezekiah became *s* and was at the
Ps 107. 17 Some were *s* through their sinful ways,
Prov 13.12 Hope deferred makes the heart *s*, but
Isa 1. 5 The whole head is *s*, and the whole
Jer 8.18 is gone, grief is upon me, my heart is *s*.
Mt 9.12 of a physician, but those who are *s*.
Lk 4.40 all those who had any who were *s* with
5.31 of a physician, but those who are *s*;
Acts 5.15 they even carried out the *s* into the
Jas 5.14 Are any among you *s*? They should call

SICKLE

Deut 23.25 you shall not put a *s* to your neighbor's
Joel 3.13 Put in the *s*, for the harvest is ripe. Go
Rev 14.15 "Use your *s* and reap, for the hour to

SICKNESS

Eccl 5.17 in much vexation and *s* and resentment.

Isa 10.16 wasting *s* among his stout warriors,
Hos 5.13 When Ephraim saw his *s*, and Judah his

SIDE

Ps 124. 1 not been the LORD who was on our *s*,
Jn 19.34 one of the soldiers pierced his *s*

SIDON

Gen 10.15 Canaan became the father of *S* his
Mt 11.21 in you had been done in Tyre and *S*,
15.21 went away to the district of Tyre and *S*.
Mk 3. 8 and the region around Tyre and *S*.
Lk 4.26 except to a widow at Zarephath in *S*,
Acts 27. 3 The next day we put in at *S*; and Julius

SIDONIANS

Deut 3. 9 (the *S* call Hermon Sirion, while the
Judg 18. 7 they were far from the *S* and had no
1 Kings 5. 6 knows how to cut timber like the *S*."
2 Kings 23.13 for Astarte the abomination of the *S*,

SIGH (SIGHING)

Ps 31.10 spent with sorrow, and my years with *s*;
90. 9 our years come to an end like a *s*.

SIGHT

Gen 6. 8 Noah found favor in the *s* of the LORD.
Deut 34. 7 his *s* was unimpaired and his vigor had
1 Kings 15.11 did what was right in the *s* of the LORD,
Eccl 6. 9 Better is the *s* of the eyes than the
Isa 65.16 are forgotten and are hidden from my *s*.
2 Cor 8.21 not only in the Lord's *s* but also in the

SIGN

Gen 9.12 "This is the *s* of the covenant that I
Ex 4. 8 first *s*, they may believe the second *s*.
31.13 for this is a *s* between me and you
Num 16.38 Thus they shall be a *s* to the Israelites.
Josh 4. 6 this may be a *s* among you. When your
Judg 6.17 then show me a *s* that it is you who
1 Sam 2.34 shall be the *s* to you—both of them
1 Kings 13. 3 He gave a *s* the same day, saying, "This
Isa 7.11 Ask a *s* of the LORD your God; let it be
7.14 the Lord himself will give you a *s*.
37.30 this shall be the *s* for you: This year eat
38. 7 "This is the *s* to you from the LORD, that
55.13 everlasting *s* that shall not be cut off.
Jer 44.29 This shall be the *s* to you, says the
Ezek 4. 3 it. This is a *s* for the house of Israel.
12. 6 the land; for I have made you a *s* for
14. 8 make them a *s* and a byword and cut
24.24 Ezekiel shall be a *s* to you; you shall do
Mt 12.39 but no *s* will be given to it except the *s*
16. 1 asked him to show them a *s* from
24. 3 what will be the *s* of your coming and
26.48 Now the betrayer had given them a *s*,
Mk 8.11 asking him for a *s* from heaven, to test
13. 4 what will be the *s* that all these things
14.44 betrayer had given them a *s*, saying,
Lk 2.12 This will be a *s* for you: you will find a
2.34 and to be a *s* that will be opposed
11.16 demanding from him a *s* from heaven.
11.29 it asks for a *s*, but no *s* will be given to
21. 7 what will be the *s* that this is about to
23. 8 was hoping to see him perform some *s*.
Jn 2.18 "What *s* can you show us for doing this?"
10.41 "John performed no *s*, but everything
Acts 4.16 a notable *s* has been done through
Rom 4.11 He received the *s* of circumcision as a
1 Cor 14.22 Tongues, then, are not a *s* for believers

SIGNS

Gen 1.14 and let them be for *s* and for seasons
Isa 8.18 whom the LORD has given me are *s*
Jer 10. 2 or be dismayed at the *s* of the heavens;
Dan 4. 3 How great are his *s*, how mighty his
Mt 16. 3 you cannot interpret the *s* of the times.
Mk 13.22 false prophets will appear and produce *s*

Mk 16.17 these *s* will accompany those who
Jn 2.11 Jesus did this, the first of his *s*, in Cana
2.23 they saw the *s* that he was doing.
4.48 "Unless you see *s* and wonders you will
6. 2 following him, because they saw the *s*
20.30 Now Jesus did many other *s* in the
Acts 5.12 Now many *s* and wonders were done
15.12 of all the *s* and wonders God had done
1 Cor 1.22 Jews demand *s* and Greeks desire
Rev 13.13 It performs great *s*, even making fire
13.14 by the *s* that it is allowed to perform on
16.14 demonic spirits, performing *s*, who go

SIGNAL

Isa 5.26 He will raise a *s* for a nation far away,
11.10 the root of Jesse shall stand as a *s* to
13. 2 On a bare hill raise a *s*, cry aloud to
18. 3 when a *s* is raised on the mountains,
Zech 10. 8 I will *s* for them and gather them in, for

SIGNET

Jer 22.24 Judah were the *s* ring on my right hand,
Dan 6.17 king sealed it with his own *s* and with

SILAS (SILVANUS)

Acts 15.22 sent Judas called Barsabbas, and *S*,
15.40 But Paul chose *S* and set out, the
16.19 they seized Paul and *S* and dragged
17. 4 were persuaded and joined Paul and *S*,
18. 5 When *S* and Timothy arrived from
2 Cor 1.19 we proclaimed among you, *S* and
1 Thess 1. 1 Paul, *S* and Timothy, To the church of
1 Pet 5.12 Through *S*, whom I consider a faithful

SILENCE (SILENCED)

1 Kings 19.12 and after the fire the sound of sheer *s*.
Esth 4.14 if you keep *s* at such a time as this,
Ps 32. 3 While I kept *s*, my body wasted away
83. 1 O God, do not keep *s*; do not hold your
Hab 2.20 let all the earth keep *s* before him.
Rom 3.19 that every mouth may be *s*, and the
1 Tim 2.11 Let a woman learn in *s* with full
Rev 8. 1 seal, there was *s* in heaven for about

SILENT

2 Kings 18.36 the people were *s* and answered him
Ps 4. 4 sin; ponder it on your beds, and be *s*.
39. 2 I was *s* and still; I held my peace to no
Prov 17.28 fools who keep *s* are considered wise;
Zeph 1. 7 Be *s* before the Lord GOD! For the day
Zech 2.13 Be *s*, all people, before the LORD; for he
Mt 26.63 But Jesus was *s*. Then the high priest
Mk 1.25 saying, "Be *s*, and come out of him!"
1 Cor 14.28 is no one to interpret, let them be *s*
14.34 women should be *s* in the churches.

SILLY

2 Tim 3. 6 and captivate *s* women, overwhelmed by

SILOAM

Lk 13. 4 were killed when the tower of *S* fell
Jn 9. 7 to him, "Go, wash in the pool of *S*"

SILVER

Ps 12. 6 are promises that are pure, *s* refined
Prov 8.19 fine gold, and my yield than choice *s*.
Isa 1.22 Your *s* has become dross, your wine is
Jer 6.30 They are called "rejected *s*," for the LORD
Hag 2. 8 The *s* is mine, and the gold is mine,
Mt 26.15 you?" They paid him thirty pieces of *s*.
27. 3 and brought back the thirty pieces of *s*
Lk 15. 8 having ten *s* coins, if she loses one
Acts 3. 6 Peter said, "I have no *s* or gold, but

SILVERSMITH

Judg 17. 4 gave it to a *s*, who made it into an idol
Acts 19.24 Demetrius, a *s*, who made silver shrines

SIMEON (Son of Jacob)

Born, Gen 29.33; with Levi, took revenge on Shechem, Gen 34; detained as a hostage, Gen 42.24; his future predicted, Gen 49.5-7.

SIMEON (the Prophet)

Lk 2.25 Jerusalem whose name was *S*; this man
2.34 Then *S* blessed them and said to his

SIMON

Mt 10. 4 *S* the Cananaean, and Judas Iscariot,
Mk 3.18 Thaddaeus, and *S* the Cananaean, and
Acts 1.13 Alphaeus, and *S* the Zealot, and Judas

SIMPLE

Ps 19. 7 of the LORD are pure, making wise the *s*;
116. 6 The LORD protects the *s*; when I was
119.130 light; it imparts understanding to the *s*.
Prov 1.22 "How long, O *s* ones, will you love
9. 4 "You that are *s*, turn in here!" To those

SIN (n)

Gen 4. 7 do not do well, *s* is lurking at the door;
31.36 What is my *s*, that you have hotly
Lev 24.15 who curses God shall bear the *s*.
Num 12.11 do not punish us for a *s* that we have so
32.23 and be sure your *s* will find you out.
1 Sam 2.17 the *s* of the young men was very great
1 Kings 8.36 forgive the *s* of your servants, your
17.18 to me to bring my *s* to remembrance,
2 Kings 21.16 besides the *s* that he caused Judah to *s*
2 Chr 6.25 forgive the *s* of your people, and bring
Job 10. 6 out my iniquity and search for my *s*,
13.23 me know my transgression and my *s*.
Ps 32. 5 Then I acknowledged my *s* to you, and I
38.18 confess my iniquity; I am sorry for my *s*.
Prov 5.22 they are caught in the toils of their *s*.
20. 9 my heart clean; I am pure from my *s*"?
24. 9 The devising of folly is *s*, and the
Eccl 5. 6 Do not let your mouth lead you into *s*,
Isa 5.18 who drag *s* as with cart ropes,
30. 1 but against my will, adding *s* to *s*;
Jer 17. 1 The *s* of Judah is written with an iron
Mic 6. 7 fruit of my body for the *s* of my soul?"
Mt 12.31 forgiven for every *s* and blasphemy, but
13.41 out of his kingdom all causes of *s*
Jn 1.29 God who takes away the *s* of the world!
8. 7 anyone among you who is without *s*
8.21 for me, but you will die in your *s*.
8.46 Which of you convicts me of *s*? If I tell
15.22 but now they have no excuse for their *s*.
16. 8 he will prove the world wrong about *s*
Acts 7.60 "Lord, do not hold this *s* against them."
Rom 3. 9 and Greeks, are under the power of *s*,
5.12 just as *s* came into the world through
6.14 For *s* will have no dominion over you,
6.23 For the wages of *s* is death, but the free
7. 7 for the law, I would not have known *s*.
7.13 It was *s*, working death in me through
14.23 does not proceed from faith is *s*.
2 Cor 5.21 he made him to be *s* who knew no *s*, so
Gal 3.22 all things under the power of *s*,
1 Tim 5.20 As for those who persist in *s*, rebuke
Heb 3.13 be hardened by the deceitfulness of *s*.
4.15 been tested as we are, yet without *s*.
12. 4 In your struggle against *s* you have not
1 Pet 2.22 "He committed no *s*; and no deceit was
1 Jn 1. 8 If we say we have no *s*, we deceive
3. 5 away sins, and in him there is no *s*.
5.16 what is not a mortal *s*, you will ask, and

SINS (n)

Lev 26.21 to plague you sevenfold for your *s*.
2 Kings 13. 6 did not depart from the *s* of the house
2 Chr 25. 4 all shall be put to death for their own *s*."
28.10 What have you except *s* against the
Ps 25. 7 Do not remember the *s* of my youth or

Ps 79. 9 deliver us, and forgive our *s*, for your
103. 10 not deal with us according to our *s*,
Isa 38.17 have cast all my *s* behind your back.
43.24 burdened me with your *s*; you have
58. 1 rebellion, to the house of Jacob their *s*.
Lam 4.13 It was for the *s* of her prophets and the
Dan 4.27 atone for your *s* with righteousness, and
Am 5.12 and how great are your *s*— you who
Mt 1.21 for he will save his people from their *s*."
Mk 2. 5 the paralytic, "Son, your *s* are forgiven."
3.28 people will be forgiven for their *s* and
Lk 5.20 said, "Friend, your *s* are forgiven you."
Jn 20.23 If you forgive the *s* of any, they are
Acts 22.16 be baptized, have your *s* washed away,
1 Cor 15.17 faith is futile and you are still in your *s*.
Gal 1. 4 who gave himself for our *s* to set us free
Eph 2. 1 were dead through the trespasses and *s*
Heb 9. 7 that he offers for himself and for the *s*
10.17 their *s* and their lawless deeds
1 Pet 2.24 He himself bore our *s* in his body on
3.18 Christ also suffered for *s* once for all,

SIN (SINS SINNING) (v)

Gen 39. 9 great wickedness, and *s* against God?"
Lev 4. 2 When anyone *s* unintentionally in any
Deut 20.18 you thus *s* against the LORD your God.
1 Sam 2.25 but if someone *s* against the LORD, who
12.23 me that I should *s* against the LORD
14.33 the troops are *s* against the LORD by
19. 4 "The king should not *s* against his
1 Kings 8.46 there is no one who does not *s*—
2 Chr 6.36 "If they *s* against you— for there is no
Job 7.20 If I *s*, what do I do to you, you watcher
10.14 If I *s*, you watch me, and do not acquit
Ps 119. 11 heart, so that I might not *s* against you.
Eccl 7.20 righteous as to do good without ever *s*.
Mt 5.29 If your right eye causes you to *s*, tear it
18.15 another member of the church *s* against
Lk 17. 3 If another disciple *s*, you must rebuke
Jn 5.14 been made well! Do not *s* any more,
1 Cor 6.18 but the fornicator *s* against the body
8.12 when it is weak, you *s* against Christ.
Heb 10.26 if we willfully persist in *s* after having
1 Jn 2. 1 things to you so that you may not *s*.
3. 6 no one who *s* has either seen him or
3. 9 who have been born of God do not *s*,

SINNED

Ex 9.27 said to them, "This time I have *s*;
32.30 "You have *s* a great sin. But now I will
Num 14.40 that God has promised, for we have *s*."
22.34 "I have *s*, for I did not know that you
Deut 1.41 "We have *s* against the LORD! We are
9.16 that you had indeed *s* against the LORD
Josh 7.11 Israel has *s*; they have transgressed my
Judg 10.10 "We have *s* against you, because we
1 Sam 7. 6 and said, "We have *s* against the LORD."
15.24 Saul said to Samuel, "I have *s*; for I
24.11 I have not *s* against you, though you are
2 Sam 12.13 to Nathan, "I have *s* against the LORD."
24.10 "I have *s* greatly in what I have done.
1 Kings 14.16 which he *s* and which he caused Israel
2 Kings 17. 7 people of Israel had *s* against the LORD
1 Chr 21. 8 David said to God, "I have *s* greatly in
Neh 1. 6 of Israel, which we have *s* against you.
Job 33.27 'I *s*, and perverted what was right, and
35. 6 If you have *s*, what do you accomplish
Ps 78.32 In spite of all this they still *s*; they did
Isa 42.24 not the LORD, against whom we have *s*,
Jer 8.14 because we have *s* against the LORD.
14. 7 are many, and we have *s* against you.
Lam 1. 8 Jerusalem *s* grievously, so she has
5. 7 Our ancestors *s*; they are no more, and
Dan 9. 5 we have *s* and done wrong, acted
Hos 10. 9 the days of Gibeah you have *s*, O Israel;
Mic 7. 9 the LORD, because I have *s* against him,
Mt 27. 4 "I have *s* in betraying innocent blood."
Lk 15.18 "Father, I have *s* against heaven and
Jn 9. 2 who *s*, this man or his parents, that he
Rom 2.12 All who have *s* apart from the law will
3.23 all have *s* and fall short of the glory of

SIN OFFERING

Ex 29.14 with fire outside the camp; it is a *s*.
Lev 4. 3 herd without blemish as a *s* to the LORD.
5. 6 from the flock, a sheep or a goat, as a *s*;
6.25 the ritual of the *s*. The *s* shall be

SINAI

Ex 19. 1 day, they came into the wilderness of *S*.
19.20 the LORD descended upon Mount *S*,
34.29 Moses came down from Mount *S*. As he
Deut 33. 2 The LORD came from *S*, and dawned
Ps 68. 8 at the presence of God, the God of *S*,
Gal 4.24 is Hagar, from Mount *S*, bearing

SINFUL

Isa 1. 4 Ah, *s* nation, people laden with iniquity,
Lk 5. 8 away from me, Lord, for I am a *s* man!
1 Tim 1. 9 for the godless and the *s*, for the unholy

SING

Num 21.17 this song: "Spring up, O well! —*S* to it!
1 Chr 16. 9 *S* to him, *s* praises to him, tell of all his
2 Chr 20.21 appointed those who were to *s* to the
Job 29.13 and I caused the widow's heart to *s* for
Ps 59.16 But I will *s* of your might; I will *s* aloud
75. 9 I will *s* praises to the God of Jacob.
81. 1 *S* aloud to God our strength; shout for
89. 1 I will *s* of your steadfast love, O LORD,
95. 1 O come, let us *s* to the LORD; let us
96. 2 *S* to the LORD, bless his name; tell of his
108. 1 is steadfast; I will *s* and make melody.
Prov 29. 6 a snare, but the righteous *s* and rejoice.
Isa 12. 5 *S* praises to the LORD, for he has done
26.19 in the dust, awake and *s* for joy!
35. 6 the tongue of the speechless *s* for joy.
38.20 and we will *s* to stringed instruments
42.10 *S* to the LORD a new song, his praise
44.23 *S*, O heavens, for the LORD has done it;
52. 8 together they *s* for joy; for in plain sight
54. 1 *S*, O barren one who did not bear; burst
65.14 servants shall *s* for gladness of heart,
Jer 20.13 *S* to the LORD; praise the LORD! For he
Zech 2.10 *S* and rejoice, O daughter Zion! For lo, I
Rom 15. 9 you among the Gentiles, and *s* praises
1 Cor 14.15 but I will *s* praise with the mind also.
Rev 14. 3 they *s* a new song before the throne and

SINGING

Song 2.12 the time of *s* has come, and the voice
Isa 14. 7 rest and quiet; they break forth into *s*.
Zeph 3.17 he will exult over you with loud *s* as on
Acts 16.25 Silas were praying and *s* hymns to God,

SINNER (SINNERS)

Ps 25. 8 therefore he instructs *s* in the way.
104. 35 Let *s* be consumed from the earth, and
Prov 13.21 Misfortune pursues *s*, but prosperity
Eccl 2.26 but to the *s* he gives the work of
Isa 13. 9 desolation, and to destroy its *s* from it.
Mt 9.10 many tax collectors and *s* came and
9.13 come to call not the righteous but *s*."
Mk 2.15 tax collectors and *s* were also sitting
2.17 come to call not the righteous but *s*."
14.41 of Man is betrayed into the hands of *s*.
Lk 6.32 For even *s* love those who love them.
6.34 Even *s* lend to *s*, to receive as much
7.37 a woman in the city, who was a *s*,
13. 2 were worse *s* than all other Galileans?
15. 2 "This fellow welcomes *s* and eats
15. 7 more joy in heaven over one *s* who
19. 7 gone to be the guest of one who is a *s*."
Jn 9.16 "How can a man who is a *s* perform
9.24 to God! We know that this man is a *s*."

Rom 3. 7 why am I still being condemned as a *s*?
5.19 disobedience the many were made *s*,
Gal 2.17 we ourselves have been found to be *s*, is
Jas 5.20 whoever brings back a *s* from wandering

SISTER (SISTERS)

Gen 12.13 Say you are my *s*, so that it may go well
20. 2 said of his wife Sarah, "She is my *s*."
26. 7 about his wife, he said, "She is my *s*";
Ex 2. 4 His *s* stood at a distance, to see what
Prov 7. 4 Say to wisdom, "You are my *s*," and call
Song 4. 9 have ravished my heart, my *s*, my bride,
8. 8 We have a little *s*, she has no breasts.
Ezek 16.48 your *s* Sodom and her daughters has
Mk 3.35 God is my brother, and *s*, and mother."
Acts 23.16 the son of Paul's *s* heard about the
1 Cor 9. 5n right to be accompanied by a *s* as wife,
1 Thess 4. 6 no one wrong or exploit a brother or *s*
1 Tim 5. 2 mothers, to younger women as *s*—
2 Jn 13 children of your elect *s* send their

SIT (SAT SITTING)

Judg 21. 2 and *s* there till evening before God, and
Ps 110. 1 "*S* at my right hand, until I make your
Isa 6. 1 I saw the Lord *s* on a throne, high and
Jer 15.17 I did not *s* in the company of
Ezek 3.15 river Chebar. And I *s* among them,
Mic 4. 4 they shall all *s* under their own vines
Mk 10.37 "Grant us to *s*, one at your right hand
12.36 said to my Lord, "*S* at my right hand,
16.19 heaven and *s* down at the right hand
Lk 7.32 are like children *s* in the marketplace
20.42 said to my Lord, "*S* at my right hand,
Acts 2.34 said to my Lord, "*S* at my right hand,
Heb 1. 3 he *s* down at the right hand of the
10.12 "he *s* down at the right hand of God,"

SIXTH

Lk 1.26 In the *s* month the angel Gabriel was

SKETCH

Heb 8. 5 is a *s* and shadow of the heavenly one;

SKILL (SKILLFUL)

1 Sam 16.16 someone who is *s* in playing the lyre;
1 Kings 7.14 he was full of *s*, intelligence, and
Ps 78.72 them, and guided them with a *s* hand.
Prov 22.29 you see those who are *s* in their work?

SKIN (SKINS)

Gen 3.21 God made garments of *s* for the man
21.14 took bread and a *s* of water, and gave it
Job 2. 4 "*S* for *s*! All that people have they will
7. 5 and dirt; my *s* hardens, then breaks out
19.20 I have escaped by the *s* of my teeth.
Jer 13.23 Can Ethiopians change their *s* or the
Mk 2.22 otherwise, the wine will burst the *s*,

SKULL

Mt 27.33 Golgotha (which means Place of a *S*),
Mk 15.22 (which means the place of a *s*).
Lk 23.33 is called The *S*, they crucified Jesus
Jn 19.17 out to what is called the Place of the *S*,

SKY (SKIES)

Gen 1. 8 God called the dome *S*. And there was
2 Kings 7. 2 LORD were to make windows in the *s*,
Ps 85.11 will look down from the *s*.
Isa 34. 4 rot away, and the *s* roll up like a scroll.
Lk 12.56 interpret the appearance of earth and *s*;
Rev 6.14 The *s* vanished like a scroll rolling itself

SLANDER (SLANDERED SLANDERS)

Ps 15. 3 who do not *s* with their tongue, and do
50.20 your kin; you *s* your own mother's child.
101. 5 who secretly *s* a neighbor I will destroy.
Prov 30.10 Do not *s* a servant to his master, or the
1 Cor 4.13 we endure; when *s*, we speak kindly.
2 Pet 2.10 they are not afraid to *s* the glorious

SLANDERER (SLANDERERS)

Lev 19.16 You shall not go around as a *s* among
Rom 1.30 they are gossips, *s*, God-haters, insolent,

SLAP

2 Cor 11.20 or puts on airs, or gives you a *s* in the

SLAUGHTER (SLAUGHTERED)

Ps 44.22 long, and accounted as sheep for the *s*.
Jer 11.19 I was like a gentle lamb led to the *s*.
Rom 8.36 we are accounted as sheep to be *s*."
Rev 6. 9 those who had been *s* for the word of
13. 8 in book of life of the Lamb that was *s*.

SLAVE (SLAVES)

Gen 9.25 "Cursed be Canaan; lowest of *s* shall he
21.10 Cast out this *s* woman with her son; for
Deut 5.15 Remember you were a *s* in the land of
6.21 "We were Pharaoh's *s* in Egypt, but the
21.14 You must not treat her as a *s*, since you
Josh 9.23 some of you shall always be *s*, hewers
Prov 19.10 luxury, much less for a *s* to rule over
Eccl 10. 7 I have seen *s* on horseback, and princes
Jer 2.14 Is Israel a *s*? Is he a homeborn servant?
34.11 and took back the male and female *s*
Lam 5. 8 *S* rule over us; there is no one to deliver
Mt 20.27 to be first among you must be your *s*;
21.34 he sent his *s* to the tenants to collect
25.14 summoned his *s* and entrusted his
25.23 'Well done, good and trustworthy *s*;
Mk 10.44 wishes be first among you must be *s*
12. 2 he sent a *s* to the tenants, to collect
14.47 struck the *s* of the high priest, cutting
Lk 17. 9 Do you thank the *s* for doing what was
19.17 "Well done, good *s*! Because you have
20.10 he sent a *s* to the tenants in order that
22.50 of them struck the *s* of the high priest
Jn 8.34 everyone who commits sin is a *s* to sin.
Rom 6.16 yourselves to anyone as obedient *s*,
7. 6 we are *s* not under the old written code
1 Cor 7.21 Were you a *s* when called? Do not be
2 Cor 4. 5 Christ as Lord and ourselves as your *s*
Gal 3.28 there is no longer *s* or free, there is no
4. 1 as they are minors, are no better than *s*,
Eph 6. 5 *S*, obey your earthly masters with fear
Col 3.22 *S*, obey your earthly masters in
Titus 2. 9 Tell *s* to be submissive to their masters
Philem 16 no longer as a *s* but more than a *s*, a
1 Pet 2.18 *S*, accept the authority of your masters
2 Pet 2.19 but they themselves are *s* of corruption;

SLAVE-GIRL

Gen 16. 2 from bearing children; go in to my *s*;

SLAVERY

Ex 20. 2 the land of Egypt, out of the house of *s*.
Deut 5. 6 the land of Egypt, out of the house of *s*.
Rom 8.15 you did not receive a spirit of *s* to fall
Gal 5. 1 and do not submit again to a yoke of *s*.
Heb 2.15 lives were held in *s* by the fear of death.

SLEEP (n)

Gen 2.21 God caused a deep *s* to fall upon the
1 Sam 26.12 a deep *s* from the LORD had fallen upon
Ps 127. 2 toil; for he gives *s* to his beloved.
132. 4 I will not give *s* to my eyes or slumber
Prov 3.24 you lie down, your *s* will be sweet.
6. 4 Give your eyes no *s* and your eyelids no
24.33 little *s*, a little slumber, a little folding
Eccl 5.12 Sweet is the *s* of laborers, whether they
Isa 29.10 poured out upon you a spirit of deep *s*,
Jer 51.39 become merry and then *s* a perpetual *s*

SLEEP (SLEEPING SLEPT)

Ps 3. 5 I lie down and *s*; I wake again, for the
13. 3 to my eyes, or I will *s* the *s* of death,
121. 4 keeps Israel will neither slumber nor *s*.
Song 5. 2 I *s*, but my heart was awake. Listen! my

Dan 12.2 of those who *s* in the dust of the earth
Mt 9.24 "Go away, for the girl is not dead but *s*."
26.40 came to the disciples and found them *s*;
Mk 5.39 and weep? The child is not dead but *s*."
14.37 He came and found them *s*; and he said
14.40 once more he came and found them *s*,
Lk 22.45 and found them *s* because of grief

SLIP (SLIPPED SLIPS)

Deut 32.35 for the time when their foot shall *s*;
Ps 17.5 fast to your paths, my feet have not *s*.
18.36 steps under me, and my feet did not *s*.
37.31 is in their hearts; their steps do not *s*.
38.16 who boast against me when my foot *s*."

SLIPPERY

Ps 35.6 Let their way be dark and *s*, with the
73.18 you set them in *s* places; you make

SLOW

Prov 16.32 who is *s* to anger is better than the
19.11 Those with good sense are *s* to anger,

SLUMBER (SLUMBERS)

Ps 121.3 be moved; he who keeps you will not *s*.
Prov 6.10 A little sleep, a little *s*, a little folding
Isa 5.27 weary, none stumbles, none *s* or sleeps,

SMALL (SMALLEST)

Job 40.4 I am of *s* account; what shall I answer
Mt 13.32 it is the *s* of all seeds, but when it has

SMASHES

Dan 2.40 just as iron crushes and *s* everything, it

SMELLED

Gen 27.27 he *s* the smell of his garments, and he

SMELT

Isa 1.25 I will *s* away your dross as with lye and

SMITH

1 Sam 13.19 there was no *s* to be found throughout
Isa 54.16 I who have created the *s* who blows the

SMITTEN

Ps 102.4 My heart is *s* and withered like grass; I

SMOKE

Gen 19.28 *s* of the land going up like the *s* of a
Ps 68.2 As *s* is driven away, so drive them away;
Prov 10.26 and *s* to the eyes, so are the lazy to
Rev 15.8 the temple filled with *s* from the glory

SMOOTH

Prov 2.16 from the adulteress with her *s* words,
Isa 30.10 speak to us *s* things, prophesy illusions,
Lk 3.5 straight, and the rough ways made *s*;

SNAKE (SNAKES)

Ex 4.3 on the ground, and it a became a *s*;
7.10 down his staff . . . , and it became a *s*.
Jer 8.17 I am letting *s* loose among you, adders
Mt 23.33 You *s*, you brood of vipers! How can you
Mk 16.18n they will pick up *s* in their hands, and if
Lk 10.19 authority to tread on *s* and scorpions,

SNARE (SNARES)

Ex 23.33 their gods, it will surely be a *s* to you.
Deut 7.16 their gods, for that would be a *s* to you.
Judg 2.3 you, and their gods shall be a *s* to you."
8.27 and it became a *s* to Gideon and to his
1 Sam 18.21 her to him that she may be a *s* for him,
Job 22.10 Therefore *s* are around you, and sudden
Ps 38.12 Those who seek my life lay their *s*;
64.5 they talk of laying *s* secretly, thinking,
69.22 their table be a trap for them, a *s* for
Prov 18.7 are their ruin, and their lips are a *s* to
22.25 their ways and entangle yourself in a *s*.
29.25 The fear of others lays a *s*, but one who
Jer 18.22 pit to catch me, and laid *s* for my feet.
50.24 You set a *s* for yourself and you were
Ezek 12.13 him and he shall be caught in my *s*;
Lk 21.35 day catch you unexpectedly, like a *s*.
1 Tim 3.7 fall into disgrace and the *s* of the devil.

SNATCH (SNATCHING)

Job 24.9 There are those who *s* the orphan child
Jn 10.28 never perish. No one will *s* them out
Jude 23 save others, by *s* them out of the fire;

SNOW (SNOWS)

2 Sam 23.20 lion in a pit on a day when *s* had fallen.
Job 38.22 you entered the storehouses of the *s*,
Ps 51.7 wash me, and I shall be whiter than *s*.
147.16 He gives *s* like wool; he scatters frost
Prov 25.13 Like the cold of *s* in the time of harvest
26.1 Like *s* in summer or rain in harvest, so
31.21 not afraid for her household when it *s*,
Isa 1.18 sins are like scarlet, they shall be like *s*;
Jer 18.14 Does the *s* of Lebanon leave the crags
Lam 4.7 Her princes were purer than *s*, whiter
Mt 28.3 lightning, and his clothing white as *s*.

SOAP

Job 9.30 If I wash myself with *s* and cleanse my

SOBER

1 Thess 5.6 do, but let us keep awake and be *s*;

SODOM

Gen 10.19 as far as Gaza, in the direction of *S*,
13.13 Now the people of *S* were wicked, great
14.12 they took Lot . . . who lived in *S*, and
19.24 LORD rained on *S* . . . sulfur and fire
Jer 50.40 As when God overthrew *S* and
Mt 10.15 it will more tolerable for the land of *S*
11.23 power done in you had been done in *S*,
Lk 17.29 on the day that Lot left *S*, it rained fire
Rev 11.8 great city that is prophetically called *S*

SOFT

Prov 15.1 A *s* answer turns away wrath, but a
Mt 11.8 out to see? Someone dressed in *s* robes?

SOIL (SOILED)

Gen 9.20 Noah, a man of the *s*, was the first to
Rev 3.4 who have not *s* their clothes; they will

SOLDIERS

Mt 28.12 to give a large sum of money to the *s*,
Lk 3.14 *S* also asked him, "And we, what should
7.8 set under authority, with *s* under me:
Jn 19.23 When the *s* had crucified Jesus, they

SOLE

Josh 1.3 Every place that the *s* of your foot will

SOLID

1 Cor 3.2 I fed you with milk, not *s* food, for you
Heb 5.12 of God. You need milk, not *s* food;

SOLOMON (SOLOMON'S)

Born, 2 Sam 12.24; anointed king, 1 Kings 1.32-40; established his kingdom, 1 Kings 2.12-46; married Pharaoh's daughter, 1 Kings 3.1; asked for wisdom, 1 Kings 3.5-15; judged wisely, 1 Kings 3.16-28; conferred with Hiram, 1 Kings 5; 7.13-14; built the temple, 1 Kings 6; 7.15-51; built his own house, 1 Kings 7.1-12; dedicated the temple, 1 Kings 8; the LORD's covenant with Solomon, 1 Kings 9.1-9; visited by the queen of Sheba, 1 Kings 10.1-13; turned from the LORD, 1 Kings 11.1-40; died, 1 Kings 11.41-43. (See also 2 Chr 1—9.)

Prov 1.1 proverbs of *S*, son of David, king of
Song 1.1 The Song of Songs, which is *S*.
Mt 6.29 even *S* in all his glory was not clothed
Lk 11.31 the earth to listen to the wisdom of *S*,
11.31 see, something greater than *S* is here.
Jn 10.23 in the temple, in the portico of *S*.

Acts 3.11 in the portico called *S* Portico, utterly

SON

Gen 18.10 and your wife Sarah shall have a *s*."
22. 2 "Take your *s*, your only *s* Isaac, whom
Deut 21.18 stubborn and rebellious *s* who will not
2 Sam 7.14 to him, and he shall be a *s* to me.
18.33 "O my *s* Absalom, my *s*, my *s* Absalom!
2 Kings 4.14 "Well, she has no *s*, and her husband is
4.16 in due time, you shall embrace a *s*."
8. 1 woman whose *s* he had restored to life,
1 Chr 17.13 to him, and he shall be a *s* to me.
Ps 2. 7 He said to me, "You are my *s*; today I
Prov 3.12 the one he loves, as a father the *s*
Isa 7.14 shall bear a *s*, and she shall name him
9. 6 has been born for us, a *s* given to us;
Jer 31.20 Is Ephraim my dear *s*? Is he the child I
Am 7.14 "I am no prophet, nor a prophet's *s*; but
Mic 7. 6 *s* treats the father with contempt, the
Mt 9.27 loudly, "Have mercy on us, *S* of David."
12.23 and said, "Can this be the *S* of David?"
13.55 Is not this the carpenter's *s*? Is not his
21.37 them saying, 'They will respect my *s*.'
22. 2 who gave a wedding banquet for his *s*,
22.42 he?" They said to him, "The *s* of David."
Mk 1.11 "You are my *S*, the Beloved; with you I
9. 7 "This is my *S*, the Beloved; listen to
9.17 "Teacher, I brought you my *s*; he has a
12. 6 He had still one other, a beloved *s*;
14.61 the Messiah, the *S* of the Blessed One?"
Lk 1.31 and bear a *s*, and you will name him
1.57 to give birth, and she bore a *s*.
7.12 mother's only *s*, and she was a widow;
9.38 "Teacher, I beg you to look at my *s*, he
12.53 be divided, father against *s* and *s*
15.21 no longer worthy to be called your *s*.'
19. 9 because he too is a *s* of Abraham.
20.13 I will send my beloved *s*; perhaps they
20.44 calls him Lord; so how can he be his *s*?"
Jn 1.14 glory as of a father's only *s*, full of grace
3.16 loved the world that he gave his only *S*,
4.47 him to come down and heal his *s*,
8.36 So if the *S* makes you free, you will be
9.20 is our *s*, and that he was born blind;
10.36 because I said, 'I am God's *S*'?
17.12n was lost except the *s* of destruction
19.26 to his mother, "Woman, here is your *s*."
Acts 13.10 "You *s* of the devil, you enemy of all
13.33 'You are my *S*; today I have begotten
Gal 1.16 was pleased to reveal his *S* to me,
4. 4 of time had come, God sent his *S*,
Col 1.13 us into the kingdom of his beloved *S*,
Heb 1. 2 last days he has spoken to us by a *S*,
3. 6 was faithful over God's house as a *s*.
5. 5 said to him, "You are my *S*, today I have
11.17 was ready to offer up his only *s*,
1 Jn 1. 3 the Father and with his *S* Jesus Christ.
2.23 No one who denies the *S* has the
4. 9 God sent his only *S* into the world so
4.14 Father has sent his *S* as the Savior of
5.12 Whoever has the *S* has life; whoever

SONS

Gen 6. 2 the *s* of God saw that they were fair;
Ps 127. 3 *S* are indeed a heritage from the LORD,
132. 12 If your *s* keep my covenant and my
144. 12 May our *s* in their youth be like plants
Jer 16. 2 not take a wife, nor shall you have *s* or
Mt 21.28 A man had two *s*; he went to the first

SON OF GOD

Mt 4. 3 "If you are the *S*, command these
8.29 "What have you to do with us, *S*?
14.33 him, saying, "Truly you are the *S*."
26.63 tell us if you are the Messiah, the *S*."
27.40 yourself! If you are the *S*, come down
Lk 1.35 will be holy; he will be called the *S*.
Jn 1.34 and have testified that this is the *S*."
3.18 not believed in the name of the only *S*.
19. 7 die because he has claimed to be the *S*."
Acts 9.20 in the synagogues, saying, "He is the *S*."
Rom 1. 4 and was declared to be *S* with power
Eph 4.13 the faith and of the knowledge of the *S*,
Heb 4.14 through the heavens, Jesus, the *S*,
6. 6 own they are crucifying again the *S*
10.29 by those who have spurned the *S*,
1 Jn 4.15 those who confess that Jesus is the *S*,
Rev 2.18 These are the words of the *S*, who has

SON OF MAN

Mt 8.20 but the *S* has nowhere to lay his head."
9. 6 know that the *S* has authority on earth
10.23 the towns of Israel, before the *S* comes.
12. 8 For the *S* is lord of the sabbath."
12.32 whoever speaks a word against the *S*
13.37 one who sows the good seed is the *S*;
16.27 *S* is to come with his angels in the glory
17.22 "The *S* is going to be betrayed into
24.27 west, so will be the coming of the *S*.
24.30 Then the sign of the *S* will appear in
25.31 "When the *S* comes in his glory, and all
26. 2 and the *S* will be handed over to be
26.24 The *S* goes as it is written of him, but
26.64 from now on you will see the *S* seated
Mk 2.10 the *S* has authority on earth to forgive
9.31 "The *S* is to be betrayed into human
14.21 For the *S* goes as it is written of him,
14.62 'you will see the *S* seated at the right
Lk 6. 5 to them, "The *S* is lord of the sabbath."
9.22 "The *S* must undergo great suffering,
9.44 your ears: The *S* is going to be betrayed
22.69 the *S* will be seated at the right hand of
Jn 3.13 one who descended from heaven, the *S*.
3.14 wilderness, so must the *S* be lifted up,
Acts 7.56 "I see the heavens opened, and the *S*
Rev 1.13 I saw one like the *S*, clothed with a
14.14 seated on the cloud was one like the *S*,

SONG (SONGS)

Ex 15. 1 the Israelites sang this *s* to the LORD:
Deut 31.19 therefore write this *s*, and teach it to
Job 30. 9 "And now they mock me in *s*; I am a
Ps 28. 7 exults, and with my *s* I give thanks
33. 3 Sing to him a new *s*; play skillfully on
40. 3 He put a new *s* in my mouth, a *s* of
69.12 and the drunkards make *s* about me.
81. 2 Raise a *s*, sound the tambourine, the
95. 2 a joyful noise to him with *s* of praise!
119. 54 Your statutes have been my *s* wherever I
137. 3 For there our captors asked us for *s*,
144. 9 I will sing a new *s* to you, O God; upon
149. 1 Sing to the LORD a new *s*, his praise in
Prov 25.20 is one who sings *s* to a heavy heart.
Isa 26. 1 On that day this *s* will be sung in the
30.29 have a *s* as in the night when a holy
Ezek 33.32 To them you are like a singer of love *s*,
Mic 2. 4 they shall take up a taunt *s* against you,
Rev 5. 9 They sing a new *s*: "You are worthy to
15. 3 they sing the *s* of Moses, the servant of

SORCERER

Ex 22.18 You shall not permit a female *s* to live.

SORROW (SORROWS)

Ps 13. 2 my soul, and have *s* in my heart all day
16. 4 choose another god multiply their *s*;
31.10 For my life is spent with *s*, and my
119. 28 My soul melts away for *s*; strengthen
Eccl 1.18 who increase knowledge increase *s*.
7. 3 *S* is better than laughter, for by sadness
Isa 35.10 gladness, and *s* and sighing shall flee
51.11 gladness, and *s* and sighing shall flee
Jer 20.18 forth from the womb to see toil and *s*,
45. 3 me! The LORD has added *s* to my pain;

Lam 1.12 Look and see if there is any *s* like my *s*,
Ezek 23.33 shall be filled with drunkenness and *s*.
Jn 16. 6 things to you, *s* has filled your hearts.
Rom 9. 2 I have great *s* and unceasing anguish in
2 Cor 2. 7 may not be overwhelmed by excessive *s*.

SORROWFUL

2 Cor 6.10 as *s*, yet always rejoicing; as poor, yet

SORRY

Gen 6. 6 LORD was *s* that he had made
1 Sam 15.35 the LORD was *s* that he had made Saul
Ps 38.18 I confess my iniquity; I am *s* for my sin.

SOSTHENES

Acts 18.17 seized *S*, the official of the synagogue,
1 Cor 1. 1 by the will of God, and our brother *S*,

SOUL (SOULS)

Deut 6. 5 all your heart, and with all your *s*,
1 Sam 18. 1 the *s* of Jonathan was bound to the *s* of
2 Chr 6.38 repent with all their heart and *s* in the
Job 7.11 will complain in the bitterness of my *s*.
30.16 now my *s* is poured out within me;
Ps 23. 3 me beside still waters; he restores my *s*.
42.11 Why are you cast down, O my *s*, and
56.13 For you have delivered my *s* from death,
103. 1 Bless the LORD, O my *s*; and all that is
Prov 21.10 The *s* of the wicked desire evil; their
27. 9 heart glad, but the *s* is torn by trouble.
Song 1. 7 Tell me, you whom my *s* loves, where
Isa 1.14 and your appointed festivals my *s* hates;
Jer 13.17 my *s* will weep in secret for your pride;
Mic 6. 7 the fruit of my body for the sin of my *s*?"
Mt 10.28 who kill the body but cannot kill the *s*;
22.37 with all your heart, and with all your *s*,
Mk 12.30 with all your heart, and with all your *s*,
Lk 1.47 Mary said, "My *s* magnifies the Lord,
12.19 say to my *s*, "*S*, you have ample goods
21.19 By your endurance you will gain your *s*.
Acts 2.27 For you will not abandon my *s* to
1 Pet 1.22 have purified your *s* by your obedience
3 Jn 2 health, just as it is well with your *s*.
Rev 18.14 fruit for which your *s* longed has gone
20. 4 I saw the *s* of those who had been

SOUND

Gen 3. 8 They heard the *s* of the LORD God
Ezek 1.24 the *s* of their wings like the *s* of mighty
Zeph 1.14 the *s* of the day of the LORD is bitter,
2 Tim 1.13 Hold to the standard of *s* teaching that
Titus 2. 2 prudent, and *s* in faith, in love, and in
2. 8 *s* speech that cannot be censured; then

SOUNDNESS

Ps 38. 3 There is no *s* in my flesh because of
Isa 1. 6 there is no *s* in it, but bruises and sores

SOVEREIGN (SOVEREIGNTY)

1 Kings 4.21 Solomon was *s* over all the kingdoms
Dan 4.17 the Most High is *s* over the kingdom
4.25 High has *s* over the kingdom of mortals,
4.32 the Most High has *s* over the kingdom
4.34 For his *s* is an everlasting *s*, and his

SOW (SOWED SOWN SOWS)

Gen 26.12 Isaac *s* in that land, and in the same
47.23 here is seed for you; *s* the land.
Ps 107. 37 they *s* fields, and plant vineyards, and
126. 5 those who *s* in tears reap with shouts
Prov 6.19 and one who *s* discord in a family.
22. 8 Whoever *s* injustice will reap calamity,
Eccl 11. 4 Whoever observes the wind will not *s*;
Isa 32.20 will you be who *s* beside every stream,
Jer 4. 3 fallow ground, and *s* not among thorns.
12.13 have *s* wheat and have reaped thorns,
31.27 when I will *s* the house of Israel and
Hos 8. 7 For they *s* the wind, and they shall reap
10.12 *S* for yourselves righteousness; reap
Mic 6.15 You shall *s*, but not reap; you shall
Mt 6.26 birds of the air; they neither *s* nor reap
13.27 'Master, did you not *s* good seed in
25.26 did you, that I reap where I did not *s*,
Mk 4. 3 "Listen! A sower went out to *s*.
Lk 12.24 the ravens: they neither *s* nor reap,
Jn 4.37 holds true, 'One *s* and another reaps.'
1 Cor 9.11 If we have *s* spiritual good among you,
15.36 What you *s* does not come to life unless
2 Cor 9. 6 one who *s* sparingly will also reap
Gal 6. 7 mocked, for you reap whatever you *s*.

SOWER

Mt 13. 3 saying: "Listen! A *s* went out to sow.
13.18 "Hear then the parable of the *s*.
Mk 4.14 The *s* sows the word.
Lk 8. 5 "A *s* went out to sow his seed; and as

SPAIN

Rom 15.24 come to you when I go to *S*. For I do
15.28 I will set out by way of you to *S*; and I

SPAN

Mt 6.27 add a single hour to your *s* of life?
Lk 12.25 add a single hour to your *s* of life?

SPARE (SPARED SPARES)

Josh 6.25 Rahab . . . Joshua *s*. Her family has
1 Sam 15. 9 Saul and the people *s* Agag, and the
24.10 some urged me kill you, but I *s* you.
2 Sam 21. 7 the king *s* Mephibosheth, the son of
Job 2. 6 well, he is in your power; only *s* his life."
21.30 that the wicked are *s* in the day of
Ps 119. 88 In your steadfast love *s* my life, so that
Prov 13.24 who *s* the rod hate their children, but
17.27 One who *s* words is knowledgeable, one

SPARROW (SPARROWS)

Ps 84. 3 Even the *s* finds a home, and the
Mt 10.29 Are not two *s* sold for a penny?
Lk 12. 6 Are not five *s* sold for two pennies? Yet

SPEAK (SPEAKING SPEAKS SPOKE SPOKEN)

Ex 20. 1 Then God *s* all these words:
20.19 but do not let God *s* to us, or we will
33. 9 tent, and the LORD would *s* with Moses.
Num 7.89 into tent of meeting to *s* with the LORD,
11.25 came down in the cloud and *s* to him,
12. 8 With him I *s* face to face —clearly, not
Deut 5. 4 The LORD *s* with you face to face at the
5.24 Today we have seen that God may *s* to
1 Sam 3. 9 "*S*, LORD, for your servant is listening.'"
1 Kings 22.14 the LORD says to me, that I will *s*."
2 Chr 18.13 lives, whatever God says, that I will *s*."
Job 33.14 For God *s* in one way, and in two,
Ps 50. 1 LORD, *s* and summons the earth from
85. 8 will *s*, for he will *s* peace to his people,
87. 3 Glorious things are *s* of you, O city of
139. 20 those who *s* of you maliciously, and lift
Eccl 3. 7 a time to keep silence, and a time to *s*;
Isa 40. 2 *S* tenderly to Jerusalem, and cry to her
Jer 1. 6 I do not know how to *s*, for I am only a
Hos 2.14 the wilderness, and *s* tenderly to her.
Mt 17.25 Jesus *s* of it first, asking, "What do you
Mk 2. 2 door, and he was *s* the word to them.
Lk 4.32 teaching, because he *s* with authority.
4.41 them and would not allow them to *s*,
12.10 everyone who *s* a word against the Son
Jn 7.46 answered, "Never has anyone *s* like this!"
Acts 2. 4 and began to *s* in other languages,
5.40 them not to *s* in the name of Jesus,
1 Tim 5. 1 Do not *s* harshly to an older man, but *s*
Heb 11. 4 he died, but through his faith he still *s*.
Jas 4.11 Whoever *s* evil against another or judges

SPEAR (SPEARS)

1 Sam 26. 8 to the ground with one stroke of the *s*;

Isa 2. 4 and their *s* into pruning hooks;
Jn 19.34 of the soldiers pierced his side with a *s*,

SPECIAL

2 Tim 2.20 clay, some for *s* use, some for ordinary.

SPECK

Mt 7. 3 do you see the *s* in your neighbor's eye,
Lk 6.41 do you see the *s* in your neighbor's eye,

SPECTACLE

Nah 3. 6 you with contempt, and make you a *s*.

SPEECH

Ex 4.10 but I am slow of *s* and of tongue."
Ps 19. 2 Day to day pours forth *s*, and night to
Prov 17. 7 Fine *s* is not becoming to a fool; still
29.20 Do you see someone who is hasty in *s*?
Ezek 3. 5 not sent to a people of obscure *s* and
Zeph 3. 9 change the *s* of the peoples to a pure *s*,
1 Cor 1. 5 enriched in him, in *s* and knowledge of
2 Cor 10.10 is weak, and his *s* is contemptible"
Col 4. 6 Let your *s* always be gracious, seasoned

SPEECHLESS

Ezek 3.26 shall be *s* and unable to reprove them;
Dan 10.15 my face toward the ground and was *s*.
Mt 22.12 without a wedding robe?' And he was *s*.
Acts 9. 7 who were traveling with him stood *s*,

SPELLBOUND

Mk 11.18 the whole crowd was *s* at his teaching.

SPEND (SPENT)

Gen 19. 2 *s* the night, and wash your feet; then
47.18 from my lord that our money is all *s*;
Ps 38. 8 I am utterly *s* and crushed; I groan

SPEWED

Jon 2.10 spoke to the fish, and it *s* Jonah out

SPICE (SPICES)

Song 4.10 the fragrance of your oils than any *s*!
Jn 19.40 wrapped it with the *s* in linen cloths

SPIES

Josh 2. 1 sent two men ecretly from Shittim as *s*,
6.23 men who had been *s* went in and
Judg 1.24 When the *s* saw a man coming out of

SPIRIT

Gen 6. 3 "My *s* shall not abide in mortals forever,
Ex 31. 3 I have filled him with divine *s*, with
Num 11.17 will take some of the *s* which is on you
11.29 the LORD would put his *s* upon them!"
27.18 son of Nun, a man in whom is the *s*,
Judg 9.23 God sent an evil *s* between Abimelech
1 Sam 19. 9 an evil *s* from the LORD came upon Saul,
28. 8 "Consult a *s* for me, and bring up for
1 Kings 22.21 until a *s* came forward and stood before
2 Kings 2.15 "The *s* of Elijah rests on Elisha."
5.26 " Did I not go with you in *s* when
Neh 9.20 You gave your good *s* to instruct them,
Job 15.13 so that you turn your *s* against God,
32. 8 But truly it is the *s* in a mortal, the
Ps 34.18 and saves the crushed in *s*.
77. 3 and I moan; I meditate, and my *s* faints.
78. 8 whose *s* was not faithful to God.
104. 30 you send forth your *s*, they are created;
106. 33 for they made his *s* bitter, and he spoke
139. 7 Where can I go from your *s*? Or where
142. 3 When my *s* is faint, you know my way.
143. 10 Let your good *s* lead me on a level
Prov 16. 2 own eyes, but the LORD weighs the *s*.
17.22 but a downcast *s* dries up the bones.
18.14 human *s* will endure sickness; but a
20.27 The human *s* is the lamp of the LORD,
Eccl 3.21 Who knows whether the human *s* goes
Isa 4. 4 its midst by a *s* of judgment and by a *s*
32.15 until a *s* from on high is poured out on
42. 1 I have put my *s* upon him; he will bring
44. 3 I will pour my *s* upon your descendants,
Ezek 1.12 wherever the *s* would go, they went,
1.20 the *s* of the living creatures was in the
8. 3 *s* lifted me up between earth and
10.17 for the *s* of the living creatures was
36.27 I will put my *s* within you, and make
37.14 I will put my *s* within you, and you
Dan 4. 8 is endowed with a *s* of the holy gods—
5.11 is endowed with a *s* of the holy gods.
Joel 2.28 I will pour out my *s* on all flesh;
Hab 2. 4 Look at the proud! Their *s* is not right
Hag 2. 5 My *s* abides among you; do not fear.
Zech 4. 6 by might, nor by power, but by my *s*,
12. 1 earth and formed the human *s* within:
Mt 4. 1 Jesus was led up by the *S* into the
5. 3 "Blessed are the poor in *s*, for theirs is
10.20 but the *S* of your Father speaking
12.18 I will put my *S* upon him, and he will
26.41 the *s* indeed is willing, but the flesh is
Mk 1.23 synagogue a man with an unclean *s*;
14.38 the *s* indeed is willing, but the flesh is
Lk 1.47 and my *s* rejoices in God my Savior,
4. 1 was led by the *S* into the wilderness,
Jn 3. 6 is flesh, and what is born of the *S* is *s*.
3.34 for he gives the *S* without measure.
6.63 It is the *s* that gives life; the flesh is
Acts 2.17 I will pour out my *S* upon all flesh, and
20.22 And now, as a captive to the *S*, I am on
Rom 1. 4 power according to the *s* of holiness
8. 2 the law of the *S* of life in Christ Jesus
8. 4 to the flesh but according to the *S*.
8. 5 those who live according to the *S* set
8. 6 is death, but to set the mind on *S* is life
1 Cor 2.10 God has revealed to us through the *S*;
3.16 temple and that God's *S* dwells in you?
12.13 For in the one *S* we were all baptized
2 Cor 1.22 giving us his *S* in our hearts as a first
Gal 4. 6 God has sent the *S* of his Son into our
6. 8 if you sow to the *S* you will reap eternal
Eph 5.18 is debauchery; but be filled with the *S*,
1 Thess 5.19 Do not quench the *S*. Do not despise
2 Tim 1. 7 rather a *s* of power and of love and of
Heb 9.14 through the eternal *S* offered himself
Jas 2.26 just as the body without the *s* is dead,
4. 5 "God yearns jealously for the *s* that he
1 Jn 3.24 in us, by the *S* which he has given us.
5. 8 the *S*, and the water, and the blood,
Rev 2. 7 listen to what the *S* is saying to the
22.17 The *S* and the Bride say, "Come." And

SPIRITS

Lk 4.36 he commands the unclean *s*, and out
Heb 1.14 not all angels *s* in the divine service,
Rev 3. 1 of him who has the seven *s* of God
4. 5 torches, which are the seven *s* of God;

SPIRIT OF GOD

Gen 1.2n while the *s* swept over the face of the
41.38 else like this— one in whom is the *s*?"
Num 24. 2 by tribe. Then the *S* came upon him,
1 Sam 11. 6 the *s* came upon Saul in power when he
19.20 the *s* came upon the messengers of
2 Chr 15. 1 The *S* came upon Azariah son of Oded.
24.20 the *S* took possession of Zechariah son
Job 27. 3 is in me and the *s* is in my nostrils,
33. 4 The *s* has made me, and the breath of
Rom 8.14 all who are led by the *S* are children
15.19 and wonders, by the power of the *S*
Phil 3. 3 circumcision, who worship in the *S* and
1 Jn 4. 2 By this you know the *S*: every spirit that

SPIRIT OF THE LORD

Judg 3.10 The *s* came upon him, and he judged
6.34 the *s* took possession of Gideon; and he
11.29 the *s* came upon Jephthah, and he

Judg 13.25 The *s* began to stir him at
15.14 the *s* rushed on him, and the ropes that
1 Sam 16.13 the *s* came mightily upon David from
1 Kings 18.12 the *s* will carry you I know not where;
22.24 "Which way did the *s* pass from me to
2 Chr 20.14 the *S* came upon Jahaziel son of
Isa 11. 2 The *S* shall rest on him, the spirit of
40.13 Who has directed the *s*, or as his
Ezek 11. 5 Then the *S* fell upon me, and he said to
Lk 4.18 "The *S* is upon me, because he has
Acts 5. 9 agreed together to put the *S* to the test?
2 Cor 3.17 Lord is the Spirit, and where the *S* is,

SPIRITUAL

Rom 2.29 of the heart— it is *s* and not literal.
7.14 we know that the law is *s*; but I am of
1 Cor 2.13 by the Spirit, interpreting *s* things
3. 1 I could not speak to you as *s* people,
10. 3 in the sea, and all ate the same *s* food,
12. 1 Now concerning *s* gifts, brothers and
15.44 a physical body, it is raised a *s* body.

SPIT (SPAT)

Deut 25. 9 *s* in his face, and declare, "This is what
Mt 26.67 Then they *s* in his face and struck him;
Mk 7.33 ears and he *s* and touched his tongue.
14.65 Some began to *s* on him, to blindfold
15.19 his head with a reed, *s* upon him,
Rev 3.16 cold not hot, I am about to *s* you out

SPLENDOR

Ps 29. 2 of his name; worship the LORD in holy *s*.
96. 9 Worship the LORD in holy *s*; tremble
Ezek 16.14 for it was perfect because of my *s*
Hag 2. 9 The latter *s* of this house shall be

SPOIL (SPOILS)

Judg 5.19 of Megiddo, they got no *s* of silver.
Ps 44.10 our foe, and our enemies have gotten *s*.
119.162 at your word like one who finds great *s*.

SPOT

Tim 6.14 the commandmant without *s* or blame

SPREAD (SPREADING)

2 Sam 5.18 Philistines had come and *s* out in the
2 Kings 19.14 of the LORD and *s* it before the LORD.
Ps 88. 9 you, O LORD; I *s* out my hands to you.
Prov 29. 5 flatters a neighbor is *s* a net for the
Ezek 16. 8 I *s* the edge of my cloak over you, and
Mt 21. 8 large crowd *s* their cloaks on the road.
Mk 11. 8 Many people *s* their cloaks on the road,
Lk 19.36 people kept *s* their cloaks on the road.
Phil 1.12 me has actually helped to *s* the gospel,

SPRING (SPRINGS)

Josh 15.19 gave her the upper *s* and the lower *s*.
Ps 104. 10 You make *s* gush forth in the valleys;
Hos 13.15 shall dry up, his *s* shall be parched.
Jas 3.11 Does a *s* pour forth from the same
2 Pet 2.17 These are waterless *s* and mists driven
Rev 21. 6 as a gift from the *s* of the water of life.

SPROUT

Num 17. 5 staff of the man whom I choose shall *s*;
Ps 92. 7 though the wicked *s* like grass and all

SPURN (SPURNED)

Lev 26.15 if you *s* my statutes, and abhor my
Heb 10.29 by those who have *s* the Son of God,

SPY (SPIED SPYING)

Gen 42.30 us, and charged us with *s* on the land.
Num 13. 2 "Send men to *s* out the land of Canaan,
13.17 sent them to *s* out the land of Canaan,
13.21 So they went and *s* out the land from
1 Chr 19. 3 search and to overthrow and to *s* out
Gal 2. 4 who slipped in to *s* on the freedom we

SQUANDER (SQUANDERED)

Prov 29. 3 company with prostitutes is to *s* one's
Lk 15.13 and there he *s* his property in dissolute

STABILITY

Prov 29. 4 By justice a king gives *s* to the land, but
Isa 33. 6 he will be the *s* of your times,

STAFF

Ex 4. 2 is that in your hand?" He said, "A *s*."
4.20 and Moses carried the *s* of God in his
Num 17. 3 and write Aaron's name on the *s* of
Judg 5.14 those who bear the marshal's *s*;
2 Kings 4.29 and lay my *s* upon the face of the child."
Mk 6. 8 nothing for their journey except a *s*;

STAGGER (STAGGERED)

Job 12.25 light; he makes them *s* like a drunkard.
Ps 107. 27 they reeled and *s* like drunkards, and

STALLS

2 Chr 9.25 Solomon had four thousand *s* for horses

STALK

Mk 4.28 of itself, first the *s*, then the head,

STAMMERING

Isa 28.11 *s* lip and with alien tongue he will
33.19 *s* in a language that you cannot

STAND (STANDING STANDS STOOD)

Gen 18.22 Abraham remained *s* before the LORD.
Num 16.48 He *s* between the dead and the living;
Deut 7.24 no one will be able to *s* against you,
10. 8 to *s* before the LORD to minister to him,
29.10 You *s* assembled today, all of you,
Josh 10.13 And the sun *s* still, and the moon
Neh 8. 5 when he opened it, all the people *s*.
Ps 5. 5 The boastful will not *s* before your eyes;
130. 3 mark iniquities, Lord, who could *s*?
135. 2 you that *s* in the house of the LORD, in
Jer 6.16 *S* at the crossroads, and look, and ask
Ezek 2. 1 O mortal, *s* up on your feet, and I will
Mt 9. 6 to the paralytic— "*S* up, take your bed
Mk 2.11 *s* up, take your mat and go to your
Lk 5.24 to you, *s* up and take up your bed and
21.36 place, and to *s* before the Son of man."
Jn 5. 8 to him, "*S* up, take your mat and walk."
Acts 7.56 and the Son of Man *s* at the right hand
1 Cor 6. 4 appoint as judges those who have no *s*
10.12 if you think you are *s*, watch out that
16.13 Keep alert, *s* firm in your faith, be
Gal 5. 1 Christ has set us free. *S* firm, therefore,
Phil 4. 1 crown, *s* firm in the Lord in this way,
1 Thess 3. 8 if you continue to *s* firm in the Lord.
2 Tim 2.19 But God's firm foundation *s*, bearing
1 Pet 5.12 is the true grace of God. *S* fast in it.
Jude 24 to make you *s* without blemish in the

STANDARD

Num 10.14 The *s* of the camp of Judah set out
Isa 31. 9 and his officers desert the *s* in panic,"
Jer 4. 6 Raise a *s* toward Zion, flee for safety, do

STAR (STARS)

Gen 1.16 light to rule the night— and the *s*.
15. 5 "Look toward heaven and count the *s*, if
22.17 your offspring as numerous as the *s*
Num 24.17 a *s* shall come out of Jacob, and a
Deut 1.10 you are as numerous as the *s* of heaven.
10.22 has made you as numerous as the *s*
28.62 once you were as numerous as the *s*
Judg 5.20 The *s* fought from heaven, from their
1 Chr 27.23 to make Israel as numerous as the *s* of
Neh 4.21 break of dawn until the *s* came out.
Job 38. 7 when the morning *s* sang together, and
Ps 147. 4 He determines the number of the *s*; he
Isa 14.12 you are fallen from heaven, O Day *S*,

Dan 8.10 some of the *s*, and trampled on them.
12. 3 many to righteousness, like the *s* forever
Mt 2. 2 For we observed his *s* at its rising, and
Heb 11.12 were born, "as many as the *s* of heaven
2 Pet 1.19 and the morning *s* rises in your hearts.
Rev 1.16 In his right hand he held seven *s*, and
8.10 a great *s* fell from heaven, blazing like a
22.16 of David, the bright morning *s*."

STARED

Isa 63. 5 I *s*, but there was no one to sustain me;

STATE

Mt 12.45 the last *s* of that person is worse than
Lk 11.26 and the last *s* of that person is worse

STATUE

Dan 2.31 O king, and lo! there was a great *s*.
Acts 19.35 the great Artemis and of the *s* that fell

STATUTE (STATUTES)

Lev 18. 5 You shall keep my *s* and my ordinances;
Num 35.29 These things shall be a *s* and ordinance
Ps 119. 48 which I love, I will meditate on your *s*.
Ezek 5. 6 against my ordinances and my *s*,

STAY (STAYED STAYING)

Ex 2.21 Moses agreed to *s* with the man, and he
16.29 each of you *s* where you are; do not
Jer 42.15 hungry for bread, and there we will *s*,'
Mt 10.11 it is worthy and *s* there until you leave.
Lk 19. 5 down; for I must *s* at your house today."
Jn 1.38 Teacher), where are you *s*?" He said to
Acts 1. 4 While *s* with them, he ordered them not
Heb 11. 9 By faith he *s* for a time in the land he

STEADFAST

Ps 57. 7 My heart is *s*, O God, my heart is *s*. I
1 Cor 15.58 be *s*, immovable, always excelling

STEADFAST LOVE

Gen 24.12 and show *s* to my master Abraham.
32.10 I am not worthy of the least of all the *s*
39.21 was with Joseph and showed him *s*;
Ex 34. 7 keeping *s* for the thousanth generation,
1 Chr 16.34 for he is good; for his *s* endures forever.
2 Chr 7. 3 he is good, for his *s* endures forever."
Ezra 7.28 who extended to me *s* before the king
Ps 17. 7 Wondrously show your *s*, O savior of
25. 6 of your mercy, O LORD, and of your *s*,
25. 7 according to your *s* remember me, for
26. 3 For your *s* is before my eyes, I walk in
36. 7 How precious is your *s*, O God! All
40.10 I have not concealed your *s* and your
63. 3 your *s* is better than life, my lips will
69.16 Answer me, O LORD, for your *s* is good;
77. 8 Has his *s* ceased forever? Are his
85.10 *S* and faithfulness will meet;
89. 2 that your *s* is established forever;
92. 2 declare your *s* in the morning, and your
100. 5 the LORD is good; his *s* endures forever,
103. 17 But the *s* of the LORD is from everlasting
107. 8 Let them thank the LORD for his *s*, for
107. 43 things, and consider the *s* of the LORD.
118. 1 for he is good; his *s* endures forever.
119. 88 In your *s* spare my life, so that I may
136. 1 for he is good, for his *s* endures forever.
Isa 63. 7 according to the abundance of his *s*.
Jer 16. 5 people, says the LORD, my *s* and mercy.
Lam 3.22 The *s* of the LORD never ceases, his
Hos 6. 6 I desire *s* and not sacrifice, the

STEADFASTNESS

Rom 15. 4 written for our instruction, so that by *s*
2 Thess 3. 5 the love of God and to the *s* of Christ.

STEAL (STEALING STEALS STOLE)

Gen 31.30 father's house, why did you *s* my gods?"
Ex 20.15 You shall not *s*.
22. 1 When someone *s* an ox or a sheep, and
Deut 5.19 Neither shall you *s*.
2 Sam 15. 6 Absalom *s* the hearts of the people of
Prov 6.30 who *s* only to satisfy their appetite
Jer 7. 9 Will you *s*, murder, commit adultery,
Mt 6.20 where thieves do not break in and *s*.
19.18 You shall not *s*; You shall not bear false
Eph 4.28 Thieves must give up *s*; rather let them

STEEP

Mt 8.32 the whole herd rushed down the *s* bank

STEP (STEPS)

1 Sam 20. 3 there is but a *s* between me and death."
Job 14.16 then you would not number my *s*, you
18. 7 Their strong *s* are shortened, and their
31. 4 not see my ways, and number all my *s*?
Ps 18.36 You gave me a wide place for my *s*
37.23 Our *s* are made firm by the LORD, when
44.18 turned back, nor have our *s* departed
73. 2 stumbled; my *s* had nearly slipped.
119.133 Keep my *s* steady according to your
Prov 16. 9 the way but the LORD directs the *s*.
20.24 All our *s* are ordered by the LORD; how
Isa 38. 8 sun on the dial of Ahaz turn back ten *s*."
Jer 10.23 as they walk cannot direct their *s*.
Lam 4.18 They dogged our *s* so that we could not
2 Cor 12.18 spirit? Did we not take the same *s*?

STEPHEN

Acts 6. 5 they chose *S*, a man full of faith and
6. 9 and Asia, stood up and argued with *S*.
7.59 While they were stoning *S*, he prayed,
8. 2 Devout men buried *S*, and made loud
11.19 persecution that took place over *S*
22.20 the blood of your witness *S* was shed,

STEWARDS

1 Cor 4. 1 of Christ and *s* of God's mysteries.

STICK (STICKS)

Num 15.32 a man gathering *s* on the sabbath day.
Prov 18.24 but a true friend *s* closer than one's
Ezek 37.16 take a *s* and write on it, "For Judah,

STIFF-NECKED

Ex 33. 3 you on the way, for you are a *s* people."
2 Chr 30. 8 Do not now be *s* as your ancestors were,
Acts 7.51 "You *s* people, uncircumcised in heart

STILL

Josh 10.13 And the sun stood *s*, and the moon
Ps 37. 7 Be *s* before the LORD, and wait patiently
39. 2 I was silent and *s*; I held my peace to
46.10 "Be *s*, and know that I am God! I am
107. 29 he made the storm be *s*, and the waves

STING

1 Cor 15.55 your victory? Where, O death, is your *s*?"

STINGERS

Rev 9.10 tails like scorpions, with *s*, and in their

STIRS (STIRRED)

Ex 35.21 they came, everyone whose heart was *s*,
2 Chr 36.22 LORD *s* up the spirit of King Cyrus of
Prov 28.25 The greedy person *s* up strife, but
Hag 1.14 the LORD *s* up the spirit of Zerubbabel
Lk 23. 5 "He *s* up the people by teaching
Jn 5.4n into the pool, and *s* up the water;
5. 7 into the pool when the water is *s* up;
Acts 6.12 They *s* up the people as well as the
2 Cor 9. 2 and your zeal has *s* up most of them.

STOCKS

Job 13.27 You put my feet in the *s*, and watch all
Jer 20. 2 prophet Jeremiah, and put him in the *s*
Acts 16.24 cell and fastened their feet in the *s*.

STOLEN

2 Sam 19.41 have the people of Judah *s* you away,

STOMACH

Mt 15.17 goes into the mouth enters the *s*,
Mk 7.19 since it enters, not the heart but the *s*,
1 Cor 6.13 is meant for the *s* and the *s* for food,"
1 Tim 5.23 take a little wine for the sake of your *s*

STONE (STONES) (n)

Ex 28.11 you shall engrave the two *s* with the
Deut 5.22 He wrote them on two *s* tablets, and
10. 1 "Carve out two *s* tablets like the former
Josh 4. 6 time to come, 'What do those *s* mean
24.26 he took a large *s*, and set it up there
1 Sam 6.18 The great *s*, beside which they set down
7.12 Samuel took a *s* and set it up between
17.40 and chose five smooth *s* from the wadi,
25.37 died within him; he became like a *s*.
Ps 118. 22 The *s* that the builders rejected has
Prov 27. 3 A *s* is heavy, and sand is weighty, but a
Isa 28.16 laying in Zion a foundation *s*, a tested *s*,
Jer 2.27 father," and to a *s*, "You gave me birth."
Ezek 11.19 I will remove the heart of *s* from their
Dan 2.35 the *s* that struck the statue became a
Hab 2.11 The very *s* will cry out from the wall,
Mt 7. 9 child asks for bread, will give him a *s*?
21.42 'The *s* which the builders rejected has
21.44 who falls on this *s* will be broken to
24. 2 I tell you, not one *s* will be left here
27.66 made the tomb secure by sealing the *s*.
Mk 12.10 the *s* which the builders rejected has
13. 2 Not one *s* will be left here upon
16. 4 looked up, they saw that the *s*, which
Lk 3. 8 is able from these *s* to raise up children
4. 3 God, command this *s* to become a loaf
11.11n bread, will give a *s*; or if your child asks
19.40 were silent, the *s* would shout out."
20.17 'The *s* which the builders rejected has
21. 6 will come when not one *s* will be left
24. 2 They found the *s* rolled away from the
Jn 8.59 they picked up *s* to throw at him, but
11.39 Jesus said, "Take away the *s*." Martha,
20. 1 and saw that the *s* had been removed
Acts 4.11 Jesus is 'the *s* that was rejected by you,
2 Cor 3. 3 not on tablets of *s* but on tablets of
1 Pet 2. 6 "See, I am laying in Zion a *s*, a

STONE (STONED STONES STONING)

Lev 24.14 and let the whole congregation *s* him.
Num 14.10 congregation threatened to *s* them.
15.36 outside the camp and *s* him to death,
Deut 13.10 *S* them to death for trying to turn you
21.21 men of the town shall *s* him to death,
Josh 7.25 And all Israel *s* him to death; they
1 Sam 30. 6 danger; for the people spoke of *s* him,
Mt 23.37 city that kills the prophets and *s* those
Jn 8. 5 Moses commanded us to *s* such women.
10.31 Jews took up stones again to *s* him.
2 Cor 11.25 beaten with rods; once I received a *s*.
Acts 7.58 him out of the city and began to *s* him;

STOP (STOPPED)

Num 11.28 men, said, "My lord Moses, *s* them!"
Job 9.12 He snatches away; who can *s* him? Who
Ps 63.11 exult, for the mouths of liars will be *s*.

STORE (STORED STORING)

Gen 41.49 So Joseph *s* up grain in such
Mt 6.19 "Do not *s* up for yourselves treasures on
1 Tim 6.19 thus *s* up for themselves the treasure of

STOREHOUSE (STOREHOUSES)

Gen 41.56 Joseph opened all the *s*, and sold to the
Job 38.22 "Have you entered the *s* of the snow, or
Ps 33. 7 sea in a bottle; he put the deeps in *s*.
Isa 39. 2 armory, all that was found in his *s*.
Jer 10.13 and he brings out the wind from his *s*.
Mal 3.10 Bring the full tithe into the *s*, so that

STORK

Lev 11.19 the *s*, the heron of any kind, the
Jer 8. 7 Even the *s* in the heavens knows its

STORM

Ps 107. 29 he made the *s* be still, and the waves of
Jer 23.19 Look, the *s* of the LORD! Wrath has gone
Jon 1.12 me that this great *s* has come upon you."

STRAIGHT

Prov 3. 6 him, and he will make *s* your paths.
11. 5 of the blameless keeps their ways *s*,
Eccl 7.13 can make *s* what he has made crooked?
Isa 45.13 and I will make all his paths *s*;
Acts 9.11 "Get up and go to the street called *S*,

STRAIGHTFORWARD

Eccl 7.29 God made human beings *s*, but they

STRAIN (STRAINING)

Mt 23.24 guides, you *s* out a gnat but swallow
Phil 3.13 and *s* forward to what lies ahead,

STRANGE

Ps 44.20 or spread out our hands to a *s* god,

STRANGER (STRANGERS)

Gen 23. 4 "I am a *s* and an alien residing among
Deut 10.18 who loves the *s*, providing them food
10.19 shall also love the *s*, for you were *s*
Job 31.32 the *s* has not lodged in the street; I
Ps 69. 8 I have become a *s* to my kindred, an
146. 9 The LORD watches over the *s*, he
Jer 14. 8 why should you be like a *s* in the land,
Lam 5. 2 inheritance has been turned over to *s*,
Joel 3.17 be holy, and *s* shall never again pass
Mt 25.35 I was a *s* and you welcomed me,
Eph 2.12 *s* to the covenants of promise, having

STRAW

Ex 5. 7 You shall no longer give the people *s* to
Job 21.18 How often are they like *s* before the
Jer 23.28 What has *s* in common with wheat?
1 Cor 3.12 silver, precious stones, wood, hay, *s*—

STREAM (STREAMS)

Gen 2. 6 but a *s* would rise from the earth, and
Ps 1. 3 They are like a trees planted by *s* of
42. 1 As a deer longs for flowing *s*, so my
119.136 My eyes shed *s* of tears because your
Isa 2. 2 the hills; all the nations shall *s* to it.
32. 2 tempest, like *s* of water in a dry place,
35. 6 in the wilderness, and *s* in the desert;

STREET (STREETS)

Ps 18.42 I cast them out like the mire of the *s*.
Acts 9.11 "Get up and go to the *s* called Straight,

STRENGTH

Ex 15. 2 The LORD is my *s* and my might, and he
Num 11. 6 but now our *s* is dried up, and there is
Deut 33.25 bronze; and as your days, so is your *s*.
Judg 16. 6 tell me what makes your *s* so great, and
2 Sam 22.40 you girded me with *s* for the battle; you
Job 6.11 What is my *s*, that I should wait? And
9.19 If it is a contest of *s*, he is the strong
18.12 Their *s* is consumed by hunger, and
35.10 'Where is God my Maker, who gives *s*
Ps 18.32 the God who girded me with *s*, and
21. 1 In your *s* the king rejoices, O LORD, and
29. 1 beings, ascribe to the LORD glory and *s*.
29.11 May the LORD give *s* to his people! May
68.28 your might, O God; show your *s*, O God,
73.26 but God is the *s* of my heart and my
81. 1 Sing aloud to God our *s*; shout for joy
84. 5 Happy are those whose *s* is in you, in
96. 6 him; *s* and beauty are in his sanctuary.

Ps 102. 23 He has broken my *s* in midcourse; he
105. 4 Seek the LORD and his *s*; seek his
118. 14 The LORD is my *s* and my might; he has
Eccl 7.19 Wisdom gives *s* to the wise more than
10.17 time—for *s*, and not for drunkeness!
Isa 10.13 "By the *s* of my hand I have done it,
30.15 quietness and in trust shall be your *s*.
40. 9 good tidings; lift up your voice with *s*,
49. 5 LORD, and my God has become my *s*—
51. 9 awake, put on *s*, O arm of the LORD!
52. 1 Awake, awake, put on your *s*, O Zion!
Jer 16.19 LORD, my *s* and my stronghold, my
Hab 3.19 GOD, the Lord, is my *s*; he makes my
Lk 1.51 He has shown *s* with his arm; he has
21.36 praying that you may have *s* to escape
1 Cor 10.13 will not let you be tested beyond your *s*,
Eph 6.10 in the Lord and in the *s* of his power.
Col 1.11 May you be made strong with all the *s*
1 Pet 4.11 do so with the *s* that God supplies,

STRENGTHEN (STRENGTHENED STRENGTHENING STRENGTHENS)

1 Sam 23.16 there he *s* his hand through the LORD.
30. 6 David *s* himself in the LORD his God.
Job 4. 3 many; you have *s* the weak hands.
Ps 89.21 with him; my arm also shall *s* him.
Isa 35. 3 *S* the weak hands, and make firm the
41.10 I will *s* you, I will help you, I will
54. 2 lengthen your cords and *s* your stakes.
Ezek 34.16 and I will *s* the weak, but the fat and
Dan 10.18 in human form touched me and *s* me.
Zech 10. 6 I will *s* the house of Judah, and I will
Acts 15.41 Syria and Cilicia, *s* the churches.
18.23 Galatia and Phrygia, *s* all the disciples.
Rom 16.25 to God who is able to *s* you according
1 Cor 1. 8 He will also *s* you to the end, so that
Eph 3.16 he may grant that you may be *s* in your
Phil 4.13 do all things through him who *s* me.
1 Thess 3. 2 to *s* and encourage you for the sake of
3.13 may he so *s* your hearts in holiness that
1 Pet 5.10 Christ, will himself restore, support, *s*
Rev 3. 2 Wake up, and *s* what remains and is on

STRETCH (STRETCHED STRETCHES)

1 Kings 17.21 he *s* himself upon the child three times,
Job 9. 8 who alone *s* out the heavens and
Ps 68.31 let Ethiopia hasten to *s* out its hands to
104. 2 You *s* out the heavens like a tent, you
Lam 1.17 Zion *s* out her hands, but there is no
Mt 12.13 he said to the man, "*S* out your hand."

STRICKEN

1 Sam 24. 5 David was *s* to the heart because he
2 Sam 24.10 David was *s* to the heart because he

STRIFE

Gen 13. 7 *s* between the herders of Abram's
Ps 55. 9 for I see violence and *s* in the city.
Prov 13.10 By insolence the heedless make *s*, but
17. 1 than a house full of feasting with *s*.
17.14 The beginning of *s* is like letting out
18. 6 A fool's lips bring *s*, and a fool's mouth
28.25 The greedy person stirs up *s*, but
29.22 One given to anger stirs up *s*, and the
30.33 blood, so pressing anger produces *s*.

STRIKE (STRUCK)

Gen 3.15 He will *s* your head, and you will *s* his
Ex 12.12 I will *s* down every firstborn in the land
12.29 the LORD *s* down all the firstborn in the
Num 20.11 lifted up his hand and *s* the rock twice
2 Sam 12. 9 You have *s* down Uriah the Hittite with
12.15 The LORD *s* the child that Uriah's wife
Ps 121. 6 The sun shall not *s* you by day, nor the
141. 5 Let the righteous *s* me; let the faithful
Isa 27. 7 Has he *s* them down as he *s* down those
53. 4 accounted him stricken, *s* down by God,
Jer 5. 3 You have *s* them, but they felt no

Hag 2.17 I *s* you and all the products of your toil
Mk 14.27 'I will *s* the shepherd, and the sheep

STRIP (STRIPPED)

Lev 19.10 You shall not *s* your vineyard bare, or
Num 20.28 Moses *s* Aaran of his vestments, and
Job 19. 9 He has *s* my glory from me, and taken

STRIVE (STRIVEN STRIVING)

Gen 32.28 but Israel, for you have *s* with God
Isa 41.11 those who *s* against you shall be as
Mt 6.33 But *s* first for the kingdom of God and
Lk 12.31 Instead, *s* for his kingdom, and these
13.24 "*S* to enter through the narrow door; for
1 Cor 12.31 But *s* for greater gifts. And I will show
14.12 for spiritual gifts, *s* to excel in them
Phil 1.27 *s* side by side with one mind for the
2 Pet 3.14 *s* to be found by him at peace, without

STRONG (STRONGER)

Judg 14.14 eat. Out of the *s* came something sweet."
2 Sam 3. 1 David grew *s* and *s*, while the house of
1 Chr 19.13 Be *s*, and let us be courageous for our
28.20 "Be *s* and of good courage, and act. Do
2 Chr 26.16 when he had become *s* he grew proud,
Ps 27.14 Wait for the LORD; be *s*, and let your
140. 7 Lord, my *s* deliverer, you have covered
Eccl 6.10 able to dispute with those who are *s*.
9.11 nor the battle to the *s*, nor bread to the
Mt 12.29 how can one enter a *s* man's house and
Lk 11.21 When a *s* man, fully armed, guards his
Rom 15. 1 *s* ought to put up with the failings of
1 Cor 1.25 weakness is *s* than human strength.
1.27 is weak in the world to shame the *s*;
Eph 6.10 Finally, be *s* in the Lord and in the
2 Tim 2. 1 my child, be *s* in the grace that is in
1 Jn 2.14 young people, because you are *s* and

STRONGHOLD

Ps 9. 9 The LORD is a *s* for the oppressed, a *s* in
18. 2 and the horn of my salvation, my *s*.
27. 1 The LORD is the *s* of my life; of whom
94.22 But the LORD has become my *s*, and my
Joel 3.16 his people, a *s* for the people of Israel.
Nah 1. 7 LORD is good, a *s* in a day of trouble;

STRUGGLE (STRUGGLING)

Prov 28. 4 but those who keep the law *s* against
Eph 6.12 our *s* is not against enemies of blood
Col 2. 1 you to know how much I am *s* for you,

STUBBLE

Ex 5.12 the land of Egypt, to gather *s* for straw.
Isa 47.14 they are like *s*, the fire consumes them;
Mal 4. 1 arrogant and and all evildoers will be *s*;

STUBBORN

Deut 9. 6 righteousness, for you are a *s* people.
29.19 safe even though we go our own *s* ways"
Judg 2.19 any of their practices or their *s* ways.
2 Kings 17.14 not listen, but were *s*, as their ancestors
Ps 81.12 So I gave them over to their *s* hearts, to
Ezek 3. 7 have a hard forehead and a *s* heart.

STUBBORNNESS

1 Sam 15.23 and *s* is like iniquity and idolatry.
Mk 16.14n them for their lack of faith and *s*,

STUDENTS

Mt 23. 8 you have one teacher, and you are all *s*.

STUDY

Ps 101. 2 I will *s* the way that is blameless. When
Eccl 12.12 and much *s* is a weariness of the flesh.

STUMBLE (STUMBLED STUMBLING)

Prov 3.23 way securely and your foot will not *s*.
4.19 they do not know what they *s* over.
Isa 3. 8 Jerusalem has *s*, and Judah has fallen,

SUPPLANT
Hos 12. 3 In the womb he tried to *s* his brother,

SUPPLICATION
2 Sam 24.25 LORD answered his *s* for the land, and
Job 8. 5 If you will seek God and make *s* to the
Ps 28. 2 Hear the voice of my *s*, as I cry to you
Isa 45.14 They will make *s* to you, saying, "God is

SUPPORT
Gen 13. 6 the land could not *s* both of them living
Ezek 30. 6 Those who *s* Egypt shall fall, and it
Mt 15. 5 'Whatever *s* you might have had from
Acts 20.35 by such work we must *s* the weak,
2 Cor 11. 8 churches by accepting *s* from them
3 Jn 8 Therefore we ought to *s* such people, so

SUPPORTERS
Job 31.21 because I saw I had *s* at the gate;

SURE
1 Jn 2. 3 by this we may be *s* that we know him,

SURROUND (SURROUNDED)
Gen 19. 4 and old, all the people . . . *s* the house;
Ps 118. 11 They *s* me, *s* me on every side; in the
Lk 8.45 "Master, the crowds *s* you and press in
Heb 12. 1 since we are *s* by so great a crowd of

SURVIVORS
Neh 1. 3 "The *s* there in the province who
Joel 2.32 among the *s* shall be those whom the
Mic 2.12 I will gather the *s* of Israel; I will set

SUSA
Neh 1. 1 year, while I was in *S* the capital,
Esth 1. 2 sat his royal throne in the citadel of *S*,
2. 5 was a Jew in the citadel of *S* whose
8.15 the city of *S* shouted and rejoiced.
9.18 the Jews who were in *S* gathered on the

SUSPENSE
Jn 10.24 "How long will you keep us in *s*? If you

SUSTAIN (SUSTAINED)
Neh 9.21 years you *s* them in the wilderness
Ps 55.22 burden on the LORD, and he will *s* you;

SWALLOW (n)
Isa 38.14 Like a *s* or a crane I clamor, I moan
Jer 8. 7 the turtledove, *s*, and crane observe the

SWALLOW (SWALLOWED SWALLOWS)
Num 16.30 ground opens its mouth and *s* them up,
Ps 35.25 Do not let them say, "We have *s* you up."
Isa 25. 7 all nations; he will *s* up death forever.
Jon 1.17 provided a large fish to *s* up Jonah;
1 Cor 15.54 "Death has been *s* up in victory."
2 Cor 5. 4 so that what is mortal may be *s* up

SWARM (SWARMS)
Gen 1.20 "Let the waters bring forth *s* of living
Ex 8.21 I will send *s* of flies on you, your
Lev 11.41 All creatures that *s* upon the earth are

SWEAR (SWEARS SWORE SWORN)
Gen 24. 3 I will make you *s* by the LORD, the God
Lev 19.12 You shall not *s* falsely by my name,
Deut 6.10 the land that he *s* to your ancestors,
Ps 110. 4 LORD has *s* and will not change his
Isa 48. 1 who *s* by the name of the LORD, and
62. 8 LORD has *s* by his right hand and by his
Jer 4. 2 if you *s*, "As the LORD lives!" in truth, in
22. 5 words, I *s* by myself, says the LORD,
44.26 Lo, I *s* by my great name, says the LORD,
Am 4. 2 GOD has *s* by his holiness: The time is
Zech 5. 3 everyone who *s* falsely shall be cut off
Mt 5.34 Do not *s* at all, either by heaven, for it
23.16 whoever *s* by the gold of the sanctuary,
Jas 5.12 do not *s*, either by heaven or by earth

SWEAT
Gen 3.19 "By the *s* of your face you shall eat
Lk 22.44 his *s* became like great drops of blood

SWEET
Judg 14.14 Out of the strong came something *s*."
Ps 119.103 How *s* are your words to my taste,

SWEPT
Gen 1. 2 a mighty wind *s* over the face of the
Isa 44.22 *s* away your transgressions like a cloud,
Mt 12.44 it finds it empty, *s*, and put in order.

SWIFT
Eccl 9.11 the race is not to the *s*, nor the battle

SWINE
Mt 8.31 cast us out, send us into the herd of *s*."
Mk 5.12 "Send us to the *s*, let us enter them."
Lk 8.32 herd of *s* was feeding; and the demons

SWORD (SWORDS)
Gen 3.24 a *s* flaming and turning to guard the
Judg 7.14 "This is no other than the *s* of Gideon
7.20 cried, "A *s* for the LORD and for Gideon!"
1 Kings 3.24 king said, "Bring me a *s*," and they
Isa 2. 4 beat their *s* into plowshares, and their
49. 2 made my mouth like a sharp *s*, in the
Jer 9.16 I will send the *s* after them, until I have
25.38 become waste because of the cruel *s*,
Ezek 21. 9 Say: A *s*, a *s* is sharpened, it is also
Joel 3.10 Beat your plowshares into *s*, and your
Mic 4. 3 they shall beat their *s* into plowshares,
Zech 13. 7 "Awake, O *s*, against my shepherd,
Mt 10.34 I have not come to bring peace, but a *s*.
26.51 on his *s*, drew it, and struck the slave of
Mk 14.47 drew his *s*, and struck the slave of the
Lk 2.35 a *s* will pierce your own soul
Eph 6.17 the *s* of the Spirit, which is the word of
Heb 4.12 sharper than any two-edged *s*, piercing
Rev 1.16 his mouth came a sharp two-edged *s*,
19.15 from his mouth comes a sharp *s* with

SYCAMORE
Am 7.14 a herdsman, and a dresser of *s* trees,
Lk 19. 4 So he ran ahead and climbed a *s* tree to

SYCHAR
Jn 4. 5 he came to a Samaritan city called *S*,

SYMPATHY
Job 42.11 they showed *s* and comforted him for
1 Pet 3. 8 all of you, have unity of spirit, *s*, love

SYNAGOGUE
Mk 5.38 to the house of the leader of the *s*,
6. 2 the sabbath he began to teach in the *s*,
Lk 7. 5 and it is he who built our *s* for us."
8.41 a man named Jairus, a leader of the *s*.
Acts 18. 4 Every sabbath he would argue in the *s*
19. 8 He entered the *s* and for three months

SYRIA
Mt 4.24 So his fame spread throughout all *S*,
Lk 2. 2 while Quirinius was governor of *S*.
Acts 15.41 He went through *S* and Cilicia,

T

TABERNACLE
Ex 25. 9 pattern of the *t* and of all its furniture,
26.30 you shall erect the *t* according to the
40. 2 you shall set up the *t* of the tent of

TABLE (TABLES)
Ex 25.23 You shall make a *t* of acacia wood, two
37.10 He also made the *t* of acacia wood, two
2 Kings 4.10 put there for him a bed, a *t*, a chair,

Ps 23. 5 You prepare a *t* before me in the
69.22 Let their *t* be a trap for them, a snare
78.19 "Can God spread a *t* in the wilderness?
Mal 1.12 you say that the LORD's *t* is polluted,
Acts 6. 2 the word of God in order to wait on *t*.
1 Cor 10.21 partake of the *t* of the Lord and the *t* of

TABLET (TABLETS)

Ex 31.18 the two *t* of the covenant, *t* of stone,
34. 1 "Cut two *t* of stone like the first; and I
Deut 9.10 LORD gave me the two stone *t* written
Isa 8. 1 Take a large *t* and write on it in
Lk 1.63 He asked for a writing *t*, and wrote,
2 Cor 3. 3 on *t* of stone but on *t* of human hearts.

TAKE (TAKEN TAKES)

Ex 25. 2 the Israelites to *t* for me an offering;
Prov 8.10 *T* my instruction instead of silver, and
11.30 a tree of life, but violence *t* lives away.
Lam 3.58 You have *t* up my cause, O Lord, you
Mt 26.26 and said, "*T*, eat; this is my body."
Mk 14.22 it to them, and said "*T*; this is my body."
Jn 14. 3 I will come again and will *t* you to
Heb 11. 5 was not found, because God had *t* him."
Rev 22.19 if anyone *t* away from the words of the

TALE

Lk 24.11 these words seemed to them an idle *t*,

TALENTS

Mt 18.24 one who owed him ten thousand *t* was
25.15 to one he gave five *t*, to another two, to

TALK (TALKED TALKING)

Job 11. 2 and should one full of *t* be vindicated?
15. 3 Should they argue in unprofitable *t*, or
Ps 71.24 my tongue will *t* of your righteous help,
Prov 4.24 speech, and put devious *t* far from you.
Zech 1.14 the angel who *t* with me said to me,
Mt 16. 8 little faith, why are you *t* about having
Lk 24.15 While they were *t* and discussing, Jesus

TAME

Jas 3. 8 no one being can *t* the tongue—a

TARSHISH

Gen 10. 4 The descendants of Javan: . . . *T*,
2 Chr 9.21 the king's ships went to *T* with the
20.36 joined him in building ships to go to *T*;
Ps 48. 7 an east wind shatters the ships of *T*.
72.10 the kings of *T* and of the isles render
Isa 23.14 Wail, O ships of *T*, for your fortress is
Jon 1. 3 Jonah set out to flee to *T* from the

TARSUS

Acts 9.11 Judas look for a man of *T* named Saul.
11.25 Barnabas went to *T* to look for Saul,
21.39 replied, "I am a Jew, from *T* in Cilicia,

TASKMASTERS

Ex 1.11 they set *t* over them to oppress them
5. 6 Pharaoh commanded the *t* of the

TASTE (TASTED)

Ps 34. 8 O *t* and see that the LORD is good;
Mt 5.13 but if salt has lost its *t*, how can its
16.28 who will not *t* death before they see the
Mk 9. 1 who will not *t* death until they see that
Lk 9.27 who will not *t* death before they see the
Acts 23.14 by an oath to *t* no food until we have
Col 2.21 not handle, Do not *t*, Do not touch"?
Heb 2. 9 of God he might *t* death for everyone.
6. 4 and have *t* the heavenly gift,
1 Pet 2. 3 indeed you have *t* that the Lord is good.

TAUNT

Ps 42.10 my adversaries *t* me, while they say to
44.13 You have made us the *t* of our
102. 8 All day long my enemies *t* me; those
Isa 14. 4 up this *t* against the king of Babylon:
Hab 2. 6 Shall not everyone *t* such people and,

TAUNT-SONGS

Lam 3.63 I am the object of their *t*.

TAX (TAXES)

Mt 9. 9 called Matthew sitting at the *t* booth;
17.24 your teacher not pay the temple *t*?"
22.17 Is it lawful to pay *t* to the emperor,
Mk 2.14 son of Alphaeus sitting at the *t* booth,
12.14 Is it lawful to pay *t* to the emperor, or
Lk 5.27 named Levi, sitting at the *t* booth;
20.22 Is it lawful for us to pay *t* to the
Rom 13. 6 also pay *t*, for the authorities are God's

TAX COLLECTOR (TAX COLLECTORS)

Mt 21.31 *t* and the prostitutes go into the
Mk 2.15 many *t* and sinners were also sitting
Lk 3.12 Even *t* came to be baptized, and they
5.30 "Why do you eat and drink with *t* and
7.29 including the *t* acknowledged the justice
7.34 and drunkard, a friend of *t* and sinners!'
18.10 pray, one a Pharisee and the other a *t*.
19. 2 Zacchaeus; he was a chief *t* and was

TEACH

Ex 4.12 I will . . . *t* you what you shall speak."
18.20 and *t* them the statutes and instructions
Lev 10.11 you are to *t* the people of Israel all the
Deut 4. 5 I now *t* you statutes and ordinances for
4.10 the earth, and may *t* their children so";
5.31 that you shall *t* them, so that they may
11.19 *T* them to your children, talking about
20.18 that they may not *t* you to do all the
31.19 write this song, and *t* it to the Israelites;
33.10 They *t* Jacob your ordinances, and
Judg 13. 8 again to us, and *t* us what we are to do
Ezra 7.10 and to *t* the statutes and ordinances in
Job 12. 7 ask the animals, and they will *t* you; the
21.22 Will any *t* God knowledge, seeing that
Ps 25. 4 your ways. O LORD; *t* me your paths.
25.12 He will *t* them the way that they should
27.11 *T* me your way, O LORD; and lead me on
34.11 to me; I will *t* you the fear of the LORD.
86.11 *T* me your way, O LORD, that I may walk
90.12 So *t* us to count our days that we may
119. 12 are you, O LORD; *t* me your statutes.
119. 33 *T* me, O LORD, the way of your statutes,
143. 10 *T* me to do your will, for you are my
Prov 9. 9 *t* the righteous and they will gain in
Isa 2. 3 that he may *t* us his ways and that we
28. 9 "Whom will he *t* knowledge, and to
Jer 31.34 No longer shall they *t* one another, or
Ezek 44.23 *t* my people the difference between the
Mic 3.11 for a bribe, its priests *t* for a price,
4. 2 that he may *t* us his ways and that we
Mt 13.54 began to *t* the people in their
Mk 4. 2 He began to *t* them many things in
6. 2 On the sabbath he began to *t* in the
8.31 began to *t* them that the Son of Man
Lk 4.15 He began to *t* in their synagogues and
11. 1 "Lord, *t* us to pray, as John taught his
12.12 for the Holy Spirit will *t* you at that very
Jn 14.26 send in my name, will *t* you everything,
Acts 4.18 ordered them not to speak or *t* at all in
5.42 they did not cease to *t* and proclaim
Rom 2.21 that *t* others, will you not *t* yourself?
Col 3.16 you richly; *t* and admonish one another
1 Tim 2.12 I permit no woman to *t* or to have
Heb 8.11 they shall not *t* one another or say to

TEACHES (TEACHING TAUGHT)

Deut 4. 1 ordinances which I am *t* you to observe,
2 Chr 15. 3 the true God, and without a *t* priest,
17. 9 They *t* in Judah, having the book of the
Ps 94.10 He who *t* knowledge to humankind,
Prov 4.11 I have *t* you the way of wisdom; I have

Isa 50. 4 my ear to listen as those who are *t*.
Jer 32.33 though I have *t* them persistently, they
Dan 1. 4 were to be *t* the literature and language
Mt 4.23 Galilee, *t* in their synagogues
7.29 for he *t* them as one having authority,
Mk 1.22 for he *t* them as one having authority,
9.31 he was *t* his disciples, saying to them,
14.49 after day I was with you in the temple *t*,
Lk 4.31 Galilee, and was *t* them on the sabbath.
Jn 6.45 'And they shall all be *t* by God.'
Acts 1. 1 wrote about all that Jesus did and *t*
5.25 prison are standing in the temple and *t*
15.35 and there, with many others, they *t*
18.25 and *t* accurately the things concerning
21.28 This is the man who is *t* everyone
Gal 6. 6 Those who are *t* the word must share in
Eph 4.21 heard about him and were *t* in him,
1 Tim 6. 3 Whoever *t* otherwise and does not agree
1 Jn 2.27 as his anointing *t* you about all things,

TEACHER (TEACHERS)

Job 36.22 in his power; who is a *t* like him?
Ps 119. 99 have more understanding than all my *t*,
Eccl 1. 1 The words of the *T*, the son of David,
Isa 30.20 your *T* will not hide himself any more,
Mt 10.24 "A disciple is not above his *t*, nor a
17.24 "Does your *t* not pay the temple tax?"
23. 8 to be called rabbi, for you have one *t*,
26.18 "The *T* says, My time is near; I will
Mk 5.35 is dead. Why trouble the *t* any further?"
Lk 5.17 Pharisees and *t* of the law were sitting
6.40 A disciple is not above the *t*, but
Jn 11.28 privately, "The *T* is here and is calling
20.16 in Hebrew, "Rabbouni!" (which means *T*).
Eph 4.11 some pastors and *t*, to equip the saints
1 Tim 1. 7 talk, desiring to be *t* of the law,

TEACHING (TEACHINGS)

Deut 32. 2 May my *t* drop like the rain, my speech
Prov 1. 8 and do not reject your mother's *t*;
13.14 The *t* of the wise is a fountain of life,
Isa 51. 7 people who have my *t* in your hearts;
Jer 6.19 and as for my *t*, they have rejected it.
Mt 16.12 of bread, but of the *t* of the Pharisees
Lk 4.32 They were astonished at his *t*, because
Jn 7.16 answered them, "My *t* is not mine, but
18.19 about his disciples and about his *t*.
Acts 2.42 devoted themselves to the apostles' *t*
5.28 you have filled Jerusalem with your *t*
17.19 "May we know what this new *t* is that
Rom 6.17 form of *t* to which you were entrusted,
1 Tim 4.13 reading of scripture, to exhorting, to *t*.
5.17 those who labor in preaching and *t*;
6. 3 *t* that is in accordance with godliness,
2 Tim 3.10 you have observed my *t*, my conduct,
3.16 and is useful for *t*, for reproof, for
2 Jn 9 who does not abide in the *t* of Christ,

TEAR (TEARS) (n)

Ps 42. 3 My *t* have been my food day and night,
56. 8 put my *t* in your bottle. Are they not in
Isa 25. 8 GOD will wipe away the *t* from all faces,
38. 5 heard your prayer, I have seen your *t*;
2 Cor 2. 4 and with many *t*, not to cause you pain,
Rev 7.17 God will wipe away every *t* from their
21. 4 he will wipe away every *t* from their

TEAR (TORN) (v)

1 Sam 15.28 "The LORD has *t* the kingdom of Israel
Mt 5.29 your right eye causes you to sin, *t* it out
Mk 15.38 curtain of the temple was *t* in two, from
Gal 4.15 you would have *t* out your eyes and

TEKOA

2 Sam 14. 2 Joab sent to *T*, and brought from there
2 Chr 20.20 and went out into the wilderness of *T*;
Jer 6. 1 Blow the trumpet in *T*, and raise a
Am 1. 1 who was among the shepherds of *T*,

TELL (TOLD)

2 Sam 1.20 *T* it not in Gath, proclaim it not in the
Neh 9.23 into the land that you had *t* their
Ps 40. 9 I have *t* the glad news of deliverance in
105. 2 to him; *t* of all his wonderful works.
Isa 41.22 bring them, and *t* us what is to happen.
Jer 33. 3 will *t* you great and hidden things that
38.15 Jeremiah said to Zedekiah, "If I *t* you,
Mt 28. 7 go quickly and *t* his disciples, 'He has
Mk 5.14 The swineherds ran off and *t* it in the
16. 7 go, *t* his disciples and Peter that he is
2 Cor 12. 4 and heard things that are not to be *t*,

TEMPEST

Prov 10.25 When the *t* passes, the wicked are no

TEMPESTUOUS

Jon 1.11 the sea was growing more and more *t*.

TEMPLE

Ps 11. 4 The LORD is in his holy *t*; the LORD's
29. 9 forest bare; and in his *t* all say, "Glory!"
48. 9 love, O God, in the midst of your *t*.
65. 4 the goodness of your house, your holy *t*.
79. 1 they have defiled your holy *t*;
Isa 44.28 of the *t*, "Your foundation shall be laid."
Jer 7. 4 in these deceptive words: "This is the *t*
Ezek 43. 5 and the glory of the LORD filled the *t*.
43.11 make known to them the plan of the *t*,
Dan 11.31 by him shall occupy and profane the *t*
Hab 2.20 the LORD is in his holy *t*; let all the
Zech 6.12 and he shall build the *t* of the LORD.
Mt 4. 5 placed him on the pinnacle of the *t*,
21.12 all who were selling and buying in the *t*,
24. 1 point out to him the buildings of the *t*.
26.61 I am able to destroy the *t* of God, and
27.40 "You who would destroy the *t* and build
Mk 11.15 he entered the *t* and began to drive out
11.16 anyone to carry anything through the *t*.
14.58 heard him say, "I will destroy this *t* that
15.29 You who would destroy the *t* and build
Lk 2.46 they found him in the *t*, sitting among
4. 9 placed him on the pinnacle of the *t*,
18.10 "Two men went up to the *t* to pray, one
19.45 he entered the *t* and began to drive out
Jn 2.14 In the *t* he found people selling cattle,
2.19 "Destroy this *t*, and in three days I will
Acts 24. 6 He even tried to profane the *t*, and so
1 Cor 3.16 not know that you are God's *t* and that
6.19 your body is a *t* of the Holy Spirit
2 Cor 6.16 For we are the *t* of the living God; as
Eph 2.21 and grows into a holy *t* in the Lord;
Rev 11. 1 "Come and measure the *t* of God and
11.19 God's *t* in heaven was opened, and the
15. 8 the *t* was filled with smoke from the
21.22 I saw no *t* in the city, for its *t* is the

TEMPORARY

2 Cor 4.18 for what can be seen is *t*, but what

TEMPT (TEMPTED)

Mk 1.13 in the wilderness forty days, *t* by Satan;
Lk 4. 2 for forty days he was *t* by the devil.
1 Cor 7. 5 so that Satan may not *t* you because of
Jas 1.13 No one, when *t*, should say, "I am being

TEMPTER

Mt 4. 3 The *t* came and said to him, "If you are
1 Thess 3. 5 that somehow the *t* had tempted you

TEN

Gen 18.32 Suppose *t* are found there." He
Deut 4.13 observe, that is, the *t* commandments;
Lk 17.12 a village, *t* lepers approached him.

TENANTS

Mt 21.33 Then he leased it to *t* and went to
Mk 12. 1 watchtower, then he leased it to *t*

Lk 20.16 come and destroy those *t* and give the

TEND (TENDED)

Ps 78.72 With upright heart he *t* them, and
1 Pet 5. 2 elders among you to *t* the flock of God

TENT (TENTS)

Gen 4.20 the ancestor of those who live in *t* and
12. 8 on the east of Bethel, and pitched his *t*,
13. 3 to the place where his *t* had been at the
Ex 29.44 I will consecrate the *t* of meeting and
33. 7 the camp; he called it the *t* of meeting.
Lev 1. 1 and spoke to him from the *t* of meeting,
Josh 18. 1 at Shiloh, and set up the *t* of meeting
2 Sam 7. 2 of cedar, but the ark of God stays in a *t*."
1 Chr 17. 1 of the covenant of the LORD is under a *t*."
Job 29. 4 the friendship of God was upon my *t*;
Ps 15. 1 O LORD, who may abide in your *t*? Who
19. 4 the heavens he has set a *t* for the sun,
Prov 14.11 but the *t* of the upright flourishes.
Isa 33.20 a quiet habitation, an immovable *t*,
40.22 like a curtain, and spreads them like a *t*
Jer 10.20 My *t* is destroyed, and all my cords are
Acts 7.44 ancestors had the *t* of testimony in the
2 Cor 5. 1 that if the earthly *t* we live in is
Heb 8. 5 when he was about to erect the *t*,
Rev 15. 5 temple of the *t* of witness in heaven

TENTH

Gen 14.20 And Abram gave him a *t* of everything.
28.22 that you give me I will surely give one *t*
Lev 27.32 All tithes of herd and flock, every *t* one
Isa 6.13 Even if a *t* remain in it, it will be
Heb 7. 2 to him Abraham apportioned "one-*t* of

TENT-MAKERS

Acts 18. 3 worked together— by trade they were *t*.

TERM

Isa 40. 2 cry to her that she has served her *t*, that

TERRIFY (TERRIFIED)

Job 15.24 distress and anguish *t* them; they
23.16 my heart faint; the Almighty has *t* me;
Ps 2. 5 in his wrath, and *t* them in his fury,
Mt 14.26 him walking on the sea, they were *t*,
27.54 they were *t* and said, "Truly this man
Lk 9.34 they were *t* as they entered the cloud.

TERROR

Lev 26.16 will do this to you: I will bring *t* on you;
Ps 91. 5 You will not fear the *t* of the night, or
Isa 2.19 of the ground, from the *t* of the LORD,
17.14 At evening time, lo, *t*! Before morning,
Jer 8.15 for a time of healing, but there is *t*
20. 4 I am making you a *t* to yourself and to
48.44 Everyone who flees from the *t* shall fall
Mk 16. 8 for *t* and amazement had seized them;

TEST (n)

Ex 15.25 and there he put them to the *t*.
Deut 6.16 not put the LORD . . . to the *t*, as you
Ps 106. 14 and put God to the *t* in the desert;
Isa 7.12 ask, and I will not put the LORD to the *t*.
Mal 3.10 and thus put me to the *t*, says the LORD
3.15 when they put God to the *t* they escape."
Mt 4. 7 not put the Lord your God to the *t*.' "
22.18 "Why are you putting me to the *t*, you
Mk 12.15 "Why put me to the *t*? Bring me a
Lk 4.12 not put the Lord your God to the *t*.' "
Acts 5. 9 to put the Spirit of the Lord to the *t*?
15.10 why are you putting God to the *t* by
1 Cor 10. 9 We must not put Christ to the *t*, as

TEST (TESTED TESTING TESTS)

Gen 22. 1 God *t* Abraham. He said to him,
42.15 Here is how you shall be *t*: as Pharaoh
Ex 17. 7 the Israelites quarreled and *t* the LORD,
Num 14.22 and yet you have *t* me these ten times
Deut 8. 2 to humble you, *t* you to know what was
13. 3 God is *t* you, to know whether you
Judg 2.22 In order to *t* Israel, whether or not they
1 Kings 10. 1 she came to *t* him with hard questions.
Job 12.11 Does not the ear *t* words as the palate
Ps 7. 9 you who *t* the minds and hearts, O
11. 5 The LORD *t* the righteous and the
66.10 for you, O God, have *t* us; you have
78.18 They *t* God in their heart by demanding
78.56 they *t* the Most High God, and rebelled
81. 7 I *t* you at the waters of Meribah.
95. 9 when your ancestors *t* me, and put me
105. 19 pass, the word of the LORD kept *t* him.
139. 23 my heart; *t* me and know my thoughts.
Prov 17. 3 is for gold, but the LORD *t* hearts.
Jer 12. 3 O LORD, know me; You see me and *t* me
17.10 "I the LORD *t* the mind and search the
20.12 O LORD of hosts, you *t* the righteous,
Lam 3.40 Let us *t* and examine our ways, and
Dan 1.12 "Please *t* your servants for ten days; Let
Mt 19. 3 and to *t* him they asked, "Is it lawful for
Mk 8.11 him for a sign from heaven, to *t* him.
Lk 11.16 Others, to *t* him, kept demanding from
Jn 6. 6 He said this to *t* him, for he himself
8. 6 They said this to *t* him, so that they
2 Cor 13. 5 you are living in the faith. *T* yourselves.
Gal 6. 4 All must *t* their own work, then that
1 Thess 5.21 but *t* everything; hold fast to what is
Heb 2.18 is able to help those who are being *t*.
4.15 has been *t* as we are, yet without sin.
1 Jn 4. 1 but *t* the spirits to see whether they are

TESTIFY (TESTIFIED TESTIFIES)

Deut 19.18 witness, having *t* falsely against another,
1 Sam 12. 3 Here I am; *t* against me before the LORD
Job 15. 6 and not I; your own lips *t* against you.
Ps 50. 7 O Israel, I will *t* against you. I am God,
Isa 59.12 you are many, and our sins *t* against us.
Jer 14. 7 Although our iniquities *t* against us, act,
Hos 5. 5 Israel's pride *t* against him; Ephraim
7.10 Israel's pride *t* against him; yet they do
Mt 23.31 Thus you *t* against yourselves that you
Lk 21.13 This will give you an opportunity to *t*.
Jn 1. 7 He came as a witness to *t* to the light,
1.34 and have *t* that this is the Son of God."
3.11 we know and *t* to what we have seen;
3.26 to whom you *t*, here he is baptizing,
3.32 He *t* to what he has seen and heard, yet
5.31 If I *t* about myself, my testimony is not
5.37 And the Father who sent me has *t* on
5.39 life; and it is they that *t* on my behalf.
7. 7 hates me because I *t* against it that its
15.26 from the Father, he will *t* on my behalf.
15.27 "You also are to *t* because you have
18.23 I have spoken wrongly, *t* to the wrong.
21.24 is the disciple who is *t* to these things
Acts 8.25 after Peter and John had *t* and spoken
14. 3 who *t* to the word of his grace by
20.21 as I *t* both to Jews and to Greeks about
26.16 to appoint you to serve and *t* to the
1 Pet 1.11 when it *t* in advance to the sufferings
1 Jn 4.14 we have seen and do *t* that the Father
3 Jn 3 and *t* to your faithfulness to the truth,
12 We also *t* for him, and you know that
Rev 1. 2 who *t* to the word of God and to the
22.20 The one who *t* to these things says,

TESTIMONY

Isa 8.16 Bind up the *t*, seal the teaching among
Mt 8. 4 that Moses commanded, as a *t* to them."
24.14 the world, as a *t* to all nations;
26.59 were looking for false *t* against Jesus
Mk 1.44 what Moses commanded, for a *t*
6.11 dust that is on your feet as a *t* against
13. 9 kings because of me, as a *t* to them.
14.55 council were looking for *t* against Jesus
Lk 5.14 for your cleansing, for a *t* to them."

Lk 9. 5 town shake the dust off your feet as a *t*
22.71 "What further *t* do we need? We have
Jn 4.39 in him because of the woman's *t*,
8.13 on your own behalf; your *t* is not valid."
8.17 that the *t* of two witnesses is valid.
1 Cor 1. 6 as the *t* of Christ has been strengthened
2 Cor 1.12 is our boast, the *t* of our conscience:
1 Jn 5. 9 If we receive human *t*, the *t* of God is
Rev 6. 9 for the word of God and for the *t* they
12.17 of God and hold the *t* of Jesus.
19.10 For the *t* of Jesus is the spirit of
22.16 to you with this *t* for the churches.

TESTING (n)

Lk 8.13 for a while and in a time of *t* fall away.
1 Cor 10.13 No *t* has overtaken you that is not
Jas 1. 3 know that the *t* of your faith produces

THADDAEUS

Mt 10. 3 James son of Alphaeus, and *T*;
Mk 3.18 *T*, and Simon the Cananaean, and Judas

THANK (THANKED)

Ps 107. 21 Let them *t* the LORD for his steadfast
Isa 38.18 For Sheol cannot *t* you, death cannot
Mt 11.25 Jesus said, "I *t* you, Father, Lord of
Lk 10.21 "I *t* you, Father, Lord of heaven and
17. 9 Do you *t* the slave for doing what was
17.16 himself at Jesus' feet and *t* him.
Jn 11.41 "Father, I *t* you for having heard me.
Acts 28.15 On seeing them, Paul *t* God and took
Rom 1. 8 First, I *t* my God through Jesus Christ
Phil 1. 3 I *t* God every time I remember you,
1 Thess 3. 9 How can we *t* God enough for you in

THANK OFFERING (THANK OFFERINGS)

Lev 7.12 you shall offer with the *t* unleavened
2 Chr 29.31 bring sacrifices and *t* to the house of
Ps 56.12 perform, O God; I will render *t* to you.
Jer 17.26 and bringing *t* to the house of the LORD.
Am 4. 5 bring a *t* of leavened bread, and

THANKS

2 Chr 7. 3 and worshiped and gave *t* to the LORD,
Neh 12.40 of those who gave *t* stood in the house
Ps 7.17 I will give to the LORD the *t* due to his
30.12 my God, I will give *t* to you forever.
75. 1 We give *t* to you, O God; we give *t*; your
92. 1 It is good to give *t* to the LORD, to sing
100. 4 praise. Give *t* to him, bless his name.
107. 1 O give *t* to the LORD, for he is good; for
138. 1 I give you *t*, O LORD, with my whole
Isa 12. 1 will say in that day: I will give *t* to you,
Dan 2.23 I give *t* and praise, for you have given
Mt 15.36 after giving *t* he broke them and gave
Acts 27.35 he took bread; and giving *t* to God in
Rom 1.21 not honor him as God or give *t* to him,
6.17 But *t* be to God that you, having once
7.25 of death? *T* be to God through Jesus
14. 6 in honor of the Lord and give *t* to God.
1 Cor 14.17 you may give *t* well enough, but the
15.57 But *t* be to God, who gives us the
2 Cor 2.14 But *t* be to God, who in Christ always
8.16 But *t* be to God who put in the heart of
Eph 1.16 I do not cease to give *t* for you as I
5.20 your hearts, giving *t* to God the Father
Col 3.17 Lord Jesus, giving *t* to God the Father
1 Thess 2.13 We also constantly give *t* to God for
5.18 ceasing, give *t* in all circumstances;
2 Thess 1. 3 We must always give *t* to God for you,

THANKSGIVING

Lev 22.29 When you sacrifice a *t* offering to the
Ps 26. 7 singing aloud a song of *t*, and telling all
50.14 Offer to God a sacrifice of *t*, and pay
50.23 Those who bring *t* as their sacrifice
69.30 with a song; I will magnify him with *t*.
116. 17 I will offer to you a *t* sacrifice and call
Isa 51. 3 be found in her, *t* and the voice of song.
Jer 30.19 Out of them shall come *t*, and the
1 Tim 4. 4 rejected, provided it is received with *t*;
Rev 7.12 glory and wisdom and *t* and honor and

THESSALONICA

Acts 17. 1 they came to *T*, where there was a
17.11 were more receptive than those in *T*,
27. 2 by Aristarchus, a Macedonian from *T*.
Phil 4.16 even when I was in *T*, you sent me help
2 Tim 4.10 world, has deserted me and gone to *T*;

THICKET

Gen 22.13 looked up and saw a ram, caught in a *t*

THIEF (THIEVES)

Ps 50.18 You make friends with a *t* when you see
Prov 6.30 *T* are not despised who steal only to
29.24 partner of a *t* is to hate one's own life;
Jer 2.26 As a *t* is shamed when caught, so the
Mt 6.19 and where *t* break in and steal;
24.43 what part of the night the *t* was coming,
Lk 12.39 known at what hour the *t* was coming,
Jn 12. 6 but because he was a *t*; he kept the
2 Pet 3.10 the day of the Lord will come like a *t*,
Rev 3. 3 I will come like a *t*, and you will not

THIGH

Gen 24. 2 that he had, "Put your hand under my *t*,

THINK (THINKING)

Ps 63. 6 when I *t* of you on my bed, and
Prov 12.15 Fools *t* their own way is right, but the
Mt 5.17 "Do not *t* that I have come to abolish
22.42 "What do you *t* of the Messiah? Whose
Lk 6. 8 he knew what they were *t*, he said
11.17 But he knew what they were *t* and said
Rom 12. 3 ought to *t*, but *t* with sober judgement,
2 Cor 12. 6 that no one may *t* better of me than
Gal 6. 3 who are nothing *t* they are something,
2 Tim 2. 7 *T* over what I say, for the Lord will give

THIRD

Mt 17.23 him, and on the *t* day he will be raised."
26.44 he went away and prayed for the *t* time,

THIRST (THIRSTS)

Ps 42. 2 My soul *t* for God, for the living God.
63. 1 my soul *t* for you, my flesh faints for
69.21 food, and for my *t* they gave me vinegar
143. 6 hands to you; my soul *t* for you like a
Isa 48.21 They did not *t* when he led them
41.17 and their tongue is parched with *t*,
55. 1 Ho, every one who *t*, come to the
Am 8.13 and the young men shall faint for *t*.
Mt 5. 6 who hunger and *t* for righteousness,
Rev 7.16 will hunger no more, and *t* no more;

THIRSTY

Prov 25.25 Like cold water to a *t* soul, so is good
Isa 29. 8 a *t* person dreams of drinking and
32. 6 and to deprive the *t* of drink.
35. 7 pool, and the *t* ground springs of water;
65.13 servants shall drink, but you shall be *t*;
Mt 25.35 I was *t* and you gave me something to
Jn 7.37 "Let anyone who is *t* come to me, and
19.28 order to fulfill the scripture), "I am *t*."
Rom 12.20 them; if they are *t*, give them something
2 Cor 11.27 hungry and *t*, often without food, cold
Rev 22.17 "Come." And let everyone who is *t* come.

THIRTY

Zech 11.12 out as my wages *t* shekels of silver.
Mt 26.15 They paid him *t* pieces of silver.
27. 3 and brought back the *t* pieces of silver

THOMAS

Mt 10. 3 Bartholomew; *T* and Matthew the tax
Mk 3.18 Matthew, and *T*, and James son of

Jn 11.16 *T*, who was called the Twin, said to his
14. 5 *T* said to him, "Lord, we do not know
20.27 he said to *T*, "Put your finger here and
21. 2 were Simon Peter, *T* called the Twin,

THONG

Mk 1. 7 down and untie the *t* of his sandals.

THORN (THORNS)

Gen 3.18 *t* and thistles it shall bring forth for
Num 33.55 barbs in your eyes and *t* in your sides;
Isa 5. 6 it shall be overgrown with briers and *t*;
Mt 13. 7 Other seeds fell upon *t*, and the *t* grew
27.29 twisting some *t* into a crown, they put it
Mk 4. 7 Other seed fell among *t* and the *t* grew
15.17 twisting some *t* into a crown, they put it
Lk 6.44 Figs are not gathered from *t*, nor are
8. 7 Some fell among *t*; and the *t* grew with
Jn 19. 5 Jesus came out, wearing the crown of *t*
2 Cor 12. 7 elated, a *t* was given me in the flesh,
Heb 6. 8 if it produces *t* and thistles, it is

THOUGHT (THOUGHTS)

Job 21.27 "Oh, I know your *t*, and your schemes
Ps 10. 4 it out"; all their *t* are, "There is no God."
40. 5 wondrous deeds and your *t* toward us;
40.17 and needy, but the LORD takes *t* for me.
56. 5 cause; all their *t* are against me for evil.
92. 5 works, O LORD! Your *t* are very deep!
94.11 The LORD knows our *t*, that they are
139. 17 How weighty to me are your *t*, O God!
Prov 1.23 I will pour out my *t* to you; I will make
12. 5 The *t* of the righteous are just; the
Isa 55. 8 For my *t* are not your *t*, nor are your
59. 7 innocent blood; their *t* are *t* of iniquity,
66.18 For I know their works and their *t*, and
Dan 2.30 you may understand the *t* of your mind.
Am 4.13 reveals his *t* to mortals, makes the
Mic 4.12 But they do not know the *t* of the LORD;
Mt 9. 4 But Jesus, perceiving their *t*, said, "Why
1 Cor 3.20 Lord knows the *t* of the wise, that they
2 Cor 10. 5 and we take every *t* captive to obey
Heb 4.12 it is able to judge the *t* and intentions

THOUSAND (THOUSANDS)

1 Sam 18. 7 has killed his *t*, and David his ten *t*."
Ps 50.10 forest is mine, the cattle on a *t* hills.
68.17 *t* upon *t*, the LORD came from Sinai into
84.10 a day in your courts is better than a *t*
Eccl 7.28 One man among a *t* I found, but a
Song 5.10 and ruddy, distinguished among ten *t*.
2 Pet 3. 8 one day is like a *t* years, and a *t* years
Rev 20. 2 and Satan, and bound him for a *t* years,

THREATS

Prov 13. 8 for a person's life, but the poor get no *t*.
Lk 3.14 "Do not extort money from anyone by *t*

THREE

Dan 6.13 he is saying his prayers *t* times a day."
Mt 17. 4 I will make *t* dwellings here, one for
1 Jn 5. 8 water and the blood, and these *t* agree.

THRESH (THRESHED THRESHES THRESHING)

Ruth 3. 2 winnowing barley tonight at the *t* floor.
Isa 41.15 you shall *t* the mountains and crush
Jer 51.33 Babylon is like a *t* floor at the time
Hos 10.11 was a trained heifer that loved to *t*,
Am 1. 3 because they have *t* Gilead with *t*
1 Cor 9.10 whoever *t* should *t* in hope of a share in

THROAT (THROATS)

Prov 23. 7 like a hair in the *t*, so are they. "Eat
Hab 2. 5 They open their *t* as wide as Sheol; like
Mt 18.28 seizing him by the *t*, he said, 'Pay what
Rom 3.13 "Their *t* are opened graves; they use

THRONE (THRONES)

1 Kings 1.13 me as king, and he shall sit upon my *t*?
1.37 make his *t* greater than the *t* of my lord
9. 5 I will establish your royal *t* over Israel
10.18 The king also made a great ivory *t*, and
1 Chr 17.12 for me, and I will establish his *t* forever.
Ps 9. 4 just cause; you have sat on the *t* giving
45. 6 Your *t*, O God, endures forever and ever.
93. 2 your *t* is established from of old; you
103. 19 LORD has established his *t* in the
132. 11 sons of your body I will set on your *t*."
Prov 16.12 to do evil, for the *t* is established by
25. 5 king, and his *t* will be established in
Isa 6. 1 died, I saw the Lord sitting on a *t*,
16. 5 a *t* shall be established in steadfast love
66. 1 Heaven is my *t* and the earth is my
Jer 3.17 time Jerusalem shall be called the *t*
17.12 O glorious *t*, exalted from the
43.10 and he will set his *t* above these stones
Lam 5.19 your *t* endures to all generations.
Dan 7. 9 As I watched, *t* were set in place, and
Mt 19.28 followed me will also sit on twelve *t*,
Lk 1.32 give to him the *t* of his ancestor David.
Acts 7.49 'Heaven is my *t*, and the earth is my
Heb 1. 8 "Your *t*, O God, is forever and ever, and
4.16 Let us therefore approach the *t* of grace
8. 1 at the right hand of the *t* of the Majesty
Rev 4. 2 there in heaven stood a *t*, with one
4. 4 twenty-four *t*, and seated on the *t* are
20. 4 Then I saw *t*, and those seated on them
20.11 I saw a great white *t* and one who sat
22. 1 as crystal, flowing from the *t* of God

THRONG

Ps 109. 30 I will praise him in the midst of the *t*.

THROW (THREW THROWN)

Isa 22.18 and *t* you like a ball into a wide land;
Mt 4. 6 are the Son of God, *t* yourself down;
8.12 heirs of the kingdom will be *t* into the
13.42 and they will *t* them into the furnace of
Lk 20.15 they *t* him out of the vineyard and

THUMMIN

Ex 28.30 shall put the Urim and the *T*, and they
Lev 8. 8 breastplate he put the Urim and the *T*.

THUNDER (THUNDERS THUNDERED)

1 Sam 12.17 the LORD, that he may send *t* and rain;
2 Sam 22.14 The LORD *t* from heaven, the Most High
Ps 18.13 LORD also *t* in the heavens, and the
29. 3 over the waters; the God of glory *t*, the
Mk 3.17 the name Boanerges, that is, sons of *t*);

TIDINGS

1 Kings 14. 6 For I am charged with heavy *t* for you.
Ps 68.11 is the company of those who bore the *t*:
Isa 40. 9 O Zion, herald of good *t*; lift up your
41.27 I give to Jerusalem a herald of good *t*.

TIGLATH-PILESER (PUL)

Received tribute from Menahem, 2 Kings 15.19-20; carried the people captive to Assyria, 2 Kings 15.29; paid homage by Ahaz, 2 Kings 16.7-10 (2 Chr 28.20-21); deported some of the tribes of Israel, 1 Chr 5.26.

TIGRIS

Gen 2.14 name of the third river is *T*, which flows
Dan 10. 4 bank of the great river (that is, the *T*),

TILL (TILLER)

Gen 2. 5 and there was no one to *t* the ground;
3.23 God sent him . . . to *t* the ground from
Zech 13. 5 "I am no prophet, I am a *t* of the soil;

TIME (TIMES)

Gen 21. 2 age, at the *t* of which God had spoken
Ex 12.40 The *t* that the Israelites had lived in
2 Kings 5.26 Is this a *t* to accept money and to
Esth 4.14 to royal dignity for such a *t* as this."
Ps 31.15 My *t* are in your hand; deliver me from

Ps 34. 1 I will bless the LORD at all *t*; his praise
89.47 Remember how short my *t* is— for what
119.126 It is *t* for the LORD to act, for your law
Eccl 3. 1 is a season, and a *t* for every matter
8. 6 For every matter has its *t* and way,
9.11 but *t* and chance happen to them all.
Ezek 12.27 years ahead; he prophesies for distant *t*."
30. 3 will be a day of clouds, a *t* of doom for
Hab 2. 3 is still a vision for the appointed *t*;
Hag 1. 2 These people say the *t* has not yet
Mt 8.29 come here to torment us before the *t*?"
26.18 'The Teacher says, My *t* is near; I will
Jn 7. 6 "My *t* has not yet come, but your *t* is
1 Cor 7.29 appointed *t* has grown short; from now
Eph 5.16 making the most of the *t*, because the
Col 4. 5 outsiders, making the most of the *t*.
Rev 1. 3 what is written in it; for the *t* is near.
12.14 she is nourished for a *t*, and *t*, and half a

TIMOTHY

Paul's son in the Lord, 1 Cor 4.17; 1 Tim 1.2,18; 2 Tim 1.2; son of a Greek father and a Jewish mother, Acts 16.1; brought up in a devout home, 2 Tim 1.5; 3.14-15; lived in Lystra (or Derbe), Acts 16.1; circumcised, Acts 16.3; accompanied Paul in his second missionary journey, Acts 16.1-4; 17.14-15; 18.5; 1 Thess 3.2-6; ordained, 1 Tim 4.14; 2 Tim 1.6; sent to the church in Corinth, 1 Cor 4.17; 16.10; accompanied Paul in the third missionary journey, Acts 20.4; in charge of the church in Ephesus, 1 Tim 1.3; 4.12; urged by Paul to visit him in prison, 2 Tim 4.9,13; imprisoned and released, Heb 13.23.

1 Cor 4.17 For this reason I sent you *T*, who is my
16.10 If *T* comes, see that he has nothing to

TITHE (TITHES)

Lev 27.31 If persons wish to redeem any of their *t*,
Num 18.21 To the Levites I have given every *t* in
18.24 Levites as their portion of the *t* of the
Deut 14.22 Set apart a *t* of all the yield of your
26.12 finished paying all the *t* of your produce
Neh 10.37 to bring to the Levites the *t* from our
Mal 3. 8 "How are we robbing you?" In your *t* and
Mt 23.23 hypocrites! For you *t* mint, dill, and
Lk 11.42 woe to you Pharisees! for you *t* mint
Heb 7. 9 who receives *t*, paid *t* through Abraham,

TITLE

Mt 22.20 "Whose head is this, and whose *t*?"
Mk 12.16 "Whose head is this, and whose *t*?"

TITUS

2 Cor 2.13 I did not find my brother *T* there.
7. 6 consoled us by the arrival of *T*,
8. 6 so that we might urge *T* that, as he had
8.23 As for *T*, he is my partner and
12.18 *T* did not take advantage of you, did
Gal 2. 1 with Barnabas, taking *T* along
2 Tim 4.10 has gone to Galatia, *T* to Dalmatia.
Titus 1. 4 To *T*, my loyal child in the faith we

TODAY (TODAY'S)

Ps 95. 7 of his hand. O that *t* you would listen
Mt 6.34 of its own. *T* trouble is enough for *t*.
Lk 23.43 I tell you, *t* you will be with me in
Heb 3.15 "*T*, if you hear his voice, do not harden

TOGETHER

Gen 22. 8 son." So the two of them walked on *t*.
Acts 2. 1 had come, they were all *t* in one place.
2.46 they spent much time *t* in the temple,
Col 1.17 all things, and in him all things hold *t*.

TOIL

Prov 14.23 In all *t* there is profit, but mere talk
Eccl 1. 3 What do people gain from all the *t* at
3.13 drink and take pleasure in all their *t*.
4. 4 I saw that all *t* and all skill in work
4. 6 with quiet than two handfuls with *t*,
Eccl 4. 8 yet there is no end to all their *t*, and
5.19 and find enjoyment in their *t*— this is
6. 7 All human *t* is for the mouth, yet the
10.15 The *t* of fools wears them out, for they
Lk 12.27 how they grow: they neither *t* nor spin;
2 Cor 11.27 in *t* and hardship, through many a
Col 1.29 For this I *t* and struggle with all the
Rev 2. 2 "I know your works, your *t* and your

TOLL

Ezra 4.13 they will not pay tribute, custom, or *t*,
7.24 custom, or *t* on any of the priests,
Mt 17.25 from whom do kings of the earth take *t*

TOMB (TOMBS)

Mt 23.27 For you are like whitewashed *t*, which
27.60 rolled a great stone to the door of the *t*
Mk 6.29 and took his body, and laid it in a *t*.
15.46 laid it in a *t* that had been hewn out of
Lk 8.27 he did not live in a house but in the *t*.
11.47 you build the *t* of the prophets whom
24. 1 they came to the *t*, taking the spices
Jn 11.31 she was going to the *t* to weep there.
19.41 and in the garden there was a new *t* in
20. 6 went into the *t*. He saw the linen

TOMORROW

Prov 27. 1 Do not boast about *t*, for you do not
Isa 22.13 "Let us eat and drink, for *t* we die."
Mt 6.30 is alive today and *t* is thrown into the
1 Cor 15.32 "Let us eat and drink, for *t* we die."
Jas 4.14 you do not even know what *t* will bring.

TONGUE (TONGUES)

Job 5.21 hidden from the scourge of the *t*, and
Ps 5. 9 are open graves; they flatter with their *t*.
31.20 under your shelter from contentious *t*.
34.13 Keep your *t* from evil, and your lips
35.28 Then my *t* shall tell of your
39. 1 my ways that I may not sin with my *t*;
45. 1 my *t* is like the pen of a ready scribe.
52. 2 Your *t* is like a sharp razor, you worker
64. 3 who whet their *t* like swords, who aim
Prov 10.20 The *t* of the righteous is choice silver;
10.31 but the perverse *t* will be cut off.
12.18 but the *t* of the wise brings healing.
18.21 Death and life are in the power of the *t*,
25.15 and a soft *t* can break bones.
Isa 45.23 knee shall bow, every *t* shall swear."
54.17 you shall confute every *t* that rises
Jer 9. 5 they have taught their *t* to speak lies;
9. 8 Their *t* is a deadly arrow; it speaks
Mk 7.35 opened, his *t* was released, and he
16.17n out demons; they will speak in new *t*;
Acts 2. 3 Divided *t*, as of fire, appeared among
19. 6 they spoke with *t* and prophesied—
Rom 3.13 graves; they use their *t* to deceive."
1 Cor 12.10 to another various kinds of *t*, to another
13. 1 If I speak in *t* of mortals and of angels,
14. 2 those who speak in a *t* do not speak to
14.21 written, "By people of strange *t* and by
14.22 *T*, then, are a sign not for believers but
Jas 1.26 and do not bridle their *t* but deceive
3. 5 the *t* is a small member, yet it boasts of

TOOTH (TEETH)

Ex 21.24 eye for eye, *t* for *t*, hand for hand, foot
Deut 19.21 eye for eye, *t* for *t*, hand for hand, foot
Job 19.20 and I have escaped by the skin of my *t*.
Prov 25.19 Like a bad *t* or a lame foot is trust in a
Song 4. 2 Your *t* are like a flock of shorn ewes
Ezek 18. 2 and the children's *t* are set on edge"?

TORCH (TORCHES)

Gen 15.17 flaming *t* passed between these pieces.
Judg 7.16 and empty jars, with *t* inside the jars,
Rev 4. 5 of the throne burn seven flaming *t*,

TORMENT (TORMENTED TORMENTS)

Job 19. 2 "How long will you *t* me, and break me
Ps 32.10 Many are the *t* of the wicked, but
Isa 50.11 from my hand: you shall lie down in *t*.
Mt 8.29 Have you come here to *t* us before the
15.22 of David; my daughter is *t* by a demon."
Mk 5. 7 God? I adjure you by God, do not *t* me."
Lk 8.28 High God? I beg you, do not *t* me"—
16.23 in Hades, where he was being *t*, he
Rev 20.10 they will be *t* day and night forever and

TOSSED (TOSSING)

Ex 14.27 the LORD *t* the Egyptians into the sea.
Job 7. 4 is long and I am full of *t* till the dawn.
Isa 57.20 wicked are like the *t* sea that cannot

TOUCH (TOUCHED TOUCHES)

Gen 3. 3 of the garden, nor shall you *t* it, or you
1 Sam 10.26 went warriors whose hearts God had *t*.
Job 4. 5 it *t* you, and you are dismayed.
5.19 troubles; in seven no harm shall *t* you.
Ps 105. 15 saying, "Do not *t* my anointed ones; do
Jer 1. 9 LORD put out his hand and *t* my mouth;
Zech 2. 8 one who *t* you *t* the apple of my eye.
Mt 8. 3 He stretched out his hand and *t* him,
8.15 he *t* her hand, and the fever left her,
9.21 "If I only *t* his cloak, I will be made
9.29 Then he *t* their eyes and said,
14.36 might *t* even the fringe of his cloak;
20.34 with compassion, Jesus *t* their eyes.
Mk 5.28 "If I but *t* his clothes, I will be made
6.56 they might *t* even the fringe of his
Lk 8.45 "Someone *t* me; for I noticed that power
1 Cor 7. 1 "It is well for a man not to *t* a woman."
2 Cor 6.17 and *t* nothing unclean; then I will
1 Jn 5.18 them, and the evil one does not *t* them.

TOWEL

Jn 13. 4 outer robe, and tied a *t* around himself.

TOWER

Gen 11. 4 let us build ourselves a city, and a *t*
Lk 13. 4 were killed when the *t* of Siloam fell
14.28 intending to build a *t*, does not first sit

TRADE (TRADED)

Ezek 27.17 Judah and the land of Israel *t* with you;
Mt 25.16 went off at once and *t* with them;
Acts 19.25 together, with the workers of same *t*,

TRADITION (TRADITIONS)

Mt 15. 2 your disciples break the *t* of the elders?
Mk 7. 5 disciples not live according to the *t* of
7. 8 of God and hold to human *t*."
2 Thess 2.15 stand firm and hold to the *t* that you

TRAIN (TRAINED TRAINING TRAINS)

Gen 14.14 taken captive, he led forth his *t* men,
Ps 144. 1 rock, who *t* my hands for war, and my
Prov 22. 6 *T* children in the right way, and when
1 Tim 1. 4 than the divine *t* that is known by faith.
4. 8 physical *t* is of some value, godliness is
Titus 2.12 *t* us to renounce impiety and worldly

TRAITOR

Lk 6.16 and Judas Iscariot, who became a *t*.

TRAMPLE (TRAMPLED)

Job 9. 8 the heavens and *t* the waves of the Sea;
Ps 56. 1 to me, O God, for people *t* on me;
Hab 3.15 You *t* the sea with your horses,

TRANCE

Dan 10. 9 of his words, I fell into a *t*, face to the

TRANSFER (TRANSFERRED)

2 Sam 3.10 to *t* the kingdom from the house of
Col 1.13 and *t* us into the kingdom of his

TRANSFIGURED

Mt 17. 2 he was *t* before them, and his face
Mk 9. 2 themselves. And he was *t* before them,

TRANSFORM (TRANSFORMED)

Rom 12. 2 be *t* by the renewing of your minds, so
2 Cor 3.18 are being *t* into the same image from
Phil 3.21 He will *t* the body of our humiliation

TRANSGRESS (TRANSGRESSED)

Deut 26.13 I have neither *t* nor forgotten any of
Josh 23.16 If you *t* the covenant of the LORD your
Judg 2.20 people have *t* my covenant that I
2 Kings 18.12 but *t* his covenant—all that Moses the
1 Chr 5.25 But they *t* against the God of their
Ps 17. 3 in me; my mouth does not *t*.
Jer 34.18 those who *t* my covenant and did not
Lam 3.42 We have *t* and rebelled, and you have
Hos 6. 7 at Adam they *t* the covenant; there they
Am 4. 4 Come to Bethel—and *t*; to Gilgal—and

TRANSGRESSION (TRANSGRESSIONS)

Lev 16.16 and because of their *t*, all their sins;
Job 31.33 if I have concealed my *t* as others do,
Ps 32. 1 Happy are those whose *t* is forgiven,
39. 8 Deliver me from all my *t*. Do not make
51. 3 For I know my *t*, and my sin is ever
89.32 I will punish their *t* with the rod and
Prov 10.19 When words are many, *t* is not lacking,
28.13 No one who conceals *t* will prosper, but
Isa 57. 4 Are you not children of *t*, the offspring
59.12 our *t* before you are many, and our sins
6 because their *t* are many, their
Ezek 18.22 None of the *t* that they have committed
39.24 to their uncleanness and their *t*,
Am 1. 3 For three *t* of Damascus, and for four, I
3.14 On the day I punish Israel for its *t*, I
Mic 1. 5 All this is for the *t* of Jacob and for the
Rom 5.14 whose sins were not like the *t* of Adam,
Gal 6. 1 if anyone is detected in a *t*, you who

TRANSGRESSOR

Gal 2.18 down, then I demonstrate that I am a *t*.

TRAVEL (TRAVELED TRAVELS)

Deut 23.14 God *t* along with your camp, to save
Ezek 27.25 The ships of Tarshish *t* for you in your
2 Cor 8.19 appointed by the churches to *t* with us

TRAVELER

Job 31.32 I have opened my doors to the *t*—

TREACHEROUS

Job 6.15 My companions are *t* like a torrent-bed,
Prov 11. 3 but the crookedness of the *t* destroys
Isa 24.16 the *t* deal treacherously, the *t* deal very
2 Tim 3. 4 haters of good, *t*, reckless, swollen with

TREACHERY

Lev 26.40 in that they committed *t* against me,
Josh 22.16 'What is this *t* that you have committed
Jer 5.27 full of birds, their houses are full of *t*;

TREAD (TREADING)

Ps 44. 5 our foes; through your name we *t* down
91.13 You will *t* on the lion and the adder,
Mic 7.19 us; he will *t* our iniquities under foot.
Hab 3.19 deer, and makes me *t* upon the heights.
Mal 4. 3 you shall *t* down the wicked, for they
1 Cor 9. 9 muzzle an ox while it is *t* out the grain."

TREASON

2 Kings 9.23 about and fled, saying to Ahaziah, "*T*,
11.14 tore her clothes and cried, "*T*! *T*!"
2 Chr 23.13 tore her clothes, and cried, "*T*! *T*!"

TREASURE (TREASURED TREASURES)

Gen 43.23 must have put *t* in your sacks for you;
1 Kings 14.26 he took away the *t* of the house of the

2 Kings 20.13 he showed them all his *t* house, the
Job 23.12 his lips; I have *t* in my bosom the words
Prov 2. 1 my words and *t* up my commandments
2. 4 and search for it as for hidden *t*—
15. 6 house of the righteous there is much *t*,
15.16 fear of the LORD than great *t* and trouble
21.20 Precious *t* remains in the house of the
Eccl 2. 8 for myself silver and gold and the *t*
Isa 33. 6 the fear of the LORD is Zion's *t*.
45. 3 give you the *t* of darkness and riches
Jer 15.13 your *t* I will give as plunder, without
20. 5 *t* of the kings of Judah into the hand of
Mic 6.10 Can I forget the *t* of wickedness in the
Hag 2. 7 so that the *t* of all nations shall come,
Mt 6.19 "Do not store up for yourselves *t* on
12.35 brings good things out of a good *t*,
13.44 of heaven is like *t* hidden in a field,
13.52 brings out of his *t* what is new and
Lk 6.45 person out of the good *t* of his heart
12.21 those who store up *t* for themselves
12.34 For where your *t* is, there your heart
2 Cor 4. 7 we have this *t* in clay jars, so that it
Col 2. 3 in whom are hidden all the *t* of wisdom

TREASURE CHESTS

Mt 2.11 opening their *t* they offered him gifts

TREASURY

Josh 6.19 they shall go into the *t* of the LORD."
Zech 11.13 "Throw it into the *t*"— this lordly price
Mk 12.41 the crowd putting money into the *t*.
Jn 8.20 he was teaching in the *t* of the temple,

TREATED

Jer 6.14 *t* the wound of my people carelessly,

TREATY

Josh 9. 6 a far country; so now make a *t* with us."
Isa 33. 8 The *t* is broken, its oaths are despised,

TREE (TREES)

Gen 2. 9 *t* of life also in the midst of the garden,
Deut 16.21 shall not plant any *t* as a sacred pole
20.19 you must not not destroy its *t* by
21.23 anyone hung on a *t* is under God's
1 Kings 19. 4 and sat down under a solitary broom *t*.
Job 14. 7 hope for a *t*, if it be cut down, that it
Ps 52. 8 I am like a green olive *t* in the house of
104. 16 The *t* of the LORD are watered
Prov 15. 4 A gentle tongue is a *t* of life, but
Jer 17. 8 like a *t* planted by water, sending out
Ezek 31. 8 no *t* in the garden of God was like it in
47. 7 I saw upon the bank a great many *t* on
Dan 4.10 there was a *t* at the center of the earth,
Mic 4. 4 own vines and under their own fig *t*,
Mt 7.17 same way, every good *t* bears good fruit,
12.33 for the *t* is known by its fruit;
Lk 6.43 "No good *t* bears bad fruit, nor again
19. 4 ahead and climbed a sycamore *t* to see
Acts 13.29 they took him down from the *t* and laid
Gal 3.13 "Cursed is everyone who hangs on a *t*"—
Rev 2. 7 to eat from the *t* of life that is in the
22. 2 the *t* of life with its twelve kinds of
22.14 they will have the right to the *t* of life

TREMBLE (TREMBLING)

Ps 99. 1 LORD is king; let the peoples *t*! He sits
Isa 13.13 I will make the heavens *t*, and the earth
14.16 "Is this the man who made the earth *t*,
24.18 and the foundations of the earth *t*.
32.11 *T*, you women who are at ease, shudder,
64. 2 the nations might *t* at your presence!
66. 5 of the LORD, you who *t* at his word:
Am 8. 8 Shall not the land *t* on this account,
Mk 5.33 happened to her, came in fear and *t*

TRESPASS (TRESPASSES)

1 Sam 25.28 Please forgive the *t* of your servant; for
Mt 6.14 For if you forgive others their *t*, your
Mk 11.26 in heaven may also forgive your *t*."
Rom 4.25 handed over to death for our *t* and was
2 Cor 5.19 not counting their *t* against them,
Col 2.13 when he forgave us all our *t*, erasing the

TRIAL (TRIALS)

Judg 6.39 let me, please, make *t* just once more;
Mt 6.13 And do not bring us to the time of *t*,
26.41 you may not come into the time of *t*;
Mk 14.38 you may not come into the time of *t*;
Lk 11. 4 And do not bring us to the time of *t*."
22.28 who have stood by me in my *t*; and I
Acts 20.19 with tears, enduring the *t* that came
2 Pet 2. 9 knows how to rescue the godly from *t*,
Rev 3.10 I will keep you from the hour of *t* that

TRIBE (TRIBES)

Judg 21. 6 and said, "One *t* is cut off from Israel
Ps 122. 4 To it the *t* go up, the *t* of the LORD, as
Jer 51.19 and Israel is the *t* of his inheritance;
Rev 7. 4 sealed out of every *t* of the people of

TRIBULATION

Lam 3. 5 and enveloped me with bitterness and *t*;

TRIBUTE

Num 31.37 the LORD's *t* of sheep and goats was six
Judg 3.15 Israelites sent *t* by him to King Eglon of

TRICKED

Gen 3.13 said, "The serpent *t* me, and I ate."

TRICKERY

Eph 4.14 wind of doctrine, by people's *t*, by their

TRIUMPH (TRIUMPHED TRIUMPHING TRIUMPHS)

Ex 15.21 to the LORD, for he has *t* gloriously;
Judg 5.11 repeat the *t* of the LORD, the *t* of his
Ps 18.50 Great *t* he gives to his king, and shows
41.11 because my enemy has not *t* over me.
Prov 28.12 When the righteous *t*, there is great
Isa 45.25 LORD all the offspring of Israel shall *t*
Col 2.15 example of them, *t* over them in him.

TRIUMPHAL

2 Cor 2.14 in Christ always leads us in *t* procession

TROAS

Acts 16. 8 passing by Mysia, they went down to *T*.
20. 5 ahead and were waiting for us in *T*;
2 Cor 2.12 When I came to *T* to proclaim the good
2 Tim 4.13 the cloak that I left with Carpus at *T*,

TROUBLE (TROUBLES) (n)

Josh 7.25 said, "Why did you bring *t* on us?
Judg 11. 7 you come to me now when you are in *t*?"
1 Kings 20. 7 See how this man is seeking *t*; for he
Job 3.26 am I quiet; I have no rest; but *t* comes."
5. 7 human beings are born to *t* just as
5.19 He will deliver you from six *t*; in seven
14. 1 of woman, few of days, and full of *t*,
Ps 27. 5 hide me in his shelter in the day of *t*;
34. 6 the LORD, and was saved from every *t*.
37.39 LORD; he is their refuge in the time of *t*.
46. 1 and strength, a very present help in *t*.
50.15 Call on me in the day of *t*; I will deliver
66.14 my mouth promised when I was in *t*.
73. 5 They are not in *t* as others are; they are
90.10 even then their span is only toil and *t*;
Prov 15.16 of the LORD than great treasure and *t*
27. 9 the heart glad, but the soul is torn by *t*.
Nah 1. 7 LORD is good, a stronghold in a day of *t*;
Mt 13.21 while and when *t* or persecution arises
Gal 6.17 From now on, let no one make *t* for me;

TROUBLE (TROUBLED) (v)

Num 33.55 they shall *t* you in the land where you

Ezek 32. 9 I will *t* the hearts of many peoples, as I
Dan 7.15 me, Daniel, my spirit was *t* within me,
Mt 26.10 "Why do you *t* the woman? She has
Mk 14. 6 why do you *t* her? She has performed a
Lk 8.49 daughter is dead; do not *t* the teacher
Jn 12.27 "Now is my soul *t*. And what should I
13.21 After saying this Jesus was *t* in spirit,
14. 1 "Do not let your hearts be *t*. Believe in

TRUE

1 Kings 11. 4 his heart was not *t* to the LORD his God,
2 Chr 15.17 Nevertheless the heart of Asa was *t* all
16. 9 those whose heart is *t* to him.
Jn 15. 1 "I am the *t* vine, and my Father is the
Rom 3. 4 everyone is a liar, let God be *t*,
Phil 1.18 way, whether out of false motives or *t*;
4. 8 Finally, beloved, whatever is *t*, whatever
Titus 1.13 That testimony is *t*. For this reason

TRUMPET (TRUMPETS)

Ex 19.16 and a blast of a *t* so loud that all the
Lev 23.24 commemmorated with *t* blasts.
Num 10. 2 "Make two silver *t*; you shall make them
Judg 7.16 put *t* into the hands of all of them, and
2 Kings 9.13 they blew the *t*, and proclaimed, "Jehu
Ps 98. 6 With *t* and the sound of the horn make
Isa 27.13 on that day a great *t* will be blown, and
Ezek 33. 5 They heard the sound of the *t* and did
Joel 2. 1 Blow the *t* in Zion; sound the alarm on
Am 3. 6 Is a *t* blown in a city, and the people
Zech 9.14 Lord GOD will sound the *t* and march
Mt 6. 2 you give alms, do not sound a *t*
1 Cor 15.52 *t* will sound, and the dead will be raised
1 Thess 4.16 with the sound of God's *t*, will descend

TRUST (n)

Deut 1.32 spite of this, you have no *t* in the LORD
Job 8.14 is gossamer, a spider's house their *t*.
31.24 "If I have made gold my *t*, or called fine
Ps 40. 4 are those who make the LORD their *t*,
146. 3 Do not put your *t* in princes, in mortals,
Prov 20. 6 loyal, but who can find one worthy of *t*?
22.19 So that your *t* may be in the LORD, I
25.19 tooth or a lame foot is *t* in a faithless
Isa 32.17 righteousness, quietness and *t* forever.
Mic 7. 5 Put no *t* in a friend, have no confidence
Heb 2.13 And again, "I will put my *t* in him." And

TRUST (TRUSTED TRUSTING TRUSTS)

Num 20.12 "Because you did not *t* in me, to show
Deut 9.23 LORD your God, neither *t* nor obeying
28.52 and fortified walls, in which you *t*,
2 Kings 18. 5 He *t* in the LORD the God of Israel; so
Job 18.14 from the tent in which they *t*, and are
Ps 13. 5 But I *t* in your steadfast love; my heart
21. 7 For the king *t* in the LORD, and through
25. 2 O my God, in you I *t*; do not let me be
31.14 But I *t* in you, O LORD; I say, "You are
33.21 in him, because we *t* in his holy name.
37. 3 *T* in the LORD, and do good; so you will
49. 6 those who *t* in their wealth and boast of
52. 7 but *t* in abundant riches, and sought
55.23 out half their days. But I will *t* in you.
62. 8 *T* in him at all times, O people; pour
84.12 hosts, happy is everyone who *t* in you.
91. 2 and my fortress; my God, in whom I *t*."
115. 8 are like them; so are all who *t* in them.
125. 1 Those who *t* in the LORD are like Mount
Prov 3. 5 *T* in the LORD with all your heart, and
11.28 Those who *t* in their riches will wither,
16.20 will prosper, and happy are those who *t*
28.25 whoever *t* in the LORD will be enriched.
Isa 26. 4 *T* in the Lord forever, for in the LORD
28.16 foundation: "One who *t* will not panic."
31. 1 who rely on horses, who *t* in chariots
42.17 put to shame—who *t* in carved images,
50.10 no light, yet *t* in the name of the LORD
Jer 7. 4 not *t* in these deceptive words: "This is
13.25 you have forgotten me and *t* in lies.
17. 5 "Cursed are those who *t* in mere
17. 7 Blessed are those who *t* in the LORD,
29.31 send him, and has led you to *t* in a lie,
48. 7 because you *t* in your strongholds and
Dan 6.23 on him, because he had *t* in his God.
Hos 10.13 Because you have *t* in your power and
Mk 10.24n for those who *t* in riches to enter the
Rom 4. 5 works *t* him who justifies the ungodly,
1 Pet 1.21 him you have come to *t* in God,

TRUSTWORTHY

Ps 111. 7 faithful and just; all his precepts are *t*.
Mt 25.21 "Well done, good and *t* slave; you have
Lk 19.17 you have been *t* in a very small thing,
1 Cor 4. 2 of stewards that they should be found *t*.
Rev 21. 5 this, for these words are *t* and true."

TRUTH

Ps 15. 2 is right and speak *t* from their heart;
Prov 12.17 Whoever speaks the *t* gives honest
23.23 Buy *t*, and do not sell it; buy wisdom,
Isa 45.19 I the LORD speak the *t*, I declare what is
48. 1 the God of Israel, but not in *t* or right.
Dan 4.37 for all his works are *t*, and his ways are
8.12 it cast *t* to the ground, and kept
Lk 1. 4 so that you may know the *t* concerning
Jn 8.32 and you will know the *t*, and the *t* will
14. 6 "I am the way, and the *t*, and the life.
18.38 my voice." Pilate asked him, "What is *t*?"
Rom 1.25 they exchanged the *t* about God for a
1 Cor 5. 8 the unleavened bread of sincerity and *t*.
13. 6 in wrongdoing, but rejoices in the *t*.
2 Cor 13. 8 against the *t*, but only for the *t*.
Eph 4.21 and were taught in him, as *t* is in Jesus.
1 Jn 2. 4 in such a person the *t* does not exist;

TRUTHFUL

Prov 12.19 *T* lips endure forever, but a lying tongue
14.25 A *t* witness saves lives, but one who

TRY (TRIED)

Job 23.10 when he has *t* me, I shall come out like
34.36 Would that Job were *t* to the limit,
Ps 17. 3 If you *t* my heart, if you visit me by
26. 2 Prove me, O LORD, and *t* me; test my
119.140 Your promise is well *t*, and your servant

TUMULT

Isa 22. 5 a day of *t* and trampling and confusion
Hos 10.14 therefore the *t* of war shall rise against

TUNIC (TUNICS)

Mk 6. 9 wear sandals and not to put on two *t*.
Lk 9. 3 bread, nor money—not even an extra *t*.

TURMOIL

Job 30.27 My inward parts are in *t*, and are never
Ps 39. 6 Surely for nothing they are in *t*; they

TURN (TURNED TURNING TURNS)

Deut 23. 5 your God *t* the curse into a blessing for
2 Kings 17.13 "*T* from your evil ways and keep my
23.25 no king like him, who *t* to the LORD
Ezra 6.22 had *t* the heart of the king of Assyria to
Ps 6. 4 *T*, O LORD, save my life; deliver me for
40. 4 who do not *t* to the proud, to those who
90. 3 to dust, and say, "*T* back, you mortals."
119. 36 *T* my heart to your decrees, and not to
119. 51 me, but I do not *t* away from your law.
Prov 4.27 or to the left; *t* your foot away from evil.
Eccl 7.25 I *t* my mind to know and to search out
Isa 2.22 *T* away from mortals, who have only
6.10 with their minds, and *t* and be healed."
45.22 *T* to me and be saved, all the ends of
53. 6 astray; we have all *t* to our own way,
Jer 5.23 heart; they have *t* aside and gone away.

Jer 15. 7 people; they did not *t* from their ways.
15.19 If you *t* back, I will take you back, and
18. 8 *t* from its evil, I will change my mind
25. 5 "*T* now, everyone of you, from your evil
31.13 I will *t* their mourning into joy, I will
35.15 '*T* now everyone of you from your evil
Ezek 14. 6 Repent and *t* away from your idols; and
33.11 *t* back from your evil ways; for why will
Mt 5.39 you on the right cheek, *t* the other also;
13.15 understand with their heart and *t*
Mk 4.12 understand; so they may not *t* again and
Lk 1.16 He will *t* many of the people of Israel to
22.32 once you have *t* back, strengthen your
Acts 14.15 should *t* from these worthless things
17. 6 who have been *t* the world upside down
28.27 understand with their heart and *t*
1 Thess 1. 9 how you *t* to God from idols, to serve a

TURTLEDOVE (TURTLEDOVES)

Gen 15. 9 "Bring me . . . a *t*, and a young pigeon."
Lev 1.14 you shall choose your offering from *t* or
Song 2.12 and the voice of the *t* is heard in our
Lk 2.24 law of the Lord, "a pair of *t*, or two

TWELVE

1 Kings 11.30 he was wearing and tore it into *t* pieces.
Mt 10. 2 These are the names of the *t* apostles:
Mk 3.14 And he appointed *t*, whom he also
6. 7 He called the *t*, and began to send
14.17 it was evening, he came with the *t*.
Lk 2.42 And when he was *t* years old, they went
6.13 called his disciples and chose *t* of them
8.42 he had an only daughter, about *t* years
Jn 6.67 So Jesus asked the *t*, "Do you also wish

TWINKLING

1 Cor 15.52 in the *t* of an eye, at the last trumpet.

TWINS

Gen 25.24 was at hand, there were *t* in her womb.
38.27 came, there were *t* in her womb.

TWO

Gen 6.19 shall bring *t* of every kind into the ark,
Eccl 4. 9 *T* are better than one, because they
Isa 6. 2 with *t* they covered their faces, and with
Mt 6.24 "No one can serve *t* masters; for a slave
18.20 where *t* or three are gathered in my
21.28 A man had *t* sons; he went to the first
24.40 Then *t* will be in the field; one will be
27.21 "Which of the *t* do you want me to
Lk 24.13 on that same day *t* of them were going
1 Cor 6.16 For it is said, "The *t* shall be one flesh."

TYPE

Rom 5.14 who is a *t* of the one who was to come.

TYRANTS

Mt 20.25 and their great ones are *t* over them.

TYRE (TYRIAN)

Josh 19.29 reaching to the fortified city of *T*;
1 Kings 5. 1 King Hiram of *T* sent his servants to
9.11 Hiram of *T* having supplied Solomon
2 Chr 2.14 of the Danite women, his father a *T*.
Ps 45.12 people of *T* will seek your favor with
Isa 23. 1 The oracle concerning *T*. Wail, O ships
Mk 3. 8 and the region around *T* and Sidon.
Lk 10.13 in you had been done in *T* and Sidon,
Acts 21. 3 left, we sailed to Syria and landed at *T*,

U

UNAWARE

1 Cor 10. 1 I do not want you to be *u*, brothers and
2 Cor 1. 8 We do not want you to be *u*, brothers

UNBELIEF

Mt 13.58 of power there, because of their *u*.
Mk 6. 6 And he was amazed at their *u*. Then he
9.24 child cried out, "I believe; help my *u*!"
Rom 11.20 were broken off because of their *u*,

UNBELIEVERS

1 Cor 6. 6 court against a believer—and before *u*
14.23 in tongues, and outsiders or *u* enter,
2 Cor 6.14 Do not be mismatched with *u*. For what

UNBELIEVING

1 Cor 7.14 the *u* husband is made holy through his
Titus 1.15 to the corrupt and *u* nothing is pure.

UNCHASTITY

Mt 5.32 his wife, except on the ground of *u*,

UNCIRCUMCISED

Ex 12.48 land. But no *u* person shall eat of it;
Judg 14. 3 and take a wife from the *u* Philistines?"
Rom 3.30 faith and the *u* through that same faith.
1 Cor 7.18 Was anyone at the time of his call *u*?

UNCLEAN

Lev 13. 3 he shall pronounce him ceremonially *u*.
13.45 cover his upper lip and cry out, "*U*, *u*."
Num 19.11 any human being shall be *u* seven days.
Isa 6. 5 me! I am lost, for I am a man of *u* lips,
52. 1 and the *u* shall enter you no more.
64. 6 all become like one who is *u*, and all
Hag 2.14 hands; and what they offer there is *u*.
Mt 12.43 "When the *u* spirit has gone of a person,
Mk 5. 2 of the tombs with an *u* spirit met him.
7.25 whose little daughter had an *u* spirit
Lk 4.33 man who had the spirit of an *u* demon,
9.42 Jesus rebuked the *u* spirit, healed the
11.24 "When the *u* spirit has gone out of a
Acts 10.14 eaten anything that is profane or *u*."
10.28 I should not call anyone profane or *u*.
1 Cor 7.14 Otherwise, your children would be *u*,

UNCLEANNESS

Lev 5. 3 when you touch human *u*—any *u* by
Ezra 9.11 have filled it end to end with their *u*.

UNCONDEMNED

Acts 16.37 "They have beaten us in public, *u*, men
22.25 you to flog a Roman citizen who is *u*?"

UNCOVERED

Mt 10.26 nothing is covered that will not be *u*,
Lk 12. 2 is covered up that will not be *u*,

UNDEFILED

Heb 7.26 blameless, *u*, separated from sinners,

UNDERGOING

1 Pet 5. 9 world are *u* the same kinds of suffering.

UNDERSTAND (UNDERSTOOD)

Gen 11. 7 they will not *u* one another's speech."
2 Kings 18.26 Aramaic language, for we *u* it; do not
Neh 8. 8 sense, so that the people *u* the reading.
Job 26.14 the thunder of his power who can *u*?"
42. 3 I have uttered what I did not *u*,
Ps 119.100 I *u* more than the aged, for I keep your
Prov 28. 5 The evil do not *u* justice, but those who
Isa 36.11 to your servants in Aramaic, for we *u* it;
Jer 9.12 Who is wise enough to *u* this? To whom
23.20 his mind. In the latter days you will *u*
Dan 8.17 "*U*, O mortal, that the vision is for the
Mt 13.14 'You will indeed listen, but never *u*,
13.51 "Have you *u* all this?" They answered,
Mk 6.52 they did not *u* about the loaves, but
7.18 "Then do you also fail to *u*? Do you not
Jn 20. 9 as yet they did not *u* the scripture, that
Acts 8.30 asked, "Do you *u* what you are reading?"
10.34 "I truly *u* that God shows no partiality,
28.27 and *u* with their heart and turn—and I
Rom 1.20 they are, have been *u* and seen through

Rom 11.25 I want you to *u* this mystery: a
2 Cor 1.14 as you have already *u* us in part—

UNDERSTANDING (n)

Deut 32.28 void of sense; there is no *u* in them.
Job 17. 4 Since you have closed their minds to *u*,
Ps 136. 5 who by *u* made the heavens, for his
147. 5 in power; his *u* is beyond measure.
Prov 2.11 watch over you; and *u* will guard you.
15.32 but those who heed admonition gain *u*.
18. 2 A fool takes no pleasure in *u*, but only
Isa 29.16 of the one who formed it, "He has no *u*?"
40.14 and showed him the way of *u*?
Jer 10.12 and by his *u* stretched out the heavens.
Hos 4.14 thus a people without *u* comes to ruin.
Mt 15.16 he said, "Are you also still without *u*?
Mk 12.33 with all the heart and with all the *u*,
Lk 2.47 him were amazed at his *u* and answers.

UNDO

Eccl 10. 4 post, for calmness will *u* great offenses.

UNDYING

Eph 6.24 with all who have an *u* love for our Lord

UNFAIR

Ezek 18.25 "The way of the Lord is *u*." Hear now, O

UNFAITHFUL (UNFAITHFULNESS)

1 Chr 10.13 So Saul died for his *u*; he was *u* to the
Lk 12.46 him in pieces, and put him with the *u*.

UNGODLY

Job 16.11 God gives me up to the *u*, and casts me
18.21 such are the dwellings of the *u*, such is
Ps 43. 1 God, and defend my cause against an *u*
Rom 5. 6 at the right time Christ died for the *u*.

UNINTENTIONALLY

Lev 4. 2 When anyone sins *u* in any of the
Num 15.24 then if it was done *u* without the
Deut 19. 4 who has killed another person *u*

UNITED

Judg 20.11 gathered against the city, *u* as one.
1 Cor 6.17 anyone *u* to the Lord becomes one
Heb 4. 2 because they were not *u* by faith with

UNITY

Ps 133. 1 it is when kindred live together in *u*!
Eph 4. 3 effort to maintain the *u* of the Spirit
4.13 until all of us come to the *u* of the faith

UNJUST (UNJUSTLY)

Lev 19.15 You shall not render an *u* judgment;
Ps 71. 4 of the wicked, from the grasp of the *u*
82. 2 "How long will you judge *u* and show
Prov 28.16 but one who hates *u* gain will enjoy a
29.27 The *u* are an abomination to the
Zeph 3. 5 without fail; but the *u* knows no shame.

UNKNOWN

Acts 17.23 with this inscription, 'To an *u* god.'
2 Cor 6. 9 as *u*, and yet are well known; as dying,

UNLEAVENED

Lev 23. 6 the festival of *u* bread to the LORD;
Deut 16. 8 days you shall continue to eat *u* bread,
2 Chr 30.21 at Jerusalem kept the feast of *u* bread

UNMARRIED

1 Cor 7. 8 To the *u* and the widows I say it is well

UNPRODUCTIVE

1 Cor 14.14 my spirit prays but my mind is *u*.
Titus 3.14 needs, so that they may not be *u*.

UNRIGHTEOUS (UNRIGHTEOUSNESS)

Jer 22.13 Woe to him who builds his house by *u*,
Mt 5.45 rain on the righteous and on the *u*.

UNROLLED

Lk 4.17 He *u* the scroll and found the place

UNSEARCHABLE

Job 5. 9 He does great things and *u*, marvelous
Ps 145. 3 greatly to be praised; his greatness is *u*.
Prov 25. 3 for depth, so the mind of kings is *u*.
Rom 11.33 How *u* are his judgments and how

UNSKILLED

Heb 5.13 infant, is *u* in the word of righteousness,

UNSTAINED

Jas 1.27 and to keep oneself *u* by the world.

UNTIE

Mk 1. 7 not worthy to stoop down and *u* the
Lk 19.30 been ridden. *U* it and bring it here.

UNTRAINED

2 Cor 11. 6 I may be *u* in speech, but not in

UNVEILED

1 Cor 11. 5 prays or prophesies with her head *u*
2 Cor 3.18 all of us, with *u* faces, seeing the glory

UNWORTHY

1 Cor 11.27 or drinks the cup of the Lord in an *u*

UPBUILDING

1 Cor 14. 3 speak to other people for their *u*

UPHOLD (UPHOLDS)

Ps 37.17 be broken, but the LORD *u* the righteous.
63. 8 clings to you; your right hand *u* me.
Jer 30.13 There is no one to *u* your cause, no

UPRIGHT (UPRIGHTLY)

Num 23.10 Let me die the death of the *u*, and let
Job 4. 7 perished? Or where were the *u* cut off?
Ps 7.10 is my shield, who saves the *u* in heart.
11. 7 deeds; the *u* shall behold his face.
32.11 and shout for joy, all you *u* in heart.
107. 42 The *u* see it and are glad; and all
Prov 2.21 For the *u* will abide in the land, and
3.32 LORD, but the *u* are in his confidence.
14. 2 Those who walk *u* fear the LORD, but

UPROAR

Ps 46. 6 The nations are in an *u*, the kingdoms
Acts 21.31 cohort that all Jerusalem was in an *u*.

UPROOT (UPROOTED)

Mt 13.29 the weeds you would *u* the wheat
15.13 Father has not planted will be *u*.

UPSTAIRS

Lk 22.12 He will show you a large room *u*,
Acts 1.13 they went to the room *u*, where they

UR

Gen 11.28 Terah in the land of his birth, in *U*
11.31 they went out together from *U* of the
15. 7 I am the LORD who brought you from *U*
Neh 9. 7 chose Abram and brought him out of *U*

URGE (URGED URGES)

2 Kings 4. 8 lived, who *u* him to have a meal.
5.23 "Please accept two talents." He *u* him
Lk 24.29 they *u* him strongly, saying, "Stay with
Acts 27.22 I *u* you now to keep up your courage,
2 Cor 5.14 the love of Christ *u* us on, because we
6. 1 we *u* you also not to accept the grace of
9. 5 it necessary to *u* the brothers to go on

URIM

Ex 28.30 shall put the *U* and the Thummin, and
Lev 8. 8 in the breastpiece he put the *U* and the
1 Sam 28. 6 answer him, not by dreams, or by *U*,

USE

Hab 2.18 What *u* is an idol once its maker has

USEFUL

2 Tim 4.11 with you, for he is *u* in my ministry.
Philem 11 you, but now he is indeed *u* both to you

UTENSILS

2 Tim 2.20 there are *u* not only of gold and silver

UZ

Gen 10.23 The descendants of Aram: *U*, Hul,
Job 1. 1 in the land of *U* whose name was Job.
Lam 4.21 Edom, you that live in the land of *U*;

UZZIAH

2 Chr 26. 1 people of Judah took *U*, who was
26.11 Moreover *U* had an army of soldiers, fit
26.18 "It is not for you, *U*, to make offering to
26.21 King *U* was leprous to the day of his
27. 2 LORD just as his father *U* had done—
Isa 1. 1 Judah and Jerusalem in the days of *U*,
6. 1 In the year that King *U* died, I saw the
Mt 1. 8 and Joram the father of *U*, and *U* the

V

VAIN

Ps 127. 1 the house, those who build it labor in *v*.
Prov 31.30 Charm is deceitful, and beauty is *v*, but
1 Cor 15.14 then our proclamation has been in *v*

VALLEY (VALLEYS)

1 Kings 20.28 of the hills but he is not a god of the *v*,'
Ps 23. 4 through the darkest *v*, I fear no evil;
Isa 22. 1 The oracle concerning the *v* of vision.
40. 4 Every *v* shall be lifted up, and every
Jer 19. 6 son of Hinnom, but the *v* of Slaughter.
Ezek 37. 1 the middle of a *v*; it was full of bones.
Joel 3.14 multitudes, in the *v* of decision!
Lk 3. 5 Every *v* shall be filled, and every

VALUE

Mt 13.46 on finding one pearl of great *v*,
Lk 12. 7 you are of more *v* than many sparrows.
1 Tim 4. 8 while physical training is of some *v*,

VANISH (VANISHED)

Judg 6.21 the angel of the LORD *v* from his sight.
Ps 78.33 So he made their days *v* like a breath,
Ezek 26.17 How you have *v* from the seas, O city
Lk 24.31 him; and he *v* from their sight.
Rev 6.14 The sky *v* like a scroll rolling itself up,

VANITY

Eccl 1. 2 *V* of vanities, says the Teacher, *v* of
2.21 toil for it. This also is *v* and a great evil.
12. 8 *V* of vanities, says the Teacher; all is *v*.

VARIETIES

1 Cor 12. 4 there are *v* of gifts, but the same Spirit;
12. 5 there are *v* of activities, but it is the

VEIL (VEILED)

Gen 24.65 So she took her *v* and covered herself.
Ex 26.33 the *v* shall separate for you the holy
34.33 with them, he put a *v* on his face;
36.35 He made the *v* of blue, purple, and
2 Cor 3.14 of the old covenant, that same *v* is still
4. 3 even if our gospel is *v*, it is *v* to those

VENGEANCE

Gen 4.15 kills Cain will suffer a sevenfold *v*."
Lev 19.18 You shall not take *v* or bear any grudge
Deut 32.35 *V* is mine, and recompense, for the time
Ps 58.10 righteous will rejoice when they see *v*
94. 1 you God of *v*, you God of *v*, shine forth!
Isa 63. 4 day of *v* was in my heart, and the year
Jer 50.15 this is the *v* of the LORD: take *v* on her,
Nah 1. 2 LORD takes *v* on has adversaries and
Rom 12.19 is written, "*V* is mine, I will repay, says
Heb 10.30 one who said, "*V* is mine, I will repay."

VERSED

Esth 1.13 all who were *v* in law and custom,
Acts 18.24 eloquent man, well-*v* in the scriptures.

VESSEL (VESSELS)

2 Kings 4. 3 borrow *v* . . . , empty *v* and not just a few.
Ps 31.12 is dead; I have become like a broken *v*.
Prov 26.23 Like the glaze covering an earthen *v* are
Isa 52.11 you who carry the *v* of the LORD.
Jer 18. 4 the *v* he was making of clay was spoiled
19.11 and this city, as one breaks a potter's *v*,
22.28 despised broken pot, a *v* no one wants?
Hos 8. 8 are among the nations as a useless *v*.

VESTMENTS

Ex 28. 2 You shall make sacred *v* for the glorious

VICTOR

Isa 41. 2 Who has roused a *v* from the east,

VICTORIOUS

Isa 41.10 I will uphold you with my *v* right hand.
Zech 9. 9 and *v* is he, humble and riding

VICTORY

Deut 20. 4 who goes with you . . . to give you the *v*."
1 Sam 2. 1 my enemies, because I rejoice in my *v*.
14.23 So the LORD gave Israel *v* that day. The
14.45 die, who has accomplished this great *v*
2 Sam 8. 6 The LORD gave *v* to David wherever he
19. 2 *v* that day was turned into mourning for
2 Kings 13.17 arrow of *v*, the arrow of *v* over Aram!
1 Chr 18. 6 The LORD gave *v* to David wherever he
2 Chr 20.17 your position, stand still, and see the *v*
Job 40.14 your own right hand can give you *v*.
Ps 20. 5 May we shout for joy over your *v*, and
44. 3 nor did their own arm give them *v*;
144. 10 the one who gives *v* to kings, who
Prov 21.31 of battle, but the *v* belongs to the LORD.
Isa 63. 5 so my own arm brought me *v* , and my
Zeph 3.17 is in your midst, a warrior who gives *v*;
Zech 12. 7 LORD will give *v* to the tents of Judah
Mt 12.20 wick until he brings justice to *v*.
1 Cor 15.54 "Death has been swallowed up in *v*."
1 Jn 5. 4 this is the *v* that conquers the world,

VIGILANCE

Prov 4.23 Keep your heart with all *v*; for from it

VILE

2 Sam 13.12 done in Israel; do not do anything so *v*!

VINDICATE (VINDICATES VINDICATING)

Deut 32.36 Indeed the LORD will *v* his people, have
1 Kings 8.32 *v* the righteous by rewarding them
2 Chr 6.23 *v* those who are in the right by
Ps 43. 1 *V* me, O God, and defend my cause
135. 14 For the LORD will *v* his people, and have
Isa 50. 8 he who *v* me is near. Who will contend

VINDICATION

Ps 24. 5 and *v* from the God of their salvation.
98. 2 he has revealed his *v* in the sight of the
103. 6 The LORD works *v* and justice for all
Mic 7. 9 me out to the light; I shall see his *v*.

VINE (VINES)

1 Kings 4.25 all of them under their *v* and fig trees.
Ps 80. 8 You brought a *v* out of Egypt; you drove
80.14 heaven, and see; have regard for this *v*,
Isa 5. 2 of stones, and planted it with choice *v*;
Ezek 19.10 Your mother was like a *v* in a vineyard
Hos 10. 1 Israel is a luxuriant *v* that yields its
Joel 1. 7 It has laid waste my *v*, and splintered
Mic 4. 4 they shall all sit under their own *v* and

Mt 26.29 never again drink of this fruit of the *v*
Mk 14.25 never again drink of the fruit of the *v*
Jn 15. 1 "I am the true *v*, and my Father is the

VINEGAR

Ps 69.21 food, and for my thirst they gave me *v*
Prov 10.26 Like *v* to the teeth, and smoke to the

VINEYARD (VINEYARDS)

Gen 9.20 of the soil, was the first to plant a *v*.
Deut 20. 6 Has anyone planted a *v* but not yet
22. 9 shall not sow your *v* with a second kind
1 Kings 21. 1 Naboth . . . had a *v* in Jezreel, beside
Song 1. 6 but my own *v* I have not kept!
2.15 ruin the *v*— for our *v* are in blossom."
Isa 5. 1 beloved my love-song concerning his *v*:
27. 2 On that day: A pleasant *v*, sing about it!
Mt 20. 1 in the morning to hire laborers for his *v*.
21.28 'Son, go and work in the *v* today.'
21.33 landowner who planted a *v*, put a fence
Mk 12. 1 them in parables. "A man planted a *v*,
Lk 20. 9 "A man planted a *v*, and leased it to

VINTAGE

Isa 32.10 for the *v* will fail, the fruit harvest will
Jer 48.32 fruits of your *v* the destroyer has
Rev 14.19 gathered the *v* of the earth, and he

VIOLATE (VIOLATED)

Job 37.23 abundant righteousness he will not *v*.
Heb 10.28 Anyone who has *v* the law of Moses

VIOLENCE

Job 16.17 though there is no *v* in my hands, and
19. 7 Even when I cry out, '*V*!' I am not
Ps 7.16 on their own heads their *v* descends.
73. 6 necklace; *v* covers them like a garment.
Jer 22. 3 do no wrong or *v* to the alien, the
Hab 1. 3 Destruction and *v* are before me; strife
Mal 2.16 and covering one's garment with *v*,
Mt 11.12 the kingdom of heaven has suffered *v*,

VOILENT

2 Sam 22.49 you delivered me from the *v*.
Acts 27.14 soon a *v* wind, called the northeaster,

VIPER (VIPERS)

Job 20.16 of asps; the tongue of a *v* will kill them.
Mt 3. 7 brood of *v*! Who warned you to flee
12.34 brood of *v*! How can you speak good
Acts 28. 3 when a *v*, driven out by the heat,

VIRGIN (VIRGINS)

Gen 24.16 The girl was very fair to look upon, a *v*,
Lev 21.14 He shall marry a *v* of his own kin,
Judg 21.12 four hundred young *v* who had never
1 Kings 1. 2 "Let a young *v* be sought for my lord
Ps 45.14 her the *v*, her companions, follow.
Jer 14.17 the *v* daughter—my people —is struck
Lam 2.13 I may comfort you, O *v* daughter Zion?
Joel 1. 8 Lament like a *v* dressed in sackcloth for
Mt 1.23 the *v* shall conceive and bear a son,
Lk 1.27 to a *v* engaged to a man whose name
1 Cor 7.28 sin, and if a *v* marries, she does not sin.
2 Cor 11. 2 to present you as a chaste *v* to Christ.
Rev 14. 4 with women, for they are *v*; these follow

VIRGINITY

Deut 22.14 her, I did not find evidence of her *v*."
22.15 the evidence of the young woman's *v*
Judg 11.38 her companions, and bewailed her *v*

VISION (VISIONS)

Gen 15. 1 word of the LORD came to Abram in a *v*,
Num 12. 6 LORD make myself known to them in *v*,
1 Sam 3. 1 in those days; *v* were not widespread.
Job 4.13 Amid thoughts from *v* of the night,
7.14 me with dreams and terrify me with *v*,
Isa 1. 1 The *v* of Isaiah the son of Amoz, which
22. 1 The oracle concerning the valley of *v*.
29.11 The *v* of all this has become for you
Jer 14.14 prophesying to you a lying *v*, worthless
23.16 They speak *v* of their own minds, not
Lam 2. 9 no more, and her prophets obtain no *v*
Ezek 1. 1 were opened, and I saw *v* of God.
7.26 shall keep seeking a *v* from the prophet;
11.24 lifted me up and brought me in a *v*
12.22 and every *v* comes to nothing"?
13. 7 Have you not seen a false *v*, and uttered
40. 2 brought me, in *v* of God, to the land of
Dan 1.17 Daniel also had insight into all *v* and
7. 2 I, Daniel, saw in my *v* by night the four
10. 7 I, Daniel, alone saw the *v*; the people
Hos 12.10 it was I who multiplied *v*, and through
Ob 1 The *v* of Obadiah. Thus says the Lord
Hab 2. 2 Write the *v*; make it plain on tablets, so
Zech 13. 4 will be ashamed, every one, of their *v*
Lk 24.23 that had indeed seen a *v* of angels who
Acts 2.17 your young men shall see *v*, and your
11. 5 praying, and in a trance I saw a *v*.
16. 9 During the night Paul had a *v*; there
18. 9 One night the Lord said to Paul in a *v*,
26.19 I was not disobedient to the heavenly *v*,
2 Cor 12. 1 but I will go on to *v* and revelations of

VISIT

Job 7.18 on them, *v* them every morning, test
Ps 65. 9 You *v* the earth and water it, you greatly
Jer 29.10 years are completed will I *v* you,

VOICE (VOICES)

Gen 27.22 "The *v* is Jacob's *v*, but the hands are
Num 7.89 he would hear the *v* speaking to him
Deut 4.12 but saw no form; there was only a *v*.
4.33 ever heard the *v* of a god speaking out
8.20 you would not obey the *v* of the LORD
1 Sam 1.13 lips moved, but her *v* was not heard;
1 Kings 19.13 Then there came a *v* to him that said,
Ps 29. 3 The *v* of the LORD is over the waters; the
68.33 listen, sends out his *v*, his mighty *v*.
81. 5 I hear a *v* I had not known: "I relieved
95. 7 O that you would listen to his *v*! Do not
Song 2. 8 The *v* of my beloved! Look, he comes,
Isa 6. 8 I heard the *v* of the Lord saying, "Whom
30.30 will cause his majestic *v* to be heard
40. 6 A *v* says, "Cry out!" And I said, "What
66. 6 A *v* from the temple! The *v* of the LORD,
Jer 7.34 mirth and gladness, the *v* of the bride
16. 9 the *v* of mirth and the *v* of gladness,
42. 6 with us when we obey the *v* of the LORD
Joel 2.11 The LORD utters his *v* at the head of his
Mic 6. 9 *v* of the LORD cries to the city (it is
Mt 3. 3 "The *v* of one crying out in the
3.17 And a *v* from heaven said, "This is my
17. 5 and from the cloud a *v* said, "This is my
Mk 1.11 And a *v* came from heaven, "You are my
9. 7 from the cloud there came a *v*, "This is
Lk 3. 4 Isaiah, "The *v* of one crying out in the
9.35 came a *v* that said, "This is my Son,
Jn 1.23 "I am the *v* of one crying out in the
5.25 the dead will hear the *v* of the Son
5.37 You have never heard his *v* or seen his
10.16 them also, and they will listen to my *v*.
Acts 4.24 they raised their *v* together to God and
7.31 to look, there came the *v* of the Lord:
12.22 "The *v* of a god, and not of a mortal!"
26.14 I heard a *v* saying to me in the Hebrew
Rom 10.18 "Their *v* has gone out to all the earth
2 Pet 1.18 heard this *v* come from heaven,
Rev 14. 2 I heard a *v* from heaven like the sound

VOID

Gen 1. 2 the earth was a formless *v* and darkness
Jer 4.23 on the earth, and lo, it was waste and *v*;
19. 7 I will make *v* the plans of Judah and

VOMIT (VOMITED)
Lev 18.25 and the land *v* out its inhabitants.
Job 20.15 swallow down riches and *v* them up
Prov 25.16 or else, having too much, you will *v* it.
26.11 Like a dog that returns to its *v* is a fool
2 Pet 2.22 "The dog turns back to its own *v*," and,

VOW (VOWS)
Gen 28.20 Then Jacob made a *v*, saying, "If God
31.13 anointed a pillar and made a *v* to me.
Lev 22.18 whether in payment of a *v* or as a
27. 2 When a person makes an explicit *v* to
Num 6. 2 make a special *v*, the *v* of a nazirite, to
21. 2 Then Israel made a *v* to the LORD and
30. 2 When a man makes a *v* to the LORD, or
Deut 23.21 If you make a *v* to the LORD your God,
Judg 11.30 Jephthah made a *v* to the LORD, and
1 Sam 1.11 She made this *v*: "O LORD of hosts, if
Ps 22.25 my *v* I will pay before those
56.12 My *v* to you I must perform, O God; I
65. 1 to you shall *v* be performed, O you who
116. 18 I will pay my *v* to the LORD in the
Eccl 5. 4 no pleasure in fools. Fulfill what you *v*.
Acts 18.18 had his hair cut, for he was under a *v*.

VOYAGE
Acts 27.10 I can see that the *v* will be with danger

VULTURES
Lk 17.37 "Where the corpse is, there the *v* will

W

WAGES
Gen 30.28 name your *w*, and I will give it."
31. 7 me and changed my *w* ten times,
Ex 2. 9 it for me, and I will give you your *w*."
Jer 22.13 and does not give them their *w*;
Hag 1. 6 earn *w* earn *w* to put them into a bag
Lk 3.14 and be satisfied with your *w*."
Rom 6.23 the *w* of sin is death, but the free gift of
1 Cor 3. 8 will receive *w* according to the labor

WAILING
Lk 8.52 they were all weeping and *w* for her;

WAIT (WAITED WAITING WAITS)
Ps 25. 3 those who *w* for you be put to shame;
25. 5 of my salvation; for you I *w* all day long.
27.14 *W* for the LORD; be strong, and let your
37. 7 Be still before the LORD, and *w* patiently
37.34 *W* for the LORD, and keep to his way,
40. 1 I *w* patiently for the LORD; he inclined
62. 1 for God alone my soul *w* in silence;
69. 3 My eyes grow dim with *w* for my God.
130. 5 I *w* for the LORD, my soul *w*, and in his
Prov 20.22 repay evil"; *w* for the LORD, and he will
Isa 8.17 I will *w* for the LORD, who is hiding his
26. 8 O LORD, we *w* for you; your name and
30.18 the LORD *w* to be gracious to you,
40.31 those who *w* for the LORD shall renew
42. 4 and the coastlands *w* for his teaching.
49.23 those who *w* for me shall not be put to
59.11 We *w* for justice, but there is none; for
60. 9 the coastlands shall *w* for me, the ships
64. 4 besides you, who works for those who *w*
Lam 3.26 It is good that one should *w* quietly for
Hos 12. 6 justice, and *w* continually for your God.
Mic 7. 7 I will *w* for the God of my salvation; my
Zeph 3. 8 Therefore *w* for me, says the LORD, for
Mk 15.43 who was also himself *w* expectantly for
Lk 8.40 him, for they were all *w* for him.
12.36 be like those who are *w* for their master
Rom 8.23 groan inwardly while we *w* for adoption,
1 Cor 1. 7 spiritual gift as you *w* for the revealing
11.33 together to eat, *w* for one another.
Gal 5. 5 by faith, we *w* eagerly for the hope of
1 Thess 1.10 to *w* for his Son from heaven, whom he
Titus 2.13 while we *w* for the blessed hope, and
2 Pet 3.12 *w* for and hastening the day of God,

WAKE
Rom 13.11 the moment for you to *w* from sleep.

WAKENS
Isa 50. 4 Morning by morning he *w*— *w* my ear

WALK
Gen 13.17 Rise up, *w* through the length and
17. 1 "I am God Almighty; *w* before me, and
24.40 LORD, before whom I *w*, will send his
Lev 26.12 And I will *w* among you, and will be
Deut 10.12 to *w* in all his ways, to love him, to
Josh 22. 5 to *w* in all his ways, to keep his
1 Kings 3.14 If you will *w* in my ways, keeping my
9. 4 if you will *w* before me, as David your
2 Kings 21.22 and did not *w* in the way of the LORD.
2 Chr 6.14 with your servants who *w* before you
7.17 for you, if you *w* before me, your father
Neh 5. 9 Should you not *w* in the fear of our
10.29 a curse and an oath to *w* in God's law,
Ps 48.12 *W* about Zion, go all around it, count
56.13 so that I may *w* before God in the light
78.10 but refused to *w* according to his law.
81.13 to me, that Israel would *w* in my ways!
82. 5 they *w* around in darkness; all the
89.15 who *w*, O LORD, in the light of your
101. 2 I will *w* with integrity of heart within
116. 9 I *w* before the LORD in the land of the
119. 1 who *w* in the law of the LORD.
138. 7 Though I *w* in the midst of trouble, you
Prov 1.15 my child, do not *w* in their way, keep
2.20 Therefore *w* in the way of the good,
8.20 I *w* in the way of righteousness, along
28. 6 Better to be poor and *w* in integrity
Eccl 2.14 in their head, but fools *w* in darkness.
Isa 2. 3 ways and that we may *w* in his paths."
8.11 warned me not to *w* in the way of this
30.21 you, saying, "This is the way, *w* in it."
33.15 Those who *w* righteously and speak
40.31 be weary, they shall *w* and not faint.
42. 5 upon it and spirit to those who *w* in it:
42.24 in whose ways they would not *w*, and
57. 2 those who *w* uprightly will rest on their
65. 2 rebellious people, who *w* in a way that
Jer 6.16 where the good way lies; and *w* in it,
10.23 that mortals as they *w* cannot direct
31. 9 I will let them *w* by brooks of water, in
Am 3. 3 Do two *w* together unless they have
Mic 4. 5 peoples *w*, each in the name of its god,
6. 8 and to *w* humbly with your God?
Zech 3. 7 If you will *w* in my ways and keep my
10.12 the LORD, and they shall *w* in his name,
Mt 9. 5 forgiven,' or to say, 'Stand up and *w*'?
Jn 5. 8 "Stand up, take your mat and *w*." At
11. 9 Those who *w* during the day do not
12.35 *W* while you have the light, so that the
Acts 3. 6 Christ of Nazareth, stand up and *w*."
Rom 6. 4 so we too might *w* in newness of life.
8. 4 who *w* not according to the flesh but
2 Cor 6.16 "I will live in them and *w* among them,
1 Jn 2. 6 in him," ought to *w* just as he walked.
Rev 3. 4 they shall *w* with me, dressed in white,

WALKS (WALKED WALKING)
Gen 3. 8 sound of the LORD God *w* in the garden
5.22 Enoch *w* with God after the birth of
6. 9 in his generation; Noah *w* with God.
Deut 30.16 *w* in his ways, and observing his
1 Kings 3. 6 David, because he *w* before you in
16.26 he *w* in all the way of Jeroboam son of
2 Kings 13. 6 he caused Israel to sin, but *w* in them;
16. 3 he *w* in the way of the kings of Israel.
17. 8 *w* in the customs of the nations whom
17.19 but *w* in the customs that Israel had

2 Chr 17. 3 was with Jehoshaphat, because he *w* in
21.12 Because you have not *w* in the ways of
Job 22.14 not see, he *w* on the dome of heaven.'
Ps 26. 1 O LORD, for I have *w* in my integrity,
55.14 company; we *w* in the house of God
128. 1 who fears the LORD, who *w* in his ways.
Prov 10. 9 Whoever *w* in integrity *w* securely, but
28.18 One who *w* in integrity will be safe, but
Isa 9. 2 The people who *w* in darkness have
Dan 3.25 unbound, *w* in the middle of the fire,
Mt 14.25 he came *w* toward them on the sea.
14.29 started *w* on the water, and came
Mk 6.48 early in the morning, *w* on the sea.
8.24 see people but they look like trees, *w*."
Jn 6.19 they saw Jesus *w* on the sea and
Rom 14.15 you eat, you are no longer *w* in love.
2 Jn 4 that my children are *w* in the truth.

WALL (WALLS)

Ex 14.22 the waters forming a *w* for them on
Deut 3. 5 these were fortress towns with high *w*,
1 Sam 25.16 they were a *w* to us both by night and
Neh 2.15 the valley by night and inspected the *w*.
6.15 So the *w* was finished on the
12.27 at the dedication of the *w* of Jerusalem
Ps 18.29 and by my God I can leap over a *w*.
Prov 18.11 in their imagination it is like a high *w*.
Isa 26. 1 he sets up victory like *w* and bulwarks.
Jer 1.18 city, an iron pillar, and a bronze *w*,
Dan 5. 5 began writing on the plaster of the *w*
Hos 2. 6 I will build a *w* against her, so that she
Zech 2. 5 I will be a *w* of fire all around it, says
Acts 9.25 him down through an opening in the *w*,
23. 3 will strike you, you white-washed *w*!
Eph 2.14 and has broken down the dividing *w*,
Heb 11.30 By faith the *w* of Jericho fell after they

WANDER (WANDERED WANDERS)

Num 32.13 he made them *w* in the wilderness for
Ps 107. 4 Some *w* in desert wastes, finding no
109. 10 May his children *w* about and beg; may
Prov 21.16 *w* from the way of understanding
Jer 14.10 they have loved to *w*, they have not
Lam 4.14 Blindly they *w* through the streets, so
Jas 5.19 if anyone among you *w* from the truth

WANT

Ps 23. 1 The LORD is my shepherd, I shall not *w*;
34. 9 ones, for those who fear him have no *w*.
Mk 14.36 me; yet, not what I *w*, but what you *w*."
1 Cor 4. 8 Already you have all you *w*! Already you

WAR (WARS)

Gen 14. 2 these kings made *w* with King Bera of
Ps 18.34 He trains my hands for *w*, so that my
27. 3 though *w* rise up against me, yet I will
46. 9 He makes *w* cease to the end of the
144. 1 who trains my hands for *w*, and my
Isa 2. 4 nation, neither shall they learn *w*
41.12 those who *w* against you shall be as
Mt 24. 6 you will hear of *w* and rumors of *w*;
Mk 13. 7 when you hear of *w* and rumors of *w*,
Lk 14.31 out to wage *w* against another king,
21. 9 "When you hear of *w* and insurrections,
2 Cor 10. 3 but we do not wage *w* according to
Rev 12. 7 And *w* broke out in heaven; Michael
12.17 went off to make *w* on the rest of her

WARFARE

2 Cor 10. 4 of our *w* are not merely human,

WARMING

Mk 14.54 sitting with the guards, *w* himself at
Jn 18.18 was standing with them and *w* himself.

WARN (WARNED WARNING)

Gen 43. 3 "The man solemnly *w* us, saying, 'You
Num 26.10 fifty men; and they became a *w*.
Deut 8.19 I solemnly *w* you today that you shall
2 Kings 6.10 than once or twice he *w* such a place
17.13 the LORD *w* Israel and Judah by every
Neh 13.15 I *w* them at that time against selling
Ps 19.11 by them is your servant *w*; in keeping
Jer 11. 7 I solemnly *w* your ancestors when I
Ezek 3.17 mouth, you shall give them *w* from me.
33. 5 of the trumpet, and did not take *w*;
Mt 2.12 having been *w* in a dream not to return
3. 7 vipers! Who *w* you to flee from the
Mk 1.43 After sternly *w* him he left him, and he
Lk 16.28 *w* them, so that they will not also come
Acts 4.17 let us *w* them to speak no more to
20.31 night or day to *w* everyone with tears.
Heb 8. 5 he was about to erect the tent, was *w*,
11. 7 By faith Noah, *w* by God about events

WARRIOR (WARRIORS)

Judg 11. 1 Jephthah . . . was a mighty *w*. Gilead
2 Sam 23. 8 the names of the *w* whom David had:
Job 16.14 and again; he rushes at me like a *w*.
Zeph 3.17 is in your midst, a *w* who gives victory;

WASH (WASHED)

Ex 29. 4 tent of meeting, and *w* them with water.
Num 5.23 and *w* them off into the water of
Deut 21. 6 elders . . . shall *w* their hands over the
23.11 comes, he shall *w* himself in water,
2 Kings 5.10 "Go, *w* in the Jordan seven times, and
Job 9.30 If I *w* myself with soap, and cleanse my
Ps 26. 6 I *w* my hands in innocence, and go
51. 2 *W* me thoroughly from my iniquity, and
73.13 clean and *w* my hands in innocence.
Isa 1.16 *W* yourselves; make yourselves clean;
4. 4 once the Lord has *w* away the filth of
Jer 2.22 Though you *w* yourself with lye and use
4.14 Jerusalem, *w* your heart clean of
Mt 6.17 fast, put oil on your head and *w* your
27.24 and *w* his hands before the crowd,
Lk 11.38 that he did not first *w* before dinner.
Jn 9. 7 to him, "Go, *w* in the pool of Siloam"
13. 5 began to *w* the disciples' feet and to
Acts 22.16 have your sins *w* away, calling on his
1 Cor 6.11 But you were *w*, you were sanctified,

WASTE

Isa 24. 1 LORD is about to lay *w* the earth and
34.10 generaton to generation it shall lie *w*;
Jer 4. 7 to make your land a *w*; your cities will
Mt 26. 8 they were angry and said, "Why this *w*?

WATCH (WATCHED WATCHING)

Gen 31.49 "The LORD *w* between you and me, when
Job 29. 2 as in the days when God *w* over me;
Ps 130. 6 than those who *w* for the morning,
Prov 15. 3 in every place, keeping *w* on the evil
Jer 1.12 for I am *w* over my word to perform it."
20.10 close friends are *w* for me to stumble.
Zech 11.11 the sheep merchants, who were *w* me,
Mt 27.36 sat down there and kept *w* over him.
1 Cor 10.12 are standing, *w* out that you do not fall.
Col 3.22 in everything, not only while being *w*

WATCHFUL

Zech 12. 4 the house of Judah I will keep a *w* eye,

WATCHPOST

Hab 2. 1 I will stand at my *w*, and station myself

WATER (WATERS) (n)

Ex 17. 1 but there was no *w* for the people
Num 5.18 the priest shall have the *w* of bitterness
20. 2 there was no *w* for the congregation;
Deut 8.15 He made *w* flow for you from flint rock,
1 Kings 18.33 "Fill four jars with *w*, and pour it on the
2 Kings 2.14 struck the *w*, saying, "Where is the
2 Chr 32.30 outlet of the *w* of Gihon and directed
Ps 18.16 took me; he drew me out of mighty *w*.

Ps 69. 1 for the *w* have come up to my neck.
Prov 11.25 and one who gives *w* will get *w*.
25.25 Like cold *w* to a thirsty soul, so is good
Song 8. 7 Many *w* cannot quench love, neither
Isa 12. 3 will draw *w* from the wells of salvation.
33.16 food will be supplied, their *w* assured.
43. 2 When you pass through the *w*, I will be
44. 3 For I will pour *w* on the thirsty land,
58.11 a spring of *w*, whose *w* never fail.
Jer 9. 1 O that my head were a spring of *w*, and
14. 3 they find no *w*, they return with their
17. 8 They shall be like a tree planted by *w*,
17.13 the fountain of living *w*, the LORD.
Ezek 36.25 I will sprinkle clean *w* upon you, and
47. 1 *w* was flowing from below the threshold
Am 5.24 let justice roll down like *w*, and
Hab 2.14 of the LORD, as the *w* cover the sea.
Zech 14. 8 On that day living *w* shall flow out from
Mt 3.11 I baptize you with *w* for repentance,
10.42 cup of cold *w* to one of these little ones
27.24 took some *w* and washed his hands
Mk 9.41 *w* to drink because you bear the name
Lk 3.16 "I baptize you with *w*; but one who is
16.24 the tip of his finger in *w* and cool my
Jn 1.26 "I baptize with *w*. Among you stands
2. 7 said to them, "Fill the jars with *w*."
3. 5 God without being born of *w* and Spirit.
4.14 those who drink of the *w* that I will give
5.3n waiting for the stirring of the *w*; for an
7.38 heart shall flow rivers of living *w*.' "
Acts 8.36 eunuch said, "Look, here is *w*! What is
10.47 "Can anyone withhold the *w* for
1 Jn 5. 6 Christ, not with the *w* only but with the
Rev 22.17 anyone who wishes take the *w* of life

WATER (WATERED) (v)

Gen 2. 6 and *w* whole face of the ground—
13.10 that the plain of the Jordan was well *w*
29.10 Jacob . . . *w* the flock of his mother's
Isa 27. 3 am its keeper; every moment I *w* it.
1 Cor 3. 6 I planted, Apollos *w*, but God gave the

WATERCOURSES

Joel 1.20 cry to you because the *w* are dried up,

WAVE (WAVES)

Ps 42. 7 cataracts; all your *w* and your billows
88. 7 and you overwhelm me with all your *w*.
Jon 2. 3 all your *w* and your billows passed over
Mt 14.24 the boat, battered by the *w*, was far
Mk 4.37 and the *w* beat into the boat, so that
Jas 1. 6 the one who doubts is like a *w* of the

WAVERING

Ps 26. 1 I have trusted in the LORD without *w*.
Heb 10.23 the confession of our hope without *w*,

WAY

Gen 3.24 to guard the *w* to the tree of life.
Num 21. 4 the people became impatient on the *w*.
Judg 2.22 take care to walk in the *w* of the LORD
1 Sam 9. 8 it to the man of God, to tell us our *w*."
2 Sam 22.31 This God—his *w* is perfect; the
1 Kings 16.26 walked in all the *w* of Jeroboam son of
Job 16.22 I shall go the *w* from which I shall not
19. 8 He has walled up my *w* so I cannot
23.10 he knows the *w* that I take; when he
28.13 Mortals do not know the *w* to it, and it
28.23 "God understands the *w* to it, and he
38.19 "Where is the *w* to the dwelling of light,
Ps 1. 6 watches over the *w* of the righteous, but
5. 8 make your *w* straight before me.
18.30 This God—his *w* is perfect; the
25. 9 is right, and teaches the humble his *w*.
37. 5 Commit your *w* to the LORD; trust in
37.23 by the LORD, when he delights in our *w*;
37.34 Wait for the LORD, and keep to his *w*,
67. 2 that your *w* may be known upon the
Ps 77.13 Your *w*, O God, is holy. What god is so
101. 6 walks in the *w* that is blameless
119. 9 can young people keep their *w* pure?
139. 24 in me, and lead me in the *w* everlasting.
Prov 2. 8 and preserving the *w* of his faithful
7.27 Her house is the *w* to Sheol, going
8.20 I walk in the *w* of righteousness, along
10.29 The *w* of the LORD is a stronghold for
13.15 but the *w* of the faithless is their ruin.
14.12 There is a *w* which seems right to a
15. 9 The *w* of the wicked is an abomination
15.19 The *w* of the lazy is overgrown with
16.25 there is a *w* which seems to be right,
22. 6 Train children in the right *w*, and when
Isa 30.21 you, saying, "This is the *w*, walk in it."
40. 3 wilderness prepare the *w* of the LORD,
40.27 "My *w* is hidden from the LORD, and my
43.16 who makes a *w* in the sea, a path in the
53. 6 astray; we have all turned to our own *w*,
57.14 said, "Build up, build up, prepare the *w*,
59. 8 The *w* of peace they do not know, and
Jer 5. 4 for they do not know the *w* of the LORD,
10.23 that the *w* of human beings is not in
21. 8 I am setting before you the *w* of life
23.12 their *w* shall be to them like slippery
Ezek 18.25 you say, "The *w* of the Lord is unfair."
33.17 say, "The *w* of the Lord is not just,"
Nah 1. 3 His *w* is in whirlwind and storm, and
Mt 3. 3 'Prepare the *w* of the Lord, make his
11.10 who will prepare your *w* before you.'
22.16 teach the *w* of God in accordance with
Mk 1. 2 before you, who will prepare your *w*;
12.14 but teach the *w* of God in accordance
Lk 3. 4 'Prepare the *w* of the Lord, make his
7.27 who will prepare your *w* before you.'
Jn 14. 6 "I am the *w*, and the truth, and the life.
Acts 9. 2 if he found any who belonged to the *W*,
16.17 who proclaim to you a *w* of salvation."
18.26 and explained the *W* of God to him
19.23 broke out concerning the *W*.
22. 4 I persecuted this *W* up to the point of
24.14 the *W*, which they call a sect, I worship
Rom 3.17 the *w* of peace they have not known."
Heb 9. 8 the *w* into the sanctuary has not yet
10.20 by the new and living *w* that he opened
2 Pet 2.21 known the *w* of righteousness than,
Rev 16.12 to prepare the *w* for the kings from the

WAYFARER

Judg 19.17 the old man looked up and saw the *w*
Jer 14. 8 in the land, like a *w* turning aside for

WAYS

2 Sam 22.22 For I have kept the *w* of the LORD, and
1 Kings 2. 3 your God, walking in his *w* and keeping
3.14 If you will walk in my *w*, keeping my
Job 21.14 We do not desire to know your *w*.
24.23 supported; his eyes are upon their *w*.
31. 4 Does not he see my *w*, and number all
Ps 18.21 For I have kept the *w* of the LORD, and
95.10 go astray, and they do not regard my *w*."
103. 7 He made known his *w* to Moses, his
Prov 5.21 For human *w* are under the eyes of the
16. 2 All one's *w* may be pure in one's own
20.24 then can we understand our own *w*?
31.27 looks well to the *w* of her household,
Isa 2. 3 that he may teach us his *w* and that we
55. 9 so are my *w* higher than your *w* and my
Jer 4.18 Your *w* and your doings have brought
16.17 my eyes are on all their *w*; they are not
17.10 to give to all according to their *w*,
Ezek 7. 3 judge you according to your *w*; I will
33.11 the wicked turn from their *w* and live;
Dan 4.37 works are truth, and his *w* are justice;
Mic 4. 2 that he may teach us his *w* and that we
Rom 11.33 judgments and how inscrutable his *w*!
Rev 15. 3 Just and true are your *w*, King of the

WEAK
Ezek 34. 4 You have not strengthened the *w*, you
Acts 20.35 we must support the *w*, remembering
Rom 5. 6 While we were still *w*, at the right time
14. 1 Welcome those who are *w* in faith, but
15. 1 to put up with the failings of the *w*,
1 Cor 1.27 God chose what is *w* in the world to
4.10 in Christ. We are *w*, but you are strong.
8. 7 their conscience, being *w*, is defiled.
9.22 To the *w* I became *w*, so that I might
2 Cor 11.29 Who is *w*, and I am not *w*? Who is
12.10 for whenever I am *w*, then I am strong.
1 Thess 5.14 hearted, help the *w*, be patient with all

WEAKNESS (WEAKNESSES)
1 Cor 1.25 and God's *w* is stronger than human
2. 3 I came to you in *w* and in fear and in
2 Cor 13. 4 he was crucified in *w*, but lives by the
Heb 4.15 is unable to sympathize with our *w*,

WEALTH
Deut 8.17 of my own hand have gotten me this *w*."
Job 31.25 if I have rejoiced because my *w* was
Ps 49. 6 those who trust in their *w* and boast of
112. 3 *W* and riches are in their houses, and
Prov 12.27 but the diligent obtain precious *w*.
13. 7 pretend to be poor, yet have great *w*.
13.11 *W* hastily gotten will dwindle, but those
13.22 sinner's *w* is laid up for the righteous.
Eccl 5.19 Likewise all to whom God gives *w* and
Song 8. 7 If one offered for love all the *w* of his
Isa 61. 6 you shall enjoy the *w* of the nations,
Jer 17.11 lay, so are all who amass *w* unjustly;
Ezek 28. 5 your heart has become proud in your *w*.
Hab 2. 5 Moreover, *w* is treacherous; the arrogant
Mt 6.24 the other. You cannot serve God and *w*.
13.22 the lure of *w* choke the word, and it
Mk 4.19 cares of the world, and the lure of *w*,
10.23 it will be for those who have *w* to enter
Lk 16. 9 for yourselves by means of dishonest *w*
2 Cor 8. 2 have overflowed in a *w* of generosity on
Heb 11.26 suffered for the Christ to be greater *w*
Rev 18.17 one hour all this *w* has been laid waste."

WEAPON (WEAPONS)
Eccl 9.18 Wisdom is better than *w* of war, but
Jer 51.20 You are my war club, my *w* of battle:
2 Cor 6. 7 with the *w* of righteousness for the right
10. 4 for the *w* of our warfare are not merely

WEAR (WEARS)
Deut 22. 5 A woman shall not *w* a man's apparel,
Prov 23. 4 Do not *w* yourself out to get rich; be
Eccl 10.15 The toil of fools *w* them out, for they
Lk 18. 5 so that she may not *w* me out by

WEARINESS
Eccl 12.12 end, and much study is a *w* of the flesh.

WEARISOME
Eccl 1. 8 All things are *w*; more than one can

WEARY (WEARIED)
2 Sam 21.15 the Philistines, and David grew *w*.
Job 3.17 troubling, and there the *w* are at rest.
Isa 1.14 burden to me, I am *w* of bearing them.
5.27 None of them is *w*, none stumbles,
7.13 to *w* mortals, that you *w* my God also?
43.22 but you have been *w* of me, O Israel!
43.24 you have *w* me with your iniquities.
47.13 are *w* with your many consultations;
57.10 You grew *w* from your many wanderings,
Jer 15. 6 destroyed you — I am *w* of relenting.
31.25 I will satisfy the *w*, and all who are
Mic 6. 3 In what have I *w* you? Answer me! For I
Mal 2.17 You have *w* the LORD with your words.
Gal 6. 9 let us not grow *w* in doing what is right,
2 Thess 3.13 do not be *w* in doing what is right.

WEATHER
Mt 16. 2 you say, 'It will be fair *w*, for the sky is

WEAVER (WEAVER'S)
Job 7. 6 My days are swifter than a *w* shuttle,
Isa 38.12 like a *w* I have rolled up my life; he

WEDDING
Mt 22. 2 to a king who gave a *w* banquet
22. 8 'The *w* is ready, but those invited were
25.10 went with him into the *w* banquet;
Lk 12.36 to return home from the *w* banquet,

WEEDS
Mt 13.25 his enemy came and sowed *w* among

WEEKS
Deut 16.10 you shall keep the festival of *w* for the
Dan 9.24 "Seventy *w* are decreed for your people

WEEP (WEEPING WEEPS WEPT)
Gen 27.38 father!" And Esau lifted his voice and *w*.
42.24 He turned away from them and *w*; then
43.30 went into a private room and *w* there.
45. 2 he *w* so loudly that the Egyptians heard
46.29 fell on his neck, and *w* on his neck a
Judg 20.23 went up and *w* before the LORD
1 Sam 30. 4 until they had no more strength to *w*.
2 Sam 18.33 up to the chamber over the gate, and *w*;
Ezra 3.12 *w* with a loud voice when they saw this
Neh 1. 4 I heard these words I sat down and *w*,
8. 9 all the people *w* when they heard the
Job 16.16 My face is red with *w*, and deep
Ps 6. 6 tears; I drench my couch with my *w*.
6. 8 the LORD has heard the sound of my *w*.
30. 5 *W* may linger for the night, but joy
137. 1 and we *w* when we remembered Zion.
Eccl 3. 4 a time to *w*, and a time to laugh; a time
Isa 15. 2 to the temple, to the high places to *w*;
Jer 13.17 not listen, my soul will *w* in secret for
22.10 Do not *w* for him who is dead, nor
31.15 bitter *w*. Rachel is *w* for her children;
Lam 1.16 For these things I *w*; my eyes flow with
2.11 My eyes are spent with *w*; my stomach
Ezek 8.14 were sitting there *w* for Tammuz.
27.31 they *w* over you in bitterness of soul,
Joel 2.17 the priests, the ministers of the LORD, *w*.
Mic 1.10 Tell it not in Gath, *w* not at all; in
Zech 12.10 *w* bitterly over him, as one *w* over a
Mt 2.18 Rachel *w* for her children;
8.12 there will be *w* and gnashing of teeth
24.51 there will be *w* and gnashing of teeth.
26.75 And he went out and *w* bitterly.
Mk 14.72 three times." And he broke down and *w*.
Lk 6.21 "Blessed are you who *w* now, for you
8.52 "Do not *w*; for she is not dead but
19.41 near and saw the city, he *w* over it,
22.62 times." And he went out and *w* bitterly.
23.28 do not *w* for me, but *w* for yourselves
Jn 11.31 she was going to the tomb to *w* there.
11.35 Jesus began to *w*.
20.11 But Mary stood *w* outside the tomb. As
20.15 "Woman, why are you *w*? Whom are you
Acts 21.13 "What are you doing, *w* and breaking
Rom 12.15 those who rejoice, *w* with those who *w*.
Rev 5. 4 I began to *w* bitterly because no one
18. 9 will *w* and wail over her when they see

WEIGH (WEIGHED WEIGHS)
1 Sam 2. 3 of knowledge, and by him actions are *w*.
Job 6. 2 "O that my vexation were *w*, and all my
31. 6 let me be *w* in a just balance, and let
Prov 16. 2 own eyes, but the LORD *w* the spirit.
21. 2 of the doer, but the LORD *w* the heart.
24.12 not he who *w* the heart perceive it?
Isa 40.12 and *w* the mountains in scales and the
Jer 32.10 and and *w* the money on scales.
Dan 5.27 TEKEL, you have been *w* on the scales

Zech 11.12 So they *w* out as my wages thirty
1 Cor 14.29 and let the others *w* what is said.

WEIGHTS

Deut 25.13 not have in your bag two kinds of *w*,
Prov 20.10 Diverse *w* and diverse measures are

WEIGHTY

Ps 139. 17 How *w* to me are your thoughts, O God!

WELCOME (WELCOMED WELCOMES)

Mt 10.40 "Whoever *w* you *w* me, and whoever *w*
18. 5 Whoever *w* one such child in my name
Mk 6.11 If any place will not *w* you and they
9.37 "Whoever *w* one such child in my name
Lk 8.40 when Jesus returned, the crowd *w* him
9. 5 Wherever they do not *w* you, as you are
9.11 he *w* them, and spoke to them about
9.48 *w* this child in my name *w* me,
10.10 enter a town and they do not *w* you,
19. 6 hurried down, and was happy to *w* him.
Acts 2.41 who *w* his message were baptized, and
28.30 expense, and *w* all who came to him,
Rom 15. 7 *W* one another, therefore, just as Christ
16. 2 so that you may *w* her in the Lord as is
Gal 4.14 me, but *w* me as an angel of God,

WELFARE

Gen 43.27 He inquired about their *w*, and said, "Is
Neh 2.10 had come to seek the *w* of the people
Ps 35.27 who delights in the *w* of his servant."
Prov 3. 2 life and abundant *w* will they give you.
Jer 29. 7 behalf, for in its *w* you will find your *w*.
38. 4 is not seeking the *w* of his people, but

WELL (WELLS) (n)

Gen 21.19 her eyes and she saw a *w* of water.
21.25 to Abimelech about a *w* of water
24.11 down outside the city by the *w* of water;
26.22 moved from there and dug another *w*,
Num 21.17 Israel sang this song: "Spring up, O *w*!
2 Sam 23.15 drew water from the *w* of Bethlehem
Song 4.15 a *w* of living water, and flowing streams
Isa 12. 3 will draw water from the *w* of salvation.
Jer 6. 7 As a *w* keeps its water fresh, so she
Lk 14. 5 child or an ox that has fallen into a *w*,
Jn 4. 6 Jacob's *w* was there, and Jesus, tired

WELL (adv)

2 Sam 18.29 "Is it *w* with the young man Absalom?"
Prov 27. 6 *W* meant are the wounds a friend
Mt 9.22 daughter; your faith has made you *w*."
Mk 5.23 so that she may be made *w*, and live."

WELL-BEING

Lev 3. 1 If the offering is a sacrifice of *w*, if you
7.11 of the sacrifice of the offering of *w*

WEST

Ps 103. 12 as far as the east is from the *w*, so far
Mt 8.11 many will come from east and *w* and
Lk 13.29 people will come from east and *w*, from

WHEAT

Judg 6.11 Gideon was beating out *w* in the wine
Jer 23.28 What has straw in common with *w*?
Mt 13.25 came and sowed weeds among the *w*,
13.29 you uproot the *w* along with them.
Lk 3.17 and to gather the *w* into his granary;
Jn 12.24 unless a grain of *w* falls into the earth

WHEEL

Jer 18. 3 and there he was working at his *w*.
Ezek 1.16 being something like a *w* within a *w*.
10.10 alike, something like a *w* within a *w*.

WHIP

Prov 26. 3 A *w* for the horse, a bridle for the
Isa 10.26 of hosts will wield a *w* against them,
Jn 2.15 Making a *w* of cords, he drove all of

WHIRLWIND

2 Kings 2.11 and Elijah ascended in a *w* into heaven.
Isa 5.28 like flint, and their wheels like the *w*.
Hos 8. 7 the wind, and they shall reap the *w*.

WHISPER

Ps 41. 7 All who hate me *w* together about me;
Isa 29. 4 and your speech shall *w* out of the dust.

WHISPERER

Prov 16.28 strife, and a *w* separates close friends.
18. 8 The words of a *w* are like delicious
26.22 The words of a *w* are like delicious

WHITE

Eccl 9. 8 Let your garments be always *w*; do not
Mk 9. 3 and his clothes became dazzling *w*,
Acts 1.10 heaven, suddenly two men in *w* robes
Rev 1.14 head and his hair were *w* as *w* wool,

WHITEWASH (WHITEWASHED)

Job 13. 4 As for you, you *w* with lies; all of you
Mt 23.27 hypocrites! For you are like *w* tombs,
Acts 23. 3 "God will strike you, you *w* wall! Are

WHOLESOME

2 Kings 2.21 the LORD, I have made this water *w*;
Prov 15.31 The ear that heeds *w* admonition will

WHORE (WHORES)

Jer 3. 1 You have played the *w* with many
Ezek 16.28 You played the *w* with the Assyrians,
23. 5 Oholah played the *w* while she was
Hos 2. 5 their mother has played the *w*; she who
Rev 17. 5 "Babylon the great, mother of *w* and of

WICK

Isa 42. 3 a dimly burning *w* he will not quench;
Mt 12.20 or quench a smoldering *w*, until he

WICKED

Gen 13.13 the people of Sodom were *w*, great
2 Chr 19. 2 "Should you help the *w* and love those
Job 9.24 earth is given into the hand of the *w*;
11.20 the eyes of the *w* will fail; all the way of
15.20 The *w* man writhes in pain all their
21.30 that the *w* are spared in the day of
27.13 "This is the portion of the *w* with God,
Ps 10.15 Break the arm of the *w* and evildoers;
37.10 little while, and the *w* will be no more;
37.35 I have seen the *w* oppressing, and
94. 3 shall the *w*, how long shall the *w* exult?
112. 10 The *w* see it and are angry; they gnash
119. 53 indignation seizes me because of the *w*,
139. 19 O that you would kill the *w*, O God,
141. 5 Never let the oil of the *w* anoint my
Prov 2.22 but the *w* will be cut off from the land,
10. 6 the mouth of the *w* conceals violence.
10.30 but the *w* will not remain in the land.
13. 6 is upright, but sin overthrows the *w*.
16. 4 even the *w* for the day of trouble.
28. 1 The *w* flee when no one pursues, but
Isa 26.10 If favor is shown to the *w*, they do not
53. 9 They made his grave with the *w* and his
Ezek 18.27 when the *w* turn away from the
33.15 if the *w* restore the pledge, give back
Dan 12.10 the *w* shall continue to act wickedly.
Mt 18.32 'You *w* slave! I forgave you all that debt
25.26 'You *w* and lazy slave! You knew, did
Acts 3.26 turning each of you from your *w* ways."
1 Cor 5.13 outside. "Drive out the *w* person from

WICKEDLY

Judg 19.23 "No, my brothers, do not act so *w*.
1 Chr 21.17 is I who have sinned and done very *w*.
Neh 9.33 dealt faithfully and we have acted *w*;

WICKEDNESS

Gen 6. 5 LORD saw that the *w* of humankind was
1 Sam 24.13 says, Out of the wicked comes forth *w*';
Job 20.12 "Though *w* is sweet in their mouth,
Prov 8. 7 truth; *w* is an abomination to my lips.
Isa 9.18 For *w* burned like a fire, consuming
Jer 6. 7 so she keeps fresh her *w*; violence and
Ezek 16.57 before your *w* was uncovered? Now you
Rom 1.18 who by their *w* suppress the truth.
1.29 They were filled with every kind of *w*,

WIDOW (WIDOWS WIDOW'S WIDOWS')

Deut 14.29 the orphans, and the *w* in your towns,
24.17 you shall not take a *w* garment in
Job 22. 9 You have sent *w* away empty-handed,
29.13 upon me, I caused the *w* heart to sing
Ps 109. 9 children be orphans, and his wife a *w*.
Prov 15.25 proud, but maintains the *w* boundaries.
Isa 1.17 defend the orphan, plead for the *w*.
10. 2 of their right, that *w* may be their spoil,
Jer 49.11 them alive; and let your *w* trust in me.
Lam 1. 1 How like a *w* has she become, she that
Mt 23.14n For you devour *w* houses and for the
Mk 12.40 They devour *w* houses and for the sake
12.42 A poor *w* came and put in two small
Lk 4.25 there were many *w* in Israel in the time
7.12 his mother's only son, and she was a *w*;
21. 2 he also saw a poor *w* put in two small
Acts 6. 1 their *w* were being neglected in the
1 Tim 5. 3 Honor *w* who are really *w*. If a *w* has

WIFE (WIFE'S WIVES)

Gen 12.12 'This is his *w*'; then they will kill me,
Num 5.12 If any man's *w* goes astray and is
Ruth 4.13 Boaz took Ruth and she became his *w*.
1 Sam 25.39 David wooed Abigail, to make her his *w*.
Job 31.10 then let my *w* grind for another, and let
Ps 128. 3 Your *w* will be like a fruitful vine within
Prov 5.18 blessed, rejoice in the *w* of your youth,
6.24 to preserve you from the *w* of another,
6.29 is he who sleeps with his neighbor's *w*;
18.22 He who finds a *w* finds a good thing,
19.13 and a *w* quarreling is a continual
19.14 but a prudent *w* is from the LORD.
31.10 A capable *w* who can find? She is far
Eccl 9. 9 Enjoy life with the *w* whom you love,
Jer 3. 1 If a man divorces his *w* and she goes
3.20 as a faithless *w* leaves her husband, so
Ezek 24.18 morning, and at evening my *w* died.
Hos 1. 2 "Go, take for yourself a *w* of whoredom
2.19 I will take you as my *w* forever; I will
12.12 Israel served for a *w*, and for a *w* he
Mal 2.14 companion and your *w* by covenant.
Mt 1.24 he took her as his *w*, but had no
5.31 "Whoever divorces his *w*, let him give
19. 5 and be joined to his *w*, and the two
27.19 judgment seat, his *w* sent word to him,
Mk 10. 2 "Is it lawful for a man to divorce his *w*?"
12.19 brother dies, leaving a *w* but no child,
Lk 17.32 must not turn back. Remember Lot's *w*.
Acts 5. 7 his *w* came in, not knowing what had
1 Cor 7. 4 the *w* does not have authority over her
7.27 Are you free from a *w*? Do not seek a *w*.
7.39 A *w* is bound as long as her husband
9. 5 to be accompanied by a believing *w*,
Eph 5.22 *W*, be subject to your husbands as you
5.31 be joined to his *w*, and the two will
Col 3.18 *W*, be subject to your husbands, as is
1 Thess 4.4n you know how to take a *w* for himself
1 Pet 3. 1 *W*, in the same way, accept the

WILD

Ex 32.25 the people were running *w* (for Aaron

WILDERNESS

Num 26.65 "They shall die in the *w*." Not one of
Deut 8.15 you through the great and terrible *w*,
1 Sam 23.14 remained in the strongholds in the *w*,
Song 3. 6 What is that coming up from the *w*, like
Isa 35. 1 *w* and the dry land shall be glad, the
41.18 I will make the *w* a pool of water, and
64.10 Your holy cities have become a *w*, Zion
Ezek 20.10 of Egypt and brought them into the *w*.
Mk 1.13 He was in the *w* forty days, tempted by
Lk 4. 1 the Spirit in the *w*, where for forty days
7.24 did you go out into the *w* to look at?

WILL (WILLS)

Ezra 7.18 may do, according to the *w* of your God.
Ps 40. 8 I delight to do your *w*, O my God; your
Isa 53.10 it was the *w* of the LORD to crush him
Mt 6.10 Your *w* be done, On earth as it is in
12.50 whoever does the *w* of my Father in
18.14 it is not the *w* of your Father in heaven
26.42 pass unless I drink it, your *w* be done."
Mk 3.35 Whoever does the *w* of God is my
Jn 4.34 "My food is to do the *w* of him who
5.30 own *w*, but the *w* of him who sent me.
6.38 own *w*, but the *w* of him who sent me.
7.17 who resolves to do the *w* of God
Acts 21.14 except to say, "The Lord's *w* be done."
Rom 1.10 by God's *w* I may somehow at last
2.18 know his *w* and determine what is best
9.16 it depends not on human *w* or exertion,
12. 2 you may discern what is the *w* of God
1 Cor 9.17 if I do this of my own *w*, I have a
2 Cor 8. 5 to the Lord and, by the *w* of God, to us,
Gal 1. 4 evil age, according to the *w* of our God
Eph 5.17 understand what the *w* of the Lord is.
Phil 2.13 you both to *w* and to work for his good
Col 4.12 fully assured in everything that God *w*.
1 Thess 4. 3 this is the *w* of God, your sanctification:
Heb 10. 7 'See, God, I have come to do your *w*, O
1 Pet 2.15 is God's *w* that by doing right you
3.17 good, if suffering should be God's *w*,
4. 2 by human desires but by the *w* of God.
1 Jn 2.17 those who do the *w* of God live forever.
Rev 4.11 and by your *w* they existed and were

WILLING (WILLINGLY)

1 Chr 29. 5 Who then will offer *w*, consecrating
Ps 110. 3 Your people will offer themselves *w* on
Lk 22.42 "Father, if you are *w*, remove this cup

WILLOWS

Lev 23.40 of leafy trees and *w* of the brook;
Ps 137. 2 On the *w* there we hung up our harps.

WIN

1 Cor 9.19 to all, so that I might *w* more of them.

WIND

Gen 1.2n while a mighty *w* swept over the face of
1 Kings 19.11 a great *w*, so strong that it was splitting
Job 26.13 By his *w* the heavens were made fair;
Ps 55. 8 myself from the raging *w* and tempest."
Eccl 8. 8 No one has power over the *w*, to
Ezek 1. 4 a stormy *w* came out of the north; a
Hos 8. 7 For they sow the *w*, and they shall reap
12. 1 Ephraim herds the *w*, and pursues the
13.15 east *w* shall come, a blast from the
Lk 8.24 And he woke up and rebuked the *w* and
Jn 3. 8 The *w* blows where it chooses, and you
Acts 2. 2 a sound like the rush of a violent *w*,

WINDOW (WINDOWS)

Gen 7.11 and *w* of the heavens were opened.
2 Kings 7. 2 if the LORD were to make *w* in the sky,
Dan 6.10 which had *w* in its upper room open
2 Cor 11.33 was let down in a basket through a *w* in

WINDSTORM

Mt 8.24 A *w* arose on the sea, so great that the
Mk 4.37 A great *w* arose, and the waves beat

WINE
Gen 9.24 Noah awoke from his *w* and knew what
19.35 they made their father drink *w* that
Lev 10. 8 Drink no *w* nor strong drink, neither
Num 6. 3 they shall separate themselves from *w*
Judg 13. 4 Now be careful not to drink *w* or strong
2 Sam 13.28 when Amnon's heart is merry with *w*,
Esth 1.10 day, when the king was merry with *w*,
Prov 20. 1 *W* is a mocker, strong drink a brawler,
23.30 Those who linger late over *w*, those who
Eccl 2. 3 mind how to cheer my body with *w*—
Song 1. 2 For your love is better than *w*, your
Isa 5.11 in the evening to be inflamed by *w*,
5.22 you who are heroes in drinking *w* and
24.11 is an outcry in the streets for lack of *w*;
56.12 "Come," they say, "let us get *w*; let us fill
Jer 35. 6 they answered, "We will drink no *w*, for
Ezek 44.21 No priest shall drink *w*, when he enters
Dan 5. 4 drank *w* and praised the gods of gold
Hos 4.11 *W* and new *w* take away the
Am 6. 6 who drink *w* in bowls, and anoint
Mt 27.34 they offered him *w* to drink, mixed with
Mk 2.22 no one puts new *w* into old wineskins;
15.23 they offered him *w* mixed with myrrh;
Lk 5.37 And no one puts new *w* into old
Jn 2. 9 tasted the water that had become *w*,
Acts 2.13 and said, "They are filled with new *w*."
Eph 5.18 Do not get drunk with *w*, for that is
1 Tim 5.23 but take a little *w* for the sake of your

WINE PRESS
Judg 6.11 beating out wheat in the *w*, to hide it
Isa 63. 3 "I have trodden the *w* alone, and from
Rev 14.19 he threw it into the great *w* of the

WINESKINS
Mt 9.17 Neither is new wine put into old *w*;
Lk 5.37 And no one puts new wine into old *w*;

WINGS
Ex 19. 4 how I bore you on eagles' *w* and
Ruth 2.12 the God of Israel, under those *w* you
Ps 17. 8 hide me in the shadow of your *w*, from
18.10 he came swiftly upon the *w* of the wind.
36. 7 take refuge in the shadow of your *w*.
55. 6 And I say, "O that I had *w* like a dove! I
61. 4 find refuge under the shelter of your *w*.
Prov 23. 5 it takes *w* to itself, flying like an eagle
Isa 6. 2 attendance above him; each had six *w*:

WINKING (WINKS)
Prov 6.13 with crooked speech, *w* the eyes,
10.10 Whoever *w* the eye causes trouble, but

WINNOW
Isa 41.16 You shall *w* them and the wind shall
Jer 51. 2 to Babylon, and they shall *w* her.

WINTER
Gen 8.22 night, summer and *w* shall not cease."
Song 2.11 away; for *w* is past, the rain is over
Acts 27.12 was not suitable for spending the *w*,
1 Cor 16. 6 with you or even spend the *w*, so that
2 Tim 4.21 Do your best to come before *w*. Eubulus
Titus 3.12 for I have decided to spend the *w* there.

WIPED
Acts 3.19 to God so that your sins may be *w* out,

WISDOM
Deut 4. 6 this will show your *w* and discernment
2 Sam 14.20 my lord has *w* like the *w* of the angel of
1 Kings 4.29 God gave Solomon very great *w*
10. 4 of Sheba observed all the *w* of Solomon,
10.23 kings of the earth in riches and in *w*.
2 Chr 1.10 Give me now *w* and knowledge to go
9. 6 of your *w* had been told to me;
Job 12. 2 are the people, and *w* will die with you.
28.12 "But where shall *w* be found? And
38.36 Who has put *w* in the inward parts, or
Ps 37.30 The mouths of the righteous utter *w*,
49. 3 My mouth shall speak *w*; the
111. 10 fear of the LORD is the beginning of *w*;
Prov 1. 2 For learning about *w* and instruction,
1.20 *W* cries out in the street; in the squares
2.10 *w* will come into your heart, and
8.11 *w* is better than jewels, and all that you
16.16 How much better to get *w* than gold! To
19. 8 To get *w* is to love oneself; to keep
21.30 No *w*, no understanding, no counsel,
24. 3 By *w* a house is built, and by
31.26 She opens her mouth with *w*, and the
Eccl 1.13 mind to seek and to search out by *w* all
7.12 For the protection of *w* is like the
9.16 yet the poor man's *w* is despised,
Isa 11. 2 him, the spirit of *w* and understanding,
Jer 49. 7 Is there no longer *w* in Teman? Has
51.15 who established the world by his *w*,
Dan 1.20 In every matter of *w* and understanding
5.11 and *w* like the *w* of the gods.
9.22 I have now come out to give you *w* and
Mt 11.19 Yet *w* is vindicated by her deeds."
12.42 the earth to listen to the *w* of Solomon,
13.54 "Where did this man get this *w* and
Lk 2.52 And Jesus increased in *w* and in years,
7.35 Nevertheless, *w* is vindicated by all her
11.31 the earth to listen to the *w* of Solomon,
21.15 I will give you words and a *w* that none
Acts 7.22 Moses was instructed in all the *w* of the
Rom 11.33 the riches and *w* and knowledge of God!
1 Cor 1.17 the gospel, and not with eloquent *w*,
1.24 is the power of God and the *w* of God.
1.30 Jesus, who became for us *w* from God,
2. 6 among the mature we do speak *w*,
3.19 the *w* of this world is foolishness with
12. 8 through the Spirit the utterance of *w*,
Eph 1.17 may give you a spirit of *w* and
3.10 that through the church the *w* of God
Jas 1. 5 If any of you is lacking in *w*, ask God,
3.17 the *w* from above is first pure, then
2 Pet 3.15 to you according to the *w* given him,

WISE
Deut 32.29 If they were *w*, they would understand
1 Kings 3.12 I give you a *w* and discerning mind; no
Job 5.13 He takes the *w* in their own craftiness;
Ps 49.10 When he looks at the *w*, they die; fool
Prov 10. 8 *w* of heart will heed commandments
13. 1 A *w* child loves discipline, but a scoffer
14. 1 The *w* woman builds her house, but the
16.14 death, and whoever is *w* will appease it.
22.17 The words of the *w*: Incline your ear
Isa 5.21 who are *w* in their own eyes, and
Jer 8. 8 How can you say, "We are *w*, and the
Dan 2.12 all the *w* men of Babylon be destroyed.
12. 3 Those who are *w* shall shine like the
Hos 14. 9 Those who are *w* understand these
Mt 2. 1 *w* men from the East came to
7.24 will be like a *w* man who built his
10.16 be *w* as serpents and innocent as doves.
11.25 have hidden these things from the *w*
24.45 "Who then is the faithful and *w* slave
1 Cor 1.20 Where is the one who is *w*? Where is
2 Cor 11.19 put up with fools, being *w* yourselves!
Eph 5.15 you live, not as unwise people but as *w*,
Jas 3.13 Who is *w* and understanding among

WISER
Ps 119. 98 Your commandment makes me *w* than
Ezek 28. 3 You are indeed *w* than Daniel; no secret

WISHES
Esth 6. 6 for the man whom the king *w* to honor?"
6.11 for the man whom the king *w* to honor."
Jas 4.15 you ought to say, "If the Lord *w*,

WITHER (WITHERED WITHERS)

Ps 37. 2 the grass, and *w* like the green herb.
Isa 40. 7 The grass *w*, the flower fades, when the
Ezek 47.12 Their leaves will not *w* nor their fruit
Mt 12.10 a man was there with a *w* hand, and
21.19 And the fig tree *w* at once.
Mk 3. 1 a man was there who had a *w* hand.
4. 6 and since it had no root, it *w* away.
11.21 The fig tree that you cursed has *w*."
Lk 6. 6 a man there whose right hand was *w*.

WITHHOLD (WITHHELD)

Gen 22.12 you have not *w* your son, your only son,
Deut 24.14 You shall not *w* the wages of poor and
Job 31.16 "If I have *w* anything that the poor
Ps 21. 2 and have not *w* the request of his lips.
84.11 No good thing does the LORD *w* from
Prov 3.27 Do not *w* good from those to whom it is
Am 4. 7 I also *w* the rain from you when there
Lk 6.29 your coat do not *w* even your shirt.
Rom 8.32 He who did not *w* his own Son, but

WITNESS (WITNESSES) (n)

Gen 21.30 that you may be a *w* for me that I dug
31.50 that God is *w* between you and me."
Ex 20.16 You shall not bear false *w* against your
Num 35.30 to death on the testimony of a single *w*.
Deut 5.20 Neither shall you bear false *w* against
17. 6 On the evidence of two or three *w* the
19.15 on the evidence of two or three *w* shall
31.19 that this song may be a *w* for me
Josh 22.27 to be a *w* between us and you, and
24.22 to serve him. And they said, "We are *w*."
Judg 11.10 LORD will be *w* between us; we will
Ruth 4.11 "We are *w*. May the LORD make the
Job 16.19 Even now, in fact, my *w* is in heaven,
Prov 14. 5 A faithful *w* does not lie, but a false *w*
14.25 A truthful *w* saves lives, but one who
19. 5 A false *w* will not go unpunished, and
24.28 Do not be a *w* against your neighbor
25.18 who bears false *w* against a neighbor.
Isa 43.10 You are my *w*, says the LORD, and my
44. 8 of old and declared it? You are my *w*!
55. 4 See, I made him a *w* to the peoples, a
Jer 29.23 I am the one who knows and bears *w*,
32.10 I signed the deed, sealed it, got *w*, and
42. 5 be a true and faithful *w* against us if we
Mic 1. 2 let the Lord GOD be a *w* against you,
Mal 2.14 the LORD was *w* between you and the
3. 5 be swift to bear *w* against the sorcerers,
Mt 18.16 by the evidence of two or three *w*.
Mk 14.63 and said, "Why do we still need *w*?
Lk 24.48 Jerusalem. You are *w* of these things.
Acts 1. 8 you will be my *w* in Jerusalem, in all
2.32 raised up, and of that all of us are *w*.
5.32 we are *w* to these things, and so is the
10.39 We are *w* to all that he did both in
14.17 yet he has not left himself without a *w*
22.15 you will be his *w* to all the world of
22.20 blood of your *w* Stephen was shed, I
23.11 you must bear *w* also in Rome."
Rom 1. 9 is my *w* that without ceasing I
8.16 Spirit bearing *w* with our spirit that we
2 Cor 13. 1 by the evidence of two or three *w*."
1 Thess 2.10 You are *w*, and God also, how pure,
Heb 12. 1 are surrounded by so great a cloud of *w*,
Rev 1. 5 Jesus Christ, the faithful *w*, the firstborn
3.14 the Amen, the faithful and true *w*, the
11. 3 I will grant my two *w* authority to
17. 6 saints and the blood of the *w* to Jesus.

WITNESS (v)

Deut 4.26 I call heaven and earth to *w* against you
30.19 I call heaven and earth to *w* against you

WOE

Job 10.15 If I am wicked, *w* to me! If I am
Isa 6. 5 "*W* is me! I am lost, for I am a man of
45. 7 I make weal and create *w*; I the LORD do
Mk 14.21 *w* to that one by whom the Son of Man
1 Cor 9.16 *w* to me if I do not proclaim the gospel!
Rev 8.13 midheaven, "*W*, *w*, *w* to the inhabitants

WOLF (WOLVES)

Isa 11. 6 The *w* shall live with the lamb, the
65.25 The *w* and the lamb shall feed together,
Acts 20.29 after I have gone, savage *w* will come in

WOMAN (WOMEN)

Gen 2.23 this one shall be called *W*, for out of
3.12 "The *w* whom you gave to be with me,
1 Kings 11. 1 Solomon loved many foreign *w* along
Prov 9.13 The foolish *w* is loud; she is ignorant
31.30 but a *w* who fears the LORD is to be
Eccl 7.26 bitter than death the *w* who is a trap,
Isa 4. 1 Seven *w* shall take hold of one man in
7.14 Look, the young *w* is with child and
32. 9 Rise up, you *w* who are at ease, hear
62. 5 For as a young man marries a young *w*,
Mt 9.20 a *w* who had been suffering from
Mk 15.40 were also *w* looking on from a distance;
Lk 7.37 And a *w* in the city, who was a sinner,
13.11 there appeared a *w* with a spirit that
17.35 will be two *w* grinding meal together;
23.49 including the *w* who had followed him
Jn 2. 4 "*W*, what concern is that to you and to
8. 3 a *w* who had been caught in adultery;
16.21 When a *w* is in labor, she has pain,
Rom 1.27 giving up natural intercourse with *w*
1 Cor 7. 1 "It is well for a man not to touch a *w*."
11. 9 created for the sake of *w*, but *w* for the
14.34 *w* should be silent in the churches.
Gal 4. 4 God sent his Son, born of a *w*, born
1 Tim 2. 9 the *w* should dress themselves modestly
Heb 11.35 *W* received their dead by resurrection.
Rev 12. 1 a *w* clothed with the sun, with the
12. 6 the *w* fled into the wilderness, where
17. 3 a *w* sitting on a scarlet beast that was

WOMB

Eccl 11. 5 comes to the bones in the mother's *w*,
Lk 11.27 "Blessed is the *w* that bore you and the
Jn 3. 4 enter a second time into the mother's *w*

WONDER (WONDERS)

Ex 3.20 So I will . . . strike Egypt with all my *w*
7. 9 Pharaoh says to you, 'Perform a *w*,'
15.11 awesome in splendor, doing *w*?
Ps 88.10 Do you work *w* for the dead? Do the
136. 4 who alone does great *w*, for his
Acts 3.12 You Israelites, why do you *w* at this, or

WONDERFUL

Gen 18.14 Is anything too *w* for the LORD? At the
Judg 13.18 "Why do you ask my name? It is too *w*."
2 Sam 1.26 your love to me was *w*, passing the love
Job 42. 3 what I did not understand, things too *w*
Ps 119.129 Your decrees are *w*; therefore my soul
139. 6 Such knowledge is too *w* for me; it is so
139. 14 wonderfully made. *W* are your works;
Prov 30.18 Three things are too *w* for me; four I do
Isa 9. 6 he is named *W* Counselor, Mighty God,
25. 1 for you have done *w* things, plans

WONDROUS

Ps 26. 7 and telling all your *w* deeds.
72.18 God of Israel, who alone does *w* things.
119. 18 I may behold *w* things out of your law.

WOOD

Ex 15.25 the LORD showed him a piece of *w*; he
Prov 25.20 Like a moth in clothing or a worm in *w*,

WOOL

Deut 22.11 not wear clothes made of *w* and linen

WORK (WORKS) (n)

Gen 2. 2 on the seventh day from all the *w*
Ex 23.12 Six days you shall do your *w*, but on
1 Chr 16. 9 to him, tell of all his wonderful *w*.
Neh 3. 5 their shoulders to the *w* of their Lord
Job 10. 3 to despise the *w* of your hands and
37.14 Job; stop and consider the wondrous *w*
Ps 28. 5 of the LORD, or the *w* of his hands,
102. 25 the heavens are the *w* of your hands.
104. 23 People go out to their *w* and to their
104. 24 O LORD, how manifold are your *w*! In
145. 10 All your *w* shall give thanks to you, O
Prov 16. 3 Commit your *w* to the LORD, and your
31.31 and let her *w* praise her in the city
Eccl 8.17 I saw all the *w* of God, that no one can
Isa 66.18 I know their *w* and their thoughts, and I
Hab 1. 5 For a *w* is being done in your days that
3. 2 and I stand in awe, O LORD, of your *w*.
Jn 5.36 *w* that the Father has given me to
9. 3 blind so that God's *w* might be revealed
10.25 The *w* that I do in my Father's name
17. 4 earth by finishing the *w* that you gave
Acts 9.36 She was devoted to good *w* and acts of
Rom 4. 5 to one who without *w* trusts him who
9.12 not by *w* but by his call) she was told,
11. 6 grace, it is no longer on the basis of *w*,
1 Cor 3.13 the *w* of each builder will become
9. 1 Are not you my *w* in the Lord? If I am
Gal 3. 2 the Spirit by doing the *w* of the law or
5.19 Now the *w* of the flesh are obvious:
Eph 2. 9 —not the result of *w*, so that no one
Phil 2.30 came close to death for the *w* of Christ,
1 Thess 5.13 very highly in love because of their *w*.
2 Thess 2.17 and strengthen them in every good *w*
1 Tim 6.18 to be rich in good *w*, generous, and
2 Tim 3.17 proficient, equipped for every good *w*.
Titus 3. 5 he saved us, not because of any *w* of
Heb 1.10 the heavens are the *w* of your hands;
Jas 2.17 So faith by itself, if it has no *w*, is dead.
2.21 our ancestor Abraham justified by *w*,
Rev 20.12 dead were judged according to their *w*,

WORK (WORKED WORKING WORKS)

Neh 4. 6 height; for the people had a mind to *w*.
Prov 31.13 and flax, and *w* with willing hands.
Jer 18. 3 house, and there he was *w* at his wheel.
Hag 2. 4 *w*, for I am with you, says the LORD of
Mt 20.12 'These last *w* only one hour, and you
Mk 16.20 while the Lord *w* with them and
Lk 5. 5 "Master, we *w* all night but we have
Jn 5.17 "My Father is still *w*, and I also am *w*."
6.27 Do not *w* for the food which perishes,
9. 4 We must *w* the works of him who sent
Rom 8.28 all things *w* together for good for those
1 Cor 3. 9 we are God's servants, *w* together; you
2 Cor 6. 1 As we *w* together with him, we urge you
Gal 2. 8 (for he who *w* through Peter making
Phil 2.12 *w* out your own salvation with fear and
2 Thess 3.10 Anyone unwilling to *w*, should not eat.

WORKER (WORKERS)

Prov 16.26 The appetite of *w* works for them; their
2 Tim 2.15 a *w* who has no need to be ashamed,

WORLD (WORLDS)

Ps 19. 4 and their words to the end of the *w*.
Mt 13.38 the field is the *w*, and the good seed
Mk 16.15n "Go into all the *w* and proclaim the
Lk 9.25 if they gain the whole *w*, but lose or
Jn 8.23 you are of this *w*, I am not of this *w*.
9.39 "I came into this *w* for judgment so
12.19 Look, the *w* has gone after him!"
16.33 In the *w* you face persecution. But take
17.14 the *w*, just as I do not belong to the *w*.
17.21 us, so that the *w* may believe that you
Acts 17. 6 have been turning the *w* upside down
Rom 5.12 as sin came into the *w* through one
1 Cor 4. 9 become a spectacle to the *w*, to angels
Heb 11. 3 the *w* were prepared by the word of
11.38 of whom the *w* was not worthy. They
1 Jn 2.15 Do not love the *w* or the things in the
3.13 and sisters, that the *w* hates you.
4. 5 They are from the *w*, therefore what

WORM (WORMS)

Ps 22. 6 But I am a *w*, and not human; scorned
Isa 41.14 Do not fear, you *w* Jacob, you insect
Mk 9.48 where their *w* never dies, and the fire is
Acts 12.23 down, and he was eaten by *w* and died.

WORRY (WORRIED WORRIES)

Mt 6.25 do not *w* about your life, what you will
10.19 do not *w* about how you are to speak or
Lk 10.41 Martha, you are *w* and distracted
12.11 do not *w* about how you are to defend
21.34 and drunkenness and *w* of this life,
Phil 4. 6 Do not *w* about anything, but in

WORSE

Ps 39. 2 my distress grew *w*, my heart became
Mt 12.45 state of the person is *w* than the first.
2 Tim 3.13 will go from bad to *w*, deceiving

WORSHIP

Gen 22. 5 we will *w*, and then we will come back
Ex 3.12 you shall *w* God upon this mountain."
20. 5 shall not bow down to them or *w* them;
24. 1 the elders of Israel, and *w* at a distance.
34.14 (for you shall *w* no other god, because
1 Sam 1. 3 go up year by year from his town to *w*
1 Chr 16.29 *W* the LORD in holy splendor; tremble
Ps 22.27 of the nations shall *w* before him.
29. 2 his name; *w* the LORD in holy splendor.
95. 6 O come, let us *w* and bow down, let us
96. 9 *W* the LORD in holy splendor; tremble
132. 7 dwelling place; let us *w* at his footstool."
Isa 2.20 which they made for themselves to *w*,
27.13 will come and *w* the LORD on the holy
36. 7 'You shall *w* before this altar'?
Jer 7. 2 Judah, you that enter these gates to *w*
Dan 3.28 serve and *w* any god except their own
Zech 14.16 go up year after year to *w* the King,
Mt 4. 9 you, if you will fall down and *w* me."
4.10 '*W* the Lord your God, and serve only
Lk 4. 7 If you, then, will *w* me, it will all be
Jn 4.21 when you will *w* the Father neither on
4.24 who *w* him must *w* in spirit and truth."
12.20 among those who went up to *w* at the
16. 2 by doing so they are offering *w* to God.
Acts 7.42 them over to *w* the host of heaven,
18.13 man is persuading people to *w* God
19.27 brought all Asia and the world to *w* her."
1 Cor 14.25 before God and *w* him, declaring, "God
Phil 3. 3 circumcision, who *w* in the Spirit of
Heb 1. 6 he says, "Let all God's angels *w* him."
Rev 7.15 throne of God, and *w* him day and night
13. 8 all the inhabitants of the earth will *w* it,
14. 7 *w* him who made heaven and earth, the
19.10 I fell down at his feet to *w* him, but he
22. 8 I fell down to *w* at the feet of the angel

WORSHIPED (WORSHIPING WORSHIPS)

Gen 24.26 man bowed his head and *w* the LORD
Ex 4.31 their misery, they bowed down and *w*.
12.27 And the people bowed down and *w*.
Deut 17. 3 going to serve other gods and *w* them
Judg 2. 7 The people *w* the LORD all the days of
3. 6 to their sons, and they *w* their gods.
10.13 have abandoned me and *w* other gods;
1 Sam 1.19 in the morning and *w* before the LORD;
2 Sam 12.20 went into the house of the LORD, and *w*;
15.32 came to the summit, where God was *w*,
2 Kings 17.33 So they *w* the LORD but also served their
2 Chr 20.18 Jerusalem fell down before the LORD, *w*
Job 1.20 his head, and fell on the ground and *w*.

Ps 66. 4 All the earth *w* you; they sing praises to
Isa 44.15 Then he makes a god and *w* it, makes it
Mt 14.33 And those in the boat *w* him, saying,
28. 9 him, took hold of his feet, and *w* him.
Lk 2.37 temple, but *w* with fasting and prayer
24.52 And they *w* him, and returned to
Jn 9.31 he does listen to one who *w* him and
9.38 He said, "Lord, I believe." And he *w* him.
Acts 10.25 met him, and falling at his feet, *w* him.
Rev 5.14 "Amen!" And the elders fell down and *w*.
13. 4 They *w* the dragon, for he had given

WORSHIPERS

2 Kings 10.21 all the *w* of Baal came, so that there

WORTH

2 Sam 18. 3 you are *w* ten thousand of us; therefore
Rom 8.18 time are not *w* comparing with the glory
Phil 2.22 But Timothy's *w* you know, how like a

WORTHLESS

Ps 60.11 against the foe, for human help is *w*.
Lk 17.10 ordered to do, say, 'We are *w* slaves;
Acts 14.15 turn from these *w* things to the living

WORTHY

Gen 32.10 I am not *w* of the least of all the
Ruth 3.11 people know that you are a *w* woman.
Prov 20. 6 loyal, but who can find one *w* of trust?
Mt 3.11 me; I am not *w* to carry his sandals.
8. 8 "Lord, I am not *w* to have you come
10.37 father or mother more than me is not *w*
Mk 1. 7 I am not *w* to stoop down and untie the
Lk 7. 4 "He is *w* of having you do this for him,
7. 6 I am not *w* to have you come under my
15.21 you; I am no longer *w* to be called
Jn 1.27 I am not *w* to untie the thong of his
Acts 5.41 were considered *w* to suffer dishonor
13.25 I am not *w* to untie the thong of the
2 Thess 1.11 our God may make you *w* of his call
Heb 3. 3 Jesus is *w* of more glory than Moses,
11.38 of whom the world was not *w*. They
Rev 3. 4 me, dressed in white, for they are *w*.
4.11 "You are *w*, our Lord and God, to
5. 2 "Who is *w* to open the scroll and break
5. 9 "You are *w* to take the scroll and to

WOUND (WOUNDED WOUNDS)

Deut 32.39 I kill and I make alive; I *w* and I heal;
1 Kings 22.34 carry me out of the battle, for I am *w*."
2 Chr 18.33 carry me out of the battle, for I am *w*."
Ps 38. 5 My *w* grow foul and fester because of
Prov 23.29 Who has *w* without cause? Who had
27. 6 Well meant are the *w* a friend inflicts,
Isa 1. 6 but bruises and sores and bleeding *w*;
53. 5 But he was *w* for our transgressions,
Jer 10.19 me because of my hurt! My *w* is severe.
15.18 is my pain unceasing, my *w* incurable,
30.12 hurt is incurable, your *w* is grievous.
Mic 1. 9 For her *w* is incurable. It has come to
Nah 3.19 assuaging your hurt, your *w* is mortal.
Zech 13. 6 "What are these *w* on your chest?" the
Lk 10.34 bandaged his *w*, having poured oil
20.12 this one they also *w* and threw out.
1 Cor 8.12 *w* their conscience when it is weak, you
Rev 13. 3 but its mortal *w* had been healed. In

WRAPPED

Lam 3.44 you have *w* yourself with a cloud so
Mk 15.46 down the body, *w* it in the linen cloth,
Lk 2. 7 son and *w* him in bands of cloth,

WRATH

2 Kings 22.13 great is the *w* of the LORD that is
Ezra 10.14 until the fierce *w* of our God on this
Job 16. 9 He has torn me in his *w*, and hated me;
Ps 76.10 Human *w* serves only to praise you,
Hos 5.10 them I will pour out my *w* like water.
Hab 3. 2 known; in *w* may you remember mercy.
3. 8 Was your *w* against the rivers, O LORD?
Zeph 2. 2 upon you the day of the LORD's *w*.
Mt 3. 7 warned you to flee from the *w* to come?
Jn 3.36 not see life, but must endure God's *w*.
Rom 2. 5 up *w* for yourself on the day of *w*,
3. 5 That God is unjust to inflict *w* on us?
4.15 for the law brings *w*; but where there is
Col 3. 6 the *w* of God is coming on those who
1 Thess 1.10 —Jesus, who rescues us from the *w*
Rev 6.16 the throne and from the *w* of the Lamb;
14.19 the great wine press of the *w* of God.

WREATH (WREATHS)

1 Kings 7.17 of checker work with *w* of chain work
1 Cor 9.25 they do it to receive a perishable *w*, but

WRESTLED (WRESTLING)

Gen 30. 8 I have *w* with my sister, and have
32.24 and a man *w* with him until daybreak.
Col 4.12 always *w* in his prayers on your behalf,

WRETCHED

Rom 7.24 *W* man that I am! Who will rescue me

WRITE (WRITTEN WROTE)

Ex 17.14 *W* this as a reminder in a book and
24. 4 Moses *w* all the words of the LORD. He
31.18 of stone, *w* with the finger of God.
34. 1 I will *w* on the tablets the words that
Deut 6. 9 *w* them on the doorposts of your house
11.20 *W* them on the doorposts of your house
17.18 a copy of this law *w* for him in the
27. 3 You shall *w* on them all the words of
31. 9 Moses *w* down this law, and gave it to
2 Chr 23.18 as it is *w* in the law of Moses, with
Neh 10.34 the LORD our God, as it is *w* in the law.
Ps 40. 7 I am; in the scroll of the book it is *w*
Prov 7. 3 *w* them on the tablet of your heart. Say
22.20 Have I not *w* for you thirty sayings of
Eccl 12.10 words, and he *w* words of truth plainly.
Jer 17. 1 The sin of Judah is *w* with an iron pen;
30. 2 *W* in a book all the words that I have
36. 2 Take a scroll and *w* on it all the words
36.18 and I *w* them with ink on the scroll."
Dan 12. 1 everyone who is found *w* in the book.
Hos 8.12 Though I *w* for him the multitude of my
Hab 2. 2 *W* the vision; make it plain on tablets,
Mk 9.12 How then is it *w* about the Son of Man,
Lk 10.20 that your names are *w* in heaven."
Jn 8. 6 Jesus bent down and *w* with his finger
19.22 answered, "What I have *w* I have *w*."
20.30 signs which are not *w* in this book.
Acts 13.33 by raising Jesus; as also it is *w* in the
Rom 15. 4 whatever was *w* in former days was *w*
Heb 8.10 minds, and *w* them on their hearts,
10.16 and I will *w* them on their minds,"
2 Pet 3.15 our beloved brother Paul *w* to you
1 Jn 5.13 I *w* these things to you who believe in
Rev 1.19 Now *w* what you have seen, what is,
3.12 I will *w* on you the name of my God,

WRITING (WRITINGS)

Ex 32.16 the *w* was the *w* of God, engraved upon
Ezek 9. 2 a man clothed in linen, with a *w* case
Lk 1.63 He asked for a *w* tablet and wrote, "His
2 Tim 3.15 you have known the sacred *w* which are

WRONG (WRONGED WRONGS)

Ex 2.13 he said to the one who was in the *w*,
Num 5. 7 shall make full restitution for his *w*,
1 Sam 26.21 Saul said, "I have done *w*; come back,
2 Kings 18.14 "I have done *w*; withdraw from me;
Job 6.24 me understand how I have gone *w*.
32. 3 they had declared Job to be in the *w*.
Ps 7. 3 done this, if there is *w* in my hands,
58. 2 No, in your hearts you devise *w*; your
Prov 30.20 her mouth, and says, "I have done no *w*."

Jer 37.18 also said to King Zedekiah, "What *w*
Mk 12.24 "Is not this the reason you are *w*, that
Lk 23.41 but this man has done nothing *w*."
Acts 25.10 I have done no *w* to the Jews, as you
1 Cor 6. 7 a defeat for you. Why not rather be *w*?
2 Cor 7. 2 we have *w* no one, we have corrupted
12.13 did not burden you? Forgive me this *w*!
Philem 18 If he has *w* you in any way, or owes you

Y

YEAR (YEARS)

Lev 16.34 atonement . . . once in the *y* for all their
Ps 102. 27 are the same, and your *y* have no end.
Prov 10.27 but the *y* of the wicked will be short.
Isa 61. 2 to proclaim the *y* of the LORD's favor,
63. 4 and the *y* for my redeeming had come.
Ezek 46.17 his to the *y* of liberty; then it shall
Lk 2.52 Jesus increased in wisdom and in *y*,
Rev 20. 6 they will reign with him a thousand *y*.

YEARNING

2 Sam 13.39 of the king went out, *y* for Absalom;

YEAST

Mt 13.33 "The kingdom of heaven is like *y* that a
16. 6 and beware of the *y* of the Pharisees
Mk 8.15 beware of the *y* of the Pharisees and the
Lk 12. 1 "Beware of the *y* of the Pharisees, that
13.21 It is like *y* that a woman took and
1 Cor 5. 6 that a little *y* leavens the whole batch
Gal 5. 9 you. A little *y* leavens the whole batch

YES

Mt 5.37 let your word be '*Y, Y*' or 'No, No';
2 Cor 1.17 ready to say "*Y, y*" and "No, no" at the
1.20 every one of God's promises is a "*Y*."

YESTERDAY

Job 8. 9 for we are but of *y*, and we know
Heb 13. 8 is the same *y* and today and forever.

YIELD

2 Chr 30. 8 but *y* yourselves to the LORD and come

YOKE

Lev 26.13 I have broken the bars of your *y* and
1 Kings 12. 4 "Your father made our *y* heavy. Now
2 Chr 10. 4 "Your father made our *y* heavy.
Isa 9. 4 For the *y* of their burden, and the bar
10.27 and his *y* will be destroyed from your
14.25 his *y* shall be removed from them, and
58. 6 to undo the thongs of the *y*, to let the
Jer 28. 2 broken the *y* of the king of Babylon.
Lam 1.14 My transgressions were bound into a *y*;
Nah 1.13 I will break his *y* from you and snap the
Mt 11.29 Take my *y* upon you, and learn from
Acts 15.10 placing on the neck of the disciples a *y*

YOUNG (YOUNGER)

Gen 25.23 the other, the elder shall serve the *y*."
1 Chr 29. 1 God has chosen, is *y* and inexperienced,
Job 30. 1 they make sport of me, those who are *y*
39.16 It deals cruelly with its *y*, as if they
Prov 1. 4 knowledge and prudence to the *y*—
Eccl 11. 9 Rejoice, *y* man, while you are *y*, and let
Dan 1. 4 *y* men without physical defect and
Mt 19.20 The *y* man said to him, "I have kept all
Mk 14.51 *y* man was following him, wearing
16. 5 entered the tomb, they saw a *y* man,
Lk 15.12 The *y* of them said to his father,
Jn 21.18 when you were *y*, you used to fasten
Acts 23.17 "Take this *y* man to the tribune, for he
Rom 9.12 was told, "The elder shall serve the *y*."
Titus 2. 6 urge the *y* men to be self-controlled.
1 Jn 2.13 I am writing to you, *y* people, because

YOUTH

Gen 8.21 of the human heart is evil from *y*;
Ps 25. 7 Do not remember the sins of my *y*, or
103. 5 that your *y* is renewed like the eagle's.
110. 3 the morning, like dew, your *y* will come
Eccl 12. 1 your creator in days of your *y*,
Isa 65.20 a hundred years will be considered a *y*,
Jer 22.21 This has been your way from your *y*, for
Mal 2.14 you and the wife of your *y*, to whom
Mk 10.20 I have kept all these from my *y*."
Lk 18.21 "I have kept all these since my *y*."
Acts 26. 4 Jews know my way of life from my *y*,
1 Tim 4.12 Let no one despise your *y*, but set the

Z

ZACCHAEUS

Lk 19. 2 named *Z*; he was a chief tax collector
19. 5 "*Z*, hurry and come down; for I must
19. 8 *Z* stood there and said to the Lord,

ZAPHON

Job 26. 7 He stretches out *Z* over the void, and

ZEAL

2 Kings 10.16 with me, and see my *z* for the LORD."
19.31 survivors. The *z* of the LORD will do this.
Ps 69. 9 It is *z* for your house that has consumed
119.139 My *z* consumes me because my foes
Isa 9. 7 The *z* of the LORD of hosts will do this.
26.11 Let them see your *z* for your people,
37.32 The *z* of the LORD of hosts will do this.
63.15 Where are your *z* and your might? The
Jn 2.17 written, "*Z* for your house will consume
Rom 10. 2 they have a *z* for God, but it is not
2 Cor 7. 7 your *z* for me, so that I rejoiced
7.12 your *z* for us might be made known to
9. 2 last year; and your *z* has stirred up most
Phil 3. 6 as to *z*, a persecutor of the church;

ZEALOUS

Num 25.13 he was *z* for his God, and made
Acts 21.20 the Jews, and they are all *z* for the law.
22. 3 being *z* for God, just as all of you are
Gal 1.14 *z* for the traditions of my ancestors.

ZEBULUN

Gen 30.20 him six sons"; so she named him *Z*.
49.13 *Z* shall settle at the shore of the sea; he
Num 26.26 The descendants of *Z* by their clans: of
Deut 33.18 of *Z* he said, "Rejoice, *Z*, in your going
Ps 68.27 in a body, the princes of *Z*, the princes
Isa 9. 1 he brought into contempt the land of *Z*
Mt 4.13 sea, in the territory of *Z* and Naphtali,
Rev 7. 8 from the tribe of *Z* twelve thousand,

ZECHARIAH

Ezra 5. 1 Now the prophets, Haggai and *Z* son of
6.14 of the prophet Haggai and *Z* son of
Zech 1. 1 word of the LORD came to the prophet *Z*
7. 1 the word of the LORD came to *Z* on the

ZEPHANIAH

Zeph 1. 1 The word of the LORD that came to *Z*

ZERUBBABEL

Ezra 2. 2 They came with *Z*, Jeshua, Nehemiah,
4. 2 they approached *Z* and the heads of the
5. 2 Then *Z* the son of Shealtiel and Jeshua
Neh 7. 7 They came with *Z*, Jeshua, Nehemiah,
Hag 1. 1 LORD came by the prophet Haggai to *Z*
2. 2 Speak now to *Z* son of Shealtiel,
Zech 4. 6 "This is the word of the LORD to *Z*: Not

ZION

Ps 2. 6 "I have set my king on *Z*, my holy hill."
48. 2 Mount *Z*, in the far north, the city of
50. 2 Out of *Z*, the perfection of beauty, God
Isa 1. 8 And daughter *Z* is left like a booth in a
2. 3 For out of *Z* shall go forth instruction,
Heb 12.22 you have come to Mount *Z* and to the

MAP INDEX

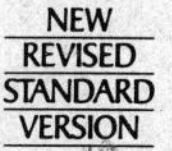

Index to Color Maps

The following index will enable you to locate places on the color maps quickly and easily. There are six maps in all: Map 1–World of the Patriarchs; Map 2–Palestine and Syria; Map 3–Kingdom of David and Solomon; Map 4–Jesus' Ministry; Map 5–Paul's Missionary Journeys; Map 6–Jerusalem in Jesus' Time. The first number of each index entry refers to the number of the map; the second one to the location of the place on that map.

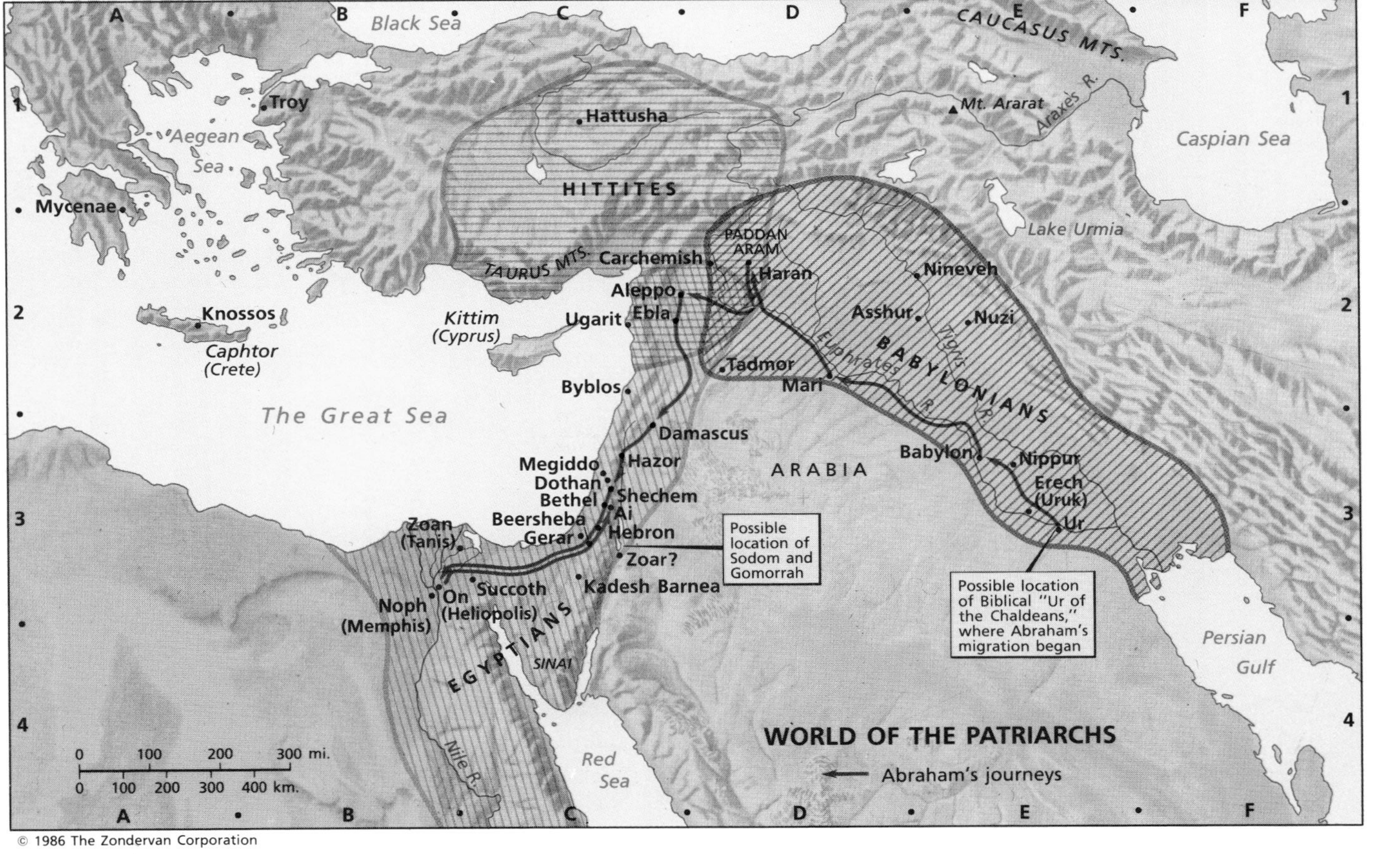
WORLD OF THE PATRIARCHS
Abraham's journeys
Black Sea
CAUCASUS MTS.
Caspian Sea
Mt. Ararat
Araxes R.
Lake Urmia
Troy
Aegean Sea
Mycenae
Hattusha
HITTITES
TAURUS MTS.
Carchemish
PADDAN ARAM
Haran
Aleppo
Ebla
Ugarit
Knossos
Caphtor (Crete)
Kittim (Cyprus)
Nineveh
Asshur
Nuzi
Tigris R.
Euphrates R.
BABYLONIANS
Tadmor
Mari
Byblos
The Great Sea
Damascus
Hazor
Megiddo
Dothan
Bethel
Shechem
Ai
Beersheba
Gerar
Hebron
Zoar?
Possible location of Sodom and Gomorrah
Kadesh Barnea
ARABIA
Babylon
Nippur
Erech (Uruk)
Ur
Possible location of Biblical "Ur of the Chaldeans," where Abraham's migration began
Zoan (Tanis)
Succoth
On (Heliopolis)
Noph (Memphis)
EGYPTIANS
SINAI
Nile R.
Red Sea
Persian Gulf
0 100 200 300 mi.
0 100 200 300 400 km.

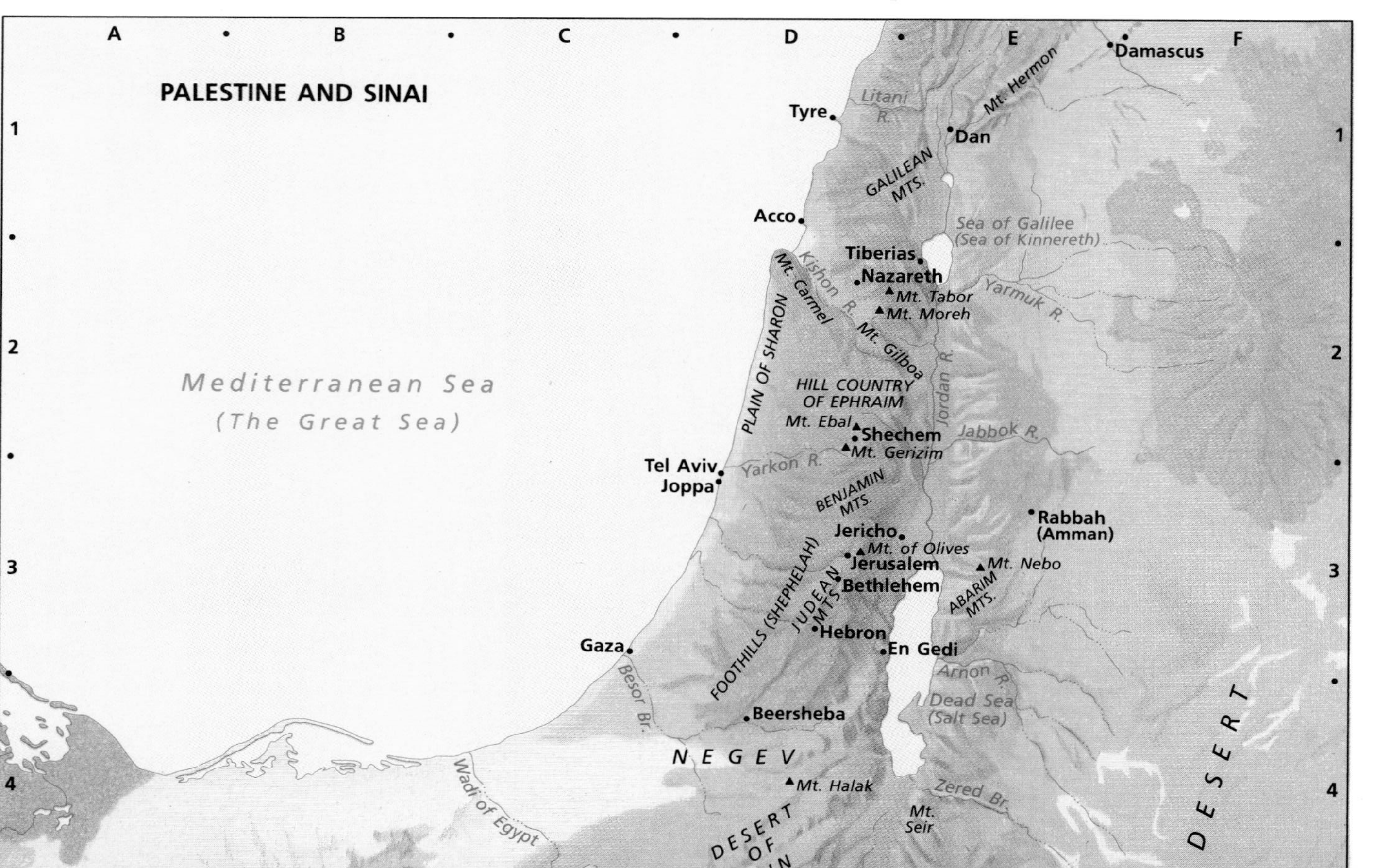
PALESTINE AND SINAI
A
B
C
D
E
F
1
2
3
4
Damascus
Mt. Hermon
Tyre
Litani R.
Dan
GALILEAN MTS.
Acco
Sea of Galilee
(Sea of Kinnereth)
Tiberias
Nazareth
Mt. Tabor
Mt. Moreh
Kishon R.
Mt. Carmel
Mt. Gilboa
Yarmuk R.
PLAIN OF SHARON
Mediterranean Sea
(The Great Sea)
HILL COUNTRY OF EPHRAIM
Jordan R.
Mt. Ebal
Shechem
Mt. Gerizim
Jabbok R.
Tel Aviv
Joppa
Yarkon R.
BENJAMIN MTS.
Rabbah
(Amman)
Jericho
Mt. of Olives
Jerusalem
Mt. Nebo
Bethlehem
FOOTHILLS (SHEPHELAH)
JUDEAN MTS.
ABARIM MTS.
Hebron
Gaza
En Gedi
Besor Br.
Arnon R.
Dead Sea
(Salt Sea)
Beersheba
NEGEV
Mt. Halak
Zered Br.
Wadi of Egypt
Mt. Seir
DESERT OF ZIN
DESERT

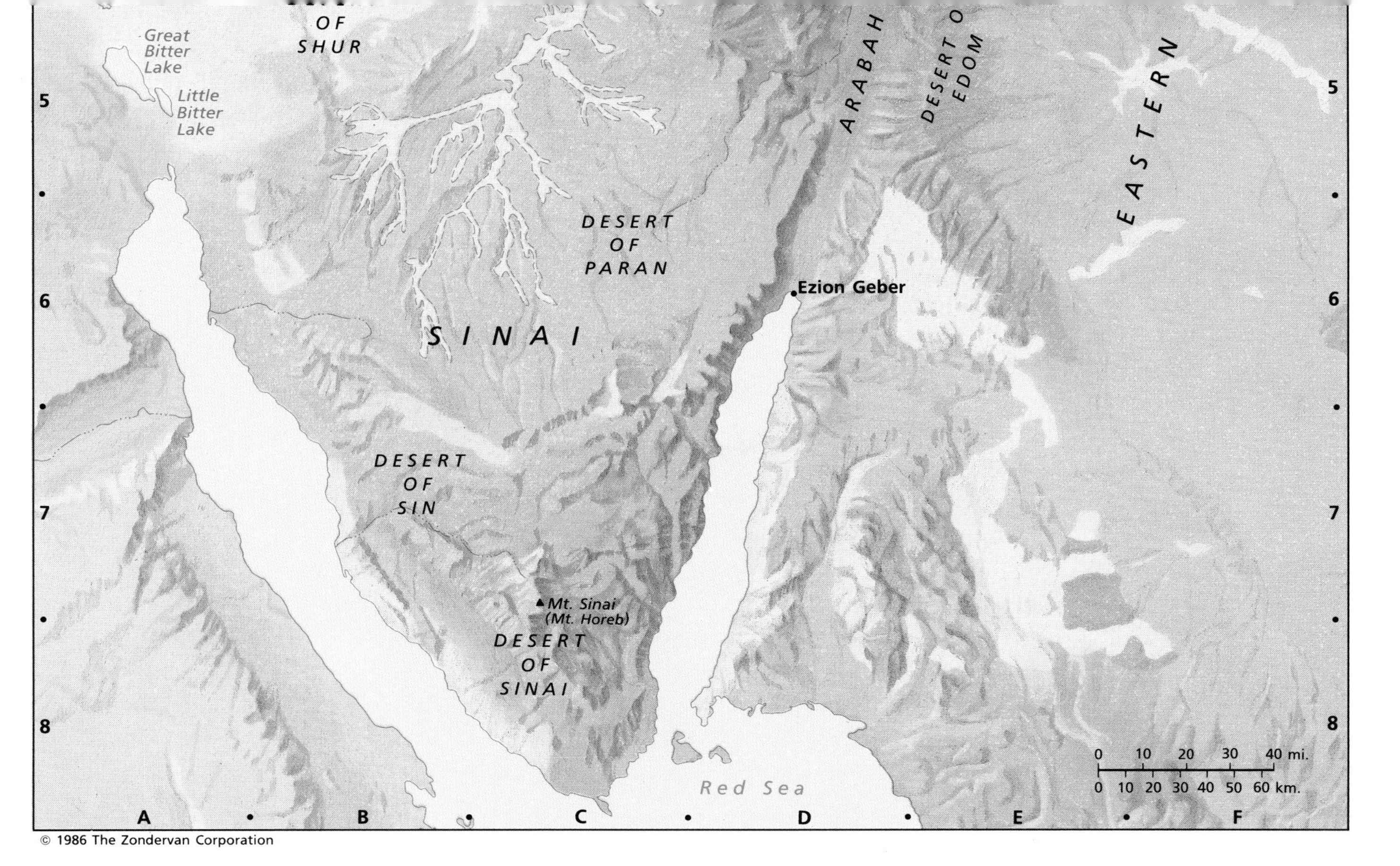
OF
SHUR
Great
Bitter
Lake
Little
Bitter
Lake
ARABAH
DESERT O
EDOM
EASTERN
DESERT
OF
PARAN
Ezion Geber
SINAI
DESERT
OF
SIN
Mt. Sinai
(Mt. Horeb)
DESERT
OF
SINAI
Red Sea
0 10 20 30 40 mi.
0 10 20 30 40 50 60 km.
5
6
7
8
A
B
C
D
E
F

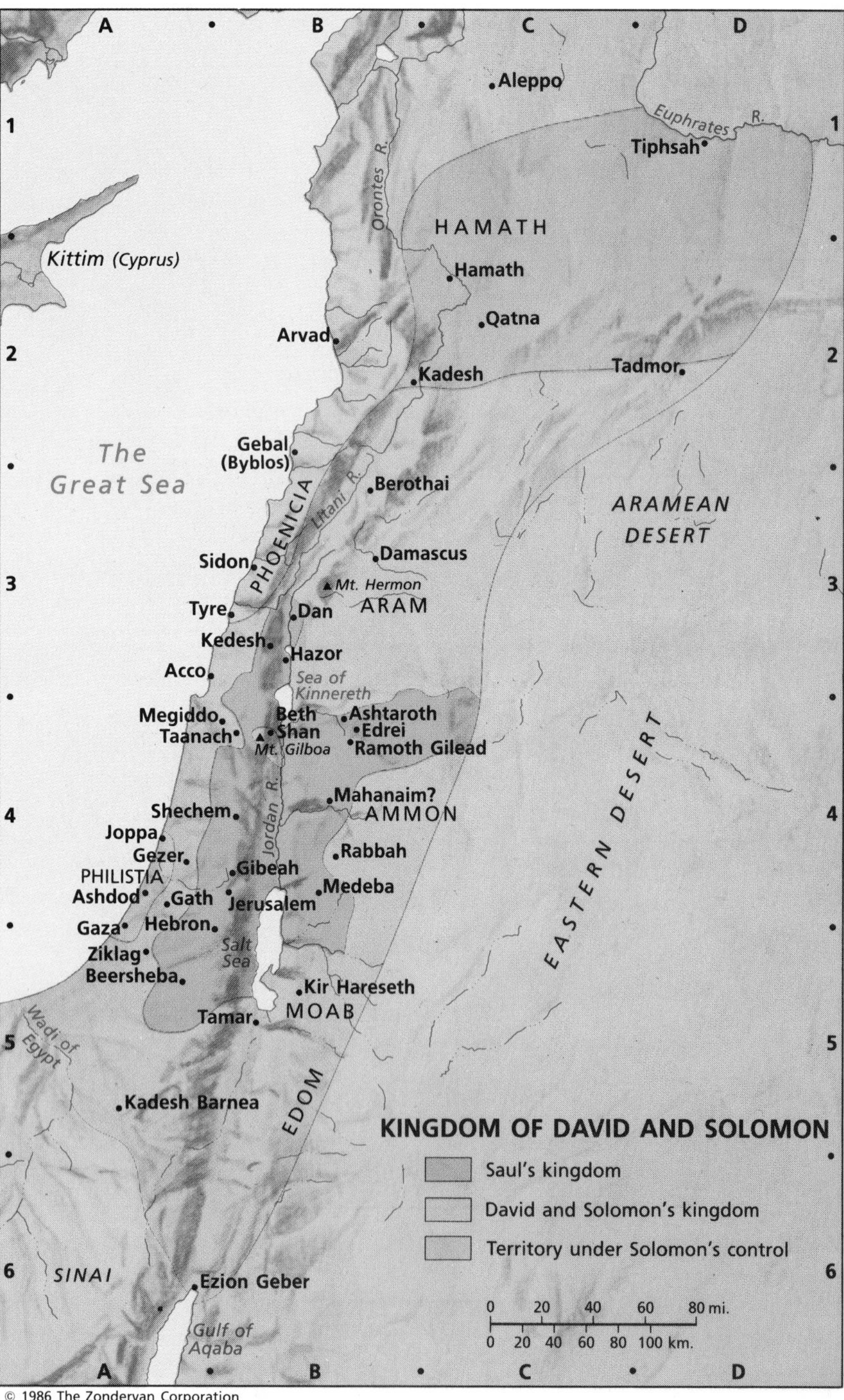
KINGDOM OF DAVID AND SOLOMON
Saul's kingdom
David and Solomon's kingdom
Territory under Solomon's control
A
B
C
D
1
2
3
4
5
6
Aleppo
Euphrates R.
Tiphsah
Orontes R.
HAMATH
Hamath
Qatna
Kittim (Cyprus)
Arvad
Kadesh
Tadmor
The Great Sea
Gebal (Byblos)
PHOENICIA
Litani R.
Berothai
ARAMEAN DESERT
Sidon
Damascus
Mt. Hermon
Tyre
Dan
ARAM
Kedesh
Hazor
Acco
Sea of Kinnereth
Megiddo
Taanach
Beth Shan
Mt. Gilboa
Ashtaroth
Edrei
Ramoth Gilead
Jordan R.
Mahanaim?
AMMON
Shechem
Joppa
Gezer
PHILISTIA
Ashdod
Gath
Gibeah
Jerusalem
Rabbah
Medeba
EASTERN DESERT
Gaza
Hebron
Salt Sea
Ziklag
Beersheba
Kir Hareseth
MOAB
Tamar
Wadi of Egypt
EDOM
Kadesh Barnea
SINAI
Ezion Geber
Gulf of Aqaba
0 20 40 60 80 mi.
0 20 40 60 80 100 km.

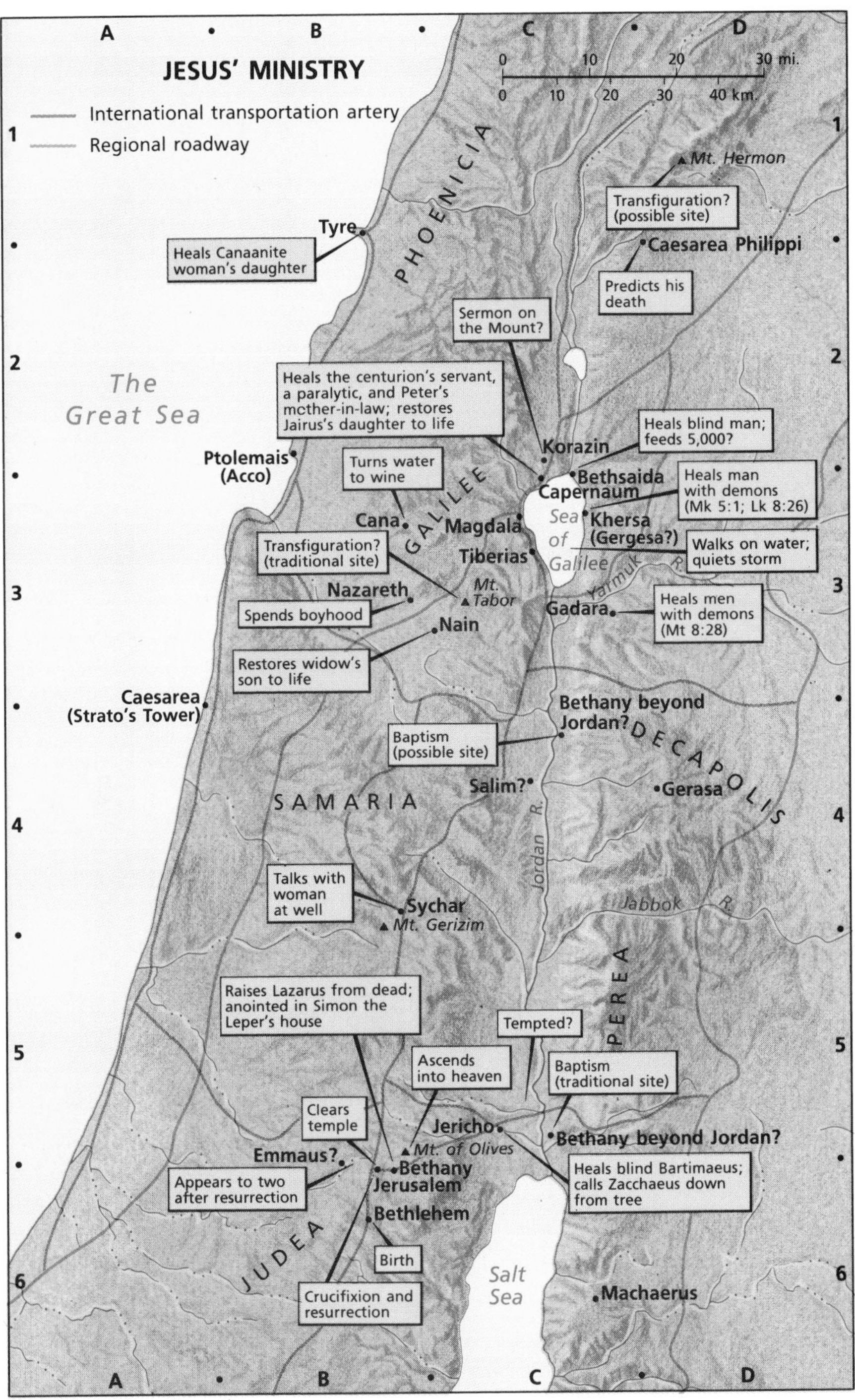
JESUS' MINISTRY
International transportation artery
Regional roadway
The Great Sea
PHOENICIA
GALILEE
SAMARIA
JUDEA
DECAPOLIS
PEREA
Mt. Hermon
Transfiguration? (possible site)
Caesarea Philippi
Predicts his death
Tyre
Heals Canaanite woman's daughter
Sermon on the Mount?
Heals the centurion's servant, a paralytic, and Peter's mother-in-law; restores Jairus's daughter to life
Heals blind man; feeds 5,000?
Korazin
Bethsaida
Capernaum
Heals man with demons (Mk 5:1; Lk 8:26)
Ptolemais (Acco)
Turns water to wine
Cana
Magdala
Sea of Galilee
Khersa (Gergesa?)
Walks on water; quiets storm
Tiberias
Transfiguration? (traditional site)
Mt. Tabor
Yarmuk R.
Nazareth
Spends boyhood
Gadara
Heals men with demons (Mt 8:28)
Nain
Restores widow's son to life
Caesarea (Strato's Tower)
Bethany beyond Jordan?
Baptism (possible site)
Salim?
Gerasa
Jordan R.
Talks with woman at well
Sychar
Mt. Gerizim
Jabbok R.
Raises Lazarus from dead; anointed in Simon the Leper's house
Tempted?
Ascends into heaven
Baptism (traditional site)
Clears temple
Jericho
Bethany beyond Jordan?
Mt. of Olives
Emmaus?
Bethany
Jerusalem
Appears to two after resurrection
Heals blind Bartimaeus; calls Zacchaeus down from tree
Bethlehem
Birth
Salt Sea
Machaerus
Crucifixion and resurrection
0 10 20 30 mi.
0 10 20 30 40 km.
A B C D
1 2 3 4 5 6

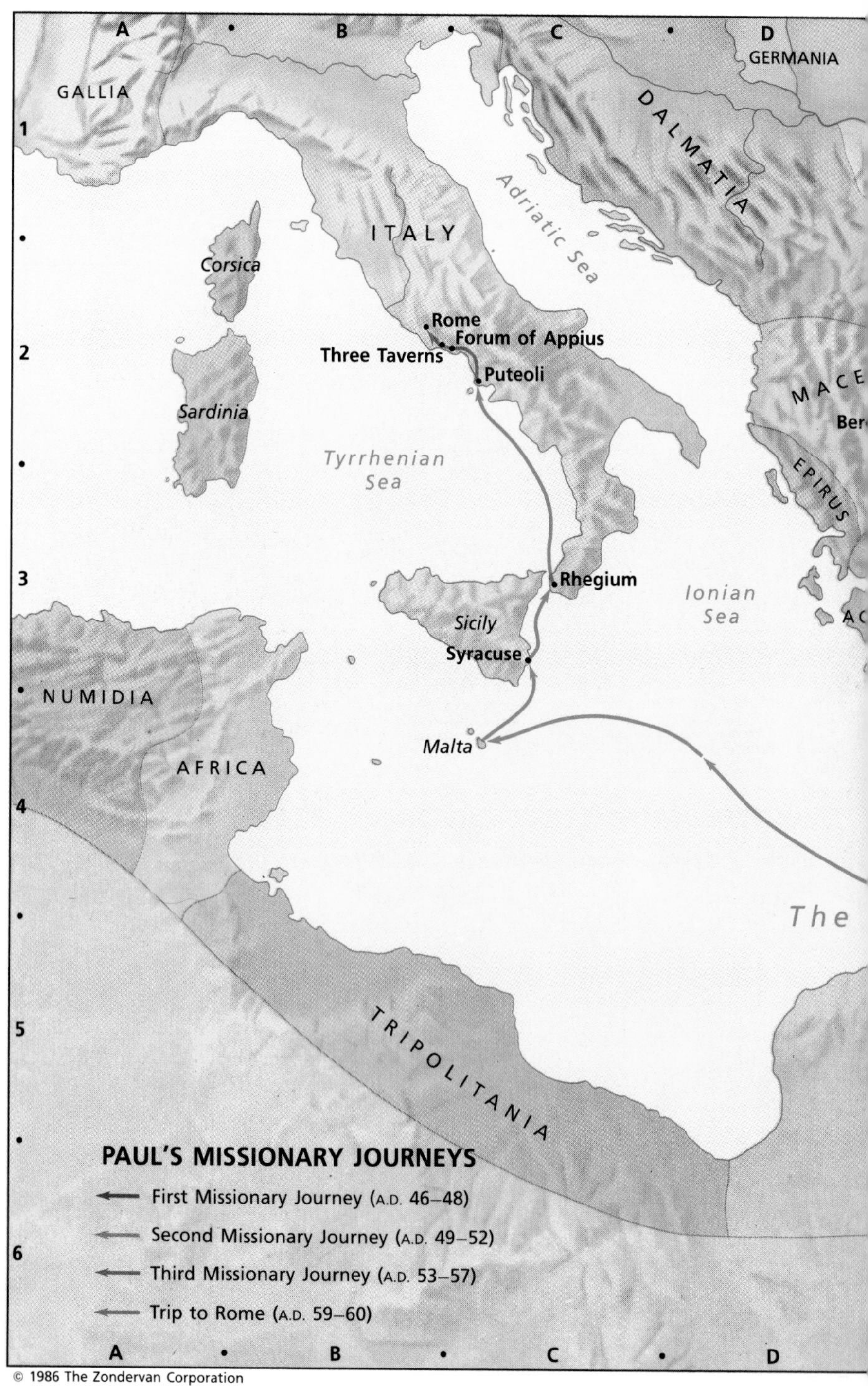
A
B
C
D
GERMANIA
GALLIA
DALMATIA
1
Adriatic Sea
ITALY
Corsica
Rome
Forum of Appius
2
Three Taverns
Puteoli
MACE
Sardinia
Ber
Tyrrhenian
Sea
EPIRUS
3
Rhegium
Ionian
Sea
AC
Sicily
Syracuse
NUMIDIA
Malta
AFRICA
4
The
5
TRIPOLITANIA
PAUL'S MISSIONARY JOURNEYS
First Missionary Journey (A.D. 46–48)
Second Missionary Journey (A.D. 49–52)
6
Third Missionary Journey (A.D. 53–57)
Trip to Rome (A.D. 59–60)
A
B
C
D